THE COLUMBIA LIPPINCOTT GAZETTEER OF THE WORLD

The Columbia Lippincott Gazetteer of the World

CONTAINS A *Supplement* IDENTIFYING THE NEW NATIONS THAT HAVE APPEARED SINCE THE ORIGINAL *Gazetteer* AND TAKING GEOGRAPHICAL ACCOUNT OF OTHER MAJOR DIFFERENCES BETWEEN THE WORLD OF 1952 AND THE WORLD OF 1961.

THE COLUMBIA LIPPINCOTT GAZETTEER OF THE WORLD

EDITED BY LEON E. SELTZER

WITH THE GEOGRAPHICAL RESEARCH STAFF OF COLUMBIA UNIVERSITY PRESS AND WITH THE COOPERATION OF THE AMERICAN GEOGRAPHICAL SOCIETY

WITH 1961 SUPPLEMENT

COLUMBIA UNIVERSITY PRESS

MORNINGSIDE HEIGHTS NEW YORK BY ARRANGEMENT WITH J. B. LIPPINCOTT COMPANY

THE KRESGE FOUNDATION

HAS GENEROUSLY PROVIDED FUNDS TO MEET PART OF THE COST OF THE RESEARCH AND OF THE PREPARATION OF THE MANUSCRIPT FOR THIS WORK.

INTERNATIONAL STANDARD BOOK NUMBER 0-231-01559-3

PRINTED IN THE UNITED STATES OF AMERICA

10 9 8 7 6

PREFACE

THE term *gazetteer*, in a geographical sense, is used to describe several kinds of works which list geographical names in alphabetical order. Such works vary greatly, however, both in scope and in the amount of information they contain. For example, indexes to maps and atlases, simply listing names and map locations, are often called gazetteers. But the comprehensive gazetteer which is an *encyclopedia of places* has a long and honorable history among reference books, and it is to this tradition that *The Columbia Lippincott Gazetteer of the World* hopes to add. The user of this book will find listed in one alphabet the places of the world—countries, regions, provinces, states, counties, cities, towns, islands, lakes, mountains, deserts, seas, rivers, canals, dams, peninsulas, capes, and like geographical features, and a good deal of information about them—variant spellings, pronunciation, population, geographic and political location, altitude, trade, industry, agriculture, mineral and other natural resources, irrigation works, river lengths, communications, history, cultural institutions and monuments, battles, and other facts pertinent to the place.

Not for many years—since the last Lippincott gazetteer was published in 1905—has the English-speaking world had a modern gazetteer of wide scope; yet at no other time has it needed one so much. The development of swift and widespread communications has drawn together the distant parts of the world, and people have become familiar with the names of a great many far-off places—names that often conceal meanings more and more imperative for the alert and anxious man to know. To Columbia University Press it seemed time, after the Second World War, to make available in convenient form and in great detail the latest knowledge about the places of the world. This, in the making of an entirely new book, the editors and publishers of *The Columbia Lippincott Gazetteer* have tried to do.

The amount and kind of information which have painstakingly been gathered together in this volume are not easily found elsewhere. A great fund of geographical knowledge has been examined to find and to clarify the information—some of it obscure, some of it nowhere set down in its proper order, some of it contradictory or hidden by insufficient exploration—which has gone into these articles, from the brief note on a small village to the essay on the source and flow of a great river. The articles here are not designed to take the place of those many-faceted essays on countries and larger places to be found in an encyclopedia; yet in the matter of geographic detail the reader will find here information he will not find in the encyclopedia. Neither is the *Gazetteer* designed to take the place of the atlas; rather, it complements the atlas, providing information largely unobtainable from maps. In this work the reader will find more up-to-date descriptive data on more places and geographic features of the world than he is likely to find elsewhere.

The criteria for the inclusion of places in this work have been designed always to embrace as many places as possible. First, the base chosen for each country or area has been made broad enough to insure that no place of importance is omitted; then to this basic list hundreds and sometimes thousands of places more have been added. A few examples will serve to indicate the scope of the work. The book includes: for the United States—every county and every incorporated place in the 1950 census, as well as several thousand unincorporated places and geographical features; for China—the seat of every county (of which there are over 2,000), as well as thousands of cross references and articles on independent cities, smaller towns, and geographical features; for France—every village of over 2,000 persons, as well as the capital of every canton, many of them hamlets of only a few hundred persons; for the Soviet Union—every city, workers' settlement or town, and county seat. While the emphasis is on the modern world, the ancient world has not been neglected. The oldest civilized areas of the world are extensively treated, and there are articles here on important biblical and archaeological sites and on ancient regions, towns, cities, and geographic features.

In the spelling of place names there is wide variance in English usage, and both reference-book editors and geographers, as well as the general public, have long been plagued with the problem. In the English-speaking world two agencies have contributed much to the elimination of this confusion—the Board on Geographic Names of the Department of the Interior, in the United States, and the Permanent Committee on Geographical Names, in Great Britain. *The Columbia Lippincott Gazetteer* has made wide use of their findings. In the United States particularly the decisions of the Board on Geographic Names have been invaluable. The Board's decisions on foreign place names have also been of great use, but these could not always be followed unmodified, for the needs upon which the Board's principles of decision are based are often very different from those of a general reference book, whose concern is with the language of history, literature, and everyday speech as well as with current linguistic and political factors.

Since this book is written in English, primarily for English-speaking readers, a place has been listed under its English name, when it clearly has one; sometimes, the common English name for a place may be out of a language different from that of the country in which the place is currently located. For example, the book uses Moscow rather than Moskva, Rome rather than Roma, Timbuktu rather than Tombouctou, and Gallipoli rather than Gelibolu. Where English usage has changed, the book reflects the change.

In languages whose accent marks are familiar to English-speaking readers and are commonly used by them, the names appear throughout this book fully accented. In languages whose accent marks are less well known, the accents are indicated in every case at least once, in italics, at the beginning of each article. Native names spelled differently from English names are fully listed as cross references. For languages which do not use the Latin alphabet (such as Arabic, Chinese, Greek, and Russian), the book provides, in addition to English names or conventional spellings, at least one—and usually two—consistent transliterations. In this matter, where English has long responded to several transliteration systems, the usefulness of this procedure will be apparent; the transliterated names in this book constitute a degree of parallel listings nowhere before attempted. Also, when other variant transliterations and common spellings out of other languages using the Latin alphabet occur, these are fully listed as cross references. Sometimes, as with *Byblos*—from whose name came the Greek word for book and, ultimately, the word for Bible—the modern name of a place may appear in many ways, in this case out of the Arabic as Jebeil, Jubeil, Jebail, Jubayl, Jbail, Djébail, Djoubeil. Such an entry demands numerous cross references, and the *Gazetteer* gives as many as are useful.

Special care has been taken to include place-name changes, the dates when the changes have taken place, and appropriate cross references. Sometimes, in addition to ordinary place-name changes, local usage prevents proper identification. For example, in China's Yunnan province the district of Lungchwan has a winter and spring capital, Shanmulung, and a summer and fall capital, Changfengkai, each of which is called simply Lungchwan during the period in which it is the seat of the local government; such areas of confusion have been clarified in the book.

The pronunciation of place names is not only often difficult to obtain, but equally difficult, without elaborate apparatus, to communicate in print. Great effort has been expended to obtain pronunciations, and these are indicated by means of a system of symbols as simple—and therefore as quickly usable—as possible. A further note on pronunciation and the key to pronunciation symbols face the first page of text.

Places have been located, unless otherwise indicated, by straight-line distances in miles from a larger feature, but geographic coordinates have been given when latitude and longitude would also be useful.

Much of the information in the book has been collected from official or otherwise authoritative sources, but this material has been carefully used. It is the business of a reference book of this kind to report the facts, but it is also its business to report doubt when the facts are uncertain. For example, there have been instances, in several countries across the world, where two or more official agencies—of parallel and equal rank and importance—have reported different figures for the same item; in such cases the book either gives both figures or reconciles the data in a way which will not mislead the reader.

Even when there is no conflict among official sources, care has been taken to present as accurate a set of facts as possible. An example or two will suffice. The altitude of Mount Carstensz in New Guinea has long been given in sources using the English system as 16,404 feet, a figure obtained by multiplying the estimated height of 5,000 meters by the conversion factor 3.2808. Since 16,404 feet seems to indicate a degree of exactitude unsubstantiated by the estimate, it was felt that *circa* 16,400 feet is a more accurate description of its known altitude. Again, in working on the altitudes of the numerous Swiss mountain peaks, the staff researchers found, in Swiss, French, German, Austrian, and Italian sources, different but equally authoritative figures for the same peaks. These discrepancies were referred to the Swiss Topographic Service, which explained that there were two reasons for the difficulty: first, the Swiss have long used in their computations a mean sea-level base 3.3 meters higher than that used by the four adjacent countries; and, secondly, the peaks themselves were being resurveyed and recomputed, and the results are gradually being republished in new maps. The figures used by the *Gazetteer* are those furnished it by the Swiss Topographic Service and reflect the current status of their corrections and changes.

In the use of population figures, too, pains have been taken to be clear. Since the meaning of terms comparable to "city, municipality, town, village, and commune" varies from country to country, the *Gazetteer* gives wherever possible figures for the agglomerated population in areas whose characteristics are as near as possible like those of cities, towns, and villages as we know them. This has not always been possible, and various devices have sometimes had to be employed in order to give an accurate indication of the size of the place. For example, in the Philippines the important villages all have the same name as the municipalities of which they are the center; the municipality—really comparable in size to a small county—also includes numerous other villages. The last available census figures of the Philippines (those of 1948) include only the population by municipalities—figures often ten and sometimes nearly a hundred times as large as the population of the village itself. The *Gazetteer* uses the 1948 municipality figures, but since it seemed also necessary to indicate in some way the actual size of the village under discussion, the village populations from the 1939 census (which *are* available) are also given. Similar devices have been used for other countries where necessary. Notes on the population figures used in the book are in a table on pages viii–ix.

The information on industry, agriculture, climate, relief, and history has been analyzed and regrouped so as to be found here, as often as possible, under the nearest specific town or feature to which it applies. In addition, however, much pertinent data is grouped under larger and more inclusive headings, and the reader will often find it useful to consult articles whose names occur in the article which has been looked up.

The information which makes up this book has been gathered not only from libraries and other resources available in this country but also—by means of a large and continuous correspondence—from hundreds of government agencies all over the world. Many of the officials of these agencies have given far more than perfunctory replies to numerous requests for various kinds of information and often went to great expense in time and effort to help the staff in its research. To thank them all by name is impossible, but to them and to the many informants in this country who generously gave of their special knowledge the staff owes countless thanks.

The many people who were closest to the work are listed elsewhere in this volume; to them belongs the credit for the long and difficult task of gathering and checking the enormous quantity of detail that went into the articles. For their tireless and painstaking efforts and for their constant enthusiasm the editor is more grateful than he can express.

Special thanks are due, too, to Miss Ena L. Yonge, Map Curator, and Miss Nordis Felland, Librarian, of the American Geographical Society; to the librarians of the many parts of the Libraries of Columbia University; to C. S. Hammond & Co., Inc., which has been most generous in allowing the staff wide use of its library; and to the United States Bureau of the Census, whose officials cooperated most considerately at a time when final census figures were required.

In a particular manner do the editor and publishers of the *Gazetteer* owe thanks to The Kresge Foundation. At the midpoint in the compilation of the *Gazetteer*, when the publishers were faced with the prospect of abandoning the project rather than either curtail its scope or lower the quality of the research, The Kresge Foundation generously granted the funds necessary to carry on the work.

The editor and the staff owe gratitude, too, to Charles G. Proffitt, Director of Columbia University Press, for his constant encouragement and confidence. Henry H. Wiggins, Manager of the Publication Department of the Press, has given much-appreciated aid and wise counsel. Thanks are also due for the support and cooperation of the J. B. Lippincott Company.

This first edition of *The Columbia Lippincott Gazetteer of the World* is now offered to the reader with the hope that it will prove to be a useful reference book and that it will serve its users as faithfully as did its honorable predecessors.

January 7, 1952 L.E.S.

ADVISORY EDITORS

JOHN K. WRIGHT
Former Director
American Geographical Society

WILLIAM BRIDGWATER
Editor
The Columbia Encyclopedia

WILLIAM B. S. SMITH
Linguistic Editor
The Columbia Encyclopedia

EDITOR

LEON E. SELTZER

ASSISTANT EDITOR: THEODORE SHABAD

STAFF

HELEN E. STROOP
PETER M. STERN
SONO ROSENBERG
LEO DEUEL
EVERETT RIPLEY

Karol N. Gess
Arthur Anthony Lawrence
Lydia B. Schanzer
Maurice Harari
Alexander Shatton
Chung-yuan Chang
Richard A. von Glatz
Walter Albee
Irene van Dongen
Jack Preston
Raymond Dickinson Ruhland
Constance Ellis
Julia Casa Rashti
Barbara Melissa Voorhis
Joan S. McQuary
Hazel H. McQuary

Pronunciation: William B. S. Smith, John Kepke, Edith Crowell Trager, Charles Noble, Morris Swadesh, Raven I. McDavid, Jr., Michael Luther, Virginia Glenn McDavid

CONTRIBUTORS

Erik Achorn
U Po Thoung Allamon
Prok Amranand
Marjorie Musolf Baclawski
Wilson C. Carter
Nelda Cassuto
Thomas W. Chu
Fred M. Colland
Eliezer Czerniak
Abdul K. Disu
Charles T. Emmett, Jr.
Frederic M. Evans
Alice Ferguson
Tilford Gaines
Horst W. R. Galley
Richard C. Goodson
Sotos E. Hadjis
Henry Hamburger
Joseph Harari
Harry W. Hazard, Jr.
Harry W. Hazard, 3d
Ma Tin Hlyne
Rafael D. Iriarte
Emeline Moore Kappel
Quentin R. Keith
John G. Kotselas
Muriel Kotselas
Peter Kotsogean
Eric G. Lassen
Richard Morgan Lawrence
Hallgrimur Ludvigsson
William R. Palmer
Geraldine Pelles
Demetrios Politis
Sarah Pomeranc
Paul F. Power
Mohammed A. Rashti
Eric P. Sandahl
Kouros Satrap
Reza Shahshahani
Jonathan Slesinger
Renée Spodheim
David Otto Tyson
John S. Ullmann
Ralph L. Veals
Gabriel Weinreich
Uriel Weinreich
Victor Winston

KEY TO POPULATION FIGURES

RECENT POPULATION FIGURES for many areas of the world are often difficult to obtain. Some countries have never taken a census; some take only partial censuses; some which do take censuses publish them completely only many years after the census is taken; some publish only part of the results of a census and some have been known to suppress all results of a census. The population figures used in this book were the best obtainable at the time of printing. The figures of the last complete census have been used wherever possible and wherever they are most useful. Recent official estimates have been used either when they were the result of careful annual corrections based on an earlier census or when there were no recent census figures. Unofficial estimates have been used only when no official figures of any kind were obtainable.

Aden. Colony—1946 census; Protectorate—unofficial estimates.
Afghanistan. Unofficial estimates.
Alaska. 1950 census, final figures for towns of over 2,500 population, preliminary figures for other towns; 1939 census figures (dated) for a few villages not listed in 1950 census.
Albania. 1945 census.
Algeria. 1948 census.
Andorra. Unofficial estimates.
Anglo-Egyptian Sudan. 1948 official estimates.
Angola. 1940 census.
Argentina. 1947 census for civil divisions and towns; unofficial estimates for small places.
Australia. 1947 census, preliminary results.
Austria. 1951 census figures (preliminary; dated) for provinces and large cities; 1948 register of population (undated) for other places.
Bahama Islands. 1943 census.
Bahrein. 1950 census.
Barbados. 1946 census.
Basutoland. 1946 census for the country as a whole and for districts; unofficial estimates for other places.
Bechuanaland. 1946 census.
Belgian Congo. 1948 official estimates.
Belgium. 1948 official estimates.
Bermuda. 1949 official estimates for the colony and its capital; 1939 census for parishes.
Bhutan. Unofficial estimate.
Bolivia. 1949 official estimates (dated) for departments and chief towns: 1948 official district estimates (undated) for other towns.
Bonin Islands. 1940 census.
Brazil. 1950 census figures (preliminary; dated) for states and the larger towns; 1940 census figures (final; undated) for small places.
British Honduras. 1946 census.
British Somaliland. Unofficial estimates.
Brunei. 1947 census.
Bulgaria. 1946 census.
Burma. 1941 census figures (dated) for districts; 1931 census figures (undated) for towns.
Cambodia. 1948 official estimates.
Cameroons, British. 1948 official estimates (dated) for the colony and its divisions; 1931 census figures (undated) for towns.
Cameroons, French. 1950 official estimates.
Canada. 1948 official estimates for each province as a whole; 1946 census for places in the Prairie Provinces (Alberta, Saskatchewan, Manitoba); 1945 census for places in Newfoundland; 1941 census for places in the other provinces; unofficial estimates for certain small places.
Cape Verde Islands. 1950 census, preliminary results.
Ceylon. 1946 census, preliminary results.
Channel Islands. 1951 census figures for each island; 1945 census figures for parishes of Jersey; 1931 census figures for parishes in Guernsey bailiwick.
Chile. 1940 census.
China. (1) 1947 and 1948 official estimates (dated) are used for all independent cities (for China, the term "city" is used in this book only with reference to such independent municipalities). (2) 1948 official estimates (undated) are used for the county seats in the 12 provinces of Chekiang, Fukien, Jehol, Kiangsi, Kiangsu, Kwangtung, Kweichow, Ningsia, Shensi, Suiyuan, Szechwan, and Yunnan. (3) County figures (undated) for all other provinces are official Chinese estimates made mostly in the 1940s but with some dating from the mid-1930s. (4) Total figures (undated) for each of the provinces are unofficial estimates.
Colombia. 1938 census.
Comoro Islands. 1948 official estimates.
Cook Islands. 1945 census.
Costa Rica. 1950 census.
Cuba. 1943 census.
Curaçao (Dutch West Indies). 1948 official estimates.
Cyprus. 1946 census.
Czechoslovakia. 1947 census.
Denmark. 1950 census figures (preliminary; dated) for country as a whole, for amts (counties), and for large cities; 1945 census figures (final; undated) for towns.
Dominican Republic. 1950 census (preliminary results) for provinces and towns; 1935 census for villages.
Ecuador. 1950 census, preliminary results.
Egypt. 1947 census.
England and Wales. 1951 census figures (preliminary; dated) for counties and urban centers; 1931 census figures (final; undated) for parishes.
Eritrea. Unofficial estimates.
Estonia. 1934 census.
Ethiopia. 1948 official estimates for the larger towns; unofficial estimates for other places.
Falkland Islands. 1946 census.
Fiji. 1946 census.
Finland. 1949 official estimates.
Formosa. 1950 census for the larger cities; 1935 census for smaller places.
France. 1946 census; figures are those for the towns and villages (agglomerated population) within the communes.
French Equatorial Africa. 1950 official estimates.
French India. 1946 census.
French Oceania. 1946 census.
French Somaliland. 1946 and 1948 official figures for the territory and its capital; unofficial estimates for other places.
French West Africa. 1946–49 official figures.
Gambia. 1948 official estimates.
Germany. West Germany—1950 census figures (preliminary; dated) for all states and cities, 1946 census figures (final; undated) for the smaller towns; East Germany—1946 census figures for all places.
Gibraltar. 1948 official estimates.
Gilbert and Ellice Islands. 1947 census.
Gold Coast. 1948 census, preliminary results.
Greece. 1951 census figures (preliminary; dated) for the country and for the larger cities; 1940 census (final; undated) for nomes and the smaller places.
Greenland. 1945 census.
Guadeloupe. 1946 census.
Guam. 1950 census, preliminary results.
Guatemala. 1950 census, preliminary results.
Guiana, British. 1946 census.
Guiana, Dutch. 1948 official estimates.
Guiana, French. 1946 census.
Haiti. 1950 census, preliminary results.
Hawaii. 1950 census, final figures for places of over 2,500 population, preliminary figures for smaller places.
Honduras. 1950 census figures (preliminary; dated) for departments; 1945 census figures (final; undated) for towns.
Hong Kong. 1949 official estimates and 1931 census.
Hungary. 1941 census.
Iceland. 1949 official estimates.
India. 1951 census figures (preliminary; dated) for states; 1941 census figures (final; undated) for all other places.
Indonesia. 1930 census.
Iran. 1940–42 census figures.
Iraq. 1947 census.
Ireland. 1946 census for places; 1951 census figure (preliminary) for country as a whole.
Israel. 1950, 1949, 1946 official estimates, all dated; 1948 official estimates, undated.
Italian Somaliland. Unofficial estimates.
Italy. 1936 census; figures are those for the towns and villages (agglomerated population) within the communes.
Jamaica. 1943 census and official estimates.
Japan. 1947 census.
Jordan. 1950 official estimate for country as whole; 1947 and 1946 official estimates for places.
Kenya. 1948 census.
Korea. North Korea—1944 census; South Korea—1949 census.
Kuwait. 1949 official estimates.
Laos. 1947 official estimates.
Latvia. 1935 census.
Lebanon. 1946 official estimates (dated) for country and large towns; 1945 official estimates (undated) for small towns.
Leeward Islands (B.W.I.). 1946 census.
Liberia. Unofficial estimates.
Libya. 1950 and 1947 official estimates (dated) for civil divisions and main cities, unofficial estimates (undated) for small places.
Liechtenstein. 1941 census.
Lithuania. 1939 official estimates.
Luxembourg. 1947 census.
Macao. 1940 census.
Madagascar. 1948 census.
Malaya. 1947 census.
Maldive Islands. 1946 census.
Malta. 1948 census.
Man, Isle of. 1951 census (preliminary) for the island; 1939 census (final) for towns.
Martinique. 1946 census.
Mauritius. 1944 census.
Mexico. 1950 census figures (preliminary; dated) for states; 1940 census figures (final; undated) for towns.
Monaco. 1946 census.
Mongolian People's Republic. 1951 unofficial estimates (dated) for the country and its capital; unofficial estimates (undated) for other places.
Morocco, French. 1947 census.
Morocco, Spanish. 1945 census.
Mozambique. 1950 census figures (preliminary; dated) for the country and some towns; 1940 census figures (final; undated) for most towns.
Nauru. 1947 census.
Nepal. 1941 and 1920 censuses.
Netherlands. 1947 census; figures are those for the towns and villages (agglomerated population) within the communes.
New Caledonia. 1944–46 official estimates (undated); 1936 census (dated).
New Guinea, Netherlands. 1930 census.
New Guinea, Territory of. 1949–50 official estimate.
New Hebrides. 1946 official estimates.
New Zealand. 1945 census.
Nicaragua. 1950 census, preliminary results.
Nigeria. 1931 census.
Niue. 1945 census.
Norfolk Island. 1947 census.
North Borneo. 1951 census (preliminary results) for the country and larger towns; official estimates for other places.
Northern Ireland. 1951 census figures (preliminary; dated) for counties,

county boroughs, and other urban centers; 1937 census figures (final; undated) for small places.
Northern Rhodesia. 1946 census.
Norway. 1946 census.
Nyasaland. 1949 official estimates for the protectorate and towns; 1945 census for provinces.
Oman. Unofficial estimates.
Pacific Islands, Trust Territory of the. 1948 official estimates.
Pakistan. 1951 census figures (preliminary; dated) for civil divisions and large cities; 1941 census figures (final; undated) for smaller places.
Panama. 1950 census figures (preliminary; dated) for civil divisions and large towns; 1940 census figures (final; undated) for other places.
Panama Canal Zone. 1950 census, final figures for towns of over 2,500 population, preliminary figures for other towns.
Papua, Territory of. 1949–50 official estimate.
Paraguay. 1947 official estimates; figures for towns are district populations.
Peru. 1940 census.
Philippines. 1948 census figures (preliminary) for provinces, municipalities, and some islands; 1939 census figures (final) for villages and other islands.
Poland. 1950 official estimates (dated) for major cities; 1946 census figures (undated) for other places.
Portugal. 1950 census figures (preliminary; dated) for country as whole and for the Azores and Madeira; 1940 census figures (final; undated) for towns and civil divisions.
Portuguese Guinea. 1940 census.
Portuguese India. 1940 census.
Puerto Rico. 1950 census, final results for towns of over 2,500 population, preliminary results for other towns.
Qatar. Unofficial estimates.
Réunion. 1946 census.
Ruanda-Urundi. 1949 official estimates.
Rumania. 1948 census figures (preliminary; dated) for major cities and towns; 1941 census figures (final; undated) for villages.
Ryukyu Islands. 1950 census, preliminary results.
Saar. 1946 census.
Saint Helena. 1946 census.
Saint Pierre and Miquelon. 1946 census.
Salvador. 1950 census figures (preliminary results; dated) for the country as whole and for the larger towns; 1948 official estimates (undated) for small towns and for departments.
Samoa, American. 1950 census, preliminary results.
Samoa, Western. 1945 census.
Sãn Marino. 1936 census.
São Tomé e Principe. 1950 census.
Sarawak. 1947 census.
Saudi Arabia. Unofficial estimates.
Scotland. 1951 census figures (preliminary; dated) for counties and urban centers; 1931 census figures (final; undated) for parishes.
Seychelles. 1947 census.
Sierra Leone. 1948 census figures (undated), except for towns of the colony (1931 census figures; dated).
Singapore. 1947 census.
Solomon Islands. Unofficial estimates.
South Africa, Union of. 1946 census.
Southern Rhodesia. 1946–48 censuses.
South-West Africa. 1946 census.
Spain. 1940 census.
Spanish Guinea. 1942 census.
Spanish Possessions in North Africa. 1940 census.
Spanish West Africa. 1940 census and later official estimates.
Sweden. 1950 census figures (preliminary; dated) for the country as a whole and for the larger cities; 1945 census figures (final; undated) for small places and for counties.
Switzerland. 1950 census figures (preliminary; dated) for cantons and major cities and towns; 1941 census figures (final; undated) for other places.
Syria. 1946 official estimates.
Swaziland. 1946 census.
Tanganyika. 1948 census.
Tangier. 1947 official estimate.
Thailand. 1947 census, preliminary results.
Tibet. Unofficial estimates.
Timor, Portuguese. 1940 census.
Togoland, British. 1948 census, preliminary results.
Togoland, French. 1947 official estimates.
Tokelau. 1945 census.
Tonga. 1948 official estimates.
Trieste, Free Territory of. 1949 official estimate (dated) for the territory as a whole; 1936 census figures (undated) for towns and villages (agglomerated population) within the communes.
Trinidad and Tobago. 1946 census.
Trucial Oman. Unofficial estimates.
Tunisia. 1946 census.
Turkey. 1950 census figures (preliminary; dated) for provinces and large towns; 1945 census figures (final; undated) for smaller towns.
Uganda. 1948 census.
Union of Soviet Socialist Republics. Population figures for all places in the Soviet Union (except in Estonia, Latvia, and Lithuania, for which see elsewhere in this table) are dated. (1) For places in pre-war Soviet Union and in the territories annexed as a result of the Second World War, certain dates apply to censuses taken by the respective countries in those years: 1926 (USSR), 1930 (Rumania), 1931 (Poland), 1939 (USSR, Germany), 1940 (Japan), and 1941 (Memel; Rumania; Hungarian census of annexed Czech territory); the 1941 figures for former Finnish territory are official estimates. (2) All other figures are estimates, of varying degrees of reliability and usefulness, gleaned from every available source.
United States. 1950 census, final figures (undated), for all states and counties, and for incorporated and unincorporated places listed in the 1950 census; 1940 census figures (dated) for places listed in 1940 census but not listed in 1950 census; unofficial estimates (undated, but indicated by the abbreviation *c.* [*circa*=about]) for small unincorporated places not included in either census.
Uruguay. Unofficial estimates.
Vatican City. Unofficial estimate.
Venezuela. 1950 census figures (preliminary; dated) for states and their capitals; 1941 census figures (final; undated) for other places.
Vietnam. 1943 and 1936 official estimates.
Virgin Islands of the United States. 1950 census, preliminary results.
Volcano Islands. 1940 census.
Windward Islands (B.W.I.). 1946 census.
Yemen. 1948 estimates.
Yugoslavia. 1948 census, preliminary results.
Zanzibar. 1948 census.

ABBREVIATIONS

acad. =academy
A.D. =*anno Domini* [in the year of our Lord]
Afr. =Africa
agr. = agriculture, agricultural
Ala. =Alabama
alt. =altitude
Alta. =Alberta
Amer. =America, American
anc. =ancient
Ariz. =Arizona
Ark. =Arkansas
assn. =association
ASSR=Autonomous Soviet Socialist Republic
Aug. =August
Ave. =Avenue
b. =born
B.C.=before Christ; British Columbia
Belg. =Belgian
bet. =between
bldg. =building
Br. =British
Bulg. =Bulgarian
B.W.I.=British West Indies
c. =*circa* (about)
Calif. =California
Can. =Canadian
Capt. =Captain
cent. =century, centuries
Co. =Company
co. =county
coed. =coeducational
col. =college
Colo. =Colorado
Conn. =Connecticut
cos. =counties
cu. =cubic
C.Z. =Canal Zone
d. =died, died in
D.C. =District of Columbia
Dec. =December
Del. =Delaware
dept. =department
dist. =district
div. =division
DP =displaced person
Dr. =Doctor
Du. =Dutch
E =east
e.g. = *exempli gratia* [for example]
elev. =elevation
ENE =east-northeast
Eng. =English
ESE =east-southeast
esp. =especially
est. =estimated, established
etc. =*et cetera* [and others, and so forth]
Eur. =European
F. =Farenheit
Feb. =February
Fin. =Finnish
Fla. =Florida
Fr. =French
ft. =foot, feet, fort
Ga. =Georgia
Gall. =Gallery
Gen. =General; Genesis
Ger. =German
Gov. =Governor
govt. =government
Gr. =Greek
hosp. =hospital
hp =horsepower
hq. =headquarters
ht. =height
Hung. =Hungarian
i.e. =*id est* [that is]
Ill. =Illinois
in. =inch, inches
inc. =incorporated
Ind. =Indiana
Inst. =Institute, Institution
isl., isls. =island, islands
Ital. (*or* It.) =Italian
Jap. =Japanese
Jan. =January
Jr. =Junior
kw =kilowatt
kwh =kilowatt hours
Ky. =Kentucky
L. =Lake
La. =Louisiana
Lab. =Labrador
Lat. =Latin
lat. =latitude
Lat. Amer. = Latin America
L.I. =Long Island
Lith. =Lithuanian
long. =longitude
Lt. =Lieutenant
Man. =Manitoba
Mass. =Massachusetts
max. =maximum
Md. =Maryland
Mex. =Mexican
mfg. =manufacturing
mi. =mile, miles
Mich. =Michigan
min. =minimum
Minn. =Minnesota
Miss. =Mississippi
Mo. =Missouri
Mont. =Montana
MS =manuscript
MSS =manuscripts
Mt. =Mount
mtn. =mountain
mts. =mounts, mountains
mus. =museum
N =north
N.Amer. =North America
natl. =national
naut. =nautical
N.B. =New Brunswick
N.C. =North Carolina
N.Dak. =North Dakota
NE =northeast
Nebr. =Nebraska
Neth. =Netherlands
Nev. =Nevada
N.F. =Newfoundland
N.H. =New Hampshire
N.J. =New Jersey
N.Mex. =New Mexico
NNE =north-northeast
NNW =north-northwest
No. =*numero* (number)
Nor. =Norwegian
Nov. =November
N.S. =Nova Scotia; New Style
N.S.W. =New South Wales
NW =northwest
N.W.T. =Northwest Territories
N.Y. =New York
N.Z. =New Zealand
Oct. =October
Okla. =Oklahoma
Ont. =Ontario
O.S. =Old Style
Pa. =Pennsylvania
P.E.I. =Prince Edward Island
P.I. =Philippine Islands
P.O. =Post Office
Pol. =Polish
pop. =population
Port. =Portuguese
P.R. =Puerto Rico
prov. =province
Que. =Quebec
R. =River
RAF =Royal Air Force
R.C. =Roman Catholic
reinc. =reincorporated
R.I. =Rhode Island
RR =Railroad
RSFSR = Russian Soviet Federated Socialist Republic
Rus. =Russian
S =south
S.Amer. =South American
Sask. =Saskatchewan
S.C. =South Carolina
S.Dak. =South Dakota
SE =southeast
sec., sect. =section
Sept. =September
Sp. (*or* Span.) =Spanish
sq. mi. =square miles
SS. =Saints
SSE =south-southeast
SSR =Soviet Socialist Republic
SSW =south-southwest
St. =Saint, Street
Ste =*Sainte* (Saint, feminine)
SW =southwest
Swed. =Swedish
temp. =temperature
Tenn. =Tennessee
T.H. =Territory of Hawaii
TVA =Tennessee Valley Authority
UN, U.N. =United Nations
Univ. =University
U. of So. Afr. =Union of South Africa
U.S. =United States
USSR =Union of Soviet Socialist Republics
Va. =Virginia
V.I. =Virgin Islands
Vt. =Vermont
W =West
Wash. =Washington
Wis. =Wisconsin
WNW =west-northwest
WSW =west-southwest
W.Va. =West Virginia
Wyo. =Wyoming
yd. =yard, yards

KEY TO PRONUNCIATION

ā f*a*te (fāt), f*ai*l (fāl), v*a*c*a*tion (vākā′shu̇n)

â c*a*re (kâr), M*a*ry (mâ′rē)

ă b*a*t (băt), *a*dd (ăd), m*a*rry (mă′rē)

ä f*a*ther (fä′dhu̇r), m*a*rble (mär′bu̇l)

ã French t*an*t (tã), C*aen* (kã), and similar sounds in some other languages

b *b*ack (băk), ca*b* (kăb)

ch *ch*ap (chăp)

d *d*ock (dŏk), co*d* (kŏd)

dh fa*th*er (fä′dhu̇r), *th*en (dhĕn). Compare with th.

ē *e*ven (ē′vu̇n), cl*ea*ring (klēr′ĭng), obv*i*ous (ŏb′vēu̇s)

ĕ *e*nd (ĕnd), m*e*t (mĕt), m*e*rry (mĕ′rē)

ẽ French v*in* (vẽ), bi*en* (byẽ), and similar sounds in some other languages

f *f*at (făt), *Ph*ilip (fĭ′lĭp)

g *g*et (gĕt), ta*g* (tăg)

h *h*at (hăt). See also ch, dh, kh, sh, th, zh, and hw.

hw *wh*ere (hwâr), *wh*at (hwŏt)

ī f*i*ne (fīn), bu*y*er (bī′u̇r)

ĭ p*i*n (pĭn), p*i*t (pĭt), sp*i*r*i*t (spĭ′rĭt), fat*e*d (fā′tĭd)

j *j*am (jăm), e*dg*e (ĕj), *g*in*g*er (jĭn′ju̇r)

k coo*k* (ko͝ok), ta*ck*le (tă′ku̇l)

kh lo*ch* (lŏkh), German Aa*ch*en (ä′khu̇n), Li*ch*t (lĭkht), and similar sounds in some other languages

l pea*l* (pēl), pu*ll* (po͝ol)

m ha*mm*er (hă′mu̇r)

n di*nn*er (dĭ′nu̇r)

ng si*ng*i*ng* (sĭng′ĭng), fi*ng*er (fĭng′gu̇r), sa*ng* (săng), sa*n*k (săngk)

ō h*o*pe (hōp), potat*o* (pu̇tā′tō)

ô *o*rbit (ôr′bĭt), f*a*ll (fôl)

ŏ h*o*t (hŏt), t*o*ddy (tŏ′dē), b*o*rrow (bŏ′rō)

õ French d*ont* (dõ), chans*on* (shãsõ′), and similar sounds in some other languages

oi b*oi*l (boil), r*oy*al (roi′u̇l)

o͞o b*oo*t (bo͞ot), l*o*se (lo͞oz)

o͝o f*oo*t (fo͝ot), p*u*rely (pyo͝or′lē), manip*u*late (mu̇nĭ′pyo͝olāt)

ou sc*ou*t (skout), cr*ow*d (kroud)

p *p*i*p*e (pīp), ha*pp*y (hă′pē)

r *r*oad (rōd), appea*r*ed (u̇pērd′), ca*r*pente*r* (kär′pu̇ntu̇r)

s *s*aw (sô), ca*s*e (kās)

sh *sh*all (shăl), na*ti*on (nā′shu̇n)

t *t*ight (tīt), ra*t*ing (rā′tĭng)

th *th*in (thĭn), my*th* (mĭth). Compare with dh.

ū f*u*me (fūm), *eu*phemism (ū′fu̇mĭ″zu̇m)

û c*u*rl (kûrl), Hamb*u*rg (hăm′bûrg), French *œu*vre (û′vru̇), p*eu* (pû), German sch*ö*n (shûn), G*oe*the (gû′tu̇), and similar sounds in some other languages

ŭ b*u*tter (bŭ′tu̇r), s*u*ds (sŭdz), h*u*rry (hŭ′rē)

u̇ *a*ffair (u̇fâr′), sōf*a* (sō′fu̇), contr*a*vene (kŏntru̇vēn′), m*o*nop*o*ly (mu̇nŏ′pu̇lē), s*u*burb*a*n (su̇bûr′bu̇n), call*ou*s (kă′lu̇s), rath*e*r (ră′dhu̇r)

ü French Cl*u*ny (klünē′), German L*ü*beck (lü′bĕk), and similar sounds in some other languages

ũ French Mel*un* (mu̇lũ′), Chambr*un* (shãbrũ′), and similar sounds in some other languages

v *v*est (vĕst), tri*v*ial (trĭ′vēu̇l)

w *w*ax (wăks)

y *y*ou (yo͞o), bun*i*on (bŭ′nyu̇n)

z *z*ipper (zĭ′pu̇r), ea*s*e (ēz), tread*s* (trĕdz)

zh plea*s*ure (plĕ′zhu̇r), a*z*ure (ă′zhu̇r)

′ primary accent, written after the vowel or syllable carrying the main stress: Nebraska (nu̇bră′sku̇), Kansas (kăn′zu̇s)

″ secondary accent: Cheltenham (chĕl′tu̇nhăm″), Colchester (kōl′chĕ″stu̇r)

– dash, replacing obvious portion of pronunciation: Ismailia (ĭz″mäĭlē′ä, ĭs″–, ēs″–, –mā–)

- hyphen, to prevent ambiguity: Erlanger (ûr′lăng-u̇r), Lachine (lu̇-shēn′)

NOTES. Pronunciation is indicated in parentheses, using the symbols above. The purpose is to give at least one acceptable way in which the name may be pronounced; but the pronunciation is omitted in many instances where it will be obvious to the English-speaking reader.

Secondary accent marks are frequently left out where their omission does not cause any ambiguity—where, for example, a native speaker of English automatically pronounces with subsidiary stress.

Where two or more names listed in succession are spelled and pronounced alike the pronunciation is ordinarily indicated for the first occurrence only.

For names of localities or geographical features in English-speaking areas the local usage of careful speakers is given preference. However, the pronunciation as shown here is normalized, for the most part, so as not to reflect mere dialect variations.

For foreign names the speaker of English desires to use a pronunciation that will be acceptable to other speakers of English (unless he is speaking in a foreign language). In many cases (e.g., Paris) there is a traditional pronunciation that resembles little the current native pronunciation, and attempts to introduce into English conversation an approximation of the native form (something like pärē′) are regarded as an affectation. It is customary with foreign names that have no conventional English form to pronounce them with English sounds approximating the foreign ones. Such an approximation is indicated in this work, whenever there is no established usage to follow.

Actual good foreign-language pronunciations can be acquired only through imitation and study. Nevertheless, Englishmen and Americans have for many years made a practice of imitating roughly five French sounds: ã, ẽ, õ, ũ, and ü. A speaker of English can attain ã by saying äng without the closure at the back of the mouth necessary to make ng, breathing through nose and mouth as well; ẽ is similarly like the beginning of ăng, õ like that of ōng, and ũ like that of ûng. To approximate ü say o͞o with vigor, then, keeping the lips rounded, change the sound quickly to ē.

The sounds here symbolized by kh are produced very much like k, though without stoppage of breath; k may be used as a substitute sound, thus lŏk instead of lŏkh, ä′ku̇n for ä′khu̇n.

For Latin names the venerable English tradition is followed [e.g., Caesar (sē′zu̇r)].

A

A (ô), Nor. *Å*. **1** Fishing village (pop. 351) in Moskenes canton, Nordland co., N Norway, on E Moskenesoy of Lofoten Isls., 50 mi. SW of Svolvaer. Sometimes spelled Aa. Formerly Aag. **2** Village in Afjord (Nor. *Åfjord*) canton (pop. 2,676), Sor-Trondelag co., central Norway, port at head of A Fjord, 36 mi. N of Trondheim; agr., lumbering, fishing; boatbuilding. Sometimes spelled Aa.

Aa, Norway: see A.

Aa, river: see AA RIVER.

Aabenraa (ô′bŭnrô′), Ger. *Apenrade*, city (1950 pop. 13,017) and port, ⊙ Aabenraa dist. of Aabenraa-Sonderborg amt, S Jutland, Denmark, on Aabenraa Fjord and 45 mi. SW of Odense; machine shops, brewery, organ factory. After 1864 in Germany until 1920 plebiscite.

Aabenraa Fjord, inlet of the Little Belt, S Jutland, Denmark; 2 mi. wide, max. depth c.145 ft.; Aabenraa city at head.

Aabenraa-Sonderborg (-sûn′ürbôr), Dan. *Aabenraa-Sønderborg*, amt (□ 475; 1950 pop. 94,051), S Jutland, Denmark; has Aabenraa dist. (□ 305; pop. 46,909; ⊙ Aabenraa) and Sonderborg dist. (□ 170; pop. 47,142; ⊙ Sonderborg); latter includes ALS isl. Agr., livestock, beekeeping. After 1864 region was in Germany until 1920 plebiscite.

Aach (äkh), village (pop. 1,007), S Baden, Germany, on AACH RIVER and 6 mi. N of Singen; cotton mfg. Danube water seeping away at Immendingen here reappears as powerful spring.

Aachen (ä′khŭn) or **Aix-la-Chapelle** (āks′-lä-shŭpĕl′, Fr. ĕks″-lä-shäpĕl′), city (1939 pop. 162,164; 1946 pop. 110,462; 1950 pop. 129,967), in former Prussian Rhine Prov., W Germany, after 1945 in North Rhine-Westphalia, 38 mi. WSW of Cologne, 77 mi. E of Brussels; 50°47′N 6°5′E. Rail hub near Belgian and Dutch borders; main entry point into Germany from W Europe; commercial and industrial center situated in coal-mining region. Noted spa, with warm sulphur springs frequented since Roman times. Mfg. of railroad cars, electric motors, machinery, needles, aniline dyes, light bulbs, textiles; food processing. It was coronation city of Ger. kings until 1531. Noted cathedral, founded by Charlemagne and containing his tomb, was rebuilt in 10th cent. Retaining parts of original structure, with later Gothic additions, it was relatively little damaged in Second World War, which devastated almost all other noteworthy bldgs. (total damage about 85%). Most churches, including 12th-cent. St. Folian's, 14th-cent. St. Nicholas', and 15th-cent. St. Paul's were demolished or heavily damaged. Gothic town hall, built on site of Charlemagne's palace and containing Emperor's Hall with noted frescoes, was badly damaged, as were the historical mus. and the 20th-cent. casino. Has technical acad., institute of engineering, conservatory for church music. Aachen, the Roman *Aquis Granum*, rose to prominence as favorite residence of Charlemagne and as his N capital. Created free imperial city c.1250; was scene of numerous important diets and, since 17th cent., of a number of peace conferences (e.g., treaty in 1668 ended War of Devolution; treaty in 1748 ended War of the Austrian Succession). Under Fr. rule after 1792, it was annexed in 1801 by France, who held it until Congress of Vienna (1814–15), when it was given to Prussia. Occupied by Allies, 1918–30. The 1st important Ger. city to be captured in Second World War, Aachen fell (Oct., 1944) to U. S. troops after days of bitter fighting.

Aach River (äkh), S Baden, Germany, rises 5 mi. N of Aach, flows 25 mi. S and E, past Singen, into the Zeller See 1.5 mi. W of Radolfzell.

Aadal, canton, Norway: see HEN.

Aadal River, Norway: see BEGNA RIVER.

Aadalsbruk, Norway: see ADALSBRUK.

Aafjord, Norway: see A FJORD.

Aag, Norway: see A, in Nordland co.

Aakirkeby (ô″kĭrkûbü′), city (pop. 1,625), Bornholm amt, Denmark, on SW Bornholm isl.; granite and black marble quarrying. Black marble church dates partly from 12th cent.

Aakra and **Aakrahavn**, Norway: see AKRAHAMN.

Aakrahamn, Norway: see AKRAHAMN.

Aal, Norway: see AL.

Aalborg (ôl′bôr), amt (□ 1,129; 1950 pop. 225,394), N Jutland, Denmark, containing most of HIMMERLAND region and small area N of Lim Fjord; ⊙ Aalborg. Other cities: Norre Sundby, Logstor. N part is low, S more hilly (highest point, 374 ft.). Soil not very fertile; large moor and forest area.

Aalborg, fourth largest city (1950 pop. 79,806) in Denmark, ⊙ Aalborg amt, N Jutland, on S Lim Fjord and 60 mi. NNW of Aarhus; 57°3′N 9°55′E. Mfg. (cement, textiles, spirits, machinery, tobacco products); port (shipyard) and airport. A 1,900-ft. pontoon bridge (Christian IX Bridge) leads across fjord to Norre Sundby. Naval school, 14th-cent. church; seat of Lutheran bishop. One of oldest cities in Denmark; dates at least from early 11th cent.

Aaland Islands, Finland: see ALAND ISLANDS.

Aalen (ä′lŭn), town (pop. 21,941), Württemberg, Germany, after 1945 in Württemberg-Baden, at N foot of Swabian Jura, on the Kocher and 30 mi. N of Ulm; 48°51′N 10°7′E. Rail transshipment point; mfg. of machinery, safes, steel furniture, nails, textiles, pharmaceuticals, candy. Pottery- and brickworks. Has 17th-cent. town hall, 18th-cent. church. Developed around Roman settlement. Created free imperial city 1360. Devastated by fire 1634.

Aalen, Norway: see ALEN.

Aalestrup (ôl′ŭstrōōp), town (pop. 1,483), Viborg amt, N Jutland, Denmark, 17 mi. N of Viborg; meat packing, mfg. (furniture, bicycles).

Aalesund, Norway: see ALESUND.

Aalfotbrae, Norway: see ALFOTBRE.

Aalgaard, Norway: see ALGARD.

Aalsmeer (äls′mār), village (pop. 10,142), North Holland prov., W Netherlands, on the Ringvaart and 10 mi. SW of Amsterdam; nursery center for flowers; lake fishing, mfg. (flower pots, artificial marble).

Aalst, Belgium: see ALOST.

Aalten (äl′tŭn), town (pop. 6,400), Gelderland prov., E. Netherlands, 6 mi. WSW of Winterswijk, near Ger. border; mfg. (combs, brushes, pipes), cotton weaving.

Aalter (äl′tŭr), village (pop. 7,110), East Flanders prov., NW Belgium, 12 mi. WNW of Ghent; textile mfg.; cattle, agr. Formerly spelled Aeltere.

Aalvik, Norway: see ALVIK.

Aamdals Verk, Norway: see AMDALS VERK.

Aamli, Norway: see AMLI.

Aandalsnes, Norway: see ANDALSNES.

Äänekoski (ă′nĕkōs″kē), town (pop. 6,009), Vaasa co., S central Finland, at S end of L. Keitele, 25 mi. N of Jyväskylä; lumber, pulp, cellulose, and paper mills; woodworking.

Aar, Switzerland: see AAR RIVER.

Aarau (ä′rou), town (1950 pop. 14,295), ⊙ Aargau canton, N Switzerland, on Aar R., at foot of the Jura, 23 mi. W of Zurich. Metalworking (electrical goods, bells, mathematical instruments), printing; shoes, flour, pastry, cotton textiles. Hydroelectric plant. Large cantonal library, several museums, late-Gothic church, town hall (18th cent.), medieval towers.

Aarburg (är′bōōrk), town (pop. 2,932), Aargau canton, N Switzerland, on Aar R. and 2 mi. S of Olten; cotton textiles, knit goods, leather; woodworking. Has 11th-cent. castle.

Aardal, Norway: see ARDALSTANGEN.

Aardenburg (är′dŭnbûrkh), town (pop. 1,260), Zeeland prov., SW Netherlands, on Flanders mainland, 10 mi. SSW of Breskens, near Belg. border; stone quarrying, dairying. Site (1672) of stubborn Dutch defense against French. Trade center in 19th cent.

Aare River, Switzerland: see AAR RIVER.

Aargau (är′gou), Fr. *Argovie* (ärgôvē′), canton (□ 542; 1950 pop. 300,442), N Switzerland; ⊙ Aarau. Traversed by Aar and Reuss rivers; has fertile valleys (cereals, orchards) and wooded hills. Hydroelectric system along the Rhine (highest capacity plant at Ryburg). Health resorts at BADEN, RHEINFELDEN. Metal products, textiles, clothes, foodstuffs; saltmining in NW. Pop. German speaking and largely Protestant. Became a canton 1803.

Aarhus (ôr′hōōs), amt (□ 310; 1950 pop. 198,267), E Jutland, Denmark, on the Kattegat; ⊙ Aarhus. Fertile agr. lowland, with industry and ¾ of pop. in Aarhus city and suburbs.

Aarhus, 2d largest city (1950 pop. 116,167) in Denmark, ⊙ Aarhus amt, E Jutland, on Aarhus Bay and 95 mi. WNW of Copenhagen; 56°9′N 10°13′E. Seaport, commercial and industrial center, rail junction. Mfg. of iron, machinery, tobacco products, candy; oil refining, meat packing, brewing. Seat of bishop (now Lutheran) since at least 12th cent. The 13th-cent cathedral has been rebuilt several times. Aarhus Univ. was opened 1928.

Aarhus Bay, inlet (c.50 ft. deep) of the Kattegat, E Jutland, Denmark; bounded S by Tuno isl., with Kalvo Bay on N, Begtrup Bay on E.

Aa River (ä), N France, rises in Artois hills 8 mi. W of Fauquembergues, flows NE to Arques (junction with Neuffossé Canal), thence NW, past Saint-Omer, forming Nord–Pas-de-Calais dept. border, to North Sea at Grand-Fort-Philippe, just below Gravelines. Length, c.50 mi.

Aa River. 1 or **Kurische Aa** [Ger.,=Courland Aa], Latvia: see LIELUPE RIVER. **2** or **Livländische Aa** [Ger.,=Livonian Aa], Latvia: see GAUJA RIVER.

Aa River, North Brabant prov., S Netherlands, rises NE of Weert, flows NW, parallel to the Zuid-Willemsvaart, past Helmond, to Dommel R. at 's Hertogenbosch.

Aa River, name of several rivers in Switzerland, including: in Aargau canton, a tributary of the Aar, traversing the Hallwilersee; in Schwyz canton, an influx of L. of Zurich, draining the WÄGGITAL; in Unterwalden canton, the SARNER AA and the Engelberger Aa, both flowing to L. of Lucerne.

Aarlanderveen (är′ländŭrvān), village (pop. 383), South Holland prov., W Netherlands, 9 mi. N of Gouda; brick mfg.; cattle raising, dairying, agr.

Aarlen, Belgium: see ARLON.

Aarlifoss, Norway: see ARLIFOSS.

Aaro (ô′rû), Dan. *Aarø*, island (□ 2.2; pop. 310) in the Little Belt, Denmark, 4 mi. ESE of mouth of Haderslev Fjord; agr. In Germany until 1920.

Aar River (är) or **Aare River** (är′ŭ), longest (183 mi.) stream entirely in Switzerland, rising in Bernese Alps and flowing to the Rhine opposite Waldshut, Germany. Emerging from Grimsel L., which is fed by Oberaar Glacier and by Unteraar Glacier (formed by Lauteraar and Finsteraar glaciers), it flows N, past Meiringen; thence W, through L. of Brienz, past Interlaken, and through L. of Thun; thence NW, past Thun and Bern (here dammed to form the Wohlensee). It enters L. Biel as Hagneck Canal and leaves it (NE) as Aar Canal at Nidau (its old, natural bed, called the Alte Aare, parallels E shore of lake), thence generally NE, past Solothurn, Olten, and Aarau, to the Rhine. The Aar is navigable from the Rhine to Thun. Number of hydroelectric plants are on it. Scenic Gorge of the Aar, Ger. *Aareschlucht* or *Aarelamm*, is at Meiringen.

Aars (ôrs), town (pop. 2,562), Aalborg amt, N Jutland, Denmark, 22 mi. SW of Aalborg; meat packing; cigars, margarine.

Aarschot (är′skhōt), town (pop. 10,611), Brabant prov., N central Belgium, on Demer R. and 9 mi. NE of Louvain; market center for vegetable-growing dist.; brewing. Has 14th-cent. church. Formerly spelled Aerschot.

Aartrijke (är′trī″kŭ), town (pop. 4,346), West Flanders prov., NW Belgium, 9 mi. SW of Bruges; agr. market (grain, stock).

Aarup (ô′rōōp), town (pop. 1,067), Odense amt, Denmark, on Fyn isl. and 13 mi. W of Odense; machinery mfg., wine.

Aarwangen (är′väng-ŭn), town (pop. 2,235), Bern canton, NW Switzerland, on Aar R. and 11 mi. E of Solothurn; woolen textiles.

Aas, Norway: see As.

Aasen, Norway: see ASEN.

Aaseral, Norway: see ASERAL.

Aasgaardstrand, Norway: see ASGARDSTRAND.

Aasvaer, Norway: see ASVAER.

Aat, Belgium: see ATH.

Aavasaksa (ä′väsäk″sä), village in Ylitornio commune (pop. 8,246), Lapi co., NW Finland, on Torne R. (Swedish border) and 40 mi. NNW of Tornio; agr., lumbering. Just E is Aavasaksa hill (728 ft.), tourist spot known for its fine view of the midnight sun. Sometimes Avasaksa.

Ab [Persian,=water, river], for names beginning thus and not found here: see under following part of the name.

Aba (ä′bä), village (1948 pop. 4,101), Eastern Prov., NE Belgian Congo, on Congo-Nile road and 165 mi. NNE of Irumu, in cotton and cattle area; trading center and customs station on Anglo-Egyptian Sudan border; repair shops for motor vehicles; rice processing. Has R.C. and Protestant missions, hosp. for Europeans.

Aba (ŏ′bŏ), town (pop. 4,199), Fejer co., W central Hungary, 12 mi. SSE of Szekesfehervar; wheat, corn, beans, dairy.

Aba (ä′bä), town (pop. 12,958), Owerri prov., Eastern Provinces, S Nigeria, on railroad and 35 mi. NE of Port Harcourt; road and trade center; palm oil and kernels, kola nuts; soap mfg. Scene of native women's riots, 1929–30.

Abacaxis River (äbŭkŭshēs′), E Amazonas, Brazil, flows c.200 mi. N to a right arm of the Amazon 80 mi. WSW of Maués.

Abaco or **Abaco and Cays**, district, Bahama Isls.: see GREAT ABACO ISLAND.

Abadan (ä″bŭdän′, äbädän′), town (1940 pop. 39,739), Sixth Prov., in Khuzistan, SW Iran, port on the Shatt al Arab (Iraq line) 30 mi. from the head of the Persian Gulf, and 30 mi. ESE of Basra; 30°20′N 48°18′E. One of world's leading oil-refining and -shipping centers, situated on N end of 40-mi.-long Abadan isl. in Shatt al Arab delta; linked by highway with Ahwaz and by pipe lines with the near-by oil fields of Khuzistan (Lali, Masjid-i-Sulaiman, Haft Kel, Agha Jari, Gach Saran); airport. Refinery and 1st pipe line were begun 1909–10, completed 1913.

Abadeh (äbädĕ'), town (1940 pop. 7,448), Seventh Prov., in Fars, S central Iran, 110 mi. N of Shiraz and on highway to Isfahan; grain, cotton, opium, fruit. Rugmaking, woodworking.

Abades (ävä'dhĕs), town (pop. 1,036), Segovia prov., central Spain, 9 mi. WSW of Segovia; cereals, livestock.

Abadia dos Dourados (äbûdē'ŭ dōōs dōrä'dōōs), town (pop. 923), W Minas Gerais, Brazil, 10 mi. W of Coromandel; rubies found here.

Abadla (äbädlä'), Saharan village, Aïn-Sefra territory, W Algeria, 50 mi. SW of Colomb-Béchar. Southernmost point reached by trans-Saharan railroad (completed to Colomb-Béchar and Kenadsa; construction of Kenadsa-Abadla strip halted in 1943).

Abadszalok (ŏ'bät-tsŏlōk), Hung. *Abádszalók*, town (pop. 7,620), Jasz-Nagykun-Szolnok co., E central Hungary, on Tisza R. and 19 mi. NW of Karcag; sawmill; fishing; agr. (corn, wheat), cattle.

Aba el Waqf or **Aba al-Waqf** (both: ä'bäl-wäkf'), village (pop. 10,685), Minya prov., Upper Egypt, on railroad and 35 mi. N of Minya; cotton ginning, woolen and sugar milling; cereals.

Abaeté (äbĭtĕ'). **1** City (pop. 3,822), W central Minas Gerais, Brazil, near upper São Francisco R., 100 mi. NW of Belo Horizonte; diamond washing. Platinum and lead deposits. **2** City, Pará, Brazil: see ABAETETUBA.

Abaetetuba (ûbĭtĭtōō'bù), city (pop. 3,054), E Pará, Brazil, port near right bank of Pará R. (Amazon delta), 27 mi. SW of Belém; mfg. of shoes, tiles; alcohol distilling, rice cleaning, vegetable-oil processing. Airfield. Road to Moju. Until 1944, Abaeté.

Abaiang (äbī'äng) or **Apia** (ä'pē'ä), atoll (□ 11; pop. 2,823), N Gilbert Isls., W central Pacific, in Br. colony of Gilbert and Ellice Isls.; 1°49'N 172°57'E. Produces copra. In Second World War, occupied (Dec., 1941) by Japanese, regained (Nov., 1943) by U.S. Formerly Charlotte Isl.

Abai-Bazar or **Abay-Bazar** (ŭbī"-bŭzär'), village (1939 pop. over 500), S South Kazakhstan oblast, Kazakh SSR, near Uzbek SSR border, c.20 mi. SW of Saryagach; cotton.

Abajo Mountains (ă'bûhō), SE Utah, near Colo. line, E of Colorado R., N of Blanding. Abajo Peak (11,357 ft.), highest point, is 7 mi. WSW of Monticello. Range lies within section of La Sal Natl. Forest.

Abak (äbäk'), town (pop. 1,365), Calabar prov., Eastern Provinces, SE Nigeria, 15 mi. SSE of Ikot Ekpene; road center; palm oil and kernels, cacao, kola nuts.

Abakaliki (äbäkä'lēkē), town (pop. 4,307), Ogoja prov., Eastern Provinces, SE Nigeria, 40 mi. ESE of Enugu; silver and lead-zinc mining center; palm oil and kernels, kola nuts. Limestone and salt deposits.

Abakan (ŭbŭkän'), city (1939 pop. 36,135), ⊙ Khakass Autonomous Oblast, Krasnoyarsk Territory, Russian SFSR, on Yenisei R., on S.Siberian RR and 150 mi. SSW of Krasnoyarsk; 53°43'N 91°20'E. Terminus of branch railroad from Achinsk; sawmilling, meat processing, metalworking. Teachers col. Site of Bronze Age tumuli and Turkic inscriptions. Founded 1707 as fortress. Known as Ust-Abakanskoye until 1931, when it became a city.

Abakan Range, part of Kuznetsk Ala-Tau mtn. system, in S Siberian Russian SFSR; forms border bet. Khakass Autonomous Oblast and Kemerovo oblast; extends 125 mi. NE from Teletskoye L.; highest point, 8,000 ft. Forms divide bet. upper Ob and Yenisei river basins.

Abakan River, SE Khakass Autonomous Oblast, Krasnoyarsk Territory, Russian SFSR, rises in 2 headstreams in Altai Mts. in S oblast, flows 350 mi. NE to Yenisei R. just S of Abakan.

Abakanskoye, Russian SFSR: see KRASNOTURANSK.

Abakansko-Zavodskoye, Russian SFSR: see ABAZA.

Abakrampa (äbäkräm'pä), town, Western Prov., S Gold Coast colony, 10 mi. N of Cape Coast; lime-growing center; lime-juice extracting.

Abal, Yemen: see UBAL.

Abalá (äbälä'), town (pop. 632), Yucatan, SE Mexico, 22 mi. S of Mérida; henequen.

Abalakskoye (ŭbŭläk'skŭyŭ), village, S Tyumen oblast, Russian SFSR, on Irtysh R. and 14 mi. SE of Tobolsk, near site of anc. Sibir; former monastery.

Aballo, France: see AVALLON.

Abalti (äbäl'tē), village, Kaffa prov., SW Ethiopia, near Omo R., 65 mi. NE of Jimma; cotton growing.

Aban (ŭbän'), village (1948 pop. over 500), S Krasnoyarsk Territory, Russian SFSR, 35 mi. NNE of Kansk, in agr. area; lumbering, metalworking.

Abana, Syria: see BARADA.

Abana (ä'bänä"), village (pop. 734), Kastamonu prov., N Turkey, port on Black Sea, 45 mi. NNE of Kastamonu; grain, hemp.

Abancay (äbängkī'), city (pop. 5,789), ⊙ Apurímac dept. and Abancay prov. (□ 1,012; pop. 39,218), S central Peru, on affluent of Apurímac R., at S foot of Cerro Jayuri, on road to Cuzco, and 300 mi. ESE of Lima; 13°35'S 72°55'W; alt. 7,871 ft. Sugar-growing and -milling center; copper mining, liquor and rum distilling; sericulture. It was a leading commercial city during colonial era.

Abangares, canton, Costa Rica: see LAS JUNTAS.

Abangares River (äbäng-gä'rĕs), NW Costa Rica, rises in the Cordillera de Guanacaste, flows 25 mi. SW, through rich gold-mining area, past Gongolona, La Sierra, and Las Juntas, to upper Gulf of Nicoya W of Manzanillo.

Abânico Dam (äbä'nēkō), Bío-Bío prov., S central Chile, in the Andes, on upper Laja R. and 90 mi. SE of Concepción; major hydroelectric plant supplies steel mills of Talcahuano and Concepción.

Abanilla (ävänē'lyä), town (pop. 3,026), Murcia prov., SE Spain, 16 mi. NNE of Murcia; esparto-growing and -processing center; olive pressing, flour milling. Wine, fruit, almonds. Mineral springs. Clay and marble quarries near by.

Abano Terme (ä'bänō tĕr'mĕ), town (pop. 1,232), Padova prov., Veneto, N Italy, 5 mi. SW of Padua. Health resort noted for its hot sulphur waters (up to 189° F.) and mud baths; plant nurseries, bottling works. In near-by Euganean Hills is a large Benedictine abbey (Convento di Praglia) founded 1080.

Abanto y Ciérvana (ävän'tō ē thyĕr'vänä), iron-mining area, Vizcaya prov., N Spain, c.10 mi. NW of Bilbao. Chief town, Gallarta (pop. 2,852).

Abapó (äbäpō'), village (pop. c.400), Santa Cruz dept., E central Bolivia, port on Río Grande, at road crossing, and 6 mi. SW of Cabezas. Former Franciscan mission.

Abarán (ävärän'), town (pop. 6,145), Murcia prov., SE Spain, on Segura R. and 3 mi. SE of Cieza; esparto processing (rope), fruit-conserve and marmalade mfg., sawmilling. Orange and lemon groves; cereals, olive oil, wine. Sheep raising.

Abaroa, Bolivia: see CHALLAPATA.

Abarqu or **Abarquh** (äbärkōō'), town (1930 pop. estimate 16,000), Tenth Prov., in Yezd, central Iran, 85 mi. SW of Yezd and on Yezd-Shiraz road; grain, opium, tobacco, cotton; goat raising. Hand-woven cotton textiles.

Abasha (ŭbŭshä'), village (1939 pop. over 2,000), W Georgian SSR, in Colchis lowland, on railroad and 25 mi. W of Kutaisi; corn, soybeans; hogs.

Abashiri (ä"bä'shĭrē), city (1940 pop. 32,732; 1947 pop. 34,850), E Hokkaido, Japan, fishing port on Abashiri Bay, 95 mi. ENE of Asahigawa; commercial center for agr., stock-raising area. Port frequently icebound in winter. Sometimes spelled Abasiri.

Abashiri Bay, Jap. *Abashiri-wan*, inlet of Sea of Okhotsk, E Hokkaido, Japan; 30 mi. long, 10 mi. wide. Abashiri is on W, Shari on S shore. Formerly sometimes called Shari Bay.

Abasiri, Japan: see ABASHIRI, city.

Abasolo (äbäsō'lō). **1** Town (pop. 1,222), Coahuila, N Mexico, in E outliers of Sierra Madre Oriental, 20 mi. N of Monclova; coal mining. **2** or **Cuitzeo de Abasolo** (kwētsä'ō dā), town (pop. 5,115), Guanajuato, central Mexico, on central plateau, 20 mi. SW of Irapuato; alt. 5,643 ft.; corn-growing center. Miguel Hidalgo y Costilla b. (1753) near by. **3** Town (pop. 263), Nuevo León, N Mexico, and 20 mi. NW of Monterrey, on railroad; grain, livestock. **4** Town (pop. 379), Tamaulipas, NE Mexico, 55 mi. NE of Ciudad Victoria; sugar, cereals, livestock.

Abastumani (ŭbäs"tōōmä'nyē), town (1926 pop. 1,244), SW Georgian SSR, in Adzhar-Imeretian Range, 33 mi. S of Kutaisi (linked by highway); mtn. health resort (alt. 4,077 ft.) with hot springs; sawmills. Astrophysical observatory. Until 1936, spelled Abastuman, Abas-Tuman, or Abbas-Tuman.

Abatskoye (ŭbät'skŭyŭ), village (1948 pop. over 2,000), SE Tyumen Oblast, Russian SFSR, on Ishim R. and 40 mi. ENE of Ishim; dairy farming.

Abau (ŭbou'), town, Territory of Papua, SE New Guinea, on coast, 115 mi. SE of Port Moresby.

Abaucán River, Argentina: see COLORADO, RÍO.

Abauj (ŏ'bou-ē), Hung. *Abaúj*, county (□ 648; pop. 93,269), NE Hungary; ⊙ Szikszo. Mountainous (Cserehat Mts. in W, Tokaj-Eperjes Mts. in E); heavily forested; drained by Hernad R. Some agr. (barley, potatoes), livestock (cattle, sheep). Hungary's most sparsely populated co. Formerly called Abauj-Torna.

Abaujszanto (ŏ'bou-ĭsän'tō), Hung. *Abaújszántó*, town (pop. 4,908), Abauj co., NE Hungary, 22 mi. NE of Miskolc; wine-trading center; flour mill. Has 13th-cent. church.

Abaya, Lake (ä'bäyä), Ital. *Abbaia* (□ 485), S Ethiopia, in Great Rift Valley, bet. lakes Awusa and Chamo, 170 mi. SSW of Addis Ababa; 6°20'N 38°E; alt. 4,160 ft.; c.45 mi. long, 7–14 mi. wide. Contains many isls. (the largest c.7 mi. long), some inhabited by fishermen and hunters. Hot springs on N bank. Chief tributary, Billate R. (N). Drains into L. Chamo (3 mi. S) during periods of exceptional flood. S portion is called Nai Chaba. Discovered in 1896 by Italians and originally named L. Margherita after their Queen.

Abay-Bazar, Kazakh SSR: see ABAI-BAZAR.

Abaza (ŭbŭzä'), village (1939 pop. over 500), S Khakass Autonomous Oblast, Krasnoyarsk Territory, Russian SFSR, on Abakan R. and 90 mi. SW of Abakan; iron mines, metalworks. Formerly Abakansko-Zavodskoye.

Abbach (ä'bäkh), village (pop. 2,739), Lower Bavaria, Germany, on the Danube and 6 mi. SSW of Regensburg; summer resort with sulphur-mineral springs. Has ruins of anc. castle where Emperor Henry II was b. Chartered 1486. Lime- and sandstone quarries in area.

Abbadia San Salvatore (äb-bädē'ä sän sälvätô'rĕ), town (pop. 5,463), Siena prov., Tuscany, central Italy, on E slope of Monte Amiata, 25 mi. NW of Orvieto; ore-processing center for near-by mercury mines. Resort (alt. 2,720 ft.); mfg. (soap, cement).

Abbai, river, Ethiopia: see BLUE NILE.

Abbakumovo, Russian SFSR: see SHCHERBAKOV.

Abbasabad (äbäs"äbäd'), town, Second Prov., in Shahrud, NE Iran, 70 mi. W of Sabzawar and on highway to Shahrud; copper mining near by. Smelter projected here.

Abbasanta (äb-bäsän'tä), village (pop. 1,613), Cagliari prov., W central Sardinia, 19 mi. NNE of Oristano. Has dolmen and numerous nuraghi, including near-by Nuraghe Losa.

Abbas-Tuman, Georgian SSR: see ABASTUMANI.

Abbaye, Point, Mich.: see HURON BAY.

Abbazia, Yugoslavia: see OPATIJA.

Abbé, Lake (äbā'), or **Abhebad** (äbhĕbäd'), salt lake on Ethiopian–Fr. Somaliland border, 90 mi. WSW of Djibouti; 15 mi. long, 15 mi. wide. Receives Awash R.

Abbehausen (ä"bāhou'zŭn), village (commune pop. 8,001), in Oldenburg, NW Germany, after 1945 in Lower Saxony, 2 mi. W of Nordenham.

Abbendun, England: see ABINGDON.

Abbeville (äbvēl'), anc. *Abbatis Villa*, town (pop. 16,098), Somme dept., N France, on canalized Somme R. 12 mi. from its estuary on English Channel, and 25 mi. NW of Amiens; road center; sugar milling, locksmithing, mfg. of carpets, biscuits, beer. Town, including late-Gothic church of St. Wolfram, was heavily damaged in Second World War. Originally fortified in 10th cent. By a treaty signed here in 1259, Henry III of England relinquished his claims to Normandy, Anjou, Maine, Poitou, and Touraine. As ⊙ of Ponthieu it was in English hands 1272–1477. Cloth and carpet mfg., introduced by Colbert, gave town great prosperity in 17th cent.

Abbeville (ă'bēvĭl, -bĭ-), county (□ 509; pop. 22,456), NW S.C.; ⊙ Abbeville. Bounded by Savannah R. (W), Saluda R. (NE). Includes part of Sumter Natl. Forest. Piedmont agr. area (cotton, oats, corn), with some mfg. Formed 1785.

Abbeville. **1** City (pop. 2,162), ⊙ Henry co., SE Ala., 85 mi. SE of Montgomery, near Chattahoochee R., in cotton and corn area; lumber milling, cotton ginning. **2** City (pop. 890), ⊙ Wilcox co., S central Ga., 27 mi. E of Cordele, near Ocmulgee R., in agr. area; also lumber, naval stores. **3** Town (pop. 9,338), ⊙ Vermilion parish, S La., on Vermilion R. and 65 mi. SW of Baton Rouge; milling and distributing center for rice-growing area which also produces sugar cane, cotton, corn; cotton ginning, sugar milling; oil wells. Fur trapping. Fisheries, sea-food canneries. Grew around R.C. chapel built 1845 by the French; inc. 1850. **4** Village (1940 pop. 275), Lafayette co., N Miss., near Sardis Reservoir, 10 mi. N of Oxford. **5** City (pop. 5,395), ⊙ Abbeville co., NW S.C., 13 mi. W of Greenwood, in piedmont cotton area; textiles, clothing, grain products, cottonseed oil, beverages. Secessionist meeting held here Nov., 1860.

Abbey Craig, hill (362 ft.), NE Stirling, Scotland, 2 mi. NE of Stirling; site of monument to Sir William Wallace.

Abbeyfeale (ă"bēfēl'), Gaelic *Mainistir na Féile*, town (pop. 1,149), SW Co. Limerick, Ireland, on Feale R. and 9 mi. ESE of Listowel; dairying, cattle raising; grain, potatoes.

Abbey Green, Scotland: see LESMAHAGOW.

Abbeyleix (ă"bēläks'), Gaelic *Mainistir Laoighise*, town (pop. 522), S Co. Laoighis, Ireland, 9 mi. SSW of Port Laoighise; agr. market (wheat, barley, potatoes, beets). Abbey (no remains) founded here 1183.

Abbeyside, Ireland: see DUNGARVAN.

Abbey Works, Wales: see PORT TALBOT.

Abbi Addi, Ethiopia: see ABI ADDI.

Abbiategrasso (äb"byätĕgräs'sô), town (pop. 13,704), Milano prov., Lombardy, N Italy, near Ticino R., 14 mi. WSW of Milan. Agr. center; dairy and meat products, macaroni, candy, soap, fertilizer, alcohol, glassware.

Abbot, agr. and lumbering town (pop. 462), Piscataquis co., central Maine, on the Piscataquis and 10 mi. WNW of Dover-Foxcroft.

Abbots Bromley (ă'bŭts brŭm'lē), agr. village and parish (pop. 1,075), E central Stafford, England, 5 mi. NE of Rugely. Scene of annual fair (Sept.) at which the 400-year old Horn Dance or Dance of the Deer Men is performed. It is connected with the legend of Robin Hood.

Abbotsbury, agr. village and parish (pop. 552), S Dorset, England, 7 mi. NW of Weymouth. Has 15th-cent. tithe barn, ruins of 11th-cent. abbey. Center of monastic life until 16th cent.

Abbotsford, village (pop. 562), SW B.C., 6 mi. S of Mission across Fraser R.; rail junction. Dairying, clay quarrying, brick making, milk canning; fruit (strawberries, raspberries), hops.

Abbotsford, locality near Melrose, N Roxburgh, Scotland, on the Tweed and 3 mi. W of Melrose; site of estate (from 1811 to 1832) of Sir Walter Scott, with large mansion, containing many relics of the author, who died here.

Abbotsford, village (pop. 1,013), on Clark-Marathon co. line, central Wis., 34 mi. W of Wausau, in dairying region; railroad junction; dairy products, cigars.

Abbotshall, Scotland: see KIRKCALDY.

Abbots Langley (lăng'lē), residential town and parish (pop. 5,553), SW Hertford, England, 3 mi. N of Watford. Nicholas Breakspear (Pope Adrian IV) b. here. Church dates from 12th cent.

Abbotstown, agr. borough (pop. 538), Adams co., S Pa., 14 mi. WSW of York.

Abbott, town (pop. 345), Hill co., central Texas, 10 mi. S of Hillsboro, in cotton area.

Abbott, Mount (3,460 ft.), E Queensland, Australia, in Great Dividing Range, near Bowen, 80 mi. SE of Townsville.

Abbottabad (ăb'ŭtăbăd″), town (pop., including cantonment area, 27,424), ⊙ Hazara dist., NE North-West Frontier Prov., W Pakistan, 95 mi. ENE of Peshawar; hill resort; trade center (wheat, corn, barley, timber, cloth fabrics), hand-loom weaving (turbans), embroidering. Col.

Abbottsburg, town (1940 pop. 157), Bladen co., S N.C., 18 mi. SE of Lumberton.

Abbyville, city (pop. 99), Reno co., S central Kansas, 16 mi. WSW of Hutchinson; wheat.

Abcoude or **Abkoude** (both: äpkou'), town (pop. 1,776), Utrecht prov., W central Netherlands, 8 mi. SSE of Amsterdam; dairying.

Abdali or **'Abdali** (ăbdälē'), sultanate (pop. 25,000) and premier tribal area of Western Aden Protectorate; ⊙ Lahej. Situated just N of Aden Colony, it is one of most fertile agr. areas of the protectorate; produces grain, fruit (bananas, citrus fruit, mangoes), coconuts, sugar cane, sesame. Pop. is entirely settled. Formerly tributary to Yemen, the Abdali broke away in 1728, seized Aden, and remained independent until the arrival of the British in 1839. The treaty signed with the British in that year was the 1st of a series of agreements leading to the formation of Aden Protectorate. One of the original Nine Cantons, Abdali was occupied by the Turks during First World War. In 1948, the Subeihi tribal area (W) came under Abdali jurisdiction.

Abdalyar, Azerbaijan SSR: see LACHIN.

Abd-el-Kader (ăbdĕlkädär'), highest peak (5,344 ft.) of the Mitidja Atlas, in N central Algeria, overlooking Blida city and Mitidja lowland (N).

Abd el Kuri (ăb'dĕl kōō'rē), island (c.22 mi. long, 3 mi. wide) in Indian Ocean, 65 mi. WSW of Socotra isl., of which it is a dependency, and c.70 mi. ENE of Cape Guardafui; fisheries.

Abdera (ăbdēr'ŭ), anc. city of W Thrace, Greece, on Aegean Sea, E of Mesta R. mouth, in rich wheat lands. Founded 650 B.C. by Clazomenae and soon destroyed by Thracians, it was rebuilt c.500 B.C. by colonists from Teos. Flourished until it fell 352 B.C. to Macedon; became free city (198 B.C.) under Roman rule. The Abderites were considered by anc. Greeks as proverbially stupid; however, Gr. philosophers Protagoras and Democritus lived here 5th cent. B.C. The modern village of Avdera or Avdhira (1928 pop. 980) is 11 mi. SSE of Xanthe, NW of the ruins of the anc. city.

Abdera, Spain: see ADRA.

Abdie (ăb'dē), parish (pop. 670, including part of NEWBURGH burgh), NW Fifeshire, Scotland. Parish church (ruins) dates from 14th cent.

Abdulino (ŭbdōō'lyĭnŭ), city (1926 pop. 13,636), NW Chkalov oblast, Russian SFSR, near Ik R., 50 mi. ENE of Buguruslan; rail junction; W terminus of S.Siberian RR; flour-milling, grain-trading center; metalworking. Became city in 1923.

Abdul Khasib (ăb'dōōl khäsēb'), town, Basra prov., SE Iraq, 11 mi. ESE of Basra, on the Shatt al Arab.

Abdulla, Mount (ăbdōōl'lä) (9,751 ft.), Harar prov., E central Ethiopia, 20 mi. NNE of Harar.

Abdullahpur (ŭbdōōl'lŭpōōr) town (pop. 3,842), Meerut dist., NW Uttar Pradesh, India, 4 mi. E of Meerut; wheat, gram, jowar, sugar, oilseeds.

Abdullapur, village, Ambala dist., E Punjab, India, on Western Jumna Canal and 4 mi. S of Jagadhri; market center for sugar cane, wheat, rice, timber; sugar milling, pulp and paper milling, starch mfg.; iron products. Sometimes spelled Abdullahpur.

Abéché (äbāshā') or **Abécher** (ăbĕsh'ŭr, äbäshĕr'), town, ⊙ Ouadai region, E Chad territory, Fr. Equatorial Africa, 400 mi. ENE of Fort-Lamy; 13°27'N 20°49'E. Center of native trade (zebu cattle, sheep, horses, camels, millet, dried fish, hides, dates, salt, indigo) on main road to Darfur (Anglo-Egyptian Sudan); also camel caravans to Kufra oases and Benghazi (Cyrenaica). Karakul-sheep raising; stud farm. Customs station. Has military camp, veterinary center, hosp., mosque. Formerly (16th–19th cent) renowned as slave market. Gustav Nachtigal visited it in 1873. Pop. has greatly declined since Fr. occupation in 1913 (1900 pop. c.30,000; 1915 pop. 6,000). Sometimes spelled Abeshr.

Ab-e-Diz, Iran: see AB-I-DIZ.

'Abeih or **'Abayh** (äbā'), Fr. *Abey*, village, central Lebanon, near the coast, 10 mi. S of Beirut; sericulture, cereals, oranges. Once an important Druse religious center. An American school founded here 1866 was later moved to Beirut.

Abejar (ävähär'), town (pop. 764), Soria prov., N central Spain, on Burgos-Soria RR and 17 mi. W of Soria; cereals, livestock, timber, resins; sawmilling, flour milling. Limestone deposits.

Abejorral (äbähôräl'), town (pop. 4,665), Antioquia dept., NW central Colombia, in the Cordillera Central, 34 mi. SSE of Medellín; alt. 7,172 ft. Coffeegrowing center; corn, sugar cane, beans, yucca, bananas, wheat, potatoes, cattle, sheep.

Abelvaer (ä'bŭlvăr), village (pop. 245), in Naeroy (Nor. *Naerøy*) canton (pop. 2,315), Nord-Trondelag co., central Norway, on a small isl. (118 acres) 1 mi. off the mainland, 21 mi. NNW of Namsos; fisheries, canneries. Formerly spelled Apelvaer or Appelvaer.

Abemama (äbämä'mä) or **Apamama** (äpämä'mä), atoll (□ 6.5; pop. 1,174), N Gilbert Isls., W central Pacific, in Br. colony of Gilbert and Ellice Isls.; 22'N 173°53'E; coconuts, pandanus fruit. Site of govt. hosp. and airfield. In Second World War, occupied (Nov., 1943) by U.S. Formerly Roger Simpson Isl.

Abenberg (ä'bŭnbĕrk), town (pop. 2,311), Middle Franconia, W central Bavaria, Germany, 7 mi. SSW of Schwabach; gold and silver lacemaking, brewing. Hops, cattle. Chartered 1299. On near-by hill is 15th-cent. castle. Sandstone quarries.

Abengibre (ävĕng-hē'brā), town (pop. 1,118), Albacete prov., SE central Spain, 22 mi. NE of Albacete; saffron, hemp, cereals, wine.

Abengourou (äbĕng-gōō'rōō), town (pop. c.3,250), SE Ivory Coast, Fr. West Africa, near Gold Coast border, 100 mi. NNE of Abidjan; cacao, coffee, kola nuts, bananas, yams, manioc. Cacao research station. R.C. mission. Gold and diamond deposits near by.

Abenójar (ävänō'här), town (pop. 3,007), Ciudad Real prov., S central Spain, 25 mi. WSW of Ciudad Real; cereals, grapes, olives, timber, livestock. Silver and silver-bearing lead mines. Has noted stalagmite-stalactite caverns.

Abensberg (ä'bŭnsbĕrk), town (pop. 3,990), Lower Bavaria, Germany, on small Abens R. and 18 mi. SW of Regensburg; brewing, lumber and flour milling. Surrounded by partly preserved medieval wall; has late-Gothic church and town hall. Chartered c.1348. Here Napoleon defeated the Austrians in April, 1809.

Abeokuta (äbā'ōkōōtä), province (□ 4,266; pop. 434,526), Western Provinces, SW Nigeria; ⊙ Abeokuta. On Dahomey border (W) in equatorial forest belt; rain forest (S), deciduous forest (N); drained by Ogun R. Native textile industry (cotton weaving, indigo dyeing); processing of cacao, palm oil and kernels. Food crops: yams, corn, cassava, plantains. Phosphate deposits. Pop. is largely Yoruba. Main centers: Abeokuta and Ilaro. Formed 1914 from former Egba kingdom.

Abeokuta, city (pop. 45,763), ⊙ Abeokuta prov., Western Provinces, SW Nigeria, on Ogun R., on railroad (Aro station), and 50 mi. N of Lagos; 7°10'N 3°20'E. Major trade center, cotton weaving, indigo dyeing; cacao, palm oil and kernels, timber. Has hospitals. Sandstone quarry (SW). Founded c.1825 as refuge against native slave raiders, it became chief town of kingdom of Egba.

Aberaman (ăbŭră'mŭn), town (pop. 15,063) in Aberdare urban dist., NE Glamorgan, Wales, on Cynon R.; coal mining.

Aberarth, Wales: see ABERAYRON.

Aberastain or **Villa Aberastain** (vē'yä äbărästĭn'), town (pop. estimate 1,000), ⊙ Pocito dept. (□ 250; 1947 census pop. 17,697), S San Juan prov., Argentina, on railroad, in San Juan R. valley (irrigation area), 9 mi. SSW of San Juan. Wine- and fruitgrowing center.

Aberavon (ăbŭră'vŭn), town (pop. 16,848) in Port Talbot municipal borough, W central Glamorgan, Wales, on Swansea Bay of Bristol Channel; metallurgical industry, tinplate and cable mfg.

Aberayron (ăbŭrī'rŭn), urban district (1931 pop. 1,155; 1951 census 1,227), W Cardigan, Wales, on Cardigan Bay of Irish Sea, at mouth of Aeron R., 13 mi. SW of Aberystwyth; agr. market, seaside resort. Just NE is woolen-milling village of Aberarth (ăbŭrärth').

Aberbargoed, England: see BEDWELLTY.

Aberbrothock or **Aberbrothwick,** Scotland: see ARBROATH.

Abercarn (ăbŭrkärn'), urban district (1931 pop. 20,551; 1951 census pop. 18,757), W Monmouth, England, on Ebbw R. and 8 mi. NW of Newport; coal mining, tinplate mfg.; agr. market.

Aberchalder (ăbŭrkôl'dŭr), agr. village, central Inverness, Scotland, on shore of Loch Oich, on Oich R. and on Caledonian Canal, 4 mi. SW of Fort Augustus.

Aberchirder (ăbŭrkûr'dŭr), burgh (1931 pop. 868; 1951 census 800), NE Banffshire, Scotland, on Isla R. and 9 mi. SSW of Banff; agr. market.

Aberconway, Wales: see CONWAY.

Abercorn (ăbŭrkôrn'), village (pop. 201), S Que., on Missisquoi R. and 26 mi. SSE of Granby, near Vt. border; dairying.

Abercorn, township (pop. 1,420), Northern Prov., NE Northern Rhodesia, near S end of L. Tanganyika, 95 mi. N of Kasama; 8°50'S 31°22'E; alt. 5,400 ft. Major coffee center and tourist resort; dairy products, livestock. Experimental silkworm industry. Airfield. A former Br. trade post, established 1889. Was ⊙ former Tanganyika prov. Kalambo Falls are 20 mi. NNW.

Abercorn, agr. village and parish (pop. 775), N West Lothian, Scotland, on Firth of Forth, 3 mi. W of Queensferry.

Abercrombie (ă″bŭrkrŏm'bē), village (pop. 244), Richland co., SE N.Dak., 30 mi. S of Fargo and on Red River of the North. Fort Abercrombie State Park is on site of U.S. post established 1858. Sheyenne Natl. Forest is W.

Abercynon (ăbŭrkŭ'nŭn), town (pop. 8,956) in Mountain Ash urban dist., E Glamorgan, Wales, on Taff R. and 3 mi. NNE of Pontypridd; coal mining.

Aberdare (ăbŭrdâr'), urban district (1931 pop. 48,746; 1951 census 40,916), NE Glamorgan, Wales, on Cynon R. and 4 mi. SW of Merthyr Tydfil; anthracite mining, mfg. of electric cables. Has 13th-cent. church.

Aberdare Range, section of E rim of Great Rift Valley, in W central Kenya, NE of Naivasha and Gilgil, just S of the equator; alt. 12–13,000 ft.

Aberdeen (ăbŭrdēn'), town (pop. 1,072), E New South Wales, Australia, 70 mi. NW of Newcastle; coal-mining center.

Aberdeen, village (pop. 251), central Sask., 22 mi. NE of Saskatoon; wheat.

Aberdeen, Chinese *Shekpaiwan* (sĕk'bī'wän'), town, SW Hong Kong isl., on Aberdeen harbor, 2½ mi. S of Victoria; shipyards.

Aberdeen or **Aberdeenshire** (–shĭr), county (□ 1,971.1; 1931 pop. 300,436; 1951 census 308,055), NE Scotland; ⊙ Aberdeen. Bounded by Kincardine, Angus, and Perthshire (S), Inverness (SW), Banff (W and NW), and the North Sea (N and E). Drained by the Dee, Don, Deveron, Ugie, and Ythan rivers. Surface is mountainous in SW (Grampian and Cairngorm mts.), leveling toward coasts. Ben Macdhui (4,296 ft.) is highest peak; several other peaks are over 3,000 ft. high. Agr., Dee salmon fisheries, and North Sea herring and whitefish fisheries are important; other industries are granite quarrying, fish curing, and food-products mfg. In Dee valley are numerous tourist resorts, including Braemar (scene of noted Highland Games) and Ballater. Balmoral Castle is chief royal residence in Scotland. Besides Aberdeen, other towns are Peterhead, Fraserburgh, Huntly, Rosehearty, and Inverurie. Old Deer is associated with the "Book of Deer." In co. is site of battle of Harlaw. Near Ythan Wells was most northerly Roman station discovered in Britain. There are numerous anc. castle ruins.

Aberdeen, Lat. *Devana*, burgh (1931 pop. 167,258; 1951 census 182,714), ⊙ Aberdeenshire, Scotland, in SE part of co. and partly in NE Kincardine, on the North Sea at mouth of the Dee, 95 mi. NE of Edinburgh; 57°8'N 2°6'W. A co. of itself, it is chief port, commercial center, and largest city of NE Scotland. With a good harbor, it is major fishing port and fish-curing center. Other industries: woolen and paper milling, tanning, machinery mfg. Aberdeen is called the Granite City; granite quarries are near by and stone polishing is an important industry; many local bldgs. are of this stone. N part of city, Old Aberdeen, is on Don R. and includes King's Col. (founded 1494 by Bishop Elphinstone) of Aberdeen Univ., and the granite cathedral of St. Machar, founded c.1136, dating mostly from 14th cent. and later. The Don is crossed by 14th-cent. Bridge of Balgownie or Auld Brig o'Don. New part of city has Marischal Col. (founded 1593 by George Keith, earl marischal of Scotland), City Cross (1686), St. Nicholas Church (13th-16th cent.), and an art gall. and mus. Aberdeen was chartered a royal burgh in 1179; 2d charter was granted (1319) by Robert the Bruce. City was involved in numerous wars up to the 1745 rising. City's suburbs include Kittybrewster and Woodside (NW), with woolen and paper mills, and fishing port of Torry (S). Near Torry the Dee is crossed by Brig o'Dee, built (1520–27) by Bishop Dunbar; in 1639 Montrose forced passage here after defeating Covenanters. Aberdeen airport is at DYCE.

Aberdeen, village (1931 pop. 645), Sierra Leone colony, near NW point of Sierra Leone Peninsula, 3 mi. W of Freetown; fishing; cassava, corn.

Aberdeen, town (pop. 4,411), SE central Cape Prov., U. of So. Afr., on the Great Karroo, 30 mi. SW of Graaff Reinet; sheep-, cattle-raising center; scene of monthly stock fairs. Airfield.

Aberdeen (ă'bŭrdēn, ăbŭrdēn'). **1** Village (pop. 1,468), Bingham co., SE Idaho, 11 mi. N of American Falls, in region irrigated by near-by American Falls Reservoir; livestock, poultry, potatoes, sugar beets. **2** Town (pop. 2,944), Harford co., NE Md., near Chesapeake Bay, 28 mi. ENE of Baltimore.

Trade, residential town near Aberdeen Proving Ground (U.S. Army ordnance test center) and Army Chemical Center (including Edgewood Arsenal), together occupying c.87,000 acres along bay near here. Has canneries, metal-furniture plant. Settled c.1800, inc. 1892. **3** City (pop. 5,290), ⊙ Monroe co., E Miss., on Tombigbee R. at head of navigation, and 24 mi. NNW of Columbus, in agr. (cotton), dairying, and timber area; lumber, clothing, dairy products, cotton-seed products. A number of fine ante-bellum homes are here. Inc. 1837. **4** Town (pop. 1,603), Moore co., central N.C., 30 mi. W of Fayetteville; trade center; shipping point for tobacco, fruit, and truck area; mfg. of hosiery, insecticides. Inc. 1893. **5** Village (pop. 551), Brown co., SW Ohio, on the Ohio (bridged), opposite Maysville, Ky. **6** City (pop. 21,051), ⊙ Brown co., NE S.Dak., 120 mi. NE of Pierre, 10 mi. W of James R.; 45°30′N 98°30′W. Rail and wholesale distribution center; farm machinery, wood products; dairy produce, flour, wheat, barley, oats, corn. State teachers col., hosp., airport. Settled 1880, inc. 1882. **7** Port city (pop. 19,653), Grays Harbor co., W Wash., 65 mi. WSW of Tacoma, at confluence of Chehalis and Wishkah rivers, and on Grays Harbor; contiguous with HOQUIAM. A jr. col. is here. Lumber, wood products; fishing, fish canning. Port of entry. Settled c.1865, inc. 1890.

Aberdeen Falls, waterfall in Hatton Plateau, S central Ceylon, on right headstream of the Kelani Ganga and 8 mi. NW of Hatton; hydroelectric station planned here.

Aberdeen Lake (□ 475), W central Keewatin Dist., Northwest Territories; 64°30′N 99°W; 50 mi. long, 2–18 mi. wide; drained E by Thelon R.

Aberdeenshire, Scotland: see ABERDEEN, county.

Aberdour (ăbûrdour′). **1** Parish, Aberdeen, Scotland: see NEW ABERDOUR. **2** Seaside resort and parish (pop. 2,055), S Fifeshire, Scotland, on the Firth of Forth, 6 mi. SW of Kirkcaldy. Has partly Norman church of St. Fillan and ruins of 17th-cent. castle.

Aberdulais (ăbûrdĭ′lŭs), town in Tonna (tô′nä) parish (pop. 1,626), W central Glamorgan, Wales, on Neath R. and 2 mi. NE of Neath; tinplate mfg. Opposite, on Neath R., is residential town of Tonna.

Aberdyfi, Wales: see TOWYN.

Abererch (ăbûrĕrkh′), agr. village and parish (pop. 1,096), W Caernarvon, Wales, on Lleyn Peninsula, just NE of Pwllheli.

Aberfeldy (ăbûrfĕl′dē), burgh (1931 pop. 1,504; 1951 census 1,523), central Perthshire, Scotland, on the Tay (18th-cent. bridge) and 23 mi. NW of Perth; woolen milling, whisky distilling, bacon and ham curing. Just S are the Falls of Moness, on small Urlar R., noted for scenic beauty.

Aberffraw (ăbûrfrou′), agr. village and parish (pop. 790), S Anglesey, Wales, near Caernarvon Bay of Irish Sea, 9 mi. WNW of Caernarvon. Anc. residence of princes of North Wales.

Aberford, agr. market village and parish (pop. 600), West Riding, central Yorkshire, England, 8 mi. ENE of Leeds.

Aberfoyle (ăbûrfoil′), agr. village and parish (pop. 1,014), SW Perthshire, Scotland, 16 mi. W of Dunblane. Some scenes of Scott's *Rob Roy* are set here. Loch Ard (2 mi. long), 3 mi. W, has remains of anc. Murdoch Castle.

Abergavenny (ăbûrgûvĕ′nē,–gĕ′nē), municipal borough (1931 pop. 8,608; 1951 census 8,844), N Monmouth, England, on Usk R. and 16 mi. N of Newport; agr. market, supplying near-by coal-mining region. Has 11th-cent. castle. The church was formerly chapel of 11th-cent. Benedictine priory. Site of Roman station of *Gobannium.* Near by is co. mental hosp.

Abergeldie Castle (ăbûrgĕl′dē), royal residence in SW Aberdeen, Scotland, on the Dee and 5 mi. W of Ballater. It was frequently visited by Edward VII when he was Prince of Wales.

Abergele and Pensarn (ăbûrgĕ′lē, pĕn′sărn), urban district (1931 pop. 2,650; 1951 census 7,539), N Denbigh, Wales; includes market town of Abergele, 10 mi. NW of Denbigh, and seaside resort of Pensarn, on Irish Sea, just N of Abergele.

Abergwili (ăbûrgwĭ′lē), town and parish (pop. 1,396), central Carmarthen, Wales, on Towy R. and 2 mi. ENE of Carmarthen; woolen milling. Site of palace of bishops of St. David's.

Abergwynfi and Blaengwynfi (ăbûrgwĭn′vē, blĭn-gwĭn′vē), town (pop. 3,488) in Glyn-corwg urban dist., N central Glamorgan, Wales; coal mining.

Aberhonddu, Wales: see BRECKNOCK.

Aberlady (ăbûrlā′dē), town and parish (pop. 1,094), N East Lothian, Scotland, on Firth of Forth, 5 mi. NW of Haddington; resort.

Aberlour (ăbûrlour′), officially Charlestown of Aberlour, burgh (1931 pop. 1,175; 1951 census 1,153), W Banffshire, Scotland, on the Spey (bridge) and 11 mi. WSW of Keith; agr. market; whisky distilling.

Abermain (ăbûrmān′), town (pop. 2,182), E New South Wales, Australia, 18 mi. WNW of Newcastle; dairying, coal-mining center.

Abermawddach, Wales: see BARMOUTH.

Abernathy (ă′bûrnăthē), city (pop. 1,692), Hale and Lubbock counties, NW Texas, on the Llano Estacado, 17 mi. N of Lubbock; agr., dairying; cotton, wheat, sugar beets; cheese factory.

Abernethy (ăbûrnĕ′thē), village (pop. 290), SE Sask., 30 mi. WSW of Melville; wheat, stock.

Abernethy (ăbûrnĕ′thē,–nē′thē). **1** Village in Abernethy and Kincardine parish (1931 pop. 1,123), E Inverness, Scotland, 4 mi. SSW of Grantown-on-Spey, near Nethy Bridge. **2** Burgh (1931 pop. 595; 1951 census 675), SE Perthshire, Scotland, 6 mi. SE of Perth; agr. market. It was an anc. Pictish ⊙ and see of bishopric until 10th cent. Has anc. round tower, 10th cent. or earlier.

Abersee, Austria: see SANKT WOLFGANGSEE.

Abersychan (ăbûrsĭ′kŭn, –sŭ′khŭn), former urban district (1931 pop. 25,748), central Monmouth, England, 11 mi. NNW of Newport; steel milling, tinplate mfg., coal mining; agr. market. In it (SSE) is tinplate-mfg. town of Pontnewynydd (pŏnt″nūwĭ′nĭdh). Abersychan was inc. (1935) in Pontypool.

Abert, Lake (ā′bûrt), S Oregon, intermittently dry lake in Lake co., N of Goose L.; bed is c.14 mi. long, 5 mi. wide.

Abertamy (ä′bĕrtămĭ), village (pop. 1,253), W Bohemia, Czechoslovakia, 10 mi. NNW of Carlsbad, in the Erzgebirge; tanning center, noted for its gloves.

Abertawe, Wales: see SWANSEA.

Abertillery (ăbûrtĭlā′rē), urban district (1931 pop. 31,803; 1951 census pop. 27,617), W Monmouth, England, on branch of Ebbw R. and 12 mi. NW of Newport; tinplate-mfg. and coal-mining center; agr. market. Urban dist. includes towns of Cwmtillery (kōōmtĭlā′rē) (pop. 10,043) and Llanhilleth (lănhĭ′thlĕth) (pop. 3,836).

Abertridwr (ăbûrtrĭ′dōōr), town (pop. 5,001) in Caerphilly urban dist., E Glamorgan, Wales, on Rhymney R.; coal mining.

Abertura (ävĕrtōō′rä), village (pop. 1,214), Cáceres prov., W Spain, 16 mi. SSE of Trujillo; cereals, some wine.

Aberystwyth (ăbûrŭst′wĭth), municipal borough (1931 pop. 9,473; 1951 census 9,323), N Cardigan, Wales, on Cardigan Bay of Irish Sea, at mouths of Rheidol R. and Ystwyth R., 35 mi. NE of Cardigan; seaside resort, with leather tanneries. Cultural center of Cardiganshire; seat of Univ. Col. of Wales, Natl. Library of Wales, and Methodist Theological Col. Has promenade and pier. In Middle Ages it was a walled and fortified town; its castle (begun 1277, destroyed by Welsh 1282, rebuilt by Edward I in 1284) was one-time stronghold of Owen Glendower. Castle was destroyed by Parliamentarians at end of Civil War.

Abeshr, Fr. Equatorial Africa: see ABÉCHÉ.

Abetone (äbĕtō′nĕ), village (pop. 820), Pistoia prov., Tuscany, central Italy, near Monte Cimone, 19 mi. NW of Pistoia. Summer resort and winter sports center in Etruscan Apennines, on Passo dell'Abetone, a pass (alt. 4,554 ft.) crossed by road bet. San Marcello Pistoiese and Pievepelago.

Abey, Lebanon: see 'ABEIH.

Abez or **Abez'** (ŭbĕs′), town (1942 pop. over 500), NE Komi Autonomous SSR, Russian SFSR, on Usa R., on N. Pechora RR and 95 mi. SW of Vorkuta, in Pechora coal basin; reindeer raising.

Abha (ăbhä′), main town of Asir, Saudi Arabia, 120 mi. SE of Qunfidha, on plateau, in upper reaches of the Wadi Bisha; alt. 8,000 ft. Caravan center of highland Asir, in agr. dist.; millet, dates, vegetables, grapes; basket mfg. Garrisoned by Turks before First World War; captured 1920 by Ibn Saud. Formerly called Manadhir or Menadir; sometimes spelled Ebha or Ibha.

Abhar (ăbhär′), town, First Prov., in Khamseh, N Iran, on railroad and 50 mi. SE of Zenjan, on Abhar R. (headstream of Shur R.); noted vineyards; wheat, fruit. Flourished under Arab rule.

Abhebad, lake, Ethiopia and Fr. Somaliland: see ABBÉ, LAKE.

Abiad, Bahr el, Anglo-Egyptian Sudan: see WHITE NILE.

Abiad, Tell, Syria: see ET TELL EL ABYAD.

Abi Addi or **Abbi Addi** (ä′bē ăd′dē), town (pop. 2,000), Tigre prov., N Ethiopia, 37 mi. S of Aduwa; agr. area (coffee, bananas, lemons); trade center.

Abiak or **Abyek** (ăbyăk′), coal-mining town, First Prov., in Kazvin, N Iran, 35 mi. ESE of Kazvin, near highway and railroad to Teheran.

Abiar, El (ĕl ăbyär′), village (pop. 130), W Cyrenaica, Libya, on railroad and 30 mi. ENE of Benghazi; caravan center.

Abibe, Serranía de (sĕrānē′ä dā ăbē′bā), NW spur of the Cordillera Occidental, in Antioquia dept., NW Colombia, extends c.60 mi. from Paramillo massif NNW partly along Bolívar dept. border.

Abid, Oued el (wĕd′ĕl ăbēd′), left tributary of the Oum er Rbia, in W central Fr. Morocco, rises in the High Atlas, flows c.150 mi. W, entering the Oum er Rbia below Dar Ould Zidouh. At Bin el Ouidane (32°7′N 6°27′W; 17 mi. S of Béni Mellal) a new irrigation dam (460 ft. high) and hydroelectric project was begun 1948.

Ab-i-Diz or **Ab-e-Diz** (both: ăb′ēdēz′), river in SW Iran, in Luristan and Khuzistan, rises in Zagros mts. NW of Burujird, flows 250 mi. S, past Burujird, Durud, and Dizful, to Karun R. 25 mi. NNE of Ahwaz. Middle valley is used by Trans-Iranian RR. Used for irrigation in lower course.

Abidjan (ăbējăn′, ăbĭjăn′), city (pop. c.56,000, of whom c.2,000 are Europeans), ⊙ Ivory Coast, Fr. West Africa, port on N shore of Ebrié Lagoon (separated by sand bar from the Atlantic), 150 mi. W of Takoradi (Gold Coast) and 540 mi. SE of Dakar; 5°10′N 3°58′W. Railroad to Bobo-Dioulasso, 200 mi. N. Major export center for productive region (cacao, coffee, cotton, peanuts, palm oil, palm kernels, hardwood, rubber), it ships mostly through its auxiliary ports, Port-Bouet (S), linked by rail, and Grand-Bassam (E). There are administrative offices, missions, educational institutions, hospitals, airfield, seaplane base. Succeeded Bingerville as ⊙ in 1935.

Abie (ā′bē), village (pop. 113), Butler co., E Nebr., 40 mi. NNW of Lincoln, near Platte R.

Ab-i-Istada or **Ab-i-Istadah** (ăb′-ĭ-ĭstä′dŭ), salt lake in E Afghanistan, 70 mi. SSW of Ghazni; 11 mi. long, 6 mi. wide; alt. 7,000 ft. Receives Ghazni R.

Abiko (ä″bē′kō), town (pop. 11,276), Chiba prefecture, central Honshu, Japan, 11 mi. N of Funabashi, on small lake; rice, raw silk, poultry.

Abila, N Africa: see CEUTA.

Abila (ă′bĭlŭ), anc. town of Syria, bet. Damascus and Baalbek; ⊙ Abilene tetrarchy of the Romans. Site is near present-day village of Suq Wadi Barada.

Abilene (ăbĭlē′nē), region of Syria, E of the Anti-Lebanon mts.; in Roman times a tetrarchy of which Abila was ⊙.

Abilene (ă′bŭlēn, ă′bĭ–). **1** City (pop. 5,775), ⊙ Dickinson co., central Kansas, on Smoky Hill R. and 22 mi. ENE of Salina; shipping point in wheat region; grain milling; mfg. of cosmetics, toys, patent medicines. Laid out 1860, inc. 1869. Grew as cattle town on Chisholm Trail. Wild Bill (James Butler) Hickok was marshal here in 1870s. State fair takes place annually in Sept. Childhood home of Gen. Dwight D. Eisenhower is here. Damaged by great flood of July, 1951. **2** City (pop. 45,570), ⊙ Taylor co., W central Texas, c.140 mi. WSW of Fort Worth; shipping, trade, distribution center for agr. (cotton, wheat), dairying, cattle-ranching, poultry-raising region; also refines and ships petroleum. Mfg. (clothing, confectionery, food products, machinery, fishing tackle, textiles). Seat of Hardin-Simmons Univ., Abilene Christian Col., McMurry Col., and a state hosp. L. Abilene (city's reservoir; fishing) is 15 mi. SW, in state park; Lytle (lĭ′tŭl) and Kirby lakes are just S. U.S. Camp Barkley (10 mi. SW) was active training center in Second World War. About 14 mi. N are ruins of old Fort Phantom Hill; 12 mi. SSW is Buffalo Gap, old frontier town. Founded 1881.

Abilene, Lake, W central Texas, impounded by dam (1922) in Elm Creek (a S tributary of Clear Fork of Brazos R.), 15 mi. SW of Abilene, to which it supplies water; c.2.5 mi. long. Fishing; state park here.

Abimva (ăbēm′vä), village, Eastern Prov., NE Belgian Congo, 32 mi. ENE of Watsa; gold-mining and trading center; rice processing.

Abingdon (ă′bĭngdŭn), Anglo-Saxon *Abbendun*, municipal borough (1931 pop. 7,241; 1951 census 10,176), N Berkshire, England, on the Thames and 6 mi. S of Oxford; agr. market; leather, agr.-machinery, textile-printing, concrete industries. Has two 15th-cent. churches and ruins of Benedictine abbey (dating from 675), an important seat of learning in Norman times.

Abingdon. **1** City (pop. 3,300), Knox co., W central Ill., 10 mi. S of Galesburg; trade and shipping center in agr. and bituminous-coal area; livestock, corn, wheat, fruit, poultry; dairy products. Mfg.: clothing, pottery, brushes, plumbing equipment. Inc. 1857. **2** Village (1940 pop. 1,119), Harford co., NE Md., near Bush R., 21 mi. ENE of Baltimore; makes clothing. Near by are Aberdeen Proving Ground and Army Chemical Center. Founded 1779 by William Paca, who was b. near by. **3** Town (pop. 4,709), ⊙ Washington co., SW Va., in the Appalachians near Tenn. line, 14 mi. NE of Bristol; mtn. resort (alt. c.2,000 ft.); trade center in tobacco and grain area; mfg. (condensed milk, clothing), handicraft industries. Experimental theater. Settled c.1765; inc. 1778. Attacked in 18th-cent. Indian uprisings; burned by Federal troops in Civil War.

Abingdon Island, Galápagos: see PINTA ISLAND.

Abinger (ă′bĭnjŭr), agr. village and parish (pop. 1,549), S central Surrey, England, 24 mi. SW of London; site of govt. magnetic observation station (51°12′N 0°24′W), moved here 1923 from Greenwich.

Abington, town in Crawfordjohn parish, S Lanark, Scotland, on the Clyde and 14 mi. SSE of Lanark; agr. market.

Abington. **1** Village, Conn.: see POMFRET. **2** Town (pop. 7,152), Plymouth co., E Mass., 18 mi. SSE of Boston, just E of Brockton; mfg. (shoes, textile machinery). Includes North Abington (1940 pop. 2,044). Settled 1668, inc. 1713. **3** Urban township (1950 pop. 28,988), Montgomery co., SE Pa., N suburb of Philadelphia; chiefly residential. Includes villages of Abington (1940 pop. 3,758), Roslyn (rŏz′lĭn) (1940 pop. 3,399), Glenside (mfg. of paints, rubber products, electrical products), North Glenside, Ardsley, McKinley, and Noble.

Abinsi (ăbĕn'shē), town (pop. 1,339), Benue prov., Northern Provinces, central Nigeria, on Benue R. and 15 mi. E of Makurdi; road center; shea nuts, sesame, cassava, yams. Br. commercial station in 19th cent.

Abinskaya (ŭbēn'skīŭ), village (1926 pop. 13,559), W Krasnodar Territory, Russian SFSR, on railroad and 35 mi. WSW of Krasnodar; food processing; flour mill, sunflower-oil press.

Ab-i-Panj, Afghanistan and USSR: see PANJ RIVER.

Ab-i-Qaisar, Afghanistan: see QAISAR RIVER.

Abiquiu (ă'bĕkū), village (pop. c.500), Rio Arriba co., N N.Mex., on Rio Chama, in N foothills of Valle Grande Mts., and 40 mi. NNW of Santa Fe; alt. 5,930 ft.; livestock, chili. Built on site of pueblo ruins.

Abiramam (ŭbĭră'mŭm), town (pop. 10,521), Ramnad dist., S Madras, India, 40 mi. SE of Madura, 12 mi. SW of Paramagudi, in cotton, palmyra, grain area; cotton weaving.

Abisko (ä'bēskōō"), village, Norrbotten co., N Sweden, on SW shore of Torne L., near Norwegian border, 50 mi. NW of Kiruna; winter-sports center.

Abita Springs (ŭbē'tŭ), town (pop. 559), St. Tammany parish, SE La., 37 mi. N of New Orleans, in agr. area.

Abitibi (ăbŭtĭ'bē), county (□ 76,725; pop. 67,689), W Que., on Ont. border; ⊙ Amos.

Abitibi, Lake (□ 350), on Que.- Ont. line, 48°50'N 79°45'W; alt. 868 ft.; 45 mi. long, up to 19 mi. wide. Drained by Abitibi R. Surrounded by gold-mining region.

Abitibi River, NE Ont., issues from L. Abitibi, flows N, past Iroquois Falls, through Abitibi Canyon (hydroelectric plant), to confluence with Moose R., which flows past Moosonee to James Bay; 340 mi. long.

Abiyan, Aden: see ABYAN.

Abja-Paluoja, Abya-Paluoya, or **Ab'ya-Paluoya** (ä'byä-päl'woiä), town (commune pop. 3,048), SW Estonia, on railroad and 19 mi. SSW of Viljandi; textile milling, varnish mfg.; railroad shops. Consists of adjoining towns of Abja (E) and Paluoja (W).

Abkhaz Autonomous Soviet Socialist Republic (ăbkăz', Rus. ŭpkhäs'), **Abkhazia**, or **Abkhasia** (both: ăbkā'zēŭ, ăbkā'zhŭ), Rus. *Abkhaziya* (ŭpkhä'zēŭ), administrative division (□ 3,300; 1946 pop. estimate 300,000) of NW Georgian SSR; ⊙ Sukhumi. Bet. Black Sea and densely wooded SW slopes of the Greater Caucasus; includes narrow subtropical littoral bet. Gagry and mouth of Ingur R. Coastal strip includes almost entire pop. (35% Georgian; 30% Abkhasian, a Moslem Caucasian people; 13% Armenian; Russians) and is principal agr. area. Main products: tobacco (Abkhazia is one of main USSR producers), corn (chief food crop), citrus fruit, tea, wine, tung, essential oils (geranium). Industry, in addition to agr. processing, is based on hydro-electric power (Sukhumi plant), forest resources (hardwood), and coal (at Tkvarcheli). Many tourist and health resorts along Black Sea coast are served by coastal railroad. Main centers: Sukhumi, Gudauty, Ochemchiri, Gagry. Region was annexed by Russia from Turkey in 1810; became autonomous SSR in 1921.

Abkoude, Netherlands: see ABCOUDE.

Abla (ä'vlä), town (pop. 1,944), Almería prov., S Spain, 27 mi. NW of Almería; olive-oil processing, flour milling; ships grapes, almonds. Sericulture.

Ablaketka (ŭblŭkyĕt'kŭ), town (1943 pop. over 500), NW East Kazakhstan oblast, Kazakh SSR, on Irtysh R., at mouth of Ablaketka R., and 12 mi. SE of Ust-Kamenogorsk, on rail spur; site of Ust-Kamenogorsk hydroelectric power plant (construction begun 1939); sawmill, lime and brickworks.

Ableman, Wis.: see ROCK SPRINGS.

Ablitas (ävlē'täs), town (pop. 2,204), Navarre prov., N Spain, 6 mi. SSW of Tudela; olive-oil processing; cereals, wine. Gypsum quarries.

Ablon (äblō'), village (pop. 212), Calvados dept., NW France, 3 mi. SE of Honfleur; dynamite factory.

Abnub (ăbnōōb'), village (pop. 9,342, largely Coptic), Asyut prov., central Upper Egypt, on E bank of the Nile and 7 mi. NNW of Asyut; pottery making, wood and ivory carving; cereals, dates, sugar cane.

Abnud (ăbnōōd'), village (pop. 9,734), Qena prov., Upper Egypt, on E bank of the Nile, on railroad, and 9 mi. SSE of Qena; cereals, sugar cane, dates.

Abo, Finland: see TURKU.

Abo (äbō'), town, Warri prov., Western Provinces, S Nigeria, at head of Niger R. delta, 55 mi. E of Warri, in oil-palm region; hardwood, rubber, cacao. An important Br. commercial station in 19th cent. Sometimes spelled Aboh.

Aboba, Bulgaria: see PLISKOV.

Abo-Bjorneborg, Finland: see TURKU-PORI.

Aboh, Nigeria: see ABO.

Abohar (ŭbō'hŭr), town (pop. 21,222), Ferozepore dist., W Punjab, India, 55 mi. SSW of Ferozepore; agr. market (gram, wheat, cotton); hand-loom weaving, cotton ginning, oilseed pressing; engineering and metalworks.

Aboisso or **Aboïsso** (äboi'sō), village (pop. c.2,000), SE Ivory Coast, Fr. West Africa, 22 mi. E of Abidjan; lumbering (exotic wood), coffee and cacao growing. R.C. mission. Rail line to Ajame.

Abolição (äbōōlēsā'ō), town (pop. 563), E Rio Grande do Sul, Brazil, on Camaquã R. and 22 mi. WSW of Camaquã. Copper mining in vicinity. Until 1944, called Patrocínio.

Abomey (ăbōmā', ŭbō'mē), town (pop. c.16,900), S Dahomey, Fr. West Africa, on railroad and 65 mi. NW of Porto-Novo; agr. center (peanuts, palm oil, palm kernels, cotton, castor beans, coffee, corn). Mfg. of bricks, butter, mats, pots. Cotton ginning. Has airfield. R.C. and Protestant missions; mosque. Former ⊙ Dahomey kingdom.

Abomey-Calavi (kälä'vē), village (pop. c.2,900), S Dahomey, Fr. West Africa, on L. Nokoué, 7 mi. NW of Cotonou; palm kernels, palm oil, corn, manioc. R.C. mission.

Abona Point (ävō'nä), SE Tenerife, Canary Isls., 25 mi. SSW of Santa Cruz de Tenerife; 28°8'N 16°25'W.

Abondance (äbōdäs'), village (pop. 209), Haute-Savoie dept., SE France, 13 mi. SE of Thonon-les-Bains, in the Chablais (Savoy Pre-Alps); *vacheries* cheese mfg. Has given its name to high-grade Alpine cattle. Winter sports.

Abonema or **Abonnema** (äbōn'ĕmä), town, Owerri prov., Eastern Provinces, S Nigeria, on Sombrero R., just S of Degema, and 17 mi. W of Port Harcourt; palm-oil mill; hardwood, rubber. Fisheries.

Abong-M'Bang or **Abong-Mbang** (ä'bông-ŭmbäng'), town, ⊙ Haut-Nyong region, S central Fr. Cameroons, on Upper Nyong R. and 120 mi. E of Yaoundé; native trade center in coffee area; communications point; brick mfg. Has leprosarium, R.C. and Protestant missions. Nyong R. is navigable bet. here and M'Balmayo.

Abonnema, Nigeria: see ABONEMA.

Abony (ŏ'bônyŭ), town (pop. 15,299), Pest-Pilis-Solt-Kiskun co., central Hungary, 9 mi. W of Szolnok; agr. center (grain), cattle, horses; flour mills, brickworks.

Abor Hills (äbôr'), hill ranges in what was Sadiya frontier tract, NE Assam, India, NW of Sadiya, astride upper Brahmaputra (Dihang) R.; rise to c.15,000 ft. Inhabited by Abor tribes. Constituted (1950) as Abor Hills tribal dist. (□ c.8,000; pop. c.218,000; ⊙ Pasighat), part of Assam's NE frontier tract.

Aborlan (äbôrlän', äbôr'län), town (1939 pop. 486; 1948 municipality pop. 6,351), on E central coast of Palawan, Philippines, 25 mi. SW of Puerto Princesa; rice, coconuts. Municipality includes Malanao Isl., just offshore.

Aboshi (ä"bō'shē), town (1945 pop. estimate 19,412), Hyogo prefecture, S Honshu, Japan, on Harima Sea, 7 mi. WSW of Himeji; mfg. center (celluloid, matches, shell buttons); saltmaking. Since c.1947, part of Himeji.

Aboso (äbō'sō), town, Western Prov., SW Gold Coast colony, on railroad and 5 mi. NNE of Tarkwa; gold mining; cacao, cassava, corn. Sometimes spelled Abosso.

Aboudouhour, Syria: see ABU ED DUHUR.

Abou Kémal, Syria: see ABU KEMAL.

Aboukir (äbōōkēr'), village (pop. 1,318), Oran dept., NW Algeria, 8 mi. SE of Mostaganem; wine.

Aboukir, Egypt: see ABUKIR.

Above Derwent (dûr'wŭnt), parish (pop. 1,132), W Cumberland, England. Includes lead-mining and sheep-raising village of Braithwaite, 2 mi. W of Keswick.

Aboyne (ŭboin'), market town in Aboyne and Glen Tanar parish (pop. 1,552), S Aberdeen, Scotland, on the Dee and 10 mi. E of Ballater; resort, and scene of annual Highland Gathering. Aboyne Castle was begun 1671. Glen Tanar or Glen Tanner is wooded valley of the Water of Tanner, 12-mi.-long tributary of the Dee.

Abqaiq or **Abqayq** (ăbkīk'), oil town (pop. 4,000) in Hasa, Saudi Arabia, 38 mi. SW of Dhahran and on railroad to Riyadh; 25°57'N 49°42'E. Largest and most prolific of Saudi Arabian oil fields; terminus of pipe line (opened 1950) to Saida (Lebanon); also linked by pipe lines with Dhahran and Ras Tanura. Discovered 1940, it rapidly reached commercial production after Second World War. The Buqqa sub-field (discovered 1947) is a N extension of the Abqaiq field, and c.25 mi. NNE of Abqaiq.

'Abr, Al, Aden: see HUSN AL 'ABR.

Abra (ä'brä), province (□ 1,471; 1948 pop. 86,600), N Luzon, Philippines, near W coast; ⊙ BANGUED. Mountainous terrain, drained by Abra R. Fertile valleys produce rice, sugar cane, corn. Lumbering is important.

Abraham, Mount (4,049 ft.), Franklin co., W central Maine, 8 mi. N of Salem.

Abraham, Plains of, plateau in SW part of Quebec city, S Que., overlooking the St. Lawrence. Here, Sept. 13, 1759, the British under Wolfe defeated the French under Montcalm and established final control over Canada. Both commanders were killed.

Abraham Lincoln National Historical Park (116.5 acres; established 1939), central Ky., 3 mi. S of Hodgenville. Includes part of Sinking Spring Farm, Abraham Lincoln's birthplace (Feb. 12, 1809). Log cabin in which he is thought to have been born is housed in memorial building designed by John Russell Pope, completed 1911.

Abraham's Bay, town (pop. 285), SE Bahama Isls., on S central Mayaguana isl., 330 mi. SE of Nassau; 22°21'N 72°58'W. Sometimes Abraham Bay.

Abrakunis (ŭbrŭkōō'nyĭs), village (1939 pop. over 500), SE Nakhichevan Autonomous SSR, Azerbaijan SSR, 13 mi. SE of Nakhichevan, in winegrowing dist.; distilling.

Abram (ā'brŭm), urban district (1931 pop. 6,660; 1951 census 6,286), S Lancashire, England, 3 mi. SSE of Wigan; coal mining.

Abramovka (ŭbrä'mŭfkŭ), village (1926 pop. 2,174), E central Voronezh oblast, Russian SFSR, 40 mi. WSW of Borisoglebsk; flour mill.

Abramtsevo, Russian SFSR: see KHOTKOVO.

Abrantes (ŭbrăn'tĭsh), city (pop. 4,170), Santarém dist., Ribatejo prov., central Portugal, on right bank of Tagus R. and 32 mi. NE of Santarém; rail junction; commercial center of fruitgrowing region; cork processing, woodworking, pottery mfg. Early fortified, it was through the centuries a strategic point on road to Lisbon. Alfonso I took it from the Moors in 1148. John I gathered his army here before battle of Aljubarrota (1385). In Napoleonic Wars, Junot won battle of Abrantes (1807), but Masséna was unable in 1810 to take city by siege. The church of Santa Maria do Castelo, atop a near-by hill, is now a mus. containing tombs of counts of Abrantes. Industrial suburb of Rossio ao Sul do Tejo is across the Tagus.

Abra Pampa (ä'brä päm'pä), village (pop. estimate 1,000), ⊙ Cochinoca dept. (□ 2,970; 1947 census pop. 6,923), N central Jujuy prov., Argentina, on railroad and 45 mi. S of La Quiaca. Gold- and tin-mining center; chinchilla breeding.

Abra River (ä'brä), N Luzon, Philippines, rises in several branches in mountainous interior of Abra prov. c.30 mi. NE of Bangued, flows 55 mi. generally SW to S.China Sea near Vigan.

Abrau-Dyurso (ŭbrou"-dyōōrsô'), town (1939 pop. over 500), W Krasnodar Territory, Russian SFSR, near Black Sea, 8 mi. WSW of Novorossisk; noted wine-making center; champagne production.

Abraveses (äbrŭvā'zĭsh), N suburb (pop. 1,164) of Viseu, Viseu dist., N central Portugal.

Abre Campo (ä'brĭ kăm'pōō), city (pop. 1,764), E Minas Gerais, Brazil, 30 mi. ENE of Ponte Nova; tobacco, coffee, sugar. Mica deposits.

Abrego (äbrā'gō), town (pop. 1,784), Norte de Santander dept., N Colombia, in Cordillera Oriental, on Gamarra-Cúcuta cableway and 15 mi. SE of Ocaña; alt. 4,606 ft. Cacao, coffee, corn. Formerly La Cruz.

Abrene, Russian SFSR: see PYTALOVO.

Abreschwiller (äbrĕsh-vēlâr'), Ger. *Alberschweiler* (äl'bĕrsh-vī"lŭr), village (pop. 1,100), Moselle dept., NE France, rail terminus on NE slope of the Vosges, 7 mi. SSE of Sarrebourg; health resort. Sawmilling.

Abrets, Les (lāzäbrā'), village (pop. 1,349), Isère dept., SE France, 7 mi. ESE of La Tour-du-Pin; road center; woodworking, silk milling, cheese mfg.

Abreus (äbrā'ōōs), town (pop. 1,446), Las Villas prov., central Cuba, 11 mi. NW of Cienfuegos, in agr. region (sugar cane, cattle). The sugar central of Constancia is 3 mi. S.

Abri (ä'brē), town, Northern Prov., Anglo-Egyptian Sudan, on right bank of the Nile and 105 mi. SSW of Wadi Halfa; cotton, wheat, barley, corn, fruits. Temple and church ruins near by.

Abricots (äbrēkō'), agr. town (1950 census pop. 617), Sud dept., SW Haiti, on the NW coast of Tiburon Peninsula, 12 mi. W of Jérémie; sugar cane. Sometimes called Les Abricots.

Abril, 27 de, Costa Rica: see VEINTISIETE DE ABRIL.

Abriola (äbrēô'lä), village (pop. 2,343), Potenza prov., Basilicata, S Italy, 9 mi. S of Potenza.

Abrolhos (äbrō'lyōōs), group of rocky shoals in the Atlantic off Brazilian coast, c.40 mi. SE of Caravelas, Bahia; 17°58'S 38°40'W; lighthouse.

Abrolhos Islands, Australia: see HOUTMAN ABROLHOS.

Abrucena (ävrōōthā'nä), town (pop. 1,936), Almería prov., S Spain, 28 mi. NW of Almería; olive-oil processing, flour milling; sericulture. Cereals, wine, fruit, livestock; ships grapes.

Abrud (äbrōōd'), Ger. *Gross-Schlatten* (grōs-shlä'-tŭn), Hung. *Abrudbánya* (ŏ'brōōdbä"nyŏ), anc. *Auraria Major*, town (1948 pop. 2,656), Cluj prov., central Rumania, in Transylvania, in the Muntii Metalici, 29 mi. NW of Alba-Iulia; rail terminus and center of gold-producing region; also summer resort (alt. 1,998 ft.); trades in lumber, livestock.

Abruzzi, Mount (ŭbrōō'zē), (10,700 ft.), SE B.C., near Alta. border, in Rocky Mts., 55 mi. SSE of Banff; 50°27'N 115°7'W.

Abruzzi e Molise (äbrōō'tsē ā mô'lēzĕ), region (□ 5,883; pop. 1,589,804), S central Italy; ⊙ Aquila. Bordered by The Marches (N), Campania and Apulia (S), Adriatic Sea (E), and Latium (W). Abruzzi (N) comprises provs. of AQUILA, CHIETI, PESCARA, and TERAMO; Molise (S) is coextensive with CAMPOBASSO prov. Traversed by most rugged part of Apennines, which culminate here in GRAN SASSO D'ITALIA and Maiella mts.; mostly mountainous and hilly. Watered by Pescara, Sangro, Trigno, and Biferno rivers. Area 16% forested.

Agr. (cereals, potatoes, grapes, sugar beets, olives, fruit) predominates, especially in reclaimed Lago FUCINO; stock raising (sheep, swine, cattle) widespread; fishing (Pescara, Francavilla al Mare, Ortona). Its few mineral resources include bauxite (Aquila prov.) and asphalt (San Valentino in Abruzzo Citeriore). Hydroelectric plants (Bussi sul Tirino, Campotosto, Piano d'Orta). Mfg. largely restricted to provincial capitals and a few other towns (Agnone, Giulianova, Lanciano, Ortona, Sulmona). Conquered by Romans in 4th cent. B.C., became part of Lombard duchy of Spoleto (6th–11th cent.), Norman Kingdom of Sicily (12th–13th cent.) and Kingdom of Naples (13th–19th cent.). Suffered numerous earthquakes (1703–1915), especially in Abruzzi. In 1945 part of territory (□ 67; pop. 10,887) transferred from Campobasso to Caserta prov.

Absaroka Range (locally, in Montana, ăbsôr'kē, elsewhere generally ăbsûrō'kŭ), range of Rocky Mts. in S Mont. and NW Wyo., bet. Yellowstone R. (W and N) and Bighorn Basin (E); extends c.150 mi. S from Yellowstone R. SW of Livingston, Mont., to Wind R. valley (Wyo.); BEARTOOTH RANGE, a NE spur, includes Granite Peak (12,850 ft.), highest peak in Mont. The Absarokas are highest at Francs Peak (13,140 ft.; sometimes Franks Peak), c.40 mi. SSW of Cody, Wyo.; other summits over 12,000 ft. include Washakie Needles (wŏ'shŭkē) (12,496 ft.), Needle Mtn. (12,130 ft.), Fortress Mtn. (12,073 ft.), Dead Indian Peak (12,253 ft.), Trout Peak (12,259 ft.), Mt. Crosby (12,435 ft.), all in Wyo.; and Cold Mtn. (12,610 ft.), in Mont. Range, which forms E boundary of Yellowstone Natl. Park, is drained by tributaries of the Bighorn and the Yellowstone; it includes Absaroka Natl. Forest and part of Custer Natl. Forest in Mont., Shoshone Natl. Forest in Wyo. Sylvan Pass (8,559 ft.), on E boundary of Yellowstone Natl. Park, and Ishawooa Pass (ī'shŭwä) (9,870 ft.), 10 mi. E of park, cross range in Wyo.

Absarokee (ăbsôr'kē), village (pop. c.350), Stillwater co., S Mont., 12 mi. SW of Columbus and on branch of Yellowstone R., in dude-ranch area.

Abscon (äpskō'), town (pop. 4,289), Nord dept., N France, 10 mi. WSW of Valenciennes, in coal-mining basin; beet-sugar refining.

Absdorf (äps'dôrf), village (pop. 1,358), E central Lower Austria, 10 mi. W of Stockerau; rail junction.

Absecon (ăbsē'kŭn), city (pop. 2,355), Atlantic co., SE N.J., on W shore of Absecon Bay and 6 mi. NW of Atlantic City; mfg. (concrete blocks, shell novelties); nursery products, poultry. Settled c.1780, inc. 1902.

Absecon Bay, SE N.J., bay (2.5 mi. long) bet. Absecon and Atlantic City; Absecon Inlet, N of Atlantic City, is principal entrance. **Absecon Beach**, 10-mi. sandbar bridged at several points to mainland, is SE of Absecon across Absecon Bay; on it are ATLANTIC CITY and other resorts. Lighthouse at N tip; landmark (1854–1932); no longer used.

Abtao Island (äptou'), islet in Gulf of Ancud, just NE of Chiloé Isl., Llanquihue prov., S central Chile, 32 mi. SW of Puerto Montt. Wheat, potatoes, livestock; fishing. On it is village (1930 pop. 267) of Codihué (kōdēwä'). Just NW, on mainland, is village of Abtao.

Abtenau (äp'tŭnou), town (pop. 3,817), Salzburg, W central Austria, 15 mi. SE of Hallein, at N foot of the Tennengebirge; lumber mills. Mineral springs near by.

Abu (ŭ'bōō) or **Mount Abu**, town (pop. 4,316), Banas Kantha dist., N Bombay, India, on SW outlier of Aravalli Range, 34 mi. NE of Palanpur, 110 mi. N of Ahmadabad. Picturesque hill resort, famous for its Jain temples, of which 2 among Delwara or Dilwara group are outstanding; built (c.1031, 1231) of white marble, both are richly ornamented and have magnificent detailed carvings. Guru Sikhar (5,650 ft.), 5 mi. N, is highest point in Aravalli Range. Abu was hq. of Resident for former Rajputana States; surrounding area (□ 6; pop. 4,680) was called Abu dist.; inc. 1950 into Banas Kantha dist. Police training col. here.

Abu, Mount, Indonesia: see AWU, MOUNT.

Abu al 'Arish, Saudi Arabia: see ABU 'ARISH.

Abu al-Zuhur, Syria: see ABU ED DUHUR.

Abu Arish, Abu 'Arish, or **Abu al 'Arish** (ă'bōō ăl ărēsh'), village in Asir, Saudi Arabia, 20 mi. ENE of Qizan, in Tihama lowland; millet, stock raising. Salt deposits near by.

Abucay (äbōō'kī, äbōōkī'), town (1939 pop. 6,485; 1948 municipality pop. 8,453), Bataan prov., S Luzon, Philippines, on E Bataan Peninsula, on Manila Bay, 32 mi. WNW of Manila; trade center for agr. area (sugar cane, rice).

Abu Deleig (ă'bōō dĕlāg') or **Abu Deleiq** (dĕlāk'), town, Kassala prov., NE Anglo-Egyptian Sudan, on road and 90 mi. ENE of Khartoum.

Abu Dhabi or **Abu Zabi** (ă'bōō dhä'bē), westernmost and largest sheikdom (□ 4,000; pop. 4,000) of TRUCIAL OMAN, extending 200 mi. along Trucial Coast of Persian Gulf bet. the Khor al Ghanadha (E) and the Khor el Odeid at base of Qatar peninsula (W); pearling, fishing. The chief town, Abu Dhabi, is on coast, 90 mi. SW of Sharja; 24°28'N 54°22'E; airfield. Town becomes an isl. at high tide. Petroleum exploration begun here 1950.

Abu Durba or **Abu Durbah** (ă'bōō dōōr'bä), town on SW coast of Sinai Peninsula, NE Egypt, on Gulf of Suez, 110 mi. SSE of Suez; its oil wells are abandoned.

Abu ed Duhur (ăbōō' ĕd-dōōhōōr') or **Abu al-Zuhur** (ĕz-zōōhōōr'), Fr. *Aboudouhour*, town, Aleppo prov., NW Syria, on railroad and 30 mi. S of Aleppo; cotton, cereals.

Abu el Matamir or **Abu al-Matamir** (both: ăbōōl' mätä'mĭr), village (1937 pop. 1,379; 1947 commune pop. 12,434), Beheira prov., Lower Egypt, 20 mi. SW of Damanhur; cotton, rice, cereals.

Abu el Numrus, Abu en Numrus, or **Abu al-Numrus** (all: ă"bōō ĕn-nōōm'rōōs), village (pop. 8,497), Giza prov., Upper Egypt, 4 mi. S of Giza; corn, cotton.

Abu Ghosh or **Abu Gosh** (both: äbōō' gōsh'), village (1949 pop. 662), E Israel, in Judaean Hills, 7 mi. WNW of Jerusalem. From Middle Ages until 18th cent., toll station for pilgrims to Jerusalem. Has anc. monastery with noted mosaics and relics of Roman occupation. Excavations (1950) have yielded finds of site believed to be biblical *Kirjath-jearim*.

Abu Habba, Iraq: see SIPPAR.

Abu Hadriya or **Abu Hadriyah** (ă'bōō hădrē'yŭ), oil town in Hasa, Saudi Arabia, 100 mi. NW of Dhahran, near Persian Gulf; 27°22'N 49°E. Oil was discovered here in 1939 at 10,000 ft.

Abu Hail or **Abu Hayl** (ă'bōō hīl'), village on Trucial Coast of Persian Gulf, 5 mi. SW of Sharja, at boundary bet. Dibai and Sharja sheikdoms. Sometimes spelled Abu Heil.

Abu Hamed or **Abu Hamad** (both: ă'bōō hă'mĕd), town, Northern Prov., Anglo-Egyptian Sudan, on right bank of the Nile, on railroad and 125 mi. NE of Merowe; cotton, wheat, barley, corn, fruits, durra; livestock. Police post. From here railroad traverses Nubian Desert to Wadi Halfa, thus cutting off great Nile bend. Captured 1897 by British in campaign against the Khalifa.

Abu Hammad (ă'bōō hämăd'), village (pop. 7,685), Sharqiya prov., Lower Egypt, on railroad and 11 mi. SE of Zagazig; cotton.

Abu Hayl, Trucial Oman: see ABU HAIL.

Abu Heil, Trucial Oman: see ABU HAIL.

Abu Hommos, Egypt: see ABU HUMMUS.

Abu Hummus (ă'bōō hōōm'mōōs), village (pop. 6,525), Beheira prov., Lower Egypt, on Mahmudiya Canal and 10 mi. WNW of Damanhur; cotton-seed-oil mill. Sometimes spelled Abu Hommos, Abu Homs.

Abuja (äbōō'jä), town (pop. 4,592), Niger prov., Northern Provinces, central Nigeria, 50 mi. SE of Minna; major tin-mining center; shea-nut processing; ginger, cassava, millet, durra.

Abu Kemal or **Abu Kamal** (both: ă'bōō kĕmăl'), Fr. *Abou Kémal*, town, Euphrates prov., E Syria, near Iraqi frontier, on right bank of Euphrates R., and 75 mi. SE of Deir ez Zor.

Abukir, Aboukir, or **Abu Qir** (all: ă"bōōkēr', ŭbōō'kŭr), village (pop. 7,086), Beheira prov., Lower Egypt, on Abukir point (W limit of ABUKIR BAY), 13 mi. NE of Alexandria. This is approximately the site of anc. CANOPUS.

Abukir Bay, Aboukir Bay, or **Abu Qir Bay**, semi-circular inlet (□ c.160) of Mediterranean Sea, NW Lower Egypt, bet. Abukir Point and Rosetta mouth of the Nile; fisheries. Connected with L. Idku by short canal, El Mac'adiya, supposed to be the old Canopic branch of the Nile. Bay was scene of famous battle (sometimes called the battle of the Nile) in which Nelson defeated (1798) the Napoleonic fleet. Nelson Isl. lies 3 mi. NE of Abukir village.

Abu Kirkas, Egypt: see ABU QURQAS.

Abuksah or **Abu Kisah** (both: ă"bōōksă'), village (pop. 12,607), Faiyum prov., Upper Egypt, on railroad and 9 mi NW of Faiyum; cotton, cereals, sugar cane, fruits.

Abukuma River (äbōō'kōōmŭ), Jap. *Abukuma-gawa*, Fukushima and Miyagi prefectures, central Honshu, Japan, rises in mts. just NW of Shirakawa, flows E, past Shirakawa, and NNE, past Koriyama, Fukushima, and Kakuda, to the Pacific 15 mi. S of Sendai; 122 mi. long. Drains extensive rice-growing area. Hydroelectric plants on small tributaries.

Abullonia, Lake, Turkey: see APULYONT, LAKE.

Abulug (äbōōlōōg'), town (1939 pop. 2,066; 1948 municipality pop. 11,433), Cagayan prov., extreme N Luzon, Philippines, on small Abulug R. and 14 mi. NW of Aparri; agr. center (rice, tobacco).

Abu Mombazi (ă'bōō mōmbä'zē), village, Equator Prov., NW Belgian Congo, on a headstream of Mongala R. and 100 mi. NNE of Lisala; cotton ginning. Has Capuchin and Franciscan mission and schools. Sometimes spelled Abu Mombassy.

Abu Musa Island (ă'bōō mōō'sŭ), in Persian Gulf, belonging to Sharja sheikdom of Trucial Oman; 25°52'N 55°2'E; 3 mi. across. Red-oxide deposits; pearling, fishing.

Abuná, province, Bolivia: see SANTA ROSA, Pando dept.

Abunã (äbōōnã'), town (pop. 338), W Guaporé territory, W Brazil, on right bank of Madeira R. (Bolivia border), on Madeira-Mamoré RR, and 120 mi. SW of Pôrto Velho. Receives rubber for transshipment from Manoa (Bolivia), 6 mi. W at mouth of Abuná R. Until 1944, Abunã was called Presidente Marques.

Abuna Josef (ä'bōōnä), peak (c.13,747 ft.), NE Ethiopia, in highlands of Wallo prov., 10 mi. NE of Lalibala; 12°10'N 39°10'E. Tsellari and Takkaze rivers rise SE.

Abuná River (äbōōnä'), Port. *Abuña* (äbōōnã'), rises on Brazil-Bolivia border near 10°S in several headstreams SW of Santa Rosa (Bolivia), flows c.200 mi. NE, through rubber-producing rain forest, to the Madeira at Manoa. Navigable.

Abu Qir, Egypt: see ABUKIR.

Abu Qurqas (ă'bōō kōōr'käs), town (pop. 7,285), Minya prov., Upper Egypt, on the Nile, on railroad, and 12 mi. SSE of Minya; woolen milling, sugar milling, cotton ginning; rice, cereals. Also spelled Abu Qirqas, Abu Kirkas, Abu Kerkas.

Aburakawa, Japan: see AOMORI, city.

Aburatsu (äbōō'rä'tsōō), town (pop. 11,558), Miyazaki prefecture, SE Kyushu, Japan, port on Philippine Sea, 23 mi. S of Miyazaki; fishing. Exports lumber.

Aburi (äbōō'rē), town, Eastern Prov., SE Gold Coast colony, in Akwapim Hills, 20 mi. NNE of Accra; road junction; cacao, palm oil and kernels. Has horticultural experiment station, botanical garden, and Scottish mission.

Abu Road (ŭ'bōō), town (pop. 9,935), Banas Kantha dist., N Bombay, India, near Banas R., 30 mi. NE of Palanpur; rail station for Abu (10 mi. NW); markets millet, corn, wheat, barley; mfg. of soap, flour, atta, spices, ice. Formerly called Kharari.

Abu Rukba (ă'bōō rōōk'bŭ) or **Abu Rukuba** (rōō'-kōōbŭ), village, Blue Nile prov., E central Anglo-Egyptian Sudan, near railroad, 50 mi. WSW of Kosti; administrative hq. for Baggara Arabs.

Abury, England: see AVEBURY.

Abus, England: see HUMBER RIVER.

Abu Shehr, Iran: see BUSHIRE.

Abu Shusha, Israel: see GEZER.

Abu Simbel (ă'bōō sĭm'bŭl) or **Abu Simbil** (–bĭl), village (pop. 2,655), Aswan prov., S Egypt, on the Nile and 33 mi. NE of Wadi Halfa. The 2 famous rock temples built (c.1250 B.C.) by Ramses II were discovered 1812. Before the principal temple stand 4 statues of Ramses II, 65 ft. high, and smaller statues of his wife and sons. Sometimes called Ipsambul.

Abu Sir or **Abu Sir Bana** (ă'bōō sēr' bănă'), village (pop. 7,734), Gharbiya prov., Lower Egypt, on Damietta branch of the Nile and 3 mi. S of Samannud; cotton.

Abu Sir el Malaq or **Abu Sir al-Malaq** (both: ĕl mă'lăk), village (pop. 6,674), Beni Suef prov., Upper Egypt, near the Nile, 16 mi. N of Beni Suef; cotton, cereals, sugar cane. Site of extensive ancient cemeteries.

Abu Suweir or **Abu Suwayr** (both: ă'bōō sŭwăr'), village (pop. 6,119), Sharqiya prov., Lower Egypt, on Ismailiya Canal, on Cairo-Ismailia RR, and 12 mi. WSW of Ismailia. Near by (S) are ruins of anc. Tell el Maskhuta, the treasure city built by Ramses II and also called Pithom or House of Atum.

Abuta (ä"bōō'tä), town (pop. 8,473), SW Hokkaido, Japan, on NE shore of Uchiura Bay, 20 mi. NW of Muroran; iron and sulphur mining, lumbering. Hot springs near by.

Abu Tig (ă'bōō tēg') or **Abu Tij** (tēzh'), town (pop. 20,100), Asyut prov., central Upper Egypt, on W banks of the Nile, on railroad, and 12 mi. SE of Asyut; cotton ginning, silk weaving, pottery making, wood and ivory carving; cereals, dates, sugar cane.

Abu Tisht (ă'bōō tĭsht'), village (pop. 3,292), Qena prov., Upper Egypt, on railroad and 11 mi. NW of Nag Hammadi; cereals, sugar cane, dates.

Abuya Myeda (ä'bōōyä myĕ'dä), highest peak (c.13,120 ft.) in Shoa prov., central Ethiopia, on NW escarpment of Great Rift Valley, 45 mi. SSE of Dessye; 10°33'N 39°51'E.

Abuyog (äbōō'yōg), town (1939 pop. 4,744; 1948 municipality pop. 46,930), E Leyte, Philippines, on Leyte Gulf, 35 mi. S of Tacloban; agr. center (coconuts, rice, corn).

Abu Zabad (ă'bōō zăbăd'), town, Kordofan prov., central Anglo-Egyptian Sudan, on road and 90 mi. SW of El Obeid; gum arabic, cotton, peanuts, sesame, corn, durra; livestock. Police post.

Abu Za'bal (ă'bōō zä'băl), village (pop. 13,398), Qalyubiya prov., Lower Egypt, on Ismailia Canal and 15 mi. NNE of Cairo city center; basalt quarries; cotton, flax, cereals, fruits.

Abu Zabi, Trucial Oman: see ABU DHABI.

Abu Zenima or **Abu Zinimah** (both: ă'bōō zĭnē'mŭ), town, Sinai peninsula, NE Egypt, on Gulf of Suez, 70 mi. SSE of Suez; manganese and iron mined in vicinity at Umm Bugma or Umm Bujmah, 14 mi. ESE. Has a small landing.

Abwong (äbwông'), village, Upper Nile prov., S central Anglo-Egyptian Sudan, on left bank of Sobat R. and 35 mi. SE of Malakal; livestock; corn, durra.

Aby (ō'bü"), Swedish *Åby*, village (pop. 1,854), Ostergotland co., SE Sweden, near head of Bra Bay, Swedish *Bråviken* (brō'vē"kŭn), 30-mi.-long inlet of Baltic, 4 mi. N of Norrkoping; rail junction; woolen milling, brick mfg.

Aby or **Abyy** (ä'bē), village, NE Yakut Autonomous SSR, Russian SFSR, N of Arctic Circle, 225 mi. WNW of Sredne-Kolymsk; trading post. Coal deposits near by.

Abyad, Bahr el, Anglo-Egyptian Sudan: see White Nile.

Abyad, Et Tell el, Syria: see Et Tell el Abyad.

Abyan (ăbyăn'), village and oasis, Fadhli sultanate, Western Aden Protectorate, on Gulf of Aden, 30 mi. NE of Aden, at mouth of the Wadi Bana; one of chief agr. areas of Aden Protectorate. Sometimes spelled Abiyan.

Abya-Paluoya, Estonia: see Abja-Paluoja.

Abydos, Egypt: see Araba el Madfuna.

Abydos (ubī'dus), anc. town of Asia Minor, in present Turkey, at narrowest part of the Hellespont (Dardanelles) opposite Sestos, where Xerxes crossed on his bridge of boats and where legend of Hero and Leander is laid. Its site is just NE of Canakkale, NW Turkey in Asia.

Abyek, Iran: see Abiak.

Abyla, N Africa: see Ceuta.

Aby Lagoon (äbē') (32 mi. long, up to 12 mi. wide), SE Ivory Coast, Fr. West Africa, 45 mi. E of Abidjan. Separated from Gulf of Guinea by narrow bar. Receives Bia and Tano rivers.

Abymes (äbēm'), town (commune pop. 12,369), W Grande-Terre, Guadeloupe, 2 mi. NE of Pointe-à-Pitre, in sugar-growing region; mfg. of molasses. Sometimes called Les Abymes.

Abyssinia: see Ethiopia.

Abzac, France: see Coutras.

Abzanovo (ŭbzä'nuvŭ), village (1939 pop. over 500), S Bashkir Autonomous SSR, Russian SFSR, 70 mi. E of Chkalov; wheat, rye, oats.

Acacías (äkäsē'äs), village, Meta intendancy, central Colombia, at E foot of Cordillera Oriental, 13 mi. SSW of Villavicencio; cattle raising.

Acadia (ukā'dēu), Fr. *Acadie* (äkädē'), former name of Atlantic coast region of North America settled by the French from 1603 onward; its possession was disputed by England. Settlement began when de Monts was granted fur-trade monopoly bet. 40° and 46°N; 1st permanent settlement was established (1605) at Port Royal. Louis XIII later granted additional territory, covering region bet. the St. Lawrence and Florida, but for practical purposes Acadia was defined within boundaries of present provinces of Nova Scotia and New Brunswick. Frequent English attacks on French settlements of Acadia were made from 1610 onward; in 1621 English settlement began in Nova Scotia, which was granted to Sir William Alexander by James I, but this region was ceded to France by Treaty of St. Germain en Laye (1632). Colonization proceeded under the Company of New France. Anglo-French warfare continued; Treaty of Ryswick (1697) again recognized French control of Acadia. In War of Spanish Succession the English captured most of French-held territory, and Treaty of Utrecht (1713) recognized British sovereignty over region, France retaining Cape Breton and Prince Edward isls. (Île Royale and Île St. Jean). Last French and Indian war (1754) resulted in deportation (1775) of French inhabitants of Acadia to coastal region bet. Maine and Georgia, causing much hardship: in literature, Longfellow's *Evangeline* is the classic account of this exodus. French stronghold of Louisburg was captured by the British, 1758, and Treaty of Paris (1763) ended existence of Acadia as political unit and closed French era in North America.

Acadia, parish (□ 662; pop. 47,050), S La.; ⊙ Crowley. Bounded W by Bayou Nezpique, S by Bayou Queue de Tortue; drained by navigable Mermentau R.; crossed by Gulf Intracoastal Waterway. Rice-growing region; also cotton, corn, sugar cane, sweet potatoes. Oil and natural-gas wells; lumber. Cotton ginning, rice milling; edible-frog industry. Formed 1805.

Acadia National Park (□ 44.6), S Maine, mainly on Mount Desert Island, with a part on Schoodic Peninsula (E) across entrance to Frenchman Bay of Atlantic Ocean, and a part on Isle au Haut (c.25 mi. SW of Mt. Desert Isl.). Mtn. area noted for scenic beauty, and rich plant and forest growth. Established as Sieur de Monts Natl. Monument 1916, as Lafayette Natl. Park 1919; name changed to Acadia Natl. Park 1929. Forests were extensively damaged by fire (1947) that destroyed much of Bar Harbor.

Acahay or **Acahaí** (äkä-äē'), town (dist. pop. 12,443), Paraguarí dept., S Paraguay, 55 mi. SE of Asunción. Agr. (tobacco, rice, corn, peanuts, cattle); tanning. Founded 1783. Cerro Acahay (1,900 ft.) is just NW. Ocher deposits near by.

Acahualco (äkäwäl'kō), officially San Antonio Acahualco, town (pop. 2,401), Mexico state, central Mexico, 8 mi. WSW of Toluca; cereals, livestock; dairying.

Acajete (äkähā'tā). **1** Town (pop. 2,813), Puebla, central Mexico, at SE foot of Malinche volcano, 17 mi. ENE of Puebla, on railroad; alt. 8,051 ft.; cereals, maguey, livestock. **2** Town (pop. 855), Veracruz, E Mexico, in Sierra Madre Oriental, on railroad and 6 mi. NW of Jalapa; alt. 6,690 ft.; coffee, corn.

Acajutla (äkähōōt'lä), town (pop. 1,574), Sonsonate dept., W Salvador, port on the Pacific, near mouth of Río Grande, 11 mi. SW of Sonsonate (linked by rail and road); 13°36'N 89°51'W. Fisheries; seashell processing; beach resort. Exports coffee, sugar, balsam of Peru. Here Sp. conquistadores defeated Indians, 1524. Town flourished in colonial period as one of chief Pacific ports of Central America.

Acala (äkä'lä), town (pop. 2,385), Chiapas, S Mexico, on upper Grijalva R. and 23 mi. ESE of Tuxtla; agr. center (mangoes, sugar cane, fruit, livestock).

Acamas, Cape, Cyprus: see Arnauti, Cape.

Acámbaro (äkäm'bärō), city (pop. 17,643), Guanajuato, central Mexico, on central plateau, on Lerma R. and 45 mi. SSW of Querétaro; alt. 6,066 ft. Rail junction; agr. center (corn, wheat, sugar, vegetables, fruit, livestock); tanneries. Founded 1526.

Acambay (äkämbī'), officially San Miguel Acambay, town (pop. 1,438), Mexico state, central Mexico, 23 mi. NE of El Oro; cereals, livestock.

Acancéh (äkänsā'), town (pop. 2,298), Yucatan, SE Mexico, 15 mi. SE of Mérida; rail junction in henequen-growing region.

Acandí (äkändē'), town (pop. 1,124), Chocó dept., NW Colombia, minor port on Caribbean coast (Gulf of Darién), 45 mi. NW of Turbo (Antioquia); banana and rice growing. Trade with Panama. Gold mines near by.

Acanthus (ukăn'thus), anc. city of Greek Macedonia, on Chalcidice Peninsula, near site of modern Hierissos, at isthmus of Acte peninsula, on Gulf of Acanthus (Hierissos) of Aegean Sea. A Persian base in Xerxes' Greek campaign, 480 B.C.; near by Xerxes' canal was cut through the isthmus in preparation of the campaign.

Acapetagua (äkäpätä'gwä), town (pop. 1,448), Chiapas, S Mexico, in Pacific lowlands, 16 mi. NW of Huixtla; sugar, coffee, cacao, fruit, livestock.

Acaponeta (äkäpōnā'tä), city (pop. 7,111), Nayarit, W Mexico, in coastal lowlands, on Acaponeta R. and 75 mi. NNW of Tepic, on railroad. Mining (gold, silver, copper), processing, and agr. center (corn, tobacco, beans, sugar cane, vegetables, fruit, cattle); mfg. of soap, tobacco products.

Acaponeta River, W Mexico, rises in Durango in W outliers of Sierra Madre Occidental, flows S into Nayarit to Acaponeta, here turning W to lagoons and marshes which drain into the Pacific; c.120 mi. long.

Acapulco (ăkupōōl'kō, Sp. äkäpōōl'kō), officially Acapulco de Juárez, city (pop. 9,993), Guerrero, SW Mexico, port on sheltered bay on the Pacific, 190 mi. SSW of Mexico city; 16°51'N 99°55'W. Major seaside resort, with fine beaches. Deep-sea fishing, processing, and agr. center (cotton, coffee, sugar cane, tropical fruit, livestock); cotton ginning, sesame-seed processing; tungsten foundry. Exports hides, timber, fruit. Radio stations, airfield. One of oldest ports on North American Pacific coast; founded 1550. Long the starting point for Sp. colonial voyages and chief port of departure for the development of the Philippines. Frequently damaged by earthquakes and hurricanes.

Acará (äkurä'), city (pop. 264), E Pará, Brazil, head of navigation on Acará R. (right tributary of Pará R.) and 50 mi. S of Belém; manioc flour, lumber, oilseed.

Acarahú, Brazil: see Acaraú.

Acaraí, Serra (sĕ'rū äkäräē'), mountain range of N South America, on Brazil–Br. Guiana border, extends c.80 mi. E-W in lat. 2°N, and forms N watershed of Amazon basin. Rises to c.1,300 ft. Formerly spelled Acarahy; in Br. Guiana, Akarai Mts.

Acarape (äkurä'pĭ), town (pop. 1,746), N Ceará, Brazil, on Fortaleza-Crato RR and 17 mi. NE of Baturité; sugar, cotton, coffee.

Acará River (äkurä'), E Pará, Brazil, rises near 4°S 49°W, flows c.200 mi. N, past Acará (head of navigation), joining the Moju 15 mi. S of Belém to form the Guajará, which at Belém enters the Pará (Amazon delta). Sometimes called the Acará Grande.

Acaraú (äkurä-ōō'), city (pop. 2,421), N Ceará, Brazil, port on the Atlantic, 40 mi. E of Camocim; ships dried and salted fish, salt, cotton, sugar. Airfield. Formerly spelled Acarahú.

Acaraú River, NW Ceará, Brazil, enters the Atlantic at Acaraú; c.150 mi. long. Not navigable.

Acaray River (äkärī'), SE Paraguay, rises E of Curuguaty, flows c.110 mi. SE to Paraná R. above Iguassú Falls. Navigable; used to transport maté and timber.

Acari (äkurē'), city (pop. 1,262), S Rio Grande do Norte, NE Brazil, on Borborema Plateau, 105 mi. WSW of Natal; mining of rare minerals (beryls, columbite), gypsum, sulphur, and saltpeter. Irrigation dam and reservoir under construction. Airfield. Formerly spelled Acary.

Acarigua (äkärē'gwä), town (pop. 6,134), Portuguesa state, W Venezuela, in llanos 36 mi. SSE of Barquisimeto; road and commercial center in agr. region (sugar cane, cotton, corn, rice, cattle); sawmilling, dairying. Airfield. Former state capital.

Acarnania (ăkurnā'nēu), or **Acarnania and Aetolia** (ētōl'yu), Gr. *Akarnania, Aitolia*, nome (□ 2,137; pop. 197,968), W central Greece; ⊙ Missolonghi. Bounded S by Gulf of Patras of Ionian Sea, W by Ionian Sea, N by Gulf of Arta and S Epirus, NE by Eurytania along the Panaitolikon, and E by Phocis; largely mountainous (Akarnanika, Arakynthos), except for Agrinion plain, drained by Achelous R. Contains L. Trichonis. Agr.: tobacco, wheat, oats, wine; livestock raising, fishing (caviar). Tobacco processing at Agrinion. Other centers are Missolonghi (with its port, Kryoneri), Naupaktos, and Amphilochia. Modern Acarnania nome (called Aetolia and Acarnania until Second World War) includes anc. Aetolia. In anc. times, the name Acarnania was restricted to the region W of the Achelous R., with the chief city Stratus. Isolated geographically, anc. Acarnania played little part in the history of classical Greece. It was allied to Athens in 5th cent. B.C. and succeeded in maintaining its independence against Corinth and Sparta. Later (390–375 B.C.) Sparta controlled the region. A new city league (formed 314 B.C.) was briefly subdued by Aetolia in 3d cent., but existed under Roman rule until 30 B.C. After break-up (1204) of Byzantine Empire, Acarnania passed to Epirus and (1480) to Turks. In 1832, it became part of independent Greece.

Acary, Brazil: see Acari.

Acasio (äkä'syō), town (pop. c.4,200), Potosí dept., W central Bolivia, 16 mi. NNW of San Pedro; grain. Sometimes Acacio.

Acate (äkä'tĕ), village (pop. 4,210), Ragusa prov., SE Sicily, near Acate R., 5 mi. NW of Vittoria. Called Biscari until c.1937.

Acatenango (äkätänäng'gō), town (1950 pop. 1,017), Chimaltenango dept., S central Guatemala, at NW foot of volcano Acatenango, 10 mi. SW of Chimaltenango; alt. 5,499 ft.; coffee, grain, sugar cane, henequen; livestock. Fuego volcano may be reached from here.

Acatenango, inactive volcano (12,992 ft.), S central Guatemala, on Sacatepéquez-Chimaltenango dept. border, just N of volcano Fuego and 10 mi. WSW of Antigua. One of its 3 craters (nearly obstructed) exudes gases. Acatenango town is at NW foot of the volcano.

Acateno or **San José Acateno** (sän hōsā' äkätä'nō), town (pop. 1,003), Puebla, central Mexico, in Gulf lowlands, 22 mi. SSE of Papantla; sugar cane, coffee, fruit.

Acate River (äkä'tĕ) or **Dirillo River** (dērēl'lō), SE Sicily, rises on Monte Lauro, flows 32 mi. SW to Mediterranean Sea 7 mi. SE of Gela.

Acatic (äkätēk'), town (pop. 1,522), Jalisco, central Mexico, on interior plateau, 30 mi. ENE of Guadalajara; grain, fruit, vegetables, livestock.

Acatitlán (äkätētlän'), town (pop. 1,707), Mexico state, central Mexico, 50 mi. WSW of Toluca; sugar cane, coffee, fruit.

Acatlán (äkätlän'). **1** Town (pop. 1,684), Hidalgo, central Mexico, 20 mi. E of Pachuca; corn, maguey, livestock. **2** Officially Acatlán de Osorio, city (pop. 5,591), Puebla, central Mexico, on central plateau, on Inter-American Highway and 60 mi. SSE of Puebla; sugar-growing and -refining center. Silver and copper mines. **3** Town (pop. 1,211), Veracruz, E Mexico, in Sierra Madre Oriental, 14 mi. NNE of Jalapa; coffee, corn, fruit.

Acatlán de Juárez (dā whä'rēs), town (pop. 2,567), Jalisco, W Mexico, on central plateau, 23 mi. SW of Guadalajara; alt. 4,429 ft.; sugar-growing center; grain, vegetables, fruit.

Acatzingo (äkätsēng'gō), officially Acatzingo de Hidalgo, town (pop. 4,403), Puebla, central Mexico, on central plateau, 27 mi. ESE of Puebla, on railroad; agr. center (cereals, maguey, vegetables, fruit).

Acaxtlahuacán (äkäksläwäkän'), town (pop. 1,118), Puebla, central Mexico, 40 mi. S of Matamoros; corn, sugar, fruit, livestock.

Acay, Nevado del (nāvä'dō dĕl äkī'), Andean mountain (20,800 ft.) in W central Salta prov., Argentina, 20 mi. SE of San Antonio de los Cobres.

Acayuca (äkīōō'kä), town (pop. 1,487), Hidalgo, central Mexico, 9 mi. SW of Pachuca; grain, maguey, livestock.

Acayucan (äkīōō'kän), city (pop. 5,143), Veracruz, SE Mexico, on Isthmus of Tehuantepec, 25 mi. W of Minatitlán; agr. center (sugar cane, tobacco, tropical fruit, livestock).

Acca, Israel: see Acre.

Accad, Mesopotamia: see Akkad.

Accadia (äk-kādē'ä), town (pop. 5,091), Foggia prov., Apulia, S Italy, 6 mi. S of Bovino; wine, olive oil, cheese.

Acceglio (ät-chā'lyô), village (pop. 275), Cuneo prov., Piedmont, NW Italy, in Cottian Alps, on Maira R. and 28 mi. WNW of Cuneo. Has hydroelectric power station. Anthracite mines, marble quarries near by.

Accettura (ät-chĕt-tōō'rä), town (pop. 4,089), Matera prov., Basilicata, S Italy, 21 mi. ESE of Potenza; wine, olive oil, cheese.

Accha (äk'chä), town (pop. 1,396), Cuzco dept., S Peru, in the Andes, 29 mi. S of Cuzco; wheat.

Accho, Israel: see Acre.

Accident, town (pop. 242), Garrett co., extreme NW Md., in the Alleghenies 30 mi. W of Cumberland. Near by are Savage R. State Forest and a trout-rearing station.

Acco, Israel: see Acre.

Accomac, county, Va.: see Accomack.

Accomac (ă'kŭmăk″), town (pop. 500), ⊙ Accomack co., E Va., on Eastern Shore, 24 mi. S of Pocomoke City, Md. Old debtors' prison, built in 1750s. Rail station at Tasley, 2 mi. SW.

Accomack or **Accomac**, county (□ 470; pop. 33,832), E Va.; ⊙ Accomac. On Eastern Shore peninsula near its S tip; bounded N by Md., W by Chesapeake Bay and its arms, Tangier and Pocomoke Sounds; off coast (E) lie barrier isls. (CHINCOTEAGUE, ASSATEAGUE, Assawaman, Metomkin, Cedar) which shelter its bays from the Atlantic. Co. includes TANGIER ISL. in Chesapeake Bay. Productive coastal plain; truck farming (potatoes, sweet potatoes, tomatoes), poultry raising, dairying, fruitgrowing. Fishing, oyster culture, crabbing are important; fish, shellfish, vegetables canned and shipped. Pine timber. Ocean bathing, game fishing, sightseeing attract tourists; many old bldgs. (some dating from 17th cent.) remain. Formed 1663.

Accord, village (1940 pop. 514), Ulster co., SE N.Y., on Rondout Creek and 15 mi. SW of Kingston, in summer-resort area.

Accotink (ă'kŭtĭngk), hamlet, Fairfax co., N Va., near the Potomac, 9 mi. SW of Alexandria. Near by is Pohick Church (completed 1774), where Washington worshipped.

Accous (äko͞os'), village (pop. 428), Basses-Pyrénées dept., SW France, on the Gave d'Aspe, in Aspe valley of Pyrenees, and 15 mi. S of Oloron-Sainte-Marie; electrometallurgy.

Accoville (ă'kōvĭl), village (pop. 2,386, with adjacent Braeholm), Logan co., SW W.Va., c.10 mi. SE of Logan, in coal-mining region.

Accra (ŭkrä', ă'krŭ, ä'krä), city (pop. 135,456), ⊙ Gold Coast and port on Gulf of Guinea, 260 mi. WSW of Lagos (Nigeria); 5°31'N 0°12'W. Administrative and commercial center; terminus of railroad to Kumasi (Ashanti). Port of entry (via surf boats and lighters); exports cacao and gold. Fishing and fish canning; large brewery. Has modern Gold Coast hosp. (1927) at Kawli Bu across Kawli Lagoon (W). City includes non-native residential section (James Town) W of port, business section (Ussher Town; center), govt. buildings at Victoriaborg (NE), and, further E, 17th-cent. Christiansborg castle (governor's residence). Outlying residential dists. include Adabraka (N) and Labadi (E). City waterworks are at Weija on Densu R. (W). Univ. Col. is at Achimota, 6 mi. N. International airport 4½ mi. NE. City grew in 19th cent. around 3 fortified posts founded in 17th cent.: Br. Ft. James (now a prison), Du. Ft. Crèvecoeur (passed 1871 to British who renamed it Ussher), and Danish Christiansborg castle (passed 1850 to British). Became ⊙ Gold Coast in 1876; developed rapidly after construction (begun 1909) of railroad into rich cacao hinterland. Damaged in 1939 earthquake. Sometimes spelled Akkra.

Accrington, municipal borough (1931 pop. 42,991; 1951 census 40,671), E central Lancashire, England, 20 mi. N of Manchester; cotton-milling center, with mfg. of textiles, textile machinery, textile soap; also mfg. of leather, paint, electrical equipment; oil distilling. Near by, clay quarrying, brick mfg., coal mining. In the borough is village of Baxenden, with cotton spinning, mfg. of chemicals.

Accumoli (äk-ko͞o'mōlē), village (pop. 475), Rieti prov., Latium, central Italy, near Tronto R., 25 mi. NNW of Aquila.

Acebal (äsābäl'), town (pop. estimate 1,000), S Santa Fe prov., Argentina, 23 mi. SSW of Rosario, in agr. area (grain, potatoes, livestock); liquor distilling.

Acebo (äthā'vō), village (pop. 2,524), Cáceres prov., W Spain, 30 mi. SSW of Ciudad Rodrigo; lace mfg., olive-oil pressing, flour milling. Orange growing in area.

Acebuchal, Spain: see ACEUCHAL.

Acedera (äthā-dhä'rä), town (pop. 241), Badajoz prov., W Spain, 14 mi. ENE of Villanueva de la Serena; cereals, olives, acorns, oranges, vegetables, livestock.

Aceguá (äsägwä'), village, Cerro Largo dept., NE Uruguay, on Yaguarón R. (Uruguay-Brazil border), on highway, and 34 mi. N of Melo. Border transit point; grain, sheep, cattle.

Acehuche (äthäo͞o'chä), town (pop. 2,311), Cáceres prov., W Spain, 27 mi. NNW of Cáceres; cereals, wine, livestock.

Aceituno, El, Honduras: see EL ACEITUNO.

Acequias, Las, Argentina: see LAS ACEQUIAS.

Acerenza (ächĕrĕn'tsä), town (pop. 4,625), Potenza prov., Basilicata, S Italy, near Bradano R., 13 mi. NE of Potenza; olive oil, cheese. Noted for its wine. Archbishopric. Has 13th-cent. cathedral.

Acerno (ächĕr'nô), town (pop. 2,870), Salerno prov., Campania, S Italy, 16 mi. ENE of Salerno.

Acerra (ächĕr'rä), anc. *Acerrae*, town (pop. 19,177) Napoli prov., Campania, S Italy, 8 mi. NNE of Naples. Agr. center (corn, potatoes, beans, hemp). Bishopric.

Acesines, India and Pakistan: see CHENAB RIVER.

Acesines, Sicily: see ALCANTARA RIVER.

Aceuchal (äthäo͞ochäl') or **Acebuchal** (äthävo͞ochäl'), town (pop. 5,137), Badajoz prov., W Spain, 5 mi. SW of Almendralejo, in the fertile Tierra de Barros (cereals, olives, grapes, garlic, livestock).

Ach, Austria: see HOCHBURG-ACH.

Achacachi (ächäkä'chē), town (pop. c.21,280), ⊙ Omasuyos prov., La Paz dept., W Bolivia, on Keka R., near L. Titicaca, at base of Achacachi Peninsula, and 45 mi. NW of La Paz; alt. 12,556 ft. Local trade; potatoes, rye; livestock (sheep, llamas).

Achacachi, Gulf of, SE inlet of L. Titicaca, W Bolivia, N of Achacachi Peninsula; 12 mi. long, 9 mi. wide. Achacachi near SE shore, Santiago de Huata on S shore.

Achacachi Peninsula or **Huata Peninsula** (wä'tä), on SE L. Titicaca, W Bolivia; extends W into lake from Achacachi, opposite Copacabana Peninsula; forms Gulf of Achacachi (N) and Strait of Tiquina (W); separating lakes Chucuito and Uinamarca); 15 mi. long, 10 mi. wide.

Achacollo, Serranía de (sĕrānē'ä dā ächäkō'yō), W outlier of Cordillera de Azanaques, in the Eastern Cordillera of the Andes Oruro dept., W Bolivia, E of Poopó; extends 15 mi. N-S; rises to c.14,500 ft. Tin-mining region, with main mines at Antequera, Totoral, and Avicaya (S).

Achaea (ŭkē'ŭ), Gr. *Achaia* or *Akhaia*, nome (□ 1,141; pop. 223,796), N Peloponnesus, Greece; ⊙ Patras. Bordered S by Erymanthos mts., E by Aroania mts., N by gulfs of Corinth and Patras; drained by Selinous, Vouraikos, and Krathis rivers. Fertile agr. region; produces Zante currants, wine, citrus fruits, olives. Livestock (sheep, goats) raised in hills. Patras is main port and industrial center and with Aigion handles most of Zante-currant export. Modern Achaea (administratively part of W central Greece) was part of Achaea and Elis nome until c.1930, when Elis became a separate nome. Anc. Achaea sent colonists to Croton, Sybaris, Metapontum, and Caulonia in S Italy. Its 12 city states, including Helice, Pellene, Aegium, Patrae, and Dyme, joined (4th cent. B.C.) to form the 1st Achaean League. After its dissolution, 10 cities formed (280 B.C.) the 2d Achaean League, which became the chief power of Greece, expanding through Peloponnesus, until conquered (146 B.C.) by Romans. Roman senatorial province of Achaea (⊙ Corinth; formed 27 B.C.) included all Greece S of Thessaly. In Middle Ages, French formed (after 1204) principality of Achaea or Morea, including nearly all Peloponnesus, until conquered (1460) by Turks. Achaea PHTHIOTIS was SE section of anc. Thessaly.

Achaguas (āchä'gwäs), town (pop. 471), Apure state, W central Venezuela, in llanos 50 mi. W of San Fernando; cattle.

Achaia, Greece: see ACHAEA.

Achala, Cumbre de (ko͞om'brä dā ächä'lä), pampean mountain range of Sierra de Córdoba, W Córdoba prov., Argentina. Cerro Champaquí, in center, rises to 9,450 ft., highest point of Sierra de Córdoba.

Achalm (äkh″älm'), height (2,313 ft.) of Swabian Jura, S Württemberg, Germany, just W of Reutlingen. Crowned by ruins of 11th-cent. castle.

Achampet, India: see AMRABAD.

Achanta (ŭchän'tŭ), town (pop. 9,462), West Godavari dist., NE Madras, India, in Godavari R. delta, 45 mi. E of Ellore; rice milling; oilseeds, tobacco, sugar cane, coconuts. Sometimes spelled Atchanta.

Achao (ächou'), village (pop. 707), ⊙ Quinchao dept. (□ 5,496; pop. 22,561), Chiloé prov., S Chile, on central QUINCHAO ISLAND, off E Chiloé Isl., 45 mi. SE of Ancud; minor port in agr. area (potatoes, grain, livestock); fishing, lumbering.

Achar (ächär'), town (pop. 460), Tacuarembó dept., N central Uruguay, on railroad and 50 mi. SSW of Tacuarembó; grain, cattle, sheep.

Acharat, Syria: see 'ASHARA, QASR EL.

Acharnai or **Akharnai** (both: äkhŭrnā'), Lat. *Acharnae* (ŭkär'nē), town (pop. 10,364), Attica nome, E central Greece, on railroad and 7 mi. N of Athens; produces textiles, soap, alcoholic beverages. Anc. Acharnae, using charcoal, supplied armor to Athens. Formerly called Menidi or Menidion.

Achauba River, India and Burma: see MANIPUR RIVER.

Achdar, Gebel el, Libya: see AKHDAR, GEBEL EL.

Achdir (ächdēr'), village, Rif territory, central Sp. Morocco, on Alhucemas Bay opposite Alhucemas Isls., 3 mi. SE of Villa Sanjurjo; truck farming. Airfield 5 mi. SE. Also spelled Ajdir.

Ache, river, Austria: see BREGENZER ACHE, river.

Achedorus River, Greece: see ECHEDOROS RIVER.

Achele Guzai, Eritrea: see ADI CAIEH, division.

Achelous River (ăkĭlō'ŭs), Gr. *Acheloos* or *Akheloos* (both: ăkhĕlō'ôs), second longest river (after the Aliakmon) of Greece, rises in central Pindus system just S of Metsovon gap, flows 132 mi. S through mtn. gorges to fertile Agrinion plain and into Ionian Sea opposite Cephalonia, 18 mi. W of Missolonghi. Hydroelectric plant. Its course forms the border bet. Epirus and Acarnania (W) and Thessaly, Eurytania, and Aetolia (E). Formerly called Aspropotamos. Achelous was the river god of the anc. Greeks.

Acheng or **A-ch'eng** (ä'chŭng'), town, ⊙ Acheng co. (pop. 287,763), W Sungkiang prov., Manchuria, 20 mi. SSE of Harbin and on railroad; flour milling, match mfg., sugar refining; brickworks. An old Manchu town, it was a leading city of N central Manchuria, until superseded by Harbin; called Ashihho until 1909.

Achen Pass, Austro-German border: see ACHENSEE.

Achensee (ä'khŭnzä), lake (□ 2.66) in Bavarian Alps of N Tyrol, W Austria, 20 mi. NE of Innsbruck; 5.5 mi. long, 233 ft. average depth, alt. 3,045 ft. Tourist center; resorts include Pertisau and Achenkirchen. Cogwheel railroad to Jenbach. Achen Pass (10 mi. NNW) leads to Tegernsee (Bavaria).

Achern (ä'khŭrn), town (pop. 4,391), S Baden, Germany, at W foot of Black Forest, 5 mi. SW of Bühl; rail junction; noted for its kirsch. Mfg. of champagne bottles, agr. implements, chairs, pottery; paper milling. Fruit and wine trade. Has 14th-cent. chapel.

Acheron River or **Akheron River** (both: ă'kŭrŏn), in S Epirus, Greece, rises in the Tomaros, flows 36 mi. SW to the Ionian Sea 6 mi. SE of Parga. In Greek mythology, the boundary stream of Hades. Formerly called Mavropotamos and Phanariotikos.

Acheux-en-Amiénois (äshû'-ānämyānwä'), agr. village (pop. 515), Somme dept., N France, 16 mi. NE of Amiens; sugar beets.

Achhibal, Kashmir: see ANANTNAG, town.

Achhnera or **Achnera** (both: ŭchnā'rŭ), town (pop. 8,069), Agra dist., W Uttar Pradesh, India, 16 mi. W of Agra; rail junction; trades in pearl millet, gram, wheat, oilseeds, cotton. Important stronghold in 18th cent., under Jats.

Achi (ŭchē'), village, SW Dzhalal-Abad oblast, Kirghiz SSR, 10 mi. E of Dzhalal-Abad; mtn. pastures.

Achicourt (äshēko͞or'), S suburb (pop. 2,068) of Arras, Pas-de-Calais dept., N France; iron foundry; building materials.

Achikulak (ŭchē″ko͞oläk'), village (1926 pop. 2,035), NW Grozny oblast, Russian SFSR, on road and 35 mi. ESE of Budennovsk; flour mill, metalworks; cotton, wheat, sheep.

Achille (ă'chŭlē), town (pop. 383), Bryan co., S Okla., 11 mi. S of Durant, in agr. area; cotton ginning.

Achilleion, Greece: see GASTOURION.

Achill Island (ă'kĭl) [Irish,=eagle], island (□ 56.5; 14 mi. long, 11 mi. wide; rises to 2,204 ft. in Slieve Mor) in the Atlantic just off W coast of Co. Mayo, Ireland, bet. Blacksod Bay (N) and Clew Bay (S), separated from mainland by narrow sound crossed by bridge. Several fishing villages on precipitous coasts. Interior is mountainous, partly boggy. Some oats and potatoes grown; pigs, cattle, poultry are raised. Chief villages: Dugort (N) and Keel (S), fishing ports and seaside resorts. At W extremity is Achill Head (53°59'N 10°15'W).

Achill Sound, Gaelic *Gob an Choire*, town (pop. 198), W Co. Mayo, Ireland, on narrow sound opposite Achill Isl., 19 mi. NW of Westport; agr. market (cattle, pigs, poultry, potatoes, oats).

Achim (ä'khēm), village (pop. 6,860), in former Prussian prov. of Hanover, NW Germany, after 1945 in Lower Saxony, 10 mi. SE of Bremen; mfg. of textiles, shoes, furniture, tobacco products; pulp milling, food processing.

Achimota (ächēmō'tä), village, Eastern Prov., S Gold Coast colony, on railroad and 6 mi. N of Accra. Educational center; site of Univ. Col. (formerly Prince of Wales Col.; opened 1927; became a univ. col. in 1948) and Achimota teachers col. Hq. (1942–45) of West African War Council, and, after 1946, of West African Council of governors.

Achin (ŭchēn'), Indonesian *Atjeh* (ä'chĕ), region of N Sumatra, Indonesia; main town, Kutaraja. A Moslem sultanate in 16th cent., it was visited (1506) by a Portuguese of da Cunha's fleet and subsequently by Dutch and English East India companies. Achin reached the height of its power in early 17th cent., but declined later. The Dutch gained control of the coast in 1873 and waged a guerrilla war until c.1910 in a partly successful effort to subdue the interior.

Achinos or **Akhinos** (both: äkhēnôs'), village (pop. 1,158), Serrai nome, Macedonia, Greece, on Struma R. and 12 mi. SE of Serrai. **Lake Achinos** (just NE) is a former flood reservoir on Struma R., drained (1930s) in connection with Struma R. canalization.

Achin River (ŭchēn', ä–) or **Atjeh River** (ä'chĕ), N Sumatra, Indonesia, rises in highlands 25 mi. SSW of Sigli, flows c.70 mi. NW, past Kutaraja, to Indian Ocean at Ule-Lue.

Achinsk (ŭchēnsk', ä'chĭnsk), city (1948 pop. over 10,000), SW Krasnoyarsk Territory, Russian SFSR, on Chulym R. (head of navigation) and 85 mi. W of Krasnoyarsk, at junction of Trans-Siberian RR and Abakan branch line; tanning, vegetable-oil industry, breweries. Manganese mining at near-by Mazulski. Founded 1621; chartered c.1782; important river-road transfer point until construction of railroad.

Achiotepec (ächyōtāpĕk'), town (pop. 1,290), Hidalgo, central Mexico, 55 mi. NE of Pachuca; corn, sugar cane, tobacco, fruit.

Achiras (ächē'räs), village (pop. estimate 1,300), W Córdoba prov., Argentina, 35 mi. W of Río Cuarto; rail terminus and camping resort, with mineral waters; agr. (corn, wheat, livestock). Silver and copper mines near by.

Achisai or **Achisay** (ŭchēsī'), town (1948 pop. over 10,000), central South Kazakhstan oblast, Kazakh

SSR, in the Kara-Tau, 33 mi. NE of Turkestan (linked by railroad). Lead- and zinc-mining center, supplying Chimkent lead works.

Achi-Su (ŭchē″-sōō′), town (1948 pop. over 2,000), E Dagestan Autonomous SSR, Russian SFSR, on Caspian coastal railroad and 25 mi. SSE of Makhachkala; oil wells, developed in late 1930s.

Achkarren (äkh′kä″rŭn), village (pop. 690), S Baden, Germany, on W slope of the Kaiserstuhl, 11 mi. NW of Freiburg; known for its wine.

Achkel, Lake (äshkĕl′), N Tunisia, at foot of the Djebel Achkel (1,667 ft.), 7 mi. N of Mateur; 9 mi. long, 4 mi. wide; marshy banks. Outlet (E) to L. of Bizerte. Also spelled Ischkeul.

Achkhoi-Martan, Russian SFSR: see NOVOSELSKOYE.

Achmetha, Iran: see HAMADAN.

Achnera, India: see ACHHNERA.

Acho, Mount, N Africa: see CEUTA.

Achocalla (ächōkä′yä), town (pop. c.3,840), La Paz dept., W Bolivia, in the Altiplano, near railroad, 6 mi. SSW of La Paz; truck produce.

Acholi, district, Uganda: see GULU.

Achonry (ă′kŏnrē), Gaelic *Achadh Chonaire*, agr. village (district pop. c.2,400), S Co. Sligo, Ireland, 15 mi. SW of Sligo; cattle raising, potato growing. Seat of R.C. bishopric, but see house is at Ballaghadereen.

Achray, Loch (lŏkh ăkrā′), lake (1 mi. long, ½ mi. wide), SW Perthshire, Scotland, 7 mi. W of Callander, and separated from Loch Katrine by the TROSSACHS. Outlet: Teith R. It is of great scenic beauty.

Achtkarspelen, Netherlands: see BUITENPOST.

Achuapa (ächwä′pä), town (1950 pop. 504), León dept., W Nicaragua, 9 mi. N of El Sauce; wheat, corn, rice, beans, sesame. Gold mining near by; iron deposits SE.

Achupallas (ächōōpä′yäs), village, Chimborazo prov., S central Ecuador, in the Andes, 7 mi. SE of Alausí; cereals, potatoes, stock; thermal springs.

Achuyevo (ŭchōō′yĭvŭ), town (1948 pop. over 500), W Krasnodar Territory, Russian SFSR, fishing port on Sea of Azov, at mouth of Protoka arm of Kuban R. delta, 35 mi. NNE of Temryuk, in marshy lagoon area; fish processing.

Achy, France: see MARSEILLE-EN-BEAUVAISIS.

Achyrochorion, Greece: see NEA VYSSE.

Achzib (ăk′zĭb) or **Akhziv** (äkhzēv′), Arabic *Ez Zib*, biblical locality, NW Palestine, on Mediterranean, 17 mi. NNE of Haifa. Arab village here was abandoned 1948.

Aci, Lake (äjŭ′), Turkish *Acı* (□ 61), SW Turkey, 34 mi. E of Denizli; 17 mi. long, 5 mi. wide; alt. 2,743 ft.

Aci Castello (ä′chē kästĕl′lô), village (pop. 1,872), Catania prov., E Sicily, port on Gulf of Catania, 4 mi. NNE of Catania. Has ruins of Norman castle (built 1297). NE, 1 mi., are 7 small Cyclopean Isls. which, according to Gr. mythology, the blinded Polyphemus hurled after the ships of Ulysses. Largest is c.230 ft. high, 2,300 ft. in circumference.

Aci Catena (ä′chē kätä′nä), village (pop. 4,087), Catania prov., E Sicily, at SE foot of Mt. Etna, 2 mi. SW of Acireale; perfume industry.

Acintal, Guatemala: see ASINTAL.

Acipayam (äjŭ′päyäm″), Turkish *Acıpayam*, village (pop. 3,109), Denizli prov., SW Turkey, 28 mi. SSE of Denizli; wheat, barley, potatoes. Formerly Garbikaraagac.

Acireale (ä″chērĕä′lĕ), town (pop. 19,440), Catania prov., E Sicily, port on Ionian Sea, at SE foot of Mt. Etna, 8 mi. NNE of Catania, in citrus-fruit and grape region. Health resort with warm sulphur springs, noted since Roman times. Produces citrus syrups, macaroni, leather goods, soap, wax, glass, cutlery, metal furniture, musical instruments; pozzuolana mining; coral fishing. Has citrus-fruit experiment station, meteorological observatory. Bishopric. Has 18th-cent. cathedral (damaged in Second World War), seminary, teachers col. Town largely rebuilt following earthquake of 1693.

Aci Sant'Antonio (ä′chē säntäntô′nyō), village (pop. 2,916), Catania prov., E Sicily, on SE slope of Mt. Etna, 2 mi. W of Acireale; linseed oil.

Ackerman, town (pop. 1,463), ⊙ Choctaw co., central Miss., 45 mi. WSW of Columbus, in timber and agr. area; lumber milling.

Ackersand, Switzerland: see STALDEN.

Ackia Battleground National Monument (ă′kyŭ) (49.15 acres; established 1938), NE Miss., 7 mi. NW of Tupelo. Marks site of battle of Ackia (May, 1736), in which Chickasaw Indians, aided by English, defeated combined force of Fr. troops and Choctaw Indians. Result was opening of region to English settlement.

Ackley, town (pop. 1,608), on Franklin-Hardin co. line, N central Iowa, near Beaver Creek, 15 mi. SSE of Hampton; rail junction; agr. trade center; corn cannery, creamery. Inc. 1858.

Acklins Island or **Acklin Island,** island (50 mi. long, 1–13 mi. wide) and district (□ 120; pop. 1,744), S Bahama Isls., just SE of Crooked Isl., c.250 mi. SE of Nassau. Exports cascarilla, timber, and sponge. Main settlement, Snug Corner.

Ackworth, Quaker town (pop. 95), Warren co., S central Iowa, 17 mi. SSE of Des Moines.

Acme, village (pop. 282), S Alta., 35 mi. W of Drumheller; grain elevators, stock.

Acme (ăk′mē). **1** Town (pop. 139), Columbus co., S N.C., 15 mi. NW of Wilmington; mfg. of clay products, fertilizer. **2** Village, Hardeman co., N Texas, 5 mi. W of Quanah; gypsum mining and processing. **3** Village (pop. 1,479, with near-by Kayford), Kanawha co., W W.Va., 23 mi. SSE of Charleston.

Acoaxet, Mass.: see WESTPORT.

Acobamba (ākōbäm′bä). **1** City (pop. 1,912), ⊙ Acobamba prov. (created 1943), Huancavelica dept., S central Peru, in Cordillera Occidental, 32 mi. E of Huancavelica; wheat, corn; cattle, sheep. **2** Town (pop. 1,351), Junín dept., central Peru, in Cordillera Central, on road, and 4 mi. N of Tarma; orchards; vegetables.

Acolla (äkō′yä), town (pop. 3,116), Junín dept., central Peru, in Cordillera Central, near Mantaro R., 4 mi. NW of Jauja; grain, alfalfa; sheep raising.

Acolman (äkōl′män), officially El Calvario Acolman, town (pop. 660), Mexico state, central Mexico, 20 mi. NE of Mexico city; maguey, cereals. Has church and monastery of San Agustín Acolman, built 1539–60.

Acoma (ă′kōmŭ), pueblo (□ 386.9), Valencia co., W central N.Mex. Acoma village (1948 pop. 1,482) is c.55 mi. WSW of Albuquerque; alt. c.7,000 ft. Pueblo Indians, who live in long terraced dwellings made of stone and adobe located on precipitous mesa 357 ft. high, engage in agr. and pottery making. Important annual festival (Sept.) honors St. Stephen. San Esteban Rey Mission is old adobe church (remodeled 1699) with walls 60 ft. high, 10 ft. thick. Village was discovered 1540 by followers of Coronado, subdued 1599 by Juan de Oñate. Participated in general Pueblo uprising (1680) against Spanish and in later revolt of 1696. Near-by point of interest is Enchanted Mesa, sandstone butte (430 ft. high), supposed by Indians to have been inhabited by ancestors. Acomita is small agr. settlement in the pueblo 10 mi. W of Acoma.

Acomayo (äkōmī′ō). **1** Town (pop. 2,355), ⊙ Acomayo prov. (□ 408; pop. 32,651), Cuzco dept., S Peru, in high Andean valley, 32 mi. SSE of Cuzco. Mining (gypsum, coal, iron) and agr. center (potatoes, grain, stock); mfg. of textile goods. **2** Town (pop. 2,742), Huánuco dept., central Peru, in Cordillera Central, near Huallaga R., 15 mi. NE of Huánuco, on highway to Tingo María; coca, coffee, cacao; cattle raising.

Acomb (ā′kŭm). **1** Town and parish (pop. 929), S Northumberland, England, near Tyne R. just N of Hexham; coal mining. Site of abandoned lead mines. **2** Residential town and parish (pop. 5,580), West Riding, central Yorkshire, England, 2 mi. W of York. Site of York waterworks. Near by the emperor Severus is said to have been cremated.

Acomita, N.Mex.: see ACOMA.

Aconcagua (äkōngkä′gwä), peak (22,835 ft.) of the Andes, in Argentina just E of Chile border, 70 mi. WNW of Mendoza, Argentina; 32°39′S 70°1′W. Highest peak of the Western Hemisphere. USPALLATA PASS is at its S foot. First ascended 1897 by Zurbriggen and Vines, members of the FitzGerald expedition, which gave its alt. as 23,080 ft.

Aconcagua, province (□ 3,940; 1940 pop. 118,049; 1949 estimate 113,531), central Chile, bet. the Pacific and the Andes; ⊙ San Felipe. In E are high mts. (e.g., Aconcagua, Juncal, Leones, and Plomo peaks) on Argentina border, and the Uspallata Pass, under which passes the Transandine RR. There are fertile valleys of subtropical vegetation. Has warm, temperate climate of considerable dryness. Rich mineral resources include copper (Catemu, Cabildo), kaolin (San Lorenzo), salt (Papudo); also lead, iron, gold, silver, and manganese ores. Agr.: cereals, alfalfa, potatoes, tobacco, fruit, wine, hemp—mostly in Ligua and Aconcagua river valleys. Cattle, sheep, mules, and goats in Andean foothills. Mining, quarrying, flour milling, wine making, tobacco processing. Processing industries at San Felipe and Los Andes. Resorts: Papudo (Pacific coast), Jahuel, Río Blanco, Portillo (Andes).

Aconcagua, town, Chile: see SAN FELIPE.

Aconcagua River, in Aconcagua and Valparaiso provs., central Chile, rises in the Andes at NW foot of Aconcagua massif, flows c.120 mi. W, past Los Andes, San Felipe, Calera, and Quillota, to the Pacific at Concón, 12 mi. NE of Valparaiso. In its fertile valley hemp, tobacco, fruit, wine, grain are grown.

Aconchi (äkōn′chē), town (pop. 996), Sonora, NW Mexico, on Sonora R. (irrigation) and 70 mi. NE of Hermosillo; wheat, corn, vegetables, sugar, livestock.

Aconi Point, promontory on the Atlantic, NE N.S., at N end of Boularderie Isl., 7 mi. NW of Sydney Mines; 46°19′N 60°17′W.

Aconquija, Nevado del (nävä′dō dĕl äkōngkē′hä), or **Nevado del Anconquija** (nävä′dō dĕl ängkōng–), pampean range on Catamarca-Tucumán prov. border, Argentina, W of Tucumán; extends c.50 mi. NNE-SSW; rises to 18,000 ft. Kaolin, silver deposits.

Acopiara (äkōōpyä′rŭ), city (pop. 2,259), S central Ceará, Brazil, on railroad and 22 mi. NW of Iguatu; livestock. Until 1944, Afonso Pena, formerly also spelled Affonso Penna.

Acora (äkō′rä), town (pop. 1,224), Puno dept., SE Peru, on the Altiplano, 16 mi. ESE of Puno; alt. 12,693 ft.; potatoes, grain, livestock.

Açôres, Portugal: see AZORES.

Acoria (äkōr′yä), town (pop. 1,440), Huancavelica dept., S central Peru, on Huancavelica R. on railroad and 15 mi. NE of Huancavelica; silver mining; grain, corn, tubers; cattle and sheep raising.

Acos (ä′kōs), town (pop. 1,735), Cuzco dept., S Peru, in Apurímac R. valley, 29 mi. S of Cuzco; grain, potatoes, stock.

Acostambo (äkōstäm′bō), town (pop. 1,029), Huancavelica dept., S central Peru, on Huancayo–Huancavelica RR, on Mantaro R. and 27 mi. NNW of Huancavelica; grain, cattle, sheep.

Acosta San Ignacio or **San Ignacio de Acosta** (sän ēgnä′syō dā äkō′stä), town (pop. 293), San José prov., W Costa Rica, at S foot of the Escazú, 11 mi. SW of San José; trading center in coffee zone; beans, corn, rice, oranges, bananas.

Acoxochitlán (äkōksōchētlän′), town (pop. 3,525), Hidalgo, central Mexico, in Sierra Madre Oriental, 30 mi. E of Pachuca; corn, maguey, livestock.

Acoyapa (äkoiä′pä), town (1950 pop. 1,148), Chontales dept., S Nicaragua, 23 mi. SE of Juigalpa, at road junction; stock-raising center. Its port on L. Nicaragua is San Ubaldo.

Acoyotla (äkoi-ōt′lä), town (pop. 1,184), Hidalgo, central Mexico, in foothills of Sierra Madre Oriental, 25 mi. W of Huejutla; corn, rice, sugar cane, tobacco, fruit.

Acoz (äkō′), town (pop. 1,289), Hainaut prov., S central Belgium, 6 mi. SE of Charleroi; metal foundries, forges.

Acqualagna (äkwälä′nyä), village (pop. 757), Pesaro e Urbino prov., The Marches, central Italy, 8 mi. SSE of Urbino.

Acquanegra sul Chiese (äkwänä′grä sōōl kyä′zĕ), village (pop. 2,856), Mantova prov., Lombardy, N Italy, near confluence of Chiese R. with the Oglio, 18 mi. W of Mantua; toy mfg. Has 12th-cent. church.

Acquapendente (äkwäpĕndĕn′tĕ), town (pop. 3,791), Viterbo prov., Latium, central Italy, 13 mi. WNW of Orvieto; bricks, tiles, pottery, wine, olive oil. Bishopric. Cathedral has terra-cotta altar (1522).

Acquarica del Capo (äkwä′rēkä dĕl kä′pô), village (pop. 3,105), Lecce prov., Apulia, S Italy, 18 mi. SE of Gallipoli.

Acquaro (äkwä′rô), village (pop. 2,592), Catanzaro prov., Calabria, S Italy, 10 mi. SE of Vibo Valentia; olive oil, wine, perfume.

Acquasanta (äkwäsän′tä), village (pop. 804), Ascoli Piceno prov., The Marches, central Italy, on Tronto R. and 10 mi. SW of Ascoli Piceno; health resort (alt. 1,280 ft.) with hot mineral waters. Cement-works.

Acquasparta (äkwäspär′tä), village (pop. 1,189), Terni prov., Umbria, central Italy, 11 mi. NNW of Terni. Has medieval walls, late 13th-cent. church, and 16th-cent. palace with mus. Mineral springs near by.

Acquaviva delle Fonti (äkwävē′vä dĕl-lĕ fôn′tē), town (pop. 11,934), Bari prov., Apulia, S Italy, 16 mi. S of Bari; agr. center (vegetables, grapes, olives, almonds); alcohol distillery.

Acquaviva Platani (plä′tänē), village (pop. 3,189), Caltanissetta prov., central Sicily, near Platani R., 21 mi. WNW of Caltanissetta. Sulphur mine is S.

Acqui (ä′kwē), anc. *Aquae* or *Aquae Statiellae*, town (pop. 9,643), Alessandria prov., Piedmont, N Italy, on Bormida R. and 18 mi. SSW of Alessandria; rail junction. Health resort, noted since Roman times for saline sulphur springs (113°–167°F.). Produces wine, macaroni, bricks, glassware, clothing, metal products. Bishopric since end of 4th cent. Has cathedral (consecrated 1067), 14th- and 15th-cent. castles. Roman ruins include baths, aqueduct.

Acra (ă′krŭ, ô′–), resort village, Greene co., SE N.Y., in the Catskills, 12 mi. WNW of Catskill.

Acre (ä′krĭ), federal territory (□ 59,139; 1940 pop. 79,768; 1950 census 116,124), westernmost Brazil; ⊙ Rio Branco. Bounded by Peru (W and S), Bolivia (SE); and by Amazonas (N). Lies within tropical rain-forest basin of the Amazon. Traversed by upper Juruá and Purus rivers, and by the Acre and Iaco (tributaries of the Purus). Some gold and tin deposits. Chief towns: Rio Branco, Cruzeiro do Sul, Sena Madureira. Air and river transport are principal means of communication. Originally part of Bolivia, Acre was turned over to Brazil in 1903, in exchange for an indemnity and the promise to build the Madeira-Mamoré RR. A leading wild rubber-growing region, it experienced a short-lived boom near turn of 20th cent.

Acre (ā′kûr, ä′kûr), Hebrew *Acco* or *Akko*, Arabic *Acca* or *'Akka*, Fr. *Saint Jean d'Acre*, called *Accho* in Old Testament, *Ptolemais* in New Testament, town (1949 pop. estimate 9,000), NW Israel, at N end of Zebulun Valley, on Bay of Acre of Mediterranean, on railroad and 9 mi. NE of Haifa. Largely evacuated by Arab pop., 1948. Its new industries include steel-rolling mill. Has citadel and remains of old fortifications, partly dating from time of Crusades. Base (405–359 B.C.) of Artaxerxes' campaign against Egypt. After Byzantine rule captured (A.D. 638) by Mohammedans; fel-

Crusaders 1104, captured by Saladin 1187. Recaptured 1191 by Crusaders, who established their chief port here. Fell (1291) to Saracens. Captured (1514) by Turks. With British aid it successfully withstood (1799) Napoleon's siege. Taken (1832) by Ibrahim Pasha for Mohammed Ali of Egypt, Acre was recaptured (1840) by Turks with British and Austrian help. Captured (1948) by Israeli forces.

Acre, Bay of, inlet (7–10 mi. wide) of Mediterranean, NW Israel; extends SW-NE bet. Haifa and Acre.

Acrefair, Wales: see CEFN MAWR.

Acre River (ä'krĭ), in Acre territory and SW Amazonas, westernmost Brazil, rises on Peru border near 11°S 70°30'W, flows E along Brazil-Peru and Brazil-Bolivia borders to Cobija and Brasiléia, then NNE, past Xapuri (head of navigation) and Rio Branco, to the Purus at Bôca do Acre. Length, c.400 mi. Also called Aquiri (old spelling, Aquiry).

Acri (ä'krē), town (pop. 5,387), Cosenza prov., Calabria, S Italy, 15 mi. NNE of Cosenza; agr. trade center (wine, olive oil, cheese, salted meats, pigs). Has anc. walls and 17th-cent. palace.

Acritas, Greece: see AKRITAS, CAPE.

Acroceraunia or **Acroceraunian Mountains** (ă"krōsĭrô'nēŭn), Albanian *Rreza e Kanalit* (rä'zä ä känälēt'), NW prong of CERAUNIAN MOUNTAINS of S Albania, extend c.25 mi. from Mt. Cike NW into KARABURUN peninsula of Strait of Otranto, terminating in Cape LINGUETTA; rise to 4,918 ft. The name Acroceraunia is also applied (mainly by the Greeks) to the entire Ceraunian system, the Karaburun peninsula, and Cape Linguetta.

Acrocorinthus (ă"krōkûrĭn'thŭs) or **Akrokorinthos** [Gr.,=high point of Corinth], a rock (1,886 ft.) in Argolis and Corinthia nome, NE Peloponnesus, Greece, overlooking Old Corinth (at N foot), 4 mi. SW of CORINTH. Site of ruins of acropolis of Corinth, it was also strongly fortified in Middle Ages. On summit stood a temple of Aphrodite, and below gushed the fountain of Pirene from which Pegasus drank, in Gr. legend.

Acs (äch), Hung. *Ács*, town (pop. 6,575), Komarom-Esztergom co., N Hungary, 17 mi. E of Györ; distilleries, sugar refineries. Wheat, rye; cattle, horses. Roman ruins.

Actaeon Islands (ăktē'ŭn), uninhabited coral group, S Tuamotu Isls., Fr. Oceania, S Pacific; 21°20'S 136°30'W; includes Maturei Vavao (formerly Melbourne Isl.), Tenarunga (formerly Minto Isl.), Vahanga (formerly Bedford Isl.), and Tenararo. Discovered 1606 by Queiros.

Acte, peninsula, Greece: see AKTE.

Acteopan (äktāō'pän), town (pop. 1,153), Puebla, central Mexico, 21 mi. SW of Atlixco; corn, sugar, fruit.

Actipán (äktēpän'), officially Actipán de Morelos, town (pop. 1,762), Puebla, central Mexico, 27 mi. ESE of Puebla; cereals, maguey, fruit.

Actium (ăk'tēŭm, ăk'shēŭm), Gr. *Aktion*, promontory and town of anc. Greece, in NW Acarnania, on S side of entrance to Gulf of Arta, opposite modern Preveza. Site of temple to Apollo, dating from 5th cent. B.C. Noted for the naval victory won offshore (31 B.C.) by Octavian (Augustus) over fleets of Antony and Cleopatra. The Actian Games organized by the Romans in memory of the victory were staged at near-by Nicopolis.

Actlazayanca (äkläsīäng'kä), town (pop. 1,165), Tlaxcala, central Mexico, 30 mi. ENE of Tlaxcala; cereals, maguey, livestock.

Acton, village (pop. 2,063), S Ont., 12 mi. ENE of Guelph; mfg. of machinery, electrical equipment, farm implements, leather, gloves, underwear, plastics, flour, feed.

Acton, residential municipal borough (1931 pop. 70,510; 1951 census 67,424), Middlesex, England, 7 mi. W of London; various light industries. One-time residence of Henry III. Center of Puritanism at time of Cromwell.

Acton. 1 Town (pop. 473), York co., SW Maine, 23 mi. W of Biddeford. **2** Town (pop. 3,510), Middlesex co., NE central Mass., 21 mi. WNW of Boston; apples; metal stampings, chemicals, wood products; granite. Includes villages of South Acton (1940 pop. 726) and West Acton (1940 pop. 883). Settled c.1680, inc. 1735.

Acton, parish (pop. 1,952), E Denbigh, Wales, just N of Wrexham; coal mining.

Acton Burnell (bûr'nŭl), agr. village and parish (pop. 218), central Shropshire, England, 7 mi. SSE of Shrewsbury. Has late-13th-cent. church and ruins of anc. castle where Edward I held a parliament in 1283.

Acton Vale, town (pop. 2,366), S Que., 50 mi. E of Montreal; woodworking, silk milling, mfg. of linen thread, shoes.

Actopan (äktō'pän). **1** Town (pop. 3,300), Hidalgo, central Mexico, on Inter-American Highway, in central plateau, and 18 mi. NW of Pachuca, on railroad; alt. 6,722 ft. Agr. center (corn, wheat, wine, beans, fruit, livestock). Has 16th-cent. Augustinian monastery with anc. frescoes. Thermal springs near by. **2** Town (pop. 1,214), Veracruz, E Mexico, in Sierra Madre Oriental foothills, 20 mi. E of Jalapa; corn, coffee, fruit.

Açu (äsōō'), city (pop. 3,748), central Rio Grande do Norte, NE Brazil, head of navigation on Piranhas R. and 40 mi. SE of Mossoró, in region growing carnauba, sugar, and cotton; important saltworks, gypsum quarries. Irrigation dam under construction. Also spelled Assu.

Acuitzeramo (äkwētsärä'mō), town (pop. 1,811), Michoacán, central Mexico, 17 mi. ENE of Zamora; cereals, fruit, livestock.

Acuitzio (äkwēt'syō), officially Acuitzio del Canje, town (pop. 2,661), Michoacán, central Mexico, 16 mi. SSW of Morelia; cereals, fruit, livestock; tanning, flour milling.

Acula (äkōō'lä), town (pop. 1,332), Veracruz, SE Mexico, in Sotavento lowlands, 19 mi. S of Alvarado; sugar, coffee, tropical fruit, livestock.

Aculco (äkōōl'kō), officially San Jerónimo Aculco, town (pop. 808), Mexico state, central Mexico, 22 mi. SE of San Juan del Río; cereals, livestock.

Acul-du-Nord (äkül-dü-nôr'), town (1950 census pop. 1,231), Nord dept., N Haiti, 9 mi. SW of Cap-Haïtien; rice, fruit. Fine harbor near by.

Aculeo, Lake (äkōōlā'ō) (□ 16), Santiago prov., central Chile, 30 mi. SSW of Santiago; known for its fishing.

Acul-Samedi (äkül-sämdē'), village (1950 census pop. 331), Nord dept., NW Haiti, on the Plaine du Nord, 25 mi. SE of Cap-Haïtien; coffeegrowing.

Acultzingo (äkōōltsēng'gō), town (pop. 1,613), Veracruz, E Mexico, in Sierra Madre Oriental, 17 mi. SW of Orizaba; coffee, sugar, fruit, corn.

Acuña, Villa, Mexico: see VILLA ACUÑA.

Açuruá, Serra do (sĕ'rŭ dōō äsōōrōōä'), plateau in W central Bahia, Brazil, extends c.70 mi. S of Santo Inácio parallel to right bank of São Francisco R. Rises to 2,500 ft. Gold and diamond mining. Formerly spelled Serra do Assuruá.

Acushnet (ŭkōōsh'nĭt), town (pop. 4,401), Bristol co., SE Mass., on estuary of Acushnet R., just N of New Bedford; rubber goods, boxes, crushed stone. Settled c.1660, inc. 1860.

Acushnet River, SE Mass., rises in SW Plymouth co., flows c.15 mi. S, past Acushnet, to Buzzards Bay bet. Fairhaven and New Bedford; lower course is wide estuary.

Acuto (äkōō'tō), village (pop. 2,126), Frosinone prov., Latium, S central Italy, 14 mi. NW of Frosinone.

Acutzilapan (äkōōtsēlä'pän), officially Santiago Acutzilapan, town (pop. 2,462), Mexico state, central Mexico, 40 mi. NW of Mexico city; grain, sugar cane, fruit, livestock.

Acworth (ăk'wûrth). **1** City (pop. 1,466), Cobb co., NW central Ga., 27 mi. NW of Atlanta; hosiery and lumber mills. Kennesaw Mtn. Natl. Battlefield Park and Allatoona Reservoir near by. Inc. 1860. **2** Town (pop. 418), Sullivan co., SW N.H., on Cold R. and 12 mi. SW of Newport. Has fine early church (1825).

Ad [Arabic,=the], for Arabic names beginning thus: see under following part of the name.

Ada (ä'dä), town (pop., including Big Ada, just NW, 5,199), Eastern Prov., SE Gold Coast colony, port on Gulf of Guinea, at mouth of Volta R. (ferry), and 60 mi. ENE of Accra; fishing center; coconuts. Important commercial station in 19th cent.

Ada (ā'dŭ), county (□ 1,140; pop. 70,649), SW Idaho; ⊙ Boise. Irrigated agr. area in Boise R. valley; bounded S by the Snake. Dairy products, hay, sugar beets, fruit, truck; mfg. at Boise. Formed 1864.

Ada. 1 City (pop. 2,121), ⊙ Norman co., NW Minn., near Wild Rice R., 31 mi. NNE of Fargo, N.Dak., in Red R. valley; trade and shipping point in grain, potato, sugar-beet area; dairy products. Founded 1874, inc. 1881. **2** Village (pop. 3,640), Hardin co., W central Ohio, 15 mi. E of Lima and on Ottawa R.; trade center for farming area (corn, onions, wheat, dairy products, poultry); greenhouses, poultry hatcheries; lumber, sporting goods, machinery, rubber products. Seat of Ohio Northern Univ. Laid out 1853, inc. 1861. **3** City (pop. 15,995), ⊙ Pontotoc co., S central Okla., c.70 mi. SE of Oklahoma City, and on Clear Boggy Creek; market and distribution center for oil and agr. area (cotton, corn, oats, hay, grain, sorghum, livestock; dairy products). Oil refining; mfg. of cement, machinery, glass, metal products, furniture, flour, feed, leather goods, tile. Seat of East Central State Col. Settled 1889.

Ada (ä'dä), village (pop. 10,414), Vojvodina, N Serbia, Yugoslavia, on Tisa R., on railroad and 9 mi. S of Senta, in the Backa.

Adabazar, Turkey: see ADAPAZARI.

Adadle (ädäd'lā), village, W Br. Somaliland, in Ogo highland, on road and 45 mi. ENE of Hargeisa; millet, corn; camels, sheep, goats.

Adah, village (pop. 1,191, with adjacent Antram), Fayette co., SW Pa., on the Monongahela and 10 mi. W of Uniontown.

Adai, district, Kazakh SSR: see FORT SHEVCHENKO.

Adai-Khokh or **Aday-Khokh** (ŭdī'-khôkh"), peak (15,239 ft.) in main range of the central Greater Caucasus, on Russian SFSR–Georgian SSR border, 27 mi. SW of Alagir; 42°47'N 43°48'E.

Adair (ŭdâr'). **1** County (□ 569; pop. 12,292), SW Iowa; ⊙ Greenfield. Drained by Middle, North, and Thompson rivers, and by Middle and East branches of the Nodaway. Rolling agr. area (corn, cattle, hogs, poultry). Bituminous-coal deposits. Formed 1851. **2** County (□ 393; pop. 17,603), S Ky.; ⊙ Columbia. Drained by Green R. and several creeks. Agr. area (livestock, grain, burley tobacco, poultry, fruit); timber; some mfg. at Columbia. Formed 1801. **3** County (□ 574; pop. 19,689), N Mo.; ⊙ Kirksville. Drained by Chariton and Salt rivers. Grain, cattle, poultry; coal; mfg. at Kirksville. Formed 1841. **4** County (□ 569; pop. 14,918), E Okla., in the Ozarks; ⊙ Stilwell. Bounded E by the Ark. line; drained by Illinois R. and small Barre Creek. Agr. (fruit, truck, livestock, grain, berries). Farm-products processing, some mfg. Stone and marble quarries; timber. Hunting, fishing. Formed 1907.

Adair. 1 Town (pop. 827), on Adair-Guthrie co. line, SW Iowa, 55 mi. W of Des Moines, in grain, poultry, dairy area; feed milling. **2** Town (pop. 299), Mayes co., NE Okla., c.45 mi. ENE of Tulsa, in rich stock-grazing and agr. region.

Adair Bay (ŭdâr'), inlet at head of Gulf of California, Sonora, NW Mexico, SE of mouth of Colorado R.

Adairsville (ŭdârz'vĭl), town (pop. 916), Bartow co., NW Ga., 14 mi. ENE of Rome; mfg. (textiles, lumber).

Adairville (ŭdâr'vĭl), town (pop. 800), Logan co., S Ky., at Tenn. line, on South Fork of Red R. and 32 mi. SW of Bowling Green, in agr., timber area; makes hosiery. Mineral springs.

Adaja River (ädhä'hä), Ávila and Valladolid provs., central Spain, rises c.30 mi. WSW of Ávila, flows E to Ávila, then N to the Duero 7 mi. ENE of Tordesillas; 120 mi. long. Receives Eresma R. 3 mi. S of Valdestillas.

Adakale, Turkey: see ARDANUC.

Ada-Kaleh (ädä-kä'lĕkh), Ger. *Neu-Orsova* (noi"-ôrsō'vä), island (pop. 579), in Danube R., SW Rumania, opposite Varciorova; 1 mi. long, ¼ mi. wide; specializes in tobacco-growing and sugar trade. Former Turkish territory (till 1912), it still preserves old Turkish buildings and fortifications, has a majority of Turkish inhabitants.

Adak Island (ā'dăk) (30 mi. long, 3–20 mi. wide), Andreanof Isls., Aleutian Isls., SW Alaska, 50 mi. WSW of Atka Isl., 9 mi. E of Kanaga Isl.; 51°49'N 176°40'W; rises to 3,900 ft. on Mt. Moffett (N). Sweeper Cove (E) is main harbor. Fox farming main native occupation. U.S. army, navy, and air bases, established here (1942) in Second World War, were important in Aleutian campaign. Bases were enlarged and made permanent after 1943; main air base at Davis, on NE coast. Just E is Kagalaska Isl.

Adal (ädäl'), arid region in Fr. Somaliland, along N shore of Gulf of Tadjoura. Forms part of Danakil desert. Nomadic grazing.

Adal, canton, Norway: see HEN.

Adalar, Turkey: see PRINCES ISLANDS.

Adalia, Turkey: see ANTALYA, city.

Adalia, Gulf of, Turkey: see ANTALYA, GULF OF.

Adal River, Norway: see BEGNA RIVER.

Adalsbruk (ô'dälsbrōōk), Nor. *Adalsbruk*, village (pop. 637) in Loten (Nor. *Løten*) canton (pop. 6,404), Hedmark co., SE Norway, on small Akersvik R. (Nor. *Åkersvik*), on railroad and 7 mi. E of Hamar; lumbering; woodworking. Sometimes spelled Aadalsbruk.

Adama, Ethiopia: see HADAMA.

Adamant Mountain (10,980 ft.), SE B.C., in Selkirk Mts. of the Rockies, 50 mi. NNE of Revelstoke; 51°43' N 117°55'W.

Adamaoua, Fr. Cameroons and Nigeria: see ADAMAWA.

Adamawa (ädämä'wä, ädä'mä'wä), Fr. *Adamaoua*, Ger. *Adamaua*, former native kingdom in W equatorial Africa, midway bet. L. Chad and Gulf of Guinea; 6°–11°N 11°–15°E. Settled by Fulah in 15th cent.; came (early 19th cent.) under control of Emir of Yola; divided c.1900 into Br. and Ger. zones. Ger. part divided bet. Br. and Fr. Cameroons after First World War. The Br. section now forms a prov. of Nigeria, while the Fr. section forms the administrative regions of Adamaoua and BENOUÉ in Fr. Cameroons. **Adamawa** province (□ 33,765; 1931 pop. 657,976), in Northern Provinces, E Nigeria, is on Fr. Cameroons border; ⊙ Yola. It includes part (□ 10,965; 1931 pop. 204,604; 1948 pop. estimate 301,700) of Br. Cameroons. Located in savanna, it includes Shebshi (SE), Alantika (E), and Mandara (NE) mts.; drained by Benue and Gongola rivers. Silver and lead mining; salt and limestone deposits. Agr. (peanuts, cassava, millet, durra, yams); cattle raising. Chief towns: Yola, Numan. Pop. largely Fulah. Section in Br. Cameroons is divided into 2 parts, separated by Benue R. valley: N dists. (□ 1,740; 1948 pop. estimate 200,400), with centers at Mubi and Madagali, and S dists. (□ 9,225; 1948 pop. estimate 101,300), with centers at Toungo and Gashaka. Formerly called Yola prov. The Fr. part constitutes **Adamawa** administrative region (□ 28,870, 1950 pop. 158,700), N central Fr. Cameroons; ⊙ N'Gaoundéré. Bounded W by Br. Cameroons, E by Fr. Equatorial Africa. Nomadic grazing. Natron springs. Pop. largely Fulah.

Adam-Clisi or **Adam-Klissi** (ädäm-klēs'), village (pop. 1,088), Constanta prov., SE Rumania, 34 mi. WSW of Constanta; noted for remains of Trajan's commemorative monument, *Tropaeum Trajani* (A.D. 109).

Adamdighi (ŭdŭm′dĭgē), village, Bogra dist., N central East Bengal, E Pakistan, 21 mi. W of Bogra; trades in rice, jute, rape and mustard, sugar cane.

Adamello (ädämĕl′lō), mountain group of S zone of Rhaetian Alps, N Italy, on Lombardy and Trentino–Alto Adige border, S of Ortles mtn. group, E of Val Camonica. Highest peaks are Monte Adamello (11,660 ft.), 31 mi. WNW of Trent, and Monte Care Alto (11,358 ft.), just SE. Contains over 50 glaciers whose waters feed Oglio, Chiese, and Sarca rivers and are used for hydroelectric power. Its N arm is La PRESANELLA.

Adaminaby (ă″dŭmĭ′nŭbē), town (pop. 552), SE New South Wales, Australia, in Australian Alps, on Snowy R. and 55 mi. SSW of Canberra; large hydroelectric plant; sheep raising.

Adami Tullo (ä′dämē tōōl′lō), village, Arusi prov., S central Ethiopia, near L. Zwai, on road and 26 mi. WNW of Asselle, in agr. (cereals, cotton) and fishing region.

Adam-jo-Tando, W Pakistan: see TANDO ADAM.

Adamov, Czechoslovakia: see BLANSKO.

Adamovka (ŭdä′mŭfkŭ), village (1939 pop. over 500), E Chkalov oblast, Russian SFSR, 60 mi. ENE of Orsk; wheat, sunflowers, livestock.

Adam Peak, Nev.: see OSGOOD MOUNTAINS.

Adams. 1 County (□ 1,247; pop. 40,234), N central Colo.; ⊙ Brighton. Irrigated agr. area, with South Platte R. in W. Sugar beets, beans, livestock. Formed 1902. 2 County (□ 1,377; pop. 3,347), W Idaho; ⊙ Council. Mtn. area bounded W by Snake R. and Oregon, watered by headstreams of Weiser and Little Salmon rivers. Livestock grazing, agr. (apples, pears, peaches, timothy). Weiser Natl. Forest extends throughout much of co. Seven Devils Mts. are in NW. Formed 1911. 3 County (□ 866; pop. 64,690), W Ill.; ⊙ Quincy. Bounded W by the Mississippi; drained by small Bear and McKee creeks. Agr. area (livestock, corn, wheat, soybeans, poultry; dairy products), with diversified mfg. Limestone quarries. Formed 1825. 4 County (□ 345; pop. 22,393), E Ind., bounded E by Ohio line; ⊙ Decatur. Farming (livestock, soybeans, grain, poultry, truck) and dairying area; timber. Diversified mfg., including the processing of dairy products and other foods. Drained by Wabash and St. Marys rivers and small Longlois Creek. Formed 1835. 5 County (□ 426; pop. 8,753), SW Iowa; ⊙ Corning. Gently rolling prairie, drained by Middle and East branches of the Nodaway, by Little Platte R., and by One Hundred and Two R. Agr. (corn, hogs, cattle, poultry). Bituminous-coal deposits, some coal mines, sand and gravel pits, limestone quarries. Formed 1851. 6 County (□ 448; pop. 32,256), SW Miss.; ⊙ NATCHEZ. Bounded W by the Mississippi (here the La. line), S by Homochitto R. Includes part of Homochitto Natl. Forest. Agr. (cotton, corn), dairying, lumbering. Oil field; clay, limestone deposits. Formed 1799. 7 County (□ 562; pop. 28,855), S Nebr.; ⊙ Hastings. Agr. area drained by Little Blue R. Mfg. at Hastings; grain, livestock, poultry produce. Formed 1871. 8 County (□ 990; pop. 4,910), SW N.Dak.; ⊙ Hettinger; drained by Cedar Creek. Coal. Formed 1907. 9 County (□ 588; pop. 20,499), S Ohio; ⊙ West Union. Bounded S by Ohio R., here forming Ky. line; drained by small creeks. Includes Serpent Mound State Park. Agr. area (livestock, dairy products, tobacco, grain); some mfg. at Manchester. Formed 1799. 10 County (□ 526; pop. 44,197), S Pa.; ⊙ GETTYSBURG. Agr. and fruitgrowing area, bounded S by Md., W and NW by South Mtn. Agr. (apples, peaches, cherries, wheat); limestone; shoe mfg., canning. Formed 1800. 11 County (□ 1,895; pop. 6,584), SE Wash., in Columbia basin agr. region; ⊙ Ritzville. Rolling prairies bounded SE by Palouse R. Wheat, alfalfa, livestock, dairy products. Formed 1883. 12 County (□ 677; pop. 7,906), central Wis.; ⊙ Friendship. Dairying, general-farming, and timber area; dairy-products processing; railroad repair shops. Drained by tributaries of Wisconsin R., which bounds co. on W; the gorge Dells of the Wisconsin is in SW. Formed 1848.

Adams. 1 Town (pop. 12,034), Berkshire co., NW Mass., in the Berkshires, on Hoosic R. and 14 mi. NNE of Pittsfield; paper mills, textiles, food products; printing; calcium quarries. Susan B. Anthony b. here. Inc. 1778. 2 Village (pop. 663), Mower co., SE Minn., near Iowa line, 15 mi. SE of Austin in grain and livestock area; dairy products, poultry. 3 Village (pop. 457), Gage co., SE Nebr., 25 mi. SSE of Lincoln and on branch of Nemaha R.; grain. 4 Village (pop. 1,762), Jefferson co., N N.Y., 13 mi. SSW of Watertown, in dairy region; mfg. (paint, patent medicines, chemicals, surgical equipment, wood products); summer resort. Inc. 1851. 5 Village (pop. 411), Walsh co., NE N.Dak., 30 mi. W of Grafton. 6 City (pop. 154), Umatilla co., NE Oregon, 13 mi. NE of Pendleton; grain elevators. 7 City (pop. 1,425), Adams co., central Wis., 30 mi. S of Wisconsin Rapids, in timber and farm area (dairying; poultry, grain, potatoes). Founded before 1860; inc. 1926.

Adams, Fort, R.I.: see NEWPORT, city.

Adams, Mount. 1 Peak, N.H.: see PRESIDENTIAL RANGE. 2 Peak (12,307 ft.), S Wash., in Cascade Range, 55 mi. SW of Yakima.

Adam's Bridge or **Rama's Bridge** (rä′mŭz), chain of shoals in Indian Ocean, bet. India and Ceylon; separate Palk Strait (N) and Gulf of Mannar (S); 18 mi. long. India-Ceylon ferry route passes N, bet. Dhanushkodi on Rameswaram Isl. (W) and Talaimannar on Mannar Isl. (E). Legendary site of causeway built by Rama, hero of the Ramayana.

Adamsburg, borough (pop. 238), Westmoreland co., SW Pa., 2 mi. SW of Jeanette.

Adams Center, village (1940 pop. 714), Jefferson co., N N.Y., 9 mi. SSW of Watertown; feed, condensed milk.

Adams Lake (□ 54), S B.C., 50 mi. NNW of Vernon; 39 mi. long, 1–2 mi. wide. Drained SE into Shuswap L. by short Adams R.

Adam's Peak, Singhalese *Sri Padastanaya* and *Samanaliya*, mountain (7,360 ft.), S central Ceylon, in SW Ceylon Hill Country, 11 mi. NNE of Ratnapura. Famous Buddhist, Hindu, and Moslem pilgrimage center; rock at summit bears impression of a foot regarded as the Buddha's by Buddhists, Siva's by Hindus, and Adam's by Moslems, who believe this to be the site of Adam's fall from Paradise.

Adams Peak (8,300 ft.), E Calif., in the Sierra Nevada, 30 mi. NNW of Reno, Nev.

Adamsthal, Czechoslovakia: see BLANSKO.

Adamstown, W suburb of Newcastle, New South Wales, Australia; coal-mining center.

Adamstown, borough (pop. 1,020), Lancaster and Berks cos., SE Pa., 10 mi. SW of Reading; settled 1739.

Adamsville, village (pop. 249), S Que., on Centre Yamaska R. and 8 mi. SSW of Granby; dairying.

Adamsville. 1 Village (pop. 1,531), Jefferson co., N central Ala., 8 mi. NW of downtown Birmingham. 2 Village (pop. 164), Muskingum co., central Ohio, 12 mi. NE of Zanesville, in agr. area. 3 Village, R.I.: see LITTLE COMPTON. 4 Town (pop. 927), McNairy co., SW Tenn., 36 mi. SE of Jackson; sawmills, cotton gins.

Adamuz (ädhämōōth′), town (pop. 5,618), Córdoba prov., S. Spain, near the Guadalquivir, 16 mi. NE of Córdoba; olive-oil processing, soap mfg., flour milling. Stock raising, lumbering; cereals.

Adana, province, Turkey: see SEYHAN.

Adana (ä′dänä″), city (1950 pop. 117,799), ⊙ Seyhan prov., S Turkey, 4th largest city in Turkey, in SE corner of Asia Minor, on railroad, on Seyhan R., and 240 mi. SSE of Ankara, 30 mi. from Mediterranean coast; 37°N 35°19′E. Commercial processing, and agr. trade center. Cotton mills, tobacco factory; agr. machinery works; wheat, oats, cotton trade. Colonized under the Romans, it prospered, declined, and was restored (A.D. c.782) by Harun-ar-Rashid.

Adancata, Ukrainian SSR: see GLYBOKA.

Adanero (ädhänā′rō), town (pop. 770), Ávila prov., central Spain, 20 mi. NNE of Ávila; cereals, vegetables, grapes, livestock; flour milling.

Adapazari (ä″däpäzärŭ′, –zä′rē), Turkish *Adapazarı*, city (1950 pop. 36,210), Kocaeli prov., NW Turkey, on Sakarya R. 24 mi. E of Izmit, near L. Sapanca; rail terminus and agr. center (wheat, corn, potatoes, poultry); mfg. of agr. implements, railroad rolling stock; zinc, iron, and copper near by. Trading center for rugs, silk, linen, tobacco. Sometimes Adabazar (ädäbäzär′).

Adare (ŭdâr′), Gaelic *Ath Dara*, town (pop. 496), N central Co. Limerick, Ireland, on Maigue R. and 10 mi. SW of Limerick; agr. market (grain, potatoes; dairying). R.C. church was part of White Abbey, founded 1230; Protestant church belonged to Austin Friary, founded c.1315. There are ruins of Franciscan Friary founded 1464. Anc. castle was rebuilt in 14th cent.

Adare, Cape (ŭdâr′), headland, Antarctica, NE extremity of Victoria Land, on the South Pacific at W edge of Ross Sea; 71°17′S 170°15′E. Discovered 1841 by Sir James C. Ross. Kristensen and Borchgrevink landed here 1895, the 1st landing on Antarctic continent. Borchgrevink returned in 1899.

Adarus, Palestine: see ATLIT.

Adasiya, El, or **Al-Adasiyah** (both: ĕl ädäsē′yŭ), village, N Jordan, on Yarmuk R. and 5 mi. S of Samakh. Olives, bananas, oranges. Tourist resort; ruins (S).

Adavad (ŭdä′vŭd), town (pop. 6,249), East Khandesh dist., NE Bombay, India, 9 mi. ESE of Chopda; local agr. market (millet, wheat). Sometimes spelled Adawad.

Adawa, Japan: see ATAWA.

Aday-Khokh, peak, USSR: see ADAI-KHOKH.

Addanki (ŭdŭng′kē), town (pop. 11,310), Guntur dist., NE Madras, India, on Gundlakamma R. and 45 mi. SW of Guntur; rice and oilseed milling, cattle raising; handicraft leather goods.

Addar, Ras, Tunisia: see BON, CAPE.

Adda River (äd′dä), anc. *Addua*, Lombardy, N Italy, rises in Rhaetian Alps 9 mi. NW of Bormio, flows SSW and E, through the VALTELLINA, and S, through L. Como and L. of Lecco, across Lombard plain, past Lodi, to Po R. 6 mi. W of Cremona. Receives Brembo and Serio rivers (left). Navigable for 30 mi. in lower course; forms boundary bet. Milano and Cremona provs. Extensively used for hydroelectric power in upper Valtellina, for irrigation on Lombard plain. Strategic line in many wars.

Ad Daro (äd dä′rō), village (pop. 1,000), Tigre prov., N Ethiopia, 40 mi. WNW of Aksum; cereals, livestock.

Addatigala (ŭdŭtē′gŭlŭ), village, East Godavari dist., NE Madras, India, in Eastern Ghats, 28 mi. NNW of Peddapuram. Bamboo, myrobalan in near-by forests; graphite deposits.

Addi Caieh, Eritrea: see ADI CAIEH, town.

Addieville, village (pop. 271), Washington co., SW Ill., 22 mi. SW of Centralia, in agr. and bituminous-coal area.

Addiewell, village in West Calder parish, SW Midlothian, Scotland; shale-oil mining.

Addingham (ă′dĭng-ŭm), town and parish (pop. 2,005), West Riding, W central Yorkshire, England, near Wharfe R., 3 mi. WNW of Ilkley; rayon milling.

Addington, England: see CROYDON.

Addington, town (pop. 174), Jefferson co., S Okla., 18 mi. S of Duncan, in farm area.

Addis, village (pop. 505), West Baton Rouge parish, SE La., 8 mi. SW of Baton Rouge; sugar mill.

Addis Ababa (ă′dĭs ă′bŭbŭ, ŭbä′bŭ, Amharic äd′dĭs ä′bäbä) [Amharic,=new flower], city (pop. c.300,000), ⊙ Ethiopia and Shoa prov.; 9°2′N 38°47′E. Connected by rail (486 mi.) with Djibuti, Fr. Somaliland, since 1917. A motor road has linked it with Eritrean towns of Massawa since 1936 and Assab since 1939. Communication and commercial center (coffee, hides, beeswax, cereals); cigarette factory, cement works, artisan industries (weaving, leatherworking, metalworking). It is a sprawling city situated on a hilly upland (c. 7,775–8,100 ft.) sheltered by mts. (N, E). Consists mainly of thatched huts, with a sprinkling of modern bldgs. Has churches, schools, hospitals, and a leprosarium. On hills SE of the city proper are the imperial palace and parliament. Founded 1887 by Menelik II, who moved the capital here in 1889 from near-by Intotto. Here, in 1896, Italians recognized Ethiopian independence. Occupied (1936–41) by Italians, who made it ⊙ Italian East Africa.

Addis Alam (äd′dĭs ä′läm), Ital. *Addis Alem*, town (pop. 1,000), Shoa prov., central Ethiopia, on road and 25 mi. W of Addis Ababa, in agr. region (cereals, bananas); lime, meat products. Founded 1900 by Menelik II, who planned to transfer the capital here but abandoned the project in 1903.

Addiscombe, England: see CROYDON.

Addison, county (□ 785; pop. 19,442), W Vt., bounded W by L. Champlain and rising to Green Mts. in E; ⊙ Middlebury. Agr. and resort region; dairying, fruit, wood products, poultry. Lake and mtn. resorts; winter sports. Includes part of Green Mtn. Natl. Forest; drained by Otter Creek, New Haven and White rivers. Organized 1787.

Addison. 1 Town (pop. 590), Winston co., NW Ala., 50 mi. NNW of Birmingham. 2 Village (pop. 813), Du Page co., NE Ill., W of Chicago and 16 mi. SE of Elgin. 3 Town (pop. 846), Washington co., E Maine, at mouth of Pleasant R., 16 mi. SW of Machias; fishing, lumbering, resorts. 4 Village (pop. 488), Lenawee co., SE Mich., 17 mi. WNW of Adrian, in grain and dairy area; flour- and sawmilling. 5 Village (pop. 1,920), Steuben co., S N.Y., on Canisteo R. and 9 mi. WSW of Corning, in dairying region; wood products, flour. Inc. 1873. 6 Borough (pop. 237), Somerset co., SW Pa., 23 mi. SW of Somerset. 7 Town (pop. 628), Addison co., W Vt., 8 mi. NW of Middlebury and on L. Champlain, here bridged to Crown Point, N.Y., at Chimney Point, site of Fr. settlement (1730) near fort built (1690) by N.Y. expedition. 8 Town, W.Va.: see WEBSTER SPRINGS.

Ad Diwaniya, Iraq: see DIWANIYA, city.

Addlestone, England: see CHERTSEY.

Addo Elephant National Park (□ 26.5), S Cape Prov., U. of So. Afr., 30 mi. N of Port Elizabeth; reserve for Addo elephants, Cape buffalo, bushbuck, duiker, and other game.

Addor (ă′dŭr), town (pop. 110), Moore co., central N.C., 19 mi. NE of Rockingham. Formerly Keyser.

Addua, Italy: see ADDA RIVER.

Addu Atoll (ädōō′), extreme S group (pop. 5,686) of Maldive Isls., in Indian Ocean, bet. 0°34′S and 0°42′S, 675 mi. SW of Ceylon, 460 mi. NNE of Diego Garcia (Chagos Archipelago). Trades with other Maldives in coconuts, coir, dried fish, palm mats, tortoise shell. Served as Br. naval anchorage in Second World War.

Addyston (ă′dĕstŭn), village (pop. 1,651), Hamilton co., extreme SW Ohio, on Ohio R. and 10 mi. W of Cincinnati; iron pipe, castings. Founded 1789. William Henry Harrison Memorial Park is near by.

Adegem (ä′dŭ-khŭm), agr. village (pop. 4,981), East Flanders prov., NW Belgium, 4 mi. WNW of Eekloo.

Adeje (ädhā′hā), town (pop. 2,437), Tenerife, Canary Isls., 38 mi. SW of Santa Cruz de Tenerife; tomatoes, bananas, cereals, grapes, cochineal, potatoes, corn. Its port is served by transoceanic fruit ships. Adeje was isl.'s ⊙ in pre-Sp. times.

Adel (ā″dĕl′). 1 City (pop. 2,776), ⊙ Cook co., S Ga., 23 mi. NNW of Valdosta; tobacco and watermelon market; food canning, milling (veneer, lumber), fertilizer mfg. Inc. 1889. 2 Town (pop. 1,799), ⊙ Dallas co., central Iowa, on Raccoon R. and 20 mi. W of Des Moines; brick and tile plant, poultry hatchery; soybean processing. Settled 1846, inc. 1887.

Adela, La, Argentina: see Río COLORADO, La Pampa natl. territory.

Adelaide, city (pop. 35,032; metropolitan Adelaide 382,604), ⊙ South Australia, near E shore of Gulf St. Vincent, at foot of Mt. Lofty Ranges; 34°55'S 138°35'E. Cultural and commercial center of state. Torrens R. divides S.Adelaide (business center) from N.Adelaide; park separates city from suburbs. Has automobile factory. Its outlet, Port Adelaide, is 7 mi. NW. Govt.-owned ammunition plants, flour and knitting mills. Seat of Univ. of Adelaide (1874), Waite Inst. of Agr. Research (1924), school of mines, St. Peter's Cathedral (Anglican), St. Francis Xavier's Cathedral (R.C.), Govt. House, art gall., Natural History Mus. (1895). Oldest settlement (1836) of state. Principal suburbs: BURNSIDE, GLENELG, HINDMARSH, KENSINGTON AND NORWOOD, MITCHAM, THEBARTON, UNLEY, WOODVILLE, WEST TORRENS.

Adelaide, town (pop. 4,156), SE Cape Prov., U. of So. Afr., on Koonap R. and 40 mi. NNW of Grahamstown, at foot of Winterberg mts.; stock-raising and market center, noted for Merino sheep; dairying, citrus fruit.

Adelaide Island (68 naut. mi. long, 20 naut. mi. wide), Antarctica, off W coast of Palmer Peninsula, NW of Marguerite Bay; 67°15'S 68°40'W. Discovered 1832 by John Biscoe, Br. navigator.

Adelaide Islands or **Queen Adelaide Islands,** Sp. *Archipiélago de la Reina Adelaida*, group off Magallanes prov., S Chile, on the Pacific at NW entrance to Strait of Magellan, separated from Muñoz Gamero Peninsula by Smyth Channel. Isls. are almost entirely uninhabited.

Adelaide Peninsula, NW Keewatin Dist., Northwest Territories, extends 60 mi. N into the Arctic Ocean, S of King William Isl.; 68°30'N 97°W. On N coast many relics of Franklin's expedition (1847–48) have been found (Grant Point, Starvation Cove).

Adelaide River, NW Northern Territory, Australia, rises in hills W of Brock's Creek, flows 110 mi. N to Adam Bay of Clarence Strait; navigable 53 mi. by steamer; mangroves.

Adelanto or **El Adelanto** (ĕl ädālän'tō), town (pop. 1,401), Jutiapa dept., SE Guatemala, in highlands, 9 mi. SSE of Jutiapa; alt. 3,300 ft. Corn, beans, livestock.

Adelboden (ä'dŭlbō'dŭn), town (pop. 2,659), Bern canton, SW central Switzerland, 19 mi. SW of Interlaken; highest commune (4,450 ft.) in Bernese Alps. Year-round resort noted for mtn. climbing, winter sports. Has 15th-cent. church.

Adelebsen (ä"dŭlĕp'sŭn), village (pop. 2,824), in former Prussian prov. of Hanover, W Germany, after 1945 in Lower Saxony, 9 mi. NW of Göttingen; flour products. Basalt quarries near by.

Adélie Coast (ă'dŭlē, ädālē'), part (□ 150,000) of coast of Wilkes Land, Antarctica, on Indian Ocean, bet. 136°20'E and 142°20'E. Discovered 1840 by Dumont d'Urville, French explorer; explored 1911–14 by Sir Douglas Mawson. Claimed by France, which maintains a meteorological station at 66°45'S 141°E; officially put under Fr. sovereignty in 1938. U.S. does not recognize claims in Antarctica. Also called Adélie Land (Fr. *Terre Adélie*).

Adeline (ă'dŭlīn), village (pop. 135), Ogle co., N Ill., 22 mi. WSW of Rockford, in rich agr. area.

Adell (ādĕl', ŭdĕl'), village (pop. 366), Sheboygan co., E Wis., 15 mi. SW of Sheboygan, in dairy and grain area.

Adelnau, Poland: see ODOLANOW.

Adelong (ă'dŭlŏng), village (pop. 738), S New South Wales, 60 mi. W of Canberra; gold-mining center; sheep.

Adelphi (ŭdĕl'fī), village (pop. 392), Ross co., S Ohio, 15 mi. NE of Chillicothe and on small Salt Creek, in agr. area.

Adelphi, The (ŭdĕl'fē), small district of Westminster, London, England, bet. S side of the Strand and N bank of the Thames, just E of Charing Cross; developed by the Adams brothers from designs mainly by Robert Adam. Among its famous residents were Garrick, Galsworthy, J. M. Barrie, G. B. Shaw, W. B. Yeats, and H. G. Wells. Since 1937 most of the bldgs. have been demolished to make way for modern office blocks.

Adelsberg, Yugoslavia: see POSTOJNA.

Adelsheim (ä'dŭls-hīm), town (pop. 2,423), N Baden, Germany, after 1945 in Württemberg-Baden, 19 mi. NNE of Heilbronn; fruit. Resort with cataphoretic baths. Has 15th-cent. church, 17th-cent. town hall.

Adem, El (ĕl ä'dĕm), village, E Cyrenaica, Libya, 15 mi. S of Tobruk; road junction. Has airport of Tobruk. Bombed (1940) and scene of fighting (1942) bet. Axis and British in Second World War.

Ademi, Russian SFSR: see ADIMI.

Ademuz (ä-dhämōōth'), town (pop. 2,589), Valencia prov., E Spain, on Turia R. and 21 mi. SSW of Teruel; linen-cloth mfg., brandy distilling; apples, cereals, nuts, sugar beets.

Aden (ā'dŭn, ä'–), fortified town (1946 pop. 56,849), ⊙ Aden Colony, port on Gulf of Aden, 100 mi. E of the strait Bab el Mandeb, on volcanic Aden peninsula (□ 21), which rises to 1,808 ft. in the Jabal Shamsan; 12°47'N 45°E. Administrative and economic center of Aden Colony and Aden Protectorate; port of call on great shipping lane linking Mediterranean Sea and Indian Ocean, and free port since 1850; entrepôt and collecting center of S Arabian Peninsula. Main industry is bunkering of ships and handling of cargo by large firms employing immigrant Yemeni Arabs. Entrepôt trade is concerned with the export of local salt and of hides, skins, coffee, gums, incense, and grain from Aden Protectorate and Yemen; and with the importation and distribution of finished goods to the hinterland. Small local mfg. produces soap, aluminum utensils, cigarettes, textiles, sesame oil and oil cake. A strategic outpost of Britain, Aden guards the S approach to the Red Sea. Its harbor on sheltered Aden Bay has numerous loading berths, and oiling and coaling installations, and admits ships of 36-ft. draught. Telegraph station at Ras Boradli. The town of Aden, known administratively as Fortress township, consists of widely separated urban nuclei on the Aden peninsula and the low Khormaksar isthmus linking it to the mainland. These divisions are CRATER (old historic Aden proper, on E shore of peninsula); TAWAHI, the overseas port, govt. and business center, on peninsula's W coast, adjoining STEAMER POINT; MAALA, the native dhow harbor and warehouse section, on peninsula's N coast; and KHORMAKSAR, site of military airfield and reservation. An important trade center since anc. times, Aden passed successively to the Ptolemies of Egypt (3d cent. B.C.), to Rome (30 B.C.), Ethiopia, and Persia (6th cent. A.D.). Following the advent of Islam (7th cent.), Aden's history became closely linked with that of Yemen. It flourished on the Europe-Asia trade route and was reported (1276) by Marco Polo to have a pop. of 80,000, but the discovery of the Cape of Good Hope marked the beginning of its decline. It was attacked in 1513 and 1516 by the Portuguese and fell in 1538 to the Turks, who held it until their evacuation of Yemen in 1630. In 1728, the Abdali governor of Lahej took Aden into his sultanate. Aden's decline continued, however, and at the time (1839) of its capture by the British its pop. was 600. The revival of the Red Sea route in mid-19th cent. and the opening (1869) of the Suez Canal rapidly regained for Aden its old importance. It became a major fueling station for coal and oil and an entrepôt for trade with Arabia, Ethiopia, and Somaliland. Town was closely threatened by a Turkish advance from Yemen during First World War. A railroad built during the war to Lahej was dismantled in 1929. During Second World War, Aden was an important air base.

Aden, Gulf of, W arm of the Arabian Sea, bet. the Somaliland "horn" of E Africa and Aden Protectorate on the S Arabian Peninsula; 550 mi. long, 300 mi. wide at mouth bet. Cape Guardafui and Ras Fartak. Connecting W via the strait Bab el Mandeb with the Red Sea, it lies on the great Mediterranean–Indian Ocean shipping lane. Chief ports are Aden and Mukalla on N coast, Djibouti and Berbera on S coast.

Adena (ŭdē'nŭ), village (pop. 1,517), Jefferson co., E Ohio, 15 mi. SW of Steubenville, in coal-mining area.

Adenau (ä'dŭnou), village (pop. 2,575), in former Prussian Rhine Prov., W Germany, after 1945 in Rhineland-Palatinate, in the Eifel, 13 mi. WNW of Mayen; rail terminus. Noted Nürburg auto race track is 3 mi. S.

Aden Bay (ā'dŭn, ä'–), inlet of Gulf of Aden, bet. Aden and Little Aden peninsulas, and constituting the harbor of Aden Colony; 8 mi. long, 4 mi. wide; opens on the gulf via 3-mi.-wide strait. Salt pans on N shore.

Aden Colony, British crown colony (□ 75; 1946 pop. 80,516; including PERIM □ 80, pop. 80,876) on SW tip of the Arabian Peninsula, on Gulf of Aden 100 mi. E of the strait Bab el Mandeb; ⊙ Aden. In addition to Perim, the KAMARAN ISLANDS (off Yemen) and KURIA MURIA ISLANDS (off the Dhofar coast of Oman) are also considered part of the colony. The colony proper consists of the developed ADEN (E) and undeveloped LITTLE ADEN (W) peninsulas of volcanic origin, joined by a narrow strip of hinterland and enclosing ADEN BAY, the harbor of the colony. Its climate, governed by the monsoons, is cool and pleasant during the NE monsoon (Oct.–April). During the summer, however, a damp, airless heat prevails, except when dispelled (July–Aug.) by the strong winds of the SW monsoon. Sandstorms are apt to occur through the summer. Rainfall is very scanty and irregular, in some years nonexistent. Pop. includes Arabs (73%), Indians (11%), Jews (9%; since 1946 largely emigrated to Israel), and Somalis (5%); it is concentrated on the Aden peninsula, site of the town of Aden and the colony's commercial and industrial hub. There is some agr. at Sheikh Othman and Hiswa on mainland. Salt, evaporated in pans on N shore of Aden Bay, is main local product. Colony has airfields at Khormaksar (military) and Bir Fadhl (civil). Aden colony is administered by a governor who is also governor of the protectorate, aided by executive and (since 1947) legislative councils. The history of the colony dates from the capture (1839) of Aden by the East India Company from Bombay, at which time Aden became a settlement directed by a resident and considered part of the presidency of Bombay. Area of the settlement was enlarged by the acquisition of Little Aden (1868) and the mainland coastal strip (1882, 1888). In 1932, the settlement was detached from Bombay and created a chief commissioner's prov. under the central Indian govt. Finally, in 1937, Aden became a separate crown colony.

Aden Protectorate, group of independent Arab tribal districts (□ 110,000; 1946 pop. 670,000) on S coast of Arabian Peninsula, in protective treaty relations with Great Britain. It was under govt. of India until 1927, when it passed under the Colonial Office, and is administered by the governor of Aden Colony. Extending along the Gulf of Aden and Arabian Sea from the strait Bab el Mandeb (W) to the cape Ras Dharbat 'Ali (limit of Oman sultanate), the protectorate is bounded inland by Yemen and the great Arabian desert Rub 'al Khali. Physiographically, it consists of an arid littoral belt, 4–40 mi. in depth and, inland, of serrated ranges and elevated plateaus. The most characteristic features of the Aden hinterland are the granitic Kaur ranges (W) and the Wadi Hadhramaut (E), the latter being deeply incised into the broad limestone tableland. The maritime plains are hot and humid in summer, cooler and drier in winter. A wider temp. range is encountered inland. Because of the irregular and insufficient precipitation, agr. is dependent on irrigation from watercourses and wells. Chief agr. dists. are: coastal Lahej, Abyan, and Ahwar oases; Mukheiras truck-gardening area on Audhali plateau; the wadies Hajr, Duan (honey), Hadhramaut; and the Gheil Ba Wazir (tobacco) oasis. Staple crops are millet, wheat, barley, sesame, lucerne, and dates. Stock raising (sheep, goats, donkeys, camels) supplies animal power, meat, and hides. Fisheries furnish important export products (dried sardines, shark, tunny, and kingfish). Guano is collected on Baraqa Isls. off Bir Ali. Weaving, dyeing, gold- and silverwork are the principal industries. The protectorate has no railways. Camel caravans are the chief means of transportation. Motor highways radiate from Aden to the Subeihi country, to Taiz and Qataba in Yemen, and to Lodar and Ahwar. A coastal road serves the protectorate in E and is linked with the Wadi Hadhramaut. Airfields are maintained (since 1928) by the British for policing purposes. Pop. is tribal Arab of the Shafa'i sect of Sunnis. Most of the small Jewish minority emigrated to Israel in late 1940s. The chief centers are Lahej (W), and Mukalla, Shihr, and Seiyun (E). Aden Protectorate has no overall govt. and is divided for administrative purposes into the Western Aden Protectorate and the Eastern Aden Protectorate. The **Western Aden Protectorate** (□ 40,000; 1946 pop. 350,000) is directed by a British political agent (hq. at Aden), whose staff advises local rulers on the administration of their areas. This territory was under the control of Yemen until the 18th cent., in the course of which the Yemeni governors of the various tribal dists., led by the Abdali sultan of Lahej, declared their independence and founded local dynasties. Following British occupation (1839) of Aden, these chiefs entered into treaty relations with Britain; and by the outbreak of the First World War, the Western Aden Protectorate had acquired its present limits. During the war, the westernmost dists. of Subeihi, Abdali, Haushabi, and Amiri were held (1915–18) by the Turks from Yemen. The boundary with Yemen, originally delimited during 1902–5, and extended in 1914 by an Anglo-Turkish convention, was modified in 1934 by the so-called "Status Quo Line," effective for 40 years. In the 1940s, a number of tribal chiefs entered into closer adviser relations with Britain. Western Aden Protectorate includes the so-called original NINE CANTONS—ABDALI, AMIRI, HAUSHABI, FADHLI, Upper and Lower YAFA, SUBEIHI, AQRABI, Upper and Lower AULAQI, and ALAWI—as well as the additional tribal areas of AUDHALI, BEIHAN, SHAIBI, DATHINA, and the RADFAN confederation (led by the Qutaibi tribe). The **Eastern Aden Protectorate** (□ 70,000; 1946 pop. 320,000), also known as the HADHRAMAUT, is directed by a British agent (hq. at Mukalla). Under uncertain Yemeni suzerainty until 1704, the territory was thereafter controlled by the powerful Kathiri tribe until the 19th cent., when the Quaiti tribe achieved supremacy with British aid. Although the original protectorate treaty with the Quaiti dates from 1888, close contact developed only in 1930s, and adviser treaties were signed in 1937 and 1939. Eastern Aden Protectorate includes the QUAITI and KATHIRI sultanates (the 2 so-called Hadhramaut states), the Wahidi sultanates of BALHAF and BIR ALI, the small coastal sheikdoms of Irqa and Haura, and the MAHRI sultanate of Qishn and SOCOTRA.

Adernò, Sicily: see ADRANO.

Adh [Arabic, =the], for Arabic names beginning thus: see under following part of the name.

Adhoi (ŭdō'ē), town (pop. 5,076), N Saurashtra, India, 45 mi. NNW of Morvi, in enclave in Cutch; markets millet, salt.

Adiaké (ädyä'kā), village, SE Ivory Coast, Fr. West Africa, on W shore of Aby Lagoon, 45 mi. E of Abidjan; lumbering, coffee and cacao growing. Meteorological station.

Adi Caieh (ädē' käyä'), administrative division, central Eritrea, bet. Ethiopia and Red Sea (Gulf of Zula); ⊙ Adi Caieh. Part of central plateau (alt. c.3–9,000 ft.) which descends abruptly to narrow coastal plain. Watered by upper Gash R. (here called Mareb R.). Some stock raising (cattle, camels, goats) and agr. (cereals, vegetables). Chief centers: Adi Caieh, Senafe, Saganeiti. Airport at Gura. Also called Achele Guzai.

Adi Caieh, town (pop. 3,600), ⊙ Adi Caieh div., central Eritrea, on road and 45 mi. SE of Asmara; alt. c.7,840 ft. Commercial center (cereals, hides, oilseeds, honey); flour milling. Near by are ruins of 2 Axumite cities. Sometimes also Addi Caieh and Addicaie.

Adichanallur, India: see SRIVAIKUNTAM.

Adícora (ädē'kōrä), town (pop. 823), Falcón state, NW Venezuela, port on E coast of Paraguaná Peninsula, 8 mi. E of Pueblo Nuevo; fisheries.

À Dieu Vat (ä dyû vä'), gold placer in Inini territory, N Fr. Guiana, 45 mi. W of Cayenne.

Adigeni (ŭdyĭgĕ'nyē), village (1939 pop. over 500), SW Georgian SSR, on S slope of Adzhar-Imeretian Range, 15 mi. WNW of Akhaltsikhe, near Turkish border; orchards.

Adige River (ä'dējĕ), Ger. *Etsch*, anc. *Athesis*, longest river (255 mi.) of Italy after the Po, rises S of Passo di Resia in 3 small Alpine lakes, flows S and E, through Val Venosta, S, through Val Lagarina, past Trento and Rovereto, SE, across Po plain, past Verona and Legnago, and E to the Adriatic 5 mi. SE of Chioggia. Navigable for 70 mi. in lower course; forms Rovigo-Padova prov. boundary. Used for irrigation and hydroelectric power. Receives Noce R. (right), Isarco and Avisio rivers (left).

Adighe Autonomous Oblast, Russian SFSR: see ADYGE AUTONOMOUS OBLAST.

Adigrat (ä'dēgrät), town (pop. 4,290), Tigre prov., N Ethiopia, near Eritrean border, on road and 80 mi. SE of Asmara, in cereal-growing and stock-raising (cattle, donkeys, goats) region; 14°15'N 39°28'E.

Adilabad (ŭdĭläbäd'), district (□ 7,294; pop. 823,622), NE Hyderabad state, India, on Deccan Plateau; ⊙ Adilabad. Bounded NW and N by Penganga, NE by Wardha, E by Pranhita, S by Godavari rivers. Hilly and thickly forested; bamboo (pulp used in Sirpur paper mill), teak. Largely sandy red soil; millet, oilseeds (chiefly peanuts, cottonseed), cotton, rice. Cotton ginning, oilseed and rice milling, coal mining (near Belampalli and Rajura), sawmilling. Main towns: Nirmal (road center), Adilabad (agr. market). Became part of Hyderabad during state's formation in 18th cent. Pop. 76% Hindu, 15% tribal (including Gonds), 6% Moslem, 1% Christian.

Adilabad, town (pop. 11,128), ⊙ Adilabad dist., NE Hyderabad state, India, 150 mi. N of Hyderabad; agr. trade center; cotton ginning, rice milling, cottonseed-oil extraction. Formerly also Edlabad.

Adimi (ŭdyĭmē'), town (1948 pop. over 10,000), NE Maritime Territory, Russian SFSR, on Sea of Japan, 190 mi. N of Ternei; fish cannery. Until c.1940, Ademi.

Adin (ā'dĭn), village (pop. c.250), Modoc co., NE Calif., 30 mi. SW of Alturas; trade center for agr. and lumbering region.

Adi Quala (ädē' kwä'lä), village (pop. 550), Adi Ugri div., central Eritrea, near Ethiopian border, on road and 18 mi. S of Adi Ugri, in cotton- and coffee-growing region; alt. c.6,740 ft.

Adirampatnam (ŭdĭräm'pŭtnŭm), since 1949 officially **Adirampattinam**, town (pop. 10,004), Tanjore dist., SE Madras, India, port on Palk Strait, 34 mi. SE of Tanjore; trades in rice, coconuts, coral, livestock; saltworks. Pop. 60% Moslem. Sometimes spelled Adirampatanam.

Adirondack (ă"dürŏn'dăk), resort village, Warren co., E N.Y., in the Adirondacks, on E shore of Schroon L., 18 mi. WSW of Ticonderoga.

Adirondack Mountains, NE N.Y., group bounded E by L. Champlain and L. George region, extending from foothills near Que. line in N to the Mohawk valley in S; mts. descend gradually to St. Lawrence valley in NW and to Black R. valley in SW. Sometimes mistakenly included in the Appalachian system, the Adirondacks are geologically a S extension of the Laurentian Plateau. Highest near E margin, where ranges trend NE–SW; high point is Mt. Marcy (alt. 5,344 ft.; highest peak in state), c.12 mi. SSE of Lake Placid village. Other notable peaks are: Mt. MacIntyre (5,112 ft.) S of L. Placid; Mt. Haystack (4,918 ft.) and Mt. Skylight (4,920 ft.), both near Mt. Marcy; and Whiteface Mtn. (4,872 ft.), N of L. Placid. Much of the region, which is noted for its beautiful scenery, forests, and its many lakes, is included in Adirondack Forest Preserve (2,177,701 acres). Noted lakes (with many summer, winter resorts) are L. George, L. Placid, and Indian, Schroon, Cranberry, Big and Little Tupper, Long, Upper and Lower Saranac, and Raquette lakes and the Fulton Chain. In the Adirondacks are sources of the Hudson, the Ausable (flowing to L. Champlain), the Black (flowing to L. Ontario), and tributaries of the St. Lawrence. Several highways cross the region, and railroads penetrate it; there are popular hiking trails and canoeing routes. Iron mining revived c.1938; millions of tons of ore were produced in Second World War. Talc, zinc, titanium (iron ore by-product) are also produced.

Adi Ugri (ädē' ōō'grē), administrative division, central Eritrea, bordering on Ethiopia; ⊙ Adi Ugri. Occupies central plateau (alt. 6–9,000 ft.); watered by upper Gash R. (here called Mareb R.). Agr. (cereals, citrus fruit, vegetables, cotton, coffee) around chief settlements of Adi Ugri, Adi Quala, Aressa, and Debarua. Stock raising. Has gold and lignite deposits. Also called Serae.

Adi Ugri, town (pop. 4,600), ⊙ Adi Ugri div., central Eritrea, on Asmara-Aduwa road and 32 mi. SSW of Asmara; alt. c.6,500 ft. Commercial center; flour mills, tannery. Lignite mine and gold deposits near by. Has missions, mosque, school of arts and crafts.

Adiyaman (ädŭ'yämän"), Turkish *Adıyaman*, town (pop. 10,192), Malatya prov., E central Turkey, 40 mi. S of Malatya; wheat, barley, chick-peas, lentils, tobacco, cotton. Formerly Hisnumansur or Husnumansur.

Adjar, in Rus. names: see ADZHAR.

Adjim (äjēm'), village, Djerba dist., SE Tunisia, fishing port on S shore of Djerba isl., facing mainland, 12 mi. SSW of Houmt-Souk; sponge market; wool milling. Orchards and olive groves.

Adjohon (äjōhōn'), town (pop. c.5,000), S Dahomey, Fr. West Africa, on Ouémé R. and 7 mi. NW of Porto-Novo; palm kernels, palm oil, corn, cotton, manioc, peanuts.

Adjud (äjōōd'), town (1948 pop. 4,028), Putna prov., E Rumania, 27 mi. N of Focsani; rail junction, agr. market, notably for livestock; mfg. of mirrors.

Adjuntas (äd-hōōn'täs), town (pop. 5,262), W central Puerto Rico, in the Cordillera Central, 13 mi. NNW of Ponce; alt. 1,622 ft.; summer resort and coffee-trading center. Garzas hydroelectric plant is 4 mi. S. Manganese deposits near by. The Alto de la Bandera resort and pass is 2½ mi. SE.

Adkot, India: see ATKOT.

Adler (ä'dlyĭr), town (1926 pop. 2,215), S Krasnodar Territory, Russian SFSR, port on Black Sea, at mouth of Mzymta R., on coastal railroad and 13 mi. SE of Sochi; health resort; subtropical agr. (tea, tobacco, citrus fruit, orchards); metalworks, quarries. Exports nuts, dried fruit.

Adlergebirge (äd'lürgübĭr"gü), Czech *Orlické Hory* (ôr'lĭch-kā hô'rĭ), Pol. *Góry Orlickie* (gōō'rĭ ôrlĭts'-kyĕ), mountain range of the Sudetes, along Czechoslovak-Pol. border; extend c.35 mi. bet. Nachod (NNW) and Kralicky (SSE); rise to 3,655 ft. in Velka Destna mtn. Extensively forested. Divocha Orlice and Ticha Orlice rivers rise near SE foot. Largely in Poland and separated from the Adlergebirge by upper Divocha Orlice R., lie the parallel HABELSCHWERDT MOUNTAINS.

Adlerkosteletz, Czechoslovakia: see KOSTELEC NAD ORLICI.

Adler River, Czechoslovakia: see ORLICE RIVER.

Adlington, urban district (1931 pop. 4,180; 1951 census 3,998), central Lancashire, England, 4 mi. SE of Chorley; cotton milling, coal mining.

Adliswil (äd'lĭsvēl), town (pop. 5,105), Zurich canton, N Switzerland, on Sihl R. and 4 mi. SSW of Zurich; textiles.

Admiral Island, B.C.: see SALTSPRING ISLAND.

Admiralty Gulf, inlet of Timor Sea, NE Western Australia, bet. Gibson Point (E) and Cape Voltaire (W); 35 mi. long, 30 mi. wide.

Admiralty Inlet, NW Baffin Isl., Northwest Territories, fjord (230 mi. long) of Lancaster Sound, bet. Brodeur and Borden peninsulas. One of the world's longest fjords, it is 2–20 mi. wide; shoreline is steep and abrupt, rising to c.1,000–1,500 ft. Inlet has several arms. On NE shore of inlet is Arctic Bay trading post.

Admiralty Inlet, Wash.: see PUGET SOUND.

Admiralty Island (□ 1,664), SE Alaska, in the Alexander Archipelago, S of Juneau; 57°44'N 134°20'W; 90 mi. long, 35 mi. wide; rises to 4,639 ft. Fishing (cannery at ANGOON), lumbering.

Admiralty Islands, small volcanic group (□ 800; pop. 12,400), Manus dist., BISMARCK ARCHIPELAGO, Territory of New Guinea, SW Pacific, 250 mi. W of New Ireland. MANUS is largest isl. and is surrounded by smaller isls. and coral reefs. Produce copra, pearls. Discovered 1616 by Willem Schouten. In Second World War, site of Jap. air base taken 1944 by Allied forces who 1st landed on Los Negros Isl. off E coast of Manus.

Admiralty Peninsula, Rus. *Poluostrov Admiralteystva*, headland on W coast of N isl. of Novaya Zemlya, Russian SFSR; 15 mi. wide, 10 mi. long; 75°N 55°45'E. Smidovich, settlement, on S shore.

Admiralty Range, Antarctica, along N coast of Victoria Land, in 71°20'S 168°30'E. Rises to 9,859 ft. in Mt. Sabine. Discovered 1841 by Sir James C. Ross.

Admiralty Sound, Sp. *Seno del Almirantazgo*, S extension of Strait of Magellan, extends 50 mi. E into W coast of main isl. of Tierra del Fuego from Dawson Isl. and Whiteside Channel; 10 mi. wide at mouth, diminishing to 3 mi. at head.

Admire (ăd'mīr), city (pop. 184), Lyon co., E central Kansas, 17 mi. N of Emporia; livestock, grain.

Admont (äd'mōnt), town (pop. 3,342), Styria, central Austria, on the Enns and 30 mi. NW of Knittelfeld; brewery; summer resort. Benedictine abbey (founded 1074) has large library.

Adnet (äd'nĕt), village (pop. 1,770), Salzburg, W central Austria, 6 mi. SE of Salzburg. Marble quarries near by.

Ado (ä'dō), town, Abeokuta prov., Western Provinces, SW Nigeria, 20 mi. SSW of Ilaro; cacao industry, indigo dyeing, cotton weaving; palm oil and kernels. Phosphate deposits.

Ado-Ekiti (ä'dō ā'kētē), town, Ondo prov., Western Provinces, S Nigeria, 25 mi. N of Akure; textile center; cacao, palm oil, timber, rubber, cotton.

Adoenara, Indonesia: see ADONARA.

Adola (ädō'lä), village, Sidamo-Borana prov., S Ethiopia, on road and 50 mi. NW of Negelli. Gold mining in near-by Dawa valley.

Adolfo Alsina. **1** District, Buenos Aires prov., Argentina: see CARHUÉ. **2** Department, Río Negro natl. territory, Argentina: see VIEDMA.

Adolphustown (ŭdŏl'fŭs-), village, SE Ont., on Adolphus Reach, inlet of L. Ontario, 20 mi. ESE of Belleville; founded 1784 by United Empire Loyalists.

Adona (ŭdō'nŭ), town (pop. 194), Perry co., central Ark., 40 mi. NW of Little Rock, near Arkansas R.

Adonara, **Adunara**, or **Adoenara** (both: ädōōnä'rä), island (□ 200; pop. 36,906), Solor Isls., Lesser Sundas, Indonesia, in Flores Sea, just E of Flores, near Lomblem (W); 20 mi. long, 10 mi. wide; mountainous, rises to 5,442 ft. Fishing, agr.

Adoni (ädō'nē), city (pop. 35,431), Bellary dist., NW Madras, India, 40 mi. NNE of Bellary; cotton-trade center; hand-loom cotton and silk weaving. Experimental farm (cotton research). Anc. fort figured in 18th-cent. wars of the Deccan.

Adony (ŏ'dônyŭ), town (pop. 3,959), Fejer co., central Hungary, on the Danube and 21 mi. E of Szekesfehervar; river port; wheat, rye, livestock.

Ador (ädhōr'), village (pop. 1,165), Valencia prov., E Spain, 5 mi. SW of Gandía; olive oil, wine, fruit, cacao.

Adorf (ä'dôrf), town (pop. 8,316), Saxony, E central Germany, in the Erzgebirge, on the White Elster and 13 mi. SSE of Plauen; frontier station near Czechoslovak border, opposite Rossbach; rail junction; cotton and woolen milling, embroidering; mfg. of carpets, mother-of-pearl articles, musical instruments.

Adour River (ädōōr'), anc. *Aturus*, in Hautes-Pyrénées, Gers, and Landes dept., SW France, rises in the central Pyrenees near the Pic du Midi de Bigorre, flows N then in wide arc W, past Bagnères-de-Bigorre, Tarbes, Aire, Saint-Sever, and Dax (head of navigation), to Bay of Biscay 3.5 mi. below Bayonne. Total length, 210 mi. Receives the Midouze (right) and the Luy, Gave de Pau, and Nive rivers (left). A shifting sandbar near mouth is a shipping hazard.

Adowa, Ethiopia: see ADUWA.

Adpar, town, SW Cardigan, Wales, on Teifi R., anc. borough, now part of Newcastle Emlyn; 1st printing press in Wales was established here 1719.

Adra (ŭ'drŭ), town (pop. 7,516), Manbhum dist., SE Bihar, India, 23 mi. NE of Purulia; rail junction; rice, corn, oilseeds, bajra, sugar cane.

Adra (ädh'rä), anc. *Abdera*, city (pop. 6,907), Almería prov., S Spain, in Andalusia, port on the Mediterranean, 32 mi. WSW of Almería. Exports lead from Berja mines; also sugar and fruit. Sugar-cane production and processing center. Fishing; mfg. of fruit conserves, brandy distilling. Cereals, almonds, fruit, wine in area. Abdera, founded by Phoenician traders, stood at foot of hill below Adra; it was last stronghold of the Moors in Spain under Boabdil.

Adrada, La (lä ädh-rä'dhä), town (pop. 1,572), Ávila prov., central Spain, in Sierra de Gredos, 24 mi. S of Ávila, in fertile valley (olives, vegetables, grapes, fruit, forage, livestock); flour milling. Forests yield timber and pine cones.

Adrados (ädhrä'dhōs), town (pop. 830), Segovia prov., central Spain, 30 mi. N of Segovia; barley, rye, wheat, grapes, livestock. Lumbering.

Adrall (ädhräl'), village (pop. 212), Lérida prov., NE Spain, on Segre R. and 3 mi. SW of Seo de Urgel; hydroelectric plant.

Adramyti, Adramyttium, Turkey: see EDREMIT.

Adranga (ädräng'gä), village, Eastern Prov., NE Belgian Congo, on right bank of Kibali R. and 105 mi. NNE of Irumu; communications point and center of native trade. Has a commemorative monument to the Congo Free State expedition (1897) against the Mahdists of Anglo-Egyptian Sudan.

Adrano (ädrä'nō), anc. *Hadranum* or *Adranum*, town (pop. 24,307), Catania prov., E Sicily, on SW slope of Mt. Etna, near junction of Simeto and Salso rivers, 18 mi. NW of Catania. Agr. center (citrus fruit, grapes). Has Norman castle (now a prison) erected by Roger I, and convent he established in 1157. Founded c.400 B.C. by Dionysius I near temple of Hadranos, a Siculian deity; conquered by Romans 263 B.C. Has ruins of necropolis, anc. wall, towers, Roman buildings. Called Adernò until 1929.

Adranos River, Turkey: see KIRMASTI RIVER.

Adranum, Sicily: see ADRANO.

Adrar (ädrär'), village (pop. 1,722) and Saharan oasis, in Aïn-Sefra territory, W central Algeria, on trans-Saharan auto track to Gao (Fr. West Africa) and 280 mi. SSE of Colomb-Béchar; 27°54'N 0°16'W. Belongs to the Touat group of oases which receive underground waters of the Oued Saoura. Date palms.

Adrar, interior region of Mauritania, Fr. West Africa, a low central massif with steep cliffs in W Sahara, extending c.250 mi. SW-NE from about 19°30'N to 21°40'N. Rises to c.800 ft. Region is watered by many streams feeding several large oases, where dates, vegetables, and cereals thrive. Atar (SW) is main settlement. The Adrar has long been a stronghold of Moorish tribes. Also called Adrar (Berber for mountain) of Mauritania to distinguish it from other Adrars of the Sahara.

Adrasan, Cape (ädräsän'), on Gulf of Antalya, SW Turkey, 40 mi. SSW of Antalya; 36°20'N 30°32'E.

Adraskan or **Adraskand,** river, Afghanistan: see HARUT RUD.

Adrasman (ŭdrŭsmän'), town (1945 pop. over 500), NE Leninabad oblast, Tadzhik SSR, on S slope of Kurama Range, 32 mi. NE of Leninabad; bismuth mining.

Adré (ädrā'), village, E Chad territory, Fr. Equatorial Africa, on Anglo-Egyptian Sudan border, opposite Geneina, 100 mi. ESE of Abéché; customs station and military outpost on main road to Darfur.

Adria (ä'drēä), anc. *Hadria, Hatria,* and *Atria,* town (pop. 9,435), Rovigo prov., Veneto, N Italy, on Tartaro R. and 13 mi. E of Rovigo; rail junction; foundries, alcohol distillery; mfg. (furniture, bricks, lye, marmalade, methane gas, cement). Navigable canal links town with near-by Po and Adige rivers and with the Adriatic. Bishopric. Has cathedral and mus. of antiquities. Once an Etruscan, later a Roman town and flourishing port on the Adriatic (now 14 mi. away) to which it gave its name.

Adrian (ā'drēŭn). **1** City (pop. 503), Johnson and Emanuel counties, E central Ga., 16 mi. WSW of Swainsboro. **2** City (pop. 18,393), ⊙ Lenawee co., SE Mich., c.60 mi. SW of Detroit. Distribution point and trade center for farm area. Mfg. of metal, paper products, wire fencing, furniture, auto parts, tools, clothing, chemicals, electrical goods, food products. Chrysanthemum growing. Seat of Adrian Col. and Siena Heights Col. Settled 1825; inc. as village 1836, as city 1853. **3** Village (pop. 1,115), Nobles co., SW Minn., on small tributary of Rock R., near Iowa line, and 18 mi. W of Worthington, in grain, livestock, poultry area; dairy products. **4** Agr. city (pop. 905), Bates co., W Mo., near South Grand R., 10 mi. N of Butler.

Adrianople (ā"drēŭnō'pŭl) or **Edirne** (ĕdĭr'nĕ), province (□ 2,241; 1950 pop. 221,125), Turkey in Europe; ⊙ Adrianople. Bordered N by Bulgaria, W by Greece (along Maritsa R.), S by Gulf of Saros. Drained by Maritsa R. and its tributaries, Tundzha and Ergene rivers. Agr. (rice, sesame, rye, wheat, canary grass, onions, sugar beets, potatoes, flax, raisins).

Adrianople or **Edirne,** anc. *Uskudama,* later *Adrianopolis* or *Hadrianopolis,* Bulgarian *Odrin,* city (1950 pop. 30,245), ⊙ Adrianople prov., Turkey in Europe, at junction of Maritsa and Tundzha rivers, 4 mi. from Greek frontier, on railroad and 130 mi. WNW of Istanbul; 41°40'N 26°35'E. Agr., trade, and mfg. center, producing silk and cotton goods. Here is the magnificent early-16th-cent. mosque of Selim. There are other mosques and ruins of the palace of the sultans. Named after Emperor Hadrian, who founded it (c.125 A.D.) on site of the older Uscudama; Byzantine writers also called it Orestia. Of great strategic importance and strongly fortified, city had turbulent history. The defeat (378) of Emperor Valens by the Visigoths at Adrianople laid Greece open to the barbarians. Later conquered by the Avars, the Bulgarians, and the crusaders, city passed to the Turks in 1361 and was residence of the sultans until fall of Constantinople in 1453. In 19th cent. the Russians captured Adrianople twice in the Russo-Turkish Wars, and in 1912 the Bulgarians took it in the Balkan Wars. Restored to Turkey by the Conference of Lausanne (1923).

Adrianovka (ŭdrēä'nŭfkŭ), village (1948 pop. over 2,000), central Chita oblast, Russian SFSR, on branch of Trans-Siberian RR and 55 mi. SE of Chita; lumbering.

Adriatic Sea (ādrēă'tĭk), arm of the Mediterranean, bet. the Italian and Balkan peninsulas; 500 mi. long, 60–140 mi. wide; max. depth 4,035 ft. (S). It extends from Gulf of Trieste at its head SE to Strait of Otranto, which leads to Ionian Sea. The Italian coast (W) is low and straight, while the Yugoslav (Dalmatian) and Albanian shores (E) are rocky, with many inlets and offshore isls. Near its head the Adriatic receives the Po and Adige rivers. An important navigation route bet. N Italy, central Europe, and the Mediterranean, the Adriatic is served by the Italian ports of Brindisi, Bari, and Venice, the free port of Trieste, the Yugoslav ports of Rijeka (Fiume), Split, Dubrovnik, and Kotor, and the Albanian ports of Durazzo and Valona. Noted for its scenery, mild climate, and blue water, the Adriatic is a popular tourist region, particularly along the picturesque Dalmatian coast. The sea is named for Adria, which, like Ravenna, was once a flourishing Adriatic port, and was later silted up by the Po delta.

Adro (ä'drô), town (pop. 2,967), Brescia prov., Lombardy, N Italy, S of Lago d'Iseo, 14 mi. WNW of Brescia; hosiery, cotton textiles, shoes, alcohol.

Adrogué (ädrōgā'), residential city (pop. 37,588), ⊙ Almirante Brown dist. (□ c.50; pop. 42,088), in Greater Buenos Aires, Argentina, 12 mi. S of Buenos Aires. Stock raising, mfg. (textiles, dairy products). Natl. col., theater.

Adrspach, Czechoslovakia: see TEPLICE NAD METUJI.

Ad Teklesan (äd tĕklĕsän'), Ital. *Ad Teclesan,* village, Asmara div., W Eritrea, on main road and 20 mi. NNW of Asmara, in gold-mining region.

Adua, Ethiopia: see ADUWA.

Adui, Russian SFSR: see LOSINY.

Adula (ädōō'lä), mountain group in Lepontine Alps, SE Switzerland, on border of Ticino and Grisons cantons. Highest peak, Rheinwaldhorn (11,173 ft.); the Güferhorn is 11,103 ft. Hinterrhein R., a headstream of the Rhine, rises here and flows E through Rheinwald valley.

Adulis, Eritrea: see ZULA.

Adunara, Indonesia: see ADONARA.

Adur River (ā'dŭr), Sussex, England, rises 3 mi. SSE of Horsham, flows 20 mi. S to the Channel at Shoreham-by-Sea. Navigable in lower course.

Aduwa or **Adowa** (both: ä'dŭwä, ä'dōōwä), Ital. *Adua,* town (pop. 6,000), Tigre prov., N Ethiopia, near Eritrean border, 80 mi. S of Asmara; 14°9'N 38°51'E; alt. c.6,250 ft.; road junction. Trade center (cereals, coffee, hides, honey, salt); artisan industries (metalworking, leatherworking, weaving). Has churches and ruins of a Jesuit mission (17th cent.). Scene of Menelik's great victory (1896) over the Italians, who later occupied it (1935–41) and made it part of Eritrea. Retaken by British 1941. Formerly ⊙ Tigre prov.

Advance (ăd'văns). **1** Town (pop. 413), Boone co., central Ind., 16 mi. ESE of Crawfordsville, in agr. area. **2** Village (pop. 1,578, with adjacent Flatwoods), Greenup co., extreme NE Ky., near Ohio R., 2 mi. SW of Ironton, Ohio. **3** City (pop. 733), Stoddard co., SE Mo., 15 mi. WSW of Chaffee. **4** Town (pop. 216), Davie co., W central N.C., 14 mi. SW of Winston-Salem.

Advent Bay, Spitsbergen: see LONGYEAR CITY.

Adventure Bay, inlet of the Pacific off Aysén prov., S Chile, bet. central Chonos Archipelago and Guamblin Isl., N of 45°S; c.20 mi. long, c.30 mi. wide.

Adventure Bay, wide inlet of Tasman Sea, E of central isthmus of Bruny isl., off SE Tasmania; 9 mi. N-S, 4 mi. E-W. Visited 1777 by Cook.

Advocate Harbour, village (pop. estimate 200), N N.S., on Minas Channel, 20 mi. W of Parrsboro; dairying, farming. Copper formerly mined here.

Adwalton Moor, England: see DRIGHLINGTON.

Adwick-le-Street (ă'dĭk-lŭ-), urban district (1931 pop. 20,257; 1951 census 18,808), West Riding, S Yorkshire, England, 4 mi. NW of Doncaster; coal mining. Has 13th-14th-cent. church. In urban dist. (N) is coal-mining suburb of Carcroft (pop. 7,897).

Adyar (ŭd'yŭr), village, Chingleput dist., E Madras, India, on right bank of Adyar R. and 5 mi. SW of Madras; residential suburb. Hq. of Theosophical Society; library has noted collection of anc. Tamil MSS. Has Besant High School, Kalakshetra (art center; noted for training in classical Hindu dance), teachers training school (Montessori method; founded 1947).

Adyar River, Chingleput dist., E Madras, India, rises 10 mi. N of Chingleput, flows c.25 mi. NE and E, past Madras (forms city's S boundary) to Bay of Bengal.

Adyge Autonomous Oblast or **Adyghe Autonomous Oblast** (ŭdĭgyĕ'), administrative division (□ 1,700; 1946 pop. estimate 300,000) of central Krasnodar Territory, S European Russian SFSR, at foot of the NW Greater Caucasus; ⊙ Maikop. Along left banks of Laba and Kuban rivers; lies largely in lowland extending S into Caucasus foothills. Winter wheat, sunflowers, tobacco (W), ambary hemp and coriander (E). Industries based on agr. (flour milling, oil pressing, fiber processing). Mfg. at Maikop. Pop. largely Adyge or Adighe (Circassian) and Russian. One of the remaining ethnic areas of Circassia (since 1864, under Russian rule), the Adyge Autonomous Oblast (formed 1922) was successively included in North Caucasus (1924), Azov-Black Sea (1934), and Krasnodar (1937) territories.

Adynkata, Urkainian SSR: see GLYBOKA.

Adzaneta (äd-thänā'tä), town (pop. 1,466), Castellón de la Plana prov., E Spain, 18 mi. NNW of Castellón de la Plana; olive-oil processing, cotton milling; livestock, wheat, vegetables, fruit.

Adzaneta de Albaida (dā älvī'dhä), village (pop. 1,219), Valencia prov., E Spain, 11 mi. S of Játiva; olive oil, wine, almonds.

Adzhamka (ŭjäm'kŭ), village (1926 pop. 10,678), central Kirovograd oblast, Ukrainian SSR, on road and 12 mi. ENE of Kirovograd; metalworks.

Adzhar Autonomous Soviet Socialist Republic (ä'jär, ŭjär', Rus. ŭjär') or **Adzharistan** (ŭjä'rĭstän", Rus. ŭjä"rēstän'), administrative division (□ 1,100; 1946 pop. estimate 200,000) of SW Georgian SSR; ⊙ Batum. On Black Sea, at W end of the Lesser Caucasus (Adzhar-Imeretian Range); bounded S by Turkey; drained by Adzharis-Tskhali R. (hydroelectric station). Sharply divided into mtn. section (E; sparsely populated; livestock, tobacco, lumbering) and narrow, humid, subtropical coastal lowland (yearly rainfall 100 in.). Littoral produces tea, citrus fruit (⅔ of Georgian production), tung and camphor oil, rubber, bamboo. Republic is chief USSR producer of tea and citrus fruit. Tourist and seaside resorts. Main towns, Batum (industrial center) and Kobuleti, served by railroad from Tiflis. Pop. 55% Adzhars (Georgians who adopted Mohammedanism under Turkish rule), 15% Georgians, and Armenians, Russians, and Greeks. Region annexed by Russia from Turkey partly in 1829, partly in 1878; became autonomous SSR in 1921. Sometimes spelled Ajar and Adjar.

Adzhar-Imeretian Range (ä'jär-ĭmürĕ'tēŭn, ŭjär'–), forested W range of the Lesser Caucasus, in SW Georgian SSR; extends c.80 mi. bet. Borzhomi (E) and Batum (W); rises to 9,350 ft. Crossed by Kutaisi-Abastumani-Akhaltsikhe road at Zekari Pass (alt. 7,100 ft.). Contains health resorts of Abastumani, Sairma, and Bakhmaro.

Adzharis-Tskhali River (ŭjä'rĭs-tsŭkhä'lyē), Adzhar Autonomous SSR, Georgian SSR, rises in Adzhar-Imeretian Range, flows c.45 mi. W to the Coruh (Chorokh) SE of Batum. On it is Adzharis-Tskhali hydroelectric station (also known as *Atsges*), at Makhuntseti, 13 mi. E of Batum.

Adzhigol, Russian SFSR: see FEODOSIYA.

Adzhikabul, Azerbaijan SSR: see KAZI-MAGOMED.

Adzhikend (ŭjēkyĕnt'), town (1945 pop. over 500), W Azerbaijan SSR, 11 mi. S of Kirovabad, in agr. dist.; summer resort.

Adzopé (ädzōpā'), town (pop. c.3,350), SE Ivory Coast, Fr. West Africa, 55 mi. N of Abidjan; coffee, cacao, bananas, hardwood.

Aebeltoft (ĕ'bŭltôft), city (pop. 2,104) and port, Randers amt, E Jutland, Denmark, on S shore of Djursland peninsula and 18 mi. E of Aarhus, on Aebeltoft Bay; fisheries, leather tanning. City dates from 14th cent. Sometimes spelled Ebeltoft.

Aebeltoft Bay, Denmark: see MOLS.

Aedipsos, Greece: see LOUTRA AIDEPSOU.

Aegadian Islands or **Aegadean Islands,** Sicily: see EGADI ISLANDS.

Aegae, Euboea, Greece: see LIMNE.

Aegaleos, Greece: see AIGALEOS.

Aegates, Sicily: see EGADI ISLANDS.

Aegean Islands (ējē'ŭn), Gr. *Aigaioi Nesoi* or *Aiyaioi Nisoi,* name generally applied to the isls. of the AEGEAN SEA. In a narrower sense, the isls. off Asia Minor, N of the Dodecanese, forming the Aegean Isls. administrative division (□ 1,506; pop. 304,022; ⊙ Mytilene) of Greece, with the nomes of CHIOS (with Psara), LESBOS (with Lemnos), and SAMOS (with Icaria).

Aegean Sea, Gr. *Aigaion Pelagos* or *Aiyaion Pelagos,* Turkish *Ege Denizi,* arm of the Mediterranean Sea bet. Greece and Asia Minor (Turkey), bounded S by Crete; c.400 mi. long, c.200 mi. wide; connected by the Dardanelles with the Sea of Marmara and the Black Sea. It is dotted with isls., nearly all belonging to Greece. These are generally grouped into the AEGEAN ISLANDS proper, the DODECANESE, the CYCLADES, the Northern SPORADES, and EUBOEA, as well as such isolated offshore isls. as THASOS, SAMOTHRACE, and the Turkish isls. of IMBROS (Imroz) and Bozcaada (Tenedos). The leading ports are Piraeus, Salonika, Volos, Mytilene, Herakleion (Crete), and Kavalla, in Greece, and Smyrna in Turkey. Formerly called Archipelago [from Gr. *archipelagos,*=chief sea]; the name of the Aegean Sea has been variously derived from Aegae (modern Limne; a town in Euboea); from Aegeus, father of Theseus; and from Aegea, an Amazon queen, who drowned in it. In anc. times, the Aegean Sea was subdivided into the Thracian Sea (N), the Icarian Sea, along the coast of Asia Minor, the Myrtoan Sea, bet. the Peloponnesus and the Cyclades, and the deep Sea of Crete (modern Sea of CANDIA), bet. the Cyclades and Crete.

Aegerisee, Ägerisee, or **Egerisee** (all: ā'gŭrēzā'), lake (□ 3), Zug canton, N central Switzerland, among mts.; alt. 2,375 ft. UNTERÄGERI and OBERÄGERI are on N shore.

Aegilia, Greece: see ANTIKYTHERA.

Aegimures, Tunisia: see ZEMBRA.

Aegina (ējī'nŭ), Gr. *Aigina* or *Aiyina* (both: ā'yēnä), island (□ 32; pop. 10,052) in Saronic Gulf of Aegean Sea, Attica nome, E central Greece, off W coast of Attica peninsula, 17 mi. SW of Athens; 37°46'N 23°26'E; 7 mi. long, 3–8 mi. wide; rises to 1,745 ft. Produces grain, wine, peanuts, figs, almonds, vegetables; fisheries, sulphur springs. Its pinewoods make it a favored summer resort. On NW shore is town of Aegina (pop. 5,820), 23 mi. SW of Athens; fishing port; pottery making, trading. A hill near NE coast, 5 mi. E of Aegina town, is site of temple (discovered 1811) with famed marble sculptures (Aeginetan marbles), dating from 5th cent. B.C. Inhabited from late neolithic times,

Aegina was conquered (c.1000 B.C.) by Dorian Greeks, struck the 1st Greek coins, and rose to great commercial importance. Athens defeated Aegina in 459 B.C. and in 431 B.C. expelled its pop.; the isl. declined thereafter. It suffered during Turkish-Venetian struggles and was settled (16th cent.) by Albanians. The town was a temporary capital of Greece in late 1820s.

Aegina, Gulf of, Greece: see Saronic Gulf.

Aegion, Greece: see Aigion.

Aegium, Greece: see Aigion.

Aeglesberg, England: see Aylesbury.

Aegospotamos (ē″gŭs-pŏ′tùmŭs), stream of anc. Thrace, flowed across Gallipoli Peninsula to the Hellespont (Dardanelles). At its mouth the Spartan Lysander destroyed the Athenian fleet in 405 B.C., ending the Peloponnesian War.

Aegviidu or **Aegvidu** (ĭg′vēdōō), town, N Estonia, on railroad and 33 mi. ESE of Tallinn; health resort.

Aegyptus, anc. name for Egypt.

Aelana, Jordan: see Aqaba.

Aelia Capitolina, Palestine: see **Jerusalem.**

Aeltere, Belgium: see Aalter.

Aemilia, Italy: see Emilia-Romagna.

Aemilianum, France: see Millau.

Aemilian Way, anc. Roman road, an extension of the Flaminian Way from Ariminium (Rimini) to the Po at Placentia (Piacenza).

Aeminium, Portugal: see Coimbra.

Aeng, Burma: see An.

Aenos or **Aenus,** Turkey: see Enos.

Aeolia, Asia Minor: see Aeolis.

Aeolian Islands, Sicily: see Lipari Islands.

Aeolis (ē′ùlĭs) or **Aeolia** (ēō′lēù), anc. region of W coast of Asia Minor, a collective term for the cities planted there by the Aeolians, a branch of the Hellenic peoples.

Aeolus, Mount (ē′ōlùs) (8,672 ft.), W Alta., near B.C. border, in Rocky Mts., in Jasper Natl. Park, 27 mi. N of Jasper; 53°16′N 118°4′W.

Aéré (ăĕ′rā), village, N Senegal, Fr. West Africa, on arm of the Senegal R. and 11 mi. S of Boghé (Mauritania), 48 mi. ESE of Podor; gum, millet.

Aerhtai, China: see Sharasume.

Aermadidi, Indonesia: see Airmadidi.

Aero (â′rû), Dan. *Ærø*, island (□ 34; pop. 10,723), Denmark, in Baltic Sea, 10 mi. S of Fyn isl.; 14 mi. long. Ports: Aeroskobing, Marstal.

Aeroskobing (â′rŭskûbĭng), Dan. *Ærøskøbing*, city (pop. 1,390) and port, Svendborg amt, Denmark, on N shore of Aero isl. and 15 mi. SSW of Svendborg; shipbuilding.

Aerschot, Belgium: see Aarschot.

Aerzen or **Ärzen** (both: âr′tsŭn), village (pop. 3,155), in former Prussian prov. of Hanover, W Germany, after 1945 in Lower Saxony, 5 mi. SW of Hameln; forestry.

Aesch (ĕsh), town (pop. 2,829), Basel-Land half-canton, N Switzerland, on Birs R. and 6 mi. S of Basel; cotton textiles (twine); metal- and woodworking.

Aeschi bei Spiez (ĕ′shē bī shpēts′), village (pop. 1,358), Bern canton, central Switzerland, near L. of Thun, 2 mi. S of Spiez; resort (alt. 2,821 ft.).

Aesepus River, Turkey: see Gonen River.

Aesis, Italy: see Iesi.

Aethalia, Italy: see Elba.

Aethiopia: see Ethiopia.

Aetna, Sicily: see Etna, Mount.

Aetolia (ētōl′yù), Gr. *Aitolia*, region of W central Greece; main town, Missolonghi. Located on N shore of Gulf of Patras, E of Achelous R., it forms part of Acarnania nome. Anc. Aetolia was primarily an inland farming and pastoral country, with chief cities at Thermum and Calydon. It was of little significance in Gr. history until the formation (314 B.C.) of the Aetolian League, a powerful confederation of cities, which gained control (3d cent.) of the Delphic Amphictyony and opposed the Achaean League and the Macedonians. Allied with Rome, the Aetolians defeated Philip V of Macedon at Cynoscephalae (197 B.C.); later they turned against Rome in alliance with Antiochus III of Syria. His defeat (189 B.C.) marked Aetolia's downfall and later incorporation into Roman Achaea. It became part of Epirus after 1204, was under Serbian domination (middle 14th cent.), and fell to Turks in 1450. It became part of independent Greece in 1832.

Aewol (ă′wŭl′), Jap. *Gaigetsu*, township (1946 pop. 29,142), N Cheju Isl., Korea, 12 mi. WSW of Cheju; barley, millet, cotton, sweet potatoes.

'Afag, Iraq: see 'Afaq.

'Afaj, Iraq: see 'Afaq.

Afanasyevo or **Afanas'yevo** (ŭfŭnä′syĭvŭ), village (1926 pop. 397), E Kirov oblast, Russian SFSR, on Kama R. and 40 mi. ENE of Omutninsk; grain, flax. Formerly Afanasyevskoye.

Afando, Afandos, Greece: see Aphantos.

Afantos, Greece: see Aphantos.

'Afaq (ä′făk), town, Diwaniya prov., SE central Iraq, 18 mi. ENE of Diwaniya; rice, dates. Site of anc. Nippur is just N. Also spelled 'Afaj and 'Afag.

Afaqa, Lebanon: see Afqa.

Afar, Ethiopia: see Danakil.

Afdem (äf′dĕm), village (pop. 700), Harar prov., E central Ethiopia, in Great Rift Valley, on railroad and 55 mi. W of Diredawa. Also spelled Afdam.

Afdera (äf′dĕrä), peak (7,300 ft.) of Danakil mts., NE Ethiopia, at Eritrean border, 20 mi. E of **L.** Egogi Bad.

Affligem, Belgium: see Hekelgem.

Afflighem, Belgium: see Hekelgem.

Affoltern am Albis (äfôl′tùrn äm äl′bĭs), town (pop. 3,053), Zurich canton, N Switzerland, 7 mi. SSW of Zurich; silk, pastry; canning, woodworking.

Affoltern bei Zürich (bī tsü′rĭkh), village, Zurich canton, N Switzerland, 4 mi. NNW of Zurich.

Affoltern im Emmental (ĭm ĕ′mĕntäl), town (pop. 1,160), Bern canton, W Switzerland, 8 mi. NW of Bern.

Affonso Claudio, Brazil: see Afonso Cláudio.

Affonso Penna, Brazil: see Acopiara.

Affreville (äfrùvēl′), town (pop. 10,042), Alger dept., N central Algeria, in middle Chéliff Valley, on railroad and 60 mi. SW of Algiers; agr. trade center (wine, cereals, cattle) and commercial outlet for Miliana (4 mi. N) and Teniet-el-Haad (30 mi. SSW); mfg. of building materials, distilling, palm-fiber processing.

Affroun, El- (ĕl-äfrōōn′), village (pop. 3,344), Alger dept., N central Algeria, in the Mitidja plain, on railroad and 11 mi. W of Blida; vineyards, citrus groves; essential-oil distilling.

Affuá, Brazil: see Afuá.

Affula, Israel: see Afula.

Afghanistan (ăfgă′nĭstăn″, ăfgä″nĭstän′), independent kingdom (□ 250,000; pop. 12,000,000) of SW Asia; ⊙ Kabul. It is land-locked and bounded N by the Tadzhik, Uzbek, and Turkmen republics of the USSR, W by Iran, S and E by Pakistan, and touches China's Sinkiang prov. at eastern most tip of the Wakhan panhandle. Afghanistan's relief is dominated by the Hindu Kush, which is highest (25,263 ft.) on the Pakistan border (NE) and fans out in many outliers constituting the central highlands, known as the Hazarajat. Among the chief outliers are the Koh-i-Baba, the Band-i-Turkestan, the Paropamisus Mts., the Safed Koh, and the Siah Koh. The rugged mtn. heart of Afghanistan is surrounded by arid lowlands extending to the N, W, and S frontiers of the country and watered by streams descending from the central highlands. The Helmand, Afghanistan's longest river, separates the S deserts of Dasht-i-Margo and Registan on its way to the Seistan depression (SW); the Farah and Hari Rud water the W plains of Farah and Herat; the Murghab, Qaisar, Sar-i-Pul, Balkh, Khulm, and Kunduz rivers irrigate Afghan Turkestan (N); the Kokcha R. drains Afghan Badakhshan (NE) and the Kabul R. the enclosed basins (E) of Kabul and Jalalabad. The Amu Darya (the anc. Oxus) forms part of the N frontier with the USSR. The country has dry continental climate, with precipitation (largely in winter and spring) varying from 10 in. annually in the central highlands to 2 in. in the S marginal deserts. Strong winds ("Wind of 120 days") in the W plains recall the climate of the adjacent Iranian plateau. The humid subtropical Jalalabad basin constitutes a special climatic province. Vegetation is differentiated vertically and ranges from true desert lowlands, through steppes in the foothills of the Hindu Kush system, to alpine mtn. meadows. True forests are found only in Nuristan (Asmar Forest) and in the Safed Koh of E Afghanistan. Pop. is densest in the Kabul, Jalalabad, and Kandahar areas, as well as in the irrigated agr. dists. and mtn. valleys. The Afghans, the basic ethnic element in the S half of the country, constitute half of total pop. They are Sunnite Moslem people and speak the Pashto (Pashtu, Pushtu) language of the Iranian group. Pashto falls into 2 main dialects: the Yusufzai or Pakhto (NE) and the more widespread and standardized Kandahari or Pashto (S). The leading Afghan tribes—1,500,000 Durani (Durrani; SW) and 1,200,000 Ghilzai (SE)— are largely settled and have an agr. economy. Smaller nomad pastoral Afghan tribes range across the frontier into W Pakistan, where they are partly settled and are generally called Pathans. Most numerous among the non-Afghan minorities, which inhabit the N half of the country, are the Tajiks (Tadzhiks), a Sunnite Moslem people of Iranian stock, constituting 15% of total pop. They are concentrated around Herat, and in Kataghan and Badakhshan, and are related to pop. of Soviet Tadzhik SSR across the upper Amu Darya. The central highlands (or Hazarajat) are so named for the Hazaras (10% of the total), a Shiite Persian-speaking people descended from the Mongol invaders of 13th–15th cent. They are adjoined W in Herat prov. of NW Afghanistan by the so-called Chahar Aimaks (Jamshidis, Firoz-Kohis, Taimanis), semi-nomadic tribes of Persian speech and Sunnite Moslem religion. In Afghan Turkestan, adjoining their respective republics of the USSR, live the Uzbeks (8%) of Mazar-i-Sharif prov. and the Turkmen (4%) of Maimana prov., both peoples of Sunnite Moslem religion and Turkic speech. Nomadic Baluch tribes live in the S deserts adjoining Pakistani Baluchistan. In the mid-1930s, Pashto replaced Persian as the official language of Afghanistan and the Afghan govt. began to encourage the diffusion of Pashto among all sections of the pop., including the Persian-speaking educated and merchant classes. Agr. and livestock raising are equally developed in Afghanistan, the former furnishing food for domestic consumption, the latter yielding the chief export products. Only 1.5% of the total area of the country is under cultivation, with half this area under irrigation. Irrigation is carried on by rivers (in Afghan Turkestan and the Herat oasis), by *karez* or *kariz* (subterranean aqueducts) in the S lowlands, and by natural springs in the hilly dists. Wheat is the most important grain, occupying nearly half the sown acreage; rice is grown along Kunduz and Khulm rivers (N) and in Kabul and Jalalabad basins; barley, millet, and corn are lesser grains. Cotton and sugar beets are the leading industrial plants, grown mainly in Afghan Turkestan (Kataghan prov.). Fruit orchards yield important export products: dried fruit (raisins, dried apricots), fresh fruit (pomegranates, peaches), almonds and pistachio nuts. Citrus fruit, bananas, and sugar cane are grown in the subtropical Jalalabad basin. Oilseeds (notably castor beans), madder, and asafetida are traditional products. In the livestock industry, the dominant position is taken by sheep (including the valuable karakul breed of Maimana prov.) and goats. Dairying is found around the large urban centers and among the Tajiks of Kataghan-Badakhshan, while mules, horses, and camels are also raised. Lumbering is important only in Nuristan and the timber floated down the Kabul R. to W Pakistan. The development of modern mfg. and processing industries began in late 1930s. The Kabul ordnance plant combines the mfg. of armaments, munitions, leather goods, textiles, and the mint. There are modern cotton mills at Pul-i-Khumri and Jabal-us-Siraj, woolen mills at Kabul and Kandahar, cotton gins, oilseed and soap factories at Kunduz, a beet-sugar refinery at Baghlan. Power is provided in part by small hydroelectric stations in the Kabul area. Most of the industrial production continues on a handicraft and cottage industry basis, including flour, oilseed, and rice milling and the weaving of carpets. Mineral resources, though abundant, are still in the earliest stages of exploitation. The main deposits are coal (Ishpushta), chrome (Logar R. valley), salt (Taliqan), petroleum (Tirpul), iron, lead-zinc, marble, talc, beryl. Badakhshan is famous for its lapis lazuli and gems. Afghanistan has no railroads and its road net consists chiefly of a circular 1,000-mi. route ringing the central highlands, via the country's chief cities, and an E-W route traversing the highlands bet. Kabul and Herat. The Afghan road net connects with Pakistan via the noted Khyber Pass to Peshawar at frontier post of Torkham and via highway to Quetta at Spinbaldak; it crosses into Iran at Islam Qala (W of Herat) and into the USSR at Torghondi (opposite the Soviet rail terminus of Kushka) and by Amu Darya ferry at Termez. Afghanistan's foreign trade passes predominantly to Pakistan and India and overseas through the port of Karachi. The bulk of Afghanistan's export trade consists of karakul skins shipped to New York, while fruit and nuts go largely to Pakistan and India. Wool, cotton, and medicinal herbs are lesser export items. Kabul and Kandahar are the primary commercial cities for trade with Pakistan and Herat and Mazar-i-Sharif for commerce with Iran and the USSR. Other centers are Jalalabad (E), Gardez and Ghazni (SE), Farah (SW), Maimana and Andkhui (N), and Kunduz and Faizabad (NE). Camel and mule caravans still play a major role in domestic transportation. Small military airfields are scattered through the country with only irregular commercial service bet. Kabul and Teheran. The country's rivers are not navigable, with the exception of the Amu Darya on the N frontier. They serve chiefly for irrigation (Girishk-Kajakai project on Helmand R.) and, in the case of the Kabul R. basin, for logging. The modern Afghanistan corresponds roughly to 4 provs. of the anc. Persian empire—Aria, Bactria, Drangiana, and Arachosia—conquered 516 B.C. by Darius I. These fell to Alexander the Great with the rest of the empire in 328 B.C. Under the Diadochi, Afghanistan fell to the Seleucid dynasty, but Bactria established itself 246 B.C. as a separate kingdom reaching from the upper Jaxartes (Syr Darya) to NW India. The Greco-Bactrian state fell (c.130 B.C.) to the nomad Sacae (Sakas), who later moved into Seistan, and to the Yuechi (Yueh-chi), which founded (1st cent. A.D.) the Kushan dynasty of NW India. Turkic successors of the Kushans were in control in Kabul in 661 when Herat fell to the Arabs, who also extended their conquest to Balkh (Afghan Turkestan) in 705. On the break-up of the Caliphate, the Arab-ruled areas of N and W Afghanistan passed to the Persian Saffarids (867–908) and to the more powerful Samanids (892–999), while E Afghanistan, with Kabul, remained (after 880) under Brahman Hindu rulers. In late 10th cent. rose the Turkic house of Ghazni, which rapidly brought all Afghanistan under its control and under Mahmud of Ghazni (997–1030) ruled an empire extending from W Persia to the Punjab. The short-lived Ghaznevid realm fell, however, to the Seljuk Turks (W and N) and, later, to the rival Afghan house of Ghor

(E). The Ghorids reached their zenith under Mohammed (1173–1206), who conquered all of N India and founded the Turko-Afghan sultanate of Delhi. After a brief period of incorporation in the realm of the Khwarizm (Khorezm) shahs, Afghanistan was overrun (1221–22) by Jenghiz Khan and remained under his successors until the advent (1398) of Tamerlane. After the latter's death (1405), the country was ruled by the Timurids until one of them, Baber (Babar), assumed power (1512), invaded NW India, overthrew the Delhi sultans and founded the Mogul empire after the 1st battle of Panipat (1526). The Mogul's Afghan possessions became of secondary importance in the new Indian realm; the Uzbeks of Bukhara annexed Afghan Turkestan; Herat and, later, Kandahar passed to the Persian Safavids; and only Kabul and Ghazni remained under Mogul rule. In 1709, the Ghilzai Afghan tribe of Kandahar rose against the Persians and conquered Persia itself in 1722. The Persian tide returned with Nadir Shah, who rapidly brought all Afghanistan under his control and sacked Delhi in 1739. After his death, Ahmed Shah, Sadozai family chief of the Durani tribe, founded modern Afghanistan with ⊙ at Kandahar. He extended his rule over Khurasan, Kashmir, Sind, and the Punjab and defeated the Mahrattas in the 3d battle of Panipat (1761). Under his successors, Kabul became capital (1773), but Afghanistan lost many of its possessions and the shahs of the Sadozai dynasty were overthrown in 1818. After an unsettled period of civil war, the Barakzai family of the Durani tribe seized power in 1835 under the leadership of Dost Mohammed, the 1st emir of the Mohammedzai dynasty. His rule saw the emergence of the 19th-cent. problem of Afghanistan, in which the rivalry bet. Britain and Russia for the Afghan buffer state resulted in the Afghan Wars. Interference of the British in Afghan affairs and their attempt to reestablish Shah Shuja, a former Sadozai ruler (1803–09), resulted in the 1st Afghan War (1839–42), marked by the notorious massacre (Jan., 1842) of the British Kabul garrison. After the war, Dost Mohammed resumed his reign (until his death, 1863) and rewon Herat (lost 1856 to Persia) and Afghan Turkestan. Afghan-British estrangement in the mid-1870s and the arrival of a Russian mission in Kabul precipitated the 2d Afghan War (1878–81), in which the Anglophile Abdur Rahman was installed. During his reign, the Afghan-Russian border was demarcated (1885–88), following the PANJDEH incident, and the Durand line was agreed upon (1893) bet. Afghanistan and India's North-West Frontier Prov. and delimited (1894–96). At the same time, the boundary in the Pamir was settled, resulting in the formation of the Afghan Wakhan panhandle. Under the rule of Habibullah (1901–19), the Anglo-Russian agreement of 1907 guaranteed the independence of Afghanistan under British influence. That influence was resented, especially during the First World War, and was ended (1919) with the 50-day 3d Afghan War (or war of independence) under the leadership of Amanullah. A pro-Westerner, Amanullah began a strong program of modernization and assumed (1926) the title of king. His reforms provoked the revolt of fanatical tribes under the leadership of the Afghan Tajik Bacha-i-Saqao, the "brigand-king," and he was forced to abdicate in 1929. After 9 months of anarchy, Mohammed Nadir Shah, one of Amanullah's ministers, ascended the throne and moderated Amanullah's reforms. Following his assassination (1933), his son, Mohammed Zahir Shah, set out to strengthen the country and build its economy. Development programs were begun, furthered by Afghan neutrality during Second World War, and aided by U.S. post-war loans. The creation (1947) of Pakistan brought about Afghan concern over the separatist aspirations of the Pathan tribes beyond the Durand line. According to the constitution of 1931, legislative power is vested in the parliament consisting of the king, a senate of 40 appointed members and a natl. assembly of 120 elected representatives. For purposes of local administration, Afghanistan was formerly divided into 5 major provinces (*Wilayat*): KABUL, KANDAHAR, HERAT, MAZAR-I-SHARIF, KATAGHAN-BADAKHSHAN; and 4 minor provs. (*Hakumat-i-Ala*): EASTERN PROVINCE, SOUTHERN PROVINCE, FARAH, and MAIMANA. Since the mid-1940s, when the Eastern and Southern provinces obtained "major province" status and Badakhshan was separated as a "minor province," Afghanistan falls accordingly into 7 major and 3 minor provinces.

Afgoi (äfgoi′), town (pop. 1,000), in the Benadir, S Ital. Somaliland, on the Webi Shebeli and 20 mi. NW of Mogadishu, in irrigated region (bananas, castor beans, cotton, maize); road junction.

Afikim, Israel: see AFIQIM.

Afikpo (äfēp′-pō), town (pop. 19,556), Ogoja prov., Eastern Provinces, SE Nigeria, 50 mi. SE of Enugu, 26 mi. E of rail station; road center; palm oil and kernels, cacao, kola nuts. Its port on Cross R. is Ndibi Beach, 5 mi. S.

Afiqim or **Afikim** (both: äfēkēm′), settlement (1949 pop. 1,039), Lower Galilee, NE Israel, near left bank of the Jordan, on railroad and 8 mi. SSE of Tiberias; mixed farming; plywood and box mfg.

Afiunkarahissar, Turkey: see AFYONKARAHISAR.

Afjord, canton, Norway: see A, Sor-Trondelag co.

A Fjord (ô′fyôrd″, ô′fyōr), Nor. *Åfjord*, inlet of the North Sea in Sor-Trondelag co., central Norway; 10 mi. long, c.1 mi. wide. At its head lies A village. Sometimes spelled Aafjord.

Aflaj (ăflăj′), district of S Nejd, Saudi Arabia, c.180 mi. S of Riyadh. Its group of oases includes Kharfa and Laila.

Aflenz or **Aflenz Land** (äf′lĕnts länt), village (pop. 1,512), Styria, E central Austria, 9 mi. N of Bruck an der Mur; mfg. (leather goods, felt, chemicals). Graphite mined in vicinity. Aflenz Kurort (pop. 957), a resort, is 1 mi. NE.

Aflou (äflōō′), village (pop. 4,313), Oran Dept., N central Algeria, in the Djebel Amour (Saharan Atlas) 100 mi. SSE of Tiaret and 50 mi. NE of Laghouat; 34°8′N 2°6′E; alt. 4,650 ft. Horse and sheep raising. Handicraft industries (wool, blankets, rugs, baskets).

Afmadu (äfmä′dōō), town (pop. 2,000), in the Benadir, S Ital. Somaliland, on road and 65 mi. NW of Kismayu; caravan center.

Afogados da Ingàzeira (äfōōgä′dōōs dä ēng-gäzā′rŭ), city (pop. 2,228), central Pernambuco, NE Brazil, 37 mi. NW of Sertânia; cotton, manioc, livestock raising.

Afognak (ăfŏg′năk), village (pop. 159), S Alaska, on SE Afognak Isl., 20 mi. NW of Kodiak; trade center for fishing, trapping region; fur farming. School. Established in early 19th cent. by Russian settlers.

Afognak Island (43 mi. long, 9–23 mi. wide), S Alaska, bet. Shelikof Strait (W) and Gulf of Alaska (E), N of Kodiak Isl.; 58°16′N 152°35′W. Rises to 2,546 ft. (NE). Afognak village, SE. Trapping, fur farming, fishing.

Afon River or **Avon River** (both: ă′vŭn), Glamorgan, Wales, rises 4 mi. W of Ystrad Rhondda, flows 15 mi. SW, past Cwmavon and Port Talbot, to Bristol Channel at Aberavon.

Afonso Cláudio (äfō′sōō klou′dyōō), city (pop. 1,126), W central Espírito Santo, Brazil, 55 mi. WNW of Vitória; coffee, bananas, rice, manioc. Formerly spelled Affonso Claudio.

Afonso Pena. **1** City, Bahia, Brazil: see CONCEIÇÃO DO ALMEIDA. **2** City, Ceará, Brazil: see ACOPIARA.

Afqa or **Afaqa** (both: ăfkä′), village, central Lebanon, 25 mi. NE of Beirut. Has grotto on a cliff 650 ft. high; near its entrance are ruins of a Roman temple.

Afragola (äfrägô′lä), town (pop. 29,281), Napoli prov., Campania, S Italy, 5 mi. NNE of Naples, in agr. region (cereals, fruit, hemp); straw-hat mfg. Has Angevin castle, now an orphanage.

Afram River (äfräm′), S Gold Coast, rises in Ashanti 10 mi. NW of Mampong, flows c.150 mi. SE, past Mankrong (canoe-traffic head), to Volta R. 30 mi. N of Akuse. Dries up in dry season (Oct.-March). Bauxite deposits near Mpraeso.

Afreda, lake, Ethiopia: see EGOGI BAD.

Afrera, lake and peak, Ethiopia: see EGOGI BAD.

Africa, 2d-largest continent (including offshore isls.: □ c.11,500,000; pop. c.200,000,000), joined to Asia by the Sinai peninsula (the Suez Canal is usually considered the dividing line) and facing Europe across the Strait of Gibraltar and the narrow straits separating Cape Bon (Tunisia) from Sicily. It is bounded by the Mediterranean (N), Red Sea (NE; linked to Gulf of Aden by Bab el Mandeb strait), Indian Ocean (E), and Atlantic Ocean (W). Extending 5,000 mi. N-S and 4,700 mi. E-W, Africa is a compact land mass almost lacking in major indentations and peninsulas. Its forbidding interior, its lack of major coastal lowlands, and its rapids-strewn streams have hindered exploration and development. Straddling the equator, and extending roughly to the same lat. N (Cape Blanc, 37°21′N) as S (Cape Agulhas, 34°52′S), Africa is a land of the tropics. It attains its greatest width near 12°N, bet. the horn of Somaliland (Ras Hafun, 51°23′E) and the W bulge (Cape Verde, 17°33′W, at Dakar), where it reaches within 1,850 mi. of South America across the narrow waist of the Atlantic. S of 5°N its width is cut in half by the Gulf of Guinea, the only major embayment. One major isl. (Madagascar), several smaller isls., and a few archipelagoes are part of the African region; these include the Seychelles, Mascarenes, Comoros, and Socotra in Indian Ocean; the isls. (São Tomé, Principe, Fernando Po, Annobón) of the Gulf of Guinea; Madeira, Canary Isls., and Cape Verde Isls. in the Atlantic off NW coast. Africa is a geologically simple unit. Underlying it is a vast platform of complex pre-Cambrian and Paleozoic rocks, partly covered by Mesozoic and Tertiary sedimentaries; as a result of gentle warping these now form basins (Congo Basin, Kalahari Basin, basins of L. Chad, middle Nile and middle Niger) and domes (Ahaggar, Tibesti). Strong folding occurred only in N, where the ATLAS mts. form an extension of the Alpine system, and in the Cape mts. at the extreme S. Topographically most of Africa is a plateau, lower in N and W, higher in E and S. Among the most prominent mtn. masses are the Ethiopian highlands, which rise above 15,000 ft., the High Atlas range in Morocco (Djebel Toubkal, 13,665 ft.), and the Drakensberg (over 11,000 ft.), part of the S African escarpment. The highest elevations are found in E Africa, where volcanic Kilimanjaro (19,565 ft.), Mt. Kenya (17,040 ft.), and Mt. Elgon (14,178 ft.), and the non-volcanic Ruwenzori (16,795 ft.) tower above the tableland. The GREAT RIFT VALLEY, a chain of mtn.-rimmed structural troughs traceable from the Red Sea to Mozambique, is a relief feature peculiar to E Africa. Here, too, are the great lakes (Rudolf, Albert, Edward, Kivu, Tanganyika, and Nyasa occupying sections of the rift valley; L. Victoria lying on the plateau bet. the 2 principal rift depressions), 2d in size only to N America's lake system. Africa also contains the world's most extensive and empty desert regions; the SAHARA, with its E extensions in the Libyan, Arabian, and Nubian deserts, spans the continent from the Atlantic to the Red Sea, isolating the densely populated sections of NW Africa from the bulk of the continent to the S. Its dry, sandy wastes give rise to scorching winds (harmattan, khamsin, simoom, sirocco) which periodically invade adjacent regions. In the S is another desert, the KALAHARI, in Bechuanaland Protectorate. The coastal NAMIB DESERT in South-West Africa owes its aridity to the cold offshore Benguela Current. Africa's great river systems make an intricate pattern, particularly in the lake dist., where both the Nile and the Congo draw part of their headwaters. The CONGO RIVER, master stream of Belgian Congo, the one major waterway of the continent flowing entirely in wet regions, receives numerous tributaries (especially Ubangi and Kasai rivers); its lower stretches, bet. Leopoldville and Matadi, are interrupted by rapids, but it remains nevertheless equatorial Africa's major traffic artery. The NILE RIVER, lifeline of Egypt, fed by the great lakes (White Nile) and by L. Tana in Ethiopia (Blue Nile), traverses 1,000 mi. of desert without benefit of any tributaries, reaching the Mediterranean in a huge delta below Cairo. The NIGER RIVER, largest in W Africa, reaches the fringes of the Sahara in its great N bend, but after spreading out in an interior delta it continues SE to the Gulf of Guinea in Nigeria; its chief tributary is the Benue. The SENEGAL RIVER reaches the Atlantic at Saint-Louis. In the S part of the continent the ZAMBEZI RIVER drains the Rhodesias and empties into Mozambique Channel NE of Beira; the Zambezi, with its famed VICTORIA FALLS and narrow Kariba Gorge, is a potential source of hydroelectricity. The LIMPOPO RIVER skirts the S African veld and enters the Indian Ocean in Mozambique, while the ORANGE RIVER, flowing in opposite direction, fringes the Kalahari on its way to the S Atlantic. Fr. North Africa's main streams are the historic Medjerda in Tunisia, the Chéliff in Algeria, and several Atlas-fed rivers in Morocco. L. Chad, at the center of an interior-drainage basin in the Sudan, is fed by the Shari. Africa's climate and vegetation adhere to a latitudinal pattern, except in the E African upland, where altitude governs. The N half of the Congo Basin and the E coast of the Gulf of Guinea are Africa's equatorial rain forest region; a warm coastal sector on the W African bulge, from Sierra Leone to Ivory Coast, has a monsoon-type equatorial climate with annual rainfall exceeding 80 in. N and S of the equator, the rain forest gradually becomes park savanna, changing to tall grass savanna and semi-arid steppe with increasing latitude. Desert conditions are reached near 17°N and 17°S. A savanna belt also follows the E African coast from Somaliland to the U. of So. Afr. Mid-latitude climate and vegetation are found in scattered upland areas, such as on the upper slopes of Ruwenzori and in the Ethiopian highlands. In general, climate ceases to be an inhibiting factor to European settlement in the African tropics above 5,000 ft. Only near its 2 extremities does Africa have regions of subtropical climate; Natal and the E part of Cape Prov. are humid subtropical, while the Cape Town dist. in S and the coastal strip of Fr. North Africa have typical Mediterranean climate. Here wine and olive and citrus trees are grown; the Atlas slopes are clad with cork oaks, Aleppo pines, cedars, and thujas; irrigation agr. is prevalent, and most of the continent's small grains (wheat, barley) are grown here. Elsewhere, commercial agr. is for the most part limited to European-run plantations; principal crops so grown are sugar cane (Natal, Mauritius, Réunion), sisal (Kenya, Tanganyika, Mozambique), coffee (Br. East Africa, Fr. West Africa, Angola; *mocha* coffee in Ethiopian highlands), tea (Kenya, Nyasaland), bananas (Fr. Guinea, Cameroons, Mozambique, Canary Isls.), rubber (Liberia), tobacco (especially in Southern Rhodesia, Nyasaland). Long-staple cotton is the principal export crop of Egypt and of Anglo-Egyptian Sudan (GEZIRA irrigation scheme); it is also grown by natives in the Macina irrigation dist. on the Niger (Fr. Sudan), in Uganda, and in Angola. Cacao is a peasant crop in the Gold Coast (world's largest producer), Nigeria, Ivory Coast, and Cameroons; a plantation crop in Belgian Congo and on the isls. in the Gulf of Guinea. Peanuts are cultivated in Fr. West Africa (especially Senegal), Gambia, Nigeria, and Belgian Congo; the Br. East African peanut scheme (begun 1947) was reduced by 1951. Palm oil and palm kernels enter world trade from Nigeria, Sierra

Leone, and the Belgian Congo. Dates are the chief export product of the Saharan oases. Corn, manioc, yams, pulses, plantains, oil seeds, millets, and sorghums are widely grown by natives for subsistence. The tsetse fly has been instrumental in barring extensive tropical regions to livestock. Most of the cattle, though highly prized by tribal natives, is of poor quality because of tropical disease and frequently overgrazed pastures. Only in the U. of So. Afr., Fr. North Africa, Southern Rhodesia, and Kenya has meat processing achieved any importance. South Africa, with its large sheep herds, is a ranking shipper of wool and mutton. Despite the depredations of the white man, Africa's parks and savannas remain a haven for wildlife. The true African fauna, distinguished by its variety of hoofed animals, includes the elephant, rhinoceros, hippopotamus, giraffe, zebra, and numerous species of antelope. Here, too, are found all of the predatory jungle animals, and the anthropoid apes whose home is the equatorial forest. Extensive reserves for wildlife protection have been established in Br. East Africa, Belgian Congo, and in the U. of So. Afr. About ¼ of the continent is in forests (mostly hardwood), of which, however, only a small part is accessible or of commercial value. Lumbering, long inhibited by transport difficulties and labor shortage, is gaining importance in Nigeria, Belgian Congo, and Fr. Equatorial Africa, with the construction of modern sawmills and veneer and plywood factories along the coast. Gums and resins are gathered in the semi-arid parts of the Sudan and Somaliland. The continent is very deficient in mineral fuels but contains an abundance of rare and strategic minerals (copper, manganese, chrome, uranium, diamonds, gold). Workable coal deposits are limited to the U. of So. Afr. (Africa's largest mines are in Natal), Southern Rhodesia, Algeria, Morocco, and Nigeria; little is of coking quality. Though prospecting for petroleum is carried on in widely scattered dists. (Tunisia, Morocco, Ethiopia), only Egypt's oil wells are in regular operation. Belgian Congo and Northern Rhodesia are among the world's leading copper producers; important quantities of cobalt are also recovered here. Manganese from the U. of So. Afr., Gold Coast, and Fr. Morocco constitutes c.20% of world output; major chromite deposits are mined in Southern Rhodesia and in U. of So. Afr.; tin in Belgian Congo, Nigeria, and Uganda; lead and zinc in Northern Rhodesia, South-West Africa, Morocco, Belgian Congo, and Tanganyika. Southern Rhodesia and the U. of So. Afr. produce asbestos, while Tunisia and Morocco supply much of the world's phosphate rock. Iron ore is mined in Transvaal (supplying the continent's only major steelworks, at Pretoria and Vanderbijl Park), in Southern Rhodesia (for the Que Que ironworks), in Algeria, Morocco, and Sierra Leone, and since 1950 in Liberia; important deposits have been blocked out near Conakry, Fr. Guinea, and in Northern Rhodesia near Lusaka. Bauxite is mined in Gold Coast since Second World War; Fr. Guinea also has deposits. Africa remains pre-eminent in its gold and diamond resources, particularly in the U. of So. Afr. Gold is also mined in substantial quantities in Southern Rhodesia, Belgian Congo, and the Gold Coast. Though Kimberley remains the world's diamond capital, Belgian Congo is now the leading producer; Angola and Tanganyika also export diamonds. Shinkolobwe in Belgian Congo is a leading source of uranium. Most tribal natives and desert nomads still live outside the modern economy. Africa's 63,000 mi. of railroads (about ½ of South America's mileage) are unevenly distributed over the continent, most of it in the U. of So. Afr. (35%), Fr. North Africa (13%), and Belgian Congo (7.5%). Africa's only trans-continental railroad links the Atlantic at Lobito (Angola) with the Indian Ocean at Beira (Mozambique); it serves the copper dists. of Belgian Congo and Northern Rhodesia, the Wankie coal mine, and the high veld regions of Southern Rhodesia. The much-discussed but wholly uneconomical Trans-Saharan RR has been completed from the Mediterranean Coast at Nemours (Algeria) only to the N edge of the Sahara below Colomb-Béchar. The typical African railroad pattern consists of unconnected spurs penetrating inland from the principal ports (e.g., Mombasa to L. Victoria, Dar es Salaam to L. Tanganyika, Djibouti to Addis Ababa, Lagos to Kano). Other lines complement river communications by circumventing rapids and falls, especially along the Congo and the Nile. Because the continent remains essentially a raw-material exporting area, its ports (many of which suffer from congestion and poor facilities) are important. Among the leading ones are Oran, Algiers, Bône, Bizerte, Tunis, Sfax, Tripoli, Alexandria, and Port Said on the Mediterranean; Suez, Port Sudan, Massawa on the Red Sea, and Djibouti at its outlet; Mombasa, Dar es Salaam, Beira, Lourenço Marques, Durban, and Port Elizabeth on the Indian Ocean; Tamatave is the chief port of Madagascar; on the Atlantic, Capetown, Lobito, Boma, and Matadi (the latter 2 near the mouth of the Congo), Douala, Port Harcourt (on Niger delta in Nigeria), Lagos, Accra, Takoradi, Abidjan, Monrovia, Freetown, Dakar, and Casablanca. Africa's pop. is unevenly distributed over the continent. With the exception of Egypt's Nile Valley (where densities reach 1,000 persons per sq. mi.), there is a fair degree of correlation bet. distribution of pop. density and mean annual precipitation. In the following regions, where pop. densities are above average, minimum rainfall exceeds 25 in.: (1) the Guinea coast and S Sudan from the Gambia to the Niger and the lower Congo, with largest concentrations near Niger delta; (2) the great lakes dist. of E Africa, especially around L. Victoria; (3) the coast of E Africa bet. Mombasa (Kenya) and Cape Town, with highest density in Natal; (4) the Mediterranean fringe of Fr. North Africa. The Sahara and N Sudan form the great divide bet. white and Negroid ethnic groups. Arabs (Semites) occupy the Mediterranean coast, N Anglo-Egyptian Sudan, and the E desert oases; they have pushed the Hamitic Berbers into the less accessible mtn. regions of NW Africa; the nomadic Tuaregs and Tibbus are also of Hamitic origin; in E Africa, the horn of Somaliland and part of Ethiopia are inhabited by the Hamitic Somali and Galla. S of the Sahara, the mixed-blood Sudanese peoples include the Wolaf, Mandingoes, Songhai, Mossi, Kru, Fulani, Ewe, Yoruba, Ibo, and Hausa; the language of the Hausa is considered the *lingua franca* of the W Sudan. The equally transitional middle Nile region is occupied by Nilotic tribes (especially the Shilluk, Nuer, Dinka); the Masai and Nandi of Br. East Africa are also partly of Hamitic stock. The Bantu Negroes, numbering over 50,000,000, occupy at least ⅓ of the continent (mostly S of equator); Swahili is the *lingua franca* of the E African native pop. Bushman and Hottentot tribes are now restricted to South-West Africa and parts of Cape Prov., while the Pygmy Negrillos, the continent's oldest inhabitants, limit their hunting activities to the equatorial forest belt. The Malagasy, of part Bantu, part Malayo-Polynesian origin, inhabit Madagascar. Largest European concentrations are found in the U. of So. Afr. (Dutch and British) and in NW Africa (French, Italian, Spanish); Southern Rhodesia and Kenya are the leading tropical areas of European settlement. Indians (brought to Africa as indentured laborers bet. 1834 and 1911) constitute important minorities in U. of So. Afr. (c.280,000), especially in Natal, in Mauritius (270,000), and in Br. East Africa (c.180,000). Islam (with over 60 million adherents in Africa) is the dominant religion N of the Sahara and among some of the Sudanic peoples. A minority (5–10%) of Egyptians are Coptic Christians, as are the Amhara, the ruling class of Ethiopia. The majority of tribal natives in tropical Africa still practice various forms of animism, but cannibalism has virtually disappeared, largely as a result of active missionary work. In the civilization of Egypt, established before 3,000 B.C., Africa may perhaps claim the most ancient settled culture in the world. In 9th cent. B.C., the Phoenicians founded Carthage and subsequently explored the continent's N and W coast. Mediterranean Africa figured prominently in the history of Rome (the name Africa was 1st given by Romans to the region about Carthage, later extended to most of NW coast), especially during the period of the Punic Wars and later as the granary of the empire. Divided among barbarians after the dissolution of the West Roman Empire, N Africa was reunited under the conquering Arabs (7th–11th cent.), who effectively propagated Islam. From here the Moors invaded the Iberian Peninsula and were not finally expelled until the 15th cent. Portugal, in search of a safe route to India, pioneered in exploring the African coast line, and a Portuguese, Bartholomew Diaz, was 1st to round (1488) the Cape of Good Hope. Vasco da Gama visited the E coast and reached India in 1499. Portugal soon established coastal stations to trade in ivory, gold, spices, and slaves. Dutch, British, and French competition severely restricted Portugal in 16th–17th cent., when slave trade reached its zenith. Penetration of the "dark continent" began in 18th cent. Among the numerous famous explorers were James Bruce, Mungo Park, John Speke, David Livingstone, and Henry Stanley. The discovery (1858) of L. Victoria by Burton and Speke marked one of the high spots of African exploration; the age-old mystery of the source of the Nile was thereby solved. Though the Dutch had colonized the Cape of Good Hope in 17th cent., and the British had founded the colony of Sierra Leone in 1808, the intense scramble for empire in Africa did not get underway until mid-19th cent., by which time the slave trade had also finally disappeared. By 1912, the major European powers had accomplished the partition of the continent, and only Ethiopia and Liberia retained at least nominal independence. After the First World War Germany's colonies were given to France and England as mandates of the League of Nations (they became U.N. trust territories after 1946) and Egypt gained (1922) her independence. The Italian empire in East Africa, built up as a result of the Ethiopian War (1935–36), collapsed during Second World War. Former Italian Somaliland became (1950) an Italian trusteeship under the U.N., to expire in 1959. Also in 1950 the U.N. agreed to a federation of formerly Italian Eritrea with Ethiopia. Libya (consisting of Tripolitania, Cyrenaica, and Fezzan) was to achieve its independence in 1952, under U.N. auspices. France controls the largest territory of all colonial powers in Africa. Units of the French Union in Africa include Algeria, the protectorates of Morocco and Tunisia, the isl. (overseas department) of Réunion, and the overseas territories of French West Africa (Dahomey, French Guinea, French Sudan, Ivory Coast, Mauritania, Niger, Senegal, Upper Volta), French Equatorial Africa (Gabon, Middle Congo, Ubangi-Shari, Chad), French Somaliland, Madagascar, and the Comoro Islands. French Togoland and French Cameroons are U.N. trust territories. The bulk of British possessions is in E Africa; here are British Somaliland, Kenya, Uganda, Tanganyika (former German East Africa, now a U.N. trust territory), Zanzibar, Nyasaland, Northern Rhodesia, and Southern Rhodesia (a self-governing colony). The Union of South Africa is a dominion of the Br. Commonwealth of Nations; former Ger. South-West Africa is administered and claimed by the U. of So. Afr.; Bechuanaland Protectorate, Basutoland, and Swaziland are Br. protectorates. In W Africa, Br. possessions form several coastal enclaves; they are Nigeria (which administers Br. Cameroons), Gold Coast (which administers Br. Togoland), Sierra Leone, and Gambia. Br. isls. in African area are Mauritius and the Seychelles in the Indian Ocean, Saint Helena, Ascension, and Tristan da Cunha in the Atlantic. The Anglo-Egyptian Sudan is a condominium jointly administered by Egypt and Britain. The once powerful Portuguese empire in Africa is now limited to Angola, Mozambique, Portuguese Guinea, São Tomé e Principe, and the Cape Verde Islands. Madeira is considered part of metropolitan Portugal. Belgian Congo, in the heart of Africa, is Belgium's only colony. Spain's colonial possessions include the protectorate of Spanish Morocco (which encloses the international zone of Tangier), Spanish West Africa (along W edge of the Sahara), and Spanish Guinea (including continental Sp. Guinea or Río Muni, and isls. of Fernando Po and Annobón). The Canary Islands are an integral part of Spain. For further information see separate articles on countries, physical features, regions, and cities.

Africa, Cape, Tunisia: see Mahdia.

African Banks, Seychelles: see African Islands.

African Islands or **African Banks,** in N Amirantes, outlying dependency of the Seychelles, 140 mi. WSW of Mahé Isl., 4°54′S 53°23′E; 3 mi. long, 1 mi. wide. Of coral formation. Uninhabited.

Afrin (ä'frēn), Fr. *Afrine* (äfrēn'), town, Aleppo prov., NW Syria, on Afrin R. and 27 mi. NW of Aleppo; cotton, cereals.

Afrin River, Fr. *Afrine,* rises in S Turkey near Gaziantep, flows S into Syria for c.45 mi., turns W into Turkey, and just NE of Antioch enters L. Amik, which drains S to the Orontes; 100 mi. long.

Afsar, India: see Nawada.

Afsin (äf-shĭn'), Turkish *Afşin,* village (pop. 4,205), Maras prov., S central Turkey, near Ceyhan R., 45 mi. N of Maras; chromium deposits; grain. Formerly Efsus, Efsuz, Elfus; also Yarpus, Yarpuz.

Afsluitdijk, Netherlands: see Ijsselmeer.

Afton. 1 Town (pop. 936), Union co., S Iowa, 9 mi. E of Creston; dairy, concrete, and wood products. **2** Village (pop. 142), Washington co., E Minn., on St. Croix L. (in St. Croix R.) and 16 mi. E of St. Paul; corn, oats, barley, potatoes, livestock. **3** Village (pop. 875), Chenango co., S central N.Y., on the Susquehanna and 22 mi. ENE of Binghamton, in agr. area; feed, lumber, burial vaults. Summer resort. **4** Town (pop. 1,252), Ottawa co., extreme NE Okla., 11 mi. ENE of Vinita, in rich farm area (grain, livestock, corn); feed milling. L. of the Cherokees lies to E and S. **5** Town (pop. 1,319), Lincoln co., W Wyo., near Idaho line, just W of Salt River Range, 70 mi. NNW of Kemmerer; alt. 6,100 ft.; dairy and trade center for Star Valley (grain, flour, timber, furs). Coal mine near. Mormon tabernacle here. Near by is Univ. of Wyoming agr. experiment station. Settled c.1885, laid out 1896, inc. 1902.

Afton River, Ayrshire, Scotland, rises at S foot of Blackcraig Hill, flows 9 mi. N to Nith R. at New Cumnock. It is the "Sweet Afton" of Burns's poem.

Afuá (äfwä'), city (pop. 789), NE Pará, Brazil, on N shore of Marajó isl., 140 mi. NW of Belém. Formerly spelled Affuá.

Afula or **Affula** (both: äfōō'lä), town (pop. 3,000), N Israel, at NE edge of Plain of Jezreel, 6 mi. S of Nazareth; rail junction, road center; flour mills, workshops. In immediate vicinity are agr. school for girls and large hosp., serving Plain of Jezreel settlements. Modern town founded 1925 on site of biblical locality of *Haophel.* Site of Crusaders' castle of La Fève was 2 mi. E. Sometimes spelled Afule or Affule.

Afyonkarahisar (äfyôn'kärähĭsär') [Turkish,=black castle of opium], province (□ 5,234; 1950 pop. 372,566), W central Turkey; ⊙ Afyonkarahisar.

Has Akar R.; Mt. Emir in N; L. Aksehir on E; L. Aci in S. Leading opium (Turkish *afyon*) producer; mohair, wool, sugar beets, wheat, vetch, pears. Sometimes simply Afyon. Formerly Afiunkarahissar.

Afyonkarahisar, city (1950 pop. 29,881), ⊙ Afyonkarahisar prov., W central Turkey, 150 mi. SW of Ankara; rail junction on lines to Smyrna and Istanbul; agr. market, the center of a large opium-poppy growing area. Also wheat, barley, potatoes, onions, vetch. Sometimes called Afyon of Karahisar (Karahissar). Formerly Afiunkarahissar.

Afzalgarh (ŭf'zŭlgŭr), town (pop. 5,759), Bijnor dist., N Uttar Pradesh, India, near the Ramnagar, 15 mi. ESE of Nagina; hand-loom cotton weaving; rice, wheat, gram, barley, sugar cane. Founded 18th cent.

Aga (ăgă') or **Aja** (ăjă'), village (pop. 6,903), Daqahliya prov., Lower Egypt, on Damietta branch of the Nile and 9 mi. SSW of Mansura; cotton, cereals.

Aga (ŭgä'), a Buryat-Mongol national okrug (□ 9,380; 1946 pop. estimate 30,000), administrative division of S Chita oblast, Russian SFSR; ⊙ Aginskoye. Drained by Aga R.; bounded S by Onon R. Branch of Trans-Siberian RR passes through E section. Pop. chiefly Buryat-Mongols. Stock raising (cattle, sheep, horses), hunting, and lumbering are important. Until 1937, part of Buryat-Mongol Autonomous SSR.

Aga, river, Russian SFSR: see AGA RIVER.

Agabama River (ägäbä'mä), central Cuba, rises in hills of Santa Clara, flows c. 60 mi. S of the Caribbean in a delta 12 mi. SE of Trinidad. Its lower course is called Manatí.

Agade (ugä'dē, ugä'dē) or **Akkad** (ä'kăd, ä'käd), anc. city of Mesopotamia, a ⊙ AKKAD, in what was to become N Babylonia; its site is in modern Iraq, perhaps near SIPPAR.

Agades, Fr. Niger, Fr. West Africa: see AGADEZ.

Agadez (ägädĕz') or **Agades** (ägädĕs'), town (pop. c.4,250), central Niger territory, Fr. West Africa, road junction and oasis at S foot of Aïr mts., 440 mi. ENE of Niamey; 17°N 7°57'W; market; exports livestock and hides to Nigeria and S Algeria. Region also produces wheat, corn, millet, tomatoes, onions, tobacco. Meteorological station; airfield. Salt deposits near. Former ⊙ a Tuareg kingdom.

Agadir (ägädēr', ăgudēr'), city (pop. 12,438), ⊙ Agadir frontier region (□ 24,205; pop. 735,080), SW Fr. Morocco, its southernmost port on the Atlantic, 5 mi. N of mouth of Sous R., 75 mi. S of Mogador; 30°26'N 9°38'W. A fishing and military supply port, opened to foreign commerce in 1930; has become gateway to the fertile Sous region (early fruits and vegetables). Its improved harbor facilities are designed to make it shipping point for minerals (molybdenum, manganese, cobalt, zinc and lead) mined in immediate hinterland. Linked with Mogador by good coastal road and with Marrakesh via Taroudant and Tizi n' Test pass. Naval air station. Commercial airport, on Casablanca-Dakar route, is 4 mi. SE. Fish salting and canning, mfg. of building materials, and small metalworking are chief industries. A massive citadel atop 720-ft. rock overlooks harbor. Occupied (1505–41) and fortified by Portuguese, who named it Santa Cruz. Closed to commerce in 1765. The presence here (1911) of German cruiser *Panther*, ostensibly to protect Ger. interests, precipitated an international crisis. Taken by French in 1913.

Agadir Tissint (tēsēnt'), Saharan outpost, Agadir frontier region, SW Fr. Morocco, in a wadi of the Djebel Bani, 40 mi. NE of Tata; 29°55'N 7°19'W.

Agadyr or **Agadyr'** (ŭgudĭr'), town (1945 pop. over 500), central Karaganda oblast, Kazakh SSR, on railroad and 105 mi. S of Karaganda. Lead-zinc and copper deposits (W).

Agaete (ägäā'tā), town (pop. 2,863), Grand Canary, Canary Isls., 18 mi. W of Las Palmas, and on isl.'s NW shore; coffee, tomatoes, bananas, fruit. Fishing. Medicinal springs.

Agaie (ägä'), town (pop. 4,814), Niger prov., Northern Provinces, W central Nigeria, 45 mi. SSW of Minna; shea-nut processing; cotton, peanuts, cassava, durra, yams.

Agalega (ägälĕ'gä), island dependency (□ 27; pop. 437) of Mauritius, in Indian Ocean, c.600 mi. N of Mauritius; 12 mi. long, 5 mi. wide; 10°25'S 56°40'E. Includes North Isl. and South Isl. (site of main settlement), linked by sand bank. Coconut plantations; horse raising. Meteorological station.

Agalta, Sierra de (syĕ'rä dā ägäl'tä), mountain range in E Honduras; extends 40 mi. SW-NE bet. Sico R. (N) and Olancho Valley (S); 8,500 ft. high.

Agalteca, Honduras: see CEDROS.

Agameto (ägämĕ'tō), village, Eastern Prov., NE Belgian Congo, near Uele R., 40 mi. NNE of Buta; cotton ginning, coffee plantations, palm groves.

Agana (ägä'nyŭ), city (1950 pop. 1,918), GUAM, on W coast, 5 mi. E of U.S. naval base at Apra Harbor. Before it was completely destroyed (1945) in Second World War, it was largest and most important town (1940 pop. 10,004) on isl., exporting copra. U.S. appropriations made (1946) for its rehabilitation.

Agano, Japan: see AKAIKE.

Agapia (ägä'pyä), village (pop. 1,070), Bacau prov., NE Rumania, in E foothills of the Moldavian Carpathians, 5 mi. SW of Targu-Neamt; climatic resort (alt. 1,575 ft.). Site of noted monastery, 1st established in 16th cent., later transformed into convent, with religious art mus.

Agapovka (ŭgä'pufkŭ), town (1942 pop. over 500), SW Chelyabinsk oblast, Russian SFSR, on Ural R. and 10 mi. SSE of Magnitogorsk; limestone works, supplying Magnitogorsk metallurgy. Formerly Agapovo.

Agar (ŭgŭr'), town (pop., including cantonment area, 8,469), central Madhya Bharat, India, 25 mi. NNW of Shajapur; rail spur terminus; agr. market (millet, cotton, wheat); cotton ginning, hand-loom weaving.

Agar (ā'gär), town (pop. 141), Sully co., central S.Dak., 10 mi. N of Onida; cattle-shipping point; grain, poultry.

Agara (ŭgŭrä'), town (1939 pop. over 500), central Georgian SSR, on Kura R., on railroad and 17 mi. WNW of Gori; fruit canning; orchards, sugar beets.

Agara-Mamballi (ŭ'gŭrŭ-mŭm'bŭlē), town (pop. 3,964), Mysore dist., S Mysore, India, 30 mi. ESE of Mysore; hand-loom silk weaving.

Agareb (ägärĕb'), village, Sfax dist., E Tunisia, 13 mi. W of Sfax; olive groves.

Aga River (ŭgä'), S Chita oblast, Russian SFSR, rises in Daurian Range, flows c.100 mi. NE, through Aga Buryat-Mongol Natl. Okrug, to Onon R. 25 mi. above its mouth.

Agaro or **Aggaro** (ä'gärō), village, Kaffa prov., SW Ethiopia, on road and 17 mi. NE of Jimma, in coffee-growing region.

Agarpara, India: see PANIHATI.

Agartala (ŭgŭr'tŭlŭ), town (pop. 17,693), ⊙ Tripura, NE India, on tributary of the Meghna and 56 mi. NE of Dacca; trade center (rice, cotton, tea, mustard, jute). Airfield.

Agashi (ŭgä'shē), village (pop. 11,128), Thana dist., W Bombay, India, on Arabian Sea, 30 mi. N of Bombay; fish-supplying center (pomfrets, jewfish); betel farming; plantains, rice. In 16th cent., Port. timber and shipbuilding port.

Agassiz (ă'gusē), village (pop. estimate 600), SW B.C., near Fraser R., 10 mi. NE of Chilliwack; mixed farming, lumbering, fruitgrowing. Site of Dominion experimental farm.

Agassiz, Lake, glacial lake which existed for c.1,000 years in Pleistocene times and was formed by melting of continental ice sheet. Was c.700 mi. long, more than 250 mi. wide; included parts of what are now Minn., N.Dak., and Manitoba. As ice disappeared, water drained N into Hudson Bay, leaving L. Winnipeg, L. Manitoba, L. Winnipegosis, Lake of the Woods, Red L., and others. L. Traverse, Big Stone L., and Minnesota R. are in channel of original S outlet (prehistoric River Warren). Fine claylike silt deposited in bed of lake is mainly responsible for fertility of rich, wheat-growing valley of Red River of the North. Lake named 1879 for Louis Agassiz.

Agassiz, Mount, peak (2,394 ft.) of White Mts., in NW N.H., just SE of Bethlehem.

Agassiz Peak, Ariz.: see SAN FRANCISCO PEAKS.

Agastiyampalli, India: see VEDARANNIYAM.

Agastya Malai (ŭgŭ'styŭ mŭlī'), peak (6,132 ft.) in S Western Ghats, in S Madras, India, 22 mi. ENE of Trivandrum; gives rise to Tambraparni R.

Agat (ä'gät), town (pop. 1,339) and municipality (pop. 4,654), NW GUAM, near Apra Harbor. Totally destroyed in Second World War; reconstruction begun in 1946.

Agatha, France: see AGDE.

Agathopolis, Bulgaria: see AKHTOPOL.

Agattu Island (ăgŭtōō') (18 mi. long, 4–9 mi. wide), Near Isls., Aleutian Isls., SW Alaska, 20 mi. SE of Attu Isl.; 52°26'N 173°34'E; rises to 2,075 ft. Uninhabited, mountainous, treeless.

Agaumdir (ägoumdĭr'), mtn. district in Gojjam prov., NW Ethiopia, bet. L. Tana and Blue Nile R. Agr. (honey, cereals) and stock raising (horses, mules). Chief centers, Dangila and Enjabara. Sometimes written Agaumeder.

Agawam (ă'gŭwăm), town (pop. 10,166), Hampden co., SW Mass., on Connecticut and Westfield rivers and 3 mi. SW of Springfield; woolens, metal products; dairying, truck. Settled 1635, inc. 1855. Includes agr. village of Feeding Hills (1940 pop. 1,443). Agawam is also the former name of IPSWICH town.

Agawam River, E Mass., small stream entering the Atlantic in Plymouth town; also former name of lower course of WESTFIELD RIVER in W Mass.

Agawa River (ă'gŭwŭ), central Ont., rises E of L. Superior, flows SW, then S, and finally W, to L. Superior 60 mi. NNW of Sault Ste Marie; 60 mi. long. At its mouth pitchblende deposits were discovered, 1948.

Agay, France: see SAINT-RAPHAËL.

Agazzano (ägätsä'nō), village (pop. 799), Piacenza prov., Emilia-Romagna, N central Italy, 11 mi. SW of Piacenza.

Agbabu (äb-bäbōō'), town, Ondo prov., Western Provinces, S Nigeria, 5 mi. NNE of Okitipupa; rubber, timber, palm oil and kernels, yams, cassava, maize, plantains.

Agbaja (äb-bäjä'), town (pop. 836), Kabba prov., Northern Provinces, S central Nigeria, near Niger R., 13 mi. NNW of Lokoha; shea nuts, palm oil and kernels; cotton, cassava, durra, yams. Iron deposits.

Agbede (äb-bā'dā), town, Benin prov., Western Provinces, S Nigeria, 15 mi. NNW of Ubiaja; palm oil and kernels, kola nuts, cacao, cotton.

Agbelouvé (ägbĕlōō'vā), village, S Fr. Togoland, on railroad and 40 mi. N of Lomé; cacao, palm oil and kernels, cotton. R.C. and Protestant missions.

Agbor (äb-bōr'), town (pop. 3,937), Benin prov., Western Provinces, S Nigeria, 40 mi. E of Benin City; road and trade center; palm oil and kernels, hardwood, rubber, kola nuts. Lignite deposits near by.

Agboville (ägbōvēl'), town (pop. c.7,550), S Ivory Coast, Fr. West Africa, on railroad and 45 mi. NNW of Abidjan; trading center for productive region; cacao, coffee, bananas, kola nuts, manioc, corn, rice, timber. Meteorological station. R.C. mission.

Agbulakh, Georgian SSR: see TETRI-TSKARO.

Agdam (ŭgdăm'), city (1932 pop. estimate 11,450), S Azerbaijan SSR, on railroad and 45 mi. SSW of Yevlakh; road center in vineyard and orchard dist.; wines; food processing. Teachers col.

Agdash (ŭgdăsh'), city (1932 pop. estimate 7,290), central Azerbaijan SSR, on road and 15 mi. ENE of Yevlakh, in cotton area; food processing; sericulture.

Agde (ägd), anc. *Agatha*, town (pop. 6,687), Hérault dept., S France, fishing port on the Canal du Midi and on Hérault R. near its mouth on the Gulf of Lion, 13 mi. E of Béziers; fertilizer mfg., shipbuilding. Wine trade. Built of basalt, it is known as the "Black Town." Has fortress-like 12th-cent. Romanesque church. Founded 6th cent. B.C. Episcopal see 5th cent. to 1790. Damaged during Second World War.

Agdenes (äg'dunās), canton (pop. 1,314), Sor-Trondelag co., central Norway, on the North Sea S of entrance to Trondheim Fjord and NE of Kristiansund; fishing, agr. Permanent defenses of Trondheim Fjord are located here and on N shore of the fjord, opposite Agdenes; beacon light.

Agdz (ägdz), village and Saharan oasis, Marrakesh region, S Fr. Morocco, on the Oued Dra S of the Djebel Sagho, 30 mi. SE of Ouarzazate; 30°43'N 6°28'W.

Agdzhabedy (ŭgjŭbyĕ'dē), village (1926 pop. 2,937), S Azerbaijan SSR, on Mili Steppe, 33 mi. ENE of Agdam; cotton; food processing.

Agedabia (äjĕdä'byä), town (1950 pop. 5,971), W Cyrenaica, Libya, near Gulf of Sidra, 95 mi. S of Benghazi; road junction for routes to interior oases. Has mosque, Roman (aqueduct, wells) and Byzantine (5th-cent. basilica) ruins. Scene of heavy fighting (1941–42) in Second World War.

Agedincum, France: see SENS.

Agedir, Ras, Tunisia and Libya: see AJDIR, RAS.

Agege (ägā'gā), town (pop. 10,993), Nigeria colony, on railroad and 14 mi. NNW of Lagos; trade center in cacao area; citrus-fruit drinks; palm oil and kernels. Has govt. experimental livestock stations.

Ageki (ä"gä'kē), town (pop. 3,140), Mie prefecture, S Honshu, Japan, 12 mi. NW of Kuwana; rice, wheat, raw silk.

Agematsu (ägā'mä'tsōō), town (pop. 8,919), Nagano prefecture, central Honshu, Japan, 20 mi. NNW of Iida; lumbering.

Agen (ä-zhē'), anc. *Aginnum*, town (pop. 26,051), ⊙ Lot-et-Garonne dept., SW France, on the Garonne and Garonne Lateral Canal, and 55 mi. NW of Toulouse; commercial center in fruit-growing region (plums, grapes, peaches); fruit and vegetable canning, mfg. of pharmaceuticals, fertilizer, biscuits, chocolates. Has largely Romanesque cathedral (begun 11th cent.). Seat of the Nitiobriges, a Gallic tribe; captured (509) by Franks, it became ⊙ of Agenais (or Agenois) countship under Carolingians, and passed to England (1154) with rest of Aquitaine. Retaken (14th-15th cent.) and inc. into Guienne prov.

Agenais, France: see AGEN.

Agency. 1 Town (pop. 524), Wapello co., SE Iowa, near Des Moines R., 6 mi. E of Ottumwa, in agr. area. Established 1838 as Indian agency. **2** Town (pop. 234), Buchanan co., NW Mo., on Little Platte R. and 8 mi. SE of St. Joseph.

Agency Lake, S Oregon, N arm of Upper Klamath L.; 6 mi. long, 3 mi. wide.

Agency Valley Dam, Oregon: see NORTH FORK.

Agenda, city (pop. 159), Republic co., N Kansas, 15 mi. NE of Concordia; corn, wheat.

Agendicum, France: see SENS.

Agenebode or **Agenebodi** (äjĕnä'bōdī), town, Benin prov., Western Provinces, S central Nigeria, port on Niger R. opposite Idah; palm oil and kernels, yams, cassava, corn, plantains.

Agenieten Islands (ägŭnē'tŭn), group of c.30 coral islets of Indonesia, in Java Sea off NW Java, 25 mi. NW of Jakarta; 5°51'S 106°36'E. Visited by fishermen and coconut pickers.

Agenosho (ä"gā'nōshō), principal town (pop. 10,593) of O-shima, Yamaguchi prefecture, Japan, on S coast of isl.; agr. center (rice, wheat, oranges); fishing.

Ageo (ä'gäō), town (pop. 10,485), Saitama prefecture, central Honshu, Japan, 5 mi. NW of Omiya, in agr. area (rice, wheat); sake, raw silk. Prefectural agr. experiment station here.

Ager (ägăr'), town (pop. 791), Lérida prov., NE Spain, in Catalonia, at S foot of the Montsech, 27 mi. NNE of Lérida, in agr. region (cereals, grapes, hemp). Medicinal springs. Has 9th-cent. Romanesque church.

Ägerisee, Switzerland: see AEGERISEE.

Ager River (ä'gür), S central Upper Austria, flows 20 mi. N, E, and NE from the Attersee to Traun R. near Lambach.

Agerso (ä'yürs-û), Dan. *Agersø*, island (□ 2.6; pop. 378), Denmark, in Smaalandsfarvand strait, just SW of Zealand isl.

Ages, village (pop., with adjacent Brookside, 1,190), Harlan co., SE Ky., in the Cumberlands, on Clover Fork of Cumberland R. and 5 mi. E of Harlan; bituminous coal.

Ageyevo (ŭgyā'ŭvŭ), town (1948 pop. over 500), W Tula oblast, Russian SFSR, 7 mi. WSW of Khanino, in Moscow Basin; lignite mining.

Agfalva (äk'fŏlvŏ), Hung. *Ágfalva*, frontier town (pop. 2,541), Sopron co., W Hungary, 3 mi. W of Sopron; rail junction on Austrian line.

Aggfors, Sweden: see MORSIL.

Aggtelek (ŏk'tĕlĕk), town (pop. 713), Borsod-Gömör co., NE Hungary, 20 mi. NNE of Ozd; entrance to Aggtelek Cave, one of BARADLA CAVES.

Aghacashel (ăkh"ŭkă'shŭl), Gaelic *Achadh Caisil*, village (district pop. 169), S central Co. Leitrim, Ireland, at foot of Slieve Ardagh, 4 mi. ENE of Drumshambo; coal mining.

Agha Jari (ägä' järē'), oil town, Sixth Prov., in Khuzistan, SW Iran, 95 mi. ENE of Abadan (linked by pipeline) and 27 mi. WNW of Behbehan; oil field opened 1944.

Aghalee (ăkhŭlē'), agr. village (district pop. 832), S Co. Antrim, Northern Ireland, on Lagan Navigation Canal and 5 mi. NE of Lurgan; mfg. of wicker goods; raises flax, potatoes, cattle.

Aghda, Iran: see AQDA.

Agheila, El (ĕl ägā'lä), village (pop. 898), W Cyrenaica, Libya, at southernmost point of Gulf of Sidra, on coastal road and 70 mi. WSW of Agedabia. Caravan track to Kufra oases. Scene of fighting in Second World War. Twice the point of farthest Br. advance during the seesaw battles of 1941, it was also the jumping-off point of Rommel's counteroffensive in Jan., 1942. Definitively captured by British in Dec., 1942, during their advance on Tripoli.

Agheressalam, Ethiopia: see HULA.

Aghia, Aghion, Aghios [Gr.,=saint], in Greek names: see HAGIA, HAGION, HAGIOS.

Aghil-Karakoram Range (ägĕl' kă'rŭkō"rŭm), N lateral range of Karakoram mtn. system, NE Kashmir; from China border at 76°E extends c.200 mi. SE to headwaters of Kara Kash R.; consists of series of ranges connected by high tablelands; average alt., c.20,350 ft. Continued NW by Muztagh Ata Range.

Aghiresu (ägērăsh'), Rum. *Aghireşu*, Hung. *Egeres* (ĕ'gĕrĕsh), village (pop. 2,034), Cluj prov., W central Rumania, in N foothills of the Apuseni Mts., on railroad and 15 mi. NW of Cluj; coal mining, mfg. of fertilizers, chemicals, bricks, flour. Large power plant. In Hungary, 1940–45.

Aghrim, Ireland: see AUGHRIM.

Aghur el Kubra (ăghōōr' ĕl kōōb'rä) or **Ajhur al-Kubra** (ăjhōōr' ăl), village (pop. 9,403), Qalyubiya prov., Lower Egypt, 20 mi. NNW of Cairo; cotton, flax, cereals, fruit.

Agigea (äjĕj'yä), village (pop. 523), Constanta prov., SE Rumania, on Black Sea, on railroad and 7 mi. S of Constanta; mfg. of bricks and tiles. Has marine research laboratories.

Agiguan, Marianas Isls.: see AGUIJAN.

Agincourt (ă'jŭnkôrt, Fr. ä-zhēkōōr'), modern Fr. *Azincourt* (äzēkōōr'), village (pop. 114), Pas-de-Calais dept., N France, 11 mi. NW of Saint-Pol. Here, on Oct. 25, 1415, Henry V won a momentous victory over the French.

Agine-Afanasyevski or **Agine-Afanasyevskiy** (ä'gēnyĕ-ŭfŭnä'syĭfskē), town (1948 pop. over 2,000), SE Lower Amur oblast, Khabarovsk Territory, Russian SFSR, 75 mi. SW of Bogorodskoye; gold mining.

Aginnum, France: see AGEN.

Aginsk-, in Russian names: see also AGA.

Aginskoye (ŭgēn'skŭyŭ). **1** Village (1939 pop. over 500), ⊙ Aga Buryat-Mongol Natl. Okrug, S Chita oblast, Russian SFSR, 75 mi. SE of Chita, in stock-raising area. **2** Village (1939 pop. over 2,000), S Krasnoyarsk Territory, Russian SFSR, 40 mi. SSE of Uyar, in hemp-growing area.

Agira (äjē'rä), anc. *Agyrium*, town (pop. 14,411), Enna prov., E central Sicily, near Salso R., 15 mi. NE of Enna; cement. Rich sulphur mines near by. One of oldest towns of interior. Has 15th-cent. church, Swabian castle with 416-ft. tower.

Aglazovo (ŭglä'zŭvŭ), village (1926 pop. 10,256), NE Tambov oblast, Russian SFSR, 15 mi. NNW of Morshansk; grain.

Aglen (ŭglĕn'), village (pop. 2,956), Pleven dist., N Bulgaria, on Vit R. and 8 mi. E of Lukovit; wheat, corn, livestock.

Agliano (älyä'nô), village (pop. 825), Asti prov., Piedmont, NW Italy, 8 mi. S of Asti, in grape-growing region; mineral springs. Gypsum quarries near by.

Agly River (äglē'), in Pyrénées-Orientales dept., S France, rises in the Corbières, flows 50 mi. generally E, past Saint-Paul, Latour-de-France, and Rivesaltes, to the Gulf of Lion at Le Barcarès.

Agmondesham, England: see AMERSHAM.

Agna (ä'nyä), village (pop. 922), Padova prov., Veneto, N Italy, 17 mi. SSE of Padua; wine making.

Agnadello (änyädĕl'lô), village (pop. 1,501), Cremona prov., Lombardy, N Italy, 9 mi. NW of Crema, in irrigated region (sericulture, livestock raising, saddle making. Here in 1509 Louis XII of France defeated the Venetians; in 1705 the duke of Vendôme defeated Prince Eugene.

Agnana Calabra (änyä'nä kä'läbrä), village (pop. 1,223), Reggio di Calabria prov., Calabria, S Italy, 5 mi. WNW of Siderno Marina; olive oil, salami, dried figs. Coal deposits and mineral springs near by.

Agnanda, Greece: see AGNANTA.

Agnano (änyä'nô), former crater lake, Campania, S Italy, in Phlegraean Fields, 5 mi. WSW of Naples. Formed in Middle Ages; drained in 1870. On S rim of crater is health resort with mineral springs and vapor baths.

Agnanta or **Agnanda** (both: ä'gnŭndŭ), village (pop. 1,616), Arta nome, S Epirus, Greece, 22 mi. NNE of Arta, at foot of the Tzoumerka; olive oil; pears, almonds.

Agnat, France: see AUZON.

Agnebilékrou, Ivory Coast: see AGNIBILÉKROU.

Agnetendorf (ägnā'tŭndôrf) or **Jagniatkow** (yägnyōt'kōōf), Pol. *Jagniątków*, village in Lower Silesia, after 1945 in Wroclaw prov., SW Poland, near Czechoslovak border, in the Riesengebirge, 8 mi. SW of Hirschberg (Jelenia Gora). Gerhart Hauptmann lived and died here.

Agnethlen, Rumania: see AGNITA.

Agnew, village (pop. c.350), Santa Clara co., W Calif., 4 mi. N of Santa Clara; state mental hosp.

Agnew Lake (ăg'nū) (21 mi. long, 1 mi. wide), SE central Ont., on Spanish R. and 30 mi. WSW of Sudbury.

Agnibilékrou (änyēbēlĕ'krōō) or **Agnebilékrou** (änyŭ–), village (pop. c.1,300), E Ivory Coast, Fr. West Africa, near Gold Coast border, 33 mi. NNE of Abengourou; cacao, coffee, kola nuts.

Agnita (ägnē'tä), Ger. *Agnethlen* (äknāt'lŭn), Hung. *Szentágota* (sĕntä'gôtŏ), village (pop. 4,834), Sibiu prov., central Rumania, in Transylvania, on railroad and 16 mi. SSE of Sighisoara; mfg. of footwear, textiles, alcohol; meat processing, flour milling. Has old church.

Agno (äg'nō), town (1939 pop. 9,533; 1948 municipality pop. 12,485), Pangasinan prov., central Luzon, Philippines, near W coast of Cape Bolinao peninsula, 29 mi. WNW of Lingayen; agr. center (copra, rice).

Agnone (änyō'nĕ), town (pop. 4,449), Campobasso prov., Abruzzi e Molise, S central Italy, 23 mi. NW of Campobasso. Rail terminus; metalworking center (bells, copper utensils, wrought-iron products, gold jewelry); macaroni mfg. Roman ruins (amphitheater, columns) near by.

Agno River (äg'nō), central Luzon, Philippines, rises in mts. in S Mountain Prov. near Mankayan, flows S into Pangasinan prov., past Alcala and Bayambang, to Lingayen Gulf; c.125 mi. long. Navigable 50 mi. by native boats. Has extensive fertile delta.

Agnousa, Greece: see OINOUSA.

Ago Bay (ä'gō), Jap. *Ago-wan*, NE inlet of Kumano Sea, in Mie prefecture, S Honshu, Japan; sheltered by small peninsula near W entrance to Ise Bay; 5 mi. E-W, 3 mi. N-S. Oyster beds (pearls). Hamajima is on NW side of entrance to bay.

Agochi, Korea: see AOJI.

Agoeng, Mount, Indonesia: see AGUNG, MOUNT.

Agogna River (ägô'nyä), N Italy, rises on Monte Mottarone, bet. lakes Maggiore and Orta, 3 mi. ESE of Omegna; flows 65 mi. S, past Novara, to Po R. 7 mi. NNW of Voghera. Crossed by Cavour Canal N of Novara.

Agogo (ägō'gō), town, Ashanti, S central Gold Coast, 37 mi. E of Kumasi; roadhead; cacao, cassava, corn. Basel mission training center.

Agon (ägō'), village (pop. 409), Manche dept., NW France, on the Channel, 6 mi. W of Coutances. Bathing resort of Courtainville-Plage (pop. 1,656), 1 mi. NW.

Agordat (ägôrdät'), administrative division, W Eritrea, bordered by Anglo-Egyptian Sudan on N and W; ⊙ Agordat. Occupies low plateau (alt. c.1,500–4,000 ft.), watered by intermittent Barka and Gash rivers. Sparsely settled steppe region devoted chiefly to nomadic grazing (cattle, goats, camels). Agr. (durum wheat, fruit, cotton, gum arabic, coffee, tobacco) around chief settlements of Agordat, Barentu, Karkabat, and Tessenei. Called Bassopiano Occidentale [Ital.,=western lowland] under Italian administration (until 1941).

Agordat, town (pop. 2,050), ⊙ Agordat div., W Eritrea, on road to Kassala (Anglo-Egyptian Sudan) and 75 mi. W of Asmara (linked by rail); alt. 2,000 ft. Trade center (livestock, cereals, cottonseed, gum arabic, coffee); button mfg., cotton ginning, flour milling, oilseed pressing. Has fort, hosp., mosque, school of arts and crafts. Italians defeated (1890, 1893) Sudan Dervishes here. Town was occupied (1941) by the British in Second World War.

Agordo (ä'gôrdô), town (pop. 1,388), Belluno prov., Veneto, N Italy, on Cordevole R. and 13 mi. NW of Belluno; rail terminus; hydroelectric plant; sawmills, shoe factory. Has school of mineralogy. Copper mines near by.

Agost (ägōst'), town (pop. 2,060), Alicante prov., E Spain, 10 mi. NW of Alicante; pottery and textile mfg.; almonds, wine, olive oil.

Agosta, Sicily: see AUGUSTA.

Agosto, 25 de (vĕntēsĭng'kō dā ägō'stō), village, Florida dept., S central Uruguay, on Santa Lucía R., on Montevideo-Florida RR and highway, and 3 mi. N of Santa Lucía. Dairy center; wheat, corn, cattle.

Agou (ä'gōō), village, S Fr. Togoland, on railroad and 50 mi. NW of Lomé; cacao plantation; palm oil and kernels, cotton. R.C. and Protestant missions.

Agoué (ägwā'), village, S Dahomey, Fr. West Africa, landing on coastal strip (Gulf of Guinea) forming enclave in Fr. Togoland, on railroad and 32 mi. ENE of Lomé; copra market. R.C. mission.

Agoulinitsa, village, Greece: see EPITALION.

Agoulinitsa, Lake of (ägōōlēnē'tsä), lagoon of Gulf of Kyparissia, W Peloponnesus, Greece, 4 mi. SSE of Pyrgos; 9 mi. long, 1 mi. wide; fisheries. Also spelled Agulinitsa; sometimes called L. of Epitalion (ĕpētä'lēōn).

Agout River (ägōō'), in Tarn dept., S France, rises in the Monts de l'Espinouze 5 mi. W of Saint-Gervais, flows 112 mi. generally W, past Castres and Lavaur, to the Tarn near Saint-Sulpice. Receives Dadou R. (right).

Agra (ä'grŭ, ŭg'rŭ), district (□1,861; pop. 1,289,774), W Uttar Pradesh, India; ⊙ Agra. In Ganges-Jumna Doab; irrigated by Agra Canal; agr. (pearl millet, gram, wheat, barley, jowar, oilseeds, cotton, corn). Main centers: Agra, Firozabad, Fatehpur Sikri, Achhnera, Itimadpur. Name Agra also designates area of Uttar Pradesh (□ 82,176; pop. 40,906,147) covering roughly all but E central portion (OUDH) of state. Mogul empire's **Agra Province,** founded by Akbar in 16th cent., embraced W dists. of present Uttar Pradesh and parts of adjacent states (W and S). During late-18th and early-19th cent., most of this area, with adjacent Br. acquisitions (E), became part of Bengal presidency; separated (1833) from Bengal to form presidency of Agra and named North-Western Provinces in 1835; joined (1877) with Oudh; union named United Provinces of Agra and Oudh in 1902.

Agra, city (pop., including S cantonment area, 284,149), ⊙ Agra dist., W Uttar Pradesh, India, on right bank of the Jumna and 120 mi. SSE of Delhi. Rail and road junction; trade (grain, oilseeds, cotton) and industrial center, producing carpets, chemicals, acids, leather goods, glass, hosiery, brassware, brushes, and noted marble and alabaster articles; cotton, flour, and oilseed mills. Iron and steel rolling mills in NE area, called Belanganj. Agra Col. (opened 1823; now part of Agra Univ.), medical school (founded 1854). Agra is famous for its magnificent mausoleums and mosques. The beautiful Taj Mahal (built 1630–48), probably the most noted mausoleum in the world, lies near the Jumna just E of the cantonment; it is of pure white marble, built on a great marble terrace, with a large central dome (58 ft. in diameter), and 4 smaller domes at each corner, flanked by 4 tall minarets. Built by Shah Jehan as a memorial to his favorite wife Arjmand Banu (Mumtaz-i-Mahal), the Taj contains cenotaphs of the emperor and his wife; it is approached through an ornate red sandstone gateway which leads into a lovely garden containing a watercourse between dual rows of cypresses. On the Jumna is the fort (built 1566 by Akbar) which contains the noted Moti Masjid or Pearl Mosque (142 ft. long, 56 ft. high; completed 1654) of Shah Jehan, the Diwan-i-Khas (private audience hall) of Aurangzeb, the Shish Mahal or Mirror Palace, and the red sandstone Jehangiri Mahal. The Jami Masjid, in Mogul-Pathan style, lies W of the fort. A noted Mogul example of marble filigree work is the tomb of Itimad-ud-daula (Jehangir's Wazir) just across the Jumna, near its left bank. Anc. Agra, on left bank, was ⊙ (1501–26) under Lodi kings and under Babar. Present city, on right bank of river, was founded 1566 as ⊙ by Akbar; ⊙ moved to Fatehpur Sikri in 1569, thence to Lahore in 1584, and back to Agra in 1601. After removal of ⊙ to Delhi by Aurangzeb in 1659, Agra declined; captured successively by Jats and Mahrattas; taken (1803) by English during Second Mahratta War. Was ⊙ North-Western Provs., 1835–59. Called Akbarabad by Shah Jehan.

Agra (ă'grŭ). **1** City (pop. 354), Phillips co., N Kansas, 11 mi. E of Phillipsburg, in corn belt; livestock. **2** Town (pop. 302), Lincoln co., central Okla., 8 mi. SW of Cushing, in agr. area.

Agra and Oudh, United Provinces of, India: see UTTAR PRADESH.

Agra Canal, irrigation system in SE Punjab and W Uttar Pradesh, India; from headworks on Jumna R., 5 mi. SE of New Delhi, it parallels river's right bank for 145 mi. S and SE to Banganga R. (tributary of the Jumna) 23 mi. SE of Agra. Divides into various branches in Muttra and Agra dists. in rich agr. area. Opened 1874.

Agraciada (ägräsyä'dä), village (pop. 250), Soriano dept., SW Uruguay, 13 mi. N of Carmelo (connected by highway); center of agr. area (wheat, corn, oats, sheep, cattle).

Agrado (ägrä'dō), town (pop. 2,925), Huila dept., S central Colombia, in upper Magdalena valley, 10 mi. WNW of Garzón; agr. center (rice, cacao, coffee, silk, stock); alum mines.

Agrakhan Peninsula (ŭgrŭkhän'), narrow tongue of land in Caspian Sea, in Dagestan Autonomous SSR, Russian SFSR, N of Makhachkala. Forms E side of Agrakhan Gulf (35 mi. long, up to 7 mi. wide). Lopatin (at N tip) and several smaller settlements are fishing centers.

Agram, Yugoslavia: see ZAGREB, city.

Agramonte (ägrämōn'tā). **1** Town (pop. 1,847), Camagüey prov., E Cuba, sugar central just S of Florida and 23 mi. WNW of Camagüey. **2** Town (pop. 2,607), Matanzas prov., W Cuba, on railroad and 38 mi. SE of Matanzas, in sugar-growing region. The Santa Rita sugar mill is just SSW.

Agramunt (ägrämōōnt'), town (pop. 2,256), Lérida prov., NE Spain, 12 mi. NW of Cervera; road center on Urgel Canal; agr. trade (cereals, sugar beets, olive oil, wine, hemp); stock raising, lumbering.

Agrate Brianza (ägrä'tĕ brēän'tsä), village (pop. 3,020), Milano prov., Lombardy, 11 mi. NE of Milan; silk; woodworking.

Ágreda (ä'grä-dhä), town (pop. 2,746), Soria prov., N central Spain, in Old Castile, on railroad and 27 mi. ENE of Soria. Resort and agr. center on fertile, high plain (cereals, grapes, nuts, hemp, fruit, livestock); apiculture; flour milling, mfg. of woolen goods. Has convent.

Agrelios, Cape, Greece: see MALEA, CAPE.

Agrelo (ägrā'lō), town (pop. estimate 500), N Mendoza prov., Argentina, on railroad and 18 mi. S of Mendoza; winegrowing.

Agrestina (ägrĭstē'nů), city (pop. 2,195), E Pernambuco, NE Brazil, 12 mi. S of Caruaru; cotton, coffee, cereals. Until 1944, called Bebedouro.

Agri (ärŭ'), Turk. *Ağrı*, prov. (□ 4,888; 1950 pop. 155,545), E Turkey; ⊙ Karakose. Bordered N by Aras Mts., E by Iran. Drained by Murat R.; mountainous and unproductive. Pop. largely Kurd. Formerly Bayazit.

Agri Dagi, Turkey: see ARARAT, MOUNT.

Agrigento (ägrējĕn'tô), province (□ 1,172; pop. 418,265), S and SW Sicily; ⊙ Agrigento. Hilly terrain, rising to 5,180 ft. in Monte Cammarata; drained by Platani and Salso rivers. Agr. (wheat, grapes, olives, almonds); livestock (sheep, goats) in W. Mining (sulphur, rock salt) in E. Fisheries (tunny, coral, sponge). Sulphur industry concentrated at Agrigento, Porto Empedocle, and Licata. Anc. ruins at Agrigento and Eraclea. Called Girgenti until 1927.

Agrigento, anc. *Agrigentum*, town (pop. 27,785), ⊙ Agrigento prov., S Sicily, 30 mi. SW of Caltanissetta; 37°18'N 13°35'E. Rail junction; sulphur market; mfg. (cement, furniture, pharmaceuticals, soap). Bishopric, with Christian catacombs (2d cent. B.C.), 14th- and 15th-cent. churches (including cathedral), seminary. Has palace, public library (1765), archaeological mus. (damaged in Second World War). Near by are neolithic necropolises, ruins of 7 Greek temples of 6th to 5th cent. B.C. (including that of Zeus; 331 ft. long; 2d largest temple of antiquity), and Roman ruins (200–100 B.C.). Founded by Greek colonists from Gela (40 mi. SW) 580–579 B.C.; occupied by Romans 210 B.C.; taken from Greeks in A.D. 828 by Saracens. Called Girgenti until 1927. Porto Empedocle, 3 mi. SW, is its port.

Agrihan (ägrēhän'), uninhabited volcanic island (□ c.18), N Marianas Isls., W Pacific, 230 mi. N of Saipan; 18°46'N 145°40'E; c.6 mi. long, 3.5 mi. wide; contains highest peak (3,166 ft.) of group. Fertile plateaus; phosphate deposits. Formerly Grigan.

Agri Hills, Denmark: see MOLS.

Agrinion (ägrē'nēôn), Lat. *Agrinium* (ŭgrĭ'nēŭm), city (1951 pop. 21,752), Acarnania nome, W central Greece, on E edge of fertile agr. lowland, on railroad and 17 mi. N of Missolonghi; tobacco-processing center; cigarette mfg; trade in tobacco, olive oil, wheat, wine, lumber. Airport. Anc. Agrinium was located on Achelous R., 5 mi. NW of modern town, which was 1st mentioned in 14th cent. (as Vrachori or Vrakhori) and became an important center under the Turks.

Agrinion, Lake, Greece: see TRICHONIS, LAKE.

Agrinium, Greece: see AGRINION.

Agrio, Río (rē'ō ä'grēō), river in central Neuquén natl. territory, Argentina, rises in Andean hills near El Huecú, flows c.100 mi. S and E, past El Huecú and Las Lajas, to Neuquén R. 40 mi. NE of Zapala.

Agri River (ä'grē), anc. *Aciris*, in Basilicata, S Italy, rises in the Apennines 12 mi. S of Potenza, flows S, past Marsico Nuovo, and E to Gulf of Taranto 16 mi. SE of Pisticci; 68 mi. long. Furnishes water (aqueduct completed 1937) to many towns in Matera prov.

Agropoli (ägrô'pôlē), town (pop. 3,548), Salerno prov., Campania, S Italy, port on Gulf of Salerno, 26 mi. SE of Salerno; bathing resort.

Agros (ägrôs'), village (pop. 1,500), Limassol dist., central Cyprus, summer resort in Olympus Mts., 26 mi. SW of Nicosia; grapes, almonds, carobs; goats.

Agros, Turkey: see ATABEY.

Agryz (ŭgrĭs'), city (1939 pop. estimate 15,400), NE Tatar Autonomous SSR, Russian SFSR, near Izh R., 22 mi. SSW of Izhevsk; rail junction; mfg. (machines, building materials), food processing; grain and egg trade. Became city in 1938.

Agto (äkh'tō), fishing settlement (pop. 108), Egedesminde dist., W Greenland, on small isl. in Davis Strait, 55 mi. SSW of Egedesminde; 67°56'N 53°37'W. Radio station.

Agua (ä'gwä), inactive volcano (12,310 ft.), in S central Guatemala, on Guatemala-Sacatepéquez dept. border, 8 mi. S of Antigua. Frequently visited for its views; usually ascended from Santa María, at NE foot. In 1541, eruption and accompanying flood destroyed CIUDAD VIEJA.

Agua, Cabo de (kä'bō dā ä'gwä), Fr. *Cap de l'Eau*, headland of E Sp. Morocco, on the Mediterranean just W of mouth of Muluya R. (Fr. Morocco border), 30 mi. SE of Melilla; 35°9'N 2°26'W. Chafarinas Isls. are just offshore, 2 mi. N.

Agua Amarga (ä'gwä ämär'gä), village (pop. 144), Almería prov., S Spain, on the Mediterranean, and 22 mi. ENE of Almería; terminus of mining railroad from Lucainena de las Torres; shipping port for iron, lead-silver ore, esparto, fruit.

Agua Blanca (ä'gwä bläng'kä), town (1950 pop. 1,281), Jutiapa dept., SE Guatemala, in highlands, 22 mi. NE of Jutiapa; corn, beans, livestock.

Agua Blanca, town (pop. 538), Hidalgo, central Mexico, 30 mi. NE of Pachuca; corn, beans, sugar, livestock.

Agua Blanca, town (pop. 681), San Martín dept., N central Peru, on affluent of Huallaga R. and 50 mi. SSE of Moyobamba; sugar cane, rice, coca.

Agua Blanca, town (pop. 1,011), Portuguesa state, W Venezuela, landing on affluent of Cojedes R. and 9 mi. NE of Acarigua; cotton, sugar cane, corn, cattle.

Água Branca (ä'gwů brāng'ků), city (pop. 1,053), W Alagoas, NE Brazil, 90 mi. W of Palmeira dos Índios; cotton, coffee, stock. Limestone, marble deposits. Paulo Afonso Falls are 20 mi. SW.

Agua Caliente (ä'gwä kälyĕn'tā), village, Cartago prov., central Costa Rica, 2 mi. SSE of Cartago; coffee, sugar cane, fodder crops. Limestone quarries; hot springs. Charcoal burning near by.

Agua Caliente. 1 Resort, Lower California, Mexico: see TIJUANA. **2** Town, Sinaloa, Mexico, near El Fuerte: see AGUA CALIENTE DE VACA.

Aguacaliente, town, Sinaloa, Mexico, near Mazatlán: see AGUACALIENTE DE GÁRATE.

Agua Caliente, village, Huánuco dept., central Peru, on Pachitea R., on highway, and 27 mi. SSW of Pucallpa; 8°48'S 74°41'W; center of Ganso Azul oil fields; refinery.

Agua Caliente, Venezuela: see UREÑA.

Aguacaliente de Gárate (ä"gwäkälyĕn'tā dā gä'rätā), town (pop. 1,417), Sinaloa, NW Mexico, in coastal lowlands, 23 mi. ESE of Mazatlán; chick-peas, corn, tobacco, fruit, vegetables. Sometimes Aguacaliente.

Agua Caliente de Vaca (dā vä'kä) or **Agua Caliente,** town (pop. 1,152), Sinaloa, NW Mexico, on the Río del Fuerte and 30 mi. NE of El Fuerte; corn, chick-peas, sugar.

Aguacatán (ägwäkätän'), town (1950 pop. 793), Huehuetenango dept., W central Guatemala, on S slope of Cuchumatanes Mts., 11 mi. E of Huehuetenango; alt. 5,128 ft. Market center; rice, avocados; textile milling.

Aguacate (ägwäkä'tā), town (pop. 3,324), Havana prov., W Cuba, on railroad and 36 mi. ESE of Havana, in agr. region (sugar cane, tobacco); stone quarrying. The sugar central Rosario is just W.

Aguacate Mountains, section of continental divide in W central Costa Rica, in area of San Ramón; rises to over 4,000 ft. Gold fields at S foot.

Aguachica (ägwächē'kä), town (pop. 2,457), Magdalena dept., N Colombia, in Magdalena basin, 13 mi. WNW of Ocaña; coffee.

Aguada (ägwä'dä), town (pop. 196), Santander dept., N central Colombia, 10 mi. S of Contratación; coffee, sugar cane, cotton, livestock.

Aguada, town (pop. 3,178), NW Puerto Rico, near the coast, on railroad and 12 mi. N of Mayagüez; sugar-milling center; mfg. of cigars. At site of pre-Columbian village (where Columbus allegedly landed), considered to be founded 1506. Manganese deposits near by. The Coloso sugar mill is 1½ mi. E.

Aguada, La (lä), Andean volcano (c.19,000 ft.) in N Catamarca prov., Argentina, 7 mi. S of Antofalla volcano.

Aguada de Pasajeros (dā päsähä'rōs), town (pop. 3,985), Las Villas prov., central Cuba, on edge of the Ciénaga de Zapata, on railroad and 30 mi. NW of Cienfuegos. Produces sugar (several mills in vicinity), timber, charcoal, livestock. Lime pits.

Aguada Grande (grän'dā), town (pop. 1,184), Lara state, NW Venezuela, in Segovia Highlands, 38 mi. NNW of Barquisimeto; sugar cane, fruit, stock.

Aguadas (ägwä'däs), town (pop. 7,631), Caldas dept., W central Colombia, in Cordillera Central, 37 mi. N. of Manizales; alt. 7,264 ft. Coffeegrowing center; sugar cane, cereals, potatoes, yucca, silk, fruit; mfg. of Panama hats. Silver and gold mines near by.

Agua de Dios (ä'gwä dā dē'ōs), town (pop. 7,213), Cundinamarca dept., central Colombia, in W foothills of Cordillera Oriental, 12 mi. ENE of Girardot; health resort with mineral springs. Leprosarium. Inc. 1873 as site of govt. hosp.

Aguadilla (ägwädē'yä), town (pop. 18,276), NW Puerto Rico, port on Mona Passage, 70 mi. W of San Juan (linked by railroad and highway); 18°26'N 67°8'W. Processing and trading center for rich agr. region (sugar cane, coffee, fruit, tobacco, cotton); mfg. of straw hats and cigars; sugar milling; fishing. Port of entry. Its small open bay used by vessels drawing 30 ft. At a near-by point, Columbus is supposed to have taken water supplies in 1493. Town was founded 1775; now a seat of a senatorial dist. The Borinquen (bōrĭng-kĕn') airfield is 5 mi. N.

Aguadores (ägwädō'rĕs), beach resort, Oriente prov., E Cuba, 3½ mi. S of Santiago de Cuba.

Agua Dulce (ä'gwä dōōl'sā), town (pop. estimate 500), E Tucumán prov., Argentina, on railroad and 18 mi. SE of Tucumán, in agr. area (corn, alfalfa, sugar cane, livestock).

Aguadulce, town (pop. 2,829), Coclé prov., central Panama, in Pacific lowland on Inter-American Highway and 21 mi. SW of Penonomé. Commercial center; agr. (sugar cane, corn, rice, beans), stock raising, salt production. Developed rapidly since 1920. Its port Puerto Aguadulce (pop. 30), 2 mi. E, was active until construction of Inter-American Highway.

Aguadulce (ägwä-dhōōl'thā), town (pop. 3,372), Seville prov., SW Spain, 6 mi. E of Osuna; processes olives, cereals. Its rail station is 2 mi. W.

Agua Dulce (ä'wů dōōl'sē), village (pop. 660), Nueces co., S Texas, 32 mi. W of Corpus Christi; rail point in agr., oil-producing area.

Agua Fría (ä'gwä frē'ä), village (pop. 430), El Paraíso dept., S Honduras, in Sierra del Chile, 7 mi. NNW of Danli; connected by road with Tegucigalpa; gold-mining center.

Agua Fria River (ä'wů frē'ů), W Ariz., intermittent stream rising E of Prescott; flows c.120 mi. generally S to join Gila R. 16 mi. W of Phoenix. Lake Pleasant Dam (256 ft. high, 2,210 ft. long; built 1927) forms L. Pleasant, 45 mi. SSE of Prescott, used for irrigation.

Aguaí (ägwäē'), city (pop. 2,473), E São Paulo, Brazil, 60 mi. N of Campinas; rail junction (spur to Águas da Prata and Poços de Caldas); coffee, cotton, potatoes, corn. Until 1944, called Cascavel.

Agua Larga (ä'gwä lär'gä), town (pop. 662), Falcón state, NW Venezuela, in N outliers of Andean spur, 13 mi. WNW of Churuguara; coffee, cacao, sugar cane.

Agualeguas (äg"wälā'gwäs), town (pop. 2,471), Nuevo León, N Mexico, 65 mi. NE of Monterrey; cotton, corn, sugar, cactus fibers; silver, lead, and zinc deposits.

Aguán or **Santa Rosa de Aguán** (sän'tä rō'sä dā ägwän'), town (pop. 1,257), Colón dept., N Honduras, on Caribbean Sea, at mouth of Aguán R., 17 mi. E of Trujillo; coconuts, corn, livestock. Sometimes called Barra de Aguán.

Aguanaval River (ägwänäväl'), N central Mexico, rises in Sierra Madre Occidental 35 mi. NW of Zacatecas, flows c. 250 mi. N, through Zacatecas, Durango, and Coahuila, past Río Grande, Nieves, and San Juan de Guadalupe, and along Durango–Coahuila border, to the Laguna de Viesca 9 mi. NW of Viesca. Its lower course is used, together with Nazas R., to irrigate fertile Laguna Dist. Its upper course is called Río Grande in Zacatecas.

Agua Negra Pass (ä'gwä nā'grä) (c.15,650 ft.), in the Andes, on Argentina-Chile border, on road bet. Rodeo (Argentina) and Coquimbo (Chile); 30°12'S 69°52'W.

Aguán River (ägwän'), N Honduras, rises in Sierra de Sulaco near Yorito, flows c.150 mi. ENE, through banana zone, past Sabá and Tocoa, to Caribbean Sea at Aguán. Middle and lower valley served by banana railroad from Trujillo. Main tributary, Yaguale R. (right).

Aguapeí River (ägwůpĭē'), W São Paulo, Brazil, rises W of Pirajuí as the Rio Feio, flows c.200 mi. WNW in a deep valley to the Paraná at 21°5'S 51°45'W. Paralleled by Tietê (N) and Peixe (S) rivers, and separated from them by a continuous narrow divide. Interrupted by rapids. Navigable in lower course. Formerly spelled Aguapehy.

Aguapey River (ägwäpā'), E Corrientes prov., Argentina, rises in low hill country 30 mi. S of Posadas, flows c.125 mi. S, through swampy region, to Uruguay R. at Alvear, opposite Itaqui, Brazil.

Água Preta (ä'gwů prā'tů), city (pop. 2,407), E Pernambuco, NE Brazil, 5 mi. ESE of Palmares; sugar, coconuts, cereals.

Agua Prieta (ä'gwä prēā'tä), city (pop. 4,106), Sonora, NW Mexico, near U.S. border, 3 mi. S of Douglas, Ariz., on railroad; alt. 3,900 ft.; livestock, corn.

Aguaragüe, Serranía de (sĕrănē'ä dä ägwärä'gwä), range in S Bolivia; extends 110 mi. N from Argentina border at Yacuiba to Cuevo; rises to c.5,000 ft. Crossed by Pilcomayo R. (center). One of main petroleum regions of Bolivia, with oil fields of Sanandita and Ñancorainza.

Aguaray (ägwärī'), town (pop. estimate 700), NE Salta prov., Argentina, on railroad and 70 mi. NNE of Orán; lumbering and agr. center (corn, sugar cane).

Aguarico River (ägwärē'kō), Napo-Pastaza prov., NE Ecuador, rises SE of Tulcán in the Andes on Colombia line, flows c.230 mi. ESE, through tropical forests, to the Napo R. at Pantoja; navigable. Lower course forms (since 1942) Peru-Ecuador line.

Aguarón (ägwärōn'), town (pop. 1,695), Saragossa prov., NE Spain, 30 mi. SW of Saragossa, in wine-growing dist.; olive-oil processing, liqueur mfg.; sheep raising, lumbering. Antimony mine near by.

Aguasabon River (ä"gwŭsä'bŭn), NW Ont., rises 20 mi. N of Schreiber, flows 45 mi. in a wide arc SE and S to L. Superior 7 mi. ESE of Schreiber. Drainage of Long L. has been diverted to this river by channel and control dam, thus diverting waters of Long L. to L. Superior.

Aguas Amargas, Guatemala: see Zunil, town.

Aguasay (ägwäsī'), town (pop. 1,022), Monagas state, NE Venezuela, 45 mi. SW of Maturín; cattle raising.

Águas Belas (ä'gwŭs bĕ'lŭs), city (pop. 3,572), central Pernambuco, NE Brazil, 50 mi. WSW of Garanhuns; livestock. Formerly spelled Águas Bellas.

Aguas Blancas, Cerro (sĕ'rō ä'gwäs bläng'käs), Andean volcano (18,960 ft.) on Argentina-Chile border, 33 mi. NNW of the Cerro Colorados; 25°43'S.

Aguas Buenas (ä'gwäs bwā'näs), town (pop. 2,671), E central Puerto Rico, in mts. 14 mi. S of San Juan, in tobacco- and fruitgrowing region. Great caves are near by.

Aguas Calientes, river, Bolivia: see San Rafael River.

Aguascalientes (ägwäskälyĕn'tĕs), state (□ 2,499; 1940 pop. 161,693; 1950 pop. 188,104), N central Mexico; ⊙ Aguascalientes. On the central plateau (alt. c.6,000 ft.), with broken ranges of the Sierra Madre Occidental W and SW. It is one of the smallest states in Mexico, bounded E, N, and W by Zacatecas, S by Jalisco. Well irrigated by San Pedro (or Aguascalientes) R. Its climate varies with alt.: mild to subtropical in SW, colder in more arid N. Its mineral resources are little exploited, but there are silver, lead, copper, and gold mines in Asientos and Tepezalá (N). Many sulphuric thermal springs, notably around capital. Predominantly an agr. region important for corn and chick-pea crops and for high-quality livestock (cattle, mules, sheep, horses). Produces wheat, barley, sweet potatoes, vegetables; sugar cane, tobacco, wine, and fruit (peaches, apricots, apples, pears, melons) in S and SW. Large expanses of forests.

Aguascalientes, city (pop. 82,234), ⊙ Aguascalientes, N central Mexico, on interior plateau near San Pedro or Aguascalientes R., on railroad and 110 mi. NE of Guadalajara, 265 mi. NW of Mexico city; 21°53'N 102°18'W; alt. 6,181 ft. Health resort, processing, trading, and agr. center (cereals, vegetables, wine, fruit, livestock). Maintains largest Mexican railroad shops (rail system developed in late 19th cent.); foundries, potteries, tanneries, flour and textile mills, tobacco factories, wineries, fruit canneries, distilleries, brewery; noted for mfg. of drawn linen and serapes. Set among volcanic hills; city has many thermal springs in its outskirts. Has fine colonial architecture, plazas, parks, govt. and municipal palace, church of San Antonio. Annual pilgrimages and fiestas. Beneath the city are immense pre-Colombian catacombs, whose origin still puzzles archaeologists. Aguascalientes was founded 1575 as silver-mining town.

Aguas Calientes, Sierra de (syĕ'rä dä), subandean mountain range on Catamarca-Salta prov. border, NW Argentina, extends c.70 mi. N–S; Cerro Gordo, WSW of Molinos, rises to over 17,500 ft.

Aguascalientes River, Mexico: see San Pedro River.

Águas da Prata (ä'gwŭs dä prä'tŭ) [Port.,=silver waters], city (pop. 1,064), E São Paulo, Brazil, on railroad and 14 mi. SW of Poços de Caldas (Minas Gerais), in bauxite- and zirconium-mining region; alt. 2,680 ft. Well-known spa, with mineral springs and modern hotels.

Aguas Virtuosas, Brazil: see Lambari.

Aguathuna (ä"gwŭthōō'nŭ), village, SW N.F., on Port au Port isthmus, 9 mi. W of Stephenville; limestone-quarrying center. Stone is shipped to steel plants of Sydney, N.S.

Aguaviva (ägwävē'vä), town (pop. 1,607), Teruel prov., E Spain, 16 mi. S of Alcañiz; olive-oil processing; wine, cereals, fruit.

Aguaytía River (ägwītē'ä), Loreto dept., E Peru, rises near Huánuco dept. border, flows c.130 mi. NE to Ucayali R. 30 mi. NNW of Pucallpa. One of its headstreams surges through the Boquerón Abad.

Aguda (ägōō'dŭ), S suburb (pop. 1,007) of Oporto, Pôrto dist., N Portugal; tileworks.

Agudo (ägōō'dhō), town (pop. 4,306), Ciudad Real prov., S central Spain, 50 mi. W of Ciudad Real; stock-raising, lumbering, agr. center (olives, cereals, cork); mfg. of wax, candles, bottle corks, cheese.

Agudos (ägōō'dōōs), city (pop. 3,644), central São Paulo, Brazil, 12 mi. SSE of Bauru; rail junction; cotton, coffee; cotton ginning.

Águeda (ä'gĭdŭ), town (pop. 2,334), Aveiro dist., N central Portugal, 12 mi. ESE of Aveiro; mfg. (ink, pottery); winegrowing.

Agueda River (ägā'dhä), Salamanca prov., W Spain, rises on N slopes of the Sierra de Gata near El Payo, flows 80 mi. NNW, past Ciudad Rodrigo, to the Duero (Douro) at Port. border near La Fregeneda. For last 15 mi. of its course, it forms Sp.-Port. boundary, flowing in deep gorge. Dam and irrigation reservoir above Ciudad Rodrigo.

Aguelmous, Fr. Morocco: see Khénifra.

Agüera, La (ägwā'rä), or **Güera** (gwā'rä), village (pop. 23), southernmost Río de Oro, Sp. West Africa, on W shore of Cap Blanc Peninsula, 6 mi. SSW of Port-Étienne (Fr. West Africa); 20°50'N 17°6'W. Trawl fisheries. Permanently occupied by Spain since 1920. Also spelled La Aguera or Guera.

Aguerbat, Syria: see 'Aqiribat.

Aguiar da Beira (ägyär' dŭ bā'rŭ), town (pop. 719), Guarda dist., N central Portugal, 24 mi. NE of Viseu; metalworks; resin, dairy products. Has many medieval buildings.

Aguijan, Aguigan, or **Aguiguan** (all: ägēhän'), uninhabited volcanic island (□ 3), Saipan dist., S Marianas Isls., W Pacific, 80 mi. NNE of Guam; 3 mi. long, 2 mi. wide.

Aguijita (ägēhē'tä), coal-mining settlement (pop. 5,069), Coahuila, N Mexico, 5 mi. NW of Sabinas.

Aguikchuk (ŭgōō'ĭkchŭk), Eskimo village, SW Alaska, on narrow channel separating Nelson Isl. from mainland, 90 mi. WSW of Bethel; trapping, fishing.

Aguilafuente (ä"gēläfwĕn'tā), town (pop. 1,549), Segovia prov., central Spain, 19 mi. N of Segovia; cereals, chick-peas, grapes, livestock; flour milling, lumbering, naval-stores mfg.

Aguilán, Pico (pē'kō ägēlän'), mountain (8,661 ft.), N Venezuela, in coastal range, 6 mi. ENE of Caracas.

Aguilar (ägēlär'), village (pop. estimate 1,000), N central Jujuy prov., Argentina, in Sierra de Aguilar, 80 mi. NNW of Jujuy; alt. c.16,000 ft.; lead-zinc-silver mining center.

Aguilar (ägēlär'), town (1939 pop. 8,178; 1948 municipality pop. 10,587), Pangasinan prov., central Luzon, Philippines, 10 mi. S of Lingayen; trade center for agr. area (rice, corn, copra). Mineral pigments are mined.

Aguilar or **Aguilar de la Frontera** (ägēlär' dā lä frōntā'rä), city (pop. 15,144), Córdoba prov., S Spain, in Andalusia, 27 mi. SSE of Córdoba. Wine-shipping center. Olive-oil and meat processing, brandy distilling, wood turning, flour milling; mfg. of soap, knitwear, furniture. Cereals, lumber. Limestone and gypsum quarries. Has ruined Moorish castle.

Aguilar (ă'gwĭlär"), city (pop. 1,038), Las Animas co., SE Colo., on Apishapa R., just E of Sangre de Cristo Mts., and 18 mi. NNW of Trinidad, in agr. and grazing region; alt. 6,700 ft. Inc. 1894.

Aguilar, Sierra de (syĕ'rä dā), subandean mountain range, N central Jujuy prov., Argentina, surrounding Aguilar; extends 25 mi. N–S; rises to c. 16,000 ft. Rich in lead, zinc, silver.

Aguilar de Campóo (ägēlär' dā kämpō'), town (pop. 2,509), Palencia prov., N central Spain, on Pisuerga R. and 53 mi. SW of Santander; flour milling, plaster mfg.; cereals, potatoes, livestock. Marble quarries. Has one Romanesque and one Gothic church and ruins of anc. walls. Near by is Premonstratensian convent (11th cent.; later rebuilt) with fine cloisters.

Aguilar de la Frontera, Spain: see Aguilar.

Aguilar del Río Alhama (dĕl rē'ō älä'mä), town (pop. 1,569), Logroño prov., N Spain, 20 mi. WSW of Tudela; cotton mill; fruit, vegetables, lumber, livestock. Iron deposits near by.

Aguilares (ägēlä'rĕs), town (pop. estimate 2,500), ⊙ Río Chico dept. (□ c.750; 1947 pop. 52,900), SW Tucumán prov., Argentina, on railroad and 45 mi. SW of Tucumán near the Río Chico; sugar-growing and stock-raising center; tanning, sugar refining, rice milling.

Águilas (ä'gēläs), town (pop. 11,636), Murcia prov., SE Spain, port on the Mediterranean, and 35 mi. WSW of Cartagena; ships iron and lead from near-by mines. Fishing, fish processing, boat building; iron founding; mfg. of esparto rope, tiles, furniture. Capers, almonds, figs, and other fruit in area. Gypsum quarries. Has ruined castle.

Aguilera, La (lä ägēlā'rä), town (pop. 979), Burgos prov., N Spain, 6 mi. NW of Aranda de Duero; grapes, fruit, hemp, stock. Has noted Franciscan hermitage.

Aguililla (ägēlē'yä), officially Aguililla de Iturbide, town (pop. 2,311) Michoacán, W Mexico, in Sierra Madre del Sur, 70 mi. SW of Uruapan; cereals, sugar, fruit; iron mining.

Agüimes (ägwē'mĕs), town (pop. 2,827), Grand Canary, Canary Isls., 14 mi. S of Las Palmas; cereals, tomatoes, sweet potatoes, olives, almonds, fruit, sugar cane, livestock. Flour mills. Saltworks. Summer resort, with near-by beach.

Aguirre, Argentina: see Pinto.

Aguirre, Chile: see Lo Aguirre.

Aguirre or **Central Aguirre** (ägē'rā), village (pop. 2,781), S Puerto Rico, on the coast, facing Puerto Jobos, 7 mi. WSW of Guayama; sugar milling.

Aguirre Bay (ägē'rā), inlet of the Atlantic in SE Tierra del Fuego natl. territory, Argentina, 25 mi. SW of Cape Buen Suceso; extends c.10 mi. W–E (5 mi. wide); 54°55'S 65°45'W.

Agusan (ägē'sän), town (1939 pop. 5,347) in Himamaylan municipality, Negros Occidental prov., W Negros isl., Philippines, on Panay Gulf, just SSE of Binalbagan; agr. center (rice, sugar cane).

Agüita Pass (ägwē'tä) (16,700 ft.), in the Andes on Argentina-Chile border, at NW foot of the Cerro de los Patos; 27°17'S 68°53'W. On road bet. Fiambalá (Argentina) and Copiapó (Chile).

Aguja, Cabo de la (kä'bō dā lä ägōō'hä), headland on Caribbean coast of Magdalena dept., N Colombia, 5 mi. NNE of Santa Marta; 11°19'N 74°13'W.

Aguja Point (ägōō'hä), Pacific cape at S end of Sechura Bay, Piura dept., NW Peru, at N foot of Cerro Illesca; 5°55'S 81°9'W.

Agujas, Point, Dominican Republic: see Falso, Cabo.

Agula (ä'gōōlä), village (pop. 958), Tigre prov., N Ethiopia, on road and 15 mi. NE of Makale; cereals, livestock.

Agulhas, Cape (ŭgŭ'lŭs) [Port.,=needles], SW Cape Prov., U. of So. Afr., S extremity of Africa, on dividing line bet. the Atlantic and Indian oceans, 110 mi. SE of Cape Town; 34°52'S 19°59'E. Rocky projection with jagged reefs; submerged rocks which extend into sea are danger to navigation. Lighthouse, signal station. Near by is Bontebok Natl. Park (□ 2.8).

Agulhas Current: see Mozambique Current.

Agulhas Negras (ägōō'lyŭs nā'grŭs), town (pop. 3,270), W Rio de Janeiro state, Brazil on left bank of Paraíba R., opposite Resende (bridge), on railroad and 80 mi. WNW of Rio; livestock, grain, coffee. Until 1943, called Campos Elísios.

Agulhas Negras, peak, Brazil: see Itatiaia.

Agulinitsa, village, Greece: see Epitalion.

Agulinitsa, Lake of, Greece: see Agoulinitsa, Lake of.

Agullent (ägōōlyĕnt'), town (pop. 1,161), Valencia prov., E Spain, 12 mi. SSW of Játiva; cheese processing, candle mfg.; wine, olive oil, cereals.

Agulo (ägōō'lō), village (pop. 1,202), Gomera, Canary Isls., 9 mi. NW of San Sebastián; bananas, tomatoes, grapes, corn, potatoes.

Agumbe (ŭgōōm'bē), village, Shimoga dist., NW Mysore, India, on pass in Western Ghats, 45 mi. SW of Shimoga; annual rainfall as high as 483 in. has been recorded here. Also spelled Agumbi.

Agung, Mount, or **Mount Agoeng** (both: ä'gōōng), highest volcanic peak (10,308 ft.) of Bali, Indonesia, 30 mi. ESE of Singaraja. On NW slope is a lake, 5 mi. long. Also called Peak of Bali.

Agusan (ägōō'sän), province (□ 4,120; 1948 pop. 126,448), N Mindanao, Philippines, on Mindanao Sea; ⊙ Butuan. Drained by Agusan R. Its swampy middle valley is flanked by mts. Coconut growing. Gold mining.

Agusan River, largest river (240 mi. long) of Mindanao, rises NE of Davao Gulf in SE part of isl., flows N in a fertile valley parallel to E coast, past Butuan, to Butuan Bay of Mindanao Sea on N coast. Navigable 20 mi. for ships of 6-ft. draught, 160 mi. for small craft.

Agutaya Island (ägōōtä'yä) (1939 pop. 2,539), one of the Cuyo Isls., Palawan prov., Philippines, in Sulu Sea, 16 mi. NNW of Cuyo Isl., NE of Palawan; 11°9'N 120°57' E. Rice, coconuts. Villafria is chief town.

Agvali (ŭgvä'lyē), village (1939 pop. over 500), W Dagestan Autonomous SSR, Russian SFSR, on Andi Koisu (river) and 10 mi. SW of Botlikh; grain, sheep. Pop. largely Andi.

Agyrium, Sicily: see Agira.

Ahaggar Mountains (ŭhä'gŭr) or **Hoggar Mountains** (ŏgär'), volcanic upland of the central Sahara, in S Algeria, bet. lat. 21° and 25°N, long. 4° and 8°E. Rise to 9,850 ft. in Tahat peak; several other summits exceed 5,000 ft. Receive somewhat more rain than surrounding desert; give rise to several wadis, notably the Oued Igharghar. Tamanrasset (on trans-Saharan auto track) is chief settlement. Mostly nomadic Tuareg pop.

Ahar (ŭhär'). **1** Village, S Rajasthan, India: see Udaipur, city. **2** Village, Bulandshahr dist., W Uttar Pradesh, India, on the Ganges and 23 mi. E of Bulandshahr; wheat, barley, oilseeds. Hindu temples.

Ahar (ähär'), town (1940 pop. 18,886), Third Prov., in Azerbaijan, NW Iran, 50 mi. ENE of Tabriz, and on road, in mountainous Arasbaran dist.; grain, fruit. Iron deposits near by.

Ahaus (ä'hous), town (pop. 6,747), in former Prussian prov. of Westphalia, NW Germany, after 1945 in North Rhine-Westphalia, 11 mi. NNW of Coesfeld; rail junction; textile mfg., tobacco processing, dairying.

Ahe (ä'hä), atoll (pop. 92), N Tuamotu Isls., Fr. Oceania, S Pacific; 14°30'S 146°20'W; its companion isl. is Manihi (pop. 73). Discovered 1765 by John Byron, who named them Prince of Wales Isl.

Ahémé, Lake (ähĕ'mā), coastal lagoon (14 mi. long, 4 mi. wide), SW Dahomey, Fr. West Africa, 10 mi. NW of Ouidah. Into it empties small Couffo R.

Ahéré, Syria: see 'AHIRE, EL.

Ahichhattra, India: see RAMNAGAR.

Ahigal (ĭgäl'), village (pop. 2,228), Cáceres prov., W Spain, 13 mi. NNW of Plasencia; olive-oil processing, ham curing, flour- and sawmilling; cereals, cork, livestock.

Ahikoy, Turkey: see YATAGAN.

Ahillones (äēlyō'nĕs), town (pop. 748), Badajoz prov., W Spain, 8 mi. E of Llerena; cereals, sheep, hogs; textile goods.

Ahiolu, Bulgaria: see POMORIYE.

'Ahirah, Al-, Syria: see 'AHIRE, EL.

Ahir Dagi (ähŭr' däŭ"), Turkish *Ahır Dağı*, highest peak (8,176 ft.) of Maras Mts., S Turkey, in E part of Taurus Mts., 12 mi. ENE of Maras.

'Ahire, El, or Al-'Ahirah (both: ĕl ä'hĭrù), Fr. *Ahéré*, town, Jebel ed Druz prov., S Syria, 14 mi. NNW of Es Suweida; cereals. Sometimes spelled 'Ahiry.

Ahirli, Turkey: see KARABURUN.

'Ahiry, Syria: see 'AHIRE, EL.

Ahjar, Wadi, Yemen: see SHIBAM.

Ahjir, Wadi, Yemen: see SHIBAM.

Ahlat (älät'), village (pop. 3,124), Bitlis prov., SE Turkey, on NW shore of L. Van, 33 mi. NE of Bitlis; grain, potatoes, sugar beets. The peak Suphan Dag is 20 mi. NE.

Ahlbeck or **Seebad Ahlbeck** (zā'bät äl'bĕk), village (pop. 5,817) in former Prussian Pomerania prov., E Germany, after 1945 in Mecklenburg, on NE shore of Usedom isl., 3 mi. NW of Swinemünde; popular seaside resort.

Ahlen (ä'lùn), town (pop. 30,049), in former Prussian prov. of Westphalia, NW Germany, after 1945 in North Rhine-Westphalia, 17 mi. SE of Münster; mfg. (enamel- and ironware, shoes, furniture). Coal mining. Has Gothic church. Chartered towards end of 12th cent. Strontium mined here in 1880s.

Ahmadabad or **Ahmedabad** (both: ä'mùdùbäd, ämŭdä'bäd), district, N Bombay, India; ⊙ Ahmadabad. Bounded by Sabarmati R. (E), Gulf of Cambay (SE), Mehsana dist. (N). Agr. (millet, cotton, wheat, rice, oilseeds); handicraft cloth weaving. Ahmadabad is major textile and commercial center; Dholera, Dholka, and Dhandhuka are cotton markets. Area annexed to Mogul empire by Akbar in 1572; under Mahrattas in 18th cent. Area of original dist. (□ 3,879; 1941 pop. 1,372,171) reduced 1949 by inter-dist. realignment. Pop. 82% Hindu, 12% Moslem, 1% Christian.

Ahmadabad or **Ahmedabad,** city (pop. 591,267; including NE cantonment area, 595,210), ⊙ Ahmadabad dist., N Bombay, India, on left bank of Sabarmati R. and 275 mi. N of Bombay, in Gujarat; 23°2'N 72°38'E. One of largest cotton-milling centers in India; transportation hub (rail and road junction; airport); agr. market (cotton, grain, oilseeds); commercial center. Mfg. of textiles, chemicals, pottery, bricks, tiles, leather goods, paper, matches, textile equipment, and hosiery; oilseed and flour milling; cloth dyeing and printing; general engineering. Noted handicrafts include jewelry, carved blackwood and ivory, stonework, carpets, cloth fabrics, gold and silver thread, lacquerware, products in copper and brass. The cultural center of Gujarat, with many outstanding mosques, tombs, temples (notably Jain), and other bldgs. in Gujarat architecture. Gujarat Col., Gandhi's Satyagraha Ashram (on W bank of the Sabarmati), law, technical, and medical cols. Scene of strong trade union movement. Industrial suburbs include Asarva (oilseed milling), Saraspur (cotton milling), and Dariapur (glue mfg.). An old wall, with 12 gateways, surrounds the city; tree-lined avenue extends 3 mi. NE to cantonments. Main rail station is just E; Ellis Bridge rail station across the Sabarmati (W) is reached via large bridge. Isls. in river here produce melons, sugar cane, potatoes. Founded 1411 by a Gujarat sultan (Ahmad Shah I), Ahmadabad fell to Akbar's forces in 1572; enjoyed over a century of prosperity under Moguls. Decline in 18th cent. was followed by establishment (early-19th cent.) of textile industry. Center of many of Gandhi's activities in 1920s and 1930s.

Ahmadgarh (ä'mŭdgŭr), town (pop. 4,368), N central Patiala and East Punjab States Union, India, 10 mi. NNW of Maler Kotla; local trade in wheat, millet, cotton.

Ahmadi (ämădē'), town in SE Kuwait, 20 mi. SSE of Kuwait town; residential community for BURGAN oil field; tank farm; water-evaporation plant. Linked by pipe lines with its port and loading terminal of MENA AL AHMADI, 5 mi. ESE. Developed after 1946.

Ahmadnagar (ä'mŭdnŭgŭr), district (□ 6,646; pop. 1,142,229), E Bombay, India, on Deccan Plateau; ⊙ Ahmadnagar. Bordered at NW corner by Western Ghats, NE by Godavari R., SW by Bhima R.; watered by tributaries of Godavari and Bhima rivers, including Pravara R. (N); irrigated by several canal systems. Cotton ginning, handicraft cloth weaving, sugar milling; trades in millet, wheat, cloth fabrics, and gur (from irrigated tracts). Ahmadnagar, Sangamner, Kopargaon, and Shevgaon are road and market centers. Formed part of 16th-cent. Deccan kingdom of Ahmadnagar. Area reduced 1950 by exchange of enclaves with Hyderabad. Pop. 85% Hindu, 6% Moslem, 5% Christian, 4% tribal. Also spelled Ahmednagar.

Ahmadnagar. 1 City (pop. 54,193; including E cantonment area, 70,418), ⊙ Ahmadnagar dist., E Bombay, India, 125 mi. E of Bombay; road center; military station; cotton market; trades in cloth fabrics, millet, wheat, sugar; cotton ginning and milling, hand-loom weaving, tanning, biri mfg., map making; copper and brass products. Missions noted for handicrafts (rope mfg., cloth and carpet weaving). Industrial schools. Founded in late-15th cent.; became ⊙ important Deccan kingdom of Ahmadnagar; captured 1600 by Akbar's forces after heroic resistance by Chand Bibi, a dowager-queen of Bijapur; taken (mid-18th cent.) by Mahrattas. The fort was used by British for political prisoners, including Nehru, 1942–45. Also spelled Ahmednagar. **2** Town, Sabar Kantha dist., Bombay, India: see HIMATNAGAR.

Ahmadpur (ä'mŭdpōōr). **1** or **Ahmedpur** (ä'mŭdpōōr), town (pop. 6,332), Bidar dist., W central Hyderabad state, India, 40 mi. SW of Nander; millet, cotton, rice. Sometimes called Rajura. Road junction of Sirur Tajband is 5.5 mi. SSE. **2** Village, Birbhum dist., West Bengal, India: see SAINTHIA.

Ahmadpur or **Ahmadpur Sial** (syäl'), town (pop. 6,248), Jhang dist., S central Punjab, W Pakistan, 50 mi. SW of Jhang-Maghiana; wheat, millet, cotton; hand-loom weaving. Sometimes spelled Ahmedpur-Syal.

Ahmadpur East, town (pop. 12,255), Bahawalpur state, W Pakistan, 30 mi. SW of Bahawalpur; trades in wheat, cotton, millet, and local products (carbonate of soda, leather goods, pottery). Sometimes called Ahmadpur.

Ahmadpur Lamma (lŭm'mŭ) or **Ahmadpur West,** town (pop. 4,758), Bahawalpur state, W Pakistan, 125 mi. SW of Bahawalpur; local market for mangoes, wheat, cotton; hand-loom weaving.

Ahmedabad, India: see AHMADABAD.

Ahmednagar, India: see AHMADNAGAR, city.

Ahmedpur, Hyderabad state, India: see AHMADPUR.

Ahmedpur-Syal, W Pakistan: see AHMADPUR.

Ahmeek (ämēk'), village (pop. 360), Keweenaw co., NW Upper Peninsula, Mich., 15 mi. NNE of Houghton, on Keweenaw Peninsula; copper mining.

Ahn (än), village (pop. 237), SE Luxembourg, on Moselle R. and 4 mi. SSW of Grevenmacher, on Ger. border; vineyards.

Ahoada (ähwä'dä), town (pop. 1,227), Owerri prov., Eastern Provinces, S Nigeria, on Sombrero R. and 25 mi. NNW of Degema; trade center; palm-oil mill; kola nuts.

Ahome (äō'mā), town (pop. 1,500), Sinaloa, NW Mexico, on the Río del Fuerte (irrigation area), near Gulf of California, and 135 mi. NW of Culiacán; agr. center (sugar, tomatoes, chick-peas, corn, fruit).

Ahoskie (ùhŏ'skē), town (pop. 3,579), Hertford co., NE N.C., 38 mi. SE of Roanoke Rapids, in agr. and timber area; sawmilling.

Ahqaf, Arabia: see RUB' AL KHALI.

Ahram or **Ahrom** (ärōm'), town, Seventh Prov., in Fars, S central Iran, 28 mi. ESE of Bushire and on road to Firuzabad.

Ahraura (ŭrou'rŭ), town (pop. 11,534), Mirzapur dist., SE Uttar Pradesh, India, 29 mi. ESE of Mirzapur; sugar milling, toy mfg.; trades in rice, gram, barley, wheat, oilseeds. Rail station of Ahraura Road is 12 mi. N.

Ahrensbök or **Ahrensböck** (both: ä'rùnsbûk), village (pop. 10,914), in Schleswig-Holstein, NW Germany, 11 mi. NNW of Lübeck; woodworking, spinning. Until 1937 in Oldenburg.

Ahrensburg (ä'rùnsbōōrk), residential town (pop. 16,450), in Schleswig-Holstein, NW Germany, 13 mi. NE of Hamburg; mfg. of machinery, tools, precision instruments, chemicals; weaving, woodworking. Potteries. Has Renaissance castle and church. Chartered 1949.

Ahrntal, Italy: see AURINA, VALLE.

Ahrom, Iran: see AHRAM.

Ahr River (är), W Germany, rises in the Eifel near Belgian border, flows 50 mi. generally E to the Rhine, 1.5 mi. NE of Sinzig. Lower valley noted for its red wine.

Ahrweiler (är'vī"lùr), town (commune pop., including Bachem and Walporzheim, 6,688), in former Prussian Rhine Prov., W Germany, after 1945 in Rhineland-Palatinate, on the Ahr and 13 mi. S of Bonn; trade center for wine region. Bachem (bä'khùm), just E, and Walporzheim (väl'pôrts-hīm"), 1 mi. SW, produce noted red wine.

Ahsa, Al, Saudi Arabia: see HASA.

Ähtäri, Finland: see INHA.

Ahtme or **Akhtme** (äkht'mä), town (1949 pop. over 500), NE Estonia, 3 mi. SE of Johvi; oil-shale distilling; power plant.

Ahuac (äwäk'), town (pop. 2,129), Junín dept., central Peru, in Mantaro R. valley, 7 mi. WSW of Huancayo; grain, alfalfa; cattle raising.

Ahuacatlán (äwäkätlän'). **1** Town (pop. 2,666), Nayarit, W Mexico, on W plateau of Sierra Madre Occidental, 43 mi. SE of Tepic, on railroad; alt. 3,380 ft.; agr. center (corn, beans, sugar, cattle). Silver and gold deposits near by. Anc. Aztec town. **2** Town (pop. 2,115), Puebla, central Mexico, in Sierra Madre Oriental, 8 mi. NE of Zacatlán; corn, tobacco, sugar, fruit.

Ahuachapán (äwächäpän'), department (□ 804; 1950 pop. 94,755), W Salvador, on the Pacific; ⊙ Ahuachapán. Bounded W by Río de la Paz (Guatemala border); traversed E-W by coastal range sloping N to Río de la Paz and S to the Pacific. Agr. (coffee, grain), livestock raising. Salt is obtained along coast. Main centers, Ahuacapán and Atiquizaya, served by railroad from Santa Ana. Formed 1869.

Ahuachapán, city (1950 pop. 10,290), ⊙ Ahuachapán dept., W Salvador, on Molino R. (small left affluent of Río de la Paz) and 45 mi. WNW of San Salvador; alt. 2,690 ft.; 13°57'N 89°51'W. Commercial and mfg. center; rail terminus and road junction; produces pottery, jewelry, soap, footwear, clothing. Agr. (sugar cane, coffee, fruit, grain), livestock raising. Thermal baths. Hydroelectric station is 2 mi. W, on Molino R.

Ahuacuotzingo (äwäkwōtsĕng'gō), town (pop. 1,107), Guerrero, SW Mexico, in Sierra Madre del Sur, 30 mi. ENE of Chilpancingo; alt. 4,970 ft.; cereals, fruit, forest products (resin, rubber, vanilla).

Ahualulco. 1 or **Ahualulco de Mercado** (äwälōōl'kō dā mĕrkä'dō), city (pop. 6,433), Jalisco, W Mexico, on central plateau, 40 mi. W of Guadalajara, on railroad. Mining center (silver, gold, lead, copper); corn, peanuts, fruit, sugar. **2** Town (pop. 1,080), San Luis Potosí, N central Mexico, on interior plateau, 20 mi. NW of San Luis Potosí; alt. 6,240 ft.; gold, silver, lead mining.

Ahuashuatepec (äwäswätāpĕk'), officially San Andrés Ahuashuatepec, town (pop. 1,455), Tlaxcala, central Mexico; grain, livestock.

Ahuatempan (äwätĕm'pän), officially Santa Inés Ahuatempan, town (pop. 2,719), Puebla, central Mexico, on central plateau, 45 mi. SSE of Puebla; alt. 5,987 ft. Rail terminus; agr. center (corn, sugar cane, fruit, livestock).

Ahuatlán (äwätlän'), town (pop. 775), Puebla, central Mexico, 12 mi. E of Matamoros; alt. 4,127 ft.; corn, sugar, livestock.

Ahuazotepec (äwäsōtāpĕk'), town (pop. 946), Puebla, central Mexico, in Sierra Madre Oriental, 13 mi. ESE of Tulancingo, on railroad; alt. 7,326 ft.

Ahuehuetitla (äwäwätēt'lä), town (pop. 1,317), Puebla, central Mexico, 31 mi. SE of Matamoros; cereals, sugar cane, tropical fruit, livestock.

Ahukini Harbor (ä'hōōkē'nē), N Kauai, T.H., on Hanalei Bay.

Ahun (ä-ū'), village (pop. 626), Creuse dept., central France, near Creuse R., 11 mi. NW of Aubusson; coal mining.

Ahunui (ähōōnōō'ē), uninhabited atoll, S. Tuamotu Isls., Fr. Oceania, S Pacific; 19°40'S 140°25'W. Formerly Byam Martin's Isl.

Ahuriri River (ähōō'rērē), central S.Isl., New Zealand, rises in Southern Alps bet. L. Ohau and L. Hawea, flows c.65 mi. SE and E, joining Tekapo R. to form WAITAKI RIVER.

Ahus (ō'hüs"), Swedish *Åhus*, town (pop. 1,933), Kristianstad co., S Sweden, seaport on Hano Bay of the Baltic, at mouth of Helge R., 9 mi. SE of Kristianstad; eel fishing; seaside resort; in important tobacco-growing region. Has 12th-cent. church and remains of medieval archbishops' castle. Commercial center in Middle Ages.

Ahvaz, Iran: see AHWAZ.

Ahvenanmaa, Finland: see ALAND ISLANDS.

Ahwar (äwär'), town, ⊙ Lower Aulaqi sultanate, Western Aden Protectorate, on coastal road and 120 mi. ENE of Aden, 5 mi. from Gulf of Aden; center of agr. area; airfield, radio station.

Ahwaz or **Ahvaz** (ähwäz'), city (1940 pop. 45,528), ⊙ Sixth Prov., SW Iran, 340 mi. SW of Teheran and 80 mi. NE of Basra; transportation center of Khuzistan, head of navigation and transshipment point on Karun R.; junction of railroads and highways from Basra, Khurramshahr, Abadan, and Bandar Shahpur; airfield; textile mills. An important agr. and trade center under Arab rule, it flourished in 12th and 13th cent., later declined. In modern times, it developed again after the opening (1888) of Karun R. to British trade, and boomed in 20th cent. with development of Khuzistan oil fields and the Trans-Iranian RR. The modern city was briefly known as Nasiri or Naseri until it assumed the name of anc. Ahwaz.

Ai, river, Russian SFSR: see AI RIVER.

Aiaktalik (īùktä'lĭk), village, S Alaska, on Aiaktalik Isl. (5 mi. long, 4 mi. wide), in Sitkinak Strait, off S Kodiak Isl.; 56°42'N 154°7'W. Natives work in Kodiak Isl. canneries during summer. Has Russian Orthodox church.

Aibak, Afghanistan: see HAIBAK.

Aibar (īvär'), town (pop. 1,454), Navarre prov., N Spain, 21 mi. SE of Pamplona; olive-oil processing; wine, cereals, sheep.

Aibling, Bad, Germany: see BAD AIBLING.
Aibonito (ībōnē'tō), town (pop. 5,126), central Puerto Rico, in the Cordillera Central, 17 mi. WSW of Caguas; summer resort in agr. region (coffee, fruit, vegetables, flowers, stock).
Aichach (īkh'äkh), town (pop. 6,342), Upper Bavaria, Germany, on Paar R. and 13 mi. NE of Augsburg; textile mfg., metalworking, printing, food processing. Has late-Gothic church. Chartered 1204. Near by stood ancestral castle of Wittelsbach family.
Aichi (ī'chē), prefecture [Jap. *ken*] (□ 1,962; 1940 pop. 3,166,592; 1947 pop. 3,122,902), central Honshu, Japan; ⊙ NAGOYA, its chief port. Bounded E by Ise Bay, S by Philippine Sea; includes Chita and Atsumi peninsulas. Large coastal plain in Nagoya area, with mountainous, forested interior. Drained by Kiso R. (important for hydroelectric power). Agr. (rice, herbs, sweet potatoes); large production of poultry and raw silk. Fish hatcheries on shores of Chita and Atsumi bays. Lignite and quartz crystal mined in W area. Mfg. of porcelain and textiles (cotton, wool, silk); metal- and woodworking. Nagoya is major industrial center. Other centers: TOYOHASHI, OKAZAKI, ICHINOMIYA, SETO, HANDA, TOYOKAWA.
Aichow, China: see AIHSIEN.
Aicota (īkō'tä), village, Agordat div., W Eritrea, on Gash R. and 36 mi. W of Barentu; road junction; alt. c.2,000 ft.; cattle raising, dom nut gathering.
Aidabul or **Aydabul'** (īdŭbōōl'), town (1948 pop. over 2,000), S Kokchetav oblast, Kazakh SSR, 40 mi. SSW of Kokchetav; distillery.
Aidar River or **Aydar River** (īdär'), W European USSR, rises in Central Russian Upland E of Veidelevka, Russian SFSR; flows c.120 mi. S, into Ukrainian SSR, through rich wheat country, past Starobelsk, to Northern Donets R. N of Voroshilovgrad.
Aidemir or **Aydemir** (īdĕmĕr'), village (pop. 2,978), Ruse dist., NE Bulgaria, in SW Dobruja, near the Danube, 4 mi. W of Silistra; wheat, flax, truck. In Rumania, 1913–40.
Aidenbach (ī'dùnbäkh), village (pop. 2,508), Lower Bavaria, Germany, 17 mi. W of Passau; wheat, barley, cattle, horses.
Aidepsos, village, Greece: see LOUTRA AIDEPSOU.
Aidepsos, Gulf of, or **Gulf of Aidhipsos** (both: ĕdhēpsôs'), inlet of Gulf of Euboea in NW Euboea; 4 mi. long, 3 mi. wide. Loutra Aidepsou is on E shore.
Aidin, Turkey: see AYDIN.
Aidonat, Greece: see PARAMYTHIA.
Aidone (īdō'nĕ), town (pop. 8,178), Enna prov., SE central Sicily, 14 mi. SE of Enna. Varied mining industry (marble, gypsum, bitumen, sulphur).
Aidunat, Greece: see PARAMYTHIA.
Aidussina, Yugoslavia: see AJDOVSCINA.
Aidyrlinski or **Aydyrlinskiy** (īdĭrlyēn'skē), town (1948 pop. over 2,000), NE Chkalov oblast, Russian SFSR, in E foothills of the S Urals, 5 mi. SE of Kvarkeno, near railroad; gold, nickel mines.
Aiea (äyā'ü), town (pop. 3,714), S Oahu, T.H., 7 mi. NW of Honolulu; center for sugar cultivation.
Aiello Calabro (äyĕl'lô kä'läbrô), village (pop. 1,182), Cosenza prov., Calabria, S Italy, 13 mi. SSW of Cosenza; raw silk, olive oil.
Aieta (äyā'tä), village (pop. 1,753), Cosenza prov., Calabria, S Italy, 8 mi. NNE of Scalea.
Aiga (ī'gä), town (pop. 4,154), Mie prefecture, S Honshu, Japan, on Kumano Sea, on E Kii Peninsula, 38 mi. SW of Uji-yamada; agr., fishing, lumbering. Until 1934, called Oka.
Aigachi (īgä'chē), town (pop. c.2,100), La Paz dept., W Bolivia, port on L. Titicaca, 32 mi. WNW of La Paz; alt. 12,933 ft.; potatoes, barley, quinoa, sheep. Also spelled Aygachi.
Aigaion Pelagos, Greece: see AEGEAN SEA.
Aigaleos (ĕgā'lāôs), Lat. *Aegaleos* (ēgā'lēŏs), mountain in Attica nome, E central Greece, W of Athens; rises to 1,535 ft. Overlooks Salamis strait, site of naval battle (480 B.C.).
Aigas (ā'gùs), rocky islet in Beauly R., N Inverness, Scotland, 6 mi. SW of Beauly; noted for scenic beauty.
Aigen (ī'gùn). **1** village (pop. 1,782), Styria, central Austria, near Enns R., 27 mi. SE of Bad Ischl; summer resort. **2** Village (pop. 2,033), N Upper Austria, on Grosse Mühl R. and 27 mi. NW of Linz, near Czechoslovak line; rail terminus; market center. Monastery of Schlägl to S.
Aighinion, Greece: see AIGINION.
Aighion, Greece: see AIGION.
Aigidik or **Aygidik** (īgĭdēk'), peak (8,587 ft.) in SW Rila Mts., W Bulgaria, 17 mi. E of Gorna Dzhumaya.
Aigina, Greece: see AEGINA.
Aiginion or **Aiyinion** (both: ĕyē'nēôn), town (pop. 3,638), Salonika nome, Macedonia, Greece, on railroad and 23 mi. WSW of Salonika; cotton, wheat, vegetables. Formerly called Libanovon; also Aighinion.
Aigion or **Aiyion** (both: ā'yēôn), Lat. *Aegium* (ē'jēùm), city (pop. 15,259), Achaea nome, N Peloponnesus, Greece, port on Gulf of Corinth, on railroad and 18 mi. E of Patras. Exports Zante currants; also olives, oranges, figs. Paper mill, alcohol distillery. The anc. city was a member of 1st Achaean League and became seat of the confederation after destruction (373 B.C.) of Helice; joined (276 B.C.) 2d Achaean League. Formerly called Vostitsa, Ital. *Vostizza.* Sometimes spelled Aegion and Aighion.
Aigle (ĕgl'ù), town (pop. 3,918), Vaud canton, SW Switzerland, in Rhone R. valley, 21 mi. SE of Lausanne; flour, beer, clothes; woodworking. Medieval castle, late-Gothic church.
Aigle, Cap de l' (käp dù lĕg'lù), or **Bec de l'Aigle** (bĕk–), rocky headland of Bouches-du-Rhône dept., SE France, on the Mediterranean, enclosing La Ciotat bay (E), 15 mi. SE of Marseilles. Cliffs (1,000 ft. high) extend NW to Cassis.
Aigle, L'. **1** Locality, Corrèze dept., France: see LAPLEAU. **2** Town, Orne dept., France: see LAIGLE.
Aignan (ānyā'), village (pop. 526), Gers dept., SW France, 20 mi. NW of Mirande; tartar mfg.
Aignay-le-Duc (ānyā'-lù-dük'), agr. village (pop. 583), Côte-d'Or dept., E central France, 15 mi. SSE of Châtillon-sur-Seine.
Aigoual, Mont (mōtägwäl'), peak (5,141 ft.) in the Cévennes, S France, on Lozère-Gard dept. border, 6 mi. SE of Meyrueis. Meteorological observatory on summit. Atlantic-Mediterranean drainage divide.
Aigre (ā'grù), village (pop. 998), Charente dept., W France, 18 mi. NNW of Angoulême; brandy distilling.
Aigrefeuille, France: see AIGREFEUILLE-SUR-MAINE.
Aigrefeuille-d'Aunis (āgrùfû'ē-dōnēs'), village (pop. 744), Charente-Maritime dept., W France, 10 mi. ESE of La Rochelle; railroad junction; distilling, dairying. Has 12th–14th-cent. church.
Aigrefeuille-sur-Maine (–sür-mĕn'), village (pop. 448), Loire-Inférieure dept., W France, on Maine R. and 12 mi. SE of Nantes; vineyards. Until 1934, Aigrefeuille.
Aiguá (īgwä'), town (pop. 3,500), Maldonado dept., S Uruguay, 30 mi. ENE of Minas; stock raising (cattle, sheep).
Aiguebelle (ĕgbĕl'), village (pop. 798), Savoie dept., SE France, in Maurienne valley near its junction with Isère R. valley, 10 mi. SSW of Albertville; electrometallurgical and electrochemical (fertilizer) works.
Aiguebelle, abbey, France: see DONZÈRE.
Aigueperse (ĕgpârz'), village (pop. 1,526), Puy-de-Dôme dept., central France, in the Limagne, 10 mi. NNE of Riom; chemical works (carbonic acid, insecticides). Has 13th-cent. church.
Aigues-Mortes (ĕg-môrt'), town (pop. 3,320), Gard dept., S France, on the Rhone-Sète Canal and 16 mi. ESE of Montpellier, amidst marshes of Rhone R. delta. The town (a seaport in Middle Ages, now silted up) was built by Louis IX, who embarked from here for his 2 crusades (1248 and 1270). A small marvel of medieval architecture, its remarkable 13th-cent. ramparts and fortified tower (Tour de Constance) have been preserved intact. A canal (4 mi. long) enters the Mediterranean at Le Grau-de-Roi. There are important saltworks. Sometimes spelled Aiguesmortes.
Aigues-Vives (–vēv'), village (pop. 863), Gard dept., S France, 12 mi. SW of Nîmes; distilling, tile mfg., winegrowing. Sometimes spelled Aiguesvives.
Aiguille, Pointe de l' (pwĕt dù lāgwē'), headland of Alpes-Maritimes dept., SE France, on the Mediterranean, 4 mi. SW of Cannes, at foot of Estérel range. Bounds Golfe de la Napoule (NE).
Aiguille de Chambeyron (āgwē' dù shābārō'), peak (11,155 ft.) of the Cottian Alps, in Basses-Alpes dept., SE France, near Ital. border, 5 mi. ENE of Saint-Paul. Glaciers.
Aiguille du Géant (dü zhāā'), peak (13,170 ft.) of Mont Blanc massif, on Fr.-Ital. border, just NE of Col du Géant, at head of Géant (or Tacul) glacier, 6 mi. SE of Chamonix.
Aiguille du Midi (dü mēdē'), peak (12,608 ft.) of the Mont Blanc massif, in Haute-Savoie dept., SE France, overlooking Chamonix (3 mi. N). Aerial tramway.
Aiguilles or **Aiguilles-en-Queyras** (āgwē'-ā-kārä'), village (pop. 273), Hautes-Alpes dept., SE France, on the Guil and 14 mi. SE of Briançon, in Cottian Alps; alt. 4,830 ft. Resort; winter sports. Cheese mfg.
Aiguilles Rouges (– rōōzh'), Alpine range of acicular peaks in Haute-Savoie dept., SE France, overlooking Chamonix valley (E), opposite Mont Blanc massif. Rise to 9,511 ft. Mont Brévent, just N of Chamonix, is southernmost peak.
Aiguille Verte (āgwē' vârt'), peak (13,540 ft.) of Mont Blanc massif, Haute-Savoie dept., SE France, bet. Argentière glacier (N) and Talèfre glacier (S), overlooking Chamonix valley (W).
Aiguillon (āgēyō'), village (pop. 1,509), Lot-et-Garonne dept., SW France, on the Lot near its mouth on Garonne R. and 15 mi. WNW of Agen; mfg. of footwear; food canning.
Aigun (īgōōn'), Chinese *Aihun* (ī'hōōn'), town (1940 pop. c.20,000), ⊙ Aigun co. (1946 pop. 75,546), N Heilungkiang prov., Manchuria, 310 mi. N of Harbin, and on right bank of Amur R. (USSR line), opposite Blagoveshchensk; major river port, rail terminus, and center of trade with USSR. Flour milling, distilling, sawmilling, brick mfg.; ship repair yards. Gold mining near by. It is the original Manchu village of Sakhalin or Sakhalin-Ula, Rus. *Sakhalyan.* Opened 1858 to foreign trade, it boomed during the Manchurian gold rush (1880s) when its pop. reached 50,000. It became known by the Chinese name of Taheiho (dä'hā'hŭ') or Taheihotun (–dōōn'), later Heiho (hā'hŭ') or Heihotun (–dōōn'). While in Manchukuo, it was reached in 1935 by railroad and was ⊙ Heilungkiang prov. (1934–46). In 1949, it adopted the name of Aigun when the co. seat was moved here from old Aigun, 20 mi. S. Old Aigun (pop. c.7,000), founded 1684, was the oldest Chinese outpost on Amur R. By the treaty of Aigun signed here (1858), the left Amur bank was ceded by China to Russia. Old Aigun became ⊙ Heilungkiang prov. and was also known as Heilungkiang-cheng until provincial ⊙ was moved to Tsitsihar. Primarily an administrative center (until 1949), it never reached the commercial prominence of new Aigun.
Aigurande (āgürād'), village (pop. 1,498), Indre dept., central France, 13 mi. SW of La Châtre; sawmilling, cattle raising. Granite quarries near.
Aihsien (Cantonese ī'yün'), Mandarin *Yaihsien* (yī'shyĕn'), town, ⊙ Aihsien co. (pop. 93,383), S Hainan, Kwangtung prov., China, on coastal railroad and 125 mi. SW of Kiungshan; center of stock-raising area; produces coconuts, betel nuts, melon seeds, wheat, rattan cane. Sugar milling. Fisheries, saltworks. Until 1912 called Aichow or Yaichow.
Aihun, Manchuria: see AIGUN.
Aija (ī'hä), city (pop. 1,562), ⊙ Aija prov. (□ 524; pop. 13,286), Ancash dept., W central Peru, in Cordillera Negra of the Andes, 18 mi. SSW of Huarás; alt. 10,531 ft. Agr. products (barley, potatoes, corn); sheep raising. Iron and coal deposits near by.
Aijal (ī'jŭl), village, ⊙ Lushai Hills dist., S Assam, India, 76 mi. S of Silchar, in Lushai Hills (extensive bamboo tracts); rice, cotton.
Aikawa (ī'käwä), principal town (pop. 8,205) on Sado Isl., Niigata prefecture, Japan, on W coast, 30 mi. W of Niigata, off N Honshu; mining center (gold, silver) since 17th cent.; pottery making.
Aiken (ā'kĭn), county (□ 1,097; pop. 53,137), W S.C.; ⊙ Aiken. At edge of piedmont region, in Sand Hills belt; bounded W by Savannah R., NE by North Fork of Edisto R.; drained by South Fork of the Edisto. Agr. (cotton, corn, fruit, truck, dairy products); number of cotton-milling towns; kaolin deposits. Noted resort area around Aiken. Part of U.S. Atomic Energy Commission installation is in S. Formed 1871.
Aiken, city (pop. 7,083), ⊙ Aiken co., W S.C., 16 mi. ENE of Augusta, Ga., in the sandhills. Popular resort; trade and industrial center (lumber milling, kaolin shipping, printing) for agr. and forest area. Facilities for all sports, but known especially for riding and polo playing. Laid out 1834, inc. 1835.
Aikenton (ā'kùntùn), town (1940 pop. 41), Jasper co., N central Ga., 9 mi. NE of Monticello.
Aikino or **Aykino** (ī'kĭnŭ), village (1926 pop. 560), W Komi Autonomous SSR, Russian SFSR, on Vychegda R. (landing) and 45 mi. NW of Syktyvkar; flax.
Ailao Pass (ī'lou') (1,345 ft.), in Annamese Cordillera, central Vietnam, 50 mi. WNW of Hue, near Laos line; used by Dongha-Savannakhet highway.
Ailet (īlĕt'), village (pop. 150), Massawa div., central Eritrea, in coastal lowland, on road and 20 mi. W of Massawa; hot mineral springs.
Ailette River (ālĕt'), Aisne dept., N France, rises N of Craonne, flows c.35 mi. WNW, past Anizy-le-Château, to the Oise below Chauny. Followed through most of its course by Oise-Aisne Canal. Scene of heavy fighting in First World War, especially in Chemin des Dames sector.
Aileu (īlĕ'ōō), town, Portuguese Timor, in central Timor, 10 mi. S of Dili; coffee, copra. Formerly Vila General Carmona.
Ailey, town (pop. 508), Montgomery co., E central Ga., 11 mi. W of Vidalia; mfg. (clothing, lumber).
Ailinginae (ī'lĭng-ēnä'ā), uninhabited atoll (□ 1), Ralik Chain, Kwajalein dist., Marshall Isls., W central Pacific, 150 mi. NW of Kwajalein; 15 mi. long; 25 islets.
Ailinglapalap (ī'lĭnglä'päläp), atoll (□ 4; pop. 706), Ralik Chain, Marshall Isls., W central Pacific, 150 mi. SE of Kwajalein; triangular, with base 25 mi. wide; 52 islets; copra. Formerly Odia Isl.
Aillant or **Aillant-sur-Tholon** (äyā'-sür-tôlō'), agr. village (pop. 1,004), Yonne dept., N central France, 12 mi. WNW of Auxerre; dairying.
Aillant-sur-Tholon, Yonne dept., France: see AILLANT.
Aillevillers (īvēlâr'), village (pop. 1,577), Haute-Saône dept., E France, at foot of the Vosges, 18 mi. NNW of Lure; railroad junction. Kirsch distilling, silk and rayon weaving, hand embroidering. Hosiery and rolling mills at near-by La Chaudeau.
Ailly-le-Haut-Clocher (äyē'-lù-ō-klôshā'), agr. village (pop. 544), Somme dept., N France, 7 mi. ESE of Abbeville. Damaged in Second World War.
Ailly-sur-Noye (–sür-nwä'), village (pop. 1,541), Somme dept., N France, 10 mi. SSE of Amiens; flour milling, dairying. Damaged in Second World War.

Ailly-sur-Somme (–sür-sôm'), village (pop. 1,827), Somme dept., N France, on left bank of Somme R. and 5 mi. WNW of Amiens; linen and jute milling.
Ailsa Craig (āl'sù), village (pop. 474), S Ont., on Ausable R. and 18 mi. NW of London; dairying, flax growing.
Ailsa Craig (ĕl'sù), rocky island (1 mi. long, 1 mi. wide; alt. c.1,100 ft.) rising strikingly out of the water at mouth of Firth of Clyde, off coast of Ayrshire, Scotland, 10 mi. W of Girvan. Composed of a kind of granite rare in Great Britain. Site of lighthouse (55°16'N 5°7'W).
Ailuk (ī'lŏŏk), atoll (□ 2; pop. 319), Ratak Chain, Kwajalein dist., Marshall Isls., W central Pacific, 160 mi. NE of Kwajalein; 20 mi. long; 35 islets.
Aim (ŭēm'), village (1939 pop. over 2,000), E Andizhan oblast, Uzbek SSR, on the Kara Darya and 18 mi. E of Andizhan; cotton.
Aimangala, India: see CHITALDRUG, town.
Aimaraes, province, Peru: see CHALHUANCA.
Aimargues (āmärg'), town (pop. 2,523), Gard dept., S France, 13 mi. SW of Nîmes; distilling; wine and olive trade.
Aimaya or **Aymaya** (īmī'ä), town (pop. c.3,700), Potosí dept., W central Bolivia, at E foot of Cordillera de Azanaques, just NW of Chayanta and 7 mi. E of Uncía; truck, grain.
Aime (ām), village (pop. 1,075), Savoie dept., SE France, in Alpine Tarentaise valley, on the Isère and 15 mi. SE of Albertville; anthracite mines. Has Roman ruins.
Aimogasta (īmōgä'stä), village (pop. estimate 1,000), ⊙ Arauco dept. (□ 645; 1947 census pop. 5,021), N La Rioja prov., Argentina, at NE foot of the Sierra de Velasco, on railroad and 60 mi. N of La Rioja, in Río Colorado irrigation area. Olive growing, olive-oil mfg.
Aimorés (īmŏŏrĕs'), city (pop. 3,853), easternmost Minas Gerais, Brazil, on the Rio Doce, at S foot of the Serra dos Aimorés, on railroad and 70 mi. NW of Vitória (Espírito Santo); exploitation of mica and beryls. Formerly spelled Aymorés.
Aimorés, Serra dos (sĕ'rù dŏŏs), range in E Brazil, along Minas Gerais–Espírito Santo border, bet. Mucuri R. (N) and the Rio Doce (S). Rises to 2,850 ft. Serra dos Aimorés region (□ 3,914; 1940 pop. 66,994; 1950 census 162,062) is disputed bet. Minas Gerais and Espírito Santo; settlement by federal govt. is pending. Formerly spelled Aymorés.
Ain (ē), department (□ 2,249; pop. 306,778), in former Burgundy prov., E France; ⊙ Bourg. Bounded by Switzerland (NE), the Rhone (S and E), and the Saône (W). The Ain, flowing S to the Rhone, bisects the dept. and separates the BRESSE and DOMBES regions (W) from the Jura (culminating in the Crêt de la Neige at 5,652 ft.), which occupies E part of dept. Intensive poultry raising and diversified agr. (cereals, wine, hemp, tobacco) in the Bresse. Fishing, hog and cattle raising in lake-studded Dombes dist. Grazing and cheese mfg. in mts. Asphalt mines N of Seyssel. Important hydroelectric installations on the Rhone at Chancy-Pougny (Swiss border), Bellegarde, and GÉNISSIAT, and on Ain R. near Bolozon. Numerous small workshops, manned by skilled artisans, engage in woodturning, watchmaking, plastics- and metal-working. Chief towns are Bourg (poultry-shipping center and regional agr. market), Oyonnax (France's leading plastics mfg. center), and Bellegarde (chemical, metallurgical industry).
Ain, river, France: see AIN RIVER.
'Ain, Wadi al (wä'dē ăl ĭn'), right tributary valley of the Wadi Duan, Quaiti state, Eastern Aden Protectorate; 15 mi. long. Joins the Wadi Duan just S of the Wadi Hadhramaut.
Aïn-Abessa (ĭn'-äbĕsä'), village (pop. 1,158), Constantine dept., NE Algeria, on S slope of Babor range, 10 mi. NW of Sétif; cereals, cork.
Aïn-Abid (ĭn'-äbĕd'), village (pop. 2,074), Constantine dept., NE Algeria, in the High Plateaus, on railroad and 21 mi. SE of Constantine; cereals.
Ainabkoi (īnäbkoi'), village, Rift Valley prov., W Kenya, on Uasin Gishu Plateau, on railroad and 30 mi. SE of Eldoret; coffee, tea, wheat, corn.
Ainabo (īnäbō'), village, SE Br. Somaliland, in plateau, 70 mi. WNW of Las Anod; stock raising.
Ainaro (ī"närŏŏ'), town (pop. 491), ⊙ Suro dist. (□ 753; pop. 68,786), Portuguese Timor, in central Timor, 30 mi. S of Dili; trade center for area producing coffee, sandalwood, fruit, sheep. Tile, brick, and pottery mfg. Formerly called Suro.
'Ainat, Aden: see 'EINAT.
Ainatpur, India: see BELAPUR.
Ainazi, Ainazhi, or **Aynazhi** (ī'nä-zhē), Lettish *Ainaži*, Ger. *Hainasch*, city (pop. 918), N Latvia, in Vidzeme, port on Gulf of Riga, 65 mi. N of Riga, on Estonian border; terminus of rail line from Valmiera; sawmilling.
Aïn-Beïda (ĭn'bādä') [Arabic,=white spring], town (pop. 12,238), Constantine dept., NE Algeria, in the High Plateaus, 60 mi. SE of Constantine; junction on Constantine-Tebessa RR (spur to Khenchela); alt. 3,300 ft. Native agr. market in fertile wheat- and barley-growing dist. Founded 1848 as Fr. military post.
Aïn-Bessem (ĭn'-bĕsĕm'), town (pop. 4,550), Alger dept., N central Algeria, on railroad and 10 mi. N of Aumale; winegrowing center; olives, cereals.
Aïn-Boucif (ĭn'-bŏŏsēf'), village (pop. 962), Alger dept., N central Algeria, in the Titteri range (Tell Atlas), 34 mi. SE of Médéa; esparto shipping, sheep raising.
Ain Dar or **'Ayn Dar** (ĭn' där'), oil field, Hasa, Saudi Arabia, 28 mi. W of Abqaiq (linked by pipe line); discovered 1948.
'Ain Diwar or **'Ayn Diwar** (ĭn' dē'wär), Fr. *Aïn Diwar*, town, Jezire prov., NE Syria, on Turkish border, 95 mi. NE of El Haseke; cereals, sheep. Oil deposits.
Aindling (īnt'lĭng), village (pop. 1,263), Upper Bavaria, Germany, 16 mi. SSE of Donauwörth; brewing. Chartered 1479.
Aïn-Draham (ĭn'-drä-äm'), town (pop. 611), Tabarka dist., NW Tunisia, in the Khroumirie section of the Tell, near Algerian border, 12 mi. S of Tabarka; livestock market; lumbering, cork processing. Lead and zinc deposits near by. Excellent climate. Summer resort of Col des Ruines just N.
Aïn el Aouda (ĭn' ĕl oudä'), village, Rabat region, NW Fr. Morocco, 15 mi. S of Rabat; center of European agr. settlement; cereals, wine.
'Ain el 'Arab or **'Ayn al-'Arab** (both: ĭn' ĕl äräb'), Fr. *Aïn el Arab*, town, Aleppo prov., N Syria, at Turkish border, on railroad, and 80 mi. NE of Aleppo; cereals.
Aïn-el-Arba (ĭn'-ĕl-ärbä'), village (pop. 3,662), Oran dept., NW Algeria, on rail spur and 24 mi. SW of Oran, near the Oran Sebkha; winegrowing.
Aïn-el-Asker (ĭn'ĕl-äskâr'), village, Tunis dist., N Tunisia, 19 mi. SSW of Tunis; vineyards.
'Ain el Beida, El, or **Al-'Ayn al-Bayda** (both: ĕl ĭn' ĕl bā'dù), town, Homs prov., central Syria, 70 mi. ESE of Homs, on the Kirkuk-Tripoli oil pipe line, W of Palmyra.
'Ain el Fije or **'Ayn al-Fijah** (both: ĭn' ĕl fē'jù), Fr. *Aïn Figeh*, village, Damascus prov., SW Syria, on railroad and 10 mi. NW of Damascus; alt. 2,820 ft.; orchards, poplars, vineyards. Ruins of old Roman temple near by.
Ain el Gazala, Cyrenaica: see GAZALA, EL.
Aïn-el-Hadjar (ĭn'-ĕl-äjär'), village (pop. 928), Oran dept., NW Algeria, on S slope of Tell Atlas, on railroad and 5 mi. S of Saïda; paper milling, winegrowing, livestock raising.
Aïn el Hamra, Fr. Morocco: see SOUK EL ARBA DU RHARB.
'Ain el Kurum or **'Ayn al-Kurum** (both: ĭn' ĕl kŏŏrŏŏm'), Fr. *Aïn Kroum*, town, Latakia prov., W Syria, 30 mi. ESE of Latakia; sericulture, cotton, tobacco, cereals.
Aïn-el-Turck (ĭn'-ĕl-türk'), village (pop. 1,474), Oran dept., NW Algeria, on the Mediterranean, 8 mi. WNW of Oran; bathing resort; winegrowing, truck gardening. Also called Aïn-el-Turck-la-Plage.
Aïn-Fekan (ĭn'-fäkän'), village (pop. 1,932), Oran dept., NW Algeria, in the Tell Atlas, 14 mi. SW of Mascara; winegrowing. Just NW is the spa of Bou-Hanifia (hot springs; known to Romans).
Aïn Figeh, Syria: see 'AIN EL FIJE.
Aïn-Galaka (ĭn'-gäläkä'), village, N Chad territory, Fr. Equatorial Africa, in SE Sahara, 40 mi. W of Largeau; oasis on trans-Saharan track to Fr. West Africa; dates, camels, wheat. Former Senussite base. Also spelled Aïn-Galakka.
Aïn Guenfouda, Fr. Morocco: see DJÉRADA.
Aïn-Kerma (ĭn'-kârmä'), village (pop. 615), Constantine dept., NE Algeria, 8 mi. NW of Constantine; antimony mine.
Aïn-Kial (ĭn'-kēäl'), village (pop. 1,584), Oran dept., NW Algeria, 7 mi. SSW of Aïn-Témouchent; wine, cereals; horse raising. Also spelled Aïn-Khial.
Aïn Kroum, Syria: see 'AIN EL KURUM.
Aïn Leuh (ĭn' lû), town (pop. 2,672), Meknès region, N central Fr. Morocco, on N slopes of the Middle Atlas and 45 mi. SSE of Meknès; lumbering center. Fr. military post established 1916.
Aïn-M'Lila (ĭn'-mùlēlä'), town (pop. 5,336), Constantine dept., NE Algeria, on railroad to Biskra, and 23 mi. S of Constantine, in cereal-growing section of the High Plateaus.
Aïn-Mokra (ĭn'-mōkrä'), village (pop. 496), Constantine dept., NE Algeria, near L. Fetzara, 18 mi. SW of Bône; cork gathering and processing; winegrowing. Iron ore formerly mined here.
Aïn-Moularès, Tunisia: see MOULARÈS.
Ainola, Finland: see JÄRVENPÄÄ.
Ainos, Turkey: see ENOS.
Ainoura, Japan: see SASEBO.
Aïn-Oussera (ĭn'-ŏŏsrä'), locality in Alger dept., N central Algeria, in the High Plateaus, 32 mi. SSE of Boghari, on railroad to Djelfa; sheep, wool.
Aïn-Rhelal (ĭn'-gäläl'), village, Bizerte dist., N Tunisia, on Tunis-Bizerte RR and 17 mi. S of Bizerte; petroleum deposits.
Ain River (ē), Jura and Ain depts., E France, rises in central Jura near Nozeroy, flows 118 mi. SSW, past Champagnole and Pont-d'Ain, to the Rhone 8 mi. S of Meximieux. Harnessed for hydroelectric power near Vescles and Bolozon. Traverses picturesque gorges in upper course. Navigable seasonally. Receives the Bienne (left).
Aïn-Roua (ĭn'-rŏŏä'), village (pop. 678), Constantine dept., NE Algeria, on S slope of Biban range (Little Kabylia), 16 mi. NW of Sétif; iron and zinc mining.
Aïn Sebaâ (ĭn' sùbä-ä'), village, Casablanca region, W Fr. Morocco, on the Atlantic, 4 mi. NE of Casablanca; truck farming. Zoological garden.
Aïn-Sebaa (ĭn'-sùbä-ä'), village, Tabarka dist., NW Tunisia, in Medjerda Mts., near the Mediterranean, 9 mi. E of Tabarka; horse raising. Zinc and iron deposits near by.
Aïn-Sefra (ĭn'-sĕfrä'), military territory (□251,024; 1948 pop. 250,894) of W Algeria, westernmost of the SOUTHERN TERRITORIES, in the Sahara; ⊙ Colomb-Béchar. Bounded by Oran dept. (N), Fr. Morocco (NW), Spanish Sahara (W), and Fr. West Africa (SW). Narrow-gauge railroad extends from Oran dept. to Colomb-Béchar (via Aïn-Sefra); from Fr. Morocco comes the trans-Saharan RR, completed in Second World War to Colomb-Béchar. Coal mined in basin of Kenadsa and Colomb-Béchar. Chief Saharan oases belong to the Gourara and Touat group. Principal export products: dates, wool, sheep, esparto.
Aïn-Sefra, town and Saharan oasis (pop. 3,500), Aïn-Sefra territory, W Algeria, in the Ksour Mts. (Saharan Atlas), on railroad from Oran to Colomb-Béchar RR and 200 mi. S of Oran; 32°45'N 0°31'W; alt. 3,600 ft. Dates, cereals. Esparto collected in area. Sheep raising. Military post.
Ainslie, Lake (ānz'lē) (12 mi. long, 5 mi. wide), NE N.S., on W Cape Breton Isl., 4 mi. SE of Inverness; 46°8'N 61°11'W. Drained by Southwest Margaree R. Fluorspar mining.
Aïn-Smara (ĭn'-smärä'), village (pop. 476), Constantine dept., NE Algeria, on the Oued Rhumel, on railroad and 9 mi. SW of Constantine; horse breeding. Zinc mine at the Djebel Felten (5 mi. SW); marble quarry.
Ainsworth, village and parish (pop. 1,969), SE central Lancashire, England, 3 mi. E of Bolton; cotton milling.
Ainsworth. 1 Town (pop. 396), Washington co., SE Iowa, 7 mi. E of Washington, in agr. area. **2** City (pop. 2,150), ⊙ Brown co., N Nebr., 135 mi. NW of Grand Island; trade center in well-watered region; dairy produce, livestock, poultry, grain. Settled 1877, inc. 1883.
Aintab, Turkey: see GAZIANTEP.
Aïn-Tagrout (ĭn'-tägrŏŏt'), village (pop. 533), Constantine dept., NE Algeria, in the Tell, 19 mi. WSW of Sétif; cereals; horse raising.
Aïn-Taya (ĭn'-täyä'), village (pop. 2,443), Alger dept., N central Algeria, on the Mediterranean, 13 mi. E of Algiers, and just E of Cape Matifou; bathing resort; truck gardening, tobacco growing. Also called Aïn-Taya-les-Bains.
Aïn-Tédelès (ĭn'-tädùlĕs'), village (pop. 2,424), Oran dept., NW Algeria, near the Chéliff, 12 mi. NE of Mostaganem; olive and winegrowing, stock raising; olive pressing.
Aïn-Témouchent (ĭn'-tāmŏŏshä'), town (pop. 18,848), Oran dept., NW Algeria, in the Tell, 40 mi. SW of Oran; rail terminus; road and commercial center in winegrowing area; oil refining, cement and furniture mfg. Trade in cereals, olives, wines, and horses. Has experimental agr. station and school.
Aïn Toura, Lebanon: see 'AIN TURA.
Aintree, village and parish (pop. 338), SW Lancashire, England, on Leeds-Liverpool Canal and 5 mi. NNE of Liverpool. Has well-known steeplechase racecourse (4½ mi. long), scene of the annual Grand Natl. race, founded in 1839.
'Ain Tura or **'Ayn Turah** (ĭn' tŏŏ'rù), Fr. *Aïn Toura*, village, central Lebanon, near the coast, 7 mi. NE of Beirut; sericulture, lemons. Here was founded (17th cent.), by the Jesuits, 1st French school in Lebanon.
Aïn-Yagout (ĭn'-yägŏŏt'), village, Constantine dept., NE Algeria, on railroad and 20 mi. NE of Batna. The Medracen (5 mi. S) is a vast cylinder-shaped mausoleum of pre-Roman origin.
Ain Zalah, Ain Zala, or **Ain Zaleh** (ĭn' zä'lù), village, Mosul prov., N Iraq, 40 mi. NW of Mosul; oil wells.
'Ain Zehalta or **'Ayn Zahalta** (ĭn' zĕhăl'tä), Fr. *Aïn Zhalta*, village (pop. 1,446), central Lebanon, 14 mi. SE of Beirut; alt. 4,000 ft.; health resort; sericulture, cereals, fruits. Has Assyrian ruins.
Ainzón (īn-thōn'), town (pop. 1,871), Saragossa prov., NE Spain, 2 mi. SSE of Borja; mfg. of alcohol, knit goods; olive-oil, flour, wine making.
Aio (ī'ō), town (pop. 10,831), Yamaguchi prefecture, SW Honshu, Japan, on Suo Sea, 11 mi. SSW of Yamaguchi; fishing port; rice-growing center; metalworking.
Aioi, Japan: see O-o.
Aion Island or **Ayon Island** (īôn'), tundra-covered island in NW Chaun Bay of E. Siberian Sea, NE Siberian Russian SFSR; site of govt. arctic station; 70°N 169°E. Forms part of Chukchi Natl. Okrug, Khabarovsk Territory.
Aïoun, El (ĕl äyŏŏn'), town (pop. 2,488), Oujda region, NE Fr. Morocco, on railroad and 34 mi. WSW of Oujda; flour and wool market; esparto processing. Manganese deposit 15 mi. S.
Aïoun du Dra, El (dü drä'), Saharan military outpost, Agadir frontier region, southwesternmost Fr. Morocco, near the Oued Dra (border of Spanish Southern Protectorate of Morocco), 100 mi. SW of Tiznit; 28°31'N 10°42'W.

Aïoun-el-Atrouss or **Aioun el Atrous** (both: ĕl ätrōōs'), village, SE Mauritania, Fr. West Africa, in the Sahara, 450 mi. E of Saint-Louis, Senegal. Trades in gum arabic. Stock raising (camels, cattle, sheep, goats).

Aipe (ī'pā), town (pop. 1,920), Huila dept., S central Colombia, landing on left bank of upper Magdalena R., opposite Villavieja, and 20 mi. N of Neiva; rice, cacao, coffee, livestock. Anc. Indian market town. Famed for undeciphered hieroglyphic inscriptions. Gold, silver, copper, coal, and petroleum deposits near by.

Ai-Petri or **Ay-Petri** (ī-pyĕ'trē), W section of Crimean Mts., S Crimea, Russian SFSR; 10 mi. long. Rises to 4,045 ft. at the Ai-Petri, 2 mi. NNW of Alupka.

Aiquile (īkē'lā), town (pop. c.9,000), ⊙ Campero prov., Cochabamba dept., central Bolivia, on S outlier of Cordillera de Cochabamba and 90 mi. SE of Cochabamba, on Camiri-Tintín oil pipe line; alt. 7,277 ft. Junction point of highways from Cochabamba to Sucre and Santa Cruz; agr. products (corn, fruit, vegetables). Sugar cane in valley of Mizque R. (E).

Aïr (īr) or **Azbine** (äzbē'nā), low massif and region of the Sahara, in N Niger territory, Fr. West Africa, continuing the Ahaggar massif southward. Rises to 5,900 ft. There are several oases; chief settlement is Agadez, 17°N 7°57'W. A former kingdom of the Tuaregs, region is now of little importance. Sometimes Asben.

Aira (ī'rä), village, Wallaga prov., W central Ethiopia, near Birbir R., 12 mi. NNW of Yubdo; mining (iron, gold).

Aira Force, England: see ULLSWATER.

Airag Nur, Mongolia: see AIRIK NOR.

Airaines (ārĕn'), village (pop. 1,072), Somme dept., N France, 11 mi. SE of Abbeville; linen bag mfg. Ruins of 2 castles, Roman entrenchments near by.

Airak Nor, Mongolia: see AIRIK NOR.

Airão (īrã'ō), town (pop. 165), NE Amazonas, Brazil, landing on right bank of the Rio Negro and 120 mi. NW of Manaus; rubber. Formerly Ayrão.

Airdrie (âr'drē), village (pop. 198), S Alta., on Nose Creek and 18 mi. N of Calgary; wheat.

Airdrie, burgh (1931 pop. 26,734; 1951 census 30,308), N Lanark, Scotland, 11 mi. E of Glasgow; coal mines, metal foundries, boilerworks, paper mills, biscuit factories. Free library was 1st established in Scotland.

Airds, The (ârdz), district of N Argyll, Scotland, bet. lochs Linnhe (N) and Creran (S), noted for scenic beauty.

Airds Moss, boggy region of central Ayrshire, Scotland, bet. Ayr R. and Lugar Water; c.5 mi. long, 3 mi. wide.

Aire, river, England: see AIRE RIVER.

Aire (âr'). **1** or **Aire-sur-l'Adour** (-sür-lädōōr'), town (pop. 2,431), Landes dept., SW France, on the Adour and 18 mi. SE of Mont-de-Marsan; road center and livestock market; meat canning (pâté de foie gras), distilling, cement mfg. Has 12th–17th-cent. church. Episcopal see until 1933. **2** or **Aire-sur-la-Lys** (-lä-lēs'), town (pop. 4,660), Pas-de-Calais dept., N France, on the Lys (head of navigation) at junction of Aire–La Bassée and Neuf-fossé canals, and 10 mi. SE of Saint-Omer; agr. trade center (flax, tobacco, sugar beets, cereals). Mfg. (plumbing fixtures, hosiery, beer); petroleum refining. Many of its 16th-cent. bldgs. and its 15th-cent. Gothic church were heavily damaged in Second World War.

Aire, Isla del (ē'slä dhĕl ī'rā), islet off SE Minorca, Balearic Isls., 6 mi. S of Mahón.

Aireborough, urban district (1951 census pop. 27,533), West Riding, central Yorkshire, England, 5 mi. NE of Bradford; woolen milling. Rawdon and Yeardon inc. (1937) in Aireborough.

Airedale, England: see AIRE RIVER.

Aire–La Bassée Canal (âr–lä bäsā'), Pas-de-Calais dept., N France, connects the Lys (at Aire) with the Deûle (4 mi. E of La Bassée). Passes Béthune. Length, c.30 mi. Scene of fighting in First World War.

Aire River (âr), Yorkshire, England, rises 4 mi. NW of Settle, flows 70 mi. SE and E, past Skipton, Bingley, Leeds, and Castleford, to the Ouse above Goole. Receives Calder R. at Castleford. Navigable below Knottingley. Its industrial valley, known as Airedale, is the place of origin of the Airedale dog.

Aire River, Meuse and Ardennes dept., N France, rises 5 mi. ENE of Ligny-en-Barrois, flows 81 mi. NNW, along E slope of the Argonne, through defile of Grandpré, to the Aisne 8 mi. SE of Vouziers. Scene of fighting in First World War.

Aire-sur-l'Adour, France: see AIRE, Landes dept.

Aire-sur-La-Lys, France: see AIRE, Pas-de-Calais dept.

Airik Nor, Airag Nur, or **Ayrig Nuur** (all: ī'rŭkh nōr', nōōr'), shallow fresh-water lake (□ 45) of W Mongolian People's Republic, just S of lake Kirgis Nor (linked by channel); 48°51'N 93°35'E; 12 mi. long, 8 mi. wide, 3 ft. deep. Receives Dzabkhan R. Also spelled Airak Nor, Ayrik Nur, or Ayrag Nur. Another Airik Nor (or Airik Kul) is in China's Sinkiang prov., in the Dzungaria, 15 mi. NE of the lake Telli Nor; 46°N 85°45'E.

Ai River or **Ay River** (ī), E European Russian SFSR, rises in the S Urals NNE of Iremel mtn., flows N past Zlatoust, SW, and NW past Bolshe-Ustikinskoye, to Ufa R. 25 mi. S of Sarana; 160 mi. long. Lumber floating. Receives Ik (right) and Satka (left) rivers.

Airlie (âr'lē), parish (pop. 687), W Angus, Scotland. The modern Airlie Castle, 10 mi. W of Forfar, incorporates remains of earlier structure burned (1640) by Argyll.

Airmadidi or **Aermadidi** (īrmädē'dē), town, NE Celebes, Indonesia, 10 mi. SE of Menado; coconut-desiccation plant. Also spelled Ajermadidi.

Airobol, Turkey: see HAYRABOLU.

Airola (īrô'lä), town (pop. 4,918), Benevento prov., Campania, S Italy, 12 mi. E of Caserta, in fruit- and vegetable-growing region.

Airole (īrô'lĕ), village (pop. 610), Imperia prov., Liguria, NW Italy, near Fr. border, on Roya R. and 7 mi. N of Ventimiglia, in olive-growing region; customhouse. Has hydroelectric plant.

Airolo (īrô'lô), town (pop. 1,719), Ticino canton, S Switzerland, on Ticino R. and 26 mi. NNW of Locarno, 9 mi. from Ital. border, at S end of St. Gotthard pass and tunnel; alt. 3,756 ft. Near by are Ritom and Lucendro lakes.

Airport. 1 Village (pop. 7,866, with near-by La Lama), Stanislaus co., central Calif. **2** Village (pop. 1,028), Yakima co., S Wash. There is also an Air Port village in Spokane co. near Spokane.

Airport Drive, town (pop. 225), Jasper co., SW Mo.

Airth (ârth), agr. village and parish (pop. 2,226), E Stirling, Scotland, on the Forth estuary and 8 mi. ESE of Stirling. Near by is 16th-cent. Airth Castle, with 14th-cent. tower.

Airvault (ârvō'), village (pop. 1,525), Deux-Sèvres dept., W France, on Thouet R. and 13 mi. NNE of Parthenay; cementworks. Has 11th-13th-cent. Romanesque church, ruins of a cloister, and 12th-cent. bridge (damaged in Second World War) spanning the Thouet.

Airy, Cape, SW extremity of Cornwallis Isl., E central Franklin Dist., Northwest Territories, on Barrow Strait, at S entrance of McDougall Sound; 74°58'N 96°40'W.

Aisch River (īsh), Bavaria, Germany, rises 2 mi. SE of Burgbernheim, flows 41 mi. NE, past Neustadt, to the Regnitz 5 mi. NNW of Forchheim.

Aiscia (ī'shä), village (pop. 600), Harar prov., E central Ethiopia, near Fr. and Br. Somaliland borders, on railroad and 95 mi. NE of Diredawa, in arid lowland.

Aisén, Chile: see AYSÉN.

Aiserey (āzrā'), village (pop. 481), Côte-d'Or dept., E central France, on Burgundy Canal and 12 mi. SE of Dijon; beet-sugar refining; osier trade.

Aishihik, village, SW Yukon, on Aishihik L., 100 mi. NW of Whitehorse; 61°35'N 137°30'W; airfield; radio and weather station.

Aishihik Lake (40 mi. long, 1–5 mi. wide), SW Yukon, 75 mi. NW of Whitehorse; 61°30'N 137°47'W. Drains S into Lewes R.

Aisne (ĕn), department (□ 2,868; pop. 453,411), N France, occupying parts of Île-de-France, Picardy, and Champagne; ⊙ Laon. Touches on Belgium (NNE). Generally level. Drained by Oise, Aisne, Marne, Somme, and Sambre rivers, interconnected by canals. Diversified agr. (sugar beets, flax, wheat, oats, potatoes). Livestock raising and dairying in Vervins area. Textile industry centered at Saint-Quentin and Bohain; metallurgy at Hirson and Guise. Saint-Gobain has noted mirror factory. Sugar distilling, tanning, woodworking. Chief towns are Saint-Quentin, Soissons, and Laon. Dept. was in battle line throughout First World War. Fighting was particularly severe along Chemin des Dames ridge, in Saint-Quentin area, and in Château-Thierry sector, where American troops participated in a successful offensive (1918).

Aisne-Marne Canal (–märn'), Marne dept., N France, connects Aisne R. at Berry-au-Bac with Marne R. (NW of Chalons-sur-Marne). Paralleling the Vesle, it passes at Rheims.

Aisne River, in Marne, Ardennes, Aisne, and Oise depts., N France, rises near Vaubecourt (Meuse dept.), flows NNW along W slopes of the Argonne past Sainte-Menehould and Vouziers, thence W, past Rethel, and Soissons, to the Oise just above Compiègne; 175 mi. long. Paralleled by Ardennes Canal from Vouziers to Asfeld, thence by a lateral canal. Connected with the Oise by Oise-Aisne Canal, with the Marne by Aisne-Marne Canal. Receives Aire R. (right), Suippe and Vesle rivers (left). Was important battle line in First World War, particularly E of Soissons.

Aïssa, Djebel, Algeria: see KSOUR MOUNTAINS.

Aistersheim (ī'stŭrs-hīm), village (pop. 809), central Upper Austria, 13 mi. W of Wels; cattle; apples, pears.

Aistratis, Greece: see HAGIOS EUSTRATIOS.

Aït Amar (īt' ämär'), locality, Casablanca region, NW Fr. Morocco, 15 mi. NNW of Oued Zem; Morocco's only iron mine in operation after Second World War. Electrified rail spur to Casablanca–Oued Zem line completed 1937.

Aitape (ītä'pē), town, Sepik dist., Territory of New Guinea, NE New Guinea, 90 mi. W of Wewak, 540 mi. NW of Port Moresby.

Aith (āth), village on W coast of Mainland isl., Shetlands, Scotland, 12 mi. NW of Lerwick; fishing port; woolens.

Aitkin (ā'kĭn), county (□ 1,824; pop. 14,327), E central Minn.; ⊙ Aitkin. Agr. area drained by Mississippi R. and watered in SW by part of Mille Lacs L. Dairy products, potatoes, deposits of marl and peat. L. Minnewawa, Sandy L., and state forest in NE. Co. formed 1857.

Aitkin, resort village (pop. 2,079), ⊙ Aitkin co., central Minn., on Mississippi R., near Mille Lacs L., and 27 mi. NE of Brainerd, in grain and potato region; shipping point for dairy products, turkeys, fruit. Numerous lakes and state forest in vicinity. Settled 1870.

Aitolia, Greece: see AETOLIA.

Aitolikon (ĕtôlĭkôn'), town (pop. 4,351), Acarnania nome, W central Greece, 6 mi. NW of Missolonghi, on isl. in inlet of Missolonghi lagoon; connected by rail causeway with mainland; fishing and trading center. A Gr. resistance center in war of independence, it was besieged and captured (1826) by Turks. In independent Greece since 1832.

Aitos or **Aytos** (ī'tôs), city (pop. 9,972), Burgas dist., E Bulgaria, on S slope of Aitos Mts. (SE spur of E Balkan Mts.), 17 mi. NW of Burgas; agr. center. Has stone-cutting and agr. schools, ruins of 14th-cent. fortress.

Aït Ourir (īt' ōōrēr'), village, Marrakesh region, SW Fr. Morocco, at N foot of the High Atlas, 20 mi. ESE of Marrakesh; palm-fiber processing, salt-working. Residence of pasha of Marrakesh.

Aitutaki (ītōōtä'kē), coral atoll (c.3,900 acres; pop. 2,357), COOK ISLANDS, S Pacific, 140 mi. N of Rarotonga; 18°52'S 159°45'W; consists of some 8 islets; exports copra, fruits.

Aiud (äyōōd'), Hung. *Nagyened* (nŏ'dyĕ"nĕd), town (1948 pop. 9,535), Cluj prov., central Rumania, in Transylvania, on Mures R., on railroad and 17 mi. NNE of Alba-Iulia; center of winegrowing region; mfg. of cutlery, knitwear, clay products, paper goods; trade in wine, grain, livestock. Seat of Protestant Seminary. Founded in 12th cent.

Aiun or **El Aiun** (ĕl äyōōn'), town (pop. 143; urban dist. pop. 2,365), ⊙ Spanish Sahara and Saguia el Hamra, Sp. West Africa, on the Saguia el Hamra 35 mi. above its mouth on the Atlantic; 26°34'N 13°2'W. Barley, corn, vegetables. Offshore fisheries are chief source of income. Modern town established 1938. Also spelled Aiún.

Aiuruoca (äyōōrōō-ô'kŭ), city (pop. 1,240), S Minas Gerais, Brazil, on N slope of Serra da Mantiqueira 20 mi. E of Caxambu, in rich agr. dist. Varied mineral deposits (gold, titanium, nickel). Formerly spelled Ayuruoca.

Aivalik, Turkey: see AYVALIK.

Aivan-i-Kai or **Eyvan-e-Key** (āvän'-ĕ-kā'), town, Second Prov., in Teheran, N Iran, 35 mi. SE of Teheran and on highway to Meshed; fruit gardens; figs, pomegranates. Formerly spelled Aivan-i-Kaif.

Aiviekste River or **Ayviekste River** (ī'vyĕkstä), Ger. *Ewst*, E central Latvia, N outlet of Lubana L.; flows 80 mi. N and SW to Western Dvina R. at Gostini.

Aix, Île d' (ēl dĕks'), island (□ ½; pop. 132), in Bay of Biscay, Charente-Maritime dept., W France, bet. mouth of Charente R. and Île d'Oléron, 10 mi. S of La Rochelle. Has fortifications built by Vauban as part of Rochefort defenses. Here Napoleon surrendered (1815) to British, prior to his exile to St. Helena.

Aix-d'Angillon, Les (lāzĕks'-dã-zhēyō'), village (pop. 1,030), Cher dept., central France, 11 mi. NE of Bourges; small grains; woodworking.

Aix-en-Othe (ĕks-ãnôt'), village (pop. 1,739), Aube dept., NE central France, 17 mi. WSW of Troyes; hosiery mills.

Aix-en-Provence (–ã-prôvãs'), anc. *Aquae Sextiae*, town (pop. 32,076), Bouches-du-Rhône dept., SE France, near Arc R., 17 mi. NNE of Marseilles, in foothills of Provence Alps; spa and commercial center with important trade in almonds, olives, fruits, wines. Fruit preserving and candying, mfg. of felt hats, carpets, matches. Cultural and art center, with faculties of law and philosophy of Aix-Marseilles Univ. A seat of medieval literary activity, it is now a favorite sojourn for painters. Archi-episcopal see since 5th cent. Chief architectural sights are 13th-14th-cent. cathedral of Saint-Sauveur (tapestries, tryptich), baroque town hall, mus. of tapestries and fine arts. The centrally located *cours* Mirabeau is lined with numerous 17th–18th-cent. mansions. Aqueduct of Roquefavour (19th cent.) 7 mi. W. Founded c.122 B.C. by Romans on site of mineral springs. Here in 102 B.C. Marius defeated Teutons. Was ⊙ Provence (though several times replaced by Arles) until in 1486 estates-general of Provence met here to approve union with Fr. crown. Seat of prov. *parlement*, 1501–1789. Cézanne b. here. Locally called Aix.

Aixe-sur-Vienne (ĕks-sür-vyĕn'), town (pop. 2,298), Haute-Vienne dept., W central France, on Vienne R. and 6 mi. WSW of Limoges; mfg. (packing paper, hosiery, shoes, handmade lace, preserves). Favorite suburban resort of Limoges.

Aix-la-Chapelle, Germany: see AACHEN.

Aix-les-Bains (ĕks-lā-bē′), town (pop. 10,720), Savoie dept., SE France, 9 mi. N of Chambéry; alt. 850 ft. Famous Alpine health resort known for its mild climate, near E shore of Lac du Bourget, with modern thermal establishment, casino, and numerous hotels. Its sulphur and alum springs (113°-116°F) were known to Romans as *Aquae Gratianae* (ruins of Roman baths). Mont Revard (5,144 ft.), 4 mi. E, reached by road and rack-and-pinion railway, is winter sports center.

Aiya, Cape, or **Cape Ayya** (ī′ŭ), on S Black Sea coast of Crimea, Russian SFSR, 6 mi. SE of Balaklava; 44°27′N 33°41′E.

Aiyaion Pelagos, Greece: see AEGEAN SEA.

'Aiyat, El, or **Al-'Ayyat** (both: ĕl äyät′), village (pop. 5,523), Giza prov., Upper Egypt, on W bank of the Nile, on railroad, and 30 mi. S of Cairo; extensive sugar plantations; cotton ginning.

Aiyelet hash Shahar or **Ayelet Hashahar** (äyĕ′lĕt häshä′här), settlement (pop. 627), Upper Galilee, NE Israel, 6 mi. NE of Safad; dairying, horticulture, grain growing, poultry raising. Founded 1918; withstood (1948) heavy Arab attacks. Sometimes spelled Aiyelet ha Shahar or Ayelet Hashachar.

Aiyetoro (īyä′tōrō), town, Abeokuta prov., Western Provinces, SW Nigeria, 23 mi. WNW of Abeokuta; cotton weaving, indigo dyeing; palm oil and kernels, cotton.

Aiyina, Greece: see AEGINA.

Aiyinion, Greece, see AIGINION.

Aiyion, Greece: see AIGION.

Aizenay (äznā′), village (pop. 1,343), Vendée dept., W France, 10 mi. NW of La Roche-sur-Yon; road junction; pottery, brick- and tileworks.

Aizpute or **Ayzpute** (īz′pōōtā), Ger. *Hasenpoth*, city (pop. 3,418), W Latvia, in Kurzeme, 25 mi. NE of Liepaja (linked by narrow-gauge railroad); sawmilling, cardboard mfg., tanning, wool processing. Chartered 1378 by Livonian Knights.

Aja, Egypt: see AGA.

Aja, Jabal, Saudi Arabia: see SHAMMAR, JEBEL.

Ajabshir or **'Ajabshir** (äjäbshēr′), village, Fourth Prov., in Azerbaijan, NW Iran, on L. Urmia, 20 mi. WNW of Maragheh, and on railroad.

Ajaccio (ŭjä′chō, Fr. äzhäksyō′, It. äyät′chô), city (pop. 27,536), ⊙ Corsica, on island's W coast, port on the Mediterranean, 65 mi. SW of Bastia and 145 mi. SE of Nice, with shipping service to Marseilles and Nice; 41°55′N 8°42′E. Commercial center (wine, olive oil, citrus, timber, chestnuts) and popular winter resort beautifully situated near head of Gulf of Ajaccio (11 mi. wide, 12 mi. deep) in an amphitheater of hills. Mfg.: tobacco and flour products, furniture, corks, olive oil; distilling. Airport 4 mi. E. House where Napoleon I was born is now a mus. There are also a Napoleonic mus., and a fine arts mus. donated by Cardinal Fesch, Napoleon's uncle. Napoleon was baptized in 16th-cent. cathedral. Ajaccio was first town of Corsica to liberate itself from Ger. occupation in Sept., 1943.

Ajaigarh (ŭjī′gŭr), town (pop. 4,746), N Vindhya Pradesh, India, 13 mi. NNE of Panna; local agr. market (wheat, gram). Just S, on hill spur, is old fort (built c.9th cent.); withstood many attacks by Moguls and Mahrattas. Town was ⊙ former princely state of Ajaigarh (□ 788; pop. 96,596) of Central India agency; founded c.1730; since 1948, merged with Vindhya Pradesh.

Ajajú River, Colombia: see APAPORIS RIVER.

Ajak (ŏ′yŏk), town (pop. 3,044), Szabolcs co., NE Hungary, 22 mi. NE of Nyiregyhaza; tobacco, rye, potatoes; hogs.

Ajalpan (ähäl′pän), town (pop. 3,716), Puebla, central Mexico, 10 mi. SE of Tehuacán; alt. 4,068 ft.; agr. center (corn, rice, sugar, fruit, livestock).

Ajalvir (ähälvēr′), town (pop. 704), Madrid prov., central Spain, 13 mi. NE of Madrid; grain, olives, livestock.

Ajame (äzhä′mā), village, SE Ivory Coast, Fr. West Africa, 55 mi. ENE of Abidjan and 10 mi. N of Aboisso, linked by rail; coffee, cacao.

Ajanta (ŭjŭn′tŭ), village (pop. 3,560), Aurangabad dist., NW Hyderabad state, India, in Ajanta Hills, 50 mi. NNE of Aurangabad; cotton ginning. Famous Buddhist caves 5 mi. WNW, excavated in side of steep, 250-ft. ravine, consist of monasteries (largest, 84 sq. ft.) and shrines containing frescoes and sculpture depicting themes of Buddhist legend. Dating from c.200 B.C. to A.D. c.600, they provide a continuous narrative of Buddhist art.

Ajanta Hills, rugged E spur of N Western Ghats, central India; extend c.250 mi. in NE and SE curve through NW Hyderabad and SW Madhya Pradesh; drained by tributaries of Godavari (S) and Tapti (N) rivers; rise to over 4,000 ft. in higher (W) portion. Studded with Mahratta and Mogul hill forts.

Ajar, in Rus. names: see ADZHAR.

Ajara, Mount, Japan: see OWANI.

Ajasse (äjäshĕ′), town (pop. 7,376), Ilorin prov., Northern Provinces, SW Nigeria, 25 mi. SE of Ilorin; road center; shea-nut processing, cotton weaving, cattle raising.

Ajax Mountain, Mont.: see BITTERROOT RANGE.

Ajay River (ŭjī′), in Bihar and West Bengal, India, rises in NE Chota Nagpur Plateau foothills, in 2 headstreams joining 5 mi. S of Deoghar; flows c.160 mi. SSE and E, through rice-growing area, to Bhagirathi R. at Katwa.

Ajdir, Sp. Morocco: see ACHDIR.

Ajdir, Ras, or **Ras Agedir** (räs′ äjdēr′), headland of N Africa on the Mediterranean, marking Tunisia-Libya border, just SE of Ben Gardane (Tunisia).

Ajdovscina (ī′dôfshchēnä), Slovenian *Ajdovščina*, Ital. *Aidussina* (īdōōs-sē′nä), Ger. *Haidenschaft* (hī′dŭnshäft), anc. *Haidovium*, village (1936 pop. 1,186), W Slovenia, Yugoslavia, 31 mi. WSW of Ljubljana, in fertile Vipava R. valley. Rail terminus (line from Gorica); cotton spinning, timber trade. Until 1947, in Italy.

Ajena, Gold Coast: see VOLTA RIVER.

Ajermadidi, Indonesia: see AIRMADIDI.

Ajhur al-Kubra, Egypt: see AGHUR EL KUBRA.

Aji Chai, Iran: see TALKHEH RIVER.

Ajigasawa (äjĭgä′säwŭ), town (pop. 6,199), Aomori prefecture, N Honshu, Japan, 18 mi. NW of Hirosaki, rice-export port on Sea of Japan; rice and charcoal collection center.

Ajijic (ähēhēk′), town (pop. 2,041), Jalisco, central Mexico, on N shore of L. Chapala, 27 mi. SSE of Guadalajara; resort; grain, fruit, livestock.

Ajiki (ä″jē′kē), town (pop. 7,009), Chiba prefecture, central Honshu, Japan, 6 mi. NW of Narita; rice, raw silk.

Ajimi, Japan: see AJIMU.

Ajimu (ä″jē′mōō) or **Ajimi** (–mē), town (pop. 4,338), Oita prefecture, N Kyushu, Japan, 23 mi. NW of Oita; rice-growing center. Sometimes Ashimi.

Ajino (ä″jē′nō), town (pop. 11,775), Okayama prefecture, SW Honshu, Japan, on strait bet. Hiuchi and Harima seas, 14 mi. SW of Okayama; salt-making center. Includes (since early 1940s) former town of Akasaki. Sometimes spelled Azino.

Ajiro (ä″jē′rō), town (pop. 4,297), Shizuoka prefecture, central Honshu, Japan, on NE Izu Peninsula, on Sagami Sea, 4 mi. SSE of Atami; fishing port.

Ajjampur (ŭ′jŭmpŏor), town (pop. 3,716), Kadur dist., W central Mysore, India, 32 mi. NNE of Chikmagalur; cotton ginning, cattle breeding. Training center for revival of handspinning and -weaving.

Ajka (oi′kŏ), town (pop. 3,322), Veszprem co., NW central Hungary, in Bakony Mts., on Torna R. and 16 mi. W of Veszprem; agr. (potatoes, corn); coal mining; glassmaking. Major electric power plant.

'Ajlun (äjlōōn′), town (pop. c.2,000), Jordan, 28 mi. NNW of Amman; alt. 2,490 ft.; grain (wheat, millet), olives, vineyards. Hematite deposits.

Ajman or **'Ajman** (äjmăn′), sheikdom (□ 25; pop. 2,000) of TRUCIAL OMAN, on Persian Gulf, forming enclave in Sharja sheikdom. Consists of Ajman town (7 mi. NE of Sharja) and environs; pearling, fishing; dates.

Ajmer (ăjmēr′, ŭjmär′), chief commissioner's state (□ 2,425; 1951 pop. 692,506), NW India; ⊙ Ajmer. Consists of 2 detached areas surrounded by Rajasthan territory. Larger W section crossed by Aravalli Range, especially SW strip (Merwara) where hills rise to c.3,000 ft. Drained by headstreams of Luni R. (flowing SW) and by tributaries of Banas R. (flowing E). Crops include millet, corn, wheat, barley, cotton. Textile milling at Ajmer and Beawar; cotton ginning, hand-loom weaving. Mica, feldspar, and building-stone deposits worked. Pushkar is noted pilgrimage center. Area settled c.11th cent. by Chauhan Rajputs; annexed to Delhi kingdom (Slave dynasty) in early 13th cent.; under Moslem rulers of Malwa, 1470–1531. A Mogul stronghold from mid-16th to late-17th cent.; held by Mahrattas in late-18th cent. until 1818, when ceded to British. Made chief commissioner's prov. in 1871; known as Ajmer-Merwara. In 1950, constituted a chief commissioner's state. Chief languages: Rajasthani, Hindi. Sometimes spelled Ajmere.

Ajmer, city (pop. 147,258), ⊙ Ajmer state, India, 215 mi. SW of New Delhi, in Aravalli Range; rail junction (large workshops); trade center (grain, salt, cotton, wool, cloth fabrics, mica); agr. market (millet, wheat, maize, oilseeds). Cotton, woolen, and oilseed milling, cotton ginning, mfg. (hosiery, soap, shoes, saddlery, pharmaceutical products, ice, inks, electric wire), handicraft cloth weaving and dyeing, wood carving; printing presses. City lies at foot of prominent hill fort (SW; alt. c.2,850 ft.). Contains several noted bldgs., including ruined 12th-cent. mosque, tomb of 13th-cent. Moslem saint (visited by pilgrims), Akbar's palace (now used as mus.), and some marble pavilions built by Shah Jahan on edge of lake (NW). Mayo Col. (opened 1875) is SE. According to tradition, founded A.D. c.145, but more probably c.1100 by a Chauhan Rajput; sacked 1193 by Muhammad of Ghor. Was popular retreat and military base against Rajputs for Mogul emperors; here, in 1616, Jahangir received Sir Thomas Roe, ambassador of James I.

Ajo (ä′hō), village (pop. 1,164), Santander prov., N Spain, near the Bay of Biscay, 10 mi. ENE of Santander; corn, cattle, lumber. Cape Ajo is near by; 43°31′N 3°36′W.

Ajo (ä′hō), village (pop. 5,817), Pima co., SW Ariz., 87 mi. SW of Phoenix; health resort; smelting center. Copper, gold, silver, and lead mines near by. Organ Pipe Cactus Natl. Monument is S.

Ajodhya (ŭjōd′yŭ), since 1948 officially **Ayodhya** (ŭyōd′yŭ), E suburb of FYZABAD city, Fyzabad dist., E central Uttar Pradesh, India, on the Gogra; rail junction. Regarded as one of 7 most sacred Hindu centers in India (3 large annual melas); mentioned as a great city in the Ramayana, when it was ⊙ Kosala kingdom under Rama Chandra. Restored A.D. c.400 by King Vikramaditya (Chandragupta II) of Ujjain; became chief city of Gupta empire. Noted temples include Hanuman's temple (16th-cent. mosque near by, built on anc. Hindu temple sites associated with life of Rama) and Jain temples (5 of which mark birthplace of 5 early Jain canonists or *tirthankaras*). Formerly called Awadh (gave its name to OUDH).

Ajofrín (ähōfrēn′), town (pop. 1,997), Toledo prov., central Spain, 11 mi. S of Toledo; olives, grapes, cereals, potatoes, sheep; tanning, cheese processing, wine making.

Ajoupa-Bouillon (äzhōōpä′-bōōyō′), town (pop. 475), N Martinique, at E foot of Mont Pelée, 15 mi. NNW of Fort-de-France; sugar growing, rum distilling.

Ajra (ŭj′rŭ), village, Kolhapur dist., S Bombay, India, 40 mi. S of Kolhapur; rice, sesame, cashew nuts; trades in teak, sandalwood, myrobalans.

Ajrestan, Afghanistan: see UJRISTAN.

Ajuchitlán (ähōōchētlän′), officially Ajuchitlán del Progreso, town (pop. 2,656), Guerrero, SW Mexico, on the Río de las Balsas and 18 mi. SE of Altamirano. Cereals, cotton, sugar cane, fruit.

Ajudá, São João Baptista de: see SÃO JOÃO BAPTISTA DE AJUDÁ; OUIDAH.

Ajusco (ähōō′skō), town (pop. 1,123), Federal Dist., central Mexico, at NE foot of Cerro Ajusco, 15 mi. S of Mexico city; cereals, vegetables, fruit, livestock.

Ajusco, Cerro (sĕ′rō), extinct volcano (c.12,900 ft.) in Federal Dist., central Mexico, 19 mi. SSW of Mexico city. Its last eruption, believed to have taken place c.5,000 B.C., buried part of the anc. Cuicuilco pyramid near Tlalpan. One of the nearby NE craters (Xitli) has shown recent activity. The peak is in the Sierra de Ajusco, which forms part of S wall of the central plateau.

Ajuterique (ähōōtärē′kā), town (pop. 1,325), Comayagua dept., W central Honduras, 7 mi. SW of Comayagua; truck produce, onions. Pop. largely Indian.

Ajuy (ä′hwē), town (1939 pop. 2,047; 1948 municipality pop. 17,448), Iloilo prov., E Panay isl., Philippines, on Guimaras Strait, 33 mi. SE of Capiz; agr. center (sugar cane, rice, coconuts); sugar milling.

Ak, Turkey: for rivers see AKCAY and AKSU; for peaks see AK DAG.

Akaba, town, JORDAN: see AQABA.

Akaba (äkä′bä), village, S Fr. Togoland, on railroad and 30 mi. N of Atakpamé; cacao, palm oil and kernels, cotton; its rail station is c.2 mi. S.

Akabira (äkä′bērä) or **Akahira** (–hērä), town (pop. 40,287), W central Hokkaido, Japan, 22 mi. SW of Asahigawa; coal-mining center.

Akademiya Nauk Range (ŭkŭdyä′mēŭ nŭōōk′) [Rus.,=academy of sciences], highest branch in central Pamir-Alai mtn. system, on border of Gorno-Badakhshan Autonomous Oblast and Garm Oblast, Tadzhik SSR. At its junction with Peter the First Range is STALIN PEAK, highest point of USSR. Other peaks over 20,000 ft. high include Molotov and Kaganovich peaks (S), Voroshilov and Kalinin peaks (N). Many glaciers, including FEDCHENKO GLACIER (E).

Akae, Japan: see MIYAZAKI, city.

Akahira, Japan: see AKABIRA.

Akaho (ä″kä′hō), town (pop. 19,342), Nagano prefecture, central Honshu, Japan, on Tenryu R. and 34 mi. S of Matsumoto, in forested area; spinning.

'Akaika or **'Ukaykah** (both: äkī′kŭ), town, Muntafiq prov., SE Iraq, at W extremity of the lake Hor al Hammar, 18 mi. ESE of Nasiriya; dates. Also spelled Akika.

Akaike (ä″kä′ēkä), town (pop. 14,686), Fukuoka prefecture, N Kyushu, Japan, 11 mi. S of Yawata; coal-mining center. Formerly Agano.

Akaishi, Mount (äkī′shē), Jap. *Akaishi-dake* (10,296 ft.), central Honshu, Japan, on Nagano-Shizuoka prefecture border, 27 mi. WSW of Kofu; alpine flora.

Akalgarh (ä′kŭlgŭr), town (pop. 6,546), Gujranwala dist., E Punjab, W Pakistan, 22 mi. WNW of Gujranwala; local trade in wheat, rice, millet; rice husking and milling.

Akalkot (ŭkŭl′kōt), town (pop. 13,810), Sholapur dist., E Bombay, India, 22 mi. SE of Sholapur; road center; agr. market (millet, peanuts, wheat, cotton); cotton ginning, hand-loom weaving, hosiery and match mfg., oilseed milling. Was ⊙ former princely state of Akalkot (□ 473; pop. 103,903) in Deccan States, Bombay; inc. 1949 into Sholapur and Satara North dists., Bombay.

Akama (ä″kä′mä), town (pop. 6,107), Fukuoka prefecture, N Kyushu, Japan, 18 mi. NNE of Fukuoka; coal mining.

Akamagaseki, Japan: see SHIMONOSEKI, city.

Akana (ä″kä′nä), town (pop. 2,986), Shimane prefecture, SW Honshu, Japan, 26 mi. S of Izumo; rice, timber, livestock.

Akan National Park, Japan: see KUTCHARO, LAKE.
Akanthou (äkänthōō'), town (pop. 1,790), Famagusta dist., NE Cyprus, at N foot of Kyrenia Mts., near the coast, 27 mi. NE of Nicosia; carobs, olive oil; sheep, goats. Noted Kantara castle and resort is 10 mi. E.
Akaoka (ä"kä'ôkä), town (pop. 6,079), Kochi prefecture, S Shikoku, Japan, on Tosa Bay, 12 mi. E of Kochi; rice, raw silk; spinning mill, fishery.
Akarai Mountains, Br. Guiana-Brazil: see ACARAÍ, SERRA.
Akarmara, Georgian SSR: see TKVARCHELI.
Akarnania, Greece: see ACARNANIA.
Akaroa, county, New Zealand: see DUVAUCHELLE.
Akaroa (ăkûrō'û), borough (pop. 487) and harbor, E S.Isl., New Zealand, on Banks Peninsula, 25 mi. SE of Christchurch; summer resort; dairying, fruitgrowing center.
Akarp (ō'kärp"), Swedish *Åkarp*, village (pop. 1,280), Malmohus co., S Sweden, 6 mi. NE of Malmo; grain, potatoes, stock. Has agr. col.
Akasaka (äkä'säkü). **1** Town (pop. 2,129), Aichi prefecture, central Honshu, Japan, 8 mi. NW of Toyohashi; rice, raw silk. **2** Town (pop. 6,602), Gifu prefecture, central Honshu, Japan, 2 mi. NW of Ogaki, in rice-growing area; pottery making.
Akasaki (äkä'sä'kē). **1** Town, Okayama prefecture, Japan: see AJINO. **2** Town (pop. 5,246), Tottori prefecture, SW Honshu, Japan, on Sea of Japan, 19 mi. ENE of Yonago; fishing port.
Akashi (ä"kä'shē), city (1940 pop. 47,751; 1947 pop. 57,390), Hyogo prefecture, S Honshu, Japan, on strait bet. Harima Sea and Osaka Bay, 15 mi. W of Kobe. Industrial center; engineering works, chemical plants, textile mills; fish canning. Bombed (1945) in Second World War.
Akaska (ûkă'skû), town (pop. 84), Walworth co., N central S.Dak., 13 mi. SSW of Selby.
Akassa (äkä'sä), town, Owerri prov., Eastern Provinces, S Nigeria, minor port on Gulf of Guinea, at mouth of Nun channel of Niger R. delta, 14 mi. W of Brass; 4°15'N 6°5'E. Exports palm oil and kernels, hardwood. Lighthouse. In late 19th cent., a major port and hq. of Royal Niger Co.
Akatani (äkä'tänē), village (pop. 4,165), Niigata prefecture, N Honshu, Japan, 20 mi. ESE of Niigata; mining (coal, gold, silver, copper, iron).
Akayu (ä"kä'yōō), town (pop. 9,027), Yamagata prefecture, N Honshu, Japan, 10 mi. NNE of Yonezawa, in fruitgrowing area (grapes, cherries); wine making. Ski resort. Hot springs near by.
Ak-Baital, river, Tadzhik SSR: see MURGAB RIVER.
Akbarabad, India: see AGRA, city.
Akbarpur (ŭk'bŭrpŏŏr). **1** Village, Cawnpore dist., S Uttar Pradesh, India, 25 mi. WSW of Cawnpore; gram, wheat, jowar, barley, mustard. **2** Town (pop. 7,376), Fyzabad dist., E central Uttar Pradesh, India, on Tons R. and 35 mi. SE of Fyzabad; handloom cotton weaving; trades in rice, wheat, gram, oilseeds, hides. Fort ruins contain 16th-cent. mosque.
Akbou (äkbōō'), village (pop. 2,330), Constantine dept., NE Algeria, in the Oued Soummam valley bet. Great and Little Kabylia, 36 mi. SW of Bougie; olive and fig growing, olive-oil pressing.
Ak-Bulak (äk"-bōōläk'), town (1948 pop. over 10,000), S Chkalov oblast, Russian SFSR, near Ilek R., on Trans-Caspian RR and 27 mi. ESE of Sol-Iletsk; lignite mining; flour milling, metalworking.
Akcaabat (äkchä'äbät"), Turkish *Akçaabat*, village (pop. 4,414), Trebizond prov., NE Turkey, on Black Sea, 9 mi. W of Trebizond; corn, tobacco. Formerly Polathane.
Akcadag (äkchädä'), Turkish *Akçadağ*, village (pop. 3,540), Malatya prov., E central Turkey, 18 mi.W of Malatya; wheat, barley, rice, millet, tobacco. Formerly Arga.
Akcakara Dag (äkchä"kärä' dä"), Turkish *Akçakara Dağ*, peak (9,645 ft.), E central Turkey, in Bitlis Mts., 31 mi. W of Mus.
Akcakoca (äkchä'kôjä"), Turkish *Akçakoca*, village (pop. 3,494), Bolu prov., NW Turkey,on Black Sea 35 mi. NW of Bolu; grain, flax, mohair goats. Formerly Akcasehir.
Akcasehir, Turkey: see AKCAKOCA.
Akcay (äkchī') or **Ak River,** Turkish *Akçay*, stream, SW Turkey, rises in Mentese Mts. 35 mi. E of Mugla, flows 85 mi. NW, past Bozdogan, to Buyuk Menderes R. 8 mi. SW of Nazilli.
Akchatau (ŭkchŭtou'), town (1944 pop. over 500), SE Karaganda oblast, Kazakh SSR, c.90 mi. NNW of Balkhash; molybdenum- and tungsten-mining center. Developed during Second World War.
Akche or **Aqche** (äkchä'), Chinese *Akoki* or *A-k'o-ch'i* (both: ä'kûchē'), town, ⊙ Akche co. (pop. 11,482), W Sinkiang prov., China, near USSR border, at S foot of the Kokshaal-Tau, on Kokshaal R. (headstream of the Aksu) and 120 mi. W of Aksu; cattle raising; grain.
Akchi-Karasu, Kirghiz SSR: see MUZTOR.
Ak Dag (äk'dä), Turkish *Ak Dağ*. **1** Peak (6,665 ft.), Amasya prov., N Turkey, 10 mi. N of Amasya. **2** Peak (10,125 ft.), Antalya prov., SW Turkey, in Bey Mts., 37 mi. SW of Antalya. **3** Peak (10,021 ft.), Antalya prov., SW Turkey, in Elmali Mts., 65 mi. WSW of Antalya. **4** Peak (8,035 ft.), Denizli prov., SW Turkey, 13 mi. E of Civril, overlooking Buyuk Menderes R. **5** Peak (7,011 ft.) and range, central Turkey, on Yozgat-Sivas prov. line, 10 mi. SE of Akdagmadeni, overlooking the Kizil Irmak. Karababa Dag (7,693 ft.) is highest in the range, which stretches 85 mi. along the river. Antimony.
Akdagmadeni (äkdä'mädĕ"nē), Turkish *Akdağmadeni*, village (pop. 2,458), Yozgat prov., central Turkey, 60 mi. SSE of Yozgat; lead mines; mohair goats.
Ak-Darya or **Ak-Dar'ya** (äk"-dŭryä'), village, S Samarkand oblast, Uzbek SSR, near the Ak Darya (S arm of Zeravshan R.), 20 mi. NW of Samarkand; cotton; metalworks.
Ak Darya, river, Uzbek SSR: see ZERAVSHAN RIVER.
Ak-Dzhar, Kazakh SSR: see AKZHAR.
Aké (äkā'), Maya ruins in Yucatan, SE Mexico, 20 mi. E of Mérida.
Akechi (ä"kā'chē), town (pop. 4,025), Gifu prefecture, central Honshu, Japan, 15 mi. E of Tajimi; spinning; pottery.
Akeley, resort village (pop. 525), Hubbard co., N central Minn., 17 mi. ENE of Park Rapids, near Leech L., in livestock area; dairy products.
Aken (ä'kûn), town (pop. 14,624), in former Prussian Saxony prov., central Germany, after 1945 in Saxony-Anhalt, port on the Elbe and 8 mi. W of Dessau; mfg. of light metals, bricks; sugar refining, shipbuilding.
Akershus (ä'kûrs-hōōs"), county [Nor. *fylke*] (□ 1,895; pop. 170,133), SE Norway; extraterritorial ⊙ Oslo. Extends N from Oslo Fjord to S end of L. Mjosa. Includes residential and industrial suburbs of Oslo; also Drobak city, Gardermoen airport, and historic Eidsvoll village. Shipping and mfg. industries are important. Aker canton, formerly part of Akershus, was inc. with Oslo co. in 1948.
Akersloot (ä'kûrslōt), village (pop. 1,514), North Holland prov., NW Netherlands, on Alkmaar L. and 5 mi. S of Alkmaar; cattle raising, dairying.
Akers styckebruk (ō"kûrs stü'kûbrük"), Swedish *Åkers styckebruk*, village (pop. 805), Sodermanland co., E Sweden, 8 mi. SSE of Strangnas; rail junction; iron- and steelworks. Gun foundry founded here 1866.
Aketi (äkĕ'tē), town (1948 pop. 8,194), Eastern Prov., N Belgian Congo, on Itimbiri R. and 60 mi. W of Buta; railroad terminus and river port, transshipment point for agr. produce of Uele area (notably cotton). Cotton ginning, palm-oil milling, rice processing, mfg. of soap; repair of automobiles. Rubber and coffee plantations in vicinity. Has R.C. mission and schools, hosp. for Europeans. Aketi port, called Port-Chaltin, dates from 1925.
Akhaia, Greece: see ACHAEA.
Akhali-Afoni (ŭkhä'lyē-ŭfô'nyē), Rus. *Novy Afon* or *Novyy Afon*, town (1939 pop. over 500), NW Abkhaz Autonomous SSR, Georgian SSR, port on Black Sea, 11 mi. NW of Sukhumi; health resort; citrus fruit, tobacco. Until 1948, Psirtskha.
Akhalkalaki (ŭkhäl"kŭlä'kē) [Georgian,=new city], city (1926 pop. 3,475; largely Armenian), S Georgian SSR, in the Lesser Caucasus, on small right affluent of the Kura, 70 mi. WSW of Tiflis, near Turkish border. Road center in livestock and potato-growing dist.; metalworking, woolen milling; limestone works. Founded in early 11th cent; passed (15th cent.) to Turks and (1829) to Russia. Formerly called Akhalkalak.
Akhalkhevi (ŭkhŭlkhyĕ'vē), village, NE Georgian SSR, on upper Argun R., on N slope of the Greater Caucasus, and 65 mi. S of Grozny; livestock, hardy grain. Until 1944 (in former Chechen-Ingush Autonomous SSR), called Itum-Kale.
Akhal-Senaki, Georgian SSR: see MIKHA TSKHAKAYA.
Akhaltsikhe (ŭkhŭltsē'khyĭ), city (1926 pop. 12,328), SW Georgian SSR, in the Lesser Caucasus, in upper Kura R. valley, on railroad and 45 mi. SSE of Kutaisi, near Turkish border. Lignite-mining center (since middle 1940s); sawmilling, handicraft industry (metal, silver, and silk goods); orchards. Site of old Turkish fortress. Strategic point at entrance to Kura valley. Until 1936, spelled Akhaltsikh.
Akhan-Garan (ŭkhän"-gŭrän'), village, S Tashkent oblast, Uzbek SSR, on Angren R. and 30 mi. SE of Tashkent; cotton, rice.
Akharnai, Greece: see ACHARNAI.
Akhaura (ŭkou'rŭ), village, Tippera dist., E East Bengal, E Pakistan, on arm of Meghna R. and 28 mi. N of Comilla; rail junction (spur to Ashuganj); jute-pressing center; rice, jute, oilseeds.
Akhdar, Gebel el, or **Gebel el Achdar** (jĕ'bĕl ĕl äkhdär') [Arabic,=green mountain], plateau (average alt. 2,000 ft.) in W Cyrenaica, Libya, W of Derna; c.100 mi. long, 20 mi. wide; rises to 2,870 ft. S of Beda Littoria. Has scattered, stunted evergreen groves. Occupies center of lower, more extensive plateau (average alt. 1,000 ft.) which rises sharply from narrow coastal plain (N) and descends gradually to the Sahara (S). Annual rainfall (mostly in winter), over 16 in.; around Cyrene, 20–24 in. This is the most promising area of Cyrenaica. Here Italians founded (1930s) the agr. settlements of Baracca, Maddalena, Oberdan, Beda Littoria, Berta, and Luigi di Savoia. Principal products: wheat, barley, olives, grapes, almonds, livestock (sheep, goats). Crossed (E-W) by roads; Barce-Benghazi railroad in W. Scene of many battles (1941–42) bet. Axis and British in Second World War.
Akhdar, Jabal, or **Jabal Akhdhar** (jă'băl), highest range of Oman, rising to 9,900 ft. in the Jabal Sham, 85 mi. WSW of Muscat. Limestone formation.
Akheloos River, Greece: see ACHELOUS RIVER.
Akheron River, Greece: see ACHERON RIVER.
Akhetaton, Egypt: see TEL EL AMARNA.
Akhinos, Greece: see ACHINOS.
Akhiok (ăk'hēŏk"), village (pop. 72), S Alaska, SW Kodiak Isl., on Alitak Bay (30 mi. long, 9 mi. wide at mouth), 90 mi. SW of Kodiak; 56°56'N 154°10'W. Aleut fishing village; cannery. Has Russian Orthodox church. Formerly also called Alitak (ă'lĭtăk).
Akhiolu, Bulgaria: see POMORIYE.
Akhirokhorion, Greece: see NEA VYSSE.
Akhisar (äk"hĭsär'), anc. *Thyatira*, town (1950 pop. 23,579), Manisa prov., W Turkey, on railroad and 31 mi. NE of Manisa; manganese; tobacco, olives, raisins, valonia, wheat, barley, cotton. Sometimes spelled Akhissar. Anc. Thyatira, a city of Lydia, was one of the Seven Churches in Asia addressed by St. John.
Akhmedly (ŭkhmyĭdlē'), town (1939 pop. over 500) in Shaumyan dist. of Greater Baku, Azerbaijan SSR, on S Apsheron Peninsula, 6 mi. E of Baku; vineyards, truck produce.
Akhmeta (ŭkhmyĕ'tŭ), village (1939 pop. over 2,000), E Georgian SSR, near Alazan R., 17 mi. NW of Telavi, in forest dist.
Akhmim (äkhmēm'), anc. *Chemmis* and *Panopolis*, town (pop. 32,071), Girga prov., Upper Egypt, on E bank of the Nile and 13 mi. NW of Girga, 55 mi. SSE of Asyut; wool and silk weaving, pottery making, sugar refining; cotton, cereals, sugar cane, dates. Sometimes spelled Ekhmim.
Akhnur (ŭk'nŏŏr), town (pop. 3,398), Jammu dist., SW Kashmir, on Chenab R. and 14 mi. NNW of Jammu; trades in timber (chir, deodar), wheat, rice, bajra, corn. Large fort, built c.1780.
Akhouat, El- (ĕl-äkhwät'), village, Teboursouk dist., N central Tunisia, 14 mi. S of Teboursouk; wheat-storage depot. Lead, zinc, and iron mining.
Akhsu (ŭkhsōō'), village (1926 pop. 548), E Azerbaijan SSR, 80 mi. W of Baku; highway junction in cotton and wheat area.
Akhta, Armenian SSR: see NIZHNYAYA AKHTA.
Akhtala (ŭkhtŭlä'), town (1939 pop. over 500), N Armenian SSR in the Lesser Caucasus, on railroad and 7 mi. ENE of Alaverdi; copper mining. Has 13th-cent. cathedral. Until 1939, Nizhnyaya Akhtala.
Akhtanizov Liman (ŭkhtŭnyē'zŭf lyĭmän'), lagoon on Sea of Azov coast, W Krasnodar Territory, Russian SFSR, just W of Temryuk; 14 mi. long, 4 mi. wide. Receives arm of lower Kuban R.
Akhtarayn, Syria: see AKHTERIN.
Akhtari, Russian SFSR: see PRIMORSKO-AKHTARSKAYA.
Akhtar Liman (ŭkhtär' lyĭmän'), inlet of Sea of Azov, Krasnodar Territory, Russian SFSR, just W of Primorsko-Akhtarskaya; 4 mi. wide, 8 mi. long. Receives branches of Protoka arm of lower Kuban R.
Akhteboli, Bulgaria: see AKHTOPOL.
Akhterin (äkhtĕrēn') or **Akhtarayn** (äkhtärān'), *Fr. Aktérine*, village, Aleppo prov., NW Syria, near Turkish border, on railroad and 25 mi. NNE of Aleppo; pistachios, cereals.
Akhtiar, Russian SFSR: see SEVASTOPOL.
Akhtme, Estonia: see AHTME.
Akhtopol (äkh'tôpôl, äkhtô'–), anc. *Agathopolis*, city (pop. 1,052), Burgas dist., SE Bulgaria, fishing port on Black Sea, 34 mi. SE of Burgas, near Turkish border; lumber and charcoal exports. Has ruins of Hellenic town with fortress and 2 churches. Called Akhteboli under Turkish rule (15th–19th cent.).
Akhtuba River (ŭkhtōō'bŭ), E arm of lower Volga R., in S European Russian SFSR, leaves main stream 13 mi. NE of Stalingrad, flows 320 mi. SE, parallel to the Volga, through Volga-Akhtuba flood plain (fertile vegetable- and melon-growing region), past Vladimirovka, Sasykoli, and Kharabali, through Volga R. delta, to Caspian Sea 50 mi. E of Astrakhan. Navigable in spring; fisheries. Its lower course, called Bigach, is main easternmost arm of Volga R. delta.
Akhty (ŭkhtē'), village (1926 pop. 3,886), S Dagestan Autonomous SSR, Russian SFSR, in the E Greater Caucasus, on Samur R. and 50 mi. SW of Derbent; health resort (hot sulphur springs near by); rug weaving; grain, irrigated orchards. Pop. largely Lezghian. An important fortress in Caucasian wars in mid-19th cent.
Akhtyrka (ŭkhtĭr'kŭ), city (1926 pop. 26,982), SE Sumy oblast, Ukrainian SSR near Vorskla R., 40 mi. S of Sumy; rail terminus; flour-milling center; metalworks. Founded by Poles; passed (1640s) to Russia.
Akhuryan (ŭkhōōryän'), village (1939 pop. over 2,000), NW Armenian SSR, 3 mi. E of Leninakan; wheat, sugar beets. Pumice and diatomite deposits near by. Until 1945, Duzkend.
Akhuryan River, Armenian SSR: see ARPA-CHAI.

Akhyritou (äkhērē'tōō), village (pop. 947), Famagusta dist., E Cyprus, 5 mi. W of Famagusta. Site of irrigation reservoir fed by Pedias R.
Akhyrokhorion, Greece: see Nea Vysse.
Akhziv, Palestine: see Achzib.
Aki (ä'kē), former province in SW Honshu, Japan; now part of Hiroshima prefecture.
Aki. 1 Town (pop. 11,913), Kochi prefecture, S Shikoku, Japan, on Tosa Bay, 21 mi. ESE of Kochi; rail terminus; mfg. center (silk textiles, sake, tea); lumber. **2** or **Aki-machi** (äkē'mächē), town (pop. 4,411), Oita prefecture, NE Kyushu, Japan, on E Kunisaki Peninsula, 17 mi. NNE of Oita, on Iyo Sea; rice, raw silk; lumber, bamboo, straw mats. Fishery.
Akiachak (äk'yŏŏchŭk, ăk'yŏŏchăk), Eskimo village (pop. 177), SW Alaska, on Kuskokwim R. and 15 mi. NE of Bethel; trapping. Sometimes spelled Akiachok.
Akiak (ă'kēăk"), Eskimo village (pop. 169), SW Alaska, on Kuskokwim R. and 22 mi. ENE of Bethel; trading and supply center; trapping; steamer landing.
Akid, India: see Colair Lake; Undi.
Akika, Iraq: see 'Akaika.
Akil (äkēl'), town (pop. 1,630), Yucatan, SE Mexico, 17 mi. SE of Ticul; henequen, sugar, fruit. Maya ruins near by.
Aki-machi, Japan: see Aki, Oita prefecture.
Akimiski Island (ăkĭmĭ'skē) (□ 898), SE Keewatin Dist., Northwest Territories, in James Bay, opposite mouths of Ekwan and Attawapiskat rivers; 53°N 81°W; 60 mi. long, 25 mi. wide.
Akimovka (ŭkē'mŭfkŭ), village (1926 pop. 5,562), SW Zaporozhe oblast, Ukrainian SSR, 14 mi. SW of Melitopol; flour mill, metalworks, railroad shops.
Akim Swedru (äkēm' swĕ'drōō), town, Eastern Prov., central Gold Coast colony, 6 mi. SW of Oda; gold mining.
Akita (ä"kē'tä), prefecture [Jap. *ken*] (□ 4,503; 1940 pop. 1,052,275; 1947 pop. 1,257,398), N Honshu, Japan; ⊙ Akita. Bounded W by Sea of Japan; generally mountainous terrain, drained by many small streams. Noshiro is chief port. Fertile lowlands produce rice, tobacco, soybeans, fruit. Extensive livestock raising and fishing. Major copper-mining area of Japan; limited mining of gold, silver, lead, zinc. Large oil field in Akita city area, on W coast.
Akita, city (1940 pop. 61,791; 1947 pop. 116,300), ⊙ Akita prefecture, N Honshu, Japan, port on Sea of Japan, at mouth of Omono R., 110 mi. NNW of Sendai; 39°43'N 140°8'E. Oil center (refineries); mfg. (silk textiles, metalwork). Principal exports: rice, oil. Fort was built here in 8th cent. for fighting against Ainus; important castle town in feudal period. Includes (since early 1940s) its former outer port Tsuchizakiminato (1940 pop. 18,047), and former towns of Araya (1940 pop. 6,686) and Terauchi (1940 pop. 5,260).
Akitio, New Zealand: see Pongaroa.
Akitsu (ä"kē'tsōō), town (pop. 16,487), Hiroshima prefecture, SW Honshu, Japan, on Inland Sea, 14 mi. ENE of Kure; includes (since early 1940s) former adjacent town of Mitsu (1940 pop. 5,242). Commercial center in rice-growing, stock-raising area; makes sake. Fishery.
Akividu, India: see Colair Lake; Undi.
Akiyoshi (äkē'yōshē), village (pop. 2,325), Yamaguchi prefecture, SW Honshu, Japan, 11 mi. WNW of Yamaguchi; tourist resort. Large cave with stalactites near by.
Akizuki (äkē'zōōkē), town (pop. 2,203), Fukuoka prefecture, N central Kyushu, Japan, 19 mi. SE of Fukuoka, near Amaki; rice, wheat, barley.
Akjoujt (äkzhōō'zhŭt), village, W central Mauritania, Fr. West Africa, 290 mi. NNE of Saint-Louis, Senegal, and 180 mi. ESE of Port-Étienne; millet, melons; goats, cattle, sheep.
Akka, Israel: see Acre.
Akka (äk-kä'), Saharan oasis and military outpost, Agadir frontier region, SW Fr. Morocco, in the Djebel Bani, 30 mi. SSW of Tata; 29°24'N 8°14'W.
Akkad or **Accad** (ă'kăd, ä'käd), region of Mesopotamia, occupying the N part of later Babylonia. The S part was Sumer. City-states began to appear in 4th millennium B.C. Akkad flourished after Sargon began (c.2800? B.C.) to spread wide his conquests, taking them from his capital, Agade (or the city of Akkad) to the Mediterranean shores and including Sumer. Later, Sumerians held sway, and the kingdom of Ur embraced both Akkad and Sumer. Elam took power toward end of 3d millennium, and by defeating the Elamites, Hammurabi was able to create Babylonia, which had its capital in Akkad.
Ak Kaleh, Iran: see Pahlevi Dezh.
Akkar or **'Akkar** (äk-kär'), village (pop. 1,583), N Lebanon, on Akkar R. and 25 mi. ENE of Tripoli; sericulture, cereals, oranges. Site of the famous castle of Akkar, built before 11th cent. and an important military objective for many centuries.
Akkerman, Ukrainian SSR: see Belgorod-Dnestrovski.
Akkermanovka, Russian SFSR: see Novo-Troitsk.
Akkeshi (äk-kä'shē) or **Atsukeshi** (ä"tsōōkä'shē), town (pop. 13,692), SE Hokkaido, Japan, fishing port on inlet of the Pacific, 24 mi. ENE of Kushiro; coal mining. Marine biological laboratory of Hokkaido Imperial Univ. here.
Akkoy, Turkey: see Bulancak.
Akkra, Gold Coast: see Accra.
Akkrum (ä'krŭm), town (pop. 2,376), Friesland prov., N Netherlands, 11 mi. S of Leeuwarden; dairying, mfg. (cattle feed, skates), meat packing.
Akkul or **Akkul'** (ŭkōōl'), village (1948 pop. over 2,000), W Dzhambul oblast, Kazakh SSR, on Assa R. and 55 mi. NW of Dzhambul; cotton, sheep.
Ak-Kurgan (äk"-kōōrgän'), village (1939 pop. over 500), S Tashkent oblast, Uzbek SSR, on Angren R. and 30 mi. SSW of Tashkent; cotton.
Aklavik (ăklä'vĭk), village (pop. estimate 200; district pop. 757), NW Mackenzie Dist., Northwest Territories, near Yukon border, on W channel of Mackenzie R. delta, 60 mi. SE of its mouth on Mackenzie Bay of the Beaufort Sea; 68°13'N 135°1'W; trading center for Northwest Territories Arctic region; Hudson's Bay Co. fur-trading post. Seaplane base, govt. radio and meteorological station, hosp., Royal Canadian Mounted Police post. Site of Anglican cathedral, seat of bishop of the Arctic, Anglican and R.C. missions, boarding school for Indian and Eskimo children. Grains, vegetables are grown, dairy cattle raised. Mean temps. are 57°F. (July), −19°F. (Jan.). Trading post was established 1912 on S bank of Mackenzie R., moved 1920 to N bank.
Aklim, Djebel (jĕ'bĕl äklēm'), highest peak (8,300 ft.) of the Anti-Atlas, SW Fr. Morocco, 45 mi. SE of Taroudant; 30°7'N 8°16'W.
Akmal-Abad, Uzbek SSR: see Gizhduvan.
Ak-Mechet (äk"-myĭchĕt'). **1** City, Kazakh SSR: see Kzyl-Orda, city. **2** City, central Crimea, Russian SFSR: see Simferopol. **3** Village, W Crimea, Russian SFSR: see Chernomorskoye.
Akmene, Lithuania: see Mazeikiai.
Akmolinsk (ŭkmŭlyēnsk'), oblast (□ 59,000; 1946 pop. estimate 400,000), N Kazakh SSR; ⊙ Akmolinsk. In NW Kazakh Hills; drained by upper Ishim and lower Nura rivers; includes black-earth steppe (N), inland Tengiz basin and dry steppe (S). Dry, continental climate. Chiefly agr.: wheat, oats, dairy products in N and E; cattle, sheep, millet, wheat in W; semi-nomadic sheep raising in SW. Food processing, mfg. of agr. machines. Mining: gold, antimony (Turgai); coal (Sary-Adyr); bauxite. Pop. chiefly Kazakhs, Russians, Ukrainians. Chief centers: Akmolinsk, Atbasar, Stepnyak, Makinsk. Oblast crossed by Trans-Kazakhstan RR (N–S), by S.Siberian RR (E–W). Formed 1939.
Akmolinsk, city (1939 pop. over 30,000), ⊙ Akmolinsk oblast, Kazakh SSR, on Ishim R., on S.Siberian RR, and 120 mi. NW of Karaganda; 51°9'N 71°25'E. Rail junction; center of agr. and stock-raising area; mfg. (agr. machinery, felt boots); tanning, wool processing, flour and sawmilling. Founded 1830 in Rus. conquest of Kazakhstan.
Akmyany, Lithuania: see Mazeikiai.
Aknasugatag, Rumania: see Ocna-Sugatag.
Aknoul (äknōōl'), village (pop. 761), Fez region, N Fr. Morocco, on SE slopes of Rif Mts., 30 mi. NNE of Taza; military outpost near Sp. Morocco border.
Ako, Formosa: see Pingtung.
Ako (äkō'), town (pop. 29,158), Hyogo prefecture, S Honshu, Japan, on Harima Sea, 18 mi. WSW of Himeji; rail terminus; saltmaking center.
Akobo (äkō'bō), town, Upper Nile prov., E central Anglo-Egyptian Sudan, at Ethiopian border, 150 mi. SE of Malakal, on Pibor R. at influx of the Akobo; peanuts, corn, durra; livestock.
Akobo River, Ital. *Acobo*, rises in highlands of SW Ethiopia in several branches bet. Wota and Maji, flows NW, forming boundary with Anglo-Egyptian Sudan, to Pibor R. near town of Akobo; total length, c.270 mi. Its valley has gold deposits.
A-k'o-ch'i, China: see Akche.
Akoki, China: see Akche.
Akola (ŭkō'lŭ), district (□ 4,093; pop. 907,742), Berar div., W Madhya Pradesh, India; ⊙ Akola. On Deccan Plateau; partly bordered (N) by central Satpura Range; lowland (N), drained by Purna R. (tributary of the Tapti); Ajanta Hills (S), drained by Penganga R. In major black-soil cotton-growing tract; also produces millet, wheat, oilseeds. Timber (teak) and gum arabic in Ajanta Hills (cattle raising). Cotton ginning, oilseed milling, soap mfg. Akola is a cotton-trade and textile center. Pop. 90% Hindu, 10% Moslem.
Akola. 1 Village (pop. 4,447), Ahmadnagar dist., central Bombay, India, on Pravara R. and 55 mi. NW of Ahmadnagar; market center for cotton, millet; cotton ginning. **2** Town (pop. 62,564), ⊙ Akola dist., W Madhya Pradesh, India, near Purna R. (tributary of the Tapti), 140 mi. WSW of Nagpur; cotton-trade and -textile center in major cotton-growing tract; oilseed milling, soap mfg. Has col. of arts, handicraft school. Experimental farm.
Akonolinga (äkōnōlĭng'gä), village, Nyong et Sanaga region, S central Fr. Cameroons, on Nyong R. and 55 mi. ESE of Yaoundé; hardwood lumbering center; palm plantations. R.C. mission.
Akora Khattak (ŭkō'rŭ khätäk'), village, Peshawar dist., E North-West Frontier Prov., W Pakistan, on Kabul R. and 7 mi. E of Nowshera, on railroad; tobacco processing.
Akosu, China: see Aksu.
Akot (ä'kōt), town (pop. 22,465), Akola dist., W Madhya Pradesh, India, 22 mi. N of Akola; trades in cotton, millet, wheat, mangoes; cotton ginning, oilseed milling. Village of Argaon, 8 mi. W, was scene (1803) of Br. victory over Mahratta forces.
Akouda (äkōōdä'), village, Sousse dist., E Tunisia, in coastal area (*sahel*) near Gulf of Hammamet, 5 mi. NW of Sousse; olive groves.
Akow, Formosa: see Pingtung.
Akpatok Island (□ 551), SE Franklin Dist., Northwest Territories, in Ungava Bay; 60°25'N 68°2'W; 27 mi. long, 15 mi. wide; rises to 930 ft.
Akrabi, Aden: see Aqrabi.
Akra Dag (äkrä'dä), Turkish *Akra Dağ*, peak (5,705 ft.), S Turkey, on Mediterranean coast just N of Syrian line.
Akra Fjord (ô'krä fyôr"), Nor. *Åkrafjord*, in Hordaland co., SW Norway; 19 mi. long, 1-2 mi. wide; extends NE from Skanevik.
Akrahamn (ô'krähämŭn), Nor. *Åkrahamn*, or **Akrehamn** (ô'krŭhämŭn), Nor. *Åkrehamn*, village (pop. 1,478) in Akra or Aakra (Nor. *Åkra*) canton (pop. 4,808), Rogaland co., SW Norway, on W shore of Karmoy, 4 mi. WSW of Kopervik; fisheries; mfg. of herring oil and meal. Sometimes spelled Aakrahamn or Aakrahavn.
Akranes (ä'kränĕs"), city (pop. 2,540), in but independent of Borgarfjardar co., W Iceland, on Faxa Bay, at tip of peninsula bet. Borgar Fjord (N) and Hval Fjord (S), 12 mi. NNW of Reykjavik; fishing port.
Akrata (äkrä'tä), village (pop. 1,182), Achaea nome, N Peloponnesus, Greece, on Krathis R. near its mouth on Gulf of Corinth, on railroad, and 32 mi. E of Patras; Zante currants, wine. Took active part in Gr. war of independence.
Akrathos (ä'kräthôs) [from Gr. *Akra Athos*,=Cape Athos] or **Cape Hagion Oros** (ä'yēôn ô'rôs), Ital. *Capo Monte Santo* (kä'pô mōn'tä sän'tō), a SE extremity of Akte (Athos) prong of Chalcidice peninsula, Greek Macedonia, on Aegean Sea, at E foot of Mt. Athos; 40°9'N 24°24'E. Also called Cape Lavra.
Akrehamn, Norway: see Akrahamn.
Akritas, Cape (äkrē'täs), Lat. *Acritas*, S tip of Messenia Peninsula, SW Peloponnesus, Greece, on Ionian Sea, W of Gulf of Messenia; 36°43'N 21°54'E. Formerly Cape Gallo.
Akrites or **Akritis** (both: äkrē'tĭs), Aegean island (□ 2.6; pop. 96) in the Dodecanese, Greece, NE of Patmos; 37°27'N 26°45'E; 3.5 mi. long, 1 mi. wide. Formerly called Arki [Ital. *Archi*].
Ak River, Turkey: see Akcay; Aksu.
Akrokeri (äkrōkĕ'rē), town, Ashanti, S central Gold Coast, on railroad and 7 mi. NNE of Obuasi; gold mining; cacao, cassava, corn.
Akrokorinthos, Greece: see Acrocorinthus.
Akron (ă'krŭn). **1** Town (pop. 684), Hale co., W Ala., 24 mi. SW of Tuscaloosa, near Black Warrior R.; lumber. **2** Town (pop. 1,605), ⊙ Washington co., NE Colo., c.100 mi. ENE of Denver; alt. 4,300 ft. Railroad div. point in agr. area; dairy products, poultry, grain. U.S. agr. experiment station near by. Founded 1882, inc. 1887. **3** Town (pop. 946), Fulton co., N Ind., 45 mi. SSE of South Bend, in agr. area; garden tools, lumber. **4** Town (pop. 1,251), Plymouth co., NW Iowa, near S.Dak. boundary (formed here by Big Sioux R.), 24 mi. NNW of Sioux City; feed mill, creamery. Platted 1871 as Portlandville; inc. 1882. **5** Village (pop. 431), Tuscola co., E Mich., 18 mi. E of Bay City, in agr. area. **6** Village (pop. 2,481), Erie co., W N.Y., 20 mi. ENE of Buffalo; shipping center for dairying and farming region; mfg. (gypsum and lime products, cement, wallboard, roofing, ivory buttons, feed, dehydrated milk, canned foods); wheat, hay, potatoes, cabbage, mushrooms. Near by is Tonawanda Indian Reservation. Inc. 1849. **7** Industrial city (pop. 274,605), ⊙ Summit co., NE Ohio, on Cuyahoga R. and 30 mi. S of Cleveland; greatest rubber-mfg. center of world, with 3 huge rubber factories and many subsidiary plants. Also produces cereals, machinery, tools, auto parts, chemicals, furniture, textiles, clay products, surgical supplies, matches. Port of entry. Has a municipal airport, an airport stadium, and a huge Zeppelin air dock. It is U.S. center for lighter-than-air craft; the dirigibles *Akron* and *Macon* were built here. Seat of Univ. of Akron and Goodyear Industrial Inst. Annual International Soap Box Derby held here. Portage Lakes are S. Settled 1807; inc. 1865 as city. Akron's early growth followed opening here (1827) of Ohio and Erie Canal. Rubber industry began in 1870, and great industrial boom came with growing demand for automobile tires after c.1910. In 1940, pop. of metropolitan dist. (including Barberton, Cuyahoga Falls, Kent, Ravenna, Tallmadge, Wadsworth, and other places) was 349,705; in the census of 1950, the metropolitan dist. (pop. 410,032) was defined as Summit co. **8** Borough (pop. 1,028), Lancaster co., SE Pa., 10 mi. NE of Lancaster; shoes. Inc. 1884.
Akropong (äkrōpông'), town, Eastern Prov., SE Gold Coast colony, in Akwapim Hills, 32 mi. NNE of Accra, on road; cacao, palm oil and kernels, cassava. Presbyterian church mission and col.

Akrotiri Bay (äkrôtē'rē), small Mediterranean inlet on coast of S Cyprus, bounded W by Akrotiri Peninsula. At its head is isl.'s principal port, Limassol, for which the bay is sometimes called.

Akrotiri Peninsula, S Cyprus, juts c.7 mi. S (c.4 mi. wide) into the Mediterranean, bounded by Episkopi Bay (W) and Akrotiri Bay (E), terminating in Cape ZEUGHARI (SW) and Cape GATA (SE). At its NE base is the port of Limassol. In its center is a salt lake.

Akrounda (äkrōōn'dä), water dam and village (pop. 260), Limassol dist., S Cyprus, 7 mi. NNE of Limassol.

Aksai or **Aksay** (ŭksī'), village (1926 pop. 3,915), S Stalingrad oblast, Russian SFSR, near railroad (Gniloaksaiskaya station), 55 mi. SSW of Stalingrad; wheat, cotton; cattle.

Aksai River or **Aksay River,** NW Dagestan Autonomous SSR, Russian SFSR, rises in Andi Range, flows c.70 mi. NNE, past Ritlyab and Babayurt, to Terek R. near Kizlyar. Waters largely used up in lower course for cotton irrigation canals in Babayurt area.

Aksaiskaya or **Aksayskaya** (ŭksī'skīŭ), village (1926 pop. 6,051) SW Rostov oblast, Russian SFSR, on Don R. and 7 mi. ENE of Rostov; truck, dairying; tomato canning, glassworking.

Aksakovo (ŭksä'kŭvŭ), town (1926 pop. 643), W Bashkir Autonomous SSR, Russian SFSR, 7 mi. S of Belebei; rail junction; grain, livestock. Sanatorium near by.

Aksaray (äksärī'), town (pop. 9,558), Nigde prov., central Turkey, 45 mi. NW of Nigde; lignite; wheat, rye, barley, vetch, beans, onions. Formerly also Akserai.

Aksarka (ŭksär'kŭ), village, NW Yamal-Nenets Natl. Okrug, Tyumen oblast, Russian SFSR, N of Arctic Circle, on Ob R. and 40 mi. NE of Salekhard; fish canning. Sometimes spelled Oksarka.

Aksay-, in Rus. names: see AKSAI-.

Aksehir (äk-shĕhĭr'), anc. *Philomelion*, Turkish *Akşehir*, town (1950 pop. 13,325), Konya prov., W central Turkey, just S of L. Aksehir, on railroad, 70 mi. WNW of Konya; carpet mfg.; wheat, barley; opium. It was probably a town of anc. Pergamum. Sometimes spelled Akshehr.

Aksehir, Lake, Turkish *Akşehir* (□ 41), W central Turkey, 45 mi. ESE of Afyonkarahisar, just N of Aksehir; 11 mi. long, 6 mi. wide; alt. 3,250 ft.

Akseki (äksĕkē'), village (pop. 3,209), Antalya prov., SW Turkey, 60 mi. ENE of Antalya, in Taurus Mts.; wheat, onions, sugar beets.

Aksel, Netherlands: see AXEL.

Aksenovo-Zilovskoye (ŭksyô'nŭvŭ-zē'lŭfskŭyŭ), town (1939 pop. over 10,000), central Chita oblast, Russian SFSR, on Trans-Siberian RR (Zilovo station) and 180 mi. NE of Chita, in lumbering area; metalworks. Formerly Zilovo-Aksenovo.

Akserai, Turkey: see AKSARAY.

Aksha (ŭkshä'), village (1948 pop. over 2,000), S Chita oblast, Russian SFSR, on Onon R. and 120 mi. S of Chita, near Mongolian border; grain and cattle market.

Ak-Sheikh, Russian SFSR: see RAZDOLNOYE, Crimea.

Akstafa (ŭkstŭfä'), city (1932 pop. estimate 2,220), W Azerbaijan SSR, on railroad and 55 mi. NW of Kirovabad, on highway to L. Sevan; cotton ginning.

Aksu or **Aqsu** (äksōō'), Chinese *Akosu* or *A-k'o-su* (both: ä'kŭsōō'), town (pop. c.20,000) and oasis (pop. 91,936), SW Sinkiang prov., China, on Aksu R. and 250 mi. ENE of Kashgar, and on road to Turfan; 41°8'N 79°56'E. Caravan center on highway S of the Tien Shan; cotton-textile and carpet mfg., jade carving, tanning. Sericulture; livestock. Copper- and metalworking on basis of near-by mines. Also called Aksu Yangi Shahr [Uigur, =Aksu new town]. Old Aksu, 10 mi. N, is now called KONA SHAHR.

Aksu (äksōō') or **Ak River,** S Turkey, flows 82 mi. from L. Egridir to Mediterranean Sea 11 mi. E of Antalya.

Aksu (ŭksōō'), village (1939 pop. over 500), central Taldy-Kurgan oblast, Kazakh SSR, on the Ak-Su (river) and 65 mi. NE of Taldy-Kurgan; irrigated agr. (wheat); sheep, cattle.

Ak-Su. 1 River, Taldy-Kurgan oblast, Kazakh SSR, rises in Dzungarian Ala-Tau, flows 160 mi. NW, through irrigated wheat area and sandy desert, past Aksu, to L. Balkhash 40 mi. W of Burlyu-Tobe. **2** River, Tadzhik SSR: see MURGAB RIVER.

Aksuat (ŭksōōät'), village (1948 pop. over 2,000), SE Semipalatinsk oblast, Kazakh SSR, 220 mi. SE of Semipalatinsk, near China frontier; irrigated agr. (wheat).

Aksu-Ayuly (ŭksōō'-ŭyōō'lē), village (1948 pop. over 500), E central Karaganda oblast, Kazakh SSR, 75 mi. SSE of Karaganda; cattle raising; copper deposits.

Aksubayevo (ŭksōōbī'ŭvŭ), village (1926 pop. 2,360), S Tatar Autonomous SSR, Russian SFSR, 37 mi. SSE of Chistopol; sawmilling; wheat, stock.

Aksum or **Axum** (äk'sōōm), town (pop. 10,000), Tigre prov., N Ethiopia, on road and 12 mi. W of Aduwa; alt. c.7,000 ft. Major religious (Coptic) center with anc. cathedral (believed to house the Ark of the Covenant) containing valuable inscriptions, monastery, and notable granite obelisks. Carries on trade in cereals, coffee, hides, honey; has artisan industries (weaving, leatherworking, metalworking). Gold deposits c.20 mi. S. Formerly (1st–6th cent. A.D.) capital of kingdom occupying much of Ethiopia and modern Anglo-Egyptian Sudan.

Aksu River or **Aqsu River** (äksōō'), W Sinkiang prov., China, formed near Aksu by headstreams rising in the Tien Shan in Kirghiz SSR, flows c.60 mi. SE, joining Yarkand R. to form the Tarim.

Aktanysh (ŭktŭnĭsh'), village (1939 pop. over 2,000), NE Tatar Autonomous SSR, Russian SFSR, near Belaya R., 39 mi. E of Menzelinsk; rye, oats, wheat, legumes.

Aktash (ŭktäsh'). **1** Village (1932 pop. estimate 3,890), SE Tatar Autonomous SSR, Russian SFSR, on Stepnoi Zai R. and 45 mi. NNW of Bugulma; grain, livestock. **2** Village (1939 pop. over 500), W Samarkand oblast, Uzbek SSR, on Trans-Caspian RR (Zirabulak station) and 8 mi. W of Katta-Kurgan; cotton ginning, sugar milling.

Ak-Tau (ŭk-tou'), range in NW Samarkand oblast, Uzbek SSR; extends 50 mi. E from Nurata; rises to 5,700 ft. Molybdenum and tungsten mining at Lyangar.

Akte or **Akti** (ăk'tē, äktē'), Lat. *Acte*, or **Hagion Oros** or **Ayion Oros** (ä'yēôn ô'rôs), Ital. *Monte Santo* (mōn'tä sän'tō), E prong of Chalcidice peninsula, Greek Macedonia, on Aegean Sea, bet. Singitic (W) and Strymonic (E) gulfs; 30 mi. long, 5 mi. wide, rises to 6,670 ft. in Mt. ATHOS; terminates in capes Nymphaion and Akrathos. Akte is coextensive with autonomous MOUNT ATHOS. Xerxes canal was cut through isthmus at its base, 480 B.C.

Ak-Tepe (äk"-tyĭpyĕ'), village, NE Tashauz oblast, Turkmen SSR on Khiva oasis, 35 mi. NW of Tashauz; cotton.

Aktérine, Syria: see AKHTERIN.

Akti, peninsula, Greece: see AKTE.

Aktogai or **Aktogay** (ŭktŭgī'), village (1939 pop. over 500), SE Karaganda oblast, Kazakh SSR, 95 mi. N of Balkhash, on dry steppe; sheep, camels.

Aktyubinsk (ŭktyōō'bĭnsk), oblast (□ 114,700; 1946 pop. estimate 300,000), NW Kazakh SSR; ⊙ Aktyubinsk. Extends S from border of Russian SFSR to Aral Sea; includes MUGODZHAR HILLS (center); drained by Irgiz and upper Emba rivers. Agr. area in N (wheat, millet, cattle); in S and E, dry steppe (sheep, goats, camels), with some desert stretches (BARSUKI). Dry, continental climate. Extensive nickel and chrome mines (Batamshinski, Khrom-Tau, Donskoye), phosphorites (Alga, Kandagach), coal (Berchogur, Kurashasaiski), petroleum fields (W; along Emba R.). Aktyubinsk ferroalloy works are important. Trans-Caspian RR crosses oblast NW-SE, intersecting Guryev-Orsk RR at Kandagach. Main centers: Aktyubinsk, Chelkar, Temir. Pop. Kazakhs, Ukrainians, Russians. Formed 1932.

Aktyubinsk, city (1936 pop. estimate 45,000), ⊙ Aktyubinsk oblast, Kazakh SSR, on Ilek R., on Trans-Caspian RR and 90 mi. SW of Orsk, 1,000 mi. WNW of Alma-Ata; 50°17'N 57°7'E. Industrial center; has ferroalloy (nickel, chrome) plant (5 mi. from city center; built in early 1940s); mfg. of electrical goods, machine repairing, wool and food (flour, meat) processing. Superphosphate produced at Alga (S). Teachers col. Pop. mainly Russian. Founded 1869 in Rus. conquest of Kazakhstan; developed rapidly after construction of railroad (1905).

Ak-Tyuz (ŭk-tyōōs'), town (1939 pop. over 500), E Frunze oblast, kirghiz SSR, on S slope of Trans-Ili Ala-Tau, on the Lesser Kemin and 75 mi. E of Frunze; lead mine, supplying Chimkent works; tin and indium ores.

Akugdlit (äkōōg'lĭt), fishing and sealing settlement (pop. 137), Christianshaab dist., W Greenland, on small Akugdlit Isl., on inlet of Disko Bay, 10 mi. S of Christianshaab; 68°40'N 15°14'W.

Akulurak (äkōō'lŭräk), Eskimo village (pop. 70), W Alaska, on Yukon R. delta, 9 mi. E of mouth of Yukon R., 130 mi. S of Nome; 62°34'N 164°33'W; trapping. Grew up around St. Mary's Jesuit Mission, Eskimo orphanage established 1918.

Akúnâk or **Akúnâq** (both: äkōō'näk), fishing settlement (pop. 167), Egedesminde dist., W Greenland, on small isl. in S part of Disko Bay, 13 mi. ENE of Egedesminde; 68°44'N 52°19'W.

Akune (ä"kōō'nä), town (pop. 30,311), Kagoshima prefecture, W Kyushu, Japan, on E.China Sea, 37 mi. NW of Kagoshima; mining center (iron, copper). Hot springs.

Akun Island (ăkōōn') (14 mi. long, 2–10 mi. wide), in Krenitzin group, Fox Isls., E Aleutian Isls., SW Alaska, bet. Akutan Isl. (W) and Unimak Isl. (ENE); 54°12'N 165°32'W; rises to 2,685 ft. on Mt. Gilbert (N), extinct volcano.

Akure (äkōō'rä), town, ⊙ Ondo prov., Western Provinces, S Nigeria, 140 mi. ENE of Lagos; 7°15'N 5°12'E. Agr. trade center; cotton weaving; cacao, palm oil and kernels, rubber, timber, cotton.

Akurenan (äkōōrä'nän), town (pop. 146), continental Sp. Guinea, near Gabon border, 85 mi. SE of Bata. Coffee, yucca.

Akureyri (ä'kürā"rē), city (pop. 7,017), in but independent of Eyjafjardar co., N Iceland, near head of the Eyja Fjord, 150 mi. NE of Reykjavik; 65°40'N 18°6'W. Chief city of N Iceland; commercial center, fishing port. Fish-oil refinery; agr. market (potatoes, vegetables; sheep). Has technical col., agr. experiment station. Inc. 1786.

Akuse (äkōō'sä), town (pop. 3,027), Eastern Prov., SE Gold Coast colony, on Volta R. and 45 mi. NE of Accra; palm oil and kernels, cacao, cotton. Its port and light-draught navigation head on Volta R. is Amedika (just NE).

Akusha (ŭkōōshä'), village (1926 pop. 2,518), central Dagestan Autonomous SSR, Russian SFSR, at SE end of Gimry Range of E Greater Caucasus, 40 mi. SSE of Buinaksk; grain, sheep raising. Pop. largely Darghin. A Rus. fortress in Caucasian wars in mid-19th cent. Formerly also Akushi.

Akutan (ăkŭtăn'), village (pop. 80), E Akutan Isl., Aleutian Isls., SW Alaska, 35 mi. ENE of Dutch Harbor; supply point for trappers and fur farmers. Whaling station until 1938.

Akutan Island (19 mi. long, 15 mi. wide), in Krenitzin group, Fox Isls., E Aleutian Isls., SW Alaska, 12 mi. NE of Unalaska Isl.; 54°8'N 165°53'W; rises to 4,244 ft. on Akutan Peak (center), active volcano (erupted 1946). Fox farming.

Akutikha (ŭkōōtyē'khŭ), town (1939 pop. over 2,000), central Altai Territory, Russian SFSR, on Obe R. and 37 mi. W of Bisk; glassworks.

Akwana (äkwä'nä), town (pop. 626), Benue prov., Northern Provinces, E central Nigeria, 45 mi. E of Makurdi; galena-mining center.

Akwanga (äkwäng'-gä), town (pop. 1,208), Plateau Prov., Northern Provinces, central Nigeria, 45 mi. S of Kafanchan; tin mining; cassava, millet, durra.

Akwapim Hills (äkwäpĕm'), SE Gold Coast, extend from Nsawam c.40 mi. NE to Volta R. near Senchi; rise to 2,500 ft. Fertile area, rich in cacao and oil palms. Main centers: Mampong, Akropong, Somanya.

Akyab (ăkyăb', äkyäb'), N district (□ 5,152; 1941 pop. 760,705) of Arakan div., NW Lower Burma; ⊙ Akyab. Bet. Bay of Bengal and Arakan Yoma, on E Pakistan border (Naaf R.). Intensive rice cultivation in coastal plains; forested inland hills. Main rivers: Mayu, Kaladan, Lemro. Pop. is 50% Burmese, 30% Indian.

Akyab, Burmese *Sittwe* (sĭt'twā), town (pop. 38,094), ⊙ Arakan div. and Akyab dist., Lower Burma; port on low-lying peninsula at mouth of Kaladan River, on Bay of Bengal, 170 mi. SSE of Chittagong (E Pakistan); 20°9'N 92°54'E. Rice-milling and exporting center; match mfg. Airfield. Originally a small fishing village, it developed after 1st Anglo-Burmese War (1826) when administrative seat was moved here from Myohaung. In Second World War, held 1942–45 by Japanese.

Akyar or **Ak'yar** (ŭkyär'), village (1948 pop. over 2,000), SE Bashkir Autonomous SSR, Russian SFSR, on Tanalyk R. and 50 mi. S of Baimak; rye, oats, livestock.

Akyazi (äkyäzŭ'), Turkish *Akyazı*, village (pop. 2,797), Kocaeli prov., NW Turkey, on Mudurnu R. and 13 mi. ESE of Adapazari; grain, potatoes.

Akyma (ŭkī'mŭ), locality, Demerara co., N central Br. Guiana, on Demerara R. and 7 mi. SSW of Mackenzie; bauxite deposits.

Akzhal (ŭkzhäl'), town (1939 pop. over 2,000), E Semipalatinsk oblast, Kazakh SSR, 10 mi. E of Zhangis-Tobe; gold-mining center.

Akzhar (ŭkzhär'), village (1948 pop. over 2,000) SW East Kazakhstan oblast, Kazakh SSR, in N foothills of Tarbagatai Range, 55 mi. W of Zaisan; irrigated agr. (wheat); cattle. Formerly spelled Ak-Dzhar.

Al [Arabic, =the], for Arabic names beginning thus: see under following part of the name.

Al (ôl), Nor. *Ål*, village and canton (pop. 4,315), Buskerud co., S Norway, in the Hallingdal, on railroad and 65 mi. NW of Honefoss; agr., stock raising, lumbering. Sometimes spelled Aal. Dyna (dü'nä) mtn. (3,975 ft.) is 7 mi. SW.

Ala (ä'lä), village (pop. 1,800), Tigre prov., N Ethiopia, 40 mi. ENE of Makale; cereals, livestock; salt market.

Ala (ä'lä), village (pop. 2,301), Trento prov., Trentino–Alto Adige, N Italy, in Val Lagarina, 9 mi. S of Rovereto; alcohol distillery. Has several notable palaces.

Ala, Sweden: see LJUSNE.

'Ala, El, Al 'Ala, or **Al 'Ula** (all: ĕl älä'), town and oasis of N Hejaz, Saudi Arabia, on coastal plateau, 180 mi. NW of Medina, and on former Hejaz railway; date-growing center; fruit (lemons, plums).

Ala, El- (ĕl-älä'), village, Kairouan dist., central Tunisia, 31 mi. WSW of Kairouan; olive groves. Lead and zinc mining on slopes of Djebel Trozza (4 mi. SE).

Alà, Monti di (môn'tē dē älä'), mountain range, N Sardinia; extends 20 mi. NE from middle course of Mannu d'Oschiri R.; rises to 3,588 ft. at Monte Lerno.

Alabama (ălŭbă'mŭ), state (land □ 51,078; with inland waters □ 51,609; 1950 pop. 3,061,743; 1940 pop. 2,832,961), S U.S., bordered by Tenn. (N), Ga. (E), Miss. (W), Fla. (S), and Gulf of Mexico

(SW); 28th in area, 17th in pop., admitted 1819 as the 22d state; ⊙ Montgomery. The "Cotton State," roughly rectangular, is c.280 mi. long (N–S), c.200 mi. wide (E–W), with an appendix c.55 mi. long and wide in the extreme SW corner bordering the Gulf. From sea level here, the state rises gradually NE to 2,407 ft. in Cheaha Mountain; has a mean alt. of 500 ft. Upper Ala., especially the NE section, is the terminus of the Appalachian highlands, while lower Ala. is a part of the Gulf coastal plain. The coastal plain is a generally hilly and forested region with the upper portion crossed (E–W) by the Black Belt prairie and a wire-grass section in the SE. It terminates at the Fall Line hills (500–600 ft. high) which mark the beginning of the Appalachian system and curve across the state bet. Colbert co. (in the NW corner) and Lee co. (in the E central part of the state, on the Ga. line). The Appalachian region includes portions of the Cumberland Plateau (N), traversed E–W by the Tennessee R.; the Great Appalachian Valley (NE), here drained chiefly by the Coosa R.; and the Piedmont (E central), whose major river is the Tallapoosa. The Appalachian plateaus are well forested and hilly with a few prominent ridges (Sand, Lookout, Talladega mts.) and many narrow valleys. The Great Appalachian Valley consists of a series of NE-SW ridges (notably Red Mountain) paralleled by more extensive valleys. Ala. has many miles of streams, making it one of the leading river states in the U.S. Except for the Tennessee and its tributaries, the rivers flow S and SW to the Gulf, chiefly through the Mobile River system, which empties into Mobile Bay. The principal streams of the Mobile system are the Tombigbee and Black Warrior, which drain the W part of the state; the Alabama, Coosa, and Cahaba, which flow through the NE and central portions; and the Tallapoosa, which crosses E central Ala. In SE Ala. are the Escambia, Conecuh, and Choctawhatchee, which flow through NW Fla. to the Gulf. Many of the rivers contain dams and locks and are extensively used for navigation and power. The Tennessee is a major traffic artery for large barges, while the Mobile system furnishes extensive waterways for shallow-draft boats from Mobile, the state's only seaport, to Montgomery and the Birmingham dist. in Ala.; and to Rome, Ga., and Columbus, Miss. The power dams have greatly aided the state's industrialization. Some of the larger are Wilson, Wheeler, and Guntersville dams (major TVA dams) in the Tennessee; Lay, Mitchell, and Jordan dams in the Coosa; and Martin and Thurlow dams in the Tallapoosa. Also important are the Langdale, Riverview, Bartletts Ferry, and Goat Rock dams in the Chattahoochee, which forms part of the Ala.-Ga. line. In addition, there are several power dams in the Conecuh and Pea rivers in lower Ala. Natural lakes are lacking and swamps are few except in some of the river bottoms, on the Mobile delta, and on the coast, where marshes alternate with sandy beaches. Forests, chiefly pine, cover c.60% of the state, making lumbering and pulp and paper milling major industries; turpentine mfg. is also carried on. Other important trees include oak, gum, and yellow poplar. The state is predominantly rural and agr. The few large towns are chiefly mfg., market, and transportation centers. They include Birmingham (the largest city), Bessemer, Gadsden, and Anniston in the Great Appalachian Valley; Decatur and Florence in the Tennessee Valley; Tuscaloosa in the Cumberland Plateau; and Montgomery, Selma, Phenix City, Dothan, and Mobile in the coastal plain. Farming is favored by the humid subtropical climate, characterized by long, hot summers and short, mild winters. The growing season is long, 200–250 days, and, in the extreme SW corner, 250–300 days. The average annual rainfall is plentiful (c.54 inches) and is well distributed, with a fall minimum, useful for harvesting. There is comparatively little mechanization. Soil depletion is widespread and c.25% of the state is severely eroded. In recent years the use of fertilizer and soil conservation methods, together with crop diversification, have made substantial progress. Ala. is one of the major U.S. producers of cotton, which, with corn, still occupies most of the cultivated land. The chief cotton regions are the Tennessee Valley and adjacent part of the Great Appalachian Valley, and the Black Belt; the valleys are also the principal fruit (peaches, apples) areas of the state. Other major crops include peanuts, grown chiefly in the wire-grass section of SE Ala.; hay, important in the wire-grass section and the Black Belt; sweet potatoes, found all over the state; and grain (especially oats). In addition, truck crops and tung and pecan nuts are grown in S Ala. Livestock and livestock products have become very important, ranking next to cotton in value. Large numbers of cattle are raised in SW Ala. and the Black Belt, while the SE is the chief hog region; other livestock includes poultry, sheep, and goats. The processing of farm products constitutes the basis of such major industries as cotton, peanut, and grain milling, and meat packing. In addition, the state has large deposits of coal, iron, and limestone, making it an important manufacturer of iron and steel products, coke, and cement. Upper Ala., especially the Cumberland Plateau and the adjacent part of the Great Appalachian Valley, is the chief mineral region. The state ranks 3d as a U.S. producer of iron ore, mining c.7% of the nation's output, and is noted as a center for cast-iron products. The Birmingham dist., where the minerals occur in close proximity, is the principal center of the iron and steel and cement industries. Another important metal-processing area is the Tennessee Valley, where there is also a major chemical (especially fertilizer) industry, based on the abundant hydroelectric power; Muscle Shoals here is a noted chemical center. Other industries include the mfg. of brick and tile (based on the large clay deposits) and rubber products. In addition, there is fishing (especially shrimp, oysters) along the coast. Although Spaniards, including De Soto, were the earliest white explorers of the region, the 1st settlement was made (1702) by the French in the Mobile area. After 1763 it belonged to the British, who ceded it to the U.S. in 1783 after the American Revolution. Substantial settlement did not begin until after the War of 1812. The Indians, decisively defeated by Andrew Jackson in 1814, were no longer a menace, and England furnished a ready market for cotton, which rapidly supplanted furs as the chief product of the region. So many settlers came from the neighboring states, especially Ga., that in 1817 Ala. was detached from Miss. and made a separate territory, becoming a state 2 years later. Large numbers of Negroes (now c.⅓ of the pop.) were used to work the plantations. During the Civil War, Ala. sided with the Confederacy, and Mobile Bay was the scene (1864) of a great naval battle won by the Federal forces under Admiral Farragut. Agr. was slow to recover after the war, although industry was gradually expanded as the mining of coal and iron increased. Cotton became less dominant when the inroads of the boll weevil and the high prices for food crops during the First World War resulted in the speeding up of crop diversification. This trend was given further impetus by the AAA programs in the '30s. Industrialization, which expanded during the Second World War, has continued to grow, leading to a more balanced economy. See also articles on the cities, towns, geographic features, and the 67 counties: Autauga, Baldwin, Barbour, Bibb, Blount, Bullock, Butler, Calhoun, Chambers, Cherokee, Chilton, Choctaw, Clarke, Clay, Cleburne, Coffee, Colbert, Conecuh, Coosa, Covington, Crenshaw, Cullman, Dale, Dallas, De Kalb, Elmore, Escambia, Etowah, Fayette, Franklin, Geneva, Greene, Hale, Henry, Houston, Jackson, Jefferson, Lamar, Lauderdale, Lawrence, Lee, Limestone, Lowndes, Macon, Madison, Marengo, Marion, Marshall, Mobile, Monroe, Montgomery, Morgan, Perry, Pickens, Pike, Randolph, Russell, Saint Clair, Shelby, Sumter, Talladega, Tallapoosa, Tuscaloosa, Walker, Washington, Wilcox, Winston.

Alabama City, Ala.: see Gadsden.

Alabama River, navigable stream formed by confluence of Coosa and Tallapoosa rivers 10 mi. N of Montgomery, Ala.; flows W, past Selma, then SW and S to Tombigbee R., with which it forms Mobile R. 30 mi. N of Mobile (45 mi., river distance); 318 mi. long. Used for shipment of sand, gravel, logs, pulpwood, cotton, gasoline. Plan for development of Alabama-Coosa river system (720 mi. long to farthest headsteam; drains □ 22,600) includes Allatoona Dam in Etowah R.

Alabashly (ülä″bŭshlē′), rail station, W Azerbaijan SSR, on main Baku-Tiflis line and 8 mi. NW of Kirovabad; junction for electrified spur line (built 1948) to Dashkesan magnetite mines.

Alabaster, village (pop. c.300), Iosco co., NE Mich., on Saginaw Bay, c.45 mi. NNE of Bay City; gypsum quarrying.

Alabat Island (äläbät′) (□ 74; 1948 pop. 5,607), Quezon prov., Philippines, just off E coast of S Luzon, bet. Lopez Bay (W) and Calauag Bay (E); 14°6′N 122°3′E. Isl. is 24 mi. long, 4 mi. wide; rises to 1,384 ft. Fishing. Chief center and port is Alabat (1939 pop. 1,514) on W coast.

Alabja, Iraq: see Halabja.

Ala-Buka (ülä″-bōōkä′), village (1939 pop. over 500), W Dzhalal-Abad oblast, Kirghiz SSR, in S foothills of Chatkal Range, 80 mi. NW of Dzhalal-Abad, in irrigated agr. (wheat) area.

Alaca (äläjä′), village (pop. 3,006), Corum prov., N central Turkey, 27 mi. SSW of Corum; wheat, beans, mohair goats. Formerly Huseyinabat.

Alacam (älächäm′), Turkish *Alaçam*, village (pop. 4,617), Samsun prov., N Turkey, near Black Sea, 45 mi. NW of Samsun; tobacco center.

Alachua (ülă′chōōü, ülō′chŭwä), county (□ 892; pop. 57,026), N Fla., bounded N by Santa Fe R.; ⊙ Gainesville. Has many lakes (Orange, Newmans, Santa Fe). Produces corn, vegetables, peanuts, cotton, tobacco, citrus fruit, nuts (pecan, tung); livestock; lumber, and naval stores. Quarries limestone, phosphate, and flint in W. Formed 1824.

Alachua, city (pop. 1,116), Alachua co., N Fla., 15 mi. NW of Gainesville; watermelon- and vegetable-shipping center. Founded 1884.

Alacrán Arrecife (äläkrän′ äräsē′fä), reef in Gulf of Mexico, 80 mi. off N Yucatan coast; 13 mi. long, c.7 mi. wide. Consists of numerous islets and rocks, among them Pérez Isl. (S), a narrow reef c.800 yards long, with fishing huts, good landing, and lighthouse; 22°24′N 90°12′W.

Alacranes (äläkrä′nĕs), town (pop. 2,157), Matanzas prov., W Cuba, on railroad and 19 mi. S of Matanzas, in agr. region (sugar cane, honey, cattle). Airfield. For a time it was called Alfonso XII. The Conchita sugar central is SE.

Alacsony Tatras, Czechoslovakia: see Low Tatra.

Alacuás (äläkwäs′), W suburb (pop. 3,702) of Valencia, Valencia prov., E Spain, in truck-farming area; mfg. of furniture, toys, candy, tartaric acid; sawmilling; cereals, olive oil, wine, hemp.

Ala Dag or **Ala Dagh** (ä′lä dä″, älä′dä), Turkish *Ala Dağ*. **1** Range in S Turkey, in SE Asia Minor, the easternmost and highest part of the Taurus Mts. proper, just SW of the Anti-Taurus; extends 45 mi. SSW-NNE W of Seyhan R.; rises to 12,251 ft. in Kaldi Dag, N of Adana. **2** Peak (7,562 ft.), S central Turkey, 25 mi. WNW of Konya. **3** Range of E Turkey extending SW from Mt. Ararat to L. Van; rises to 11,545 ft.

Ala Dagh (älä′ däg′), Persian *Kuh-i-Aleh* (kōō′-hēälĕ′), one of the Turkmen-Khurasan ranges, in NE Iran; rises to 10,000 ft. in the Shah Jehan, 110 mi. NW of Meshed. Continued SE by Binalud Range.

Aladag River, Turkish *Aladağ*, N central Turkey, rises in Koroglu Mts. 12 mi. ESE of Bolu, flows 70 mi. S to Sakarya R. 20 mi. SE of Nallihan.

Aladdin. **1** Town (pop. 19), Madison co., E central Ind., W suburb of Alexandria. **2** Village, Crook co., NE Wyo., near S.Dak. line and Black Hills, 19 mi. NE of Sundance. Hq. of Bear Lodge Dist. of Black Hills Natl. Forest here.

Alaejos (äläā′hōs), town (pop. 3,404), Valladolid prov., N central Spain, 16 mi. W of Medina del Campo; alcohol distilling; cereals, wine.

Alafors (ä″läfôrs′, -fōsh′), village (pop. 683), Alvsborg co., SW Sweden, near Gota R., 6 mi. NE of Kungalv; textile milling.

Alag (ŏ′lŏg), town (pop. 3,801), Pest-Pilis-Solt-Kiskun co., N central Hungary, near the Danube, 9 mi. N of Budapest. Has 14th-cent. church; race track.

Alaganuck, Alaska: see Alakanuk.

Alagar Hills, India: see Sirumalai Hills.

Alagez (ŭlŭgyôs′), village (1939 pop. over 500), NW Armenian SSR, on N slope of Mt. Aragats, 24 mi. ESE of Leninakan; livestock (winter pastures).

Alagez, Mount, Armenian SSR: see Aragats, Mount.

Alagi, peak, Ethiopia: see Alaji.

Alagir (ŭlŭgēr′), city (1926 pop. 4,192; 1944 pop. over 10,000), central North Ossetian Autonomous SSR, Russian SFSR, on Ardon R. and 23 mi. W of Dzaudzhikau; rail terminus; N end of Ossetian Military Road; machine mfg., sawmilling, woodworking, cement making (local marl deposits). Health resort. Became city in 1938.

Alagna (älä′nyä), village (pop. 1,219), Pavia prov., Lombardy, N Italy, near Terdoppio R., 13 mi. W of Pavia.

Alagna Valsesia (välsā′zyä), village (pop. 142), Vercelli prov., Piedmont, N Italy, on S slope of Monte Rosa, 21 mi. NNW of Biella. Resort (alt. 3,906 ft.), point of ascent for Monte Rosa. Gold mines 1 mi. N. Iron, lead, zinc deposits near by.

Alagnon River or **Allagnon River** (älänyō′), in Cantal, Haute-Loire, and Puy-de-Dôme depts., central France, rises in Massif du Cantal near Le Lioran, flows 50 mi. NE, past Murat and Massiac, to the Allier 7 mi. SSE of Issoire.

Alagoa de Baixo, Brazil: see Sertânia.

Alagoa do Monteiro, Brazil: see Monteiro.

Alagoa Grande (älŏgō′ŭ grän′dĭ), city (pop. 4,103), E Paraíba, NE Brazil, 50 mi. W of João Pessoa; W terminus of rail spur from Camarazal; sugar cane, cotton, fruit (pineapples, bananas, oranges).

Alagoa Nova (nō′vŭ), city (pop. 2,378), E central Paraíba, NE Brazil, 13 mi. NE of Campina Grande; agave fibers, tobacco, beans, fruit. Called Laranjeiras, 1939–43.

Alagoas (älŏgō′ŭs), state (□ 11,016; 1940 pop. 951,300; 1950 census 1,106,454), NE Brazil; ⊙ Maceió. Of triangular shape, it is bounded E by the Atlantic, N by Pernambuco, S by lower São Francisco R. (Sergipe border). Its coastal plain, merging in S with São Francisco lowland, rises toward interior upland (*sertão*) in NW. Tropical temperatures (average, 80° F.) somewhat relieved by SE trade winds; March-July is rainy season. The São Francisco (interrupted by the Paulo Afonso Falls and 60 mi. of rapids; navigable below Piranhas) is state's only important river. Coastal area is dotted with inter-connected salt-water lagoons cut off from the Atlantic by sandy barrier beaches. Chief agr. products are sugar, cotton, rice, pineapples, and tobacco. Castor beans, fibers, dyewood, and livestock are also shipped. Sugar milling (in numerous local plants), alcohol distilling, and textile weaving are principal industries. State will benefit from completion (early 1950s) of large hydroelectric installations at Paulo Afonso Falls. Chief cities are Maceió and Penedo (port on lower São Francisco R.). Maceió is linked by rail with Recife (Pernambuco) and Palmeira dos Índios (in the interior). As part of captaincy of Pernambuco (until 1817), Alagoas was occupied by the Dutch in 17th cent. Became prov. of Brazilian empire in 1823, and state of federal republic in 1889.

Alagoas, city, Brazil: see MARECHAL DEODORO.

Alagoinhas (älŭgoi'nyŭs), city (1950 pop. 21,605), Bahia, Brazil, 60 mi. N of Salvador, in tobacco-growing region; rail junction on Salvador-Aracaju line (branch to Juàzeiro); ships tobacco, sugar, leather, mangabeira rubber, livestock.

Alagón (älägōn'), town (pop. 6,130), Saragossa prov., NE Spain, bet. the Ebro and the Imperial Canal, 15 mi. NW of Saragossa; sugar milling, chocolate mfg.; lumbering, stock raising. Cereals, fruit grown in area. Has Jesuit church, and parish church with octagonal tower.

Alagón River, in Salamanca and Cáceres prov., W Spain, chief tributary of the Tagus; rises in NE spurs of the Peña de Francia, flows 130 mi. SW to the Tagus near Alcántara. Trout fishing. Irrigation reservoir.

Alah or **Allah** (älä'), town (1939 pop. 1,490), Cotabato prov., S Mindanao, Philippines, 75 mi. SE of Cotabato near upper Alah R. (tributary of Pulangi R.), in rich rice-growing area. Land settlement project begun here 1950.

Alahyar-jo-Tando, Pakistan: see TANDO ALLAHYAR.

Alai, range, Kirghiz SSR: see ALAI RANGE.

Alaid Island (ŭlīēt'), Jap. *Araido-to* or *Araito-to,* northernmost (50°56'N 155°42'E; □ 48) of main Kurile Isls. group, Russian SFSR; separated from Paramushir Isl. (E) by 12-mi.-wide Alaid Strait; 8 mi. in diameter. Rises to 7,657 ft. in Alaid volcano, Jap. *Oyakoba-yama,* highest in the Kuriles. Has small fishing pop.

Alaigne (älā'nyŭ), village (pop. 296), Aude dept., S France, 7 mi. WNW of Limoux; fruit- and wine-growing. Cereals.

Alai Range or **Alay Range** (ŭlī'), one of W ranges of Tien Shan mountain system, in S Osh oblast, Kirghiz SSR; extends from upper reaches of the Kara Darya on China border 200 mi. W to Sokh R. headwaters; rises to c.16,500 ft. Osh-Khorog highway crosses (N–S) at Taldyk Pass (11,980 ft.). Just S, the KYZYL-SU drains **Alai Valley,** a fertile, elevated pasture area, with some wheat cultivation, lying N of Trans-Alai Range.

Alais, France: see ALÈS.

Alaiye, Turkey: see ALANYA.

Alájar (älä'här), town (pop. 1,501), Huelva prov., SW Spain, in the Sierra de Aracena, 6 mi. W of Aracena, in agr. region (corn, acorns, fruit, olives, livestock); flour- and sawmilling, chocolate mfg. Has mineral springs, marble quarry.

Alajeró (älähārō'), village (pop. 428), Gomera, Canary Isls., 9 mi. W of San Sebastián; cereals, bananas, potatoes, beans, tomatoes, figs, fruit, almonds, chick-peas, livestock.

Alaji (ä'läjē), Ital. *Alagi,* peak (11,279 ft.), N Ethiopia, in Tigre prov., at W edge of Great Rift Valley, 36 mi. S of Makale.

Alajuela (älä-whā'lä), province (□ 3,700; 1950 pop. 148,850) of N Costa Rica; ⊙ Alajuela. Located largely in tropical lowlands drained by the Río Frío (Guatuso Lowland) and San Carlos R., it extends from Nicaragua border S across the Central Cordillera (Poás volcano) onto the central plateau and the Tárcoles valley. Agr.: coffee, sugar cane, corn, beans, rice, pineapples. Stock raising and lumbering in lowlands. Gold mining in Aguacate hills near San Mateo. Served by railroad and Inter-American Highway on central plateau section. Main centers are Alajuela, San Ramón, Grecia, Orotina, and Villa Quesada.

Alajuela, city (1950 pop. 13,903), ⊙ Alajuela prov., central Costa Rica, on central plateau, on Inter-American Highway, on railroad and 12 mi. NW of San José; alt. 3,225 ft.; 10°2'N 84°12'W. Commercial center; mfg. of vegetable oils, textiles, canned goods, beverages, soaps; coffee processing, lumber milling. Livestock fair; grain trade. Has cathedral, weaving school, and flower gardens. The westernmost city on central plateau, it developed as trading center for San Carlos and Turrúcares lowlands. Declined after construction of railroad to Puntarenas, which by-passed it (S).

Alajuela, Panama Canal Zone: see MADDEN DAM.

Alajuelita (älä-whālē'tä), town (1950 pop. 622), San José prov., central Costa Rica, on central plateau, 2.5 mi. SSW of San José, in coffee area; vegetables; pottery making. Its church with Christ of Esquipulas is annual pilgrimage center.

Alakanuk (ălŭkă'nŭk), village (pop. 146), W Alaska, near Bering Sea, 10 mi. NE of mouth of Yukon R., 120 mi. S of Nome; trading center for trappers and prospectors. Sometimes spelled Alaganuck.

Alaknanda River (ä'lŭknŭn'dŭ), headstream of the Ganges, in N Uttar Pradesh, India; formed in W Kumaun Himalayas by junction of 2 headstreams rising E and W of Kamet mtn. and joining at Joshimath; flows c.75 mi. SW, past Chamoli and Srinagar, joining Bhagirathi R. at Devaprayag to form Ganges R. One of the sacred rivers of India.

Alakshan, China: see ALASHAN.

Ala-Kul or **Ala-Kul'** (ŭlä"-kōōl'), salt lake (□ 890), E Kazakh SSR, near China frontier, on border of Semipalatinsk and Taldy-Kurgan oblasts, 100 mi. E of L. Balkhash; 154 ft. deep. Valley connected with Ebi Nor, lake in Sinkiang prov., China, by DZUNGARIAN GATES. Receives Urdzhar R. (N). Also known as Ala-Kol.

Alakurtti (ä'lŭkōōrtyē), village, N Karelo-Finnish SSR, on railroad and 60 mi. WSW of Kandalaksha. Finnish frontier post until 1940, when it passed to USSR.

Alalakeiki Channel (ä'läläkāē'kē), bet. Kahoolawe and Maui isls., T.H., 6 naut. mi. wide.

Alamagan (älämägän'), uninhabited volcanic island (□ 4), N Marianas Isls., W Pacific, c.270 mi. NNE of Guam; 2.8 mi. long, 1.6 mi. wide; extinct crater with 2 peaks (higher is 2,441 ft.).

Alamanas River, Greece: see SPERCHEIOS RIVER.

Alamance (ă'lŭmăns), county (□ 434; pop. 71,220), N central N.C.; ⊙ Graham. Piedmont area; crossed by Haw R. Tobacco, corn, hay, dairy products; timber. Mfg. of textiles, furniture; sawmilling. Formed 1849.

'Alamayn, Al-, Egypt: see ALAMEIN.

Alambagh, India: see LUCKNOW, city.

Alambazar, India: see BARANAGAR.

Alameda (ălŭmē'dŭ), town (pop. 246), SE Sask., 34 mi. ENE of Estevan; grain elevators, stock.

Alameda (älämā'dhä), city (pop. 5,865), Málaga prov., S Spain, in the Sierra de Yeguas, 14 mi. NNW of Antequera; olive-oil industry; liquor distilling, sawmilling, tanning, mfg. of esparto goods (baskets).

Alameda (ălŭmē'dŭ), county (□ 733; pop. 740,315), W Calif.; ⊙ Oakland. Stretches from San Francisco Bay E across Coast Ranges to touch San Joaquin Valley (in NE); includes Livermore Valley (wines). Cities of East Bay residential, port, industrial region (OAKLAND, ALAMEDA, BERKELEY, industrial Emeryville)| are linked to San Francisco (W) by San Francisco-Oakland Bay Bridge; in S, bay is spanned by San Mateo Toll Bridge near Hayward. Growing of flowers, nursery plants; agr. (truck, grain, hay; fruit, especially grapes; nuts); poultry, dairy products, livestock. Salt and bromine production; sand, gravel, clay quarrying; magnesite mining, stone quarrying. Formed 1853.

Alameda. 1 (ălŭmē'dŭ) City and port (pop. 36,256), Alameda co., W Calif., on isl. (6½ mi. long) in E San Francisco Bay, across an estuary (deepwater harbor) from Oakland, with which it is connected by Posey Tube (completed 1928) and several bridges. Includes Bay Farm Isl., tip of a mainland peninsula (just S). Residential, industrial; large shipping terminals, shipyards, canneries, foundries, lumber mills, borax refineries, railroad shops. Seat of large U.S. naval air station (formerly Benton Field), a U.S. coast guard base, and a U.S. maritime school. Has fine parks, beaches, yacht harbor. Inc. as town in 1854, as city in 1884. **2** (ălŭmē'dŭ) Village (pop. 4,694), Bannock co., SE Idaho, residential suburb of Pocatello. Laid out 1912, known as Fairview until 1920, inc. 1924. **3** (ălŭmē'dŭ, –mā'dŭ) Village (pop. 1,792), Bernalillo co., central N.Mex., on Rio Grande and 8 mi. N of Albuquerque, in irrigated agr. region; alt. c.5,000 ft.; grain, chili, fruit. Sanitarium here. Sandia Mts. and part of Cibola Natl. Forest are E, Sandia Pueblo Indian village just N.

Alameda de la Sagra, La (lä älämā'dhä dhā lä sä'grä), town (pop. 1,575), Toledo prov., central Spain, near the Tagus, 28 mi. S of Madrid; olive-oil factories; gypsum quarries. Cereals, grapes, livestock.

Alamedilla (älämā-dhē'lyä), village (pop. 1,854), Granada prov., S Spain, 20 mi. NNW of Guadix; flour milling, lumbering; olives, cereals, sugar beets.

Alamein (ălŭmān', ä–, ä'lŭmān, ä'–), **El Alamein,** or **Al-'Alamayn** (both: ĕl älämān'), village, N Egypt, in Western Desert prov., on coastal railroad and 65 mi. W of Alexandria; site of one of the decisive battles of Second World War. Here the British halted their retreat before Rommel's pursuing army and established (June, 1942) a defense line extending c.35 mi. S to the QATTARA DEPRESSION. Out of this defensive position broke the British under Montgomery and Alexander in the great battle of Oct. 23–Nov. 3, 1942, routing the Axis forces and removing the threat to Alexandria and the Suez Canal.

Alamillo (älämē'lyō), town (pop. 2,014), Ciudad Real prov., S central Spain, in N Sierra Morena, 7 mi. SSE of Almadén. Grain and olive growing, sheep raising, flour milling.

Alaminos (älämē'nōs), town (1939 pop. 2,130; 1948 municipality pop. 26,240), Pangasinan prov., central Luzon, Philippines, on Cape Bolinao peninsula, 18 mi. WNW of Lingayen; agr. center (rice, corn, copra).

Alamitos Bay (ălŭmē'tŭs), S Calif., many-armed lagoon at mouth of San Gabriel R. on the Pacific, just E of Long Beach; pleasure-craft anchorage. Sheltered by sandspit, with parks, fine beaches.

Álamo (ä'lämō), town (pop. 2,977), Veracruz, E Mexico, in Gulf lowlands, 17 mi. NW of Tuxpan; corn, sugar, coffee, fruit. Petroleum wells near by. Sometimes Temapache.

Alamo (ă'lŭmō). **1** Town (pop. 800), Wheeler co., SE central Ga., 27 mi. SSE of Dublin. **2** Town (pop. 163), Montgomery co., W Ind., near Sugar Creek, 9 mi. SW of Crawfordsville, in agr. area. **3** Village (pop. 192), Williams co., NW N.Dak., 31 mi. N of Williston. **4** Town (pop. 1,501), ⊙ Crockett co., W Tenn., 20 mi. NW of Jackson, in cotton, grain, livestock, truck region; cotton ginning. **5** City (pop. 3,017), Hidalgo co., extreme S Texas, in the lower Rio Grande valley, 7 mi. E of McAllen, in rich irrigated truck, citrus, cotton area; fruit, vegetable canning, cotton ginning. Inc. 1924.

Álamo, El (ĕl ä'lämō), town (pop. 1,096), Madrid prov., central Spain, 21 mi. SW of Madrid; cereals, grapes, chick-peas, carobs. Wine making (*mistela*), mfg. of cream of tartar.

Alamo, The, Texas: see SAN ANTONIO.

Alamo Canal, Calif. and Lower Calif.: see IMPERIAL VALLEY.

Alamogordo (ălŭmŭgôr'dŭ, –dō), town (pop. 6,783), ⊙ Otero co., S N.Mex., just W of Sacramento Mts., 85 mi. NNE of El Paso, Texas; alt. c.4,300 ft. Trade center and health resort in agr. and livestock region; sawmills, railroad repair shops, marble works. Town settled 1898 with arrival of railroad. State school for blind, hq. of Lincoln Natl. Forest here. Part of Lincoln Natl. Forest is just E; Mescalero Indian Reservation is NE. White Sands Natl. Monument, White Sands Proving Grounds for rockets, and Holloman Air Force Base are SW. First atomic bomb was exploded (July 16, 1945) c.50 mi. NW in desert region W of SIERRA OSCURA.

Alamogordo Dam, N.Mex.: see PECOS RIVER.

Alamo Heights (ă'lŭmō), city (pop. 8,000), Bexar co., S central Texas; a N residential suburb of San Antonio. Inc. 1926.

Alamor (älämôr'), town (1950 pop. 1,256), Loja prov., S Ecuador, in the Andes, 7 mi. NW of Celica; cereals, cattle. Also called Puyango.

Álamos (ä'lämōs), city (pop. 2,921), Sonora, NW Mexico, in mtn. valley, 135 mi. SE of Guaymas; mining center (silver, zinc, gold, copper). Iron deposits near by. Lumbering.

Alamos, Los, Chile: see LOS ALAMOS.

Alamosa (ălŭmō'sŭ), county (□ 720; pop. 10,531), S Colo.; ⊙ Alamosa. Irrigated agr. area, watered by Rio Grande; bounded E by Sangre de Cristo Mts. Livestock, hay, potatoes. San Luis Valley extends N–S. Part of Great Sand Dunes Natl. Monument and San Isabel Natl. Forest in NE. Formed 1913.

Alamosa, city (pop. 5,354), ⊙ Alamosa co., S Colo., on Rio Grande, in San Luis Valley, and 90 mi. SW of Pueblo; alt. 7,500 ft. Shipping and processing center, with railroad shops, for San Luis Valley; dairy and meat products, potatoes; mfg. (flour, beverages, oil products). State teachers col. here. Near by is state soldiers' and sailors' home. Blanca Peak is ENE, Great Sand Dunes Natl. Monument NE. City founded and inc. 1878 with coming of railroad.

Alampur (ä'lŭmpōōr). **1** Town (pop. 5,703), Raichur dist., S Hyderabad state, India, on Tungabhadra R. and 55 mi. SE of Raichur; sugar cane, mangoes, tamarind; rice and oilseed milling, cotton ginning. **2** Village, NE Madhya Bharat, India, 42 mi. ESE of Lashkar; gram, millet. Malhar Rao Holkar, founder of house of Indore, died here in 1766.

Alamut (älämōōt'), village, First Prov., in Kazvin, N Iran, in Elburz mts., 35 mi. ENE of Kazvin. Castle here was hq. of the Ismailian terrorist sect of Assassins, who fought the Crusaders throughout the 12th cent. until destroyed by the Seljuk Turks in mid-13th cent.

Aland or **Alland** (both: ŭlŭnd'), town (pop. 13,041), Gulbarga dist., W Hyderabad state, India, 24 mi. NW of Gulbarga; millet, cotton, wheat; flour milling.

Alandi (ŭlŭn'dē), town (pop. 2,170), Poona dist., central Bombay, India, 11 mi. N of Poona; Hindu pilgrimage center.

Aland Islands (ä'lŭnd, ô'–), Swedish *Åland* (ō'länd), Finnish *Ahvenanmaa* (ä'vĕnänmä'), archipelago coextensive with Aland co. (□ 572; including water area, □ 581; pop. 23,056) of Finland, in the Baltic Sea at entrance to Gulf of Bothnia, bet. mainlands of Sweden and Finland; ⊙ Mariehamn, a port on Aland isl. The archipelago consists of c.6,500 granite isls. and skerries, of which 80 are inhabited. Largest isl. is Aland (□ 285; pop. 15,259); other larger isls. are Eckero, Lemland, Lumparland, and Vardo. Pop. is entirely Swedish-speaking and enjoys a degree of autonomy. Fishing is chief industry; agr. (rye, barley, flax, vegetables) and cattle raising are carried on under difficult conditions. Many windmills are still in use. Tourist trade is important. In 19th cent. the isls., and especially port of Mariehamn, were home of important fleet of sailing vessels engaged in Australian grain trade, but after Second World War the last of these was laid up. Inhabited in prehistoric times, Aland Isls. were christianized in 12th cent. by Swedes. Seized (1714) by Peter the Great after his naval victory, near by, over Swedes; restored (1721) to Sweden. Passed (1809) with Finland to Russia. In Crimean War shelled (1854) by Anglo-French fleet; demilitarized (1856) under Treaty of Paris. Fortified (1915) by Russians with British and French consent. During Finnish war of independence (1918) isls. were captured by Finns, then occupied by Swedes, Germans, and again by Finns. Strong pro-Swedish secessionist movement led to grant of local autonomy. Finnish sovereignty confirmed (1921) by League of Nations, which at same time neutralized archipelago and guaranteed the islanders special rights. Sometimes spelled Aaland.

Alandroal (ălăndrōōăl′), town (pop. 1,733), Évora dist., S central Portugal, 30 mi. ENE of Évora; grain, cheese; iron deposits. Has interesting 13th-cent. castle.

Alandur (ălŭn′dōōr), town (pop. 13,213), Chingleput dist., E Madras, India, residential suburb of Madras, 5 mi. SSW of city center.

Alange (ălăn′hā), town (pop. 2,764), Badajoz prov., W Spain, 10 mi. SE of Mérida, in agr. region (cereals, olives, truck, livestock). Known for its mineral springs since Roman times. Sometimes Alanje.

Alangudi (ä′lŭng-gōōdē), town (pop. 2,959), Trichinopoly dist., S Madras, India, 11 mi. E of Pudukkottai; millet, peanuts, rice.

Alanís (älänēs′), town (pop. 4,054), Seville prov., SW Spain, in the Sierra Morena, 45 mi. NNE of Seville; agr. center (olives, vegetables, livestock); lumbering, charcoal burning, flour milling. Has old castle.

Alanje (ălăn′hā), village (pop. 506), Chiriquí prov., W Panama, in Pacific lowland, on railroad and 8 mi. WSW of David; commercial center; coffee bananas, cacao, livestock. One of oldest towns of W Panama.

Alanje, Spain: see ALANGE.

Alanno (ălăn′nô), village (pop. 1,143), Pescara prov., Abruzzi e Molise, S central Italy, 11 mi. WSW of Chieti; mfg. (bricks, asphalt).

Alano di Piave (ălä′nô dē pyä′vē), village (pop. 1,160), Belluno prov., Veneto, N Italy, near Piave R., 7 mi. S of Feltre; silk mill.

Alanskoye (ŭlăn′skŭyŭ), village (1939 pop. over 2,000), N North Ossetian Autonomous SRR, Russian SFSR, 10 mi. SSW of Malgobek; wheat. Petroleum deposits. Until 1944 (in Chechen-Ingush Autonomous SSR), called Psedakh.

Alanson (ŭlăn′sŭn), village (pop. 319), Emmet co., NW Mich., 10 mi. NE of Petoskey, bet. Burt and Crooked lakes, in resort area.

Alantika Mountains (ăläntē′kä), range in W central Africa, on Nigeria–Fr. Cameroons border, just S of Benue R. valley.

Alanya (ä′län″yä), town (pop. 5,884), Antalya prov., SW Turkey, port on Mediterranean Sea, 75 mi. ESE of Antalya; copper, chromium; barley, wheat, onions, cotton. Formerly Alaya, Alaia, or Alaiye.

Alao Island (ălou′) (□ 4.2; pop. 574), off E coast of Chiloé Isl., Chiloé prov., S Chile, 25 mi. ESE of Castro; 4 mi. long; potatoes, livestock; fishing.

Alaotra, Lake (ălăō′trŭ) (□ 70), NE central Madagascar, 110 mi. NE of Tananarive; 25 mi. long, 8 mi. wide; alt. 2,460 ft. Drains NE to Indian Ocean via Maningory R. (c.60 mi. long). Largest lake of Madagascar. The surrounding agr. area (rice, manioc, tobacco, geraniums) is being extended by drainage of vast swamps to W and SW. The region is connected to main trunk Tananarive-Tamatave by Ambatosoratra-Moramanga railroad. L.Alaotra agr. station (1926) experiments on rice, manioc, peanuts. Fishing in lake waters.

Alaouites, Territory of the, Syria: see LATAKIA, province.

Alap (ŏ′lŏp), town (pop. 3,152), Fejer co., W central Hungary, 30 mi. SSE of Szekesfehervar; wheat, corn; cattle.

Alapaha (ŭlă′pŭhô″), town (pop. 505), Berrien co., S Ga., 18 mi. ESE of Tifton, near Alapaha R.

Alapaha River, rises in SE corner of Dooly co., S Ga., flows SSE, past Willacoochee and Statenville, into N Fla. to Suwannee R. 10 mi. SW of Jasper; 190 mi. long.

Alapayevsk (ŭlŭpī′ŭfsk), city (1926 pop. 12,148; 1932 pop. estimate 30,000), S central Sverdlovsk oblast, Russian SFSR, in E foothills of the central Urals, on Neiva R. and 60 mi. E of Nizhni Tagil; rail junction; a major metallurgical center (based on local iron and charcoal), producing steel and pig iron; mfg. of prefabricated houses, woodworking. Refractory-clay quarries, charcoal burners, limestone and peat works near by. Extensive bauxite, siderite, and limonite deposits. Ironworks date from 1702; became city in 1933. Was childhood home of Tchaikovsky.

Alapillai, India: see SIRONCHA.

Alaplie, Turkey: see ALPULLU.

Alapulai, India: see ALLEPPEY.

Alapur (ä′läpōōr), town (pop. 7,914), Budaun dist., central Uttar Pradesh, India, 11 mi. SE of Budaun; trades in wheat, pearl millet, mustard, barley, gram. Founded 15th cent. Has 17th-cent. mosque.

Alaquines (äläkē′nēs), city (pop. 864), San Luis Potosí, N central Mexico, 30 mi. NE of Río Verde; alt. 4,268 ft.; corn, wheat, cotton, maguey.

Alaraz (äläräth′), village (pop. 1,653), Salamanca prov., W Spain, 25 mi. SE of Salamanca; meat processing, flour milling. Mineral springs.

Alarcón (älärkōn′), town (pop. 572), Cuenca prov., E central Spain, in New Castile, on Júcar R. and 36 mi. S of Cuenca; cereals, grapes, saffron, honey, sheep. Woolen-goods mfg. Picturesque old town; has ruins of Romanesque castle, and Gothic Santa María church. Site of hydroelectric project.

Alar del Rey (älär′ dhĕl rā′), town (pop. 1,129), Palencia prov., N central Spain, on Pisuerga R. and 47 mi. NNE of Palencia; woolen mills. Starting point of the Canal of Castile.

Alaró (älärō′), town (pop. 3,686), Majorca, Balearic Isls., rail terminus 12 mi. NE of Palma; agr. center (olives, almonds, carobs, sheep, goats). Lumbering, olive-oil pressing; marble quarrying, coal mining. Mfg. of shoes and cement.

Alasehir (ălă′shĕhĭr″), Turk. *Alaşehir*, town (1950 pop. 10,738), Manisa prov., W Turkey, on railroad near Gediz R. and 60 mi. ESE of Manisa; raisins, valonia, barley, wheat, sugar beets; hot mineral springs. Near site of anc. PHILADELPHIA. Sometimes spelled Alashehir.

Alashan Desert (ălăshän′), in Ningsia section of Inner Mongolia, China, bet. Alashan Mts. and Yellow R. (E) and the river Etsin Gol (W); inhabited by the West Mongol tribe of the Alashan Eleut (Ölöt). Sometimes called Alakshan.

Alashan Mountains or **Holan Mountains** (hŭ′län′), SE Ningsia prov., China, extend parallel to Yellow R., separating Ningsia agr. dist. (E) from Alashan Desert (W); rise to over 10,000 ft. 40 mi. NW of Yinchwan. Sometimes called Alakshan.

Alash River, Honduras: see JICATUYO RIVER.

Alaska (ŭlă′skŭ), U.S. territory (□ 571,065; with water area □ 586,400; 1939 pop. 72,524; 1950 pop. 128,643), NW North America; ⊙ JUNEAU. ANCHORAGE is largest city. Alaska is a huge block of land at NW extremity of the continent bet. the Arctic Ocean (N) and Pacific Ocean (S). Its rugged coastline in W thrusts in Seward Peninsula to Bering Strait, which separates it by 55 mi. from the Asiatic USSR. The strait opens S on Bering Sea and N on Chukchi Sea. S of Seward Peninsula is Norton Sound, and further S, Bristol Bay, just N of the long Alaska Peninsula which is continued by the ALEUTIAN ISLANDS to the USSR boundary near 172°E. Isls. to N of the Aleutians include PRIBILOF ISLANDS, SAINT LAWRENCE ISLAND, and NUNIVAK ISLAND. S shore of Alaska is deeply indented by Cook Inlet and Prince William Sound, with the Kenai Peninsula bet. them running SW; it is continued by KODIAK ISLAND. Prince William Sound is itself a part of the wide Gulf of Alaska. Where the coast runs SE from the Gulf of Alaska lies the narrow Panhandle of Alaska, cutting into the Canadian prov. of British Columbia; off the panhandle coast is the ALEXANDER ARCHIPELAGO. Except for the panhandle, the E boundary of Alaska is with Yukon Territory. Not only the rough coast but the high mtn. ranges of Alaska cut the territory into 3 well-defined geographic regions: (1) the Pacific slope, which includes the panhandle and S central and SW Alaska; (2) interior Alaska, which extends from the N slope of the coastal ranges to the S slopes of the Brooks Range in the N; and (3) arctic Alaska, which extends N of Brooks Range to the Arctic Ocean. The climate of Alaska is generally mild, the Japan Current and the high mts. combining to make the coast extremely wet. Here, too, are fjords and great glacier fields, such as Malaspina Glacier. The Stikine and Copper rivers here reach the coast. Average annual precipitation, reaching 150 in., has nourished lush vegetation and dense forests throughout the coastal and isl. sections. Average winter temp. is c.32°F., summer 50–60°F. The S Alaska valleys near Anchorage, Homer, and Palmer are cooler and drier than the SE and S central region. SW Alaska is mountainous and of recent volcanic origin; the Aleutian Mts. extend the length of Alaska Peninsula. Active volcanic phenomena include Katmai Volcano and the Valley of Ten Thousand Smokes in Katmai Natl. Monument. N portion of this region is forested, but Aleutian Isls. are treeless, being covered with low bushes and grasses. Here heavy fog is added to the typical Pacific climate, and there are occasional violent winds (the williwaws). N of the Pacific slope and coastal mtn. ranges is the Alaska Range, rising to the highest peak in North America, Mt. McKinley in Mt. McKinley Natl. Park. N and W of the Alaska Range is interior Alaska, extending W from the Canadian border and N to the Brooks Range. This is the drainage basin of the Kuskokwim R. and the great Yukon R. Interior Alaska is a high plateau, sloping gradually towards deltas of the Yukon and Kuskokwim on Bering Sea. River valleys have park-like forest growth; uplands are tundra covered. Climate is continental, with warm summers and extremely cold winters, and dry with average annual rainfall from 15–20 in. In arctic Alaska, N of Brooks Range, there are no forests. Tundra covered, it is a flat, uninteresting expanse cut by many shallow streams flowing N to the Arctic Ocean. Short summers thaw only 1–2 ft. of permanently frozen surface; winters are long and cold, prevented from being exceedingly severe by proximity of the sea. Largest river in region is Colville R.; northernmost point is Point Barrow. The difficulties of communication are one of the most troublesome problems of Alaska; air transport is answering it in part, and all Alaskan towns have their much-used airports. Communications are difficult even in the panhandle, the most populous of the regions, with the capital and others of the best-known towns—KETCHIKAN, old SITKA, WRANGELL, and SKAGWAY. It is connected with Seattle by steamships plying the Inside Passage and is more "civilized," although tourists find the villages of Haida, Tlingit, and Tsimshian Indians exotic and remote. (There are Athapascan Indians in the interior of Alaska, but Eskimos compose the bulk of Alaska's natives.) The chief economic reliance of the people is upon fish, notably the Alaska salmon, and also herring, halibut, crab, shrimp. Some riches still come from the mines that were the spur for founding most of the towns. Principal gold areas are Fairbanks (interior), Juneau (SE), and Nome (W). Other minerals are coal (Matanuska, Healy River) and platinum (Goodnews Bay); also mercury, copper, antimony, tungsten, nickel, tin, iron, lead, zinc, jade, asbestos. The 3d of the Alaskan trilogy of wealth (fish, minerals, furs) was formerly of great importance. Trapping and fur farming are carried on throughout the Territory; chief furs yielded are seal (from Pribilof Isls.), mink, beaver, fox, otter, muskrat, and marten. The Pribilof blue fox is sought but is no longer plentiful. Of the estimated 2,000,000 acres of arable land, only c.12,000 acres are in production; main crops are potatoes, truck vegetables, berries, and dairy products—all for domestic consumption. The land is generally so steep in the Pacific area that agr. is minimal. This is not true of S central Alaska. There, bet. the mts. of the coast and the wide curve of the Alaska Range, are wide valleys that can support farms; here is the much publicized MATANUSKA VALLEY, with its market center at Palmer. Anchorage, the metropolis of the region and the largest and most rapidly growing town of Alaska, is the center for the Matanuska Valley and, more important, the center for the Alaska RR, for airways, and for U.S. defense installations; it is also connected with the Alaska Highway and continued its wartime boom after the Second World War was over. The Kenai Peninsula also has farmlands being developed near Homer. S of Fairbanks is the TANANA VALLEY. There are great stands of timber in Chugach and Tongass natl. forests. The principal cities—besides Juneau and Anchorage are Fairbanks, Sitka, Ketchikan, Petersburg, Wrangell, Cordova, Nome, Whittier, Palmer, Valdez—are, because of communications difficulties, largely self-contained entities, with banking and commercial facilities, newspapers, hotels, radio stations, stores, and activities commonly found only in larger cities in the U.S. Seward, on Kenai Peninsula, having lost its commanding position as terminus of the Alaska RR to Whittier, fell back upon the development of a highway. Valdez on Prince William Sound is enhanced by the RICHARDSON HIGHWAY to Fairbanks (linked with the Alaska Highway). Cordova, which formerly was the port for the big Kennecott copper mine up the Copper R., was injured by the closing of the mine and the railroad to it in 1938 and took recourse only to the sea communications; the products of its fish canning are taken away by steamer. Kodiak on Kodiak Isl. also depends upon the ocean lanes. The native Aleuts of the Aleutian Isls. were the 1st to feel the pressure of white civilization when Russian fur traders came in the 18th cent. When the hunting of the sea otter declined in the 19th cent. so did the importance of the isls., only to be reawakened when Japanese attack in the Second World War showed their prime significance in strategy. Bloody fighting took place on them (notably on ATTU), and Dutch Harbor became a major key of the U.S. defense system. Alaska was 1st reached by Vitus Bering and Aleksandr Chirikov in 1741. Though Capt. James Cook made the 1st survey of the coast bet. Sitka and Bering Strait in 1778 and the SE coast was charted by Capt. George Vancouver in 1791, the settlement of the land was in the hands of the Russians; 1st permanent settlement was established 1784 at Three Saints Bay on Kodiak Isl. by Grigori Shelekhov. Sitka was founded 1799 by Aleksandr Baranov, who headed the Russian America Co., a monopoly. Sitka was rebuilt after destruction by the Indians in 1802. From a "castle" at Sitka Baranov ruled, extending the Russian trade far down the coast. But Canadian fur traders pushed across the continent in the wake of Sir Alexander Mackenzie, and the American Lewis and Clark expedition was followed by the founding of the short-lived post at Astoria. A clash of interests occurred. In 1824 negotiations with Great Britain and the U.S. set the limit of the Russian colony definitely at 54°40′ N. Already the Russians had begun to withdraw from the American coast, and Alaska settled into a long period of decline. In 1867 the territory was bought by the U.S. for $7,200,000. The purchase was made also solely through the determined energy of Secretary of State William H. Seward, and for many years afterward—even after Alaska had begun to return fortunes in gold and fish—the land was sometimes derisively called Seward's Folly or Seward's Icebox. Alaska was neglected.

The U.S. army officially had it in charge until 1876. After a small lapse of govt. altogether except for customs men, the navy was given charge in 1879. Most of the territory was not even known, although the British (notably Sir John Franklin and Capt. F. W. Beechey) had early explored the Arctic coast and the Hudson's Bay Co. men, Robert Campbell and Alexander Murray had explored the Yukon, where Fort Yukon was founded in 1847. It was not until gold was discovered in the Juneau region in 1880 that Alaska was given a governor and a feeble local administration was established by the Organic Act of 1884. Missionaries, who had come to the region in the late '70s, exercised considerable influence. Most influential of them was Sheldon Jackson, best known for his introduction of reindeer to help the Alaskan Eskimo, beggared by the wanton destruction of the fur seals. The sealing was the subject of a long international controversy which was not ended until after gold had changed Alaska permanently. Paradoxically, the 1st finds that had tremendous influence on Alaska were not in Alaska at all, but in Canada. The development at Fortymile Creek and in the upper Yukon area prepared the way for the great Klondike strike of 1896, which brought a stampede. Most of the miners were from the U.S. and most of them came through Alaska. The big discoveries in Alaska itself followed—Nome in 1889, Fairbanks in 1902. The miners and prospectors—the sourdoughs—took over Alaska, and the era of the rough mining camps reached its height; this was the Alaska of Jack London, Rex Beach, and romance. It was also lawless, and a criminal code was belatedly applied in 1899. Not until 1906 did Alaska get a Territorial representative in Congress. The boundary bet. the Panhandle of Alaska and British Columbia was settled in 1903. A new era began for Alaska with the establishment of local govt. in 1912 (Juneau had officially replaced Sitka as capital in 1900 and had begun to function as capital in 1906). The building of the Alaska RR from Seward to Fairbanks was commenced with govt. funds in 1915. Already, however, the flush of gold fever had begun to die and Alaska receded into one of its periods of lull. The fishing industry, quietly going forward in the noise of gold rushes, had become the major Alaskan industry, which it still remains. Mining was revived by use of the deep-dredging process in the 1920s. Alaska's latest lull was ended by its greatest boom with the approach of the Second World War, when U.S. defense bases were built. The Japanese did actually get a foothold in the Aleutian Isls. and were ousted only after hard fighting in 1943. More important, Alaska became an arsenal, and money poured in for creation of army camps, naval bases, and air bases. Besides those in the Aleutians, U.S. air bases were built at Ladd Field and Eielson Air Force Base near Fairbanks, Elmendorf Field near Anchorage, and Mark Field near Nome. The Alaska Highway was built, supplying a still-weak but much-needed link in communication. Univ. of Alaska was chartered 1917 and opened 1922 as Alaska Agr. Col. and School of Mines; it is at College, 5 mi. from Fairbanks. With Alaska's post-war growth and the development of its natural resources, there was increasing sentiment for statehood for Alaska, both in the territory itself and in the U.S.

Alaska, Gulf of, broad N inlet of Pacific Ocean, on S coast of Alaska, bet. Alaska Peninsula (W) and Alexander Archipelago (E). Includes Kodiak Isl. Chief ports are Anchorage, Seward, and Valdez.

Alaska Current, branch of Aleutian Current, flowing counterclockwise in Gulf of Alaska.

Alaska Highway, road (1,527 mi. long) to Alaska in W Canada, beginning at railhead at Dawson Creek, B.C., through the Yukon, to Fairbanks, Alaska. Built (March–Oct., 1942) under very difficult conditions by U.S. Army engineers to provide overland supply route to American Forces in Alaska. Canadian section of highway was turned over to Canada, April 1, 1946. Formerly called Alaska Military Highway, Alaskan International Highway, and, unofficially, Alcan Highway. Serves Fort St. John, Fort Nelson, Teslin, Whitehorse, Snag, and Northway. In S, at Dawson Creek, the highway joined an existing road (468 mi. long) to Edmonton, Alta. In N the highway is joined by other roads which serve Haines, Valdez, and Anchorage (see Haines Cut-off, Tok Cut-off, Richardson Highway, Glenn Highway).

Alaska Juneau Camp (jo͞o'nō), village (1940 pop. 79), SE Alaska, 2 mi. S of Juneau; gold mine with mill.

Alaska Military Highway: see Alaska Highway.

Alaskan International Highway, Alaska: see Alaska Highway.

Alaska Peninsula, SW Alaska, extends 500 mi. SW from mainland, near 59°30'N 155°W, bet. Bristol Bay of Bering Sea (NW) and the Pacific (SE). Aleutian Range runs length of peninsula; includes many volcanoes, including those in Katmai National Monument (NE). Native villages on both shores; fishing, trapping. Largely unsurveyed. Weather is wet, cool, and foggy throughout year. Aleutian Isls. extend SW from tip of peninsula.

Alaska Range, mountain range, S central Alaska, extends c.400 mi. E–W in a crescent S of Fairbanks and N of Cook Inlet, Kenai Peninsula, and Prince William Sound. It is NW continuation of the Coast Mts. system, and is in turn continued by the Aleutian Range. Highest peak is Mt. McKinley (20,270 ft.); other high peaks are Mt. Foraker (17,280 ft.), Mt. Hunter (14,960 ft.), Mt. Hayes (13,740 ft.), Mt. Silverthrone (13,130 ft.), and Mt. Gerdine (12,600 ft.). Range separates S Alaska coastal region from tundra prairie of interior.

Alassio (äläs'syô), town (pop. 5,609), Savona prov., Liguria, NW Italy, port on Gulf of Genoa and 11 mi. NE of Imperia, in flower, hemp, flax region; wine making. Resort of Riviera di Ponente; noted for fine villas, luxuriant gardens. Has Gothic church (1507).

Alat (ülät'), village (1939 pop. over 500), SW Bukhara oblast, Uzbek SSR, on Trans-Caspian RR and 40 mi. SW of Bukhara; cotton.

Ala-tau (ä'lä-tou') [Turkic, =mottled mountains], generic name of several ranges of the Tien Shan system, in the USSR, so named for their patches of snow. The principal ranges are the Dzungarian Ala-Tau, Trans-Ili Ala-Tau, Kungei Ala-Tau, Terskei Ala-Tau, and Talas Ala-Tau. The Kuznetsk Ala-Tau is an outlier of the Altai Mts.

Alatna (ŭlăt'nŭ), Indian village (pop. 31), N central Alaska, on Koyukuk R., at mouth of Alatna R., and 100 mi. N of Tanana, on Arctic Circle; trapping, placer gold mining. Airstrip.

Alatna River, N central Alaska, rises on S slope of Brooks Range near 67°51'N 155°10'W; flows c.200 mi. SE to Koyukuk R. at Alatna.

Alatoz (älätōth'), town (pop. 1,402), Albacete prov., SE central Spain, 22 mi. NW of Almansa; olive-oil and wine processing; saffron, honey.

Alatri (älä'trē), town (pop. 4,702), Frosinone prov., Latium, S central Italy, 6 mi. N of Frosinone; rail terminus; cotton and woolen mills, wax industry. Bishopric. Has anc. fortifications, including polygonal walls.

Alattyan (ŏ'lŏt-tyän), Hung. *Alattyán*, town (pop. 2,570), Jasz-Nagykun-Szolnok co., E central Hungary, on Zagyva R. and 7 mi. NW of Jaszladany; wheat, barley; hogs.

Alatyr or **Alatyr'** (ŭlŭtĭr'), city (1932 pop. estimate 25,560), SW Chuvash Autonomous SSR, Russian SFSR, port on Sura R., at mouth of Alatyr R., and 95 mi. SSW of Cheboksary, on railroad (locomotive and car-building shops); lumber-, livestock-, and grain-trading center; sawmilling, metalworking, mfg. of clothing and knitwear, food processing (flour, potatoes). Founded 1552.

Alatyr River or **Alatyr' River,** E central European Russian SFSR, rises W of Tashino, Gorki oblast; flows 190 mi. E, past Ardatov, to Sura R. at Alatyr city; lumber floating.

Alausí (älousē'), town (1950 pop. 4,812), Chimborazo prov., S central Ecuador, in Andean valley, on Guayaquil-Quito RR and 39 mi. SSW of Riobamba; alt. c.7,500 ft. Mtn. resort and sulphur-mining center, in agr. region (cereals, potatoes, flowers, stock). Mfg. of cotton cloth.

Álava (ä'lävä), province (□ 1,175; pop. 112,876), N Spain, one of the Basque Provs.; ⊙ Vitoria. Bounded SW by Ebro R.; occupied by wide plain crossed by outlying ranges of E Cantabrian Mts. Drained by Ebro R. and tributaries (e.g., Zadarra R.). Anthracite and lignite mines (S); limestone, asphalt quarries. Essentially agr.: cereals, sugar beets, wine, potatoes, vegetables, livestock. Industries (including metalworks) located in Vitoria, the only important town. In prov. are 2 enclaves, Treviño (a part of Burgos prov.) and Orduña (Vizcaya prov.). Basque language is still spoken in some areas.

Alava, Cape (ă'lŭvŭ), Clallam co., NW Wash., westernmost point of continental U.S., on the Pacific 15 mi. S of Cape Flattery; 48°10'N 124°44'W.

Alaverdi (ŭlŭ"vyĭrdyē'), city (1944 pop. over 10,000), N Armenian SSR, on railroad and 45 mi. ENE of Leninakan; major copper-mining center; electrolytic smelting, chemical (superphosphate, sulphuric-acid) works. City includes former towns (S) of Manes (1926 pop. 891) and Sanain (1926 pop. 663; site of 10th-cent. monastery), inc. c.1940. Until 1936, spelled Allaverdy.

Alawakhawa, E. Pakistan: see Thakurgaon.

Alawi or **'Alawi** (ä'lăwē), small tribal area (pop. 1,200) of Western Aden Protectorate, bet. Amiri and Haushabi areas; ⊙ Al Qasha. One of original Nine Cantons; protectorate treaty concluded in 1895.

Alawites, Territory of the, Syria: see Latakia, province.

Alawoona (ă"lŭwo͞o'nŭ), village, SE South Australia, 110 mi. E of Adelaide; rail junction; wheat, wool.

Alaya, Turkey: see Alanya.

'Alayh, Lebanon: see 'Aleih.

Alayor (äläyōr'), city (pop. 3,944), Minorca, Balearic Isls., 7 mi. NW of Mahón. Important shoe and cheese industry. Limekilns. Also liquor distilling, wine making, tanning, sawmilling; mfg. of hardware, candles, shoe polish. Region grows cereals, tubers, potatoes, grapes, livestock.

Alay Range, Kirghiz SSR: see Alai Range.

Alazan Bay, Texas: see Baffin Bay.

Alazan River or **Alazan' River** (ŭlŭzän'yŭ), in Transcaucasia, USSR, rises on S slope of Mt. Barbalo in the Greater Caucasus, flows 270 mi. SE to Mingechaur Reservoir on Kura R. Drains Kakhetia; forms part of Georgia-Azerbaijan border in lower course.

Alazeya Plateau (ŭlŭzyä'ŭ), NE Yakut Autonomous SSR, Russian SFSR, bet. Indigirka R. (W) and Alazeya and Kolyma rivers (E); rises to c.1,700 ft. **Alazeya River** rises here, flows 550 mi. NE and N to E.Siberian Sea.

Alba (älbä'), anc. *Alba Augusta*, village (pop. 396), Ardèche dept., S France, 8 mi. W of Montélimar; silk throwing. Formerly called Aps.

Alba (äl'bä), anc. *Alba Pompeia*, town (pop. 11,072), Cuneo prov., Piedmont, NW Italy, on Tanaro R. and 16 mi. SSE of Asti; agr. trade center (grapes, white truffles, nuts, raw silk, livestock). Mfg. (automobile chassis, agr. machinery, bricks, wine, macaroni). Tourist industry. Has viticulture school, mus. Bishopric; cathedral dates from 1486.

Alba (ăl'bŭ). **1** City (pop. 352), Jasper co., SW Mo., on Spring R. and 12 mi. NNE of Joplin. **2** Borough (pop. 190), Bradford co., N Pa., 27 mi. S of Elmira, N.Y. **3** Town (pop. 547), Wood co., NE Texas, near Sabine R., 35 mi. NW of Tyler; cotton gin, grain mill; lignite mines.

Albacete (älvāthā'tā), province (□ 5,738; pop. 374,472), SE central Spain, in Murcia; ⊙ Albacete. Occupies SE end of central plateau of Spain; consists (NW) of barren high plain (a part of the La Mancha) and of mountainous and hilly dists. (S) crossed by irregular ranges. The Júcar (N) and the Segura (S) form several reservoirs used for irrigation and power. In W is chain of lagoons connected by the Alto Guadiana, one of headstreams of the Guadiana. Sulphur mines (Hellín); some zinc, iron, and lignite deposits, only partly exploited; gypsum, clay, and limestone quarries; saltworks and mineral springs. Predominantly agr., with anc. methods of cultivation still prevailing. Poor communications. Saffron, widely exported, is characteristic product; cereals, wine, olive oil, esparto, hemp, honey, truck; rice growing and sericulture in S. Stock raising, especially sheep and mules. Olive-oil and esparto processing, wine and brandy distilling, flour milling, tanning, wool spinning; also mfg. of cutlery (Albacete) and chemicals (Hellín). Chief towns: Albacete, Hellín, Villarrobledo, La Roda.

Albacete, city (pop. 50,567), ⊙ Albacete prov., SE central Spain, in Murcia, 140 mi. SE of Madrid; 38°59'N 1°52'W. Agr. center in irrigated plain yielding wine, saffron, esparto, cereals. Long noted for its mfg. of daggers and knives; also mfg. of chemicals, cement, pottery and tiles, furniture, soap, flower extracts, leather goods, bonnets, candy; meat processing, alcohol distilling, flour- and sawmilling. Ships saffron and wine. Consists of old section on hill, with some 16th–17th cent. houses, and lower-lying modern town rapidly expanding. Only notable bldgs. are 16th-cent. church and the palace of counts de Pino Hermoso. Probably of Moorish origin, Albacete was scene of 2 bloody battles bet. Christians and Moors. Since surrounding swamps were drained (19th cent.) and irrigation canal was built, city has revived. Has military airport and aviation school.

Albacutya, Lake (ălbŭko͞o'tyŭ) (□ 23), W central Victoria, Australia, 200 mi. ESE of Adelaide, N of L. Hindmarsh; 7 mi. long, 3 mi. wide; shallow, frequently dry.

Alba de Tormes (äl'vä dhä tôr'mĕs), town (pop. 2,943), Salamanca prov., W Spain, on Tormes R. and 13 mi. SE of Salamanca; mfg. of chemical fertilizers, ceramics; tanning, flour- and sawmilling; cereals, livestock. Carmelite convent has tomb of St. Theresa of Jesus who died here. Ruins of castle of dukes of Alba on hill near by.

Albaida (älvī'dhä), city (pop. 3,417), Valencia prov., E Spain, 10 mi. S of Játiva; wax-processing center; textile mfg. Cereals, olive oil, wine. Has medieval palace. Founded by Moors, liberated (1248) by James I.

Albaida de Aljarafe (dhä älhärä'fā), town (pop. 1,016), Seville prov., SW Spain, 10 mi. W of Seville; olives, grapes, cereals.

Alba-Iulia (äl'bä-yo͞o'lyä), Ger. *Karlsburg* (kärlz'bo͝ork), former Ger. *Weissenburg* (vī'sŭnbo͝ork), Hung. *Gyulafehérvár* (dyo͞o'lŏfĕ"hârvär), anc. *Apulum*, city (1948 pop. 14,420), Hunedoara prov., central Rumania, in Transylvania, on Mures R. and 170 mi. NW of Bucharest; 46°4'N 23°35'E. Rail junction and historic center in a winegrowing region; mfg. (soap, furniture, footwear); trade in wine, grain, fowl, fruit. Its citadel was built 1716–35 by Charles VI. Most important landmarks are 12th-cent. Romanesque R.C. church partly restored in late Gothic, with the tombs of Hunyadi family; 17th-cent. baroque city gate; Batthyaneum bldg., which contains valuable incunabula and other collections; church erected 1922 for the coronation of Ferdinand I and Queen Marie; archaeological mus. Built on ruins of Apulum, ⊙ Roman Dacia, Alba-Iulia became in 11th cent. an Orthodox bishop's see and the residence of the Transylvanian princes; later it became R.C. bishopric. Union of Transylvania, Moldavia, and Walachia under Michael the Brave (1599) and union of

Transylvania with Rumania (1918) were both proclaimed here.

Albal (älväl'), S suburb (pop. 3,494) of Valencia, Valencia prov., E Spain, in truck-farming area; textile mfg., brandy distilling, meat processing; rice, peanuts, cereals.

Albalá (älvälä') or **Albalat** (älvälät'), village (pop. 3,267), Cáceres prov., W Spain, 19 mi. SE of Cáceres; olive-oil processing; cereals, wine, livestock.

Albaladejo (älvälä-dhā'hō), town (pop. 2,773), Ciudad Real prov., S central Spain, 32 mi. ESE of Valdepeñas; cereals, olives, grapes, livestock; plaster mfg.

Albaladejo del Cuende (dhĕl kwĕn'dā), town (pop. 886), Cuenca prov., E central Spain, 19 mi. SSW of Cuenca; saffron, cereals, vegetables, potatoes, olives, grapes, sheep.

Albalat, Cáceres prov., Spain: see ALBALÁ.

Albalat de la Ribera (älvälät'dhä lä rēvä'rä), town (pop. 3,180), Valencia prov., E Spain, on Júcar R. and 4 mi. NE of Alcira; rice mills; wheat, oranges, apples.

Albalat dels Sorélls (dhĕls sōrāls'), N suburb (pop. 1,730) of Valencia, Valencia prov., E Spain; oranges, wheat, potatoes.

Albalate de Cinca (älvälä'tā dhā thĭng'kä), town (pop. 1,223), Huesca prov., NE Spain, on Cinca R. and 17 mi. NW of Fraga; olive-oil processing, lumbering; wine, sugar beets, fruit.

Albalate del Arzobispo (dhĕl är-thōvē'spō), town (pop. 3,682), Teruel prov., E Spain, 18 mi. WNW of Alcañiz; olive-oil processing, woolen milling, soap mfg., lumbering; trade in livestock, wine, fruit, saffron.

Albalate de las Nogueras (dhā läs nōgā'räs), town (pop. 1,015), Cuenca prov., E central Spain, 22 mi. NNW of Cuenca; cereals, grapes, saffron, olives, fruit, vegetables, sheep. Lumbering, olive-oil extracting, flour milling.

Albalate de Zorita (dhā thōrē'tä), town (pop. 1,307), Guadalajara prov., central Spain, near Tagus R., 28 mi. SE of Guadalajara; olives, cereals, hemp, sugar beets; apiculture. Flour milling, olive-oil pressing, mfg. of stockings.

Alba Longa (ăl'bù lông'gù), city of anc. Latium, central Italy, on W shore of L. Albano, SE of Rome, near Castel Gandolfo. Traditionally founded by Ascanius, son of Aeneas, and legendary birthplace of Romulus and Remus, it was the mother city of Rome, by whose king, Tullus Hostillus, it was supposedly razed in 665 B.C. There are anc. tombs and fragments of an imperial villa.

Albán (älvän'), village (pop. 997), Cundinamarca dept., central Colombia, 32 mi. NW of Bogotá; sugar cane, tobacco, coffee, fruit, livestock.

Alban (älbä'), village (pop. 664), Tarn dept., S France, 16 mi. E of Albi; fluorspar quarries.

Albánchez (älvän'chĕth), town (pop. 1,231), Almería prov., S Spain, 35 mi. NE of Almería; olive-oil processing, flour milling; almonds, oranges. Gypsum quarries, lignite mines.

Albánchez de Úbeda (dhā ōō'vädhä), town (pop. 2,424), Jaén prov., S Spain, 18 mi. E of Jaén; olive-oil processing; sheep raising.

Albanel (älbùnĕl'), village (pop. 426), S central Que., 9 mi. W of Dolbeau; dairying, pig raising.

Albanel, Lake (50 mi. long, 6 mi. wide), central Que., 5 mi. SE of L. Mistassini, into which it drains; alt. 1,289 ft.

Alban Hills (ôl'bùn), Ital. *Colli Laziali* or *Monti Albani,* in Latium, central Italy, 10 mi. SE of Rome. Volcanic in origin, they surround a large crater containing in center the chief peaks, Monte Faete (3,136 ft.) and Monte Cavo (3,113 ft.). On W slopes are lakes Albano and Nemi. Noted as resort and winegrowing region.

Albania, in anc. geography, a country bet. Armenia and the Caspian Sea, corresponding approximately to the modern Azerbaijan SSR. The Albanian or Caspian Gates are probably identical with the Iron Gates at DERBENT.

Albania (ălbā'nyù, -nēù), in the 2 Albanian dialects, Gheg *Shqipni* or *Shqipnija,* Tosk *Shqipri* or *Shqipriја,* republic (□ 10,632; 1945 pop. 1,122,044), SE Europe; ⊙ TIRANA. Smallest and most backward of the Balkan states, across the Adriatic and the Strait of Otranto from Italy, it is bordered N and E by Yugoslavia (with which it shares L. SCUTARI, L. OCHRIDA, and L. PRESPA) and S by Greece (with which it disputes a large section of EPIRUS). Albania extends about 210 mi. N-S, averaging 50 mi. in width. As a region, Albania is often understood to reach deeply into SW Yugoslavia (Kosovo-METOHIJA) and, to a lesser extent, into NW Greece; in both these countries there are considerable Albanian minorities. Save for the marshy alluvial lowlands along the coast—fertile but feverous—Albania is rugged and mountainous, traversed by S spurs of the Dinaric system, notably the NORTH ALBANIAN ALPS (N); ⅔ of the territory is above 3,000 ft. Highest peak, KORAB (9,066 ft.), lies E on Yugoslav line. In the productive intramontane basins, such as that around KORITSA, live most of the predominantly (77%) rural people. The country is crossed by numerous rivers, among them DRIN RIVER, SEMENI RIVER, VIJOSA RIVER. The SHKUMBI RIVER, in center, is considered the dividing line bet. the Gheg-speaking North and the Tosk-speaking South. Most rivers are seasonal, running dry in summer, but being transformed into torrents during the winter. Apart from BUJUNA RIVER, outlet of L. Scutari along Yugoslav border (NW), none is navigable. The climate is of the mild Mediterranean type in the littoral, permitting cultivation of citrus fruit, olives, and figs. The E mts. are continental, with considerable extremes. Precipitation—largely in winter—amounts to 80–100 inches in N mts., 40–48 inches on the coast. Though they are as yet of little economic importance, Albania has substantial mineral resources, principally petroleum fields of PATOS and KUCOVË (since 1950 called Stalin). The latter is linked by pipe line with the port of VALONA, which has coal and oil-bunkering piers. Among minerals exported are bitumen (SELENICË), copper (PUKË, RRUBIG), chromite (LABINOT), bauxite. Other deposits include iron ore, lignite, rock salt. Large tracts of the mtn. slopes—c.30% of the entire area—are covered by forests (oak, walnut, chestnut, beech, pine, fir), giving way above 1,400 ft. to meadows, where extensive stock raising (sheep, goats, cattle, donkeys, mules), still the principal occupation, is carried on. Wool, hides, furs, and some cheese are shipped. An estimated 13% is cultivated land, chiefly in Koritsa and ARGYROKASTRON region, and largely devoted to corn (⅗), followed by wheat, oats, rye, and barley. Industrial crops are increasingly grown: cotton, tobacco (for export), sunflowers, sugar beets (in reclaimed MALIQ dist.); olives in W lowlands. Industries are based on these products. Processing and trading at Valona, Koritsa, Argyrokastron, BERAT, ELBASAN, and Tirana. Tirana is also seat of a technical col. DURAZZO is the leading port, linked by railroad with Tirana and Elbasan. SCUTARI serves as trading center of the N, mfg. cement, textiles, cigarettes, soap. There are several textile mills, including one huge plant near Tirana. Koritsa has a brewery. The post-Second World War govt. has undertaken an ambitious program for the introduction of new crops and industries, and for the construction of highways and railroads. A hydroelectric plant is at Selitë. However, textiles, most consumer goods, and some wheat and corn have to be imported. The Albanian people belong to the old Illyrian race, noted for their social organization into clans. The great majority, about ⅔, are Moslems, c.200,000 are Orthodox Christians, c.100,000 R.C. Illiteracy is still high. The interior formed an independent kingdom that reached its height in 3d cent. B.C. Greek colonies were founded on the coast from Corfu and Corinth. Region came under nominal Roman rule by 1st cent. A.D., though the mtn. tribes were never fully subdued. Occupied (5th cent.) by Ostrogoths, Albania was reconquered (535) for Byzantine Empire by Justinian I. Venice established colonies at Scutari and Durazzo. Inroads were made (1082) by the Normans under Robert Guiscard. In 1272 Charles I of Naples was proclaimed king of Albania. The 14th cent. saw Serb and Turkish conquests. Stout resistance against the Turks was led by Scanderbeg, who has become a national legend. But in 1478 Albania passed under the Ottoman rule that influenced the country deeply and was to last until 1912, when independence was proclaimed and an international control commission established its boundaries. In Second Balkan War (1913) Albania was occupied by the Serbs. In 1914, William, Prince of Wied, accepted the crown, only to be soon expelled. During First World War Albania was variously held by Serbs, Montenegrins, Greeks, Italians, Bulgarians, Austrians, and French. The borders of 1913 were subsequently re-established with minor changes. A former premier and president of the republic, Zog, made himself king in 1928. In April, 1939, Italy, which had come to exert a virtual protectorate over the country, occupied Albania and united it with the Italian crown. From here Italians launched their 1940 attack on Greece. During the Second World War guerilla warfare was waged by anti-fascist forces, as whose strong man emerged the leftist Enver Hoxha. When Allied forces landed late in 1944, partisans seized most of Albania and established a republic. Under Hoxha's presidency a Communist one-party govt. was set up, strictly adhering to the Cominform policy, and eventually clashing with British, Greek, and Yugoslav interests. The isl. of SASENO was returned (1947) by Italy. The country is administratively divided into 22 cities and 26 rural dists. For further information see individual articles on towns, cities, and physical features.

Albano, Lake (älbä'nō), picturesque crater lake (□ 2), Latium, central Italy, in Alban Hills, 13 mi. SE of Rome; c.6 mi. in circumference, 2 mi. long, alt. 784 ft., max. depth 558 ft. Drained by anc. tunnel (W), supposedly built in late 4th cent. B.C., flowing to an affluent of the Tiber. Near its shores, site of ALBA LONGA (W), are resorts of Albano Laziale and Castel Gandolfo.

Albano di Lucania (dē lōōkä'nyä), village (pop. 2,462), Potenza prov., Basilicata, S Italy, 13 mi. ESE of Potenza.

Albano Laziale (lätsyä'lĕ), town (pop. 9,414), Roma prov., Latium, central Italy, near L. Albano, 15 mi. SE of Rome; wine making, alcohol distilling, marble working. Summer resort with beautiful villas, convents, and Roman ruins (amphitheater). Bishopric. Badly damaged by air bombing (1944) in Second World War.

Albany (ôl'bùnē), municipality and port (pop. 4,759), SW Western Australia, 240 mi. SSE of Perth and on Princess Royal Harbour of King George Sound; rail terminus; butter factory. Exports fruit. Oldest settlement (1826) of state; founded as penal colony.

Albany, town (pop. 1,590), St. Mary parish, N Jamaica, on railroad and 5 mi. W of Annotto Bay; bananas.

Albany, anc. and literary name of Scotland. Variants are Alban and Albin. ALBION usually refers to England.

Albany. 1 County (□ 531; pop. 239,386), E N.Y.; ⊙ ALBANY (the state capital). Bounded E by the Hudson, partly N by Mohawk R. and the Barge Canal. Includes the Helderbergs and part of the Catskills (resorts). Dairying, farming (clover, grain, fruit, truck), stock and poultry raising. Extensive mfg. at Albany, Watervliet, Cohoes. Formed 1683. **2** County (□ 4,400; pop. 19,055), SE Wyo.; ⊙ Laramie. Grain, livestock area bordering on Colo.; watered by Laramie R. and Wheatland Reservoir. Oil. Migratory bird refuge, parts of Medicine Bow Natl. Forest and Medicine Bow Mts. in SW. Laramie Mts. in E. Formed 1868.

Albany. 1 Residential city (pop. 17,590), Alameda co., Calif., on San Francisco Bay, just N of Berkeley. A U.S. Dept. of Agr. chemurgic research laboratory is here. Inc. 1908 as Ocean View, renamed 1909. **2** City (pop. 31,155), ⊙ Dougherty co., SW Ga., on Flint R., at head of navigation, and c.80 mi. SE of Columbus. Major market and processing center for pecans and peanuts; mfg. (thread, sheeting, hosiery, lumber, fertilizer, candy, cottonseed oil, farm machinery); meat packing. Albany State Col. here; Turner Air Force Base near. Chehaw State Park near by on reservoir (c.10 mi. long) formed by power dam in Flint R. Founded 1836, inc. 1841. **3** Village (pop. 544), Whiteside co., NW Ill., on the Mississippi, just S of Clinton (Iowa), in agr. and hunting area. Natl. wildlife refuge is near by. **4** Town (pop. 1,846), Delaware co., E Ind., near Mississinewa R., 12 mi. NE of Muncie; livestock, grain; tinware, tools, wire products. **5** Town (pop. 1,920), ⊙ Clinton co., S Ky., in Cumberland foothills near Tenn. line, 40 mi. SW of Somerset, in agr. (livestock, poultry, dairy products), coal-mine, timber area; lumber and flour milling; concrete blocks. Fishing near by. Wolf Creek Dam is N, Dale Hollow Reservoir is SW. Area settled c.1800. **6** Township (pop. 242), Oxford co., W Maine, on Crooked R. and c.30 mi. WNW of Auburn, partly in White Mtn. Natl. Forest. Feldspar, beryl mines at Lynchville village. **7** Village (pop. 1,196), Stearns co., central Minn., 20 mi. WNW of St. Cloud, in livestock and poultry area; small trading point for near-by lake resorts; dairy products. **8** City (pop. 1,850), ⊙ Gentry co., NW Mo., on East Fork of Grand R. and 43 mi. NE of St. Joseph; grain, livestock, poultry. Founded c.1845. **9** Town (pop. 154), Carroll co., E central N.H., on Swift R., in White Mtn. Natl. Forest, and just W of Conway. **10** City (pop. 134,995), ⊙ N.Y. and Albany co., E N.Y., on W bank of the Hudson at head of deepwater navigation, and 130 mi. N of New York city; 42°39'N 73°45'W; alt. 18 ft. Port of entry, and a major shipping point for grain, petroleum, lumber. Transportation center, linked by Hudson R. and Erie division of the Barge Canal to Great Lakes ports, and to the St. Lawrence by waterway following the Hudson, the Champlain division of the Barge Canal, and Richelieu R. Has railroad shops, important express-transfer and wholesale warehouses. Chief industries: oil refining, printing and publishing, meat packing; mfg. of machinery, chemicals, paper and wood products, heaters, foundry products, felt and textile products, clothing, foodstuffs, equipment for billiards and other games. Seat of N.Y. State Col. for Teachers; the observatory (Dudley Observatory) and schools of pharmacy, law, and medicine of Union Univ.; and Col. of St. Rose. Points of interest: the capitol (built 1867–98); State Office Bldg.; N.Y. State Mus.; Albany Inst. of History and Art; Schuyler Mansion (1762), now a mus. John Boyd Thacher State Park is c.10 mi. W, in the Helderbergs. Albany's site was visited (1609) by Henry Hudson. Fort Nassau, 1st trading post in vicinity, was built in 1614 by the Dutch. Permanent settlers from Holland came to Fort Orange (Dutch) in 1623; settlement was renamed Albany when English took control in 1664. Chartered 1686 as city, after becoming fur-trading center of the colonies. The Albany Congress met here, 1754. Albany was made ⊙ N.Y. in 1797. City grew as commercial center and as port for clippers and canal boats after opening of Champlain and Erie canals in 1820s; 1st railroad came in 1831. Great lumbering industry of Civil War period was replaced in importance in late-19th cent. by mfg. Opening in 1932 of docks for deep-draught vessels again made city a seaport. **11** Village (pop. 525)

Athens co., SE Ohio, 9 mi. SW of Athens, in limestone-quarrying area. **12** City (pop. 10,115), ⊙ Linn co., W Oregon, on Willamette R. at mouth of Calapooya R., and 20 mi. S of Salem; rail, trade, and poultry-shipping center for farm and orchard area; food processing (meat, dairy products), mfg. (lumber, leather goods, furniture). Founded 1848, inc. 1864. **13** City (pop. 2,241), ⊙ Shackelford co., N central Texas, 31 mi. NE of Abilene; market, shipping center in cattle-ranching, agr., oil-producing area; petroleum refining, cotton processing, poultry packing. Old Fort Griffin (state park here) is 14 mi. N. **14** Rural town (pop. 704), including Albany village (pop. 196), Orleans co., N Vt., on Black R. and 16 mi. SW of Newport; potatoes. Granted 1782. **15** Village (pop. 839), Green co., S Wis., 13 mi. NE of Monroe, and on Sugar R., in agr. area; hardware mfg.

Albany River, N central Ont., issues from L. St. Joseph, flows 610 mi. E and NE to James Bay at Fort Albany. Formerly important fur-trade route. At its mouth is Fort Albany, trading post.

Alba Pompeia, Italy: see ALBA.

Alba Posse (äl′bä pō′sä), town (pop. estimate 500), S Misiones natl. territory, Argentina, on Uruguay R. (Brazil border) opposite Evangelista, and 75 mi. E of Posadas. Agr. center (corn, sugar cane, grapes, cassava, livestock); sawmills, tannery.

Albardón (älbärdōn′), town (1947 pop. 3,611), ⊙ Albardón dept. (□ c.350; 1947 pop. 10,494), S San Juan prov., Argentina, in San Juan R. valley (irrigation area), on railroad and 7 mi. N. of San Juan. Winegrowing center. Marble quarries; sawmills.

Albaredo d'Adige (älbärā′dô dä′dējĕ), village (pop. 1,394), Verona prov., Veneto, N Italy, on Adige R. and 16 mi. SE of Verona, in sericulture region.

Albares (älvä′rĕs), town (pop. 1,026), Guadalajara prov., central Spain, 37 mi. E of Madrid; cereals, olives, potatoes, sugar beets, grapes, hemp, sheep. Flour milling, wool washing, olive-oil pressing.

Albarico (älbärē′kō), town (pop. 940), Yaracuy state, N Venezuela, at NE foot of Sierra de Aroa, 6 mi. NE of San Felipe; copper and platinum mining.

Albarracín (älvärä-thēn′), city (pop. 1,044), Teruel prov., E Spain, on the Turia and 18 mi. WNW of Teruel; wool spinning, flour milling. Cereals, fruit, sheep in area. Has old cathedral, now a collegiate church. Iron, coal, silver deposits near.

Albat, Russian SFSR: see KUIBYSHEVO, Crimea.

Albatera (älvätā′rä), town (pop. 3,646), Alicante prov., E Spain, 11 mi. SW of Elche; rail junction; olive-oil processing, alcohol distilling; hog raising; dates, almonds, figs, cereals.

Albatross Bay, inlet of Gulf of Carpentaria, W Cape York Peninsula, N Queensland, Australia; 23 mi. long (N-S), 10 mi. wide (E-W).

Albay (älbī′), province (□ 996; 1948 pop. 394,694), SE Luzon, Philippines, bounded E by Lagonoy Gulf and Albay Gulf, W by Burias Pass; ⊙ LEGASPI. Includes SAN MIGUEL ISLAND, CAGRARAY ISLAND, BATAN ISLAND, RAPU-RAPU ISLAND. Mountainous, rising to 7,926 ft. in Mt. Mayon. Chief product is abacá (Manila hemp); other crops are rice and coconuts. Copper is mined on Rapu-Rapu Isl. Until 1946, Albay included the subprov. of CATANDUANES, now a separate prov., embracing Catanduanes isl., just E across Maqueda Channel.

Albay, municipality, Philippines: see LEGASPI.

Albay Gulf, inlet of Philippine Sea, SE Luzon, Philippines, separated from Lagonoy Gulf (N) by San Miguel, Cagraray, Batan, and Rapu-Rapu isls.; 30 mi. E-W, 5-13 mi. N-S. Port of Legaspi is on W shore.

Albbruck (älp′rŏŏk), village (pop. 1,646), S Baden, Germany, at S foot of Black Forest, near the Rhine, 5 mi. WSW of Waldshut; cellulose mfg., metal- and woodworking. Bet. here and Dogern is hydroelectric plant Albbruck-Dogern.

Albee (ôl′bē), town (pop. 75), Grant co., E S.Dak., 12 mi. SSE of Milbank.

Albelda (älvĕl′dä), town (pop. 1,301), Huesca prov., NE Spain, on the Aragon and Catalonia Canal and 18 mi. NNW of Lérida; olive-oil processing; wine, fruit.

Albelda de Iregua (dhā ērä′guä), town (pop. 1,485), Logroño prov., N Spain, 8 mi. S of Logroño; olive-oil processing, canning (fruit, vegetables). Cattle, hogs, lumber in area.

Albemarle (ăl′bůmärl), county (□ 739; pop. 26,662), central Va.; co. courthouse is at CHARLOTTESVILLE, in but independent of co. W part is in the piedmont and rises to the Blue Ridge (W); bounded SW by Rockfish R., S by James R.; drained by headstreams of the Rivanna and by short Hardware R. Includes part of Shenandoah Natl. Park. Known for historic estates (notably MONTICELLO); Univ. of Virginia at Charlottesville. Agr. (wheat, tobacco, apples, peaches, corn, hay); cattle, sheep, horses, poultry; dairying. Soapstone, slate. Formed 1774.

Albemarle, town (pop. 11,798), ⊙ Stanly co., S central N.C., 37 mi. ENE of Charlotte; mfg. of textiles, hosiery, yarn, furniture; lumber and flour mills. Morrow Mtn. State park is near. Inc. 1842.

Albemarle and Chesapeake Canal, SE Va., a section (c.10 mi. long) of Intracoastal Waterway connecting a branch of Elizabeth R. (entering Hampton Roads at Norfolk) with short North Landing R. (entering Currituck Sound, N.C., which communicates with Albemarle Sound, S).

Albemarle Island, Galápagos: see ISABELA ISLAND.

Albemarle Sound, an arm of the Atlantic piercing NE N.C. for c.50 mi. (E-W); 5-15 mi. wide. Its seaward end (Kitty Hawk Bay), sheltered from ocean by Kitty Hawk barrier beach, joins Currituck (N), Croatan and Roanoke (S) sounds, and is crossed by Intracoastal Waterway. Receives PASQUOTANK, ALLIGATOR, Chowan, and Roanoke rivers. Bridged (W) near Edenton. Elizabeth City (on the Pasquotank) is chief port.

Albenga (älbĕng′gä), anc. *Albium Ingaunum,* town (pop. 5,848), Savona prov., Liguria, NW Italy, port on Gulf of Genoa, near mouth of Centa R., 22 mi. SW of Savona. Horticultural center (noted for its peaches); resort of Riviera di Ponente. Produces hemp, linen, wine, olive oil, canned tomatoes, pharmaceuticals. Exports fruit and vegetables. Marble quarries. Bishopric since 4th cent.; 5th-cent. baptistery, early Romanesque chapel (10th cent.), cathedral of San Michele (12th cent.). Islet of Gallinaria near by.

Albenga River, anc. *Albinia,* Tuscany, central Italy, rises in the Apennines, 5 mi. W of Santa Fiora, flows 40 mi. S and SW to Tyrrhenian Sea 5 mi. N of Orbetello. At its mouth are saltworks.

Albens (älbĕs′), village (pop. 770), Savoie dept., SE France, 12 mi. SW of Annecy.

Alberbury (ôl′bůrbůrē), agr. village in Alberbury with Cardeston parish (pop. 809), W Shropshire, England, 8 mi. W of Shrewsbury. Near by are remains of a medieval abbey and 15th-cent. tower of Rowton Castle. There is a Norman church. Agr. village of Cardeston is 6 mi. W of Shrewsbury.

Alberca, La (lä älvĕr′kä), village (pop. 1,754), Salamanca prov., W Spain, 24 mi. ESE of Ciudad Rodrigo; cereals, chestnuts, fruit, lumber. Iron mining near by.

Alberca de Záncara, La (dhā thäng′kärä), town (pop. 2,263), Cuenca prov., E central Spain, in La Mancha, 50 mi. NW of Albacete; cereals, olives, grapes, saffron, livestock; apiculture.

Alberche River (älvĕr′chā), Castile, central Spain, rises in the Sierra de Gredos N of Arenas de San Pedro, flows E through fertile valley of Ávila prov., then SW, past Escalona, through La Sagra plain to the Tagus 3 mi. E of Talavera de la Reina; c.110 mi. long. Used for irrigation, hydroelectricity.

Alberdi, department, Argentina: see CAMPO GALLO.

Alberdi (älbĕr′dē), NW suburb of Rosario, SE Santa Fe prov., Argentina, on Paraná R.; flax, wheat, corn. Agr. research station.

Alberdi, town (dist. pop. 3,130), Ñeembucú dept., S Paraguay, on Paraguay R. opposite Formosa (Argentina), and 70 mi. SSW of Asunción; fruitgrowing (citrus, bananas) and cattle-raising center.

Albères, Monts (mōzälbĕr′), Sp. *Montes Alberes* (mōn′tĕs älvā′rĕs), easternmost chain of the Pyrenees on Franco-Sp. border, extending c.20 mi. from vicinity of Céret (France) to the Mediterranean at Cape Cerbère. Average alt. 3,000 ft. Crossed by road at Perthus pass (915 ft.). Towns on rocky, seaward slope: Collioure, Port-Vendres, Banyuls-sur-Mer, Cerbère (all in France), and Port Bou (Spain). Subtropical vegetation on lower N slopes.

Albergaria-a-Velha (älbĕrgůrē′ů-vĕ′lyů), town (pop. 2,389), Aveiro dist., N central Portugal, on branch railroad and 10 mi. ENE of Aveiro; mfg. (paper, ceramics); lumbering (eucalyptus and pine trees), winegrowing.

Alberhill, village (1940 pop. 550), Riverside co., S Calif., in Santa Ana Mts., 19 mi. S of Riverside; large clay mines.

Alberique (älvärē′kä), town (pop. 6,764), Valencia prov., E Spain, on Júcar R. and 5 mi. SW of Alcira; terminus of branch railroad from Valencia. Agr. trade center (rice, cereals, fruit, olive oil, tobacco); rice milling, meat processing, brick mfg.

Alberite (älvärē′tä), town (pop. 1,322), Logroño prov., N Spain, 4 mi. S of Logroño; wine, olive oil, cereals, fruit.

Alberndorf (äl′bĕrndôrf), village (pop. 2,021), N Upper Austria, 8 mi. NNE of Linz, N of the Danube; potatoes, rye.

Alberni (ălbûr′nē), city (pop. 1,807), S central Vancouver Isl., SW B.C., at head of Alberni Canal, just N of Port Alberni, 90 mi. NW of Victoria, in lumbering, fishing, and mining (gold, silver, copper, lead, zinc) area.

Alberni Canal, fjord (23 mi. long, 1 mi. wide) of Barkley Sound, SW B.C., in SW Vancouver Isl., extending NE and N to Port Alberni and Alberni, in lumbering, fishing, farming, and mining area. Navigable for ocean-going ships. Also called Alberni Inlet.

Albernoa (älbĕrnō′ů), village (pop. 2,404), Beja dist., S Portugal, 12 mi. SSW of Beja; grain, sheep, timber.

Alberobello (älbĕrôbĕl′lô), town (pop. 6,222), Bari prov., Apulia, S Italy, 12 mi. S of Monopoli; mfg. (agr. machinery, wax products).

Alberona (älbĕrô′nä), village (pop. 3,459), Foggia prov., Apulia, S Italy, 22 mi. WSW of Foggia, in agr. region (cereals, grapes, olives).

Alberschweiler, France: see ABRESCHWILLER.

Albersdorf (äl′bůrsdôrf), village (pop. 3,684), in Schleswig-Holstein, NW Germany, 8 mi. SE of Heide, in the S Dithmarschen; resort with radioactive mineral spring; woodworking.

Albersweiler (äl′bůrsvī″lůr), village (pop. 2,260), Rhenish Palatinate, W Germany, on E slope of Hardt Mts., on the Queich and 4 mi. WNW of Landau; wine. Cherries, tobacco.

Albert, county (□ 681; pop. 8,421), SE N.B., on the Bay of Fundy, bounded N and E by Petitcodiac R. estuary; ⊙ Hopewell Cape.

Albert, village (pop. estimate c.250), SE N.B., near Petitcodiac R., 16 mi. SSE of Moncton, in albertite, gypsum, oil-shale, manganese mining district.

Albert (älbâr′), town (pop. 8,742), Somme dept., N France, on the Ancre and 17 mi. ENE of Amiens; mfg. of agr. machinery, machine tools, hardware. Aircraft factory at Méaulte (1.5 mi. S). Changed hands 4 times and was completely destroyed in First World War. Numerous Br. cemeteries and memorials near by. Damaged again in Second World War. Called Ancre until 1619.

Albert, city (pop. 218), Barton co., central Kansas, on Walnut Creek and 15 mi. WNW of Great Bend; wheat. Oil and gas fields near by.

Albert, Cape, E Ellesmere Isl., NE Franklin Dist., Northwest Territories, E extremity of Bache Peninsula, on Kane Basin; 79°2′N 74°15′W.

Albert, Lake, or **Albert Nyanza** (nīăn′zů, nē-, nyän′zä), lake (□ 2,064) in E central Africa, on Belgian Congo–Uganda border, NW of L. Victoria; 100 mi. long, 25 mi. wide; alt. 2,030 ft. Receives Semliki R. (SW) and the Victoria Nile (NE). The Albert Nile issues from its N end, just W of Victoria Nile mouth. It is the northernmost of the great central African lakes in W Great Rift Valley, and is bordered in W and E by precipitous forested cliffs. Highlands on Belgian Congo side are noted as a major region of European agr. settlement (coffee plantations; vegetables, cattle). Lake waters abound in fish. Crocodile grounds in S. Main ports are Kasenyi and Mahagi Port (Belgian Congo), Butiaba (Uganda). Murchison Falls on the Victoria Nile may be reached by steamer from Butiaba. Lake was discovered 1864 by Samuel Baker and named for Queen Victoria's consort. Both Henry Stanley and Emin Pasha established forts here (1885–90). A dam at N end is planned for long-range storage of Nile waters.

Albert, Lake, lagoon (□ 66), SE South Australia, 60 mi. SE of Adelaide, connected with L. Alexandrina (NW) by small passage; 14 mi. long, 8 mi. wide, 5–10 ft. deep.

Albert, Lake, Hamlin and Kingsbury counties, E S.Dak., S of Watertown; 4 mi. long, 2 mi. wide.

Albert, Mount (3,550 ft.), SE Que., on N side of Gaspé Peninsula, 60 mi. E of Matane, in Shickshock Mts.

Alberta (älbĕrtä′), village, Equator Prov., N Belgian Congo, on right bank of Congo R. and 60 mi. E of Lisala; large palm-oil mills. Agr. institute for natives, hosp. for Europeans, trade schools; R.C. mission.

Alberta (ălbûr′tů), province (land area □ 248,800, total □ 255,285; 1946 pop. 803,330; 1948 estimate 846,000), W Canada, westernmost of the Prairie Provs.; ⊙ Edmonton. Extends E from the Continental Divide of the Rocky Mts., bounded by Mont. (S), B.C. (W), Mackenzie Dist. (N), and Sask. (E). Surface consists of a large plateau, rising W to the Rockies and broken by distinctive foothill formations. S part of prov. is undulating prairie land; drained by Red Deer, Oldman, St. Marys, Bow, and Milk rivers. Central Alberta has parklike country, partly wooded, broken by ridges and wide valleys, with many small lakes and streams; drained by North Saskatchewan R. and its tributaries. N part of prov. alternates bet. prairie and woodland; drained by Peace, Athabaska, Pembina, and Hay rivers. Largest lakes are Athabaska, Claire, Lesser Slave, Beaverhill, Gull, Buffalo, Sullivan, and McGregor lakes. Highest peaks of the Rockies in Alberta are mts. Athabaska, Balfour, Columbia, Temple, Hector, Saskatchewan, Assiniboine, Alberta, and The Twins, most of them on Alta.-B.C. border. Main mtn. passes into B.C. are Kicking Horse, Vermilion, Crowsnest, and Yellowhead passes. Average summer max. temp. is 75°F.; minimum winter temp. range from 18°F. (Calgary) to 3°F. (Fort Chipewyan). Mean annual rainfall is 15–20 inches; heaviest in central and N part of prov. Snowfall ranges from 30–35 inches (S) to 40–50 inches (N). Soil is generally fertile; in the Calgary-Lethbridge region it is irrigated by extensive system of canals and dams. Chief agr. products are wheat and other cereals, stock (cattle, sheep), wool, and dairy produce. Sugar beets have been introduced in S part of prov. Alberta is Canada's chief coal-mining region; mining centers are Lethbridge and Drumheller. Natural gas and oil deposits are extensive; main fields are in Turner Valley, Edmonton, Leduc, Wainwright, Medicine Hat, and Bow Island region. Other minerals are bituminous sands, gypsum, clay. Chief industries are meat packing, oil refining, dairying, lumbering, textile milling, mfg. of iron and steel products. Besides

Edmonton, other cities are Calgary, Lethbridge, Medicine Hat, Red Deer, Drumheller, and Wetaskiwin. Banff, Jasper, and Lake Louise are important tourist centers. In Alberta are the Jasper, Banff, Elk Island, Wood Buffalo, and Waterton Lakes natl. parks. Alberta was 1st reached by French traders from Quebec in mid-18th cent., followed by Hudson's Bay Co. representatives. North West Co. began trading operations, 1779. Early trading posts included Fort McMurray, Fort Chipewyan, Fort Edmonton, Jasper House, and Rocky Mountain House. Territory was ceded to Canada by the Hudson's Bay Co. in 1870 and inc. in the Northwest Territories; the Canadian Pacific RR reached the area in 1883. Area was named Alberta and created a district in 1882; prov. of Alberta was organized in 1905; its greatest population increase took place bet. 1901 (pop. 73,022) and 1911 (pop. 374,295). In Second World War Edmonton was S focal point of Alaska Highway traffic.

Alberta. 1 Village (pop. 139), Stevens co., W Minn., 7 mi. W of Morris, in corn, oat, and barley area. 2 Town (pop. 430), Brunswick co., S Va., 36 mi. SW of Petersburg; agr., lumber milling.

Alberta, Mount (11,874 ft.), W Alta., near B.C. border, in Rocky Mts., in Jasper Natl. Park, 50 mi. SE of Jasper; 52°17′N 117°29′W.

Albert Canal (81 mi. long), NE Belgium, extends from the Meuse at Liége to the Scheldt (Escaut) at Antwerp, links Liége and the Meuse industrial area with port of Antwerp; serves Hasselt (by short branch canal) and Herentals. Joined by Canal d'Embranchement 2.5 mi. NE of Tessenderloo. Navigable by ships to 2,000 tons. Completed 1939, it was named for Albert I, who started it in 1930. Its steep, reinforced walls and its location made it part of Belgium's E defenses, but it was quickly crossed by Germans in Second World War. The speedy capture of Fort Eben Emael near Liége was particularly spectacular. Near Herentals it joins the Liége-Meuse Junction Canal and at Maastricht the Zuid-Willemsvaart, which extends N into the Netherlands.

Albert City, town (pop. 736), Buena Vista co., NW Iowa, 30 mi. E of Cherokee; mfg. (grease guns, pumps, livestock equipment).

Albert Edward, Lake, central Africa: see EDWARD, LAKE.

Albert Edward, Mount, New Guinea: see OWEN STANLEY RANGE.

Albertfalva (ŏl'bĕrtfŏl"vŏ), S suburb (pop. 4,762) of Budapest, Pest-Pilis-Solt-Kiskun co., N central Hungary; textiles (wool, silk, cotton), hats, chemicals, rubber goods.

Alberti (älbĕr'tē), town (pop. 4,482), ⊙ Alberti dist. (□ c.435; pop. 14,980), N central Buenos Aires prov., Argentina, near the Río Salado, 20 mi. SW of Chivilcoy. Agr. center: wheat, corn, sunflowers; stock raising.

Albertin or **Al'bertin** (ŭlbyĕr'tyĭn), Pol. *Albertyn*, town (1939 pop. over 500), SW Baranovichi oblast, Belorussian SSR, 3 mi. ESE of Slonim; mfg. (paper, textiles, bricks), flour milling, sawmilling. Developed in 18th cent. as textile and carpet mfg. center.

Albertine Rift, Africa: see GREAT RIFT VALLEY.

Albertinia (ălbûrtĭ'nēŭ), town (pop. 1,222), S Cape Prov., U. of So. Afr., 30 mi. W of Mossel Bay; cattle, wheat; dairying; honey; lime. Yellow-ocher deposits worked near by.

Albert Lea, city (pop. 13,545), ⊙ Freeborn co., S Minn., on Fountain L. and L. Albert Lea, near Iowa line, c.90 mi. S of Minneapolis; rail and industrial center in diversified farming area; mfg. (oil burners, clothing, agr. and electrical equipment); meat and dairy products, beverages. Marl deposits near by. Settled 1855, platted 1856.

Albert Lea, Lake, S Minn., extends E from Albert Lea city; 7 mi. long, 1 mi. wide. Drains into Shell Rock R.

Albert National Park (□ c.3,900; 1st established 1925), mostly in Kivu prov., E Belgian Congo, near Uganda border; a small SE section is in Ruanda-Urundi. Bounded S by L. Kivu, N by 1°N lat., E and W by the escarpments of the Albertine Rift. Most important of Belgian Congo natl. parks. Most of Semliki R., RUWENZORI range, the Belgian shores of L. EDWARD, Ruindi R. and Rutshuru R. plains, and VIRUNGA volcanoes are parts of the park. Administrative hq. at RUMANGABO.

Albert Nile, name given to section of the upper Nile in NW Uganda; issues from N end of L. Albert just W of mouth of VICTORIA NILE; flows 130 mi. N, past Pakwach, Rhino Camp, and Laropi, to Anglo-Egyptian Sudan border at Nimule, here becoming the BAHR EL JEBEL. Navigable for entire course.

Albert Nyanza, central Africa: see ALBERT, LAKE.

Alberton, town (pop. 554), NW P.E.I., on Cascumpeque Bay, 30 mi. NNW of Summerside; fishing port. Fox fur-farms near by.

Alberton, residential town (pop. 14,264), S Transvaal, U. of So. Afr., on Witwatersrand, 6 mi. SE of Johannesburg. Rand Airport just E.

Alberton. 1 Village, Md.: see DANIELS. 2 Town (pop. 326), Mineral co., W Mont., 25 mi. WNW of Missoula and on the Clark Fork.

Albert Peak (10,008 ft.), SE B.C., in Selkirk Mts., 15 mi. E of Revelstoke; 51°2′N 117°51′W.

Albert-Plage, Belgium: see KNOKKE.

Albert River, N Queensland, Australia, formed by junction of 2 headstreams (Barclay R., Beames Creek); flows 40 mi. NE, past Burketown, to Gulf of Carpentaria. Navigable 30 mi. below Burketown by small craft carrying meat, wool.

Albertson, village (1940 pop. 1,238), Nassau co., SE N.Y., on W Long Isl., 2 mi. N of Mineola; mfg. (electric fixtures, concrete pipe).

Albert Town, town (pop. 101), S Bahama Isls., on Long Cay or Fortune Isl., 250 mi. SE of Nassau; 22°37′N 74°22′W. Sisal, stock, salt.

Albert Town, town (pop. 1,650), Trelawny parish, W central Jamaica, 30 mi. NW of May Pen; tropical fruit, spices.

Albertville (älbĕrvēl'), town (1948 pop. 9,930), ⊙ Tanganyika dist. (□ 52,120; 1948 pop. c.353,000), Katanga prov., E Belgian Congo, on W shore of L. Tanganyika, just S of the outlet of Lukuga R., 420 mi. NNE of Elisabethville; main base of navigation on the Tanganyika, head of railroad to Kindu, and commercial center; customs station. Mfg. of textiles, lime, and pharmaceuticals; ship repairing, stone quarrying. Albertville harbor (dating from 1916) handles most of imports to Belgian Congo coming via Indian Ocean coast and Dar-es-Salaam to Kigoma railroad; also exports some of E Belgian Congo produce. Has R.C. and Protestant missions, hospitals for Europeans and natives, and airport. Founded 1891, besieged by Arab slave-traders 1892–93.

Albertville (älbĕrvēl'), town (pop. 5,536), Savoie dept., SE France, on left bank of Arly R. just above its influx into the Isère, at W end on TARENTAISE valley, 20 mi. SE of Annecy, in Savoy Alps; commercial and communications center at junction of 4 Alpine valleys. Apple growing and beekeeping in area. Electrometallurgical works at near-by Ugine and Venthon. La Girotte dam (built 1942–48) in mts. above city is highest dam site in W Europe. Laid out (1845) on a regular plan by Charles Albert of Sardinia, town faces stronghold of Conflans (on hill) which preserves 12th-cent. residence of counts of Savoy, and is topped by a fort (alt. 5,570 ft.).

Albertville. 1 City (pop. 5,397), Marshall co., NE Ala., 20 mi. NW of Gadsden, in cotton and corn area; lumber milling, bottling. 2 Village (pop. 238), Wright co., E Minn., near Mississippi R., 27 mi. NW of Minneapolis; corn, oats, barley.

Albesa (älvä'sä), town (pop. 1,499), Lérida prov., NE Spain, 10 mi. N of Lérida, in irrigated agr. area; wine, olive oil; cattle, sheep, mules.

Albestroff (älbùstrôf'), Ger. *Albesdorf* (äl'bùsdôrf), village (pop. 312), Moselle dept., NE France, 16 mi. NW of Sarrebourg.

Albettone (älbĕt'tônĕ), village (pop. 433), Vicenza prov., Veneto, N Italy, 13 mi. S of Vicenza; cement works.

Albi (älbē'), anc. *Albiga*, town (pop. 27,185), ⊙ Tarn dept., S France, on left bank of Tarn R. and 40 mi. NE of Toulouse; industrial and commercial (cereals, wine, livestock) center in coal-mining dist. Glassworks, slaked-lime works, foundries, rayon and woolen factories; flour milling, distilling, macaroni and fertilizer mfg. An attractive town built of red brick, it has a remarkable fortresslike Gothic cathedral (13th–14th cent.); a 13th–15th cent. archiepiscopal palace; and an 11th-cent. bridge which leads to the industrial suburb of La Madeleine. An episcopal see since 5th cent., Albi was ruled by its bishops (archbishops after 1678) from 12th cent. to French Revolution. It gave its name to the Albigensian Heresy, which led to the Albigensian Crusade and the establishment of the Inquisition (1229).

Albia (ăl'bēŭ), city (pop. 4,838), ⊙ Monroe co., S Iowa, near Cedar R., c.60 mi. SE of Des Moines, in bituminous-coal-mining area; rail junction; mfg. (farm equipment, concrete blocks). Founded as Princeton; inc. 1859.

Albiate (älbyä'tĕ), village (pop. 3,062), Milano prov., Lombardy, N Italy, on Lambro R. and 5 mi. N of Monza; ribbon factories.

Albidona (älbēdô'nä), village (pop. 1,937), Cosenza prov., Calabria, S Italy, 16 mi. NNE of Castrovillari; wine making, domestic weaving.

Albignasego (älbēnyä'sĕgō), village (pop. 757), Padova prov., Veneto, N Italy, 4 mi. S of Padua.

Albin, town (pop. 208), Laramie co., SE Wyo., near Nebr. line, 45 mi. NE of Cheyenne.

Albina (älbē'nä), town (pop. 411), ⊙ Marowijne dist. (□ 15,508; pop. 16,455), NE Du. Guiana, port on Marowijne or Maroni R. opposite Saint-Laurent (Fr. Guiana), and 80 mi. ESE of Paramaribo; ships lumber and gold.

Albinea (älbēnā'ä), village (pop. 1,595), Reggio nell'Emilia prov., Emilia-Romagna, N central Italy, 7 mi. S of Reggio nell'Emilia.

Albino (älbē'nô), town (pop. 4,256), Bergamo prov., Lombardy, N Italy, on Serio R. and 7 mi. NE of Bergamo; silk, woolen, and cotton mills; foundry; mfg. (textile machinery, cement). Has 14th-cent. church. Sandstone quarries near by.

Albion (ăl'bēŭn), anc. and literary name of Britain. It is usually restricted to England and is perhaps derived from the chalk cliffs [Latin *albus*=white]. ALBANY generally designates Scotland.

Albion. 1 Village (pop. 610), Cassia co., S Idaho, 15 mi. SE of Burley; alt. 4,750 ft. 2 City (pop. 2,287), ⊙ Edwards co., SE Ill., 16 mi. W of Mount Carmel, in agr. area (livestock, poultry, fruit); mfg. (clothing, flour, brick). Founded 1818 by English settlers led by Morris Birkbeck and George Flower; inc. 1869. Several early houses are preserved. 3 Town (pop. 1,341), ⊙ Noble co., NE Ind., 26 mi. NNW of Fort Wayne, in scenic lake region; agr. (livestock, soybeans, grain, poultry, fruit; dairy products); mfg. (furniture, lumber, tile, flour). Laid out 1847. "Limberlost," home of Gene Stratton Porter, is near by. 4 Town (pop. 492), Marshall co., central Iowa, 6 mi. NNW of Marshalltown, in agr. area. 5 Agr. town (pop. 992), Kennebec co., S Maine, 10 mi. E of Waterville. Elijah Lovejoy b. here. Inc. 1804. 6 City (pop. 10,406), Calhoun co., S Mich., on Kalamazoo R. and 18 mi. W of Jackson. Mfg. of trucks, water heaters, bakery equipment, boats, wire; railroad shops. Seat of Albion Col. Starr Commonwealth home for delinquent boys is near by. Settled 1833; inc. as village 1855, as city 1885. 7 City (pop. 2,132), ⊙ Boone co., E central Nebr., 40 mi. SW of Norfolk and on Beaver Creek; beverages, dairy and poultry produce, livestock, grain. Settled 1871, inc. 1873. 8 Village (pop. 4,850), ⊙ Orleans co., W N.Y., on Barge Canal and 30 mi. W of Rochester; canning; mfg. of packers' supplies, textiles, feed, machinery; printing. Summer resort. Stone quarries. A state training school for women is here. Inc. 1828. 9 Town (pop. 178), Pushmataha co., SE Okla., c.40 mi. ESE of McAlester, in Ouachita Mts.; lumbering. 10 Borough (pop. 1,729), Erie co., NW Pa., 22 mi. SW of Erie; metal products; railroad shops. Settled 1815, inc. 1861. 11 Mill village in Lincoln and Cumberland towns, Providence co., NE R.I., on Blackstone R. (bridged here) and 9 mi. N of Providence; cotton textiles. 12 Town (pop. 256), Whitman co., SE Wash., 8 mi. SE of Colfax and on South Fork of Palouse R., in agr. region.

Albis (äl'bĭs), mountain range, N Switzerland, just SSW of Zurich. The Albishorn (3,000 ft.) is one of its peaks. Albis Tunnel (2 mi. long), at S end of range, carries railroad bet. Zurich and Zug.

Albisola Marina or **Albissola Marina** (both: älbēs-sô'lä mārē'nä), village (pop. 1,830), Savona prov., Liguria, NW Italy, port on Gulf of Genoa and 2 mi. NE of Savona, in fruit and vegetable region. Noted for ceramics. Just N is **Albisola Superiore** (sōopĕ-rēō'rĕ) village (pop. 1,803), birthplace of Pope Julius II.

Albium Ingaunum, Italy: see ALBENGA.

Albizzate (älbētsä'tĕ), village (pop. 1,498), Varese prov., Lombardy, N Italy, 5 mi. N of Gallarate; mfg. (motorcycles, bicycles, cotton textiles, cork products, chemicals).

Alblasserdam (älblä'sùrdäm), town (pop. 4,755), South Holland prov., W Netherlands, on Noord R. and 9 mi. ESE of Rotterdam; shipbuilding, mfg. (industrial oxygen, cigars, wire, rope).

Albocácer (älvōkä'thĕr), town (pop. 2,115), Castellón de la Plana prov., E Spain, 26 mi. N of Castellón de la Plana; olive-oil processing, flour milling; sheep raising; cereals, almonds, honey. Has remains of medieval castle of Knights Templars, to whom city belonged (1294–1312).

Albolodúy (älvōlōdh-wē'), town (pop. 1,395), Almería prov., S Spain, 16 mi. NW of Almería; olive-oil and esparto processing, flour milling; ships grapes, oranges, almonds. Gypsum quarries.

Albolote (älvōlō'tā), town (pop. 3,055), Granada prov., S Spain, 5 mi. NW of Granada; flour mills. Olive oil, cereals, wine.

Albona d'Istria, Yugoslavia: see LABIN.

Alborán, El (ĕl älvōrän'), islet of Spain, in the SW Mediterranean, 135 mi. E of Gibraltar; 35°57′N 3°2′W. Lighthouse.

Alboraya (älvōrī'ä), NE suburb (pop. 3,599) of Valencia, Valencia prov., E Spain; mfg. of willow baskets, flour milling; agr. trade (cereals, vegetables, fruit, tobacco).

Alborea (älvōrā'ä), town (pop. 2,194), Albacete prov., SE central Spain, 32 mi. NE of Albacete; alcohol distilling, plaster mfg. Public granary. Cereals, wine, saffron. Gypsum and marble quarries near by.

Alborz, Iran: see ELBURZ.

Al-Bostan, Turkey: see ELBISTAN.

Albox (älvōks', -ôsh'), town (pop. 4,266), Almería prov., S Spain, near Almanzora R., 40 mi. NNE of Almería; olive-oil and cheese processing; mfg. of linen and hemp cloth, furniture, pottery, fruit conserves. Cereals, almonds, apricots, livestock. Has anc. castle.

Albrechtice (äl'brĕkhtyĭtsĕ), Ger. *Olbersdorf* (ôl'-bĕrsdôrf), town (pop. 1,900), N Silesia, Czechoslovakia, 7 mi. NW of Krnov; oats.

Albreda (älbrĕ'dä), village (pop. 176), Western Div., Gambia, on right bank of Gambia R. and 15 mi. ESE of Bathurst; fishing; coconuts, cassava, corn. Fr. trading post 1681–1857; ceded to Britain for resettlement of repatriated slaves. It is part of Gambia colony, but is administered under the protectorate.

Albret, France: see LABRIT.
Albright (ôl'brīt), town (pop. 396), Preston co., N W.Va., on Cheat R. 3 mi. NE of Kingwood.
Albristhorn (äl'brĭst-hôrn), peak (9,072 ft.) in Bernese Alps, SW central Switzerland, 3 mi. W of Adelboden.
Albrook Field, military reservation, Balboa dist., Panama Canal Zone, adjoining Balboa Heights. U.S. air base. Commercial aviation activities were transferred (1949) to Tocumen airport, 12 mi. NE of Panama city.
Albudeite (älvōō-dhā'tā), town (pop. 1,225), Murcia prov., SE Spain, 15 mi. WNW of Murcia; esparto processing; citrus fruit, almonds, cereals.
Albuera, La (lä älvwā'rä), town (pop. 1,909), Badajoz prov., W Spain, on small Albuera R. and 14 mi. SE of Badajoz; cereals, vegetables, livestock. Site of victory (1811) of combined British-Spanish-Portuguese forces over the French led by Soult.
Albuera River, Badajoz prov., W Spain, rises near Salvatierra de los Barros, flows c.30 mi. N to the Guadiana 7 mi. E of Badajoz.
Albufeira (älbōōfā'rů), town (pop. 3,043), Faro dist., S Portugal, port on the Atlantic, 19 mi. WNW of Faro; fishing and canning (mainly tuna); almonds, carobs, figs, olives; resort. Its castle was last Moorish stronghold in Portugal.
Albufera (älvōōfā'rä), lagoon (□ 13; 11 mi. long, 5 mi. wide), Valencia prov., E Spain, 10 mi. SSE of Valencia. Two narrow channels which communicate with the Mediterranean are closed artificially 2 months a year so that the lagoon's level is raised to overflow surrounding rice fields. Waterfowl hunting grounds.
Albuixech (älvwē-shĕk'), N suburb (pop. 2,019) of Valencia, Valencia prov., E Spain, in truck-farming area; rice, wheat, wine.
Albula Alps (äl'bōōlä), mountain group in Rhaetian Alps in Grisons canton, E Switzerland, N of St. Moritz; crossed by **Albula Pass** (alt. 7,597 ft.), which leads from Upper Engadine to Albula valley. **Albula River,** rising in mts. 5 mi. N of St. Moritz, flows 22 mi. NW to the Hinterrhein N of Thusis; hydroelectric plant here. **Albula Tunnel** (4 mi. long) carries railroad.
Albuñol (älvōōnyōl'), city (pop. 2,811), Granada prov., S Spain, near the Mediterranean, 18 mi. ENE of Motril; brandy distilling, flour milling. Ships almonds, raisins, dried figs, grapes. Wine and cereals. La Rábita (pop. 1,446; 3 mi. SSW) is its port.
Albuñuelas (älvōōnyōōā'läs), village (pop. 1,365), Granada prov., S Spain, 17 mi. S of Granada; olive-oil processing, essential-oil mfg., flour milling; esparto, wine, lumber. Lead, cobalt, and nickel mines.
Albuquerque (ăl'bůkûr"kē), city (pop. 96,815), ⊙ Bernalillo co., central N.Mex., on upper Rio Grande, near Sandia and Manzano Mts., 55 mi. SW of Santa Fe; 35°4'N 106°38'W; alt. 4,943 ft. Largest city in state; commercial and industrial center and railroad div. point in agr., livestock, coal-mining region. Food processing (meat and dairy products, flour), fruit canning; lumber mills, wool warehouses, railroad shops, sawmills, sheet-metal works; mfg. of metal appliances, cement, bricks, tiles, wood fixtures, Indian handicrafts. City consists of new town and old town. Old Albuquerque, founded 1706 by Sp. settlers, was named San Felipe de Alburquerque after Philip V of Spain and Duke of Alburquerque (1st *r* later dropped from name of city). New town (platted 1880, inc. as city 1890) grew with development of rail transportation and became important as wool center and food-processing point. City is health resort, with U.S. veterans hosp., U.S. Indian hosp., many sanitariums. Univ. of N.Mex., Catholic Teachers Col. of N.Mex., hq. of Cibola Natl. Forest, U.S. Indian school, United Pueblos Agency are here. Kirtland Air Force Base and Sandia Base (guided-missiles experiment station) are here. Points of interest in Old Town are plaza and church of San Felipe de Nerí (1706). Numerous Indian pueblos in vicinity; part of Cibola Natl. Forest 8 mi. E.
Albuquerque Cays (älbōōkĕr'kā), coral reef in the Caribbean c.120 mi. off Mosquito Coast of Nicaragua, belonging to Colombia, in SAN ANDRÉS Y PROVIDENCIA intendancy; 12°10'N 81°50'W.
Albuquerque Lins, Brazil: see LINS.
Albur, Portugal: see ALVOR.
Alburg (ôl'bûrg), town (pop. 1,402), including Alburg village (pop. 563), Grand Isle co., NW Vt., on peninsula jutting into L. Champlain from Que. line; port of entry; dairy products. Fr. settlers before 1750, permanent settlers 1782. Bridge (built 1937) to Rouses Point, N.Y.
Alburnett, town (pop. 254), Linn co., E Iowa, 12 mi. N of Cedar Rapids; limestone quarries.
Alburquerque (älvōōrkĕr'kā), town (pop. 9,787), Badajoz prov., W Spain, near Port. border, 23 mi. N of Badajoz; trading center for agr. region (olives, wheat, cork, grapes, wool, sheep, hogs). Mfg. of olive oil, cork articles, flour, meat products, red wine, chocolate, charcoal; limekilns. Phosphate mines near by. Has an old castle. Ruins of a sanctuary are 4 mi. E.
Alburtis (ălbûr'tĭs), borough (pop. 979), Lehigh co., E Pa., 9 mi. SW of Allentown.
Albury (ăl'bůrē), municipality (pop. 14,412), S New South Wales, Australia, near Victoria border, on Murray R. and 135 mi. WSW of Canberra; gold-mining and wool-trading center; wheat, wine, fruit, dairy products. Hume Reservoir is near by.
Albury (ôl'bůrē), residential town and parish (pop. 1,145), central Surrey, England, 3 mi. E of Guildford. Has partly ruined Normal church. Home of duke of Northumberland, here, was rebuilt by Pugin.
Albuzzano (älbōōtsä'nô), village (pop. 1,160), Pavia prov., Lombardy, N Italy, 6 mi. E of Pavia.
Alby or **Alby-sur-Chéran** (älbē'-sür-shārā'), village (pop. 206), Haute-Savoie dept., SE France, on the Chéran and 7 mi. SW of Annecy, in Savoy Pre-Alps; foundry; cheese mfg.
Alby (äl'bü"), village (pop. 1,008), Vasternorrland co., NE Sweden, on Ljunga R. and 50 mi. SE of Ostersund; chemical works, hydroelectric station.
Alby-sur-Chéran, France: see ALBY.
Alcabón (älkävōn'), town (pop. 1,217), Toledo prov., central Spain, 21 mi. WNW of Toledo; cereals, olives, sheep.
Alcácer (älkä'thĕr), town (pop. 4,230), Valencia prov., E Spain, 8 mi. SW of Valencia; olive-oil processing; citrus and other fruit; mulberry trees. Trades in cereals, vegetables, wine.
Alcácer do Sal (älkä'sĕr dōō säl'), anc. *Salacia Imperatoria*, town (pop. 3,639), Setúbal dist., S central Portugal, at head of Sado R. estuary, on railroad and 25 mi. SE of Setúbal, amidst rice fields; saltworks. Agr. trade center (rice, grain, cork, sheep). Has archaeological mus. and ruined castle. An important imperial city under Romans, it later became a Moorish stronghold (*El Kasr*). After repeated assaults during 12th cent., it was definitively recaptured by Alfonso II in 1217. Was 1st hq. of the Order of São Tiago.
Alcáçovas (älkä'sōōvůsh), town (pop. 3,165), Évora dist., S central Portugal, 18 mi. SW of Évora; flour milling, cow-bell mfg.; trade in olives, cork, sheep. Of importance under the Moors.
Alcains (älkä'ēnsh), town (pop. 3,714), Castelo Branco dist., central Portugal, on railroad and 6 mi. NNE of Castelo Branco; agr. trade; hat mfg., dairying.
Alcalá (älkälä'), town (pop. 1,707), Valle del Cauca dept., W Colombia, on Armenia-Manizales RR, in Cauca valley, and 9 mi. SE of Cartago; alt. 4,232 ft.; coffee, tobacco, sugar cane, corn, stock.
Alcala (älkälä'). **1** Town (1939 pop. 2,114; 1948 municipality pop. 13,214), Cagayan prov., N Luzon, Philippines, on Cagayan R. and 20 mi. NNW of Tuguegarao; agr. center (tobacco, rice). **2** Town (1939 pop. 1,516; 1948 municipality pop. 17,064), Pangasinan prov., central Luzon, Philippines, on Agno R. and 18 mi. SE of Dagupan; rice, corn, copra.
Alcalá de Chisvert or **Alcalá de Chivert** (both: älkälä' dhā chēvĕrt'), town (pop. 4,399), Castellón de la Plana prov., E Spain, 26 mi. NE of Castellón de la Plana; olive-oil processing, flour- and sawmilling; ships oranges, almonds, wine. Bathing beach on the Mediterranean is 4 mi. SE. Coal mining near by.
Alcalá de Guadaira (gwä-dhī'rä), city (pop. 17,758), Seville prov., SW Spain, in Andalusia, on Guadaira R. and 8 mi. SE of Seville (linked by rail). Resort on undulating, wooded plain; known for its fine parks, healthy climate, and artistic interest. Also has important processing plants, chiefly for mfg. of olive oil, flour, and bread. Its ruined castle, mirroring the style of several historic periods, notably 13th and 16th cent., was made (1925) a natl. monument.
Alcalá de Gurrea (gōōrā'ä), village (pop. 909), Huesca prov., NE Spain, 16 mi. WSW of Huesca. Sotonera irrigation reservoir (2 mi. N) fed by canal from Gállego R.
Alcalá de Henares (ānä'rĕs), city (pop. 18,013), Madrid prov., central Spain, in New Castile, on Henares R. and 17 mi. E of Madrid, and on treeless plateau where chiefly wheat, potatoes, olives, and chick-peas are grown. Has railroad shops and some small mfg. plants (ceramics, candles, soap, leather, ice, meat products, flour, chocolate, marzipan, candied almonds). Famous for its many associations with Sp. history and culture, reflected in its typical Castilian character. Among outstanding bldgs. are the Colegio Mayor de San Ildefonso, the renowned old univ. inaugurated 1508 and transferred to Madrid in 1836; the royal archives housed in former archiepiscopal palace; Gothic church La Magistral; the parochial church of Santa María, where Cervantes, b. in the city, was baptized. Also notable are 17th-cent. Bernardine monastery and remains of 12th-cent. wall. The Cortes met here under Alfonso XI. An airport is just N. Across the river was the Roman town *Complutum*, for which the polyglot *Biblia Complutensis*, published here under auspices of Cardinal Jiménez (who founded the univ.), is named.
Alcalá de la Vega (lä vā'gä), town (pop. 775), Cuenca prov., E central Spain, on Cabriel R. and 33 mi. E of Cuenca; sheep raising, flour milling.
Alcalá del Júcar (dhĕl hōō'kär), town (pop. 1,480), Albacete prov., SE central Spain, on Júcar R. and 26 mi. NE of Albacete; olive-oil processing, wool spinning; cereals, wine, fruit.
Alcalá de los Gazules (dhā lōs gäthōō'lĕs), city (pop. 6,135), Cádiz prov., SW Spain, in Andalusia, 32 mi. E of Cádiz; lumbering, stock raising, flour milling, jasper quarrying; produces cork. Has sulphur springs and abandoned coal mines.
Alcalá del Río (dhĕl rē'ō), town (pop. 3,407), Seville prov., SW Spain, on the Guadalquivir and 9 mi. N of Seville; cereals, tubers, chick-peas, oranges, olives, livestock; apiculture. Has Roman and Arab ruins.
Alcalá del Valle (vä'lyä), town (pop. 4,023), Cádiz prov., SW Spain, in N spur of the Cordillera Penibética, 11 mi. N of Ronda; cereals, olives, grapes, acorns, timber, livestock; flour milling. Has mineral springs.
Alcalá la Real (lä rääl'), city (pop. 8,437), Jaén prov., S Spain, in Andalusia, 23 mi. SSW of Jaén; industrial and agr. trade center. Mfg. of pianos, furniture, soap, footwear, knit goods, baskets; olive-oil and meat processing, flour milling, brandy and liqueur distilling, wood turning. Cereals and wine. Tourist industry. Mineral springs. Has remains of anc. castle, and has 2 notable churches. Alfonso IX of Castile, who recovered it from Moors, added *la Real* [the royal] to its name. Scene of Fr. victory (1810) over Spaniards.
Alcalde (ălkăl'dā), village (pop. c.350), Rio Arriba co., N N.Mex., on Rio Grande, in San Juan Pueblo land grant, 28 mi. NNW of Santa Fe; alt. c.5,700 ft.; trading point. Sangre de Cristo Mts. just E.
Alcamo (äl'kämô), town (pop. 38,129), Trapani prov., W Sicily, 23 mi. SW of Palermo; agr. trade center; grapes, corn, sumac, dairy cattle. Has castle, 14th-cent. church. Founded by Saracens in 9th cent.
Alcampel (älkämpĕl'), town (pop. 1,966), Huesca prov., NE Spain, 22 mi. NNW of Lérida; sawmilling, olive-oil processing; wine, fruit, almonds.
Alcanadre (älkänä'dhrā), town (pop. 1,767), Logroño prov., N Spain, near Ebro R., 18 mi. ESE of Logroño; fruit, olive oil, wine, cereals, livestock. Sodium sulphate deposits near by.
Alcanadre River, Huesca prov., NE Spain, rises on S slopes of the central Pyrenees c.25 mi. NE of Huesca, flows c.60 mi. S to Cinca R. 10 mi. NW of Fraga.
Alcanar (älkänär'), city (pop. 5,040), Tarragona prov., NE Spain, 5 mi. N of Vinaroz, near the Mediterranean; olive-oil processing; shipping of fish and almonds; oranges, fruit, wine.
Alcanede (älkänā'dĭ), town (pop. 249), Santarém dist., central Portugal, 14 mi. NNW of Santarém; pottery mfg.
Alcanena (älkänā'nů), town (pop. 2,140), Santarém dist., central Portugal, 15 mi. N of Santarém; tanning center; cheese mfg.
Alcan Highway, Alaska: see ALASKA HIGHWAY.
Alcanhões (älkänyō'ĭsh), town (pop. 2,171), Santarém dist., central Portugal, 4 mi. NNE of Santarém; trade center for fertile agr. region in lower Tagus valley (rice, wheat, corn).
Alcañices (älkänyē'thĕs), town (pop. 1,272), Zamora prov., NW Spain, 35 mi. WNW of Zamora, near Port. line; flour milling, cotton spinning; livestock, cereals, flax, honey.
Alcañiz (älkänyēth'), city (pop. 7,753), Teruel prov., E Spain, in Aragon, on Guadalope R. and 38 mi. WNW of Tortosa, 60 mi. SE of Saragossa; road junction in fertile oasis. Olive-oil production center; mfg. of tiles, cement, chocolate, soap, lubricants. Trades in cereals, livestock, fruit. Has fine town hall and medieval castle. In 212 B.C. the Carthaginians under Hasdrubal here defeated the Romans.
Alcañizo (älkänyē'thō), village (pop. 941), Toledo prov., central Spain, 15 mi. W of Talavera de la Reina; lumbering, stock raising; grain, olives, wine.
Alcântara (älkän'tůrů), city (pop. 1,358), N Maranhão, Brazil, shallow port on W shore of São Marcos Bay, opposite São Luís Isl., 12 mi. NW of São Luís, in cotton dist. Lighthouse. One of state's oldest towns, it flourished in 17th cent.
Alcántara (älkän'tärä), anc. *Norba Caesarea*, town (pop. 4,404), Cáceres prov., W Spain, in Estremadura, on Tagus R. near Port. border, and 32 mi. NW of Cáceres; olive presses, flour mills; cereals, vegetables, sheep. Has famous Roman bridge (A.D. 105; 617 ft. long, 26 ft. wide) with triumphal arch; Gothic church (13th cent.); and ruined monastery and church of San Benito (16th cent.). Belonged to military-religious order of Knights of Alcántara, to whom town was given (13th cent.) by Alfonso IX of Castile. Was stronghold against Moors and later against Portuguese.
Alcantara River (älkän'tärä), anc. *Acesines*, NE Sicily, rises in Nebrodi Mts. near Floresta, flows S, past Randazzo, thence E, along N base of Mt. Etna, to Ionian Sea 2 mi. S of Cape Schiso; 30 mi. long. Most utilized river of isl.; furnishes E Sicily with hydroelectric power from dam near Francavilla di Sicilia; supplies water for irrigation.
Alcantarilla (älkäntärēl'yä), town (pop. 10,744), Murcia prov., SE Spain, near Segura R., 5 mi. WSW of Murcia; rail junction. Fruit-conserve processing; mfg. of soap, hardware, cotton tex-

tiles. Stock raising; citrus and other fruit, pepper, cereals, vegetables in area.

Alcaracejos (älkärä-thā'hōs), town (pop. 1,748), Córdoba prov., S Spain, 7 mi. WNW of Pozoblanco; olive-oil processing, soap mfg.; cereals, sheep. Lead mining near by.

Alcara li Fusi (älkä'rä lē fōō'zē), village (pop. 3,336), Messina prov., NE Sicily, in Nebrodi Mts., 20 mi. ENE of Mistretta.

Alcaraz (älkäräs'), village (pop. estimate 700), N central Entre Ríos prov., Argentina, on railroad and 60 mi. ENE of Paraná; wheat, flax, corn, livestock (cattle, sheep, hogs, poultry); dairying, flour milling, processing of palm fibers.

Alcaraz (älkäräth'), city (pop. 3,041), Albacete prov., SE central Spain, 30 mi. SW of Albacete; mfg. of tin articles, tanning, wool spinning, flour milling; lumbering, stock raising; truck-farming products. Has fine town hall. Mineral springs. Salt works, copper mining near by.

Alcarraz (älkäräth'), village (pop. 2,597), Lérida prov., NE Spain, 7 mi. SW of Lérida, near the Segre, in irrigated agr. area (cereals, wine, olive oil, alfalfa); stock raising.

Alcarria (älkä'ryä), tableland in S Guadalajara and N Cuenca provs., central Spain, forming part of the great Castilian plateau (Meseta), and occupying fertile country along the upper Tagus; also watered by Henares and Tajuña rivers. Known for its fine honey and aromatic plants.

Alcatraz (ăl'kutrăz"), rocky island in San Francisco Bay, W Calif., c.1 mi. N of San Francisco. "The Rock," as the Federal prison here is nicknamed, became (1933) the last stop for the most vicious and incorrigible inmates of Federal prisons. There is no pardon from Alcatraz. The isl. has been a Spanish fort and U.S. military prison.

Alcatrazes (älkutrā'zĭs), rocky shoals in the South Atlantic, off São Paulo coast of SE Brazil, 40 mi. ESE of Santos; 24°6'S 45°42'W. Lighthouse.

Alcaucín (älkou-thēn'), town (pop. 1,099), Málaga prov., S Spain, 21 mi. NE of Málaga; raisins, olives, figs, oranges, cereals, goats.

Alcaudete (älkou-dhā'tā), city (pop. 8,598), Jaén prov., S Spain, 20 mi. SW of Jaén; mfg. of cement, soap, cotton textiles, footwear; olive-oil and cheese processing, flour- and sawmilling, wood turning, fruit canning. Cereals, fruit, lumber. Has ruined Moorish castle, and 16th-cent. church; and several houses built in black marble.

Alcaudete de la Jara (dhā lä hä'rä), town (pop. 2,906), Toledo prov., central Spain, 12 mi. S of Talavera de la Reina; agr. center (olives, fruit, cereals; olive-oil pressing, tile mfg.

Alcázar del Rey (älkä'thär dhĕl rā'), town (pop. 829), Cuenca prov., E central Spain, 50 mi. ESE of Madrid; grain, wine. Stone quarrying.

Alcázar de San Juan (dhā sän'hwän'), city (pop. 23,083), Ciudad Real prov., S central Spain, in New Castile, 45 mi. NE of Ciudad Real. Rail junction and trading center in La Mancha plain. The region produces forage, wheat, olives, grapes, livestock. Industries include alcohol and liquor distilleries, saltpeter factories. Known for its sweet wines, pastry, and cheese. It was the Celtiberian *Alce.* Was once residence of the St. John of Jerusalem order.

Alcazarén (älkä-thärĕn'), town (pop. 1,195), Valladolid prov., N central Spain, 20 mi. S of Valladolid; sheep, cattle; cereals, wine.

Alcazarquivir (älkäsär'kēvēr'), Arabic *El Qsar el Kbir* or *El Ksar el Kebir* [=the great wall], city (pop. 35,786), Lucus territory, W Sp. Morocco, on Lucus R. and 55 mi. S of Tangier; 35°N 5°54'W; rail junction on Tangier-Fez RR (spur to Larache, 20 mi. NW), and customs station near Fr. Morocco border. Agr. trade center of irrigated Lucus Valley (wheat, vegetables, citrus fruit). Trade in hides and skins, wool, hardwoods. Artisan industries (cabinet-making, pottery mfg.). Beautiful gardens surround city. In a decisive battle fought near by in 1578, King Sebastian of Portugal was routed and killed by the Moors. After 2 centuries of internal struggles, Alcazarquivir was occupied by Spain in 1912. Also called Alcazar by Spaniards.

Alcester (ôl'stur), town and parish (pop. 2,195), SW Warwick, England, on Arrow R. at mouth of Alne R., 7 mi. W of Stratford-on-Avon; agr. market with flour mills. Has church dating from 14th cent. Was site of Roman station *Alauna.*

Alcester (ăl'sĕstur), city (pop. 585), Union co., SE S.Dak., 24 mi. N of Elk Point; dairy products, livestock, poultry, corn.

Alchani, Greece: see THETIDEION.

Alchester, England: see CHESTERTON.

Alchevsk, Ukrainian SSR: see VOROSHILOVSK, Voroshilovgrad oblast.

Alchi, Kashmir: see KHALATSE.

Alcira (äl-thē'rä), anc. *Suero* or *Saetabicula,* city (pop. 20,951), Valencia prov., E Spain, on isl. in Júcar R., 23 mi. S of Valencia; citrus-fruit shipping center. Mfg. of cement, paper, cotton cloth, burlap, knit goods, insecticides, candy, artificial flowers; rice processing, flour- and sawmilling; processing of essential oils, orange juice. Sericulture; cattle raising; rice, cereals, fruit, esparto in area; also pinewoods. Limestone quarries near by. Irrigation dates from Moorish times. Has Roman bridge spanning the Júcar. Was Carthaginian colony. Taken by Moors (8th cent.); liberated 1242 by James I, who granted it great privileges; declined after expulsion (1609) of Moriscos.

Alcluith, Scotland: see DUMBARTON.

Alcoa (ălkō'u). **1** Village, Ill.: see ALORTON. **2** Industrial city (pop. 6,355), Blount co., E Tenn., 15 mi. S of Knoxville; large aluminum-reduction plants. Founded 1913 by Aluminum Co. of America; inc. 1919.

Alcoba (älkō'vä), town (pop. 928), Ciudad Real prov., S central Spain, 35 mi. NW of Ciudad Real; cereals, carobs, chick-peas, livestock; lumbering, dairying.

Alcobaça (älkōōbä'su). **1** City (pop. 1,540), SE Bahia, Brazil, on the Atlantic, 12 mi. NNE of Caravelas; ships coffee, cacao, tapioca, copaiba oil, lumber. Graphite deposits. **2** City, Pará, Brazil: see TUCURUÍ.

Alcobaça, town (pop. 4,016), Leiria dist., W central Portugal, 17 mi. SSW of Leiria in fruitgrowing dist.; textile milling, mfg. of ceramics, fruit preserving, distilling. Became a center of the Cistercians in reign of Alfonso I, and its abbey (begun c.1150, completed 1222) is the finest example of medieval architecture in Portugal. The early kings of Portugal are buried here.

Alcocer (älkō-thār'), town (pop. 1,456), Guadalajara prov., central Spain, 32 mi. ESE of Guadalajara; olives, cereals, sheep; flour milling, tile mfg.

Alcochete (älkōōshā'tĭ), town (pop. 3,114), Setúbal dist., S central Portugal, on E bank of Tagus estuary, 8 mi. E of Lisbon; fisheries; alcohol distilling, mfg. of pottery, cordage.

Alcoentre (älkwān'trĭ), village (pop. 1,308), Lisboa dist., central Portugal, 15 mi. W of Santarém; olives, cork.

Alcolea (älkōlā'ä). **1** Town (pop. 1,495), Almería prov., S Spain, 9 mi. N of Berja; olive-oil processing, flour milling; cereals, fruit, lumber, livestock. Ships grapes. **2** Village (pop. 2,728), Córdoba prov., S Spain, 7 mi. NE of Córdoba. Near-by bridge on the Guadalquivir was scene (1868) of victory of Serrano over troops of Isabella II, which led to her abdication.

Alcolea de Calatrava (dhā käläträ'vä), town (pop. 2,337), Ciudad Real prov., S central Spain, 10 mi. W of Ciudad Real; cereals, chick-peas, sheep, hogs.

Alcolea de Cinca (thĭng'kä), town (pop. 1,770), Huesca prov., NE Spain, on Cinca R. and 18 mi. NW of Fraga; olive oil, wheat, livestock.

Alcolea del Río (dhĕl rē'ō), town (pop. 3,115), Seville prov., SW Spain, on the Guadalquivir and 23 mi. NE of Seville; agr. center (wheat, barley, corn, olives, livestock).

Alcolea de Tajo (dhā tä'hō), town (pop. 806), Toledo prov., central Spain, on the Tagus and 20 mi. WSW of Talavera de la Reina; olives, cereals.

Alcollarín (älkōlyärēn'), village (pop. 1,155), Cáceres prov., W Spain, 17 mi. SSE of Trujillo; flour mills; wheat, olive oil, wine.

Alcolu (ăl'kulōō), village (1940 pop. 797), Clarendon co., E central S.C., 14 mi. SSE of Sumter.

Alcona (ălkō'nu), county (□ 677; pop. 5,856), NE Mich.; ⊙ Harrisville. Bounded E by L. Huron; drained by Au Sable and Pine rivers. Farm area (potatoes, grain, corn, livestock); fisheries, nurseries. Includes part of Huron Natl. Forest. Hubbard L. (resort) is in N. Organized 1869.

Alconchel (älkōnchĕl'), town (pop. 4,263), Badajoz prov., W Spain, 25 mi. SSW of Badajoz; agr. center (cereals, olives, livestock); flour milling, olive-oil pressing, lumbering.

Alconchel de la Estrella (dhā lä ĕstrĕ'lyä), town (pop. 815), Cuenca prov., E central Spain, 34 mi. SW of Cuenca; cereals, sheep; flour milling.

Alconera (älkōn-thā'rä), town (pop. 1,328), Badajoz prov., W Spain, 16 mi. E of Jerez de los Caballeros; cereals, olives, grapes, livestock. Marble quarries; limekilns; mfg. of plaster, tiles.

Alcora (älkō'rä), town (pop. 3,276), Castellón de la Plana prov., E Spain, 12 mi. NW of Castellón de la Plana. Noted for its colored tiles and porcelain; cotton milling; cereals, wine, oranges.

Alcorcón (älkōrkōn'), town (pop. 523), Madrid prov., central Spain, on railroad and 9 mi. SW of Madrid; grain growing, stock raising.

Alcorisa (älkōrē'sä), town (pop. 3,313), Teruel prov., E Spain, 16 mi. SW of Alcañiz; olive-oil and wine center; flour mill. Irrigation reservoir near by.

Alcorn (ôl'kôrn, ăl'–), county (□ 405; pop. 27,158), NE Miss., bordering N on Tenn.; ⊙ Corinth, farm-products processing center. Drained by Hatchie and Tuscumbia rivers. Agr. (cotton, corn, dairy products, soybeans, livestock), lumbering. Formed 1870.

Alcorn, village, Claiborne co., SW Miss., near the Mississippi, 27 mi. NNE of Natchez. Seat of Alcorn Agr. and Mechanical Col. (founded 1871).

Alcorta (älkôr'tä), town (pop. estimate 3,000), S Santa Fe prov., Argentina, 50 mi. SW of Rosario; agr. center (corn, flax, wheat, alfalfa, vegetables, fruit, livestock); mfg. of agr. implements.

Alcoutim (älkō'tēn), town (pop. 453), Faro dist., S Portugal, on the Guadiana (Sp. border) opposite Sanlúcar de Guadiana and 20 mi. N of Vila Real de Santo António; grain. Has Renaissance church.

Alcova Dam, central Wyo., on N.Platte R. and 30 mi. SW of Casper; earthfill dam 265 ft. high, 763 ft. long; finished 1938 as unit in Kendrick project for land reclamation. Diverts water from Pathfinder Reservoir and N.Platte R. into Casper Canal, which irrigates area in vicinity of Casper.

Alcover (älkōvär'), town (pop. 2,220), Tarragona prov., NE Spain, 8 mi. NNE of Reus; mfg. (knit goods, ceramics); olive-oil processing; agr. trade (wine, cereals, fruit, hemp).

Alcovy River (ăl'kōvē), N central Ga., rises 5 mi. NE of Lawrenceville, flows c.50 mi. SE and S to LLOYD SHOALS RESERVOIR 13 mi. NE of Jackson.

Alcoy (älkoi'), city (pop. 42,519), Alicante prov., E Spain, in Valencia, industrial center 25 mi. N of Alicante; wool and paper (chiefly cigarette paper) milling are chief industries. Also metalworking (iron and steel tubing; textile, farm, and other machinery; electrical equipment); mfg. of cement, matches, footwear, knit and leather goods, cotton textiles, burlap, felt hats, candy; distilling (brandy and liqueur), sawmilling. Agr. trade (wine, cereals, olive oil). Lignite deposits near by. Has some baroque churches and many educational and welfare institutions.

Alcozauca (älkōsou'kä), officially Alcozauca de Guerrero, town (pop. 758), Guerrero, SW Mexico, in Sierra Madre del Sur, near Oaxaca border, 15 mi. SE of Tlapa; cereals, livestock.

Alcubierre (älkōōvyĕ'rä), village (pop. 1,139), Huesca prov., NE Spain, 24 mi. S of Huesca; wine, almonds, cereals, livestock.

Alcubillas (älkōōvē'lyäs), town (pop. 2,088), Ciudad Real prov., S central Spain, 14 mi. E of Valdepeñas; grain- and winegrowing.

Alcublas (älkōōv'läs), town (pop. 1,973), Valencia prov., E Spain, 14 mi. NW of Liria; olive-oil processing; wheat, wine, figs.

Alcudia (älkōōdh'yä), city (pop. 2,809), Majorca, Balearic Isls., 31 mi. NE of Palma, in agr. region (rice, truck, livestock). Lumbering, lobster fishing; rug mfg. Anc. fortified city, with Roman walls. Saltworks and lignite deposits near by. On the sea (on fine Alcudia Bay), 1½ mi. SE, is Puerto de Alcudia.

Alcudia de Carlet (dhā kärlĕt'), town (pop. 5,157), Valencia prov., E Spain, 6 mi. NW of Alcira; rice milling, brandy distilling, olive- and peanut-oil processing; cereals, wine, oranges.

Alcudia de Crespíns (krĕspēns'), town (pop. 2,092), Valencia prov., E Spain, 4 mi. WSW of Játiva; mfg. of woolen and cotton cloth, tiles, soap, insecticides, nougat; sawmilling; cereals, peanuts, fruit.

Alcudia de Guadix (gwä-dhēks'), town (pop. 1,915), Granada prov., S Spain, 3 mi. SE of Guadix; iron foundries, flour mills; wine, sugar, hemp, tobacco.

Alcuéscar (älkwā'skär), town (pop. 4,459), Cáceres prov., W Spain, 22 mi. SSE of Cáceres; hog and sheep raising; olive oil, cereals, oranges and other fruit.

Alda, village (pop. 190), Hall co., SE central Nebr., 5 mi. SW of Grand Island, near Wood R. Stolley State Park near by.

Aldabra Island (äldä'bru), outlying atoll dependency (pop. 47) of the Seychelles, in Indian Ocean, 250 mi. NW of Madagascar and 750 mi. SW of Mahé Isl. (in Seychelles proper); 9°25'S 46°20'E. The atoll, largest (21 mi. long, 8 mi. wide) of the Seychelles, encloses a lagoon (□ 50). Turtle hunting; copra industry. Habitat of giant land tortoise. The Aldabra group includes Assumption, Astove, and Cosmoledo isls.

Aldama (äldä'mä). **1** Town (pop. 2,818), Chihuahua, N Mexico, on Chuviscar R. and 18 mi. NE of Chihuahua, on railroad; alt. 4,140 ft.; silver and copper mining; cereals, fruit, cattle. **2** Town (pop. 1,559), Tamaulipas, NE Mexico, on Gulf plain, 50 mi. NNW of Tampico; sugar, citrus fruit, livestock.

Aldama, Villa, Mexico: see VILLA ALDAMA.

Aldamas, Los, Mexico: see LOS ALDAMAS.

Aldan (ŭldän'), city (1939 pop. over 10,000), SE Yakut Autonomous SSR, Russian SFSR, in E Siberia, on Aldan Plateau, 265 SSW of Yakutsk, and on Yakutsk-Never highway. Major gold-mining center, in Aldan gold basin (developed after 1923). Called Nezametny until 1939, when it became a city. Was (1939–47) ⊙ former Aldan administrative okrug.

Aldan (ôl'dun), borough (pop. 3,430), Delaware co., SE Pa., SW suburb of Philadelphia.

Aldan Plateau (ŭldän'), S Yakut ASSR, Russian SFSR, N of Stanovoi Range; mainly gneiss, some granite formations; alt. 2,500–3,300 ft. Important gold-mining area.

Aldan River, S Yakut Autonomous SSR, Russian SFSR, rises in W Stanovoi Range, flows N and E, around Aldan Plateau, past Tommot (head of navigation; c.1,000 mi. from mouth) and Chagda, thence N, past Ust-Maya, and NW to Lena R. 100 mi. N of Yakutsk; 1,767 mi. long. Receives Amga (left), Uchur and Maya (right) rivers.

Aldaya (äl-dhī'ä), W suburb (pop. 4,467) of Valencia, Valencia prov., E Spain, in rich truck-farming area; mfg. (toys, furniture, fans). Olive oil, hemp, wine in area.

Aldborough (ôld'buru, ôl'buru), agr. village and parish (pop. 543), West Riding, central Yorkshire, England, on Ure R. and 7 mi. ESE of Ripon. Said to be site of Roman station *Isurium*. Has some remains of anc. city wall.

Aldbourne (ôld'bôrn, ô'bûrn), agr. village and parish (pop. 1,028), E Wiltshire, England, 6 mi. NE of Marlborough. Has 15th-cent. church.

Aldbrough (ôl'brŭ, ô'brōōf), agr. village and parish (pop. 741), East Riding, SE Yorkshire, England, near North Sea, 10 mi. NE of Hull. Has 13th–15th-cent. church.

Aldeacentenera (äl-dhäā-thĕntänä'rä), village (pop. 2,469), Cáceres prov., W Spain, 14 mi. ENE of Trujillo; meat processing; stock raising; cereals, vegetables.

Aldeadávila de la Ribera (äl-dhä"ä-dhä'vēlä dhä lä rēvä'rä), town (pop. 2,032), Salamanca prov., W Spain, near the Duero, 55 mi. WNW of Salamanca; flour milling, brandy distilling, wool and linen milling; cereals, fruit, lumber.

Aldea del Cano (äl-dhä'ä dhĕl kä'nō), village (pop. 2,177), Cáceres prov., W Spain, 14 mi. S of Cáceres; meat processing; stock raising; cereals.

Aldea del Rey (rā'), town (pop. 4,521), Ciudad Real prov., S central Spain, 18 mi. SSE of Ciudad Real; agr. center (cereals, grapes, olives, truck, pepper, livestock). Basalt quarrying; cheese making. Has mineral springs.

Aldea de Trujillo (dhä trōōhē'lyō), village (pop. 1,488), Cáceres prov., W Spain, 7 mi. N of Trujillo; cereals.

Aldeamayor de San Martín (äl-dhä"ämīōr' dhä sän' märtēn'), town (pop. 1,129), Valladolid prov., N central Spain, 10 mi. SSE of Valladolid; lumbering; sheep raising; cereals, sugar beets, wine.

Aldeanueva de Barbarroya (äl-dhä'ä nwä'vä dhä bärväroi'ä), village (pop. 2,445), Toledo prov., central Spain, near the Tagus, 17 mi. SW of Talavera de la Reina; cereals, olives, livestock; flour milling, olive-oil extracting, meat packing.

Aldeanueva de Ebro (ä'vrō), town (pop. 2,648), Logroño prov., N Spain, near Ebro R., 6 mi. SE of Calahorra; olive-oil and wine processing, alcohol distilling; cereals, fruit, hogs.

Aldeanueva de la Vera (lä vä'rä), town (pop. 3,093), Cáceres prov., W Spain, 22 mi. ENE of Plasencia; olive-oil and cheese processing; mfg. of soap, honey, wax; stock raising; wine, peppers, figs, nuts. Near by is Yuste monastery.

Aldeanueva del Camino (dhĕl kämē'nō), village (pop. 1,982), Cáceres prov., W Spain, 18 mi. NE of Plasencia; produces sweet and pickled peppers; olive-oil processing, flour milling; wine, livestock.

Aldeanueva de San Bartolomé (dhä sän' bärtōlōmā'), village (pop. 1,288), Toledo prov., central Spain, 27 mi. SW of Talavera de la Reina; cereals, olives, onions, livestock; lumbering.

Aldeaquemada (äl-dhä"ä kämä'dhä), town (pop. 1,340), Jaén prov., S Spain, 18 mi. NE of La Carolina; stock raising; cereals, olive oil.

Aldea Real (äl-dhä'ä rääl'), town (pop. 813), Segovia prov., central Spain, 15 mi. N of Segovia; cereals, grapes, livestock; lumbering.

Aldeburgh (ôld'bûrŭ, ôl'brŭ), municipal borough (1931 pop. 2,479; 1951 census 2,684), E Suffolk, England, on narrow spit bet. North Sea and Alde R. estuary, 20 mi. ENE of Ipswich; seaside resort and fishing port. Has 15th-cent. church and 16th-cent. Moot Hall. George Crabbe b. here.

Aldeia da Ponte (äldä'ŭ dä pōn'tĭ), agr. village (pop. 1,542), Guarda dist., N central Portugal, near Sp. border, 24 mi. SE of Guarda; rye, potatoes, wine, livestock.

Aldeia Nova or **Aldeia Nova de São Bento** (nô'vŭ dĭ sä'ō bän'tōō), town (pop. 4,861), Beja dist., S Portugal, 25 mi. ESE of Beja, near Sp. border; agr. trade center (grain, olives, sheep); pottery.

Aldeia Velha (vĕ'lyŭ), village (pop. 1,378), Guarda dist., N central Portugal, near Sp. border, 25 mi. SE of Guarda; rye, potatoes, olives, wine.

Aldeire (äl-dhä'rä), town (pop. 1,983), Granada prov., S Spain, 10 mi. SSE of Guadix; cereals, fruit, chestnuts. Mineral springs. Zinc, lead, antimony mines in area.

Alden (ôl'dŭn). **1** Town (pop. 829), Hardin co., central Iowa, on Iowa R. and 5 mi. W of Iowa Falls; livestock, grain. Limestone quarries near by. **2** City (pop. 286), Rice co., central Kansas, 24 mi. NW of Hutchinson, near Arkansas R.; wheat. **3** Village (pop. 668), Freeborn co., S Minn., near Iowa line, 11 mi. W of Albert Lea, in livestock, grain, and poultry area; dairy products, alfalfa meal. **4** Resort village (pop. 1,252), Erie co., W N.Y., 18 mi. E of Buffalo; mineral wells, natural-gas wells; mfg. (machinery, sheet-metal products, feed); truck farming. Inc. 1869.

Aldenham (ôl'dŭnŭm), residential town and parish (pop. 5,379), SW Hertford, England, 2 mi. NE of Watford. Has 13th-cent. church.

Aldeno (äldä'nō), village (pop. 1,783), Trento prov., Trentino-Alto Adige, N Italy, near the Adige, 6 mi. S of Trent; wine making.

Alder (ôl'dŭr), village (pop. c.150), Madison co., SW Mont., 50 mi. SSE of Butte and on Ruby R., just NE of Snowcrest Mts.; shipping point for livestock, farm produce, gold ore.

Alder Dam, Wash.: see NISQUALLY RIVER.

Alderetes (äldärä'tēs), town (pop. estimate 700), ⊙ Cruz Alta dept. (□ c.600; 1947 pop. 66,597), central Tucumán prov., Argentina, on railroad and 4 mi. E of Tucumán, across Salí R.; sugar-cane center.

Aldergrove, village (pop. estimate 300), SW B.C., near Wash. border, 30 mi. ESE of Vancouver; lumbering, dairying; fruit, vegetables.

Aldergrove, village, S Co. Antrim, Northern Ireland, 6 mi. S of Antrim; air base.

Alde River (äld), Suffolk, England, rises 5 mi. N of Framlingham, flows 30 mi. SE, past Aldeburgh and Orford, to North Sea 5 mi. SW of Orford. Called Ore R. below Orford.

Alderley Edge (ôl'–), urban district (1931 pop. 3,145; 1951 census 3,689), E central Cheshire, England, 8 mi. SSW of Stockport; market town, with mfg. of agr. machinery. Near by is Chorley Hall, a 16th-cent. mansion.

Aldermaston, village, S Berkshire, England, 10 mi. WSW of Reading; site of atomic-energy plant (construction begun 1950).

Aldermen, The, uninhabited volcanic group of 3 isls. and scattered islets in Bay of Plenty, N N. Isl., New Zealand; largest isl. is ½ mi. long.

Alderney (ôl'dûrnē), Fr. *Aurigny* (ōrēnyē'), anc. *Riduna*, island (1,962 acres; 1951 pop. 1,319), one of Channel Isls., off Normandy coast, 28 mi. W of Cherbourg, separated from Cotentin Peninsula by 10-mi.-wide Race of Alderney; 4 mi. long, 1 mi. wide; ⊙ Saint Anne. Cattle breeding, potato and grain growing. In 1940 isl. was demilitarized and partly evacuated prior to occupation by Germans. It was liberated in 1945.

Alderney, Race of, Fr. *Raz Blanchart* (räz blä-shär'), strait (10 mi. wide) bet. Alderney isl. of the Channel Isls. and Cape La Hague; dangerously swift tidal races.

Aldersbach (äl'dûrsbäkh), village (pop. 1,574), Lower Bavaria, Germany, 17 mi. W of Passau; brewing, woodworking. Has former Cistercian monastery (founded 1146) with baroque church.

Aldershot (ôl'–), municipal borough (1931 pop. 34,280; 1951 census pop. 36,184), Southampton, NE Hampshire, England, 8 mi. W of Guildford, 35 mi. SW of London; site of largest military training center in United Kingdom, with extensive barracks and military installations. Among industries are brewing and flour milling. Has church dating from 13th cent. Aldershot was a small village until establishment of military camp in 1854.

Alderson (ôl'dûrsŭn). **1** Town (pop. 311), Pittsburg co., SE Okla., 5 mi. SE of McAlester, in farm area. **2** Town (pop. 1,489), Monroe and Greenbrier counties, SE W.Va., on Greenbrier R. and 12 mi. WSW of Lewisburg, in agr. area. Federal reformatory for women here. Settled 1777.

Aldie (ôl'dē), village, Loudoun co., N Va., 10 mi. SSW of Leesburg. Near by is "Oak Lawn" (1823), home of James Monroe.

Aldinga, village, SE South Australia, 26 mi. S of Adelaide; dairy products, livestock.

Aldingbourne (ăl'dĭngbôrn ăln'bôrn), agr. village and parish (pop. 1,319), SW Sussex, England, 4 mi. N of Bognor Regis. Medieval church.

Aldonā (äldō'nā), town (pop. 8,045), N Goa dist., Portuguese India, 6 mi. NNE of Pangim; rice, mangoes, coconuts.

Aldora, town (pop. 591), Lamar co., W central Ga., 2 mi. W of Barnesville.

Aldrich (ôl'–). **1** Village (1940 pop. 728), Shelby co., central Ala., 28 mi. S of Birmingham. **2** Village (pop. 131), Wadena co., central Minn., on small affluent of Crow Wing R. and 35 mi. W of Brainerd, in grain and livestock area; dairy products. Inc. 1938. **3** Town (pop. 198), Polk co., SW central Mo., in the Ozarks, on Little Sac R. and 9 mi. SW of Bolivar.

Aldridge, urban district (1951 census pop. 29,167), S Staffordshire, England, 3 mi. ENE of Walsall; coal mining; brick and tile mfg.

Aldridge (ôl'drĭj), village (1940 pop. 857), Walker co., N Ala., 28 mi. NW of Birmingham.

Aldwincle or **Aldwinkle** (ä'nĭkŭl), agr. parish (pop. 316), E Northampton, England, on Nene R. and 2 mi. NNE of Thrapston. Includes adjoining villages of Aldwincle Saint Peter (Thomas Fuller b. here) and Aldwincle All Saints (Dryden b. here).

Aledo (ŭlē'dō), city (pop. 2,919), ⊙ Mercer co., NW Ill., 23 mi. SSW of Rock Island; trade and shipping center in agr. and bituminous-coal area; corn, oats, wheat, soybeans, livestock, poultry; dairy products. Mfg. (brick, feed). Has Roosevelt military acad. Inc. 1885.

Aleg (älĕg'), village, SW Mauritania, Fr. West Africa, 180 mi. ENE of Saint-Louis, Senegal; millet, gum arabic; sheep, goats.

Alegazovo, Russian SFSR: see BOLSHE-USTIKINSKOYE.

Alegranza Island (älägrän'thä), uninhabited islet (□ c.4.5; 3 mi. long), northernmost of Canary Isls., 145 mi. NE of Las Palmas; extinct volcanoes rise over 800 ft. Lighthouse at Point Delgada; 29°25'N 13°29'W. Sometimes Allegranza.

Alegre (älä'grĭ), city (pop. 4,773), S Espírito Santo, Brazil, on railroad and 28 mi. W of Cachoeiro de Itapemirim, in coffee dist.; coffee hulling, cotton ginning, sawmilling.

Alegrete (älĭgrē'tĭ), city (1950 pop. 20,160), Rio Grande do Sul, Brazil, 120 mi. W of Santa Maria; rail junction; livestock center (cattle, sheep, horses); meat processing, shipping of wool and hides. Agates mined near by. Airfield.

Alegrete, town (pop. 729), Portalegre dist., central Portugal, 7 mi. SE of Portalegre, near Sp. border; wine, olives, grain; chestnuts. Has old castle.

Alegria (älägrē'ä), town (1939 pop. 898; 1948 municipality pop. 13,676), S Cebu isl., Philippines, 20 mi. NE of Tanjay, across Tañon Strait; corn, coconuts. Oil deposits.

Alegría (älägrē'ä), city (pop. 2,148), Usulután dept., E central Salvador, on N slope of volcano Tecapa, 12 mi. NNW of Usulután; coffee growing.

Aleh, Kuh-i-, Iran: see ALA DAGH.

'Aleih or **'Alayh** (älä'), Fr. *Aley*, town (pop. 5,271), central Lebanon, 6 mi. SE of Beirut, and on Damascus RR; alt. 2,800 ft.; summer resort.

Alei River or **Aley River** (ŭlyä'), central Altai Territory, Russian SFSR, rises in Kolyvan Range of Altai Mts., flows c.330 mi. W, past Lokot, and NE, along Turksib RR, past Rubtsovsk and Aleisk, to Ob R. 25 mi. S of Barnaul.

Aleisk or **Aleysk** (ŭlyäsk'), city (1939 pop. over 10,000), central Altai Territory, Russian SFSR, on Turksib RR, on Alei R. and 70 mi. SSW of Barnaul; flour mill, sugar refinery.

Alejandro or **Alejandro Roca** (älāhän'drō rō'kä), town (pop. 2,507), S central Córdoba prov., Argentina, on Río Cuarto and 24 mi. W of La Carlota; agr. center (cereals, flax, sunflowers); cattle raising, flour milling, dairying.

Alejandro Stefenelli (stäfänĕ'lē), village (pop. estimate 500), N Río Negro natl. territory, Argentina, on railroad, on Río Negro and 4 mi. E of Fuerte General Roca; alfalfa, wine, fruit, sheep, goats; wine making. Gypsum deposits.

Alejo Ledesma (älä'hō lädäz'mä), town (pop. 2,452), SE Córdoba prov., Argentina, 70 mi. SSW of Marcos Juárez; wheat, flax, corn, alfalfa, sunflowers, cattle.

Alekhovshchina (ŭlyĭkhôf'shchĭnŭ), village, NE Leningrad oblast, Russian SFSR, on Oyat R. and 24 mi. SSE of Lodeinoye Pole; coarse grain.

Aleknagik (ŭlĕk'nŭgĭk), village (pop. 103), SW Alaska, on Aleknagik L. (20 mi. long), 16 mi. NNW of Dillingham; supply point for trappers; fishing; cannery.

Aleksandrinka (ŭlyĭksŭndrēn'kŭ), town (1926 pop. 4,568), central Stalino oblast, Ukrainian SSR, in the Donbas, 15 mi. SSW of Stalino; refractory clays.

Aleksandriskaya, Aleksandriiskaya, or **Aleksandriyskaya** (–drē'skīŭ), village (1926 pop. 7,289), S Stavropol Territory, Russian SFSR, on left bank of Kuma R. and 8 mi. WNW of Georgiyevsk; flour mill, metalworks; truck, vineyards, wheat.

Aleksandriya (–drē'ŭ). ⊙ **1** City (1926 pop. 18,705), E Kirovograd oblast, Ukrainian SSR, on Ingulets R. and 40 mi. ENE of Kirovograd. Center of lignite-mining area (developed after 1945); mfg. (mining machinery, excavators, chemicals), woodworking, flour milling. Granite quarries. Dates from mid-18th cent.; originally an agr. trade center. In Second World War, held (1941–43) by Germans. **2** Pol. *Aleksandrja* (älĕksän'drēä), village (1931 pop. 1,780), central Rovno oblast, Ukrainian SSR, on Goryn R. and 8 mi. NNE of Rovno; flour milling, sawmilling, tanning; truck gardening.

Aleksandro-Grigoryevka or **Aleksandro-Grigor'yevka** (ŭlyĭksän'drŭ-grĭgô'ryŭfkŭ), town (1939 pop. over 500), central Stalino oblast, Ukrainian SSR, in the Donbas, 5 mi. N of Stalino; coal mines.

Aleksandro-Nevski or **Aleksandro-Nevskiy** (–nyĕf'skē), town (1948 pop. over 2,000), S Ryazan oblast, Russian SFSR, 17 mi. SSE of Ryazhsk; flour, tobacco products.

Aleksandropol, Armenian SSR: see LENINAKAN, city.

Aleksandrov (–drŭf), city (1926 pop. 12,655), NW Vladimir oblast, Russian SFSR, on left tributary of Klyazma R. and 65 mi. WNW of Vladimir. Rail junction on Moscow outer belt line; mfg. (radio equipment, clothing), cotton milling, food processing. Famous Uspenski convent (16th–17th cent.), formerly used as place of exile, here. Known since early 16th cent. Ivan the Terrible resided here (1564–81) and organized the Oprichnina, political police. Chartered 1778.

Aleksandrovac, Aleksandrovats, Aleksandrovac Krusevacki, or **Aleksandrovats Krushevachki** (älĕksän'drôväts krōō'shĕvächkē), Serbo-Croatian *Aleksandrovac Kruševački*, village (pop. 1,535), Zupa co., S central Serbia, Yugoslavia, 16 mi. SW of Krusevac; winegrowing.

Aleksandrov-Gai or **Aleksandrov-Gay** (ŭlyĭksän'drŭf-gī'), village (1926 pop. 8,049), SE Saratov oblast, Russian SFSR, on Greater Uzen R. and 30 mi. SE of Novouzensk, near Kazakh SSR border; rail terminus; flour milling; wheat, cattle, sheep.

Aleksandrovka (–kŭ). **1** City, Amur oblast, Russian SFSR: see KUIBYSHEVKA. **2** Village (1948 pop. over 2,000), N Chkalov oblast, Russian SFSR, 65 mi. NW of Chkalov; wheat, sunflowers, livestock. **3** Village (1926 pop. 8,033), SW Rostov oblast, Russian SFSR, 30 mi. SW of Azov; flour mill, metalworks; wheat, sunflowers, castor beans, cotton; cattle raising. **4** Town, Ukrainian SSR:

see ORDZHONIKIDZE, Dnepropetrovsk oblast. **5** Village (1926 pop. 5,149), N Kirovograd oblast, Ukrainian SSR, 30 mi. N of Kirovograd; sugar mill. **6** Agr. town (1926 pop. 4,479), central Stalino oblast, Ukrainian SSR, in the Donbas, 11 mi. SW of Stalino. **7** Village (1926 pop. 1,503), NW Stalino oblast, Ukrainian SSR, on Samara R. and 15 mi. SSW of Barvenkovo; metalworks. **8** Town (1939 pop. over 500), S central Voroshilovgrad oblast, Ukrainian SSR, on Lugan R. and 4 mi. W of Voroshilovgrad; woodworking. **9** Village, NW Voroshilovgrad oblast, Ukrainian SSR; see LOZNO-ALEKSANDROVKA.

Aleksandrovo (älĕksän'drôvô). **1** Village (pop. 3,496), Pleven dist., N Bulgaria, on Osam R. and 14 mi. NE of Lovech; wheat, corn, livestock. Formerly Kara Khasan. **2** Village (pop. 3,061), Stara Zagora dist., central Bulgaria, in Kazanlik Basin, on Tundzha R. and 16 mi. W of Kazanlik; roses, mint, grain. Formerly Okchilav.

Aleksandrovsk (ŭlyĭksän'drŭfsk). **1** City, Murmansk oblast, Russian SFSR: see POLYARNY. **2** or **Aleksandrovsk on Sakhalin** (să'kŭlēn, -ĭn, säkälēn'), Rus. *Aleksandrovsk-Sakhalinski* (-sŭkhŭlyēn'skē), city (1948 pop., including suburbs, over 100,000), on W coast of N Sakhalin, Russian SFSR, port on Tatar Strait, 275 mi. N of Yuzhno-Sakhalinsk; 50°53'N 142°10'E. Port of entry to N Sakhalin; ships coal, lumber; receives food products, finished goods. Coal-mining center (mines at suburbs of Due, Mgachi, and Oktyabrski); sawmilling, fish canning; power plant. Founded 1881 as tsarist exile center; later developed into port and industrial town; became city in 1927. Was (1932–47) ⊙ Sakhalin oblast. **3** City, Zaporozhe oblast, Ukrainian SSR: see ZAPOROZHE, city.

Aleksandrovskaya, Kabardian Autonomous SSR, Russian SFSR: see TEREK, town.

Aleksandrovsk-Grushevski, Russian SFSR: see SHAKHTY, Rostov oblast.

Aleksandrovski or **Aleksandrovskiy** (-drŭfskē). **1** Town (1926 pop. 1,580), central Kursk oblast, Russian SFSR, 22 mi. SE of Oboyan; flour milling. Meat packing at adjoining Prokhorovka village. **2** Town (1926 pop. 3,281), E central Molotov oblast, Russian SFSR. 8 mi. NNW of Kizel, on railroad (Kopi station); mfg. (machine tools, building materials). Until 1928, Aleksandrovski Zavod. Became city in 1951, renamed Aleksandrovsk.

Aleksandrovski Zavod or **Aleksandrovskiy Zavod** (zŭvôt'), village (1926 pop. 2,097), SE Chita oblast, Russian SFSR, on Gazimur R. and 75 mi. NE of Borzya; silver and lead mines. Former silver-mining center.

Aleksandrovskoye (-skŭyŭ). **1** Village, Kirghiz SSR: see KIROVSKOYE. **2** Village (1926 pop. 13,287), S central Stavropol Territory, Russian SFSR, on Stavropol Plateau, on left branch of Kuma R. and 55 mi. SE of Stavropol; flour mill, metalworks; dairying; wheat, sunflowers. Quarrying. **3** Village (1939 pop. over 500), NW Tomsk oblast, Russian SFSR, on Ob R. and 165 mi. NW of Narym, in agr. area. **4** Village, SE Tomsk oblast, Russian SFSR, on Tomsk-Asino RR (near Tugan station) and 20 mi. NE of Tomsk, in agr. area.

Aleksandrow (älĕksän'drōōf), Pol. *Aleksandrów*, Rus. *Aleksandrov* (ŭlyĭksän'drŭf). **1** or **Aleksandrow Kujawski** (kōōyäf'skē), town (pop. 7,577), Bydgoszcz prov., central Poland, on railroad and 10 mi. SSE of Torun; brick mfg., flour milling. Until First World War, Rus. frontier station on Ger. border on main Berlin-Moscow line. **2** or **Aleksandrow Lodzki** (wōōt'skē), Pol. *Aleksandrów Łodzki*, town (pop. 6,926), Lodz prov., central Poland, 8 mi. WNW of Lodz city center; weaving, hosiery mfg., flour milling.

Alekseyevka (ŭlyĭksyā'ŭfkŭ). **1** Town (1948 pop. over 2,000), N Akmolinsk oblast, Kazakh SSR, near railroad (Ak-Kul station), 60 mi. NNW of Akmolinsk; cotton ginning; mfg. of construction materials. **2** Village (1948 pop. over 2,000), SE East Kazakhstan oblast, Kazakh SSR, on China border, S of Marka-Kul (lake), 70 mi. NNE of Zaisan; gold placers. **3** Town (1926 pop. 2,027), central Kuibyshev oblast, Russian SFSR, on railroad (Padovka station) and 5 mi. WNW of Kinel; asphalt and sulphur mining; bitumen works. **4** Village (1926 pop. 3,622), SE Kuibyshev oblast, Russian SFSR, 33 mi. S of Pavlovka; flour milling, metalworking; wheat, livestock. **5** Town (1948 pop. over 2,000), N Saratov oblast, Russian SFSR, on right bank of Volga R. and 14 mi. SSW of Khvalynsk; metalworking center. **6** Town (1926 pop. 11,712), SW Voronezh oblast, Russian SFSR, on Tikhaya Sosna R. and 21 mi. SW of Ostrogozhsk; essential-oil extraction; sunflower-oil press.

Alekseyevo-Druzhkovka (-ŭvŭ-drōōshkôf'kŭ), town (1939 pop. over 500), N central Stalino oblast, Ukrainian SSR, in the Donbas, 4 mi. SE of Druzhkovka; fire clays.

Alekseyevo-Lozovskoye (-lŭzôf'skŭyŭ), village (1926 pop. 2,190), NW Rostov oblast, Russian SFSR, 22 mi. E of Chertkovo; metalworks; wheat, sunflowers, cattle.

Alekseyevo-Orlovka (-ŭrlôf'kŭ), town (1926 pop. 3,929), E Stalino oblast, Ukrainian SSR, in the Donbas, 9 mi. WNW of Chistyakovo; coal mines.

Alekseyevsk (-ŭfsk). **1** Town, Russian SFSR: see SVOBODNY, Amur oblast. **2** Town (1939 pop. over 500), N Irkutsk oblast, Russian SFSR, on Lena R. (landing) and 12 mi. NE of Kirensk; lumbering.

Alekseyevskaya (ŭlyĭksyā'ŭfskīŭ), village (1926 pop. 2,441), NW Stalingrad oblast, Russian SFSR, on Buzuluk R., near its confluence with Khoper R., and 25 mi. SW of Novo-Annenski; metalworks, flour mill; wheat, sunflowers.

Alekseyevskoye (-skŭyŭ). **1** Village (1932 pop. estimate 2,530), W central Tatar Autonomous SSR, Russian SFSR, near Kama R., 21 mi. W of Chistopol; dairying (powdered milk), metalworking. **2** Village (1926 pop. 5,468), central Kharkov oblast, Ukrainian SSR, 38 mi. S of Kharkov; dairying.

Aleksikovo, Russian SFSR: see NOVO-NIKOLAYEVSKAYA.

Aleksin (ŭlyĕk'sĭn), city (1926 pop. 3,942), NW Tula oblast, Russian SFSR, on right bank of Oka R. and 30 mi. NW of Tula; limestone works, flour mills. Founded 1348.

Aleksinac or **Aleksinats** (both: älĕk'sēnäts), town (pop. 7,383), E central Serbia, Yugoslavia, on the Southern Morava and 17 mi. NNW of Nis. Brown-coal mine (just N) is connected with railroad across river by ropeway. Truck gardening, tobacco growing in vicinity. Site of Turkish victory (1876) over Serbs. Formerly spelled Alexinatz.

Alella (älā'lyä), village (pop. 1,395), Barcelona prov., NE Spain, 10 mi. NE of Barcelona, in wine-growing area.

Alemania (älāmä'nyä), mining settlement (1930 pop. 1,937), Antofagasta prov., N Chile, on railroad and 45 mi. NE of Taltal; nitrate production.

Além Paraíba (älĕn' pŭräē'bŭ), city (pop. 9,598), southernmost Minas Gerais, Brazil, on Paraíba R. (Rio de Janeiro border), on railroad and 80 mi. NE of Rio de Janeiro; industrial center (textiles, paper); ships coffee, lumber, dairy products. Formerly spelled Além Parahyba.

Alemquer, Brazil: see ALENQUER.

Alemquer, Portugal: see ALENQUER.

Alemtejo, Portugal: see ALENTEJO.

Alen (ô'lŭn), Nor. *Ålen*, village and canton (pop. 2,480), Sor-Trondelag co., central Norway, on the Gaula, on railroad and 19 mi. N of Roros; pyrite-mining center, with near-by mines of Killingdal and Kjoli (Nor. *Kjøli*). Formerly spelled Aalen. Storli (stôr'lē) Village is 2 mi. NW; novelist Jonas Lie b. here.

Alencar (älĕngkär'), town (pop. 668), SW Ceará, Brazil, 10 mi. E of Iguatu, on Fortaleza-Crato RR at junction of Orós spur, near large irrigation reservoir. Magnesite mined in area. Formerly called José de Alencar.

Alençon (äläsõ'), town (pop. 16,692), ⊙ Orne dept., NW France, in Normandy, on the Sarthe and 110 mi. WSW of Paris; road and commercial center (horses, grain), long known for its lace manufactures ("point d'Alençon"). Textile milling (linen and woolen cloth; bleaching and printing), mfg. of auto chassis, mining equipment, footwear, brick. In fertile agr. plain surrounded by wooded hills: Forest of Écouves (N; □ 30; alt. 1,368 ft.), Forest of Perseigne (E; □ 20; alt. 1,115 ft.), and the ALPES MANCELLES (SW). Has 14th-18th-cent. church of Notre Dame; 15th-cent. Ozé mansion (containing mus.); remains of 15th-cent. castle; and 18th-cent. town hall (with mus. of paintings). Was ⊙ of county, later duchy, of Alençon, which passed to Fr. crown in 1525. Heavily damaged in Second World War.

Alenquer (älĕngkĕr'), city (pop. 2,801), W central Pará, Brazil, on left branch of the lower Amazon and 30 mi. N of Santarém; cattle, nuts, fish (arapaima). Limestone and lead deposits in area. Formerly spelled Alemquer.

Alenquer, town (pop. 2,262), Lisboa dist., central Portugal, 25 mi. NNE of Lisbon; winegrowing center; wool and paper mills. Has 13th-cent. Franciscan convent and ruins of a medieval castle. Formerly spelled Alemquer.

Alentejo (äläntā'zhōō) [Port.,=beyond the Tagus], former province (□ 9,179; 1940 pop. 669,766), central and S Portugal; old ⊙ Évora. It contained Beja, Évora, and Portalegre dists. Bounded by Spain (E), and by the Tagus (N), it has a short Atlantic coastline S of Cape Sines. It also borders on old Estremadura prov. (W) and on Algarve (S). Drained by the Guadiana, which forms part of its boundary with Spain. Although only part of the land is arable, Alentejo is known as the granary of Portugal. The region's second great resource is its cork forests. Sheep, horses, cattle, and hogs are raised, and, in addition to grain, olives and fruit (grapes, figs, lemons, pomegranates) are grown. Copper mined at Aljustrel and Mina de São Domingos. Olive-oil and cork processing, pottery mfg. and leatherworking are principal industries. Prov. figured in reconquest of Portugal from the Moors; after the battle of Ourique (1139), Alfonso I proclaimed himself King of Portugal. Region played an even more important part in the many wars with Castile (14th and 17th cent.). In 1936 Alentejo was divided into 2 new provinces (ALTO ALENTEJO, ⊙ Évora; BAIXO ALENTEJO, ⊙ Beja) which together slightly exceed area of old prov. by including S portion of old Estremadura prov. Old spelling, Alemtejo.

Alenuihaha Channel (ä'lānōō"ēhä'hä), bet. Maui and Hawaii isls., T.H., 26 naut. mi. wide.

Aleppo (ŭlĕ'pō), Arabic *Haleb* or *Halab* (both: hälĕb'), Fr. *Alep* (älĕp'), province (□ 7,980; 1946 pop. 911,855), NW Syria; ⊙ Aleppo. Bounded N and W by Turkey and Latakia prov., E by the Euphrates. Agr. (corn, millet, cotton, wheat, pistachios), textile and carpet mfg.; dairying, stock raising. Much of its produce goes to Iraq and Turkey, and there is a busy exchange through the Mediterranean ports of Latakia and Tripoli. Main urban centers: Aleppo, El Hamidiya, Jerablus, Jisr esh Shughur, Ma'arret en Nu'man.

Aleppo, Arabic *Haleb* or *Halab*, biblical *Beroea* or *Berea*, Fr. *Alep*, largest city (1946 pop. 337,777) of Syria, ⊙ Aleppo prov., NW Syria, 70 mi. E of the Mediterranean, 25 mi. from Turkish border, on railroad, and 75 mi. NNE of Hama, 55 mi. E of Antioch; 36°10'N 37°10'E; alt. 1,050 ft. Chief commercial and industrial center of N Syria, producing silks, cotton textiles, carpets, yarn, vegetable oils, soap, sugar. Trades also in wheat, cereals, wool, olive oil, livestock, dairy products. Has heavy trade with Turkey and Iraq. An ancient city on the main caravan route across Syria to Baghdad, it was center of a kingdom of the Hittites before 1,000 B.C. and was taken by the various conquerors of Syria. Its importance was enhanced after the fall of Palmyra in A.D. 272. A flourishing city of the Byzantine Empire, it was taken by Arabs in 7th cent., recovered by Byzantines in 10th cent., and retaken by Seljuk Turks late in 11th cent. The Crusaders formally besieged it, but without success, in 1124. Saladin took it in 1183 and made it his stronghold. It was conquered by the Mongols in 1260 and again by Tamerlane in 1401, but was not long held. In 1517 the Ottoman Turks made it a part of their empire, and it was a great commercial center. Ibrahim Pasha took it (1832) for Mohammed Ali of Egypt who was forced to give it up in 1840. Its importance declined with the establishment of new trade routes, but it recovered after First World War when Syria was established as a French mandate and, later, became independent. It has often been severely damaged by earthquake. A notable landmark is the great citadel built in late 4th cent. B.C. on a hill commanding the city.

Alerce (älĕr'sā), village (1930 pop. 301), Llanquihue prov., S central Chile, on railroad and 4 mi. N of Puerto Montt, in agr. area (grain, potatoes, livestock); dairying, lumbering.

Alerces, Los, Argentina: see LOS ALERCES.

Aleria (älārēä', It. älā'rēä), agr. village (pop. 734), E Corsica, on Tavignano R. near its mouth into Tyrrhenian Sea, and 23 mi. SE of Corte, on site of anc. Phocean and Roman colonies. Aleria plain, extending c.25 mi. along the coast, is Corsica's only important lowland. Insalubrious climate. Also spelled Aléria.

Alert Bay, village (pop. estimate 400), SW B.C., on Cormorant Isl. (□ 2), at entrance to Johnstone Strait just off N coast of Vancouver Isl., 100 mi. NW of Courtenay; 50°35'N 126°55'W; port of entry; lumber and fish-shipping port; fish canning, lumbering. Site of Dominion radio station and Indian mission.

Alès (älĕs'), town (pop. 20,027), Gard dept., S France, on the Gardon d'Alès and 25 mi. NW of Nîmes, at foot of the Cévennes; center of industrial and coal-mining region. Has blast furnaces, steel mills, glass- and metalworks, chemical and silk-spinning factories. Iron ore, pyrite, zinc, silver, and antimony are also mined in area. Heavy industry extends into N suburb of Les Tamaris. By the Peace of Alais (1629), French Protestants lost their political power. Alès was formerly called Alais.

Ales (ä'lĕs), village (pop. 1,492), Cagliari prov., W Sardinia, 15 mi. SE of Oristano; rail terminus. Bishopric. Also called Ales Sardo.

Alesanco (äläsäng'kō), town (pop. 1,190), Logroño prov., N Spain, 19 mi. WSW of Logroño, in rich winegrowing area.

Alesd (ä'lĕsht), Rum. *Aleşd*, Hung. *Élesd* (ā'lĕsht), village (pop. 2,353), Bihor prov., W Rumania, on Rapid Körös R., on railroad and 22 mi. E of Oradea; lumbering; mfg. of bricks, tiles, terra-cotta stoves; large limekilns. In Hungary, 1940–45.

Aleshki, Ukrainian SSR: see TSYURUPINSK.

Aleshtar, Iran: see ALISHTAR.

Alesia, France: see ALISE-SAINTE-REINE.

Aleskirt, Turkey: see ELESKIRT.

Alesk River, SW Yukon and S Alaska, rises on E slope of St. Elias Mts. near 60°30'N 137°W, flows 160 mi. SSW in a winding course to Dry Bay of the Gulf of Alaska at 59°5'N 138°30'W.

Alessandra (älĕs-sän'drä), village (pop. 200), in the Benadir, S Ital. Somaliland, on Juba R. opposite Gelib; agr. experiment station (castor beans, tobacco, cayenne pepper, peanuts, bananas).

Alessandria (älĕs-sän'drēä), province (□ 1,386; pop. 493,698), Piedmont, N Italy; ⊙ Alessandria. Hilly terrain, rising to 5,581 ft. in Mt. Ebro (SE), predominates, almost enclosing Tanaro R. plain; drained by Tanaro, Bormida, and Scrivia rivers. Agr. (wheat, grapes); stock raising. Limestone quarries near Casale Monferrato. Mfg. at Alessandria, Casale Monferrato, Tortona, Novi Ligure. Area reduced in 1935 to form Asti prov.

Alessandria, city (pop. 51,949), ⊙ Alessandria prov., Piedmont, N Italy, on Tanaro R., near mouth of the Bormida, and 48 mi. SE of Turin; 44°55′N 8°37′ E. Rail and road junction; industrial center with railroad shops, foundries; mfg. of felt hats especially; also automobile chassis, motorcycles, bicycles, iron beds, aluminum, cork, glass, furniture, fertilizer, shoes; food canning; alcohol distilling; sugar refining; clothing mills. Bishopric since 1175. Has cathedral (rebuilt 1805), 17th-cent. palaces, citadel (1728), mus., picture gall. Founded 1168 as stronghold against Frederick Barbarossa by Lombard League under auspices of Pope Alexander III, whose name it bears. Battlefield of Marengo is 2 mi. SE. In Second World War, bombed (1942–44).

Alessandria del Carretto (dĕl kär-rĕt′tô), village (pop. 1,602), Cosenza prov., Calabria, S Italy, 14 mi. NNE of Castrovillari; wine, cheese.

Alessandria della Rocca (dĕl-lä rôk′kä), town (pop. 6,112), Agrigento prov., SW central Sicily, 19 mi. NNW of Agrigento.

Alessano (älĕs-sä′nô), town (pop. 3,824), Lecce prov., Apulia, S Italy, 22 mi. SE of Gallipoli; agr. center; wine, olive oil; tobacco, figs.

Ales Sardo, Sardinia: see ALES.

Alessio, Albania: see LESH.

Alesund (ô′lusŏŏn), Nor. *Ålesund*, city (pop. 18,143), More og Romsdal co., W Norway, port built on 3 isls. off the mainland at mouth of Stor Fjord, 70 mi. SW of Kristiansund; 62°28′N 6°8′E. Fishing, sealing, and whaling center, with Norway's largest fishing harbor. Has freezing, smoking, and cold-storage plants; fish-oil refineries. Industries also produce boats and motors, textiles and clothing, fishing equipment, meat and agr. products. Besides its cod and herring fleets, it is a base for arctic fishing. City rebuilt in stone after severe fire in 1904. Sometimes spelled Aalesund.

Alet or **Alet-les-Bains** (älĕt′-lā-bē′), village (pop. 538), Aude dept., S France, on Aude R. and 4 mi. SSE of Limoux; mineral springs. Its ruined church was part of medieval abbey. Episcopal see (1317–1790).

Aletsch Glacier (ä′lĕch), largest (□ 66) in the Alps, S central Switzerland, W and S of the Aletschhorn; composed of Great Aletsch Glacier, Upper Aletsch Glacier (with Upper Aletsch Hütten at 8,672 ft.), and Middle Aletsch Glacier. Great Aletsch Glacier descends in 10-mi.-long stream of ice from Concordia Platz (N), where it meets Great Aletsch Firn and Jungfrau Firn, to Aletschwald (S), a nature reserve. Belalp and Riederalp are noted resorts. The **Aletschhorn** (13,774 ft.), 8 mi. SSE of Mürren, is one of highest peaks in Bernese Alps.

Aleutian Current (ùlōō′shùn, ùlū′-) or **Subarctic Current,** cold current of North Pacific Ocean, bet. Aleutian Isls. and 42°N; formed by union of Japan and Okhotsk currents at 40°N 160°E, it flows E and branches (c.140°W) into ALASKA CURRENT and CALIFORNIA CURRENT. One branch enters Bering Sea, where it flows counterclockwise before becoming part of Okhotsk Current.

Aleutian Islands, chain of volcanic islands, SW Alaska, extending c.1,100 mi. SW from tip of Alaska Peninsula bet. the N Pacific (S) and the Bering Sea (N); 53°–55°N 163°20′W–172°25′E. Main groups (E–W) are the FOX ISLANDS, ANDREANOF ISLANDS, RAT ISLANDS, and NEAR ISLANDS. Partially submerged peaks of the Aleutian Range, isls. are rugged, mountainous, treeless, and covered with grass and sedges; sheep are reared on several isls. Inhabited by Aleuts, an Eskimo race. Fishing and fur trapping are main occupations. Mean temp. ranges (Kiska Isl.) from 28.4°F. (Jan.) to 47.8°F. (August); average annual rainfall 33.21 in. Fog is prevalent, and dangerous sea currents course along the chain and its many uncharted surrounding rocks. Main navigational channels or passes through the chain are Unimak Pass, Umnak Pass, Amukta Pass, and Seguam Pass. Among main volcanic peaks are Shishaldin Volcano, Unimak Isl.; Mt. Makushin, Unalaska Isl.; Mt. Vsevidof, Umnak Isl.; and Mt. Gareloi, Gareloi Isl. Isls. were discovered 1741 by Vitus Bering; later, fur traders established themselves here and severely exploited native Aleuts; at end of 18th cent. center of fur-trading operations shifted to Kodiak. Isls. were purchased 1867 by the U.S. as part of Alaska; fishing and fur industry now under govt. control. In Second World War Japanese opened attack on Aleutian Isls. with bombing (June 3, 1942) of Dutch Harbor; two weeks later Kiska and Attu isls. were occupied and inhabitants deported to Japan. Natives of other isls., evacuated 1942 by U.S. Navy, were repatriated 1945. U.S. bases were established on Adak and Amchitka isls.; from here and from Kodiak and Cold Bay Japanese positions were heavily attacked. Air and naval bases were later established on Shemya and Umnak isls. U.S. forces landed (May, 1943) on Attu and captured isl. after 3 weeks of bitter fighting; Japanese had in meantime evacuated Kiska Isl. Since the war, isls. have assumed new strategic importance and permanent bases have been expanded on Umnak, Adak, Atka, Amchitka, Shemya, and Attu isls.; Shemya is important airport on N route bet. U.S. and Far East.

Aleutian Range, mountain range, SW Alaska, extends c.600 mi. NE–SW along entire Alaska Peninsula from W end of Alaska Range to head of Cook Inlet, continued (SW) by Aleutian Isls., partially submerged peaks of the range. Of volcanic origin, it includes some of world's largest volcanoes, including KATMAI VOLCANO and Veniaminof Crater.

Aleutian Trench, submarine depression of North Pacific Ocean, on S side of the Aleutian Isls. arc. The greatest depth was long considered to be 24,225 ft. E of Attu Isl. A near-by sounding of 24,420 ft. was reported in 1950.

Alex-, in Rus. names: see names beginning ALEKS-.

Alex (ă′lĭks), town (pop. 563), Grady co., central Okla., 13 mi. SE of Chickasha, and on Washita R.; cotton ginning.

Alexander, village (pop. estimate 500), SW Man., 15 mi. W of Brandon; grain elevators; dairying.

Alexander. 1 County (□ 224; pop. 20,316), extreme S Ill.; ⊙ Cairo. Bounded W and S by Mississippi R. and SE by Ohio R.; drained by Cache R. Agr. area (cotton, fruit, corn), with some mfg. (lumber products; cottonseed and soybean processing; shoes, beverages). Includes part of Shawnee Natl. Forest. Formed 1819. **2** County (□ 255; pop. 14,554), W central N.C.; ⊙ Taylorsville. Piedmont area; bounded S by Catawba (Wateree) R. (hydroelectric dams and reservoirs); drained by small South Yadkin R. Farming (tobacco, cotton, corn, grain, hay, fruit); timber (pine). Textile mfg., sawmilling. Formed 1847.

Alexander. 1 Town (pop. 194), on Pulaski-Saline co. line, central Ark., 12 mi. SW of Little Rock. **2** Town (pop. 278), Franklin co., N central Iowa, 15 mi. WNW of Hampton; livestock. **3** City (pop. 188), Rush co., central Kansas, on Walnut Creek and 40 mi. W of Great Bend; wheat, livestock. **4** Town (pop. 282), Washington co., E Maine, in hunting, fishing area, 12 mi. SW of Calais. **5** Village (pop. 304), Genesee co., W N.Y., on Tonawanda Creek and 7 mi. SSW of Batavia; cans vegetables. **6** Village (pop. 302), McKenzie co., W N.Dak., 17 mi. W of Watford City.

Alexander, Cape, NE Mackenzie Dist., Northwest Territories, on Dease Strait, at N extremity of Kent Peninsula; 68°56′N 105°50′W.

Alexander, Cape, W extremity of Greenland, on NW coast, on Smith Sound; 78°9′N 73°8′W.

Alexander, Lake, Morrison co., central Minn., 18 mi. SW of Brainerd; 4.5 mi. long, 1.5 mi. wide. Drains through small lake and stream into Long Prairie R.

Alexander Archipelago, SE Alaska, large group of islands just off coast S of Juneau, extending from Icy Strait and Cross Sound (58°25′N) to Dixon Entrance (54°40′N). Largest isls., N–S: CHICHAGOF ISLAND, ADMIRALTY ISLAND, BARANOF ISLAND, KUPREANOF ISLAND, KUIU ISLAND, MITKOF ISLAND, WRANGELL ISLAND, PRINCE OF WALES ISLAND, and REVILLAGIGEDO ISLAND. Chief towns are KETCHIKAN (on Revillagigedo) and SITKA (on Baranof). Industries: lumbering, fishing, fish processing, fur farming, gold mining. Discovered by Russians in 1741 and later explored by England, Spain, and U.S. A remnant of a submerged mtn. system, the isls. rise steeply from the sea, with irregular shore lines, and are separated from each other and from the mainland by deep, narrow channels, making part of the Inside Passage.

Alexander Bay, Afrikaans *Alexanderbaai* (ălĕksän″-dùrbī′), village (pop. 669), NW Cape Prov., U. of So. Afr., on South-West Africa border, on the Atlantic at mouth of Orange R., 200 mi. SW of Keetmanshoop; 28°37′S 16°29′E. In diamond-mining region, discovered 1929. Airport.

Alexander City, city (pop. 6,430), Tallapoosa co., E Ala., 45 mi. NE of Montgomery, near Martin L.; milling center in cotton, corn, and dairying area; cotton goods, clothing, drainage castings, lumber products. Settled mid-19th cent. as Youngville, inc. 1873 as Alexander City.

Alexander I Island (c.235 naut. mi. long, 50–100 naut. mi. wide), Antarctica, in Bellingshausen Sea just off W coast of Palmer Peninsula, from which it is separated by George VI Sound and Marguerite Bay; 71°S 71°W. Discovered 1821 by Bellingshausen and called Alexander I Land until it was proved an isl. by U.S. expedition of 1940.

Alexander Mills, town (pop. 885), Rutherford co., SW N.C., 4 mi. S of Forest City.

Alexander Range, Kirghiz SSR: see KIRGHIZ RANGE.

Alexandersbad, Germany: see WUNSIEDEL.

Alexandra, town (pop. 1,258), central Victoria, Australia, on Goulburn R. and 60 mi. NE of Melbourne; rail terminus; livestock center in forested area; dairy plant, sawmills.

Alexandra, borough (pop. 1,028), S central S.Isl., New Zealand, 70 mi. NW of Dunedin and on Clutha R.; fruitgrowing.

Alexandra, residential town (pop. 52,170), S Transvaal, U. of So. Afr., on Witwatersrand, 6 mi. NE of Johannesburg. Almost entire pop. consists of native gold miners.

Alexandra, Mount, second highest summit (16,750 ft.) of the RUWENZORI, E central Africa, on Belgian Congo–Uganda border. First ascended by duke of Abruzzi and his expedition in 1906; named for the queen of Edward VII of England.

Alexandra Land, Rus. *Zemlya Aleksandry*, westernmost island of Franz Josef Land, Russian SFSR, in Arctic Ocean; 70 mi. long, 10–30 mi. wide; culminates SW in Cape Mary Harmsworth; separated from George Land (E) by Cambridge Strait.

Alexandra Nile, Africa: see KAGERA RIVER.

Alexandretta, city, Turkey: see ISKENDERUN.

Alexandretta, sanjak of (ă″lĭgzăndrĕ′tù, sänjäk′), former name of HATAY prov. (□2,205; pop. 254,141), S Turkey, bet. the Mediterranean and Syria. In it are cities of ANTIOCH (capital) and its port, Alexandretta (now ISKENDERUN). Has mixed population, with high percentage of Syrian Christians. Awarded to Syria in 1920, it became in 1936 subject of a complaint to League of Nations by Turkey, which claimed that Turkish minority privileges in the sanjak were being infringed. An agreement bet. France (then mandatory power in Syria) and Turkey was effected (1937) by the League, and Alexandretta was given autonomous status. Riots bet. Turks and Arabs resulted (1938) in establishment of joint French and Turkish military control; finally, in 1939, France transferred dist. to Turkey.

Alexandria, municipality (pop. 8,060), E New South Wales, Australia, 4 mi. S of Sydney, in metropolitan area; textile mills; mfg. (matches, soap, candles, cordials.)

Alexandria (älĭshăn′drĭù), city (pop. 765), SW Rio Grande do Norte, NE Brazil, near Paraíba border, 95 mi. SSW of Mossoró; cattle raising.

Alexandria, town (pop. 2,175), SE Ont., 20 mi. NNE of Cornwall; woodworking, glove mfg., agr. (dairying; cattle, poultry). Seat of R.C. diocese, with cathedral.

Alexandria, Arabic *Al-Iskandariyah*, city (□ 95; pop. 925,081), coextensive with Alexandria governorate, the chief seaport of Egypt, on a narrow strip of land bet. the Mediterranean Sea and L. Maryut (Mareotis), 110 mi. NW of Cairo; 31°12′N 29°54′E. The city serves as the summer ⊙ Egypt. Exports chiefly raw cotton. Industries: cotton ginning, leather tanning, cottonseed-oil pressing; metalworks; mfg. of paper, soap, matches, boots, shoes, stockings, cigarettes, beer. SW are limestone quarries. The E harbor of Alexandria, known as the Great Harbor in anc. times, when it was sheltered by a mole, is now used only for fishing. The modern harbor is to W, and has been developed and enlarged mainly since 1871. Excellent rail connections with Cairo and various points in the Nile delta; airports at Dikheila (S) and Abukir (N). SW is the suburb of MEX and important saltworks; along the coast, N, are the popular summer resort and beach Ramleh, the royal palace El Muntazah, and, beyond the city limits, ABUKIR and site of anc. CANOPUS. Founded in 332 B.C. by Alexander the Great on the westernmost mouth (Canopic) of the Nile, partly on the mainland and partly on PHAROS, Alexandria was ⊙ (304 B.C.–30 B.C.) of the Ptolemies and as a commercial center soon outgrew Carthage and became the largest city in the West. It was the great center of Hellenistic and Jewish culture (the Septuagint was prepared here) and had 2 celebrated royal libraries, said to contain about 490,000 different rolls or, counting duplicates, 700,000 rolls. Around the museum, which housed one of the libraries, arose a great university which attracted many scholars, including Aristarchus of Samothrace and Euclid. Julius Caesar occupied (47 B.C.) the city and when Octavian (later Augustus), after the suicide of Antony and Cleopatra, entered it in 30 B.C., it formally became part of the Roman Empire. It was the greatest of provincial capitals, with a pop. of c.300,000 free persons and an even larger number of slaves. Became a center of Christian learning under Byzantine Empire, and a patriarchate was established here. The famous libraries were destroyed over the years, and although a decline in shipping had hurt the city's economy, it still had 300,000 inhabitants when it fell (A.D. 642) to the Arabs. They moved the ⊙ Egypt to Cairo, and Alexandria's decline continued, especially in the 14th cent. when the canal to the Nile silted up. By the time Napoleon took it (1798; retaken 1801 by the British), it was nothing but a small town. It regained its importance under Mohammed Ali, who ordered the construction (1819) of Mahmudiya Canal to the Nile; this brought it most of the Nile trade and made possible the irrigation of large areas in the city's vicinity. Of anc. Alexandria very little remains: the ruins at Pharos, Pompey's Pillar (tall granite shaft), and catacombs. The famous museum has a vast collection of antiquities and volumes. Farouk Univ. is here.

Alexandria, town, St. Ann parish, N central Jamaica, 10 mi. SW of St. Ann's Bay, in rich agr. region (citrus fruit, corn, pimento, coffee, cattle). Germans settled here 1836–42.

Alexandria (ălĕksän′drēù), town (1948 pop. 17,840), Teleorman prov., S Rumania, in Walachia, on railroad and 26 mi. NE of Turnu-Magurele; trading center (mainly in grain); woodworking, flour milling; machine shops. Has agr. school.

Alexandria, town in Bonhill parish, central Dumbarton, Scotland, on Leven R. and 3 mi. N of Dumbarton; textile printing and dyeing.

Alexandria, county, Va.: see ARLINGTON, co.

Alexandria. 1 City (pop. 5,147), Madison co., E central Ind., on small Pipe Creek and c.40 mi. NE of Indianapolis, in agr. area; limestone quarries supply city's rock-wool industry. Mfg. of boilers, thermos ware, canvas gloves, asbestos and magnesium products. **2** Town (pop. 465), Clark co., NE Mo., 5 mi. SW of Keokuk, Iowa. **3** Town (pop. 536), a ⊙ Campbell co., N Ky., 14 mi. SSE of downtown Cincinnati. **4** City (pop. 34,913), ⊙ Rapides parish, central La., 95 mi. NW of Baton Rouge, and on Red R., opposite Pineville, its sister city; railroad and machine shops, foundries, creosoting works, cotton- and cottonseed-processing plants; lumber, building materials, naval stores, batteries, paint, oil-well supplies, chemicals; packed meat, dairy products; ski mfg. Commercial fisheries. Has R.C. cathedral (1898). A state park is near by. Laid out 1810, inc. 1818. **5** City (pop. 6,319), ⊙ Douglas co., W Minn., in lake region c.45 mi. SE of Fergus Falls; resort; tourist and trade center in grain and potato region; dairy products, beverages. Kensington Rune Stone is here. Settled 1857, laid out 1865. **6** Village (pop. 317), Thayer co., SE Nebr., 10 mi. ENE of Hebron and on branch of Little Blue R.; dairy produce, livestock, grain. **7** Town (pop. 402), Grafton co., central N.H., on Newfound L. and 30 mi. NNW of Concord; mica quarries. **8** Village (pop. 464), Licking co., central Ohio, 11 mi. W of Newark and on Raccoon Creek, in agr. area. **9** Borough (pop. 443), Huntingdon co., central Pa., 6 mi. NW of Huntingdon; bricks, flour. **10** City (pop. 714), ⊙ Hanson co., SE S.Dak., 15 mi. ESE of Mitchell, near James R.; dairy products, building stone, corn, wheat. **11** Town (pop. 372), De Kalb co., central Tenn., 17 mi. SE of Lebanon. Annual co. fair here. **12** City (pop. 61,787), independent of any co., N Va., on the Potomac (bridged), just S of Washington, D.C. Chiefly residential, with many historic landmarks; a port of entry; large railroad shops and freight yards, naval ordnance plant; mfg. of chemical fertilizers, concrete and metal products. Points of interest: Gadsby's Tavern (1752); Carlyle House (1752), where Washington received his major's commission from Gen. Braddock; Christ Church (1767–73); Ramsey House (1749–51); George Washington Masonic Natl. Memorial Temple (1923–32), housing Washington mementoes. Nearby "Woodlawn," a Washington family estate, was made a natl. shrine in 1949. An Episcopal seminary and Mt. Vernon are near by. Alexandria patented 1657; permanently settled in early-18th cent.; part of Dist. of Columbia, 1789–1847; inc. as town 1779, as city 1852. In Civil War, Federal operational base for N Va.

Alexandria Arachosiorum, Afghanistan: see KANDAHAR.

Alexandria Ariorum, Afghanistan: see HERAT, city.

Alexandria Bay, resort village (pop. 1,688), Jefferson co., N N.Y., on the St. Lawrence and 25 mi. N of Watertown; a gateway to the Thousand Isls.; port of entry. Mfg. (clothing, wood products, machinery, boats); sturgeon fisheries; dairying. Thousand Islands International Bridge (1938) spans the St. Lawrence near by. Inc. 1878.

Alexandria Troas, Turkey: see TROAS.

Alexandrina, Lake, lagoon (□ 220), SE South Australia, at mouth of Murray R., 40 mi. SE of Adelaide; 23 mi. long, 13 mi. wide, 5–15 ft. deep. Connects with the Coorong (S) and L. Albert (SE).

Alexandroupolis (ălĕksändrōō'pôlēs), city (pop. 19,411), ⊙ Hevros nome, W Thrace, Greece, port on NW shore of Gulf of Ainos (inlet of Aegean Sea), 65 mi. SW of Adrianople (Edirne), near Maritsa R. delta (Turkish border); trade center linked by rail with Salonika and Adrianople; wheat, cotton, silk, sesame, rice, tobacco, dried fruit, dairy products; fisheries, salt pans. Air field. Bishopric (moved here 1889 from Enos). Originally called Dedeagach, it developed from small fishing village after 1871, supplanting older port of Enos upon completion (1896) of Salonika-Istanbul RR. When it became a part of Greece after First World War, it was renamed for the Gr. king Alexander.

Alexandrovsk, Alaska: see ENGLISH BAY.

Alexinatz, Yugoslavia: see ALEKSINAC.

Alexis, village (pop. 821), on Mercer-Warren co. line, NW Ill., near Henderson Creek, 11 mi. NW of Galesburg, in agr. and bituminous-coal area.

Alexisbad, Germany: see HARZGERODE.

Alexishafen (ălĕk'sĭshä'fŭn), small harbor, NE New Guinea, on N shore of Astrolabe Bay. In Second World War, site of Jap. air base taken 1944 by Allied forces. Sometimes called Sek Harbour.

Aley, Lebanon: see 'ALEIH.

Aley River; Aleysk; Russian SFSR: see ALEI RIVER; ALEISK.

Alezio (ălĕt'syô), anc. *Aletium,* town (pop. 5,511), Lecce prov., Apulia, S Italy, 4 mi. E of Gallipoli; wine, olive oil.

Alfacar (ălfäkär'), NE suburb (pop. 1,889) of Granada, Granada prov., S Spain; olive-oil processing, flour milling; cereals, fruit, wine. Lignite mines; gypsum and stone quarries.

Alfafar (ălfäfär'), S suburb (pop. 3,464) of Valencia, Valencia prov., E Spain, in truck area; rice milling, furniture mfg.; mulberry trees.

Alfaiates (ălfäyä'tĭsh), village (pop. 1,694), Guarda dist., N central Portugal, 22 mi. SE of Guarda, near Sp. border; rye, potatoes, olives, wine, livestock.

Alfajarín (ălfähärēn'), town (pop. 1,235), Saragossa prov., NE Spain, 10 mi. ESE of Saragossa; sugar beets, cereals, alfalfa, esparto, fruit.

Alfajayucan (ălfähīōō'kän), town (pop. 736), Hidalgo, central Mexico, 45 mi. NW of Pachuca; alt. 6,227 ft.; cereals, maguey, beans, livestock.

Alfalfa (ăl'făl'fŭ), county (□ 884; pop. 10,699), N Okla.; ⊙ Cherokee. Bounded N by Kansas line. Intersected by Salt Fork of Arkansas R., impounded in co. by GREAT SALT PLAINS DAM (with wildlife refuge); and drained also by Medicine Lodge R. and Turkey Creek. Agr. (wheat, barley, cotton, alfalfa, livestock, poultry). Mfg. at Cherokee. Formed 1907.

Alfambra (ălfäm'brä), town (pop. 1,224), Teruel prov., E Spain, 15 mi. NNE of Teruel; produces hemp, cereals, saffron, sugar beets. Iron and manganese mines near by.

Alfamén (ălfämĕn'), village (pop. 1,334), Saragossa prov., NE Spain, 24 mi. SW of Saragossa; sheep raising; wine, cereals, watermelons.

Alfandega da Fé (ălfăndā'gŭ dä fā'), town (pop. 1,344), Bragança dist., N Portugal, on S slope of Serra de Bornes, 35 mi. SSW of Bragança; wine, olives, figs.

Alfaques, Puerto de los (pwĕr'tō dhā lōs ălfä'kēs), bay of the Mediterranean on Catalonia coast, NE Spain, c.15 mi. SE of Tortosa, on S side of Ebro delta and almost enclosed by sandspit. On N shore of spit are extensive saltworks. San Carlos de la Rápita is on W shore.

Alfara del Patriarca (ălfä'rä dhĕl pätrēär'kä), N suburb (pop. 2,272) of Valencia, Valencia prov., E Spain, in truck-garden area (melons); paper mfg.; also trades in wheat, olive oil, wine.

Alfarelos (ălfŭrā'lōōsh), agr. village (pop. 1,154), Coimbra dist., N central Portugal, 12 mi. WSW of Coimbra; rail junction; pottery mfg.

Alfarnate (ălfärnä'tā), town (pop. 2,376), Málaga prov., S Spain, in spur of the Cordillera Penibética, 20 mi. NNE of Málaga; olives, cereals, chick-peas, livestock; mfg. of textile and esparto goods.

Alfarnatejo (ălfärnätā'hō), town (pop. 441), Málaga prov., S Spain, 19 mi. NNE of Málaga; olives, cereals, livestock.

Alfaro, Ecuador: see DURÁN.

Alfaro (ălfä'rō), city (pop. 8,067), Logroño prov., N Spain, in Old Castile, near the Ebro, 40 mi. SE of Logroño, in fertile plain yielding pepper, cereals, wine, sugar beets, fruit. Canneries (vegetables, fruit), distilleries (alcohol, brandy), sugar and flour mills; sandal mfg. Mineral springs. Irrigation reservoir near by.

Alfaro Ruíz, canton, Costa Rica: see ZARCERO.

Alfarp (ălfärp'), village (pop. 1,347), Valencia prov., E Spain, 11 mi. NW of Alcira; cereals, esparto; cattle raising. Gypsum quarries near by.

Alfarrás (ălfärăs'), village (pop. 1,446), Lérida prov., NE Spain, 15 mi. NNW of Lérida, and on the Noguera Ribagorzana, in irrigated agr. area.

Alfatar (ălfätär'), village (pop. 3,446), Ruse dist., NE Bulgaria, in SW Dobruja, 10 mi. S of Silistra; wheat, corn, sheep. In Rumania (1913–1940).

Alfedena (ălfĕdā'nä), village (pop. 1,706), Aquila prov., Abruzzi e Molise, S central Italy, near Sangro R., 14 mi. NW of Isernia. Partly destroyed by heavy fighting in Second World War. Near by are ruins of anc. *Aufidena.*

Alfeite (ălfā'tĭ), village (pop. 1,010), Setúbal dist., S central Portugal, on S shore of Tagus estuary, 2 mi. S of Lisbon. Site of former royal estate.

Alfeld (äl'fĕlt), town (pop. 12,287), in former Prussian prov. of Hanover, NW Germany, after 1945 in Lower Saxony, on the Leine and 12 mi. SW of Hildesheim; mfg. of machinery, tools, precision instruments, textiles, shoes, furniture; woodworking. Has 16th-cent. town hall.

Alfen, Netherlands: see ALPHEN.

Alfen aan den Rijn, Netherlands: see ALPHEN AAN DEN RIJN.

Alfenas (ălfā'nŭs), city (pop. 7,422), SW Minas Gerais, Brazil, on railroad and 50 mi. NE of Poços de Caldas; alt. 2,800 ft. Agr. trade center (coffee, sugar, dairy products, cereals). Healthful climate. Has school of pharmacy and dentistry.

Alferrarede (ălfĕrŭrā'dĭ), town (pop. 2,026), Santarém dist., central Portugal, a NE suburb of Abrantes, on railroad near right bank of Tagus R.; mfg. (pottery, olive oil, resins).

Alfianello (ălfyänĕl'lô), village (pop. 2,025), Brescia prov., Lombardy, N Italy, near Oglio R., 11 mi. NE of Cremona.

Alfios River, Greece: see ALPHEUS RIVER.

Alfkarleby, Sweden: see ALVKARLEBY.

Alföld (ŏl'fûld) or **Great Hungarian Plain,** mostly in central and E Hungary, partly in N Yugoslavia and W Rumania; level, very fertile region bounded N by S foothills of the Carpathians, S by Balkan highlands; extends W from Rumania to the Dunantul. Most fertile sections, the BANAT and BACSKA, were taken from Hungary at Trianon. Extensive irrigation projects, started by Hungary in late 19th cent., have increased arable areas, as has draining of swamps in central and E parts. Main products: wheat, corn, alfalfa, hemp, flax; livestock. Arid grasslands, called *puszta,* on which large numbers of cattle formerly grazed, have almost completely disappeared; preserved only in the HORTOBAGY, near Debrecen.

Alfonsine (ălfônsē'nĕ), town (pop. 4,158), Ravenna prov., Emilia-Romagna, N central Italy, on Senio R. and 10 mi. NW of Ravenna; agr. machinery, vinegar. Trade in cereals, hemp, sugar beets. Vincenzo Monti b. here. Damaged in Second World War.

Alfonso XII, Cuba: see ALACRANES.

Alfonso XIII, town (1939 pop. 1,300), on SW coast of Palawan, Philippines.

Alford (ôl'fŭrd), urban district (1931 pop. 2,227; 1951 census 2,218), Parts of Lindsey, E Lincolnshire, England, 11 mi. SE of Louth; agr. market. Has 14th-cent. church, rebuilt 1869.

Alford (ä'fŭrd), town and parish (pop. 1,336), central Aberdeen, Scotland, near Don R., 13 mi. WSW of Inverurie; agr. market. Near by the Covenanters were defeated by Montrose in 1645. There are ruins of anc. Balfluig Castle.

Alford (ôl'fŭrd). **1** Town (pop. 375), Jackson co., NW Fla., 10 mi. WSW of Marianna; pecans. **2** Town (pop. 212), Berkshire co., W Mass., 17 mi. SSW of Pittsfield, in the Berkshires, near N.Y. line; summer resort.

Alfordsville (ăl'fŭrdzvĭl), town (pop. 101), Daviess co., SW Ind., 33 mi. ESE of Vincennes.

Alforja (ălfōr'hä), town (pop. 1,498), Tarragona prov., NE Spain, 8 mi. WNW of Reus; olive-oil processing, lumbering, stock raising; agr. trade (wine, cereals, filbert nuts).

Alfortville (ălfôrvēl'), town (pop. 27,940), Seine dept., N central France, a SE suburb of Paris, 4.5 mi. from Notre Dame Cathedral, in triangle formed by junction of Seine and Marne rivers; mfg. (rubber, paper, glass, hosiery); metalworks.

Alfotbre (ôl'fōtbrā), Nor. *Ålfotbre,* glacier (□ 40) in Sogn og Fjordane co., W Norway, bet. the North Sea and Nord Fjord; rises to 5,350 ft. 24 mi. ENE of Floro. Formerly spelled Aalfotbrae.

Alfred, village (pop. estimate 750), SE Ont., 40 mi. ENE of Ottawa; dairying.

Alfred. 1 Town (pop. 1,112), ⊙ York co., SW Maine, 12 mi. W of Biddeford. Settled 1764, inc. 1794. **2** Village (pop. 2,053), Allegany co., W N.Y., 8 mi. SW of Hornell; agr. (dairy products; poultry, potatoes); machinery; sand and gravel. Seat of Alfred Univ. (1857), with a state agr. and technical institute; and state col. of ceramics.

Alfred, Cape, SE extremity of Victoria Isl., S Franklin Dist., Northwest Territories, on Victoria Strait, at entrance of Albert Edward Bay; 69°39'N 101°W.

Alfredo Chaves (ălfrā'dōō shä'vĭs). **1** City (pop. 1,071), S central Espírito Santo, Brazil, 32 mi. SW of Vitória; coffee, rice; horse and mule trade. **2** City, Rio Grande do Sul, Brazil: see VERANÓPOLIS.

Alfredo M. Terrazas (ălfrā'dō ā'mā tĕrä'säs), town (pop. 1,302), San Luis Potosí, E Mexico, on fertile gulf plain, 38 mi. SSE of Valles; tobacco, sugar, coffee, fruit, livestock. Formerly Axtla.

Alfreton (ôl'frĭtŭn), urban district (1931 pop. 21,234; 1951 census 23,388), E Derby, England, 9 mi. WSW of Mansfield; coal-mining center (since 16th cent.) and agr. market. Has church dating from 12th cent. In urban dist. are towns of: Somercotes and Riddings (pop. 8,589), with coal mines, foundries, potteries, knitting mills; Ironville (pop. 1,457), with metalworks; and Swanwick (pop. 3,804), with hosiery mills.

Alfsborg, Sweden: see ALVSBORG.

Alfta (ălf'tä"), village (pop. 808), Gavleborg co., central Sweden, on Voxna R. and 10 mi. W of Bollnas; sawmilling, woodworking; mfg. of electrical equipment.

Alga (äl'gä), Ital. *Alghe,* village (pop. 400), Sidamo-Borana prov., S Ethiopia, on road and 40 mi. NNE of Yavello, in stock-raising region. Formerly Kuku.

Alga (ŭlgä'), town (1939 pop. over 2,000), N Aktyubinsk oblast, Kazakh SSR, on Trans-Caspian RR, on Ilek R. and 22 mi. S of Aktyubinsk; phosphorite-mining center, producing superphosphate, sulphuric acid, calcium phosphate; power plant.

Algaba, La (lä ălgä'vä), town (pop. 5,539), Seville prov., SW Spain, on the Guadalquivir and 4 mi. N of Seville; agr. center (cereals, cotton, sugar beets, tobacco, licorice). Fisheries.

Algaida (ălgī'dhä), town (pop. 2,413), Majorca, Balearic Isls., Spain, on railroad and 13 mi. E of Palma, in fertile agr. region (almonds, figs, wheat, barley, tubers, wine, livestock).

Algamarca (ălgämär'kä), village (pop. 557), Cajamarca dept., NW Peru, in Cordillera Occidental, 14 mi. W of Cajabamba; silver and copper mining.

Algámitas (ălgä'mētäs), town (pop. 1,497), Seville prov., SW Spain, in NW spur of the Cordillera Penibética, 8 mi. NE of Olvera (Cádiz prov.); cereals, olives, chick-peas, livestock; timber. Mfg. of olive oil and plaster.

Algar (ălgär'). **1** Town (pop. 3,167), Cádiz prov., SW Spain, 36 mi. E of Cádiz, in agr. region (wheat, olives, fruit, livestock); liquor distilling. Has mineral springs. **2** NE suburb (pop. 2,529) of Cartagena, Murcia prov., SE Spain; truck-farming produce.

Algard (ôl′gôr), Nor. *Ålgård*, village (pop. 1,271) in Gjestal (formerly Gjesdal) canton (pop. 2,696), Rogaland co., SW Norway, 14 mi. SSE of Stavanger; terminus of railroad spur from Ganddal. Woolen milling, dairying, mfg. of agr. tools and wooden shoes in canton. Sometimes spelled Aalgaard. Woolen milling at Oltedal (ôl′tûdäl) village (pop. 503), 7 mi. NE.

Algarinejo (älgärēnä′hō), town (pop. 3,357), Granada prov., S Spain, 11 mi. N of Loja; olive-oil processing, flour milling; cereals, fruit, wine.

Algarrobal (älgärōväl′), village (1930 pop. 193), Atacama prov., N central Chile, 30 mi. N of Vallenar; rail junction.

Algarrobo (älgärō′vō). **1** Mining settlement (1930 pop. 259), Atacama prov., N central Chile, on railroad and 24 mi. NNE of Vallenar; copper and gold mining. **2** Village (1930 pop. 189), Valparaiso prov., central Chile, on the Pacific, 22 mi. S of Valparaiso; resort.

Algarrobo, town (pop. 2,340), Málaga prov., S Spain, in coastal lowland 22 mi. E of Málaga; sugar cane, raisins, figs, olives, almonds.

Algarrobo del Águila (dĕl ä′gēlä), village (pop. estimate 300), ⊙ Chical-có dept. (1947 pop. 1,197), NW La Pampa prov., Argentina, on W arm of Atuel R. 160 mi. W of Santa Rosa, in stock-raising area (goats, sheep, cattle).

Algarrobo Verde, Argentina: see VILLA SANTA ROSA.

Algarve (älgär′vĭ), Arabic *Al Gharb* [=the West], southernmost province (□ 1,958; 1940 pop. 317,628) of Portugal; ⊙ Faro. It is coextensive with Faro dist. Bounded by the Atlantic (S and W) and by the lower Guadiana (E; Sp. border), it is separated from the rest of Portugal by low hill ranges (chiefly the Serra de Monchique) which terminate in Cape St. Vincent, the southwesternmost point of Portugal and of continental Europe. Algarve's coastal area, S of barren hill country, has a subtropical climate and grows an abundance of Mediterranean fruit (almonds, carobs, olives, figs, pomegranates, citrus, and even dates). Active tuna and sardine fisheries off shore. Chief exports are dried and fresh fruit, canned fish, wine, and salt. Principal cities are Faro, Silves, Lagos, Portimão, and Tavira. First settled by Phoenicians, region later absorbed Roman civilization and throve under Byzantines (6th–7th cent.), briefly under Visigoths, and especially under Moors, who made it their last stronghold in Portugal. Made into a Moorish kingdom in 1140 (⊙ Silves), its reconquest was completed 1249 by Alfonso III, who took the title of King of Portugal and of the Algarve. Regional architecture and agr. irrigation methods reveal strong Moorish influence. Pop. has a long seafaring tradition; near Cape St. Vincent, Prince Henry the Navigator founded his well-known school for navigators. Prov. was severely damaged by earthquake of 1755.

Algatocín (älgätō-thēn′), town (pop. 992), Málaga prov., S Spain, at S foot of the Sierra de Ronda, 12 mi. SSW of Ronda; oranges, chestnuts, figs, potatoes, olives, wax.

Algäu, Germany: see ALLGÄU.

Algäu Alps, Austria and Germany: see ALLGÄU ALPS.

Algeciras (ăljŭsĭ′rŭs, Sp. älhä-thē′räs), city (pop. 20,226), Cádiz prov., SW Spain, in Andalusia, Mediterranean seaport on Algeciras Bay, opposite Gibraltar, 55 mi. ESE of Cádiz, 310 mi. SSW of Madrid; 36°8′N 5°27′W. Terminus of railroad express from Paris, and transoceanic port trading chiefly with North Africa. Its fine location and mild winters, and near-by beaches and Fuente Santa mineral springs, have made it a popular resort. Chief exports are crude and processed cork; fishing and fish salting are its major industries. Has shipyards. The surrounding fertile region produces cereals, tobacco, truck, hogs and cattle. Founded 713 by the Moors, probably at site of anc. Roman town, it was wrested from them by Alfonso XI of Castile in 1344 and destroyed in a renewed Moorish attack from Granada. Practically refounded (1704) by Sp. refugees from Gibraltar. Scene (1801) of naval engagement in which British defeated combined Fr. and Sp. fleets. Here was held (1906) the Algeciras Conference, settling dispute of Eur. powers over Morocco. Moorish aqueduct near by.

Algeciras Bay or **Gibraltar Bay,** Mediterranean inlet (6 mi. by 4 mi.), Cádiz prov., S Spain, opening S off Strait of Gibraltar, and bounded SE by Rock of Gibraltar. Algeciras is on its W shore, Gibraltar on E, and La Línea on NE.

Algemesí (älhämäsē′), town (pop. 15,443), Valencia prov., E Spain, near Júcar R., 3 mi. N of Alcira, in fertile garden area. Canning (vegetables, jams and marmalades), flour and rice milling, olive-oil processing; orange and lemon juice, essential oils; insecticide mfg. Ships citrus and other fruit, peanuts, vegetables.

Algenrodt, Germany: see IDAR-OBERSTEIN.

Alger (älzhā′), N central department (□ 21,182; 1948 pop. 2,765,898) of Algeria, on the Mediterranean bet. depts. of Oran (W) and Constantine (E); ⊙ Algiers. Traversed WSW-ENE by parallel ranges of the Tell Atlas (Dahra, Mitidja Atlas, Ouarsenis Massif, Titeri) culminating in the Djurdjura range (highest peak, Lella Khedidja, 7,572 ft.) of Great Kabylia. S of the TELL are the semi-arid High Plateaus and the Saharan Atlas. Just inland from a hilly coastal strip flanking the city of ALGIERS lies the fertile MITIDJA plain, the heart of European agr. settlement in Algeria. Agr. also in the lower valley of CHÉLIFF RIVER and in the valleys of the Isser and Sebaou wadis. Wheat, oats, and barley are chief crops; wine, citrus fruit, truck produce, tobacco, and perfume flowers are grown in the Mitidja and other irrigated sections. Olives are the main product of Great KABYLIA (NE). In the High Plateaus sheep and goats are raised and esparto grass grown. Mineral deposits (iron, copper, lead, zinc) are scattered and mostly unexploited. From the E-W trunk railroad linking Fr. Morocco with Tunisia, a spur extends S to Djelfa (Territory of Ghardaïa). Good roads serve the Tell and reach Bou-Saâda oasis. Agr. processing is concentrated in Algiers area. Blida and Boufarik are agr. centers of the Mitidja; Affreville, Miliana, and Orléansville of Chéliff valley. Tizi-Ouzou is the chief town of Great Kabylia. Cherchel, Ténès, and Dellys are secondary ports. Over 85% of dept.'s pop. is Moslem. Most of the non-Moslems are in Algiers and in Mitidja lowland. Alger dept. was created 1848, when Fr. occupation of N Algeria was completed.

Alger, city, Algeria: see ALGIERS.

Alger (ăl′jŭr), county (□ 913; pop. 10,007), N Upper Peninsula, Mich.; ⊙ Munising. Bounded N by L. Superior; drained by Whitefish and small Sturgeon rivers, and by affluents of Manistique R. Includes Grand Isl. Part of Hiawatha Natl. Forest in co. Dairying, agr. (livestock, poultry, potatoes, grain, fruit); some mfg. at Munising; lumbering, commercial fishing. Resorts. Contains Pictured Rocks, several waterfalls, and small lakes. Organized 1885.

Alger, village (pop. 943), Hardin co., W central Ohio, 14 mi. E of Lima, in agr. area; canning.

Algeria (ălgē′rēŭ), Fr. *Algérie* (älzhārē′), government-general (□ 846,124; pop. 8,681,785) of the French Union, in N Africa; ⊙ ALGIERS. Comprises 3 depts. (ORAN, ALGER, CONSTANTINE) which constitute N Algeria, and the SOUTHERN TERRITORIES (nearly 10 times the N part in area) in the SAHARA. Occupies the central and largest portion of Fr. North Africa's bulge, bet. Fr. Morocco (W) and Tunisia (E). Its rocky Mediterranean coast line is 750 mi. long. In the Sahara it borders on Fezzan (Libya; E), Fr. West Africa (S), and Sp. West Africa (W). Including the Southern Territories, Algeria extends from 19°N to 37°N and from 8°30′W to 12°20′E. The ATLAS MOUNTAINS cross the entire length of N Algeria; near the coast are the well-watered ranges of the Tell Atlas interrupted by a few sub-coastal lowlands (MITIDJA; Oran, Philippeville, Bône basins; lower Chéliff valley) where most of agr. land and pop. are concentrated. The highest ranges of the Tell Atlas are in KABYLIA (Lella Khedidja, 7,572 ft.). Further S are the semi-arid High Plateaus whose interior drainage basins contain playa lakes (Chott ech Chergui, Chott el Gharbi, Chott el Hodna); bounding them on the S, the Saharan Atlas, which also runs parallel to the coast, marks the N limit of the Sahara Desert. The Atlas Mts. are thus a formidable topographic and climatic barrier bet. the Mediterranean and the Sahara. N Algeria has a Mediterranean climate (delightful winters, hot summers), while in the Sahara extreme diurnal range and very hot summers are typical. While certain coastal ranges in Constantine dept. receive up to 50 in. of rainfall annually, the large region S of the Saharan Atlas receives less than 8 in. The name TELL has therefore been given to the region N of the 12-in. isohyet where Mediterranean agr. is possible; this belt includes all of the Tell Atlas and the E part of the High Plateaus where cereals (wheat, barley, oats) are the chief crop. Wine, citrus, early fruits and vegetables (tomatoes, beans, artichokes), tobacco, and perfume flowers are grown in coastal lowlands, and cotton cultivation has been begun in irrigated valley of CHÉLIFF RIVER, Algeria's largest stream. Largest concentrations of olive groves are in Kabylia (where figs are also grown), and in areas of Guelma, Tlemcen, and Sidi-bel-Abbès. Cork is the chief product of the densely forested coast ranges of Kabylia and of Constantine dept. around Bône. Evergreen oak and thuya forests are most abundant in the Saïda and Tlemcen Mts. of Oran dept., while the AURÈS massif of the Saharan Atlas is noted for its Aleppo pines and cedars. Esparto grass, the typical vegetation of the W and central High Plateaus, is collected for export to European paper mills; the N Saharan oases (Biskra, Touggourt, Ouargla, El-Oued) yield dates (especially the Deglet Nur variety) for export. Sheep and goats (very numerous), and camels are raised in the drier interior, cattle and horses in the Tell. There are active sardine, anchovy, tunny, and sprat fisheries. With certain exceptions, Algeria's mineral resources are scattered and therefore not fully exploited. Phosphates are mined in E Algeria near TEBESSA (Djebel Kouif and Djebel Dir mines) and exported from Bône; in the same area is country's largest iron mine (Djebel Ouenza). Iron (especially pyrites) is also shipped from smaller mines in Béni-Saf area (Oran dept.). Extensive but poorly located coal deposits are worked at Kenadsa and shipped by rail to Oran or Nemours. Zinc, copper, lead, and barite production is of minor importance. Algeria's hydroelectric development is limited to the valleys of Chéliff and Rhumel rivers, which supply power to Algiers and Constantine respectively. The majority of industrial plants are wineries, flour mills, distilleries, perfume and tobacco factories, all processing local produce. Algiers has metal- and cementworks, Oran produces fertilizer, and both cities make non-durable consumer goods. Handicraft industry is best preserved in Tlemcen and Constantine. Algeria's principal ports are Algiers, Oran (with the naval base of Mers-el-Kebir), Bône, Philippeville, Bougie, and Mostaganem. Constantine is the largest city of the interior; Mascara, Sidi-bel-Abbès (Oran dept.); Blida, Miliana, Orléansville, Tizi-Ouzou (Alger dept.); Tebessa, Sétif, and Guelma (Constantine dept.) are smaller inland towns of N Algeria. Country's rail net (c.2,800 mi.) has grown around a trunk E-W line linking Tunisia with Morocco; N spurs serve principal ports, while S spurs (Constantine–Biskra–Touggourt; Algiers–Djelfa; Perrégaux–Colomb-Béchar) cross the High Plateaus and the Saharan Atlas and connect with the N termini of trans-Saharan auto and caravan tracks. The completed section of a long-planned trans-Saharan RR links Nemours (on the Mediterranean) with Colomb-Béchar (Aïn-Sefra territory), traversing E Fr. Morocco. N Algeria has a well-developed road net. In Southern Territories the principal trans-Saharan routes lead from Colomb-Béchar across the TANEZROUFT to the great bend of the Niger in Fr. Sudan; from Djelfa and Touggourt, past In-Salah and across the AHAGGAR to Niamey and Zinder in Niger territory and to Nigeria. Trans-Saharan airlines touch at Aoulef and Tindouf. N Algeria's main airfields are at Algiers (Maison-Blanche), Oran, and Bône. Country's leading exports are wines for consumption in France (*vins ordinaires*), esparto grass, phosphates, iron ore, potatoes, and early vegetables. Algeria has long been a mecca for tourists; attractions include the old quarter of Algiers surrounding the *casbah*, the picturesque site of Constantine and Tlemcen, the rugged topography of Kabylia and the Aurès, and the many Roman remains (especially ruins at Lambèse, Djemila, and Timgad in Constantine dept.). Pop., of mixed Berber and Arab stock, is Mohammedan; pure Berber elements remain in the less accessible parts of the Tell Atlas and in the Aurès; the Mzabites, a heretic Moslem sect, are found in a group of Saharan oases centered on Ghardaïa; the nomadic Tuareg tribes make their hq. in the Ahaggar. In 1948, the non-Moslem pop. of Algeria (960,107) included 876,686 French (c.10% of total pop.) concentrated in the Mitidja lowland, at Algiers and at Oran. European farmers own c.⅓ of all land under cultivation. The area of Algeria (the name of the present political unit dates from French occupation) was 1st dominated by Carthage. The richness of the Tell attracted Roman conquerors, who after taking part in wars of Numidia and Mauretania, occupied coastal belt, making it the granary of Rome. In the Christian days of the empire, St. Augustine was bishop at Hippo Regius (now Bône). Conquered by Vandals (A.D. 430–31) and by Byzantines (534), region was Islamized after the Arab conquest in 7th cent. For many centuries minor rulers vied for supremacy without achieving effective or lasting control over the whole area. In 1518, Algiers was seized by Turks, but Turkish power never extended beyond the Tell. Coastal cities (especially Algiers) became pirate strongholds and European punitive expeditions were dispatched against them. At beginning of 18th cent., the dey (ruler) of Algiers became virtually independent of Turks, maintaining himself from proceeds of piracy. His defiance of foreigners led in 2d decade of 19th cent. to the so-called Algerine War. French forces occupied Algiers in 1830, and conquered most of N Algeria 1830–1847, against opposition led by Abd-el-Kader; Kabylia was occupied by 1870, and the Saharan area was pacified 1900–09. French colonization and development in N Algeria exceeded that in any other Fr. overseas possession. During Second World War, Br. naval action at Oran resulted in virtual destruction of Fr. fleet in N Africa; in Nov., 1942, Allied landings at Oran and Algiers paved the way for the Allied victory over Axis forces in neighboring Tunisia (May, 1943). Algiers then became the seat of Charles de Gaulle's provisional Fr. govt. Politically, Algeria occupies a privileged position within the Fr. Union. It is ruled by a governor-general who directs most public services independently of Paris, and prepares a special budget for Algeria; by the statute of 1947, Algerians in the 3 northern depts. were granted universal franchise and elected (1948) their own legislative assembly. Algeria is also heavily represented in the parliament of the Fr. republic. The Southern Territories (divided into the 4 territories of AÏN-SEFRA, GHARDAÏA, TOUGGOURT, and SAHARAN OASES) are under a central military administration at Algiers, but are to be incorporated into N Algeria's depts. For further details see articles on administrative divisions, cities, towns, and physical features.

Algés (älzhĕsh'), town (pop. 7,836), a W suburb of Lisbon, central Portugal, on Tagus R. estuary, 5 mi. from city center; bathing resort; textiles.

Algete (älhā'tā), town (pop. 1,169), Madrid prov., central Spain, near Jarama R., 15 mi. NE of Madrid, in grain-growing region; also grapes, olives, fruit, livestock.

Alghe, Ethiopia: see ALGA.

Alghena, Eritrea: see ELGHENA.

Alghero (älgā'rô), town (pop. 14, 579), Sassari prov., NW Sardinia, port on Mediterranean Sea, 17 mi. SW of Sassari. Rail terminus; fruit canning, sawmilling; fishing (lobster, coral); olive oil. Copper and cadmium mines near by. Bishopric. Has cathedral built 1510 (badly damaged in Second World War). Founded 1102. Necropolis of Anghelu Ruju, with neolithic tombs, near by. In Second World War, bombed (1941).

Algiers (ăljērz'), Fr. *Alger* (älzhā'), Arabic *Al-Jezair,* city (1948 pop. 266,165; with suburbs 473,261), ⊙ Algeria and Alger dept., French North Africa's chief port on the Mediterranean, on W shore of semi-circular Algiers Bay, c.500 mi. SSW of Marseilles; 36°47'N 3°4'E. Commercial and cultural center of Algeria, seat of governor-general, and popular tourist and winter resort. Its industries, aside from cement and metalworks (agr. machinery, cables, electrical equipment, tools) consist mainly of plants processing the agr. output of fertile MITIDJA lowland. They include wineries, distilleries, perfume and tobacco factories, flour mills. Other products are footwear, paints and varnishes, corks and metal bottlecaps, barrels and crating. The modern port (continually expanded since 1890), which extends for 3 mi. and is sheltered by overlapping breakwaters, ships wine, fruits and vegetables, cereals, cork, tanbark, tobacco, sheep, and wool, mainly to metropolitan France. Iron, zinc, and lead are exported in small quantities. Algiers is also an important coaling and refueling station, and fishing port; has frequent passenger service to Fr. Mediterranean ports, especially Marseilles. Hydroplane base. Stretching along bay for 10 mi. in the shape of an amphitheater at foot and on slopes of coastal hills (*sahel*), Algiers presents a brilliant white appearance from the sea. From the Place du Gouvernement (faced by 16th-cent. Djama Djedid mosque), the old town, with its labyrinthine pattern of narrow, arcaded streets, and steep dead-end alleys, nestles at the foot of the *casbah* (citadel). The present citadel, erected by Turks in 16th cent., was residence of last 2 deys of Algiers. Beyond the *casbah* rises the 1,335-ft. Bouzaréa hill. Also of note are the great mosque (near waterfront), probably dating from 11th cent., with a 14th-cent. minaret; the 19th-cent. cathedral, governor's palace, and archiepiscopal palace, all lining Place Malakoff; and the natl. library, a fine 18th-cent. Moorish building. The modern, predominantly European part of Algiers includes the former S suburb of Mustapha, and dists. of Agha-Saulière, Isly, Belcourt. Here are the univ. (founded 1909 by combining several faculties), the mus. of antiquities, the governor's summer palace (in Mustapha-Supérieur dist.). Near city's S end is the noted Jardin d'Essai, a public park, botanical garden, and native plant nursery. Beyond it Algiers merges with its populous suburbs of Kouba, Hussein-Dey, Maison-Carrée (agr. inst.), and Maison-Blanche airport (9 mi. SE). Other suburbs are El-Biar (W) and Saint-Eugène (N). Algiers has a typical Mediterranean climate with rainfall (27 inches per year) concentrated in fall and winter, and an average temp. of 64°F. Founded in 10th cent. by the Berbers on site of Roman *Icosium,* it became important after Turkish rule was established (1518) by Barbarossa, who built a mole connecting mainland with off-shore islet (Peñon). City became a base for Barbary pirates and was visited by many European punitive expeditions, notably by Charles V (1541), by Abraham Duquesne's Fr. fleet (1682–83), by Stephen Decatur's force (1815), and by the Anglo-Dutch fleet under Lord Exmouth (1816). During 18th cent., the dey of Algiers had virtually sovereign power. The French conquest of Algeria began with capture of Algiers (1830), after initial landings at near-by Cape Sidi-Ferruch. In Second World War, city surrendered to Allies (Nov. 8, 1942) after offering token resistance. It became hq. of Allied forces and of De Gaulle's provisional French govt. Rapidly growing Moslem element accounted (1948) for c.40% of city's total pop.

Algiers, La.: see NEW ORLEANS.

Alginet (älhĕnĕt'), town (pop. 6,705), Valencia prov., E Spain, 8 mi. NNW of Alcira, in agr. area (strawberries, oranges); olive-oil processing, brandy distilling, rice milling; sericulture.

Algoa (ălgō'ŭ), town (pop. 73), Jackson co., NE Ark., 11 mi. SE of Newport.

Algoa Bay (ălgō'ŭ) (15 mi. long, 50 mi. wide at mouth), S Cape Prov., U. of So. Afr., inlet of the Indian Ocean; extends ENE from Cape Recife and Port Elizabeth, both on W side of entrance. Receives Sundays R. Discovered in late 15th cent. by Portuguese explorers, it became departure point for Goa colony. British settlers arrived here 1820 and founded Port Elizabeth.

Algodonales (älgō-dhōnä'lĕs), town (pop. 5,163), Cádiz prov., SW Spain, in N spur of the Cordillera Penibética, 17 mi. NW of Ronda; agr. center (cereals, olives, grapes, fruit, livestock); olive-oil pressing, liquor distilling.

Algoma (ălgō'mŭ), district (□ 19,320; pop. 52,002), central Ont., on L. Superior; ⊙ Sault Ste Marie.

Algoma. 1 Mining village (pop. 1,100 with adjoining Elkridge), McDowell co., S W.Va., 9 mi. E of Welch; semibituminous coal. **2** City (pop. 3,384), Kewaunee co., E Wis., on Door Peninsula, on L. Michigan, 27 mi. ENE of Green Bay city, in lake-resort area; dairy plants, woodworking and hammock factories. A co. normal school is near by. Inc. 1879.

Algona (ălgō'nŭ), city (pop. 5,415), ⊙ Kossuth co., N Iowa, on East Des Moines R. and 40 mi. N of Fort Dodge; rail junction; poultry packing, grain milling; rendering plants, creameries, machine shops, concrete works. Sand pits near by. State park is SW. Settled 1854, inc. 1872.

Algonac (ăl'gŭnăk), resort village (pop. 2,639), St. Clair co., E Mich., 25 mi. SSW of Port Huron, and on St. Clair R. (Ont. boundary) just above its delta mouth on L. St. Clair. Mfg. of gas engines, fishing tackle; boatbuilding. Truck farming. State park near by. Inc. 1867.

Algonquin, village (pop. 1,223), McHenry co., NE Ill., on Fox R. (bridged here) and 8 mi. N of Elgin, in dairying and lake-resort area.

Algonquin Provincial Park (ălgŏng'kĭn, –kwĭn) (□ 2,741), SE Ont., W of Pembroke. Established 1893, it is hilly, with numerous lakes; Opeongo L. is largest. Camping, fishing, canoeing. Forms watershed bet. Ottawa R. and Georgian Bay.

Algood (ăl'go͝od), town (pop. 729), Putnam co., central Tenn., 5 mi. NE of Cookeville; lumber, wood products, bricks.

Algorta (älgōr'tä), town (pop. 7,667), Vizcaya prov., N Spain, 8 mi. NW of Bilbao, and on E shore of Bilbao Bay of Bay of Biscay, just outside of Bilbao breakwater. Metalworks; mfg. of cement, ceramics, tiles. Popular bathing resort.

Algorta, town (pop. 650), Río Negro dept., W Uruguay, in the Cuchilla de Haedo, 70 mi. NE of Fray Bentos, 40 mi. E of Paysandú; rail junction.

Algrange (älgräzh'), Ger. *Algringen* (äl'grĭng-ŭn), town (pop. 7,801), Moselle dept., NE France, 6 mi. W of Thionville; iron-mining center.

Alguada Reef (älgwä' dä, –dŭ), Lower Burma, in Andaman Sea, off Bassein R. mouth of Irrawaddy delta; 15°45'N 94°15'E; lighthouse.

Alguaire (älgwī'rā), town (pop. 2,248), Lérida prov., NE Spain, 8 mi. NNW of Lérida, in irrigated area (cereals, olive oil, wine); livestock.

Alguazas (älgwä'thäs), town (pop. 1,539), Murcia prov., SE Spain, near the Segura, 8 mi. NW of Murcia; fruit-conserve processing, sawmilling; olive oil, fruit, cereals; sericulture.

Algueña (älgwā'nyä), town (pop. 1,502), Alicante prov., E Spain, 20 mi. NW of Elche; olive pressing; wine, cereals, almonds.

Algund, Italy: see LAGUNDO.

Algyö (ŏl'dyû), Hung. *Algyő,* town (pop. 4,964), Csongrad co., S Hungary, on Tisza R. and 6 mi. NNE of Szeged; agr.

Algyogyalfalu, Rumania: see GEOAGIU.

Alhama or **Alhama de Granada** (älä'mä dhā gränä'-dhä), city (pop. 7,308), Granada prov., S Spain, 24 mi. SW of Granada; olive-oil and cheese processing, flour- and sawmilling. Cereals, wine, fruit; stock raising; lumbering. Lignite deposits. Has warm mineral springs, known to Romans and Moors. Played important role in Christian conquest (15th cent.) of kingdom of Granada, as one of keys to capital city; conquered (1482) by the Catholic Kings. Seriously damaged (1884) in earthquake, but soon rebuilt.

Alhama de Almería (dhā älmärē'ä), town (pop. 2,614), Almería prov., S Spain, 10 mi. NW of Almería; processes sulphur from near-by mines; produces cereals, olive oil, fruit, esparto; ships grapes. Mineral springs. Black-marble quarries in vicinity.

Alhama de Aragón (dhā ärägōn'), village (pop. 1,918), Saragossa prov., NE Spain, on Jalón R. and 14 mi. WSW of Calatayud; mfg. (ceramics, soap); grows sugar beets, wine, cereals, pears. Has warm mineral springs, noted since Roman times, when called *Aquae Bilbilitanae.* Nine mi. SW are remains of former Cistercian monastery (built in 12th cent., restored in 17th) with 13th-cent. church and cloisters.

Alhama de Murcia (dhā mo͞or'thyä), town (pop. 5,955), Murcia prov., SE Spain, 20 mi. SW of Murcia; a spa noted since anc. times. Olive-oil processing, flour- and sawmilling, mfg. of sweetmeats and alcohol; ships grapes. Gypsum and limestone quarries. Has ruins of Moorish castle.

Alhambra (äläm'brä), town (pop. 2,329), Ciudad Real prov., S central Spain, 19 mi. ESE of Manzanares; cereals, vegetables, fruit, potatoes, grapes, olives, livestock. Gravel pits, grindstone quarries, mineral springs. In Roman times, center of Oretania region. Became, during Middle Ages, 2d of 3 capitals of Campo Montrel.

Alhambra, Moorish palace, Spain: see GRANADA, city.

Alhambra (ălhăm'brŭ). **1** City (pop. 51,359), Los Angeles co., S Calif., suburb c.5 mi. E of downtown Los Angeles; residential; mfg. (oil-refining equipment, felt, clay products, aircraft). Founded 1881, inc. 1903. **2** Village (pop. 476), Madison co., SW Ill., 28 mi. NE of East St. Louis, in agr. area.

Alhandra (älyän'drŭ), town (pop. 4,310), Lisboa dist., central Portugal, on lower Tagus R. near head of its estuary, 15 mi. NNE of Lisbon; textile milling, cement mfg., fish canning. Saltworks.

Alhaurín de la Torre (älourēn' dhā lä tô'rā), town (pop. 2,345), Málaga prov., S Spain, on railroad and 8 mi. WSW of Málaga; potatoes, corn, sugar beets, almonds, raisins, olives; flour milling. Marble quarries and lead mines near by.

Alhaurín el Grande (ĕl grän'dā), town (pop. 8,234), Málaga prov., S Spain, in Andalusia, at N foot of Penibética spur, on railroad and 15 mi. WSW of Málaga. Situated in hilly, wine- and fruitgrowing (figs, olives, oranges) region, it is a spa and processing center. Flour milling, liquor distilling, olive-oil processing, raisin drying; mfg. of soap, shoes, toys, furniture, cork articles. Has Arab and Roman remains. Marble, granite, jasper quarries near by.

Alhendín (älĕndēn'), town (pop. 3,079), Granada prov., S Spain, 5 mi. SW of Granada; agr. trade (cereals, sugar, olive oil, hemp, truck produce).

Alhos Vedros (ä'lyo͞osh vā'dro͞osh), village (pop. 1,840), Setúbal dist., S central Portugal, near S bank of Tagus estuary, 7 mi. SE of Lisbon; cork processing.

Alhucemas Bay (älo͞othā'mäs), semi-circular inlet of the W Mediterranean, on coast of Sp. Morocco, 50 mi. W of Melilla; 8 mi. wide, 5 mi. long. Villa Sanjurjo is on W shore. **Alhucemas Islands,** a group of 3 islets near head of bay, less than 1 mi. from mainland, are a possession of Spain, under its direct sovereignty. The largest isl. (pop. 148) has a garrison. Occupied by Spain in 1673. Bombarded (1923) by Abd-el-Krim in Rif revolt.

Alhué (älwā'), village (pop. 699), Santiago prov., central Chile, 50 mi. SW of Santiago; agr. center (grain, potatoes, fruit, livestock).

Alì (älē'), commune (pop. 4,026), Messina prov., NE Sicily, near Cape Alì, 14 mi. SSW of Messina; citrus fruit. Comprises villages of Alì Marina (on coast; sulphur baths) and Alì Superiore (2 mi. N.)

A-li, Tibet: see NGARI.

Alì, Cape (älē'), on NE coast of Sicily, at S end of Strait of Messina; 38°1'N 15°27'E.

Alia (ä'lyä), town (pop. 7,271), Palermo prov., N central Sicily, near Torto R., 14 mi. S of Termini Imerese; agr. center.

Alía (älē'ä), town (pop. 3,341), Cáceres prov., W Spain, 38 mi. E of Trujillo; linen- and woolen-cloth mfg., olive-oil processing; stock raising; cereals, wine, fruit.

Alia, El- (ĕl-älyä'), village, Bizerte dist., N Tunisia, 11 mi. SE of Bizerte; olives, oranges.

Aliabad (älē'äbäd''), W suburb of Kabul, Afghanistan, in the Chahardeh, at foot of Asmai Hill; tuberculosis sanatorium; dairy farm.

Aliabad or **'Aliabad** (älē''äbäd'). **1** Town, Second Prov., in Gurgan, NE Iran, 30 mi. ENE of Gurgan and on road to Gunbad-i-Qawus. Formerly called Katul. **2** Town, in Mazanderan, Iran: see SHAHI.

Aliaga (älyä'gä), town (1939 pop. 1,911; 1948 municipality pop. 12,594), Nueva Ecija prov., central Luzon, Philippines, 8 mi. W of Cabanatuan; rice, corn.

Aliaga, town (pop. 603), Teruel prov., E Spain, on Guadalope R. and 32 mi. NE of Teruel; cereals, livestock. Coal mines in vicinity.

Aliaguilla (älyägē'lyä), town (pop. 1,510), Cuenca prov., E central Spain, near Valencia prov. border, 50 mi. ESE of Cuenca; cereals, grapes, olives, saffron, livestock. Hydroelectric plant.

Aliakmon River (älēäk'môn), anc. *Haliacmon* (hälēăk'mŭn), Macedonian *Bistritsa* (bĭstrē'tsä, vĭs–), longest river of Greece, in Macedonia; 195 mi. long. Rises in the Grammos on Albanian border 25 mi. WSW of Kastoria, flows SE in intermontane basin, past Nestorion and Argos Orestikon, and NE, bet. Vermion and Pieria mts., and through Giannitsa lowland to Gulf of Salonika of Aegean Sea 20 mi. SW of Salonika. Hydroelectric plants E of Kozane. Formerly also called Vistritsa; known as Inje-Kara-Su under Turkish rule.

Aliança (älēä'sŭ), city (pop. 1,524), E Pernambuco, NE Brazil, on railroad and 40 mi. NW of Recife; sugar, coffee, manioc. Formerly spelled Alliança.

Aliano (älyä'nô), village (pop. 1,574), Matera prov., Basilicata, S Italy, 6 mi. S of Stigliano.

Alibag (ä'lēbäg), town (pop. 6,526), ⊙ Kolaba dist., W Bombay, India, on Arabian Sea, 20 mi. S of Bombay, in the Konkan; market center for rice, coconuts, mangoes; tanning, fishing (mackerel, pomfrets).

Ali-Bairamly or **Ali-Bayramly** (ŭlyē'-bīrăm'lē), town (1948 pop. over 2,000), E Azerbaijan SSR, on Shirvan Steppe, on lower Kura R. and 55 mi. SW of Baku; rail junction; cotton ginning; metalworks.

Alibei Lagoon or **Alibey Lagoon** (ŭlyibyā'), Black Sea coast lagoon, SE Izmail oblast, Ukrainian SSR, just NE of Shagany Lagoon; 8 mi. long, 4 mi. wide.

Alibotush Mountains (ä″lēbō′to͝osh), Gr. *Ali Butus* (älē′ bĭtēs′), sometimes *Ordelos* or *Ordhilos* in Macedonia, on Bulgarian-Greek border, at S end of Pirin Mts., 8 mi. SSW of Nevrokop; rise to 7,257 ft. Karstlike formations; sparse vegetation.

Alibunar (ä′lēbo͞onär″), Hung. *Alibunár* (ŏ′lĭbo͞onär″), village (pop. 13,586), Vojvodina, NE Serbia, Yugoslavia, 20 mi. NE of Pancevo, in the Banat; rail junction.

Alicante (ălĭkăn′tē, Sp. älēkän′tā), province (□ 2,264; pop. 607,562), E Spain, in Valencia on the Mediterranean; ⊙ Alicante. Mountainous in N and NW with some fertile valleys; coastal plain widening in S; picturesque, rocky coast in N, low and sandy with salt lagoons in S. Watered by the Segura and a few short, intermittent rivers used for irrigation. Has little rainfall; pleasant climate in winter, very hot in summer. Its barren areas contrast with densely populated, irrigated garden regions (Alicante, Elche, Orihuela, Alcoy) containing palms, orange and lemon groves, fruit and vegetable orchards, and vineyards; other products are cereals, olive oil, hemp, esparto. Sericulture is important, as are fishing (S coast) and lumbering (N, W). Marble, gypsum and clay quarries. Processes wine (widely exported for blending with other wines), olive oil, hemp (Orihuela), and esparto (Crevillente); fruit canning. Other mfg.: textiles, cigarette paper, metal products (Alicante, Alcoy), sweets and candy (Jijona, Cocentaina), footwear (Elda). The salt industry at Torrevieja leads in Spain.

Alicante, anc. *Lucentum*, city (pop. 83,140), ⊙ Alicante prov., E Spain, in Valencia, on bay of the Mediterranean, 225 mi. SE of Madrid; 38°22′N 0°28′W. Its fine harbor, protected by 2 breakwaters, exports wine, almonds, olive oil, fruit. Oil refinery, tobacco factory, metal and chemical works; mfg. of cement, cotton textiles, knit goods, pottery and tiles, footwear, soap, essential oils, nougat candy, firecrackers. Also fruit canning, marble processing, flour- and sawmilling. Irrigated surrounding plain yields wine (largely used for blending with other wines), almonds, cereals, truck produce. On isolated rock (E) dominating the city is Castle of Santa Barbara, commanding fine view; the ruins of Castle of San Fernando are on hill farther inland. Fine promenade lined with palms skirts harbor. The fine climate makes Alicante a popular winter resort. Has largely restored Gothic church, 17th-cent. collegiate church, and baroque town hall. Airport is 5 mi. SSW. After reconquest (c.1250) from Moors, city was contested by Castile and Aragon, until it went (1309) to Aragon. Bombarded by Archduke Charles (1706) in War of Spanish Succession and by insurgent planes in civil war of 1936–39.

Alice, town (pop. 3,433), SE Cape Prov., U. of So. Afr., on upper Keiskama R. and 40 mi. NE of Grahamstown, at foot of Amatola Range; lumbering center; woodworking; stock, grain. Just N is Fort Hare, site of South African Native Col.; 2 mi. NW is Lovedale native mission col.

Alice. **1** Village (pop. 162), Cass co., SE N.Dak., 20 mi. SW of Casselton. **2** City (pop. 16,449), ⊙ Jim Wells co., S Texas, c.40 mi. W of Corpus Christi; railroad division point, shipping much cattle; supply center for oil field. Oil refining, cotton ginning, cottonseed-oil milling, mfg. of cheese, beverages, clay products, oil-field machinery; natural-gas recycling plant; sulphur mining. Inc. 1910.

Alice, Punta dell' (po͞on′tä dĕl-lälē′chĕ), S Italy, point on SW coast of Gulf of Taranto, 23 mi. N of Crotone; 39°24′N 17°10′E.

Alice Arm, village, W B.C., near Alaska border, on Alice Arm, branch of Observatory Inlet of the Pacific, 90 mi. NE of Prince Rupert; port, shipping copper and pyrites, refined at ANYOX; gold, silver, lead, and zinc mining.

Alicedale, village (pop. 1,193), SE Cape Prov., U. of So. Afr., on Bushmans R. and 25 mi. W of Grahamstown; rail junction and construction camp; stock, grain, feed crops.

Alice Springs, town (dist. pop. 2,078), S central Northern Territory, Australia, 800 mi. SSE of Darwin, in Macdonnell Ranges; 23°42′S 133°50′E; alt. 1,900 ft. N terminus of Central Australian RR; tourist center of state; livestock, opals. Was (1926–31) ⊙ Central Australia, a former subdivision of Northern Territory. Formerly Stuart.

Alice Town, town (pop. 238), NW Bahama Isls., on spit of North Bimini isl., 55 mi. E of Miami, Fla., 130 mi. WNW of Nassau. Resort; fishing, growing of sisal, coconuts, corn. Bailey's Town is just N.

Aliceville, town (pop. 3,170), Pickens co., W Ala., c.35 mi. WSW of Tuscaloosa, near Tombigbee R.; textiles, lumber.

Alichur River (ŭlyēcho͞or′), SE Tadzhik SSR, rises in Alichur Range of the Pamir, N of Zor-Kul (lake), flows c.65 mi. N and W to YASHIL-KUL (lake).

Alicia (älē′syä), town (pop. estimate 1,500), E Córdoba prov., Argentina, 40 mi. SSW of San Francisco; agr. (wheat growing, stock raising, dairying).

Alicia (ŭlĭ′shŭ), town (pop. 299), Lawrence co., NE Ark., 22 mi. WNW of Jonesboro.

Alicudi (älēko͞o′dē), anc. *Ericusa*, island (□ 2; pop. 594), westernmost of Lipari Isls., in Tyrrhenian Sea off N Sicily, W of Filicudi, 55 mi. NW of Milazzo; 2 mi. long; rises to 2,185 ft. in SW. Vineyards; fisheries. Sometimes spelled Alicuri.

Alife (älē′fĕ), town (pop. 3,331), Caserta prov., Campania, S Italy, in Volturno R. valley, 18 mi. N of Caserta, in cereal- and olive-growing region.

Aliganj (ä′lēgŭnj), town (pop. 6,378), Etah dist., W Uttar Pradesh, India, 30 mi. E of Etah; trades in wheat, pearl millet, barley, corn, jowar, oilseeds, cotton. Founded 18th cent. by a eunuch.

Aliganj Siwan, India: see SIWAN.

Aligarh (ä′lēgŭr), district (□ 1,940; pop. 1,372,641), W Uttar Pradesh, India; ⊙ Aligarh. In Ganges-Jumna Doab; agr. (wheat, barley, bajra, gram, corn, jowar, cotton, mustard, sugar cane). Main centers: Aligarh, HATHRAS, Atrauli, SIKANDRA RAO.

Aligarh. **1** Village, E Rajasthan, India, 22 mi. SE of Tonk; millet, wheat. Formerly called Rampura. **2** City (pop., including old city of Koil, 112,655), ⊙ Aligarh dist., W Uttar Pradesh, India, 70 mi. SE of Delhi. Rail and road junction; important trade center (wheat, barley, pearl millet, gram, cotton, corn, mustard, sugar cane); cotton milling, ginning, and pressing; mfg. of glass, locks, brass fittings; oilseed milling; dairy products. Has noted Aligarh Muslim Univ. (until 1920, Anglo-Oriental Col.) and soil survey laboratory. Annual fair. Fort (just N; built 1524) was important stronghold under Jats, Afghans (defeated Jats c.1776 and changed name of fort from Ramgark to Aligarh), and Mahrattas (defeated by English in 1803). Old city of Koil is W of railroad; anc. Hindu and Buddhist temple remains have been found in ruined fort, on which 18th-cent. mosque now stands.

'Ali Gharbi (ä′lē gär′bē), town, 'Amara prov., E Iraq, on Tigris R. and 50 mi. NNW of 'Amara; rice, dates, corn, millet.

Aligudarz (älēgo͞odärz′), town (1942 pop. 8,459), Sixth Prov., in Luristan, SW Iran, 65 mi. SE of Burujird; grain, opium, fruit. Has tribal Bakhtiari pop. Sometimes spelled Ali Gudar.

Alija de los Melones (älē′hä dhä lōs mälō′nĕs), town (pop. 1,360), Leon prov., NW Spain, 24 mi. SE of Astorga; agr. center noted for its melons; cereals, flax, hemp; marble quarries. Has castle and palace.

Alijó (älēzhô′), town (pop. 1,588), Vila Real dist., N Portugal, 15 mi. ESE of Vila Real; winegrowing, sheep and goat raising. Airfield just N.

Alijos Rocks (älē′hōs), 3 tiny desolate islets in the Pacific, c.200 mi. off Lower California, NW Mexico; 24°57′N 115°45′W. Rise to 112 ft.

Alikher (ä′lĭkär) or **Hallikhed** (hŭl′lĭkād), town (pop. 5,426), Bidar dist., W Hyderabad state, India, 18 mi. WSW of Bidar; millet, cotton, oilseed, rice.

Alikovo (ä′lyĭkŭvŭ), village (1932 pop. estimate 290), central Chuvash Autonomous SSR, Russian SFSR, 35 mi. SW of Cheboksary; flax retting; grain.

Alima, region, Fr. Equatorial Africa: see DJAMBALA.

Alima River (älēmä′), central Middle Congo territory, Fr. Equatorial Africa, rises in Crystal Mts. 35 mi. W of Djambala, flows c.300 mi. in a wide curve E to Congo R. 25 mi. SSW of Mossaka. Navigable for 200 mi. upstream. Known as the Leketi (lĕkĕ′tē) in its upper course. Explored (1878) by de Brazza.

Alimena (älēmā′nä), town (pop. 5,083), Palermo prov., central Sicily, near Salso R., 16 mi. WSW of Nicosia. Rock-salt quarries near by.

Alimnia (älēmnēä′), Ital. *Alinnia* (älēn′nēä), Aegean island (□ 3; pop. 29) in the Dodecanese, Greece, off W coast of Rhodes; 36°46′N 27°42′E.

Alimodian (älēmōdyän′), town (1939 pop. 5,654; 1948 municipality pop. 16,886), Iloilo prov., SE Panay isl., Philippines, 12 mi. NW of Iloilo; agr. center (rice, coconuts).

Alindao (älēndou′), village, S Ubangi-Shari, Fr. Equatorial Africa, 70 mi. SSE of Bambari; trading center; cotton ginning. Gold is mined in vicinity.

Aline (ŭlēn′), town (pop. 385), Alfalfa co., N Okla., 33 mi. WNW of Enid, in agr., stock-raising, and dairying area.

Aline, Loch (lŏkh ă′lĭn, –lēn, ălēn′), small inlet on SW coast of Morven peninsula, Argyll, Scotland, extends 3 mi. NNE from the Sound of Mull.

Alinghar River, Afghanistan: see LAGHMAN.

Aling Kangri (ä′lĭng käng′grē) or **Alung Gangri** (ä′lo͝ong gäng′grē), Chinese *A-ling-kang-li* (ä′lĭng′ gäng′lē′), mountain range of NW Trans-Himalayas, W Tibet; extends c.480 mi. WNW–ESE. Highest point, Aling Kangri peak (24,000 ft.), is 80 mi. NNE of Gartok, in extreme W. Gold mines at Thok Jalung.

Alingsas (ä″lĭngsōs′), Swedish *Alingsås*, city (1950 pop. 12,783), Alvsborg co., Sweden, on L. Mjor, 25 mi. NE of Goteborg; textile milling, tanning, metalworking, brewing; mfg. of clothing, leather goods, chocolate. Has mus. Inc. 1619.

Alinnia, Greece: see ALIMNIA.

Alipore (ä′lēpôr, ä′lēpo͞or), residential suburban ward (pop. 46,332) in Calcutta municipality, ⊙ 24-Parganas dist., SE West Bengal, India, 3 mi. S of city center; general engineering works; printing and bookbinding, cement mfg., oilseed milling. Zoological and horticultural gardens. Also Alipur.

Alipur (ä′lēpo͝or), town (pop. 4,829), Muzaffargarh dist., SW Punjab, W Pakistan, 50 mi. SSW of Muzaffargarh; agr. market (wheat, dates, millet, sugar cane); small trade in molasses, indigo.

Alipura (ŭlē′po͞orŭ), village, NW Vindhya Pradesh, India, 10 mi. NW of Nowgong. Was ⊙ former petty state of Alipura (□ 73; pop. 17,735) of Central India agency; since 1948, merged with Vindhya Pradesh.

Alipur Duar (ä′lēpo͞or dwär′), village, Jalpaiguri dist., N West Bengal, India, 50 mi. E of Jalpaiguri; rice milling; trades in rice, tea, mustard, tobacco, jute.

Aliquippa (ălŭkwĭ′pŭ), borough (pop. 26,132), Beaver co., W Pa., 18 mi. NW of Pittsburgh and on Ohio R. Grew after expansion of steel mills in 1909; lead and glass products, barrels, boxes, paints.

Alirajpur (ŭlē′räjpo͞or), town (pop. 6,117), SW Madhya Bharat, India, 65 mi. WSW of Dhar; local market for millet, maize, timber; cotton ginning. Also called Rajpur. Was ⊙ former princely state of Alirajpur (□ 849; pop. 112,754) of Central India agency; since 1948, merged with Madhya Bharat.

Ali-Sabieh (älē′-säbyĕ′), village (pop. 250), SE Fr. Somaliland, on railroad and highway to Ethiopia, 45 mi. SW of Djibouti; administrative post and hill station (alt. 2,300 ft.). Trading center of Issa Somalis. Also spelled Ali-Sabiet.

Alisal, village (pop. 16,714), Monterey co., W Calif., near Salinas.

Alisar Huyuk (ălĭ-shär″ hüyük′), Turkish *Alişar Hüyük*, site of excavations of Hittite tablets in central Turkey, 30 mi. SE of Yozgat, on small Kanak R., tributary of Delice R.

Aliseda (älēsä′dhä), town (pop. 3,908), Cáceres prov., W Spain, 18 mi. W of Cáceres; olive-oil processing, flour milling; stock raising; cereals, honey, fruit.

Alise-Sainte-Reine (älēz′-sĕt′-rĕn′), village (pop. 497), Côte-d'Or dept., E central France, 9 mi. SE of Montbard. Atop near-by Mont Auxois (1,370 ft.) was anc. Alesia, where Caesar in 52 B.C. succeeded in starving out the besieged Gallic garrison under Vercingetorix. The fall of Alesia marked virtual end of Gallic resistance to Rome. A colossal statue of Vercingetorix was erected here by Napoleon III in 1863.

Ali Shan (ä′lē shän′), Jap. *Ari San* (ä′rē sän′), scenic forested mountain (8,140 ft.) in central Formosa, 21 mi. E of Kiayi (linked by lumber railroad); summer resort; lumbering dist. Meteorological observatory. Also called Tuikao Shan.

Alishang River, Afghanistan: see LAGHMAN.

'Ali Sharqi (ä′lē shär′kē), town 'Amara prov., SE Iraq, on Tigris R. and 31 mi. NW of 'Amara; dates, rice, corn, millet, sesame.

Alishtar or **Aleshtar** (ălĕshtär′), town, Sixth Prov., in Luristan, SW Iran, 25 mi. NNW of Khurramabad.

Alistrate or **Alistrati** (both: älēsträ′tē), town (pop. 4,951), Serrai nome, Macedonia, Greece, on road and 11 mi. SW of Drama, at SE end of the Menoikion; cotton center; tobacco, beans.

Alitak, Alaska: see AKHIOK.

Alitus, Lithuania: see ALYTUS.

Aliverion (älēvĕ′rēôn), town (pop. 3,364), S central Euboea, Greece, port on Gulf of Euboea, 23 mi. ESE of Chalcis; lignite-mining center; wheat, wines. Large power plant.

Aliwal (ă′lĭwŭl, älē′väl), village, Ludhiana dist., central Punjab, India, 14 mi. W of Ludhiana. Br. victory was won (1846) over the Sikhs, here, in 1st Sikh war.

Aliwal North (ă′lĭwŭl), Afrikaans *Aliwal-Noord* (ä′lĭväl-no͝ort′), town (pop. 8,783), E Cape Prov., U. of So. Afr., on Orange Free State border, on Orange R. (bridge) and 110 mi. SSE of Bloemfontein; alt. 4,650 ft.; rail junction; dairying, flour milling, furniture mfg., stoneworking. Resort with mineral springs. Airport. Treaty of Aliwal North (1869) defined boundary bet. Orange Free State and Basutoland.

Aliwal South, a former name of MOSSEL BAY, Cape Prov., U. of So. Afr.

Alix, village (pop. 428), S central Alta., on small Alix L., 28 mi. ENE of Red Deer; coal mining, lumbering, dairying, stock raising.

Aliyabad, India: see KOLAMBUR.

Aljaraque (älhärä′kā), town (pop. 1,881), Huelva prov., SW Spain, on Odiel R. estuary, opposite and 4 mi. W of Huelva; wheat, olives, grapes, figs, almonds, oranges.

Aljezur (äl-zhĭzo͞or′), town (pop. 1,926), Faro dist., S Portugal, 16 mi. NNW of Lagos; rice, grain, horse beans; cork production.

Aljojuca (älhōho͞o′kä), town (pop. 2,427), Puebla, central Mexico, 10 mi. NNW of Serdán; cereals, maguey, livestock.

Aljubarrota (äl-zho͞obŭrô′tŭ), village (pop. 531), Leiria dist., W central Portugal, 14 mi. SSW of Leiria. Here was fought, in 1385, the momentous battle in which the Portuguese aided by English archers defeated the forces of King John I of Castile, thus assuring Port. independence and making possible the vigorous administration of John I of Portugal.

Aljucén (älhōō-thĕn'), town (pop. 512), Badajoz prov., W Spain, 9 mi. N of Mérida, and on Guadiana R.; cereals, chick-peas, livestock.

Aljustrel (äl-zhōōstrĕl'), town (pop. 5,433), Beja dist., S Portugal, on rail spur and 19 mi. SW of Beja; Portugal's chief copper-mining center; watering place known for its arsenic springs.

Alkali Lakes, Calif.: see SURPRISE VALLEY.

Alkaline Lake or **Lake Arthur,** Kidder co., S N.Dak.; comprises 2 small bodies of water (one 3 mi. long, one 2 mi. long), connected by small creek and fed intermittently by short stream.

Alkhani, Greece: see THETIDEION.

Alkmaar (älk'mär), town (pop. 37,837), North Holland prov., NW Netherlands, on North Holland Canal and 20 mi. NNW of Amsterdam, 6 mi. E of North Sea coast. Rail junction; iron foundries; mfg. (furniture, paper, shoes, cigars, chocolate), food canning, vegetable growing. Market center for N part of prov., with cheese and cattle markets. Has 15th-cent. church. Chartered 1254; besieged (1573) by Spaniards. Scene of 1799 convention, under which British evacuated the Netherlands after defeat by French at Castricum.

Alkmaar Lake, Du. *Alkmaardermeer* (älk'märdŭrmär"), North Holland prov., NW Netherlands, 13 mi. NNW of Amsterdam; 3 mi. long, 1 mi. wide. On it are Uitgeest and Akersloot.

Alkoven (äl'kōfŭn), town (pop. 3,565), central Upper Austria, 9 mi. W of Linz; grain, cattle.

Allaben (ô'lŭbŭn), resort village, Ulster co., SE N.Y., in the Catskills, on Esopus Creek and 23 mi. NW of Kingston.

Allada (äl-lä'dä), town (pop. c.7,400), S Dahomey, Fr. West Africa, on railroad and 35 mi. WNW of Porto-Novo; agr. center (palm kernels, palm oil, copra, coffee, corn, manioc). R.C. and Protestant missions.

Allagadda (ŭl'ŭgŭdŭ), village, Kurnool dist., N Madras, India, 55 mi. SE of Kurnool; rice, turmeric, betel, cotton.

Allagash (ă'lŭgăsh), plantation (pop. 680), Aroostook co., N Maine, at junction of St. John and Allagash rivers, 25 mi. SW of Fort Kent.

Allagash Lake, Piscataquis co., N central Maine, 57 mi. N of Greenville, in wilderness recreational area; 4 mi. long, 2–3 mi. wide. Connected by stream to Chamberlain L. to SE.

Allagash River, N Maine, rises in Allagash L., N Piscataquis co.; flows c.80 mi. NE, joining other lakes, through wilderness, to St. John R. at Allagash.

Allagnon River, France: see ALAGNON RIVER.

Allah, Philippines: see ALAH.

Allahabad (ä"lŭhŭbäd', ŭl-lŭhä'bäd), district (□ 2,798; pop. 1,812,981), SE Uttar Pradesh, India; ⊙ Allahabad. On Ganges Plain and Ganges-Jumna Doab; foothills of Kaimur Hills in SE. Chief crops: gram, rice, barley, wheat, pearl millet, jowar, oilseeds, sugar cane, cotton. Glass-sand deposits in SW area. Main centers: Allahabad, Mau Aimma, Phulpur. Archaeological landmarks include KOSAM, BHITA, and JHUSI. Area S of Jumna and Ganges rivers formerly part of Br. BUNDELKHAND.

Allahabad, city (pop., including cantonment, 260,630), ⊙ Uttar Pradesh and Allahabad dist., SE Uttar Pradesh, India, on N bank of Jumna R. just NW of its entrance to the Ganges, 350 mi. SE of New Delhi; 25°28'N 81°52'E. Rail and road junction; trade center (grain, oilseeds, sugar cane, ghee, cotton); flour and woolen mills; mfg. of hosiery, soap, bricks. Airport at suburb of Bamrauli (W). Modern city, with industrial and residential sections, extends W and NW; has civil aviation training center, Univ. of Allahabad (founded 1887), and Anand Bhawan (early home of Jawaharlal Nehru; now a hq. of Indian Natl. Congress). Towards rivers' confluence is the old city (built 1583 by Akbar); has large fort, containing city's earliest monument, an Asokan pillar with inscriptions (c.242 B.C.) of edicts of Asoka and other inscriptions from 4th to 17th cent. A. D. Just S of fort, a garden (Khusru Bagh), originally planned by Jehangir, includes noted 17th-cent. tomb of Jehangir's son, Khusru. On rivers' banks, in area called Tribeni (for union of mythical Saraswati R. with the Jumna and Ganges), large Hindu religious festivals are held, including annual Magh Mela and, every 12th year, a festival known as Kumbh Mela (held in succession every 3 years at HARDWAR, Allahabad, NASIK, and UJJAIN), which is attended by as many as 4,000,000 pilgrims. Allahabad was site of anc. Aryan holy city of Prayag or Prag, visited by Hsüan-Tsang in 7th cent. A.D. Conquered by Afghans in 1194. Held by Mahrattas, 1739–50, when it was sacked by nawab of Farrukhabad. In 1765, Treaty of Allahabad signed here; Shah Alam II (ruler of disintegrating Mogul empire) granted to East India Co. (represented by Clive) the administration of Bengal, Bihar, and Orissa. Finally ceded to English in 1801. Scene of fighting in Sepoy Rebellion of 1857. Although Allahabad is officially ⊙ Uttar Pradesh, many state legislative offices are in Lucknow. Glass mfg., sugar processing, oilseed milling at S suburb of Naini.

Allahabad, town (pop. 2,182), Bahawalpur state, W Pakistan, 55 mi. SW of Bahawalpur; local market for rice, dates, wheat; rice husking.

Allahuekber Dag (älä"hōōĕkbĕr'dä"), Turkish *Allahuekber Dağ*, peak (10,246 ft.), NE Turkey, 22 mi. W of Kars.

Allaikha or **Allaykha** (ŭlīkhä'), village (1948 pop. over 500), N Yakut Autonomous SSR, Russian SFSR, on left bank of Indigirka R. and 250 mi. NW of Sredne-Kolymsk; reindeer raising. Just N is settlement of CHOKURDAKH.

Allaire (ălâr'), agr. village (pop. 338), Morbihan dept., W France, 27 mi. E of Vannes. Megalithic monuments near by.

Allais (ă'lāz"), mining village (1940 pop. 579), Perry co., SE Ky., in Cumberland foothills, near North Fork Kentucky R. just N of Hazard; bituminous coal.

Allakaket (ălŭkă'kĭt), Indian village (pop. 77), N central Alaska, on Koyukuk R. at mouth of Alatna R., and 100 mi. N of Tanana; supply base for trappers and gold prospectors. Indian mission; airfield.

Allakh-Yun or **Allakh-Yun'** (ŭläkh'-yōōn"yŭ), town (1939 pop. over 2,000), SE Yakut Autonomous SSR, Russian SFSR, on Allakh-Yun R. (right affluent of Aldan R.) and 275 mi. E of Yakutsk, on Yakutsk-Okhotsk highway. Center of gold-mining region developed after 1932.

Allalinhorn (älälēn'hôrn), peak (13,224 ft.) in Pennine Alps, S Switzerland, 7 mi. ENE of Zermatt. **Allalin Pass** (11,703 ft.) is SW of peak.

Allal Tazi (äl-läl'täzē'), village, Rabat region, NW Fr. Morocco, in the Rharb lowland, on Sebou R. and 24 mi. NE of Port-Lyautey.

Allamakee (ă"lŭmŭkē'), county (□ 639; pop. 16,351), extreme NE Iowa, bounded by Minn. (N) and Wis. (E; line here formed by the Mississippi); ⊙ Waukon. Rolling prairie area drained by Upper Iowa R.; has hilly, forested "Little Switzerland" dist. in E; rich dairying region, producing also hogs, poultry, corn, grass seed. Limestone quarries; lead, zinc, and iron deposits. Some mfg. Formed 1847.

All-American Canal, irrigation canal, S Calif., largest in U.S.; built (1934–40) by the Bureau of Reclamation. The canal (80 mi. long, c.200 ft. wide, 22 ft. deep) taps Colorado R. at IMPERIAL DAM c.15 mi. N of Yuma (Ariz.) and flows W to a point W of Calexico. From it, 3 main canals supply water to IMPERIAL VALLEY. The Coachella Main Canal, completed 1948, branches from the All-American 36 mi. from its head and carries water 123 mi. N and E to the COACHELLA VALLEY. Water is also supplied to Yuma irrigation project; power is generated by plants on main canal.

Allamoore, Texas: see ALLAMORE.

Allamore (ă'lŭmôr), village, Hudspeth co., extreme W Texas, 11 mi. W of Van Horn, in mtn. region; alt. 4,619 ft. Shipping point for livestock. Sometimes spelled Allamoore.

Allan, village (pop. 386), S central Sask., 30 mi. ESE of Saskatoon; wheat, dairying.

Allanche (älāsh'), village (pop. 821), Cantal dept., S central France, in the Monts du Cézallier, 16 mi. NNW of Saint-Flour; resort; cattle, cheese.

Alland (äl'länt), village (pop. 1,623), SE Lower Austria, on Schwechat R. and 8 mi. WNW of Baden; vineyards.

Alland, India: see ALAND.

Allanmyo (ălŭnmyō', ä"länmyō'), town (pop. 12,511), Thayetmyo dist., Upper Burma, on left bank of Irrawaddy R. (opposite Thayetmyo) and 35 mi. N of Prome; cotton-milling center; experimental cotton farms. Named after Maj. Grant Allan who demarcated boundary bet. Upper and Lower Burma (1853).

Allansford, village (pop. 583), SW Victoria, Australia, on Hopkins R. and 135 mi. WSW of Melbourne, near Warrnambool; livestock; cheese factory, dairy plant.

Allan Water, river in Stirling and Perthshire, Scotland, rises 6 mi. SW of Auchterarder, flows 20 mi. W, SW, and S, past Dunblane and Bridge of Allan, to the Forth 2 mi. N of Stirling.

Allapilli, India: see SIRONCHA.

Allard, Lake (11 mi. long, 2 mi. wide), E Que., 15 mi. N of Havre St. Pierre; 50°31'N 63°31'W. Drains into the St. Lawrence. Here are world's largest ilmenite deposits.

Allariz (älyärēth'), town (pop. 1,819), Orense prov., NW Spain, 10 mi. SSE of Orense; tanning, flour milling; makes and ships almond sweets. Fruit, wine, flax in area. Has fine church of Santa Clara convent.

Allas-les-Mines (äläs'-lā-mēn'), village (pop. 128), Dordogne dept., SW France, on the Dordogne and 8 mi. WSW of Sarlat; cement factory.

Allassac (äläsäk'), village (pop. 1,633), Corrèze dept., S central France, near the Vézère, 7 mi. NNW of Brive-la-Gaillarde; calcium carbide mfg., fruit, vegetable and meat preserving, flour milling. Slate quarries near by. Large hydroelectric plants at Le Saillant on the Vézère (1.5 mi. NNW).

Allatoona Dam, Bartow co., NW Ga., in ETOWAH RIVER, 34 mi. NW of Atlanta, near Cartersville; 190 ft. high, 1,250 ft. long; concrete, gravity construction. Completed 1950; used for flood control, power, and navigation. Dam is initial project in comprehensive plan for development of Alabama-Coosa river system. Impounds Allatoona Reservoir (□ 32; capacity 722,000 acre-feet) in Bartow, Cherokee, and Cobb counties; extends 36 mi. up Etowah R.; has recreation facilities.

Allauch (alōsh'), town (pop. 2,532), Bouches-du-Rhône dept., SE France, 6 mi. NE of Marseilles; nougat mfg. Bauxite mines in Chaîne de l'Étoile (N). Old Gr. colony.

Allaverdy, Armenian SSR: see ALAVERDI.

Allaykha, Russian SFSR: see ALLAIKHA.

Alle, river, Poland and USSR: see LYNA RIVER.

Allegan (ă'lĭgăn), county (□ 829; pop. 47,493), SW Mich.; ⊙ Allegan. Bounded W by L. Michigan; drained by Kalamazoo and 2 Black rivers. Fruit-growing (apples, peaches); dairying; agr. (onions, grain, hay, livestock). Mfg. at Allegan, Otsego, and Plainwell. Fisheries. Has resorts, art colony, Allegan State Forest. Organized 1835.

Allegan, city (pop. 4,801), ⊙ Allegan co., SW Mich., on Kalamazoo R. and 22 mi. NW of Kalamazoo, in farm area (livestock, dairy products, poultry, grain, corn, fruit). Mfg. of auto parts, drugs, excelsior, chairs, cement blocks, bedding, flour. Resort. Settled 1834; inc. as city 1907.

Allegany (ă'lŭgā"nē, ă"lŭgā'nē). **1** County (□ 426; pop. 89,556), W Md.; ⊙ Cumberland. Bounded N by Pa. line, S by the Potomac and its North Branch (forms W.Va. line here); drained by Evitts, Wills, other creeks. Appalachian ridge and valley country (E and central) includes Wills Mtn.; the Alleghenies (W) include Dans Mtn. and Big Savage Mtn. (NW corner). Bituminous coal mines, limestone quarries, clay pits, timber; mfg. at Cumberland. Agr. in fertile valleys (apples, corn, wheat, dairy products). Hunting, fishing. Co. includes Green Ridge State Forest (E) and Cumberland Narrows across Wills Mtn. Formed 1789. **2** County (□ 1,048; pop. 43,784), W N.Y., bounded S by Pa. line; ⊙ Belmont. Dairying, oil (refineries), and natural-gas area; diversified mfg., especially at Wellsville. Also produces maple sugar, potatoes, fruit, truck, buckwheat, stock and poultry. Resorts on small lakes. Includes part of Oil Spring Indian Reservation. Drained by Genesee and Canisteo rivers, Canaseraga Creek, and small Angelica Creek. Formed 1806.

Allegany, village (pop. 1,738), Cattaraugus co., W N.Y., on Allegheny R., just W of Olean; dairy products, cutlery, lumber; oil wells and refinery; sand and gravel pits. Agr. (hay, wheat, potatoes). St. Bonaventure Col. (1875) and St. Elizabeth's Acad. for girls (1859) are at adjacent St. Bonaventure village. Allegany State Park and Allegany Indian Reservation are W. Inc. 1906.

Alleghany: see also ALLEGHENY.

Alleghany (ă'lŭgā"nē, ă"lŭgā'nē). **1** County (□ 230; pop. 8,155), NW N.C., on Va. line; ⊙ Sparta. In the Blue Ridge; drained by New R. Farming (corn, wheat, hay, tobacco, potatoes); livestock-raising; sawmilling (oak). Included in Yadkin Natl. Forest. Formed 1859. **2** County (□ 451; pop. 23,139), W Va.; ⊙ Covington. In the Alleghenies; bounded W by W.Va.; drained by Jackson and Cowpasture rivers. Includes part of Jefferson Natl. Forest. CLIFTON FORGE is in but independent of co. Agr. (grain, hay), dairying, fruitgrowing, livestock raising; mfg. (especially paper and rayon) at Covington. Iron and coal mining, limestone quarrying. Formed 1822.

Alleghe (äl'lĕgĕ), village (pop. 410), Belluno prov., Veneto, N Italy, on small lake, 21 mi. NW of Belluno, in the Dolomites; resort (alt. 3,212 ft.); cutlery factory.

Alleghenies, U.S.: see ALLEGHENY MOUNTAINS.

Allegheny (ă'lŭgā"nē, ă"lŭgā'nē), county (□ 730; pop. 1,515,237), W Pa.; ⊙ Pittsburgh. Industrial area drained by Allegheny and Monongahela rivers (which form Ohio R. at Pittsburgh) and by Youghiogheny R. Great steel center. Industrial development due: to navigable rivers which lead to Mississippi basin and the sea; to bituminous coal beds; to early settlement and start in iron mfg. Metal products, food, chemicals, paper, machinery, railroad supplies; bituminous coal, natural gas, oil, clay, limestone, sandstone; grain, apples. Formed 1788.

Allegheny Mountains or **Alleghenies,** E U.S., a part of the ALLEGHENY PLATEAU of the Appalachians, extending for more than 500 mi. on E part of the plateau from N central Pa. into S W.Va. and SW Va. Southwestward from West Branch of Susquehanna in Pa. an escarpment known in various sections as the Allegheny Front (in Pa. and again in W.Va.), Dans Mtn. (in Md.), and Allegheny Mtn. (in W.Va. and along W.Va.–Va. line) marks the E edge of the Alleghenies and overlooks the ridge-and-valley country of the Folded Appalachians to E; escarpment is highest (over 4,800 ft.) in W.Va. On the W, the mtn. belt merges with rough country of the plateau region. The Alleghenies include several generally parallel NE–SW ridges (Laurel Hill, Chestnut Ridge, Rich, Cheat, and Shavers mts., Negro Mtn.), and the highest points in Pa. (Mt. Davis, 3,213 ft.) and W.Va. (Spruce Knob, 4,860 ft.). Formed by folding of the E edge of the Paleozoic sedimentary rocks composing the plateau, the mts. are a rugged near-wilderness belt with large tracts of timber (mainly hardwoods) and deposits of bituminous coal, iron, petroleum, natural gas, and clay. Parts (particularly in W.Va.) are noted for scenic beauty. North Branch of the Potomac and New R. have cut gorges through the Alleghenies. The name Alleghenies is also often applied to much of the adjoining plateau region (W). Formerly spelled Alleghany.

Allegheny Plateau, E U.S., a W section of the APPALACHIAN MOUNTAINS system; extends SW from Mohawk R. valley and L. Ontario and L. Erie lowlands on the NE, across much of N.Y., most of Pa., E Ohio, nearly all of W.Va. (name Kanawha Plateau is sometimes applied to W.Va. and Ohio portion), and SW Va., to meet Cumberland Plateau in S W.Va. and SE Ky. On E, adjoins the Folded Appalachians; on W, meets the interior plain. Generally sloping from E to W, it has mountainous belts in E: CATSKILL MOUNTAINS are in N.Y., POCONO MOUNTAINS in Pa.; ALLEGHENY MOUNTAINS extend from N central Pa. to S W.Va. and SW Va. Except in N, where surface underwent glaciation and is now gently rolling, plateau surface is rugged and deeply dissected by streams; thus the name Allegheny Mts. or the Alleghenies is often applied to much of the region outside of the E mtn. belt. Underlain by Paleozoic sedimentary rocks which are bedded horizontally except in Allegheny Mts., where folding has occurred, the plateau is rich in minerals; it includes the great Appalachian bituminous coal field (in W Pa., W.Va., Va., Ohio), and produces petroleum and natural gas (Pa., W.Va., Ky.), clay, and salt. Its timber stands (mainly hardwood) are valuable. Drainage of N part is into the Delaware, Allegheny, and Susquehanna rivers; S part drains into the Ohio system. Formerly spelled Alleghany.

Allegheny River, in Pa. and N.Y., rises in Potter co., N Pa.; flows NW, past Coudersport, Pa., and Olean and Salamanca, N.Y., thence SW into Pa., past Warren, Oil City, and Franklin, and generally S, past Kittanning, to Pittsburgh, here joining Monongahela R. to form Ohio R.; 325 mi. long; drains □ 11,700. Important channel of commerce before advent of railroads; still used in transport of some bulky freight. Several navigation locks and dams above Pittsburgh. Allegany Indian Reservation is along its shores in Cattaraugus co., N.Y.; Cornplanter Indian Reservation in Warren co., Pa. River formerly sometimes spelled Alleghany.

Allegranza Island, Canary Isls.: see ALEGRANZA ISLAND.

Allègre (älĕ'grù), village (pop. 900), Haute-Loire dept., S central France, at N end of Monts du Velay, 14 mi. NW of Le Puy; lacemaking, woodworking.

Allemond or **Allemont** (älmõ'), village (pop. 176), Isère dept., SE France, in OISANS valley at foot of Belledonne range, 16 mi. ESE of Grenoble; Alpine resort. Slate quarries.

Allen (ä'lĕn), town (1947 census 3,277), N Río Negro natl. territory, Argentina, in Río Negro valley (irrigation area), on railroad and 17 mi. WNW of Fuerte General Roca. Alcohol distilleries, wineries, sawmills, limekilns, food canneries. Agr. (alfalfa, wine, fruit, sheep, goats). Gypsum deposits near by.

Allen. 1 County (□ 671; pop. 183,722), NE Ind.; ⊙ FORT WAYNE. Bounded E by Ohio line; drained by Maumee, St. Joseph, and St. Marys rivers. Farming (grain, corn, soybeans), stock raising, dairying. Formed 1823. **2** County (□ 505; pop. 18,187), SE Kansas; ⊙ Iola. Rolling prairie area, drained by Neosho R. Stock and grain raising, dairying. Oil and gas fields. Formed 1855. **3** County (□ 364; pop. 13,787), S Ky.; ⊙ Scottsville. Bounded S by Tenn., NE by Barren R.; drained by Trammel Fork. Agr. area (livestock, grain, burley tobacco, fruit, poultry, dairy products); oil wells, hardwood timber. Some mfg. at Scottsville. Formed 1815. **4** Parish (□ 755; pop. 18,835), SW central La.; ⊙ Oberlin. Drained by Calcasieu R. Pulp, paper, and lumber milling; also rice and feed mills, cotton gins. Agr. (rice, corn, cotton, sweet potatoes, citrus fruit, livestock). Formed 1910. **5** County (□ 410; pop. 88,183), W Ohio; ⊙ LIMA. Intersected by Ottawa and Auglaize rivers. Extensive mfg. at Lima. Diversified farming (livestock, grain, poultry, soybeans). Oil wells, limestone quarries. Formed 1831.

Allen. 1 City (pop. 241), Lyon co., E central Kansas, 15 mi. N of Emporia, in livestock and grain region; feed milling. **2** or **Allen City,** town (pop. 421), Floyd co., E Ky., in the Cumberlands, on Levisa Fork and 15 mi. NW of Pikeville. **3** Village (pop. 374), Dixon co., NE Nebr., 20 mi. W of Sioux City, Iowa. **4** Town (pop. 1,215), on Pontotoc-Hughes co. line, S central Okla., 17 mi. ENE of Ada, near Canadian R.; cotton ginning, mfg. of petroleum products.

Allen, Bog of, extensive morass and peat-bog region (□ c.375) in Ireland, covering parts of E Co. Offaly, N Co. Laoighis, and NW Co. Kildare; drained by the Boyne. There are patches of cultivable land.

Allen, Lough (lŏkh), lake (8 mi. long, 3 mi. wide) on borders of Co. Leitrim and Co. Roscommon, Ireland, on the Shannon N of Drumshambo.

Allen, Port, T.H.: see PORT ALLEN.

Allenburg, Russian SFSR: see DRUZHBA.

Allenby Bridge, Arabic *Jisr Allenby,* road bridge over Jordan R., in N central Jordan, on main Jerusalem-Amman road, 5 mi. ENE of Jericho. Until 1948, customs point bet. Palestine and Transjordan.

Allenc (älã'), village (pop. 202), Lozère dept., S France, 7 mi. ENE of Mende; silver-bearing lead mines.

Allen City, Ky.: see ALLEN.

Allendale, town and parish (pop. 2,218), S Northumberland, England, on small tributary of the South Tyne, 8 mi. SW of Hexham; lead-mining center; agr. market. In parish (7 mi. S) is lead- and zinc-mining town of Allenheads.

Allendale, county (□ 418; pop. 11,773), SW S.C.; ⊙ Allendale. Bounded W by Savannah R.; drained SE by Coosawhatchie R. Watermelons, truck, livestock, timber; hunting draws tourists. Formed 1919.

Allendale. 1 Village (pop. 442), Wabash co., SE Ill., 8 mi. NNE of Mount Carmel, in agr. area. **2** Town (pop. 142), Worth co., NW Mo., 32 mi. ENE of Maryville. **3** Borough (pop. 2,409), Bergen co., NE N.J., 3 mi. N of Ridgewood. Settled 1740, inc. 1894. **4** Town (pop. 2,474), ⊙ Allendale co., SW S.C., 45 mi. SW of Orangeburg, in agr. area noted for watermelons; lumber, veneer, beverages, confectionery. Tourist center for hunters.

Allende (äyĕn'dā) or **Valle de Allende** (vä'yä dā). **1** Town (pop. 2,400), Chihuahua, N Mexico, 16 mi. E of Hidalgo del Parral; alt. 5,091 ft.; silver, gold, lead, copper mining. **2** City (pop. 5,613), Coahuila, N Mexico, 30 mi. SW of Piedras Negras; rail junction; agr. center (cereals, cotton, livestock); flour milling, cotton processing. **3** City, Guanajuato, Mexico: see SAN MIGUEL DE ALLENDE. **4** Town, Mexico state, Mexico: see VILLA ALLENDE. **5** Town (pop. 1,296), Nuevo León, N Mexico, on Inter-American Highway and 33 mi. SE of Monterrey; oranges, sugar.

Allende, Villa, Mexico: see VILLA ALLENDE, Chiapas.

Allendorf, Germany: see BAD SOODEN-ALLENDORF.

Allenheads, England: see ALLENDALE.

Allenhurst, resort borough (pop. 758), Monmouth co., E N.J., on the coast just N of Asbury Park. Deal L. is near.

Allen Park, village (pop. 12,329), Wayne co., SE Mich., residential suburb just SW of Detroit. Settled 1776; inc. 1927.

Allenport, borough (pop. 923), Washington co., SW Pa., 4 mi. SE of Charleroi and on Monongahela R.; steel.

Allenstein (ä'lŭn-shtīn) or **Olsztyn** (ôl'shtĭn), city (1939 pop. 50,396; 1946 pop. 29,053) in East Prussia, after 1945 ⊙ Olsztyn prov., NE Poland, on Lyna (Alle) R. and 65 mi. S of Kaliningrad; 53°47'N 20°29'E. Rail junction; commercial center; popular health resort; cattle market; sawmilling, woodworking; power station. Seat of R.C. bishop of Warmia. Has fairs; agr. col. In Second World War, c.45% destroyed. Town hall now houses part of Torun univ. Founded 1348 by Teutonic Knights, who built castle here; chartered 1353. Passed 1466 to Poland, 1772 to Prussia; retained by Germany after 1920 plebiscite. Entirely resettled by Poles after Second World War. Copernicus lived here for some time.

Allenstown, rural town (pop. 1,540), Merrimack co., S N.H., on the Suncook and 7 mi. SE of Concord; textiles. Settled before 1748, inc. 1831.

Allensville, town (pop. 337), Todd co., S Ky., near Tenn. line, 26 mi. ESE of Hopkinsville.

Allenton. 1 Textile-milling village (pop. c.900) in North Kingstown town, Washington co., S central R.I., 20 mi. S of Providence; woolens. **2** Village (pop. c.350), Washington co., E Wis., on tributary of Rock R. and 33 mi. NW of Milwaukee; dairy products.

Allen Town, town (1931 pop. 352), Sierra Leone colony, on Sierra Leone Peninsula, 9 mi. SE of Freetown, on railroad. Ilmenite mining (S).

Allentown. 1 Borough (pop. 931), Monmouth co., central N.J., 10 mi. ESE of Trenton; nursery products, truck. Imlay mansion (c.1790) here. **2** City (pop. 106,756), ⊙ Lehigh co., E Pa., 50 mi. NNW of Philadelphia and on Lehigh R.; steel products, automobiles, cement, machinery, electrical appliances, textiles, clothing, tobacco products. Seat of Muhlenberg Col. and Cedar Crest Col. Liberty Bell brought here (1777) for safekeeping during Revolutionary War. Laid out c.1752 as Allentown; inc. as borough 1811 and renamed Northampton; renamed Allentown 1838; inc. as city 1867.

Allentsteig (äl'ĕntshtīk), town (pop. 2,364), NW central Lower Austria, 23 mi. NNW of Krems; rye, potatoes.

Allenville, village (pop. 253), Moultrie co., central Ill., near Kaskaskia R., 10 mi. NW of Mattoon, in agr. area.

Allenwood, resort village, Monmouth co., E N.J., near Manasquan R., 7 mi. SW of Asbury Park. Has co. tuberculosis sanatorium.

Alleppey (ŭlĕ'pē), locally *Alapulai* (ŭlŭ'pōōlī), city (pop. 56,333), W Travancore, India, port on Malabar Coast of Arabian Sea, 80 mi. NW of Trivandrum; connected with Cochin (N) and Quilon (S) by lagoon-canal system. Exports coir, copra, coconuts, timber; mfg. of coir products (rope, mats), copra, jute gunney bags, rubber goods, electrical supplies; rice and sawmilling, cashew-nut processing. Col., affiliated with Univ. of Travancore.

Aller (ô'lùr), agr. village and parish (pop. 348), central Somerset, England, 8 mi. SE of Bridgwater.

Allerby, England: see OUGHTERSIDE AND ALLERBY.

Alle River, Poland and USSR: see LYNA RIVER.

Aller River (ä'lùr), NW Germany, rises 5 mi. N of Oschersleben, flows c.160 mi. N and WNW, past Celle (head of navigation), to the Weser 2 mi. NW of Verden. Oil fields in valley (below Celle).

Aller River (älyär'), Oviedo prov., NW Spain, rises in Cantabrian Mts. 16 mi. ENE of Pajares Pass, flows 25 mi. WNW, across rich coal- and iron-mining region, to Lena R.

Allersberg (ä'lùrsbĕrk), village (pop. 2,558), Middle Franconia, central Bavaria, Germany, 15 mi. SSE of Nuremberg; toy and wire mfg., brewing; hops, cabbage. Chartered 1323.

Allersheim (ä'lùrs-hīm), village (pop. 499), Lower Franconia, W Bavaria, Germany, 11 mi. SSW of Würzburg; wheat, cattle.

Allerton, England: see BRADFORD.

Allerton. 1 Village (pop. 244), on border of Vermilion and Champaign cos., E. Ill., 22 mi. SW of Danville, in agr. and bituminous-coal area. **2** Town (pop. 761), Wayne co., S Iowa, 25 mi. W of Centerville; dairy products. **3** Village, Mass.: see HULL.

Allerton Point, Mass.: see NANTASKET BEACH.

Allery (älùrē'), village (pop. 943), Somme dept., N France, 10 mi. SSE of Abbeville; jute and linen weaving.

Alle-sur-Semois (äl-sür-sùmwä'), village, Namur prov., SE Belgium, on Semois R. and 20 mi. W of Neufchâteau, in the Ardennes; quarrying.

Allevard (älvär'), town (pop. 1,841), Isère dept., SE France, on the Bréda and 14 mi. SSE of Chambéry, in Belledonne range of Dauphiné Alps; spa with sulphur springs. Has important electrometallurgical works (steel, ferroalloys) processing locally mined iron.

Alley (ă'lē), town (pop. 1,780), Clarendon parish, S Jamaica, on left bank of Minho R. near its mouth, and 11 mi. S of May Pen, in irrigated sugar region. Its church is allegedly oldest on the isl. Former ⊙ now-dissolved Vere parish.

Alleyton, village, Colorado co., S Texas, on Colorado R. and 4 mi. E of Columbus; sand, gravel mining.

Allgäu or **Algäu** (both: äl'goi), region in SW Germany, N of Allgäu Alps, bet. upper Lech R. and L. of Constance; noted for its cattle and dairying. Main town: Kempten.

Allgäu Alps or **Algäu Alps,** Ger. *Allgäuer Alpen* or *Algäuer Alpen,* N division of Central Alps along Austro-Ger. border; extend E from L. Constance to Lech R. valley; highest peak, Mädelegabel (8,678 ft.). Lech and Iller rivers rise here. Bregenzerwald is lower part (W) overlooking L. Constance. Allgäu Alps sometimes considered W outliers of Bavarian Alps.

Allhallows (ôlhă'lōz), parish (pop. 747), W Cumberland, England. Includes coal-mining village of Fletchertown, 5 mi. SW of Wigton, and dairying village of Baggrow.

Aliança, Brazil: see ALIANÇA.

Alliance, village (pop. 243), SE central Alta., 110 mi. SE of Edmonton; coal mining, mixed farming, dairying; grain elevators.

Alliance (äleän'sù), village (pop. 397), Commewijne dist., N Du. Guiana, on Commewijne R. and 20 mi. E of Paramaribo; sugar milling.

Alliance. 1 City (pop. 7,891), ⊙ Box Butte co., NW Nebr., 45 mi. NE of Scotts Bluff, in Great Plains region; railroad repair shops; ships seed potatoes, grain, cattle; beverages, dairy and poultry produce. U.S. testing ground for plants is here. Rodeo in June. Founded 1888. **2** City (pop. 26,161), Stark co., E central Ohio, 16 mi. ENE of Canton and on Mahoning R.; industrial, distribution, and rail center. Mfg.: iron and steel, aircraft, mill machinery, electrical equipment, brick, tile, pottery, office machines, tools, clothing. Coal mining. Mount Union Col. is here. Laid out 1838 as Freedom; inc. 1854 as village, 1889 as city.

Allier (älyā'), department (□ 2,850; pop. 373,381), in old Bourbonnais prov., central France; ⊙ Moulins. Lies athwart N spurs of the Massif Central; drained by the Loire (E), Allier (center), and Cher (W) rivers which cross dept. S-N. NE portion occupied by lake-studded SOLOGNE BOURBONNAISE. Agr. (wheat, barley, potatoes, wine and vegetables) predominates in the Allier lowland (LIMAGNE). Hogs and poultry extensively raised. Coal mines at Commentry, Buxières-les-Mines, Noyant-d'-Allier, and Bert; gypsum and kaolin quarries near Lurcy-Lévy. Industry concentrated in Montluçon-Commentry dist. (at S end of Berry Canal, near coal mines), where iron, steel, rubber tires and glass are produced. Dept. has important health resorts, led by Vichy, which exports its mineral waters on a large scale. Chief towns: Montluçon, Moulins, Vichy, Commentry, Cusset.

Allier River, central France, rises in Mercoire forest (N of Mont Lozère), Lozère dept., flows 255 mi. NNW, past Langogne, Issoire, Vichy, and Moulins, to the Loire below Nevers. Parallels upper course of Loire R., and crosses (S-N) the fertile LIMAGNE. Navigable below Issoire; irregular volume. Receives the Alagnon and Sioule (left), the Dore (right).

Alligator, town (pop. 214), Bolivar co., NW Miss., 11 mi. SW of Clarksdale, in agr. area.

Alligator Lake, Hyde co., E N.C., in swamplands (Alligator Swamp) 13 mi. N of Swanquarter; c.4 mi. long.

Alligator Pond, town (pop. 1,800), Manchester parish, S Jamaica, on fine bay and beach, 10 mi. S of Mandeville; fishing.

Alligator-Pungo River Canal, N.C.: see ALLIGATOR RIVER.

Alligator River, Australia: see SOUTH ALLIGATOR RIVER.

Alligator River, NE N.C., S arm of Albemarle Sound extending 25 mi. S and E into Alligator Swamp; forms Dare-Tyrrell co. line; 2–5 mi. wide. Its head is connected with Pungo R. (SW) by Alligator-Pungo R. Canal (c.20 mi. long), forming part of Intracoastal Waterway.

Alligerville, N.Y.: see KYSERIKE.

Allihies (ăl'ĭhēs'), Gaelic *Aillighthe*, village, SW Co. Cork, Ireland, on the Atlantic at foot of Slieve Miskish mts., 6 mi. W of Castletown Bere; copper mining.

Allinagaram (ŭl-lĭnŭg'ŭrŭm), town (pop. 13,123), Madura dist., S Madras, India, 7 mi. SW of Periyakulam. Teni or Theni, road center 1 mi. S, trades in products of Cardamom Hills (W) and Palni Hills (N).

Allingaabro (ä'lĭng-ôbrō″), town (pop. 1,072), Randers amt, E Jutland, Denmark, 10 mi. E of Randers; machinery mfg.

Allinge-Sandvig (ä'lĭngŭ-săn'vē), city (pop. 2,195), Bornholm amt, Denmark, on N shore of Bornholm isl.; comprises Allinge (pop. 1,513) and Sandvig (pop. 682) communities, with separate ports; seafaring. Granite quarry.

Allington (ăl'-), agr. village and parish (pop. 114), central Kent, England, on Medway R. just N of Maidstone; stone quarrying. Has remains of old castle. Thomas Wyatt b. here.

Allington, agr. parish (pop. 1,303), E Denbigh, Wales, 6 mi. NE of Wrexham.

Allingtown, Conn.: see WEST HAVEN.

Allison. 1 Town (pop. 771), ⊙ Butler co., N central Iowa, 29 mi. NW of Waterloo; creamery. Limestone quarry, sand and gravel pit near by. **2** Village (pop. 1,764), Fayette co., SW Pa., 10 mi. NW of Uniontown, in bituminous-coal area.

Allison Gap, village (pop. 1,015), Smyth co., SW Va., on Holston R. and 14 mi. WNW of Marion. Sometimes Allisons Gap.

Allison Island, N.Y.: see MURPHY ISLAND.

Allisons Gap, Va.: see ALLISON GAP.

Alliste (äl-lē'stĕ), village (pop. 3,654), Lecce prov., Apulia, S Italy, 10 mi. SSE of Gallipoli; olive oil, wine.

Alliston (ă'lĭstŭn), town (pop. 1,733), S Ont., on Boyne R. near Nottawasaga R. and 40 mi. NW of Toronto; mfg. of agr. machinery; woolen milling, woodworking, agr. (dairying; tobacco, potatoes).

Allithwaite, England: see LOWER ALLITHWAITE.

Allmallojekna, Sweden: see SULITJELMA, mountain range, Norway.

Allo (ä'lyō), town (pop. 1,613), Navarre prov., N Spain, 8 mi. S of Estella; olive-oil processing; wine, wheat.

Alloa (ă'lōŭ), burgh (1931 pop. 13,323; 1951 census 13,436), Clackmannan, Scotland, at head of Firth of Forth, 6 mi. E of Stirling; seaport, agr. market, and mfg. town; hosiery and yarn mills, agr. machinery works, bottle works, whisky distilleries, and noted ale breweries. Suburb of South Alloa has large timber yards. Coal mines in vicinity. Near by is Alloa Park, seat of earl of Mar, with 13th-cent. Alloa Tower.

Allock (ă'lŏk″), mining village (1940 pop. 998), Perry co., SE Ky., in Cumberland foothills, 7 mi. ESE of Hazard; bituminous coal.

Allomata (äl-lō'mätä), village (pop. 1,850), Wallo prov., NE Ethiopia, on road and 10 mi. SSE of Quoram, in agr. region (durra, corn, cotton).

Allonah, village and port, NW S.Bruny, Tasmania, on D'Entrecasteaux Channel; dairying center.

Allonby (ă'lŭnbē), village and parish (pop. 461), W Cumberland, England, on Allonby Bay of Solway Firth, 5 mi. NE of Maryport; dairy farming.

Allong Bay, Vietnam: see ALONG BAY.

Allonim, Israel: see ALONIM.

Allons (ă'lŭnz), town (pop. 270), Overton co., N Tenn., 4 mi. N of Livingston, near Dale Hollow Reservoir.

Allos (älôs'), village (pop. 232), Basses-Alpes dept., SE France, on Verdon R. and 10 mi. S of Barcelonnette, in Provence Alps; alt. 4,675 ft. Tourist and winter-sport resort. Col d' Allos, a pass (alt. 7,382 ft.), is 5 mi. NNW. Scenic Allos L. (alt. 7,316 ft; 1 mi. long) is 4 mi. E, at foot of Mont Pelat.

Allouagne (älwä'nyŭ), town (pop. 2,576), Pas-de-Calais dept., N France, 6 mi. W of Béthune; market in fertile agr. area (wheat, sugar beets, tobacco). Brewing.

Allouez (ă'lōōā). **1** Village (pop. c.335), Keweenaw co., NW Upper Peninsula, Mich., 8 mi. NE of Houghton, in copper-mining region. **2** Village (pop. 4,094), Brown co., E Wis., just S of Green Bay. There is also a suburb of Superior city called Allouez.

Allouez Bay, Wis.: see SUPERIOR BAY.

Alloway, Scotland: see AYR, burgh.

Alloway Creek, SW N.J., rises E of Salem, flows c.25 mi. SW, past Quinton and Hancocks Bridge, to Delaware R. 6 mi. SW of Salem. Navigable to Quinton.

Alloza (älyō'thä), village (pop. 1,711), Teruel prov., E Spain, 20 mi. WSW of Alcañiz; cereals, wine, olive oil, lumber.

All Pines, village (pop. 538), Stann Creek dist., central Br. Honduras, small Caribbean port 12 mi. SSW of Stann Creek; bananas, coconuts, citrus fruit; fisheries. Lighthouse.

All Saints, village (pop. 1,544), central Antigua, B.W.I., 5 mi. SE of St. John's; sugar cane, sea-island cotton.

All Saints Bay, Brazil: see TODOS OS SANTOS BAY.

Allschwil (älsh'vēl), town (pop. 7,315), Basel-Land half-canton, N Switzerland, Custom station on Fr. border, opposite Hegenheim, 3 mi. WSW of Basel; paper, shoes, tiles; metal and woodworking.

Allstedt (äl'shtĕt), town (pop. 4,445), in former Prussian Saxony prov., central Germany, after 1945 in Saxony-Anhalt, at E end of Goldene Aue region, on the Helme and 7 mi. SE of Sangerhausen; sugar refining, malting, metalworking. Has medieval former imperial castle; remains of Romanesque church destroyed in Peasants' War. Chartered 935.

Allston, Mass.: see BOSTON.

Allumette Island (ălūmĕt') or **Île aux Allumettes** (ēl'ōzälümĕt'), island (16 mi. long, 3-7 mi. wide), SW Que., in an expansion of Ottawa R. called L. Allumette, opposite Pembroke.

Allumiere (äl-lōōmyā'rĕ), town (pop. 3,580), Roma prov., Latium, central Italy, in Tolfa Hills, 7 mi. NE of Civitavecchia; alum mining; mfg. of chemicals.

Allur or **Alluru** (ŭlōō'rōō), town (pop. 12,058), Nellore dist., E Madras, India, 19 mi. NNE of Nellore; rice milling; palmyra sugar; cashew and Casuarina plantations. Saltworks E, on Coromandel Coast of Bay of Bengal. Rail station (workshops) 8 mi. WNW, at Bitragunta.

Alluru Kottapatnam (ŭlōō'rōō kŏt'ŭpŭtnŭm) or **Kottapatnam,** town (pop. 8,663), Guntur dist., NE Madras, India, on Bay of Bengal, near Buckingham Canal, 8 mi. SE of Ongole; palmyra and betel palms. Also spelled Allurukothapatnam or Kottapatam.

Ally, France: see LAVOÛTE-CHILHAC.

Alma (älmä'), village (pop. 1,824), Alger dept., N central Algeria, near the Mediterranean, 20 mi. E of Algiers; tobacco, wine, truck.

Alma (ăl'mŭ), village (pop. estimate 500), S Ont., 18 mi. NW of Guelph; dairying, mixed farming.

Alma, river, Crimea: see ALMA RIVER.

Alma (ăl'mŭ). **1** Town (pop. 1,228), Crawford co., NW Ark., 13 mi. NE of Fort Smith; ships strawberries, truck. **2** Town (pop. 149), Park co., central Colo., on South Platte R., in Rocky Mts., and 12 mi. E of Leadville; alt. 10,300 ft. Gold mines. Mt. Lincoln, Quandary Peak, and Hoosier Pass near by. **3** City (pop. 2,588), ⊙ Bacon co., SE central Ga., 22 mi. NNW of Waycross; naval stores, lumber, cotton. Inc. 1906. **4** Village (pop. 404), Marion co., S central Ill., 18 mi. NE of Centralia, in agr., oil-producing, and bituminous-coal area. **5** City (pop. 716), ⊙ Wabaunsee co., E central Kansas, on small affluent of Kansas R. and 33 mi. W of Topeka; grain, livestock. **6** City (pop. 8,341), Gratiot co., central Mich., on Pine R. and 36 mi. W of Saginaw, in agr. area (beans, sugar beets, corn). Mfg. of trailers, bicycle rims, furniture; oil and beet-sugar refineries. Has Alma Col. and Mich. Masonic Home. Settled 1853; inc. as village 1872, as city 1905. **7** City (pop. 357), Lafayette co., W central Mo., near Missouri R., 19 mi. ESE of Lexington. **8** City (pop. 1,768), ⊙ Harlan co., S Nebr., 60 mi. SW of Hastings and on Republican R., near Kansas line; trade center for agr. region; dairy and poultry produce, grain, livestock. Founded 1871. **9** City (pop. 1,068), ⊙ Buffalo co., W Wis., on the Mississippi and 40 mi. SW of Eau Claire, at foot of bluffs; dairy products, timber. Federal dam here completed in 1935. Settled c.1852, inc. 1885.

Alma-Ata (ăl'mŭ-ă'tä,–ätä', Rus. ŭlmä″-ŭtä') [Kazakh, =father of apples], oblast (□ 41,700; 1946 pop. estimate 500,000), SE Kazakh SSR; ⊙ Alma-Ata. Extends (70–80 mi. wide) from L. Balkhash along Ili R. to China border; mountainous in S (Trans-Ili Ala-Tau); sandy desert in NW, along lower Ili R. Entirely agr., with sheep and camel breeding in NW; along mtn. foothills extensive irrigation produces basic wheat and sugar-beet crops, tobacco, opium, and rubber-bearing, fiber-producing, and medicinal plants. Garden fruit (apples, grapes) grown on mtn. slopes. Some lumbering in mtn. forest zone. Fisheries along L. Balkhash shore. Food and other products processed at Alma-Ata and Ili. Turksib RR crosses central section. Pop. ⅔ Kazakhs; others are Russians, Ukrainians, Taranchi, Uigurs. Formed 1932.

Alma-Ata, city (1926 pop. 45,395; 1939 pop. 230,528), ⊙ Kazakh SSR and Alma-Ata oblast, in N foothills of Trans-Ili Ala-Tau, on short Malaya Almatinka R., on spur of Turksib RR and 430 mi. ENE of Tashkent, 2,000 mi. ESE of Moscow; 43°15'N 77°E. Center of agr. and orchard area (sugar beets, wheat, tobacco, apples, grapes); mfg. of heavy machinery; railroad repair shops, spinning mills; fruit preserving, meat packing, sugar, wine, and tobacco processing; tanning, sawmilling, metalworking. Has univ. (founded 1928), Kazakh Acad. of Sciences (founded 1945), medical, veterinary, agr., metallurgical, and teachers colleges. Large library, conservatory, Kazakh and Rus. opera houses, theaters, museums, motion-picture studios. Laid out in rectangular plan; resorts on slopes of the Trans-Ili Ala-Tau (S). Founded 1854 as Rus. fortress Verny on site of Kazakh settlement of Alma-Ata; became ⊙ former Semirechye (after 1922, DZHETYSU). Destroyed by earthquakes (1887, 1910). Renamed Alma-Ata 1927. Developed rapidly after transfer (1927–29) of ⊙ from Kzyl-Orda and construction of Turksib RR.

Almacellas (älmä-thä'lyäs), village (pop. 2,840), Lérida prov., NE Spain, 13 mi. NW of Lérida; meat, olive-oil processing; cattle, sheep, cereals, wine.

Alma Center, village (pop. 441), Jackson co., W central Wis., 40 mi. SE of Eau Claire, in dairying region.

Almácera (älmä'thärä), N suburb (pop. 2,625) of Valencia, Valencia prov., E Spain, in truck-farming area; porcelain mfg.; cereals, wine.

Almáchar (älmä'chär), town (pop. 2,342), Málaga prov., S Spain, 12 mi. ENE of Málaga, in wine-growing region; produces raisins.

Almada (älmä'dŭ), town (pop. 5,724), Setúbal dist., S central Portugal, on S bank of Tagus estuary, opposite Lisbon, and adjoining Cacilhas; cork processing, fish canning, pottery mfg. Has wine depots. Overlooked by a castle and an old convent (fine view of Lisbon).

Alma Dag, Turkey: see AMANOS MOUNTAINS.

Almadén (älmä-dhĕn'), city (pop. 12,468), Ciudad Real prov., S central Spain, in New Castile, in N spur of the Sierra Morena (Sierra de Almadén), 50 mi. WSW of Ciudad Real. Renowned as center of one of the world's richest mercury-mining regions, worked since Roman and Moorish times. Also raises cereals and livestock. Flour mills, shoe factories. Has mining school.

Almaden (ălmŭdĕn'), village (pop. c.250), Santa Clara co., W Calif., 11 mi. S of San Jose; quicksilver mines (since 1845). New Almaden is just S.

Almadén de la Plata (dhä lä plä'tä), town (pop. 3,685), Seville prov., SW Spain, in the Sierra Morena near Huelva prov. border, 34 mi. N of Seville; cork, cereals, timber (eucalyptus, poplar), livestock. Marble quarrying, iron and copper mining. Abandoned silver mines.

Almadenejos (älmä-dhĕnä'hōs), town (pop. 1,383), Ciudad Real prov., S central Spain, in New Castile, on railroad and 7 mi. ESE of Alamdén; mercury, silver, lead mines. Also raises grain, sheep, hogs. Flour milling.

Almadies, Cape (älmä'dyĕs), westernmost point of Africa, at tip of Cape Verde, W Senegal, Fr. West Africa, 9 mi. NW of Dakar; 14°45'N 17°33'W.

Almafuerte (älmäfwĕr'tä), town (pop. 2,509), central Córdoba prov., Argentina, on Río Tercero and 60 mi. WNW of Villa María; agr. center (cereals, flax, peanuts, livestock).

Almagrera, Sierra de (syĕ'rä dhä älmägrä'rä), range in Almería prov., S Spain, near E Mediterranean coast. Iron and silver-bearing lead mines.

Almagro (älmä'grō), city (pop. 8,551), Ciudad Real prov., S central Spain, in New Castile, on railroad and 13 mi. ESE of Ciudad Real. Spa, textile and agr. center in fertile region of La Mancha (cereals, grapes, olives, anise, fruit, livestock). Alcohol and liquor distilling, wine making, olive-oil pressing, flour milling, tanning, cheese processing; basalt quarrying. Mfg. of silk lace, embroideries, woolen goods, shoes, furniture, meat products, plaster, soap. Historic city, preserving fine bldgs. such as former palace of the Knights of Calatrava, Dominican convents, and San Agustín, San Bartolomé el Real, and Madre de Dios churches. Its univ., founded in 16th cent., was suppressed in 19th cent.

Almagro Island, Chile: see CAMBRIDGE ISLAND.

Almagro Island (□ 8; 1939 pop. 3,300), Samar prov., Philippines, in Samar Sea, 6 mi. N of Maripipi Isl., bet. Masbate and Samar isls.; 11°55'N 124°18'E; 5 mi. long, 2 mi. wide. Mountainous, rising to 1,824 ft. Coconut growing.

Almaguer (älmägĕr'), town (pop. 830), Cauca dept., SW Colombia, in Cordillera Central, 40 mi. SSW of Popayán; alt. 7,585 ft.; coffee, sugar cane, cereals, fruit, stock. Founded 1541.

Almahilla, Sierra de (syĕ'rä dhä älmäē'lyä), hill range in Almería prov., S Spain, NE of Almería. Iron and some zinc mines.

Alma Island or **Île d'Alma** (ēl'dälmä'), island (8 mi. long, 3 mi. wide), S central Que., at E end of L. St. John, bet. 2 outlets of the Saguenay, opposite St. Joseph d'Alma.

Almalyk (ŭlmŭlĭk'), town (1945 pop. over 500), NE Tashkent oblast, Uzbek SSR, on N slope of Kurama Range, 40 mi. SE of Tashkent; copper-mining center; smelter. Developed in late 1940s.

Almanor, Lake (ăl'mŭnôr") (c.10 mi. long), Plumas co., NE Calif., in the Sierra Nevada, 5 mi. SW of Westwood; impounded by Lake Almanor Dam (135 ft. high, 1,250 ft. long; for power) on North Fork Feather R. Resort, noted for trout fishing; campgrounds.

Almansa (älmän'sä), city (pop. 14,358), Albacete prov., SE central Spain in Murcia, 45 mi. ESE of Albacete; agr. center, on fertile plain yielding cereals, saffron, olives, grapes. Mfg. of footwear, bells, tiles, plaster; tanning, wine and olive-oil processing, flour- and sawmilling, alcohol and liqueur distilling. Honey, livestock in area. Mineral springs. Ruins of Moorish castle and tower on hill near by. In War of Spanish Succession, French and Spaniards, fighting for Philip V under Berwick, defeated (1707) near here troops of Archduke Charles.

Almanzor, Plaza del Moro, Spain: see PLAZA DEL MORO ALMANZOR.

Almanzora River (älmän-thō'rä), Almería prov., S Spain, rises on NW slope of the Sierra de los Filabres, flows c.80 mi. E and SE to the Mediterranean 5 mi. E of Vera. Near its mouth the French defeated (1810) the Spaniards.

Almaraz (älmäräth'), town (pop. 1,035), Cáceres prov., W Spain, on Tagus R. and 27 mi. SE of Plasencia; olive oil, cereals. Has fine 16th-cent. bridge.

Almaraz de Duero (dhā dhwā'rō), village (pop. 1,093), Zamora prov., NW Spain, 9 mi. WSW of Zamora; stock raising, lumbering; cereals, wine. Tin mines near by.

Almarcha, La (lä älmär'chä), town (pop. 1,261), Cuenca prov., E central Spain, 29 mi. SSW of Cuenca; saffron, cereals, grapes, olives, sheep. Medicinal springs.

Almargen (älmär'hĕn), town (pop. 2,564), Málaga prov., S Spain, at SW foot of the Sierra de Yeguas, on railroad and 17 mi. NNE of Ronda; grapes, olives, vegetables, stock; olive-oil pressing, flour milling, liquor distilling. Mineral springs.

Alma River or **Al'ma River** (ăl'mŭ, Rus. äl'mŭ), S Crimea, Russian SFSR, rises in Crimean Mts. W of Alushta, flows c.45 mi. WNW and W to Black Sea 16 mi. N of Sevastopol. Along lower course, allied Fr. and Turkish troops in Crimean War defeated (Sept., 1854) Russians.

Almasfüzitö (ŏl'mäsh-füzĭtŭ), Hung. *Almásfüzitő*, suburb (pop. 597) of Szöny, Komarom-Esztergom co., N Hungary; starch; oil refinery.

Almaskamaras (ŏl'mäsh-kŏmŏräsh), Hung. *Almáskamarás*, town (pop. 2,465), Csanad co., SE Hungary, 16 mi. S of Bekescsaba; grain, onions; cattle.

Almatret (älmätrĕt'), village (pop. 1,110), Lérida prov., NE Spain, 24 mi. SW of Lérida; almond shipping, olive-oil processing, sheep raising. Lignite deposits near by.

Almaville (ăl'mŭvĭl), village (pop. 2,282), S Que., on St. Maurice R., opposite Shawinigan Falls, in dairying, cattle- and pig-raising region.

Almazán (älmä-thän'), town (pop. 3,197), Soria prov., N central Spain, in Old Castile, on Duero (Douro) R. (crossed by fine bridge), on railroad and 20 mi. S of Soria, in fertile agr. region (cereals, sugar beets, livestock); apiculture. Lumbering, flour milling, tanning, woolen milling. Airfield, hydroelectric plant. Has Romanesque San Miguel church and palace of the counts of Altamira; and remains of old wall. Severely damaged (1810) by French during Peninsular War.

Almaznaya (ŭlmäz'nīŭ), town (1926 pop. 2,971), SW Voroshilovgrad oblast, Ukrainian SSR, in the Donbas, 4 mi. SW of Kadiyevka; metallurgical works.

Almazora (älmäthō'rä), town (pop. 7,804), Castellón de la Plana prov., E Spain, in Valencia, on Mijares R. and 3 mi. S of Castellón de la Plana; hardware mfg., liqueur distilling, flour- and sawmilling; agr. trade (citrus and other fruit, peppers, flax); sericulture. Founded by Moors; liberated in 1234 by James I of Aragon.

Almedina (älmä-dhē'nä), town (pop. 1,465), Ciudad Real prov., S central Spain, 25 mi. ESE of Valdepeñas; cereals, grapes, olives, potatoes, livestock; liquor distilling, olive-oil pressing.

Almedinilla (älmä-dhēnē'lyä), town (pop. 1,821), Córdoba prov., S Spain, 18 mi. SE of Baena; olive-oil processing, flour- and sawmilling; cereals, fruit, lumber, livestock.

Almeida (älmā'dŭ), town (pop. 1,401), Guarda dist., N central Portugal, near Sp. border, 25 mi. NE of Guarda; agr. processing (olive oil, cheese). Strongly fortified in 18th cent., it was scene of a battle in Peninsular War (1810–11).

Almeida (älmā'dhä), village (pop. 1,382), Zamora prov., NW Spain, 24 mi. SW of Zamora; cork processing, brandy distilling, blanket mfg.; cereals, potatoes, vegetables. Mineral springs.

Almeirim (älmā'rēn), city (pop. 119), central Pará, Brazil, on left bank of the Amazon and 160 mi. ENE of Santarém.

Almeirim, town (pop. 6,704), Santarém dist., central Portugal, 4 mi. SE of Santarém; center of fruit- and winegrowing region; olive-oil and cheese mfg., distilling, textile milling. Several Cortes were held here.

Almelo (äl'mŭlō), town (pop. 40,118), Overijssel prov., E Netherlands, at junction of Overijssel Canal and Almelo-Nordhorn Canal, 9 mi. NW of Hengelo; rail junction; textile center (spinning, weaving, dyeing); dry-cleaning industry; mfg. of engines, trucks, mattresses, furniture; meat packing. Huis te Almelo castle (E). Sometimes spelled Almeloo.

Almelo-Nordhorn Canal (–nôrt'hôrn), Overijssel prov., E Netherlands, runs 21 mi. E–W, bet. Almelo (here joining Overijssel Canal) and Nordhorn (Germany); 17 mi. are in the Netherlands. Netherlands part opened 1889, Ger. part 1904.

Almena (ălmē'nŭ). **1** City (pop. 616), Norton co., NW Kansas, on Prairie Dog Creek and 10 mi. ENE of Norton; grain, livestock, poultry; silica mines. **2** Village (pop. 406), Barron co., NW Wis., 16 mi. WSW of Rice Lake; dairy products.

Almenar (älmānär'). **1** Town (pop. 2,827), Lérida prov., NE Spain, 13 mi. NNW of Lérida, in irrigated agr. area (cereals, wine, olive oil, linen, hemp); sawmilling. **2** or **Almenar de Soria** (dhā sō'ryä), town (pop. 714), Soria prov., N central Spain, 15 mi. ESE of Soria; cereals, sheep, cattle.

Almenara (älmĭnä'rŭ), city (pop. 2,603), NE Minas Gerais, Brazil, on left bank of navigable Jequitinhonha R., near Bahia border, and 120 mi. NNE of Teófilo Otoni; semiprecious stones. Until 1944, called Vigia.

Almenara (älmänä'rä), town (pop. 2,100), Castellón de la Plana prov., E Spain, 6 mi. NNE of Sagunto; rice mill; cereals, oranges, olive oil, flax; sericulture. Has some ruins of Roman temple and remains of Moorish castle. Here James I of Aragon routed (1238) the Moors, and Charles V's troops defeated (1521) the *communeros* of Valencia.

Almendares River (älmĕndä'rĕs), Havana prov., W Cuba, rises E of Tapaste, flows 27 mi. W and N to the Gulf of Mexico 3½ mi. W of Havana Harbor. Serves as water supply for Havana. Cascades (Husillo) along its course.

Almendra (älmān'drŭ), village (pop. 1,526), Guarda dist., N central Portugal, near the Douro, 35 mi. NNE of Guarda; grows wine (port), olives, figs, almonds, oranges.

Almendral (älmĕndräl'). **1** Suburb (pop. 1,391) of San Felipe, Aconcagua prov., central Chile. **2** SE suburb of VALPARAISO, Valparaiso prov., Chile.

Almendral, town (pop. 3,253), Badajoz prov., W Spain, 20 mi. SSE of Badajoz; olive-oil pressing, flour milling, lumbering; cork.

Almendral de la Cañada (dhā lä känyä'dhä), town (pop. 940), Toledo prov., central Spain, in S spur of the Sierra de Gredos, 14 mi. NNE of Talavera de La Reina; grapes, figs, olives, livestock. Flour milling, olive-oil pressing.

Almendralejo (älmĕndrälā'hō), city (pop. 21,071), Badajoz prov., W Spain, 16 mi. S of Mérida; center of the fertile Tierra de Barros (cereals, grapes, olives, saffron, livestock); alcohol and liquor distilling, wine making, flour milling, olive-oil extracting, meat packing; mfg. of ceramics, meat products, barrels, soap, sweets. Noted for its collection of antiquities housed in the mansion of the marquis of Monsalud.

Almendro (älmĕn'drō), town (pop. 1,072), O'Higgins prov., S central Chile, on railroad, just NE of Coltauco.

Almendro, El (ĕl), town (pop. 843), Huelva prov., SW Spain, 25 mi. NW of Huelva; grain, stock.

Almendros (älmĕn'drōs), town (pop. 1,156), Cuenca prov., central Spain, 9 mi. SE of Tarancón; grain, olives, grapes, livestock.

Almenêches (älmŭnĕsh'), village (pop. 327), Orne dept., NW France, 7 mi. SE of Argentan; horse raising. Has Renaissance church (part of former Benedictine abbey).

Almenevo or **Al'menevo** (ŭlmyĕ'nyĭvŭ), village (1926 pop. 1,853), SW Kurgan oblast, Russian SFSR, 20 mi. SSE of Shumikha; cattle raising.

Almenno San Salvatore (älmĕn'nô sän sälvätô'rĕ), village (pop. 2,212), Bergamo prov., Lombardy, N Italy, near Brembo R., 5 mi. NW of Bergamo; cement making. Has 12th-cent. church.

Almensilla (älmĕnsē'lyä), town (pop. 1,274), Seville prov., SW Spain, 9 mi. SW of Seville; olives, cereals, grapes, timber; limekilns.

Almería (älmārē'ä), province (□ 3,388; pop. 359,730), S Spain, in Andalusia; ⊙ Almería. Bounded (S, SE) by the Mediterranean; mostly mountainous, crossed by several irregular ranges separated by fertile valleys; drained by Almanzora R. E coast high and rocky to Cape Gata; S coast forms Gulf of Almería. Has hot climate with little rainfall. An important mineral region with iron, silver-bearing lead, sulphur, zinc, and gold mines, and minor copper, magnesite, and platinum mines. Deposits are in Filabres, Almagrera, Alhamilla, Gádor, and Gata ranges, and in E spurs of Sierra Nevada. Marble, gypsum, and stone quarries; mineral springs. Stock raising (mainly sheep) and fishing. Chief agr. products: esparto (Almería is leading Sp. producer), fruit (especially white grapes), olives, cereals, sugar cane, vegetables, potatoes, and wine. Minerals, esparto, and white grapes are exported from ports of Almería, Adra, Garrucha. Has few industries, almost all derived from agr.: esparto and olive-oil processing, sugar and flour milling, fruit canning; some iron foundries and sulphur refineries. Almería is prov.'s only large city; other centers are Berja, Adra, Vélez Rubio, Huércal-Overa.

Almería, city (pop. 69,824), ⊙ Almería prov., S Spain, in Andalusia, seaport on Gulf of Almería on the Mediterranean, 260 mi. SSE of Madrid; 36°50'N 2°30'W. Harbor is safe (breakwaters) and deep enough to accommodate large vessels; has 2 ore-shipping piers at terminus of mining railroad from Sierra Alhamilla; exports iron, lead, silver, sulphur, esparto, and its noted white grapes. Seismological and wireless station. Oil and sulphur refineries, tanneries. Mfg. of shoes, furniture, cement, tiles, felt hats, canvas, flour products; esparto processing, fruit canning. City extends bet. sea and hills to W, on which rise ruins of San Cristóbal castle and of Moorish fort (*alcazaba*) with towers. Narrow, tortuous streets and white houses give it an Oriental aspect. Pleasant climate in winter, very hot in summer. Has 16th-cent. Gothic cathedral, church of Santiago with 16th-cent. tower, episcopal palace, and seminary. Occupied by Carthaginians and Romans; prospered under Moors (8th–15th cent.) as important trade center and for a time as capital of petty independent kingdom and stronghold of powerful pirates; liberated (1489) by the Catholic Kings. In 1937, during the civil war, city was shelled by German warships and seriously damaged.

Almesbury, England: see AMESBURY.

Almet'yevo or **Al'met'yevo** (ŭlmä'tyĭvŭ), village (1926 pop. 2,778), SE Tatar Autonomous SSR, Russian SFSR, on Stepnoi Zai R. and 32 mi. NNW of Bugulma; grain, livestock.

Almhult (ĕlm'hŭlt"), Swedish *Älmhult*, town (pop. 3,128), Kronoberg co., S Sweden, at S end of L. Mockel, 35 mi. N of Kristianstad; rail junction; stone quarrying, woodworking; mfg. of glass, furniture. Tourist resort.

Almina, Punta (pōōn'tä älmē'nä), headland of NW Africa, just E of Ceuta (Sp. possession), marking E limit of Strait of Gibraltar; 35°54'N 5°17'W; lighthouse. It forms extremity of a peninsula (c.2 mi. long) extending E from Ceuta harbor; rises to 636 ft. at Mt. Acho.

Almino Afonso (älmē'nōō äfō'sōō), town (pop. 712), SW Rio Grande do Norte, NE Brazil, near Paraíba border, 70 mi. SSW of Mossoró; terminus (1949) of rail line from Mossoró to be extended to Souza (Paraíba).

Almira (ălmī'rŭ), town (pop. 395), Lincoln co., E central Wash., 20 mi. S of Grand Coulee Dam, in Columbia basin agr. region; ships wheat.

Almirantazgo, Seno del, Chile: see ADMIRALTY SOUND.

Almirante (älmērän'tā), town (pop. 1,566), Bocas del Toro prov., W Panama, in Caribbean lowland, railhead and port on Almirante Bay of Caribbean Sea, 10 mi. WSW of Bocas del Toro. Abacá and cacao center. Major banana-shipping port until abandonment in 1929 of Sixaola and Changuinola R. plantations.

Almirante Brown, Argentina: see ADROGUÉ.

Almirante Montt Gulf (mōnt'), inlet of the Pacific in Magallanes prov., S Chile, N of Muñoz Gamero Peninsula; 20 mi. long, c.8 mi. wide. Puerto Natales is on its NE shore.

Almirón Island (älmērōn'), in Uruguay R., Paysandú dept., NW Uruguay, 4 mi. WSW of Paysandú, 1 mi. offshore; 4 mi. long, ½ mi. wide; 32°23'S 58°11'W.

Almiros, town, Greece: see HALMYROS.

Almiros, Gulf of, Crete: see ALMYROS, GULF OF.

Almissa, Yugoslavia: see OMIS.

Almkerk (älm'kĕrk), village (pop. 694), North Brabant prov., W central Netherlands, 4 mi. S of Gorinchem; cattle raising, agr.

Almoçageme (älmōōsäzhā'mĭ), village (pop. 1,100), Lisboa dist., central Portugal, near Atlantic coast at Cape Roca, 20 mi. W of Lisbon; winegrowing. Beaches and rocky shoreline attract tourists and painters.

Almodôvar (älmōōdō'vŭr), town (pop. 2,836), Beja dist., S Portugal, 35 mi. SSW of Beja; grain milling, cheese mfg., leatherworking.

Almodóvar del Campo (älmō-dhō'vär dhĕl käm'pō), city (pop. 8,488), Ciudad Real prov., S central Spain, in New Castile, on railroad and 23 mi. SW of Ciudad Real; stock-raising and agr. center in fertile valley (tubers, chick-peas, cereals, olives, grapes, forage). Lead mining, basalt and lime quarrying. Among processing industries are liquor and alcohol distilling, wine making, cheese processing, meat packing. Has ruins of fort (built 745). Was a cultural center during Middle Ages. Juan de Ávila b. here.

Almodóvar del Pinar (pēnär'), town (pop. 1,048), Cuenca prov., E central Spain, 27 mi. SSE of Cuenca; cereals, resins, livestock; apiculture.

Almodóvar del Río (rē'ō), town (pop. 4,358), Córdoba prov., S Spain, on the Guadalquivir and 16 mi. WSW of Córdoba; agr. trade center (cereals, cork, honey, livestock). Olive-oil processing, sawmilling. Has Moorish castle fortified by Peter the Cruel to hold his treasury.

Almogía (älmōhē'ä), town (pop. 2,275), Málaga prov., S Spain, on small Campanillas R. and 9 mi. NNW of Málaga, in agr. region (almonds, figs, olives, cereals); flour milling, olive-oil pressing, straw-hat making, plaster mfg.

Almoguera (älmōgā'rä), town (pop. 1,374), Guadalajara prov., central Spain, near the Tagus, 37 mi. ESE of Madrid; cereals, vegetables, grapes.

Almohaja (älmōä'hä), village (pop. 201), Teruel prov., E Spain, 25 mi. NW of Teruel. Extensive iron mines near by.

Almoharín (älmōärēn'), town (pop. 3,923), Cáceres prov., W Spain, 21 mi. SW of Trujillo; olive-oil processing, ceramics and wax mfg. Cereals, livestock in area.

Almoines (älmoi'nĕs), village (pop. 1,604), Valencia prov., E Spain, 2 mi. S of Gandía; fruitgrowing (oranges, apricots, peaches); silk spinning.

Almolda, La (lä älmōl'dä), town (pop. 1,047), Saragossa prov., NE Spain, 36 mi. ESE of Saragossa; sheep raising; cereals.

Almolonga (älmōlōng'gä), town (1950 pop. 3,183), Quezaltenango dept., SW Guatemala, 2 mi. SE of Quezaltenango, at NE foot of Cerro Quemado; alt. 6,808 ft. Truck produce, grain.

Almoloya (älmōloi'ä). **1** Town (pop. 1,327), Hidalgo, central Mexico, 38 mi. SE of Pachuca, on railroad; maguey. **2** Officially Almoloya de Alquisiras, town (pop. 1,798), Mexico state, central Mexico, 31 mi. SSW of Toluca; coffee, sugar, fruit. **3** Officially Almoloya de Juárez, town (pop. 696), Mexico state, central Mexico, 31 mi. SW of Mexico city; grain, livestock. **4** Officially Almoloya del Río, town (pop. 2,702), Mexico state, central Mexico, 13 mi. SE of Toluca; agr. center (cereals, vegetables, livestock); dairying.

Almonacid de la Sierra (älmōnä-thēdh' dhā lä syĕ'rä), town (pop. 1,674), Saragossa prov., NE Spain, 17 mi. ENE of Calatayud, in winegrowing dist.; mfg. (alcohol, tartaric acid); trades in livestock, cereals, olive oil.

Almonacid del Marquesado (dhĕl märkäsä'dhō), town (pop. 1,059), Cuenca prov., E central Spain, 38 mi. WSW of Cuenca; cereals, grapes.

Almonacid de Toledo (dhā tōlā'dhō), town (pop. 1,591), Toledo prov., central Spain, 11 mi. SE of Toledo; cereals, grapes, olives, sheep; processing of cheese and meat products. Site of Sp. defeat (Aug., 1809) during Peninsular War.

Almonacid de Zorita (thōrē'tä), town (pop. 1,272), Guadalajara prov., central Spain, near the Tagus, 28 mi. SE of Guadalajara, in fertile agr. region (cereals, grapes, olives, hemp, sugar beets, anise, potatoes, beans, truck, livestock); olive-oil pressing.

Almonaster la Real (älmōnästär' lä rääl'), town (pop. 865), Huelva prov., SW Spain, in the Sierra de Aracena, 12 mi. W of Aracena; copper mining. Cork, chestnuts, hogs. Has mineral springs.

Almond. **1** (ä'mŭnd) Village (pop. 659), on Allegany-Steuben co. line, W N.Y., 5 mi. W of Hornell, in agr. area. **2** (ăl'mŏnd) Village (pop. 435), Portage co., central Wis., 19 mi. SSE of Stevens Point, in dairy and farm area.

Almondbank (ä'mŭndbăngk″), village, SE Perthshire, Scotland, on Almond R. and 6 mi. W of Perth; textile bleaching.

Almondbury, England: see HUDDERSFIELD.

Almond River (ä'mŭnd). **1** In Lanark, West Lothian, and Midlothian, Scotland, rises near Kirk of Shotts, flows 24 mi. E, past Mid Calder, to the Firth of Forth at Cramond. **2** In Perthshire, Scotland, rises 8 mi. E of Killing, flows 30 mi. E, through the GLENALMOND, to the Tay 2 mi. N of Perth.

Almondsbury (ä'mŭnzbŭrē), town and parish (pop. 2,795), SW Gloucester, England, 7 mi. N of Bristol; agr. market; brickworks. Has 14th-cent. church. Site of Roman defenses.

Almont (ăl'mŏnt″). **1** Hamlet, Gunnison co., W central Colo., in Rocky Mts., 9 mi. NNE of Gunnison, at head of Gunnison R.; alt. 8,000 ft. Fishing resort. **2** Village (pop. 1,035), Lapeer co., E Mich., 16 mi. SE of Lapeer, in farm area (fruit, grain, dairy products); mfg. of auto parts, locks. Inc. 1855. **3** Village (pop. 190), Morton co., S central N.Dak., 35 mi. WSW of Bismarck and on Muddy Creek.

Almonte (ăl'mŏnt), town (pop. 2,543), SE Ont., on Mississippi R. and 26 mi. WSW of Ottawa; woolen, flannel, tweed milling; dairying; woodworking; mfg. of soap, agr. implements, castings.

Almonte (älmōn'tä), town (pop. 8,516), Huelva prov., SW Spain, in Andalusia, 24 mi. E of Huelva; agr. center (cereals, grapes, olives, stock); wine making, alcohol distilling, flour- and sawmilling, dairying. Limekilns. Shrine to the Virgin near by.

Almonte River, Cáceres prov., W Spain, rises on N slopes of the Sierra de Guadalupe, flows 75 mi. WNW to the Tagus 4 mi. E of Garrovillas.

Almopia (älmôpē'ä), region of Greek Macedonia, near Yugoslav border, bet. Voras and Paikon massifs. Chief town, Ardea.

Almora (ălmō'rŭ, ŭlmō'rŭ), district (□ 5,502; pop. 687,286), Kumaun div., N Uttar Pradesh, India; ⊙ Almora. In E Kumaun Himalayas (rising to 25,645 ft. in Nanda Devi; N); bounded E by Nepal and Kali (Sarda) R., N by Tibet (border undefined). Agr. (rice, wheat, barley, corn, buckwheat, fruits) mainly along tributaries of the Kali; tea, extensive sal jungles in Kumaun Himalayas (copper deposits). Main towns: Almora, Ranikhet, Pithoragarh. Important trade route to Gartok (Tibet) through Anta Dhura pass.

Almora, town (pop. 10,995), ⊙ Almora dist., N Uttar Pradesh, India, 160 mi. ENE of Delhi, in E Kumaun Himalaya foothills (alt. c.5,500 ft.); road terminus; mfg. of copper utensils; trades in rice, wheat, barley, corn. Was ⊙ Chand Rajputs in 16th cent.; captured 1744 by Rohillas. During Gurkha War, decisive Gurkha defeat (1815) by British at Sitoli (just N).

Almoradí (älmōrä-dhē'), town (pop. 3,648), Alicante prov., E Spain, in fertile truck-farming area near the Segura, 12 mi. SW of Elche; canning (fruit and vegetables), olive-oil processing, mfg. of chemical fertilizers. Produces also hemp, rice, and wine; ships oranges, pepper. Gypsum and stone quarries.

Almorchón (älmōrchōn'), village (pop. 659), Badajoz prov., W Spain, 14 mi. E of Castuera; rail junction on Madrid-Badajoz RR, which here branches off to Córdoba. Has ruins of old castle.

Almorox (älmōrōks'), town (pop. 2,624), Toledo prov., central Spain, on S slopes of the Sierra de Gredos, rail terminus 31 mi. NW of Toledo; cereals, grapes, figs, pine cones, livestock. Olive-oil pressing, liquor distilling. Has 16th-cent. church with fine plateresque portal.

Almosd (äl'môzhd), Hung. *Álmosd*, agr. town (pop. 2,425), Bihar co., E Hungary, 17 mi. ESE of Debrecen. Ferencz Kazinczy b. here.

Almudébar (älmōō-dhā'vär), town (pop. 2,954), Huesca prov., NE Spain, 11 mi. SW of Huesca, in irrigated agr. area (cereals, wine, sugar beets); flour milling, sheep raising.

Almuñécar (älmōōnyā'kär), city (pop. 5,258), Granada prov., S Spain, on islet in delta of small Verde R., on the Mediterranean, and 10 mi. W of Motril; fishing and boat building; alcohol distilling, sugar refining. Cereals, wine, olive oil, sugar cane, and fruit in area. Bathing beach. Has ruined Moorish castle.

Almunia de Doña Godina, La (lä älmōō'nyä dhā dō'nyä gō-dhē'nä), town (pop. 3,461), Saragossa prov., NE Spain, in Jalón R. valley, 28 mi. SW of Saragossa; olive-oil processing, brandy distilling; sheep raising; agr. trade (wine, fruit, cereals).

Almunia de San Juan, La (sän'hwän'), town (pop. 1,033), Huesca prov., NE Spain, on Aragon and Catalonia Canal and 9 mi. SE of Barbastro, in agr. area (sugar beets, wine, cereals); olive-oil processing; sheep raising.

Almuradiel (älmōōrä-dhyĕl'), town (pop. 1,255), Ciudad Real prov., S central Spain, on railroad and highway to Granada, and 18 mi. SSW of Valdepeñas; cereals, grapes, olives, livestock.

Almusafes (älmōōsä'fĕs), town (pop. 3,034), Valencia prov., E Spain, in irrigated area 13 mi. S of Valencia; rice-growing center. Olive-oil processing, flour milling; cattle raising; sericulture.

Almyra (ălmī'rŭ), town (pop. 235), Arkansas co., E central Ark., 10 mi. SE of Stuttgart, in agr. area.

Almyros, town, Greece: see HALMYROS.

Almyros, Gulf of, or **Gulf of Almiros** (both: älmērôs'), broad inlet of Aegean Sea on N coast of central Crete, 10 mi. wide, 5 mi. long. Rethymnon is on S shore.

Aln, river, England: see ALN RIVER.

Alna (ôl'nŭ), town (pop. 350), Lincoln co., S Maine, on Sheepscot R. and 16 mi. NE of Bath. Meetinghouse, here, built 1789. Includes Head Tide village.

Alnashi (ŭlnŭshē'), village (1948 pop. over 2,000), S Udmurt Autonomous SSR, Russian SFSR, 21 mi. SE of Mozhga; wheat, rye, oats, livestock.

Alne, Sweden: see JARVED.

Alne River (ôn, ôln), Warwick, England, rises c.10 mi. S of Birmingham, flows 15 mi. S and SW, past Henley-in-Arden, to Arrow R. at Alcester.

Alness (ăl'nĕs), agr. village and parish (pop. 849), E Ross and Cromarty, Scotland, on Alness R. (16 mi. long), near its mouth on Cromarty Firth, 3 mi. W of Invergordon.

Alney Island (ôl'nē), N central Gloucester, England, in Severn R., just WNW of Gloucester; 2 mi. long.

Alnmouth (ăl'mouth, ăln'–), town and parish (pop. 631), E Northumberland, England, on North Sea at mouth of Aln R., 4 mi. ESE of Alnwick; small seaport and resort.

Alno, Swedish *Alnön* (äl'nûn″), island (□ 25; pop. 5,496) in Gulf of Bothnia, E Sweden, 3 mi. E of Sundsvall, across narrow channel; 7 mi. long, 3 mi. wide. Vii (W) is largest village. Lumber and pulp milling, brick mfg. Has 13th-cent. parish church.

Aln River (ăln), Northumberland, England, rises in several branches in the Cheviot Hills 12 mi. W of Alnwick, flows 16 mi. E, past Alnwick, to North Sea at Alnmouth.

Alnwick (ă'nĭk), urban district (1931 pop. 6,883; 1951 census 7,366), E Northumberland, England, on Aln R. and 30 mi. N of Newcastle-upon-Tyne; agr. market, with agr.-machinery works. Site of Alnwick Castle, belonging to the dukes of Northumberland, and remains of 13th-cent. Hulne Priory. Has 15th-cent. church, Hotspur Tower (1450), and 14th-cent. remains of Alnwick Abbey. Town hall was built 1771.

Alofi (älō'fē), uninhabited volcanic island, HOORN ISLANDS, SW Pacific, 5 mi. SE of Futuna; 6 mi. long, 3 mi. wide; rises to 1,200 ft. Timber; coconuts.

Aloha (ŭlō'ŭ, –hŭ), village (1940 pop. 712), Washington co., NW Oregon, 10 mi. W of Portland in dairying and agr. area (fruit, truck).

Alon (ă'lōn'; Burmese ŭlōn'), village, Lower Chindwin dist., Upper Burma, on left bank of Chindwin R., 6 mi. NNW of Monywa, on railroad to Yeu. Depot for timber rafts.

Along Bay (ä'lông'), Fr. *Baie d'Along*, N Vietnam, arm of Gulf of Tonkin bet. mainland of Quangyen prov. and Catba Isl.; c.20 mi. long, 5–10 mi. wide. Strewn with thousands of limestone rocks and islets, scrub covered, forming grottoes and known for their beauty. Also spelled Allong, Halong, or Dalong.

Alonim or **Allonim** (älōnēm'), settlement (pop. 506), NW Israel, at NW end of Plain of Jezreel, 10 mi. SE of Haifa; flute mfg.; dairying, fruitgrowing. Site of teachers' seminary and of youth reception center. Founded 1938.

Alonnisos, Greece: see HALONNESOS.

Alonso de Ibáñez, Bolivia: see SACACA.

Alor (ă'lôr, ä'–) or **Ombai** (ōmbī'), largest island (□ 810; pop. 68,029) of Alor Isls., Lesser Sundas, Indonesia, 15 mi. N of Timor across Ombai Strait; 55 mi. long, 20 mi. wide. Mountainous, rising to 5,791 ft. On W coast is chief town and port of Kalabahi (käläbä'hē), exporting copra. Fishing, agr. (corn, cotton, rice, coconuts).

Alor, W Pakistan: see AROR.

Álora (ä'lōrä), city (pop. 5,614), Málaga prov., S Spain, on Guadalhorce R. (irrigation) and 17 mi. WNW of Málaga (linked by rail). Resort picturesquely situated in E outliers of the Sierra de Ronda; center of fruitgrowing region (oranges, lemons, almonds, pomegranates, olives). Liquor distilling, flour milling; mfg. of food preserves, olive oil, soap, straw hats. Cement factory near by. Has ruined castle. The El Chorro gorge (c.10 mi. long, 200 ft. high) and hydroelectric works are near by, 3 mi. N.

Alor Gajah (ä'lôr gä'jä), town (pop. 1,446), Settlement of Malacca, SW Malaya, on railroad and 13 mi. N of Malacca; rice, rubber.

Alor Islands (ă'lôr, ä'–), group (□ 1,126; pop. 90,616), Lesser Sundas, Indonesia, in Flores Sea, 15 mi. N of Timor across Ombai Strait; 8°17'S 124°46'E. Consist of 2 isls. (ALOR and PANTAR) surrounded by several small isls. Fishing, agr. (corn, cotton, coconuts).

Alor Pongsu (ä'lôr pōng'sōō), village (pop. 403), NW Perak, Malaya, on railroad and 16 mi. NW of Taiping, in Krian rice dist.

Alor Star (ä'lôr stär'), town (pop. 32,424), ⊙ Kedah, NW Malaya, on Kedah R., 6 mi. from Strait of Malacca, and 50 mi. N of George Town, on railroad; residence of sultan and Br. adviser; major rice-trading center. Has noted mosque. Airport at Kepala Batas, 6 mi. NNE.

Alorton (ŭlôr'tŭn), village (pop. 2,547), St. Clair co., SW Ill., SE of East St. Louis, within St. Louis metropolitan dist. Inc. 1944. Formerly Alcoa.

Alosno (älō'snō), town (pop. 2,439), Huelva prov., SW Spain, 22 mi. NNW of Huelva, in agr. region (cereals, vegetables, fruit, stock); mining (copper, manganese, iron-copper pyrite).

Alost (älôst'), Flemish *Aalst* (älst), town (pop. 42,193), East Flanders prov., N central Belgium, on Dender R. and 15 mi. WNW of Brussels; textile center (cotton and linen weaving, silk lingerie); shoes, leather goods, matches; market for poultry, hops, oil seed. Electric-power station. Has church of St. Martin and town hall (both 15th cent.)

Alot (ŭlōt'), town (pop. 5,678), W central Madhya Bharat, India, 45 mi. NNW of Ujjain; millet, wheat, cotton; sugar milling, cotton ginning. Sometimes spelled Alote.

Alotenango (älōtänäng'gō), town (pop. 2,811), Sacatepéquez dept., S central Guatemala, on Guacalate R., bet. Fuego (W) and Agua (E) volcanoes, and 8 mi. SSW of Antigua; alt. 4,514 ft. Coffee, sugar cane. The Fuego may be ascended from here.

Alouette Lake (ălōōĕt') (11 mi. long, 1 mi. wide), SW B.C., 27 mi. E of Vancouver. Drained SW by Alouette R. (15 mi. long; hydroelectric power) into Pitt R.

Aloxe-Corton (älôks-kôrtō'), village (pop. 230), Côte-d'Or dept., E central France, on E slope of the Côte d'Or, 3 mi. N of Beaune; Burgundy wines.

Alozaina (älō-thäē'nä), town (pop. 2,781), Málaga prov., S Spain, in W spur of the Cordillera Penibética, 25 mi. W of Málaga, in fruitgrowing and agr. region (olives, figs, oranges, grapes, chick-peas, wheat, livestock); olive-oil pressing, flour milling, liquor distilling.

Alpachiri (älpächē'rē), town (pop. estimate 1,000), E La Pampa natl. territory, Argentina, on railroad and 60 mi. SSE of Santa Rosa; wheat, rye, alfalfa, corn, livestock.

Alpalhão (älpŭlyä'ō), village (pop. 2,784), Portalegre dist., central Portugal, 13 mi. NW of Portalegre; road junction; produces noted cheese; ships cork, olive oil, wine.

Alpandeire (älpändä'rā), town (pop. 915), Málaga prov., S Spain, on SE slope of the Sierra de Ronda, 7 mi. S of Ronda; olives, cereals, cork, grapes, figs, livestock; liquor distilling, olive-oil extracting, flour milling. Has idle coal and platinum mines. Crypt of its parochial church contains mummies.

Alpar (ŏl'pär), Hung. *Alpár*, town (pop. 4,866), Pest-Pilis-Solt-Kiskun co., S central Hungary, on the Tisza and 15 mi. ESE of Kecskemet; corn, wheat; horses, hogs.

Alpargatal, Dominican Republic: see VICENTE NOBLE.

Alpatlahua (älpätlä'wä), town (pop. 948), Veracruz, E Mexico, at NE foot of the Pico de Orizaba, 8 mi. WSW of Huatusco; fruit.

Alpbach (älp'bäkh), village (pop. 1,414), Tyrol, W Austria, 17 mi. SW of Kufstein; cattle, sheep.

Alpe d'Huez, L', France: see HUEZ.

Alpe di Succiso (äl'pĕ dē sōōt-chē'zō), peak (6,617 ft.) in Etruscan Apennines, N central Italy, 16 mi. ESE of Pontremoli. Source of Secchia R.

Alpedrete (älpādrā'tā), town (pop. 592), Madrid prov., central Spain, on E slopes of the Sierra de Guadarrama, on railroad and 25 mi. NW of Madrid; grain, cattle, sheep; granite quarrying.

Alpedrinha (älpĭdrē'nyü) anc. *Petratinia*, village (pop. 1,493), Castelo Branco dist., central Portugal, on railroad and 19 mi. N of Castelo Branco at E foot of Serra da Guardunha; surrounded by orchards, olive groves, and pinewoods. Has Roman remains.

Alpena (ăl pē'nü), county (□ 568; pop. 22,189), NE Mich.; ⊙ Alpena. Bounded E by L. Huron; drained by Thunder Bay R. and its affluents. Dairy and farm area (livestock, potatoes, grain, raspberries). Mfg. at Alpena. Limestone quarries, fisheries; timber. Summer and winter resort. Includes a state forest and a hunting area. Long L. is NE. Organized 1857.

Alpena. 1 or **Alpena Pass,** town (pop. 304), Boone co., N Ark., 11 mi. WNW of Harrison, in the Ozarks. **2** City (pop. 13,135), ⊙ Alpena co., NE Mich., at mouth of Thunder Bay R. on Thunder Bay of L. Huron, and c.105 mi. NNE of Bay City. Mfg. of paper, cement, machinery, leather, textiles, clothing, dairy products, flour, beverages; meat packing. Limestone quarries, fisheries; timber. Agr. (fruit, potatoes). Resort for summer and winter sports. Laid out 1856 as Fremont, renamed 1859; inc. as city 1871. **3** City (pop. 426), Jerauld co., SE central S.Dak., 15 mi. SW of Huron; dairy produce, livestock, poultry, grain.

Alpera (älpā'rä), town (pop. 2,924), Albacete prov., SE central Spain, 35 mi. E of Albacete; flour milling, alcohol distilling; cereals, saffron, wine, fruit; stock raising. Stone quarries. Stalagmite and stalactite caves. Reservoir (built by Moors) and dam near by.

Alperton, England: see WEMBLEY.

Alpes, Basses-, France: see BASSES-ALPES.

Alpes, Hautes-, France: see HAUTES-ALPES.

Alpes Mancelles (älp mäsĕl'), hills in Sarthe dept., W France, c.10 mi. SW of Alençon, crossed in a gorge by Sarthe R. Resort: Saint-Léonard-des-Bois.

Alpes-Maritimes (–märētēm'), southeasternmost department (□ 1,442—before 1947; pop. 448,973) of France; ⊙ Nice. Bounded by Italy (E) and by the Mediterranean (S). Surrounds principality of Monaco. Mountainous throughout, with Maritime Alps (E) and Provence Alps W of Var R. Other coastal streams: Loup, Paillon, Roya. Agr. restricted to narrow coastal belt (Fr. Riviera) where flowers for perfume mfg. (especially in Grasse area) and subtropical vegetation thrive thanks to unusually mild winter climate. Tourist industry is foremost along RIVIERA. Mfg.: perfumes and essences, olive oil, flour products; canning, distilling. Principal resorts are Nice, Cannes, Menton, Antibes, Juan-les-Pins, Villefranche, Beaulieu-sur-Mer. Dept. formed 1860 from county of Nice (then acquired by France) and Grasse dist., which was detached from Var dept. In Second World War Allies landed (Aug., 1944) W of Cannes. By Fr.-Ital. peace treaty of 1947, dept. acquired a frontier strip (□ 202; 1936 pop. 4,274), including villages of La Brigue, Tende, and Saint-Dalmas-de-Tende, thus moving frontier northward to follow crest of Maritime Alps.

Alpha (ăl'fü). **1** Village (pop. 630), Henry co., NW Ill., 16 mi. N of Galesburg, in agr. and bituminous-coal area. **2** Village (pop. 378), Iron co., SW Upper Peninsula, Mich., 13 mi. ESE of Iron River city, in dairy and poultry area. **3** Village (pop. 230), Jackson co., SW Minn., 6 mi. E of Jackson, near Iowa line, in agr. area; dairy products. **4** Borough (pop. 2,117), Warren co., W N.J., near Delaware R., 3 mi. SE of Phillipsburg; mfg. (radio and electronic equipment, textiles). Inc. 1911.

Alpharetta, town (pop. 917), Fulton co., NW central Ga., 22 mi. NNE of Atlanta; clothing mfg.

Alpheios River, Greece: see ALPHEUS RIVER.

Alphen or **Alfen** (äl'fün), agr. village (pop. 1,224), North Brabant prov., S Netherlands, 6 mi. SW of Tilburg.

Alphen aan den Rijn or **Alfen aan den Rijn** (än dün rīn'), town (pop. 15,763), South Holland prov., W Netherlands, on the Old Rhine and 7 mi. E of Leiden; rail junction; mfg. (asphalt, bricks, roofing tiles, ship's machinery, motors, washing machines, paper, leather products, jam, fruit juices and pulp); shipbuilding; dairying, truck gardening. Du. hq. during 1673 winter campaign against French.

Alpheus River (ălfē'üs), Gr. *Alpheios* or *Alfios* (both: älfēōs'), main stream of Peloponnesus, Greece, rises in the Taygetus, flows 69 mi. NW, past Olympia, to Gulf of Kyparissia 4 mi. S of Pyrgos. Receives Erymanthos and Ladon rivers. In Gr. mythology, it was supposed to flow partly underground and was used by Hercules to clean stables of Augeas. The Ladon and the lower Alpheus were formerly known as the Rouphia, Ruphia, or Roufias (rōōfēäs').

Alphington (ăl'fĭngtün), town and parish (pop. 1,280), E central Devon, England, 2 mi. S of Exeter; agr. market. Has 15th-cent. church.

Alphonse Island (ăl'fŏnz, älfōs'), outlying dependency (pop. 83) of the Seychelles, in Indian Ocean, 450 mi. NE of N tip of Madagascar and 250 mi. SW of Mahé Isl. (in the Seychelles proper); 7°1'S 52°45'E; 1½ mi. long, ½ mi. wide. Of coral origin. Copra; fisheries. The Alphonse group also includes Bijoutier and St. François isls.

Alphubel (älp'hōōbül), peak (13,809 ft.) in the Mischabelhörner of Valaisian Alps, S Switzerland, 6 mi. NE of Zermatt. Alphubeljoch, a pass (12,418 ft.), is SE of peak.

Alpiarça (älpyär'sü), town (pop. 6,254), Santarém dist., central Portugal, 6 mi. ENE of Santarém, in fertile fruit- and winegrowing area; distilling, olive-oil pressing, flour milling, cheese mfg.

Alpignano (älpēnyä'nō), village (pop. 2,522), Torino prov., Piedmont, NW Italy, on Dora Riparia R. and 8 mi. WNW of Turin; iron- and steelworks.

Alpilles, France: see ALPINES.

Alpine (ăl'pīn), county (□ 723; pop. 241), E Calif.; ⊙ Markleeville. Along crest of the Sierra Nevada S of L. Tahoe, mostly within El Dorado, Mono, and Stanislaus natl. forests; bounded NE by Nev. line. Includes Sonora Peak (11,429 ft.) and Stanislaus Peak (11,202 ft.). Mts. are crossed here by Kit Carson Pass and Ebbetts Pass (highways). Drained by Mokelumne R., a headstream of the Stanislaus, and by forks of Carson R. Hunting, fishing, camping; includes Alpine and Blue lakes, mineral springs. Little agr., chiefly hay; beef-cattle and sheep grazing. Some gold mining. Had silver boom from 1850s to 1870s; ruins of silver towns (Silver Mountain, Silver King, Monitor) remain. Formed 1864.

Alpine. 1 Borough (pop. 644), Bergen co., NE N.J., near Hudson R. (ferry to Yonkers), 3 mi. NE of Bergenfield. Includes part of Palisades Interstate Park. **2** Town (pop. 5,261), ⊙ Brewster co., extreme W Texas, in mts. N of Big Bend of the Rio Grande; alt. 4,481 ft. Railroad junction; shipping point for cattle, sheep; resort, with dude ranches and state parks near by. Big Bend Natl. Park is c.70 mi. S. Sul Ross State Teachers Col., with historical mus., is here. Founded 1882 with coming of railroad. **3** City (pop. 571), Utah co., N central Utah, 22 mi. S of Salt Lake City; farming.

Alpine, Lake, Alpine co., E Calif., in the Sierra Nevada, 20 mi. SW of Markleeville; c.1 mi. long. Lake Alpine (summer resort) is on its shore.

Alpine Lake, Marin co., W Calif.: see LAGUNITAS.

Alpine Peak, Utah: see DRAPER.

Alpines (äl'pēn') or **Apilles** (älpē'), isolated limestone range in Bouches-du-Rhône dept., SE France, extending c.15 mi. ESE-WNW bet. Salon and Tarascon, overlooking Crau lowland (S). Rises to 1,266 ft. Near its crest is ruined village of Les Baux. Saint-Rémy is on N slope. Bauxite deposits.

Alpirsbach (äl'pērsbäkh"), town (pop. 2,773), S Württemberg, Germany, after 1945 in Württemberg-Hohenzollern, in Black Forest, on the Kinzig and 8 mi. S of Freudenstadt; woodworking. Climatic health resort (alt. 1,427 ft.). Has remains of 11th-cent. Benedictine monastery, with rebuilt church.

Alplaus (ôl'plôs, ăl'–), village (1940 pop. 505), Schenectady co., E N.Y., on Mohawk R. and the Barge Canal, and 4 mi. N of Schenectady.

Alpnach (älp'näkh), commune (pop. 2,714), Obwalden half-canton, central Switzerland, near L. of Alpnach (a SW arm of L. of Lucerne). Includes villages of **Alpnach** or **Alpnach Dorf** (woodworking), 3 mi. N of Sarnen, and **Alpnach Stad** (N), rail and steamer station at foot of the Pilatus.

Alpoca (ălpō'kü), village (pop. 1,056, with adjacent Bud), Wyoming co., S W.Va., 14 mi. ENE of Welch, in coal-mining region.

Alportel, Portugal: see SÃO BRAZ DE ALPORTEL.

Alpoyeca (älpoiä'kä), town (pop. 604), Guerrero, SW Mexico, in Sierra Madre del Sur, 13 mi. N of Tlapa; cereals, fruit.

Alps, great mountain system of S central Europe, extending in a SW-NE arc (about 680 mi. long) from the Mediterranean coast of S France and NW Italy, along Fr.-Ital. border, across S and central Switzerland, along N frontier of Italy, through most of Austria and into S Germany (where it reaches its northernmost extension), E along Austro-Yugoslav border, and SE along Adriatic coast of Yugoslavia into Albania. The Alps thus form a great physiographic barrier separating the Po valley of N Italy from lowlands of France (W and NW), Germany (N), and Danubian plain (NE), covering c.80,000 sq. mi. Although some of the continent's highest peaks are found here (culminating in Mont Blanc, 15,781 ft.), the Alps are easily crossed at numerous low passes and do not present a climatic divide, although S slopes are milder because of Mediterranean influence. Geologically, the Alps are the result of extensive folding and overthrusting due to pressure exerted from S and SE. Uplift probably began in the Mesozoic and culminated in the Pleistocene epoch of the Cenozoic, exposing crystalline rock formations which constitute the central zone of high peaks. The lower ranges flanking the central zone are predominantly limestone formations. The Alpine uplift represents but one of a vast mtn. system extending SE to the Caucasus and the mts. of central Asia, NW to the Jura, SW to the Pyrenees, and S to the Atlas range of North Africa. Alpine waters drain, through 3 master streams rising here, to the North Sea (Rhine), to the W Mediterranean (Rhone), to the Adriatic (Po), and feed tributaries of the Danube which flows to the Black Sea. Due to the relatively low base level and to the sheerness of the glacier-shaped topography (horns, arêtes, cirques, U-shaped and hanging valleys), the region is remarkable for its magnificent scenery enhanced by many glaciers (Mer de Glace, Aletsch, Gorner, Pasterze) and lakes (Geneva, Thun, Lucerne, Brienz, Zürich, Maggiore, Lugano, Como, Iseo, Garda). Bet. the perpetual snow line (8–10,000 ft.) and valley bottoms, several vegetation zones are encountered. Characteristic Alpine flora (e.g., edelweiss) is found above timber line and in rocky mtn. crags. The sparse fauna includes chamois and marmots. Cattle and goat grazing and dairying are chief occupations in high Alps. Agr. is confined to valley floors, foothills, and milder S slopes on which wine and other Mediterranean crops are grown. Industry, until recently limited to skilled handicraft, is growing because of increased utilization of region's hydroelectric potential. Tourism is by far the chief source of income and has received added impetus from greater popularity of mountaineering and skiing. Among the numerous internationally known resorts are Chamonix (France); Zermatt, Interlaken, St. Moritz, Davos, Arosa (Switzerland); Sankt Anton, Innsbruck, Kitzbühel, Salzburg, Bad Gastein (Austria); Garmisch-Partenkirchen, Berchtesgaden (Germany); Cortina d'Ampezzo, Bolzano (Italy); and Bled (Yugoslavia). The Alps have been variously subdivided according to geological structure or geographical position. They have been arbitrarily divided into Western Alps (from the Mediterranean to Great St. Bernard Pass), Central Alps (in Switzerland, N Italy, S Germany, and W Austria to Brenner Pass and Inn valley beyond Innsbruck), and Eastern Alps (reaching the Danube at Vienna, and the Balkans in S Yugoslavia and Albania). The Western Alps comprise (S-N) the LIGURIAN ALPS (which link up with the Apennines at Cadibona Pass), the MARITIME ALPS, COTTIAN ALPS, GRAIAN ALPS, and MONT BLANC group (along Fr.-Ital. border); and the PROVENCE ALPS, DAUPHINÉ ALPS, and SAVOY ALPS (entirely in France). Highest peaks are the Mont Blanc, Barre des Écrins (13,461 ft.), and Gran Paradiso (13,323 ft.). Chief passes in Western Alps: TENDA PASS, MADDALENA PASS, MONTGENÈVRE PASS, MONT CENIS, and LITTLE SAINT BERNARD PASS. The Central Alps include in 2 parallel WSW-ENE groupings, a S section (PENNINE ALPS, LEPONTINE ALPS, RHAETIAN ALPS, ÖTZTAL ALPS) and a N section (BERNESE ALPS, Alps of the FOUR FOREST CANTONS, GLARUS ALPS, ALLGÄU ALPS, and BAVARIAN ALPS). Highest peaks, Dufourspitze in MONTE ROSA group (15,203 ft.), MATTERHORN (14,701 ft.), Finsteraarhorn (14,032 ft.), JUNGFRAU (13,653 ft.), Piz Bernina (13,304 ft.), and Monte Leone (11,683 ft.). Chief passes in Central Alps: GREAT SAINT BERNARD PASS, SIMPLON PASS, SAINT GOTTHARD PASS, MALOJA PASS, STELVIO PASS, SPLÜGEN PASS (Switzerland to Italy); LÖTSCHBERG PASS, GRIMSEL PASS, FURKA PASS (in Switzerland); and ARLBERG (W Austria). The Eastern Alps consist (W-E) of the ZILLERTAL ALPS, HOHE TAUERN, NIEDERE TAUERN and outliers which terminate (E) in the WIENER WALD; flanked (N) by the SALZBURG ALPS and the SALZKAMMERGUT dist., and (S) by the DOLOMITES, CARNIC ALPS (continued eastward by the KARAWANKEN), and NORIC ALPS. Also in the Eastern Alps, the JULIAN ALPS form a link bet. the Carnic Alps and the DINARIC ALPS (including the KARST) which form the long SE spur of the Alpine system. Highest peaks, GROSSGLOCKNER (12,460 ft.), Wildspitze (12,379 ft.), Marmolada (10,964 ft.), Hochkönig (9,639 ft.), Triglav (9,395 ft.), Kellerwand (9,219 ft.). Principal crossings in the Eastern Alps: BRENNER PASS, KATSCHBERG PASS, SEMMERING. Among Alpine peoples the word *Alp* or *Alm* designates not the summits or ranges, but the high pastures above timber line. The name *Alps* has been given to other ranges elsewhere in the world (e.g., Australian Alps, Japanese Alps).

Alpstein (älp'shtīn), mountain in the Alps, NE Switzerland. SÄNTIS, its highest peak, is SSW of Appenzell.

Alpujarras (älpōōhä'räs), a mountainous area of Andalusia, S Spain, in Granada and Almería provs., bet. the Sierra Nevada and the Mediterranean. Has deep valleys, woodlands, and pastures. Vineyards. Iron, lead, and quicksilver mines. Chief cities: Órjiva, Ugíjar. Noted for strong resistance of Moorish pop. after fall (1492) of Granada; completely subdued only in 1571.

Alpullu (älpōōlōō'), village (pop. 1,811), Kirklareli prov., Turkey in Europe, on railroad and 5 mi. SSE of Babaeski; sugar refinery. Formerly Alaplie.

Alpuyeca (älpōōyä'kä), town (pop. 1,357), Morelos, central Mexico, 13 mi. S of Cuernavaca; sugar, rice, coffee, fruit, vegetables.

Alqosh or **Alqush** (both: älkōōsh'), village, Mosul prov., N Iraq, 25 mi. N of Mosul; wheat, barley, fruits. A religious center of a Chaldean sect. Sometimes called Kosh.

Alquería de la Condesa (älkārē'ä dhä lä kōndä'sä), village (pop. 1,469), Valencia prov., E Spain, 3 mi. SE of Gandía; vegetables, fruit, mulberry trees.

Alquife (älkē'fä), town (pop. 1,219), Granada prov., S Spain, on slopes of the Sierra Nevada, 8 mi. S of Guadix; iron-mining center.

Alquízar (älkē'sär), town (pop. 6,360), Havana prov., W Cuba, on railroad and 27 mi. SSW of Havana; sugar cane, tomatoes, tobacco, potatoes, pineapples, vegetables. Charcoal burning, lumbering.

Alqush, Iraq: see ALQOSH.

Alresford, England: see NEW ALRESFORD.

Alright Island (ôl'–), (8 mi. long, 3 mi. wide), in Gulf of St. Lawrence, E Que., one of Magdalen Isls., 65 mi. NNE of Prince Edward Isl. House Harbour (SW) is chief settlement. Fisheries.

Alro (äl'rû), Dan. *Alrø*, island (□ 2.9; pop. 305), Denmark, at mouth of Horsens Fjord, off E Jutland; farming, fishing.

Als (äls), Ger. *Alsen* (äl'zûn), island (□ 121; pop. 34,294), in the Little Belt, Denmark; separated from Sundeved peninsula, S Jutland, by Als Sound. Sonderborg, main city; Nordborg and Augustenborg, towns. Fertile soil; agr., fruitgrowing. Isl. belonged to Germany until 1920 plebiscite.

Alsace (ăl'săs, –săs, Fr. älzäs'), Ger. *Elsass* (ĕl'zäs), anc. *Alsatia*, region and former province of E France along the Rhine border with Germany, bet. the Vosges (W) and the Rhine (E), now administratively divided into Bas-Rhin and Haut-Rhin depts., and Territory of Belfort. Agr. in Alsatian lowland (cereals, hops, tobacco, potatoes, vegetables, fruit). Winegrowing on E slopes of the Vosges. Potash mines near Mulhouse, oil wells at Merkwiller-Péchelbronn. Chief industries concentrated in Mulhouse-Colmar area (cotton textiles, chemicals) and near Strasbourg (metallurgy). Principal communications with Fr. areas W of the Vosges via Belfort and Saverne gaps and over some minor Vosges passes. Chief cities are Strasbourg, Mulhouse, Colmar, Belfort. Pop. can speak French, but also retains its own Alemannic dialect. Part of Roman prov. of Upper Germany, Alsace fell to Alemanni (5th cent.) and to Franks (496). Treaty of Verdun (843) included it in Lotharingia, the Treaty of Mersen (870) in Kingdom of East Franks (later Germany). Its chief towns gained virtual independence in 13th cent. as free imperial cities. They accepted Reformation, but rural areas remained mostly Catholic. After receiving part of Alsace from Austria in 1648, Louis XIV forcibly took control of entire prov., including Strasbourg, 1680–97. Treaty of Ryswick (1697) confirmed France in its new possessions. Mulhouse, allied with Switzerland, was not annexed until French revolution. Alsace, with own *parlement* at Colmar retained favored fiscal and religious status until 1790, when it was divided into depts. of Haut-Rhin and Bas-Rhin. In 1871, all of Alsace, except Territory of Belfort, was incorporated into Germany. With part of Lorraine, it formed the "imperial land" (*Reichsland*) of Alsace-Lorraine. Returned to France by Treaty of Versailles (1919), Alsace developed a strong particularist movement for autonomy, enhanced by religious motives (Concordat of 1801, which had been ended in France in 1905, was still valid in Alsace). Occupied by Germany in 1940, it was again considered part of the Reich, and Alsatians were drafted into Ger. army. After long and difficult fighting (especially in Colmar pocket and along Ger. border N of Haguenau) Alsace was completely liberated by Allies in Jan., 1945.

Alsace, Ballon d' (bälō' dälzäs'), Ger. *Welscher Belchen* (vĕl'shûr bĕl'khûn) or *Elsässer Belchen* (ĕl'zĕsûr), rounded summit (c.4,100 ft.) of the S Vosges, E France, on Haut-Rhin–Vosges dept. border, 13 mi. N of Belfort. Winter sports hotel on S slope. Ballon Pass (alt. 3,865 ft., just W) is on Belfort-Remiremont road.

Alsace-Lorraine (ăl'săs-lûrān', –săs, Fr. älzäs'-lôrĕn'), Ger. *Elsass-Lothringen* (ĕl'zäs-lō'trĭng-ûn), frontier region bet. France (W), Germany (N and E), and Switzerland (S), bounded by the Rhine on E. Long disputed by France and Germany, it was incorporated into Germany in 1871, and recovered by France in 1919. Now administratively divided into Fr. depts. of Haut-Rhin, Bas-Rhin, and Moselle. It was again under Ger. administration 1940–44 during Second World War.

Alsager (ôl'sûjûr), urban district (1931 pop. 2,852; 1951 census 5,574), SE Cheshire, England, 5 mi. E of Crewe; agr. market. Christ's Church dates from 1789.

Alsask (ălsăsk'), town (pop. 206), SW Sask., on Alta. border, 40 mi. W of Kindersley; sodium-sulphate mining; grain elevators, dairying.

Alsasua (älsä'swä), town (pop. 3,060), Navarre prov., N Spain, 17 mi. SSW of Tolosa; road and rail junction; iron foundry, sawmills. Agr. trade (corn, chestnuts, potatoes, cattle).

Alsatia (ălsā'shû), district of Whitefriars, London, England, on N side of the Thames, just NE of Charing Cross. Carmelite White Friars monastery, founded here 1241, was dissolved 1538, but the precincts continued to provide sanctuary to debtors until 1697.

Alsatia, France: see ALSACE.

Alsdorf (äls'dôrf), town (pop. 18,421), in former Prussian Rhine Prov., W Germany, after 1945 in North Rhine-Westphalia, near Dutch border, 7 mi. NNE of Aachen; coal-mining center; coke byproducts (ammonia, benzol, gas, tar).

Alsea River (ălsē'û), W Oregon, rises in Coast Range SW of Corvallis, flows 27 mi. W to the Pacific at Waldport.

Alsek River (ăl'sĕk), SE Alaska, rises in the Yukon near 60°50'N 137°40'W, flows 150 mi. S to the Pacific at Dry Bay 50 mi. SE of Yakutak.

Alsen, Denmark: see ALS.

Alsen (äl'sûn), village (pop. 114), Cavalier co., N N.Dak., 17 mi. SW of Langdon.

Alsenborn (äl'zûnbôrn), village (pop. 1,708), Rhenish Palatinate, W Germany, 7 mi. ENE of Kaiserslautern; grain, potatoes.

Alseno (älsā'nô), village (pop. 392), Piacenza prov., Emilia-Romagna, N central Italy, 17 mi. SE of Piacenza; cement.

Alsenz (äl'zĕnts), village (pop. 1,740), Rhenish Palatinate, W Germany, 20 mi. N of Kaiserslautern; winegrowing; fruit, grain.

Alsergrund (äl'sûrgrŏŏnt), district (□ 1; pop. 79,695) of Vienna, Austria, just N of city center.

Alsey (ăl'zē), village (pop. 294), Scott co., W central Ill., 15 mi. SW of Jacksonville, in agr. area.

Alsfeld (äls'fĕlt), town (pop. 8,191), central Hesse, W Germany, in former Upper Hesse prov., 28 mi. ENE of Giessen; textile mfg., lumber milling. Has late-Gothic town hall.

Alsh, Loch (lŏkh ălsh'), sea inlet in SW Ross and Cromarty, Scotland, separating Skye from mainland; extends 8 mi. E from the Inner Sound at Kyle; up to 3 mi. wide. Continued E by Loch DUICH; in S narrow Kyle Rhea, 3 mi. long, connects loch with Sound of Sleat.

Alsheim (äls'hīm), village (pop. 2,100), Rhenish Hesse, W Germany, 9 mi. N of Worms; wine.

Alsina, Lake (älsē'nä), salt lake (□ 25) in W Buenos Aires prov., Argentina, 40 mi. NE of Carhué, in lake dist.; 14 mi. long, 1–2 mi. wide.

Alsip, village (pop. 1,228), Cook co., NE Ill., S suburb of Chicago, just W of Blue Island.

Alsleben or **Alsleben an der Saale** (äls'lā"bûn än dĕr zä'lû), town (pop. 5,066), in former Prussian Saxony prov., central Germany, after 1945 in Saxony-Anhalt, on the Saxonian Saale and 7 mi. SSW of Bernburg; flour milling, sugar refining; limestone quarrying.

Alsoarpas, Rumania: see ARPASUL-DE-JOS.

Alsojara, Rumania: see IARA.

Alsokubin, Czechoslovakia: see DOLNI KUBIN.

Alsonemedi (ŏl'shōnāmĕdē), Hung. *Alsónémedi*, town (pop. 8,726), Pest-Pilis-Solt-Kiskun co., N central Hungary, 13 mi. S of Budapest; grain, potatoes, poultry, honey.

Alsosag (ŏl'shō-shäg), Hung. *Alsóság*, town (pop. 3,378), Vas co., W Hungary, 24 mi. E of Szombathely; wheat, potatoes.

Alsoszopor, Rumania: see SUPURUL-DE-JOS.

Alsotatrafüred, Czechoslovakia: see DOLNI SMOKOVEC.

Alsoviso, Rumania: see VISEUL-DE-JOS.

Alsovizkoz, Czechoslovakia: see SVIDNIK.

Als Sound or **Als Fjord** (äls), Denmark, strait connecting Aabenraa Fjord (N) with Flensburg Fjord (S), and separating Als isl. from Sundeved peninsula (S Jutland). Width varies from 2.5 mi. at N end to 750 ft. at S end, here crossed by pontoon bridge (built 1856) connecting Sonderborg, city on both sides of S Als Sound. On Augustenborg Fjord (SE branch; 4 mi. long) is Augustenborg town.

Alstadhaug. **1** Village and canton, Nordland co., Norway: see ALSTAHAUG. **2** Village, Nord-Trondelag co., Norway: see SKOGN.

Alstahaug (äl'stähoug), village and canton (pop. 1,706), Nordland co., N central Norway, at S end of Alsten Isl., 20 mi. W of Mosjoen; fishing, fish canning and packing; cattle raising. Formerly spelled Alstadhaug.

Alstead (ăl'stĭd), town (pop. 851), Cheshire co., SW N.H., on Cold R. and 17 mi. NNW of Keene; mica products; feldspar. State's 1st paper mill built here, 1793. Inc. 1772.

Alsten Island (äl'stûn), Nor. *Alstenøy* (□ 59; pop. 3,447), Nordland co., N central Norway, separated from mainland by Vefsn Fjord, 16 mi. NW of Mosjoen; 66°N 13°E; 20 mi. long (NE-SW), 5 mi. wide. It is mountainous, with 7 peaks called the Seven Sisters (highest is Stortind: 3,497 ft.), celebrated in legend. Chief villages on isl. are ALSTAHAUG (S) and SANDNESSJOEN (N).

Alsterbro (äl'stûrbrōō"), village (pop. 629), Kalmar co., SE Sweden, on Alster R. and 14 mi. N of Nybro; glass mfg., woodworking.

Alster River (äl'stûr), NW Germany, rises 4 mi. SE of Kaltenkirchen, flows c.30 mi. generally S to Hamburg (here dammed since early Middle Ages), entering the Elbe in 2 parallel canals which separate historic Old City (E) from 17th-cent. New City. When new fortifications were built (17th cent.), the Alster basin was divided into large Aussenalster [=outer Alster] (408 acres) and small Binnenalster [=inner or inland Alster], which is bordered (S) by the noted Jungfernstieg, Hamburg's "Fifth Avenue."

Alster River, Swedish *Alsterån* (äl'stûrōn"), SE Sweden, rises SW of Aseda, flows 80 mi. generally E to Kalmar Sound of Baltic at Pataholm.

Alston (ôl'stûn), town in Alston with Garrigill parish and rural district (pop. 2,678), E Cumberland, England, 16 mi. NE of Penrith, in the Pennines; steel furnaces; mfg. of hosiery; limestone quarrying.

Alston (ôl'stûn), town (pop. 147), Montgomery co., E central Ga., 10 mi. SSW of Vidalia.

Alstonville (ôl'stûnvĭl, ŏl'–), town (pop. 643), NE New South Wales, Australia, 95 mi. S of Brisbane, near Lismore; dairying and agr. center.

Alta (äl'tä), village and canton (pop. 4,992), Finnmark co., N Norway, at head of Alta Fjord, at mouth of Alta R., 50 mi. SSW of Hammerfest; fishing port; seaplane base. Dairying, agr. First settled 1714 by Finns.

Alta, river, Norway: see ALTA RIVER.

Alta. **1** Resort village, Placer co., E Calif., in the Sierra Nevada foothills, 25 mi. NE of Auburn. **2** Town (pop. 1,348), Buena Vista co., NW Iowa, near Storm L., 13 mi. ESE of Cherokee; dairy products, cement blocks. Sand pits near by. Has municipal hosp. Inc. 1878. **3** Winter resort, Salt Lake co., N central Utah, in Wasatch Mts. 17 mi. SE of Salt Lake City; alt. 8,583 ft.; skiing.

Altadena (ăltûdē'nû), unincorporated residential town (1940 pop. 23,558), Los Angeles co., S Calif., on lower slopes of San Gabriel Mts., just N of Pasadena; citrus-fruit, avocado groves; light mfg. Christmas Tree Lane of giant deodars is illuminated at holiday season.

Alta Fjord (äl'tä), Nor. *Altafjord* or *Altefjord*, Finnmark co., N Norway, inlet (20 mi. long, 7–11 mi. wide) of Norwegian Sea, with which it is connected by sounds on either side of isls. Seiland and Stjernoy. At its head are Alta, Bossekop, and Elvebakken villages. Receives Alta R. Sometimes called Alten Fjord.

Alta Gracia (äl'tä grä'syä), city (pop. 12,058), ⊙ Santa María dept. (□ c.1200; pop. 40,002), W central Córdoba prov., Argentina, 23 mi. SW of Córdoba. Railhead; mining, commercial, and agr. center; tourist resort. Quarrying of lime and granite. Tungsten, mica, and marble deposits near by. Tanning, dairying, bottling of mineral waters, grain growing and livestock raising. Hydroelectric station on near-by affluent of Río Segundo. Once a center of Jesuit Indian missions. Has baroque church.

Altagracia (ältägrä'syä). **1** Village (pop. 782), Camagüey prov., E Cuba, on railroad and 14 mi. ENE of Camagüey, in agr. region (fruit, cattle); manganese deposits. Also spelled Alta Gracia. **2** or **Central Altagracia**, sugar-mill village (pop. 1,147), Oriente prov., E Cuba, 35 mi. NW of Santiago de Cuba.

Alta Gracia (äl'tä grä'syä), town (1950 pop. 1,184), Rivas dept., SW Nicaragua, on Ometepe Isl. in L. Nicaragua, at N foot of volcano Concepción, 18 mi. NE of Rivas, principal town on isl.; mfg. (hats, mats); coffee, tobacco, cotton, sesame.

Altagracia (ältägrä'syä). **1** Town (pop. 2,371), on Margarita Isl. (N), Nueva Esparta state, NE Venezuela, 6 mi. NNW of La Asunción; cotton, sugar cane, beans, corn, coconuts; sugar milling. **2** Town (pop. 3,257), Zulia state, NW Venezuela, port on narrows of L. Maracaibo, across from and 7 mi. NE of Maracaibo. Terminus of railroad and pipe line from El Mene oil fields, 35 mi. E. Fishing and agr. center (corn, beans, bananas, coconuts, cotton).

Altagracia, La, province, Dominican Republic: see LA ALTAGRACIA.

Altagracia de Orituco (dā ōrētōō'kō), town (pop. 3,395), Guárico state, N central Venezuela, in S outliers of coastal range, on Orituco R. and 60 mi. SE of Caracas. Cattle, corn, sugar cane, fruit, cotton.

Al Tahoe (tä'hō), resort village, El Dorado co., E Calif., on S shore of L. Tahoe, in the Sierra Nevada; alt. 6,225 ft.

Altai, mountains, Asia: see ALTAI MOUNTAINS.

Altai, China: see SHARASUME.

Altai or **Altay** (both: ăltī', ăl'tī, ältī', Rus. ŭltī'), territory [Rus. *krai* or *kray*] (□ 101,000; 1946 pop. estimate 2,400,000) in S Siberian Russian SFSR; ⊙ Barnaul. Includes GORNO-ALTAI AUTONOMOUS OBLAST. Has wooded ALTAI MOUNTAINS (SE) and dry KULUNDA STEPPE (NW); includes richest black-earth area of Siberia; drained by upper Ob R. Produces chiefly wheat, sugar beets, flax, dairy products. Textile (cotton, linen) and food industries (sugar, pork products) are important. Chief towns: BARNAUL, BISK, RUBTSOVSK, SLAVGOROD, ALEISK. Traversed by Turksib RR and connected with Mongolia by Chuya highway. One of the most densely populated areas of Siberia; 1st settled by Russians in early-18th cent. Formed 1937 out of W Siberian Territory. An earlier Altai govt. existed 1917-25.

Altai or **Altay,** village (1948 pop. over 500), E Khakass Autonomous Oblast, Krasnoyarsk Territory, Russian SFSR, on Yenisei R. and 25 mi. SE of Abakan, in agr. area.

Altai Mountains or **Altay Mountains,** major mountain system of central Asia, at junction of USSR (Russian SFSR and Kazakh SSR), China, and Mongolia, and containing the headwaters of the Irtysh, the Ob, and the tributaries of the upper Yenisei; range rises just inside Mongolian People's Republic to 15,266 ft. in the Tabun Bogdo mtn. knot (49°10'N 87°55'E). The highest peak within the USSR is the Belukha (15,157 ft.), in the Katun Alps. These constitute, with the Chuya Alps (E), the highest glaciated ranges of the Russian Altai. Of the numerous lakes, Teletskoye L. and Marka-Kul are the largest. Among the main outliers are the Salair Ridge and the Kuznetsk Ala-Tau, which enclose the Kuznetsk Basin. The Altai Mts. consist of much-folded Paleozoic strata, later peneplained and reelevated; region has continental climate, with rainy summers and cold, dry winters. Dense forests extend up to 6,500 ft., with alpine meadows to the snow line at 8,200 ft. The mts. are noted for their lead-silver-zinc deposits, mined chiefly on the Kazakh slopes at Leninogorsk and Zyryanovsk, and for mercury mined at Chagan-Uzun. Pop. consists of Turkic Altaic tribes (hunting, livestock and maral breeding) in higher reaches, and Russians and Kazakhs in foothills. Politically the Russian Altai falls largely within the Gorno-Altai Autonomous Oblast, a division of Altai territory. The **Mongolian Altai,** Mongolian *Altayn Nuruu,* a southeasterly extension of the Altai Mts., starts in the Tabun Bogdo mtn. knot and lies within W Mongolian People's Republic. It becomes progressively lower in alt. and drier in climate toward the E as it enters the Gobi desert and at about lat. 98°E takes the name Gobi Altai. The **Gobi Altai** section consists of a series of parallel ranges rising to over 13,000 ft. in the Ikhe Bogdo and nearly devoid of any but semi-desert vegetation. One of the easternmost ranges of the Gobi Altai is the Gurban Saikhan, in the area of Dalan Dzadagad.

Altaiskaya, Russian SFSR: see CHESNOKOVKA.

Altaiskoye or **Altayskoye** (ŭltī'skŭyŭ), village (1926 pop. 7,555), central Altai Territory, Russian SFSR, 40 mi. S of Bisk; sawmilling.

Alta Italia (äl'tä ētä'lyä), town (pop. estimate 1,200), NE La Pampa natl. territory, Argentina, on railroad and 30 mi. NW of General Pico; wheat, corn, alfalfa, flax, livestock; dairying, flour milling.

Alta Loma (ăltŭ lō'mŭ), village (pop. c.3,000), San Bernardino co., S Calif., in foothill citrus belt, just E of Upland.

Altamachi River, Bolivia: see SANTA ELENA RIVER.

Altamaha River (ăl'tŭmŭhô"), SE Ga., formed by confluence of Oconee and Ocmulgee rivers 7 mi. NNE of Hazelhurst, flows 137 mi. SE, past Darien, to the Atlantic through Altamaha Sound (2 mi. wide) at N end of St. Simon Isl. Dredged and navigable, with its branches, for c.200 mi. for boats of light draft.

Altamahaw (ăl'tŭmŭhô"), village (pop. c.300), Alamance co., N central N.C., on Haw R. and 17 mi. ENE of Greensboro; hosiery mfg.

Altamira (ältŭmē'rä), city (pop. 1,573), central Pará, Brazil, on left bank of Xingu R. (not navigable here) and 140 mi. ESE of Santarém; rubber, medicinal oils.

Altamira (ältämē'rä), officially San José de Altamira, town (1950 pop. 705), Puerto Plata prov., N Dominican Republic, in Cordillera Setentrional, on railroad and 13 mi. SW of Puerto Plata, in agr. region (coffee, cacao, fruit).

Altamira, town (pop. 1,387), Tamaulipas, NE Mexico, on Gulf plain, 12 mi. NNW of Tampico, on railroad; agr. (henequen, citrus fruit, bananas, tomatoes). Saltworks.

Altamira (ältämē'rä), town (pop. 507), Barinas state, W Venezuela, in Andean foothills, on upper Santo Domingo R. and 23 mi. NW of Barinas; corn, coffee, stock.

Altamira Cave (ăltŭmĭ'rŭ, Sp. ältämē'rä), cave near Santillana, 2.5 mi. NW of Torrelavega, Santander prov., N Spain, where Old Stone Age colored drawings and relics were discovered in 1879.

Altamirano (ältämērä'nō). **1** Town (pop. 492), Chiapas, S Mexico, on affluent of Jatatė R. and 33 mi. ENE of San Cristóbal de las Casas; corn, fruit. **2** or **Ciudad Altamirano** (syōōdädh'), city (pop. 4,046), Guerrero, SW Mexico, on Cutzamala R. (Michoacán border) near its confluence with the Río de las Balsas, and 70 mi. W of Iguala. Agr. center (cereals, tobacco, coffee, sugar cane, tropical fruit, resin, vanilla). Pungarabato until 1936.

Altamirano Sud (sōōdh'), town (pop. estimate 700), central Entre Ríos prov., Argentina, 85 mi. ESE of Paraná; grain and livestock center; leather processing. Village of Altamirano Norte adjoins it.

Altamont (ăl'tŭmŏnt). **1** City (pop. 1,580), Effingham co., SE central Ill., 12 mi. WSW of Effingham; railroad junction; wheat-shipping point; mfg. (clothing, egg cases). Agr. (corn, wheat; dairy products; poultry, livestock). Inc. as village in 1872, as city in 1901. **2** City (pop. 652), Labette co., SE Kansas, 8 mi. SSE of Parsons; trading and shipping point in stock-raising, dairying, and agr. region. Coal mines, oil and gas wells in vicinity. **3** Town (pop. 178), Daviess co., NW Mo., near Grand R., 40 mi. ENE of St. Joseph; agr., livestock, dairy farms. **4** Village (pop. 1,127), Albany co., E N.Y., at base of the Helderbergs, 14 mi. WNW of Albany, in dairying and grain area. Summer resort; lakes near by. **5** Village (pop. 1,022, with adjacent Cresmont), Schuylkill co., E Pa. **6** Town (pop. 76), Deuel co., E S.Dak., 6 mi. N of Clear Lake.

Altamonte Springs (ăl'tŭmŏnt), town (pop. 858), Seminole co., E central Fla., 8 mi. N of Orlando.

Altamount, town (pop. 296), ⊙ Grundy co., SE central Tenn., 35 mi. NW of Chattanooga, in the Cumberlands; lumbering.

Altamura (ältämōō'rä), town (pop. 31,099), Bari prov., Apulia, S Italy, in Apennine foothills, 26 mi. SW of Bari. Rail junction; agr. center (cereals, grapes, almonds, livestock); mfg. (macaroni, fertilizer). Bishopric. Has cathedral begun 1232.

Altan Bulak or **Altan Bulag** (äl'tän bōō'läkh), city (pop. over 2,000), ⊙ Selenga aimak, N Mongolian People's Republic, on USSR border (opposite Kyakhta), on highway and 165 mi. NNW of Ulan Bator; major trading center on USSR-Mongolia route. Formerly called Maimachen or Maimachin, it developed (early-18th cent.) as a customs station, on main Russia-China trade route, handling tea, wool, and hides. Partly superseded by newer trade center of Sukhe Bator, 15 mi. WSW.

Altan-Tepe, Rumania: see TOPOLOG.

Altar (ältär'), town (pop. 1,137), Sonora, NW Mexico, on Altar R. irrigation; affluent of Magdalena R. and 65 mi. SW of Nogales, in agr. (wheat, corn, cotton, beans) and mining (copper, zinc) area.

Altar, Cerro (sĕ'rō ältär') or **Capac-Urcu** (käpäk'-ōōr'kōō), Andean massif on Chimborazo–Santiago Zamora prov. border, central Ecuador, 15 mi. E of Riobamba; 1°40'S 78°25'W. Extinct volcano, with 2 snow-capped peaks, which resembles an altar; highest cone rises to 17,300 ft.

Altare (ältä'rĕ), village (pop. 2,404), Savona prov., Liguria, NW Italy, near Cadibona Pass, 8 mi. WNW of Savona. Known for its glass industry.

Altare, Colle di, Italy: see CADIBONA PASS.

Altarejos (ältärä'hōs), town (pop. 1,044), Cuenca prov., E central Spain, 16 mi. SW of Cuenca; grain- and winegrowing, stock raising.

Alta River (äl'tä), Nor. *Altaelv,* Finnmark co., N Norway, rises on Finnish border S of Kautokeino, flows c.120 mi. N, past Kautokeino, to head of Alta Fjord at Alta. Noted for its salmon. Upper course called Kautokeino R., Nor. *Kautokeinoelv.*

Altata (ältä'tä), town (pop. 115), Sinaloa, NW Mexico, minor port on shallow bay of Gulf of California, 35 mi. WSW of Culiacán; oyster fishing.

Altaussee (ält'ous'zā), summer resort (pop. 2,484), Styria, central Austria, on small lake of same name (alt. 2,325 ft.) in the Salzkammergut, and 8 mi. SE of Bad Ischl. Salt mined near by.

Alta Vela (äl'tä vä'lä), islet off S Hispaniola isl., just S of Beata Isl.

Alta Verapaz (äl'tä väräpäs'), department (□ 3,353; 1950 pop. 194,321), central Guatemala; ⊙ Cobán. In N highlands (Sierra de Chamá), sloping N into Petén lowlands; bounded by Chixoy R. (W) and Sierra de las Minas (SE); drained by Polochic and Cahabón rivers. Mainly agr. (coffee, corn, beans, sugar cane, cacao, vanilla, tropical fruit; livestock; lumbering, chicle collecting (N). Coffee processing, matting, weaving, pottery making are local industries. Main trade route is Verapaz RR (bet. Pancajché and Panzós), continued by Polochic R. route. Chief urban centers: Cobán, San Cristóbal, Carchá.

Altavilla Irpino (ältävēl'lä ērpē'nō), town (pop. 5,632), Avellino prov., Campania, S Italy, 6 mi. N of Avellino; mfg. (explosives, cement). Sulphur mines near by.

Altavilla Milicia (mēlē'chä), village (pop. 3,779), Palermo prov., N Sicily, 3 mi. SE of Bagheria. Norman church, founded 1077, near by.

Altavilla Silentina (sēlĕntē'nä), village (pop. 1,752), Salerno prov., Campania, S Italy, 8 mi. SSE of Eboli.

Alta Vista. 1 Town (pop. 312), Chickasaw co., NE Iowa, 16 mi. NE of Charles City, in corn, hog, and dairy area. **2** City (pop. 420), Wabaunsee co., E central Kansas, 22 mi. S of Manhattan, in livestock and grain region; poultry packing.

Altavista, industrial town (pop. 3,332), Campbell co., S central Va., on Roanoke R. and 21 mi. S of Lynchburg, in agr. area (tobacco, grain); rail junction; mfg. (cedar chests, cotton and rayon textiles). Inc. 1910; rechartered 1936.

Altay, in Rus. names: see ALTAI.

Alt-Berun, Poland: see BIERUN.

Altbreisach, Germany: see BREISACH.

Altbunzlau, Czechoslovakia: see STARA BOLESLAV.

Altdamm, Poland: see DABIE, Szczecin prov.

Altdorf (ält'dôrf"). **1** Village (pop. 1,177), S Baden, Germany, at W foot of Black Forest, 5 mi. SSW of Lahr; tobacco. **2** Town (pop. 5,306), Middle Franconia, N central Bavaria, Germany, 13 mi. ESE of Nuremberg; textile mfg., metal- and woodworking, brewing. Chartered 1400. Site of univ. (1623–1814).

Altdorf (ält'dôrf") or **Altorf** (ält'ôrf), town (pop. 5,692), ⊙ Uri canton, central Switzerland, SSE of L. of Uri, E of Reuss R. and 9 mi. S of Schwyz; cables, rubber goods; woodworking. Scene of traditional exploits of William Tell; Tell Monument, Tell Theater, historical mus.

Altea (ältā'ä), town (pop. 3,456), Alicante prov., E Spain, on the Mediterranean, and 25 mi. ESE of Alcoy; dried-fish processing, flour milling, olive pressing. Citrus fruit, wine, raisins, almonds. Ophite quarries. Has anc. castle.

Alte Aare River, Switzerland: see AAR RIVER.

Alte Elde River, Germany: see ELDE RIVER.

Altefähr (äl"tŭfâr'), village (pop. 1,445), in former Prussian Pomerania prov., N Germany, after 1945 in Mecklenburg, on SW Rügen isl., on narrow Bodden strait of the Baltic, 2 mi. NE of Stralsund. Until 1936, when Rügen Dam was completed, it was terminus of train ferry from Stralsund.

Altefjord, Norway: see ALTA FJORD.

Altels (äl'tŭls), peak (11,918 ft.) in Bernese Alps, S Switzerland, 8 mi. NNW of Leuk.

Altena (äl'tŭnä), town (pop. 20,085), in former Prussian prov. of Westphalia, W Germany, after 1945 in North Rhine-Westphalia, on the Lenne and 5 mi. S of Iserlohn; ironworks, wire mills; mfg. of electrical goods. Has large 12th-cent. castle. Chartered 1367.

Altenahr (äl'tünär), village (pop. 1,402), in former Prussian Rhine Prov., W Germany, after 1945 in Rhineland-Palatinate, on the Ahr and 5 mi. W of Ahrweiler; tourist center known for its red wine. Anc. ruined castle towers above village.

Altenau (äl'tŭnou), town (pop. 2,744), in former Prussian prov. of Hanover, W Germany, after 1945 in Lower Saxony, in the upper Harz, on the Oker (near its source) and 5 mi. E of Clausthal-Zellerfeld; rail terminus; summer resort and winter-sports center (alt. 1,610 ft.) at NW foot of the Bruchberg; sawmilling, brewing.

Altenbeken (äl'tŭnbā"kŭn), village (pop. 3,306), in former Prussian prov. of Westphalia, NW Germany, after 1945 in North Rhine-Westphalia, 8 mi. ENE of Paderborn; rail junction.

Altenberg (äl'tŭnbĕrk"), town (pop. 1,796), Saxony, E central Germany, in the Erzgebirge, 16 mi. SW of Pirna, near Czechoslovak border; tin and wolframite mining and smelting; woodworking. Winter-sports resort. Mining begun in 15th cent.

Altenberge (äl'tŭnbĕr"gŭ), village (pop. 5,123), in former Prussian prov. of Westphalia, NW Germany, after 1945 in North Rhine-Westphalia, 9 mi. NW of Münster; linen weaving.

Altenbreitungen, Germany: see BREITUNGEN.

Altenbruch (äl'tŭnbrōōkh), village (pop. 4,735), in former Prussian prov. of Hanover, NW Germany, after 1945 in Lower Saxony, on Elbe estuary, 4 mi. SE of Cuxhaven; metalworking. Bathing resort.

Altenburg (äl'tŭnbōōrk), city (pop. 51,805), Thuringia, central Germany, on the Pleisse and 25 mi. S of Leipzig; 50°59'N 12°27'E. Textile-milling center, in lignite- and clay-mining region; also mfg. of machinery, sewing machines, glass, carpets, leather, hats, playing cards, tobacco products; metal- and woodworking, food canning, brewing. Rail junction; airfield. Towered over by former ducal castle (11th-12th cent.; rebuilt 15th-18th cent.; now mus.). Has 15th-cent. castle church and 16th-cent. town hall. First mentioned as town in 976; became imperial city in 12th cent. Passed in 1243 to house of Wettin. Was ⊙ duchy of Saxe-Altenburg (1603–72; and again, 1826–1918).

Altenburg (ăl'tŭnbûrg), town (pop. 272), Perry co., E Mo., near Mississippi R., 5 mi. W of Grand Tower, Ill.

Altenburg, Ungarisch-, Hungary: see MOSONMAGYAROVAR.

Altendorf (äl'tŭndôrf), residential district (since 1901) of ESSEN, W Germany, 2 mi. W of city center; site of Krupp workers' colonies (Alfredshof, Kronenhof, Schederhof).

Altenessen (äl'tŭnĕ'sŭn), industrial district (since 1915) of ESSEN, W Germany, port on Rhine-Herne Canal and 3.5 mi. N of city center; coal mining.

Alten Fjord, Norway: see ALTA FJORD.

Altengamme, Germany: see VIERLANDE.

Altenkessel (äl'tŭn-kĕ'sŭl), town (pop. 7,993), S Saar, near Fr. border, 4.5 mi. WNW of Saarbrücken, near Saar R.; coal mining.

Altenkirchen (äl"tŭnkĭr'khŭn), town (pop. 3,567), in former Prussian Rhine Prov., W Germany, after 1945 in Rhineland-Palatinate, in the Westerwald, 20 mi. SW of Siegen; rail junction; iron and lead mines.

Altenkunstadt (äl"tŭn-kōōn'shtät), village (pop. 2,695), Upper Franconia, N Bavaria, Germany, on the Main and 8 mi. ESE of Lichtenfels; glass mfg., metal- and leatherworking, tanning.

Area in square miles is indicated by the symbol □, capital city or county seat by the symbol ⊙.

Altenmarkt (äl'tunmärkt). **1** Village (pop. 2,199), Lower Bavaria, Germany, near the Danube, 9 mi. SE of Plattling; glass and textile mfg. Has former Benedictine monastery (c.737–1783). **2** Village (pop. 2,437), Upper Bavaria, Germany, on the Alz and 10 mi. NNW of Traunstein; textile mfg., metal- and woodworking. Has former Augustinian monastery, with early-12th-cent. church (rebuilt 1756).

Altenoythe (äl'tunoi"tu), village (commune pop. 6,683), in Oldenburg, NW Germany, after 1945 Lower Saxony, 14 mi. NNW of Cloppenburg.

Altensteig (äl'tun-shtīk"), town (pop. 3,003), S Württemberg, Germany, after 1945 in Württemberg-Hohenzollern, in Black Forest, on Nagold R. and 6 mi. WNW of Nagold; rail terminus; furniture mfg. Summer resort.

Altentreptow (äl'tuntrāp'tō), town (pop. 8,604), in former Prussian Pomerania prov., N Germany, after 1945 in Mecklenburg, on Tollense R. and 10 mi. N of Neubrandenburg; agr. center (grain, potatoes, sugar beets, stock). Has 14th-cent. church and old town gates. Chartered 1190. For several years residence of novelist Reuter. Until 1940s called Treptow or Treptow an der Tollense.

Altenweddingen (äl'tunvĕ'dĭng-un), village (pop. 3,549), in former Prussian Saxony prov., central Germany, after 1945 in Saxony-Anhalt, 11 mi. SSW of Magdeburg; lignite mining.

Alte Oder River, Germany: see ODER MARSHES.

Altepexi (ältāpĕk'sē), town (pop. 2,771), Puebla, central Mexico, 8 mi. SE of Tehuacán, on railroad; alt. 4,104 ft. Textile milling; corn, sugar, fruit, livestock.

Alter do Chão (ältĕr' dōō shā'ō), town (pop. 256), W Pará, Brazil, on right bank of the Tapajós above its influx into the Amazon, and 15 mi. SW of Santarém.

Alter do Chão, town (pop. 4,960), Portalegre dist., central Portugal, 14 mi. SW of Portalegre; cheese-mfg. center; grain milling, olive-oil pressing, horse raising, cork shipping. Has castle built 1359.

Alter Rhein River (äl'tur rīn') [=Old Rhine], old arm of the upper Rhine below its influx into L. of Constance; flows c.7 mi., past St. Margrethen and Rheineck, to L. of Constance about 5 mi. W of the Rhine's present mouth.

Alt Gaarz, Germany: see RERIK.

Altha, town (pop. 434), Calhoun co., NW Fla., 10 mi. NNW of Blountstown.

Althaldensleben, Germany: see HALDENSLEBEN.

Altham (ôl'thum, ăl'tum, ôl'tum), village and parish (pop. 902), E Lancashire, England, 4 mi. W of Burnley; coal mining; mfg. of chemicals.

Altheide, Bad, Poland: see POLANICA ZDROJ.

Altheim (ält'hīm), town (pop. 3,887), W Upper Austria, 9 mi. E of Braunau; furniture mfg.

Altheim, village (pop. 437), SE Saar, near Fr.-Ger. borders, 6 mi. SSW of Zweibrücken; stock, grain.

Altheimer (ôlt'hī"mur), town (pop. 680), Jefferson co., central Ark., 11 mi. NE of Pine Bluff, near Arkansas R.

Althofen (ält'hōfun), town (pop. 2,905), Carinthia, S Austria, near Gurk R., 18 mi. NNE of Klagenfurt; summer resort; mfg. of chemicals. Lignite mined near by (N).

Althorp (ôl'thôrp), agr. village and parish (pop. 71), central Northampton, England, 6 mi. NW of Northampton. Althorp Manor, owned by Spencer family, has fine library.

Altimir (ältĭmēr'), village (pop. 2,954), Vratsa dist., N Bulgaria, on Skat R. and 15 mi. SSW of Oryakhovo; vineyards, grain.

Altin Dag (ältün'dä"), Turkish *Altın Dağ*, peak (10,836 ft.), SE Turkey, in Hakari Mts., 15 mi. SE of Beytussebap.

Altinho (ältē'nyōō), city (pop. 1,238), E Pernambuco, NE Brazil, 15 mi. SSW of Caruaru; coffee, sugar; horse raising.

Altinópolis (ältēnô'pōōlēs), city (pop. 2,031), NE São Paulo, Brazil, near Minas Gerais border, on railroad and 29 mi. ENE of Ribeirão Prêto; furniture and pottery mfg.; agr. (coffee, grain, cotton).

Altinozu (ältün'üzü"), Turkish *Altınözü*, village (pop. 2,822), Hatay prov., S Turkey, 10 mi. SE of Antioch; grain.

Altiplano (ältēplä'nō), high intermontane plateau (c.12,000 ft.) bet. the Western and Eastern cordilleras (Cordillera Occidental, Cordillera Oriental) of the Andes, situated largely in W Bolivia and extending N into SE Peru and S into extreme NW Argentina. Its principal interior basins are occupied by lakes Titicaca and Poopó (linked by the Desaguadero) and the salares de Uyuni and Coipasa. PUNA vegetation and economy. Copper mining (Corocoro). Main centers are Puno (Peru), La Paz, Oruro, and Uyuni (Bolivia).

Altkirch (ältkērsh', Ger. ält'kĭrkh), town (pop. 3,565), Haut-Rhin dept., E France, on the Ill and 10 mi. SSW of Mulhouse; road center; mfg. (cement, footwear, cotton goods, tobacco products), iron founding.

Alt Landsberg or **Altlandsberg** (ält'länts'bĕrk), town (pop. 5,606), Brandenburg, E. Germany, 14 mi. ENE of Berlin; market gardening.

Altleiningen (ält'lī'nĭng-un), village (pop. 1,371), Rhenish Palatinate, W Germany, in Hardt Mts., 5 mi. NW of Bad Dürkheim; woodworking; winegrowing. Castle (12th cent.) was razed by French in 1689.

Altlengbach (ält'lĕng'bäkh), village (pop. 1,946), central Lower Austria, 20 mi. W of Vienna; wheat, cattle, fruit.

Altlünen (ält'lü'nun), village (pop. 5,747), in former Prussian prov. of Westphalia, NW Germany, after 1945 in North Rhine-Westphalia, just N of Lünen; grain, cattle, hogs.

Altlussheim (ält'lōōs'hīm"), village (pop. 3,036), N Baden, Germany, after 1945 in Württemberg-Baden, on the Rhine and 3 mi. ESE of Speyer; tobacco, sugar beets, strawberries.

Altmannstein (ält'män-shtīn"), village (pop. 1,063), Upper Palatinate, central Bavaria, Germany, 14 mi. NE of Ingolstadt; flour and lumber milling, brewing. Chartered 1331.

Altmar (ălt'mär"), village (pop. 299), Oswego co., N central N.Y., on Salmon R. and 25 mi. E of Oswego; wood products.

Altmittweida (ält'mĭt'vī"dä), village (pop. 3,356), Saxony, E central Germany, 10 mi. N of Chemnitz; textile milling, leather mfg.

Altmühl River (ält'mül), Bavaria, Germany, rises 7 mi. NE of Rothenburg, flows 137 mi. SE and E, past Eichstätt, to the Danube at Kelheim. Receives Ludwig Canal (left) at Dietfurt (head of navigation for small vessels).

Altmünster (ältmün'stur), town (pop. 7,760), S Upper Austria, on NW shore of L. Traun and 2 mi. SW of Gmunden; well-known summer resort.

Alto (ăl'tō). **1** Town (pop. 302), Habersham and Banks counties, NE Ga., 17 mi. NE of Gainesville. **2** Town (pop. 1,021), Cherokee co., E Texas, 30 mi. NW of Lufkin; trade center in tomato, cotton region; canneries; woodworking. Inc. 1909.

Alto, El: for Latin American towns, see EL ALTO.

Alto, El, Bolivia: see LA PAZ, city.

Alto, Pico, Azores: see SANTA MARIA ISLAND.

Alto, Sierra del (syĕ'rä dĕl äl'tō). **1** or **Sierra de Ancasti** (ängkä'stē), subandean range in Aconquija system in SE Catamarca prov., Argentina, extends c.100 mi. S from area of El Alto nearly to the Salinas Grandes; rises to 5,000 ft. N section is usually known as Sierra del Alto and S section as Sierra de Ancasti. **2** or **Sierra San Antonio** (sän äntō'nyō) or **Sierra del Río Seco** (dĕl rē'ō sā'kō), subandean mountain range along Bolivia-Argentina border, N of Orán (Salta prov.), Argentina; extends c.45 mi. N-S; rises to c.3,500 ft.

Alto Alentejo (äl'tōō älāntā'zhōō), province (□ 4,888; 1940 pop. 375,511), central Portugal, formed 1936 from old Alentejo prov.; ⊙ Évora. It contains Évora dist. and major part of Portalegre dist.

Alto Amazonas, province, Peru: see YURIMAGUAS.

Alto Araguaia (äl'tōō ärugwī'u), city (pop. 537), E Mato Grosso, Brazil, on left bank of upper Araguaia R. (Goiás border) and 220 mi. SE of Cuiabá; cattle raising. Diamond washings.

Alto Cedro (äl'tō sā'drō), town (pop. 679), Oriente prov., E Cuba, 37 mi. NNW of Santiago de Cuba; rail junction picturesquely set in Sierra de Nipe foothills. The Alto Cedro sugar mill is 3 mi. N.

Alto Chicapa (äl'tōō shēkä'pu), village, Malange prov., N central Angola, on central plateau, 115 mi. SW of Vila Henrique de Carvalho. Kasai, Kwango, Kwilu, and Chicapa rivers rise near by.

Alto de la Bandera or **El Alto de la Bandera** (ĕl äl'tō dā lä bändā'rä), resort and pass (c.2,500 ft.), W central Puerto Rico, in the Cordillera Central, 2½ mi. SE of Adjuntas. Sometimes Alto Bandera.

Alto de Sierra (äl'tō dā syĕ'rä), town (pop. estimate 800), S San Juan prov., Argentina, on San Juan R. (irrigation area), on railroad and 6 mi. ESE of San Juan. Winegrowing center; apiculture, fruit growing, stock raising, seed cultivation.

Altofonte (ältôfôn'tē), village (pop. 4,947), Palermo prov., N Sicily, 6 mi. SSW of Palermo. Called Parco before 1931.

Altofts, former urban district (1931 pop. 4,981), West Riding, S central Yorkshire, England, 4 mi. NE of Wakefield; coal mining. Inc. 1938 in Normanton.

Alto Longá (äl'tōō lōng-gä'), city (pop. 378), N central Piauí, Brazil, 40 mi. ESE of Teresina, in cattle-raising region; babassu nuts, carnauba wax, sugar.

Alto Lucero (äl'tō lōōsā'rō), town (pop. 2,704), Veracruz, E. Mexico, in Sierra Madre Oriental, 14 mi. NE of Jalapa; corn, sugar, coffee, tobacco, fruit.

Alto Madeira (äl'tōō mudā'rū), village (pop. 61), N Guaporé territory, W Brazil, on right bank of Madeira R. (at Santo Antônio rapids), on Madeira-Mamoré RR, and 5 mi. SW of Pôrto Velho. Founded 1728, it was head of navigation on the Madeira until, with completion of railroad, it was superseded by Pôrto Velho as rubber-shipping center. Formerly called Santo Antônio. In Mato Grosso until formation (1943) of Guaporé territory.

Alto Molócuè (äl'tōō mōōlō'kwĕ), village, Zambézia prov., N central Mozambique, on road and 160 mi. NNE of Quelimane; corn, beans, manioc, tea.

Altomonte (ältômôn'tē), village (pop. 2,044), Cosenza prov., Calabria, S Italy, 3 mi. S of Lungro; wine, olive oil.

Altomünster (äl'tōmün"stur), village (pop. 2,102), Upper Bavaria, Germany, 12 mi. NW of Dachau; metalworking, brewing. Former Benedictine abbey (founded c.730) has mid-18th-cent. church.

Alton (ôl'tun), village (pop. estimate 500), S Ont., on Credit R. and 5 mi. SSE of Orangeville; dairying, mixed farming.

Alton, urban district (1931 pop. 6,188; 1951 census 8,636), E Hampshire, England, 16 mi. ENE of Winchester; agr. market, with breweries and storage-battery works. Has 15th-cent. church.

Alton. **1** City (pop. 32,550), Madison co., SW Ill., on bluffs above the Mississippi (bridged) c.4 mi. above mouth of the Missouri, 17 mi. N of downtown St. Louis, of whose metropolitan area it is part. Trade, distributing (river, rail, highway), and mfg. center (steel, clay, glass, lead, and brass products; farm and mine tools, chemicals, clothing, shoes, beverages, ammunition, leather, paper, textiles, flour and other food products, boats). Oil refinery; stone quarries. Seat of Shurtleff Col., Monticello Col., and a boys' military acad. Principia Col. is near by, at Elsah. Has monument to Elijah P. Lovejoy, killed here in 1837; scene of last Lincoln-Douglas debate (1858) is marked. Pere Marquette State Park is near by. Alton lock and dam in the Mississippi here are among largest in the river. Laid out 1817 in region visited (1673) by Jolliet and Marquette; inc. 1821. **2** Town (pop. 71), Crawford co., S Ind., on Ohio R. and 35 mi. WSW of New Albany, in agr. area. **3** Town (pop. 1,038), Sioux co., NW Iowa, on Floyd R. and c.40 mi. NNE of Sioux City; cement and rendering works. Gravel pits near by. Inc. 1883. **4** City (pop. 317), Osborne co., N Kansas, on South Fork Solomon R. and 14 mi. W of Osborne; trading point for livestock and grain region. **5** Town (pop. 314), Penobscot co., S central Maine, just NW of Old Town; agr., lumbering. **6** Town (pop. 571), ⊙ Oregon co., S Mo., 26 mi. E of West Plains; agr. trade. **7** Town (pop. 1,189), Belknap co., E central N.H., 23 mi. NE of Concord and on Merrymeeting R., near S end of L. Winnipesaukee. Its resort village of Alton Bay is on narrow neck of lake. Settled 1770, inc. 1796. **8** Town (pop. 154), Kane co., S Utah, 27 mi. N of Kanab, in scenic mtn. region called the Pink Cliffs; alt. 6,875 ft. Inc. 1935.

Altona (ăltō'nu), town (pop. 2,807), S Victoria, Australia, 8 mi. SW of Melbourne, on N shore of Port Phillip Bay; agr. center (oats, barley), truck gardening. Oil refinery.

Altona, village (pop. 1,065), SE Man., 60 mi. SSW of Winnipeg, near N.Dak. border; grain, stock; flour milling.

Altona (äl'tōnä), major fishing port (1933 pop. 241,970) of Hamburg, NW Germany, on right bank of the Norderelbe, adjoining Sankt Pauli (E) and Eimsbüttel (N) dists.; important fish-processing industry; mfg. of machine tools. Active trade: fish, grain, tropical products, cattle, coal. Heavily damaged in Second World War. First mentioned in 16th cent.; passed 1640 to Holstein. Chartered in 1664, it became 1st free port of N Europe. In 1889 it inc. industrial Ottensen (W), with grave of Klopstock. Stellingen (NW), site of world-renowned Hagenbeck zoo, was inc. in 1927. Altona itself was inc. into Hamburg in 1938. The noted Elbchaussee, a scenic road bordered by large estates, leads along steep Elbe shore to Blankenese, 5 mi. W.

Altona (ăltō'nu). **1** Village (pop. 462), Knox co., NW central Ill., 16 mi. NE of Galesburg, in agr. and bituminous-coal area. **2** Town (pop. 344), De Kalb co., NE Ind., 19 mi. N of Fort Wayne, in agr. area. **3** Town (pop. 13), Bates co., W Mo., near South Grand R., 11 mi. NNE of Butler.

Alton Bay, N.H.: see ALTON.

Altoona (ăltōō'nu). **1** Town (pop. 860), Etowah co., NE central Ala., 18 mi. W of Gadsden. **2** Town (pop. 763), Polk co., central Iowa, 8 mi. ENE of Des Moines; corn cannery. **3** City (pop. 582), Wilson co., SE Kansas, on Verdigris R. and 16 mi. SW of Chanute; trading and shipping point in livestock, poultry, dairy, and grain region. Oil wells in vicinity. **4** Industrial city (pop. 77,177), Blair co., central Pa., 80 mi. E of Pittsburgh, in bituminous-coal region. Railroad shops; textiles, clothing, electrical products, automobile parts, metal products, food; Governor's conference here 1862 pledged support to Lincoln. Just W is scenic Horseshoe Curve of Pennsylvania RR. Settled c.1769, laid out 1849, inc. as borough 1854, as city 1868. **5** City (pop. 1,713), Eau Claire co., W central Wis., 3 mi. E of Eau Claire, in farming and stock-raising area. Settled 1882, inc. 1887.

Alto Paraná (äl'tō päränä'), department (□ 7,817; pop. 3,998), SE Paraguay; ⊙ Hernandarias. Bordered (E) by the Paraná, along Brazil and Argentina borders. Forested hill country, including outliers of central Brazilian plateau. The Paraná is navigable to impressive Guairá Falls on Brazil line. Has subtropical vegetation, high rainfall. Produces maté and lumber.

Alto Paraná River, Brazil-Paraguay-Argentina: see PARANÁ RIVER.

Alto Park, village (pop. 1,195), Floyd co., NW Ga.

Alto Parnaíba (äl'tōō pärnä-ē'bu), city (pop. 822), S Maranhão, Brazil, on left bank of Parnaíba R. (Piauí line), diagonally opposite Santa Filomena; cattle, carnauba wax, babassu nuts. Until 1944, Vitória do Alto Parnaíba.

Altopascio (ältôpä'shô), village (pop. 972), Lucca prov., Tuscany, central Italy, 9 mi. ESE of Lucca; cement mfg.

Alto Pass, village (pop. 462), Union co., S Ill., 22 mi. SW of Herrin, in Ill. Ozarks.

Alto Pencoso (äl'tō pĕngkō'sō), village (pop. estimate 700), W San Luis prov., Argentina, at S foot of Sierra del Alto Pencoso, on railroad and 35 mi. WSW of San Luis. Lumbering, stock raising, gypsum quarrying.

Alto Pencoso, Sierra del (syĕ'rä dĕl), pampean mountain range in NW San Luis prov., Argentina, 20 mi. W of San Luis. A W spur of Sierra de Córdoba, it extends c.45 mi. N from Alto Pencoso; rises to c.3,500 ft.

Altorf, Switzerland: see ALTDORF.

Alto Rio Doce (äl'tōō rē'ōō dō'sĭ), city (pop. 1,249), S Minas Gerais, Brazil, in the Serra do Espinhaço near source of the Rio Doce, 35 mi. SE of Conselheiro Lafaiete; tobacco, sugar, dairy products.

Altorricón (ältôrēkōn'), village (pop. 1,150), Huesca prov., NE Spain, 17 mi. NW of Lérida, in irrigated agr. area (rice, cereals, sugar beets, flax, fruit, olives).

Altos (äl'tōōs), city (pop. 2,437), N central Piauí, Brazil, 25 mi. ENE of Teresina, in cattle-raising area; ships babassu nuts, hides and skins.

Altos (äl'tōs), town (dist. pop. 12,462), La Cordillera dept., S central Paraguay, in Cordillera de los Altos, 28 mi. E of Asunción; agr. center (oranges, maté, melons, livestock). Founded 1538.

Altos, Cordillera de los (kôrdĭyä'rä dā lōs äl'tōs), hilly range in Paraguarí and La Cordillera depts., S central Paraguay, 30 mi. E of Asunción; c. 60 mi. long NW-SE; rises to c.2,000 ft.

Altos, Los, Venezuela: see LOS ALTOS.

Altos de Chipión (äl'tōs dā chēpyōn'), village (pop. estimate 1,000), NE Córdoba prov., Argentina, 37 mi. NNW of San Francisco; wheat, flax, oats, livestock; dairy products.

Alto Songo (äl'tō sōng'gō), town (pop. 4,276), Oriente prov., E Cuba, on railroad and 13 mi. NE of Santiago de Cuba; agr. center (tobacco, coffee, cacao, fruit); cattle raising, apiculture.

Altotonga (ältōtōng'gä), city (pop. 4,478), Veracruz, E Mexico, in Sierra Madre Oriental, 28 mi. NW of Jalapa; agr. center (corn, coffee, sugar, tobacco, fruit).

Altötting (ält'û'tĭng), town (pop. 8,529), Upper Bavaria, Germany, near the Inn, 42 mi. SW of Passau; metalworking, printing. Has anc. pilgrimage chapel with shrine of Holy Virgin, and late-Romanesque church containing tomb of Tilly.

Alto Uruguai (äl'tōō ōōrōōgwī'), town (pop. 234), Rio Grande do Sul, Brazil, on Uruguay R., opposite Monteagudo (Argentina), and 65 mi. N of Santo Ângelo.

Alto Verde (äl'tō vĕr'dā), E suburb (pop. estimate 1,500) of Santa Fe, E central Santa Fe prov., Argentina, on arm of Paraná R.; stock-raising and dairying center.

Altragusa, Yugoslavia: see CAVTAT.

Altranstädt (ält'rän'shtĕt), village (pop. 1,817), in former Prussian Saxony prov., central Germany, after 1945 in Saxony-Anhalt, 10 mi. W of Leipzig. In treaty signed here (Sept., 1706) with Charles XII of Sweden, Augustus the Strong of Saxony abandoned Polish throne.

Altrincham (ôl'trĭng-ùm), municipal borough (1931 pop. 21,356; 1951 census 39,787), N Cheshire, England, 8 mi. SW of Manchester; metalworks (refrigeration and weighing machinery, machine tools); mfg. of abrasives. Truck-gardening center for Manchester. Chartered in 1290. Sometimes spelled Altringham.

Altrip (ält'rēp'), village (pop. 3,159), Rhenish Palatinate, W Germany, on the Rhine and 4 mi. SE of Ludwigshafen; chemicals. Grain, sugar beets, tobacco. Roman remains excavated near by.

Alt Ruppin (ält' rōō'pĭn), town (pop. 3,369), Brandenburg, E Germany, at N tip of Ruppin L., 3 mi. NE of Neuruppin; potatoes, grain, stock; dairying; forestry.

Alt Sandec, Poland: see STARY SACZ.

Altschmecks, Czechoslovakia: see STARY SMOKOVEC.

Alt-Schwanenburg, Latvia: see GULBENE.

Altsohl, Czechoslovakia: see ZVOLEN.

Altstadt, Czechoslovakia: see STARE MESTO.

Altstätten (ält'shtĕ'tùn), town (pop. 8,213), St. Gall canton, NE Switzerland, 8 mi. ESE of St. Gall; embroideries, chemicals, leather, foodstuff.

Alt Thann, France: see VIEUX-THANN.

Altukhovo (ŭltōō'khùvŭ), town (1946 pop. over 500), SE Bryansk oblast, Russian SFSR, 38 mi. S of Bryansk; sawmilling.

Altun Köprü (äl'tōōn kû'prû) or **Altun Kopri** (kō'prē), village, Kirkuk prov., NE Iraq, on Little Zab R. and 25 mi. NW of Kirkuk; barley, wheat, fruit, sheep.

Altura (ältōō'rä), town (pop. 2,804), Castellón de la Plana prov., E Spain, 18 mi. NW of Sagunto; olive-oil processing, mfg. of cotton textiles and burlap; cereals, vegetables, fruit, and wine; sericulture. Lead and silver mining, marble quarrying near by.

Altura (ăltōō'rù), village (pop. 269), Winona co., SE Minn., near Mississippi R., 15 mi. W of Winona; dairy products.

Alturas (ăltōō'rùs), city (pop. 2,819), ⊙ Modoc co., NE Calif., on Pit R. and c.90 mi. SE of Klamath Falls, Oregon; shipping and trade center for stock-raising, farming, lumbering region. Hq. of Modoc Natl. Forest. Hunting, fishing near by. Warner Mts. are just E. Inc. 1901.

Altus (ăl'tùs). **1** Town (pop. 431), Franklin co., NW Ark., 37 mi. ENE of Fort Smith, near Arkansas R. **2** City (pop. 9,735), ⊙ Jackson co., SW Okla., 70 mi. NW of Wichita Falls (Texas), bet. Salt Fork (3 mi. W) and North Fork (11 mi. E) of Red R.; rail junction; market and processing center for agr. region (mainly cotton; also wheat, alfalfa, livestock). Cotton ginning and compressing, meat packing, dairying; feed, flour, and cottonseed-oil milling; railroad shops. Mfg. also of canvas, metal, and concrete products; cotton-gin equipment, machine-shop products. Seat of Altus Col. N of city, on North Fork of Red R., is W. C. Austin reclamation project, chief unit of which is ALTUS DAM. Founded c.1892, inc. 1901.

Altus Dam, SW Okla., 18 mi. N of Altus, on North Fork of Red R.; c.100 ft. high, 1,112 ft. long; reservoir capacity 151,650 acre-ft. Chief unit of W. C. Austin project (begun 1941) for irrigation of c.50,000 acres, flood control, and water supply to Altus. Occupies site of Lugert Dam and old L. Altus reservoir (1927).

Altvater Gebirge, Czechoslovakia: see JESENIKY.

Altweier, France: see AUBURE.

Altwies (ält'vēs), village (pop. 389), SE Luxembourg, 9 mi. SSE of Luxembourg city, on Fr. border; stone quarrying; fruitgrowing (plums, cherries).

Alty-Agach (ŭltē"-ŭgäch'), village (1939 pop. over 2,000), NE Azerbaijan SSR, at SE end of the Greater Caucasus, 60 mi. NW of Baku; livestock, lumber.

Alty-Aryk (ŭltē"-ŭrĭk'), village (1926 pop. 5,706), SE Fergana oblast, Uzbek SSR, 15 mi. W of Fergana, in cotton area; silk milling. Formerly also called Lyailyak-Khana.

Altynai or **Altynay** (ŭltĭnī'), town (1943 pop. over 500), S Sverdlovsk oblast, Russian SFSR, 11 mi. N of Sukhoi Log, on railroad; anthracite-mining center; gold mines. Formerly called Antratsit and Irbitskiye Vershiny.

Altyn-Kol, Russian SFSR: see TELETSKOYE LAKE.

Altyn-Kul or **Altyn-Kul'** (ŭltĭn"-kōōl'), village (1939 pop. over 500), NW Andizhan oblast, Uzbek SSR, near the Kara Darya, c.10 mi. WNW of Andizhan; cotton.

Altyn Tagh (ältün' täg'), N branch of the Kunlun mtn. system, S Sinkiang prov., China, extends over 500 mi. WSW-ENE bet. 84° and 94°E, along S edge of Tarim basin and Taklamakan Desert; rises to 17,000 ft. It is continued E by the Nan Shan. Also called Astin Tagh and Ustun Tagh.

Alucra (älōōchrä'), village (pop. 711), Giresun prov., N Turkey, 45 mi. SSE of Giresun; corn, sugar beets. Formerly Mesudiye.

Aluksne (ä'lōōksnā), Latvian *Alūksne*, Ger. *Marienburg*, city (pop. 4,385), NE Latvia, in Vidzeme, 45 mi. SE of Valga, on S shore of small Aluksne L. (isl. has castle ruins); sawmilling, wool and flax spinning; oilseed mill, brewery.

Alula (älōō'lä), town (pop. 2,000), in the Mijirtein, N Ital. Somaliland, port on Gulf of Aden, 120 mi. ENE of Bender Kassim; 11°58'N 50°45'E; fishing (tunny), mother of pearl, frankincense gathering.

Alum Bank, Pa.: see PLEASANTVILLE, Bedford co.

Alum Bay, England: see NEEDLES, THE.

Aluminé (älōōmēnā'), town (pop. estimate 500), ⊙ Aluminé dept. (1947 pop. 2,650), W Neuquén natl. territory, Argentina, on Aluminé R. and 50 mi. SW of Zapala; stock raising (sheep, goats); sawmills.

Aluminé, Lake, Andean lake (□ 22; alt. 3,580 ft.) in W Neuquén natl. territory, Argentina, 8 mi. S of Arco Pass, near Chile border; 11 mi. long. Outlet, **Aluminé River,** flows c.75 mi. S, joining Catán-Lil R. to form Collón Curá R.

Alung Gangri, Tibet: see ALING KANGRI.

Alupka (ŭlōōp'kŭ), city (1926 pop. 2,974), S Crimea, Russian SFSR, port on Black Sea coast, at S foot of the Ai-Petri, 7 mi. SW of Yalta. Major tourist and health resort; numerous sanatoriums and rest homes. Has 100-acre park with former Vorontsov castle (built 1840s in late English Gothic style; now a mus. and rest home); residence of Winston Churchill during 1945 Yalta Conference.

Alur (älōōr'). **1** Village, Bellary dist., NW Madras, India, 17 mi. S of Adoni; cotton, millet, peanuts. **2** Town (pop. 2,133), Hassan dist., W Mysore, India, 8 mi. WSW of Hassan; local agr. trade center (rice, sugar cane, millet); rice milling.

Alushta (ŭlōōsh'tŭ), city (1926 pop. 4,759), S Crimea, Russian SFSR, port on Black Sea coast, 17 mi. NE of Yalta; health resort (rest homes, bathing beach) in winegrowing and tobacco area. Originally called Aluston; dates from 6th-5th cent. B.C.; became important fortress in 6th cent. A.D. under Justinian I. Commercial center in Genoese times (13th-14th cent.).

Alustante (älōōstän'tā), town (pop. 1,040), Guadalajara prov., central Spain, 19 mi. SE of Molina; lumbering, stock raising; grows grain, potatoes, vegetables. Mfg. of slate pencils.

Aluta River, Rumania: see OLT RIVER.

Alutgama (ŭlōōtgä'mŭ), village (pop. 3,010), Western Prov., Ceylon, on SW coast, at mouth of the small Bentota Ganga, 35 mi. SSE of Colombo; trades in graphite, tea, rubber, rice, vegetables, cinnamon.

Alutnuwara (ŭlōōt"nōōvä'rŭ), village (pop. 1,008), Uva Prov., central Ceylon, on the Mahaweli Ganga and 25 mi. E of Kandy; rice, vegetables; rubber plantation. Site of one of oldest stupas in Ceylon; Buddhist pilgrimage center. Of strategic importance in anc. times. Formerly called Mahiyangana.

Aluwihare, Ceylon: see MATALE.

Alva (ăl'vù), burgh (1931 pop. 3,820; 1951 census 4,107), Clackmannan, Scotland, near Devon R., 3 mi. N of Alloa, at foot of Ochil Hills; woolen milling, coal mining. Near by is Alva Glen (valley) with small picturesque waterfall, in former silver-mining region.

Alva (ăl'vù). **1** Mining village (pop. 1,341), Harlan co., SE Ky., in the Cumberlands, 19 mi. ENE of Middlesboro; bituminous coal. **2** City (pop. 6,505), ⊙ Woods co., NW Okla., on Salt Fork of Arkansas R. and 50 mi. NW of Enid; commercial and processing center for agr. area (especially wheat). Mfg. of dairy products, flour, feed, mattresses. Northwestern State Col. is near by. Settled 1893.

Alva B. Adams Tunnel (13.07 mi. long; alt. 8,400 ft.), N Colo., in Rocky Mtn. Natl. Park. Important unit in Colorado–Big Thompson project; conducts water ENE from Grand L. (supplied from GRANBY Reservoir) through Front Range to point 6 mi. SW of Estes Park; 9.75 ft. in diameter. Makes water available for irrigation and power on E slope of Continental Divide. Temporary pipe line connects E portal with BIG THOMPSON RIVER.

Alvah, Scotland: see KIRKTOWN OF ALVAH.

Alvaiázere (älväyä'zĭrĭ), town (pop. 294), Leiria dist., W central Portugal, 24 mi. ENE of Leiria, in olive-growing area.

Alvalade (älvùlä'dĭ), town (pop. 1,803), Setúbal dist., S central Portugal, on Sado R., on railroad and 30 mi. WSW of Beja; cork industry.

Alvan, Ill.: see ALVIN.

Alvand, Iran: see ALWAND.

Alvarado, Argentina: see GENERAL ALVARADO, Salta prov.

Alvarado, Costa Rica: see PACAYAS.

Alvarado (älvärä'dō), city (pop. 5,776), Veracruz, E Mexico, port on peninsula bet. Alvarado Lagoon and Gulf of Campeche, 38 mi. SE of Veracruz. Rail terminus; fishing center (pearls, turtles, crabs, oysters), supplying the Mexico city market. Preserves character of 16th-cent. fishing village. Has old church (built 1779). Pedro de Alvarado, a lieutenant of Cortés, landed here in 1518.

Alvarado. 1 (ălvùrä'dō) Village (1940 pop. 776), Alameda co., W Calif., 18 mi. SE of Oakland; beet-sugar, salt refining. **2** (ălvùrā'dō) Village (pop. 317), Marshall co., NW Minn., on Snake R., near Red R., and 20 mi. NNE of Grand Forks, N.Dak., in grain area. **3** (ălvùrā'dù) City (pop. 1,656), Johnson co., N central Texas, 24 mi. S of Fort Worth; trade point in cotton, grain area; cotton ginning, poultry packing; mfg. (furniture, clothing).

Alvarado Lagoon (älvärä'dō), NW Honduras, salt-water lagoon off Gulf of Honduras, just SE of Puerto Cortés; 2.5 mi. long, 1.5 mi. wide. Connected by canals with lower Chamelecón R. (E) and Cortés Bay (W). Fisheries.

Alvarado Lagoon, Veracruz, SE Mexico, in Sotavento lowlands; 20 mi. long, up to 3 mi. wide. Port of Alvarado is at its opening on Gulf of Campeche. Receives united Papaloápam and San Juan rivers.

Alvarães (älvùrä'ĭs), town (pop. 315), central Amazonas, Brazil, on right bank of the Amazon and 13 mi. NW of Tefé. Until 1944, Caiçara (old spelling, Caissara).

Álvares Machado (äl'vùrĭs mùshä'dōō), city (pop. 2,125), W São Paulo, Brazil, on railroad and 7 mi. WNW of Presidente Prudente; coffee, rice, fruit, corn, timber.

Álvarez (äl'värĕs), town (pop. estimate 1,500), S Santa Fe prov., Argentina, 15 mi. SW of Rosario; agr. center (corn, flax, potatoes, livestock); liquor distilling, tanning.

Alvarez, Villa de, Mexico: see VILLA DE ALVAREZ.

Álvaro Obregón (äl'värō ōbrāgōn'). **1** City (pop. 2,788), Guanajuato, central Mexico, 55 mi. E of Guanajuato; alt. 6,627 ft.; cereals, sugar, alfalfa, fruit, livestock. Formerly Iturbide. **2** Town (pop. 1,504), Michoacán, central Mexico, 14 mi. NE of Morelia; cereals, vegetables, livestock. Formerly San Bartolo. **3** City (pop. 7,439), Tabasco, SE Mexico, port at mouth of Grijalva and Usumacinta rivers, 6 mi. inland from the Gulf of Campeche, 40 mi. NNE of Villahermosa, 120 mi. ENE of Coatzacoalcos. Trading, processing, and agr. center (sugar, tobacco, corn, rice, beans, cacao, bananas, livestock; timber). Tanning, sawmilling, vegetable-oil pressing; mfg. of soap, footwear. Exports fruit, wood. Airfield. Sometimes called Frontera. **4** Town, Zacatecas, Mexico: see NORIA DE ANGELES.

Alvartirunagari, India: see ALWAR TIRUNAGARI.

Alvaston and Boulton (bōl'tùn), residential former urban district (1931 pop. 3,280), S Derby, England, on Derwent R. and 3 mi. SE of Derby.

Alvastra (äl'västrä"), locality, Ostergotland co., S Sweden, on E shore of L. Vatter, 18 mi. W of Mjolby. Here are ruins of Sweden's oldest Cistercian monastery (mid-12th cent.). Tourist resort.

Alvaton (ăl'vŭtŭn), town (pop. 95), Meriwether co., W Ga., 19 mi. WSW of Griffin, near Flint R.

Alvdal (älv' däl), village (pop. 349; canton pop. 2,535), Hedmark co., E Norway, at head of the Osterdal, on Glomma R., at mouth of small Folla R., on railroad and 40 mi. SW of Roros; transshipment point for Folldal copper-pyrite mines (cable railroad to Folldal).

Alvdalen (ĕlv'dä"lŭn), Swedish *Älvdalen*, village (pop. 1,070), Kopparberg co., central Sweden, on East Dal R. and 70 mi. NW of Falun; porphyry quarrying, sawmilling; tourist resort. Noted for its old customs and dialect. Has 16th-cent. church, mus. Includes Ostermycklang (û'stûrmük"lĕng), Swedish *Östermyckläng*, village.

Alvear (älvā-är'). **1** town (pop. 3,697), E Corrientes prov., Argentina, port on Uruguay R., opposite Itaqui (Brazil), at mouth of Aguapey R., on railroad and 95 mi. E of Mercedes. Agr. center (rice, corn, peanuts, tobacco, flax, citrus fruit). **2** Town (pop. estimate 600), S Santa Fe prov., Argentina, 10 mi. S of Rosario; rail junction in grain and livestock area.

Alveley (ăv'lē), agr. village and parish (pop. 822), SE Shropshire, England, near Severn R., 7 mi. NW of Kidderminster; gravel quarrying. Has church (mainly 13th cent.).

Alvenas, Sweden: see VALBERG.

Alverca (älvĕr'kŭ), village (pop. 1,417), Lisboa dist., central Portugal, on lower Tagus R. and 13 mi. NNE of Lisbon; airport. Saltworks.

Alveringem (äl'vŭrĭng"ŭm), agr. village (pop. 2,128), West Flanders prov., NW Belgium, 5 mi. SSE of Furnes. Formerly spelled Alveringhem.

Alversdorf (äl'fŭrsdôrf), village (pop. 2,143), in Brunswick, NW Germany, after 1945 Lower Saxony, 5 mi. S of Helmstedt, in sugar-beet region.

Alverstoke, England: see GOSPORT.

Alverstone, Mount (ôl'vŭrstŭn) (14,500 ft.), SW Yukon, on Alaska border, in St. Elias Mts.; 60°21'N 139°4'W.

Alverstraumen, Norway: see ALVERSUND.

Alversund (äl'vŭrsoon), village and canton (pop. 1,968), Hordaland co., SW Norway, port on narrow sound off North Sea, 13 mi. NNW of Bergen; sawmill, biscuit factory; exports dairy and agr. products. In the canton is Alverstraumen village, on Radoy 1 mi. W across the sound, with fish and meat canneries.

Alves (ăl'vŭs), agr. village and parish (pop. 888), N Moray, Scotland, 5 mi. W of Elgin.

Alvesta (äl'vŭstä"), town (pop. 4,047), Kronoberg co., S Sweden, at N end of Sal L., Swedish *Salen* (sä'lŭn) (8 mi. long, 1 mi. wide), 9 mi. W of Vaxjo; rail junction; mfg. of machinery, glass, furniture; woolen mills. Has old church.

Alvie (ăl'vē), agr. village and parish (pop. 541), E Inverness, Scotland, on small Loch Alvie (1 mi. long, ½ mi. wide), near the Spey, 9 mi. NE of Kingussie.

Alvignano (älvēnyä'nô), village (pop. 2,368), Caserta prov., Campania, S Italy, 12 mi. N of Caserta.

Alvik (ôl'vĭk, -vēk), Nor. *Ålvik*, village (pop. 796) in Kvam canton (pop. 5,232), Hordaland co., SW Norway, on Hardanger Fjord, 37 mi. E of Bergen; metallurgical center (iron alloys, pig iron). Bjolvefoss near by. Sometimes spelled Aalvik.

Alvik, Sweden: see VII.

Alvin. **1** Village (pop. 287), Vermilion co., E Ill., on North Fork of Vermilion R. and 10 mi. N of Danville. Sometimes Alvan. **2** City (pop. 3,701), Brazoria co., S Texas, 24 mi. S of Houston; trade center in oil and sulphur-producing, dairying, truck-farming area; flower nurseries.

Alvinc, Rumania: see VINTUL-DE-JOS.

Alvinópolis (älvēnô'poolēs), city (pop. 2,218), SE central Minas Gerais, Brazil, 30 mi. NNW of Ponte Nova; sugar-cane growing. Lignite deposits.

Alvinston (ăl'vĭnstŭn), village (pop. 699), S Ont., on Sydenham R. and 30 mi. ESE of Sarnia; flax and flour milling, fruit and vegetable canning.

Alviso (ălvē'sō), town (pop. 652), Santa Clara co., W Calif., 6 mi. NNW of Santa Clara; farming. Duck hunting in marshes (N).

Alvito (älvē'tô), village (pop. 1,847), Frosinone prov., Latium, S central Italy, 7 mi. ESE of Sora.

Alvito (älvē'too), town (pop. 2,610), Beja dist., S Portugal, near railroad, 18 mi. NNW of Beja; trades in grain, citrus fruit, cork, sheep; cheese mfg. Has old castle (c.1500).

Alvkarleby (ĕlv'kär"lŭbü", ĕlvkär'lŭbü"), Swedish *Älvkarleby*, village (pop. 3,159), Uppsala co., E Sweden, on Dal R. (falls; 52 ft. high, 257 ft. wide) and 13 mi. SE of Gavle; hydroelectric station. Formerly spelled Elfkarleby and Alfkarleby, Swed. *Älfkarleby*.

Alvkarleo (ĕlv'kär"lŭû", ĕlvkär'lŭû"), Swedish *Älvkarleö*, village (pop. 478), Uppsala co., E Sweden, on Dal R., near its mouth on Gulf of Bothnia, 13 mi. SE of Gavle; metalworking. Near by is hydroelectric station of Alvkarleby.

Alvo, village (pop. 190), Cass co., SE Nebr., 15 mi. E of Lincoln.

Alvon, village, Greenbrier co., SE W.Va., 9 mi. NNE of White Sulphur Springs, in Monongahela Natl. Forest. Near by is Blue Bend Recreation Area.

Alvor (älvōr'), anc. *Portus Hannibalis*, town (pop. 1,979), Faro dist., S Portugal, on the Atlantic (S coast), 3 mi. W of Portimão; seaside resort; fish canning. Its Moorish castle is in ruins since 1755 earthquake. Captured 1189 from Moors, who had named it Albur.

Alvord (ăl'vŭrd). **1** Town (pop. 263), Lyon co., NW Iowa, 9 mi. SW of Rock Rapids, in agr. area. **2** Town (pop. 735), Wise co., N Texas, c.45 mi. NW of Fort Worth, near West Fork of Trinity R., in agr., cattle area.

Alvordton (ăl'vŭrtŭn), village (pop. 335), Williams co., extreme NW Ohio, near Mich. line, 14 mi. NNE of Bryan.

Alvoy (älv'ûü), Nor. *Alvøy*, village (pop. 395) in Laksevag (Nor. *Laksevåg*) canton, Hordaland co., SW Norway, ferry station on narrow sound off North Sea, 6 mi. SW of Bergen; mfg. (paper, glue, food products).

Alvsborg (ĕlfs'bôr"yŭ), Swedish *Älvsborg*, county [Swedish *län*] (□ 4,918; 1950 pop. 358,506), SW Sweden; ⊙ Vanersborg. In Dalsland and in Vastergotland, co. includes W part of L. Vaner. Generally low and level, surface rises toward SE; co. is drained by Gota, Viska, Atra, and many smaller rivers. Lakes include Mjor, Stora Le, and Asmund. Agr. (wheat, rye, oats), cattle raising, dairying, are important. Industries include textile, paper, and pulp milling. Cities are Trollhattan (major power station; heavy industry), Vanersborg, Boras, Alingsas, Ulricehamn, and Amal. Formerly spelled Elfsborg and Alfsborg, Swed. *Älfsborg*.

Alvsbyn (ĕlfs'bün"), Swedish *Älvsbyn*, village (pop. 1,446), Norrbotten co., N Sweden, on Pite R. and 20 mi. SW of Boden; rail junction; tree nurseries; woodworking. Sometimes spelled Alvsby, Swedish *Älvsby*.

Alwand or **Alvand** (äl'vänd), anc. *Orontes* (ōrŏn'tēz), mountain (11,640 ft.) in W central Iran, rising just S of Hamadan; snow-capped, with picturesque valleys. Chiefly composed of quartz; graphite deposits. Tuisarkan is on S slopes. Sometimes spelled Elvend.

Alwand (äl'wänd), small E suburb of Khanaqin, Diyala prov., E Iraq, at Iran line, in an oil-producing area; has small refinery.

Alwar (ŭl'vŭr, ŭl'wŭr), former princely state (□ 3,158; pop. 823,055) in Rajputana States, India; ⊙ was Alwar. A Rajput state, founded in 1770s by Pratap Singh; soon after, overrun by Mahrattas. Treaty concluded with British in 1803. In 1949, joined union of Rajasthan. Sometimes spelled Alwur.

Alwar, city (pop. 54,143), ⊙ Alwar dist., E Rajasthan, India, 65 mi. NE of Jaipur; market for millet, gram, oilseeds, cotton fabrics, cattle; handicraft cloth weaving, oilseed and flour milling; mfg. of ice, aerated water, iron safes, paint, varnish, pottery, glass-bangles. Situated at foot of low hill range, city contains some fine palaces, armory, col., and library (valuable Oriental MSS). Was ⊙ former Rajputana state of Alwar.

Alwar Tirunagari or **Alvartirunagari** (äl'vär tĭroonŭg'ŭrē), town (pop. 6,284), Tinnevelly dist., S Madras, India, on Tambraparni R. and 19 mi. ESE of Tinnevelly; carpet weaving, sugar refining. Seasonal cattle-trade center during temple pilgrimage festivals. Also spelled Alwarthirunagari.

Alwaye (ŭlvŭ'yĕ), city (pop. 9,744), NW Travancore, India, on Periyar R. and 37 mi. NNW of Kottayam; aluminum works; mfg. of cotton textiles; glassworks (lenses, tableware, sheet glass), chemical fertilizer plant; electroplating, rice milling, cashew-nut processing. Construction begun 1950 on plant to process monazite ore for thorium. Col. (affiliated with Univ. of Travancore). Health resort; bathing.

Alyaty (ŭlyŭtē'), town (1939 pop. over 500), E Azerbaijan SSR, on Caspian Sea, 30 mi. SW of Baku; rail junction; fishing port. Oil wells and gas deposits near by.

Alygdzher (ŭlĭgjĕr'), village (1948 pop. over 500), SW Irkutsk oblast, Russian SFSR, in Eastern Sayan Mts., on upper Chuna R. (Uda R.) and 165 mi. SSW of Nizhneudinsk; trading point and cultural center for local Karagass (Tofalar) nomads. Mica deposits near by. Also known as Kultbaza Alygdzher.

Alyn River (ă'lĭn), Denbigh and Flint, Wales, rises 5 mi. NW of Llangollen, flows 50 mi. NE and E, past Clwydian Hills, and past Hope and Mold, to the Dee 6 mi. S of Chester.

Alyth (ā'lĭth), burgh (1931 pop. 1,662; 1951 census 2,072), E Perthshire, Scotland, 5 mi. ENE of Blairgowrie; linen and woolen milling; agr. market. Near by is Airlie Castle; present structure dates from 18th cent.

Alytus or **Alitus** (ălētoos'), Ger. and Pol. *Olita*, fortified city (pop. 9,207), S Lithuania, on Neman R. and 33 mi. S of Kaunas; rail terminus; sawmilling and wood-cracking center; mfg. of lubricating oils, turpentine, tar, pulp, paper; flour milling, tanning, canning, wool spinning. Regional mus. City dates from 14th cent.; passed 1795 to Prussia, 1815 to Rus. Poland; in Suvalki govt. until 1920.

Alzaga (äl-thä'gä), outer NW suburb (pop. 6,047) of Bilbao, Vizcaya prov., N Spain, on Nervión R.; mfg. of metal cables, machinery, naval equipment, and also ceramics and canned foods.

Alzamai or **Alzamay** (ŭlzŭmī'), town (1948 pop. over 2,000), W Irkutsk oblast, Russian SFSR, on Trans-Siberian RR and 35 mi. SE of Taishet; lumbering.

Alzano Maggiore (ältsä'nô mäd-jô'rē), village (pop. 3,814), Bergamo prov., Lombardy, N Italy, on Serio R. and 3 mi. NE of Bergamo; silk industry.

Alzatate or **San Carlos Alzatate** (sän kär'lōs älsätä'tā), town (1950 pop. 1,420), Jalapa dept., E central Guatemala, at SE foot of volcano Alzatate (9,020 ft.), 13 mi. SSW of Jalapa; corn, beans, livestock.

Alzenau or **Alzenau in Unterfranken** (äl'tsŭnou ĭn oon'tŭrfräng"kŭn), village (pop. 3,678), Lower Franconia, NW Bavaria, Germany, on small Kahl R. and 9 mi. NNW of Aschaffenburg; tanning, brewing, lumber and flour milling. Tobacco- and winegrowing. Has 18th-cent. church.

Alzette River (ălzĕt'), S and central Luxembourg, rises 2.5 mi. WNW of Esch-sur-Alzette, flows 40 mi. E and N, past Esch-sur-Alzette, Bettembourg, Luxembourg, and Mersch, to the Sûre at Ettelbruck, just below mouth of Wark R. Not navigable.

Alzey (älts'ī"), town (pop. 9,005), Rhenish Hesse, W Germany, 13 mi. NW of Worms; rail junction; mfg. (machinery, shoes); market center for wine and agr. region. Remains of fortifications. Roman artifacts in mus. Was a residence of electors palatine. Passed to Hesse in 1815.

Alzon (älzō'), village (pop. 252), Gard dept., S France, 8 mi. WSW of Le Vigan; dairying; lead and copper mining.

Alzonne (älzōn'), village (pop. 1,015), Aude dept., S France, on Fresquel R. and 9 mi. WNW of Carcassonne; cereal- and winegrowing, distilling.

Alz River (älts), Bavaria, Germany, rises in the Chiemsee, flows 33 mi. NE to the Inn, 8 mi. ENE of Altötting.

Am [Arabic,=the], for Arabic names in Aden Protectorate beginning thus: see under following part of the name.

Ama (ä'mä), town (pop. 5,946), Hyogo prefecture, Japan, on SW coast of Awaji-shima, 13 mi. SW of Sumoto; rice, wheat, truck. Tile making; fishing.

Amacueca (ämäkwā'kä), town (pop. 1,900), Jalisco, W Mexico, on L. Sayula, 45 mi. SE of Ameca; grain, alfalfa, sugar, fruit, livestock.

Amacuro River (ämäkoo'rō), in Venezuela and British Guiana, rises on international boundary at 7°53'N 60°22'W, flows NE along international line for half its course, then NW, to fall into the Atlantic at one of the mouths of the Orinoco (Boca Grande or Boca de Navíos) at San José de Amacuro; length, c.100 mi. Upper course not navigable because of rapids.

Amacuzac (ämäkoosäk'), town (pop. 897), Morelos, central Mexico, 24 mi. SSW of Cuernavaca; rice, tropical fruit, vegetables. Airfield near by. Hydroelectric plant, supplying Federal Dist., is on Amacuzac R. tributary of Río de las Balsas.

Amadeus, Lake (ŭmă'dēŭs) (□ 340), SW Northern Territory, Australia, 170 mi. SW of Alice Springs; 76 mi. long, 12 mi. wide; usually dry; salt.

Amadi (ämä'dē), town, Equatoria prov., S Anglo-Egyptian Sudan, 100 mi. WNW of Juba; road junction; cotton, peanuts, sesame, corn, durra; livestock. Hq. Moru dist., inhabited by Sudanese tribe.

'Amadiya or **'Amadiyah** (ämädē'yŭ) town, Mosul prov., N Iraq, in mts. of Kurdistan, near Turkish frontier, 60 mi. NNE of Mosul; wheat, barley, fruits.

Amadjuak (ŭmă'jooăk), Eskimo settlement, S Baffin Isl., SE Franklin Dist., Northwest Territories, on Hudson Strait; 64°1'N 72°39'W.

Amadjuak Lake (50 mi. long, 28 mi. wide), SW Baffin Isl., SE Franklin Dist., Northwest Territories; 65°N 71°W; borders W on the Great Plain of the Koukdjuak. Drains N into Nettilling L. by Amadjuak R. (c.50 mi. long).

Amador (ă'mŭdôr"), county (□ 594; pop. 9,151), central and E Calif.; ⊙ Jackson. Extends from Sacramento Valley (W) to the Sierra Nevada (E), where Mokelumne Peak rises to 9,371 ft. Bounded N by Mokelumne R., S by Cosumnes R. Partly in El Dorado Natl. Forest. Includes part of Pardee Reservoir. Mother Lode gold-mining region, made famous in the tales of Mark Twain and Bret Harte, centers around Jackson; many old gold camps survive. Lode-gold mining; clay, sand, and gravel quarrying. Stock grazing (cattle, sheep), some farming (chiefly hay), dairying, poultry raising. Lumbering, lumber milling. Recreational region (trout fishing, lakes, winter sports). Formed 1854.

Amadora (ämŭdô'rŭ), residential suburb (pop. 6,158) of Lisbon, central Portugal, on railroad and 6 mi. NW of city center; fruit preserving.

Amador City or **Amador,** city (pop. 151), Amador co., central Calif., 37 mi. ESE of Sacramento, in Mother Lode region; gold.

Amagá (ämägä'), town (pop. 2,306), Antioquia dept., NW central Colombia, in valley of Cordillera Central, on railroad and 18 mi. SW of Medellín, in agr. area (coffee, tobacco, sugar cane); alt. 4,567 ft. Coal and iron mining; mfg. of agr. implements.

Amagansett (ă″mŭgăn′sĭt), resort and fishing village (1940 pop. 974), Suffolk co., SE N.Y., near S shore of E Long Isl., 14 mi. ENE of Southampton.

Amagasaki (ämä″gä′säkē), city (1940 pop. 181,011; 1947 pop. 233,183), Hyogo prefecture, S Honshu, Japan, on Osaka Bay, on Yodo R. just NNW of Osaka. Industrial center; chemical and metallurgical plants, engineering works, textile mills; glass, pottery, beer. Exports metalwork, drugs, dyes, pottery, woodwork. Bombed (1945) in Second World War.

Amager (ä′măyŭr), island (□ 25.1; pop. 150,775), Denmark, in the Oresund, bet. Koge Bay and Drogden strait; truck produce. In N is part of COPENHAGEN city; in S half are Taarnby, Kastrup, and Dragor towns. Royal park at SW tip.

Amagi, Japan: see AMAKI.

Amagon (ă′mŭgŏn″), town (pop. 181), Jackson co., NE Ark., 11 mi. ESE of Newport.

Amaguaña (ämägwä′nyä), village, Pichincha prov., N central Ecuador, in the Andes, on Guaillabamba R. and 11 mi. S of Quito; cotton-textile milling; cereals, fruit.

Amaichá (ämīchä′), village (pop. estimate 1,000), NW Tucumán prov., Argentina, at W foot of the Cumbres Calchaquíes, 45 mi. NW of Tucumán; alt. 6,300 ft.; agr. center: corn, alfalfa, grapes, tomatoes, pepper, livestock. Sometimes Amaichá del Valle.

Amaki (ä″mä′kē) or **Amagi** (-gē), town (pop. 11,754), Fukuoka prefecture, N central Kyushu, Japan, 19 mi. SE of Fukuoka; rail terminus; commercial center for agr. area (rice, wheat, barley); textile mill.

Amaknak Island (ŭmăk′năk), islet in Unalaska Bay, NE Unalaska Isl., Fox Isls., Aleutian Isls., SW Alaska; site of DUTCH HARBOR. Also spelled Umaknak.

Amakusa Islands (ämä′kōōsä), Jap. *Amakusa-to*, island group (□ 341; 1940 pop. 192,595; 1947 pop. 260,854), in E.China Sea, Japan, off W coast of Kyushu, bet. Amakusa Sea (W) and Yatsushiro Bay (E); comprises c.70 isls. and islets. SHIMO-JIMA (largest isl.), KAMI-SHIMA, and OYANO-SHIMA are in Kumamoto prefecture; NAGA-SHIMA and SHISHI-JIMA in Kagoshima prefecture. Mountainous, fertile. Hot springs on Shimo-jima. Chief products: rice, fish.

Amakusa Sea, Jap. *Amakusa-nada*, NE arm of E.China Sea, bet. Nomo Peninsula (W) and Shimo-jima (E), Japan; c.20 mi. wide. N arm is called TACHIBANA BAY, NE arm, SHIMABARA BAY.

Amal (ō′mōl), Swedish *Åmål*, city (pop. 7,312), Alvsborg co., SW Sweden, on W shore of L. Vaner, 35 mi. SW of Karlstad; rail junction, lake port. Railroad shops; mfg. of rubber products, electrical equipment, furniture, pianos, clothing. Inc. 1643. Suffered destructive fire, 1901.

Amalapuram (ŭmŭlä′pōōrŭm), town (pop. 14,527), East Godavari dist., NE Madras, India; road center in Godavari delta mouth, 30 mi. SSW of Cocanada; rice milling, coir-rope mfg.; sugar cane, tobacco, oilseeds.

Amalfi (ämäl′fē), town (pop. 3,232), Antioquia dept., NW central Colombia, in E foothills of Cordillera Central, 24 mi. E of Yarumal; alt. 5,250 ft. Agr. (corn, sugar, coffee, yucca, rice, bananas, cattle); gold mining.

Amalfi (ämäl′fē), town (pop. 4,259), Salerno prov., Campania, S Italy, port on Gulf of Salerno, 24 mi. SE of Naples. Tourist center noted for its climate and scenery; bathing resort; mfg. (paper, macaroni, nets), fishing. Archbishopric. Has fine 10th-cent. cathedral (many times restored) with 11th-cent. bronze doors (cast in Constantinople), 13th-cent. campanile, and picturesque cloister (chiostro del Paradiso). First (9th cent.) of Ital. maritime republics; became a duchy in 953 and rivaled Pisa, Venice, and Genoa. Established a maritime code, the *Tavole Amalfitane*, used in the Mediterranean until 16th cent. Taken by the Normans (1131) and sacked by Pisans (1135, 1137). Suffered landslides (1343, 1924).

Amalga, town (pop. 225), Cache co., N Utah, 9 mi. N of Logan.

Amalias (ämälēäs′), city (pop. 15,321), Elis nome, W Peloponnesus, Greece, on railroad and 10 mi. NNW of Pyrgos; commercial center for local agr. production (Zante currants, olives, wine) and dairy products.

Amalinda (ămŭlĭn′dŭ), residential town (pop. 2,802), SE Cape Prov., U. of So. Afr., 7 mi. NW of East London.

Amalner (ŭ′mŭlnăr), town (pop. 34,694), East Khandesh dist., NE Bombay, India, 32 mi. W of Jalgaon; road center; trades in cloth fabrics, millet, wheat; cotton ginning and milling, tanning, oilseed milling. Has Indian Inst. of Philosophy (founded 1916).

Amambahy, Serra de, Brazil: see AMAMBAÍ, SERRA DE.

Amambaí (ämämbäē′), city (pop. 1,100), southernmost Mato Grosso, Brazil, near Paraguay border, 45 mi. SE of Ponta Porã, in maté-growing region. Formerly called Patrimônio União. In Ponta Porã territory, 1943–46.

Amambaí, Serra de (sĕ′rŭ dĭ), Sp. *Sierra de Amambay* (syĕ′rä dā ämämbī′), range of central Brazilian plateau in S Mato Grosso and along Brazil-Paraguay border; extends c.200 mi. SSW from Campo Grande, forming divide bet. tributaries of Paraguay R. (W) and Paraná R. (E); rises to c.2,300 ft. Chief towns are Ponta Porã (Brazil) and Pedro Juan Caballero (Paraguay). Formerly spelled Serra de Amambahy.

Amambaí River, southernmost Mato Grosso, Brazil, rises in the Serra de Amambaí near Paraguay border, flows 150 mi. ESE to the Paraná 60 mi. above Guaíra Falls. Used for barge shipments of maté from Ponta Porã region to Paraguay and Argentina. Formerly spelled Amambahy.

Amambay (ämämbī′), department (□ 4,997; pop. 18,024), E Paraguay; ⊙ Pedro Juan Caballero. Borders Brazil, with Apa R. on N and mts. on E. In fertile, forested outliers of central Brazilian plateau. Has humid, subtropical climate. Predominantly cattle-raising and maté-growing area.

Amambay, Sierra de, Brazil and Paraguay: see AMAMBAÍ, SERRA DE.

Amami-gunto (ä″mä′mē-gōōntō), N island group (□ 498; 1950 pop. 219,024) of Ryukyu Islands, bet. E.China Sea (W) and Philippine Sea (E), 180 mi. S of Kyushu; 27°3′-29°58′N 128°26′-129°55′E. Its 200-mi. chain comprises AMAMI-O-SHIMA (largest), TOKUNO-SHIMA, OKINOERABU-SHIMA, KIKAI-SHIMA, YORON-JIMA, TOKARA-GUNTO, and many scattered islets. Generally mountainous and fertile (sugar cane, sweet potatoes). Extensive fishing industry. Sometimes Anglicized as Amami Isls. Formerly sometimes called Hokubu-shoto.

Amami-O-shima (ä″mä′mē-ō′shĭmä), largest island (□ 333; 1950 pop. 107,940, including offshore islets) of isl. group Amami-gunto, in Ryukyu Islands, bet. E.China Sea (W) and Philippine Sea (E), 150 mi. S of Kyushu; 28°19′N 129°25′E; 38 mi. long, 15 mi. wide. Hilly; fertile (sugar cane extensively grown). Tuna fishing. Chief products: silk textiles, sugar. Naze is chief town and port. Isl. is sometimes called O-shima.

Amamlu (ŭmŭmlōō′), village (1939 pop. over 2,000), NW Armenian SSR, on railroad and 22 mi. E of Leninakan, in sugar-beet and grain area; sugar refinery; limestone quarries.

Amana, Syria: see BARADA.

Amana (ă′mŭnŭ, ŭmă′nŭ), village, Iowa co., E central Iowa, chief village of the **Amana Society**, corporate name of a group of 7 small communities (total pop. c.1,400), near Iowa R., c.20 mi. WNW of Iowa City, in livestock, grain, fruit, truck-farming area; mfg. (woolen textiles, furniture, refrigeration equipment, meat and bakery products, feed). The first village, Amana, was settled 1855 by members of the Community of True Inspiration, a German religious sect. By 1861 they had laid out 5 more villages—East Amana, West Amana, High Amana, Upper South Amana, Lower South Amana—and had purchased Homestead. Settlers developed a successful communal way of life. Society was made a cooperative corporation, with separation of religious and economic administration, in 1932. The quaint villages, where craft culture has been preserved through the Amanite pattern of economic self-sufficiency, attract many visitors.

Amanalco (ämänäl′kō), officially Amanalco de Becerra, town (pop. 533), Mexico state, central Mexico, 23 mi. W of Toluca; cereals, livestock.

Amaná River (ämänä′), NE Venezuela, rises at SE foot of Cerro Peonia, flows c.125 mi. E, through the llanos, to Guanipa R. 35 mi. E of Maturín. Petroleum wells situated in middle course.

Amance (ämãs′), village (pop. 648), Haute-Saône dept., E France, 13 mi. NNW of Vesoul; lumbering.

Amancey (ämãsā′), village (pop. 501), Doubs dept., E France, in the Jura, 14 mi. S of Besançon; cheese mfg.

Amanda, village (pop. 587), Fairfield co., central Ohio, 9 mi. WSW of Lancaster, in agr. area; mfg. of hardware.

Amandas, Southern Rhodesia: see CONCESSION.

Amandola (ämän′dōlä), village (pop. 1,235), Ascoli Piceno prov., The Marches, central Italy, on Tenna R. and 14 mi. NW of Ascoli Piceno; rail terminus; resort (alt. 1,804 ft.).

Amangeldy or **Amangel'dy** (ŭmŭn-gyĕl′dē), village (1939 pop. over 500), SE Kustanai oblast, Kazakh SSR, on the Kara-Turgai (headstream of Turgai R.) and 70 mi. ENE of Turgai, in millet area. Until 1936, Batbakkara.

Amani (ämä′nē), village, Tanga prov., NE Tanganyika, 30 mi. W of Tanga; sisal, cotton, copra. Site of East African Agr. Research Inst., experimental stock farm and tung plantation.

Ama-no-hashidate, Japan: see MIYAZU.

Amanos Mountains (ümä′nŭs), **Gavur Mountains** (gyävōōr′), Turkish *Gâvur*, or **Alma Dag** (älmä′-dä″), Turkish *Alma Dağ*, anc. *Amanus*, range, S Turkey, an outlier of Taurus Mts. extending c.110 mi. NNE along E shore of Gulf of Iskenderun. Peaks include Migir Tepe (7,418 ft.), Ikiz Tepe (5,580 ft.), and Musa Dag (4,445 ft.). Town of Osmaniye on W slope. Range once formed boundary with Syria. Belen Pass crosses it. Also called Hatay or Nur Mts.

Amanpur (ŭmăn′pōōr), town (pop. 1,486), Etah dist., W Uttar Pradesh, India, 9 mi. SE of Kasganj; wheat, pearl millet, braley, corn, oilseeds.

Amantea (ämäntā′ä), town (pop. 4,623), Cosenza prov., Calabria, S Italy, on Tyrrhenian Sea, 15 mi. SSW of Cosenza; fishing port; bathing resort; wine, olive oil. Damaged by earthquakes in 1637–38 and 1905.

Amanzimtoti (ämänzēmtō′tē), town (pop. 2,532), E Natal, U. of So. Afr., on Indian Ocean, 18 mi. SW of Durban; seaside resort.

Amapá (ämŭpä′), federal territory (□ 53,057; 1950 census pop. 38,374), northernmost Brazil; ⊙ Macapá. Bounded by Fr. Guiana (N), Pará (W and S), Amazon delta and Atlantic Ocean (SE and E). Crossed by equator. Lies in tropical rain-forest zone. Mangrove forests in marshy coastal area. High-grass savannas on higher ground in interior. Chief products: hardwood, medicinal plants, skins of wild animals, rubber, Brazil nuts, fish. Some cattle pastures. Gold found in rivers in Amapá city area. Iron and manganese deposits recently discovered. Chief towns: Macapá, Amapá, and Mazagão. Long a territory disputed by France and Brazil, Amapá remained administratively part of Pará state until created a separate federal territory in 1943.

Amapá, city (pop. 444), NE Amapá territory, N Brazil, near the Atlantic, 140 mi. N of Macapá, in mangrove forest area; ships timber, Brazil nuts, fibers. Manganese and gold found in area. Airport near by.

Amapala (ämäpä′lä), town (pop. 2,809), Valle dept., S Honduras, port on NW Tigre Isl., in Gulf of Fonseca, 19 mi. SW of Nacaome; 13°17′N 87°39′W. Main Pacific port of Honduras; serves coastal and overseas trade. Launch service to San Lorenzo on mainland. Mfg. (soap, furniture, bricks, beverages); tanning, tortoise-shell processing. Exports lumber, coffee, hides, livestock. Airfield. Founded 1833.

Amapari, town, Brazil: see FERREIRA GOMES.

Amapari River (ämŭpŭrē′), Amapá territory, N Brazil, a tributary of the Araguari. Manganese deposits recently discovered along its course.

'Amara or **'Amarah** (ämä′rŭ), province (□ 7,247; pop. 308,108), SE Iraq, bordering E on Iran; ⊙ 'AMARA. The Tigris traverses it NNW–SSE, its flood plain forming large marshes and rich agr. lands. Dates, rice, corn, millet, sesame. At Al 'Azair is the alleged tomb of the prophet Ezra.

'Amara or **'Amarah**, town (pop. 48,915), ⊙ 'Amara prov., SE Iraq, on the Tigris and 19 mi. SE of Baghdad; rice, dates, corn, millet, giant millet, sesame. Taken 1915 by British in their Mesopotamia campaign.

Amara, Rumania: see SLOBOZIA.

Amaraji (ämŭrŭzhē′), city (pop. 1,876), E Pernambuco, NE Brazil, 45 mi. SW of Recife; sugar, cereals. Formerly spelled Amaragy or Amaragi.

Amaraleja (ämŭrŭlā′zhŭ), town, Beja dist., S Portugal, 13 mi. NE of Moura, near Sp. border; grain, olive oil. Airfield.

Amaralina (ämŭrŭlē′nŭ), suburban seaside resort of Salvador, E Bahia, Brazil, on the Atlantic.

Amarante (ämŭrăn′tĭ), city (pop. 1,748), central Piauí, Brazil, port on right bank of Parnaíba R. (Maranhão border) at influx of Canindé R., opposite Iguaratinga, and 80 mi. S of Teresina. Ships carnauba wax, hides and skins, sugar, and maniçoba rubber. Airfield.

Amarante, town (pop. 2,497), Pôrto dist., N Portugal, on Tâmega R. and 30 mi. ENE of Oporto; wool milling. Has 16th-cent. Dominican church.

Amarapura (ämärä′pōōrä′, Burmese ŭmŭyä′ pōōyä″), town (pop. 8,254), Mandalay dist., Upper Burma, on left bank of Irrawaddy R. (rail bridge, 3 mi. SW), 5 mi. S of Mandalay, on Mandalay–Myitkyina RR. Govt. silk-weaving works; mfg. of tile, pottery, baskets. Weaving school. An anc. ⊙ Burma, it has ruins of old palace, fortifications, pagodas, colossal image of Buddha. Founded 1783, it supplanted Ava as ⊙ Burma under Bodawpaya, and remained (except 1823–37) seat of govt. until abandoned (1860) for Mandalay.

Amaravati (ŭmŭrä′vŭtē), village, Guntur dist., NE Madras, India, on right bank of Kistna R. and 20 mi. NNW of Guntur. Site of well-known Buddhist archaeological remains; stupa of 1st cent. A.D. had base diameter of 192 ft.; several beautiful marble carvings now in British Mus., London, and in Central Mus., Madras. Was ⊙ Buddhist Andhra dynasties of early Christian era.

Amaravati River, S central Madras, India, formed in Anaimalai Hills by junction of streams rising in Travancore-Cochin; flows NE through fertile agr. valley, past Dharapuram, and E past Karur to Cauvery R. 7 mi. E of Karur; c.130 mi. long.

'Amar el Kubra, El, or **Al-'Amar al-Kubra** (both: ĕl ämär′ ĕl kōōb′rä), village (pop. 7,848), Qalyubiya prov., Lower Egypt, 25 mi. NNW of Cairo; cotton, flax, cereals, fruit.

Amares (ämä′rĭsh), town, Braga dist., N Portugal, 6 mi. NE of Braga; livestock, pottery.

Amargosa (ämärgō′zŭ), city (pop. 4,264), E Bahia, Brazil, 55 mi. W of Nazaré; W terminus of railroad from São Roque do Paraguaçu; ships coffee, tobacco, cotton, cattle. Jade deposits.

Amargosa Desert (ă″märgō′sŭ), S Nev., along Calif.-Nev. line, NE of Death Valley, Calif.; crossed by Amargosa R.

Amargosa Range, in E Calif. and S Nev., barren range forming E wall of Death Valley; extends c.110 mi. SSE from Grapevine Peak (8,705 ft.), on state line, to Amargosa R. Funeral Peak (6,397 ft.) is near center. Sections of range (N–S) are locally called Grapevine Mts., Funeral Mts., and Black Mts. Amargosa Desert is E.

Amargosa River, S Nev. and E Calif., intermittent stream rising in Pahute Mesa, Nev.; flows S, then NW, to sink into Death Valley, Calif.

Amarillas (ämärē'yäs), town (pop. 1,579), Matanzas prov., W Cuba, on railroad and 40 mi. SE of Cárdenas; sugar cane, fruit, stock.

Amarillo (ămurĭ'lō), city (pop. 74,246), ⊙ Potter co., extreme N Texas, on high plains of the Panhandle, c.245 mi. W of Oklahoma City, Okla.; commercial, industrial, transportation (rail, air, highway) center of the Panhandle region (natural gas, oil, wheat, cattle). Meat packing, flour milling, oil refining, zinc smelting; mfg. of carbon black, synthetic rubber, farm implements, iron and steel products, machinery, oil-field supplies, brick, tile, wood products, sports equipment, leather, cottonseed oil, clothing, bedding, canvas goods, food products; railroad shops. Large helium plants at near-by Exell and Soncy. Oil and gas supply center, with pipe lines to several states. Has jr. col. and a veterans' hosp. Annual music festival. Palo Duro Canyon State Park is SE. Settled 1887 with coming of railroad; at first a buffalo-hunters' center, later a cow town, became market for wheat farms in 20th cent. and became industrially important after discovery of oil and gas near by. Inc. 1892.

Amarinthos, Greece: see AMARYNTHOS.

Amarkantak (ŭmŭrkŭn'tŭk), village, extreme SE Vindhya Pradesh, India, 130 mi. SSE of Rewa, on plateau (alt. c.3,400 ft.) at E junction of Vindhya and Satpura ranges; noted Hindu pilgrimage center at source of Narbada R.

Amarnagar, India: see THANA DEVLI.

Amarnath (ŭmŭr'nät) or **Ambarnath** (ŭm'bŭrnät), village (pop. 721), Thana dist., central Bombay, India, 5 mi. SE of Kalyan; small industrial settlement; chemical and match mfg., textile milling; ordnance factory. Has 11th-cent. Sivaite temple. Also spelled Ambernath.

Amarnath Cave, Kashmir: see PAHLGAM.

Amaro, Monte (môn'tĕ ämä'rô), second highest peak (9,170 ft.) in the Apennines, in Maiella mtn. group, Abruzzi e Molise, S central Italy, 9 mi. ENE of Sulmona.

Amarousion (ämäroo'sēôn), town (pop. 12,744), Attica nome, E central Greece, on railroad, and 7 mi. NNE of Athens, in Athens metropolitan dist.; pottery-making center; summer resort. Formerly called Marousi.

Amarração, Brazil: see LUÍS CORREIA.

Amarume (ämä'roomä), town (pop. 8,862), Yamagata prefecture, N Honshu, Japan, on Mogami R. and 9 mi. NNE of Tsuruoka; rice, raw silk, cattle.

Amarvik, Greece: see KAMVOUNIA.

Amarwara (ŭmŭrvä'rŭ), village, Chhindwara dist., central Madhya Pradesh, India, 22 mi. NE of Chhindwara; sunn-hemp retting, essential-oil (*rosha* or Andropogon) extraction; wheat, rice, oilseeds. Lac cultivation in near-by forested hills.

Amarynthos or **Amarinthos** (both: ämä'rĭnthôs), town (pop. 2,405), S central Euboea, Greece, port on S arm of Gulf of Euboea, 17 mi. ESE of Chalcis; wheat; wine; livestock; fisheries. Formerly called Kato Vathia [Gr.,=lower Vathia].

Amasia, Turkey: see AMASYA.

Amasiya (ŭmŭsē'ŭ), village (1932 pop. estimate 650), NW Armenian SSR, on the Western Arpa-Chai and 12 mi. NNW of Leninakan; livestock, wheat, flax.

Amasra (ämäs'rä), town (pop. 1,379), Zonguldak prov., N Turkey, port on Black Sea, 37 mi. ENE of Zonguldak.

Amasya or **Amasia** (ämä'syä, ă"mūsī'ŭ), province (□ 1,886; 1950 pop. 163,494), N central Turkey; ⊙ Amasya. Bordered on N by Canik Mts.; drained by Yesil Irmak and Cekerek R. Lead ore with gold and silver in it found at Gumushacikoy in NW. Opium, wool, apples, tobacco, hemp, sugar beets.

Amasya or **Amasia,** town (1950 pop. 14,446), ⊙ Amasya prov., N central Turkey, on railroad, on Yesil Irmak, and 90 mi. NW of Sivas, 50 mi. SSW of Samsun; known for its tiles, made here since Seljuk period. Trade in apples, tobacco, wheat, onions, opium. Important city in kingdom of Pontus and under Byzantines and Seljuks. Strabo b. here. Old castle on high hill.

Amatán (ämätän'), town (pop. 1,077), Chiapas, S Mexico, near Tabasco border, in foothills of Sierra Madre, 13 mi. NNW of Simojovel.

Amatauraá (ämŭtourä'), town (pop. 353), W Amazonas, Brazil, on right bank of the Amazon and 70 mi. E of São Paulo de Olivença. Formerly spelled Maturá.

Amatenango (ämätänäng'gō). **1** Officially Amatenango de la Frontera, town (pop. 398), Chiapas, S Mexico, in Sierra Madre, 3 mi. NE of Motozintla; sugar. **2** Officially Amatenango del Valle, town (pop. 1,317), Chiapas, S Mexico, in Sierra de Hueytepec, 20 mi. SE of San Cristóbal de las Casas; alt. 6,046 ft.; corn, fruit.

Amatepec (ämätäpĕk'), town (pop. 984), Mexico state, central Mexico, 21 mi. SW of Sultepec; sugar, coffee, fruit. Silver and gold deposits near by.

Amates, Los, Guatemala: see LOS AMATES.

Amathus (ă'mŭthŭs), ruined city, Limassol dist., S Cyprus, on Akrotiri Bay, c.4 mi. E of Limassol. Founded c.1100 B.C. by the Phoenicians. Famous in Roman times for its cult of Aphrodite. Had temples to Aphrodite and to Adonis. Other ruins include Byzantine church, a stone vessel from the Acropolis, and a Necropolis, which yielded valuable works of art. Sometimes spelled Amathous.

Amatique, Bay of (ămŭtē'kē), inlet of Gulf of Honduras of Caribbean Sea, on Guatemala–Br. Honduras border, bounded E by Cabo de Tres Puntas; 10 mi. wide, 25 mi. long. Puerto Barrios is on S shore, Lívingston (at mouth of the Río Dulce) on SW shore. Br. Honduras ports on NW shore are Baranco and Punta Gorda. Also receives Sarstoon and Moho rivers.

Amatitán (ämätētän'), town (pop. 2,201), Jalisco, W Mexico, 25 mi. NW of Guadalajara; alt. 4,200 ft.; grain, beans, sugar, tobacco, fruit.

Amatitlán (ämätētlän'), city (1950 pop. 6,683), Guatemala dept., S central Guatemala, in central highlands, at W end of L. Amatitlán (on its outlet, the Michatoya), 14 mi. SW of Guatemala, on railroad; alt. 3,871 ft. Major year-round resort; wool milling; sugar cane, coffee, grain, fruit. Has 16th-cent. church (damaged in 1773 earthquake). Formerly a cochineal-producing center; was ⊙ Amatitlán dept. (abolished c.1935).

Amatitlán, town (pop. 821), Veracruz, SE Mexico, on Papaloápam R., in Sotavento lowlands, and 25 mi. W of San Andrés Tuxtla; sugar cane, tropical fruit. Amatlán until 1938.

Amatitlán, Lake, volcanic lake, S central Guatemala, 11 mi. SSW of Guatemala; 7 mi. long, 3 mi. wide, c.130 ft. deep; alt. 4,085 ft. Inlet: Villalobos R. (NE). Outlet: MICHATOYA RIVER (W), at Amatitlán. Popular summer and weekend resort for Guatemala city. Hot springs on S shore.

Amatlán (ämätlän'). **1** Officially Amatlán de los Reyes, town (pop. 2,036), Veracruz, E Mexico, in Sierra Madre Oriental, 3 mi. S of Córdoba, on railroad. Anc. Indian settlement with Aztec remains. Picturesque market. **2** or **Amatlantepetl** (ämätlän"täpĕ'tŭl), town (pop. 1,280), Veracruz, E Mexico, in Gulf lowland, 33 mi. NW of Tuxpan; corn, sugar, fruit. Petroleum wells. **3** Town, Veracruz, E Mexico, near San Andrés Tuxtla: see AMATITLÁN.

Amatlán de Cañas (dā kä'nyäs), town (pop. 1,963), Nayarit, W Mexico, near Ameca R. (Jalisco border), 55 mi. SE of Tepic; corn, sugar, cattle.

Amatlantepetl, Mexico: see AMATLÁN.

Amatola Range (ămŭtō'lŭ), SE Cape Prov., U. of So. Afr., extends 30 mi. in a semicircle W and SW from Stutterheim; rises to 6,360 ft. on Hogsback mtn., 25 mi. W of Stutterheim.

Amatongaland or **Tongaland** (ă"mŭ–, –tŏng'gŭlănd), region of N ZULULAND, NE Natal, U. of So. Afr., annexed to Natal 1897, merged with Zululand 1898.

Amatrice (ämätrē'chĕ), town (pop. 1,352), Rieti prov., Latium, central Italy, 20 mi. NNW of Aquila, in livestock and agr. (cereals, potatoes) region.

Amatsu (ă"mä'tsoo), town (pop. 7,819), Chiba prefecture, central Honshu, Japan, on SE coast of Chiba Peninsula, 20 mi. NE of Tateyama; fishing.

Amaxac (ämähäk'), officially San Barnabé Amaxac de Guerrero, town (pop. 2,066), Tlaxcala, central Mexico, 4 mi. NE of Tlaxcala; grain, alfalfa, maguey, livestock.

Amay (ämā'), town (pop. 6,507), Liége prov., E central Belgium, 14 mi. SW of Liége, near Meuse R.; ceramics, paving blocks.

Amayuca (ämīoo'kä), town (pop. 1,321), Morelos, central Mexico, 12 mi. SE of Cuautla; rice, sugar, coffee, fruit.

Amazar (ŭmŭzär'), town (1948 pop. over 2,000), E Chita oblast, Russian SFSR, on Amazar R. (short left branch of Amur R.), on Trans-Siberian RR and 45 mi. E of Mogocha; sawmilling. Another Amazar (1926 pop. 746) is on the Amur, at mouth of Amazar R., and 90 mi. ESE of Mogocha.

Amazon, river, South America: see AMAZON RIVER.

Amazonas (ämŭzō'nŭs), state (□ 614,913; 1940 pop. 438,008; 1950 census 530,920), NW Brazil; ⊙ Manaus. Bounded by Venezuela (N), Colombia (NW), Peru (W); by Acre and Guaporé territories (S), states of Mato Grosso (S) and Pará (E), and Rio Branco territory (N). Largest state of Brazil. Crossed W–E by the middle Amazon (called the Solimões above influx of the Rio Negro). Lies wholly within tropical rain-forest basin (commonly known as Amazonia) of the Amazon, bet. lat. 10°S and 2°N. Though erroneously considered one of the world's hottest areas, high humidity and small temperature range render climate uncomfortable for white settlers. Abundant rainfall (c.80 inches) seasonally floods large parts of the Amazon basin. Region characterized by monotonous expanse of dense forests, with human settlement limited to river banks. Chief navigable tributaries of the Amazon in this state are the Javari, Jutaí, Juruá, Tefé, Purus, and Madeira (right), and the Japurá and Rio Negro (left). Chief products, exported via the Amazon, are Brazil nuts, rubber, medicinal plants, hardwood, cacao, tobacco, hides and skins, and miscellaneous roots and fibers. Mfg. limited to handicraft industries. River navigation and air transport (chiefly hydroplane) are chief means of communication. State has no hard-surfaced roads or railroads. Principal towns are Manaus (economic and cultural center of Amazonia) on the Rio Negro; Parintins, Itacoatiara, Coari, and Tefé on the Amazon; Borba, Manicoré on the Madeira; and Lábrea on the Purus. Amazonas was made a prov. in 1850, and a state in 1889, when Brazil became a federal republic. Early 20th-cent. rubber boom brought pop. increase to region and great prosperity to Manaus. In decline since First World War, Amazonas remains today one of the world's largest unexploited areas. Rio Branco territory and part of Guaporé territory were carved out of Amazonas in 1943. A region (□ 1,232) along E border of state is disputed (1949) bet. Pará and Amazonas.

Amazonas (ämäsō'näs), commissary (□ 48,008; 1938 pop. 6,414; 1950 estimate 6,480), SE Colombia; ⊙ LETICIA. Lies just S of the equator, bordering S on Peru, largely along Putumayo R. and partly on the Amazon; Brazil is E. Cut by Caquetá R. and bordered NE by Apaporis R. Has hot, humid climate. It largely comprises vast, densely forested lowlands, mostly unexplored and almost entirely undeveloped. It was administered as an intendancy until 1944.

Amazonas, department (in 1940: □ 13,948; enumerated pop. 69,560, plus estimated 20,000 Indians), N Peru, bordering on Ecuador; ⊙ Chachapoyas. Situated at W edge of the Amazon basin, it is crossed by E ridges of the Andes. Drained by Marañón, Santiago, and Utcubamba rivers. Climate is generally hot and humid. There is some gold washing; also sulphur, salt, and coal deposits. An undeveloped and partly unexplored region, it grows some sugar cane, cacao, potatoes, coffee, coca, tobacco, yucca, flax, fruit, grain in fertile upland valleys. The densely forested lowlands yield rubber, resin, vanilla, tropical timber. Main industries are liquor and alcohol distilling, tanning, mfg. of straw hats. Dept. was set up 1832, but its boundaries have frequently been changed.

Amazonas, river, South America: see AMAZON RIVER.

Amazonas, territory (□ 67,857; 1941 pop. 3,728; 1950 census pop. 6,945, excluding 40,000 Indians), S Venezuela; ⊙ Puerto Ayacucho. Bordered W by Colombia (Orinoco R., Atabapo R., Río Negro), S and SE by Brazil (Sierra Parima). Largely unexplored territory; consists of vast jungle forests. Includes W outliers of Guiana Highlands; there, near Brazil border, rises the Orinoco, linked by Casiquiare R., a natural channel, with Río Negro, part of the Amazon system. Hot, tropical climate, with heavy rains (May–Sept.). Rubber, balata gum, and vanilla are gathered from wild trees; some yucca and sugar cane are cultivated.

Amazonia (ămŭzō'nēŭ), town (pop. 308), Andrew co., NW Mo., on Missouri R. and 9 mi. N of St. Joseph.

Amazon River (ă'mŭzŏn, –zŭn), Sp. and Port. *Amazonas* (Sp. ämäsō'näs, Port. ämŭzō'nŭs), great river of N central South America, and the world's largest if measured by volume of water carried. Rises in 2 major headstreams—MARAÑÓN and UCAYALI—in the Andes of Peru within c.100 mi. of the Pacific, traverses the lowlands of NE Peru, and flows E across N Brazil, just S of the equator, to the Atlantic in a delta 200 mi. wide. With its tributaries, numbering over 500, and including the Tocantins—not strictly an affluent of the Amazon proper—it drains a basin of c.2,700,000 sq. mi. (only a little smaller than continental U.S.), which, extending from 5°N (source of the Rio Branco) to 20°S (headstreams of the Mamoré), covers not only N half of Brazil, but also E part of Bolivia, Peru, Ecuador, Colombia, and S Venezuela, with the world's largest tropical rain forest [Port. *selva*]. The Amazon's length is usually estimated at c.3,300 mi. with the Marañón (generally considered Amazon proper), and at bet. 3,700 and 3,900 mi. with the Ucayali (including its longest headstream, the Apurímac). Receiving its name at junction (4°30'S 73°27'W) of its two NE-flowing Andean headstreams, the Amazon (by then a sluggish, lowland stream with an extremely low gradient) passes Iquitos (Peru), turns E, and after forming S boundary of Leticia Trapezium (Colombia-Peru line), enters Brazil at Sapurara (formerly Tabatinga), attaining width of 2 mi. here. Meandering through a flood plain c.50 mi. wide and forming an intricate network of channels separated by jungle-covered isls., the river (called Solimões bet. Brazil border and influx of the Rio Negro) receives its largest tributaries in Brazil, especially those from the S. Below Manaus (actually located on the Rio Negro just above the Amazon), the wide valley narrows until, near Santarém, the Guiana (N) and Brazilian highlands (S) come to within c.150 mi. of each other, and the main stream is squeezed to a width of 1¼ mi. (and to a depth of 250 ft.) bet. flood-plain bluffs at Óbidos. Below influx of the Xingu, the valley widens again near apex of the great delta. The delta's N branch, a maze of isls. and channels, is separated from its S arm (named PARÁ RIVER) by MARAJÓ isl. On the latter, below influx of the Tocantins, is the seaport of Belém, serving as commercial outlet for the Amazon basin (often called Amazonia). The river's silt-laden discharge into the Atlantic is visible 200 mi. out to sea, and is swept by currents to the Guiana coast line. Because of river's low gradient, the tide can be felt 500 mi. upstream beyond Santarém; it is preceded by a tidal bore (locally called *pororóca*), up to 15 ft. high. While the main stream presents no obstacles to navigation to as far as the foothills of the Andes, many of its tributaries are obstructed by falls and rapids at edge of N Brazilian highlands. The Amazon's principal affluents are, from the N, the Napo, Putumayo (or Içá), Caquetá (or Japurá), Rio Negro (with its tributary, the Rio Branco), Jamundá, and Trombetas. Among the generally longer S tributaries are the Javari (on Brazil-Peru border), Juruá, Purus, Madeira (formed by junction of Mamoré and Beni rivers), Tapajós, Xingu, and Tocantins (emptying with its affluent, the Araguaia, into Pará R.). Ocean-going vessels of up to 5,000 tons ascend the Amazon to Manaus (c.1,000 mi. upstream), and Iquitos (2,300 mi. from the sea) is head of navigation for ships of less than 14-ft. draught. Smaller boats ascend the Marañón to Pongo de Manseriche gorge, the Ucayali beyond Pucallpa (whence a road leads to the Pacific coast at Lima), and the principal tributaries for varying distances. Chief ports along the Amazon are now linked by air and hydroplane service. The Amazon is at the center of a great interlocking hydrographic system linking South America's 3 major drainage basins. In the N, through the Rio Negro and the CASIQUIARE, it connects with the upper Orinoco; while in the S, short portages from the headwaters of the Guaporé (a subtributary of the Madeira) form the link with the Paraguay-Paraná. Economically, these communications are as yet of little importance because of the region's backwardness and low pop. density. The vast tropical forest, which receives upward of 80 inches of rainfall in E and W parts of the basin, appears monotonous from the air, but contains a wide variety of evergreens (often more than 100 different species of trees in 1 sq. mi.), including valuable hardwoods (mahogany, rosewood). The fauna, unlike that of African forests, includes few large animals. Monkeys, squirrels, snakes, exotic birds (multicolored parakeets) and insects live in the treetops. Tapirs, turtles, manatees, fresh-water porpoises, and numerous species of fish (notably the *pirarucu*) are found in or near the streams. The Amazon was probably 1st seen (1500) by Vicente Yáñez Pinzón, who navigated its lower course. Real exploration began with voyage of Francisco de Orellana down from the Napo in 1540–41; his fanciful stories of female warriors gave river its name. During 1637–39, Pedro Teixeira led the voyage upstream that really opened the Amazon to world knowledge. The valley, sparsely peopled by Indian tribes (mostly of the Guaraní-Tupi linguistic stock and of meager material culture), remains for the most part unsettled today. In 1850, regular navigation on the river was authorized by Dom Pedro II, and some immigrants arrived (notably Confederate veterans from the U.S.) at Santarém; but except for the Belém region (settled early), little exploitation occurred until the wild-rubber boom on the upper Amazon in late 19th and early 20th cent. From this period date the construction of the Madeira-Mamoré RR, the only rail line in the interior now in existence, and the renewal of scientific expeditions, notably those of Roosevelt and Rondon (1913–14), and of Rice. With the collapse of the rubber boom (resulting from the region's inability to compete with SE Asia's newly developed rubber plantations), Amazonia entered a period of decline, only slightly relieved by a mild boom during Second World War. The experimental rubber plantations, established after 1927 by an American company at Fordlândia and Belterra along the Tapajós, and taken over by Brazil after Second World War, have not as yet pointed the way to a large-scale rubber development, although tires and other rubber products are now made in Brazil from domestic latex. The *selva* yields, however, in commercial quantities, cabinet woods, Brazil nuts, babassu nuts, gums, ipecac roots, sarsaparilla, tonka beans, copaiba, and the skins of rare animals. Cacao and sugar cane are cultivated in isolated clearings, and Japanese settlers (established here since First World War) are largely responsible for building up jute production. Livestock is raised in 2 areas, along the upper Rio Branco and on Marajó isl. In 1940s, Braz. govt. established a health service (chiefly by launch) for region, and appropriated funds for the development of this, one of the world's largest unsettled areas.

Amb (ŭmb), petty state (□ 174; pop. 47,916), NE North-West Frontier Prov., W Pakistan, in Malakand agency, on both banks of the Indus; chief village, Amb. Agr. (wheat, corn, barley).

Amb, village, Amb state, NE North-West Frontier Prov., W Pakistan, on Indus R. and 23 mi. NW of Abbottabad; hand mfg. of mtn. guns, rifles, ammunition.

Amba, India: see MOMINABAD.

Ambabo (ämbä'bō), village, Fr. Somaliland, on N shore of Gulf of Tadjoura, 25 mi. NW of Djibouti; small fishing port; formerly had flourishing caravan trade.

Ambad (ŭm'bŭd), village (pop. 5,062), Aurangabad dist., NW Hyderabad state, India, 35 mi. E. of Aurangabad; millet, wheat, oilseeds; cotton ginning. Formerly spelled Ambarh.

Ambadi, Lake (ämbä'dē), in swampy Sudd region of the Nile system, S central Anglo-Egyptian Sudan, 100 mi. NE of Wau; 30 mi. long. Formed by flood waters of Jur and Tonj rivers, it gives rise to the BAHR EL GHAZAL. Navigable July-March to Meshra er Req, at S end.

Ambah (ŭmbä'), town (pop. 4,897), NE Madhya Bharat, India, 35 mi. N of Lashkar; local market for gram, millet, wheat.

Ambahta (ŭmbä'tŭ), town (pop. 5,111), Saharanpur dist., N Uttar Pradesh, India, 15 mi. SW of Saharanpur; wheat, rice, rape, mustard, gram. Built (14th cent.) as cantonment for Mogul troops by Firoz Shah Tughlak; has two 16th-cent. mosques. Also spelled Ambehta.

Ambala (ŭmbä'lă), district (□ 1,851; pop. 847,745), E Punjab, India; ⊙ Ambala. Bounded NW by Sutlej R.; lies mainly bet. Patiala and East Punjab States Union (SW, N) and Himachal Pradesh (NE), with an enclave in each. Drained by seasonal streams; agr. (wheat, gram, corn, cotton, rice, sugar cane). Chief towns: Ambala, Jagadhri, Rupar (headworks of Sirhind Canal). Projected new ⊙ Punjab near Chandigarh village. Sometimes spelled Umballa. Air Force Acad. here.

Ambala, city (pop. 44,964; including cantonment area, 107,383), ⊙ Ambala dist., E Punjab, India, 95 mi. SE of Jullundur. Military station; commercial center; rail junction; airport; trades in grain, cotton, spices, timber, metal; cotton ginning, making of fruit juices and preserves, flour milling, mfg. of machine tools, food processing; glassworks, glue factory. Govt. Metal Work Inst. Cantonment, 3 mi. SE, is one of largest in India; mfg. of chemicals, glass, scientific apparatus, machinery, aerated water, ice, flour, curry powder, dairy products; handicraft cloth weaving and bamboo-furniture making.

Ambalangoda (ŭmbŭlŭng-gō'dŭ), town (pop. 9,952), Southern Prov., Ceylon, on SW coast, 18 mi. NW of Galle; fishing center; trades in vegetables, rice, tea, coconuts, cinnamon.

Ambalantota (ŭmbŭlŭntō'tŭ), village, Southern Prov., Ceylon, on the Walawe Ganga and 6 mi. W of Hambantota; rice milling; rice, tomatoes, chili. Rice research station.

Ambalavao (ämbälävou'), town, Fianarantsoa prov., E Madagascar, on highway and 25 mi. SSW of Fianarantsoa; mfg. of paper. R.C. and Protestant missions, hosp.

Ambalema (ämbälā'mä), town (pop. 3,167), Tolima dept., W central Colombia, landing on Magdalena R., on railroad and 50 mi. WNW of Bogotá. Tobacco center in agr. region also producing corn, rice, bananas, sugar cane, yucca, livestock; mfg. of tobacco products, pottery; sugar refining. Petroleum deposits near by. Founded 1776.

Ambam (äm'bäm), village, N'Tem region, S Fr. Cameroons, near Sp. Guinea and Fr. Equatorial Africa borders, 40 mi. SSE of Ebolowa; trading post in cacao-growing area.

Ambana (ämbä'nä), town (pop. c.4,000), La Paz dept., W Bolivia, in the Eastern Cordillera of the Andes, 18 mi. ENE of Puerto Acosta; *oca*, barley, potatoes.

Amban Ganga (ŭm'bŭn gŭng'gŭ), river, central Ceylon, rises in N Ceylon Hill Country, in several headstreams joining N of Matale; flows N and NE, past Elahera, to the Mahaweli Ganga 6 mi. SE of Polonnaruwa; c.60 mi. long. Land reclamation project at ELAHERA.

Ambanja (ämbän'dzŭ), town, Majunga prov., N Madagascar, on highway and 115 mi. SW of Diégo-Suarez, in rice region; mfg. of tapioca and cassava starch, cacao plantations; sugar cane, lemon groves. Has business school. Airfield.

Ambarawa (ämbärä'wä), town (pop. 6,345), central Java, Indonesia, 20 mi. S of Semarang, at foot of Mt. Merbabu; trade center for agr. and forested area (rice, coffee, corn, cassava, rubber, cacao, cinchona bark). Has textile mills. Also spelled Ambarava.

Ambarchik (ŭmbär'chĭk), village (1948 pop. over 500), NE Yakut Autonomous SSR, Russian SFSR, port on E.Siberian Sea just E of Kolyma R. mouth, 270 mi. NE of Sredne-Kolymsk; govt. observation post; supply port on Arctic sea route.

Ambarh, India: see AMBAD.

Ambaritsa (ämbä'rĕtsä), peak (7,104 ft.) in Troyan Mts., N central Bulgaria, 5 mi. NNW of Karlovo. Also called Levski.

Ambarnath, India: see AMARNATH.

Ambasamudram (ŭmbä'sŭmōōdrŭm), town (pop. 17,540), Tinnevelly dist., S Madras, India, on Tambraparni R. opposite Kallidaikurichi and 16 mi. WSW of Tinnevelly; agr. center; trades in cotton goods, oil cake, coffee, cardamom, onions; cotton weaving. Industrial development furthered by Papanasam hydroelectric project. Rice research station. Near-by bell-metal industry supplies bells and idols to Madras temples.

Ambas Bay (äm'bŭs), inlet (5 mi. wide, 2 mi. long) of Gulf of Guinea, in Br. Cameroons; 4°N 9°10'E. In it are small, rocky Ambas Isls. On NW shore is port of Victoria, overlooked by Cameroon Mtn.

Ambato, Argentina: see LA PUERTA, Catamarca prov.

Ambato (ämbä'tō), city (1950 pop. 33,908), ⊙Tungurahua prov., Ecuador, in high Andean valley, near NE foot of the Chimborazo, on Pan American Highway, on Guayaquil-Quito RR and 70 mi. S of Quito; 1°14'S 78°37'W; alt. c.8,400 ft. Pleasant temperate climate. Among the country's leading commercial and communication centers, Ambato is also noted for the variety of fruit grown in its outskirts (strawberries, peaches, apples, pears, grapes, oranges); other crops of the fertile region include: sugar cane, corn, wheat, barley, cinchona, vegetables. It has tanneries, canneries, flour and textile mills, wineries, a rubber factory, and machine shops; mfg. of furniture, buttons, and leather articles. The picturesque garden city is a favorite resort, with Miraflores suburb visited by wealthy Guayaquil families. Among its fine bldgs. is a Renaissance cathedral; a mausoleum and other structures commemorate Juan Montalvo, noted Latin American poet, who was b. here (1833). Near Ambato in 1821, Sucre, at first defeated by Sp. royalists, later achieved victory after receiving help from San Martín; this victory led to the decisive battle of Pichincha. The city has been frequently damaged by volcanic eruptions and earthquakes, most recently in 1949.

Ambato, Sierra de (syĕ'rä dā), subandean range in SE Catamarca prov., Argentina, extends c.100 mi. SSW from area of Andalgalá to the Río Colorado, forming divide bet. the Salar de Pipanaco (W) and Catamarca valley (E); rises to c.11,000 ft. N section is sometimes known as Sierra de Manchao.

Ambato-Boéni (ämbä'tōō-bwĕ'nē), town, Majunga prov., NW Madagascar, on Betsiboka R. and 60 mi. SSE of Majunga; agr. market and rice center with large rice mills. Has R.C. and Protestant missions, trade school, veterinary center.

Ambatofinandrahana (ämbä"tōōfēnändrä'hänŭ), town, Fianarantsoa prov., E central Madagascar, 70 mi. NNW of Fianarantsoa; alt. 4,706 ft.; quartz and amethyst mining.

Ambatolampy (–läm'pē), town (1948 pop. 4,674), Tananarive prov., central Madagascar, on railroad and 30 mi. S of Tananarive; horse-breeding center; rice, corn, pulse, potatoes, swine; graphite mining near by. Has R.C. and Protestant missions, small seminary and jr. col.

Ambatondrazaka (ämbä"tōōndräzä'kŭ), town, Tamatave prov., E Madagascar, on railroad, S of L. Alaotra and 70 mi. WNW of Tamatave; rice center. Rice processing, mfg. of tapioca and corn starch. Airport. Agr. school, hosp. Also rice processing at Manakambahiny (mänäkämbähē'nē), 15 mi. ENE.

Ambatosoratra (–sōōrä'trŭ), village, Tamatave prov., NE central Madagascar, on SE shore of L. Alaotra, 90 mi. NE from Tananarive; terminus of railroad from Moramanga. Rice milling, mfg. of tapioca and starch at Andreba (ändrĕ'bŭ) just SW.

Ambawela (ŭmbŭvā'lŭ), village, Central Prov., Ceylon, on Hatton Plateau (alt. 6,064 ft.), 7 mi. SSE of Nuwara Eliya; tea, vegetables; govt. cattle-breeding farm. Elgin Falls (projected hydroelectric station) is 2.5 mi. W, on right tributary of the Mahaweli Ganda.

Ambazac (ãbäzäk'), village (pop. 995), Haute-Vienne dept., W central France, 10 mi. NE of Limoges; mfg. of porcelain. Two hydroelectric plants on Taurion R. (3 mi. SE and 4 mi. S).

Ambazac, Monts d' (mõ däbäzäk'), hill range in Massif Central, Haute-Vienne dept., W central France, extending c.15 mi. NNE from Limoges. Alt. 2,300 ft. Its kaolin quarries supply the renowned Limoges porcelain factories.

Ambelakia, Greece: see AMPELAKIA.

Ambeno, Portuguese Timor: see OE-CUSSE.

Amber (ŭm'bär), town (pop. 5,130), E central Rajasthan, India, 5 mi. N of Jaipur. Taken by Kachwaha Rajputs in mid-12th cent. and made their ⊙ until 1728, when Jaipur was founded. Old palace is noted example of Rajput architecture; contains beautiful apartments with mosaics and marble sculptures.

Amber, Cape, Madagascar: see AMBRE, CAPE.

Amberg (äm'bĕrk), city (1950 pop. 38,794), Upper Palatinate, N central Bavaria, Germany, on the Vils and 32 mi. NNW of Regensburg; 49°27'N 11°52'E. Rail junction; mfg. of precision instruments, textiles, porcelain; cement and enameling works. Large iron-ore deposits near by (NW) have been mined since Middle Ages. Has Gothic church, 15th-cent. town hall. Was ⊙ Upper Palatinate until 1810. Archduke Charles of Austria here defeated (1796) the French under Jourdan.

Ambergris Cay (ăm'bŭrgrēs, –rĭs), island (pop. 421) in Caribbean Sea, Belize dist., N Br. Honduras, 28 mi. NNE of Belize; 25 mi. long, 5 mi. wide. Coconut plantations. San Pedro is on SE shore.

Ambérieu or **Ambérieu-en-Bugey** (äbärēû'-äbüzhä'), town (pop. 5,120), Ain dept., E France, at foot of the S Jura, near the Albarine, 18 mi. SSE of Bourg; railroad center, with workshops. Iron foundry, silk mill. Airport.

Amberley, township (pop. 465), ⊙ Kowai co. (□ 157; pop. 1,747), E S.Isl., New Zealand, 27 mi. N of Christchurch; center of agr., sheep-raising area; phosphate.

Amberley, village (pop. 885), Hamilton co., extreme SW Ohio, a NE suburb of Cincinnati.

Ambert (äbâr'), town (pop. 5,036), Puy-de-Dôme dept., central France, on the Dore and 35 mi. SE of Clermont-Ferrand; specializes in religious articles. Other mfg.: lace, ribbons, razor blades, furniture.

Ambès (äbĕs'), village (pop. 267), Gironde dept., SW France, on tongue of land bet. Garonne and Dordogne rivers, 12 mi. N of Bordeaux; petroleum refinery, vineyards. At the **Bec d' Ambès** (point 4 mi. NW) the Dordogne joins the Garonne to form the Gironde estuary.

Ambia (ăm'bēū), town (pop. 356), Benton co., W Ind., near Ill. line, 34 mi. WNW of Lafayette, in agr. area.

Ambidedi (ämbēdĕ'dē), village, SW Fr. Sudan, Fr. West Africa, landing on Senegal R., on Dakar-Niger RR, and 22 mi. WNW of Kayes; sisal growing; stockraising. Sometimes Ambidédi.

Ambikapur (ŭmbē'käpōōr), town (pop. 8,517), ⊙ Surguja dist., E Madhya Pradesh, India, 100 mi. NE of Bilaspur; rice, oilseeds. Was ⊙ former princely states of Surguja, of Chhattisgarh States. Lac cultivation in near-by dense sal forests (bamboo, khair, myrobalan). Coal deposits (NW). Sometimes called Bisrampur.

Ambil Island (ämbēl') (1939 pop. 294), one of the Lubang Isls., Mindoro prov., Philippines, in S. China Sea, just E of Lubang Isl., off SW Luzon; 4 mi. in diameter; rises to 2,477 ft. Rice growing. Chromite deposits.

Ambilly (äbēyē'), town (pop. 2,224), Haute-Savoie dept., SE France, just NW of Annemasse, on Swiss border, 4 mi. E of Geneva; printing, meat and cheese processing.

Ambilobe (ämbēlōō'bä), town, Majunga prov., N Madagascar, on Mahavavy R., near W coast, 60 mi. SSE of Diégo-Suarez; agr. center (notably for rice) and communications point; mfg. of tapioca and cassava starch, rice processing, woodworking. Copra, sugar cane, essential oils produced in vicinity. Leprosarium. Airfield.

Ambite (ämbē'tä), town (pop. 850), Madrid prov., central Spain, on Tajuña R., on railroad and 27 mi. E of Madrid; olives, cereals, beans, potatoes, sugar beets. Olive-oil extracting, flour milling, liquor distilling.

Ambitle, Bismarck Archipelago: see FENI ISLANDS.

Ambla (äm'blä), town (pop. 523), N Estonia, 5 mi. SW of Tapa; agr. market (potatoes).

Amblainville (äblēvēl'), village (pop. 541), Oise dept., N France, 16 mi. S of Beauvais; mother-of-pearl buttons.

Amble, urban district (1931 pop. 4,205; 1951 census 4,677), E Northumberland, England, on North Sea at mouth of Coquet R., 7 mi. SE of Alnwick; coal mining, shipbuilding.

Amblecote, urban district (1931 pop. 3,099; 1951 census 3,165), S Stafford, England, 8 mi. S of Wolverhampton; glass mfg.

Ambler, borough (pop. 4,565), Montgomery co., SE Pa., 14 mi. NNW of Philadelphia; asbestos, metal products, chemicals; quarrying; agr. School of horticulture. Inc. 1888.

Ambler Highlands, village (pop. 1,864, with adjacent Fort Washington), Montgomery co., SE Pa.

Ambleside, former urban district (1931 pop. 2,343), W Westmorland, England, in the Lake District, near N end of L. Windermere, 11 mi. NW of Kendal; tourist resort and agr. market in cattle- and sheep-raising area. Parish church (built 1854 by Sir Gilbert Scott) has stained-glass windows contributed by English and American admirers of Wordsworth. Known as a literary center in 19th cent. Has excavations of Roman fort built A.D. 79 by Agricola. Included 1935 in new urban dist. of The Lakes.

Ambleteuse (äblûtûz'), village (pop. 562), Pas-de-Calais dept., N France, on English Channel, 6 mi. N of Boulogne; small beach resort; oysters, lobsters. Ruins of port built by Vauban and remodeled by Napoleon I.

Amblève River (äblĕv'), E Belgium, rises near Ger. border SE of Malmédy, flows 35 mi. W, past Stavelot, Remouchamps, and Aywaille, to Ourthe R. just N of Comblain-au-Pont. Receives Warche R. just E of Stavelot.

Ambo (äm'bō), village (pop. 600), Shoa prov., central Ethiopia, on road and 40 mi. W of Addis Alam; hot mineral springs (86°F.).

Ambo (äm'bō), city (pop. 1,338), ⊙ Ambo prov. (□ 743; pop. 32,299), Huánuco dept., central Peru, on E slopes of Cordillera Central, on Huallaga R., on highway, and 14 mi. SE of Huánuco; alt. 6,768 ft. Agr. products: sugar cane, coffee, grain; cattle.

Amboanio, Madagascar: see MAJUNGA, town.

Amboasary (ämbwäsä'rē), village, Tamatave prov., E central Madagascar, on railroad and 25 mi. N of Moramanga; sisal center; also rice.

Ambodifototra, Madagascar: see SAINTE MARIE ISLAND.

Ambohidratimo (ämbōōhēdrätē'mōō), town, Tananarive prov., E central Madagascar, on highway and 10 mi. NW of Tananarive; native market. Insane asylum.

Ambohimahasoa (–mähä'swŭ), town, Fianarantsoa prov., E central Madagascar, 30 mi. NNE of Fianarantsoa; alt. 4,264 ft. Food-processing center (beef, pork, poultry, fruit, rice), highway junction. R.C. and Protestant missions, hosp.

Ambohimanga (ämbōōhēmäng'gŭ), town, Tananarive prov., central Madagascar, 10 mi. NNE of Tananarive; as the home and former necropolis of Imerina kings, it is the holy city of Malagasys. Ruins of old fortress.

Amboim, Angola: see PÔRTO AMBOIM.

Amboina (ămboi'nŭ) or **Ambon** (äm'bōn), important island (□ 314; pop. 66,821) of the MOLUCCAS, Indonesia, in Banda Sea, 7 mi. S of SW coast of Ceram; 3°29'–3°48'S 127°54'–128°25'E; 32 mi. long, 10 mi. wide. Generally hilly, rising to 3,405 ft., with fertile coastal plain. Chief products: nutmeg, cloves, rice, sugar, fish. Natives in N are Moslem, those in S are Christians. The Amboinese, many of whom fought for years in Du. army, opposed Indonesian independence. On Laitimor Peninsula in S is port town of Amboina (pop. 17,334), shipping copra and spices; was free port 1854–1904. Isl. was visited 1512 by the Portuguese; Francis Xavier came 1546 and won many converts. The Dutch, arriving in 1600, captured (1605) Port. fortress here, thus becoming dominant power on isl. Br. settlement here was destroyed 1623 by the Du. in the so-called massacre of Amboina. Early in Second World War, Amboina was major Allied naval base, taken (Feb., 1942) by the Japanese. Amboina led a brief revolt in 1950 against the state of Indonesia. Sometimes spelled Amboyna.

Amboise (äbwäz'), town (pop. 4,224), Indre-et-Loire dept., W central France, on left bank of Loire R. and 14 mi. E of Tours; mfg. (footwear, radios, photographic equipment, agr. implements). Trade in wine and woolens. Its noted late-Gothic castle (with Renaissance additions) was a royal residence from the reign of Charles VIII (who was born and died here) to that of Francis II. Leonardo da Vinci, who probably worked on it, is said to be buried in its chapel. Abd-el-Kader was confined here (1848–52) when castle served as state prison. Amboise gave its name to the conspiracy of Amboise (1560), a Huguenot plot against the Guise family, and the edict of Amboise (1563) in which Catherine de' Medici guaranteed liberty of worship to Protestant nobility.

Ambon, Indonesia: see AMBOINA.

Ambonnay (äbônä') village (pop. 780), Marne dept., N France, on SE slope of Montagne de Reims, 10 mi. ENE of Épernay; winegrowing (champagne).

Ambositra (ämbōōsē'trŭ), town (1948 pop. 4,636), Fianarantsoa prov., E Madagascar, on highway and 65 mi. NNE of Fianarantsoa; alt. 4,296 ft. Rice processing; copper, quartz, and graphite mining; coffee plantations. R.C. mission, hosp.

Ambouli (ämbōō'lē), oasis and SW suburb of Djibouti, Fr. Somaliland, on Gulf of Tadjoura; truck gardening. Pumping station supplies Djibouti with water.

Ambovombe (ämbōōvōōm'bä), town, Tuléar prov., S Madagascar, near S coast, on highway and 55 mi. WSW of Fort-Dauphin; agr. center with sheep stud farm, experimental station for dry farming (manioc, millet, sorghum, corn); also cattle raising. R.C. and Lutheran missions.

Amboy (ăm'boi). **1** Desert hamlet, San Bernardino co., S Calif., c.75 mi. ESE of Barstow. Near by is Amboy Crater, a volcanic cone. **2** City (pop. 2,128), Lee co., N Ill., on Green R. (bridged here) and 11 mi. SSE of Dixon, in agr. area; railroad shops; mfg. of dairy products, gasoline filters. Inc. 1857. **3** Town (pop. 414), Miami co., N central Ind., 13 mi. SE of Peru, in agr. area. **4** Village (pop. 585), Blue Earth co., S Minn., near Blue Earth R., 21 mi. SSW of Mankato, in grain, livestock, poultry area; dairy products.

Amboyna, Indonesia: see AMBOINA.

Ambra (äm'brä), village (pop. 585), Arezzo prov., Tuscany, central Italy, 14 mi. WSW of Arezzo; broom mfg.

Ambracia, city, Greece: see ARTA, city.

Ambracia, Lake (ămbrā'shŭ) (□ 5), in Acarnania nome, W central Greece, S of Amphilochia, at SE end of Gulf of Arta; 6 mi. long, 2 mi. wide. Formerly called L. Limeni.

Ambracian Gulf, Greece: see ARTA, GULF OF.

Ambrakia, Greece: see ARTA, city.

Ambre, Cape, or **Cape Amber**, Fr. *Cap d' Ambre* (käp dä'brŭ), N tip of Madagascar; 11°55'S 49°15'E. Lighthouse.

Ambre, Mount, Fr. *Mont d'Ambre* (mõ'), N Madagascar, 26 mi. SW of Diégo-Suarez; rises to 4,460 ft.; of volcanic origin. Forests, cinchona plantations.

Ambridge, borough (pop. 16,429), Beaver co., W Pa., 16 mi. NW of Pittsburgh and on Ohio R.; structural steel, metal products, electrical equipment, building supplies, canned goods, flour, paint; bituminous coal, oil, gas. Harmony Society established here the communistic settlement Economy (1825–1906), on site of Indian village. Some of Economy's bldgs. remain.

Ambrières-le-Grand (äbrēâr'-lù-grä), village (pop. 949), Mayenne dept., W France, on Varenne R. and 7 mi. N of Mayenne; sawmilling; quarrying. Has 11th-cent. church. Formerly Ambrières.

Ambrim, New Hebrides: see AMBRYM.

Ambriz (ämbrēsh'), town (pop. 2,196), Congo prov., NW Angola, small port on the Atlantic, 70 mi. N of Luanda. Ships cotton, palm oil and kernels, manioc. Airfield.

Ambrizete (ämbrēzĕ'tĭ), town (pop. 1,147), Congo prov., NW Angola, small port on the Atlantic, 110 mi. N of Luanda; 7°15'S 12°55'E. Ships cotton, oil seeds; salt pans, fisheries. Airfield. Road to Uíge.

Ambrolauri (ŭmbrŭlŏō'rē), town (1939 pop. over 500), N Georgian SSR, on Rion R. and 29 mi. NE of Kutaisi; vineyards. Hydroelectric station (W). Called Yenukidze in mid-1930s.

Ambronay (äbrônä'), village (pop. 483), Ain dept., E France, at foot of the S Jura, 15 mi. SSE of Bourg; wood veneering. Has 13th-15th-cent. church and cloister.

Ambrose, city (pop. 286), Divide co., NW N.Dak., port of entry 9 mi. WNW of Crosby, near Canada line.

Ambrosio, Campo (käm'pō ämbrō"syō), oil field in Zulia state, NW Venezuela, on NE shore of L. Maracaibo, near Cabimas.

Ambrym (ăm'brĭm,-brēm'), volcanic island (□ c.230; pop. c.4,500), New Hebrides, SW Pacific, 65 mi SE of Espiritu Santo; 25 mi. long, c.15 mi. wide; coffee, cocoa. Active volcano, Mt. Benbow (3,720 ft.). Sometimes spelled Ambrim.

Ambulong Island (ämbōōlông') (3 mi. long, 1.5 mi. wide; 1939 pop. 284), Mindoro prov., Philippines, just off S coast of Mindoro isl. adjacent to Ilin Isl.; rice growing.

Ambur (ŭmbōōr'), town (pop. 33,700), North Arcot dist., central Madras, India, on Palar R. and 33 mi. WSW of Vellore, in agr. area; trades in products (tanbark, tamarind, nux vomica, hemp narcotics) of Javadi Hills (E), hides and skins; tannery. Sugar mill at Mailpatti or Melpatti, 7 mi. NE.

Amchitka Island (ămchĭt'kŭ) (40 mi. long, 2–5 mi. wide), Rat Isls., Aleutian Isls., SW Alaska, 50 mi. ESE of Kiska Isl.; 51°31'N 179°1'E; rises to 1,335 ft. Site of U.S. air base in Second World War; operations against Attu and Kiska were carried on from here.

Amchitka Pass, sea passage (60 mi. wide), Aleutian Isls., SW Alaska, bet. Delarof Isls., at W end of Andreanof Isls. (E) and Rat Isls. (W); 51°45'N 179°25'W. Steamer route from N Pacific to Bering Sea.

'Amd, Wadi (wä'dē ä'md), left tributary valley of the Wadi Duan, Quaiti state, Eastern Aden Protectorate; 60 mi. long. Joins the Wadi Duan just S of the Wadi Hadhramaut. Chief town, Hureidha.

Amdals Verk (ôm'däls vărk"), Nor. *Åmdals Verk*, village (pop. 150) in Mo canton, Telemark co., S Norway, 55 mi. WNW of Skien; copperworks. Mining since 16th cent., regular working since 1915. Sometimes spelled Aamdals Verk.

Am-Dam (äm-däm'), village, E central Chad territory, Fr. Equatorial Africa, 80 mi. SSW of Abéché, on road to Darfur (Anglo-Egyptian Sudan).

Amderma (äm'dyĭrmŭ), town (1940 pop. over 500), E Nenets Natl. Okrug, Archangel oblast, Russian SFSR, port on Kara Sea, 260 mi. NE of Archangel; govt. observation station, air transport center; fluorspar mine.

Amdo, China: see TSINGHAI.

Amealco (ämā-äl'kō), town (pop. 1,729), Querétaro, central Mexico, 33 mi. SSE of Querétaro; alt. 6,807 ft.; agr. center (corn, wheat, beans, lentils, sugar, alfalfa, livestock).

Ameca (ämā'kä), city (pop. 13,003), Jalisco, W Mexico, on central plateau, on Ameca R. and 45 mi. WSW of Guadalajara; alt. 4,019 ft. Rail terminus; agr. center (grain, sugar, chick-peas, beans, alfalfa); tanning.

Amecameca (ämā"kämā'kä), officially Amecameca de Juárez, city (pop. 7,573), Mexico state, central Mexico, on central plateau, near foot of Ixtacihuatl and Popocatepetl, on railroad and 30 mi. SE of Mexico city; alt. 8,015 ft. Agr. center (cereals, vegetables, livestock); yarn and flour mills. Old Aztec town. Has 16th-cent. parish church. Famed sanctuary of Sacro Monte, one of Mexico's most venerated places of pilgrimage, is on near-by hill. Amecameca is also the usual starting point for ascent of volcanoes Popocatepetl and Ixtacihuatl.

Ameca River (ämā'kä), W Mexico, rises in Jalisco 14 mi. W of Guadalajara, flows c.140 mi. W, past Ameca, along Nayarit-Jalisco border, to the Pacific at Banderas Bay 5 mi. NW of Puerto Vallarta.

Amedika, Gold Coast: see AKUSE.

Ameghino (ämāgē'nō), town (pop. 2,772), NW Buenos Aires prov., Argentina, 33 mi. N of General Pinto; agr. center: wheat, corn, flax, livestock; dairying.

Ameglia (ämā'lyä), village (pop. 1,000), La Spezia prov., Liguria, N Italy, near mouth of Magra R., 7 mi. SE of Spezia.

Ameixial (ämāshäl'), village, Évora dist., S central Portugal, 6 mi. NW of Estremoz. Here Spaniards (under John of Austria) were defeated by Portuguese and British in 1663.

Ameland (ä'mulänt), island (□ 22; pop. 2,258), one of West Frisian Isls., Friesland prov., N Netherlands, bet. North Sea (N) and the Waddenzee (S); 14 mi. long, 2.5 mi. wide. Separated from Terschelling isl. (W) by the Borndiep or the Amelander Gat, from Schiermonnikoog isl. (E) by the Pinkegat and the Friesche Gat, from mainland (S) by the Waddenzee. N shore is protected by dunes. Horse breeding; truck gardens. Lighthouse (NW). Chief villages: HOLLUM, NES OP AMELAND, Ballum, Buren, and Bliek (or Blijke). Ferry from Nes to Holwerd, on mainland. Breakwater built from mainland (1875) to collect silt, forming base of a dam; now partly submerged.

Amelander Gat, Netherlands: see BORNDIEP.

Amelia (ämä'lyä), anc. *Ameria,* town (pop. 2,583), Terni prov., Umbria, central Italy, 12 mi. W of Terni; mfg. (agr. tools, metal furniture, electrical apparatus, cement, rope, macaroni). Travertine quarries near by. Bishopric. Has anc. walls (Roman, medieval), cathedral with campanile (1050), and 13th cent. church.

Amelia (ämä'lyä), village (pop. 32), Loreto dept., NE Peru, on Javarí R., opposite Remate de Males (Brazil); 4°21'S 70°9'W. Formerly Nazareth.

Amelia (ümēl'yü), county (□ 366; pop. 7,908), central Va.; ⊙ Amelia Court House. Bounded N and E by Appomattox R., SE by small Namozine Creek. Agr. (mainly tobacco; also corn, wheat, hay), dairying, livestock raising; extensive lumbering, lumber milling; feldspar, mica, pegmatite deposits. Formed 1735.

Amelia, village (pop. 601), Clermont co., SW Ohio, 17 mi. ESE of Cincinnati; makes furniture.

Amelia Court House or **Amelia,** village (pop. c.800), ⊙ Amelia co., central Va., 32 mi. WSW of Richmond; timber, agr.

Amelia Island, Nassau co., NE Fla., one of the Sea Isls. in Atlantic Ocean, separated from the mainland by salt marshes (bridged by road and railroad); extends 13.5 mi. S from mouth of St. Marys R. and is c.2 mi. wide. In N part of isl. are Fernandina, Fort Clinch State Park, and a lighthouse (30°40'N 81°27'W).

Amélie-les-Bains (ämälē'-lā-bē'), village (pop. 1,677), Pyrénées-Orientales dept., S France, in the VALLESPIR of E Pyrenees, on Tech R. and 4 mi. WSW of Céret; spa with noted hot sulphur springs and tuberculosis sanatoriums. Paper milling, plaster mfg. Hydroelectric plant. Ruins of Gallo-Roman thermae. Formerly called Fort-les-Bains and Les Bains-d'Arles.

Amendolara (ämĕndôlä'rä), village (pop. 1,680), Cosenza prov., Calabria, S Italy, near Gulf of Taranto, 23 mi. NE of Castrovillari; wine making.

Amenia (ümē'nēü). **1** Village (1940 pop. 1,052), Dutchess co., SE N.Y., near Conn. line, 20 mi. NE of Poughkeepsie, in dairying area; mfg. (vinegar, machinery). Thomas Lake Harris had his Brotherhood of the New Life sect here, 1863–67. **2** Village (pop. 127), Cass co., E N.Dak., 21 mi. WNW of Fargo; grain elevator.

Ameni Island, India: see AMINI ISLAND.

Amer, river, Netherlands: see BERGSCHE MAAS RIVER.

Amer (ämär'), town (pop. 1,486), Gerona prov., NE Spain, 12 mi. W of Gerona; olive oil, wine, livestock, lumber. Hydroelectric plant is on the Ter, 2 mi. S.

America or **the Americas** [for Amerigo Vespucci], the lands of the Western Hemisphere—North America, Central America, South America, and the West Indies, but not including Greenland. First used (1507) by the German geographer Martin Waldseemüller in an account of Vespucci's travels, the name America originally referred only to the lands (West Indies, Central and South America) discovered (1492–1502) by Columbus. Mercator extended its use (1538) to the entire New World. The term America is frequently used as a synonym for the United States of America.

América (ämä'rēkä), town (pop. 4,850), ⊙ Rivadavia dist. (□ 1,350; pop. 14,680), W Buenos Aires prov., Argentina, 36 mi. NNW of Trenque Lauquén, in agr. area (sunflowers, corn, barley, livestock); flour milling, mfg. of soap and ceramics.

América or **Central América** (sĕnträl'), sugar-mill village (pop. 1,585), Oriente prov., E Cuba, 35 mi. NW of Santiago de Cuba.

Americana (ämĭrēkä'nü), city (pop. 5,794), E central São Paulo, Brazil, near Piracicaba R., on railroad and 21 mi. NW of Campinas; silk milling, mfg. of synthetic fertilizer, assembling of farm machinery. Has new hydroelectric plant. Settled 1868 by U.S. immigrants from the former Confederate states. Until mid-1930s, called Villa Americana.

American Falls, city (pop. 1,874), ⊙ Power co., SE Idaho, on Snake R., at S end of American Falls Reservoir, and 21 mi. WSW of Pocatello; alt. 4,330 ft.; wheat-shipping center for irrigated agr. area (wheat, livestock, poultry, potatoes). AMERICAN FALLS DAM (unit in Minidoka irrigation project) and large hydroelectric plant are here. City grew after arrival of railroad (1892). Moved to present site after construction (1927) of dam, reservoir of which inundated former site. Trout hatchery and American Falls (c.50 ft. high; in Snake R.) are near by.

American Falls Dam, SE Idaho, on Snake R. at American Falls. Concrete, gravity dam (89 ft. high, 5,227 ft. long; completed 1927), unit in Minidoka project, serves hydroelectric plant and forms American Falls Reservoir (capacity 1,700,000 acre-ft.; 21 mi. long, max. width 9 mi.), storing surplus water for 90,000 acres in project and for 600,000 acres of privately irrigated land.

American Fork, city (pop. 5,126), Utah co., N central Utah, just N of Utah L. (on one of its tributaries), 27 mi. S of Salt Lake City; alt. 4,566 ft.; resort and poultry center in agr. area (poultry, potatoes, sugar beets); dairy products, flour. Served by Provo R. irrigation project. Settled 1850, inc. 1853. Timpanogos Cave Natl. Monument is near by.

American Highland, upland portion of Antarctica back of Ingrid Christensen Coast, in 72°S 79°E; alt. c.7,500 ft. Discovered 1939 by Lincoln Ellsworth.

American River, village, E Kangaroo Isl., South Australia, on small inlet of Backstairs Passage of Indian Ocean, 11 mi. SSE of Kingscote across Nepean Bay; barley, eucalyptus oil, sheep.

American River, N central Calif., formed by its North and South forks c.3 mi. NE of Folsom, flows c.30 mi. SW to Sacramento R. at Sacramento. Its headstreams rise in the Sierra Nevada, flow generally SW through deep canyons. After 1848, much gold was taken along river's banks. In 1948, construction was begun on FOLSOM DAM, a unit of Central Valley project.

American Samoa: see SAMOA.

Americus (ümĕ'rĭkŭs). **1** City (pop. 11,389), ⊙ Sumter co., SW central Ga., c.50 mi. SE of Columbus and on Muckalee Creek; trade and processing center for agr. and timber area; mfg. of clothing, cottonseed oil, stoves, lumber, boxes; food canning, peanut processing. Has state jr. col. Inc. 1832. **2** City (pop. 339), Lyon co., E central Kansas, near Neosho R., 8 mi. NW of Emporia, in cattle and grain region.

Amern (ä'mürn), village (pop. 5,083), in former Prussian Rhine Prov., W Germany, after 1945 in North Rhine-Westphalia, 4 mi. WSW of Dülken; grain, cattle.

Amerongen (ä'mürōng"ün), village (pop. 2,235), Utrecht prov., central Netherlands, near the Lower Rhine, 16 mi. SE of Utrecht, in tobacco-growing area. First refuge of William II of Germany in 1918. Has 17th-cent. castle (*Zuijlestein*).

Amerrique, Cordillera, or **Cordillera Amerrisque** (kôrdĭyä'rä ämĕrē'kä,–skä), section of main continental divide in S central Nicaragua; extends c.30 mi. SE from Comoapa.

Amer River, Netherlands: see BERGSCHE MAAS RIVER.

Amersfoort (ä'mürsfōrt), town (pop. 55,996), Utrecht prov., central Netherlands, on Eem R. and 12 mi. ENE of Utrecht; rail junction; industrial center; mfg. of chemicals, dyes, heating equipment, motors, bicycles; auto assembly plant; carpet weaving, brewing, canning, tobacco processing; poultry raising, truck gardening. John van Oldenbarneveldt b. here. Has 14th-cent. water gate (*Koppelpoort*), 15th-cent. Gate of Our Lady (*Onze Lieve Vrouwen Toren*). During First World War, site of camp for refugees from Belgium.

Amersham (ă'mürshŭm), residential town and parish (pop. 6,121), S Buckingham, England, 7 mi. ENE of High Wycombe; agr. market, producing also some metal products. Has 17th-cent. market hall and 13th-cent. church. Town is associated with the Drake family. Town formerly called Agmondesham. Near by is agr. village of Coleshill; Edmund Waller b. here.

Amery (ā'mürē), city (pop. 1,625), Polk co., NW Wis., on Apple R. and 53 mi. NW of Eau Claire, in lake-resort area; dairy products, canned peas, flour, poultry; grain elevators. Settled 1884, inc. 1919.

Amery, Mount (ā'mürē) (10,940 ft.), SW Alta., near B.C. border, in Rocky Mts., in Banff Natl. Park, 75 mi. SE of Jasper; 52°2'N 116°59'W.

Ames. 1 City (pop. 22,898), Story co., central Iowa, on Skunk R. and 30 mi. N of Des Moines; rail junction. Atomic-energy laboratory. Mfg. of hats, laboratory aprons, metal products, concrete blocks, veterinary supplies, feed; canned vegetables. Laid out 1864, inc. 1869. Hq. of state highway commission here. Near by is Iowa State Col. of Agr. and Mechanic Arts. **2** Village (pop. 193), Montgomery co., E central N.Y., 22 mi. WSW of Amsterdam. **3** Town (pop. 263), Major co., NW Okla., 20 mi. WSW of Enid, in grain and livestock area.

Amesbury, town and parish (pop. 2,488), E Wiltshire, England, on the Avon and 7 mi. N of Salisbury; agr. market. Its church is Norman to 13th cent. Amesbury is the Almesbury of Arthurian legend. STONEHENGE is 2 mi. W.

Amesbury, town (pop. 10,851), including Amesbury village (pop. 9,711), Essex co., NE Mass., on the Merrimack and 15 mi. NE of Lawrence; hats, boats, heels, castings, metal products, shoes. Former shipbuilding center. Settled 1654, inc. 1668.

Ames Range, Antarctica, W of Hobbs Coast, in Marie Byrd Land, in 75°30'S 132°W. Discovered 1940 by U.S. expedition.

Amestratus, Sicily: see MISTRETTA.

Amesville, village (pop. 269), Athens co., SE Ohio, 9 mi. ENE of Athens, in livestock and coal area.

Amethi (ŭmä'tē). **1** Town (pop. 7,038), Lucknow dist., central Uttar Pradesh, India, 15 mi. SE of Lucknow city center; cotton weaving; wheat, rice, gram, millet. Held by Rajputs until Moslem advent, c.1550. **2** Village, Sultanpur dist., E central Uttar Pradesh, India, 18 mi. SW of Sultanpur; rice, wheat, gram, barley.

Ametista (ämĭtē'stü), city, NW Espírito Santo, Brazil, claimed as **Barra do Ariranha** by Minas Gerais, in disputed Serra dos Aimorés region, 60 mi. W of São Mateus.

Amettla de Mar, La (lä ämät'lä dhä mär'), village (pop. 2,819), Tarragona prov., NE Spain, 15 mi. ENE of Tortosa, and on the Mediterranean; olive-oil processing; carob beans.

Ameur-el-Aïn (ämûr'-ĕl-ēn'), village (pop. 1,722), Alger dept., N central Algeria, in Mitidja plain, 15 mi. W of Blida; winegrowing; essential-oil processing. Traprock quarries.

Amfiklia, Greece: see AMPHIKLEIA.

Amfilokhia, Greece: see AMPHILOCHIA.

Amfissa, Greece: see AMPHISSA.

Amfreville-la-Campagne (äfrüvēl'-lä-käpä'nyü), village (pop. 189), Eure dept., NW France, 17 mi. SSW of Rouen; apple orchards; dairying.

Amfreville-la-Mi-Voie (–lä-mē-vwä'), village (pop. 1,868), Seine-Inférieure dept., N France, on Seine R. and 4 mi. SSE of Rouen; cable mfg., textile printing.

Amga (ŭmgä'), village (1948 pop. over 500), SE Yakut Autonomous SSR Russian SFSR, on Amga R., on Yakutsk-Ayan highway and 110 mi. SE of Yakutsk, in agr. area. Oil deposits upstream. Civil war battle, 1923.

Amga River, S Yakut Autonomous SSR, Russian SFSR, rises on W Aldan Plateau, flows 1,025 mi. NE, past Amga, parallel to Aldan R., which it enters 170 mi. ENE of Yakutsk.

Amginski Perevoz or **Amginskiy Perevoz** (ŭmgēn'-skē pĕrĭvôs'), village, SE Yakut Autonomous SSR, Russian SFSR, on Amga R. and 145 mi. E of Yakutsk; ferry on Yakutsk-Okhotsk highway.

Amguid (ämgēd'), Saharan outpost, Saharan Oases territory, S central Algeria, 190 mi. ESE of In-Salah; caravan center and junction of auto tracks; 26°25'N 5°21'E.

Amgun River or **Amgun' River** (ŭmgōōn'yü), S Khabarovsk Territory, Russian SFSR, rises E of Chekunda in Bureya Range, flows 490 mi. NNE, past Imeni Poliny Osipenko (head of navigation), to Amur R. above Nikolayevsk. Navigable for 265 mi. above its mouth. Gold found along its upper course and along its main (left) affluent, the Kerbi.

Amhara (ămhä'rü, äm'härä), a former major province of Ethiopia, now largely included in BEGEMDIR and GOJJAM provs. Its rulers dominated much of Ethiopia 12th–19th cents., and the Amharic language and culture were widespread among the upper classes. Gondar was the capital in 17th–19 cents. and again under Italian rule (1936–41) when the prov. was reconstituted.

Amherst (ă'mürst), Burmese *Kyaikkami* (chĭk'-kümē"), central district (□7,410; 1941 pop. 593,-490), Tenasserim div., Lower Burma; ⊙ Moulmein. Bet. Gulf of Martaban (W) and Thaungyin R. (Thailand border) in Dawna Range (E). Rice in coastal plain; timber (teak) in mts. Large salt (brine) production. Antimony, tungsten, iron ore present but not exploited. Served by Ye-Moulmein RR and linked to Thailand via Three Pagodas Pass. Pop. is 45% Mon, 20% Karen, 15% Burmese.

Amherst, village, Amherst dist., Lower Burma, in Tenasserim, minor Andaman Sea port on headland at S mouth of Salween R., and 30 mi. SSW of Moulmein. Pilot station and seaside resort; small coastal trade. Founded 1826 and named for Lord Amherst.

Amherst (ă'mürst, ăm'hürst). **1** Town (pop. 8,620), ⊙ Cumberland co., N N.S., near Cumberland Basin (arm of Chignecto Bay), 55 mi. NW of Truro; iron founding, woolen milling, mfg. of railroad cars, machinery, boilers, shoes. Near by are ruins of Fort Lawrence and Fort Beauséjour (1750–51), on opposite sides of former French-English boundary. **2** Village, Que.: see HAVRE AUBERT.

Amherst, county (□ 467; pop. 20,332), W central Va.; ⊙ Amherst. Mainly in the piedmont; rises NW to the Blue Ridge, (here traversed by Blue Ridge Parkway, Appalachian Trail); bounded SW, S, and SE by James R. and drained by its tributaries. W and NW area in George Washington Natl. Forest. Chiefly agr. (tobacco; also hay, fruit); dairying. Titanium ore deposits. Formed 1761.

Amherst. 1 Agr. town (pop. 151), Hancock co., S Maine, 21 mi. E of Bangor. **2** Town (pop. 10,856), including Amherst village (pop. 7,900), Hampshire co., W central Mass., 7 mi. NE of Northampton; small mfg. Seat of Amherst Col. and Univ. of Mass. Settled 1703, inc. 1775. Includes villages of Cushman (kōōsh'mün) and North Amherst (1940 pop. 885). Emily Dickinson b. here. **3** Village (pop. 219), Buffalo co., S central Nebr., 15 mi. NW of Kearney and on Wood R. **4** Town (pop. 1,461), Hillsboro co., S N.H., 12 mi. SW of Manchester near the Souhegan. Horace Greeley b. here. Settled c.1733, inc. 1760. **5** Village (pop. 3,542), Lorain co., N Ohio, 5 mi. SW of Lorain, near L. Erie, in sandstone-quarrying and fruitgrowing area; metal products, machinery, crates. Settled c.1810. **6** City (pop. 922), Lamb co., NW Texas, on the Llano Estacado, c.45 mi. NW of Lubbock; retail point for agr. area. Waterfowl hunting, fishing in near-by lakes. **7** Town (pop. 1,038), ⊙ Amherst co., central Va., in Blue Ridge foothills, 13 mi. NNE of Lynchburg; fruit, tobacco. **8** Village (pop. 608), Portage co., central Wis., on small Tomorrow R. and 14 mi. ESE of Stevens Point; trade center in dairy, timber, and farm area (poultry, truck).

Amherstburg, town (pop. 2,853), S Ont., on Detroit R., near L. Erie, 16 mi. S of Detroit; food canning, distilling, lumbering, textile knitting, chemical mfg.; resort. In limestone-quarrying, tobacco, corn-growing region. Fort Malden, later Fort Amherstburg, was built here (1796) by the British after their evacuation of Detroit. In War of 1812 it was British garrison and naval station, later captured by Americans.

Amherstdale, village (1940 pop. 2,910), Logan co., SW W.Va., 10 mi. SE of Logan; coal mining.

Amherst Island. 1 Island (□ 22.8), SE Ont., one of the Thousand Isls., at head of L. Ontario, near entrance to the St. Lawrence, 7 mi. WSW of Kingston; 11 mi. long, 5 mi. wide. Popular resort. Granted to La Salle by Louis XIV; originally called Île de Tonti. **2** Island (10 mi. long, 4 mi. wide), in Gulf of St. Lawrence, E Que., southernmost of the Magdalen Isls., 50 mi. N of Prince Edward Isl. and 5 mi. S of Grindstone Isl.; 47°13'–47°17'N 60°46'–62°2'W. Havre Aubert (E) is chief town. Fisheries.

Amherst Junction, village (pop. 185), Portage co., central Wis., 13 mi. ESE of Stevens Point and 2 mi. N of Amherst; railroad junction.

Ami, China: see KAIYÜAN, Yunnan prov.

Amiãis de Baixo (ämyā'ĭsh dĭ bī'shōō), town (pop. 2,039), Santarém dist., central Portugal, 15 mi. NNW of Santarém, in olive, fruit- and winegrowing area. Formerly spelled Amiãos de Baixo.

Amiandos or **Pano Amiandos** (pä'nō ämē'ändôs), village (pop. 656), Limassol dist., S central Cyprus, in Olympus Mts., 23 mi. SW of Nicosia; alt. 4,500 ft. Quarries asbestos, which is transported by 19-mi. aerial ropeway to the coast, whence it is shipped.

Amiata, Monte (môn'tĕ ämyä'tä), extinct volcano (5,689 ft.) in the Apennines, Tuscany, central Italy, 8 mi. W of Radicofani. Has mercury mines (Abbadia San Salvatore, Piancastagnaio), sulphur springs; several ski runs.

Amicalola Falls (ă"mĭkŭlō'lŭ), in the Blue Ridge, Dawson co., N Ga., 15 mi. W of Dahlonega, in Amicalola Falls State Park. Highest falls (729 ft.) in the state, formed by 7 cascades of a mtn. stream.

Amicano (ämēkä'nō), officially San Pablo Amicano, town (pop. 1,089), Puebla, central Mexico, 6 mi. SSW of Acatlán; sugar, corn, fruit, livestock.

Amida, Turkey: see DIYARBAKIR, city.

Amidon (ă'mĭdŏn), village (pop. 82), ⊙ Slope co., SW N.Dak., 37 mi. SW of Dickinson. Lignite mine near by.

Amieira (ämyā'rŭ), village (pop. 1,492), Portalegre dist., central Portugal, near the Tagus, 25 mi. NW of Portalegre; grain, olive oil, wine, cork.

Amiens (ă'myŭnz, Fr. ämyē'), anc. *Samarobriva*, city (pop. 79,807), ⊙ Somme dept., N France, on swampy and braided Somme R. and 70 mi. N of Paris; 59°53'N 2°18'E; important communications (8 rail lines) and textile center known for diversity of its products: cotton and linen cloth, velvet, velveteen, plush, satin and moleskin fabrics, woolens, carpets and tapestries, rayon, ready-to-wear clothing, and hats. Other mfg.: machinery, machine and precision tools, chemicals, perfumes, furniture, chocolates, and flour products. Intensive truck gardening in suburban marshlands (locally called *hortillonnages*). Jute and flax spinning in Somme R. valley on both sides of Amiens. Trade in grain, beet-sugar, wool, oil-seeds, and leather. The Cathedral of Notre Dame (damaged in First World War; undamaged in Second World War) is largest and one of finest French Gothic cathedrals. Begun in 1220, it is 470 ft. long, has nave 140 ft. high. Transepts were added in 14th cent., spire (360 ft. high) and large rose window in 16th cent. Near by is statue of Peter the Hermit (b. here). Important Gallo-Roman town (chief city of Ambiani tribe). Episcopal see since 4th cent. Historical ⊙ PICARDY. Overrun and captured by many invaders. Treaty of Amiens, signed here in 1802, marked brief pause in Napoleonic wars. Occupied by Prussians in 1870. Taken and lost by Germans in 1914, it became important Br. military base, and was again threatened and bombarded by Germans in 1918; 60% of city destroyed in Second World War.

Amik, Lake (ämĭk') (□ 39), S Turkey, 9 mi. NE of Antioch, near Syrian line; 9 mi. long, 6 mi. wide; alt. 460 ft. Drains S into Orontes R.

Amiktok Island (ă'mĭktŏk") (2 mi. long, 1 mi. wide), NE Labrador, in Seven Islands Bay; 59°25'N 63°42'W. Just NE is Avigalik or Whale Isl.

Aminabad (ämēn"äbäd'), village, Tenth Prov., in Isfahan, central Iran, 70 mi. SSE of Isfahan and on highway to Shiraz; airfield.

Amindaion, Greece: see AMYNTAION.

Amin Divi Islands or **Amindivi Islands** (ŭmĭndē've), N group (pop. 6,177) of LACCADIVE ISLANDS, India, in Arabian Sea, bet. 11°–12°N and 72°–73°E; administered by South Kanara dist. of Madras. Include Amini, Cardamum, Chetlat, and Kiltan isls. (all inhabited). Main products: coir, copra, fish.

Aminga (äming'gä), village (pop. estimate 600), ⊙ Castro Barros dept. (□ 540; 1947 census pop. 3,496), N La Rioja prov., Argentina, at NE foot of Sierra de Velasco, in irrigated area, 40 mi. N of La Rioja. Agr. center (wine, corn, olives, goats, sheep, cattle). Cultivation of olives was introduced by Jesuits in 18th cent.

Amingaon (ŭmĭn'goun), village, Kamrup dist., W Assam, India, on Brahmaputra R. (rail ferry) opposite Pandu, and 4 mi. W of Gauhati.

Amini Island (ŭmĭ'nē), coral island of Amin Divi group of Laccadive Isls., India, in Arabian Sea; 11°5'N 72°45'E. Administered by South Kanara dist., Madras; coconuts; mfg. of coir and copra. Formerly spelled Ameni.

Aminnagar Sarai (ŭmēn'nŭgŭr sŭrī'), town (pop. 2,944), Meerut dist., NW Uttar Pradesh, India, 18 mi. W of Meerut; wheat, gram, jowar, sugar cane, oilseeds.

Amino (ä"mē'nō), town (pop. 8,778), Kyoto prefecture, S Honshu, Japan, on Sea of Japan, 24 mi. NW of Maizuru, in rice-growing area; raw silk, bamboo ware, textiles. Fishing.

Amioun, Lebanon: see AMYUN.

Amir or **'Amir** (ämēr'), settlement (pop. 350), Upper Galilee, NE Israel, in Hula swamp region, on headwaters of the Jordan, 16 mi. NE of Safad; fish breeding, irrigated farming. Has hosp. Village founded 1939.

Amiradzhany (ŭmērŭjä'nē), town (1939 pop. over 500) in Ordzhonikidze dist. of Greater Baku, Azerbaijan SSR, on S Apsheron Peninsula, 8 mi. ENE of Baku, on small lake; chemical industry; marlpits.

Amirante Isles, Seychelles: see AMIRANTES.

Amirantes (ă'mĭrănts) or **Amirante Isles** (ă'mĭrănt), archipelago in Indian Ocean, an outlying dependency of the Seychelles, 500 mi. NNE of N tip of Madagascar and 150 mi. WSW of Mahé Isl.; 4°50'–6°17'S 52°50'–53°25'E; 100 mi. long (N–S). Includes African Isls., Daros, Desneuf, St. Joseph, Poivre, and Marie Louise isls. Copra is chief product.

Amiri (ămē'rē), tribal area (pop. 27,000) of Western Aden Protectorate, on Yemen border; ⊙ Dhala. A mountainous dist., situated bet. middle Wadi Bana and the upper Wadi Tiban; pastoral and agr. (wheat) pop., ruled by an amir (emir). One of the original Nine Cantons, Amiri concluded a protectorate treaty in 1904 and entered into closer adviser relations with Aden in 1944. Exercises loose suzerainty over the RADFAN tribal confederation.

'Amiriya, El, or **Al-'Amiriyah** (both: ĕl ä"mĭrē'yŭ), village (pop. 3,814), Western Desert frontier prov., NW Egypt, on coastal railroad and 12 mi. SSW of Alexandria. Good road to Cairo. Has hosp. Was important British base during the Western Desert campaigns (1940–42).

Amish, village, Johnson co., E Iowa, 16 mi. SW of Iowa City. Amish settlement.

Amisk Lake (□ 111), NE Sask., on Man. border, 11 mi. SW of Flin Flon; 23 mi. long, 12 mi. wide. Contains Missi Isl. (7 mi. long, 6 mi. wide).

Amisus, Turkey: see SAMSUN, city.

Amite (ŭmēt'), county (□ 729; pop. 19,261), SW Miss.; ⊙ Liberty. Borders S on La.; drained by Homochitto, Tangipahoa, Amite and Tickfaw rivers. Agr. (cotton, corn, truck), dairying, lumbering. Includes part of Homochitto Natl. Forest. Formed 1809.

Amite, town (pop. 2,804), ⊙ Tangipahoa parish, SE La., 45 mi. NE of Baton Rouge and on Tangipahoa R.; ships truck produce, strawberries; cotton, corn, dairy products. Cotton gins, grain mills; mfg. of cotton gins, canning machinery. Gravel, sand pits near by. Settled 1836, inc. 1861.

Amite River, in Miss. and La., rises in SW Miss. in West and East forks, joining near La. line; flows c.100 mi. S and E, past Denham Springs, La., to L. Maurepas; navigable for c.37 mi. of lower course.

Amity. 1 Town (pop. 591), Clark co., S central Ark., 24 mi. NW of Arkadelphia, in agr. area; cotton ginning, sawmilling; cinnabar mines near. **2** Town (pop. 300), Aroostook co., E Maine, 15 mi. S of Houlton, near N.B. line; agr., lumbering. **3** Town (pop. 128), De Kalb co., NW Mo., 23 mi. ENE of St. Joseph. **4** City (pop. 672), Yamhill co., NW Oregon, 35 mi. SW of Portland in grain-growing and dairying area.

Amityville (ă'mĭtēvĭl), residential village (pop. 6,164), Suffolk co., SE N.Y., on S shore of W Long Isl., 9 mi. E of Freeport; summer resort. Mfg.: wood products, textiles, aircraft parts, pipes, novelties, cement blocks. Settled 1780, inc. 1894.

Amixtlán (ämēslän'), town (pop. 1,207), Puebla, central Mexico, in SE foothills of Sierra Madre Oriental, 18 mi. SE of Huauchinango; sugar, coffee, fruit. Has pre-Columbian stone idols.

Amizmiz (ämēzmēz'), village, Marrakesh region, SW Fr. Morocco, on N slope of the High Atlas, 32 mi. SSW of Marrakesh; hill resort (alt. 3,180 ft.). Center of mining area: lead and zinc at Asif el Mal (just NW) and Talaat n'Yakoub (20 mi. S), molybdenum at Azegour mine (6 mi. SSW). Oued N'Fis dam is NE.

Amjhera (ŭmjā'rŭ), village, SW Madhya Bharat, India, 12 mi. WSW of Dhar, in Vindhya Range; corn, rice.

Amjorby (ăm'yûrbü"), Swedish *Amjörby*, village (pop. 742), Varmland co., W Sweden, on Klar R. and 60 mi. NW of Filipstad; grain, stock. Includes villages of Munkebol (mŭng'kŭbōōl") and Manas (mō'nĕs"), Swedish *Månäs*.

Amla, Norway: see SOGNDAL, Sogn og Fjordane co.

Amlekhganj (ŭmlākh'gŭng), town, S central Nepal, in the Terai, at foot of Siwalik Range, 35 mi. SSW of Katmandu; rail terminus; transfer point to Katmandu on main India-Katmandu road; trades in rice, wheat, corn, barley, oilseeds, jute, hides.

Amli (ôm'lē), Nor. *Åmli*, village and canton (pop. 1,887), Aust-Agder co., S Norway, on Nid R., on railroad and 24 mi. NNW of Arendal; iron deposits (S); lumbering. Sometimes spelled Aamli.

Amlia Island (ăm'lēŭ) (46 mi. long, 3–9 mi. wide), Andreanof Isls., Aleutian Isls., SW Alaska, just E of Atka Isl.; 52°5'N 173°30'W; rises to 2,020 ft.

Amloh (ŭmlō'), town (pop. 2,184), E central Patiala and East Punjab States Union, India, 21 mi. NNW of Patiala; agr. (millet, gram, wheat, sugar cane); food processing, hand-loom weaving; metalware.

Amlwch (ăm'lŏŏkh, –lōōk), urban district (1931 pop. 2,562; 1951 census 2,700), N Anglesey, Wales, on Irish Sea, 14 mi. ENE of Holyhead; agr. market, with slate quarrying. Former copper-mining center (deposits were at Parys Mtn., S) and port. Point Lynas (lĭ'nŭs), 2 mi. E, is site of lighthouse (53°25'N 4°17'W).

Ammaia, Portugal: see PORTALEGRE, city.

Amman or **'Amman** (ämän', ăm-măn', ăm–), city (pop. c.90,000), ⊙ Jordan, in N central part of the country, on upper reaches of the Wadi Zerqa' (Jabbok R.), on Hejaz RR, and 50 mi. ENE of Jerusalem; alt. 2,460 ft.; road junction, airfield. Tourist resort (ruins). Industrial center of Jordan: mfg. of textiles, tobacco products, leather, flour, biscuits, cement, tiles. Power plant and printing shops. Has govt. school of arts and crafts. Phosphate extraction (N), clay. It was the anc. Rabbah or Rabbath Ammon, capital of the Ammonites. Rebuilt and called Philadelphia by the Greeks, it was one of the cities of the Decapolis.

Ammanford, urban district (1931 pop. 7,164; 1951 census 6,578), SE Carmarthen, Wales, bet. Loughor R. and Amman R., 11 mi. NE of Llanelly; coal mining.

Am Masharij, Aden: see MASHARIJ, AM.

Ammatti (ŭm-mŭt'tē), village (pop. 282), S Coorg, India, 15 mi. SSE of Mercara; road center in coffee-estate area; oranges. Teak, sandalwood, rubber plantations (E).

Ammayanakkanur or **Ammayanakanur** (ŭm"mŭyŭnŭkŭnōōr'), village, Madura dist., S Madras, India, on railroad (Kodaikanal Road station) and 23 mi. NW of Madura; trade center for agr. products of Palni Hills (W); transfer point for health resort of Kodaikanal, 29 mi. W.

Ammeberg (ô"mŭbĕr'yŭ), Swedish *Åmmeberg*, village (pop. 794), Orebro co., S central Sweden, on small bay at N extremity of L. Vatter, 17 mi. SSW of Kumla; zinc and lead mining and smelting.

Ammeloe (ä'mŭlō, –lōō), village (pop. 7,066), in former Prussian prov. of Westphalia, NW Germany, after 1945 in North Rhine-Westphalia, 19 mi. NW of Coesfeld, near Dutch border; dairying.

Ammenas, Sweden: see ROSENFORS.

Ammendorf (ä'mŭndôrf), town (pop. 18,723), in former Prussian Saxony prov., central Germany, after 1945 in Saxony-Anhalt, near Saxonian Saale, 4 mi. S of Halle; lignite-mining center; mfg. of railroad cars, chemicals, dyes; paper milling, metalworking.

Ammerland, Germany: see WESTERSTEDE.

Ammer River (ä'mŭr), Bavaria, Germany, rises in the Bavarian Alps c.9 mi. W of Füssen, flows 45 mi. N, past Oberammergau and Weilheim, to the AMMERSEE just E of Diessen.

Ammersee (ä'mŭrzā"), lake (□ 17), Upper Bavaria, Germany, 19 mi. WSW of Munich; 10 mi. long, 1½–4 mi. wide, 271 ft. deep; alt. 1,749 ft. Inlet, AMMER R.; outlet, AMPER R. Resorts: Diessen (SW tip), Herrsching (E shore).

Ammerstol (ä'mŭrstōl), village (pop. 1,093), South Holland prov., W Netherlands, on Lek R. and 14 mi. E of Rotterdam; salmon fishing, cattle raising. Founded 1321.

Ammi-Moussa (äm-mē'-mōōsä'), village (pop. 1,074), Oran dept., N Algeria, on N slope of Ouarsenis Massif, 32 mi. ENE of Relizane; livestock, cereals.

Ammochostos, Cyprus: see FAMAGUSTA, city.

Ammoedara, Tunisia: see HAÏDRA.

Ammon, village (pop. 447), Bonneville co., SE Idaho, 4 mi. SE of Idaho Falls; alt. 4,710 ft.

Ammonium, Egypt: see SIWA.

Ammonoosuc River or **Lower Ammonoosuc River** (ămŭnōō'sŭk), NW N.H., rises in White Mts. N of Mt. Washington, flows c.55 mi. generally W and SW to the Connecticut at Woodsville. Wild Ammonoosuc R., rising in Kinsman Notch, flows c.15

mi. NW to the Ammonoosuc at Bath. UPPER AMMONOOSUC RIVER enters the Connecticut c.50 mi. N.

Ammouliane or **Ammouliani** (both: ämōōlēänē'), Greek island (□ 2.5; pop. 615) at head of Singitic Gulf of Aegean Sea, Chalcidice nome, Macedonia, 24 mi. E of Polygyros; 3 mi. long, 1.5 mi. wide. Village on NE coast. Formerly called Moulara.

Amne Machin Mountains (äm'nä' mä'chĭn'), Chinese *Chi-shih Shan*, W spur of the Kunlun system, SE Tsinghai prov., China, in hairpin bend of upper Yellow R.; mts. rise to c.25,000 ft. 190 mi. SW of Sining.

Amnéville (ämnävēl'), town (pop. 5,422), Moselle dept., NE France, on the Orne and 7 mi. SSW of Thionville, in iron-mining dist.; metalworking, bronze smelting, Portland cement mfg.

Amnicon River (ăm'nĭkŏn"), extreme NW Wis., rises in small lake c.20 mi. S of Superior, flows c.30 mi. generally NE, through James Bardon Park, to L. Superior 11 mi. E of Superior. Waterfalls (highest: 35 ft.) in park.

Amnok-kang, Korea and Manchuria: see YALU RIVER.

Amo (ā'mō), town (pop. 354), Hendricks co., central Ind., on Mill Creek and 25 mi. WSW of Indianapolis, in agr. area.

Amo Chu, river, Tibet and Bhutan: see TORSA RIVER.

Amod (ŭmōd'), town (pop. 7,088), Broach dist., N Bombay, India, 22 mi. NNW of Broach; market center for cotton, wheat, millet, rice; cotton ginning, handicraft cloth weaving; iron products (knives, razors).

Amoerang, Indonesia: see AMURANG.

Amol, Iran: see AMUL.

Amole Peak, Ariz.: see TUCSON MOUNTAINS.

Amoles or **Pinal de Amoles** (pēnäl' dā ämō'lĕs), town (pop. 687), Querétaro, Mexico, at E foot of Cerro Pingüicas, 25 mi. NE of Tolimán; cereals, sugar, tropical fruit, maguey.

Amöneburg (ämû'nûbŏŏrk), town (pop. 1,233), in former Prussian prov. of Hesse-Nassau, W Germany, after 1945 in Hesse, 7 mi. E of Marburg. Seat (8th–12th cent.) of noted Benedictine convent.

Amora (ämō'rů), village, Setúbal dist., S central Portugal, on S inlet of Tagus estuary, 6 mi. S of Lisbon; mfg. of explosives.

Amorbach (ä'môrbäkh"), town (pop. 3,754), Lower Franconia, W Bavaria, Germany, 4 mi. SW of Miltenberg; textile mfg., woodworking. Mid-18th-cent. church of former Benedictine monastery (founded in 10th cent.; secularized 1803) has two 12th-cent. Romanesque towers.

Amorebieta (ämōrāvyā'tä), village (pop. 1,128), Vizcaya prov., N Spain, road junction 10 mi. ESE of Bilbao; metalworking; mfg. of auto accessories, paints and varnishes, cement. Damaged in civil war of 1936–39.

Amoreira (ämŏŏrā'rů), village (pop. 1,160), Leiria dist., W central Portugal, near railroad and 36 mi. SE of Leiria; oranges, wheat, wine; potatoes, beans.

Amoret (ă'mûrĕt), town (pop. 255), Bates co., W Mo., near Marais des Cygnes R., 14 mi. W of Butler.

Amorgopoula, Greece: see ANYDROS.

Amorgos (ŭmôr'gûs, ämôrgôs'), easternmost island (□ 44; pop. 3,069) of the Cyclades, Greece, in Aegean Sea, SE of Naxos; 36°50'N 26°E; 18 mi. long (NE–SW), 4 mi. wide; rises to 2,695 ft. in the Krikelos. Produces figs, olive oil, wine, tobacco, barley, vegetables, cheese. Bauxite deposits. Chief town, Amorgos (pop. 820), is on E shore. Colonized in antiquity by Milesians (N) and Samians (S). Under Turkish rule, 1537–1832.

Amorita (ămûrē'tů), town (pop. 125), Alfalfa co., N Okla., 22 mi. ENE of Alva, near Kansas line; mfg. of farm machinery.

Amorosi (ämôrô'zē), village (pop. 1,687), Benevento prov., Campania, S Italy, near Calore R. mouth, 12 mi. NE of Caserta; tomato canning.

Amory (ā'mûrē), city (pop. 4,990), Monroe co., E Miss., near Tombigbee R., 35 mi. N of Columbus; clothing, lumber, cottonseed and dairy products. Trade and shipping center for agr. (cotton), dairying, and timber area. Founded 1887.

Amos (ā'mûs), town (pop. 2,862), ⊙ Abitibi co., W Que., 50 mi. ENE of Rouyn; mining center (gold, copper, molybdenum, zinc, lead); lumbering, woodworking, furniture mfg. Inc. 1914.

Amoskeag Falls, N.H.: see MANCHESTER.

Amot, canton, Norway: see RENA.

Amot, village, Norway: see GEITHUS.

Amotape (ämōtä'pä), town (pop. 901), Piura dept., NW Peru, on coastal plain, on Chira R., on Pan-American Highway and 15 mi. NNE of Paita, in irrigated area; cotton, fruit.

Amotfors (ōmōōt'fôrs", –fôsh"), Swedish *Åmotfors*, village (pop. 1,037), Varmland co., W Sweden, on the lake *Nysockensjö* (nü'sō"kŭnshû") (7 mi. long, ½ mi. wide), 10 mi. NW of Arvika, near Norwegian border; lumber and paper milling, metalworking, explosives mfg.

Amou (ämōō'), village (pop. 584), Landes dept., SW France, on Luy de Béarn R. and 17 mi. ESE of Dax; cereals, dairy produce.

Amouda, Syria: see 'AMUDE.

Amour, Djebel (jĕ'bĕl ämōōr'), range of the Saharan Atlas in N central Algeria, extending c.80 mi. SW–NE from Géryville area (Aïn-Sefra territory) to Aflou (S Oran dept.), bet. the High Plateaus (N) and Sahara Desert (S). Highest peaks are Djebel Ksel (6,588 ft.) and Djebel Touïla (6,466 ft.). Shrub-oak forests.

Amour Point, cape on Strait of Belle Isle, SE Labrador, on NE side of entrance of Forteau Bay; 51°27'N 56°51'W; lighthouse.

Amoy (ŭmoi'), Mandarin *Hsia-men* (shyä'mŭn'), second-largest city (1948 pop. 158,271) of Fukien prov., China, on SW shore of Amoy isl. (10 mi. across), in Amoy Bay of Formosa Strait, off Lung R. estuary, 135 mi. SW of Foochow; 24°27'N 118°4'E. A leading industrial and commercial center of SE China coast; mfg. of chemicals, machinery, paper, noodles, wine. Its fine harbor, located on coastwise shipping lanes, suffers from the lack of an extensive natural hinterland—it is restricted to Lung R. basin of SE Fukien. It exports mainly sugar, tobacco, fruit (longans), tea, and paper products. Seat of a univ. (financed by emigrants to Malaya). Opposite Amoy proper, across the inner harbor, is the isl. of Kulangsü or Kulanghsü (1.5 mi. long, 1 mi. wide), the former foreign settlement and a fine residential section. The 1st Chinese port to trade (18th cent.) with British and Dutch, it supplanted Changchow (Lungki), up Lung R. Amoy was occupied (1841) by the British, and by the Treaty of Nanking (1842) became one of the original ports opened to foreign trade. It had a flourishing tea trade (which declined in late-19th cent.) and was a Chinese emigration port, mainly for SE Asia. During Sino-Japanese War, it was held (1938–45) by the Japanese. City passed in 1949 to Communist control. Formerly also known as Szeming.

Amozoc (ämōsōk'), officially Amozoc de Mota, town (pop. 3,810), Puebla, central Mexico, on central plateau, 10 mi. E of Puebla; alt. 7,595 ft.; rail junction and sheep-grazing center. Noted for woolen goods (serapes), silver inlaid spurs, and ceramics. Many colonial churches.

Ampang (äm'päng), town (pop. 5,948), E central Selangor, Malaya, on rail spur and 4 mi. E of Kuala Lumpur; tin mining.

Ampanihy (ämpä'nēhē), town, Tuléar prov., S Madagascar, 105 mi. SE of Tuléar; agr. market; livestock. Industrial garnets found near by.

Amparo (ämpä'rōō), city (pop. 9,548), E São Paulo, Brazil, 23 mi. NE of Campinas; rail junction; wine-growing center; coffee, cotton, wheat. Has experimental viticultural station.

Amparo, El, Venezuela: see EL AMPARO.

Ampato, Nudo de (nōō'dō dā ämpä'tō), Andean massif (20,670 ft.), Arequipa dept., S Peru, in Cordillera Occidental, 40 mi. NW of Arequipa.

Ampegama (ŭmpā'gŭmŭ), village (pop. 1,813), Southern Prov., Ceylon, 7 mi. ESE of Ambalangoda; graphite-mining center; vegetables, tea, rubber, coconuts, cinnamon, rice.

Ampelakia or **Ambelakia** (both: ämbĕlä'kēä), town (pop. 1,477), Larissa nome, NE Thessaly, Greece, 17 mi. NNE of Larissa, at NW foot of Mt. Ossa, overlooking Vale of Tempe; cotton spinning and dyeing. Was a noted cotton center in Middle Ages, known for its cooperative labor methods.

Ampenan (äm'pünän), chief port of Lombok, Indonesia, on W coast of isl., on Lombok Strait, 3 mi. WNW of Mataram; 8°34'S 116°5'E; exports rice.

Ampère (ãpâr'), village (pop. 1,959), Constantine dept., NE Algeria, in the Hodna Mts., 26 mi. SSE of Sétif; cereals, sheep, wool.

Amper River (äm'pùr), Bavaria, Germany, rises in the AMMERSEE, flows 55 mi. NE, past Dachau, to the Isar 2 mi. NE of Moosburg.

Ampersand Lake (ăm'pûrsănd"), Essex co., NE N.Y., in the Adirondacks, 12 mi. WSW of Lake Placid village; c.1¼ mi. long. Just N is **Ampersand Mountain** (3,365 ft.), a peak of the Adirondacks, 16 mi. NW of Mt. Marcy.

Ampezzo (ämpĕt'tsô), village (pop. 1,436), Udine prov., Friuli–Venezia Giulia, NE Italy, near Tagliamento R. 11 mi. W of Tolmezzo; resort (alt. 1,837 ft.)

Ampfelwang (ämp'fùlväng), town (pop. 3,588), S central Upper Austria, 7 mi. NW of Vöcklabruck. Lignite mine near by.

Ampfing (äm'pfĭng), village (pop. 2,294), Upper Bavaria, Germany, on the Isen and 5 mi. W of Mühldorf; sheep, barley, rye. Near by, in 1322, took place the battle of MÜHLDORF.

Amphikleia or **Amfiklia** (both: ämfē'klēä), town (pop. 4,114), Phthiotis nome, E central Greece, on railroad and 20 mi. SSE of Lamia; summer resort; agr. center (wheat, tobacco, barley). Formerly called Dadi.

Amphilochia or **Amfilokhia** (both: ämfēlōkhē'ä), town (pop. 3,642), Acarnania nome, W central Greece, port on SE shore of Gulf of Arta 36 mi. NNW of Messolonghi; olive oil, wine, dairy products; cattle, sheep, goats, hogs; fisheries. Also spelled Amphilokhia and Amfilochia. Formerly called Karavassara or Karvasaras.

Amphion, France: see PUBLIER.

Amphipolis (ămfĭ'pùlĭs), main anc. Greek city on N Aegean Sea, in Macedonia 27 mi. SW of modern Drama, on Strymonic Gulf at mouth of Struma (Strymon) R. Founded 437 B.C. as an Athenian colony in Edoni territory, it developed as center for gold-mining and lumbering operations in the Pangaion (Pangaeus), later succeeded by Philippi; captured (424 B.C.) in Peloponnesian War by Spartans under Brasidas, who died in defeating the Athenians near by in 422. Became independent after Peace of Nicias (421 B.C.); passed 357 B.C. to Philip II of Macedon, and, following battle of Pydna, was capital (168–148 B.C.) of Macedonia Prima, one of the Roman republics. Near by is modern Gr. village of Amphipolis or Amfipolis (1928 pop. 282), formerly called Neokhorion and, under Turkish rule, Yeni-Koi.

Amphissa or **Amfissa** (both: ămfĭ'sů), town (pop. 5,466), ⊙ Phocis nome, W central Greece, at W foot of the Parnassus, 80 mi. NW of Athens; road center; trades in wheat, olives and olive oil, wine; cattle and sheep raising. Bauxite deposits (SE). Its port is Itea on Bay of Galaxeidion (or Amphissa or Salona) of Gulf of Corinth. Medieval ruins on acropolis. The chief town of W (Ozolean) Locris, Amphissa was usually allied with Thebes and opposed to Phocis. Its attempt (340 B.C.) to resettle Crisa in the plain sacred to Apollo precipitated the fourth Sacred (Amphissean) War (339–338 B.C.), in which Philip II of Macedon overwhelmed all Greece and the city itself was destroyed. Under French rule (13th cent.), the medieval city became known as Salona (sùlō'nù), a name it retained for centuries.

Amphitheater, suburb (pop. 12,664) of Tucson, Pima co., SE Ariz.

Amphitrite Group (ămfĭtrī'tē), Chinese *Süante* or *Hsüan-te* (both: shüăn'dŭ'), northeasternmost group of the Paracel Isls., China, in S.China Sea, 180 mi. SE of Hainan; 16°55'N 112°18'E. Includes WOODY ISLAND and Rocky Isl. (S), Tree Isl. and other small isls. (N).

Amphoe or **Amphur,** a civil division in Thailand: for Thai names beginning thus, see under following proper name.

Ampier (äm'pĕr), town (pop. 2,474), Plateau Prov., Northern Provinces, Central Nigeria, 17 mi. E of Pankshin; tin mining; cassava, millet, durra.

Ampin, Formosa: see ANPING.

Amplepuis (ãplùpwē'), town (pop. 4,044), Rhône dept., E central France, in the Monts du Beaujolais, 13 mi. ESE of Roanne; textile milling (blankets, muslins, surgical supplies) and dyeing, mirror mfg. Silk trade.

Ampollino River (ämpôl-lē'nô), Calabria, S Italy, rises in La Sila mts. on S slope of Montenero, flows 15 mi. E, parallel to ARVO RIVER, to Neto R. 6 mi. SE of SAN GIOVANNI IN FIORE. Dammed (Trepido dam) near its source to form large reservoir (Lago Ampollino; 6 mi. long, .5 mi. wide); used for power (Orichella hydroelectric plant). Forms part of Catanzaro–Cosenza prov. boundary.

Amposta (ämpō'stä), city (pop. 7,348), Tarragona prov., NE Spain, in Catalonia, on the Ebro and 8 mi. SSE of Tortosa, at W edge of Ebro delta; olive-oil processing; rice-, flour-, and sawmilling; soap mfg., gypsum processing. Agr. trade (livestock, wine, cereals, fruit). Has castle built (11th cent.) by counts of Barcelona to defend Tortosa.

Ampsin (ãpsē'), town (pop. 2,794), Liége prov., E central Belgium, on Meuse R. and 3 mi. ENE of Huy; zinc processing.

Ampthill (ăm'tĭl, ămt'hĭl), urban district (1931 pop. 2,168; 1951 census 2,873), central Bedford, England, 7 mi. S of Bedford; agr. market. A cross in Ampthill Park marks site of castle where Katherine of Aragon lived, pending her divorce. The 14th-cent. church contains monument to Richard Nicolls, 1st English governor of New York.

Ampudia (ämpōōdh'yä), town (pop. 1,556), Palencia prov., N central Spain, 15 mi. SW of Palencia; cereals, vegetables, wine, livestock. Has medieval castle.

Ampuero (ämpwä'rō), town (pop. 1,031), Santander prov., N Spain, 20 mo. ESE of Santander; mfg. of leather goods; cereals, lumber, cattle.

Ampuis (ãpwē'), village (pop. 941), Rhône dept., E central France, on right bank of Rhone R. and 4 mi. SW of Vienne; biscuit mfg. Apricot orchards and noted vineyards.

Ampur, a civil division in Thailand: for Thai names beginning thus, see under following proper name.

Ampurdán (ämpōōr-dhän'), fertile coastal plain, Gerona prov., NE Spain, in Catalonia, bet. Pyrenees and Ter R. Chief city, Figueras. Drained by Ter and Fluviá rivers. Forests and pastures; horse breeding; vineyards.

Ampurias (ämpōō'ryäs), hamlet (pop. 32), Gerona prov., NE Spain, in Catalonia, 1.5 mi. N of La Escala, on Gulf of Rosas of the Mediterranean. On site of anc. Greek town of *Emporion* (Latin *Emporium* or *Emporiae*); excavations.

Amqui (ăm'kwē) or **Saint Benoît Joseph Labre** (sē bùnwä' zhōzĕf' lä'brů), village (pop. 1,593), ⊙ Matapedia co., E Que., at base of Gaspé Peninsula, on Matapedia R., near SE end of L. Matapedia, 50 mi. E of Rimouski; lumbering, dairying.

Amrabad (ŭmräbäd'), town (pop. 5,032), Mahbubnagar dist., S Hyderabad state, India, 60 mi. SE of Mahbubnagar; millet, rice. Teak, ebony, and gum arabic in forest area (S). Sometimes called Achampet (name applied to village 13 mi. W).

Amran or **'Amran** (ämrän'), town (pop. 5,000), Sana prov., N central Yemen, 26 mi. NW of Sana, in main watershed ridge.

Amraoti (ŭmrou'tē), district (□ 4,715; pop. 988,524), Berar div., W Madhya Pradesh, India, on Deccan Plateau; ⊙ Amraoti. Partly bordered by Tapti R. (NW) and Wardha R. (E); highland plain, crossed (N) by central Satpura Range; drained by Purna R. (tributary of the Tapti) and tributaries of the Wardha. In major cotton-growing tract (cotton over 50% of sown area); also produces millet, wheat, oilseeds. Timber (teak) in N hills (cattle raising). Cotton ginning, oilseed milling. Amraoti and Ellichpur are cotton-trade centers, Badnera a cotton-milling center. Pop. 90% Hindu, 10% Moslem.

Amraoti, town (pop. 61,971), ⊙ Berar div. and Amraoti dist., W Madhya Pradesh, India, 85 mi. W of Nagpur; major cotton-trade center in important Indian cotton-growing tract; cotton ginning, oilseed milling. Col. of arts. Served by rail spur from cotton-milling center of Badnera, 6 mi. SSW.

Amreli (ŭmrā'lē), district (created 1949), NW Bombay, India; ⊙ Amreli. Consists of scattered enclaves on Kathiawar peninsula; main group is in S central area; W section lies at extreme tip of peninsula, with ports at Okha and Dwarka (sacred Hindu city); E section is just S of Bhaunagar, with Gogha roadstead on Gulf of Cambay. Agr. (millet, oilseeds, cotton); hand-loom weaving. Dist. formed 1949 by merger of Amreli div. of former Baroda state and detached S part of Ahmadabad dist. (Bombay).

Amreli, town (pop. 25,485), ⊙ Amreli dist., NW Bombay, India, on Kathiawar peninsula, 60 mi. WSW of Bhaunagar; agr. market (millet, oilseeds, cotton); hand-loom weaving, cotton ginning, tanning, dyeing; silverworks.

Am Rija, Aden: see RIJA, AM.

Amriswil (äm'rĭsvēl), town (pop. 5,377), Thurgau canton, NE Switzerland, 9 mi. NNW of St. Gall; knit goods, pastry.

Amrit or **'Amrit** (ămrēt'), anc. *Marathus*, village, Latakia prov., W Syria, on the Mediterranean 28 mi. N of Tripoli. Here was an anc. Phoenician city (settled from isl. of Ruad, a few mi. N), still flourishing in time of Alexander the Great.

Amritsar (ŭmrĭt'sŭr), district (□ 1,976; pop. 1,621,138), W Punjab, India; ⊙ Amritsar. In Bari Doab, bet. Ravi R. (NW) and Beas R. (E); bordered W by Pakistan Punjab, E by Patiala and East Punjab States Union. Irrigated by Upper Bari Doab Canal system; agr. (wheat, cotton, gram, oilseeds); hand-loom weaving. Played prominent part in Sikh history. Original dist. (□ 1,572; 1941 pop. 1,413,876) enlarged 1947 by inc. of small E portion of Lahore dist., Pakistan.

Amritsar, city (pop., including NW cantonment area, 391,010), ⊙ Amritsar dist., W Punjab, India, 45 mi. NW of Jullundur, 31 mi. E of Lahore; 31°38'N 74°52'E. Rail and road junction; airport; major commercial and mfg. center, with large textile industry; trades extensively in wool, cotton, silk, hides and skins, timber, piece goods, metal products; agr. market (wheat, gram, rice, oilseeds, sugar cane). Cotton, woolen, sugar, and oilseed milling, silk weaving, tanning, flour and rice milling, fruit canning, food processing, mfg. of carpets, hosiery, rayon goods, chemicals, glass, machinery, electrical apparatus, abrasive products, varnish, glue, soap, ice. Noted handicrafts include silk and woolen fabrics (especially pashm), ivory trinkets, gold and silver thread, copper- and brassware, cutlery, combs, leather goods. Has Khalsa Col. (founded 1882), arts, medical, and technical cols., textile institute, several high schools. Religious center of the Sikhs; founded 1577 by Ram Das (the 4th guru) around a sacred tank (Sanskrit *amrita saras*,=pool of immortality), now in center of city proper. In middle of tank is celebrated Golden Temple (completed by Arjun, the 5th guru; redecorated by Ranjit Singh), which is approached by causeway of white marble; under gold and copper dome the Granth Sahib (sacred book of Sikh scriptures) is kept. In W section is fort of Govindgarh, built 1809 by Ranjit Singh. Growth of trade and of shawl industry accompanied rise of Sikh power; after annexation (1849) to Br. India, city became famous for its carpets. On April 13, 1919, at park of Jallianwala (Jallewallian) Bagh, occurred the notorious Amritsar Massacre, when hundreds of Gandhi's followers were killed and thousands wounded when fired on by troops under British control.

Amroha (ŭmrō'hŭ), city (pop. 55,957), Moradabad dist., N central Uttar Pradesh, India, 19 mi. WNW of Moradabad; hand-loom cotton-weaving center; sugar processing, pottery mfg.; trades in wheat, rice, pearl millet, sugar cane. Extensive mosques, including former Hindu temple (now a Moslem pilgrimage site). Moguls defeated (1304) by Afghans near by.

Amrum (äm'rōōm), North Sea island (□ 7.9; 1939 pop. 925; 1946 pop. 2,838) of North Frisian group, NW Germany, 17 mi. off Schleswig-Holstein coast; 6 mi. long (N-S), c.3 mi. wide (E-W). Resort; harbor at Wittdün (S tip); main village, Nebel.

Amsele (ōm'sā"lŭ), Swedish *Åmsele*, village (pop. 326), Vasterbotten co., N Sweden, on Vindel R. and 20 mi. ESE of Lycksele; stock; dairying.

Am Shat, Aden: see SHAT, AM.

Amsteg (äm-shtāk'), hamlet, Uri canton, central Switzerland, on Reuss R. and 8 mi. S of Altdorf; hydroelectric plant. St. Gotthard railway viaduct and tunnels here.

Amstel River (äm'stŭl), North Holland prov., W Netherlands; formed at Uithoorn by 2 small tributaries; flows 12 mi. N to the Ij (inlet of the Ijsselmeer) at Amsterdam. Navigable.

Amstelveen (äm'stŭlvān), village (pop. 1,064), North Holland prov., W Netherlands, 5 mi. S of Amsterdam, near Amstel R.; water-sports center.

Amstenrade (äm'stŭnrädŭ), town (pop. 2,539), Limburg prov., SE Netherlands, 4 mi. NW of Heerlen; coal-mining center. Emma coal mine and coke plant is SE.

Amsterdam (ăm'stŭrdăm, Du. äm'stŭrdäm'), city (pop. 803,847), constitutional ⊙ and largest city of the Netherlands, in North Holland prov., on the Ij at mouth of Amstel R., and 30 mi. NE of The Hague; 52°23'N 4°54'E. Major port and commercial center; seat of an important stock exchange and of most Netherlands commercial, industrial, banking and insurance companies; art trade center. Extensive port installations are located on S bank of the Enclosed Ij (Du. *Afgesloten IJ*), central part of the Ij. Main docks are E of the Central Station (central point of city). Merwede Canal entrance is on S bank of the Ij and 2.5 mi. ENE of the Central Station; North Holland Canal entrance is on N bank of the Ij and opposite the Central Station; entrance to North Sea Canal (linking city with North Sea) is 4 mi. NW. Chief imports: sugar, tea, coffee, tobacco, rubber, hides, cacao and cacao butter, kapok, wood. Exports are mostly manufactured goods, seeds, paper. Important transit trade in timber, ores, coal, grain goes mainly to and from Germany via Merwede Canal and branches of the Rhine. Has auction marts for imported colonial products. Railroad center; large airport at SCHIPHOL, 5 mi. SW. Mfg. center (consumer goods, railroad and bridging material, heavy machinery, power plants, aircraft, clothing); shipbuilding, brewing, food processing, sugar refining. Center of diamond-cutting and -polishing industry. Main streets are the Dam, on which are 15th-cent. church (*Nieuwe Kerk*); 17th-cent. Dam Palace (Du. *Paleis op den Dam*), formerly town hall, since 1808 a royal palace; and the Damrak, on which is the stock exchange (Du. *Beurs*). Kalvertstraat and Leidschestraat are chief shopping centers; former has many silversmith shops. Other notable buildings: 13th-cent. church (*Oude Kerk*); 15th-cent. weighhouse; 16th-cent. town hall; 17th-cent. Beguine Court (*Begijnenhof*); Rembrandt's house. Has many museums, notably National Mus. (*Rijksmuseum*), founded by Louis Napoleon and containing one of largest and finest collections of Du. and Flemish paintings, including Rembrandt's "Night Watch." Town Mus. (Du. *Stedelijks Museum*) has 19th-cent. and modern paintings. Rembrandt's house is a mus., containing several of his paintings and illustrations. Univ. (in 18th-cent. building), Royal Academy of Sciences. Because of soft ground, city is built on piles and is transected by a large number of concentric and radial canals flanked by streets and crossed by some 400 bridges. It lies mainly on S bank of the Ij; industrial suburbs lie E and W. Birthplace of philosopher Baruch Spinoza, painters Salomon and Philips Konink, Adriaen van de Velde, Meindert Hobbema; residence (1639–56) of Rembrandt. Dam on Amstel R. from which city takes its name was built in 13th cent. Amsterdam 1st mentioned in 1275 when it received certain tax exemptions; chartered in 1300; joined Hanseatic League in 1369. Having accepted the Reformation, the people of Amsterdam in 1578 expelled their pro-Spanish magistrates and joined the rebellious Netherlands provinces. The commercial ruin of Antwerp and Ghent and a large influx of refugees from all nations (notably of Flemish merchants, of Jewish diamond-cutters from Portugal and Spain, and of French Huguenots) contributed to the rapid growth of Amsterdam after late 16th cent. Peace of Westphalia (1648), by closing the Scheldt (Escaut) to navigation, further stimulated the prosperity of Amsterdam at expense of Spanish Netherlands. Taken (1795) by the French, Amsterdam became ⊙ of the kingdom of the Netherlands under Louis Bonaparte. The constitution of 1814 made it ⊙ of the Netherlands. However, The Hague remains seat of the governments and of the sovereigns, who are merely sworn in at Amsterdam. Because of silting up of the Ijsselmeer in 19th cent., North Holland Canal was built (1819–24); proved insufficient for traffic requirements, and in 1876 North Sea Canal, accommodating largest ocean-going ships, was opened. Occupied in Second World War by German troops, 1940–45, Amsterdam suffered severe hardship and (after the premature Dutch rising late in 1944) even famine.

Amsterdam. **1** Town (pop. 160), Bates co., W Mo., 14 mi. WNW of Butler. **2** Industrial city (pop. 32,240), Montgomery co., E central N.Y., on Mohawk R. and the Barge Canal, and 30 mi. NW of Albany; important rug- and carpet-mfg. center; also makes clothing, pearl buttons, brooms, bedding, linseed oil, paper and wood products. Guy Park, a colonial house, is mus. of Indian and historic relics. At Fort Johnson, just W, is home (now a mus.) of Sir William Johnson. Settled in late-18th cent.; inc. 1885. Carpet industry began 1842. **3** Village (pop. 1,048), Jefferson co., E Ohio, 17 mi. WNW of Steubenville, and on small Yellow Creek, in agr. and coal-mining area. Settled 1830, inc. 1904.

Amsterdam Island, outlying dependency (□ 16) of Madagascar, in S Indian Ocean 2,800 mi. off SE coast of Africa, c.1,200 mi. NE of Kerguelen Isls. and N of Saint Paul Isl.; 37°50'S 77°34'E; 6 mi. long, 4 mi. wide. Mountainous and of volcanic origin, rises to 2,760 ft. Wild cattle herds; sea lions. Discovered 1522; named 1633 by Van Diemen, Dutch explorer; claimed 1843 by France. Occasionally visited by fishermen and whalers. Meteorological station installed 1950. Also known as New Amsterdam, Fr. *Nouvelle-Amsterdam*.

Amsterdam Island, islet (1 mi. long), just off Vogelkop peninsula, NW New Guinea, in the Pacific, just N of Middleburg Isl., 17 mi. W of Cape of Good Hope; 0°20'S 132°10'E.

Amsterdamoya (äm'stŭrdäm-ŭ"yä), Nor. *Amsterdamøya*, island (5 mi. long, 1–3 mi. wide; rises to 1,650 ft.), Spitsbergen group, in Arctic Ocean, just off NW West Spitsbergen; 79°45'N 10°55'E. In 17th and 18th cent., SE coast was site of important Dutch whaling settlement of Smeerenburg.

Amstetten (äm'shtĕtŭn), city (pop. 11,429), W Lower Austria, near Ybbs R., 21 mi. ENE of Steyr; ironworks, railroad shops.

Amston, Conn.: see HEBRON.

Am-Timan (äm-tēmän'), town, ⊙ Salamat region (□ 37,050; 1950 pop. 94,500), E central Chad territory, Fr. Equatorial Africa, 350 mi. ESE of Fort-Lamy; native market for millet, cattle, sheep.

Amuay, Venezuela: see LAS PIEDRAS.

Amu Darya (ä'mōō där'yŭ, ŭmōō' dŭryä'), anc. *Oxus* (ŏk'sŭs), Arabic *Jaihun* or *Jayhun* (jīhōōn'), one of the chief rivers of Central Asia; length, 872 mi.; including PANJ RIVER headstream, 1,577 mi. Formed by junction of Vakhsh and Panj rivers 18 mi. SW of Nizhni Pyandzh (head of navigation) on USSR-Afghanistan line, it forms the border for 200 mi., flowing past Termez to Kham-i-Ab—Bossaga, then NW through Turkmen SSR, past Kerki and Chardzhou, and through Uzbek SSR, past Turtkul and Nukus, to Aral Sea, where it forms large delta mouth with 2 main branches. Channel shifts handicap navigation. Extensive irrigation along its course, notably in Khiva oasis and delta. Receives Kafirnigan and Surkhan Darya (right), but is not reached by Zeravshan R. Lower course separates the deserts Kyzyl-Kum and Kara-Kum. Construction on the TURKMEN CANAL through the Kara-Kum to the Caspian Sea was begun 1950 at Takhia-Tash, SE of Nukus.

'Amude or **'Amudah** (both: ämōō'dŭ), Fr. *Amouda*, town, Jezire prov., NE Syria, on Turkish border, on railroad, and 40 mi. NNE of El Haseke; sheep raising. Oil deposits.

'Amudiyah, Aden: see MUDIA.

Amuku Lake (ämōōkōō'), small lake, Rupununi dist., SW Br. Guiana, near Brazil line, on W bank of Rupununi R., in an extensive savanna; 3°43'N 59°25'W. Supposed site, in early colonial days, of fabled golden city Manoa and of Raleigh's El Dorado.

Amul or **Amol** (ämōl'), town (1941 pop. 14,166), Second Prov., in E Mazanderan, N Iran, 75 mi. NE of Teheran across Elburz mts., and on Haraz R. (short Caspian coastal stream); orange groves, rice. Coal and iron deposits. An old town with anc. ruins.

Amund Ringnes Island (□ 1,764), Sverdrup Isls., N Franklin Dist., Northwest Territories, in the Arctic Ocean; 77°53'–78°49'N 95°30'–98°55'W; separated from Ellef Ringnes Isl. (W) by Hassel Sound, from Meighen Isl. (N) and Axel Heiberg Isl. (E) by Good Friday Gulf, and from Cornwall Isl. (S) by Hendriksen Strait. Isl. is 70 mi. long, 20–45 mi. wide; surface rises to over 2,000 ft.

Amundsen Gulf (ä'mōōnsŭn, ă'mŭnsŭn), Northwest Territories, arm (250 mi. long) of the Arctic Ocean in 70°N 120°W, opening off Beaufort Sea (W) bet. Mackenzie and Franklin dists. Leading E is Dolphin and Union Strait (SE), which is continued E by Coronation Gulf, Dease Strait, and Queen Maud Gulf, eventually leading to Baffin Bay via several other straits. Separates Banks Isl. (N) and Mackenzie Dist. mainland (S), and washes W shore of Victoria Isl. Amundsen Gulf is westernmost section of the Northwest Passage through the Arctic Isls.; passage was 1st completed by Roald Amundsen's expedition, 1903–06.

Amundsen Sea, part of the South Pacific off coast of Antarctica, W of Ross Sea, bet. Thurston Peninsula (71°20'S 98°W) and Cape Dart (73°15'S 123°W). Explored and named 1929 by Nils Larsen, a Norwegian.

Amur (ämōōr', Rus. ŭmōōr'), oblast (□ 139,000; 1946 pop. estimate 575,000) in SE Siberian Russian SFSR, in the Soviet Far East; ⊙ Blagoveshchensk. Bounded S by Amur R. (Manchuria border), N by Stanovoi Range; mainly hilly (NW); includes fertile Zeya-Bureya Plain (SE), chief agr. region (wheat, coarse grain, soybeans, livestock) of Soviet Far East. Gold mining in upper Selemdzha and Zeya river valleys. Agr. industries (flour milling, dairying, distilling, tanning). Lignite mining at Raichikhinsk. Other centers (served by Trans-Siberian RR): Skovorodino, Shimanovski, Svobodny, Kuibyshevka. Formed 1948 out of greater portion of Amur oblast (formed 1932 as part of Khabarovsk Territory) and NE section of Chita oblast.

Amur, river, USSR and China: see AMUR RIVER.

Amurang or **Amoerang** (ämo͞oräng'), town, NE Celebes, Indonesia, on inlet of Celebes Sea, 30 mi. SW of Menado; coconut-desiccation plant.

Amur Bay or **Amur Gulf**, inlet of Peter the Great Bay of Sea of Japan, Russian SFSR, W of Muravyev-Amurski Peninsula; 35 mi. long, 8 mi. wide. Vladivostok is on E shore. Receives Suifun R. (N). Fisheries.

Amuri, New Zealand: see CULVERDEN.

Amuria (ämo͞o'ryä), town, Eastern Prov., Uganda, 20 mi. N of Soroti; cotton, peanuts; livestock.

Amur-Nizhne-Dneprovsk, Ukrainian SSR: see DNEPROPETROVSK, city.

Amur River (ämo͝or'), Chinese *Hei Ho* (hā' hŭ') [black river], *Heilung Kiang* or *Heilung Chiang* (both: hā'lo͝ong' jyäng') [black dragon river], Manchu *Sakhalin Ula*, one of the great rivers of NE Asia, formed on USSR-China line by union of Shilka and Argun rivers; it flows 1,100 mi. SE, along international line, past Moho, Blagoveshchensk (opposite Aigun), and Tungkiang, and turns NE, going through the Khabarovsk Territory of the Russian SFSR, past Khabarovsk (Trans-Siberian RR crossing), Komsomolsk (rail ferry), and Nikolayevsk, to Tatar Strait opposite N Sakhalin isl., near Sea of Okhotsk, forming 10-mi.-wide estuary. Navigable in entire course during ice-free season (May-Nov.). Its total length is 1,767 mi.; including the Shilka and its headstream, the Onon, 2,703 mi.; including the Argun, 2,621 mi. It receives the Zeya, Bureya, and Amgun rivers (left), and the Sungari and Ussuri rivers (right). The Amur region [Rus. *Priamurye* or *Priamur'ye*] became the scene (17th cent.) of conflicting Russo-Chinese interests. It was adjudged Chinese territory by the treaty of Nerchinsk (1689). By the treaty of Aigun (1858), the left bank passed to Russian control.

Amurzet (ŭmo͝orzyĕt'), village (1948 pop. over 500), S Jewish Autonomous Oblast, Khabarovsk Territory, Russian SFSR, on Amur R. and 70 mi. WSW of Leninskoye; grain, soybeans. Iron deposits (N).

Amvrakia, Greece: see ARTA, city.

Amvrakikos Kolpos, Greece: see ARTA, GULF OF.

Amvrosiyevka (ŭmvrô'sēŭfkŭ), city (1939 pop. over 10,000), SE Stalino oblast, Ukrainian SSR, in the Donbas, 34 mi. ESE of Stalino; cementworks; chalk quarries. Until 1944, Donetsko-Amvrosiyevka.

Amwas, Palestine: see EMMAUS.

Amyclae (ŭmī'klē), anc. town of Laconia nome, S Peloponnesus, Greece, 4 mi. SSE of Sparta. Once⊙ kingdom of Menelaus, it has ruins of Apollo temple. On site is modern village of Amiklai or Amyklai (pop. 1,494).

Amyin (ŭmyĭn'), village, Sagaing dist., Upper Burma, on left bank of Chindwin R. and 12 mi. S of Monywa.

Amyntaion or **Amindaion** (both: ämĭn'dāyôn), town (pop. 2,889), Phlorina nome, Macedonia, Greece, on railroad and 13 mi. SE of Phlorina; road junction; agr.; lignite mining. Formerly called Sorovits.

Amyun (ămyo͞on'), Fr. *Amioun*, village (pop. 3,701), N Lebanon, near the coast, 20 mi. S of Tripoli; known for its excellent olive oil; sericulture, cotton, cereals, olives, oranges.

An [Arabic,=the], for Arabic names beginning thus and not found here: see under following part of the name.

An (än), village, Kyaukpyu dist., Lower Burma, in Arakan, on An R. (short coastal stream) and 40 mi. NE of Kyaukpyu, on road over An Pass of the Arakan Yoma. Formerly spelled Aeng.

Ana or **'Anah** (ä'nŭ), village, Dulaim prov., W Iraq, on the Euphrates and 100 mi. NW of Ramadi; dates, livestock. Sometimes spelled Anna.

Anaa (ä'nä'), atoll (pop. 411) of 11 islets, Tuamotu Isls., Fr. Oceania, S Pacific, c.40 mi. S of Fakarava. Formerly Chain Isl.

Anabar River (ŭnŭbär'), NW Yakut Autonomous SSR, Russian SFSR, rises on Central Siberian plateau, flows 560 mi. N, past Saskylakh, through reindeer country, to Laptev Sea of Arctic Ocean E of Nordvik, forming a narrow estuary. Navigable for c.100 mi.

Anabuki (änä'bo͝okē), town (pop. 4,398), Tokushima prefecture, E central Shikoku, Japan, on Yoshino R. and 22 mi. W of Tokushima; rice, wheat, barley; artisan fan industry. It is starting point for ascent of Mt. Tsurugi.

Anacapa Island, Calif.: see SANTA BARBARA ISLANDS.

Anacapri (änäkä'prē), town (pop. 2,613) on isl. of Capri, Napoli prov., Campania, S Italy, 1 mi. W of town of Capri; tourist center (alt. 902 ft.).

Anacetaba (änŭsĭtä'bŭ), city (pop. 1,224), N Ceará, Brazil, 35 mi. W of Fortaleza; carnauba wax. Until 1944, called São Gonçalo.

Anaconda (ănŭkŏn'dŭ), city (pop. 11,254), ⊙ Deer Lodge co., SW Mont., 25 mi. WNW of Butte and on branch of the Clark Fork, just NE of Anaconda Range of Continental Divide; alt. c.1 mi. Smelting (copper, zinc); by-products of smelting (arsenic, sulphuric acid, phosphate fertilizer), bricks, metal castings, beverages; dairy products, livestock, potatoes. Mine offices of Anaconda Copper Mining Company are here. Washoe Smelter has stack 585 ft. high, 1 of largest in world. Winter sports carnival takes place annually. Founded as Copperopolis 1883, inc. as Anaconda 1888.

Anaconda Range, in SW Mont., rises near Anaconda as portion of Continental Divide in Rocky Mts.; extends W and SW to Idaho line. Highest point, Mt. Evans (10,635 ft.).

Anacortes (ă"nŭkôr'tez, -tĕz, -tŭs), port city (pop. 6,919), Skagit co., NW Wash., on Fidalgo Isl. (bridged to mainland) and 20 mi. SSW of Bellingham. Port of entry. Lumber, wood products, fish, food processing. Settled c.1860, platted 1876.

Anacostia River (ănŭkŏs'chŭ, ănŭkŏ'stēŭ), in central Md. and Dist. of Columbia, is formed by branches at Hyattsville, Md., flows c.12 mi. SW, past Bladensburg, Cottage City, and Colmar Manor, Md., and through S part of Washington, to the Potomac. Part of Washington harbor occupies lower part. Along river (much of it bordered by parks) in Washington are a naval air station, naval gun factory, and naval receiving station.

Anadarko (ănŭdär'kō), city (pop. 6,184), ⊙ Caddo co., W central Okla., c.50 mi. WSW of Oklahoma City, and on Washita R.; trade and processing center for rich agr. region (cotton, grain, alfalfa, livestock, poultry). Dairying, cotton ginning; flour, feed, and cottonseed milling; meat packing. Oil wells near by. Hq. of Western Okla. Consolidated Indian Agency; seat of a U.S. school for Indians. Holds annual Indian exposition. Founded 1901.

Ana de Chaves Bay (ä'nŭ dĭ shä'vĭsh), on NE coast of São Tomé Isl., São Tomé e Príncipe, in Gulf of Guinea; 0°20'N 7°16'W. On it is port of São Tomé. Formerly spelled Anna de Chaves.

Anadia (änŭdē'ŭ), city (pop. 2,009), central Alagoas, NE Brazil, 37 mi. W of Maceió; sugar, cotton, cereals. Rock-crystal and mica quarries.

Anadia, town (pop. 1,187), Aveiro dist., N central Portugal, near railroad, 18 mi. SE of Aveiro; wine-growing (sparkling wines), distilling.

Anadyr or **Anadyr'** (ŭnŭdĭr'), town (1948 pop. over 2,000), ⊙ Chukchi Natl. Okrug, Kamchatka oblast, Khabarovsk Territory, Russian SFSR, port on estuary of Anadyr R., on Bering Sea, and 1,050 mi. NE of Petropavlovsk; 64°43'N 177°28'E. Fish canning, tanning. Lignite mining. Until c.1930, Novo-Mariinsk.

Anadyr Bay or **Anadyr Estuary**, W inlet of Anadyr Gulf in NE Siberia, Russian SFSR; receives Anadyr R. at Anadyr. Onemen Gulf, formed by confluence of Anadyr and Bolshaya rivers, is SW section of Anadyr Bay, W of Anadyr.

Anadyr Gulf, inlet of NW Bering Sea, NE Siberia, Russian SFSR; extends from Cape Navarin N to Cape Chaplin; includes Anadyr Bay (W) and Krest Gulf (N). Whaling ground.

Anadyr Range or **Chukchi Range** (cho͞ok'chē), NE Siberian Russian SFSR, bet. E.Siberian Sea and Anadyr R. basin; extends c.500 mi. from Cape Shelagski E into Chukchi Peninsula, ending at Kolyuchin Bay; rises to 6,500–7,500 ft. in central portion.

Anadyr River, NE Siberian Russian SFSR, rises on plateau at N end of Kolyma Range, flows 694 mi. S and E, through wooded tundra, past Markovo, Ust-Belaya, and Anadyr, to Anadyr Bay of Bering Sea. Receives Belaya (left) and Bolshaya (right) rivers. Coal and gold found along banks.

Anafi, Greece: see ANAPHE.

Anaga Point (änä'gä), NE headland of Tenerife, Canary Isls., 11 mi. NE of Santa Cruz de Tenerife; 28°33'N 16°6'W. Lighthouse.

Anagni (änä'nyē), town (pop. 6,590), Frosinone prov., Latium, S central Italy, 13 mi. NW of Frosinone; olive oil, wine. Bishopric. Has 11th-cent. cathedral (remodeled 13th cent.) and 13th-cent. town hall. In medieval times a papal residence. Several popes, including Boniface VIII, b. here.

'Anah, Iraq: see 'ANA.

Anaheim (ă'nŭhīm), city (pop. 14,556), Orange co., S Calif., 23 mi. SE of Los Angeles, on coastal plain; packing, processing plants (citrus fruit, walnuts), fruit canning; mfg. of canning equipment, chemicals, wire, military range finders. Founded 1857 by Germans as cooperative community. Inc. 1870, reincorporated 1888.

Anaho Island, Nev.: see PYRAMID LAKE.

Anáhuac (änä'wäk), region in central Mexico, bet. Sierra Madre Oriental (E) and Sierra Madre Occidental (W), N of volcanic E-W range. Commonly refers to the part of the central plateau of Mexico comprising the most densely populated agr. and industrial area of the country (Mexico state and Federal Dist.). Includes the valleys of the Pánuco and Lerma river systems. Once the name for an Aztec empire, it means "near the water," because of the many lakes in the Valley of Mexico, such as Texcoco, Zumpango, Chalco, and Xochimilco, now mostly dry.

Anáhuac, city (pop. 2,771), Nuevo León, N Mexico, on Río Salado (irrigation area) and 45 mi. SW of Nuevo Laredo; cotton-growing and -ginning center. Its railroad station, Rodríguez, is S across the river.

Anahuac (ă'nŭwăk), city (pop. 1,284), ⊙ Chambers co., SE Texas, on Galveston Bay (here called Trinity Bay) at mouth of Trinity R., c.40 mi. E of Houston. Port, on channel connecting with Houston ship channel; fishing; tourist trade. Oil refinery, natural-gas recycling plant. Oil wells, timber, agr. (rice, truck), cattle ranching in area. An important early port, it was scene (1832, 1835) of clashes in which Anglo-American settlers successfully opposed Mex. officials. Ruins of old Fort Anahuac (1830) are near. Inc. after 1940.

Anaimalai (ŭnī'mŭlī), village, Coimbatore dist., SW Madras, India, 7 mi. SW of Pollachi; depot for teak from Anaimalai Hills (S); mfg. of railway sleepers, cotton pressing; quinine and tea factories.

Anaimalai Hills, northernmost area (□ c.1,600) of S section of Western Ghats, S India, bet. PALGHAT GAP (N) and CARDAMOM HILLS (S), in NE Travancore-Cochin; rise to over 8,000 ft. in E peaks. Noted as important source of teak, tea, coffee, rubber, cinchona, and lac. Main shipping centers: Pollachi, Udamalpet. Sometimes spelled Anamalai.

Anai Mudi (ŭnī' mo͞o'dē), peak (8,841 ft.) in S Western Ghats, in Travancore-Cochin, India, 55 mi. ENE of Cochin; highest point in peninsular India.

Anaiza, 'Anaiza, 'Unaiza, or **'Unayzah** (all: änā'zŭ), town and oasis, ⊙ Qasim prov. of Nejd, Saudi Arabia, 200 mi. NW of Riyadh, near the Wadi Rima; 26°5'N 43°58'E. Caravan center; palm groves; domestic crafts (metalwork); stock raising. Dating from Middle Ages, Anaiza has periodically contested supremacy over Qasim area with Buraida.

Anajás (änŭzhäs'), city (pop. 364), E Pará, Brazil, in center of Marajó isl., 95 mi. WNW of Belém; cattle raising.

Anajatuba (änŭzhŭto͞o'bŭ), city (pop. 1,137), N Maranhão, Brazil, at mouth of Mearim R. on São Marcos Bay, near São Luís–Teresina RR, 45 mi. S of São Luís; cotton, sugar, rice.

Anak (än'äk'), Jap. *Angaku*, township (1944 pop. 25,185), Hwanghae prov., central Korea, N of 38°N, 15 mi. SSE of Chinnampo, in iron-mining area. Near by are hot springs.

Anakapalle (ŭnŭkŭpŭ'lē), city (pop. 29,249), Vizagapatam dist., NE Madras, India, 20 mi. W of Vizagapatam; road and agr. trade center; sugar, rice, and oilseed milling, jaggery mfg.; mango groves. Agr. research station (fruit, cotton, chili, tobacco). Buddhist stupa near by.

Anaklia (ŭnä'klyēŭ), village (1939 pop. over 2,000), W Georgian SSR, small port on Black Sea, at mouth of Ingur R., 60 mi. WNW of Kutaisi; citrus fruit. Sometimes spelled Anakliya.

Anaktuvuk Pass (ănŭkto͞o'vŭk), village (pop. 65), N Alaska, in pass of Brooks Range, near upper Anaktuvuk R.; 68°10'N 151°40'W.

Anaktuvuk River, N Alaska, rises in N Brooks Range near 68°N 150°45'W, flows c.130 mi. N to Colville R. at 69°31'N 151°30'W.

Analalava (änälälä'vŭ), town, Majunga prov., NW Madagascar, cabotage port on Mozambique Channel, at mouth of large lagoon, 120 mi. NE of Majunga; trades in fibers, waxes, mangrove bark, hardwoods; saltworks, rice fields. Meteorological station. R.C. mission. Airfield.

Analândia (änŭlän'dyŭ), city (pop. 1,044), E central São Paulo, Brazil, 20 mi. NNW of Rio Claro; rail-spur terminus; mfg. of agr. tools; coffee, cotton, grain. Until 1944, called Anápolis (old spelling, Annapolis).

Anamã (änŭmä'), town (pop. 147), central Amazonas, Brazil, on left bank of the Amazon and 90 mi. WSW of Manaus; rubber.

Anamabu (änämä'bo͞o), town, Western Prov., S Gold Coast colony, on Gulf of Guinea, 5 mi. WSW of Saltpond; fishing center; cassava, corn. A Du. trading post, founded early 17th cent.; passed 1872 to British.

Anamalai Hills, India: see ANAIMALAI HILLS.

Ana María, Gulf of (ä'nä märē'ä), Caribbean inlet of E Cuba, 40 mi. W of Camagüey; shallow sea, fringed by reefs (Ana María keys) and bounded by marshy coastland; c.20 mi. N-S.

Anambar River, W Pakistan: see NARI RIVER.

Anambas Islands (änäm'bäs), group (pop. 12,371), Indonesia, in S.China Sea, bet. Borneo and Malay Peninsula, 165 mi. NE of Singapore; 3°19'N 106°16'E. Comprise 3 isls. surrounded by numerous islets. Jemaja or Djemadja (both: jāmä'jä), the largest, is 15 mi. long, 10 mi. wide, with irregular coastline. Other main isls. are Siantan, with town of Terempa, and Matak. Hilly and wooded. Lumbering, fishing, copra producing.

Anamizu (änä'mēzo͞o), town (pop. 8,353), Ishikawa prefecture, central Honshu, Japan, on E Noto Peninsula, on inlet of Toyama Bay, 13 mi. NNW of Nanao; rice growing.

Anamoose (ă'nŭmo͞os), city (pop. 542), McHenry co., central N.Dak., 55 mi. ESE of Minot; livestock, dairy produce, poultry, grain, wheat, rye, oats.

Anamosa (ănŭmō'sŭ), city (pop. 3,910), ⊙ Jones co., E Iowa, on Wapsipinicon R., at mouth of Buffalo

Creek, and 21 mi. ENE of Cedar Rapids; work clothes, packed poultry and eggs, dairy products, concrete blocks. Limestone quarries near by. Wapsipinicon State Park just S. Has state reformatory for men. Grant Wood b. near Anamosa. First named Dartmouth, then Lexington; inc. 1856.

Anamur (änämŏŏr'), village (pop. 2,734), Icel prov., S Turkey, port on the Mediterranean, near Cape Anamur, 110 mi. WSW of Mersin; zinc and iron industry; barley, wheat, sesame, millet.

Anamur, Cape, S Turkey, on Mediterranean Sea, 5 mi. SSW of Anamur; southernmost point of Anatolia; 36°2'N 32°48'E.

Anand (ŭnŭnd'), town (pop. 17,154), Kaira dist., N Bombay, India, 22 mi. SE of Kaira; rail junction; market center (millet, wheat, rice, cotton); dairy farming, match mfg., cotton ginning, handicraft cloth weaving. Several Christian missions; agr. and tobacco research institutes.

Anandpur (ŭnŭnd'pŏŏr). **1** Village, Keonjhar dist., NE Orissa, India, on Baitarani R. and 45 mi. SE of Keonjhargarh; local trade in rice, salt, timber, lac. **2** Village, Hoshiarpur dist., N central Punjab, India, near Sutlej R., 40 mi. SE of Hoshiarpur; wheat, corn. Residence (c.1665–75) of 9th Sikh guru. Annual religious fair.

Ananev or **Ananiev,** Ukrainian SSR: see ANANYEV.

Ananindeua (änünĕndĕ'wŭ), city (pop. 461), E Pará, Brazil, on Belém-Bragança railroad and 9 mi. NE of Belém.

Anantapur (ŭnŭn'tŭpŏŏr), district (□ 6,734; pop. 1,171,419), W Madras, India; ⊙ Anantapur. On Deccan Plateau; drained by Penner R. Agr.: millet, oilseeds (extensive peanut and castor-bean growing), rice, cotton. Bamboo, satinwood, tanbark in dispersed forest hills (sheep grazing). Barite and steatite (near Tadpatri), corundum (near Hindupur, Kalyandrug, Madakasira), and gold (near Uravakonda) mines. Main towns: Anantapur, Guntakal, Hindupur.

Anantapur, city (pop. 21,482), ⊙ Anantapur dist., W Madras, India, 210 mi. NW of Madras; peanut and castor-bean milling. Engineering col.

Anantnag (ŭnŭnt'näg) or **Kashmir South** (kăshmēr', kăsh'mēr) district (□ 2,814; pop. 851,616), Kashmir prov., SW central Kashmir; ⊙ Anantnag. Mainly in W Punjab Himalayas, with Vale of Kashmir in center; drained by Jhelum R. Agr. (rice, corn, oilseeds, wheat, saffron, barley); iron ore deposits in SE. Main centers: SRINAGAR, Anantnag, Bijbihara, Shupiyan, Pampur. Many resort areas, including Dal L., Manasbal L., Pahlgam, and Vernag. Archaeological landmarks include Anantnag town, Harwan, Pandrethan, Srinagar, Awantipur. Pilgrimage centers at Amarnath Cave and Nara Nag. Prevailing mother tongue, Kashmiri. Pop. 91% Moslem, 8% Hindu.

Anantnag or **Islamabad** (ĭslä'mäbäd"), town (pop. 11,985), ⊙ Anantnag dist., SW central Kashmir, in Vale of Kashmir, on tributary of upper Jhelum R. and 30 mi. SE of Srinagar; rice, corn, oilseeds, wheat. S head of navigation for larger boats in Vale of Kashmir. One of largest springs in Kashmir is 5 mi. SE, at Achhibal village; gardens; pisciculture. At Kother (or Kuther), 8 mi. SE, is sacred spring and extensive 10th- or 11th-cent. temple ruins. At Martand, 4 mi. ENE, is largest (63 ft. long, 70 ft. high) and finest example of anc. Kashmir temple architecture; built (8th cent. A.D.; on base of earlier temple) by King Lalitaditya and dedicated to Hindu sun god; largely destroyed in 14th cent. by Moslem ruler.

Ananuri (ŭnŭnōō'rē), village (1939 pop. over 500), central Georgian SSR, on Aragva R., on Georgian Military Road and 30 mi. NNW of Tiflis. Site of fortress (built 1704). Formerly spelled Ananur.

Ananyev or **Anan'yev** (ŭnä'nyĭf), city (1926 pop. 18,230), N central Odessa oblast, Ukrainian SSR, 90 mi. NNW of Odessa; distilleries, cottonseed-oil press, flour and cotton mills; clothing mfg. In Moldavian Autonomous SSR (1924–40).

Ananyevo or **Anan'yevo** (ŭnä'nyĭvŭ), village (1939 pop. over 2,000), N Issyk-Kul oblast, Kirghiz SSR, on N shore of Issyk-Kul (lake), 40 mi. NW of Przhevalsk; wheat, opium; fisheries. Until 1942, Sazanovka.

Anapa (ŭnä'pŭ), city (1926 pop. 13,380), W Krasnodar Territory, Russian SFSR, port on Black Sea, 25 mi. NW of Novorossisk, in winegrowing region; children's health resort; wine-making center; distilling, food processing, cotton ginning. Exports wheat.

Anaparti, India: see BIKKAVOLU.

Anaphe or **Anafi** (both: änä'fē), Aegean island (□ 12; pop. 785), in the Cyclades, Greece, E of Thera; 36°2'N 25°50'E; 7 mi. long, 3.5 mi. wide; wheat, olive oil, honey. Main town, Anaphe (pop. 579), is on S shore.

Anápolis (ănä'pŏŏlēs). **1** City (pop. 8,091), S Goiás, central Brazil, 40 mi. NE of Goiânia, 400 mi. NW of Belo Horizonte (Minas Gerais). Pioneer center at NW terminus of rail line which penetrates Braz. interior from Rio de Janeiro and São Paulo. Ships region's agr. produce (livestock, jerked beef, coffee, mangabeira rubber, corn, and more recently wheat) and minerals found in state (rock crystals, nickel, gold, diamonds). Important rutile deposits in area. Airport. Formerly spelled Annapolis. **2** City, São Paulo, Brazil: see ANALÂNDIA. **3** City, Sergipe, Brazil: see SIMÃO DIAS.

Anapo River (ä'näpô), SE Sicily, rises on Monte Lauro, flows 28 mi. generally E, past Palazzolo Acreide (hydroelectric plant), to Ionian Sea S of Syracuse.

Anapu River (ănŭpōō'), E central Pará, Brazil, enters Pará R. (S distributary of Amazon delta) NE of Portel after a N course of c.400 mi. Navigable in lower course.

Anapurna, massif, Nepal: see ANNAPURNA.

Anar (änär'), village, Eighth Prov., in Kerman, S central Iran, 90 mi. SE of Yezd and on road to Kerman; grain, cotton, pistachios.

Anarajapura, Ceylon: see ANURADHAPURA.

Anarak (änäräk'), town (1930 pop. estimate 1,270); Tenth Prov., in Yezd, central Iran, near railroad; 110 mi. NNW of Yezd, in mineralized desert area; lead-mining center, producing also nickel, copper, antimony.

Anardarah or **Anardarrah** (ŭnär'dŭrŭ), village (pop. over 500), Farah prov., W Afghanistan, 35 mi. NW of Farah and on the Harut Rud.

Anas, river, Spain: see GUADIANA RIVER.

Añasco (änyä'skō), town (pop. 3,463), W Puerto Rico, near the coast, on Añasco R., on railroad and 5 mi. N of Mayagüez; sugar center. Scene of last Indian rebellion (1511).

Añasco River or **Río Grande de Añasco,** W Puerto Rico, rises in the Cordillera Central W of Adjuntas, flows c.40 mi. W to Mona Passage 4 mi. NNW of Mayagüez. In its basin are new reservoirs and hydroelectric projects.

Anaset (ō'nĕ"sŭt), Swedish *Ånäset*, village (pop. 609), Vasterbotten co., N Sweden, near Gulf of Bothnia, 30 mi. S of Skelleftea; stock, dairying. Noted for cheese made here.

Anastasia Island (ănŭstā'shŭ, –zhŭ), barrier beach in St. Johns co., NE Fla., on the Atlantic, sheltering Matanzas R. (W); c.14 mi. long, ½–2½ mi. wide; N end connected with St. Augustine by bridge. Coquina quarries.

Anastasiyevka (ŭnŭstä'sēŭfkŭ), village (1926 pop. 2,742), SW Rostov oblast, Russian SFSR, 31 mi. NW of Taganrog; wheat, sunflowers, cattle.

Anatahan (ä'nätähän'), uninhabited volcanic island Saipan dist., N Marianas Isls., W Pacific, 190 mi. NNE of Guam; 5 mi. long, 2 mi. wide. Extinct crater with peak (2,585 ft.).

Anatolia (ănŭtō'lēŭ, –lyŭ) [Gr.,=sunrise], Asiatic part (□ 287,117; 1950 pop. 19,308,441) of TURKEY; its area covers 97% of all Turkey. Anatolia, the westernmost part of Asia, is a predominantly mountainous peninsula bet. Black Sea (N), Aegean Sea (W), and the Mediterranean (S). It is almost identical with, and is sometimes used to mean, ASIA MINOR.

Añatuya (änyätōō'yä), town (pop. 9,252), ⊙ General Taboada dept. (□ 2,360; pop. 24,432), S central Santiago del Estero prov., Argentina, 95 mi. SE of Santiago del Estero, in Río Salado irrigation area. Rail junction; cotton, sunflowers, livestock, lumbering, cotton ginning, flour milling. Dept. formerly called Veintiocho (28) de Marzo.

Anau, Turkmen SSR: see ANNAU.

Anauá River (änou-ä'), Rio Branco territory, northernmost Brazil, rises in the Serra Uassari at Br. Guiana border, flows c.175 mi. WSW to the Rio Branco (left bank) above Catrimani.

Anawalt, village (pop. 1,383), McDowell co., S W.Va., 11 mi. SE of Welch; coal mining.

Anaypazari, Turkey: see GULNAR.

Ançã (ãsã'), village (pop. 2,015), Coimbra dist., N central Portugal, 6 mi. NW of Coimbra; agr. processing (rice, olive oil).

Ancarano (ängkärä'nō), village (pop. 529), Teramo prov., Abruzzi e Molise, S central Italy, near Tronto R., 9 mi. ESE of Ascoli Piceno, in cerealgrowing region.

Ancash (äng'käsh), department (□ 14,705; pop. 465,135), W central Peru; ⊙ Huarás. Bordered by the Pacific (W) and Marañón R. (E). Cordillera Occidental crosses dept. NW-SE, and branches out into Cordillera Blanca (E) and Cordillera Negra (W), forming valley of Callejón de Huaylas, drained by Santa R. Grain, vegetables, potatoes, cattle in mts. and upper Santa R. valley; sugar in coastal plain, along lower Santa R.; also cotton, rice. Lead, copper, silver, gold mined in the Andes in area of Huarás, Carás, and Recuay. Along Santa R. are rich iron and coal deposits. Dept. is served by railroad connecting its main Pacific port of Chimbote with mtn. dists. Formed 1836. Formerly Ancachs.

Ancaster (ăng'kŭstŭr), village (pop. c. 500), S Ont., 7 mi. W of Hamilton; fruitgrowing, dairying.

Ancaster, agr. village and parish (pop. 758), Parts of Kesteven, W Lincolnshire, England, 7 mi. NE of Grantham; limestone quarrying. Many relics of a Roman station on Ermine Street have been found here. Its church has 14th-cent. tower.

Ancasti (ängkä'stē), village (pop. estimate 300), ⊙ Ancasti dept. (□ 960; pop. 3,900), SE Catamarca prov., Argentina, in Sierra de Ancasti, 27 mi. SE of Catamarca, in stock-raising area; alt. 2,975 ft.

Ancasti, Sierra de, Argentina: see ALTO, SIERRA DEL.

Ancell (ăn'sŭl), town (pop. 295), Scott co., SE Mo., near Mississippi R., just W of Illmo.

Ancenis (ãsnē'), town (pop. 4,244), Loire-Inférieure dept., W France, on Loire R. and 21 mi. NE of Nantes; road center (bridge across the Loire); lumber and livestock market; mfg. (bricks, furniture, vinegar); winegrowing. Coal deposits in Ancenis-Teillé area (NW). Birthplace of Joachim du Bellay near by.

Ancerville (ãsĕrvēl'), village (pop. 1,380), Meuse dept., NE France, near Marne R., 4 mi. E of Saint-Dizier; known for its kirsch. Precision metalworks. Cherry, pear, apple orchards.

Anchau (ä'ĕchou), town (pop. 2,852), Zaria prov., Northern Provinces, N central Nigeria, 45 mi. ESE of Zaria; cotton, peanuts, ginger. Surrounding dist. cleared of tsetse flies in connection with pop. resettlement scheme. Another Anchau is on railroad, 30 mi. NE of Zaria. Sometimes spelled Anchao.

Anchi (än'jē'), town (pop. 11,029), ⊙ Anchi co. (pop. 82,485), NW Chekiang prov., China, near Anhwei line, 40 mi. NW of Hangchow, NW of the Mokan Shan; tea, rice, wheat, bamboo.

An-ch'i, Fukien prov., China: see ANKI.

Anchialus, Bulgaria: see POMORIYE.

Anchicayá River (änchēkīä'), coastal stream in Valle del Cauca dept., SW Colombia, flows c.50 mi. from hills W of Cali to the Pacific S of Buenaventura. Upper course is site of hydroelectric project.

Anchieta (äshyĕ'tŭ). **1** City, Bahia, Brazil: see PIATÃ. **2** City (pop. 1,437), S Espírito Santo, Brazil, port on the Atlantic, 30 mi. E of Cachoeiro de Itapemirim; exploitation of monazitic sands; coffee, sugar. Founded in 16th cent. as Benevente.

An-ch'ing, China: see ANKING.

An-ch'iu, China: see ANKIU.

Ancho (ăn'chō), village (pop. c.100), Lincoln co., central N.Mex., 22 mi. NNE of Carrizozo, just NW of Jicarilla Mts.; alt. c.6,100 ft. Trade center in gold-mining, livestock region. Part of Lincoln Natl. Forest near by.

Anchorage, city (1939 pop. 3,495; 1950 pop. 11,254), S Alaska, at head of Cook Inlet, 260 mi. SSW of Fairbanks and on Alaska RR (division hq.); 61°10'N 149°55'W. Largest city of Alaska, an important defense center, and commercial, communications, and distribution center for a wide area. It is also a fishing port (canning) and has sawmills and railroad shops. Terminus of the Glenn Highway (which connects with Alaska Highway), it serves the Matanuska Valley (agr. developments, coal fields, timber stands), and the Kuskokwim Valley and Willow Creek mining regions. Has Federal hosp., new Federal bldg., and numerous facilities of a modern city. Anchorage was founded 1915 (1st bldgs. arrived 1914) as hq. of the Alaska RR (built 1915–23). It boomed as a defense center in the Second World War. Fort Richardson (NW) became U.S. Army hq. for Alaska, 1941. Elmendorf Field, 4 mi. NE, is military air base and commercial airport, with connections to the U.S., interior of Alaska, and Far East.

Anchorage, town (pop. 883), Jefferson co., NW Ky., residential E suburb of Louisville; makes whisky.

Anchorage Island: see SUWARROW.

Anchor Bay, Mich.: see SAINT CLAIR, LAKE.

Anchor Bay Gardens, village (pop. 1,127), Macomb co., SE Mich.

Anchor Island, New Zealand: see DUSKY SOUND.

Anchor Point, village (pop. 61), S Alaska, W Kenai Peninsula, on Cook Inlet, 12 mi. NW of Homer; supply point for farming and fishing region. Anchor Point headland is at 59°46'N 151°52'W.

Anchorville, resort village, St. Clair co., E Mich., on Anchor Bay of L. St. Clair, and 12 mi. NE of Mt. Clemens.

Anchovy, town (pop. 1,650), St. James parish, NW Jamaica, on Kingston–Montego Bay RR and 3½ mi. S of Montego Bay; bananas, sugar cane.

Anchuras (änchōō'räs), town (pop. 759), Ciudad Real prov., S central Spain, in enclave of Toledo prov., 34 mi. S of Talavera de la Reina; cereals, cork, timber, livestock; flour milling, cheese processing. Antimony, lead, silver-bearing lead, and sulphur deposits.

Ancião (ãsyã'ō), town (pop. 936), Leiria dist., W central Portugal, 24 mi. NE of Leiria; olives, wine; textile dyeing.

Ancienne Lorette (ãsēĕn' lôrĕt'), village (pop. estimate 1,000), S central Que., on short Lorette R. (waterfalls) and 7 mi. W of Quebec; shoe mfg., dairying, truck gardening; resort. Founded 1673 by Jesuits. Near by is Loretteville.

Ancizes-Saint-Georges, Les, France: see MANZAT.

Anclote Keys (ăng'klōt), W Fla., several small islands in Gulf of Mexico, opposite mouth of Anclote R., 6 mi. WNW of Tarpon Springs; largest is 2½ mi. long. Natl. wildlife refuge.

Anclote River, W Fla., rises in SW Pasco co., flows c.17 mi. WSW, past Tarpon Springs, to Gulf of Mexico opposite Anclote Keys.

Anco, mining village (1940 pop. 848), Knott co., E Ky., in Cumberland foothills, 8 mi. E of Hazard; bituminous coal.

Ancober, Ethiopia: see ANKOBER.

Ancohuma, Bolivia: see ILLAMPU.

Ancón (ängkōn'), oil town in Guayas prov., W Ecuador, on W Santa Elena Peninsula, 70 mi. W of Guayaquil; linked by pipe line with La Libertad, refining center 10 mi. NW. The petroleum deposits were discovered 1923.

Ancon (ăng'kŏn), Sp. *Ancón* (ängkōn'), town (pop. 1,695), Balboa dist., Panama Canal Zone, on transisthmian railroad and 1½ mi. ENE of Balboa, virtually a suburb of Panama city (E). Residential and medical center of the zone.

Ancón, town (pop. 1,097), Lima dept., W central Peru, Pacific port on Ancón Bay (4 mi. wide, 1 mi. long), on spur of Pan American Highway, on Lima-Huacho RR and 20 mi. NNW of Lima. Fisheries; beach resort. A treaty was signed here (1883) ending the War of the Pacific bet. Chile and Peru.

Ancona (ängkô'nä), province (□ 748; pop. 372,229), The Marches, central Italy; ⊙ Ancona. Borders on the Adriatic; hill and mtn. terrain, watered by Esino and Musone rivers. Chief activities are agr. (wheat, corn, grapes, olives, raw silk), stock raising, and fishing. Sulphur mining at Belliso Solfare. Mfg. at Ancona, Fabriano, Iesi, Osimo, and Senigallia. Contains noted pilgrimage center of Loreto.

Ancona, city (pop. 57,100), ⊙ The Marches and Ancona prov., central Italy, seaport on the Adriatic, 130 mi. NE of Rome; 43°37'N 13°31'E. Mfg. center; shipbuilding, mfg. of furniture, cement, soap, pharmaceuticals, shoes, hats, majolica, glass, cartridges, macaroni. Exports sulphur and asphalt. Archbishopric. Has white marble arch of Trajan, Byzantine-Romanesque cathedral (11th–13th cent.; severe war damage repaired), and Natl. Mus. of The Marches, with valuable archaeological mus. (both badly damaged). Founded in late 4th cent. B.C. by Greek refugees from Syracuse; prospered under Romans. Under direct papal rule from 1532 to 1860, except for period of Fr. domination (1797–1815). Severely damaged (1943–44) in Second World War by numerous air raids and artillery bombardments, and 2 naval shellings.

Anconquija, Nevado del, Argentina: see ACONQUIJA, NEVADO DEL.

Ançor, El- (ĕl-änsôr'), village (pop. 1,790), Oran dept., NW Algeria, 13 mi. W of Oran; winegrowing. Les Andalouses estate (truck, wine) just NE.

Âncora or **Vila Praia de Âncora** (vē'lù prä'yù dĭ ăng'kōōrù), village (pop. 1,374), Viana do Castelo dist., N Portugal, on the Atlantic, on railroad and 7 mi. N of Viana do Castelo; fishing port (sardines) and small bathing resort.

Ancoraimes (ängkōrī'mĕs), town (pop. c.11,900), La Paz dept., W Bolivia, near L. Titicaca, 70 mi. NW of La Paz; alt. 12,697 ft.; trade center (agr. products, livestock).

Ancos (äng'kōs), village (pop. 128), Ancash dept., W central Peru, in Cordillera Occidental, 8 mi. SW of Cabana; coal (high-grade anthracite) deposits.

Ancre River (ā'krù), Somme dept., N France, rises in Artois hills S of Bapaume, flows 20 mi. SW, past Albert, to the Somme below Corbie. Gave name to battle (1916) in First World War.

Ancroft, town and parish (pop. 1,410), N Northumberland, England, 5 mi. S of Berwick-upon-Tweed; agr. market; stone quarrying.

Ancrum (ăn'krùm), agr. village and parish (pop. 858), N central Roxburgh, Scotland, on Teviot R. and 3 mi. NNW of Jedburgh. Ancrum Moor, 2 mi. N, is scene of defeat (1545) of English under Lord Evers by Scots under Archibald Douglas. At edge of moor is Lilliard's Edge, with grave of Maiden Lilliard, a heroine of the battle.

Ancud (ängkōōdh'), town (pop. 4,078), ⊙ Chiloé prov. and Ancud dept. (□ 1,434; pop. 27,278), S Chile, on N coast of Chiloé Isl., on Ancud Bay of the Pacific, 55 mi. SW of Puerto Montt, 600 mi. SSW of Santiago; 41°52'S 73°52'W. Port, resort, commercial and agr. center (potatoes, wheat, livestock). Exports timber; has brewery. Has cathedral (bishopric), govt. bldgs., hosp. Narrow-gauge railroad to Castro, 45 mi. S. Founded 1769, town was one of the last Sp. royalist strongholds. Near by are ruins of anc. forts: San Antonio, Santa Bárbara, and Agüí. Formerly San Carlos de Ancud.

Ancud, Gulf of, inlet of the Pacific bet. NE Chiloé Isl. and the mainland of Chile; c.40 mi. W–E, 30 mi. N–S. It is continued NE by Reloncaví Sound and connected with ocean by Chacao Strait (NW).

Ancy-le-Franc (ãsē'-lù-frã'), village (pop. 780), Yonne dept., N central France, on Armançon R. and Burgundy Canal, and 10 mi. SE of Tonnerre; cementworks, metalworks. Has handsome Renaissance château.

Ancyra, Turkey: see ANKARA, city.

Anda, Norway: see ANDOY.

Anda (än'dä), town (1939 pop. 1,681; 1948 municipality pop. 11,213), on W coast of Cabarruyan Isl., Pangasinan prov., Philippines, on small inlet of Lingayen Gulf; rice-growing center.

Andabamba (ändäbäm'bä), town (pop. 913), Huancavelica dept., S central Peru, on Mantaro R. and 30 mi. ENE of Huancavelica; wheat, alfalfa; cattle, sheep.

Andacollo (ändäkō'yō), village (pop. estimate 500), ⊙ Minas dept. (1947 pop. 5,299), NW Neuquén natl. territory, Argentina, on Neuquén R., at SW foot of the Cordillera del Viento, and 25 mi. NW of Chos Malal. Wheat, corn, alfalfa, livestock.

Andacollo, village (1930 pop. 922), Coquimbo prov., N central Chile, 23 mi. SSE of Coquimbo; gold placer mining. Place of pilgrimage to the Virgen del Rosario de Andacollo shrine.

Andagoya, Colombia: see ISTMINA.

Andahuaillillas (ändäwīlē'yäs), town (pop. 1,119), Cuzco dept., S Peru, on Vilcanota R., on railroad and 22 mi. ESE of Cuzco; grain, alfalfa, stock.

Andahuaylas (ändäwī'läs), town (pop. 2,507), ⊙ Andahuaylas prov. (□ 2,864; pop. 116,958), Apurímac dept., S central Peru, in Andean spur, 38 mi. W of Abancay; alt. 9,590 ft. Trading and agr. center (corn, fruit, sugar cane, stock).

Andal or **Ondal** (ŭndäl'), town (pop. 9,856), Burdwan dist., W West Bengal, India, in Damodar Valley, near the Damodar, 5 mi. ESE of Raniganj; rail junction serving extensive coal-mining area; large rail workshops; cement and pottery mfg.; electrical engineering works, breweries.

Andalaly (ŭndùlä'lē), village (1926 pop. 735), NW Dagestan Autonomous SSR, Russian SFSR, 15 mi. SW of Khasavyurt; wheat, livestock. Until 1944 (in Chechen-Ingush Autonomous SSR), called Nozhai-Yurt.

Andale, city (pop. 316), Sedgwick co., S central Kansas, 18 mi. WNW of Wichita, in wheat region.

Andalgalá (ändälgälä'), town (pop. 4,956), ⊙ Andalgalá dept. (□ 3,190; pop. 10,513), central Catamarca prov., Argentina, on short Andalgalá R., at S foot of the Nevado del Aconquija, and 70 mi; NNW of Catamarca; alt. 3,133 ft. Rail terminus; agr. center in irrigated area (grain, alfalfa, wine, stock). Hydroelectric station. Earthquake zone.

Andalsnes (ôn'däls-nās"), Nor. *Åndalsnes*, village (pop. 1,346) in Grytten canton (pop. 2,834), More og Romsdal co., W Norway, at head of Romsdal Fjord, at mouth of the Rauma, 40 mi. S of Kristiansund; terminus of railroad to Lillehammer and Oslo; fishing and domestic industries. Site of Allied landing (1940); heavily damaged by shelling. Sometimes spelled Aandalsnes. Formerly called Nes. Suburb (pop. 318) of Veblungsnes (vĕ'blōōngs-nās") is 1 mi. SW.

Andalucía (ändälōōsē'ä), town (pop. 3,171), Valle del Cauca dept., W Colombia, in Cauca valley, on railroad and 5 mi. NNE of Tuluá; agr. center (tobacco, coffee, sugar cane, cacao, corn, livestock). Coal deposits near by.

Andalusia (ăndùlōō'zhù,–shù), Sp. *Andalucía* (ändälōōthē'ä), anc. *Baetica*, region (□ 33,675; pop. 5,219,362), S and SW Spain, on the Mediterranean and Strait of Gibraltar (S) and the Atlantic (SW), bordering W on Portugal. It consists of 8 provs., named for their chief cities, those S of the Guadalquivir being referred to customarily as Lower Andalusia (CÁDIZ, MÁLAGA, GRANADA, ALMERÍA), and those extending N from the all-important Guadalquivir to the Sierra Morena called Upper Andalusia (HUELVA, SEVILLE, CÓRDOBA, JAÉN). Physiographically a well-defined region, though of great variety, Andalusia differs from the rest of Spain in its climate (mild winters, hot summers in interior lowlands) and soil conditions, as well as in its racial make-up and cultural heritage, all of which have considerable affinity with Africa. It is separated from the great central Meseta (plateau) of Spain by the Sierra Morena, and is traversed in S by the Cordillera Penibética, which, rising steeply from the Mediterranean coast, reaches Alpine grandeur in the rugged, snow-capped Sierra Nevada (Mulhacén, 11,411 ft., is highest peak in Spain). Bet. the 2 ranges lies the fertile Andalusian plain, formed by the Guadalquivir (navigable to Seville) and its numerous affluents. Along the Mediterranean coast stretches a narrow strip of land, off which open a few interior valleys in the adjoining sierras, and which is a favorite resort area noted as well for its subtropical vegetation (sugar cane, palm trees; also excellent wine). Uninhabited marshes (Las Marismas), fringed by dunes, extend along the Atlantic shore. Though there occur large barren tracts in the region's interior, the irrigated Guadalquivir valley is one of the most productive in Spain, making Andalusia, which is Spain's largest region, also its most populous. Covered by olive groves, it also grows wheat, corn, barley, grapes, figs, almonds, peaches, citrus and other fruit, sugar beets, vegetables, cotton. Cattle, bulls for the ring, and fine horses are bred. Hogs, sheep, and goats are chiefly raised on the mtn. slopes, which also yield cork, chestnuts, acorns, walnuts, and timber. One of Andalusia's principal sources of wealth since anc. times has been its mines (e.g., at Ríotinto, Tharsis, La Carolina, Linares, Peñarroya-Pueblonuevo, Bélmez), rich in copper, iron, galena, tin, zinc, nickel, sulphur, antimony, tungsten, coal, pyrite, manganese, jasper, marble, lime, gypsum. Fisheries, chiefly of tunny and sardines, along Atlantic and Mediterranean shores. Industries depend to a large degree on agr. and grazing, and include flour milling, wine making, alcohol and brandy distilling, olive-oil extracting, fruit and fish canning, meat and fish salting, sugar refining. Famous wines like sherry (from Jerez), amontillado (from Montilla), and Málaga have achieved international fame. Its goods are exported through many ports, such as Almería, Málaga, La Línea, Algeciras, Cádiz, Jerez, Seville, Huelva, Ayamonte. Railroads are relatively few; the chief line links Madrid with Cádiz via Córdoba and Seville. As one of Europe's most historic and colorful regions, it has a varied history. The Phoenicians settled here in the 11th cent., attracted by the mineral resources, and founded coastal colonies, notably Gadir (now Cádiz) and, supposedly, the inland town of Tartessus (sometimes identified with the biblical Tarshish). Greeks, Ligurians, and Carthaginians followed. The latter were expelled (3d cent. B.C.) by the Romans, who merged S Spain into the prov. of Baetica. During that period a high cultural level was achieved, and Baetica contributed philosophers, poets, soldiers, and even emperors to the Roman Empire. Yet it reached its unsurpassed peak under the Moors, who crossed (711) the Strait of Gibraltar (named for their leader Tarik) and defeated the Visigoths (who were preceded by the Vandals and Suevi) in the battle of Guadelete at the present-day Laguna de Janda. Here they established their western emirate and formed the 4 kingdoms of Córdoba, Seville, Jaén, and Granada. While the 3 former were conquered by the kings of Castile in 13th cent., Granada held out until 1492. Of the Moorish period remain bldgs. of oriental splendor, in Mudejar (Mozarabic) style, among them the Alhambra of Granada, and the Alcazar and Giralda of Seville. From the 16th cent. Andalusia declined, though the discoveries in the New World brought great riches, which chiefly passed through the ports of Seville, and later Cádiz. Gibraltar was ceded to Britain in 1713. Most of Andalusia fell early during Sp. civil war (1936–39) into hands of the Nationalist forces. The semioriental, Moorish influence is still noticeable in the character, language, and in some customs of its temperamental people, dramatized in the bull fighter and smuggler.

Andalusia (ăn"dùlōō'zhù). **1** City (pop. 9,162), ⊙ Covington co , S Ala., 75 mi. S of Montgomery, near Conecuh R.; milling and processing center for agr. area; shirts, underwear, lumber, naval stores, cottonseed oil; peanuts, meat products. Settled in early 19th cent. as New Site. Inc. 1901. **2** Village (pop. 510), Rock Island co., NW Ill., on the Mississippi and 10 mi. WSW of Rock Island; makes pearl buttons.

Andaman and Nicobar Islands (ăn'dùmùn, –măn; nĭkōbär', nĭ'kōbär), chief commissioner's state (□ 3,143; 1951 pop. 30,963), India, in E Bay of Bengal, comprising ANDAMAN ISLANDS (N) and NICOBAR ISLANDS (S); ⊙ Port Blair. Isl. chain extends 500 mi. roughly N–S, bet. SW Burma (Pagoda Point) and NW Sumatra, enclosing Andaman Sea (E). The isls. represent summits of submarine range connected with Arakan Yoma in W Burma. In 1872, Andamans and Nicobars were formed into chief commissionership under govt. of India; in 1950, became constituent state of republic of India, administered by chief commissioner (with advisory council) at Port Blair and by assistant commissioner on Car Nicobar Isl.

Andaman Archipelago, Andaman Isls.: see RITCHIE'S ARCHIPELAGO.

Andaman Islands, group of isls. (□ 2,508; 1941 pop. 21,316) in E Bay of Bengal, forming N part of Indian state of ANDAMAN AND NICOBAR ISLANDS. Main group is N–S band of isls. (c.160 mi. long), very close together and comprising 5 large isls. of Great Andaman group (North Andaman, Middle Andaman, Baratang, South Andaman, Rutland) and many smaller isls. lying just off their shores. Just E, across Diligent Strait, is Ritchie's Archipelago; S, across Duncan Passage, is Little Andaman Isl. The Andamans consist mostly of hilly terrain, rising to 2,400 ft. in Saddle Peak on N. Andaman Isl., and many narrow valleys, although there are few perennial streams; shorelines deeply indented. Climate is monsoon tropical, characterized by mean temp. of 85°F. and heavy annual rainfall (90–130 in.; mostly June–Sept.); cyclones in Bay of Bengal sometimes originate near by. Dense tropical forests (redwood, gurjun, bamboo; coconut palms in S) cover most of area, although more land is being cleared and cultivated with rice, pulse, coffee, fruit, and rubber. From Port Blair, the Andamans' administrative center and only town, timber and copra are exported to India, but bulk of islanders' foodstuffs and luxuries are imported. The Andamanese tribes are Negritos and are probably allied to other SE Asian aborigines. Now numbering only a few hundred, they stand bet. 4 ft. 6 in. and 4 ft. 11 in. in height, are very dark-skinned, and have experienced an extremely isolated and retarded development; animism is their religion. Of other inhabitants—mainly ex-convicts of Port Blair penal colony and recent settlers from Indian mainland—Hindus comprise 40%, Moslems 35%, Buddhists 13%, and Christians 7%. Hindustani is the lingua franca. Lying on sea routes bet. India and the Far East, the Andamans have been known to travelers since 7th cent. A.D.; modern history of isls. has been associated with PORT BLAIR (founded 1789 by British) and adjacent penal settlement (discontinued 1945). In Second World War, under Jap. occupation (1942–45) and partly administered by rebel Indian natl. army.

Andaman Sea (□ 300,000; mean depth 2,850 ft.), arm of Indian Ocean, bounded N by coast of Lower Burma, E by Burma's Tenasserim coast and Thailand section of Malay Peninsula, S by Sumatra, and W by Andaman and Nicobar isls.; over 600 mi. long N–S, 400 mi. wide. Joined SE by Strait of Malacca to South China Sea, W by channels separating the Andamans and Nicobars with Bay of Bengal and Indian Ocean proper. The southernmost of these, the Great Channel, is on Colombo-Singapore shipping lane to the Far East. Andaman Sea receives Irrawaddy (delta), Sittang, and Salween rivers in Burma, where it forms the Gulf of Martaban. Rocky Mergui Archipelago lies off the Tenasserim coast. Chief ports: in Burma, Rangoon, Bassein (in Irrawaddy delta), Moulmein, Tavoy, and Mergui; in Andaman Isls., Port Blair; in Sumatra, Sabang.

Andamarca (ändämär'kä), town (pop. c.3,200), Oruro dept., W Bolivia, in the Altiplano, near W shore of L. Poopó, 65 mi. SW of Oruro; alt. c.12,000 ft.; potatoes, alpaca.

Andamarca. 1 Village (pop. 2,024), Ayacucho dept., S Peru, on E slopes of Cordillera Occidental, 34 mi. N of Puquio; beans, grain, livestock. **2** Town (pop. 1,576), Junín dept., central Peru, in Cordillera Central, 50 mi. E of Jauja; sugar, corn, fruit.

Andancette (ädäsĕt'), village (pop. 467), Drôme dept., SE France, on right bank of Rhone R. and 22 mi. NNW of Valence; mfg. (flour products, porcelain insulators).

Andapa (ändä'pŏŏ), town (1948 pop. 4,705), Tamatave prov., NE Madagascar, at foot of Tsaratanana Massif, 165 mi. S of Diégo-Suarez; vanilla processing; coffee.

Andarab, Afghanistan: see BANU.

Andaraí (ändŏŏräē'), city (pop. 4,244), central Bahia, Brazil, near upper Paraguaçu R., 200 mi. W of Salvador; 12°48'S 41°25'W. Important diamond-mining center. Formerly spelled Andarahy. Itaetê (26 mi. SE) is W terminus of railroad to Salvador.

Andaray (ändärī'), town (pop. 588), Arequipa dept., S Peru, in W foothills of Cordillera Occidental, 15 mi. WNW of Aplao; gold mining. Archaeological remains near by.

Andarkot (ŭn'dŭrkōt), village, Baramula dist., W central Kashmir, in Vale of Kashmir, 6 mi. NE of Patan. Has anc. Buddhist monastery, Hindu temple ruins, 7th- or 8th-cent. A.D. Hindu sculptures. Was (9th cent. A.D.) ⊙ King Jayapida. Here last anc. Hindu ruler of Kashmir, Queen Kotadevi, surrendered 1339 to Moslems.

Andau (än'dou), town (pop. 2,926), Burgenland, E Austria, near Hung. border, 21 mi. ENE of Sopron, Hungary; sugar beets.

Andebu (än'nŭbōō), village and canton (pop. 3,103), Vestfold co., SE Norway, 10 mi. WNW of Tonsberg; lumbering, dairying.

Andechs, Germany: see HERRSCHING.

Andeer (ändâr'), town (pop. 614), Grisons canton, E Switzerland, on the Hinterrhein and 7 mi. S of Thusis.

Andelfingen (än'dŭlfĭng-ŭn), district (pop. 18,043), Zurich canton, N Switzerland. Among its communes are Grossandelfingen (pop. 881), on Thur R. and 7 mi. N of Winterthur, and Kleinandelfingen (pop. 932), across the river; former produces flour, tower clocks.

Andelle River (ädĕl'), Seine-Inférieure and Eure depts., NW France, rises near Forges-les-Eaux, flows 30 mi. SSW, past Fleury-sur-Andelle and Pont-Saint-Pierre, to the Seine 4 mi. above Pont-de-l'Arche.

Andelot (ädùlō'), village (pop. 608), Haute-Marne dept., NE France, 12 mi. NE of Chaumont; chair mfg.

Andelsbuch (än'dùlsbōōkh), village (pop. 1,335), Vorarlberg, W Austria, on river Bregenzer Ache and 10 mi. SE of Bregenz; hydroelectric works.

Andelys, Les (lāzädùlē'), town (pop. 3,735), Eure dept., NW France, 20 mi. SE of Rouen, consisting of Le Petit Andely (hugging right bank of picturesque Seine R. meander) and Le Grand Andely (1 mi. ENE; heavily damaged in Second World War); metal- and glassworks; hosiery and candy mfg., silk spinning, printing. Le Grand Andely has a 13th–17th-cent. Gothic and Renaissance church (severely hit 1939–45) and 2 monuments of Poussin (b. near by). Le Petit Andely is dominated by impressive ruins of Château Gaillard, a fortress built 1196 by Richard Coeur de Lion for defense of Normandy, and starved into submission (1204) by Philip II of France.

Andematunum, France: see LANGRES.

Andenes (än'nùnās), village (pop. 1,670; canton pop. 2,795), Nordland co., N Norway, at N tip of Andoy of the Vesteralen group, 40 mi. NNW of Harstad; fisheries; lighthouse. Fishing village (pop. 497) of Bleik (blāk) is 5 mi. SW, on W shore of isl., under overhanging rocks. Bleiksoy (Nor. *Bleiksøy*), islet off Bleik, has cliffs extremely productive of bird feathers and down.

Andenne (ädĕn'), town (pop. 7,882), Namur prov., S central Belgium, on Meuse R. and 10 mi. E of Namur; chalk quarrying; mfg. (ceramics, bricks, drainage pipes, chemicals, paper); metal foundries. Town belonged to 1st Carolingian kings; here St. Begga, daughter of Pepin of Héristal, founded a nunnery (692) which passed to Namur in 1785.

Anderacha (ändĕrä'chä), Ital. *Anderaccia*, village, Kaffa prov., SW Ethiopia, on an affluent of Omo R. and 5 mi. SE of Bonga; coffee growing.

Anderida, England: see PEVENSEY.

Anderlecht (än'dùrlĕkht), town (pop. 86,484), Brabant prov., central Belgium, on Charleroi-Brussels Canal and 3 mi. SW of Brussels; industrial and residential suburb; mfg. (textiles, leather, tanning fluid, chemicals, lumber, paper, glassware, food products). Has 14th-cent. Gothic church.

Anderlues (ädĕrlü'), town (pop. 12,636), Hainaut prov., S Belgium, 8 mi. W of Charleroi; coal mining; coke plants.

Andermatt (än'dùrmät), village (pop. 1,496), Uri canton, S central Switzerland, near the Reuss, 14 mi. S of Altdorf; summer health resort (alt. 4,737 ft.), winter sports center. Late-Gothic church, 17th-cent. church, 18th-cent. chapel. St. Gotthard Tunnel is beneath village; roads lead to St. Gotthard Pass (S), to Furka and Grimsel passes (W), and to Oberalp Pass (E).

Andernach (än'dùrnäkh), town (pop. 13,869), in former Prussian Rhine Prov., W Germany, after 1945 in Rhineland-Palatinate, on left bank of the Rhine (steamer landing; ferry) and 10 mi. NW of Coblenz; rail junction; mfg. of chemicals, malting. Pottery works. Exports millstones. Has 13th-cent. church, 15th-cent. watchtower, 16th-cent. town hall. Was Roman garrison (*Antunnacum*). Belonged 1167–1801 to archbishopric of Cologne.

Andernos-les-Bains (ädĕrnō'-lā-bē'), town (pop. 2,041), Gironde dept., SW France, on N shore of Arcachon Basin, 27 mi. WSW of Bordeaux; small bathing resort; oyster culture; mfg. of fertilizer and fishing equipment. Sanatoria.

Anderny (ädĕrnē'), village (pop. 304), Meurthe-et-Moselle dept., NE France, 7 mi. NNW of Briey; iron mining.

Anderslov (än'dùrslûv"), Swedish *Anderslöv*, village (pop. 766), Malmohus co., S Sweden, 8 mi. SE of Trelleborg; metalworking; grain, potatoes, sugar beets, stock.

Anderson. 1 County (□ 577; pop. 10,267), E Kansas; ⊙ Garnett. Gently rolling agr. area watered by Pottawatomie Creek. Stock and grain raising, dairying. Oil and natural-gas fields. Formed 1855. **2** County (□ 206; pop. 8,984), central Ky.; ⊙ Lawrenceburg. Bounded E by Kentucky R., SW by Beech Fork; drained by Salt R. Gently rolling upland agr. area (burley tobacco, dairy products, poultry, horses, corn, hay) in Bluegrass region. Some mfg. at Lawrenceburg. Formed 1827. **3** County (□ 776; pop. 90,664), NW S.C.; ⊙ Anderson. Bounded W by Tugaloo and Savannah rivers, E by Saluda R.; drained by Seneca R. Many cotton mills; diversified agr. (cotton, grain, fruit, vegetables). Formed 1826. **4** County (□ 338; pop. 59,407), E Tenn.; ⊙ Clinton. NW part is in the Cumberlands, remainder of co. in ridge-traversed Great Appalachian Valley; drained by Clinch R. Includes Norris Reservoir (Norris Dam) and communities of NORRIS (a TVA center) and OAK RIDGE, center for nuclear research and atomic-materials production. Bituminous-coal mining; lumbering; livestock raising, dairying, agr. (fruit, tobacco, corn, hay). Formed 1801. **5** County (□ 1,068; pop. 31,875), E Texas; ⊙ PALESTINE, transportation, processing center. Bounded W by Trinity R., E by Neches R.; partly wooded (extensive lumbering). Oil, natural gas, asphalt, lignite, clay produced; coal, salt deposits. Diversified agr., livestock area; truck, fruit, legumes, cotton, cattle, hogs, poultry; dairying. Hunting, fishing attract visitors. Formed 1846.

Anderson. 1 Village (pop. 1,501), Shasta co., N Calif., near Sacramento R., 11 mi. SE of Redding; lumber, dairy products. **2** Industrial city (pop. 46,820), ⊙ Madison co., E central Ind., on West Fork of White R. and 34 mi. NE of Indianapolis; mfg. of castings, pumps, tools, auto parts, glass-making and other machinery, wire and metal products, ranges, ceramics, glass, paperboard products; furniture); meat packing, oil refining. Here are Anderson Col. and Theological Seminary, a tuberculosis hosp., and Mounds State Park (with mus. and prehistoric Indian mounds). Platted 1823; inc. as town in 1838, as city in 1865. A Moravian mission for Indians was near by, 1801–06. **3** City (pop. 1,073), McDonald co., extreme SW Mo., in the Ozarks, on branch of Elk R., 16 mi. S of Neosho; tomatoes, strawberries, grapes; timber. **4** City (pop. 19,770), ⊙ Anderson co., NW S.C., 28 mi. SW of Greenville; textile-milling center, with surrounding mill villages; printing; mfg. (beverages, ice, clothing, mattresses, roofing, fertilizer); foundries; cotton, fruit, vegetables. Anderson Jr. Col. here. Near by, on Seneca R., is early hydroelectric plant (built c.1895). Laid out 1827, inc. 1882. **5** Village (1940 pop. 559), ⊙ Grimes co., E central Texas, 9 mi. NE of Navasota; trade, shipping point in agr., timber area.

Anderson Bay, inlet of Bass Strait, N Tasmania, bet. Croppies Point (W of Ringarooma Bay) and East Sandy Cape; 15 mi. E-W, 5 mi. N-S.

Anderson Lake (□ 52), S central B.C., in Coast Mts., 16 mi. W of Lillooet; 16 mi. long, 1-2 mi. wide. Drains NE into Fraser R. through Seton L.

Anderson Ranch Dam, SW Idaho, on South Fork of Boise R. and 40 mi. SE of Boise. Earth-fill dam (456 ft. high, 1,350 ft. long; completed 1950), used for power, irrigation and flood control.

Anderson River, N Mackenzie Dist., Northwest Territories, rises c.30 mi. N of Great Bear L., flows NW in a winding course to Liverpool Bay of the Beaufort Sea at Stanton; 465 mi. long.

Anderson Valley, Calif.: see BOONVILLE.

Andersonville, village (pop. 281), Sumter co., SW central Ga., 10 mi. NNE of Americus; meat packing, bauxite mining. Natl. cemetery contains the graves of 13,741 Union soldiers, most of whom died here (1864–5) in crowded Confederate stockade (now a state park).

Anderstorp (än'dùrstôrp"). **1** Village (pop. 1,250), Jonkoping co., S Sweden, near Nissa R., 17 mi. NW of Varnamo; metalworking, furniture mfg. **2** Village (pop. 379), Halland co., SW Sweden, 9 mi. SE of Goteborg; grain, flax, sugar beets, stock.

Anderten (än'dùrtŭn), village (pop. 3,668), in former Prussian prov. of Hanover, W Germany, after 1945 in Lower Saxony, near Weser-Elbe Canal (lock; level difference: 49 ft.), 4.5 mi. E of Hanover city center.

Andes (ăn'dēz), Sp. *Los Andes* or *Cordillera de los Andes* (kôrdĕyä'rä dā lōs än'dās), great mountain system (over 4,000 mi. long) of South America, extending parallel to the Pacific coast from Tierra del Fuego northward through Argentina, Chile, Bolivia, Peru, and Ecuador, to the Caribbean coasts of Colombia and Venezuela, and forming the backbone of the entire continent. In the N, through spurs reaching into the Isthmus of Panama, it connects with the Central American ranges, and thus with the Sierra Madre and the Rocky Mts. of North America. In the S, after its submergence in Drake Passage, the system continues along Palmer Peninsula of Antarctica. Though scarcely 200 mi. wide (except in Bolivia, where its width is doubled), the Andes form one of the world's most prominent mtn. masses, loftier than any outside of the Himalayas. Its summits, many of which are higher than Mt. McKinley (highest in North America), include ACONCAGUA (22,835 ft.), the highest in the Americas. Other well-known peaks (including active or quiescent volcanoes) are LLULLAILLACO, ILLIMANI, ILLAMPU, EL MISTI, HUASCARÁN, CHIMBORAZO, COTOPAXI. Structurally, the Andes are composed of several rather closely jointed units which appear either as a single chain (in S), or as several parallel ranges (cordilleras) N of Chilean border. In general, the mts. were formed by folding and faulting, but in 3 distinct sections (S Colombia and Ecuador, central and S Peru, and along Chile-Bolivia border) there are important volcanic formations. As formidable a topographic feature as the Andean barrier must be expected to exert a decisive influence on the continent's climate, drainage pattern, and human geography. Closely following the S coast line of Tierra del Fuego, the Andes turn N at the Strait of Magellan, forming Chile-Argentina border. In S section (as far N as 42°S lat.), the W slopes are drowned in the sea, giving the shore line an indented fjordlike appearance; while on E margin, large glacier-fed finger lakes (Argentino, Viedma, San Martín, Pueyrredón, Buenos Aires) form the transition to the Patagonian plateau (E). The noted alpine resort dists. of LLANQUIHUE and NAHUEL HUAPÍ are bet. 40° and 42°S lat. From here on N, the single Andean range overlooks the Central Valley of Chile. Only N of 35°S lat. do the Andes exceed 10,000 ft. Bet. the high peaks of Aconcagua and TUPUNGATO, the barrier is crossed by the Transandine RR in a tunnel underneath USPALLATA PASS. Farther N, the Andes traverse a dry belt, where only the E slopes receive any (and scanty) rainfall. In this section (especially in lat. 25°S) are the 3 parallel ranges: the Cordillera de Domeyko (W), overlooking Chile's Atacama Desert; the central range along Chile-Argentina border; and the Sierra de Calalaste (E), supported by lower parallel ranges in Argentina. This region of dry slopes and high intermontane tablelands with salt pans is known as the Puna de Atacama. It is traversed (since 1948) by the Transandine RR of the North from Antofagasta (Chile) to Salta (Argentina), crossing the central range at SOCOMPA PASS. Near 23°S lat. (where Argentina, Bolivia, and Chile meet), the Andean system widens to form the ALTIPLANO, enclosed bet. 2 main ranges—the volcanic Western Cordillera [Sp. *Cordillera Occidental*] along Chile-Bolivia border and in S Peru (main peaks: Sajama, El Misti, Chachani), and the Eastern Cordillera [Sp. *Cordillera Oriental*], in W Bolivia (main peaks: Illimani, Illampu). The Altiplano contains the fresh-water L. TITICACA, salty L. POOPÓ, and several large salt pans (Salar de Coipasa, Salar de Uyuni). It is reached by the railroads bet. Antofagasta and Bolivia and bet. Arica and La Paz, and by the Southern RR of Peru (Mollendo-Puno). Near 18°S lat., where the Andes attain their max. width, they assume a northwesterly direction, paralleling the Pacific coast. Beyond the Nudo de Vilcanota (Vilcanota Knot), where the marginal ranges are reunited, the Andes of S and central Peru have been recognized as an uplifted peneplain, heavily dissected. Here short, intermittent streams flow W to the Pacific, while the ranges of the E watershed are cut by the deep gorges of the Amazon's headwaters and tributaries.

The Central RR (Lima–La Oroya) of Peru, which climbs the W range in this section and reaches alt. of 15,665 ft., is highest rail crossing in the Andes. N of the Nudo de Pasco, where the ranges are again drawn together into a knot, the narrower Andes are dissected by the valleys of the Marañón (E) and Santa (W) rivers. The snow-covered Cordillera Blanca, bet. these 2 valleys, contains the highest peaks of the Peruvian Andes (Huascarán). In Ecuador, 2 parallel cordilleras are connected by several cross-ranges which divide the upland into a series of intermontane basins linked by a longitudinal railroad (Quito-Guayaquil). Here the anc., deeply eroded Andean uplift has been buried beneath great lava flows, topped by symmetrical volcanoes (over 15 exceeding an alt. of 15,000 ft.), among which are the Chimborazo and Cotopaxi. Just inside Colombia, the Andes fan out into 3 ranges separated from each other by the structural valleys of the Magdalena and its principal tributary, the Cauca. These ranges are the Cordillera Occidental (bet. the Pacific and Cauca R.), with its westernmost outlier (Serranía de Baudó) extending into Panama; the high, volcanic Cordillera Central (bet. Cauca and Magdalena rivers), with Tolima and Huila peaks; and the Cordillera Oriental (E of the Magdalena), which encloses several high basins, including the Sabana de Bogotá. Near Cúcuta (at Colombia-Venezuela border), the last-mentioned range bifurcates into the Sierra Nevada de Mérida (which extends NE to the Caribbean and is continued in the coastal ranges of Venezuela to the N shore of Trinidad) and the Sierra de Perijá (which reaches the Caribbean in the Guajira peninsula and is linked to the granitic block of the Sierra Nevada de Santa Marta). Bet. these 2 forks lies the oil-rich Maracaibo depression. Geologically, the Andes consist of a complex folded series of sedimentary and extrusive formations supported by extensive granitic intrusions. The instability resulting from intensive and recurring tectonic activity is manifested in the steady development of volcanoes and in the frequent occurrence of earthquakes along the Andean uplift, which coincides generally with the Tertiary orogeny of the Alpine and Himalayan systems. As the Andes extend over 65° of lat., the processes of erosion and of denudation, which have sculptured the surface, differ widely from S to N. The southernmost sections, heavily glaciated during the Ice Age, are still covered by extensive glaciers descending to 2,500 ft. in S Patagonia and to the head of the fjords on the Pacific coast. Near 15°S lat., the perpetual snow line rises to c.17,500 ft. in the Western Cordillera, while at the equator its position is paradoxically c.15,500 ft. Recent evidence seems to prove that even the highest peaks in tropical latitudes, not now covered by ice masses, have been sculptured by glaciers. The Andes are a major storehouse of important nonferrous metals, which are to be found, for the most part, at relatively inaccessible altitudes. Chief resources are copper (mined at Chuquicamata, Potrerillos and El Teniente in Chile; Cerro de Pasco in Peru), tin (in the Eastern Cordillera of Bolivia), antimony (in Bolivia), and gold and silver in smaller quantities throughout the range. Salt and borax are recovered from the salt pans of the Altiplano and the Puna de Atacama. Typical of all tropical and subtropical upland regions, climatic and vegetation zones occur in a vertical pattern. At the E base of the Andes, including the hot, humid lowland and the foothill slopes up to 3,000 ft., is the *tierra caliente* zone of luxuriant tropical vegetation. Above it (3-7,000 ft.) is the *tierra templada*, with generally uniform temperatures (annual range not exceeding 5 degrees of Fahrenheit). The *tierra fría*, above 7,000 ft., is the zone most favorable for European settlement. The plateaus and high basins of the *tierra fría* have been peopled since remote times and have seen the rise of the Inca and other great Indian civilizations. Here are coniferous forests which, at higher altitudes, give way to scrub and grassland resulting from less rainfall and lower temperatures. Temperate-climate crops (e.g., wheat) and the indigenous tubers (potato, quinoa, *oca*) are cultivated in the *tierra fría*, and animals native to the Andes (llamas, guanacos, vicuñas, and alpacas) are grazed in the extensive pastures. The bleaker zone, bet. 10,000 and 13,000 ft., is called the *puna*. Here temperatures tend to extremes, with sudden transition from hot days to cold nights. Only the hardiest crops (barley, potatoes) can be grown. Above the *puna*, extending to the snow line, are the paramos, a desolate area of tundra vegetation. Characteristic of Andean fauna (in addition to animals mentioned) are the *vizcacha*, puma (or cougar), as well as the famous condor. Among the best-known ascents of the Andes are those of the Chimborazo by Humboldt (1802) and Whymper (1880), and of the Aconcagua by Zurbriggen and Vines (1897).

Andes (än'dās), town (pop. 5,991), Antioquia dept., NW central Colombia, in valley of Cordillera Occidental, 45 mi. SSW of Medellín; alt. 4,452 ft. Coffeegrowing center; also sugar, corn, beans, tobacco, cacao, livestock. Founded 1852.

Andes, Italy: see PIETOLE.

Andes (ăn'dĭz), village (pop. 430), Delaware co., S N.Y., 22 mi. SE of Oneonta, in a resort area of the Catskills.

Andes, Lake (ăn'dēz), Charles Mix co., S S.Dak.; 14 mi. long, c.2 mi. wide; fed by 3-mi. canal. Waterfowl refuge. City of Lake Andes and state fish hatchery are on it.

Andes, Los, Argentina: see LOS ANDES.

Andes, Los, Bolivia: see PUCARANI.

Andes, Los, town, Chile: see LOS ANDES.

Andeville (ädüvēl'), village (pop. 1,068), Oise dept., N France, 13 mi. SSE of Beauvais; button mfg.

Andevoranto (ändĕvōōrän'tōō), town, Tamatave prov., E Madagascar, on coast and Canal des Pangalanes, 60 mi. SSW of Tamatave; native market; mfg. of carbonated drinks.

Andheri (ŭndä'rē), town (pop., including S village of Ville Parle, 38,493), Bombay Suburban dist., W Bombay, India, on Salsette Isl., 13 mi. N of Bombay city center; mfg. (chemicals, electrical appliances, matches, tobacco products), stone crushing, palmyra-tree tapping; motion picture studios. Has several colleges. At Mogre (N) mfg. of silver thread, fireworks, paints, varnish.

Andhra (ŭn'drŭ) or **Telingana** (tä"lĭng-gä'nŭ), historical and linguistic region of peninsular India, comprising the country now occupied by N and NE Madras and S and E Hyderabad, where Telugu, a Dravidian tongue, is predominantly spoken. The anc. Andhra kings, Buddhists by religion, ruled (3d cent. B.C.–3d cent. A.D.) over much of this area. Its chief cities are Hyderabad, Warangal, Bezwada (Vijayavada), Rajahmundry, and Vizagapatam.

Andhra River (ŭn'drŭ), central Bombay, India, rises in Western Ghats SE of Bhivpuri, flows 16 mi. SE to right tributary of Bhima R. 2 mi. NE of Vadgaon. Dammed in upper course to form lake; supplies BHIVPURI power plant of Andhra valley hydroelectric project.

Andifli, Turkey: see KAS.

Andijk (ändīk'), village (pop. 4,523), North Holland prov., NW Netherlands, on the Ijsselmeer and 9 mi. NE of Hoorn; cauliflower, garden seeds, tulip bulbs. Sometimes spelled Andyk.

Andikaros, Greece: see ANTIKAROS.

Andikithira, Greece: see ANTIKYTHERA.

Andi Koisu, river, Russian SFSR: see KOISU.

Andilanatoby (ändēlänätōō'bē), village, Tamatave prov., E central Madagascar, on railroad, SW of L. Aloatra and 17 mi. SW of Ambatondrazaka; rice center.

Andimakhia, Greece: see ANTIMACHEIA.

Andimilos, Greece: see ANTIMELOS.

Andimishk or **Andimeshk** (ändēmĕshk'), town, Sixth Prov., in Khuzistan, SW Iran, on Trans-Iranian RR and 80 mi. NNW of Ahwaz; railroad maintenance point and station for Dizful (10 mi. SE); oranges, rice. Formerly known as Salehabad. Sometimes spelled Andimeshg.

Andino (ändē'nō), village (pop. estimate 800), S Santa Fe prov., Argentina, on left bank of Carcarańa R. and 23 mi. NNW of Rosario; hydroelectric station; paper milling.

Andiparos, Greece: see ANTIPAROS.

Andipatti (ŭn'dĭpŭ"tē), town (pop., including Jakkampatti, 1.5 mi. WNW, 7,944), Madura dist., S Madras, India, 35 mi. WNW of Madura; trades in products of Cardamom Hills (W), Palni Hills (N).

Andipatti Hills, India: see VARUSHANAD HILLS.

Andipaxoi, Greece: see ANTIPAXOS.

Andipsara, Greece: see ANTIPSARA.

Andirá (ändērä'), city (pop. 1,234), N Paraná, Brazil, on railroad and 25 mi. WSW of Ourinhos (São Paulo), in coffee zone; manioc, rice, tung oil. Until 1944, called Ingá.

Andi Range (än'dyē), N spur of the E Greater Caucasus in W Dagestan Autonomous SSR, Russian SFSR; extends c.50 mi. NE from main divide; forms watershed bet. the Andi Koisu (SE) and Aksai R. (NW); rises to c.9,000 ft.

Andirin (ändŭrŭn'), Turkish *Andırın*, village (pop. 1,192), Maras prov., S central Turkey, 32 mi. W of Maras; wheat, beans.

Andirrion, Cape, Greece: see ANTIRRION, CAPE.

Andissa, Greece: see ANTISSA.

Andizhan (ăn"dĭzhăn', Rus. ŭndyĭzhän'), oblast (□ 1,600; 1946 pop. estimate 600,000), E Uzbek SSR; ⊙ Andizhan. In E Fergana Valley; drained by the Kara Darya; extensive irrigation. Major part of territory under cotton cultivation; some wheat; sericulture; cattle and horses. Sheep breeding in non-irrigated areas. Industry based on cotton and silk production: cotton-ginning plants, silk mills. Oil and gas fields at Palvantash, Yuzhny Alamyshik, and Andizhan town. Railroads radiate from Andizhan city. Pop. chiefly Uzbeks; some Kirghiz. Formed 1941.

Andizhan, city (1939 pop. 83,691), ⊙ Andizhan oblast, Uzbek SSR, in Fergana Valley, 165 mi. ESE of Tashkent; 40°47'N 72°20'E. In cotton area; sericulture. Junction of railroads from Kokand, Namangan, Karasu, and Kokan-Kishlak; cotton-ginning center; cottonseed-oil extraction, food processing, metalworking. Teachers col. Served by rail depots Andizhan I (on E outskirts) and Andizhan II (5 mi. N). Many earthquakes (latest in 1902). Known since 9th cent. The oil town of Andizhan (1945 pop. over 500; developed during Second World War) is E of Leninsk, 12 mi. S of Andizhan city (linked by gas pipe line).

Andkhui (ŭnd-khōō'ē), town (pop. 25,000), Maimana prov., N Afghanistan, in Afghan Turkestan, on lower Qaisar R. and 115 mi. W of Mazar-i-Sharif; center of irrigated area (fruit, wine); karakul trade, rug weaving. Linked by road with Kerki (USSR) via Imam-Nezer. Pop. is largely Turkmen. Also spelled Andkhoi.

Andlau or **Andlau-au-Val** (ädlō'-ō-väl'), village (pop. 1,352), Bas-Rhin dept., E France, on the Andlau (small tributary of the Ill), at E foot of the Vosges, and 9 mi. NNW of Sélestat; granite quarrying. Has restored Romanesque church.

Andlau-au-Val, France: see ANDLAU.

Andoain (ändwīn'), town (pop. 2,179), Guipúzcoa prov., N Spain, 7 mi. SSW of San Sebastián; metal- and woodworking, cotton milling and printing; mfg. of textile machinery, handsaws, paper.

Andoas (ändō'äs), town (pop. 189), Loreto dept., N Peru, landing on Pastaza R., in Amazon basin, and 90 mi. E of Macas (Ecuador), 275 mi. WNW of Iquitos; 2°15'S 76°50'W. Cacao, tobacco.

Andolsheim (ädôlzĕm', Ger. än'dôls-hīm), agr. village (pop. 645), Haut-Rhin dept., E France, on the Ill and 3 mi. ESE of Colmar.

Andomski Pogost or **Andomskiy Pogost** (ŭndôm'skē pŭgôst'), village (1932 pop. estimate 160), NW Vologda oblast, Russian SFSR, near L. Onega, 17 mi. NNE of Vytegra; coarse grain; fire clays.

Andong (än'dông'), Jap. *Anto*, town (1949 pop. 41,061), N.Kyongsang prov., S Korea, 50 mi. NNE of Taegu; rail junction; commercial center in stock-raising and agr. area (rice, hemp, cotton, tobacco).

Andorf (än'dôrf), town (pop. 5,027), NW Upper Austria, on Pram R. and 9 mi. SE of Schärding; mfg. of knives.

Andorno Micca (ädôr'nō mēk'kä), formerly Andorno Cacciorna, commune (pop. 8,576), Vercelli prov., Piedmont, N Italy, on Cervo R. just N of Biella. Chief villages: Andorno Cacciorna (pop. 2,400) and Sagliano Micca (sälyä'nō) (pop. 1,558), producing hats, cotton textiles, alcohol.

Andorra (ăndô'rŭ), Fr. *Andorre* (ädôr'), tiny state (□ 191; pop. c.5,200) high in the E Pyrenees bet. Ariège and Pyrénées Orientales depts. of France and Lérida prov. of Spain; ⊙ Andorra or Andorra la Vella. Situated bet. 42°26'–42°39'N and 1°25'–1°48'E, it extends c.18 mi. W-E, 16 mi. N-S. Drained by VALIRA RIVER, Andorra comprises several narrow mtn. valleys and gorges, bounded by high peaks, of which the Puig de la Coma Pedrosa (9,665 ft.) is highest. It attracts summer visitors. Its rigorous but healthful climate is characterized by cold winters and cool summers. Passes are snowbound for about 8 months of the year. Some subsistence crops (oats, barley), fruit, and tobacco are grown. Sheep grazing is the principal occupation, though income is also derived from smuggling. Andorra has iron mines, argentiferous lead deposits, marble quarries, thermal springs, and extensive pine groves. Its few minor industries include wool combing, spinning, tobacco processing, sandal mfg., chiefly centered at SAN JULIÁN DE LORIA. Andorra is noted for its powerful radio station. Since valleys open to S side of the Pyrenees, communication is easier with Spain. A highway via Envalira Pass (7,897 ft.) links the main localities—San Julián de Loria, Andorra, Les Escaldes (spa; hydroelectric plant), Encamp, Canillo, Sordeu (near-by iron mines)—with Spain and France; a branch now leads to Ordino, site of Moorish ruins. There is no railroad. The people are Catalan in race and speech, R.C. in religion. A unique and archaic political creation, Andorra is properly speaking not an independent land but a fief under the joint suzerainty of the president of France and the bishop of Urgel (Spain), paying nominal tribute of 960 francs and 450 pesetas annually. Autonomous status is reputed to date from Carolingian era (8th to 9th cent.). In accordance with 1278 treaty—still in force—sovereign title over the valleys was shared bet. the count of Foix and the bishop of Urgel. The rights of the former were transmitted by inheritance to Henry IV of France and passed from the Fr. kings to the Fr. presidents. Both the Fr. president and bishop of Urgel act as "co-princes," controlling through their representatives (*viguiers*) judicial matters. Public services are supervised by the prefect of Pyrénées Orientales dept. Andorra is administered by a council of 24, elected for 4 years by the heads of families and presided over by a syndic. A 1933 revolution enforced universal male suffrage, which was, however, again abolished (1941). Politically a semi-feudal state, Andorra's quaint medievalism is also reflected in its communal agrarian organization. The republic is administratively divided into 6 parishes or dists. named for the principal localities.

Andorra or **Andorra la Vella** (lä vĕ'lyä), Sp. *Andorra la Vieja* (ändô'rä lä vyā"hä), Fr. *Andorre-la-Vieille* (ädôr-lä-vyā'), town (pop. c.950), ⊙ Andorra, on Valira R., 11 mi. NNE of Seo de Urgel (Spain), and 31 mi. S of Foix (France); alt. 3,510 ft. Sheep raising, subsistence agr. Radio transmitter. A 16th-cent. bldg. houses the Council-General, Mayor's office, court of justice, school and prison.

Andorra (ändô'rä), town (pop. 2,956), Teruel prov., E Spain, 16 mi. WSW of Alcañiz; plaster and soap mfg.; produces olive oil, wine, cereals. Coal mine near by.

Andosilla (ändōsē'lyä), town (pop. 2,308), Navarre prov., N Spain, 17 mi. SW of Tafalla; olive-oil processing; grain, sugar beets, wine.

Andouillé (ädwēyā'), village (pop. 634), Mayenne dept., W France, 7 mi. N of Laval; asbestos quarries.

Andover (ăn'–), village (pop. estimate c.300), W N.B., on St. John R. (bridge), opposite mouth of Tobique R., 18 mi. ENE of Presque Isle, Maine, in potato region; angling center. Formerly also called Tobique.

Andover, municipal borough (1931 pop. 9,692; 1951 census 14,661), NW Hampshire, England, 12 mi. NW of Winchester; agr. market and flour-milling center, with metalworks. Site of baptism (994) of King Olaf I Tryggvason by St. Alphege. Remains of Saxon and Roman camps have been found near by. Enham, village for disabled soldiers, is 2 mi. N.

Andover (ăn'dōvŭr). **1** Town (pop. 1,034), Tolland co., E central Conn., on Hop R. and 16 mi. E of Hartford, in agr. area. Small Andover L. is resort. Settled 1718, inc. 1848. **2** Village (pop. 256), Henry co., NW Ill., 17 mi. SE of Moline, in agr. and bituminous-coal area. **3** Town (pop. 80), Clinton co., E Iowa, 10 mi. N of Clinton. Limestone quarry near by. **4** Town (pop. 756), Oxford co., W Maine, 12 mi. WNW of Rumford, in resort area; skiing. Makes wood products. **5** Town (pop. 12,437), Essex co., NE Mass., just S of Lawrence; woolens, soap, rubber goods. Seat of Phillips Acad. and Abbot Acad. State forest. Merrimack R. skirts township (W). Settled 1643, inc. 1646. Includes Shawsheen Village, model "company town." **6** Rural town (pop. 1,057), Merrimack co., S central N.H., 22 mi. NW of Concord. East Andover village, on small lake, is resort. Settled 1761, inc. 1779. **7** Borough (pop. 560), Sussex co., NW N.J., 5 mi. S of Newton. Ore deposit near by furnished iron in Revolution. **8** Village (pop. 1,351, Allegany co., W N.Y., 14 mi. SSW of Hornell; oil and gas wells; dairy products, potatoes, hay. Inc. 1892. **9** Village (pop. 1,102), Ashtabula co., extreme NE Ohio, 21 mi. SSE of Ashtabula, near Pa. line, in agr. area; electric lamps, baskets, powdered milk. Pymatuning Reservoir (recreation) is just E. **10** City (pop. 277), Day co., NE S.Dak., 30 mi. E of Aberdeen; market town for rich farming region. **11** Town (pop. 185), Windsor co., S central Vt., 20 mi. SW of Windsor, in Green Mts.

Andover Dam, Conn.: see HOP RIVER.

Andoy (än'ûü), Nor. *Andøy*, marshy, hilly island (□ 150; pop. 5,925) in Norwegian Sea, Nordland co., N Norway, northernmost of the Vesteralen group, NW of Harstad, within the Arctic Circle; 69°N 16°E; 35 mi. long, 7 mi. wide. Fishing (cod, herring, salmon, halibut, haddock). Coal deposits. Sometimes called Anda or Anna. Chief villages: ANDENES (N), BJORNSKINN (S), Risoyhamn (S).

Andradas (ändrä'dûs), city (pop. 2,346), SW Minas Gerais, Brazil, near São Paulo border, 20 mi. S of Poços de Caldas; coffeegrowing, dairying. Zirconium deposits.

Andrade (ăndrā'dē), hamlet, Imperial co., S Calif., in Yuma Indian Reservation, on Colorado R. and 6 mi. W of Yuma, Ariz.; port of entry from Mexico.

Andradina (ändrûdē'nû), city (pop. 2,123), NW São Paulo, Brazil, near Paraná R., on railroad and 24 mi. ESE of Três Lagoas (Mato Grosso); pioneer agr. settlement (established 1928) and cattle-fattening center; mfg. of pottery and tiles, sawmilling. Diversified agr. (rice, corn, cotton, manioc, fruit).

Andraitx (ändrĭch', -äch'), town (pop. 3,301), Majorca, Balearic Isls., 11 mi. W of Palma. Trades in products of fertile region (carobs, almonds, olives, figs, barley, timber); olive-oil pressing, sawmilling, cheese processing, lime and gypsum quarrying, cement milling, hog raising. Also a resort. Has fine harbor 2 mi. S.

Andrapa, Turkey: see KIRSEHIR, town.

Andravida or **Andravidha** (both: ändrûvē'dhû), town (pop. 3,378), Elis nome, NW Peloponnesus, Greece, on railroad and 18 mi. NW of Pyrgos; Zante currants, figs, wheat; raising of cattle and sheep. Ruins of St. Sophia and other churches (13th cent.). Under French rule became seat (after 1204) of Prince of Morea.

Andreanof Islands (ăndrēă'nôf, ändrĕä'nôf), group of Aleutian Isls., SW Alaska, bet. Pacific (S) and Bering Sea (N), extending c.275 mi. bet. Rat Isls. (W) and Fox Isls. (E); near 52°N 172°57'–179°9' W. Largest isls. are Amlia, Atka, Adak, Kanaga, and Tanaga. Treeless and windswept, isls. are usually fogbound. Sheep ranching, fox farming, trapping are carried on by native Aleuts. Named for Russian navigator who explored them, 1760–64. Isls. were site of several important U.S. bases during Second World War; bases at Adak were enlarged and made permanent after 1943.

Andreapol or **Andreapol'** (ŭndrăä'pûl), town (1948 pop. over 2,000), E Velikiye Luki oblast, Russian SFSR, on Western Dvina R. and 70 mi. ENE of Velikiye Luki; dairying; brickworks. Limestone quarries; lignite mining.

Andreas, Cape (ändrä'äs), NE tip of Cyprus and Karpas Peninsula, on the Mediterranean; 35°40'N 34°36'E. Apostolos Andreas monastery is 3 mi. S.

Andreasberg, Sankt, Germany: see SANKT ANDREASBERG.

Andreba, Madagascar: see AMBATOSORATRA.

André Delpit, Fr. Morocco: see KHOURIBGA.

Andrelândia (ăndrĭlăn'dyû), city (pop. 2,340), S Minas Gerais, Brazil, on N slope of Serra da Mantiqueira, on railroad and 40 mi. S of São João del Rei; rutile mining.

Andrés Ibáñez, Bolivia: see SANTA CRUZ, city.

Andrésy (ädrāsē'), town (pop. 2,775), Seine-et-Oise dept., N central France, port on right bank of the Seine just below influx of Oise R. and 16 mi. NW of Paris.

Andretta (ändrĕt'tä), town (pop. 2,810), Avellino prov., Campania, S Italy, 28 mi. E of Avellino; machinery mfg.

Andréville, Que.: see SAINT ANDRÉ DE KAMOURASKA.

Andrew, village (pop. 369), central Alta., near Whiteford L. (4 mi. long), 50 mi. ENE of Edmonton; mixed farming, dairying.

Andrew, county (□ 430; pop. 11,727), NW Mo.; ⊙ Savannah. Bounded W by Nodaway R., SW by the Missouri; drained by One Hundred and Two R. and Little Platte R. Agr. region (corn, oats, wheat), livestock, poultry. Formed 1841.

Andrew, town (pop. 280), Jackson co., E Iowa, 25 mi. S of Dubuque, in agr. area.

Andrew Jackson, Mount (13,750 ft.), Antarctica, in S part of Palmer Peninsula; 71°31'S 63°34'W.

Andrew Johnson National Monument, Tenn.: see GREENEVILLE.

Andrews, county (□ 1,504; pop. 5,002), W Texas; ⊙ Andrews. On S Llano Estacado, bounded W by N.Mex. line; alt. 3–5,000 ft. Cattle-ranching region; one of state's leading oil-producing counties; also natural gas, minerals (salt, potash, sodium compounds, drilling mud); some agr., hogs, sheep, poultry. Includes Shafter L., other shallow lakes (fishing); hunting. Formed 1876.

Andrews. 1 Town (pop. 1,083), Huntington co., NE central Ind., near Wabash R., 6 mi. WSW of Huntington, in agr. area. **2** Town (pop. 1,397), Cherokee co., extreme W N.C., 14 mi. NE of Murphy, in Nantahala Natl. Forest; lumber milling; mfg. of tanning extract, rugs, wood products. Nantahala Gorge is NE. **3** Town (pop. 2,702), Georgetown and Williamsburg counties, E S.C., 15 mi. WNW of Georgetown, in agr. area; lumber, furniture, veneer. **4** City (pop. 3,294), ⊙ Andrews co., W Texas, on S Llano Estacado, 35 mi. NW of Midland; shipping, trading point for rich oil-producing, cattle-ranching region, with some agr. (corn, cotton, grain sorghums). Shafter L. (fishing) is 7 mi. NW.

Andrews Air Force Base, Md.: see CAMP SPRINGS.

Andreyev, Poland: see JEDRZEJOW.

Andreyeva, Imeni (ē'mĭnyē ŭndrā'ûvŭ), village (1939 pop. under 500), NE Tashauz oblast, Turkmen SSR, on Khiva oasis, 8 mi. ESE of Tashauz; cotton. Until c.1940, Taza-Bazar. Also called Imeni A. A. Andreyeva.

Andreyevka (ŭndrā'ûfkŭ). **1** Village (1948 pop. over 2,000), NE Taldy-Kurgan oblast, Kazakh SSR, in Dzungarian Ala-Tau, W of Ala-Kul (lake), 125 mi. ENE of Taldy-Kurgan; sheep, grain. **2** Village (1939 pop. over 2,000), SW Chkalov oblast, Russian SFSR, on Buzuluk R. and 35 mi. SSW of Buzuluk; metalworking; wheat, livestock. **3** Town (1939 pop. over 500), E Stalino oblast, Ukrainian SSR, in the Donbas, 6 mi. NNW of Snezhnoye; coal mines. **4** Town (1939 pop. over 500), N Stalino oblast, Ukrainian SSR, in the Donbas, near Slavyansk. **5** Village (1926 pop. 5,783), SE Zaporozhe oblast, Ukrainian SSR, 25 mi. NNW of Osipenko; cotton. Feldspar, mica deposits near by.

Andreyevka Pervaya (pyĕr'vīŭ) [Rus.,=Andreyevka No. 1], town (1926 pop. 9,849), central Kharkov oblast, Ukrainian SSR, on the Northern Donets and 34 mi. SE of Kharkov; flour milling. Andreyevka Vtoraya (ftŭrī'ŭ) [Rus.,=Andreyevka No. 2] is just SE.

Andreyevo (ŭndrā'ûvŭ), town (1939 pop. over 500), central Vladimir oblast, Russian SFSR, 12 mi. E of Sudogda; sawmilling.

Andreyevo-Ivanovka (–ēvä'nûfkŭ), village (1939 pop. over 500), central Odessa oblast, Ukrainian SSR, 16 mi. SE of Ananyev; metalworks. Formerly called Chernovo.

Andreyevsk (ŭndrā'ûfsk), town (1948 pop. over 500), NE Irkutsk oblast, Russian SFSR, 18 mi. N of Bodaibo; gold mines.

Andreyevskoye (ŭndrā'ûfskŭyû). **1** Village (1948 pop. over 2,000), SW Novosibirsk oblast, Russian SFSR, 22 mi. SSW of Bagan. Formerly called Voskrenskoye. **2** Village (1939 pop. over 500), NE Smolensk oblast, Russian SFSR, 18 mi. SW of Sychevka; flax.

Andrézieux (ädrāzyû'), village (pop. 1,769), Loire dept., SE central France, in Forez Plain, on the Loire and 9 mi. NW of Saint-Étienne; produces small arms, tools, clothing, laces, braids.

Andria (än'drēä), city (pop. 54,438), Bari prov., Apulia, S Italy, 30 mi. WNW of Bari; wine, olive oil, flour, macaroni, cheese, cotton textiles. Bishopric. A favorite residence of Frederick II, who built imposing Castel del Monte near by.

Andriba (ändrē'bû), town, Majunga prov., N central Madagascar, on highway to Tananarive and 110 mi. SSE of Majunga; mfg. of tapioca and cassava starch, rice processing; gold mining in vicinity. Annual cattle fairs held here.

Andrichau, Poland: see ANDRYCHOW.

Andries, Sint, Netherlands: see SINT ANDRIES.

Andrijevica or **Andriyevitsa** (ändrē'ĕvĭtsä), town (pop. 1,928), E Montenegro, Yugoslavia, on Lim R. and 33 mi. NE of Titograd; local trade center. Dates from 1877; named after old local church of St. Andrija.

Andrimont (ädrēmõ'), town (pop. 6,940), Liége prov., E Belgium, 2 mi. NE of Verviers; wool spinning and weaving.

Andritsaina (ŭndrē'tsĕnŭ), village (pop. 1,756), Elis nome, W Peloponnesus, Greece, on N slope of Minthes mts., 27 mi. SE of Pyrgos; summer resort; livestock raising (sheep, goats); wine. Ruins of temple of Pan. Sometimes spelled Andritsaena and Andritsena.

Andriyevitsa, Yugoslavia: see ANDRIJEVICA.

Androka (ändrō'kû), village, Tuléar prov., S Madagascar, on SW coast, 40 mi. SW of Ampanihy; castor beans, corn, sorghum; cattle.

Andronovskoye (ŭndrô'nûfskŭyû), village, NE Leningrad oblast, Russian SFSR, on Oyat R. and 45 mi. E of Lodeinoye Pole; coarse grain.

Andros (ăn'drŏs), northernmost island (□ 145; pop. 17,926) of the Cyclades, Greece, in Aegean Sea, bet. Euboea (NW) and Tenos (SE; separated by 1-mi.-wide Andros Channel); 37°45'N 24°40'E; 25 mi. long, 10 mi. wide; rises to 3,294 ft. in Mt. Kouvarion (Kouvara). Produces grain, figs, tobacco, olives, silk, citrus fruit, wine; fishing; manganese and marble deposits. Chief town, Andros (pop. 3,028), is on E shore. Originally dependent (8th cent. B.C.) on Eretria, Andros submitted 490 B.C. to Persians, revolted 410 from Athens, and was occupied 200 B.C. by Pergamum and Rome. In Middle Ages it belonged (after 1204) to the Venetians, then to the Turks until 1913.

Androscoggin (ăndrûskŏ'gĭn), county (□ 478; pop. 83,594), SW Maine; ⊙ Auburn. The "Twin Cities" of Lewiston and Auburn, on the Androscoggin, are centers of state's shoe and textile industries. Other mfg.: paper, wood products, linoleum. Rich agr., dairying area; cans and ships fruit, vegetables. Androscoggin and Little Androscoggin rivers furnish power; several lakes are recreational centers. Formed 1854.

Androscoggin Lake, SW Maine, 16 mi. NE of Lewiston on Androscoggin-Kennebec co. line; c.3 mi. long, 1–2.5 mi. wide. Drains through Dead R. into Androscoggin R.

Androscoggin River, N.H. and Maine, formed by junction of Magalloway R. and short outlet of Umbagog L. in N N.H. at c.1,200 ft.; flows c.175 mi. generally SE, through Maine, furnishing power at Rumford, Auburn, Lewiston, and Brunswick, joining Kennebec R. below Augusta to form Merrymeeting Bay. Used for logging.

Andros Island (ăn'drŏs, –drûs), island (c.100 mi. long, up to 45 mi. wide) and district (□ 1,600; pop. 6,718), W Bahama Isls., 20 mi. W of New Providence Isl., and equidistant (c.100 mi.) from Florida (WNW) and Cuba (S). It is really an archipelago, intersected by narrow, navigable channels. Has the only river in the Bahamas, the 15-mi. Goose R. Along its coast are a number of inhabited cays. The isl. is largely wooded. Main products: timber (pine, mahogany, lignum vitae, etc.), pineapples, sponge. Principal settlements: Mangrove Cay (E), Kemp's Bay (SE), Nicholls' Town and Staniard Creek (NE), Fresh Creek or Coakley Town (E). The isl. was called Espiritu Santo by the Spaniards. It was permanently settled in 1787.

Androsovo (ŭndrô'sûvŭ), village (1939 pop. over 500), W Smolensk oblast, Russian SFSR, 40 mi. SW of Smolensk; flax. Treaty concluded here (1667) bet. Poland and Russia gave Smolensk, the Ukraine on left bank of Dnieper R., and city of Kiev to Russia. Formerly Andrusovo.

Androth Island (ăndrōt'), coral island of Laccadive Isls., India, in Arabian Sea; 10°40'N 73°40'E. Administered by Malabar dist., Madras; coconuts; mfg. of coir and copra.

Andrushevka (ŭndrŏŏshôf'kŭ, ŭndrŏŏ'shĭfkŭ), town (1926 pop. 4,921), SE Zhitomir oblast, Ukrainian SSR, 22 mi. SE of Zhitomir; sugar refinery, distillery.

Andrusovo, Russian SFSR: see ANDROSOVO.

Andrychow (ändrĭkh'ŏŏf), Pol. *Andrychów*, Ger. *Andrichau* (ändrĭkh'ou), town (pop. 5,055), Krakow prov., S Poland, on railroad and 30 mi. WSW of Cracow; textile mfg., flour milling, sawmilling; brickworks; farming.

Andújar (ändŏŏ'här), city (pop. 22,924), Jaén prov., S Spain, in Andalusia, on Guadalquivir R. and 24 mi. NW of Jaén; pottery making is chief industry; water-cooling jars (alcarrazas) made here are used throughout Spain. Other mfg.: soap, wax, honey, glycerin, textiles, sandals; olive-oil processing, tanning, flour- and sawmilling. Mineral springs near by. Has Gothic church with plateresque façade, 13th-cent. Mudejar tower, and remains of Moorish walls. Ruins of Iberian settlement in vicinity. Airfield near by.

Anduk Dag (ändōōk'dä), Turkish *Anduk Dağ*, peak (9,285 ft.), E central Turkey, in Bitlis Mts., 16 mi. SW of Mus.

Andulo (ändōō'lō), town (pop. 2,631), Bié prov., central Angola, on Bié Plateau, 70 mi. NNW of Silva Pôrto; coffee, wheat, corn, beans.

Anduze (ãdüz'), village (pop. 1,526), Gard dept., S France, on the Gardon d'Anduze, 7 mi. SW of Alès; hosiery and pottery mfg. Has 16th- or 17th-cent. citadel.

Andyk, Netherlands: see ANDIJK.

Andzhiyevski or **Andzhiyevskiy** (ŭnjēĕf'skē), town (1926 pop. 1,433), S Stavropol Territory, Russian SFSR, on railroad and 3 mi. WNW of Mineralnye Vody; quarries.

Aneby (ä'nübü"), village (pop. 1,137), Jonkoping co., S Sweden, on Svart R. (waterfalls near by) and 13 mi. NNE of Nassjo; sawmilling, woodworking.

Anécho (änā'chō), town (pop. 6,887), S Fr. Togoland, small port on Slave Coast of Gulf of Guinea, on a strip of land bet. a lagoon and the sea, 27 mi. ENE of Lomé (linked by rail); lagoon transport to Grand-Popo (Dahomey; E); commercial center; exports cacao, palm oil and kernels, cotton, corn, coffee, copra. Manioc and tapioca processing. Airfield; hosp.; R.C. mission. Formerly Petit-Popo or Little Popo.

Anegada (ănùgä'dù), islet (□ c.13; pop. 274), Br. Virgin Isls., northernmost of the Lesser Antilles, 25 mi. NE of Tortola isl.; 18°45'N 64°20'W. Low and flat, surrounded by reefs, it is 10 mi. long (W–E), up to 2 mi. wide. Fishing and salvaging.

Anegada, Point (änägä'dä), headland at N tip of main isl. of Tierra del Fuego, Chile, on Strait of Magellan; 52°27'S 69°29'W.

Anegada Bay (änägä'dä), inlet of the Atlantic in SW Buenos Aires prov., Argentina, S of delta of the Río Colorado. With adjoining Unión (N) and San Blas (S) bays, it is 50 mi. wide. Contains Flamenco, Gama, Césares, and Riachos isls.

Anegada Passage (ănùgä'dù), channel (c.40 mi. wide) in the West Indies, bet. the Atlantic and the Caribbean, separating Anegada and Virgin Gorda of Br. Virgin Isls. (W) from SE Leeward Isls.

Anegasaki, Japan: see ANEZAKI.

Aneityum (ănē'ĭtyùm), volcanic island (□ c.25; pop. 192), southernmost isl. of New Hebrides, SW Pacific; 20°12'S 169°46'E; circular, c.35 mi. in circumference; kauri pine.

'Aneiza, Jordan: see 'INAZA.

Aneiza, Saudi Arabia: see ANAIZA.

'Aneiza, Jebel, or **Jabal 'Unayzah** (both: jĕ'bĕl ùnā'zù), mountain (3,084 ft.) in Syrian Desert, marking junction of Jordan, Iraq, and Saudi Arabia borders; 32°5'N 39°10'E.

Anekal (ŭnĕkŭl'), town (pop. 7,048), Bangalore dist., E Mysore, India, 20 mi. SSE of Bangalore; road center in silk-growing and sugar-cane area; handicraft lacquerware.

Añelo (änyä'lō), village, ⊙ Añelo dept. (1947 pop. 658), E Neuquén natl. territory, Argentina, on Neuquén R. and 55 mi. NW of Neuquén; alfalfa, livestock. Formerly called Tratayén.

Aneroid, village (pop. 281), S Sask., 45 mi. SE of Swift Current; wheat, livestock.

Anet (änā'), village (pop. 1,244), Eure-et-Loir dept., NW central France, near the Eure, 8 mi. NNE of Dreux; mfg. (tin cans, cartons). Has remains of 16th-cent. Renaissance château built by Delorme for Diane de Poitiers.

Anet, Switzerland: see INS.

Aneta (ùnĕ'tù), city (pop. 469), Nelson co., E central N.Dak., 50 mi. SW of Grand Forks.

Anethou, Pic d', NE Spain: see ANETO, PICO DE.

Aneto, Pico de (pē'kō dhā änā'tō), Fr. *Pic de Néthou* or *Pic d' Anethou* (pēk dānàtōō'), highest peak (11,168 ft.) of the Pyrenees (central range) in the Maladetta group, NE Spain, near Fr. border, 10 mi. SW of Viella.

Anezaki (änā'zä'kē) or **Anegasaki** (änā"gä'säkē), town (pop. 9,104), Chiba prefecture, central Honshu, Japan, on W Chiba Peninsula, on Tokyo Bay, 10 mi. SW of Chiba; agr. (rice, peaches, pears); fishing.

Anfa, Fr. Morocco: see CASABLANCA.

Anfu (än'fōō'). **1** Town, Hunan prov., China: see LINLI. **2** Town (pop. 11,564), ⊙ Anfu co. (pop. 111,183), W Kiangsi prov., China, 20 mi. NW of Kian; rice, cotton, wheat; mfg. (straw hats, bamboo paper). Anthracite mines, limestone quarries.

Anfuchen (än'fōō'jŭn'), town, S Szechwan prov., China, 5 mi. WSW of Jungchang and on Chungking-Chengtu RR; pottery center. Formerly known as Shaochiufang.

Anga (ŭn-gä'), village (1939 pop. over 500), SE Irkutsk oblast, Russian SFSR, on Anga R. (right affluent of the Lena) and 12 mi. E of Kachuga, in agr. area.

Angaco, dept., Argentina; see VILLA DEL SALVADOR.

Angaco Norte (äng-gä'kō nôr'tä), town (pop. estimate, including VILLA DEL SALVADOR, 2,000), S San Juan prov., Argentina, in San Juan R. valley (irrigation area), adjoining (SW) Villa del Salvador, on railroad, and 7 mi. NE of San Juan. Agr. center (alfalfa, corn, wine, fruit, livestock); wine making, fruit drying. Formerly Kilómetro 924.

Angaco Sud (sōōdh'), town (pop. estimate 1,000), ⊙ San Martín dept. (□ c.190; 1947 pop. 7,726), S San Juan prov., Argentina, on railroad, on San Juan R. and 7 mi. ESE of San Juan. Wine- and fruitgrowing center; wineries, lime kilns.

Angaku, Korea: see ANAK.

Angamacutiro (äng-gämäkōōtē'rō), officially Angamacutiro de la Unión, town (pop. 2,845), Michoacán, central Mexico, on affluent of Lerma R. and 14 mi. WNW of Puruándiro; cereals, livestock.

Angangki or **Ang-ang-ch'i** (both: äng'äng'chē'), town, W central Heilungkiang prov., Manchuria, 10 mi. SSW of Tsitsihar; rail junction on Chinese Eastern RR.

Angangueo (äng-gäng-gä'ō), town (pop. 8,196), Michoacán, central Mexico, on central plateau, 45 mi. NW of Toluca, on railroad; alt. 8,530 ft. Lumbering and mining center (silver, lead, copper); sawmills.

Angaraes, Peru: see LIRCAY.

Angara River (äng"gärä', Rus. ŭn-gùrä'), in SE Siberian Russian SFSR, in Irkutsk oblast and Krasnoyarsk Territory; outlet (SW) of L. Baikal; flows NNW, past Irkutsk and Bratsk, and W to Yenisei R. 35 mi. SSE of Yeniseisk; 1,151 mi. long. Chief waterway bet. Baikal and Yenisei areas. Navigable above and below 50-mi. rapids below Bratsk. These and other rapids at L. Baikal outlet are points of potential hydroelectric power development. Receives Irkut, Belaya, Oka, Taseyeva (left) and Ilim (right) rivers. Also known as Upper Tunguska R., Rus. *Verkhnyaya Tunguska*, below mouth of Ilim R. UPPER ANGARA RIVER enters L. Baikal in NE.

Angareb River (äng'gärĕb), Begemdir prov., NW Ethiopia, rises in highlands near Davark, flows c.170 mi. W and NW to Atbara R. just inside Anglo-Egyptian Sudan.

Angarsk (ŭngärsk'), city (1951 pop. over 10,000), Irkutsk oblast, Russian SFSR, on Angara R. SE of Irkutsk. Industrial boom city, founded in late 1940s.

Angaston (ăng'gùstùn), town (pop. 1,218), SE South Australia, 38 mi. NNE of Adelaide; rail terminus; wine center; wheat, fruit. Limestone and marble quarries.

Angat (äng-gät'), town (1939 pop. 3,417; 1948 municipality pop. 12,776), Bulacan prov., S central Luzon, Philippines, 22 mi. N of Manila; agr. center (rice, sugar cane, corn); foundry clay. Iron is mined near by. Sometimes called Santa Cruz.

Angatuba (ãng-gùtōō'bù), city (pop. 1,630), S São Paulo, Brazil, 25 mi. WNW of Itapetininga; processes dairy products, cotton, coffee, manioc.

Angaur (äng"our'), coral island (□ c.3; c.2.5 mi. long), southernmost of Palau isls., W Caroline Isls., W Pacific; 6°53'N 134°8'E. Chalk cliffs; known for phosphate deposits.

Angduphodang, Bhutan: see WANGDU PHODRANG.

Ange (ông'ù), Swedish *Ånge*, town (pop. 2,651), Vasternorrland co., NE Sweden, on Ljunga R. and 55 mi. W of Sundsvall; rail junction; trade center in lumbering, dairying region.

Angediva Island (änzhädē'vù), small outlying dependency (□ c.½) of Goa dist., Portuguese India, in Arabian Sea, 55 mi. SSE of Pangim, 4 mi. S of Karwar (Bombay state). Used by Arab traders in 15th cent.; visited by Vasco da Gama in 1498; taken by Portuguese in 1505. For some time a penal settlement. Also spelled Anjidiv.

Ange Gardien (ãzh gärdyẽ'), village (pop. estimate 350), S Que., on the St. Lawrence and 11 mi. NE of Quebec; dairying.

Angeja (ãzhā'zhù), village (pop. 1,861), Aveiro dist., N central Portugal, on Vouga R. and 6 mi. NE of Aveiro; pottery, lumbering (pine and eucalyptus trees), winegrowing.

Angel, El, Ecuador: see EL ANGEL.

Ángel Albino Corzo, Mexico: see JALTENANGO.

Ángel de la Guarda Island (än'hĕl dā lä gwär'dä) (□ 330), in Gulf of California, NW Mexico, 10 mi. off coast of Lower California, across the strait Canal de las Ballenas, N of 29°N; 50 mi. long, 2–10 mi. wide. Barren, uninhabited; rises to 4,315 ft.; serves as seasonal fishing base (pearls, sharks, seals, whales). Sometimes Angel de la Guardia.

Angeles (ăn'jùlùs, Sp. än'hĕlĕs), town (1939 pop. 3,377; 1948 municipality pop. 37,558), Pampanga prov., central Luzon, Philippines, on railroad and 10 mi. NW of San Fernando; agr. center (rice, sugar cane).

Ángeles (än'hĕlĕs), village, W central Puerto Rico, in N hills of the Cordillera Central, 13 mi. SSW of Arecibo, in tobacco-growing region.

Ángeles, Cerro de los (sĕ'rō dhā lōs än'hĕlĕs), hill in Madrid prov., central Spain, 7 mi. S of Madrid, just E of Getafe; considered geographical center of Spain. Atop it is a shrine.

Ángeles, Los, Chile: see LOS ÁNGELES.

Ángeles, Los, Mexico: see LOS ÁNGELES.

Angel Fall, waterfall in Bolívar state, SE Venezuela, on affluent of Caroní R.; drops from plateau in Guiana Highlands; 5°57'N 62°33'W. Said to be highest uninterrupted waterfall in world; drop estimated to be bet. 3,300 and 5,000 ft.

Angelholm (ĕng"ùlhôlm'), Swedish *Ängelholm*, city (pop. 6,928), Kristianstad co., SW Sweden, on Ronne R., near its mouth on Kattegat, 30 mi. NE of Halsingborg; rail junction; sugar refining, tanning, metalworking. Has old town hall and remains of medieval church. Chartered c.1470. Bathing beach is just W, on Skalderviken bay.

Angélica (änhä'lēkä), town (pop. estimate 800), central Santa Fe prov., Argentina, 50 mi. WNW of Santa Fe; grain-growing and stock-raising center; mfg. of harvesters, dairy products.

Angelica (ănjĕ'lĭkù), village (pop. 928), Allegany co., W N.Y., on small Angelica Creek and 19 mi. W of Hornell; shock absorbers; agr. (dairy products; potatoes).

Angelina (ănjùlē'nù), county (□ 857; pop. 36,032), E Texas; ⊙ LUFKIN, commercial, mfg. center. Bounded N and NE by Angelina R., W and S by Neches R. Includes parts of Angelina and Davy Crockett Natl. Forests. Heavily wooded, in heart of E Texas pine region; industries center on forest products (newsprint, lumber, creosoted wood, other wood products). Also dairying, livestock (cattle, poultry, hogs); some agr. (peanuts, truck, fruit, corn, potatoes, sugar cane). Some oil, natural gas; clay, fuller's earth, lignite, iron deposits. Hunting, fishing. Formed 1846.

Angelina River, E Texas, rises S of Tyler, flows c.200 mi. generally SE to Neches R. 12 mi. W of Jasper. Near its mouth is site of proposed McGee Bend Dam and Reservoir, a unit in Neches R. flood-control, water-supply plan.

Angel Island, largest island (c.1½ mi. long) in San Francisco Bay, W Calif., N of San Francisco; politically part of Marin co. From 1863 to 1946, it was U.S. Army base; was long the site of a quarantine station (established 1892) and immigration station (established 1909). In Second World War, an internment camp for enemy nationals was here.

Angell Peak, Oregon: see ELKHORN RIDGE.

Angeln (äng'ùln), peninsular region (□ 330) of NE Schleswig-Holstein, NW Germany, bounded by Flensburg Firth (N), the Baltic (E), and the Schlei (S). Hilly, agr. (wheat) region, with stock (cattle, hogs) raising. Main village: Süderbrarup. Many prehistoric finds. Traditionally home of the Angles who migrated to Britain in 5th cent.

Angelokastron, Lake, Greece: see LYSIMACHIA, LAKE.

Angelópolis (änhĕlō'pōlēs), town (pop. 902), Antioquia dept., NW central Colombia, on W slopes of Cordillera Central, on railroad and 14 mi. SW of Medellín; alt. 6,447 ft. Coal mining, lumbering. Fertile agr. area (coffee, corn, beans, sugar cane, yucca, bananas).

Angels Camp, city (pop. 1,147), Calaveras co., central Calif., c.45 mi. E of Stockton, in Sierra Nevada foothills. Holds annual Jumping Frog Jubilee, honoring Mark Twain's story. Lumbering, gold mining, stone quarrying, stock raising. Founded after gold was discovered here in 1848; inc. 1912. Official name, Angels. Rail station is Valley Springs (18 mi. NW).

Angera (änjä'rä), village (pop. 2,044), Varese prov., Lombardy, N Italy, port on SE shore of Lago Maggiore, 13 mi. WSW of Varese; mfg. (motorcycles, bicycles, toys), alcohol distilling, marble working. Pietro Martire d'Anghiera b. here.

Angerapp, Russian SFSR: see OZERSK.

Angerapp River (äng'ùräp), Pol. *Węgorapa* (vĕgôrä'-pä), left headstream of Pregel R., in East Prussia, after 1945 in NE Poland and Kaliningrad oblast, Russian SFSR, rises in Mamry L., flows generally NNE, past Wegorzewo and Ozersk, and W, joining Inster R. just below Chernyakhovsk to form Pregel R. Receives Goldap and Pissa rivers (right).

Angerburg, Poland: see WEGORZEWO.

Angerlo (äng'ùrlō), village (pop. 399), Gelderland prov., E Netherlands, on Ijssel R. and 10 mi. E of Arnhem; cattle raising, agr.

Angermanland (ông'ùrmänländ"), Swedish *Ångermanland*, historic province [Swedish *landskap*] (□ 8,135; pop. 187,570), NE Sweden, on Gulf of Bothnia. Included in Vasterbotten co. (N) and Vasternorrland co. (S).

Angerman River, Swedish *Ångermanälven* (ông'-ùrmänĕl"vùn), N Sweden, rises on Norwegian border mts., near 65°15'N 14°30'E, flows 280 mi. in winding course generally SSE, past Vilhelmina, Asele, Solleftea, and Kramfors, to Gulf of Bothnia 10 mi. NE of Harnosand. It has several falls (power stations). Navigable below Solleftea; important logging. On its 20-mi.-long estuary are numerous lumber and pulp mills. Noted for scenic beauty.

Angermund (äng"ùrmōōnt'), town (pop. 1,919), in former Prussian Rhine Prov., W Germany, after 1945 in North Rhine-Westphalia, 7 mi. S of Düsseldorf; grain.

Angermünde (äng"ùrmün'dù), town (pop. 10,813), Brandenburg, E Germany, on small lake, 40 mi. NE of Berlin; rail junction; agr. market (grain, tobacco, sugar beets); dairying, metalworking; forestry. Has 13th-cent. church.

Angers (ã-zhā'), village (pop. 359), SW Que., on Ottawa R. and 6 mi. SW of Buckingham; lumbering, dairying.

Angers (ăn'jùrz, ăn'jĕrz', Fr. ã-zhā'), anc. *Juliomagus*, city (pop. 86,083), ⊙ Maine-et-Loire dept., W France, on Maine R. and 165 mi. SW of Paris; commercial, industrial, and food-processing center known for its sparkling wines; river port; has cable and wire mills, and factories producing agr. machinery, chemical fertilizer, shoes, hosiery, umbrellas; vegetable and fruit preserving, liqueur distilling. Important slate quarries at near-by Trélazé (5 mi. ESE) and Saint-Barthélemy-d'Anjou (3 mi. E). Has 12th-13th-cent. Gothic Cathedral of Saint-Maurice and several museums, one of them with a fine collection of 14th–18th-cent. tapestries. Of Pre-Roman origin, Angers became the Roman Juliomagus; later seat of powerful counts of Anjou (870–1204). Episcopal see since 3d cent. Although its univ. (reorganized 1875) was suppressed in French Revolution and its military acad. removed to Saumur, the city remains a seat of higher learning and an art center. Excavations made in 1937 revealed important Roman and early medieval remains. The 13th-cent. pentagon-shaped castle and 15th-cent. house of Olivier Barrault were among the many bldgs. damaged in Second World War. David d'Angers and René Bazin b. here.

Angerville (äzhĕrvēl'), village (pop. 1,389), Seine-et-Oise dept., N central France, 11 mi. SW of Étampes; agr. market (cereals, truck, poultry).

Anghiari (äng-gyä'rē), village (pop. 1,820), Arezzo prov., Tuscany, central Italy, 10 mi. NE of Arezzo; agr. tools. Has church with Della Robbia Madonna.

Angicos (äzhē'kōōs), city (pop. 807), central Rio Grande do Norte, NE Brazil, terminus (1949) of railroad from Natal (95 mi. E); carnauba wax, cotton, cheese.

Angie (ăn'jē), village (pop. 230), Washington parish, SE La., 14 mi. NNE of Bogalusa, near Miss. line, in agr. area.

Angier (ăn'jŭr), town (pop. 1,182), Harnett co., central N.C., 21 mi. SSW of Raleigh; fertilizer mfg., lumber milling.

Angistri (äng-gē'strē) or **Angistrion** (äng-gē'strēôn) island (□ 4; 1940 pop. 764), in Saronic Gulf of Aegean Sea, Attica nome, Greece, 4 mi. off W coast of Aegina; 37°42'N 23°20'E; 3 mi. long, 1.75 mi. wide; stock raising (sheep, goats); fisheries. On N shore is village (1928 pop. 382) of Angistri (formerly Megalochori), 28 mi. SW of Athens.

Angistron, Greece: see TSINGELION.

Angites River or **Angitis River** (both: äng-gē'tĭs), in Macedonia, Greece, rises on Bulg. line in Alibotush Mts., flows SE, cutting underground channel through Phalakron massif, through Drama lowland and SW to the Struma; 50 mi. long. A canalized affluent drains marshy Philippi plain.

Angka Peak, Thailand: see INTHANON PEAK.

Angkor (ăng'kôr, ängkôr'), great collection of Khmer ruins, NW Cambodia, 4 mi. N of Siemreap, near N shore of lake Tonle Sap. Extending over an area of 40 sq. mi., the ruins contain some of the most imposing and best-preserved monuments of anc. Cambodia. **Angkor Thom** (tōm') [=the great Angkor], an anc. Khmer capital, occupies a conspicuous place among the ruins. It is moated and surrounded by a square wall (nearly 8 mi. in perimeter) pierced by 5 identical gates (surmounted by 4-faced heads) from which wide avenues lead to the central Bayon, a temple with a main tower rising to over 150 ft. and about 50 smaller pyramidal towers. Just NW of the Bayon is the Royal Palace, and there are numerous other temples, buildings, and monuments, all decorated with elaborate stone carvings depicting scenes of Khmer life and episodes from the Hindu epics. Just S of Angkor Thom is **Angkor Wat** or **Angkor Vat** (both: wät, vät) [=Angkor temple], the best-preserved monument (sculptures, bas reliefs) of Khmer Art. Dedicated to Vishnu, the temple consists of a three-storied rectangular pyramid surmounted by 5 main towers over 200 ft. high, the entire complex being enclosed by a rectangular moated wall 6,000 yds. in perimeter. Begun in 9th cent. as Yasodharapura, the Angkor complex was completed in 12th cent. with the erection of Angkor Wat. Raided (1178) by the Chams and (1357 and 1404) by the Thai, it was abandoned 1443 in favor of Pnompenh. The ruins were discovered (1860) in thick jungle, cleared after 1908 and converted into a park.

Anglais, Les (lāz äglā'), village (1950 census pop. 1,052), Sud dept., SW Haiti, on SW coast of Tiburon Peninsula, 33 mi. W of Les Cayes; banana growing.

Ang-la-ling Hu, Tibet: see NGANGLARING TSO.

Angle Inlet, Minn.: see LAKE OF THE WOODS, lake.

Anglès (äglĕ'), village (pop. 340), Tarn dept., S France, 16 mi. ESE of Castres; stock raising.

Anglés (äng-glās'), town (pop. 2,477), Gerona prov., NE Spain, 10 mi. WSW of Gerona; agr. and stock-raising center; lumbering.

Anglesey or **Anglesea** (both: ăng'gŭlsē), island and county (□ 275.1; 1931 pop. 49,029; 1951 census 50,637), in Irish Sea, NW Wales, separated from mainland (Caernarvon) by narrow Menai Strait; c.20 mi. N-S, c.25 mi. E-W; ⊙ HOLYHEAD. Co. includes HOLY ISLAND. Surface is flat and low; agr., sheep raising, fishing, woolen milling are chief industries. Holyhead is port on main route from London to Ireland; other towns are Amlwch, Beaumaris, Menai Bridge. Two bridges link isl. with mainland. Anglesey has played part in most phases of British history and was known to the Romans (often identified with *Mona*); it was finally subdued by Edward I.

Anglesola (äng-gläsō'lä), town (pop. 1,956), Lérida prov., NE Spain, 10 mi. W of Cervera, near Urgel Canal, in irrigated agr. area; sawmilling; trades in cereals, wine, olive oil.

Anglet (äglā'), W suburb (pop. 942) of Bayonne, Basses-Pyrénées dept., SW France, connecting Bayonne and Biarritz; woodworking, cellulose mfg. Airport.

Angleton (ăng'gŭltŭn), city (pop. 3,399), ⊙ Brazoria co., S Texas, c.40 mi. S of Houston; rail shipping center in oil-producing and agr. area (cotton, rice, cattle, truck); cotton and moss gins, fig-processing plant. Settled 1896, inc. 1912.

Angleur (äglûr'), town (pop. 10,645), Liége prov., E Belgium, at confluence of Vesdre R. and Ourthe R., 2 mi. SE of Liége; rail junction; blast furnaces; zinc mining.

Anglia: see ENGLAND.

Angliers (äng-glēā'), village (pop. estimate 250), W Que., on L. des Quinze, at head of Rapide des Quinze, short torrential stream, 20 mi. ENE of Haileybury; hydroelectric power center, supplying Rouyn-Noranda mining region.

Anglo-Egyptian Sudan (sōōdăn'), territory (□ 967,-500; 1948 pop. estimate 8,053,669), NE Africa, a condominium under joint Egyptian and Br. rule; ⊙ KHARTOUM. Bounded N by Egypt, NW by Libya, W by Fr. Equatorial Africa, S by Belgian Congo, Uganda, and Kenya, and E by Ethiopia and Eritrea. In NE there is a 500-mi. frontage on the Red Sea. Extending over 1,250 mi. N-S from 22°N to 4°N, it lies in the vast plain of aggradation built up by the Nile system. Aside from a few isolated heights in center (Nuba Mts.), mts. are found only along territory's periphery: Ethiopian highlands (E), Etbai range (NE, along Red Sea coast), Marra Mts. (W, along Nile-Chad watershed), and Imatong Mts. (S, at edge of E African highlands). Climate and vegetation reflect the transition typical of the SUDAN. In S, annual rainfall reaches 50 in.; length of rainy season (summer) and amount of precipitation decrease northward; N of 18°N rainfall is negligible; here the Libyan and Nubian deserts flank the Nile valley. Vegetation ranges from park savanna and patches of tropical forest in S to low grass, scrub, and xerophytic desert plants in N. The Nile system is the country's principal physiographic feature and transport artery. The Albert Nile, here called BAHR EL JEBEL enters the Sudan at NIMULE, traverses the marshy SUDD region and unites with the BAHR EL GHAZAL to form the WHITE NILE. At Khartoum, the latter joins the BLUE NILE (which emerges from Ethiopian highland), and the main Nile continues northward, describing a huge S-curve below Atbara, to the Egyptian border at WADI HALFA. Two important right tributaries, the Sobat and the Atbara, contribute greatly to the Nile's volume. Agr. in well-watered S is negligible because of region's backwardness and poor drainage. Farther N irrigation is necessary; the GEZIRA above Khartoum (watered from SENNAR dam), and the KASSALA and TOKAR areas are therefore the only regions of commercial agr. Here long-staple cotton (chief export crop) and a variety of food crops are grown. Cotton is also cultivated in narrow strips along the main Nile. Elsewhere natives grow durra, peanuts, corn, and oilseeds. Semi-arid Kordofan prov. (center) supplies most of the world's gum arabic, gathered from wild acacias. Livestock raising, chiefly nomadic, is the occupation of majority of pop. Gold deposits are worked at Gebeit (near Red Sea) and salt is produced at Port Sudan. Railroads (c.2,000 mi.) link principal towns and supplement river navigation. Khartoum, North Khartoum, and OMDURMAN, at hub of communications, are connected with El OBEID (gum arabic and oilseed center), Sennar, Kassala, and PORT SUDAN (through which cotton, gum arabic, hides, and skins are exported). A railroad also parallels the Nile northward and by-passes the river's great bend to Wadi Halfa. Both Nile branches are navigable above Khartoum, the White Nile to Juba, the Bahr el Ghazal to Wau, and the Blue Nile to Roseires. Below Khartoum are 5 cataracts, but a stretch bet. Merowe and Kerma is also navigable. Situated astride the Cape-to-Cairo air route, Anglo-Egyptian Sudan has airfields at Wadi Halfa, Dongola, Khartoum, El Obeid, Malakal, and Juba. An important cultural boundary running approximately along 11°N separates Arabic-speaking N Sudan (peopled largely by Moslem whites) from the predominantly negroid S, where pagan tribes (Dinka, Nuer, Shilluks) preserve numerous distinct languages and dialects. The territory's early history is associated with that of NUBIA (N Sudan). Unification in 19th cent. began with conquest (1820–22) by Mohammed Ali. He was followed in 1870s by Sir Samuel Baker and Charles Gordon (both in Egyptian service) who suppressed slave trade and established military posts on the upper Nile. The Mahdist revolt (1881–98), in which the Mahdis gained the victory at Khartoum (1885), resulted in evacuation of Egyptian forces. The rule of the dervishes was brought to an end in 1898 by Lord Kitchener's victory near Omdurman. Joint Br. and Egyptian administration was established in 1899 after Fr. claims to S Sudan were settled as a result of the Fashoda incident (see KODOK). The condominium was reaffirmed by Anglo-Egyptian treaty of 1936. During Second World War, territory was briefly invaded (1940–41) by Italians from Eritrea. It is administered by a governor-general appointed by Egypt with assent of Great Britain. A predominantly elective legislative assembly and an executive council (at least ½ Sudanese) were established in 1948. Anglo-Egyptian Sudan is divided for administration into 9 provs.: BAHR EL GHAZAL, BLUE NILE, DARFUR, EQUATORIA, KASSALA, KHARTOUM, KORDOFAN, NORTHERN, and UPPER NILE.

Anglure (äglür'), village (pop. 618), Marne dept., N France, on the Aube and 6 mi. NE of Romilly-sur-Seine; flour milling, cheese mfg.

Angmagssalik (ängmäkh'shälĭk), settlement (dist. pop. 1,121), SE Greenland, on S coast of Angmagssalik Isl. (25 mi. long, 12–20 mi. wide); 65°36'N 37°36'W. Fishing (salmon, Greenland shark) and hunting (polar bear). Meteorological and radio station. Has old-age home. Founded 1894. Here in 1472 or 1473 landed the 1st Europeans to arrive in Greenland after early Middle Ages. The isl. rises to 4,336 ft.

Ango (äng'gō), village, Eastern Prov., N Belgian Congo, on a tributary of Uele R. and 115 mi. NE of Buta; cotton ginning. R.C. mission.

Ango-Ango (äng'gō-äng'gō), village, Leopoldville prov., W Belgian Congo, on left bank of Congo R., adjacent to Nóqui (Angola) and 4 mi. SW of Matadi; liquid-fuels port (storage tanks), linked by rail with Matadi and by pipe line with Leopoldville.

Angoche, Mozambique: see ANTÓNIO ENES.

Angol (äng-gōl'), town (pop. 12,398), ⊙ Malleco prov. and Angol dept. (□ 1,083; pop. 52,535), S central Chile, on Rehue R. near its junction with Malleco R., on railroad and 70 mi. SSE of Concepción, 320 mi. SSW of Santiago; 37°48'S 72°43'W. Fruitgrowing center (chiefly apples); also wheat, barley, wine; cattle. Flour milling, brewing, tanning, lumbering. The town, a former outpost against Araucanian Indians, was founded 1862.

Angola (ăng-gō'lŭ) or **Portuguese West Africa**, Port. colony (□ 481,351; 1940 pop. 3,738,010), SW Africa, on the Atlantic S of Gulf of Guinea; ⊙ Luanda. CABINDA exclave, N of Congo estuary, is part of Angola. Bounded by Belgian Congo (N and E), Northern Rhodesia (E), South-West Africa (S). Its 1,000-mi.-long Atlantic coast line extends from 6°S (mouth of Congo R.) to 17°S (mouth of Cunene R.); territory attains greatest width (over 700 mi.) bet. Lobito (13°30'E) and Northern Rhodesia border (24°E). Physiographically, Angola consists of a coastal lowland (60 mi. wide in N; less than 20 mi. wide in S), and of a vast dissected tableland (average alt. 6,000 ft.) rising abruptly from the coastal strip, then sloping gently E toward the Congo and Zambezi basins. This central plateau (called Bié Plateau in high section near Nova Lisboa), is one of Africa's major watersheds. From it the Congo's left tributaries (Kwango, Kwilu, Kasai) flow N, the upper Zambezi's right tributaries (Lungwebungu, Luanginga) flow E, the Kwando and Okovanggo drain SE into N Bechuanaland's interior basins, and several shorter streams (Cuanza, Cunene) empty directly into the Atlantic. Coastal region N of Lobito has unhealthful tropical climate (mean annual temp. 75°–80°F.); further S, the heat is tempered by cold Benguela Current offshore, which however prevents rainfall from reaching coast. The more salubrious upland (mean annual temp. 65°–70°F.) receives up to 60 in. of precipitation (Sept.–April). Commercial agr. is limited to tropical lowland plantations yielding sugar, cacao (especially in Cabinda dist.), and cotton, and to European enterprises on central plateau which produce coffee, sisal, and beeswax for export. Subsistence crops (manioc, beans, rice) and corn are grown chiefly by natives, who also gather wild rubber, sesame, and palm products for export. Cattle is increasingly raised in plateau sections not threatened by tse-tse fly. Of Angola's mineral deposits (copper in Bembe area, iron, lignite), only diamonds are commercially exploited, in Chicapa valley (Lunda dist.) of NE Angola. Railroad construction is important factor in development of extensive interior. Two short lines (Luanda-Malange in N, Mossâmedes-Sá da Bandeira in S) tap coast's immediate hinterland, while the Benguela RR (completed 1929 in Angola) traverses colony's entire width from Lobito on the Atlantic to copper-rich Katanga prov. of Belgian Congo. New roads radiate from larger towns along railroad. Airlines link coastal cities with Fr. Equatorial Africa, Belgian Congo, and Northern Rhodesia. W Africa's coast has few natural harbors; one of the best, sheltered by an elongated sandspit, is LOBITO, Angola's chief port. Other Angola ports, mostly open roadsteads, are (N-S): Santo António do Zaire, Ambrizete, Ambriz, LUANDA, Pôrto Amboim, Novo Redondo, BENGUELA, and Mossâmedes. Principal centers of the interior are Nova Lisboa (laid out as future ⊙ Angola), Sá da Bandeira, Malange, Silva Pôrto, Uíge. Agr. processing is chief industry. Fishing, fish preserving, and salt panning are carried on in coastal towns. There are tobacco factories, sawmills, potteries, and brickworks, and modern railroad shops (at Nova Lisboa). The great majority of Angola's pop. are natives of Bantu stock, with several tribes of Bushmen in SE. European pop. (1940) was 44,000. Angola's N coast was discovered 1482 by Port. navigator Diogo Cão, and several points were occupied after 1505. Luanda was founded 1575. Occupied by Dutch 1641–48. Colony's prosperity in 17th–19th cent. depended on lucrative slave trade with Brazil. Angola's frontiers are result of several agreements with France (1886), Germany (for South-West Africa border, 1886), England (1891), Belgian Congo (1927). A governor-general resides at Luanda. In 1946 the colony was administratively divided into 5 provinces (Congo, Malange, Benguela, Bié, Huíla) and 16 dists.

Angola (ăng-gō'lù, ăn"–). **1** Resort city (pop. 5,081), ⊙ Steuben co., extreme NE Ind., 40 mi. N of Fort Wayne, in hilly lake region; agr., and some mfg. (feed, brick, tile, flour, condensed milk, automobile and aircraft parts). Tri-State Col. (coeducational) is here. Pokagon State Park is near by. **2** Village (pop. 1,936), Erie co., W N.Y., near L. Erie, 20 mi. SSW of Buffalo; summer resort; mfg. (machinery, wood containers, canned foods). Inc. 1873.

Angola Swamp, N.C.: see HOLLY SHELTER SWAMP.

Angoon (ăn-gōōn'), village (pop. 410), SE Alaska, on W coast of Admiralty Isl., on Chatham Strait at mouth of Hood Bay, 65 mi. S of Juneau; fishing; cannery.

Angora, Turkey: see ANKARA.

Angostura (äng-gōstōō'rä), railroad station, Cochabamba dept., central Bolivia, on Cochabamba-Arani RR and 12 mi. SE of Cochabamba. Tamborada R. (branch of Rocha R.) here crossed by Angostura Dam.

Angostura, town (pop. 1,704), Antioquia dept., NW central Colombia, in Cordillera Central, 45 mi. NNE of Medellín; alt. 5,371 ft. Agr. region (coffee, sugar cane, yucca, bananas, cattle, hogs); forest products (timber, resins); mfg. of methylated alcohol, dairying.

Angostura, town (pop. 1,241), Sinaloa, NW Mexico, on Mocorito R., in Gulf of California lowland, and 60 mi. NW of Culiacán; chick-peas, sugar, corn, tomatoes, fruit.

Angostura, Venezuela: see CIUDAD BOLÍVAR.

Angostura, La. 1 Village, Neuquén natl. territory, Argentina: see VILLA LA ANGOSTURA. **2** Village, Río Negro natl. territory, Argentina: see LA ANGOSTURA.

Angostura Dam, S.Dak.: see CHEYENNE RIVER.

Angoulême (ãgōōlĕm'), city (pop. 39,987), ⊙ Charente dept., W France, atop rocky limestone promontory (240 ft. high) overlooking Charente R. and 65 mi. NNE of Bordeaux; communications and paper-milling center; brandy distilleries, natl. explosives factory; mfg. of small motors, electrical equipment, felt slippers, hosiery, fertilizer; brewing, mushroom preserving, printing. Has restored Romanesque cathedral and medieval ramparts. Of pre-Roman origin and early episcopal see, it became (9th cent.) seat of counts of Angoumois, vassals of dukes of Aquitaine. Recovered from England in 1373, it became an appanage of Orléans-Angoulême branch of house of Valois. Francis I made Angoulême a titular duchy. Margaret of Valois b. here.

Angoumois (ãgōōmwä'), region and former province, W France, now occupying most of Charente and part of Dordogne depts.; old ⊙ Angoulême. Cattle and poultry raising in NE; winegrowing along Charente R. Famous brandy distilled in Cognac area. Ruled by counts of Angoulême, the last of whom, upon becoming king of France in 1515 as Francis I, incorporated it into royal domain.

Angra de Cintra (äng'grä dā sēn'trä), bay on Atlantic coast of Río de Oro, Sp. West Africa, 50 mi. SSW of Villa Cisneros; 5 mi. long, 12 mi. wide. Entrance obstructed by reefs. Uninhabited desert shore. Also called Bahia de Cintra.

Angra do Heroísmo (äng'grù dōō ĭrwēz'mōō), district (□ 268; pop. 78,109) of the central Azores, covering TERCEIRA ISLAND, GRACIOSA ISLAND, and SÃO JORGE ISLAND; ⊙ Angra do Heroísmo (on Terceira).

Angra do Heroísmo, city (pop. 9,435), ⊙ Angra do Heroísmo dist., central Azores, on S shore of TERCEIRA ISLAND, 100 mi. NW of Ponta Delgada (on São Miguel Isl.); 38°39'N 27°13'W. Seaport, exporting wine, pineapples, dairy products; fish canning, embroidering, tanning, tobacco processing. Episcopal see with 16th-cent. cathedral. The 17th-cent. castle of St. John the Baptist overlooks city. Founded 1534. Resisted Sp. invasions in late 16th cent. Administrative ⊙ Azores until 1832.

Angra dos Reis (äng'grù dōōs rās'), city (pop. 4,622), SW Rio de Janeiro state, Brazil, fishing port on Ilha Grande Bay of the Atlantic, 70 mi. W of Rio; terminus of branch railroad; rum distilling, flour milling, fish processing, mfg. of caustic soda. Exports coffee and minerals (shipped here from Minas Gerais). City preserves Portuguese-colonial aspect; has ruined monastery and 17th-cent. baroque church of Our Lady of Carmo.

Angra Pequena, South-West Africa: see LÜDERITZ.

Angre (ã'grù), village (pop. 1,094), Hainaut prov., SW Belgium, 13 mi. WSW of Mons, near Fr. border; chicory.

Angren (ŭn-gryĕn'), city (1948 pop. over 10,000), NE Tashkent oblast, Uzbek SSR, on Angren R. and 45 mi. ESE of Tashkent (linked by railroad); 41°N 70°7'E. Major coal-mining center of Soviet Central Asia; ceramic industry; coal-gas plant (pipe line to Tashkent). Developed in Second World War on site of small village of Dzhigiristan; became city in 1946. Large-scale production began in 1947.

Angren River, Tashkent oblast, Uzbek SSR, rises in Chatkal Range, flows c.130 mi. W, past Angren coal mines, Ak-Kurgan, and Soldatskoye, to the Syr Darya 10 mi. SSE of Chinaz.

Angrezabad, India: see ENGLISH BAZAR.

Angri (äng'grē), town (pop. 11,851), Salerno prov., Campania, S Italy, 11 mi. WNW of Salerno; cotton milling, tomato canning, mfg. of vegetable oils.

Angshui, China: see SANSUI.

Angtassom (ängtäsôm'), town, Takeo prov., SW Cambodia, 40 mi. SSW of Pnompenh, on road.

Angthong (ängtông'), town (1947 pop. 8,527), ⊙ Angthong prov. (□ 414; 1947 pop. 150,304), S Thailand, on Chao Phraya R. and 55 mi. N of Bangkok; trade center; rice, corn. Sometimes spelled Angtong.

Anguiano (äng-gēä'nō), town (pop. 1,122), Logroño prov., N Spain, 22 mi. SW of Logroño; flour mills; cereals, nuts, livestock, lumber; trout fishing.

Anguiatú (äng-gēätōō'). **1** Village (pop. 155), Chiquimula dept., E Guatemala, on Salvador border, 6 mi. S of Concepción; corn, wheat. **2** Rail frontier station, Jutiapa dept., SE Guatemala, 7 mi. E of Asunción Mita, NNW of L. Güija.

Anguil (äng-gēl'), town (pop. estimate 1,000), E central La Pampa natl. territory, Argentina, on railroad and 17 mi. ENE of Santa Rosa; grain, livestock center; dairying.

Anguilla (ăng-gwĭ'lù), coral island (□ 35; pop. 5,037), dependency of St. Kitts-Nevis presidency, Leeward Isls., B.W.I., just N of St. Martin and 55 mi. NNW of St. Kitts; 18°15'N 63°10'W; 16 mi. long, 3 mi. wide; flanked by many islets. Healthy climate, though water is scarce. Main products: sea-island cotton, salt; also livestock, coconuts, sisal. Discovered 1493 by Columbus, it was colonized by the British in 1650.

Anguilla, town (pop. 601), Sharkey co., W Miss., 33 mi. SSE of Greenville.

Anguillara Sabazia (äng-gwēl-lä'rä säbät'syä), village (pop. 1,849), Roma prov., Latium, central Italy, on SE shore of L. Bracciano, 18 mi. NW of Rome. Has castle.

Anguillara Veneta (vā'nĕtä), village (pop. 2,648), Padova prov., Veneto, N Italy, on Adige R. and 7 mi. NE of Rovigo.

Anguille, Cape (ăng-gwĭl', ăng'gĭl', ăng'gwĭl), westernmost point of Newfoundland, 24 mi. NW of Port aux Basques, 47°54'N 59°27'W.

Anguille Mountains, range in SW N.F., extending 40 mi. NE from Cape Anguille along St. George Bay; rises to 1,759 ft.

Anguita (äng-gē'tä), village (pop. 721), Guadalajara prov., central Spain, on Tajuña R. and 15 mi. E of Sigüenza; cereals, vegetables, livestock. Timber, naval stores.

Angul (ŭng'gōōl), former district of Bihar and Orissa prov., India; ⊙ was Angul. Comprised 2 detached sections, N and S of Mahanadi R. After creation in 1936 of separate Orissa prov., S subdivision (□ 800; pop. 86,779) was inc. into Ganjam dist. and in 1949 transferred to newly-created Baudh dist., while N subdivision (□ 881; pop. 165,856) was inc. into Cuttack dist. and in 1949 transferred to newly-created Dhenkanal dist.

Angul, village, Dhenkanal dist., central Orissa, India, 35 mi. WNW of Dhenkanal; market center (rice, tobacco, timber); biri mfg., hand-loom weaving, basket making. Was ⊙ former Angul dist.

Angumu (äng-gōō'mōō), village, Eastern Prov., E Belgian Congo, 150 mi. ESE of Stanleyville; gold-mining center.

Angus (ăng'gùs), village (pop. estimate 400), S Ont., near Nottawasaga R., 11 mi. WSW of Barrie; dairying, mixed farming.

Angus (ăng'gùs), formerly **Forfar** (fôr'fùr) or **Forfarshire** (–shĭr), county (□ 873.5; 1931 pop. 270,190; 1951 census 274,870), E Scotland; ⊙ Forfar. Bounded by Firth of Tay (S), Perthshire (W), Aberdeen (N), Kincardine (NE), and the North Sea (E). Drained by North Esk, South Esk, and Isla rivers. Surface is wild, picturesque, and mountainous in SW (Sidlaw Hills) and NW (Grampian Mts.), separated by the fertile Strathmore valley. Farming, stock raising, and fishing are carried on. Co. is noted for its granite and building stone; jute milling is important (Dundee). Other industries are shipbuilding, iron founding, mfg. of food products and textiles. Dundee is largest city. Forfar has jute and linen mills. Other towns are Arbroath, Montrose, Brechin (with cathedral), Monifieth, and Kirriemuir. Co. was part of S Pictavia. Glamis Castle figures in *Macbeth.*

Angus, village (pop. 34), Nuckolls co., S Nebr., 5 mi. NNE of Nelson and on Little Blue R.

Angwin, Calif.: see SAINT HELENA.

Anhai (än'hī'), town, SE Fukien prov., China, minor port on Formosa Strait, 20 mi. SSW of Tsinkiang; handles most of Tsinkiang's maritime trade.

Anhalt (än'hält), former state (□ 898; 1939 pop. 432,289), central Germany, after 1945 included in SAXONY-ANHALT; ⊙ was Dessau. Formed almost complete enclave in former Prussian Saxony prov., bordered (E) by Brandenburg. Level region except for outliers of lower Harz (W); drained by the Elbe. Until 1918, Anhalt was ruled by one of the most anc. houses of Germany, descending from a son of Albert the Bear. Divided most of the time into several principalities ruled by the various branches of the family. United (1863) into single duchy; joined German Empire in 1871. Became republic in 1918 and joined Weimar Republic. Catherine II of Russia was a princess of Anhalt-Zerbst.

Anhanga (ănyăng'gù), city (pop. 581), E Pará, Brazil, on Belém-Bragança RR and 50 mi. NE of Belém.

Anhée (ănā'), village (pop. 1,322), Namur prov., S Belgium, on Meuse R. and 4 mi. NNW of Dinant; marble quarrying.

Anhembi, Brazil: see PIRAMBÓIA.

Anhialo, Bulgaria: see POMORIYE.

Anhilvada, India: see PATAN, Mehsana dist., Bombay.

Anhoa (än'hwä'), town, Mytho prov., S Vietnam, 8 mi. SE of Mytho, across Mekong R. delta arm; rice, sericulture.

Anholt (än'hôlt), island (□ 8.4; pop. 218), Denmark, in the Kattegat, 30 mi. NE of Djursland, Jutland; 6 mi. long, 2.5 mi. wide. In W are low hills.

Anholt (än'hôlt), town (pop. 2,012), in former Prussian prov. of Westphalia, NW Germany, after 1945 in North Rhine-Westphalia, on Issel R. and 8 mi. W of Bocholt, near Dutch border; cattle.

An-hsi, China: see ANSI, Kansu prov.

An-hsiang, China: see ANSIANG.

Anhsien (än'shyĕn'), town (pop. 22,043), ⊙ Anhsien co. (pop. 243,147), NW Szechwan prov., China, 50 mi. NW of Santai; paper milling, tea and medicinal-herbs processing. Agr: rice, millet, wheat, sweet potatoes, rapeseed.

An-hsin, China: see ANSIN.

An-hua, China: see ANHWA.

An-hui, China: see ANHWEI.

Anhwa or **An-hua** (both: än'hwä'). **1** Town, ⊙ Anhwa co. (pop. 632,891), N central Hunan prov., China, 80 mi. W of Changsha, in antimony-mining region; tea-processing center. **2** Town, Kwangsi prov., China: see IPEH. **3** Town, Kweichow prov., China: see TEHKIANG.

Anhwei or **An-hui** (both: än'hwā'), province (□ 54,000; pop. 25,000,000) of E China; divided administratively after 1949 into North Anhwei [Chinese *Hwanpeh* or *Hwanpei*] (□ 40,000; pop. 21,000,000; ⊙ Hofei) and South Anhwei [Chinese *Hwannan*] (□ 14,000; pop. 4,000,000; ⊙ Wuhu), respectively N and S of Yangtze R. Bounded N by Shantung and Pingyuan, W by Honan and Hupeh, S by Kiangsi, SE by Chekiang, and E by Kiangsu, Anhwei is a zone of transition bet. the S Yangtze hills and the N China plain and, as a result, falls into N and S zones, distinct in nearly every respect. Hills predominate S of the Yangtze, rising to 8,694 ft. in the Hwang Mts.; N of the Yangtze are the Tapieh Mts. along the Hupeh line and the low Hwan Mts. along the Yangtze-Hwai divide. Elsewhere, alluvial lowlands studded with lakes prevail in the Yangtze valley (S center), and especially on the Hwai plain (N). The climate in the S hills and valleys is generally mild, with hot, wet summers. The N plain, however, is exposed to cold W winds and receives little rain. These climatic differences are reflected in agr. land use. Rice, cotton, ramie, and silk are produced in S, while N production is restricted largely to wheat, beans, and various millets. Anhwei produces about 60% of China's tea, which is grown in the Tunki-Kimen area (S; known for the Keemun variety) and in the Liuan area (N; known for the sunglo leaf). Pine forests in S hills furnish India ink (Siuning), a traditional local product. Among mineral resources, coal is mined at Suhsien, Shunkengshan (SW of Pengpu), and near Ningkwo; iron at Tayao Shan (near Tangtu) and Taochung, and copper at Tungling. The leading industrial centers are Pengpu (N) and Wuhu (S); other important cities are Hofei, Anking (the historical ⊙), and the tea center of Tunki. In addition to the E-W navigation routes of Yangtze (ocean-going vessels) and Hwai rivers, the prov. is served by Nanking-Wuhu-Kiangsi railroad (S) and by the Hwainan (Tienkiaan-Yüki) and Tientsin-Pukow lines (N). Anhwei's Chinese pop. speaks primarily the Lower Yangtze Mandarin in a broad belt on both sides of the stream and N Mandarin on Hwai R. plain. The isolated Hweichow dialect is spoken in the Sihsien-Tunki hill area on the Kiangsi-Chekiang line. Originally part of the anc. prov. of Kiangnan, Anhwei (named for the cities of Anking and Hweichow) was separated (1667) from it under the Manchu dynasty. It was occupied (1938–45) by the Japanese during Second World War. Prov. passed 1949 to the Chinese Communists, who divided it into 2 administrative regions. Anhwei's traditional name is Hwan or Huan.

Ani (än'yē'). **1** Town (pop. 7,798), ⊙ Ani co. (pop. 66,181), NW Kiangsi prov., China, 18 mi. NW of Nanchang; rice, cotton, wheat, beans. **2** Town, Shansi prov., China: see ANYI.

Ani (ä'nē, änē'), town (pop. 399), Kars prov., NE Turkey, 25 mi. E of Kars, near the Arpa-Chai (USSR line). Here are ruins of the anc. city of Ani, the ⊙ of medieval Armenia; it was often besieged by Turks, Georgians, and Mongols, and was finally destroyed by earthquake in 17th cent. Notable are ruins of a cathedral and several churches (11th–13th cent.), and remnants of double walls.

Ani, Armenian SSR: see ANI-PEMZA.

Aniai (ä"nē'ī), town (pop. 5,450), Akita prefecture, N Honshu, Japan, 25 mi. NE of Akita; agr., lumbering; mining (gold, copper).

Aniak (ă'nēăk), village (pop. 145), W Alaska, on Kuskokwim R. at mouth of Aniak R., and 100 mi. NE of Bethel; 61°45'N 159°40'W; trapping and fur trading; supply point for prospectors. Airfield, radio station.

Aniakchak Crater (ănēăk'chăk), SW Alaska, on Alaska Peninsula, 40 mi. N of Chignik; 56°54'N 158°8'W; active volcano (4,420 ft.) with crater 6 mi. in diameter. Discovered 1923; believed to be extinct until it erupted May 1, 1931.

Aniak River, W Alaska, rises near 60°21'N 159°13'W, flows 100 mi. N to Kuskokwim R. at Aniak.

Aniane (änyän'), village (pop. 1,679), Hérault dept., S France, near the Hérault, 15 mi. WNW of Montpellier; distilling, olive preserving.

Aniche (änēsh'), town (pop. 8,277), Nord dept., N France, 8 mi. ESE of Douai; coal-mining center; glassworks. Briquet mfg.

Anicuns (änēkōōns'), city (pop. 1,335), S Goiás, central Brazil, 40 mi. NW of Goiânia; ships hides, tobacco. Gold and mica deposits.

Anidhros, Greece: see ANYDROS.

Anié (änē'ā), village, S Fr. Togoland, on right bank of Anié R. (right arm of Mono), on railroad and 15 mi. N of Atakpamé; cotton center.

Anie, Pic d' (pēk' dänē'), summit (8,215 ft.) in W Pyrenees, SW France, near Sp. border, 6 mi. WSW of Accous.

Aniene River (änyā'nē), anc. *Anio*, Latium, central Italy, rises in the Apennines 10 mi. SW of Avezzano, flows NW past Subiaco, SW past Tivoli, and W to the Tiber just above Rome; 61 mi. long. Has furnished water to Rome since anc. times; now also used for hydroelectric power (Castel Madama, Tivoli). Below Tivoli, where it forms a noted waterfall, also called Teverone River.

Anif (ä'nēf), village (pop. 2,158), Salzburg, W central Austria, 4 mi. S of Salzburg. Near by is Hellbrunn château (1613–15) with fine fountains.

Anikshchyai, Lithuania: see ANYKSCIAI.

Animas, Chile: see LAS ANIMAS.

Animas, Cerro (sĕ'rō ä'nēmäs), Andean peak (13,917 ft.), SW Colombia, in Cordillera Central, 40 mi. NE of Pasto.

Animas, Sierra de las (syĕ'rä dā läs), hilly range (12 mi. long), Maldonado dept., S Uruguay, 45 mi. E of Montevideo. Mirador Nacional mtn. (1,644 ft.) is highest point in Uruguay.

Animas City (ă'nĭmŭs), town (1940 pop. 712), La Plata co., SW Colo., on Animas R., in W foothills of San Juan Mts., just N of Durango, in livestock and farming region; alt. 6,500 ft. Gold, silver, coal mines near by.

Animas River, SW Colo. and NW N.Mex., rises in several branches in San Juan Mts. N of Silverton, Colo.; flows c.110 mi. S, past Animas City and Durango, and SW to San Juan R. at Farmington, N.Mex. Hydroelectric plant 20 mi. N of Durango.

Anina, Rumania: see STEIERDORFANINA.

Aniñón (änēnyōn'), village (pop. 1,768), Saragossa prov., NE Spain, 8 mi. NNW of Calatayud, in olive- and winegrowing area; sheep raising.

Anio, Italy: see ANIENE RIVER.

Ani-Pemza (ä"nyē-pyĕm'zŭ), town (1932 pop. estimate 1,060), NW Armenian SSR, on the Western Arpa-Chai (Turkish border) and 25 mi. SSW of Leninakan, on short rail spur; pumice [Rus. *pemza*] quarries. Near by are ruins of Ani, ⊙ Bagratide kingdom of Armenia (10th cent.); sacked (1064) by Seljuk Turks; deserted since 1319 earthquake.

Anir, Bismarck Archipelago: see FENI ISLANDS.

Anisakan (ŭnē'sŭkän'), village, Mandalay dist., Upper Burma, on railroad and 20 mi. E of Mandalay.

Anita (ŭnē'tŭ), town (pop. 1,112), Cass co., SW Iowa, 13 mi. E of Atlantic, in livestock and grain area. Platted 1869, inc. 1875.

Aniva (ŭnyē'vŭ), city (1940 pop. 7,404), S Sakhalin, Russian SFSR, minor port on Aniva Gulf, 18 mi. SSW of Yuzhno-Sakhalinsk, in agr. area; a S terminus of E coast railroad; fish canning, sawmilling. Under Jap. rule (1905–45), called Rutaka (rōō"tä'kä).

Aniva, Cape, Jap. *Naka-shiretoko-misaki* (nä'kä shērā'tō'kō mēsä'kē), S extremity of Sakhalin, Russian SFSR, on E side of Aniva Gulf; 46°1'N 143°25'E.

Aniva Gulf, Jap. *Aniwa-wan* (änē'wä-wän), inlet of Sea of Okhotsk on S coast of Sakhalin, Russian SFSR, bet. capes Aniva (E) and Crillon (W); 65 mi. wide, 50 mi. long. Chief port, Korsakov.

Anivorano or **Anivorano-du-Sud** (änēvōōrä'nōō-dü-süd'), town, Tamatave prov., E central Madagascar, on railroad and 50 mi. SSW of Tamatave; graphite and gold mining, stone quarrying, coffee plantations; mfg. of carbonated drinks.

Aniwa (ä'nēwä'), small coral island (pop. 186), New Hebrides, SW Pacific, 15 mi. E of Tanna; 7 mi. long, 2 mi. wide.

Aniwa (ă'nŭwä), village (pop. 257), Shawano co., E central Wis., 21 mi. ENE of Wausau; dairying.

Aniwa-wan, Russian SFSR: see ANIVA GULF.

Anizy-le-Château (änēzē'-lù-shätō'), village (pop. 960), Aisne dept., N France, on Ailette R. and Oise-Aisne Canal, and 9 mi. WSW of Laon; metalworks; sugar-beet growing.

Anja (änzhä'), Saharan military outpost, Agadir frontier region, southwesternmost Fr. Morocco, near Ifni enclave (Spanish), 35 mi. S of Tiznit; 29°12'N 9°51'W. Also Aneja.

Anjad (ŭn'jŭd), town (pop. 6,594), SW Madhya Bharat, India, 10 mi. E of Barwani, in Narbada R. valley; markets cotton, millet, wheat, rice; cotton ginning, hand-loom weaving. Sometimes called Anjar.

Anjala (än'yälä), village (commune pop. 5,004), Kymi co., SE Finland, on Kymi R. (rapids) and 16 mi. NNW of Kotka; pulp and paper mills; hydroelectric station.

Anjangaon (ŭn'jŭngoun), town (pop. 17,797), Amraoti dist., W Madhya Pradesh, India, 35 mi. NW of Amraoti, in major cotton-growing tract; millet, wheat, oilseeds; cotton ginning.

Anjar (ŭnjär'). **1** Town (pop., including suburban area, 16,773), S Cutch, India, 25 mi. SE of Bhuj; rail junction; trade center (wheat, cotton, barley); cotton ginning and milling, embroidering, match mfg. **2** Town, SW Madhya Bharat, India: see ANJAD.

Anjen (än'rŭn'). **1** Town, ⊙ Anjen co. (pop. 142,175), SE Hunan prov., China, 40 mi. ESE of Hengyang; rice-growing center. Graphite mining (W). **2** Town, Kiangsi prov., China: see YÜKIANG.

Anjengo (ŭnjĕng'gō), village (pop. 4,963), SW Travancore, India, on Arabian Sea, 18 mi. NW of Trivandrum; coir rope and mats; fishing. One of earliest (1684) English trading stations in India. With the village of Tangasseri (pop. 2,201), 20 mi. NW, Anjengo was administered by Malabar dist. (Madras) until 1906, when it passed to Travancore; later (1927–49) temporarily under Tinnevelly dist. (Madras).

Anjidiv Island, Portuguese India: see ANGEDIVA ISLAND.

Anjiro or **Anjiro-Sabotsy** (ändzē'rōō-säbōō'tsē), town, Tamatave prov., E central Madagascar, on railroad and 30 mi. E of Tananarive; mfg. of starch and tapioca, hardwoods; lumbering. Sometimes called simply Sabotsy.

Anjo (änjō'), town (pop. 34,162), Aichi prefecture, central Honshu, Japan, 4 mi. W of Okazaki; poultry and agr. (rice, wheat, citrus fruit, pears) center; mfg. (cotton textiles, fireworks, tiles), food canning. Agr. and forestry schools.

Anjo, Korea: see ANSONG.

Anjou (ăn'jōō, Fr. äzhōō'), old province of W France now forming Maine-et-Loire and parts of adjoining depts.; ⊙ Angers. Crossed by broad valley of the Loire (Val d'Anjou) and of its tributaries, the Mayenne, Sarthe, Loir, and Thouet. Has extensive vineyards from which the renowned Vouvray and Saumur sparkling wines are made. Conquered by Caesar, Anjou fell (5th cent.) to the Franks under Clovis and became (9th cent.) a countship under Charlemagne. Often attacked by the dukes of Brittany and the Norsemen, it acquired prominence during 11th and 12th cent. under Fulk Nerra and Geoffrey Martel. Anjou then passed to England until Philip II recaptured it (1204) from John of England. In 1246 it was given in appanage to the counts of Provence. Philip VI of France reunited Anjou to the crown, made it a duchy (1360) and gave it to Louis I of Naples, his son. Finally, in 1480, under Louis XI, it was reannexed to the royal domain. It was given in appanage at various periods during 16th cent., its last duke being Francis of Alençon and Anjou. In 1790, Anjou was administratively divided into present depts.

Anjouan Island (äzhwä', änjōōän') or **Johanna Island** (jōhă'nŭ), island (□ 138; pop. c.49,000), one of 4 main isls. of Comoro Isls., in Mozambique Channel of Indian Ocean, bet. Mayotte Isl. and Grande Comore Isl., off NW Madagascar; 20 mi. long, 18 mi. wide. Picturesque isl., rising to 5,165 ft. in Mt. Tingue. Produces coffee, vanilla, copra, essential oils; also grows manioc, sweet potatoes, peanuts. Industries include sisal treating, sugar milling; handicrafts (notably doll making). Main town and port, Mutsamudu, is on NW coast. Formerly the most frequented of the Comoro Isls. and noted as a slave market, Anjouan was long subject to a strong Arab influence. Local dynasty of sultans was founded c. 1506 by Moslems from Shiraz and ruled intermittently over other Comoro Isls. Made part of Fr. protectorate 1886.

Anjou Islands, Russian SFSR: see NEW SIBERIAN ISLANDS.

Anju (än'jōō'), Jap. *Anshu*, town (1944 pop. 21,861), S.Pyongan prov., N Korea, on Chongchon R. and 40 mi. NNW of Pyongyang, in coal-mining area.

Anjum (än'yŭm), village (pop. 1,002), Friesland prov., N Netherlands, near Lauwers Zee, 6 mi. NE of Dokkum; dairying.

Anjuna (änzhōō'nŭ), town (pop. 5,688), N Goa dist., Portuguese India, 8 mi. NNW of Pangim; local market for rice, fish, coconuts.

Ankaizina (ängkäzē'nŭ), mountainous region (alt. c.3,250 ft.), N Madagascar, S of Tsaratana massif; noted for coffee plantations.

Ankang or **An-k'ang** (än'käng'), town, ⊙ Ankang co. (pop. 211,591), S Shensi prov., China, 110 mi. S of Sian and on Han R.; commercial center; exports lacquer, tung oil, paper, hides, wool, sheepskins; cotton weaving. Gold washing. Asbestos quarrying near by. Until 1913, Hingan.

Ankara (ăng'kŭrŭ, äng'–, Turk. äng'kärä"), prov. (□ 11,442; 1950 pop. 818,271), central Turkey; ⊙ Ankara. Bordered N by Koroglu Mts., E by portions of Delice and Kizil Irmak rivers, S by L. Tuz, W by Sakarya R.; drained also by Cubuk, Ankara, Kirmir, and Aladag rivers. Lignite in S, lead at Denek in SE. Rich agr. prov. (wheat, barley, rice, sugar beets, dye plants, vetch, apples, apricots, raisins). Mohair goats, sheep. It has long been known for Angora wool. Produces textiles and gum tragacanth. Formerly Angora.

Ankara, formerly known as **Angora** (ăng-gô'rŭ, ăn–), anc. *Ancyra*, city (1950 pop. 286,781), ⊙ Turkey and Ankara prov., central Anatolia, at junction of Cubuk and Ankara rivers, on railroad and c.225 mi. ESE of Istanbul; 39°55'N 32°50'E; alt. 2,910 ft. Processing and trade center for agr. region long known for its longhaired goats and production of Angora wool or mohair. Market for grain and other agr. products; makes textiles, cement, tiles, beer, vaccines, leather goods. Airport. The anc. town was an important commercial center from very early times; in 1st cent. A.D. it became ⊙ Roman prov. Galatia Prima. Flourished under Augustus, from whose reign dates the marble temple in the ruins of which was found the *Monumentum Ancyranum*, an inscription valuable as a record of Augustan history. Here in 1402 Tamerlane defeated and captured Sultan Bajazet I. Ankara declined and was a small town of no importance when, in 1920, Kemal Ataturk chose it to establish the Turkish Nationalist govt. In 1923 govt. was transferred here from Istanbul, partly so as to break with past tradition, partly because of central situation of Ankara. The city grew with amazing speed (1924 pop. c.35,000; 1927 pop. 74,553), so that today it is second in size only to Istanbul in Turkey. Except for the ruins of an ancient castle atop a high rock, it is completely modern, with impressive public buildings, wide streets, theaters, an opera, and a univ. (founded 1946 out of several faculties established in 1920s).

Ankara River, central Turkey, rises on Elma Dagi, 10 mi. SSE of Ankara, flows 85 mi. W, past Cankaya and Ankara, to Sakarya R. 20 mi. E of Mihaliccik. Receives Cubuk and Ova rivers (right).

Ankaratra Highlands (äng-kärä'trä), mountainous region (□ c.2,000), central Madagascar, extending to SW of Tananarive and NW of Antsirabe; rises to 8,552 ft. Potatoes, coffee.

Ankarsrum (äng'kärsrŭm"), village (pop. 1,677), Kalmar co., SE Sweden, 13 mi. WSW of Vastervik; ironworks, founded 1665.

Ankavandra (ängkävän'drŭ), village, Tuléar prov., W central Madagascar, 120 mi. W of Tananarive; trading center for near-by goldfields (E). Hosp., airport. Former military post.

Ankazoabo (ängkäzwä'bōō), town, Tuléar prov., SW Madagascar, 90 mi. NE of Tuléar; native market; cattle raising.

Ankazobe (ängkäzōō'bŭ), town, Tananarive prov., central Madagascar, on highway and 40 mi. NW of Tananarive; rice center. Trade school for natives.

Ankenbälli (äng'kŭnbĕ"lē), peak (11,838 ft.) in Bernese Alps, S central Switzerland, 5 mi. E of Grindelwald.

Ankeny (ăng'kŭnē), town (pop. 1,229), Polk co., central Iowa, 10 mi. N of Des Moines, in agr. area.

Anker River, Warwick, England, rises just E of Bulkington, flows 20 mi. NW, past Nuneaton, Atherstone, and Polesworth, to Tame R. at Tamworth.

Ankhe (än'khā'), town, Kontum prov., central Vietnam, in Moi Plateaus, on the upper Song Ba, 50 mi. SE of Kontum, on road from Quinhon; coffee, tea, rubber plantations; cattle raising.

Ankhialo, Bulgaria: see POMORIYE.

Ankhor or **Onkhor** (äng'kōr), village, Br. Somaliland, minor port on Gulf of Aden, 85 mi. E of Berbera; gums; fisheries; oil deposits.

Anki or **An-ch'i** (both: än'chē'), town (pop. 5,584), ⊙ Anki co. (pop. 299,418), S Fukien prov., China, 60 mi. WSW of Putien; sweet potatoes, rice, wheat, beans. Iron, lead, and coal mines near by.

Anking or **An-ch'ing** (both: än'chĭng'), formerly **Hwaining** (hwī'nĭng'), city (1932 pop. 121,379), S Anhwei prov., China, port on left bank of Yangtze R. and 150 mi. SW of Nanking; the historical ⊙ Anhwei, it was replaced (1940s) by Hofei. Trades in rice, cotton, wheat. Weaving and tanning industry. Has military acad.; mint. An old city, dating from 13th-cent. Sung dynasty. Ravaged 1852 by the Taipings. Became (1902) treaty port of call. It is ⊙ Hwaining co. (1936 pop. 663,088), and was known by that name from 1912 until it became a separate municipality in 1949.

Ankiu or **An-ch'iu** (both: än'chyō'), town, ⊙ Ankiu co. (pop. 560,374), central Shantung prov., China, 20 mi. SSE of Weifang; kaoliang, millet, peanuts.

Anklam (äng'kläm), town (pop. 19,449), in former Prussian Pomerania prov., N Germany, after 1945 in Mecklenburg, on the Peene and 45 mi. NW of Stettin; mfg. of machinery, furniture; sugar refining, metalworking, shipbuilding. During Second World War its synthetic-oil plants and aircraft works were very heavily bombed (1944–45). Aeronautical pioneer Lilienthal b. here. Has 13th–15th-cent. church, 15th-cent. town gate.

Anklesvar (ŭngklā'svŭr), town (pop. 14,187), Broach dist., N Bombay, India, near Narbada R., 4 mi. S of Broach; trade center for cotton, wheat, millet, bamboo, timber (from forests in E part of dist.); cotton ginning and weaving, soap mfg., stone cutting. Other spellings: Ankleswar, Ankleshwar.

Ankober or **Ancober** (ăngkō'bûr, Amharic äng'kōbûr), town (pop. 3,000), Shoa prov., central Ethiopia, on high escarpment overlooking Great Rift Valley, 75 mi. NE of Addis Ababa; 9°34'N 39°45'E. Founded in mid-18th cent. and former ⊙ Shoa kingdom. Until building of Djibuti–Addis Ababa railroad, served as important caravan center on route to the sea. Its flourishing trade and industries (silverworking, weaving, tanning) have since declined. Sometimes spelled Ankobar.

Ankobra River (ängkō'brä), SW Gold Coast, rises NE of Wiawso, flows c.120 mi. S, past Prestea, to Gulf of Guinea just W of Axim. Navigable by steam launches 50 mi. above mouth. Until construction (1910–11) of railroad, it was major access route to Prestea gold mines.

Ankogel (äng'kōgŭl), peak (10,705 ft.) of the Hohe Tauern, S Austria, on Carinthia-Salzburg line NW of Spittal. The Hochalmspitze (11,007 ft.) rises just SE.

Ankola (ŭngkō'lŭ), village (pop. 4,104), Kanara dist., S Bombay, India, on Arabian Sea, 16 mi. SSE of Karwar; rice, coconuts, betel nuts; handloom cotton weaving.

Ankole, district, Uganda: see MBARARA.

Ankoro (ängkō'rō), village, Katanga prov., SE Belgian Congo, on Lualaba R. opposite mouth of Luvua R. and 170 mi. WSW of Albertville; steamboat landing, trading center. R.C. mission.

Ankovo or **An'kovo** (änyŭkô'vŭ), village (1926 pop. 1,463), W Ivanovo oblast, Russian SFSR, 38 mi. WSW of Ivanovo; garment mfg.

An-kuang, Manchuria: see ANKWANG.

An-kuo, China: see ANKWO.

Ankwang or **An-kuang** (än'gwäng'), town, ⊙ Ankwang co. (pop. 114,385), SW Heilungkiang prov., Manchuria, 40 mi. E of Taonan; soda-extracting center; kaoliang, livestock.

Ankwo or **An-kuo** (än'gwô'), town, ⊙ Ankwo co. (pop. 204,789), SW central Hopeh prov., China, 30 mi. SSW of Paoting; medicinal herbs, wheat, rice, millet. Until 1914, Chichow.

Anlongthnot, Cambodia: see KRAKOR.

Anlu (än'lōō'). **1** Town (pop. 13,073), ⊙ Anlu co. (pop. 240,411), E central Hupeh prov., China, 60 mi. NW of Hankow; rice, wheat, cotton, indigo. Until 1912 called Teian. **2** Town, Hupeh prov., China: see CHUNGSIANG.

Anlung (än'lŏŏng'), town (pop. 8,713), ⊙ Anlung co. (pop. 106,504), SW Kweichow prov., China, 125 mi. SW of Kweiyang; alt. 4,708 ft.; cotton textiles, embroidered goods; rice, sugar, hides. Manganese deposits, coal deposits, kaolin quarry near by. Called HINGI until 1913, and Nanlung, 1913–31.

Anmoore, village (pop. 1,388), Harrison co., N W.Va., 3 mi. SE of Clarksburg, in coal, timber, petroleum, livestock region.

Ann, Cape, NE Mass., N of Massachusetts Bay, 30 mi. NE of Boston; E extremity of Essex co.; 42°38'N 70°35'W. Noted for old fishing villages resorts, and artists' colonies, especially GLOUCESTER and ROCKPORT. Shelters Ipswich Bay. Gloucester Harbor indents S shore, Annisquam Harbor (ăn'ĭskwăm) N shore; Annisquam R., a navigable passage c.4 mi. long, connects them. Small Thacher Isl. is off E shore.

Anna, Iraq: see 'ANA.

Anna (ä'nä), town (pop. 1,229), Valencia prov., E Spain, 8 mi. WNW of Játiva; wool and cotton spinning; olive oil, vegetables, fruit.

Anna (än'nŭ), village (1926 pop. 3,634), N central Voronezh oblast, Russian SFSR, 50 mi. ESE of Voronezh; rail terminus; sunflower-oil extraction, distilling.

Anna. 1 City (pop. 4,380), Union co., S Ill., 32 mi. N of Cairo, in Ill. Ozarks; ships fruit, truck, wheat, corn; mfg. (wood products, shoes); marble and granite works. A state insane asylum is here. Inc. 1865. **2** Village (pop. 554), Shelby co., W Ohio, 8 mi. N of Sidney, in agr. area. **3** Town (pop. 525), Collin co., N Texas, 20 mi. S of Sherman, in cotton, truck area.

Annabella, town (pop. 263), Sevier co., central Utah, 4 mi. SSE of Richfield, near Sevier R.

Annaberg (ä'näbĕrk), town (pop. 19,584), Saxony, E central Germany, in the Erzgebirge, 18 mi. S of Chemnitz, near Czechoslovak border, in mining region (uranium, bismuth, cobalt, tin); textile center (silk, lace, ribbon, braid, hosiery). Mfg. of glass, electrical equipment, cardboard. Winter-sports resort. Has 16th-cent. church. Founded 1496 as silver-mining settlement; silver mining ceased 1892. Lace and braid making were introduced in mid-16th cent.

Annabessacook, Lake (ă"nŭbĕ'sŭkŏŏk), Kennebec co., S Maine, just S of Winthrop; 3.5 mi. long.

Annaburg (ä'näbŏŏrk), town (pop. 5,184), in former Prussian Saxony prov., central Germany, after 1945 in Saxony-Anhalt, 12 mi. N of Torgau; pottery mfg. Has 16th-cent. castle.

Annada (ă'nā"dŭ), town (pop. 93), Pike co., E Mo., near Mississippi R., 21 mi. ESE of Bowling Green.

Annadale, SE N.Y., a section of Richmond borough of New York city, in S Staten Isl.

Annagh (ănä', ă'nä). **1** Island (627 acres; 2 mi. long), off W Co. Mayo, Ireland, bet. Achill Isl. and mainland, separated from both by narrow channels. **2** Islet in N part of Lough Conn, N central Co. Mayo, Ireland, 5 mi. SW of Ballina.

An Najaf, Iraq: see NAJAF.

Annaka (än-nä'kä), town (pop. 10,608), Gumma prefecture, central Honshu, Japan, 6 mi. W of Takasaki; mulberry and rice fields. Mineral springs.

Annalee River (–lē'), cos. Monaghan and Cavan, Ireland, rises 7 mi. W of Carrickmacross, flows 30 mi. W, past Cootehill, to N end of Lough Oughter at outlet of Erne R.

Annalong (ănŭlŏng'), fishing village (district pop. 1,112), S Co. Down, Northern Ireland, on the Irish Sea, 6 mi. ENE of Kilkeel.

Annam (ŭnăm', ă'năm", än'näm'), former empire and Fr. protectorate (□ 57,840; 1943 pop. 7,183,500) in E central Indochina, constituting (after 1945–46) central VIETNAM; ⊙ Hue. Situated bet. Tonkin (N) and Cochin China (S), Annam extends nearly 800 mi. in a long, narrow ribbon bet. the South China Sea (E) and the mtn. backbone of the Annamese Cordillera, which separates it from Laos and Cambodia (W). At its S end, the Annamese Cordillera forms the MOI PLATEAUS, placed after 1946 under separate administration. Along the sharply indented coast, mtn. spurs reaching to the sea separate numerous narrow coastal plains formed by the deltas of short, torrential rivers (Song Ba, Song Ca, Song Ma). These small areas supply a deficit rice crop, as well as cinnamon (in Tramy area), cotton, and raw silk. Weaving of textile fibers and fish processing are the chief industries. The principal cities (Hue, Vinh with its port of Benthuy, Tourane, and Quinhon) are served by the longitudinal Saigon-Hanoi RR and highway. Of the various peoples, most important are the Annamese (85% of total pop.) and the indigenous Moi (over 10%) of the plateaus. The origins of the Annamese state may be traced to the peoples of Chinese culture of Red River valley of Tonkin, which fell (3d cent. B.C.) under Chinese rule and formed a kingdom subject to China from 939 until 1428 when the Annamese established an independent state. The original area of Annam was expanded 1472 with the annexation of the kingdom of the Chams or Champa (a state of Indian origins which had existed in S Annam since A.D. 192). Following a dynastic division (16th cent.) bet. the Le line ruling from TONKIN (modern Hanoi) and the Nguyen line of Hue, Annam fell into 2 domains to which the first European missionaries and navigators gave the names of Tonkin and Cochinchina. The Hue dynasty pushed S in 17th and early 18th cent., annexing the remainder of Champa and the Cambodian provs. on the lower Mekong (modern Cochinchina). In late 18th cent. the dynasties of Hue and Tonkin were overthrown, but all Annamese lands were reunited (1802) under the restored Hue dynasty as the empire of Annam. In return for their aid in restoring the unified empire, the French had obtained (1787) from Annam the port of Tourane and admission for their missionaries and traders. Subsequent Annamese attempts to withdraw into isolation, mistreatment of Fr. nationals and Annamese Christian converts opened the way to French military operations beginning in 1858, which led to the seizure of present-day Cochinchina and Tonkin, and to the Fr. protectorate (1883–84) over Annam, which joined (1887) the Union of Indochina. After the Second World War, Annam became part (1945–46) of Vietnam.

Annam, Porte d', Vietnam: see ANNAM GATE.

Annamalainagar, India: see CHIDAMBARAM.

Anna Maria, resort city (pop. 345), Manatee co., SW Fla., 18 mi. SSW of St. Petersburg, on Anna Maria Key (c.8 mi. long), at mouths of Tampa and Sarasota bays.

Annamese Cordillera, main mtn. range of Indochina and Vietnam, forming divide bet. Mekong R. basin and rivers draining into South China Sea; extends c.700 mi. NW–SE along the coast, rising to 10,500 ft. in the Ngoc Ang, at 15°N. Includes (N) TRANNINH PLATEAU, is crossed in lower central portion by Mugia and Ailao passes, and rises to its highest point in S igneous massif. The chain drops sharply on the coast side, but slopes gently (W) toward the Mekong, forming in S section the MOI PLATEAUS.

Annam Gate, Fr. *Porte d'Annam* (pôrt' dänäm'), low pass (522 ft.) in coastal spur of Annamese Cordillera, N central Vietnam, on South China Sea, 35 mi. NNW of Donghoi; crossed by coastal highway. Marked S limit of original Annamese state (roughly modern Tonkin) prior to conquest (1472) of the Chams.

Annan, China: see TSINGLUNG, Kweichow prov.

Annan (ă'nŭn), burgh (1931 pop. 3,959; 1951 census 4,631), S Dumfries, Scotland, on Annan R. (bridged) near its mouth on Solway Firth, 15 mi. ESE of Dumfries; agr. market, with hosiery and flour mills, tanneries, distilleries, marine equipment works, fertilizer works, and nursery gardens. Edward Irving b. here. At the Old Academy, Carlyle and Irving were pupils. Church (18th cent.) is on site of old castle.

Annandale (ă'nŭndăl), municipality (pop. 12,396), E New South Wales, Australia, 2 mi. SW of Sydney; mfg. center (chemicals, sheet metal, furniture).

Annandale. 1 Village (pop. 899), Wright co., S central Minn., near Clearwater L., c.45 mi. WNW of Minneapolis; resort; trading point in livestock, grain, poultry region; dairy products. **2** Village (1940 pop. 551), Hunterdon co., W N.J., 17 mi. ESE of Phillipsburg, in farm area.

Annandale-on-Hudson, village (pop. c.150), Dutchess co., SE N.Y., on E bank of the Hudson and 17 mi. S of Hudson. Seat of Bard Col.

Annan River (ă'nŭn), Dumfries, Scotland, rises in Moffat Hills 5 mi. NNW of Moffat, flows 49 mi. S, past Moffat and Anna, to Solway Firth 2 mi. S of Annan.

Annapes (änäp'), town (pop. 2,656), Nord dept., N France, 4 mi. E of Lille; textile milling, sugar-beet distilling.

Annapolis. 1 City, Goiás, Brazil: see ANÁPOLIS. **2** City, São Paulo, Brazil: see ANALÂNDIA.

Annapolis, county (□ 1,285; pop. 17,692), W N.S., on Bay of Fundy; ⊙ Bridgetown.

Annapolis (ŭnă'pŭlĭs). **1** City (pop. 10,047), ⊙ Md. and Anne Arundel co., central Md., on Severn R. near its mouth on Chesapeake Bay and 23 mi. S of Baltimore. Residential town, noted for its historic bldgs. and colonial charm, it is seat of U.S. Naval Acad. (c.235 acres), opened 1845 as Naval School and renamed 1850; acad. bldgs. include Bancroft Hall (dormitory), Dahlgren Hall (armory), chapel containing crypt of John Paul Jones, and mus. of naval history; acad. was used as military hosp. in Civil War. City is a port of entry and a trade and shipping center for truck- and fruitgrowing region; has seafood industry (fish, crabs, oysters), boatyards. Seat of St. Johns Col. (chartered 1784, opened 1789; for men), successor to King William's School (established 1696). In the state house (built 1772–4), the "Association of Freemen" passed pre-Revolutionary resolutions against taxation without representation; here the Congress, meeting Nov. 26, 1783, to June 3, 1784, received (Dec. 23, 1783) Washington's resignation as commander-in-chief, the Revolutionary War peace treaty was ratified (1784), and the Annapolis Convention was held (1786), preliminary to the Federal Constitutional Convention. Other points of interest: the Old Treasury (c.1695); the library (1737); St. Anne's Church (Episcopal), built 1859 on site of church of 1704. In vicinity are naval engineering and radio stations, a natl. cemetery, and summer resorts along the bay. Settled c.1648 as Providence by Va. Puritans; later called Anne Arundel, it was named Annapolis 1695, after ⊙ Md. was removed here (1694) from St. Marys City. Chartered 1708 by Queen Anne, inc. as city 1796. Escaped British attack in Revolution. Fort Severn (1808) which guarded city in War of 1812, later became nucleus of Naval Acad. First newspaper in Md. published here, 1745. **2** Town (pop. 490), Iron co., SE central Mo., in the St. Francois Mts. 14 mi. N of Piedmont. **3** Village (pop. 1,538, with adjacent Retsil), Kitsap co., W Wash., adjacent to Port Orchard.

Annapolis Basin, tidal arm of Bay of Fundy, W N.S., extends 16 mi. NE–SW bet. Digby and Annapolis Royal, where it receives Annapolis R.; up to 4 mi. wide. Its entrance is narrow Digby Gut, bordered by 500-ft. cliffs.

Annapolis River, in W N.S., rises SW of Kentville, flows 75 mi. NW, past Middleton and Bridgetown, to the Annapolis Basin at Annapolis Royal. Fertile valley is noted for its apples.

Annapolis Royal, town (pop. estimate c.800), W N.S., at head of Annapolis Basin, at mouth of Annapolis R., 16 mi. NW of Digby; market in applegrowing region. Originally established 1605 by de Monts on N side of Annapolis Basin, and called Port Royal, settlement was abandoned 1607, reoccupied 1610; destroyed 1614 (O.S. 1613) by the British under Samuel Argall; resettled 1620 by Scottish colonists. Treaty of St. Germain (1632) restored it to the French, who subsequently abandoned the place. In 1635 new settlement of Port Royal was established on site of present town. Temporarily taken by the British in 1654 and 1690, it was finally captured (1710) by New England force under Francis Nicholson, and renamed in honor of Queen Anne. Until 1749 it was ⊙ Nova Scotia. In 1744–45 it resisted French and Indian attacks. In 1917 ground (c.30 acres) of ruined Fort Anne became Dominion natl. park. Officers' Quarters (built 1797–98) of fort have been restored as mus.

Annapurna (ŭn-nŭpŏŏr'nŭ), 35-mi.-long massif of central Nepal Himalayas, N central Nepal, at 28°35'N 84°E. Rises to Annapurna I (26,502 ft.; W) and Annapurna II (26,041 ft.; E). Annapurna I was 1st climbed (1950) by Fr. expedition led by Maurice Herzog; as of 1950, highest mtn. climbed by man. Sometimes spelled Anapurna.

Ann Arbor, city (pop. 48,251), ⊙ Washtenaw co., SE Mich., on Huron R. and 35 mi. W of Detroit. The seat of Univ. of Michigan, it is a college community and trade center for large agr. and fruit-growing area. Mfg. of tools, metal products, chemicals, precision instruments, cameras, auto parts, machinery, food products, electrical goods, tents, awnings. Hq. here of Mich. Municipal League. Annually, the May Music and Dramatic Festivals held at univ. Nichols Arboretum is famous for its lilacs and peonies. Laid out 1824; inc. as village 1833, as city 1851.

Anna Regina (rŭjī'nŭ), village (pop. 848), Essequibo co., N Br. Guiana, on Atlantic coast, c.4 mi. N of Queenstown; coconut plantations.

Anna's Hope, agr. station, St. Croix Isl., U.S. Virgin Isls., 2 mi. SW of Christiansted, in sugar-growing region.

An Nasiriya, Iraq: see NASIRIYA.

Annau (ŭnou'), village, S Ashkhabad oblast, Turkmen SSR, at foot of the Kopet-Dagh, on Trans-Caspian RR and 5 mi. SE of Ashkhabad. Site of 15th-cent. mosque, citadel, burial mounds, and other ruins. Anc. center dating from c.3000 B.C. Also spelled Anau.

Annawan (ă'nuwăn), village (pop. 592), Henry co., NW Ill., 33 mi. ESE of Moline, in bituminous-coal and livestock area.

Annay (ānā'), town (pop. 2,655), Pas-de-Calais dept., N France, near Haute-Deûle Canal, 3 mi. NE of Lens, in coal-mining dist.; furniture mfg. Also called Annay-sous-Lens.

Annbank, village in Tarbolton parish, W Ayrshire, Scotland, 5 mi. ENE of Ayr; coal mining.

Anne, Cape, NW Somerset Isl., central Franklin Dist., Northwest Territories, on Barrow Strait, at N end of Peel Sound; 74°3'N 95°W.

Anne Arundel (ăn" ŭrŭn'dŭl, ŭră'nŭl), county (□ 417; pop. 117,392), central Md.; ⊙ Annapolis. Bounded E by Chesapeake Bay, N and NE by Patapsco R., W by Patuxent R. Truck, fruit, tobacco, poultry, livestock, dairy products; seafood industry (fish, oysters, crabs); boatworks. Pine timber (in SE). Chesapeake shore has many small resorts, especially in vicinity of Magothy, Severn, South rivers (tidal estuaries). In N are residential suburbs of Baltimore. Includes U.S. Naval Acad. at Annapolis, Fort George G. Meade (in W; c.17,000 acres; permanent Army post, established 1917), Friendship International Airport (airfield for Baltimore), state park at Sandy Point. Formed 1650.

Annecy (ănsē'), town (pop. 24,414), ⊙ Haute-Savoie dept., SE France, 21 mi. S of Geneva, in Savoy Pre-Alps; popular summer resort and excursion center at N end of L. of Annecy; mfg. (jewelry, ball bearings, metal watchbands, chocolate, slaked lime), cotton milling, tanning. Aluminum and paper mills in suburban Cran-Gevrier. Of medieval aspect, town is crossed by narrow canals. Dominated by 12th–14th cent. castle of counts of Geneva and by new (20th cent.) monastery of the Visitation (yearly pilgrimage). Became (1535) seat of bishop of Geneva. St. Francis of Sales (b. here) was bishop (1602–22), and, together with St. Joan of Chantal, founded 1st convent of the Visitation. Annecy is now a diocese in its own right.

Annecy, Lake of, in Haute-Savoie dept., SE France, c.25 mi. S of Geneva, bet. Bauges (S) and Bornes (NE) massifs of Savoy Pre-Alps; □ 10; 9 mi. long, ½–2 mi. wide, separated into N and S parts by narrows bet. Talloire and Duingt. Its steep shores are lined with resorts and orchards. Annecy is at NNW end. Its outlet (2 mi. long) is tributary of the Fier.

Annecy-le-Vieux (–lŭ-vyū'), village (pop. 247), Haute-Savoie dept., SE France, 2 mi. NNE of Annecy; bell foundry; cheese and biscuit mfg.

Annemasse (ănmäs'), town (pop. 7,337), Haute-Savoie dept., SE France, near the Arve, 4 mi. E of Geneva; customs station near Swiss border; watch-mfg. center. Also makes shoes, stockings, pencils, synthetic jewels. Resort.

Annenfeld, Azerbaijan SSR: see SHAMKHOR, city.

Annenski Most or **Annenskiy Most** (ä'nyĭnskē môst"), village (1939 pop. over 500), NW Vologda oblast, Russian SFSR, on Kovzha R., at S end of Mariinsk Canal, and 145 mi. NW of Vologda; coarse grain.

Annequin (änkē'), town (pop. 2,012), Pas-de-Calais dept., N France, 4 mi. ESE of Béthune; coal mines.

Annesley Bay, Eritrea: see ZULA.

Annette, village (pop. 284), SE Alaska, on SW Annette Isl., near U.S. air base.

Annette Island (20 mi. long, 7–10 mi. wide), SE Alaska, Gravina Isls., Alexander Archipelago, 5 mi. SSE of Ketchikan across Revillagigedo Channel; 55°8'N 131°27'W; rises to 3,610 ft. Reserve of Tsimshian Indians; site of METLAKAHTLA town, established 1887. Site (W) of U.S. air base, built in Second World War; commercial airport for Ketchikan.

Annezin (änzē'), W suburb (pop. 3,528) of Béthune, Pas-de-Calais dept., N France.

Annfield Plain, former urban district (1931 pop. 15,931), N Durham, England, 9 mi. SW of Newcastle-upon-Tyne; coal-mining center. Inc. 1937 in Stanley.

Annicco (än-nĕk'kō), village (pop. 2,229), Cremona prov., Lombardy, N Italy, 11 mi. NW of Cremona; silk mills, saddle factory.

Annieopsquotch Mountains (ă"nēŏp'skwŏch"), range (40 mi. long) in SW N.F., SW of Red Indian L.; rises to over 2,000 ft.

Annigeri (ŭn'nĭgărē), town (pop. 8,091), Dharwar dist., S Bombay, India, 29 mi. E of Dharwar; millet, cotton; cotton ginning. Large 12th-cent. temple. Sometimes spelled Annigari.

Anning (än'nĭng'), town (pop. 4,236), ⊙ Anning co. (pop. 58,503), central Yunnan prov., China, 15 mi. SW of Kunming; alt. 6,152 ft. Rice milling, iron smelting; rice, wheat, millet, beans. Iron mines and bauxite deposits near by.

Annino, Azerbaijan SSR: see SHAMKHOR, city.

Annisquam, village, Mass.: see GLOUCESTER.

Annisquam Harbor, Mass.: see ANN, CAPE.

Annisquam River, Mass.: see ANN, CAPE.

Anniston (ă'nĭstŭn, –nŭs–). **1** City (pop. 31,066), ⊙ Calhoun co., E Ala., 55 mi. E of Birmingham, in foothills of Appalachian Mts. Trade, industrial center for iron-mining and agr. area. Mfg. of cast-iron soil pipe and pipe fittings, clothing, yarn, mattresses, and awnings, industrial castings and machine parts, chemicals, prefabricated houses, concrete building material, lumber, bakery products. U.S. ordnance depot. Founded 1872 as iron-mfg. town, inc. 1883. Fort McClellan near by. **2** Town (pop. 377), Mississippi co., extreme SE Mo., near Mississippi R., 8 mi. S of Charleston.

Annitsford, England: see WEETSLADE.

Anniviers, Val d' (väl dänēvyā'), valley and resort area, Valais canton, S Switzerland, extending c.8 mi. along small tributary of the Rhone, S of Sierre. Chippis hydroelectric plants in N. Vissoie or Vissoye (vēswä') is main village (pop. 277).

Annobón (änōbōn'), volcanic island (□ 6½; pop. 1,379) in Gulf of Guinea, c.200 mi. WSW of Cape Lopez (Gabon, Fr. Equatorial Africa), forming part of insular Sp. Guinea; 1°25'S 5°37'E. Rises to 2,200 ft. Fishing, lumbering. San Antonio (on N shore) is chief settlement. Administered from Fernando Po isl.

Annoeullin (änûlē'), town (pop. 4,926), Nord dept., N France, 9 mi. SW of Lille; mfg. (work clothing, hosiery, soap, chicory), cloth bleaching.

Annona, town (pop. 392), Red River co., NE Texas, 38 mi. E of Paris, in agr. area.

Annonay (änōnā'), town (pop. 13,092), Ardèche dept., S France, in the Monts du Vivarais, 19 mi. SE of Saint-Étienne; tanning and paper-milling center; wool washing, silk processing, straw-hat mfg. Important trade in hides and skins.

Annonyme Island, Seychelles: see ANONYME ISLAND.

Annopol or **Annopol'** (ŭnô'pŭl), village (1926 pop. 1,897), N Kamenets-Podolski oblast, Ukrainian SSR, 10 mi. N of Slavuta; distilling; wheat.

Annot (änō'), village (pop. 885), Basses-Alpes dept., SE France, in the Provence Alps, 11 mi. NE of Castellane; resort. Has picturesque 16th–17th-cent. houses.

Annotto Bay (ŭnŏ'tŭ, ŭnŏ'tō), town (pop. 2,805), St. Mary parish, N Jamaica, banana port on right bank of Wag Water R. mouth, on railroad to Port Antonio and 21 mi. N of Kingston. Trades also in coconuts, coffee, cacao, dyewood, sugar cane. Sugar milling.

Ann's Grove, village (pop., including adjacent Two Friends, 1,415), Demerara co., N Br. Guiana, on Atlantic coast, on Georgetown-Rosignol RR (Clonbrook station) and 15 mi. ESE of Georgetown; rice, sugar cane, fruit, stock.

Annville, village (pop. 3,564), Lebanon co., SE central Pa., 4 mi. W of Lebanon; textiles, shoes; dairying; limestone. Has Lebanon Valley Col. Indiantown Gap Military Reservation (established 1935) is NW. Settled c.1745, laid out 1765.

Annweiler (än"vī'lŭr), town (pop. 4,230), Rhenish Palatinate, W Germany, in Hardt Mts., on the Queich and 7 mi. W of Landau; mfg. of enamel goods, measuring sticks, pasteboard; woodworking. Chartered 1219. Ruins of anc. castle of Trifels near by.

Ano Archanai or **Ano Arkhanai** (both: ä'nô ärkhä'nĕ), town (pop. 3,361), Herakleion nome, central Crete, 7 mi. SSE of Candia; raisins, potatoes, citrus fruits, olive oil.

Anogeia or **Anoyia** (both: ŭnô'yēŭ), town (pop. 3,072), Rethymne nome, central Crete, 25 mi. ESE of Rethymnon; carobs, almonds, wine, olive oil. Also spelled Anoghia.

Anoka (ŭnō'kŭ), county (□ 425; pop. 35,579), E Minn.; ⊙ Anoka. Agr. area bounded SW by Mississippi R. and drained by Rum R. Dairy products, livestock, grain, poultry; deposits of marl and peat. Formed 1857.

Anoka. 1 City (pop. 7,396), ⊙ Anoka co., E Minn., on Mississippi R., at mouth of Rum R., and 17 mi. NNW of Minneapolis. Resort; farm trade center in grain, livestock, and poultry region; dairy products; mfg. (ammunition, furniture, household appliances, beverages). Settled 1844, laid out 1853, inc. 1878. State hosp. for insane is here. **2** Village (pop. 60), Boyd co., N Nebr., just N of Butte and on Ponca Creek, near S.Dak. line.

Ano Kouphonesos or **Ano Koufonisos** (both: ä'nô-kōōfônē'sôs), Aegean island (□ 2.2; pop. 234) in the Cyclades, Greece, 1 mi. off SE end of Naxos isl.; 34°55'N 26°10'E; 2 mi. long, 1 mi. wide.

Anolaima (änōlī'mä), town (pop. 2,459), Cundinamarca dept., central Colombia, on W slopes of Cordillera Oriental, 29 mi. WNW of Bogotá; sugar cane, tobacco, yucca, coffee, fruit, stock; noted for pineapples. Has pilgrimage chapel.

Año Nuevo, Islas, Argentina: see NEW YEAR'S ISLANDS.

Año Nuevo Point (ă'nō nōōā'vō), promontory on coast of San Mateo co., W Calif., 20 mi. NW of Santa Cruz; New Year's Point Lighthouse here. Named by Vizcaino, who sighted it soon after New Year's Day, 1603.

Anonyme Island or **Annonyme Island,** one of the Seychelles, in Indian Ocean, off E coast of Mahé Isl., 5½ mi. SE of Victoria; 4°39'S 55°3'E; ⅓ mi. long, ⅓ mi. wide; granite formation.

Anopino (ŭnô'pĕnŭ), town (1944 pop. over 500), S Vladimir oblast, Russian SFSR; 6 mi. NNW of Gus-Khrustalny; glassworking.

Ano Porroia (ä'nô pôrô'yŭ), town (pop. 3,129), Serrai nome, Macedonia, Greece, 22 mi. NNE of Kilkis, at foot of the Belasica (Bulg. border); tobacco, barley, beans.

Anor (änôr'), industrial village (pop. 1,416), Nord dept., N France, near Belg. border, 3 mi. SE of Fourmies; rail junction; edge-tool mfg.

Añora (änyō'rä), town (pop. 2,974), Córdoba prov., S Spain, 4 mi. NW of Pozoblanco; sheep raising, lumbering; cereals, olive oil.

Anori (änōōrē'), town (pop. 418), central Amazonas, Brazil, on left bank of the Amazon and 120 mi. WSW of Manaus. Formerly spelled Anory and Anouri.

Anorí (änōrē'), town (pop. 1,826), Antioquia dept., NW central Colombia, in Cordillera Central, 18 mi. ENE of Yarumal; alt. 5,036 ft. Gold mining. Agr. region (sugar cane, coffee, corn, beans, yucca, rice, bananas, cacao, cattle, hogs).

Anosibe (änōōsē'bā), village, Tamatave prov., E central Madagascar, 55 mi. SE of Tananarive; gold mining, cattle raising.

Anou Islands, Tuamotu Isls.: see DUKE OF GLOUCESTER ISLANDS.

Anould (änōō'), village (pop. 284), Vosges dept., E France, on the Meurthe and 7 mi. S of Saint-Dié; paper mill near by.

Añover de Tajo (änyōvär'dhä tä'hō), town (pop. 2,589), Toledo prov., central Spain, on the Tagus and 30 mi. S of Madrid, on La Sagra plain; cereals, asparagus, potatoes, sugar beets, sheep, cattle.

Anoyia, Crete: see ANOGEIA.

An Pass (ăn), crossing (alt. 4,000 ft.) of Arakan Yoma, Upper Burma, on route bet. Minbu on Irrawaddy R. and An (Kyaukpyu dist.); 19°58'N 94°14'E.

Anpeh or **Anpei** (both: än'bā'), town (pop. 1,959), ⊙ Anpeh co. (pop. 39,178), W central Suiyuan prov., China, on railroad and 50 mi. NW of Paotow; cattle raising; wheat, millet, licorice. Phosphate deposits. Until 1925 called Tashetai.

Anpei, China: see ANPEH.

Anpin, Formosa: see ANPING.

Anping or **An-p'ing** (än'pĭng'). **1** Town, ⊙ Anping co. (pop. 172,893), SW central Hopeh prov., China, 55 mi. ENE of Shihkiachwang and on Huto R.; cotton, wheat, kaoliang, millet. **2** Town, Yunnan prov., China: see MAKWAN.

Anping or **An-p'ing,** Jap. *Anpin* or *Ampin* (äm'pēn), town (1935 pop. 6,353), W central Formosa, on W coast, outer port (2 mi. W) of Tainan and seaside resort; saltworks; fish hatchery. Historical mus. Site of Dutch Fort Zeelandia or Zelandia (built 1630), later replaced by Chinese castle (ruins).

Anrath (än'rät), village (pop. 6,291), in former Prussian Rhine Prov., W Germany, after 1945 in North Rhine-Westphalia, 5 mi. SW of Krefeld; cattle.

An River (ăn), short coastal stream in Arakan, Lower Burma, rises in the Arakan Yoma, flows 50 mi. SSW, past An and Sakanmaw (head of navigation), to Bay of Bengal opposite Ramree Isl.

Ans (äs), town (pop. 16,156), Liége prov., E Belgium, 2 mi. NW of Liége; coal mining; metal industry.

Ansai, China: see ANSI, Shensi prov.

Ansbach (äns'bäkh), city (1950 pop. 33,134), ⊙ Middle Franconia, W Bavaria, Germany, on the Franconian Rezat and 24 mi. WSW of Nuremberg; 49°18'N 10°34'E. Rail transshipment point; metal (cars, motors, electrical equipment) and textile (linen, clothing, cotton and silk thread) industries; plastics. Also lumber and paper milling, printing, woodworking, brewing. Has 12th-cent. Romanesque church of St. Gumbertus (rebuilt in 15th cent.), and late-Gothic church containing vault with numerous tombs of margraves. The 14th-cent. palace was rebuilt several times in 18th cent. Ansbach developed around 8th-cent. Benedictine abbey. City was residence of Franconian branch of Hohenzollern line from 1331 until deeded to

Prussia in 1791. Passed to Bavaria in 1806. Poet Platen b. here. Formerly also spelled Anspach.

Anse (ãs), village (pop. 961), Rhône dept., E central France, on Azergues R., near its mouth on the Saône, and 4 mi. S of Villefranche; winegrowing, distilling. Has 11th-cent. castle.

Anse-à-Foleur (ãs-ä-fôlûr'), town (1950 census pop. 932), Nord-Ouest dept., N Haiti, on the coast, 14 mi. E of Port-de-Paix; rice, cacao, fruit.

Anse Amour, L', or **Lance Amour** (both: lăns ùmōōr'), or **Anse aux Morts** (ãs ō môr'), village (pop. 40), SE Labrador, on Forteau Bay of Strait of Belle Isle, 45 mi. WSW of Cape Norman, N.F.; 51°28'N 56°52'W.

Anse-à-Pitre (ãs-ä-pē'trů), town (1950 census pop. 549), Ouest dept., SE Haiti, on the coast, on Dominican Republic border opposite Pedernales, 50 mi. SE of Port-au-Prince; coffee, timber.

Anse au Loup, L', or **Lance au Loup** (both: lăns ō lōō'), village (pop. 223), SE Labrador, on Anse au Loup, bay of Strait of Belle Isle, 40 mi. WSW of Cape Norman, N.F.; 51°31'N 56°49'W; fishing port.

Anse aux Morts, Labrador: see ANSE AMOUR, L'.

Anse Aux Pins (ãs ō pē'), village on E coast of Mahé Isl., Seychelles, anchorage on the Anse Aux Pins (inlet of Indian Ocean), 7 mi. SE of Victoria; copra, essential oils; fisheries.

Anse-à-Veau (ãs-ä-vō'), town (1950 census pop. 923), Sud dept., SW Haiti, minor port on N coast of Tiburon Peninsula, 65 mi. W of Port-au-Prince; oranges, cotton.

Anseba River (änsĕ'bä), N Eritrea, rises on central plateau near Asmara, flows 215 mi. NW to Barka R. 75 mi. SW of Karora, near Anglo-Egyptian Sudan border; seasonally dry. Along its banks grow dom palms (furnish vegetable ivory). Gold deposits worked near Asmara and Keren.

Anse-Bertrand (ãs-bĕrtrã'), town (commune pop. 8,047), N Grande-Terre, Guadeloupe, 15 mi. N of Pointe-à-Pitre; sugar growing and milling; alcohol distilling.

Anse Boileau (ãs bwälō'), village on W coast of Mahé Isl., Seychelles, anchorage on the Anse Boileau (inlet of Indian Ocean), 6½ mi. S of Victoria; copra, essential oils; fisheries.

Anse-d'Hainault (ãs-dĕnō'), town (1950 census pop. 1,779), Sud dept., SW Haiti, minor port on W tip of Tiburon Peninsula, 50 mi. WNW of Les Cayes; coffee-, cacao-growing. Copper, iron deposits near by.

Anse Etoile (ãs ätwäl'), village on E coast of Mahé Isl., Seychelles, anchorage on the Anse Etoile (inlet of Indian Ocean), 2 mi. N of Victoria; copra, essential oils; fisheries.

Anse Forbans (ãs fôrbã'), village on E coast of Mahé Isl., Seychelles, on the Anse Forbans (inlet of Indian Ocean), 11 mi. SSE of Victoria; copra, essential oils; fisheries.

Anse-la-Raye (äns"-lä-rā'), village (pop. 1,530), W St. Lucia, B.W.I., 5 mi. SW of Castries; sugar growing; fishing.

Anselmo, village (pop. 316), Custer co., central Nebr., 20 mi. NW of Broken Bow; grain.

Anse Major (ãs mäzhôr'), village on W coast of Mahé Isl., Seychelles, on the Anse Major (inlet of Indian Ocean), 4 mi. W of Victoria; copra, essential oils; fisheries.

Anserma (änsĕr'mä), town (pop. 5,458), Caldas dept., W central Colombia, in Cordillera Occidental, 22 mi. NW of Manizales; alt. 6,027 ft. Agr. center (coffee, sugar cane, cereals, fruit). Coal deposits near by.

Ansermanuevo (änsĕrmänwā'vō), town (pop. 3,196), Valle del Cauca dept., W Colombia, in Cauca valley, 5 mi. NW of Cartago; agr. center (coffee, tobacco, sugar cane, cacao, corn, stock).

Anse-Rouge (ãs-rōōzh'), village (1950 pop. 665), Artibonite dept., W Haiti, on Gulf of Gonaïves, 26 mi. NW of Gonaïves, surrounded by salt marshes.

Anse Royale (ãs rwäyäl'), village on E coast of Mahé Isl., Seychelles, on the Anse Royale (inlet of Indian Ocean), 9 mi. SSE of Victoria; copra, essential oils; fisheries. Has a leper settlement, hosp.

Anses-d'Arlets (ãs-därlā'), town (pop. 858), SW Martinique, 8 mi. S of Fort-de-France; coffee, cacao, sugar cane.

Ansfelden (äns'fĕldůn), town (pop. 9,069), central Upper Austria, near Krems R., 6 mi. S of Linz; grain, cattle.

Anshan (än'shän'), city (1946 pop. 219,715; 1947 pop. 165,988) in, but independent of, Liaotung prov., Manchuria, on South Manchuria RR and 55 mi. SW of Mukden; leading metallurgical center of Manchuria and China, with integrated iron and steel industry based on local and Kungchuling iron ore. Mfg. of pipes, steel beams, firebrick, coke, chemicals, cement. A steel plant was 1st built here in 1918 on the basis of rich (60–65% iron content) but limited local iron-ore reserves. Under Manchukuo regime, the plant was rebuilt and greatly enlarged to process the more extensive, though poorer (35–40% iron) Kungchuling reserves. In the course of this expansion, the city's pop. increased a hundredfold bet. 1930 and 1945. Called Shaho or Shahochen until 1934, when it became an independent municipality, Anshan was subordinated in 1949 directly to the central govt.

Anshu, Korea: see ANJU.

Anshun (än'shōōn'), town (pop. 41,396), ⊙ Anshun co. (pop. 200,518), W central Kweichow prov., China, 50 mi. WSW of Kweiyang; alt. 4,557 ft.; cotton weaving, pottery mfg.; embroideries. Coal deposits. Hot springs (N). Projected railroad junction.

Ansi. 1 or **An-hsi** (both: än'shē'), town, ⊙ Ansi co. (pop. 20,820), NW Kansu prov., China, on Shuleh R. and 145 mi. WNW of Kiuchüan; alt. 3,877 ft.; junction on Silk Road to Sinkiang. **2** or **Ansai** (both: än'sī'), town, ⊙ Ansi co. (pop. 8,516), N Shensi prov., China, 12 mi. NW of Yenan; wheat, beans, kaoliang.

Ansiang or **An-hsiang** (both: än'shyäng'), town, ⊙ Ansiang co. (pop. 207,410), N Hunan prov., China, on N shore of Tungting L., 40 mi. NE of Changteh; fisheries; boatbuilding.

Ansilta, Cordillera de (kōrdĭyā'rä dā änsēl'tä), Andean range in SW San Juan prov., Argentina, 30 mi. W of Tamberías; extends c.35 mi. N-S; rises to c.19,000 ft.

Ansin or **An-hsin** (both: än'shĭn'), town, ⊙ Ansin co. (pop. 138,669), central Hopeh prov., China, 17 mi. E of Paoting, on W shore of small Siting L.; cotton, wheat, rice, beans.

Ansley (ănz'lē), town and parish (pop. 2,071), NE Warwick, England, 4 mi. E of Nuneaton; coal mining. Church has 15th-cent. tower.

Ansley, village (pop. 711), Custer co., central Nebr., 15 mi. SE of Broken Bow and on Mud Creek.

Ansó (änsō'), town (pop. 945), Huesca prov., NE Spain, in the central Pyrenees, 20 mi. NW of Jaca; summer resort; trout fishing.

Anson (ăn'sůn), county (□ 533; pop. 26,781), S N.C.; ⊙ Wadesboro. Bounded S by S.C., E by Pee Dee R. (Blewett Falls L.), N by Rocky R. In piedmont region; sand hills in SE. Agr. (cotton, corn, hay, fruit, dairying); pine and oak timber. Dairy products, cotton textiles; sawmilling. Formed 1749.

Anson. 1 Residential town (pop. 2,199), Somerset co., central Maine, on Kennebec R. opposite Madison and 9 mi. W of Skowhegan; wood products. Inc. 1798. **2** City (pop. 2,708), ⊙ Jones co., W central Texas, 23 mi. NNW of Abilene; trade, shipping center for cotton, cattle-ranching area; cotton gins, mfg. (farm tools, cement, machine-shop products, feed); oil wells near. Has annual Cowboys' Christmas Ball. Ruins of old Fort Phantom Hill and Fort Phantom L. (fishing) are SE. Settled 1880, inc. 1904.

Anson Bay, inlet of Joseph Bonaparte Gulf of Timor Sea, NW Northern Territory, Australia, SSW of Darwin; 21 mi. long, 15 mi. wide. Receives Daly R. Peron Isl. at N entrance.

Ansong (än'sŭng'), Jap. *Anjo,* town (1949 pop. 19,356), Kyonggi prov., central Korea, S of 38°N, 40 mi. SSE of Seoul; rice, silk cocoons.

Ansongo (änsông-gō'), village (pop. c.400), E Fr. Sudan, Fr. West Africa, landing on left bank of the Niger (near-by rapids) and 50 mi. SE of Gao; rice, millet, livestock; fishing. Dispensary. Antimony deposits in vicinity.

Ansonia (ănsō'nēů). **1** Industrial city (pop. 18,706), coextensive with Ansonia town, New Haven co., SW Conn., on the Naugatuck and 8 mi. WNW of New Haven. Brass, copper, and bronze center, also mfg. electrical equipment, tools, machinery, textiles, wire and sheet-metal products. Settled 1651; inc. as town 1889, as city 1893. **2** Village (pop. 877), Darke co., W Ohio, 7 mi. N of Greenville and on Stillwater R.; grain, livestock, dairy products, tobacco; mfg. (burial garments, food products).

Ansonville, town (pop. estimate 3,200), NE Ont., on Abitibi R., adjoining Iroquois Falls, and 27 mi. SE of Cochrane; pulp, paper, sulphite milling. Near by are waterfalls and hydroelectric station.

Ansonville (ăn'sůnvĭl), town (pop. 545), Anson co., S N.C., 9 mi. N of Wadesboro.

Anspach, Germany: see ANSBACH.

Ansted, town (pop. 1,543), Fayette co., S central W.Va., 30 mi. ESE of Charleston; trade center for bituminous-coal-mining region. Has 18th-cent. tavern. Hawks Nest State Park is near by. Settled 1790.

Anstey (ăn'stē), town and parish (pop. 3,174), central Leicester, England, 4 mi. NW of Leicester; hosiery, shoes. Has 14th-cent. bridge over small brook. In early 19th cent. one Ned Ludd here broke up stocking frames in protest against mechanization, and gave his name to the Luddite Riots which took place later over wide areas of England.

Anstruther (ăn'strůdh-ůr), village, E Fifeshire, Scotland, on the Firth of Forth near its entrance on North Sea, 8 mi. SE of St. Andrews; composed of Anstruther Easter (1931 pop. 682) and Anstruther Wester (1931 pop. 521), which, together with adjacent KILRENNY, form a single burgh (1931 pop. 3,325; 1948 estimate 3,184). Fishing port, seaside resort. Thomas Chalmers b. at Anstruther Easter.

Ansu, China: see SÜSHUI.

Ant (ănt), atoll, Senyavin Isls., Ponape dist., E Caroline Isls., W Pacific, 5.5 mi. W of Ponape; 15 coral islets on reef 6 mi. long, 3.5 mi. wide.

Anta, Argentina: see PIQUETE, Salta prov.

Anta (än'dä'), town, ⊙ Anta co. (pop. 132,147), S central Heilungkiang prov., Manchuria, 90 mi. SE of Tsitsihar; soybeans, kaoliang, rye, corn, buckwheat, millet. Its rail-station settlement, Antachan (–jän'), 20 mi. SW on Chinese Eastern RR, is a major food-processing center, 2d only to Harbin in N Manchuria; it has oilseed and flour mills, and ships soybeans and soybean oil and cake.

Anta (än'tä), town (pop. 1,713), ⊙ Anta prov. (□ 627; pop. 43,736), Cuzco dept., S central Peru, in high Andean valley, 16 mi. WNW of Cuzco; alt. 11,270 ft. Copper mining, marble and sand quarrying; agr. region (potatoes, grain).

Antabamba (äntäbäm'bä), town (pop. 2,309), ⊙ Antabamba prov. (□ 834; pop. 14,812), Apurímac dept., S central Peru, on affluent of Pachachaca R., in Andean spur, and 50 mi. S of Abancay; alt. 11,926 ft. Gold-mining center in agr. region (grain, potatoes, livestock).

Anta Dhura or **Unta Dhura** (ŭn'tů dōō'rů), pass (alt. c.17,590 ft.) in E Kumaun Himalayas, on Tibet-India border, 10 mi. NNE of Milam, India; 30°35'N 80°10'E. Leads from Almora dist. into Tibet, on most direct trade route from Tanakpur to Gyanyima and Gartok. Kungribingri is name given to its N entrance. Also called Kyunam La.

Antagarh (ŭn'tŭgŭr), village, Bastar dist., S Madhya Pradesh, India, 25 mi. SW of Kanker, in dense forest area (sal, bamboo, myrobalan; lac cultivation).

Antakya, Turkey: see ANTIOCH.

Antalaha (äntälä'hů), town (1948 pop. 7,323), Tamatave prov., NE Madagascar, on coast, 190 mi. SSE of Diégo-Suarez; cabotage port, important vanilla center (⅓ of world's production). Also exports coffee, cloves, vetiver, rosewood.

Antalfalva, Yugoslavia: see KOVACICA.

Antalo (än'tälō), village (pop. 400), Tigre prov., N Ethiopia, 15 mi. S of Makale; cereals, honey, legumes.

Antalya (äntäl'yä), province (□ 7,771; 1950 pop. 312,102), SW Turkey, on the coast; ⊙ Antalya. Bordered NE by Taurus Mts., W by Elmali Mts. Drained by lower course of Kopru and Aksu rivers. Copper and chromium in E, manganese at Finike in W; gram, sesame, legumes, cotton; camels.

Antalya or **Adalia** (ùdä'lēü, –lyü), city (1950 pop. 27,478), ⊙ Antalya prov., SW Turkey, on Gulf of Antalya of Mediterranean, 120 mi. SW of Konya; 36°52'N 30°45'E. Seaport, rail terminus, and grain market; wheat, millet, sesame. Sericulture. Picturesque town built on slope of a high hill. Its ancient wall remains. Known in anc. times as Attalia (or Attaleia) and in Middle Ages as Satalia (or Satalieh), it is mentioned in Acts 14.25 as the port whence Paul and Barnabas sailed to Antioch.

Antalya, Gulf of, or **Gulf of Adalia,** inlet of Mediterranean Sea in SW Turkey; 130 mi. wide, 50 mi. long. Town of Antalya on N shore, Alanya on NE shore.

Antananarivo, Madagascar: see TANANARIVE, town.

Antanifotsy (äntänēfōō'tsē), village, Tananarive prov., central Madagascar, on railroad and 18 mi. NE of Antsirabe; graphite mining. R.C. and Protestant missions.

Antaradus, Syria: see TARTUS.

Antarctica (ăntärk'tĭků, –är'tĭků), continent (bet. 5,000,000 and 6,000,000 sq. mi.), surrounding the South Pole. The waters about the continent are sometimes called the Antarctic Ocean but actually are only the southernmost parts of the Atlantic, Pacific, and Indian oceans. The seas, whipped by cold, violent winds, and clogged with drifting ice, icepacks and mountainous icebergs, also show extreme and rapid variability that makes them doubly dangerous to navigation. The continent was therefore completely unknown until modern times and is still imperfectly known. Its roughly circular outline is broken by 2 deeply indenting seas, the Ross Sea on the Pacific side and Weddell Sea on the Atlantic side, and by a long narrow land projection, the PALMER PENINSULA, which stretches toward South America, some 650 mi. away. The other southernmost lands, Africa and Australia and New Zealand, are much farther away, and the great southern continent is isolated by distance as well as difficulty of access. The coasts are protected from intruders by belts of pack ice, sometimes hundreds of miles wide, and by hanging ice shelves, which end in sheer ice cliffs 50 to 200 ft. high. These ice barriers and the glaciers that come from the mountains and thrust tongues of ice into the sea "calve," making enormous icebergs (many 30 mi. or more long). Beneath the ice shelves there are some small isls., but Antarctica has only a few large isls., and those are near the Palmer Peninsula. Off the tip of the peninsula are the South Shetlands. The South Orkneys and South Georgia in the Atlantic and Macquarie in the Pacific are farther away. The Falklands, which show antarctic conditions, lie closer to South America, NE of Tierra del Fuego. Antarctica is upheaved in great mtn. ranges, some with peaks rising over 15,000 ft. high; notable are mts. MARKHAM, SIPLE, LISTER, KIRKPATRICK, EREBUS (active volcano). The central area is a high plateau hidden under a perpetual icecap. Almost all of the continent, (with an estimated average altitude of 6,000 ft., almost twice that of any other continent) is, indeed, covered by a vast ice sheet. It has unassailably the severest climate on earth, with winter temp. dropping to −70°F. and even −80°F., and in the brief, unthawing Antarctic summers temp. remains at an average of 15°F. lower than those of the ARCTIC REGIONS. In broad general plan the 2 ends of the earth are in truly antipodal contrast—in the north a circumpolar landlocked sea, in the south a circumpolar ocean-surrounded land mass. From this difference comes the much more intense cold in the south and the graver dangers and difficulties of exploration. Although there was for centuries a tradition that another land lay south of the known world, attempts to find it were defeated by the ice. Navigators—notably Capt. James Cook in 1774—made their way into antarctic waters, and the British mariner William Smith discovered the South Shetlands in Feb., 1819, and confirmed his discovery the following autumn. The discovery of Antarctica itself came as a by-product of the search by whalers for new whaling grounds, although the question as to who made it is still in some dispute. An American, Capt. Nathaniel Palmer, in Nov., 1820, sighted an unknown coast. He told the Russian voyager, Admiral Bellingshausen, who, speaking of it to others, called it Palmer's Land. An Englishman, Capt. Edward Bransfield, sailed between the South Shetlands and the continent in Jan., 1821, and probably saw the continent. In 1830 another Englishman, John BISCOE sighted high mts.; 2 years later he landed on an isl. and thinking it part of the mainland, called it and the near-by peninsula Graham Land. Hence the double name for the peninsula which Americans call Palmer Peninsula and the British call Graham Land. The British also question Palmer's log and consider either Bransfield or Biscoe the discoverer. The voyages of James Weddell, John Balleny, Dumont d'Urville, Charles Wilkes, and James C. Ross followed in the first half of the 19th cent. That of Ross was important in opening the Ross Sea approach. Then for nearly a half century interest in polar exploration turned toward the arctic region. A renewed turn to the south was marked by the explorations of the Belgian, Adrien de Gerlache, in 1897–99; his expedition was the first to winter in the area of Antarctica. As the 20th cent. began scientific interest quickened and led to a number of well-equipped expeditions, notably those of E. E. Borchgrevink, William Bruce, Erik von Drygalski, Otto Nordenskjöld, Robert Scott, Jean B. Charcot, and Douglas Mawson; all these wintered in the Antarctic. Extensive scientific surveys were made. Several expeditions were fired by the desire to reach the South Pole; E. H. Shackleton failed (1908–9), but Roald Amundsen succeeded (Dec. 14, 1911) to be followed almost immediately (Jan. 18, 1912) by Robert Scott. Considerable knowledge of the interior of Antarctica was gained, but the World War interrupted the search. When interest was resumed, the airplane provided a new method of exploration, with George Hubert Wilkins and Richard E. Byrd as the pioneers. The years just before and after 1937 were highly productive, with the British expedition (1934–37) under John Rymell, the Norwegian expedition (1936–37) of Lars Christensen, the 4th antarctic journey (1938–39) of Lincoln Ellsworth, and the voyage (1937–39) of the British *Discovery II*, the 5th on her 2-year commission to investigate the distribution and the feeding grounds of whales. In 1939–41, the U.S. Antarctic Service, with Richard E. Byrd in command, pursued research from 2 bases 2,000 mi. apart, one on Little America on the Bay of Whales, the other on Palmer Peninsula. A British expedition under J. W. S. Moor in 1944 evolved plans for systematic study of the peninsula and the mainland coast, including the establishment of meteorological stations. In the years 1946–48 knowledge of Antarctica was tremendously increased by 3 U.S. expeditions. The U.S. navy's "Operation Highjump," led by Byrd, was much the largest, most completely organized, and most thoroughly mechanized expedition ever sent to Antarctica. Topographical knowledge was greatly broadened by exploratory flights, recorded by moving pictures. Unfrozen areas were found, especially a warm-lake region in the quadrant toward Australia; many new lofty peaks were noted; and isls. under the Ross ice shelf were indicated by the magneto-meter. Photo-mapping clarified old knowledge and added new. A smaller naval expedition in 1947–48 supplemented the work. The expedition (1946–48) led by Finn Ronne centered at the base of the Palmer Peninsula and cooperated with the British Falkland Islands Dependencies Survey. Many discoveries were made, including a mountain range running SE from the Palmer Peninsula to the high, snow-covered central plateau, which was shown to be a continuation of the Andes. It was demonstrated that the theory that a strait between Ross Sea and Weddell Sea cuts Antarctica is almost certainly false. In 1947 Australia sent an official expedition into the antarctic regions. Chile and Argentina, the USSR, Norway (cooperating with Britain and Sweden), and Japan all showed interest in Antarctica in the years after the Second World War. The wide range of national interest reflects a wide range of conflicting claims to antarctic territory. The various claims on Antarctica cut the continent and its surrounding waters like pieces of a pie that has as its circumference the circle of lat. 60°S. Beginning at long. 20°W and reading clockwise, the claims are: Norway, 20°W–45°E (QUEEN MAUD LAND); Australia, 45°E–160°E (AUSTRALIAN ANTARCTIC TERRITORY), except for the Adélie Coast (French) bet. 136°E and 142°E; New Zealand, 160°E–150°W (ROSS DEPENDENCY); officially unclaimed, but explored by U.S. expeditions, 150°W–90°W; and the area of overlapping claims—Chile, 90°W–53°W, Argentina, 74°W–25°W, Great Britain, 80°W–50°W south of lat. 58°S and 50°W–20°W south of lat. 50°S. The USSR, while making no specific claims, insists upon rights by reason of Bellingshausen's work. The U.S. recognizes no claims in Antarctica and makes no official claims although U.S. explorers have dropped flags on areas they have explored. One of the usual requisites for establishing claims to a territory—that of settlement—has thus far proved impossible. The antarctic regions are definitely not friendly to man. Though the Antarctic Circle is drawn the same distance (23°30′ of latitude) from the South Pole that the Arctic Circle is from the North Pole, the area of antarctic weather conditions is much greater than that of arctic weather conditions. The cold is intensified by the incredibly strong winds that blow mainly outward from the central plateau of Antarctica and drive the melting shore ice and the great icebergs to sea and extend the area of cold to lat. 50°S. While the arctic regions have a rapid and varied summer vegetation, some year-round and abundant summer animal life, and human inhabitants, the antarctic regions have only moss, lichens, and algae as vegetation, no year-round land animal life except a wingless insect about ½ in. long and microscopic organisms, and no human inhabitants. What animal life there is is based on the sea and is found only in the sea and directly on the coast. There are however a surprising number of birds: the emperor penguin is the only year-round resident, but Adélie penguins and smaller birds are summer visitors. In that season whales and seals also arrive. Many scientists say, however, that Antarctica may have been tropical or temperate millions of years ago and may again be habitable millions of years hence.

Antarctic Archipelago, Antarctica: see PALMER ARCHIPELAGO.

Antarctic Ocean, name sometimes given to those parts of the Pacific, Atlantic, and Indian oceans which surround Antarctica; usually includes the vast frozen sea whose drift ice generally reaches c.55°S but which, off S Africa, extends to c.48°S. The waters are extremely cold and dangerous. Greatest depth is BYRD DEEP (28,152 ft.).

Antas, Rio das, Brazil: see TAQUARI RIVER.

Antassawamock Neck, Mass.: see MATTAPOISETT.

An Teallach or **Teallach** (chă'lŭkh), mountain (3,483 ft.), NW Ross and Cromarty, Scotland, 7 mi. SW of Ullapool, near head of Little Loch Broom.

Antela, Lake (äntā'lä), Orense prov., NW Spain, 15 mi. SE of Orense; 4 mi. long, 3 mi. wide. Limia (Lima) R. rises here.

Antelao (äntĕlä'ô), second highest peak (10,705 ft.) in the Dolomites, N Italy, 22 mi. N of Belluno. Has small glaciers.

Antelat (äntĕlät'), village W Cyrenaica, Libya, 35 mi. NE of Agedabia; caravan center. Scene of fighting (1942) bet. Axis and British in Second World War.

Antella (äntā'lyä), village (pop. 1,852), Valencia prov., E Spain, on Júcar R. and 10 mi. SW of Alcira; rice, oranges, esparto.

Antelope or **Antelope Mine,** township (pop. 668), Bulawayo prov., SW Southern Rhodesia, in Matabeleland, 60 mi. S of Bulawayo; gold-mining center.

Antelope, county (□ 853; pop. 11,624), NE Nebr.; ⊙ Neligh. Agr. area drained by Elkhorn R. Livestock, grain. Formed 1871.

Antelope, city (pop. 60), Wasco co., N Oregon, 50 mi. SSE of The Dalles; livestock.

Antelope Hills, Okla.: see ROGER MILLS, county.

Antelope Island (□ 36.2; c.15 mi. long, 4 mi. wide), N Utah, largest isl. in Great Salt L., 20 mi. NW of Salt Lake City; stock grazing. Buffalo herd here.

Antelope Peak, Nev.: see MONITOR RANGE.

Antelope Range, central Nev., c.35 mi. SW of Eureka; Sharp Peak (10,100 ft.), highest point.

Antelope Valley, Calif.: see MOJAVE DESERT.

Antenor Navarro (äntĭnôr' nŏovä'rōō), city (pop. 1,667), W Paraíba, NE Brazil, on railroad at junction of spur to Cajàzeiras (13 mi. SW); ships cotton, rice, sugar. Formerly called São João do Rio Peixe.

Antep, Turkey: see GAZIANTEP.

Antequera (äntākä'rä), village (pop. c.1,000), Oruro dept., W Bolivia, at S end of Serranía de Achacollo, 8 mi. SSE of Poopó; alt. 13,117 ft.; tin-mining center.

Antequera, town (dist. pop. 2,177), San Pedro dept., central Paraguay, on Paraguay R. and 6 mi. SW of San Pedro; minor port and agr. center (oranges, maté, livestock); processing of oil of petitgrain.

Antequera, town (1939 pop. 1,129; 1948 municipality pop. 16,070), W Bohol isl., Philippines, 10 mi. NNE of Tagbilaran; agr. center (rice, coconuts).

Antequera, anc. *Anticaria* or *Antiquaria,* city (pop. 23,218), Málaga prov., S Spain, in Andalusia, at N foot of El Torcal peak, near the Guadalhorce, on railroad and 21 mi. NNW of Málaga. Inland trading and processing center in fertile region (olives, cereals, sugar beets, fruit, livestock); tanning, liquor distilling, sugar refining, olive-oil pressing, flour and textile milling; iron foundries. Mfg. of chocolate, food preserves, soap, plaster, fertilizers. The historic city has ruins of Moorish castle, Roman remains, Santa María arch (1585), Mocha Tower, San Sebastián church. The Cueva de Menga, large prehistoric cairns ½ mi. E, were discovered in 1842; others have been found more recently.

Antero, Mount (ăntĕ'rō) (14,245 ft.), in Sawatch Mts., central Colo., 15 mi. NW of Salida.

Antero Park Reservoir, central Colo., on small affluent of South Platte R., in Rocky Mts., and c.70 mi. SW of Denver; 4 mi. long, 2.5 mi. wide; alt. over 9,000 ft. Formed by earth-fill dam (35 ft. high). Unit in water-supply system of Denver.

Anthemous (ănthĕmōōs'), town (pop. 2,961), Chalcidice nome, Macedonia, Greece, 10 mi. NW of Polygyros; magnesite mining. Formerly named Galatista.

Anthisnes (ätēn'), village (pop. 1,437), Liége prov., E central Belgium, 11 mi. SSW of Liége; granite quarrying.

Anthon (ăn'thŭn), town (pop. 770), Woodbury co., W Iowa, on Little Sioux R. and 29 mi. ESE of Sioux City, in livestock and grain area.

Anthony (ăn'thŭnē). **1** City (pop. 2,792), ⊙ Harper co., S Kansas, 50 mi. SW of Wichita; trade center for grain and livestock area; flour milling. Founded 1878, inc. 1879. **2** Village, R.I.: see COVENTRY.

Anthony's Lagoon, settlement (dist. pop. 86), E central Northern Territory, Australia, 400 mi. NNE of Alice Springs; airport; cattle. Sometimes spelled Anthony Lagoon.

Anthony's Nose, SE N.Y., promontory (alt. c.1,200 ft.) on E bank of the Hudson, opposite Bear Mtn., c.6 mi. NNW of Peekskill.

Anthracite, village, SW Alta., in Rocky Mts., in Banff Natl. Park, 4 mi. E of Banff; coal.

Anti-Atlas, Fr. Morocco: see ATLAS MOUNTAINS.

Antibes (ätēb'), anc. *Antipolis,* town (pop. 13,778), Alpes-Maritimes dept., SE France, port on Fr. Riviera, 11 mi. SW of Nice; horticultural center exporting flowers, oranges and olives; mfg. (perfumes, chocolate, cement pipes), petroleum refining. Its port, fortified in 17th cent. is commanded by late-16th-cent. Fort Carré (square fort). Antibes was founded in 4th cent. B.C. as a Gr. colony and preserves remains of Roman town (just S of port). Slightly damaged during Allied invasion (Aug., 1944) in Second World War. *Cap d'Antibes,* near S tip of a peninsula of same name, 2.5 mi. S of Antibes, is a fashionable seaside resort in the midst of subtropical vegetation. Juan-les-Pins is 1 mi. SSW of Antibes on Juan Gulf.

Anticosti Island (ăntĭkŏ'stē) (140 mi. long, 30 mi. wide; pop. 424), in the Gulf of St. Lawrence, E Que., at mouth of the St. Lawrence, 50 mi. NE of Gaspé Peninsula and separated from Que. mainland (N) by Mingan Passage (30 mi. wide); 49°4′–49°57′N 61°41′–64°31′W. Generally level, with ranges of low hills along N coast, rising to 625 ft. Chief settlement, Port Menier, on SW coast. Lumbering is main industry; there are some fur farms. Discovered (1534) by Jacques Cartier, isl. was granted to Jolliet by Louis XIV and remained property of his heirs until 1763, when it came under Newfoundland jurisdiction. It was returned (1774) to Canada. Attempts made to colonize isl. in 1874 and 1884 failed. In 1895 Anticosti was sold to Henri Menier, French chocolate manufacturer; it was sold 1926 to Canadian paper interests.

Anticythera, Greece: see ANTIKYTHERA.

Antietam (ăntē'tŭm), village, Washington co., W Md., 7 mi. N of Harpers Ferry, W.Va. and on the Potomac at mouth of **Antietam Creek,** which rises in S Franklin co., Pa., flows c.40 mi. S, through Hagerstown Valley. On its banks just SE of Sharpsburg and c.3 mi. NE of Antietam is **Antietam National Battlefield Site** (183.33 acres; established 1890), commemorating Civil War battle (Sept. 17, 1862) of Antietam (often called battle of Sharpsburg in the South), bloodiest day's fighting of war, which resulted in Lee's abandonment of his 1st invasion of the North; both Lee's and McClellan's forces suffered heavy losses. Antietam Natl. Cemetery (established 1862) is near.

Antifer, Cape (ätēfâr'), rounded headland of Seine-Inférieure dept., N France, on English channel, 13 mi. N of Le Havre; 49°42′N 0°9′E. Cliff rises to c.360 ft. Terminus of submarine cable to England.

Antignano (äntēnyä'nô), village (pop. 2,322), Livorno prov., Tuscany, central Italy, on coast of Ligurian Sea, 4 mi. S of Leghorn; bathing resort.

Antigo (ăn'tĭgō), city (pop. 9,902), ⊙ Langlade co., NE Wis., on tributary of Eau Claire R. and 26 mi. NE of Wausau, in dairying and potato-growing area; mfg. (cheese, wood products, shoes). Has several cooperatives. The co. historical society has mus. here. Settled 1876, inc. 1885.

Antigonish (ăn″tĭgōnĭsh′), county (□ 541; pop. 10,545), E central N.S., on Northumberland Strait and George Bay; ⊙ Antigonish.

Antigonish, town (pop. 2,157), ⊙ Antigonish co., NE N.S., at head of Antigonish Bay (6 mi. long; inlet of George Bay), 30 mi. E of New Glasgow; woolen milling, dairying, fishing, lumbering; exports dairy produce and fish. Seat of R.C. bishop; has Cathedral of St. Ninian (1867), St. Francis Xavier Univ. (which has promoted a notable cooperative here), and Mount St. Bernard Col.

Antigua (äntē′gwä), village (pop. 528), Fuerteventura, Canary Isls., 11 mi. WSW of Puerto de Cabras, in fertile region (fruit, barley, alfalfa, cochineal, potatoes, tomatoes, corn, wheat; livestock). Lime quarries and kilns.

Antigua or **Antigua Guatemala** (gwätämä′lä) [Sp.,=old Guatemala], city (1950 pop. 10,691), ⊙ Sacatepéquez dept., S central Guatemala, in central highlands, on Pensativo R. (branch of the Guacalate) and 15 mi. WSW of Guatemala; 14°34′N 90°43′W; alt. 5,029 ft. Commercial center in rich agr. area (coffee, sugar cane, grain, fodder crops); pottery making, metalworking; trading in fruit and vegetables. Sulphur baths near by. A major tourist center; has remains of many churches, monasteries, and public bldgs., including cathedral (begun 1543), palace of captains-general of Guatemala, city hall, 17th-cent. univ. (now a colonial mus.). Founded 1542 following destruction of CIUDAD VIEJA, 3 mi. SSW; became ⊙ Guatemala. Flourished in 17th cent. as one of the New World's richest capitals; became center of learning, arts, and crafts; in 18th cent. pop. reached 80,000. Continually subject to floods, volcanic eruptions, and earthquakes; almost completely destroyed (1773) by earthquakes; capital removed (1776) to present Guatemala city. The volcanoes Agua, Acatenango, and Fuego are near by.

Antigua (ăntē′gŭ, –gwŭ, ăntĭ′gwŭ), island (□ 108; pop. 40,778), Leeward Isls., B.W.I., 40 mi. E of Nevis, 40 mi. N of Guadeloupe; 17°5′N 61°50′W. Its chief city, St. John's, is ⊙ Antigua presidency (□ 170.5; pop. 41,757), which, besides Antigua isl., includes REDONDA and BARBUDA as dependencies. Antigua isl. (13 mi. long, 10 mi. wide) is of volcanic origin in SW, of coral in N and E; rises to 1,329 ft. Has dry, pleasant climate; water is scarce; occasional hurricanes in summer. Antigua's mainstays are sugar cane and sea-island cotton; also raises tropical fruit, vegetables, tobacco, livestock. Processing industries: sugar refining, rum distilling, cotton ginning. Some barite ores are shipped to Trinidad. Fishing for local consumption. The isl. was discovered 1493 by Columbus, who named it after a church in Seville. Colonized 1632 by the English from St. Kitts. Shortly thereafter occupied by the French, it was confirmed as British by Peace of Breda (1667). Nelson served (1784–87) at historic dockyard of English Harbour. In 1941 a site on NE coast was leased to the U.S. for naval and military base.

Antigua, Salina (sälē′nä äntē′gwä), salt desert (□ 200) in E La Rioja prov., Argentina, c.40 mi. SE of La Rioja, W of the Salinas Grandes; c.40 mi. long, 3–5 mi. wide. Contains sodium and potassium salts. Sometimes Salina Rioja.

Antigua Guatemala, Guatemala: see ANTIGUA.

Antigua Morelos (mōrā′lōs), town (pop. 683), Tamaulipas, NE Mexico, on Inter-American Highway and 85 mi. S of Ciudad Victoria; cereals, fruit, livestock.

Antigua Veracruz, Mexico: see JOSÉ CARDEL.

Antigüedad (äntē″gwädh-ädh′), town (pop. 1,349), Palencia prov., N central Spain, 22 mi. ESE of Palencia; flour mills; cereals, livestock.

Antiguos, Los, Argentina: see LOS ANTIGUOS.

Antikaros or **Andikaros** (both: ŭndē′kŭrôs), Aegean island (□ 0.4; 1928 pop. 7), in the Cyclades, Greece, SE of Naxos isl.; 36°50′N 25°41′E. Also called Antikeros or Andikeros.

Antikythera or **Andikithira** (both: ŭndĭkē′thērŭ), anc. *Aegilia* (ējĭ′lēŭ) or *Anticythera* (ăntĭsĭthē′rŭ), Ital. *Cerigotto* (chārēgôt′tō), island (□ 8.5; 1940 pop. 246) in Mediterranean Sea, SE of Peloponnesus and 20 mi. NW of Cape Vouxa (Crete); part of Attica nome, Greece; 35°52′N 28°18′E; 6 mi. long, 2 mi. wide. Wheat, stock raising (sheep, goats). Chief village, Potamos (1928 pop. 57), on NE shore. Inhabited by Cretans since Turkish conquest of Crete. Anc. bronze and marble objects were recovered after 1900 from wreck offshore.

Anti-Lebanon (ăn″tē-lĕ′bŭnŭn), Fr. *Anti-Liban* (ãtē-lēbã′), Lat. *Anti-Libanus* (ăn′tē-lĭbā′nōōs), mountain range, on Syrian-Lebanese line, running parallel to and E of the Lebanon range, from which it is separated by the Bekaa valley. Rises to 9,232 ft. in Mt. HERMON. Barren and stony, it is much less heavily populated than the Lebanon mts. Its Arabic name is *Jebel esh Sharqi, Jebel el Sharqi,* or *Jabal al-Sharqi.*

Antilla (äntē′yä), town (pop. 5,786), Oriente prov., E Cuba, sugar port on N shore of landlocked Nipe Bay, 60 mi. N of Santiago de Cuba. Rail terminus, airfield, and seaplane anchorage. Has extensive docks; located in fertile agr. region (sugar cane, tropical fruit). Sawmilling. Near by are iron mines and sugar mills.

Antilles (ăntĭ′lēz), main island group of the WEST INDIES, curving for c.2,500 mi. from Florida to N coast of Venezuela, and forming a natural breakwater separating the Atlantic from the Gulf of Mexico and the Caribbean. The Antilles include all the isls. of the West Indies except the Bahamas, although the name Antilles is sometimes used to designate all the West Indies. They form 2 large groups: the Greater Antilles comprise CUBA, JAMAICA, HISPANIOLA (HAITI and DOMINICAN REPUBLIC), and PUERTO RICO; the Lesser Antilles (sometimes called Caribbees) comprise the VIRGIN ISLANDS (geologically a part of the Greater Antilles), LEEWARD ISLANDS, WINDWARD ISLANDS, BARBADOS, TRINIDAD, and TOBAGO, and the Dutch (Curaçao) and Venezuelan (Margarita) isls. off NE coast of South America. Apart from the independent states of Cuba, Haiti, and the Dominican Republic, the isls. are owned by foreign powers (Great Britain, France, the Netherlands, U.S.).

Antilles Current, N branch of North Equatorial Current in North Atlantic Ocean, flowing NW along N (Atlantic) side of the Greater Antilles. It joins the current emerging from the Gulf of Mexico via the Straits of Florida to form the Florida Current, the 1st section of the Gulf Stream system.

Antimacheia or **Andimakhia** (both: ŭndēmä′khēä), Ital. *Antimachia,* town (pop. 1,870), Kos isl., in the Dodecanese, Greece, 12 mi. W of Kos.

Antímano (äntē′mänō), town (pop. 2,746), Federal Dist., N Venezuela, on Guaire R., on railroad and 5 mi. WSW of Caracas, in agr. region (sugar cane, cacao, coffee, corn).

Antimelos or **Andimilos** (both: ändē′mĭlôs), uninhabited Aegean island (□ 3) of the Cyclades, Greece, NW of Melos; 36°48′N 24°4′E. Also called Eremomelos or Erimomilos.

Antimony (ăn′tĭmō″nē), town (pop. 187), Garfield co., S Utah, 15 mi. SE of Junction and on East Fork of Sevier R.; alt. 6,500 ft.; antimony deposits near.

Anting. **1** Town, Kansu prov., China: see TINGSI. **2** Town, Shensi prov., China: see CHANGTZE.

Antioch (ăn′tēŏk), Lat. *Antiochia,* Turkish *Antakya* (äntäk′yä), city (1950 pop. 30,385), ⊙ Hatay, S Turkey, on Orontes R., 20 mi. from Mediterranean coast, and 55 mi. W of Aleppo (Syria); 36°10′N 36°10′E. Founded c.300 B.C. by Seleucus I near 2 already existing Greek colonies, and named for his father, Antiochus; the pop. was largely Macedonian. Lying at the crossroads from the Euphrates to the sea and from BEKAA to Asia Minor, it soon grew into one of the largest commercial centers and most sumptuous cities of the world; the 2 main streets at right angles to each other were lined with marble colonnades and adorned with temples, palaces, and statues. City was surrounded by a thick wall the remains of which as well as those of the aqueduct, theater, and castle are still visible. It was here that the followers of Jesus were 1st called Christians after having severed themselves from the synagogue (see Acts 11.26 & 13.1). Antioch is one of the 3 ancient patriarchates. Aurelian, who recovered it from Shapur I of Persia, erected more magnificent buildings and churches. St. Chrysostome estimated the population (4th cent. A.D.) at 200,000. In 538 Antioch fell to the Persians, in 637 to the Arabs. Nicephorus I reconquered it (969) for the Byzantine Empire, but in 1085, it fell, through treason, to the Seljuk Turks. The army of the First Crusade laid siege to Antioch in 1097 and conquered it in 1098. Bohemond I was made prince of Antioch. His principality, which extended from Iskenderun southward beyond Latakia, was one of the most powerful of the crusaders' states. In 1108 Bohemond was forced to recognize Emperor Alexius I of Byzantium as his suzerain; but the Byzantines could not for long enforce their claims and Bohemond's successor held Antioch as a virtually independent fief from the Latin kingdom of Jerusalem. After its fall (1268) to the Mamelukes of Egypt, Antioch declined; in 1516 it was conquered by the Ottoman Turks. With the sanjak of ALEXANDRETTA, Antioch was transferred to Syria in 1920 and restored to Turkey in 1939. City suffered many severe earthquakes; most destructive earthquake in recent times was in 1872. Modern Antioch occupies but a fraction of the ancient city, but it remains commercial center of a fertile area (cotton, olives, grain) and has some processing industries.

Antioch. **1** Town (pop. 11,051), Contra Costa co., W Calif., on San Joaquin R. and 30 mi. ENE of Oakland; industrial, fruit- and vegetable-shipping point; canning (especially asparagus); mfg. of fiberboard, glass containers. Has a power plant of Central Valley project. Founded 1849–50, inc. 1872. **2** Village (pop. 1,307), Lake co., extreme NE Ill., near Wis. line, 16 mi. NW of Waukegan, in dairying, farming, and lake-resort area; dairy products, flour, feed. Several lakes and Chain-O'-Lakes State Park are near by. Settled 1836, inc. 1857. **3** Village (pop. 112), Monroe co., E Ohio, 7 mi. SSE of Woodsfield, in agr. area.

Antioche, Pertuis d' (pĕrtwē′ dätēōsh′), inlet of Bay of Biscay, off Charente-Maritime dept., W France, bet. Île de Ré and Île d'Oléron; 24 mi. long, 16 mi. wide; contains small isls. (Aix, Madame) off mouth of the Charente, which form part of fortifications of Rochefort. La Rochelle, with outer port of La Pallice, on NE shore.

Antioquia (äntyō′kyä), department (□ 25,409; 1938 pop. 1,188,587; 1950 estimate 1,486,270), NW central Colombia; ⊙ Medellín. A mountainous area, it extends along fertile Cauca valley, flanked by Cordillera Central and Cordillera Occidental. Bounded W by Atrato R., E by Magdalena R., NW by Gulf of Urabá (inlet of the Caribbean). Lowlands are humid, unhealthy, and tropical; the settled uplands are more temperate, with 2 wet and 2 dry periods, the main rainy season starting in March. Commercially the most progressive dept. of Colombia, it leads in gold mining, coffeegrowing, and textile milling. Agr. crops also include sugar cane, cotton, corn, rice, fique and yucca fibers, tobacco, cacao, fruit. Cattle and hogs are raised in the highlands. Dense forests yield fine timber, resins, rubber, vanilla, cinchona and medicinal plants. Petroleum is drilled for on the Magdalena; other mineral resources include iron and coal (Amagá), silver, platinum, copper, cinnabar, lime, marble, salt. Medellín, the principal industrial city of Colombia, has textile, metalworking, and food-processing industries. Puerto Berrío, on the Magdalena, joined by rail with Medellín, is linked by steamers with Barranquilla, and handles most of Antioquia's imports and exports. Long an isolated region, it developed rapidly with the construction of railroads during 19th cent. and the development of coffee plantations after 1918.

Antioquia, town (pop. 3,810), Antioquia dept., NW central Colombia, on Cauca R., on highway, and 27 mi. NW of Medellín; alt. c.2,300 ft. Agr. center (corn, beans, sugar cane, coffee, fruit; horses). Old gold-mining town with fine colonial cathedral. Bridge across the Cauca is near by. Founded 1541, it was until 1826 the dept. capital.

Antiparos (ăntĭpä′rŏs) or **Andiparos** (ŭndē′pŭrôs), anc. *Oliarus* (ōlī′ŭrŭs), Aegean island (□ 13; pop. 606) in the Cyclades, Greece, just SW of Paros isl.; 37°2′N 24°56′E; 8 mi. long, 3 mi. wide; corn, wine; lead deposits. It has a noted stalactite cave.

Antipatris (ăntĭ′pŭtrĭs), anc. city, W Palestine, in Plain of Sharon, 10 mi. ENE of Tel Aviv, 3 mi. NE of Petah Tiqva. Founded by Herod the Great; Paul was brought here on way to Caesarea. Ruins extant.

Antipaxos (ăntĭpăk′sŏs), **Antipaxoi,** or **Andipaxoi** (both: ŭndĭpäk′sē), island (□ 2.5; pop. 153) in Ionian Sea, Greece, in Corfu nome, just SE of Paxos; 39°8′N 20°9′E; 3 mi. long, .5 mi. wide, rises to 350 ft. Oil-shale deposits. Formerly also called Antipaxo.

Antiphilippoi, Greece: see PALAIOKHORION.

Antipodes Islands (ăntĭp′ūdēz), rocky uninhabited group (□ 24), S Pacific, one of outlying isl. groups of New Zealand, 450 mi. SE of Dunedin; 49°41′S 178°43′E.

Antipolis, France: see ANTIBES.

Antipolo (äntēpō′lō), town (1939 pop. 4,093; 1948 municipality pop. 7,604), Rizal prov., S Luzon, Philippines, 13 mi. E of Manila; rice, fruit. Here is the image of Virgin of Peace and Good Voyage brought from Mexico in early 17th cent.

Antipsara or **Andipsara** (both: ŭndĭp′sŭrŭ), uninhabited Greek Aegean island (□ 1.5), off SW Psara isl., in Chios nome; 38°33′N 25°24′E.

Antique (äntē′kä), province (□ 1,034; 1948 pop. 233,506), W Panay isl., Philippines, bounded W by Cuyo East Pass; ⊙ SAN JOSE DE BUENAVISTA. Includes SEMIRARA ISLANDS. Mountainous terrain, drained by many small streams. Agr. (rice, sugar cane); copper and coal mining.

Antirrion, Cape, or **Cape Andirrion** (both: ŭndē′rēôn), W central Greece, on N side of strait linking Gulfs of Corinth (E) and Patras (W), opposite Cape Rion; 38°19′N 38°20′E. Also spelled Antirhion.

Antisana (äntēsä′nä), Andean volcano (18,714 ft.), N central Ecuador, 30 mi. SE of Quito; 0°30′S 78°13′W. A large snow-capped massif, the crater of which is still active, emitting sulphurous gases. The village of Antisana (alt. over 13,000 ft.) is on its W slope.

Antissa (ăntĭ′sŭ) or **Andissa** (än′dĭsŭ), town (pop. 3,261), on W Lesbos isl., Lesbos nome, Greece, 31 mi. WNW of Mytilene; olive oil, wine. Anc. Antissa was destroyed 168 B.C. by Rome. Formerly called Telonia.

Anti-Taurus, Turkey: see TAURUS MOUNTAINS.

Antium, Italy: see ANZIO.

Antivari, Yugoslavia: see BAR.

Antler, city (pop. 217), Bottineau co., N N.Dak., port of entry 39 mi. WNW of Bottineau, near Antler R. and Can. line.

Antler Peak, Nev.: see BATTLE MOUNTAIN.

Antlers, town (pop. 2,506), ⊙ Pushmataha co., SE Okla., c.45 mi. ENE of Durant, and on Kiamichi R.; lumber-milling town; also mfg. of mattresses, feed, wood products, canned foods, machine-shop products. Inc. 1903.

Anto, Korea: see ANDONG.

Antofagasta or **Antofagasta de la Sierra** (än′tō fägä′-stä dā lä syĕ′rä), village, ⊙ Antofagasta de la Sierra dept. (□ 11,600; pop. 677), N Catamarca prov., Argentina, in the Puna de Atacama, 150 mi. SW of Salta; alt. 11,320 ft. Small salt lake near by. In Los Andes territory until 1943.

Antofagasta, province (□ 47,515; 1940 pop. 145,147; 1949 estimate 188,664), N Chile, bet. the Andes and the Pacific, bordering on Argentina and Bolivia; ⊙ Antofagasta. Largely a desert area, with dry, moderate climate, it includes part of the Atacama Desert and towering peaks of the Andes (e.g., Llullaillaco, Socompa, Azufre Volcano, Ollagüe). Loa R. waters the oases. Primarily a mineral-producing region, it abounds in nitrates: at María Elena, Pedro de Valdivia, Santa Luisa (W); iodine is by-product of the nitrates. Also borax on large scale (Ascotán, Punta Negra), copper (Chuquicamata), silver (Caracoles), sulphur (Ollagüe), marble (Calama). At the few oases are grown grain, alfalfa, potatoes, citrus fruit, wine, and sheep are raised: Quillagua, Calama, Toconao, San Pedro de Atacama. Llamas, vicuñas, and alpacas raised on Andean slopes. Mfg. concentrated at Antofagasta and Tocopilla; high explosives at Calama. The prov. was ceded (1882) to Chile by Bolivia after the War of the Pacific.

Antofagasta, city (1940 pop. 49,106; 1949 estimate 43,318), ⊙ Antofagasta prov. and Antofagasta dept. (□ 15,883; 1940 pop. 68,958), N Chile, port on the Pacific, on railroad and 700 mi. N of Santiago; 23°38′S 70°29′W. Most important of Chile's northern cities, it is an international commercial center and outlet for the Bolivian and Chilean mining regions, exporting nitrates, copper (from Chuquicamata), sulphur, borax, and other metals. It has highway and rail connections to Bolivia, Argentina, and S Chile; in 1948 the new Transandine RR of the North was opened over Socompa Pass, bet. Antofagasta and Salta, Argentina. Industries: nitrate and metal processing, sulphur refining, brewing, mfg. of coal-tar products, fish canning, textile milling, soap and paint mfg. Has airport, theaters, administrative bldgs. It has extremely dry, moderate, unvarying climate; water is brought by aqueduct from Calama. Founded 1870 by Chileans to exploit nitrate deposits in the Atacama Desert, then belonging to Bolivia, the city was occupied 1879 by Chilean troops, beginning the War of the Pacific; after the war it was ceded to Chile, and its fortunes fluctuated with the demand for nitrates and copper. Pre-Columbian ruins of Lasana are near by.

Antofalla, Salar de (sälär′ dā äntōfä′yä), salt desert (□ 375; alt. 11,350 ft.) in the Puna de Atacama, NW Catamarca prov., Argentina, extends c.100 mi. NNE-SSW in valley (2–5 mi. wide) along W foot of Sierra de Calalaste. Contains sodium, magnesium, and aluminum salts. Antofalla volcano (21,100 ft.) is 50 mi. NW of Antofagasta, Argentina.

Antoine (ăn′twĭn), town (pop. 209), Pike co., SW Ark., 39 mi. SW of Hot Springs and on Antoine Creek.

Antoine, Lake (ăntwän′), NE Grenada, B.W.I., 12 mi. NE of St. George's, in an extinct crater.

Antoine Creek (ăn′twĭn), SW Ark., rises in N Pike co., flows c.40 mi. SE, past Graysonia and Antoine, to Little Missouri R. 11 mi. N of Prescott.

Antoing (ãtwẽ′), town (pop. 3,503), Hainaut prov., SW Belgium, on Scheldt R. and 3 mi. SE of Tournai; electric-power station; cement making, barge building. Chalk quarries.

Antola, Monte (mōn′tĕ än′tōlä), peak (5,243 ft.) in Ligurian Apennines, N Italy, 16 mi. NNE of Genoa.

Antón (äntōn′), town (pop. 1,491), Coclé prov., central Panama, in Pacific lowland, on Inter-American Highway, on Antón R. (25-mi.-long coastal stream) and 10 mi. SE of Penonomé. Stock raising center.

Anton (ăn′tŏn), city (pop. 934), Hockley co., NW Texas, on the Llano Estacado, 20 mi. NW of Lubbock; shipping and ginning point for agr. area (cotton, grain, dairy products, livestock).

Anton Chico (ăn′tŏn chē′kō), village (pop. c.400), Guadalupe co., central N.Mex., on Pecos R. and 27 mi. S of Las Vegas; alt. c.5,200 ft. Outfitting point in ranching, livestock region. Sangre de Cristo Mts. are NW.

Antongil Bay, Fr. *Baie d'Antongil* (bā dãtôNyē′), inlet of Indian Ocean on NE coast of Madagascar, adjacent to Masoala Peninsula; 40 mi. long, 20 mi. wide; 15°20′S 49°50′E. Maroantsetra port is on N shore.

Antonina (äntōōnē′nŭ), city (pop. 5,632), E Paraná, Brazil, port at head of Paranaguá Bay, 33 mi. E of Curitiba; rail-spur terminus; iron smelter (using local magnetite deposits); maté and rice processing, woodworking, mfg. of rope and soap, sugar and flour milling.

Antoninus, Wall of (ăn″tŭnī′nŭs), Roman earthwork, extending 37 mi. E-W across Scotland, bet. the Firth of Clyde, near Dumbarton, and the Firth of Forth, built A.D. 140 by Antoninus Pius. It is believed to have been c.20 ft. high and was paralleled by ditch; military stations were built along the wall.

Antoniny (ŭntŭnyĕ′nē), village (1926 pop. 2,569), central Kamenets-Podolski oblast, Ukrainian SSR, 25 mi. SSW of Shepetovka; metalworks; wheat, sugar beets.

Antonio Amaro (äntō′nyō ämä′rō), town (pop. 1,816), Durango, N Mexico, 50 mi. NE of Durango; grain, fruit, vegetables, stock.

Antônio Enes (äntô′nyōō ĕ′nĭsh), town (1940 pop. 11,979), Niassa prov., E Mozambique, port on Mozambique Channel of Indian Ocean, 100 mi. SSW of Mozambique city; ships cotton, sisal, peanuts, copra. Airfield. Founded by Portuguese in 17th cent. Formerly called Angoche. Angoche isl. is 3 mi. S.

Antonio Escobedo (äntō′nyō ĕskōbā′dō), town (pop. 1,875), Jalisco, W Mexico, on E shore of L. Magdalena, 40 mi. WNW of Guadalajara; grain, maguey, beans, livestock. Formerly San Juanito.

Antônio Pereira (äntō′nyōō pĭrā′rŭ), town (pop. 423), SE central Minas Gerais, Brazil, 5 mi. N of Ouro Prêto; manganese mine.

Antônio Prado (prä′dōō), city (pop. 1,994), NE Rio Grande do Sul, Brazil, near Taquari R., on S slope of the Serra Geral, 75 mi. N of Pôrto Alegre; flour milling, cheese mfg., lard processing.

Antônio Vaz, island, Brazil: see RECIFE.

Antonito (ăntŭnē′tŭ), town (pop. 1,255), Conejos co., S Colo., near Conejos R., in SE foothills of San Juan Mts., 28 mi. SSW of Alamosa; alt. 7,888 ft. Shipping point in San Luis Valley; potatoes, grain, livestock. Inc. 1889. Just NW is Conejos (founded 1854), one of oldest towns in Colo.

Antón Lizardo Point (äntōn′ lēsär′dō), cape on Gulf coast of Veracruz, E Mexico, 15 mi. SE of Veracruz; 19°4′N 95°59′W.

Antono-Kodintsevo, Ukrainian SSR: see KOMINTERNOVSKOYE.

Antonovka (ŭntô′nŭfkŭ), village (1939 pop. over 500), W Tatar Autonomous SSR, Russian SFSR, on right bank of Volga R. (landing) and 33 mi. S of Kazan; apple orchards. Gypsum deposits near by.

Anton River, Hampshire, England, rises just N of Andover, flows 7 mi. SE, past Andover, to Test R. 4 mi. S of Andover.

Antony, agr. village and parish (pop. 1,033), SE Cornwall, England, 5 mi. W of Plymouth. Has 15th-cent. church; 2 mi. NE is 18th-cent. Antony House, with noted paintings.

Antony (ãtônē′), residential town (pop. 20,903), Seine dept., N central France, an outer SSW suburb of Paris, 7 mi. from Notre Dame Cathedral. Brickworks, printshops; mfg. (flour products, toys). Has 12th-cent. church.

Antopol or **Antopol'** (ŭntô′pŭl), town (1931 pop. 2,210), E Brest oblast, Belorussian SSR, 18 mi. E of Kobrin; flour milling, flaxseed processing. Has ruins of old monastery.

Antraigues (ãtrĕg′), village (pop. 352), Ardèche dept., S France, on volcanic ridge 12 mi. W of Privas; silk throwing.

Antrain (ãtrẽ′), village (pop. 1,187), Ille-et-Vilaine dept., W France, on Couesnon R. and 15 mi. WNW of Fougères; tanning, flour milling; 16th-cent. château near by.

Antram, village (pop. 1,191, with adjacent Adah), Fayette co., SW Pa., on the Monongahela and 10 mi. W of Uniontown.

Antratsit, Russian SFSR: see ALTYNAI.

Antrea, Russian SFSR: see KAMENNOGORSK.

Antri (ŭn′trē), village, NE Madhya Bharat, India, 10 mi. SSE of Lashkar; agr. (millet, gram, wheat). Betel gardens near by. Tomb of Abul Fazl, author of *Ain-i-Akbari*, is 1 mi. W.

Antrim (ăn′trĭm), county (□ 1,098.3; 1937 pop. 197,266; 1951 census 231,099, excluding Belfast), Ulster, NE Northern Ireland; ⊙ Belfast. Bounded by Lough Neagh (SW), Co. Londonderry (W), Co. Down (S), the Atlantic (N), North Channel and the Irish Sea (E). Drained by Bann, Lagan, and several minor streams. Surface consists of extensive basalt plateau, rising to 1,817 ft. on Trostan, leveling toward coasts and Bann R. valley. On N coast are the remarkable basalt-rock formations of the Giant's Causeway. Chief headlands are Benbane Head, Benmore or Fair Head, and Garron Point. Isls. include Rathlin, The Skerries, and The Maidens. Oats, potatoes, flax are grown; cattle, pigs, sheep are raised. Sea fisheries are important; rock salt is mined in Carrickfergus region. Leading industries are linen milling, shipbuilding (Belfast), cotton and woolen milling, bauxite refining (Larne), cattle shipping. Chief towns are Belfast, Larne, Lisburn, Ballymena, Ballyclare.

Antrim, town (pop. 1,627), S central Co. Antrim, Northern Ireland, on NE shore of Lough Neagh, at mouth of the Six Mile Water, 14 mi. NW of Belfast; linen milling; agr. market in flax-growing region. Antrim Castle, built 1662, burned down 1922. Round tower here, dating from c.900, is one of the most perfect in Ireland.

Antrim, county (□ 477; pop. 10,721), NW Mich.; ⊙ Bellaire. Bounded W by Grand Traverse Bay; intersected by Torch L., and drained by short Jordan R. Livestock, dairy products, poultry, fruit, truck, potatoes, beans, alfalfa. Mfg. at Mancelona and Antrim. Flour- and sawmills. Resorts. Elk, Round, Intermediate, and Bellaire lakes are in co. Organized 1863.

Antrim. 1 Village (1940 pop. 610), Antrim co., NW Mich., "company town" adjacent to Mancelona, 28 mi. NE of Traverse City; iron furnace, sawmill. **2** Town (pop. 1,030), Hillsboro co., S N.H., on the Contoocook and 23 mi. SW of Concord. Mfg. (wood products, cutlery, hardware); resorts, agr. Settled 1741, inc. 1777.

Antrodoco (äntrôdô′kô), town (pop. 3,993), Rieti prov., Latium, central Italy, on Velino R. and 11 mi. E of Rieti; macaroni mfg. Has 12th-cent. church, cathedral (rebuilt 1712). Mineral baths near by.

Antropovo (ŭntrô′pŭvŭ), town (1939 pop. over 500), central Kostroma oblast, Russian SFSR, 55 mi. E of Bui; flax; lumber.

Antruong (än′trŭng), town (1936 pop. 1,100), Travinh prov., S Vietnam, in Mekong delta, 10 mi. NW of Travinh; rice. Also known as Canglong.

Antsakabary (äntsäkäbä′rē), village, Majunga prov., N Madagascar, 150 mi. SSW of Diégo-Suarez; center of coffee trade.

Antsalova (äntsälōō′vŭ), town, Tuléar prov., W central Madagascar, near W coast, 320 mi. NNE of Tuléar; cattle raising; sawmilling.

Antseh or **An-tse** (än′dzŭ′), town, ⊙ Antseh co. (pop. 72,863), S Shansi prov., China, 25 mi. NE of Linfen, in Taiyo Mts.; wheat, millet, kaoliang. Until 1914 called Yoyang.

Antsirabe (äntsērä′bā), town (1948 pop. 15,281), Tananarive prov., central Madagascar, 70 mi. SSW of Tananarive; health resort (alt. 4,166 ft.), with thermal springs; rail terminus. Mfg. of cigarettes, brushes, food preserves, carbonated drinks, tiles and bricks. Rice and meat processing; fish hatcheries; corn, pulse, potatoes, swine. Has a racecourse, sport facilities, hosp. for Europeans, technical col. for natives. Large annual fairs held here. Antsirabe agr. station specializes in temperate-climate cereals, fruit trees. Seat of vicar apostolic.

Antsirane, Madagascar: see DIÉGO-SUAREZ.

Antsla (änt′slä), city (pop. 1,558), Ger. *Anzen*, S Estonia, on railroad and 19 mi. ENE of Valga; agr. market; oats, flax, orchards, livestock.

Antsohihy (äntsōōhē′hē), town, Majunga prov., N Madagascar, at head of a W coast lagoon, 100 mi. NE of Majunga; rice center. Airfield.

Antu or **An-t'u** (än′tōō′), town, ⊙ Antu co., (pop. 16,464), SE Kirin prov., Manchuria, on headstream of Sungari R. and 65 mi. WSW of Yenki, in Changpai Mts.; lumbering center; wood-pulp mill. Antimony deposits.

Antuco (äntōō′kō), village (1930 pop. 500), Bío-Bío prov., S central Chile, on Laja R., at W foot of the Andes, and 40 mi. ENE of Los Angeles; wheat, rye, wine; lumbering. Antuco Volcano is 18 mi. ESE.

Antuco, Cerro (sĕ′rō), Andean volcano (19,000 ft.) in W Salta prov., Argentina, 25 mi. WSW of San Antonio de los Cobres; 24°16′S.

Antuco Volcano, Andean peak (9,810 ft.) in Bío-Bío prov., S central Chile, on W bank of L. Laja, 55 mi. E of Los Angeles. Inactive. Winter sports.

Antung (än′dōōng′). **1** Town, Kiangsu prov., China: see LIENSHUI. **2** City (1946 pop. 315,242; 1947 pop. 271,115), ⊙ Liaotung prov., Manchuria, port on right bank of Yalu R. (Korea line), opposite Sinuiju (rail bridge), on railroad and 125 mi. SSE of Mukden; industrial center, powered by SUPUNG hydroelectric plant on Yalu R. Lumber milling, paper and match mfg., nonferrous-metal refining (aluminum), cotton and silk weaving, agr. processing (soybean oil, flour); ship repair yards. A battleground during Sino-Japanese (1894–95) and Russo-Japanese (1904–05) wars, Antung developed after the coming (1907) of the railroad; it was opened to foreign trade and became a major rail-water transfer point. Although it accommodated some ocean-going vessels, its outer harbor of Tatungkow remained its deepwater port. Main exports are grain, coal, and lumber. City consists of old city (upstream) and modern port and commercial section (downstream). In Manchukuo, it was ⊙ Antung prov. (□ 10,234; 1940 pop. 2,231,-507) during 1934–45. Under Nationalist rule (1946–49), the ⊙ was moved to TUNGHWA. When Antung became (1949) ⊙ Liaotung prov., the seat of Antung co. (1946 pop. 292,542) was moved to the outer Yellow Sea port of Tatungkow, 25 mi. SW at mouth of Yalu R., thereafter also called Antung.

Antwerp (ăn′twûrp), Flemish *Antwerpen* (ănt′-vĕrpŭn), Fr. *Anvers* (ãvĕr′, in Belgium commonly ãvĕrs′), province (□ 1,104; pop. 1,296,687), N Belgium; ⊙ Antwerp. Bounded by the Netherlands (N), Limburg prov. (E), Brabant prov. (S), East Flanders prov. (W). Level, cultivated plain drained by Scheldt (Escaut), Dyle, Nèthe, and Rupel rivers and Albert Canal. Agr. (beets, potatoes, oats, flax, fodder); cattle raising, dairying. Machine mfg. (Antwerp, Mechlin); brick mfg. (Boom, Turnhout), food processing, sugar refining. Important towns: Antwerp, Mechlin, Lierre, Turnhout, Herentals, Mol. Prov. mainly Flemish-speaking. Antwerp formerly part of old duchy of Brabant.

Antwerp, Flemish *Antwerpen*, Fr. *Anvers*, city (pop. 266,636; with suburbs 599,240), ⊙ Antwerp prov., N Belgium, on Scheldt (Escaut) R. and 26 mi. N of Brussels, at E end of Scheldt-Meuse Junction Canal; 51°13′N 4°24′E. Leading Belgian port and commercial center, rivaled only by Rotterdam as largest port of continental Europe, it is also a world center of the diamond trade and industry; an industrial center (oil refineries, automobile assembly plants, motorcycle factories, flour mills); and one of the great historical and artistic cities of Europe. Imports cotton, grain, and (from Belgian Congo) copper and other unrefined metals. Chief exports are machinery, textiles, and other manufactured products; considerable transit trade to and from Germany, notably the Ruhr area. Port installations consist largely of basins off Scheldt R., in N section of city. The airport is at DEURNE. City's chief thoroughfare is a succession of avenues bisecting it and running parallel to site of its old ramparts. The 14th–15th-cent. Gothic cathedral of Notre Dame, with a spire 400 ft. high, is famous; it contains several Rubens paintings. Notable are 16th-cent. Gothic church of St. Paul, and church of St. James, completed in 17th cent. and containing tombs of Rubens and his family, and several of his paintings. Stock Exchange (*Bourse* or *Beurs*), founded 1460, was built (1868–72) to replace original 16th-cent. bldg. destroyed by fire. Town hall dates from 16th cent. Many old guild houses line the *Groote Markt* (market place). Has mus. of fine arts; Plantin Mus. (in house of 16th-cent. printer Christopher Plantin); botanical and zoological gardens. Birthplace of the painter Van Dyck. Known in 660, Antwerp became a Norman fort in 9th cent. Held by counts of Bouillon in 11th cent.; later under sovereignty of counts of Flanders and dukes of Burgundy. Antwerp's commercial importance increased in 15th cent. with the decline of Bruges and Ghent; in 1460 it received Europe's 1st stock exchange and became the commercial and financial hub of Europe, with a population of c.200,000. Its busy docks were the marvel of the day. The diamond industry, established in 15th cent., expanded greatly after the arrival of Jewish craftsmen expelled from Portugal. Antwerp's prosperity suffered a fatal blow when the city was sacked by mutinous Spanish troops in 1576 (the "Spanish fury"), but Antwerp resisted for 14 months (1584–85) before surrendering to the Spanish. The academy of painting, founded by Philip the Good in 1454, gave the initial impetus to the Flemish school of painting. A quiet period at beginning of 16th cent. made it into an art center, largely under leadership of Rubens. The Peace of Westphalia (1648) closed the Scheldt to navigation and Antwerp declined rapidly, until the Scheldt was reopened (1795) to further Napoleon's plans against England. Under the Dutch-Belgian treaty of separation (1839), the Netherlands received right to collect a toll on Scheldt shipping; Antwerp's modern era as a major port began only in 1863 when Belgium redeemed this treaty right by a cash payment. In First World War Antwerp was besieged by the Germans, taken in Oct., 1914, and suffered great hardship. When, in Second World War, it came into Allied hands (1944), it became a major supply base and was heavily attacked with rocket weapons by the Germans; certain areas suffered considerable destruction.

Antwerp. 1 Village (pop. 846), Jefferson co., N N.Y., on Indian R. and 22 mi. NE of Watertown; makes cheese. **2** Village (pop. 1,162), Paulding co., NW Ohio, on Maumee R., near Ind. line, and 22 mi. ENE of Fort Wayne, Ind.; dairy, livestock, grain; cheese making.

Antwerp Island, Antarctica: see ANVERS ISLAND.

Antwerp-Turnhout Canal (ăn'twûrp-tûrn'hout), N Belgium, runs 24 mi. generally ENE from Albert Canal (4.5 mi. ENE of Antwerp) to Canal d'Embranchement (at Turnhout). Serves Sint-Lenaarts.

Antze or **An-tz'u** (both: än'tsŭ'), town, ⊙ Antze co. (pop. 183,851), N Hopeh prov., China, 40 mi. SSE of Peking, near railroad to Tientsin; wheat, kaoliang, corn. Until 1914 called Tungan.

An Uaimh or **Navan** (nă'vŭn), urban district (pop. 4,102), central Co. Meath, Ireland, on the Boyne at mouth of the Blackwater, and 26 mi. NW of Dublin; woolen milling, tobacco processing, mfg. of clothing, carpets, furniture. It was site of abbey and has remains of town walls; both were destroyed by Cromwell.

Anuchino (ŭnoo'chĭnŭ), village (1939 pop. over 500), S Maritime Territory, Russian SFSR, on Daubikhe R. and 60 mi. E of Voroshilov, in agr. area (rice, soybeans, grain).

Anunghoi (ä'noong'hoi'), island at mouth of Canton R., Kwangtung prov., China, E of the Boca Tigris, N of Chuenpi isl., 35 mi. SE of Canton. Sometimes spelled Anunghoy.

Anupgarh (ŭnoop'gŭr), village, N Rajasthan, India, 80 mi. N of Bikaner; rail spur terminus; millet, gram; hand-loom weaving, camel breeding.

Anupnagar, India: see ASANSOL.

Anupshahr (ănoop'shä), town (pop. 8,315), Bulandshahr dist., W Uttar Pradesh, India, on the Ganges and 24 mi. E of Bulandshahr; trades in wheat, sugar, oilseeds, barley. Flourished during 18th cent. Founded 16th cent.

Anupshahr Branch, canal, India: see GANGES CANALS.

Anuradhapura (ŭnoor'ŭdŭpoor"ŭ), town (pop. 12,287), ⊙ North Central Prov. and Anuradhapura dist. (coextensive with prov.), Ceylon, on the Aruvi Aru and 105 mi. NNE of Colombo; road center; rice plantations, vegetable gardens. Meteorological observatory. Most famous of anc. ruined cities of Ceylon; Buddhist pilgrimage center. Town and surrounding area contain vast Buddhist ruins, including 4 chief stupas of Abhayagiriya (founded 87 B.C.), Jetavanarama (built 3d cent. A.D. by King Maha Sena; one of largest stupas in Buddhist world; original height c.300 ft.), Ruanvelli (founded 137 B.C.), and the Mirisvetiya (built 2d cent. B.C.). Oldest stupa (307 B.C.) is the Thuparama. Other ruins include rock temple of Issurumuniya (built 4th cent. B.C.; extensive Buddhist sculptures), Brazen Palace (built 2d cent. B.C.), bathing pools, and moonstones (intricately carved, semi-circular granite blocks). Pipal (Bo) tree, brought as a branch from original pipal tree at Buddh Gaya in India and planted either 288 B.C. or 245 B.C., is regarded as oldest historical tree extant. Hq. of archaeology dept.; mus. Founded 437 B.C.; was ⊙ Ceylon from 4th cent. B.C. to 8th cent. A.D., when ⊙ passed to Polonnaruwa following invasions by Tamils. Rediscovered by British in mid-19th cent. Near by are 3 anc. irrigation lakes: Nuwarawewa (3 mi. long, 2 mi. wide; built c.1st cent. A.D.), Tissawewa (built c.300 B.C.), and Bassawakkulama (reputedly constructed 505 B.C.). Formerly spelled Anarajapura.

Anuu, American Samoa: see AUNUU.

Anvers, Belgium: see ANTWERP.

Anversa degli Abruzzi (änvĕr'sä dĕlyäbroo'tsē), village (pop. 1,243), Aquila prov., Abruzzi e Molise, S central Italy, on Sagittario R. (branch of Pescara R.) and 7 mi. SW of Sulmona; hydroelectric plant.

Anvers Island (ăvâr'), Antarctica, largest isl. (40 naut. mi. long, 30 naut. mi. wide) of Palmer Archipelago, in South Pacific just off NW coast of Palmer Peninsula; 64°30'S 63°30'W. Rises to 9,412 ft. Discovered 1898 by Adrien de Gerlache, Belgian explorer. Sometimes Antwerp Isl.

Anvik (ăn'vĭk), village (pop. 97), W Alaska, on Yukon R. at mouth of Anvik R., and 35 mi. NNW of Holy Cross; trapping, fishing. Site of Episcopal mission, school. Athapaskan Indian village, discovered by Russians in 1834.

Anvik River, W Alaska, SE of Norton Sound, rises near 63°39'N 160°8'W, flows c.125 mi. generally S to Yukon R. at Anvik.

Anvil, Mich.: see RAMSAY.

Anvil Island (□ 4), SW B.C., in Howe Sound, 20 mi. NNW of Vancouver; 3 mi. long, 1 mi. wide; rises to 2,475 ft.

Anxious Bay, inlet of Great Australian Bight, W Eyre Peninsula, S South Australia, bet. Cape Radstock (NW) and Cape Finniss (SE); 42 mi. long, 13 mi. wide. Waldegrave Isls. at S end. Opens into 2 lagoons: Baird Bay (NW) and Venus Bay (ENE; site of Port Kenny).

Anxur, Italy: see TERRACINA.

Anyang (än'yäng'), city (1922 pop. estimate 60,000), ⊙, but independent of, Anyang co. (1937 pop. 613,-388), NW Pingyuan prov., China, on Hopeh line, 55 mi. NNE of Sinsiang, and on Peking-Hankow RR; center of coal-mining dist. (mines at LIUHOKOW); cotton weaving, agr. processing. Bronze Age excavations were made here (1928) on the site of Hsiang, residence (1534–1525 B.C.) of the Shang dynasty. Called Changteh until 1913, the city was in Honan prov. until 1949.

Anydros or **Anidhros** (both: ä'nĭdhrôs), small Aegean island of the Cyclades, Greece, SW of Amorgos; 36°37'N 25°40'E. Formerly called Amorgopoula.

Anyi or **Ani** (both: än'yē'), town, ⊙ Anyi co. (pop. 99,537), S Shansi prov., China, 45 mi. ENE of Yüngtsi and on railroad; salt-extracting center, based on Lutsun salt pan (S); wheat, millet, dates, grapes. The name Anyi was applied 1915–18 to Yüncheng, 3 mi. SW, another salt center. Anyi was an anc. Chinese imperial residence.

Anyinam (änyēnäm'), town, Eastern Prov., central Gold Coast colony, on railroad and 16 mi. N of Kibi; cacao, cassava, corn.

Anyksciai, Anikshchyai, or **Anikshchyay** (änēk'-shchī), Lith. *Anykščiai*, Rus. *Onikshty*, city (pop. 4,362), E central Lithuania, on Sventoji R. and 19 mi. W of Utena; mfg. (felt goods, shoes, fruit wines). In Rus. Kovno govt. until 1920.

Anyo (än'yō'), town (pop. 10,379), ⊙ Anyo co. (pop. 663,154), central Szechwan prov., China, 60 mi. WNW of Hochwan; olives, rice, sweet potatoes, wheat, cotton, beans. Saltworks near by.

Anyox (ă'nēŏks"), village, W B.C., near Alaska border, on Observatory Inlet of the Pacific, 80 mi. NNE of Prince Rupert; copper-mining and smelting center, with large pyrite smelter. Hydroelectric power. Near by is port of Alice Arm.

Anyüan (än'yüăn'). **1** Town (pop. 3,704), ⊙ Anyüan co. (pop. 107,822), S Kiangsi prov., China, 65 mi. S of Kanchow, N of Kiulien Mts.; tungsten and bismuth mines; rice, timber. **2** Town, W Kiangsi prov., China, 5 mi. ESE of Pingsiang and on spur of Chekiang-Kiangsi RR; major coal-mining center.

Anyui or **Anyuy** (ŭnyoo'ē), two rivers and their watershed ranges in NE Siberian Russian SFSR. Greater Anyui R. (S; 420 mi. long) and Lesser Anyui R. (N; 340 mi. long) rise on plateau at N end of Kolyma Range, flow W, separated by Southern Anyui Range, joining to form Anyui R. just before entering Kolyma R. at Nizhne-Kolymsk. Northern Anyui Range (up to 6,000 ft.) forms right (N) watershed of the Lesser Anyui.

Anza Desert State Park (□ c.639), S Calif., occupying most of E San Diego co.; a tract of the Colorado Desert, notable for its desert plants and colorful canyons, some of them containing palm groves. Includes former Borego Desert State Park.

Anzaldo (änsäl'dō), town (pop. c.8,700), Cochabamba dept., central Bolivia, on S slopes of Cordillera de Cochabamba, 15 mi. SSE of Tarata; barley, livestock. Until 1900s, Paredón.

Anzánigo (än-thä'nēgō), village (pop. 258), Huesca prov., NE Spain, on Gállego R. and 13 mi. SSW of Jaca. Two hydroelectric plants and Peña reservoir near by.

Anzano di Puglia (änzä'nō dē poo'lyä), village (pop. 2,372), Foggia prov., Apulia, S Italy, 10 mi. SSW of Bovino, in cereal-growing region. Formerly Anzano degli Irpini.

Anza River (än'tsä), N Italy, rises on E slope of Monte Rosa 3 mi. W of Macugnaga, flows 20 mi. E to Toce R. 7 mi. S of Domodossola.

Anzat-le-Luguet, France: see ARDES.

Anzegem (än'sĕkh-ĕm), town (pop. 3,896), West Flanders prov., NW Belgium, 10 mi. E of Courtrai; textile milling.

Anzen, Estonia: see ANTSLA.

Anzhero-Sudzhensk (ŭnzhĕ"rŭ-soojĕnsk'), city (1926 pop. 30,199; 1939 pop. 71,079), N Kemerovo oblast, Russian SFSR, on Trans-Siberian RR (Anzherskaya station) and 50 mi. N of Kemerovo; oldest and one of largest coal-mining centers of Kuznetsk Basin, in exploitation since 1898. Formed 1928 out of towns of Anzherka and Sudzhenka; became city in 1931.

Anzi (än'tsē), village (pop. 2,731), Potenza prov., Basilicata, S Italy, 11 mi. SE of Potenza, in grape- and cereal-growing region.

Anzin (ăzē'), NW suburb (pop. 14,235) of Valenciennes, Nord dept., N France; important coal-mining and metallurgical center; blast-furnaces, forges (mining equipment and rolling stock, iron and steel tubes, furnaces), glassworks, breweries. Produces refractories. Damaged in Second World War.

Anzio (ăn'zēō, It. änd'syô), anc. *Antium*, town (pop. 5,989), Roma prov., Latium, S central Italy, port on Tyrrhenian Sea, 33 mi. S of Rome; bathing resort; fishing center; sardine canning, boatbuilding. A Volscian town, it later became a favorite Roman resort. Nero was b. here, and among the ruins of his villa were found the famous statues of Apollo of Belvedere and the Girl of Anzio. Severely damaged in Second World War. In Jan., 1944, Allied troops landed here and at near-by Nettuno to draw Germans from Cassino and thus permit a break-through to Rome. The large beachhead forces absorbed repeated fierce German attacks and held out until contact with main body of U.S. Fifth Army was established in May.

Anzoátegui (änswä'tāgē), state (□ 16,720; 1941 pop. 155,746; 1950 census 238,082), NE Venezuela, on the Caribbean; ⊙ Barcelona. Bounded S by Orinoco R. (Bolívar state border). Consists almost entirely of llanos; contains also some outliers of coastal range (NW and NE). Watered by Unare, Neverí, Orinoco rivers. Tropical climate, with rainy season (May-Oct.). Possesses rich mineral resources: petroleum at El Tigre (Oficina field), El Roble, San Joaquín, and Santa Ana fields; and coal at Naricual. Primarily a cattle-grazing region; produces also cotton, cacao, coffee, sugar cane, corn, coconuts, bananas, yucca, rice, tobacco. Barcelona, its main trading center, has processing industries. Main shipping centers are ports of Guanta and Puerto La Cruz.

Anzola dell'Emilia (äntsō'lä dĕlĕmē'lyä), village (pop. 775), Bologna prov., Emilia-Romagna, N central Italy, 8 mi. WNW of Bologna; fertilizer, explosives, lime and cement.

Ao (ä'ō), town (pop. 3,217), Mie prefecture, S Honshu, Japan, 7 mi. SSE of Ueno; rice, wheat, sake, raw silk.

Aoba (äō'bä), volcanic island (□ c.95; pop. c.4,000), New Hebrides, SW Pacific, 30 mi. E of Espiritu Santo; 24 mi. long, 9 mi. wide; copra. Sometimes called Leper Isl.

Aoga-shima (äögä'shĭmä), island (□ 2; pop. 441) of isl. group Izu-shichito, Greater Tokyo, Japan, in Philippine Sea, 40 mi. S of Hachijo-jima; 2 mi. long, 1.5 mi. wide. Has active volcano (1,390 ft. high). Produces charcoal, raw silk; livestock raising; fishing.

Aogata (äō'gätä) or **Aokata** (–kätä), town (pop. 6,867), on Nakadori-shima of isl. group Goto-retto, Nagasaki prefecture, Japan, 3 mi. W of Arikawa, on E.China Sea; agr. center (rice, sweet potatoes).

Aohori (äō'hōrē) or **Ohori** (ō'hōrē), town (pop. 6,644), Chiba prefecture, central Honshu, Japan, on W Chiba Peninsula, on Tokyo Bay, 4 mi. SW of Kisarazu; rice, wheat. Mineral springs.

Aoiz (äōēth'), town (pop. 1,419), Navarre prov., N Spain, 14 mi. E of Pamplona; sawmilling, acetone processing; wine, cereals, potatoes, beans. Hydroelectric plant near by.

Aoji (ä'ō'jē'), Jap. *Agochi*, town (1944 pop. 39,616), N.Hamgyong prov., N Korea, on Tumen R. and 25 mi. NNE of Najin; coal-mining center; mfg. of chemicals.

Aokata, Japan: see AOGATA.

Aomi (äō'mē) or **Omi** (ō'mē), town (pop. 11,171), Niigata prefecture, central Honshu, Japan, on Toyama Bay, 25 mi. WSW of Takada, in rice-growing area; raw-silk culture. Limestone quarrying.

Aomi-shima, Japan: see OMI-SHIMA, Yamaguchi prefecture.

Aomori (äō'mōrē), prefecture [Jap. *ken*] (□ 3,719; 1940 pop. 1,000,509; 1947 pop. 1,180,245), N Honshu, Japan; ⊙ Aomori, its chief port. Bounded N by Tsugaru Strait, W by Sea of Japan, E by the Pacific. Largely mountainous; many small streams drain fertile lowlands. Major apple-growing dist. of Japan; also produces rice, soybeans. Lumbering, fishing, livestock raising; mfg. (cement, textiles, lacquer ware, chemicals), woodworking. Principal centers: Aomori, HACHINOHE, HIROSAKI.

Aomori, northernmost city (1940 pop. 99,065; 1947 pop. 90,828) of Honshu, Japan, ⊙ Aomori prefecture, port on Aomori Bay, 180 mi. N of Sendai; 40°49'N 140°45'E. Commercial center for lumbering area. Port connected by ferry service with Hakodate on Hokkaido and protected by breakwaters from winter monsoon; opened 1906 to foreign trade. Chief exports: rice, textiles, metalware, tobacco, oil, canned goods. Includes (since 1939) former town of Aburakawa. Bombed (1945) in Second World War.

Aomori Bay, Jap. *Aomori-wan,* inlet of Tsugaru Strait, Aomori prefecture, N Honshu, Japan; merges E with Mutsu Bay; 12 mi. long, 10 mi. wide. Aomori is on S shore.

Aonach Beag (ŭ"nŭkh bāg'), peak (4,060 ft.), SW Inverness, Scotland, 2 mi. E of Ben Nevis.

Aonla (oun'lŭ), town (pop. 16,660), Bareilly dist., N central Uttar Pradesh, India, 16 mi. WSW of Bareilly; road junction; sugar refining; trades in wheat, rice, gram, sugar cane, oilseeds, pearl millet. Tomb and fort of 1st great Rohilla leader, Ali Mohammed. In mid-18th cent., was ⊙ Rohilkhand under Ali Mohammed.

Aoos River (ä-ôs'), Lat. *Aous,* Albanian *Vijosë* (vēyô'sŭ) or *Vijosa* (vēyô'sä), Ital. *Voiussa* (voiyōōs'sä), in N Epirus, Greece, and S Albania, rises in the Pindus N of Metsovon, flows c.125 mi. NW, past Konitsa, Përmet, Këlcyrë, and Tepelenë to the Strait of Otranto, 15 mi. NW of Valona. Flows through deep gorges in upper course. Receives Drin R. (left).

Aorai, Mount (ou'rī'), peak (6,788 ft.), W Tahiti, Society Isls., S Pacific; 2d highest mtn. of isl. group.

Aorangi, New Zealand: see COOK, MOUNT.

Aoshima (äō'shĭmä), town (pop. 14,331), Shizuoka prefecture, central Honshu, Japan, just SW of Fujieda, 11 mi. SW of Shizuoka, in agr. area (rice, tea); paper milling.

Aosta (äō'stä), anc. *Augusta Praetoria,* town (pop. 13,466), ⊙ VAL D'AOSTA region, NW Italy, at junction of Great and Little St. Bernard roads, on Dora Baltea R. and 50 mi. NNW of Turin; 45°44'N 7°19'E. Metallurgical industry (iron, steel, aluminum), alcohol distillery, brewery; large hydroelectric station. Bishopric since 5th cent. Has medieval Gothic cathedral, church with 12th-cent. cloister, palace (1606), seminary (1774), mus. A chief town of the Salassi; captured by Romans 25 B.C. Important Roman remains include arch of Augustus, praetorian gate, town walls, theater, and amphitheater. St. Anselm b. here. Aosta became regional capital in 1945.

Aosta, Val d', Italy: see VAL D'AOSTA.

Aouaj, Syria: see A'WAJ.

Aouana, El- (ĕl-äwänä'), village, Bizerte dist., N Tunisia, on railroad and 23 mi. NNE of Béja; zinc mines. Iron and lead deposits.

Aoua River, Fr. and Du. Guiana: see MARONI RIVER.

Aouina, El- (ĕl-äwēnä'), NE suburb of Tunis, N Tunisia, 5 mi. from city center. Site of international airport.

Aouïnet (äwēnĕt'), village, Gabès dist., E Tunisia, on Tunis-Gabès RR and 9 mi. NNW of Gabès; olive and palm trees.

Aouïnet, El, Fr. Morocco: see DJÉRADA.

Aouïnet Torkoz, Saharan oasis and military outpost, Agadir frontier region, southwesternmost Fr. Morocco, near the Oued Dra, 85 mi. S of Tiznit; 28°29'N 9°52'W.

Aoûk, river, Fr. Equatorial Africa: see BAHR AOÛK.

Aoulef (oulĕf'), oasis and airfield, Saharan Oases territory, central Algeria, one of the Tidikelt oases, 90 mi. WSW of In-Salah; 26°58'N 1°4'E. Used as stopover by Algiers-Gao trans-Saharan airlines. Also called Aoulef Arab.

Aouli, Fr. Morocco: see MIDELT.

Aoullouz (oul-lōōz'), village, Marrakesh region, SW Fr. Morocco, on S slope of the High Atlas and W of the Djebel Siroua, 60 mi. ENE of Taroudant; manganese mine.

Aourioura (ouryōōrä'), military outpost, Agadir frontier region, southwesternmost Fr. Morocco, on the Atlantic, NE of Cape Dra and 90 mi. SW of Tiznit; 28°49'N 10°51'W.

Aous River, Greece-Albania: see AOOS RIVER.

Aouste-sur-Sye (ōōst-sür-sē'), anc. *Augusta,* village (pop. 800), Drôme dept., SE France, on Drôme R. and 17 mi. SSE of Valence; silk and paper milling.

Aoya (äō'yä), town (pop. 5,048), Tottori prefecture, SW Honshu, Japan, on Sea of Japan, 14 mi. W of Tottori; summer resort; rice, raw silk, shellfish, edible seaweed.

Apach (äpäsh', Ger. ä'päkh), village (pop. 388), Moselle dept., NE France, on right bank of Moselle R. and 12 mi. NE of Thionville; customs station on Saar border opposite Perl.

Apache (ŭpă'chē), county (□ 11,174; pop. 27,767), E Ariz.; ⊙ St. Johns. Mtn. area bordering on N.Mex. and Utah, crossed by Zuni, Little Colorado, and Puerco rivers. Carrizo and Chuska Mts. in NE, White Mts. in SW, in Fort Apache Indian Reservation. Navajo Indian Reservation occupies N half of co. Canyon de Chelly Natl. Monument is W of Chuska Mts., near N.Mex. line. Part of Petrified Forest Natl. Monument is in W, on Navajo co. line. NE tip of Apache co. is only point in U.S. common to 4 states (Ariz., N.Mex., Colo., Utah). Small dam on Little Colorado R. near St. Johns provides water for irrigated area producing alfalfa, truck, and grain. Livestock raising and dairying are important activities. Co. formed 1879.

Apache, town (pop. 1,190), Caddo co., W central Okla., 25 mi. WSW of Chickasha, and on Cache Creek, in agr. and oil area. Produces fertilizer, packed meat, feed, trailers, crushed rock; cotton ginning. Settled and inc. 1901.

Apache Mountains, W Texas, NW-SE range in Culberson co., c.25 mi. ENE of Van Horn; rises to 5,657 ft. in Apache Peak.

Apache Pass (5,115 ft.), SE Ariz., historic passage bet. Dos Cabezas Mts. and Chiricahua Mts., c.20 mi. ESE of Willcox; on 19th-cent. immigrant road to Calif.

Apache Peak (7,684 ft.), SE Ariz., in Whetstone Mts., c.20 mi. N of Fort Huachuca.

Apahida (äpähē'dä), village (pop. 2,064), Cluj prov., W central Rumania, on Little Somes R. and 8 mi. ENE of Cluj; rail junction and agr. center. In Hungary, 1940–45.

Apalachee (ă"pŭlă'chē), town (pop. 178), Morgan co., N central Ga., 19 mi. S of Athens, near Apalachee R.

Apalachee Bay, NW Fla., a bight (c.30 mi. wide) of the Gulf of Mexico, c.25 mi. S of Tallahassee; receives Aucilla, Ochlockonee, and St. Marks rivers. Its marshy coast is a natl. wildlife refuge.

Apalachee River, N central Ga., rises NE of Lawrenceville, flows c.65 mi. SE, past High Shoals, to Oconee R. 6 mi. WSW of Greensboro.

Apalachia Dam (ăpŭlă'chŭ), Cherokee co., SW N.C., in Hiwassee R., 15 mi. WNW of Murphy, near Tenn. line. A major TVA dam (150 ft. high, 1,308 ft. long; completed 1943); concrete construction; for hydroelectric power and flood control. Impounds narrow reservoir (□ c.2; capacity c.10 mi. long; 58,570 acre-ft).

Apalachicola (ă"pŭlăchĭkō'lŭ), city (pop. 3,222), ⊙ Franklin co., NW Fla., c.65 mi. SW of Tallahassee, on Apalachicola Bay (bridged here), at mouth of Apalachicola R.; port of entry and fishing center (oysters, shrimp); exports lumber, naval stores, crushed oyster shells; mfg. of fish meal and oil, seafood canning. Founded c.1820, inc. 1838. Civil War blockade ended city's position as a leading cotton-shipping port after 1830. Monument here commemorates J. W. Gorrie, who invented ice-making process (1845).

Apalachicola Bay, NW Fla., an arm of the Gulf of Mexico, bet. St. George (E) and St. Vincent (W) sounds, and sheltered by St. George Isl.; c.15 mi. long, 7 mi. wide; receives Apalachicola R. Connected with St. Andrew Bay by Gulf Intracoastal Waterway, which extends c.6 mi. up the mouth of Apalachicola R. and through L. Wimico.

Apalachicola River, NW Fla., formed at SW corner of Ga. on Fla. line by confluence of Flint and Chattahoochee rivers near Chattahoochee, flows 112 mi. S, across NW Fla., into Apalachicola Bay at Apalachicola; has dredged channel. Receives Chipola R. From farthest headstream (N Ga.), 500 mi. above mouth, drains □ 19,500.

Apalit (äpä'lēt), town (1939 pop. 2,286; 1948 municipality pop. 14,576), Pampanga prov., central Luzon, Philippines, on Pampanga R. and 7 mi. SE of San Fernando; agr. center (rice, sugar cane); fishing. Sometimes called San Juan.

Apam (äpäm'), town, Western Prov., S Gold Coast colony, on Gulf of Guinea, 8 mi. WSW of Winneba; gold placers; fishing. A Du. trading post, founded 17th cent.; passed 1872 to British.

Apam (äpäm'), city (pop. 4,972), Hidalgo, central Mexico, on central plateau, on railroad and 34 mi. SE of Pachuca; alt. 8,205 ft.; maguey-growing and pulque-distilling center.

Apamama, Gilbert Isls.: see ABEMAMA.

Apamea, Turkey: see DINAR.

Apanasenkovskoye, Russian SFSR: see DIVNOYE.

Apaneca (äpänā'kä), town (pop. 2,362), Ahuachapán dept., W Salvador, at N foot of the volcano Apaneca (6,083 ft.), 5 mi. SSE of Ahuachapán; coffee-growing center; noted flower gardens.

Apango (äpäng'gō), town (pop. 1,922), Guerrero, SW Mexico, on N slopes of Sierra Madre del Sur, 18 mi. NE of Chilpancingo; cereals, sugar, fruit, forest products (resin, vanilla).

Apapa (äpä'pä), town (pop. 2,251) in Lagos township, Nigeria colony, port on Lagos Lagoon, opposite Lagos; rail terminus; modern harbor facilities (docks, transit sheds, warehouses, drydock); petroleum tanks; soap mfg.

Apaporis River (äpäpō'rēs), SE Colombia, rises SE of the Cordillera Macarena, flows SE c.550 mi. to the Caquetá (at Brazil line), which from there on is called the Japurá in Brazil. Belongs to Amazon system. Its upper course is called the Ajajú. Obstructed by rapids.

Aparados da Serra (äpŭrä'dōōs dä sĕ'rŭ), city (pop. 1,809), NE Rio Grande do Sul, Brazil, in the Serra Geral, 35 mi. ESE of Vacaria; dairying, fruitgrowing, lumbering. Copper deposits. Until 1944, Bom Jesus.

Aparan (ŭpŭrän'), village (1939 pop. over 2,000), NW Armenian SSR on NE slope of Mt. Aragats, on the Abaran-Su (left affluent of the Aras) and 30 mi. NNW of Erivan; livestock, wheat, rugs.

Aparecida (äpärĭsĕ'dŭ). **1** City, Piauí, Brazil; see BERTOLÍNIA. **2** City (pop. 5,016), SE São Paulo, Brazil, on Paraíba R. and 5 mi. SW of Guaratinguetá; paper and cardboard mfg.; agr. (corn, rice, manioc). Has noted basilica. Formerly, Aparecida.

Aparecida do Tabuado (dōō täbwä'dōō), city (pop. 534), easternmost Mato Grosso, Brazil, on right bank of Paraná R. (São Paulo border) just below junction of Rio Grande and Paranaíba rivers, and 60 mi. NE of Três Lagoas; cattle.

Apa River (ä'pŭ), in SW Brazil and N Paraguay, rises in S Mato Grosso on W slope of Serra de Amambaí, flows c.160 mi. W, past Bela Vista, beyond which it forms Brazil-Paraguay border until its influx into the Paraguay at San Lázaro. Not navigable.

Aparri (äpä'rē), town (1939 pop. 12,458; 1948 municipality pop. 24,974), Cagayan prov., N Luzon, Philippines, port at mouth of Cagayan R. on Babuyan Channel, 50 mi. N of Tuguegarao; 18°22'N 121°38'E. Trade center for lumbering and agr. area (tobacco, rice). It is chief tobacco-exporting port of Luzon. A Jap. invasion force landed here Dec. 10, 1941.

Apasapan, Mexico: see APAZAPAN.

Apaseo (äpäsä'ō), city (pop. 3,780), Guanajuato, central Mexico, on Apaseo R. and 7 mi. E of Celaya, on railroad; grain center.

Apaseo El Alto (ĕl äl'tō), town (pop. 3,240), Guanajuato, central Mexico, 12 mi. ESE of Celaya; grain, alfalfa, fruit, vegetables, livestock.

Apaseo River, central Mexico, rises NW of Amealco (Querétaro), flows c.80 mi. NW and W, past Apaseo and Cortazar (Guanajuato), to Lerma R. 4 mi. SE of Salamanca.

Apastepeque (äpästāpā'kā), city (pop. 3,282), San Vicente dept., central Salvador, 2 mi. N of San Vicente; grain, sugar cane; hog raising.

Apastovo (ŭpä'stŭvŭ), village (1948 pop. over 2,000), W Tatar Autonomous SSR, Russian SFSR, near Sviyaga R., 18 mi. NNE of Buinsk; wheat, legumes, livestock.

Apataki (ä'pätä'kē), atoll (pop. 155), Tuamotu Isls., Fr. Oceania, S Pacific, c.65 mi. NW of Fakarava; most important of Palliser Isls., which also include Arutua, Kaukura, Toau. Lagoon is 15 mi. long, 18 mi. wide. Site of chief village of Tuamotu Isls. Formerly Hegemeister Isl.

Apatfalva (ŏ'pätfŏlvŏ), Hung. *Apátfalva,* agr. town (pop, 5,773), Csanad co., SE Hungary, on Maros R. and 6 mi. SE of Mako; rail junction; frontier station on Rum. line.

Apatin (ä'pätĭn), village (pop. 13,537), Vojvodina, N Serbia, Yugoslavia, on the Danube, on railroad and 10 mi. SW of Sombor, on Croatian border, in the Backa; fishing. Handicraft (willow baskets) in vicinity.

Apatity (ŭpŭfyē'tē), town (1939 pop. over 2,000), central Murmansk oblast, Russian SFSR, on Kola Peninsula, on L. Imandra, 95 mi. S of Murmansk; junction on Murmansk RR (spur to Kirovsk). Site of truck and dairy farm of Industriya.

Apatzingán (äpätsēng-gän'), officially Apatzingán de la Constitución, town (pop. 2,080), Michoacán, W Mexico, 32 mi. SW of Uruapan; rice, sugar, coffee, fruit.

Apaxco (äpä'skō), officially Apaxco de Ocampo, town (pop. 2,079), Mexico state, central Mexico, on railroad and 38 mi. N of Mexico city; cement milling.

Apaxtla (äpä'slä), town (pop. 2,455), Guerrero, SW Mexico, on S slope of central plateau, 30 mi. SW of Iguala; cereals, sugar, coffee, tropical fruit.

Apayao, Philippines: see MOUNTAIN PROVINCE.

Apazapan (äpäsä'pän), town (pop. 980), Veracruz, E Mexico, in Sierra Madre Oriental, 17 mi. SE of Jalapa; corn, coffee, fruit. Sometimes Apasapan.

Apco, Ohio: see RAVENNA.

Ape (ä'pā), Ger. *Hoppenhof,* city (pop. 922), NE Latvia, in Vidzeme, on Estonian border, 30 mi. SE of Valga; sawmilling, tanning.

Apecchio (äpĕk'kyō), village (pop. 704), Pesaro e Urbino prov., The Marches, central Italy, 16 mi. SW of Urbino; agr. tools.

Apel, Ter, Netherlands: see TER APEL.

Apeldoorn (ä'pŭldōrn), town (pop. 62,876), Gelderland prov., E central Netherlands, 17 mi. N of Arnhem; rail junction on edge of Suren forest; mfg. of pharmaceuticals, refrigeration machinery, paper products. Many sanitaria in vicinity. Het Loo, royal summer palace, on N outskirts.

Apelvaer, Norway: see ABELVAER.

Apen (ä'pün), village (commune pop. 8,323), in Oldenburg, NW Germany, after 1945 Lower Saxony, 17 mi. WNW of Oldenburg city, in peat region.

Apennines (ă'pünīnz), Ital. *Appennino*, mountain system (c.840 mi. long, c.80 mi. wide), Italy, S of the Po valley. Constitutes major part of Ital. peninsula, traversing its entire length from Cadibona Pass, where it meets Ligurian Alps, S to Strait of Messina; mts. of Sicily are a continuation. N division runs SE to Scheggia Pass; includes Ligurian, Etruscan (Tuscan), and Umbrian groups, in which, respectively, rise Monte Maggiorasca (5,915 ft.), Monte Cimone (7,096 ft.), and Monte Catria (5,584 ft.). From its N slopes to Po R. and Adriatic Sea flow Scrivia, Trebbia, Taro, Secchia, Panaro, Reno, Santerno, Ronco, and Savio rivers. On its S slopes rise Magra, Serchio, Arno, and Tiber rivers, which descend to Ligurian and Tyrrhenian seas. Major passes include Bocchetta, Giovi, Scoffera, La Cisa, Cerreto, Abetone, La Futa, and Bocca Serriola. In Apuane Alps (NW) are the famous quarries of Carrara marble. Central division continues S along the Adriatic to Sella di Vinchiaturo pass. Contains highest groups in the Apennines: GRAN SASSO D'ITALIA rises to 9,560 ft. in Monte Corno, and the MAIELLA to 9,170 ft. in Monte Amaro. From its E slope, which falls abruptly to the Adriatic, flow Chienti, Tronto, Pescara, Sangro, Biferno, and Fortore rivers. Gentler W slope gives rise to Liri (Garigliano) and Volturno rivers, which flow to Tyrrhenian Sea, and Nera R., a tributary of the Tiber. Contains crater lakes (Bolsena, Bracciano, Albano, Vico), mineral springs, fumaroles, and volcanic hills (Alban, TOLFA). N and central divisions contain, bet. Arno and Fiora rivers, the Tuscan hills and the Maremma district, which have valuable deposits of iron, copper, tin, mercury, lignite, marble, and borax. They rank with Sardinia as the richest mineral region of Italy. S division runs S to Gulf of Taranto, curving SE to "toe" of Italy. Rises to 7,451 ft. in the POLLINO. Other major groups, also on the "toe," are La SILA (6,392 ft.) in center and ASPROMONTE (6,417 ft.) at S tip. From E slope to Gulf of Taranto flow Bradano, Basento, Agri, Sinni, Crati, and Neto rivers; only one major river, the OFANTO flows to the Adriatic. Chief river descending W slope is the SELE. Near Naples are a volcanic region (PHLEGRAEAN FIELDS) and the famed VESUVIUS, which like Mt. ETNA in Sicily is still active. There are many mineral springs. The S division, particularly the "toe", has suffered many earthquakes, the worst occurring in 1783 and 1908. The forests (chestnut, birch, oak, pine) of the Apennines have been greatly reduced and reforestation is slowly progressing. Despite the resulting erosion and frequent landslides, towns are situated on hills above rivers because of seasonal floods, narrow valleys, malaria, and, historically, because they were more easily defended. There are extensive pastures, and the lower slopes are covered with olive groves, vineyards, orchards, nut trees, and cereals. Many hydroelectric plants.

Apenrade, Denmark: see AABENRAA.

Apetatitlán (äpätätētlän'), officially San Pablo Apetatitlán, town (pop. 743), Tlaxcala, central Mexico, on railroad and 3 mi. ENE of Tlaxcala; grain, maguey, alfalfa, livestock.

Apetlon (ä'pĕtlōn), village (pop. 2,104), Burgenland, E Austria, near Neusiedler L., 11 mi. ENE of Sopron, Hungary; sugar beets.

Apex (ā'pĕks), town (pop. 1,065), Wake co., central N.C., 12 mi. WSW of Raleigh; drug mfg., lumbering.

Aphantos or **Afandos** (both: ä'fändôs), Ital. *Afando*, town (pop. 2,313), Rhodes isl., Greece, on NE shore, 10 mi. S of Rhodes. Also spelled Afantos.

Aphrodisium, Tunisia: see ENFIDAVILLE.

Aphroditopolis, Egypt: see KOM ISHQAW.

Api (ä'pē), village, Eastern Prov., N Belgian Congo, on a tributary of Uele R. and 75 mi. NE of Buta; cotton plantations, cotton ginning. Known as the 1st African elephant taming and training center (established in 1902). The present elephant taming center is at Gangala na Bodio. R.C. mission.

Api (äpē'), mountain (23,399 ft.) in main range of W Nepal Himalayas, NW Nepal, at 30°1'N 80°57'E.

Apía (äpē'ä), town (pop. 3,312), Caldas dept., W central Colombia, in Cordillera Occidental, 30 mi. W of Manizales; coffeegrowing.

Apia, Gilbert Isls.: see ABAIANG.

Apia (ä'pēü), town (pop. c.10,000), ⊙ Western Samoa, port on N coast of UPOLU; since 1923, port of entry for TOKELAU; site of govt. hosp.

Apiaí (äpyäē'), city (pop. 1,433), S São Paulo, Brazil, in the Serra Paranapiacaba, near Paraná border, 65 mi. NNE of Curitiba; has Brazil's only electrolytic lead smelter. Sugar milling, rum distilling. Lead and silver mine at near-by Furnas. Arsenic, gold, cadmium deposits near by. Formerly spelled Apiahy.

Apiao Island (äpyou') (□ 5; pop. 710), off E coast of Chiloé Isl., Chiloé prov., S Chile, 30 mi. ESE of Castro; 5 mi. long, 1–2 mi. wide; agr. (potatoes, livestock), fishing.

Apice (ä'pēchĕ), village (pop. 1,769), Benevento prov., Campania, S Italy, near Calore R., 8 mi. E of Benevento.

Apipé Grande (äpēpā' grän'dā), island (pop. estimate 1,000), N Corrientes prov., Argentina, in Paraná R., 55 mi. W of Posadas, at Paraguay border; 20 mi. long, 10 mi. wide. Extensive rapids here. On E coast of isl. is town of Apipé or Apipé Grande, an agr. center (corn, alfalfa, sugar cane, tobacco, manioc, livestock). Just SE is isl. of Apipé Chico (chē'kō), 8 mi. long, 2 mi. wide.

Apishapa River (ŭpĭ'shüpü), SE Colo., rises in Sangre de Cristo Mts., flows 117 mi. NE, past Aguilar, to Arkansas R. W of Rocky Ford.

Ap-Iwan, Cerro (sĕ'rō äpē'wän), peak (7,580 ft.) in Patagonian Andes, on Argentina-Chile border, 10 mi. N of L. Buenos Aires; 46°9'S.

Apizaco (äpēsä'kō), city (pop. 6,768), Tlaxcala, central Mexico, on central plateau, 65 mi. E of Mexico city. Rail junction; agr. center (corn, wheat, barley, maguey, alfalfa, beans, livestock); pulque distilling, tanning, flour milling, mfg. of ceramics; iron foundry. Airfield. Formerly Barrón Escandón, still the name for the municipio.

Aplao (äplou'), town (pop. 865), ⊙ Castilla prov. (□ 1,471; pop. 23,918), Arequipa dept., S Peru, on W slopes of Cordillera Occidental, on Majes R. (irrigation) and 70 mi. WNW of Arequipa, in fertile agr. region (cotton, sugar cane, rice, fruit); wine and liquor distilling. Silver and gold mines near by.

Aplerbeck (ä'plürbĕk"), district (since 1929) of Dortmund, W Germany, 5 mi. ESE of city center; coal mining. Has 12th-cent. church.

Aplington, town (pop. 702), Butler co., N central Iowa, on Beaver Creek and 28 mi. WNW of Waterloo; feed, concrete products. Limestone quarries, sand and gravel pits near by.

Apo, Mount (ä'pō), active volcano (9,690 ft.) in S central Mindanao, Philippines, 25 mi. WSW of Davao; highest peak in the Philippines. Sulphur deposits.

Apodaca (äpōdä'kä), town (pop. 1,344), Nuevo León, N Mexico, on railroad and 10 mi. NE of Monterrey; chick-peas, barley, stock.

Apodi (äpōōdē'), city (pop. 787), W Rio Grande do Norte, NE Brazil, on E slope of Apodi plateau (extends N–S along Ceará border), 45 mi. SW of Mossoró; carnauba wax, cattle. Aquamarines found near by. Formerly spelled Apody.

Apodi River, W Rio Grande do Norte, NE Brazil, rises near Paraíba border, flows c.150 mi. NE, past Mossoró (head of navigation), to the Atlantic at Areia Branca. Intermittent-flowing river. Important salt deposits near mouth. Also called Mossoró R. in its lower course below city of that name. Formerly spelled Apody.

Apody, Brazil: see APODI.

Apoera (äpōō'rä), village (pop. 80), Nickerie dist., W Du. Guiana, on Courantyne or Corantijn R. (Br. Guiana border) and 55 mi. SSW of Nieuw Nickerie; timber, balata.

Apo Island (ä'pō), islet off SW coast of Mindoro, Philippines, just S of Apo Reef, in Mindoro Strait; 12°39'N 120°24'E. Apo East Pass and Apo West Pass flank the reef.

Apolda (äpôl'dä), city (pop. 33,439), Thuringia, central Germany, near the Ilm, 20 mi. E of Erfurt; 51°1'N 11°32'E. Woolen knitting and milling, bell casting; mfg. of machinery, fire extinguishers, chemicals, leather and food products. Of industrial importance since 16th cent.

Apolima (ä'pōlē'mä), small island (□ c.2; pop. 204), Western Samoa, under N.Z. mandate; in 10-mi. strait separating Upolu from Savaii; composed of tuff crater (472 ft. high).

Apollo, borough (pop. 3,015), Armstrong co., W central Pa., on Kiskiminetas R. opposite Vandergrift; steel mill, chemicals, cement, beverages; bituminous coal, gas, clay, limestone; agr. Laid out 1815, inc. 1848.

Apollo Bay, village (pop. 708), S Victoria, Australia, on Apollo Bay (inlet of Bass Strait), 95 mi. SW of Melbourne; tourist resort; dairy plant. Sometimes called Krambruk.

Apollonia (ăpülō'nēü), ruins of anc. city, S central Albania, 5 mi. W of Fier, near Seman R.; remains (excavated 1923–29 by French) include ruins of city wall and necropolis. Founded 588 B.C. as a colony of Corcyra (Corfu), it became an important commercial center exporting grain of the Myzeqe plain; passed 229 B.C. to Rome and was (1st cent. B.C.) an educational center for Roman patrician youths. Declined with the coming of the Barbarian invasions. Just S of the ruins is 14th-cent. Byzantine monastery of Pojan or Pojani.

Apollonia, Bulgaria: see SOZOPOL.

Apollonia, Greece: see SIPHNOS.

Apollonia, Arabic *Marsa Susa*, town (pop. 1,000), W Cyrenaica, Libya, port on Mediterranean Sea, on coastal road and 40 mi. WNW of Derna; flour milling, domestic weaving. Has Greek and Roman ruins (walls, theater) and remains of 5th-cent. Christian basilica. Anciently the port of near-by CYRENE, it flourished in 4th cent. B.C. Reestablished 1897 by Moslem refugees from Crete.

Apollonia, Lake, Turkey: see APULYONT, LAKE.

Apollonia Sozusa, Palestine: see ARSUF.

Apollonopolis Magna, Egypt: see IDFU.

Apollonskaya, Russian SFSR: see NOVO-PAVLOVSKAYA.

Apolo (äpō'lō), town (pop. c.4,620), ⊙ Caupolicán prov., La Paz dept., W Bolivia, 125 mi. NNW of La Paz; road center in tropical agr. area (coffee, cacao, coca); rubber plantations; cattle raising. Airport. Oil deposits at San José de Uchupiamomas (NE).

Apolobamba, Nudo de (nōō'dō dā äpōlōbäm'bä), Andean massif in Cordillera Oriental, on Peru-Bolivia border, 45 mi. SW of Huancané; rises to 18,924 ft. in the Palomaní.

Apopa (äpō'pä), city (pop. 2,939), San Salvador dept., W central Salvador, on railroad and 7 mi. N of San Salvador; sugar cane, grain. Sugar mill at El Angel (just NW).

Apopka (üpŏp'kü), city (pop. 2,254), Orange co., central Fla., 12 mi. NW of Orlando, near L. Apopka; shipping center for citrus fruit and truck; box mfg. Settled 1856.

Apopka, Lake, central Fla., on Orange-Lake co. line; nearly circular, and c.8-9 mi. in diameter; popular fishing area, with Winter Garden on SE shore. Connected by waterways with extensive central Fla. lake system, L. Apopka may be regarded as extreme head of OKLAWAHA RIVER.

Apoquindo (äpōkēn'dō), village (1930 pop. 35), Santiago prov., central Chile, in Andean foothills, 7 mi. E of Santiago; has thermal alkaline waters which are bottled commercially.

Aporo (äpō'rō), town (pop. 1,460), Michoacán, central Mexico, on railroad and 9 mi. SE of Hidalgo; corn, beans, sugar, fruit, livestock.

Apostle Islands, Ashland co., extreme N Wis., in SW L. Superior, near entrance to Chequamegon Bay, 10 mi. NNE of Ashland; comprise c.20 isls., the largest being Madeline Isl. (13 mi. long, 3 mi. wide). Known for wave-eroded cliffs, the group has abundant wild game (including deer, mink, muskrat, beaver), and numerous wild duck. The only settlement is LA POINTE, on Madeline Isl. Group is visited by tourists in summer.

Apostles Islands, Chile: see EVANGELIST ISLANDS.

Apóstoles (äpō'stōlĕs), town (1947 pop. 3,055), ⊙ Apóstoles dept. (1947 pop. 17,669), S Misiones natl. territory, Argentina, at SE foot of Sierra de Apóstoles (a low mtn. range), 38 mi. SSE of Posadas. Road and milling center in agr. area (maté, rice, cotton, corn). Founded by Jesuits in early 17th cent.

Apostolovo (ŭpô'stülŭvŭ), town (1926 pop. 5,189), SW Dnepropetrovsk oblast, Ukrainian SSR, 23 mi. SE of Krivoi Rog; rail junction; metalworking, food processing. Formed c.1940 by amalgamation of rail settlement of Apostolovo (in middle 1930s called Kosiorovo) and adjoining (N) village of Pokrovskoye.

Apoyo, Lake (äpoi'ō), SW Nicaragua, on Masaya-Granada dept. border, 4 mi. WSW of Granada. Located in anc. crater 2½ mi. across. Salt water. Another L. Apoyo is on Chiltepe Peninsula.

Apozol (äpōsōl'), town (pop. 1,708), Zacatecas, N central Mexico, on Juchipila R. and 55 mi. NNE of Guadalajara; alt. 4,645 ft.; grain, fruit, vegetables, livestock.

Appalachia (ă"pülă'chü), town (pop. 2,915), Wise co., SW Va., in the Cumberlands near Ky. line, 4 mi. N of Big Stone Gap; rail junction; coal-mining center in agr., dairying, orchard area. Settled 1890; inc. 1906.

Appalachian Mountains (ăpülā'chün,–chēün,–lăch'–), great mtn. system of E. North America, extending in wide belt generally parallel to the coast line for more than 1,600 mi., from the St. Lawrence in Quebec on the NE to the Gulf Coast plain in central Ala. on the SW, and lying mainly bet. the Coastal Plains and Interior Plains. Representing the much-eroded remnant of an enormous mtn. mass formed at the close of the Paleozoic period in the mtn.-making revolution which bears their name, the Appalachians embrace the major ranges (except for the Adirondack Mts.) E of the Mississippi; their highest point is in the S—at Mt. Mitchell (6,684 ft.) in the Black Mts. of N.C.; Mt. Washington (6,288 ft.), in the White Mts. of N.H., is highest peak in N portion. On basis of structure and topography, the system is divisible into 3 major longitudinal bands: the Older Appalachians (with highest peaks in system) on the E, the Folded, or Newer, Appalachians (including Great Appalachian Valley) in the center, and the Appalachian Plateau (including Catskill, Allegheny, and Cumberland mts.) on the W. The E band, the Older Appalachians, is composed of strongly-folded and metamorphosed Paleozoic rocks, with granitic and other igneous intrusions; in Canada, it is represented by the Acadian uplands (including the Shickshock and Notre Dame mts.), in NE U.S. by the New England upland, including the WHITE MOUNTAINS in N.H., GREEN MOUNTAINS in Vt., TACONIC MOUNTAINS in Vt. and Mass., and Berkshire Hills in Mass. From the New England upland, 2 prongs swing SW across N.Y. and N.J. to meet the BLUE RIDGE in Pa.; the prongs partly embrace the Triassic Lowland region (c.175 mi. NE-SW; composed of worn-down sandstones and shales), which is an important E-W transportation route. The Blue Ridge, continuing S to Mt. Oglethorpe in Ga., is bordered on the E by the PIEDMONT, underlain by the same formations, which slopes to merge with the coastal plain to E. The Blue Ridge includes highest peaks of E U.S.; with its associated ranges to the W, it widens to c.70 mi. in N.C. The Folded, or Newer, Appalachians, lying to W of the Older Appalachians, include a great composite lowland (GREAT APPALACHIAN VALLEY) along the E margin. This valley is represented in the N by the St. Lawrence lowland, the L. Champlain lowland (and Richelieu R. valley, which connects L. Champlain with the St. Lawrence), and the valley of the Hudson R.; from the Hudson, a chain of longitudinal valleys (best known is the beautiful Shenandoah Valley of Va.) continues SW to end in Ala. with merging of the Coosa valley with the Gulf Coast plain. Generally to W of the great valley, which contains fine agr. land, are the long even-crested ridges of the Newer Appalachians, cited by physiographers as classic examples of folded mts. Composed of folded Paleozoic strata which have undergone little metamorphism, the belt reaches greatest width (c.80 mi.) in E Pa., in its course across S N.Y., NW N.J., E Pa., W Md., E W.Va., W and SW Va., E Tenn., NW Ga., and NE Ala. Limestone-floored valleys of this region are valuable for agr. Westernmost part of the Appalachian system is the Appalachian Plateau (or Plateaus), beginning on N at the Mohawk R. valley of N.Y., and extending to the vicinity of Birmingham, Ala., where it meets the Gulf Coast plain. Occupying parts of N.Y., Pa., Ohio, W.Va., Ky., Tenn., and Ala., the plateau is a rugged, maturely-dissected, westward-sloping region, underlain by generally horizontal Paleozoic strata; its generally steep E escarpment overlooks the valleys of the Folded Appalachians. In the N, the plateau is known as the ALLEGHENY PLATEAU; along its E margin in N.Y., the CATSKILL MOUNTAINS rise above the Hudson valley; in Pa., W.Va. and Va., the rugged E portion of the Allegheny Plateau is known as the Allegheny Mts. In W.Va., most of which lies upon the plateau, the name Kanawha Plateau is sometimes applied. Southwesternmost portion of the plateau and of the entire Appalachian system is the CUMBERLAND PLATEAU, whose E margin is known as Cumberland Mts. in Ky. and Tenn., and by other local names as it continues SW. The Appalachians have been glaciated only in the Canadian and New England portions and on the N part (notably in W N.Y.) of the Allegheny Plateau. Valuable mineral resources of the Appalachians include the great anthracite field of E Pa. (in the Newer Appalachians), the bituminous fields of the plateau portion (in W Pa., W.Va., SW Va., E Ky., E central Tenn., and N Ala.), the petroleum and natural-gas fields of Pa. and W.Va., and the iron ore (basis of Birmingham's steel industry) of Ala.; other mineral production includes salt, bauxite, fluxing stone, clay, talc, mica, cement, and silica sand. Forests, despite much lumbering, remain valuable; timber stands are chiefly mixed hardwoods, except in New England and Canada, where conifers prevail. Hydroelectric development has been considerable in the South; the great TVA project in the basin of the TENNESSEE RIVER, with many reservoirs in Appalachian valleys, has stimulated the economy of a wide region of the southern mts. The great mtn. system was a formidable barrier to early westward expansion from seaboard settlements; when region had been penetrated, settlement and travel tended to follow the longitudinal valleys. S of New York, where the Mohawk valley was a much-traveled route, principal breaks in the E belt are the Delaware R. gap on the N.Y.-N.J. line, the valley of the Susquehanna R. in Pa., the gorge of the Potomac at Harpers Ferry, and the gorges of the James and the Roanoke in Va.; the formidable E face of the plateau portion, however, is virtually unbroken in the N (making railroad construction difficult), but in the S the Kanawha and Tennessee gorges and Cumberland Gap are natural breaks. The Appalachians, particularly in the South (where the name Appalachia is often given to the region) are rich in natural beauty; Shenandoah and Great Smoky Mts. natl. parks, many natl. forests and resort areas are visited by vacationers. Remote settlements in mtn. valleys, many of them inhabited by descendants of Scotch-Irish settlers of pre-Revolutionary and Revolutionary times, have preserved old ways of life more than any other region of the U.S.; here speech showing Elizabethan origins, ancient ballads, and handicrafts have survived despite improved communications.

Appalachian Trail, E U.S., mtn. footpath for hikers extending 2,050 mi. along crests of ranges of the Appalachian system, from Mt. Katahdin, Maine, to Mt. Oglethorpe, Ga.

Appalachian Valley, Great, U.S.: see GREAT APPALACHIAN VALLEY.

Appanoose (ăpŭnōōs', ă'pŭ-), county (□ 523; pop. 19,683), S Iowa, on Mo. line; ⊙ Centerville. Prairie agr. region (hogs, cattle, poultry, corn, soybeans, hay) and bituminous-coal-mining area drained by Chariton R.; limestone quarries. Has state park. Formed 1843.

Apparecida, Brazil: see BERTOLÍNIA.

Appelvaer, Norway: see ABELVAER.

Appennino, Italy: see APENNINES.

Appenweier (ä'pŭnvī"ŭr), village (pop. 2,029), S Baden, Germany, 8 mi. ESE of Kehl; rail junction; metal- and woodworking, lumber milling.

Appenzell (ä'pŭntsĕl), canton, NE Switzerland, surrounded by St. Gall canton. Mostly meadowland; pastures on Alpine hills (S); forests. Produces textiles (silk, cotton, embroideries); some tourism. Pop. German speaking. In 1597 Appenzell split into 2 independent half-cantons. **Appenzell Ausser Rhoden,** Fr. *Appenzell Rhodes Extérieures,* also known as Appenzell Outer Rhodes (□ 94; 1950 pop. 48,026), ⊙ Herisau, accepted the Reformation. **Appenzell Inner Rhoden,** Fr. *Appenzell Rhodes Intérieures,* also known as Appenzell Inner Rhodes (□ 67; 1950 pop. 13,448), ⊙ Appenzell, remained Catholic.

Appenzell, town (1950 pop. 4,983), ⊙ Appenzell Inner Rhoden half-canton, NE Switzerland, on Sitter R., 7 mi. S of St. Gall; alt. 2,589 ft.; produces embroidery. Castle with historical mus.; Col. of St. Anton with embroidery and lace collections.

Apperley Bridge, town in Bradford county borough, West Riding, SW Yorkshire, England, on Aire R.; woolen milling; mfg. of electrical equipment.

Apperson (ă'pŭrsŭn), town (pop. 21), Osage co., N Okla., 25 mi. W of Pawhuska.

Appiano (äp-pyä'nō), Ger. *Eppan,* commune (pop. 7,061), Bolzano prov., Trentino–Alto Adige, N Italy. Commune seat is San Michele (pop. 1,646), near Adige R., 5 mi. SW of Bolzano; wine.

Appiano Gentile (jĕntē'lĕ), village (pop. 2,266), Como prov., Lombardy, N Italy, 7 mi. SW of Como; silk mills.

Appian Way (ă'pēŭn), Latin *Via Appia,* great road built (312 B.C.) under Appius Claudius Caecus. It connected Rome with Capua and was later extended to Beneventum (Benevento), Tarentum (Taranto), and (by mid-3d cent. B.C.) Brundisium (Brindisi); it was later paved. Total length was more than 350 mi. The substantial construction of cemented stone blocks has preserved it to the present.

Appin, mountainous district of N Argyll, Scotland, extending 15 mi. NE–SW along SE shore of Loch Linnhe, bet. lochs Leven and Creran; c.7 mi. wide. District includes GLENCOE and is of great scenic beauty. Slate quarrying is chief industry. Leading villages: Ballachulish, Duror, Port Appin.

Appingedam (ä"pĭng-ŭdäm'), town (pop. 5,902), Groningen prov., NE Netherlands, 14 mi. NE of Groningen; horse and cattle market; mfg. (agr. and ship machinery, truck bodies, strawboard, linseed oil); flax.

Appleby. 1 Town, Lincolnshire, England: see SCUNTHORPE. **2** Municipal borough (1931 pop. 1,618; 1951 census 1,704), ⊙ Westmorland, England, in NE part of county, on Eden R. and 12 mi. SE of Penrith; agr. market. Has Appleby Castle (of Norman origin, rebuilt in 17th cent.) and 16th-cent. grammar school.

Apple Creek, village (pop. 548), Wayne co., N central Ohio, 6 mi. SE of Wooster; grain products, lumber.

Apple Creek, W Ill., rises SW of Springfield, flows c.60 mi. WSW, through Morgan and Greene counties, to Illinois R. c.12 mi. NW of Carrollton.

Applecross, fishing village and parish (pop. 1,034), SW Ross and Cromarty, Scotland, on the Inner Sound, opposite Raasay isl., 12 mi. WNW of Lochcarron. In 673 a church was founded here, one of earliest centers of Christianity in NW Highlands.

Appledore, town (pop. 2,367) in Northam urban dist., NW Devon, England, on Barnstaple Bay, at mouth of Torridge R. and Taw R. estuaries, 3 mi. N of Bideford; fishing port, agr. market, seaside resort.

Appledore Island, Maine: see ISLES OF SHOALS.

Applegate, village (pop. 244), Sanilac co., E Mich., on Black R. and 28 mi. NNW of Port Huron, in agr. area.

Apple River, village (pop. 431), Jo Daviess co., NW Ill., on Apple R., near Wis. line, and 23 mi. NW of Freeport, in agr. area. Apple River Canyon State Park is near by.

Apple River. 1 In NW Ill., rises in Jo Daviess co. near Wis. line, flows c.40 mi. generally SW and S, past Hanover (dammed here), to the Mississippi NW of Savanna. Its upper canyon, near Nora, is site of state park (c.150 acres). **2** In NW Wis., rises in Barron co., flows c.50 mi. SW through lake region, past Amery, to St. Croix R. 7 mi. NE of Stillwater, Minn.

Appleton. 1 Town (pop. 671), Knox co., S Maine, 12 mi. NW of Rockland; center of apple-growing region. **2** Village (pop. 2,256), Swift co., SW Minn., on Pomme de Terre R. near its mouth on Minnesota R. and 22 mi. WSW of Benson; farm trade center in grain, livestock, and poultry region; dairy products, flour. Hydroelectric plant is here. Near by are Marsh L. and Lac qui Parle. Settled 1869, laid out 1870, inc. 1881. **3** Town (pop. 120), Cape Girardeau co., SE Mo., near Mississippi R., 13 mi. SE of Perryville. **4** Town (1940 pop. 198), Allendale co., SW S.C., 4 mi. NW of Allendale. **5** City (pop. 34,010), ⊙ Outagamie co., E Wis., on Fox R. near its exit from L. Winnebago, and 26 mi. SW of Green Bay city, in dairying, stock-raising, and farming area; mfg. center (paper, machinery, woodwork, woolen goods, textiles; breweries, canneries). A large power plant is fed by Fox R. The 1st hydroelectric plant in the U.S. was built here in 1882. Seat of Lawrence Col. and of Inst. of Paper Chemistry. Harry Houdini was b. here. Settled before 1850; inc. c.1857.

Appleton City, city (pop. 1,150), St. Clair co., W Mo., 18 mi. SW of Clinton; ships grain, livestock. Inc. 1871.

Appleton Mills, textile-mill village (pop. 5,413, with adjacent Equinox), Anderson co., NW S.C., near Anderson.

Appletreewick, village and parish (pop. 191), West Riding, W Yorkshire, England, on Wharfe R. and 7 mi. NE of Skipton; lead mining, paper milling.

Applewold, borough (pop. 500), Armstrong co., W central Pa., on Allegheny R. opposite Kittanning.

Appleyard, village (pop. 1,479), Chelan co., central Wash., on the Columbia and 2 mi. S of Wenatchee.

Appley Bridge, England: see PARBOLD.

Appling, county (□ 514; pop. 14,003), SE Ga.; ⊙ Baxley. Bounded NE by Altamaha R., SW by Little Satilla R. Coastal plain agr. (tobacco, corn, melons, peanuts, livestock) and forestry (lumber, naval stores) area. Formed 1818.

Appling, agr. village (pop. c.300), ⊙ Columbia co., E Ga., 20 mi. WNW of Augusta.

Appomattox (ă"pŭmă'tŭks), county (□ 343; pop. 8,764), central Va.; ⊙ Appomattox. Bounded NW by James R.; drained by Appomattox R. Includes Appomattox Court House Natl. Monument (at Appomattox) and part of a state forest. Agr. (especially tobacco; hay, livestock), dairying, lumbering. Formed 1845.

Appomattox, town (pop. 1,094), ⊙ Appomattox co., central Va., 18 mi. E of Lynchburg; tobacco market; lumberyards; flour milling, mfg. of batteries, clothing. Inc. 1925. Near by is Appomattox Court House, site of Lee's surrender (April 9, 1865) to Grant. After Sheridan's victory at Five Forks, Lee retreated W, abandoning PETERSBURG and Richmond. His plan to join Johnston's army in N.C. was defeated, and his surrender here virtually terminated Civil War. Appomattox Court House Natl. Monument (968.3 acres; established 1940) includes old village of Appomattox Court House and McLean House (reconstructed 1949), in which articles of surrender were signed.

Appomattox River, E Va., rises in Appomattox co., flows 137 mi. generally E past Petersburg (head of navigation), to James R. at Hopewell.

Apponaganset, Mass.: see DARTMOUTH.

Apponaug (ă'pŭnôg), village (pop. c.2,000), administrative center of WARWICK city, Kent co., E R.I., on Greenwich Bay, 9 mi. S of Providence; textile finishing, rubber goods.

Apprieu (äprēŭ'), village (pop. 1,493), Isère dept., SE France, 5 mi. NW of Voiron; electrometallurgy, forges; paper milling.

Approuague (äprōōäg'), district (pop. 294) of Inini territory, commune, and small village, N Fr. Guiana. Village of GUISAMBOURG is also called Approuague; RÉGINA is ⊙ Approuague commune and dist.

Approuague River, central and NE Fr. Guiana, rises in outliers of Guiana Highlands at 3°5'N 53°7'W, flows c.175 mi. NE, through tropical forests, to the Atlantic in a wide, navigable estuary at Point Béhague. Gold placers near its mid-course.

Apra Harbor or **Port Apra** (ä'prŭ), W Guam, 5 mi. N of Agana, only good harbor on isl.; port of entry; closed to foreign vessels except by permit. U.S. naval base here.

Aprelevka (ŭpryĕ'lyĭfkŭ), town (1939 pop. over 500), central Moscow oblast, Russian SFSR, 25 mi. SW of Moscow; metal- and brickworks; mfg. of phonograph records.

Aprelsk or **Aprel'sk** (ŭpryĕlsk'), town (1948 pop. over 500), NE Irkutsk oblast, Russian SFSR, 20 mi. NE of Bodaibo; gold mines.

Aprelya, 28 (ŭpryĕ'lyŭ) [Rus.,=28th of April], town (1946 pop. over 500), central Azerbaijan SSR, on railroad (Mingechaur station) and 8 mi. W of Yevlakh; junction of rail spur to Mingechaur.

Apremont (äprŭmō'). **1** Village (pop. 221), Ardennes dept., N France, on E slope of the Argonne, 16 mi. SE of Vouziers. **2** Village (pop. 199), Meuse dept., NE France, in the Côtes de Meuse, 5 mi. ESE of Saint-Mihiel. Demolished by Allied shelling in First World War. Also called Apremont-la-Forêt.

Aprica Pass (äprē'kä) (alt. 3,875 ft.), N Italy, in Bergamasque Alps, bet. Val Camonica and Valtellina, 14 mi. E of Sondrio. Crossed by road bet. Edolo and Tresenda. Summer resort and winter-sports area.

Apricena (äprēchā'nä), town (pop. 8,869), Foggia prov., Apulia, S Italy, 8 mi. NNE of San Severo; macaroni, wine, cheese; fireworks. Largely destroyed by earthquakes in 1627.

Aprigliano (äprēlyä'nō), village (pop. 1,937), Cosenza prov., Calabria, S Italy, near upper Crati R., 5 mi. SE of Cosenza; wine making.

Aprilia (äprē'lyä), village (pop. 1,500), Latina prov., Latium, S central Italy, in reclaimed PONTINE

MARSHES, 10 mi. N of Anzio. Agr. settlement established 1937 and rebuilt after its destruction (1944) in Second World War.

Apsheron Peninsula (ŭpshĭrôn'), site of BAKU oil fields in E Azerbaijan SSR; extends about 40 mi. into SW Caspian Sea, terminating at Cape Shakhov. Forms low E extremity of the Greater Caucasus, consisting of tertiary sediments rich in petroleum deposits, mud volcanoes, natural-gas wells, and salt lakes. One of chief petroleum regions of USSR (c.15% of world reserves); principal fields at Balakhany, Sabunchi, Surakhany (developed in late-19th cent.), Kara-Chukhur, Kala, fields SW of Baku (dating from 1930s), and at Mashtagi and Buzovny (tapped during Second World War). Peninsula is included in Baku city limits; Baku proper lies on SW shore. Oil centers are linked by electric railroad and pipe lines to Baku. Port Apsheron is oil-loading port on E coast, opposite Artem Isl. A dry, subtropical area, the peninsula is watered (since late 1940s) by Samur-Divichi Canal. Agr. (fruit, truck, vineyards, olives).

Apsheron-Port, town (1939 pop. over 2,000) in Azizbekov dist. of Greater Baku, Azerbaijan SSR, Caspian port on E shore of Apsheron Peninsula, opposite Artem Isl., 26 mi. ENE of Baku; oil-loading installations.

Apsheronsk (ŭpshĭrônsk'), city (1939 pop. over 10,000), S central Krasnodar Territory, Russian SFSR, at N foot of the W Greater Caucasus, on rail spur and 20 mi. WSW of Maikop; petroleum center; lumber milling, tanning. Power station. Developed in late 1930s; became city in 1947.

Apsley Strait, Australia: see MELVILLE ISLAND.

Apt (äpt), town (pop. 5,209), Vaucluse dept., SE France, on the Coulon and 30 mi. ESE of Avignon, bet. Monts de Vaucluse (N) and Montagne du Lubéron (S); agr. trade center (almonds, wine, black truffles, fruits) in ocher-quarrying region. Fruit preserving and candying, lavender distilling, flour milling; artistic pottery, faïence, and phosphate mfg. Sulphur mines near by. Has 12th-cent. Romanesque church (former cathedral).

Apuane Alps (ä'pūän), division (□ 800) of Etruscan Apennines in Tuscany, central Italy; extend c.35 mi. along coast, bet. Magra (N) and Serchio (S) rivers. Rise to 6,384 ft. in Monte Pisanino. Noted for rich quarries of Carrara marble, worked since anc. times.

Apuania, Italy: see MASSA E CARRARA.

Apucarana (äpo͝okŏorä'nŭ), city (1948 pop. estimate 5,750), N Paraná, Brazil, 23 mi. SW of Londrina; railhead (1948) of line from Ourinhos (São Paulo); trade center of pioneer settlements in recently cleared coffee zone. Other crops: rice, cotton, potatoes, wheat. Sawmilling, coffee processing, distilling.

Apuka, village and river, Russian SFSR: see OLYUTORSKOYE.

Apulco, Mexico: see SAN PEDRO APULCO.

Apulia (ŭpū'lēŭ), Ital. *Puglia* (po͞ol'lyä), region (□ 7,469; pop. 2,642,076), S Italy; ⊙ Bari. Bordered by Abruzzi e Molise (N), Campania and Basilicata (W), Adriatic Sea (E), and Gulf of Taranto (S). Comprises 5 provs.: BARI, BRINDISI, FOGGIA, IONIO, LECCE. Occupies approximately the southern third of E coast of Italy, opposite Albania. Its southernmost tip, a peninsula bet. Strait of Otranto and Gulf of Taranto, forms the "heel" of Italy. Predominantly hilly, with narrow coastal plain widening in S (around Lecce) and large lowland in N (around Foggia). Forests cover c.5% of area. Practically semi-arid, with annual rainfall of 20–24 in. (in some places up to 30 in.); only rivers (Candelaro, Carapelle, Cervaro, OFANTO) are in N. Water supply is supplemented by *Acquedotto Pugliese* (built 1905–28), which conducts water from SELE RIVER (via 9-mi. tunnel through the Apennines) to all provs. of Apulia by means of a main aqueduct (143 mi.) and side aqueducts (1,507 mi.). Predominantly agr.; a leading producer of Italy's olive oil (over ⅓), wine, wheat, flax, almonds, figs, tobacco, and vegetables. Stock raising (sheep, goats) is widespread. Fishing (TARANTO, Manfredonia, Brindisi). Extensive salt-works at Margherita di Savoia. Bauxite mining on promontory of GARGANO. Mfg. chiefly in Bari prov. and prov. capitals. Occupied by several Italic peoples and Greek colonists before Roman conquest (4th cent. B.C.). After fall of Rome, held by Goths, Lombards, and Byzantines. Became part of kingdom of Sicily (1130–1282) and of kingdom of Naples (1282–1860). United with Italy in 1861. Feudal system long prevailed in rural areas. Social and agrarian reforms have proceeded slowly since 19th cent.

Apulo (äpo͞o'lō), town (pop. 2,555), Cundinamarca dept., central Colombia, in W foothills of Cordillera Oriental, on railroad and 35 mi. W of Bogotá; cement plant.

Apulyont, Lake (äpo͝olyônt'), anc. *Apollonia* or *Abullonia* (□ 60), NW Turkey, 18 mi. W of Bursa; 14 mi. long, 8 mi. wide. Kirmasti (Rhyndacus) R. enters S, leaves W. Sometimes spelled Apolyont.

Apure (äpo͞o'rā), inland state (□ 29,535; 1941 pop. 70,560; 1950 census 84,806), W central Venezuela; ⊙ San Fernando. Bordered S and SW by Colombia (Arauca and Meta rivers), and by Apure (N) and Orinoco (E) rivers. Consists of vast llanos in Orinoco basin, with virgin unexploited forests (W). Crossed W–E to Orinoco R. by numerous rivers. Extremely hot and tropical climate, with heavy rains (May–Sept.). Predominantly a cattle-raising region; also some horse breeding. Agr. crops, produced mainly along rivers, include corn, yucca, sugar cane, rice, tobacco, cotton, cacao. Rivers and lagoons yield great numbers of fish. Main products for export are cattle, dairy products, hides, dried fish, egret feathers. San Fernando is leading commercial center and river port. Apurito, Bruzual, and Palmarito (all on the Apure), and El Amparo (on the Arauca) are among other landings on state's navigable streams.

Apure River, W central Venezuela; formed by union of its headstreams, the Uribante and Sarare rivers, rising in the Andean Cordillera Oriental of Colombia, in Apure state 4 mi. NNE of Guadualito, flows c.350 mi. NE and E through the llanos, past Palmarito, Bruzual, Puerto de Nutrias, Apurito, and San Fernando, to the Orinoco 75 mi. ESE of San Fernando; c.500 mi. long, with headstreams. Main tributaries are the Portuguesa and Santo Domingo. Cattle are raised, and some corn, cotton, sugar cane, yucca, and fruit are produced, along its course. Navigable for river steamers its entire length from the Orinoco.

Apure Viejo (vyā'hō), S arm of Apure R., Apure state, W central Venezuela; 75 mi. long; unites with the Caño Ruende W of San Fernando.

Apurímac (äpo͞orē'mäk), department (□ 8,189; pop. 280,213), S central Peru, in the Andes; ⊙ Abancay. Crossed by numerous spurs of Cordillera Occidental. Watered by Apurímac R. and its affluents, the Pachachaca and Pampas rivers. Has temperate climate, cool in high sierras. Gold, copper, lead, and salt mines; also silver, coal, and marble deposits. Primarily a stock-raising (sheep, cattle, mules, alpacas, llamas) and agr. region (corn, barley, wheat, potatoes, sugar cane, fruit, cotton). Main industries are mining, sugar milling, liquor distilling, dairying. Wool is exported. Dept. was set up 1873.

Apurímac River, S central Peru, rises in small lake at N foot of Cordillera de Chilca SW of Cailloma (Arequipa dept.), flows c.550 mi. NW and NNW through Andean ranges, past Puerto Bolognesi (where it receives the Mantaro) and Puerto Prado (where it receives the Perené), to join the Urubamba in forming the Ucayali, one of the main headstreams of the Amazon. In its lower course, the part (80 mi.) bet. Puerto Bolognesi and Puerto Prado is called the Ene (ā'nā) and the part (80 mi.) bet. Puerto Prado and the confluence with the Urubamba, the Tambo (täm'bō). Main tributaries, Pampas and Pachachaca rivers.

Apurito (äpo͞orē'tō), town (pop. 327), Apure state, W central Venezuela, landing on Apure R. and 70 mi. W of San Fernando, in cattle country.

Apuseni Mountains (äpo͞oshān'), Rum. *Apuşeni* [=west mts.], large mountain massif in W central Rumania, mostly in Transylvania; extends c.55 mi. SSE–NNW (40 mi. wide) bet. Rapid Körös R. (N) and Mures R. (S); rises to 6,071 ft. in Bihor peak. Highly mineralized. Highest parts (W), the Bihor Mts., are mostly devoid of settlements; iron, manganese, and bauxite are mined at their W foot. Muntii Metalici [=metal mts.] to S, chiefly of volcanic formation, are Rumania's foremost producer of precious metals (Zlatna, Brad), the so-called "Gold Square"; some deposits have been worked since Roman times. There are also copper mines. White Körös R. rises here.

Aqaba, Akaba, El 'Aqaba, or **Al-'Aqabah** (all: ä'käbŭ, ĕl), anc. *Aelana* (ēlā'nŭ), town (pop. c.1,000), S Jordan, port at N tip of Gulf of Aqaba, 60 mi. SW of Ma'an. Jordan's only outlet to the sea, and trading center for hinterland Bedouins; fisheries; exports shells. Airfield. It was probably the biblical Elath; the modern town of ELATH in Israel is near by. Near by is site of biblical port of Ezion-geber.

Aqaba, Gulf of, anc. *Sinus Aelaniticus,* Arabic *Khalij al-Aqabah,* NE arm of Red Sea, bet. Egypt's Sinai peninsula (W) and northernmost Hejaz (E), and touching Israel and Jordan at its head; 100 mi. long, 12-17 mi. wide. Principal ports are Aqaba (Jordan) and Elath (Israel). Saudi Arabia's Tiran and Sanafir isls. bar entrance to gulf, which forms part of Great Rift Valley.

Aqchah (äk'chŭ), town (pop. 10,000), Mazar-i-Sharif prov., N Afghanistan, in Afghan Turkestan, 55 mi. WNW of Mazar-i-Sharif; road center in irrigated area (Balkh R. oasis). Since 1855 under Afghan control.

Aqche, China: see AKCHE.

Aqda (äkdä'), village (1930 pop. estimate 3,000), Tenth Prov., in Yezd, central Iran, 65 mi. NW of Yezd; noted for its pomegranates; dates and barley. Also spelled Aghda.

Aqiq (äkēk'), village, Kassala prov., NE Anglo-Egyptian Sudan, minor port on Red Sea, on road and 120 mi. SSE of Port Sudan; fishing.

'Aqiribat (äkērē'bät), Fr. *Aguerbat,* village, Hama prov., W Syria, 40 mi. ESE of Hama; cotton, cereals.

Aq Qaleh, Iran: see PAHLEVI DEZH.

Aqrabi or **'Aqrabi** (äk'räbē), small tribal area (pop. 1,200) of Western Aden Protectorate, adjoining NW Aden Colony; ⊙ Bir Ahmad. One of the original Nine Cantons, inhabited by peaceful pastoral and agr. pop. Protectorate treaty concluded in 1888. Sometimes spelled Akrabi.

Aqsu, China: see AKSU.

Aquae, Italy: see ACQUI.

Aquae Augustae, France: see DAX.

Aquae Borvonis, France: see BOURBONNE-LES-BAINS.

Aquae Calidae, England: see BATH.

Aquae Flaviae, Portugal: see CHAVES.

Aquae Gratianae, France: see AIX-LES-BAINS.

Aquae Sextiae, France: see AIX-EN-PROVENCE.

Aquae Solis or **Aquae Sulis,** England: see BATH.

Aquae Statiellae, Italy: see ACQUI.

Aquae Tacapitanae, Tunisia: see HAMMA, EL-.

Aquae Tarbellicae, France: see DAX.

Aquara (äkwä'rä), village (pop. 2,885), Salerno prov., Campania, S Italy, 16 mi. SSE of Eboli.

Aquarius Plateau, high tableland in Wayne and Powell counties, S central Utah. Largely in Dixie Natl. Forest. Includes several small lakes. Rises to 11,253 ft. in BLUE BELL KNOLL.

Aquebogue (ă'kwĭbŏg"), village (1940 pop. 791), Suffolk co., SE N.Y., on NE Long Isl., near Flanders Bay, 3 mi. NE of Riverhead, in summer-resort area.

Aqueduct Race Track, N.Y.: see QUEENS.

Aquia (ä'kyä), town (pop. 1,041), Ancash dept., W central Peru, in Cordillera Occidental, 50 mi. SE of Huarás; alt. 10,991 ft. Grain, potatoes, alfalfa. Mining of silver and copper near by.

Aquia (ă'kwēŭ), village, Stafford co., NE Va., 12 mi. NNE of Fredericksburg. Aquia Church, here, built 1757.

Aquia Creek, NE Va., rises near Stafford-Fauquier co. line, flows c.25 mi. E and SE to the Potomac 5 mi. SE of Stafford; navigable in lower reaches.

Aquidabã (äkēdŭbä'), city (pop. 2,488), N Sergipe, NE Brazil, 18 mi. SW of Propriá; rice, sugar, cotton. Formerly spelled Aquidaban.

Aquidabán River or **Aquidabán-mi River** (äkēdäbän'-mē), in Concepción and Amambay depts., N Paraguay, rises at W foot of Sierra de Amambay (Brazil border), flows c.150 mi. SW and W to Paraguay R. 20 mi. NW of Concepción. Navigable c.20 mi. On its banks the dictator Marshal López was killed (1870) by the Brazilians.

Aquidauana (äkēdou-ä'nŭ), city (pop. 5,773), S Mato Grosso, Brazil, on São Paulo–Corumbá RR and 75 mi. W of Campo Grande; commercial center in stock-raising area; ships wool, hides, dried meat. Manganese deposits.

Aquidneck (ŭkwĭd'nĭk), Indian and early colonial name of RHODE ISLAND in Narragansett Bay, largest isl. of R.I.

Aquila or **Aquila degli Abruzzi** (ä'kwēlä dĕlyäbro͞o'tsē), province (□ 1,943; pop. 365,716), Abruzzi e Molise, S central Italy; ⊙ Aquila. Mtn. terrain bordering on Gran Sasso d'Italia (NE); watered by upper courses of Pescara (here called Aterno), Sangro, and Liri rivers. Abruzzo Natl. Park (□ c.110) in SE. Agr. (cereals, potatoes, grapes, fruit) and sheep raising predominate; reclaimed area of Lago FUCINO is chief agr. region. Bauxite mining (Ovindoli, Lecce ne'Marsi, Villa Vallelonga). Hydroelectric plants (Anversa degli Abruzzi, Campotosto, Capistrello). Mfg. at Aquila, Avezzano, Sulmona. Suffered several earthquakes, including one in 1915. Area reduced (1927) to help form Pescara prov.

Aquila or **Aquila degli Abruzzi,** town (pop. 20,573), ⊙ Abruzzi e Molise and Aquila prov., S central Italy, on Pescara R. (here called Aterno) and 43 mi. WSW of Pescara; 42°21'N 13°24'E. Rail junction; resort (alt. 2,365 ft.); chief point of departure for near-by Gran Sasso d'Italia. Mfg. (furniture, copper goods, glass, wax, hats, macaroni); trade in agr. products, livestock. Archbishopric. Despite several earthquakes, it retains its medieval ramparts and gates, 16th-cent. castle, and many old houses and fine churches. Anciently a castle; achieved importance in 13th cent.; later became 2d city of kingdom of Naples. Damaged by air bombing (1943–44) in Second World War.

Aquila (äkē'lä), town (pop. 597), Veracruz, E Mexico, in Sierra Madre Oriental, 15 mi. WSW of Orizaba; fruit.

Aquileia (äkwēlā'yä), town (pop. 1,116), Udine prov., Friuli–Venezia Giulia, NE Italy, 21 mi. S of Udine, near the Adriatic. Has 11th-cent. Romanesque basilica with 4th-cent. mosaic floor. Archaeological mus. has mosaics and sculptures of Roman period. Attained great military and commercial importance under the Romans. Sacked by Attila in 452. Became (6th cent.) seat of powerful patriarchate. In 1420 fell to Venice and rapidly declined.

Aquiles Serdán (äkē'lĕs sĕrdän'), mining settlement (pop. 7,368), Chihuahua, N Mexico, 12 mi. ESE of Chihuahua. Rail terminus; smelting and mining center (silver, gold, lead, copper, zinc, kaolin, fluorspar, vanadium). Formerly Santa Eulalia. The mining camp Francisco Portillo (pop. 2,675), formerly Santo Domingo, is near by.

Aquilla, village (pop. 386), Geauga co., NE Ohio, just S of Chardon.

Aquin (äkē'), town (1950 census pop. 1,799), Sud dept., SW Haiti, minor port on S coast of Tiburon Peninsula, 23 mi. ENE of Les Cayes; logwood, cotton. Has well-protected harbor.

Aquincum, Hungary: see BUDAPEST.

Aquino (äkwē'nô), anc. *Aquinum*, village (pop. 1,697), Frosinone prov., Latium, S central Italy, 3 mi. NNE of Pontecorvo. Has 12th-cent. Romanesque church and Roman ruins (temple, amphitheater). Juvenal b. here. St. Thomas Aquinas b. near by, at Roccasecca.

Aquiraz (äkērās'), city (pop. 996), N Ceará, Brazil, near the Atlantic, 15 mi. SE of Fortaleza; sugar, cotton, carnauba wax. Manganese deposits.

Aquiri River, Brazil: see ACRE RIVER.

Aquismón (äkēzmōn'), town (pop. 590), San Luis Potosí, E Mexico, 25 mi. S of Valles; cotton, sugar, cereals, fruit, livestock.

Aquitaine (ăk'wĭtān, äkētĕn'), anc. *Aquitania* (ăkwĭtā'nyù), region of SW France, known as GUIENNE prov. after Hundred Years War, and now comprised in Gironde, Dordogne, Lot, Aveyron, Lot-et-Garonne, and Tarn-et-Garonne depts. Inhabited by Iberians in Gallic times, it was conquered by Caesar's army in 56 B.C. and under Augustus came to include all territory bet. Garonne and Loire rivers. Occupied by Visigoths (5th cent.), Franks (6th cent.), it became a duchy c.670, and an independent kingdom under Charlemagne's heirs. It passed to England in 1154, but was reconquered by France (1453) to become Guienne prov.

Aquitaine Basin, second largest lowland of France (SW), bounded by the Pyrenees (S), the Massif Central (N and NE), and the Bay of Biscay (W); traversed by the Garonne and drained by its numerous tributaries. A very fertile plain, it has extensive wheat and corn fields and grows wines (Bordelais, Charente, Armagnac), fruits (Agenais), and vegetables. It supplies France with poultry, horses, and mules and is self-sufficient in cattle. Mineral resources are scarce and industry is of secondary importance, chiefly of the food-processing type. Unlike the Paris Basin, it has no economic center, the 2 largest cities (Bordeaux and Toulouse) being on the periphery. Other towns are Angoulême, Périgueux, Agen, Montauban, and Bayonne. Administratively, it was formerly included in Guienne and Gascony provinces. Parts of at least 12 depts. are in Aquitaine Basin.

Aquitania, France: see AQUITAINE.

Aquitanicus Sinus: see BISCAY, BAY OF.

Aquixtla (äkē'slä), town (pop. 431), Puebla, central Mexico, 7 mi. SE of Chignahuapan; corn, maguey.

Aquone Lake, N.C.: see NANTAHALA RIVER.

Ar [Arabic,=the], for Arabic names beginning thus: see under following part of the name.

Ara, Cape (ä'rä), Jap. *Ara-saki*, southernmost point of Okinawa, in the Ryukyu Isls., Japan, in E.China Sea; 26°4'N 127°40'E.

'Ara, Ras, or **Ras al Ara,** or **Ras al-'Arah** (räs' ăl ä'rù), cape of Western Aden Protectorate, on Gulf of Aden, 75 mi. W of Aden; airfield.

Arab, town (pop. 1,592), Marshall co., NE Ala., 11 mi. W of Guntersville, near Guntersville Reservoir.

Arab, Bahr el, Anglo-Egyptian Sudan: see BAHR EL ARAB.

Arab, Shatt al, Iraq and Iran: see SHATT AL ARAB.

Araba or **Arabah** (both: ä'räbä, ă'rùbù), depression, S Palestine, along a valley (Arabic *Wadi 'Araba*) extending over 100 mi. S from the Dead Sea to Gulf of Aqaba; it lies along the Jordan-Israel border. It is a continuation of the Jordan trough, of which the GHOR, N of the Dead Sea, is a part; all are part of the GREAT RIFT VALLEY. The section on Dead Sea (below sea level) has deposits of bituminous limestone, salt, potash.

Araba el Madfuna or **'Araba al-Madfunah** (ärä'bäl mădfōō'nù), village (pop. 14,177), Girga prov., central Upper Egypt, 6 mi. SW of El Balyana, near the Nile, 100 mi. below site of anc. Thebes. Near by are the ruins of anc. *Abydos*, site of temples dating from the I to the XXV dynasty and of tombs of many Egyptian rulers. Some of the temples were dedicated to Osiris. Two of the most important temples were built by Seti I and Ramses II. Tablets, one of which is in the British Museum, list the names of anc. Egyptian rulers.

Arabat Tongue (ŭrùbät'), Rus. *Arabatskaya Strelka* (ŭrùbät'skīù strĕl'kŭ), narrow spit of land of E Crimea, Russian SFSR, separating Sea of Azov (E) and E Sivash lagoon; extends from village of Arabat (20 mi. NNE of Feodosiya), 70 mi. NNW to Genichesk (separated by narrow Genichesk Strait). Saltworks near S end.

Arabayona (äräviō'nä), town (pop. 1,015), Salamanca prov., W Spain, 16 mi. ENE of Salamanca; wheat, livestock.

Arabi (ă'rùbē). **1** Town (pop. 376), Crisp co., S central Ga., 9 mi. SSE of Cordele. **2** Village (1940 pop. 1,982), St. Bernard parish, SE La., on E bank (levee) of the Mississippi, just below New Orleans; automobile assembly plants, stockyards, meatpacking, and by-products plants. Chalmette Natl. Historical Park is near.

Arabia or **Arabian Peninsula,** large peninsular region (□ 1,000,000; pop. 12,000,000) of SW Asia. Bounded N by Syrian Desert, E by Persian Gulf and Gulf of Oman, S by Arabian Sea and Gulf of Aden, and W by Red Sea, it extends bet. 12°–32°N and 35°–60°E. It is shaped roughly like a trapezoid with its long axis oriented NW-SE and is divided politically into SAUDI ARABIA (which occupies ⅔ of the area and has ½ of pop.) and, along the S and E margins, into YEMEN, ADEN COLONY and ADEN PROTECTORATE, OMAN, TRUCIAL OMAN, QATAR, and KUWAIT. Geologically, Arabia is a gigantic block of anc. crystalline rocks, covered by later sediments, notably limestone and sandstone. This platform is defined on all sides by a series of fault-scarps, particularly along the Red Sea, where the uptilting and buckling has produced the peninsula's highest mts., rising to 9,000 ft. in N Hejaz and to over 12,000 ft. in Yemen, and overlooking the TIHAMA coastal plain of the Red Sea. Mts. also rise along the S coast in the so-called Kaur ranges of the Aden Protectorate, and in the SE bulge in the folded Jabal Akhdar (9,900 ft.) of Oman, related to the Zagros of Iran. From its uptilted W edge along the Red Sea, the Arabian plateau slopes gradually E toward the Persian Gulf. In the interior (mean alt. 2–3,000 ft.) are alternating steppe and desert, the latter of the NAFUD (N) and DAHANA (E) types and including the vast S desert of RUB' AL KHALI. The generally level interior (NEJD) is interrupted by the N highlands of Jebel SHAMMAR (N) and a N-S belt of escarpments (Jabal TUWAIQ, ARMA PLATEAU) in E central section. Although no perennial rivers now exist, the entire Arabian Peninsula is dissected by numerous deep wadies, formed apparently both by tectonic action and former fluvial erosion. The principal such valley depressions are the wadies Sirhan, Rima, Hanifa, and Dawasir, all of which follow the slope of the plateau from W to E. Arabia has a uniform low-latitude desert climate with high summer temperatures and rainfall of c.4 inches annually. Only the marginal mts. receive more rain, particularly the highlands of Asir, Yemen, and Oman, where 20–40 inches fall annually in a well-marked monsoonal rainy season (July–Sept.). These highlands, consequently, constitute the largest continuous agr. dists. of the peninsula, noted for the growing of coffee and kat (*qat*), a narcotic stimulant. Elsewhere, agr. is possible only in isolated oases, frequently strung along wadies, where dates are the staple crop, followed by grain (millet, wheat, barley), fruit, and vegetables. About ⅕ of the pop. lives the nomadic life of the Bedouin, seeking grazing lands for its camels, goats, and sheep, and subsisting on a diet of dates and camel's milk. Frankincense is a product characteristic of the MAHRI coast. Mineral exploitation is virtually nonexistent, with the exception of the petroleum resources of HASA, whose development (since 1938) has revolutionized the economy of the region. Except for Riyadh and Hail in the interior, most of Arabia's large urban centers are on or near the coast: Jidda, and the pilgrimage centers of Mecca and Medina in Hejaz; Sana and Hodeida in Yemen; Aden; Mukalla in the Hadhramaut; Muscat and Matrah in Oman; Hofuf, Abqaiq, and Dhahran in Hasa; Manama on offshore Bahrein; and Kuwait. Communications are chiefly by sea and by camel caravan. Long one of the least-known areas of the world, Arabia has been the goal of adventurers and explorers. The 1st modern expedition was that of Karsten Niebuhr, 18th-cent. German traveler, who penetrated Yemen. Joseph Halévy later (1869–70) explored the Jauf and Najran oases of the Yemen hinterland, discovering important Sabaean inscriptions. John L. Burckhardt (1814–15) and Richard Burton (1853–54) were the 1st to reach Mecca and Medina. A classic account of Arabian exploration was written by C. M. Doughty (*Travels in Arabia Deserta*). Most recently Bertram Thomas (1931) and H. St. J. B. Philby (1932) traversed the great S desert Rub' al Khali, one of the last remaining blank spots on the world map. In anc. times, Arabia was divided into Arabia Petraea [=rocky Arabia], the extreme NW section, including the Sinai Peninsula, which became a Roman prov. in A.D. 106; Arabia Deserta [=desert Arabia], the N interior; and Arabia Felix [=fertile Arabia], generally restricted to Yemen, but extended by Ptolemy to most of the peninsula. The earliest recorded civilization on the peninsula is that of the Minaean, Sabaean (see SHEBA), and Himyaritic states of modern Yemen, which fell twice (4th and 6th cent. A.D.) under Ethiopian rule and passed (575) to the Persians. This SW Arabian area was linked by the so-called incense trade route along the Red Sea with NW Arabia, where the Nabataean kingdom flourished (6th cent. B.C.–1st cent. A.D.) with its center at Petra. This was later supplanted by Palmyra, which reached its height in 3d cent. A.D. Arabian unity was not achieved until the rise of Islam under Mohammed, who came from Mecca but fled (622) to Medina in the hegira, which marks the beginning of the Mohammedan era. His dynamic faith unified the separate Arab tribes and sent them out on conquest beyond the confines of Arabia proper. Under Mohammed's immediate successors, the orthodox caliphs, Syria fell (633–36), Egypt followed (639–42), and Persia's fate was sealed in the battle of Nehavend (642). To facilitate the administration of this vast new empire, the seat of the new Moslem dominions was shifted (661) from Medina to Damascus by the Omayyad caliphs and again (750) to Baghdad by the Abbasids. With the decline of the caliphate in 9th cent., Arabia lost its political cohesion, and independent emirates began to arise in Yemen, Oman, and elsewhere. Unity was briefly reestablished (10th cent.) by the Karmathians, a terrorist Moslem sect. Thereafter, Arabia was vaguely dominated by the Egyptian Mamelukes, and after 1517 by the Turks, who resisted attempts by European powers to gain foot-holds on the Arabian coast, particularly in Oman and Yemen. Modern Arabian history begins with the Wahabi movement in mid-18th cent. This ascetic reform sect started in Nejd under the leadership of the Saudi tribe. Its army of fanatical Bedouins rapidly gained control over the entire Arabian Peninsula against Turkish resistance, occupying Mecca and Medina in 1803–4. An Egyptian punitive force, however, organized by the Turks, drove the Wahabis back (1811–18) into the desert and destroyed their capital, Deraya. The Wahabis rallied, established their new seat at Riyadh, and maintained control over Nejd (central Arabia) to the mid-century. While the Turks consolidated their hold through 19th cent. on the margins of Arabia, notably in Hejaz, Yemen, and Hasa, Britain gained a foothold at Aden and established treaty relations with Oman, Trucial Oman, Qatar, Bahrein, and Kuwait. In latter half of 19th cent., Saudi supremacy in central Arabia was challenged by the Rashid dynasty of Hail in Jebel Shammar, which gained outright control in the closing decades. However, Ibn Saud, then in exile in Kuwait, rallied his forces after 1900 and rapidly regained control over Nejd (1905) and Hasa (1913–14). During First World War, the Turkish hold on Arabia was broken by Ibn Saud, and by his rival Husein ibn Ali of Mecca, whose Arab forces were directed (1916–18) by T. E. Lawrence. After the war, Ibn Saud resumed his conquest of the peninsula and swept through Jebel Shammar (1921), Hejaz (1924–25), and Asir (1926), thus laying the foundations of the new state of Nejd and Hejaz (after 1932 Saudi Arabia), the dominant state of the peninsula. Saudi Arabia is bounded N by Jordan, along an undefined frontier dating from the 1925 Hadda treaty; by Iraq, along a line dating from the 1921 Muhammerah (Khurramshahr) treaty, which provided for a rhomboid neutral zone (□ 3,000; bet. 28°45'–29°28'N and 44°43'–46°34'E); and by Kuwait, along a border dating from the 1922 Oqair treaty, which also provided for a coastal neutral zone (□ 1,800; 29°–28°14'N). Yemen has a border agreement with Saudi Arabia dating from the 1934 Taif treaty. The S and SE marginal states (Aden Protectorate, Oman, Trucial Oman, Qatar), under treaty relations with Britain, are separated from Saudi Arabia by the great S desert Rub' al Khali and have undetermined inland frontiers, although an Anglo-Turkish convention of 1914 assigned the Rub' al Khali to the British sphere of influence.

Arabian Desert, large desert in E Egypt, bet. the Nile valley (W) and the Red Sea and Gulf of Suez (E), N of Anglo-Egyptian Sudan. Borders S on the Nubian Desert. In Egypt it is also called the Eastern Desert. The name Arabian Desert has also been popularly applied to the desert of the Arabian Peninsula.

Arabian Peninsula, SW Asia: see ARABIA.

Arabian Sea, broad arm of Indian Ocean, on S coast of Asia, bet. India and Arabia; 1,800 mi. wide bet. Cape Guardafui at horn of Africa and Cape Comorin at S tip of India. Contains Laccadive Isls. off India, Socotra off Africa, and Kuria Muria Isls. of Arabia. Its NW inlet, the Gulf of Oman (continued by the Persian Gulf), and the Gulf of Aden (continued by the Red Sea) enclose the Arabian Peninsula. Sea's main ports are Bombay and Cochin (India), Karachi (Pakistan), and Aden.

Arabis River, W Pakistan: see PORALI RIVER.

Arabistan, Iran: see KHUZISTAN.

Arabkir, Turkey: see ARAPKIR.

Arabo Konak Pass, Bulgaria: see BOTEVGRAD PASS.

Arabos, Los, Cuba: see LOS ARABOS.

Arac (äräch'), Turkish *Araç*, village (pop. 1,862), Kastamonu prov., N Turkey, on Arac R. and 25 mi. WSW of Kastamonu; spelt, wheat, hemp.

Araca (ärä'kä), town (pop. c.2,700), La Paz dept., W Bolivia, at NW end of Cordillera de Tres Cruces, 45 mi. SE of La Paz; alt. 11,811 ft.; tin-mining center.

Araçá, Brazil: see MARI.

Aracaju (ärùkùzhōō'), city (1950 pop. 68,686), ⊙ Sergipe, NE Brazil, port on right bank of Cotinguiba R. just above its mouth on the Atlantic, and 175 mi. NE of Salvador (Bahia); 10°54'S 37°3'W. Exports sugar, cotton, coconuts, rice, salt, timber, vegetable oil, hides. Industries: sugar and textile mills, tanneries, limekilns, soap factory. Sand bars render access to harbor difficult for larger vessels. City is linked by railroad with Salvador (Bahia) and Propriá (on lower São Francisco R.). Airport. Climate is tropical (average temp. 78°F.) but relieved by SE trade winds. The new govt. palace and the normal school are chief bldgs. Formerly spelled Aracajú.

Aracar, Cerro (sĕ'rō äräkär'), Andean peak (19,950 ft.), in W Salta prov., Argentina, near Chile border, 30 mi. ENE of Cerro Socompa; 24°17'S.

Araçariguama (ärüsürēgwä'mù), town (pop. 248), S São Paulo, Brazil, 28 mi. WNW of São Paulo; gold formerly mined here. Has Jesuit church, col.

Aracataca (äräkätä'kä), town (pop. 3,898), Magdalena dept., N Colombia, on railroad and 32 mi. S of Ciénaga; bananas.

Aracati (ärùkùtē'), city (pop. 6,731), NE Ceará, Brazil, commercial port on right bank of Jaguaribe R. 12 mi. above its mouth on the Atlantic, and 80 mi. SE of Fortaleza. Exports cotton, carnauba wax, salt, hides. Cotton-thread and -cloth mfg., straw and rubber processing. Hydroplane landing. Founded 1747. Formerly spelled Aracaty.

Araçatuba (ärùsùtōō'bù), city (1950 pop. 27,692), NW São Paulo, Brazil, near Tietê R., on railroad, 115 mi. NW of Bauru; commercial center in pioneer agr. region; cotton ginning, coffee roasting, alcohol distilling, sawmilling, dairying, meat packing, and animal by-products processing. Airfield. Several Japanese settlements in area.

Araceli, Philippines: see Dumaran Island.

Aracena (ärä-thā'nä), town (pop. 5,668), Huelva prov., SW Spain, in Andalusia, in wooded S part of the Sierra Morena (Sierra de Aracena), 45 mi. NW of Seville. Lumbering and agr. center (olives, acorns, chestnuts, cork, fruit, grapes, cereals, livestock). Copper-pyrite mining, jasper quarrying, sawmilling; mfg. of cheese, meat products, bottle corks, candles, ceramics. Known for its immense stalagmite caverns, Gruta de las Maravillas, visited by tourists. Has 13th-cent. church built by Knights Templars.

Aracena, Sierra de (syĕ'rä dhā), low W spur of the Sierra Morena, Huelva prov., SW Spain, extends c.50 mi. E-W. Town of Aracena at its center. Rich in pasture land and timber. In S outliers are major mineral deposits of Ríotinto and Tharsis.

Arachosia (ăr"ùkō'zhù), province of anc. Persian Empire, corresponding roughly to Kandahar prov. of modern Afghanistan. It was watered by the Arghandab R. (anc. *Arachotus*) and had its ⊙ at Kandahar (anc. *Alexandria Arachosiorum*).

Arachotus, Afghanistan: see Arghandab River.

Arachova or **Arakhova** (both: ùrä'khôvù), town (pop. 3,595), Boeotia nome, E central Greece, at S foot of the Parnassus, 16 mi. W of Levadia; summer resort; grapes, cheese. The Parnassus is climbed from here. Site of battle (1826) in Gr. war of independence.

Arachthos River or **Arakhthos River** (both: ä'räkhthôs), Lat. *Arachthus*, sometimes *Aracthus* (both: ărăk'thùs), in S Epirus, Greece, rises in the Pindus near Metsovon, flows 89 mi. S, past Arta, to the Gulf of Arta 10 mi. S of Arta. Formed part of the Greek-Turkish frontier, 1881–1913. Formerly called Arta R.

Aracoiaba (ärùkōōyä'bù), city (pop. 2,293), N Ceará, Brazil, on railroad and 5 mi. ESE of Baturité; cotton ginning, rice milling; ships hides and skins, tobacco. Formerly spelled Aracoyaba.

Araçoiaba da Serra (ärùsùyä'bù dä sĕ'rù), city (pop. 1,137), S central São Paulo, Brazil, 10 mi. W of Sorocaba; processes cotton and manioc; mfg. of starch. Until 1944, Campo Largo.

Arac River (äräch'), Turkish *Araç*, N Turkey, rises in Ilgaz Mts. 12 mi. SW of Kastamonu, flows 60 mi. W, past Arac, to Yenice R. 5 mi. SW of Safranbolu.

Aracruz (ärùkrōōs'), city (pop. 458), central Espírito Santo, Brazil, on the Atlantic, 30 mi. NNE of Vitória; coffee, sugar cane. Projected port and terminus of railroad from Minas Gerais iron mines. Until 1944, called Santa Cruz.

Aracthus River, Greece: see Arachthos River.

Aracua (ärä'kwä), town (pop. 615), Falcón state, NW Venezuela, 32 mi. SSE of Coro; coffee, cacao.

Araçuaí or **Arassuaí** (ärùswäē'), city (pop. 4,117), NE Minas Gerais, Brazil, on Araçuaí R. (right tributary of the Jequitinhonha) and 65 mi. NNW of Teófilo Otoni; W terminus of railroad from Caravelas and Ponta d'Areia (on Bahia coast). Mining center for semiprecious stones; diamonds washed in river bed; graphite deposits. Formerly spelled Arassuahy.

Araçuaí River, Minas Gerais, Brazil, rises in the Serra da Penha E of Diamantina, flows 150 mi. NE to the Jequitinhonha below Araçuaí city. Formerly spelled Arassuahy.

Arad (ä'räd), city (1948 pop. 87,291), ⊙ Arad prov., W Rumania, in Crisana-Maramures, on right bank of Mures R. opposite Aradul-Nou, near Hung. border, and 265 mi. NW of Bucharest; 46°11'N 21°19'E. Rail hub with railroad workshops, commercial and industrial center. Airport. Specializes in mfg. of textiles (notably silks), electrical products, and knitwear; sugar refining, cabinetmaking, liquor and champagne production; metalworking, tanning, flour milling, sawmilling. Large trade in grain, cattle, alcohol, wines. Has a theological seminary, 2 teachers colleges, conservatory of music. Principal buildings are mostly modern. Noted "Cultural Palace" contains several museums, library, concert hall, art gallery. The 18th-cent. citadel, built by Maria Theresa and former site of execution of Hung. revolutionary leaders (1849), is across Mures R. to E. City dates from 11th cent.; was a Turkish fortress (1542–1699). It passed then to Hungary and played an important part in Hung. struggle for independence (1848–49). National Council of Rumanians of Transylvania was established here (1918) before legal transfer of Crisana to Rumania by the Treaty of Trianon (1920). About 40% of pop. is Magyar.

Arada (ärä'dä), town (pop. 1,598), Santa Bárbara dept., W Honduras, 7 mi. SW of Santa Bárbara; mfg. of harvest hats; coffee, corn, beans.

Arada (ärä'dù), village (pop. 1,088), Aveiro dist., N central Portugal, 1 mi. S of Aveiro; pottery mfg.

Aradan (ärädän'), village, Second Prov., in Teheran, N Iran, 65 mi. ESE of Teheran and on highway to Meshed; alt. 2,898 ft. Has anc. fort ascribed to Zoroastrians. Village largely supplanted by rail center of Garmsar, 5 mi. SW.

Aradeo (ärädā'ô), town (pop. 5,772), Lecce prov., Apulia, S Italy, 10 mi. NE of Gallipoli; wine, olive oil.

Aradhippou (ärädhē'pōō), village (pop. 3,164), Larnaca dist., SE Cyprus, 4 mi. NW of Larnaca; wheat, barley, almonds, olives; sheep, goats.

Araduey River, Spain: see Valderaduey River.

Aradul-Nou (ä"rädōōl-nō'), Hung. *Újarad* (ōō'yŏrŏd), village (pop. 6,126), Arad prov., W Rumania, on railroad and on Mures R. opposite Arad; mfg. of automobile bodies; truck gardening. Founded during Turkish wars (17th cent.), it was mostly settled by Ger. colonists.

Aradus, Syria: see Ruad.

Arafali (äräfä'lē), village (pop. 450), Adi Caieh div., central Eritrea, fishing port on Gulf of Zula, 45 mi. SSE of Massawa; trade center. Pozzolana deposits and hot springs near by.

'Arafat, Jabal (jă'băl äräfăt'), granite hill, 25 mi. E of Mecca, Saudi Arabia; visited by pilgrims.

Arafo (ärä'fō), village (pop. 2,612), Tenerife, Canary Isls., 14 mi. SW of Santa Cruz de Tenerife; potatoes, grapes, tomatoes, onions, oranges, fruit.

Arafura Sea (äräfōō'rä), part of the Pacific, merging W with Timor Sea and connected with Coral Sea (E) by Torres Strait, bet. New Guinea (N) and Australia (S); contains Aru Isls.

Aragarças, Brazil: see Barra do Garças.

Aragats, Mount (ărùgäts', Rus. ŭrùgäts'), or **Mount Alagez** (ŭlùgyôs'), Turkish *Alagöz* (älägûz'), extinct volcano (13,435 ft.) in NW Armenian SSR, in the Lesser Caucasus, 30 mi. NW of Erivan. Slopes, covered with andesite, volcanic-tuff, obsidian, and pumice deposits, abound in sulphur springs. Has astrophysical research center at c.5,000 ft.

Arago, Cape (ùrä'gō, ăr'ùgō), W Oregon, 33 mi. N of Cape Blanco and just SW of Coos Bay.

Arago Lake (ă'rùgō) or **Potato Lake**, Hubbard co., NW central Minn., 4 mi. N of Park Rapids; 4 mi. long. Small resorts.

Aragon (ă'rùgŏn), Sp. *Aragón* (ärägōn'), region (□ 18,382; pop. 1,058,806) and former kingdom, NE Spain, comprising the provs. of Huesca, Teruel, and Saragossa; chief city, Saragossa. Bounded by France (N), Navarre and Castile (W), Valencia (S), and Catalonia (E). Comprises central portion of Ebro basin, limited N by S slopes of the Pyrenees (reaching here their highest point) and S by Iberian Mts. Drained by Ebro R. and its tributaries (Cinca, Gállego, Aragon, Jalón). Except for some fertile valleys and oases and irrigated areas, region is barren, sparsely populated, and poor, with little rainfall, extreme temperatures, and high winds. There is some irrigation (the Imperial and Tauste canals along the Ebro are most important), and the area raises sugar beets, wheat, wine, olives, fruit, hemp. Sheep are raised extensively, and some cattle are grazed on the mtn. slopes. Mineral resources include important iron and sulphur (Ojos Negros) and lignite (Utrillas, Montalbán) deposits; also marble and limestone quarries. Mineral springs. Besides agr. processing (principally sugar refining and olive-oil processing), other mfg. includes textiles, chemicals, machinery, cement, paper, soap, furniture, mostly centered in Saragossa. There are poor communications. The area, occupied by Romans and later (5th cent.) by the Visigoths, fell (8th cent.) to the Moors, under whom the central and S portions became the emirate of Saragossa (1017–1118), while the NW territories formed (1035) Christian kingdom of Aragon. Aragon expanded southward and by 12th cent. had absorbed Saragossa. The kingdom was united in 1137 with Catalonia and in the succeeding centuries held, at various times, parts of S France, the Balearic Isls., Sicily, and Naples. In 1479 it was joined with Castile after the marriage (1474) of Ferdinand and Isabella. The Aragonese, mostly poor and deeply religious, have remained secluded in their small towns, jealously preserving their ancient traditions. Chief cities, besides Saragossa, are Huesca, Teruel, Calatayud, Jaca.

Aragon (ă'rùgŏn). **1** Village (pop. 1,272), Polk co., NW Ga., 11 mi. E of Cedartown. **2** Village (pop. c.250), Catron co., W N.Mex., on headstream of Tularosa R., in Apache Natl. Forest, 18 mi. NE of Reserve; alt. 6,687 ft. Trading point in irrigated livestock region. Pueblo ruins in vicinity.

Aragona (äräḡô'nä), town (pop. 10,840), Agrigento prov., S Sicily, 7 mi. N of Agrigento, in almond-growing region. Sulphur mines near by. Low mud volcano (Macaluba or Maccaluba) is 3 mi. SW.

Aragon and Catalonia Canal, in Huesca and Lérida provs., NE Spain, leaves Esera R. 3 mi. NNE of its influx into the Cinca, flows c.100 mi. generally S to the Segre 6 mi. NNE of Mequinenza; used for irrigation.

Aragon River (ă'rùgŏn), Sp. *Aragón* (äräḡōn'), Huesca, Saragossa, and Navarre provs., N Spain, rises in the central Pyrenees above Canfranc near Fr. border, flows 120 mi. generally SW, past Jaca, to the Ebro 14 mi. NW of Tudela. Receives Arga R. Used for irrigation (Bárdenas and Jaca canals) and to produce hydroelectric power.

Aragua (ärä'gwä), state (□ 2,160; 1941 pop. 138,235; 1950 census 192,555), N Venezuela, on the Caribbean; ⊙ Maracay. A mountainous region of coastal range, containing fertile valleys and the E basin of L. Valencia, it has a tropical climate along coast and in interior valleys; rainy season (May–Aug.). Forms part of Venezuela's leading agr. region: coffee, cacao, sugar cane, corn, tobacco, rice, bananas, coconuts. Considerable cattle grazing.

Araguacema (ärùgwùsā'mù), city (pop. 493), N Goiás, N central Brazil, on right bank of Araguaia R. (Pará border), opposite Conceição do Araguaia (Pará). Gold placers near by. Until 1944, called Santa Maria do Araguaia.

Araguaçu, Brazil: see Paraguaçu Paulista.

Aragua de Barcelona (ärä'gwä dā bärsĕlō'nä), town (pop. 3,090), Anzoátegui state, NE Venezuela, 50 mi. SSW of Barcelona; commercial and agr. center (cotton, tobacco, sugar cane, corn, fruit, stock); lumbering; cattle trade with Orinoco region and the coast; mfg. (shawls, hammocks, *aguardiente*).

Aragua de Maturín (dā mätōōrēn'), town (pop. 749), Monagas state, NE Venezuela, 26 mi. NW of Maturín; cacao, sugar cane, livestock.

Araguaiana (ärùgwīä'nù), town (pop. 429), E Mato Grosso, Brazil, on left bank of Araguaia R. (Goiás border) and 180 mi. WNW of Goiânia; cattle hides. Diamond washings in area. Formerly called Registro do Araguaya.

Araguaia River (ärägwī'ù), central Brazil, rises on interior plateau near 18°S 53°W, flows NNE to the Tocantins (at São João do Araguaia), forming (throughout its course) W border of Goiás state (with Mato Grosso and Pará). Length estimated at 1,100–1,500 mi. In its middle course (bet. 13°S and 10°S lat.), it separates into 2 branches enclosing Bananal Island. Navigable for small craft; obstructed by rapids near mouth. Diamond washings. No important towns (except Indian settlements) along its banks. Chief tributary, Garças R. (left). Formerly spelled Araguaya.

Araguaito, Caño (kä'nyō ärägwī'tō), arm of Orinoco R. delta, Delta Amacuro territory, NE Venezuela; branches off from the main arm of the Orinoco, the Río Grande, and flows c.60 mi. NE to the Caño Araguao.

Araguao, Boca (bō'kä ärägwou'), mouth of Orinoco R. delta on the Atlantic, Delta Amacuro territory, NE Venezuela, 70 mi. E of Tucupita; receives the Caño Araguao and other Orinoco arms; 18 mi. long, up to 4 mi. wide.

Araguao, Caño (kä'nyō), arm of Orinoco R. delta, Delta Amacuro territory, NE Venezuela; branches off from the main arm of the Orinoco, the Río Grande, flows c.75 mi. NE to the Atlantic through the Boca Araguao.

Araguari (ärùgwùrē'), city (1950 pop. 25,789), W Minas Gerais, Brazil, in Triângulo Mineiro, on railroad and 20 mi. NNE of Uberlândia; stock-raising and -shipping center; rice hulling, tanning, meat processing. Diamonds found in area. Airfield. Formerly spelled Araguary.

Araguari River, Amapá territory, N Brazil, rises near Fr. Guiana border, flows c.250 mi. generally E to the Atlantic N of the Amazon delta. Navigable below Ferreira Gomes. Receives Amapari R.

Aragua River (ärä'gwä), Aragua state, N Venezuela, rises in coastal range, flows c.50 mi. S and W, past La Victoria, San Mateo, Cagua, Santa Cruz, and Palo Negro, to L. Valencia. In its fertile valley coffee, cacao, corn, sugar cane, tobacco, and fruit are produced and cattle raising is carried on.

Araguatins (ärùgwùtēns'), city (pop. 609), northernmost Goiás, N central Brazil, on right bank of Araguaia R. and 60 mi. ESE of Marabá (Pará). Diamonds and rock crystals found in area. Until 1944, called São Vicente.

Aragüita (ärägwē'tä), town (pop. 504), Miranda state, N Venezuela, on Tuy R. and 36 mi. SE of Caracas; cacao, sugar.

Aragure (ä'rägōōrä), village (pop. 700), Tigre prov., N Ethiopia, 14 mi. E of Makale; cereals, livestock.

Aragva River (ŭrăg'vù), central Georgian SSR, rises in the central Greater Caucasus NW of Pass of the Cross, flows c.60 mi. S, past Pasanauri, to Kura R. at Mtskheta. Georgian Military Road runs through its valley.

Arahal, El (ĕl äräl'), city (pop. 11,932), Seville prov., SW Spain, on railroad and 25 mi. ESE of Seville; processing and agr. center (olives, cotton, cereals, livestock, timber). Liquor distilling, flour milling, olive-oil processing; mfg. of soap and meat products. Has mineral springs.

Arahama (ärä'hä'mä) town (pop. 5,427), Miyagi prefecture, N Honshu, Japan, on Abukuma R. and 8 mi. NE of Kakuda; fishing.

Ara Hangay, Mongolia: see NORTH KHANGAI.

Arai (ärī'). **1** Town (pop. 11,923), Niigata prefecture, central Honshu, Japan, 6 mi. S of Takada; rice-growing center. Winter sports. **2** Town (pop. 12,128), Shizuoka prefecture, central Honshu, Japan, on SW shore of L. Hamana, near its outlet, 7 mi. ESE of Toyohashi; rice, raw silk. Fishery.

Araido-to, Russian SFSR: see ALAID ISLAND.

Araioses (ärīô'zĭs), city (pop. 3,001), NE Maranhão, Brazil, near mouth of Parnaíba R. (Piauí border) on the Atlantic, 9 mi. W of Parnaíba; ships sugar, rice, cattle. Formerly spelled Arayoses.

Araíporanga (äräē"pōōräng'gù), city (pop. 403), N Paraná, Brazil, 45 mi. SE of Londrina; hog raising. Until 1944, called São Jerônimo.

Araira (ärī'rä), town (pop. 679), Miranda state, N Venezuela, 30 mi. ESE of Caracas; coffee, cacao, corn.

Araish, El, Sp. Morocco: see LARACHE.

Araito-to, Russian SFSR: see ALAID ISLAND.

Ara Jovis, Spain: see ARANJUEZ.

Arak (äräk'), city (1941 pop. 51,365), First Prov., W central Iran, 150 mi. SW of Teheran, on road and on Trans-Iranian RR; 34°6'N 49°42'E; alt. 5,952 ft. Main center of former Arak prov. and a railroad division point, in grain-producing area; rugmaking; match mfg., beet-sugar refining, liquor distilling. Has small colony of Armenians. Airfield. Founded in early-19th cent. and called Sultanabad until mid-1930s, the city was ⊙ former prov. of IRAQ, later spelled Arak. Since 1938, Arak prov. forms part of Iran's First Prov. (see GILAN.)

Arakabesan (ä'räkäbä'sän), wooded volcanic island, Palau, W Caroline Isls., W Pacific, just NW of Koror; 7°21'N 134°27'E; 2 mi. long, ¾ mi. wide. In Second World War site of Jap. army base.

Arakaka (ärùkä'kù), village, Essequibo co., NW Br. Guiana, on upper Barima R. and 65 mi. SE of Morawhanna; 7°35'W 60°2'W. Gold-washing and -dredging center.

Arakan (ăr'ùkăn'), Burmese *Yakhaing* (yùkīn'), NW division (□ 14,194; 1941 pop. 1,152,733) of Lower Burma, on Bay of Bengal; ⊙ Akyab. Extends along W slopes of the Arakan Yoma from E Pakistan border (Naaf R.) to Bassein area of Irrawaddy delta. Divided into dists. of Akyab, Kyaukpyu, and Sandoway. Monsoon climate with rains May–Oct. (200 in. yearly). Cultivated area is largely under rice; other crops are fruit, tobacco. Oak and bamboo forests in hills. Served by coastal and river vessels and An and Taungup pass routes over Arakan Yoma. Pop. is 60% Burmese, including Arakanese with Bengali admixture and own dialect, 25% Indian, 5% Chin. Under Indian influence in 9th cent.; inc. into unified Burma in 11th cent. under Anawrata; independent kingdom after 15th cent.; passed to Burma in 1784 under Bodawpaya. Ceded to Br. East India Company after 1st Anglo-Burmese War (1826) and merged 1862 in Br. (Lower) Burma. In Second World War held 1942–45 by Japanese.

Arakan Hill Tracts, former dist. (□ 3,228; 1941 pop. 34,005) of Arakan div., Lower Burma; ⊙ Paletwa. On India and Pakistan borders and at N end of the Arakan Yoma; drained by Kaladan R. Pop. was 80% Chin, 10% Burmese. In accordance with 1947 Burma Constitution, dist. was inc. into the CHIN HILLS div. of Upper Burma.

Arakan Yoma (ărùkăn' yō'mù), range of mountains in SW Burma, bet. Arakan coast on Bay of Bengal and Irrawaddy valley, extending from Chin Hills (N) to Irrawaddy delta; rises to over 6,500 ft. A notable climatic barrier, it cuts off central Burma from SW monsoon, thus creating a dry zone of 25–45 in. annual rainfall. Crossed by An and Taungup passes. Also called Arakan Roma in Arakanese dialect.

Ara Khangai, Mongolia: see NORTH KHANGAI.

Arakhova, Greece: see ARACHOVA.

Arakhthos River, Greece: see ARACHTHOS RIVER.

Arakinthos, Greece: see ARAKYNTHOS.

Araks River, Transcaucasia: see ARAS RIVER.

Arakynthos or **Arakinthos** (both: ùrä'kĭnthôs), mountain massif in Acarnania nome, W central Greece, bet. L. Trichonis and Gulf of Patras; 20 mi. long; rises to 3,094 ft. 6 mi. NNE of Messolonghi. Formerly called Zygos or Zigos.

Aral, town, Tadzhik SSR: see KUIBYSHEVSK.

Aral Kara-Kum (ŭräl' kŭrä"-kōōm'), sandy desert NE of Aral Sea, in NW Kzyl-Orda oblast, Kazakh SSR.

Aral Sea (ă'rŭl, Rus. ŭräl'), Kazakh *Aral Tengiz* [= island sea], Rus. *Aralskoye More,* one of largest (□ 24,635) inland seas of the world; in the USSR, in Kazakh SSR and Kara-Kalpak Autonomous SSR of Uzbek SSR, 175 mi. E of Caspian Sea; 230 mi. long, 175 mi. wide, alt. 170 ft., average depth 55 ft. (223 ft. on W shore); slight salinity (1.03%). W and N shores are rocky escarpments (Ust-Urt plateau); on E are sandy desert areas (Kyzyl-Kum). N portion frozen for c.3 months. Fed by 2 great rivers: Syr Darya (NE) and Amu Darya (S); there is no outlet. Many isls., including Kug-Aral (N; □ 105) and Vozrozhdeniye Isl. (W center; □ 83). Navigation hindered by storms and shallowness; only route is bet. Muinak and Aralsk. Shores sparsely inhabited; densest pop. in Aralsk-Kazalinsk area (NE) and the Amu Darya delta mouth (S), sites of fishing industry (sturgeon, carp, perch). Fish types show former connection with Caspian Sea. First mentioned by Arab geographers as Khwarazm Sea, Rus. *Khorezmiyskoye More.* Reached by Russians in 1840s.

Aralsk or **Aral'sk** (ŭrälsk'), city (1939 pop. over 10,000), NW Kzyl-Orda oblast, Kazakh SSR, on N shore of Aral Sea, on Trans-Caspian RR and 230 mi. NW of Kzyl-Orda; fish canning, salt extracting, metalworking. Lake shipping to Muinak. Founded 1905 as railroad construction settlement. Formerly called Aralskoye More. Just S, on Aral Sea shore, is **Aralsulfat** or **Aralsul'fat** (ŭräl"sōōlfät'), town (1948 pop. over 2,000); Glauber-salts extracting.

Araluen (ă"rùlōō'ĭn). **1** Village (pop. 122), SE New South Wales, 45 mi. SE of Canberra; gold-mining center. **2** Village, SW Western Australia, 18 mi. SSE of Perth and on Canning R.; orchards. Canning Dam (in Darling Range) near by.

Aram (ā'răm), anc. country of SW Asia, roughly identifiable with Syria. Movement of Arameans westward to Syria apparently took place before 1200 B.C. The Bible records constant contacts bet. the Hebrews and Aram, mentioning states of Damascus, Beth-rehob, Geshur, Maachah, and Zoba.

Aramac (ă'rùmăk), village (pop. 488), central Queensland, Australia, 330 mi. W of Rockhampton; rail terminus; sheep.

Arambagh (ŭräm'băg), town (pop. 8,992), Hooghly dist., S central West Bengal, India, on Rupnarayan R. and 37 mi. W of Hooghly; trades in rice, jute, pulse, potatoes. Formerly called Jahanabad. Rice milling 12 mi. ESE, at Champadanga; rail-spur terminus.

Aramberri (ärämbĕ'rē), city (pop. 1,057), Nuevo León, N Mexico, 55 mi. SSW of Linares; alt. 3,633 ft.; grain, fruit, stock.

Aramboli (ŭrŭmbō'lē), town (pop. 7,166), S Travancore, India, 8 mi. NE of Nagercoil; coir rope and mats, palmyra jaggery; hand-loom weaving. Also spelled Aramboly.

Aramecina (ärämäsē'nä), town (pop. 631), Valle dept., S Honduras, near Goascarán R. (Salvador border), 10 mi. NNE of Goascarán; corn, rice. A gold- and silver-mining center in Sp. colonial times.

Aramil or **Aramil'** (ŭrùmēl'), town (1926 pop. 5,098), S Sverdlovsk oblast, Russian SFSR, on Iset R. and 12 mi. SE of Sverdlovsk, near railroad; woolen-milling center; mfg. of machines, felt boots. Aramil village and rail station (9 mi. WSW) has stone quarries.

Aramits (ärämēts'), village (pop. 282), Basses-Pyrénées dept., SW France, in W Pyrenees, 8 mi. SW of Oloron-Sainte-Marie; sawmilling, sheep and mule raising.

Aramon (ärämõ'), village (pop. 1,171), Gard dept., S France, on right bank of Rhone R. and 8 mi. SW of Avignon; fruitgrowing and processing; olive trees.

Arampampa (ärämpäm'pä), town (pop. c.3,500), ⊙ General Bilbao prov., Potosí dept., W central Bolivia, near Caine R., 21 mi. N of San Pedro; grain.

Arán, Valle de (vä'lyä dhä ärän'), Fr. *Val d'Aran* (väl därä'), valley in Lérida prov., NE Spain, near Fr. border, at foot of the Maladetta group in the central Pyrenees; Garonne R. rises here and flows N to France; chief town, Viella. Has some mineral deposits and mineral springs. Tourist trade. Although on Fr. side of main Pyrenean divide, it has remained in Spain through its omission in treaty of Corbeil (1258), repeated in Peace of the Pyrenees (1659).

Arañado, El, Argentina: see EL ARAÑADO.

Aranda de Duero (ärän'dä dhä dhwā'rō), town (pop. 8,073), Burgos prov., N Spain, in Old Castile, on right bank of the Duero or Douro (crossed by fine bridge), on Burgos-Madrid highway, and 75 mi. N of Madrid. Communications hub in fertile valley (cereals, grapes, vegetables, sheep); dairying, liquor distilling, beet-sugar and flour milling, lumbering; mfg. of resins, pottery, tiles, chocolate; flour mills, iron foundries. Has remains of anc. walls and fine parochial church.

Aranda de Moncayo (mōng-kī'ō), town (pop. 1,081), Saragossa prov., NE Spain, 18 mi. NW of Calatayud, in olive- and winegrowing area.

Arandas (ärän'däs), town (pop. 7,254), Jalisco, central Mexico, 40 mi. NE of Ocotlán; wheat- and bean-growing center.

Arandelovac, Yugoslavia: see ARANDJELOVAC.

Arándiga (ärän'dēgä), town (pop. 1,230), Saragossa prov., NE Spain, 13 mi. NE of Calatayud; olive-oil processing; agr. trade (wine, cereals, sheep).

Arandjelovac or **Arandyelovats** (ärän'dyĕlōväts), Serbo-Croatian *Arandelovac,* village (pop. 4,806), central Serbia, Yugoslavia, on railroad and 35 mi. S of Belgrade, in the Sumadija; center of lignite-mining area; ships plums. Mineral waters. Clay deposits, winegrowing in vicinity.

Arang (ŭrŭng'), town (pop. 6,719), Raipur dist., E Madhya Pradesh, India, 22 mi. E of Raipur; rice milling; oilseeds (chiefly flax).

Aranguren (äräng-gōō'rĕn), town (pop. estimate 1,000), W Entre Ríos prov., Argentina, on railroad and 40 mi. SE of Paraná; flax, wheat, corn, alfalfa, livestock; flour milling.

Arani (ärä'nē), town (pop. c.7,800), ⊙ Arani prov., Cochabamba dept., central Bolivia, on S slopes of Cordillera de Cochabamba, 30 mi. ESE of Cochabamba; alt. 9,058 ft. Transshipment point on railroad from Cochabamba; on highway to Sucre and to Santa Cruz; barley, corn, potatoes.

Arani (ä'rŭnē), town (pop. 5,508), Chingleput dist., E Madras, India, 20 mi. NW of Madras; rice, tamarind, sesame. Also spelled Arni.

Aran Island (ă'rùn) (4,356 acres; 4 mi. long, 3 mi. wide, rises to 750 ft.) in the Atlantic, off W coast of Co. Donegal, Ireland, 5 mi. WNW of Dungloe. At NW end of isl. is lighthouse (55°1'N 8°35'W).

Aran Islands or **Arran Islands** (ă'rùn), group of 3 islands (□ 18.1; pop. c.2,000), off SW coast of Co. Galway, Ireland, in the Atlantic at entrance to Galway Bay; 53°1'–53°8'N 9°31'–9°53'W. The isls., INISHMORE (largest), INISHMAAN, and INISHEER, with numerous monastic remains and prehistoric forts, are rocky and bleak; a little agr. is carried on with great difficulty. Also fishing.

Aranjuez (äränhwāth'), anc. *Ara Jovis,* town (pop. 21,771), Madrid prov., central Spain, in New Castile, in fertile region, on left bank of the Tagus near influx of Jarama R., and 27 mi. S of Madrid. Communications and agr. center, chiefly known as former residence of Sp. kings. Favored by a fine climate, the region grows sugar beets, asparagus, strawberries, cereals, vegetables, fruit. There are some important consumer industries, such as beet-sugar mills (pulp and molasses), match factories; mfg. of glue, gelatins, fertilizers, textiles, belts, elastics, precision instruments. Has agr. school. The splendid palace (built by Juan de Herrera and damaged several times by fire) is surrounded by gardens rivaling Versailles and has paintings by Velázquez. Once a hq. of the Knights of Santiago, though dating back to pre-Christian era, Aranjuez was selected by Charles V as royal resort. Major bldgs. were started under Philip II, and the place has been associated with Sp. Hapsburg and Bourbon kings ever since. Here was ratified (1805) the Treaty of Aranjuez bet. Spain and Napoleon. In 1808 Charles IV signed his abdication at Aranjuez.

Aranjuez (äränghwās'), village (pop. 3,117), NW Trinidad, B.W.I., 3½ mi. E of Port of Spain, in agr. region (coconuts, sugar cane).

Aran Mawddwy (ă'rùn moudh'wē), mountain (2,970 ft.), S Merioneth, Wales, 10 mi. SW of Bala.

Aranmore, Ireland: see INISHMORE.

Aran-na-naomh, Ireland: see INISHMORE.

Aransas (ŭrăn'zùs), county (□ 276; pop. 4,252), S Texas; ⊙ Rockport. On Gulf coast, here indented by Aransas, Copano, and St. Charles bays; traversed by Gulf Intracoastal Waterway. Includes St. Joseph Isl. and a natl. wildlife refuge (wintering grounds of rare whooping cranes). Cattle raising, truck farming, fisheries (shrimp, shellfish, fish); tourist trade (fishing, beaches). Some dairying, poultry; some oil, natural gas. Aransas Pass (on deep-water channel) and Rockport are ports (oil, seafood shipping). Formed 1871.

Aransas Bay, S Texas, inlet (c.25 mi. long, c.5 mi. wide) of Gulf of Mexico, bet. the mainland and St. Joseph Isl. Traversed by Gulf Intracoastal Waterway, which connects it with Corpus Christi Bay (SW), San Antonio Bay (NE). Principal ports are Rockport and Aransas Pass, with access to the Gulf through Aransas Pass channel. Copano Bay (kō'pŭnō), NW arm of Aransas Bay, receives Aransas R. (c.50 mi. long) and Mission R. from NW, Copano Creek (c.20 mi. long) from N. St. Charles Bay (11 mi. long, 1–3 mi. wide) is NE arm.

Aransas Pass, city (pop. 5,396), San Patricio and Aransas counties, S Texas, on Aransas Bay and 17 mi. NE of Corpus Christi; a port on deepwater ship channel to the Gulf, passing SE through land cut across Harbor Isl. (port facilities) and through Aransas Pass. Ships oil; resort; fisheries, oil refineries (supplied by local fields and pipelines), carbon-black plant. Truck farming in area. Settled 1890, inc. 1910.

Aransas Pass, channel, S Texas, leading from Gulf of Mexico bet. Mustang Isl. (S), St. Joseph Isl. (N), and connecting with Gulf Intracoastal Waterway and other channels leading into Corpus Christi Bay (NW), to Aransas Pass city (N), Aransas Bay (NE). Port Aransas is on S shore; Aransas Pass lighthouse is inside pass on Harbor Isl., which separates Corpus Christi and Aransas bays.

Aransas River, Texas: see ARANSAS BAY.

Arantangi (ŭrŭntăng'gē), village (pop. 3;383), Tanjore dist., SE Madras, India, 45 mi. SSW of Tanjore; rail terminus, with branch to laterite quarry, 3 mi. WNW (road metal, building stone); silk weaving and dyeing.

Aranuka (ärănōō'kä), atoll (□ 5.9; pop. 366), N Gilbert Isls., W central Pacific; 0°11'N 173°39'E. Formerly Nanouki.

Aranyaprathet (ärän"yäprätăt'), village (1937 pop. 5,124), Prachinburi prov., SE Thailand, on Cambodia frontier, and on Bangkok–Pnompenh RR, 135 mi. E of Bangkok, near Poipet (Cambodia). Sometimes spelled Aranyapradesa.

Aranyosbanya, Rumania: see BAIA-DE-ARIES.

Aranyosgyeres, Rumania: see CAMPIA-TURZII.

Aranyosmarot, Czechoslovakia: see ZLATE MORAVCE.

Aranyos River, Rumania: see ARIES RIVER.

Aranzazu (äränsä'sōō), town (pop. 3,551), Caldas dept., W central Colombia, on W slopes of Cordillera Central, 14 mi. N of Manizales; alt. 6,443 ft. Terminus of aerial tramway from Manizales; coffee-growing center; silk, sugar cane, cereals, fruit. Coal deposits near by.

Arao (ärä'ō), city (pop. 51,448), Kumamoto prefecture, W Kyushu, Japan, on the Ariakeno-umi, 30 mi. NW of Kumamoto; coal-mining center.

Araouan (äräwän'), village, central Fr. Sudan. Fr. West Africa, on a Saharan trail and 150 mi. NNW of Timbuktu. Radio and climatological station. Sometimes Arouane.

Aráoz (ärous'), town (pop. estimate 500), E Tucumán prov., Argentina, on railroad and 24 mi. SE of Tucumán; corn, sugar cane, livestock.

Arapahoe (ůră'pùhō), county (□ 827; pop. 52,125), N central Colo., bordering Denver; ⊙ Littleton. Agr. area, bounded W by South Platte R. Dairy products, wheat. Formed 1861.

Arapahoe. 1 City (pop. 1,226), Furnas co., S Nebr., 50 mi. SW of Kearney and on Republican R.; dairy and poultry produce, grain, livestock. Platted 1871. **2** Town (pop. 273), Pamlico co., E N.C., 13 mi. SE of New Bern. **3** Town (pop. 311), ⊙ Custer co., W Okla., 4 mi. N of Clinton, in agr. area (grain, alfalfa, cotton, livestock, poultry; dairy products). **4** Village (pop. c.100), Fremont co., W central Wyo., on Popo Agie R. and 15 mi. NE of Lander; alt. c.5,200 ft. Trading point for Wind River Indian Reservation. Indians process corn, vegetables in near-by U.S. cannery.

Arapahoe Peak or **Arapaho Peak** (13,506 ft.), N Colo., in Front Range, c.20 mi. W of Boulder. Arapahoe glacier is on E face of peak.

Arapawa Island, New Zealand: see QUEEN CHARLOTTE SOUND.

Arapey or **Parada Arapey** (pärä'dä äräpä'), village, Salto dept., NW Uruguay, on Arapey R., on railroad and 33 mi. NE of Salto; cereals, livestock.

Arapey River or **Arapey Grande River** (grän'dā), Salto dept., NW Uruguay, rises at junction of Cuchilla de Haedo, Cuchilla de Belén, and Cuchilla Negra, at Uruguay-Brazil border, 32 mi. SW of Rivera; flows 125 mi. W, past Arapey, to Uruguay R. 10 mi. NNE of Constitución. Receives Arapey Chico R. (right).

Arapicos (äräpē'kōs), village, Santiago-Zamora prov., E central Ecuador, on E slopes of the Andes, 30 mi. NNE of Macas (connected by road); tiger and puma hunting.

Arapiles (äräpē'lēs), village (pop. 536), Salamanca prov., W Spain, 5 mi. SSE of Salamanca; the scene of a battle (commonly known as the "battle of Salamanca") in which Wellington defeated (1812) the French under Marmont.

Arapiraca (ärŭpērä'kä), city (pop. 2,443), central Alagoas, NE Brazil, 21 mi. S of Palmeira dos Índios; cotton, fruit. Mineral springs; phosphate deposits.

Arapis, Greece: see SALAMIS.

Arapkir (äräpkĭr'), Turkish *Arapkır*, town (pop. 6,684), Malatya prov., E central Turkey, 50 mi. NNE of Malatya; wheat, potatoes, fruit; silk and cotton goods. On trade route bet. Aleppo and Trebizond. Sometimes spelled Arabkir or Arabgir.

Araple or **Arapli,** Greece: see LACHANOKEPOS.

Arapongas (ärŭpông'gŭs), city (1948 pop. estimate 4,000), N Paraná, Brazil, on railroad and 20 mi. SW of Londrina, in recently cleared pioneer coffee zone; cotton, potatoes.

Arapsun (äräpsōōn'), village (pop. 1,763), Nigde prov., central Turkey, near the Kizil Irmak, 45 mi. W of Kayseri; lignite; grain. Formerly Gulsehir.

Arapuni (ărŭpōō'nē), township (pop. 381), N central N.Isl., New Zealand, 28 mi. SE of Hamilton and on Waikato R.; site of largest hydroelectric plant on N.Isl.

Araq, Iran: see IRAQ, province.

Araquari (ärŭkwŭrē'), city (pop. 806), NE Santa Catarina, Brazil, near the Atlantic, opposite São Francisco isl., on railroad and 10 mi. SE of Joinvile; meat and fish preserving, lumbering. Until 1944, called Parati (formerly Paraty).

Araqueda (äräkā'dä), village (pop. 1,326), Cajamarca dept., NW Peru, in Cordillera Occidental, 10 mi. W of Cajabamba; silver and copper mining.

Arar, France: see SAÔNE RIVER.

Arara, Netherlands New Guinea: see ARARE.

Araranguá (ärŭrăng-gwä'), city (pop. 3,239), SE Santa Catarina, Brazil, near the Atlantic, 55 mi. SW of Laguna; coal-mining center and terminus of railroad from Laguna, whence coal is shipped to Volta Redonda steel plant (Rio de Janeiro). Manioc, rice, sugar. Settled 1891 by Italians. Old name, Campinas.

Araraquara (ärŭrŭkwä'rŭ), city (1950 pop. 34,671), central São Paulo, Brazil, 50 mi. SSW of Ribeirão Prêto; road, rail junction; commercial and agr.-processing center of one of state's most productive areas. Ships coffee to Santos for export, and cattle and cotton to São Paulo. Processing of milk products and cottonseed; mfg. of oil cake; sugar milling, alcohol distilling.

Araras (ärä'rŭs), city (pop. 7,282), E central São Paulo, Brazil, on railroad and 40 mi. NNW of Campinas; dairying center; mfg. of condensed milk, meat packing, brandy distilling, textile milling, manioc processing.

Araras, Serra das (sĕ'rŭ däs). **1** Range of central Brazilian plateau, in E Mato Grosso, bet. 18° and 19° S lat., forming divide bet. tributaries of Paraguay R. (W) and Paraná R. (SE). Average alt. 2,000 ft. **2** Range in W Paraná, Brazil, extending W from Guarapuava, and forming divide bet. Piquiri (N) and Iguassú (S) rivers. Rises to c.5,000 ft.

Ararat (ă'rŭrăt), municipality (pop. 5,957), SW central Victoria, Australia, 110 mi. WNW of Melbourne; rail junction; commercial center for livestock area; dairy plant, winery. Gold mining in vicinity.

Ararat (ŭrŭrät'), town (1939 pop. over 2,000), S Armenian SSR, at E foot of Mt. Ararat, on railroad and 26 mi. SSE of Erivan, near Aras R.; cement works; distilling (wines, brandies). Formerly called Davalu.

Ararat, Mount (ă'rŭrăt), Turkish *Ağrı Dağı* or *Büyük Ağrı Dağı* (büyük" ărŭ' däü"), Armenian *Massis*, Persian *Kuh-i-Nuh*, highest peak (16,945 ft.) in Turkey, at its E frontier, c.10 mi. from Iran line and c.20 mi. from USSR line; 39°42'N 44°18'E. Just SE of the main peak (called Great Ararat; *büyük* means great) is its 2d summit (12,877 ft.), Little Ararat (Turkish *Küçük Ağrı Dağı*). Ararat is traditional landing place of Noah's Ark. The Ararat region is identified with Armenia in many anc. records. In anc. Assyrian inscriptions Ararat appears as Urartu. It was 1st climbed in modern times in 1829.

Arare or **Arara** (ärä'rä), village, Netherlands New Guinea, on N coast of isl., 130 mi. WNW of Hollandia. In Second World War U.S. troops landed here May, 1944.

Arari (ärŭrē'), city (pop. 4,019), N Maranhão, Brazil, port on lower Mearim R. and 65 mi. S of São Luís, in cotton, rice, and sugar dist. Formerly spelled Arary.

Araripe (ärŭrē'pĭ), city (pop. 876), SW Ceará, Brazil, on N slope of the Serra do Araripe, 55 mi. W of Crato; hides, cotton, maniçoba rubber. Talc quarry.

Araripe, Serra do (sĕ'rŭ dōō), plateau in uplands of NE Brazil, on Ceará-Pernambuco border, in lat. 7°30'S. Separates drainage of São Francisco (S) and Jaguaribe (N) rivers. Rising to c.3,000 ft., in its higher parts it remains unexplored. Stock grazing. Gypsum deposits.

Araripina (ärŭrēpē'nŭ), city (pop. 1,084), westernmost Pernambuco, NE Brazil, in the Serra do Araripe, near Piauí border; 40°35'W 7°30'S; livestock. Until 1944, São Gonçalo.

Arariúna (ärŭrēōō'nŭ), city (pop. 1,549), E Pará, Brazil, in E part of Marajó isl., 45 mi. NW of Belém; stock-raising center. Until 1944, Cachoeira.

Araro (ä'rärō), Ital. *Arero*, village, Sidamo-Borana prov., S Ethiopia, near an affluent of Dawa R., 60 mi. NE of Mega. Formerly also Meta Gafersa.

Araró (ärärō'), town (pop. 1,686), Michoacán, central Mexico, on E shore of L. Cuitzeo, on railroad and 25 mi. NE of Morelia; cereals, fruit, livestock.

Araruama (ärŭrōōä'mŭ), city (pop. 1,761), S Rio de Janeiro state, Brazil, on N shore of Araruama Lagoon, on railroad and 55 mi. E of Rio; saltworking, brandy distilling; limekilns.

Araruama Lagoon, tidewater lake on SE coast of Brazil, in Rio de Janeiro state, connected by a channel at Cabo Frio (E end) with the open Atlantic; 22 mi. long. Araruama city near W extremity. Extensive saltworks on S shore for Cabo Frio chemical industry. Shells collected for limekilns. Fisheries. Navigable for small vessels. The sand bar separating it from the sea is called Massambaba Beach (bathing).

Araruna (ärŭrōō'nŭ), city (pop. 1,606), Paraíba, NE Brazil, near Rio Grande do Norte border, 70 mi. NW of João Pessoa; cotton, agave fibers, fruit. Kaolin deposits.

Arasan (äräsän'), Chinese *Wenchüan* or *Wen-ch'üan* (both: wŭn'chüän'), town, ⊙ Arasan co. (pop. 10,473), NW Sinkiang prov., China, near USSR border, 80 mi. N of Kuldja, at S foot of the Dzungarian Ala-Tau; tungsten mining.

Arasbaran, Iran: see AHAR.

Aras River (äräs'), anc. *Araxes* (ărăk'sēz), Rus. *Araks*, Persian and Turkish *Aras*, stream (666 mi. long) bet. USSR (N) and Turkey and Iran (S); rises in Turkish Armenia S of Erzurum, flows generally E past Mt. Ararat and Dzhulfa, forming parts of borders bet. Turkish and Soviet Armenia and bet. Soviet and Iranian Azerbaijan. In Azerbaijan SSR part of the stream (its old course) joins the Kara at Sabirabad, while the rest of it flows (since 1896; canalized 1909) directly to the Caspian Sea at Kirov Bay. Since much of its course is rapid and tumultuous, it is not navigable but is used extensively for irrigation (cotton). Receives the Western Arpa-Chai, Zanga, Eastern Arpa-Chai, and the Qara Su.

Arassuahy or **Arassuaí,** Brazil: see ARAÇUAÍ.

Arata (ärä'tä), town (pop. estimate 1,000), NE La Pampa natl. territory, Argentina, on railroad and 35 mi. W of General Pico; grain, livestock.

Aratano (ärä'tä'nō), town (pop. 6,544), Tokushima prefecture, E Shikoku, Japan, 21 mi. S of Tokushima; agr. center (rice, oranges, pears); canned bamboo shoots, charcoal, tiles.

Araticu (ärŭtēkōō'), city (pop. 117), E Pará, Brazil, near right bank of Pará R. (Amazon delta), 100 mi. WSW of Belém. Until 1944, Oeiras.

Arato (ä"rä'tō), town (pop. 6,181), Yamagata prefecture, N Honshu, Japan, on Mogami R. and 14 mi. WSW of Yamagata; raw silk, rice, charcoal.

Aratu (ärŭtōō'), village, E Bahia, Brazil, on Todos os Santos Bay of the Atlantic, 12 mi. NNE of Salvador; oil and natural-gas wells.

Aratuípe (ärŭtwē'pĭ), city (pop. 1,308), E Bahia, Brazil, 7 mi. SW of Nazaré; ships coffee, tobacco, manioc flour, rapeseed; makes ceramics. Formerly spelled Aratuhype.

Arau (ärou'), town (pop. 1,081), Perlis, NW Malaya, on W coast railroad and 5 mi. E of Kangar; residence of raja. Site of irrigation headworks for rice-growing dist.

Arauá (ärou-ä'), city (pop. 949), S Sergipe, NE Brazil, 17 mi. WSW of Estância; sugar, coffee, tobacco.

Arauca (ärou'kä), commissary (□ 9,973; 1938 pop. 11,156; 1950 estimate 11,280), E Colombia; ⊙ Arauca. Borders N and E on Venezuela, with Arauca R. on N, Casanare R. on S. Except for outliers of Cordillera Oriental in W, it consists mainly of low llano grasslands, sparsely populated. Climate is tropical, with moderate rainfall. Cattle raising; some cacao, yucca, bananas, corn, and fruit are grown. Forests yield wood, resins, gums. Trade is mostly with Venezuela, to which are shipped, via Orinoco waterways, hides, timber, rubber, resins.

Arauca, town (pop. 1,871), ⊙ Arauca commissary, E Colombia, landing on Arauca R., opposite El Amparo (Venezuela), and 280 mi. NE of Bogotá, in llano lowlands; 7°5'N 70°45'W. Trading post in agr. region (corn, cacao, sugar cane, rice, cattle); ships furs, hides, rubber, resins via Arauca and Orinoco rivers to Venezuela. Airport, customhouse.

Araucania (ärôkā'nēŭ, Sp. ärouká'nyä), region of Chile S of Bío-Bío R., inhabited by the Araucanian Indians, whose territory once included almost all of Chile. A warlike people, they resisted Sp. and Chilean rule until 1870. Their final revolt ended with treaty of Temuco (1881).

Araucária (ärouká'rēŭ), city (pop. 763), SE Paraná, Brazil, on Iguassú R., near railroad, and 15 mi. SW of Curitiba; lard processing, distilling, mfg. of tomato paste; potato and winegrowing.

Arauca River (ärou'kä), in Venezuela and Colombia, rises E of Bucaramanga, N central Colombia, in Cordillera Oriental, flows E c.500 mi. through llano lowlands, along border of Arauca intendancy (Colombia) and Apure state (Venezuela), past Arauquita, El Amparo, and Arauca, into Venezuela, and to Orinoco R. 70 mi. ESE of San Fernando de Apure. Navigable for small craft.

Arauco, Argentina: see AIMOGASTA.

Arauco (ärou'kō), province (□ 2,222; 1940 pop. 66,107; 1949 estimate 70,856), S central Chile; ⊙ Lebu. On the Pacific; bordered E by Cordillera de Nahuelbuta. Has important coal mines (centers are Curanilahue, Colico, and the ports of Lebu and Arauco). Stock raising (cattle, sheep, horses); agr. (wheat, corn, oats, peas, beans, lentils; some wine in N). Rich in timber, which is exported. Lakes include Lanalhue and Lleu-Lleu. Mocha Isl. is off the coast. Prov. set up 1875.

Arauco, town (pop. 2,707), ⊙ Arauco dept. (□ 866; pop. 28,153), Arauco prov., S central Chile, on a bay on the Pacific, and 35 mi. SSW of Concepción; 37°15'S 73°20'W. Rail terminus, beach resort, coal-mining center. Also produces grain, leguminous vegetables, timber.

Arauco Gulf, inlet of the Pacific in Concepción and Arauco provs., S central Chile. On its shore are ports of La Boca, Coronel, Lota, and Arauco. Santa María Isl. is at its SW entrance. Receives Bío-Bío R. Submarine coal deposits.

Arauquita (ärouké'tä), village (pop. 361), Arauca commissary, E Colombia, landing on Arauca R. (Venezuela border) and 45 mi. W of Arauca, in llano lowlands; cacao, bananas, yucca, corn, cattle.

Araure (ärou'rā), town (pop. 1,939), Portuguesa state, W Venezuela, adjoining Acarigua (N), 35 mi. SSE of Barquisimeto (connected by highway); cotton-growing center; sugar cane, corn, cattle.

Arausio, France: see ORANGE.

Aravaca (äräva'kä), town (pop. 495), Madrid prov., central Spain, resort 5 mi. W of Madrid; also grain growing, mfg. of soap and lace.

Aravalli Range (ŭră'väl-lē), hill system in NW India, extending from N Gujarat plain c.350 mi. NE, through Rajasthan and Ajmer states, to just N of Khetri; isolated offshoots continue NE to S of Delhi. Separates vast Thar Desert (W) from upland region (E). N section is narrow and broken, but below Ajmer it widens to c.25 mi. and at S end spreads out c.100 mi. into confused mass of hills and valleys. General height, c.1,500–3,000 ft.; rises to 5,650 ft. in Guru Sikhar peak, near Abu (SW). Gives rise to several streams, including Sabarmati, Banas, and Luni rivers. Wild game (leopards, tigers) common in forests. S end inhabited by Bhil tribes.

Aravan (ŭrŭvän'), village (1939 pop. over 2,000), NE Osh oblast, Kirghiz SSR, in Fergana Valley, 14 mi. W of Osh; cotton; metalworks.

Aravankadu, India: see WELLINGTON.

Aravis, Col des, France: see CLUSAZ, LA.

Araxá (ärüshä'), city (pop. 10,040), W Minas Gerais, Brazil, in the Serra da Canastra, on railroad and 65 mi. ENE of Uberaba; alt. 3,200 ft. Resort with warm sulphur springs, and dry, healthful climate (mean temp. 66°F.). Spa recently improved with luxurious new hotels. Dairying. Airport. In 1947, large apatite deposits (for fertilizer industry) were discovered near by.

Araxes River, Transcaucasia: see ARAS RIVER.

Araxos, Cape, Greece: see PAPAS, CAPE.

Araya, Japan: see AKITA, city.

Araya (ärī'ä), village (pop. 1,070), Álava prov., N Spain, 19 mi. ENE of Vitoria; metalworks.

Araya Peninsula, Sucre state, NE Venezuela, in the Caribbean N of Gulf of Cariaco, 15 mi. S of Margarita Isl.; 45 mi. long W-E from Araya Point (10°38'N 64°18'W) to its base near L. Campona; up to 11 mi. wide. Has extensive salt deposits and provides good fishing grounds.

Arayat (ärä'yät), town (1939 pop. 1,269; 1948 municipality pop. 22,783), Pampanga prov., central Luzon, Philippines, on Pampanga R. and 10 mi. NE of San Fernando, near Mt. Arayat; terminus of spur of Manila–San Fernando RR; sugar milling.

Arayat, Mount, cone-shaped extinct volcano (3,378 ft.), Pampanga prov., central Luzon, Philippines, near Arayat, 45 mi. NNW of Manila.

Arayit Dag (äräyŭt' dä), Turkish *Arayıt Dağ*, peak (5,970 ft.), W central Turkey, in Sivrihisar Mts., 15 mi. SE of Sivrihisar.

Arayoses, Brazil: see ARAIOSES.

Arazdayan Steppe (ŭräz"dŭyän'), in S Armenian SSR, on Aras R. and 30 mi. SE of Erivan, on Nakhichevan Autonomous SSR border. For centuries a swampy, malarial dist.; became (after Second World War) site of reclamation project.

Arba (är'bä), village (pop. 500), Harar prov., E central Ethiopia, in Great Rift Valley, on railroad and 14 mi. NE of Awash.

Arba, L' (lärbä'), town (pop. 6,517), Alger dept., N central Algeria, in the Mitidja plain at foot of the Tell Atlas, 16 mi. SSE of Algiers; agr. trade center (wine, tobacco, citrus). Zinc deposits (S).

Arbai Khere or **Arbay Heere** (är'bī khĕ'rä), town, ⊙ South Khangai aimak, central Mongolian People's Republic, at SE foot of Khangai Mts., on the Ongin Gol and 225 mi. WSW of Ulan Bator. Formerly called Ubur Khangaün or Obör Hangayin.

Arbanasi (ärbänä'sē), village (pop. 574), Gorna Oryakhovitsa dist., N Bulgaria, 2 mi. N of Tirnovo; summer resort; horticulture. Has two 19th-cent. monasteries, five 17th- and 18th-cent. churches with frescoes, ruins of fortified houses. Founded in 15th cent. by Albanians.

Arbaoua (ärbäwä'), village, Rabat region, N Fr. Morocco, customs station on Tangier-Fez RR at Sp. Morocco border, 6 mi. S of Alcazarquivir.

Arbatax (ärbätäks'), village (pop. 264), Nuoro prov., E Sardinia, on Tyrrhenian coast and 33 mi. SSE of Nuoro; rail terminus; lobster fisheries. Port for near-by Tortolì. Only port in 100 mi. bet. capes Comino (N) and Carbonara (S).

Arbatax di Tortolì, Sardinia: see TORTOLÌ.

Arbatski or **Arbatskiy** (ŭrbät'skē), town (1940 pop. over 500), W Sverdlovsk oblast, Russian SFSR, 12 mi. NNW of Kushva; peat digging, lumbering.

Arbay Heere, Mongolia: see ARBAI KHERE.

Arbazh (ŭrbäsh'), village (1926 pop. 300), SW Kirov oblast, Russian SFSR, 40 mi. S of Kotelnich; flax processing.

Arbe, Yugoslavia: see RAB ISLAND.

Arbeca (ärvā'kä), town (pop. 2,948), Lérida prov., NE Spain, 16 mi. ESE of Lérida, and on Urgel Canal; olive-oil processing and exporting, almond shipping; soap mfg.; cereals, livestock.

Arbela, Assyria: see ERBIL, town.

Arbela (ärbĕ'lŭ), town (pop. 87), Scotland co., NE Mo., on South Wyaconda R. and 8 mi. E of Memphis.

Arbeláez (ärbälīs'), town (pop. 1,056), Cundinamarca dept., central Colombia, on W slopes of Cordillera Oriental, 33 mi. SW of Bogotá; corn, tobacco, sugar cane, coffee, fruit, stock. Resort.

Arbent (ärbā'), village (pop. 334), Ain dept., E France, in the Jura, 10 mi. NNE of Nantua; wood turning.

Arbil, Iraq: see ERBIL.

'Arbina or **'Arbinah** (ärbē'nŭ), Fr. *Arbine*, village (pop. c.5,000), Damascus prov., SW Syria, 4 mi. ENE of Damascus, in the Ghuta valley; pears, olives.

Arboga (är'bō"gä), city (pop. 7,094), Vastmanland co., central Sweden, on Arboga R. and 30 mi. SW of Vasteras; mfg. of machinery, chemicals, metal alloys, electrical equipment. Has 12th- and 15th-cent. churches and 15th-cent. town hall. Inc. 1330, it was of great importance in Middle Ages; meeting place of several parliaments. Its trade declined in 17th cent., when opening of Hjalmar Canal (3 mi. E) provided new trade route, by-passing city.

Arbogar, Russian SFSR: see KHOLBON.

Arboga River, Swedish *Arbogaån* (är"bō'gäōn"), S central Sweden, rises as Hork R., Swedish *Hörksälven* (hûrks'ĕl"vŭn), W of Grangesberg, flows 100 mi. generally SE, past Kopparberg, Lindesberg, and Arboga, to L. Malar at Kungsor. Connected (3 mi. E of Arboga) with L. Hjalmar by 8-mi.-long Hjalmar Canal.

Arbois (ärbwä'), town (pop. 3,151), Jura dept., E France, on W slopes of the Jura, 18 mi. SE of Dôle; known for its wines. Mfg. of tools and hosiery; wood turning.

Arbois, Mont d' (mõ därbwä'), summit (c.6,000 ft.) of the Savoy Alps, 10 mi. WNW of Mont Blanc. Aerial tramways from Mégève (2 mi. W) and Saint-Gervais-les-Bains (3 mi. NNE). Winter sports.

Arboleda, La (lä ärvōlā'dhä), village (pop. 2,245), Vizcaya prov., N Spain, 7 mi. WNW of Bilbao. Iron mines near by.

Arboledas (ärbōlā'däs), town (pop. 1,926), Norte de Santander dept., N Colombia, 27 mi. SW of Cúcuta; alt. 3,303 ft.; coffee, corn, cacao, tobacco, fique fibers; cigar mfg.

Arboletes Point (ärbōlā'tēs), headland in Caribbean Sea, NW Colombia, on Antioquia–Bolívar dept. border, 60 mi. NNE of Turbo; 8°56'N 76°27'W. Village of Arboletes is 3 mi. S.

Arbon (ärbō'), town (pop. 7,897), Thurgau canton, NE Switzerland, on L. Constance, 6 mi. NNE of St. Gall, on site of Roman *Arbor Felix*. Motorcars, leather, foodstuffs. Old castle, 18th-cent. church, historical mus.

Arbore (är'bôrā), village (pop. 5,605), Suceava prov., N Rumania, 5 mi. NE of Solca; lumber center. Has 16th-cent. church with frescoes.

Arborea (ärbôrā'ä), village (pop. 571), Cagliari prov., W Sardinia, near Gulf of Oristano, 9 mi. S of Oristano; canned foods. Agr. settlement, established 1928 on land reclaimed from near-by Stagno di Sassi. Originally named Villaggio Mussolini; changed c.1935 to Mussolinia di Sardegna; became Arborea c.1944.

Arborfield, village (pop. 446), E Sask., 25 mi. NE of Tisdale; dairying, wheat.

Arbor Terrace, town (pop. 1,150), St. Louis co., E Mo., just W of St. Louis. Inc. 1936.

Arbós (ärvōs'), town (pop. 1,289), Tarragona prov., NE Spain, 5 mi. NE of Vendrell; lace mfg.; agr. trade (olive oil, wine, cereals, vegetables). Its three-towered church has sculptured façade.

Arbra (är'brō"), Swedish *Arbrå*, village (pop. 1,057), Gavleborg co., E Sweden, on Ljusna R. and 8 mi. N of Bollnas; foundries, woolen mills; metal- and woodworking.

Arbre Broyé, L' (är'brŭ brwäyā'), village, Haut-Donnai prov., S central Vietnam, in Moi Plateaus, on railroad and 10 mi. SE of Dalat; hill resort (alt. 4,931 ft.); tea plantations.

Arbresle, L' (lärbrĕl'), town (pop. 2,598), Rhône dept., E central France, on the Brévenne, bet. Monts du Lyonnais (S) and Monts du Beaujolais (NW), 12 mi. NW of Lyons; silk and velvet weaving. Ruins of 11th-cent. castle.

Arbroath (ärbrōth'), **Aberbrothock** (ăbŭrbrŏ'thŭk), or **Aberbrothwick** (-thĭk), burgh (1931 pop. 17,635; 1951 census 19,503), SE Angus, Scotland, on North Sea, 16 mi. ENE of Dundee; fishing port, seaside resort, agr. market; with mfg. of shoes, tar, sailcloth. Has anc. abbey church and remains of abbey founded 1178 by William the Lion. Town is the Fairport of Scott's *Antiquary*. Just SW is Elliot, with textile-bleaching and asphalt works. Just N, in village of St. Vigeans (vĭ'jŭnz), is 11th-cent. church containing the Droston Stone, with old inscriptions.

Arbucias (ärvōōth'yäs), town (pop. 2,167), Gerona prov., NE Spain, 20 mi. SW of Gerona; livestock, wine, charcoal, lumber.

Arbuckle (är'bŭ"kŭl), village (1940 pop. 624), Colusa co., N central Calif., 13 mi. S of Colusa; almonds, grain, fruit.

Arbuckle Mountains, S Okla., low range rising c.700 ft. above surrounding plain, in S Murray co. and N Carter co., N of Ardmore; □ c.300. Vacation area; includes Turner Falls with park. Noted for interesting geological formations. Near by are Platt National Park (NE), and L. Murray with state park (S).

Arbus (är'bōōs), village (pop. 5,557), Cagliari prov., SW Sardinia, 15 mi. NNE of Iglesias; lead, zinc, silver mines of Gennamare (or Gennamari; 6 mi. WSW) and Ingurtosu (5 mi. W). Molybdenum near by.

Arbutus (är"bū'tŭs), suburban village (1940 pop. 9,773, with adjacent residential Halethorpe), Baltimore co., central Md., just SW of Baltimore; makes motors, crates, industrial gases, metal products.

Arbuzinka (ŭrbōō'zĭnkŭ), village (1926 pop. 7,058), NW Nikolayev oblast, Ukrainian SSR, 24 mi. N of Voznesensk; flour mill.

Arbyrd (är'bûrd), city (pop. 679), Dunklin co., extreme SE Mo., in Mississippi flood plain, 17 mi. SW of Kennett.

Arc or **Arc-lès-Gray** (ärk-lā-grā'), N suburb (pop. 2,578) of Gray, Haute-Saône dept., E France, on right bank of Saône R.; glucose mfg., woodworking.

Arc, river, France: see ARC RIVER.

Arcachon (ärkäshõ'), town (pop. 13,931), Gironde dept., SW France, on S shore of Arcachon Basin near its channel into Bay of Biscay, 32 mi. WSW of Bordeaux; popular bathing resort (summer) and health resort (winter); oyster and deep-sea fishing port. It is well laid out amidst pine groves. Has laboratory of maritime zoology and aquarium.

Arcachon Basin, bay on Atlantic Ocean, in Gironde dept., SW France, enclosed by sand dunes and pine forests of the Landes except for channel (2 mi. wide) S of Cape Ferret; 8 mi. wide, 11 mi. long. Fishing and oyster culture. Arcachon (on S shore) and Andernos-les-Bains (on N shore) are resorts.

Arcade. 1 City (pop. 114), Jackson co., NE central Ga., 12 mi. NW of Athens. **2** Village (pop. 1,818), Wyoming co., W N.Y., on Cattaraugus Creek and 35 mi. SE of Buffalo, in dairying region; summer resort; mfg. (wood products, clothing). Settled c.1800, inc. 1871.

Arcadia (ärkā'dēŭ), Gr. *Arkadia* or *Arkadhia*, nome (□ 1,671; pop. 171,062), central Peloponnesus, Greece; ⊙ Tripolis. Bordered N by Aroania and Erymanthos and Alpheus rivers, SE by Gulf of Argolis; mostly mountainous (Arcadia and Megalopolis plateaus). Livestock and agr. region; wheat, tobacco, potatoes, wine; raising of sheep and goats. Industry at Tripolis. Summer resorts. Anc. region of Arcadia (known for its peaceful pastoral and hunting people speaking an Arcado-Cyprian dialect) had no coast line; it included the cities of Megalopolis, Mantinea, and Tegea. Dominated by Sparta (6th cent. B.C.–371 B.C.), the Arcadian cities later formed a short-lived confederacy (⊙ Megalopolis) under Theban tutelage. Later the area was split bet. Achaean and Aetolian leagues and bet. Spartan and Macedonian influence. Slav influx (8th cent. A.D.) was followed by French rule (1204–1460) and by Turkish domination until Gr. war of independence.

Arcadia, village, Greece: see KYPARISSIA.

Arcadia. 1 Residential city (pop. 23,066), Los Angeles co., S Calif., 13 mi. ENE of downtown Los Angeles, at base of San Gabriel Mts.; citrus fruit, walnuts, truck, poultry, rabbits. Site of Santa Anita race track. Inc. 1903. **2** City (pop. 4,764), ⊙ De Soto co., S central Fla., on Peace R. and c.60 mi. SE of Tampa; trade and shipping center for extensive cattle and citrus-fruit area; citrus-fruit packing houses and canneries. Holds annual rodeos, cattle show. **3** Town (pop. 1,073), Hamilton co., central Ind., near Cicero Creek, 29 mi. N of Indianapolis, in agr. area. **4** Town (pop. 425), Carroll co., W central Iowa, 9 mi. W of Carroll, in agr. area. **5** City (pop. 572), Crawford co., SE Kansas, at Mo. line, 16 mi. NNE of Pittsburg, in diversified agr. and coal-mining area. **6** Town (pop. 2,241), ⊙ Bienville parish, NW La., 50 mi. E of Shreveport, in cotton-producing area; cotton ginning, cottonseed processing, lumber milling. Natural-gas wells. Training school for Negroes here. **7** Village (pop. c.500), Manistee co., NW Mich., on L. Michigan and 17 mi. N of Manistee, in farm and resort area; furniture mfg. **8** Resort town (pop. 414), Iron co., SE central Mo., in St. Francois Mts. just S of Ironton. **9** Village (pop. 574), Valley co., central Nebr., 15 mi. SW of Ord and on Middle Loup R.; livestock, grain, dairy and poultry produce. **10** Village (pop. 529), Hancock co., NW Ohio, 8 mi. ENE of Findlay and on South Branch of Portage R. **11** Village, Oklahoma co., central Okla., 17 mi. NE of Oklahoma City, in oil-producing area. **12** Mill village (pop. 2,554), Spartanburg co., NW S.C., 5 mi. W of Spartanburg; cotton textiles. **13** City (pop. 1,949), Trempealeau co., W Wis., on Trempealeau R. and 33 mi. NNW of La Crosse, in dairy and livestock area; beer, dairy products; nursery; timber. Inc. 1925.

Arcadia, Gulf of, Greece: see KYPARISSIA, GULF OF.

Arcahaie (ärkäī'), agr. town (1950 census pop. 1,631), Ouest dept., W Haiti, on the Gulf of Gonaïves, 20 mi. NW of Port-au-Prince, on railroad; sugar cane, bananas. Sometimes L'Arcahaie.

Arcangelo, Greece: see ARCHANGELOS.

Arcanum (ärkā'nŭm), village (pop. 1,530), Darke co., W Ohio, 8 mi. SSE of Greenville, in diversified-farming area; mfg. of tennis racquets, lumber milling; tobacco warehouses.

Arcata (ärkā'tŭ), coast city (pop. 3,729), Humboldt co., NW Calif., 6 mi. NE of Eureka, at N end of Humboldt Bay; lumbering, mfg. of barrels; dairying. Seat of Humboldt State Col. Bret Harte lived here, 1857–60. Founded 1850, inc. 1903.

Arc Dome, Nev.: see TOIYABE RANGE.

Arce, Bolivia: see PADCAYA.

Arce (är'chĕ), town (pop. 1,937), Frosinone prov., Latium, S central Italy, 12 mi. ESE of Frosinone.

Arceburgo (ärsĭbōōr'gōō), city (pop. 2,043), SW Minas Gerais, Brazil, on São Paulo border, 16 mi. WSW of Guaxupé; coffeegrowing, dairying.

Arcelia (ärsā'lyä), town (pop. 3,139), Guerrero, SW Mexico, in Río de las Balsas basin, 25 mi. ESE of Altamirano; silver, gold, lead, copper mining. Airfield.

Arc-en-Barrois (ark-ã-bärwä'), agr. village (pop. 752), Haute-Marne dept., NE France, 13 mi. SSW of Chaumont; lumbering.

Arcene (är'chĕnĕ), village (pop. 1,803), Bergamo prov., Lombardy, N Italy, 8 mi. SSW of Bergamo.

Arcetri (är'chătrē), village, Tuscany, Italy, just S of Florence. Residence (1634–42) of Galileo after his trial by the Inquisition.

Arc-et-Senans (ärk-ā-sůnā'), village (pop. 1,010), Doubs dept., E France, near the Loue, 14 mi. ESE of Dôle, S of Forêt de Chaux; railroad junction; metalworking, dairying.

Arcevia (ärchā'vyä), town (pop. 1,445), Ancona prov., The Marches, central Italy, 11 mi. N of Fabriano; mfg. (silk textiles, cement, bicycles, motorcycles). Has church with works of Luca Signorelli and terra-cotta altar by G. della Robbia.

Archanai, Ano, Crete: see ANO ARCHANAI.

Archangel (ärk'ān"jůl), Rus. *Arkhangelsk* or *Arkhangel'sk* (ŭrkhän'gĭlsk), oblast (□ 229,400, including Arctic isls.; 1946 pop. estimate 1,050,000) in N European Russian SFSR; ⊙ Archangel. Includes mainland section of oblast proper (half of total area), NENETS NATIONAL OKRUG, and isl. dependencies of SOLOVETSKIYE ISLANDS, KOLGUYEV ISLAND, MATVEYEV ISLAND, VAIGACH ISLAND, NOVAYA ZEMLYA, and FRANZ JOSEF LAND. Mainland is a plain drained by Onega, lower Northern Dvina, Mezen, and Pechora rivers; forested except for tundra in extreme N. Some grain, flax, and dairy farming in alluvial river valleys; fur trapping in N forests; reindeer raising in tundra; fishing, seal and bird hunting along coast and on Arctic isls. Foremost lumbering and sawmilling region of USSR; plywood, pulp, and paper milling, wood distillation (tar, resin, alcohol) along rail lines and at main ports (Archangel, Onega, Mezen, Naryan-Mar); mfg. of prefabricated houses, shipbuilding. Archangel, Kotlas, and Molotovsk are main centers. Archangel-Vologda RR, with branches to Belomorsk and Kotlas, and Northern Dvina R. are chief transportation arteries. Oblast exports lumber, tar, resin, furs, hog bristles; imports machinery, grain, mfg. products. Formed 1937 out of Northern Oblast.

Archangel, Rus. *Arkhangelsk* or *Arkhangel'sk,* city (1926 pop. 76,774; 1939 pop. 281,091), ⊙ Archangel oblast, Russian SFSR, major port at head of the Northern Dvina delta mouth, 25 mi. from White Sea, 700 mi. NNE of Moscow; 64°34'N 40°34'E. Largest sawmilling and lumber-exporting center of USSR; rail terminus; supply point for Arctic sea route; shipyards, sawmills, rope mills, tanneries; processing center for White Sea fisheries. During brief navigation season (June-Oct.), exports lumber, resin, turpentine, furs, and hog bristles. Has cathedral of Archangel Michael (1685–99), regional and fisheries mus., lumber institute, medical and teachers colleges. Central section lies on right bank of the Northern Dvina across from rail station. Beyond Kuznechikha branch of delta (N) is suburb of Solombala, a naval base until 1863; present site of shipyards, docks, paper and pulp mills. City extends in narrow band, hemmed in by marshes, over 10 mi. N along Maimaksa branch (a deep-draught channel of delta; sawmills) to outer port of Ekonomiya, 15 mi. from the sea. Founded (1583) as Novo-Kholmogory (later renamed Arkhangelsk) following establishment of Anglo-Muscovite trade. Flourished as only Rus. port during 16th and 17th cent.; declined after founding (1703) of St. Petersburg. Regained importance after construction of railroad (1897) and played major role as supply port during First and Second World wars. Occupied by Allies (1918–20). An important lend-lease port during Second World War. Was ⊙ Archangel govt. (until 1929); later, ⊙ Northern Territory (after 1936, oblast).

Archangel Bay, Russian SFSR: see DVINA BAY.

Archangelos or **Arkhangelos** (both: ärkhäng'gĕlôs), Ital. *Arcangelo* (ärkän'jĕlô), town (pop. 2,438), Rhodes isl., Greece, near E shore, 18 mi. S of Rhodes.

Archar (ärchär'), village (pop. 4,127), Vidin dist., NW Bulgaria, on the Danube (landing) and 13 mi. W of Lom; vineyards, grain; fisheries. Has ruins of Roman town of Ratiaria (aqueduct, stone tombs).

Archbald, industrial borough (pop. 6,304), Lackawanna co., NE Pa., 9 mi. NE of Scranton and on Lackawanna R.; anthracite mining; textiles, clothing. Settled 1831, inc. 1877.

Archbold (ärch'bōld), village (pop. 1,486), Fulton co., NW Ohio, 13 mi. ENE of Bryan; agr. (sugar beets, hay, wheat); mfg. of agr. machinery, furniture, wood products; slaughterhouse.

Archdale, town (pop. 1,218), Randolph co., central N.C., 4 mi. SE of High Point. Founded 1773 by Quakers.

Archeda, Russian SFSR: see FROLOVO.

Archena (ärchā'nä), town (pop. 5,149), Murcia prov., SE Spain, on the Segura and 13 mi. NW of Murcia; esparto processing, fruit-conserve mfg., sawmilling. Citrus and other fruit; livestock. Warm sulphur springs near by noted since Roman times.

Archennes (ärshĕn'), Flemish *Eerken* (ār'kůn), town (pop. 772), Brabant prov., central Belgium, 4 mi. NE of Wavre; mfg. of storage batteries.

Archer, county (□ 917; pop. 6,816), N Texas; ⊙ Archer City. Drained by West Fork of Trinity R., Little Wichita and Wichita rivers; includes L. Kickapoo, parts of Diversion and Wichita lakes. Agr. (wheat, oats, grain sorghums, corn, cotton), dairying; cattle ranching; some poultry, hogs, sheep. There are oil and natural-gas fields. Formed 1858.

Archer. 1 City (pop. 586), Alachua co., N Fla., 15 mi. WSW of Gainesville; rail junction; lumber milling, mfg. of mining machinery. **2** Town (pop. 167), O'Brien co., NW Iowa, 7 mi. SE of Sheldon; livestock, grain.

Archer City, city (pop. 1,901), ⊙ Archer co., N Texas, 22 mi. S of Wichita Falls; trade center for oil-producing, cattle ranching, agr. area (grain, poultry, dairy products). Settled c.1880, inc. 1910.

Arches (ärsh), village (pop. 1,148), Vosges dept., E France, on Moselle R. and 6 mi. SE of Épinal; paper milling.

Arches National Monument (□ 53; established 1929), SE Utah, on Colorado R. just N of Moab. Sandstone has been shaped by erosion into huge vertical slabs in which arches and windows have been cut by weathering. South Window is 65 ft. high; Landscape Arch, in Devil's Garden (N), is a natural bridge more than 100 ft. high, 291 ft. long. Other formations include gigantic towers, balanced rocks, and pinnacles.

Árchez (är'chāth), town (pop. 674), Málaga prov., S Spain, 26 mi. ENE of Málaga; raisins; also grapes and olives.

Archi, Greece: see AKRITES.

Archi (är'kē), village (pop. 1,288), Chieti prov., Abruzzi e Molise, S central Italy, near Sangro R., 10 mi. S of Lanciano.

Archiac (är-shēäk'), village (pop. 478), Charente-Maritime dept., W France, 8 mi. WNW of Barbezieux; winegrowing, brandy distilling. Dolmens near by.

Archico, Eritrea: see HARKIKO.

Archidona (ärchē-dhō'nä), village, Napo-Pastaza prov., E central Ecuador, on E slopes of the Andes, on affluent of Napo R. and 5 mi. N of Tena; zinc deposits. Formerly ⊙ Oriente prov.

Archidona, city (pop. 6,495), Málaga prov., S Spain, in spur of the Cordillera Penibética, 26 mi. N of Málaga; agr. center (cereals, olives, grapes, stock); olive-oil pressing, liquor distilling, sawmilling, soap making. Iron and gypsum deposits. Outside the city (N) is the Cueva de las Granjas (cave).

Archie, town (pop. 300), Cass co., W Mo., near South Grand R., 12 mi. S of Harrisonville.

Archipelago (ärkĭpĕ'lůgō), a former name for the Aegean Sea; it was later applied to the numerous isls. in the Aegean, and now means any cluster of isls.

Archman (ŭrchmän'), health resort, S Ashkhabad oblast, Turkmen SSR, on N slope of the Kopet-Dagh, 75 mi. WNW of Ashkhabad and on Trans-Caspian RR.

Archuleta (är"chůlē'tů), county (□ 1,364; pop. 3,030), SW Colo.; ⊙ Pagosa Springs. Agr. area on N.Mex. line; drained by San Juan R.; bounded E by San Juan Mts. Livestock. Includes parts of San Juan and Rio Grande natl. forests. Formed 1885.

Arcidosso (ärchēdôs'sô), town (pop. 1,605), Grosseto prov., Tuscany, central Italy, near Monte Amiata, 23 mi. ENE of Grosseto; woolen mill. Manganese mines near by.

Arcila or **Arzila** (both: ärthē'lä, –sē'lä), anc. *Zilis,* city (pop. 17,201), Lucus territory, W Sp. Morocco, small fishing port on the Atlantic, on Tangier-Fez RR and 25 mi. SSW of Tangier. Trades in wheat, barley, beans, corn, sheep, cattle. Vegetable-fiber processing. Preserves 15th-16th-cent. Portuguese walls. Built on site of Phoenician settlement, it later fell to Romans; it suffered numerous incursions during Middle Ages. Occupied after 1471 by Portuguese, then by Spaniards (who evacuated it 1589), city has been in Sp. hands since 1911.

Arcisate (ärchēzä'tĕ), village (pop. 1,856), Varese prov., Lombardy, N Italy, 3 mi. NNE of Varese; cement mfg.

Arcis-sur-Aube (ärsē'sůr-ōb'), town (pop. 2,176), Aube dept., NE central France, on Aube R. and 17 mi. N of Troyes; hosiery mfg. Its 15th-16th-cent. church was heavily damaged in Second World War. Scene of battle (1814) bet. Napoleon I and Allies. Danton b. here.

Arciz, Ukrainian SSR: see ARTSIZ.

Arc-lès-Gray, Haute-Saône dept., France: see ARC.

Arco (är'kô), town (pop. 3,448), Trento prov., Trentino–Alto Adige, N Italy, near N end of Lago di Garda, on Sarca R. and 3 mi. NNE of Riva; olive-oil refinery, alcohol distillery, shoe factory. Famous health resort (alt. 299 ft.). Has palace (1501), church (1603–18), ruins of castle, and monument to Giovanni Segantini, who was b. here.

Arco (är'kō). **1** Resort village (pop. 961), ⊙ Butte co., SE central Idaho, c.70 mi. NW of Pocatello in mtn. region; alt. 5,318 ft.; trade center for agr. (grain, livestock) and mining (silver, lead) area; hq. for Craters of the Moon Natl. Monument. Lost River atomic-energy reactor testing station (8 mi. E), begun 1949. **2** Village (pop. 178), Lincoln co., SW Minn., 6 mi. SSE of Ivanhoe, in grain area.

Arco del Diablo (är'kō dĕl dēä'blō), peak (7,400 ft.) in Florida Mts., SW N.Mex., 13 mi. SE of Deming.

Arcola (ärkō'lů), town (pop. 572), SE Sask., 60 mi. E of Weyburn; grain elevators, lumber and flour mills; resort.

Arcola (är'kôlä), village (pop. 1,562), La Spezia prov., Liguria, N Italy, near Magra R., 4 mi. E of Spezia. Has 15th-cent. church.

Arcola (ärkō'lů). **1** City (pop. 1,700), Douglas co., E central Ill., 13 mi. N of Mattoon; ships broomcorn, makes brooms; poultry hatchery. Platted 1855, inc. 1865. An Amish colony is near by. **2** Town (pop. 413), Washington co., W Miss., on small Deer Creek and 15 mi. SE of Greenville.

Arcole (är'kôlĕ), village (pop. 1,945), Verona prov., Veneto, N Italy, 15 mi. SE of Verona. Scene of victory of Napoleon over Austrians in 1796.

Arconate (ärkônä'tĕ), village (pop. 2,464), Milano prov., Lombardy, N Italy, 11 mi. NNW of Abbiategrasso; cotton.

Arco Pass (c.4,500 ft.), in the Andes, on Argentina-Chile border, 60 mi. W of Zapala; 38°46'S 71°5'W.

Arcore (är'kôrĕ), village (pop. 3,851), Milano prov., Lombardy, N Italy, 4 mi. NE of Monza; mfg. (rubber goods, ribbon).

Arcos, Los, or **Losarcos** (lōs är'kōs), town (pop. 2,045), Navarre prov., N Spain, 11 mi. SW of Estella; olive-oil, brandy mfg.; cereals, wine, livestock.

Arcos de Canasí, Cuba: see CANASÍ.

Arcos de Jalón (är'kōs dhā hälōn'), town (pop. 1,324), Soria prov., N central Spain, on Madrid-Saragossa RR and 40 mi. SSE of Soria; grain growing, flour milling, stock raising, clay quarrying. Hydroelectric plant on small Jalón R.

Arcos de la Frontera (lä frōntā'rä), city (pop. 10,919), Cádiz prov., SW Spain, in Andalusia, on right bank of Guadalete R. and 31 mi. NE of Cádiz. Processing, lumbering, and agr. center in fertile region (cereals, vegetables, cork, olives, cattle, hogs, goats); apiculture. Dairying, flour milling, liquor and wine distilling; mfg. of cork and cork plugs, olive oil, esparto goods. Has sulphur mines. Picturesquely situated atop rocky hill, it has notable old bldgs. and mansions. Ruins of castle of the duke of Arcos.

Arcos de Valdevez (är'kŏŏsh dĭ väldā'vĭzh), town (pop. 1,468), Viana do Castelo dist., N Portugal, 21 mi. N of Braga; produces ceramics. Noted for battle (1140) bet. Alfonso I and Alfonso VII of Leon.

Arcot, district, India: see NORTH ARCOT; SOUTH ARCOT.

Arcot (är'kŏt, –kůt), Tamil *Arkadu* (ŭr'kŭdōō), town (pop. 16,583), North Arcot dist., E central Madras, India, on Palar R. and 13 mi. E of Vellore; rice, sugar cane, peanuts; cotton weaving. Became ⊙ Carnatic in 1712. Captured by Clive (1751); variously held by French, English, Mysore sultans, and Nawabs of Arcot until finally ceded 1801 to English.

Arcoverde (ärkōōvĕr'dĭ), city (pop. 4,176), central Pernambuco, NE Brazil, on railroad and 75 mi. W of Caruaru; ships cotton, coffee, tobacco. Asbestos deposits near by. Until 1944, called Rio Branco.

Arcozelo (ärkōōzā'lōō), agr. village (pop. 1,661), Guarda dist., N central Portugal, 18 mi. SE of Viseu; some winegrowing.

Arc River (ärk). **1** In Bouches-du-Rhône dept., SE France, rises near Saint-Maximin (Var dept.), flows c.45 mi. W to the Étang de Berre 4 mi. NW of Berre-l'Étang. W of Aix-en-Provence it is spanned by 19th-cent. Roquefavour aqueduct (1,230 ft. long, 270 ft. high) built to carry Durance R. waters to Marseilles. **2** In Savoie dept., SE France, rises in Graian Alps near Ital. border, flows c.90 mi. NW in a great arc through MAURIENNE valley of Savoy Alps, past Lanslebourg, Modane, Saint-Jean-de-Maurienne, and Aiguebelle, to the Isère near Saint-Pierre-d'Albigny. Navigable below La Chambre. Its 18 hydroelectric plants activate important metal and chemical works. Its valley followed by railroad and road to Italy via Mont Cenis.

Arcs, Les (lāzärk'), town (pop. 2,167), Var dept., SE France, 5 mi. S of Draguignan, near the Argens; rail junction (spur to Draguignan); cork mfg., sericulture.

Arctic, village, Alaska: see ARCTIC VILLAGE.

Arctic (är'tĭk), industrial village in West Warwick town, Kent co., central R.I., on Pawtuxet R. and 10 mi. SSW of Providence; textiles; trade center for agr., mfg. area.

Arctic Archipelago or **Arctic Islands** (ärk'tĭk), large Canadian isls. in Arctic Ocean, almost coextensive with FRANKLIN Dist., Northwest Territories.

Arctic Bay, trading post, N Baffin Isl., SE Franklin Dist., Northwest Territories, on E side of Admiralty Inlet; 73°3'N 85°12'W; radio and meteorological station. Site of R.C. mission. Fur-trading post was established 1926, later abandoned, reestablished 1936.

Arctic Contractors, village (pop. 44), E central Alaska, near Fairbanks.

Arctic Current: see LABRADOR CURRENT.

Arctic Institute Islands, Russian SFSR: see ARKTICHESKI INSTITUT ISLANDS.

Arctic Ocean, virtually landlocked sea (□ 5,440,000) at top of the world, extending from North Pole to c.70°N, regarded as a subsidiary of the Atlantic Ocean and sometimes called Arctic Sea or North Polar Sea. Bounded by Norway, USSR, Alaska, and Canada, it communicates with the Atlantic Ocean on both sides of Greenland—via BAFFIN BAY, DAVIS STRAIT, and LABRADOR SEA (W); and GREENLAND SEA and NORWEGIAN SEA (E). It is connected with the Pacific by Bering Strait. It consists of an elliptical, deep basin, surrounded by generally shallow, marginal seas (600 ft. deep) overlying the bordering continental shelf. The shelf seas are BARENTS SEA, KARA SEA, LAPTEV SEA, EAST SIBERIAN SEA, and CHUKCHI SEA, while the marginal BEAUFORT SEA is part of the deep basin. The greatest depth (17,850 ft.) was recorded in 1927 by Sir Hubert Wilkins c.400 mi. N of Herald Isl. at 77°45'N 175°W. Its depth in vicinity of North Pole is 14,350 ft.; average depth of the Arctic Ocean is 4,200 ft. Within the fringing shelf seas are the isls. of Canada's ARCTIC ARCHIPELAGO, and WRANGEL ISLAND, HERALD ISLAND, NEW SIBERIAN ISLANDS, SEVERNAYA ZEMLYA, NOVAYA ZEMLYA, FRANZ JOSEF LAND, and SPITSBERGEN. The influx of major rivers (Mackenzie, Lena, Yenisei, Ob) and the reduced evaporation in the Arctic Regions create a strong outflow of Arctic water into the connecting oceans. By far the greatest exchange in the water balance takes place with the Atlantic bet. Greenland and Norway, in the form of the cold EAST GREENLAND CURRENT and the warm NORTH ATLANTIC CURRENT. A much weaker outflow through Baffin Bay forms the LABRADOR CURRENT W of Greenland. Most of the Arctic Ocean is covered during the greater part of the year by broken, piled-up pack ice varying in thickness from 10 ft. in winter to 7 ft. in summer. Small icebergs are found in the vicinity of Severnaya Zemlya, Franz Josef Land, and Spitsbergen. Most icebergs of large size originate in the Greenland glaciers and are carried S by the East Greenland and Labrador currents. The salinity (33 per mill) of the Arctic Ocean is the lowest of the world's oceans. Fauna is found—in the form of polar bears, arctic hare, and gulls—as is plankton. For an account of Arctic exploration, see ARCTIC REGIONS.

Arctic Red River, village (district pop. 129), NW Mackenzie Dist., Northwest Territories, on Mackenzie R., at mouth of Arctic Red R., and 70 mi. SSE of Aklavik; 67°27'N 133°45'W; radio station, Royal Canadian Mounted Police post; site of R.C. mission. Fur-trading post was established c.1900 by Hudson's Bay Co.

Arctic Red River, NW Mackenzie Dist., Northwest Territories, rises in Mackenzie Mts. near 64°20'N 131°40'W, flows 230 mi. N to Mackenzie R. at Arctic Red River village.

Arctic Regions, northernmost area of the earth, centered about the North Pole and the Arctic Ocean. The determination of its imprecise limits varies according to definition: the Arctic Circle (66°17'N) is sometimes used as the arbitrary boundary; the parallel of lat. 70°N is also used; and the boundary defined by the weather—a wavy line changing with the seasons—is frequently employed. By all definitions, the land area in the largely oceanic arctic includes the Canadian ARCTIC ARCHIPELAGO in FRANKLIN Dist., bet. Baffin Bay and Beaufort Sea; from ⅔ to ¾ of Greenland; SPITSBERGEN and the other isls. of SVALBARD; FRANZ JOSEF LAND; NOVAYA ZEMLYA, SEVERNAYA ZEMLYA, TAIMYR PENINSULA, NEW SIBERIAN ISLANDS, WRANGEL ISLAND, and N Siberia; and northernmost Alaska, at least the area N of Brooks Range. N Canada is sometimes included. The most northerly point of land is the N tip of Greenland, Cape Morris Jesup (83°39'N 34°12'W), 440 mi. from the North Pole. In summer the coldest areas are on the ice-cap in N Greenland and in the never-melting region about the North Pole. In winter the lowest temperatures are in N Siberia and N central Canada. The cold loses its full grip on the Arctic Regions in summer; everywhere there is at least one month with a temp. above freezing. Under the "midnight sun" temperatures mount and vegetation springs to life in the BARREN GROUNDS and the tundras wherever the soil can give sufficient nourishment. The flowers of the arctic meadows have pleased the eyes of many explorers. The abundant animal life has many fur bearers and many animals with a high food value for man. There are seal, walrus, and whale and many fish. Duck and other water fowl light on the summer lakes. On the rocky coasts are rookeries of auks, terns, and other sea birds. The Eskimo has used this abundant animal life to adapt himself to arctic conditions. Arctic explorers have generally succeeded in so far as they have learned what the Eskimo can teach, as did Vilhjalmur Stefansson. The 1st explorers in the arctic regions were the Norsemen, the Vikings. Much later the search for the NORTHWEST PASSAGE and the NORTHEAST PASSAGE to reach the reaches of the Orient from Europe spurred exploration to the N. This activity began in 16th cent. and continued in 17th, but the hardships suffered and the more or less negative results obtained by early explorers—among them Martin Frobisher (1576–78), John Davis (1585–87), Henry Hudson (1607–11), William Baffin (1615–16), and William Barentz (1594–96)—caused interest to wane. The fur traders in Canada did not begin serious explorations across the Barren Grounds until later part of 18th cent. Alexander Mackenzie undertook extensive exploration after the beginnings made by Samuel Hearne, Philip Turnor, and others. In the region of NE Asia and W Alaska the Russian explorations under Vitus Bering and others and the activities of the *promyshlennyki* [fur traders] had already begun to make the arctic coasts known. After the Napoleonic Wars, Br. naval officers, inspired by the efforts of John Barrow, took up the challenge of the North. Sir John Franklin, F. W. Beechey, John Ross and James Ross, W. E. Parry, P. W. Dease, Thomas Simpson, George Back, John Rae—each name carries its own story of courage, hardship, and adventure. The disappearance of Franklin on his expedition of 1845–48 gave rise to more than 40 searching parties, English and American. The general outlines of the arctic Canadian coast and the archipelago N of Canada were made known. Otto Sverdrup, D. B. Macmillan, and Vilhjalmur Stefansson added significant knowledge. Meanwhile Franz Josef Land was discovered in 1873, Novaya Zemlya was explored. The Northeast Passage was finally navigated 1878–79 by N. A. E. Nordenskjold. Roald Amundsen, who went through the Northwest Passage in 1903–6, also went through the Northeast Passage in 1918–20. Greenland attracted some explorers, and others were fired with the desire to be 1st at the North Pole. The credit went to Robert E. Peary in 1909. Fridtjof Nansen in the brilliantly conceived drift of his vessel *Fram* in the ice in 1893–96 failed to reach the North Pole but reached 85°57'N, or within 280 mi. of the Pole, and added enormously to the knowledge of the Arctic Ocean. Air exploration of the regions began with the tragic balloon attempt of S. A. Andrée in 1897. In 1926 Richard E. Byrd and Floyd Bennett flew over the North Pole and Amundsen and Lincoln Ellsworth flew from Spitsbergen to Alaska across the North Pole and unexplored regions N of Alaska. In 1928 Sir Hubert Wilkins flew from Alaska to Spitsbergen. The use of the "great circle" route for world air travel increased the importance of Arctic Regions, while new ideas of the agr. and other possibilities of arctic and near-arctic regions led to many projects of development. The USSR was particularly active. In 1937 and 1938 many field expeditions were sent out by British, Danish, Norwegian, Russian, Canadian, and American groups to learn more of the North. The Soviet group under Ivan Papinin, set down on an ice floe near the North Pole, drifted with the current for 274 days. Valuable hydrological, meteorological, and magnetic observations were made. The four men were taken off the floe at 70°48'N 19°48'W, after having drifted from 89°26'N 78°W. Arctic drift was further explored (1937–40) by the Russian icebreaker *Sedov*, and the existence of Sannikov Isl. was proved a myth. In 1938 air photographs by Danish explorers over N Greenland proved the much-sought PEARY CHANNEL to be only a fjord. Before the Second World War the USSR had established many meteorological and radio stations in the arctic, and the war itself saw new developments. Russian activity (not only in developing meteorological stations but also in practical exploitation of resources) pointed the way to the development of the arctic regions; thus, Igarka, at the mouth of the Yenisei above the Arctic Circle, was built up to develop the mineral and timber resources of the region. Bet. 1940 and 1942 the Canadian Mounted Police vessel, the *St. Roch*, made the 1st W-E journey through the Northwest Passage.

Arctic Sea: see ARCTIC OCEAN.

Arctic Stream: see LABRADOR CURRENT.

Arctic Village, Indian village (pop. 141), NE Alaska, on Chandalar R. and 110 mi. N of Fort Yukon; 68°10'N 145°40'W; gold placer mining; trapping. Formerly Arctic.

Arcturus (ärktū'rŭs), village, Salisbury prov., NE central Southern Rhodesia, in Mashonaland, 20 mi. ENE of Salisbury; tobacco, wheat, corn, citrus fruit, dairy products. Gold, tin, arsenic mining.

Arcueil (ärkû'ē), town (pop. 16,206), Seine dept., N central France, a S suburb of Paris, 4 mi. from Notre Dame Cathedral, just S of Gentilly; precision metalworks; mfg. (biscuits, vinegar). Has 13th-cent. Gothic church and remains of 3d-cent. Roman aqueduct.

Arcy-sur-Cure (ärsē'-sür-kür'), village (pop. 519), Yonne dept., N central France, on Cure R. and 11 mi. NW of Avallon; lumbering. In near-by stalactite caverns prehistoric remains have been found.

Ard, Loch, Scotland: see ABERFOYLE.

Arda, river, Bulgaria and Greece: see ARDA RIVER.

Ardabil, Iran: see ARDEBIL.

Ardagh (är'dä, är'dŭ), Gaelic *Árdachadh*, agr. village (pop. 77), central Co. Longford, Ireland, 6 mi. SE of Longford; dairying, cattle raising, potato growing.

Ardahan (ärdähän'), town (pop. 6,182), Kars prov., NE Turkey, in Armenia, on Kura R. and 40 mi. NNW of Kars; barley. Fortified town often disputed bet. Russians and Turks in 19th cent.

Ardakan (ärdäkän'). **1** Town (1945 pop. estimate 4,500), Seventh Prov., in Fars, S Iran, 55 mi. NW of Shiraz; grain, cotton, sugar beets. **2** Town (1933 pop. estimate 10,000), Tenth Prov., in Yezd, central Iran, 35 mi. NW of Yezd and on railroad; grain, cotton, pomegranates, melons; noted for its pistachios. Hand-woven cotton textiles.

Ardales (ärdhä'lĕs), town (pop. 4,365), Málaga prov., S Spain, on affluent of the Guadalhorce and 26 mi. NW of Málaga; agr. center (olives, wheat, almonds, livestock). Has sulphur springs.

Ardalstangen (ôr'dälstäng"ŭn), Nor. *Årdalstangen*, village (pop. 445) in Ardal (Nor. *Årdal*) canton (pop. 2,182), Sogn og Fjordane co., W Norway, 21 mi. E of Sogndal, at head of Ardal Fjord (Nor. *Årdalsfjord*), a 12-mi. extension of Sogne Fjord; aluminum works; cattle raising, marble quarrying; tourist center. Sometimes spelled Aardalstangen.

Ardanuc (ärdänōōch'), Turkish *Ardanuç*, village (pop. 606), Coruh prov., NE Turkey, 13 mi. ESE of Artvin; grain. Also called Adakale.

Ardara (ärdŭrä'), Gaelic *Árda Ráth*, town (pop. 444), W Co. Donegal, Ireland, at head of an Atlantic inlet, 15 mi. NW of Donegal; woolen milling.

Arda River (är'dä), Gr. *Ardas* or *Ardhas* (both: är'dhŭs), S Bulgaria and Greece, rises in central Rhodope Mts. near Smolyan, flows 180 mi. E, past Kirdzhali and Ivailovgrad (Bulgaria) and into Greek Thrace to the Maritsa just W of Adrianople (Edirne), on Turkish border. Its drainage basin corresponds approximately to the area of W Thrace that remained in Bulgaria by the treaty of Neuilly (1919).

Arda River (är'dä), N central Italy, rises in Ligurian Apennines, 4 mi. NNW of Bardi, flows 40 mi. NNE, past Fiorenzuola d'Arda and Cortemaggiore, to Po R. 8 mi. SSE of Cremona.

Ardasa, Turkey: see TORUL.

Ardatov (ŭrdä'tŭf). **1** or **Ardatovo** (ŭrdä'tŭvŭ), village (1926 pop. 3,225), SW Gorki oblast, Russian SFSR, 30 mi. WSW of Arzamas; potatoes, wheat. **2** City (1926 pop. 5,880), NE Mordvinian Autonomous SSR, Russian SFSR, on Alatyr R. and 15 mi. W of Alatyr; sawmilling, agr.-processing (hides, grain) center; match mfg. Founded 1588.

Ardchattan (ärdkă'tŭn), mountainous district of N Argyll, Scotland, on both sides of Loch Etive, coextensive with parish (pop. 2,083) of Ardchattan and Muckairn. Chief village, BONAWE.

Ardea or **Ardhea** (both: ärdhā'ŭ), town (pop. 3,825), Pella nome, Macedonia, Greece, 12 mi. N of Edessa; center of Almopia lowland; wine, red peppers, silk, cotton. Formerly called Suboskon.

Ardeal, Rumania: see TRANSYLVANIA.

Ardebil or **Ardabil** (ärdŭbēl'), city (1940 pop. 63,406), Third Prov., in Azerbaijan, NW Iran, 110 mi. E of Tabriz, and on road to Astara, near USSR border and Caspian Sea; situated on intermontane plain at E foot of the Savalan; grain, dried fruit; rug weaving. Airfield. Mineral springs near by. Has mausoleum of Sheikh Sefiuddin, 14th-cent. religious leader, and of Shah Ismail (1480–1524), founder of Safavid dynasty. City flourished in 8th cent. under Arab rule and later as early capital of Safavid dynasty. Occupied 1827 by Russians, who acquired valuable manuscripts for St. Petersburg library.

Ardèche (ärdĕsh'), department (□ 2,145); pop. 254,598), in former Languedoc prov., S France; ⊙ Privas. Bounded by Rhone R. (E); traversed SSW–NNE by the Monts du VIVARAIS; drained by short tributaries of the Rhone (Ariège, Doux, Érieux). A leading silkworm- and sheep-raising dept. In addition to mulberry and chestnut trees, there are fine vineyards (Saint-Péray) and orchards along right bank of the Rhone. Cereals and potatoes are also grown. Has iron mines near Privas and important limestone quarries and cementworks near Le Teil, Cruas, and La Voulte-sur-Rhône. Silk is processed in almost every village; chief spinning centers: Aubenas and Tournon. Leading industrial town is Annonay (paper mills, tanneries). Privas is known for its glazed marrons, and Vals-les-Bains for its mineral springs. Medieval countship of Vivarais roughly occupied what is now Ardèche dept.

Ardèche River, Ardèche dept., S France, rises in the Monts du Vivarais near Saint-Étienne-de-Lugdarès, flows 70 mi. generally SE, past Aubenas, to the Rhone above Pont-Saint-Esprit. Near Vallon it is spanned by the Pont d'Arc, a natural bridge. Receives the Chassezac (right).

Arded (är'dĕd), Hung. *Erdőd* (ĕr'dût), village (pop. 4,927), Baia-Mare prov., NW Rumania, 10 mi. S of Satu-Mare; rail junction and agr. center. Has ruins of 15th-cent. fortress. In Hungary, 1940–45.

Ardee (ärdē') [town on the Dee], Gaelic *Baile Átha Fhirdhiadh*, town (pop. 2,346), W Co. Louth, Ireland, on Dee R. and 13 mi. NW of Drogheda; agr. market (wheat, barley, potatoes; cattle); mfg. of agr. implements, furniture. In 13th cent. Roger de Pippart here founded Crutched Friary, Carmelite Friary, and castle; the latter was taken (1315) by Edward Bruce, by O'Neill (1538), and by the Irish and again by the English in 1641. In war of 1689–90 town was hq. of forces of James II and later of those of William III.

Ardeer, Scotland: see STEVENSTON.

Ardelan, Iran: see KURDISTAN.

Ardelthan, town (pop. 565), S central New South Wales, Australia, 145 mi. WNW of Canberra; tinmining center.

Arden (är'dŭn), town (pop. 1,341), Aalborg amt, N Jutland, Denmark, 19 mi. S of Aalborg; cement, peat.

Arden. **1** Residential village (1940 pop. 612), New Castle co., N Del., 6 mi. N of Wilmington; art, theatrical, and literary center; handicrafts. Founded 1900 as single-tax colony. Post office name formerly Grubbs. **2** Town (1940 pop. 1,187), Richland co., central S.C.; N residential suburb of Columbia.

Arden, Forest of, former extensive woodland centered in Warwickshire, England, scene of Shakespeare's *As You Like It.*

Ardenicë (ärdānē'tsü) or **Ardenica** (–tsä), Ital. *Ardenizza* (ärdānēt'tsä), monastery, S central Albania, 6 mi. N of Fier; dates partly from 15th cent. Its church was restored (18th cent.). Petroleum deposits near by.

Ardenne, Château d' (shätō' därdĕn'), former royal castle, Namur prov., S Belgium, in the Ardennes, 6 mi. SE of Dinant; purchased by Leopold I, who established model farms on estate, it became favorite royal hunting lodge. Now resort hotel.

Ardennes (ärdĕn'), department (□ 2,028; pop. 245,335), N France; ⊙ Mézières. Bounded N by Belgium. Contains S part of the Ardennes and N part of the Argonne. Drained by the Meuse and the Aisne, which are connected by Ardennes Canal. Agr. only in Aisne valley. Lumbering and stock raising in uplands. Important state quarries near Fumay and Rimogne. Leading industry is metalworking, concentrated in numerous small plants along the Meuse bet. Charleville and Givet. Sedan area is known for its woolen cloth manufactures. Chief towns are twin cities of Charleville and Mézières; Sedan; and Rethel. In 1815 and 1870, dept. was scene of Fr. military disasters. Completely occupied by Germans during First World War. Near Sedan Germans broke through once again in May, 1940, thus launching the "battle of France."

Ardennes or **Forest of Ardennes** (ärdĕn', –dĕnz'), Fr. ärdĕn'), anc. *Arduenna Silva,* wooded plateau (1,600–2,300 ft.) E of Meuse R., partly in Ardennes dept., N France, but mostly in SE Belgium (Luxembourg and Liége provs.) and in grand duchy of Luxembourg. Rises to 2,283 ft. in the Botrange (Belgium), highest point of the HOHE VENN section. Heavily dissected by entrenched rivers (Semois, Amblève, Ourthe). Population, chiefly Walloon, is pastoral. Larger cities (Sedan, Mézières, Namur, Liége) in Meuse valley; industrial centers (Arlon, Longwy, Pétange, Verviers) at SE and N edges. Chief towns (road junctions) on plateau are Bastogne, Neufchâteau, Saint-Vith. In Germany (E), the Ardennes are continued by the Eifel. A traditional battleground, the Ardennes were scene of bitter fighting (1914 and 1918) in First World War, and of "Battle of the Bulge" (Dec., 1944–Jan., 1945) in Second World War.

Ardennes Canal, in Ardennes dept., N France, connects the Aisne with the Meuse, paralleling the Aisne bet. Asfeld and Vouziers, crossing the Argonne near Le Chesne, and following Bar R. to its mouth on the Meuse near Dom-le-Mesnil. Length, 61 mi. Transports lumber, iron.

Ardenno (ärdĕn'nô), village (pop. 824), Sondrio prov., Lombardy, N Italy, in the Valtellina, 11 mi. W of Sondrio; hydroelectric plant.

Ardentes (ärdãt'), village (pop. 1,242), Indre dept., central France, on the Indre and 8 mi. SE of Châteauroux; woodworking, cattle raising. Has 12th-cent. church.

Ardenza (ärdĕn'tsä), town (pop. 3,833), Livorno prov., Tuscany, central Italy, on Ligurian Sea, 2 mi. S of Leghorn; bathing resort; mfg. (industrial furnaces, ventilators, driers).

Arderin (ärdĕ'rĭn), mountain (1,733 ft.), W Co. Laoighis, Ireland, 15 mi. W of Port Laoighise; highest peak of the Slieve Bloom.

Ardersier (ärdûrsēr') or **Campbelltown,** village and parish (pop. 1,760), N Inverness, Scotland, on Moray Firth, 9 mi. NE of Inverness, in fertile region (called Carse of Ardersier) bet. Moray Firth and Nairnshire border. Fishing port and resort. Near by is FORT GEORGE.

Ardes or **Ardes-sur-Couze** (ärd-sür-kōōz'), village (pop. 810), Puy-de-Dôme dept., central France. in Monts du Cézallier, 11 mi. SW of Issoire; cattle raising. Antimony mine at nearby Anzat-le-Luguet.

Ardestan, Iran: see ARDISTAN.

Ardewan Pass (ŭr'dûwän) (alt. 5,250 ft.), in Paropamisus Mts., NW Afghanistan, 25 mi. N of Herat, and on road to Afghan frontier post of Torghondi, opposite Kushka (USSR).

Ardfert (ärd'fûrt), Gaelic *Ård Fhearta,* town (pop. 126), W Co. Kerry, Ireland, near the Atlantic, 5 mi. NW of Tralee; agr. market (potatoes, grain; dairying). Has 12th-cent. Temple-na-Hoe church and Gothic Temple-na-Griffin church. There are remains of 13th-cent. cathedral and of Franciscan abbey, founded 1253. Episcopal see of Ardfert, now united with Limerick and Aghadoe, was founded in 6th cent. by St. Brendan.

Ardfinnan (ärdfĭ'nün), Gaelic *Ård Fhionáin,* town (pop. 253), S Co. Tipperary, Ireland, on Suir R. and 8 mi. WSW of Clonmel; agr. market (dairying, cattle raising; potatoes, beets); woolen milling. Remains of castle built by King John.

Ardglass (ärdglăs'), town (pop. 1,413), E Co. Down, Northern Ireland, on the Irish Sea, 6 mi. SE of Downpatrick; 54°16'N 5°37'W; herring-fishing center. It was formerly chief port of Co. Down, protected by 5 fortified bldgs., of which there are some remains. Port entrance is marked by lighthouse.

Ardgowan, Scotland: see INVERKIP.

Ardhas River, Bulgaria and Greece: see ARDA RIVER.

Ardhea, Greece: see ARDEA.

Ardibbo, Lake (ärdĭb'bō), Wallo prov., NE Ethiopia, near L. Haik, 12 mi. ENE of Dessye; alt. 6,890 ft.; 4 mi. long, 2 mi. wide.

Ardino (är'dēnô), village (pop. 1,469), Khaskovo dist., S Bulgaria, in E Rhodope Mts., 13 mi. WSW of Kirdzhali; processes tobacco. Lead deposits 2 mi. SE. Until 1934, Yegri-Dere, sometimes spelled Iridere.

Ardistan or **Ardestan** (ärdĕstän'), town (1942 pop. 5,669), Tenth Prov., in Isfahan, W central Iran, on road and 65 mi. NE of Isfahan, near Teheran-Yezd RR; wheat, barley, opium, pistachios, almonds, pomegranates, figs.

Ardjoeno, Mount, or **Mount Ardjuno,** Indonesia: see ARJUNO, MOUNT.

Ardleigh (ärd'lē), town and parish (pop. 1,515), NE Essex, England, 5 mi. NE of Colchester; agr. market.

Ardley, village (pop. estimate 100), S central Alta., 25 mi. E of Red Deer; coal mining.

Ardlui (ärdlōō'ē), village in Arrochar parish, NW Dumbarton, Scotland, at N end of Loch Lomond, 15 mi. ENE of Inveraray; tourist resort, terminal of loch steamers.

Ardmore (ärdmôr'), Gaelic *Ård Mór,* town (pop. 149), SW Co. Waterford, Ireland, on the Atlantic, 11 mi. SSW of Dungarvan; fishing port and resort. Has 11th-13th-cent. cathedral, anc. round tower, and oratory of St. Declan, who founded Irish Col. here in 7th cent. Just E is Ardmore Head.

Ardmore (ärd'mōr). **1** Town (pop. 408), Limestone co., N Ala., on Tenn. line, 22 mi. NW of Huntsville. **2** City (pop. 17,890), ⊙ Carter co., S Okla., c.90 mi. S of Oklahoma City; commercial, shipping, and mfg. center of rich agr. (cotton, hay, truck, livestock), and asphalt- and oil-producing region. Oil refining; flour, feed, and cottonseed-oil milling; cotton ginning; mfg. of oil-field equipment, machinery, metal and concrete products, leather, butane-gas appliances, dairy and other food products. A state hosp. and Carter Seminary (U.S. school for Indians) are here. Near by are the Arbuckle Mts. (c.10 mi. N) and L. Murray (just S; state park), which are recreation areas. Settled 1887, inc. 1898. **3** Village (pop. 9,015), center of LOWER MERION township, Montgomery co., SE Pa.; W suburb of Philadelphia; mfg. of motor vehicles. Settled c.1800. **4** Town (pop. 107), Fall River co., SW S.Dak., 30 mi. SSW of Hot Springs and on Hat Creek, at Nebr. line. **5** Town (pop. 157), Giles co., S Tenn., at Ala. line, 17 mi. SE of Pulaski; hosiery, cheese.

Ardmore Head, promontory, SW Co. Waterford, Ireland, 11 mi. SSW of Dungarvan; 51°57'N 7°42'W.

Ardnacrusha (ärdnûkrŭ'shü), Gaelic *Ard na Croise,* locality in SE Co. Clare, Ireland, on the Shannon and 2 mi. N of Limerick; site of major hydroelectric power station.

Ardnadam (ärdnă'dûm), a resort village near Dunoon, Argyll, Scotland.

Ardnamurchan (ärdnûmûrkh'ün), peninsula and parish (pop. 1,139), NW Argyll, Scotland. Peninsula extends 16 mi. E–W, bet. the Sea of the Hebrides (N) and Loch Sunert and the Sound of Mull (S); it is up to 7 mi. wide; rises to 1,729 ft. Chief village is fishing port of Kilchoan (kĭl-khōn'), on S coast, 6 mi. N of Tobermory. At W extremity of peninsula is the Point of Ardnamurchan, with lighthouse (56°44'N 6°13'W), westernmost point of isl. of Great Britain. Near by are remains of old Mingary Castle.

Ardnaree, Ireland: see BALLINA.

Ardoch (är'dŏkh), parish (pop. 1,029), S Perthshire, Scotland, 6 mi. S of Crieff. Includes agr. village of Braco. Grounds of Ardoch House here are site of remains of Roman camp of *Lindum,* the most perfectly preserved in Great Britain.

Ardoch (är'dŏk), village (pop. 137), Walsh co., NE N.Dak., 25 mi. NNW of Grand Forks.

Ardon (ŭrdôn'), village (1926 pop. 5,547), central North Ossetian Autonomous SSR, Russian SFSR, on railroad, on Ardon R. and 23 mi. WNW of Dzaudzhikau; fruit and vegetable canning, bastfiber (hemp) processing.

Ardon River, in North Ossetian Autonomous SSR, Russian SFSR, rises in main range of the central Greater Caucasus SE of the Adai-Khokh, flows c.70 mi. N, past Mizur, Alagir, and Ardon, to Terek R. near Darg-Kokh. Valley used by Ossetian Military Road.

Ardooie (ärdô'yû), town (pop. 7,152), West Flanders prov., W Belgium, 4 mi. NE of Roulers; textiles, shoes; agr. market. Formerly spelled Ardoye.

Ardore (ärdô'rĕ), town (pop. 1,715), Reggio di Calabria prov., Calabria, S Italy, near Ionian Sea, 6 mi. SW of Locri; olive oil.

Ardouan, Greece: see KOKKINOVRACHOS.

Ardova Caves, Czechoslovakia: see SLOVAKIAN KARST.

Ardoye, Belgium: see ARDOOIE.

Ardres (är'drů), village (pop. 1,349), Pas-de-Calais dept., N France, 8 mi. SE of Calais; sugar refining. The celebrated meeting of the "Field of the Cloth of Gold" bet. Henry VIII and Francis I was held at near-by Balinghem in 1520.

Ardrishaig (ärdrĭ'shĭg, –shĕg), fishing port in South Knapdale parish (pop. 2,188), S central Argyll, Scotland, on Loch Gilp, 21 mi. WNW of Dunoon; whisky distilling. SE terminus of CRINAN CANAL.

Ardrossan (ärdrŏ'sün), village and port (pop. 558), S South Australia, on E coast of Yorke Peninsula, 50 mi. NW of Adelaide across Gulf St. Vincent; wheat, wool; limestone.

Ardrossan, burgh (1931 pop. 6,889; 1951 census 8,799), NW Ayrshire, Scotland, on Firth of Clyde, 14 mi. NW of Ayr; port and beach resort, with oil refinery and iron foundries. At port entrance is lighthouse (55°39'N 4°50'W). Just WNW, in Firth of Clyde, is small Horse Isl.

Ards, The, peninsula (c.20 mi. long, 5 mi. wide) and former barony in E Co. Down, Northern Ireland, bet. the Irish Sea (E) and Strangford Lough (W).

Ardsley, former urban district (1931 pop. 9,216), West Riding, S central Yorkshire, England. Here are Ardsley East, 3 mi. NNW of Wakefield, and, just W, Ardsley West; coal mining, woolen milling, metalworking. Inc. 1937 in Morley.

Ardsley. **1** Residential village (pop. 1,744), Westchester co., SE N.Y., just NE of Dobbs Ferry, in New York city suburban area; mfg. of chemicals. Has large arboretum maintained by Columbia Univ. Ardsley-on-Hudson is c.1 mi. NW, on E bank of the Hudson. **2** Village, Pa.: see ABINGTON.

Ardsley-on-Hudson, N.Y.: see ARDSLEY.

Arduan, Greece: see KOKKINOVRACHOS.

Arduenna Silva, Belgium, Luxembourg, and France: see ARDENNES.

Ardusat (är'dōōshät), Rum. *Ardușat,* Hung. *Erdőszáda* (ĕr'dûsä"dŏ), village (pop. 1,777), Baia-Mare prov., NW Rumania, on railroad and 25 mi. SE of Satu-Mare. In Hungary, 1940–45.

Ardvorlich, Scotland: see EARN, LOCH.

Ardwick, E suburb of Manchester, SE Lancashire, England; mfg. of clothing, aluminum, chemicals, paint.

Are (ō'rů), Swedish *Åre,* village (pop. 428), Jamtland co., NW Sweden, in mts. near Norwegian border, at foot of the peak Areskutan, on Indal R. and 50 mi. WNW of Ostersund; summer and winter-sports resort. Has medieval Lapp church. Site of several sanitaria. Near by are the falls Tannforsen.

Areado (ărēä'dōō), city (pop. 2,410), SW Minas Gerais, Brazil, on railroad and 8 mi. NW of Alfenas; dairying, coffeegrowing.

Areal (ărēäl'), town (pop. 1,097), N Rio de Janeiro state, Brazil, 11 mi. SE of Três Rios; rail junction; coffee. New hydroelectric plant.

Arebi, Belgian Congo: see WATSA.

Arechavaleta (ärächävälä'tä), town (pop. 1,058), Guipúzcoa prov., N Spain, on Deva R. and 16 mi. NE of Vitoria; iron and aluminum founding; cider distilling. Mineral springs.

Arecibo (ärāsē'bō), town (pop. 28,659), N Puerto Rico, port on small open bay of the Atlantic, at mouth of the Arecibo, on railroad and 40 mi. W of San Juan; 18°28'N 66°44'W. Port of entry; processing center in agr. region (sugar cane, coffee, tobacco, fruit); sugar milling, alcohol and rum distilling; mfg. of needlework, clothing, furniture, agr. machinery. Has U.S. customhouse, R.C. and Presbyterian churches. An old colonial city, settled 1556. Site of Br. defeat (1702). Adjoining it are fine beaches. Further inland are the Dos Bocas (9 mi. S) and Caonillas (13 mi. S) hydroelectric plants. Arecibo airport is 3 mi. E.

Arecibo River or **Río Grande de Arecibo,** W central Puerto Rico, rises in the Cordillera Central, flows c.40 mi. N to the Atlantic just E of Arecibo. On its mid-course is the large Dos Bocas dam, reservoir, and hydroelectric plant (completed 1943). With the Dos Bocas project is now linked the new Caonillas dam (230 ft. high, 780 ft. long) on the small Caonillas R., an affluent.

Aredale (är'dāl), town (pop. 204), Butler co., N central Iowa, 25 mi. SSE of Mason City.

Arefino (ŭryĕ'fēnŭ), village (1926 pop. 160), N central Yaroslavl oblast, Russian SFSR, on small Ukhra R., near Rybinsk Reservoir, 18 mi. NE of Shcherbakov; flax processing, clothing industry.

Areguá (ärāgwä'), town (dist. pop. 7,410), Central dept., S Paraguay, on railroad, on L. Ypacaraí and 18 mi. E of Asunción. Resort and processing center (vegetable oil, cotton goods, liquor, ceramics, sweets, sausages). Founded 1538.

Aregue (ärā'gā), town (pop. 574), Lara state, NW Venezuela, on affluent of Tocuyo R., in Segovia Highlands, and 5 mi. NE of Carora.

Areia (ără'ů). **1** City, Bahia, Brazil: see UBAÍRA. **2** City (pop. 3,318), E Paraíba, NE Brazil, on E slope of Borborema Plateau, 55 mi. WNW of João Pessoa; cattle-raising center; ships cotton, potatoes, agave fibers. Has agr. school.

Areia Branca (brăng'ků), city (pop. 5,792), W Rio Grande do Norte, NE Brazil, port on the Atlantic at mouth of Apodi R., and 19 mi. NNE of Mossoró; chief salt-producing and -shipping center of Brazil; also exports carnauba wax. Hydroplane landing. Kaolin deposits in area. Pôrto Franco (on left bank of the Apodi, 3 mi. SSW) is N terminus of railroad to Mossoró and the interior.

Areias (ärā'ŭs), city (pop. 934), extreme SE São Paulo, Brazil, near Paraíba R., 15 mi. E of Cruzeiro; distilling; butter and cheese processing; cattle raising.

Arelas, France: see ARLES.

Arena (ärā'nä), village (pop. 2,917), Catanzaro prov., Calabria, S Italy, 9 mi. SE of Vibo Valentia; wine, olive oil.

Arena, village (pop. 296), Iowa co., S Wis., near Wisconsin R., 27 mi. WNW of Madison, in dairying region. Tower Hill State Park is near by.

Arena, La, Panama: see LA ARENA

Arena, La, Peru: see LA ARENA.

Arena, La (lä ärā'nä), village (pop. 1,851), Oviedo prov., NW Spain, port on Bay of Biscay at mouth of Nalón R., 17 mi. NW of Oviedo; fishing and fish processing (anchovies), boat building.

Arena, Point, Calif.: see POINT ARENA.

Arenac (â'rŭnăk), county (□ 368; pop. 9,644), E Mich.; ⊙ Standish. Bounded SE by Saginaw Bay; drained by Rifle, Pine, and Au Gres rivers. Livestock, dairy products, potatoes, corn, sugar beets, grain. Flour mill, grain elevator, milk-products plant. Commercial fishing. Resorts (hunting, fishing, bathing). State forest is in NW. Formed 1831.

Arenal (ärānäl'), extinct volcano (5,092 ft.) in the Cordillera de Guanacaste, NW Costa Rica, 10 mi. E of L. Arenal.

Arenal, Campo del (käm'pō dĕl), desert plateau (alt. c.7,000 ft.) in E Catamarca prov., Argentina, bet. Nevado del Aconquija (E) and Sierra Chango-real (W), N of Andalgalá; large sand dunes. Crossed by Belén–Santa María road. Sometimes called "Sahara Argentino."

Arenal, El, Mexico: see EL ARENAL.

Arenal, El (ĕl), town (pop. 2,196), Ávila prov., central Spain, in fertile valley of the Sierra de Gredos, 34 mi. SW of Ávila; fruit, beans, chestnuts, potatoes, onions, olives, grapes. Lumbering, flour milling.

Arenal, Lake, marshy lake in NW Costa Rica, in the Arenal depression in the Cordillera de Guanacaste; 7 mi. long, 2 mi. wide; alt. 1,575 ft. Outlet: **Arenal River** (left affluent of the San Carlos).

Arenales, Argentina: see GENERAL ARENALES.

Arenas (ärā'nās), town (pop. 832), Málaga prov., S Spain, 22 mi. ENE of Málaga; grapes, raisins, almonds, olives.

Arenas, town (pop. 663), Sucre state, NE Venezuela, in coastal range, 20 mi. SE of Cumaná; sugar.

Arenas, Las (läs), town (pop. 7,302), Vizcaya prov., N Spain, on right bank of Nervión R. at its mouth on Bilbao Bay (inlet of Bay of Biscay), opposite Portugalete (transporter bridge), and 7 mi. NW of Bilbao; metal industries; paper mfg., fishing-boat construction. Bathing resort.

Arenas, Punta de (pōōn'tä dā), or **Point Arenas,** cape on NE coast of main isl. of Tierra del Fuego, Argentina, at N edge of San Sebastián Bay, 40 mi. SE of Cape Espíritu Santo; 53°8'S 68°12'W.

Arenas del Rey (dĕl rā'), town (pop. 1,255), Granada prov., S Spain, 22 mi. SW of Granada; resin mfg. Cereals, olive oil, fruit, lumber. Lignite mines near by.

Arenas de San Juan (dā sän' hwän'), town (pop. 1,477), Ciudad Real prov., S central Spain, on Gigüela or Záncara R., and 28 mi. NE of Ciudad Real; cereals, grapes, olives, goats, sheep.

Arenas de San Pedro (pā'dhrō), town (pop. 4,297), Ávila prov., central Spain, in Old Castile, at S foot of the Sierra de Gredos, 36 mi. SW of Ávila. Beautiful Castilian resort town, surrounded by peaks, in fertile valley irrigated by Tiétar R. Subtropical vegetation, yielding grapes, all kinds of fruit, chestnuts, olives, honey. Lumbering, flour milling. Mfg. of soap, resins, dairy products, soft drinks, tiles. Outside the walls is convent of San Pedro de Alcántara, named for saint who d. here.

Arendal (ä'rŭndäl), city (pop. 11,570), ⊙ Aust-Agder co., S Norway, port on Tromoy Sound (inlet of the Skagerrak) at mouth of Nid R., 120 mi. SSW of Oslo; 58°27'N 8°45'E. Excellent harbor, protected by isls. Tromoy and Hisoy; rail terminus and important shipping center for coastwise trade. Car ferry to Grenaa, Denmark; terminus of cables to Newbiggin, England, and to Hirtshals, Denmark. Lumber, floated down Nid R., is milled and exported; iron and aluminum smelting, mfg. of electrical appliances; poultry hatching; production of beer, tobacco products. Has historic 4-story, wooden city hall; and a navigation school. A port since 14th cent., it had the largest fleet in Norway just before the steamship era.

Arendal River, Norway: see NID RIVER.

Arendonk (ä'rŭndŏngk), town (pop. 7,960), Antwerp Prov., N Belgium, 6 mi. E of Turnhout; dynamite mfg. Formerly spelled Arendonck.

Arendsee (ä'rŭntzā"). **1** Resort, Mecklenburg, N Germany: see KÜHLUNGSBORN. **2** Town (pop. 3,240), in former Prussian Saxony prov., central Germany, after 1945 in Saxony-Anhalt, on Arend L. (□ 2), 14 mi. SW of Wittenberge; health resort. Has 13th-cent. church of former Benedictine monastery.

Arendtsville (â'rŭntsvĭl), borough (pop. 409), Adams co., S Pa., 7 mi. NNW of Gettysburg.

Arenig Fach (ăr'ĕ'nĭg väkh'), mountain (2,264 ft.), N Merioneth, Wales, 8 mi. ESE of Blaenau-Ffestiniog.

Arenig Fawr (–vour'), mountain (2,800 ft.), N Merioneth, Wales, 6 mi. W of Bala.

Arenillas (ärānē'yäs), village, El Oro prov., S Ecuador, on railroad and 21 mi. SSW of Machala, in coastal agr. region (cacao, coffee, stock).

Arensburg, Estonia: see KURESSAARE.

Arenys de Mar (ärā'nēs dhā mär'), Catalan *Arénys de Mar,* town (pop. 5,178), Barcelona prov., NE Spain, in Catalonia, on the Mediterranean, 24 mi. NE of Barcelona; mfg. of knitwear, woolens, laces, liqueurs; cork processing; shipyards. Summer and winter resort. Has naval school.

Arenys de Munt (mōōnt'), Catalan *Arénys de Munt,* village (pop. 2,662), Barcelona prov., NE Spain, 7 mi. NE of Metaró; mfg. (laces, towels, brandy). Cork, oranges, wine in area.

Arenzano (ärĕnzä'nō), village (pop. 2,319), Genova prov., Liguria, N Italy, port on Gulf of Genoa and 12 mi. W of Genoa; paper, cotton, and jute mills; cork and cutlery factories. Bathing and winter resort.

Arenzville (â'rĭnzvĭl, ä'–), village (pop. 513), Cass co., W central Ill., 12 mi. NNW of Jacksonville, in agr. area.

Areopagus (ărēŏ'pŭgŭs) [by incorrect etymology assumed by the Greeks to mean *hill of Ares*], rocky hill (370 ft.) NW of the Acropolis of Athens, Greece, famous as sacred meeting place of the prime council of anc. Athens.

Areopolis (ŭrāô'pôlĭs), town (pop. 1,379), Laconia nome, S Peloponnesus, Greece, on Gulf of Messenia, at W foot of the Taygetus, 28 mi. SSW of Sparta; fisheries. Formerly Tsimova.

Arequipa (ärākē'pä), department (□ 21,662; pop. 270,996), S Peru, on the Pacific; ⊙ Arequipa. Crossed by Cordillera Occidental NW-SE, it includes many snow-capped volcanic peaks (El Misti, Pichu Pichu, Chachani). Watered by Tambo, Vitor, Majes, and Ocoña rivers, used for irrigation in the arid but fertile coastland. Climate is semitropical and practically rainless near the ocean, cooler in the mts. Though predominantly agr., it is rich in mineral resources: gold, silver, copper, lead, antimony, mica, borax (Laguna de Salinas), marble. The river valleys and elevated oasis around Arequipa city grow cotton, sugar cane, wheat, barley, corn, rice, grapes, fruit, vegetables. Cattle and alpaca raising in the high sierras. Rural industries: cotton ginning, cottonseed-oil extracting, alcohol distilling, wine making, flour milling, mining. Arequipa city is a major textile-milling and -processing center, and an important wool market. The ocean port of Mollendo is being gradually replaced by the safer Matarani (completed 1941). There are many noted thermal springs (Jesús, Yura) and archaeological remains. Arequipa was set up as dept. in 1822.

Arequipa, city (pop. 79,185), ⊙ Arequipa dept. and Arequipa prov. (□ 3,529; pop. 132,686), S Peru, in Chili R. valley, at foot of the perfectly shaped cone of El Misti volcano, on Pan American Highway, and 55 mi. NE of its port Mollendo, 95 mi. SE of Lima; 16°24'S 71°32'W; alt. 7,800 ft. The 3d largest city of the country and commercial center of S Peru and N Bolivia, it has a mild, dry, climate (mean temp. 59°F) and is situated in a fertile irrigated region (cotton, corn, wheat, potatoes, yucca, vegetables, fruit, stock) surrounded by an arid *pampa.* A busy trading and distributing center, it is a market chiefly for wool (sheep and alpaca). Among its industries are textile mills, tanneries, shoe factories, iron foundries, food canneries, flour mills, cotton gins, brewery, dairy plants. Airport. Formerly an Inca city, it was founded by the Spanish in 1540. Bishopric. Has a univ.; also a cathedral (founded 1612), many churches, convents, and 2 observatories (on the El Misti). Famed for its colorful Indian markets and beautiful location towered over by snow-capped peaks, Arequipa is one of the most picturesque cities of Peru. Though frequently damaged by earthquakes (disastrously in 1868), its outstanding bldgs., of white sillar lava stone, have been reconstructed. In the vicinity are several bathing resorts and thermal springs, as well as pre-Columbian remains.

Arequito (ärākē'tō), town (pop. estimate 2,500), S Santa Fe prov., Argentina, 50 mi. WSW of Rosario; wheat, flax, barley, alfalfa, fruit, cattle, poultry; dairying, flour milling.

Arero, Ethiopia: see ARARO.

Arês (ärās'), city (pop. 2,108), E Rio Grande do Norte, NE Brazil, on a lagoon of the Atlantic, 25 mi. S of Natal; saltworks; carnauba palms. Formerly spelled Arez.

Ares or **Arés** (ärās'), town (pop. 2,103), La Coruña prov., NW Spain, fishing port on Ares Bay, 10 mi. NE of La Coruña; fish and meat processing, boatbuilding; stock raising, lumbering.

Areskutan, Swedish *Åreskutan* (ō'rŭskü"tän), peak (4,659 ft.), NW central Sweden, near Norwegian border, 50 mi. WNW of Ostersund; 63°27'N 13°5'E. Overlooks upper Indal R.

Arestinga Lagoon (ärĕstēng'gä), inlet of the Caribbean in Margarita Isl., Nueva Esparta state, NE Venezuela.

Arethusa (ărĭthū'sŭ), celebrated fountain in Sicily, in city of Syracuse, on Ortygia isl. In Greek mythology Arethusa was a nymph who fled the attentions of the river-god Alpheus and was changed into a fountain. He pursued and caught her, whence the story that the waters of the Alpheus R. in Greece flow beneath the sea to reappear in Syracuse in the fountain of Arethusa.

Arethusa, Syria: see RASTAN, ER.

Areuse River (ärûz'), W Switzerland, rises in the Jura W of Fleurier, flows 19 mi. NE and E, draining Val de Travers, to L. of Neuchâtel 4 mi. SW of Neuchâtel.

Arévalo (ärā'välō), city (pop. 3,999), Ávila prov., central Spain, in Old Castile, on Segovia prov. border, on Madrid–La Coruña RR and 39 mi. N of Ávila. Agr. market of the prov., on N plains (*Moraña*), where chiefly wheat, chick-peas, carobs, potatoes, fruit, and grapes are grown, and livestock is raised. Also exports wool, and pine cones. Flour milling, tanning, meat packing; mfg. of naval stores, soap, tiles; limekilns. Historic city with old Santa María church, and with medieval castle in which Blanche of Bourbon was held prisoner by Pedro the Cruel. Also has fine aqueduct and a lofty tower on the wall gate. Taken from Moors by Alfonso VI.

Arez, Brazil: see ARÊS.

Arezzo (ärĕ'tsô), province (□ 1,247; pop. 319,754), Tuscany, central Italy; ⊙ Arezzo. Mtn. and hill terrain, including portions of the Pratomagno and Monti Chianti; watered by upper courses of Arno and Tiber rivers and the Chiana. Agr. (grapes, olives, cereals, raw silk, fruit) and livestock raising (cattle, sheep) predominate. Lignite mining (San Giovanni Valdarno, Pratovecchio, Castiglion Fiorentino). Mfg. at Arezzo, San Giovanni Valdarno, and Montevarchi.

Arezzo, anc. *Arretium,* town (pop. 24,411), ⊙ Arezzo prov., Tuscany, central Italy, in upper Arno valley, 38 mi. SE of Florence; 43°28'N 11°53'E. Rail junction; agr. trade center (cereals, wine, olive oil, silk, cattle); mfg. (metal furniture, wine and olive oil, machinery, musical instruments, silverware, woolen textiles, paper, alcohol, macaroni). Bishopric. Has fine Gothic cathedral (completed 1510), and notable churches, including Romanesque Santa Maria della Pieve (roof damaged), San Francesco (begun 1332; important frescoes by Piero de'Franceschi), and Renaissance Santa Maria delle Grazie (altar by A. della Robbia). Palazzo della Fraternità (1375–1460; damaged 1943) houses art gall. and mus. An Etruscan town; later under the Romans, became famous for its red clay Aretini vases. In late Middle Ages noted as a center of learning and arts. Distinguished men b. here include Guido d'Arezzo, Petrarch, Aretino, and Vasari. Parts of town badly damaged by air bombing (1943–44) in Second World War.

Arfak Mountains (är'fäk), E Vogelkop peninsula, NW New Guinea, S of Manokwari; c.30 mi. long, rise to 9,643 ft.

Arfersiorfik (äkhfĕkhsyôkh'fĭk), fjord (95 mi. long, 1–15 mi. wide), W Greenland, 30 mi. S of Egedesminde; 68°15'N 52°W. Extends E from Davis Strait to edge of inland icecap, where its several arms receive large glaciers, including Nordenskjöld Glacier (N). Niarkornârssuk settlement on N shore, near mouth. Fjord was starting point (1883) of Nordenskjöld expedition.

Arga, Turkey: see AKCADAG.

Argaeus, Mount, Turkey: see ERCIYAS DAGI.

Argalaste or **Argalasti** (both: ärgŭlŭstē'), town (pop. 3,021), Magnesia nome, SE Thessaly, Greece, 19 mi. SE of Volos, at SE foot of the Pelion; olive oil; stock raising (sheep, goats); fisheries. Also spelled Arghalasti.

Argamasilla de Alba (ärgämäsē'lyä dhä äl'vä), town (pop. 6,537), Ciudad Real prov., S central Spain, in New Castile, on the Alto Guadiana and 45 mi. ENE of Ciudad Real. Processing and agr. center on La Mancha plain. Produces grapes, cereals, beans, potatoes, corn, sheep. Lumbering, liquor distilling, wine making, flour milling, dairying (cheese). Hydroelectric plant. Its railroad station is called Cinco Casas. Cervantes is believed to have begun his *Don Quixote* in a local jail.

Argamasilla de Calatrava (käläträ'vä), town (pop. 4,069), Ciudad Real prov., S central Spain, on railroad and 19 mi. SW of Ciudad Real; agr. center (cereals, truck, grapes, olives, sheep, goats). Olive-oil extracting, liquor distilling, vegetable canning; lime quarrying.

Argana (ärgänä'), village, Agadir frontier region, SW Fr. Morocco, at SW end of the High Atlas, 38 mi. NE of Agadir; argan trees.

Arganda (ärgän'dä), town (pop. 4,447), Madrid prov., central Spain, on railroad and 15 mi. SE of Madrid; agr. center (grapes, olives, cereals, truck produce, vegetables, sugar beets, forage, livestock). Olive-oil extracting, alcohol and liquor distilling, wine making, sugar refining; plaster, clay, and stone quarrying. Adjoined by industrial (sugar, molasses) suburb of La Poveda (pop. 357).

Arganil (ärgŭnēl'), town (pop. 1,086), Coimbra dist., N central Portugal, 20 mi. E of Coimbra; mfg. (brooms, ceramics); trades in grain, corn, wine. Hydroelectric plant near by.

Argao (ärgä'ō, ärgou'), town (1939 pop. 3,502; 1948 municipality pop. 33,596), central Cebu isl., Philippines, 35 mi. SW of Cebu city, port on Bohol Strait; agr. center (corn, coconuts).

Argaon, India: see AKOT.

Argapoera, Mount, Indonesia: see ARGAPURA, MOUNT.

Argapura, Mount, or **Mount Argapoera** (both: är"gäpōō-rä), peak (10,131 ft.), E Java, Indonesia, just W of Bondowoso. Also spelled Argopuro.

Arga River (är'gä), Navarre prov., N Spain, rises in W Pyrenees near Fr. border NNE of Pamplona, flows 100 mi. generally S, past Pamplona, to Aragon R. 6 mi. above its influx into the Ebro.

Argayash (ŭrgŭyäsh'), town (1932 pop. estimate 2,360), N central Chelyabinsk oblast, Russian SFSR, on railroad and 30 mi. NW of Chelyabinsk; quarrying; metalworking, flour milling. Until 1934, in detached section of Bashkir Autonomous SSR.

Argegno (ärjā'nyô), resort village (pop. 780), Como prov., Lombardy, N Italy, port on SW shore of L. Como, 10 mi. N of Como.

Argelès-Gazost (ärzhŭlĕs'-gäzôst'), village (pop. 1,893), Hautes-Pyrénées dept., SW France, in central Pyrenees, near Gave de Pau R., 18 mi. SSW of Tarbes; resort with thermal establishment; woodworking, wool combing.

Argelès-sur-Mer (-sür-mâr'), town (pop. 2,588), Pyrénées-Orientales dept., S France, at foot of Monts Albères, near the Gulf of Lion, 12 mi. SSE of Perpignan; cork mfg.; winegrowing. Beach 2 mi. E.

Argenau, Poland: see GNIEWKOWO.

Argens River (ärzhã'), Var dept., SE France, rises in Lower Provence Alps, flows 72 mi. E, in fertile valley bet. coastal Monts des Maures and Estérel, to the Mediterranean 2 mi. S of Fréjus.

Argenta (ärjĕn'tä), town (pop. 3,684), Ferrara prov., Emilia-Romagna, N central Italy, on Reno R. and 18 mi. SE of Ferrara; agr. trade center (cereals, hemp, sugar beets, tobacco); macaroni mfg.

Argenta (ärjĕn'tŭ), village (pop. 575), Macon co., central Ill., 21 mi. NE of Decatur; corn, wheat, soybeans.

Argentan (ärzhãtã'), town (pop. 4,936), Orne dept., NW France, on the Orne and 23 mi. NNW of Alençon; road and market center (poultry, horses, grain); sawmilling. Lacemaking school. Heavily damaged (including 15th–17th-cent. church of St. Germain) during battle of Falaise-Argentan pocket (Aug., 1944) in Second World War.

Argentario, Monte (môn'tē ärjĕntä'rēô), outlier of the Apennines, Tuscany, central Italy, promontory in Tyrrhenian Sea, bordering on lagoon of ORBETELLO; 7 mi. long, 6 mi. wide; rises to 2,083 ft. (S). Formerly an isl., now connected with mainland by 2 tombolos and a causeway (1 mi. long) from Orbetello. Chief town, Porto Santo Stefano (N). Has manganiferous iron mines (E).

Argentat (ärzhãtä'), town (pop. 2,320), Corrèze dept., S central France, on the Dordogne (at S end of its gorge) and 14 mi. SE of Tulle; agr. trade center. Coal deposits near by.

Argenteau (ärzhãtō'), village (pop. 845), Liége prov., E Belgium, on Meuse R. and 7 mi. NNE of Liége; market center for fruitgrowing region.

Argentera (ärjĕntä'rä), village (pop. 105), Cuneo prov., Piedmont, NW Italy, 3 mi. SE of Maddalena Pass, near Fr. border, on Stura di Demonte R. and 31 mi. W of Cuneo; customs station.

Argentera, Colle dell': see MADDALENA PASS.

Argentera, Punta (pōōn'tä), or **Rocca dell'Argentera** (rôk'kä dĕl-lärjĕntä'rä), NW Italy, highest peak (10,817 ft.) in Maritime Alps, in Piedmont, 2 mi. N of Fr. border, 8 mi. SSW of Valdieri.

Argenteuil (ärzhãtû'ē), county (□ 783; pop. 22,670), SW Que., on Ont. border; ⊙ Lachute.

Argenteuil (ärzhãtû'ē), city (pop. 53,513), Seine-et-Oise dept., N central France, a NW suburb of Paris, 8 mi. from Notre Dame Cathedral, on right bank of the Seine; industrial center with large metalworks (aircraft motors, tractors, electrical apparatus, rolling stock, automobile parts). Other mfg.: rayon, rubber, pharmaceuticals, plaster, carton); ozocerite refining. Supplies Paris with asparagus and strawberries. Railroad yards. City grew around convent (founded 7th cent., destroyed in Fr. Revolution) in which Héloise became prioress. The Seamless Tunic, said to have been worn by Christ and given to convent by Charlemagne, is now enshrined in 19th-cent. church. City heavily damaged in Second World War.

Argentia (ärjĕn'shŭ, – shēŭ), village, SE N.F., on W coast of Avalon Peninsula, on Placentia Bay, 65 mi. WSW of St. John's; 46°42'N 53°59'W. Here is large U.S. base, obtained 1940 on 99-year lease from Great Britain. In August, 1941, the Atlantic Charter was signed by President Roosevelt and Winston Churchill aboard ships offshore. Argentia was formerly a herring- and salmon-fishing port.

Argentiera, Greece: see KIMOLOS.

Argentiera, Cape (ärjĕntyâ'rä), NW Sardinia, 25 mi. W of Sassari; 40°44'N 8°21'E. Lead and zinc mines.

Argentiera-Nurra (–nōō'rä) or **Argentiera e Nurra** (ā), village (pop. 3,394), Sassari prov., NW Sardinia, 18 mi. WNW of Sassari, on Cape Argentiera; lead and zinc mining.

Argentière or **Argentières** (ärzhãtyâr'), Alpine village of Haute-Savoie dept., SE France, resort in Chamonix valley, 5 mi. NNE of Chamonix, at NW foot of Mont Blanc massif; alt. 4,111 ft. Mountain climbing, winter sports. The Aiguille d'Argentière (12,818 ft.) rises 5 mi. ESE on Franco-Swiss border. From it and neighboring Mont Dolent descends the Argentière glacier (6 mi. long) to within 1 mi. of village.

Argentière, Col de l': see MADDALENA PASS.

Argentière-la-Bessée, L' (lärzhãtyâr'-lä-bĕsā'), Alpine commune (pop. 2,008), Hautes-Alpes dept., SE France, on the upper Durance and 9 mi. SSW of Briançon, at SE foot of Massif du Pelvoux; aluminum works. Silverbearing galena mined near by. Until 1941, called L'Argentière.

Argentina (ärjŭntē'nŭ) or the **Argentine** (är'jŭntēn), republic (□ 1,073,699; with water surface, □ 1,084,359; pop. 15,893,827), S South America; ⊙ BUENOS AIRES. The 2d largest nation of South America, Argentina is more than ⅓ the size of the U.S. Bet. the Andes on the W and the Atlantic on the E, it is an enormous triangle, stretching from the broad base near the Tropic of Capricorn southward c.2,300 mi. to the isl. tip of Tierra del Fuego, which points toward Antarctica. In the Atlantic off the far south are the Falkland Isls. (Sp. *Islas Malvinas*), claimed by Argentina but administered by the British. There are also large Argentine claims in Antarctica. Argentina in the NE fronts on the Río de la Plata, one of the major waterways of the Western Hemisphere, which separates Argentina from Uruguay. The tributary rivers also act as international boundaries of Argentina—the Uruguay, with Uruguay and Brazil; the Paraná and the Pilcomayo, with Paraguay. In the NW the land borders with Bolivia are in the arid Andean highlands and the semitropical CHACO. The W boundary with Chile follows the line of the Andes, in the highest elevations of the globe outside central Asia. The kingly ACONCAGUA (22,835 ft.) has at its foot USPALLATA PASS and the TRANSANDINE RAILWAY; it is only the highest of many snow-capped volcanoes, including LLULLAILLACO, MERCEDARIO, TUPUNGATO, and MAIPO. The climate of Argentina is as varied as its topography. Humidity, lowest in the rain-shadow of the eastern Andean slopes, increases markedly across plains of the PAMPA, the heart of Argentina, and across the "Wet Pampa" near the Atlantic, to reach its peak (over 60 in.) in the alluvial lowlands of the N and NE. In N Argentina, the Chaco and the physiographically similar Mesopotamia (bet. the Paraná and Uruguay rivers) are predominantly flat, but in the extreme NE the country reaches into the Brazilian highland and converges with Brazil and Paraguay at IGUASSÚ FALLS. The northern country—savannas and dense forests, interspersed with swamps—yields quebracho and mate as well as lumber, tung nuts, and castor beans; agr. produce (flaxseed, cotton, rice, and citrus fruits) comes chiefly from the cleared sections of the Mesopotamia in Entre Ríos and Corrientes provs. Only here and in the Andean highlands is the native Indian element still strong, and some place names still testify to the enterprise of the Jesuits who created reductions (Sp. *reducciones*) in the Chaco in the 17th cent. Pioneer settlements of East Europeans were planted in the 1930s and later, gaining considerable success in exploiting this neglected northern land. Just to the S the Pampa owes most of its fabulous success to hard-working Italian immigrants, who began to come there in numbers in the late 19th cent. Yet the gaucho, the nomadic herdsman of an earlier day—depicted in Martín Fierro, the great Argentine folk epic by José Hernández—is still a legendary natl. symbol. The vast, somewhat monotonous plain lies bet. the Chaco and Colorado R. (roughly 30°S to 40°S) and is some 400 mi. wide from the Atlantic to the Andean foothills; it comprises Buenos Aires prov., parts of Santa Fe, Santiago del Estero, Córdoba, and San Luis provs., and La Pampa natl. territory. Its deep soil is the basic wealth of the republic, for commerce and industry rely upon the products of its farms and ranches. As exporter of wheat, corn, and flaxseed, beef, mutton, hides, and wool, Argentina rivals the U.S., Canada, and Australia. Alfalfa, the leading crop, is grown to feed the cattle herds, which are among the world's finest. Truck gardening, dairying, and fruitgrowing grow more important about the city of Buenos Aires (coextensive with the federal dist.). Most of the principal cities of Argentina are on the Pampa, and Buenos Aires is leader of them all. The largest city of South America, cosmopolitan Buenos Aires is one of the great ports of the world, connected by rail not only to other cities of the Pampa and S Argentina, but also to Paraguay, Uruguay, and Brazil, to Chile by 2 routes (the Transandine, via Mendoza, and the Transandine of the North, via Salta, and to Bolivia via Tucumán. These lines, a road net, natl. and international airlines, and a small Argentine merchant marine built up in the Second World War give the nation the best communications system of the continent, with Buenos Aires in the hub. Industries center in the city, mostly processing plants but also some factories—meat-packing plants (*frigoríficos*), flour mills, sugar refineries, oil refineries, wineries, dairy plants, chemical works, textile mills, cement plants, machine shops, and printing plants. Near by are several industrial cities such as Avellaneda, Quilmes, and Lomas de Zamora. Elsewhere on the Pampa are La Plata, capital of Buenos Aires prov., supreme in meat packing; Rosario, 2d largest Argentine city, a huge grain port on the Paraná, nearly 250 mi. from the sea; Santa Fe, another Paraná port; Mar del Plata, a resort and fishing center on the Atlantic; and Bahía Blanca, the largest port directly on the Atlantic, acting with its 5 subports as gateway to the S part of the Pampa, the Plaza Huincul oil fields in Neuquén territory, and the Patagonian lake dist. On the W edge of the Pampa is the 3d city of the republic, picturesque Córdoba, with its old univ. and its trade in fruits and grain from the region irrigated by San Roque Dam. Córdoba shows the transition from the "Dry Pampa" to the desolation of the arid Andean foothills, mostly useful only for pasturing goats. In the great arid stretches there are, however, small but remarkably productive oases, settled from Peru and Upper Peru (Bolivia) in the 2d half of the 16th cent.—MENDOZA, SAN JUAN, TUCUMÁN, and SALTA. The oases produce wine, sugar, and all kinds of fruit. The minerals of this NW region (coal, salt, borates, quartz, mica, onyx, gypsum, wolfram, zinc, tin, copper, lead, and silver), exploited to a small extent earlier, have been subject to more development. The oil fields of Mendoza and Salta provs. in 1951 were of far greater economic value. They in turn were surpassed by the oil fields of PATAGONIA, in the COMODORO RIVADAVIA military dist.; these supply about 70% of Argentina's oil output, and a pipe line linking them with Buenos Aires was completed in 1950. Except for the oil fields, Argentine Patagonia is largely undeveloped, although in the NW section there is a region of blue lakes cupped in the Andes. Here NAHUEL HUAPÍ Natl. Park (established 1934), adjoining the Chilean lake dist., is a resort area, attractive both in winter and summer. Elsewhere Patagonia sweeps S c.1,000 mi. from the Colorado R. to Tierra del Fuego in bleak, wind-bitten plateaus, supporting little more than sheep grazing. Like Siberia in diversity, it also has gained a bad name from use as a penal colony. Mining (coal, kaolin, and gold) is negligible, and agr. is restricted to some subsistence farms in irrigated valleys. On the Atlantic a few small, river-mouth ports have fishing fleets, lumberyards, and processing plants—Viedma on the Río Negro, Rawson on the Chubut, Santa Cruz on the Santa Cruz, and Río Gallegos on the Gallegos. USHUAIA on Beagle Channel is called the southernmost town in the world. Into this forbidding country Welsh, Scottish, and English sheep ranchers came after 1880, and after the Second World War many Ital. immigrants arrived, while the influx of Chileans has always been tied to boundary disputes. Only a scant few of the native Indians remain. These once-warlike tribes were even lower in the scale of material culture than most of the Indians of Argentina. Only in NW Argentina was there an agr. people, under the influence of the Incas. They are recalled by ruins N of Jujuy, but their importance was eclipsed in later times by the immigration of Araucanian Indians from Chile. Elsewhere there were fierce warriors, who did much to hamper settlement but disappeared under white warfare and white pressure. Argentina, unlike most of the Latin American nations, has a population that is overwhelmingly of European descent. The Europeans probably 1st arrived in the region in 1502 in the voyage of Amerigo Vespucci (if the possibility of Phoenician discovery in anc. times is disregarded altogether). The search for a Southwest Passage to the Orient brought Juan Díaz de Solís to the Río de la Plata in 1516, but he was killed by Indians when he landed near the present Maldonado, Uruguay. Magellan entered (1520) the estuary, and Sebastian Cabot ascended the Paraná and the Paraguay. His delight in native ornaments may be responsible for the name of Río de la Plata [silver river] and the name of Argentina [of silver]. Pedro de Mendoza in 1536 founded the 1st settlement of the present Buenos Aires, but Indian attacks forced abandonment of the settlement, and Asunción became the unquestioned leading city of the Río de la Plata region. The settlement of Argentina, therefore, moved from W to E, in the opposite course from that of the U.S., for towns were established on the NW oases in direct connection with Spanish colonies in Peru and Chile before Buenos Aires was refounded in 1580 by Juan de Garay. His son-in-law, Hernando Árias de Saavedra (Hernandarias), one of the ablest of Spanish colonial administrators, secured the division of the Río de la Plata territories, and Buenos Aires achieved a sort of semi-independence under the viceroyalty of Peru. The mercantilist system favored by Spain and the other imperial nations, however, placed Buenos Aires under severely hampering commercial conditions, and smuggling became an accepted profession, particularly in commerce with the Portuguese in Brazil and with the British. While the cities of present W and NW Argentina grew by supplying the mining towns of the Andes, Buenos Aires was threatened by the activities of the Portuguese in the Banda Oriental. The disparate development of the cities foreshadowed the separatist tendencies of the provinces after the republic was created. In 1776 the Sp. govt. finally made Buenos Aires a free port and the capital of a viceroyalty that included present Argentina, Uruguay, Paraguay, and (briefly) Bolivia. From this combination grew the idea of a Greater Argentina to include all the Río de la Plata countries. This was the fundamental plan at the beginning, when the movement for independence from Spain got under way. Two Br. assaults in Buenos Aires (1806, 1807) were repelled by Argentine militia and helped to build up Creole self-confidence. On May 25, 1810 (May 25 is the Argentine natl. holiday), revolutionists, acting nominally in favor of the Bourbons dethroned by Napoleon, deposed the viceroy, and the govt. was controlled by a junta. The result was war against the royalists. The patriots under Manuel Belgrano won (1812) a victory at Tucumán. On July 9, 1816, a congress in Tucumán proclaimed the independence of the United Provs. of La Plata. Other patriot generals were Mariano Moreno and Juan Martín de Pueyrredón and, above all, that great liberator, José de San Martín. URUGUAY and PARAGUAY went their own way despite hopes of reunion, while in Argentina virtually permanent civil war followed independence, with countless coups d'état and ephemeral triumphs of regional, social, or political factions. Anarchy was not ended by the election of Bernardino Rivadavia in 1826, for the unitarians who favored a centralized govt. dominated by Buenos Aires were opposed to the federalists, who opposed the oligarchy of Buenos Aires and were backed by autocratic *caudillos* with gaucho troops. The unitarians temporarily triumphed when Argentinians combined to help the Uruguayans repel Brazilian conquerors in the battle of Ituzaingó (1827), which led to the independence of Uruguay. The internal conflict was, however, soon resumed and was not even quelled when Juan Manuel de Rosas, the most notorious *caudillo* of them all, established a dictatorship that lasted until 1852. He was overthrown (1852) by Justo José de Urquiza, who called a constituent assembly at Santa Fe, and a constitution was adopted (1853) based on the principles enunciated by Juan Bautista Alberdi. Mitre, denouncing Urquiza as a *caudillo*, brought about the secession of Buenos Aires prov. and the downfall of the Urquiza plans. Under the administrations of Mitre (1862–68), Sarmiento (1868–74), and Nicolás de Avellaneda (1874–80), schools were built, public works started, and liberal reforms instituted. The War of the Triple Alliance brought little advantage to Argentina. In 1880 the enemies of Buenos Aires triumphed. The city remained capital, but the federal dist. was cut up, and Buenos Aires prov. was given La Plata as its capital. Conquest of the Indians by Gen. Julio A. Roca made colonization of the region in the S and the SW possible. Already the Pampa had begun to undergo its agr. transformation, urged on particularly by the federalists. The immigration of Italians, Spanish (including Basques), French, Germans, British, Swiss, and East Europeans helped to fill the land and to make Argentina one of the world's granaries. Establishment of refrigerating plants for meat made expansion of commerce possible. The British not only were prime consumers of Argentine products but also invested substantially in building factories, public utilities, and railroads (which were nationalized in 1948). Efforts to end the power of the great creole landowners, however, were not genuinely successful, and the military tradition continued to play a part in politics, the army frequently combining with the conservatives and later with the growing ranks of labor to alter the govt. by coup d'état. A serious boundary dispute with Chile was settled in 1902, and perpetual peace bet. the 2 nations was symbolized in the Christ of the Andes, a statue in Uspallata Pass. A "palace revolt" in 1944 resulted in power residing in a group of army colonels, chief among them Juan Perón. Argentina belatedly (March, 1945) entered the Second World War on the side of the Allies and became a member of the U.N. Perón, who was overwhelmingly victorious in the election of Feb., 1946, established a type of popular dictatorship new to Latin America, based on support from reactionaries, workers, the army, nationalists, and the clerical groups. His regime promptly showed most of the characteristics of the European fascist governments. To cure Argentina's serious economic ills a program of economic self-sufficiency was inaugurated. The speed of industrialization was, however, limited by lack of power resources and machine tools. For further information, see special articles on cities, regions, physical features, and the following territorial units: provs. of BUENOS AIRES, CATAMARCA, CÓRDOBA, CORRIENTES, ENTRE RÍOS, JUJUY, LA RIOJA, MENDOZA, SALTA, SAN JUAN, SAN LUIS, SANTA FE, SANTIAGO DEL ESTERO, TUCUMÁN; territories of CHACO, CHUBUT, FORMOSA, LA PAMPA, MISIONES, NEUQUÉN, RÍO NEGRO, SANTA CRUZ, TIERRA DEL FUEGO; and military dist. of COMODORO RIVADAVIA. Chaco and La Pampa became provs. in 1951.

Argentina River, Italy: see TAGGIA RIVER.

Argentine (ärzhätēn'), village (pop. 308), Savoie dept., SE France, in Alpine Maurienne valley, near the Arc, 13 mi. SSW of Albertville; calcium carbide mfg., talc quarrying.

Argentine, Kansas: see KANSAS CITY, Kansas.

Argentine Mountain (10,000 ft.), SE B.C., in Selkirk Mts., on W edge of Hamber Provincial Park, 40 mi. NNE of Revelstoke; 51°33' N117°55'W.

Argentine Pass (är'jùntēn) (13,132 ft.), central Colo., in Front Range, bet. Clear Creek and Summit counties. Once crossed by wagon road, 1st used 1872; now crossed by trail. Grays Peak near by.

Argentino, Lake (ärhäntē'nō), large fresh-water lake (□ 546; alt. 613 ft.) in S Patagonian Andes of SW Santa Cruz natl. territory, Argentina; extends c.65 mi. E from Chile border. Its outlet (E) is Santa Cruz R. Its several W arms are fed by Andean glaciers. Lake is in a natl. park.

Argenton or **Argenton-sur-Creuse** (ärzhätō'-sür-krûz'), town (pop. 5,316), Indre dept., central France, on Creuse R. and 18 mi. SSW of Châteauroux; road and tourist center; textile milling (lingerie, woolen yarn), tanning, printing. Has two 15th-cent. churches, a restored 11th-cent. chapel, and ruins of a feudal castle overlooking Creuse valley. Region made famous by George Sand.

Argentona (ärhĕntō'nä), village (pop. 2,721), Barcelona prov., NE Spain, 2 mi. WNW of Mataró; mfg. (brandy, knitted goods). Wine, hemp, cereals, fruit in area. Mineral springs. Granite quarries, copper deposits near by.

Argenton-Château (ärzhätō'-shätō'), village (pop. 908), Deux-Sèvres dept., W France, on Argenton R. (tributary of Thouet R.) and 21 mi. ESE of Cholet; granite quarries. Has ruins of castle once lived in by Philippe de Comines.

Argenton-sur-Creuse, France: see ARGENTON.

Argentoratum, France: see STRASBOURG.

Argentré (ärzhäträ'), village (pop. 435), Mayenne dept., W France, 6 mi. E of Laval; woodworking.

Argentré-du-Plessis (-dü plĕsē'), village (pop. 867), Ille-et-Vilaine dept., W France, 18 mi. W of Laval; cider making, horse breeding. Near-by 14th-cent. Château des Rochers (restored 17th–18th cent.) was home of Mme. de Sévigné.

Argent-sur-Sauldre (ärzhä'-sür-sō'drù), village (pop. 1,425), Cher dept., central France, on Grande Sauldre R. and 12 mi. SW of Gien; metalworks; mfg. (pottery, shirts, footwear). Has a 15th-cent. church and a turreted castle.

Arges, province, Rumania: see PITESTI.

Arges River (är'jĕsh), Rum. *Arges*, S Rumania, in Muntenia, formed by 2 headstreams on S slopes of the Fagaras Mts., flows S past Curtea-de-Arges and SE past Pitesti, to Danube R. just W of Oltenita; 180 mi. long. Receives Dambovita R. (left). Used for logging. Linked (1949) with Bucharest by 13-mi. canal, supplying water to the capital.

Arghalasti, Greece: see ARGALASTE.

Arghana, Turkey: see ERGANI.

Arghandab River (ŭr'gŭndäb), anc. *Arachotus*, S Afghanistan, rises in S outliers of the Hindu Kush 110 mi. SW of Kabul, flows c.350 mi. SW, past Kandahar oasis, to Helmand R. at Qala Bist. Receives Arghastan R. (left). Irrigates rich section of Kandahar prov.

Arghastan River (ŭrgŭstän'), SE Afghanistan, formed c.100 mi. E of Kandahar, flows c.170 mi. W, past Maruf, to Arghandab R. 30 mi. WSW of Kandahar. Receives Tarnak R. (right).

Arghos Orestikon, Greece: see ARGOS ORESTIKON.

Arginusae (ärjĭnū'sē), anc. name of 3 islets off W coast of Asia Minor, near Lesbos, where the Athenians defeated the Spartans in 406 B.C.

Argirocastro, Albania: see ARGYROKASTRON.

Argo or **Argo Khandaq** (är'gō khän'däk), town, Northern Prov. Anglo-Egyptian Sudan, on left bank of the Nile, opposite N end of Argo isl. and 25 mi. N of Dongola; cotton, wheat, barley, corn, fruits, durra; livestock. Police post.

Argo, Ill.: see SUMMIT.

Argoed, England: see BEDWELLTY.

Argo Island, long narrow island in Nile R., N Anglo-Egyptian Sudan, opposite Argo and 10 mi. N of Dongola; 25 mi. long, 2 mi. wide. Cotton.

Argolas (ärgô'lùs), S suburb (pop. 7,039) of Vitória, central Espírito Santo, Brazil, across Espírito Santo Bay. Has capital's railroad station, airport.

Argolicus Sinus, Greece: see ARGOLIS, GULF OF.

Argolis (är'gùlĭs), region of Greece, in the NE Peloponnesus, roughly identical with the Argive plain around city of ARGOS; part of ARGOLIS AND CORINTHIA nome; its chief town is Nauplia.

Argolis, Gulf of, Gr. *Argolikos Kolpos*, Lat. *Argolicus Sinus*, inlet of Aegean Sea in E Peloponnesus, Greece, SW of Argolis Peninsula; 20 mi. wide, 30 mi. long. Receives Xerias R. Contains several small isls., including Spetsai at its entrance. Nauplia is on NW shore. Formerly called Gulf of Nauplia or Nauplion.

Argolis and Corinthia (kùrĭn'thēù) or **Argolis and Korinthia**, nome (□ 1,762; pop. 191,735), NE Peloponnesus, Greece; ⊙ NAUPLIA. Includes isls. off SE coast in Gulf of Argolis (SPETSAI isl). Mainland is bordered N by Gulf of Corinth, E and SE by Aegean Sea, SW by Arcadia, W by Achaea. Chief Zante-currant region of Greece; vegetables, tobacco, wheat; livestock raising (sheep, goats, hogs). Fisheries and sponge fishing along coast. Tourist trade. Industry centered at Argos. Main ports are Nauplia and Corinth. Anc. regions of ARGOLIS (S) and Corinthia (N) included cities of ARGOS, CORINTH, NEMEA, MYCENAE, and TIRYNS. Modern nome (administratively in E central Greece) is also called Argolis and Corinth; after Second World War it was divided into 2 nomes, Argolis (pop. 80,188) and Corinthia (pop. 111,547).

Argolis Peninsula, in E Peloponnesus, Greece, on Aegean Sea bet. Gulf of Argolis (SW) and Saronic Gulf (NE); terminates SE in Cape Skyllaion; 45 mi. long, 12–20 mi. wide. Except for E section (part of Attica nome), it is in Argolis and Corinthia nome. Nauplia on SW coast.

Argonia, city (pop. 562), Sumner co., S Kansas, on Chikaskia R. and 39 mi. SW of Wichita; grain.

Argonne (är'gŏn, Fr. ärgôn'), also called **Argonne Forest**, wooded ridge in N France, extending c.45 mi. SSE-NNW along Meuse-Marne dept. border and into Ardennes dept., forming natural barrier bet. Lorraine and Champagne regions. Flanked by Aisne R. (W). Cut by several gaps used by roads and railroads. Chief towns are Sainte-Menehould (S) and Vouziers (N), both on W slope. Its importance is mainly strategic. Here, in 1792, the French repulsed the Prussians at Valmy. Area was battleground throughout First World War. In Allied victory drive of Sept.–Nov., 1918, the Meuse-Argonne sector was carried by Americans. Regional name is also applied to larger area bet. the Aisne (W) and the Meuse (E).

Argonne, locality, Ill.: see LEMONT.

Argopuro, Mount, Indonesia: see ARGAPURA, MOUNT.

Argos (är'gŏs, är'gùs), city (pop. 13,503) of S (Argolis) section of Argolis and Corinthia nome, NE Peloponnesus, Greece, 23 mi. SSW of Corinth near head of Gulf of Argolis, in the Argive plain; rail and road center; trades in vegetables, tobacco, wheat, corn; vegetable canning, cigarette mfg. Occupied since early Bronze Age, Argos is reputed to be the oldest city of Greece. It was the center of anc. Argolis and dominated much of the Peloponnesus under Pheidon (8th–7th cent. B.C.) until the rise of Sparta; later Argos often sided with Athens. It had a school of fine arts in 5th cent. B.C. under Polycletus. Argos joined Achaean League in 229 B.C., continued to flourish after capture by Rome (146 B.C.), and through French, Venetian, and Turkish rules. Early seat of Gr. natl. assemblies. A prominent city in Gr. mythology, Argos was center of worship of the goddess Hera; ruins of a theater and a temple, the Heraeum, are 4 mi. NNE. W is the acropolis of Larissa.

Argos (är'gùs), town (pop. 1,284), Marshall co., N Ind., 30 mi. S of South Bend; dairying, lumber milling. Has fish hatchery. L. Maxinkuckee is WSW.

Argos Orestikon (är'gŏs ôrĕstĭkôn'), town (pop. 4,292), Kastoria nome, Macedonia, Greece, on Aliakmon R. and 5 mi. S of Kastoria; lumbering; charcoal burning; skins. Formerly called Khroupista. Also spelled Arghos Orestikon.

Argostoli (ärgôstôlē') or **Argostolion** (ärgôstô'lēōn), city (pop. 10,183), ⊙ Cephalonia nome, Greece, port on SW shore of Cephalonia isl., on 10-mi. long Argostoli Bay (opposite Lexourion), 90 mi. W of Patras. Trade center for currants, wine, olive oil; flour mills (powered by sea current). Seat of Gr. metropolitan. Ruins of anc. Cranii (SE).

Argovie, Switzerland: see AARGAU.

Arguedas (ärgā'dhäs), town (pop. 2,934), Navarre prov., N Spain, near the Ebro, 8 mi. N of Tudela; plaster mfg., flour milling; trades in sugar beets, cereals, alfalfa, vegetables.

Argueil (ärgû'ē), village (pop. 312), Seine-Inférieure dept., N France, 20 mi. ENE of Rouen; furniture.

Arguello, Point (ärgwĕ'lō), SW Calif., coastal promontory and westernmost point of Santa Barbara co., 12 mi. WSW of Lompoc; lighthouse.

Arguenon River (ärgnō'), Côtes-du-Nord dept., W France, rises in Landes du Méné E of Collinée, flows c.30 mi. N, past Broons and Jugon, to English Channel below Plancoët.

Arguin Bay (ärgwēn'), sheltered Atlantic inlet of W Mauritania, Fr. West Africa, 40 mi. ESE of Cap Blanc. Well-known fishing ground, chiefly for lobster. Cape Arguin is at SW entrance; 20°34'N 17°4'W.

Arguis (ärgēs'), village (pop. 204), Huesca prov., NE Spain, 12 mi. N of Huesca. Dam (1st built 1584) and hydroelectric plant near by.

Argungu (ärgōōng-gōō'), town (pop. 6,547), Sokoto prov., Northern Provinces, NW Nigeria, on Kebbi R. and 55 mi. WSW of Sokoto; agr. trade center (cotton, millet, rice); timber; cattle and skins. Limestone deposits.

Argun River or **Argun' River** (ärgōōn', ärgōō'nyù), right headstream of Amur R., on Manchuria-USSR line, rises as the Hailar in the Great Khingan Mts., flows W, past Hailar, along Chinese Eastern RR, to USSR frontier, where it has intermittent connections (S) with lake HULUN NOR. As the Argun proper, it forms 500-mi. section of international frontier until it joins the Shilka to form the Amur. Total length, including Hailar section, 950 mi. Silver-lead ore and coal are found along its banks.

Argun River (ŭrgōōn′), in Georgian SSR and Grozny oblast, Russian SFSR, rises in Georgian section of the Greater Caucasus, 25 mi. ESE of Mt. Kazbek; flows 100 mi. NNE, past Akhalkhevi, Sovetskoye, and Predgornoye, to Sunzha R. 12 mi. ENE of Grozny.

Argusville, village (pop. 126), Cass co., E N.Dak., 14 mi. NNW of Fargo.

Argyle (är′gīl). **1** Town (pop. 244), Clinch co., S Ga., 20 mi. WSW of Waycross. **2** Township (pop. 133), Penobscot co., S central Maine, on the Penobscot just above Old Town; agr., lumbering. **3** Village (pop. 846), Marshall co., NW Minn., on Middle R. and 10 mi. N of Warren, in grain area; dairy products, beverages. **4** Town (pop. 162), Osage co., central Mo., 21 mi. SSE of Jefferson City. **5** Village (pop. 351), Washington co., E N.Y., 5 mi. ESE of Fort Edward, in dairying area. Lakes near by. **6** Village (pop. 702), Lafayette co., S Wis., on East Branch of Pecatonica R. and 35 mi. SW of Madison, in agr. area; cheese, sorghum, canned vegetables.

Argyll or **Argyllshire** (ärgīl′, –shĭr), county (□ 3,110.1; 1931 pop. 63,050; 1951 census 63,270), W Scotland; ⊙ Inverary. Bounded by Buteshire (S), the Atlantic and North Channel (W), Inverness (N), and Perthshire and Dumbarton (E). Drained by several small rivers, has deeply indented coastline, and includes numerous isls., among them S part of the Inner Hebrides (Mull, Coll, Tiree, Colonsay, Oronsay, Iona, Islay, and others) and Kintyre peninsula. Surface is wild and mountainous, rising to Ben Cruachan (3,689 ft.). The county's beautiful scenery has made it the setting of many literary works, and it has numerous tourist resorts. Main sea inlets are lochs Shiel, Linnhe, Leven, and Fyne; Loch Awe is largest inland lake. Agr. is limited to coastal areas; oats, barley, and hay are chief crops; sheep and cattle grazing. Herring fisheries are important. Granite and slate are quarried; industries include aluminum processing (Kinlochleven), woolen milling, and whisky distilling (Islay and Campbeltown). Other towns are Dunoon, Oban, Tarbert, and Lochgilphead. There are many anc. castles and monastic ruins; Iona has noted church and relics of early Christian civilization. Dunstaffanage Castle, near Oban, was seat of government of the Scots from c.500 until after their union with the Picts in 844. Argyll was setting of many clan wars, and is 2d-largest co. of Scotland.

Argyllshire, Scotland: see ARGYLL.

Argyrokastron (är′jĭrōkă″strŏn) or **Aryirokastron** (Gr. äryērô′kästrôn) [Gr., =silver castle], Albanian Gheg *Gjinokastër* or *Gjinokastra* (gyēnôkäs′trŭ,–rä), Albanian Tosk *Gjirokastrë* or *Gjirokastra*, Ital. *Argirocastro*, Turkish *Eregri-Kasri*, city (1945 pop. 10,910), S Albania, 45 mi. SE of Valona, on the Drin (left tributary of Vijosë R.); commercial center; dairy products, tobacco, vineyards; silversmithing, tanning. Airport. Center of the Bektashi (Moslem sect). Has 18th-cent. mosques, Orthodox cathedral (1774), and citadel (rebuilt in 19th cent. on Venetian foundations). Built near site of anc. Adrianopolis, the city dates probably from 4th cent., passed to Venetians and (1460) to Turks. Captured (1811) by Ali Pasha; was (late 19th cent.) center of Albanian resistance against Turks. Under Ital. occupation (1915–20); an independent Albania under Ital. protection was proclaimed here (1917). During Second World War, held (1940–41) by Gr. troops.

Arheilgen (är″hīl′gŭn), N suburb (pop. 10,255) of Darmstadt, W Germany, 2.5 mi. N of city center. Inc. 1937 into Darmstadt.

Aria (â′rēŭ, ŭrī′ŭ), province of anc. Persian Empire, astride the river Arius (modern Hari Rud) and corresponding roughly to Herat prov. of modern Afghanistan.

Ariake Bay (ä″rē′ä′kē), Jap. *Ariake-wan*, inlet of Philippine Sea, SE Kyushu, Japan, bet. Cape Toi (E) and Osumi Peninsula (W); 3 mi. long, 3 mi. wide. Uchinoura on SW shore. Sometimes called Shibushi Bay.

Ariakeno-umi (ärē′ä′kānō-ōō″mē), gulf of Amakusa Sea, NW Kyushu, Japan, bet. Hizen Peninsula (W) and mainland (E); merges S with Shimabara Bay; 20 mi. long N-S, 17 mi. wide E-W. Omuta on E shore.

Arial (â′rēŭl), mill village (pop. 1,098), Pickens co., NW S.C., just NW of Easley. Post office name, Ariail.

Arial Khan River (är′yäl khän′), in East Bengal, E Pakistan, a distributary of Ganges Delta, leaves Padma R. 15 mi. E of Faridpur, flows c.150 mi. generally S, past Madaripur and Barisal, here dividing into several distributaries, to Bay of Bengal W of Meghna R. mouth. Main distributaries include Bishkhali and Patuakhali rivers. Navigable for entire course by river steamers.

Ariana or **Aryana** (ărēä′nŭ, –ä′nŭ), region of anc. Persian Empire, corresponding roughly to the Iranian plateau, but extending N to the river Oxus (modern Amu Darya) and E to the Indus.

Ariana or **El-Ariana** (ĕl äryänä′), N residential suburb (pop. 9,668) of Tunis, N Tunisia; woolen mill; orange and olive groves, vineyards.

Ariancoupom, Fr. India: see ARIYANKUPPAM.

Ariankavu (ŭrēŭngkä′vōō), pass (alt. c.1,000 ft.) in Western Ghats, S India, just W of Shencottah; 18 mi. long E-W; used for rail tunnel.

Ariano (ärēä′nô), village (pop. 1,566), Salerno prov., Campania, S Italy, 3 mi. NW of Eboli; paper milling. Hydroelectric plant near by.

Ariano Irpino (ērpē′nô), town (pop. 9,473), Avellino prov., Campania, S Italy, 17 mi. ENE of Benevento; mfg. (cement, pottery, macaroni, textiles); wine, olive oil. Bishopric. Has cathedral, castle, and ruins of medieval walls. Gypsum mines near by. Formerly Ariano di Puglia.

Ariano nel Polesine (nĕl pôlā′zēnĕ), village (pop. 2,552), Rovigo prov., Veneto, N Italy, on Po R. delta mouth and 8 mi. SSE of Adria; rail terminus; agr.-machinery factories.

Ariany (äryänē′), village (pop. 1,125), Majorca, Balearic Isls., 25 mi. ENE of Palma; grain growing. Has Franciscan nunnery.

Ariari River (ärēä′rē), Meta intendancy, E central Colombia, rises at SE foot of Páramo de Sumapaz near Cundinamarca border, flows c.160 mi. SE, through llano grasslands, to Guaviare R. 9 mi. W of San José del Guaviare. Some gold placers in its valley.

Árias (är′yäs), town (pop. 2,726), SE Córdoba prov., Argentina, 70 mi. SSW of Marcos Juárez; grain, cattle.

Ari Atoll, central group (pop. 3,760) of Maldive Isls., in Indian Ocean, bet. 3°30′N and 4°18′N, just W of Male Atoll.

Arica (ärē′kä), town (pop. 14,064), ⊙ Arica dept. (□ 6,379; pop. 21,836), Tarapacá prov., N Chile, port on the Pacific at mouth of the Quebrada de Azapa, just S of Peru border, 125 mi. N of Iquique, at N edge of the Atacama Desert; 18°28′S 70°19′W. Rail terminus (Since 1913) of line from La Paz (Bolivia) and of branch from Tacna (Peru). Trading, fishing, and mfg. center. Exports tin, copper, tungsten ores, sulphur, borax, hides, and llama wool from Bolivia and N Chile. Cotton gins, spaghetti factories, wool-packing plants. Some agr. in irrigated area (olives, oranges, vegetables, cotton, alfalfa) and in adjoining Lluta and Azapa valleys. It is a beach resort for Bolivian society. Maintains customhouses for Bolivia and Peru, for which Arica is a free port. The town is built at the foot of El Morro headland, where in 1880, during War of the Pacific, the Chileans were victorious over Peruvians. Arica was severely damaged in 1868 earthquake. Like the greater part of N Chile, it has an almost completely rainless climate, but the cool Peruvian current keeps the temp. moderate. Town dates from pre-Columbian days and was conquered by the Incas in 1250. A Peruvian port during colonial times, it was occupied 1880 by Chile and (with Tacna) awarded to Chile by treaty of Ancón (1883). The Tacna-Arica dispute was finally settled 1929, when Tacna was awarded to Peru while Chile retained Arica.

Aricagua (ärēkä′gwä), town (pop. 859), Sucre state, NE Venezuela, in coastal range adjoining Cumanacoa, 24 mi. SE of Cumaná; sugar cane, coffee, cacao.

Ariccia (ärēt′chä), resort town (pop. 4,854), Roma prov., Latium, central Italy, near L. Albano, 6 mi. WNW of Velletri; soap mfg.; stone quarrying. Badly damaged in Second World War.

Aricha, El- (ĕl-ärēshä′), village, Oran dept., NW Algeria, on border of Aïn-Sefra territory, 45 mi. S of Tlemcen, in the High Plateaus; road junction and military post.

Arichat (ă′rŭshät″, ărĭshät′), village (pop. estimate 750), ⊙ Richmond co., E N.S., on S coast of Madame Isl., just S of Cape Breton Isl., 18 mi. ESE of Port Hawkesbury; 45°31′N 61°1′W; fishing port; lumbering. First settled by the French c.1730; raided by John Paul Jones during American Revolution.

Arichuna (ärēchōō′nä), town (pop. 830), Apure state, W central Venezuela, in llanos 30 mi. SE of San Fernando; cattle.

Arico or **Lomo de Arico** (lō′mō dhā ärē′kō), town (pop. 575), Tenerife, Canary Isls., 24 mi. SW of Santa Cruz de Tenerife; cereals, potatoes, tomatoes, bananas, oranges, wine, honey, goats; cheese processing.

Aride Island (pop. 25), one of the Seychelles, in Indian Ocean, 5 mi. NNW of Praslin Isl.; 4°13′S 55°40′E; 1 mi. long, ⅓ mi. wide; granite formation. Copra; fisheries.

Aridh, 'Aridh, or **'Arid** (ä′rĭdh), district of Nejd, Saudi Arabia; chief town, Riyadh. Group of oases constituting political center of Nejd and the heart of Wahabism.

Arie (ä″rē′ä), town (pop. 9,848), Nagasaki prefecture, W Kyushu, Japan, on SE Shimabara Peninsula, 25 mi. ESE of Nagasaki; health resort (hot springs).

Ariège (ärēĕzh′), department (□ 1,893; pop. 145,956), S France, formerly part of county of Foix and of Languedoc prov.; ⊙ Foix. Bounded by Spain and Andorra (S). Occupied by central Pyrenees (in S is Pic de Montcalm, 10,105 ft. high) and their ramifications. The valleys of Ariège and Salat rivers (flowing S-N) provide only access to the crest of Pyrenees. Lumbering and grazing in mts. Agr. (corn, wheat, potatoes, fruits, wine) along rivers and in N lowlands. Iron, lead, bauxite mines; marble, talc, stone quarries. Hydroelectric plants power important electrometallurgical industry (Tarascon, Perles-et-Castelet, Pamiers), chemical works (Auzat, Mercus-Garrabet), paper mills (Saint-Girons area), textile factories (Lavelanet, Foix, Saverdun). The Hers R. valley specializes in comb mfg. Chief towns: Pamiers, Foix, Saint-Girons. Ax-les-Thermes is leading resort.

Ariège River, Ariège and Haute-Garonne depts., S France, rises in E Pyrenees on Andorra border, flows 106 mi. generally NNW, past Ax-les-Thermes, Tarascon, Foix, and Pamiers, to the Garonne 6 mi. above Toulouse; activates numerous hydroelectric plants. Its upper valley provides access to the Col de Puymorens and to Spain. Receives the Hers (right).

Ariel Dam, Wash.: see LEWIS RIVER.

Arienzo (ärēĕn′tsô), town (pop. 3,144), Caserta prov., Campania, S Italy, 17 mi. NE of Naples; shoe mfg.

Aries River (ä′rēēsh), Rum. *Arieş*, Hung. *Aranyos* (ŏ′rŏnyōsh), in W central and central Rumania, Transylvania, rises in Apuseni Mts. at E foot of Bihor, flows 80 mi. E, past Campeni, Baia-de-Aries, and Turda, to Mures R. 3 mi. W of Ludus. Noted for its gold-bearing sands exploited for centuries.

Arifiye (ärĭ′fĭyĕ″), village (pop. 1,999), Kocaeli prov., NW Turkey, 5 mi. SSW of Adapazari; rail junction.

Arifwala (ŭrĭfvä′lŭ), town (pop. 7,553), Montgomery dist., SE Punjab, W Pakistan, 25 mi. S of Montgomery; wheat, cotton, millet; cotton ginning. Forest plantation 10 mi. N. Sometimes written Arif Wala.

Arigna, Gaelic *Airgneach*, village, Co. Leitrim, Ireland, near Lough Allen, 11 mi. NE of Boyle; coal mining. Iron mines here are now closed down.

Ariguanabo, Lake (ärēgwänä′bō) (5 mi. long, 2½ mi. wide), Havana prov., W Cuba, in Ariguanabo depression, 18 mi. SW of Havana. Largest inland body of water of the isl.

Arija (ärē′hä), town (pop. 1,631), Burgos prov., N Spain, on railroad and 34 mi. SSW of Santander; cereals, potatoes, fruit. Sand quarrying.

Arikaree River (ărĭkâ′rē), Colo. and Nebr., rises in several branches in N Lincoln co., Colo.; flows 129 mi. ENE to Haigler, SW Nebr., here joining North Fork Republican R. to form Republican R. Intermittent flow in Colo.

Arikawa (ärē′käwŭ), town (pop. 11,058), on Nakadori-shima of isl. group Goto-retto, Nagasaki prefecture, Japan, on E.China Sea. Chief town of isl.; whaling, fishing.

Arild (ä′rĭld″), fishing village (pop. 276), Malmohus co., S Sweden, on Skalder Bay of the Kattegat, on E coast of Kullen peninsula, 17 mi. NNW of Halsingborg; seaside resort. Has 11th-cent. chapel.

Arilje or **Arilye** (ä′rĭlyĕ), village (pop. 759), W Serbia, Yugoslavia, on Western Morava R. and 15 mi. SE of Titovo Uzice.

Arima (ŭrē′mŭ), town (pop. 8,069), N Trinidad, B.W.I., on railroad and 16 mi. E of Port of Spain, at head of extensive plain. Once flourishing cacao center, the town has recovered through establishment of adjoining (E) Fort Read, U.S. army base. Originally a native Indian village and mission.

Arimalam (ŭrĭmŭlŭm′), town (pop. 6,620), Trichinopoly dist., S Madras, India, 9 mi. SE of Pudukkottai; fiber-basket weaving; rice, palmyra palms.

Arimao River (ärēmou′), Las Villas prov., central Cuba, flows c.50 mi. WSW to the Caribbean just E of Cienfuegos Bay. Receives Hanabanilla R., noted for its waterfall.

Arimatsu (ä″rē′mätsōō), town (pop. 3,502), Aichi prefecture, central Honshu, Japan, just SE of Nagoya; rice, wheat, raw silk.

Ariminum, Italy: see RIMINI.

Arimo (â′rĭmō), village (pop. 337), Bannock co., SE Idaho, 25 mi. SE of Pocatello; alt. 4,736 ft. Wheat, oats, potatoes, livestock.

Aringay (ärēng′ī, –gī), town (1939 pop. 1,576; 1948 municipality pop. 13,079), La Union prov., N central Luzon, Philippines, on railroad and 16 mi. W of Baguio, near Lingayen Gulf; rice, gypsum.

Ariño (ärē′nyō), town (pop. 1,205), Teruel prov., E Spain, 24 mi. W of Alcañiz; olive oil, wine, honey. Sulphur springs. There are lignite mines near by.

Arinos River (ärē′nōōs), N Mato Grosso, Brazil, rises near 14°30′S 56°15′W along the Amazon-Paraguay watershed, flows c.400 mi. NNW to the Juruena. Considered longest headstream of Tapajós R. Interrupted by rapids.

Arinthod (ärētō′), village (pop. 720), Jura dept., E France, in the Jura, 14 mi. W of Saint-Claude; wood turning. Has 12th-cent. church.

Ario (är′yō). **1** Officially Ario de Bayón, town (pop. 2,304), Michoacán, central Mexico, on railroad and 5 mi. NW of Zamora; cereals, sugar cane, vegetables, livestock. Sometimes Santa Mónica Ario. **2** or **Ario de Rosales** (dā rōsä′lĕs), town (pop. 5,924), Michoacán, central Mexico, on SW edge of central plateau, 20 mi. SE of Uruapan; alt. 6,700 ft. Agr. center (cereals, tobacco, sugar cane, tropical fruit). Lumbering.

Arion, town (pop. 220), Crawford co., W Iowa, on Boyer R. and 30 mi. WSW of Carroll.

Aripo, Mount (ŭrĭ'pō), or **Cerro de Aripo** (sĕ'rō dā ärē'pō), peak (3,085 ft.), N Trinidad, B.W.I., highest peak of the Br. colony of Trinidad and Tobago, 19 mi. ENE of Port of Spain.

Aripuanã (ärēpwŭnä'), city, NW Mato Grosso, Brazil, on upper Aripuanã R. and 400 mi. S of Manaus (Amazonas); 9°45'S 59°40'W.

Aripuanã River, SE Amazonas, Brazil, rises in NW Mato Grosso, flows c.400 mi. N to the Madeira (right bank) 75 mi. NE of Manicoré. Receives Roosevelt R. (left). Navigable in lower course, which is sometimes called the Roosevelt.

Ariquemes (ărēkä'mĭs), town, Guaporé territory, W Brazil, on Cuiabá-Pôrto Velho telegraph line; 9°55'S 63°7'W.

Ariranha (ărērä'nyŭ), city (pop. 1,116), N central São Paulo, Brazil, 45 mi. SE of São José do Rio Prêto; coffee processing, distilling, sugar milling, pottery mfg.

Arisaig (ă'rĭsăg), fishing village in Arisaig and Moidart parish (pop. 1,175), W Inverness, Scotland, on the Atlantic, 29 mi. WNW of Fort William.

Ari San, Formosa: see ALI SHAN.

Arish, El, or **Al-'Arish** (both: ĕl ärēsh'), anc. *Rhinocolura*, town (pop. 10,791), ⊙ Sinai prov., NE Egypt, on Mediterranean Sea, on Cairo-Haifa RR, and 90 mi. E of Port Said. Has a hospital and several schools. Here, the French signed (1800) the treaty by which they undertook to evacuate Egypt. In First World War it was taken (1916) by the British.

Arismendi (ärēzmĕn'dē), town (pop. 378), Barinas state, W Venezuela, on Guanare R. and 45 mi. WNW of La Unión; cattle.

Arispe, Mexico: see ARIZPE.

Arispe (ŭrĭs'pē), town (pop. 110), Union co., S Iowa, on Grand R. and 10 mi. SE of Creston.

Arissa, Lake (ä'rēsä), in salt marshes of AUSSA dist., NE Ethiopia, near French Somaliland border, 10 mi. NE of L. Abbé; c.5 mi. long.

Arista (ärē'stä), town (pop. 432), San Luis Potosí, N central Mexico, 35 mi. NNE of San Luis Potosí; alt. 5,410 ft.; wheat, corn, beans, cotton, maguey.

Aristazabal Island (ă'rĭstăzŭbăl'), (□ 149; 28 mi. long, 10 mi. wide), W B.C., in Hecate Strait, just W of Princess Royal Isl. across Laredo Channel; 52°40'N 128°8'W. Wooded surface is hilly, rises to 1,085 ft. (S). Just N is small Rennison Isl.

Arita (ä"rē'tä), town (pop. 8,103), Saga prefecture, W Kyushu, Japan, on central Hizen Peninsula, 11 mi. E of Sasebo; rail junction in agr. area (rice, wheat); known for porcelain ware.

Aritao (ärētä'ō, -tou'), town (1939 pop. 1,633; 1948 municipality pop. 7,322), Nueva Vizcaya prov., central Luzon, Philippines, on Cagayan R. and 11 mi. SSW of Bayombong; rice-growing center.

Ariton (ă'rŭtŭn), farming town (pop. 620), Dale co., SE Ala., 21 mi. SE of Troy.

Aritzo (ärēt'tsō), village (pop. 2,445), Nuoro prov., central Sardinia, 26 mi. SSW of Nuoro; wood carving.

Arius, Afghanistan: see HARI RUD.

Arivechi (ärēvä'chē), town (pop. 944), Sonora, NW Mexico, on affluent of Yaqui R. and 110 mi. E of Hermosillo; corn, beans, cattle.

Arivonimano (ä"rēvōonēmä'nōō), town, Tananarive prov., central Madagascar, on highway and 22 mi. WSW of Tananarive; alt. 4,850 ft; cattle market. Site of airport for Tananarive.

Ariyalur (ŭrĭyŭlōōr'), town (pop. 10,018), Trichinopoly dist., S Madras, India, 32 mi. NE of Trichinopoly; cotton pressing and weaving, peanut-oil extraction, sheep raising; cattle market.

Ariyankuppam (ŭrĭyăng'kōōpŭm), Fr. *Ariancoupom* (äryäkōōpō'), town (commune pop. 18,793), Pondicherry settlement, Fr. India; suburb of Pondicherry, 5 mi. SSW of city center; betel farming; mango gardens.

Ariyanur, India: see VIRAPANDI, Salem dist., Madras.

Ariza (ärē'thä), town (pop. 2,544), Saragossa prov., NE Spain, on Jalón R. and 23 mi. WSW of Calatayud, in agr. area (sugar beets, wine, cereals); mfg. (linen cloth, tiles, glass). In rocks near by are pre-Moorish cave dwellings.

Arizaro, Salar de (sälär' dā ärēsä'rō), salt desert (□ 1,700; alt. 12,000 ft.) in the Puna de Atacama, W Salta prov., Argentina; c.100 mi. N-S (c.50 mi. wide). Contains sodium and carbonate salts.

Arize River (ärēz'), Ariège and Haute-Garonne depts., S France, rises in the Plantaurel range, flows 25 mi. generally N, past Le Mas-d'Azil (where it traverses a cavern) and Rieux, to the Garonne above Carbonne.

Arizgoiti, Spain: see BASAURI.

Arizona (ă"rĭzō'nŭ), state (land □ 113,580; with inland waters □ 113,909; 1950 pop. 749,587; 1940 pop. 499,261), SW U.S., bordered S by Mexico, E by N.Mex., N by Utah, W by Nev. and Calif.; 5th in area, 37th in pop.; admitted 1912 as 48th state; ⊙ Phoenix. The state, whose extreme dimensions are 395 mi. N-S and 345 mi. E-W, consists of high plateaus, deep chasms, short mtn. ranges, and desert plains. It is wholly within drainage basin of COLORADO RIVER, which cuts through NW corner and then bends S to form most of W boundary. N Ariz. lies on the COLORADO PLATEAU, an extensive upland region (here c.5-7,000 ft. high), marked by spectacular gorges, colorful buttes and mesas, lava flows, and volcanic cones. Most prominent feature is the famous GRAND CANYON of the Colorado, isolating the Kaibab and Kanab plateaus (NW) from the rest of the state. In NE section, drained by Little Colorado R., chief features are the BLACK MESA, PAINTED DESERT, METEOR CRATER, and San Francisco Peaks, culminating in Humphreys Peak (12,655 ft.), highest point in the state. The plateau region terminates (S) in several deeply eroded escarpments (including Mogollon Rim), which overlook a mtn. belt 70-150 mi. wide and stretching NW-SE across center of the state; average elevation of mts. is 4-5,000 ft., with some peaks rising to 8-10,000 ft. In S Ariz., the desert plains form an extension of the Great Basin prov. of Nev. and S Calif., although most of the section drains to the sea (Gulf of Calif.) via GILA RIVER, a tributary of the Colorado. The block mtn. ranges in the SW are widely separated and rarely over 3,000 ft. in alt., while those in the SE are more compact and attain heights of 7-9,000 ft. Arizona's dry, salubrious climate is characterized by low humidity, clear air, and many days (c.80%) of sunshine; rainfall varies from less than 5 in. in SW and 8-15 in. in N to 25-30 in. on higher mtn. slopes, where there is also a winter snowfall. Phoenix (S center) has mean temp. of 52°F. in Jan. and 90°F. in July, with annual rainfall of c.8 in. Flagstaff (N center) has mean temp. of 27°F. in Jan. and 65°F. in July, with 21 in. of rainfall. The arid conditions are reflected in the predominantly desert type of vegetation, represented by cacti, yuccas, and creosote bushes in subtropical S and by juniper and piñon in N tablelands; along edge of Colorado Plateau and in E mtn. section—beginning at alt. of c.7,000 ft.—is an extensive belt of valuable evergreen forests. Of state's land area, 73% is in federal ownership, including vast stretches of range land (where beef cattle and sheep are raised) and c.12,000,000 acres of natl. forest reserves. Agr., depending almost entirely upon irrigation, has been limited by the available water supply. Although small areas of dry farming exist (mainly at alt. of c.5,000 ft.), the bulk of cropland is concentrated in the valleys of SALT RIVER and Gila, Santa Cruz, Verde, and Agua Fria rivers, where federal and state projects, such as Roosevelt; Coolidge, and Horse Mesa storage dams and numerous wells irrigate over 800,000 acres. Farming is intensive and highly commercialized. Chief crops are cotton (both long and short staple), picked by Indians, Mexicans, and migratory workers from other states, and barley, alfalfa, grain sorghums, wheat, hay, oats, lettuce, cantaloupes, carrots, citrus fruit, and dates. Main distributing centers are Phoenix, Yuma, Glendale, Temple, and Casa Grande. In the higher mtn. areas are large forests of ponderosa pine (c.85%), Douglas fir, white fir, and Engelmann spruce, supplying timber for sawmills in Flagstaff, Williams, and McNary. Arizona's considerable mineral wealth is based largely on copper (35-40% of natl. output), gold, silver, lead, and zinc. Other reserves include asbestos, molybdenum, tungsten, manganese, building stone, and helium (near Holbrook). Chief copper mining dists., near which are reduction and smelting plants, are Miami, Bisbee, Morenci, Globe, Ajo, Jerome, Ray, and Superior. Primary smelting and refining comprise state's main industry; lumbering, meat packing, food processing, cotton ginning, flour milling, and tanning are also important. Phoenix, Tucson, Douglas, Prescott are principal mfg. centers Winter tourists, attracted by Arizona's dry, healthful climate, constitute important source of revenue. Points of interest include Grand Canyon Natl. Park and Petrified Forest, Organ Pipe Cactus, Chiricahua, Tuzigoot, and Navajo natl. monuments, old mining towns such as TOMBSTONE and Wickenburg, and the larger resorts of Phoenix, Tucson, and Flagstaff. Handicraft items (blankets, rugs, leather goods, wood novelties, baskets, pottery) are produced for the tourist trade, especially by the Indian pop. (over 55,000), who are mainly Navahos, Apaches, and Hopis (Pueblo Indians) living on reservations. Archaeological discoveries (from cliff and pueblo dwellings) in many places throughout Ariz. have shed much light on the early Indian cultures of the Southwest. The 1st white men to reach what is now Ariz. were Spanish explorers, including Francisco Coronado (1540-42), and missionaries, notably the Jesuit Father Kino (1690s). After Mexican war of independence from Spain, area became (1824) part of territory of Nuevo Mexico (⊙ Santa Fe); about this time American trappers such as Bill Williams began to make their way along the lower Colorado and Gila rivers. By Treaty of Guadalupe Hidalgo (1848) and Gadsden Purchase (1853) Ariz. was ceded to the U.S., forming W half of N.Mex. territory until 1863, when it was made a separate territory. In 1850s gold, silver, and copper were discovered, followed by mining booms (e.g., at Bisbee and Tombstone) in the '70s and '80s; and many settlers arrived with the completion (1880s) of the transcontinental railroads. Fierce Apache uprisings were quelled in 1862 and 1886. After withdrawal of recall-of-judges clause in draft constitution because of presidential objection, Ariz. became a state in 1912; recall provision restored later that year. Of major concern to the state is the efficient use of both river and underground water for irrigation. The Univ. of Ariz. is at Tucson, Ariz. State Col. at Tempe. For further information see articles on cities, towns, physical features, and the 14 counties: APACHE, COCHISE, COCONINO, GILA, GRAHAM, GREENLEE, MARICOPA, MOHAVE, NAVAJO, PIMA, PINAL, SANTA CRUZ, YAVAPAI, YUMA.

Arizpe (ärē'spä), city (1,126), Sonora, NW Mexico, on Sonora R. and 100 mi. NNE of Hermosillo; mining center (silver, gold, copper); agr. (wheat, corn, sugar, livestock). Anc. colonial ⊙ of Sonora and Sinaloa Sometimes Arispe.

Arjang (ôr'yĕng"), Swedish *Årjäng*, town (pop. 1,338), Varmland co., W Sweden, at N end of L. Sil, 25 mi. SW of Arvika; rail junction; agr. market (grain, stock). Resort.

Arjay, village (1940 pop. 890), Bell co., SE Ky., in the Cumberlands, 14 mi. N of Middlesboro, in bituminous-coal mining area.

Arjeplog (är'yŭplōōg"), village (pop. 830), Norrbotten co., N Sweden, bet. lakes Hornavan and Uddjaur, 100 mi. W of Boden; Lapp trading center, scene of annual fair. Site of Lapp school and old-age home.

Arjish, village, Turkey: see ERCIS.

Arjona (ärhō'nä), town (pop. 10,416), Bolívar dept., N Colombia, in Caribbean lowlands, on railroad and 18 mi. SE of Cartagena; commercial town in sugar and cattle region; sugar refinery; rail point for sugar plantations.

Arjona, city (pop. 10,169), Jaén prov., S Spain, 19 mi. NW of Jaén; agr. trade center. Mfg. of pottery, soap, olive oil; tanning, flour milling. Cereals, vegetables, livestock in area. Clay quarries.

Arjonilla (ärhōnē'lyä), town (pop. 6,042), Jaén prov., S Spain, 24 mi. NW of Jaén; olive-oil processing, wine distilling; trades in cereals.

Arjuno, Mount, Mount Ardjuno, or **Mount Ardjoeno** (all: ärjōō'nō), volcanic peak (9,968 ft.), E Java, Indonesia, 40 mi. SSW of Surabaya. Also Arjuna.

Arkabutla (ärkŭbŭt'lŭ), village (pop. 207), Tate co., NW Miss., c.30 mi. S of Memphis (Tenn.), on SW shore of Arkabutla Reservoir.

Arkabutla Dam, Miss.: see COLDWATER RIVER.

Arkadak (ŭrkŭdäk'), town (1939 pop. over 10,000), W Saratov oblast, Russian SFSR, near Khoper R., on railroad and 30 mi. NNE of Balashov; distilling, flour milling, sunflower-oil extraction.

Arkadelphia (är"kŭdĕl'fēŭ), city (pop. 6,819), ⊙ Clark co., S central Ark., 26 mi. S of Hot Springs and on Ouachita R. (head of navigation), in timber, diversified farm area; mfg. of wood products, flour, candy, feed; lumbering, cotton ginning. Seat of Ouachita Col. and a state teachers col. First settled c.1807, inc. 1836.

Arkadhia, Greece: see ARCADIA.

Arkadia, Greece: see ARCADIA.

Arkaig, Loch (lŏkh ärkăg'), lake (12 mi. long, 1 mi. wide; 359 ft. deep), SW Inverness, Scotland, extends W from S end of Loch Lochy, into which it drains.

Arkalgud (ŭr'kŭlgōōd), town (pop. 5,091), Hassan dist., W Mysore, India, 11 mi. S of Hassan; grain, rice, tobacco.

Arkansas (är'kŭnsô), state (land □ 52,725; with inland waters □ 53,102; 1950 pop. 1,909,511; 1940 pop. 1,949,387), S central U.S., bordered N by Mo., E by Tenn. and Miss., S by La., SW by Texas, W by Okla.; 26th in area, 30th in pop.; admitted 1836 as 25th state; ⊙ Little Rock. The "Bear State" (or "Bowie State") is 245 mi. N-S and 275 mi. E-W at its widest points. Lying wholly within the drainage basin of the Mississippi R., whose course forms most of E boundary, Ark. may be divided into 2 well-defined topographical sections by a line running from the NE through Little Rock to the Okla. border in the SW: to the N and W are highlands, while in the S and E are plains. In the E is the 30-80-mi.-wide Mississippi alluvial plain, a fertile, low-lying tract subject to occasional flood (despite protective levees), and locally called the Delta Its chief features are several ox-bow lakes, such as L. CHICOT (S), the broad St. Francis R. basin (N), and the long, low CROWLEY'S RIDGE. S Ark. lies in the Gulf coastal plain, here a gently SE-sloping region (200-700 ft. high), well timbered, and broken in the W by a series of NW-facing escarpments. It is drained by the lower ARKANSAS RIVER, Saline R., Ouachita R., and Red R. The state's highland area consists of 2 parts, separated by the upper Arkansas R. valley (from Fort Smith to Little Rock). In the W central section, S of Arkansas R., the OUACHITA MOUNTAINS extend c.120 mi. E-W in several parallel folded ridges, rising to 2,850 ft. in Blue and Magazine mts., the state's highest points. In the NW and N are the OZARK MOUNTAINS, mostly rugged plateau country, with an alt. of c.1,000 ft., reaching c.2,300 ft in the BOSTON MOUNTAINS, which overlook the Arkansas valley on the S; here rises the White R., an affluent of the Mississippi. Ark. has a generally humid subtropical climate, characterized by long, hot summers, short, mild winters, an average relative humidity of 45–65%, and an annual rainfall ranging from 45 in. in N and SW to c.55 in. in SE parts; on the higher hill slopes annual snowfall rarely exceeds 10 in. Little Rock (center) has mean temp. of 42°F. in Jan., 81°F. in July, and 47 in. of annual rainfall; El Dorado (S) has mean temp. of 47°F. in Jan., 82°F. in July, and 51 in. of rain. The crop season varies from 180 days in the NW to 240 days in the SE. Native vegetation consists of mixed stands of cypress, tupelo, and red gum in the Mississippi basin and other river-bottom lands, oak and hickory in the N and NW, and mostly oak and pine elsewhere. Soil erosion is a major problem, especially on lower hill slopes and in coastal plain section. Ark. is predominantly an agr. state, with some 17,500,000 acres or over 50% of its area in farm and range land. The growing of cotton, the major cash crop, dominates rural life, Ark. ranking 3d in natl. production. Over ⅓ of the field crop total of c.6,000,000 acres is in cotton, with the heaviest concentration in the St. Francis basin, Arkansas R. valley, and SW counties. Corn is raised (for grain and fodder) throughout the state, but especially in the NE and the Arkansas valley. Other crops are oats, hay, rice (c.⅓ of U.S. output; in E irrigated dists.), and soybeans. Vegetables (mostly potatoes, tomatoes) and fruit (apples, strawberries, grapes, peaches), grown mainly in extreme NW section, are important. Cattle and hogs are raised. Dairy farming is centered chiefly in the upper Arkansas valley. Over 20,000,000 acres are classified as forest land, Ark. ranking 2d in the South in hardwood timber stands; natl. forest reserves, in Ouachita and Ozark mts., comprise 3,589,550 acres. Chief commercial species include shortleaf and loblolly pine, oak, red gum, cypress, tupelo, cottonwood, ash, and hickory. Lumbering and the mfg. of wood products (furniture, paper, etc.) are the state's leading industries. Petroleum and natural gas fields are located in S Ark., with oil refineries at EL DORADO, Smackover, and Magnolia. Coal—mainly poor quality bituminous, though some anthracite occurs—is mined in the upper Arkansas valley. Bauxite deposits (used primarily for aluminum production), just S of Little Rock, yield over 90% of U.S. supply. Other minerals are manganese (near Batesville), cinnabar (mercury ore), building stone, quartz, sand and gravel, zinc, rutile, and barite. The country's only diamond mine, now closed, is near Murfreesboro (Pike co.). Zinc is smelted at Fort Smith and Van Buren; an aluminum plant is near Malvern. Industries consist largely of the processing of raw materials. Besides woodworking and petroleum refining, there is cotton ginning, cottonseed-oil milling, fruit and vegetable canning, bottling, rice and flour milling; also mfg. of textiles, light machinery, bricks and tiles, glass, pottery. Principal industrial and commercial centers are LITTLE ROCK, FORT SMITH, North Little Rock, PINE BLUFF, TEXARKANA, BLYTHEVILLE, Helena, Hot Springs, Camden, Paragould, and Hope. Flood control and power projects include Carpenter, Remmel, Norfork, Blue Mtn., and Bull Shoals dams, whose reservoirs are also recreational areas. Popular resorts are the many mtn. spas, notably HOT SPRINGS and its adjoining natl. park. The Univ. of Ark. is at Fayetteville. The country now comprising Ark. was inhabited by Quapaw or Arkansas Indians at the time of the early white expeditions into the region —De Soto (1541–42), Marquette and Jolliet (1673), and La Salle (1682). La Salle claimed the vast Mississippi valley (known as Louisiana) for France. ARKANSAS POST, 1st white settlement in Ark., was founded by the French in 1686. Spain acquired the Louisiana country by treaty in 1763, and soon afterwards several fur-trading posts were set up along the Mississippi. France regained the region in 1800, but ceded it to the U.S. in 1803 by the Louisiana Purchase. Ark. was part of Louisiana Territory 1804–12 and of Missouri Territory from 1812 to 1819, when it became a separate territory. Cotton planters, homesteaders, and lumbermen, as well as the advent of the early Mississippi and Arkansas river steamboats, all contributed to the rapid settlement of the land. After statehood was achieved (1836), development proceeded apace with the search for mineral wealth and the coming of the stagecoach, Fort Smith flourishing as the E terminus of the mid-19th cent. overland routes to Santa Fe and Fort Bliss, near El Paso, Texas. Ark. seceded from the Union in 1861 and was the scene of several Confederate defeats during the Civil War, such as the battles of Pea Ridge (1862), Prairie Grove (1862), and Arkansas Post (1863). The war caused great social and economic distress in the state, and the Reconstruction period was marked by the corrupt regime of carpetbaggers and scalawags. In the '70s and '80s the railroads opened up much of the interior sections and lumbering and fruitgrowing became important. Oil was discovered near El Dorado in the early 1920s. The state has a sizable Negro minority (c.25%). It has an essentially cotton economy, and in recent years many workers have moved to the industrial North. See also articles on cities, towns, geographic features, and the 75 counties: ARKANSAS, ASHLEY, BAXTER, BENTON, BOONE, BRADLEY, CALHOUN, CARROLL, CHICOT, CLARK, CLAY, CLEBURNE, CLEVELAND, COLUMBIA, CONWAY, CRAIGHEAD, CRAWFORD, CRITTENDEN, CROSS, DALLAS, DESHA, DREW, FAULKNER, FRANKLIN, FULTON, GARLAND, GRANT, GREENE, HEMPSTEAD, HOT SPRING, HOWARD, INDEPENDENCE, IZARD, JACKSON, JEFFERSON, JOHNSON, LAFAYETTE, LAWRENCE, LEE, LINCOLN, LITTLE RIVER, LOGAN, LONOKE, MADISON, MARION, MILLER, MISSISSIPPI, MONROE, MONTGOMERY, NEVADA, NEWTON, OUACHITA, PERRY, PHILLIPS, PIKE, POINSETT, POLK, POPE, PRAIRIE, PULASKI, RANDOLPH, SAINT FRANCIS, SALINE, SCOTT, SEARCY, SEBASTIAN, SEVIER, SHARP, STONE, UNION, VAN BUREN, WASHINGTON, WHITE, WOODRUFF, YELL.

Arkansas, county (□ 1,035; pop. 23,665), E central Ark.; ⊙ Stuttgart and De Witt. Bounded S by Arkansas R.; drained by White R. and small Bayou Meto. Agr. (cotton, rice, corn, oats, soybeans, hay, lespedeza; livestock); lumbering, rice and cotton processing, commercial fishing; ships pecans. Has Ark. Post State Park (recreational area). Duck, quail hunting. Formed 1813.

Arkansas City. 1 (är'kŭnsô) Town (pop. 1,018), ⊙ Desha co., SE Ark., c.60 mi. SE of Pine Bluff and on the Mississippi. Founded c.1873. 2 (ärkăn'zŭs) City (pop. 12,903), Cowley co., S Kansas, on Arkansas R. at mouth of Walnut R., and 45 mi. SSE of Wichita, near Okla. line; trade and shipping center (with railroad repair shops) for oil-producing and agr. area; oil refining, flour milling, meat packing, dairying. Laid out 1870, inc. 1872. Served in 1893 as point of departure for settlement of near-by Cherokee Strip. Growth stimulated by discovery (1914) of oil in vicinity.

Arkansas Post (är'kŭnsô), village, Arkansas co., E central Ark., c.40 mi. ESE of Pine Bluff and on Arkansas R. Oldest white settlement in state, founded 1686 by the French as trading post. Important river port for a time, it became territorial ⊙ in 1819, and in the Civil War was a Confederate stronghold until 1863, when Union forces made a successful attack. The Ark. Post State Park (recreational area) is adjacent.

Arkansas River (är'kŭnsô, ärkăn'zŭz), S central U.S., flows 1,450 mi. generally ESE from the Rocky Mts. of central Colo., through Kansas, Okla., and Ark., to Mississippi R. N of Greenville, Miss. Rises as mtn. stream in small lakes near Leadville (Colo.), flows 171 mi. SSE and E, through ROYAL GORGE, to Pueblo (Colo.), then 460 mi. generally E to Hutchinson (Kansas), and 819 mi. SE, past Wichita (Kansas), Tulsa (Okla.), and Fort Smith and Little Rock (Ark.), entering Mississippi R. in Desha co., Ark.; drains □ 160,500; has total fall of 11,400 ft. from source to mouth; navigable to mouth of Neosho R., 475 mi. upstream. Crosses the Great Plains in SE Colo. (E of Pueblo), S Kansas, and NE Okla.; flows bet. Boston Mts. (N) and Ouachita Mts. (S) in W Ark.; and drains alluvial plain in central and SE Ark. Receives principal tributaries—Canadian, Cimarron, Neosho, and Verdigris rivers—in E Okla., and the Salt Fork of the Arkansas R. in N Okla.; and is connected near its mouth with White R. by short cutoff formed as result of backwater from Mississippi R. Power is developed at 25 plants in river basin, and 750,000 acres in SW Kansas and SE Colo. are under irrigation. The volume of water is extremely variable, and disastrous floods have occurred (chiefly below Tulsa), necessitating construction of levees along much of lower course. Important control works are JOHN MARTIN DAM on main stream in Colo., FORT GIBSON DAM and GRAND RIVER DAM on Neosho R. in Okla., and Blue Mountain and Wister dams, on minor tributaries. Agr. and stock raising are important activities in the river valley. Cotton and rice are grown in area around mouth, wheat and cotton in Okla., wheat in Kansas; and sugar beets, grain, and fruit in irrigated regions of SW Kansas and SE Colo. Food processing is the leading occupation in the larger river cities. Oil refining is the major industry in parts of basin in S Kansas and Okla.; and coal is mined in E Okla. and W Ark. The Arkansas is believed to have been crossed (1541) near site of Dodge City by Coronado and was probably ascended in part of lower course (Ark.) by De Soto in early 1540s. It was explored in 1806 in upper course (Colo.) by Zebulon Pike. In 19th cent. it served as important route for trade and travel, and is now used for transportation of sand and gravel, logs, and farm supplies. There is a plan for river improvement to make possible 9-ft. navigability along lower third of main stream and part of Verdigris R.

Arkari (ŭrkä'rē), village, Chitral state, N North-West Frontier Prov., W Pakistan, 150 mi. N of Peshawar, in the Hindu Kush, SW of Tirich Mir; corn, millet, fruit. Lead mining near by.

Arkhangelo-Pashiski Zavod, RSFSR: see PASHIYA.

Arkhangelos, Greece: see ARCHANGELOS.

Arkhangelsk, Russian SFSR: see ARCHANGEL.

Arkhangelskaya or **Arkhangel'skaya** (ŭrkhän'gĭlskīŭ), village (1926 pop. 11,394), E Krasnodar Territory, Russian SFSR, 13 mi. SE of Tikhoretsk; metalworks, flour mill; fish hatchery.

Arkhangelskoye or **Arkhangel'skoye** (–skŭyŭ). 1 Village (1926 pop. 4,084), E central Bashkir Autonomous SSR, Russian SFSR, 40 mi. SE of Ufa; wheat, oats, livestock. Former site (until c.1930) of ironworks called Arkhangelsk or Arkhangelski Zavod. 2 Village, Moscow oblast, Russian SFSR: see KRASNOGORSK. 3 Settlement on W coast of N isl. of Novaya Zemlya, Russian SFSR; 75°52'N 59°10'E; airfield. 4 Village (1926 pop. 10,768), E Stavropol Territory, Russian SFSR, on Kuma R. and 12 mi. SSW of Budennovsk; flour milling, metalworking; cotton, wheat. 5 Village (1926 pop. 1,552), SE Tula oblast, Russian SFSR, 18 mi. NW of Yefremov; wheat. 6 Village (1926 pop. 9,708), N Voronezh oblast, Russian SFSR, 45 mi. W of Borisoglebsk; wheat, sunflowers, sugar beets.

Arkhara (ŭrkhä'rŭ), village (1926 pop. 2,147), SE Amur oblast, Russian SFSR, on Trans-Siberian RR and 125 mi. ESE of Blagoveshchensk, in agr. area (grain, soybeans).

Arkhipovka (ŭrkhē'pŭfkŭ), town (1948 pop. over 500), S Ivanovo oblast, Russian SFSR, 14 mi. SSW of Shuya; cotton weaving.

Arkhon (ŭrkhôn'), peak (13,957 ft.) in N front range of the central Greater Caucasus, Russian SFSR, 21 mi. SSW of Alagir.

Arkhonskaya (ŭrkhôn'skīŭ), village (1926 pop. 5,855), central North Ossetian Autonomous SSR, Russian SFSR, near Gizeldon R., 10 mi. NW of Dzaudzhikau; wheat, corn, truck produce.

Arki, Greece: see AKRITES.

Arki (ŭr'kē), village, W Himachal Pradesh, India, 13 mi. WNW of Simla; local market for maize, wheat, rice, ginger, potatoes. Was ⊙ former Punjab Hill state of Baghal.

Arkinda (ärkĭn'dŭ), town (pop. 92), Little River co., extreme SW Ark., 35 mi. NW of Texarkana, at Okla. line.

Arkley, England: see BARNET.

Arklow (ärk'lō), Gaelic *Inbhear Mor*, urban district (pop. 4,915), SE Co. Wicklow, Ireland, on the Irish Sea at mouth of Avoca R., 14 mi. SSW of Wicklow; 52°48'N 6°9'W; fishing town, resort, and seaport, serving near-by mining area (copper, lead, bog-iron, china-clay); also mfg. of explosives. Has remains of anc. castle of the Ormonds. In 1798 General Needham here won final victory over insurgent United Irishmen.

Arkoe (är'kō), town (pop. 48), Nodaway co., NW Mo., on One Hundred and Two R. and 6 mi. SSE of Maryville.

Arkoma (ärkō'mŭ), town (pop. 1,691), Le Flore co., SE Okla., at state line 3 mi. S of Fort Smith, Ark.

Arkona (ärkō'nŭ), village (pop. 406), S Ont., 9 mi. E of Forest; dairying, flax growing.

Arkona (ärkō'nä), cape, N Germany, N extremity of Rügen isl., on the Baltic, 15 mi. NW of Sassnitz; 54°41'N 13°26'E. Lighthouse. Has remains of anc. fortifications; once site of Wendish temple, destroyed in 12th cent.

Arkonam (ŭrkō'nŭm), town (pop. 15,484), North Arcot dist., E central Madras, India, 40 mi. W of Madras; rail junction (workshops).

Arkoudi or **Arkoudhi** (both: ärkōō'dhē), uninhabited island (□ 1.5) of Ionian group, Greece, 3 mi. off SE Leukas isl., in Leukas nome; 38°33'N 20°43'E. Sometimes spelled Arkudi.

Arkport, village (pop. 701), Steuben co., W N.Y., 18 mi. WNW of Bath.

Arksey, England: see BENTLEY WITH ARKSEY.

Arkticheski Institut Islands or **Arkticheskiy Institut Islands** (ŭrktyē'chĭskē ĭnstyētōōt') [Rus., =arctic institute], in Kara Sea of Arctic Ocean, 75 mi. off NW Taimyr Peninsula, in Krasnoyarsk Territory, Russian SFSR; 75°15'N 81°45'E.

Arkudi, Greece: see ARKOUDI.

Arkul or **Arkul'** (ŭrkōōl'), town (1926 pop. 946), S Kirov oblast, Russian SFSR, on Vyatka R. and 20 mi. SSE of Molotovsk; shipyards.

Arkwright. 1 Village in Arkwright town (1940 pop. 688), Chautauqua co., extreme W N.Y., 7 mi. SE of Dunkirk. 2 Village, R.I.: see COVENTRY. 3 Village (pop. 1,266), Spartanburg co., NW S.C., just S of Spartanburg.

Arlanc (ärlä'), village (pop. 1,713), Puy-de-Dôme dept., central France, near the Dore, 9 mi. S of Ambert; ribbon and lace making.

Arlanza River (ärlän' thä), N Spain, rises in escarpment of central plateau, flows c.75 mi. W, past Salas de los Infantes and Lerma in Burgos prov., to Pisuerga R. 12 mi. E of Palencia; joined by Arlanzón R. 8 mi. above its mouth.

Arlanzón River (ärlän-thōn'), N Spain, rises in escarpment of central plateau, flows c.70 mi. W and SW, past Burgos, to Pisuerga R. 12 mi. E of Palencia; joined by Arlanza R. 8 mi. above its mouth. Used for hydroelectric power.

Arlberg (ärl'bĕrk), peak and pass (5,910 ft.) at N end of Rhaetian Alps, in W Austria; winter sports center. **Arlberg Tunnel** (built 1880–84) carries railroad (electrified 1923) bet. Langen (Vorarlberg) and Sankt Anton (Tyrol); 6⅓ mi. long; highest point c.1,600 ft. below road traversing pass.

Arlecdon and Frizington (är'lŭkdŭn, frĭ'–, frī'–), former urban district (1931 pop. 4,328), W Cumberland, England. Includes market town of Arlecdon, 5 mi. ENE of Whitehaven; the town of Frizington, 5 mi. ESE of Whitehaven, with iron-ore mining and mfg. of shoes; and the village of Rowrah, just SE of Frizington, with granite quarries and disused iron mines.

Arlee, village (pop. c.300), Lake co., W Mont., on branch of Flathead R. and 20 mi. N of Missoula; trading point.

Arles (ärlz, Fr. ärl), anc. *Arelas*, town (pop. 20,138), Bouches-du-Rhône dept., SE France, on left bank of the Grand Rhône, and 45 mi. NW of Marseilles, at NW terminus of Arles-Port-de-Bouc Canal; commercial center near head of Rhone delta, with trade in products of Crau (E; olives) and Camargue (S; livestock, wine, salt) dists. Metalworking, boat building, sulphur refining; mfg. (newsprint, hats, sausages, goat cheese). A flourishing Roman town and metropolis of Gaul in late empire. Here Constantine I convoked (314) a synod which condemned Donatism. Constantine II b. here. Archiepiscopal see, 4th cent. to 1790. Became (879) seat of kings of Cisjurane Burgundy (or Provence) and (933) of Kingdom of Arles. Town soon obtained substantial self-government and retained a special political status until French Revolution. Though heavily damaged in Second World War (especially right bank port dist. of Trinquetaille, and approaches to railroad bridge), most historical monuments were spared. They include a Roman arena (2d cent. A.D.) seating 26,000 and now used for bullfights; a Roman theater (1st or 2d cent. A.D.) where Venus of Arles was unearthed; the Aliscamps [i.e. Elysian fields], remains of Roman necropolis; church (former cathedral) and cloister of Saint-Trophime (11th–15th cent.); 17th-cent. townhall; *Museon-Arlaten*, a mus. of Provençal culture and folklore established in a 16th-cent. mansion by poet Mistral (b. near by); and museums of pagan and Christian art. Benedictine abbey of Montmajour (suppressed 1786) with 12th-cent. church and cloister and 14th-cent. keep is 3 mi. NE. Arles has attracted many painters.

Arlesey, town and parish (pop. 2,468), E Bedford, England, 6 mi. S of Biggleswade; brick and concrete works. Has 13th-cent. church. Iron Age relics have been found here.

Arlesheim (är'lùs-hīm"), town (pop. 3,360), Basel-Land half-canton, N Switzerland, 5 mi. S of Basel; silk textiles; metal- and woodworking. Has 17th-18th-cent. church.

Arles-Port-de-Bouc Canal (ärl-, pôr-dù-bōōk'), Bouches-du-Rhône dept., SE France, connects the Rhone at Arles with the Gulf of Fos of the Mediterranean at Port-de-Bouc; 29 mi. long. Together with Étang de BERRE and ROVE Tunnel, it forms Rhone-Marseilles shipping canal.

Arles-sur-Tech (-sür-tĕsh'), village (pop. 1,678), Pyrénées-Orientales dept., S France, in the VALLESPIR of E Pyrenees, on the Tech and 6 mi. WSW of Céret; agr. market; mfg. of sandals and woolens. Apple orchards. Loading point for iron ore mined at Batère (3 mi. NW in the Massif du Canigou). Has 11th–12th-cent. abbatial church.

Arleux (ärlû'), village (pop. 1,463), Nord dept., N France, on Sensée Canal and 6 mi. S of Douai, in cereal and sugar-beet area. Sometimes called Arleux-du-Nord.

Arley, town and parish (pop. 3,751), N Warwick, England, 8 mi. NNW of Coventry; coal mining. Has 14th-cent. church.

Arlifoss (ôr'lĭfôs), Nor. *Årlifoss*, falls (56 ft.) on Tinne R., Telemark co., S Norway, 10 mi. NNW of Notodden; hydroelectric plant. Sometimes spelled Aarlifoss.

Arlington, village (pop. 1,231), SE Orange Free State, U. of So. Afr., 30 mi. WNW of Bethlehem; alt. 5,154 ft.; rail junction; grain elevator; stock, dairying.

Arlington, urban county (□ 24; pop. 135,449), N Va., along the Potomac opposite Washington, D.C., with which it is connected by Arlington Memorial Bridge (1926–32) and 4 other spans. Without civil divisions, co. is governed as a unit. Alexandria city adjoins on S. Composed mainly of residential suburbs, including villages of Arlington, Clarendon (a business center), Fort Myer Heights, Rosslyn (rŏz'lĭn). Points of interest include Arlington Natl. Cemetery (408 acres; established 1864), with graves of c.60,000 American war dead, the tomb of the Unknown Soldier, and a notable marble amphitheater; cemetery is part of "Arlington," the former estate of Custis and Lee families, and includes Arlington House, now preserved as Lee Mansion Natl. Memorial (established 1925; 2.71 acres). In co. are also U.S. Fort Myer, Natl. Airport (airport for Washington), Pentagon Bldg. (Dept. of Defense), and other military and naval installations and govt. offices. Some industries (bldg. materials, foundry and glass products, geophysical instruments); truck and dairy farming, horticulture. Renamed 1920 from Alexandria.

Arlington. **1** Urban area, Calif.: see RIVERSIDE, city. **2** Village (1940 pop. 749), Duval co., NE Fla., on St. Johns R., opposite Jacksonville. **3** City (pop. 1,382), Calhoun and Early counties, SW Ga., 32 mi. WSW of Albany; mfg. of cottonseed oil, peanut products, veneer, barrel staves. Inc. as village 1881, as city 1923. **4** Village (pop. 247), Bureau co., N Ill., 12 mi. NNW of La Salle, in agr. and bituminous-coal area. **5** Town (pop. 661), Fayette co., NE Iowa, 13 mi. ENE of Oelwein; dairy products, livestock remedies. Limestone quarry (N). **6** City (pop. 405), Reno co., S central Kansas, 18 mi. SW of Hutchinson, in wheat area. **7** Town (pop. 584), Carlisle co., SW Ky., 31 mi. SW of Paducah, in agr. area. **8** Residential town (pop. 44,353), Middlesex co., E Mass., 6 mi. NW of Boston; mfg. (textile machinery, wood products, leather goods), agr. trade (truck, celery, dairying). Settled c.1630. Includes villages of East Arlington and Arlington Heights. **9** Village (pop. 1,313), Sibley co., S Minn., on small affluent of Minnesota R. and c.55 mi. SW of Minneapolis, in grain, livestock, poultry area; dairy products, canned corn. **10** Village (pop. 593), Washington co., E Nebr., 25 mi. NW of Omaha and on Elkhorn R.; grain. **11** Village, N.J.: see KEARNY. **12** Village (pop. 5,374), Dutchess co., SE N.Y., adjoining Poughkeepsie (W). Seat of Vassar Col. **13** Village (pop. 5,085), Gaston co., S N.C., 2 mi. W of Gastonia. **14** Town (pop. 525), Yadkin co., N N.C., 4 mi. SSE of Elkin, near Yadkin R. Inc. 1930. **15** Village (pop. 825), Hancock co., NW Ohio, 10 mi. S of Findlay; limestone, concrete, plaster, lumber. **16** City (pop. 686), Gilliam co., N Oregon, 50 mi. E of The Dalles and on Columbia R.; hunting. **17** Village, R.I.: see CRANSTON. **18** Village, Spartanburg co., NW S.C., 16 mi. W of Spartanburg; textile mill. **19** City (pop. 1,096), Kingsbury co., E S.Dak., 60 mi. NNW of Sioux Falls, in lake region; livestock, dairy products, grain. Founded 1880. **20** Town (pop. 463), Shelby co., SW Tenn., near Loosahatchie R., 23 mi. NE of Memphis. **21** City (pop. 7,692), Tarrant co., N Texas, 12 mi. E of Fort Worth; seat of North Texas Agr. Col. Market center in agr. area (truck, fruit, poultry); rose growing, poultry hatching; iron- and wood-working; mineral water. Founded near by 1873, moved to railroad 1876, inc. 1896. **22** Town (pop. 1,463), Bennington co., SW Vt., on Batten Kill and 14 mi. N of Bennington, in area of country estates and summer homes; furniture, wood products. Scene on Vt. state seal is view from Thomas Chittenden home. Settled 1762. **23** Village, Arlington co., Va.: see ARLINGTON, county. **24** Village (pop. 4,124, with near-by Kenwood and Five Forks), Prince George co., E Va., a suburb of Hopewell. **25** Town (pop. 1,635), Snohomish co., NW Wash., on Stillaguamish R. and 15 mi. N of Everett; lumber, dairy products, poultry, truck. **26** Village (pop. 255), Columbia co., S central Wis., 19 mi. N of Madison; fruit and vegetable canning.

Arlington Heights. **1** Residential village (pop. 8,768), Cook co., NE Ill., NW suburb of Chicago, 15 mi. E of Elgin, in dairying and truck-farming area; mfg. (desks, chairs, beverages, wooden cases). Arlington Park Race Track is here. Resort, camping area near by. Settled in 1830s; inc. 1887. **2** Village (pop. 1,312), Hamilton co., extreme SW Ohio, a N suburb of Cincinnati.

Arlo (ŏr'lō), Hung. *Arló*, town (pop. 3,147), Borsod-Gömör co., NE Hungary, 3 mi. S of Ozd; coal mined near by.

Arlod (ärlō'), village (pop. 1,052), Ain dept., E France, on the Rhone, at foot of the Jura, and 11 mi. ESE of Nantua; calcium-carbide mfg.

Arlon (ärlõ'), Flemish *Aarlen* (är'lùn), anc. *Orolaunum*, town (pop. 11,384), ⊙ Luxembourg prov., SE Belgium, in the Ardennes 100 mi. SE of Brussels, near border of grand duchy of Luxembourg; 55°20' N 3°85'E. Agr. and livestock market; mfg. (briar pipes, cigars). Part of pop. employed in near-by steel plants, including those in Luxembourg and France. Provincial mus. in town hall. Ruined Cistercian abbey of Clairfontaine near by. A Roman settlement on road from Treves to Rheims, Arlon was fortified in 4th cent.; became co. center in 10th cent. Suffered repeated attacks in 16th, 17th, and 18th cents.; fortifications dismantled by French in 1670. In 1830 became provisional ⊙ Luxembourg prov.; status confirmed in 1839.

Arlov (är'lûv"), Swedish *Arlöv*, village (pop. 3,439), Malmohus co., S Sweden, on the Oresund, 3 mi. NE of Malmo; sugar refining, metalworking, paper milling.

Arltunga, settlement, S central Northern Territory, Australia, 55 mi. ENE of Alice Springs; gold mining, mica, tungsten.

Arluno (ärlōō'nô), village (pop. 4,265), Milano prov., Lombardy, N Italy, 12 mi. WNW of Milan; foundry, electric motorcar factory.

Arly River (ärlē'), Savoie dept., SE France, rises in Savoy Alps near Mégève, flows c.20 mi. SSW, past Ugine, to the Isère below Albertville. Receives the Doron de Beaufort. Powers electrometallurgical works.

Arma, city (pop. 1,334), Crawford co., SE Kansas, near Mo. line, 10 mi. N of Pittsburg; shipping point for coal-mining and agr. region. Inc. 1909.

Armação de Pêra (ärmŭsã'ō dĭ pā'rù), village (pop. 1,391), Faro dist., on the Atlantic (S coast) and 11 mi. ESE of Portimão; popular beach resort; fishing (sardines, lobsters, crabs, clams).

Armada (ärmā'dù), village (pop. 961), Macomb co., SE Mich., 16 mi. N of Mt. Clemens, in grain, sugar-beet, and bean-producing area; nursery.

Armadale (är'mùdāl), town (pop. 1,046), SW Western Australia, 17 mi. SSE of Perth; residential.

Armadale (är'mùdāl), burgh (1931 pop. 4,854; 1951 census 5,803), SW West Lothian, Scotland, 2 mi. W of Bathgate; coal and shale-oil mining, steel milling, mfg. of chemicals, tiles.

Armadillo, Mexico: see VILLA MORELOS, San Luis Potosí.

Armageddon, Palestine: see MEGIDDO.

Armagh (är'mù), village (pop. estimate 400), S Que., 35 mi. E of Quebec; lumbering, dairying, stock raising.

Armagh (ärmä'), county (□ 488.7; 1937 pop. 108,815; 1951 census 114,226), Ulster, S Northern Ireland; ⊙ Armagh. Bounded by cos. Lough and Monaghan, Ireland (S and SW); Co. Tyrone (NW); Lough Neagh (N); and Co. Down (E). Drained by Bann, Newry, and Blackwater rivers. Level and fertile in N, surface becomes hilly in S, rising to 1,893 ft. on Slieve Gullion. Potatoes are chief crop; cattle are raised. There is some granite quarrying. Linen milling is leading industry; also mfg. of carpets, clothing, rope. Armagh is ecclesiastical center for all Ireland. Other towns are Lurgan, Portadown, Keady. Navan Fort was site of Emania, for many centuries ⊙ Ulster.

Armagh, urban district (1937 pop. 7,064; 1951 census 9,279), ⊙ Co. Armagh, Northern Ireland, 35 mi. SW of Belfast; 54°21'N 6°40'W; linen milling, bacon and ham curing. From 5th cent. it has been the religious center of Ireland, St. Patrick having been made archbishop of Armagh in 445. It is seat of Protestant and R.C. archbishops. Features are Protestant cathedral (dating mainly from 18th cent.), R.C. cathedral (1840–73), observatory (1791), Royal School (1627; founded by Charles I), and St. Patrick Diocesan Col. The "Book of Armagh" is copy of New Testament in Latin, with documents relating to life of St. Patrick. Town became important educational center; it was subjected to several Danish raids. After battle of Clontarf (1014), Brian Boru and his son were buried here. In 1566 Shane O'Neill destroyed Armagh, and in 1642 it was burned. Just W of Armagh is Navan Fort, large elliptical mound, on site of Emania, legendary ⊙ Ulster.

Armagh (är'mù), borough (pop. 176), Indiana co., SW central Pa., 11 mi. NW of Johnstown.

Armagnac (ärmänyäk'), hilly region, former countship of SW France, now included in W Gers, S Lot-et-Garonne, and E Landes dept.; Auch was the capital. Its white grapes make famed Armagnac brandy, with chief centers at Condom, Vic-Fezensac, Lannepax, Montréal, and Fleurance. The counts of Armagnac became powerful in 15th cent. In 1607, Henry IV incorporated Armagnac into royal domain as part of Gascony prov.

Armagon (är'mùgŏn), lighthouse, on Sriharikota isl., Nellore dist., E Madras, India, 34 mi. NNW of Pulicat. Site of English settlement founded c.1625. Formerly spelled Armeghon and Armugam.

Armamar (ärmùmär'), town (pop. 743), Viseu dist., N central Portugal, 6 mi. W of Lamego, in wine growing region (port wine); olives, figs, almonds, oranges.

Armançon River (ärmäsõ'), Côte-d'Or and Yonne depts., E central France, rises 3 mi. SW of Pouilly-en-Auxois, flows 108 mi. generally NW, past Semur-en-Auxois and Tonnerre, to the Yonne 5 mi. above Joigny. In its upper course and again from influx of Brenne R. to its mouth, it is accompanied by the Burgundy Canal.

Armant (är'mănt), anc. *Hermonthis* (hûrmŏn'thĭs), town (1937 pop. 3,360; 1947 commune pop. 16,260), Qena prov., Upper Egypt, on W bank of the Nile and 8 mi SW of Luxor, in sugar-cane growing region; cereals, dates; sugar milling, pottery making. Sometimes spelled Erment. Across the Nile, on railroad, is the town of **Armant el Waburat** or **Armant al-Waburat** (ĕl wăbōō'rät) (1947 commune pop. 9,412). Also called El Idisat.

Arma Plateau (är'mù) or **Aruma Plateau** (ä'rōōmù) (1,800 ft.), in E Nejd, Saudi Arabia; extends parallel to and E of the Jabal Tuwaiq. W scarp rises 400 ft. above the plain. Area contains some of most populated dists. of Nejd.

Armavir (ärmùvēr', Rus. ŭrmùvēr'), city (1939 pop. 83,677), E Krasnodar Territory, Russian SFSR, on Kuban R. at mouth of the Urup, and 100 mi. E of Krasnodar, in rich grain and livestock region. Junction of railroads from Rostov to Baku and Tiflis; workshops. Industrial center; agr. processing (flour, vegetable oils, meat, alcohol, wool, cotton), mfg. of agr. and other machines, wires, nails; foundry. Oil pipe-line pumping station. Founded 1848. During Second World War, held (1942-43) by Germans.

Armeghon, India: see ARMAGON.

Armenia (ärmē'nēù), Armenian *Hayastan*, Georgian *Somkheti*, Rus. *Armeniya*, Turkish *Ermenistan*, region and former kingdom of Asia Minor. Its boundaries varied widely in the course of history, but as a region it is generally understood to include E Turkey and the ARMENIAN SOVIET SOCIALIST REPUBLIC. It thus forms a continuation of the Anatolian plateau. Mt. ARARAT, the highest point, is in Turkey, as are the sources of Euphrates, Tigris, and Aras rivers and L. VAN. Trebizond, on the Black Sea, Erzurum and Kars are chief cities of Turkish Armenia, which, unlike Soviet Armenia, has no official standing. Armenian history is extremely ancient. According to tradition, the kingdom was founded in the region of L. Van by Haig or Haik, a descendant of Noah, and was ruled for centuries by Haig's successors. Frequently invaded by the Assyrians, in whose inscriptions it is mentioned as Urartu (Ararat). A battleground of Assyrians, Medes, and Persians it was, by 6th cent. B.C., a Persian satrapy. Conquered (4th cent. B.C.) by Alexander the Great, it became after his death part of the kingdom of Seleucus I and his descendants. Later became (189 B.C.) an independent state (⊙ Artaxata) until Tigranes II lost it to Rome. The Romans distinguished bet. Greater and Lesser Armenia, respectively E and W of the Euphrates. Christianity was introduced early; Armenia is oldest Christian state. In 3d cent. A.D. the Sassanidae came to power in Persia and overran Armenia. After partition (384) of kingdom bet. Persia and Rome, Armenia was the constant prey of Persians, Byzantines, White Huns, Khazars, and Arabs. From 885 to 1046 the kingdom enjoyed autonomy under native rulers, the Bagratids (⊙ Ani); it then was reconquered by the Byzantines, who promptly lost it to the Seljuk Turks. Pushed westward, a number of Armenians established kingdom of Little Armenia in Cilicia. In 1375 the Mamelukes conquered and destroyed kingdom of Little Armenia. Shortly afterward (1386–94) Tamerlane seized Greater Armenia and massacred a large part of population. The Ottoman Turks followed, and by 16th cent. held all Armenia. Eastern Armenia was chronically disputed bet. Turkey and Persia. It was from Persia that Russia, in 1828, acquired the area of present Armenian SSR. There remains a considerable Armenian minority in NW Iran. The Congress of Berlin (1878) also assigned the Kars, Ardahan, and Batum dists. to Russia, which restored Kars and Ardahan to Turkey in 1921. The Armenian people underwent one of the worst trials in its history bet. 1894 and 1915. A systematic plan for its extermination was put into action by the Turks and was sporadically resumed, notably in 1915. The Armenians rose in revolt at Van, which they held until relieved by Russian troops. The Treaty of Brest-Litovsk (1918) made Russian Armenia an independent republic under German auspices. It was superseded by the Treaty of Sèvres (1920), which created an independent Greater Armenia, comprising both the Turkish and the Russian parts. In same year, however, the Communists gained control of Russian Armenia and proclaimed it a Soviet republic, and in 1921 the Russo-Turkish Treaty established present boundaries, thus ending Armenian independence. Before 1914 there were c.2,500,000 Armenians in Russia, Turkey, and Iran. Of these a large percentage were massacred or fled abroad.

Armenia (ärmä'nyä), city (pop. 29,673), Caldas dept., W central Colombia, on W slopes of Cordillera Central, 39 mi. SSW of Manizales; alt. 4,878 ft. Railroad terminus (connected with Buenaventura and Manizales), transfer point for traffic to Bogotá via Ibagué highway across Quindío Pass (9 mi. SE). Major coffee center and processing point in fertile Quindío agr. region (principally coffee, but also corn, beans, sugar cane, silk, fruit, cattle); mfg. of chocolate, carbonated beverages, native earthenware; pasteurizing plant. Coal deposits near by.

Armenia, city (pop. 18,898), Sonsonate dept., W Salvador, on railroad and 20 mi. W of San Salvador; coffee, grain; stock raising.

Armenian Highland, Rus. *Armyanskoye Nagor'ye,* mountainous section of Transcaucasia, in USSR and Turkey, separated from the Greater Caucasus by Rion (Colchis) and Kura lowlands; average alt. 5,000–6,500 ft. Its N edge is formed by the Lesser CAUCASUS. Essentially a series of plateaus covered by lava flows, the highland rises in Mt. Ararat and in the extinct volcano Mt. Aragats (Alagez). The Aras and Kura rivers rise here.

Armenian Soviet Socialist Republic, sometimes called simply **Armenia** (ärmē'nēù), constituent republic (□ 11,500; 1947 pop. estimate 1,345,000) of the USSR, in S Transcaucasia; ⊙ Erivan (Yerevan). Bounded by Georgia (N), Azerbaijan SSR (E), Iranian Azerbaijan and Turkey (S and W; partly along Aras R.); encloses (S) Nakhichevan Autonomous SSR, exclave of Azerbaijan SSR. Mountainous country (rising to 13,432 ft. in Mt. Aragats), consisting mainly of high plateaus surrounded by elevated mtn. ranges (Zangezur Range) and descending N toward Kura R. valley and S to Aras R. Dry continental climate, with humid, cool summers in the plateau and hot, dry summers in Aras R. valley; mean temp., 14°–20° F. (Jan.), 62°–77°F. (July). Yearly rainfall, 12–28 in. Soils, largely of volcanic origin, are fertile, but require irrigation in low-rainfall areas. Hydroelectric potential, notably in Sevan-Zanga river system, is considerable. Pop. consists of Armenians (85%; a Japhetic language group of Armeno-Gregorian religion), Azerbaijani Turks, Georgians, Russians, Kurds, and Assyrians. Administratively, the republic falls into independent cities and *raions* (*rayons*). Agr. varies with respect to alt.: grazing (wool, meat, hides) and dairy farming (butter, Swiss-type cheese) on high plateaus, which also serve as summer pastures for adjacent republics; wheat, barley, sugar beets, orchards in Leninakan and Lori steppes (3–6,000 ft.); rice, vineyards, subtropical fruit, cotton in Aras R. valley (irrigation and drainage systems). Chief mineral resources: copper (Alaverdi, Kafan), molybdenum (Kadzharan), volcanic tuff (Artik), pumice (Ani-Pemza), and marble. Hydroelectric industries (developed during 1940s) produce aluminum, synthetic rubber, and nitrate fertilizers at Erivan. Other industrial centers; Leninakan, Kirovakan. Main exports are copper, building stone, cotton, cognac, wool, hides, cheese. The Armenian SSR was formed out of former Rus. Erivan and Yelizavetpol govts. in 1920 and joined (1922) the USSR as a member of the Transcaucasian SFSR; became a separate constituent republic in 1936. Efforts have been made, particularly after Second World War, to absorb Armenian refugees from all over the world into Soviet Armenia. See the article on ARMENIA.

Armenierstadt, Rumania: see GHERLA.

Armentières (ärmätyâr'; in the song, är"mùntërz'), town (pop. 18,691), Nord dept., N France, on the Lys and 9 mi. WNW of Lille, near Belg. border; major linen-weaving center, with velvet, hosiery, underwear, and clothing manufactures. Breweries. Completely destroyed in heavy First World War fighting. Captured (1918) by Germans in battle of the Lys. Became famous through many versions of the song *Mademoiselle from Armentières.* Rebuilt, it was damaged in Second World War.

Armería (ärmärē'ä), town (pop. 1,456), Colima, W Mexico, on Pacific coastal plain, on Armería R., 5 mi. inland and 26 mi. SSW of Colima; rice, corn, sugar cane, coffee, tropical fruit.

Armería River, W Mexico, rises in Jalisco S of Ameca, flows SE, past Ayutla, and S into Colima, past Armería, to the Pacific 7 mi. SE of Cuyutlán; c.140 mi. long. Called Ayutla in upper course (Jalisco), San Pedro in middle course. Used for irrigation.

Armero (ärmā'rō), town (pop. 6,401), Tolima dept., W central Colombia, in Magdalena valley, on railroad and 60 mi. NW of Bogotá; tobacco-growing center; also corn, rice, cotton, coffee, sugar cane, bananas; rice, corn, and coffee milling, cotton ginning, vegetable-oil extracting. Thermal springs. Tobacco experiment station near by.

Armi, Cape (är'mē), on S coast of Calabria, S Italy, 6 mi. WNW of Melito di Porto Salvo; 37°57'N 15°41'E.

Armidale (är'mĭdāl), municipality (pop. 7,809) E New South Wales, Australia, 170 mi. N of Newcastle; gold-mining center; wool, dairy products. Seat of New England Univ. Col. (1938), teachers col., Anglican and R.C. cathedrals.

Armijo (ärmē'hō) village (pop. 4,516), suburb of Albuquerque, Bernalillo co., central N.Mex.

Armilla (ärmē'lyä), SW suburb (pop. 2,414) of Granada, Granada prov., S Spain; sugar mill. Olive oil, cereals, truck produce. Has race tracks. Airport near by.

Armington. **1** Village (pop. 314), Tazewell co., central Ill., 19 mi. SW of Bloomington, in agr. area. **2** Village (pop. c.75), Cascade co., central Mont., on branch of Missouri R. and 20 mi. SE of Great Falls; coal-mining point.

Armizonskoye (ŭrmēzôn'skŭyù), village (1926 pop. 656), S Tyumen oblast, Russian SFSR, 65 mi. WSW of Ishim, in agr. area (grain, livestock).

Armley and New Wortley, town (pop. 20,181), in Leeds county borough, West Riding, S central Yorkshire, England, on Aire R. just SW of Leeds; woolen milling and printing, leather tanning and mfg.; clothing mills, chemical works.

Armona (ärmō'nù), village (pop. 1,274), Kings co., S central Calif., 3 mi. W of Hanford; ships fruit.

Armonk (är'mŏngk), residential village (pop. c.2,000), Westchester co., SE N.Y., 7 mi. NNE of White Plains, in diversified-farming area; mfg. of putty.

Armori (ŭrmō'rē), town (pop. 7,367), Chanda dist., S Madhya Pradesh, India, near Wainganga R., 60 mi. NE of Chanda; rice, millet, flax. Hematite deposits near by.

Armorica (ärmô'rĭkù) [Breton,=on the sea], anc. name of NW part of France, and identified with Brittany during the Middle Ages. Older spelling, Aremorica.

Armorican Massif (ärmô'rĭkùn), Fr. *Massif Armoricain,* upland of W France, extending from Paris Basin into Brittany. Heavily eroded and generally infertile, it rises to c.1,200 ft. in Montagnes d'Arrée and Montagnes Noires in Finistère dept.

Armour (är'mùr), city (pop. 900), ⊙ Douglas co., SE S.Dak., 57 mi. NW of Yankton; shipping center for grain, livestock, poultry. Founded 1886.

Armstrong, town (pop. estimate 2,500), S central Santa Fe prov., Argentina, 55 mi. WNW of Rosario; agr. center (wheat, corn, flax); grain elevators.

Armstrong, city (pop. 977), S B.C., 13 mi. NNE of Vernon; fruit and vegetable growing, dairying, woodworking, alfalfa and flour milling. Known for celery grown here.

Armstrong. **1** County (□ 660; pop. 80,842), W Pa.; ⊙ Kittanning. Coal-mining and mfg. area, drained by Allegheny R.; bounded SW by Kiskiminetas R. Bituminous coal; glass, metal, clay products; oil, gas; limestone, sand. Formed 1800. **2** County (□ 518; pop. 52), central S.Dak.; unorganized and attached to Stanley co. for judicial purposes; in Cheyenne River Indian Reservation; cattle-raising area bounded S by Cheyenne R., E by Missouri R. Formed 1883. **3** County (□ 909; pop. 2,215), extreme N Texas; ⊙ Claude. In high plains of the Panhandle, with part of Cap Rock escarpment in E; alt. 2,400–3,000 ft. Cattle ranching area, with some agr. (wheat, sorghum, dairy products, poultry). Duck hunting in small prairie lakes. Includes part of Palo Duro Canyon State Park along Prairie Dog Town Fork of Red R. Formed 1876.

Armstrong. **1** Town (pop. 943), Emmet co., NW Iowa, on East Des Moines R. and 18 mi. E of Estherville; feed mills, creamery. Gravel pit near by. **2** City (pop. 424), Howard co., central Mo., near Missouri R., 9 mi. N of Fayette, in grain and livestock area.

Armstrong, Fort, U.S. army post, Honolulu, T. H., at harbor entrance; established 1907.

Armstrong, Mount (9,161 ft.), on Alta.-B.C. border, in Rocky Mts., 55 mi. SW of Calgary.

Armstrong, Port, Alaska: see PORT ALEXANDER.

Armstrong Redwoods State Park (c.400 acres), Sonoma co., W Calif., near Russian R., just NW of Guerneville. Virgin redwood forest.

Armstrong Station, village (pop. estimate 400), W Ont., near NW end of L. Nipigon, 130 mi. E of Sioux Lookout; gold mining, lumbering. Airport, radio station.

Armthorpe, town and parish (pop. 6,135), West Riding, S Yorkshire, England, 3 mi. ENE of Doncaster; coal mining.

Armugam, India: see ARMAGON.

Armunia (ärmōō'nyä), village (pop. 2,098), Leon prov., NW Spain, on Bernesga R. and 2 mi. S of Leon; flour mills; cereals, stock, vegetables.

Armur (ŭrmōōr'), town (pop. 8,683), Nizamabad dist., N central Hyderabad state, India, 14 mi. NE of Nizamabad; rice, millet, sugar cane, oilseeds; silk weaving.

Armyansk (ŭrmyänsk'), village (1926 pop. 2,670), N Crimea, Russian SFSR, on Perekop Isthmus, on railroad and 45 mi. NW of Dzhankoi; flour milling, vegetable canning; wheat, livestock. Pop. largely Armenian and Greek. Formerly an active trading center called Armyanski Bazar [Rus.,=Armenian bazaar].

Arnac-Pompadour (ärnäk'-pōpädōōr'), village (pop. 995), Corrèze dept., S central France, 19 mi. NNW of Brive-la-Gaillarde; stud farms. Has 15th-cent. castle bestowed upon Marquise de Pompadour by Louis XV.

Arnaia (ärnä'ù), town (pop. 2,657), Chalcidice nome, central Macedonia, Greece, 11 mi. NE of Polygyros, at E foot of the Cholomon; timber; olive oil; wine. Formerly called Laringovi.

Arnas Dag (ärnäs' dä), Turkish *Arnas Dağ,* peak (11,645 ft.), E Turkey, in Van Mts., 9 mi. SW of Satak.

Arnau, Czechoslovakia: see HOSTINNE.

Arnaudville (är'nùvĭl), village (pop. 872), on St. Landry–St. Martin parish line, S central La., at head of navigation on Bayou Teche, 14 mi. SE of Opelousas; agr. (sugar cane, cotton); sugar milling, cotton ginning.

Arnauti, Cape (ärnäōō'tē), anc. *Acamas,* W tip of Cyprus, at NW gate of Khrysokhou Bay; 35°6'N 32°18'E. The Baths of Aphrodite are 5 mi. SE.

Arnavutkoy (ärnä'vōōtkû'ē), Turkish *Arnavutköy,* N section (pop. 9,832) of Istanbul, Turkey, on European side of the Bosporus; American Col. for Girls (1871) here.

Arnay-le-Duc (ärnä'-lù-dük'), village (pop. 1,840), Côte-d'Or dept., E central France, 15 mi. NE of Autun; tools, biscuits.

Arne (our'nä), Icelandic *Árne,* county [Icelandic *sýsla*] (pop. 5,506), SW Iceland; ⊙ Selfoss. Extends along SW part of Atlantic coast. Includes wide fertile valley formed by Olfusa R. and its affluents. Thingvallavatn lake in N. Sheep and cattle raising, dairying, fruit and vegetable growing. Chief towns are Selfoss, Eyrarbakki, and Hveragerdi; co. includes historic localities of Thingvellir and Skalholt. In N part of co. is noted Geysir hot spring.

Arneburg (är'nùbōōrk), town (pop. 3,073), in former Prussian Saxony prov., central Germany, after 1945 in Saxony-Anhalt, on the Elbe and 8 mi. NE of Stendal; grain, potatoes, livestock.

Arnedillo (ärnā-dhē'lyō), town (pop. 799), Logroño prov., N Spain, 21 mi. SE of Logroño; cotton mills; noted mineral springs. Coal mining near by.

Arnedo (ärnā'dhō), city (pop. 6,008), Logroño prov., N Spain, 24 mi. SE of Logroño; center of shoe industry; tanning, olive-oil processing, vegetable canning, rubber pressing, soap and chocolate mfg. Wine, pepper, truck products in area. Has anc. cave dwellings.

Arnegard (är'nùgärd), village (pop. 206), McKenzie co., W N.Dak., 8 mi. W of Watford City; potatoes, turkeys.

Arnemuiden (är'nùmoi'dùn), town (pop. 2,608), Zeeland prov., SW Netherlands, on Walcheren isl., 2 mi. E of Middelburg, near Sloe inlet of the Western Scheldt; fishing; shipbuilding.

Arnes (är'nĕs), town (pop. 1,095), Tarragona prov., NE Spain, 15 mi. NW of Tortosa; olive-oil processing; agr. trade (wine, cereals, vegetables, potatoes, almonds).
Arnesby, village and parish (pop. 282), central Leicester, England, 8 mi. SSE of Leicester; hosiery. Has Norman church.
Arnett (är'nĕt), town (pop. 690), ⊙ Ellis co., NW Okla., 30 mi. SW of Woodward, in agr. area (wheat, sorghums, livestock, poultry; dairy products). Wildlife refuge near by.
Arnhem (är'nŭm), Ger. *Arnheim*, city (pop. 97,350), ⊙ Gelderland prov., E Netherlands, port on the Lower Rhine and 36 mi. ESE of Utrecht; rail junction with rail bridge (WSW, on the Lower Rhine); mfg. of textiles (artificial silk, clothing, knitted goods), leather goods, chemicals, pharmaceuticals, engineering industry (engines, metal products, radio and electrical components); shipbuilding; tin smelting. Object of major Allied airborne landing (1944) in Second World War.
Arnhem, Cape, NE Northern Territory, Australia; NW point of Gulf of Carpentaria; 12°16'S 137°E.
Arnhem Bay, inlet of Arafura Sea, Arnhem Land, N Northern Territory, Australia; separated from Buckingham Bay (NW) by Flinders Point peninsula; 20 mi. E-W, 15 mi. N-S. Contains several small islets; Mallison Isl. at entrance.
Arnhem Land (□ c.31,200), aboriginal reservation, N Northern Territory, Australia, extends 200 mi. S from Cobourg Peninsula and 285 mi. E from Van Diemen Gulf to Gulf of Carpentaria; rugged; many bays. Archaeological expedition was made here (1948) by American and Australian scientists.
Arnho, Marshall Isls.: see ARNO.
Arni (ŭr'nē). **1** Town, Chingleput dist., Madras, India: see ARANI. **2** Town (pop. 19,668), North Arcot dist., E central Madras, India, 20 mi. SE of Vellore; road center in agr. area (rice, cotton, peanuts); cotton and silk weaving; peanut-oil works.
Arni Road, India: see KOLAMBUR.
Arnis (är'nĭs), town (pop. 977), in Schleswig-Holstein, NW Germany, on the Schlei, 17 mi. NE of Schleswig, in the Angeln; fishing; summer resort. Founded 1667.
Arnissa (är'nēsŭ), village (pop. 2,915), Pella nome, Macedonia, Greece, on railroad and 11 mi. W of Edessa, at N shore of L. Vegoritis. Formerly called Ostrovon.
Arniston Engine, town in Cockpen parish, E Midlothian, Scotland, on South Esk R. and 4 mi. S of Dalkeith; coal mining.
Arno (är'nō), atoll (□ 5; pop. 1,014), Ratak Chain, Majuro dist., Marshall Isls., W central Pacific, 300 mi. SE of Kwajalein; 26 mi. long; 83 islets; copra. Sometimes spelled Arnho.
Arno Bay, village and port, on E Eyre Peninsula, S South Australia, 100 mi. SW of Port Pirie across Spencer Gulf; agr. center; exports wheat.
Arnold, residential urban district (1931 pop. 14,470; 1951 census 21,474), S central Nottingham, England, 4 mi. NNE of Nottingham; hosiery industry. Has church dating from 12th cent.
Arnold. 1 Village (pop. 936), Custer co., central Nebr., 30 mi. W of Broken Bow and on S.Loup R.; livestock, grain, dairy and poultry produce. **2** Borough (pop. 10,263), Westmoreland co., W central Pa., on Allegheny R., adjoining New Kensington; glass. Inc. 1895.
Arnold City, village (pop. 3,219, with adjacent Fairhope), Fayette co., SW Pa.
Arnold Dam, Texas: see ROY INKS DAM.
Arnold Mills, R.I.: see CUMBERLAND.
Arnolds Park, town (pop. 1,078), Dickinson co., NW Iowa, near West Okoboji L., 16 mi. N of Spencer; mfg. (boxes, molds, castings). Sand and gravel pit near by. Summer resort in vicinity of several state parks. Has monument commemorating Spirit Lake Indian massacre (1857) of early settlers of region.
Arnoldstein (är'nōltshtīn), town (pop. 5,302), Carinthia, S Austria, 8 mi. SW of Villach, near Gail R., in Carnic Alps; rail junction; lead and zinc smelting; spa. Ruins of Arnoldstein cloister near by.
Arnon River (ärnō'), Cher dept., central France, rises 5 mi. N of Boussac, flows 85 mi. N, past Lignières, Chârost, and Lury-sur-Arnon, to the Cher 2 mi. below Vierzon. Receives (left) the Théols which flows past Issoudun.
Arnon River, Jordan: see MUJIB, WADI EL.
Arno River (är'nô), anc. *Arnus*, Tuscany, central Italy, rises in Etruscan Apennines on Monte Falterona, at alt. of 4,455 ft.; flows SSE and NNW, forming a loop around the PRATOMAGNO, past Pontassieve, and W, past Florence, Signa, Empoli, Pontedera, and Pisa, to Ligurian Sea 7 mi. SW of Pisa; length 150 mi., of which 19 mi. are navigable. Chief affluents: Sieve, Pesa, Elsa, and Era rivers. Connected with Tiber R. by the CHIANA and Paglia. Its valley, Val d'Arno, W of the Pratomagno, is noted for its fertility and scenic beauty and for numerous fossil bones of prehistoric animals found there. Its upper valley, E of the Pratomagno, is called the Casentino.
Arnota, Rumania: see HOREZU.
Arnouville-lès-Gonesse (ärnōovēl'-lā-gônĕs'), town (pop. 6,481), Seine-et-Oise dept., N central France, an outer NNE suburb of Paris, 9 mi. from Notre Dame Cathedral; precision metalworks; mfg. of plastics.
Arnprior (ärnprī'ŭr), town (pop. 3,895), SE Ont., on L. des Chats (widening of Ottawa R.) at mouth of Madawaska R., and 32 mi. W of Ottawa; woolen, felt, paper, pulp, and lumber milling; dairying; mfg. of bricks, tiles; resort. Iron is mined near by.
Arnsberg (ärns'bĕrk), town (pop. 16,675), in former Prussian prov. of Westphalia, W Germany, after 1945 in North Rhine-Westphalia, on a bend of the Ruhr and 15 mi. E of Iserlohn; paper milling. Summer resort. Has ruined 11th-cent. castle; 13th–14th-cent. church. Chartered 1238. Was main seat of Westphalian Vehmic courts (15th–16th cent.).
Arnsdorf, Czechoslovakia: see NOVY BOR.
Arnsdorf (ärns'dôrf), town (pop. 4,374), Saxony, E central Germany, 12 mi. ENE of Dresden; metalworking; mfg. of glass, furniture, parquet flooring, lead products.
Arnside, village and parish (pop. 1,154), S Westmorland, England, on Kent R., near Lancashire boundary, and 9 mi. SSW of Kendal; limestone quarrying; sheep, agr. Has Arnside Tower, a fortified 15th-cent. house.
Arnskrone, Poland: see WALCZ.
Arnstadt (ärn'shtät), city (pop. 27,846), Thuringia, central Germany, on Gera R. and 10 mi. SSW of Erfurt; 50°50'N 10°57'E. Rail junction; mfg. of gloves, shoes, machinery, radio equipment, precision instruments; tanning, rayon milling, woodworking. Fluorspar and manganese mined near by. Has 17th-cent. church of St. Boniface (J. S. Bach was organist here, 1703–05 and 1706–07); also two 13th-cent. churches, 16th-cent. town hall, 18th-cent. palace. First mentioned 704. Chartered 1266.
Arnstein (ärn'shtīn), town (pop. 2,527), Lower Franconia, NW Bavaria, Germany, 12 mi. N of Würzburg; brewing, tanning, flour milling. Has Gothic pilgrimage church.
Arnswalde, Poland: see CHOSZCZNO.
Arntfield, village (pop. estimate 400), W Que., 11 mi. WSW of Rouyn; mining (gold, copper, molybdenum, zinc, lead).
Arnultovice, Czechoslovakia: see NOVY BOR.
Arnus, Italy; see ARNO RIVER.
Aroa (ärō'ä), town (pop. 2,117), Yaracuy state, N Venezuela, at NW foot of Sierra de Aroa, 60 mi. W of Puerto Cabello; copper-mining center. Pyrite deposits consist of equal parts of iron and copper sulphides. Mines date from early colonial period (1632) and were once owned by Bolívar; now are badly flooded. Railroad connects Aroa with port of Tucacas on the Caribbean.
Aroa, Sierra de (syĕ'rä dā), range in Yaracuy state, N Venezuela, W of San Felipe; NE section (c.50 mi. long) of great Andean spur; rises to 5,866 ft. Has deposits of copper (Aroa), platinum (Albarico), lead (Chivacoa), gold.
Aroania (ärōä'nēŭ), mountain massif in N Peloponnesus, Greece, extends 25 mi. along border bet. Argolis and Corinthia nome and Achaea nome; rises to 7,725 ft. 33 mi. SE of Patras. Formerly called Chelmos or Khelmos.
Aroa River (ärō'ä), N Venezuela, rises S of Aroa (Yaracuy state), flows c.60 mi. ENE to Triste Gulf 7 mi. S of Tucacas.
Aroche (ärō'chā), town (pop. 5,659), Huelva prov., SW Spain, 45 mi. N of Huelva, in W spur of the Sierra Morena (Picos de Aroche), 45 mi. N of Huelva; copper, manganese, and graphite mining. Agr. products include cereals, fruit, olives, tubers; livestock. Lumbering, flour milling.
Aroe Bay, Indonesia: see ARU BAY.
Aroe Islands, Indonesia: see ARU ISLANDS.
Arolla (ärôl'lä), village and resort, Valais canton, S Switzerland, 15 mi. SSE of Sion, in Pennine Alps; alt. 6,570 ft.
Arolsen (är'ôl"zŭn), town (pop. 4,726), in former Prussian prov. of Hesse-Nassau, W Germany, after 1945 in Hesse, 10 mi. NE of Korbach; summer resort. Has baroque castle. Founded 1719. Until 1929 it was ⊙ former Waldeck principality. Sculptor Rauch and painter Kaulbach b. here.
Aroma (ärō'mä), village, Kassala prov., NE Anglo-Egyptian Sudan, on railroad and 30 mi. NNW of Kassala; cotton; livestock. Old Turkish fort.
Aroma, Bolivia: see SICASICA.
Aroma Park (ŭrō'mŭ), village (pop. 544), Kankakee co., NE Ill., at junction of Kankakee (bridged here) and Iroquois rivers, 3 mi. SE of Kankakee, in agr. area.
Aromashevo (ŭrŭmä'shĭvŭ), village (1939 pop. over 2,000), S Tyumen oblast, Russian SFSR, on Vagai R. and 30 mi. N of Katyshka, in agr. area (grain, livestock).
Arona (ärō'nä), village (pop. 384), Tenerife, Canary Isls., 38 mi. SW of Santa Cruz de Tenerife; tomatoes, wheat, barley, bananas, potatoes, grapes, fruit, livestock. Its port Los Cristianos (pop. 781) is 3 mi. SW.
Arona (ärô'nä), town (pop, 5,667), Novara prov., Piedmont, N Italy, port on SW shore of Lago Maggiore, 22 mi. N of Novara. Rail junction; commercial center; mfg. (cotton textiles, alcohol, sausage, toys, jewelry, cutlery, fountain pens). Limestone quarries near by. Has church of Santa Maria (15th–17th cent.; with altar piece by Gaudenzio Ferrari), 15th-cent. palace, Benedictine abbey, and ruins of Borromean castle. On near-by hill is a large copper and bronze statue (1624) of St. Charles Borromeo, who was b. here 1538.
Arona (ŭrō'nŭ), borough (pop. 482), Westmoreland co., SW Pa., 6 mi. WSW of Greensburg.
Aron River (ärō'), Nièvre dept., central France, rises S of Châtillon-en-Bazois, flows c.25 mi. SW to the Loire at Decize. Followed throughout its course by Nivernais Canal.
Aroostook (ŭrōō'stŏŏk), village (pop. estimate c.300), W N.B., on St. John R. at mouth of Aroostook R., at Maine border 16 mi. NE of Presque Isle, in potato region. Site of hydroelectric power station.
Aroostook (ŭrōō'stŏŏk, -stŭk), largest county (□ 6,805; pop. 96,039) in Maine, bordering on Que. and N.B.; ⊙ Houlton. One of nation's richest agr. areas, producing c.15% of U.S. potato crop. Large tracts of lake-studded wilderness furnish lumber and offer hunting, fishing, canoeing. Manganese deposits. Mfg.: wood products, farm machinery, fertilizers. Drained by Allagash, Aroostook, Fish, Little Madawaska, Machias, Mattawamkeag, Meduxnekeag, and St. John rivers. Formed 1839.
Aroostook River, Maine and N.B., rises in N Penobscot co., Maine; winds c.140 mi. generally E, through Aroostook co., to St. John R. in N.B., 6 mi. E of Fort Fairfield, Maine.
Aror (ŭrōr'), village, Sukkur dist., NE Sind, W Pakistan, 5 mi. SE of Rohri. Site of anc. Alor, ⊙ Hindu dynasty; visited (A.D. c.640) by Hsüan-Tsang.
Arorae (ärô'rī), atoll (□ 5; pop. 1,558), Kingsmill Group, S Gilbert Isls., W central Pacific; 2°38'S 176°49'E; produces copra.
Aroroy (ärōroi'), town (1939 pop. 4,177; 1948 municipality pop. 23,888), N Masbate isl., Philippines, on Masbate Pass; fishing and agr. center (rice, coconuts).
Arosa (ärō'zä), village (pop. 1,980), Grisons canton, E Switzerland, on Plessur R. and 8 mi. SE of Chur; one of highest (alt. c.6,000 ft.) health resorts and leading winter sports centers in Switzerland.
Arosa Bay (ärō'sä), Sp. *Ría de Arosa* (rē'ä dhä), inlet of the Atlantic in N Spain, on W coast of Galicia, at mouth of Ulla R., bet. La Coruña and Pontevedra provs.; 16 mi. long, 2–12 mi. wide. At entrance is Salvora Isl. (lighthouse), near center is Arosa Isl. Fishing ports and bathing resorts (Vilagarcía, Carubados, Puebla de Caramiñal) dot deeply indented shores.
Aroser Rothorn (ärō'zŭr rōt'hôrn), peak (9,788 ft.) in the Alps, E Switzerland, 4 mi. SW of Arosa.
Arouca (ärō'kŭ), town (pop. 599), Aveiro dist., N central Portugal, 30 mi. NE of Aveiro, in barren hilly region. Has 8th-cent. convent.
Arouca (ŭrōō'kŭ), village (pop. 3,661), N Trinidad, B.W.I., on railroad and 12 mi. E of Port of Spain; sugar growing.
Aroussa, El- (ĕl-ärōōsä'), village, Medjez-el-Bab dist., N Tunisia, on Siliana R. and 12 mi. ESE of Teboursouk, in wheat-growing region.
Arp, city (pop. 909), Smith co., E Texas, 17 mi. SE of Tyler; oil refinery; trade center in oil, agr. area.
Arpacay (ärpächī'), Turkish *Arpaçay*, village (pop. 881), Kars prov., NE Turkey, on the Arpa-Chai and 20 mi. NE of Kars; wheat, barley, potatoes. Formerly Zarusat.
Arpa-Chai or **Arpa-Chay** (ärpä-chī'), two left affluents of Aras R. in Armenian SSR. The Western [Rus. *zapadny*] Arpa-Chai, Turkish *Arpa Çayı*, Armenian *Akhuryan*, rises in a small lake in the Lesser Caucasus 20 mi. NW of Leninakan, flows 85 mi. S through ARPALICH GORGE, past Leninakan, forming USSR-Turkey line to its confluence with the Aras 45 mi. W of Erivan. The Eastern [Rus. *vostochny*] Arpa-Chai rises in Karabakh Upland SE of L. Sevan, flows c.70 mi. W and SW, past Mikoyan and Bash-Norashen, to the Aras below Norashen; used for irrigation in lower course.
Arpaia (ärpä'yä), village (pop. 1,708), Benevento prov., Campania, S Italy, 14 mi. SW of Benevento.
Arpajon (ärpä-zhō'), town (pop. 4,134), Seine-et-Oise dept., N central France, 19 mi. SSW of Paris; agr. trade center (especially beans, cherries); shoe mfg. Has wooden 17th-cent. market hall.
Arpaklen (ŭrpŭklyĕn'), village, SW Ashkhabad oblast, Turkmen SSR, on SW slope of the Kopet-Dagh, 45 mi. SSE of Kizyl-Arvat; barite and witherite quarries.
Arpalich Gorge (ŭrpä'lyĭch), defile in the Lesser Caucasus, NW Armenian SSR, on the upper Western Arpa-Chai, 15 mi. N of Leninakan; alt. 7,200 ft. Here the Arpa-Chai, contained by 300-ft.-long dam, forms storage reservoir (□ 8) for irrigation of Shiraki Steppe.
Arpasul-de-Jos (ärpä'shōōl-dā-zhôs'), Rum. *Arpaşul-de-Jos*, Hung. *Alsóárpás* (ŏl'shōär"päsh), village (pop. 1,301), Sibiu prov., central Rumania, on railroad and 14 mi. SW of Fagaras; agr. center noted for colorful regional costumes. Has 18th-cent. church.
Arpino (ärpē'nô), anc. *Arpinum*, town (pop. 2,613), Frosinone prov., Latium, S central Italy, 13 mi. E of Frosinone; woolen mill. Has anc. walls, remains

of medieval castle. Agrippa, Marius, and Cicero b. here. Anciently a Volscian, later (305 B.C.) a Roman town.

'Arqa, Aden: see IRQA.

Arquà Petrarca (ärkwä' pĕträr'kä), village (pop. 684), Padova prov., Veneto, N Italy, in Euganean Hills, 12 mi. SW of Padua. Has house and tomb of Petrarch, who died here in 1374.

Arquà Polesine (pōlā'zēnĕ), village (pop. 1,547), Rovigo prov., Veneto, N Italy, 5 mi. SSW of Rovigo, in cereal-growing region. Has castle rebuilt in 13th cent.

Arquata del Tronto (ärkwä'tä dĕl trôn'tô), village (pop. 267), Ascoli Piceno prov., The Marches, central Italy, on Tronto R. and 16 mi. WSW of Ascoli Piceno; resort.

Arquata Scrivia (skrē'vyä), village (pop. 2,485), Alessandria prov., Piedmont, N Italy, on Scrivia R. and 7 mi. SSE of Novi Ligure; rail junction; silk and jute mills.

Arque (är'kā), town (pop. c.6,300), ⊙ Arque prov., Cochabamba dept., central Bolivia, on S slopes of Cordillera de Cochabamba, 31 mi. SSW of Cochabamba, and on railroad from Oruro; alt. 8,858 ft. In tin-mining region; corn, orchards. Berenguela tin mines 6 mi. S.

Arquennes (ärkĕn'), agr. village (pop. 1,978), Hainaut prov., S central Belgium, on Charleroi-Brussels Canal and 3 mi. SW of Nivelles.

Arques (ärk), ESE suburb (pop. 5,161) of Saint-Omer, Pas-de-Calais dept., N France, at junction of Aa R. and Neuffossé Canal; crystal and glass-mfg. center; paper milling, jute spinning, distilling.

Arques-la-Bataille (-lä-bätī'), town (pop. 2,429), Seine-Inférieure dept., N France, on the Arques and 4 mi. SSE of Dieppe; rayon mfg., woodworking. Has ruined castle (12th cent.) of dukes of Normandy. Here, in 1589, Henry IV defeated Catholic League under duke of Mayenne.

Arques River, Seine-Inférieure dept., N France, formed by the Béthune and 2 other streams near Arques-la-Bataille, flows 4 mi. NW to English Channel at Dieppe.

Arquillos (ärkē'lyōs), town (pop. 2,607), Jaén prov., S Spain, 13 mi. NE of Linares; olive-oil processing, stock raising.

Arrabalde (äräväl'dā), village (pop. 1,003), Zamora prov., NW Spain, 14 mi. NW of Benavente; linseed-oil processing; cereals, vegetables.

Arrabal de Jesús (äräväl' dhā hāsōōs'), NNW suburb (pop. 3,261) of Tortosa, Tarragona prov., NE Spain, on right bank of the Ebro; olive-oil processing, soap and fertilizer mfg.

Arrabal de San Lázaro (sän' lä'thärō), S suburb (pop. 1,682) of Tortosa, Tarragona prov., NE Spain; olive-oil processing.

Arrábida, Serra da (sĕ'rŭ därä'bēdŭ), range of S central Portugal, in S Estremadura prov., overlooking the Atlantic coast bet. Cape Espichel (W) and Setúbal (E). Rises to 1,640 ft. in the Formosinho (panorama). At alt. of 940 ft. is the ruined convent of Arrábida directly above the sea.

Arracourt (äräkōōr'), village (pop. 333), Meurthe-et-Moselle dept., NE France, 7 mi. S of Château-Salins; cattle.

Arraga (ärä'gä), village (pop. estimate 500), W central Santiago del Estero prov., Argentina, on railroad and 15 mi. S of Santiago del Estero. Wheat, corn, cotton, alfalfa, watermelons; stock raising, lumbering, charcoal burning, flour milling.

Arrah (ŭ'rŭ), city (pop. 53,122), ⊙ Shahabad dist., W Bihar, India, on Ganges Plain, on Arrah Canal and 31 mi. W of Patna; rail and road junction; trades in rice, wheat, gram, oilseeds, barley, corn, sugar cane; oilseed milling. Figured in Sepoy Rebellion of 1857. Mfg. of sugar-mill accessories 7 mi. W, at village of Bihiya, formerly also spelled Beheya.

Arrah Canal, India: see SON CANALS.

Arraial do Cabo (ärīäl' dōō kä'bōō), town (pop. 1,768), E Rio de Janeiro state, Brazil, on Cabo Frio, 75 mi. W of Rio; saltworking.

Arraias (ärī'ŭs), city (pop. 1,001), E central Goiás, central Brazil, 260 mi. NNE or Anápolis; cattle, corn, rice, mangabeira rubber. Rock-crystal, gold, and platinum deposits in area. Formerly spelled Arrayas.

Arraiján (ärīhän'), village (pop. 1,298), Panama prov., central Panama, on Inter-American Highway and 7 mi. W of Panama city, at Canal Zone border; agr. center (bananas, oranges); stock raising.

Arraiolos (ärŭyō'lōōsh), town (pop. 2,391), Évora dist., S central Portugal, on railroad and 10 mi. NNW of Évora; noted for its carpet manufactures (Moorish style); also makes cheese, smoked sausages, flour products, footwear. Has ruined castle and remnants of town walls and gates.

Arran (ă'rŭn), island (□ 165.8; pop. 4,506), largest in Buteshire, Scotland, in the Firth of Clyde, separated from Kintyre peninsula (W) by Kilbrannan Sound and from Bute isl. (NE) by Sound of Bute; 20 mi. long, 10 mi. wide. Wild and mountainous, rising to 2,866 ft. on Goat Fell (NE). Chief town is BRODICK, on E coast; LAMLASH is 4 mi. S of Brodick. Isl. has fine scenery and extensive deer forests; hunting and fishing attract many tourists. In 12th cent. the Scots took Arran from Norway and it became a royal hunting ground.

Arran Islands, Ireland: see ARAN ISLANDS.

Arras, England: see MARKET WEIGHTON AND ARRAS.

Arras (ă'rŭs, Fr. äräs'), anc. *Nemetacum* and *Nemetocenna,* town (pop. 30,065), ⊙ Pas-de-Calais dept., N France, on the Scarpe (canalized) and 27 mi. SSW of Lille; important road center; beet-sugar and vegetable-oil processing, metalworking, brewing, hosiery and agr. tool mfg. Trade in grains and in plants yielding oil and dyes. Formerly noted for its tapestry manufactures. Despite destruction of 2 wars, Arras retains aspect of a 17th-cent. Sp.-Flemish town. Its Renaissance town hall and 18th-cent. cathedral were heavily damaged in First World War, restored after 1919, and again hit in Second World War. The restored 18th-cent. abbey of St. Vaast (now housing mus.) was left intact in 1939–45. City is of Gallo-Roman origin (chief city of Atrebates); became ⊙ Artois, and, sharing its history, passed in turn to Burgundy, France, and Spain, being definitively reconquered by France in 1640. Gives its name to treaty of 1435, bet. Charles VII of France and Philip the Good of Burgundy, and to treaty of 1482, bet. Louis XI of France and Maximilian of Austria. Subjected to heavy front-line shelling in First World War (town center destroyed), Arras resisted Ger. assaults and gave its name to Br. offensive of April–May 1917, in which Canadians distinguished themselves at Vimy Ridge (6 mi. N). Second World War damages heaviest in S part of town. Robespierre b. here.

Arrayanes (ärīä'nĕs), N suburb (pop. 2,402) of Jaén, Jaén prov., S Spain; important lead mines.

Arrayas, Brazil: see ARRAIAS.

Arre (är), village (pop. 408), Gard dept., S France, 5 mi. WSW of Le Vigan; silk-hosiery mfg.

Arreau (ärō'), village (pop. 832), Hautes-Pyrénées dept., SW France, on Neste R. and 15 mi. SE of Bagnères-de-Bigorre; road junction and railroad terminus; commercial center of AURE VALLEY. Has 15th–16th-cent. church with Romanesque portal.

Arrecife (ärā-thē'fā), city (pop. 7,692), chief town and port of Lanzarote isl., Canary Isls., 125 mi. ENE of Las Palmas; 28°58'N 13°33'W. Roads radiate to all parts of the isl. The spacious harbor has busy foreign trade. Region produces onions, cereals, potatoes, chick-peas, grapes, fruit. Fishing. Saltworks, fish canneries. Mfg. of embroidery.

Arrecifes (äräsē'fĕs), town (pop. 7,550), ⊙ Bartolomé Mitre dist. (□ 659; pop. 32,066), N Buenos Aires prov., Argentina, on Arrecifes R. and 30 mi. SE of Pergamino, in agr. region (corn, wheat, flax, livestock).

Arrecifes River, N Buenos Aires prov., Argentina, formed just W of Arrecifes by union of 2 headstreams, flows c.60 mi. E and NE, past Arrecifes, to Baradero R. (arm of the lower Paraná) 5 mi. NW of Baradero.

Arrée, Montagnes d' (mōtä'nyŭ därā'), low granitic mountains in Finistère dept., W France, in the eroded Armorican Massif; extend 30 mi. SW–NE across dept.; rise to 1,283 ft. Also called Monts d'Arrée and Montagne d'Arré.

Arresa (ärĕ'sä), village, Adi Ugri div., central Eritrea, 37 mi. SW of Asmara, in cotton- and coffee-growing region; alt. 6,630 ft.

Arreskov Lake (ä'rŭskou) or **Fleninge Lake** (flĕn'-ĭng-ŭ), S Fyn isl., Denmark; largest (2 mi. long, 1 mi. wide) on Fyn isl.

Arreso (ä'rŭsû), Dan. *Arresø,* largest lake (5 mi. long, 5 mi. wide) of Denmark, on N Zealand isl.; joined by canal to Roskilde Fjord.

Arretium, Italy: see AREZZO, town.

Arrhoe, Turkey: see URFA, city.

Arriaga (äryä'gä). **1** City (pop. 4,511), Chiapas, S Mexico, in Pacific coastal lowland, on railroad and 13 mi. NW of Tonalá; processing and agr. center (tropical fruit, sugar cane, tobacco, cereals, livestock); tanning, furniture making. Airfield. **2** Town (pop. 1,791), San Luis Potosí, N central Mexico, on interior plateau, 32 mi. SW of San Luis Potosí; alt. 7,212 ft.; grain, beans, fruit, livestock.

Arriate (äryä'tā), town (pop. 3,696), Málaga prov., S Spain, in Sierra de Ronda, on railroad and 4 mi. N of Ronda; olives and olive oil, grapes, liquor, flour, fruit. Mfg. of meat products.

Arriba (ŭrī'bŭ), town (pop. 367), Lincoln co., E Colo., 22 mi. E of Limon; alt. 5,239 ft. Livestock, grain, poultry.

Arrieta (äryā'tä), landing (pop. 108), Lanzarote, Canary Isls., 11 mi. NNE of Arrecife. Sometimes Puerto de Arrieta.

Arrigorriaga (ärēgōryä'gä), village (pop. 2,268), Vizcaya prov., NE Spain, on Nervión R. and 4 mi. SSE of Bilbao; paper, explosives, nails. Iron mines.

Arris (ärē'), village (pop. 107), Constantine dept., NE Algeria, in the Aurès massif, 23 mi. SSE of Batna; sheep raising. Mercury mined near by.

Arroba (ärō'vä), village (pop. 1,053), Ciudad Real prov., S central Spain, 24 mi. WNW of Piedrabuena; cereals, chick-peas, tubers, fruit.

Arrochar (ă'rŏkh-ŭr), agr. village and parish (pop. 670), NW Dumbarton, Scotland, at N end of Loch Long, 14 mi. N of Helensburgh; tourist resort.

Arrochar (ă'rōkär), SE N.Y., a section of Richmond borough of New York city, in E Staten Isl., S of St. George. U.S. Fort Wadsworth is near by.

Arroio do Meio (äroi'ōō dōō mā'ōō), city (pop. 1,077). E central Rio Grande do Sul, Brazil, on Taquari R. and 7 mi. N of Estrêla; hogs, lard, grain. Semiprecious stones found in area.

Arroio dos Ratos (dōōs rä'tōōs), town (pop. 6,332), E Rio Grande do Sul, Brazil, 30 mi. WSW of Pôrto Alegre; important coal-mining center. Coal is taken by rail to Jacuí R. (10 mi. NE), thence by barge to Pôrto Alegre and its seaports.

Arroio Grande (grăn'dĭ), city (pop. 2,619), S Rio Grande do Sul, Brazil, 50 mi. SW of Pelotas; rice, fruit, wool.

Arromanches-les-Bains (ärômăsh'-lā-bē'), village (pop. 270), Calvados dept., NW France, resort on the Channel, 5 mi. NE of Bayeux. In Second World War, Br. troops landed near by (June 6, 1944) in Normandy invasion.

Arrôniz (ärō'nēth), town (pop. 1,940), Navarre prov., N Spain, 6 mi. SW of Estella; olive-oil processing. Wine, cereals in area.

Arroscia River (är-rô'shä), NW Italy, rises in Ligurian Alps 2 mi. E of Mt. Saccarello, flows 23 mi. E, joining Neva R. (14 mi. long) to form Centa (chĕn'-tä) R., which flows 2 mi. E to Gulf of Genoa near Albenga.

Arrouch, El- (ĕl-ärōōsh'), village (pop. 3,318), Constantine dept., NE Algeria, in irrigated Saf-Saf valley, 16 mi. S of Philippeville; olive-oil pressing, flour milling; tobacco and winegrowing. Zardézas Dam is 4 mi. SE.

Arroux River (ärōō'), Côte-d'Or and Saône-et-Loire depts., E central France, rises near Arnay-le-Duc, flows 75 mi. SSW, past Autun, Toulon-sur-Arroux, and Geugnon (head of canalization), to the Loire just below Digoin. Receives the Bourbince (left).

Arrow, Lough (lŏkh), lake (5 mi. long, 2 mi. wide), E Co. Sligo, Ireland, 14 mi. SSE of Sligo, drained N by Unshin R. There are numerous isls.

Arrowhead, Lake, San Bernardino co., S Calif., resort lake (2½ mi. long) in San Bernardino Mts., 11 mi. NNE of San Bernardino; alt. c.5,100 ft. Lake Arrowhead village is center of summer- and winter-resort region.

Arrowhead Hot Springs, Calif.: see SAN BERNARDINO, city.

Arrowhead Peak (4,216 ft.), S Calif., a W foothill summit of San Bernardino Mts., just N of San Bernardino; slope is marked by 7½-acre arrowhead-shaped rock outcrop.

Arrow Lake (15 mi. long, 2 mi. wide), W Ont., on Minn. border, 40 mi. WSW of Fort William; alt. 1,510 ft. Drains SE into L. Superior.

Arrow Lakes, S B.C., 2 expansions of Columbia R., bet. Revelstoke and U.S. border; total □ 150. Upper Arrow L. is 47 mi. long, 1–3 mi. wide; Lower Arrow L. is 53 mi. long, 2 mi. wide. Both lakes lie bet. high mtn. ranges and are noted for their scenic beauty. Steamers of the Canadian Pacific RR ply the lakes, and a branch line connects Arrowhead, at head of the upper lake, with Revelstoke on the main line.

Arrow River. 1 In Worcester and Warwick, England, rises just N of Alvechurch, flows 11 mi. S, past Redditch and Alcester, to Avon R. 5 mi. NE of Evesham. Receives the Alne at Alcester. **2** In Wales and England, rises in Radnor 7 mi. W of Kington, flows 25 mi. E into Hereford, past Kington, to Lugg R. just SSE of Leominster.

Arrow Rock, town (pop. 170), Saline co., central Mo., on Missouri R. and 14 mi. ESE of Marshall.

Arrowrock Dam, SW Idaho, on Boise R. and 14 mi. E of Boise. Concrete, arch-gravity dam (350 ft. high, 1,150 ft. long) completed 1915 as unit in Boise irrigation project. Forms Arrowrock Reservoir (capacity 286,500 acre-ft.), used in irrigation of c.170,000 acres.

Arrowsic (ŭrou'sĭk), farming and fishing town (pop. 172), Sagadahoc co., SW Maine, just below and across Kennebec R. from Bath.

Arrowsmith, village (pop. 316), McLean co., central Ill., 18 mi. E of Bloomington, in grain-growing area.

Arrowtown, borough (pop. 201), S central S.Isl., New Zealand, 100 mi. WNW of Dunedin; agr.

Arrowwood, village (pop. 206), S Alta., near Bow R., 50 mi. ESE of Calgary; wheat.

Arroyito (äroi-ē'tō), town (pop. 2,984), E central Córdoba prov., Argentina, on the Río Segundo and 70 mi. E of Córdoba; wheat, flax, oats, peanuts, sunflowers, livestock.

Arroyo (äroi'ō), town (pop. 4,980), SE Puerto Rico, sugar port 4 mi. ESE of Guayama, surrounded by sugar plantations; port of entry, rail terminus; sugar milling, rum and alcohol distilling. Acetone-butyl alcohol plant. Adjoining E is a U.S. military reservation. The large Lafayette sugar mill is just N. Hematite deposits in vicinity.

Arroyo Aguiar, Argentina: see ASCOCHINGA.

Arroyo Arenas (äroi'ō ărä'näs), town (pop. 2,123), Havana prov., W Cuba, 13 mi. SW of Havana; tobacco, vegetables, fruit, livestock.

Arroyo de la Luz (dhā lä lōōth'), town (pop. 10,228), Cáceres prov., W Spain, in Estremadura, 11 mi. W of Cáceres; agr. trade center. Mfg. of footwear, cotton textiles, knit goods, chocolate; cork processing, flour milling, olive pressing. Active wool trade. Cereals, wine, vegetables, livestock in area. Has fine town hall and mansion of counts of Benavente. Formerly called Arroyo del Puerco.

Arroyo del Puerco, Spain: see ARROYO DE LA LUZ.

Arroyo de San Serván (sän' sĕrvän'), town (pop. 2,953), Badajoz prov., W Spain, 7 mi. SW of Mérida; cereals, grapes, olives, fruit.
Arroyo Grande (grän'dā), village (pop. c.1,000), Pando dept., NW Bolivia, on Arroyo Grande R. (branch of Tahuamanu R.) and 75 mi. WSW of Puerto Rico; rubber.
Arroyo Grande (ŭroi'ō grăn'dē), city (pop. 1,723), San Luis Obispo co., SW Calif., 12 mi. SSE of San Luis Obispo; grows flower and vegetable seeds, truck, grain; cattle. Oil field near by. Founded 1877, inc. 1911.
Arroyo Grande (äroi'ō grän'dā), town (pop. 1,000), Flores dept., SW Uruguay, 33 mi. SSW of Trinidad, on Soriano-Colonia dept. border.
Arroyo Hondo (ŭroi'ō ŏn'dō), village (1940 pop. 541), Taos co., N N.Mex., 10 mi. NNW of Taos, near the Rio Grande, in Sangre de Cristo Mts.; alt. 6,775 ft.; agr., livestock. Part of Carson Natl. Forest near by.
Arroyomolinos de la Vera (äroi"ōmōlē'nōs dhā lä vā'rä), village (pop. 1,143), Cáceres prov., W Spain, 12 mi. ENE of Plasencia; cattle raising; olive oil, wine.
Arroyomolinos de León (lāōn'), town (pop. 2,245), Huelva prov., SW Spain, in the Sierra Morena, 12 mi. NE of Aracena; cork and olive center; also fruit, acorns, cereals, livestock. Mfg. of meat products.
Arroyomolinos de Montánchez (mōntän'chĕth), town (pop. 2,203), Cáceres prov., W Spain, 23 mi. SE or Cáceres; olive pressing, sheep and hog raising; cereals, wine, fruit. Near here the English and Spanish defeated (1811) the French.
Arroyo Naranjo (äroi'ō närän'hō), town (pop. 2,755), Havana prov., W Cuba, 7 mi. S of Havana (linked by rail); dairying; fruit, vegetables.
Arroyo Pareja or **Puerto Arroyo Pareja** (pwĕr'tō, pärā'hä), town (pop. estimate 1,000), SW Buenos Aires prov., Argentina, at mouth of the inlet Arroyo Pareja of the Bahía Blanca (bay), 2 mi. S of Punta Alta. One of the ports of Bahía Blanca with harbor installations extending onto 1-mi.-long embankment (S); grain elevators. Beach resort at base of embankment. Sand and gravel quarries near by.
Arroyo Seco (sä'kō), town (pop. estimate 2,500), SE Santa Fe prov., Argentina, near Paraná R., 15 mi. SSE of Rosario; agr. center (potatoes, corn, flax); viticulture; flour milling, winemaking, fish canning.
Arroyo Seco, town (pop. 576), Querétaro, central Mexico, 25 mi. NNW of Jalpan; cereals, sugar.
Arroyos y Esteros (äroi'ōs ē ĕstā'rōs), town (dist. pop. 12,840), La Cordillera dept., S central Paraguay, 40 mi. NE of Asunción; stock-raising center; sugar refining, liquor distilling.
Arruda dos Vinhos (ärōō'dŭ dōosh vē'nyōosh), town (pop. 1,039), Lisboa dist., central Portugal, 18 mi. N of Lisbon, winegrowing center. Has 16th-cent. churches.
Arru Islands, Indonesia: see ARU ISLANDS.
Ars or **Ars-en-Ré** (ärzä-rā'), village (pop. 835), on W coast of Île de Ré, Charente-Maritime dept., W France, 18 mi. WNW of La Rochelle; saltworks; truck gardening.
Arsache (ärsä'kā), village (pop. 4,364), Bucharest prov., S Rumania, 13 mi. SW of Giurgiu; grain, vegetables.
Arsenal, Ark.: see PINE BLUFF.
Ars-en-Ré, France: see ARS.
Arsenyevo or **Arsen'yevo** (ŭrsyĕ'nyĭvŭ), village (1948 pop. over 500), SW Tula oblast, Russian SFSR, 21 mi. ESE of Belev; rye, oats.
Arshan (ŭrshän'), village (1948 pop. over 500), SW Buryat-Mongol Autonomous SSR, Russian SFSR, on S slope of Eastern Sayan Mts., 85 mi. WSW of Irkutsk; tuberculosis sanatorium; tourist center.
Arsia, Yugoslavia: see RASA.
Arsiè (ärsyā') village (pop. 1,537), Belluno prov., Veneto, N Italy, 10 mi. N of Bassano; wine making.
Arsiero (ärsyā'rō), town (pop. 2,140), Vicenza prov., Veneto, N Italy, 20 mi. NNW of Vicenza. Industrial center; paper and woolen mills, ironworks, furniture factory. Reconstructed following heavy fighting (1916) here in First World War.
Arsikere (ŭr'sĭkĕrē), town (pop. 7,051), Hassan dist., W central Mysore, India, 24 mi. NNE of Hassan; rail junction (workshops); road and agr. trade center; cotton ginning, furniture mfg. Has 12th-cent. Chalukyan temple. Experimental farm. Kaolin works at near-by Bageshpur village.
Arsinga, Turkey: see ERZINCAN, town.
Arsinoë, Cyprus: see FAMAGUSTA.
Arsinoë, Cyrenaica: see TOCRA.
Arsinoë (ärsĭ'nōē). **1** Anc. city of Upper Egypt, W of the Nile; its extensive ruins are at site of modern Faiyum. First called Crocodilopolis, it was renamed and developed by Ptolemy II. **2** Anc. city of Egypt, near modern Suez. Founded by Ptolemy II, it was terminus of a canal from the Pelusiac arm of the Nile to the Gulf of Suez and became an important port. Later called Cleopatris.
Arsk (ärsk), town (1926 pop. 2,638), NW Tatar Autonomous SSR, Russian SFSR, 35 mi. NE of Kazan, on railroad; metalworking, food processing.
Arsoli (är'sōlē), village (pop. 1,550), Roma prov., Latium, central Italy, 13 mi. ENE of Tivoli. Has castle (rebuilt 16th cent.).
Ars-sur-Moselle (ärsür-mōzĕl'), town (pop. 2,213), Moselle dept., NE France, on left bank of Moselle R. and 6 mi. SW of Metz; mfg. (explosives, bolts, cement pipes), canning. Near by are remains (several arches) of a Roman aqueduct which crossed the Moselle here.
Arsuf (ärsōōf'), anc. *Apollonia Sozusa*, anc. city, W Palestine, in Plain of Sharon, on Mediterranean, 9 mi. NNE of Tel Aviv. As Arsur it was important during Crusades as ⊙ seigneurie. Richard Coeur de Lion here defeated (1191) Saladin. Remains of 13th-cent. fortifications.
Arsuk (äkh'sōōk), settlement (pop. 274), Frederikshaab dist., SW Greenland, on the coast, at mouth of Arsuk Fjord (20 mi. long), 65 mi. SE of Frederikshaab; 61°10'N 48°27'W; fishing, sheep raising. Radio station. IVIGTUT cryolite mine near by.
Arsur, Palestine: see ARSUF.
Artá (ärtä'), town (pop. 5,076), Majorca, Balearic Isls., rail terminus 38 mi. ENE of Palma; agr. center (almonds, carobs, figs, fruit, grapes, olives, livestock). Olive-oil presses, limekilns. Renowned for near-by stalactite caves (5 mi. ESE on coast) and prehistoric monuments.
Arta (är'tŭ), nome (□ 672; pop. 65,175), Epirus, Greece; ⊙ Arta. Bounded N by the Tzoumerka massif, W by Louros R., S by Gulf of Arta, and E by the Achelous R., it is drained by Arachthos R. Agr.: corn, barley, cotton, citrus fruit, almonds, pears. Fisheries in lagoons on Gulf of Arta.
Arta, anc. *Ambracia* (ămbrā'shŭ), city (pop. 9,441), ⊙ Arta nome, S Epirus, Greece, on Arachthos R. 10 mi. from its mouth and 36 mi. SSE of Ioannina; trade center for cotton, grain, citrus fruit, olives, almonds, tobacco, fish; textile, leather, and embroidery mfg. Seat of Gr. metropolitan. Has Byzantine remains. Originally founded 7th cent. B.C. as a Corinthian colony, it passed 338 B.C. to Philip II of Macedon and 294 B.C. to Pyrrhus, who made it ⊙ Epirus. It joined Aetolian League in 229 B.C. and declined after its conquest (189 B.C.) by Rome. Largely deserted (31 B.C.) when pop. was settled in newly founded Nicopolis. Rebuilt as Arta in Byzantine times, it was taken (1083) by the Normans, was (13th–14th cent.) in independent Epirus where it succeeded Ioannina as capital and passed (1430) to the Turks, who called it Narda. It was annexed to Greece in 1881 and was on frontier of European Turkey until 1913.
Arta, Gulf of, or **Ambracian Gulf** (ămbrā'shŭn), Gr. *Amvrakikos Kolpos*, large Ionian inlet in W central Greece, bet. S Epirus and Acarnania; 20 mi. long, 5–10 mi. wide. Nearly enclosed, it communicates with Ionian Sea via 1-mi.-wide channel at Preveza. Other small ports are Vonitsa and Amphilochia on S (Acarnanian) shore. The Gulf receives Arachthas and Louros rivers. Also called Gulf of Ambrakia (Amvrakia).
Artajona (ärtähō'nä), town (pop. 2,297), Navarre prov., N Spain, 17 mi. SSW of Pamplona; center for olive-oil and wine production; chocolate, brandy mfg. Sugar beets, potatoes, cereals in area.
Artaki, Turkey: see ERDEK.
Artana (ärtä'nä), town (pop. 2,183), Castellón de la Plana prov., E Spain, 14 mi. SW of Castellón de la Plana; cork processing, basket making, lumbering; olive oil, cereals, fruit, hemp.
Arta Plateau (är'tä), basaltic plateau (2,460 ft.) of Fr. Somaliland, on S coast of Gulf of Tadjoura, 25 mi. W of Djibouti; hill station.
Arta River, Greece: see ARACHTHOS RIVER.
Artashat (ŭrtŭshät'), town (1926 pop. 2,505), S Armenian SSR, in irrigated Aras R. valley, on railroad and 15 mi. S of Erivan; distilling (wines, brandies); viti- and sericulture; cotton, wheat. Called Kamarlu or Kamarlyu until 1945, when it was renamed Artaxata for anc. ⊙ Armenia (2d–1st cent. B.C.), whose ruins are near by.
Artaxata, Armenian SSR: see ARTASHAT.
Arteaga (ärtā-ä'gä). **1** Town (pop. 1,632), Coahuila, N Mexico, in Sierra Madre Oriental, 8 mi. ENE of Saltillo; alt. 5,282 ft. Rail terminus; corn, beans, istle fibers, candelilla wax, cattle. Silver, lead deposits near by. **2** Town (pop. 1,332), Michoacán, W Mexico, in foothills, 70 mi. SSW of Uruapan; cereals, coffee, sugar, fruit.
Artegna (ärtā'nyä), town (pop. 2,514), Udine prov., Friuli–Venezia Giulia, NE Italy, 12 mi. NNW of Udine; shoe factory.
Arteijo (ärtā'hō), commune of La Coruña prov., NW Spain, in Galicia, 7 mi. SW of La Coruña. Its chief village (pop. 219), Bayuca (bīū'kä), a spa known for its thermal springs, is sometimes called Arteijo.
Artek, Russian SFSR: see AYU-DAG.
Artelny or **Artel'nyy** (ŭrtyĕl'nē), town (1933 pop. over 500), W Sverdlovsk oblast, Russian SFSR, in the central Urals, on left branch of Tura R. and 6 mi. NW of Is, on rail spur; gold placers.
Artem (ŭrtyôm'), city (1947 pop. c.50,000), S Maritime Territory, Russian SFSR, 20 mi. N of Vladivostok, on branch of Trans-Siberian RR; major lignite-mining center; power plant. Developed during 1930s, when it overtook Suchan as main mining center in Vladivostok area. Satellite mining towns (SW) are Uglovoye and Trudovoye.
Artema, Imeni (ē'mĭnyē urtyô'mŭ). **1** N iron-mining suburb (1926 pop. 1,303) of Krivoi Rog, Dnepropetrovsk oblast, Ukrainian SSR, 3 mi. NNE of city center and on right bank of Saksagan R. Formerly called Galkovski (after c.1926 Artemovski) Rudnik. **2** City (1926 pop. 4,369), central Stalino oblast, Ukrainian SSR, in the Donbas, 2 mi. SE of Dzerzhinsk; coal mines. Formerly called Artemovski Rudnik.
Artemisa (ärtāmē'sä), town (pop. 13,084), Pinar del Río prov., W Cuba, on Central Highway, on railroad and 35 mi. SW of Havana; trading and processing center in agr. region (sugar cane, tobacco, pineapples, fruit); mfg. of liquor and soap. Has 2 sugar refineries in outskirts.
Artemision (ärtĕmē'sēôn), Lat. *Artemisium* (är"tŭmĭ'shēŭm), mountain massif in NE Peloponnesus, Greece; rises to 5,813 ft. 8 mi. W of Argos.
Artemision, Cape, Lat. *Artemisium*, N extremity of Euboea, Greece, on Aegean Sea; 39°2'N 23°16'E. Noted for naval battle bet. Greeks and Persians in 480 B.C.; site of ruins of temple of goddess Artemis.
Artem-Ostrov (ŭrtyôm'-ŏ"strŭf) [Rus.,=Artem isl.], town (1939 pop. over 2,000) in Artem dist. of Greater Baku, Azerbaijan SSR, on N end of Artem Isl. (in Caspian Sea, off Apsheron Peninsula; linked since 1941 by causeway), 27 mi. ENE of Baku; oil wells (developed 1902).
Artemovka (ŭrtyô'mŭfkŭ). **1** Town (1926 pop. 5,339), N central Kharkov oblast, Ukrainian SSR, 12 mi. SW of Kharkov; distilling. **2** Town (1926 pop. 2,191), E Poltava oblast, Ukrainian SSR, 25 mi. NE of Poltava; sugar refining, distilling.
Artemovsk (ŭrtyô'mŭfsk). **1** City (1939 pop. over 10,000), S Krasnoyarsk Territory, Russian SFSR, 85 mi. NE of Minusinsk; gold-mining center. Founded 1860; called Olkhovski or Ol'khovskiy until 1939, when it became a city. **2** City (1939 pop. 55,165), NE Stalino oblast, Ukrainian SSR, in the Donbas, 40 mi. NNE of Stalino. Industrial center in salt-mining region; ironworks (wire, nails), silicate and glassworks, clothing mills, food industry. Teachers col. City founded 1571; until 1923, Bakhmut. **3** Town (1926 pop. 3,153), SW Voroshilovgrad oblast, Ukrainian SSR, in the Donbas, 4 mi. SW of Voroshilovsk; coal-mining center. Formerly Rudnik Imeni Artema.
Artemovski or **Artemovskiy** (–fskē). **1** Town (1939 pop. over 2,000), NE Irkutsk oblast, Russian SFSR, 25 mi. NE of Bodaibo; gold mines. Formerly called Feodosiyevski. **2** City (1948 pop. over 10,000), S central Sverdlovsk oblast, Russian SFSR, in E foothills of the central Urals, on railroad and 60 mi. NE of Sverdlovsk. Rail junction (Yegorshino station); bituminous-coal-mining center; mfg. (radio equipment, building materials), metalworking, food processing. Developed before First World War; became city in 1938. Until 1928, called Yegorshino or Yegorshinskiye Kopi.
Artemus (ärtē'mŭs), village (1940 pop. 635), Knox co., SE Ky., in the Cumberlands, on Cumberland R. and 17 mi. NNW of Middlesboro.
Artenara (ärtänä'rä), village (pop. 293), Grand Canary, Canary Isls., 15 mi. SW of Las Palmas; cereals, almonds, oranges.
Artenay (ärtŭnā'), agr. village (pop. 998), Loiret dept., N central France, in the Beauce, 13 mi. N of Orléans; hosiery.
Artern (är'tŭrn), town (pop. 7,601), in former Prussian Saxony prov., central Germany, after 1945 in Saxony-Anhalt, on the Unstrut and 8 mi. S of Sangershausen; potash mining; machinery mfg., sugar refining, malting, brewing. Resort with saline springs. Has 13th-cent. church.
Artés (ärtās'), town (pop. 2,175), Barcelona prov., NE Spain, 9 mi. NE of Manresa; cotton mills. Wine, olive oil, fruit in area.
Artesa de Lérida (ärtā'sä dhā lā'rēdhä), village (pop. 1,097), Lérida prov., NE Spain, 6 mi. SE of Lérida; olive-oil processing; agr. trade (wine, almonds, alfalfa).
Artesa de Segre (sĕ'grā), city (pop. 1,636), Lérida prov., NE Spain, 14 mi. NE of Balaguer, and on Segre R. and Urgel Canal; road center in irrigated agr. area (livestock, cereals, hemp).
Artesia (ärtē'zhŭ). **1** Town (1940 pop. 5.837), Los Angeles co., S Calif., 16 mi. SE of downtown Los Angeles, near Long Beach; dairying, truck and poultry farming. **2** Town (pop. 281), Moffat co., NW Colo., near Utah line, 75 mi. WSW of Craig. **3** Town (pop. 594), Lowndes co., E Miss., 14 mi. WSW of Columbus; ships hay. **4** City (pop. 8,244), Eddy co., SE N.Mex., near Pecos R. and L. McMillan, 30 mi. NNW of Carlsbad; trade center in livestock, cotton, alfalfa region; oil refining; wool, mechanical appliances, beverages. Discovery of oil (1923) stimulated growth. Surrounding region irrigated by artesian wells. Settled 1903, inc. 1930.
Artesian, village (pop. 380), S Alaska, near Anchorage.
Artesian, city (pop. 429), Sanborn co., SE central S.Dak., 18 mi. ESE of Woonsocket; center of large artesian water basin; trading point for farming region; dairy produce, livestock, corn, wheat.
Arth (ärt), town (pop. 5,146), Schwyz canton, central Switzerland, at S end of L. of Zug, 7 mi. WNW of Schwyz; silk textiles. Goldau, to SE, is a railway junction; lamp mfg.; scene of the Goldau landslip which in 1806 descended from the Rossberg, burying 4 villages.

Arthabaska (är″thŭbă′skŭ), county (□ 666; pop. 30,039), S Que., on Nicolet R.; ⊙ Arthabaska.
Arthabaska, town (pop. 1,883), ⊙ Arthabaska co., S Que., on Nicolet R. and 45 mi. N of Sherbrooke; lumbering, dairying center; mfg. of furniture, shirts.
Arthès (ärtĕs′), village (pop. 1,241), Tarn dept., S France, on the Tarn opposite Saint-Juéry, 4 mi. NE of Albi; wool spinning, slaked-lime mfg.
Arthez (ärtĕz′), village (pop. 613), Basses-Pyrénées dept., SW France, 9 mi. ESE of Orthez; meat canning (chiefly pâté de foie gras), poultry raising.
Arthington, village, Montserrado co., W Liberia, on St. Paul R. and 17 mi. N of Monrovia, on road; palm oil and kernels, coffee.
Arthur, village (pop. 937), S Ont., 24 mi. NW of Guelph; woolen milling, dairying, lumbering; mfg. of shoes, castings.
Arthur, county (□ 706; pop. 803), W central Nebr.; ⊙ Arthur. Plains region devoted to livestock raising. Formed 1888.
Arthur. 1 Village (pop. 1,573), on Douglas-Moultrie co. line, E central Ill., 16 mi. NNW of Mattoon, in agr. area (corn, wheat, soybeans, broomcorn; dairy products; livestock, poultry). Mfg.: brooms, road machinery, cheese, powdered milk, oil tanks, burial vaults, caskets, office equipment. Platted 1873, inc. 1877. Large Amish colony is near by. **2** Town (pop. 243), Ida co., W Iowa, 7 mi. E of Ida Grove, in livestock and grain area. **3** Village (pop. 176), ⊙ Arthur co., W central Nebr., 55 mi. NW of North Platte; livestock. **4** Town, N.C.: see BELLARTHUR. **5** Village (pop. 380), Cass co., E N.Dak., 25 mi. NW of Fargo.
Arthur, Lake. 1 In La.: see MERMENTAU RIVER. **2** In N.Dak.: see ALKALINE LAKE.
Arthuret, England: see LONGTOWN.
Arthur Kill, SE N.Y. and NE N.J., narrow channel (c.14 mi. long) connecting Raritan and Newark bays; separates Staten Isl. from N.J. shore; bridged at Elizabeth and Perth Amboy, N.J.
Arthur Lakes, lake (□ 14), central Tasmania, near Great Lake, 60 mi. NNW of Hobart; nearly divided by tongue of land into 2 equal parts (each c.4 mi. long, 2 mi. wide).
Arthur River, NW Tasmania, rises in Mt. Bischoff near Waratah, flows 63 mi. WNW to Indian Ocean 7 mi. S of West Point.
Arthur's Pass (alt. 3,109 ft.), in Arthur Pass Natl. Park, Southern Alps, W central S.Isl., New Zealand, 70 mi. NW of Christchurch; links E with W coast. E opening of OTIRA tunnel near by; winter sports.
Arthur's Seat, hill (822 ft.), Midlothian, Scotland, 2 mi. E of Edinburgh. Its geologic structure has given rise to much discussion.
Arthur's Stone, anc. cromlech on Cefn Bryn (kĕ′vŭn brĭn′), a hill (581 ft.) on Gower peninsula, SW Glamorgan, Wales, 11 mi. WSW of Swansea. It is block of millstone, 14 x 7 ft., weighing 25 tons.
Arthur's Town, town (pop. 450), central Bahama Isls., on N Cat Isl., 115 mi. ESE of Nassau; 24°38′N 75°42′W. Fruit, sisal.
Arthurstown, Gaelic *Colmán*, town (pop. 103), SW Co. Wexford, Ireland, on E shore of Waterford Harbour, 7 mi. E of Waterford; fishing port.
Arti (ŭrtyē′), town (1926 pop. 8,725), SW Sverdlovsk oblast, Russian SFSR, in SW foothills of the central Urals, near Ufa R., 85 mi. WSW of Sverdlovsk; metallurgical center (pig iron). Until 1929, Artinski Zavod.
Artibonite, department, Haiti: see GONAÏVES.
Artibonite Plain (ärtēbōnēt′), fertile basin in W central Haiti, along lower Artibonite R., extending from the coast (Gulf of Gonaïves) 60 mi. inland to Mirebalais. Main cities along the coast are Gonaïves and Saint-Marc. Grows bananas, rice, coffee, cotton, sugar cane, tobacco.
Artibonite River, Sp. *Artibonito* (ärtēbōnē′tō), largest stream of Hispaniola isl., rises in Dominican Republic in Cordillera Central near Haiti line SW of Santiago, flows SW, W, and NW, partly along international border, and into Haiti, through fertile Artibonite Plain, past Mirebalais and Petite-Rivière-de-l'Artibonite, to Gulf of Gonaïves 10 mi. NNW of Saint-Marc; c.150 mi. long. Navigable for small boats c.100 mi. upstream. Used for irrigation. Principal affluent, Guayamouc R.
Artificio (ärtēfē′syō), town (pop. 1,262), Valparaiso prov., central Chile, 2 mi. N of Calera.
Artigas (ärtē′gäs), SW suburb (pop. 1,666) of Badalona, Barcelona prov., NE Spain.
Artigas, department (□ 4,393; pop. 56,423), NW Uruguay; ⊙ Artigas. Bordered by Brazil (N and NE, across Cuareim R.) and Argentina (W, across Uruguay R.). The Cuchilla de Belén crosses dept. SE–NW. Drained by the Arroyo Tres Cruces Grande and Arroyo Cuaró Grande. Stock raising (cattle, sheep, horses), agr. (grain, vegetables). Quartz and amethysts are found in area of the Arroyo Catalán Grande. Dept. served by a railroad net branching off at Isla Cabellos, and by highway from Salto. Main centers: Artigas, Bella Unión, Tomás Gomensoro. Dept. was formed 1884.
Artigas. 1 City (pop. 16,500), ⊙ Artigas dept., NW Uruguay, on Cuareim (or Quaraí) R., opposite Quaraí (Brazil), and 110 mi. NE of Salto, 300 mi. NNW of Montevideo; 30°23′S 56°28′W. Rail terminus; airport. Trade and export center for cattle, charqui, fats, wool, cereals, and fruit; *saladero*. Has govt. house, public schools, parochial church. Founded 1852, it became capital on creation of dept. in 1884. Until 1930s, called San Eugenio. **2** Town, Cerro Largo dept., Uruguay: see RÍO BRANCO.
Artik (ŭrtyĕk′), city (1932 pop. estimate 4,430), NW Armenian SSR, at NW foot of Mt. Aragats, 13 mi. SSE of Leninakan (linked by rail); building-stone quarrying center; volcanic tuff, pumice; wheat, sugar beets. Developed during Second World War.
Artillery Lake (50 mi. long, 1–9 mi. wide), E Mackenzie Dist., Northwest Territories, NE of Great Slave L.; 63°10′N 107°55′W. Drains SW into Great Slave L.
Artois (ärtwä′), region and former province of N France, now included in Pas-de-Calais dept.; ⊙ Arras. Bounded by Flanders (NE) and Picardy (S and W). Traversed by low hills. Primarily agr. Contains W section of Franco-Belgian coal basin. Possession of counts of Flanders until annexed (12th cent.) to France by Philip II. Passed (14th cent.) to Burgundy. Ruled (16th cent.) by Austria, later by Spain. Reconquered for France by Louis XIII in 1640. A battleground for centuries, Artois was scene of heavy First World War fighting. Gave its name to artesian wells, used here.
Artos Dag (ärtôs′dä), Turkish *Artos Dağ*, peak (11,400 ft.), E Turkey, in Van Mts., 3 mi. SE of Gevas.
Artova (är′tôvä″), village (pop. 376), Tokat prov., N central Turkey, 16 mi. S of Tokat; wheat, barley, potatoes. Formerly Ciftlik.
Artsiz (ŭrtsēs′), Rum. *Arciz* (ärchēz′), village (1930 pop. 2,951; 1941 pop. 587), central Izmail oblast, Ukrainian SSR, in Bessarabia, on Kogalnik R. and 45 mi. WSW of Belgorod-Dnestrovski; rail junction (repair shops); mfg. (textiles, agr. implements). Founded, after 1812, as Ger. agr. colony; Ger. pop. repatriated in 1940. Spelled Artsyz, 1940–44.
Art-sur-Meurthe (är-sür-mûrt′), village (pop. 409), Meurthe-et-Moselle dept., NE France, on Meurthe R. and 5 mi. SE of Nancy; soda mfg.
Artsyz, Ukrainian SSR: see ARTSIZ.
Artukainen (är′tōōkī″nĕn), suburb of Turku, Turku-Pori co., SW Finland, 3 mi. W of city center; site of Turku airport.
Artvin, province, Turkey: see CORUH.
Artvin (ärtvĭn′), Turkish *Artvin*, village (pop. 3,986), ⊙ Coruh prov., NE Turkey, on Coruh R. and 90 mi. NNE of Erzurum, 18 mi. S of USSR line; tobacco, grain; copper near by.
Aru (ä′rōō), village, Eastern Prov., NE Belgian Congo, on Uganda border opposite Arua and 120 mi. NE of Irumu; customs station and center of cattle-raising region; dairying; coffee plantations in vicinity. Protestant mission.
Arua (ä′rōōä), town (pop. c. 8,000), NW Uganda, at Belgian Congo border, opposite Aru, 100 mi. WNW of Gulu; cotton, coffee, tobacco; livestock.
Aruanã (ärwŭnä′), town (pop. 613), W Goiás, central Brazil, on right bank of Araguaia R. (Mato Grosso border) at influx of the Rio Vermelho; road terminus; cattle raising. Until 1944, called Leopoldina.
Aruba (ärü′bä), island (□ 67.56; 1948 pop. estimate 50,000), Du. West Indies; chief town, Oranjestad. Situated 20 mi. N of Paraguaná Peninsula, Venezuela, and 45 mi. W of Curaçao isl.; 19 mi. long, up to 4 mi. wide; bet. 12°25′–12°38′N and 69°53′–70°4′W. Tropical, semiarid climate. Economically important as transshipment and refining center for Venezuelan petroleum, centered at Oranjestad. Produces divi-divi, sisal; raises goats, sheep. Its gold and phosphate deposits are not worked. Oil industry introduced 1925.
Aru Bay or **Aroe Bay** (both: ä′rōō), inlet (10 mi. long, 8 mi. wide) of Strait of Malacca, N Sumatra, Indonesia. On S shore is port of Pangkalan Susu. Oil fields near its shores.
Arucas (ärōō′käs), city (pop. 4,112, commune pop., 21,804), Grand Canary, Canary Isls., 6 mi. WNW of Las Palmas; agr. center in fertile agr. region (bananas, sugar cane, cochineal, potatoes, tomatoes, cereals, grapes). Important for its sugar industry. Stone quarrying, wine making, flour milling, sawmilling, stock raising.
Arudy (ärüdē′), village (pop. 1,571), Basses-Pyrénées dept., SW France, on the Gave d'Ossau and 11 mi. SE of Oloron-Sainte-Marie; iron foundry, cotton mill, limekilns; tanning, lumbering. Marble quarried and worked near by.
Aru Islands or **Aroe Islands** (both: ä′rōō), group (□ 3,306; pop. 18,176), S Moluccas, Indonesia, in Arafura Sea, c.80 mi. S of isthmus on W New Guinea; 6°10′S 134°20′E. The 5 main isls., fringed with c.80 islets, form an almost solid block of land (110 mi. long) separated by 4 narrow channels. Principal isls. ranging N–S are Kola (20 mi. long, 12 mi. wide), Wokam (pop. 2,025; 35 mi. long, 25 mi. wide), Kobror, Kobroor, or Kobrur (pop. 3,028; 35 mi. long, 30 mi. wide), Maikoor or Makor (pop. 589; 28 mi. long, 7 mi. wide), and Trangan (pop. 5,192; 55 mi. long, 28 mi. wide). Off W coast of Wokam is small Wamar isl. (pop. 1,774; 6 mi. long, 4 mi. wide), site of DOBO, chief town of Aru Isls. The 5 principal isls. are sometimes considered as being 1 isl., called Tanabesar. Group is generally fertile, with swampy coastal area. Agr. products: sago, rice, corn, sugar, tobacco, coconuts. Most important products: pearls, mother-of-pearl, tortoise shell, trepang. Natives are of mixed Papuan and Malayan stock. Has fauna related to that of Australia, and not to that of other Indonesian isls. Group was discovered 1606 by the Dutch who began colonization after 1623. Also spelled Arru.
Aruma Plateau, Saudi Arabia: see ARMA PLATEAU.
Arumuganeri, India: see KAYALPATNAM.
Arundel (ă′rŭndŭl, ŭrŭn′dŭl), village (pop. estimate 350), SW Que., in the Laurentians, 30 mi. WNW of St. Jérôme; dairying; skiing resort. Kaolin mined near by.
Arundel (ă′rŭndŭl), municipal borough (1931 pop. 2,490; 1951 census 2,680), SW Sussex, England, on Arun R. and 8 mi. WNW of Worthing. It is on hillside below 12th-cent. Arundel Castle, seat of dukes of Norfolk. Has 14th-cent. church. Formerly a timber-trade center.
Arundel-on-the-Bay (ŭrŭn′dŭl–), resort village, Anne Arundel co., central Md., on Chesapeake Bay and 5 mi. SE of Annapolis.
Arun River (ă′rŭn), Sussex, England, rises in 2 branches in S Surrey, flows 37 mi. S, past Arundel, to the Channel at Littlehampton. Navigable below Arundel. Receives Rother R. 7 mi. N of Arundel.
Arun River, Nepal: see KOSI RIVER.
Arunta Desert, Australia: see SIMPSON DESERT.
Aruppukkottai or **Aruppu-Kottai** (both: ŭrōōp′pōō-kōt′tī), town (pop. 35,001), Ramnad dist., S Madras, India, 28 mi. S of Madura, in cotton area; trade center. Also spelled Arupukottai.
Arure or **Vega de Arure** (bā′gä dhā ärōō′rā), village (pop. 407), Gomera, Canary Isls., 13 mi. WNW of San Sebastián; cereals, bananas, tomatoes, potatoes, cattle, sheep; flour milling.
Arusha (ärōō′shä), town (pop. 5,320), ⊙ Northern Prov. (□ 32,165; pop. 586,226), Tanganyika, at S foot of Mt. Meru, 200 mi. NW of Tanga; alt. 4,620 ft.; 3°22′S 36°42′E. Terminus (since 1929) of railroad from Tanga, via Moshi. Agr. center amidst European coffee plantations; papain, pyrethrum grown on slopes of Mt. Meru; livestock raising. Pozzuolana deposits. Airfield. Masai Steppe is S.
Arusi or **Arussi** (ä′rōōsē), province (□ c.14,000), S central Ethiopia; ⊙ Asselle. Bordered by Awash (NE) and Omo (W) rivers. Forested mtn. region rising to c.14,240 ft. in Mt. Enkwolo (E). Traversed (N–S) by Great Rift Valley containing lakes Zwai, Hora Abyata, Langana, and Shala. Drained by Billate R. Pop. largely Galla. Agr. (coffee, cereals, potatoes, beans), cattle raising, and fishing. Has iron deposits. Crossed by road (N–S) from Addis Ababa.
Aruvankadu, India: see WELLINGTON.
Aruvi Aru (ärōō′vē ä′rōō), river, NW Ceylon, rises in N extension of Ceylon Hill Country, near Dambulla; flows 104 mi. NNW, past Anuradhapura, to Gulf of Mannar 12 mi. S of Mannar; 2d longest river of Ceylon. In middle course, called Malwatu (or Malvatu) Oya; it is used in a land reclamation scheme (□ 37).
Aruwimi River (ärōōwē′mē), right tributary of Congo R. in N and NE Belgian Congo. Rises as the Ituri (ētōō′rē) in rich gold-mining region of Kilo-Moto 20 mi. S of Adranga and flows c.300 mi. S and W, past Irumu and Penge to Avakubi, where it takes the name Aruwimi and flows c.320 mi. further, past Panga and Banalia, to Congo R. at Basoko. Navigable in its lower course only as far as Yambuya, 75 mi. upstream; its upper and middle courses abound in rapids, particularly upstream of Avakubi and near Panga. The deep equatorial forests of Ituri are well-known as haunts of Pygmies and as hunting grounds for okapis. The Aruwimi-Ituri was explored by Stanley (1887–89).
Arva or **Arvagh** (both: är′vä), Gaelic *Ármhach*, town (pop. 399), W Co. Cavan, Ireland, 10 mi. SW of Cavan; agr. market (cattle, pigs, potatoes).
Arvada (ärvă′dŭ), town (pop. 2,359), Jefferson co., N central Colo., on Ralston Creek, just NW of Denver, E of Front Range; alt. 5,300 ft. Livestock, poultry, grain, sugar beets, truck produce; beverages, flour. Inc. 1904.
Arva River, Czechoslovakia: see ORAVA RIVER.
Arve Prinsen Island (är′vŭ prĭn′sŭn), Dan. *Arve Prinsens Ejland* (29 mi. long, 6–19 mi. wide), W Greenland, at head of Disko Bay, near SE end of the Vaigat, 13 mi. E of Disko isl.; 69°43′N 51°7′W. Separated from mainland by Atâ Sound (4 mi. wide). Mountainous, rising to 2,759 ft. Settlements are Ritenbenk (W) and Atâ (E).
Arve River (ärv), Haute-Savoie dept., SE France and Switzerland, rises at Col de la Balme in Mont Blanc massif, flows SW through Chamonix valley, thence generally NW, through alternating gorges and basins, past Sallanches, Cluses, Bonneville, and S suburbs of Geneva, to the Rhone 1.5 mi. below its exit from L. Geneva; c.60 mi. long. Activates several hydroelectric plants. Followed by Geneva–Chamonix–Martigny-Ville RR. Receives the Giffre (right). Its valley below Servoz called FAUCIGNY.
Arverne (är′vûrn″), SE N.Y., a residential and shore-resort section of S Queens borough of New York city, on Rockaway Beach; boatbuilding, furniture mfg.

Arvert, Pointe d' (pwēt därvâr'), headland on the Pertuis de Maumusson of Bay of Biscay, Charente-Maritime dept., W France, opposite S end of Île d'Oléron, c.13 mi. SSW of Rochefort; 45°48'N 1°15'W.

Arveyron River, France: see MER DE GLACE.

Arvi (ŭr'vē), town (pop. 16,228), Wardha dist., central Madhya Pradesh, India, 29 mi. NW of Wardha; rail spur terminus; cotton-trade center; cotton ginning; millet, wheat, oilseeds; orange and plantain orchards. Cattle raising in near-by forested hills (teak, sal).

Arvida (ärvī'dů, ärvē'dů), city (pop. 4,581), S central Que., on Saguenay R. and 5 mi. W of Chicoutimi; great aluminum-production center, with bauxite-reduction plants, abrasives mfg. Near by are hydroelectric plants.

Arvidsjaur (är'vĭtsyour"), village (pop. 1,699), Norrbotten co., N Sweden, 70 mi. WNW of Pitea; rail junction; sawmilling. Site of Lapp settlement.

Arvier (ärvyā'), village (pop. 113), Val d'Aosta region, NW Italy, on Dora Baltea R. and 8 mi. W of Aosta; hydroelectric plant.

Arvika (är'vē"kä), city (1950 pop. 15,154), Varmland co., W Sweden, on NE shore of Glaf Fjord, 35 mi. NW of Karlstad; rail junction; mfg. of agr. machines, pianos, tobacco products; textile milling.

Arvin, unincorporated town (pop. 5,007), Kern co., S central Calif., 15 mi. SE of Bakersfield; trade, shipping, and processing center in agr. area (fruit, cotton, potatoes).

Arvonia (ärvō'nēů), village, Buckingham co., central Va., near James R., 24 mi. SSE of Charlottesville; slate quarries.

Arvo River (är'vô), Calabria, S Italy, rises in La Sila mts. on S slope of Botte Donato, flows 20 mi. E, parallel to AMPOLLINO RIVER, to Neto R. just S of San Giovanni in Fiore. Dammed (Nocelle dam) near its source to form large reservoir (Lago Arvo or Lago Arvo Nocelle; 5 mi. long, .5 mi. wide); used for hydroelectric power.

Arwad, Syria: see RUAD.

Aryana, Iran: see ARIANA.

Aryirokastron, Albania: see ARGYROKASTRON.

Aryk-Balyk (ŭrĭk"-bŭlĭk'), village (1948 pop. over 2,000), SW Kokchetav oblast, Kazakh SSR, 50 mi. WSW of Kokchetav; wheat; horse breeding.

Arys, Poland: see ORZYSZ.

Arys or **Arys'** (ŭrĭs'), town (1939 pop. over 10,000), S South Kazakhstan oblast, Kazakh SSR, at junction of Trans-Caspian and Turksib railroads, 40 mi. WNW of Chimkent; freight and switchyards; cotton; cattle, horse breeding.

Arys River or **Arys' River**, in South Kazakhstan oblast, Kazakh SSR, rises in the Talass Ala-Tau, flows 140 mi. W, through cotton area, past Arys, to the Syr Darya 10 mi. W of Timur; important for irrigation.

Arzachena (ärdzäkā'nä), village (pop. 1,567), Sassari prov., NE Sardinia, 50 mi. NE of Sassari.

Arzacq-Arraziguet (ärzäk'-äräzēgā'), village (pop. 546), Basses-Pyrénées dept., SW France, 16 mi. N of Pau; cereals, wine; horse raising.

Arzamas (ŭrzůmäs'), city (1926 pop. 19,203), S Gorki oblast, Russian SFSR, on Tesha R. (right affluent of Oka R.) and 65 mi. S of Gorki; agr.-processing center (distilling, fruit canning, flour milling); woolen milling, tanning. Teachers col. Rail junction (Arzamas II), 3 mi. N. Has numerous old churches and monasteries. Of Mordvinian origin; fortress of Moscow domain after 1393; chartered 1578.

Arzana (ärdzä'nä), village (pop. 2,575), Nuoro prov., E Sardinia, 29 mi. SSE of Nuoro.

Arzano (ärzänō'), village (pop. 400), Finistère dept., W France, 5 mi. ENE of Quimperlé; apple orchards.

Arzano (ärdzä'nô), town (pop. 10,819), Napoli prov., Campania, S Italy, 4 mi. N of Naples, in agr. region (grapes, hemp, fruit).

Arzberg (ärts'běrk), town (pop. 6,540), Upper Franconia, NE Bavaria, Germany, in the Fichtelgebirge, 8 mi. ENE of Wunsiedel; mfg. of porcelain, textiles, nails; brewing, tanning, lumber and flour milling. Chartered 1400.

Ärzen, Germany: see AERZEN.

Arzen River (ärzěn') or **Arzeni River** (ärzě'nē), in central Albania, rises 15 mi. E of Tirana, flows c.50 mi. to the Adriatic 9 mi. N of Durazzo. Also spelled Erzen or Erzeni.

Arzew (ärzů'), town (pop. 3,566), Oran dept., NW Algeria, port on W shore of sheltered Gulf of Arzew (Mediterranean Sea), 20 mi. NE of Oran; exports esparto grass shipped here from the interior, with which it is linked by rail (southern terminus, Colomb-Béchar); refines sulphur (for vineyards). Saltworks at El Mellaha salt flat (10 mi. S; narrow-gauge railroad). Has a hydroplane landing and recently improved harbor facilities. Town was (12th cent.) a maritime arsenal of Abd-el-Moumen. Taken by French in 1833. Also spelled Arzeu.

Arzew, Gulf of, wide inlet of the Mediterranean, Oran dept., NW Algeria, bet. Cape Carbon (W) and Cape Ivi (E); 30 mi. wide, 10 mi. long. On its shores are ports of Arzew (W) and Mostaganem (E). The Chéliff empties into it.

Arzgir (ŭrzgēr'), village (1926 pop. 12,683), NE Stavropol Territory, Russian SFSR, near Manych Depression, 40 mi. N. of Budennovsk, in wheat and cotton area; road center; flour mill, metalworks.

Arzignano (ärdzēnyä'nô), town (pop. 4,597), Vicenza prov., Veneto, N Italy, on Chiampo R. and 10 mi. W of Vicenza; mfg. (motors, pumps, agr. machinery); tanneries, silk and woolen mills. Quarries (basalt, limestone) near by.

Arzila, Sp. Morocco: see ARCILA.

Arzl (ärtsůl), village (pop. 1,501), Tyrol, W Austria, near Inn R., 10 mi. NE of Landeck.

Arzni (är'znyē), village (1939 pop. over 500), central Armenian SSR, on Zanga R. and 10 mi. NNE of Erivan; alt. c.4,000 ft. Health resort; mineral springs.

Arzúa (är-thōō'ä), town (pop. 1,268), La Coruña prov., NW Spain, 19 mi. E of Santiago; cheese processing, cattle raising, lumbering; potatoes.

As [Arabic,=the], for Arabic names beginning thus: see under following part of the name.

As (äsh), Czech *Aš*, Ger. *Asch* (äsh), town (pop. 11,378), W Bohemia, Czechoslovakia, 12 mi. NNW of Cheb, in the Smrciny, near Ger. border. Rail junction; mfg. of cotton, silk, and woolen textiles; linen, lace, embroidery. Exodus of former large Ger. pop. began in 1933 and reached culminating point after Second World War.

As (ôs), Nor. *As*, village (pop. 799; canton pop. 4,405), Akershus co., SE Norway, on railroad and 16 mi. S of Oslo; seat of agr. col. Sometimes spelled Aas.

Asa (ä'sä), town (pop. 17,209), Yamaguchi prefecture, SW Honshu, Japan, 8 mi. NW of Ube; agr. center (rice, wheat, sweet potatoes). Coal mines near by.

Asa (ō'sä"), Swedish *Åsa*, village (pop. 225), Halland co., SW Sweden, on the Kattegat, 9 mi. S of Kungsbacka; seaside resort.

Asaa (ä'sô), town (pop. 1,137), Hjorring amt, NE Jutland, Denmark, 27 mi. SE of Hjorring, near E coast; mfg. (agr. machinery).

Asaba (äsäbä'), town (pop. 5,474), Benin prov., Western Provinces, S Nigeria, on right bank of Niger R., opposite Onitsha (ferry), and 75 mi. E of Benin City; agr. trade center; palm oil and kernels, kola nuts. Lignite deposits. Richard Lander captured here (1830) by natives and later ransomed. Town was a Br. commercial station in 19th cent.

Asaca River (äsä'kä), coastal stream of SW Morocco, rises in spurs of the Anti-Atlas, flows generally W to the Atlantic, forming in its lower course the S border of Ifni territory (Sp. enclave in Fr. Morocco). Often called Uad Nun, Fr. *Oued Noun*. Also spelled Assaka.

Asadabad (äsäd"äbäd'), town, Fifth Prov., in Hamadan, W Iran, 23 mi. W of Hamadan, and on highway to Kermanshah, at foot of Shah (Asadabad) Pass; grain, opium, tobacco, cotton. Sometimes spelled Assadabad.

Asafabad or **Asifabad** (both: ä"sĭfäbäd'), village (pop. 3,480), Adilabad dist., NE Hyderabad state, India, 55 mi. ESE of Adilabad; millet, oilseeds, rice.

Asagi Dag (äsä'ŭ dä), Turkish *Aşağı Dağ*, peak (10,730 ft.), E Turkey, 10 mi. SSE of Kagizman.

Asahan River (äsůhän'), NE Sumatra, Indonesia, rises in L. Toba, in Barisan Mts., flows c.80 mi. NE, past Tanjungbalai, to Strait of Malacca 7 mi. NE of Tanjungbalai.

Asahi (ä"sä'hē), town (pop. 10,858), Chiba prefecture, central Honshu, Japan, 10 mi. W of Choshi; rice, wheat, poultry.

Asahi-dake (ä"sä'hē-dä'kā), highest peak (7,513 ft.) of Hokkaido, Japan, in Daisetsu-zan Natl. Park, 25 mi. ESE of Asahigawa; volcanic; rare alpine flora on slopes.

Asahigawa (äsähē'gäwů) or **Asahikawa** (–käwů), city (1940 pop. 87,514; 1947 pop. 107,508), W central Hokkaido, Japan, on Ishikari R. and 70 mi. NE of Sapporo, in sawmilling and rice-growing area; rail junction; mfg. (machinery, chemical and ceramic products), spinning, sake brewing.

Asai (äsī') or **Azai** (äzī'), town (pop. 6,957), Aichi prefecture, central Honshu, Japan, just N of Ichinomiya; rice, raw silk, poultry; textiles.

Asaka (ä"sä'kä), town (pop. 11,313), Saitama prefecture, central Honshu, Japan, 6 mi. W of Kawaguchi; agr. (rice, wheat, sweet potatoes); metal-working.

Asakawa (äsä'käwů). **1** Town (pop. 7,463), Fukushima prefecture, central Honshu, Japan, 12 mi. ESE of Shirakawa; rice, silk cocoons. **2** Town (pop., 7,127), Greater Tokyo, central Honshu, Japan, just SW of Hachioji, in agr. area; silk.

Asalu, Iran: see NABAND BAY.

Asama, Mount (ä"sä'mä), Jap. *Asama-yama* (c.8,200 ft.), central Honshu, Japan, on Nagano-Gumma prefecture border, 90 mi. NW of Tokyo. Most violent and highest of the active volcanoes in Japan, with crater c.¾ mi. in circumference. Eruption of 1783 killed thousands of people.

Asamai (ä"sä'mī), town (pop. 8,046), Akita prefecture, N Honshu, Japan, 5 mi. SSW of Yokote; rice, silk cocoons, dyes.

Asamankese (äsämängkě'sä), town, Eastern Prov., S central Gold Coast colony, 22 mi. WNW of Nsawam; cacao, palm oil and kernels, cassava. Sometimes spelled Asamangkese.

Asama-yama, Japan: see ASAMA, MOUNT.

Asamushi, Japan: see NONAI.

Asan (ă'săn), town (pop. 622) and municipality (pop. 3,093), W Guam, on coast; livestock, rice, coconuts.

Asane, canton, Norway: see SALHUS.

Asángaro, Peru: see AZÁNGARO.

Asansol (ŭsŭnsōl'), city (pop. 55,797), Burdwan dist., W West Bengal, India, in Damodar Valley, 65 mi. WNW of Burdwan; main coal-trade center of Raniganj coal field; major Indian locomotive workshop; mfg. of bricks, tiles, furniture; general and electrical engineering works. A coal-mining center 9 mi. NE, at Churulia. Aluminum extraction 7 mi. E, at village of J. K. Nagar (also written Jaykaynagar) or Anupnagar.

Asari, Latvia: see RIGAS JURMALA.

Asarum (ä'särŭm"), village (pop. 1,692), Blekinge co., S Sweden, 3 mi. NNW of Karlshamn; copper works, cotton mills.

Asarva, India: see AHMADABAD, city.

Asba Tafari (äs'bä tä'färē), town (pop. 2,000), Harar prov., E central Ethiopia, 90 mi. W of Harar, in agr. region (coffee, cereals); connected with railroad (at Miesso) by road. A major center (founded c.1934) of Chercher highland. Under Ital. administration (1936–41) called Asba Littoria.

Asben, Fr. West Africa: see AÏR.

Asbest (ŭzbyěst'), city (1926 pop. 7,587; 1932 pop. estimate 36,500), S Sverdlovsk oblast, Russian SFSR, in E foothills of the central Urals, 33 mi. ENE of Sverdlovsk; rail spur terminus; leading asbestos-mining center of USSR. Developed before First World War; became city in 1933. Until 1928, Asbestovye Rudniki [Rus.,=asbestos mines].

Asbestos, town (pop. 5,711), S Que., on Southwest Nicolet R. and 26 mi. N of Sherbrooke; asbestos-mining and mfg. center; textile mill, woodworking.

Asbestos Mountains, N Cape Prov., U. of So. Afr., extend c.120 mi. NNE from Orange R. near Prieska, forming W edge of Kaap Plateau; rise to 6,070 ft. at N end of range. Asbestos mines. Continued N by Kuruman Hills, which extend 30 mi. N-S.

Asbestovski or **Asbestovskiy** (ŭzbyěs'tůfskē), town (1941 pop. over 500), S central Sverdlovsk oblast, Russian SFSR, 13 mi. SW (under jurisdiction) of Alapayevsk; asbestos mining, lumbering.

Asbury (ăz'–). **1** Town (pop. 52), Dubuque co., E Iowa, 3 mi. WNW of Dubuque. **2** Town (pop. 210), Jasper co., SW Mo., near Spring R., 15 mi. NNW of Joplin.

Asbury Park, resort city (pop. 17,094), Monmouth co., E N.J., on the coast and 6 mi. S of Long Branch; recreational facilities include excellent beach, municipal auditorium, boardwalk, pier. Mfg. (clothing, window shades, electrical products, confectionery, beverages); seafood, fruit, truck. Founded 1869, inc. 1897; adopted commission govt. 1915, municipal manager plan 1933.

Ascalon (ăs'kůlŏn) or **Ashkelon** (ăshkělŏn'), anc. city, W Palestine, in Judaean Plain, on the Mediterranean, 12 mi. N of Gaza. A Canaanite city, it was captured by Ramses II; later held in succession by Philistines, Assyrians, and Persians. A center of worship of the goddess Astarte. Major port in Roman era; Herod the Great b. here. Episcopal see in Byzantine times. Called Escalone during Crusades; Godfrey of Bouillon won major battle near by, 1099. Captured 1153 by Baldwin III, retaken 1187 by Saladin; captured 1191 by Richard Coeur de Lion; surrendered to Saladin, 1192; destroyed 1270. Considerable Roman and Crusaders' remains extant. Sometimes spelled Askalon.

Ascanius, Lake, Turkey: see IZNIK, LAKE.

Ascención (äsěnsyōn'), village (pop. c.1,500), Santa Cruz dept., E central Bolivia, 80 mi. NW of Concepción; airport; cotton growing. Franciscan mission until 1938. Sometimes spelled Ascensión.

Ascensión, Bolivia: see ASCENCIÓN.

Ascensión (äsěnsyōn'), town (pop. 1,104), Chihuahua, N Mexico, on Casas Grandes R. (irrigation) and 100 mi. SW of Ciudad Juárez; alt. 4,255 ft. Cotton, cereals, cattle; silver, gold, copper mining.

Ascension, parish (□ 300; pop. 22,387), SE La.; ⊙ Donaldsonville. Intersected by Mississippi R.; also drained by Amite R. Agr. (sugar cane, corn, rice, hay, truck, sweet potatoes, strawberries). Some mfg., including farm-products processing. Oil and natural-gas wells; timber. Formed 1807.

Ascensión Bay, Quintana Roo, SE Mexico, inlet of Caribbean Sea on E coast of Yucatan Peninsula, 10 mi. N of Espíritu Santo Bay, E of Felipe Carrillo Puerto; 13 mi. long N-S, 15 mi. wide. Vigía Chico is on NW shore.

Ascension Island, British island (□ 34; 1948 pop. 191), a dependency (since 1922) of SAINT HELENA, in S Atlantic, c.700 mi. NW of St. Helena; 7°56'S 14°22'W. Main settlement, Georgetown, is an international cable station. Volcanic islet is 7½ mi. long, 6 mi. wide. Rises to 2,870 ft. in Green Mtn. Has a tropical, though healthful climate, moderated by SE trade winds. Annual mean temp. is 85°F. at sea level, 75°F. on Green Mtn. The uplands have sufficient rainfall—c.30 in.—to support vegetation and livestock (cattle, sheep). Its shores are known for turtles, and the surrounding waters abound in fish. Isl. was discovered by Portuguese on Ascension Day, 1501. William Dampier was wrecked (1701) here. After arrival (1815) of exiled Napoleon in St. Helena, British maintained a small naval station on the until then uninhabited isl. During Second World War the U.S. built an airfield here to guard S Atlantic sealanes. All American forces were withdrawn by 1947.

Ascension Island, Caroline Isls.: see PONAPE.

Ascensión Island, Chile: see GUAITECAS ISLANDS.

Asch, Czechoslovakia: see As.

Aschach or **Aschach an der Donau** (ä'shäkh än dĕr dō'nou), town (pop. 2,310), N central Upper Austria, on the Danube and 13 mi. WNW of Linz; rail terminus; summer resort; mfg. (potato starch). Parish church with baroque interior.

Aschaffenburg (ä-shä'fŭnbŏŏrk), city (1950 pop. 44,919), Lower Franconia, NW Bavaria, Germany, port on right bank of the Main (canalized) and 24 mi. ESE of Frankfurt; 49°59'N 9°9'E. Industrial and commercial center; mfg. of textiles, special paper for export, precision and optical instruments. Also metal (motors, machine tools, agr. and household implements) and chemical (paint, varnish, cellulose, soap, cosmetics) industries. Trades in lumber, coal, wine, and fruit. Developing on site of a Roman garrison, Aschaffenburg came to electors of Mainz in 10th cent. Changed hands several times in Thirty Years War; stormed by Fr. troops under Turenne in 1672. Passed to Bavaria in 1814. Captured by U.S. troops in April, 1945. Second World War destruction (40%) included 12th–13th-cent. church of SS. Peter and Alexander, Renaissance Jesuit church (1619–21), and Renaissance castle (1605–14; former summer residence of archbishops of Mainz).

Ascheberg (ä'shŭbĕrk). **1** Village (pop. 3,335), in Schleswig-Holstein, NW Germany, on W shore of Plön L., 3 mi. W of Plön; summer resort; woodworking. **2** Village (pop. 5,541), in former Prussian prov. of Westphalia, NW Germany, after 1945 in North Rhine-Westphalia, 11 mi. S of Münster; grain, cattle, hogs.

Aschendorf (ä'shŭndôrf), village (pop. 4,473), in former Prussian prov. of Hanover, NW Germany, after 1945 in Lower Saxony, near the Ems, 3 mi. SW of Papenburg, in fenland.

Aschersleben (ä'shŭrslā"bŭn), city (pop. 42,196), in former Prussian Saxony prov., central Germany, after 1945 in Saxony-Anhalt, 30 mi. SSW of Magdeburg; 51°45'N 11°28'E. Center of potash- and lignite-mining region; textile milling, sugar refining; mfg. of steel products, machine tools, chemicals, blankets, paper products. Has 15th-cent. church, 16th-cent. town hall, and remains of old fortifications. Chartered 1175. Was seat of Ascanian counts (ancestral castle of Ascanians stood here) until it passed (1315) to bishopric of Halberstadt, with which it fell to Brandenburg in 1648.

Asciano (äshä'nô), town (pop. 2,075), Siena prov., Tuscany, central Italy, near Ombrone R., 13 mi. SE of Siena; travertine quarrying. Has 14th-cent. fortifications and several old churches. Near by is famous Benedictine monastery of Monte Oliveto Maggiore (early 14th cent.), adorned with frescoes by L. Signorelli and Sodoma.

Ascó (äskō'), town (pop. 1,953), Tarragona prov., NE Spain, on the Ebro and 12 mi. NE of Gandesa; soap mfg., olive-oil processing; almond shipping; agr. trade (cereals, livestock, wine, vegetables).

Ascochinga (äskōchēng'gä). **1** Village (pop. estimate 500), Córdoba prov., Argentina, at E foot of Sierra Chica, 32 mi. N of Córdoba; fashionable summer and winter resort in Córdoba hills. Site of a Jesuit mission, with picturesque old bldgs. **2** Town (pop. estimate 1,000), E central Santa Fe prov., Argentina, 15 mi. N of Santa Fe; agr. center (alfalfa, flax, corn, livestock). Adjoining is Arroyo Aguiar, its railroad and postal station.

Ascoli Piceno (ä'skōlē pēchā'nô), province (□ 807; pop. 303,869), The Marches, central Italy, bordering on the Adriatic; ⊙ Ascoli Piceno. Crossed by the Apennines; watered by Tronto, Tenna, and Aso rivers. Agr. (cereals, grapes, potatoes, raw silk, olives); stock raising. Fishing (San Benedetto del Tronto). Hydroelectric plants on Tronto R. Mfg. at Ascoli Piceno, Fermo, San Benedetto del Tronto, Porto San Giorgio.

Ascoli Piceno, anc. *Asculum Picenum,* town (pop. 20,665), ⊙ Ascoli Piceno prov., The Marches, central Italy, on Tronto R. and 43 mi. NW of Pescara; 42°51'N 13°35'E. Rail terminus; mfg. (macaroni, canned tomatoes, woolen textiles, majolica, shoes, paper, carbide, electrodes). Bishopric. Has cathedral, 12th-cent. octagonal baptistery, medieval bldgs., and Roman remains.

Ascoli Satriano (sätrēä'nô), anc. *Asculum,* town (pop. 7,989), Foggia prov., Apulia, S Italy, near Carapelle R., 18 mi. S of Foggia; agr. trade center (grain, wool, cheese); shoe factory. Bishopric. Here Pyrrhus defeated Romans in 279 B.C.; his heavy losses here led to the term "Pyrrhic victory."

Ascona (äskô'nä), resort town (pop. 2,314), Ticino canton, S Switzerland, on Lago Maggiore, near mouth of Maggia R., and 1 mi. SW of Locarno. Has 15th- and 16th-cent. churches.

Ascope (äskō'pā), city (pop. 3,727), Libertad dept., NW Peru, in W foothills of Cordillera Occidental, in irrigated Chicama R. valley, 27 mi. NNW of Trujillo. Rail terminus; sugar cane, rice, fruit; cattle raising.

Ascot (ă'skŭt), NE suburb (pop. 16,865) of Brisbane, SE Queensland, Australia.

Ascot (ă'skŭt), village in parish of Sunninghill, E Berkshire, England, 6 mi. SW of Windsor. On Ascot Heath, here, is racecourse, scene of annual (June) races instituted by Queen Anne in 1711.

Ascotán (äskōtän'), village (1930 pop. 68), Antofagasta prov., N Chile, in the Andes (alt. 12,980 ft.), on railroad and 65 mi. NE of Calama, at S edge of Salar de Ascotán, a salt desert (20 mi. long, 2–10 mi. wide) considered to be one of the world's largest borax deposits.

Ascq (äsk), town (pop. 3,485), Nord dept., N France, 5 mi. E of Lille; textile and flour milling, beet-sugar distilling, chicory mfg.

Ascra (ă'skrŭ), anc. town of Boeotia, central Greece, at E foot of Zagora section of the Helicon, 11 mi. WSW of Thebes. The home of the poet Hesiod (8th cent. B.C.), it was destroyed by Thespiae. On site is modern village of Palaiopanagia or Palaiopanayia (pop. 1,392).

Asculum, Italy: see ASCOLI SATRIANO.

Ascutney, village, Vt.: see WEATHERSFIELD.

Ascutney, Mount (ŭskŭt'nē), isolated peak (3,144 ft.), SE Vt., near the Connecticut, just S of Windsor; granite quarries. State park here.

Asebu (äsĕ'bōō), town, Western Prov., S Gold Coast colony, 8 mi. NE of Cape Coast; lime growing.

Aseda (ōs'ā"dä), Swedish *Åseda,* town (pop. 1,761), Kronoberg co., S Sweden, 30 mi. NE of Vaxjo; rail junction; sawmilling, furniture mfg.

Asekeyevo (ŭsyĭkyā'ŭvŭ), village (1926 pop. 2,649), NW Chkalov oblast, Russian SFSR, on Greater Kinel R., on railroad and 13 mi. ESE of Buguruslan; metalworking; wheat, sunflowers.

Asele (ō'sŭlŭ), Swedish *Åsele,* village (pop. 1,509), Vasterbotten co., N Sweden, on Angerman R. and 70 mi. NW of Ornskoldsvik; market center in cattle-raising, dairying region.

Aselle, Ethiopia: see ASSELLE.

Asembo (äsĕm'bō), village, Nyanza prov., W Kenya, on Kavirondo Gulf of L. Victoria, 30 mi. WSW of Kisumu; fishing center; cotton, peanuts, sesame, corn. Also called Asembo Bay and sometimes spelled Asembu.

Asen (ō'sŭn), Nor. *Åsen,* village and canton (pop. 1,999), Nord-Trondelag co., central Norway, on railroad and 24 mi. NE of Trondheim; produces wool textiles, organs, explosives, lumber, wooden goods. Sometimes spelled Aasen.

Asenovgrad (äsĕ'nôvgrăd), city (pop. 20,920), Plovdiv dist., S central Bulgaria, at N foot of E Rhodope Mts., on Asenovitsa R. and 12 mi. SE of Plovdiv; rail spur terminus; processing center in tobacco, silk, and fruitgrowing dist.; cigarette mfg. Has ruins of 13th-cent. castle, 16th-cent. churches. Once a Bulg. stronghold; became commercial town under Turkish rule (15th–19th cent.). Until 1934, Stanimaka. Asenitsa hydroelectric station completed here 1951.

Asenovitsa River (äsĕnô'vĕtsä), S central Bulgaria, rises in central Rhodope Mts. S of Chepelare, flows N, past Chepelare, and NNE, past Asenovgrad, to Maritsa R. 10 mi. E of Plovdiv; 55 mi. long. Also called Chaya R. and Chepelare R.

Asensbruk (ō"sŭnsbrŭk'), Swedish *Åsensbruk,* village (pop. 569), Alvsborg co., SW Sweden, on small bay on W shore of L. Vaner, 20 mi. SSW of Amal; paper and pulp milling.

Aseral (ô'sŭräl), Nor. *Åseral,* village and canton (pop. 1,124), Vest-Agder co., S Norway, 40 mi. N of Mandal; agr., cattle raising, lumbering, fishing, deer hunting. Sanatorium is N. Sometimes spelled Aaseral.

Aserei, Monte (môn'tĕ äzĕrā'), peak (4,695 ft.) in Ligurian Apennines, N central Italy, 4 mi. NNW of Ferriere.

Aseri (ä'sĕrē), town (1949 pop. over 500), NE Estonia, port on Gulf of Finland, 20 mi. NE of Rakvere; rail terminus (spur from Sonda); cement-milling center.

Aserradores Island, Nicaragua: see CORINTO.

Aserrí (äsĕrē'), town (pop. 172), San José prov., central Costa Rica, on central plateau, 5 mi. SSW of San José (linked by road); coffee, sugar cane, beans, corn. The near-by (S) Aserrí stone, a huge rock (100 ft. long, 30 ft. wide), attracts tourists.

Asfeld (äsfĕld'), village (pop. 768), Ardennes dept., N France, on the Aisne, on Ardennes Canal, and 12 mi. WSW of Rethel; cheese mfg.

Asfi, Fr. Morocco: see SAFI.

Asfun, El Mata'na, Asfun El Mata'na, or **Asfun al-Mata'nah** (äsfōōn' ĕl-mätä'nŭ), anc. *Asphyrus,* town (pop. 9,465), Qena prov., Upper Egypt, on W bank of the Nile, 6 mi. NNW of Isna, in sugar-cane-growing region; sugar mill, pottery works. Railway station of El Mata'na is across Nile R. Sometimes El Mataana.

Asgardstrand (ôs'gôrstrăn), Nor *Åsgårdstrand,* town (pop. 522), Vestfold co., SE Norway, on W shore of Oslo Fjord, 5 mi. NNE of Tonsberg; seaside resort. Sometimes spelled Aasgaardstrand.

Ash [Arabic, =the], for Arabic names beginning thus: see under following part of the name.

Ash, town and parish (pop. 2,094), E Kent, England, 3 mi. W of Sandwich; agr. market. Has 13th-cent. church.

Asha (ä'shä), village (pop. 2,041), Famagusta dist., E Cyprus, 13 mi. E of Nicosia; wheat; barley, cotton, olives; sheep, cattle.

Asha (ŭshä'), city (1932 pop. estimate 24,800), W Chelyabinsk oblast, Russian SFSR, in the S Urals, on railroad (Vavilovo station) and 55 mi. ENE of Ufa; metallurgical center, based on Bakal iron mines; wood cracking, charcoal burning. Gypsum quarries near by (S). Became city in 1933; until c.1928, called Asha-Balashevski Zavod.

Ashammar (ōs'hä"mär), Swedish *Åshammar,* village (pop. 726), Gavleborg co., E Sweden, 7 mi. WNW of Sandviken; grain, flax, potatoes, stock.

Ashan, China: see SHARASUME.

Ash and Normandy, residential and agr. parish (pop. 6,108), W Surrey, England. Includes town of Ash, 2 mi. E of Aldershot; agr. market, with part-Norman church. Normandy is agr. village.

Ashangi, Lake (ä'shäng-gē), N Ethiopia, in Tigre prov., 65 mi. S of Makale; 12°32'N 39°35'E; alt. c.7,900 ft.; 3 mi. long, 2.5 mi. wide. Bet. here and Mai Chio (N) a decisive battle was won (1936) by the Italians in Italo-Ethiopian War.

Ashanti (ŭshăn'tē, ä"shäntē', äshän'tē), British protectorate (□ 24,560; pop. 823,672), central Gold Coast; ⊙ Kumasi. Bounded W by Ivory Coast of Fr. West Africa, N by Northern Territories (along Black Volta R.), E by Togoland (along Volta R.), and S by Gold Coast colony. Main mtn. range of Gold Coast (including Mampong Scarp) crosses region NW-SE, separating Volta drainage basin (Pru and Afram rivers; N) from coastal drainage area (Tano, Ofin, and Pra rivers; S). Tropical forest (S of main range). Chief products: cacao (around Kumasi), kola nuts (Sunyani, Goaso), hardwood, rubber. Food crops (cassava, corn, yams) grown in savanna N of main range. Gold mining at Obuasi, Konongo, Juaso. Area is served by railroads (S) and roads (N) converging on Kumasi. A native kingdom (⊙ Kumasi) founded 1697 by Osei Tutu who subdued rival tribes. During 18th and 19th cent. the Ashanti Confederacy developed into strong military power, making frequent incursions into coastal area. Friction bet. British and Ashanti resulted in several wars (1824–26, 1873–74) during which Kumasi was twice occupied by British. In 1896, area was placed under Br. protection and the king deposed. A revolt in 1900 was quelled. In 1901, Ashanti came under Gold Coast administration. The Ashanti Confederacy (dissolved 1901) was restored in 1935. A chief commissioner represents the governor of Gold Coast. Human sacrifice has been abolished, but fetishism is still prevalent among the Ashanti. The pop. engages in handicraft weaving and the working of precious metals.

'Ashar (ä'shär), the old port for Basra, SE Iraq, on the Shatt al Arab, just NE of Basra, for which it is also the commercial section.

'Ashara, Qasr el, or **Qasr al-'Asharah** (both: kä'sür ĕl-ä'shärŭ), Fr. *Acharat,* village, Euphrates prov., E Syria, on Euphrates R. and 37 mi. SE of Deir ez Zor.

Asharoken (ăshŭrō'kŭn), resort village (pop. 116), Suffolk co., SE N.Y. on N shore of W Long Isl., on Eatons Neck, 5 mi. NE of Huntington.

Ashaway (ă'shŭwā), village (pop. 1,022) in Hopkinton town, Washington co., SW R.I., 34 mi. SSW of Providence, in agr. area; mfg. (textiles, fish line, twine).

Ashbourne (ăsh'bôrn), urban district (1931 pop. 4,506; 1951 census 5,440), W Derby, England, on Dove R. near mouth of Henmore R., 13 mi. NW of Derby; cotton milling, milk canning, mfg. of pharmaceuticals. Has Elizabethan grammar school, 13th-cent. church containing monument by Thomas Banks. In urban dist. (WSW) is cotton-milling town of Mayfield.

Ashburn. 1 City (pop. 2,918), ⊙ Turner co., S central Ga., 19 mi. NNW of Tifton; trade and processing for agr. and timber area; mfg. of cottonseed products, clothing, naval stores; peanut shelling, sawmilling. Founded 1889. **2** Town (pop. 153), Pike co., E Mo., on Mississippi R. and 15 mi. SE of Hannibal.

Ashburnham (ăsh'bûrnhăm), town (pop. 2,603), Worcester co., N Mass., 7 mi. NW of Fitchburg; furniture mfg.; dairying, fruit. State forest. Settled 1736, inc. 1765.

Ashburton (ăsh'bûrtŭn), urban district (1931 pop. 2,505; 1951 census 2,704), S Devon, England, 17 mi. SW of Exeter; agr. market. Has 15th-cent. church and 14th-cent. grammar school.

Ashburton, borough (pop. 7,550), ⊙ Ashburton co. (□ 2,459; pop. 10,204), E S.Isl., New Zealand, 50 mi. SW of Christchurch; agr. center; woolen and flour mills.

Ashburton River, NW Western Australia, rises in hills 140 mi. SSW of Nullagine, flows 220 mi. NW, through mountainous region, to Indian Ocean at Onslow near entrance to Exmouth Gulf; intermittent. Hardey and Henry rivers are the main tributaries.

Ashbury, S suburb of Pretoria, S central Transvaal, U. of So. Afr.

Ashby. 1 Agr. town (pop. 1,464), Middlesex co., N Mass., 7 mi. N of Fitchburg, near N.H. line; makes small toy parts. Settled c.1676, inc. 1767. **2** Village (pop. 443), Grant co., W Minn., near Pelican and Christina lakes, 18 mi. SE of Fergus Falls, in agr. area; dairy products, feed.

Ashby-de-la-Zouch (ăsh'bē-dŭ-lă-zōōsh'), urban district (1931 pop. 5,091; 1951 census 6,406), W Leicester, England, 16 mi. WNW of Leicester; hosiery, chemical, and soap industries. Site of Ashby Castle, built in 15th cent., and scene of imprisonment of Mary Queen of Scots in 1569. The 15th-cent. church contains tombs of Huntingdon family. Town figures largely in Scott's *Ivanhoe.*

Ashby Woulds (wōldz), urban district (1931 pop. 3,351; 1951 census 3,418), W Leicester, England. Includes coal-mining town of Moira, 3 mi. W of Ashby-de-la-Zouch, with pottery works.

Ashcroft, village (pop. estimate 750), S B.C., on Thompson R. and 40 mi. W of Kamloops; potatoes, tomatoes, stock; distributing center for mining and agr. region. Cariboo Road, built 1862–65, during Cariboo gold rush, to the Fraser R. gold mines, begins here.

Ashdod (ăshdŏd') or **Azotus** (ŭzō'tŭs), anc. locality, W Palestine, in Judaean Plain, near Mediterranean, 13 mi. SW of Rehovot. Philistine stronghold, it withstood 29-year-siege by Psamtik I. Was seat of worship of Dagus. Destroyed by Maccabees, restored by Romans, it became early center of Christianity and episcopal see. In antiquity also called Hippenus. On site is modern village of Ashdod, Arabic *Isdud.*

Ashdot Ya'aqov or **Ashdot Yaakov** (both: äshdōt' yä-äkōv'), settlement (pop. 1,200), Lower Galilee, NE Israel, near Jordan border, bet. Jordan R. (W) and Yarkon R. (SE), on railroad and 9 mi. SSE of Tiberias; mixed farming; canning (fruit and vegetable juices, preserves). Founded 1933.

Ashdown, Berkshire, England: see WHITE HORSE VALE.

Ashdown, city (pop. 2,738), ⊙ Little River co., extreme SW Ark., 18 mi. N of Texarkana, in cotton-growing and truck-farming area; cotton processing, lumber milling. Founded 1892, inc. as city 1937.

Ashdown Forest, Sussex, England, a former forest, now heathland, bet. East Grinstead and Uckfield.

Ashe (ăsh), county (□ 427; pop. 21,878), NW N.C.; ⊙ Jefferson. In the Blue Ridge; bounded N by Va., W by Tenn.; drained by headstreams of New R. Included in Yadkin Natl. Forest. Farming (tobacco, corn, white potatoes, hay, grain), cattle, sheep; sawmilling. Formed 1799.

Asheboro (ăsh'bŭrŭ), town (pop. 7,701), ⊙ Randolph co., central N.C., 24 mi. S of Greensboro, in the piedmont; mfg. center (hosiery, textiles, furniture); lumber and flour mills. In 1936, a prehistoric Keyauwee Indian burial ground was excavated near by. Founded 1779; chartered 1796; inc. 1843.

Asher (ă'shŭr), town (pop. 420), Pottawatomie co., central Okla., 23 mi. S of Shawnee, near Canadian R.

Asherton, town (pop. 2,425), Dimmit co., SW Texas, c.65 mi. N of Laredo; a shipping point in irrigated truck-growing area. Inc. 1925.

Asheville (ăsh'vĭl), city (pop. 53,000), ⊙ Buncombe co., W N.C., on a plateau (alt. c.2,000 ft.) of the Blue Ridge, on French Broad R. and 100 mi. WNW of Charlotte, N.C., 80 mi. ESE of Knoxville, Tenn. Chief transportation and commercial center of W N.C.; a noted resort and tourist center near Great Smoky Mts. Natl. Park, Pisgah Natl. Forest, and Mt. Mitchell (6,684 ft.); mfg. of cotton, rayon, hosiery, furniture, rugs, leather and metal products; lumber mills. Has 2 jr. colleges. Founded after 1791; inc. 1797.

Ashey, agr. parish (pop. 1,499), on Isle of Wight, Hampshire, England, 3 mi. SSW of Ryde.

Ashfield, municipality (pop. 44,761), E New South Wales, Australia, 5 mi. WSW of Sydney, in metropolitan area; chemicals, clothing.

Ashfield, agr. town (pop. 977), Franklin co., W Mass., 10 mi. WSW of Greenfield. Seat of Sanderson Acad.

Ash Flat, town (pop. 265), Sharp co., N Ark., 30 mi. N of Batesville.

Ashford (ăsh'fŭrd). **1** Urban district (1931 pop. 15,248; 1951 census 24,777), E central Kent, England, on Great Stour R. and 13 mi. SW of Canterbury; railroad shops, tanneries, knitting mills, breweries, agr.-machinery works. Has 15th-cent. church. **2** Town, Middlesex, England: see STAINES.

Ashford. 1 Town (pop. 1,400), Houston co., extreme SE Ala., 10 mi. SE of Dothan in farming area; naval stores. **2** Town (pop. 845), Windham co., NE Conn., 11 mi. N of Willimantic; center of agr. area in which farmers' cooperative plan has developed. Includes villages of Warrenville (with 18th-cent. houses), Westford. State forests here.

Ash Fork or **Ashfork,** village (1940 pop. 675), Yavapai co., NW central Ariz., 47 mi. W of Flagstaff in livestock area; alt. 5,144 ft.; lumber products. Onyx and sandstone quarries near by.

Ash Grove, city (pop. 970), Greene co., SW Mo., in the Ozarks, on Sac R. and 18 mi. WNW of Springfield; agr. trading center; lead mine.

Ashibetsu (äshĭbä'tsōō), town (pop. 38,784), W central Hokkaido, Japan, 20 mi. SSW of Asahigawa; coal-mining center.

Ashiestiel, Scotland: see CLOVENFORDS.

Ashigara, Japan: see ODAWARA.

Ashigashiya (ăshēgä'shēä), town (pop. 1,195), N Br. Cameroons, administered as part of Bornu prov. of Nigeria, on Fr. Cameroons border, 65 mi. S of Dikwa; peanuts, millet, cotton; cattle, skins.

Ashihho, Manchuria: see ACHENG.

Ashikaga (äshĭkä'gä), city (1940 pop. 48,310; 1947 pop. 51,309), Tochigi prefecture, central Honshu, Japan, 30 mi. SW of Utsunomiya; textile center (silk, rayon). Great center of Chinese learning in 15th cent. Sometimes spelled Asikaga.

Ashimi, Japan: see AJIMU.

Ashimori (äshĭmō'rē), town (pop. 3,102), Okayama prefecture, SW Honshu, Japan, 8 mi. NW of Okayama, in agr. area.

Ashingdon, agr. village and parish (pop. 504), SE Essex, England, 5 mi. N of Southend-on-Sea. Reputed site of battle of Assandun (1016) in which Canute defeated Edmund Ironside.

Ashington, urban district (1931 pop. 29,418; 1951 census 28,723), central Northumberland, England, 15 mi. N of Newcastle-upon-Tyne; coal-mining center, with metal foundries. In urban dist. (W) is coal-mining town of Hirst (pop. 19,623).

Ashino (äshē'nō), town (pop. 4,856), Tochigi prefecture, central Honshu, Japan, 11 mi. NE of Otawara; rice, tobacco, silk cocoons.

Ashio (äshē'ō), town (pop. 19,107), Tochigi prefecture, central Honshu, Japan, 26 mi. WNW of Utsunomiya, in mtn. area; major copper-mining center. School of mines.

Ashiya (ä"shē'yä), sometimes spelled Asiya. **1** Town (1947 pop. 11,286), Fukuoka prefecture, N Kyushu, Japan, 7 mi. WNW of Yawata, on Hibiki Sea; coal-mining center. **2** City (1940 pop. 39,137; 1947 pop. 37,033), Hyogo prefecture, S Honshu, Japan, on Osaka Bay, bet. Nishinomiya (E) and Mikage (W); fashionable residential area for Kobe and Osaka.

Ashizuri Point (ä"shē'zōōrē), Jap. *Ashizuri-zaki,* cape in Kochi prefecture, SW Shikoku, Japan, in Philippine Sea, at W side of Tosa Bay; 32°43'N 133°2'E; lighthouse.

Ashkelon, Palestine: see ASCALON.

Ashkhabad (ăsh'kŭbăd", äsh"kŭbäd', Rus. ŭsh-khŭbät'), oblast (□ 87,600; 1946 pop. estimate 550,000), W Turkmen SSR; ⊙ Ashkhabad. Bounded S by Iran (along the KOPET DAGH), W by Caspian Sea; includes large section of the desert Kara-Kum, Balkhan ranges, and the Kara-Bogaz-Gol (gulf). Irrigated and dry farming (orchards, wheat, cotton) on N slopes of the Kopet-Dagh and on Tedzhen R. oasis. Glauber's salt extracted at Kara-Bogaz-Gol. Coal (Yagman, Tuar-Kyr), natural gas (N of Chikishlyar), sulphur (Darvaza, Serny Zavod). Fisheries along Caspian Sea coast (Gasan-Kuli, Kizyl-Su). Industry centered at Ashkhabad, Krasnovodsk, Kizyl-Arvat. Pop.: Turkmen, Russians. Formed 1939; it absorbed (1947) Krasnovodsk oblast.

Ashkhabad, largest city (1926 pop. 51,593; 1939 pop. 126,580; 1948 pop. estimate 167,000) and ⊙ Turkmen SSR and Ashkhabad oblast, on Trans-Caspian RR, at foot of the Kopet-Dagh, near Iran border, and 320 mi. ESE of Krasnovodsk, 1,550 mi. SE of Moscow; 37°58'N 58°22'E. Center of fertile oasis (vineyards, orchards); cotton ginning and milling, silk spinning, glass mfg., meat packing, wine making, food processing (meat, flour, canned goods). Railroad shops. Site of Turkmen univ. (1950), mus., scientific research institute, agr., medical, and teachers colleges, branch of USSR Acad. of Sciences. Moving-picture studios. Founded (1881) as Askhabad by Russians; from c.1920 to 1927 it was called Poltoratsk; after 1927 spelled Ashkhabad. Partly destroyed by earthquake (1948).

Ashkirk, agr. village and parish (pop. 308), E Selkirk, Scotland, 5 mi. S of Selkirk.

Ashkum, village (pop. 420), Iroquois co., E Ill., 16 mi. SSW of Kankakee, in rich agr. area.

Ashland. 1 County (□ 426; pop. 33,040), N central Ohio; ⊙ Ashland. Drained by forks of Mohican R. Includes Mohican State Forest (recreation area), with a flood-control dam. Agr. area (livestock, grain, hay, fruit); mfg. at Ashland and Loudonville; gravel pits. Formed 1846. **2** County (□ 1,037; pop. 19,461), extreme N Wis., bounded N by L. Superior; ⊙ Ashland. Includes Apostle Isls., just N of Chequamegon Bay. Part of Gogebic Range (source of iron ore) is in co. Drained by Bad R. Has section of Chequamegon Natl. Forest. The Bad River Indian Reservation is largely wasteland. Lumbering, iron mining, dairying; mfg. at Ashland. Copper Falls State Park is here. Formed 1860.

Ashland. 1 Town (pop. 1,593), ⊙ Clay co., E Ala., 26 mi. S of Anniston; cotton ginning. **2** Village (pop. 1,039), Cass co., W central Ill., 20 mi. WNW of Springfield; ships grain; dairy products, livestock, poultry. Inc. 1869. **3** City (pop. 1,493), ⊙ Clark co., SW Kansas, 40 mi. SSE of Dodge City, in grain and cattle region. Oil wells near by. Founded 1884, inc. 1886. **4** City (pop. 31,131), Boyd co., NE Ky., on left bank (levee) of Ohio R. (toll bridge to Ohio) and 11 mi. WNW of Huntington, W.Va. Chief city of E Ky. and part of Huntington-Ashland metropolitan dist.; rail and river shipping point; airport. Iron and steel mills, coke works, oil and gasoline refineries; mfg. of bricks, ballast, heat-resistant equipment, chemicals, leather, shoes, food products; lumbering. Has jr. col. Surrounding hilly region has coal mines, oil and gas wells, clay pits, limestone and sandstone quarries, hardwood timber, iron deposits (1st iron furnace set up 1826; local deposits no longer worked). State fish hatchery and large Central Park, with Indian burial mounds, here. In Ohio R. are U.S. navigation lock and dam. Near by is "Traipsin' Woman's Cabin," scene of annual American Folk Song Festival. Raceland (7 mi. NW) has noted race track. Settled 1815; laid out 1850; inc. as village 1858, as city 1870. **5** Town (pop. 2,370), Aroostook co., NE Maine, on Aroostook R. and 19 mi. W of Presque Isle; ships starch, potatoes, lumber. Settled c.1837, inc. 1862. **6** Town (pop. 3,500), Middlesex co., E central Mass., 3 mi. SW of Framingham; metal and electrical products. Settled c.1750, inc. 1846. **7** Village (pop. 328), ⊙ Benton co., N Miss., c.55 mi. ESE of Memphis (Tenn.), in agr. area; lumber. **8** Town (pop. 416), Boone co., central Mo., near Missouri R., 14 mi. NNW of Jefferson City. **9** Village (pop. c.100), Rosebud co., SE Mont., 60 mi. SSW of Miles City and on Tongue R. Div. hq. of Custer Natl. Forest; trading point in livestock region. **10** City (pop. 1,713), Saunders co., E Nebr., 23 mi. NE of Lincoln, near Platte R.; grain. Settled 1863, inc. 1886. **11** Town (pop. 1,599), Grafton co., central N.H., on the Pemigewasset and 35 mi. N of Concord, just SW of Squam L.; paper, wood products, textiles, agr., poultry, dairy products. Set off from Holderness 1867. **12** City (pop. 14,287), ⊙ Ashland co., N central Ohio, 13 mi. NE of Mansfield, in agr. area (corn, wheat, hay); mfg. of machinery, hardware, rubber goods, metal products; printing; also makes clothing, drugs, heaters. Seat of Ashland Col. Laid out 1815. **13** Town (pop. 104), Pittsburg co., SE Okla., 21 mi. WSW of McAlester, in farm area. **14** City (pop. 7,739), Jackson co., SW Oregon, on small affluent of Rogue R., near Calif. line, and 11 mi. SE of Medford; resort with mineral springs; trade center for fruit, grain, lumbering area; canned goods. Granite quarries, gold mines near by. Has Southern Oregon Col. of Education. Mt. Ashland (7,535 ft.) is 8 mi. S in Siskiyou Mts. Founded 1852, inc. 1874. Shakespearean Festival takes place annually in Aug. **15** Borough (pop. 6,192), Columbia and Schuylkill counties, E central Pa., 10 mi. NW of Pottsville; anthracite; metal products, clothing. Settled 1845, laid out 1847, inc 1857. **16** Town (pop. 2,610), Hanover co., E central Va., 16 mi. N of Richmond, in dairying, truck-farming region; mfg. of shirts; flour and lumber milling. Seat of Randolph-Macon Col. Patrick Henry and Henry Clay b. near by. "Scotchtown," Patrick Henry's home (1771–77) and later the home of Dolly Madison, is also near. Settled 1848; inc. 1858. **17** City (pop. 10,640), ⊙ Ashland co., extreme N Wis., port of entry on Chequamegon Bay of L. Superior, 60 mi. E of Superior; railroad center; mfg. of paper, woodwork, tile, briquettes; ironworks. Harbor is icebound Dec.–April; port ships iron ore (mined in Gogebic Range), coal, lumber. Northland Col. is here. French explorers visited (17th cent.) the bay shore; and a French mission was founded (1665) near Ashland by Father Allouez. Settled 1854, the city grew as iron-mining and lumbering center, and as terminus for 1st railroad in northern Wisconsin (1877). Inc. in 1887.

Ashland City, town (pop. 1,024), ⊙ Cheatham co., N central Tenn., on Cumberland R. and 18 mi. NW of Nashville, in tobacco, grain, livestock area; makes hosiery, weed cutters; sawmilling.

Ashley, New Zealand: see LOBURN.

Ashley (ăsh'lē), county (□ 933; pop. 25,660), SE Ark.; ⊙ Hamburg. Bounded S by La. line, W by Saline and Ouachita rivers; drained by Bayou Bartholomew. Agr. (cotton, corn, hay). Mfg., processing industries at Crossett. Contains state game refuge. Formed 1849.

Ashley. 1 City (pop. 738), Washington co., SW Ill., 13 mi. S of Centralia, in agr. and bituminous-coal area; corn, wheat, fruit, livestock, poultry; dairy products. **2** Town (pop. 680), on De Kalb–Steuben co. line, NE Ind., 33 mi. N of Fort Wayne, in agr. area; canned goods, cement. **3** Village (pop. 449), Gratiot co., central Mich., 31 mi. SW of Saginaw, in farm area. **4** City (pop. 1,423), ⊙ McIntosh co., S N.Dak., 85 mi. SE of Bismarck, near S.Dak. line. Dairy products, flour, livestock, poultry, grain. Moved from near-by lake to present location on railroad in 1888. Inc. 1920. **5** Village (pop. 798), Delaware co., central Ohio, 15 mi. SSE of Marion; makes furniture, heating equipment. **6** Borough (pop. 5,243), Luzerne co., NE central Pa., just S of Wilkes-Barre; anthracite; metal products, lace; railroad shops. Settled 1810, inc. 1870.

Ashley Falls, Mass.: see SHEFFIELD.

Ashley River, SE S.C., rises near Ridgeville, flows 40 mi. SE, joining Cooper R. at Charleston to form Charleston Harbor. Partly navigable.

Ashmant, Egypt: see Ishmant.

Ashmore, village (pop. 406), Coles co., E Ill., 18 mi. E of Mattoon, in rich agr. area.

Ashmore and Cartier Islands, Territory of, dependency of Australia, in Indian Ocean, c.300 mi. N of Broome, Western Australia. Ashmore Isls. comprise 3 coral islets (each c.½ mi. wide) enclosed by a reef Cartier Isl., c.½ mi. wide, is sandy and also surrounded by a reef.

Ashmun (ăshmōōn'), town (pop. 19,229; with suburbs, 23,135), Minufiya prov., Lower Egypt, on railroad and 25 mi. NW of Cairo, in rich agr. area; cotton ginning, cigarette mfg.; cereals, cotton, flax.

Ashmunein, El, or **Al-Ashmunayn** (both: ĕl-ăshmōō'nān), anc. *Hermopolis Magna,* village (pop. 6,150), Asyut prov., central Upper Egypt, 22 mi. S of Minya; cereals, dates, sugar cane. Site of temple built by Seti II (1200 B.C.). Sometimes spelled Eshmunein.

Ashokan (ŭshō'kŭn), village Ulster co., SE N.Y., on N shore of Ashokan Reservoir, in resort area of the Catskills, 12 mi. WNW of Kingston.

Ashokan Reservoir (□ c.13), Ulster co., SE N.Y., part of New York city water-supply system; impounded by Olive Bridge (or Ashokan) Dam (4,650 ft. long, 252 ft. high; completed 1912), in Esopus Creek 6 mi. NW of Kingston; filling completed 1916. Receives water from Schoharie Reservoir (N) via 18-mi. Shandaken Tunnel to Esopus Creek upstream from Ashokan Reservoir. Ashokan water, after aeration here, is carried to New York city by Catskill Aqueduct.

Ashover (ăsh'ōvŭr), town and parish (pop. 2,419), central Derby, England, 6 mi. SSW of Chesterfield; agr. market. It was once a lead-mining place. Has 15th-cent. church.

Ashraf, Iran: see Behshahr.

Ash Shamiya, Iraq: see Shamiya, Ash.

Asht, Tadzhik SSR: see Shaidan.

Ashta (ŭsh'tŭ). **1** Town (pop. 5,640), W Bhopal state, India, on upper Parbati R and 45 mi. WSW of Bhopal; agr. market center (wheat, gram, cotton, millet, oilseeds); handicraft cloth weaving and dyeing; local trade in opium. **2** Town (pop. 9,973), Satara South dist., S Bombay, India, 12 mi. NW of Sangli; markets millet, peanuts, wheat; handloom weaving.

Ashtabula (ăsh"tŭbū'lŭ), county (□ 706; pop. 78,695), extreme NE Ohio; ⊙ Jefferson. Bounded N by L. Erie; intersected by Grand and Ashtabula rivers and Conneaut and Pymatuning creeks. Includes part of Pymatuning Reservoir (recreation area). Agr. (livestock; dairy products; fruit, truck, hay, grain); mfg. at Ashtabula and Conneaut; greenhouses, apiaries, wineries. Lake resorts. Formed 1811.

Ashtabula, city (pop. 23,696), Ashtabula co., extreme NE Ohio, on harbor at mouth of Ashtabula R., on L. Erie, c.55 mi. NE of Cleveland; important lake-rail transshipment point: unloads L. Superior iron ore for Youngstown-Pittsburgh steel dists., ships coal. Port of entry. Ferry to Port Burwell, Ont. Mfg. of foundry products, communications equipment, agr. tools, leather goods, metal products, chemicals. Railroad shops, oil refineries; fisheries; hothouse fruit, vegetables. Settled c.1801 by New Englanders; inc. as village in 1831, as city in 1891.

Ashtabula River, NE Ohio, rises in E Ashtabula co., flows N and W into L. Erie at Ashtabula; c.40 mi. long.

Ashtarak (ŭshtŭräk'), village (1926 pop. 4,853), W central Armenian SSR, at SE foot of Mt. Aragats, 12 mi. NW of Erivan (linked by road); road center; distilling (wines, brandies); vineyards, wheat, livestock.

Ashtarnian (äshtärnēän'), town, Sixth Prov., in Luristan, SW Iran, 10 mi. NW of Burujird.

Ashtead, residential town and parish (pop. 4,783), central Surrey, England, just NE of Leatherhead; mfg. of leather cloth, paint, electrical appliances. Church includes Roman tiles.

Ashti (ŭsh'tē). **1** Town (pop. 5,741), Bir dist., NW Hyderabad state, India, 40 mi. WSW of Bir; trades in cotton, wheat, millet, oilseeds. **2.** Town (pop. 6,457), Wardha dist., central Madhya Pradesh, India, 40 mi. NW of Wardha; cotton, millet, wheat, oilseeds. Cattle raising in near-by forested hills (teak, sal).

Ashton. 1 Resort village (pop. 1,256), Fremont co., E Idaho, near Henrys Fork, 14 mi. NE of St. Anthony; alt. 5,256 ft.; trading point in irrigated agr. area (wheat, seed peas, potatoes); lumbering; hydroelectric plant. Inc. 1906. Dude ranches near by. Yellowstone and Grand Teton natl. parks are E. **2** Village (pop. 913), Lee co., N Ill., 13 mi. E of Dixon, in rich agr. area; makes cheese, cement vaults. **3** Town (pop. 588), Osceola co., NW Iowa, 10 mi. NNE of Sheldon, in livestock and grain area. **4** Village (pop. 381), Sherman co., central Nebr., 10 mi. E of Loup City and on branch of Middle Loup R. **5** Village, R.I.: see Cumberland. **6** City (pop. 222), Spink co., NE central S.Dak., 8 mi. N of Redfield, near James R.

Ashton-in-Makerfield, urban district (1931 pop. 20,546; 1951 census 19,053), SW Lancashire, England, 15 mi. ENE of Liverpool; cotton milling, coal mining.

Ashton-under-Lyne, municipal borough (1931 pop. 51,573; 1951 census 46,490), SE Lancashire, England, on Tame R. and 6 mi. E of Manchester; cotton milling, coal mining, mfg. of hats, leather and leather goods, plastics, soap, machine tools; metallurgy and machine making; baking. Has church dating from 14th cent.

Ashton-upon-Mersey (–ŭpŭn-mûr'zē), town in Sale municipal borough, N Cheshire, England, on Mersey R. and 6 mi. SW of Manchester; steel center.

Ashuanipi River, Labrador, upper course of the Hamilton River.

Ashuapmuchuan River (ăshwäp"mōōchwän'), central Que., rises SSE of Chibougamau L., flows 170 mi. SE in a winding course, through Ashuapmuchuan L. (8 mi. long), to L. St. John. Upper course is called Ducharme R.

Ashuelot River (ăsh"ūē'lŭt, ăsh'wĭlŏt), W N.H., rises in Ashuelot Pond, S Sullivan co.; flows SW through Cheshire co. to the Connecticut at Hinsdale, furnishing power at Keene, Swanzey, Winchester, Hinsdale, and other towns along 50-mi. course.

Ashuganj (ŭsh'ōōgŭnj), village, Tippera dist., E East Bengal, E Pakistan, on Meghna R (rail ferry to Bhairab Bazar) and 40 mi. NNW of Comilla; rail spur terminus.

Ashur (ä'shŭr, ä'shōōr) or **Assur** (ä'sŭr, ä'sōōr), anc. city and original ⊙ Assyrian Empire; its site is on a rocky promontory on right bank of the Tigris, in Mosul prov., N Iraq, 60 mi. S of Mosul, near the modern Sharqat. It was later replaced by Calah and Nineveh. Many archaeological treasures have been unearthed here in 20th cent.

Ashuradeh Islands (äshōō"rädĕ'), in SE Caspian Sea, NE Iran, off E tip of Miyan Kaleh Peninsula, at entrance to Gurgan Lagoon; naval station.

Ashville. 1 Town (pop. 494), St. Clair co., NE central Ala., on branch of Coosa R. and 18 mi. SW of Gadsden; cotton ginning, lumber milling. **2** Village (pop. c.450), Chautauqua co., extreme W N.Y., near Chautauqua L., 7 mi. W of Jamestown; lumber. **3** Village (pop. 1,303), Pickaway co., S central Ohio, 17 mi. S of Columbus; food products, mops. **4** Borough (pop. 441), Cambria co., SW central Pa., 11 mi. ENE of Ebensburg.

Asi, river, Syria and Turkey: see Orontes River.

Asia, anc. Roman prov. embracing W part of Asia Minor; established 133 B.C., it included Mysia, Lydia, Ionia, and Caria; Phrygia was inc. into the prov. in 116 B.C.

Asia, largest continent (including offshore isls.: □ c.16,900,000; pop. c.1,300,000,000), forming with Europe the Eurasian land mass. Asia constitutes one-twelfth of the surface of the globe and one-third of the earth's land area. Asia's W land boundary with Europe lies along the Ural Mts., the Ural R., and the Greater Caucasus. Asia Minor, the continent's extreme W peninsula, bet. the Mediterranean and Black seas, is separated from Europe by the Turkish Straits (Bosporus, Dardanelles). Asia is also joined (W) to Africa by the Sinai Peninsula, the Suez Canal being usually considered the dividing line. The continent is bounded by the Arctic (N), Pacific (E), and Indian (S) oceans, whose secondary seas (sometimes virtually inland seas) form major indentations separated by large peninsulas and frequently closed off by major offshore isl. groups. Thus, the Arctic seas—Kara, Laptev, E. Siberian and Chukchi seas—are separated from each other by the Taimyr Peninsula, the isl. group Severnaya Zemlya, New Siberian Isls., and Wrangel Isl. On the Pacific side, the Bering Sea is bounded by the Chukchi and Kamchatka peninsulas and North America's Aleutian chain; the Sea of Okhotsk by Sakhalin and the Kurile Isls.; the Sea of Japan by Korea and Japan; the E. China Sea with the Yellow Sea by the Ryukyu Isls. and Formosa; and the S. China Sea by the Philippines, Indonesia, and the Indochinese and Malay peninsulas. On the Indian Ocean, 2 major indentations—the Bay of Bengal and the Arabian Sea—separate the Indochinese, Indian (with offshore Ceylon), and Arabian peninsulas. Situated entirely in the N hemisphere, mainland Asia extends N from Tanjong Piai (1°16'N) to Cape Chelyuskin (77°41'N) and E from Cape Baba (26°4'E) to Cape Dezhnev (169°40'W), which faces Alaska across Bering Strait. Geologically, Asia consists essentially of anc. blocks of complex pre-Cambrian rocks—the Arabian and Indian peninsulas (S) and the Central Siberian Plateau (N)—which enclose a central zone of folded ranges uplifted during the great Tertiary (Alpine) orogenesis. In accordance with this underlying structure, Asia falls into the following major physiographic provinces: the N lowlands covering W central Asia and most of Siberia; the vast central highland zone of high plateaus (rising to 15,000 ft. in Tibet) enclosed by Asia's mightiest ranges (Himalayas, Karakorum, Kunlun, Tien Shan, Hindu Kush); and the S peninsular plateaus of India and Arabia, merging, respectively, into the great Indo-Gangetic and Tigris-Euphrates plains. Another major division is that of the lowlands of E Asia, separated by mtn. spurs of the central highland zone and flanked on the outside by the succession of mts. characteristic of the continent's easternmost margins. Asia's rivers, among the longest in the world, rise generally in the high plateaus and break through the great chains toward the peripheral lowlands. They are the Ob, Yenisei, and Lena in Siberia's Arctic drainage basin; the Amur, Yellow R., Yangtze, West R., and Mekong of E and SE Asia's Pacific basin; and the Salween, Irrawaddy, Brahmaputra, Indus, Tigris, and Euphrates of S and SW Asia's Indian Ocean drainage. Central Asia has vast areas of interior drainage, including the Amu Darya, Syr Darya, Ili, and Tarim rivers, which drain into inland lakes (Aral, Balkhash) or disappear in desert sands. The great plateaus form the most important climatic divide. N and W of this divide the most important climatic influences are the temperate westerlies characteristic of most of Europe but greatly modified by Asia's extreme continentality. S and E are the monsoon lands whose climate is governed by great temperature and pressure changes in the interior, bringing cool, dry out-blowing winds in winter and hot, moist in-blowing winds in summer. In the complex vegetation cover, 2 major forest realms are discernible, each corresponding to one of the major climatic divisions. These forest belts—the Siberian coniferous taiga and the varied wet evergreen and deciduous monsoon forests—are separated by the great interior belt of steppes and barren desert plateaus. Because of extremes in climate and topography, much of Asia is thus unattractive for human settlement, less than 10% being under cultivation. By far the most important food crop is rice, which is grown for home consumption in countries with large populations (China, India, Pakistan, and Japan), while countries with smaller populations (Burma, Thailand, Vietnam) are major rice exporters. Other grains are wheat, grown chiefly in China, Siberia, and Pakistan, and various coarse grains, such as kaoliang and other types of millet. Fats and oils (soybeans, peanuts, sesame, copra) and sugar cane play a major role in monsoonal Asia, with the largest production in China and India, where they are used domestically, and in Indonesia and Philippines, who are the leading exporters. Among non-food crops, cotton and jute are exported from India and Pakistan and silk from Japan. The large production of cotton in Soviet Central Asia and of cotton and silk in China is largely consumed domestically. Other typical industrial export products of monsoonal Asia are rubber (chiefly in Malaya and Indonesia) and tea (in India and Ceylon) and, among the forest resources, the teak of Burma and Thailand. Siberia's vast forest resources remain largely untouched. Asia's economy is predominantly agricultural and only a few regions—where there are power facilities, trained labor, modern transport and access to raw materials—have developed industrially. Japan and her former overseas empire (Manchuria, Korea, Formosa), and Soviet Asia are distinguished by their industrial development. Industrialization is progressing too in India and China. Contributing greatly to the income of these countries are vital mineral exports: petroleum in Iran, Iraq, Saudi Arabia, Kuwait, Indonesia, Burma, and British Borneo, and tin in Malaya and Indonesia. Iron and steel industry has developed in Japan, N Korea, Manchuria, India, Turkey, and in Soviet Asia on the basis of coal and iron resources. In these areas, heavy industry is associated with mfg. of machinery, chemicals (fertilizers), and cement The principal industrial output of Asia is cotton textiles, produced chiefly in Japan, China, and India. Jute in India and rayon in Japan rank 2d to cotton in the milling of fibers. In addition to oil and tin, Asia has valuable export minerals in manganese (India), chromite (Turkey, Philippines), and iron ore (Malaya, Philippines), while China is one of the world's leading producers of antimony and tungsten. The development of railroads is greatest in the industrialized countries, with India, Japan, China, Soviet Asia, and Pakistan each exceeding 5,000 mi. of lines. River navigation is significant only on the Yangtze and West rivers in China, and, to a lesser degree, on the Irrawaddy in Burma. The Siberian streams (except the Amur) are handicapped by the long winter season, while rapids and an irregular regime render navigation difficult on the other great Asian streams. Because of the difficult inland connections, international trade moves mostly by sea. The principal ports are Vladivostok, Dairen, Tientsin, Shanghai, Canton, Hong Kong, Singapore, Rangoon, Calcutta, Madras, Bombay, Karachi, and Aden on the mainland, Yokohama, Manila, Jakarta, and Colombo on the offshore isls. The distribution of Asia's pop., the largest of any continent, is determined primarily by climate and topography, with the monsoon and fertile alluvial plains determining the greatest density. Such are the Ganges Plain of India and the Yangtze and North China plains of China, the small alluvial plains of Japan, and the fertile volcanic soils of Java. Urbanization, which develops with industrialization, is greatest in Japan, India, China, and Soviet Asia. Two-thirds of the native pop. of Asia belongs to the Mongoloid groups (N and E), the rest to the Caucasoid groups (SW). Primitive hunting and fishing economies prevail in N, nomadic pastoralism in center, while more highly developed cultures are found in S and E. In religion, Asia's pop. today follows largely the practices of Hinduism (in India), Buddhism (in Ceylon, Burma, Thailand, Cambodia in its simple form; in Tibet and Mongolia as Lamaism; in China as an eclectic mixture with Confucianism and Taoism; and in Japan as a mixture with Confucianism and Shinto), Islam (in Indonesia, W central and SW Asia), and Roman Catholicism in the Philippines. Asia harbored some of the world's oldest civilizations. In the West flourished the empires of the Sumerian, Babylonian, Assyrian, Median, Persian, Greek, Roman, and Arab civilizations and in the East the cultures of China, India, and Japan. Later, in N and central Asia, primitive nomadic tribes (Huns, Tatars, Turks) gave rise to the great Westward migrations. Their tribal, military state organization reached its highest form under the Mongols (13th-14th cent.), whose court was visited by the 1st European travelers, notably Marco Polo. Vasco da Gama reached India by sea in 1498. In N Asia, Russian Cossacks traversed Siberia and reached the Pacific by 1640. With the formation of the English, French, Dutch, and Portuguese trading companies in 17th cent., great trade rivalry developed along the coasts of India and China and resulted in increasing European colonial control of Asian lands. In 19th cent., China and Japan were the last to open their doors to foreign trade, with Japan rapidly rising to a world industrial and military power. Following the First World War, which left Asia largely untouched, progress was made in developing and modernizing the Asian economy, notably in areas under the rule of Japan. The Second World War and the conflicts of its aftermath hit Asia heavily. After Japan's defeat and the reduction of her empire, Asia assumed an increasing role in the world scene and gradually broke her ties with Europe. After 1945, the major developments were the independence of numerous major states in SW, S, and SE Asia, the simmering revolts against European rule in Malaya and Vietnam, the Communist revolution in China, and the Korean war. The independent states of Asia are as follows: in SW Asia are TURKEY, SYRIA, LEBANON, ISRAEL, JORDAN, IRAQ, IRAN, AFGHANISTAN, and the states of the Arabian Peninsula (SAUDI ARABIA, YEMEN, OMAN, TRUCIAL OMAN, QATAR, BAHREIN, KUWAIT); in the Indian peninsula are PAKISTAN and INDIA, associated along their N margins with the Himalayan states of NEPAL, SIKKIM, and BHUTAN, and off the peninsula's tip with insular CEYLON; in SE Asia are BURMA, THAILAND (Siam), INDONESIA, and the PHILIPPINES; in E Asia are CHINA (and offshore FORMOSA), KOREA, JAPAN, and the MONGOLIAN PEOPLE'S REPUBLIC; the N third of Asia is in the UNION OF SOVIET SOCIALIST REPUBLICS. Vestiges of the once great European holdings are as follows: Britain—the colonies of ADEN, CYPRUS, HONG KONG, SINGAPORE, SARAWAK, and NORTH BORNEO, the protected state of BRUNEI, the ADEN PROTECTORATE, the Federation of MALAYA, and the MALDIVE ISLANDS; France—FRENCH INDIA and the associated Indochinese states of VIETNAM, CAMBODIA, and LAOS; the Netherlands—Netherlands NEW GUINEA; Portugal—MACAO, PORTUGUESE INDIA, and Portuguese TIMOR.

Asiago (äzyä'gô), town (pop. 3,051), Vicenza prov., Veneto, N Italy, 23 mi. N of Vicenza, on Asiago plateau (S foothill of the Alps, rising to 7,680 ft. in Cima Dodici; also known as Sette Comuni). Resort (alt. 3,278 ft.); mfg. (liquor, cheese, wood and marble products). Has mus. of antiquities. Astronomical observatory near by. Completely reconstructed (1919–24) after heavy fighting here and on its plateau in First World War.

Asia Minor, the great peninsula of extreme W Asia, called also ANATOLIA, bet. Black Sea (N), the Mediterranean (S), and Aegean arm of the Mediterranean (W). The Black Sea and the Aegean are linked by the Sea of Marmara and the 2 straits of the Bosporus and the Dardanelles (anc. Hellespont)—one of the most famous waterways of the world. Near S coast of Asia Minor are Taurus Mts., and the rest of the peninsula is occupied by the mountain-crossed, lake-dotted Anatolian Plateau. Corresponds to most of TURKEY in Asia. Asia Minor was chief meeting place of Oriental and Occidental civilization in ancient times, for it was connected with Mesopotamia by Tigris and Euphrates rivers and with Greece by its coasts. After the decline of the Hittites, Greek colonies were begun on the coastlands, and the Greeks thus came into contact with Lydia and Phrygia and more especially with Troy. The conquest of Asia Minor by the Persians led to the Persian Wars. Alexander the Great incorporated the region in his empire, and after his death in the wars of the Diadochi it was divided into small states. It was reintegrated by the Romans, but was subject to almost constant attack by invaders under the Byzantine Empire, falling to the Arabs and the Seljuk Turks. It was temporarily reconquered for the West by the Crusaders, who set up ephemeral states. Taken by the Ottoman Turks in the 13th-15th cent., it was thereafter in the Ottoman Empire. The principal anc. divisions of Asia Minor were: Bithynia, Paphlagonia, and Pontus on N coast; Mysia, Lydia, and Caria on W coast; Lycia, Pamphylia, and Cilicia on S coast; and Phrygia, Galatia, Cappadocia, Lycaonia, and Pisidia in the interior.

Asid Gulf (äsēd'), arm of Visayan Sea, Philippines, deeply indents S coast of Masbate isl.; c.40 mi. E-W (at entrance), c.20 mi. N-S. Milagros is on N shore.

Asientos (äsyĕn'tōs), town (pop. 1,847), Aguascalientes, N central Mexico, on railroad and 28 mi. NNE of Aguascalientes; silver, gold, lead, copper mining.

Asientos, Los, Panama: see LOS ASIENTOS.

Asifabad, India: see ASAFABAD.

Asif el Mal, Fr. Morocco: see AMIZMIZ.

Asikaga, Japan: see ASHIKAGA.

Asile or **L'Asile** (läzēl'), town (1950 pop. 300), Sud dept., SW Haiti, on Tiburon Peninsula, 22 mi. NE of Les Cayes; coffee, oranges.

Asilomar, Calif.: see MONTEREY PENINSULA.

Asinara, Gulf of (äzēnä'rä), inlet of Mediterranean Sea, NW Sardinia, bet. Asinara Isl. (W) and Point Falcone (E); 40 mi. wide; fisheries (tunny, lobster). Receives Coghinas and Mannu rivers. Chief port, Porto Torres.

Asinara Island (□ 20; pop. 567), just off NW Sardinia, in Sassari prov., W of Gulf of Asinara; 10 mi. long; separated from Cape Falcone by 1-mi.-wide strait; rises to 1,335 ft. Livestock. Penal colony, quarantine station here.

Asingan (äsĕng'än), town (1939 pop. 2,703; 1948 municipality pop. 24,701), Pangasinan prov., central Luzon, Philippines, 22 mi. E of Dagupan; agr. center (rice, corn, copra).

Asino, Salvador: see ILOPANGO, LAKE.

Asino (ä'sēnŭ), town (1939 pop. over 2,000), SE Tomsk oblast, Russian SFSR, on Chulym R. and 55 mi. NE of Tomsk (linked by railroad); river port; lumber milling.

Asintal or **El Asintal** (ĕl äsēntäl'), town (pop. 294), Retalhuleu dept., SW Guatemala, in Pacific piedmont, 4 mi. NW of Retalhuleu; sugar cane, corn, rice. Sometimes spelled Acintal.

Asir or **'Asir** (äsēr'), SW dependency (□ 25,000; pop. 1,000,000) of Nejd, Saudi Arabia; main town, Abha. Situated on Red Sea, bet. Hejaz (N) and Yemen (S), and bounded E by Nejd; consists of arid Tihama coastal plain (20–30 mi. wide), and of E highlands rising in an abrupt escarpment to 9,000 ft. and sloping gradually eastward to the great interior desert. Moderate summer rainfall in the highlands feeds a number of intermittent streams around whose upper courses savanna grassland prevails. This precipitation renders Asir one of the chief agr. areas of Saudi Arabia. On the upper valley slopes grow millet, wheat, bananas, dates (Bisha), coffee; while in the drier piedmont, millet and the nuts of the *daum* (*dom*) palm are the chief products. Stock (cattle, sheep, goats, camels) is raised widely, though settled agr. pop. predominates. Basketwork is typical of the region, which also makes pottery, vases, and water pipes. Although stone bldgs. prevail in the highlands, beehive-shaped huts of straw and clay are typical of the Tihama lowland. Pop. belongs largely to Shafai branch of the Sunni sect, though Wahabism is popular in NE. Main centers are Abha (in highlands), Sabya (in lowlands), and Qizan (the chief port). Asir successfully repelled an Egyptian expedition in 1834, but was occupied by the Turks in 1872 and became a sanjak of Turkish Yemen. In late-19th cent., the Idrisi dynasty of Sabya revolted against the Turks and by 1910 had control over most of the prov. After First World War, while the Idrisi briefly held the Tihama lowland of Yemen, upland Asir came (1920) under Wahabi control; and the entire prov. accepted Ibn Saud's suzerainty in 1926. Yemen's objection to complete integration (1933) of Asir into Saudi Arabia led to a brief war (1934), in the course of which Ibn Saud's forces ranged S to Hodeida in Yemen's Tihama. By the treaty of Taif, Asir and Najran were declared part of Saudi Arabia. Asir falls administratively into the provs. of Asir or Upper Asir (chief town, Abha) and Asir Tihama (chief town, Sabya).

Asirgarh, fortress, India: see BURHANPUR.

Asi River, Turkey: see ORONTES RIVER.

Asiya, Japan: see ASHIYA.

Aska (ŭs'kŭ), town (pop. 5,794), Ganjam dist., SE Orissa, India, on Rushikulya R. and 22 mi. NNW of Berhampur; road junction; market center (rice, sugar cane, timber); sugar mill, distillery.

Askale (äsh"kälĕ'), Turkish *Aşkale*, village (pop. 1,962), Erzurum prov., NE Turkey, on railroad, on Euphrates R., and 30 mi. W of Erzurum; grain.

Askalon, Palestine: see ASCALON.

Askaniya-Nova (ŭskä'nyēŭ-nô'vŭ), town (1939 pop. over 500), S Kherson oblast, Ukrainian SSR, in steppe region, 50 mi. WNW of Genichesk; zoological reserve used for scientific research.

Askarovo (ŭskä'rŭvŭ), village (1926 pop. 619), E Bashkir Autonomous SSR, Russian SFSR, in the S Urals, 25 mi. WSW of Magnitogorsk; lumbering; livestock, grain. Jasper deposits near by (NE).

Askeaton (ăskē'tŭn), Gaelic *Eas Géiphtine*, town (pop. 461), NW Co. Limerick, Ireland, on Deel R. near its mouth on the Shannon, and 16 mi. WSW of Limerick; agr. market (grain, potatoes; dairying). Has ruins of Desmond Castle, dating from c.1200. Parish church incorporates parts of 13th-cent. commandery of the Knights Templars. There are 15th-cent. remains of Franciscan friary.

Askern, town and parish (pop. 6,477), West Riding, S Yorkshire, England, 7 mi. N of Doncaster; coal mining. Spa resort with medicinal springs.

Askersund (äs"kûrsŭnd'), city (pop. 2,166), Orebro co., S central Sweden, on small bay at N extremity of L. Vatter, 30 mi. SSW of Orebro; metalworking, hosiery knitting. Has 17th-cent. church, mus. Fishing port and trade center since pagan times. Chartered 1643.

Askhabad, Turkmen SSR: see ASHKHABAD, city.

Askim (äs'kĭm), village (pop. 3,744; canton pop. 8,049), Ostfold co., SE Norway, near Glomma R., on railroad and 20 mi. NE of Moss; lumber and construction industries; mfg. of rubber products, glass wool.

Askim (äs'kēm"), residential village (pop. 1,033), Goteborg och Bohus co., SW Sweden, near the Kattegat, 4 mi. S of Goteborg.

Askino (ä'skēnŭ), village (1926 pop. 2,699), N Bashkir Autonomous SSR, Russian SFSR, 60 mi. SW of Krasnoufimsk, in woodland; wood cracking.

Askion, Greece: see SINIATSIKON.

Askival, Scotland: see RUM.

Askiz (ŭskēs'), village (1926 pop. 741), S Khakass Autonomous Oblast, Krasnoyarsk Territory, Russian SFSR, on Abakan R. and 55 mi. SW of Abakan; coal and barite mining; chemical industry. Formerly Askysskoye or Askyzskoye.

Askja (äs'kyä), inactive volcano (4,754 ft.), E central Iceland, 60 mi. SE of Akureyri; 65°2'N 16°45'W. Highest peak of the short Dyngjufoll (dĕng'gyüfû"tûl), Icelandic *Dyngjufjöll*, range; its crater is filled with water. Last major eruption 1875. N of volcano extends the Odadahraun (ō'doudhähûrû"ün), Icelandic *Ódáðahraun*, lava field (□ 1,422), which covers large part of NE Iceland.

Asko (äsk'û), Dan. *Askø*, island (□ 1.1; pop. 238), Denmark, in Smaalandsfarvand strait, 2 mi. N of Lolland isl.

Askov (ă'skŏv), village (pop. 387), Pine co., E Minn., c.50 mi. SW of Duluth; rutabagas, dairy products, eggs.

Askoy (äsk'ûû), Nor. *Askøy*, island (□ 34; pop. 7,613) in North Sea, Hordaland co., SW Norway, 3 mi. NW of Bergen; 14 mi. long, 5 mi. wide; fishing, fish canning and salting. Formerly Spelled Askö. At village of Strusshamn (strōōs'hämûn), on S shore: mfg. of woolen yarn, shoddy. At village of Skiftesvik (shĭf'tûsvēk) on E shore: mfg. of tar products. At village of Kleppesto (klĕp'pûstû), Nor. *Kleppestø*, on SW shore: mfg. of agr. equipment. Isl. includes Askoy canton (pop. 6,714).

Askrigg, agr. village and parish (pop. 488), North Riding, NW Yorkshire, England, on Ure R. and 19 mi. NNE of Settle; cheese market. Has 14th-cent. church, bridge built in 1150, and 15th-cent. mansion.

Askysskoye or **Askyzskoye,** Russian SFSR: see ASKIZ.

Asl (ă'sûl), oil-mining settlement, Sinai, Egypt, on NE coast of Gulf of Suez, 40 mi. SSE of Suez, S of Sudr.

Asljunga (ōs'yŭng"ä), Swedish *Åsljunga*, village (pop. 586), Kristianstad co., S Sweden, 18 mi. NW of Hassleholm; grain, potatoes, stock.

Asluj, Israel: see HALUTSA.

Asmar (ŭsmär'), town (pop. over 2,000), Eastern Prov., Afghanistan, on Kunar R. and 70 mi. NE of Jalalabad, near Pakistan line; junction on roads to Chitral and Dir. The **Asmar Forest** (W) is a wild region, in E Afghanistan, on S slopes of the Hindu Kush, in the Nuristan. Timber (80% of country's production) is floated down Alishang and Alinghar rivers to Kabul R. and Peshawar dist.

Asmara (äsmä'rä, äz–), administrative division, central Eritrea; ⊙ Asmara. Chief center of population, communications, and industry in Eritrea. Occupies one of highest (c.7–9,000 ft.), most fertile, and healthful parts of central plateau; watered by affluents of Barca and Anseba rivers. Agr. (cereals, fruit, vegetables, coffee, agave, oilseeds). Cattle raising. Has large auriferous area and several mines near Asmara. Industry at Asmara and Decamere. Crossed by Massawa-Bisha railroad and highways. Also Known as Hamasien.

Asmara, city (1947 pop. c.95,000), ⊙ Eritrea and Asmara div., central Eritrea, 40 mi. SW of Massawa, its port on Red Sea; 15°19'N 38°55'E; alt. c.7,700 ft. Administrative center and hub of communications on Massawa-Bishe RR, on Massawa-Kassala cross-country highway, and on roads to Addis Ababa (Ethiopia), and Port Sudan (Anglo-Egyptian Sudan); also linked with its port by aerial cable (c.45 mi. long) built 1935–37 to haul freight. Airport. Radio transmitter. Industries include meat canning, tanning, milling (flour, lumber), coffee and vegetable fiber processing, vegetable-oil extracting, perfume distilling; mfg. of buttons, glass, brick, cement. Gold and copper mining near by. Receives power from Belesa hydroelectric plant and water by aqueduct from near-by reservoirs. Has modern European quarter with fine public bldgs. and residences. Has cathedral (built 1922), Coptic church, mosque, forts, hosp., stadium, theaters, technical and professional school. Near by are agr. experiment and animal vaccine stations. Taken by Italians in 1889; in 1897 capital transferred here from Massawa. Occupied (1941) by British in Second World War.

Asminerod, Denmark: see FREDENSBORG.

Asnaes (ăs″nĕs′), town (pop. 1,024), Holbaek amt, Zealand, Denmark, 11 mi. NW of Holbaek; machinery mfg.

Asnaes, peninsula, Denmark: see KALUNDBORG FJORD.

Asnelles or **Asnelles-sur-Mer** (änĕl′-sür-mâr′), village (pop. 308), Calvados dept., NW France, resort on the Channel, 7 mi. N of Bayeux. Here, on June 6, 1944, Br. troops landed in Normandy invasion during Second World War.

Asni (äsnē′), village, Marrakesh region, SW Fr. Morocco, on N slopes of the High Atlas, on Tizi n'Test pass road, and 27 mi. S of Marrakesh; alt. 4,250 ft. Hill resort. Near-by Oukaïmedem height, just NE of the Djebel Toubal, is winter-sports center (alt. 8,630 ft.).

Asnières or **Asnières-sur-Seine** (änyâr′-sür-sĕn′), city (pop. 72,035), Seine dept., N central France, a NW industrial suburb of Paris, 5 mi. from Notre Dame Cathedral, on left bank of Seine R. (and within its large N bend) opposite Clichy; metallurgy; mfg. (automobiles, electrical and radio equipment, hosiery, glass, perfumes, chemicals and pharmaceuticals, photographic materials). Has animal cemetery.

Asnières-sur-Oise (–sür-wäz′), village (pop. 740), Seine-et-Oise dept., N central France, 19 mi. N of Paris; rubber mfg.

Aso (ä′sō), town (pop. 6,015), Ibaraki prefecture, central Honshu, Japan, on E shore of lagoon Kasumi-ga-ura, 7 mi. NW of Choshi; fish processing, sawmilling.

Asoda (ŭsō′dŭ), town (pop. 7,458), East Khandesh dist., NE Bombay, India, 3 mi. NE of Jalgaon; market center for cotton, linseed, millet.

Asola (ä′zôlä), town (pop. 3,908), Mantova prov., Lombardy, N Italy, on Chiese R. and 19 mi. WNW of Mantua; silk mills, toy factory.

Asolo (ä′zôlô), town (pop. 760), Treviso prov., Veneto, N Italy, 19 mi. NW of Treviso; agr.-machinery factory, tannery, silk mill. Has medieval walls, 15th-cent. palace with archaeological mus. Eleanora Duse buried here.

Aso National Park (ä′sō) (□ 263), central Kyushu, Japan, includes parts of Kumamoto and Oita prefectures. Its principal feature is volcanic Aso-san; also contains Mt. Kuju, highest peak of Kyushu. Hot springs.

Asopos River (ŭsôpôs′), Lat. *Asopus* (ŭsō′pŭs). **1** In Boeotia and Attica, E central Greece, rises in the Cythaeron massif, flows 34 mi. E to S Gulf of Euboea 12 mi. SE of Chalcis. Formerly called Vourgenis. **2** In N Peloponnesus, Greece, rises near Nemea, flows 20 mi. N to Gulf of Corinth 10 mi. WNW of Corinth. Asopus was a Gr. river god.

Aso River (ä′zô), The Marches, central Italy, rises in Monti Sibillini 16 mi. W of Ascoli Piceno, flows 35 mi. ENE to the Adriatic 7 mi. SE of Fermo, near Pedaso.

Asosa (ä′sōsä), town, Wallaga prov., W central Ethiopia, 75 mi. NW of Nejo; 10°2′N 34°31′E. Chief trade center (coffee, beeswax, hides, gold) of Beni Shangul dist. Gold placer mining near by.

Aso-san (ä′sō-sän), group of 5 volcanic cones in Kumamoto prefecture, central Kyushu, Japan, 22 mi. ENE of Kumamoto; principal feature of Aso Natl. Park. Highest cone, Taka-dake (c.5,225 ft.). All inactive except Naka-dake (4,340 ft.). Crater floor (15 mi. N-S, 10 mi. E-W) is largest in world.

Asososca (äsōsō′skä), W Nicaragua, extinct volcano (2,651 ft.) in Cordillera de los Marabios, 14 mi. E of León.

Asososca, Lake, SW Nicaragua, small crater lake 2 mi. WSW of Managua; over 1,500 ft. deep. Reservoir for Managua's water supply. On E shore is Las Piedrecitas, parklike residential suburb of Managua.

Asotin (ŭsō′tŭn), county (□ 627; pop. 10,878), extreme SE Wash.; ⊙ Asotin. Plateau and rolling hill area rising to Blue Mts. in SW and bordering on Oregon and Idaho. Watered by Grande Ronde and Snake rivers. Includes part of Umatilla Natl. Forest. Wheat, fruit, dairy products, livestock; lumbering. Formed 1883.

Asotin, town (pop. 740), ⊙ Asotin co., SE Wash., 28 mi. SSE of Pullman and on Snake R. Wheat, grapes, fruit, dairy products, wool.

Aspach (ä′späkh), town (pop. 2,670), W Upper Austria, 14 mi. SE of Braunau; brewery.

Aspadana, Iran: see ISFAHAN, city.

Aspang Markt (ä′späng märkt), town (pop. 2,642), SE Lower Austria, on Pitten R. and 11 mi. S of Neunkirchen; vineyards.

Aspatria (äspā′trēŭ), former urban district (1931 pop. 3,239), W Cumberland, England, on Ellen R. and 18 mi. WSW of Carlisle; coal mining, metal-working, mfg. of agr. machinery. Site of agr. col.

Aspavé Highlands (äspävā′), Sp. *Altos de Aspavé*, on Panama-Colombia border, near Pacific coast; rise to c.3,500 ft. Sometimes spelled Espavé.

Aspe (äs′pā), town (pop. 7,567), Alicante prov., E Spain, 7 mi. NW of Elche; footwear-mfg. center; also makes furniture, pottery, soap, plaster, flour Citrus fruit, olive oil, wine. Clay and marble quarries, coal deposits near by. Irrigation reservoir is 2 mi. E.

Aspe, Gave d' (gäv däsp′), river, Basses-Pyrénées dept., SW France, rises in the Pyrenees near Somport pass (Sp. border), flows 35 mi. N, through deep picturesque Aspe valley, past Urdos and Accous, joining the Gave d'Ossau at Oloron-Sainte-Marie to form the Gave d'Oloron. Used for hydroelectric power. Paralleled by trans-Pyrenean road and railroad.

Aspelt (äspĕlt′), village (pop. 536), SE Luxembourg, 7 mi. SSE of Luxembourg city, near Fr. border; building-stone quarrying; fruit growing (cherries).

Aspen, city (pop. 916), ⊙ Pitkin co., W central Colo., on Roaring Fork R., just W of Sawatch Mts., and 30 mi. W of Leadville; alt. 7,850 ft. Winter resort; silver and lead mines; livestock, grain, potatoes, timber. Once a rich silver-mining camp with pop. of 15,000. Castle Peak and Snowmass Mtn. near by. Founded 1878, inc. 1881. In 1949 was scene of international gathering in honor of 200th anniversary of birth of Goethe.

Aspenas, Sweden: see LERUM.

Aspendus (ăspĕn′dŭs), anc. ruined town of SW Turkey, 25 mi. E of Antalya, near Serik, on the Kopru (anc. Eurymedon); once a chief city of Pamphylia, its remains include a very large theater.

Asperen (äs′pŭrŭn), town (pop. 1,656), South Holland prov., W Netherlands, 7 mi. ENE of Gorinchem; horse-breeding center; brick mfg. Town taken 1204 by Count Willian I of Holland, 1480 by Duke of Burgundy, 1574 by Spaniards, and 1672 by French.

Asperg (äs′pĕrk), town (pop. 5,239), N Württemberg, Germany, after 1945 in Württemberg-Baden, 2.5 mi. W of Ludwigsburg; wine. Site was settled in prehistoric times. Small fortress of Hohenasperg (just N) is now a prison.

Aspermont (ă′spŭrmŏnt), town (pop. 1,062), ⊙ Stonewall co., NW central Texas, 55 mi. NW of Abilene; trade, and shipping center for agr. and cattle-ranching region, producing grain, cotton, fruit, dairy products, poultry; some oil.

Aspern (ä′spŭrn), E suburb (pop. 5,834) of Vienna, Austria, 5 mi. E of city center, in Grossenzersdorf dist.; airport. Near by, Archduke Charles defeated Napoleon, May 21–22, 1809. Until 1938 in Floridsdorf dist.

Aspero (äs′pŭrû″), Swedish *Asperö*, fishing village (pop. 226), Goteborg och Bohus co., SW Sweden, on isl. (232 acres) of same name, in the Kattegat, 5 mi. WSW of Goteborg.

Aspet (äspā′), village (pop. 541), Haute-Garonne dept., S France, 7 mi. SSE of Saint-Gaudens; livestock market; marble quarrying and working.

Aspetuck River (ăs′pĭtŭk″), Fairfield co., SW Conn., rises SE of Danbury, flows c.20 mi. S to Saugatuck R. N of Westport. WEST ASPETUCK RIVER and EAST ASPETUCK RIVER, branches of Housatonic R., are N, in Litchfield co.

Asphaltites, Lacus, Palestine: see DEAD SEA.

Aspindza (ŭspēndzä′), village (1932 pop. estimate 840), SW Georgian SSR, in the Lesser Caucasus, on Kura R. and 15 mi. ESE of Akhaltsikhe; orchards.

Aspinwall, Panama: see COLÓN, city.

Aspinwall. 1 Town (pop. 107), Crawford co., W Iowa, 17 mi. SW of Carroll, in agr. area. **2** Residential borough (pop. 4,084), Allegheny co., SW Pa., on Allegheny R. opposite N Pittsburgh. Settled 1796, inc. 1893.

Aspiran (äspērä′), village (pop. 1,122), Hérault dept., S France, near Hérault R., 13 mi. SSE of Lodève; fiber processing, winegrowing.

Aspiring, Mount (9,975 ft.), W central S.Isl., New Zealand, in Southern Alps, near L. Wanaka.

Aspland Island, islet, South Shetland Isls., off Palmer Peninsula, Antarctica; 61°30′S 55°55′W.

Aspley Guise (ăs′plē-gīz′), agr. village and parish (pop. 1,105), W Bedford, England, 2 mi. N of Woburn.

Aspo, island, Sweden: see DROTTNINGSKAR.

Aspres-sur-Buëch (ä′sprû-sür-bwĕsh′), village (pop. 532), Hautes-Alpes dept., SE France, on the Grand Buëch and 16 mi. WSW of Gap, in arid S Dauphiné Alps; rail and road junction.

Aspromonte (äsprômôn′tĕ), range (□ c.640) of S Apennines, in Reggio di Calabria prov., S Italy, near S extremity of Calabria, bet. Strait of Messina and Ionian Sea. Chief peak, MONTALTO (6,417 ft.). On its slopes and along the coast citrus fruit, olives, grapes, figs, almonds, and cereals are grown. Livestock raising (sheep, goats) and forestry are also carried on. A major earthquake region of Italy; suffered severe shocks in 1783, 1857, 1883, 1905, and 1908. Here Garibaldi was defeated and taken prisoner (1862) by Victor Emmanuel II.

Aspropotamos River, Greece: see ACHELOUS RIVER.

Aspropyrgos or **Aspropirgos** (both: äsprô′pĭrgôs), town (pop. 4,880), Attica nome, E central Greece, on railroad and 9 mi. WNW of Athens; trading center for local dairy products (milk, cheese), wheat, straw, olive oil, vegetables, wine. Formerly called Kalyvia or Kalyvia Khasias.

Aspull (ă′spŭl, ă′spŭ), urban district (1931 pop. 7,193; 1951 census 6,522), S central Lancashire, England. Includes coal-mining and cotton-spinning village of Aspull Moor, 3 mi. NE of Wigan.

Asquam Lake, N.H.: see SQUAM LAKE.

Asquith, town (pop. 222), S central Sask., 24 mi. W of Saskatoon; wheat, dairying.

Assa (äsä′), Saharan oasis and military outpost, Agadir frontier region, southwesternmost Fr. Morocco, near the Oued Dra, 80 mi. SSE of Tiznit; 28°36′N 9°27′W.

Assab (äsäb′), administrative division, SE Eritrea; ⊙ Assab. Borders Red Sea (E), Ethiopia (W), and Fr. Somaliland (S). Occupies part of DANAKIL desert, plain in E and volcanic highlands in W. Nomadic grazing (camels, goats, cattle). Has scattered oases (date and dom palms, acacia). Fishing. Chief settlements along coast include Assab, Beilul, Edd, Raheita. Caravan routes are principal means of communication. Called Dancalia Meridionale [Ital.,=southern Dankalia] under Ital. administration (until 1941).

Assab, town (pop. 8,000), ⊙ Assab div., SE Eritrea, port on Red Sea, 50 mi. NW of Bab el Mandeb strait, opposite Mocha (Yemen) and 275 mi. SE of Massawa, in hot, arid coastal plain; 13°1′N 42°45′E. Commercial and caravan center (hides, livestock, honey, cereals, coffee); extensive salt-works, water distillation plant, power station. Airfield. Linked by road with Addis Ababa via Dessye. Acquired (1869) by Italian shipping interests as a coaling station. Taken over by Ital. govt. 1882; formed nucleus of Ital. colonization in Eritrea.

Assabet River (ŭsă′bĭt), in E Mass., rises in E Worcester co., flows c.30 mi. NE, past Hudson and Maynard (water power), joining Sudbury R. to form Concord R. in Concord town.

Assadabad, Iran: see ASADABAD.

Assahoun or **Assahun** (äsähōōn′), village, S Fr. Togoland, on railroad and 32 mi. NW of Lomé; cacao, palm oil and kernels, cotton. R.C. and Protestant missions.

Assahun, Fr. Togoland: see ASSAHOUN.

Assaí (äsäē′), city (pop. 1,241), N Paraná, Brazil, on road, and 23 mi. ESE of Londrina; sawmilling; grows coffee, cotton, rice. Settled by Japanese.

Assainvillers (äsēvēlâr′), village (pop. 112), Somme dept., N France, 3 mi. SE of Montdidier. Scene of heavy First World War fighting (1918).

Assaka River, Morocco: see ASACA RIVER.

Assake, city, USSR: see LENINSK, Uzbek SSR.

Assal, Lake (äsäl′), salt lake (□ c.40), Fr. Somaliland, in Danakil desert, 55 mi. W of Djibouti; 10 mi. long, 4 mi. wide; c.500 ft. below sea level. Consists of salt flats in W portion. Surrounded by volcanic mts.

Assam (ăsăm′), constituent state (□ 54,084; 1951 pop. 9,129,442, with frontier tribal areas not in census, □ 82,276, pop. 9,690,073), extreme NE India; ⊙ Shillong. Bordered E by Burma and Indian state of Manipur, N by Tibet, NW by Bhutan, W by West Bengal (India) and East Bengal (E Pakistan), and SW by Tripura (India). Topography dominated by mtn. ranges and intervening valleys of BRAHMAPUTRA RIVER and SURMA RIVER. In N, large mtn. mass comprises E ASSAM HIMALAYAS, rising to 20,000-ft. peaks on Tibetan border; in NE, beyond Brahmaputra bend, are Mishmi Hills. Along E boundary Patkai Range, NAGA HILLS, Manipur Hills, LUSHAI HILLS, and Chin Hills extend from N to S. In center of state, running E-W bet. Brahmaputra and Surma valleys, is Assam Range (4–6,000 ft.), including Khasi Hills and Shillong Plateau. Brahmaputra valley is fertile, alluvial strip (c.50 mi. wide) extending 425 mi. across state; main Brahmaputra affluents in Assam are Subansiri, Luhit, Burhi Dihing, and Manas rivers. Climate is monsoon tropical with especially heavy rainfall, averaging 75–85 in. on Shillong Plateau, 110–120 in. in Brahmaputra valley, 125–150 in. in Surma Valley, and over 400 in. on S slopes of Khasi Hills, where, at Cherrapunji (annual average 450 in.), one of world's heaviest precipitations has been recorded—over 900 in. reputed to have fallen in 1861. Mean temp. ranges from 62°F. in Jan. to 84°F. in July. Region is subject to severe earthquakes and floods; notable were those of 1897 and 1950. Mts. and valleys clothed with dense tropical forests (chiefly sal and bamboo), with temperate evergreens (live oak and pine) at higher altitudes. Elephants, rhinoceroses, tigers, leopards, bears abound. State is predominantly rural and agr. (85% of pop.), with cultivation concentrated in broad river valleys. Rice is widely grown, while other crops include jute, oilseeds, sugar cane, short staple cotton, and, in Assam Range, potatoes and oranges. Produces c.60% of India's tea, with over 440,000 acres under cultivation in Brahmaputra and Surma valleys. Lumber is valuable resource, but large remote and inaccessible tracts remain undeveloped; other forest products include lac, silkworms, and some wild rubber. India's only petroleum fields are in Lakhimpur and Cachar dists.; refinery at Digboi. Coal mined in

Lakhimpur dist. and Assam Range; limestone quarries in Khasi Hills. Industries, on small scale, consist mostly of agr. processing (tea, rice, oilseeds); match factory at Dhubri, tin-can factory at Tinsukia. Handicrafts include cotton and silk weaving, tea-box making, boat building, pottery and metalware mfg. Principal towns: GAUHATI, SHILLONG, Dibrugarh, Jorhat, Dhubri, Silchar, Tezpur, Nowgong, Barpeta. Turbulent streams and thick jungles impede communications. The Brahmaputra (unbridged) has important steamer service; 2 rail lines connect upper Assam with Bengal. Trade with Burma is insignificant; main routes run through Manipur state and Chaukan Pass; Ledo Road, built in Second World War, is now little used. Gauhati and Dibrugarh are linked by air with Calcutta. Pop. consisted (1941) of Hindus (42%), Moslems (31%), and several Tibeto-Burman tribes (26%)—mainly Kacharis, Ahoms, Nagas, Garos, and Khasis—who are mostly animists; after the creation of Pakistan in 1947 many Moslems left, and the densely populated dist. of Sylhet, which went to Pakistan, was predominantly Moslem. Chief languages: Assamese, Bengali. Assam was part of old Aryan area *Kamarupa* and later under Buddhist Pal and Hindu Sen dynasties; tantric form of Hinduism probably originated in Assam. Visited A.D. c.640 by Hsüan-tsang, who supplied 1st reliable account of region. In early 13th-cent., invaded by Ahoms, a Shan tribe (later converted to Hinduism), who by 16th cent. had established themselves by defeating Chutiya, Kachari, and Koch kingdoms. Although Ahom power was on the wane in 17th cent., they were able to resist invasions by Moguls from Bengal. Ahoms enlisted English aid (1792) in suppressing local rebellions; after Br. withdrawal Burmese troops moved in, resulting in 1st Anglo-Burmese War (1824–26), in which Burmese were expelled and, by treaty of Yandabo (1826), were forced to cede Assam to East India Co. Soon various outlying tracts were inc. into Br. territory, administered as part of Bengal. Was chief commissioner's prov., 1874–1921, except for period (1905–12) when it formed part of Eastern Bengal and Assam prov.; made governor's prov. in 1921; became constituent state of Indian republic in 1950. During Second World War, westward advance of Japanese was repulsed in Kohima section (E). Upon partition of India (1947), predominantly Moslem dist. of Sylhet—except for small E part—inc. into E Pakistan; Khasi States merged with Assam. State comprises 7 dists. of Cachar, Darrang, Goalpara, Kamrup, Lakhimpur, Nowgong, and Sibsagar; and, under the administration of the central govt., 6 autonomous dists. (Garo Hills, Khasi and Jaintia Hills, Lushai Hills, Mikir Hills, Naga Hills, and North Cachar Hills), the North East Frontier Agency (comprising Balipara and Tirap frontier tracts, Abor Hills and Mishmi Hills tribal dists.), and Naga Tribal Area.

Assam Himalayas (hĭmä'lŭyŭz, hĭmŭlā'yŭz), E subdivision of the HIMALAYAS, S central Asia, in the great bend of Brahmaputra R.; from upper Tista R. in Sikkim (India) extend 450 mi. E, through Bhutan and N Assam, along Tibet border, to the Brahmaputra near Namcha Barwa, highest peak (25,445 ft.). Divided into subsidiary DONGKYA and BLACK MOUNTAIN ranges (W) and DAFLA, MIRI, and ABOR hills (E), rising sharply from the plains. Main peaks, other than Namcha Barwa, are KULA KANGRI (24,780 ft.), Kangri (24,740 ft.), CHOMO LHARI (23,997 ft.), and Kangto (23,260 ft.). Range gives rise to Subansiri, Manas, Sankosh, Raidak, and Jaldhaka rivers, all flowing to N bank of the Brahmaputra. Main towns (W): Gangtok, Kalimpong (commands main India-Tibet trade route leading into CHUMBI VALLEY via Natu La and Jelep La passes), Punakha, Paro, Tashi Chho, Byakar, and Chirang. Other W passes include TANG LA, PELE LA, and BUM LA. Geological and structural features indicate Assam Himalayas extend E beyond the Brahmaputra, turning sharply S into Burma.

Assam Range, hill range, W and central Assam, India, separating Brahmaputra valley (N) from Surma Valley (S); comprises GARO HILLS, KHASI HILLS, JAINTIA HILLS, and SHILLONG PLATEAU.

Assam States, former political agency (□ 12,408; pop. 725,655), situated within Assam, India. Comprised group of 25 petty Khasi States (in W Assam; inc. 1948 into Khasi and Jaintia Hills dist.) and Manipur (on India-Burma border; acceded to India 1949 as a chief commissioner's state).

Assandun, England: see ASHINGDON.

Assaré (äsŏorĕ'), city (pop. 1,451), SW Ceará, Brazil, on N slope of Serra do Araripe, 45 mi. NW of Crato; cattle raising; ships hides, maniçoba rubber. Gypsum deposits.

Assaria (ŭsâ'rēŭ), city (pop. 221), Saline co., central Kansas, 11 mi. S of Salina, in wheat and livestock area.

Assa River (ŭsä'). **1** In Dzhambul oblast, Kazakh SSR, rises in the S Kara-Tau, flows c.100 mi. N into the Muyun-Kum (desert); it enters and leaves the Bilikul (lake W of Dzhambul) at c.1,500 ft. Forms 8-mi.-long Ters-Ashchibulak irrigation reservoir in lower course. **2** In Grozny oblast, Russian SFSR, rises in main range of the central Greater Caucasus, E of Mt. Kazbek; flows N, past Pervomaiskoye, and E to Sunzha R. 12 mi. WSW of Grozny; c.80 mi. long.

Assateague Island (ă'sŭtēg), narrow barrier isl. c.35 mi. long, off Atlantic shore (Delmarva Peninsula) of SE Md. and E Va.; to W lie Sinepuxent and Chincoteague bays. Abundant wildlife includes wild ponies, rounded up annually for auction at Chincoteague, Va. Inhabited only by Coast Guard crews, isl. is visited by hunters, fishermen. Said to have been explored 1524 by Verrazano.

Assawaman Island (ă'sŭwŏ"mŭn), E Va., barrier island off Atlantic shore of Accomack co., 8 mi. NE of Accomac; c.4 mi. long. Assawaman Inlet is at N, Gargathy Inlet at S end. Sometimes spelled Assawoman.

Assawoman Bay, tidal lagoon (c.4 mi. long, 2 mi. wide), Worcester co., SE Md., just S of Del. line; opens on the Atlantic through Ocean City Inlet.

Assawompsett Pond (ăsŭwŏmp'sĭt), Plymouth co., SE Mass., 9 mi. ESE of Taunton, in lake region; c.3 mi. long. Joined by streams to Long Pond (SW) and Great Quittacas Pond (SE).

Assay Creek, S central Utah, rises in Markagunt Plateau, flows c.25 mi. N, joining Panguitch Creek just N of Panguitch to form Sevier R.

Assaye, India: see BHOKARDAN.

Assche, Belgium: see ASSE.

Asse (ä'sŭ), town (pop. 11,254), Brabant prov., central Belgium, 8 mi. NW of Brussels; market center for hop- and fruitgrowing area. Formerly spelled Assche.

Assebroek (ä'sŭbrŏŏk), town (pop. 5,815), West Flanders prov., NW Belgium, SE suburb of Bruges.

Assel (ä'sŭl), village (pop. 4,276), in former Prussian prov. of Hanover, NW Germany, after 1945 in Lower Saxony, near Elbe estuary, 6 mi. N of Stade; mfg. of chemicals.

Asselborn (ä'sŭlbôrn), village (pop. 382), N Luxembourg, in the Ardennes, 9 mi. N of Wiltz; slate quarrying; lumbering, sawmills.

Asselle (äsĕ'lā), Ital. *Aselle*, village (pop. 500), ⊙ Arusi prov., S central Ethiopia, bet. L. Zwai and Mt. Badda, 85 mi. SSE of Addis Ababa, in livestock region; 7°50'N 39°7'E; road terminus, sawmilling.

Assembléia, Brazil: see VIÇOSA, Alagoas.

Assemini (äs-sä'mēnē), village (pop. 4,150), Cagliari prov., S Sardinia, 8 mi. NNW of Cagliari; ceramics.

Assen (ä'sŭn), town (pop. 19,859), ⊙ Drenthe prov., NE Netherlands, at NE end of the Smildervaart, 15 mi. S of Groningen; rail junction; mfg. (brushes, clothing, caps), food canning and processing; pig and egg market; prov. butter-control station. Has 17th- cent. town hall (once chapel of an abbey), neo-Gothic prov. govt. building. Prehistoric stone monuments near by.

Assendelft (ä'sŭndĕlft), village (pop. 6,044), North Holland prov., W Netherlands, 9 mi. NW of Amsterdam.

Assenede (äsĕ'nŭdŭ), agr. village (pop. 5,491), East Flanders prov., NW Belgium, near Netherlands border, 12 mi. N of Ghent.

Assens (ăs'sŭns). **1** City (pop. 4,826) and port, Odense amt, Denmark, on W Fyn isl. and 22 mi. SW of Odense, on the Little Belt; sugar refinery, meat-packing plant, iron foundry. **2** Town (pop. 1,556), Randers amt, NE Jutland, Denmark, 14 mi. N of Randers; cement plant.

Asse River (äs), Basses-Alpes dept., SE France, rises in Provence Alps above Barrême, flows 40 mi. WSW to the Durance 6 mi. NE of Manosque.

Assern, Latvia: see RIGAS JURMALA.

Assi-bou-Nif (äsē'-bōō-nēf'), village (pop. 1,388), Oran dept., NW Algeria, 8 mi. E of Oran; wine, truck; dairying.

Assiniboia (ŭsĭnŭboi'ŭ), town (pop. 1,585), S Sask., 55 mi. SSW of Moose Jaw; alt. 2,436 ft.; railroad shops, coal and oil depot, grain elevators, lumber and flour mills; in coal-mining region.

Assiniboine, Mount (ŭsĭ'nŭboin) (11,870 ft.), on Alta.-B.C. border, in Rocky Mts., in Mt. Assiniboine Park, 22 mi. S of Banff; 50°56'N 115°42'W. First climbed by Sir James Outram, 1901.

Assiniboine River, Sask. and Man., rises in E Sask. N of Yorkton, flows SE, past Kamsack, to mouth of Qu'Appelle R., then flows E through S Man., past Brandon and Portage la Prairie, to Red R. at Winnipeg; c.600 mi. long. Principal tributary is the Souris. The Assiniboine valley is Canada's chief wheat-growing region. River was discovered and explored by the La Vérendryes, 1736; subsequently forts were built on sites of the present Winnipeg and near the present Portage la Prairie; later river became important transportation route for fur traders and then for westward expansion of settlement. Named for Assiniboin, or Stone, Indians, and was formerly called Stone Indian R.

Assinie (äsēnē'), Atlantic landing, SE Ivory Coast, Fr. West Africa, on spit S of Aby Lagoon, near Gold Coast border, 45 mi. ESE of Abidjan. Ships hardwood. Coffee growing. Pitch deposits near by.

Assir, Ras, Ital. Somaliland: see GUARDAFUI, CAPE.

Assis (äsēs'), city (pop. 8,964), W São Paulo, Brazil, on railroad and 70 mi. SE of Presidente Prudente; rice, coffee, and cotton processing; cattle raising. Sometimes spelled Assiz.

Assisi (ŭsē'zē, It. äs-sē'zē), town (pop. 4,686), Perugia prov., Umbria, central Italy, 12 mi. ESE of Perugia, on hill in the Apennines; hemp mill; wrought-copper products, pumps, fertilizer. Bishopric. Famous as birthplace (1182) of St. Francis of Assisi, above whose tomb 2 churches were superimposed (1228–53; frescoes by Cimabue and Giotto depicting life of St. Francis). In Gothic church of Santa Chiara (1257–60) is tomb of St. Clare, also b. here. Other notable churches include 12th-cent. cathedral, San Damiano, and Santa Maria della Minerva, converted from anc. Temple of Minerva. In the plain below Assisi is imposing late-Renaissance church of Santa Maria degli Angeli (begun 1569), built around chapel of Porziuncula, cradle of the Franciscan order.

Assiut, Egypt: see ASYUT, city.

Asslar (äs'lär), village (pop. 4,929), in former Prussian prov. of Hesse-Nassau, W Germany, after 1945 in Hesse, on the Dill and 3 mi. NNW of Wetzlar; building materials; woodworking.

Assling, Yugoslavia: see JESENICE.

Assmannshausen (äs"mäns-hou'zŭn), village (pop. 1,504), in former Prussian prov. of Hesse-Nassau, W Germany, after 1945 in Hesse, in the Rheingau, at W foot of the Taunus, on right bank of the Rhine and 17 mi. WSW of Wiesbaden; noted for its red wine. Warm alkaline spring near by.

Asso (äs'sô), village (pop. 1,238), Como prov., Lombardy, N Italy, on Lambro R. and 10 mi. ENE of Como; resort; mfg. (silk and cotton textiles, cutlery).

Assomada (ŭsŏŏmä'dŭ), town, Cape Verde Isls., near center of São Tiago Isl., 17 mi. NW of Praia, Coffee and orange growing.

Assonet, Mass.: see FREETOWN.

Assoro (äs-sô'rô), village (pop. 3,876), Enna prov., central Sicily, near Dittaino R., 9 mi. NE of Enna; alabaster and sulphur mining. Has 15th-cent. church. Ruins of anc. castle near by. In Second World War, scene of heavy fighting (1943).

Assos (ă'sŏs) or **Assus** (-sŭs), anc. city, Mysia, NW Asia Minor, on Gulf of Adramyttium (Edremit) opposite Lesbos. Extensive ruins. Aristotle was a member of a 4th cent. B.C. school here. St. Paul passed through Assos.

Assouan, Egypt: see ASWAN.

Assu, Brazil: see AÇU.

Assuan, Egypt: see ASWAN.

Assumar (äsōō'mär), village (pop. 1,402), Portalegre dist., central Portugal, on railroad and 10 mi. SSE of Portalegre in hilly, forested region.

Assumption, parish (□ 357; pop. 17,278), SE La.; ⊙ Napoleonville. Bounded W partly by Grand R.; intersected by Bayou Lafourche (navigable). Agr. (sugar cane, corn, rice, truck). Sugar refining, canning, moss ginning. Furs; lumber. Oil and gas fields. Includes L. Verret (fishing, boating). Formed 1807.

Assumption, city (pop. 1,466), Christian co., central Ill., 22 mi. SSW of Decatur; mfg. (clothing, bedding); bituminous-coal mining; agr. (corn, wheat, soybeans). Inc. 1902.

Assumption Island, Marianas Isls.: see ASUNCION.

Assumption Island, outlying dependency of the Seychelles, one of the Aldabra group, in Indian Ocean, 225 mi. NW of N tip of Madagascar; 9°46'S 46°34'E. Of coral origin. Guano. Also spelled Assomption.

Assur, Iraq: see ASHUR.

Assuruá, Brazil: see SANTO INÁCIO.

Assweiler (äs'vī"lŭr), village (pop. 578), SE Saar, 6 mi. SE of St. Ingbert; stock, grain.

Assy, Plateau d', France: see PASSY.

Assynt (ă'sĭnt), extensive parish (□ 172; 1931 pop. 1,342; 1947 estimate 1,000), in SW Sutherland, Scotland. Includes agr. village of Inchnadamph (ĭnch"nŭdămf'), at SE end of Loch Assynt (8 mi. long, 1 mi. wide), 19 mi. NNE of Ullapool. Angling, fishing. There are ruins of 15th-cent. Ardvreck Castle, scene of capture of Montrose in 1650. Peak of Ben More Assynt (3,273 ft.) is 5 mi. E of Inchnadamph.

Assyria (ŭsĭ'rēŭ), anc. empire of W Asia. It developed around city of ASHUR or Assur in Mesopotamia on the upper Tigris and S of the later capital, Nineveh. Apparently the nucleus of a Semitic state was forming by beginning of 3d millennium B.C., but it was inconsiderable, and its eponymous god, Ashur, was little honored while the kings of BABYLON and the Hittites were powerful. Briefly in 17th cent. B.C. it expanded, but it soon relapsed into weakness. CALAH became ⊙ after c.1300 B.C.; the 13th cent. B.C. saw Assyria threatening the surrounding states, and under Tiglath-pileser III (reign c.1115–c.1102 B.C.), Assyrian soldiers entered the kingdom centered about Urartu (Ararat; see ARMENIA), took BABYLONIA, and crossed N Syria to reach the Mediterranean. This empire was, however, only ephemeral, and Assyrian greatness was to wait until the 9th cent., when Ashurnasyal III entered on his career. He pushed his conquests N to Urartu and W to Lebanon and the Mediterranean. Shalmaneser III continued the Assyrian conquests, which was further pushed by Tiglath-pileser III, who reigned from 745 to

728 B.C. He subdued Babylonia, defeated the king of Urartu, attacked the Medes, established control over Syria, and, as an ally of Ahaz of Judah (who became his vassal), defeated his Aramaic-speaking enemies centered at Damascus. His successors, particularly Sargon, expanded Assyria. The great victory of Sargon at Raphia (720 B.C.) and his invasions of Armenia, Arabia, and other lands made Assyria indisputably one of the greatest of ancient empires. His son Sennacherib is particularly remembered in the West for his warfare against his rebellious vassal, Hezekiah of Judah. His successor, Esar-Haddon (reign 681–668 B.C.) defeated the Chaldaeans and carried his conquests to Egypt. Under Esar-Haddon's son, Assur-bani-pal, Assyria reached its zenith and approached its fall. An Egyptian revolt under Psamtik I was successful. The rapid decline of Assyria had begun, but the reign of Assur-bani-pal (669?–626? B.C.) saw the Assyrian capital at its height of splendor. The big library of cuneiform tablets he collected ultimately proved to be one of the most important historical sources of antiquity. Assyrian culture owed much to earlier Babylonian civilization. It was not long after the death of Assur-bani-pal that Assyria fell. The king of the Medes, Cyaxares, and the ruler of Damascus, Nabopolassar, joined forces to take Nineveh in 612 B.C. Under the son of Nabopolassar, Nebuchadnezzar, Babylonia was renewed in power, and the great-grandson of Cyaxares, Cyrus the Great, was to establish the Persian Empire, which owed much to the earlier Assyrian state.

Asta, Cima d' (chē'mä dä'stä), peak (9,345 ft.) in the Dolomites, N Italy, 18 mi. NW of Feltre.

Astacinga (ästäsĕng'gä), town (pop. 770), Veracruz, E Mexico, 19 mi. S of Orizaba; coffee, fruit.

Astacus, Turkey: see IZMIT.

Astaffort (ästäfôr'), village (pop. 898), Lot-et-Garonne dept., SW France, on Gers R. and 9 mi. S of Agen; wheat, orchards.

Astakos (ästäkôs'), town (pop. 2,992), Acarnania nome, W central Greece, small port on Gulf of Astakos (inlet of Ionian Sea), 22 mi. NW of Missolonghi; dairying, stock raising; fisheries. Formerly Dragomesto.

Astaneh (ästänĕ'), village, First Prov., in Gilan, N Iran, 23 mi. E of Resht and on the lower Sefid Rud; tea, oranges, silk, tobacco.

Astara (ästärä'), town, Third Prov., in Azerbaijan, NW Iran, port on Caspian Sea, on road and 145 mi. ENE of Tabriz, at mouth of small Astara R., just S of Astara (USSR); handles much of Iranian Azerbaijan's export trade.

Astara (ä"stürä', Rus. ŭstŭrä'), city (1932 pop. estimate 2,770), SE Azerbaijan SSR, port on Caspian Sea, at mouth of short Astara R. (Iran. border), 20 mi. S of Lenkoran; rail terminus opposite Astara, Iran; fisheries; subtropical agr. (tea, citrus fruit, tung oil). Iron ore near by.

Astarabad, Iran: see GURGAN.

Astatula (ăstūtōō'lū), town (pop. 255), Lake co., central Fla., 25 mi. WNW of Orlando, near L. Harris.

Asten (äs'tŭn), village (pop. 4,199), North Brabant prov., SE Netherlands, 6 mi. SE of Helmond; strawboard mfg., beer; cattle raising, dairying.

Asten, Kahle, Germany: see KAHLE ASTEN.

Astenet, Belgium: see WALHORN.

Asterabad, Iran: see GURGAN.

Asti (ä'stē), province (□ 584; pop. 245,764), Piedmont, NW Italy; ⊙ Asti. Consists largely of MONTFERRAT hills (2,772 ft. high in S); drained by Tanaro R. Agr. (grapes, vegetables, fruit), stock raising (cattle, swine, goats). Gypsum quarries near Agliano. Mfg. at Asti. Formed 1935 from Alessandria prov.

Asti anc. *Hasta,* city (pop. 26,476), ⊙ Asti prov., Piedmont, NW Italy, near Tanaro R., 28 mi. SE of Turin, in grape- and vegetable-growing region; rail junction; industrial and commercial center noted for its wine. Market center for grapes, silkworm cocoons, livestock, vegetables. Has distilleries, sulphur refinery, barrel and bottle works, silk and rayon mills, ironworks; food canning; mfg. of pottery, bricks. Bishopric since A.D. 932. Has Gothic cathedral (rebuilt 1309–48), 12th-cent. baptistry. Important in medieval times; has several churches, palaces, towers of the period. The poet Vittorio Alfieri lived here. Asti became capital when prov. was formed 1935.

Asti (ŏ'stē), village, Sonoma co., W Calif., in Russian R. valley, 27 mi. NW of Santa Rosa; shipping center of winegrowing dist. Settled in 1880s as Italian-Swiss colony.

Astico River (ä'stēkô), N Italy, rises in Alpine foothills 9 mi. E of Rovereto, flows 35 mi. SE to Bacchiglione R. 4 mi. SE of Vicenza. In lower course called Tesina River.

Asticou, Maine: see MOUNT DESERT.

Astillero (ästīyä'rō), village, Puno dept., SE Peru, landing on Tambopata R. and 65 mi. NNW of Sandia; rubber; lumbering.

Astillero, El (ĕl ästēlyä'rō), village (pop. 2,453), Santander prov., N Spain, at head of inlet of Bay of Biscay, 4 mi. S of Santander; metalworking; oil refinery; sandal mfg. Bathing beaches.

Astin Tagh, China: see ALTYN TAGH.

Astipalaia, Greece: see ASTYPALAIA.

Astley, town and parish (pop. 4,584), S Lancashire, England, 9 mi. W of Manchester; coal mining, cotton milling.

Astley Bridge, town in Bolton borough, S central Lancashire, England; cotton milling.

Astol (ō'stōōl"), Swedish *Åstol,* fishing village (pop. 538), Goteborg och Bohus co., SW Sweden, on islet of same name in the Skagerrak, 20 mi. NNW of Goteborg.

Astolat, England: see GUILDFORD.

Aston, NE industrial suburb (pop. 35,612) of Birmingham, NW Warwick, England. Site of Aston Hall (scene of Civil War action), now mus. Until 1911 it was an independent municipal borough.

Aston Clinton, agr. village and parish (pop. 1,494), E central Buckingham, England, 4 mi. ESE of Aylesbury. Has 14th-cent. church.

Astor (ŭstōr'), district (□ 1,632; pop. 17,026), Kashmir prov., W Kashmir; ⊙ Bunji. In extreme N Punjab Himalayas; bounded N by the Indus. Agr. (pulse, wheat, corn). Main villages: Bunji, Astor. Was part of former Gilgit dist., divided (1934) into Gilgit leased area and Gilgit Wazarat; latter name changed to Astor dist. soon thereafter. Held since 1948 by Pakistan. Prevailing mother tongue, Shina. Also spelled Astore.

Astor, village, Astor dist., W Kashmir, in N Punjab Himalayas, on Astor R. (left tributary of the Indus) and 45 mi. SE of Gilgit; pulse, wheat, corn. Fort. Former residence of a Dard raja. Also spelled Astore.

Astorga (ästôr'gä), anc. *Asturica Augusta,* city (pop. 14,523), Leon prov., NW Spain, 26 mi. WSW of Leon; agr. trade center, noted for its chocolate and cookies; flour and sawmilling, tanning, meat processing; mfg. of ceramics, hats, soap. Episcopal see since 3d cent. Has Roman walls and towers, an imposing cathedral (15th–17th cent.) with cloisters, a seminary, a 17th-cent. town hall, and a modern episcopal palace. Important military road center under Romans; taken by and soon liberated from Moors (8th cent.); rebuilt by Ordoño I (9th cent.), became one of chief cities of Asturian kingdom; sacked again by Moors (10th cent.). Fell to French (1810) after heroic resistance; freed in 1812.

Astoria (ăstō'rēū). **1** Town (pop. 1,308), Fulton co., W central Ill., 28 mi. SSW of Canton; trade center in agr. and bituminous-coal area; feed mill. Inc. 1839. **2** A commercial, industrial, and residential section of NW Queens borough of New York city, connected with the Bronx and Manhattan by Triborough Bridge and with the Bronx by Hell Gate railroad bridge; mfg. (clothing, wood products, leather goods, machine parts, truck bodies and parts). Settled as Hallett's Cove in 17th cent.; renamed for John Jacob Astor and inc. in 1839. Has several 18th-cent. houses. Astoria Park is here. **3** City (pop. 12,331), ⊙ Clatsop co., NW Oregon, on S bank of Columbia R. (here forming part of Wash. line) near its mouth on the Pacific, and c.70 mi. NW of Portland; port of entry. River and coastal port with salmon and tuna fisheries and canneries, flour and lumber mills, and dairy industry. Exports lumber and lumber products, wheat, flour, salmon, and dried fruit. Has agr. experiment station of Oregon State Col. Site of Fort Clatsop, Lewis and Clark camp (1805–06), is near by. First settlement on site of Astoria was fur-trading post (Fort Astoria) established (1811) by expedition sent out by John Jacob Astor. Became important factor in U.S. claim to Oregon Territory. Was sold (1813) to North West Company, but restored by British to U.S. in 1818. Refounded in 1843 by immigrants who had come W on Oregon Trail; inc. 1865. Grew as trade center and later attracted Scandinavian settlers. Much of old city destroyed by fire (1922); later rebuilt. **4** Town (pop. 206), Deuel co., E S.Dak., 15 mi. SSE of Clear Lake, near Minn. line.

Astorp (ōs'tôrp"), Swedish *Åstorp,* town (pop. 4,160), Kristianstad co., SW Sweden, 11 mi. NE of Halsingborg; rail junction; stone quarrying; mfg. of bricks, furniture.

Astove Island, outlying dependency (pop. 36) of the Seychelles, one of the Aldabra group, in Indian Ocean, 150 mi. NW of Madagascar; 10°6'S 47°45'E; 2 mi. long, 1¼ mi. wide. Of coral origin. Guano.

Astra (ä'strä), oil town (pop. estimate 500), E Comodoro Rivadavia military zone, Argentina, 10 mi. N of Comodoro Rivadavia; rail terminus, until 1946 in Chubut natl. territory.

Astrabad, Iran: see GURGAN.

Astradamovka (ŭstrŭdäm'ŭfkŭ), village (1926 pop. 3,099), NW Ulyanovsk oblast, Russian SFSR, 30 mi. SE of Alatyr; grain, potatoes; orchards.

Astrakhan or **Astrakhan'** (ă'strŭkăn", Rus. ä'strŭkhŭnyŭ), oblast (□ 37,200; 1946 pop. estimate 750,000) in S European Russian SFSR; ⊙ Astrakhan. In Caspian Lowland; drained by lower Volga R.; bordered by Yergeni Hills (W), Manych Depression (SW), and Caspian Sea (E). Steppe (W) and desert (E) climate. Mineral resources: salt (Baskunchak L.), gypsum (Nizhni Baskunchak), natural gas (Privolzhski), petroleum (S). Major fishing region (roach, herring, sturgeon, salmon). Grazing (sheep, horses, camels) in steppe. Agr., with vegetables, melons (Volga R. delta and Volga-Akhtuba flood plain), wheat (N), mustard (W), cotton, millet (along W edge of Volga R. delta). Fish processing and preserving, with floating canneries on Caspian Sea; shipbuilding (Astrakhan), saltworking (Vladimirovka, Nizhni Baskunchak), sawmilling (Astrakhan, Privolzhski). Light mfg. and agr. processing in main urban centers (Astrakhan, Stepnoi). Served by Moscow-Astrakhan-Gudermes RR and by navigation on the Volga (chief outlet for Astrakhan fish and for Baku oil exports). Formed 1943 out of major part of dissolved Kalmyk Autonomous SSR and SE panhandle (Volga-Akhtuba flood plain and Volga R. delta) of Stalingrad oblast.

Astrakhan or **Astrakhan',** city (1939 pop. 253,655; 1946 pop. estimate 300,000), ⊙ Astrakhan oblast, Russian SFSR, major Caspian Port, on Volga R. delta mouth, 40 mi. inland from Caspian Sea, 800 mi. SE of Moscow; 70 ft. below sea level; 46°22'N 48°6'E. One of greatest fish and caviar-preserving and exporting centers of USSR; transshipment point for Baku oil, N European timber, Central Asian and Iranian dried fruit. Shipbuilding, food processing (fish oil, meat, flour, hops, vegetables); mfg. of chemicals, shoes, glass, fish nets, soap; metal- and woodworking (barrels), cotton milling; cold-storage plants. Has walled kremlin (1589–1662), regional and ichthyological mus., picture gall., fishery school, medical and teachers colleges. A univ. existed here briefly in 1920s. City proper is on left bank of main (Bakhtemir) arm of Volga R. delta mouth, bet. secondary Bolda (N; lumber port) and Tsarev (S) channels. Across the main Volga arm lies suburb of Trusovo (linked by bridge; terminus of railroad built during Second World War from Kizlyar). Earth dikes protect low-lying city against Volga floods. A ship channel leads from Astrakhan, along Bakhtemir arm of the Volga, to Caspian Sea. The deepwater "12-foot roadstead" (85 mi. SSW of Astrakhan), a major floating freight-transfer point bet. Caspian Sea and Volga R. vessels, handles southbound lumber, grain, metals, finished goods, and northbound oil, cotton, rice, fruit, silk; has floating storage houses, repair shops, and fish-processing plants. Astrakhan developed in 13th cent. under Mongols on right Volga R. bank, near site of anc. Khazar city of Itil (8th–10th cent.). Was ⊙ Tatar khanate until captured (1556) by Ivan the Terrible. Rus. kremlin erected on left bank formed nucleus of new city which developed rapidly in 17th cent. as a commercial center (Central Asian and Persian trade), shipping, among other goods, Astrakhan fur. New impetus given its growth by opening (1870s) of Baku oil fields and start of Volga R. oil transportation. During civil war (1917–20), Astrakhan remained in Soviet hands; served as base for conquest (1920) of Caspian Sea and the Caucasus. During Second World War, an objective (1942) of Germans, who were stopped, however, 100 mi. W. A govt. ⊙ until 1928; also ⊙ former Kalmyk autonomous oblast from 1920 until founding of Elista (now Stepnoi) in 1928.

Astrakhan-Bazar (ä'strŭkhŭn-bŭzär'), village (1932 pop. estimate 760), SE Azerbaijan SSR, 35 mi. NW of Lenkoran; wheat, livestock.

Astrakhanka (ŭstrŭkhän'kŭ), village, central Akmolinsk oblast, Kazakh SSR, near S.Siberian RR, 75 mi. NW of Akmolinsk; bauxite deposits.

Astrida (ästrēdä', ästrē'dä), town (1949 pop. 1,915), central Ruanda-Urundi, in Urundi, 44 mi. SSW of Kigali; alt. 5,736 ft.; educational center with school for sons of African chiefs and medical school for natives. Tree nurseries, cinchona plantations near by. Also trading center. Has hospitals for Europeans and natives. Research laboratory of tropical medicine. Airfield. Its native name is Butare (bōōtä'rä), from an adjoining village. Astrida was founded 1927 as prospective ⊙ of Ruanda-Urundi and named for Queen Astrid of Belgium.

Astro, Greece: see ASTROS.

Astrolabe Bay (ă'strŭlăb), NE New Guinea, N of Huon Peninsula; site of Madang and Alexishafen harbors.

Astrolabe Field, Papua: see PORT MORESBY.

Astropalia, Greece: see ASTYPALAIA.

Astros (ä'strôs), village (pop. 1,953), Arcadia nome, E Peloponnesus, Greece, on Gulf of Argolis, 20 mi. ESE of Tripolis; wine, almonds, olive oil, tobacco, wheat; livestock (sheep, goats). Site of medieval castle. The 2d natl. Gr. assembly (1823) was held near by. Sometimes called Astro.

Astudillo (ästōō-dhe'lyō), town (pop. 2,426), Palencia prov., N central Spain, in fertile agr. area near Pisuerga R., 18 mi. NE of Palencia; a leading grain market; mfg. of woolens, threshing machines, dairy products; flour milling.

Asturias (ăstōō'rēŭs, Sp. ästōōr'yäs), town (1939 pop. 1,999; 1948 municipality pop. 29,932), central Cebu isl., Philippines, on Tañon Strait, 22 mi. NW of Cebu city; agr. center (corn, coconuts).

Asturias, region (□ 4,207; pop. 836,642) and former kingdom, NW Spain, on the Bay of Biscay, coextensive with OVIEDO prov. Bounded by Galicia (W), Leon (S), Old Castile (E). Here the Cantabrian Mts. rise to their highest peak, Picos de Europa (SE), and slope to the sea, forming deep valleys. Drained by numerous, short, swift rivers —Nalón, Lena, Navia, Sella. The high, rocky coast has several good ports: Gijón, Avilés, Llanes, Ribadesella. Coal mines, richest in Spain, have been worked since Roman times, and mining is the chief industry (Langreo, Quirós, Aller, Mieres dists.), yielding 70% of Spain's bituminous coal; also anthracite, iron, zinc, lead, manganese, and copper. The metallurgical works of Oviedo have developed greatly since late 19th cent. Mfg. of iron and steel, chemicals, glass, processed foods (fish and meat, dairy products), and cider. Extensive forests (lumbering) and fine pastures (cattle raising) in interior, favored by abundant rainfall. Agr.: corn, vegetables, apples and other fruit. Fishing and fish processing along coast. Chief cities: Oviedo, Gijón, Avilés, Mieres. Historically the cradle of the Sp. kingdom, Asturias, settled by an old Celtiberian people, was conquered by the Romans (3d–2d cent. B.C.) and by the Visigoths (5th cent. A.D.), but during the Moorish invasion became the refuge of the Christian nobles. Here they founded the 1st Christian kingdom, defeated the Moors, and started the reconquest of Spain. Kingdom of Asturias became (10th cent.) kingdom of Asturias and Leon, which united (1230) with kingdom of Castile. Heir presumptive to Sp. throne bore title of prince of Asturias after 1388. The Asturians are noted for their stubborn courage and independence—traits shown in the warfare against Napoleon, in various uprisings against the Sp. govt., and in the Sp. civil war of 1936–39.

Asturica Augusta, Spain: see ASTORGA.

Astypalaia or **Astipalaia** (both: ästĭpä'lēä), Ital. *Stampalia* (stämpä'lēä), Lat. *Astypalaea* (ăstĭpūlē'ŭ), Aegean island (□ 37; pop. 1,791) in the Dodecanese, Greece, WSW of Kos; 36°35'N 26°20'E; rises to 1,414 ft. (SW). Barley, beans, wine, olive oil; sponge fishery. Main town, Astypalaia (pop. 1,467), is on SE shore. Also called Astropalia.

Asuansi or **Asuantsi** (äswän'sē), town, Western Prov., S Gold Coast colony, 13 mi. N of Cape Coast (linked by road); lime-growing center; palm oil and kernels, cassava. Has modern hosp., agr. experiment station (livestock), and trade training center (opened 1948).

Asuke (ä"sōō'kä), town (pop. 4,350), Aichi prefecture, central Honshu, Japan, 14 mi. ESE of Seto; charcoal, lumber, raw silk.

Asum, Bahr, Anglo-Egyptian Sudan and Fr. Equatorial Africa: see BAHR SALAMAT.

Asunción (äsōōnsyōn'), village, Pando dept., NW Bolivia, on Madre de Dios R. and 130 mi. WSW of Riberalta; rubber.

Asuncion, uninhabited volcanic island (□ 3), N Marianas Isls., W Pacific, c.300 mi. N of Saipan; 19°40'N 145°24'E; c.2 mi. in diameter; conelike, rising to 2,923 ft. Formerly Assumption Isl.

Asunción, Mexico: see ASUNCIÓN DONATO GUERRA.

Asunción, city (pop. 113,598; with suburbs, 144,327), ⊙ Paraguay and ⊙ (but independent of) Central dept., principal port on Paraguay R. (Argentina border) and 625 mi. N of Buenos Aires; 25°16'S 57°41'W. Major inland port, rail terminus; commercial, industrial, and cultural center. It dominates all phases of Paraguayan life, having one-tenth of the country's pop. and handling c.75% of its exports and 90% of its imports. Processes agr. and forest products: cotton, wool, and rayon mills; flour mills, furniture factories, vegetable-oil mills, sugar refineries, alcohol and liquor distilleries, breweries, tanneries, shoe factories, match factories, shipbuilding yards, railroad shops. Outlet for rich agr. hinterland (sugar cane, cotton, subtropical fruit, cereals, tobacco, livestock). Ships hardwood, hides, oranges, maté. Linked through river steamers and railroad (via Encarnación across the upper Paraná) with Buenos Aires and the Atlantic. An old Sp. town, retaining much of its colonial aspect, it is laid out in rectangular fashion. Noteworthy bldgs. include: Natl. Palace, the Renaissance cathedral and archbishop's residence, municipal theater, Godoi Mus., the Hall of Congress, Encarnación Church, the Natl. Univ. and other schools and colleges. The Panteón Nacional has the remains of Francisco Solano López and the tomb of the unknown soldier. The site of the city may have been visited by Ayolas, but the town, called Nuestra Señora de la Asunción [Our Lady of the Assumption], seems to have been founded in August of 1536 or 1537 by Juan de Salazar and Gonzalo de Mendoza. A trading post on the route to Peru, it flourished under the governorship of Domingo Martínez de Irala and became the most important town in the La Plata region. Its leadership was destroyed by the rise of Buenos Aires in 17th cent. In 1811 Paraguay here declared its independence. Asunción suffered internal and external conflicts (during the War of the Triple Alliance, 1865-1870, it was bombarded by Brazilians and had to be temporarily evacuated), but has grown steadily in recent years. TRINIDAD, RECOLETA, Villa Morra, and LAMBARÉ are the most important suburbs.

Asunción, Venezuela: see LA ASUNCIÓN.

Asunción Donato Guerra (dōnä'tō gĕ'rä) or **Asunción,** town (pop. 614), Mexico state, central Mexico, 30 mi. W of Toluca; grain, fruit, livestock.

Asunción Mita (mē'tä), town (1950 pop. 2,791), Jutiapa dept., SE Guatemala, in highlands, 13 mi. ENE of Jutiapa, on Inter-American Highway; corn, beans, livestock. Indian burial mounds near.

Asunción River, Mexico: see MAGDALENA RIVER.

Asungate, Cordillera de (kôrdēyä'rä dā äsōōngä'tā), NW spur of Cordillera de CARABAYA, in Cordillera Occidental of the Andes, SE Peru, extends from area of Macusani 100 mi. NW to Cordillera de Vilcanota; rises to 20,187 ft. in the peak Asungate (13°47'S 71°15'W).

Asvaer (ôs'văr), Nor. *Åsvaer*, group of small islands, Nordland co., N central Norway, 6 mi. NW of Donna isl., 55 mi. W of Mo; 66°15'N 12°13'E; cod fisheries; lighthouse (N). Sometimes spelled Aasvaer.

Asvestochorion or **Asvestokhorion** (both: äsvĕstôkhô'rēôn), town (pop. 4,004), Salonika nome, Macedonia, Greece, 4 mi. E of Salonika; wheat, tobacco, silk. Tuberculosis sanatarium.

Aswan (äswän', ăswăn') province (□ 363; pop. 286,854), S Egypt, in Nile valley; ⊙ Aswan. Bounded S by the Anglo-Egyptian Sudan, E by the Arabian Desert, N by Qena prov., W by Libyan Desert. Agr. (cereals, dates). Main urban centers: Aswan (site of the great dam), IDFU, KOM OMBO. Rail line runs along E bank of Nile R. Prov. is of great archaeological importance; here are the rock temples of ABU SIMBEL, the Roman temple of Kalabsha, the temples of Kom Ombo and Idfu, the ruins on the isl. of PHILAE, and ruins of anc. Nekheb. Also spelled Assuan and Assouan.

Aswan, anc. *Syene*, town (pop. 25,397), ⊙ Aswan prov., S Egypt, on E bank of the Nile and just below 1st cataract, on railroad, and 60 mi. S of Idfu; 24°5'N 32°54'E. Trading center and winter resort; wool spinning and weaving, tanning, shoe making; cereals, dates. Opposite Aswan is ELEPHANTINE, a fertile isl. with important archaeological remains. Near Aswan are the original syenite quarries. The great **Aswan Dam,** 3 mi. upstream, is 1¼ mi. long. Built of syenite, it was completed 1902. Height of the dam was raised to 146½ ft. in 1912, affecting the river level for 174 mi. upstream; it was raised another 30 ft. in 1933, increasing the length of the reservoir to 230 mi. The roadway over the dam is 26 ft. wide. There is a series of locks on the west side. Except from July to October, when the sluices are open, the isl. and temple of PHILAE are submerged. Hydroelectrical power is planned for Aswan Dam. Also spelled Assuan and Assouan.

Asylum, Pa.: see BRADFORD, county.

Asyut (ăsyōōt'), province (□ 812; pop. 1,378,904), central Upper Egypt, in Nile valley; ⊙ Asyut. Bounded S by Girga prov., E by Arabian Desert, N by Minya prov., and W by Libyan Desert. Pottery making, wood and ivory carving; agr. (cereals, sugar cane, dates). Main urban centers, besides Asyut, are Abu Tig, Dairut, Mallawi, Manfalut. Served by railway running along W bank of Nile R. The Asyut Barrage provides the prov. N of Asyut with summer irrigation. The IBRAHIMIYA CANAL, which starts at Asyut, serves the BAHR YUSUF at Dairut. Of special archaeological interest are the ruins of TEL EL AMARNA.

Asyut, anc. *Lycopolis* (lĭkŏ'pùlis), largest city (pop. 88,730) of Upper Egypt, ⊙ Asyut prov., on W bank of the Nile, on railroad, and 235 mi. S of Cairo; 27°11'N 31°11'E. Industrial and trading center, connected by road to the oases of Bahariya, Farafra, Dakhla, and Kharga; cotton spinning, wood and ivory carving, mfg. of shoes, pottery, refrigerants. Agr: cereals, dates, sugar cane. The Asyut Barrage, built (1902) across the Nile below the head of the Ibrahimiya Canal and 1 mi. N of Asyut, is 2,730 ft. long, 41 ft. high; remodeled 1938; used for irrigation. Also spelled Assiut and, formerly, Siut.

Aszar (ä'sär), Hung. *Ászár*, town (pop. 1,556), Komarom-Esztergom co., N Hungary, 20 mi. SW of Györ; starch mfg., brickworks. Prehistoric, Celtic, and Roman remains found near by.

Aszod (ŏ'sōd), Hung. *Aszód*, town (pop. 5,695), Pest-Pilis-Solt-Kiskun co., N central Hungary, 20 mi. NE of Budapest; mfg. of furniture, tiles, and bricks. Reform school for boys.

At [Arabic, =the], for Arabic names beginning thus: see under following part of the name.

Atâ (ätä), fishing and hunting settlement (pop. 44), Jokobshavn dist., W Greenland, on E coast of Arve Prinsen Isl., on Atâ Sound (30-mi. arm of Disko Bay) which separates isl. from mainland, 70 mi. E of Ritenbenk; 69°46'N 50°58'W.

Ata (ä'tä'), uninhabited island, S Tonga, S Pacific, 85 mi. SSW of Tongatabu; rises to 1,165 ft. Extinct volcanoes. Formerly Pylstaert Isl.

Atabapo River (ätäbä'pō), Amazonas territory, S Venezuela, flows c.150 mi. NNW, almost entirely along Colombia–Venezuela border, to Guaviare R. at San Fernando de Atabapo, just before joint stream enters Orinoco R.

Atabey (ätäbā'), village (pop. 2,801), Isparta prov., W central Turkey, 14 mi. N of Isparta; rose petals. Formerly Agros.

Atacama (ätäkä'mä), province (□ 30,843; 1940 pop. 84,312; 1949 estimate 76,363), N Chile, bet. the Pacific and the Andes; ⊙ COPIAPÓ. Watered by the Quebrada del Salado, Copiapó R., and Huasco R. Has a dry, mild climate. Includes part of the Atacama Desert. In E are some of highest peaks of the Andes (Potro, Tres Cruces, San Francisco); and several salt deserts (Maricunga and Pedernales). Predominantly a mining region: copper (Potrerillos, Tierra Amarilla), gold (Domeyko, Algarrobo), borax (Pedernales). Agr. in irrigated valleys of Copiapó and Huasco rivers: alfalfa, clover, corn, subtropical fruit, wine. Sheep, goats, cattle (S and E). Mining, smelting, wine making, dairying. Prov. was set up 1843. The Pacific isls. of San Félix and San Ambrosio, as well as Easter Isl., are dependencies of Atacama prov.

Atacama, Puna de (pōō'nä dā), high Andean tableland (above 10,000 ft.) on Argentina-Chile border, traversed by the Eastern Cordillera. Marked by dry, cold climate and sparse scrub vegetation; has many salt pans (salares of Arizaro, Pocitos, Hombre Muerto, and Antofalla, and the Salinas Grandes in Argentina, and the Salar de Atacama in Chile). The chief urban centers are San Antonio de los Cobres (Argentina) and San Pedro de Atacama (Chile). Since 1948 it is crossed (W–E) by the Transandine RR of the North. The high-alt. Puna de Atacama is often confused with the low-lying Chilean Atacama Desert, from which it is separated by the Cordillera de Domeyko.

Atacama, Salar de (sälär' dā), salt desert (alt. c.7,875 ft.) in the Puna de Atacama, Antofagasta prov., N Chile, extends c.60 mi. N–S along main Andean cordillera, bet. 23° and 24°S; 3–25 mi. wide. Borax deposits.

Atacama Desert, arid region of N Chile, extends c.600 mi. S from Peru border to area of Copiapó (Atacama prov.). The desert proper (c.2,000 ft. above sea level) is a series of dry salt basins bounded W by the Pacific coastal range (c.2,500 ft.) and E by the Cordillera de Domeyko, a flanking range of the Andes separating the desert from the Puna de Atacama, its highland counterpart. There is practically no vegetation; in many places rain has never been recorded. Of the coastal streams descending from the Andes, only the Loa R. reaches the Pacific. Arica, Iquique, Antofagasta, and Taltal are the chief ports. The Atacama has been known chiefly for its fabulous nitrate wealth. Production (begun 2d half of 19th cent.) reached a peak c.1900, but declined following the development during First World War of synthetic nitrates. Ceded 1883–84 by Peru and Bolivia to Chile, the region now forms Tarapacá, Antofagasta, and Atacama provs.

Atacama Trench, submarine depression in South Pacific Ocean, off W coast of South America. The greatest depth (25,049 ft.) is the Richards Deep, off Atacama Desert at 25°42'S 71°30'W.

Atacames (ätäkä'mĕs), town, Esmeraldas prov., NW Ecuador, minor Pacific port, 13 mi. SW of Esmeraldas, in tropical forest (balsa wood, tagua nuts, mangrove, bananas, coco).

Atacazo, Cerro (sĕ'rō ätäkä'sō), extinct Andean volcano (14,623 ft.), Pichincha prov., N central Ecuador, 12 mi. SW of Quito.

Ataco or **Concepción de Ataco** (kōnsĕpsyōn' dā ätä'kō), town (pop. 3,526), Ahuachapán dept., W Salvador, in crater of extinct volcano Ataco (4,872 ft.), 4 mi. S of Ahuachapán; basket weaving; coffee, grain, truck.

Atafu (ätäfōō'), NW atoll (600 acres; pop. 451), TOKELAU, S Pacific, 310 mi. N of Western Samoa; 8°34'S 172°30'W; c.62 islets on reef 3 mi. long, 2.5 mi. wide; coconuts. Formerly Duke of York Isl.

Atajate (ätähä'tä), town (pop. 277), Málaga prov., S Spain, in the Sierra de Ronda, on railroad and 8 mi. SW of Ronda, in agr. region (cereals, oranges, olives, timber, cork, livestock).

Atajo, Sierra (syĕ'rä ätä'hō), subandean range in E central Catamarca prov., Argentina, 15 mi. N of Andalgalá. A SW spur of the Nevado del Aconquija, it extends c.25 mi. E-W, rising to 12,000 ft. Copper mining at Capillitas; gold deposits. Also called Sierra Capillitas.

Ataka, Japan: see KOMATSU, Ishikawa prefecture.

Ataka Gebel, Egypt: see ATAQA, GEBEL.

Ataki (ŭtä'kē), Rum. *Otaci* (ôtä'chē), village (1941 pop. 2,570), N Moldavian SSR, on Dniester R. (Ukrainian border), opposite Mogilev-Podolski, on railroad; agr. center; flour and oilseed milling. Until Second World War, pop. largely Jewish.

Atakora Mountains (ätäkō'rä), low range (up to c.2,500 ft.) in NW Dahomey, Fr. West Africa, running c.130 mi. NE-SW along Upper Volta and Fr. Togoland border, forming divide bet. drainage systems of Oti R. (W) and Ouémé R. (E).

Atakpamé (ätäkpä'mā), town (pop. 6,005), S Fr. Togoland, on the railroad, and 100 mi. N of Lomé; commercial and agr. center; cacao, palm oil and kernels, cotton, coffee. Cotton ginning. Has a hosp., R.C. and Protestant missions. Chromite, serpentine, and asbestos deposits near by.

Atalaia (ätŭlä'yù), city (pop. 1,462), E Alagoas, NE Brazil, on railroad and 20 mi. WNW of Maceió; sugar and cotton growing. Sugar mills near by.

Atalandi, Greece: see ATALANTE.

Atalante or **Atalandi** (both: ŭtülän'dē), town (pop. 4,041), Phthiotis nome, E central Greece, near Gulf of Euboea, 35 mi. ESE of Lamia; wheat, cotton; wine. Also spelled Atalanti. Its landing 3 mi. ENE on Gulf of Euboea is sheltered by small Atalante isls.

Atalanti, Greece: see ATALANTE.

Atalaya, Argentina: see MAGDALENA.

Atalaya (ätälī'ä), village (pop. 598), Veraguas prov., W central Panama, in Pacific lowland, 6 mi. SE of Santiago; sugar cane, livestock.

Atalaya, town (pop. 1,114), Loreto dept., E central Peru, at union of Apurímac (Tambo R.) and Urubamba rivers, 80 mi. ESE of Puerto Bermúdez (Pasco dept.); 10°42'S 73°43'W; sugar cane, bananas, yucca.

Atalaya, town (pop. 618), Badajoz prov., W Spain, 16 mi. E of Jerez de los Caballeros; cereals, olives, acorns, fruit, livestock.

Atalaya, La (lä), village (pop. 1,559), Grand Canary, Canary Isls., near Guía de Gran Canaria, in agr. region (bananas, tomatoes, cereals, livestock). Built on terraces of a mtn. slope.

Atalayasa (ätälīä'sä), highest peak (1,558 ft.) of Iviza, Balearic Isls., 8 mi. W of Iviza city.

Ataléia, Minas Gerais, Brazil: see JOEIRANA, Espírito Santo.

Atalissa (ă"tùlĭ'sù), town (pop. 204), Muscatine co., SE Iowa, 11 mi. NNW of Muscatine.

Atami (ä"tä'mē). **1** Town (1947 pop. 8,470), Fukushima prefecture, central Honshu, Japan, 22 mi. SW of Fukushima, on small tributary of Abukuma R. (hydroelectric plant); gold and silver mining. Hot springs. Formerly Takagawa. **2** City (1940 pop. 24,477; 1947 pop. 34,754), Shizuoka prefecture, central Honshu, Japan, at base of Izu Peninsula, on W shore of Sagami Bay, 12 mi. E of Numazu; hot-springs resort; textiles, camellia oil. Near by is islet Hatsu-shima, known for its forest of camellia trees.

Atamisqui or **Villa Atamisqui** (vē'yä ätämē'skē), town (pop. estimate 800), ⊙ Atamisqui dept. (□ 830; 1947 pop. 14,190), S central Santiago del Estero prov., Argentina, near the Río Dulce, 27 mi. SE of Loreto. Agr. center (wheat, corn, alfalfa, livestock).

Atanasovo (ätänä'sôvô), N suburb (pop. 1,674) of Burgas, E Bulgaria, on W shore of Atanasovo L. (□ 6.6), a salt lagoon off Gulf of Burgas. Formerly Atanaskoi.

Atangmik (ätäng'mĭk), fishing settlement (pop. 159), Sukkertoppen dist., SW Greenland, on headland in Davis Strait, 45 mi. NNW of Godthaab; 64°47'N 52°10'W.

Atanik (ŭtä'nĭk), Eskimo village (1939 pop. 19), NW Alaska, on Arctic Ocean, 20 mi. NE of Wainwright.

Ataqa, Gebel, or **Jabal 'Ataqah** (both: jĕ'bĕl ätä'kä), range, NE Egypt, c.7 mi. W of Suez; rises to 2,770 ft. Sometimes spelled Ataka.

Ataquines (ätäkē'nĕs), town (pop. 1,508), Valladolid prov., N central Spain, 11 mi. SE of Medina del Campo; cereals, vegetables, lumber.

Atar (ätär'), town (pop. c.4,000), W central Mauritania, Fr. West Africa, oasis on caravan trail in Adrar mtn. region, 260 mi. E of Port-Étienne and 380 mi. NE of Saint-Louis, Senegal. Produces dates, millet, grain, barley, watermelons; goats, sheep, cattle. Has airfield, meteorological station, school for native tapestry.

Ataran River (ätärän'), in Tenasserim, Lower Burma, rises in Tenasserim Range (Thailand line) near Three Pagodas Pass, flows c.150 mi. NW, past Kya-in Seikkyi (head of navigation), to Salween R. at Moulmein. Navigable for 73 mi. Called Zami R. (zä'mē) in upper course.

Atarasquillo or **Santa María Atarasquillo** (sän'tä märē'ä ätäräskē'yō), town (pop. 1,780), Mexico state, central Mexico, 22 mi. WSW of Mexico city; cereals, livestock.

Atarfe (ätär'fā), NW suburb (pop. 4,683) of Granada, Granada prov., S Spain; mfg. of chemical fertilizers, soap, cement, coal briquettes; sugar milling, olive-oil processing. Lumbering and stock raising; also cereals, sugar beets, tobacco in area. Mineral springs 2 mi. NW. Ruins of anc. Elvira in vicinity.

Atarjea (ätärhā'ä), town (pop. 319), Guanajuato, central Mexico, 45 mi. E of San Luis de la Paz; alt. 4,068 ft.; grain, maguey, sugar, livestock.

Atarra (utŭr'rŭ), town (pop. 5,947), Banda dist., S Uttar Pradesh, India, 20 mi. SE of Banda; gram, jowar, wheat, oilseeds, rice. Sometimes called Atarra Buzurg.

Atarsumba (ŭtŭrsōōm'bŭ), town (pop. 2,453), Kaira dist., N Bombay, India, 23 mi. E of Ahmadabad; agr. market (millet, pulse, rice). Sometimes spelled Attarsumba.

Atascadero (ŭtăskùdâ'rō), village (pop. 3,443), San Luis Obispo co., SW Calif., 15 mi. N of San Luis Obispo and on Salinas R.; poultry center.

Atascosa (ătùskō'sù), county (□ 1,206; pop. 20,048), SW Texas; ⊙ Jourdanton. Drained by Atascosa R. Agr. (especially peanuts; also truck, strawberries, corn, grain sorghums, broomcorn, hay, cotton); cattle ranching; dairying. Oil, natural-gas wells; clay, sand deposits. Formed 1856.

Atascosa River, S Texas, rises near Atascosa, flows c.90 mi. generally SE to Frio R. just above its mouth on the Nueces, S of Three Rivers.

Atasuski or **Atasuskiy** (ŭtùsōō'skē), town (1948 pop. over 2,000), central Karaganda oblast, Kazakh SSR, on railroad (Zhana Arka station), on branch of the Sary-Su and 135 mi. SW of Karaganda; iron-mining center, supplying Temir-Tau metallurgical plant. Developed in early 1940s.

Atauro (ätou'rōō), island (□ 72; pop. 4,059), dependency of Portuguese Timor, in Ombai Strait, 15 mi. N of Dili; 14 mi. long, 6 mi. wide; hilly. Fishing. Has airport. Also called Pulo Cambing and Kambing.

Atawa (ä"tä'wä) or **Adawa** (ä"dä'wä), town (pop. 4,682), Mie prefecture, S Honshu, Japan, on Kumano Sea, on SE Kii Peninsula, 5 mi. NNE of Shingu; rice, wheat; fishing.

Atbara (ăt'bärä), town (pop. 37,750), Northern Prov., Anglo-Egyptian Sudan, on right bank of Atbara R. at its junction with the Nile, 10 mi. N of Ed Damer; 17°42'N 33°58'E; important rail junction for Port Sudan (NE), Khartoum (S), Egypt (N). Has large railroad workshops and technical school; commercial and agr. center with trade in cotton, wheat, barley, corn, fruit, durra, and livestock. Administrative hq. of Sudan Govt. Railways. Cement plant near by. Airport. Here Kitchener defeated the Khalifa's troops, 1898.

Atbara River, NE Anglo-Egyptian Sudan, rises on W slopes of Ethiopian highlands W of Gondar, flows c.500 mi. NNW, past Khashm el Girba and Goz Ragab to the Nile at Atbara. It is the Nile's only tributary bet. Khartoum and the sea. Navigable in flood season (June-Aug.). Dries to a series of pools after Aug. During flood it contributes 22% of main Nile volume, but its flow is very erratic. Receives Setit and Angareb rivers.

Atbasar (ŭtbŭsär'), city (1926 pop. 6,746), NW Akmolinsk oblast, Kazakh SSR, on S.Siberian RR, on Ishim R. and 135 mi. WNW of Akmolinsk, in cattle and grain area; livestock market, tanning industry. Founded 1846 in Rus. conquest of Kazakhstan.

Atbashi (ŭtbŭshē'), village (1948 pop. over 2,000), SW Tyan-Shan oblast, Kirghiz SSR, on At-Bashi R., on N slope of At-Bashi Range, and 18 mi. SW of Naryn; on road to Kashgar (China); agr.; saw-milling.

Atbashi Canal, irrigation waterway in Chu valley, in N Frunze oblast, Kirghiz SSR; flows c.50 mi. parallel to CHU RIVER below Chumysh Dam.

At-Bashi Range, range of Tien Shan mountain system, in Tyan-Shan oblast, Kirghiz SSR; extends from Chatyr-Kul (lake) c.100 mi. NE to headwaters of At-Bashi R., (left tributary of Naryn R.); rises to 15,000 ft.

Atchafalaya Bay (ùchă'fùlī"ù), arm of the Gulf of Mexico, S La., 15 mi. S of Morgan City, at mouth of Atchafalaya R.; c.21 mi. long NW-SE, 10 mi. wide. Point Chevreuil (shùvrāl') is at NW side of entrance; at SE side is Point Au Fer (ō fâr'), with shell reef extending c.10 mi. NW. On the reef c.3 mi. offshore is Eugene Isl., site of Point Au Fer Reef lighthouse (29°22'N 91°23'W). Four League Bay (c.11 mi. long) is Atchafalaya Bay's SE arm, with channel into Gulf from SE end.

Atchafalaya River, La., a distributary of Red R., branches to SW from main stream in W Pointe Coupee parish at point where Old R. (c.7 mi. long) carries part of Red R. waters SE to the Mississippi; winds c.170 mi. S and SE, past Simmesport and Morgan City, to Atchafalaya Bay of Gulf of Mexico; navigable. Above Morgan City (where it intersects Gulf Intracoastal Waterway), it widens into Grand L. (c.35 mi. long, 2-6 mi. wide). The extensive guide-levee systems of West Atchafalaya Floodway (W of river) and Morganza Floodway (E) have made its valley a route to the Gulf for high-water runoff of Red and Mississippi rivers.

Atchanta, India: see ACHANTA.

Atchison. 1 County (□ 421; pop. 21,496), NE Kansas; ⊙ Atchison. Gently rolling agr. area, bounded E by Missouri R. and Mo.; drained by Delaware R. Livestock, corn, apples. Formed 1855. **2** County (□ 549; pop. 11,127), extreme NW Mo.; ⊙ Rockport. On Missouri R. (W); drained by Tarkio and Nishnabotna rivers. Corn, livestock region. Formed 1845.

Atchison, city (pop. 12,792), ⊙ Atchison co., NE Kansas, on Missouri R. (here forming Mo. line) and 40 mi. NW of Kansas City, Kansas; trade center (with railroad repair shops) in grain, livestock, and apple region. Flour milling; mfg. of locomotive parts, industrial alcohol, plumbing supplies, steel and wire products, leather goods; bottling. Limestone quarrying. St. Benedict's Col. (R.C.; 1859), Mt. St. Scholastica Col. (R.C.; 1863), and state orphans' home are here. Bridge across Missouri R. was finished in 1938. Settled 1854, inc. 1855. Grew as river port, rail terminus (Atchison, Topeka, and Santa Fe RR), and outfitting point for travelers to West.

Atco. 1 Village (pop. 1,443), Bartow co., NW Ga., just NW of Cartersville; mfg. of tire-cord fabric. **2** Village (1940 pop. 1,308), Camden co., SW N.J., 16 mi. SE of Camden; makes brooms.

Ateca (ätä'kä), town (pop. 3,327), Saragossa prov., NE Spain, on Jalón R. and 8 mi. WSW of Calatayud, in agr. area (olives, wine, sugar beets, fruit, hemp); stock raising. Has remains of Moorish towers and medieval castle; 10 mi. SW is ruined former monastery (dates from 12th cent.; restored in 17th).

'Ateibe, El (ĕl ätā'bù), or **Al-'Utaybah** (ĕl-ōōtā'bù), Fr. *Outeïba*, lake, SW Syria, 18 mi. E of Damascus, in the Ghuta valley. Has no outlet but receives the waters of the Barada which are used for irrigation. On S shore is the village of El 'Ateiba. Wheat, corn, millet, fruit grown near by.

Ateleta (ätĕlā'tä), village (pop. 1,122), Aquila prov., Abruzzi e Molise, S central Italy, near Sangro R., 18 mi. N of Isernia.

Atella (ätĕl'lä), town (pop. 1,568), Potenza prov., Basilicata, S Italy, 8 mi. S of Melfi, in agr. (cereals, olives) and livestock region. Hot mineral baths near by.

Atella di Caserta (dē käzĕr'tä), commune (pop. 12,128), Caserta prov., Campania, S Italy, 3 mi. ESE of Aversa and 8 mi. N of Naples. Site of anc. Oscan town of Atella where Roman comedies (*Atellanae*) originated. In Napoli prov. 1927-45, and then called Atella di Napoli.

Atemajac de Brizuela (ätämähäk' dā brēswä'lä), town (pop. 2.049), Jalisco, W Mexico, 40 mi. SW of Guadalajara; grain, beans, sugar, alfalfa.

Atemajac del Valle (dĕl vä'yä), town (pop. 1,658), Jalisco, central Mexico, 4 mi. N of Guadalajara; cereals, peanuts, sugar cane, fruits, vegetables, livestock.

Atempan (ätĕm'pän), town (pop. 707), Puebla, central Mexico, 5 mi. W of Teziutlán; corn, coffee, fruit.

Atena Lucana (ä'tĕnä lōōkä'nä), village (pop. 1,740), Salerno prov., Campania, S Italy, 5 mi. NNW of Sala Consilina.

Atenango del Río (ätänäng'gō dĕl rē'ō), town (pop. 897), Guerrero, SW Mexico, on affluent of the Mezcala (Río de las Balsas system) and 34 mi. ESE of Iguala; cereals, sugar, fruit.

Atenas (ätä'näs), city (1950 pop. 638), Alajuela, W central Costa Rica, on Tárcoles plain, 15 mi. WSW of Alajuela, on road from Río Grande rail station; agr. and commercial center; vegetables (beans, potatoes), grain, fodder; stock raising.

Atenayuca (ätänīōō'kä), town (pop. 1,631), Puebla, central Mexico, 45 mi. SE of Puebla; corn, sugar, livestock.

Atencingo (ätĕnsēng'gō), village (pop. 2,390), Puebla, central Mexico, on central plateau, on railroad and 12 mi. SW of Matamoros; agr. center (corn, rice, sugar, fruit, livestock); sugar refining.

Atenco (ätĕng'kō). **1** Officially San Mateo Atenco, town (pop. 4,330), Mexico state, central Mexico, 9 mi. ESE of Toluca; agr. center (cereals, fruit, livestock); dairying. **2** Officially San Salvador Atenco, town (pop. 1,650), Mexico state, central Mexico, 16 mi. NE of Mexico city; cereals, maguey, livestock. **3** Officially San Juan Atenco, town (pop. 1,641), Puebla, central Mexico, 45 mi. E of Puebla; cereals, maguey.

Atengo (ätĕng'gō). **1** Town (pop. 1,262), Hidalgo, central Mexico, on Tula R. and 40 mi. W of Pachuca; corn, beans maguey, livestock. **2** Town (pop. 1,169), Jalisco, W Mexico, 20 mi. SW of Ameca; sugar, cotton, rice, tobacco.

Atenguillo (ätĕng-gē'yō), town (pop. 1,377), Jalisco, W Mexico, 30 mi. WSW of Ameca; alt. 4,452 ft.; bananas, rice, sugar cane, tobacco, cotton.

Atenquique (ätĕngkē'kā), village, Jalisco, W Mexico, at E foot of the Colima peaks, 7 mi. W of Tuxpan; lumbering center; soda, wood-pulp mills.

Atentze, China: see TEHTSIN.

Aterazawa (ätä"rä'zäwù), town (pop. 7,910), Yamagata prefecture, N Honshu, Japan, on Mogami R. and 11 mi. NW of Yamagata; raw-silk culture, goldfish breeding.

Aterno River, Italy: see PESCARA RIVER.

Atescatempa (ätĕskätĕm'pä), town (1950 pop. 1,019), Jutiapa dept., SE Guatemala, in highlands, 12 mi. SE of Jutiapa, near Salvador line; corn, beans, rice; livestock. **Lake Atescatempa** (25 ft. deep) is 4 mi. NE; drains, via Atescatempa R., NE into L. Güija. Dried up 1893; later reappeared.

Atessa (ätĕs'sä), town (pop. 3,515), Chieti prov., Abruzzi e Molise, S central Italy, 12 mi. SSE of Lanciano; rail terminus; mfg. (macaroni, bricks, pottery, leather goods).

Ateste, Italy: see ESTE.

Ateuf, El-, or **El-Atteuf** (ĕl-ätûf'), Saharan village, Ghardaïa territory, central Algeria, one of the Mzab oases, 5 mi. E of Ghardaïa; date palms. Founded in 11th cent.

Atexcal (ätĕskäl'), officially San Martín Atexcal, town (pop. 730), Puebla, central Mexico, 23 mi. WSW of Tehuacán; alt. 6,184 ft.; corn, sugar, livestock.

'Atf, El, or **Al-'Atf** (both: ĕl-ätf'), village (pop. 2,500), Beheira prov., Lower Egypt, on Rosetta branch of the Nile, contiguous (N) with El Mahmudiya. Has steam pumps which raise water into Mahmudiya Canal when the Nile is low.

Atfih (ätfē'), village (pop. 8,717), Giza prov., Upper Egypt, on the Nile and 42 mi. S of Cairo; corn, cotton, sugar cane. Site of anc. Aphroditopolis.

Atglen, borough (pop. 668), Chester co., SE Pa., 8 mi. WSW of Coatesville.

Ath [Arabic, =the], for Arabic names beginning thus: see under following part of the name.

Ath, Flemish *Aat* (both: ät), town (pop. 10,284), Hainaut prov., SW Belgium, on Dender R. and 17 mi. E of Tournai; sugar-refining center; furniture, chemicals, silk. Formerly had cotton and lace industry. Has 12th-cent. tower, 14th-cent. church, 17th-cent. town hall.

Athabaska (ă″thúbă′skú), town (pop. 747), central Alta., on Athabaska R. and 80 mi. N of Edmonton; grain elevators, lumbering, mixed farming, stock raising. In area are oil, gas, silica-sand deposits.

Athabaska, Lake (□ 3,058), NW Sask. and NE Alta.; 59°N 110′W. Crescent shaped, it is c.200 mi. long, 5–36 mi. wide. Receives Athabaska and Peace rivers in SW and is drained NW by Slave R. into Great Slave L., thence by Mackenzie R. into the Arctic Ocean. On the edge of the Laurentian Plateau, lake is connected with Churchill R. by canoe route via Wollaston and Reindeer lakes. Chief settlements on lake are Fort Chipewyan, Goldfields, and Fond du Lac; in summer they are connected by steamers of the Hudson's Bay Co. Lake was 1st surveyed and mapped (1790–92) by Philip Turnor.

Athabaska, Mount (11,452 ft.), SW Alta., near B.C. border, in Rocky Mts. bet. Jasper and Banff natl. parks, 60 mi. SE of Jasper; 52°11′N 117°12′W. On edge of Columbia Icefield and surrounded by Athabaska and Saskatchewan glaciers. North Saskatchewan R. rises here. First climbed 1898 by J. N. Collie.

Athabaska Pass (5,736 ft.), in Rocky Mts., on Alta.-B.C. border, 35 mi. S of Jasper; 52°22′N 118°11′W. Leads from headwaters of Athabaska R. across the Continental Divide to upper Columbia R. Discovered c.1811 by David Thompson or one of his agents, it was for 50 years chief route for Hudson's Bay Co. fur trade with Columbia R. country, until coming of the railroad.

Athabaska River, Alta., most southerly tributary of Mackenzie R., rises in Rocky Mts. in the Columbia Icefield near Mt. Columbia, flows N through Jasper Natl. Park to Jasper, then NE through Jasper L. and Brûlé L. to Mirror Landing E of Lesser Slave L.; here it turns sharply E and then S, to Athabaska, where it turns sharply once more, flowing N through a series of rapids, past Fort McMurray, through a delta to SW end of L. Athabaska opposite Fort Chipewyan; 765 mi. long. Chief tributaries are Pembina, Lesser Slave, La Biche, and Clearwater rivers. An important route to the Mackenzie valley, river was for many years used by the Hudson's Bay Co.; goods were sent overland to Athabaska, thence by scow to the series of rapids above Fort McMurray, and then by tramway to steamers below the falls.

Athalia (úthāl′yú), village (pop. 307), Lawrence co., S Ohio, on the Ohio and 10 mi. NE of Huntington, W.Va.

Athalmer (ŭtăl′mŭr) or **Lake Windermere** (wĭn′-dŭrmēr), resort village, SE B.C., on slope of Rocky Mts., on Columbia R., at N end of Windermere L., 50 mi. SSW of Banff; alt. 2,624 ft.

Athamanika, Greece: see TZOUMERKA.

Athani, India: see ATHNI.

Athapapuska Lake (ă″thúpúpŭ′skú) (□ 104), NW Man., on Sask. border, 12 mi. SE of Flin Flon; 20 mi. long, 20 mi. wide.

Atharabanki River, E Pakistan: see PUSUR RIVER.

Athboy (ăth-boi′), Gaelic *Baile Átha Buidhe,* town (pop. 462), W Co. Meath, Ireland, 7 mi. NW of Trim; market in agr. area (cattle, horses; potatoes). Just E is Hill of Ward (307 ft. high), site of anc. Palace of Tlachtga, once scene of important annual fair.

Athea, Gaelic *Baile Átha an tSléibhe,* town (pop. 242), W Co. Limerick, Ireland, on Galey R. and 9 mi. E of Listowel; agr. market (potatoes, grain; dairying).

Athelney, Isle of (ă′thŭlnē), small marshy tract, central Somerset, England, near junction of the Tone and the Parrett, 5 mi. SSE of Bridgwater. Alfred the Great hid here in 878 after his defeat by Danes, and in 888 founded a Benedictine abbey here. Among relics found is "Alfred jewel," now in Ashmolean Mus. at Oxford.

Athelstan (ă′thŭlstăn), town (pop. 115), Taylor co., SW Iowa, at Mo. line, on Little Platte R. and 11 mi. SE of Bedford, in agr. area.

Athelstaneford (ă′thŭlstŭnfŏrd″), agr. village and parish (pop. 945), N central East Lothian, Scotland, 3 mi. NNE of Haddington. Robert Blair and John Home were parish ministers here.

Athena (úthē′nú), city (pop. 750), Umatilla co., NE Oregon, 18 mi. NE of Pendleton; pea canning.

Athenry (ăth-ŭnrī′), Gaelic *Baile Átha an Ríogh,* town (pop. 1,153), central Co. Galway, Ireland, 13 mi. E of Galway; agr. market (sheep; potatoes, beets); jute milling. There are remains of 13th-cent. walls, castle, and Dominican abbey, and of 15th-cent. Franciscan Friary.

Athens (ă′thĭnz), village (pop. 722), SE Ont., 14 mi. W of Brockville; dairying, lumbering; resort.

Athens, Gr. *Athenai* or *Athinai* (both: äthē′nē), Lat. *Athenae,* city (1940 pop. 481,225; 1951 pop. 559,250; Greater Athens: 1,124,109 in 1940; 1,368,142 in 1951), ⊙ Greece and Attica nome, 190 mi. SSE of Salonika; 37°58′N 23°43′E. The political, economic, and cultural center of Greece, Athens lies near the Saronic Gulf of the Aegean Sea, in the chief Attic plain (drained by Cephisus and Ilissus rivers) bet. the Aigaleos (W) and Hymettus (E) hills. The plain is broken by limestone ridges, of which the precipitous Acropolis (412 ft.) and the Lycabettus (909 ft.) dominate the city. Athens is connected by interurban railway with its port, Piraeus, by the main Greek trunk railroad with Salonika, and by narrow-gauge lines with Laurion and with Corinth and the Peloponnesus. One of the chief highway approaches is from Eleusis (W) via the anc. Sacred Way. The city's airports are at Dekeleia (Tatoi; military) and Ellenikon (civil). The city has a univ. (founded 1837), polytechnic institute, academy of sciences, natl. library, and natl. archaeological mus., and schools of classical studies. It is the see of Gr. metropolitan, who presides over the Holy Synod of the Greek Orthodox Church. With Piraeus, Athens forms the economic heart of Greece, accounting for 60–70% of the country's industrial output; it has (with its suburbs) mfg. of cotton, wool, and silk textiles; rugs, leather goods, machine tools, chemicals and munitions, wines and brandy, furniture, millinery, shoes and cigarettes. There is a considerable publishing industry. Water is supplied by the Marathon reservoir and electric power by coal-fed plants at Hagios Georgios Keratsiniou and Neon Phaleron. Other industrial and residential suburbs, included with Piraeus in the Athens metropolitan conurbation, are Kallithea, Nea Smyrna, Nea Ionia, and Palaion Phaleron. On the Saronic Gulf (S) is the "Attic Riviera" with the seaside resorts of Glyphada and Vouliagmene. Athens has a moderate, healthy climate with mean temperatures of 47°F (Jan.) and 80°F (July) and yearly precipitation of 20 in. While the anc. city lay in a ring around the Acropolis and to the W, the heart of modern Athens is built in rectilinear fashion mostly on the N and E sides of the Acropolis, covering the depression that extends to the Lycabettus (NE). Constitution (Syntagma) Square and Concordia (Omonia) Square are the main traffic hubs, connected by the parallel Stadion (Churchill) Street (shopping center) and University (Venizelos) Blvd. (academic quarter). The former Royal Palace (built 1834–38; since 1930s, Parliament), off Constitution Square, lies in the NW corner of Athens' largest park, consisting (N) of the royal garden and (S) of the Zappion garden with exhibition hall. Further S, across the Ilissus, is the Panathenaic stadium (begun 330 B.C.; restored 1896–1906), scene of the 1st modern Olympic games (1896). Adjoining (S) the park is the Olympieum, where 15 gigantic columns (56.5 ft. high) remain of one of the greatest anc. temples (begun 530 B.C.; completed under Hadrian (117–138 A.D.), whose arch (near by) marked the limit of a new quarter added by Hadrian to anc. Athens. Clustering at S foot of the Acropolis are the Dionysus theater (6th cent. B.C.; the oldest Gr. theater, where anc. Gr. dramas were 1st performed) and the Odeon (theater) of Herodes Atticus (A.D. 167). The Acropolis itself (accessible from the W) is crowned by the Parthenon, an edifice of white Pentelic marble, 228 by 101 ft., with an outer framework of 46 Doric columns, 34.5 ft. high. The building was erected (447–432 B.C.) under Pericles with ornamentation by Phidias or his school. Other edifices on the Acropolis are the Erechtheum (421–407 B.C.), the most notable Ionic structure, with the portico of the Caryatids, the temple of Athena Nike (Wingless Victory), the Propylaea (437–432 B.C.), a monumental winged gateway, and the Acropolis mus. (1878). W and N of the Acropolis are the Theseum or Hephaesteum (5th cent. B.C.), the best preserved temple of anc. Greece, the Dipylon, the main gate of anc. Athens, with near-by anc. cemetery, the Roman Agora (market), and the Roman octagonal Tower of the Winds (1st cent. B.C.). In the hills W of the Acropolis are the modern observatory (1842), the Pnyx, meeting-place of the Athenian ecclesia, and the Areopagus hill. To these monuments are drawn thousands of tourists and students yearly. The cultural legacy of anc. Athens is incalculable, and to Athens, which, more than any other Greek city state, created the golden period of anc. Greece, is owed much of the Greek heritage and Hellenistic culture that abounds in the writings of Western Europe. Until the 6th cent. B.C., however, there were few signs of what Athens would become. It was an old city, named in honor of its patron-goddess Athena (Minerva), and was traditionally ruled (until c.1000 B.C.) by Ionian kings who had gained suzerainty over all Attica after the legendary fusion (1300 B.C.) of the separate Attic states by Theseus. The succeeding control by aristocrats, marked by the Draconian code (621 B.C.), ended with Solon's democratic reforms (594 B.C.). These were retained under the tyranny of Pisistratus and his sons until 511 when Cleisthenes established the true democracy that continued during most of Athens' greatness. Commerce and the making of pottery for export had already begun to enrich the Athenians, and literature and art had started their growth. It remained, however, for the Persian Wars (500–449 B.C.) to place Athens at the head of the Greek nation. Its leaders won decisive victories over the Persians: Miltiades at Marathon (490 B.C.), and Themistocles at Salamis (480 B.C.). The powerful Athenian navy made possible Athenian hegemony (after 478–477 B.C.) in the Delian League until the successful completion of the Persian Wars. During this period, under Pericles (443–429 B.C.) Athens reached its apogee. These were the days of Socrates, Aeschylus, Sophocles, and Euripides. The Parthenon was erected; sculpture and painting flourished. Piraeus, the new port of Athens, was linked to the city by the famous Long Walls. At the peak of Athenian power, the long-standing rivalry with Sparta led to the Peloponnesian War (431–404 B.C.). Abandoned by its allies and unsuccessful in its campaigns, Athens was compelled to bow to Sparta, reduce her fleet, tear down the Long Walls, and accept the govt. of the Thirty Tyrants. However, as the result of an astonishingly rapid recovery, Athens regained (403) her democracy under Thrasybulus, rebuilt her fleet, and recreated 378–377 the 2d Delian League against Sparta, which lost power in the battle of Leuctra (371). The new Athenian power was short-lived. The coming of the Macedonian conqueror Philip II spelled Athens' political doom, as well as that of all Greece, consummated at the battle of Chaeronea (338 B.C.). Throughout this period, Athenian achievements in philosophy, drama, and art had continued, with Aristophanes, Plato, and Aristotle the leading figures, but this glory waned in 3d cent. B.C. as Athens' contributions were spread over the world in Hellenistic culture. Macedonian rule was followed (197 B.C.) by Roman control. Having chosen to support Mithridates VI of Pontus against Rome, Athens was sacked (86 B.C.) by Sulla. Yet, Athens had a period of Roman prosperity (notably in 2d cent. A.D.), from which many of today's Roman remains date. In 395 it was taken by the Visigoths and continued under Byzantine rule as a center of religious learning. Following the creation (1204) of the Latin Empire of Constantinople, Athens passed (1205) to French noblemen who took the title of dukes of Athens in 1258. Following a confused period when Catalans, Aragonese, Florentines, and Venetians rapidly succeeded each other in control through 14th and early 15th cents., Athens fell to the Turks in 1458. Under Ottoman rule, the city was briefly recaptured by Venice in 1466 and in 1687–88, when a bombardment destroyed the Parthenon. The city changed hands (1822–1830) several times during the Gr. war of independence and, as an insignificant little town, became ⊙ Greece in 1834. A period of intensive urban reconstruction followed in which the new N and E city quarters were built. After the First World War, the pop. was swelled by refugees from Turkey. Occupied (1941–44) by the Germans during Second World War, Athens escaped damage then (although it suffered great hardship) and in the civil troubles that followed its liberation, but experienced another great pop. boom in the influx of refugees from devastated rural areas.

Athens, county (□ 504; pop. 45,839), SE Ohio; ⊙ Athens. Bounded SE by Ohio R., here forming W. Va. line; intersected by Hocking R., small Shade R., and small Sunday and Federal creeks. Agr. (livestock, truck, fruit, grain); mfg. at Nelsonville and Athens; coal mines, limestone quarries. Formed 1805.

Athens. 1 City (pop. 6,309), ⊙ Limestone co., N Ala., 15 mi. N of Decatur, near Tenn. line, in cotton, corn, and dairying area; hosiery and lumber mills; bakery products, work clothing. Has fine ante-bellum homes. Seat of Athens Col. Settled 1814, inc. 1818. Sacked and occupied by Federal troops 1862, recaptured 1864 by Gen. N. B. Forrest. **2** Town (pop. 57), Howard co., SW Ark., 26 mi. NNW of Nashville. **3** City (pop. 28,180), ⊙ Clarke co., NE central Ga., c.60 mi. ENE of Atlanta and on Oconee R. Cotton market and mfg. center (textiles, tire fabric, fertilizer, cottonseed oil, metal and wood products, canned foods). Has notable ante-bellum houses. Founded 1801 as site for Univ. of Georgia; inc. as city 1872. **4** City (pop. 1,048), Menard co., central Ill., near Sangamon R., 10 mi. N of Springfield; bituminous-coal mines; ships grain; mfg. of radiator guards. Inc. 1892. **5** Village (pop. 487), Claiborne parish, N La., 45 mi. ENE of Shreveport; agr.; cotton gins. **6** Agr. town (pop. 725), Somerset co., central Maine, 10 mi. NNE of Skowhegan. **7** Village (pop. 768), Calhoun co., S Mich., 22 mi. SE of Kalamazoo, in orchard and farm area; mfg. of fruit baskets. **8** Village (pop. 1,545), Greene co., SE N.Y., on W bank of the Hudson and 27 mi. S of Albany, in limestone-quarrying area; summer resort. Mfg. (bricks, boats, cider). Settled 1686, inc. 1805. **9** City (pop. 11,660), ⊙ Athens co., SE Ohio, on Hocking R. and 35 mi. W of Marietta, in livestock and coal area; meat products, machinery, printed matter, tools. Seat of Ohio Univ. and a state hosp. for the insane. Surveyed 1795–96 and settled shortly thereafter; inc. as city, 1912. **10** Borough (pop. 4,430), Bradford co., NE Pa., on Susquehanna R., near mouth of Chemung R., just below Sayre; clothing; wood, metal, dairy products; agr. Indian village originally. Settled c.1778, laid out 1786, inc. 1831. **11** City (pop. 8,618), ⊙ McMinn co., SE Tenn., 50 mi. NE of Chattanooga; rail junction; trade center for timber, cotton, tobacco region; mfg. of woolens, furniture, hosiery, farm machinery, stoves, paper and wood products. Seat of Tenn. Wesleyan Col. (jr.; coeducational). Laid out 1821. **12** City (pop. 5,194), ⊙ Henderson co., E Texas, 34 mi. WSW of Tyler; shipping center of rich oil and agr. area (fruit, truck, cotton, poultry), mfg. (brick, tile, pottery, canned goods, cottonseed oil, clothing). Annual Old Fiddlers Contest. Founded c.1850, inc. 1901. **13** (also ā'–) Town (pop. 139), Windham co., SE Vt., 19 mi. N of Brattleboro. **14** Town (pop. 935), Mercer co., S W.Va., 6 mi. NE of Princeton, in coal-mining and agr. area. Concord Col. (state teachers col.) here. **15** Village (pop. 823), Marathon co., central Wis., 22 mi. WNW of Wausau, in dairying, lumbering, and farming area; makes cheese, wood products, agr. implements, canned goods.

Atherley, village (pop. estimate 250), S Ont., bet. L. Simcoe (S) and Couchiching L. (N), 3 mi. E of Orillia; resort; dairying, mixed farming.

Atherstone (ă'thûr–), town and parish (pop. 6,245), N Warwick, England, on Anker R. and 5 mi. NW of Nuneaton; agr. market; granite quarrying. In parish (W) is agr. village of Merevale (mĕ'rĭvŭl), site of 12th-cent. Merevale Abbey.

Atherton (ă'thûrtŭn), town (pop. 1,989), NE Queensland, Australia, 30 mi. SW of Cairns, on Atherton Tableland; dairying, agr. (corn, sugar cane, rice) center.

Atherton, urban district (1931 pop. 19,989; 1951 census 20,591), S Lancashire, England, 11 mi. WNW of Manchester; cotton milling, coal mining; mfg. of electrical equipment, machinery.

Atherton, residential town (pop. 3,630), San Mateo co., W Calif., c.25 mi. SSE of San Francisco, bet. Redwood City (NW) and Menlo Park. Inc. 1923.

Atherton Plateau, Australia: see ATHERTON TABLELAND.

Atherton Tableland, tropical plateau (□ 12,000), NE Queensland, Australia; extends c.230 mi. SSE from Laura to Ingham, parallel with NE coast; alt. 2,000 ft. Timber, dairy products; some sugar cane and rice. Chief towns: Atherton, Herberton. Sometimes called Atherton Plateau.

Athesis, Italy: see ADIGE RIVER.

Athgarh (ŭt'gŭr), village, Cuttack dist., E Orissa, India, near Mahanadi R., 15 mi. WNW of Cuttack. Was ⊙ former princely state of Athgarh (□ 163; pop. 55,498) in Orissa States, along left bank of river; inc. 1949 into Cuttack dist.

Athiémé (ätyĕ'mā), town (pop. 7,700), S Dahomey, Fr. West Africa, rail terminus on Togoland border, 65 mi. W of Porto-Novo; agr. center (palm kernels, palm oil, cacao, corn, castor beans, copra, cotton, coffee, shea nuts). Meteorological station; R.C. and Protestant missions.

Athienou (äthēĕ'nōō), town (pop. 3,169), Larnaca dist., E central Cyprus, 13 mi. SE of Nicosia; wheat, almonds, carobs, olive oil; sheep, cattle.

Athi River (ä'tē), village, Central Prov., S central Kenya, on Athi R., on railroad, and 15 mi. SSE of Nairobi; 1°38'S 37°12'E. Meat-packing, mfg. of beef products, dairying; coffee, wheat, corn.

Athi River, S Kenya, rises in Kikuyu Escarpment S of Nairobi, flows c.350 mi. SE, past Athi River village, to Indian Ocean N of Malindi. Also called Galana R. in lower reaches.

Athis (ätēs'), village (pop. 528), Orne dept., NW France, 18 mi. E of Vire; cheese mfg.

Athis-Mons (ätēs'-mõs'), town (pop. 8,414), Seine-et-Oise dept., N central France, on left bank of the Seine and 10 mi. S of Paris; large metalworks.

Athleague (ăth-lēg'), Gaelic *Átha Liag*, town (pop. 177), SW Co. Roscommon, Ireland, on Suck R. and 6 mi. SW of Roscommon; agr. market (cattle, sheep; potatoes).

Athlit, Israel: see ATLIT.

Athlone (ăthlōn'), Gaelic *Áth Luain*, urban district (pop. 8,379), SW Co. Westmeath, Ireland, on the Shannon (bridged) and 70 mi. W of Dublin; tweed and cotton milling, canvas mfg. Site of largest Irish radio transmitter, and of extensive barracks. Has remains of town walls (1576) and (on E bank of the Shannon) of 13th-cent. Franciscan abbey. Here John de Grey built a castle (c.1210) which became of strategic importance and was besieged unsuccessfully (1641) by the Connaughtmen and, later, by forces of William III. It was taken 1691 by General de Ginkell, later earl of Athlone.

Athmallik (ŭtmŭ'lĭk), village, Dhenkanal dist., central Orissa, India, on Mahanadi R. and 70 mi. W of Dhenkanal; local market for timber, rice, oilseeds. Formerly called Kaintira. Was ⊙ former princely state of Athmallik (□ 723; pop. 72,765) in Orissa States, on left bank of Mahanadi R.; inc. 1949 into newly-created Dhenkanal dist.

Athmera, Djebel el, Tunisia: see LONG STOP HILL.

Athna (äth'nä), village (pop. 1,986), Famagusta dist., E Cyprus, 25 mi. ESE of Nicosia; wheat, barley, potatoes; sheep, goats.

Athni (ŭt'nē), town (pop., including suburban area, 17,954), Belgaum dist., S Bombay, India, 70 mi. NE of Belgaum; road junction; trade center for cotton, peanuts, jaggery, wheat, millet; cotton ginning, handicraft blanket making; noted for its wheelwrights. Sometimes spelled Athani.

Athok (ŭthŏk'), village, Bassein dist., Lower Burma, in Irrawaddy delta, on railroad and 35 mi. NE of Bassein.

Athol. 1 (ă'thŏl) Village (pop. 226), Kootenai co., N Idaho, 20 mi. N of Coeur d'Alene. **2** (ă'thŏl) City (pop. 203), Smith co., N Kansas, 7 mi. W of Smith Center, in corn belt; grain, livestock. **3** (ă'-thŏl, ă'thŭl) Town (pop. 11,554), including Athol village (pop. 9,708), Worcester co., N Mass., on Millers R. and 22 mi. W of Fitchburg; machinery, castings, precision tools, furniture, artificial leather. Settled 1735, inc. 1762. **4** (ă'thôl") Summer-resort village, Warren co., E N.Y., in the Adirondacks, near the Hudson, 16 mi. NW of Glens Falls.

Athole, Scotland: see ATHOLL.

Atholl or **Athole** (both: ă'thŭl), mountainous district (□ 450) of Grampian Mts., N Perthshire, Scotland. Castle at Blair Atholl is seat of dukes of Atholl. Extensive deer forest (□ c.150).

Athos, Cape, Greece: see AKRATHOS.

Athos, Mount (ă'thŏs, ā'thŏs), **Hagion Oros**, or **Ayion Oros** (both: ä'yēôn ô'rôs), highest point (6,670 ft.) on Chalcidice peninsula, Greek Macedonia, at SE end of AKTE prong, in autonomous monastic dist. of MOUNT ATHOS.

Athus (ätüs'), town (pop. 5,641), Luxembourg prov., SE Belgium, 8 mi. S of Arlon, near borders of France and grand duchy of Luxembourg; rail junction; blast furnaces, foundries.

Athy (ŭthī'), Gaelic *Baile Átha h-Í*, urban district (pop. 3,639), SW Co. Kildare, Ireland, on Barrow R., on branch of Grand Canal, and 11 mi. NNW of Carlow, 40 mi. SW of Dublin; agr. market (cattle, horses; potatoes), with iron foundries. Woodstock Castle (1190) was besieged (1649) by Confederates under General Preston. White Castle, guarding river crossing, was built c.1500.

Ati (ätē'), town, ⊙ Batha region, central Chad territory, Fr. Equatorial Africa, on Batha R. and 230 mi. ENE of Fort-Lamy; native trade center and military outpost on road to Darfur (Anglo-Egyptian Sudan); stud farm.

Atibaia (ätēbī'ŭ), city (pop. 4,151), SE São Paulo, Brazil, on railroad and 30 mi. N of São Paulo; meat packing, distilling, textile mfg.

Atico (ä'tēkō), town (pop. 373), Arequipa dept., S Peru, minor Pacific port at mouth of Atico R., on Pan American Highway and 33 mi. SSW of Caravelí; cotton, fruit, grain; fishing. Airfield.

Atienza (ätyĕn'thä), anc. *Titia* or *Tythia*, town (pop. 1,408), Guadalajara prov., central Spain, in New Castile, near Soria prov. border, 45 mi. SW of Soria, in stock-raising and lumbering region; also fruit, truck, tubers, cereals. Flour milling; mfg. of dies, arms, plaster. Has notable churches of Trinidad and San Juan. In the outskirts are remains of fortifications and castle. A Roman colony, it was taken (718) by Moors, conquered (877) by Alfonso III.

Atifi or **'Atifi** (ätēfē'), petty sheikdom of SUBEIHI tribal area, Western Aden Protectorate; ⊙ Huwairib. Protectorate treaty concluded 1889.

Atig (ŭtyēk'), town (1926 pop. 3,392), SW Sverdlovsk oblast, Russian SFSR, in the central Urals, on small lake, on railroad and 4 mi. ENE of Nizhniye Sergi; metalworking. Until 1929, Atigski Zavod.

Atikameg Lake (ătĭ'kŭmĕg) (□ 90), NW Man., near Sask. border, 10 mi. NNE of The Pas; 19 mi. long, 3 mi. wide. Drains into Saskatchewan R.

Atikokan (ătĭkō'kŭn), village (pop. estimate 1,000), W Ont., on Atikokan R., near its mouth on Seine R., and 120 mi. WNW of Fort William; alt. 1,284 ft.; center of Steep Rock Lake iron-mining region.

Atil (ätēl'), town (pop. 392), Sonora, NW Mexico, on affluent of Magdalena R. (irrigation) and 50 mi. SW of Nogales; wheat, corn, beans, cotton.

Atima (ätē'mä), town (pop. 1,228), Santa Bárbara dept., W Honduras, 17 mi. W of Santa Bárbara, on N slope of Sierra de Atima; tobacco, sugar cane, corn.

Atima, Sierra de (syĕ'rä dā), range in Santa Bárbara–Lempira depts., W Honduras, S of Atima; extends c.15 mi. E-W, forming S watershed of Jicatuyo R.; rises to over 3,500 ft.

Atimonan (ätēmō'nän), town (1939 pop. 6,477; 1948 municipality pop. 21,474), Quezon prov., S Luzon, Philippines, on Lopez Bay, 40 mi. ESE of San Pablo; agr. center (coconuts, rice); fishing.

Atina (ätē'nä), town (pop. 1,843), Frosinone prov., Latium, S central Italy, 23 mi. E of Frosinone; soap mfg.

Atina, Turkey: see PAZAR.

Atiquipa (ätēkē'pä), town (pop. 115), Arequipa dept., S Peru, near Pacific coast, on Pan-American Highway and 7 mi. W of Chala, in irrigation area (cotton, grain, fruit).

Atiquizaya (ätēkēsī'ä), city (pop. 6,497), Ahuachapán dept., W Salvador, on railroad and 7 mi. NE of Ahuachapán; pottery making, basket weaving; coffee, grain.

Atitalaquia (ätētälä'kyä), town (pop. 378), Hidalgo, central Mexico, 32 mi. W of Pachuca; corn, vegetables, fruit.

Atitlán or **Santiago Atitlán** (säntyä'gō ätētlän'), town (1950 pop. 7,209), Sololá dept., SW central Guatemala, on S shore of L. Atitlán, 10 mi. SSW of Sololá; alt. 4,675 ft. Market; coffee, grain; beekeeping. Before Sp. conquest, principal town of Zutugil Indians. Sometimes called Santiago.

Atitlán, inactive volcano (11,565 ft.), Sololá dept., SW central Guatemala, near L. Atitlán, 5 mi. SSW of San Lucas. Was active 1524–1843.

Atitlán, Lake (□ 53), Sololá dept., SW central Guatemala, in central highlands, 40 mi. W of Guatemala; 16 mi. long, 11.5 mi. wide, c.1,050 ft. deep; alt. c.4,500 ft. One of most picturesque lakes of Central America; thought to lie in anc. valley dammed by volcanic ash. On its shores are inactive volcanoes Atitlán and Tolimán (S), San Pedro and Santa Clara (SW). Main towns: Panajachel, with its tourist resorts of Tzunjuyú and Monterrey (N shore); Atitlán and San Lucas (S shore). Predominantly Indian pop. engages in fishing (small fish, crabs) and in cotton and woolen weaving.

Atiu (ätēōō'), coral island (6,950 acres; pop. 1,114), COOK ISLANDS, S Pacific, c.115 mi. NE of Rarotonga; 20°2'S 158°7'W; rises to 394 ft.; exports fruits, copra.

Atizapán (ätēsäpän'). **1** Officially Atizapán de Zaragoza, town (pop. 1,437), Mexico state, central Mexico, on railroad and 12 mi. NW of Mexico city; cereals, livestock. **2** or **Santa Cruz Atizapán** (sän'tä krōōs'), town (pop. 1,454), Mexico state, central Mexico, 10 mi. SE of Toluca; cereals, livestock.

Atjeh, region Indonesia: see ACHIN.

Atjeh River, Indonesia: see ACHIN RIVER.

Atka (ăt'kŭ), village (pop. 107), SW Alaska, on Atka Isl., Aleutian Isls.; 52°12'N 174°12'W. Has Russian Orthodox church and Federal school for natives. Fox farming and basket weaving; supply point. Sometimes called Nazan.

Atka (ät'kŭ), village, N Khabarovsk Territory, Russian SFSR, 95 mi. N of Magadan, on Magadan-Kolyma highway; auto-repair plant, brickworks.

Atka Island (65 mi. long, 2–20 mi. wide), Andreanof Isls., Aleutian Isls., SW Alaska, 50 mi. ENE of Adak; 52°7'N 174°30'W; rises to 4,852 ft. on Korovin Volcano (NE). Atka village (E). Fox farming; basket weaving. Air base established during Second World War, later expanded.

Atkarsk (ŭtkärsk'), city (1926 pop. 19,348), W central Saratov oblast, Russian SFSR, near Medveditsa R., 50 mi. NW of Saratov; rail junction; agr. center (dairying, flour milling, sunflower-oil extraction); metalworking. Chartered 1780.

Atkins. 1 Town (pop. 1,291), Pope co., N central Ark., 11 mi. E of Russellville, near Arkansas R., in diversified farm area, vegetable canning, lumber milling. Settled 1840, inc. 1878. **2** Town (pop. 387), Benton co., E central Iowa, 10 mi. W of Cedar Rapids; feed milling.

Atkinson, Br. Guiana: see HYDE PARK.

Atkinson, county (□ 318; pop. 7,362), S Ga.; ⊙ Pearson. Bounded W by Alapaha R.; drained by Satilla R. Coastal plain agr. (cotton, corn, peanuts, tobacco, livestock) and forestry (lumber, naval stores) area. Formed 1917.

Atkinson. 1 Village (pop. 825), Henry co., NW Ill., 27 mi. ESE of Moline, in agr. and bituminous-coal-mining area. **2** Town (pop. 400), Piscataquis co., central Maine, on Piscataquis R. and 8 mi. ESE of Dover-Foxcroft. **3** City (pop. 1,372), Holt co., N Nebr., 18 mi. WNW of O'Neill and on Elkhorn R.; grain, dairy produce. Settled 1876, inc. 1884. **4** Town (pop. 492), Rockingham co., SE N.H., at Mass. line, 19 mi. SE of Manchester. **5** Town (pop. 294), Pender co., SE N.C., 13 mi. W of Burgaw; sawmilling.

Atkot (ŭt'kōt), village, central Saurashtra, India, 30 mi. SE of Rajkot; cotton ginning. Sometimes spelled Adkot.

Atlacomulco (ätläkōmōōl'kō). **1** Town (pop. 1,779), Mexico state, central Mexico, 22 mi. ESE of El Oro; grain, fruit, livestock. **2** Town, Morelos, Mexico: see CUERNAVACA.

Atlahuilco (ätläwēl'kō), town (pop. 361), Veracruz, E Mexico, 10 mi. S of Orizaba; coffee.

Atlamajalcingo (ätlämähälsēng'gō), officially Atlamajalcingo del Monte, town (pop. 235), Guerrero, SW Mexico, in Sierra Madre del Sur, 20 mi. SSW of Tlapa.

Atlangatepec (ätläng-gätāpĕk'), town (pop. 733), Tlaxcala, central Mexico, 15 mi. NNE of Tlaxcala; maguey.

Atlanta (ŭtlăn'tŭ, ăt–). **1** City (pop. 331,314), ⊙ Ga. and Fulton co., in Fulton and De Kalb counties, NW central Ga., 135 mi. E of Birmingham, Ala., near Chattahoochee R.; 33°45'N 84°25'W; alt. 1,050. Largest city in state; chief rail center of the South, with large railroad shops, and one of its principal distributing, industrial, and cultural centers. Mfg. of textiles, clothing, mattresses, furniture, pencils, fertilizer, paint, cottonseed oil, asphalt products, foundry products, machinery, electrical goods, paper, shoes, pharmaceuticals; printing and publishing, meat packing, and auto assembling are important. A leading U.S. mule market. Seat of: Sixth District Federal Reserve Bank, federal penitentiary (1899), U.S. veterans' hosp., a naval air station, and near-by Fort McPherson (U.S. Army post). City is also a port of entry. Points of interest include: the capitol (1889), housing the state library; city hall (1929); Cyclorama Bldg. containing the painting "Cyclorama of the Battle of Atlanta"; the state archives bldg., the large stockyards and state farmers' market; co-cathedral of Christ the King (R.C.); and High Mus. of Art. Educational institutions: Atlanta division of Univ. of Ga., a part of Emory Univ., Ga. Inst. of Technology, Oglethorpe Univ. (8 mi. NNE), Morris Brown Col. (Negro; 1885), Gammon Theological Seminary, John Marshall Law School, Southern Col. of Pharmacy, Woodrow Wilson Col. of Law, Atlanta Law School, and the Atlanta Univ. System (Negro; organized 1929) including Atlanta Univ., Atlanta Univ. School of Social Work, Clark Col., Morehouse Col., and Spelman Col. First settled in 1833; founded 1837 as Terminus, the end of the railroad line; inc. 1843 as Marthasville; named Atlanta (1845); inc. as city 1847. In the Civil War, Atlanta was an important Confederate center for communications and supplies; it fell to Sherman on Sept. 2, 1864. Most of the city was burned on Nov. 15, before Sherman began his march to the sea. Strategic point in his route is marked by Atlanta Campaign Natl. Historic Site (21 acres; established 1944), 45 mi. NW of city. Development as a rail, commercial, and industrial center was rapid, especially after the Reconstruction. A number of conventions and expositions in the 19th and 20th cent. drew attention to Atlanta's strategic distributory position. It has been capital since 1868 (chosen permanently by popular vote 1877). **2** City (pop. 1,331), Logan co., central Ill., 18 mi. SW of Bloomington, in agr. and bituminous-coal-mining area; dairy products. Founded 1854 as Xenia; inc. 1869. **3** Town (pop. 613), Hamilton co., central Ind., near Cicero Creek, 32 mi. N of Indianapolis, in agr. area. **4** City (pop. 309), Cowley co., SE Kansas, 33 mi. SE of Wichita, in cattle and grain area. **5** Village, ⊙ Montmorency co., N Mich., on branch of Thunder Bay R. and 35 mi. W of Alpena, in hunting and fishing region. **6** City (pop. 438), Macon co., N central Mo., 11 mi. N of Macon; grain, livestock. **7** Village (pop. 147), Phelps co., S Nebr., 5 mi. SW of Holdrege. **8** City (pop. 3,782), Cass co., NE Texas, c.23 mi. SSW of Texarkana, near meeting of La., Ark., Texas boundaries; trade, processing center in truck-farming, lumbering area; lumber milling, brick mfg., vegetable canning. Rodessa oil field (in La.) is SE.

Atlantic, county (□ 575; pop. 132,399), SE N.J., on the coast; ⊙ Mays Landing. Many coast resorts (notably ATLANTIC CITY) along its isl.-dotted shore. Farming (truck, dairy products, grain, fruit, poultry); mfg. (textiles, glassware, clothing, furniture, bricks, boats, concrete blocks, food products); fishing. Includes part of pine barrens region (timber, cranberries, huckleberries). Drained by Great Egg Harbor and Mullica rivers. Formed 1837.

Atlantic. 1 City (pop. 6,480), ⊙ Cass co., SW Iowa, on East Nishnabotna R. (hydroelectric plant) and 45 mi. ENE of Council Bluffs; trade and processing center; poultry-packing plants, corn and pumpkin canneries; mfg. of feed, beverages, popcorn, wood and sheet-metal products, saws. Inc. 1869. **2** or **Atlantic Mine,** village (1940 pop. 812), Houghton co., NW Upper Peninsula, Mich., 4 mi. SW of Houghton, in copper-mining area. **3** Town (pop. 844), Carteret co., E N.C., 25 mi. ENE of Morehead City; fishing, net mfg.

Atlantic Beach. 1 Resort town (pop. 1,604), Duval co., NE Fla., on the Atlantic, adjacent to Neptune Beach and 15 mi. E of Jacksonville. **2** Resort village (1940 pop. 545), Nassau co., SE N.Y., on barrier beach off S shore of Long Isl., across Rockaway Channel (bridged) from Far Rockaway. Coast guard station. **3** Resort town (pop. 49), Carteret co., E N.C., on Bogue Isl. in Bogue Sound (bridged), S of Morehead City. Just E is Fort Macon State Park, with fort built c.1826–35, restored 1936.

Atlantic City. 1 City (pop. 61,657), Atlantic co., SE N.J., 60 mi. SE of Philadelphia, 100 mi. SSW of New York, on 10-mi. sandbar called ABSECON BEACH. Popular resort and convention city, known for its hotel- and shop-lined boardwalk (7 mi. long, 40–60 ft. wide), amusement piers, municipal auditorium (main hall seats 40,000), bathing and yachting facilities. Diverse mfg. (confections, glassware, paint, hosiery, furniture, boats); dairy, poultry, and fruit products; distilleries. Naval air station. Ships seafood. Fishing village until coming of railroad (1854). First boardwalk built 1870. Inc. 1854. **2** Village, Fremont co., W central Wyo., in foothills of Wind River Range, 24 mi. S of Lander; alt. 7,655 ft. Gold mining; busy mining point in 1870.

Atlantic Highlands, resort borough (pop. 3,083), Monmouth co., NE N.J., on Sandy Hook Bay, 8 mi. NW of Long Branch; residential; truck farming. NAVESINK HIGHLANDS (just E) are often called Atlantic Highlands. Settled before 1675, inc. 1887.

Atlantic Mine, Mich.: see ATLANTIC.

Atlántico (ätlän'tēkō), department (□ 1,340; 1938 pop. 268,409; 1950 estimate 406,530), N Colombia; ⊙ BARRANQUILLA. Located on Caribbean Sea, bounded by upper Magdalena R. (E) and Canal del Dique (S). Tropical, humid region, consisting largely of thickly forested lowlands with many lagoons and rivulets. Densely populated. Main crops are cotton and sugar cane; also corn, beans, yucca, bananas, rice, cacao, timber; cattle. Some coal, gold, petroleum (Tubará), and gypsum deposits. Barranquilla, on the Magdalena, is an important Caribbean port and industrial center (mainly textile milling).

Atlantic Ocean [Latin,=of Atlas; probably as being beyond Atlas Mts.], second-largest ocean (□ 31,-830,000; with adjoining seas, including Arctic Ocean, □ 41,000,000). It extends from the Arctic to the Antarctic regions bet. the Americas (W) and Europe and Africa (E), and is divided by the equator into the North Atlantic Ocean (□ 14,000,000) and the South Atlantic Ocean (□ 18,000,000). Principal subsidiary seas of the Atlantic, all in the N part, are the Gulf of Mexico and Caribbean Sea in the Americas, the Arctic Ocean, the North and Baltic seas in Europe, and the Mediterranean Sea bet. Europe and Africa. The Atlantic is connected with the Pacific by the Panama Canal and, S of Cape Horn, by Drake Passage; and with the Indian Ocean by the Suez Canal and, S of Cape of Good Hope, across 20°E. Greatest depth recorded is the Milwaukee Depth (30,246 ft.) in the North Atlantic off N coast of Puerto Rico; mean depth of the Atlantic Ocean is 12,900 ft. Salinity of the tropical Atlantic Ocean is 37 per mill, the highest of the world's oceans. The general pattern of Atlantic currents is that of a clockwise movement (North Equatorial, Gulf Stream, Canaries currents) in North Atlantic, and of a counterclockwise flow (South Equatorial, Brazil, Benguela currents) in South Atlantic. The Labrador Current of Arctic origin, with its floating icebergs, is a constant menace to the shipping routes of the North Atlantic. A notable feature of Atlantic submarine topography is the mid-Atlantic ridge extending parallel to the continental margins and rising c.6,000 ft. above the ocean floor. The ridge appears as the isls. of the Azores, St. Paul Rocks, Ascension, St. Helena, and Tristan da Cunha. Other isl. groups are the Cape Verde Isls., Canaries, Madeira, and isls. of the Gulf of Guinea, off Africa; the British Isles and Iceland, in Europe; and Newfoundland, the West Indies, Bermuda, Falkland Isls., South Georgia, South Orkney Isls., off the Americas. The shortest distance across the Atlantic is 1,850 mi. bet. Dakar, Africa, and the bulge of Brazil. Commerce bet. the Mediterranean Sea and the NE Atlantic was initiated by the Carthaginians. From c.7th cent. A.D., Scandinavians sailed the Atlantic; they probably reached North America c.1000. Trade routes along the coast of Africa were opened by the Portuguese in 15th cent. Following the voyages of Columbus to the Western Hemisphere, the North Atlantic rapidly acquired the world's most active shipping lanes, linking Europe and North America. The 1st crossing by air was made in 1919, and regularly scheduled air routes were opened in 1939.

Atlantic Peak, Wyo.: see WIND RIVER RANGE.

Atlántida (ätlän'tēdä), department (□ 1,914; 1950 pop. 70,646), N Honduras, on Caribbean Sea; ⊙ La Ceiba. On coast E of Ulúa R.; drained by Leán R.; rises from litoral lowlands (N) to Sierra de Nombre de Dios (S) on Yoro dept. border. Agr. (rice, coconuts, abaca, citronella, plantains, sugar cane, corn, beans, fruit). Mfg. at La Ceiba. Served by network of plantation railroads. Major centers and ports: La Ceiba, Tela. Formed 1902.

Atlántida, town (pop. 5,000), Canelones dept., S Uruguay, beach resort on the Río de la Plata, and 25 mi. ENE of Montevideo.

Atlapexco (ätläpĕ'skō), agr. town (pop. 421), Hidalgo, central Mexico, 9 mi. SSE of Huejutla.

Atlapulco or **San Gregorio Atlapulco** (sän grägōr'yō ätläpōōl'kō), town (pop. 4,102), Federal Dist., central Mexico, just E of Xochimilco, 13 mi. S of Mexico city; cereals, fruit, flowers, livestock.

Atlas, village (pop. 3,090), Northumberland co., E central Pa.

Atlasburg, village (pop. 1,885, with adjacent Slovan), Washington co., SW Pa., 20 mi. WSW of Pittsburgh.

Atlas Mountains, folded mountain system of NW and N Africa, extending c.1,500 mi. WSW-ENE across Morocco, N Algeria (where it is widest, c.250 mi.), and Tunisia, roughly parallel to the Mediterranean coast, from the Atlantic coast of SW Morocco to the Cape Bon peninsula of NE Tunisia. Geologically contemporary with Europe's great Alpine uplifts, the Atlas may be linked with Spain's Cordillera Penibética via the RIF mts. and is manifested in the Atlantic by the Canary Isls. A massive, corrugated mtn. system composed of a maze of lofty ranges, high plateaus, and broken block mts., culminating in the Djebel Toubkal (13,665 ft.) of Morocco, the Atlas Mts. are a topographic and climatic barrier bet. the Sahara and the Mediterranean. In Morocco, facing the Atlantic, are the highest and most continuous ranges: the High or Great Atlas (Fr. *Grand Atlas*), which extends 400 mi. SW-NE from Cape Guir toward the Algerian border; some of the peaks are snow-capped, and here is the clearest evidence of past glaciation. NE is the shorter Middle Atlas (Fr. *Moyen Atlas*) overlooking the Moroccan meseta toward the coast and extending NE to the Taza corridor; it rises to 10,794 ft. in the Djebel Bou Naceur. SW of the High Atlas, the Anti-Atlas reaches the Atlantic at the Ifni enclave; enclosing the SOUS lowland, it is linked to the High Atlas by the volcanic Djebel Siroua (10,840 ft.). In Algeria, there are 3 well-marked physiographic divisions: the coastal Tell Atlas (Fr. *Atlas tellien*) or Maritime Atlas, the Saharan Atlas (Fr. *Atlas saharien*) overlooking the Sahara, and, bet. these 2 chains, the High Plateaus. The Tell Atlas, a series of ranges grouped into 2 roughly parallel chains and separated by narrow valleys and basins, contains (W-E) the Tlemcen Mts., Tessala Mts., Saïda Mts., Ouarsenis Massif, Titeri range, Mitidja Atlas, the mts. of KABYLIA (including DJURDJURA range, rising to 7,572 ft. in the Lella Khedidja), the Biban range, Hodna Mts., Constantine Mts., and Medjerda Mts. Bet. these ranges there are several mtn.-fringed coastal lowlands (MITIDJA; Oran, Philippeville, Bône basins; lower Chéliff valley) which contain most of Algeria's cities and agr. land. Abundant orographic winter rainfall (up to 50 in. annually) supports intensive Mediterranean agr. (citrus, wine, olives). S of the Tell Atlas, the semi-arid High Plateaus (average alt. 3,000 ft.) hold several playa lakes (Chott ech Chergui, Chott el Gharbi, Chott el Hodna). Esparto grass and wool are chief products in W; wheat in more humid E. The Saharan Atlas, bet. the High Plateaus and the Sahara, consists of a discontinuous chain traceable from the Moroccan border to Tunisia; principal ranges (W-E) are Ksour Mts., Djebel Amour, Ouled-Naïl Mts., Zab Mts., AURÈS massif (rising to 7,641 ft. in the Djebel Chélia, highest peak in N Algeria), Nemencha Mts., and Tebessa Mts. In Tunisia, the Tell Atlas, along N coast, terminates near Bizerte. The Saharan Atlas S of the Medjerda valley is reduced to isolated block mts. (highest, Djebel Chambi, 5,066 ft.), terminating in NE Tunisia's Cape Bon peninsula. The well-watered coastal Atlas ranges are forested (oak trees, Aleppo pines, cedars, thuyas); cork is the chief forest product (especially in Kabylia). Several perennial streams drain these N ranges to the Atlantic and the Mediterranean; principal rivers are the Oum er Rbia, Sebou, Tensift, Sous, and Moulouya in Morocco; the Chéliff in Algeria; and the Medjerda in NE Algeria and N Tunisia. Intermittent streams flowing southward from the High Atlas and the Saharan Atlas lose themselves in the Sahara after watering a string of oases. The Atlas is a veritable mineral storehouse; iron is mined along Algeria-Tunisia border (especially at Djebel Ouenza), at Aït Amar in Fr. Morocco, and at Beni bu Ifrur in Sp. Morocco; manganese at Bou Arfa and in Ouarzazate area of Morocco; lead chiefly at Bou Beker, Morocco; molybdenum at Azegour, Morocco; cobalt at Bou Azzer, Morocco; coal at Djérada, Morocco; zinc, copper, antimony, and mercury in scattered deposits. Of Fr. North Africa's extensive phosphate deposits, only those in the Tebessa area (Algeria) are within the confines of the Atlas. The Moroccan Atlas ranges have 3 main passes (Tizi n'Talghemt, Tizi n'Test, Tizi n'Tichka) traversed by N-S roads. In Algeria N-S rail lines across the Atlas link Oran with Colomb-Béchar, Algiers with Djelfa, and Constantine with Biskra; there is also a good road net. The relatively inaccessible ranges have long been strongholds of the proudly independent and fierce Berber pop. Pacification of the Moroccan Atlas by Fr. forces was not completed until 1930s, while in Algeria the tribes of the Aurès massif resisted Fr. penetration for over 40 yrs. Scientific exploration of the Atlas was not undertaken until the 2d half of 19th cent.

Atlatlahuca (ätlätläōō'kä), town (pop. 1,880), Mexico state, central Mexico, 16 mi. SSE of Toluca; cereals, livestock.

Atlatlahucan (–kän), town (pop. 1,749), Morelos, central Mexico, 22 mi. E of Cuernavaca; sugar, fruit, vegetables, livestock.

Atlautla (ätlout'lä), officially San Miguel Atlautla, town (pop. 2,712), Mexico state, central Mexico, at W foot of Popocatepetl, on railroad and 38 mi. SE of Mexico city; cereals, fruit, stock.

Atlazalalpan (ätläsäläl'pän), officially San Pablo Atlazalalpan, town (pop. 1,837), Mexico state, central Mexico, 21 mi. SE of Mexico city; cereals, fruit, maguey, livestock.

Atlequizayan (ätlākēsī'än), town (pop. 1,023), Puebla, central Mexico, in SE foothills of Sierra Madre Oriental, 28 mi. ESE of Huauchinango; corn, sugar, fruit.

Atlin (ăt'lĭn), village (pop. estimate 500), NW B.C., near Alaska border, on Atlin L., 90 mi. NNE of Juneau; lumbering; in mining (gold, silver, lead, zinc, coal) region. Resort.

Atlin Lake (□ 308), NW B.C. and S Yukon, near Alaska border, 60 mi. NNE of Juneau; 66 mi. long, 2–6 mi. wide. On E shore is Atlin village, in gold-mining region. Drains N into Lewes R.

Atlit or **Athlit** (both: ätlēt'), settlement (pop. 500), NW Israel, on Mediterranean, on railroad, and 8 mi. SSW of Haifa; salt pans, stone quarries; seaside resort. Large immigrants' camp was British detention camp until May, 1948. Modern village founded 1903. Just NW are remains of Crusaders' castle (1217) of Athlit (*Chastiau Pelerin* or *Castrum Peregrinorum*), stronghold of Knights Templars until abandoned (1291) after fall of Acre; built on site of Phoenician town of *Adarus* which in Roman times became one of last outposts (A.D. c.130) of Jewish independence in Palestine. Iron Age pottery excavated here.

Atlixco (ätlē'skō), city (pop. 17,034), Puebla, central Mexico, on central plateau, 18 mi. SW of Puebla; alt. 6,000 ft. Rail junction; processing and agr. center famous for grain (corn, wheat) and fruit (oranges, limes, mangoes); sugar cane and coffee. Tanneries, flour mills; mfg. of cotton yarn and fabrics, silverware, pharmaceuticals. Airfield.

Atlixtac (ätlēstäk'), town (pop. 476), Guerrero, SW Mexico, in Sierra Madre del Sur, 20 mi. E of Chilapa; alt. 5,451 ft.; cereals, livestock.

Atmakur (ŭt'mŭkōōr). **1** Town (pop. 9,609), Kurnool dist., N Madras, India, 36 mi. E of Kurnool; cotton ginning. Timber, bamboo, dyewood (red sandalwood), and fibers in Eastern Ghats (E). Noted Sivaite temple 23 mi. NE, at Srisailam (on Kistna R.); scene of large annual pilgrimage. **2** Village, Nellore dist., E Madras, India, 27 mi. NW of Nellore; rice, millet, cashew. Mica quarrying near.

Atmore, city (pop. 5,720), Escambia co., SW Ala., 40 mi. NE of Mobile, in agr. area (corn, cotton, strawberries); lumber milling, cotton ginning, bottling. Inc. 1907. State prison farm near by.

Atocha (ätō'chä), town (pop. c.3,300), Potosí dept., SW Bolivia, 50 mi. SE of Uyuni, on Villazon-Uyuni RR; alt. 11,926 ft. Ore-concentration plant and shipping point for Quechisla mines.

Atocha, town, Tungurahua prov., central Ecuador, N suburb of Ambato, in high Andean valley; fruit (apples, citrus, pears), sugar cane, cereals. In 1949 earthquake zone.

Atocongo (ätōkōng'gō), village (pop. 606), Lima dept., W central Peru, 13 mi. SE of Lima; cement.

Atoka (ūtō'kū), county (□ 992; pop. 14,269), SE Okla.; ⊙ Atoka. Drained by the Muddy Boggy and Clear Boggy creeks. Stock raising, agr. (cotton, corn, truck, grain, sorghums); lumber milling; stone quarrying; timber. Formed 1907.

Atoka. 1 City (pop. 2,653), ⊙ Atoka co., SE Okla., 31 mi. NNE of Durant, and on Muddy Boggy Creek, in agr. area (cotton, corn, oats); lumber and flour milling. Timber. Founded 1867. An agreement ending Choctaw and Chickasaw Indian tribal govt. was signed here in 1897. **2** Town (pop. 334), Tipton co., W Tenn., 25 mi. NNE of Memphis, in cotton-growing region.

Atoleiros, Portugal: see FRONTEIRA.

Atolinga (ätōlēng'gä), town (pop. 549), Zacatecas, N central Mexico, near Jalisco border, 8 mi. SW of Tlaltenango; grain, fruit, livestock. Airfield.

Atomic City, city (1951 pop. c.500), Bingham co., SE Idaho, c.20 mi. NW of Blackfoot. Grew after establishment (1949) of U.S. atomic-reactor testing station (just N); inc. 1950.

Atotonilco el Alto or **Atotonilco** (ätōtōnēl'kō ĕl äl'tō), city (pop. 9,249), Jalisco, central Mexico, on interior plateau, 55 mi. ESE of Guadalajara. Rail terminus; agr. center (grain, cotton, chick-peas, oranges, livestock); flour milling, tanning, vegetable-oil pressing, wine making.

Atotonilco el Bajo (ĕl bä'hō), town (pop. 1,610), Jalisco, W Mexico, on L. Atotonilco, 30 mi. SW of Guadalajara; oranges, chick-peas, livestock.

Atotonilco el Grande (ĕl grän'dä), town (pop. 2,614), Hidalgo, central Mexico, on central plateau, 12 mi. NNE of Pachuca; alt. 6,890 ft.; corn, beans, fruit, maguey, livestock. Thermal springs near by. MINERAL DEL CHICO, formerly called Atotonilco, is just S.

Atotonilco Tula (tōō'lä), town (pop. 584), Hidalgo, central Mexico, 33 mi. WSW of Pachuca; corn, fruit, vegetables.

Atotonilquillo (ätōtōnēlkē'yō), town (pop. 1,699), Jalisco, central Mexico, on Santiago R. and 26 mi. SE of Guadalajara, on railroad; grain, beans, vegetables, fruit.

Atouguia da Baleia (ätōgē'ū dū bŭlĕ'yū), town (pop. 1,190), Leiria dist., W central Portugal, 3 mi. SE of Peniche; wheat, corn, wine; pottery. Has 15th-cent. church (art treasures) and ruined castle.

Atoyac (ätoiäk'). **1** Officially Atoyac de Alvarez, city (pop. 2,147), Guerrero, SW Mexico, in Pacific lowland, 40 mi. NW of Acapulco; rice, sugar, fruit, livestock. **2** Town (pop. 4,999), Jalisco, W Mexico, on E shore of L. Sayula, on central plateau, 45 mi. SSW of Guadalajara; agr. center (alfalfa, grain, fruit, livestock). **3** Town (pop. 1,349), Veracruz, E Mexico, in Sierra Madre Oriental foothills, on railroad and 10 mi. E of Córdoba; coffee, sugar, fruit. Notable waterfalls near by.

Atoyac River. 1 In central Mexico, upper course (largely in Puebla) of the Río de las BALSAS. **2** In Oaxaca, S Mexico, rises on Mixtecapán plateau (Sierra Madre del Sur) NE of Oaxaca, flows c.200 mi. S, W, and SW, past Oaxaca, to the Pacific 19 mi. S of Jamiltepec. Called Río Verde in lower course.

Atoyatempan (ätoiätĕm'pän), town (pop. 2,068), Puebla, central Mexico, 25 mi. SE of Puebla; cereals, vegetables, stock.

Atpadi (ŭtpä'dē), village (pop. 7,626), Satara South dist., S central Bombay, India, 45 mi. NNE of Sangli; market center for millet, oilseeds, wheat, sugar cane.

Atraf-i-Balda (ŭträf'-ē-bŭl'dŭ), district (□ 2,626; pop. 612,493), central Hyderabad state, India, on Deccan Plateau; ⊙ Hyderabad. In hilly area (cattle raising), drained by Musi R. Sandy red soil; millet, rice, oilseeds (chiefly peanuts). Surrounds Hyderabad, its only important town; noted Golconda fort is just W of Hyderabad. Formerly the personal estate of the Nizam; nationalized by Indian govt. in 1949. Pop. 83% Hindu, 13% Moslem.

Atrai (ŭtrī'), village, Rajshahi dist., W East Bengal, E Pakistan, on Atrai R. and 29 mi. NE of Rajshahi; rice milling, jute pressing; rice, jute, oilseeds, wheat.

Atrai River, in West Bengal (India) and East Bengal (Pakistan), rises at foot of SE Nepal Himalayas, 6 mi. NNE of Siliguri; flows S, through rich agr. area (rice, jute, mustard, pulse, tobacco), past Balurghat and Atrai, and SE, through Chalan Bil, to Jamuna R. (main course of the Brahmaputra) 6 mi. SE of Bera; c.240 mi. long. In upper course, called Karatoya; in lower course, also called Baral. Main tributaries: another Karatoya (mouth 3 mi. NNW of Bera) and another Jamuna (mouth 11 mi. S of Naogaon).

Atrak River, Iran: see ATREK RIVER.

Atranos, Turkey: see ORHANELI.

Atra River (ĕ'trän"), Swedish *Ätran*, SW Sweden, rises E of Ulricehamn, flows 145 mi. generally SW, past Ulricehamn, Svenljunga, and Atran, to the Kattegat at Falkenberg. Logging route; salmon.

Atrato River (äträ'tō), Chocó dept., W Colombia, rises in Cordillera Occidental E of Quibdó, flows c.375 mi. N, past Quibdó, in meandering course, forming part of Antioquia border, and by a wide delta enters the Caribbean in Gulf of Urabá, the S part of Gulf of Darien. While its estuary is obstructed by sandbars, its upper course is navigable, and ships ascend it to Quibdó. Fed by incessant rains, its valley has lush forests yielding hardwood, tagua nuts, palms, kapok, balata gum, resins. Its head is Colombia's primary platinum-mining region. The river has been considered for construction of an interoceanic route.

Atrauli (ŭtrou'lē), town (pop. 16,323), Aligarh dist., W Uttar Pradesh, India, 16 mi. NE of Aligarh; wheat, barley, pearl millet, gram, cotton, sugar cane.

Atraulia (ŭtroul'yŭ), town (pop. 2,196), Azamgarh dist., E Uttar Pradesh, India, 23 mi. NNW of Azamgarh; rice, wheat, barley, sugar cane. Also spelled Atrauliya.

Atrek River or **Atrak River** (both: äträk', Rus. ätryĕk'), in NE Iran, rises in Turkmen-Khurasan mts. near Quchan, flows over 300 mi. W, past Quchan, Shirvan, and Moraveh Tappeh, to its confluence with Sumbar R. at Turkmen SSR (USSR) border, then follows border to Caspian Sea just S of Gasan-Kuli. Used for irrigation.

Atreucó, Argentina: see MACACHÍN.

Atri (ä'trē), town (pop. 3,837), Teramo prov., Abruzzi e Molise, S central Italy, 15 mi. ESE of Teramo; mfg. (flour, macaroni, terra cotta, licorice); market for wine, olive oil, cheese, livestock. Bishopric. Has cathedral (13th-14th cent.).

Atria, Italy: see ADRIA.

Atrio del Cavallo, Italy: see VESUVIUS.

Atripalda (ätrēpäl'dä), town (pop. 4,767), Avellino prov., Campania, S Italy, 2 mi. E of Avellino; tannery, cementworks, macaroni factories.

Atrisco (ătrĭ'skō), village (pop. 7,367, with near-by Five Points), Bernalillo co., central N.Mex., near Albuquerque.

Atropatene, Iran: see AZERBAIJAN.

Atru (ŭt'rōō), village, SE Rajasthan, India, 55 mi. ESE of Kotah; wheat, millet; distillery. Headworks of minor irrigation canal 2 mi. NNE, on Parbati R.

Atsabe (ätsä'bā), town, Portuguese Timor, in central Timor, 25 mi. SSW of Dili; coffee.

Atsugi (ä"tsōō'gē), town (pop. 10,782), Kanagawa prefecture, central Honshu, Japan, 8 mi. N of Hiratsuka; collection center (rice, raw silk). Large airfield; after Jap. surrender (1945) in Second World War, U.S. troops first landed here.

Atsukeshi, Japan: see AKKESHI.

Atsuma (ätsōō'mä), village (pop. 9,749), S Hokkaido, Japan, 16 mi. ENE of Tomakomai; oil wells; rice fields.

Atsumi (ätsōō'mē), town (pop. 11,427), Yamagata prefecture, N Honshu, Japan, on Sea of Japan, 15 mi. WSW of Tsuruoka; hot-springs resort. Sometimes spelled Atumi.

Atsumi Bay, Jap. *Atsumi-wan*, E arm of Ise Bay, central Honshu, Japan; bounded S by Atsumi Peninsula; merges NW with Chita Bay; 15 mi. E-W, 10 mi. N-S. Toyohashi on E shore.

Atsumi Peninsula, Jap. *Atsumi-hanto*, Aichi prefecture, central Honshu, Japan, bet. Atsumi Bay (N) and Philippine Sea (S), just W of L. Hamana; 20 mi. long, 5 mi. wide; hilly, fertile. Main centers: Tawara, Fukue. Sometimes spelled Atumi.

Atsuta, Japan: see NAGOYA.

Attafs, Les (lāzätäf'), village (pop. 779), Alger dept., N central Algeria, in irrigated Chéliff valley, on railroad and 20 mi. ENE of Orléansville; cereals. Hydroelectric plant.

Attaia, El-, Tunisia: see KERKENNAH.

Attala (ă'tùlù), county (□ 724; pop. 26,652), central Miss.; ⊙ Kosciusko. Bounded W by Big Black R.; intersected by Yockanookany R. and Lobutcha Creek. Agr. (corn, cotton, hay), dairying, stock raising, lumbering. Formed 1833.

Attalia, Turkey: see ANTALYA, city.

Attalla (ùtă'lù), city (pop. 7,537), Etowah co., NE Ala., on branch of Coosa R. and just W of Gadsden; rail junction in iron-mining and agr. area; foundry products (chiefly screw machinery and cast-iron soil pipe), cotton goods, lumber, concrete blocks. Founded 1870, inc. 1872.

Attapulgus (ătùpŭl'gùs), town (pop. 457), Decatur co., SW Ga., 12 mi. SSE of Bainbridge, near Fla. line; fuller's-earth mining.

Attard (ät-tärd'), village (parish pop. 2,480), central Malta, 4 mi. W of Valletta. Attard and near-by LIJA and BALZAN are called the "Three Villages." Has fine parish church (1631) and domed church (1725). In outskirts is St. Anton Palace, a residence of the governor of Malta, built c.1625.

Attarsumba, India: see ATARSUMBA.

Attatba (ätätbä'), village (pop. 1,082), Alger dept., N central Algeria, in Mitidja plain, 11 mi. NW of Blida; winegrowing.

Attawapiskat River (ă"tùwùpĭ'skĭt), N Ont., issues from Attawapiskat L., midway bet. L. Nipigon and Hudson Bay, flows 465 mi. E to James Bay opposite Akimiski Isl. At its mouth is trading post of Attawapiskat.

Attawaugan, Conn.: see KILLINGLY.

Attean Mountain (ă'tēùn) (2,442 ft.), Somerset co., W Maine, 7 mi. SW of Jackman, in recreational area.

Attean Pond, Somerset co., W Maine, 3 mi. S of Jackman, in hunting, fishing area; 5 mi. long, 2 mi. wide.

Attendorn (ä'tùndôrn), town (pop. 7,850), in former Prussian prov. of Westphalia, W Germany, after 1945 in North Rhine-Westphalia, 13 mi. SE of Lüdenscheid; iron and limestone works. Has 14th-cent. church. Chartered 1222. Was member of Hanseatic League. Large stalactite cave NE.

Atterbury, Camp, Ind.: see COLUMBUS.

Atterbury Air Force Base, Ind.: see COLUMBUS.

Attercliffe, town (pop. 22,975) in Sheffield county borough, West Riding, S Yorkshire, England, just NE of Sheffield; steel-milling center; also chemical and shoe industries.

Attersee (ät'ùrzā), village (pop. 1,328), SW Upper Austria, on W shore of the Attersee and 8 mi. SW of Vöcklabruck; rail terminus; summer resort; wood carving.

Attersee or **Kammersee** (käm'ùrzā), picturesque lake (□ 18) in the Salzkammergut, SW Upper Austria, 10 mi. W of Gmunden; 12 mi. long, 2 mi. wide, max. depth 560 ft., alt. 1,525 ft. Outlet: Ager R., which flows to the Traun.

Attert (ätâr'), agr. village (pop. 735), Luxembourg prov., SE Belgium, 5 mi. N of Arlon.

Atteuf, El-, Algeria: see ATEUF, EL-.

Attica (ă'tĭkù), Gr. *Attike* or *Attiki*, nome (□ 1,310; pop. 1,300,271), E central Greece; ⊙ Athens. Includes mainland section of anc. Attica, N coastal belt of E Argolis Peninsula (including POROS, HYDRA, DOKOS isls.), isls. in Saronic Gulf (SALAMIS, AEGINA, ANGISTRI), MAKRONESOS (northwesternmost of the Cyclades), and far-off isls. bet. SE Peloponnesus and NW Crete (KYTHERA, ANTIKYTHERA). Mainland Attica constitutes SE extremity of Attica peninsula, bet. the Gulf of Euboea (N) and Gulf of Corinth and Saronic Gulf (S); it is separated from Boeotia by Cithaeron and Parnes mts. Agr. (wheat, olive oil, wine, almonds, figs) in Athens and Eleusis lowlands. Mfg. industries in ATHENS-PIRAEUS metropolitan area; lead-zinc and iron mining at Laurion, lignite at Oropos. The Pentelikon and Hymettus massifs are known for their marble. According to tradition, Theseus combined 12 Attic townships into the Athenian state. Until the 6th cent. B.C. the country districts had a largely independent life, but with the development (5th cent. B.C.) of an aggressive Athenian foreign policy, the Attic countryside became a mere appendage of Athens and shared its subsequent history.

Attica. 1 City (pop. 3,862), Fountain co., W Ind., on the Wabash and 21 mi. WSW of Lafayette; trading center in agr. and bituminous-coal area; mfg. (cement products, brick, steel castings, canned goods, overalls, railroad equipment). Settled 1825, inc. 1866. Bear Creek Canyon and a natural stone arch are near by. **2** City (pop. 622), Harper co., S Kansas, 12 mi. NW of Anthony, in wheat region; poultry hatchery. **3** Village (pop. 2,676), Wyoming co., W N.Y., on Tonawanda Creek and 10 mi. SSW of Batavia, in agr. area; summer resort. Mfg. (patent medicines, wood products, automatic stokers, plastics). Attica State Prison is here. Settled 1804, inc. 1837. **4** Village (pop. 858), Seneca co., N Ohio, 15 mi. ESE of Tiffin; rubber gloves, wood products, flour.

Attichy (ätēshē'), village (pop. 656), Oise Dept., N France, on the Aisne and 10 mi. E of Compiègne; glue mfg.

Attigny (ätēnyē'), village (pop. 1,195), Ardennes dept., N France, on the Aisne, on Ardennes Canal, and 8 mi. NW of Vouziers; sugar-beet refining, dairying, horse raising. Anc. residence of Carolingian kings.

Attike, Greece: see ATTICA.

Attiki, Greece: see ATTICA.

Attikuppa, India: see KRISHNARAJPET.

Attili (ŭt'ĭlē), town (pop. 9,811), West Godavari dist., NE Madras, India, in Godavari R. delta, on rail spur and 33 mi. E of Ellore; rice and oilseed milling; tobacco, sugar cane. Sometimes spelled Attile.

Attimis (ät'tēmēs), village (pop. 1,084), Udine prov., Friuli-Venezia Giulia, NE Italy, 9 mi. NNE of Udine; cementworks.

Attingal (ŭting'gŭl), city (pop. 16,237), SW Travancore, India, 17 mi. NW of Trivandrum; rope and mats of coconut and palmyra fiber; cashew-nut processing; cassava, rice, mangoes. Also spelled Attungal.

Attleboro (ă'tŭlbŭrŭ), city (pop. 23,809), Bristol co., SE Mass., 11 mi. NE of Providence, R.I.; jewelry (since 1780), bleaching and dyeing, paper and metal specialties, optical goods, tools, machinery. Settled 1634, inc. as town 1694, as city 1914.

Attleboro Falls, Mass.: see NORTH ATTLEBORO.

Attleborough, town and parish (pop. 2,608), S central Norfolk, England, 14 mi. SW of Norwich; agr. market, with cider-bottling works. Church has Saxon foundation and Norman tower.

Attnang-Puchheim (ät'näng-pōōkh'hīm), town (pop. 6,581), S central Upper Austria, on Ager R. and 3 mi. E of Vöcklabruck; rail junction.

Attock (ŭtŏk'), dist. (□ 4,148; 1951 pop. 723,000), Punjab, W Pakistan; ⊙ Campbellpur. On Potwar Plateau; bounded N and NW by Indus R., S by Salt Range, NE by W offshoots of Punjab Himalayas. Wheat, millet, gram grown in fertile N plain. Hand-loom weaving, horse breeding; wood products. Petroleum fields at Khaur and Dhulian, cement works near Wah. Alexander the Great believed to have crossed the Indus c.10–15 mi. NE of Attock town in 326 B.C.

Attock, town (pop. 1,574), Attock dist., NW Punjab, W Pakistan, on Indus R. and 11 mi. NW of Campbellpur; local agr. market (wheat, millet). Scenic hill fort, built (1581) by Akbar, formerly of some importance; seized (1812) by Ranjit Singh and later by British. Rail and road bridge 1 mi. S, across the Indus.

Attogon (ätōgōn'), village, S Dahomey, Fr. West Africa, on railroad and 35 mi. NW of Porto-Novo; palm kernels, palm oil, copra. R. C. mission.

Attopeu (ät-tō'pû'), town, Champassak prov., S Laos, 70 mi. ESE of Pakse.

Attoyac Bayou (ŭtoi'yăk bī'ō), E Texas, rises in Rusk co., flows generally SSE c.65 mi. to Angelina R. 24 mi. ESE of Lufkin.

Attu (ă'tōō, ă"tōō'), village (1939 pop. 44), on NE Attu Isl., Aleutian Isls., SW Alaska, at head of Holtz Bay; 52°56'N 173°14'E; trading post; fox farming, basket weaving. Natives evacuated by Japanese invaders in 1942, repatriated in 1945.

Attu Island (30 mi. long, 8–15 mi. wide), westernmost of the Aleutians, SW Alaska, largest of Near Isls.; 52°55'N 172°57'E. Rugged, barren, and fog-bound; rises to c.4,100 ft. Some trapping and fox farming. In Second World War isl. was occupied (1942) by Japanese forces, who removed inhabitants (41 Aleuts, 2 Americans) to Japan and fortified isl. (surviving natives were repatriated 1945). U.S. troops landed (May 11, 1943) at Holtz Bay (NE) and Massacre Bay (SE) and after 3 weeks of bitter fighting captured isl. (June 1, 1943). It later became important base (air base on Massacre Bay) for Aleutian campaign and is important link in N Pacific defense system.

Attungal, India: see ATTINGAL.

Attur or **Atur** (ŭtōōr'), town (pop. 15,656), Salem dist., S central Madras, India, on Vellar R. and 30 mi. E of Salem; road center in agr. valley; trades in rice, cotton, sugar, castor oil; mfg. of culinary vessels; steatite workings in Kalrayan Hills (N) and Pachaimalai and Kollaimalai hills (S, SW; bamboo, sandalwood, fruit).

Attymon, Gaelic *Áth Díomáin*, village, central Co. Galway, Ireland, 16 mi. W of Ballinasloe; peat-digging center.

Atuabo (ätwä'bō), village, Western Prov., SW Gold Coast colony, on Gulf of Guinea, 23 mi. WNW of Axim; fishing; rice, cassava, corn, coconuts. Just W is Beyin, once a Port. trading post, founded 16th cent.

Atuana, Marquesas Isls.: see ATUONA.

Atuel River (ätwĕl'), Mendoza prov., W Argentina, rises in the Andes on Chile border near Molina Pass, flows SE, curving ENE and NE, and, S of San Rafael, E and SE, past General Alvear, to the Río Salado in La Pampa natl. territory 6 mi. SE of Santa Isabel; c.300 mi. long. Near the confluence, the arms of the Atuel enclose a marshy tract known as the Bañados del Atuel. Hydroelectric plant at El Sosneado. The irrigation dam at Nihuil was begun 1942.

Atuel Sud, Argentina: see JAIME PRATS.

Atulapa (ätōōlä'pä), village, Chiquimula dept., E Guatemala, on Honduras border, near Lempa R., 5 mi. ESE of Esquipulas; corn, wheat, livestock.

Atumi, Japan: see ATSUMI.

Atuntaqui (ätōōntä'kē), town (1950 pop. 2,670), Imbabura prov., N Ecuador, in the Andes, 8 mi. W of Ibarra; textile-milling center in agr. region (cereals, cotton, sugar cane, fruit, livestock).

Atuntze, China: see TEHTSIN.

Atuona (ätwō'nä) or **Atuana** (ätwä'nä), town (pop. 618), ⊙ Marquesas Isls., Fr. Oceania, S Pacific, on S coast of Hiva Oa, overlooking Bay of Traitors. Grave of Gauguin is here.

Atur, India: see ATTUR.

Atura (ätōō'rä), town, Northern Prov., Uganda, landing on the Victoria Nile (ferry) and 4 mi. WSW of Lira; cotton, peanuts, sesame.

Atures Rapids (ätōō'rĕs), on Venezuela-Columbia border, obstacle to navigation on upper Orinoco R., S of PUERTO AYACUCHO; 6 mi. long. Together with Maipures Rapids further S, they are circumvented by a road.

Aturus, France: see ADOUR RIVER.

Atushih or **A-t'u-shih** (both: ä'tōō'shû'), town, ⊙ Atushih co. (pop. 46,786), W Sinkiang prov., China, on Turugart Pass road and 20 mi. NNW of Kashgar; cattle raising; agr. products; saltworks. Barite quarrying near by.

Atwater. **1** City (pop. 2,856), Merced co., central Calif., in San Joaquin Valley, 7 mi. WNW of Merced; irrigated agr. (sweet potatoes, peaches, melons), dairying. Inc. 1922. **2** Village (pop. 880), Kandiyohi co., S central Minn., 14 mi. E of Willmar, in grain and livestock area; flour, dairy products. Gravel pits near by.

Atwood, village (pop. estimate 600), S Ont., 22 mi. N of Stratford; dairying, mixed farming.

Atwood. **1** Village (pop. 661), on Douglas-Piatt co. line, E central Ill., 26 mi. E of Decatur; dairy products, soybeans, corn, wheat. **2** City (pop. 1,613), ⊙ Rawlins co., NW Kansas, on Beaver Creek and 27 mi. N of Colby; grain, livestock. Founded 1878, inc. 1885. **3** Borough (pop. 110), Armstrong co., W central Pa., 14 mi. ESE of Kittanning.

Atwood Cay, Bahama Isls.: see SAMANA ISLAND.

Atwood Reservoir, E Ohio, impounded in a small tributary of Tuscarawas R., c.5 mi. W of Carrollton; capacity 49,700 acre-ft.; for flood control.

Atyashevo (ŭtyä'shĭvŭ), village (1926 pop. 2,808), E Mordvinian Autonomous SSR, Russian SFSR, on railroad and 25 mi. SW of Alatyr; hemp retting; agr. (hemp, wheat, potatoes).

Atyrá (ätērä'), town (dist. pop. 7,949), La Cordillera dept., S central Paraguay, in the Cordillera de los Altos, 32 mi. E of Asunción; agr. center (tobacco, cotton, sugar cane, fruit, livestock); distilling, tanning. Founded 1538.

At-Yuryakh (ät"-yōōryäkh'), river, right affluent of Taskan R., in N Khabarovsk Territory, Russian SFSR, in Kolyma gold-mining dist., bet. 62°30' and 62°45'N; 45 mi. long. Gold mining along its course.

Atyuryevo or **Atyur'yevo** (ŭtyōōr'yĭvŭ), town (1926 pop. 4,776), W Mordvinian Autonomous SSR, Russian SFSR, 20 mi. WSW of Krasnoslobodsk; grain, legumes, hemp. Until c.1938, spelled Atyurevo.

Atzacán (ätsäkän'), town (pop. 2,547), Veracruz, E Mexico, at SE foot of Pico de Orizaba, 4 mi. NNE of Orizaba; coffee, fruit.

Atzala (ätsä'lä), town (pop. 1,602), Puebla, central Mexico, 18 mi. W of Puebla; cereals, beans, maguey.

Atzalán (ätsälän'), town (pop. 768), Veracruz, E Mexico, 29 mi. NW of Jalapa; cereals, coffee, fruit.

Atzendorf (ä'tsŭndôrf), village (pop. 3,760), in former Prussian Saxony prov., central Germany, after 1945 in Saxony-Anhalt, 5 mi. N of Stassfurt; lignite mining; lime processing.

Atzgersdorf (äts'gŭrsdôrf), industrial town (pop. 7,372), after 1938 in Liesing dist. of Vienna, Austria, 5 mi. SW of city center.

Atzitzihuacán (ätsētsēwäkän'), officially Santiago Atzitzihuacán, town (pop. 492), Puebla, central Mexico, 30 mi. SW of Puebla; cereals, sugar, vegetables.

Atzizintla (ätsēsēn'tlä), town (pop. 1,476), Puebla, central Mexico, near Veracruz border, on railroad and 15 mi. WNW of Orizaba; cereals, maguey, fruit.

Atzompa (ätsōm'pä). **1** Officially San Gregorio Atzompa, town (pop. 1,106), Puebla, central Mexico, on railroad and 10 mi. W of Puebla; cereals, fruit, livestock. **2** Officially San Juan Atzompa, town (pop. 511), Puebla, central Mexico, 24 mi. SE of Puebla; cereals, livestock. **3** Town, Veracruz, Mexico: see SOLEDAD.

Au or **Au in der Hallertau** (ou' ĭn dĕr hä'lŭrtou), village (pop. 2,473), Lower Bavaria, Germany, on small Abens R. and 19 mi. W of Landshut; brewing; hops, wheat. Chartered 1349.

Au (ou), town (pop. 2,297), St. Gall canton, NE Switzerland, 12 mi. E of St. Gall, near Austrian border and the Rhine; embroideries, knit goods, foodstuffs; wood-and metalworking, printing.

Auasa, Lake, Ethiopia: see AWUSA, LAKE.

Auau Channel (ou'ou'), bet. Lanai and Maui isls., T.H., 7 naut. mi. wide.

Aub (oub), town (pop. 1,577), Lower Franconia, W Bavaria, Germany, 13 mi. SW of Kitzingen; brewing, flour milling. Wheat, barley, beets, cattle. Has late-17th-cent. town hall. Sandstone quarries near by.

Aubagne (ōbä'nyŭ), town (pop. 6,627), Bouches-du-Rhône dept., SE France, 10 mi. E of Marseilles, in small, hill-surrounded lowland; rail and road junction; mfg. (bricks and tiles, optical instruments, corks), meat processing. Ships strawberries and cherries. Chemical works at near-by Camp-Major-Charrel.

Aubange (ōbäzh'), residential village (pop. 2,354), Luxembourg prov., SE Belgium, 8 mi. S of Arlon.

Aubarre (ou'bärā), village (pop. 1,000), Harar prov., E central Ethiopia, near Br. Somaliland border, 39 mi. ENE of Jijiga.

Aube (ōb), department (□ 2,327; pop. 235,237), in Champagne, NE central France; ⊙ Troyes. On perimeter of Paris Basin; central and NW part occupied by Champagne badlands (*Champagne pouilleuse*). SE part is forested and more fertile. Drained SE-NW by Seine and Aube rivers. Agr. (rye, barley, wheat), sheep raising. Hosiery mfg. only important industry, with centers at Troyes, Romilly-sur-Seine, Arcis-sur-Aube, and Aix-en-Othe. Woodworking at Bar-sur-Aube.

Aube, river, France: AUBE RIVER.

Aubel (ōbĕl'), village (pop. 3,086), Liége prov., E Belgium, 13 mi. ENE of Liége.

Aubenas (ōbŭnä'), town (pop. 4,636), Ardèche dept., S France, near the Ardèche, 13 mi. SW of Privas; trades in raw and spun silk; silk throwing, rayon processing, mfg. of clothing and pharmaceuticals. Known for its glazed marrons. Its 13th–17th-cent. castle houses the town hall.

Aubenton (ōbätō'), agr. village (pop. 647), Aisne dept., N France, 13 mi. E of Vervins.

Auberive (ōbŭrēv'), village (pop. 324), Haute-Marne dept., NE France, in Plateau of Langres, 14 mi. WSW of Langres and on Aube R.; woodworking.

Aube River (ōb), Haute-Marne and Aube depts., NE central France, rises in Plateau of Langres above Auberive, flows 140 mi. NW, past Bar-sur-Aube and Arcis-sur-Aube, to the Seine 3 mi. N of Romilly-sur-Seine. Navigable.

Aubervilliers (ōbĕrvēlyā'), industrial NNE suburb (pop. 52,766) of Paris, Seine dept., N central France, 4 mi. from Notre Dame Cathedral; chemical works (fertilizer, paints, varnishes), metalworks (steel mill, foundries); petroleum refinery. Other mfg.: boilers and plumbing fixtures, leather goods, electromagnets, perfumes, biscuits.

Aubeterre or **Aubeterre-sur-Dronne** (ōbtâr'-sür-drôn'), agr. village (pop. 478), Charente dept., W France, on Dronne R. and 21 mi. SE of Barbezieux. Paper mills near by.

Aubière (ōbyâr'), SE residential suburb (pop. 3,960) of Clermont-Ferrand, Puy-de-Dôme dept., central France; winegrowing.

Aubigny or **Aubigny-en-Artois** (ōbēnyē'-ãnärtwä'), village (pop. 863), Pas-de-Calais dept., N France, 9 mi. WNW of Arras; tobacco, hops, sugar beets.

Aubigny-sur-Nère (–sür-nâr'), town (pop. 2,354), Cher dept., central France, 17 mi. SW of Gien; road center; mfg. (electric motors, biscuits, shirts), tanning. Has 12th–14th-cent. church and 15th-cent. wooden houses.

Aubin (ōbĕ'), town (pop. 4,574), Aveyron dept., S France, 12 mi. ESE of Figeac; coal-mining center.

Aubois River (ōbwä'), Cher dept., central France, rises 5 mi. above Sancoins, flows 25 mi. N, past La Guerche and Jouet-sur-l'Aubois, into the Loire 14 mi. below Nevers. Followed throughout its length by the Berry Canal.

Auboué (ōbwā'), town (pop. 2,450), Meurthe-et-Moselle dept., NE France, in Briey iron basin, on Orne R. and 3 mi. SSE of Briey; iron mining; pig-iron production, mfg. of mining explosives.

Aubrac, Monts d' (mō' dōbräk'), basaltic mountain range in the Massif Central, S central France; S outlier of Auvergne Mts., extending c.30 mi. NNW-SSE along Aveyron-Cantal-Lozère dept. borders, bounded by Massif du Cantal and Truyère R. (N), Viadène Plateau (W), and Lot R. (S). Rises to 4,826 ft. Cattle raising, cheese making.

Aubrais, Les, France: see FLEURY-LES-AUBRAIS.

Aubrey, town (pop. 491), Denton co., N Texas, 38 mi. N of Dallas, in farm area.

Aubrives (ōbrēv'), village (pop. 758), Ardennes dept., N France, on the Meuse and 4 mi. SSW of Givet, near Belgian border; iron foundry.

Aubry Lake (ô'brē) (40 mi. long, 1–13 mi. wide), NW Mackenzie Dist., Northwest Territories, NW of Great Bear L.; 67°25'N 126°28'W.

Aubure (ōbür'), Ger. *Altweier* (ält'vīŭr), village (pop. 310), Haut-Rhin dept., E France, resort in the Vosges, 5 mi. W of Ribeauvillé; alt. c.2,650 ft. Cheese mfg. Sanatorium.

Auburn (ô'bŭrn). **1** Municipality (pop. 21,902), E New South Wales, Australia, on S shore of Parramatta R. and 10 mi. W of Sydney, in metropolitan area; industrial center; mfg. (woodwork, pottery, chemicals, confectioneries), iron foundry. **2** Village (pop. 494), SE South Australia, 60 mi. N of Adelaide; wheat, wool, livestock, dairy products.

Auburn, village (pop. estimate 200), SW Ont., on Maitland R. and 10 mi. E of Goderich; dairying, mixed farming.

Auburn or **Lissoy** (lĭsoi′), agr. village (district pop. 519), S Co. Westmeath, Ireland, near Lough Ree, 7 mi. NNE of Athlone; scene of *The Deserted Village*, by Goldsmith, who spent his youth here.

Auburn (ô′bûrn). **1** City (pop. 12,939), Lee co., E Ala., 50 mi. ENE of Montgomery; lumber products, cotton goods. Alabama Polytechnic Inst. here. Settled c.1836. **2** City (pop. 4,653), ⊙ Placer co., central Calif., in Sierra Nevada foothills, 30 mi. NE of Sacramento, and on North Fork of American R.; shipping center for orchard, poultry, and livestock region; resort. Seat of Placer Col. Old New Orleans Hotel here. Early mining camp (gold, discovered 1848, soon gave out). Inc. 1860. **3** Town (pop. 301), Barrow co., NE central Ga., 8 mi. WNW of Winder. **4** City (pop. 1,963), Sangamon co., central Ill., 15 mi. SSW of Springfield; bituminous-coal mines; corn, wheat, oats, livestock, poultry, dairy products. Inc. 1865. **5** City (pop. 5,879), ⊙ De Kalb co., NE Ind., 21 mi. N of Fort Wayne; trading center in agr. area (livestock; dairy products; soybeans, grain); mfg. (automobiles and automotive parts, foundry products, rubber specialties, lumber, oil burners, stationery). Settled 1836. **6** Town (pop. 350), Sac co., W Iowa, 13 mi. N of Carroll; livestock, grain. **7** Town (pop. 994), Logan co., S Ky., 18 mi. WSW of Bowling Green, in agr. area; stone quarries; mfg. of hosiery, leather products, ax handles); flour and feed mills. **8** City (pop. 23,134), ⊙ Androscoggin co., SW Maine, on W bank of Androscoggin R. (at mouth of Little Androscoggin R.) opposite LEWISTON, with which it is joined by highway and railroad bridges. Shoe-mfg. center (industry dates from c.1835); canneries. Settled c.1786, town inc. 1842, city 1869; city-manager plan adopted 1917, 1st in state. L. Auburn, here, is source of "Twin Cities" water. **9** Residential town (pop. 8,840), Worcester co., S central Mass., 6 mi. S of Worcester; concrete and metal products. Settled 1714, inc. 1837. Includes villages of West Auburn (1940 pop. 689) and Stoneville (1940 pop. 2,904). **10** City (pop. 869), Bay co., E Mich., 9 mi. W of Bay City, in agr. area. **11** City (pop. 3,422), ⊙ Nemaha co., SE Nebr., 55 mi. SE of Lincoln and on Little Nemaha R., near Missouri R.; flour, fruit, dairy produce, grain. Sheridan (founded 1868) and Calvert (founded 1881) united as Auburn in 1882. **12** Town (pop. 1,158), Rockingham co., SE N.H., on Massabesic L., just E of Manchester. **13** City (pop. 36,722), ⊙ Cayuga co., W central N.Y., in Finger Lakes region, at N end of Owasco L., 22 mi. WSW of Syracuse; locomotive works; mfg. of farm machinery, rope, shoes, food products, wagons, auto accessories, textiles, clothing, plastics; wood, rubber, metal, and paper products; surgical instruments, chemicals. Trade center of agr. area. Here are Auburn State Prison, where Auburn penal system originated; and the home and grave of William H. Seward, whose records, books, and Indian relics are in city mus. Harriet Tubman lived here. Settled 1793, inc. 1848. **14** Borough (pop. 994), Schuylkill co., E central Pa., 8 mi. SE of Pottsville and on Schuylkill R.; bricks. **15** Village, R.I.: see CRANSTON. **16** City (pop. 6,497), King co., W central Wash., 10 mi. ENE of Tacoma; railroad junction and trade center for agr. region. Platted c.1887. **17** Town (pop. 149), Ritchie co., W W.Va., 40 mi. ESE of Parkersburg. **18** Village (pop. c.300), Lincoln co., W Wyo., bet. Idaho line and Salt R., 6 mi. NNW of Afton; alt. c.6,300 ft. Dairy products, grain, livestock. Hot springs, salt and sulphur deposits near by. Salt River Range just E.

Auburndale. 1 City (pop. 3,763), Polk co., central Fla., 10 mi. E of Lakeland, on several small lakes; citrus-fruit shipping center, with large packing houses and canneries; also mfg. of boxes, asphalt, brick. Founded 1884, inc. 1911. **2** Village, Mass.: see NEWTON. **3** Village (pop. 325), Wood co., central Wis., 9 mi. ESE of Marshfield, in dairying and agr. area.

Auburn Heights, village (1940 pop. 1,809), Oakland co., SE Mich., just E of Pontiac, on Clinton R.

Auburntown (ô′bûrntoun), town (pop. 273), Cannon co., central Tenn., 9 mi. N of Woodbury.

Aubusson (ōbüsõ′), town (pop. 4,935), Creuse dept., central France, on the Creuse and 21 mi. SE of Guéret; noted carpet and tapestry mfg. center. Also has light-metalworks, brewery, precision instrument factory. Carpets 1st made here in 15th cent. Cardinal Aubusson b. here.

Auby (ōbē′), town (pop. 5,417), Nord dept., N France, on Haute-Deûle Canal and 3 mi. NNW of Douai; chemical works (fertilizer, saltpeter), lead and zinc smelters.

Aucanquilcha, Cerro (sĕ′rō oukängkēl′chä), Andean peak (20,275 ft.) in Antofagasta prov., N Chile, near Bolivia border; 21°13′S. Has sulphur deposits.

Auce or **Autse** (out′sä), Ger. *Autz*, city (pop. 3,320), SW Latvia, in Zemgale, 35 mi. WSW of Jelgava, near Lith. border; woodworking.

Auch (ōsh), anc. *Elimberris*, town (pop. 11,489), ⊙ Gers dept., SW France, on the Gers and 40 mi. W of Toulouse; road and market center; important trade in Armagnac brandy, wine, grain. Food processing (pâté de foie gras, biscuits), flour milling, mfg. of furniture, sandals, hosiery, and construction materials. The 15th-17th-cent. Gothic cathedral (with classic façade) contains fine stained-glass windows and wooden stalls. The upper and lower town are connected by a monumental flight of steps. One of chief towns of Roman Gaul, Auch became an archiepiscopal see (9th cent.), capital of ARMAGNAC and, later (18th cent.), of Gascony.

Auchel (ōshĕl′), town (pop. 10,614), Pas-de-Calais dept., N France, 8 mi. WSW of Béthune; coal-mining center.

Auchenblae, Scotland: see FORDOUN.

Auchencairn, Scotland: see RERRICK.

Auchenheath (ŏkh-ŭnhēth′), village in Lesmahagow parish, central Lanark, Scotland, 5 mi. W of Lanark; coal mining.

Auchi (ouchē′), town, Benin prov., Western Provinces, S central Nigeria, 32 mi. W of Idah; cotton textiles; palm oil and kernels, cotton, kola nuts, cacao.

Auchinblae, Scotland: see FORDOUN.

Auchincruive (ŏkh-ĭnkrōōv′), agr. village in Ayr parish, W Ayrshire, Scotland, 3 mi. NE of Ayr; site of West of Scotland Agr. Col., located in Auchincruive House, former experimental farm, given to nation in 1930. Also site of Hannah Research Inst.

Auchinleck (ŏkh-ĭnlĕk′), town and parish (pop. 6,626), E central Ayrshire, Scotland, 13 mi. E of Ayr; coal mining. James Boswell, b. at near-by Auchinleck House, is buried in churchyard here.

Auchleven (ŏkhlē′vŭn), village, central Aberdeen, Scotland, 2 mi. S of Insch; woolen milling.

Auchmithie (ŏkhmĭ′thē), fishing village, SE Angus, Scotland, on the North Sea, 4 mi. NE of Arbroath.

Auchmuty (ôkmū′tē), village, central Fifeshire, Scotland, just W of Markinch; paper milling.

Auchterarder (ŏkhtŭrär′dŭr), burgh (1931 pop. 2,254; 1951 census 2,434), S Perthshire, Scotland, on Ruthven Water (9-mi.-long tributary of Earn R.) and 13 mi. SW of Perth; agr. market. Scene of origin of dispute (1834) which led to secession of Free Church of Scotland.

Auchterderran (ŏkhtŭrdĕ′rŭn), town and parish (pop. 16,665, including part of Lochgelly burgh), S central Fifeshire, Scotland, 5 mi. WNW of Kirkcaldy; coal mining.

Auchtergaven, Scotland: see BANKFOOT.

Auchterhouse Hill, Scotland: see SIDLAW HILLS.

Auchterless (ŏkhtŭrlĕs′), agr. village and parish (pop. 1,458), N Aberdeen, Scotland, 4 mi. S of Turriff. Farmhouse incorporates remains of Tolly Castle (c.1300). Near by are remains of anc. Hatton Castle.

Auchtermuchty (ŏkhtŭrmŭkh′tē, ôktŭrmŭk′tē), burgh (1931 pop. 1,252; 1951 census 1,330), N Fifeshire, Scotland, 9 mi. WSW of Cupar; agr. market, with hosiery mills and whisky distilleries. John Glas b. here. Just SE is agr. village of Dunshelt.

Auchy-les-Mines (ōshē′-lā-mēn′), town (pop. 3,336), Pas-de-Calais dept., N France, on Aire–La Bassée Canal, 6 mi. E of Béthune; coal mining. In front lines during First World War. Formerly named Auchy-lès-Labassée.

Aucilla River (ôsĭ′lŭ), S Ga. and NW Fla., rises 5 mi. NE of Thomasville, Ga., flows SE into Fla., thence SSW into E end of Apalachee Bay (Gulf of Mexico) 25 mi. WSW of Perry, Fla.; c.75 mi. long.

Auckland (ŏk′lŭnd), provincial district (□ 25,400; pop. 640,971), N N.Isl., New Zealand; site of Auckland, former ⊙ dominion. Fertile coastal plain, mtn. range in W, kauri forest in N. Hot springs; health resorts. Chief harbors: Waitemata, Manukau, Kaipara. Quartz, gold mines. Produces dairy foods, timber, kauri gum. Area roughly divided into 2 land dists., N Auckland and Auckland.

Auckland, city (pop. 123,457; metropolitan Auckland 263,370), New Zealand, on N N.Isl., bet. Waitemata Harbour (N) and Manukau Harbour (S), 1,280 mi. ESE of Sydney; 36°51′S 174°45′E. Chief port of dominion; former ⊙ (1841–65) New Zealand. Many volcanic cones in plains surrounding city; Mt. Eden (644 ft.), highest. Seat of Auckland War Memorial Mus. (Maori collection), Auckland University Col., Anglican and R.C. cathedrals. Naval base. Shipyards, sugar refinery, ammunition plants, canneries. Exports dairy products, hides, timber, gold, wool. Auckland is ⊙ Waitemata co. (□ 607; pop. 19,973), ⊙ Manukau co. (□ 240; pop. 13,076), and ⊙ Eden co. (□ 14; pop. 16,730), but city forms independent unit. Founded 1841.

Auckland Islands, uninhabited group (□ 234), S Pacific, one of outlying isl. groups of New Zealand, 300 mi. S of Invercargill; 50°32′S 166°13′E. Comprise c.6 isls.; largest (27 mi. long, 15 mi. wide) rises to 2,000 ft. Fur seals. Discovered 1806.

Auckland Saint Andrew, England: see SAINT ANDREW AUCKLAND.

Auckland Saint Helen, England: see SAINT HELEN AUCKLAND.

Aucun (ōkŭ′), village (pop. 157), Hautes-Pyrénées dept., SW France, in central Pyrenees, 5 mi. WSW of Argelès-Gazost; corn, vegetables, cattle.

Aude (ōd), department (□ 2,449; pop. 268,889) in Languedoc, S France; ⊙ Carcassonne. Bounded by Gulf of Lion (E), the CORBIÈRES (S), and Massif Central (N). Drained by Aude R. Predominantly a winegrowing region with some agr. (wheat, oats, fruit, livestock) W of Carcassonne. Important gold, arsenic, and silver mines at Salsigne and Villanière. Saltworks near coast. Felt-hat industry (Couiza, Espéraza). Chief towns: Carcassone (tourist center), Narbonne (wine trade), Castelnaudary, Limoux (nougats, sparkling wines).

Audegle (oudĕg′lä), town (pop. 2,500), in the Benadir, S Ital. Somaliland, on the Webi Shebeli and 35 mi. W of Mogadishu; road junction. Agr. and livestock center.

Audenarde, Belgium: see OUDENAARDE.

Audenge (ōdäzh′), village (pop. 1,308), Gironde dept., SW France, on E shore of Arcachon Basin, 24 mi. WSW of Bordeaux; shipping of pit props; oyster beds.

Audenshaw (ô′–), urban district (1931 pop. 8,461; 1951 census 12,656), SE Lancashire, England, 5 mi. E of Manchester; mfg. of leather, pharmaceuticals, metal products. Site of Manchester water reservoirs.

Auderghem (ōdûrgĕm′), Flemish *Oudergem* (ou′dûrkhĕm), residential town (pop. 18,660), Brabant prov., central Belgium, SE suburb of Brussels. Has remains of anc. Augustine monastery, founded 1368; here the painter Hugo van der Goes lived and died. In anc. times locality was favorite hunting resort of dukes of Brabant.

Aude River (ōd), Pyrénées-Orientales and Aude depts., S France, rises in the Pyrenees near Pic de Carlitte, flows N, past Quillan and Limoux, to Carcassonne, then swings E, entering the Gulf of Lion 12 mi. E of Narbonne; 138 mi. long. Upper course harnessed for hydroelectric power. Paralleled by Canal du Midi below Carcassonne. Receives the Fresquel (left).

Audeux (ōdû′), agr. village (pop. 95), Doubs dept., E France, 7 mi. W of Besançon.

Audhali, 'Audhali, or **'Awdali** (ou′dhälē), sultanate (pop. 10,000) of Western Aden Protectorate, on Yemen "Status Quo Line"; chief town, Lodar (sultan's residence, Zara). Dominated by granitic ridge of Kaur al AUDHILLA; includes major agr. dist. of MUKHEIRAS, on N slope. Protectorate treaty concluded 1912. Sometimes called Audhilla, 'Audhillah, or 'Awdillah; also Audilla or 'Audillah.

Audhilla, Kaur al, or **Kaur al 'Audhillah,** or **Kawr al-'Awdillah** (kour′ ăl oudhĭl′lŭ), W section of granitic Kaur ranges in Aden hinterland, along Yemen "Status Quo Border"; rises to 8–9,000 ft., constituting highest part of the Audhali country. Lodar and Zara are at S foot; Mukheiras agr. area at N foot. Sometimes spelled Audilla or 'Audillah.

Audierne (ōdyârn′), town (pop. 3,890), Finistère dept., W France, 20 mi. WNW of Quimper; port and bathing resort on Bay of Biscay, with sardine and lobster fisheries; fish canning and drying, lace and tulle weaving; saltworks.

Audierne, Bay of, on Bay of Biscay, in Finistère dept., W France, bet. Pointe du Raz (NW) and Pointe de Penmarch (SE), c.15 mi. W of Quimper; 24 mi. wide, c.5 mi. long; sardine fisheries.

Audilla or **'Audillah,** sultanate, Aden: see AUDHALI.

Audilla, Kaur al, or **'Audillah, Kaur al,** Aden: see AUDHILLA, KAUR AL.

Audincourt (ōdĕkōōr′), town (pop. 8,656), Doubs dept., E France, 3 mi. SE of Montbéliard and part of its industrial dist., on Doubs R. Forges, automobile and textile plants.

Audley (ôd′lē), former urban district (1931 pop. 13,621), NW Stafford, England, 6 mi. NW of Stoke-on-Trent; coal mines, metalworks. Has church with 14th-cent. tower.

Audna River (oud′nä), Nor. *Audna* or *Audnedalselv*, Vest-Agder co., S Norway, rises in lake region near Grindheim, flows 30 mi. S through the Audnedal, past Vigmostad, to an inlet of North Sea 8 mi. W of Mandal. Sometimes called Undalselv.

Audorf, Germany: see SCHACHT-AUDORF.

Audrain (ôdrān′), county (□ 692; pop. 23,829), NE central Mo.; ⊙ Mexico. Drained by South Fork of Salt R. and West Fork of Cuivre R. Agr. (corn, oats, barley, soy beans), cattle, poultry; mfg. at Mexico and Vandalia; fire-clay deposits, coal, lumber. Formed 1836.

Audruicq (ōdrüĕk′), village (pop. 1,843), Pas-de-Calais dept., N France, 11 mi. ESE of Calais; chicory.

Audubon (ô′dŭbŏn), county (□ 448; pop. 11,579), W central Iowa; ⊙ Audubon. Prairie agr. area (cattle, hogs, poultry, corn, hay, oats) drained by East Nishnabotna R.; coal deposits. Formed 1851.

Audubon. 1 City (pop. 2,808), ⊙ Audubon co., W central Iowa, on East Nishnabotna R. (hydroelectric plant) and 22 mi. N of Atlantic; canned corn, hybrid seed corn, feed. Platted 1878, inc. 1880. **2** Village (pop. 275), Becker co., W Minn., 7 mi. WNW of Detroit Lakes, in lake region; dairy products. **3** (ô′dŭbŏn) Borough (pop. 9,531), Camden co., SW N.J., 4 mi. SE of Camden; wire cloth, concrete blocks; truck, dairy products. Large cooperative housing project here. Inc. 1905.

Audubon, Mount, Colo.: see FRONT RANGE.

Audubon Memorial State Park (c.400 acres), Henderson co., W Ky., near the Ohio just N of Henderson. Memorial to Audubon, who hunted and studied birds here; includes bird refuge, mus., and camp facilities.

Audubon Park. 1 Town (pop. 1,790), Jefferson co., N Ky., a suburb of Louisville. **2** Borough (pop.

1,859), Camden co., SW N.J., just W of Audubon and near Camden. Inc. after 1940.

Audun-le-Roman (ōdū′-lŭ-rômā′), town (pop. 2,641), Meurthe-et-Moselle dept., NE France, 9 mi. N of Briey, in important iron-mining area.

Audun-le-Tiche (-lü-tēsh′), Ger. *Deutsch-Oth* (doich′-ōt′), town (pop. 5,701), Moselle dept., NE France, near Luxembourg border, 12 mi. NW of Thionville, in iron-mining dist.; blast furnaces.

Aue (ou′ü), town (pop. 25,567), Saxony, E central Germany, in the Erzgebirge, on the Zwickauer Mulde and 13 mi. SE of Zwickau; center of important uranium-mining region (developed after 1945), with concentrating plant. Mfg. of cotton and wool textiles, knitwear, machine tools, cutlery, silver articles, pianos, matches, chemicals, pharmaceuticals. Distributing center for important wood-working region. Hydroelectric power station. Chartered 1629.

Auer, Italy: see ORA.

Auerbach (ou′ürbäkh). **1** Town (pop. 6,353), Upper Palatinate, NE Bavaria, Germany, 20 mi. NW of Amberg; textile mfg. Has late-17th-cent. church. Iron ore mined in area. **2** N suburb (pop. 6,108) of Bensheim, S Hesse, W Germany; wine. Has anc. ruined castle. Inc. into Bensheim after 1939. **3** Town (pop. 18,708), Saxony, E central Germany, in the Erzgebirge, on Göltzsch R. and 16 mi. SSW of Zwickau; cotton milling, hosiery knitting; mfg. of carpets, lace, curtains, embroidery, machinery, paper. Tuberculosis sanitariums near by. **4.** Village (pop. 4,152), Saxony, E central Germany, in the Erzgebirge, 10 mi. S of Chemnitz; hosiery knitting.

Auerbakhovski Rudnik, Russian SFSR: see RUDNICHNY, Sverdlovsk oblast.

Auersperg, Yugoslavia: see VISNJA GORA.

Auerstedt (ou′ür-shtĕt), village (pop. 924), in former Prussian Saxony prov., central Germany, after 1945 in Saxony-Anhalt, 2 mi. NW of Bad Sulza. French under Davout here defeated (Oct. 14, 1806) Prussians under Duke Charles of Brunswick.

Auerswalde (ou′ürsväl″dü), village (pop. 3,816), Saxony, E central Germany, 5 mi. N of Chemnitz; hosiery knitting, cigar mfg.

Au Fer, Point, La.: see ATCHAFALAYA BAY.

Aufidus, Italy: see OFANTO RIVER.

Aufkirchen (ouf′kĭr″khün), village (pop. 560), Middle Franconia, W Bavaria, Germany, on the Wörnitz and 8 mi. E of Dinkelsbühl; cattle, sheep, hogs.

Augathella, village (pop. 624), S central Queensland, Australia, on Warrego R. and 50 mi. NNE of Charleville; livestock.

Auge Valley (ōzh), Calvados dept., NW France, a marshy, delta-like region drained by lower Dives R. and its tributary, the Vie, extending c.15 mi. inland from Channel coast bet. mouth of Orne R. (W) and Cabourg (E). On its excellent pastures Normandy cattle and horses are raised.

Augevand, Norway: see OGGE LAKE.

Auggen (ou′gün), village (pop. 1,290), S Baden, Germany, at W foot of Black Forest, 12 mi. NNW of Lörrach; known for its white Markgräfler wine.

Augher (ŏkh′ür), agr. village (district pop. 729), S Co. Tyrone, Northern Ireland, on Blackwater R. and 15 mi. WSW of Dungannon, near Clogher; oats, flax, potatoes; cattle.

Aughnacloy (ŏkh″nükloi′), town (pop. 780), S Co. Tyrone, Northern Ireland, on Irish border, 10 mi. SW of Dungannon; agr. market (cattle; flax, oats, potatoes).

Aughrabies Falls (ōkhrä′bēs, ōgrä′bēs) or **King George's Falls,** on Orange R., NW Cape Prov., U. of So. Afr., 60 mi. WSW of Upington; drops 480 ft. after cataract fall of 140 ft.

Aughrim (ŏkh′rĭm, ôg′–). **1** or **Aghrim,** Gaelic *Eachdhruim*, town (pop. 109), E Co. Galway, Ireland, 4 mi. WSW of Ballinasloe; agr. market (cattle, sheep; potatoes, beets). Scene of important victory (1691) of forces of William III under Gen. Ginkel over those of James II under Gen. St. Ruth. **2** Gaelic *Eachdhruim Ui Bhroin*, town (pop. 345), S Co. Wicklow, Ireland, on Aughrim R. and 8 mi. WNW of Arklow; granite quarrying.

Aughris Head (ŏkh′rĭs), promontory, N Co. Sligo, Ireland, on Sligo Bay, 12 mi. W of Sligo; 54°17′N 8°45′W.

Aughrus Point (ŏkh′rŭs), promontory, NW Co. Galway, Ireland, 9 mi. WNW of Clifden; 53°32′N 10°12′W.

Aughton (ô′tŭn), agr. village and parish (pop. 2,918), SW Lancashire, England, 2 mi. SW of Ormskirk.

Augila (oujē′lä), oasis (pop. 1,500), W Cyrenaica, Libya, 20 mi. WNW of Gialo oasis, near N end of Libyan Desert; dates, figs, olives, barley; goats. Sometimes considered part of Gialo oasis.

Auglaize (ôglāz′), county (□ 400; pop. 30,637), W Ohio; ⊙ Wapakoneta. Drained by Auglaize and St. Marys rivers; part of Grand L. is in W. Agr. area (livestock, grain, poultry; dairying); mfg. at St. Marys, Wapakoneta, Minster, New Bremen. Sand, gravel, and clay pits; hunting, fishing. Formed 1848.

Auglaize River, NW Ohio, rises SE of Lima, flows SW to Wapakoneta, then N, past Fort Jennings, joining the Maumee at Defiance; c.100 mi. long. Tributaries are Ottawa and Blanchard rivers (E), Little Auglaize R. (W).

Augpilagtok or **Augpilagtoq** (both: oukhpĭläkh′tôk). **1** Fishing settlement (pop. 129), Nanortalik dist., S Greenland, on Ilua Fjord, channel of Prince Christian Sound Passage, 70 mi. ESE of Julianehaab; 60°8′N 44°16′W. **2** Fishing and hunting settlement (pop. 116), Upernavik dist., W Greenland, on small isl. in Baffin Bay, on S side of Upernavik Ice Fjord, 14 mi. ENE of Upernavik; 72°53′N 55°35′W.

Au Gres (ō grā′), city (pop. 442), Arenac co., E Mich., on Au Gres R. near its mouth on Saginaw Bay, and 33 mi. NNE of Bay City. Farming, commercial fishing. Resort. Has public hunting grounds and state forest.

Au Gres River, E Mich., rises in lake in E Ogemaw co., flows c.45 mi. SE, past Au Gres, to Saginaw Bay. Chief tributary is East Branch (c.30 mi. long).

Augsburg (ouks′bŏŏrk), anc. *Augusta Vindelicorum*, city (1939 pop. 185,374; 1946 pop. 160,055; 1950 pop. 184,712), ⊙ Swabia, W Bavaria, Germany, at N tip of the Lechfeld, on the Lech, near mouth of the Wertach, and 34 mi. WNW of Munich; 48°22′N 10°54′E. Important rail junction; textile center of S Germany (cotton, linen, jute; cloth, thread, yarn; clothing, hats, tents). Has metal industry (Diesel motors, rotary presses, refrigerators, agr. machinery, sheet metal, machine tools, cog wheels, nails, saws, springs). Produces also precision instruments (microscopes), chemicals (synthetic fiber; fertilizer; soap, paint); paper mfg., printing, leatherworking, brewing. Airplane and U-boat-engine mfg. center until 1945. Has Romanesque cathedral (994–1065) with Gothic additions completed 1432; R.C. St. Ulrich church (1475–1604); Fugger House (1512–15); Renaissance-baroque Zeughaus; several medieval gates; 3 early-17th-cent. fountains. A Roman colony founded by Augustus in 15 B.C., Augsburg became (6th cent.) episcopal see. Besieged by Magyars 955. Created free imperial city 1276. The home of Fugger and Welser families and birthplace of Holbein and Burgkmair, it was Europe's commercial and banking center in 15th and 16th cent., and a rallying point of Ger. art and science. Scene of important religious agreements during Reformation, but city remained Catholic. Declined during Thirty Years War. Captured by U.S. troops in spring, 1945. Second World War destruction (40–50%) included city hall (1615–20), many noteworthy churches, several Fugger residences; the well-known Fuggerei, an early-16th-cent. housing project for R.C. poor, was heavily damaged.

Augst or **Baselaugst** (bä′zŭl-oukst′), village (pop. 592), Basel-Land half-canton, N Switzerland, on the Rhine (Ger. border), at mouth of Ergolz R., and 6 mi. ESE of Basel, opposite Wyhlen. Site of Augst-Wyhlen hydroelectric plant. Roman settlement (*Augusta Raurica*) with remains of Roman theater just S. Just NE of Augst, on the Rhine, in Aargau canton, is village of Kaiseraugst (pop. 748).

Augusta (ôgŭ′stü), village (pop. 142), SW Western Australia, 170 mi. SSW of Perth, at mouth of Blackwood R. Starting point for tour of limestone caves; Moondyne Cave near by.

Augusta (ougōō′stä), town (pop. 17,716), Siracusa prov., E Sicily, port on small peninsula in Ionian Sea, 12 mi. NNW of Syracuse; salt, soap, cement, and brick industries; tunny fisheries. Exports mineral oil, clay, salt. Has 17th-cent. palace, 18th-cent. cathedral, Swabian castle (now a penitentiary; badly damaged in Second World War). Founded 42 B.C. by Romans; devastated by Barbarians and Saracens; reestablished 1232 by Frederick II; largely destroyed by earthquake of 1693. Long a naval station. Known as Agosta for several centuries before 1860. Anc. Greek colony of Megara Hyblaea, founded 728 B.C. by Megara, was just SW.

Augusta (ôgŭ′stü, ügŭ′–), county (□ 999; pop. 34,154), NW Va.; co. courthouse is at STAUNTON, in but independent of co. Mainly in S Shenandoah Valley; Shenandoah Mtn. in W and NW, Blue Ridge in SE and E. Includes parts of Shenandoah Natl. Park, George Washington Natl. Forest, Appalachian Trail, Blue Ridge Parkway. Drained by Middle and South rivers (headstreams of the Shenandoah), Maury and Calfpasture rivers. Agr. (fruit, wheat, corn, hay), livestock raising (cattle, hogs, poultry), dairying. Lumbering; manganese mining; rock quarrying. Mfg. at Staunton, Waynesboro. Formed 1745.

Augusta. 1 City (pop. 2,317), ⊙ Woodruff co., E central Ark., c.65 mi. NE of Little Rock and on White R., in agr. area (cotton, corn, hay); cotton ginning, gristmilling, sawmilling; commercial fishing, mussel-shell gathering. Settled 1846, inc. as city 1931. **2** City (pop. 71,508), ⊙ Richmond co., E Ga., c.65 mi. SW of Columbia, S.C., head of navigation on Savannah R. (212 mi. upstream), at the fall line; 30°28′N 81°59′W. Cotton market and commercial center with important textile-milling, clay-mining, and processing industries; mfg. of fabrics, clothing, brick, tile, chemicals, fertilizer, cottonseed oil, food products, paper products, lumber, machinery; meat packing and canning. A govt. lock and dam below the city (completed 1937) aids port facilities. Ships cotton, lumber, naval stores. Its mild climate makes Augusta a winter resort. Here are: Univ. of Ga. School of Medicine, Paine Col., Haines Inst. (Negro), U.S. arsenal (1819), and a veterans' hosp. Here, too, are the boyhood home of Woodrow Wilson and many old houses of Georgian and classic-revival design. U.S. Camp Gordon is 8 mi. WSW. City was laid out 1735 as a trading post by James Oglethorpe and named for mother of George III; inc. as town 1789, as city 1798. Augusta changed hands many times during the Revolutionary War and was finally taken (1781) by Continental forces under Andrew Pickens and "Light-Horse Harry" Lee. Was state capital, 1785–95. Site of largest Confederate powder works during Civil War. Construction (begun 1951) of Atomic Energy Commission's huge Savannah River Plant, across river in Aiken and Barnwell counties, S.C., caused large pop. influx. **3** Village (pop. 945), Hancock co., W Ill., 30 mi. NE of Quincy; agr. (livestock, grain); bituminous-coal mining; poultry hatchery. **4** City (pop. 4,483), Butler co., S Kansas, on Walnut R. and 19 mi. E of Wichita; trading and shipping point for livestock, grain, and oil region; mfg. of gasoline, auto trailers. Stone quarries and oil wells near by. State park in vicinity. Settled c.1868, inc. 1871. **5** City (pop. 1,599), Bracken co., N Ky., port on left bank (levee) of the Ohio and 37 mi. SE of Cincinnati; ships burley tobacco; mfg. of shoes, cement blocks, metal stampings, carriages. Was site of Augusta Col. (c.1800), one of 1st Methodist schools in U.S. City founded c.1792. **6** City (pop. 20,913), ⊙ Maine (since 1831) and Kennebec co., on the Kennebec and c.45 mi. from its mouth, at head of navigation; alt. 120 ft.; 44°19′N 69°50′W. Paper and textile milling, shoe making, printing; mfg. of wood products. Seat of domed state capitol (1829), James G. Blaine's home (now governor's mansion), U.S. arsenal, state hosp. for insane. Near by are soldiers' home, Belgrade Lakes (N), and L. Cobbosseecontee (W). Begun on Indian site (Cushnoc) as a Plymouth Company trading post (1628); later was site of Fort Western (1754; partly restored) and was included in town of HALLOWELL until 1797, when it was inc. as town; city inc. 1849. Settlement around fort developed as shipbuilding and shipping port; dam (built 1837) stimulated mfg. **7** Village (pop. 898), Kalamazoo co., SW Mich., on Kalamazoo R. and 12 mi. ENE of Kalamazoo, in farm area (corn, wheat, oats, fruit); flour, baskets. **8** Town (pop. 218), St. Charles co., E Mo., near Missouri R., 35 mi. W of St. Louis; agr. **9** Village (pop. c.450), Lewis and Clark co., W central Mont., 50 mi. W of Great Falls and on branch of Sun R., in agr. region. Near-by Gibson Dam, on short N fork of Sun R., forms Willow Creek Reservoir, used for irrigation. **10** City (pop. 1,458), Eau Claire co., W central Wis., on small tributary of Eau Claire R. and 20 mi. SE of Eau Claire, in dairying, stock-raising, and farming area (grain, cranberries); creameries, feed mill, cannery. Inc. 1885.

Augusta, Cape (ougōō′stä), on Caribbean coast of Atlántico dept., N Colombia, at mouth of Magdalena R. opposite Gómez Isl., 8 mi. NW of Barranquilla; 11°5′N 74°50′W.

Augusta, Mount (14,070 ft.), on Yukon-Alaska border, in St. Elias Mts., 190 mi. W of Whitehorse, on S edge of Seward Glacier; 60°18′N 140°27′W.

Augusta Praetoria, Italy: see AOSTA.

Augusta Raurica, Switzerland: see AUGST.

Augusta Suessionum, France: see SOISSONS.

Augusta Taurinorum, Italy: see TURIN.

Augusta Veromanduorum, France: see SAINT-QUENTIN.

Augusta Vindelicorum, Germany: see AUGSBURG.

Augustenborg (ăv′gōōstŭnbôr), town (pop. 1,502), Aabenraa-Sonderborg amt, Denmark, on Als isl. and 4 mi. NE of Sonderborg, on Augustenborg Fjord. Founded around castle built 1651.

Augustenborg Fjord, Denmark: see ALS SOUND.

Augustine Island (7 mi. long, 7 mi. wide), S Alaska, in Kamishak Bay, at mouth of Cook Inlet, 60 mi. W of Seldovia; 59°22′N 153°26′W. Rises to 3,970 ft. (active volcano).

Augustobona, France: see TROYES.

Augustodunum, France: see AUTUN.

Augustonemetum, France: see CLERMONT-FERRAND.

Augustoritum Lemovicensium, France: see LIMOGES.

Augusto Severo (ougōō′stōō sĭvĕ′rōō), city (pop. 461), W Rio Grande do Norte, NE Brazil, 45 mi. S of Mossoró; carnauba wax, sugar, tobacco.

Augustow (ougōō′stōōf), Pol. *Augustów*, Rus. *Avgustov* (ŭvgōō′stŭf), town (pop. 8,338), Bialystok prov., NE Poland, on Augustow Canal, on railroad and 50 mi. N of Bialystok; mfg. of cement, bricks; tanning, flour milling, sawmilling. Scene of severe battle in First World War. During Second World War, under administration of East Prussia. Augustow Forest extends E from the town into Belorussian SSR as far as Neman R.

Augustow Canal, Pol. *Kanal Augustowski* (kä′nou ougōōstôf′skē), Rus. *Kanal Avgustovskiy* (kŭnäl′ ŭvgōō′stôfskē), Bialystok prov., Poland, linking Biebrza and Czarna Hancza rivers; 63 mi. long. From Biebrza R. runs N past Augustow, and E through several small lakes, to the Czarna Hancza near Belorussian SSR border. Built 1824–39; numerous water locks; used chiefly for logging.

Augustusburg (ougŏŏ'stŏŏsbŏŏrk"), town (pop. 3,330), Saxony, E central Germany, in the Erzgebirge, 8 mi. E of Chemnitz; hosiery knitting, climatic and winter-sports resort. Has 16th-cent. castle.

Au in der Hallertau, Germany: see AU.

'Auja, El, or **'Auja** (ou'jŭ, ĕl), village, S Palestine, in W part of the Negev, on Egyptian border, 30 mi. SW of Beersheba. Papyri from 6th cent. found here. Under Israeli-Egyptian armistice (1949) in neutral zone.

Auke Bay (ôk), SE Alaska, small inlet on N shore of Stephens Passage, at NW end of Douglas Isl., 10 mi. NW of Juneau; 58°22'N 134°40'W; fishing. On N side of entrance is Indian fishing village (pop. 196).

Aulad Isma'il or **Awlad Isma'il** (oulăd' ĭsmä'ĭl), village (pop. 8,149), Girga prov., central Upper Egypt, 8 mi. SSE of Tahta; cotton, cereals, dates, sugar.

Aulander (ô'lăn"dŭr), town (pop. 1,112), Bertie co., NE N.C., 18 mi. N of Williamston; sawmilling.

Aulanko (ou'längkō), recreation area and resort, Häme co., S Finland, in lake region, 2 mi. N of Hämeenlinna, surrounded by forest reservation.

Aulaqi, 'Aulaqi, or **'Awlaqi** (ou'läkē), easternmost tribal area of Western Aden protectorate, bordered E by Eastern Aden Protectorate and extending from Gulf of Aden to Yemen "Status Quo Line." One of the original Nine Cantons, it consists of the Lower Aulaqi, S of the Kaur al Awaliq, and the Upper Aulaqi on the N plateau. The **Lower Aulaqi** is a sultanate (pop. 12,000) with ⊙ at Ahwar. The sultan concluded a protectorate treaty in 1888 and an adviser agreement in 1944. The **Upper Aulaqi** is a loose confederation (pop. 53,000), ruled partly by a sultan (⊙ Nisab) in treaty relations with Britain since 1904, and partly by a sectional sheik (⊙ Yeshbum) in treaty relations since 1903.

Aulas (ōlä'), village (pop. 409), Gard dept., S France, 2 mi. NW of Le Vigan; silk-hose mfg.

Aulatsivik Island (12 mi. long, 9 mi. wide), just off NE Labrador; 59°50'N 64°W. Mainly mountainous, rising to 3,100 ft. (S).

Auldearn (ôldûrn'), agr. village and parish (pop. 1,193), Nairnshire, Scotland, 3 mi. E of Nairn. In 1645 Montrose here defeated a superior Covenanters' force.

Aulella River, Italy: see MAGRA RIVER.

Aulenbach, Russian SFSR: see KALINOVKA, Kaliningrad oblast.

Aulestad, Norway: see AULSTAD.

Auletta (oulĕt'tä), village (pop. 2,313), Salerno prov., Campania, S Italy, on Tanagro R. and 20 mi. ESE of Eboli.

Aulie-Ata, Kazakh SSR: see DZHAMBUL, city.

Aulis (ô'lĭs), anc. town of Boeotia, E central Greece, on Gulf of Euboea; on its site is modern village of VATHY AULIDOS, 4 mi. S of Chalcis. In Greek legend, Aulis was the port where Iphigenia was sacrificed, and from which Agamemnon and the Greek fleet set out for Troy.

Aulla (äŏŏl'lä), town (pop. 1,755), Massa e Carrara prov., Tuscany, central Italy, in the Lunigiana, on Magra R., at mouth of Aulella R., and 9 mi. NE of Spezia; rail junction; agr. market; macaroni, fertilizer, jute products. Old fort here.

Aullène (ōlĕn'), town (pop. 2,050), S central Corsica, 12 mi. NNE of Sartène; alt. 2,725 ft.

Aullville (ôl'vĭl), town (pop. 123), Lafayette co., W central Mo., 16 mi. SE of Lexington.

Aulnay or **Aulnay-de-Saintonge** (ōnā'-dŭ-sĕtōzh'), village (pop. 916), Charente-Maritime dept., W France, 10 mi. NE of Saint-Jean-d'Angély; cattle raising, dairying, distilling. Has 12th-cent. Romanesque church noted for its portal and square tower.

Aulnay-sous-Bois (-sōō-bwä'), town (pop. 32,223), Seine-et-Oise dept., N central France, a residential NE suburb of Paris, 9 mi. from Notre Dame.

Aulneau Peninsula (ôl'nō), W Ont., on E shore of L. of the Woods, 20 mi. S of Kenora; 30 mi. long, 16 mi. wide.

Aulne River (ōn), Finistère dept., W France, rises in Montagnes d'Arrée 16 mi. ESE of Morlaix, flows 100 mi. SW and W, past Châteauneuf-du-Faou and Châteaulin to Brest Roads (inlet of the Atlantic) 13 mi. SE of Brest. Forms section of Brest-Nantes Canal.

Aulnoye (ōnwä'), town (pop. 4,523), Nord dept., N France, near the Sambre, 7 mi. NW of Avesnes; rail junction; iron and steel products. Granite quarries.

Aulon (ōlō'), village (pop. 525), Haute-Garonne dept., S France, 7 mi. NE of Saint-Gaudens; oil wells.

Aulon or **Avlon** (both: ävlôn'), town (pop. 2,231), Attica nome, E central Greece, on railroad and 19 mi. N of Athens; wheat, olive oil; sheep and goat raising. Formerly called Salesi.

Aulonarion or **Avlonarion** (both: ävlônä'rēōn), town (pop. 2,298), E central Euboea, Greece, 27 mi. ENE of Chalcis; stock raising (sheep, goats).

Aulowönen, Russian SFSR: see KALINOVKA, Kaliningrad oblast.

Aulstad (oul'stä) or **Aulestad** (ou'lŭstä), village in Vestre Gausdal canton (pop. 2,850), Opland co., S central Norway, in the Gausdal (tributary valley of the Gudbrandsdal), 20 mi. NW of Lillehammer. Estate of poet Bjornson (Nor. *Bjørnson*) is now natl. monument.

Ault (ō), village (pop. 1,605), Somme dept., N France, on English Channel, 17 mi. W of Abbeville; copper founding; lock mfg. Near-by Bois-de-Cise (SW) and Onival (N) are small beach resorts.

Ault (ôlt), town (pop. 866), Weld co., N Colo., 10 mi. N of Greeley; alt. 4,940 ft. Sugar beets, livestock, dairy.

Ault Hucknall (ôlt hŭk'nŭl), town and parish (pop. 2,553), NE Derby, England, 7 mi. ESE of Chesterfield; agr. market. Thomas Hobbes died here.

Aulus-les-Bains (ōlüs'-lā-bē'), village (pop. 482), Ariège dept., S France, in central Pyrenees near Sp. border, on the Garbet (small tributary of Salat R.) and 16 mi. SE of Saint-Girons; spa with mineral springs. Chemical fertilizer mfg., sawmilling. Until 1938, called Aulus.

Auly (ŭōō'lē), town (1926 pop. 4,643), central Dnepropetrovsk oblast, Ukrainian SSR, 10 mi. WNW of Dneprodzerzhinsk; quarrying.

Auma (ou'mä), town (pop. 4,609), Thuringia, central Germany, 15 mi. SW of Gera; textile milling, woodworking; mfg. of machinery, pumps, china. Power station.

Aumale (ōmäl'), anc. *Auzia,* town (pop. 3,461), Alger dept., N central Algeria, in the Tell Atlas (Titeri range), 55 mi. SE of Algiers; alt. 2,900 ft.; terminus of rail spur from Bouïra; trades in wines, cereals, horses. A garrison town under Romans, Turks, and (since 1846) French.

Aumale, village (pop. 1,568), Seine-Inférieure dept., N France, on the Bresle and 24 mi. S of Abbeville; tanning, petroleum refining, glass-bottle mfg. Has 15th-16th-cent. late-Gothic church. Heavily damaged in Second World War.

Aumetz (ōmĕs', Ger. ou'mĕts), village (pop. 1,799), Moselle dept., NE France, 11 mi. WNW of Thionville; iron mines.

Aumont-Aubrac (ōmōtōbräk'), village (pop. 753), Lozère dept., S France, bet. the Monts d'Aubrac (SW) and the Montagnes de la Margeride (NE), 17 mi. NW of Mende; pottery mfg., woodworking. Until 1937, Aumont.

Aumsville, town (pop. 281), Marion co., NW Oregon, 10 mi. SE of Salem; fruit, nuts, milk.

Aumühle-Billenkamp (ou'mü"lŭ-bĭ'lŭn-kämp"), residential village (pop. 3,510), in Schleswig-Holstein, NW Germany, 12 mi. E of Hamburg city center; woodworking. Bismarck memorial church near by.

Auna (ounä'), town (pop. 1,436), Niger prov., Northern Provinces, W Nigeria, 45 mi. S of Yelwa; gold-mining center; shea-nut processing, cotton weaving; cassava, durra, yams.

Aunay-sous-Crécy (ōnā'-sōō-krāsē'), village (pop. 338), Eure-et-Loir dept., NW central France, 5 mi. SSW of Dreux; chemical fertilizer mfg.

Aunay-sur-Odon (-sür-ōdō'), village (pop. 185), Calvados dept., NW France, on the Odon and 17 mi. SW of Caen; cheese mfg. Damaged in Second World War.

Aundah, India: see HINGOLI.

Aundh (ound), town (pop. 4,423), Satara North dist., central Bombay, India, 25 mi. SE of Satara; market center for millet, ghur, peanuts, timber. Was ⊙ formerly princely state of Aundh (□ 488; pop. 88,723) in Deccan States, Bombay; inc. 1949 into dists. of Satara North, Satara South, and Bijapur.

Auneau (ōnō'), village (pop. 1,602), Eure-et-Loir dept., N central France, in the Beauce, 13 mi. E of Chartres; agr. machinery mfg.

Auneuil (ōnû'ē), village (pop. 918), Oise dept., N France, 6 mi. SW of Beauvais; brick- and tileworks.

Aungban (oung'băn'), village, Hsamonghkam state, Southern Shan State, Upper Burma, 25 mi. ESE of Taunggyi, on road and railroad to Thazi; junction for roads to Lawksawk (N) and Pinhmi (S).

Aunis (ōnēs'), small region and former province of W France, on Bay of Biscay, N of lower Charente R., forming, with Saintonge, the modern Charente-Maritime dept., including isls. of Ré and Oléron. A part of Aquitaine, it was incorporated (1371) into Fr. royal domain, and remained last important Protestant stronghold in France. Chief city: La Rochelle.

Auñón (ounyōn'), town (pop. 1,052), Guadalajara prov., central Spain, 22 mi. ESE of Guadalajara; olives, grapes, cereals, sheep; vegetable oils.

Aunrai, India: see GOPIGANJ.

Aunus, Karelo-Finnish SSR: see OLONETS.

Aunuu (ounōō'ōō), island (pop. 400), American Samoa, S of E end of Tutuila; has circular crater c.275 ft. high. Sometimes written Anuu.

Aups (ōps), village (pop. 1,087), Var dept., SE France, in Provence Alps, 14 mi. NW of Draguignan; mfg. (olive oil, turpentine), beekeeping.

Aur (our), atoll (□ 2; pop. 399), Ratak Chain, Majuro dist., Marshall Isls., W central Pacific, 225 mi. SE of Kwajalein; 15 mi. long, 10 mi. wide; 42 islets. Formerly Calvert Isls.

'Aura, Masna'a (mäs'nä ou'rŭ), or **Masna'at al Aura** (mäs'nä ăl ou'rŭ), town, ⊙ Duan prov. of Quaiti state, Eastern Aden Protectorate, in the upper Wadi Duan, 65 mi. NW of Mukalla. Has governor's castle. Near by is Khoreiba airfield.

Aurai, India: see GOPIGANJ.

Auraiya (ourī'yŭ), town (pop. 9,840), Etawah dist., W Uttar Pradesh, India, near Lower Ganges Canal, 37 mi. SE of Etawah; road center; trades in pearl millet, wheat, barley, corn, gram, oilseeds, cotton. Has 18th-cent. Rohilla mosques. Founded 16th cent. Sometimes spelled Auriya.

Aurangabad (ou"rŭng-gäbäd'), district (□ 6,212; pop. 1,071,950), NW Hyderabad state, India, on Deccan Plateau; ⊙ Aurangabad. Bordered N by Ajanta Hills, S by Godavari R. Mostly highland (drained by Purna R. In black-soil area; cotton, wheat, millet, oilseeds (chiefly peanuts), tobacco. Cotton ginning, flour and oilseed milling, tanning, biri mfg.; cattle raising. Main trade centers: Aurangabad (cotton- and silk-weaving center), Jalna. Archaeological landmarks include famous rock-cut shrines at Ajanta and Ellora. Dist. became part of Hyderabad during state's formation in 18th cent. Pop. 78% Hindu, 16% Moslem, 1% Christian. Sometimes spelled Aurungabad.

Aurangabad. 1 Town (pop. 8,878), Gaya dist., W central Bihar, India, 40 mi. W of Gaya; rice, gram, oilseeds, wheat; leather mfg. Saltworks 8 mi. NNW, near Palmerganj. **2** City (pop., including cantonment, 50,924), ⊙ Aurangabad dist., NW Hyderabad state, India, 175 mi. ENE of Bombay; road junction; cotton- and silk-milling center; agr. trade center (chiefly millet, wheat, peanuts); biri mfg.; iron and steel products. Industrial schools. Was hq. (with important hill fortress at Daulatabad, 8 mi. WNW) of Aurangzeb's govt. in mid-17th cent. Just N are 7th-cent. Buddhist cave temples; famous rock-cut shrines of Ellora 14 mi. NW.

Aurangabad Saiyid (sī'yĭd), town (pop. 5,354), Bulandshahr dist., W Uttar Pradesh, India, 9 mi. NE of Bulandshahr; wheat, oilseeds, barley, sugar cane, jowar, corn. Founded 1704. Also called Aurangabad. Agr. col. 2.5 mi. NNE, at village of Lakhaoti.

Auranitis, Syria: see HAURAN.

Aurapushekaru (ou'räpōōshākä'rōō), coral island, S Palau, W Caroline Isls., W Pacific; 7°18'N 134°30'E; 3 mi. long; rises to 613 ft.

Auraria (ûrâ'rēŭ), village (pop. c.200), Lumpkin co., N Ga., 15 mi. NW of Gainesville, in gold-mining area.

Aura River, Finnish *Aurajoki* (ou'räyō"kē), SW Finland, rises W of Loimaa, flows 40 mi. generally SW to inlet of Gulf of Bothnia at Turku.

Aura River (ou'rä), in Opland and More og Romsdal counties, W Norway, issues from small lake of same name in the Dovrefjell 25 mi. NW of Dombas, flows c.30 mi. NW, over several falls, through Eikesdal L. (12 mi. long), to head of Lang Fjord (E arm of Molde Fjord) at Nauste.

Auras, Poland: see URAZ.

Auray (ōrā'), town (pop. 8,038), Morbihan dept., W France, port on Auray R. estuary and 11 mi. W of Vannes; furniture and lace mfg., oyster breeding. Preserves numerous medieval houses. Basilica of SAINTE-ANNE-D'AURAY is 4 mi. NE. Near by, Charles of Blois was killed during a battle (1364) of the War of the Breton Succession. At the *Champ des Martyrs* 800 Royalists, who had landed at Quiberon, were massacred by Republicans in 1795.

Aurea, Chersonesus, Malaya: see MALAY PENINSULA.

Aureilhan (ōrāyā'), NE suburb (pop. 3,703) of Tarbes, Hautes-Pyrénées dept., SW France; brick factory, sawmills.

Aurelia (ourā'lyä), village (pop. 286), Roma prov., Latium, central Italy, 3 mi. N of Civitavecchia; aluminum industry.

Aurelia (ûrēl'yŭ), town (pop. 807), Cherokee co., NW Iowa, 6 mi. ESE of Cherokee, in livestock and grain area.

Aurelianum, France: see ORLÉANS.

Aure River (ōr), Calvados dept., NW France, rises in Normandy Hills near Caumont, flows N, past Bayeux, thence W, past Trévières, to the Vire 1 mi. below Isigny and just above its mouth on English Channel. Length, c.35 mi.

Aurès (ōrĕs'), anc. *Aurasius Mons,* strongly folded mtn. massif in Constantine dept., NE Algeria, forming a unit of the Saharan Atlas and containing Algeria's highest summits. Bounded by the High Plateaus (N), the Hodna depression (W), the Nemencha Mts. (E), its S slopes border steeply on the Sahara. Highest peaks (Djebel Chélia, 7,641 ft.; Kef Mahmel, 7,615 ft.) are snow-covered part of the year. Because of adequate rainfall at higher elevations, the massif is covered with Aleppo pine and oak forests, while the lower slopes have only xerophytic vegetation. The Aurès is crossed (near W edge) by 1 major natural route (known to Romans; used by Batna-Biskra road and railroad) through the El-Kantara defile. Difficult of access, the Aurès has long been a retreat of semi-nomadic Berber tribes. Though first occupied by French in 1845, it was not completely pacified until 1879.

Aureum, Spain: see ORENSE, city.

Aure Valley (ōr), Hautes-Pyrénées dept., SW France, bet. Vielle-Aure and La Barthe-de-Neste; drained by Neste R. Has electrometallurgical factories at SARRANCOLIN, BEYRÈDE-JUMET, and HÈCHES.

Aurich (ou'rĭkh), town (pop. 10,925), in former Prussian prov. of Hanover, NW Germany, after 1945 in Lower Saxony, in East Friesland, on Ems-Jade Canal and 13 mi. NE of Emden; noted for its annual horse fair; textile mfg. Has castle (restored

1852). Of anc. origin. Chartered 1539. Was ⊙ county, later duchy, of East Friesland.

Auriesville (ô'rēzvĭl), village, Montgomery co., E central N.Y., on Mohawk R. and the Barge Canal, and 6 mi. W of Amsterdam. Here is R.C. Shrine of Our Lady of Martyrs, commemorating St. Isaac Jogues and other French missionaries killed in 1640s by the Iroquois.

Aurignac (ōrēnyăk'), village (pop. 834), Haute-Garonne dept., S France, 11 mi. NE of Saint-Gaudens; horse breeding. Prehistoric tools and animal relics found in near-by caves have given name to Aurignacian period.

Aurigny, Channel Isls.: see ALDERNEY.

Aurillac (ōrēyăk'), anc. *Aureliacum*, town (pop. 18,957), ⊙ Cantal dept., S central France, on SW slope of Massif du Cantal, on the Jordanne and 65 mi. SSW of Clermont-Ferrand; road and commercial center; noted for its umbrella factories; mfg. of fishnets, men's clothing, footwear, copperware, bricks and tiles; brewing, distilling, processing and shipping of Cantal cheese. Pope Sylvester II and Paul Doumer b. here.

Aurina, Valle (väl'lĕ ourē'nä), Ger. *Ahrntal*, lateral valley of the Pustertal, Bolzano prov., N Italy; extends from Vetta d'Italia c.20 mi. S to Campo Tures. Formed by upper course of Aurino R. Forestry, cattle raising, poppy growing.

Aurine, Alpi, Italy: see ZILLERTAL ALPS.

Aurino River (ourē'nô), N Italy, rises in Alps near Vetta d'Italia peak, flows 30 mi. S, through Valle Aurina, past Campo Tures, to Rienza R. near Brunico.

Auriol (ōrēôl'), village (pop. 1,883), Bouches-du-Rhône dept., SE France, 14 mi. ENE of Marseilles, in hilly region; resins, olive oil.

Auriol, Mount, peak (7,580 ft.), S Yukon territory, Canada, overlooking Alaska Highway, SE of Kluane L.; 60°35'N 137°30'W. Named 1951 for president of France.

Aurisina (ourēzē'nä), Slovenian *Nabrežina* (nä'-brĕzhēnä), village (pop. 972), N Free Territory of Trieste, on Gulf of Trieste, on railroad and 9 mi. NW of Trieste; rail junction; seaside resort. Marble quarries. Placed 1947 under Anglo-American administration. Until c.1920, called Nabresina.

Auriya, India: see AURAIYA.

Aurizona (ourēzō'nù), town (pop. 1,383), northernmost Maranhão, Brazil, near the Atlantic, 130 mi. NW of São Luís, in gold-mining area. Formerly called Presidente Vargas.

Aurland (our'län) or **Aurlandsvangen** (our'läns-väng"ùn), village (pop. 439; canton pop. 2,372), Sogn og Fjordane co., W Norway, on Aurlands Fjord, 75 mi. NE of Bergen; barrel mfg. Tourist center in the FLAMSDAL. Has 14th-cent. stone church.

Aurlands Fjord (our'läns), S arm of Sogne Fjord, Sogn og Fjordane co., W Norway; c.20 mi. long. On it is Aurland village. Branches into NAEROY FJORD (SW).

Aurlandsvangen, Norway: see AURLAND.

Aurolzmünster (ou'rōltsmüns"tùr), town (pop. 2,706), W Upper Austria, just NNW of Ried im Innkreis; brewery.

Auron (ōrō'), village in Maritime Alps, Alpes-Maritimes dept., SE France, near head of Tinée R. valley above Saint-Étienne-de-Tinée; alt. 5,276 ft. Winter sports.

Auron River, Cher dept., central France, rises 6 mi. W of Lurcy-Lévy, flows 52 mi. NW, past Dun-sur-Auron, to Bourges where it joins the Yèvre. Followed along most of its course by N section of Berry Canal.

Auronzo (ourôn'tsô), commune (pop. 3,827), Belluno prov., Veneto, N Italy. Commune seat is Villagrande (pop. 1,878), 31 mi. NNE of Belluno, in the Dolomites; resort (alt. 2,835 ft.); soap factory.

Aurora (ourô'rù), city (pop. 1,946), S Ceará, Brazil, on Fortaleza-Crato RR and 37 mi. NE of Crato; cotton, tobacco, sugar, rice.

Aurora (ùrô'rù). **1** Village (pop. 290), Essequibo co., N Br. Guiana, on the Atlantic at mouth of Essequibo R., 26 mi. WNW of Georgetown; rice and coconut growing, stock raising. **2** Gold mine, Essequibo co., N Br. Guiana, on Cuyuni R., and 85 mi. WNW of Bartica; served by river boats.

Aurora (ùrō'rù, ôrō'–), town (pop. 2,726), S Ont., 22 mi. N of Toronto; tanning, mfg. of shoes, farm implements, flour products. School for boys.

Aurora, Society Isls.: see MAKATEA.

Aurora (ùrō'rù), county (□ 711; pop. 5,020), SE central S.Dak.; ⊙ Plankinton. Level farming area watered by intermittent creeks. Livestock, dairy products, poultry, wheat, corn. Formed 1879.

Aurora. 1 Residential city (pop. 11,421), Adams and Arapahoe counties, N central Colo., just E of Denver; alt. 5,400 ft. Huge U.S. Fitzsimons General Hosp. near by. Inc. 1903. **2** Industrial city (pop. 50,576), Kane co., NE Ill., on Fox R. (bridged here) and 36 mi. W of Chicago, in dairying and stock-raising area; railroad shops, machine shops, foundries. Mfg. of aluminum goods, iron and steel products; conveying, pumping, and construction machinery; fire escapes, elevators, furniture, textiles, office supplies, clocks, auto accessories, paper and fiber boxes, clothing, hardware. Seat of Aurora Col. Settled 1834, inc. 1837. Was 1st Ill. town with electrical street lighting (1881). **3** City (pop. 4,780), Dearborn co., SE Ind., on Ohio R. and 22 mi. WSW of Cincinnati (Ohio), in agr. area (livestock, tobacco, truck); lumber milling; mfg. of coffins, furniture, cement vaults, clothing. Laid out 1819. Inundation by flood in 1937 caused much damage. **4** Town (pop. 225), Buchanan co., E Iowa, 13 mi. NE of Independence. **5** City (pop. 221), Cloud co., N Kansas, 11 mi. SE of Concordia, in wheat region. **6** Town (pop. 91), Hancock co., S Maine, 24 mi. ENE of Bangor, in hunting, fishing area. **7** Village (pop. 1,371), St. Louis co., NE Minn., near St. Louis R., at E end of Mesabi iron range, 14 mi. E of Virginia. Open-pit iron mines near by. Experimental plant here concentrates low-grade ore (taconite). Parts of Superior Natl. Forest in vicinity. Inc. 1903. **8** City (pop. 4,153), Lawrence co., SW Mo., in the Ozarks, 28 mi. SW of Springfield; agr.; mfg. (shoes, grain products); lead, zinc mines. Laid out 1870. **9** City (pop. 2,455), ⊙ Hamilton co., SE central Nebr., 20 mi. E of Grand Island and on branch of Big Blue R.; flour; livestock, grain, dairy produce. Founded 1872, inc. 1877. **10** Town, Nev.: see HAWTHORNE. **11** Village (pop. 711), Cayuga co., W central N.Y., in Finger Lakes region, on E shore of Cayuga L., 35 mi. SW of Syracuse in agr. area (dairy products, poultry, grain). Resort. Seat of Wells Col. for women (1869). **12** Fishing town (pop. 525), Beaufort co., E N.C., 19 mi. NE of New Bern, on an inlet of Pamlico R. estuary. **13** Village (pop. 571), Portage co., NE Ohio, 22 mi. SE of Cleveland and on branch of Chagrin R.; sandstone quarry. **14** City (pop. 242), Marion co., NW Oregon, 10 mi. SW of Oregon City; hops. Founded 1855 as Christian communistic colony. **15** Town (pop. 202), Brookings co., E S.Dak., 6 mi. E of Brookings; grain elevators. **16** Town (pop. 614), Sevier co., central Utah, near Sevier R., 4 mi. SW of Salina. **17** Town (pop. 951), Florence co., extreme NE Wis., 5 mi. SW of Iron Mountain, Mich.; lumbering.

Aurora Island, New Hebrides: see MAEWO.

Auros (ōrō'), village (pop. 354), Gironde dept., SW France, 16 mi. W of Marmande; winegrowing, cattle raising.

Aursund (our'sŏŏn), lake (□ 17) on the Glomma, in Sor-Trondelag co., central Norway, 8 mi. NNE of Roros; 12 mi. long. Klinkenberg pyrite mine is N.

Aurungabad, India: see AURANGABAD.

Aus (ous), town (pop. 529), SW South-West Africa, on edge of inland plateau, near Namib Desert, 70 mi. E of Lüderitz; alt. 4,742 ft.; sheep raising.

Ausa or **Owsa** (both: ou'sŭ), town (pop. 7,504), Osmanabad dist., W Hyderabad state, India, 12 mi. SSW of Latur; road center; millet, wheat, cotton. Owsa Road, rail station, is 10 mi. NNW. Also spelled Ousa.

Ausable Chasm (ôsā'bùl), Essex co., NE N.Y., gorge of lower Ausable R. above Keeseville, near river mouth on L. Champlain; c.1½ mi. long, 20–50 ft. wide, 100–200 ft. deep; has waterfalls, rapids, odd rock formations. Crossed by stone bridge (1842) near Keeseville. Ausable Chasm village is tourist resort.

Au Sable Forks, village (pop. 1,643), on Clinton-Essex co. line, NE N.Y., at junction of East and West branches here forming Ausable R., 21 mi. SSW of Plattsburg, in timber, agr., and resort area; mfg. (paper, pulp); granite quarries. Ausable Chasm of Ausable R. is NE.

Ausable Lakes, NE N.Y., 2 small lakes (Upper Ausable, c.1 mi. long; Lower Ausable, c.2 mi. long) in the Adirondacks, 15 mi. SSE of Lake Placid village. Connected and drained by East Branch of Ausable R.

Au Sable Point, Mich.: see SAGINAW BAY.

Au Sable River, NE Mich., formed by several branches near Crawford-Oscoda co. line, flows c.80 mi. SE, past Mio, to L. Huron at Oscoda (Iosco co.). Power dams in lower course, North Branch flows c.30 mi. SE from Otsego co. Middle Branch (c.33 mi. long) rises SW of Otsego L., flows S and E, past Grayling. South Branch rises in L. St. Helen, flows N, past Roscommon; c.37 mi. long.

Ausable River, NE N.Y., formed by East Branch (c.30 mi. long) and West Branch (c.25 mi. long), both rising in the Adirondacks and flowing generally NE to their junction at Au Sable Forks village; thence the stream flows c.20 mi. NE, through AUSABLE CHASM in its lower course, to L. Champlain 10 mi. S of Plattsburg.

Auscha, Czechoslovakia: see USTEK.

Auschwitz, Poland: see OSWIECIM.

Ausejo (ousā'hō), town (pop. 1,399), Logroño prov., N Spain, 17 mi. ESE of Logroño; wine, olive oil, fruit, cereals.

Ausim or **Awsim** (ousēm'), town (pop. 15,016), Giza prov., Upper Egypt, 8 mi. NW of Cairo city center; silk weaving. Site of anc. Letopolis.

Auskerry (ôskĕ'rē), island (pop. 4) of the Orkneys, Scotland, 3 mi. S of Stronsay; 1 mi. long. Lighthouse (59°1'N 2°33'W).

Auspitz, Czechoslovakia: see HUSTOPECE.

Aussa (ou'sä), S dist. of the DANAKIL region, in Harar and Wallo provs., NE Ethiopia, near Fr. Somaliland border. Malarial lowland containing salt marshes with several lakes (Gamarri, Arissa, Abbé) which are fed by the Awash (used for irrigation). Pastoralism (camels, cattle, sheep, goats); salt extracting, cereal growing. Chief centers, Sardo and Hadele Gubo.

Aussee, Austria: see BAD AUSSEE.

Aussenalster, Germany: see ALSTER RIVER.

Aussig, Czechoslovakia: see USTI NAD LABEM.

Aust-Agder (oust'-äg'dùr), county [Nor. *fylke*] (□ 3,609; pop. 74,861), S Norway; ⊙ Arendal. Includes a narrow lowland along Skagerrak coast. Inland are highlands passing into the Bykle Mts., traversed by the valley Setesdal. Nickel and low-grade iron ore are mined. Most of co. is forested; agr. is scarce; there is lumbering, cattle raising, dairying. Timber is floated to coastal cities where it is milled and exported. Active fishing and lobster industries. Co. abounds in burial mounds and excavation sites dating from Stone and Iron ages, as well as from Viking period. Its main centers are: Risor, Tvedestrand, Arendal, Grimstad, Lillesand. Until 1918, co. (then called *amt*) was named Nedenes.

Austell (ôstĕl'), city (pop. 1,413), Cobb co., NW central Ga., 15 mi. WNW of Atlanta. Inc. as town 1885, as city 1929.

Austerlitz (ô'stùrlĭts, Ger. ow'–), Czech *Slavkov* or *Slavkov u Brna* (släf'kôf ŏŏ'bùrnä), town (pop. 4,451), S central Moravia, Czechoslovakia, on railroad and 12 mi. ESE of Brno; agr. center (barley, wheat). Here, in "battle of the three emperors," Napoleon I defeated (Dec. 2, 1805) combined Russian and Austrian armies under Tsar Alexander I and Emperor Francis II; Napoleon's most brilliant and complete victory. A famous description of it is in Tolstoy's *War and Peace.* Austerlitz has notable 18th-cent. castle, church, and cenotaph with chapel on site of battle.

Austin, county (□ 662; pop. 14,663), S Texas; ⊙ Bellville. Bounded E by Brazos R.; also drained by San Bernard R. Agr. (cotton, peanuts, corn, hay, pecans, truck); livestock (cattle, hogs, poultry); dairying. Lumbering; oil, natural-gas wells. State park at San Felipe, founded 1823 as hq. of Stephen F. Austin's colony. Co. formed 1836.

Austin. 1 Town (pop. 154), Lonoke co., central Ark., 25 mi. NE of Little Rock. **2** Village (pop. c.150), Delta co., W Colo., on Gunnison R. and 7 mi. ENE of Delta; alt. 5,070 ft. Shipping point for fruit and dairy products. Black Canyon of the Gunnison ends here. Fruit Growers Dam, 3 mi. N, on small branch of Gunnison R., is unit in Fruit Growers irrigation project. **3** Village (pop. 2,906), Scott co., SE Ind., 32 mi. N of New Albany, in agr. area; tin cans, canned foods. **4** City (pop. 23,100), ⊙ Mower co., SE Minn., on Cedar R., near Iowa line, and 35 mi. SW of Rochester; railroad-div. point, with repair shops, and trade and industrial center for agr. area; food processing (meat and dairy products); canned vegetables, beverages. Junior col. is here, state park near by. Settled 1853, platted 1856, inc. 1876. **5** Village (pop. c.700), ⊙ Lander co., central Nev., in W foothills of Toiyabe Range, 60 mi. W of Eureka; alt. 6,147 ft.; distributing center; silver, gold; cattle, sheep, wool. **6** Town (pop. 39), Grant co., NE Oregon, 35 mi. WSW of Baker. **7** Borough (pop. 804), Potter co., N Pa., 11 mi. SSW of Coudersport; paper mill. **8** City (pop. 132,459), ⊙ Texas and Travis co., S central Texas, on both banks of Colorado R. and c.70 mi. NE of San Antonio; 30°16'N 97°45'W; alt. 650 ft. State's governmental and educational center (seat of Univ. of Texas, St. Edward's Univ., Austin Presbyterian Theological Seminary, Lutheran Concordia Col., Samuel Huston Col., Tillotson Col.); commercial and distribution center for wide region (cattle, cotton, pecans, mohair, dairy products, poultry). Near-by hydroelectric dams on the Colorado supply power to several counties and to industries here: furniture, brick, tile, and other clay products, food products (especially Mex. foods), beverages, cut stone, machinery, wood and metal products. Here are a state mental hosp. and state institutions for the deaf, dumb, and blind. Points of interest: the capitol (1885) and other govt. bldgs.; Univ. of Texas campus; house of O. Henry (now a mus.), Elizabeth Ney's studio (also a mus.), and old Fr. embassy. Near by are recreation areas (Barton Springs, L. Austin Park, others). U.S. fish hatchery and U.S. military airfield (Bergstrom Air Force Base) are near. Laid out 1838 as Waterloo; chosen as capital site 1839 and renamed in honor of Stephen F. Austin. Evacuated (1842–45) by govt. because of Indian raiders and the Mex. occupation of San Antonio; became seat of state govt. (1845) on annexation of Texas by U.S.; made permanent capital, 1870. Industrial growth stimulated by harnessing (since 1934) of river by power and flood-control projects of Lower Colorado R. Authority.

Austin, Lake (□ 320), W central Western Australia, 310 mi. NNE of Perth; 43 mi. long, 6 mi. wide; usually dry.

Austin, Lake, Texas: see TOM MILLER DAM.

Austin Dam, Texas: see TOM MILLER DAM.

Austin Lake, village (pop. 2,032), Kalamazoo co., SW Mich., 6 mi. S of Kalamazoo.

Austinville. 1 Town (pop. 1,110), Morgan co., N Ala., 3 mi. SW of Decatur, near Tennessee R. **2** Village (1940 pop. 713), Wythe co., SW Va., on New R. and 10 mi. SE of Wytheville; lead and zinc mining.

Australasia (ô″strůlā′zhů, –shů), islands of the S Pacific including Australia, New Zealand, New Guinea, and adjacent isls. Term sometimes covers all Oceania.

Australes, Îles (ēl′ ōsträl′), outlying dependencies (since 1924) of Madagascar, in S Indian Ocean and mostly in subantarctic zone. Comprise KERGUELEN ISLANDS, CROZET ISLANDS, SAINT PAUL ISLAND, AMSTERDAM ISLAND, and ADÉLIE COAST. For the group of Fr. Oceania in the Pacific called Austral, see TUBUAI ISLANDS.

Australia (ôstrā′lyů) [Latin,=southern], island continent (□ 2,948,366) bet. the Indian and Pacific oceans and SE of Asia, bounded W and S by Indian Ocean, N by Torres Strait, Timor Sea, and Arafura Sea, E by Coral and Tasman seas; bet. 10°41′-39°8′S and 119°9′-153°39′E. It is 2,400 mi. E-W, 2,000 mi. N-S. With the island prov. of TASMANIA off E part of its S coast, the continent makes up the Commonwealth of Australia, a British dominion (□ 2,974,581; pop. 7,579,358, excluding aborigines). There are 5 continental states (QUEENSLAND, NEW SOUTH WALES, VICTORIA, SOUTH AUSTRALIA, and WESTERN AUSTRALIA) as well as the NORTHERN TERRITORY and the AUSTRALIAN CAPITAL TERRITORY (cut out of New South Wales, with CANBERRA, the federal capital). Australia also has jurisdiction of the Territory of PAPUA, NORFOLK ISLAND, and the AUSTRALIAN ANTARCTIC TERRITORY. The Territory of New Guinea (see NEW GUINEA, TERRITORY OF) is governed by Australia under U.N. trusteeship, and NAURU, also under U.N. trusteeship, is governed jointly by Australia, the United Kingdom, and New Zealand. The continent itself (the smallest continent or the largest isl. of the world, according to definition) is nearly as large as the continental United States. It is on the whole excessively dry, supposedly because there are no mts. in the interior to precipitate rainfall. Up from the narrow coast in the W the land rises abruptly in what seems from the sea to be mtn. ranges but are actually the escarpment of a plateau that occupies all the W part of Australia. It is 1–2,000 ft. high and has no permanent rivers or lakes. Here in W central Australia are the vast Great Sandy, Gibson, and Victoria deserts. In the SW corner of Western Australia there is a fertile area, but the rest of the state is arid and valuable chiefly for its gold mines. To the N the Timor Sea separates this dry land from Indonesia; the NW corner is hottest part of Australia, with mean annual temp. of 90°F. The Territory of Northern Australia also belongs to the arid plateau, with tropical temperatures. Its northernmost section, Arnhem Land (principally given over to reservations for aborigines) faces the Arafura Sea in the N and the huge Gulf of Carpentaria on the E. Across the gulf is the long spit of land called CAPE YORK PENINSULA, the northernmost section of Queensland; this, far from being dry is wet jungle land (parts of the coast have 160 in. of rain). Off the NE coast of the continent stretches the GREAT BARRIER REEF. In the extreme E of Australia, hugging the coast, are the mts. of the Great Dividing Range, which runs down the whole E coast and then parallels the SE coast, through Queensland, New South Wales, and Victoria. It rises to Mt. Kosciusko (7,305 ft.), highest in Australia, in the S part of the range, called the Australian Alps. This E area is more temperate, with a range of 45°–85°F. The rivers on the E and S slopes run to the Coral and Tasman seas through narrow but rich coastal plains. The rivers on the W flow either N to the Gulf of Carpentaria or SW to the Indian Ocean. The longest of all Australian river systems, that of the MURRAY RIVER and its tributaries the DARLING RIVER and the MURRUMBIDGEE RIVER (with the Lachlan) drain the S part of the interior basin that lies bet. the mts. and the waterless plateau. The Murray is the only permanent river of Australia and is used for hydroelectric power and irrigation. The interior basin is not well supplied with water but in the Great Artesian Basin of S Queensland wells can be sunk to obtain water for sheep ranching. Hume Dam in the Murray on the New South Wales–Victoria border creates a reservoir that irrigates a large agricultural area. Large interior rivers, such as the BARCOO RIVER, are usually dry. The largest lakes (Mackay, Amadeus, Eyre, in central region) have no outlet and are usually dry. Most of the good farming areas and the good ports are in the E and particularly the SE (except for the area about Perth in SW Western Australia), where the climate is most temperate. Victoria is the smallest but by far the most densely populated of the continental states. Its ⊙, MELBOURNE, is surpassed in size only by SYDNEY, the ⊙ New South Wales, while BRISBANE, the ⊙ Queensland (in the extreme SE of the state), and ADELAIDE, the ⊙ South Australia, are also large. Stock raising and grain production (wheat, barley, oats) have long been staple occupations of Australia, and there are many vineyards. Tropical and subtropical products—citrus fruits, sugar cane, tobacco, cotton, and tropical fruits (mostly from the NE)—are also important, and there is considerable dairying; some lumbering is done in the E and SE. Besides the gold fields of Western Australia there are coal mines in New South Wales. Gold and coal are also found elsewhere, as well as lead, silver, zinc, and tin. A pearling industry is active on NW coast. Industries have developed in the large cities. The principal exports are wool, meat, grain, dairy products, fruit, raw sugar, lead, and zinc. Australia, remote from any other continent, has many distinctive forms of plant life, notably species of giant eucalyptus, of animal life, including the kangaroo, the flying opossum, the wallaby, the wombat, the platypus, the spiny anteater, and many unusual birds, such as the lyrebird and the emu. Foreign animals when introduced have frequently done well. Rabbits, brought into the land in 1788, have done entirely too well, multiplying until by the middle of the 19th cent. they were a distinct menace to sheep raising. In 1907 a fence 1,000 mi. long was built from the N coast to the S to prevent the rabbits from invading Western Australia. When Europeans 1st reached Australia they found 2 general groups of natives, speaking entirely different languages and having completely different customs—those in the N resembling the Negroid Western Papuans and those in the S supposedly related to the Dravidians of India. The material culture of both groups was low and they did not offer much opposition to white settlement. Today they are some 75,000 in number and are concentrated on reservations in the northern, torrid area of the continent. White settlement was slow in coming. It seems probable that Australia was 1st sighted by a Portuguese, Manuel Godhino de Eredia, in 1601 and may have been sighted by a Spaniard, Luis Vaez de Torres (1605–6). In the century following it was visited by the Dutch, who named it New Holland. In 1688 the British William Dampier landed at King Sound on NW coast. Nearly a century later Capt. James Cook reached Botany Bay (1770) and sailed N to Cape York, claiming the coast for Great Britain. Not long afterward in 1788 the 1st Br. settlement was made —a penal colony on the shores of Port Jackson where Sydney now stands. By 1829 the whole continent was a Br. dependency. Exploration, begun before the 1st settlement was founded, was continued by such men as Sir Matthew Flinders (1798), Ludwig Leichhardt (lost with all his party in 1848) and John McDouall Stuart (1st to cross the continent, 1862). Sheep raising was introduced early and before the middle of the 19th cent. wheat had become important enough to prompt the races of the "grain ships" taking their precious cargo half way around the world to England. A gold strike in Victoria in 1851 brought a rush to that region and caused it to be separated from New South Wales. With minerals, sheep, and grain forming the base of the economy, Australia developed. The colonial administration was shifted, but confederation did not come until a constitution drafted in 1891 was approved by the British Parliament and was put in operation in 1901; by it the colonies of New South Wales, Victoria, Queensland, South Australia, and Tasmania were federated. The Northern Territory was transferred to the federation in 1911. In that same year territory was acquired from New South Wales for building a new capital, Canberra, which was later built; Parliament began meeting there in 1927. The executive power is vested in a governor general (representing the British sovereign), a cabinet presided over by a prime minister representing the party or a coalition given a majority in popular elections. The Parliament consists of 2 houses. The distribution of federal and state powers is roughly like that of the U.S. From its early years, the federal government has been noted for its liberal legislation—woman suffrage was adopted in 1910, old-age pensions were provided in 1909, invalid pensions in 1910, maternity allowances in 1912, a subsidy to parents for each child born after the first (1941), and unemployment and sickness benefits in 1944. The literacy rate is high. Government grants have aided in the establishment of state universities—the Univ. of Sidney (1852), the Univ. of Melbourne (1854), the Univ. of Adelaide (1874), and the Univ. of Queensland (in Brisbane, 1909). The railroad systems are also owned by the separate states and there is no uniformity. A railroad crosses the continent E to W, but a projected line N to S has never been finished. Air service is greatly aiding the communications system. Australians were notable in service in the First World War, and were also in arms in great numbers in the Second World War. Australia declared war on Germany Sept. 3, 1939, and on Japan Dec. 9, 1941, The continent seemed in imminent danger of attack by the Japanese early in 1942, but the threat was averted by Allied victory in the battle of the Coral Sea.

Australian Alps, chain of mountain ranges, SE Australia, forming S part of Great Dividing Range; extend c.200 mi. SW from Australian Capital Territory to Goulburn R., Victoria. Comprise several ranges: MUNIONG RANGE (largest); Bowen Mts. and Barry Mts., Victoria. Rise to 7,305 ft. in Mt. Kosciusko, highest peak of Australia; forested slopes; winter sports.

Australian Antarctic Territory (□ 2,472,000), the part of Antarctica claimed by Australia; includes isls. and all territory (except Adélie Land, claimed by France) S of 60°S lat. bet. 45° and 160°E long. Placed under Australia in 1933. U.S. does not recognize claims in Antarctica.

Australian Capital Territory (□ 911; pop. 16,905), SE Australia, within state of New South Wales; site of CANBERRA, ⊙ of the Commonwealth. This area, formerly known as Yass-Canberra, was surrendered 1911 by New South Wales to the Commonwealth and was called Federal Capital Territory; name changed 1938 to Australian Capital Territory. Part of JERVIS BAY area ceded 1915 by New South Wales to the Commonwealth.

Austral Islands (ô′strůl), group in Fr. Oceania, in the Pacific: see TUBUAI ISLANDS. For the names of certain other Fr. possessions, in the S Indian Ocean, which are also called Austral by the French, see AUSTRALES, ÎLES.

Austrasia (ôstrā′zhů), E part of the Morovingian kingdom of the Franks in 6th, 7th, and 8th cent., comprising, in general, parts of E France, W Germany, and the Netherlands, with its capital at Metz. It was formed by the 511 partition among sons of Clovis I. Later temporarily reunited with NEUSTRIA.

Austratt (oust′rôt), Nor. *Austrått*, castle in Orland (Nor. *Ørland*) canton (pop. 3,963), Sor-Trondelag co., central Norway, on Stjorn Fjord, 28 mi. NW of Trondheim. Founded in 12th cent.; palace built on same site (1654). Formerly spelled Ostraat, Nor. *Østråt* or *Østraat*.

Austrheim, Norway: see FEDJE.

Austria, Ger. *Osterreich* (ûs′tûrīkh), federal republic (□ 32,375; 1951 pop. 6,918,959), central Europe; ⊙ VIENNA. Divided administratively into 9 autonomous provs. [Ger. *Bundesländer*]: VORARLBERG and TYROL (in W panhandle), SALZBURG and UPPER AUSTRIA (N central), CARINTHIA (S central), BURGENLAND, LOWER AUSTRIA, STYRIA, and VIENNA (E). Situated almost completely in the Alps, it extends bet. 46°30′–49°N (40 mi. wide in W, 160 mi. wide in E) and 9°30′–17°E (360 mi. long). The Rhine valley and L. of Constance form W border with Liechtenstein and Switzerland, from which Austria is also separated by the Rhaetian Alps (extreme SW). In the south, the ÖTZTAL ALPS, the ZILLERTAL ALPS, and the CARNIC ALPS form border with Italy, and the KARAWANKEN with Yugoslavia. E border towards Hungary follows W rim of Carpathian basin; Czechoslovakia borders NE. Lower valley of Inn and Salzach rivers, SALZBURG ALPS, BAVARIAN ALPS, and ALLGÄU ALPS separate Austria from Germany (N). Due to its diversified topography (high mountains, low valleys, hilly regions), the country's climate is extremely varied; mean annual temp. in Vienna is 49°F. After Switzerland, Austria is Europe's most mountainous state (average height above sea level 3,000 ft.), traversed in general W-E direction by ranges of Central and Eastern Alps, which reach the Danube at Vienna in the WIENER WALD. Spectacular glaciers crown the ranges along the Italian border and the HOHE TAUERN (which rise to 12,460 ft. in the Grossglockner). The N border and the central ranges (KITZBÜHEL ALPS, NIEDERE TAUERN, TOTES GEBIRGE, STEINERNES MEER, ENNSTAL ALPS) do not rise above 10,000 ft. Many passes (BRENNER PASS, ARLBERG, GLOCKNERSTRASSE, KATSCHBERG PASS, SEMMERING PASS) facilitate transportation. Beautiful mountain regions, picturesque valleys and villages, and numerous mineral springs have made tourism an important industry. Vienna is the country's leading tourist center, but the world-renowned music festivals at SALZBURG, the neighboring SALZKAMMERGUT resort region, and the Tyrol also attract thousands of visitors each year. Kitzbühel, Sankt Anton am Arlberg, Seefeld, Mariazell, and Zürs are popular skiing resorts; among the many spas Bad Ischl, Baden, Bad Gastein, and Bad Hall are perhaps the best known. The warm lakes of Carinthia (Millstättersee, Ossiachersee, Wörthersee) have become favorite water-sports areas (boating, swimming). The country is rich in mineral resources. Styria possesses vast iron ore deposits (ERZBERG), on which the Austrian steel industry is based. Over 80% of the country's lignite needs are supplied by local mines (Köflach, Voitsberg, Fohnsdorf, Thomasroith, Wolfsegg). Salt is gained at Solbad Hall, Hallstatt, Hallein, and in the Altaussee region. Copper is mined at Schwaz and Brixlegg (Tyrol), lead and zinc at Bleiberg and magnesite at Radenthein (both in Carinthia). Some gold and silver is found in the valleys on the N slopes of the Hohe Tauern. With its Zistersdorf fields Austria ranks after USSR and Rumania among Europe's petroleum producers. Despite relatively heavy destruction, Austria emerged from the Second World War with greater industrial plant capacity than before 1938, development being greatest in the production of iron and steel, aluminum, machine tools, chemicals, and artificial fibers. Styria (Graz, Leoben-Donawitz, Kapfenberg, Judenburg) and Upper Austria (Linz, Braunau, Steyr, Wels) are centers of heavy industry, while most of the country's finishing and processing industries are located in and around Vienna (Wiener Neustadt, Amstetten, Neunkirchen, Sankt Pölten). Other mfg. towns are Klagenfurt, Spittal, and Villach. Vorarlberg is noted for its textiles (Bludenz, Dornbirn, Feldkirch) and hand-made embroidery. By 1950 only a small percentage of Austria's high potential in hydroelectric power had been realized. Hydroelectric stations are located on all major rivers (the Danube and its tributaries, Drau, Enns, Ill, Inn, Mur), but most power is gained from plants located in the steep Alpine valleys (Kaprun, Mallnitz, Spullersee). Almost ¾ of the country's arable land (c.20% of total area) is in Upper and Lower Austria and in the Burgenland. Self-sufficient in the production of potatoes and sugar, Austria is forced to import grain, fats, animal and vegetable oils. Meadows and pastures occupy c.30% of total area; stock raising is an important source of livelihood in the mtn. provs., and much of the dairy produce is exported. Forests (mostly spruce) cover almost 40% of the country; and Austria is one of the few European states exporting lumber and paper. Resin is derived from the black pine forests SW of Vienna. Over the centuries the word Austria has designated various political and geographic concepts. In its narrowest sense it only included Upper and Lower Austria (with Vienna); in its widest meaning it symbolized imperial Hapsburg power. The region of German-speaking Austria (present meaning, dating only from 1918) was conquered (15 B.C.-A.D. 10) from the Celts by the Romans. Overrun and devastated by Huns and Germanic tribes after the 5th cent., the region was conquered (788) by Charlemagne, who set up the 1st Austrian (i.e., Eastern) March in present Upper and Lower Austria. After the Magyar invasions Emperor Otto I reconstituted the march and in 976 Austria was given to the Babenberg family, who ruled it until the extinction of their line in 1246. After a short period of conflict Austria (created a duchy in 1156), Styria (acquired by the Babenbergs in 1192), and Carinthia were incorporated (1278) into the domains of the German king Rudolf of Hapsburg. The house of Hapsburg ruled Austria with only 2 minor interruptions until 1918. As Austrian dukes, the Hapsburgs added (1363) Tyrol, among other territories, to their possessions. From 1438 until 1806 the Hapsburgs were also Holy Roman Emperors and the archduchy (since 1453) of Austria generally shared the fate of the empire. The union of Austria, Bohemia, and Hungary, lasting until 1918, came into being in 1526, 3 years before the 1st Turkish siege of Vienna. The ravages of the Thirty Years War by-passed the archduchy, but Hapsburg power in Germany was considerably weakened by the conflict. The Holy Roman Empire continued as a mere shadow and Hapsburg interests focused more and more on their personal lands. Shortly after the 2d Turkish siege of Vienna (1683) most of Hungary was liberated from Ottoman rule and, together with Bohemia and Moravia, was subjected to intensive Germanization. Emperor Charles VI (1711–40) secured by means of the Pragmatic Sanction the succession to the Hapsburg lands for his daughter Maria Theresa, under whose reign (1740–80) the real struggle bet. Austria and Prussia over supremacy in Germany began. Except for the loss of Silesia, Maria Theresa held her own in her wars against Frederick II of Prussia. With the partitions (1772, 1793, and 1795) of Poland, Austria renewed its eastward expansion. The advent of Napoleon spelled the final doom of the Holy Roman Empire, and in 1804 Francis II took the title "Francis I, Emperor of Austria." After the humiliations at Pressburg (1805) and Schonbrunn (1809), Austria was forced into a French alliance, but in 1813 it again joined the coalition against Napoleon. The Congress of Vienna (1814–15) did not restore to Austria its former possessions in the Netherlands and in Baden, but awarded it Lombardy, Venetia, Istria, and Illyria. As the leading power both of the German Confederation and the Holy Alliance, Austria under the reactionary Metternich ministry dominated European politics. The European revolution of 1848–49 shook the Hapsburg empire and drove out Metternich. A liberal constitution was granted, but Emperor Ferdinand was soon forced to abdicate in favor of his nephew Francis Joseph (1848–1916). Absolutism returned, heightening racial tension within the empire. However, economic prosperity was promoted by the suppression of internal tariff barriers, and several reforms dating from 1848 were upheld, notably the complete abolition of serfdom. After the military and political weakness of the empire had been demonstrated by the Austrian loss of Lombardy in the Italian War of 1859, Prussia struck a final blow at its rival. Austria was crushed in the Austro-Prussian War of 1866, was expelled from the German Confederation, and lost Venetia to Italy. A reorientation toward the east and a reorganization of the government became inevitable, and in 1867 a compromise (Ger. *Ausgleich*) established a dual state, the Austro-Hungarian Monarchy. Constitutional government returned, but failure to provide a satisfactory status for the Slavs and the disastrous part of Austria in bringing about the First World War, caused the collapse of the monarchy in 1918, two years after Francis Joseph's death. His successor, Charles I, abdicated; on Nov. 12, after a peaceful revolution staged by the Socialist and Pan-German parties, German Austria was proclaimed a republic and a part of Greater Germany. The Treaty of Saint-Germain (1919) fixed the present Austrian borders and forbade (as did the Treaty of Versailles) any kind of political or economic union with Germany. Austria, the former focal point of the practically self-sufficient Dual Monarchy, entered the post-war period shaken by political unrest and economic instability. Conflict between Socialist Vienna and the "Black" (i.e., clericalist) rural population mounted; National Socialism gained rapidly and soon absorbed the Pan-German party. During the fascistic regime of Chancellor Engelbert Dollfuss a serious Socialist revolt occurred (1934), which was bloodily suppressed by the army. In July, 1934, the National Socialists assassinated Dollfuss but failed to seize the government. Under Chancellor Kurt von Schuschnigg German pressure for unification increased, and in 1938 National Socialists, who had been outlawed in 1934, were included in the cabinet. In March, 1938, the *Anschluss* to Germany became a reality; in 1940 Austria was fully incorporated into Germany. Captured early in 1945 by Soviet and U.S. troops, Austria was divided into 5 zones of military occupation: Vorarlberg and Tyrol (French zone); Salzburg and W Upper Austria (U.S. zone); E Upper Austria, Lower Austria, and Burgenland (Soviet zone); Carinthia and Styria (British zone); and Vienna, jointly occupied by the 4 powers. In Jan., 1946, Austria was formally recognized by the Western powers, but a peace treaty had not yet been signed by mid-1951.

Austria, Lower, province: see LOWER AUSTRIA.

Austria, Upper, province: see UPPER AUSTRIA.

Austrian Sound, Rus. *Avstriyskiy Proliv*, strait of Arctic Ocean in E Franz Josef Land, Russian SFSR; separates Wilczek Land (E) from Hall and other central isls. (W); 70 mi. long, 10 mi. wide.

Austur-Skaftafell, (û'üstür-skäf'täfĕ"tŭl), county [Icelandic *sýsla*] (pop. 1,139), SE Iceland; ⊙ Vik i Myrdal. On narrow coastal strip bet. Atlantic and SE edge of Vatnajokull glacier region. Drained by several short glacier streams. Sheep raising, potato growing, fishing. Hofn is largest village.

Austvagoy (oust'vôg-û"ü), Nor. *Austvågøy*, largest island (□ 203; pop. 8,041) of the Lofoten Isls., in Norwegian Sea, in Nordland co., N Norway, 55 mi. W of Narvik and separated from Hinnoy (E) by a narrow strait; 33 mi. long (SW-NE), 11 mi. wide; rises to 3,458 ft. Chief occupation, fishing. SVOLVAER, on SE coast, is main town. Sometimes spelled Ostvagoy or Ostvaagoy, Nor. *Østvågøy*.

Austwell, city (pop. 228), Refugio co., S Texas, 28 mi. E of Refugio and on Hynes Bay, an arm of San Antonio Bay.

Autauga (ôtô'gŭ), county (□ 599; pop. 18,186), central Ala.; ⊙ Prattville. In the Black Belt, bounded S by Alabama R., W by Mulberry R. Farming area (cotton, vegetables, potatoes) with gently rolling land, forest. Formed 1818.

Autaugaville, town (pop. 459), Autauga co., central Ala., 20 mi. WNW of Montgomery; wood products.

Auterive (ōtrēv'), village (pop. 1,674), Haute-Garonne dept., S France, on the Ariège and 17 mi. S of Toulouse; hosiery and custom-jewelry mfg.

Auteuil (ōtû'ē), old town, France, now comprised in 16th *arrondissement* of Paris, bet. the Seine and the Bois de Boulogne. Site of a fashionable steeplechase track. Favorite residence of Boileau, Molière, and La Fontaine.

Authie River (ōtē'), N France, rises in Artois hills N of Acheux (Somme dept.), flows c.60 mi. WNW, forming Somme–Pas-de-Calais dept. border, past Doullens and Auxi-le-Château, to English Channel, forming Authie bay 10 mi. SW of Montreuil.

Authon-du-Perche (ōtō-dü-pârsh'), village (pop. 712), Eure-et-Loir dept., NW central France, in the Perche hills, 9 mi. SSE of Nogent-le-Rotrou; stock raising, wooden-shoe mfg.

Autissiodurum, France: see AUXERRE.

Autlán (outlän'), officially Autlán de Navarro, city (pop. 10,915), Jalisco, W Mexico, in W outliers of Sierra Madre Occidental, 55 mi. NW of Colima; alt. 3,018 ft. Agr. center (corn, wheat, sugar, cotton, fruit, livestock); tanneries.

Autol (outōl'), town (pop. 3,367), Logroño prov., N Spain, 6 mi. SSW of Calahorra; agr. trade center (wine, fruit, vegetables, cereals). Olive-oil processing, vegetable canning, alcohol distilling.

Autrey-lès-Gray (ōtrā' lā grā'), village (pop. 480), Haute-Saône dept., E France, 5 mi. WNW of Gray; dairying.

Autricum, France: see CHARTRES.

Autryville (ô'trēvĭl), town (pop. 151), Sampson co., SE central N.C., on South R. and 15 mi. ESE of Fayetteville.

Autse, Latvia: see AUCE.

Autun (ōtû'), anc. *Augustodunum*, town (pop. 11,767), Saône-et-Loire dept., E central France, on Arroux R. and 29 mi. WNW of Chalon-sur-Saône; road center. Produces industrial oils, dyes, fertilizer, furniture; tanning, metalworking. Has noteworthy Roman remains (gateways, amphitheater), a 12th-cent. cathedral, and a Gallo-Roman mus. Founded by Augustus to replace BIBRACTE, it became a Roman center of learning and seat of first dukes of Burgundy. Modern town, smaller than anc. city, does not fully occupy area within old walls.

Autz, Latvia: see AUCE.

Auvelais (ōvŭlā'), town (pop. 8,196), Namur prov., S central Belgium, on Sambre R. and 9 mi. ENE of Charleroi; steel foundries; mfg. (machinery, glass, sulphuric acid); power station.

Auvergne (ōvûrn', Fr. ōvâr'nyù), region and former province, central France, in the Massif Central, forming present depts. of Cantal, Puy-de-Dôme, and part of Haute-Loire; ⊙ Clermont-Ferrand. Traversed (N-S) by Auvergne Mts. (highest peak: Puy de Sancy, 6,187 ft.), which are flanked by basaltic plateaus. Near center is fertile Limagne lowland. Drained by Allier and Dordogne rivers. Numerous hot mineral springs (notably at Mont-Dore, La Bourboule, Royat), and the strange volcanic scenery of the region attract tourists. Chief cities are Clermont-Ferrand (rubber-mfg. center), Riom, Thiers, Aurillac. The Auvergnats are descendants of the Arverni (Celtic tribe) whose leader, Vercingetorix, headed the revolt against Caesar. Unable to support themselves with stock-raising, dairying, and handicraft industries, they have tended to migrate in large numbers during the winter, working as street-vendors or chimney sweeps, formerly in Spain and, even now, in Paris. As part of Aquitaine, Auvergne passed (1152) to the English. Divided by feudal quarrels into several lordships, it passed, in part, to French crown in 1204; another section (duchy of Auvergne) passed (1416) to dukes of Bourbon, and was annexed to France (1527) by Francis I. By 1610, Auvergne was fully incorporated in royal domain.

Auvergne Mountains, Fr. *Monts d'Auvergne*, highest section of the Massif Central, central France, in Puy-de-Dôme and Cantal depts.; bounded by upper Dordogne valley (W), the Limagne lowland (E), and the Truyère gorge (S). Consists of 4 groups of volcanic peaks, N-S: Monts Dôme, Monts Dore, Monts du Cézallier, Massif du Cantal. Highest peak, Puy de Sancy (6,187 ft.) in the Monts Dore. Other summits: Plomb du Cantal (6,096 ft.), Puy de Dôme (4,806 ft.). Region is distinguished by hundreds of extinct cones (some with perfectly preserved craters), vast intrusions of basalt, and lava flows. Tourists are attracted by the grandiose scenery and by numerous mineral hot springs (notably at Mont-Dore, La Bourboule, Royat). Region is gaining in popularity as a winter-sports area. There is no evidence of volcanic activity in historical times.

Auvers-sur-Oise (ōvâr'-sür-wäz'), town (pop. 2,678), Seine-et-Oise dept., N central France, on right bank of the Oise and 3 mi. ENE of Pontoise; fruit and mushroom shipping.

Auvézère River (ōväzâr'), Corrèze and Dordogne depts., W central France, rises N of Uzerche, flows c.55 mi. WSW to the Isle 7 mi. above Périgueux. Sometimes called Haute-Vézère.

Auvillar (ōvēlär'), village (pop. 484), Tarn-et-Garonne dept., SW France, on the Garonne and 10 mi. W of Castelsarrasin; limekilns.

Aux Cayes, Haiti: see CAYES, LES.

Auxerre (ōsâr'), anc. *Autissiodurum*, town (pop. 20,809), ⊙ Yonne dept., N central France, on Yonne R. and 40 mi. SW of Troyes; commercial center, with extensive trade in Chablis and other lower Burgundy wines. Produces well-known candies; processes locally quarried ocher into paints and dyes; distilling, printing, metalworking. Has 13th-16th-cent. Gothic cathedral; former abbatial church of St. Germain-en-Auxerrois (built on 6th-cent. crypts and containing early medieval relics); and 13th-cent. prefecture (former episcopal palace) with Romanesque arcade. Boulevards occupy site of anc. walls. Town gave its name to medieval county of Auxerrois. Acquired by Burgundy under Treaty of Arras (1435). Damaged in Second World War. St. Germanus (5th-cent. bishop of Auxerre) b. here.

Auxey-Duresses (ōsā'-dürĕs'), village (pop. 271), Côte-d'Or dept., E central France, on SE slope of the Côte d'Or, 5 mi. SW of Beaune; distilling. Burgundy wines.

Auxier (ôk'shûr), village (1940 pop. 707), Floyd co., E Ky., in Cumberland foothills, on Levisa Fork and 23 mi. NW of Pikeville.

Auxi-le-Château (ōksē'-lù-shätō'), town (pop. 2,821), Pas-de-Calais dept., N France, on the Authie and 16 mi. NE of Abbeville, in dairying region; shoe and furniture mfg.

Auximum, Italy: see OSIMO.

Auxois, Mont, France: see ALISE-SAINTE-REINE, Côte-d'Or dept.

Auxonne (ōsôn'), town (pop. 3,023), Côte-d'Or dept., E central France, on the Saône and 19 mi. SE of Dijon; foundries. Preserves and ships fruits (chiefly melons), vegetables.

Aux Sources, Mont, U. of So. Africa: see MONT-AUX-SOURCES.

Auxvasse (ō'vôz, ōvôz'), town (pop. 507), Callaway co., central Mo., 12 mi. N of Fulton; grain, stone quarry.

Auzances (ōzäs′), village (pop. 1,259), Creuse dept., central France, near the Cher, 17 mi. ENE of Aubusson; pork processing.

Auzat (ōzä′), village (pop. 900), Ariège dept., S France, in central Pyrenees, on Vicdessos R. (small tributary of the Ariège) and 15 mi. SSW of Foix; electrochemical factory. Hydroelectric plant.

Auzon (ōzō′), village (pop. 700), Haute-Loire dept., S central France, near the Allier, 7 mi. N of Brioude; mfg. of chemicals (arsenic). Copper deposits at Agnat (1.5 mi. S).

Ava (ä′vä; Burmese ûwä′), village, Sagaing dist., Upper Burma, 10 mi. SW of Mandalay and on left bank of Irrawaddy R. opposite Sagaing (Myitkyina-Mandalay RR bridge, 5,894 ft. long). Founded 1364, it was long a ⊙ Burma, notably 1635–1751 under Toungoo dynasty; 1763–83, when it was succeeded by Amarapura; and 1823–37, following destruction by fire of Amarapura. Only ruins remain of its wall, palace, and pagodas.

Ava (ā′vů). **1** City (pop. 734), Jackson co., SW Ill., 26 mi. WNW of Herrin, in bituminous-coal-mining and agr. region. **2** City (pop. 1,611), ⊙ Douglas co., S Mo., in the Ozarks, 39 mi. SE of Springfield, in resort, timber, and agr. region; cheese factory, lumber and grain products. Founded 1864.

Avacha, Sopka (sôp′kŭ ŭvä′chŭ) or **Avachinskaya Sopka** (ŭvä′chĭnskīŭ sôp′kŭ), active volcano (8,960 ft.) in E mtn. range of S Kamchatka Peninsula, Russian SFSR, 18 mi. N of Petropavlovsk. Has secondary active cone rising within old crater (2.5 mi. across).

Avacha Bay (ŭvä′chŭ), sheltered inlet of Pacific Ocean, on SE coast of Kamchatka Peninsula, Russian SFSR; receives Avacha River, 100 mi. long. Petropavlovsk lies on bay's NE shore.

Avachinskaya Sopka, Russian SFSR: see AVACHA, SOPKA.

Avadi, India: see VILLIVAKKAM.

Avaí (ävăē′), city (pop. 1,941), W central São Paulo, Brazil, on railroad and 20 mi. NW of Bauru; cotton and coffee processing. Formerly Avahy.

Availles-Limouzine (ävī′-lēmōōzēn′), village (pop. 894), Vienne dept., W central France, on Vienne R. and 7 mi. N of Confolens; cattle raising.

Avaj, Iran: see AVEH.

Avakubi (ävākōō′bē), village, Eastern Prov., E Belgian Congo, on left bank of Ituri R. bet. 2 sections of rapids and 170 mi. ENE of Stanleyville; cotton ginning, rice processing; rubber plantations in vicinity. Has R.C. mission. Below Avakubi, Ituri R. becomes Aruwimi R.

Aval: see BAHREIN.

Avala (ä′välä), mountain (1,676 ft.), N Serbia, Yugoslavia, 9 mi. S of Belgrade; magnesite, mercury, and galena deposits. Memorial to Unknown Soldier, designed by Mestrovic, stands on summit.

Avaldsnes (ä′välsnäs), village and canton (pop. 3,835), Rogaland co., SW Norway, on NE shore of Karmoy, 4 mi. SSE of Haugesund; fishing; woolen milling. Has stone church (c.1250). VISNES village (pop. 340) is in canton.

Avallon (ävälō′), anc. *Aballo,* town (pop. 5,102), Yonne dept., N central France, on Cousin R. and 27 mi. SE of Auxerre, in the Morvan; road and tourist center. Tanneries; mfg. (agr. machines, furniture, biscuits, cement); asbestos processing.

Avaloirs, Mont des (mõ dăzävälwär′), one of a series of hills in Mayenne dept., highest point (1,368 ft.) of W France, 2 mi. E of Pré-en-Pail.

Avalon, England: see GLASTONBURY.

Avalon (ă′vůlŏn). **1** City (pop. 1,506), Los Angeles co., S Calif., on SE SANTA CATALINA ISLAND, overlooking Avalon Bay; steamer connections with Wilmington (Los Angeles Harbor); airport. Center of isl.'s resort and sport activities; has an Indian mus., a bird sanctuary, and a casino and theater. Founded 1888, inc. 1913. **2** Town (pop. 151), Stephens co., NE Ga., 9 mi. ESE of Toccoa, near S.C. line. **3** Village, Md.: see TILGHMAN ISLAND. **4** Resort borough (pop. 428), Cape May co., S N.J., on Seven Mile Beach isl. (bridged to mainland) and 24 mi. SW of Atlantic City, on the Atlantic. **5** Village (pop. 2,195), Butler co., SW Ohio. **6** Residential borough (pop. 6,463), Allegheny co., SW Pa., NW suburb of Pittsburgh, on Ohio R. Settled 1802, inc. 1874.

Avalon, Isle of, England: see GLASTONBURY.

Avalon Dam, N.Mex.: see PECOS RIVER.

Avalon Peninsula (ă′vůlŏn) (□c.4,000; pop. c.125,000), SE N.F., connected with mainland (NW) by 4-mi.-wide isthmus, bounded N by Trinity Bay, S by Placentia Bay. It is 110 mi. long, up to 60 mi. wide; rises to 950 ft. on hilly E coast. Conception Bay (N) and St. Mary's Bay (S) deeply indent the peninsula in the middle. Chief towns are St. John's, Carbonear, Harbour Grace, Markland, and Placentia. On W coast is the U.S. base ARGENTIA. Most densely populated part of Newfoundland, Avalon contains c.45% of total pop. of isl. Fishing, iron mining (on Bell Isl.), lumbering, mfg. are chief sources of employment. Subsistence agr. is carried on; important berry crop is exported.

Avalos or **Fundición de Ávalos** (fōōndēsyōn′ dā ä′välōs), town (pop. 4,128), Chihuahua, N Mexico, 4 mi. SE of Chihuahua; lead- and silver-smelting center.

Avanashi (ŭvŭnä′shē), town (pop. 6,096), Coimbatore dist., SW Madras, India, 9 mi. NNW of Tiruppur; hand-loom cotton weaving.

Avanhandava (ävůnyăndä′vů), city (pop. 1,643), NW São Paulo, Brazil, on railroad and 20 mi. NW of Lins; coffee processing, pottery mfg., distilling. Hydroelectric plant at falls on Tietê R. (16 mi. N) inaugurated 1946.

Avanigadda (ŭvŭ′nĭgŭdŭ), village, Kistna dist., NE Madras, India, in Kistna R. delta, 18 mi. SW of Masulipatam; rice, tobacco, coconuts.

Avanos (ävänôs′), village (pop. 4,583), Kirsehir prov., central Turkey, on the Kizil Irmak and 50 mi. SE of Kirsehir; wheat, linseed, mohair goats.

Avant (ā′vănt), town (pop. 389), Osage co., N Okla., 20 mi. SE of Pawhuska, and on Bird Creek.

Avanti, India: see UJJAIN.

Avantipur, Kashmir: see AWANTIPUR.

Avants, Les, Switzerland: see MONTREUX.

Avarau: see PALMERSTON.

Avard (ā′värd), town (pop. 96), Woods co., NW Okla., 9 mi. SW of Alva, in wheat-growing and stock-raising area.

Avaré (ävůrĕ′), city (pop. 10,382), S central São Paulo, Brazil, on railroad and 35 mi. SW of Botucatu; cotton ginning, and mfg. of cottonseed oil, corn meal, agr. implements, furniture, leather; sawmills.

Avaricum, France: see BOURGES.

Avaris (ůvâ′rĭs), anc. city of Egypt, in E part of Nile delta, ⊙ Hyksos dynasty; identified possibly with Tanis or Pelusium.

Avar Koisu, river, Russian SFSR: see KOISU.

Avarua, Cook Isls.: see RAROTONGA.

Avasaksa, Finland: see AAVASAKSA.

Avasfelsöfalu, Rumania: see NEGRESTI.

Avdeyevka Pervaya (ŭvdyā′ufkŭ pyĕr′vīŭ) [Rus., =Avdeyevka No. 1], town (1926 pop. 3,822), central Stalino oblast, Ukranian SSR, in the Donbas, on railroad and 9 mi. NNW of Stalino; metalworks, food industries. Avdeyevka Vtoraya [Rus., =Avdeyevka No. 2], town (1926 pop. 4,945), lies just E.

Avdotino or **Avdot'ino** (ŭvdô′tyĭnŭ), town (1926 pop. 2,359), central Stalino oblast, Ukranian SSR, in the Donbas, on railroad (Karavannaya station) and 5 mi. SSE of Stalino; food processing.

Avebury or **Abury** (both: ā′bůrē), agr. village and parish (pop. 561), N central Wiltshire, England, on Kennet R. and 6 mi. W of Marlborough. Has Saxon and Norman church. Village lies within Avebury Circle, neolithic group of upright stones, older and larger than Stonehenge. In 1943 village and circle became natl. property. Near by is artificial mound of Silbury Hill, oldest and largest prehistoric structure in Great Britain.

Avedore (ä′vůdhûrů), Dan. *Avedøre,* town (pop. 1,026), Copenhagen amt, NE Zealand, Denmark, 3 mi. SW of Copenhagen.

Aveh (ävĕ′), town, First Prov., in Kazvin, NW central Iran, 65 mi. SW of Kazvin and on highway to Hamadan. Sometimes spelled Avej or Avaj.

Aveiras de Cima (ävā′rŏsh dĭ sē′mů), village (pop. 1,916), Lisboa dist., central Portugal, 14 mi. SW of Santarém; fruit- and winegrowing.

Aveiro (ävā′rōō), town (pop. 210), W Pará, Brazil, on right bank of Tapajós R. and 60 mi. SSW of Santarém. Near by are the Ford rubber plantations of Belterra and Fordlândia (now Brazilian-owned).

Aveiro, district (land □ 1,046, including Aveiro lagoon 1,070; pop. 429,870), N central Portugal, in Beira Litoral prov. and S part of Douro Litoral prov.; ⊙ Aveiro. Borders on the Atlantic; drained by lower Vouga R., which forms a lagoon (salt marshes) at its mouth. Sardine fishing, saltworking, porcelain mfg. Agr. products: wine, corn, rice. Lumbering.

Aveiro, anc. *Talabriga,* city (pop. 11,247), ⊙ Aveiro dist., Beira Litoral prov., N central Portugal, at mouth of Vouga R. (Aveiro lagoon) and 36 mi. S of Oporto; sardine-fishing port and saltworking center connected by canal across lagoon and sand bar with the open Atlantic; fish canning, pottery and porcelain mfg. (especially at Vista Alegre just S); agr. trade (wine, olive oil, grain, fruit). Airfield. Mus. in former convent contains 17th-cent. marble tomb of St. Joanna (daughter of Afonso V). City became known in 16th cent. as the base from which João Afonso dispatched his cod-fishing fleets to Newfoundland. Aveiro lagoon (□ 24), a malarial area until drained in 19th cent., has been partially reclaimed for agr.

Avej, Iran: see AVEH.

Avelgem (ä′vůlkhěm), town (pop. 5,110), West Flanders prov., W Belgium, near Scheldt R., 9 mi. ESE of Courtrai; textile industry. Formerly spelled Avelghem.

Avella (ävĕl′lä), town (pop. 4,260), Avellino prov., Campania, S Italy, 20 mi. ENE of Naples. Near by is site of anc. Abella.

Avella, village (pop. 1,356), Washington co., SW Pa., 27 mi. WSW of Pittsburgh, near W.Va. line, in coal-mining region.

Avellaneda. 1 Department, Río Negro natl. territory, Argentina: see CHOELE-CHOEL. **2** Department, Santiago del Estero prov., Argentina: see HERRERA.

Avellaneda (ävěyänä′dä). **1** City (pop. estimate 100,000), ⊙ Avellaneda dist. (□ 19; pop. 282,054), in Greater Buenos Aires, Argentina, separated from federal dist. by Riachuelo R. Major rail and industrial center; oil refineries, meat-packing plants, plywood factories, lead mills; hides, wool, chemicals, clothing, cement. Exports foodstuffs, leather goods, minerals. Argentina's most important industrial town, formerly called Barracas al Sud, it was named 1904 after President Nicolás Avellaneda. Its port, DOCK SUD, is located NE at mouth of Riachuelo R. on Río de la Plata. **2** Town (pop. estimate 1,000), NE Santa Fe prov., Argentina, on railroad (Ewald station) and 3 mi. NNW of Reconquista; agr. center (flax, corn, cotton, peanuts, sunflowers); flour milling, cotton ginning, peanut-oil pressing.

Avellino (ävĕl-lē′nô), province (□ 1,082; pop. 446,412), Campania, S Italy; ⊙ Avellino. Mtn. and hill terrain, watered by Calore and upper courses of Sele and Ofanto rivers. Agr. (cereals, olives, grapes, fruit); stock raising (sheep, swine). Sulphur mining (Altavilla Irpino, Tufo). Industry at Avellino, Ariano Irpino, and Solofra (tanning).

Avellino, town (pop. 20,578), ⊙ Avellino prov., Campania, S Italy, in the Apennines, 28 mi. ENE of Naples; 40°55′N 14°48′E. Sulphur refinery, alcohol distillery, foundry, hat factory, cream of tartar and candy (*torrone*) industries. Schools of viticulture and industrial arts. Bishopric. On a mtn. 4 mi. NW is Benedictine convent and shrine of Monte Vergine (alt. 4,167 ft.; founded 1119), visited yearly by thousands of pilgrims.

Avena, Argentina: see SAN MARTÍN DE LAS ESCOBAS.

Avenal (ă′vĭnůl), village (pop. 3,982), Kings co., S central Calif., c.50 mi. SW of Fresno; supply center in Kettleman Hills oil field.

Aven Armand, France: see MEYRUEIS.

Avenay (ävnā′), village (pop. 836), Marne dept., N France, on S slope of Montagne de Reims, 5 mi. NE of Épernay; winegrowing (champagne).

Avenches (ävăsh′), Ger. *Wifflisburg* (vĭf′lĭsbŏŏrk), anc. *Aventicum,* town (pop. 1,565), Vaud canton, W Switzerland, 8 mi. NW of Fribourg, in Avenches dist. (pop. 4,764), an enclave in Fribourg canton. An anc. town, with estimated pop. of 80,000 in 100 B.C., it grew and flourished as chief town of Helvetia under Romans in 1st and 2d cent. A.D. Remains of Roman theater, amphitheater, and town walls (4 mi. long). Roman tower, Corinthian column, and medieval castle still stand; mus. has numerous antiquities. Remains of aqueduct SW.

Avenières, Les (lāzävůnyâr′), village (pop. 1,419), Isère dept., SE France, near left bank of the Rhone, 7 mi. NE of La Tour-du-Pin; shoe mfg., silk spinning.

Avenio, France: see AVIGNON.

Aven River (ävĕ′), Finistère dept., W France, rises in Montagnes Noires, flows 25 mi. S, past Rosporden (where it forms lake 1 mi. long) and Pont-Aven, to Bay of Biscay in narrow estuary.

Aventicum, Switzerland: see AVENCHES.

Aventine Hill (ă′vůntīn), one of the 7 hills of Rome.

Avenwedde (ä′fůnwĕ″dů), village (pop. 5,731), in former Prussian prov. of Westphalia, NW Germany, after 1945 in North Rhine-Westphalia, 3 mi. ENE of Gütersloh; pumpernickel; hog raising.

Avenza (ävĕn′tsä), town (pop. 5,007), Massa e Carrara prov., Tuscany, central Italy, near Ligurian Sea, 2 mi. SW of Carrara; rail junction; macaroni, clothing, rubber shoes, emery products. Exports marble from Carrara.

Avera (ůvē′rů), town (pop. 230), Jefferson co., E Ga., 36 mi. SW of Augusta.

Averill Park (ā′vůrĭl″), village (1940 pop. 647), Rensselaer co., E N.Y., 9 mi. SE of Troy; fur dressing, mfg. of knit goods.

Ave River (ä′vĭ), N Portugal, rises in Serra da Cabreira c.5 mi. E of Vieira do Minho, flows 53 mi. SW to the Atlantic at Vila do Conde. Not navigable.

Averno (ävĕr′nô), anc. *Avernus,* small crater lake, Campania, S Italy, near Gulf of Pozzuoli, in Phlegraean Fields, 10 mi. W of Naples; circular, .6 mi. wide. In anc. times its sulphurous vapors were said to kill all birds flying over it, and Romans regarded it as the entrance to hell. Just W are ruins of Cumae.

Averoy (ä′vůr-û″ü), Nor. *Averøy,* island (□ 62; pop. 4,303) in North Sea, More og Romsdal co., W Norway, just SW of Kristiansund; 13 mi. long, 11 mi. wide; fishing. Chief villages, BREMSNES and KVERNES.

Aversa (ävĕr′sä), town (pop. 26,538), Caserta prov., Campania, S Italy, 9 mi. NNW of Naples. Rail junction; agr. center (cereals, hemp, fruit); macaroni, soap, chemicals. Noted for its white wine. Bishopric. Founded 1029 by Normans; their 1st possession in Italy.

Avery (ā′vůrē), county (□ 247; pop. 13,352), NW N.C.; ⊙ Newland. In the Blue Ridge; bounded W by Tenn.; in Pisgah Natl. Forest; drained by small North Toe R. Farming (corn, potatoes, hay, vegetables, apples), cattle raising; lumbering; mining (mica, feldspar, kaolin). Formed 1911.

Avery, town (pop. 442), Red River co., NE Texas, c.45 mi. ESE of Paris; trade, shipping point in fruit, truck area.

Avery Island, one of the Five Isls., in Iberia parish, S La., a salt dome (alt. c.200 ft.) in sea marshes and swamps c.9 mi. SW of New Iberia. Rock-salt mines (producing since 1791); pepper-sauce mfg. Oil wells and pipeline are near by. Here are the noted sanctuary for birds (especially egrets) and the Jungle Gardens, with many rare plants. Prehistoric Indian relics have been found here.

Avesa (ävä'zä), village (popp. 2,205), Verona prov., Veneto, N Italy, near Adige R., 2 mi. N of Verona.

Aves Island (ä'väs) or **Bird Island**. **1** Uninhabited Caribbean islet, dependency of Venezuela, 145 mi. W of Dominica, Windward Isls.; 15°42'N 63°38'W. **2** Uninhabited Caribbean reefs, dependency of Venezuela, 105 mi. NNW of Caracas; 12°N 67°30' W. Guano deposits.

Avesnelles (ävĕnĕl'), SE suburb (pop. 2,341) of Avesnes, Nord dept., N France; wool spinning, dairying.

Avesnes or **Avesnes-sur-Helpe** (ävĕn'-sür-ĕlp'), town (pop. 4,770), Nord dept., N France, 34 mi. NE of Saint-Quentin; dairying center in stock-raising area. Wool spinning, brewing. Orchards in area. Formerly fortified. Church (13th-16th cent.) damaged in Second World War.

Avesnes-le-Comte (–lü-kōt'), agr. village (pop. 1,361), Pas-de-Calais dept., N France, 11 mi. W of Arras; brewing, furniture mfg.

Avesnes-les-Aubert (–lāzōbâr'), town (pop. 4,165), Nord dept., N France, 7 mi. ENE of Cambrai, in sugar-beet area; cambric and linen handkerchief-mfg. center. Also spelled Avesnes-lès-Aubert.

Avesnes-sur-Helpe, Nord dept., France: see AVESNES.

Avesta (ä'vüstä"), city (pop. 6,474), Kopparberg co., central Sweden, in Bergslag region, on Dal R. and 40 mi. SE of Falun; mfg. of steel, aluminum, stainless steel. Formerly (1636–1869) a copper-mining center, with copper works and mint.

Avetrana (ävĕträ'nä), village (pop. 3,543), Ionio prov., Apulia, S Italy, 6 mi. SE of Manduria; wine, olive oil.

Aveyron (ävārō'), department (□ 3,386; pop. 307,717), S France, in former Guienne prov., and co-extensive with ROUERGUE dist.; ⊙ Rodez. Mountainous area in the Massif Central, bounded by the Monts d'Aubrac and Viadène Plateau (N), and the Cévennes (SE). It contains much of the CAUSSES, and the Ségala Plateau (center). Drained E-W by the Lot and Truyère (N), Aveyron and Viaur (center), and Tarn R. (S). Agr. on Ségala Plateau (wheat, rye, potatoes) and in sheltered river gorges (fruits, vegetables, wine). Sheep, whose milk and skin are locally processed, in the Causses, cattle in N uplands. Coal mines at Decazeville, Aubin, and Cransac; minor copper, lead, and iron deposits. Chief industrial towns are Millau (gloves), Decazeville (metallurgy), Viviez (zinc smelting), and famous cheese-making village of Roquefort. Rodez, Villefranche-de-Rouergue, and Capdenac-Gare are food-processing centers.

Aveyron River, Aveyron and Tarn-et-Garonne depts., S France, rises in the Causse de Sauveterre 2 mi. SE of Sévérac-le-Château, flows 155 mi. generally W, past Rodez and Villefranche-de-Rouergue, to the Tarn 6 mi. below Montauban. Receives Viaur R.

Avezzano (ävĕtsä'nô), town (pop. 15,003), Aquila prov., Abruzzi e Molise, S central Italy, just W of reclaimed Lago Fucino, 22 mi. S of Aquila. Rail junction; agr. center; beet-sugar refinery, alcohol distillery, sawmills, macaroni factory. Bishopric. Rebuilt after earthquake of 1915, which had its epicenter here. Badly damaged (1943–44) in Second World War.

Avgorou (ävgô'rōō), village (pop. 1,770), Famagusta dist., SE Cyprus, 27 mi. ESE of Nicosia; wheat, oats, potatoes; sheep, hogs.

Avgustov, Poland: see AUGUSTOW.

Aviano (ävyä'nô), village (pop. 1,199), Udine prov., Friuli-Venezia Giulia, 8 mi. NNW of Pordenone; agr. tools, hosiery. Stone quarries near by.

Aviá Terai (ävyä' tärī'), town (pop. estimate 500), central Chaco natl. territory, Argentina, 20 mi. WNW of Presidencia Roque Sáenz Peña. Rail junction and agr. center (corn, alfalfa, cotton, livestock).

Avicaya (ävēkī'ä), village (pop. c.850), Oruro dept., W Bolivia, at S end of Serranía de Achacollo, 12 mi. SSE of Poopó; alt. c.13,000 ft.; tin mining.

Aviemore (ăvĭmôr'), agr. village, E Inverness, Scotland, on the Spey and 13 mi. SW of Grantown-on-Spey, at foot of Cairngorm Mts.; tourist resort. Just N is Craigellachie rock, former meeting place of Clan Grant.

Avigait (ävĭgīt'), Eskimo *Kuanit*, fishing settlement (pop. 90), Frederikshaab dist., SW Greenland, on small isl. in the Atlantic, 17 mi. NW of Frederikshaab; 62°13'N 49°53'W.

Avigalik Island or **Whale Island** (2 mi. long, 2 mi. wide), NE Labrador, in Seven Islands Bay; 59°27'N 63°40'W. Just SW is Amiktok Isl.

Avigliana (ävēlyä'nä), village (pop. 2,940), Torino prov., Piedmont, NW Italy, near Dora Riparia R., 14 mi. W of Turin; ironworks, chemical plant; mfg. of varnish, enamel, explosives, textiles. Has 12th-cent. church of San Pietro (remodeled 15th cent.).

Avigliano (ävēlyä'nô), town (pop. 4,485), Potenza prov., Basilicata, S Italy, 8 mi. NW of Potenza; woolen mill, dyeworks, soap factory.

Avignon (ăvē'nyō, Fr. ävēnyō'), anc. *Avenio*, city (pop. 47,111), ⊙ Vaucluse dept., SE France, on left bank of the Rhone, and 55 mi. NNW of Marseilles; commercial and transportation center with important trade in wines (*Côtes-du-Rhône*), fruits, and silkworm eggs. Metalworks; mfg. of chemical fertilizer, dyes, paper, rayon, candied fruit, beeswax, clothing, furniture, tiles, playing cards. Located in (but never a part of) the Comtat Venaissin, Avignon was papal see during "Babylonian captivity" (1309–77), and residence of several antipopes (1378–1408). After end of Great Schism, it was officially ruled by papal legates, though actually enjoying self-government. Became archiepiscopal see in 1475. Incorporated into France in 1791, after a plebiscite. Here, in 1808, Pope Pius VII was briefly imprisoned by Napoleon I. Papal sojourn left strong imprint on Avignon and gave it considerable prosperity. It is a city of numerous churches dominated by huge papal palace, built in 14th-cent. as residence, fortress, and place of worship. Rocky height overlooking the Rhone just N of palace is now a public garden (*Promenade du Rocher des Domes*). The famed 12th-cent. bridge of St. Bénézet (subject of popular song) reaches only half-way across the Rhone since 17th cent. City still retains its massive 14th-cent. ramparts (slightly damaged in Second World War); modern districts, including railroad station and main highways, extend E and S of walled town. Avignon and near-by Fontaine-de-Vaucluse were celebrated by Petrarch, who resided at court of Clement VI.

Avignonet (ävēnyônā'), village (pop. 4), Isère dept., SE France, 16 mi. S of Grenoble, in Dauphiné Alps; hydroelectric plant on the Drac.

Avihayil or **Avihail** (both: ävēhĭl'), settlement (pop. 600), W Israel, in Plain of Sharon, near Mediterranean, 2 mi. NE of Natanya; mixed farming. Founded 1932; later absorbed adjacent settlement of Ein Haoved.

Ávila (ä'vēlä), province (□ 3,107; pop. 234,671), central Spain; ⊙ Ávila. The westernmost part of Old Castile prov., it is separated by the Sierra de Guadarrama from Madrid prov. (E), and by the Sierra de Gredos (rising in Plaza del Moro Almanzor to 8,504 ft.) from Toledo prov. (S). Segovia prov. is NE, Valladolid prov. N, and Cáceres prov. W. Its N flat section is part of the central plateau (Meseta); the S is rugged and mountainous, with fertile valleys formed by the Alberche, Adaja, and Tiétar rivers. Generally rigorous, continental climate (hot, dry, summers; cold winters); the S valleys are much warmer, remindful of Andalusia in their vegetation (olives, oranges, grapes, tobacco, leguminous vegetables, spices, hemp, figs, etc.). All kinds of grain (wheat, rye, barley) are grown widely, constituting with livestock, chiefly Merino sheep, and forest products (timber, naval stores), its mainstay. Industries, apart from a few textile plants, are almost entirely restricted to agr. processing. The historic city of Ávila, though an important communications point, is surpassed as agr. market by Arévalo. Ávila prov. is traversed by the Madrid–La Coruña RR. It is today only a shadow of what it was in the Middle Ages. Industries and commerce were disrupted with expulsion of the Moriscos by Philip II in early 17th cent. St. Theresa, St. John of the Cross, San Pedro de Alcántara, and Queen Isabella were b. here. Ávila prov. was occupied by Nationalist forces in 1st year (1936) of Sp. civil war.

Ávila, officially *Ávila de los Caballeros*, anc. *Avela* or *Abula*, city (pop. 19,590), ⊙ Ávila prov., central Spain, in Old Castile, on Adaja R. and 55 mi. WNW of Madrid; alt. c.3,700 ft.; 40°39'N 4°42'W. Communications center situated on a precipitous ridge, surrounded by peaks of the Sierra de Gredos (S), Sierra de Guadarrama (E), and outliers. An old, typically Castilian city, it is a veritable mus. of medieval architecture, (attracting tourists), but has now little economic importance. The region produces chick-peas, cereals, carobs, livestock. Among its few industries are tanneries, flour mills, brewery; mfg. of soft drinks, meat products, tiles, cement articles, chocolate, soap, resins, woolen goods. Bishopric. Has a provincial mus., military school, and meteorological observatory. Its well-preserved, dark-granite walls, built in 11th cent., have many turrets and imposing gates. Against the wall nestles the fortress-like Gothic cathedral (13th-14th cent.). The basilica San Vicente is one of the finest Romanesque bldgs. in Spain. There are a number of other superb churches such as San Pedro, Santo Tomás, and San Segundo. In the convent of Encarnación lived St. Theresa, who was b. (1515) in the city. Other notable edifices include remains of an alcazar, chapel Mosén Robí, and palatial mansions of Castilian aristocrats. Probably of Phoenician origin, Ávila formed part of the Roman Lusitania. After Moorish invasion, it was several times taken by Christian forces, until finally occupied (1088) by Alfonso VI, who rebuilt it. Has decayed since expulsion of the Moriscos in early 17th cent., when commerce and industry suffered a severe blow.

Avilés, Bolivia: see URIONDO.

Avilés (ävēlās'), town (pop. 10,695), Oviedo prov., NW Spain, in Asturias, fishing port on estuary of Avilés R. 2 mi. S of Bay of Biscay, and 14 mi. NNW of Oviedo; large coal exports. Zinc and lead processing, coal briquettes, cement mfg., boat-building; chemical works (fertilizers, sulphuric acid); food industries (cured hams, processed fish, cheese, candy); brandy and cider distilling. Has several medieval bldgs. and modern church with 2 high towers. Summer resort with beaches at Salinas, 2 mi. NW.

Avilez, Bolivia: see URIONDO.

Avilla (ŭvĭ'lŭ). **1** Town (pop. 669), Noble co., NE Ind., 21 mi. NNW of Fort Wayne, in agr. area. **2** Town (pop. 142), Jasper co., SW Mo., 10 mi. E of Carthage.

Avinger (ă'vĭnjŭr), town (pop. 546), Cass co., NE Texas, 26 mi. NNW of Marshall, in agr. area.

Avintes (ävēn'tĭsh), town (pop. 1,537), Pôrto dist., N Portugal, on left bank of Douro R. and 5 mi. SE of Oporto; shoe mfg.

Avinyó (ävēnyō'), village (pop. 1,195), Barcelona prov., NE Spain, 13 mi. NE of Manresa; cotton mills. Livestock, wine, olive oil, fruit in area. Lignite and potassium mines near by.

Avio (ä'vyō), village (pop. 1,417), Trento prov., Trentino–Alto Adige, N Italy, near the Adige, 12 mi. SSW of Rovereto; wine making, alcohol distilling.

Avion (ävyō'), S suburb (pop. 16,072) of Lens, Pas-de-Calais dept., N France; coal-mining center. In front lines during battle of Arras (1917), its coal mines were systematically flooded by Germans.

Avioth, France: see MONTMÉDY.

Avirons (ävērō'), town and commune (pop. 3,364), near SW coast of Réunion isl., 11 mi. NW of Saint-Pierre; sugar-cane center.

Avis, Portugal: see AVIZ.

Avis (ā'vĭs), borough (pop. 1,193), Clinton co., N central Pa., 8 mi. ENE of Lock Haven; railroad shops.

Avisio River (ävē'zyō), N Italy, rises in the Dolomites on Marmolada peak, flows 50 mi. SW, through Val di Fiemme, past Predazzo and Cavalese, to Adige R. 4 mi. N of Trent.

Avissawella or **Avisawella** (ŭvĭsŭvĕl'lŭ), town (pop. (pop. 2,633), Western Prov., Ceylon, 24 mi. E of Colombo; trades in tea, rubber, rice, coconuts, areca nuts, cardamom. Includes anc. Singhalese city of SITAWAKA.

Aviston (ā'vĭstŭn), village (pop. 503), Clinton co., S Ill., 26 mi. W of Centralia, in agr., bituminous-coal-mining, and oil-producing area.

Aviz (ävēzh'), town (pop. 1,424), Portalegre dist., central Portugal, 29 mi. SW of Portalegre; cork, grain, sheep and hogs. Gives its name to the order of the Knights of Aviz, and after accession of John I, to the ruling dynasty of Portugal (until 1580). Ruined 12th-cent. castle overlooks town. Also spelled Avís.

Avize (ävēz'), village (pop. 1,711), Marne dept., N France, 6 mi. SSE of Épernay; noted vineyards and champagne storage caves.

Avlon, Greece: see AULON.

Avlona, Albania: see VALONA.

Avlonarion, Greece, see AULONARION.

Avning (ou'nĭng), town (pop. 1,226), Randers amt, E Jutland, Denmark, 13 mi. ESE of Randers.

Avoca (ŭvō'kŭ), town (pop. 959), central Victoria, Australia, on Avoca R. and 95 mi. WNW of Melbourne, in agr. region; eucalyptus oil, wine.

Avoca or **Ovoca** (both: ŭvō'kŭ), Gaelic *Abhainn Mhór*, town (district pop. 599), SE Co. Wicklow, Ireland, on Avoca R. and 5 mi. NW of Arklow; sulphur mining, woolen milling.

Avoca, village (pop. 301), E central Tasmania, 39 mi. SE of Launceston and on South Esk R.; livestock, oats; coal.

Avoca. **1** Town (pop. 1,595), Pottawattamie co., SW Iowa, 31 mi. ENE of Council Bluffs; rail junction; mfg. of dairy products, feed. Inc. 1875. **2** Village (pop. 281), Murray co., SW Minn., 6 mi. ESE of Slayton, in corn, oat, barley area. **3** Village (pop. 196), Cass co., SE Nebr., 35 mi. SSW of Omaha and on small branch of Missouri R. **4** Village (pop. 952), Steuben co., S N.Y., on Cohocton R. and 25 mi. NW of Corning, in agr. area; canned foods, wood products. Settled 1843, inc. 1883. **5** Residential borough (pop. 4,040), near coal mines, Luzerne co., NE Pa., 7 mi. SW of Scranton. Inc. 1889. **6** Village (pop. 424), Iowa co., SW Wis., near Wisconsin R., 18 mi. NNW of Dodgeville, in dairying region.

Avoca River, W central Victoria, Australia, rises in Great Dividing Range E of Ararat, flows 140 mi. generally N past Avoca and Charlton, to small lake W of Kerang; shallow.

Avoca River or **Ovoca River**, Co. Wicklow, Ireland, formed by the Avonbeg (16 mi. long) and the Avonmore (14 mi. long) at "The Meeting of the Waters," 5 mi. WNW of Arklow; flows 9 mi. SE to the Irish Sea at Arklow. Scenic beauty of valley is celebrated in Moore's *The Meeting of the Waters*.

Avoch (ă'vŭkh), fishing village and parish (pop. 1,408), SE Ross and Cromarty, Scotland, on Moray Firth, 2 mi. WSW of Fortrose.

Avocourt (ävôkōōr'), village (pop. 45), Meuse dept., NE France, 11 mi. WNW of Verdun. Scene of fierce Franco-German fighting in battle of Verdun, 1916–17.

Avoid Bay, inlet of Great Australian Bight, SW Eyre Peninsula, S South Australia, bet. Point Whidbey (W) and Point Avoid of Coffin Bay peninsula; 14 mi. long, 5 mi. wide. Whidbey Isls. at entrance.

Avola (ä'vôlä), town (pop. 21,461), Siracusa prov., SE Sicily, 14 mi. SW of Syracuse; almond growing and exporting; bell foundry. Damaged by 1693 earthquake (some ruins extant).

Avon (ävō'), E suburb (pop. 4,192) of Fontainebleau, Seine-et-Marne dept., N central France, near left bank of the Seine, resort in Forest of Fontainebleau; sand quarrying, mfg. of electrical equipment.

Avon. 1 (ā'vŏn) Town (pop. 3,171), Hartford co., central Conn., on Farmington R. and 8 mi. W of Hartford; agr. Avon Old Farms school for boys here. Inc. 1830. **2** (ā'vŏn") Village (pop. 870), Fulton co., W central Ill., 20 mi. S of Galesburg; grain, dairy products, livestock, poultry. **3** (ā'vŏn") Town (pop. 391), Franklin co., W central Maine, on Sandy R. and 11 mi. NW of Farmington. **4** (ā'vŏn") Town (pop. 2,666), Norfolk co., E Mass., just N of Brockton; residential and mfg. (shoe parts, moccasins, dies, rubber goods). Settled c.1700, inc. 1888. **5** (ā'vŏn") Village (pop. 386), Stearns co., central Minn., 14 mi. WNW of St. Cloud; small trading point for near-by lake resorts; dairy products. Marl deposits in vicinity. **6** (ā'vŏn") Village (pop. c.100), Powell co., W Mont., 27 mi. W of Helena and on branch of the Clark Fork; supply point in livestock and mining region. **7** (ā'vŭn, ā'-) Village (pop. 2,412), Livingston co., W central N.Y., on Genesee R. and 18 mi. SSW of Rochester; mfg. (canned foods, alfalfa meal, macaroni, refrigeration machinery); farming, dairying. Horse show held annually. Inc. 1867. **8** (ā'vŭn) Village (pop. c.500), Dare co., E N.C., 9 mi. N of Cape Hatteras, on barrier beach (Hatteras Isl.) bet. Pamlico Sound and the Atlantic; commercial fishing; truck gardens, vineyards. **9** (ā'vŏn") Village (pop. 2,773), Lorain co., N Ohio, 7 mi. E of Lorain, near L. Erie, in agr. area. Settled c.1814, inc. 1918. **10** (ā'vŏn") City (pop. 692), Bon Homme co., SE S.Dak., 10 mi. W of Tyndall; dairy products, livestock, poultry, corn, wheat.

Avonbridge (ā'vŭn-), town in Muiravonside parish, SE Stirling, Scotland, on Avon R. and 5 mi. NW of Bathgate; coal and iron mining.

Avon by the Sea (ā'vŭn), resort borough (pop. 1,650), Monmouth co., E N.J., on the coast, at mouth of Shark R., 3 mi. S of Asbury Park. Inc. 1900.

Avondale (ā'vŭndāl, ā'-), parish (pop. 5,529), W Lanark, Scotland. Includes STRATHAVEN.

Avondale (ā'vŭndāl). **1** Town (pop. 2,505), Maricopa co., S central Ariz., near Gila R., 18 mi. W of Phoenix. Inc. 1946. **2** City (pop. 532), Clay co., W Mo., just N of North Kansas City. **3** Textile village (pop. 3,494, with adjacent Caroleen and Henrietta), Rutherford co., SW N.C., c.15 mi. W of Shelby. **4** Borough (pop. 941), Chester co., SE Pa., 13 mi. NW of Wilmington, Del. **5** Village, R.I.: see WESTERLY.

Avondale Estates, city (pop. 1,070), De Kalb co., NW central Ga., residential suburb 9 mi. E of Atlanta; cotton milling. Inc. 1927.

Avondhu River, Scotland: see FORTH RIVER.

Avon Lake (ā'vŏn"), village (pop. 4,342), Lorain co., N Ohio, 16 mi. W of Cleveland, on L. Erie; bathing beaches. Makes chemicals, wood products.

Avonlea (ā'vŭnlē'), village (pop. 286), S Sask., 35 mi. SE of Moose Jaw; wheat.

Avonmore (ā'vŭnmôr), borough (pop. 1,367), Westmoreland co., SW central Pa., 27 mi. ENE of Pittsburgh and on Kiskiminetas R. Inc. 1893.

Avonmouth (ā'vŭn-), port and district of Bristol, SW Gloucester, England, on Severn R. estuary at mouth of Avon R., 6 mi. NW of Bristol; has important dock installations and petroleum refineries, flour mills, chemical- and metalworks.

Avon Park (ā'vŏn"), city (pop. 4,612), Highlands co., S central Fla., c.40 mi. SE of Lakeland, in lake region; packing and shipping center for citrus fruit. Air Force base near. Settled c.1885.

Avon River, Australia: see SWAN RIVER.

Avon River (ā'vŭn), W central N.S., rises in small lake 16 mi. SW of Windsor, flows 40 mi. N, past Windsor, to the Minas Basin.

Avon River (ā'vŭn, ă'-). **1** or **Bristol Avon River** or **Lower Avon River,** in Gloucester, Wiltshire, and Somerset, England. Rises at Tetbury, flows S, past Malmesbury, Chippenham, Lacock, and Melksham, to Bradford-on-Avon, thence NW, past Bath and Bristol, to the Severn at Avonmouth; 75 mi. long. Navigable below Bath, and for sea-going ships below Bristol. **2** or **East Avon River,** in Wiltshire and Hampshire, England. Rises 3 mi. E of Devizes, flows 48 mi. E and S, past Salisbury and Ringwood, to the Channel at Christchurch; navigable below Salisbury. **3** or **Upper Avon River,** in Northampton, Leicester, Warwick, and Worcester, England. Rises 2 mi. SW of Naseby, Northampton, flows 96 mi. SW, past Rugby, Warwick, Stratford-on-Avon, and Evesham, to the Severn at Tewkesbury; receives Alne and Stour rivers.

Avon River (ăn, ā'vŭn, ā'-). **1** In Banffshire, Scotland, rises on Ben Macdhui in the Cairngorms, flows 30 mi. N to the Spey at Ballindalloch. **2** In Lanark, Scotland: see AVON WATER. **3** In Stirling and West Lothian, Scotland, rises 4 mi. WSW of Slamannan, flows 18 mi. E, past Avonbridge, to Firth of Forth 3 mi. ESE of Grangemouth.

Avon River, Wales: see AFON RIVER.

Avon Water (ā'vŭn, ā'-), river in Lanark, Scotland, rises 5 mi. SE of Darvel, near Ayrshire border, flows 28 mi. NE, past Strathaven, Larkhall, and Hamilton, to the Clyde just E of Hamilton.

Avoyelles (ŭvoilz'), parish (□ 826; pop. 38,031), E central La.; ⊙ Marksville. Partly bounded N and E by Red R., and partly on E by Atchafalaya R. Agr. (cotton, corn, hay, rice, sugar cane, sweet potatoes), stock raising. Moss and cotton ginning, sugar and lumber milling; commercial fisheries. Includes Eola oil and natural-gas field. Has several lakes. Formed 1807.

Avramov Pass (ävrä'môf) (alt. 4,774 ft.), in W Rhodope Mts., SW Bulgaria, 10 mi. W of Velingrad, crossed by rail and highway bet. Velingrad and Razlog.

Avranches (ävrăsh'), town (pop. 6,693), Manche dept., NW France, on hill overlooking mouth of Sée R. on Bay of Saint-Michel (English Channel), 30 mi. E of Saint-Malo, at SW base of Cotentin Peninsula; agr. trade center (fruit, grain, dairy produce); cider distilling, fishing (salmon trout), tanning. From botanical garden is splendid view of MONT-SAINT-MICHEL, 8 mi. SW. Town is of Roman origin. Devastated during Hundred Years War and Wars of Religion. Its capture (July 31, 1944) marked beginning of Patton's sweep into Brittany and across France in Second World War.

Avre River (ä'vrŭ). **1** In Somme dept., N France, rises above Roye, flows 37 mi. NW, past Moreuil, to the Somme above Amiens. Scene of heavy fighting (March-May, 1918) during First World War, in which Haig abandoned Péronne and Bapaume. **2** In NW France, rises 6 mi. NNE of Mortagne (Orne dept.), flows 45 mi. ENE, past Verneuil and Nonancourt, forming Eure–Eure-et-Loire dept. border, to the Eure 3 mi. N of Dreux. Supplies Paris with water via aqueduct (starting near Verneuil). Also called Avre Normande.

Avrig (ä'vrēg), Hung. *Felek* (fĕ'lĕk), village (pop. 3,963), Sibiu prov., central Rumania, in N foothills of the Fagaras Mts., on Olt R., on railroad and 12 mi. SE of Sibiu; mfg. of glass; climatic resort. Has sanatorium and old church.

Avsa Island (äv-shä'), Turkish *Avşa*, island (pop. 615), NW Turkey, in Sea of Marmara S of Marmara Isl.; Turkeli (Turkish *Türkeli*) or Avsa is its village.

Avuka or **Avuqa** (both: ävōōkä'), settlement (pop. 150), NE Israel, in Jordan valley, 2 mi. SE of Beisan; grain, fruit, vegetables; dairying, poultry; fish breeding. Founded 1941. Sometimes spelled Avukah or Avuqah.

Awa (ä'vŭ), town (pop. 2,593), Etah dist., W Uttar Pradesh, India, 13 mi. SW of Etah; wheat, pearl millet, barlet, corn, oilseeds. Also spelled Awah.

Awa (ä'wä). **1** Former province in central Honshu, Japan; now part of Chiba prefecture. **2** Former province in E Shikoku, Japan; now Tokushima prefecture.

Awabil (ăwăbĭl'), town, ⊙ Shaibi sheikdom, Western Aden Protectorate, near Yemen "Status Quo Line," 3 mi. S of Bakhal and 70 mi. N of Aden; 13°50'N 44°52'E. Sheik's residence was moved here (1948) from Bakhal.

Awadh, India: see AJODHYA.

Awadji, Japan: see AWAJI-SHIMA.

A'waj (ā'wăj, ä'wăj), Fr. *Aouaj*, stream of SW Syria, rising on Mt. Hermon and flowing c.75 mi. E to water the region S of Damascus. Fruits and vegetables are grown in its lower valley. It is sometimes identified with the biblical Pharpar, one of the "rivers of Damascus."

Awaji-shima (äwä"jē'shĭmä), island (□ 228; pop. 190,385), Hyogo prefecture, Japan, bet. Harima Sea (E section of Inland Sea) and Osaka Bay, bet. S coast of Honshu and NE coast of Shikoku; roughly triangular; 32 mi. long, 3–17 mi. wide. Relatively flat, with fertile soil; no rivers. Produces rice, wheat, truck, flowers; mfg. (pottery, tiles), woodworking; poultry raising, fishing. Principal center, Sumoto. Sometimes spelled Awazi, and, formerly, Awadji.

Awal: see BAHREIN.

Awali (ăwälē'), main residential oil settlement of Bahrein, at N end of central depression and 10 mi. S of Manama; hq. of oil company. Developed in 1930s; given a former name of Bahrein.

Awaliq, Kaur al, or **Kawr al-'Awaliq** (kour' ăl äwälĭk'), E section of granitic Kaur ranges of Aden hinterland; rises to c.5,000 ft. Separates Upper Aulaqi country (N) from Lower Aulaqi area (S).

Awang (äwäng'), town (1939 pop. 1,077), Cotabato prov., central Mindanao, Philippines, 6 mi. S of Cotabato; rice growing.

Awano (ä"wä'nō), town (pop. 5,369), Tochigi prefecture, central Honshu, Japan, 12 mi. W of Utsunomiya; rice, wheat.

Awa-no-Naruto, Japan: see NARUTO STRAIT.

Awans, Belgium: see BIERSET.

Awantipur or **Avantipur** (both: ŭvŭn'tĭpŏŏr), village, Anantnag dist., W central Kashmir, in Vale of Kashmir, on Jhelum R. and 15 mi. SE of Srinagar; rice, corn, oilseeds. Important in anc. times; was ⊙ under King Avantivarnam (A.D. 855–883), who built 2 near-by temples (now in ruins), with larger dedicated to Siva, smaller and more ornate to Vishnu. At Payar, 5 mi. WNW, is best-preserved Hindu (Sivaite) temple of medieval (c.9th cent. A.D.) Kashmir; contains Siva lingam. At Narastan, c.12 mi. NNE, is ruined temple with unique treatment of trefoil arches on temple walls.

Awara (ä"wä'rä), town (pop. 6,223), Fukui prefecture, central Honshu, Japan, 12 mi. N of Fukui; rice, sweet potatoes, tobacco. Hot springs.

Awasa, Lake, Ethiopia: see AWUSA, LAKE.

Awash (ä'wäsh), village, Shoa prov., central Ethiopia, near Awash R., on railroad and 95 mi. E of Addis Ababa; trade center.

Awash River, E Ethiopia, rises 25 mi. W of Addis Alam on N escarpment of Great Rift Valley, flows NE along the valley in a deep gorge, past town of Awash, and, through the AUSSA dist., to L. Abbé; total length, c.500 mi. Forms boundaries of Shoa, Harar, and Arusi provs. Formerly also Hawash.

Awaso (äwä'sō), town, Western Prov., W Gold Coast colony, 40 mi. NW of Dunkwa (linked by rail); bauxite-mining center developed during Second World War.

Awatabe (äwä'tä'bā), town (pop. 3,714), Fukui prefecture, central Honshu, Japan, 4 mi. ENE of Takebu; textiles, paper.

Awatere, New Zealand: see SEDDON.

Awati or **A-wa-t'i** (both: ä'wä'tē'), town and oasis (pop. 33,607), SW Sinkiang prov., China, 35 mi. S of Aksu and on Aksu R.; carpets, cotton textiles; sericulture; cattle. Lead mines near by.

Awazi, Japan: see AWAJI-SHIMA.

'Awdali, Aden: see AUDHALI.

'Awdillah, sultanate, Aden: see AUDHALI.

'Awdillah, Kawr al-, Aden: see AUDHILLA, KAUR AL.

Awe (äwĕ'), town (pop. 2,335), Benue prov., Northern Provinces, E central Nigeria, 50 mi. NW of Wukari; road junction; salt springs; cassava, durra.

Awe, Loch (lŏkh ô'), lake, central Argyll, Scotland, extending 23 mi. NE-SW, up to 1½ mi. wide. Receives Orchy R. at its NE end, near Dalmally. Drains into Loch Etive by 4-mi.-long Awe R.

Aweil (ăwāl'), town (pop. 1,300), Bahr el Ghazal prov., S Anglo-Egyptian Sudan, on road and 90 mi. NW of Wau; cotton, corn, durra; livestock.

Awemba, former province, Northern Rhodesia: see KASAMA.

Awendaw (ō'ĭndô"), village, Charleston co., E S.C., on Bull Bay, 26 mi. NE of Charleston; ships oysters.

Awgu (ô'gōō), town, Onitsha prov., Eastern Provinces, S Nigeria, 26 mi. S of Enugu; palm oil and kernels, kola nuts.

Awirs (äwĭrs'), village (pop. 2,403), Liége prov., E central Belgium, 7 mi. WSW of Liége; chalk quarrying.

Awish el Hagar (ăwēsh' ĕl hä'gär) or **Awish al-Hajar** (ĕl-hä'jär), village (pop. 6,830), Daqahliya prov., Lower Egypt, on Damietta branch of the Nile and 5 mi. SW of Mansura; cotton, cereals.

Awka (ô'kä), town, Onitsha prov., Eastern Provinces, S Nigeria, 20 mi. E of Onitsha; agr. trade center; wood carving; palm oil and kernels, kola nuts. Lignite. Church of England mission.

Awlad Isma'il, Egypt: see AULAD ISMA'IL.

'Awlaqi, Aden: see AULAQI.

Awlaylah, Egypt: see ULEILA.

Awlu, Nigeria: see ORLU.

Awoe, Mount, Indonesia: see AWU, MOUNT.

Awoi (ăwoi'), village, Upper Nile prov., S central Anglo-Egyptian Sudan, on road and 115 mi. SSW of Malakal. Also spelled Awai.

Awre (ôr), former urban district (1931 pop. 1,033), W Gloucester, England, on Severn R. and 10 mi. SW of Gloucester; agr. market. Has 13th-cent. church.

Awsim, Egypt: see AUSIM.

Awu, Mount, or **Mount Awoe** (both: ä'wōō), active volcano (6,002 ft.), N Sangi isl., Sangi Isls., Indonesia; disastrous eruption in 1892. Also called Abu.

Awunaga (äwōōnä'gä), town, Eastern Prov., SE Gold Coast colony, on strip of land bet. Keta Lagoon and Gulf of Guinea; fishing; saltworking, cotton weaving; coconuts, cassava.

Awusa, Lake (ä'wōōsä), or **Lake Awasa** (ä'wäsä) (□ 60), Ital. *Auusa* or *Auasa*, Sidamo-Borana prov., S central Ethiopia, in Great Rift Valley, bet. lakes Shala and Abaya, 135 mi. SSW of Addis Ababa; 7°5'N 38°25'E; alt. 5,604 ft., 12 mi. long, 6 to 12 mi. wide. Has clear, slightly brackish water and contains hot mineral springs (195°–210°F.).

Axapusco (ähäpōō'skō), town (pop. 1,040), Mexico state, central Mexico, 32 mi. NE of Mexico city; maguey, corn, livestock.

Axar Fjord, Icelandic *Axarfjörður* (äkh'särfyûr"-dhür), inlet (7 mi. long, 17 mi. wide at mouth) of Greenland Sea, NE Iceland, on W side of Melrakkasletta, peninsula; 66°13'N 16°45'W. Receives the Jokulsa.

Axat (äksä'), village (pop. 723), Aude dept., S France, in foothills of E Pyrenees, on the Aude and 17 mi. S of Limoux; lumbering, sawmilling are carried on.

Axbridge, town and parish (pop. 1,017), N Somerset, England, 8 mi. ESE of Weston-super-Mare; agr. market in dairying and strawberry-growing region. Has 15th-cent. church.

Axel or **Aksel** (both: äk'sul), town (pop. 4,496), Zeeland prov., SW Netherlands, on Flanders mainland and 6 mi. SE of Terneuzen; textile mfg., building stone, woodworking; center of grain area. First mentioned in 1105.

Axel Heiberg Island (□ 13,583), largest of Sverdrup Isls., N Franklin Dist., Northwest Territories, in the Arctic Ocean; 78°8'–81°22'N 85°45'–95°15'W; separated from Amund Ringnes Isl. (SW) by Good Friday Gulf, from Meighen Isl. (NW) by Sverdrup Channel, and from Ellesmere Isl. (E) by Nansen and Eureka sounds. Isl. is 220 mi. long, 20–100 mi. wide; coastline is indented by several deep fjords. Surface consists of plateau rising to over 3,000 ft. in S and to over 6,000 ft. in NE. Isl. is named after patron of Sverdrup expedition, 1898–1902.

Axenstrasse (äk'sun-shträ'su), road along E shore of L. of Uri, central Switzerland; leads from Brunnen to Flüelen; mainly hewn in rock. It passes mtn. hamlets of Axenstein, Axenfels, and Axen (also known as Axenberg).

Axe River, England, rises in Dorset 3 mi. N of Beaminster, flows 21 mi. SW, through Devon, past Axminster, to the Channel at Seaton. Navigable 4 mi. above mouth.

Axholme, Isle of (äks'hōm), lowland area (c.18 mi. long, 5 mi. wide) in Parts of Lindsey, NW Lincolnshire, England; bounded by Trent R. (E), Idle R. (S), and Yorkshire border (W). A former marsh, it was drained in 17th cent. and became very productive. Chief town, Epworth.

Axial, village (pop. c.50), Moffat co., NW Colo., on branch of Yampa R. and 20 mi. SW of Craig; alt. 6,413 ft. Coal-mining point. Rich coal deposits near by.

Axim (äshĕm', äk'sĭm), town (pop. 4,635), Western Prov., SW Gold Coast colony, on Gulf of Guinea, 38 mi. W of Takoradi; rubber, coconuts, oil palms, hardwood, rice. Alluvial gold deposits. Lighthouse on Bobowasi Isl., just offshore. Site of Fort Antony. Originally a Port. trading post; passed 1642 to Dutch, 1872 to British.

Axios River, Yugoslavia and Greece: see VARDAR RIVER.

Axioupolis (äksēōō'pôlĭs), town (pop. 2,712), Kilkis nome, Macedonia, Greece, 17 mi. W of Kilkis, on Vardar R. (opposite Polykastron); cotton, tobacco, rice, silk. Formerly called Boemitsa.

Axius River, Yugoslavia and Greece: see VARDAR RIVER.

Axixá (äshē-shä'), city (pop. 1,192), N Maranhão, Brazil, on lower Monim R. (navigable) and 32 mi. SE of São Luís; cotton, rice, babassu nuts.

Ax-les-Thermes (äks'-lā-târm'), village (pop. 1,285), Ariège dept., S France, in E Pyrenees, on the Ariège and 20 mi. SE of Foix; resort with hot sulphur springs.

Axminster, urban district (1931 pop. 2,326; 1951 census 2,673), E Devon, England, on Axe R. and 24 mi. E of Exeter; agr. market. Formerly known for Axminster carpets, 1st made here 1755, now manufactured at Wilton. Has 13th-cent. church.

Axmouth (äks'mùth), village and parish (pop. 641), E Devon, England, on Axe R., near the Channel, just NE of Seaton; fishing port, tourist resort. Has 15th-cent. church and 16th-cent. manor house.

Axochiapan (ähōchyä'pän), town (pop. 3,198), Morelos, central Mexico, 20 mi. WSW of Matamoros; agr. center (sugar, rice, fruit, vegetables, livestock).

Axocuapan, Mexico: see TLALTETELA.

Axtell. **1** City (pop. 510), Marshall co., NE Kansas, 20 mi. E of Marysville, in corn and wheat area. **2** Village (pop. 352), Kearney co., S Nebr., 10 mi. W of Minden; grain.

Axtla, Mexico: see ALFREDO M. TERRAZAS.

Axum, Ethiopia: see AKSUM.

Axutla (ähōōt'lä), town (pop. 1,042), Puebla, central Mexico, 30 mi. S of Matamoros; corn, rice, sugar, livestock.

Axvall (äks'väl"), village (pop. 367), Skaraborg co., S central Sweden, 5 mi. E of Skara; rail junction; grain, stock. Has remains of medieval castle.

Ay (ī), town (pop. 4,031), Marne dept., N France, on the Marne and its lateral canal, 3 mi. NE of Épernay; noted champagne wine center.

Ay, river, Russian SFSR: see AI RIVER.

Aya (ä'yä), town (pop. 8,558), Miyazaki prefecture, E Kyushu, Japan, 11 mi. NW of Miyazaki; sawmills; charcoal, rice, wheat.

Ayabaca (īäbä'kä), city (pop. 2,620), ⊙ Ayabaca prov. (□ 2,734; pop. 75,068), Piura dept., NW Peru, on W slopes of Cordillera Occidental, near Peru–Ecuador border, 70 mi. NE of Piura; alt. 8,907 ft. Trade center; wheat, alfalfa, hides; cattle raising. Sometimes Ayavaca.

Ayabe (ä"yä'bā), town (pop. 15,361), Kyoto prefecture, S Honshu, Japan, 35 mi. NW of Kyoto; rail junction; spinning.

Ayachi, Djebel (jĕ'bĕl äyäshē'), peak (12,300 ft.) of the High Atlas, in central Fr. Morocco, 18 mi. SW of Midelt. Seasonally snow covered; 32°28'N 4°56'W.

Ayacucho, department, Argentina: see SAN FRANCISCO, San Luis prov.

Ayacucho (īäkōō'chō), town (pop. 9,163), ⊙ Ayacucho dist. (□ 2,606; pop. 21,575), E central Buenos Aires prov., Argentina, 38 mi. ENE of Tandil. Rail junction, sheep-raising center; linen milling; oats, wheat, flax, cattle. Hydroelectric plant.

Ayacucho, town (pop. c.2,700), Santa Cruz dept., central Bolivia, on road and 10 mi. SW of Santa Cruz; sugar cane, rice, corn.

Ayacucho, department (□ 18,190; enumerated pop. 394,208, plus estimated 20,000 Indians), S central and S Peru; ⊙ Ayacucho. Bordered by Mantaro R. (N), Apurímac R. (NE), Pampas R., and Cordillera de Huanzo (E). Crossed by cordilleras Occidental and Central. Includes L. Parinacochas. Grain, corn, potatoes, and livestock in the Andes; coca, coffee, cacao, sugar cane on E slopes; vineyards at Huanta and Ayacucho, where there is also silver, lead, copper mining. Main centers: Ayacucho, Huanta, Coracora, Puquio. Formed 1822, it was named Huamanga until 1825, after the victory of Ayacucho, when Peru won its independence.

Ayacucho, city (pop. 18,275), ⊙ Ayacucho dept. and Huamanga prov. (□ 8,699; pop. 67,211), S central Peru, on E slopes of Cordillera Occidental of the Andes, on Huancayo-Cuzco highway and 100 mi. SE of Huancayo, 200 mi. ESE of Lima; 13°10'S 74°14'W; alt. 9,029 ft. Silversmithing, tanning, mfg. of textiles, flour milling. Local trade in agr. products (grain, alfalfa); vineyards; cattle and sheep raising. Silver and lead mining near by. Bishopric. Has Superior Court of Justice; univ., cathedral, colonial style churches and bldgs. Founded 1539 by Pizarro, its name Huamanga was changed (1825) to Ayacucho after Sucre's victory (Dec. 9, 1824) in the near-by valley of Ayacucho (12 mi. NE) secured independence of Peru.

Ayadaw (ùyä'dô), village, Lower Chindwin dist., Upper Burma, 24 mi. ENE of Monywa.

Ayaguz (īŭgōōs'), city (1936 pop. estimate 30,000), S Semipalatinsk oblast, Kazakh SSR, on Turksib RR, on Ayaguz R. and 165 mi. S of Semipalatinsk; major road-rail transfer point for China trade; mfg. (metalware, construction materials); meat and other food products. Highway SE to Bakhty on China-USSR border and to Chuguchak, Sinkiang prov., China. Created (c.1930) as Turksib RR construction settlement; combined with old adjacent (S) trading center of Sergiopol, founded 1847 as fortress in Rus. conquest of Kazakhstan.

Ayaguz River, in Semipalatinsk and Taldy-Kurgan oblasts, Kazakh SSR, rises in Tarbagatai Range, flows 165 mi. NW and S, past Ayaguz, to E end of L. Balkhash.

Ayahualulco (īäwälōōl'kō), town (pop. 1,126), Veracruz, E Mexico, at S foot of Cofre de Perote, 20 mi. SW of Jalapa; corn, coffee, fruit.

Ayakhta (ŭyäkh'tŭ), town (1939 pop. over 500), S central Krasnoyarsk Territory, Russian SFSR, 85 mi. NE of Yeniseisk, in Yenisei Ridge; gold mines.

Ayakudi or **Ayakkudi** (ŭyŭk'kōōdē), town (pop. 15,903), Madura dist., S Madras, India, 3 mi. E of Palni; grain, tobacco.

Ayala (īä'lä), town (pop. 1,195), Morelos, centra Mexico, 3 mi. SW of Cuautla; sugar, rice, fruit.

Ayamonte (īämōn'tā), city (pop. 8,387), Huelva prov., SW Spain, on Guadiana R. estuary, opposite Vila Real de Santo António (Portugal), and 25 mi. W of Huelva (linked by rail). Important fishing center (chiefly tuna, sardines). Fish salting and canning, olive-oil processing, liquor distilling, mfg. of fertilizers. Customhouse. Ruins on near-by hill.

Ayan (ŭyän'), village (1948 pop. over 10,000), central Lower Amur oblast, Khabarovsk Territory, Russian SFSR, fishing port on Sea of Okhotsk, 250 mi. NW of Nikolayevsk, on highway to Yakutsk; fisheries. Gold placers near by.

Ayancik (äyänjŭk'), Turkish *Ayancık*, village (pop. 2,552), Sinop prov., N Turkey, port on Black Sea 30 mi. WSW of Sinop; corn, olives.

Ayanot (äyänōt'). **1** Settlement (pop. 400), W Israel, in Judaean Plain, 3 mi. WNW of Rehovot; site of girls' agr. training school and farm. Founded 1930. **2** Settlement, NW Israel: see RAMAT DAVID.

Ayapango (īäpäng'gō), town (pop. 914), Mexico state, central Mexico, on railroad and 30 mi. SE of Mexico city; cereals, livestock.

Ayapel (īäpĕl'), town (pop. 1,624), Bolívar dept., N Colombia, in San Jorge R. valley, on a lake and 60 mi. SE of Montería; cattle raising.

Ayapel, Serranía de (sĕrănē'ä dā), NE spur of Cordillera Central, N central Colombia, along Antioquia-Bolívar dept. border, extends c.80 mi. NNE from Paramillo massif.

Ayapunga, Cerro (sĕ'rō īäpōōng'gä), Andean peak (15,416 ft.), S central Ecuador, 23 mi. ESE of Alausí; 2°14'S.

Ayarza, Lake (īär'sä), Santa Rosa dept., S Guatemala, 13 mi. ENE of Cuilapa; 3 mi. long, 2 mi. wide, 1,150 ft. deep; alt. c.6,500 ft. Has no surface inlet or outlet.

Ayas (äyäsh'), Turkish *Ayaş*, village (pop. 3,420), Ankara prov., central Turkey, 28 mi. W of Ankara; grain, fruit, cotton; mohair goats.

Ayat or **Ayat'** (ŭyät'yù), town (1944 pop. over 500), W central Sverdlovsk oblast, Russian SFSR, near Iset R., on railroad and 32 mi. S of Nevyansk; peat digging. Until 1944, Ayatskoye.

Ayavaca, Peru: see AYABACA.

Ayaviri (īävē'rē), city (pop. 6,586), ⊙ Melgar prov. (□ 1,709; pop. 47,809), Puno dept., SE Peru, on the altiplano, on Pucará R., on railroad and 75 mi. NNW of Puno; alt. 14,677 ft. Local wool market; potatoes, grain; sheep and cattle raising.

Aycliffe, town (1951 pop. 594), S Durham, England, on Skerne R. and 5 mi. N of Darlington; limestone quarrying. Nucleus of model residential area (pop. c.10,000) for steelworkers of Darlington. Has 13th-cent. church.

Aydabul, Russian SFSR: see AIDABUL.

Aydar River, Ukrainian SSR: see AIDAR RIVER.

Aydemir, Bulgaria: see AIDEMIR.

Ayden (ā'dùn), town (pop. 2,282), Pitt co., E N.C., 10 mi. S of Greenville, in agr. (tobacco, cotton, corn) area; furniture mfg.; lumber.

Aydin (ĭdŭn', īdĕn'), Turkish *Aydın*, province (□ 2,953; 1950 pop. 337,977), W Turkey, on Aegean Sea; ⊙ Aydin. Bordered N by Aydin Mts., S by Mentese Mts.; drained by Buyuk Menderes and Akcay rivers. Emery, arsenic, antimony, magnesite, mercury, copper, iron, lignite; cotton, tobacco, valonia, olives, figs, raisins, millet. Sometimes spelled Aidin.

Aydin, Turkish *Aydın*, anc. *Tralles*, town (1950 pop. 20,421), ⊙ Aydin prov., W Turkey, on railroad near Buyuk Menderes R. (anc. Maeander) and 55 mi. SE of Smyrna; magnesite, lignite, and arsenic; figs, olives, cotton, valonia, wheat, millet. Sometimes spelled Aidin.

Aydin Mountains, Turkish *Aydın*, W Turkey, extend 100 mi. W of Cal bet. Kucuk Menderes R. (N) and Buyuk Menderes R. (S); rise to 6,040 ft. in Buyuk Cokeles. Town of Buldan on N slope. Emery, iron, copper, and lignite in W; lignite, arsenic, copper, and emery in E.

Aydyrlinskiy, Russian SFSR: see AIDYRLINSKI.

Ayelet Hashahar, Israel: see AIYELET HASH SHAHAR.

Ayelo de Malferit (īä'lō dhā mälfärĕt'), town (pop. 2,479), Valencia prov., E Spain, 9 mi. SW of Játiva; liqueur distilling, olive-oil processing; wine, corn, beans.

Ayen (äyã'), village (pop. 318), Corrèze dept., S central France, in Brive Basin, 12 mi. WNW of Brive-la-Gaillarde; grains, cattle, fruit, nuts.

Ayent (äyã'), agr. town (pop. 2,247), Valais canton, S Switzerland, 4 mi. NE of Sion; alt. 3,400 ft.

Ayer (âr), town (pop. 5,740), including Ayer village (pop. 3,107), Middlesex co., N Mass., 11 mi. ESE of Fitchburg; textile machinery, knives, chairs; agr. (apples, truck). Settled before 1670, inc. 1871. U.S. Fort Devens and state pheasant farm near by.

Ayer Baloi (ī'ùr bäloi'), village (pop. 799), S Johore, Malaya, on Strait of Malacca, 28 mi. WNW of Johore Bharu; coconuts; fisheries.

Ayerbe (īĕr'vā), town (pop. 2,157), Huesca prov., NE Spain, 17 mi. NW of Huesca; agr. trade center (wine, olive oil, fruit); brandy mfg., flour milling. Has medieval palace and Romanesque tower. Irrigation reservoir is 2 mi. NE.

Ayer Hitam (ī'ùr hĭ'täm), village (pop. 766), central Johore, Malaya, 18 mi. E of Bandar Penggaram; road center in rubber-growing dist.

Ayer Itam (ī'ùr ē'täm), town (pop. 13,478) on Penang isl., NW Malaya, 5 mi. WSW of George Town; rubber, coconuts, fruit; Chinese temple.

Ayer Kuning (ī'ùr kōō'nĭng"), village (pop. 627), S central Perak, Malaya, 3 mi. W of Tapah Road; rubber.

Ayers Cliff, village (pop. 465), S Que., on L. Massawippi, 17 mi. SW of Sherbrooke; dairying.

Ayer Tawar (ī'ùr tä'wär), village (pop. 1,181), W Perak, Malaya, 10 mi. NE of Lumut; rubber.

Aygachi, Bolivia: see AIGACHI.

Aygidik, Bulgaria: see AIGIDIK.

Aygues River (āg), Drôme and Vaucluse depts., SE France, rises in the Baronnies, flows c.55 mi. SW, past Nyons, to the Rhone 4 mi. W of Orange. Also spelled Aigues and Eygues.

Ayia, Ayion, Ayios [Gr.,=saint], for Gr. names beginning thus and not found here: see HAGIA, HAGION, HAGIOS.

Ayinkasir, Turkey: see KURTALAN.

Ayios Amvrosios (ä'yôs ämbrô'syôs), village (pop. 1,779), Kyrenia dist., N Cyprus, 17 mi. NE of Nicosia; carobs, olives; sheep, goats.

Ayios Dhometios (dhômĕt'yôs), W suburb (pop. 2,532) of Nicosia, N central Cyprus; wheat, barley, oats; sheep, goats.

Ayios Seryios (sĕr'yôs), village (pop. 1,663), Famagusta dist., E Cyprus, near Famagusta Bay of the Mediterranean and 28 mi. E of Nicosia; barley, oats, velches; sheep, hogs, cattle. The Apostelos Varnavos monastery is 1½ mi. S.

Ayios Theodoros (thäô'dôrôs). **1** Village (pop. 852), Famagusta dist., E Cyprus, 40 mi. ENE of Nicosia; grain, fruit; livestock. **2** Village (pop. 1,402), Larnaca dist., S Cyprus, 25 mi. S of Nicosia; wheat, carobs, olive oil; sheep, goats.

Aykino, Russian SFSR: see AIKINO.

Aylesbury (ālz'bùrē), municipal borough (1931 pop. 13,387; 1951 census 21,054), ⊙ Buckinghamshire, England, in center of co., 35 mi. NW of London; 51°49'N 0°49'W; agr. market for upper Thames valley, with dairy-products industry, flour mills, and, near by, silica-sand quarries. Town is famous for its ducks. Formerly known for its lace. Church, dating from 13th cent., was restored by Sir Gilbert Scott; there are also a mus. and several old inns. Town dates from Saxon times, when it was called *Aeglesberg*. Near by is Hartwell House, residence (1808–14) of Louis XVIII.

Aylesford (ālz′fürd), town and parish (pop. 3,644), central Kent, England, on Medway R. and 3 mi. NW of Maidstone; agr. market, with cement works. Has 14th-cent. bridge and 15th-cent. church. Near by is a large anc. stone tomb known as Kit's Coty. There are remains of 13th-cent. Carmelite monastery.

Aylesworth, Mount (9,310 ft.), on Alaska-B.C. border, in St. Elias Mts. 40 mi. NE of Yakutat; 59°55′N 138°48′W.

Ayllón (īlyōn′), town (pop. 1,222), Segovia prov., central Spain, near Burgos prov. border, in NE spur of the Sierra de Guadarrama, 50 mi. NE of Segovia; cereals, grapes, truck. Historic mtn. town, once residence of court of John II. Has Romanesque church, ruins of convent.

Ayllón, Sierra de (syĕ′rä dhä), NE subrange of the Sierra de Guadarrama, central Spain, SE of Riaza; extends c.10 mi. NE along Guadalajara-Segovia border; rises to 7,231 ft. Quesera pass is in SW, on road to Riaza.

Aylmer (āl′mür). **1** Town (pop. 2,478), S Ont., 11 mi. E of St. Thomas; food and milk canning, leather, shoe mfg., woodworking, lumbering, dairying, marble processing. **2** Residential town (pop. 3,115), SW Que., on Ottawa R., at NW end of L. Deschênes, 8 mi. W of Ottawa.

Aylmer, Lake. 1 Lake (□ 340; according to some sources □ 612), E Mackenzie Dist., Northwest Territories, NE of Great Slave L.; 64°5′N 108°30′W; c.40 mi. long, 4–40 mi. wide. Drained NE by Back R.; connected E with Clinton-Colden L. **2** Lake (9 mi. long, 4 mi. wide), S Que., on St. Francis R., 27 mi. NW of Megantic. At N end of lake is Disraeli town.

Aylmer, Mount (10,375 ft.), SW Alta., near B.C. border, in Rocky Mts., in Banff Natl. Park, 12 mi. NE of Banff, overlooking L. Minnewanka.

Aylsham (īl′shüm), town and parish (pop. 2,646), NE Norfolk, England, on Bure R. and 11 mi. N of Norfolk; agr. market. Once a worsted-weaving center.

Aylwin (āl′wĭn), village, SW Que., on Gatineau R. and 40 mi. NNW of Hull; feldspar mining.

Aymangala, India: see CHITALDRUG, town.

Aymaraes, province, Peru: see CHALHUANCA.

Aymaya, Bolivia: see AIMAYA.

Aymorés, Serra dos, Brazil: see AIMORÉS, SERRA DOS.

Ayna (ī′nä), town (pop. 1,735), Albacete prov., SE central Spain, 21 mi. W of Hellín; wool spinning, lumbering; cereals, esparto, olive oil, fruit. Mineral springs.

Aynac (änäk′), village (pop. 690), Lot dept., SW France, 15 mi. NW of Figeac; sawmilling, woodworking.

'Ayn al-'Arab, Syria: see 'AIN EL 'ARAB.

'Ayn al-Fijah, Syria: see 'AIN EL FIJE.

'Ayn al-Kurum, Syria: see 'AIN EL KURUM.

'Aynat, Aden: see 'EINAT.

Aynazhi, Latvia: see AINAZI.

'Ayn Dar, Saudi Arabia: see AIN DAR.

'Ayn Diwar, Syria: see 'AIN DIWAR.

Aynor (ā′nür), agr. town (pop. 551), Horry co., E S.C., 13 mi. NW of Conway.

Ayntab, Turkey: see GAZIANTEP.

'Ayn Turah, Lebanon: see 'AIN TURA.

'Ayn Zahalta, Lebanon: see 'AIN ZEHALTA.

Ayoayo (ïōï′ō), town (pop. c.4,420), La Paz dept., W Bolivia, in the Altiplano, 40 mi. S of La Paz, on La Paz–Oruro RR; alt. 12,959 ft.; barley, sheep.

Ayodhya, India: see AJODHYA.

Ayo el Chico (ī′ō ĕl chē′kō), town (pop. 3,329), Jalisco, central Mexico, 10 mi. E of Atotonilco el Alto; alt. 5,426 ft. Agr. center (wheat, corn, chick-peas, beans, fruit, stock).

Ayolas (īō′läs), town (dist. pop. 3,296), Misiones dept., S Paraguay, port on the upper Paraná (Argentina line) and 65 mi. W of Encarnación; agr. center (fruit, maté, cattle); tanning.

Ayon Island, Russian SFSR: see AION ISLAND.

Ayopaya, province, Bolivia: see INDEPENDENCIA.

Ayopaya River, Bolivia: see COTACAJES RIVER.

Ayora (īō′rä), town (pop. 6,258), Valencia prov., E Spain, 30 mi. W of Játiva; olive-oil processing, flour milling, footwear mfg.; wine, saffron, fruit, honey, cereals, sheep. Mineral springs. Copper mining near by.

Ayos (ä′yōs), village, Nyong et Sanaga region, S central Fr. Cameroons, on Nyong R. and 70 mi. E of Yaoundé; palm plantations. Has large leprosarium, medical assistants' school for natives.

Ayotla (īōt′lä), town (pop. 1,519), Mexico state, central Mexico, on railroad and 18 mi. SE of Mexico city; cereals, maguey, livestock.

Ayotoxco (īōtō′skō), officially Ayotoxco de Guerrero, town (pop. 494), Puebla, E Mexico, in SE foothills of Sierra Madre Oriental, 25 mi. S of Papantla; sugar, fruit.

Ayot Saint Lawrence (ā′yŭt), agr. village and parish (pop. 93), N central Hertford, England, 4 mi. NW of Welwyn Garden City. The house of George Bernard Shaw is national property.

Ay-Petri, Crimea, Russian SFSR: see AI-PETRI.

Ayr (âr), town (pop. 4,626), E Queensland, Australia, 45 mi. ESE of Townsville, on coast; agr. center (sugar cane).

Ayr, village (pop. 761), S Ont., on Nith R. and 9 mi. SE of Galt; dairying, lumbering; mfg. of cereal foods, agr. implements.

Ayr or **Ayrshire** (âr, âr′shĭr,–shür), county (□1,131.6; 1931 pop. 285,217; 1951 census 321,184), SW Scotland; ⊙ Ayr. Bounded by Wigtown (S), the Firth of Clyde (W), Renfrew (N), Lanark and Dumfries (E), and Kirkcudbright (SE). Drained by Ayr, Irvine, Doon, Water of Girvan, and Stinchar rivers. Loch Doon is largest lake. Surface is hilly in S and E, mountainous in SE, sloping toward level coastline. Dairying and cattle breeding (Ayrshire cattle) are important; grain and potatoes are grown. Coal, iron, limestone, sandstone are worked. Mfg. includes leather, woolen and cotton milling, pottery making, ironworking, shipbuilding (Ayr), mfg. of machinery and explosives, oil refining (Ardrossan). Other towns are Kilmarnock, Irvine, New Cumnock, Cumnock, Girvan, Troon, Saltcoats, Largs, Darvel, Galston, Newmilns. Prestwick has major airport. There are many anc. castles and abbey ruins, and literary and historical associations. Turnberry was home of Robert Bruce. Burns was b. at Alloway; many features and historical events of co. are celebrated in his poetry. Battle of Largs (1263) resulted in decline of Norse influence in Scotland.

Ayr, burgh (1931 pop. 36,783; 1951 census 43,011), ⊙ Ayrshire, Scotland, on Firth of Clyde, at mouth of Ayr R., and 30 mi. SSW of Glasgow; 55°28′N 4°39′W; seaport and commercial center, with mfg. of mining and agr. machinery, switchgear, asphalt, and leather goods; also resort with beach, esplanade, and racecourse. Two bridges over Ayr R., 13th-cent. Auld Brig (rebuilt) and New Bridge (1788), are subject of Burns's poem "Twa Brigs." Other features: 12th-cent. church of St. John the Baptist; 17th-cent. Old Church; remains of Fort Castle, built 1652 by Cromwell to replace an earlier castle; and Burns monument. In burgh (S), at mouth of Doon R. (bridged by Brig O'Doon), is village of Alloway, where Robert Burns was born. His parental cottage has been restored; adjoining are Burns Mus. and statue of poet. There are ruins of anc. church, Alloway's Auld Haunted Kirk. Just NNE of Ayr is large airport of PRESTWICK. Burgh includes suburbs of Newton-on-Ayr (NE) and Wallacetown (E).

Ayr. 1 Village (pop. 121), Adams co., S Nebr., 10 mi. S of Hastings and on Little Blue R. **2** Village (pop. 104), Cass co., E N.Dak., 16 mi. NW of Casselton.

Ayrag Nur, Mongolia: see AIRIK NOR.

Ayrão, Brazil: see AIRÃO.

Ayre, Point of (âr), promontory at N extremity of Isle of Man, England, 19 mi. NNE of Douglas; 54°25′N 4°22′W; lighthouse.

Ayrig Nuur or **Ayrik Nur**, Mongolia: see AIRIK NOR.

Ay River, Russian SFSR: see AI RIVER.

Ayr River (âr), Ayrshire, Scotland, rises 4 mi. E of Muirkirk, flows 38 mi. W, past Sorn and Tarbolton, to Firth of Clyde at Ayr. Receives Lugar Water just SSW of Mauchline.

Ayrshire, county, Scotland: see AYR.

Ayrshire (âr′shür), town (pop. 334), Palo Alto co., NW Iowa, 17 mi. ESE of Spencer, in livestock and grain area.

Aysén (īsĕn′), province (□ 34,357; 1940 pop. 17,014, 1949 estimate 21,779), S Chile; ⊙ Puerto Aysén. Rugged, sparsely settled region bet. the Andes and the Pacific; a little-explored area of mts., glaciers, fjords, sounds, and isls., with sheep-raising and lumbering activities. Its climate is cool and wet. Notable features are: TAITAO PENINSULA, CHONOS ARCHIPELAGO, L. SAN RAFAEL and its impressive glacier on W slopes of Cerro SAN VALENTÍN, and the Andean lakes shared with Argentina: L. Buenos Aires, L. General Paz, L. San Martín, and L. Cochrane (W part of L. Pueyrredón). Aysén was formed 1929 from neighboring provs. and is coextensive with Aysén dept. Formerly also spelled Aisén.

Aysén, town, Chile: see PUERTO AYSÉN.

Aysén River, Aysén prov., S Chile, formed by 2 headstreams ESE of Puerto Aysén, flows c.20 mi. W, past Puerto Aysén, to fjordlike estuary on Moraleda Channel; navigable for c.5 mi. With its principal headstream, it is 110 mi. long.

Aysgarth (āz′gärth), agr. village and parish (pop. 299), North Riding, NW Yorkshire, England, on Ure R. and 19 mi. NE of Settle; site of sanitarium. Here is Aysgarth Force, a well-known waterfall of the Ure.

Ayton (ā′tŭn), village (pop. estimate 500), S Ont., on South Saugeen R. and 35 mi. S of Owen Sound; dairying, farming, fruitgrowing.

Ayton, town and parish (pop. 1,413), E Berwick, Scotland, on Eye Water and 6 mi. NW of Berwick-on-Tweed; paper milling. Modern mansion is on site of anc. border fortress of Ayton Castle.

Aytona (ītō′nä), town (pop. 2,172), Lérida prov., NE Spain, 12 mi. SW of Lérida, near Segre R., in irrigated area (livestock, cereals, alfalfa); olive-oil processing. Hydroelectric plant near by.

Aytos, Bulgaria: see AITOS.

Ayu-Dag (īōō″-däk′), massive laccolite rock (1,785 ft.) in S Crimea, Russian SFSR, on Black Sea, 9 mi. ENE of Yalta. Artek children's camp is at its foot.

Ayudhaya, Thailand: see AYUTTHAYA.

Ayukawa (ä″yōō′käwŭ), town (pop. 6,879), Miyagi prefecture, N Honshu, Japan, on S Ojika Peninsula, fishing port on Ishinomaki Bay, 14 mi. SE of Ishinomaki; lumbering.

'Ayun, Saudi Arabia: see 'UYUN.

Ayuñgon (äyōō′nyŭgōn), town (1939 pop. 1,327; 1948 municipality pop. 14,357), Negros Oriental prov., E Negros isl., Philippines, on Tañon Strait, 31 mi. SE of Binalbagan; agr. (corn, coconuts).

Ayuruoca, Brazil: see AIURUOCA.

Ayuthia or **Ayuthya**, Thailand: see AYUTTHAYA.

Ayutla (īōōt′lä), town (1950 pop. 1,645), San Marcos dept., SW Guatemala, on Suchiate R. opposite Suchiate (Mexico) and 18 mi. W of Coatepeque. Rail terminus; customs station; sugar cane, rice, grain, beans.

Ayutla. 1 Officially Ayutla de los Libres, city (pop. 2,519), Guerrero, SW Mexico, in Pacific lowland, 45 mi. E of Acapulco; agr. center (sugar cane, cotton, coffee, tropical fruit, cereals, livestock). The Plan of Ayutla (a program to remove dictator Santa Anna) was drawn up here in 1854. The Revolution of Ayutla (1855) drove Santa Anna into exile and established a liberal govt. **2** Town (pop. 3,470), Jalisco, W Mexico, 28 mi. SSW of Ameca; agr. (cotton, sugar cane, tobacco, fruit, grain).

Ayutthaya (ŭyŏŏt′tŭyä) or **Krung Kao** (krŏŏng′ kou′) [Thai,=anc. capital] or, officially, **Phra Nakhon Si Ayutthaya** (prä′ näkôn′ sē′ ŭyŏŏt′tŭyä), town (1947 pop. 15,821), ⊙ Ayutthaya prov. (□990; 1947 pop. 362,761), S Thailand, on Lopburi R. (arm of the Chao Phraya), at mouth of Pa Sak R., on railroad and 40 mi. N of Bangkok; trading (floating market) and agr. center. Intensive rice cultivation; also corn, tobacco, sesame, fruit; hog raising; fisheries. An old ⊙ Thailand, Ayutthaya is situated on an isl. formed by the river arms and criss-crossed by canals; its ruins, among the few remains of early Thai civilization, include the royal palace (1577), numerous temples and pagodas. Founded 1349, it remained the capital until its destruction (1767) by the Burmese and the transfer of the seat of govt. to Bangkok. Also spelled Ayuthia, Ayuthya, or Ayudhaya.

Ayvacik (īväjŭk′), Turkish *Ayvacık*, village (pop. 2,406), Canakkale prov., NW Turkey, 38 mi. S of Canakkale; major producer of valonia from extensive oak forests; cereals; iron deposits.

Ayvalik (īvälŭk′), Turkish *Ayvalık*, anc. *Heraclea*, town (pop. 13,650), Balikesir prov., NW Turkey, Aegean port on Mytilene Channel opposite Lesbos isl., 27 mi. SW of Edremit; olives, olive oil, soap, valonia. Also spelled Aivalik and Aivali.

Ayviekste River, Latvia: see AIVIEKSTE RIVER.

Aywaille (äwī′), town (pop. 3,453), Liége prov., E central Belgium, on Amblève R. and 12 mi. SSE of Liége; stone quarrying; tourist resort.

Ayya, Cape, Russian SFSR: see AIYA, CAPE.

Ayyampettai (īyŭmpät′tī) or **Ayyampet** (ī′yŭmpāt), town (pop. 7,546), Tanjore dist., SE Madras, India, on arm of Cauvery R. delta and 7 mi. NNE of Tanjore; silk weaving, rush-mat mfg.; betel farms.

'Ayyat, El, Egypt: see 'AIYAT, EL.

Ayzpute, Latvia: see AIZPUTE.

Az [Arabic,=the], for Arabic names beginning thus: see under following part of the name.

Azacualpa, Guatemala: see SAN JOSÉ ACATEMPA.

Azae (äzä′ä) or **Azai** (äzī′), town (pop. 3,250), Okayama prefecture, SW Honshu, Japan, 27 mi. NW of Okayama, in agr. area (rice, wheat, peppermint); raw silk, charcoal.

Azagra (ä-thä′grä), town (pop. 2,697), Navarre prov., N Spain, near the Ebro, 23 mi. NW of Tudela; vegetable canning; trades in sugar beets, pepper, wine, cereals, fruit; horse breeding. Gypsum quarries and mineral springs.

Azai. 1 Town, Aichi prefecture, Japan: see ASAI. **2** Town, Okayama prefecture, Japan: see AZAE.

'Azair, Al, or **Al-'Uzayr** (both: äl äzīr′), village, 'Amara prov., SE Iraq, on Tigris R., near Iran border, 25 mi. SSE of 'Amara; dates, rice, corn, millet, sesame. Reputedly site of the tomb of the prophet Ezra. Also spelled Al Uzair.

Azambuja (äzämbōō′zhŭ), town (pop. 2,057), Lisboa dist., central Portugal, on railroad and 28 mi. NNE of Lisbon; wine, cork. Lumbering in surrounding pine forest.

Azambujeira (äzämbōōzhā′rŭ), village (pop. 280), Santarém dist., central Portugal, 6 mi. NW of Santarém; grows wine, olives, figs, oranges.

Azamgarh (ŭz′ŭmgŭr), district (□ 2,217; pop. 1,822,893), E Uttar Pradesh, India; ⊙ Azamgarh. On Ganges Plain; bounded N by the Gogra. Agr. (rice, barley, wheat, sugar cane, gram, mustard, corn); dhak jungle and mango groves (N). Main towns: Mau, Azamgarh, Mubarakpur.

Azamgarh, town (pop. 24,307), ⊙ Azamgarh dist., E Uttar Pradesh, India, on Tons R. and 50 mi. NNE of Benares; road junction; hand-loom cotton-weaving center; sugar milling. Founded c.1665.

Azanaques, Cordillera de (kôrdĭyā′rä dā äsänä′kĕs), range in the Eastern Cordillera of the Andes, W

Bolivia, on Oruro-Potosí dept. border, bet. Cordillera de Tres Cruces (N) and Cordillera de Los Frailes (S); extends c.90 mi. S from point 30 mi. ENE of Oruro to Mt. Azanaque, c.15 mi. SE of Challapata. Rises to 17,060 ft. at Morococala peak. Main tin-mining region of Bolivia, with mines of Catavi, Llallagua, and Uncía (E slope), Huanuni (W slope).

Azángaro (äsäng'gärō), city (pop. 3,039), ⊙ Azángaro prov. (□ 11,216; pop. 112,613), Puno dept., SE Peru, on the Altiplano, 65 mi. NNW of Puno; alt. 12,661 ft. Salt deposits; barley, potatoes, livestock. Also Asángaro.

Azanja or **Azanya** (ä'zä'nyä), village (pop. 9,353), central Serbia, Yugoslavia, 6 mi. NW of Palanka.

Azapa (äsä'pä), village (pop. 117), Tarapacá prov., N Chile, on the Quebrada de Azapa (irrigation) and 9 mi. SE of Arica; cotton, olives, oranges, alfalfa, vegetables.

Azapa, Quebrada de (kābrä'dä dā), river in N Chile, formed 8 mi. WNW of Belén, flows 55 mi. SW and W, past Azapa, to the Pacific at Arica. In its lower irrigated reaches are grown cotton, grain, fruit.

Azarbaijan, Iran: see AZERBAIJAN.

Azare (äz'ārā), town (pop. 3,853), Bauchi prov., Northern Provinces, N Nigeria, 110 mi. ESE of Kano; agr. center; cotton, peanuts, millet, durro. Has hosp., leper colony.

Azarichi, Belorussian SSR: see OZARICHI.

Azarshahr (äzär"shä'hûr), town (1940 pop. 11,890), Third Prov., in Azerbaijan, NW Iran, on road and 30 mi. SSW of Tabriz, near L. Urmia; center of Dehkharegan (Dekharegan) agr. area, for which town is sometimes named; grain, fruit, tobacco, cotton; rugmaking.

Azay-le-Ferron (äzā'-lŭ-fĕrō'), village (pop. 415), Indre dept., central France, 15 mi. N of Le Blanc; footwear mfg.

Azay-le-Rideau (-lŭ-rēdō'), village (pop. 1,387), Indre-et-Loire dept., W central France, on Indre R. and 12 mi. NE of Chinon; winegrowing, woodworking. Noted for 16th-cent. early Renaissance château (surrounded by a park and mirrored in Indre R.) which now contains mus. of Renaissance furniture and art.

A'zaz or **Azaz** (ä'zăz), town, Aleppo prov., NW Syria, near Turkish border, 27 mi. NNW of Aleppo; cotton, cereals.

Azazga (äzäzgä'), village (pop. 930), Alger dept., N central Algeria, in Great Kabylia, 18 mi. E of Tizi-Ouzou; olives, figs.

Azbi (äz'bē), town (pop. 2,000), Tigre prov., N Ethiopia, 34 mi. NE of Makale; cereals, livestock; salt market.

Azbine, Fr. West Africa: see AÏR.

Azcapotzalco (äskäpōtsäl'kō), town (pop. 31,496), Federal Dist., central Mexico, NW residential suburb of Mexico city, on railroad; petroleum-refining center; metal and food industries. Was an important Aztec center. Has 17th-cent. church on site of anc. slave market.

Azcoitia (äth-koi'tyä), Basque town (pop. 4,772), Guipúzcoa prov., N Spain, 18 mi. WSW of San Sebastián; textile milling; mfg. of sandals, berets, chocolate; cider distilling, flour and sawmilling. Limestone quarries. Mineral springs near by. St. Ignatius of Loyola was baptized in parochial church here.

Azdavay (äzdävī'), village (pop. 178), Kastamonu prov., N Turkey, on Koca R. and 30 mi. NW of Kastamonu; grain. Formerly Carsamba.

Azegour (äzgōōr'), locality, Marrakesh region, SW Fr. Morocco, on N slope of the High Atlas, 37 mi. SSW of Marrakesh; molybdenum mined since 1932. Copper deposits. Also spelled Azgour.

Azemmour (äzĕmōōr'), city (pop. 14,623), Casablanca region, W Fr. Morocco, on the Oum er Rbia just above its mouth on the Atlantic, 45 mi. SW of Casablanca and 9 mi. ENE of Mazagan; ships early fruits and vegetables. Ocean vessels cannot reach city because of sand bar. Almost untouched by European influences, Azemmour preserves the sleepy, picturesque appearance of a walled Moslem community, unchanged through the ages. An agr. penal colony is 3 mi. SW. Occupied by Portuguese 1513–41.

Azerbaijan or **Azarbaijan** (ä"zûrbījän', ä"zûr-), former province (□ 41,000; 1940 pop. 2,734,973) of NW Iran; main city, Tabriz. Bounded N by Soviet Azerbaijan (along Aras R.), W by Turkey and Iraq, S by Kurdistan, Garus, and Khamseh, and E by Gilan and Caspian Sea. An extensive stony plateau (average alt. 4,000 ft.) with imposing volcanic cones (Savalan, Sahand) and the large L. Urmia basin, and cut by river gorges. Continental climate, hot and arid in summer, cold in winter. Permanent pop. (largely Turkic) is restricted to broader valleys, where wheat, barley, tobacco, cotton, opium, and fruit are raised. Salt and coal mining; sulphur deposits (Shahin Dezh). Served by railroad from Teheran, through Tabriz, to Julfa on Aras R. (Soviet border) and with branch to Urmia lake port of Sharifkhaneh. Besides Tabriz, the main centers are Ardebil, Rizaiyeh, Khoi, Maragheh, Sarab, Mianeh, and Maku. Mahabad is a center of the Kurd country. Main Caspian port is Astara. In remote times, W Azerbaijan was part of the Urartu (Armenian) kingdom (9th–8th cent. B.C.); E section was settled by the Medes, became prov. of Media Minor of Persian Empire, and later was known as Media Atropatene, or simply Atropatene. It was ruled by the Parthians, and after A.D. 226 by the Persian Sassanian dynasty. Under Arab rule (after 7th cent.), and again (13th cent.) under Hulagu, the 1st Ilkhan, the regional center was Maragheh. This was moved to Tabriz after the conquest by Tamerlane in 14th cent. It was out of Ardebil that the Safavid dynasty arose (c.1500). Through 16th and 17th cent., Azerbaijan, including the region N of the Aras, was disputed by Turkey and Persia. The latter finally wrested control under Nadir Shah, but was forced to cede the section N of the Aras to Russia by the treaties of Gulistan (1813) and Turkmanchai (1828). The remainder was organized as a Persian prov. In 1928, it was divided into E and W Azerbaijan, which became (1938) Iran's Third (⊙ Tabriz) and Fourth (⊙ Rizaiyeh) provs., respectively. After Second World War, when Iranian Azerbaijan was occupied by Soviet troops, a Soviet-supported Turkic autonomous movement was suppressed in 1946.

Azerbaijan, Azerbaidzhan, or **Azerbaydzhan** (all: ä"zûrbījän', ä"zûr-, Rus. ä"zĭrbījän'), fully **Azerbaijan Soviet Socialist Republic**, constituent republic (□ 33,100; 1947 pop. estimate 3,100,000) of the USSR, in E Transcaucasia; ⊙ Baku. Includes NAKHICHEVAN AUTONOMOUS SOVIET SOCIALIST REPUBLIC (separated from Azerbaijan proper by Armenian SSR) and NAGORNO-KARABAKH AUTONOMOUS OBLAST (with predominant Armenian pop.). Azerbaijan is bounded by Dagestan (N), Georgia (NW), Armenia (W), Iranian Azerbaijan (S; in part along Aras R.), Caspian Sea (E). Central hot, dry Kura and Aras lowland steppes are enclosed by the Greater Caucasus (N) and E outliers of the Lesser Caucasus (SW). At S end of Caspian coastal plain is subtropical Lenkoran lowland. Generally dry continental climate varies with alt. Rivers (non-navigable except for shallow craft on lower Kura R.) are important for irrigation and hydroelectric power (Mingechaur). Pop. consists mainly of Azers or Azerbaijani Turks (63%; Shiite Moslems of Persian culture), Armenians (12%), Russians (10%), Georgians, and Tats and Talysh (2 Persian groups). Administratively, Azerbaijan falls into independent cities and *raions* (*rayons*). Main industry based on exploitation of rich petroleum resources of Apsheron Peninsula (centered on Baku) and Neftechala, with associated oil-refining, chemical, and machine-mfg. industries. Crude and refined petroleum products are shipped, via Caspian Sea and Astrakhan, up the Volga, by pipe line to Batum, and by rail from Baku. Other mineral resources: magnetite (Dashkesan), alunite (Zaglik), copper (Kedabek), arsenic, molybdenum, cobalt, cement rock (Tauz) rock salt (near Nakhichevan). Cotton (rotated with lucerne) is leading agr. product in irrigated Mugan, Mili, and Shirvan steppes. Other crops are grain (rice, corn, wheat), tobacco and walnuts (Zakataly), fruit (Kuba), and grapes. Sericulture in Nukha-Shemakha area. Subtropical crops (tea, citrus, almonds, pomegranates, pecans) flourish in Lenkoran Lowland, saffron and olives on Apsheron Peninsula. Non-irrigated steppe is used for winter pasture (mainly sheep), mts. for summer grazing. Leading industrial centers: Baku with its suburb of Sumgait, Kirovabad, Shemakha, Nukha, Lenkoran. Known to the ancients as Albania, the region was divided into several principates, following domination by Arabs, Turks, and Mongols, and was disputed bet. Turkey and Persia until ceded (1813, 1828) by the latter to Russia. The Azerbaijani people had developed after 11th cent. out of merger of local Albanian stock and invading Kuman and Turkmen tribes. After First World War, Azerbaijan had a counter-revolutionary govt. (1918–20) and, following establishment of Soviet rule, Azerbaijan SSR was formed out of Baku and Yelizavetpol (greater part) govts. and Zakataly okrug. Joined (1922) the USSR as a member of Transcaucasian SFSR; became a separate constituent republic in 1936.

Azergues River (äzârg'), Rhône dept., E central France, rises in the Monts du Beaujolais, flows 34 mi. generally SSE to the Rhone below Anse. Its valley is followed by Paris-Lyons RR.

Azero, province, Bolivia: see MONTEAGUDO.

Azero River (äsä'rō), Chuquisaca dept., S central Bolivia, rises S of Tomina, flows SE, past Sopachuy, and N, to Río Grande 27 mi. ENE of Padilla; 100 mi. long.

Azgour, Fr. Morocco: see AZEGOUR.

Azhikal, India: see CANNANORE, city.

Azib, El- (ĕl-äzēb'), village, Bizerte dist., N Tunisia, on E shore of L. Bizerte, 6 mi. SE of Bizerte; truck-gardens.

Azilal (äzēläl'), village (pop. 374), Marrakesh region, central Fr. Morocco, on N slope of the High Atlas, 90 mi. ENE of Marrakesh; alt. 4,688 ft. Military post.

Azimabad, India: see PATNA, city.

Azimganj (ŭzēm'gŭnj), town (pop., including Jiaganj, just W across river, 15,223), Murshidabad dist., central West Bengal, India, on the Bhagirathi and 9 mi. N of Berhampore; rail junction; trade (rice, gram, oilseeds, jute, barley). Jain temples.

Azincourt, France: see AGINCOURT.

Azinhaga (äzēnyä'gŭ), agr. village (pop. 1,162), Santarém dist., central Portugal, near the Tagus, 11 mi. NE of Santarém; rice, wheat, corn.

Azino, Japan: see AJINO.

Aziscohos Lake (ŭzĭs'kōōs), W Maine, artificial lake (c.12 mi. long) formed by dammed Magalloway R. in N Oxford co. Sometimes spelled Aziscoos.

Azizbekov (ŭzēs"byĭkôf'). **1** Village (1939 pop. over 500), central Armenian SSR, near the Eastern Arpa-Chai, 65 mi. SE of Erivan; livestock; irrigated orchards. Until c.1935, Pashalu. **2** District of Greater Baku, Azerbaijan SSR, on E Apsheron Peninsula; oil fields. Main centers: Bina, Imeni Kalinina, Mardakyany.

Azizia (ăzēzē'yŭ), town, W Tripolitania, Libya, on Tripoli-Garian railroad, 25 mi. SSW of Tripoli, in hilly agr. (cereals, lucerne, olives, fruit) and livestock region; alt. 380 ft.; road junction. Chief center of the GEFARA; esparto grass processing, alabaster quarrying. Has mosque, R.C. church, and restored Turkish fort. Received Ital. agr. settlers in late 1930s. Highest temp. in Africa (136°F.) recorded here.

'Aziziya, Al, or **Al-'Aziziyah** (äl äzēzē'yŭ), town, Kut prov., E Iraq, on Tigris R., on railroad, and 50 mi. SE of Baghdad; dates, millet, sesame, corn.

'Aziziya, El, or **Al-'Aziziyah** (both: ĕl-), village (pop. 10,151), Sharqiya prov., Lower Egypt, on railroad and 8 mi. ENE of Benha; cotton.

Aziziye. **1** Town, Afyonkarahisar prov., Turkey: see EMIRDAG. **2** Town, Kayseri prov., Turkey: see PINARBASI.

Azki, Oman: see IZKI.

Azna (äznä'), village, Sixth Prov., in Luristan, SW Iran, on Trans-Iranian RR and 45 mi. SSW of Arak; road-rail transfer point for highway to Isfahan.

Aznakayevo (ŭznŭkī'ŭvŭ), village (1926 pop. 2,225), SE Tatar Autonomous SSR, Russian SFSR, 25 mi. NNE of Bugulma; wheat, livestock.

Aznalcázar (äthnälkä'thär), town (pop. 2,333), Seville prov., SW Spain, on affluent of the Guadalquivir and 16 mi. WSW of Seville; olives, grain, wine; lumbering.

Aznalcóllar (äthnälkō'lyär), town (pop. 4,427), Seville prov., SW Spain, 18 mi. WNW of Seville (linked by rail); copper mining. Also trades in cereals, olives, cork, timber, livestock. Has iron-pyrite deposits.

Azogues (äsō'gĕs), town (1950 pop. 6,579), ⊙ Cañar prov., S central Ecuador, in the Andes, on Pan American Highway and 15 mi. NE of Cuenca, 175 mi. S of Quito; 2°44'S 78°50'W. Situated in high Andean valley, where corn and livestock are raised, it is a mfg. center for Panama hats; also tanning and flour milling. In the vicinity are silver and copper mines and mercury, asphalt, and ruby deposits.

Azores (ùzōrz', āzōrz'), Port. *Açôres* (ùsō'rĭsh) [=hawks], archipelago (□ 888; 1950 pop. 318,686) in the N Atlantic, 900–1,200 mi. W of Lisbon, politically part of Portugal. Consist of 9 main isls. falling into 3 natural divisions: SE group (SÃO MIGUEL ISLAND, SANTA MARIA ISLAND), central group (TERCEIRA ISLAND, GRACIOSA ISLAND, SÃO JORGE ISLAND, FAIAL ISLAND, PICO ISLAND), and NW group (FLORES ISLAND, CORVO ISLAND). Administratively, the Azores consist of 3 districts (named after chief port cities—PONTA DELGADA, ANGRA DO HEROÍSMO, HORTA) which, however, do not coincide with the physical grouping. The archipelago extends c.300 mi. E–W and 130 mi. N–S bet. 36°55'N 25°1'W (Castelo Point, Santa Maria Isl.) and 39°43'N 31°7'W (N tip of Corvo Isl.). The isls. are mostly mountainous with steep, rugged coast line, and all but Santa Maria reveal their volcanic origin by the presence of eruptive cones (active and quiescent), calderas, crater lakes, lava flows, small geysers, and mineral springs. Pico (7,611 ft.) on Pico Isl. is highest peak. Severe earthquakes and eruptions have occurred frequently, as late as 1926 (especially on Faial and São Miguel isls.). The Azores are known for their mild year-round climate with little seasonal change (Feb. average 57°F., Aug. 72°F.), but are rainier (35–45 in. per year) than equally balmy Madeira. Meteorological data compiled here are essential contribution to European weather forecasts. The fauna and flora are essentially European, with some African species. The vegetation is almost tropical in its luxuriance and variety. While coniferous forests cover mtn. slopes, such trees and plants as laurel, chestnut, eucalyptus, ferns, and bamboos are commonly found. Agr. crops, ranging from tropical to temperate, include pineapples, tea, tobacco, oranges, early vegetables, deciduous fruit, cereals, corn, and potatoes. Winegrowing, after a period of decline due to blight, is again widespread on Pico and Faial isls. Livestock is extensively raised, especially for dairying. The surrounding seas abound in fish, and whaling is still important. Industries are limited to agr. processing, straw- and woodworking, embroidering, and mfg. of crude earthenware. While their fine scenery and healthful climate have made the Azores a winter resort for Europeans, their paramount importance stems from strategic location as trans-Atlantic stepping stones. They are a hub of submarine cables, and have developed into a center of communications with the increase of scheduled trans-Atlantic flights. Two major airports were built in Second World War at Lajes on Terceira Isl. and on Santa Maria Isl.; Ponta Delgada and Horta became Allied naval and seaplane bases. Coins found on Corvo Isl. show that Carthaginians probably reached the Azores in 4th cent. B.C. Isls. 1st appeared on an Italian map in 1351. Visited by Port. navigators (1427–31); Gonçalo Velho Cabral landed on Santa Maria Isl., perhaps in 1431–32. Port. settlement began c.1450. Flemish immigrants arrived following gift of Faial Isl. to Isabella of Burgundy (1466). The Azores served as a place of exile and played important part in Port. history, notably in resisting (1580–83) the accession of Philip II of Spain, and in supporting Dom Pedro against Dom Miguel (1830–31). They are also known for the famous naval battle (1591) bet. the *Revenge* under Grenville and the Sp. fleet.

Azotus, Palestine: see ASHDOD.

Azov (ă'zŏv, –zŏf, ā'–, Rus. ŭzôf'), anc. *Tanaïs*, city (1926 pop. 17,545), SW Rostov oblast, Russian SFSR, fishing port on S arm of Don R. delta mouth near Sea of Azov, and 16 mi. WSW of Rostov; rail terminus; fish processing, lumber milling; mfg. (flour products, apparel, leather goods). Located on site of Gr. colony of Tanaïs (founded 3d cent. B.C.); a Genoese settlement (13th cent.) and under Turkish rule (15th–18th cent.). Taken (1696) by Peter the Great after epic siege; temporarily held (1696–1711) by Russia; conditionally annexed (1739) as a dismantled fortress; secured definitely in 1774. Declined following rise of Rostov.

Azov, Sea of, anc. *Palus Maeotis*, shallow N arm (□ 14,000) of Black Sea, in USSR. Bounded SW by Crimea, N by Ukraine SSR, E by the Kuban delta lowland; connected with Black Sea by Kerch Strait, with Sivash lagoon (W) through Genichesk Strait; 200 mi. long (SW–NE), 80 mi. wide, max. depth 49 ft. Counterclockwise currents have created characteristic sandspits [Rus. *kosa*] on N and E coasts and the long Arabat Tongue (W), separating Sea of Azov from Sivash lagoon. Salinity of water is reduced through heavy discharge of tributary streams: Don R. (emptying into Taganrog Gulf, a NE inlet); Mius and Kalmius rivers (N); Yeya and Kuban rivers (E). Shore reaches only are frozen (Dec.-March). Fisheries (sturgeon, pike, carp, herring) are important, especially along S coast. Principal ports: Rostov (on the Don just above its mouth); Taganrog, Zhdanov, Osipenko (on N coast); Kerch (inside Kerch Strait); fishing centers of Yeisk and Temryuk (on E coast). Iron ore and coal transported bet. interdependent metallurgical centers of Kerch and Zhdanov.

Azov-Black Sea Territory, *Azovo-Chernomorskiy Kray*, former administrative division of S European Russian SFSR; ⊙ was Rostov. Formed 1934 out of Northern Caucasus Territory, it included Adyge Autonomous Oblast; dissolved 1937 into Krasnodar Territory and Rostov oblast.

Azovo (ŭzô'vŭ), village (1926 pop. 787), S Omsk oblast, Russian SFSR, 25 mi. SW of Omsk; flour milling.

Azovskoye (ŭzôf'skŭyŭ), village (1939 pop. over 500), NE Crimea, Russian SFSR, on railroad and 12 mi. SE of Dzhankoi; flour mill; wheat, cotton, livestock. Until 1944, Kolai.

Azov Upland (ă'zŏv, –zŏf, ā'–), Rus. *Priazovskaya Vozvyshennost'*, arc-shaped hilly region in SE Ukrainian SSR; extends from Dnieper R. c.100 mi. parallel to Sea of Azov; merges (E) with Donets Ridge; rises to 1,007 ft.; dry steppe (wheat, sunflowers).

Azoyú (äsoiōō'), town (pop. 2,178), Guerrero, SW Mexico, in Pacific lowland, 19 mi. W of Ometepec; sugar, coffee, fruit, livestock.

Azpeitia (äthpā'tyä), Basque town (pop. 6,082), Guipúzcoa prov., N Spain, on Urola R. and 16 mi. SW of San Sebastián; mfg. of furniture, organs, sandals, chocolate; flour- and sawmilling. Jasper, marble, and limestone quarries near by. Has old walls and Gothic church of St. Sebastián. Loyola (1 mi. SW) has imposing convent of St. Ignatius of Loyola (b. in near-by house), a 17th-cent. church, and a hospice.

Azra', Syria: see IZRA'.

Azraq, Bahr el, Anglo-Egyptian Sudan: see BLUE NILE.

Azrou (äzrōō'), town (pop. 8,541), Meknès region, N central Fr. Morocco, on N slopes of the Middle Atlas, 37 mi. SE of Meknès; alt. 4,365 ft. Road junction; sheep and wool market; sawmilling. Winter sports. Founded 17th cent. as a Berber fortress.

Aztalan Mound Park, Wis.: see LAKE MILLS.

Aztec (ăz'tĕk"), village (pop. 885), ⊙ San Juan co., NW N.Mex., on Animas R., near Colo. line, in foothills of Rocky Mts., and 31 mi. SSW of Durango, Colo.; alt. 5,590 ft. Trade center in fruit-growing region; grain. Aztec Ruins Natl. Monument is just N.

Aztec Ruins National Monument (27.14 acres; established 1923), in San Juan co., NW N.Mex., on Animas R., just N of village of Aztec. Ruins of pre-Columbian Pueblo Indian town built of masonry and timber. Main ruin (12th cent. A.D.) was constructed around plaza; once included 500 rooms and 36 kivas, one of which (the Great Kiva) has been restored. Inhabitants practiced irrigated agr. and used implements of stone, wood, and bone.

Azua (ä'swä), province (□ 936; 1935 pop. 35,080; 1950 pop. 50,166), S Dominican Republic, on the Caribbean; ⊙ Azua. Mountainous, semiarid region, bounded N by the Cordillera Central (including Monte TINA, and crossed by the Sierra de Ocoa). Main crops (irrigation): coffee, tobacco, sugar cane, cereals, vegetables. Lumbering. Has petroleum deposits. Prov. was set up 1845; formerly comprised larger area.

Azua, officially Azua de Compostela, city (1935 pop. 5,767; 1950 pop. 7,419), ⊙ Azua prov., SW Dominican Republic, 3 mi. from its port on the Caribbean (Ocoa Bay), at S foot of the Sierra de Ocoa, 55 mi. W of Ciudad Trujillo; 18°27'N 70°43'W. Leading town of the SW; trades in agr. products (sugar cane, coffee, rice, beans, corn, resin, fruit, medicinal plants, timber). Has international airport; also ruins of anc. convent. Founded near by in 1504; later moved to present site after an earthquake destroyed previous one.

Azuaga (äth-wä'gä), town (pop. 15,413), Badajoz prov., W Spain, in N Sierra Morena, 13 mi. W of Fuenteovejuna (Córdoba prov.); mining (silver-bearing lead), processing, and agr. center (cereals, olives, vegetables, grapes, livestock). Alcohol and liquor distilling, flour- and sawmilling; mfg. of meat products, textile goods, shoes, soap. Anc. Miramontes castle near by (SE) contains graves of 2 daughters of Trajan.

Azuara (äth-wä'rä), town (pop. 2,520), Saragossa prov., NE Spain, 24 mi. S of Saragossa; olive-oil processing, flour milling, lumbering; cereals, saffron, fruit.

Azuay (äswī'), prov. (□ 3,443; 1950 pop. 243,920), S Ecuador, in the Andes; ⊙ CUENCA. Mountainous region intersected by fertile valleys, with semi-tropical humid climate; main rains: Dec.-April. Rich in ores (gold, silver, mercury, platinum) and marble quarries. Predominantly agr., it produces sugar cane, coffee, cereals, subtropical fruit, cotton. Sheep and cattle grazing; dairying. Exports cinchona bark from trans-Andean Amazon basin. Mfg. of Panama hats is a prominent urban industry. Cuenca, 3d largest city of Ecuador, is a leading commercial, cultural, and mfg. center.

Azuchi (ä"zōō'chē), village (pop. 5,699), Shiga prefecture, S Honshu, Japan, 25 mi. ENE of Kyoto; rice. Site of tomb of Oda Nobunaga, 16th-cent. military dictator of Japan.

Azuero Peninsula (äswā'rō), W central Panama, on Pacific Ocean, forms W side of Gulf of Panama; 60 mi. wide, 50 mi. long; rises to 3,067 ft. in Canajagua peak, 10 mi. SW of Las Tablas. Terminates in Mala Point (SE). Includes Herrera (NE), Los Santos (SE), and part of Veraguas (W) provs. Sometimes called Los Santos Peninsula. Old Azuero prov. (formed 1850) was divided 1855 into Los Santos and Herrera provs.

Azuer River (äth-wăr'), Ciudad Real prov., S central Spain, in New Castile, formed by headstreams 7 mi. N of Infantes, flows c.50 mi. WNW, past Manzanares, to Ojos del Guadiana marshes, where Guadiana R. emerges.

Azueta, Villa, Mexico: see VILLA AZUETA.

Azufrales, Venezuela: see EL PILAR, Sucre state.

Azufre, Cerro, or **Cerro Copiapó** (sĕ'rō äsōō'frā, kōpyäpō'), Andean peak (19,950 ft.), Atacama prov., N Chile, 75 mi. E of Copiapó; 27°19'S.

Azufre, Cerro del, Andean peak (17,965 ft.) on Atacama-Antofagasta prov. border, N Chile, 25°23'S 68°53'W.

Azufre, Paso del (pä'sō dĕl), pass (14,720 ft.), in the Andes, on Argentina-Chile border, on road bet. Antofagasta (Argentina) and Taltal (Chile); 25°7'S 68°27'W.

Azufre Norte, Paso del (nôr'tā), or **Paso de la Chapetona** (dā lä chäpātō'nä), Andean pass (11,955 ft.) on Argentina-Chile line, on road bet. San Juan (Argentina) and Los Vilos (Chile); 31°18'S. Just S is Paso del Azufre Sud (12,018 ft.)

Azufre Volcano or **Lastarria Volcano** (lästär'yä), Andean volcano (18,635 ft.) on Argentina-Chile border, 32 mi. S of Cerro Llullaillaco; 25°10'S. Sulphur deposits and sulphurous springs.

Azuga (äzōō'gä), village (pop. 2,763), Prahova prov., S central Rumania, on Prahova R., on railroad and 6 mi. N of Sinaia; mtn. resort (alt. 3,280 ft.) in the Carpathians; noted for woolen textiles; mfg. of glass, cement, cheese; brewing.

Azul (äsōōl'), city (pop. 27,082), ⊙ Azul dist. (□ 2,520; pop. 44,373), central Buenos Aires prov., Argentina, 150 mi. NW of Mar del Plata. Cattle center in hilly grazing and dairying area; grain and poultry farming. Supplies limestone for cement production; brewing, tanning, meat packing, flour milling, mfg. of ceramics, soap. Natl. col.

Azul, Cordillera (kôrdĭyā'rä), E Andean ridge in N central Peru, 60 mi. NE of Huánuco, extends c.120 mi. NE bet. 9°25'S and 8°S; rises to 8,261 ft. The Boquerón Abad gorge is a gateway to Amazon basin.

Azul, Río, Guatemala, Mexico, British Honduras: see HONDO, Río.

Azul, Serra (sĕ'rŭ äsōōl'), range of central Mato Grosso, Brazil, forming part of the Amazon-Paraguay drainage divide in lat. 14°30'S, c.30 mi. NE of Cuiabá. Average alt. 2,300 ft.

Azulita, La, Venezuela: see LA AZULITA.

Azuma, Japan: see NINOMIYA, Kanagawa prefecture.

Azumini (äzōō'mēnē), town, Owerri prov., Eastern Provinces, S Nigeria, on branch of Imo R. and 15 mi. SSE of Aba; trade center; palm oil and kernels, kola nuts.

Azuqueca de Henares (äth-ōōkā'kä dhā änä'rĕs), town (pop. 826), Guadalajara prov., central Spain, near Henares R., 7 mi. SW of Guadalajara; wheat, barley, sugar beets, grapes, truck produce, sheep; lumbering.

Azurduy (äsōōrdōō'ē), town (pop. c.8,960), ⊙ Azurduy prov., Chuquisaca dept., S central Bolivia, 80 mi. SE of Sucre; corn, wheat, barley. Until 1900s, Pomabamba.

Azure Lake (16 mi. long, 1–2 mi. wide), E B.C., in Cariboo Mts., in Wells Gray Provincial Park, 120 mi. N of Kamloops, at foot of Azure Mtn. (8,191 ft.). Drains W into North Thompson R. through Clearwater L.

Azusa (ŭzōō'sŭ), city (pop. 11,042), Los Angeles co., S Calif., at base of San Gabriel Mts., 13 mi. E of Pasadena; packs, ships citrus fruit; also produces nuts, avocados, poultry, dairy foods. Mfg. (chemicals, pipe, aircraft equipment). Seat of Pacific Bible Col. of Azusa. Founded 1887, inc. 1898.

Azuzaquí (äsōōsäkē'), town (pop. c.2,000), Santa Cruz dept., central Bolivia, 11 mi. NNE of Warnes; sugar cane, rice, corn. Also spelled Azusaquí.

Azzah, Palestine: see GAZA.

Azzan or **'Azzan** (äz-zăn'), town (pop. 600), Wahidi sultanate of Balhaf, Eastern Aden Protectorate, 50 mi. NW of Balhaf and on the Wadi Meifa'a; center of agr. oasis (pop. 2,400); airfield. Tribal-guard hq. Was formerly a separate Wahidi sultanate. Sometimes spelled Izzan.

Azzanello (ätsänĕl'lō), village (pop. 1,305), Cremona prov., Lombardy, N Italy, near Oglio R., 13 mi. NNW of Cremona; mfg. (silk textiles, saddles).

Azzano Decimo (ätsä'nō dā'chēmō), village (pop. 1,388), Udine prov., Friuli-Venezia Giulia, NE Italy, 6 mi. SE of Pordenone; alcohol distillery.

Azzega, Eritrea: see HAZZEGA.

B

Ba, Fiji: see MBA.

Ba, Song (shông' bä'), river, S central Vietnam, rises in Annamese Cordillera E of Kontum, flows 200 mi. S and E, past Ankhe, to South China Sea at Tuyhoa.

Baa, Indonesia: see ROTI.

Ba'abda or **Baabda** (bäb'dă), village (pop. 2,350), ⊙ Mt. Lebanon prov., central Lebanon, near Mediterranean Sea, 5 mi. S of Beirut and on Beirut–Damascus RR; alt. 2,300 ft.; sericulture, cotton, cereals, oranges.

Baago (bô'wŭ), Dan. *Baagø*, island (□ 2.4; pop. 149), Denmark, in the Little Belt just W of Fyn isl.; until 1861 belonged to city of Assens. Baago By, town. Formerly also spelled BOGO, the name of another Danish isl. off S Zealand.

Baaklin, Lebanon: see BA'AQLIN.

Baalbek, Ba'albek, or **Ba'albak** (all: bäl'bĕk), anc. *Heliopolis* (hēlēō'pŭlĭs), town (pop. 8,691), central Lebanon, at W foot of the Anti-Lebanon, on Beirut-Aleppo RR, and 35 mi. NNW of Damascus, 40 mi. ENE of Beirut; 34°N 36°11'E; alt. 3,800 ft. Summer resort and tourist center overlooking the Bekaa valley. Here was an important city of ancient times, where the Phoenicians built their temple to the sun-god Baal or Bel [thus the Gr. name Heliopolis, =city of the sun], later identified by the Romans with Jupiter. It was very prominent in Roman times, and among its extensive ruins are the remains of the large temple of Jupiter. Baalbek was repeatedly sacked by invaders and also suffered heavily in an earthquake in 1759.

Baan, China: see PAAN.

Baao (bä'ou), town (1939 pop. 4,083; 1948 municipality pop. 16,485), Camarines Sur prov., SE Luzon, Philippines, on railroad and 11 mi. SE of

Naga; agr. center (rice, abacá, corn). Near-by L. Baao (□ 3) is 2 mi. long, 1.5 mi. wide.

Ba'aqlin or **Ba'aqalin** (both: bä'klēn), Fr. *Baaklin* or *Baakleen*, village (pop. 3,687), central Lebanon, 16 mi. SSE of Beirut; alt. 2,800 ft.; sericulture, cotton, cereals, oranges. Seat of one of the 3 Druse religious heads.

Baar (bär), town (pop. 6,193), Zug canton, N central Switzerland, 1 mi. NNE of Zug; cotton textiles, flour. Has 14th-cent. church.

Baard (bärt), village (pop. 284), Friesland prov., N Netherlands, 6 mi. SE of Franeker, in commune (pop. 5,283) of Baarderadeel; dairying.

Baarle-Hertog (bär'lŭ-hĕr'tōkh), Fr. *Baerle-Duc* (bärlŭ-dük'), town (pop. 1,761), Antwerp prov., Belgium; an enclave in North Brabant prov., S Netherlands, 9 mi. N of Turnhout (Belgium); agr. market; strawboard mfg. A Belg. possession since 1479, when town of Baarle was divided into Baarle-Nassau (Netherlands), and Baarle-Hertog (Belgium). Status of enclave confirmed by Belgian-Netherlands treaty of separation (1839). Formerly spelled Baerle-Hertog.

Baarle-Nassau (-nä'sou), town (pop. 1,174), North Brabant prov., S Netherlands, 12 mi. SE of Breda; with Belg. enclave of BAARLE-HERTOG, it forms town of Baarle; mfg. (cigars, strawboard); egg market.

Baarn (bärn), residential town (pop. 15,400), Utrecht prov., central Netherlands, 5 mi. ESE of Hilversum; rail junction. Plant-disease research station, botanical gardens of Utrecht Univ. here.

Baasmoen, Norway: see BASMOEN.

Baasrode (bäs'rōdŭ), town (pop. 6,506), East Flanders prov., N Belgium, on Scheldt R. and 3 mi. E of Dendermonde; cotton, metallurgical industries; lace making; agr. market. Formerly spelled Baesrode.

Bab, El, or **Al-Bab** (both: ĕl băb'), town, Aleppo prov., NW Syria, 22 mi. NE of Aleppo; pistachios, cereals.

Baba (bä'bä), town (1950 pop. 500), Los Ríos, W central Ecuador, in tropical lowlands, on tributary of the Guayas system, and 13 mi. W of Babahoyo; trading center in fertile agr. region (cacao, sugar cane, rice, tropical fruit and woods, stock); rice milling.

Baba, peak (4,900 ft.) in Cordillera Isabelia, N Nicaragua, 35 mi. W of Bonanza.

Baba (bä'bä). **1** Gr. *Varnous* (värnōōs'), mountain in the Pindus system, on Yugoslav-Greek border, bet. Pelagonija valley and L. Prespa. Highest peak, the Perister (8,530 ft.), is in Yugoslavia, 8 mi. WSW of Bitolj; peak Varnous or Garvani (7,657 ft.) is on Yugoslav-Greek border, 10 mi. NW of Phlorina. **2** Mountain (5,688 ft.) in Dinaric Alps, E Herzegovina, Yugoslavia, 8 mi. SW of Gacko.

Baba, Cape (bäbä'), NW Turkey, on Aegean Sea opposite Lesbos, 20 mi. WSW of Ayvacik; westernmost point of Anatolian mainland and hence of the continent of Asia; 39°29'N 26°4'E.

Babaatik, Turkey: see BABAESKI.

Baba Budan Range (bä'bŭ bōōdŭn'), outlier of Western Ghats, in Kadur dist., W Mysore, India, NW of Chikmagalur; extends c.40 mi. in a horseshoe curve, with opening on W; c.5 mi. wide. Rises to 6,310 ft. in S, in Mulainagiri or Mulliangiri peak; highest point in Mysore. Extensive coffee plantations on slopes form basis of Mysore's noted coffee industry; cardamom and pepper estates. Important iron mines (sometimes called Kemmanugundi), mostly on N curve, supply iron- and steelworks at Bhadravati. Numerous Hindu and Moslem pilgrimage shrines. Originally called Chandragiri, range was renamed in 17th cent. for Baba Budan, Moslem pilgrim who introduced coffee growing in India (Eur. methods introduced c.1840). Sometimes written Bababudan.

Babadag (bäbädäg'), town (1948 pop. 4,022), Constanta prov., SE Rumania, in Dobruja, on W shore of small L. Babadag, on railroad, and 20 mi. S of Tulcea; trade in fish and grain; flour milling. Excursion center for near-by sites of anc. places.

Baba-Dag (bŭbä"-däk'), peak (c.11,930 ft.) in the SE Greater Caucasus, Azerbaijan SSR, 32 mi. NW of Shemakha.

Babaeski (bäbä'ĕskē"), town (pop. 5,936), Kirklareli prov., Turkey in Europe, on railroad and 22 mi. SSW of Kirklareli; important sugar-beet center; refinery at Alpullu (SSE). Also spelled Baba Eski or Eski Baba; sometimes called Babaatik or Babaiatik.

Baba Gurgur (bä'bä gōōr'gōōr), oil-mining NW suburb of Kirkuk, N Iraq, at head of oil pipe lines to the Mediterranean; refinery. The natural-gas seepages here are linked by tradition with the biblical fiery furnace of Shadrach, Meshach, Abednego.

Babahoyo (bäbä-oi'ō), city (1950 pop. 9,045), ⊙ Los Ríos prov., W central Ecuador, in tropical lowlands, at head of navigation of the Guayas system, on Babahoyo R. (one of the headstreams), 40 mi. NE of Guayaquil, 125 mi. SSW of Quito; 1°46'S 79°27'W. Processing and trading center; transshipment point for fertile agr. region (cacao, rice, pineapple, oranges, melons, tagua nuts, balsa wood); rice and sugar milling; stock raising. Near by is govt. distillery for alcohol, ether, perfumes.

Babai or **Babay** (bŭbī'), S suburb (1926 pop. 3,039) of Kharkov, Kharkov oblast, Ukrainian SSR, 6 mi. SSW of city center; distilling.

Babai, lignite basin, Russian SFSR: see YERMOLAYEVO.

Babali, Turkey: see PERSEMBE.

Babanka (bŭbän'kŭ), village (1926 pop. 4,432), SW Kiev oblast, Ukrainian SSR, 12 mi. ESE of Uman; flour mill. Formerly also called Babanovka.

Babar Islands (bä'bär), group (□ 314; pop. 11,712), S Moluccas, Indonesia, in Banda Sea, bet. Timor and Tanimbar Isls.; 7°55'S 129°43'E. Consist of 1 large isl. surrounded by 5 islets. Largest isl., Babar (pop. 6,050), is roughly circular, 20 mi. in diameter and rises to 2,733 ft.; on it is the chief town, Tepa. Group is forested, with fertile coastal strips. Produces sago, corn.

Babati (bäbä'tē), town, Northern Prov., Tanganyika, 85 mi. SW of Arusha; coffee; livestock.

Babayevo (bŭbī'ŭvŭ), city (1926 pop, 3,209), SW Vologda oblast, Russian SFSR, on railroad and 70 mi. W of Cherepovets; metalworks.

Babayurt (bŭbŭyōōrt'), village (1932 pop. estimate 780), N Dagestan Autonomous SSR, Russian SFSR, on Aksai R. and 25 mi. NNE of Khasavyurt, in irrigated cotton area; livestock (horses, sheep). Pop. largely Kumyk.

Babbacombe, England: see TORQUAY.

Babbitt. 1 Village, St. Louis co., NE Minn., c.50 mi. ENE of Hibbing; concentrating plant here processes low-grade iron ore (taconite) from large deposits near by. **2** Village (pop. 2,464), Mineral co., W Nev., at S end of Walker L., 5 mi. NW of HAWTHORNE.

Babcock, town (1940 pop. 22), Miller co., SW Ga., 15 mi. N of Bainbridge.

Babcock State Park (c.3,200 acres), Fayette co., S central W.Va., in the Alleghenies, 20 mi. NNE of Beckley. Clifftop village is near entrance.

Bab el Mandeb (băb ĕl măn'dĕb) [Arabic,=gate of tears], strait linking Red Sea and Gulf of Aden of Arabian Sea, and separating Asia's Arabian Peninsula from Africa's Fr. Somaliland; 17 mi. wide. A major shipping route, it contains Perim isl.

Babelsberg (bä'bŭlsbĕrk), E suburb of Potsdam, Brandenburg, E Germany, on the Havel, at W end of Teltow Canal; 52°24'N 13°6'E. Textile milling; mfg. of locomotives, phonographs, records, carpets. Until Second World War, center of Ger. motion-picture industry. Site of observatory of Berlin Univ. (at Neubabelsberg, N). Has 19th-cent. former summer palace of Emperor William I. Called Nowawes (nōvä'vĕs, nō'vävĕs) until 1938, when it was united with Neubabelsberg. Inc. into Potsdam in early 1940s.

Babelthuap (bä'bŭltōō'äp), volcanic island (□ 143), largest of Palau isls., W Caroline Isls., W Pacific; c. 23 mi. long; wooded hills, chalk cliffs; bauxite. Ngardok L. (1,000 yd. long, 400 yd. wide) in NE.

Babenhausen (bä"bŭnhou'zŭn). **1** Village (pop. 3,493), Swabia, SW Bavaria, Germany, on the Günz and 12 mi. NNE of Memmingen; rail terminus; dairying (cheese), brewing, printing, woodworking. Had mid-16th-cent. castle of Fugger family. **2** Town (pop. 3,343), S Hesse, W Germany, in former Starkenburg prov., on the Gersprenz and 8 mi. W of Aschaffenburg; woodworking.

Baberu (bŭbä'rōō), village, Banda dist., S Uttar Pradesh, India, 24 mi. ENE of Banda; gram, jowar, wheat, oilseeds, rice.

Babeyru, Belgian Congo: see BAYENGA.

Babhnan, India: see SWAMI NARAYAN CHHAPIA.

Babia Gora (bä'byä gōō'rä), Czech *Babí Hora* (bä'bē hô'rä), Pol. and Slovak *Babia Góra*, highest peak (5,659 ft.) in the Beskids, on Czechoslovak-Pol. border, 12 mi. NNE of Namestovo, 12 mi. SSW of Sucha; one of highest peaks in Poland.

Babilafuente (bävē"läfwĕn'tä), town (pop. 1,311), Salamanca prov., W Spain, 12 mi. E of Salamanca; wine, vegetables. Was burned in 1812 by French retreating from Salamanca.

Babimbi (bäbēm'bē), village, Sanaga-Maritime region, SW Fr. Cameroons, 70 mi. NE of Edéa.

Babimost (băbī'môst), Ger. *Bomst* (bômst), town (1939 pop. 2,190; 1946 pop. 1,264) in Brandenburg, after 1945 in Zielona Gora prov., W Poland, 20 mi. NE of Grünberg (Zielona Gora); grapes, hops. Founded c.1000; chartered 1334. Passed 1793 to Prussia; in Grand Duchy of Warsaw, 1807–13. Briefly occupied by Poles in 1919. Until 1939, Ger. frontier station on Pol. border, SW of Zbaszyn. In Second World War, c.35% destroyed.

Babinda (băbĭn'dŭ), town (pop. 1,730), E Queensland, Australia, 35 mi. SSE of Cairns, on coast; sugar-producing center.

Babine Lake (bŭbēn', bă'bēn) (□ 249), central B.C., 110 mi. WNW of Prince George; 95 mi. long, 1–6 mi. wide. Drained NW by Babine R. (c.60 mi. long) into Skeena R.

Babine Mountains, range, central B.C., extends c.100 mi. NW-SE bet. Babine R. (N), Babine L. (E), and Bulkley R. (S and W); rises to 7,827 ft. on Cronin Mtn., 16 mi. NE of Smithers.

Babin-nos Mountains (bä'bĭn-nôs"), NW part of W Balkan Mts., on Bulg.-Yugoslav border; extend N-S bet. Timok R. and Belogradchik Pass. Highest peak, Babin-nos (3,437 ft.), 12 mi. SSW of Kula (Bulgaria). Crossed by Vrashka-chuka Pass.

Babino (bä'bēnŭ), town (1942 pop. over 500), W Gorki oblast, Russian SFSR, on Oka R. and 6 mi. ESE of Dzerzhinsk; metalworks.

Babintsy (bŭbēntsē'), town (1939 pop. over 500), N central Kiev oblast, Ukrainian SSR, 25 mi. NW of Kiev; peat bogs.

Babocsa (bŏ'bōchŏ), Hung. *Babócsa*, town (pop. 2,891), Somogy co., SW Hungary, 42 mi. W of Pecs; wheat.

Babol, Iran: see BABUL.

Babolna, Hungary: see BANA.

Babolsar, Iran: see BABULSAR.

Baboosic Lake, Hillsboro co., S N.H., resort lake near Amherst, 10 mi. SW of Manchester; 1.5 mi. long.

Baboquivari Mountains (bä"bōkēvä'rē), Pima co., S Ariz., extend c.40 mi. N from Mex. line; rise to 7,730 ft. in Baboquivari Peak, c.50 mi. NW of Nogales. In section of Coronado Natl. Forest.

Babor or **Babors** (both: bäbôr'), coastal range of the Tell Atlas, in Little Kabylia, NE Algeria, extending c.40 mi. along the Gulf of Bougie. Highest peaks are Djebel Babor (6,575 ft.) and Djebel Tababor (6,430 ft.). Cork-oak forests.

Baborow (bäbô'rōōf), Pol. *Baborów*, Ger. *Bauerwitz* (bou'ŭrvĭts), town (1939 pop. 4,536; 1946 pop. 3,345) in Upper Silesia, after 1945 in Opole prov., S Poland, 11 mi. NW of Ratibor (Raciborz); rail junction; sugar refining, brick mfg., flour milling. After 1945, briefly called Baworow, Pol. *Baworów*.

Babors, Algeria: see BABOR.

Baboua (bäbwä'), village, NW Ubangi-Shari, Fr. Equatorial Africa, near Fr. Cameroons border, 110 mi. WSW of Bozoum; customs station in cotton-growing and gold-mining region.

Babouch (bäbōōsh'), village, Tabarka dist., NW Tunisia, in Medjerda Mts., 11 mi. SSW of Tabarka; custom house on Algerian border. Summer resort.

Babugarh (bä'bōōgŭr), town (pop. 1,195), Meerut dist., NW Uttar Pradesh, India, 20 mi. SSE of Meerut; wheat, gram, jowar, sugar cane, oilseeds.

Babul or **Babol** (both: bäbōōl', bäbōl'), town (1941 pop. 33,656), Second Prov., in E Mazanderan, N Iran, 90 mi. NE of Teheran across Elburz mts., and on Babul R. (short Caspian coastal stream); its Caspian port is Babulsar. Agr. center; rice, cotton, flax, oranges; cotton gins. Replaced Sari as ⊙ Mazanderan in 19th cent. Until 1930s called Barfurush.

Babulsar or **Babolsar** (bäbōlsär'), town, Second Prov., in E Mazanderan, N Iran, Caspian port 12 mi. NNW of Babul, at mouth of short Babul R.; fishing center, noted for caviar production; seaside resort. Until 1930s called Meshed-i-Sar.

Babuna River (bä'bōōnä), central Macedonia, Yugoslavia, rises on SE slope of the Solunska Glava, flows c.50 mi. generally E and NE to Vardar R. 2 mi. SSE of Titov Veles. **Babuna Mountains**, Serbo-Croatian *Babuna Planina*, rise near lower right bank of river; highest point (2,614 ft.) is 12 mi. S of Titov Veles.

Babushkin (bä'bōōshkĭn). **1** City (1926 pop. 2,570), SW Buryat-Mongol Autonomous SSR, Russian SFSR, on Trans-Siberian RR (Mysovaya station), on SE L. Baikal, and 75 mi. W of Ulan-Ude; shipbuilding, sawmilling. Iron and oil deposits near by. Prior to 1941, Mysovsk. **2** Residential city (1926 pop. 15,634; 1939 pop. 70,480), central Moscow oblast, Russian SFSR, adjoining (NE) Moscow; locomotive works, chemical plant; food processing, textiles. Became city in 1925; until 1939, Losinoostrovskaya.

Babushkina, Imeni (ē'mĭnyē bä'bōōshkēnŭ), village (1939 pop. over 2,000), SE Vologda oblast, Russian SFSR, 20 mi. SE of Totma; flax processing; health resort (mineral springs). Until c.1940, Ledengskoye.

Babusnica or **Babushnitsa** (both: bäbōōsh'nĭtsä), Serbo-Croatian *Babušnica*, village (pop. 4,516), SE Serbia, Yugoslavia, 11 mi. SW of Pirot.

Babuyan Channel, Philippines: see LUZON STRAIT.

Babuyan Island (bäbōōyän') (□ 28), one of the Babuyan Isls., Cagayan prov., Philippines, in Luzon Strait, forming S boundary of Balintang Channel, 21 mi. NE of Calayan; roughly circular, 6 mi. in diameter. Mountainous, rising in central area to 3,569 ft. at Mt. Pangasun (active volcano). Rice growing, fishing.

Babuyan Islands, Sp. *Babuyanes*, volcanic group (1939 pop. 3,292), Cagayan prov., Philippines, in Luzon Strait, bet. Babuyan and Balintang channels, 17 mi. N of Luzon; 19°10'N 121°55'E. Includes CALAYAN ISLAND (largest), CAMIGUIN ISLAND, DALUPIRI ISLAND, FUGA ISLAND, Babuyan Isl., and several islets. Generally mountainous. Rice growing, fishing.

Babyak (bä'byäk), village (pop. 6,211), Gorna Dzhumaya dist., SW Bulgaria, on W slope of W Rhodope Mts., 15 mi. NE of Razlog; flour milling; truck, livestock. Sometimes spelled Babjak.

Babylon (bă'bĭlŭn), anc. city of Mesopotamia, on the Euphrates; its site is in S Iraq, in Hilla prov., c.10 mi. from the Euphrates, just NNE of Hilla and c.55 mi. S of Baghdad. It was N of the cities that flourished in S Mesopotamia in 3d millennium B.C., and it was not until Hammurabi (c.2100 B.C.) made it ⊙ of his kingdom of Babylonia that it took on great importance. Its city god Marduk (identical with Bel) became a leading god of the Near East and the city became wealthy from commerce. It was destroyed (7th cent. B.C.) by the Assyrians under Sennacherib, and its real splendor belongs to the later period of Babylonia after the city was rebuilt—especially under Nebuchadnezzar (d.562 B.C.), from whose time most of the excavated ruins date. The Hanging Gardens became one of the Seven Wonders of the World. Its walls and its brick-built palace and towered temples were adorned with color. Under the rule of Nabonidus the city was captured by the Persians under Cyrus the Great in 538 B.C., and its glory ended. After the conquest of Alexander the Great, its trade was largely taken by Seleucia. Near by are the ruins of anc. KISH (E) and BORSIPPA (S).

Babylon, resort and residential village (pop. 6,015), Suffolk co., SE N.Y., on S Long Isl., on Great South Bay, 14 mi. E of Freeport; yachting; produces beeswax, cider, candy, machinery, greeting cards, knit goods, boats. Ferries to Fire Isl. Just NW is Belmont Lake State Park. Inc. 1893.

Babylonia (băbĭlō'nēŭ), ancient empire of Mesopotamia, the region bet. the Euphrates and Tigris now mostly in central Iraq. The name is sometimes given to the whole civilization of S Mesopotamia, including the states established by the city rulers of Lagash, Agade (or Akkad), Erech, and Ur in the 3d millennium B.C. Usually it is limited to the civilization of the valley after the fall of Sumer and the rise of the Semitic states after the triumph of Sargon. In its narrowest sense it applies only to the great state built by Hammurabi c.2100 B.C. with the city of BABYLON as its capital. Early in 18th cent. B.C. the Hittites captured Babylon and held it briefly. The nomadic Cassites or Kassites took the city c.1746 B.C. and held it precariously for centuries. There were constant wars and conquests until Babylonia became a subsidiary state of the Assyrian Empire and once more flourished. So important did it become that it was a key area in the attempted uprising against the Assyrian king Sennacherib (reign 705–687 B.C.) and Babylon was sacked (c.689 B.C.). Later, under Nabopolassar, Babylonia established (625) its independence once more and with the Medes and Persians helped to bring about the capture of Nineveh and the fall of the Assyrian Empire. Nabopolassar established what is generally known as the Chaldaean or New Babylonian Empire, and under his son, Nebuchadnezzar, the new empire reached its height, Babylon achieving a splendor that was never forgotten. The recalcitrant Hebrews were defeated and punished with the Babylonian Captivity. Egypt had already been defeated by Nebuchadnezzar in the great battle of Carchemish (605 B.C.) while Nabopolassar was still alive. But the steady growth of Persian power spelled the end of Babylonia, and in 538 B.C. the last of the Babylonian rulers surrendered to Cyrus the Great. Babylonia became an unimportant region of the Persian Empire.

Babynino (bŭbĭ'nyĭnŭ), village (1939 pop. over 500), central Kaluga oblast, Russian SFSR, 20 mi. SW of Kaluga; coarse grain.

Bac or **Bach** (both: bäch), Serbo-Croatian *Bač*, Hung. *Bács*, village (pop. 5,004), Vojvodina, NW Serbia, Yugoslavia, 12 mi. NW of Palanka, in the Backa.

Baca (bä'kä), town (pop. 1,955), Yucatan, SE Mexico, 18 mi. NE of Merida; rail terminus in henequen-growing area.

Baca (bā'kŭ), county (□ 2,565; pop. 7,964), SE Colo.; ⊙ Springfield. Grain and livestock region bordering on Okla. and Kansas; drained by branches of Cimarron R. Formed 1889.

Bacabal (bŭkŭbäl'), city (pop. 4,162), N central Maranhão, Brazil, on Mearim R. (navigable), in lake dist., and 120 mi. SSW of São Luís; cotton, tobacco, cereals, babassu nuts.

Bacacay (bäkäkī'), town (1939 pop. 2,244; 1948 municipality pop. 26,504), Albay prov., SE Luzon, Philippines, on Tabaco Bay (small inlet of Lagonoy Gulf), 12 mi. NNE of Legaspi; agr. center (abacá, rice, coconuts).

Bacadéhuachi (bäkädā'wächē), town (pop. 1,053), Sonora, NW Mexico, in W outliers of Sierra Madre Occidental, 120 mi. ENE of Hermosillo; livestock, wheat, corn.

Bacalar (bäkälär'), town (pop. 619), Quintana Roo, SE Mexico, E Yucatan Peninsula, on W bank of L. Bacalar, 23 mi. NW of Chetumal; chicle, henequen, fruit, hardwood.

Bacalar, Lake, Quintana Roo, SE Mexico, in E Yucatan Peninsula, 20 mi. W of Chetumal; 30 mi. long, 1–4 mi. wide. Connected with Río Hondo by small river.

Bacanora (bäkänō'rä), town (pop. 990), Sonora, NW Mexico, on affluent of Yaqui R. and 95 mi. E of Hermosillo, silver, lead, copper mining; wheat, corn, cattle.

Bacarra (bäkä'rä), town (1939 pop. 6,400; 1948 municipality pop. 15,851), Ilocos Norte prov., NW Luzon, Philippines, 4 mi. NNE of Laoag; rice-growing center.

Bacau (bäkû'ōō), Rum. *Bacău*, city (1948 pop. 34,461), ⊙ Bacau prov., E central Rumania, in Moldavia, on Bistrita R. and 150 mi. NE of Bucharest; rail junction, industrial and commercial center. Mfg. of woolen textiles, blankets, ribbons, leather goods, clay products, hardware, machinery, glue, confectionery, vinegar; woodworking; meat processing; flour milling. Specializes in marketing of petroleum products, fruit and nuts. Has two 15th-cent. churches. Airport. Was R. C. bishopric until 1813 and hq. of Rumanian army command in First World War. Occupied (1944) by USSR troops. Before Second World War, about half pop. were Jews. Major paper and pulp mills of Letea or Letea-Veche are just SE.

Baccalieu Island (bă'kŭlōō), (pop. 13; 4 mi. long, 1 mi. wide), N.F., off NE Avalon Peninsula, at entrance of Conception Bay; 48°8'N 52°48'W.

Baccarat (bäkärä'), town (pop. 4,639), Meurthe-et-Moselle dept., NE France, on Meurthe R. and 15 mi. SE of Lunéville; renowned for its mfg. of decorative crystal; mfg. (kitchen ranges, gloves), brewing, hand embroidering.

Baccaro Point (bă'kŭrō), promontory on the Atlantic, SW N.S., southernmost point of Nova Scotia mainland, 23 mi. SSW of Shelburne; 43°27'N 65°28'W.

Bacchiglione River (bäk-kēlyô'nĕ), N Italy, formed 5 mi. N of Vicenza, near Dueville, by confluence of 2 streams; flows 65 mi. SE, past Vicenza and Padua, to enter the Adriatic with the Brenta. Canalized in lower course and called Canale di Pontelongo. Navigable for 25 mi. Receives Astico R. (right).

Bacchus (bă'kŭs), town, Salt Lake co., N Utah, 10 mi. WSW of Salt Lake City; explosives.

Bacchus Marsh, town (pop. 1,705), S Victoria, Australia, 32 mi. WNW of Melbourne; fruit-growing center. Lignite mines near by.

Bacerac (bäsäräk'), town (pop. 950), Sonora, NW Mexico, on Bavispe R., in W outliers of Sierra Madre Occidental, 85 mi. SE of Douglas, Ariz.; copper, silver, gold, platinum mining; livestock, corn, wheat.

Bacesti (bächĕsht'), Rum. *Băcești*, village (pop. 1,978), Bacau prov., NE Rumania, on Barlad R., on railroad and 16 mi. SE of Roman; orchards, vineyards; soda-water mfg.

Bacgiang, province, Vietnam: see PHULANGTHUONG.

Bach, Yugoslavia: see BAC.

Bachan or **Batjan** (both: bächän'), island (□ 913; pop. 7,553), N Moluccas, Indonesia, in Molucca Passage, 10 mi. SW of Halmahera; 0°29'S 127°24'E; 50 mi. long, 25 mi. wide; mountainous, rising to 6,925 ft. in S. Lignite, copper, gold deposits. Chief products: timber, copra, spices, resin. Rice and tobacco are crops for local use. Chief port is LABUHA on W coast. Isl. was visited 1558 by the Portuguese who were followed by the Spaniards. The Dutch established 1st settlement here 1609; gained complete control of isl. 1667. In Second World War Bachan was site of important Jap. naval base. Also spelled Batyan.

Bachaquero (bächäkā'rō), town (pop. 1,066), Zulia state, NW Venezuela, on E shore of L. Maracaibo and 17 mi. SSE of Lagunillas; in Bachaquero oil field, extending into lake.

Bacharach (bäkh'äräkh), town (pop. 1,962), in former Prussian Rhine Prov., W Germany, after 1945 in Rhineland-Palatinate, on left bank of the Rhine (dangerous narrows) and 19 mi. NW of Bingen; noted for its wine. Surrounded by medieval fortifications; has late-Romanesque church. Was property of electors palatine until 1803.

Bachelor Butte (9,060 ft.), central Oregon, peak in Cascade Range just S of the Three Sisters.

Bachem, Germany: see AHRWEILER.

Bache Peninsula (bāch), locality on E coast of Ellesmere Isl., NE Franklin Dist., Northwest Territories, on S side of Bache Peninsula, on Buchanan Bay (inlet of Kane Basin); 79°4'N 76°10'W. Site (1926–33) of Royal Canadian Mounted Police post that was most northerly habitation in the world, within 800 mi. of North Pole.

Bachergebirge, Yugoslavia: see POHORJE.

Bachhraon (bŭch'roun), town (pop. 8,411), Moradabad dist., N central Uttar Pradesh, India, 33 mi. W of Moradabad; wheat, rice, pearl millet, oilseeds, sugar cane.

Bachhrawan (bŭchrä'vän), town (pop. 3,145), Rae Bareli dist., central Uttar Pradesh, India, 18 mi. NNW of Rae Bareli; rice, grains, gram, jowar.

Bachi Channel, Philippines-Formosa: see BASHI CHANNEL.

Bachíniva (bächē'nēvä), town (pop. 708), Chihuahua, N Mexico, 70 mi. W of Chihuahua; corn, beans, fruit, cattle.

Bachinski, Russian SFSR: see STALINO, village, Krasnoyarsk Territory.

Bachka, Bachki, Bachko, for Yugoslav names beginning thus and not found here: see under following part of the name.

Bachka, region, Yugoslavia: see BACKA.

Bachkovo (bäch'kôvô), village (pop. 1,386), Plovdiv dist., S central Bulgaria, on Asenovitsa R. and 14 mi. SSE of Plovdiv; tobacco, sericulture. Bachkovo monastery (pop. 84), just S, founded in 11th cent., has library and mus.

Bachmai (bĭk'mī'), S suburb of Hanoi, N Vietnam; radio station, airport, zoo.

Bachnea, Rumania: see BAHNEA.

Bachok (bä'chôk), village (pop. 718), N Kelantan, Malaya, port on South China Sea, 12 mi. ESE of Kota Bharu; rice, coconuts; fisheries.

Backa, Backi, Backo, for Yugoslav names beginning thus and not found here: see under following part of the name.

Backa or **Bachka** (both: bäch'kä), Serbo-Croatian *Bačka*, Hung. *Bácska* (bäch'kŏ), region of Vojvodina, N Serbia, Yugoslavia; bounded by the Danube (S, W), the Tisa (E), Hung. border (N). Fertile plain, producing corn, hemp, cabbages, paprika, and (in S) hops. Natural-gas wells in higher areas. Traversed by Danube-Tisa and Novi Sad–Mali Stapar canals. Chief cities: NOVI SAD, SUBOTICA, SOMBOR. Villages in N section are unusually large. Mineral water at TOPOLA, ZMAJEVO, and other places. Under Turkish rule until 1699; until First World War, part of Hung. co. BACS-BODROG; reoccupied (1941–44) by Hungary.

Backan (bäk'kän'), town, ⊙ Backan prov. (□ 2,000; 1943 pop. 69,500), N Vietnam, on the Song Cau and 75 mi. N of Hanoi; rice growing, forestry, cattle raising. Zinc mining at Chodien, 20 mi. NW.

Back Bay, small, shallow inlet of Arabian Sea, India, bet. S prongs of Malabar Hill (W) and Colaba (E) of Bombay city; c.3 mi. by 2 mi. in area. Along shore are several recreation grounds; land-reclamation project in Colaba section.

Back Bay, Mass., a residential section of BOSTON.

Back Bay, salt-water lagoon, SE Va., sheltered from the Atlantic by barrier beach which continues S to Cape Hatteras; c.12 mi. long; opens (S) into Currituck Sound, N.C. Back Bay village on W shore. Waterfowl hunting; fishing.

Backbone Mountain, ridge of the Alleghenies mainly in NW Md., rising to 3,360 ft. (highest point in state) 10 mi. S of Oakland; extends from Savage R. W of Westernport c.35 mi. SW into Tucker co., W.Va. Sometimes called Great Backbone Mtn.

Backegruvan (bĕ'kŭgrü"vän), Swedish *Bäckegruvan*, village (pop. 341), Vastmanland co., central Sweden, in Bergslag region, 14 mi. SSW of Fagersta; iron mining.

Backen (bä'kŭn), village (pop. 1,921), Vasterbotten co., N Sweden, on Ume R. and 2 mi. W of Umea.

Backergunge, E Pakistan: see BAKARGANJ.

Backnang (bäk'näng), town (pop. 15,412), N Württemberg, Germany, after 1945 in Württemberg-Baden, 11 mi. ENE of Ludwigsburg; rail junction; has noted leather industry (since 17th cent.), with large tanneries. Mfg. of construction machinery, trucks, autos, furniture; cotton and wool spinning. Has Romanesque church with late-Gothic choir; paneled town hall. Chartered in 13th cent.

Back River, Mackenzie and Keewatin dists., Northwest Territories, issues from L. Aylmer, flows in winding course generally NE, through lakes Pelly, Garry, Macdougall, and Franklin, to head of Chantrey Inlet; 600 mi. long. Originally called Great Fish R., it was discovered (1833–35) by Sir George Back; subsequently renamed in his honor. Sometimes called Backs R.

Back River, industrial suburb, Baltimore co., central Md., 7 mi. E of downtown Baltimore and on navigable Back R., a 12-mi. arm of Chesapeake Bay; large plant makes stainless steel.

Backs River, Canada: see BACK RIVER.

Backstairs Passage, channel of Indian Ocean, forms SE entrance to Gulf St. Vincent, SE South Australia, bet. NE coast of Kangaroo Isl. and Fleurieu Peninsula; merges with Investigator Strait (W); 15 mi. long, 12 mi. wide.

Backus, resort village (pop. 367), Cass co., central Minn., on small lake and 20 mi. S of Walker, in grain area; dairy products. State forest just W.

Backwell, agr. village and parish (pop. 1,449), N Somerset, England, 7 mi. WSW of Bristol. Has 12th–17th-cent. church.

Backworth, England: see EARSDON.

Bacles (bŭ'klĕsh), Rum. *Băcleș*, agr. village (pop. 2,023), Gorj prov., SW Rumania, 23 mi. ESE of Turnu-Severin.

Baclieu (bäk'lyō'), town (1936 pop. 13,749), ⊙ Baclieu prov. (□ 2,800; 1943 pop. 317,200), S Vietnam, in Cochin China, near South China Sea coast, 120 mi. SW of Saigon, in marshy lands; center of an intensive rice-growing area, salt extraction along coast, fisheries; mat making.

Bacninh (bäk'nĭng'), town (1936 pop. 10,000), ⊙ Bacninh prov. (□ 400; 1943 pop. 543,500), N Vietnam, in Tonkin, on Hanoi-Nacham RR and 20 mi. NE of Hanoi. Served by Song Cau river port of DAPCAU. Silk center; sericulture, spinning, weaving; mfg. of pottery, bricks. Spanish R.C. mission. Has Annamese citadel (military garrison). Captured 1884 by French.

Baco, Ethiopia; see BAKO.

Bacoachi (bäkwä'chē), town (pop. 783), Sonora, NW Mexico, on plateau (alt. 3,500 ft.), on Sonora R. and 75 mi. SE of Nogales; wheat, corn, cattle. Silver, copper, gold deposits near by.

Bacoli (bä'kôlē), town (pop. 5,506), Napoli prov., Campania, S Italy, port on Gulf of Pozzuoli, 10 mi. WSW of Naples; extracts and exports pozzuolana.

Bacolod (bäkō'lōd, -lōdh), city (1939 pop. 26,562; 1948 metropolitan area pop. 101,432), ⊙ NEGROS OCCIDENTAL prov., W Negros isl., Philippines, port on Guimaras Strait, c.300 mi. SSE of Manila; 10°40'N 122°56'E. Trade center for agr. area (rice, sugar cane). Sugar milling; fishing. Exports sugar.

Bacolor (bäkōlōr'), town (1939 pop. 1,015; 1948 municipality pop. 22,920), Pampanga prov., central Luzon, Philippines, 3 mi. SW of San Fernando; sugar cane, rice.

Bacon (bäkōn'), town (1939 pop. 3,324; 1948 municipality pop. 22,859), Sorsogon prov., extreme SE Luzon, Philippines, on Albay Gulf, 22 mi. ESE of Legaspi; agr. center (abacá, coconuts, rice).

Bacon, county (□ 293; pop. 8,940), SE central Ga.; ⊙ Alma. Bounded NE by Little Satilla R.; drained by affluents of Satilla R. Coastal plain agr. (tobacco, cotton, corn, peanuts) and forestry (lumber, naval stores) area. Formed 1914.

Bacone (bākōn'), village, Muskogee co., E Okla., just E of Muskogee; seat of Bacone Jr. Col.

Bacons Castle, village, Surry co., SE Va., near the James, 12 mi. S of Williamsburg. Bacon's Castle, a Jacobean house built c.1655, was seized and held (1676) by followers in Bacon's Rebellion.

Baconton, town (pop. 500), Mitchell co., SW Ga., 14 mi. S of Albany, near Flint R.; pecan processing.

Bacoor (bäkō-ōr'), town (1939 pop. 2,704; 1948 municipality pop. 20,453), Cavite prov., S Luzon, Philippines, on Bacoor Bay, 10 mi. SSW of Manila; fishing, agr. (rice, fruit, coconuts).

Bacoor Bay, inlet (3 mi. long, 2 mi. wide) of Manila Bay, Luzon, Philippines, sheltered N by narrow Cavite peninsula.

Bacquang (bäk'kwäng'), town, Hagiang prov., N Vietnam, on Clear R. and 25 mi. SSW of Hagiang.

Bacqueville-en-Caux (bäkvēl'-ā-kō'), village (pop. 984), Seine-Inférieure dept., N France, 10 mi. SSW of Dieppe; dairying. Formerly called Bacqueville.

Bacs, Yugoslavia: see BAC.

Bacsalmas (bä'chŏlmăsh), Hung. *Bácsalmás*, town (pop. 13,310), Bacs-Bodrog co., S Hungary, 18 mi. ESE of Baja; rail center; hemp, flour mills; wine in vicinity.

Bacs-Bodrog (bäch'-bô'drôg), Hung. *Bács-Bodrog*, county (□ 739; pop. 122,427), S Hungary; ⊙ BAJA. Flat region in SW part of the Alföld, drained by Danube and Kigyos rivers. Grain, livestock (cattle, pigs, sheep), garden products (fruit, paprika, onions); wine. Artificial fishponds contain carp and pike.

Bacsbokod (bäch'bôkôd), Hung. *Bácsbokod*, town (pop. 4,262), Bacs-Bodrog co., S Hungary, 10 mi. ESE of Baja; corn, onions, hogs.

Bacsfeketehegy, Yugoslavia: see FEKETIC.

Bacsföldvar, Yugoslavia: see GRADISTE, Vojvodina, Serbia.

Bacska, Yugoslavia: see BACKA.

Bacskeresztur, Yugoslavia: see RUSKI KRSTUR.

Bacskossuthfalva, Yugoslavia: see STARA MORAVICA.

Bacsszentivan, Yugoslavia: see PRIGREVICA.

Bactra, Afghanistan: see BALKH.

Bactrang (bäk'träng'), town, Travinh prov., S Vietnam, in Mekong delta, 17 mi. SW of Travinh, in rice-growing area.

Bactria (băk'trēŭ), region of central Asia, bet. upper reaches of the Oxus (Amu Darya) and the Hindu Kush; ⊙ was Bactra (modern BALKH). A satrapy of the anc. Persian Empire, it was conquered (328 B.C.) by Alexander the Great. Under the Seleucidae, it declared (246 B.C.) its independence and became the powerful Greco-Bactrian state, which reached from the upper Jaxartes (Syr Darya) to NW India. It fell (c.130 B.C.) to the nomad Sacae (Sakas). It corresponds to modern Afghan Turkestan.

Bacu, river, Moldavian SSR: see BYK RIVER.

Bacu Abis, Sardinia: see GONNESA.

Bacuit (bäkwēt'), town (1939 pop. 1,386; 1948 municipality pop. 2,306), N Palawan isl., Philippines, on W coast at entrance to Bacuit Bay on S. China Sea.

Bácum (bä'kōōm), town (pop. 1,624), Sonora, NW Mexico, on Yaqui R. (irrigation), on railroad and 55 mi. ESE of Guaymas; rice, wheat, corn, fruit, vegetables, cattle.

Bacup (bā'kŭp), municipal borough (1931 pop. 20,590; 1951 census 18,374), E Lancashire, England, near Yorkshire boundary 16 mi. NNE of Manchester; cotton mills, iron and brass foundries, shoe factories. Surrounding country is moorland. Coal mining at STACKSTEADS village.

Bacuranao (bäkōōränou'), town (pop. 1,182), Havana prov., W Cuba, 7 mi. E of Havana; dairying. Petroleum deposits.

Bacuri, Brazil: see SANTA QUITÉRIA DO MARANHÃO.

Bacu River, Moldavian SSR: see BYK RIVER.

Bada Barabil, India: see NOAMUNDI.

Badacsony, Mount (bŏ'dŏchônyŭ) (1,437 ft.), Zala co., W Hungary, in Bakony Mts., near L. Balaton; basalt quarries; vineyards on slopes. Ruins from 12th cent.

Badacsonytomaj (bŏ'dŏchônyŭtô"moi), town (pop. 2,719), Zala co., W Hungary, on L. Balaton and 27 mi. SW of Veszprem; red wine.

Badagara (bŭ'dŭgŭrŭ), town (pop. 17,924), Malabar dist., SW Madras, India, port on Arabian Sea, 27 mi. NNW of Calicut; fishing center; copra, coir products (rope, mats), pepper, timber; sardine-oil extraction.

Badagri or **Badagry** (bädä'grē), town (pop. 5,134), Nigeria colony, port on coastal lagoon, 38 mi. W of Lagos; market center; fisheries; cacao, palm oil and kernels, rice. A Br. trade station in 19th cent.

Bad Aibling (bät" īp'lĭng), town (pop. 8,502), Upper Bavaria, Germany, 5 mi. W of Rosenheim; textile mfg., metalworking, lumber milling; resort with mud baths. Has Gothic church. Chartered 1321. Peat bogs in area.

Badajoz (bädhähōs'), town (1939 pop. 1,180; 1948 municipality pop. 14,425), on NE Tablas Isl., Philippines, on Romblon Pass; agr. center (rice, coconuts).

Badajoz (bä-dhähōth'), province (□ 8,360; pop. 742,547), W Spain; ⊙ Badajoz. It constitutes Lower ESTREMADURA. Borders on Portugal, with which it maintains an active trade; Cáceres prov. is N, Ciudad Real prov. E, Córdoba prov. SE, Seville and Huelva provs. S. Guadiana R. crosses it E-W. A region of low ranges and interior plains (La Serena, Tierra de Barros), with its S and SE sections bounded by the Sierra Morena. Climate is very dry, with hot summers and cold winters. Though the largest prov. of Spain, it is one of its most backward, supporting a relatively small pop., impoverished by a feudal landholding system. Predominantly pastoral (sheep, hogs, goats, and some cattle). Main agr. products: olives, grapes, cereals, cork, chick-peas, tubers, thriving best in the fertile Tierra de Barros. The extensive forests yield timber (oak, chestnut, walnut, pine, etc.) and acorns. Mineral deposits are of secondary importance; among those mined or quarried are lead, iron, coal, lime, building materials. Industries based on agr. (olive-oil pressing, liquor and alcohol distilling, wine making, flour milling, tanning, dairying, meat salting and packing, food canning), centered in the chief cities, Badajoz, Mérida, Jerez de los Caballeros, Castuera, Don Benito, Almendralejo, Puebla de Alcocer, Zafra, Fuente de Cantos, Villanueva de la Serena. Badajoz prov. once formed part of Lusitania; and flourished under the Moors, when it was for some time a kingdom. It fell to the Nationalists early (Aug., 1936) in Sp. civil war.

Badajoz, anc. *Pax Augusta*, city (pop. 32,604; with suburbs 55,869), ⊙ Badajoz prov., in Estremadura, W Spain, on left bank of the Guadiana (crossed by superb Roman bridge), 4 mi. from the Port. frontier, and 120 mi. E of Lisbon, 200 mi. SW of Madrid; 38°52'N 6°58'W. The strategically placed, fortified city is an important gateway to Portugal, with which it has an active trade. Situated in a region which produces olives, grapes, cereals, cork, wax, sheep, and hogs. Its processing industries include flour milling, liquor distilling, brewing, tanning, sawmilling, slaughtering, meat packing. Badajoz lies on hilly plain above which tower the ruins of an old Moorish castle. There still remain walls of city's substantial fortifications, backing the bishop's palace, Puerta las Palmas. Though Badajoz is of great antiquity, few distinguished bldgs. are left: among them are the cathedral, begun in 13th cent. (overlaid by various styles), with notable choir; and the Espantaperros tower, 16th-cent. Pósito (former Consistorium), monastery, and theater. In Middle Ages Badajoz was capital of a Moorish kingdom (1010-c.1230), set up after the dismemberment of the Córdoba caliphate. Finally inc. (c.1230) into Christian Castile. Besieged several times by the Portuguese, it was occupied in 1811 by the French under Soult and captured by Wellington in 1812. In Sp. civil war, Badajoz' occupation (Aug., 1936) by the Nationalists was followed by the slaughter of hundreds of people. The painter Luis Morales was b. here. Rail station (pop. 5,414) is across the Guadiana. San Roque suburb is just S.

Badakhshan (bŭdŭkhshän'), province (□ 20,000; pop. 450,000), NE Afghanistan; ⊙ Faizabad. Bounded N and E by Tadzhik SSR (along Panj R.) and SE by Pakistan, it includes the WAKHAN panhandle extending E to China's Sinkiang prov. Generally mountainous (N spurs of the Hindu Kush), it descends NW toward Afghan Turkestan and is drained by Kokcha R. (irrigation). Prov. is noted for its lapis lazuli deposits (near Zebak), rubies, and emeralds. Irrigated agr. in valleys yields wheat, rice, corn, and cotton; while barley and leguminous crops are raised in hills. Livestock is raised for wool and skins. Pistachio nuts are gathered and there is sericulture in W. Pop. is primarily Tadzhik (Tajik), with urban centers at Faizabad, Rustak, Zebak, Kishm, and Jurm. Long ruled by its own mirs, Badakhshan passed in 1840 to Kataghan and in 1859 became tributary to Kabul. Its local autonomy was abolished in 1881. In 1895, the Russo-Afghan border was established along Panj R., thus separating Afghan Badakhshan from Russian Badakhshan in the Pamir, organized since 1927 as the GORNO-BADAKHSHAN AUTONOMOUS OBLAST. Afghan Badakhshan was administered until middle 1940s as part of Kataghan prov.

Badakhshan, Tadzhik SSR: see GORNO-BADAKHSHAN.

Badalona (bä-dhälō'nä), anc. *Baetulo*, outer industrial suburb (pop. 37,373) of Barcelona, NE Spain, in Catalonia, on the Mediterranean, 6 mi. NE of city center. Mfg. includes chemicals (fertilizer, dyes, paints and varnishes, disinfectants, mineral oils, tartaric acid), textiles (cotton, silk, wool), knitted and leather goods, motors, brandy, perfumes, optical goods, flour products; hemp and cork processing, tanning. Winegrowing in area. The 15th-cent. monastery of San Jerónimo de la Murtra is on hill near by.

Badalucco (bädälōōk'kô), village (pop. 2,114), Imperia prov., Liguria, NW Italy, on Taggia R. and 8 mi. NNE of San Remo.

Badalung, Thailand: see PHATTHALUNG.

Badami (bä'dämē), village (pop. 5,403), Bijapur dist., S Bombay, India, 65 mi. S of Bijapur; peanuts, millet, cotton. Sandstone and limestone deposits near by. Site of early Chalukyan ⊙; has noted Brahmanic and Jain cave temples (c.7th cent. A.D.).

Badami Bagh, Kashmir: see SRINAGAR.

Badami Bagh, W Pakistan: see LAHORE, city.

Badana or **Badanah** (bă'dănŭ), settlement, northernmost Saudi Arabia, near Iraq border, 100 mi. NE of Jauf; 30°55'N 41°E. Oil-pumping station on pipe line from Abqaiq to Saida.

Badanaval, India: see NANJANGUD.

Badarah, Iraq: see BADRA.

Badarán (bä-dhärän'), town (pop. 1,271), Logroño prov., N Spain, 20 mi. WSW of Logroño; meat processing, flour milling; wine, cereals, potatoes.

Badarganj (bŭdŭr'gŭnj), village, Rangpur dist., N East Bengal, E Pakistan, 13 mi. WSW of Rangpur; rice, dal, and flour milling; jute, tobacco, oilseeds.

Badari, El, or **Al-Badari** (both: ĕl bădä'rē), village (pop. 17,256), Asyut prov., central Upper Egypt, on E bank of the Nile and 20 mi. SE of Asyut; pottery making, wood and ivory carving; cereals, dates, sugar cane.

Badarpur (bŭdŭr'pōōr'), village, Cachar dist., S Assam, India, on Barak (Surma) R. and 15 mi. W of Silchar; rice, tea, rape and mustard. Oil wells near by; rail junction just W. Until 1947, in Sylhet dist.

Bad Aussee (bät" ous'zā), village (pop. 5,709), Styria, central Austria, in the Salzkammergut, 10 mi. SE of Bad Ischl; brewery; spa. Salt mined near by.

Badawai or **Badaway** (bădăwī'), village (pop. 6,306), Daqahliya prov., Lower Egypt, just E of Damietta branch of the Nile, 10 mi. NNE of Mansura; cotton, cereals.

Bad Axe, city (pop. 2,973), ⊙ Huron co., E Mich., c.55 mi. NE of Saginaw. Trade center for agr. area (beans, sugar beets, chicory, grain, livestock); flour and feed milling, chicory drying and packing; creameries. Settled c.1860; inc. as village 1885, as city 1905.

Bad Axe River, Vernon co., SW Wis., rises c.5 mi. NW of Viroqua, flows c.25 mi. SW to the Mississippi, nearly opposite Minn.-Iowa line, 20 mi. S of La Crosse. Near its mouth Black Hawk was defeated in 1832.

Badayun, India: see BUDAUN.

Bad Berka (bät" bĕr'kä), town (pop. 4,995), Thuringia, central Germany, on Ilm R. and 6 mi. SSW of Weimar; spa. Founded 1813 under Goethe's sponsorship.

Bad Bertrich (bät" bĕr'trĭkh), village (pop. 673), in former Prussian Rhine Prov., W Germany, after 1945 in Rhineland-Palatinate, 7.5 mi. SW of Cochem; resort with alkaline springs.

Bad Bibra (bät" bē'brä), town (pop. 2,541), in former Prussian Saxony prov., central Germany, after 1945 in Saxony-Anhalt, 11 mi. WNW of Naumburg; spa.

Bad Blankenburg (bät" blăng'kŭnbōōrk), town (pop. 6,601), Thuringia, central Germany, at foot of Thuringian Forest, on Schwarza R. and 5 mi. W of Rudolstadt; spa. Woolen and paper milling, woodworking; mfg. of precision instruments, electrical equipment. Towered over by ruins of Greifenstein castle (1st mentioned 1137). Has 18th-cent. church with 14th-cent. tower; 18th-cent. town hall. During residence here (1837–45), Fröbel founded (1840) 1st kindergarten.

Bad Bramstedt (bät" bräm'shtĕt), town (pop. 6,139), in Schleswig-Holstein, NW Germany, 15 mi. E of Itzehoe; resort with saline and mud baths. Friedrich Leopold von Stolberg b. here.

Bad Brückenau, Germany: see BRÜCKENAU.

Badcall (bădkôl'), agr. village, W Sutherland, Scotland, on Eddrachillis Bay, 30 mi. N of Ullapool.

Bad Cannstatt (bät" kän'shtät), NE suburb (pop. 48,723) of STUTTGART, N Württemberg, Germany, on the Neckar (head of navigation); noted resort with mineral springs, frequented since Middle Ages. An anc. settlement, it was an important Roman road center. Passed to counts of Württemberg in 13th cent. Chartered 1330. Inc. into rapidly growing Stuttgart in 1905. The seat of many of Stuttgart's industries, Bad Cannstatt was heavily damaged in Second World War.

Badda, Mount (bäd'dä), peak (13,560 ft.), S central Ethiopia, in Arusi prov., E of L. Zwai, at E edge of Great Rift Valley, 23 mi. ENE of Asselle; 7°55'N 39°27'E.

Baddeck (bădĕk'), village (pop. estimate 500), ⊙ Victoria co., NE N.S., central Cape Breton Isl., on Great Bras d'Or, at entrance to St. Patrick Channel, 27 mi. W of Sydney; fishing port, summer resort. Alexander Graham Bell lived here, and organized 1st flight in British territory, made by J. A. D. McCurdy on Feb. 23, 1909.

Baddegama (bŭd-dä'gŭmŭ), village (pop. 1,775), Southern Prov., Ceylon, on the Gin Ganga and 10 mi. NNW of Galle; vegetables, tea, rubber, rice, coconuts. Oldest mission station of Church of England, with church consecrated 1825.

Bad Deutsch Altenburg (bät" doitsh' ält'ŭnbŏŏrk) or **Deutsch Altenburg,** village (pop. 1,513), E Lower Austria, on the Danube and 9 mi. W of Bratislava, Czechoslovakia. Sulphur baths, known since Roman times; site of anc. Carnuntum, with amphitheater, is near by. Has fine 13th-cent. church.

Bad Ditzenbach (bät" dĭ'tsŭnbäkh), resort (pop. 633), N Württemberg, Germany, after 1945 in Württemberg-Baden, on the Fils and 6 mi. WSW of Geislingen; mineral springs.

Bad Doberan (bät"dōbŭrän'), town (pop. 10,957), Mecklenburg, N Germany, near Mecklenburg Bay of the Baltic, 10 mi. W of Rostock; spa; chemical mfg. Church (13th-14th cent.) formerly belonged to Althof monastery, which was founded (1171) near by, moved to site of present town in 1186, and secularized in 16th cent. Chartered 1879. In 1936 it inc. Baltic resort of Heiligendamm, 4 mi. NW.

Bad Driburg (bät" drē'bŏŏrk), town (pop. 7,135), in former Prussian prov. of Westphalia, NW Germany, after 1945 in North Rhine-Westphalia, 11 mi. E of Paderborn; resort with mineral springs.

Bad Düben (bät" dü'bŭn), town (pop. 6,599), in former Prussian Saxony prov., central Germany, after 1945 in Saxony-Anhalt, on the Mulde and 12 mi. E of Bitterfeld; spa. Mfg. of kid leather, rubber products, bricks, alum; metalworking, basket weaving. Until 1948 called Düben.

Bad Dürkheim (bät" dürk'hīm), town (pop. 9,680), Rhenish Palatinate, W Germany, on E slope of Hardt Mts., 8 mi. NNE of Neustadt; saltworks. Mfg. of shoes and sparkling wine; flour milling. Well-known resort, with saline springs (frequented since Roman times) and grape cure. Has 14th-cent. church. Chartered bet. 1359–79.

Bad Dürrenberg (bät" dü'rŭnbĕrk), town (pop. 13,823), in former Prussian Saxony prov., central Germany, after 1945 in Saxony-Anhalt, on the Saxonian Saale and 5 mi. SE of Merseburg; spa. Potash mining, in lignite-mining region. Power station.

Bad Dürrheim (bät" dür'hīm), village (pop. 2,183), S Baden, Germany, in Black Forest, 4 mi. SE of Villingen; rail terminus; spa (alt. 2,300 ft.), with salt mines and baths.

Badeggi (bädäjē'), town (pop. 1,328), Niger prov., Northern Provinces, W central Nigeria, on railroad and 10 mi. E of Bida; shea-nut processing, twine, sackmaking; roofing timber; cotton, cassava, durra.

Bad Eilsen (bät" īl'zŭn), village (pop. 711), in former Schaumburg-Lippe, W Germany, after 1945 in Lower Saxony, 2 mi. SW of Obernkirchen; resort with sulphur springs and mud baths.

Bad Elster (bät" ĕl'stŭr), town (pop. 3,657), Saxony, E central Germany, at NW foot of the Erzgebirge, on the White Elster and 15 mi. SSE of Plauen, near Czechoslovak border; popular resort with mineral springs. Mfg. of musical instruments.

Bad Ems (bät" ĕms') or **Ems,** town (pop. 8,454), in former Prussian prov. of Hesse-Nassau, W Germany, after 1945 in Rhineland-Palatinate, on the Lahn and 7 mi. ESE of Coblenz. One of the most famous and oldest spas in Europe; its mineral springs are probably those described by Pliny. Has casino (1913) with large park.

Baden or **Baden bei Wien** (bä'dŭn bī vēn'), resort city (pop. 20,528), E Lower Austria, picturesquely situated on Schwechat R. and 15 mi. SSW of Vienna; alt. 763 ft. World-renowned spa with sulphur springs (72°–97°F.) frequented from Roman times. Became hq. of Soviet occupation zone in 1945.

Baden (bā'dŭn), village (pop. estimate 1,000), S Ont., 10 mi. WSW of Kitchener; dairying, mixed farming.

Baden (bä'dŭn), former state (1939 □ 5,818; 1939 pop. 2,502,442) of SW Germany; ⊙ was Karlsruhe. Bounded S and W by the Rhine (Swiss, French, and Rhenish Palatinate borders), N by Hesse, NE by Bavaria, and E by Württemberg. Includes (S) the Black Forest and L. of Constance, and the Odenwald (N); drained by Rhine and Neckar rivers. Until French Revolution, region was an agglomeration of petty landgraviates and ecclesiastic estates (bishoprics of Constance, Mainz, Speyer, and Strasbourg). The BREISGAU belonged to Austrian Hapsburgs, the Mannheim-Heidelberg region to Rhenish Palatinate. Margraviates of Baden-Baden and Baden-Durlach were united (1771) under same branch of anc. Zähringen family. Margrave Charles Ferdinand became (1803) elector; assumed (1806) title of grand duke, and with Napoleon's aid acquired (1803–10) the entire state. Liberal constitution was granted to grand duchy in 1818. Revolution of 1848–49 was suppressed with help of Prussian troops. A member of German Empire from 1871, Baden became a republic in 1918 and joined Weimar Republic. After its capture (spring, 1945) by U.S. and Fr. troops, Baden was divided into 2 parts: N section (N of Karlsruhe) was put into U.S. zone of occupation and joined with N Württemberg into state of WÜRTTEMBERG-BADEN; S Baden [Ger. *Südbaden*] (S of Rastatt) was put into Fr. zone of occupation and constituted into separate state of **Baden** (□ 3,842; 1946 pop. 1,190,841; including displaced persons, 1,197,865; 1950 pop. 1,335,458); ⊙ Freiburg. With exception of the Rhine plain, it is completely mountainous (BLACK FOREST, SW portion of SWABIAN JURA); includes (S) L. of Constance. Drained by the Rhine and headstreams of the Danube. Agr. (grain, hemp, tobacco) in Rhine plain (noted for its mild climate) and on shores of L. of Constance; intensive wine- and fruitgrowing (Breisgau, KAISERSTUHL, MÄRKGRÄFLER LAND); cattle raising, forestry, and woodworking in mts. The Black Forest, a popular tourist region (BADEN-BADEN, SANKT GEORGEN, TODTNAU, TRIBERG), is noted for its clock mfg. Industries (textiles, chemicals, paper) centered at CONSTANCE, LAHR, LÖRRACH, OFFENBURG, and RASTATT. FREIBURG is cultural center with noted univ. A new constitution was drawn up in 1947. Baden joined (1949) the German Federal Republic.

Baden, village (pop. 2,824), in former Prussian prov. of Hanover, NW Germany, after 1945 in Lower Saxony, on right bank of the Weser and 14 mi. SE of Bremen; tobacco products.

Baden (bä'dŭn), town (1950 pop. 11,595), Aargau, N Switzerland, on Limmat R. and 13 mi. NW of Zurich; resort noted for curative hot springs, known to the Romans as *Aquae Helveticae* and much visited in the Middle Ages. Produces aluminum, pastry, biscuits, beer, clothes, chemicals; metal- and woodworking, printing. Old castle of Stein (dismantled) was a Hapsburg residence; in former castle of provincial governors (right bank) is collection of antiquities; tower (15th cent.), church (late Gothic), and city hall (seat of Swiss Diet, 1424-1712) remain. Baden was ⊙ of Baden canton, which existed 1798–1803.

Baden. 1 (bā'dŭn) Village, Prince Georges co., S Md., 22 mi. SE of Washington. St. Paul's Protestant Episcopal Church, built 1733 on site of church built c.1695, has historic treasures. **2** (bā'dŭn) Residential borough (pop. 3,732), Beaver co., W Pa., on Ohio R. opposite Aliquippa. Laid out c.1839, inc. 1868.

Baden-Baden (bä'dŭn-bä'dŭn), city (1950 pop. 37,007), S Baden, Germany, extending picturesquely along middle course of the Oos, 18 mi. SSW of Karlsruhe; 48°45'N 8°14'E. Most frequented spa and tourist center of Black Forest, with numerous mineral springs visited since Roman times (there are remains of Roman baths). Large casino is surrounded by a splendid park. Old and new castles tower above old section of town. An anc. settlement, it was residence of margraves of Baden-Baden until early 18th cent. Since 19th cent., one of Germany's most popular resorts. Captured by Fr. troops in April, 1945. After 1945, seat of military govt. for Fr. zone of occupation.

Baden bei Wien, Austria: see BADEN.

Badenoch (bă'dŭnŏkh), wild, mountainous, forested highland district in E and SE Inverness, Scotland, traversed by the Spey; extends 45 mi. SW-NE along borders of Perth, Aberdeen, and Banff; c.20 mi. wide. KINGUSSIE is chief town.

Baden-Powell, Mount, Calif.: see SAN GABRIEL MOUNTAINS.

Badenweiler (bä"dŭnvī'lŭr), village (pop. 2,366), S Baden, Germany, on W slope of Black Forest, 13 mi. N of Lörrach; rail terminus; climatic health resort (alt. 1,384 ft.), with mineral springs known to Romans. Has 16th-cent. former grand-ducal castle. Extensive remains of Roman bathing establishment were excavated here in 1784.

Bad Essen (bät" ĕ'sŭn), village (pop. 2,370), in former Prussian prov. of Hanover, NW Germany, after 1945 in Lower Saxony, at N foot of Wiehen Mts., near Ems-Weser Canal, 24 mi. W of Minden; resort with saline baths.

Bad Fischau (bät" fĭsh'ou), village (pop. 1,531), E Lower Austria, 4 mi. W of Wiener Neustadt; rail junction; warm springs.

Bad Frankenhausen (bät' fräng"kŭnhou'zŭn), town (pop. 9,094), Thuringia, central Germany, on S slope of the Kyffhäuser, 25 mi. N of Erfurt; spa in salt- and potash-mining region. Sugar refining; mfg. of leather, buttons, tobacco products. Has remains of old fortifications, 17th–18th-cent. palace. Scene (May, 1525) of defeat of *Bundschuh* forces under Thomas Münzer in Peasants' War.

Bad Freienwalde (bät' frī"ŭnväl'dŭ), town (pop. 10,667), Brandenburg, E Germany, at NW edge of Oder Marshes, near the Oder, 35 mi. NE of Berlin; lignite mining; spa. Mfg.: machinery, bricks, malt, mustard. Has 18th-cent. palace with large park. Chartered in 14th cent.

Bad Friedrichshall (bät" frē'drĭkhs-häl), village (pop. 6,531), N Württemberg, Germany, after 1945 in Württemberg-Baden, on the canalized Neckar, at mouth of Jagst and Kocher rivers, and 6 mi. N of Heilbronn; rail junction; salt mining. Foundries; mfg. of fire apparatus and bells; woodworking. Limestone quarry. Has 16th-cent. town hall and 2 castles. Formed 1933 through unification of Hagenbach, Jagstfeld, and Kochendorf.

Bad Gandersheim (bät" gän'dŭrs-hīm), town (pop. 5,350), Brunswick, NW Germany, after 1945 in Lower Saxony, 19 mi. S of Hildesheim; rail junction. Mfg. of chemicals; metal, paper, and wood products; toys. Food processing. Resort with salt baths (just NE). Known for its former abbey (founded c.850), where the nun Hroswitha (10th cent.) wrote her Latin poems and dramas.

Bad Gastein (bät" gä'stīn) or **Gastein,** town (pop. 5,573), Salzburg, W central Austria, in GASTEIN VALLEY, on river Gasteiner Ache and 50 mi. S of Salzburg; well-known resort (alt. 3,320 ft.) with radioactive thermal springs. The Gasteiner Ache forms the Gastein Falls (the upper, 207 ft., the lower, 280 ft. high) in the town. Has 14th-cent. church. Thermal water is piped to BAD HOFGASTEIN. By treaty of Gastein (1865) Austria assumed control of Holstein and Prussia of Schleswig.

Badger. 1 Town (pop. 301), Webster co., central Iowa, 8 mi. N of Fort Dodge; livestock, grain. **2** Village (pop. 448), Roseau co., NW Minn., 13 mi. SW of Roseau in grain, stock, poultry area; dairy products. **3** Town (pop. 180), Kingsbury co., E S.Dak., 19 mi. ENE of De Smet.

Badger Lake, oxbow lake (c.6 mi. long), in Monona co., W Iowa, near Missouri R., 10 mi. NW of Onawa.

Badger Pass, Calif.: see YOSEMITE NATIONAL PARK.

Badghis or **Badghes** (bäd'gĭs), arid district in Herat prov., NW Afghanistan, at N foot of Paropamisus Range, extending N to USSR border. Pop.: Persian-speaking Jamshidis; Turkmen nomads.

Bad Gleichenberg (bät" glī'khŭnbĕrk) or **Gleichenberg,** village (pop. 1,132), Styria, SE Austria, 25 mi. SE of Graz; resort. Mineral springs, known since Roman times.

Bad Godesberg (bät" gō'dŭsbĕrk), residential town (pop. 38,743), in former Prussian Rhine Prov., W Germany, after 1945 in North Rhine-Westphalia, on left bank of the Rhine (landing), adjoining (S) Bonn; spa with radioactive mineral springs; mfg. of pharmaceuticals. Has ruined 12th-cent. castle; baroque casino. Developed as resort since late-19th cent. Chartered 1935. Scene (Sept., 1938) of preliminary conference bet. Chamberlain and Hitler, leading to Munich Pact.

Badgom or **Badgam** (bŭd'gŭm), village, Baramula dist., W central Kashmir, in Vale of Kashmir, 7 mi. SW of Srinagar; rice, corn, wheat, oilseeds. Coal deposits S.

Bad Gottleuba (bät" gôt'loi"bä), town (pop. 3,188), Saxony, E central Germany, in Saxonian Switzerland, 8 mi. S of Pirna, spa near Czechoslovak border; metal- and woodworking. Iron formerly mined.

Bad Griesbach (bät" grēs'bäkh), village (pop. 778), S Baden, Germany, in Black Forest, 8 mi. W of Freudenstadt; rail terminus; health resort (alt. 1,667 ft.), with mineral springs known since 15th cent.

Bad Grund (bät" grŏŏnt'), town (pop. 4,124), in former Prussian prov. of Hanover, W Germany, after 1945 in Lower Saxony, in the upper Harz, 4 mi. W of Clausthal-Zellerfeld; lead, zinc, silver mining. Summer resort. Mines worked since 2d half of 12th cent.; iron mining discontinued 1885.

Bad Hall (bät" häl') or **Hall,** town (pop. 4,144), E Upper Austria, 10 mi. W of Steyr; well-known spa with one of Europe's strongest iodine springs (known since 9th cent.).

Bad Harzburg (bät" härts'bŏŏrk), town (pop. 12,606), in Brunswick, NW Germany, after 1945 in Lower Saxony, on N slope of the upper Harz, 6 mi. ESE of Goslar; fashionable spa with mineral springs; winter resort. Mfg. of pharmaceuticals, artificial fiber, textiles, toys; leather-, metal-, and woodworking; food processing. Excursion point to the Grosser Burgberg (1,585 ft.), with ruined 11th-cent. castle, and to the Brocken.

Bad Hofgastein (bät"hōf"gä'stīn), town (pop. 3,947), Salzburg, W central Austria, in GASTEIN VALLEY, on the Gasteiner Ache and 45 mi. S of Salzburg; resort (alt. 2,930 ft.). Thermal water of BAD GASTEIN is piped here. Gold mined in vicinity. Until 1936 called Hofgastein.

Bad Homburg, Bad Homburg vor der Höhe (bät" hôm'bŏŏrk fôr dĕr hû'ŭ), or **Homburg,** city (pop. 24,714), in former Prussian prov. of Hesse-Nassau, W Germany, after 1945 in Hesse, on S slope of the Taunus, 8 mi. N of Frankfurt (connected by tramway); main city of upper Taunus [Ger. *Obertaunus*] dist.; 50°13'N 8°37'E. Well-known fashionable spa, with numerous mineral springs. Mfg. of motorcycles, machinery, optical instruments, radios, electrical goods, pharmaceuticals, biscuits; tire retreading, glassworking. Has casino with large park; 17th-cent. castle. The Saalburg, a Roman fortress (2d-3d cent. A.D.), excavated and reconstructed in 19th cent., is near by. First mentioned in 12th cent., city frequently changed hands. Passed to house of Hesse in 1521; was ⊙ independent Hessen-Homburg, 1622–1866.

Badian (bädyän'), town (1939 pop. 1,895; 1948 municipality pop. 19,078), S Cebu isl., Philippines,

30 mi. NE of Tanjay across Tañon Strait, sheltered by small Badian Isl. (1½ mi. long, ¾ mi. wide; 1939 pop. 492); agr. center (corn, coconuts).

Badia Polesine (bädē'ä pôlā'zēnĕ), town (pop. 3,739), Rovigo prov., Veneto, N Italy, on Adige R. and 15 mi. W of Rovigo; mfg. (organs, shoes, hosiery, furniture), beet sugar, flour.

Badiet esh Sham, SW Asia: see SYRIAN DESERT.

Badikaha, (bädēkä'hä), village, N Ivory Coast, Fr. West Africa, on railroad and 100 mi. N of Bouaké; sisal-growing center.

Badin (bŭdĭn'), village, Hyderabad dist., S Sind, W Pakistan, 60 mi. SE of Hyderabad; rail terminus; rice milling. Salt deposits (S).

Badin (bā'dĭn), village (pop. 2,126), Stanly co., central N.C., 6 mi. NE of Albemarle, on Badin L. (c.5 mi. long, 1–3 mi. wide), formed by Yadkin Dam (217 ft. high, 1400 ft. long; completed 1919 for power) in Yadkin R. A "company town" built around a large aluminum reduction plant.

Badiraguato (bädērägwä'tō), town (pop. 753), Sinaloa, NW Mexico, 40 mi. NNW of Culiacán; in corn and sugar area.

Bad Ischl (bät" ĭ'shŭl) or **Ischl,** city (pop. 14,004), S Upper Austria, center of the SALZKAMMERGUT, on Traun R. and 28 mi. ESE of Salzburg; well-known health resort, with baths of salt, iodine, and other mineral waters; alt. 1,535 ft. Salt mined at near-by Ischler Salzberg.

Badjil, Yemen: see BAJIL.

Bad Kissingen (bät" kĭ'sĭng-ŭn), city (1950 pop. 14,318), Lower Franconia, NW Bavaria, Germany, on the Franconian Saale and 12 mi. NW of Schweinfurt; rail junction; well-known spa since 16th cent. Chemical mfg., metalworking, printing, food processing, brewing. Has meteorological institute. First mentioned in 801, its mineral springs were already known. Chartered before 1317. Scene (1874) of attempt on Bismarck's life.

Bad Kleinen (bät" klī'nŭn), village (pop. 1,973), Mecklenburg, N Germany, on N side of Schwerin L., 9 mi. S of Wismar; rail junction; spa.

Bad Kleinkirchheim (bät" klīn"kĭrkh'hīm) or **Klein Kirchheim,** village (pop. 1,237), Carinthia, S Austria, 14 mi. E of Spittal; summer resort (alt. 3,519 ft.) with radioactive thermal springs.

Bad Klosterlausnitz (bät' klō"stŭrlous'nĭts), village (pop. 3,864), Thuringia, central Germany, 10 mi. WNW of Gera; health resort; china mfg., woodworking. Has church (1152–80; later rebuilt) of former Augustinian monastery.

Bad Kohlgrub, Germany: see KOHLGRUB.

Bad König (bät" kû'nĭkh), village (pop. 3,343), S Hesse, W Germany, in former Starkenburg prov., in the Odenwald, on the Mümling and 4 mi. N of Michelstadt; resort with mineral springs. First mentioned 820.

Bad Königswart, Czechoslovakia: see LAZNE KYNZVART.

Bad Kösen (bät" kû'zŭn), town (pop. 6,193), in former Prussian Saxony prov., central Germany, after 1945 in Saxony-Anhalt, on the Saxonian Saale and 12 mi. WSW of Weissenfels; spa; doll-mfg. center; fruitgrowing, viticulture Cement mfg. Overlooking the Saxonian Saale, 2 mi. SSW, are ruins of noted 12th-cent. castles of Rudelsburg and Saaleck, both destroyed in Thirty Years War.

Bad Köstritz (bät" kû'strĭts), town (pop. 4,498), Thuringia, central Germany, on the White Elster and 5 mi. NW of Gera; spa; chemical mfg. Noted for dark beer brewed here. Has 17th-cent. palace.

Bad Kreuznach (bät" kroits'näkh), town (pop. 26,557), in former Prussian Rhine Prov., W Germany, after 1945 in Rhineland-Palatinate, on the Nahe and 21 mi. SW of Mainz; 49°51'N 7°52'E. Rail junction; noted spa with saline springs containing bromine, iodine, and radium salts. Mfg. of machinery, optical and precision instruments, chemicals, leather goods; food processing, tanning. Wine trade. Bathing establishments are located on 2 isls. in the Nahe. A Celtic settlement, it became a Roman camp. Chartered 1290. Developed as resort in 19th cent. Seat of Ger. general hq., 1916–18. Occupied by French after World War.

Bad Krozingen (bät" krō'tsĭng-ŭn), village (pop. 2,349), S Baden, Germany, 8 mi. SW of Freiburg; rail junction; metal- and woodworking. Resort with warm mineral springs (discovered 1911).

Badlands, SW S.Dak., E of Black Hills; arid plateau (150–300 ft. above surrounding countryside), c.120 mi. long, 30 to 50 mi. wide, bounded S by White R., crossed by Bad R. Characterized by numerous ridges and mesas cut by erosion into colorful peaks, pinnacles, and valleys, with scanty vegetation. Region's name has become generic term for areas of similar aspect. Rich in deposits of prehistoric fossils. Part of region (□ 192.2) in Pennington and Jackson counties was set aside (1939) as **Badlands National Monument.** Similarly eroded region is in SW N.Dak., extending N–S along right bank of Little Missouri R.; part of it is included in Theodore Roosevelt Natl. Memorial Park.

Bad Langensalza, Germany: see LANGENSALZA.

Bad Lauchstädt (bät" loukh'shtĕt), town (pop. 5,498), in former Prussian Saxony prov., central Germany, after 1945 in Saxony-Anhalt, 6 mi. WNW of Merseburg; spa. Sometimes spelled Bad Lauchstedt.

Bad Lausick (bät" lou'zĭk), town (pop. 6,785), Saxony, E central Germany, 17 mi. SE of Leipzig; spa; lignite mining; mfg. of building materials. Has 12th-cent. church. Formerly spelled Bad Lausigk.

Bad Lauterberg or **Bad Lauterberg im Harz** (bät" lou'tŭrbĕrk ĭm härts'), town (pop. 10,298), in former Prussian prov. of Hanover, W Germany, after 1945 in Lower Saxony, in the upper Harz, 12 mi. SE of Osterode; climatic health resort with hydropathic establishments; metal- and woodworking, paper milling.

Bad Liebenstein (bät" lē'bŭn-shtīn), village (pop. 3,259), Thuringia, central Germany, in Thuringian Forest, 12 mi. S of Eisenach; spa; metalworking. Has remains of medieval castle.

Bad Liebenwerda (bät" lē'bŭnvĕr"dä), town (pop. 6,472), in former Prussian Saxony prov., central Germany, after 1945 in Saxony-Anhalt, on the Black Elster and 15 mi. NNE of Riesa; spa; also mfg. of drawing and measuring instruments. Has remains of old castle.

Bad Liebenzell (bät" lē'bŭntsĕl"), town (pop. 1,947), S Württemberg, Germany, after 1945 in Württemberg-Hohenzollern, in Black Forest, on the Nagold and 8 mi. S of Pforzheim; resort with hot mineral springs. Has ruined castle.

Bad Lippspringe (bät' lĭp"shprĭng'ŭ), town (pop. 7,734), in former Prussian prov. of Westphalia, NW Germany, after 1945 in North Rhine-Westphalia, on the Lippe near its source, and 5 mi. NE of Paderborn; climatic health resort at SE foot of Teutoburg Forest; mineral springs.

Bad Meinberg (bät" mīn'bĕrk), village (pop. 2,941), in former Lippe, NW Germany, after 1945 in North Rhine-Westphalia, on N slope of Teutoburg Forest, on the Werre and 5 mi. SE of Detmold; resort with mineral springs and mud baths.

Bad Mergentheim, Germany: see MERGENTHEIM.

Badminton, England: see GREAT BADMINTON.

Bad Münder or **Bad Münder am Deister** (bät" mün'dŭr äm dī'stŭr), town (pop. 6,794), in former Prussian prov. of Hanover, W Germany, after 1945 in Lower Saxony, 16 mi. SW of Hanover; resort.

Bad Münster am Stein (bät" mün'stŭr äm shtīn'), town (pop. 1,484), in former Prussian Rhine Prov., W Germany, after 1945 in Rhineland-Palatinate, on the Nahe and 2 mi. S of Bad Kreuznach; rail junction; resort with radioactive salt springs.

Bad Müritz, Germany: see GRAAL-MÜRITZ.

Bad Nauheim (bät" nou'hīm), town (pop. 12,909), central Hesse, W Germany, in former Upper Hesse prov., on NE slope of the Taunus, 17 mi. NNE of Frankfurt; noted spa with carbon-dioxide and salt baths. Saltworks.

Badnawar (bŭdnä'vŭr), town (pop. 5,863), SW Madhya Bharat, India, 29 mi. N of Dhar; millet, cotton, oilseeds; cotton ginning.

Bad Nenndorf (bät" nĕn'dôrf), village (pop. 3,170), in former Prussian prov. of Hanover, W Germany, after 1945 in Lower Saxony, 15 mi. W of Hanover; resort with mineral springs, mud and saline baths. Founded 1787. Belonged to former Prussian prov. of Hesse-Nassau until 1932.

Badnera (bŭdnā'rŭ), town (pop. 16,037), Amraoti dist., W Madhya Pradesh, India, 6 mi. SSW of Amraoti; rail junction (branch to Amraoti); cotton-trade and -milling center; oilseed milling.

Bad Neuenahr (bät' noi'ünär'), village (pop. 5,322), in former Prussian Rhine Prov., W Germany, after 1945 in Rhineland-Palatinate, on the Ahr and 13 mi. S of Bonn; resort with hot mineral springs.

Bad Neustadt or **Bad Neustadt an der Saale** (bät" noi'shtät än dĕr zä'lŭ), town (pop. 5,926), Lower Franconia, NW Bavaria, Germany, on the Franconian Saale and 19 mi. N of Schweinfurt; rail junction; mfg. of precision instruments, brewing, flour and lumber milling. Includes Bad Neuhaus an der Saale, with mineral (carbonic acid) springs. Chartered 1232. Just E are ruins of anc. castle Salzburg, with 12th-cent. watchtower.

Badnur, India: see BETUL, town.

Badoc (bädōk'), town (1939 pop. 2,220; 1948 municipality pop. 13,573), Ilocos Norte prov., NW Luzon, Philippines, 20 mi. SSW of Laoag; rice-growing center.

Badoeng Passage, Indonesia: see BADUNG PASSAGE.

Bad Oeynhausen (bät" ŭn'hou"zŭn), town (pop. 6,652), in former Prussian prov. of Westphalia, NW Germany, after 1945 in North Rhine-Westphalia, on the Werre and 8 mi. NE of Herford; saltworks. Spa with hot and cold saline springs. Founded 1845. After 1945, seat of administration for Br. zone of occupation.

Badolato (bädôlä'tô), town (pop. 4,367), Catanzaro prov., Calabria, S Italy, near Gulf of Squillace, 24 mi. S of Catanzaro; wine, olive oil, silk. Badly damaged by earthquakes (1640, 1649, 1783).

Badolatosa (bä-dhōlätō'sä), town (pop. 2,804), Seville prov., SW Spain, on Genil R. (Córdoba prov. border) and 24 mi. E of Osuna; olives, cereals, fruit, vegetables, esparto, goats.

Bad Oldesloe (bät" ôl'dŭslō), town (pop. 14,123), in Schleswig-Holstein, NW Germany, on the Trave (head of barge navigation) and 13 mi. WSW of Lübeck; main town of Stormarn dist.; rail junction; resort with sulphur and mud baths. Foundry; mfg. of agr. machinery, armatures, dyes, furniture, textiles, wallpaper, leather goods; flour milling, meat processing. Town was heavily damaged in Second World War.

Badon (bä'dôn'), town, Quangbinh prov., N central Vietnam, 25 mi. NW of Donghoi; cattle-trading center; rice, timber, silk.

Badong, Vietnam: see CAUNGAN.

Badonviller (bädōvēlär'), village (pop. 1,916), Meurthe-et-Moselle dept., NE France, 19 mi. ESE of Lunéville; faïence works.

Bad Orb (bät" ôrp'), town (pop. 6,517), in former Prussian prov. of Hesse-Nassau, W Germany, after 1945 in Hesse, 20 mi. E of Hanau; salt baths; graduation works; tobacco mfg.

Badou (bä'dōō), village, S Fr. Togoland, on Br. Togoland border, 35 mi. W of Atakpamé; cacao, palm oil and kernels, cotton.

Badovinci or **Badovintsi** (bä'dôvĭntsē), village (pop. 5,626), W Serbia, Yugoslavia, near Drina R. (Bosnia border), 16 mi. W of Sabac, in the Macva.

Bad Peterstal (bät" pā'tŭrs-täl"), village (pop. 1,728), S Baden, Germany, in Black Forest, 10 mi. WSW of Freudenstadt; lumber milling. Climatic health resort (alt. 1,289 ft.); mineral springs known since 13th cent.

Bad Pyrmont (bät" pĭrmônt', pĭr'mônt), town (pop. 16,534), in former Prussian prov. of Hanover, W Germany, after 1945 in Lower Saxony, 9 mi. SW of Hameln; noted spa with mineral springs and mud baths. Has 18th-cent. castle. Medieval county of Pyrmont was united with county of WALDECK in late-17th cent. Annexed 1922 by Prussia.

Badr (bă'dŭr), village, N central Hejaz, Saudi Arabia, 20 mi. SW of Medina. Here Mohammed and his followers scored their 1st victory (A.D. 624) over Mecca following the hegira.

Badra or **Badarah** (both: bä'drŭ), village, Kut prov., E Iraq, near Iran border, 45 mi. N of Kut; cotton, dates.

Bad Radein, Yugoslavia: see SLATINA RADENCI.

Bad Ragaz (bät" rä'gäts), town (pop. 2,337), St. Gall canton, E Switzerland, on the Rhine, at mouth of Tamina R., and 20 mi. E of Glarus; health resort with mineral baths; paper products. Has 18th-cent. church, medieval castle ruins. Formerly Ragaz.

Bad Rappenau (bät" rä'pŭnou), village (pop. 2,688), N Baden, Germany, after 1945 in Württemberg-Baden, 10 mi. ESE of Sinsheim; saltworks. Resort with saline baths. Has early-17th-cent. castle.

Badrashein, El, or **Al-Badrashayn** (both: ĕl bădrăshān'), village (pop. 11,621), Giza prov., Upper Egypt on railroad, on the Nile, and 15 mi. S of Cairo; corn, cotton. It is on part of site of anc. MEMPHIS. Sometimes spelled Bedrashen.

Bad Rehburg, Germany: see REHBURG.

Bad Reichenhall (bät' rī"khŭnhäl'), city (1950 pop. 13,213), Upper Bavaria, Germany, in Salzburg Alps, on the Saalach and 10 mi. WSW of Salzburg; salt-mining center since Roman times; well-known summer and winter resort (alt. 1,542 ft.), with mineral springs. Completely rebuilt after fire of 1834.

Badrinath (bŭ'drēnät), village, Garhwal dist., N Uttar Pradesh, India, on headstream of the Alaknanda and 60 mi. NE of Pauri, in central Kumaun Himalayas; alt. c.10,000 ft. Noted Vishnuite temple (pilgrimage center); closed during winter. Badrinath peak (23,190 ft.) is 13 mi. W.

Bad Rippoldsau (bät" rĭ'pôlts-ou"), village (pop. 1,033), S Baden, Germany, in Black Forest, 5 mi. WSW of Freudenstadt; climatic health resort (alt. 1,840 ft.), with mineral springs (waters also exported) and mud baths.

Bad River. 1 In central Mich., rises S of Ithaca in Gratiot co., flows c.30 mi. E, past St. Charles, to Shiawassee R. just SW of Saginaw. **2** In S.Dak., rises in SW central S.Dak. near Badlands Natl. Monument, flows E 139 mi. to Missouri R. at Fort Pierre. Deposits of manganese and fuller's earth in basin. **3** In Ashland co., N Wis., rises in lake region near Mellen, flows c.45 mi. generally N, past Mellen, to L. Superior 12 mi. E of Ashland.

Bad Rothenfelde (bät' rō"tŭnfĕl'dŭ), village (pop. 2,681), in former Prussian prov. of Hanover, NW Germany, after 1945 in Lower Saxony, 12 mi. SSE of Osnabrück; resort with mineral springs.

Bad Sachsa (bät" zäk'sä), town (pop. 5,809), in former Prussian Saxony prov., W Germany, after 1945 in Lower Saxony, at S foot of the upper Harz, 12 mi. NW of Nordhausen; metal- and woodworking. Summer resort.

Bad Salzdetfurth (bät' zälts"dĕt'fōōrt), village (pop. 4,868), in former Prussian prov. of Hanover, NW Germany, after 1945 in Lower Saxony, 6 mi. SSE of Hildesheim; saltworks; potash mining. Resort with saline baths.

Bad Salzelmen, Germany: see SCHÖNEBECK.

Bad Salzig (bät" zäl'tsĭkh), village (pop. 2,410), in former Prussian Rhine Prov., W Germany, after 1945 in Rhineland-Palatinate, on left bank of the Rhine and 2.5 mi. SE of Boppard; resort with mineral springs. Cherries.

Bad Salzschlirf (bät' zälts"shlĭrf'), village (pop. 3,072), in former Prussian prov. of Hesse-Nassau, W Germany, after 1945 in Hesse, 9 mi. NW of Fulda; resort with mineral springs whose bottled water is exported.

Bad Salzuflen (bät' zälts"ŏŏf'lŭn), town (pop. 14,199), in former Lippe, NW Germany, after 1945 in North Rhine-Westphalia, near the Werre, 4 mi. SW of Herford; mfg. of rice starch. Spa with warm salt and mineral springs.

Bad Salzungen (bät" zälts'ŏŏng-ŭn), town (pop. 7,878), Thuringia, central Germany, at S foot of Thuringian Forest, on the Werra and 12 mi. SSW of Eisenach; spa; saltworks. Machine-tool and cigar mfg., metalworking, brewing. First mentioned in 8th cent.

Bad Sankt Leonhard im Lavanttale (bät' zängkt lā'ōnhärt ĭm lä'fänt-tälŭ), village (pop. 1,712) Carinthia, S Austria, on Lavant R. and 9 mi. NNW of Wolfsberg; radioactive springs. Gothic church (14th and 15th cent.). Until 1935 called Sankt Leonhard.

Bad Sauerbrunn, Austria: see SAUERBRUNN.

Bad Schallerbach (bät" shä'lŭrbäkh) or **Schallerbach,** village (pop. 1,594), central Upper Austria, 18 mi. WSW of Linz; resort with thermal spring. Developed after 1920.

Bad Schandau (bät" shän'dou), town (pop. 5,095), Saxony, E central Germany, in Saxonian Switzerland, on the Elbe and 10 mi. ESE of Pirna, near Czechoslovak border; popular health resort.

Bad Schmiedeberg (bät" shmē'dŭbĕrk), town (pop. 4,713), in former Prussian Saxony prov., central Germany, after 1945 in Saxony-Anhalt, 13 mi. SSE of Wittenberg; spa; textile milling, woodworking.

Bad Schwalbach (bät" shväl'bäkh), town (pop. 4,982), in former Prussian prov. of Hesse-Nassau, W Germany, after 1945 in Hesse, in the Taunus, 8 mi. NW of Wiesbaden; main town of lower Taunus [Ger. *Untertaunus*] dist.; resort with mineral springs and mud baths. Also called Langenschwalbach.

Bad Schwartau (bät" shvär'tou), town (pop. 15,152), in Schleswig-Holstein, NW Germany, on the Trave, at mouth of small Schwartau R., and 4 mi. N of Lübeck city center; rail junction; resort with saline springs. Sugar refining; mfg. of marmalade, chemicals, textiles, wood products. Seed-selection station. First mentioned 1215. Chartered 1912. Until 1937 in Oldenburg.

Bad Segeberg (bät" zā'gŭbĕrk), town (pop. 11,737), in Schleswig-Holstein, NW Germany, on the Trave and 16 mi. NW of Lübeck, on a small lake; resort with saline and mud baths. Mfg. (textiles, pharmaceuticals, furniture, sweets). Has Romanesque church. Large limestone caves near by. Chartered 1244. Before 1924, called Segeberg.

Badshahpur, India: see MUNGRA-BADSHAHPUR.

Bad Soden (bät" zō'dŭn). **1** or **Bad Soden am Taunus** (äm tou'nŏŏs) town (pop. 5,673), in former Prussian prov. of Hesse-Nassau, W Germany, after 1945 in Hesse, at S foot of the Taunus, 8 mi. W of Frankfurt; resort with warm saline springs. **2** or **Bad Soden bei Salmünster** (bī zäl'mün"stŭr), town (pop. 2,199), in former Prussian prov. of Hesse-Nassau, W Germany, after 1945 in Hesse, 8 mi. WSW of Schlüchtern; resort with salt baths.

Bad Sooden-Allendorf (bät" zō'dŭn-ä'lŭndôrf), town (pop. 6,227), in former Prussian prov. of Hesse-Nassau, W Germany, after 1945 in Hesse, on the Werra and 6.5 mi. NNW of Eschwege; saline springs at Bad Sooden (left bank). Poet Waldis b. at Allendorf.

Bad Steben (bät" shtā'bŭn), village (pop. 2,674), Upper Franconia, NE Bavaria, Germany, in Franconian Forest, 13 mi. WNW of Hof; rail terminus; resort with radioactive springs.

Bad Suderode (bät' zōō"dŭrō'dŭ), village (pop. 3,228), in former Prussian Saxony prov., central Germany, after 1945 in Saxony-Anhalt, at N foot of the lower Harz, 5 mi. S of Quedlinburg; spa.

Bad Sulza (bät" zŏŏl'tsŭ), town (pop. 5,510), Thuringia, central Germany, on Ilm R. and 7 mi. NE of Apolda; spa; potash mines; knitting mill. Sometimes called Stadtsulza.

Bad Sülze (bät" zül'tsŭ), town (pop. 3,222), Mecklenburg, N Germany, on Recknitz R. and 22 mi. E of Rostock; spa.

Bad Tarasp, Switzerland: see TARASP.

Bad Tatzmannsdorf (bät" täts'mänsdôrf) or **Tatzmannsdorf,** Hung. *Tarcsa* (tŏr'chŏ), village (pop. 487), Burgenland, E Austria, 19 mi. WNW of Szombathely, Hungary; resort, mineral spring.

Bad Teinach (bät" tī'näkh), village (pop. 530), S Württemberg, Germany, after 1945 in Württemberg-Hohenzollern, in Black Forest, 3 mi. SW of Calw; handwoven rugs. Climatic health resort, with mineral springs already known in 14th cent.

Bad Tennstedt (bät" tĕn'shtĕt), town (pop. 4,351), in former Prussian Saxony prov., central Germany, after 1945 in Thuringia, 15 mi. NW of Erfurt; spa.

Bad Tölz (bät" tûlts') or **Tölz,** town (pop. 12,854), Upper Bavaria, Germany, on N slope of the Bavarian Alps, on the Isar and 26 mi. S of Munich; woodworking; mfg. of lace trimmings, soap, beer; wood trade. Summer and winter resort with mineral springs. Has late-Gothic church. Chartered 1331. Petroleum deposits near by.

Bad Tönnisstein, Germany: see BURGBROHL.

Bad Überkingen (bät" ü'bûrkĭng"ŭn), resort (pop. 1,142), N Württemberg, Germany, after 1945 in Württemberg-Baden, on the Fils and 2 mi. WSW of Geislingen; alkaline springs.

Badulla (bŭdŏŏl'lŭ), town (pop. 13,231), ⊙ Uva Prov. and Badulla dist. (coextensive with prov.), S central Ceylon, in Uva Basin, on right tributary of the Mahaweli Ganga and 36 mi. SE of Kandy; rail terminus; trade (tea, rubber, rice, vegetables, oranges, pineapples) center. Meteorological observatory. Has 2 large Buddhist temples, anc. stupa. Was ⊙ old principality of Uva. Limestone quarries near by. Dunhinda Falls (projected hydroelectric station) are 2 mi. N.

Badung Passage or **Badoeng Passage** (bädŏŏng'), W arm (20 mi. long, 8–20 mi. wide) of LOMBOK STRAIT, bet. Bali (W) and Penida (E). In Second World War, scene (Feb. 19, 1942) of naval battle bet. Allied and Jap. units.

Baduria (bä'dŏŏryŭ), town (pop. 14,527), 24-Parganas dist., SE West Bengal, India, on upper Jamuna (Ichamati) R. and 30 mi. ENE of Calcutta; cotton weaving; trades in rice, jute, pulse, dates, betel nuts, potatoes.

Badus, Switzerland: see SIX MADUN.

Badvel (bŭdvāl'), town (pop. 5,723), Cuddapah dist., central Madras, India, 25 mi. NE of Cuddapah; peanuts, turmeric.

Bad Vöslau (bät" fûs'lou) or **Vöslau,** town (pop. 5,373), E Lower Austria, 3 mi. S of Baden; textiles, wine; warm springs.

Bad Wiessee (bät" vēs'zā") or **Wiessee,** village (pop. 4,692), Upper Bavaria, Germany, in Bavarian Alps, on W shore of the Tegernsee, 8 mi. ESE of Bad Tölz; paper milling. Summer resort (alt. 2,395 ft.), with Germany's strongest iodine and sulphur spring.

Bad Wildungen (bät" vĭl'dŏŏng-ŭn), town (pop. 10,773), in former Prussian prov. of Hesse-Nassau, W Germany, after 1945 in Hesse, 20 mi. SW of Kassel; resort with mineral springs. Until 1929 in former Waldeck principality.

Bad Wilsnack (bät" vĭls'näk), town (pop. 3,661), Brandenburg, E Germany, on small Karthen R., near its mouth on the Elbe, and 9 mi. ESE of Wittenberge; spa. Has 14th-cent. church, until the Reformation a point of pilgrimage. Near by is moated Plattenburg castle, former summer residence of bishops of Havelberg.

Bad Wimpfen (bät" vĭm'pfŭn), town (pop. 4,891), W Germany, after 1945 in Württemberg-Baden, on canalized Neckar R. and 7 mi. NNW of Heilbronn; saltworks. Noted resort with strong salt baths. Church of St. Peter is one of earliest works of Ger. Gothic. Was Roman camp. Free imperial city from late-14th cent. until Thirty Years War. Until 1945 it formed an exclave, bet. Baden and Württemberg, of former Hessian prov. of Starkenburg.

Bad Wörishofen (bät" vû'rĭs-hō"fŭn), spa (pop. 7,174), Swabia, SW Bavaria, Germany, 19 mi. E of Memmingen; dairying, printing, metal- and woodworking. Has late-Gothic church. Sebastian Kneipp developed his hydrotherapeutic treatments here.

Bad Zwischenahn, Germany: see ZWISCHENAHN.

Baelen, Belgium: see BALEN.

Baena (bää'nä), city (pop. 19,787), Córdoba prov., S Spain, in Andalusia, agr. trade center 32 mi. SE of Córdoba; olive-oil processing, brandy distilling, flour- and sawmilling, soap and knitwear mfg. Cereals and wine; horse breeding. Has remains of anc. walls and ruined Moorish castle. Stone quarries and iron mines near by.

Baependi (bīpĕndē'), city (pop. 2,308), S Minas Gerais, Brazil, on N slope of Serra da Mantiqueira, on railroad and 45 mi. N of Cruzeiro (São Paulo); ships coffee, liqueurs, dairy produce. Limestone quarries. Has old cathedral. Spa of Caxambu is 4 mi. WSW. Formerly spelled Baependy.

Baerl, Germany: see REPELEN-BAERL.

Baerle-Duc, Belgium: see BAARLE-HERTOG.

Baerle-Hertog, Belgium: see BAARLE-HERTOG.

Baerum, Norway: see LYSAKER.

Baesrode, Belgium: see BAASRODE.

Baesweiler (bäs'vī"lŭr), village (pop. 6,656), in former Prussian Rhine Prov., W Germany, after 1945 in North Rhine-Westphalia, 10 mi NNE of Aachen; grain.

Baetica, Roman name for present-day ANDALUSIA, Spain.

Baetic Cordillera, Spain: see PENIBÉTICA, CORDILLERA.

Baetis, river, Spain: see GUADALQUIVIR RIVER.

Bâez (bīs), town (pop. 2,060), Las Villas prov., central Cuba, on railroad and 9 mi. SW of Placetas; tobacco, fruit, cattle.

Baeza (bää'sä), village, Napo-Pastaza prov., E central Ecuador, on E slopes of the Andes, 45 mi. ESE of Quito; alt. 6,260 ft.; livestock.

Baeza (bää'thä), anc. *Beatia,* city (pop. 16,453), Jaén prov., S Spain, in Andalusia, 24 mi. NE of Jaén; agr. trade center, terminus of branch railroad from Linares. Mfg. of soap, pottery, felt hats, plaster; olive-oil processing, tanning, flour milling, brandy distilling. Grapes and cereals in area; breeds noted horses. Tourist industry. Was episcopal see till 1824. Has anc. walls, gates, and tower. Also has Gothic cathedral (restored 16th cent.), town hall (1556) with Renaissance façade, former univ. palace (1533), and late-Gothic Benavente mansion, now housing a seminary. Of anc. origin; prospered in Middle Ages, 1st under Moors as ⊙ small Moorish kingdom, then under Christians; Ferdinand III sacked it c.1237.

Bafa, Lake (bäfä') (□ 25), SW Turkey, 30 mi. SW of Aydin; 10 mi. long, 5 mi. wide. Connected with the Buyuk Menderes (Maeander).

Bafang (bä'fäng), village, Bamileké region, W Fr. Cameroons, 22 mi. SSE of Dschang; alt. 4,230 ft.; climatic station; coffee plantations. R.C. mission.

Bafatá (bŭfŭtä'), town, central Port. Guinea, head of navigation on Geba R. and 65 mi. ENE of Bissau; 12°10'N 14°39'W. Ships almonds, coconuts, rubber; cattle raising. Airfield.

Baffa (bŭf'fŭ), town (pop. 7,988), Hazara dist., NE North-West Frontier Prov., W Pakistan, 19 mi. N of Abbottabad; market center for corn, wheat, barley; weaving of cloth and woolen blankets; mule breeding. Beryl crystals near by (NW).

Baffin Bay, arm (c.700 mi. long, 70–400 mi. wide) of the N Atlantic, bet. Northwest Territories (W) and Greenland (E), near 70°–78°N 55°–80°W. Opens S on the Atlantic via Davis Strait; connected N with the Arctic via Smith Sound, and W with the Arctic by Lancaster and Jones sounds, which lead to water routes through the Arctic Archipelago. Its W shoreline includes Ellesmere, Devon, Bylot, and Baffin Isls. On Greenland shore are trading posts of Thule, Upernavik, and Umanak. It is 200–1,500 fathoms deep and covered with ice for most of the year; the Labrador Current passes through it, bringing many icebergs. Navigable passages open up during summer months. On barren, rugged coastlines sea fowl and fur-bearing animals abound; in bay there are whale fisheries. Discovered 1616 by William Baffin.

Baffin Bay, S Texas, inlet of Laguna Madre, 33 mi. S of Corpus Christi; c.15 mi. long, 4 mi. wide. Grullo Bayou (grŭ'lō bī'ō), c.20 mi. long, ½–2 mi. wide, enters from NW. Alazan Bay (ălŭzăn'), c.12 mi. long, 1–3 mi. wide, is NE arm.

Baffin Island (□ 197,754), largest and most easterly of the Canadian Arctic Archipelago, SE Franklin Dist., Northwest Territories, in the Arctic Ocean; 61°52'–73°51'N 61°19'–90°11'W. Geographically and geologically N continuation of Labrador; separated from Quebec and Labrador mainland (S) by Hudson Strait, from Keewatin Dist. mainland (SW) by Foxe Channel, from Melville Peninsula (W) by Foxe Basin and the Fury and Hecla Strait, from Boothia Peninsula and Somerset Isl. (NW) by Gulf of Boothia and Prince Regent Inlet, from Devon Isl. (N) by Lancaster Sound, and from Greenland (E) by Baffin Bay and Davis Strait. Isl. is c.1,000 mi. long, 130–450 mi. wide. Irregular coastline is indented by several deep bays: Frobisher Bay and Cumberland Sound (SE), Eclipse Sound (NE), and Admiralty Inlet (NW), one of the world's longest fjords. Surface consists generally of plateau, rising to c.3,000 ft.; in E part of isl. are several mtn. regions, with glaciers and snow fields, rising to c.8,000 ft. Foxe Peninsula and adjoining Great Plain of the Koukdjuak (SW) are level and partly marshy tundra areas. In SW part of isl. are Nettilling L. and Amadjuak L. Isl. has several peninsulas: Brodeur (NW), Borden (N), Cumberland (E), Hall (SE), and Foxe (SW). Settlements include Cape Dorset, Amadjuak, Lake Harbour, Frobisher Bay, Pangnirtung, River Clyde, Pond Inlet, and Arctic Bay. Air bases at Crystal II, near Frobisher Bay, and Crystal III, on Padloping Isl., off SW coast of Baffin Isl. Climatic data: for Pangnirtung (SE) mean temp. range is –21°F. (Jan.) to 46°F. (July), annual average rainfall 17.6 inches; for Pond Inlet (N) mean temp. range is –29°F. (Jan., Feb.) to 42°F. (July), annual average rainfall 6.3 inches. Eskimos form bulk of population; whaling, hunting, and trapping are chief occupations. Eskimo population in 1941 was 2,247. Isl. was 1st visited by Martin Frobisher, 1576–78; named after William Baffin. Among important surrounding isls. are Bylot Isl. (N) and Resolution Isl. (SE).

Baffo, Cyprus: see PAPHOS.

Bafia (bäfē'ä), town, ⊙ M'Bam region, W central Fr. Cameroons, 65 mi. NNW of Yaoundé; native trade center; rice processing, cotton weaving. R. C. and Protestant missions.

Bafing River (bäfĭng', bäfē'), headstream of Senegal R., Fr. West Africa, rises in Fouta Djallon massif of Fr. Guinea S of Timbo, flows c.350 mi. NE and N to Bafoulabé, Fr. Sudan, where it joins Bakoy R. to form the Senegal. Not navigable.

Baflo (bäflō'), village (pop. 1,209), Groningen prov., N Netherlands, 3 mi. N of Winsum; agr.

Bafoulabé (bäfōōläbā'), town (pop. c.1,000), SW Fr. Sudan, Fr. West Africa, at confluence of Bafing and Bakoy rivers, which here form the Senegal, on Dakar-Niger RR and 55 mi. SE of Kayes; millet, peanuts, beeswax, rice, corn; livestock (cattle, sheep, goats). Airfield. Also Bafulabe.

Bafoussam (bäfōō'säm), village, Bamileké region, W Fr. Cameroons, 25 mi. E of Dschang; trading center, notably for native-grown coffee and kola nuts. Has trade school, R.C. and Protestant missions.

Bafq (bäfk), town (1930 pop. estimate 6,000), Tenth Prov., in Yezd, central Iran, 65 mi. SE of Yezd, in desert area; dates, grain, cotton, gums. Coal and lead mining near by.

Bafra (bäfrä′), town (1950 pop. 14,146), Samsun, N Turkey, on the Kizil Irmak and 29 mi. NW of Samsun; tobacco center.

Bafra, Cape, N Turkey, on Black Sea, at mouth of the Kizil Irmak, 36 mi. NNW of Samsun.

Baft (bäft), town (1942 pop. 8,693), Eighth Prov., in Kerman, SE Iran, 80 mi. SSW of Kerman city, in forested hills of Lalehzar Mts.; irrigated agr. (dates, grain, opium); gums (asafetida, gum arabic), almonds, pistachio nuts. Coal, iron, and copper deposits near by.

Bafulabe, Fr. Sudan: see BAFOULABÉ.

Bafwasende (bäfwäsĕn′dä), village, Eastern Prov., NE Belgian Congo, on Lindi R. and 135 mi. ENE of Stanleyville, in palm-growing area; cotton gins and rice mills; rubber plantations near by. Previously known for its fearsome African secret society of killers, the Anyotos or "human-leopards."

Bagabag (bägäbäg′), volcanic island (□ 14), Madang dist., Territory of New Guinea, SW Pacific, 30 mi. N of Madang; sunken crater.

Bagabag, town (1939 pop. 2,299; 1948 municipality pop. 10,288), Nueva Vizcaya prov., central Luzon, Philippines, 11 mi. NE of Bayombong; rice-growing center. Manganese deposits.

Bagac (bägäk′), town (1939 pop. 2,191; 1948 municipality pop. 2,745), Bataan prov., S Luzon, Philippines, on W Bataan Peninsula, on small Bagac Bay (inlet of S.China Sea), 40 mi. W of Manila; sugar cane, rice.

Bagaces (bägä′sĕs), town (1950 pop. 706), Guanacaste prov., NW Costa Rica, on Inter-American Highway and 14 mi. SE of Liberia; corn, rice, beans, sugar cane; stock raising, lumbering. Flourished in 19th cent. as cotton and indigo center. Suffered in 1941 earthquake.

Bagadó (bägädō′), village (pop. 388), Chocó dept., W Colombia, on affluent of Atrato R. and 27 mi. SE of Quibdó; platinum- and gold-placer mines.

Bagagem River (bŏŏgä′zhĕm), W Minas Gerais, Brazil, left tributary of Paranaíba R., rises SE of Estrêla do Sul; length, 50 mi. Diamond washings.

Bagalkot (bŭgŭl′kōt), town (pop. 24,521), Bijapur dist., S Bombay, India, on Ghatprabha R. and 45 mi. S of Bijapur; market center (cotton, peanuts, millet, wheat); cotton ginning, handicraft cloth and blanket weaving, peanut milling, paper mfg.; metalware. Slate and flagstone quarried near by. Has col. Sometimes spelled Begalkot.

Bagamoyo (bägämō′yō), town, Eastern Prov., Tanganyika, minor port on Zanzibar Channel of Indian Ocean, 35 mi. NW of Dar es Salaam; 6°26′S 38°55′E. Sisal, cotton, copra. Salt deposits. R.C. bishopric. Formerly an important slave market, starting point for caravans to Ujiji (on L. Tanganyika), and (until 1891) ⊙ Tanganyika (then German East Africa). 1948 pop. c.4,000.

Bagan (bŭgän′), village (1948 pop. over 2,000), SW Novosibirsk oblast, Russian SFSR, on Baraba Steppe, on railroad and 100 mi. SE of Tatarsk, in agr. area.

Bagana, Mount (bägä′nä), peak (6,560 ft.), Crown Prince Range, S Bougainville, Solomon Isls., SW Pacific; active volcano.

Bagan Datoh (bägän′ dätō′), town (pop. 1,725), SW Perak, Malaya, minor fishing port on Strait of Malacca at mouth of Perak R., 45 mi. SW of Ipoh; coconut-growing center.

Baganga (bägäng′gä), town (1939 pop. 2,253; 1948 municipality pop. 10,002), Davao prov., E Mindanao, Philippines, on the coast, 75 mi. ENE of Davao; abacá, coconuts.

Bagan Serai (bägän′ sürī′), town (pop. 4,945), NW Perak, Malaya, on railroad and 17 mi. NW of Taiping, on Kurau R., in Krian rice dist.

Bagansiapiapi (bägän′sēä′pēä′pē), town (pop. 15,321), E Sumatra, Indonesia, port at mouth of Rokan R. on Strait of Malacca, 180 mi. SE of Medan; 2°10′N 100°48′E. Ships rubber, copra, dried fish and shrimp. Pop. is predominantly Chinese.

Bagan Tiang (bägän′ tēäng′), village (pop. 542), NW Perak, Malaya, in Krian rice dist., 28 mi. NW of Taiping, near W coast and Penang line.

Bagara (bŭgŭrä′), village, S South Kazakhstan oblast, Kazakh SSR, c.5 mi. from Ilich, in irrigated Golodnaya Step; cotton area.

Bagaryak (bŭgŭryäk′), village (1939 pop. over 2,000), N Chelyabinsk oblast, Russian SFSR, 20 mi. SW of Kamensk-Uralski; road center; grain, livestock. Graphite deposits. Mfg. of ceramics, distilling 5 mi. WNW, at Boyevo. Metalworking 14 mi. E, at Bagaryak rail station.

Bagasra (bŭg′ŭsrŭ), town (pop. 9,611), S Saurashtra, India, 31 mi. E of Junagadh; rail spur terminus; market center for grain, cotton, timber; handicraft cloth weaving. Sometimes spelled Bagasara.

Bagayevskaya (bŭgŭyĕf′skīŭ), village (1926 pop. 6,860), SW Rostov oblast, Russian SFSR, on left bank of Don R. and 15 mi. ESE of Novocherkassk; flour milling; truck, fruit. Pop. largely Cossack.

Bagdad, Iraq: see BAGHDAD.

Bagdad (bŭgdät′), village (1926 pop. 1,444), S Fergana oblast, Uzbek SSR, 15 mi. E of Kokand; cotton. Formerly spelled Bagdat. Just SW, on railroad, is Serovo village; metalworks, flour mill.

Bagdad, village (1940 pop. 809), Santa Rosa co., NW Fla., 17 mi. NE of Pensacola, near mouth of Blackwater R. on Blackwater Bay; lumbering.

Bagdadi or **Bagdati,** Georgian SSR: see MAYAKOVSKI.

Bagdarin (bŭgdä′rĭn), village, E Buryat-Mongol Autonomous SSR, Russian SFSR, on Vitim Plateau, 160 mi. N of Chita; gold mines. Formerly spelled Bogdarin.

Bagdogra, India: see BAGHDOGRA.

Bagé (bäzhĕ′), city (1950 pop. 35,340), S Rio Grande do Sul, Brazil, on railroad, 110 mi. WNW of Pelotas; livestock center (meat packing, beef jerking); woolshearing. Trades in horses, sheep, alfalfa, corn, potatoes, and hides. Has govt. wheat and cattle experiment stations. Airfield. Also spelled Bajé.

Bâgé-le-Châtel (bäzhā′-lù-shätĕl′), agr. village (pop. 429), Ain dept., E France, in the Bresse, 5 mi. E of Mâcon; poultry.

Bagenalstown, Ireland: see MUINE BHEAG.

Bagepalli (bä′gĕpŭlē), town (pop. 2,162), Kolar dist., E Mysore, India, 50 mi. NNW of Kolar; tile mfg., hand-loom woolen weaving.

Bagerhat, E Pakistan: see BAGHERHAT.

Bagerovo (bä′gyĭrŭvŭ), town (1941 pop. over 500), E Crimea, Russian SFSR, on Kerch Peninsula, on railroad and 8 mi. W of Kerch; limestone works, coquina quarries.

Bageshpur, India: see ARSIKERE.

Bageswar, India: see BAIJNATH.

Bagevadi (bä′gävä″dē), village (pop. 8,026), Bijapur dist., S Bombay, India, 24 mi. SE of Bijapur; markets millet, cotton, linseed, wheat. Alleged birthplace of founder of Lingayat cult. Sometimes spelled Bagewadi.

Baggrow, England: see ALLHALLOWS.

Baggs, town (pop. 206), Carbon co., S Wyo., on Little Snake R., near Colo. line, and 60 mi. SSW of Rawlins; alt. 6,245 ft.

Bagh (bäg), village, SW Madhya Bharat, India, 36 mi. WSW of Dhar, in Vindhya Range. Noted Buddhist cave monasteries near by, cut in side of sandstone hill, date from 6th or 7th cent. A.D.

Bagh, village, Punch jagir, W Kashmir, in W foothills of Pir Panjal Range, on tributary of the Jhelum and 23 mi. NW of Punch; corn, wheat, rice.

Bagh, village, Khyber agency, W North-West Frontier Prov., W Pakistan, 48 mi. WSW of Peshawar, in Tirah; local trade in corn, wheat, barley.

Bagha (bä′gŭ), village, Rajshahi dist., W East Bengal, E Pakistan, 20 mi. SE of Rajshahi; rice, jute. Sericulture research station near by.

Baghal (bä′gŭl), former princely state (□ 120; pop. 27,529) of Punjab Hill States, India, NW of Simla; ⊙ was Arki. Since 1948, merged with Himachal Pradesh.

Baghashwa or **Baghashwah** (băgăsh′wŭ), village, Quaiti state, Eastern Aden Protectorate, on Gulf of Aden, 33 mi. ENE of Shihr, on the cape Ras Baghashwa.

Baghat (bŭgät′), former princely state (□ 33; pop. 11,022) of Punjab Hill States, India, SW of Simla. Since 1948, merged with Himachal Pradesh.

Baghat, district (□ 414; pop. 90,415), S central Hyderabad state, India, on Deccan Plateau; ⊙ Hyderabad. In hilly area (cattle raising); sandy red soil; millet, rice, oilseeds (chiefly peanuts). Includes town of Ibrahimpatan. Situated within limits of Atraf-i-Balda dist.; formerly under administration of Medak dist.; became separate dist. in 1930s. Pop. 84% Hindu, 12% Moslem, 1% Christian.

Baghdad or **Bagdad** (băg′dăd, bägdäd′), province (□ 7,730; pop. 805,293), central Iraq, along the Tigris valley; ⊙ Baghdad, capital of Iraq. Dates, sesame, millet, apples, oranges, plums; also stock raising. In the prov. are sites of great anc. cities: CTESIPHON, SELEUCIA, SIPPAR, AGADE, SAMARRA.

Baghdad or **Bagdad,** city (pop. 364,049), ⊙ Iraq and ⊙ Baghdad prov., central Iraq, on both banks of the Tigris and only 20 mi. from the Euphrates, on railroad, and 280 mi. NW of Basra, 430 mi. WSW of Teheran (Iran), 540 mi. E of Haifa (Israel); 33°20′N 44°25′E. Trade, communications, and tourist center, with some mfg. (arrack distilling, leather tanning, book binding, mfg. of ice, cement, cigarettes, silk clothing). It is head of shallow-draught navigation on the Tigris, has rail lines to Basra, Kirkuk, and Mosul (and on to Turkey) and good air facilities; see BAGHDAD RAILWAY. From Sumerian times the site was a nodal point of desert travel and trade. The present city was founded (A.D. 762) on W bank of the river by the Abbasid caliph Mansur. From then on its commercial position generally was unrivaled. In a zone of gardens, it justified its claim to be the "Abode of Peace" when under the caliph Harun-al-Rashid it rose to be one of the greatest cities of Islam. It was the home of eminent scholars and artists, and it enjoyed great wealth through the sale of its silks and tiles. This period of its greatest glory is reflected in the *Thousand and One Nights,* in which many of the tales are set in Baghdad. After the death of Harun the seat of the caliph was moved to Samarra, and when the caliphate did return to Baghdad it was weakened by internecine struggles and could not restore the city entirely. The caliphate held on until 1258, when the Mongols under Hulagu Khan sacked the city. It rose twice again only to be destroyed by Tamerlane (1400) and by Shah Ismail of Persia (1524) and to fall prey to warring Turks and Persians. By 1638, when it became part of the Ottoman Empire, its population was only c.14,000. Few antiquities remain, but the city is still enclosed on 3 sides by anc. walls, and some of the citadel in the northern frontier survives. Baghdad was captured by Br. forces in 1917. In 1921 it became the capital of the newly constituted kingdom of Iraq.

Baghdad Railway, railroad of international importance linking Europe with Asia Minor and the Middle East. With its last link completed in 1940, it connects Haidarpasha, opposite Istanbul, Turkey, with Basra, Iraq. With alternate lines and branch lines it connects with N Iran, the USSR, Syria, and Israel. Financed chiefly by Ger. capital, its Anatolian sections were completed in 1896. The project was planned to carry the railroad to Baghdad, but protests were made to Turkey by France, Russia, and, particularly, Great Britain, which saw in the projected line a direct threat to its empire in India. Operations were held up for several years, but in 1911 work was resumed. By the end of the First World War only a stretch bet. Mosul and Samarra remained to be completed; it was built largely with Br. capital.

Baghdogra or **Bagdogra** (bägdō′grŭ), village, Darjeeling dist., N West Bengal, India, 24 mi. S of Darjeeling; airfield.

Baghelkhand (bŭg′gŭlkhŭnd), region of central India, S of Jumna R.; adjoins Bundelkhand (W); comprises E portion of Vindhya Pradesh. Crossed by E Vindhya Range; consists of elevated plain and forested hills; drained by Son R. Settled c.13th cent. by Baghela clan of Rajputs. **Baghelkhand Agency,** a subdivision of former CENTRAL INDIA agency, was created in 1871 (included Rewa, Baraunda, Nagod, Maihar, and other states) with hq. at Satna; merged with BUNDELKHAND AGENCY in 1931.

Bagherhat or **Bagerhat** (bä′gärhät), town (pop. 12,696), Khulna dist., SW East Bengal, E Pakistan, on distributary of lower Madhumati (Baleswar) R. and 17 mi. SE of Khulna; rail spur terminus; rice, flour, and oilseed milling, soap and cotton-cloth mfg. Annual fair. Has 15th-cent. ruins of Gaur kingdom.

Bagheria (bägä′rēä), town (pop. 23,809), Palermo prov., N Sicily, SSW of Cape Zaffarano, 8 mi. E of Palermo, in citrus-fruit and grape region; canned tomatoes, macaroni; cement. Has 18th-cent. villas. Near by are scanty ruins (dating from 1st cent. B.C.) of Soluntum, originally a Phoenician settlement. Also known as Bagaria in early 1900s.

Baghirmi, Chad territory, Fr. Equatorial Africa: see BAGUIRMI.

Baghlan (bäg′län), town (pop. 20,000), ⊙ Kataghan prov., NE Afghanistan, in Afghan Turkestan, on Kunduz R. and 40 mi. SW of Khanabad, on highway to Kabul; industrial center in sugar-beet area; beet-sugar refinery. Capital of prov. was moved here (middle 1940s) from Khanabad.

Baghmati River (bäg′mŭtē), E Nepal and N Bihar, India, rises in several headstreams around Katmandu in Nepal Valley, flows S through Siwalik Range and the Terai into Bihar, then SE to Burhi Gandak R. 13 mi. SE of Samastipur; 225 mi. long.

Baghpat (bäg′pŭt), town (pop. 5,519), Meerut dist., NW Uttar Pradesh, India, on the Jumna and 30 mi. W of Meerut; trades in sugar, wheat, gram, oilseeds. Former chief center of sugar trade from Punjab.

Baginbun Head cape, SW Co. Wexford, Ireland, at entrance to Bannow Bay, 14 mi. ESE of Waterford; 52°11′N 6°50′W.

Bagirmi, Fr. Equatorial Africa: see BAGUIRMI.

Bagirpasa Dagi (bäŭr″ pä-shä′ däŭ), Turkish *Bağırpaşa Dağı,* peak (10,768 ft.), E central Turkey, in Mercan Mts., 12 mi. E of Pulumur.

Baglarbasi, Turkey: see YERKOY.

Bagley. 1 Town (pop. 392), Guthrie co., W central Iowa, 17 mi. W of Perry; feed milling. **2** Resort village (pop. 1,554), ⊙ Clearwater co., NW Minn., on Clearwater R., just NE of White Earth Indian Reservation, and 24 mi. W of Bemidji in lake and forest region; lumber mills; dairy products, potatoes, grain. Settled 1898, inc. 1900. **3** Village (pop. 329), Grant co., extreme SW Wis., on Mississippi R. and 9 mi. S of Prairie du Chien, in livestock and dairy region.

Baglung (bä′glŏŏng), town, central Nepal, on the Kali Gandaki and 24 mi. W of Pokhara; cloth weaving; rice, wheat, corn, vegetables, mustard, millet, fruit.

Bagmanlyar (bŭgmŭnlyär′), suburb of Kirovabad, Azerbaijan SSR.

Bagnacavallo (bänyäkäväl′lō), town (pop. 3,886), Ravenna prov., Emilia-Romagna, N central Italy, 11 mi. W of Ravenna; agr. machinery, lumber, vegetable oils, vinegar. Has anc. church with 14th-cent. frescoes.

Bagna Odry, Poland and Germany: see ODER MARSHES.

Bagnara Calabra (bänyä′rä kä′läbrä), town (pop. 9,088), Reggio di Calabria prov., Calabria, S Italy, port on Gulf of Gioia, 15 mi. NE of Reggio di Calabria, in citrus-fruit region; fishing; silk milling, wine making. Severely damaged by earthquake of 1908.

Bagnasco (bänyä'skô), village (pop. 1,388), Cuneo prov., Piedmont, NW Italy, on Tanaro R. and 13 mi. SE of Mondovì.

Bagneaux-sur-Loing (bänyō'-sür-lwē'), village (pop. 635), Seine-et-Marne dept., N central France, on the Loing and 12 mi. S of Fontainebleau; glass milling.

Bagnell (băg'nùl), town (pop. 74), Miller co., central Mo., 8 mi. S of Eldon. **Bagnell Dam**, near by, impounds Osage R. to form LAKE OF THE OZARKS; built 1929–31, it is state's largest power dam (2,543 ft. long; 148 ft. high).

Bagnères-de-Bigorre (bänyâr'-dù-bēgôr'), anc. *Vicus Aquensis*, town (pop. 8,499), Hautes-Pyrénées dept., SW France, on Adour R. and 12 mi. SSE of Tarbes; railroad terminus; important resort and thermal station of central Pyrenees; mfg. of woolens and electrical equipment, metalworking, sawmilling, marble cutting. Slate and marble quarries near by. Has 38 mineral springs in use since Roman times. Splendid view of the PIC DU MIDI DE BIGORRE.

Bagnères-de-Luchon, France: see LUCHON.

Bagnes (bä'nyù), commune (pop. 3,601), Valais canton, SW Switzerland; extends along Vallée de Bagnes, through which flows Drance de Bagnes R.; tourist center; wool. Le Châble (lù shäbl'ù), main village, is 12 mi. SW of Sion.

Bagneux (bänyû'), town (pop. 12,262), Seine dept., N central France, a SSW suburb of Paris, 5 mi. from Notre Dame Cathedral; foundries; brick and tileworks; truck gardens. Has 12th-cent. Gothic church and a cemetery of Paris.

Bagni della Porretta, Italy: see PORRETTA TERME.

Bagni di Casciana (bä'nyē dē käshä'nä), village (pop. 1,617), Pisa prov., Tuscany, central Italy, 17 mi. SE of Pisa. Health resort with chalybeate-sulphur springs (97°F.); stone quarries.

Bagni di Lucca (lōōk'kä), town (pop. 1,116), Lucca prov., Tuscany, central Italy, on Lima R., near its confluence with the Serchio, and 12 mi. NNE of Lucca. Resort with hot mineral springs (99°–129°F.); paper mills, toy factory.

Bagni San Giuliano, Italy: see SAN GIULIANO TERME.

Bagno a Ripoli (bä'nyô ä rē'pôlē), village (pop 564), Firenze prov., Tuscany, central Italy, near the Arno, 2 mi. SE of Florence; pottery, cement, paper, shoes, macaroni.

Bagno di Romagna (dē rômä'nyä), village (pop. 734), Forlì prov., Emilia-Romagna, N central Italy, on Savio R. and 12 mi. NE of Bibbiena. Hot mineral springs (113°F.).

Bagnoles-de-l'Orne (bänyôl'-dù-lôrn'), village (pop. 587), Orne dept., NW France, in a wooded gorge, 25 mi. WNW of Alençon; fashionable watering place (slightly damaged in 1944) known for its thermal springs. Numerous hotels extend along small Vée R. and Bagnoles L. to Tessé-la-Madeleine (1 mi. SW; pop. 590), also a spa. Andaine Forest (□ 15) just W.

Bagnolet (bänyôlā'), industrial town (pop. 25,059), Seine dept., N central France, just E of Paris, 3 mi. from Notre Dame Cathedral, N of Vincennes; foundries; mfg. (auto chassis, tools, furniture, cartons, celluloid, perfumes, hats).

Bagnoli del Trigno (bänyô'lē dĕl trē'nyô), town (pop. 4,134), Campobasso prov., Abruzzi e Molise, S central Italy, near Trigno R., 14 mi. NW of Campobasso; wine, olive oil. Sulphur springs.

Bagnoli di Sopra (dē sô'prä), village (pop. 672), Padova prov., Veneto, N Italy, 15 mi. S of Padua; wine presses, hydraulic pumps. Noted for its wine.

Bagnoli Irpino (ērpē'nô), village (pop. 3,435), Avellino prov., Campania, S Italy, 16 mi. ESE of Avellino; livestock, agr. (cereals, grapes, hemp) region.

Bagnolo in Piano (bänyô'lô ēn pyä'nô), village (pop. 990), Reggio nell'Emilia prov., Emilia-Romagna, N central Italy, 5 mi. NNE of Reggio nell'Emilia; rail junction; wine making.

Bagnolo Mella (mĕl'lä), town (pop. 4,969), Brescia prov., Lombardy, N Italy, near Mella R., 8 mi. SSW of Brescia. Mfg. center; foundry, hosiery and silk mills; fertilizer, linseed oil, wine, pottery. Iron mine near by.

Bagnols or **Bagnols-les-Bains** (bänyôl'-lā-bē'), village (pop. 320), Lozère dept., S France, on the Lot and 8 mi. E of Mende; mineral springs.

Bagnols-sur-Cèze (–sür-sĕz'), town (pop. 4,002), Gard dept., S France, near the Cèze, 18 mi. NW of Avignon; black-truffle trade; fruit and vegetable shipping; distilling. Has mus.

Bagnone (bänyô'nĕ), village (pop. 655), Massa e Carrara prov., Tuscany, central Italy, 7 mi. SE of Pontremoli.

Bagnoregio (bänyôrä'jô), town (pop. 1,863), Viterbo prov., Latium, central Italy, 15 mi. N of Viterbo; hosiery factories. Bishopric. St. Bonaventure b. here. Called Bagnorea until 1922.

Bago (bä'gō). **1** Town (1939 pop. 2,908) in Davao city, Davao prov., S central Mindanao, Philippines, 6 mi. SW of Davao proper. **2** Town (1939 pop. 4,291; 1948 municipality pop. 56,693), Negros Occidental prov., W Negros isl., Philippines, on Guimaras Strait, 12 mi. SW of Bacolod; agr. center (rice, sugar cane); sugar milling.

Bagolino (bägōlē'nô), town (pop. 3,940), Brescia prov., Lombardy, N Italy, near Lago d'Idro, 23 mi. NNE of Brescia. Resort (alt. 2,336 ft.); lumbering, dairying.

Bagot (bă'gùt, băgō'), county (□ 346; pop. 17,642), S Que., on Richelieu R.; ⊙ St. Liboire.

Bagotville (bă'gùtvĭl), village (pop. 1,031), Demerara co., N Br. Guiana, on left bank of lower Demerara R. and 5 mi. SSW of Georgetown; sugar cane, rice, stock.

Bagotville, town (pop. 3,248), S central Que., on Ha Ha Bay of the Saguenay, 10 mi. SE of Chicoutimi; pulp-milling center and shipping point; dairying.

Bagrach Kol or **Bagrash Köl** (both: bägräsh' kûl), Chinese *Po-ssu-t'eng Hu*, salt lake in central Sinkiang prov., China, S of the Tien Shan, 120 mi. S of Urumchi; 41°57'N 86°45'E. Kara Shahr is near W shore.

Bagrad (bŭgrät'), village (1948 pop. over 2,000), E Khakass Autonomous Oblast, Krasnoyarsk Territory, Russian SFSR, 40 mi. NNW of Abakan; flour mills. Formerly Sukhaya Tes.

Bagradas, Tunisia: see MEDJERDA RIVER.

Bagrakot (bä'gräkōt), village, Jalpaiguri dist., N West Bengal, India, on tributary of the Tista and 26 mi. NNW of Jalpaiguri, at foot of W Assam Himalayas; rail spur terminus; extensive tea gardens (tea processing); rice, mustard, tobacco. Coal deposits near by.

Bagram or **Begram** (bùgräm'), village, Kabul prov., E Afghanistan, 5 mi. E of Charikar, near confluence of Panjshir and Ghorband rivers. A major archaeological site, identified with anc. city of *Kapisa*, destroyed 6th cent. B.C. by Cyrus the Great and later supplanted by Kabul.

Bagrasi (bŭgrä'sē), town (pop. 5,918), Bulandshahr dist., W Uttar Pradesh, India, 22 mi. NE of Bulandshahr; wheat, oilseeds, cotton, barley, corn. Also spelled Bugrasi.

Bagrationovsk (bùgrŭtyēô'nùfsk), city (1939 pop. 7,485), SW Kaliningrad oblast, Russian SFSR, 22 mi. SSE of Kaliningrad, on Pol. border, in fertile wooded dist.; iron foundry; bricks, flour. Obelisk commemorates undecisive battle fought here (Feb. 7–8, 1807), bet. French under Napoleon and Russians and Prussians, in which Bagration participated. Chartered 1335. Until 1945, in East Prussia and called Eylau or Preussisch Eylau (proi'sĭsh ī'lou).

Bagri (bä'grē), town (pop. 4,730), central Rajasthan, India, 9 mi. ESE of Sojat; markets millet, wheat, barley; metalwork.

Bagru River (bä'grōō), SW Sierra Leone, rises N of Sembehun (head of navigation), flows 30 mi. SE and SW to Sherbro R. 12 mi. NNW of Bonthe.

Bagsar, India: see BAKSAR.

Bagshot, England: see WINDLESHAM.

Bagua (bä'gwä), town (pop. 223), ⊙ Bagua prov. (created 1940), Amazonas dept., N Peru, landing on Utcubamba R. and 17 mi. E of Jaén; sugar growing. Ships cattle by raft down Marañón R. Called Bagua Chica until 1940, when it was made capital of the new prov. Bagua Grande (pop. 87) is 11 mi. SE on the Utcubamba.

Báguanos (bä'gwänōs), town (pop. 1,503), Oriente prov., E Cuba, 15 mi. SE of Holguín; sugar growing and milling.

Báguena (bä'gänä), village (pop. 1,446), Teruel prov., E Spain, on Jiloca R. and 6 mi. SE of Daroca; wine, nuts, cereals, fruit. Ruins of medieval fort near by.

Baguio (bă'gēō, Sp. bägyō'). **1** Town (1939 pop. 11,042), part of Davao city, Davao prov., S central Mindanao, Philippines, 15 mi. NW of Davao proper; abacá, coconuts. **2** City (1948 pop. 29,692) in but independent of Benguet sub-prov., Mountain Prov., N Luzon, Philippines, 125 mi. NNW of Manila; 16°24'N 120°36'E; alt. c.5,000 ft.; mean annual temp. 64°F. Chief mtn. resort of the Philippines, serving as the summer capital, and a gold-mining center near the principal gold mines of the Philippines. A charming city, planned by Daniel H. Burnham, its mtn. site is connected with the main Luzon highways by a 28-mi. road completed in 1913. Baguio was badly damaged in Second World War during severe fighting in 1945.

Baguirmi (bägērmē'), former sultanate of N central Africa, roughly coextensive with present Chari-Baguirmi administrative region (□ 36,300; 1950 pop. 251,800), W Chad territory, Fr. Equatorial Africa, adjacent to Fr. Cameroons; ⊙ Fort Lamy; former ⊙ was Massénya. Lies SE of L. Chad, bet. Shari R. (S and W), the former Kanem and Wadai states (N), and Salamat region (E). Steppe-like plateau rising to SE; most rivers are sand-obstructed channels. Livestock, millet, sesame, wild rice, cotton, indigo. Ostrich breeding, apiculture. Natives mine iron, weave and dye cotton. Baguirmese (of Negroid-Arab stock) arrived from E Sudan in early 12th cent., subdued the local Fulah and Arabs, and were converted to Islam (1600). From 17th to 19th cent. they waged incessant war on their neighbors and raided territories to S (as far as Ubangi R.) to obtain slaves. In 1871, country was conquered by sultan of Wadai, and later (1890) overrun by Rabah el Zobeir, sultan of Bornu. The French were repulsed until their victory (1900) at Kousseri. In First World War Baguirmi was used by France as base for operations against Ger. Cameroons. Also spelled Bagirmi and Baghirmi.

Bagur, El, or **Al-Bajur** (both: ĕl bă'jōōr), town (pop. 4,756; with suburbs 12,306), Minufiya prov., Lower Egypt, on railroad and 7 mi. ESE of Minuf; cereals, cotton, flax.

Bagura, E Pakistan: see BOGRA.

Baguriya Canal (băgōōrē'yù) or **Bajuriyah Canal** (băjōō–), navigable canal of the Nile delta, Lower Egypt, extending N c.55 mi. from a point on the Damietta branch S of Benha to the Rosetta branch.

Bagworth, town and parish (pop. 1,568), W central Leicester, England, 9 mi. WNW of Leicester; coal mining.

Bah (bä), town (pop. 4,738), Agra dist., W Uttar Pradesh, India, 40 mi. SE of Agra; rail spur terminus; pearl millet, gram, wheat, barley, oilseeds, cotton. Large annual cattle fair at village of Batesar, 6 mi. NW.

Bahadarpur (bŭhä'dŭrpŏŏr), town (pop. 5,120), Baroda dist., N Bombay, India, 22 mi. ESE of Baroda; cotton, millet; cotton ginning.

Bahadrabad, India: see HARDWAR.

Bahadurabad Ghat (bŭhä"dōōräbäd' gät), village, Mymensingh dist., N East Bengal, E Pakistan, on Jamuna R. (main course of the Brahmaputra; rail ferry) opposite Bharat Khali and 50 mi. NW of Mymensingh; rail terminus.

Bahadurgarh (bŭhä'dŏŏrgŭr), town (pop. 8,206), Rohtak dist., SE Punjab, India, 25 mi. SE of Rohtak; local trade in millet, gram, salt, wheat.

Bahadur Khel (kāl'), village, Kohat dist., E central North-West Frontier Prov., W Pakistan, 40 mi. SW of Kohat; grain growing. Rock-salt quarries just S; valuable deposits extend c.40 mi. E in outcrops of limestone hill range. Large gypsum deposits near by.

Bahadurpur (–pŏŏr), town (pop. 3,945), E Rajasthan, India, 10 mi. NE of Alwar; millet, gram. Sometimes spelled Bahadarpur.

Bahama Banks, Bahama Isls.: see GREAT BAHAMA BANK; LITTLE BAHAMA BANK.

Bahama Islands (bùhä'mù, bùhā'mù), archipelago and Br. colony (□ 4,403.5; pop. 68,846), in the West Indies; ⊙ NASSAU. Consist of c.700 isls. and islets (of which 20 are inhabited) and more than 2,000 rocks, reefs, and cays, bet. 20°50'–27°25' N and 72°37'–80°32'W; crossed by the Tropic of Cancer. Beginning within 50 mi. of SE Florida, they stretch SE for c.750 mi., N of and generally parallel to Cuba, to within 70 mi. of Haiti. Cay Sal Bank (W) lies S of the Florida Keys; at the SE end of the chain the TURKS AND CAICOS ISLANDS belong (since 1873) politically to Jamaica. Formed largely of calcareous matter derived from shells and coral, the isls. are physiographically related to Florida. They rest on a vast submerged limestone plateau, of which the most prominent sections are the Great Bahama Bank and Little Bahama Bank, the banks themselves rising from great ocean depths. Mangrove swamps and ponds abound in the low, honeycombed, riverless limestone ground. Principal isls. are NW-SE: GRAND BAHAMA ISLAND, GREAT ABACO ISLAND, BIMINI ISLANDS, BERRY ISLANDS, NEW PROVIDENCE ISLAND (on which is Nassau), ANDROS ISLAND (largest of the Bahamas), ELEUTHERA ISLAND, CAT ISLAND (with highest elevation, c.400 ft.), GREAT EXUMA ISLAND, SAN SALVADOR ISLAND or Watling Isl. (where Columbus is said to have landed), LONG ISLAND, CROOKED ISLAND, ACKLINS ISLAND, MAYAGUANA isl., Little Inagua and GREAT INAGUA ISLAND. The Bahamas have a subtropical, salubrious climate famed for mild winters. Mean annual temp. of Nassau is 77.2°F.; rainy season May-Oct., with an annual rainfall of c.50 inches. The isls. are sometimes visited in the fall by hurricanes, causing considerable damage, while proximity of the Gulf Stream keeps frosts away. For their vivid scenery, fine beaches, and climatic conditions, the Bahamas rank high as a winter resort. Also known for deep-sea fishing (sailfish, kingfish, muttonfish, amber jack, barracuda, etc.) in surrounding waters. Fishing for tortoises, crawfish, shells, and sponge is an important source of income, though sponge fishing has declined (since 1939) because of disease. Apart from shells, the main exports are tomatoes and other vegetables, pineapples, citrus fruit, sisal, bananas, coconuts, some timber (logwood, mahogany, lignum vitae), and cascarilla bark. To the thin layer of soil, fertilizers have to be added. There is limited stock raising (horses, cattle, sheep, hogs, poultry). Industries include salt panning, lumbering, charcoal burning. Nassau, the only city of the archipelago (though there are a number of towns), is also the leading port, tourist and commercial center. The aboriginal Lucayos, for whom the archipelago is sometimes called, were a mild, gentle, primitive people, who vanished (partly deported to Cuba) within 20 years of the coming of the Spanish. It was here, most likely at present-day San Salvador or Watling Isl., that Columbus made his 1st landfall in the New World (Oct. 12, 1492), on an isl. then called Guanahani. The Spanish do not seem to have made a permanent settlement. Early in 17th cent., Br. settlers arrived from Bermuda. The company of Eleutherian Adventurers was formed (1647) in London to attempt a systematic colonization; Cromwell made them proprietors of the isls. (1649), though the group had **been**

previously granted (1629) to Sir Robert Heath. Charles II gave the Bahamas to 6 of the Lords Proprietors of Carolina (1670), who did not relinquish their claim until 1787. Under 1st royal governor, appointed in 1717, the pirates (notably Blackbeard), for whom the isls. served as a principal rendezvous, were driven off. Frequent incursions were made by the Spanish and French, who disputed the English claim. An American Revolutionary force held Nassau shortly in 1776, and the isls. surrendered to the Spanish in 1781 but were soon retaken by a Br. force. The Br. possession was confirmed by the Treaty of Versailles (1783). After the American Revolution, many loyalists settled in the Bahamas, but with the abolition of slavery (1833) their plantations decayed. During the Civil War, blockade runners from the South operated here, enriching the islanders; and during the prohibition era in the U.S., the isls. became a base for rumrunning. In 1940 sites were leased to U.S. for naval bases. From 1940 to 1945 the duke of Windsor was the governor. By agreement with the U.S., some of the islanders were sent (1943–44) to Florida to relieve the manpower shortage. The Bahamas enjoy partial self-government, with a House of Assembly and Legislative Council. The pop. is about 85% Negro. English is spoken throughout.

Bahamdun, Lebanon: see BHAMDUN.

Bahar (bähär'), town, Fifth Prov., in Hamadan, W Iran, on road and 10 mi. NW of Hamadan; grain, fruit (melons).

Bahariya or **Bahariyah** (băhûrē'yù), oasis (pop. 6,743), in the Libyan Desert, central Egypt, c.200 mi. SSW of Alexandria. Connected by numerous caravan routes with the Mediterranean coast, the Nile valley, and Farafra oasis. Lies in a basin c.60 mi. long, 25 mi. wide, and is surrounded by hills. In its small cultivated area (□ 4) are grown dates, olives, apricots, oranges, grapes, wheat, rice. Main village is El Bawiti, E of which is an airfield. Sometimes spelled Baharia.

Bahau (bùhou'), town (pop. 2,436), E Negri Sembilan, Malaya, on E coast railroad and 32 mi. E of Seremban; rubber, oil palm.

Bahauddin, W Pakistan: see MANDI BAHAUDDIN.

Bahawalnagar (bŭhä'vŭlnŭgŭr), town (pop. 8,587), Bahawalpur state, W Pakistan, 105 mi. NE of Bahawalpur; rail junction; wheat, millet; pottery mfg.

Bahawalpur (–pŏŏr), princely state (□ 15,918; 1951 pop. 1,820,000), W Pakistan; ⊙ Bahawalpur. On edge of Thar Desert; bounded NW by Pakistan Punjab and by Sutlej, Panjnad, and Indus rivers, S and E by Rajasthan, NE by Indian Punjab. Has 2 enclaves in NE Sind. Mainly a sandy waste, with fertile riverbank tract irrigated (SW) by Panjnad Canal and (NE) by canals of lower Sutlej valley system; wheat, dates, cotton, rice, and millet grown. Hand-loom weaving, pottery mfg., rice husking, camel breeding. Chief towns: Bahawalpur, Ahmadpur East, Khanpur, Rahimyar Khan. Established after breakup of Afghan empire in late-18th cent.; independence recognized by treaties with Sikhs and British in early 19th cent. After 1921, attached to Punjab States agency; in 1947, acceded to Pakistan. Sometimes Bhawalpur.

Bahawalpur, town (pop. 40,015), ⊙ Bahawalpur state, W Pakistan, near Sutlej R., 55 mi. SSE of Multan; trade center for wheat, cotton, millet, rice, piece goods; cotton ginning, rice husking, oilseed and flour milling, soap mfg.; metalware, embroidery, pottery; agr. (dates, mangoes). Has col. of arts. Samasata rail junction is 8 mi. SW.

Bahbit el Higara, Behbit el Hagara (both: bĕ'bĭt ĕl hä'gûrù), or **Bihbit al-Hajarah** (bĭ'bĭt ĕl hä'jùrù), small village, Gharbita prov., Lower Egypt, 6 mi. WSW of Mansura. Site of anc. Hebet, the Iseum of Roman times. For Greeks and Romans, Isis was the divinity of the city and the site has extensive XXX dynasty and Ptolemaic ruins. Notable is the spendid temple of Isis (built c.270 B.C.).

Bahce (bächĕ'), Turkish *Bahçe*, village (pop. 884), Seyhan prov., S Turkey, on railroad and 70 mi. ENE of Adana; cereals, vetch, tobacco. Also called Bulanik.

Baheri (bŭhä'rē), town (pop. 9,994), Bareilly dist., N central Uttar Pradesh, India, 29 mi. N of Bareilly; sugar processing; rice, wheat, gram, corn, sugar cane.

Bahgura (bägōō'rù) or **Bahjurah** (bäjōō'rù), village (pop. 14,784), Qena prov., Upper Egypt, on railroad and 2 mi. WNW of Nag Hammadi; cereals, sugar cane, dates. Sometimes Bahgoura.

Bahi (bä'hē), town, Central Prov., central Tanganyika, on railroad and 30 mi. WNW of Dodoma; peanuts, gum arabic, beeswax.

Bahía [Sp.,=bay], for names beginning thus and not found here: see under following part of the name.

Bahia or **Baía** (bäē'ù), coastal state (□ 217,688; 1940 pop. 3,918,112; 1950 census 4,900,419) of E Brazil; ⊙ SALVADOR. Bounded by states of Sergipe (NE), Pernambuco and Piauí (N), Goiás (W), Minas Gerais (S), and Espírito Santo (SE). Consists of a coastal plain c.50 mi. wide, adjoined (W) by a broad N–S range (alt. c.3,000 ft.) which constitutes a N outlier of the Serra do Espinhaço and which contains the diamond-rich Chapada Diamantina. Further W, Bahia is traversed SSW-NNE by the middle course of São Francisco R. Westernmost Bahia is part of central Brazilian plateau and rises to 3,000 ft. in the Serra Geral de Goiás along Goiás border. The São Francisco and its tributaries form chief drainage system. Minor coastal streams (Itapicuru, Paraguaçu, Rio de Contas, Rio Pardo) flow E to the Atlantic. Humid, tropical climate along coast, dry and cooler in the interior; max. of yearly rainfall in summer. Two coastal regions of state are noted for their fertility: the RECÔNCAVO, near Salvador, produces sugar, tobacco, cotton, fruit, and subsistence crops (manioc, beans, rice); and in the SE 95% of Brazil's cacao crop is grown. Products of the interior are caroa fibers, carnauba wax, castor beans, mangabeira rubber. Bahia is a leading cattle-, sheep-, and hog-raising state; the livestock is sold for packing and export at large fairs at Feira de Santana. Cabinet wood is also exported. Bahia yields most of Brazil's black industrial diamonds, has gold placers (headwaters of the Rio de Contas, Brumado R.), and manganese, chromium, rock-crystal, and semiprecious-stone deposits. Hydroelectric power is in course of development at Paulo Afonso Falls on São Francisco R. Coastal areas well served by roads and railroads. Chief rail lines to the interior connect Salvador with Juàzeiro (on São Francisco R.), with diamond dist. near Andaraí, and with the Rio de Contas gold-mining area. In SE, a railroad links Caravelas (near coast) with Arassuaí in Minas Gerais. Chief ports are Salvador on Todos os Santos Bay, and the cacao-shipping center of Ilhéus. Other important towns: Cachoeira, Nazaré, Santo Amaro, Belmonte, Juàzeiro, Senhor do Bonfim. Cotton milling, sugar distilling, cacao processing, and mfg. of tobacco products are principal industries. Monte Pascoal (SSW of present Pôrto Seguro) was 1st land sighted by the discoverer Cabral in 1500. Under Tomé de Souza (who founded present city of Salvador in 1549), Bahia became a unified captaincy, and the center of 17th- and 18th-cent. colonization and plantation agr. based on imported Negro slave labor. In 1823 it became a prov. of the Brazilian empire, and in 1889 a state of the federal republic.

Bahia, city, Brazil: see SALVADOR.

Bahía, Ecuador: see BAHÍA DE CARÁQUEZ.

Bahía, Islas de la, Honduras: see BAY ISLANDS.

Bahía Blanca (bäē'ä bläng'kä), city (pop., including Ingeniero White, 93,122), ⊙ Bahía Blanca dist. (□ 880; pop. 104,229), SW Buenos Aires prov., Argentina, on the Arroyo Napostá Grande, near head of the Bahía Blanca (bay) and 350 mi. SW of Buenos Aires. Principal outlet for S Pampa. Rail (workshops), commercial, and industrial center with several satellite ports, including INGENIERO WHITE, PUERTO GALVÁN, GENERAL CERRI (near Bahía Blanca), and PUERTO BELGRANO and ARROYO PAREJA (near Punta Alta), shipping grain, wool, meat, hides, and importing petroleum products, agr. machinery, lumber. Industries include meat packing, flour milling, dairying, tanning, wool processing, oil refining. Fisheries. City is centered on Plaza Rivadavia, a park bordered by city hall, courthouse, banks, and neoclassic church of Our Lady of La Merced. Founded 1828 as fort against Brazilian invasions, it was settled after 1838 largely by Italian immigration. Rapid development came in 20th cent. with increasing settlement and output of the pampas.

Bahía Blanca, bay of Atlantic Ocean in SW Buenos Aires prov., Argentina, just S of city of Bahía Blanca; 33 mi. wide at mouth, 40 mi. long. Includes inlets of Bahía Falsa (W) and Rada Monte Hermoso (NE). Contains Trinidad, Bermejo, and Wood isls. N shore is lined with ports of Bahía Blanca city: Puerto Galván, Ingeniero White, and Arroyo Pareja. Receives Sauce Chico R. and the Arroyo Napostá Grande.

Bahía de Caráquez or **Bahía** (bäē'ä dā kärä'kĕs), town (1950 pop. 7,993), Manabí prov., W Ecuador, Pacific port at mouth of Chone R., on Caráquez Bay, and 30 mi. N of Portoviejo, connected by rail with Chone, 23 mi. E. In a fertile region, it exports cacao, coffee, tagua nuts, rubber, balsa wood, hides. Airfield, customhouse.

Bahia de Todos os Santos, Brazil: see TODOS OS SANTOS BAY.

Bahía Honda (ōn'dä), town (pop. 2,006), Pinar del Río prov., W Cuba, on small Bahía Honda, 50 mi. WSW of Havana; sugar cane, coffee, fruit, livestock. Bay has seaplane anchorage.

Bahía Negra (nä'grä), town (dist. pop. 600), Olimpo dept., N Paraguay, in the Chaco, on Paraguay R. (Brazil border) near mouth of Otuquis R., and 60 mi. NNW of Fuerte Olimpo. Military garrison in cattle and quebracho area.

Bahiret el Biban (bähē'rĕt ĕl bēbän'), coastal lagoon of SE Tunisia, near Tripolitanian border, just N of Ben Gardane; c.20 mi. long, 5 mi. wide; sheltered by narrow sand bar. Fisheries.

Bahjoi (bä'jōē), town (pop. 5,049), Moradabad dist., N central Uttar Pradesh, India, 13 mi. SSE of Sambhal; glass mfg.; wheat, rice, millet, sugar cane.

Bahjurah, Egypt: see BAHGURA.

Bahla or **Bahlah** (bälä'), town (pop. 3,000), Oman Proper, 40 mi. W of Izki, at S foot of the Jabal Akhdar; dates, grain. Was ⊙ Oman in 17th cent.

Bahlil, El (ĕl bälēl'), town (pop. 5,538), Fez region, N central Fr. Morocco, on N slope of the Middle Atlas, 3 mi. NW of Sefrou; fruit orchards, olive groves. Also spelled El Bhalil.

Bahluliye, El, or **Al-Bahluliyah** (both: ĕl-bălōōlē'yù), Fr. *Bahloulié*, town, Latakia prov., W Syria, 13 mi. NE of Latakia; sericulture, cotton, tobacco, cereals.

Bahnasa, El, Egypt: see OXYRHYNCUS.

Bahnea or **Bachnea** (both: bäkh'nyä), Hung. *Bonyha* (bô'nyŭhŏ), village (pop. 1,604), Mures prov., central Rumania, on railroad and 30 mi. NE of Blaj.

Bahon (bäō'), town (1950 pop. 663), Nord dept., N Haiti, on Grande Rivière du Nord, 23 mi. SSE of Cap-Haïtien, on railroad; coffeegrowing.

Bahoruco (bäōrōō'kō), province (□ 1,347; 1935 pop. 49,219; 1950 pop. 39,655), SW Dominican Republic, on Haiti border; ⊙ Neiba. Bounded by Sierra de Neiba (N) and Sierra de Bahoruco (S), watered by the Yaque del Sur. In its center is the salt lake Enriquillo, c.150 ft. below sea level. In the fertile, irrigated depression are grown coffee, corn, rice, sugar cane, bananas, vegetables. Rich in fine tropical wood. Fishing and hunting at L. Enriquillo. Large salt deposits near Neiba. Formerly a part of Barahona prov., it was set up 1943.

Bahoruco, Sierra de (syĕ'rä dā), range, SW Dominican Republic, parallel to the Cordillera Central and forming S watershed of L. Enriquillo; extends c.50 mi. E from Haiti border to the Caribbean just S of Barahona. Rises to 5,348 ft.

Bahour, Fr. India: see BAHUR.

Bahra or **Bahrah** (bä'rù), village, central Hejaz, Saudi Arabia, in the Wadi Fatima, 20 mi. W of Mecca, and on highway to Jidda.

Bahraich (bä'rīch), district (□ 2,654; pop. 1,240,569), N Uttar Pradesh, India; ⊙ Bahraich. Bounded N by Nepal, W by Gogra R.; drained by the Rapti. Agr. (rice, wheat, corn, gram, oilseeds, barley); extensive sal jungle (N). Main towns: Bahraich, Nanpara, Bhinga.

Bahraich, town (pop. 39,963), ⊙ Bahraich dist., N Uttar Pradesh, India, on tributary of the Gogra and 65 mi. NNW of Fyzabad; sugar processing; trades in grain, oilseeds, timber, tobacco. Has 13th-cent. tomb of Afghan invader, Saiyid Salar Masud, who was killed near by in 1033. Large annual fair.

Bahrain: see BAHREIN.

Bahr al Hadri, Oman: see MASIRA BAY.

Bahramabad, Iran: see RAFSINJAN.

Bahr Aoûk or **Aoûk** (bä'hûr ä-ōōk'), intermittent tributary of Shari R. in S Chad territory, Fr. Equatorial Africa, rises at Anglo-Egyptian Sudan border 50 mi. N of Birao, flows c.350 mi. SW and W to Shari R. 40 mi. SE of Fort-Archambault.

Bahrayn: see BAHREIN.

Bahr Azoum, Anglo-Egyptian Sudan and Fr. Equatorial Africa: see BAHR SALAMAT.

Bahrdar or **Bahrdar Giyorgis** (bä'hûrdär gĭyôr'gĭs), village, Gojjam prov., NW Ethiopia, at S end of L. Tana, near efflux of Blue Nile, 70 mi. S of Gondar, in agr. (coffee, cereals) and fishing region. Airfield.

Bahrein, Bahrain, or **Bahrayn** (bärān', bù–), island in Gulf of Bahrein (bet. Hasa coast of Saudi Arabia and Qatar peninsula) of Persian Gulf, forming with near-by isls.—MUHARRAQ, SITRA, UMM NASAN—the archipelago and independent Arab sheikdom of Bahrein (□ 231; 1950 pop. 109,650), under British protection; 26°N 50°30'E; ⊙ Manama. The main isl. of Bahrein, 28 mi. long (N-S) and 10 mi. wide, consists of a limestone plateau (100–200 ft.) with a central eroded basin (12 mi. long, 4 mi. wide) in which rises the Jabal Dukhan (445 ft.). Largely arid (yearly rainfall 4–5 inches), it has a cool winter (Dec.–Feb.) and a hot, oppressive summer at the height of which (June–Sept.) the temp. exceeds 100°F. Artesian-well irrigation makes agr. possible along N shore, producing dates, citrus fruit, alfalfa, millet, wheat. There are salt swamps on SW shore. Pearling, fishing (shrimp, barracuda), boatbuilding, weaving, and reed matting are the principal native industries. Since early 1930s, the central depression has been converted into a producing oil field, linked by pipe line with refinery near isl.'s NE shore and with loading terminal on Sitra isl. Refinery also receives crude oil by pipe line from Dhahran. Main urban centers are Manama and Muharraq town (airport); Awali is principal oil-workers camp. Pop. is predominantly Arab, with ruling urban elements being of the Sunni sect and rural pop. of Shiah sect. There are also Negroes (partly slaves), Persians, and Indians. Sometimes identified with the anc. *Tylos* or *Tylus*, Bahrein was formerly known as Awal or Aval, while the name Bahrein was applied to Hasa. Occupied in 1507 by Portuguese and in 1602 by Persian Shiite Arabs under Shah Abbas. The present ruling family, the Sunni Khalifah, came into power in 1783. It has been in direct relations with the British since 1805, under treaty since 1820, and under British protection since 1861. A Briton is adviser to the Bahrein govt. and there is a British political agent. Until development of its oil resources, Bahrein was noted as the center of Persian Gulf pearl trade. Following the granting of an oil concession to U.S. company in 1925 (renewed in 1940), oil was 1st obtained in 1932 and large-scale production begun in 1934. Bahrein has been claimed intermittently by Iran.

Bahr el Abiad, Anglo-Egyptian Sudan: see WHITE NILE.

Bahr el Abyad, Anglo-Egyptian Sudan: see WHITE NILE.

Bahr el Arab (bä'hŭr ĕl äräb'), intermittent river in SW Anglo-Egyptian Sudan, rises in Marra Mts. (Nile-Congo watershed) on border of Fr. Equatorial Africa, flows c.500 mi. ESE to the Bahr el Ghazal (Nile tributary) at Wankai. Nonnavigable. Floods in summer.

Bahr el Azraq, river, Anglo-Egyptian Sudan and Ethiopia: see BLUE NILE.

Bahr el Gebel, Anglo-Egyptian Sudan: see BAHR EL JEBEL.

Bahr el Ghazal (ĕl găzăl'), province (□ 77,820; 1948 pop. estimated 729,728), S Anglo-Egyptian Sudan; ⊙ Wau. Bordered by Fr. Equatorial Africa (W) and Sudd swamps (E). Consists of a vast clay plateau drained by Tonj and Jur rivers (headstreams of the Bahr el Ghazal). Agr. and livestock region: cotton, peanuts, sesame, corn, durra; cattle, sheep, goats. Main centers are Wau and Tonj. Prov. was amalgamated (1935) with Mongalla prov. and again separated in 1948.

Bahr el Ghazal, left tributary of the White Nile, in Upper Nile prov., S central Anglo-Egyptian Sudan, rises in L. AMBADI (in W SUDD swamps) which gathers flood waters of Jur and Tonj rivers, flows 150 mi. NE, past Wankai, and joins the Bahr el Jebel in L. No to form the WHITE NILE proper. Navigable July-March for steamers to Meshra er Req, and July-Oct. to Wau (on Jur R.). Because of extensive evaporation and dispersal in the Sudd, the Bahr el Ghazal's contribution to main Nile volume is negligible. Receives Bahr el Arab (left).

Bahr el Ghazal, largely dry arm of L. Chad, W central Chad territory, Fr. Equatorial Africa, meandering for 300 mi. generally SW from SE edge of the Sahara to E shore of L. Chad, just past Massakory. Main desert road to Tibesti closely follows Bahr el Ghazal ravine, because of underground water reached by wells. Also known as Soro (sōrō').

Bahr el Huleh, Israel: see HULA, LAKE.

Bahr el Jebel (jĕ'bĕl), section of the White Nile in S Anglo-Egyptian Sudan, so named below Nimule, where it enters the Sudan from Uganda as the ALBERT NILE; flows 594 mi. N, past Juba (head of navigation), Mongalla, Bor, and Jonglei, through the SUDD swamps, and joins the Bahr el Ghazal in L. No to form the WHITE NILE proper. Navigable in entire course at all seasons, except in stretch of rapids bet. Juba and Nimule (road service). Loses half its water in the Sudd region through dispersal and evaporation. A projected canal would by-pass the Sudd from Jonglei to area of Malakal. Sometimes spelled Bahr el Gebel.

Bahr el Saghir, Bahr es Saghir, or **Bahr al-Saghir** (all: bä'hŭr ĕs-sägēr'), navigable irrigation canal in Nile delta, Daqahliya prov., Lower Egypt; extends 40 mi. ENE from Mansura to Manzala.

Bahr el Zeraf or **Bahr ez Zeraf** (both: bä'hŭr ĕz-zĕräf'), nonnavigable arm of the White Nile, in the SUDD region, S central Anglo-Egyptian Sudan; formed in swamps N of Shambe, diverting part of waters of the Bahr el Jebel, it flows c.150 mi. N, past Fangak, to White Nile 35 mi. W of Malakal.

Bahret Lut, Palestine: see DEAD SEA.

Bahret Tabariya, Palestine: see GALILEE, SEA OF.

Bahr ez Zeraf, Anglo-Egyptian Sudan: see BAHR EL ZERAF.

Bahr Hadus (bä'hŭr hă'dōōs), navigable canal of the Nile delta, Lower Egypt, extends c.30 mi. from a point c.10 mi. N of Kafr Saqr to L. Manzala.

Bahr Muweis or **Bahr Muways** (mōōwās'), navigable canal of the Nile delta, E Lower Egypt, extends c.45 mi. N from a point 3 mi. NE of Benha to the Bahr Saft.

Bahr Nashart (năshärt'), navigable canal in Gharbiya prov., N Lower Egypt, extends 25 mi. N from Nashart to L. Burullus.

Bahror, India: see BEHROR.

Bahr Saft (säft), navigable canal of the Nile delta, Lower Egypt, extends c.75 mi. from the Damietta branch of Nile to L. Manzala. Used for irrigation.

Bahr Salamat (sälämät'), intermittent tributary (c.520 mi. long) of Shari R., in W Anglo-Egyptian Sudan and SW and S Chad territory, Fr. Equatorial Africa; rises in Darfur as the Bahr Asum or Azoum (äzōōm') 90 mi. WSW of El Fasher, flows c.400 mi. W and SW to Am-Timan, and, thencefrom known as Bahr Salamat, flows 120 mi. further SW through a region of swamps to Shari R. 30 mi. NW of Fort-Archambault.

Bahr Sara (särä'), river in W and N Ubangi-Shari and S Chad territories, Fr. Equatorial Africa, rises as Ouham R. (ōōhäm') 45 mi. NE of Baboua, flows 185 mi. W, past Bozoum and Bossangoa (where it takes the name Bahr Sara) and then NE, W, and NNE past Batangafo and Moïssala to Shari R. 8 mi. NW of Fort-Archambault; total length, c.420 mi. Navigable for steamboats part of the year for 175 mi. below Batangafo. Sometimes considered the main headstream of Shari R.

Bahr Shibin (shĭbēn'), navigable canal, Gharbiya and Minufiya provs., Lower Egypt; the anc. Sebennytic arm of the Nile and N prolongation of the Raiyah Minufiya; extends c.65 mi. from the Damietta branch of the Nile (6 mi. SW of Benha) to Nabaroh, where it becomes the Bahr Basandila and continues to the Mediterranean. Irrigates much of Gharbiya prov.

Bahr Yusuf (yōō'sōōf) or **Bahr Yusef** (yōō'sŭf) [=Joseph's canal or river], watercourse, Upper Egypt, a former dry bed of the Nile extending c.150 mi. from Dairut (Asyut prov.) to Faiyum. Used for irrigation, it makes fertile Faiyum prov.

Bahur (bŭhōōr'), Fr. *Bahour* (bäōōr'), town (commune pop. 20,591), Pondicherry settlement, Fr. India, 10 mi. SW of Pondicherry; rice, sugar cane. Lignite deposits near by. Also spelled Bahoor.

Bahuriband, India: see SIHORA.

Bai (bī), Chinese *Paicheng* (bī'jŭng'), town and oasis (pop. 71,985), W central Sinkiang prov., China, 95 mi. ENE of Aksu, and on highway S of the Tien Shan; carpets, bronze articles; wheat, millet. Copper mines, saltworks near by.

Baía, state, Brazil: see BAHIA.

Baia (bä'yä), anc. *Baiae*, village (pop. 962), Napoli prov., Campania, S Italy, port on Gulf of Pozzuoli, 10 mi. W of Naples; bathing resort; pozzuolana extracting and exporting. A favorite bathing resort of anc. Romans; has fragmentary remains of their sumptuous villas and huge baths.

Baia, village, Rumania: see FALTICENI.

Baia-de-Arama (bä'yä-dä-ärä'mŭ), Rum. *Baia-de-Aramă*, anc. Greek *Chalcis*, town (1948 pop. 1,513), Gorj prov., SW Rumania, 26 mi. NNE of Turnu-Severin; old copper-production center; lumbering, flour milling. Has wooden 18th-cent. church.

Baia-de-Aries (-ä'rēēsh), Rum. *Baia-de-Arieş*, Hung. *Aranyosbánya* (ŏ'rŏnyôsh-bä"nyŏ), village (pop. 1,219), Cluj prov., NW central Rumania, in the Apuseni Mts., on Aries R., on railroad and 26 mi. SW of Turda; gold-mining center.

Baia-de-Cris (-krēsh'), Rum. *Baia-de-Criş*, Hung. *Körösbánya* (kû'rûsh-bä"nyŏ), village (pop. 877), Hunedoara prov., W central Rumania, on White Körös R., on railroad and 22 mi. NNW of Deva; gold and silver mining; also tourist center.

Baía dos Tigres (bäē'ŭ dōōsh tē'grĭsh), village, Huíla prov., SW Angola, on peninsula (25 mi. long) enclosing Tigres Bay (also called Great Fish Bay), near South-West Africa border, 100 mi. SSW of Mossâmedes; fishing port. Airfield.

Baiae, Italy: see BAIA.

Baia-Mare (bä'yä-mä'rā), Hung. *Nagybánya* (nŏ'-dyûbä'nyŏ), town (1948 pop. 20,959), ⊙ Baia-Mare prov., NW Rumania, in Crisana-Maramures, 34 mi. SE of Satu-Mare; rail junction and metallurgical center, based on local lead, zinc, gold, and silver. Major chemical industry produces sulphuric acid and fertilizers; agr. tools, furniture, toys; trades in grain, fruit, nuts, wine, poultry, livestock. Long residence of a Gr. Catholic bishop. Gold and silver are mined in vicinity. Popular and picturesque health resort, much patronized by artists. Has 14th-cent. St. Stephen tower, old mint, mus. Half pop. are Magyars. In Hungary, 1940–45.

Baião (bīā'ō), city (pop. 1,191), E Pará, Brazil, landing on right bank of Tocantins R. and 115 mi. SSW of Belém; ships rubber, Brazil nuts, cacao, and copaiba oil.

Baia-Sprie (bä'yä-sprē'yĕ), Hung. *Felsőbánya* (fĕl'-shûbä'nyŏ), town (1948 pop. 3,968), Baia-Mare prov., NW Rumania, 5 mi. E of Baia-Mare; rail terminus, mining and smelting center (lead, silver, zinc, copper, gold); trade in lumber and fruit. Has old church and monastery. Most of pop. is Magyar. In Hungary, 1940–45.

Baiazeh, Iran: see BIABANAK.

Baibiene (bībyā'nā), town (pop. estimate 500), S central Corrientes prov., Argentina, on railroad and 30 mi. S of Mercedes; cattle, sheep, horses.

Baïbokoum (bībōkōōm'), village, SW Chad territory, Fr. Equatorial Africa, on M'Béré R., near Fr. Cameroons border, 60 mi. SSW of Moundou; cotton ginning; millet. Until 1946 in Ubangi-Shari colony.

Baiburt, Turkey: see BAYBURT.

Baichunas or **Baychunas** (bīchōōnäs'), oil town (1948 pop. over 2,000), N Guryev oblast, Kazakh SSR, 15 mi. S of Dossor, in Emba oil fields.

Baichurovo or **Baychurovo** (bīchōōrô'vŭ, bīchōō'-rŭvŭ), village (1939 pop. over 500), E Voronezh oblast, Russian SFSR, 25 mi. E of Borisoglebsk; wheat.

Baicoi (bŭēkoi'), Rum. *Băicoi*, town (pop. 6,040), Prahova prov., S central Rumania, in Walachia, on railroad and 10 mi. NW of Ploesti; major petroleum-production center; machine shops. Connected by oil pipe line with Moreni.

Baidarata Bay or **Baydarata Bay** (both: bī"dŭrä'tŭ), Rus. *Baydaratskaya Guba* (bī"dŭrŭtskī'ŭ gōōbä'), inlet of Kara Sea, in NW Siberian Russian SFSR, W of Yamal Peninsula; 115 mi. long, 34 mi. wide. Receives Kara R. (W).

Baidarik River, Baydarik River, or **Baydarag River** (bī'därŭkh), Mongolian *Baydarag Gol* (gōl), W central Mongolian People's Republic, rises on S slopes of Khangai Mts. 125 mi. E of Uliassutai, flows 180 mi. S, the main right arm entering lake Bon Tsagan Nor.

Baidary or **Baydary** (bīdä'rē), village (1939 pop. over 500), S Crimea, Russian SFSR, in Baidar Valley, at W end of Crimean Mts., 15 mi. SE of Sevastopol; tourist excursion center. In a pass (2 mi. S; alt. 1,729 ft.) is Baidar Gate, a stone structure built 1848, offering fine view of S Crimean coast.

Baidkaro (bīd'kŭrō), town (pop. 7,509), Hazaribagh dist., central Bihar, India, SE of Hazaribagh, in Bokaro coal field; rice, rape and mustard, oilseeds, corn, sugar cane.

Baidyabati (bīdyŭbä'tē), town (pop. 25,825), Hooghly dist., S central West Bengal, India, on Hooghly R. and 10 mi. SSW of Hooghly, 15 mi. N of Calcutta city center; rice and jute milling, rope mfg.; trades in rice, jute, potatoes, sugar cane. Rail junction just SE.

Baidyanathdham, India: see DEOGHAR, Santal Parganas dist., Bihar.

Baidzhansai or **Baydzhansay** (bījŭnsī'), town (1945 pop. over 500), E South Kazakhstan oblast, Kazakh SSR, on S slope of the Kara-Tau, 60 mi. NNE of Chimkent.

Baie [Fr.,=bay], for names beginning thus and not found here: see under following part of the name.

Baie, La (lä bā'), or **Baieville** (bā'vĭl), village (pop. 512), S Que., 8 mi. SW of Nicolet; dairying, pig raising.

Baie Comeau (bā kō'mō), town (pop. 1,548), E Que., on the St. Lawrence, at mouth of Manicouagan R., and 55 mi. NNE of Rimouski; pulp and paper milling, lumbering; in mica-mining region. Inc. 1937.

Baie-de-Henne (bā-dŭ-ĕn'), town (1950 census pop. 430), Nord-Ouest dept., NW Haiti, on Gulf of Gonaïves, 36 mi. WNW of Gonaïves, in cotton-growing region.

Baie de Shawinigan, Que.: see BAIE SHAWINIGAN, LA.

Baie du Cap (bā'dü kăp'), village (pop. 902), S Mauritius, port on Indian Ocean, 10 mi. WNW of Souillac; sugar cane.

Baie d'Urfé (bā dürfā'), town (pop. 236), S Que., on SW shore of Montreal Isl., on L. St. Louis, 18 mi. WSW of Montreal; dairying, market gardening; resort.

Baie Lazare (bā' läzär'), village on W coast of Mahé Isl., Seychelles, on the Baie Lazare (inlet of Indian Ocean), 9 mi. S of Victoria; copra, essential oils; fisheries. Also spelled Baie Lazarre.

Baie-Mahault (bā-mä-ō'), town (commune pop. 5,912), NE Basse-Terre, Guadeloupe, 5 mi. NW of Pointe-à-Pitre; sugar, cacao, coffee; distilling.

Baienfurt (bī'ŭnfōōrt), village (pop. 3,064), S Württemberg, Germany, after 1945 in Württemberg-Hohenzollern, 3.5 mi. NNE of Ravensburg; paper milling.

Baiersbronn (bī'ŭrsbrôn), village (pop. 7,268), S Württemberg, Germany, after 1945 in Württemberg-Hohenzollern, in Black Forest, on small Forbach R. near its confluence with the Murg, and 3 mi. NNW of Freudenstadt; lumber milling, woodworking. Summer resort and winter-sports center (alt. 1,916 ft.).

Baiersdorf (bī'ŭrsdôrf), village (pop. 2,202), Middle Franconia, N central Bavaria, Germany, on Ludwig Canal and Regnitz R., and 4 mi. N of Erlangen; hydroelectric station; woodworking, brewing. Hops, horse-radish. Chartered 1353.

Baie Saint Paul (bā' sānt" pôl', Fr. bā sē pôl'), village (pop. 3,500), ⊙ Charlevoix West co., SE central Que., on the St. Lawrence and 55 mi. NE of Quebec, opposite Île aux Coudres; lumbering, dairying; potato, tobacco growing; poultry raising, fox-fur farming. Founded 1681. Iron mined near by.

Baie Shawinigan, La, or **Baie de Shawinigan** (lä bā' dŭ shŭwĭ'nĭgŭn), village (pop. 1,255), S Que., on St. Maurice R., N suburb of Shawinigan Falls.

Baie Verte (bā vûrt', vârt'), inlet (15 mi. long, 18 mi. wide at mouth) of Northumberland Strait, bet. SE N.B. and N N.S., extending W from Cape Tormentine. At its head is Port Elgin. Smelt and lobster fisheries.

Baieville, Que.: see BAIE, LA.

Baignes-Sainte-Radegonde (bĕ'nyŭ-sĕt-rädgōd'), village (pop. 534), Charente dept., W France, 7 mi. SSW of Barbezieux; casein mfg., tanning.

Baigneux-les-Juifs (bĕnyû'-lā-zhwēf'), village (pop. 350), Côte-d'Or dept., E central France, near the Seine, 15 mi. E of Montbard; cattle.

Baihan, Aden: see BEIHAN.

Baihar (bī'hŭr), village, Balaghat dist., central Madhya Pradesh, India, 31 mi. NE of Balaghat, in E Satpura Range, in dense sal-forest area; cattle raising. Bauxite and mica workings near by.

Baiima (bīē'mä), town (pop. 1,089), South-Eastern Prov., E Sierra Leone, near Moa R., on railroad and 6 mi. NE of Daru; palm oil and kernels, cacao, coffee.

Baijnath (bĭj'nät), village, Almora dist., N Uttar Pradesh, India, 21 mi. NNW of Almora; rice, wheat. Anc. Kali temple; inscriptions date from A.D. 1202. Was ⊙ anc. Hindu kingdom. Tea plantations near by. Pilgrimage center 11 mi. SE, at Bageswar village; has 15th-cent. temple and tombs.

Baikadam or **Baykadam** (bīkŭdäm'), village (1939 pop. over 500), W Dzhambul oblast, Kazakh SSR, on edge of Muyun-Kum (desert), 90 mi. NW of Dzhambul; sheep.

Baikaim or **Baykaim** (bīkēm'), S suburb of Leninsk-Kuznetski, W Kemerovo oblast, Russian SFSR, in Kuznetsk Basin; coal mines.

Baikal or **Baykal** (bīkäl'), town (1948 pop. over 500), S Irkutsk oblast, Russian SFSR, on L. Baikal, at efflux of Angara R., on Trans-Siberian RR and 2 mi. SE of Irkutsk.

Baikal, Lake, or **Lake Baykal,** largest fresh-water lake (□ 12,150) of Eurasia and the world's deepest (5,712 ft. in central section), in SE Siberia Russian SFSR; forms border bet. Irkutsk oblast and Buryat-Mongol Autonomous SSR. The lake is 395 mi. long (NE-SW), up to 49 mi. wide; average alt. 1,486 ft. Occupies graben-type depression, bordered by Baikal (W), Barguzin (E), and Khamar-Daban(S) ranges. Its 336 affluents include Selenga, Barguzin, and Upper Angara rivers; its only outlet is Angara R. Largest of its 27 isls. is Olkhon Isl. (fish processing). Lake has moderating effect on local climate. Water, well aerated and transparent to depth of 132 ft., freezes Jan.-April. Lake is habitat of varied and unusual marine fauna and flora (75% of forms are endemic), including Baikal seal, viviparous deep-sea fish *golomyanka, omul* of the salmon family (chief food fish), and numerous types of mollusks. Trans-Siberian RR skirts (since 1905) rocky S shore. Steamer services link main ports of Listvyanka, Babushkin, Ust-Barguzin, and Nizhne-Angarsk. Region bet. L. Baikal and upper Amur R. is known as TRANSBAIKALIA.

Baikal-Amur Railroad (-ämōōr'), Rus. *Baikal-Amur Magistral,* abbr. *BAM,* projected railroad in E Siberia, Russian SFSR, branching from Trans-Siberian RR at Taishet and aligned N of L. Baikal with Komsomolsk on Amur R. Construction, begun in late 1930s, was interrupted in Second World War.

Baikalovo or **Baykalovo** (bīkä'lŭvŭ). **1** Village (1926 pop. 2,105), SE Sverdlovsk oblast, Russian SFSR, 33 mi. SE of Irbit; dairying; wheat. **2** Village (1926 pop. 560), S Tyumen oblast, Russian SFSR, near Tobol R., 35 mi. SSW of Tobolsk, in agr. area (grain, livestock).

Baikal Range or **Baykal Range** (bīkäl'), E Irkutsk oblast, Russian SFSR, on W shore of L. Baikal; rises to 5,800 ft. near source of Lena R. Divides Lena R. and L. Baikal basins. The Littoral Range, Rus. *Primorskiy Khrebet,* is contiguous (S); ranges are sometimes considered as one and are then called either Baikal or Littoral.

Bai-Khak or **Bay-Khak** (bī-khäk'), agr. village (1948 pop. over 500), E Tuva Autonomous Oblast, Russian SFSR, on road and 35 mi. S of Kyzyl.

Baikibashevo or **Baykibashevo** (bīkēbä'shĭvŭ), village (1926 pop. 2,088), N Bashkir Autonomous SSR, Russian SFSR, near Ufa R., 80 mi. NNE of Ufa; rye, oats, livestock.

Baikit or **Baykit** (bīkēt'), village, S Evenki Natl. Okrug, Krasnoyarsk Territory, Russian SFSR, on Stony Tunguska R., at mouth of Chunya R., and 195 mi. SW of Tura; Evenki trading and cultural center.

Baikonur or **Baykonur** (bīkŭnōōr'), town (1942 pop. over 500), W Karaganda oblast, Kazakh SSR, 30 mi. W of Karsakpai (linked by railroad); coal mining.

Baikovo or **Baykovo** (bīkô'vŭ), main village on Shumshu Isl., N main Kurile Isls. group, Russian SFSR, port on SW shore, opposite Severo-Kurilsk (across Second Kurile Strait); fish cannery; ship-repair yard, naval installations, airfield. Under Jap. rule (until 1945), called Kataoka (kätä'ō'kä).

Baikunthpur (bī'kōōntpōōr), village, Surguja dist., E Madhya Pradesh, India, 40 mi. WNW of Ambikapur. Was ⊙ former princely state of Korea, one of Chhattisgarh States; state ⊙ moved here, c.1930, from village of Sonhat, 15 mi. N. Lac growing in surrounding dense sal forests (bamboo, khair).

Bailadores (bīlädō'rĕs), town (pop. 434), Mérida state, W Venezuela, in Andean spur, on Pan-American Highway and 55 mi. SW of Mérida; alt. 5,689 ft.; coffeegrowing.

Bailan Pass, Turkey: see BELEN.

Baildon, urban district (1931 pop. 7,792; 1951 census 10,132), West Riding, W central Yorkshire, England, 5 mi. N of Bradford; woolen milling, mfg. of chemicals.

Baile Átha Cliath, Ireland: see DUBLIN, city.

Baile-Bugaz, Ukrainian SSR: see BUGAZ.

Baile-Episcopiei, Rumania: see ORADEA.

Baile-Felix, Rumania: see ORADEA.

Baile-Govora, Rumania: see GOVORA.

Baile-Herculane (bû'ēlā-hĕrkōōlä'nā), Rum. *Băile-Herculane,* Hung. *Herkulesfürdö* (hĕr'kōōlĕsh-für"-dû), Ger. *Herkulesbad* (hĕr'kōōlĕsbät"), village (pop. 442), Gorj prov., W Rumania, in S foothills of the Transylvanian Alps, on railroad and 60 mi. SE of Lugoj; noted health resort with sulphurous and saline thermal springs. Has military sanatorium, archaeological mus. Known as spa since Roman times. Destroyed during First World War and entirely rebuilt in 1919.

Baile-Moneasa, Rumania: see SEBIS.

Bailén (bīlĕn'), city (pop. 9,727), Jaén prov., S Spain, in Andalusia, 23 mi. N of Jaén; pottery and soap mfg., olive-oil processing, sawmilling, fruit canning. Mineral springs. Copper mine near by. Reservoir, dam, and small hydroelectric plant 5 mi. NW. Celebrated victory, won (1808) here in the Peninsular War by the Spaniards under Castaños, resulted in the surrender of 17,000 Fr. troops under Dupont. Sometimes Baylen, in English.

Baile-Slanic (bû'ēlā-slŭnēk'), Rum. *Băile-Slănic,* town (1948 pop. 2,157), Bacau prov., E central Rumania, on E slopes of the Moldavian Carpathians, 11 mi. W of Targu-Ocna; popular health resort (alt. 1,772 ft.) with mineral springs. Stone quarrying. Also called Slanic-Moldova.

Bailesti (bûēlĕsht'), Rum. *Băileşti,* town (1948 pop. 15,289), Dolj prov., S Rumania, in Walachia, on railroad and 30 mi. SW of Craiova; trading center (grain, livestock); flour milling, tanning, edible-oil processing.

Bailey, Ireland: see HOWTH, HILL OF.

Bailey (bā'lē), county (□ 832; pop. 7,592), NW Texas; ⊙ Muleshoe. On the Llano Estacado and bounded W by N.Mex. line; alt. 3,700–4,100 ft. Crossed by intermittent Double Mtn. Fork of Brazos R. Diversified agr. (grain sorghum, cotton, wheat, alfalfa, corn, potatoes, truck, dairy products, poultry); beef cattle, hogs. Has several lakes and a migratory waterfowl refuge. Formed 1876.

Bailey. 1 or **Baileys,** town (pop. 743), Nash co., E central N.C., 11 mi. WNW of Wilson; lumber milling. **2** Town (pop. 198), Fannin co., NE Texas, 10 mi. S of Bonham, in agr. area.

Bailey Island, Maine: see HARPSWELL.

Bailey Islands, Jap. *Haha-jima-retto,* southernmost group of Bonin Isls., W Pacific, 30 mi. E of Chichi-jima; 26°37'N 142°10'E; 11-mi. chain of volcanic isls. HAHA-JIMA is largest and Plymouth Isl. (Muko-shima) 2d largest (□ .5). Formerly Coffin Isls.

Baileys Harbor, village (pop. c.300), Door co., NE Wis., on Door Peninsula, on small inlet of L. Michigan, 20 mi. NE of Sturgeon Bay, in resort and fishing area. A coast guard station is here. Kangaroo L. (c.3 mi. long) is near by.

Bailey's Town, town (pop. 421), NW Bahama Isls., on spit of North Bimini isl., just N of Alice Town, 55 mi. E of Miami, Fla., and 130 mi. WNW of Nassau. Resort; fishing. Just N is the Lerner Marine Laboratory (under auspices of Amer. Mus. of Natural History).

Baileyton, town (pop. 224), Greene co., NE Tenn., 11 mi. N of Greeneville.

Baileyville, town (pop. 1,821), Washington co., E Maine, on St. Croix R. just above Calais. Includes Woodland, paper-milling village. Inc. 1828.

Bailhongal or **Bail Hongal** (bīl' hŏng'gŭl), town (pop. 10,913), Belgaum dist., S Bombay, India, 23 mi. E of Belgaum; market center for cotton, millet, peanuts, wheat, rice; cotton ginning, handicraft cloth weaving. Annual fair. Also called Hongal.

Bailieborough (bā'lēbŭrŭ), Gaelic *Cill Chathlaigh,* town (pop. 783), E Co. Cavan, Ireland, 16 mi. ESE of Cavan; agr. market (cattle, pigs; potatoes); mfg. of agr. implements.

Bailique (bīlē'kĭ), island and town in northernmost channel of the Amazon delta, Amapá territory, N Brazil, 100 mi. NE of Macapá; 1°N 50°W. Lighthouse.

Bailleul (bäyûl'), town (pop. 6,392), Nord dept., N France, near Belg. border, 16 mi. WNW of Lille; cotton and linen cloth mfg., lacemaking, dairying. Destroyed (1918) in First World War, it was rebuilt in traditional Flemish style, and damaged once more in Second World War.

Baillie, trading post, N Mackenzie Dist., Northwest Territories, on Beaufort Sea of the Arctic Ocean; 70°32'N 128°25'W; radio station. Just N is Cape Bathurst, northernmost point of Canadian mainland; 4 mi. WNW are the 2 Baillie Isls., larger of which is 10 mi. long, 2–7 mi. wide.

Baillie Hamilton Island (17 mi. long, 7–11 mi. wide), N central Franklin Dist., Northwest Territories, at N end of Wellington Channel, bet. Cornwallis Isl. (S), Devon Isl. (E and N), and Bathurst Isl. (W); 75°50'N 94°45'W.

Baillieston, town in Old Monkland parish, N Lanark, Scotland, 7 mi. E of Glasgow; coal mining.

Baillif (bäyēf'), town (commune pop. 3,828), SW Basse-Terre, Guadeloupe, 2½ mi. NNW of Basse-Terre; vanilla. Sometimes called Le Baillif.

Bailovo (bīē'lŭvŭ), suburb in Greater Baku, Azerbaijan SSR, on SW Apsheron Peninsula, 2 mi. S of Baku, on Caspian Sea; oil wells (developed in 19th cent.). Naval base of Baku. Offshore are submerged ruins of Arab fortress of Salkhim, inundated by 13th-cent. earthquake.

Bailundo, Angola: see VILA TEIXEIRA DA SILVA.

Baily, Ireland: see HOWTH, HILL OF.

Baimaclia, Moldavian SSR: see BAIMAKLIYA.

Baimak or **Baymak** (bīmäk'), city (1939 pop. over 10,000), SE Bashkir Autonomous SSR, Russian SFSR, on E slope of the S Urals, at headwaters of Tanalyk R., 95 mi. S of Beloretsk; copper-mining and -smelting center. Until 1944, Baimak-Tanalykovo.

Baimakliya or **Baymakliya** (bīmäk'lyēŭ), Rum. *Baimaclia* (bīmäk'lyä), village (1941 pop. 2,020), S Moldavian SSR, 22 mi. NNE of Kagul; corn, barley; sheep raising.

Baimok, Yugoslavia: see BAJMOK.

Bainbridge. 1 City (pop. 7,562), ⊙ Decatur co., SW Ga., 34 mi. W of Thomasville and on Flint R.; trade and industrial center for farm and timber area; mfg. (clothing, lumber, boxes, naval stores, paper, bottle-washing machinery); peanut shelling. Founded 1823, inc. 1829. **2** Town (pop. 455), Putnam co., W central Ind., 35 mi. W of Indianapolis, in agr. area. **3** Village, Md.: see PORT DEPOSIT. **4** Village (pop. 1,505), Chenango co., S central N.Y., on the Susquehanna and 25 mi. NE of Binghamton, in dairying and farming area; dairy products, milk plastics, feed, wood products. Settled before 1790, inc. 1829. **5** Village (pop. 964), Ross co., S Ohio, 17 mi. WSW of Chillicothe and on Paint Creek; trade center for farm area. Seip Mound State Park is near by. **6** Village (1940 pop. 585), Lancaster co., SE Pa., on Susquehanna R. and 16 mi. SE of Harrisburg.

Bainbridge, Port, inlet (15 mi. long, 3 mi. wide) of Gulf of Alaska on SE Kenai Peninsula, S Alaska, 35 mi. E of Seward; 60°4'N 148°21'W.

Bainbridge Island (15 mi. long, 1–6 mi. wide), S Alaska, in Gulf of Alaska, E of Kenai Peninsula, from which it is separated by Port Bainbridge, 40 mi. E of Seward; 60°5'N 148°10'W; rises to 2,351 ft.

Bainbridge Island, NW Wash., in Puget Sound, W of Seattle; 11 mi. long. Residential and resort isl., with game preserve, farms; berries, hothouse flowers. Includes villages of Port Madison, Winslow, and Port Blakeley.

Bain-de-Bretagne (bē-dû-brŭtä'nyû), village (pop. 1,746), Ille-et-Vilaine dept., W France, 19 mi. S of Rennes; iron mining, cider making.

Baindir, Turkey: see BAYINDIR.

Bainet (bänā'), town (1950 census pop. 956), Ouest dept., S Haiti, on the coast, 14 mi. W of Jacmel, in cotton- and fruitgrowing region. Just S is Cape Bainet.

Bain Khongor, Mongolia: see BAYAN KHONGOR.

Bainoa (bīnō'ä), town (pop. 580), Havana prov., W Cuba, on railroad and 28 mi. ESE of Havana; sugar cane, cattle.

Bains-les-Bains (bē'-lā-bē'), village (pop. 1,106), Vosges dept., E France, near the Canal de l'Est, 15 mi. SW of Épinal; resort known for its thermal springs. Nail and wire mfg., kirsch distilling.

Bain Tumen, Mongolia: see CHOIBALSAN, city.

Bain Ulegei, Mongolia: see BAYAN ULEGEI.

Bainville (bān'vĭl), town (pop. 356), Roosevelt co., NE Mont., near Missouri R. and N.Dak. line, 45 mi. E of Poplar; livestock, grain, lignite. Near by is site of Fort Union, former army post and fur-trading point.

Baiocasses, France: see BAYEUX.

Bairak, Ukrainian SSR: see KALININSK, Stalino oblast.

Bairam-Ali or **Bayram-Ali** (bīräm"-ŭlyē'), city (1939 pop. over 10,000), central Mary oblast, Turkmen SSR, on Murgab oasis, on Trans-Caspian RR and 18 mi. E of Mary; cotton-ginning center; cotton-seed-oil extraction. Has climatic sanatorium. On site of anc. Merv (see MARY, city).

Bairat (bī'rät), town (pop. 5,135), E Rajasthan, India, 42 mi. NNE of Jaipur; millet, barley. An anc. site, with Asokan rock inscription (NE) and ruins of circular Buddhist temple (3d cent. B.C.). Visited A.D. 634 by Hsüan-tsang; sacked by Mahmud of Ghazni in early 11th cent. Sometimes spelled Bairath.

Baird (bârd), city (pop. 1,821), ⊙ Callahan co., central Texas, 20 mi. E of Abilene; processing, trade, shipping point in grain, cotton, fruit, oil area; oil refining, flour milling, cotton ginning. Settled 1880, inc. 1891.

Baird, Cape, NE Ellesmere Isl., NE Franklin Dist., Northwest Territories, on Hall Basin, on S side of entrance of Lady Franklin Bay; 81°32'N 64°30'W; NE extremity of Judge Daly promontory.

Baird Glacier (bârd), in Coast Range of SE Alaska and NW B.C.; 57°8'N 132°46'W. Drains into Frederick Sound 17 mi. N of Petersburg.

Baird Inlet (70 mi. long, 1–18 mi. wide), W Alaska, bet. mouths of Yukon and Kuskokwim rivers E of Nelson Isl.; 60°53'N 163°42'W. Surrounding region largely uncharted.

Baird Mountains, NW Alaska, bet. Kotzebue Sound and Kobuk R. (S) and Noatak R. (N and W); extend c.120 mi. E–W; 158°–162°25'W 67°35'N. Rise to 5,100 ft.

Bairdstown, village (pop. 188), Wood co., NW Ohio, 9 mi. NNE of Findlay.

Baire (bī'rā), town (pop. 2,181), Oriente prov., E Cuba, on Central Highway, on railroad and 40 mi. WNW of Santiago de Cuba, in fruit- and sugar-growing region. Scene (Feb. 24, 1895) of opening battle of Cuban war of independence.

Baireuth, Germany: see BAYREUTH.

Bairia (bĭr'yŭ), town (pop. 8,971), Ballia dist., E Uttar Pradesh, India, 20 mi. E of Ballia; cotton-cloth weaving, shoe mfg.; trades in rice, gram, barley, oilseeds, sugar cane.

Bairnsdale (bârnz'dāl), town (pop. 4,604), SE Victoria, Australia, on Mitchell R. and 145 mi. E of Melbourne; agr. center (fruit, corn, potatoes); vegetable-dehydration plant.

Bairoil, village (pop. c.300), Sweetwater co., S central Wyo., 36 mi. NNW of Rawlins; alt. 6,860 ft. Gas-producing areas near by.

Bais (bĕ), village (pop. 586), Mayenne dept., W France, 12 mi. ESE of Mayenne; flour milling.
Bais (bä'ēs), town (1939 pop. 3,148; 1948 municipality pop. 17,869), Negros Oriental prov., E Negros Isl., Philippines, on Tañon Strait, 7 mi. NNW of Tanjay; agr. center (corn, sugar cane). Sugar mill, distillery, paper mill. Exports sugar.
Baisan, Israel: see BEISAN.
Baïse River (bäēz'), in Hautes-Pyrénées, Gers, and Lot-et-Garonne depts., SW France, rises in Lannemezan Plateau, flows 118 mi. N, past Mirande, Condom, and Nérac, to the Garonne 5 mi. NW of Port-Sainte-Marie. Intermittently navigable from Condom. Receives Gélise R. (left).
Baisieux (bāzyû'), town (pop. 2,533), Nord dept., N France, near Belg. border, 9 mi. E of Lille; customhouse on Lille-Tournai road; mfg. (linen and cotton fabrics, linoleum, malt).
Baisun or **Baysun** (bīsōōn'), village (1926 pop. 3,255), W Surkhan-Darya oblast, Uzbek SSR, on E slope of the Baisun-Tau, 70 mi. N of Termez; cotton milling. Coal and iron deposits near by.
Baisun-Tau or **Baysun-Tau** (-tou'), range in SE Uzbek SSR; forms SW continuation of Gissar Range, along border of Kashka-Darya and Surkhan-Darya oblasts; rises to 10,500 ft.
Baiswan, India: see BESWAN.
Bai-Syut or **Bay-Syut** (bī-syōōt'), town (1945 pop. over 500), central Tuva Autonomous Oblast, Russian SFSR, on the Lesser Yenisei and 38 mi. E of Kyzyl.
Baita (bû'ētä), Rum. *Băita*, Hung. *Láposbánya* (lä'pōsh-bä"nyŏ), village (pop. 2,148), Baia-Mare prov., NW Rumania, 5 mi. NW of Baia-Mare; mining center (pyrites, gold, silver, lead, zinc). In Hungary, 1940–45.
Baitadi (bī'tŭdē), town, W Nepal, near Kali (Sarda) R. (India border), 13 mi. E of Pithoragarh (India); wheat, rice, barley, vegetables, fruit. Nepalese military station.
Baitak Bogdo, Baitik Bogdo, or **Baydag Bogdo** (all: bī'tŭkh bŏg'dō), Chinese *Peita Shan* (bā'dä' shän'), mountain range on China-Mongolia border; 45°15'N 91°E; rises to 10,456 ft. Scene of frontier incident (1947).
Bait al Falaj, Beit el Felej, or **Bayt al-Falaj** (all: bāt' ĕl fĕlĕj'), village, N Oman, 4 mi. SW of Muscat, on Hajar slope; site of Muscat airfield. Summer residences.
Bait al Faqih or **Bayt al-Faqih** (bāt' ăl fäkē'), town (pop. 12,000), Hodeida prov., W Yemen, 30 mi. SE of Hodeida, on Tihama coastal plain; trading center for coffee and cotton; cotton weaving, indigo dyeing, tanning, and sandal mfg. A well-built town, dominated by fortresslike citadel. Sometimes spelled Beit el Faqih and Beyt el Fekih.
Baitarani River (bī'tŭrŭnē), NE Orissa, India, rises in hills SW of Keonjhargarh, flows N to Bihar border, SSE past Jajpur, and E forming 12-mi.-long joint outlet with Brahmani R., to Bay of Bengal at Palmyras Point; total length, c.250 mi. Associated with legend of Rama in Hindu mythology.
Baithuong or **Baituong** (both: bī'tŭng'), town, Thanhhoa prov., N central Vietnam, on the Song Chu and 25 mi. WNW of Thanhhoa; irrigation canal and dam.
Baitik Bogdo, Mongolia: see BAITAK BOGDO.
Baiut (bû'yōōts), Rum. *Băiuţ*, Hung. *Erzsebétbánya* (ĕr'zhăbĕt-bä"nyŏ), village (pop. 1,366), Baia-Mare prov., N Rumania, 37 mi. N of Dej; gold, silver, copper, lead mining. In Hungary, 1940–45.
Baix (bā, bāks), village (pop. 373), Ardèche dept., S France, on Rhone R. and 8 mi. E of Privas; fruit preserving.
Baixada Fluminense (bīshä'dŭ flōōmēnĕn'sĭ), marshy coastal lowland (□ c.6,500) of Rio de Janeiro state, Brazil, at foot of great escarpment (Serra do Mar). Extends from Sepetiba Bay (SW) to Paraíba R. delta (NE), and includes areas surrounding Guanabara Bay and Cabo Frio. In 1935, the federal govt. began a large-scale reclamation project of the poorly drained, disease-breeding region. Intensive agr. and truck gardening have started in vicinity of Rio de Janeiro, fostered by new natl. agr. institute established NW of the capital.
Baixas (bāksäs'), village (pop. 1,756), Pyrénées-Orientales dept., S France, 5 mi. NW of Perpignan; canning, leather-working, winegrowing. Lime kilns and marble quarries near by.
Baixau (bī'sou'), village, Soctrang prov., S Vietnam, near Bassac arm of Mekong delta, 4 mi. SE of Soctrang; rice milling, distilling.
Baixa Verde (bī'shŭ vĕr'dĭ), city (pop. 2,274), E Rio Grande do Norte, NE Brazil, on railroad and 50 mi. WNW of Natal; cotton, manioc, cereals.
Baixio (bīsh'yōō), city (pop. 631), SE Ceará, Brazil, on Cedro-Patos RR, near Paraíba border, and 40 mi. SE of Iguatu; cattle, carnauba.
Baixo Alentejo (bī'shōō ălĕntā'zhōō), province (□ 5,318; 1940 pop. 355,771), S Portugal, formed 1936 from old Alentejo prov. and from S portion of old Estremadura prov.; ⊙ Beja. It contains Beja dist. and S part of Setúbal dist.
Baixo Guandu (gwăndōō'), city (pop. 1,703), central Espírito Santo, Brazil, near Minas Gerais border, on the Rio Doce, on railroad and 70 mi. NW of Vitória; gem cutting, pottery mfg., coffee hulling.
Baixo Mearim, Brazil: see VITÓRIA DO MEARIM.
Baja (bŏ'yŏ), city (□ 77; pop. 32,309), ⊙ but independent of Bacs-Bodrog co., S Hungary, on the Danube (railroad bridge) and 90 mi. S of Budapest; rail center, river port. Mfg. of chemicals, furniture, machines, textiles (hemp, flax, wool); distilleries, flour mills, brickworks. Market center for agr. (wheat, corn, onions), livestock (cattle, hogs).
Bajabonico, Dominican Republic: see IMBERT.
Baja California, Mexico: see LOWER CALIFORNIA.
Bajada del Paraná, Argentina: see BAJADA GRANDE.
Bajada de Santa Fe, Argentina: see PARANÁ, city.
Bajada Grande (bähä'dä grän'dā), village (pop. estimate 500), W Entre Ríos prov., Argentina, port on Paraná R., on railroad and 2 mi. NW of Paraná. Mfg., fishing, and trading center; lime, cement, and ceramic factories. Serves as port for Paraná. Formerly called Bajada del Paraná.
Bajakeui, Bulgaria: see DOLNO YEZEROVO.
Bajana (bäjä'nä), village, Western Div., Gambia, on a creek leading into Gambia R. near Brefet, c.20 mi. SE of Bathurst. It is part of Gambia colony, but is administered under the protectorate.
Bajana (bŭjä'nŭ), town, NE Saurashtra, India, 22 mi. ENE of Dhrangadhra; markets cotton, salt, millet. Was ⊙ former Eastern Kathiawar state of Bajana (□ 183; pop. 13,996) of Western India States agency; merged 1948 with Saurashtra.
Baja Point (bä'hä), on Pacific Ocean, in Lima dept., W central Peru, 7 mi. SSW of Huacho; 11°18'S 77°39'W.
Bajaur (bä'jour), region of NW North-West Frontier Prov. (W Pakistan) and E Afghanistan, bet. Kunar R. (W) and Panjkora R. (E); surrounded by S offshoots of the Hindu Kush. Wheat, barley, corn cultivated; iron deposits. Inhabited by Pathan tribes. Sometimes spelled Bajour.
Baja Verapaz (bä'hä väräpäs'), department (□ 1,206; 1950 pop. 65,434), central Guatemala; ⊙ Salamá. In N highlands; bounded by upper Motagua R. (S), Chixoy R. (NW); crossed E-W by Sierra de Chuacús. Agr. (corn, beans, coffee, sugar cane, fruit, vineyards); livestock. Gold and mica mining near Motagua R. Main cities: Salamá, Rabinal.
Baj-Baj, India: see BUDGE-BUDGE.
Bajé, Brazil: see BAGÉ.
Bajgiran (bäj"gērän'), village, Ninth Prov., in Khurasan, NE Iran, 35 mi. NNW of Quchan, on highway to Ashkhabad and on USSR border, opposite Gaudan; customhouse.
Bajil (bä'jĭl), town (pop. 3,000), Hodeida prov., W Yemen, on Tihama coastal plain, 25 mi. ENE of Hodeida; market place on main road to Sana. Sometimes Badjil.
Bajina Basta or **Bayina Bashta** (both: bä'yēnä bä'shtä), Serbo-Croatian *Bajina Bašta*, village (pop. 3,595), W Serbia, Yugoslavia, 16 mi. NW of Titovo Uzice, near Drina R. (Bosnia border). Tobacco growing in vicinity.
Bajitpur (bä'jĭtpōōr), town (pop. 14,394), Mymensingh dist., E East Bengal, E Pakistan, near Meghna R., 45 mi. SSE of Mymensingh; handloom cotton-weaving center; rice, jute, oilseeds. Formerly noted for hand-woven muslins.
Bajmok, Baimok, or **Baymok** (all: bī'môk), village, Vojvodina, N Serbia, Yugoslavia, on railroad and 14 mi. SW (suburb) of Subotica, in the Backa.
Bajna (bäj'nŭ), village, W Madhya Bharat, India, 26 mi. W of Ratlam; grain; hand-loom weaving.
Bajna (boi'nŏ), town (pop. 2,007), Komarom-Esztergom co., N Hungary, 12 mi. SW of Esztergom. Metternich castle here.
Bajo Amazonas, province, Peru: see IQUITOS.
Bajo Boquete, Panama: see BOQUETE.
Bajo Nuevo, reef, Colombia: see SAN ANDRÉS Y PROVIDENCIA.
Bajos, Los, Chile: see LOS BAJOS.
Bajour, W Pakistan and Afghanistan: see BAJAUR.
Bajranggarh (bŭj'rŭng-gŭr), town (pop. 2,395), N Madhya Bharat, India, 4 mi. SSW of Guna; millet, gram, oilseeds.
Bajur, Al-, Egypt: see BAGUR, EL.
Bajuriyah Canal, Egypt: see BAGURIYA CANAL.
Bakal (bŭkäl'), city (1939 pop. over 10,000), W Chelyabinsk oblast, Russian SFSR, in the S Urals, 10 mi. SW of Satka, on rail spur; iron-mining center. Siderite and limonite deposits (exploited since 1817) used for quality steel production, supply metallurgical plants of Asha, Kasli, Katav-Ivanovsk, and Chelyabinsk. Until 1928, Bakalski Zavod.
Bakala (bäkälä'), village, central Ubangi-Shari, Fr. Equatorial Africa, 50 mi. NW of Bambari; center of trade in cotton region.
Bakaly (bŭkä'lē), village (1926 pop. 2,392), W Bashkir Autonomous SSR, Russian SFSR, on left tributary of Belaya R. and 90 mi. WNW of Ufa; wheat, rye, oats, livestock.
Bakan, Japan: see SHIMONOSEKI, city.
Bakanas (bŭkŭnäs'), village (1939 pop. over 500), NE Alma-Ata oblast, Kazakh SSR, in the Sary-Ishik-Otrau (desert), on Ili R. (head of downstream navigation) and 115 mi. NNW of Alma-Ata; sheep.
Bakaner (bäkä'när), village, SW Madhya Bharat, India, 30 mi. SSW of Dhar; cotton ginning.
Bakar (bä'kär), Ital. *Buccari* (bōōk-kä'rē), village, NW Croatia, Yugoslavia, port on Adriatic Sea, 5 mi. E of Rijeka (Fiume), on steep mtn. slopes and on well-sheltered, oval-shaped Bay of Bakar (3 mi. long; connected with sea by narrow channel). Rail branch terminus; summer resort; cement mfg., fishing. Exports lumber, cattle. Has naval acad., mus. One of oldest Croatian towns; has parts of its anc. walls, 11th-12th-cent. houses with Latin and Glagolitic inscriptions, church with Romanesque belfry, and ruined castle.
Bakarganj or **Backergunge** (bä'kŭrgŭnj), district (□ 3,783; 1951 pop. 3,647,000), East Bengal, E Pakistan, in Ganges Delta; ⊙ Barisal. Bounded E by Meghna R. and its Shahbazpur R. delta arm, W by Madhumati R.; drained by river arms of Ganges Delta; E section of the Sundarbans in S (extensive jungle; habitat of Bengal tigers). Alluvial soil; rice, oilseeds, jute, sugar cane, gram, tobacco, betel nuts and leaves; bamboo, sundari, areca and coconut palms. Extensive swamps (N). Rice and oilseed milling at Barisal, Jhalakati, and Nalchiti, mfg. of bricks, soap, and ice at Barisal, match mfg. at Patuakhali. Raided continually by Arakanese in 17th and 18th cent.; ceded to English by Moguls in 1765. Part of former Br. Bengal prov. until inc. 1947 into new Pakistan prov. of East Bengal, following creation of Pakistan.
Bakau (bäkou'), town (pop. 2,521), Gambia colony, in Kombo St. Mary dist., on Atlantic Ocean, on left bank of Gambia R. estuary at Cape St. Mary, 7 mi. WNW of Bathurst (linked by road); tomatoes, truck. Police post.
Bakchar (bŭkchär'), village, central Tomsk oblast, Russian SFSR, on Chaya R. (head of navigation), at mouths of Bakchar and Parbig rivers, and 55 mi. SSW of Kolpashevo. Formerly Selivanovo.
Bakchar River, Russian SFSR: see CHAYA RIVER.
Bakebe (bäkä'bā), village (pop. 285), S Br. Cameroons, administered as part of Eastern Provinces of Nigeria, 16 mi. SE of Mamfe; cacao, bananas, palm oil and kernels.
Bakel (bäkĕl'), town (pop. c.2,400), E Senegal, Fr. West Africa, landing on left bank of the Senegal (Mauritania border), and 320 mi. E of Dakar; gum, millet, corn, livestock.
Baker. 1 County (□ 585; pop. 6,313), N Fla., on Ga. line (N, E); ⊙ Macclenny. Largely a flatwoods area; W part included in Okefenokee Swamp and Osceola Natl. Forest. Agr. (corn, vegetables, peanuts, cotton) and forestry (lumber, naval stores). Formed 1861. **2** County (□ 355; pop. 5,952), SW Ga.: ⊙ Newton. Bounded SE by Flint R.; drained by Ichawaynochaway Creek. Coastal plain agr. (corn, peanuts, sugar cane, pecans), livestock, and lumber area. Formed 1825. **3** County (□ 3,084; pop. 16,175), NE Oregon; ⊙ Baker. Bounded E by Snake R. and Idaho; drained by Powder R. Lumber, wheat; gold, silver, copper. Blue Mts. are in W, Wallowa Mts. in N. Formed 1862.
Baker. 1 Village (pop. 762), East Baton Rouge parish, SE central La., 10 mi. N of Baton Rouge. **2** City (pop. 1,772), ⊙ Fallon co., E Mont., near N.Dak. line, 75 mi. E of Miles City; farm trading point in large gas field; gas wells; livestock, grain. Settled as Lorraine, renamed Baker 1908, inc. 1914. **3** Village, White Pine co., E Nev., near Utah line, c.45 mi. ESE of Ely. Hq. for Lehman Caves Natl. Monument (5 mi. W). **4** City (pop. 9,471), ⊙ Baker co., NE Oregon, on Powder R., near Elkhorn Ridge, and c.80 mi. SE of Pendleton; alt. 3,449 ft.; trade and shipping center for agr., stock-raising, lumbering, and mining area; hq. Whitman Natl. Forest; lumber, flour, dairy products. Gold, silver, copper mines near by. Laid out 1865 after discovery of gold (1861–62) in area, inc. 1874.
Baker, Fort, Calif.: see SAUSALITO.
Baker, Mount (10,750 ft.), N Wash., in Cascade Range, 30 mi. E of Bellingham, in Mt. Baker Natl. Forest.
Baker Island (□ 1), central Pacific, 40 mi. S of Howland Isl., U.S. naval base, near equator, on air route to Australia; 0°13'N 176°31'W; coral, arid. Claimed 1857 by U.S.; later worked for guano by both U.S. and Great Britain; colonized by Americans from Hawaii 1935; placed under Dept. of Interior 1936. In Second World War, captured by Japanese 1942, regained by U.S. 1944. Formerly worked for guano along with Jarvis and Howland isls.
Baker Island, Maine: see CRANBERRY ISLES.
Baker Lake, trading post (district native pop. 266), central Keewatin Dist., Northwest Territories, at NW end of Baker L., at mouth of Thelon R.; 64°19'N 96°5'W; airfield, govt. radio, meteorological, and scientific-research stations; Royal Canadian Mounted Police post. Site of Anglican and R.C. missions.
Baker Lake (□ c.1,000), central Keewatin Dist., Northwest Territories, at head of Chesterfield Inlet; 64°10'N 95°20'W; 70 mi. long, 7–18 mi. wide. Receives Thelon R. and Kazan R.
Baker Lake, NW Wash., in the Cascades just SE of Mt. Baker; c.1 mi. in diameter. Fish hatchery, campgrounds.
Baker River, Aysén prov., S Chile, rises in L. Bertrand, a SW arm of L. Buenos Aires, flows c.100 mi. SW through Patagonian Andes to fjord-like Baker Channel, which skirts Merino Jarpa Isl. and empties into Gulf of Peñas; total length, 275 mi. Navigable for c.45 mi. upstream.

Baker River, NW Wash., rises in Mt. Baker Natl. Forest; flows c.28 mi. generally SW to Shannon Dam (completed 1925; 263 ft. high, 493 ft. long), forming L. Shannon (7 mi. long), thence 2 mi. S to Skagit R. at Concrete.

Bakersfield. 1 City (pop. 34,784), ⊙ Kern co., S central Calif., on Kern R., at S end of San Joaquin Valley, and c.100 mi. NNW of Los Angeles; commercial and industrial center of important oil and natural-gas fields; oil refining, pipeline and rail shipping, mfg. of oil tools; railroad shops. Packs, processes, and ships produce from wide region (cattle, citrus and deciduous fruit, cotton, grain, truck). Mfg. of paint, chemicals, metal products, farm equipment. Seat of Bakersfield Col. Gold was found near by (1885), but oil (discovered here 1889) developed the city. Near by is one of world's deepest oil wells, 15,044 ft. deep. Laid out 1869, inc. 1898. **2** Town (1940 pop. 177), Ozark co., S Mo., in the Ozarks, near North Fork of White R., 22 mi. SW of West Plains. **3** Town (pop. 779), Franklin co., NW Vt., 14 mi. E of St. Albans; lumber, dairy, and maple products.

Bakers Island, NE Mass., in the Atlantic, c.6 mi. E of Salem; c.½ mi. long. Has lighthouse (42°32'N 70°47'W).

Bakersville. 1 Residential village (1940 pop. 587), Cochise co., SE Ariz., near Mex. line, 4 mi. SE of Bisbee. **2** Town (pop. 428), ⊙ Mitchell co., NW N.C., 8 mi. NW of Spruce Pine; mica mining, lumbering.

Bakersville and Elandsputte (ĕ'läntspŭ"tŭ), town (pop. 1,241), SW Transvaal, U. of So. Afr., 13 mi. NNW of Lichtenburg; alluvial-diamond mining center. Its deposits, discovered 1926, were scene of major diamond rush.

Bakerton, village (pop. 1,141), Cambria co., W central Pa., 10 mi. NNE of Nanty Glo.

Bakewell, urban district (1931 pop. 3,028; 1951 census 3,350), N central Derby, England, on the Wye R. and 10 mi. E of Buxton; spa with mineral springs and baths, fishing resort. Has 8th-cent. Saxon cross in churchyard of 14th-15th-cent. church. CHATSWORTH, seat of duke of Devonshire, is 3 mi. ENE; and HADDON HALL, seat of duke of Rutland, is 2 mi. SE.

Bakgatla (bäkgä'tlä) or **Mochudi** (mōchōō'dē), district (pop. 20,224), SE Bechuanaland Protectorate, bounded E by Transvaal, U. of So. Afr.; ⊙ Mochudi. Coextensive with Bakgatla native reserve, established 1899. Formerly called Kgatleng.

Bakhada Dam, Algeria: see MINA, OUED.

Bakhal (băkhäl'), town, Shaibi sheikdom, Western Aden Protectorate, on Yemen "Status Quo Line," 70 mi. N of Aden; 13°52'N 44°52'E. Was sheik's residence until transfer to Awabil in 1948.

Bakharden (bŭkhŭrdyĕn'), town (1948 pop. over 2,000), S Ashkhabad oblast, Turkmen SSR, on Trans-Caspian RR and 60 mi. WNW of Ashkhabad; woolen mill, rug weaving.

Bakhchisaray or **Bakhchisarai** (bŭkhchē"sŭrī') [Tatar, =garden palace], city (1939 pop. over 10,000), S Crimea, Russian SFSR, on railroad and 18 mi. SW of Simferopol, in deep gorge of the Churuk-Su (right affluent of the Kacha), in tobacco- and fruit-growing area. Handicraft center (copper- and brassware, jewelry, morocco-leather goods); fruit canning, knitting, distilling, flour milling. Limestone deposits near by. Exports tobacco, fruit, truck produce, handicraft articles. Of typical Oriental design; site of former 16th-cent. palace (twice restored; now a mus.) of Crimean khans, with white marble fountains (celebrated by Pushkin and Mickiewicz) and tombs of khans. City formerly had over 30 mosques. In cliffs (alt. over 1,600 ft.), 2 mi. SE, are abandoned cave dwellings of Chufut-Kale [Tatar, =Jews' city], center of Karaite Jews until 18th cent. Bakhchisarai was ⊙ Crimean khanate from 15th cent. to 1783, when it passed to Russia. Until Tatar deportation at end of Second World War, pop. was 70% Tatar.

Bakhmach (bäkh'mŭch), city (1948 pop. over 10,000), E Chernigov oblast, Ukrainian SSR, 65 mi. ESE of Chernigov; rail junction; meat packing, woolen milling.

Bakhmaro (bäkh'mŭrŭ), village, SW Georgian SSR, in Adzhar-Imeretian Range, 17 mi. ESE of Makharadze; mtn. resort (alt. 4,300 ft.).

Bakhmut, Ukrainian SSR: see ARTEMOVSK, Stalino.

Bakhoy River, Fr. West Africa: see BAKOY RIVER.

Bakhtegan Lake, Iran: see NIRIZ LAKE.

Bakhtemir (bŭkhtyĭmēr'), village (1926 pop. 2,116), E Astrakhan oblast, Russian SFSR, 16 mi. SW of Astrakhan and on Bakhtemir arm (westernmost; 40-mi.-long chief navigable channel) of Volga R. delta mouth; fisheries; fruit, cotton. Sometimes spelled Bakhtimir.

Bakht er Ruda (bäkht' ĕr rōō'dŭ), village, Blue Nile prov., E central Anglo-Egyptian Sudan, on the White Nile and 70 mi. S of Khartoum. Has teachers col. (founded 1934).

Bakhtiari (bäkh"tēärē'), mountainous tribal region of SW Iran, in NW Fars, W Isfahan, NE Khuzistan, and Luristan; inhabited by nomadic Bakhtiari tribes; main town is Izeh. Agr. in fertile valleys (grain, fruit); sheep raising; rugmaking. A warlike people, noted for their aggressiveness against the central govt. of Iran.

Bakhtigan Lake, Iran: see NIRIZ LAKE.

Bakhty, Kazakh SSR: see AYAGUZ, city.

Bakinskikh Komissarov, Imeni 26, (ē'mĭnyē dvŭ-tsŭtyē'shĭstyē' bŭkēn'skĭkh kŭmēsä'rŭf), oil town (1941 pop. over 500), W Ashkhabad oblast, Turkmen SSR, at N foot of Greater Balkhan Range, 20 mi. NNE of Nebit-Dag.

Bakirkoy (bäkŭrkû'ē), Turkish *Bakırköy*, city (pop. 29,870), SW section of Istanbul, Turkey in Europe, on Sea of Marmara; cotton goods, cement.

Bakir River (bäkŭr'), Turkish *Bakır Cayı*, anc. *Caicus*, NW Turkey, rises 20 mi. SW of Balikesir, flows 75 mi. SW, past Bergama, to Gulf of Candarli 14 mi. SE of Dikili. A left branch joins it 8 mi. W of Soma.

Bakka, Norway: see NAEROY FJORD.

Bakka Bay, Icelandic *Bakkaflói* (bä'käflō"ē), inlet (15 mi. long, 20 mi. wide at mouth) of Atlantic, NE Iceland, on E side of Langanes peninsula; 66°5'N 14°55'W.

Bakke, Norway: see NAEROY FJORD.

Bakkyo, Korea: see POLGYO.

Bakli, China: see PAKLI.

Bakloh (bŭk'lō), town (pop., including cantonment area, 4,061), Gurdaspur dist., N Punjab, India, in small enclave near Chamba (Himachal Pradesh), 43 mi. NE of Gurdaspur; military station; wheat, rice.

Bako (bä'kō), Ital. *Baco* or *Bacco*, village (pop. 1,200), Gamu-Gofa prov., S Ethiopia, 60 mi. WNW of Gardula.

Bakoeng, Indonesia: see LINGGA ARCHIPELAGO.

Bakonde, Belgian Congo: see HEMPTINNE-SAINT-BENOIT.

Bakonszeg (bŏ'kônsĕg), town (pop. 2,131), Bihar co., E Hungary, on Berettyo R. and 25 mi. SSW of Debrecen; wheat, corn, cattle.

Bakonycsernye (bŏ'kônyŭ-chĕrnyĕ), town (pop. 3,065), Veszprem co., NW central Hungary, in Bakony Mts., 18 mi. NW of Szekesfehervar; wine, potatoes, sheep.

Bakonyjako (bŏ'kônyŭyä"kō), Hung. *Bakonyjákó*, town (pop. 1,777), Veszprem co., NW central Hungary, in Bakony Mts., 10 mi. SE of Papa; agr., cattle, hogs.

Bakony Mountains (bŏ'kônyŭ), NW central Hungary, extend 70 mi. ENE from Zala R., bet. L. Balaton (S) and Raba R. (NW); rise to 2,339 ft. at Mt. Köris; densely forested. Excellent vineyards on slopes, especially near L. Balaton. Deposits of bauxite (Nyirad, Epleny), manganese (Epleny, Urkut), lignite (Varpalota), coal (Ajka). In 19th cent. the forests (Ger. *Bakonyer Wald*) were resort of highwaymen. City of Veszprem is on S slope.

Bakouma (bäkōōmä'), village, E Ubangi-Shari, Fr. Equatorial Africa, 65 mi. N of Bangassou; trading center in cotton region. Near-by Fadama (fädämä'), 9 mi. W, has sisal plantations.

Bakov nad Jizerou (bä'kôf näd' yĭ"zĕrō), Ger. *Bakow* or *Bakow an der Iser* (bä'kôf än dĕr ē'zŭr), village (pop. 3,215), N Bohemia, Czechoslovakia, on Jizera R. and 20 mi. SSW of Liberec; rail junction; mfg. of bast and osier articles; barley, potatoes.

Bakoy River (bäkoi'), headstream of Senega, R. in Fr. West Africa, rises NW of Siguiri in Fouta Djallon massif of Fr. Guinea, flows c.250 mi. N and NNW to Bafoulabé, Fr. Sudan, where it joins the Bafing R. to form the Senegal. Not navigable. Sometimes spelled Bakhoy. Chief affluent is Baoulé R.

Bakr-Uzyak (bŭ'kŭr-ōōzyäk'), town (1948 pop. over 2,000), E Bashkir Autonomous SSR, Russian SFSR, in the S Urals, 35 mi. SSW of Magnitogorsk; copper mining.

Baksan (bŭksän'), village (1939 pop. over 2,000), N Kabardian Autonomous SSR, Russian SFSR, on Baksan R. and 14 mi. NNW of Nalchik; wheat, corn, sunflowers, orchards. Hydroelectric power station (*Baksanges*) is 7 mi. WSW, on Baksan R.

Baksan River, Kabardian Autonomous SSR, Russian SFSR, rises in the central Greater Caucasus at S foot of Mt. Elbrus, flows c.100 mi. NE, past Baksan, to Malka R. just SE of Prokhladny. Has hydroelectric station (*Baksanges*) 7 mi. WSW of Baksan. Receives Chegem and Cherek rivers.

Baksar (bŭk'sŭr), town (pop. 2,222), Meerut dist., NW Uttar Pradesh, India, on distributary of Upper Ganges Canal and 24 mi. SE of Meerut; wheat, gram, jowar, sugar cane, oilseeds. Also called Baksarkhera. Formerly spelled Bagsar.

Baksheyevo (bŭkshā'ŭvŭ), town (1939 pop. over 500), E Moscow oblast, Russian SFSR, 15 mi. NE of Shatura; peat works.

Baktaloranthaza (bŏk'tŏlōränt-hä"zō), Hung. *Baktalórántháza*, town (pop. 2,700), Szabolcs co., NE Hungary, 17 mi. ENE of Nyiregyhaza; petroleum refinery; tobacco, fruit; hogs, sheep.

Baku (bäkōō', Rus. bŭkōō'), city (1939 pop. of Greater Baku, 809,347), ⊙ Azerbaijan SSR, port and naval base (at BAILOVO) on SW coast of APSHERON PENINSULA, on Caspian Sea, 1,200 mi. SSE of Moscow and 100 mi. N of Iranian border; 40° 21'N 49°51'E. Fifth-largest city and chief petroleum-producing center of USSR; one of main Caspian ports, trading with Iran and Soviet Central Asia. Baku is connected by rail spur with Baladzhary, junction of lines to Rostov and Tiflis. Center of petroleum-refining industry and head of oil and kerosene pipe lines to Batum; produces heavy oils, kerosene, gasoline, and other petroleum products; machine mfg. (ballbearings, oil-drilling equipment); auto, tractor, and rail repair shops; shipyards; chemical, textile, and food industries. Baku proper (rising in an amphitheater around semi-circular Baku Bay) consists of the Old City (SW), the Tatar-Persian fortress of Bad-Kube [Persian, = breath of the wind], with 12th-cent. Maiden's Tower and 15th-cent. Khan's palace; and the New City (center; dating from 19th cent.) with public bldgs., rail station, and residential quarters. Adjourning (E) are the Black City [Rus. *Cherny Gorod*] and the newer White City [Rus. *Bely Gorod*], site of refining and cracking installations. An important cultural center, Baku is seat of Azerbaijan state univ., industrial, economics, rail, and medical institutes. Has museums, theaters, conservatory. Administrative city of Baku or Greater Baku extends far beyond Baku proper, including entire Apsheron Peninsula, with its oil fields and industrial towns linked by electric railroad to Baku. Chief satellite centers: Baladzhary (rail hub), Balakhany and Sabunchi (original 19th-cent. oil centers), Surakhany, Sumgait (industrial center developed after 1945), Mashtagi and Buzovny (oil production begun during Second World War). Baku was first known in 5th cent.; mentioned as port in 10th cent. Its oil and gas wells were long venerated by the Ghebers (Zoroastrian fire-worshippers). Successively ruled by Arabs, Turks, and Persians, Baku became ⊙ former Baku khanate, conquered (1806) by Russians. Grew rapidly after development of oil industry (1870s). Abortive Bolshevik uprising (1918) was followed (to 1920) by anti-Soviet regime. Became (1920) ⊙ Azerbaijan SSR.

Baku, Second, Russian SFSR: see SECOND BAKU.

Bakuba, Iraq: see BA'QUBA.

Bakum (bä'kōōm), village (commune pop. 5,580), in Oldenburg, NW Germany, after 1945 Lower Saxony, 4 mi. WNW of Vechta, in peat region.

Bakung, Indonesia: see LINGGA ARCHIPELAGO.

Bakuriani (bŭkōōrēä'nyē), town (1926 pop. 823), S central Georgian SSR, 10 mi. SE of Borzhomi (linked by narrow-gauge railroad); health and ski resort in Trialet Range (alt. 5,510 ft.).

Bakury (bŭkōō'rē), village (1926 pop. 6,304), NW Saratov oblast, Russian SFSR, on Serdoba R. (left branch of Khoper R.) and 22 mi. ESE of Serdobsk; wheat, sunflowers.

Bakwanga (bäkwäng'gä), village, Kasai prov., S Belgian Congo, on Bushimaie R. and 60 mi. WSW of Kabinda; leading center of diamond-mining operations in Bushimaie area, employing c.6,500 workers. Produces mainly industrial diamonds and is one of the world's main suppliers. Has large hospitals; trade schools for Africans.

Bala (bä'lŭ, bă'lŭ), town (pop. 404), S Ont., on Muskoka R., on SW bay of Muskoka L., and 15 mi. W of Bracebridge; resort. Hydroelectric plant.

Bala (bä'lä), village, E Senegal, Fr. West Africa, on Dakar-Niger RR and 40 mi. ENE of Tambacounda; peanuts, timber, subsistence crops.

Bala (bälä'), Turkish *Bâlâ* or *Bâlâ*, village (pop. 1,142), Ankara prov., central Turkey, 30 mi. SE of Ankara; wheat, fruit; mohair goats.

Bala (bă'lŭ), urban district (1931 pop. 1,395; 1951 census 1,508), NE Merioneth, Wales, on the Dee at NE end of Bala L., 19 mi. NE of Dolgelley; agr. market and tourist resort; woolen milling. Site of theological col., founded 1837.

Balabac Island (bälä'bäk) (□ 125; pop. c.2,000; in 1948, including near-by isls., 3,355), Palawan prov., Philippines, 20 mi. S of S tip of Palawan; 8°N 117°E. It is c.20 mi. long; town of Balabac (1939 pop. 577) is on E coast. Rice, coconuts.

Balabac Strait, connects Sulu Sea and S.China Sea, bet. Balabac Isl. (N) of the Philippines and Balembangan (S) of North Borneo; 30 mi. wide.

Balabalagan Islands (bä"lŭbä'lŭgŭn) or **Little Paternoster Islands,** group of uninhabited islets, Indonesia, off SE coast of Borneo, in Macassar Strait; 2°25'S 117°50'E. Visited by fishermen.

Balabanovo (bŭlŭbä'nŭvŭ), town (1939 pop. over 500), NE Kaluga oblast, Russian SFSR, 6 mi. ESE of Borovsk; cotton milling.

Balabino (bŭlŭbē'nŭ), town (1926 pop. 2,267), NW Zaporozhe oblast, Ukrainian SSR, 3 mi. S of Zaporozhe.

Balaci (bäläch'), village (pop. 2,194), Teleorman prov., S Rumania, 44 mi. NNE of Turnu-Magurele; orchards. Has 17th-cent. church.

Balacita (bŭlŭchē'tsä), Rum. *Bălăcița*, village (pop. 2,363), Dolj prov., SW Rumania, 26 mi. SE of Turnu-Severin.

Balaclava (bă"lŭklă'vŭ), town (pop. 1,290), St. Elizabeth parish, W Jamaica, on Kingston-Montego Bay RR and 30 mi. WNW of May Pen; cassava, tropical fruit and spices, livestock. Noted Oxford Caves are near by.

Bala-Cynwyd (bă'lŭ-kĭn'wĭd), village (1940 pop. 4,907), in LOWER MERION township, Montgomery co., SE Pa.; W suburb of Philadelphia.

Balad (bä'läd), town, Baghdad prov., central Iraq, on Tigris R., on railroad, and 50 mi. N of Baghdad; dates, sesame, millet. Sometimes spelled Beled.

Balad (bälăd'), town (pop. 1,500), in the Benadir, S Ital. Somaliland, on the Webi Shebeli and 20 mi. N of Mogadishu, in agr. region (durra, corn, sesame, cotton).

Baladiz (bälädüz'), Turkish *Baladız*, village (pop. 643), Isparta prov., W central Turkey, 11 mi. NW of Isparta; rail junction.

Balad Ruz (bä'läd rōōz'), town, Diyala prov., E Iraq, near Iran line, 50 mi. NE of Baghdad; dates, fruit, livestock.

Baladzhary (bŭlŭjä'rē), town (1939 pop. over 2,000) in Dzerzhinski dist. of Greater Baku, Azerbaijan SSR, on Apsheron Peninsula, 5 mi. NNW of Baku; rail hub of Greater Baku, at junction of lines from Rostov and Tiflis; rail repair shops; food processing, metalworking.

Baladzholski or **Baladzholskiy** (bŭlŭjôl'skē), town (1948 pop. over 2,000), E Semipalatinsk oblast, Kazakh SSR, 50 mi. ESE of Zhangis-Tobe; gold mining.

Balaganj (bä'lägŭnj), village, Sylhet dist., E East Bengal, E Pakistan, on Kusiyara R. and 16 mi. S of Sylhet; trades in rice, tea, oilseeds, salt; handicraft mat weaving.

Balagansk (bŭlŭgänsk'), village (1926 pop. 1,179), S Irkutsk oblast, Russian SFSR, on Angara R. and 40 mi. N of Cheremkhovo, in agr. area. Founded 1653 as fortress on Siberian colonization route. Before 1924, ⊙ Balagansk dist. of Irkutsk govt.

Balaghat (bä'lägät), district (□ 3,614; pop. 634,350), central Madhya Pradesh, India, on Deccan Plateau; ⊙ Balaghat. Mainly in E Satpura Range, divided in W portion of dist. by broad, alluvial valley of Wainganga R. Rice, oilseeds (chiefly flax), wheat, corn, and millet in river valley; mango groves. Dense sal forests in NW hills (bauxite and mica workings; copper and red ocher deposits; bamboo, lac, myrobalan). An important source of India's manganese; mines mainly at Balaghat and near Ramrama Tola and Tirodi. Rice, oilseed, and flour milling; sugar milling at Balaghat (trade center). Pop. 76% Hindu, 22% tribal (mainly Gond), 2% Moslem.

Balaghat, town (pop. 11,482), ⊙ Balaghat dist., central Madhya Pradesh, India, on Wainganga R. and 85 mi. NE of Nagpur; trade and manganese-mining center (mines at rail junction just NE), with rail spurs to mines 17 mi. WNW, near Ramrama Tola, and to shipping point 25 mi. W at Katangi; sugar milling. Formerly called Burha.

Balagny-sur-Thérain (bälänyē'-sür-tārē'), village (pop. 975), Oise dept., N France, on the Thérain and 13 mi. NW of Senlis; wool combing and spinning, wall-paper mfg.

Balaguer (bälägĕr'), city (pop. 5,991), Lérida prov., NE Spain, in Catalonia, on the Segre and 15 mi. NE of Lérida; road center; olive-oil and hemp processing, sawmilling, linen and hat mfg. In well-irrigated area (livestock, cereals, sugar beets, wine).

Balaju (bŭlä'jōō), village, central Nepal, in Nepal Valley, 2 mi. NNW of Katmandu city center; resort with partially-submerged statue of Vishnu and long row of noted stone waterspouts. Hindu pilgrimage center. Gunpowder mfg. near by. Also spelled Balaji.

Balakhany (bŭlŭkhŭnē'), town (1939 pop. over 10,000) in Lenin dist. of Greater Baku, Azerbaijan SSR, on central Apsheron Peninsula, on electric railroad and 8 mi. NE of Baku; oil wells (developed after 1870s).

Balakhchin (bŭlŭkhchēn'), town (1939 pop. over 500), W Khakass Autonomous Oblast, Krasnoyarsk Territory, Russian SFSR, 90 mi. NW of Abakan, in the Kuznetsk Ala-tau; gold mines.

Balakhna (bŭlŭkhnä'), city (1939 pop. over 10,000), W Gorki oblast, Russian SFSR, on Volga R. and 18 mi. NW of Gorki on rail spur; paper milling; truck produce. Ruins of 12th-cent. monastery; 2 churches (17th cent). Dates from 1536; became shipbuilding center in 17th cent. Electric power station (GIDROTORF) and paper mills (PRAVDINSK) near by.

Balakhta (bŭläkh'tŭ), village (1926 pop. 3,027), S Krasnoyarsk Territory, Russian SFSR, on Chulym R., 70 mi. E of Uzhur; dairy farming; coal mining.

Balaklava (bă"lŭklä'vŭ), town (pop. 1,053), SE South Australia, 55 mi. N of Adelaide; rail junction; wheat-growing center.

Balaklava (bă"lŭklä'vŭ, Rus. bŭlŭklä'vŭ), city (1926 pop. 2,323), S Crimea, Russian SFSR, fishing port on Black Sea, 8 mi. SSE of Sevastopol (linked by railroad); beach and health resort (grape therapy) in winegrowing dist.; fish and vegetable canning. Limestone quarrying (shipped to Kerch metallurgical works), marble cutting. Has marine salvage operations school and (S) ruins of Genoese fortress (14th–15th cent.). Pop. largely Russian and Greek. An anc. city, founded (late 2d cent. B.C.) by Scythians; later passed to Greeks, who named it Symbalon. Known as Cembalo under the Genoese; renamed (after 1475) Balaklava by Turks. The charge of the Light Brigade, in Russo-English engagement fought here (Oct., 1854), was celebrated by Tennyson.

Balakleya (bŭlŭklyä'ŭ), city (1948 pop. over 10,000), central Kharkov oblast, Ukrainian SSR, on the Northern Donets and 45 mi. SE of Kharkov; dairying, metalworking. Neolithic and Bronze Age excavations near by.

Balakovo (bŭlŭkô'vŭ), city (1926 pop. 19,131), N central Saratov oblast, Russian SFSR, on left bank of Volga R. and 15 mi. E of Volsk; mfg. of heavy machinery, flour milling, boatbuilding. Became city in 1918. Formerly an important wheat-shipping point.

Bala Lake (bă'lŭ), Welsh *Llyn Tegid* (lĭn tĕ'gĭd), lake (1,084 acres), E central Merioneth, Wales, on the Dee; extends 4 mi. SW from Bala; 1 mi. wide; largest lake in North Wales.

Balamban (bälämbän'), town (1939 pop. 2,224; 1948 municipality pop. 34,488), central Cebu isl., Philippines, on Tañon Strait, 19 mi. NW of Cebu city; agr. center (corn, coconuts).

Bala Murghab (bä'lŭ mōōrgäb'), town (pop. 10,000), Herat prov., NW Afghanistan, on Murghab R. and 105 mi. NE of Herat, near USSR line; alt. 1,540 ft.; road center on trade routes from Herat to Afghan Turkestan and Turkmenia. Also spelled Bala Morghab.

Balan (bälã'), SE suburb (pop. 1,197) of Sedan, Ardennes dept., N France; wool combing, weaving.

Balan, Rumania: see SANDOMINIC.

Balancán (bälängkän'), officially Balancán de Domínguez, city (pop. 1,703), Tabasco, SE Mexico, on Usumacinta R. and 95 mi. E of Villahermosa; rubber, rice, tobacco, fruit. Airfield.

Balanda (bŭlŭndä'), town (1926 pop. 10,070), SW Saratov oblast, Russian SFSR, on Balanda R. (right affluent of the Medveditsa) and 34 mi. SW of Atkarsk (connected by rail spur); agr. center; food processing (flour, dairy products), distilling, metalworking.

Balandra Bay (bŭlăn'drŭ), NE Trinidad, B.W.I., small open bay 35 mi. E of Port of Spain; known for its fine surf.

Balanga (bäläng'gä), town (1939 pop. 4,582; 1948 municipality pop. 12,379), ⊙ BATAAN prov., S Luzon, Philippines, on E Bataan Peninsula, near Manila Bay, 31 mi. WNW of Manila; agr. center; sugar milling.

Balangala (bäläng-gä'lä), village, Equator Prov., W Belgian Congo, on right bank of Ikelemba R. and 45 mi. S of Basankusu; terminus of navigation.

Balangero (bälänjā'rô), village (pop. 2,107), Torino prov., Piedmont, NW Italy, 16 mi. NNW of Turin; paper mill. Asbestos, antimony mines near by.

Balangiga (bälänghē'gä), town (1939 pop. 3,546; 1948 municipality pop. 21,621), S Samar isl., Philippines, on Leyte Gulf, 55 mi. SE of Catbalogan; agr. center (coconuts, hemp).

Balangoda (bŭlŭngō'dŭ), town (pop. 2,142), Sabaragamuwa Prov., S central Ceylon, in Ceylon Hill Country, 20 mi. E of Ratnapura; tea, rubber, rice, cacao, vegetables. Iron-ore deposits near by.

Balanguingui Island (bäläng-gēng'gē) (□ .7), Samales Group, Sulu prov., Philippines, at NE end of Sulu Archipelago, 15 mi. E of Jolo Isl.

Balanod (bälänō'), village (pop. 306), Jura dept., E France, 14 mi. SSE of Louhans; marble working, wool spinning.

Balanyá or **Santa Cruz Balanyá** (sän'tä krōōs', bälänyä'), town (pop. 1,721), Chimaltenango dept., S central Guatemala, 5 mi. NW of Chimaltenango; alt. 5,085 ft.; corn, wheat, black beans.

Balaoan (bälou'än), town (1939 pop. 2,396; 1948 municipality pop. 14,274), La Union prov., N central Luzon, Philippines, near W coast, 15 mi. NNE of San Fernando; rice-growing center.

Balapitiya (bŭlŭpĭt'ĭyŭ), village, Southern Prov., Ceylon, on SW coast, 3 mi. N of Ambalangoda; fishing center; vegetables, coconut-palm plantations. Training col.

Balapur (bä'läpōōr), town (pop. 12,512), Akola dist., W Madhya Pradesh, India, 15 mi. WSW of Akola; millet, wheat, oilseeds; cotton ginning. Was a Deccan military hq. under Akbar.

Balarampur or **Bairampur** (both: bŭlrăm'pōōr), town (pop. 7,725), Manbhum dist., SE Bihar, India, on railroad (Barabhum station) and 20 mi. SW of Purulia; road center; rice, corn, oilseeds, bajra; silk growing. Also called Rangadih. Extensive lac growing, shellac mfg. 14 mi. SW, at Chandil (soapstone quarries, gold mining near by). Ochre mining 10 mi. ESE, near another Barabhum (village).

Balaruc-les-Bains (bälärük'-lā-bē'), village (pop. 811), Hérault dept., S France, on N shore of Étang de Thau, 3 mi. N of Sète; fertilizer mfg., sulphur refining. Mineral hot springs. Damaged during Second World War.

Balasan (bälä'sän), town (1939 pop. 2,266; 1948 municipality pop. 15,490), Iloilo prov., NE Panay isl., Philippines, 24 mi. ESE of Capiz; agr. center (corn, rice).

Balasfura or **Balasfurah** (bălăsfōō'rŭ), village (pop. 10,585), Girga prov., central Upper Egypt, on railroad and 3 mi. SE of Sohag; cotton, cereals, dates, sugar cane.

Balashikha (bŭlŭshē'khŭ), city (1939 pop. over 10,000), E central Moscow oblast, Russian SFSR, on rail spur and 15 mi. ENE of Moscow; textiles, paper mfg. Became city in 1939.

Balashov (bŭlŭshôf'), city (1939 pop. c.50,000), SW Saratov oblast, Russian SFSR, on Khoper R. and 120 mi. W of Saratov; agr. and industrial center in wheat and sunflower region; mfg. (aircraft, metal products, clothing); agr. processing (flour, canned goods, dairy products, alcohol). Teachers col. Chartered 1780.

Balasinor (bälä'sĭnōr), village, Kaira dist., N Bombay, India, 45 mi. NE of Kaira; agr. market (grain, cotton); cement factory. Was ⊙ former princely state of Balasinor (□ 195; pop. 61,151) in Gujarat States, Bombay; inc. 1949 into Kaira dist.

Balasore (bŭl'ŭsōr), district (□ 2,457; pop. 1,102,539), NE Orissa, India; ⊙ Balasore. In coastal strip bet. Bay of Bengal (E) and hills (W); bounded NE by West Bengal, S by Baitarani R. Largely flat, alluvial land, drained by several hill streams; rice is chief crop. Rice milling, fishing (mackerel, seer-fish, hilsa, mahseer, whitebait), hand-loom weaving; sal and bamboo in forests (W central). Main towns: Balasore, Bhadrakh. Original dist. (□ 2,194; pop. 1,029,430) enlarged by inc. (1949) of former princely state of Nilgiri.

Balasore, town (pop. 19,405), ⊙ Balasore dist., NE Orissa, India, on Burhabalang R. and 100 mi. NE of Cuttack; small trade in rice, fish, nux vomica, ghee, hardware, cotton piece goods, kerosene, and salt; rice milling, biri and bell-metal mfg., fish curing, hand-loom weaving. Has col. Chandipur, 6 mi. ESE, on Bay of Bengal, has ordnance testing station. Balasore was site (1633) of early English settlement; French, Dutch, and Danish trading posts were established later; last 2 ceded 1846 to British; Fr. *loge* (just NE of present town) given 1947 to India.

Balassagyarmat (bŏ'lŏsh-shŏdyŏr'mŏt), city (pop. 12,347), ⊙ Nograd-Hont co., N Hungary, on Ipoly R. and 40 mi. N of Budapest; rail junction; agr. market. Wine center; distilleries, brickworks, dairies. Vineyards; rye, potatoes; sheep raising.

Balat (bălăt'), village (pop. 2,698) in Dakhla oasis, S central Egypt, 26 mi. ESE of El Qasr; dates, oranges, wheat, barley.

Balat, Turkey: see DURSUNBEY.

Balaton (bă'lŭtŭn), resort village (pop. 723), Lyon co., SW Minn., on small lake, near Cottonwood R., and 15 mi. S of Marshall, in grain and poultry region; dairy products.

Balaton, Lake (bŏ'lŏtôn), Ger. *Plattensee*, W central Hungary, 56 mi. SW of Budapest, largest lake (□ 230.95) of Central Europe; 48 mi. long, average width 8 mi., 11 ft. deep. Abounds in fish; navigable by steamboat. Vineyards along shores; figs, peaches on N shore; peat bogs. Main tributary is Zala R.; outlet: Sio R., which flows to the Danube. Recreation center; tourist and health resorts (Keszthely, Siofok, Balatonfüred).

Balatonalmadi (bŏ'lŏtŏnŏl"mädē), Hung. *Balatonalmádi*, resort town (pop. 2,280), Veszprem co., W central Hungary, on L. Balaton and 7 mi. SE of Veszprem; wine, poultry.

Balatonboglar (bŏ'lŏtŏnbô"glär), Hung. *Balatonboglár*, resort town (pop. 2,970), Somogy co., SW central Hungary, on S shore of L. Balaton and 29 mi. N of Kaposvar; wine.

Balatonföldvar, Hungary: see KÖRÖSHEGY.

Balatonfüred (bŏ'lŏtŏnfü"rĕd) or **Füred,** resort town (pop. 3,826), Veszprem co., W central Hungary, on L. Balaton and 9 mi. S of Veszprem; mineral springs; wine-producing area.

Balatonfüzfő, Hungary: see FÜZFŐ.

Balatonkenese (bŏ'lŏtŏng-kĕ"nĕshĕ), resort town (pop. 3,264), Veszprem co., W central Hungary, on L. Balaton and 10 mi. SSE of Veszprem; wine, corn, flax; hogs.

Balatonkiliti (bŏ'lŏtŏngkĭ"lĭtē), town (pop. 2,882), Somogy co., W central Hungary, 37 mi. NNE of Kaposvar; wheat, wine.

Balatonlelle (bŏ'lŏtŏnlĕl"lĕ), resort town (pop. 2,613), Somogy co., SW central Hungary, on S shore of L. Balaton, 29 mi. N of Kaposvar.

Balawali, India: see NAJIBABAD.

Balayan (bäläyän'), town (1939 pop. 5,433; 1948 municipality pop. 18,305), Batangas prov., S Luzon, Philippines, on Balayan Bay, 30 mi. NW of Batangas; fishing and agr. center (rice, sugar cane, corn, coconuts).

Balayan Bay, inlet, S Luzon, Philippines, connected with S.China Sea (W) by Verde Isl. Passage, separated from Batangas Bay (E) by narrow peninsula S of L. Taal; c.15 mi. long, 13 mi. wide. Cape Santiago is at W side of entrance; Balayan and Lemery are on N shore.

Balazote (bäläthō'tä), town (pop. 2,074), Albacete prov., SE central Spain, 18 mi. WSW of Albacete; flour mills; cereals, saffron.

Balazsfalva, Rumania: see BLAJ.

Balbagar, Russian SFSR: see KURBA RIVER.

Balbi, Mount (băl'bē), peak (10,170 ft.), Emperor Range, N Bougainville, Solomon Isls., SW Pacific; highest mtn. of Solomons; active volcano.

Balbirnie, Scotland: see MARKINCH.

Balboa (bălbō'ŭ), U.S. naval station and town (pop. 4,168), ⊙ Balboa dist. (□ 222; pop. 37,271), S Panama Canal Zone, port near Pacific end of Panama Canal, on transisthmian railroad, just W of Panama city. Has extensive harbor installations, drydock, marine and railroad repair shops, warehouses, coaling plant, quarantine station. Ferry service across the canal. La Boca, at foot of Sosa Hill, adjoins SW.

Balboa, beach resort (pop. c.3,300), Orange co., S Calif., adjacent to Newport Beach, on peninsula bet. Newport Bay and the Pacific; fisheries; boat yards; yachting. Balboa Isl. (residential; resort) is in bay.

Balboa Heights, town (pop. 364), Balboa dist., S Panama Canal Zone, W of Panama city (beyond Ancon), adjoined S by Balboa. Seat of governor of Panama Canal Zone; also hq. of transisthmian railroad.

Balbriggan (bălbrĭ'gŭn), Gaelic *Baile Brig in*, town (pop. 2,537), N Co. Dublin, Ireland, on the Irish Sea, 20 mi N of Dublin; fishing port and textile center, noted for its hosiery; also shirt mfg., linen milling.

Balbunar, Bulgaria: see KURBAT.

Balby, England: see DONCASTER.

Balcarce (bälkär'sā), city (pop. 14,808), ⊙ Balcarce dist. (□ 1,591; pop. 32,470), SE BuenosAires prov., Argentina, 40 mi. WNW of Mar del Plata, in hilly country. Industrial and agr. center (oats, potatoes, wheat, livestock); dairying, flour milling; mfg. of furniture, ceramics. Kaolin deposits. Resort.

Balcarres (bălkă'rĭs), village (pop. 464), SE Sask., near the Fishing Lakes, 19 mi. N of Indian Head; grain elevators.

Balcesti (bŭlchĕsht'), Rum. *Bălceşti*, village (pop. 953), Valcea prov., S central Rumania, 38 mi. SW of Ramnicu-Valcea; orchards.

Balchik (bäl'chĭk, bälchēk'), anc. *Dionysopolis*, Rum. *Balcic*, city (pop. 6,011), Stalin dist., NE Bulgaria, port (grain and cattle exports) on Black Sea, in S Dobruja, 19 mi. NE of Stalin; summer resort; flour milling. Has former royal palace and residential villas. Under Turkish rule (15th–19th cent.). In Rumania (1913–40).

Balclutha (bălklōō'thŭ), borough (pop. 1,692), ⊙ Clutha co. (□ 990; pop. 5,985), SE S.Isl., New Zealand, 45 mi. SW of Dunedin and on Clutha R.; livestock. Kaitangata coal mines are near by.

Balcombe (bôl'kŭm), agr. village and parish (pop. 1,323), N central Sussex, England, 4 mi. NNW of Haywards Heath, on edge of Balcombe Forest. Has 13th-cent. church.

Balcones Escarpment (bălkō'nĭs), Texas, dissected fault scarp c.200 mi. long, separating EDWARDS PLATEAU (SE extension of the Great Plains) from the Gulf coastal plain; extends E and NE from the Rio Grande near Del Rio to region NE of Austin; c.1,000 ft. high in SW, c.300 ft. high near Austin.

Balcones Heights, town (pop. 376), Bexar co., SW central Texas.

Balcony Falls, Va.: see JAMES RIVER.

Balde or **El Balde** (ĕl bäl'dā), village (pop. estimate 500), W San Luis prov., Argentina, on railroad and 18 mi. W of San Luis; agr. and lumbering center; saltworks; alfalfa, corn, livestock.

Bald Eagle Creek, central Pa., rises in Allegheny Mts. in SW Centre co., flows 50 mi. NE, along NW slope of Bald Eagle Mtn., to West Branch Susquehanna R. 2 mi. E of Lock Haven.

Bald Eagle Lake, Lake co., NE Minn., 12 mi. ESE of Ely in Superior Natl. Forest; 8 mi. long; max. width 2 mi. Fed by small stream, drained by South Kawishiwi R. NW half of lake sometimes known as Gabbro L. or Gabro L.

Bald Eagle Mountain, central Pa., NE-SW ridge (1,700–2,000 ft.), runs c.85 mi. NE from just E of Tyrone to W Branch Susquehanna R. opposite Muncy; sandstone, quartzite.

Baldeggersee (bäl'dĕgŭrzā'), lake (□ 2), Lucerne canton, N Switzerland; 3.5 mi. long. Remains of prehistoric lake dwellings (N). Baldegg hamlet is on SE shore.

Baldenburg, Poland: see BIALY BOR.

Baldeo (bŭl'dāō), town (pop. 3,182), Muttra dist., W Uttar Pradesh, India, 11 mi. SE of Muttra; gram, wheat, jowar, cotton, oilseeds; pilgrimage center. Noted Vishnuite temple. Also called Dauji.

Bald Head, cape, SW Western Australia, in Indian Ocean, on peninsula forming SW shore of King George Sound; 35°6'S 118°1'E.

Bald Head, SW Maine, headland 3 mi. SE of Ogunquit.

Bald Hills, N suburb (pop. 1,172) of Brisbane, SE Queensland, Australia.

Bald Knob, town (pop. 2,022), White co., central Ark., c.55 mi. NE of Little Rock; trade, shipping center for agr. area (cotton, strawberries, potatoes). Cotton ginning, sawmilling; mfg. of handles, lumber.

Bald Knob, W.Va.,: see SHAVERS MOUNTAIN.

Bald Mountain (2,080 ft.), N central N.B., 32 mi. ENE of Grand Falls.

Bald Mountain. 1 Peak (13,964 ft.), in Rocky Mts., Summit co., N central Colo. **2** Peak, Idaho: see SALMON RIVER MOUNTAINS. **3** Peak (2,572 ft.), Franklin co., W Maine, 6 mi. SE of Weld. **4** Peak, Knox co., Maine: see CAMDEN HILLS. **5** Peak, Nev.: see TOQUEMA RANGE.

Bald Mountains, range of the Appalachians, along N.C.-Tenn. state line, NE of Great Smoky Mts. Natl. Park, bet. Nolichucky (N) and Pigeon (S) rivers. On state line are Big Bald (5,516 ft.) and Big Butt (4,889 ft.), 22 and 13 mi. SE of Greeneville, Tenn., respectively. SW portion sometimes called Max Patch Mts.; entire range sometimes considered part of Unaka Mts.

Baldo, Monte (mŏn'tĕ bäl'dō), mountain chain (24 mi. long N-S; average alt. 2,848 ft.), N Italy, bet. Lago di Garda (W) and Adige R. (E). Highest peak, Cima Val Dritta (7,277 ft.). Marble quarries in NE (Brentonico region).

Baldock (bôl'dŏk), residential urban district (1931 pop. 3,170; 1951 census 5,967), in N Hertford, England, on Ivel R. just ENE of Letchworth; hosiery; electrical industry. Church is mainly 14th cent.

Baldone (bäl'dōnä), Ger. *Baldohn*, village (commune pop. 2,140), central Latvia, 20 mi. SE of Riga; major health resort, amid pinewoods; sulphur springs, mud baths.

Baldoon (–dōōn'), locality, S Ont., near the present Chatham. Lord Selkirk founded Scottish settlement here, 1804; its failure decided Selkirk to sponsor Scottish colonization of the western prairies.

Baldovce, Czechoslovakia: see SPISSKE PODHRADIE.

Baldoyle (băldoil'), Gaelic *Baile Dubhghaill*, town (pop. 892), E Co. Dublin, Ireland, on the Irish Sea, 7 mi. NE of Dublin; fishing port and seaside resort, with racecourse.

Baldur (bôl'dŭr), village (pop. estimate 600), S Man., 45 mi. SE of Brandon; livestock center; grain elevators.

Baldwin. 1 County (□ 1,613; pop. 40,997), SW Ala., on Mobile Bay and Gulf of Mexico; ⊙ Bay Minette. Rich, level farm land; subtropical fruits, potatoes, sugar cane, pecans, vegetables, gladiolus bulbs, timber. Delta region affords good hunting and fishing. Drained by Alabama R. (NW), Little R. (N), Tensaw R. (W), and Perdido R. (E). Formed 1809. **2** County (□ 265; pop. 29,706), central Ga.; ⊙ Milledgeville. Piedmont agr. area (cotton, corn, truck, pecans, fruit, livestock), drained by Oconee R. Formed 1803.

Baldwin. 1 Village (pop. c.150), Gunnison co., W central Colo., in E foothills of West Elk Mts., on branch of Gunnison R. and 16 mi. NNW of Gunnison; alt. c.8,600 ft. Coal-mining point in livestock region. **2** Town (pop. 1,048), Duval co., NE Fla., 19 mi. W of Jacksonville; rail junction in timber and livestock area. **3** Town (pop. 490), Habersham and Banks counties, NE Ga., 14 mi. WSW of Toccoa; clothing mfg. **4** Village (pop. 354), Randolph co., SW Ill., 33 mi. SSE of East St. Louis, in agr. and bituminous-coal-mining area. **5** Town (pop. 208), Jackson co., E Iowa, 9 mi. W of Maquoketa; concrete blocks. **6** Town (pop. 1,138), St. Mary parish, S La., 23 mi. NW of Morgan City. Hunting, fishing near by. **7** Town (pop. 725), Cumberland co., SW Maine, on the Saco and 26 mi. WNW of Portland. **8** Village (pop. 835), ⊙ Lake co., W central Mich., 33 mi. SW of Cadillac. Resort. Many lakes and streams (fishing) in region. Indian village sites and mounds near by. **9** Residential suburban village (1940 pop. 15,507), Nassau co., SE N.Y., on small Baldwin Bay, on S shore of W Long Isl., 6 mi. S of Mineola; gas burners, aircraft parts, clothing, radio and electrical equipment, wood products, brushes, cement blocks, food products. Fisheries. Summer resort. **10** Village, S.C.: see BALDWIN MILLS. **11** Village (pop. 1,100), St. Croix co., W Wis., 23 mi. WNW of Menomonie; dairy products, poultry.

Baldwin City, city (pop. 1,741), Douglas co., E Kansas, 13 mi. S of Lawrence, in livestock and grain area; dairy products. Oil and gas wells near by. Baker Univ. (Methodist; 1858) is here. Laid out 1855, inc. 1870. Scene of battle (1856) bet. proslavery settlers and Free Staters.

Baldwin Mills or **Baldwin,** textile-mill village (pop. 1,440), Chester co., N S.C., just W of Chester.

Baldwin Park, unincorporated town (1940 pop. 7,572), Los Angeles co., S Calif., 16 mi. E of downtown Los Angeles; residential; fruit, truck, poultry farming; some mfg.

Baldwin Peninsula, NW Alaska, extends 45 mi. NW bet. Kotzebue Sound (SW) and Hotham Inlet (NE), N of Seward Peninsula; 65°25'–65°55'N 161°40'–162°35'W; 1–12 mi. wide. Fur farming.

Baldwinsville. 1 Village, Mass.: see TEMPLETON. **2** Village (pop. 4,495), Onondaga co., central N.Y., on Seneca R. and 12 mi. NW of Syracuse; resort and shipping center, with mfg. of knives, paper products, machinery, feed, flour; timber; agr. (potatoes, cabbage). Settled 1796, inc. 1847.

Baldwyn, town (pop. 1,567), on Lee-Prentiss co. line, NE Miss., 18 mi. N of Tupelo, in agr. area; mfg. of wagons, shirts, brick; lumber and feed milling; grain elevator. Near by is Brices Cross Roads Natl. Battlefield Site (1 acre; established 1929), which commemorates Civil War battle (June 10, 1864) in which Confederates under Gen. Nathan Bedford Forrest brilliantly routed a Union force.

Baldy, peak, Colo.: see OLD BALDY.

Baldy, Mount, Calif.: see SAN ANTONIO PEAK.

Baldy Mountain (2,727 ft.), W Man., 36 mi. NW of Dauphin; highest point of Duck Mtn. range.

Baldy Peak. 1 Peak (11,590 ft.), E Ariz., in White Mts., 20 mi. SE of McNary. **2** Peak (12,491 ft.), in E Sangre de Cristo Mts., N N.Mex., 18 mi. NW of Cimarron. **3** Peak (12,623 ft.), in SW Sangre de Cristo Mts., N central N.Mex., 15 mi. NE of Santa Fe. **4** Peak, Texas: see LIVERMORE, MOUNT.

Baldzhuan, Tadzhik SSR: see BOLDZHUAN.

Bâle, Switzerland: see BASEL.

Bale, Mount (bä'lā) (c.11,250 ft.), Harar prov., S central Ethiopia, near Goba.

Balearic Islands (bălēă'rĭk), Sp. *Baleares* (bäläā'rĕs), archipelago and province (□ 1,936; pop. 407,497) of Spain, in the W Mediterranean, 50 to 190 mi. off Sp. E coast; ⊙ PALMA. Group consists of 4 large, densely inhabited isls.: MAJORCA, MINORCA, IVIZA, FORMENTERA, and numerous small, mostly uninhabited, adjacent islets. Archipelago extends c.180 mi. NE-SW bet. 40°5'N–38°39'N and 3°21'E–1°12'E. The isls. have indented coast lines, and undulating surfaces; highest point is the Torrellas or Puig Mayor of Majorca (largest of the Balearics), rising to 4,741 ft. Noted for scenery and year-round mild climate, the archipelago is visited by many tourists. Fishing and agr. are main occupations. Among leading crops are olives, grapes, cereals, almonds, carobs, citrus fruit, capers, hemp, vegetables. Hogs and sheep are grazed widely. Mineral resources include lignite, marble, lead, salt, gravel. Extensive pine forests yield timber. The industries, principally on Majorca, include mfg. of shoes, ceramics (majolica), and metalware. Processing and trading centers besides Palma are Mahón, Iviza, Ciudadela, Manacor, La Puebla, Pollensa, Sóller, Inca. Attesting to the archipelago's great cultural antiquity are abundant prehistoric (Cyclopean) remains. The isls. were successively occupied by Iberians, Phoenicians, Greeks, Carthaginians, Romans, Byzantines. The Moors conquered isls. in 8th cent. and established in 11th cent. an independent kingdom which became seat of powerful pirates, harassing Mediterranean trade. James I of Aragon conquered the Balearics in 1229; they were included (1276–1343) in the independent kingdom of Majorca and reverted to the Aragonese crown. At the outbreak of Sp. civil war (1936), Majorca and Iviza went over to the Nationalists, while Minorca remained in hands of the Loyalists until 1939.

Balearis Major, Balearic Isls.: see MAJORCA.

Balearis Minor, Balearic Isls.: see MINORCA.

Balei or **Baley** (bŭlyä'), city (1939 pop. over 10,000), SE Chita oblast, Russian SFSR, 38 mi. S of Nerchinsk; gold-mining center. Until 1938, called Novo-Troitskoye.

Baleizão (bŭläzä'ō), village (pop. 2,167), Beja dist., S Portugal, 7 mi. E of Beja, in agr. area; grain, sheep, timber. Sometimes spelled Baleisão.

Balembangan (bälĕmbäng'än), island (15 mi. long, 1–6 mi. wide) in S.China Sea, off N tip of Borneo, 20 mi. N of Kudat; fishing. Inhabited by seafaring tribes. Trading post established here 1773 was abandoned 1775 and reestablished briefly in 1803.

Balen (bä'lŭn), town (pop. 10,935), Antwerp prov., N Belgium, 14 mi. SE of Turnhout; zinc- and lead-processing center; dynamite, glass products. Formerly spelled Baelen.

Baler (bälĕr'), town (1939 pop. 2,247; 1948 municipality pop. 17,182), Quezon prov., central Luzon, Philippines, 45 mi. ENE of Cabanatuan, on Baler Bay; fishing, agr. (coconuts, rice).

Balerna (bälĕr'nä), town (pop. 2,408), Ticino canton, S Switzerland, 4 mi. NW of Como, Italy; watches, tobacco, tiles.

Balerno (bŭlûr'nō), town in Currie parish, W central Midlothian, Scotland, on Water of Leith (14th-cent. bridge) and 7 mi. SW of Edinburgh; paper milling.

Baleshare or **Balishare** (bă"lĭ-shâr'), island (pop. 136), Outer Hebrides, Inverness, Scotland, just off S coast of North Uist; 4 mi. long.

Balestrand (bä'lüsträn), village (pop. 189; canton pop. 2,097), Sogn og Fjordane co., W Norway, on N shore of Sogne Fjord, at mouth of Fjaerlands Fjord, 20 mi. W of Sogndal; resort and tourist center; boat landing proper is sometimes called Balholm. Across the fjord is VANGSNES.

Balestrate (bälĕsträ'tĕ), village (pop. 4,691), Palermo prov., NW Sicily, port on Gulf of Castellammare, 7 mi. ENE of Castellammare del Golfo; wine making.

Baleswar River, E Pakistan: see MADHUMATI RIVER.

Balete Pass (bälā'tā), Philippines, pass through Caraballo Mts. in central Luzon, bet. Solano and San Jose.

Balezino (bŭlyĭzē'nŭ), town (1948 pop. over 2,000), N Udmurt Autonomous SSR, Russian SFSR, on Cheptsa R., on railroad and 18 mi. SE of Glazov; flax processing, mfg. (cinder blocks). At Pibanshur (5 mi. SE) is rail junction of line to Izhevsk, built during Second World War.

Balf (bŏlf), resort town (pop. 1,450), Sopron co., W Hungary, on Neusiedler L., 4 mi. SE of Sopron; sulphur springs.

Balfate (bälfä'tā), town (pop. 349), Colón dept., N Honduras, on Caribbean Sea, 29 mi. E of La Ceiba; rail terminus; coconuts, rice, sugar cane.

Balfour (băl'fôr), village (pop. 2,159), S Transvaal, U. of So. Afr., 17 mi. SE of Heidelberg; alt. 5,275 ft.; rail junction; grain, stock; grain elevator. Sometimes called Balfour North.

Balfour (băl'fŭr, –fōōr). **1** or **Smyth,** village (pop. 1,788, with near-by Druid Hills), Henderson co., SW N.C., just N of Hendersonville; cotton milling. **2** or **Balfours,** village (pop. 1,936), Randolph co., central N.C., 2 mi. N of Asheboro; residential;

hosiery mfg. 3 City (pop. 162), McHenry co., central N.Dak., 40 mi. ESE of Minot.

Balfour, Mount (10,741 ft.), SW Alta., near B.C. border, in Rocky Mts., in Banff Natl. Park, 50 mi. NW of Banff; 51°34'N 116°27'W.

Balfours, N.C.: see BALFOUR, Randolph co.

Balfourya or **Balfouria** (both: bälfo͝oryä'), settlement (pop. 300), N Israel, at N edge of Plain of Jezreel, 2 mi. NNE of Afula; mixed farming. Founded 1922.

Balfron (băl'frŏn), agr. village and parish (pop. 1,200), Stirling, Scotland, 9 mi. N of Milngavie.

Balgach (bäl'gäkh), town (pop. 2,402), St. Gall canton, NE Switzerland, 10 mi. E of St. Gall; embroideries, woolen textiles, foodstuffs; mineral baths.

Balgarka (bŭlgär'kä), highest peak (3,875 ft.) in E Balkan Mts., E central Bulgaria, 4 mi. N of Sliven. Sometimes spelled Bolgarka and Blgarka.

Balgarovo (–gä'rôvô), village (pop. 2,929), Burgas dist., E Bulgaria, 11 mi. NW of Burgas, in Aitos R. valley; sugar beets, vineyards. Formerly Urum-yeni-koi, Urum-Jenikoi, or Urum-Jenikeui.

Balgonie (bălgō'nē), town (pop. 121), S Sask., 16 mi. E of Regina; wheat.

Balgonie, Scotland: see MARKINCH.

Balhaf or **Belhaf** (both: bĕlhăf'), Wahidi sultanate (□ 5,500; pop. 25,000) of Eastern Aden Protectorate; ⊙ Balhaf. Situated just E of the Aulaqi country, it extends from the coast c.30 mi. inland to the plateau; drained by the Wadi Meifa'a; agr. and pastoral pop. Chief centers are Balhaf on the coast and the inland towns of Azzan and Habban. Protectorate treaty was concluded in 1905 and adviser agreements in 1938 and 1949. Prior to consolidation, the area was a confederation consisting of the sultanates of Balhaf, Habban, and Azzan.

Balhaf or **Belhaf**, town, ⊙ Wahidi sultanate of Balhaf, Eastern Aden Protectorate, port on Gulf of Aden, on road and 75 mi. SW of Mukalla; coastal trade; airfield. Distribution center for goods to interior of sultanate.

Balhannah (bălhă'nŭ), village (pop. 358), SE South Australia, 15 mi. ESE of Adelaide; rail junction; dairy products, livestock; bismuth.

Bal Harbour, town (pop. 224), Dade co., S Fla., near Miami Beach.

Balharshah, India: see BALLALPUR.

Balholm, Norway: see BALESTRAND.

Bali (bä'lē), town (pop. 11,879), S Br. Cameroons, administered as part of Eastern Provinces of Nigeria, in Bamenda highlands, on road and 10 mi. WSW of Bamenda; cattle raising; durra, millet.

Bali (bä'lē). 1 Town (pop. 7,044), S central Rajasthan, India, 75 mi. SSE of Jodhpur; millet, wheat; cotton-cloth dyeing. 2 Town, West Bengal, India: see BALLY.

Bali (bä'lē), island (□ 2,243; pop. 1,074,925, including offshore islets), Lesser Sundas, Indonesia, bet. Java Sea (N) and Indian Ocean (S), just E of Java across Bali Strait (2–15 mi. wide), 20 mi. W of Lombok across Lombok Strait; 7°54'–8°52'S 114°25'–115°42'E; 90 mi. long, 55 mi. wide. Although relatively small, Bali is culturally and economically one of most important isls. of Indonesia. Largely mountainous, isl. rises to 10,308 ft. in Mt. Agung; in S area is a large plain. Has moderate climate with little rainfall on N coast; rainfall in S part is heavy during monsoon periods. Wild animals include tigers and deer. Bali is known for giant waringin trees (held sacred by the Balinese). There are small teak forests. Chief products: copra, rice, coffee, tobacco, livestock (pigs, cattle). Important handicraft industries: wood carving, metalworking, weaving. Principal centers are SINGARAJA, near its port BULELENG, and DENPASAR. The Balinese (Malayan group closely related to the Javanese) are known for their physical beauty and high level of culture. Unlike Java, the predominant religion is Hinduism which spread to Bali in 7th cent.; Javanese Hindus migrated to Bali in 9th and 10th cent. Intermittently isl. was ruled (10th–15th cent.) by the Javanese. First visited 1597 by the Dutch, trade was begun in early 17th cent. by Du. East India Co. Bali was under Br. rule 1811–1816; Du. rule was not firmly established until 1908.

Bali, Peak of, Indonesia: see AGUNG, MOUNT.

Baliana, Egypt: see BALYANA, EL.

Baliapatam, India: see CANNANORE, city.

Balibo (bä"lēbo͞o'), town, ⊙ Cova-Lima dist. (□ 587; pop. 16,767), Portuguese Timor, in central part of isl., near border of Indonesian Timor, 45 mi. SW of Dili; sandalwood, copra, rice.

Balik, Lake (bälŭk'), Turkish *Balık*. 1 Lake (□ 14), N Turkey, 23 mi. NW of Samsun; 9 mi. long, 3 mi. wide. 2 Lake (□ 9), E Turkey, 26 mi. E of Karakose, in the mts. W of Mt. Ararat; 7 mi. long, 4 mi. wide; alt. 7,350 ft.

Balikesir (bälŭ'kĕsir"), Turkish *Balıkesir*, province □ 5,982; 1950 pop. 563,100), NW Turkey, on the Aegean; ⊙ Balikesir. Bordered N by Sea of Marmara, S by Kozak and Demirci Mts. Drained by Kirmasti, Koca, Gonen, and Simav rivers. Heavily forested; W half rich in minerals—lead with silver, manganese, iron, copper, zinc, antimony, arsenic, chromium; also coal and lignite. Major Merino sheep and agr. area (beans, cereals, olives, tobacco, cotton, onions, garlic).

Balikesir, Turkish *Balıkesir*, city (1950 pop. 36,001), ⊙ Balikesir prov., NW Turkey, railroad junction 110 mi. SSW of Istanbul; center of agr. dist. (sugar beets, cereals, beans, vetch, opium, tobacco); Merino sheep. Formerly a silk-mfg. city.

Balikpapan (bä"lĭkpä'pän), town (pop. 29,843), E Borneo, Indonesia, port on Macassar Strait, 210 mi. NE of Banjermasin; 1°15'S 116°50'E; chief oil center of isl. Has airport. In Second World War, the Japanese landed here in early 1942 after suffering severe losses in naval battle fought offshore. Oil installations destroyed before Jap. landing were subsequently rebuilt.

Balik Pulau (bä'lĭk po͞olou'), town (pop. 2,141) on Penang isl., NW Malaya, 12 mi. SW of George Town; rubber, coconuts.

Balilihan (bälēlē'hän), town (1939 pop. 2,267; 1948 municipality pop. 23,937), W Bohol isl., Philippines, 10 mi. NE of Tagbilaran; agr. center (rice, coconuts).

Baling (bälĭng'), town (pop. 2,599), E Kedah, Malaya, on road and 29 mi. E of Sungei Patani, near Perak line; rubber and rice plantations.

Balingasag (bälĕng-gäsäg'), town (1939 pop. 3,990; 1948 municipality pop. 26,270), Misamis Oriental prov., N Mindanao, Philippines, on Macajalar Bay, 20 mi. NNE of Cagayan; corn, coconuts.

Balingen (bä'lĭng-ŭn), town (pop. 6,831), S Württemberg, Germany, after 1945 in Württemberg-Hohenzollern, 12 mi. NE of Rottweil; rail junction; mfg. (precision instruments, electrical goods, shoes, leather gloves). Has late-Gothic church. First mentioned in 9th cent. Chartered 1255.

Balinghem, France: see GUÎNES.

Balinhard, Mount (10,270 ft.), W Alta., in Rocky Mts., in Jasper Natl. Park, 35 mi. ESE of Jasper.

Balint (bälēnts'), Rum. *Balinț*, Hung. *Bálinc* (bä'lēnts), village (pop. 1,102), Timisoara prov., W Rumania, on Bega R., on railroad and 10 mi. N of Lugoj; flour milling.

Balintang Channel, Philippines: see LUZON STRAIT.

Balipara (bälĭpä'rŭ), frontier tract (□ 12,034; 1950 pop. estimate 350,000; pop. of 6,512 g ven in 1941 census covered only 571 sq. mi. of the tract), N Assam, India; ⊙ Charduar. Bounded N by China and Tibet, W by Bhutan, E by Subansiri R. N and W frontiers are undefined. Mainly in Assam Himalayas and their extensions (Miri Hills, NE; Dafla Hills, SE); Brahmaputra valley in extreme S; drained by Subansiri R. and tributaries of the Brahmaputra. Agr. (rice, rape and mustard, tea, jute, sugar cane). Pop. 39% Hindu, 58% Animist tribes (including Miris, Daflas, and Akas).

Balipara, village, Darrang dist., N central Assam, India, 14 mi. NNW of Tezpur; rail spur terminus; tea, rice, rape and mustard, sugar cane, jute. Extensive tea gardens near by.

Balis, Syria: see MESKENE.

Balisa (bŭlē'zŭ), city (pop. 1,090), SW Goiás, central Brazil, on right bank of the Araguaia (Mato Grosso border) at influx of Garças R., in diamond-washing region. Head of navigation for small craft.

Balishare, Scotland: see BALESHARE.

Balisna (bŭlĭs'nŭ), town (pop. 5,103), Mehsana dist., N Bombay, India, 17 mi. NW of Mehsana; millet, cotton, oilseeds; cattle breeding. Also spelled Balisana.

Baliuag (bälē'wäg), town (1939 pop. 1,478; 1948 municipality pop. 30,670), Bulacan prov., S central Luzon, Philippines, 25 mi. NNW of Manila, just W of Bustos; rice milling. Known for handmade buri-palm hats.

Balivanich, Scotland: see BENBECULA.

Baliwasan (bälēwä'sän), town (1939 pop. 2,478) in Zamboanga dist., Zamboanga prov., W Mindanao, Philippines, 7 mi. NE of Zamboanga proper; fish cannery.

Bali-yefendi, Bulgaria: see KNYAZHEVO.

Balk (bä'lŭk), town (pop. 1,334), Friesland prov., N Netherlands, 10 mi. SSW of Sneek, near Sloter Meer (small lake); mfg. of drainage and pumping machinery.

Balkan, mining village (1940 pop. 799), Bell co., SE Ky., in the Cumberlands, near Cumberland R., 13 mi. NE of Middlesboro; bituminous coal.

Balkan Mountains (bôl'kŭn), Bulg. *Stara Planina* [=old mountain], anc. *Haemus*, major mtn. range of Balkan Peninsula and Bulgaria; extend c.350 mi. from upper Timok R. (W; Yugoslav border) to Cape Yemine on Black Sea (E); 12–30 mi. wide. Major divide bet. Danube (N) and Maritsa (S) rivers. Rise to 7,793 ft. at Botev Peak; crossed by c.20 highway passes, 3 rail lines, and by Iskar R. Climatic border (N limit of Mediterranean climatic influence). Mineral resources include lignite, anthracite, graphite, and metallic ores (iron, zinc, copper, lead) deposits; mineral and thermal springs. Alpine meadows in upper sections, coniferous and deciduous forests on slopes. Subdivided into 3 sections: **Western Balkan Mountains** extend c.125 mi. bet. Timok R. (W) and Botevgrad Pass (E); rise to 7,113 ft. at Midzhur peak; crossed by Sveti Nikola and Petrokhan passes, and by Iskar R. Includes Chiporov, Berkovitsa, Vratsa, and Murgash mts. Main centers: Belogradchik, Berkovitsa, Vratsa. **Central Balkan Mountains** extend c.125 mi. bet. Botevgrad Pass (W) and Vratnik Pass (E); rise to 7,793 ft. at the Botev Peak; crossed by Zlatitsa, Troyan, Shipka, and Tvarditsa passes. Include Yetropole, Troyan, Kalofer, Shipka, and Yelena mts. Main centers: Yetropole, Teteven, Troyan, Gabrovo. **Eastern Balkan Mountains** extend c.90 mi. bet. Vratnik Pass (W) and Cape Yemine of Black Sea (E); rise to 3,875 ft. at Balgarka peak; crossed by Kotel and Varbitsa passes. Include Lisa, Varbitsa, Aitos, and Yemine mts. Main centers: Targovishte, Omortag.

Balkan Peninsula, large peninsula of SE Europe bet. the Adriatic Sea (W), Ionian Sea (SW), Mediterranean Sea proper (S), Aegean Sea (SE), and the Black Sea (E); the c.200-mi.-long combined waterway of the Bosporus, the Sea of Marmara, and the Dardanelles separate it in SE from Turkey in Asia. The lower Danube and its tributary the Sava are generally considered its N limit, with an imaginary line terminating at Rijeka (Fiume). From here, at its broadest (c.800 mi.) base, the peninsula extends c.650 mi. S, gradually narrowing down to the Peloponnesus, whose S tip is Cape Matapan (36°23'N 22°29'E). It comprises GREECE, TURKEY in Europe, BULGARIA, ALBANIA, most of YUGOSLAVIA, and RUMANIA. Off the heavily indented coast line are many isls., particularly along DALMATIA and in the Aegean. Chalcidice, the Peloponnesus, and Gallipoli form sub-peninsulas. The topographic complexity of the Balkan Peninsula, dominated by the mts. and long marked by difficult communications, is reflected in the region's ethnic diversity and in its turbulent history and unstable politics. Several inhospitable ranges crisscross the area, carving out the few isolated plains which are agriculturally productive (cereals, tobacco, cotton, olives, flax, soybeans, grapes, hemp, poppies, roses, etc.). Among these plains are: the lowland sections of the SE—Thrace, S Macedonia, Attica, and Thessaly; Dalmatia and the important Yugoslav granary of VOJVODINA, which is contiguous with the Hungarian ALFÖLD; the ZETA plain of Montenegro; the DOBRUJA of Rumania and Bulgaria; and the THRACIAN PLAIN of Bulgaria. Apart from the barren KARST and the eroded highlands of Greece, the mts. are densely forested. Principal ranges related to the Carpathians and Alps are the BALKAN MOUNTAINS (E) —which give the peninsula its name—the Pindus (S), the Dinaric Alps and North Albanian Alps (W), and, in SE, the largely crystalline Rhodope Mts., most formidable of them all, rising to 9,596 ft. in the Stalin or Musala Peak. Apart from the Danube, none of the rivers—some running dry during the summer—can be used by commercial shipping. Main streams are the Morava, flowing N to the Danube, and the Vardar, draining S to the Aegean; together they form an important N-S furrow, followed by transcontinental railroad to Salonika Other rivers flowing to the Aegean are the Aliakmon, Struna, Mesta, and Maritsa. The Drina is tributary to the Sava, while the lower Danube receives the Isker. There are a few larger lakes, such as L. Scutari, L. Ohrid, L. Prespan, L. Copais, and L. Voveis. The climate is almost entirely continental, i.e., long, severe winters, hot, rainy summers. Only the S has a true Mediterranean type of climate (mild winters, dry summers). The great majority of its rural people are engaged in agr. and pastoral activities. Mining is of increasing importance in Bulgaria (coal, copper, manganese) and Yugoslavia (bauxite, lead, antimony, mercury, copper, zinc, etc.). Greece exports some iron ore, magnesite, chromite, and emery. Scattered oil and natural gas deposits occur. Spas abound in the mts. As a political concept the **Balkan States** extend beyond the conventional Danube border to include all of Yugoslavia and Rumania, i.e., all those SE European countries which were once under the complete control of the Ottoman Empire. Though some of the West's oldest (Mycenaean) and most glorious civilizations flourished in Greece, the peninsula is today among Europe's most backward areas. This entire region, open in the N to invasion from Asia and Central Europe, has always been a historic crossroads, where different races passed, met, merged, and clashed. In its recesses tribes and clans could entrench themselves. During prehistoric times it was settled by Illyrians and Thracians, antedating—and presumably related to—the various Greek strains of the Achaeans, Aeolians, Ionians, and Dorians. The Greeks encountered the already flourishing (before 1100 B.C.) Mycenaean and Minoan cultures of S Greece and Crete. All of Greece was won (338 B.C.) by Philip II of Macedon at Chaeronea. After 3d cent. B.C. the region came to be controlled by Rome and was divided into the provs. of Dalmatia, Macedonia, Epirus, Achaea, Upper and Lower PANNONIA, Upper and Lower MOESIA, Thrace, and DACIA; most of them were later united in the Prefecture of Illyricum and became (A.D. 395) a part of the East Roman Empire. In 6th cent. began the invasions of Slav and Turk (Bulgar) tribes. Though Rumanians claim Latin descent and the modern Greeks can boast of an even more noble lineage, the Slavonic element achieved dominance. These evolved as Serbs, Croats, Slovenes, Macedonians, and Albanians, and later came Magyars, Slovaks, Ruthenians, Germans, Jews, and even Circassians, Armenians, and Gypsies. Conflicting religious adherence (R.C., Orthodox Eastern, Uniate, Protestant, Moslem), cultural traditions, and natl. ambitions soon set in to turn the region into that heterogeneous area of contiguous antagonisms for which the Balkans have become a byword. Following the Barbarian invasions, the Bulgars (at their peak in 9th and 13th cent.) and the Serbs (in 14th cent.) rose to be the leading Balkan powers, challenging the Byzantine Empire, which was gradually engulfed by the rising Ottoman Empire. An independent Serbian kingdom flourished briefly under Stephen Dushan (1331–55), who ruled over Bosnia, Macedonia, Epirus, and Albania, and proclaimed himself emperor of Serbs and Greeks. The victories of Kossovo (1389) and Nikopol (1397) brought most of the peninsula under a Turkish control which was to last for almost half a millenium (see also OTTOMAN EMPIRE). It held sway in the 15th cent. over Rumelia, Bulgaria, Macedonia, Thessaly, Serbia, Herzegovina, most of Albania and Montenegro (resisting in the mts.), and the despotats of Athens, Mistra, and Patras. Sections of the Dalmatian coast remained, however, under Venetian control. From the end of the 17th cent. Ottoman power started to decline, while Austria and Russia emerged as aggressive forces, vying for the spoils. Serbia was temporarily held (1718–39) by Austria. Russia, appointing itself a defender of the enslaved Slav nations, gained in 18th cent. a temporary foothold in Moldavia and Walachia, but the princes reverted to Ottoman suzerainty, while TRANSYLVANIA remained most of the time under Magyar rule. As an outcome of the Russo-Turkish War (1828–29) and the Treaty of Adrianople, Russia obtained control of the Danube mouths, Moldavia and Walachia became a Russian protectorate nominally within the Ottoman Empire, and Greece was recognized (1829) as an independent principality (but without Thessaly and Epirus, which Greece acquired in 1881). After Turkey's defeat in the Russo-Turkish War of 1877–78 (terminated by Treaty of San Stefano) and the intervention of foreign powers at the Congress of Berlin, Rumania, Serbia, and Montenegro gained full independence, Bosnia and Herzegovina were occupied by Austria (who annexed them in 1908), Bulgaria achieved virtual independence (complete sovereignty declared in 1908), and EASTERN RUMELIA (annexed by Bulgaria in 1885) and most of Macedonia remained under Turkish control, as did Albania (until 1912). In the 2 Balkan Wars (1912–13) Turkey was reduced to a small foothold in Europe, and the Balkan countries turned immediately against each other, making the peninsula the powderkeg that was shortly to unloose the First World War among the proud and ambitious large nations of Europe. During the hostilities (1914–18), in which Bulgaria sided with the Central Powers and Turkey, most of the peninsula (except for Greece) were taken by the Central Powers but later liberated by the Allies. The history of the Balkans since then is essentially that of its separate countries. After the war emerged an independent Yugoslavia (comprising Serbia, Slovenia, Bosnia and Herzegovina, Montenegro, and part of Macedonia). Just before and during the Second World War the political boundaries of the Balkan countries were changed and rechanged; after the Second World War, however, the boundaries were approximately those established after the First World War. The once prominent French and Anglo-Saxon influence, typified in the Balkan Entente (1934), which sought to preserve the independence and identity of the several nations, gave way after the Second World War to Russian control in the "people's republics" (Bulgaria, Rumania, Albania, Yugoslavia). As usual, however, Balkan differences continued. Greece, which had to fight a civil war, became a bastion of the West, and Yugoslavia, though Communist, broke with the Russian bloc: the "Balkan problem" remained as explosive as ever. For further information see separate articles on countries, historic provs., political units, and physical features.

Balkanski Priisk, Russian SFSR: see BALKANY.

Balkany (bŏl'kănyŭ), Hung. *Balkány*, town (pop. 7,387), Szabolcs co., NE Hungary, 18 mi. NNE of Debrecen; wheat, tobacco; cattle, hogs.

Balkany (bŭlkä'nē), town (1939 pop. over 2,000), SW Chelyabinsk oblast, Russian SFSR, 20 mi. E of Magnitogorsk; tungsten-mining center. Until 1929, Balkanski Priisk.

Balkar, in Rus. names: see KABARDIAN AUTONOMOUS SOVIET SOCIALIST REPUBLIC.

Balkashino (bŭlkä'shĭnŭ), village (1948 pop. over 2,000), N Akmolinsk oblast, Kazakh SSR, 50 mi. NNE of Atbasar; wheat; cattle.

Balkassar (bŭlkŭs'sŭr), village, Jhelum dist., N Punjab, W Pakistan, on Potwar Plateau, 12 mi. W of Chakwal; petroleum wells, in operation since 1946. Oil from here and from field near Joya Mair (c.10 mi. NE; worked since 1944) goes via pipe line to Chakwal, thence by rail to refinery at Rawalpindi.

Balkh (bälkh, bŭlkh), anc. *Bactra* (băk'trēŭ), town (pop. 10,000), Mazar-i-Sharif prov., N Afghanistan, in Afghan Turkestan, 13 mi. WNW of Mazar-i-Sharif, in Balkh R. oasis. The capital of anc. Bactria, Balkh is sometimes referred to as "the mother of cities" and, according to one tradition, as the home of Zoroaster. It attained its greatest importance as ⊙ Bactrian satrapy of the old Persian Empire (5th cent. B.C.), was conquered in 328 B.C. by Alexander the Great, and flourished again as ⊙ Greco-Bactria (3d cent. B.C.). It passed in A.D. 705 to the Arabs and was the original home of the Barmecides, rivals of the caliph Harun al-Rashid. Sacked in 1221 by Jenghiz Khan, it never regained its former importance. Only weathered ruins remain of the old city. The new town, an agr. center, inhabited largely by Uzbeks, came (1850) under Afghan control.

Balkhan (bŭlkhän'), two mountain ranges in W Ashkhabad oblast, Turkmen SSR. Greater Balkhan Range extends 40 mi. E from Dzhebel, N of the Uzboi; rises to 6,120 ft. Lesser Balkhan Range, S of the Uzboi, rises to 1,975 ft.

Balkhash (bŭlkhäsh'), city (1945 pop. 70,000), SE Karaganda oblast, Kazakh SSR, on N shore of L. Balkhash, 230 mi. SSE of Karaganda; rail terminus in irrigated desert area. Large copper-smelting center for Kounradski ore; linked to mines (15 mi. N) by electric railroad; metalworking, salt extraction, sawmilling; power plant. Lake port; navigation to Burlyu-Tobe (E) and Burlyu-Baital (S). Formerly named Bertys for bay on which it was founded (1929); later renamed Pribalkhash, and, after 1937, Balkhash.

Balkhash, Lake (□ 6,680), SE Kazakh SSR, bet. Kazakh Hills (N) and the Sary-Ishik-Otrau (desert, S), 100 mi. W of China border, c.600 mi. E of Aral Sea; 375 mi. long, 15–55 mi. wide, alt. 1,115 ft., average depth 20 ft. (deepest in E, 87 ft.). Low, sandy S shore; high, rocky N shore. Salt content increases toward E, with fresh water (W) near Ili R. delta mouth, its chief inlet; it has no outlet. Freezes c.5 months a year. Receives Ili, Kara-Tal, Ak-Su, Lepsa, and Ayaguz rivers in S and E. Salt extraction (E) and fishing (since 1930; carp, perch) are important. Extensive copper deposits on N shore (Kounradski). Main ports: Balkhash (N), Burlyu-Tobe (E), Burlyu-Baital (SW).

Balkh River (bälkh, bŭlkh), Afghan Turkestan, N Afghanistan, rises in W outlier of the Hindu Kush in 2 headstreams which join 40 mi. SSW of Mazar-i-Sharif, flows c.40 mi. N, fanning out into an irrigation canal network, and irrigating Mazar-i-Sharif, Balkh, and Aqchah oases.

Balkonda (bäl'kōndŭ), town (pop. 5,040), Nizamabad dist., N central Hyderabad state, India, 21 mi. NE of Nizamabad; rice, millet, sugar, oilseeds.

Ball, Mount (10,865 ft.), SW Alta., near B.C. border, in Rocky Mts., in Banff Natl. Park, 19 mi. W of Banff; 51°9'N 116°W.

Balla, India: see KHOWAI.

Balla (bă'lŭ), Gaelic *Ball Áluinn*, town (pop. 264), S central Co. Mayo, Ireland, 8 mi. ESE of Castlebar; agr. market (cattle; potatoes).

Ballaarat, Australia: see BALLARAT.

Balla Balla (bä'lä bä'lä), village, Bulawayo prov., SW Southern Rhodesia, in Matabeleland, on railroad and 35 mi. SE of Bulawayo; alt. 3,603 ft. Serves Filabusi mining area. Tobacco, corn, citrus fruit; livestock; dairy products.

Ballabgarh (bŭl'lŭbgŭr), town (pop. 5,108), Gurgaon dist., SE Punjab, India, 19 mi. ESE of Gurgaon; millet, wheat, gram, cotton.

Ballachulish (bălŭhōō'lĭsh), town in Lismore and Appin parish (pop. 3,575), N Argyll, Scotland, in Appin district, on Loch Levin at foot of Beinn a'Bheitir mountain (3,362 ft.), 22 mi. NE of Oban. Extensive slate quarries. Near by is GLENCOE.

Ballaghaderreen (bă"lŭhŭdŭrēn'), Gaelic *Bealach an Doirín*, town (pop. 1,252), NW Co. Roscommon, Ireland, 25 mi. NW of Roscommon; agr. market (cattle, sheep, pigs; potatoes); bacon and ham curing.

Ballah, El, or **Al-Ballah** (both: ĕl băl-lä'), village, Canal Governorate, NE Egypt, on Suez Canal, on Cairo-Haifa RR, and 6 mi. S of El Qantara; important gypsum quarries near by. Airfield 3 mi. SW. S is the bed of former L. Ballah, through which passes the Suez Canal.

Ballalpur (bŭl-läl'pŏŏr) or **Ballarpur** (bŭl-lär'pŏŏr), town (pop., including E railway settlement of Balharshah, 8,712), Chanda dist., S Madhya Pradesh, India, on Wardha R. and 8 mi. SSE of Chanda; collieries here and across river in Hyderabad; sawmilling (teak in near-by forests); ceramics. Sandstone deposits near by.

Ballan (bă'lŭn), town (pop. 678), S Victoria, Australia, 45 mi. WNW of Melbourne; agr. center.

Ballancourt (bälăkōōr'), town (pop. 1,948), Seine-et-Oise dept., N central France, near the Essonne, 8 mi. SSW of Corbeil; paper milling (newsprint).

Ballangen (bäl'läng"ŭn), village (pop. 388; canton pop. 4,382), Nordland co., N Norway, on inlet of Ofot Fjord, 16 mi. WSW of Narvik; mining (iron, copper, pyrites, lead, zinc).

Ballantrae (bălŭntrā'), fishing village and parish (pop. 1,076), S Ayrshire, Scotland, on Firth of Clyde at mouth of Stinchar R., 11 mi. SW of Girvan; seaside resort.

Ballantyne Strait, W Franklin Dist., Northwest Territories, arm (80 mi. long, 35–60 mi. wide) of the Arctic Ocean, bet. Prince Patrick Isl. (SW) and Brock and South Borden isls. (NE); 77°–78°N 113°–116°30'W.

Ballao (băl-lä'ō), village (pop. 1,327), Cagliari prov., SE Sardinia, on Flumendosa R. and 26 mi. NE of Cagliari; antimony mine.

Ballarat (bă'lŭrăt), city (pop. 38,140; metropolitan Ballarat 40,181), S central Victoria, Australia, 65 mi. WNW of Melbourne; rail junction; industrial center; woolen mills, brass foundries, brewery. School of mines, Anglican and R.C. cathedrals. Founded 1851 with gold rush; formerly important gold-mining town. Includes S suburb of Sebastopol (pop. 2,041). Also spelled Ballaarat.

Ballarat (bă'lŭrăt), ghost mining town, Inyo co., E Calif., in Panamint Valley, W of Death Valley.

Ballard (bă'lŭrd), county (□ 259; pop. 8,545), SW Ky.; ⊙ Wickliffe. Bounded SW by the Mississippi (Mo. line), W, NW, and N by the Ohio (Ill. line), S by Mayfield Creek. Gently rolling upland rises above flood plains along river. Agr. (especially dark tobacco; also corn, potatoes), clay pits, timber. Has chain of small lakes. Formed 1842.

Ballard, Mount (7,500 ft.), highest peak in Mule Mts., SE Ariz., 3 mi. W of Bisbee.

Ballarpur, India: see BALLALPUR.

Ballas, El, or **Al-Ballas** (both: ĕl băl-läs'), village (pop. 10,201), Qena prov., Upper Egypt, on W bank of the Nile and 10 mi. SSE of Qena; pottery making; cereals, sugar cane, dates.

Ballater (bă'lŭtŭr), burgh (1931 pop. 1,198; 1951 census 1,301), S Aberdeen, Scotland, on the Dee and 36 mi. WSW of Aberdeen; resort with mineral springs.

Ballclub Lake, Itasca co., N central Minn., in Greater Leech Lake Indian Reservation and Chippewa Natl. Forest, 18 mi. WNW of Grand Rapids; 5.5 mi. long, 1.5 mi. wide. Drains into Mississippi R. Has small resorts. Sometimes written Ball Club.

Ballena (bäyā'nä), village, Guanacaste prov., NW Costa Rica, port on Tempisque R., opposite Bolsón (head of navigation), and 10 mi. SE of Filadelfia; coastal trade.

Ballena Point, headland, Maldonado dept., S Uruguay, at Atlantic mouth of the Río de la Plata, 4 mi. W of Maldonado; 34°55'S 55°2'W. Has fine beach and park.

Ballenas, Canal de las (känäl' dā läs bäyā'näs) [Sp.,=channel of whales], in Gulf of California, NW Mexico, bet. E coast of Lower California and Angel de la Guarda Isl.; c.55 mi. long, 10–15 mi. wide.

Ballenberg (bă'lŭnbĕrk), town (pop. 666), N Baden, Germany, after 1945 in Württemberg-Baden, 23 mi. NE of Heilbronn; grain.

Ballenstedt (bä'lŭn-shtĕt), residential town (pop. 10,538), in former Anhalt state, central Germany, after 1945 in Saxony-Anhalt, at N foot of the lower Harz, 6 mi. SE of Quedlinburg; climatic health resort. Has 18th-cent. church with grave of Albert the Bear. Oldest domain of Ascanian counts (later margraves of Brandenburg). Chartered 1512. Residence (1765–1863) of dukes of Anhalt-Bernburg. At 12th-cent. Falkenstein castle (4 mi. S), the Sachsenspiegel, early German law code, was translated from Latin into German after 1230.

Balleny Islands (bă'lŭnē), glaciated, volcanic group N of Antarctica, 150 mi. off Victoria Land, S of New Zealand; 66°15'–67°40'S 162°15'–164°45'E. Largest are Sturge Isl. and Young Isl. Discovered 1839 by John Balleny, Br. sealer.

Balleroy (bälrwä'), village (pop. 873), Calvados dept., NW France, at E edge of Forest of Cerisy, 9 mi. SW of Bayeux; woodworking, cider distilling.

Ballerup (bă'lŭrōōp), town (pop. 2,949), Copenhagen amt, NE Zealand, Denmark, 8 mi. NW of Copenhagen; truck produce; mfg. (chemicals, cement).

Ballestero, El (ĕl bälyĕstă'rō), town (pop. 1,617), Albacete prov., SE central Spain, 35 mi. WSW of Albacete; livestock, cereals, saffron.

Ballesteros (bäyĕstă'rōs), town (pop. 2,552), E central Córdoba prov., Argentina, 18 mi. SE of Villa María; wheat, flax, corn, alfalfa, livestock; dairying.

Ballesteros or **Ballesteros de Calatrava** (bälyĕstărōs dhā käläträ'vä), town (pop. 1,561), Ciudad Real prov., S central Spain, 10 mi. S of Ciudad Real; olives, cereals, chick-peas, vegetables, grapes, stock; olive-oil extracting.

Balleza, town, Mexico: see SAN PABLO BALLEZA.

Balleza River (bäyä'sä), Chihuahua, N Mexico, rises in Sierra Madre Occidental of Durango near Chihuahua border, flows c.75 mi. N, past San Pablo Balleza, to Conchos R. 13 mi. N of Valle de Olivos. Usually called San Juan R. in upper course.

Ball Ground, town (pop. 700), Cherokee co., NW Ga., 9 mi. NE of Canton; mfg. (monuments, lumber, cotton goods).

Ballia (bŭl'yŭ), district (□ 1,183; pop. 1,053,880), E Uttar Pradesh, India; ⊙ Ballia. On Ganges Plain, bounded S by Ganges, N by Gogra rivers. Agr. (rice, gram, barley, oilseeds, sugar cane, wheat, corn, millet); sugar refining, cotton weaving. Main towns: Ballia, Chit Baragaon, Rasra, Bansdih.

Ballia, town (pop. 23,520), ⊙ Ballia dist., E Uttar Pradesh, India, near the Ganges, 80 mi. ENE of Benares; sugar refining, cotton weaving; trades in grains, oilseeds, sugar cane, ghee. Annual fair.

Balliguda (bŭl'lĭgo͝odŭ), village, Ganjam dist., S central Orissa, India, in Eastern Ghats, 85 mi. NW of Berhampur.

Ballina (bă'lŭnŭ), municipality and port (pop. 3,202), NE New South Wales, Australia, at mouth of Richmond R., 105 mi. SSE of Brisbane; dairying center; exports bananas, dairy products. Platinum mine near by.

Ballina (bă'lĭnŭ), Gaelic *Béal Átha an Fheadha*, urban district (pop. 6,045), NE Co. Mayo, Ireland, on Moy R., near its mouth on Killala Bay, at mouth of Deel R., 19 mi. NNE of Castlebar; 54°7'N 9°10'W; salmon-fishing and agr. market center in cattle-raising, potato-growing area. E suburb of Ardnaree is site of modern R.C. cathedral, house of bishop of Killala, and ruins of 1427 Augustinian friary. In 1798 town was captured by the French.

Ballinagh (bălĭnä') or **Bellananagh** (bĕ"lŭnŭnä'), Gaelic *Béal Átha na nEach*, town (pop. 329), W Co. Cavan, Ireland, 5 mi. SSW of Cavan; agr. market (cattle, pigs; potatoes).

Ballinakill (bă"lĭnŭkĭl'), Gaelic *Baile na Coille*, town (pop. 318), S Co. Laoighis, Ireland, 11 mi. S of Port Laoighise; agr. market (wheat, barley, potatoes, beets). Has remains of anc. castle, destroyed 1641 by Cromwell.

Ballinamore (bă"lĭnŭmôr'), Gaelic *Béal an Átha Móir*, town (pop. 718), SE Co. Leitrim, Ireland, 14 mi. NE of Carrick-on-Shannon; agr. market (dairying, cattle; potatoes).

Ballinamuck (bă"lĭnŭmŭk'), Gaelic *Baile na Muc*, agr. village (district pop. 1,750), N Co. Longford, Ireland, 11 mi. NNE of Longford; dairying, cattle raising, potato growing. In 1798 the French under General Humbert here surrendered to the English.

Ballinasloe (bă"lĭnŭslō'), Gaelic *Béal Átha na Sluagh*, urban district (pop. 5,421), E Co. Galway, Ireland, on Suck R., on branch of the Grand Canal, and 35 mi. E of Galway; agr. market (cattle, sheep; potatoes, beets); limestone quarrying. Has noted annual livestock fairs.

Ballincollig (bă"lĭnkŏ'lĭg), Gaelic *Baile an Chullaigh*, town (pop. 300), S central Co. Cork, Ireland, near Lee R., 5 mi. W of Cork; agr. market (potatoes, oats, dairying). Has 14th-cent. castle.

Ballindalloch (bă"lĭndă'lŭkh), village, W Banffshire, Scotland, on the Spey at mouth of Avon R., and 10 mi. WSW of Dufftown; whisky distilling. Has modernized castle.

Ballindine (bă"lĭndīn'), Gaelic *Baile an Daingin*, town (pop. 231), SE Co. Mayo, Ireland, 4 mi. SSE of Claremorris; agr. market (cattle; potatoes).

Ballingarry (bă"lĭngă'rē), Gaelic *Baile an Gharrdha*, town (pop. 308), central Co. Limerick, Ireland, 17 mi. SW of Limerick; agr. market (grain, potatoes; dairying).

Ballinger (bă'lĭnjŭr), city (pop. 5,302), ⊙ Runnels co., W central Texas, at mouth of Elm Creek on Colorado R. and 36 mi. NE of San Angelo; trade, processing center in livestock, agr. area; ships wool, cotton, grain; dairying (milk, cheese); mfg. of mattresses. Near-by reservoir (capacity 2,000 acre-ft.) on Elm Creek is unit of Colorado R. flood-control project. Laid out 1886, inc. 1892.

Ballingry, town and parish (pop. 10,353, including part of Lochgelly burgh), S central Fifeshire, Scotland, 5 mi. WNW of Kirkcaldy; coal mining.

Ballinrobe (bă"lĭnrōb'), Gaelic *Baile an Ródhba*, town (pop. 1,293), S Co. Mayo, Ireland, on Robe R., near its mouth on Lough Mask, and 17 mi. S of Castlebar; agr. market (cattle; potatoes).

Ballinskelligs (bă"lĭnskĕ'lĭgz), Gaelic *Baile na Sgealg*, fishing village (district pop. 796), SW Co. Kerry, Ireland, on Ballinskelligs Bay (7 mi. long, 5 mi. wide) of the Atlantic, 10 mi. S of Cahirciveen; site of cable station to U.S. Has remains of anc. castle and abbey.

Ballintogher (bă"lĭntŏkh'ŭr), Gaelic *Baile an Tóchair*, town (pop. 87), E Co. Sligo, Ireland, 7 mi. SE of Sligo; agr. market (cattle; potatoes).

Ballisodare, Ireland: see BALLYSADARE.

Ballobar (bälyōvär'), village (pop. 1,967), Huesca prov., NE Spain, at influx of Alcanadre R. into Cinca R., 10 mi. NW of Fraga; cereals, olive oil, wine, figs.

Balloch (bă'lŭkh), agr. village in Bonhill parish, S Dumbarton, Scotland, at S end of Loch Lomond, on Leven R., just N of Bonhill; resort and S terminal of lake steamers.

Ballochmyle (bălŭkh-mīl'), agr. village in Mauchline parish, central Ayrshire, Scotland. Ballochmyle House is scene of poems by Burns.

Balloki (bŭl-lō'kē), village, Lahore dist., E Punjab, W Pakistan, 36 mi. SW of Lahore; local agr. market (wheat, cotton). Aqueduct and headworks of Lower Bari Doab Canal 2 mi. NW, on Ravi R.

Ballon (bälō'), village (pop. 720), Sarthe dept., W France, 13 mi. N of Le Mans; hemp.

Ballon de Guebwiller, France: see GUEBWILLER, BALLON DE.

Ballon de Servance, France: see SERVANCE, BALLON DE.

Ballon Pass, France: see ALSACE, BALLON D'.

Ballots (bälō'), village (pop. 430), Mayenne dept., W France, 17 mi. SW of Laval; knitwear.

Ball's Bluff, Va.: see LEESBURG.

Ballsh (bälsh) or **Ballshi** (bäl'shē), anc. *Byllis*, village (1930 pop. 450), S central Albania, in Mallakastër range, 15 mi. NE of Valona; ruins of 14th-cent. cathedral. Destroyed (late 15th cent.) by Turks.

Ballsta, Sweden: see VALLENTUNA.

Ballstad (bäl'stä), village (pop. 591) in Buksnes canton (pop. 4,434), Nordland co., N Norway, at S tip of Vestvagoy of the Lofoten Isls., 30 mi. WSW of Svolvaer; cod-fishing center; summer resort; lighthouse. Sometimes spelled Balstad.

Ballston Lake (bôl'stŭn), resort and residential village, Saratoga co., E N.Y., on Ballston L. (c.2 mi. long), 7 mi. S of Ballston Spa.

Ballston Spa (spä), village (pop. 4,937), ⊙ Saratoga co., E N.Y., 6 mi. SSW of Saratoga Springs; mfg. (knit goods, gloves, leather, confectionery, condiments). Mineral springs; formerly a popular resort. Settled 1771, inc. 1807.

Balltown, town (pop. 49), Dubuque co., E Iowa, near Mississippi R., 12 mi. NW of Dubuque.

Ballum, Netherlands: see AMELAND.

Bally (bä'lē), town (pop. 50,397), Howrah dist., S West Bengal, India, on Hooghly R. and 4.5 mi. NNE of Howrah, 5 mi. N of Calcutta city center; jute milling, mfg. of chemical fertilizer, cotton cloth, bricks, glass; iron and steel rolling works. Willingdom Bridge, across river to Baranagar, opened 1931. Also spelled Bali.

Bally (bă'lē), borough (pop. 753), Berks co., SE Pa., 16 mi. SW of Allentown; mfg. (wood products, hosiery, refrigerators).

Ballybay (bă"lĕbā'), Gaelic *Béal Átha Beithe*, town (pop. 938), central Co. Monaghan, Ireland, 9 mi. SSE of Monaghan; agr. market (flax, oats, potatoes); linen milling.

Ballybofey (bă"lĕbō'fē), Gaelic *Baile Átha Féich*, town (pop. 780), Co. Donegal, Ireland, on Finn R. and 13 mi. W of Lifford, opposite Stranorlar; agr. market (grain, flax); shirt mfg.

Ballybunion or **Ballybunnion** (bă"lĕbŭn'yŭn), Gaelic *Baile an Bhuinneanáigh*, fishing village (pop. 942), N Co. Kerry, Ireland, at mouth of the Shannon, 10 mi. WNW of Listowel; resort.

Ballycastle (bălĕkă'sŭl), urban district (1937 pop. 2,209; 1951 census 2,558), N Co. Antrim, Northern Ireland, on Ballycastle Bay of the North Channel, 17 mi. ENE of Coleraine; coal and iron mining; seaport. Has ruins of anc. Dunanynie Castle.

Ballyclare (bălĕklâr'), urban district (1937 pop. 3,777; 1951 census 3,982), S central Co. Antrim, Northern Ireland, on the Six Mile Water and 11 mi. NNW of Belfast; linen and paper milling; agr. market.

Ballydehob (bă"lĕdŭhŏb'), Gaelic *Béal Átha Dá Chab*, town (pop. 301), SW Co. Cork, Ireland, on Roaringwater Bay, 8 mi. W of Skibbereen; copper and barite mining.

Ballygawley (bălĕgô'lē), town (pop. 368), S Co. Tyrone, Northern Ireland, 11 mi. WSW of Dungannon; woolen milling.

Ballygunge (bä'lĭgŭnj), residential suburban ward (pop. 62,519) in Calcutta municipality, SE West Bengal, India, 3.5 mi. SE of city center; general engineering works; hosiery mfg. Science col.

Ballyhaise (bă"lĕhās'), Gaelic *Béal Átha hÁthais*, town (pop. 113), N Co. Cavan, Ireland, on Annalee R. and 4 mi. NNE of Cavan; agr. market (cattle, pigs; potatoes).

Ballyhalbert (bălĕhăl'bŭrt), fishing village (district pop. 1,436), NE Co. Down, Northern Ireland, on the Irish Sea 12 mi. ESE of Newtownards. Just ESE is Burr Point.

Ballyjamesduff (bălĕjāmzdŭf'), Gaelic *Baile Shéamuis Duibh*, town (pop. 516), S Co. Cavan, Ireland, 11 mi. SE of Cavan; cattle, pigs; potatoes.

Ballykennedy, Northern Ireland: see GRACEHILL.

Ballylongford (bă"lĕlŏng'fŭrd), Gaelic *Béal Átha Longphuirt*, town (pop. 510), N Co. Kerry, Ireland, near the Shannon, 7 mi. N of Listowel; agr. market (dairying, cattle raising; potatoes).

Ballymacarret (bă"lĕmŭkă'rŭt), suburb of Belfast, Co. Down, Northern Ireland, across the Lagan.

Ballymahon (bă"lĕmŭho͞on',–mŭhŏn'), Gaelic *Baile Mathghamhna*, town (pop. 691), S Co. Longford, Ireland, on the Inny, on the Royal Canal and 12 mi. S of Longford; agr. market in dairying, cattle-raising, potato-growing region. It was last Irish residence of Oliver Goldsmith, who was probably b. at near-by Pallas.

Ballymena (bălĕmē'nŭ), municipal borough (1937 pop. 12,928; 1951 census 14,165), central Co. Antrim, Northern Ireland, on Braid R. and 23 mi. NW of Belfast; linen- and woolen-milling center; mfg. of shoes and embroidery; iron mining; bacon and ham curing. Near by is Moravian settlement founded 1746.

Ballymoe (bă"lĕmō'), Gaelic *Béal Átha Mogha*, town (pop. 148), NE Co. Galway, Ireland, on Suck R. and 12 mi. WNW of Roscommon; agr. market (sheep; potatoes, beets); furniture mfg.

Ballymoney (bălĕmŭ'nē), urban district (1937 pop. 3,228; 1951 census 3,306), NW Co. Antrim, Northern Ireland, 8 mi. ESE of Coleraine; linen milling; dairying, bacon and ham curing.

Ballymore Eustace (bă"lĕmôr' ū'stĭs), Gaelic *Baile Mór na nIústasach*, town (pop. 329), W Co. Kildare, Ireland, on the Liffey and 6 mi. SSW of Naas; agr. market (cattle, horses; potatoes).

Ballymote (bă"lĕmōt'), Gaelic *Baile an Mhóta*, town (pop. 765), central Co. Sligo, Ireland, 14 mi. S of Sligo; agr. market (cattle; potatoes). Has remains of castle built 1300 by Richard de Burgh, and of Franciscan Friary, famous for *Book of Ballymote*, written here.

Ballynahinch (bălĕnŭhĭnch'), town (pop. 1,917), central Co. Down, Northern Ireland, 13 mi. S of Belfast; iron mining; agr. market (flax, oats), with medicinal springs.

Ballyragget (bă"lĕră'gĭt), Gaelic *Béal Átha Raghad*, town (pop. 469), N Co. Kilkenny, Ireland, on Nore R. and 11 mi. NNW of Kilkenny; agr. (cattle; barley, potatoes). Has anc. castle.

Ballyronan (bălĕrō'nŭn), agr. village (district pop. 1,092), SE Co. Londonderry, Northern Ireland, on W shore of Lough Neagh, 5 mi. SE of Magherafelt; growing of flax, potatoes, oats; pollan fishing.

Ballysadare, **Ballisodare**, or **Ballysodare** (all: bă"lĕsŭdâr'), Gaelic *Baile Easa Dara*, town (pop. 143), NE central Co. Sligo, Ireland, at head of Ballysadare Bay, at mouth of Unshin R., 5 mi. SSW of Sligo; salmon-fishing center. There are remains of abbey founded (c.645) by St. Fechin.

Ballysadare Bay, narrow inlet (8 mi. long) of Sligo Bay, N central Co. Sligo, Ireland.

Ballyshannon (bă"lĕshă'nŭn), Gaelic *Béal Átha Seanaigh*, town (pop. 2,514), S Co. Donegal, Ireland, on Donegal Bay at mouth of Erne R., 12 mi. SSW of Donegal; salmon- and eel-fishing center; seaside resort. Site of noted salmon leap. There are remains of anc. castle, scene of defeat (1597) of English besiegers.

Ballysitteragh, mountain (2,050 ft.), W Co. Kerry, Ireland, 3 mi. N of Dingle.

Ballysodare, Ireland: see BALLYSADARE.

Ballywalter (bălĕwôl'tŭr), fishing village (district pop. 1,317), NE Co. Down, Northern Ireland, on the Irish Sea 9 mi. ESE of Newtownards.

Balmaceda (bälmäsä'dä), village (1930 pop. 290), Aysén prov., S Chile, in the Andes, on Argentina border, 65 mi. SE of Puerto Aysén; sheep raising. Radio station.

Balmaclellan (bălmŭklĕ'lŭn), agr. village and parish (pop. 627), central Kirkcudbright, Scotland, 2 mi. NE of New Galloway.

Balmain (bălmān'), municipality (pop. 28,398), E New South Wales, Australia, on S shore of Parramatta R. and 2 mi. W of Sydney, in metropolitan area; drydocks, shipyards; mfg. (toilet articles, soap, furniture). Coal mines.

Balmat (băl'măt"), mining village, St. Lawrence co., N N.Y., 7 mi. SSE of Gouverneur; zinc, lead, pyrites.

Balmazujvaros (bŏl'mŏzo͞oĭvä"rôsh), Hung. *Balmazújváros*, town (pop. 16,318), Hajdu co., E Hungary, 14 mi. WNW of Debrecen; market center for grain, cattle region; home pottery industry.

Balme, Col de (kôl dŭ bälm'), pass (7,221 ft.) on Franco-Swiss border, at N end of Mont Blanc massif, 7 mi. SW of Martigny-Ville. Frequented by tourists from Chamonix valley (SSW).

Balme-les-Grottes, La (lä bälm-lā-grôt'), village (pop. 184), Isère dept., SE France, near the Rhone, 25 mi. ENE of Lyons. Stalactite caverns.

Balmerino (bălmŭrē'nō), agr. village and parish (pop. 599), NE Fifeshire, Scotland, on the Tay and 5 mi. SW of Dundee. Has ruins of Balmerino Abbey, founded 1229.

Balmhorn (bälm'hôrn), peak (12,179 ft.) in Bernese Alps, S Switzerland, 8 mi. NNE of Leuk.

Balmoral Castle (bălmŏ'rŭl), royal residence in Braemar dist., SW Aberdeenshire, Scotland, on right bank of the Dee and 7 mi. W of Ballater. Built of white granite by Queen Victoria in 1854 and has extensive grounds. On near-by hills are memorial cairns to Prince Albert and other members of royal family.

Balmorhea (bălmŭrā'), village (1940 pop. 588), Reeves co., extreme W Texas, 34 mi. SSW of Pecos, near NE base of Davis Mts.; center of Balmorhea irrigation project (water from creeks, San Solomon and Phantom L. springs); cotton, hay, melons. State park near.

Balnearia (bälnäär'yä), town (pop. 4,234), NE Córdoba prov., Argentina, near S shore of Mar Chiquita, 95 mi. ENE of Córdoba. Resort and agr. center; grain, flax, livestock. Airport.

Balod (bŭlōd'), village, Drug dist., E central Madhya Pradesh, India, 31 mi. S of Drug; rice, oilseeds (canal irrigation). Hematite and ceramic clay deposits (SW).

Baloda Bazar (bŭlō'dŭ bŭzär'), village, Raipur dist., E Madhya Pradesh, India, 45 mi. NE of Raipur; rice milling; oilseeds.

Baloi (bäloi'), municipality (1948 pop. 14,498), Lanao prov., Philippines, in W central Mindanao. Includes villages of Balut, Momungan, Pantar.

Balonne River (bŭlŏn'), S Queensland, Australia, rises in McPherson Range, flows NW, past Warwick, and SW, past Surat and St. George, to Dirranbandi, where it divides into 2 branches, the Culgoa (flowing to Barwon or Darling R.) and the Narran (flowing to L. Terewah); 495 mi. long.

Drains W slopes of Darling Downs. Maranoa R., main tributary. Known as Condamine R. in upper course.

Balotina, Moldavian SSR: see BOLOTINO.

Balotra (bä'lōtrŭ), town (pop. 7,765), W central Rajasthan, India, on Luni R. and 55 mi. WSW of Jodhpur; rail junction; trades in salt, millet, wheat, gram, cotton, and cattle; hand-loom weaving, cloth dyeing and printing.

Balovale (bälōvä'lā), township (pop. 328), Western Prov., W Northern Rhodesia, on Zambezi R. and 120 mi. N of Mongu; beeswax; corn, millet; hardwood. Airfield. Transferred 1946 from Kaonde-Lunda prov.

Balquhidder (băl-hwĭ'dŭr), agr. village and parish (pop. 619), SW Perthshire, Scotland, at E end of Loch Voil (5 mi. long), 10 mi. NW of Callander. Rob Roy buried here.

Balrampur (bŭlräm'po͝or). **1** Town, Manbhum dist., SE Bihar, India: see BALARAMPUR. **2** Town (pop. 35,461), Gonda dist., NE Uttar Pradesh, India, 25 mi. NNE of Gonda; road junction; sugar processing, rice milling; trades in rice, wheat, corn, gram, oilseeds. Founded 17th cent.

Balranald (bălră'nŭld), municipality (pop. 1,249), S New South Wales, Australia, on Murrumbidgee R. and 220 mi. SSE of Broken Hill; rail terminus; sheep and agr. center.

Bals (bälsh), Rum. *Balș*, town (1948 pop. 6,128), Dolj prov., S Rumania, on railroad and 21 mi. NW of Caracal; agr. trade center (grain, livestock); flour milling, mfg. of tinware.

Balsall (bôl'zôl, bôl'sŭl), town and parish (pop. 1,883), central Warwick, England, 7 mi. W of Coventry; furniture works.

Balsall Heath (bôl'sŭl hēth'), S industrial suburb (pop. 34,805) of Birmingham, NW Warwick, England.

Balsam Cone, peak, N.C.: see BLACK MOUNTAINS.

Balsam Lake (□ 17), Kawartha Lakes, S Ont., 65 mi. NE of Toronto; 10 mi. long, 1–5 mi. wide. Drains W into L. Simcoe through Trent canal. Coboconk village at N end.

Balsam Lake (bôl'sŭm), resort village (pop. 488), ⊙ Polk co., NW Wis., on small Balsam L., 35 mi. W of Rice Lake; dairying, farming.

Balsam Mountain, W N.C., ridge (an E extension of Great Smoky Mts.) extending c.40 mi. SE from point near Tenn. line, partly along Haywood-Swain co. line. Includes Richland Balsam (6,540 ft.) 8 mi. S of Waynesville, and Black Mtn. (6,275 ft.) 5 mi. farther S.

Balsamo (bäl'sämô), village (pop. 2,757), Milano prov., Lombardy, N Italy, 6 mi. N of Milan; glassware mfg.

Balsan (bŭlsän'), former princely state (□ 57; pop. 6,649) of Punjab Hill States, India, E of Simla. Since 1948, merged with Himachal Pradesh.

Balsapuerto (bälsäpwĕr'tō), town (pop. 102), Loreto dept., N central Peru, in E Andean foothills, on Moyobamba–Yurimaguas road, and 30 mi. W of Yurimaguas; bananas, yucca. On Cachiyacu R. (small affluent of the Huallaga) near by are large waterfalls.

Balsar, India: see BULSAR.

Balsareny (bälsärānē'), village (pop. 1,848), Barcelona prov., NE Spain, on Llobregat R. and 11 mi. NNE of Manresa. Wine, lumber in area.

Balsas (bäl'sŭs), city (pop. 2,165), S Maranhão, Brazil, on Balsas R. and 110 mi. E of Carolina; ships skins, feathers, cattle, manioc, rice, and corn. Roads to Carolina and Caxias. Airfield. Until 1944, Santo Antônio de Balsas.

Balsas, Río de las (rē'ō dā läs bäl'säs), river in S central Mexico, one of Mexico's largest streams, rises in N Puebla and Tlaxcala, and as the Atoyac (ätoiäk') flows S and SW through Puebla, curving W into Guerrero (where it is called Mexcala, Mezcala, or Mescala [all: mĕskä'lä]), and continues W and S along Guerrero-Michoacán border, reaching the Pacific at 17°55'N 102°10'W; total length, c.450 mi. Numerous rapids make it unnavigable. Its valley (partly irrigated) is a fertile area producing corn, coffee, cotton, sugar cane, tropical fruit, vegetables, sesame seed.

Balsas River (bäl'sŭs), S Maranhão, Brazil, rises in the Serra das Mangabeiras on Goiás border, flows c.200 mi. NE, past Balsas (head of seasonal navigation) and Loreto, to the Parnaíba at Benedito Leite.

Balsta (bōl'stä"), Swedish *Bålsta*, village (pop. 814), Uppsala co., E Sweden, 12 mi. W of Sigtuna; grain, stock.

Balstad, Norway: see BALLSTAD.

Balsthal (bäls'täl), town (pop. 4,774), Solothurn canton, N Switzerland, 11 mi. NE of Solothurn; paper, metal products, tobacco.

Balta (bôl'tŭ), island of the Shetlands, Scotland, just off E coast of Unst isl. across Balta Sound; 1½ mi. long.

Balta (bäl'tŭ), city (1926 pop. 23,034), NW Odessa oblast, Ukrainian SSR, 110 mi. NNW of Odessa, 4 mi. N of Balta station; mfg. (clothing, furniture), wine making, food processing; metalworks. From 1924 until 1940 in Moldavian Autonomous SSR, of which it was ⊙ (1924–28).

Balta (bôl'tŭ), village (pop. 196), Pierce co., N central N.Dak., 14 mi. S of Rugby.

Baltai or **Baltay** (bŭltī'), village (1926 pop. 3,444), N Saratov oblast, Russian SFSR, 17 mi. NNE of Bazarny Karabulak; flour milling, distilling, metalworking.

Baltanás (bältänäs'), town (pop. 2,783), Palencia prov., N central Spain, 16 mi. ESE of Palencia; agr. trade center (cereals, wine, sheep).

Baltasi (bŭltŭsē'), village (1939 pop. over 2,000), NW Tatar Autonomous SSR, Russian SFSR, 22 mi. NE of Arsk; grain, livestock.

Baltatesti (bŭltsŭtĕsht'), Rum. *Băltătești*, village (pop. 1,708), Bacau prov., NE Rumania, 6 mi. S of Targu-Neamt; health resort (alt. 1,558 ft.) with iodine and bromine springs. The 18th-cent. Rasboeni monastery, erected on site of victory by Stephen the Great over the Turks (1476), is 11 mi. E. Varatec convent (18th cent.) and climatic resort (alt. 1,476 ft.) is 3 mi. NW.

Baltesti (bŭltĕsht'), Rum. *Băltești*, village (pop. 952), Prahova prov., S central Rumania, 14 mi. NNE of Ploesti.

Balti, Moldavian SSR: see BELTSY.

Baltic. 1 Village, Conn.: see SPRAGUE. **2** Village (1940 pop. 584), Houghton co., NW Upper Peninsula, Mich., 5 mi. SW of Houghton, in copper-mining region. **3** Village (pop. 493), Tuscarawas co., E Ohio, 14 mi. WSW of New Philadelphia; clay products, lumber. **4** Town (pop. 255), Minnehaha co., E S.Dak., 15 mi. N of Sioux Falls and on Big Sioux R.; stone quarry, govt. nursery; livestock, dairy produce, poultry, corn, oats, barley.

Baltic-North Sea Canal, Germany: see KIEL CANAL.

Baltic Port, Estonia: see PALDISKI.

Baltic Sea, anc. *Mare Suevicum*, Ger. *Ostsee* (ôst'zā"), sea (including KATTEGAT, □ 163,000) indenting N Europe, an arm of Atlantic Ocean, enclosed by Denmark, Sweden, Finland, Russian SFSR, Estonia, Latvia, Lithuania, Poland, and Germany. It is linked with North Sea by the Danish straits (ORESUND, GREAT BELT, LITTLE BELT), the Kattegat, and the SKAGERRAK, as well as by the KIEL CANAL through NW Germany. Structurally an extension of the North Sea, it is a shallow body of water (mean depth 180 ft.), reaching its greatest depth (1,519 ft.) off the Swedish isl. of Gotland. Other isls. are Oland (Sweden), the insular part of Denmark, Fehmarn and Rügen (Germany), Saare and Hiiumaa (USSR), Aland Isls. (Finland). The northernmost arm of the Baltic Sea is the Gulf of Bothnia bet. Finland and Sweden; the easternmost arm is the Gulf of Finland bet. Finland and Estonia. Other major inlets are the Gulf of Riga, the Gulf of Danzig, and Mecklenburg Bay. The Baltic Sea receives on the mainland side the rivers Neva (outlet of L. Ladoga), the Narva (outlet of L. Peipus), the Western Dvina, the Neman, the Vistula, the Oder; and on the Scandinavian side, the Dal, Angerman, Ume, and Torne rivers. As a result of the great influx of fresh river water, the salinity of the Baltic Sea is much reduced, ranging from 15 per mill (W, near North Sea) to 5 per mill and less (E). Because of the low salinity and the general shallowness, large parts of the Baltic, notably in inner (NE) reaches, freeze over in winter for 3–5 months. Its tides are insignificant, but considerable level changes are brought about by storms. Navigated since anc. times, the Baltic has long been known as the world's source of amber, found in the area of the Samland peninsula of former East Prussia. In late Middle Ages, its commerce was dominated by the Hanseatic League. Chief Baltic ports are: in Scandinavia—Copenhagen, Stockholm, Helsinki; in USSR—Leningrad, Tallinn, Paldiski, Riga, Liepaja, Kaliningrad; in Poland—Danzig, Gdynia, Stettin; and in Germany—Rostock, Lübeck, and Kiel. In addition to its Kiel Canal link with the North Sea, the Baltic is connected with the White Sea by the WHITE SEA–BALTIC CANAL and with Volga R. by the MARIINSK CANAL system.

Baltic States, collective name applied to the countries of ESTONIA, LATVIA, and LITHUANIA, on E coast of Baltic Sea. Formed 1918 (confirmed by treaties in 1920) out of Rus. Baltic provs. or govts. of Estonia (Estland), Livonia (Livland), and Courland (Kurland), and parts of the govts. of Pskov, Vitebsk, Kovno, Vilna, and Suvalki. Remained independent republics until their annexation (1940) by the USSR. During Second World War, held (1941–44) by German troops and, with Belorussia, constituted Ger. Ostland.

Baltic-White Sea Canal, Karelo-Finnish SSR: see WHITE SEA–BALTIC CANAL.

Baltiisk, USSR: see BALTISK.

Baltim (bältēm'), village (pop. 8,862), Gharbiya prov., Lower Egypt, at NE end of L. Burullus, 53 mi. N of Tanta; fisheries.

Baltimore, village, S Ont., 5 mi. N of Cobourg; fruit, dairying, mixed farming.

Baltimore, Gaelic *Dún na Sead*, town (pop. 302), SW Co. Cork, Ireland, on the Atlantic, 7 mi. SW of Skibbereen; 51°29'N 9°22'W; fishing center, with fish-curing works. Site of Industrial Fishery School. Has ruins of anc. stronghold of the O'Driscolls. Just offshore is Sherkin isl.

Baltimore (bôl'tĭmôr, –mŭr), county (□ 610; pop. 270,273), N Md.; ⊙ Towson. Almost surrounds independent Baltimore city. Co. is bounded N by Pa. line, SE by Gunpowder R. and Chesapeake Bay, S and SW by Patapsco R.; also drained by Gunpowder Falls (stream), in which are Prettyboy and Loch Raven dams. Contains suburbs of Baltimore; mfg. of steel and ships (Sparrows Point, Back River), aircraft (Middle River), communications equipment, electric tools, scientific instruments (all at Towson). Truck, fruit, dairy farms supply Baltimore market. Deeply indented bay shore (extreme SE) has summer resorts and industrial areas. In central part are estates (including Hampton Natl. Historic Site near Towson) in dist. known for horse racing (especially cross-country races), fox hunting, and jousting tournaments. Includes part of Patapsco State Park and L. Roland. Formed 1659; Baltimore co. and Baltimore city were separated 1851.

Baltimore. 1 City (□ 85.6; 1940 pop. 859,100; 1950 pop. 949,708), ⊙ Md., in but independent of Baltimore co., N Md., at head of Patapsco R. estuary c.15 mi. above Chesapeake Bay and c.210 mi. above the Atlantic, 35 mi. NE of Washington, c.90 mi. WSW of Philadelphia; 39°18'N 76°37'E; alt. sea level to 445 ft. Largest city in Md. and 6th largest in U.S., a major seaport (ranking high among U.S. ports in total tonnage handled and in total foreign trade), port of entry, and the commercial, industrial, governmental, transportation, and educational hub of Md. Its port is served by 2 lanes to the Atlantic: the route through Chesapeake Bay, and via the CHESAPEAKE AND DELAWARE CANAL. A rail, air, and highway center, situated on the principal N-S routes of the E seaboard, and terminus of important routes from the West. It is served by Friendship International Airport (c.9 mi. S; opened 1950). The harbor, consisting of the Patapsco and 3 of its inlets (Northwest Branch, Middle Branch, Curtis Bay) has c.40 mi. of water frontage, and is adjoined by extensive industrial districts. Terminal facilities include ore and coal piers, grain elevators, shipbuilding and repair plants (including drydocks and graving docks); at near-by SPARROWS POINT are enormous shipyards and nation's largest steel mill on tidewater. Baltimore is a principal port for foreign iron ore, especially from Venezuela, Chile, Liberia, and Labrador; also imports other ores (chrome, zinc, and manganese), sugar, petroleum, rubber, coffee, tea, and spices, cork, tropical fruits, copra, fertilizers, woodpulp. Leading exports are grain, flour, coal, iron and steel, cement, lumber, fertilizer, and manufactured goods, esp. machinery and automobiles. Internal bay commerce deals mostly in vegetables, fruits, sea food (esp. oysters). Mfg. of tin cans, machinery, automobiles, tractors, railroad equipment, refractories, cement, chemicals and pharmaceuticals, fertilizers, glass products, lumber, soap, scientific instruments and electric tools, aircraft (especially at MIDDLE RIVER), textiles, clothing, straw hats, paper; has large copper smelter, printing and publishing plants (Otto Mergenthaler perfected the linotype here 1876–85), railroad repair shops, canneries, sugar and petroleum refineries, coffee-roasting and meat-packing plants. Seat of The Johns Hopkins Univ. (opened 1876), Johns Hopkins Hosp. (1889), the schools of medicine, law, dentistry, and pharmacy of Univ. of Md., Univ. of Baltimore, Col. of Notre Dame of Md., Loyola Col., Morgan State Col., St. Mary's Seminary and Univ., Coppin Teachers Col., Ner Israel Rabbinical Col., Peabody Inst. (noted conservatory of music), Maryland Institute (1826), St. Agnes Col. (in suburban Mt. Washington). Goucher Col., founded here, moved to Towson in 1950. Other points of interest are Walters Art Gall., Enoch Pratt Free Library, Md. Historical Society hq., Municipal Mus. (founded 1813), Flag House (mus. of the War of 1812), Baltimore Mus. of Art, Fort McHenry Natl. Monument (47.64 acres; established 1939 to preserve old fort built in 1790s and restored 1933), Cathedral of the Assumption of the Blessed Virgin Mary (1st R.C. cathedral in the U.S.; designed by Latrobe and built 1806–21), Washington Monument (designed by Robert Mills; built 1809–29), Lexington Market, operated since 1803, Westminster Churchyard, with grave of Edgar Allen Poe, state penitentiary, St. Mary's Industrial School for Boys, Md. Workshop for the Blind, a U.S. Marine Hosp. (1936), Loudon Park and Baltimore natl. cemeteries, U.S. Fort Holabird, Pimlico Race Track (where the Preakness is run annually). Near by are Fort Howard (SE), Edgewood Arsenal, Aberdeen Proving Ground, Hampton Natl. Historic Site, L.Roland and Loch Raven reservoirs (N), Patapsco State Park, U.S. Coast Guard shipbuilding and repair depot. Baltimore's municipal symphony orchestra is well known. Baltimore, whose location near the Mason-Dixon Line makes it a "border city" both Southern and Northern in atmosphere, is known for a flavor compounded of its monuments (which have earned it the sobriquet "Monumental City"), its distinctive cuisine, social traditions (including the Bachelors' Cotillion, established in 1796), the narrow, crowded streets of its downtown dist., the solid blocks of "row houses," each with its scrubbed white doorstep, and its many old mansions. City also has considerable communities of Polish, Italian, German, and Russian descent, and a sizable Negro section. First settlement here was made in mid-17th cent., but town was not established until 1729; clustered around the Basin (upper end of Northwest Branch), it soon became a colonial shipping center for grain and tobacco. It was inc. as a town in 1745, as city in 1797; became ⊙ Baltimore co. in 1768, but city and co. became separate administrative divisions in 1851. Shipbuilding, begun here c.1750, flourished in the Revolution, again in the War of 1812, and was important in 1st and 2d World Wars. The *Constellation*, oldest existing U.S. navy ship, was launched here in 1797; the famous clippers built here were queens of the seas in the 19th cent. When the British occupied Philadelphia (1776), Baltimore became the meeting place of the Continental Congress (Dec., 1776–March, 1777), and remained a supply base for the rest of the Revolution. In War of 1812, the gallant defense (Sept. 13–14, 1814) of Fort McHenry inspired Francis Scott Key to write *The Star-spangled Banner*. During the Civil War, Baltimore, an important Union supply depot, was so violently divided in its sympathies that martial law was maintained. Although completion (1825) of the Erie Canal endangered city's hold on the trans-Allegheny trade, Baltimore, with construction (begun 1829) of the Baltimore and Ohio RR, ultimately strengthened its commercial position. Industry, which had been confined mainly to flour milling until the Civil War, expanded rapidly thereafter, until it has come to rival shipping in importance. A disastrous fire (1904) destroyed much of the downtown dist. **2** Village (pop. 1,843), Fairfield co., central Ohio, 9 mi. N of Lancaster, in agr. area; paper boxes, cement blocks. Annexed adjacent Basil (1940 pop. 766) in 1945. **3** Town (pop. 89), Windsor co., SE Vt., 12 mi. SW of Windsor.

Baltinglass, Gaelic *Mainistir an Bhealaigh*, town (pop. 813), W Co. Wicklow, Ireland, on Slaney R. and 12 mi. NE of Carlow; agr. market (dairying; cattle, sheep; potatoes). Has remains of Cistercian abbey founded c.1150.

Baltischport, Estonia: see PALDISKI.

Baltisk, Baltiisk, or **Baltiysk** (bŭltyēsk'), city (1939 pop. 12,379), W Kaliningrad oblast, Russian SFSR, fortified outer port (25 mi. WSW) of Kaliningrad (linked by 20-mi. deep-water channel), on outlet linking (since 1497) Vistula Lagoon with Baltic Sea; naval base (shipyards); fish and fish-oil processing. Has 100-ft.-high lighthouse. Developed as fortified port under Frederick William, the Great Elector of Brandenburg; chartered 1725. Until 1945, in East Prussia, and called Pillau (pĭ'lou).

Baltiski or **Baltiski Port,** Estonia: see PALDISKI.

Baltistan (bŭl'tĭstän) or **Little Tibet** (tĭbĕt'), tract in W Ladakh dist., Kashmir; ⊙ Skardu. Comprises all of Skardu tahsil in N and part of Kargil tahsil (N of 34° and W of 77°) in S. Highest peaks of Karakoram mtn. system in NE, including K^2, Gasherbrum I, and Broad Peak. Last of independent rajas (or *gialpos*) defeated 1840 by Dogras. Inhabited by Baltis (Moslem tribes of Tibetan origin).

Baltit (bŭl'tĭt), village, ⊙ Hunza state, Gilgit Agency, NW Kashmir, on Hunza R. and 35 mi. NNE of Gilgit. Fort. Residence of mir of Hunza near by. Also called Hunza.

Baltoro Glacier (bältō'rō), a great glacier in Karakoram mtn. system, N Kashmir, bet. K^2 (N), Gasherbrum (E), and Masherbrum (S) peaks; c.35 mi. long (W-E), bet. 35°40'N 76°7'E and 35°45'N 76°40'E. Height of snout, 11,580 ft.

Baltra Island (bäl'trä), island (□ 8) of the Galápagos Isls., Ecuador, in the Pacific, off N coast of Chaves Isl.; landing field.

Baltrum (bäl'trōōm), North Sea island (□ 3.5; pop. 301) of East Frisian group, Germany, 4 mi. N of Nessmersiel; 3 mi. long (E-W), 1 mi. wide (N-S). Nordseebad Baltrum (W) is seaside resort.

Baltser, Russian SFSR: see KRASNOARMEISK, Saratov oblast.

Balu Chaung, Burma: see PILU, NAM.

Baluchistan (bŭlōō'chĭstän", bŭlōō"chĭstăn', –stän'), arid region (□ 200,000; pop. 1,100,000) of SE Iran and W Pakistan, inhabited by Iranian-speaking Baluch nomads, on N coast of the Arabian Sea. Its coastal section is known as MAKRAN. The anc. Gedrosia (⊙ Pura) of the Persian and Macedonian empires, Baluchistan was crossed (325 B.C.) by Alexander the Great on his return from India. During 7th–10th cent. A.D., Arabs held most of area. The Baluch tribes apparently came to the region in 11th and 12th cent. when they were driven from Persia by the Seljuks. Baluchistan was partly under Mogul control in early-17th cent. and disputed by Persia and Afghanistan through 18th cent. Under British influence (beginning in early-19th cent.), the area was divided bet. Persia and India, with the final boundary fixed in 1895–96. For the detailed geography and economy of Iranian Baluchistan (W) and Indian (since 1947, Pakistani) Baluchistan (E), see the following 2 articles.

Baluchistan, former province (□ 60,000; 1940 pop. 215,000) of SE Iran; ⊙ was Bampur. Its coastal dist. on Gulf of Oman of Arabian Sea is known as MAKRAN. Bounded NW by Kerman, N by Seistan, and E by Pakistani Baluchistan; arid mountainous plateau, with short seasonal rivers which supply a few irrigated agr. areas (dates, grain, cotton); camel breeding. Pop. is predominantly Baluch. Main towns are Zahidan (rail terminus), Khash, Iranshahr, and the small Makran coast ports of Jask, Chahbahar, and Gwatar. Under semiautonomous khans until it passed (mid-19th cent.) to Persian rule. Baluchistan prov. was inc. 1938 into Iran's Eighth Prov. (see KERMAN).

Baluchistan, mountainous region (□ 134,139; 1951 pop. 1,178,000) of W Pakistan; bordered N by Afghanistan, W by Iran, S by Arabian Sea, E by Sind and Punjab (Pakistan), NE by North-West Frontier Prov. Consists of 2 distinct sections: in N is Baluchistan proper (□ 52,900; 1951 pop. 622,000; under chief commissioner; ⊙ Quetta; summer hq. at Ziarat), comprising Chagai, Loralai, Quetta-Pishin, Sibi, and Zhob dists. and Bolan subdivision; remaining area (□ 81,239; 1951 pop. 556,000) comprises princely states of KALAT, KHARAN, LAS BELA, and MAKRAN. Small area around town of Gwadar on SW coast belongs to Oman. Mostly a mountainous country, with long, barren ridges separating arid deserts and valleys; chief ranges include Sulaiman (N), Central Brahui (center; crossed by Bolan Pass), Kirthar (SE), and Makran (S). Since annual rainfall averages only 3–10 in., almost all rivers are seasonal; Hingol, Nari, Dasht, Hab, and Pishin Lora rivers exceed 250 mi. in length. Hamun-i-Mashkel and Hamun-i-Lora depressions in W are inland drainage basins. Some valleys (mainly N) produce fair crops of wheat, barley, millet, and rice; melons, grapes, pomegranates, apricots cultivated in N highlands, dates in Makran. Raising of camels, horses, sheep, goats a major occupation; also hand-loom weaving, fishing (off S coast; catfish), palm-mat and basket making, embroidering, handicrafts (felt, leather goods). Extensive mineral resources include coal (chiefly near Khost, Shahrig, and Harnai in Sibi dist.), gypsum, chromite (near Hindubagh), limestone, sulphur (notably on the Koh-i-Sultan), brine salt, and lead. Has few roads and railways. Quetta is largest town and main trade center (carpets, wool, fruit, hides, leather goods, grain). Other towns: Sibi, Fort Sandeman, Chaman, Kalat, Mastung, Nushki, Pasni. Although many invaders of India have crossed Baluchistan, few sites of archaeological interest remain. Return route of Alexander the Great (325 B.C.) led through S coastal region to Persia. During 7th–10th cent. A.D., Arabs held most of area; in early-17th cent., under Mogul control; later ruled by tribal chiefs, most important of whom was khan of Kalat. British connections with country began during Afghan Wars; by treaties of 1876, 1879, and 1891, the N sections were placed under Br. control (became known as British Baluchistan) and a military base established at Quetta. Inc. 1947–48 into Pakistan. Pop. 92% Moslem, 6% Hindu, 1% Sikh; includes Baluch (27%), Pathan (22%), and Brahui (15%) tribes. Chief languages: Baluchi and Pashto (Iranian), and Brahui (Dravidian). Sometimes spelled Beluchistan.

Baludan, Syria: see BLUDAN.

Balun, India: see DALHOUSIE.

Balungao (bälōōng-gä'ō, –gou'), town (1939 pop. 1,115; 1948 municipality pop. 12,773), Pangasinan prov., central Luzon, Philippines, on railroad and 25 mi. ESE of Dagupan; rice, corn, copra.

Balurghat (bä'lōōrgät), village, ⊙ West Dinajpur dist., N West Bengal, India, on Atrai R. and 15 mi. WSW of Hilli; rice, jute, sugar cane, rape and mustard.

Balut Island (bälōōt') (□ 23; 1939 pop. 1,377), Davao prov., Philippines, off S tip of Mindanao across Sarangani Strait, just W of Sarangani Isl.; volcano, rising to 2,895 ft. Sulphur.

Balvano (bälvä'nô), village (pop. 2,481), Potenza prov., Basilicata, S Italy, 16 mi. W of Potenza, in olive- and fruit-growing region. Has ruined Norman castle.

Balvi (bäl'vē), Ger. *Bolwa*, city (pop. 2,024), NE Latvia, in Latgale, 20 mi. ESE of Gulbene, in flax area; wool processing, tanning, flour milling.

Balya (bälyä'), village (pop. 1,702), Balikesir prov., NW Turkey, on Koca R. and 17 mi. WNW of Balikesir; mining center; lead (with some silver), zinc, manganese, arsenic.

Balyana, El, or **Al-Balyana** (both: ĕl bălyănä'), town (pop. 16,315), Girga prov., central Upper Egypt, on W bank of the Nile, on railroad, and 20 mi. NW of Nag Hammadi; cottonseed-oil pressing; cotton, cereals, dates, sugar cane. Also spelled Baliana. The ruins of anc. Abydos are 5 mi. W, at ARABA EL MADFUNA.

Balykchi (bŭlĭkchē'), village (1926 pop. 3,281), NW Andizhan Oblast, Uzbek SSR, on the Kara Darya, near its junction with Naryn R., and 26 mi. NW of Andizhan; cotton.

Balyklei, Russian SFSR: see GORNY BALYKLEI.

Balyksa (bŭlĭk'sŭ), town (1948 pop. over 2,000), W Khakass Autonomous Oblast, Krasnoyarsk Territory, Russian SFSR, 100 mi. W of Abakan, in the Kuznetsk Ala-Tau; gold mines.

Balykshi (bŭlĭkshē'), SW suburb (1939 pop. over 500) of Guryev, Guryev oblast, Kazakh SSR, on right bank of Ural R.

Balzan (bälzän'), village (parish pop. 2,637), central Malta, 3 mi. W of Valletta. Balzan and near-by LIJA and ATTARD are called the "Three Villages." Among its churches, little St. Roch (1593) is the most notable. Bosso and Testaferrata palaces.

Balzapamba (bälsäpäm'bä), village, Bolívar prov., central Ecuador, on W slopes of the Andes, 16 mi. WSW of Guaranda; cereals, potatoes, fruit.

Balzar (bälsär'), town (1950 pop. 3,015), Guayas prov., W Ecuador, landing on the Daule R., in tropical lowlands, and 55 mi. N of Guayaquil; agr. center (cacao, rice, sugar cane, coffee, tobacco, rubber, cattle); rice milling.

Balzar, Cordillera de (kôrdĭyä'rä dā), hilly coastal range in Manabí prov., W Ecuador, 20 mi. E of Portoviejo; c.60 mi. long, NE-SW.

Balzer, Russian SFSR: see KRASNOARMEISK, Saratov oblast.

Balzers (bäl'zûrs), village (pop. 1,415), SW Liechtenstein, near the Rhine (Swiss border), 6 mi. S of Vaduz; corn, potatoes, livestock. Has remains of prehistoric fort; ruined castle; old parochial church.

Balzola (bäl'tsôlä), village (pop. 2,234), Alessandria prov., Piedmont, N Italy, 4 mi. NNW of Casale Monferrato, in rice-growing area. Roman tombs near by.

Bam (bäm). **1** Town (1942 pop. 13,938), Eighth Prov., in Kerman, SE Iran, on road to Zahidan and 115 mi. SE of Kerman, on W edge of the Dasht-i-Lut, on small intermittent Bam R.; trade center in henna-growing region; dates, fruit, camel raising. Has fortress held in 18th cent. by Afghans **2** Village, Ninth Prov., in Khurasan, NE Iran, 50 mi. NNE of Sabzawar, in the Ala Dagh.

Bam (bäm), village, NW Amur oblast, Russian SFSR, on Trans-Siberian RR and 15 mi. NW of Skovorodino; junction for railroad to Tyndynski

Bama (bä'mä), town (pop. 4,367), N Br. Cameroons, administered as part of Bornu prov. of Nigeria, 45 mi. SE of Maiduguri; road junction; trade center; peanuts, millet, cotton; cattle.

Bamako (bämäkō'), city (pop. c.60,150, of which c.3,450 are Europeans), ⊙ Fr. Sudan, Fr. West Africa, road junction and inland port on the Niger, on Dakar-Niger RR (extended to Koulikoro), 70 mi. NE of Fr. Guinea border and c.650 mi. ESE of Dakar; 12°38'N 8°W. Trading and distributing center for SW Sudan. Exports shea-nut products, kapok, peanuts, cotton, tobacco, sisal, hides, skins. Region produces also millet, corn, rice, manioc, beans, potatoes, livestock (sheep, goats, cattle, donkeys). Mfg. of vegetable oil and soap; also tanning, icemaking. Has airport, meteorological station, cathedral, schools of medicine, pharmacy, native artistry, and flying. The Sotuba rapids are c.2 mi. downstream, where there are also irrigation canals.

Bamania (bämän'yä), village, Equator Prov., W Belgian Congo, on Ruki R. and 5 mi. SE of Coquilhatville, in rice-growing region. Has R.C. missions and schools, including school for mulattoes.

Bamanwas (bä'mŭnväs), town (pop. 4,185), E Rajasthan, India, 50 mi. SE of Jaipur; millet, gram, rice.

Bamaur (bŭmour') or **Banmore** (băn'môr), village, NE Madhya Bharat, India, 10 mi. NNE of Lashkar; cement works, bone-fertilizer mill. Limestone quarries near by.

Bambak, Armenian SSR: see PAMBAK.

Bambamarca (bämbämär'kä), city (pop. 2,162), Cajamarca dept., NW Peru, in Cordillera Occidental, on highway, on Llaucán R. and 33 mi. N of Cajamarca; agr. products (barley, corn); cattle.

Bambang (bämbäng'), town (1939 pop. 2,952; 1948 municipality pop. 11,188), Nueva Vizcaya prov., central Luzon, Philippines, on Magat R. and 7 mi. SSW of Bayombong; rice-growing center.

Bambari (bämbärē'), town, ⊙ Ouaka-Kotto region (□ 29,750; 1950 pop. 242,300), central Ubangi-Shari, Fr. Equatorial Africa, on Ouaka R. and 160 mi. NE of Bangui; trading center (notably for cotton and rubber); road communications point; cotton ginning, cotton weaving; experimental sisal plantations. Has military and quarantine camp, R.C. mission and schools.

Bamber Bridge, town in Walton-le-Dale urban dist., W central Lancashire, England, 3 mi. SSE of Preston; cotton milling, mfg. of chemicals, batteries. Has 16th-cent. inn.

Bamberg (băm'bûrg, Ger. bäm'bĕrk), city (pop. 74,733), Upper Franconia, N Bavaria, Germany, on canalized Regnitz R. (head of navigation) just above its mouth on the Main, at N terminus of Ludwig Canal, and 31 mi. NNW of Nuremberg; 49°57'N 11°34'E. Important industrial and commercial center; cotton spinning; metal industry (heavy machinery; tin and bronze smelting); mfg. of spark plugs, light bulbs, tar paper, tobacco. Also brewing and malting, tanning, woodworking. Trades in hops, vegetables, fruit, flowers, wood, cattle. The splendid Romanesque and early-Gothic cathedral (started in 1004) contains tombs of Emperor Henry II, of his wife St. Kunigunde, and of Pope Clement II, and is decorated with excellent early-Gothic relief. St. Michael's church (of former Benedictine abbey) is 11th-cent. Romanesque and 13th–14th cent. Gothic. There are 2 episcopal palaces: the Renaissance Old Residence, built on site of anc. Babenberg castle; and 18th-cent. New Residence, housing gallery of baroque painters. Former Jesuit univ. (1753–1802; founded as col. in

1648) is now theological acad. City has observatory. Developing around ancestral castle of counts of Babenberg (later rulers of Austria), Bamberg was (1007–1802) capital of powerful ecclesiastic state, whose bishops were raised to princely rank in 15th cent. Became archbishopric in 1817. Was temporary seat of Bavarian govt. (1919). Captured by U.S. troops in April, 1945.

Bamberg, county (□ 395; pop. 17,533), S central S.C.; ⊙ Bamberg. Bounded N by South Fork of Edisto R. Agr. area (watermelons and other truck), livestock; timber. Formed 1897.

Bamberg, town (pop. 2,954), ⊙ Bamberg co., S central S.C., 17 mi. SSW of Orangeburg; market center for agr. area (watermelons, livestock); textiles, lumber. Boys' military school.

Bambesa (bämbĕ'sä), village, Eastern Prov., N Belgian Congo, 70 mi. ENE of Buta; center of cotton research; cotton ginning, palm-oil milling. Also rubber plantations.

Bambey (bämbā'), town (pop. c.6,650), W Senegal, Fr. West Africa, on railroad to the Niger and 55 mi. E of Dakar; peanut-growing center. Experimental and meteorological stations.

Bambili (bämbē'lē), village, Eastern Prov., N Belgian Congo, on right bank of Uele R. opposite the mouth of Bomokandi R., on Congo-Nile highway, and 110 mi. NE of Buta; trading post in palm and cotton area. Protestant mission.

Bamble, Norway: see ODEGARDENS VERK.

Bamboi (bämboi'), town, Northern Territories, W Gold Coast, on Black Volta R. (Ashanti border) and 30 mi. N of Wenchi, on road; millet, durra, yams. Ferry station.

Bamboo River, China: see SUI RIVER.

Bamborough, England: see BAMBURGH.

Bambouk (bämbōōk'), region, SW Fr. Sudan, Fr. West Africa, along right bank of lower Falémé R. and Senegal border, just W of Kayes. Renowned for its gold placers. Also has iron, mercury, arsenic, and manganese deposits. Peopled by Mandingoes. Sometimes Bambuk.

Bambous, Canal des (känäl' dā bäbōō'), delta arm of Red R., N Vietnam, connects Red R. near Hungyen with the Thaibinh R. SE of Haiduong; 40 mi. long.

Bambu, Belgian Congo: see KILO-MINES.

Bambuí (bämbwē'), city (pop. 2,930), SW central Minas Gerais, Brazil, on railroad and 65 mi. NE of Passos; ships dried meat, dairy products, cereals. Formerly spelled Bambuhy.

Bambuk, region in Fr. West Africa: see BAMBOUK.

Bamburgh (băm'bŭrŭ), agr. village and parish (pop. 438), NE Northumberland, England, on North Sea, 14 mi. N of Alnwick. Site of castle dating from Norman times, containing 14,000-volume Crewe library. Has 13th-cent. church, built on site of a church founded 651. In 547 it became capital of kings of Northumbria, its name being *Bebhamburh,* and was a center of early English Christianity. Grace Darling b. and died here. Sometimes spelled Bamborough.

Bamenda (bämĕn'dä), town (pop. 2,264), S Br. Cameroons, administered as part of Eastern Provinces of Nigeria, in Bamenda highlands (rise to over 8,000 ft. near Fr. Cameroons border), 140 mi. NNE of Buea; trade center; durra, millet, cattle raising; exports hides. Has hosp., leper settlement.

Bamfield, village, SW B.C., on SW Vancouver Isl., on Barkley Sound, 32 mi. SSW of Port Alberni; port of entry, with cable station. Terminal of cables to Australia and New Zealand, laid 1902.

Bamford. 1 Town and parish (pop. 956), N Derby, England, 9 mi. WSW of Sheffield; cotton milling. **2** Town, Lancashire, England: see BIRTLE-CUM-BAMFORD.

Bami (bŭmē'), village, SW Ashkhabad oblast, Turkmen SSR, on Trans-Caspian RR and 100 mi. WNW of Ashkhabad; cotton.

Bamian, Bamyan, or **Bamiyan** (bŭmyän', bä"mēyän'), town (pop. 8,000), Kabul prov., central Afghanistan, at N foot of the Koh-i-Baba, 80 mi. WNW of Kabul; alt. 8,348 ft. Major archaeological site of Afghanistan, noted for its 2 huge rock-hewn Buddha figures (174 and 115 ft. high), as well as many rock sanctuaries and cells. Tourist center; hotel. An anc. commercial and cultural center, it was visited in A.D. 630 by the Chinese traveler Hsüan Tsang and was destroyed in 1222 by Jenghiz Khan. Scene of fighting (1840) in 1st Afghan War. Sometimes called Qala Sarkari.

Bamileké (bämēlĕkā'), administrative region (□ 2,700; 1950 pop. 439,102), W Fr. Cameroons; ⊙ Dschang. Bordered W by Br. Cameroons. Mountainous (alt. 3,000–4,500 ft.) and covered with park savanna, it is the most densely settled and one of the most picturesque regions of Fr. Cameroons. Trade in native-grown coffee and kola nuts. Cinchona and aleurite plantations. Manioc, yams, corn, and millet are also cultivated on large scale.

Bamingui River (bämĭng-gē'), headstream of Shari R. in central and N Ubangi-Shari, Fr. Equatorial Africa, rises c.100 mi. WSW of Ouadda, flows 160 mi. W and NW to join with Gribingui R. 100 mi. W of N'Délé to form the Shari.

Bamiyan, Afghanistan: see BAMIAN.

Bam La (bäm'lä'), pass (alt. 14,500 ft.) in E Tibet, near the Yangtze, 50 mi. SSW of Paan, and on main road to Chamdo, on historic border bet. Tibet and China.

Bammental (bä'mŭntäl"), village (pop. 3,098), N Baden, Germany, after 1945 in Württemberg-Baden, on the Elsenz and 5 mi. SE of Heidelberg; paper milling.

Bamoun (bä'mōōn), administrative region (□ 2,895, 1950 pop. 82,100), W Fr. Cameroons; ⊙ Foumbou. Bordered W by Br. Cameroons, E by M'Bam R. Hilly and mostly under open savanna. Coffee cultivation both by natives and on European plantations. Picturesque native handicrafts still widespread here amongst its Moslem pop.

Bampton. 1 Former urban district (1931 pop. 1,392), Devon, England, 7 mi. N of Tiverton; agr. market; limestone quarries. Annual sheep and pony fair. Has 15th-cent. church. **2** Town and parish (pop. 1,167), W Oxfordshire, England, 12 mi. W of Oxford; agr. market. Has Norman 14th-cent. church. Town is noted for its Morris dancing, especially in procession on Whit Monday. **3** Village and parish (pop. 1,011), N Westmorland, England, 8 mi. S of Penrith; cattle, sheep.

Bampur (bämpōōr'), village, Eighth Prov., in Baluchistan, SE Iran, 300 mi. SE of Kerman and on intermittent Bampur R. (irrigated agr.); former ⊙ Iranian Baluchistan, and a fortress, road, and trade center, it declined in early-20th cent. and was largely replaced by IRANSHAHR, 15 mi. E.

Bamra (bäm'rŭ), former princely state (□ 1,974; pop. 178,277), in Orissa States, India; ⊙ was Deogarh. Inc. 1949 into Sambalpur dist., Orissa.

Bamra, village, Sambalpur dist., NW Orissa, India, on railroad and 45 mi. NNE of Sambalpur; sawmills; mfg. of bobbins, spools.

Bamrauli, India: see ALLAHABAD, city.

Bam Tso or **Bam Tsho** (both: bäm' tsō'), Chinese *Pa-mo Hu* (bä'mô' hōō'), lake, E central Tibet, on Chang Tang plateau, 120 mi. N of Lhasa; 31°15'N 91°E.

Bamu Island, Fr. Equatorial Africa: see STANLEY POOL.

Bamyan, Afghanistan: see BAMIAN.

Ban, Czechoslovakia: see BANOVCE NAD BEBRAVOU.

Ban [Thai, =village]: for names in Thailand beginning thus and not found here, see under following part of name.

Bana (bŏ'nŏ), town (pop. 3,264), Komarom-Esztergom co., N Hungary, 13 mi. E of Györ; ruins of Roman *Castrum Bana.* Near by is Babolna stud farm, established in 1780s by Joseph II.

Bana (bä'nä'), village, Quangnam prov., central Vietnam, 15 mi. W of Tourane; hill resort in Annamese Cordillera; alt. 4,813 ft.

Bana, Wadi (wă'dē bănă'), coastal stream of Western Aden Protectorate, rises in Yemen near Yarim, flows 100 mi. SE to Gulf of Aden 30 mi. NE of Aden. Irrigates Abyan and Khanfar oases near mouth.

Banaba: see OCEAN ISLAND.

Bañado de Ovanta (bänyä'dō dā ōvän'tä), village (pop. estimate 400), ⊙ Santa Rosa dept. (□ 1,020; pop. 5,954), SE Catamarca prov., Argentina, 35 mi. NE of Catamarca, in cattle-raising area.

Bañado de Rocha (rō'chä), village, Tacuarembó dept., N Uruguay, on the Bañado de Rocha (left affluent of the Arroyo Tres Cruces Grande) and 10 mi. NE of Tacuarembó, on railroad. Uruguay's only railroad tunnel is near by.

Bañados, Cerro de los (sĕ'rō dā lōs bänyä'dōs), Andean peak (17,520 ft.), on Argentina-Chile border, 45 mi. WNW of Rodeo, Argentina; 30°3'S.

Banagher (bă'nŭkh-ŭr), Gaelic *Beannchar na Sionna,* town (pop. 636), W Co. Offaly, Ireland, on the Shannon (bridge) and 8 mi. NNW of Birr; malting center and agr. market (hops, barley, potatoes; cattle), with alcohol distilling.

Banagüises (bänägwē'sĕs), town (pop. 2,110), Matanzas prov., W Cuba, on railroad and 29 mi. ESE of Cárdenas; sugar cane, fruit, vegetables; apiculture.

Banahao, Mount (bänä'hou), extinct volcano (7,177 ft.), S Luzon, Philippines, SE of Manila, on border bet. Laguna and Quezon provs.

Bañalbufar (bänyälbōōfär'), town (pop. 698), Majorca, Balearic Isls., on NW coast, 10 mi. NW of Palma; tomatoes, olives, wine, fruit. Fishing, olive-oil pressing, wine making (malmsey), cement mill.

Banalia (bänä'lyä), village, Eastern Prov., N Belgian Congo, on Aruwimi R. and 65 mi. N of Stanleyville; cotton ginning, rice processing. Has R.C. mission. Also called Banalia-Sainte-Elisabeth.

Banam (bänäm'), town, Preyveng prov., S Cambodia, on left bank of Mekong R. and 30 mi. SE of Pnompenh; important river port (boat building) and trading center; distillery (rice alcohol).

Banámichi (bänä'mēchē), town (pop. 814), Sonora, NW Mexico, on Sonora R. and 80 mi. NE of Hermosillo; wheat, corn, cattle. Santa Elena gold mines near by.

Banana (bänä'nä) or **Banane** (bänän'), town, Leopoldville prov., SW Belgian Congo, on Atlantic, on N side of Congo R. estuary (Angola border), opposite Santo António do Zaire and 45 mi. WSW of Boma; seaport and old trading center; customs, quarantine, and pilot stations; service station for submarine cables. Has R.C. mission. European trading establishments in Banana area date from beginning of 19th cent.

Banana Islands, 2 islands belonging to Sierra Leone colony, in the Atlantic off Cape Shilling, 3 mi. SW of Kent, and 25 mi. S of Freetown. Larger isl. is 5 mi. long, 1½ mi. wide. Fishing. Ceded to the Crown in 1820.

Bananal (bŭnŭnäl'), city (pop. 1,641), extreme SE São Paulo, Brazil, in the Serra do Mar, 12 mi. SW of Barra Mansa (Rio de Janeiro); rail-spur terminus; resort (founded 1783); stock raising, dairying (especially cheese), distilling.

Bananal Island, central Brazil, formed by Araguaia R. (W Goiás), which for 200 mi. (bet. 13°S and 10°S lat.) separates into 2 branches. Max. width, 35 mi. Inhabited by Indian tribes. Natural vegetation of babassu palms.

Banana River, shallow lagoon (c.30 mi. long, 3 mi. wide) in E Fla., bet. Merritt Isl. and Cape Canaveral barrier beach, which separates it from the Atlantic. Connected by channels at N and S ends with Indian R. lagoon.

Bananeiras (bŭnŭnā'rŭs), city (pop. 2,187), E Paraíba, NE Brazil, terminus of rail spur from Guarabira, and 55 mi. NW of João Pessoa; agr. center (bananas, pumpkins, sugar, cotton, rice, tobacco).

Bananera (bänänā'rä), town (pop. 1,122), Izabal dept., E Guatemala, just NW of Morales, on railroad; hq. of banana plantations along lower Motagua R. Modern residential settlement.

Bananito (bänänē'tō), village, Limón prov., E Costa Rica, on railroad and 8 mi. S of Limón; cacao, livestock.

Banapura, India: see SEONI-MALWA.

Banaras, India: see BENARES.

Banas, Ra's, Egypt: see BENAS, RAS.

Banas Kantha (bŭnäs' kän'tŭ), district (created 1949–50), N Bombay, India; ⊙ Palanpur. Bounded NW by Thar Desert, W by Rann of Cutch, S by Mehsana dist., E by Sabarmati R.; E section crossed by S offshoots of Aravalli Range; watered (center) by Banas R. Largely a sandy, treeless plain; agr. (millet, oilseeds, cotton, sugar cane, tobacco). Hand-loom weaving, oilseed milling, salt mfg. (W). Has famous hill resort of Abu; trade centers at Palanpur and Abu Road. Dist. formed (1949–50) by merger of former Rajputana states of Palanpur, Danta, and SE section of Sirohi, and of several former Western India states, mainly of Sabar Kantha Agency.

Banas River. 1 In E Rajasthan, India, rises in Aravalli Range S of Kumbhalgarh fortress, flows c.310 mi. E, NE, and E to Chambal R. 16 mi. N of Sheopur. Fishing (mahseer) in places. **2** In N Bombay, India, rises in S Aravalli Range just E of Sirohi, flows c.165 mi. SW into Little Rann of Cutch, SW of Radhanpur.

Banat (bänät') [i.e., territory governed by a ban], specifically applied only to the former **Banat of Temesvar** (tĕ'mĕshvär"), a fertile low-lying region bet. the Transylvanian Alps and the Danube, Tisza, and Mures rivers; ⊙ was Temesvar (Timisoara). Ruled by Hungary after 11th cent., it was 1st constituted (1441) a banat under John Hunyadi. Held by Turks after 1552, it became (1718) an Austrian military frontier zone, settled by Serbs and Germans. Returned 1779 to Hungary, where it remained until 1919, except for its brief existence (1849–60) as an Austrian crownland. By the treaty of Trianon (1920) it was divided bet. Yugoslavia and Rumania, except for small Hung. triangle near Szeged. The Rumanian **Banat,** a historical province (□ 6,975; 1948 pop. 948,596; ⊙ was TIMISOARA), includes the region around Lugoj, Oravita, and Timisoara. The Yugoslav **Banat** (chief city, Zrenjanin) is a region of Vojvodina, N Serbia, bounded by Tisa (Tisza) R. (W) and the Danube (S). It was in Danube banovina (1929–41) and remained in Serbia during Second World War.

Banatski Karlovac, Yugoslavia: see RANKOVICEVO, Vojvodina, Serbia.

Banatsko Novo Selo, Yugoslavia: see NOVO SELO.

Banau Brycheiniog, Wales: see BRECKNOCK VAN.

Banaue (bänä'wā), town (1939 pop. 2,258; 1948 municipality pop. 15,311), Ifugao sub-prov., Mountain Prov., N Luzon, Philippines, 42 mi. NE of Baguio; lumbering, rice growing.

Banau Sir Gaer, Wales: see CARMARTHEN VAN.

Banavar (bä'nävŭr), town (pop. 2,462), Hassan dist., W central Mysore, India, 27 mi. N of Hassan; cotton ginning. Also spelled Banavara.

Banbasa (bŭnbä'sŭ), village, Naini Tal dist., N Uttar Pradesh, India, near Sarda Canal (headworks 2 mi. NE), 6 mi. SSW of Tanakpur. Hydroelectric plant (installed capacity 41,400 kw.) is 7 mi. SW, at village of Kathima.

Banbridge (bănbrĭj'), urban district (1937 pop. 5,640; 1951 census 6,098), W Co. Down, Northern Ireland, on Bann R. and 22 mi. SW of Belfast; linen-milling center, with mfg. of shirts, rope, and fish nets; agr. market.

Ban Bung Sai (bän' bōōng' sī), town, Saravane prov., S Laos, on the Se Done and 12 mi. W of Saravane.

Banbury, municipal borough (1931 pop. 13,953; 1951 census 18,917), N Oxfordshire, England, on Cherwell R. and 21 mi. N of Oxford; agr. market, with mfg. of metal products, chemicals, electrical equipment; textile printing. Since 17th cent. the town has been famous for its cakes. The Banbury Cross of the nursery rhyme was destroyed by Puritans in 1602; a new cross took its place in 19th cent. There are many old houses and inns and some traces of a 12th-cent. castle built by a bishop of Lincoln.

Banchory (băng'kůrē), burgh (1931 pop. 1,690; 1951 census 1,958), N Kincardine, Scotland, on the Dee and 16 mi. WSW of Aberdeen; agr. market and resort.

Banchory-Devenick, agr. village and parish (pop. 1,335), NE Kincardine, Scotland, on the Dee and 3 mi. SW of Aberdeen.

Banckspolder, Netherlands: see SCHIERMONNIKOOG.

Banco, El, Colombia: see EL BANCO.

Bancroft, village (pop. 1,094), SE Ont., on York R. and 60 mi. NNE of Peterborough; woolen milling, dairying, lumbering; marble, limestone quarrying; resort.

Bancroft. **1** Village (pop. 495), Caribou co., SE Idaho, 30 mi. ESE of Pocatello; alt. 5,423 ft.; grain, livestock. **2** Town (pop. 901), Kossuth co., N Iowa, near East Des Moines R., 15 mi. N of Algona, in livestock and grain area. **3** Town (pop. 165), Aroostook co., E Maine, on Mattawamkeag R. and 33 mi. SW of Houlton, in agr. area. **4** Village (pop. 615), Shiawassee co., S central Mich., 21 mi. SW of Flint, in farm area. **5** Village (pop. 596), Cuming co., NE Nebr., 15 mi. NNE of West Point and on Logan Creek; grain, livestock. **6** Town (pop. 100), Kingsbury co., E central S.Dak., 12 mi. NW of De Smet.

Band (bänd), Hung. *Mezőbánd* (mĕ'zû-bänt"), village (pop. 3,071), Mures prov., central Rumania, 9 mi. WNW of Targu-Mures; rail junction; agr. market.

Banda (bän'dŭ), district (□ 2,913; pop. 722,568), S Uttar Pradesh, India; ⊙ Banda. Bounded N by Jumna R.; drained by the Ken. Foothills of Vindhya Range in S. A major gram-producing area of state; also jowar, wheat, rice, sesame, pearl millet, mustard, barley; mahua plantations. Important glass-sand deposits near Mau village. Main towns: Banda, Karwi, Rajapur. Archaeological sites at KALINJAR and Chitrakut. Formerly part of Br. BUNDELKHAND.

Banda. **1** Town (pop. 3,554), Ratnagiri dist., W Bombay, India, 90 mi. SSE of Ratnagiri; rice, betel nuts, coconuts. Near-by teak forests. **2** Village, Saugor dist., N Madhya Pradesh, India, 21 mi. NE of Saugor; wheat, millet, oilseeds. **3** Town (pop. 27,070), ⊙ Banda dist., S Uttar Pradesh, India, near Ken R., 70 mi. S of Cawnpore; road center; trades in cotton, gram, jowar, oilseeds, rice. Extensive mosques and Hindu temples. Ruins of 18th-cent. fort, captured 1804 by English, near by.

Banda, La, Argentina: see LA BANDA.

Bandai-san (bän'dī-sä) ,group of 4 volcanic cones in Fukushima prefecture, N central Honshu, Japan, 25 mi. WSW of Fukushima, near L. Inawashiro; highest cone rises to 5,968 ft. Eruption in 1888 devastated area of 27 sq. mi.

Banda Islands (băn'dů, bän'dä), group (□ c.40; pop. 13,036), S Moluccas, Indonesia, in Banda Sea, 75 mi. S of Ceram; 4°31'S 129°55'E. Consist of 1 large isl. (BANDALONTAR) surrounded by c.10 islets, including GUNUNG API (with active volcano) and BANDANAIRA. Chief products: copra, fish, sago, nutmeg. Visited 1599 by the Dutch who gained control of isl. in 1619. Formerly a major nutmeg-producing center.

Bandajuma (bändäjōō'mä), town (pop. 628), South-Western Prov., SE Sierra Leone, on Waanje R. and 15 mi. N of Pujehun; palm oil and kernels, piassava, rice.

Bandak (bän'näk, bän'däk), lake (□ 24) in Telemark co., S Norway, 45 mi. WNW of Skien, at NW end of Bandak-Norsja Canal; 18 mi. long, c.1 mi. wide. Dalen and Lastein, on W shore, are at head of canal route.

Bandak-Norsja Canal (–nôr'shô), Nor. *Bandak-Norsjå*, 65-mi.-long waterway in Telemark co., S Norway, extends from Skien on the seaboard into the uplands in Lardal canton to Dalen and Lastein. Passes through the lakes Nor (Nor. *Norsjå*, formerly *Norsjø*), Kviteseid, and Bandak. Rises 187 ft. by means of 15 locks. Small steamers ply it. Busy tourist route.

Bandaksli (bän'näkslē, –däk–), village in Mo canton (pop. 1,698), Telemark co., S Norway, on S shore of Bandak lake, 55 mi. WNW of Skien; copper and molybdenite mines. Sawmills, flour mills near by.

Bandalontar (bän"dälōn'tär), largest island (□ 17; pop. 3,148) of BANDA ISLANDS, S Moluccas, Indonesia, in Banda Sea, 75 mi. S of Ceram; 4°31'S 129°55'E; 9 mi. long, 2 mi. wide, rising to 1,758 ft. Chief products: copra, nutmeg, fish. Sometimes called Great Banda.

Bandama, Caldera de (käldā'rä dhä bändä'mä), extinct crater, Grand Canary, Canary Isls., c.4 mi. S of Las Palmas. Forms a gigantic amphitheater, roughly 3,500 ft. in diameter, 650 ft. deep.

Bandama River (bändä'mä), rises as the White Bandama in N highlands of Ivory Coast, Fr. West Africa, just W of Korhogo and near source of the Red Bandama, which joins it 20 mi. ESE of Bouaflé; flows generally S to Gulf of Guinea at Grand-Lahou; c.450 mi. long. Navigable by small vessels c.60 mi. upstream. Main affluent, Nzi.

Bandamir River, Iran: see KUR RIVER.

Bandanaira or **Bandaneira** (bändůnä'rů), island (c.2 mi. long, 1 mi. wide), Banda Isls., S Moluccas, Indonesia, in Banda Sea, bet. Bandalontar (E) and Gunung Api (W); fishing. Sometimes called Naira or Neira.

Bandaneira, Indonesia: see BANDANAIRA.

Banda Oriental (bän'dä ōryĕntäl') [Sp.,=eastern shore], region in S Uruguay, along the Río de la Plata; an alluvial plain where nearly all of Uruguay's agr. products (wheat, flax, linseed, oats, barley) are raised and most of the pop. is concentrated. So called because it was E of the original settlement about Buenos Aires, Banda Oriental was the term applied to Uruguay in Sp. colonial period.

Bandar, India: see MASULIPATAM.

Bandar Abbas or **Bandar 'Abbas** (bändär' äbäs') [Persian,=harbor of Abbas], town (1941 pop. 14,278), Eighth Prov., in Kerman, SE Iran, port on Strait of Hormuz, 22 mi. SSW of Kerman; 27°11'N 56°17'E. Fishing center with sardine cannery; cotton spinning. Customhouse. Exports fruit from Minab area. Pop. declines in hot summer season to c.10,000. The successor of HORMUZ as the leading commercial center of the Persian Gulf area, the port was built in 1623 by Abbas the Great on the site of the village of Gombrun. It flourished through 17th cent. until supplanted by Bushire in 18th cent. Under Persian rule since 1868.

Bandar Abu Shehr, Iran: see BUSHIRE.

Bandarawela (bŭndŭrŭvā'lŭ), town (pop. 3,005), Uva Prov., S central Ceylon, in Uva Basin, 18 mi. SE of Nuwara Eliya; tea-transport center; tea processing; rice plantations. A noted hill station (alt. 4,036 ft.); said to enjoy most equable climate in Ceylon.

Bandarban (bän'dŭrbŭn), village, Chittagong Hill Tracts dist., SE East Bengal, E Pakistan, on Sangu R. and 31 mi. S of Rangamati; trades in rice, cotton, oilseeds, tobacco.

Bandar Bharu or **Bandar Bahru** (bändär' bä'rōō), village (pop. 912) southernmost Kedah, Malaya, at Penang line, 22 mi. SE of George Town, and on Krian R. (Perak border) opposite Parit Buntar; rubber.

Bandar Bushehr, Iran: see BUSHIRE.

Bandar Dilam, Bandar Deilam, or **Bandar Deylam** (all: däläm'), town (1945 pop. estimate 3,130), Sixth Prov., in Khuzistan, S Iran, minor port on Persian Gulf, 90 mi. NNW of Bushire; coastwise trade. Serves Behbehan.

Bandar Endau, Malaya: see ENDAU.

Bandar Ganaweh or **Bandar Gonaveh** (gōnävĕ'), town, Seventh Prov., in Fars, S Iran, minor port on Persian Gulf, 45 mi. NNW of Bushire.

Bandar Gaz (gäz'), town, Second Prov., in Gurgan, NE Iran, port on Gurgan Lagoon of SE Caspian Sea, on railroad and 28 mi. W of Gurgan; fishing; rice milling. Former port for Gurgan, it became shallow as result of Caspian Sea recession and was replaced by Bandar Shah.

Bandar Gonaveh, Iran: see BANDAR GANAWEH.

Bandar Jissah, Oman: see JISSA.

Bandar Khairan, Oman: see KHAIRAN.

Bandar Khumair, Bandar Khomeir, or **Bandar Khomeyr** (all: khōmär'), town, Seventh Prov., in Fars, S Iran, minor port on Persian Gulf, 15 mi. NE of Lingeh.

Bandar Lingeh, Iran: see LINGEH.

Bandar Maharani (bändär' mähärä'nē), commonly called **Muar** (mōō'är), town (pop. 32,228), NW Johore, SW Malaya, port on Strait of Malacca at mouth of Muar R. and 90 mi. NW of Johore Bharu; rubber, coconuts, bananas; fisheries. Ferry service across Muar R.; airfield.

Bandar Mashur or **Bandar Ma'shur** (mäshōōr'), town (1942 pop. estimate 700), Sixth Prov., in Khuzistan, SW Iran, 55 mi. ENE of Abadan; oil-loading port on the Khor Musa (tidal inlet of Persian Gulf); linked by pipe line with Agha Jari oil field.

Bandar Pahlavi, Iran: see PAHLEVI.

Bandar Penggaram (bändär' pĕng-gä'räm), commonly called **Batu Pahat** (bä'tōō pä'hät), town (pop. 26,506), W Johore, Malaya, port on Strait of Malacca at mouth of small Batu Pahat R. (ferry), 60 mi. NW of Johore Bharu; fishing and agr. center; rubber, coconuts, fruit. Iron and bauxite mining near Yong Peng, 14 mi. NE.

Bandar Rig (rēg'), town (1945 pop. estimate 2,250), Seventh Prov., in Fars, S Iran, minor port on Persian Gulf, 37 mi. NNW of Bushire.

Bandar Shah (shä'), town, Second Prov., in Gurgan, NE Iran, port on Gurgan Lagoon of SE Caspian Sea, 20 mi. W of Gurgan; rail terminus and fishing center; airfield. First jetty built in 1926; port expanded in Second World War during lend-lease shipments to USSR; has replaced shallower port of Bandar Gaz (SW).

Bandar Shahpur (shäpōōr'), town, Sixth Prov., in Khuzistan, SW Iran, 34 mi. E of Abadan; terminus of Trans-Iranian RR and port on the Khor Musa (tidal inlet of Persian Gulf); cargo terminal and transshipment point; airfield. Opened in 1932, the port played a major role in Second World War on lend-lease supply route to USSR. It has been partly supplanted by Khurramshahr.

Bandar Shuwaikh, Kuwait: see SHUWAIKH.

Banda Sea (băn'dů, bän'dä), section (□ 285,000) of Pacific Ocean, in E Indonesia, surrounded by the semicircular arc of the South Moluccas group (Buru, Ceram, Kai, Tanimbar, Babar, Kisar, and Wetar isls.). Merges with Flores Sea (SW), Molucca Sea (NW), Ceram Sea (N), Arafura Sea (SE), and Timor Sea (S). It is 600 mi. long, 300 mi. wide; reaches greatest depth (more than 21,000 ft.) W of Kai Isls.

Bandawe (bändä'wā), village, Northern Prov., Nyasaland, on W shore of L. Nyasa, 5 mi. S of Chinteche; fishing; cassava, corn. Former mission station; African hosp., school.

Banded Peak (9,626 ft.), SW Alta., near B.C. border, in Rocky Mts., 40 mi. SE of Banff.

Banded Peak (12,760 ft.), in San Juan Mts., SW Colo., near N.Mex. line, 24 mi. SE of Pagosa Springs.

Bandeira, Pico da (pē'kōō dä bändā'rů), highest mountain (9,462 ft.) of Brazil, in the Serra do Caparaó, on Minas Gerais–Espírito Santo border, 200 mi. NNE of Rio de Janeiro.

Bandeirantes (bändärän'tĭs), city (pop. 2,247), N Paraná, Brazil, on railroad and 50 mi. ENE of Londrina, in coffee- and cotton-growing area; coffee roasting, corn and rice milling.

Ban-de-la-Roche (bã-dů-lä-rôsh'), Ger. *Steinthal* (shtīn'täl), upper valley of Bruche R., in the Vosges, Bas-Rhin dept., E France, above Fouday, made famous by works of Oberlin

Bandelier National Monument (bănddůlēr') (□ 42.2; established 1916), N central N.Mex., on the Rio Grande and 20 mi. WNW of Sante Fe. Ruins of Pueblo Indian villages (mostly 16th cent.) in cliffs and canyons of Pajarito Plateau. Inhabitants, who numbered 1,500–2,000, raised corn, beans, and pumpkins, and made pottery. Chief ruins are those of Tyuonyi Pueblo (on floor of Frijoles Canyon) and Otowi Pueblo, in detached part of monument, 6 mi. NE.

Bandera (bändā'rä), town (pop. estimate 1,500), ⊙ Belgrano dept. (□ 1,370; 1947 census pop. 6,755), SE Santiago del Estero prov., Argentina, 45 mi. SE of Añatuya. Rail junction, agr. center (cereals, sunflowers, cotton, stock); flour milling, dairying.

Bandera (bănděr'ů), county (□ 765; pop. 4,410), SW Texas; ⊙ Bandera. On Edwards Plateau; alt. c.1,000–2,000 ft.; drained by Sabinal and Medina rivers. Part of Medina L. (irrigation, recreation) is in SE. Hilly ranching area (cattle, sheep, goats), with guest ("dude") ranches; some agr. (grain sorghums, hay, corn, pecans, poultry); hunting, fishing; some timber. Formed 1856.

Bandera, village (pop. 1,036), ⊙ Bandera co., SW Texas, on Edwards Plateau, 40 mi. NW of San Antonio and on Medina R., in agr., ranching area; tourist trade; timber. Has mus. of pioneer relics. Medina L. (irrigation, recreation) is 7 mi. SE. Founded 1854 by Mormons and later turned into a Polish settlement.

Bandera, Alto, Hispaniola: see TINA, MONTE.

Banderas, Las, Nicaragua: see LAS BANDERAS.

Banderas Bay (bändā'räs), Pacific inlet, in Nayarit and Jalisco, W Mexico, just N of Cape Corriente; 27 mi. long, c.25 mi. wide. Receives Ameca R. The little port of Puerto Vallarta is at its head.

Banderilla (bändärē'yä), town (pop. 2,095), Veracruz, E Mexico, in Sierra Madre Oriental, on railroad and 4 mi. NNW of Jalapa; corn, coffee, fruit.

Bandhogarh (bän'dōgŭr), old Rajput hill fort, SE Vindhya Pradesh, India, 60 mi. SSW of Rewa; resisted Lodi attacks in late-15th cent.; taken 1597 by Akbar's forces.

Bandiagara (bändyägärä'), town (pop. c.3,700), S Fr. Sudan, Fr. West Africa, 37 mi. ESE of Mopti, in agr. region (rice, millet, livestock). Noted for its escarpments with curious dwellings, mosque, and sacred sites. Medical post.

Bandiat River (bädyä'), Dordogne and Charente depts., W France, rises 4 mi. S of Oradour-sur-Vayres, flows c.45 mi. NW, past Nontron, to the Tardoire below La Rochefoucauld. Depleted through seepage, its waters reappear near Magnac-sur-Touvre to form spring of the TOUVRE.

Bandikui (bän'dĭkōōē), village, E Rajasthan, India, 7 mi. S of Baswa, rail junction (workshops); millet, wheat.

Bandirma (bändŭrmä'),Turk. *Bandırma*, anc. *Panormus*, town (1950 pop. 18,986), Balikesir prov., NW Turkey, on an inlet of Sea of Marmara, 50 mi. N of Balikesir; rail terminus and market town (wheat, oats, beans, sheep). Boracite and pandermite (named for this place) found near by. Formerly Panderma.

Band-i-Turkestan or **Band-i-Turkistan** (bŭnd'-ĭ-tōōr'kĭstän"), W outlier of the Hindu Kush, in N Afghanistan, extending 100 mi. E-W along right (N) watershed of Murghab R.; rises to 11,590 ft. in the Zangilak, 45 mi. SW of Maimana.

Bandjermasin, Indonesia: see BANJERMASIN.

Bando (bändō') or **Banto** (–tō'), town (pop. 6,699), Tokushima prefecture, NE Shikoku, Japan, on Yoshino R. and 6 mi. NNW of Tokushima; commercial center in agr. area (rice, wheat). Site of 3 Buddhist temples and a Shinto shrine.

Bandoeng, Indonesia: see BANDUNG.
Bandol (bädôl'), town (pop. 2,478), Var dept., SE France, resort on the Mediterranean, 9 mi. W of Toulon; saltworks. Olive and winegrowing.
Bandon, Gaelic *Droichead na Banndan,* town (pop. 2,613), S Co. Cork, Ireland, on Bandon R. and 16 mi. SW of Cork; agr. market (dairying; oats, potatoes), with tanneries, breweries, distilleries. Founded c.1608 as fortified town by earl of Cork; in 1688 walls were dismantled. Sometimes called Bandonbridge.
Ban Don or **Bandon,** Thailand: see SURATTHANI.
Bandon, city (pop. 1,251), Coos co., SW Oregon, on Pacific coast, at mouth of Coquille R., 12 mi. WSW of Coquille; salmon fisheries; lumber, dairy products. Inc. 1891. Largely destroyed by forest fire (1936); later replanned and rebuilt.
Bandonbridge, Ireland: see BANDON.
Bandon River, Co. Cork, Ireland, rises in Shehy Mts., flows 40 mi. E, past Bandon, to the Atlantic at Kinsale Harbour.
Bandra (bän'drŭ), city (pop. 71,789), ⊙ Bombay Suburban dist., W Bombay, India, on Arabian Sea, on SW Salsette Isl., 9 mi. N of Bombay city center; residential area; chemical mfg., tanning, fishing (pomfrets, mackerel, jewfish, Bombay duck), palmyra-tree tapping; bakeries, slaughterhouse (SE). Govt. Tanning Inst.
Bandundu, Belgian Congo: see BANNINGVILLE.
Bandung or **Bandoeng** (both: bändŏŏng', bän'–), principal city (pop. 166,815) of Preanger region, W Java, Indonesia, 75 mi. SE of Jakarta; 6°55'S 107°36'E; alt. 2,346 ft. Industrial center (quinine, textiles, chemicals, rubber goods, machinery). Climate is cool and healthful. Has airport and a powerful radio station. There is engineering col., textile institute, Pasteur Institute. Formerly hq. of Du. East Indies Army.
Baneasa (bŭnyä'sä), Rum. *Băneasa,* outer N urban suburb (1948 pop. 8,315) of Bucharest, S Rumania, near Baneasa L.; agr. center (dairying, grain); experimental tobacco and agr. station; race-horse breeding; fisheries. It is also one of the recreation centers of Bucharest, with a race course. Site of municipal airport.
Baned, India: see SUNDARNAGAR.
Baneh (bänĕ'), town, Fifth Prov., in Kurdistan, W Iran, 27 mi. SW of Saqqiz, near Iraq border; tobacco, wheat, gums; sheep raising.
Banera (bŭnā'rŭ), town (pop. 4,919), S Rajasthan, India, 11 mi. NNE of Bhilwara; millet, gram; cotton ginning.
Bañeres (bänyā'rĕs), town (pop. 2,930), Alicante prov., E Spain, 10 mi. W of Alcoy; mfg. of paper, footwear, wool flannels, cotton cloth, knit goods; olive-oil processing, flour milling.
Banes (bä'nĕs), town (pop. 14,097), Oriente prov., E Cuba, 35 mi. ENE of Holguín; agr. center trading in sugar cane, bananas and other tropical fruit, which are exported through its port Embarcadero de Banes 3 mi. SSE on Banes Bay. The sugar central Boston is 4 mi. S.
Banes Bay, landlocked inlet (5 mi. long, 5 mi. wide) of the Atlantic, Oriente prov., E Cuba, 35 mi. E of Holguín; linked with sea by narrow channel. Embarcadero de Banes, the port for Banes, is on its N shore.
Bañeza, La (lä bänyā'thä), city (pop. 5,935), Leon prov., NW Spain, on Órbigo R. and 26 mi. SW of Leon; agr. trade center (cereals, wine, potatoes, livestock); flour- and sawmills, tanneries, sugar refinery; mfg. of wax, hats.
Banff (bămf), town (1946 pop. 2,081), SW Alta., near B.C. border, in Rocky Mts., in S part of Banff Natl. Park, on Bow R. and 65 mi. W of Calgary; alt. 4,538 ft.; surrounded by several peaks over 9,000 ft. high. Famous summer and winter tourist center and resort, with hot sulphur springs; railroad station (on Canadian Pacific RR) for Banff Natl. Park. Has mus., zoological garden, wild-animal paddock, several noted hotels, and sanitarium. Has annual winter carnival. Banff School of Fine Arts, extension of Univ. of Alberta, has held summer courses here since 1933. Industries include mfg. of pharmaceuticals and, near by, coal mining.
Banff or **Banffshire** (bămf', –shĭr, –shŭr), county (□ 629.8; 1931 pop. 54,907; 1951 census 50,135), NE Scotland; ⊙ Banff. Bounded by Inverness and Moray (W), Moray Firth and the North Sea (N), and Aberdeen (E and S). Drained by Deveron, Spey, Avon rivers. Surface generally mountainous or hilly (in S are Grampian and Cairngorm mts.), leveling to narrow fertile coastal strip. In foothills of the Grampians the valleys are also under cultivation. Cattle raising, sea fisheries, salmon fishing (in Deveron and Spey rivers), quarrying of granite, slate, and limestone, whisky distilling (Glenlivet). Other towns are Keith, Buckie, Macduff, Dufftown, Aberlour, Portsoy.
Banff, burgh (1931 pop. 3,489; 1951 census 3,359), ⊙ Banffshire, Scotland, in NE part of co., on Banff Bay of Moray Firth, at mouth of Deveron R., 40 mi. NNW of Aberdeen; fishing port, seaside resort, agr. market. There are remains of anc. castle, occupied for a time by Edward I. Bridge, built 1779, links Banff with MACDUFF.
Banff National Park (□ 2,564), SW Alta., on B.C. border, in Rocky Mts., 60 mi. W of Calgary; 130 mi. long, 30 mi. wide. It is noted for its spectacular scenery, which includes some of the highest peaks of the Canadian Rockies (Mts. Hector, Saskatchewan, Murchison, Patterson, Temple, Willingdon, Ball, St. Bride, Sir Douglas, and several other peaks over 10,000 ft. high), icefields, and many mtn. lakes. Within the park are the famous resorts of Banff and Lake Louise. On W boundary of park is Kicking Horse Pass. Park was established 1885 and subsequently enlarged. Borders N on Jasper Natl. Park and W on Yoho and Kootenay natl. parks, B.C. Crossed by Trans-Canada Highway.
Banffshire, Scotland: see BANFF, county.
Banffy-Hunyad, Rumania: see HUEDIN.
Bânfield, residential town (pop. 31,280) in Greater Buenos Aires, Argentina, adjoining Lomas de Zamora, 8 mi. SSW of Buenos Aires. Mfg. of textiles, ceramics, cement articles, hats; tanneries, sawmills.
Banfora (bänfō'rä), town (pop. c.2,100), SW Upper Volta, Fr. West Africa, on railroad and 45 mi. SW of Bobo-Dioulasso, in agr. region (peanuts, rice, shea nuts, sesame, livestock). Has experiment station for rice- and fruitgrowing. Mfg. of bricks; rice-milling. Clinic for sleeping sickness. Formerly (1919–32) part of the Ivory Coast.
Banga (băngä') or **Banja** (bänjä'), village (pop. 9,637), Girga prov., central Upper Egypt, 2 mi. NNW of Tahta; cotton, cereals, dates, sugar cane.
Banga (bŭng'gŭ), town (pop. 9,112), Jullundur dist., central Punjab, India, 26 mi. ESE of Jullundur; market center for wheat, sugar, corn; handicraft brassware, carpentry.
Banga (bäng'gä, bäng'ä), town (1939 pop. 1,393; 1948 municipality pop. 17,977), Capiz prov., N Panay isl., Philippines, 29 mi. W of Capiz; agr. center (rice, coconuts, sugar cane).
Banga, Thailand: see PHANGNGA.
Bangalore (băng'gŭlôr, băng-gŭlôr'), district (□ 3,082; pop. 1,447,059), E Mysore, India; ⊙ Bangalore. On Deccan Plateau; undulating tableland, bordered S by Cauvery R. Agr. (silk, millet, tobacco, sugar cane); bamboo, sandalwood, lac in dispersed hills. Rice, flour, and oilseed milling, cattle and sheep grazing. Handicrafts (silk and cotton weaving, lacquer- and metalware, pottery, biris); diversified industries centered in and around Bangalore city. Other chief towns: Channapatna, Closepet, Dodballapur.
Bangalore, city (□ 26; pop., including cantonment area, 406,760), administrative ⊙ Mysore and ⊙ Bangalore dist., S India, 180 mi. W of Madras, 520 mi. SE of Bombay; 12°58'N 77°35'E. Communications hub (road and rail junction; airport at N suburb of Jakkur); industrial, commercial, and cultural center. An important textile center (silk, cotton, wool, gold lace), Bangalore is also noted for its mfg. of porcelain and glassware, sandalwood soap and perfume, agr. machinery, chemicals (industrial and medical), cigarettes, telephones, and radios. India's 1st aircraft assembly plant, opened here in 1941, reconditioned Br., Indian, and U.S. planes in Second World War; in 1948, trainer aircraft were produced and the plant was organized for mfg. of commercial planes and railway coaches. City's other industries include vegetable-oil processing, chrome tanning, mfg. of tiles and bricks, asbestos products, electrical appliances, neon signs, plywood, and plastics. Motion picture studios are in E suburb of Whitefield. Industries are powered by hydroelectric works near Sivasamudram isl. (50 mi. SSW). Bangalore, at alt.of c.3,000ft., has pleasant climate; mean temp. ranges from 87°F. in May to 69°F. in Dec. Well planned city with numerous parks and wide streets; most industries located on outskirts, largely in NW area of Yesvantpur (or Yeswantpur or Jeswantpur). Cantonment area (□ 13; pop. 158,426), lying E and N of city proper, has most of city's fine residences, modern govt. bldgs. and hospitals, and a palace of the maharaja; large military hq. Remains of a palace of Tippoo Sahib and a noted botanical garden are in city proper. Bangalore is seat of one of the 2 centers of Univ. of Mysore (founded 1916; other center is in Mysore city); Bangalore center includes medical and engineering colleges. Well-known Indian Inst. of Science (founded 1911), in area of Malleswaram (NW), has courses in aeronautical, chemical, and electrical engineering, and metallurgy. Other technological institutes train radio mechanics and motion-picture technicians. Civil aviation training center in area of Jalahalli (N). Bangalore, founded 16th cent. by present Mysore dynasty, was taken c.1760 by Hyder Ali; restored to original rulers by British after Br. defeat of Hyder Ali's son, Tippoo Sahib, at Seringapatam in 1799; administration of state taken over by British from 1831 until 1881, when they reinvested maharaja with ruling power but retained Bangalore's cantonment area as a military station (under Br. administration). The cantonment area was returned to Mysore on the Br. withdrawal from India in 1947. Although Mysore city has always been dynastic ⊙ state, Bangalore has been administrative ⊙ since 1831. Agr. col. and experimental farm at N suburb of Hebbal.
Banganapalle (bŭng"gŭnŭpŭ'lĕ), town (pop. 4,255), Kurnool dist., N Madras, India, 36 mi. SSE of Kurnool; handloom cotton weaving; lacquer ware. Was ⊙ former princely state of Banganapalle (□ 259; pop. 44,592) in Madras States, India; since 1948, inc. into Kurnool dist.
Banganga River (băng'gŭng-gŭ), seasonal stream in E Rajasthan and W Uttar Pradesh, India, rises S of Karauli, flows NNW and generally E, past Khairagarh, to Jumna R. 10 mi. SE of Fatehabad (Agra dist.); c.210 mi. long. Sometimes called Utangan R. Former upper course (still known as Banganga) rises near Bairat, flows c.135 mi. S and E, disappearing SW of Bharatpur, just N of course of E Banganga R.
Bangangté (bäng-gäng'tā), village, Bamiléké region, W Fr. Cameroons, 40 mi. SE of Dschang; alt. 4,590 ft.; native trade center; coffee growing. R.C. and Protestant missions, hosp.
Bangaon or **Bongaon** (bŭn'goun), town (pop. 8,990), 24-Parganas dist., E West Bengal, India, on upper Jamuna (Ichamati) R. and 45 mi. NNE of Calcutta; rail junction; trades in rice, jute, linseed, sugar cane. Until 1947, in Jessore dist. of Br. Bengal prov. Formerly called Bongong.
Bangar (bŭng-ŭr'), town, in E section of Brunei, NW Borneo, on small Temburong R. (35 mi. long) and 15 mi. SE of Brunei town; rice, rubber, cassava; stock raising, fishing. Also called Temburong.
Bangar (bäng-gär'), town (1939 pop. 1,677; 1948 municipality pop. 14,988), La Union prov., N central Luzon, Philippines, near W coast, 20 mi. NNE of San Fernando; rice growing.
Bangarmau (băng'gŭrmou), town (pop. 5,921), Unao dist., central Uttar Pradesh, India, 29 mi. NNW of Unao; wheat, barley, rice, gram. Has 14th-cent. Moslem tombs. Ruins (14th cent.) near.
Bangassou (bäng-gäsōō'), town, ⊙ M'Bomou region (□ 65,650; 1950 pop. 120,500), S Ubangi-Shari, Fr. Equatorial Africa, on Bomu R. (Belgian Congo border) and 290 mi. ENE of Bangui; cotton gins. Airfield; customs station. Has R.C. and Protestant missions.
Bangbro (bông'brōō"), Swedish *Bångbro,* village (pop. 1,205), Orebro co., S central Sweden, in Bergslag region, on Arboga R. and 19 mi. S of Ludvika; ironworking.
Bangda (bäng'dä'), town, Travinh prov., S Vietnam, in Mekong delta, 6 mi. SE of Travinh; rice.
Bange (bäng'gä), town (pop. 7,899), Fukushima prefecture, N central Honshu, Japan, 8 mi. NW of Wakamatsu; rice, wheat, soybeans, silk cocoons.
Banggai (bŭng"gī'), second largest island (□ 112; pop. 5,290) of Banggai Archipelago, Indonesia, in Molucca Sea, just SE of Peleng, at N side of entrance to Gulf of Tolo; 1°35'S 123°30'E; 15 mi. long, 10 mi. wide; generally level. Fishing, agr. (sago, rice). On NW coast is Banggai, chief town and port of group.
Banggai Archipelago (□ 1,222; pop. 49,836), Indonesia, in Molucca Sea, off E coast of Celebes, at N side of entrance to Gulf of Tolo; 1°50'S 123°15'E; comprises PELENG (largest), BANGGAI (site of Banggai, chief town of group), and c.100 islets. Peleng is the only mountainous isl. of group. Forest products (resin, rattan), tortoise shell, trepang, agr. products (rice, sago).
Banggi or **Banguey** (both: bäng'gē), island (23 mi. long, 15 mi. wide) in S.China Sea, off N tip of Borneo, 17 mi. NE of Kudat; fishing. Inhabited by seafaring tribes.
Banghoi, Vietnam: see BANGOI.
Bangi (bäng'ē), village (pop. 399), SE Selangor, Malaya, on railroad, 5 mi. S of Kajang; rubber,rice.
Bangil (bäng-ēl'), town (pop. 20,236), E Java, Indonesia, near Madura Strait, 25 mi. S of Surabaya; agr. trade center (sugar, rice, corn); textile mills.
Bangistan: see PAKISTAN.
Bangka or **Banka** (both: bäng'kä, băng'kŭ), island (□ 4,611; pop. 205,363, including offshore islets), Indonesia, in Java Sea, off SE coast of Sumatra across Bangka Strait (10–20 mi. wide); 1°30'N–3°8'S 105°5'–106°50'E; irregularly shaped, 140 mi. long, 70 mi. wide. Generally hilly, with low, swampy coastal areas. Off SE coast are isls. of Lepar and Liat. Bangka is one of principal tin-producing centers of world; miners are Chinese. Also has deposits of iron, manganese, gold, lead, copper, wolfram. Chief town is PANGKALPINANG; chief port, MUNTOK. In 1688 the Dutch were offered sovereignty over isl. by a native chieftain, whose authority however was weaker than that of Sumatran sultan of Palembang. Isl. became important c.1710 with discovery of tin. The British gained control of isl. in 1812; ceded it to the Dutch in 1814. In Second World War isl. was seized 1942 by the Japanese. Formerly sometimes spelled Banca.
Bangkalan (bäng"kŭlän'), town (pop. 12,359) on W coast of Madura, Indonesia, 15 mi. N of Surabaya; trade center in agr. area (rice, corn, cassava). Has noted mosque.
Bangkaru, Indonesia: see BANYAK ISLANDS.
Bangkok (băng'kŏk, băngkŏk', bäng'kôk'), officially **Krung Thep** (krŏŏng tĕp') [Thai,=new capital] or **Phra Nakhon** (prä' näkôn') [Thai,=capital of state], city (1947 pop. 688,832; with THONBURI, 855,878), ⊙ Thailand and Phra Nakhon prov. (□ 343; 1947 pop. 884,197), seaport on left bank of

Chao Phraya R. (the Mae Nam or Menam) opposite Thonburi and 15 mi. from Gulf of Siam; 13°45'N 100°30'E. Leading seaport and center of natl. economy, education (univ.), and culture of Thailand, Bangkok is also a major transportation hub of SE Asia, linked by rail with Chiangmai (N Thailand), the cities of Ubon and Udon (in Korat Plateau), Pnompenh (Cambodia), and with Malaya. Electric interurban lines link Bangkok with the Gulf of Siam fishing ports of Samutprakan, Samutsakhon, and Samutsongkhram. Accessible to ocean-going vessels drawing less than 12.5 ft. (large vessels anchor at Ko SICHANG, an isl. in Gulf of Siam), Bangkok handles four-fifths of Thai foreign trade, exporting rice, teak, rubber, salt fish, hides, gold, and silver. International aviation hub (airport at DON MUANG). An important industrial center with rice, paper, and sawmills and match factories along river front, and modern industries in outlying suburbs (aircraft mfg. at BANG SU, mfg. of rolling stock at MAKKASAN, petroleum refining at KHLONG TOEI). The nucleus of Bangkok, around which the city expanded concentrically, is formed by the 18th-cent. royal town, with old royal palaces, the royal temple of Wat Phra Kaeo (founded 1785; restored 1848 and 1882), govt. offices, and natl. library and mus. Adjoining the royal town are the quarters of Samsen (paper mill) and Dusit (NE), with vast park and parliament building, the Chinese quarter of Sampeng (SE), and beyond, the modern business dist. of Bangrak. Founded 1782 by Rama I on site of small fort, Bangkok succeeded the temporary govt. seat of Thonburi as ⊙ Thailand, following fall (1767) of Ayutthaya. Originally a walled city crossed by numerous canals, Bangkok was modernized after 1890s; many buildings were constructed in European style. The name Bangkok was originally applied to a small right-bank village on the site of present Thonburi, with which Bangkok forms a single urban complex. Following the establishment of the capital on left bank, the name Bangkok denoted the entire conurbation. Since 1937, when Thonburi became a separate municipality, the name Bangkok has been restricted, officially, to Krung Thep.

Banglong (bäng'lông'), town, Soctrang prov., S Vietnam, in Mekong delta, on Bassac R. and 10 mi. E of Soctrang; rice.

Bang Nara, Thailand: see NARATHIWAT.

Bangnga, Thailand: see PHANGNGA.

Bangoi or **Banghoi** (bä'ngoi'), town, Khanhhoa prov., S central Vietnam, in Annam, port on Camranh Bay of South China Sea, 23 mi. SSW of Nhatrang, on spur of Saigon-Hanoi RR; 11°55'N; port of call for ships of 18-ft. draught; wharves, railroad shops; naval base. Fisheries.

Bangor (băng'gôr, băng'gůr), municipal borough (1937 pop. 15,769; 1951 census 20,615), NE Co. Down, Northern Ireland, on S coast of Belfast Lough, near its mouth on the Irish Sea, 12 mi. ENE of Belfast; 54°40'N 5°40'W; seaport and popular seaside resort; yachting center, scene of annual regatta. There are 3 piers, forming artificial harbor. A missionary abbey, founded here c.555 by St. Comgall, was destroyed by Danes in 9th cent.; rebuilt in 1120, it was taken over by Franciscans in 1469 and dissolved in 1542. There are some remains of abbey church. Bangor Castle dates from Elizabethan times.

Bangor (băng'gôr). **1** Municipal borough (1931 pop. 10,960; 1951 census 12,822), N Caernarvon, Wales, on Menai Strait, 9 mi. NE of Caernarvon; 53°14'N 4°7'W; agr. market; religious and educational center of N Wales, site of several colleges, including Univ. Col. of N Wales. It was center of "Bangorian Controversy," 18th-cent. pamphlet war. Has 15th-16th-cent. cathedral, developed from Norman church. Municipal borough includes districts of Glanadda (pop. 2,332), Hirael (pop. 1,884), and important slate-shipping port of Port Penrhyn (E), outlet for slate from Penrhyn quarries near BETHESDA. **2** or **Bangor-on-Dee**, or **Bangor Isycoed** (ĭsĭkoid'), agr. village and parish (pop. 533) in detached section of Flint, Wales, on Dee R. and 5 mi. SE of Wrexham. Reputed site of oldest British monastery, founded c.180, destroyed 607 by Æthelfrid of Northumbria. Believed to be site of Roman station of *Bovium*.

Bangor (băng'gôr, băn'–, băng'gůr). **1** City (pop. 31,558), ⊙ Penobscot co., S Maine, on W bank of the Penobscot, at head of navigation, at mouth of Kenduskeag Stream, opposite Brewer; alt. 100 ft.; 44°48'N 68°46'W. Third largest city in Maine; mainly a commercial center with varied industries supplementing once-dominant lumbering and paper milling; printing, lumber processing, mfg. (shoes, dental supplies, tools, machinery, furniture, clothing, food products). Port of entry. Ships lumber, woodpulp, paper. Gateway to Mt. Desert Isl. and to an extensive resort area of many lakes. Seat of Bangor Theological Seminary and Northern Conservatory of Music. Settled 1769 on site probably visited (1604) by Champlain; town inc. 1791, city 1834. Developed in 19th cent. as flourishing shipping center handling lumber, furs, fish, ice. **2** Village (pop. 1,694), Van Buren co., SW Mich., on Black R and 27 mi. W of Kalamazoo, in orchard and farm region. Mfg. of spray guns, valves, bakelite products; fruit packing. Settled c.1837; inc. 1877. **3** Borough (pop. 6,050), Northampton co., E Pa., 12 mi. N of Easton; slate quarrying; textiles, clothing. Founded 1773, inc. 1875. **4** Village (pop. 941), La Crosse co., W Wis., near La Crosse R., 13 mi. ENE of La Crosse; butter, cheese; ships livestock.

Bangor Isycoed, Wales: see BANGOR, Flint.

Bang Pa-in (bäng' pä-ĭn'), village (1937 pop. 3,254), Ayutthaya prov., S Thailand, on Lopburi R. and on railroad, 30 mi. N of Bangkok; rice mills. Royal country residence.

Bang Pakong (bäng' päkŏng'), village (1937 pop. 2,232), Chachoengsao prov., S Thailand, on Bang Pakong R. near mouth on Gulf of Siam, 35 mi. ESE of Bangkok. Local name, The Saan.

Bang Pakong River, S Thailand, rises in San Kamphaeng Range and meanders c.120 mi. W and S, past Kabinburi (head of navigation during rains), Prachinburi, and Chachoengsao (head of navigation for small sea-going ships), to Gulf of Siam at Bang Pakong. Main tributary, Nakhon Nayok. Sometimes called Prachinburi R.

Bang Pla Soi, Thailand: see CHONBURI.

Bangrod (bäng'grōd), village, W Madhya Bharat, India, 7 mi. NNE of Ratlam; oilseed milling; iron- and steelworks.

Bangs, town (pop. 935), Brown co., central Texas, 9 mi. W of Brownwood, in farm area; cotton ginning, feed milling.

Bang Saphan or **Bang Saphan Yai** (bäng' sŭpän' yī'), village (1937 pop. 3,362), Prachuabkhirikhan prov., S Thailand, on railroad and Gulf of Siam, 45 mi. SSW of Prachuabkhirikhan; gold-mining center. Also spelled Bang Sapan or Bang Span.

Bangs Lake, Ill.: see WAUCONDA.

Bang Su (bäng'sŭ'), N industrial suburb (1947 pop. 12,310) of Bangkok, in Phra Nakhon prov., S Thailand, on left bank of Chao Phraya R. (railroad bridge); aircraft and cement factories; large railroad yards. Sometimes spelled Bang Sue.

Bangsund (bäng'sŏŏn), village (pop. 367) in Klinga canton (pop. 2,143), Nord-Trondelag co., central Norway, on S inlet of Nams Fjord, 6 mi. SSW of Namsos; lumber milling.

Bangued (bäng-gād', -gādh'), town (1939 pop. 6,274; 1948 municipality pop. 14,792), ⊙ Abra prov., N Luzon, Philippines, 40 mi. S of Laoag, near Abra R.; 17°35'N 120°36'E. Trade center for agr. area (rice, sugar cane, corn).

Banguey, North Borneo: see BANGGI.

Bangui (bäng-gē'), town (1950 pop. 41,100), ⊙ Ubangi-Shari and Ombella-M'Poko region (□13,500; 1950 pop. 104,100), Fr. Equatorial Africa, on Ubangi R. opposite Zongo (Belgian Congo) and 640 mi. NNE of Brazzaville; 4°23'N 18°35'E. Main interior commercial center of Fr. Equatorial Africa; navigation terminus and transshipment point for cotton, coffee, livestock from Chad territory and for imported goods; palm-oil milling, food processing, woodworking; coffee plantations. Customs station. Airport. Also has military camp, hosp., leprosarium, school for native administrators, and school for mulattoes. Seat of vicar apostolic of Ubangi. Founded 1890.

Bangweulu, Lake (bängwäōō'lōō) (□ 3,800, including swamps), N Northern Rhodesia, E of Fort Rosebery; 60 mi. long, 25 mi. wide; alt. 3,765 ft. Its open-water area varies with rainfall; extensive swamps (traversed by Chambezi R.) adjoin S and SE. Drained S by Luapula R. Discovered 1868 by Livingstone.

Banha, Egypt: see BENHA.

Banhatti (bŭn'hŭt-tē), town (pop. 9,282), Bijapur dist., S Bombay, India, 45 mi. SW of Bijapur; market for peanuts, wheat, cotton; hand-loom weaving.

Banhida (bän'hĭdŏ), Hung. *Bánhida*, town (pop. 11,763), Komarom-Esztergom co., N Hungary, 33 mi. WNW of Budapest; rail center; electric-power plant. Lignite mined extensively near by. Szelimluk Cave, containing Ice Age remains (discovered 1934), is near by.

Ban Houei Sai (bän' hwā' sī'), town, ⊙ Haut-Mekong prov. (□ 5,000; 1947 pop. 46,000), NW Laos, on left bank of Mekong R. (head of navigation) opposite Chiang Khong (Thailand), and 230 mi. NW of Vientiane. Trading center (cattle). Ruby mines near by. Teak pagoda. Formerly called Fort Carnot.

Bani: for Arabic names beginning thus, see BENI.

Baní (bänē'), town (1935 pop. 7,374; 1950 pop. 10,048), ⊙ Trujillo Valdez prov., S Dominican Republic, 3 mi. from Caribbean coast, on highway, and 30 mi. WSW of Ciudad Trujillo; 18°16'N 70°20'W. In its fertile surroundings, coffee, rice, and bananas are grown. Birthplace of Cuban liberator Maximo Gómez.

Bani (bä'nē, bänē'), town (1939 pop. 1,531; 1948 municipality pop. 18,402), Pangasinan prov., central Luzon, Philippines, on Cape Bolinao peninsula, 26 mi. WNW of Lingayen; rice, corn, copra.

Bani, Djebel (jĕ'bĕl bä'nē), narrow folded mtn. range in SW Fr. Morocco, at N edge of the Sahara. Extending over 300 mi. parallel to lower course of the Oued Dra, it crosses the latter SE of Zagora and continues NW almost to junction with the Djebel Sagho. Rises to over 5,000 ft.

Banialuka, Yugoslavia: see BANJA LUKA.

Banias, Syria: see BANIYAS.

Bánica (bä'nēkä), town (1950 pop. 441), San Rafael prov., W Dominican Republic, near Haiti border, on Artibonito R. and 50 mi. S of Monte Cristi, in agr. region (rice, cotton; goats; timber). Founded 1503 as Real Villa de Bánica, rebuilt 1759. The ruined Haitian fort Biassou is near by.

Banihal (bŭnĭhäl') or **Gund** (gŏŏnd), village, Doda dist., W central Kashmir, in Pir Panjal Range, 20 mi. S of Anantnag; corn, rice. Sheep breeding and research farm. Slate deposits SE. **Banihal Pass** (alt. 9,290 ft.) is 5 mi. N; here main Jammu-Srinagar road passes through tunnel (closed Nov.-May to motor traffic).

Banija (bä'nēä), region in N Croatia, Yugoslavia, extending along lower Glina R.; devastated in Second World War.

Bani River (bänē'), principal Niger affluent (right), S Fr. Sudan, Fr. West Africa, formed by confluence (100 mi. E of Bamako) of several headstreams (among them Baoulé R.) which rise in mts. of N Ivory Coast. Bani proper flows c.230 mi. NE to the Niger at Mopti in Macina depression. Partly navigable.

Banister River, S Va., rises in W Pittsylvania co. N of Chatham, flows c.65 mi. E and SE, past Halifax (hydroelectric dam), to Dan R. 6 mi. E of South Boston.

Bani Suwayf, Egypt: see BENI SUEF.

Banitsa, Greece: see VENE.

Baniyas or **Banias** (bä"nĭyăs'). **1** Village, anciently in Palestine, now in Damascus prov., SW Syria, 40 mi. SW of Damascus, at foot of Mt. Hermon, near Palestine-Lebanon line. Here, at the spring which is the legendary source of the Jordan, the Greeks had the place known as Paneas (for the god Pan) and the Romans later built a temple, naming the town Caesarea Philippi. A citadel here figured in the Crusades. **2** Town, Latakia prov., W Syria, on the Mediterranean, 25 mi. S of Latakia; sericulture, cereals, olives; terminus of oil pipe line from Kirkuk (construction begun 1950). Castle here also figured in the Crusades.

Banja, Egypt: see BANGA.

Banjak Islands, Indonesia: see BANYAK ISLANDS.

Banja Koviljaca, Yugoslavia: see KOVILJACA.

Banja Luka or **Banya Luka** (both: bä'nyä lōō'kä), city (pop. 33,191), ⊙ Banja Luka oblast (formed 1949), N Bosnia, Yugoslavia, on Vrbas R. (at emergence from narrow valley onto a wide plain) and 90 mi. NW of Sarajevo. Rail terminus; road hub; trade center; mfg. (textiles, beer, tobacco and dairy products); hydroelectric plant, brown-coal mine. Site of former Turkish fortress, Eastern Orthodox cathedral, 16th-cent. mosque, theater, mus. Traces of Roman baths near by. First mentioned in 15th cent.; was temporary (1588–1638) Turkish capital of Bosnia (permanent ⊙ was Travnik). Frequent scene of battles bet. Austrians and Turks. Was ⊙ Vrbas banovina (1929–41). Formerly spelled Banialuka. Slatina Ilidze or Slatina Ilidzhe, Serbo-Croatian *Slatina Ilidže* [=salt spring hot baths], health resort, is 7 mi. NE.

Banjari, India: see SASARAM.

Banja Rusanda, Yugoslavia: see MELENCI.

Banjermasin or **Bandjermasin** (bän"jûrmä'sĭn), town (pop. 65,698), SW Borneo, Indonesia, port on Barito R., 10 mi. above its mouth, at its junction with the Martapura, 580 mi. ENE of Jakarta; 3°20'S 114°35'E. Trade center for rich Barito basin; oil refining. On swampy land; houses are largely built on piles. Exports oil, timber, rattan, rubber, gutta-percha, diamonds, gold, iron, coal. Dutch began trading here in 1606, established a settlement 1711.

Banjoemas, Indonesia: see BANYUMAS.

Banjoewangi, Indonesia: see BANYUWANGI.

Banjumas, Indonesia: see BANYUMAS.

Banjuwangi, Indonesia: see BANYUWANGI.

Bank (bän-k'), town (1926 pop. 1,164), SE Azerbaijan SSR, on Kura R., near its mouth, and 50 mi. NNE of Lenkoran; fishing center; fish canning. Until 1939 called Imeni Narimanova; later, briefly, Imeni Kirova.

Banka, Indonesia: see BANGKA.

Banka Pahari (bäng'kŭ pŭhä'rē), former petty state (□ 5; pop. 1,241) of Central India agency. In 1948, merged with Vindhya Pradesh; in 1950, inc. into Jhansi dist. of Uttar Pradesh.

Bankapur (bŭng'käpŏŏr), town (pop. 7,209), Dharwar dist., S Bombay, India, 40 mi. SSE of Dharwar; road center; millet, cotton, rice, peanuts.

Banke, Nepal: see NEPALGANJ.

Bankeryd (bäng'kûrüd"), village (pop. 1,483), Jonkoping co., S Sweden, at S end of L. Vatter, 5 mi. N of Jonkoping; metalworking.

Banket (băng'kĭt), village (pop. 235), Salisbury prov., N Southern Rhodesia, in Mashonaland, on railroad and 13 mi. E of Sinoia; alt. 4,249 ft. Tobacco, cotton, peanuts, citrus fruit. Sometimes Banket Junction.

Bankfoot, town in Auchtergaven parish (pop. 2,193), E Perthshire, Scotland, 8 mi. NNW of Perth; agr.

Ban Khai, Laos: see MUONG SOUI.

Banki (bŭng'kē), village, Cuttack dist., E Orissa, India, on Mahanadi R. and 22 mi. WSW of Cuttack; rice, oilseeds; sugar milling, handicraft cloth weaving. Sometimes called Bankigarh.

Bankipore, India: see Patna, city.

Bankot (bäng'kōt), village, Ratnagiri dist., W Bombay, India, small port on Arabian Sea, 70 mi. NNW of Ratnagiri; trades in rice and myrobalans; fish curing (mackerel, sardines, pomfrets). In 18th cent., an important port under Mahrattas and British. Formerly called Fort Victoria.

Ban Krut (bän' kro͝ot'), village (1937 pop. 2,924), Prachuabkhirikhan prov., S Thailand, on coast of Gulf of Siam and on railroad, 36 mi. SSW of Prachuabkhirikhan; tin-mining center.

Banks, county (□ 231; pop. 6,935), NE Ga.; ⊙ Homer. Piedmont agr. area (cotton, corn, hay, sweet potatoes, fruit) drained by headstreams of Broad R. Formed 1858.

Banks. 1 Town (pop. 222), Pike co., SE Ala., 7 mi. E of Troy; farming. **2** Town (pop. 240), Bradley co., S Ark., 33 mi. NE of El Dorado. **3** Village, Boise co., SW Idaho, 23 mi. NE of Emmett. Inc. after 1950. **4** City (pop. 376), Washington co., NW Oregon, 10 mi. NW of Hillsboro.

Banks, Cape, E New South Wales, Australia, in Pacific Ocean; forms N side of entrance to Botany Bay; 34°S 151°13'E.

Banks, The, N.C.: see Outer Banks.

Bankside, district of Southwark, London, England, on S bank of the Thames, just E of Charing Cross. In 16th and 17th cent. it was amusement center, site of Globe Theater and other places associated with Shakespeare. Here also was palace of Bishop of Winchester, the Clink (famous prison), and White Hart Inn.

Banks Island (□ 35), in Torres Strait 32 mi. N of Cape York Peninsula, N Queensland, Australia, just E of Mulgrave Isl.; circular, 28 mi. in circumference; rises to 1,310 ft. Fertile, wooded; pearl shell, trepang.

Banks Island. 1 Island (□ 388; 45 mi. long, 6–11 mi. wide), W B.C., in Hecate Strait, separated from Pitt and McCauley isls. by Principe Channel; 53°N 130°W. Rises to 1,760 ft. Lumbering. **2** Island (□ c.26,000; 250 mi. long, 110–180 mi. wide), westernmost of the Arctic Archipelago, SW Franklin Dist., Northwest Territories, in the Arctic Ocean; 71°5'–74°30'N 115°5'–125°35'W; separated from Victoria Isl. (SE) by Prince of Wales Strait (10–20 mi. wide), from mainland (S) by Amundsen Gulf, and from Melville Isl. (NE) by McClure Strait. Mainly hilly plateau, rising to over 2,000 ft. in S, becoming rolling, prairie-like country up to 1,500 ft. high toward N; numerous lakes. Its insularity was discovered 1851 by Sir Robert McClure; Stefansson explored interior, 1914–17.

Banks Islands, small group (pop. 2,322), New Hebrides, SW Pacific, 50 mi. NE of Espiritu Santo. Comprises Vanua Lava, Gaua, Mota, Ureparapara, Motalava, and several smaller isls.; volcanic, fertile (copra, cocoa). Polynesian natives. Discovered 1793 by Capt. Bligh.

Banks Peninsula, E S.Isl., New Zealand; 30 mi. E-W, 17 mi. N-S. Lyttelton harbor is in N, Akaroa harbor in S.

Banks Strait, channel bet. NE coast of Tasmania and Clarke Isl. of Furneaux Isls.; joins Bass Strait (W) with Tasman Sea (E); 13 mi. wide. Contains Swan Isl. (2 mi. long) and many smaller islets.

Bankston, town (pop. 40), Dubuque co., E Iowa, 15 mi. W of Dubuque.

Bankstown, municipality (pop. 42,646), E New South Wales, Australia, 11 mi. WSW of Sydney, in metropolitan area; industrial center; brass foundry, brickyards; mfg. (aluminum ware, clothing).

Bankura (bäng'ko͝orŏ), district (□ 2,646; pop. 1,289,640), W West Bengal, India; ⊙ Bankura. Bounded N by Damodar R., W by Bihar; drained by Dwarkeswar (Rupnarayan) and Kasai rivers. Lateritic soil in W (foothills of Chota Nagpur Plateau in extreme W; extensive lac cultivation), alluvial soil E. Agr. (rice, wheat, corn, gram, mustard, barley, sugar cane); sal, pipal, bamboo in dispersed forest areas. Silk-weaving center at Bishnupur; lac trade center at Khatra; cotton weaving (Bankura, Sonamukhi, Patrasaer), rice and oilseed milling; metalware, pottery, cutlery, and tool mfg. Part of 8th-cent. A.D. Hindu dynasty, with ⊙ at Bishnupur; ceded 1760 to English.

Bankura, town (pop. 46,617), ⊙ Bankura dist., W West Bengal, India, on Rupnarayan R. and 95 mi. WNW of Calcutta; rail junction (workshops); road and trade (rice, corn, wheat, mustard, gram, potatoes, sugar cane) center; rice and oilseed milling, cotton weaving, metalware mfg. Leper asylum.

Bankya (bän'kyä), village (pop. 1,978), Sofia dist., W Bulgaria, at foot of NW spur of Vitosha Mts., 8 mi. W of Sofia. Rail terminus; noted health resort; fruit, truck. Medieval monastery near by.

Bankyo, Formosa: see Pankiao.

Banmauk (bänmouk'), village, Katha dist., Upper Burma, 35 mi. WNW of Katha; teak and bamboo forests.

Ban Mee, Thailand: see Ban Mi.

Banmethuot (bän'mä'to͝ot'), town, ⊙ Darlac prov. (□ 8,300; 1943 pop. 81,400), S central Vietnam, in Annam, 55 mi. NNW of Dalat, in Moi Plateaus; airport; chief town of Darlac Plateau; tea, coffee, rubber plantations; big-game hunting. Pop. of area is largely Rade, one of Moi tribes.

Ban Mi (bän' mē'), village (1937 pop. 5,012), Lopburi prov., S Thailand, on Bangkok–Chiangmai RR and 17 mi. NNW of Lopburi; rice and sawmilling. Also spelled Ban Mee.

Banmore, India: see Bamaur.

Bannack (bă'nĭk), ghost town, Beaverhead co., SW Mont., 18 mi. W of Dillon and on branch of Beaverhead R. in Jefferson R. system. Oldest town in state (founded 1862, when gold was discovered here), and 1st territorial ⊙ (1864–65). Declined when miners left it for richer fields of Virginia City.

Bannalec (bänälĕk'), village (pop. 1,879), Finistère dept., W France, 19 mi. ESE of Quimper; fruit and vegetable preserving.

Bannang Sata (bännäng' sŭtä'), village (1937 pop. 1,455), Yala prov., S Thailand, in Malay Peninsula, on Pattani R., on road and 20 mi. S of Yala; tin and lead mining.

Banner, county (□ 738; pop. 1,325), W Nebr.; ⊙ Harrisburg. Agr. area bordering on Wyo.; drained by branches of N.Platte R. Highest point in Nebr. (5,340 ft.) in SW. Livestock, grain. Formed 1888.

Banner, village (pop. 215), Fulton co., central Ill., 7 mi. ESE of Canton, in agr. and bituminous-coal area. Near by are Rice, Big, and Goose lakes, bayou lakes near Illinois R.

Banner Elk, town (pop. 462), Avery co., NW N.C., 11 mi. WSW of Boone; mtn. resort; seat of Lees-McRae Col. (jr.; coeducational).

Banner Hill, village (pop. 2,873), Unicoi co., NE Tenn.

Bannertown, residential village (pop. 2,937, with near-by Cross Road), Surry co., NW N.C., suburb S of Mt. Airy.

Bannesdorf (bä'nŭsdôrf'), village (pop. 3,339), in Schleswig-Holstein, NW Germany, on Fehmarn isl., 2 mi. NNE of Burg; grain, potatoes, cabbage, beets.

Bannewitz (bä'nŭvĭts), town (pop. 4,100), Saxony, E central Germany, 4 mi. S of Dresden; coal mine.

Banning, city (pop. 7,034), Riverside co., S Calif., 20 mi. SE of Redlands, on broad floor of San Gorgonio Pass; almond orchards; rest homes, sanatoriums. Morongo Indian Reservation is adjacent. Laid out 1883, inc. 1913.

Banningville (bänĭngvĕl'), town (1946 pop. c.4,600), Leopoldville prov., W Belgian Congo, on right bank of Kwango R. just above its influx into Kasai R. and 120 mi. SW of Inongo; commercial center in rice and palm region. Has R.C. missions, sailors' sanitarium, hosp. for Europeans, airport with customs station. Also known as Bandundu (bändo͞on'do͞o). Wombali (wŏmbä'lē), on left bank of Kwango R. and just NW, has small seminary and mission schools.

Bannock, county (□ 1,820; pop. 41,745), SE Idaho; ⊙ Pocatello. Mtn. area drained by Bear and Portneuf rivers. Irrigated fields produce wheat, alfalfa, sugar beets; livestock, dairying; mfg. at Pocatello. Manganese deposits. Formed 1893.

Bannockburn, village in St. Ninians parish, NE Stirling, Scotland, 2 mi. SSE of Stirling; coal mining, woolen milling. Near by, on the Bannock (tributary of the Forth), is field on which was fought (June 23–24, 1314) battle of Bannockburn, in which Robert the Bruce decisively defeated the English under Edward II.

Bannockburn, village (pop. 249), Lake co., extreme NE Ill., 25 mi. NNW of Chicago.

Bannock Creek, rises in mtn. region of SE Idaho, flows c.40 mi. N, through Power co., to American Falls Reservoir NE of American Falls. Used for irrigation.

Bannovski or **Bannovskiy** (bä'nŭfskē), town (1939 pop. over 500), N Stalino oblast, Ukrainian SSR, in the Donbas, on the Northern Donets and 13 mi. N of Slavyansk.

Bann River (băn), Northern Ireland, rises as Upper Bann R. in Mourne Mts. 6 mi. ENE of Warrenpoint, S Co. Down, flows 40 mi. NW, through cos. Down and Armagh, past Banbridge, Gilford, and Portadown, to S shore of Lough Neagh. It leaves the lake at its N shore as Lower Bann R., flows 40 mi. N, forming border bet. cos. Antrim and Londonderry, past Coleraine, to the Atlantic. Navigable below Coleraine; lower course has important salmon fisheries.

Bannu (bŭn'no͞o), district (□ 1,695; 1951 pop. 306,000), North-West Frontier Prov., W Pakistan; ⊙ Bannu. Enclosed by spurs jutting E from N end of Sulaiman Range; drained by Kurram R. and its tributaries. Agr. (wheat, gram, corn, barley); local handicrafts (cloth weaving, leather goods). Conquered 1738 by Nadir Shah; later part of Dera Ismail Khan dist.; constituted a separate dist. in 1861. Exercises political control over contiguous tribal area (pop. c.27,000). Pop. 87% Moslem, 10% Hindu, 2% Sikh.

Bannu, town (pop., including cantonment area, 38,504), ⊙ Bannu dist., S central North-West Frontier Prov., W Pakistan, on Kurram R. and 90 mi. SW of Peshawar; rail terminus; trade center for wheat, millet, wool, livestock, tobacco; handicraft cloth weaving, fodder pressing; ordnance factory, engineering workshops. Has col. Formerly called Edwardesabad.

Bannur (bŭ'no͞or), town (pop. 5,683), Mysore dist., S Mysore, India, 14 mi. E of Mysore city center, near Cauvery R.; millet, cotton, sugar cane; silk growing, hand-loom weaving.

Bano, Afghanistan: see Banu.

Bañobárez (bänyōvä'rĕth), town (pop. 1,183), Salamanca prov., W Spain, 18 mi. NNW of Ciudad Rodrigo; cattle, sheep raising.

Bañolas (bänyō'läs), city (pop. 5,709), Gerona prov., NE Spain, 10 mi. NNW of Gerona; mfg. of cement, paper, textiles, leather; center of rich agr. area (livestock, olive oil, wine, hemp).

Banon (bänō'), village (pop. 473), Basses-Alpes dept., SE France, on S slope of Montagne de Lure (Provence Alps), 16 mi. NE of Apt; honey.

Baños (bä'nyōs), town (1950 pop. 2,768), Tungurahua prov., Ecuador, in the Andes, at N foot of active Tungurahua volcano, on upper Pastaza R. and 17 mi. SE of Ambato. Ecuador's leading spa, noted for its medicinal waters and alpine scenery. A gateway to the Amazon region. In cattle-grazing and fruitgrowing region. February fiesta attracts many pilgrims. Hard hit by 1949 earthquake.

Baños, town (pop. 679), Huánuco dept., central Peru, in Cordillera Occidental, 35 mi. WSW of Huánuco; corn, barley, sheep.

Baños, village (pop. 1,670), Cáceres prov., W Spain, 7 mi. SW of Béjar; olive oil, wine. Mineral springs.

Banosa, India: see Daryapur.

Baños de Catillo, Chile: see Catillo.

Baños de Cauquenes, Chile: see Cauquenes, O'Higgins prov.

Baños de Coamo, Puerto Rico: see Coamo.

Baños de Jahuel, Chile: see Jahuel.

Baños de la Encina (bä'nyōs dhä lä ĕn-thē'nä), town (pop. 3,194), Jaén prov., S Spain, 10 mi. NW of Linares; olive-oil production. Lead-silver ore deposits. Dam and reservoir 4 mi. SW.

Baños de la Laja, Argentina: see La Laja.

Baños del Inca, Peru: see Jesús, Cajamarca dept.

Baños de Panimávida, Chile: see Panimávida.

Baños de Río Tobía (dhä rē'ō tōvē'ä), town (pop. 1,346), Logroño prov., N Spain, 18 mi. SW of Logroño; meat-processing center; wine, olive oil, cereals, hogs. Mineral springs.

Baños de Soco, Chile: see El Soco.

Baños de Valdearados (väldhäärä'dhōs), town (pop. 1,161), Burgos prov., N Spain, 40 mi. S of Burgos; flour milling, wine making.

Banovce nad Bebravou (bä'nôftsĕ näd' bĕ"brävō), Slovak *Bánovce nad Bebravou*, Hung. *Bán* (bän), town (pop. 3,563), W Slovakia, Czechoslovakia, on railroad and 29 mi. NNE of Nitra; lumbering. Lace making near by. Uhrovec (o͞o'hrôvĕts) sawmills are 4 mi. NE.

Banovici or **Banovichi** (both: bä'nôvĕchē), Serbo-Croatian *Banovići*, village, E Bosnia, Yugoslavia, 40 mi. N of Sarajevo, in Tuzla coal area; rail terminus; brown-coal mine.

Ban Pai, Thailand: see Ban Phai.

Ban Phachi (bän' pä'chē'), village, Ayutthaya prov., S Thailand, 13 mi. NE of Ayutthaya; major rail junction on lines to Chiangmai (N) and Korat Plateau (E). Also spelled Ban Phaji.

Ban Phai (bän' pī'), village, Khonkaen prov., E Thailand, in Korat Plateau, on railroad and 25 mi. S of Khonkaen; road center. Also spelled Ban Pai.

Ban Phaji, Thailand: see Ban Phachi.

Ban Pong (bän' pông'), village (1937 pop. 7,493), Ratburi prov., S Thailand, on Mae Klong R. and railroad, 45 mi. W of Bangkok, in rice-growing area; rice milling. Junction for railroad to Thambyuzayat (Burma), built in Second World War.

Banquete (băn"kĕ'tē), village (pop. c.350), Nueces co., S Texas, 25 mi. W of Corpus Christi; rail point in oil, agr. area.

Banreve (bän'rāvĕ), Hung. *Bánréve*, town (pop. 1,095), Borsod-Gömör co., NE Hungary, on the Sajo and 6 mi. N of Ozd, on Czechoslovak line; rail center.

Ban-Saint-Martin (bã-sẽ-märtẽ'), NW suburb (pop. 2,352) of Metz, Moselle dept., NE France, on left bank of the Moselle; fruit preserving, soap mfg.; truck gardening.

Bansang (bän'säng), town (pop. 719), MacCarthy Isl. div., central Gambia, on left bank of Gambia R. (wharf and ferry) and 9 mi. SE of Georgetown; fishing; peanuts, palm oil and kernels, rice. Has a hospital.

Bansara (bă'särä), town, Ogoja prov., Eastern Provinces, SE Nigeria, on Ewayong R. (right tributary of Cross R.) and 22 mi. SW of Ogoja; palm oil and kernels, cacao, kola nuts.

Bansbaria (bänsbär'yŭ), town (pop. 23,716), Hooghly dist., S central West Bengal, India, on Hooghly R. and 7 mi. N of Hooghly; jute milling. Large Sivaite temples. Also spelled Bansberia. Rice milling 3 mi. NW, at village of Magra.

Bansda (bäns'dŭ), village, Surat dist., N Bombay, India, 45 mi. SE of Surat, at NW foot of Western Ghats; trades in handicrafts (mats, baskets, carpets), rice. Was ⊙ former princely state of Bansda (□ 212; pop. 54,735) in Gujarat States, Bombay; inc. 1949 into Surat dist.

Bansdih (bäns'dē), town (pop. 8,974), Ballia dist., E Uttar Pradesh, India, 11 mi. NNE of Ballia; rice, gram, barley, oilseeds, sugar cane.

Bansei (bänsā') or **Mansei** (mänsā'), town (pop. 13,829), Kagoshima prefecture, SW Kyushu, Japan, on W Satsuma Peninsula, 18 mi. SW of Kagoshima; livestock and agr. center; rice, raw silk. Sometimes called Osaki.

Bansgaon (bäns'goun), town (pop. 8,216), Gorakhpur dist., E Uttar Pradesh, India, 14 mi. S of Gorakhpur; rice, wheat, barley, oilseeds, sugar cane.

Banshiden, Formosa: see FANTZETIEN.

Bansi (bän'sē), village, Basti dist., NE Uttar Pradesh, India, on the Rapti and 30 mi. NNE of Basti; rice, wheat, barley, sugar cane. Sugar processing 23 mi. NNW, at village of Barhni.

Bansin or **Seebad Bansin** (zā'bät bänzēn'), village (pop. 1,979) in former Prussian Pomerania prov., E Germany, after 1945 in Mecklenburg, on NE shore of Usedom isl., 6 mi. NW of Swinemünde; popular seaside resort. Just inland is Bansin village (pop. 453).

Bansi Paharpur (bän'sē pŭhär'pŏŏr), village, E Rajasthan, India, 19 mi. S of Bharatpur. Sandstone quarried near by.

Banska Bela, Czechoslovakia: see BANSKA STIAVNICA.

Banska Bystrica (bän'skä bĭ'strĭtsä), Slovak *Banská Bystrica*, Ger. *Neusohl* (noi'zōl), Hung. *Besztercebánya* (bĕ'stĕrtsĕbä'nyŏ), town (pop. 12,230), ⊙ Banska Bystrica prov. (□ 3,578; pop. 486,683), central Slovakia, Czechoslovakia, in SW foothills of the Low Tatra, on Hron R. and 100 mi. NE of Bratislava; 48°45'N 19°9'E. Rail junction; former gold-mining center; now a popular summer resort; mfg. (furniture, matches, paper, knit goods, woolen textiles), metalworks, mining (copper, silver). Fairly modernized; still has 14th-cent. castle (now mus.) with 15th- and 18th-cent. chapels, 17th-cent. cathedral, 18th-cent. Chapter House with extensive archives. R.C. bishopric. Founded in 13th cent. Famous as center of uprising against Germans in 1944.

Banska Stiavnica (shtyäv'nyĭtsä), Slovak *Banská Štiavnica*, Ger. *Schemnitz* (shĕm'nĭts), Hung. *Selmec* or *Selmec-És-Bélabánya* (sĕl'mĕts-āsh-bā'lŏbänyŏ), town (pop., including Banska Bela, 11,870), S Slovakia, Czechoslovakia, in SW spur of the Carpathians, 22 mi. SSW of Banska Bystrica; rail terminus; footwear mfg., tobacco processing, woodworking, lace making. Though production has now declined, some gold, silver, lead, zinc, copper, and semi-precious stones are still mined in vicinity. Has 13th-cent. Ger. church, 15th-cent. Slovak church, old castle (now a mus. with armory and dungeons), 16th-cent. castle. Banska Bela (bĕ'lä), Slovak *Banská Belá*, Hung. *Bélabánya*, now part of Banska Stiavnica, is 2 mi. NE.

Bansko (bän'skô), city (pop. 6,161), Gorna Dzhumaya dist., SW Bulgaria, in Pirin Mts., on rail spur and 25 mi. SE of Gorna Dzhumaya; sawmilling; livestock. Has old church. Important commercial center (Struma R. valley cotton exports) in 18th cent.

Banso, Br. Cameroons: see KUMBO.

Banstead (băn'stĭd), residential urban district (1951 census pop. 33,526), E central Surrey, England, 3 mi. E of Epsom; pharmaceutical industry. Has 12th-cent. church.

Banswada (bäns'vädŭ), town (pop. 5,863), Nizamabad dist., central Hyderabad state, India, 19 mi. S of Bodhan; sugar cane, rice, oilseeds.

Banswara (bänsvä'rŭ), town (pop. 12,772), S Rajasthan, India, 85 mi. SSE of Udaipur; market center for corn, rice, millet, wheat; cotton ginning, flour milling, hand-loom weaving, wood carving. Was ⊙ former princely state of Banswara (□ 1,606; pop. 258,760) in Rajputana States, India, which was formed c.1530 out of original Dungarpur state and in 1948 merged with Rajasthan.

Bant, Germany: see RÜSTRINGEN.

Bantaeng, Indonesia: see BONTHAIN.

Bantam (băn'tŭm, bän"täm'), ruined town of W Java, Indonesia, on small Bantam Bay, c.10 mi. NW of Serang, near NW point of Java. Ruins include remains of Dutch fort and trading factory, 16th-cent. mosque, and palace of Bantam sultans. A flourishing trade center from 16th through 18th cent., Bantam was visited by Portuguese (1545), Dutch (1596), English (1603), and was after 1683 under exclusive Dutch control. In early 19th cent. it was supplanted by Serang. The Bantam Moslem sultanate, which in its heyday (16th cent.) controlled parts of Borneo and Sumatra, became a vassal of the Dutch in 1683 and was completely annexed by the Dutch in 1809. It remained a residency (□ 3,000; pop. 1,000,000) of Java until the founding of the republic of Indonesia.

Bantam, Conn.: see LITCHFIELD, town.

Bantam Lake, Litchfield co., W Conn., resort lake near Litchfield; 2.5 mi. long. Receives from N, discharges NW, **Bantam River,** which rises in 2 branches in NW Conn., flows 7 mi. S and SW from junction near Litchfield to Bantam L., thence 15 mi. NW and SW to Shepaug R. above Washington.

Bantay (băntī', bän'tī), town (1939 pop. 2,322; 1948 municipality pop. 12,714), Ilocos Sur prov., N Luzon, Philippines, just N of Vigan, near W coast; rice-growing center.

Bantayan Island (băntäyän') (□ 45; 1939 pop. 28,602), Cebu prov., Visayan Isls., Philippines, in Visayan Sea, c.10 mi. off NW coast of Cebu isl.; 11°13'N 123°44'E; 11 mi. long, 4 mi. wide. Generally low. Corn and coconut growing, fishing. On SW coast is Bantayan town (1939 pop. 4,782; 1948 municipality pop. 25,351).

Banté (băn'tā), village, S central Dahomey, Fr. West Africa, on road to Upper Volta, 36 mi. NNE of Savalou; cotton, corn, millet.

Banthat Range, Thailand-Cambodia: see CARDAMOM MOUNTAINS.

Banting (băntĭng'), village (pop. 1,221), SW Selangor, Malaya, 27 mi. SW of Kuala Lumpur, on Langat R.; rubber.

Banto, Japan: see BANDO.

Bantolmacs, Rumania: see TALMACIU.

Banton Island (băntōn') (□ 11; 1948 pop. 5,542), Romblon prov., Philippines, bet. Tablas Strait and Sibuyan Sea, 16 mi. S of Marinduque isl.; 4.5 mi. long, 4 mi. wide. Rice, coconuts.

Bantry (băn'trē), Gaelic *Beanntraighe*, town (pop. 2,453), SW Co. Cork, Ireland, at head of Bantry Bay, 45 mi. WSW of Cork; seaport, with woolen (tweed) milling, barite mining, slate quarrying. Formerly noted for pilchard fisheries.

Bantry, village (pop. 125), McHenry co., N central N.Dak., 14 mi. NW of Towner.

Bantry Bay, inlet (21 mi. long, 4 mi. wide) of the Atlantic, on SW coast of Co. Cork, Ireland. It is one of Europe's best natural anchorages. At head of bay is Bantry town. Whiddy Isl. and Bear Isl. are in the bay. In 1689 Bantry Bay was scene of indecisive Anglo-French naval battle.

Bantva (bänt'vŭ), town (pop. 18,323), dist., SW Saurashtra, India, 25 mi. W of Junagarh; agr. market (cotton, millet); handicraft cloth weaving. Was ⊙ former princely state of Manavadar. Sometimes spelled Bantwa

Bantval (bŭntväl'), town (pop. 5,807), South Kanara dist., W Madras, India, on Netravati R. and 13 mi. ENE of Mangalore; rice milling. Kaolin-clay pits near by. Also spelled Bantwal.

Banu or **Bano** (bä'nōō), fortress town (pop. over 2,000), Kataghan prov., NE Afghanistan, at N foot of the Hindu Kush, 75 mi. N of Kabul, in the Andarab (Indirab) valley for which it is sometimes named.

Banwell, agr. village and parish (pop. 1,581), N Somerset, England, 5 mi. E of Weston-super-Mare. Has 14th-16th-cent. church. Near by are Banwell Caves, where bones of extinct animals have been found.

Banya (bä'nyä) [Bulg.,=bath]. **1** Village (pop. 1,819), Gorna Dzhumaya dist., SW Bulgaria, on N slope of Pirin Mts., 4 mi. E of Razlog; flour milling; livestock. Has thermal springs and baths. **2** Village, Sofia dist., Bulgaria: see DOLNA-BANYA.

Banyak Islands or **Banjak Islands** (both: bän'yäk), group (pop. 1,731) off W coast of Sumatra, Indonesia, in Indian Ocean, 35 mi. N of Nias; 2°10'N 97°16'E. Comprises numerous small isls., the largest being Tuangku or Toeangkoe (both: tōō-äng'kōō; pop. 1,015), 20 mi. long, 6 mi. wide. Other isls. are Bangkaru or Bangkaroe (băng"-kŭrōō') and Ujungbatu or Oedjoengbatu (ōō"-jōōngbä'tōō). Coconut groves.

Banya Kovilyacha, Yugoslavia: see KOVILJACA.

Banya Luka, Yugoslavia: see BANJA LUKA.

Banyennhan (bän'yĕn'nyŭn'), village, Hungyen prov., N Vietnam, 15 mi. SE of Hanoi.

Banyo (băn'yō), NE suburb (pop. 3,064) of Brisbane, SE Queensland, Australia.

Banyo (bä'nyō), village, Adamaoua region, W Fr. Cameroons, near Br. Cameroons border, 125 mi. WSW of N'Gaoundéré; native trade center; stock raising. Tin deposits.

Banyuls-sur-Mer (bänyül'-sür-mâr'), town (pop. 3,245), Pyrénées-Orientales dept., S France, at foot of Monts Albères, on Gulf of Lion, 19 mi. SE of Perpignan; fishing port and resort. Produces fine Roussillon wines, ships sardines, anchovies. Has laboratory of marine zoology established 1887 by Univ. of Paris. Damaged in Second World War.

Banyumas, Banjumas, or **Banjoemas** (all: bän'yōō-mäs"), town (pop. 6,686), central Java, Indonesia, 75 mi. WNW of Jogjakarta; 7°31'S 109°16'E; trade center in agr. area (sugar, rice, tobacco, corn, peanut, cassava); tobacco processing.

Banyuwangi, Banjuwangi, or **Banjoewangi** (all: bän"-yōōwäng'ē), town (pop. 25,185), E Java, Indonesia, port on Bali Strait, opposite Bali, 120 mi. SE of Surabaya; 8°12'S 114°23'E; sawmilling; exports copra, lumber, rubber. Terminus of cables to Australia and Singapore.

Banz, Germany: see WEINGARTEN.

Banzai (bän'zī), town (pop. 8,186), Tokushima prefecture, NE Shikoku, Japan, 7 mi. NW of Tokushima; rail junction; agr. center (rice, wheat), poultry; sake brewing. Also called Itanoishi.

Banzare Coast (băn'zâr, –zär), part of Wilkes Land, Antarctica, on Indian Ocean, bet. 121° and 127°E. Discovered 1931 by Sir Douglas Mawson.

Banzi (bän'tsē), village (pop. 2,057), Potenza prov., Basilicata, S Italy, 1 mi. NW of Genzano di Lucania; wine making.

Banzyville (bänzēvĕl'), village, Equator prov., NW Belgian Congo, on Ubangi R. (Fr. Equatorial Africa border), opposite Mobaye, 145 mi. NNW of Lisala; customs station and trading center; cotton ginning. Has Capuchin mission and mission schools. Ubangi R. is navigable bet. here and Yakoma.

Baoebaoe, Indonesia: see BAUBAU.

Baoha (bou'hä'), town, Yenbay prov., N Vietnam, on Red R. and Hanoi-Kunming RR, 35 mi. SE of Laokay.

Baolac (bou'läk'), town, Caobang prov., N Vietnam, 40 mi. NW of Caobang, near China border.

Baoma (bäō'mä), town (pop. 884), South-Western Prov., S central Sierra Leone, near Sewa R., 22 mi. E of Bo, on railroad; palm oil and kernels, cacao, coffee.

Baoni (bou'nē), former princely state (□ 122; pop. 25,256) of Central India agency; in 1948, merged with Vindhya Pradesh; in 1950, transferred to Uttar Pradesh.

Baoulé River. 1 In SW Fr. Sudan, Fr. West Africa, rises 30 mi. WSW of Bamako, flows in wide sweep c.300 mi. N and W to Bakoy R. (Senegal R. headstream) 65 mi. ESE of Bafoulabé. Not navigable. **2** In S Fr. Sudan, headstream of BANI RIVER, E of Bamako.

Bapatla (bä'pŭtlŭ), town (pop. 16,679), Guntur dist., NE Madras, India, in Kistna R. delta, 27 mi. S of Guntur; rice milling, tobacco, palmyra and betel palms. Agr. col. (affiliated with Madras Univ.). Casuarina plantations S, on Bay of Bengal; mangrove swamp.

Bapaume (bäpōm'), town (pop. 2,564), Pas-de-Calais dept., N France, 13 mi. SSE of Arras; road junction and agr. trade center. Scene of Fr. victory (1871) over Prussians, and of several battles in First World War, when it changed hands repeatedly and was completely destroyed.

Bapeaume-lès-Rouen, France: see CANTELEU.

Ba'quba (bäkōō'bä), town (pop. 42,356), ⊙ Diyala prov., central Iraq, on Diyala R., on railroad, and 25 mi. NNE of Baghdad; dates, fruits, livestock. Sometimes spelled Bakuba.

Baquedano (bäkādä'nō), village (1930 pop. 780), Antofagasta prov., N Chile, 40 mi. NE of Antofagasta; rail junction, airport, in nitrate area.

Baquerizo Moreno, Galápagos: see PUERTO BAQUERIZO.

Baqur (bă'kōōr), village (pop. 7,713), Asyut prov., central Upper Egypt, 4 mi. NNW of Abu Tig; cereals, dates, sugar cane.

Bar (bär), village (pop. 49), Corrèze dept., S central France, on the Corrèze and 6 mi. NW of Tulle; hydroelectric plant.

Bar, river, France: see BAR RIVER.

Bar (bär), city (1926 pop. 9,430), W Vinnitsa oblast, Ukrainian SSR, 37 mi. WSW of Vinnitsa; sugar refining, distilling, machine mfg., woolen milling. Anti-Russian Confederation of Bar organized here (1768) by Polish nobility.

Bar (bär), Ital. *Antivari* (äntēvä'rē), anc. *Antebarium*, town (pop. 3,168), SW Montenegro, Yugoslavia, port on Adriatic coast opposite Bari (Italy), 25 mi. SSW of Titograd, at W foot of the Rumija; summer resort; terminus of narrow-gauge railway to Vir. Center of fruit growing (figs, olives) and bauxite area. Consists of Stari Bar (old town; mostly in ruins) and Novi Bar (new town; has good harbor). Anc. Roman settlement; once seat of primate of Serbia. Passed 1421 to Venice; under Turkish rule (after 1571) in Albania; annexed 1878 by Montenegro.

Bar, Le, or **Le Bar-sur-Loup** (lübär'sür-lōō'), village (pop. 846), Alpes-Maritimes dept., SE France, overlooking Loup R. gorge, and 5 mi. NE of Grasse; ships olive oil and orange peels.

Bara (bä'rŭ), town, Kordofan prov., central Anglo-Egyptian Sudan, on road and 35 mi. NNE of El Obeid; gum arabic, sesame, corn, durra; livestock.

Bara (bä'rŭ), town (pop. 5,963), Ghazipur dist., E Uttar Pradesh, India, on the Ganges and 17 mi. ESE of Ghazipur; rice, barley, gram, oilseeds, wheat. In 1539, Mogul emperor Humayun was defeated (just E) by the Afghan Sher Shah.

Bara (bŭ'rä), Rum. *Bâra*, village (pop. 849), Roman prov., NE Rumania, 10 mi. NE of Roman.

Bara Banki (bä'rŭ bŭn'kē), district (□ 1,722; pop. 1,162,508), central Uttar Pradesh, India; ⊙ Bara Banki. On Ganges Plain; bounded NE by Gogra R.; drained by the Gumti. Agr. (rice, gram, wheat, oilseeds, corn, sugar cane, barley, jowar); extensive mango groves; hand-loom cotton weaving. Main towns: Nawabganj, Rudauli, Zaidpur, Fatehpur.

Bara Banki, town (pop. 4,633), ⊙ Bara Banki dist., central Uttar Pradesh, India, 16 mi. ENE of Lucknow; road center; grains, sugar cane. Nawabganj is just NE.

Barabar Hill (bŭrä'bŭr), isolated hill (1,017 ft.) on Ganges Plain, central Bihar, India, 16 mi. N of Gaya. Hindu temple on peak; Asokan cave inscriptions and carvings; annual fair. Buddhist ruins near by. Iron-ore smelting in the vicinity.

Barabash (bŭrŭbäsh'), village (1939 pop. over 500), SW Maritime Territory, Russian SFSR, on branch of Trans-Siberian RR, 20 mi. W of Vladivostok, across Amur Bay; grain, soybeans, rice.

Baraba Steppe (bă'rŭbä', bä"–, Rus. bŭrŭbä'), Rus. *Barabinskaya Step'*, SE section of W.Siberian Plain, in Novosibirsk oblast, Russian SFSR; borders on Vasyuganye marshes (N), on Kulunda Steppe along Karasuk R. (S). Includes black-earth depression on Ob-Irtysh river divide, with several large lakes (L. CHANY, UBINSKOYE LAKE, L. SARTLAN); average alt. 350 ft. Pop. (mainly Russians, some Tatars) engaged in agr., livestock breeding (dairying is important), fishing. Main towns are along Trans-Siberian RR (TATARSK, BARABINSK, KUIBYSHEV). Acquired by Russia in 17th and early-18th cents.; colonization began in mid.-18th cent.

Barabhum, India: see BALARAMPUR.

Barabinsk (bŭrŭbēnsk'), city (1939 pop. over 10,000), central Novosibirsk oblast, Russian SFSR, on Baraba Steppe, on Trans-Siberian RR and 180 mi. W of Novosibirsk. Grain and livestock marketing center; flour milling, distilling, tanning, dairying. Developed in 1890s at rail station of Kainsk (now KUIBYSHEV), which it supplanted in early 20th cent. as economic center of Baraba Steppe; chartered 1917.

Baraboo (bă'rŭbōō, bâr'ŭbōō), city (pop. 7,264), ⊙ Sauk co., S central Wis., on Baraboo R. and 32 mi. NW of Madison, in hilly resort, agr., and timber region; mfg. (textiles, lumber, barn equipment, railway cars, concrete products, canned foods, hammocks, beer, butter, feed); rock quarries. Ringling Brothers' circus began here. Devils Lake State Park, the Dells of the Wisconsin, and Indian mounds are near by.

Baraboo Range, in Columbia and Sauk counties, S central Wis., an almost circular ridge of old crystalline rock (quartzite) just SW of Portage, bet. Baraboo and Wisconsin rivers; c.25 mi. in diameter; highest point: 1,620 ft. Devils Lake State Park here.

Baraboo River, central Wis., formed by branches rising in Monroe and Juneau counties, flows c.70 mi. generally SE, past Elroy, Reedsburg, and Baraboo, to Wisconsin R. just S of Portage.

Baracaldo (bärákäl'dō), industrial area (commune pop. 36,165), Vizcaya prov., N Spain, in the Basque Provs., NW of Bilbao, on left bank of Nervión R.; with Sestao (NE), it is the leading iron and steel center of Spain. Includes industrial agglomerations of Desierto (pop. 12,672), San Vicente de Baracaldo (pop. 4,396; seat of commune), and Landaburu. Terminus of mining railroads from near-by iron mines; ore-shipping docks ½ mi. long. Has blast furnaces and steel mills; also mfg. of steel tubing, rolling stock, shipbuilding equipment, machinery. First blast furnace built 1854.

Baracca (bäräk'kä), village (pop. 1,700), W Cyrenaica, Libya, on highway and 12 mi. W of Barce; agr. settlement (cereals, olives, grapes) founded 1938–39 by the Italians.

Baracci, Corsica: see PROPRIANO.

Barachois de Malbaie (bärăshwä' dŭ mälbā'), village (pop. estimate 500), E Que., E Gaspé Peninsula, on Mal Bay of the Gulf of St. Lawrence, 18 mi. SE of Gaspé; fishing port, resort.

Baracoa (bärákō'ä), town (pop. 10,395), Oriente prov., E Cuba, port on N coast, 20 mi. WNW of Cape Maisí, 90 mi. ENE of Santiago de Cuba. Exports tobacco, cacao, bananas, coconuts, and other tropical fruit. Makes coconut oil, cigars, and chocolate. Has seaplane anchorage. Founded 1511–12, by Diego de Velázquez, it was 1st white settlement in Cuba. Has 18th cent. fort and a church which was the cathedral of Cuba's 1st diocese. Set in picturesque scenery, with near-by El YUNQUE (an old navigation landmark), waterfalls, and hunting grounds. Iron deposits in vicinity.

Baracoa, village (pop. 836), Cortés dept., NW Honduras, on Chamelecón R. and 7 mi. SE of Puerto Cortés; rail junction in banana zone.

Baracs (bŏ'rŏch), town (pop. 3,043), Fejer co., W central Hungary, near the Danube, 31 mi. SE of Szekesfehervar; agr., sericulture.

Barada (bärädă', bä'rŭdŭ), biblical *Abana* or *Amana*, anc. Gr. *Chrysorrhoas*, river of SW Syria, 52 mi. long, rises in the Anti-Lebanon mts., flows S, past Zebdani and Tekiye (hydroelectric plant), then SE through Damascus to the marshy lake El 'Ateibe. Its waters, used for irrigation for centuries, make the Damascus region a green oasis. A branch of the Barada may have been the biblical Pharpar.

Barada (bĕr'ŭdŭ), village (pop. 83), Richardson co., extreme SE Nebr., 10 mi. N of Falls City, near Missouri R.

Baradères (bärädĕr'), town (1950 census pop. 902), Sud dept., SW Haiti, on Tiburon Peninsula, 34 mi. ESE of Jérémie; coffee, cotton.

Baradero (bärädā'rō), town (pop. 8,213), ⊙ Baradero dist. (□ 440; pop. 21,382), N Buenos Aires prov., Argentina, port on Baradero R. (an arm of the lower Paraná) and 35 mi. NW of Zárate, in agr. area (corn, alfalfa, flax, fruit); linen and paper milling, distilling. Founded 1778 by Spaniards.

Baradla Caves (bŏ'rŏdlŏ), NE Hungary and S Czechoslovakia, c.25 mi. NNW of Miskolc; group of 3 stalactite caverns, 2 in Hungary—Aggtelek (opened 1825) and Josvafö (opened 1929), and 1 in Czechoslovakia—Hosszuaszo (opened 1925). Combined length of caves is c.15 mi., greatest height 492 ft. There are 2 subterranean rivers, the Acheron and the Styx. Largest stalactite is 82 ft., high 26 ft. in diameter.

Baraga (bă'rŭgŭ), county (□ 904; pop. 8,037), NW Upper Peninsula, Mich.; ⊙ L'Anse. Partly bounded N by Keweenaw and Huron bays; drained by Sturgeon R. and small Silver R. Dairy, orchard, and farm area; lumbering, commercial fishing. Resorts. Contains L'Anse Indian Reservation, a state park, and many small lakes. Formed 1875.

Baraga, village (pop. 942), Baraga co., NW Upper Peninsula, Mich., on Keweenaw Bay, and 3 mi. NW of L'Anse. Resort; fishing. Indian relics found in vicinity. Baraga State Park near by (camping, bathing, fishing).

Baragaon (bŭ'rŭgoun). **1** Village, Patna dist., N central Bihar, India, 38 mi. SSE of Patna. Site of Nalanda Univ., center (4th–12th cent. A.D.) of Buddhist learning; extensive ruins include stupas, temples, and monasteries. Rail station at Nalanda, 2 mi. SSE. **2** Town, Uttar Pradesh, India: see CHIT BARAGAON.

Baragharia Nawabganj, E Pakistan: see NAWABGANJ.

Baraguá or **Central Baraguá** (sĕnträl' bärägwä'), town (pop. 1,299), Camagüey prov., E Cuba, sugar mill 13 mi. SE of Ciego de Ávila.

Baragua (bärä'gwä), town (pop. 639), Lara state, NW Venezuela, on affluent of Tocuyo R., in Segovia Highlands, and 55 mi. NW of Barquisimeto; corn, goats.

Baragua, Sierra de (syĕ'rä dā bärä'gwä), Lara state, NW Venezuela, N offshoot of great Andean spur, N of Carora; extends c.50 mi. WSW–ENE; rises to more than 3,500 ft. Cinnabar deposits at La Mesa, at S foot. Sometimes considered part of Segovia Highlands.

Barahona (bäräō'nä), province (□ 1,340; 1935 pop. 46,130; 1950 pop. 62,032), SW Dominican Republic; ⊙ Barahona. Largely a peninsula jutting into the Caribbean S of Sierra de Bahoruco; includes mouth of the Yaque del Sur on Neiba Bay, and L. Rincón. Arid area, fertile in irrigated regions, where sugar cane and coffee are grown on large scale. Extensive forests yield fine hardwood. Rock salt, gypsum, and clay deposits. Set up 1888 as maritime dist.; from it was separated Bahoruco prov. in 1943.

Barahona, city (1935 pop. 8,367; 1950 pop. 14,690), ⊙ Barahona prov., SW Dominican Republic, Caribbean port on Neiba Bay, at E foot of the Sierra de Bahoruco, and 80 mi. WSW of Ciudad Trujillo; 18°13'N 71°6'W. Sugar-milling and -trading center; exports sugar cane, molasses, coffee, tropical hardwood, fruit. Gateway to Dominican lake dist. Coastal fishing. Has airfield. A sugar central is at outskirts. Salt beds near by. City damaged by 1842 earthquake.

Barahona, village (pop. 564), Soria prov., N central Spain, 15 mi. SW of Almazán; cereals, sheep; flour milling. Airfield.

Barahpur, India: see DUMRAON.

Barai (bărī'), village, Kompong Thom prov., central Cambodia, on main road and 55 mi. NNE of Pnompenh; rubber plantations.

Baraili, India: see BARELI.

Barail Range (bŭrīl'), hill range, central Assam, India, NE of Silchar; connects Jaintia Hills (W) and Manipur Hills (E); forms part of Assam Range bet. Brahmaputra valley (N) and Surma Valley (S); extends c.110 mi. NE-SW; rises to c.9,825 ft. Evergreen and bamboo jungle; cotton; silk growing. Inhabited mainly by Kachari tribes.

Baraimi, Biraimi, Buraimi, or **Buraymi** all: (bŭrī'mē), village and oasis (pop. 5,500), ⊙ Jau dist. of Independent OMAN, 80 mi. SSE of Sharja; road and caravan center; date palms, orchards; grain cultivation. Sheep and camel raising on surrounding plain.

Barajas de Madrid (bärä'häs dhä mädrēdh'), town (pop. 1,790), Madrid prov., central Spain, 6 mi. ENE of Madrid. Site of international airport. Region raises cereals, grapes, olives, truck produce, and bulls for the ring.

Barajas de Melo (mā'lō), town (pop. 2,224), Cuenca prov., central Spain, 45 mi. ESE of Madrid; agr. center (olives, grain, truck produce, sugar beets, hemp, livestock). Lumbering, flour milling, olive-oil pressing.

Baraka (bärä'kä), village, Kivu prov., E Belgian Congo, on NW shore of L. Tanganyika, 110 mi. SSE of Costermansville; small lake port in cotton-growing area; cotton ginning. Has Protestant mission.

Barakahshetra (bŭrŭk-shā'trŭ), village, SE Nepal, on KOSI RIVER and 29 mi. NNW of Biratnagar, at 26°52'N 87°10'E. Vishnuite temple; Hindu pilgrimage center. Here is planned a 770-ft.-high dam for Kosi project which will impound a large lake for irrigation and hydroelectric power.

Barakar (bŭrä'kŭr), town (pop. 9,771), Burdwan dist., W West Bengal, India, in Damodar Valley, 7 mi. WNW of Asansol, in Raniganj coal field; rice. Coal mining near by.

Baraka River, Eritrea and Anglo-Egyptian Sudan: see BARKA RIVER.

Barakar River, India: see DAMODAR RIVER.

Barakat (bäräkăt'), village, Blue Nile prov., E central Anglo-Egyptian Sudan, in the Gezira, on left bank of the Blue Nile, on railroad and 10 mi. S of Wad Medani; cotton, wheat, barley, corn, fruits, durra; livestock. Hq. Sudan Plantations Syndicate.

Baraki Rajan (bŭ'rŭkē rä'jŭn), village, Kabul prov., E Afghanistan, on Logar R. and 45 mi. SSW of Kabul.

Barakovo, Bulgaria: see KOCHERINOVO.

Barak River (bŭräk'). **1** Branch of Kusiyara R. arm of Surma R. system, E Pakistan; 42 mi. long. **2** Name applied to upper course of Surma R. in Manipur and Cachar dist., Assam, India.

Bara Lacha La (bärä' lächä' lä'), mountain pass (alt. c.16,000 ft.) in Punjab Himalayas, in Kangra dist., NE Punjab, India, 75 mi. NE of Dharmsala, on caravan route to SE Kashmir. Headstreams (Chandra and Bhaga) of Chenab R. rise near by.

Baral River, E Pakistan: see ATRAI RIVER.

Barama River (bärä'mŭ), NW Br. Guiana, rises near Venezuela border at 7°10'N 60°37'W, flows c.120 mi. E and NE to Waini R. at 7°38'N 59°15'W. Navigable for smaller vessels. In gold region of the North West Dist. Waterfalls on its upper course. Bet. Barama and Barima rivers are manganese deposits.

Baramati (bärä'mŭtē), town (pop., including suburban area, 16,366), Poona dist., central Bombay, India, on N canal of Nira R. and 50 mi. SE of Poona; rail spur terminus; trades in cotton, sugar, millet; oilseed pressing, gur processing, tanning, hand-loom weaving; slate factory.

Baramba (bŭräm'bŭ), village, Cuttack dist., E Orissa, India, on left bank of Mahanadi R. and 34 mi. W of Cuttack; trades in rice, timber. Was ⊙ former princely state of Baramba (□ 143; pop. 52,924) in Orissa States, inc. 1949 into Cuttack dist.

Baram Point (bäräm', bä'–), NW Borneo, in S.China Sea, in NW Sarawak, just W of Brunei border; 4°35'N 113°59'E; lighthouse.

Baram River, N Sarawak, in NW Borneo, rises in Iran Mts., flows 250 mi. W and NW to S.China Sea at Baram Point.

Baramula (bärŭmōō'lŭ) or **Kashmir North** (kăshmēr', kăsh'mēr), district (□ 3,317; pop. 612,428), Kashmir prov., W central Kashmir; ⊙ Baramula. In W Punjab Himalayas (Pir Panjal Range along W border); drained by Jhelum R. Part of N section of Vale of Kashmir in S. Agr. (rice, corn, wheat, oilseeds, pulse, barley); coal deposits (SW). Main towns: Baramula, Sopur, Tsrar Sharif, Patan. Noted hill resort at Gulmarg, archaeological remains at Andarkot. Pop. 96% Moslem, 3% Hindu. Prevailing mother tongue, Kashmiri. Also spelled Baramulla.

Baramula, town (pop.12,724), ⊙ Baramula dist., W central Kashmir, at main N entrance to Vale of Kashmir, on Jhelum R. and 27 mi. WNW of Srinagar; mfg. of matches, chemicals; sawmilling; rice, corn, wheat, oilseeds. N head of navigation for larger boats in Vale of Kashmir. Noted Vishnuite temple ruins. Largely destroyed in fighting of 1947, during India-Pakistan struggle for control. Also spelled Baramulla. Just E is village of Ushkar, built 2d cent. A.D. by Kushan king Huvishka; important in medieval times; ruins include Buddhist stupa, 2 large lingams, and sculptured heads of Gandhara school.

Baran, Br. Somaliland: see BURAN.

Baran (bä'rŭn). **1** Town (pop. 14,087), SE Rajasthan, India, 42 mi. E of Kotah; trade center (wheat, millet, gram, cotton); handicraft cloth weaving and dyeing. **2** Town, Uttar Pradesh, India: see BULANDSHAHR, town.

Baran or **Baran'** (bŭrän'yŭ), town (1926 pop. 883), S Vitebsk oblast, Belorussian SSR, 5 mi. WSW of Orsha; mfg. of sewing machines. In 1920s, also called Krasnyy Oktyabr.

Baranagar (bŭr'ŭnŭgŭr), town (pop. 54,451), 24-Parganas dist., S West Bengal, India, on Hooghly R. (bridged) and 4.5 mi. N of Calcutta city center; jute milling, cotton milling, ginning, and baling, mfg. of chemicals, matches, agr. and industrial machinery. Originally a Portuguese settlement, then Dutch; ceded 1795 to English. Alambazar is N suburb.

Baranchinski or **Baranchinskiy** (bŭrŭnchēn'skē), town (1932 pop. estimate 9,500), W Sverdlovsk oblast, Russian SFSR, on railroad and 9 mi. SSW of Kushva; mfg. of transformers. Until 1928, Baranchinski Zavod.

Baranco (bŭrăng'kō), town (pop. 322), Toledo dist., S Br. Honduras, port on Bay of Amatique, 10 mi. SW of Punta Gorda. Banana plantations; coconuts, citrus fruit.

Barand (bä'ränd), Hung. *Báránd*, town (pop. 3,798), Bihar co., E Hungary, 14 mi. E of Karcag; corn, wheat, hogs.

Baranello (bäränĕl'lō), town (pop. 1,010), Campobasso prov., Abruzzi e Molise, S central Italy, 5 mi. WSW of Campobasso.

Barang (bŭ'rŭng), village, Cuttack dist., E Orissa, India, 4 mi. SSW of Cuttack; glassworks.

Barania Gora (bärä'nyä gōō'rä), Pol. *Barania Góra*, mountain (2,983 ft.) in W Beskids, S Poland, 5 mi. SW of Zywiec.

Baranja (bä'rănyä), Hung. *Baranya*, agr. region, NE Croatia, Yugoslavia; bounded by the Danube (E), the Drava (S), and Hungary (W). Industry at BELI MANASTIR and BELJE. Formed part of BARANYA co., Hungary, until 1920 and, later, 1941–44.

Baranoa (bäränō'ä), town (pop. 6,899), Atlántico dept., N Colombia, in Caribbean lowlands, 16 mi. SW of Barranquilla; cotton center; sugar, corn, beans, tropical fruit, livestock.

Baranof (bă'rŭnŏf), village (1939 pop. 10), SE Alaska, on Chatham Strait, NE Baranof Isl., 20 mi. E of Sitka; fish canning.

Baranof Island (□ 1,607), SE Alaska, in Alexander Archipelago S of Chichagof Isl., bet. Chatham Strait (E) and Gulf of Alaska (W); center near 57°N 135°W; 100 mi. long, 30 mi. wide; rises to 7,000 ft. Largest town, SITKA. Fishing, fish processing, lumbering. Discovered 1741 by Russians, Baranof Isl. was center of Russian activity in North America, 1799–1867, and hq. of Russian fur-trading interest represented by Aleksandr Baranov.

Baranovichi (bŭrä'nŭvēchē), oblast (□ 5,300; 1946 pop. estimate 800,000), W Belorussian SSR; ⊙ Baranovichi. In lowland bounded by Neman R. (NW) and extending into Pripet Marshes (S); drained by Neman and Shchara rivers. Humid continental climate (short summers). Heavily forested (includes Naliboki forest). Agr. (rye, oats, barley, potatoes, flax), livestock; fisheries. Industries based on lumber (sawmilling, pitch processing, woodworking) and agr. (wool, flax, and food processing, tanning). Mfg. of cement (Baranovichi, Novogrudok, Nesvizh, Gorodishche), concrete blocks (Novogrudok, Ivenets), textiles (Baranovichi, Albertin), paper (Albertin), agr. machinery (Slonim). Main centers: Baranovichi, Slonim, Novogrudok, Nesvizh. Well developed rail net; river navigation (Neman R.), lumber floating. Formed 1939 out of Pol. prov. of Nowogrodek, following Soviet occupation of E Poland. Held by Germany 1941–44.

Baranovichi, Pol. *Baranowicze* (bäränôvē'chĕ), city (1931 pop. 22,848), ⊙ Baranovichi oblast, Belorussian SSR, 85 mi. SW of Minsk; 53°7'N 26°E. Rail junction (5 lines); mfg. center (aluminum ware, fire pumps, cement, bricks, grindstones, glass, textiles, soap, candles); tanning, meat canning, dairying, flour milling, distilling. Has teachers col. Developed under Rus. rule in 19th cent.; passed (1921) to Poland; became (1939) ⊙ Baranovichi oblast, following Soviet occupation of E Poland. During Second World War, held (1941–44) by Germany.

Baranovka (bŭrä'nŭfkŭ). **1** Village (1932 pop. estimate 2,200), SW Ulyanovsk oblast, Russian SFSR, 23 mi. ESE of Kuznetsk; grain, legumes. **2** Town (1926 pop. 5,367), W Zhitomir oblast, Ukrainian SSR, on Sluch R. and 20 mi. S of Novograd-Volynski; ceramic industry.

Baranovski or **Baranovskiy** (bŭrŭnôf'skē), railway station, SW Maritime Territory, Russian SFSR, 10 mi. S of Voroshilov; junction of Trans-Siberian RR and branch line SW to Kraskino.

Baranow or **Baranow Sandomierski** (bärä'nōōf sändômyĕr'skē), Pol. *Baranów Sandomierski*, town (pop. 1,169), Rzeszow prov., SE Poland, on the Vistula and 15 mi. SSW of Sandomierz. Castle.

Baranowicze, Belorussian SSR: see BARANOVICHI, city.

Baran River (bä'rŭn), in W Sind, W Pakistan, rises in S Kirthar Range, flows c.100 mi. SE, through S Lakhi Hills, to Indus R. 9 mi. S of Kotri. Seasonal.

Baranya (bŏ'rŏnyŏ), county (□ 1,522; pop. 253,803), S Hungary; ⊙ Pecs. Mostly mountainous and heavily forested, except in S; includes MECSEK MOUNTAINS (center) and VILLANY MOUNTAINS (S); drained by Danube and Drava rivers. Agr. (grain, hemp, nuts, plums, peaches); livestock, poultry; sericulture, wine, honey. Industry at PECS and MOHACS. Coal mined in Mecsek Mts., bauxite deposits in Villany Mts. Formerly the co. included a small region (Serbo-Croatian BARANJA) now in Yugoslavia.

Baranya Mountains, Hungary: see MECSEK MOUNTAINS.

Barão de Cocais (bŭrã'ō dĭ kōkīs'), city (pop. 2,285), S central Minas Gerais, Brazil, in the Serra do Espinhaço, on railroad and 28 mi. E of Belo Horizonte; metallurgical center (blast furnaces, steel-rolling mill, machine shops) using Itabira iron ore and locally mined manganese. Refractory-brick plant. Until 1944, called Morro Grande.

Barão de Grajaú (dĭ grŭzhäōō'), city (pop. 791), SE Maranhão, Brazil, head of navigation on left bank of Parnaíba R. (Piauí border), opposite Floriano; carnauba wax, babassu nuts. Formerly spelled Barão de Grajahú.

Baraolt (bä'rä-ôlt'), Hung. *Barót* (bŏ'rōt), village (pop. 2,905), Stalin prov., central Rumania, 18 mi. NW of Sfantu-Gheorghe; lignite production; mfg. of cheese and alcohol. In Hungary, 1940–45.

Baraqa Islands or **Barraqa Islands** (bärä'kŭ), group of islets in Gulf of Aden off Bir Ali, Eastern Aden Protectorate, 60 mi. SW of Mukalla; guano deposits.

Baraque Fraiture (bäräk' frätür'), mountain (2,139 ft.) of the Ardennes, Luxemburg prov., SE Belgium, 9 mi. NNW of Houffalize.

Baraque Michel (mē-shĕl'), mountain (2,211 ft.) in the Hohe Venn (N section of the Ardennes), Liége prov., E Belgium, 7 mi. NNE of Malmédy; 2nd highest point in Belgium.

Baras (bäräs'), town (1939 pop. 1,179; 1948 municipality pop. 10,275), E Catanduanes isl., Philippines, 11 mi. NE of Virac; coconuts, hemp.

Barasat (bärä'sŭt), town (pop. 11,230), 24-Parganas dist., SE West Bengal, India, 13 mi. NE of Calcutta city center; rail and road junction; cotton weaving; rice, jute, pulse, sugar cane, potatoes, coconuts. Annual fair.

Barashi (bŭrä'shē), village (1926 pop. 3,878), W central Zhitomir oblast, Ukrainian SSR, on Uzh R. 19 mi. NE of Novograd-Volynski; flax, potatoes.

Baratang Island (bärätăng'), one of Andaman Islands, in Bay of Bengal, in center of Great Andaman group; 17 mi. long N–S, 2–7 mi. wide.

Barataria (bărŭtă'rēŭ, –tâ'rēŭ), village (pop. 9,140), NW Trinidad, B.W.I., 2½ mi. E of Port of Spain; agr. area (sugar, coconuts, fruit); lime-oil factory.

Barataria (bărŭtă'rēŭ), village (1940 pop. 796), Jefferson parish, extreme SE La., on Gulf Intracoastal Waterway and 13 mi. S of New Orleans; shrimping port.

Barataria, Bayou, La.: see BARATARIA BAY.

Barataria Bay, lagoon (c.12 mi. N-S, c.15 mi. E-W) in extreme SE La., c.35 mi. S of New Orleans, cut off from the Gulf of Mexico on S by Grand Terre and Grand isls., which are on either side of Barataria Pass (channel from Gulf). With irregular shores and many marshy isls., bay is center of the "Barataria country," low-lying region with innumerable waterways, situated S of New Orleans and W of the Mississippi delta. Center of state's shrimp industry, area is known for its picturesque "platform villages." Muskrat trapping. Oil and gas wells. Navigation channel from Barataria Pass leads N through bay and connecting waterways (including Bayou Barataria) into Gulf Intracoastal Waterway system S of New Orleans. In early-19th cent., region was hq. for pirates headed by the Lafitte brothers, and is still sometimes called the "Lafitte country."

Baratieri Falls (bärätyä'rē), in S Ethiopia, on Ganale Dorya R. and 45 mi. ENE of Negelli; 460 ft. high.

Baratka, Rumania: see BRATCA.

Baraunda (bŭroun'dŭ), village, N Vindhya Pradesh, India, 35 mi. NE of Panna; millet, wheat. Ochre worked near by. Was ⊙ former princely state of Baraunda (□ 228; pop. 17,306) of Central India agency, since 1948 merged with Vindhya Pradesh. Also spelled Baraundha.

Barauni (bä'rounē), town (pop., including adjacent Phulwaria, 9,554), Monghyr dist., N central Bihar, India, near the Ganges (rail ferry), 32 mi. WNW of Monghyr; rail junction; rice, wheat, corn, gram, barley. Sometimes called Phulwaria for former adjacent village. Also spelled Baruni and Beruni; formerly also called Jhuldabhaj.

Baraut (bŭrout'), town (pop. 11,464), Meerut dist., NW Uttar Pradesh, India, on Eastern Jumna Canal and 27 mi. WNW of Meerut; mfg. of iron implements; wheat, millet, sugar cane, oilseeds.

Barba (bär'bä), city (1950 pop. 709), Heredia prov., Costa Rica, on central plateau, at S foot of Barba volcano, 1.5 mi. NNW of Heredia; coffee, sugar cane, potatoes, cereals, livestock. Andesite deposits near by.

Barba, extinct volcano (9,567 ft.) in the Cordillera Central, central Costa Rica, 7 mi. N of Heredia; 10°8'N 84°26'W.

Barbacena (bärbŭsā'nŭ), city (1950 pop. 25,768), S Minas Gerais, Brazil, bet. Mantiqueira and Espinhaço mtn. ranges, on railroad and 120 mi. NNW of Rio de Janeiro; 21°13'S 43°48'W; alt. 3,675 ft. Industrial center with several textile mills (notably silk). Other mfg.: ceramics, tobacco and dairy products, footwear, preserves, candy, glass. Flowers for Rio market grown here. Has silk institute.

Barbacena, village (pop. 1,778), Portalegre dist., central Portugal, 9 mi. NW of Elvas; olives, grain, beans.

Barbacoas (bärbäkō'äs), town (pop. 3,739), Nariño dept., SW Colombia, landing on affluent of Patía R., in Pacific lowlands, and 40 mi. ESE of Tumaco. Trading and agr. center (cacao, sugar cane, rice, coffee, corn, cotton, bananas, yucca, livestock; gums, resins, other forest products). Accessible to ships from the sea. Founded 1600, it was once a rich gold-mining town (mines are near by).

Barbacoas. 1 Town (pop. 724), Aragua state, N Venezuela, in llanos, on Guárico R. and 70 mi. S of Caracas; cattle. **2** Town (pop. 558), Lara state, NW Venezuela, 18 mi. W of Tocuyo; coffee, sugar cane, cereals.

Barbadillo (bärvä-dhē'lyō), village (pop. 1,197), Salamanca prov., W Spain, 12 mi. W of Salamanca; cereals.

Barbados (bärbā'dōz), island (21 mi. long, 14 mi. wide) and Br. colony (□ 166.33; pop. 192,841), B.W.I., in the Atlantic; ⊙ Bridgetown. Most easterly of the West Indies, 100 mi. E of St. Vincent (Windward Isls.) and 175 mi. NNE of Trinidad, bet. 13°2'–13°21'N and 59°–59°12'W. Largely composed of coral limestone, overlaid by volcanic ash, presumably originating from St. Vincent. Almost entirely encircled by coral reefs. Rises in terraces toward highest point at center, Mt. Hillaby (1,104 ft.). There are no rivers to speak of; water has to be pumped from subterranean basins. Climate is one of most healthful in the West Indies, tempered by NE trade winds Dec.-June. Average annual temp. is 79.8°F. Rainfall, mostly during hot season (June-Dec.), varies from 50 inches at the coast to c.75 inches in the hills. Almost out of the track of hurricanes. Because of its equable temp. and fine beaches, Barbados is a popular tourist and winter resort. Sugar cane, planted throughout the isl., is its most important export, along with molasses and rum. Ships also cotton, tamarinds, soap, margarine, arrowroot, spices, vegetables. Other industries include mfg. of cigarettes, bay rum, ice, cassava starch, edible oils, biscuits. Though there are indications of petroleum deposits, so far only manjak has been exploited (NE). Forest resources have been depleted. Coastal fisheries are of increasing importance, a special feature being the flying-fish fleets stationed at Oistins and Speightstown. Bridgetown dominates the colony as trading and processing center, ranking highly as transoceanic port and international cable station; it does considerable trade with Br. Guiana and the neighboring isls. Originally inhabited by Arawak Indians, Barbados was presumably 1st visited by the Portuguese and named Los Barbados for the bearded fig trees they encountered. The English, landing in 1605 at Holetown, claimed the isl., which, unlike most of the other West Indian territories, has since then been continuously held by one European power. It was included (1627) in grant to earl of Carlisle. When the Br. Windward Isls. colony was constituted (1885), Barbados was set up as a separate colony. For administrative purposes it is divided into 11 parishes. The pop. is predominantly Negro. English is spoken universally. Isl.'s greatest problem is its pop. density (1,161 per sq. mi.), highest in the Caribbean area and Central and South America. To ease this tension the govt. started (1939) a settlement near Vieux Fort, S St. Lucia, Windward Isls.

Barbalha (bärbä'lyŭ), city (pop. 3,396), S Ceará, Brazil, on N slope of Serra do Araripe, 12 mi. SE of Crato; cattle-raising center; cotton. Gypsum deposits.

Barbalissus, Syria: see MESKENE.

Barbalo, Mount (bŭrbŭlô'), peak (10,807 ft.) in main range of the E Greater Caucasus, Georgian SSR, 25 mi. N of Akhmeta. A nodal mtn. mass; gives rise to Alazan and Iora rivers (S), Argun R. and the Andi Koisu (N).

Barbarena (bärbärā'nä), town (pop. 3,302), Santa Rosa dept., S Guatemala, in Pacific piedmont, 5 mi. NW of Cuilapa, on Inter-American Highway; alt. 3,999 ft.; coffee, corn, cattle. Temporary dept. capital, 1913–20.

Barbareta Island (bärbärā'tä), in Bay Islands dept., N Honduras, in Caribbean Sea, 2 mi. E of Roatán Isl.; 3 mi. long, 1 mi. wide. Coconuts; livestock.

Barbarons or **Barbarrons** (bärbärō'), village on W coast of Mahé Isl., Seychelles, 4½ mi. S of Victoria; copra, essential oils; fisheries.

Barbary Coast, Calif.: see SAN FRANCISCO.

Barbary States (bär'bŭrē), term used for North African states of Tripolitania, Tunisia, Algeria, and usually also Morocco—which were semi-independent under Turkish rule from 16th cent. until occupation by European powers in 19th cent. Moors expelled from Spain and Turkish corsairs conducted large-scale piracy, preying on Mediterranean shipping and sporadically attacking coastal towns. Their activities led to European punitive expeditions, notably that of Charles V (16th cent.), and, at beginning of 19th cent., to the Tripolitan War. Despite further expeditions, piracy was not completely ended until Fr. occupation of Algiers in 1830.

Barbas, Cape (bär'bäs), headland, Río de Oro, Sp. West Africa, 100 mi. SSW of Villa Cisneros; 22°20'N 16°43'W. S limit of St. Cyprian Bay.

Barbaste (bärbäst'), village (pop. 717), Lot-et-Garonne dept., SW France, on the Baïse and 4 mi. NW of Nérac; woodworking.

Barbastro (bärvä'strō), city (pop. 8,125), Huesca prov., NE Spain, in Aragon, near Cinca R., 27 mi. ESE of Huesca; olive-oil center. Meat processing, tanning, flour- and sawmilling; mfg. of chocolate, soap, tiles. Stock raising (cattle, hogs, sheep). Agr. trade (wine, almonds, cereals, fruit). Has 16th-cent. Gothic cathedral.

Barbate (bärvä'tā), town (pop. 7,932), Cádiz prov., SW Spain, minor Atlantic port at mouth of Barbate R., 32 mi. SE of Cádiz; fishing industry. Cape Trafalgar is 6 mi. W.

Barbate River, Cádiz prov., SW Spain, rises near Málaga prov. border, flows c.40 mi. SW, through the Laguna de JANDA, to the Atlantic at Barbate. Formerly called Guadibeca.

Barbazan (bärbäzã'), village (pop. 371), Haute-Garonne dept., S France, near the Garonne, 7 mi. SW of Saint-Gaudens; small spa; marble quarries near by.

Barber, county (□ 1,146; pop. 8,521), S Kansas; ⊙ Medicine Lodge. Rolling plain, bordered S by Okla.; drained by Medicine Lodge R. Livestock, wheat. Gas and oil fields, gypsum mines. Formed 1873.

Barber, N.J.: see PERTH AMBOY.

Barberine (bärbŭrēn'), hamlet (alt. 6,519 ft.), Valais canton, SW Switzerland, 7 mi. SW of Martigny-Ville, near Fr. border. Near by are Lac de Barberine (a small reservoir with dam), Col de Barberine (a pass; alt. 8,150 ft.), and Barberine hydroelectric plant.

Barberino di Mugello (bärbĕrē'nô dē mōōjĕl'lô), village (pop. 2,535), Firenze prov., Tuscany, central Italy, 15 mi. N of Florence; woolen textiles, hosiery, liquor, pharmaceuticals.

Barberino Val d'Elsa (väl dĕl'sä), village (pop. 710), Firenze prov., Tuscany, central Italy, 16 mi. SSW of Florence, in grape- and olive-growing region. Francesco da Barberino b. here.

Barbers Point, SW end of Oahu, T.H., 8 mi. W of Pearl Harbor; 21°18'N 158°6'W; naval air base.

Barberton, town (pop. 5,279), SE Transvaal, U. of So. Afr., near Swaziland border, 100 mi. W of Lourenço Marques; rail terminus; mining center (gold, asbestos, talc, nickel, barites, magnesite); cotton, fruit, vegetable growing. Airfield. Gold discovered 1875, mining begun in region 1882; town founded 1886 during major gold rush.

Barberton (bär'bùrtùn), city (pop. 27,820), Summit co., NE Ohio, just SW of Akron; metal products, chemicals, matches, rubber products, porcelain, sporting goods, boilers. Laid out 1891, inc. 1892.

Barberyn, Ceylon: see BERUWALA.

Barbezieux (bärbùzyû'), town (pop. 3,000), Charente dept., W France, 17 mi. SSE of Cognac; road center and cattle market; brandy distilling, paper milling, mfg. of agr. machinery, and *pâté de foie gras* with truffles.

Barbières (bärbyâr'), village (pop. 225), Drôme dept., SE France, 12 mi. ENE of Valence; kaolin quarries.

Barbigha (bŭr'bĭgŭ), town (pop. 9,513), Monghyr dist., N central Bihar, India, 50 mi. WSW of Monghyr; rice, wheat, corn, gram, barley.

Barbis (bär'bĭs), village (pop. 2,810), in former Prussian prov. of Hanover, W Germany, after 1945 in Lower Saxony, at S foot of the upper Harz, 11 mi. SE of Osterode; woodworking.

Barbizon (bär'bĭzŏn", Fr. bärbēzō'), village (pop. 758), Seine-et-Marne dept., N central France, 7 mi. SSW of Melun, resort at NW edge of Forest of Fontainebleau. Frequented by painters in 19th cent., it has given its name to the Barbizon school.

Barbosa (bärbō'sä). **1** Town (pop. 1,740), Antioquia dept., NW central Colombia, on railroad, on Porce R. and 20 mi. NE of Medellín; alt. 4,587 ft. Gold mining; cattle raising, sugar growing; corn, beans, yucca, bananas, coffee. **2** Village (pop. 4,731), Santander dept., N central Colombia, on Suárez R., in Cor illera Oriental, and 28 mi. NNE of Chiquinquirá; alt. 4,265 ft.; terminus of rail line from Bogotá.

Barbotan-les-Thermes, France: see CAZAUBON.

Barbour (bär'bùr). **1** County (□ 899; pop. 28,892), SE Ala., in Black Belt; ⊙ Clayton and Eufala. Bounded on E by Chattahoochee R. and Ga., on W by Pea R. Cotton, peanuts, livestock, potatoes; textiles. Founded 1832. **2** County (□ 341; pop. 19,745), N W.Va.; ⊙ Philippi. On Allegheny Plateau; includes part of Laurel Ridge; drained by Tygart R. Includes part of Tygart R. Reservoir and state park around it. Coal-mining and agr. (livestock, dairy products, fruit, truck, tobacco) area; lumbering; natural-gas and oil wells. Some industry at Philippi, Belington. Formed 1843.

Barboursville (bär'bùrzvĭl). **1** Village (pop. c.200), Orange co., N central Va., on railroad and 15 mi. NE of Charlottesville, in agr., livestock region. **2** Town (pop. 1,943), Cabell co., W W.Va., on Guyandot R., at Mud R. mouth, and 8 mi. E of Huntington, in agr. area. State hosp. here. Coal, natural-gas, and oil near by. Chartered 1813.

Barbourville (bär'bùrvĭl), city (pop. 2,926), ⊙ Knox co., SE Ky., in the Cumberlands, on Cumberland R. and 21 mi. NNW of Middlesboro, in region producing bituminous coal, horses, vegetables, strawberries, sorghum, hardwood timber; mfg. of wood and concrete products, corsets. Seat of Union Col. Near by are Dr. Thomas Walker State Park, containing replica of cabin built 1750 (1st home of white people in Ky.) and a small mtn. resort lake. Founded 1800.

Barbuda (bärbū'dù), island (□ 62; pop. 979), dependency of Antigua presidency, Leeward Isls., B.W.I., 28 mi. N of Antigua isl., 60 mi. ENE of St. Kitts. Low, oval-shaped isl. (15 mi. long, up to 8 mi. wide), formed by coral limestone; large lagoon in NW. Though the climate is healthful and the soil fertile, there is a shortage of water. Produces sea-island cotton, sugar cane, livestock, charcoal, and salt on small scale. Sparsely populated (it was privately owned 1691–1872), it is a noted sportsman's paradise, abounding in deer, wild pigs, guinea fowl, pigeons, and ducks. Only village is Codrington, in center. Pop. is mostly Negro.

Barby or **Barby an der Elbe** (bär'bü än dĕr ĕl'bù, bär'bē), town (pop. 7,788), in former Prussian Saxony prov., central Germany, after 1945 in Saxony-Anhalt, on the Elbe, near mouth of the Saxonian Saale, and 16 mi. SE of Magdeburg; mfg. of agr. machinery. Agr. market (grain, sugar beets, potatoes, vegetables, livestock). Site (1749–1809) of colony of Moravian Brothers.

Barca, Cyrenaica: see BARCE.

Barca (bûr'kä), Rum. *Bârca*, village (pop. 5,315), Dolj prov., S Rumania, 25 mi. SSW of Craiova.

Barca, La, Mexico: see LA BARCA.

Barca de Alva (bär'kù däl'vù), village (pop. 523), Guarda dist., N central Portugal, head of navigation on the Douro, on railroad and 38 mi. NNE of Guarda; customs station on Sp. border opposite La Fregeneda.

Barcai, Hatsor, or **Hatsor-Barcai** (hätsôr'-bärkī'), settlement (pop. 350), SW Israel, in Judaean Plain, 10 mi. SW of Rehovot; mfg. of radio equipment; mixed farming. Founded 1946; heavily shelled by Arabs, 1948. Formerly called Bnaya or Benaya; sometimes spelled Hazor-Barcai.

Barcaldine (bärkùldēn'), town (pop. 1,682), central Queensland, Australia, 330 mi. W of Rockhampton; rail junction; wool center.

Barcarena (bärkùrä'nù), city (pop. 191), E Pará, Brazil, on right bank of Pará R. (Amazon delta) and 15 mi. W of Belém; fishing.

Barcarès, Le, France: see SAINT-LAURENT-DE-LA-SALANQUE.

Barca River, Eritrea and Anglo-Egyptian Sudan: see BARKA RIVER.

Barcarozsnyo, Rumania: see RASNOV.

Barcarrota (bärkärō'tä), town (pop. 7,947), Badajoz prov., W Spain, 25 mi. SSE of Badajoz; agr. center (cereals, chick-peas, grapes, hogs, sheep, cattle); flour milling, liquor distilling. Hernando de Soto b. here.

Barce (bär'chā), Arabic *Barqa* or *Barqah*, anc. *Barca* (bär'kä), town (1950 pop. 10,566), W Cyrenaica, Libya, 55 mi. ENE of Benghazi, on plateau; rail terminus and road junction. Resort (alt. c.930 ft.) and agr. center; flour, macaroni, olive oil, meat products. Has restored Turkish fort (built 1842), mosque, hosp., power station. Colonized by Greeks in mid-6th cent. B.C.; declined under the Ptolemies. Its port was Ptolemais. Agr. settlements founded by Italians in vicinity during late 1930s. Scene of fighting (1941–42) bet. Axis and British in Second World War; bombed 1942.

Barcelinhos (bärsĭlē'nyŏŏsh), village (pop. 1,151), Braga dist., N Portugal, on Cávado R. opposite Barcelos, to which it is linked by 15th-cent. bridge.

Barcellona Pozzo di Gotto (bärchĕl-lô'nä pô'tsô dē gôt'tô), commune (pop. 27,134), Messina prov., NE Sicily, 18 mi. WSW of Messina. Principal towns: Barcellona (pop. 8,454) and adjacent Pozzo di Gotto (pop. 5,061). Agr. centers (citrus fruit, olives, wine), cattle markets.

Barcellos, Brazil: see BARCELOS.

Barcellos, Portugal: see BARCELOS.

Barcelona (bärsùlō'nù, Sp. bärthälō'nä), province (□ 2,975; pop. 1,931,875), NE Spain, in Catalonia, on the Mediterranean; ⊙ Barcelona. Occupied by S slopes and spurs of E Pyrenees, by coastal range, and by the fertile plains of Barcelona and Vich; drained by Llobregat R. and its tributaries. Coast mostly low and sandy with fine bathing resorts. Temperate climate except in high mtn. valleys; some forests and pastures (cattle raising) in N. Potash, salt, lignite mines; limestone, gypsum quarries. Chief crops are olives, grapes, almonds, fruit, cork, vegetables, and some cereals. Most densely populated and highly industrialized prov. of Spain, with heaviest concentration in Barcelona area. Chief industry: textiles. Other mfg.: machinery, chemicals (fertilizers, paints and dyes, pharmaceuticals), paper, knitwear, leather goods, glass, ceramics, brandy; printing and publishing (Barcelona). Prov. leads Spain in cement production. Makes and ships table wine and sparkling wine. Imports raw materials, exports manufactured goods, mostly through port of Barcelona. Chief cities, besides Barcelona, are Sabadell, Tarrasa, Manresa, and Mataró.

Barcelona, anc. *Barcino*, city (pop. 1,076,601), ⊙ Barcelona prov. and chief city of Catalonia, NE Spain, on the Mediterranean, 300 mi. ENE of Madrid; 41°23'N 2°11'E. Second largest city in Spain, and its largest seaport and chief industrial and commercial center. Including its suburbs, Barcelona extends, on fertile coastal plain, from mouth of Llobregat R. to that of the Ter; and overlooking it in S is the hill of Montjuich (575 ft.), crowned by a citadel. The favorable location of the city is supplemented by a fine, mild climate (mean temp. in Jan. is 47.5°F., in Aug. 75.5°F.). The excellent harbor, repeatedly enlarged and modernized, is protected by breakwaters; has dry docks and several piers; hq. of many shipping lines. Exports textiles, machinery, wine, cork, glass, fruit, potash, pyrites; imports cotton, grain, coal, metals, mineral oils, rubber. Textile milling is chief industry; also metallurgical industries (textile and farm machinery, rolling stock, automobiles, airplane and marine engines), printing and publishing. Other mfg.: chemicals (fertilizers, dyes, paints, pharmaceuticals), precision instruments, glassware, plastics, knitwear, leather goods, cosmetics. Breweries, oil refineries, distilleries. Bishopric. Seat of univ. (founded 1450), and of many other educational institutions. Center of city is Plaza de Cataluña; from here the Rambla promenades run S to the harbor across the old city, ending in a large square (monument to Columbus 200 ft. high). In the old city, with its narrow, irregular streets are: imposing Gothic cathedral of Santa Eulalia (14th–15th cent.; damaged, 1937, in civil war), with fine cloisters; episcopal palace (16th cent.; restored 18th cent.); 14th-cent. town hall and exchange; former chapel of royal palace (13th cent.), housing prov. mus. Notable churches: San Pablo del Campo (10th cent.; restored in 12th cent.), and Santa María and Santa María del Mar (both 14th cent.). In the former royal palace is archaeological and art mus. The new town, extending N and E from the old town, has regular streets and fine modern bldgs. A strong tradition holds that Barcelona was founded by the Carthaginians, deriving its name from the great Barca family of Carthage. It flourished under the Romans and the Visigoths, fell to the Moors (early 8th cent.), was taken (801) by Charlemagne and included in the Spanish March. In 9th and 10th cent. the march became independent under the leadership of the powerful counts of Barcelona, who wrested lands to the S from the Moors, thus acquiring all Catalonia. In 12th cent. Catalonia was united with Aragon, and Barcelona flourished as capital of kings of Aragon, expanding its trading, banking, and shipping activities. It reached its peak c.1400 and later shared the general decline of Catalonia. It was repeatedly (1640–52, 1715, 1808–14) occupied by the French. City was always a stronghold of Catalan separatism, and later became center of socialist and anarchist movements; it was scene of frequent insurrections (19th-20th cent.) against Sp. monarchy. Became ⊙ Catalan autonomous govt. (1932–39) and was seat of the Loyalist govt. from Oct., 1938, until it fell to Franco, Jan. 26, 1939. Repeatedly bombed during the civil war; some of its finest historic bldgs. were damaged.

Barcelona, fishing village, Chautauqua co., extreme W N.Y., on L. Erie, 16 mi. SW of Dunkirk.

Barcelona, city (1941 pop. 12,370; 1950 census 26,446), ⊙ Anzoátegui state, NE Venezuela, port on W bank of Neverí R., 3 mi. inland from the Caribbean, and 40 mi. SW of Cumaná, 150 mi. ESE of Caracas; 10°8'N 64°41'W. Connected by railroad with its port Guanta (10 mi. NE) and with Naricual coal fields. It is the commercial center for a region rich in coal, salt, cattle, cotton, cacao, sugar cane, tobacco. Trades also in hides, skins, petroleum, coffee. Mfg. (jerked beef, leather goods); cotton ginning. Airport. Founded 1671.

Barceloneta (bärsĕlōnā'tä), town (pop. 1,032), N Puerto Rico, landing on Manatí R., near the coast, on railroad and 27 mi. W of San Juan, in sugar-growing and cattle-raising region. Adjoining N is the Plazuela sugar mill. The village, cape, and fort of Palmas Altas is 3 mi. NW.

Barceloneta (bärthālōnā'tä), E harbor section of BARCELONA, NE Spain. Has foundries, machine shops, piers, wharves. Also bathing.

Barceloneta, Venezuela: see LA PARAGUA.

Barcelonnette (bärsùlônĕt'), town (pop. 2,344), Basses-Alpes dept., SE France, in Alpine Ubaye valley, 29 mi. NE of Digne; northernmost town of Provence, on road to Maddalena Pass; alt. 3,714 ft. Tourist and winter-sports resort. Mfg. (felt hats, flour products), marble cutting. Founded as Barcelone in 1231 by Raymond-Bérenger V, count of Provence. Many of its inhabitants migrated to Mexico in 19th cent.

Barcelos (bärsä'lŏŏsh), city (pop. 567), N Amazonas, Brazil, landing on right bank of the Rio Negro and 240 mi. NW of Manaus; rubber, cereals. Established as Salesian mission; it was ⊙ São José de Rio Negro captain generalcy until 1825. Formerly spelled Barcellos.

Barcelos, city (pop. 4,719), Braga dist., N Portugal, on Cávado R., on railroad and 10 mi. W of Braga; agr. trade center noted for its livestock and ceramics fairs; mfg. (cement, paper, knitwear, soft drinks). Has many bldgs. dating from 15th cent., when it became seat of dukes of Braganza (ruined castle). Formerly spelled Barcellos.

Barcika, Hungary: see KAZINCBARCIKA.

Barcillonnette (bärsēlônĕt'), village (pop. 77), Hautes-Alpes dept., SE France, 12 mi. SW of Gap.

Barcin (bär'tsēn), Ger. *Bartschin* (bär'chĭn), town (pop. 1,939), Bydgoszcz prov., central Poland, on Notec R. and 13 mi. WNW of Inowroclaw; flour milling; cattle and horse trade.

Barcino, Spain: see BARCELONA, city.

Barclay (bär'klē), town (pop. 108), Queen Annes co., E Md., 18 mi. W of Dover, Del.

Barco, Colombia: see PETRÓLEA.

Barco, El, Argentina: see EL BARCO.

Barco, El (ĕl bär'kō), village (pop. 2,054), Orense prov., NW Spain, in Galicia, in fruitgrowing dist. on Sil R., and 22 mi. WSW of Ponferrada; metal-working (small arms, hardware), meat processing, brandy distilling. Ships wine, chestnuts, nuts, fruit, medicinal herbs. Limestone quarries.

Barco de Ávila (bär'kō dhā ä'vēlä), town (pop. 2,113), Ávila prov., central Spain, in Old Castile, on Tormes R. (crossed by 2 Roman bridges), at NW foot of the Sierra de Gredos, and 45 mi. SW of Ávila. Bean-growing and sheep-raising center. Flour milling, woolen milling; trout fishing. Hydroelectric plant. Excursion point for small lake region of the Sierra de Gredos. Old town with Romanesque church, 12th-cent. walls, and Valdecorneja castle.

Barcombe (bär'kùm), agr. village and parish (pop. 1,248), central Sussex, England, near Ouse R., 3 mi. N of Lewes. Has partly Norman church.

Barcoo River (bärkōō') or **Cooper's Creek,** E central Australia, rises in Great Dividing Range E of Blackall, Queensland, flows 880 mi. generally SW, past Blackall and Innamincka, to L. Eyre, South Australia. Queensland portion drains livestock area; South Australia portion frequently dry. Thomson R., main tributary.

Barcs (bŏrch), town (pop. 8,224), Somogy co., SW Hungary, on Drava R. and 37 mi. WSW of Pecs, on Yugoslav line; rail and market center; sawmills, flour mills, alcohol refinery, brickworks, tobacco market.

Barczewo (bär-chĕ'vô), Ger. *Wartenburg* (vär'tŭnbŏŏrk"), town (1939 pop. 5,843; 1946 pop. 1,782) in East Prussia, after 1945 in Olsztyn prov., NE Poland, in Masurian Lakes region, 9 mi. ENE of Allenstein (Olsztyn); grain and cattle market. Founded 1325 by Teutonic Knights; chartered 1364. After 1945, briefly called Wartembork.

Bard (bärd), village (pop. 180), Val d'Aosta region, NW Italy, on Dora Baltea R. and 12 mi. NNW of Ivrea; hydroelectric plant. On near-by hill is 15th-cent. Fort Bard (rebuilt 1830), taken by Napoleon in 1800.

Barda (bŭrdä'). **1** City (1932 pop. estimate 2,770), central Azerbaijan SSR, on Terter R. and 15 mi. S of Yevlakh; cotton. Site of anc. Partav, ⊙ anc. Caucasian state of Albania, conquered (7th cent.) by Arabs. **2** Village (1926 pop. 2,447), S Molotov oblast, Russian SFSR, on left tributary of Kama R. and 26 mi. S of Osa; food processing; rye, oats, flax, livestock.

Bardaï (bärdī'), village, N Chad territory, Fr. Equatorial Africa, in E Sahara and Tibesti Mts. 285 mi. NW of Largeau; caravan junction near Libyan border.

Bardastrandar or **Bardhastrandar** (bär'dhästrän"-tär), Icelandic *Barðastrandar*, county [Icelandic *sýsla*] (pop. 2,708), NW Iceland; ⊙ Patreksfjordur. Covers S part of Vestfjarda Peninsula, on N shore of Breidi Fjord. Mountainous. Fishing.

Bardejov (bär'dyĕyôf), Ger. *Bartfeld* (bärt'fĕlt), Hung. *Bártfa* (bärt'fŏ), town (pop. 6,394), NE Slovakia, Czechoslovakia, on Topla R. and 21 mi. N of Presov; rail terminus. Founded in 13th cent.; noted for numerous late-Gothic and Renaissance structures, 13th-cent. church, 15th-cent. town hall (now mus.). Formerly gold and silver mined in vicinity. Popular health resort of Bardejovske Kupele (bär'dyĕyôfskā kōō'pĕlĕ), Slovak *Bardejovské Kúpele*, with alkaline and ferruginous springs and peat baths, is 2 mi. NNW.

Bardenberg (bär'dŭnbĕrk), village (pop. 5,109), in former Prussian Rhine Prov., W Germany, after 1945 in North Rhine-Westphalia, near Dutch border, 4 mi. NNE of Aachen. Coal mined near by.

Barden Reservoir, R.I.: see PONAGANSET RIVER.

Bardera (bärdĕ'rä), town (pop. 3,500), SW Ital. Somaliland, on Juba R. and 185 mi. N of Kismayu, in agr. region (durra, corn); 2°20'N 42°18'E. Road junction; head of navigation for dhows. Mosque.

Bardhastrandar, Iceland: see BARDASTRANDAR.

Bardi (bär'dē), town (pop. 1,190), Parma prov., Emilia-Romagna, N central Italy, near Ceno R., 18 mi. SW of Salsomaggiore; flour, lumber mills.

Bardia (bärdē'ŭ, bär'dyä), town (pop. 2,370), E Cyrenaica, Libya, near Egyptian border, port on Mediterranean Sea, 70 mi. ESE of Tobruk, 15 mi. NNW of Salum. Airfield. Scene of seesaw fighting (1940–42) bet. Axis and British in Second World War. Changed hands several times until finally taken by British in Nov., 1942.

Bardia (bŭrd'yŭ), village, SW Nepal, in the Terai, 23 mi. NW of Nepalganj; rice, oilseeds, jute, millet. Kumbher is 3 mi. SE; police station.

Bardis (bärdēs'), village (pop. 7,948), Girga prov., central Upper Egypt, on railroad and 5 mi. SE of Girga; cotton, cereals, dates, sugar.

Bardney, town and parish (pop. 1,444), Parts of Lindsey, central Lincolnshire, England, 10 mi. E of Lincoln; beet-sugar refining. Site of Benedictine abbey of St. Oswald, founded in late 7th cent., destroyed by the Danes c.870, and restored 1086.

Bardo (bär'dô), Ger. *Wartha* (vär'tä), town (1939 pop. 1,736; 1946 pop. 2,891) in Lower Silesia, after 1945 in Wroclaw prov., SW Poland, at S foot of the Eulengebirge, on the Glatzer Neisse and 6 mi. NNE of Glatz (Klodzko); cellulose mfg. Has noted 17th-cent. church, object of pilgrimage. After 1945, briefly called Warta.

Bardo, village, Harlan co., SE Ky., 5 mi. S of Harlan; coal mining.

Bardo, Le (lŭ bärdō'), residential W suburb (pop. 7,085) of Tunis, N Tunisia; metalworking, tanning. Orange groves. Has noted archaeological mus. (founded 1888) containing Roman and early Christian excavations. Here, in 1881, the Bey of Tunis accepted French protectorate over Tunisia.

Bardoli (bärdō'lē), town (pop. 7,385), Surat dist., N Bombay, India, 18 mi. ESE of Surat; road center; trades in cotton, millet, wheat, timber.

Bardolino (bärdôlē'nô), village (pop. 1,185), Verona prov., Veneto, N Italy, port on SE shore of Lago di Garda, 15 mi. NW of Verona; wine, marmalade.

Bardolph (bär'dôlf), village (pop. 246), McDonough co., W Ill., 5 mi. ENE of Macomb, in agr. and bituminous-coal area; corn, wheat, oats, livestock.

Bardonecchia (bärdônĕk'kyä), village (pop. 630), Torino prov., Piedmont, NW Italy, near Fr. border, at S entrance of Mont Cenis tunnel, 18 mi. W of Susa; hydroelectric plant. Summer resort (alt. 4,303 ft.); winter sports.

Bardowick (bär'dōvĭk), village (pop. 3,269), in former Prussian prov. of Hanover, NW Germany, after 1945 in Lower Saxony, on the Ilmenau and 4 mi. N of Lüneburg; furniture mfg.

Bardsey (bärd'zē), Welsh *Ynys Enlli* (ŭ'nĭs ĕn'-thlē), island (444 acres; pop. 54), Caernarvon, Wales, off SW tip of Lleyn Peninsula, 18 mi. WSW of Pwllheli and separated from mainland by 2-mi.-wide Bardsey Sound; 1½ mi. long, 1 mi. wide, rising to 548 ft.; agr. and fishing. There are ruins of abbey reputedly founded 516 by St. Cadvan; former place of pilgrimage. Site of lighthouse (52° 45'N 4°48'W).

Bardsley, village and parish (pop. 2,013), SE Lancashire, England, 2 mi. S of Oldham; coal mining, cotton milling, mfg. of pharmaceuticals.

Bardstown, city (pop. 4,154), ⊙ Nelson co., central Ky., near Beech Fork, 35 mi. SSE of Louisville, in outer Bluegrass agr. area (livestock, dairy products, grain, burley tobacco). Mfg. of whisky, concrete blocks; flour, feed, and lumber mills. Cathedral of St. Joseph (built 1816–19; has paintings said to have been given by Louis Philippe of France), monument to John Fitch, who is buried here, and many early-19th-cent. houses here. Near by are "Federal Hill" (built 1795–1818), where Stephen Foster is said to have written *My Old Kentucky Home;* "Wickland," home of 3 Ky. governors, built 1813 by Charles A. Wickliffe; Nazareth Col. and Acad. (established 1814; for women); Abbey of Our Lady of Gethsemani, a Trappist monastery founded 1848; St. Catharine Jr. Col.; and Loretto Jr. Col. In Civil War, occupied (Sept., 1862) by Gen. Braxton Bragg's Confederate army. Settled 1778; inc. 1788.

Bardwell. **1** Town (pop. 1,033), ⊙ Carlisle co., SW Ky., 28 mi. WSW of Paducah; trade center for agr. area (livestock, dairy products, poultry, grain, dark tobacco, cotton, apples); canned foods. **2** City (pop. 229), Ellis co., N Texas, 17 mi. NW of Corsicana, in agr. area.

Barèges (bärĕzh'), village (pop. 203), Hautes-Pyrénées dept., SW France, in central Pyrenees at foot of the Pic du Midi de Bigorre, 11 mi. SE of Argelès-Gazost; alt. 4,068 ft.; popular resort with powerful sulphur springs. Military hosp. Winter sports. The gorge-like valley is subject to snow avalanches. The TOURMALET pass is 5 mi. E.

Bareilly (bŭrā'lē), district (□ 1,591; pop. 1,176,197), Rohilkhand div., N central Uttar Pradesh, India; ⊙ Bareilly. On Ganges Plain; drained by the Ramganga; irrigated by Sarda Canal system. Agr. (wheat, rice, gram, sugar cane, sesame and mustard oilseeds, pearl millet, corn, jowar, barley); a major Indian sugar-processing dist. Main centers: Bareilly, Aonla, Faridpur, Baheri.

Bareilly, city (pop., including cantonment, 192,688), ⊙ Rohilkhand div. and Bareilly dist., N central Uttar Pradesh, India, near the Ramganga, 120 mi. NE of Agra; rail and road junction; trade center (grains, sugar cane); mfg. of carpets, soap, shellac, furniture; sugar processing, cotton ginning and pressing. Mfg. of matches and bobbins and catechu processing at Clutterbuckganj, just NW, on railroad. Indian Veterinary Research Inst. and rail workshops 2 mi. N at village of Izatnagar. Has col., soil survey laboratory. City founded 1537. Was ⊙ Rohilkhand under Moguls in 1657. Important under Rohillas; with surrounding country passed (1774) to nawab of Oudh following combined British and Oudh defeat of the Rohillas. Ceded 1801 to British. Figured in Sepoy Rebellion of 1857.

Barejadi (bŭrā'jŭdē), village (pop. 415), Ahmadabad dist., N Bombay, India, 9 mi. SSE of Ahmadabad; local market center; chemical and paper mfg.

Barelas (bărĕ'lŭs), village (pop. 1,846), Bernalillo co., central N.Mex., near Albuquerque.

Bareli (bŭrā'lē), town (pop. 3,748), SE Bhopal state, India, 55 mi. ESE of Bhopal; markets wheat, cotton, millet. Sometimes spelled Baraili.

Barendrecht (bä'rŭndrĕkht), town (pop. 2,668), South Holland prov., SW Netherlands, on Ijsselmonde isl. and 5 mi. SE of Rotterdam; fruit and vegetable market, with canneries; mfg. (furniture, washing machines). Agr. col.

Bärenstein (bâ'rŭn-shtīn"). **1** Town (pop. 1,693), Saxony, E central Germany, in the Erzgebirge, 13 mi. SW of Pirna, near Czechoslovak border; woodworking. Climatic health and winter-sports resort. **2** Village (pop. 4,232), Saxony, E central Germany, in the Erzgebirge, 6 mi. S of Annaberg, on Czechoslovak border, opposite Vejprty; cotton and rayon milling, knitting, and dyeing; embroidering.

Barentin (bärätē'), town (pop. 4,594), Seine-Inférieure dept., N France, 10 mi. NW of Rouen; cotton and linen milling.

Barenton (bärätō'), village (pop. 569), Manche dept., NW France, 16 mi. S of Vire; horse raising.

Barentsburg (bä'rŭntsbŏŏrg), coal-mining settlement and port, on W coast of West Spitsbergen, Spitsbergen group, on Gront Fjord (Nor. *Grønt-fjorden*, 10-mi.-long S arm of Is Fjord), 10 mi. WSW of Longyear City; 78°4'N 14°3'E. Mines operated by USSR; pop. (entirely Russian) in winter 1948–49 was c.600. In Second World War, settlement was destroyed (July, 1943) by German navy; later rebuilt.

Barents Island (băr'ŭnts, bä'rŭnts, Nor. *Barentsøya* (bä'rŭnts-û"yä), island (□ 514) in the Spitsbergen group, in Barents Sea of Arctic Ocean, off E coast of West Spitsbergen, N of Edge Isl.; 78°25'N 21°25'E. It is 30 mi. long, 20–30 mi. wide; rises to 1,302 ft. Largely uncharted.

Barents Land (bă'rŭnts), name sometimes applied to N portion of N isl. of Novaya Zemlya, USSR.

Barents Sea, Rus. *Barentsovo More*, Norwegian *Barents Havet*, portion of Arctic Ocean N of Norway and European USSR; bounded by Spitsbergen and Franz Josef Land (N), by Novaya Zemlya (E); 800 mi. long, 650 mi. wide. Connects with Norwegian Sea (W) at 20°E, bet. North Cape and Spitsbergen, and with Kara Sea (E), bet. Franz Josef Land and Novaya Zemlya and through straits Matochkin Shar, Karskiye Vorota, and Yugorski Shar. A shallow sea, warmed in SW by the Gulf Stream. Named for Willem Barentz, 16th-cent. Du. navigator. SE portion, at mouth of Pechora R., sometimes called Pechora Sea.

Barentu (bärĕn'tōō), town (pop. 1,000), Agordat div., W Eritrea, on highway and 34 mi. SW of Agordat; alt. c.3,215 ft. Commercial center (gum arabic, oilseeds, cereals, fruit, cattle). Gold mining near by. Founded 1903 by Italians.

Bäretswil (bâ'rŭtsvēl), town (pop. 2,317), Zurich canton, N Switzerland, 15 mi. E of Zurich; textiles, metalworking.

Barfak or **Barfaq** (bŭr'fŭk), village, Kataghan prov., NE Afghanistan, on N slopes of the Hindu Kush, 35 mi. SW of Doshi, and on Surkhab R., in coal-mining area. Ishpushta mine is 4 mi. SW.

Barfleur (bärflûr'), village (pop. 958), Manche dept., NW France, fishing port on the Channel, 16 mi. E of Cherbourg. **Barfleur Point**, a headland forming NE tip of Cotentin Peninsula, is 2 mi. N; 49°42'N 1°16'W. Lighthouse.

Barfurush, Iran: see BABUL.

Barga (bär'gä), town (pop. 2,362), Lucca prov., Tuscany, central Italy, in the Garfagnana, near Serchio R., 16 mi. N of Lucca; paper mills. Has Romanesque cathedral.

Barga (bärgä'), Chinese *Pa-erh-hu* (bär'hŭ'), Mongolian league of Manchuria, in N Inner Mongolian Autonomous Region; main city, Hailar. Bounded W by USSR (along Argun R.), S by Mongolian People's Republic, and E by the Great Khingan Mts., the Barga is essentially a steppe plateau in S (average alt. 2,000 ft.) and mountainous taiga in N. It contains the lakes Hulun Nor and Buir (Bor) Nor, for which it is sometimes called Hulunbuir. The Mongol pop. is engaged in stock raising (mainly sheep, horses, cattle), with wool and hides the chief export products. Chinese agr. colonization has proceeded along the Chinese Eastern RR, with main centers at Hailar, Manchouli, Pokotu, and Yalu. There are small Tungus minorities: Orochon (N), Solon (S). The TREKHRECHYE is a Russian agr. dist. Coal is mined at Chalainor, and there are mineral springs at Wenchüan. The Barga passed to China in late-17th cent. and remained a nomadic grazing area until rail construction and ensuing Chinese colonization (after 1900). When in Manchukuo, it was constituted as North Hsingan prov.; and was inc. 1946 into Hsingan prov. Part of the Inner Mongolian Autonomous Region after 1949, it was joined with Buteha to form Huna league.

Bargal (bärgäl'), village (pop. 400), in the Mijirtein, N Ital. Somaliland, port on Indian Ocean, 50 mi. N of Hordio; mother of pearl, tunny.

Barganny, Scotland: see DAILLY.

Bargarh (bŭr'gŭr). **1** Town (pop. 8,236), Sambalpur dist., W Orissa, India, 24 mi. WSW of Sambalpur; agr. market (rice, oilseeds); hand-loom weaving. **2** Village, Uttar Pradesh, India: see MAU, Banda dist.

Bargas (bär'gäs), village (pop. 3,404), Toledo prov., central Spain, 6 mi. N of Toledo; agr. center (olives, grapes, cereals; goats); olive-oil extracting, dairying; mfg. of pottery, furniture.

Barge (bär'jĕ), village (pop. 1,909), Cuneo prov., Piedmont, NW Italy, 10 mi. NW of Saluzzo; rail terminus; mushroom industry. Quarries (flagstone, gneiss) near by.

Barge Canal, N.Y.: see NEW YORK STATE BARGE CANAL.

Bargersville (bär'gŭrzvĭl), town (pop. 413), Johnson co., central Ind., 17 mi. S of Indianapolis, in agr. area.

Bargias, Piz, Switzerland: see RINGELSPITZ.

Bargiri, Turkey: see MURADIYE.

Bargny (bärnyē'), village, W Senegal, Fr. West Africa, 15 mi. E of Dakar; mfg. of lime and cement. Airfield used by U.S. during Second World War.

Bargoed (bärgoid'), town (pop. 12,177) in Gelligaer urban dist., E Glamorgan, Wales, on Rhymney R.; coal mining.

Bargou, Djebel (jĕ'bĕl bärgōō'), mountain (alt. 4,154 ft.), Maktar dist., N central Tunisia, 25 mi. NE of Maktar.

Bargteheide (bärk'tŭhī"dŭ), residential village (pop. 6,489), in Schleswig-Holstein, NW Germany, 16 mi. NE of Hamburg; mfg. of machine tools, brushes, furniture; weaving, woodworking.

Barguzin (bŭrgōōzēn'), village (1926 pop. 2,263), W Buryat-Mongol Autonomous SSR, Russian SFSR, on Barguzin R. and 150 mi. NNE of Ulan-Ude, 17 mi. E of L. Baikal; lumbering. Sable reserve (N). An old Rus. colonization center, founded 1648. Had gold-mining boom in 1870s.

Barguzin Range, NW Buryat-Mongol Autonomous SSR, Russian SFSR, bet. NE shore of L. Baikal and Barguzin R.; alpine granite formation. Its wooded slopes rise to 8,400 ft. Sable reserve on SW slopes.

Barguzin River, W Buryat-Mongol Autonomous SSR, Russian SFSR, rises on Vitim Plateau, flows 437 mi. SW, past Barguzin, to L. Baikal at Ust-Barguzin. Navigable for 160 mi. above mouth.

Barh (bär), town (pop. 11,341), Patna dist., N central Bihar, India, on Ganges R. and 34 mi. ESE of Patna; trades in rice, gram, oilseeds, wheat, barley, corn, millet; jasmine-oil extraction.

Barhaj (bŭr′hŭj), town (pop., including W suburb of Gaura, 14,582), Gorakhpur dist., E Uttar Pradesh, India, on the Gogra and 40 mi. SE of Gorakhpur; sugar milling; trades in rice, wheat, barley, oilseeds, gram, timber. Founded c.1770. Also called Gaura-Barhaj.

Barhalganj (bŭr′hŭlgŭnj) or **Chillupar** (chĭl-lōō′pär), town (pop. 3,446), Gorakhpur dist., E Uttar Pradesh, India, on the Gogra and 33 mi. SSE of Gorakhpur; trades in rice, gram, wheat, sugar cane.

Barhampur, India: see DUMRAON.

Bar Harbor, town (pop. 3,864), including Bar Harbor village (pop. 2,572), Hancock co., S Maine, on MOUNT DESERT ISLAND, 40 mi. SE of Bangor; summer resort on Frenchman Bay. Port of entry. Near by are Roscoe B. Jackson Laboratory for Cancer Research and a marine biological laboratory (at Salsbury Cove). Settled 1763, inc. 1796 as Eden, renamed 1918. A forest fire destroyed most of the town in 1947.

Bar Harbour Island (□ 5; pop. 131), SE N.F., in Placentia Bay, 30 mi. NNW of Argentia; 4 mi. long, 2 mi. wide. Fishing.

Barhimi (bärhē′mē), petty sheikdom of SUBEIHI tribal area, Western Aden Protectorate; ⊙ Khor 'Umeira. Protectorate treaty concluded in 1889. Also spelled Bruhimi.

Barhni, India: see BANSI.

Bari (bä′rē). **1** Town (pop. 2,363), SE Bhopal state, India, 45 mi. ESE of Bhopal, at foot of Vindhya Range; center of large agr. land reclamation project (launched 1950). **2** Town (pop. 11,935), E Rajasthan, India, 17 mi. WSW of Dholpur; market center for millet, gram, wheat, sandstone (quarries near by). Fort allegedly built in late-13th cent. by Firoz Shah of Ghor.

Bari (bä′rē), province (□ 1,980; pop. 1,010,907), Apulia, S Italy, bordering on the Adriatic; ⊙ Bari. Consists of Apennine foothills and a narrow coastal plain, watered by a few small streams. Predominantly agr.; a major producer of Italy's almonds and carob beans; also grows grapes, olives, fruit, and cereals. Sheep raising. Fishing. Mfg. and commerce along coast (Bari, Barletta, Molfetta, Monopoli); some mfg. inland (Altamura, Andria, Bitonto, Corato). Formerly also Bari delle Puglie.

Bari, anc. *Barium*, city (pop. 162,238), ⊙ Apulia and Bari prov., S Italy, port on the Adriatic, 50 mi. NW of Taranto, 135 mi. E of Naples; 41°8′N 16°52′E. Industrial and commercial center; steelworks, foundries, petroleum refinery, food canneries, textile and flour mills; mfg. of machinery, automobile chassis, electrical apparatus, furniture, soap, sulphur oils, wax, tobacco products, macaroni, wine, olive oil. Exports wine, olive oil, almonds, carob beans, figs, soap. Substantial trade with the Orient. Archbishopric. Has 11th-cent. cathedral with anc. baptistery, Romanesque basilica containing relics of St. Nicholas of Bari (a major pilgrimage center), medieval castle, mus. of antiquities, meteorological observatory, and univ. (founded 1924). A Roman colony, later ruled by Goths, Lombards, and Byzantines. Conquered 1071 by Normans. Became chief city of Apulia; a sailing port for the Crusades. In Second World War, port heavily bombed and damaged by ammunition explosions (1943, 1945). Formerly also called Bari delle Puglie.

Baria, India: see BARIYA.

Baria (bäryŭ′), town, ⊙ Baria prov. (□ 800; 1943 pop. 65,700), S Vietnam, on South China Sea, in Dongnai delta, 40 mi. SE of Saigon, in corn- and rubber-growing area; trading center; timber, fisheries, salt extraction.

Baricella (bärēchĕl′lä), village (pop. 494), Bologna prov., Emilia-Romagna, N central Italy, 14 mi. NE of Bologna; alcohol distillery.

Barichara (bärēchä′rä), town (pop. 2,474), Santander dept., N central Colombia, near Suárez R., 12 mi. N of Socorro; alt. 4,383 ft. Tobacco, corn, sugar cane, fique fibers, vegetables, fruit, cattle, hogs. Mfg. of cigars, fique bags, straw hats. Caverns and copper deposits near by.

Bari Doab (bä′rē dō′äb), large alluvial area in Indian and Pakistan Punjab, bet. Beas and Sutlej rivers (E) and Ravi and Chenab rivers (W). Irrigated by Upper and Lower Bari Doab canal systems and by right-bank canals of Sutlej valley system; agr. (wheat, gram, cotton, corn, rice). Comprises Multan, Montgomery, Lahore, Amritsar, and most of Gurdaspur dists.

Bari Doab Canal, Lower, large irrigation channel in SE Punjab, W Pakistan; continuation of Upper CHENAB CANAL; from aqueduct over Ravi R. near Balloki (Lahore dist.) it runs c.185 mi. SW, along river's left bank; numerous distributaries. Irrigates large parts of Lahore, Montgomery, and Multan dists. in Bari Doab. Opened 1913.

Bari Doab Canal, Upper, irrigation channel in Punjab, India, and Punjab, W Pakistan; from left bank of Ravi R. (headworks at Madhopur, Gurdaspur dist.) runs c.165 mi. SW to a point 11 mi. W of Chunian. Has 3 main branches (N branch flows through city of Lahore) and numerous distributaries. Irrigates large areas of Gurdaspur, Amritsar, and Lahore dists. in Bari Doab. Opened 1859.

Barigazzo (bärēgä′tsô), village (pop. 124), Modena prov., Emilia-Romagna, N central Italy, 27 mi. NW of Pistoia, in Etruscan Apennines. Has hot springs, used to make methane gas.

Barika (bärēkä′), village (pop. 2,948), Constantine dept., NE Algeria, in the Hodna depression, 40 mi. NNW of Biskra; sheep raising, esparto gathering.

Barile (bärē′lĕ), town (pop. 4,028), Potenza prov., Basilicata, S Italy, 4 mi. SSE of Melfi; wine, olive oil. Albanians established colony here in 15th cent.

Barili (bärē′lē), town (1939 pop. 2,622; 1948 municipality pop. 27,267), central Cebu isl., Philippines, 30 mi. SW of Cebu city, near W coast; agr. center (corn, coconuts); fishing.

Barillas or **Santa Cruz Barillas** (sän′tä krōōs′, bärē′yäs), town (pop. 1,231), Huehuetenango dept., W Guatemala, on E slope of Cuchumatanes Mts., 11 mi. ESE of San Mateo Ixtatán; alt. 4,800 ft.; coffee, sugar cane, grain; livestock.

Bariloche, Argentina: see SAN CARLOS DE BARILOCHE.

Barima, Point (bärē′mä), Atlantic headland in NE Venezuela, at mouth of the Boca Grande, largest mouth of Orinoco R.; 8°36′N 60°25′W.

Barima River, NW Br. Guiana and NE Venezuela, rises near international line at 7°29′N 60°42′W, flows c.250 mi. in large curve E, N, and WNW to the Boca Grande of the Orinoco estuary (Venezuela) at Point Barima. Navigable for 52 mi. upstream, it affords access to rich gold region of the North West Dist. of Br. Guiana. Head of navigation is Morawhanna, which is also linked through short Mora Passage with mouth of Waini R. on the Atlantic. For the greater part of the year vessels can go as far as Arakaka.

Barinas (bärē′näs), state (□ 13,590; 1941 pop. 62,959; 1950 census 80,503), W Venezuela; ⊙ Barinas. Situated in llano region N of Apure and Uribante rivers; extends E from the Andes to Portuguesa R. Drained by numerous secondary tributaries of Orinoco R., including Guanare, Santo Domingo, and Apure rivers. Climate tropical and wet in lowlands; rainy season (May–Dec.). Primarily a stock-raising state; ranks 2d as producer of cattle in Venezuela. Coffee produced in uplands; other minor crops, grown mainly along rivers, include cacao, sugar cane, tobacco, rice, corn, yucca, bananas. Its virgin forests remain unexploited. Fishing and hunting flourish. Main processed produce comprise dairy products, hides, fiber goods.

Barinas, town (1941 pop. 2,485; 1950 census 7,672), Barinas state, W Venezuela, in llanos at foot of Andean outliers, on Santo Domingo R. and 43 mi. SW of Guanare, 260 mi. SW of Caracas; 8°38′N 70°13′W. Trading center in cattle-raising region; dairy products; cacao and tobacco also produced. Airport.

Baring (bâr′ĭng), town (pop. 274), Knox co., NE Mo., near South Fabius R., 6 mi. N of Edina.

Baring, Cape (bâ′rĭng, bă′–), SW Victoria Isl., SW Franklin Dist., Northwest Territories, on Amundsen Gulf; W extremity of Wollaston Peninsula, at entrance of Prince Albert Sound; 70°1′N 116°58′W.

Baringo (bärĭng′gō), town (1948 pop. c.200), W central Kenya, E of L. Baringo (in Great Rift Valley), on road and 65 mi. NNE of Nakuru; corn.

Baringo, Lake (□ 72), W central Kenya, in Great Rift Valley, 12 mi. W of Baringo; 12 mi. long; 6 mi. wide; 25 ft. deep, alt. 3,150 ft. Waters are strongly alkaline; fish and small crocodiles abound.

Barinitas (bärēnē′täs), town (pop. 2,070), Barinas state, W Venezuela, on Santo Domingo R., in Andean foothills, and 17 mi. WNW of Barinas; coffee-growing center.

Baripada (bŭrĭpä′dŭ), town (pop. 8,281), ⊙ Mayurbhanj dist., NE Orissa, India, on Burhabalang R. and 115 mi. NNE of Cuttack; market center for rice, timber, honey, hides, lac; hosiery mfg., handloom weaving, pottery making; distillery. Technical institute, archaeological mus.

Bariri (bŏŏrērē′), city (pop. 5,426), central São Paulo, Brazil, near Tietê R., 15 mi. NNW of Jaú; rail-spur terminus in coffee zone; agr. processing (coffee, cotton, rice); cattle raising, lumbering. Formerly spelled Bariry.

Baris, Egypt: see BERIS.

Barisa, India: see SOUTH SUBURBAN.

Bari Sadri (bŭr′ē sä′drē), town (pop. 5,705), S Rajasthan, India, 34 mi. SSW of Chitor, 14 mi. WNW of Chhoti Sadri; corn, millet, wheat.

Barisal (bŏŏkĭsäl′), city (pop. 61,316), ⊙ Bakarganj dist., S East Bengal, E Pakistan, on Arial Khan R. (arm of Ganges Delta) and 70 mi. S of Dacca; trade center (rice, oilseeds, jute, sugar cane, betel nuts); rice, oilseed, and flour milling, mfg. of bricks, soap, ice; general engineering factory.

Barisan Mountains (bärēsän′), volcanic range, Sumatra, Indonesia, extends c.1,000 mi. through almost the whole length of the isl., parallel with W coast; highest peak is Mt. KERINCHI (12,467 ft.). Central part of range is known as PADANG HIGHLANDS, site of coal fields.

Barisciano (bärēshä′nô), town (pop. 2,737), Aquila prov., Abruzzi e Molise, S central Italy, at S foot of Gran Sasso d'Italia, 10 mi. ESE of Aquila.

Baritnaya, Russian SFSR: see MEDVEDEVKA.

Barito River (bärē′tō), Borneo, Indonesia, rises in central part of isl., near Sarawak border, c.180 mi. WNW of Samarinda, flows c.550 mi. generally S, through a marshy delta, past Banjermasin, to Java Sea 16 mi. SSW of Banjermasin. Navigable by ocean-going vessels to Banjermasin.

Bariya (bä′rĭyŭ), village, Panch Mahals dist., N Bombay, India, 20 mi. ESE of Godhra; rail depot for timber, corn. Also called Devgad Bariya (Baria). Was ⊙ former princely state of Bariya (□ 810; pop. 189,062) in Gujarat States, Bombay; inc. 1949 into Panch Mahals dist. Sometimes spelled Baria.

Barjac (bär-zhäk′), village (pop. 702), Gard dept., S France, 19 mi. NE of Alès; lignite and asphalt mining.

Barjols (bär-zhôl′), town (pop. 2,085), Var dept., SE France, in Lower Provence Alps, 23 mi. W of Draguignan; tanning, shoe and varnish mfg. Has 15th-cent. church and numerous fountains.

Barka or **Barkah** (bärkä′), town (pop. 5,000), Batina dist., N Oman, on Gulf of Oman, 40 mi. WNW of Muscat; fishing; date cultivation.

Barka Kana (bŭr′kŭ kä′nŭ), village, Hazaribagh dist., S Bihar, on Chota Nagpur Plateau, near Damodar R., 20 mi. NNE of Ranchi. Coal mines 3 mi. NW.

Barkal (bŭr′kŭl), village, Chittagong Hill Tracts dist., SE East Bengal, E Pakistan, on Karnaphuli R. and 14 mi. ENE of Rangamati; trades in rice, cotton, oilseeds.

Barkal, Jebel, hill, Anglo-Egyptian Sudan: see NAPATA.

Barka River (bär′kä) or **Baraka River** (bä′räkä), Ital. *Barca* or *Baraca*, in Eritrea (c.275 mi.) and Anglo-Egyptian Sudan (c.125 mi.), rises 15 mi. SW of Asmara, flows N, past Agordat and Karkabat, toward Red Sea (reached only during exceptional floods). Seasonally dry, it loses its waters in coastal plain near Tokar. Irrigates cotton fields of Tokar and Karkabat. Along its banks grow dom palms (furnish vegetable ivory). Receives Anseba R.

Barker. 1 Village (1940 pop. 634), Wyandotte co., NE Kansas, on Missouri R. (here forming Mo. line); NW suburb of Kansas City, Kansas. **2** Village (pop. 523), Niagara co., W N.Y., 35 mi. NNE of Buffalo, in fruitgrowing area; flour, canned foods, machinery.

Barker Heights, residential suburb (pop. 1,569) of Hendersonville, Henderson co., W N.C.

Barker Point, N.Y.: see MANHASSET NECK.

Barkerville, village (pop. estimate 300), S central B.C., in Cariboo Mts., 80 mi. SE of Prince George; gold, silver mining. Terminal of Cariboo Road, built 1862–65 from Ashcroft and Yale.

Barkha (bär′kä), Chinese *Pa-erh-k'o* (bär′kô′), village, SW Tibet, in Kailas Range, on main Leh-Lhasa trade route and 80 mi. SE of Gartok; alt. 15,050 ft. Handles pilgrim trade for near-by (S) Manasarowar and Rakas lakes. Also spelled Porkha and Parkha.

Barkhamsted (bärk″hăm′stĭd), town (pop. 946), Litchfield co., N Conn., 18 mi. NW of Hartford and on West and East branches of Farmington R.; dam on East Branch, here, forms Barkhamsted Reservoir (8 mi. long). Includes villages of Pleasant Valley and Riverton (Hitchcock chairs made here after 1818). State forests. Inc. 1779.

Barkhan (bär′khän), village, Loralai dist., NE Baluchistan, W Pakistan, 65 mi. ESE of Loralai; wheat, barley; handicrafts (handbags, saddlebags, embroideries); horse raising.

Barking or **Barking Town,** residential municipal borough (1931 pop. 51,270; 1951 census 78,197), SW Sussex, England, on Roding R. and 10 mi. ENE of London. Site of important pumping station for part of London's water system. Industries include mfg. of chemicals, electrical and radio equipment. There are remains of Benedictine abbey founded c.670.

Barkisland (bär′kĭslŭnd, bäslŭnd), former urban district (1931 pop. 1,552), West Riding, SW Yorkshire, England, 4 mi. SW of Halifax; woolen milling. Inc. 1937 in Ripponden.

Barkley Sound, inlet (16 mi. long, 15 mi. wide) of the Pacific in SW Vancouver Isl., SW B.C., in herring-fishing area; its head is near 49°N 125°W. Alberni Canal extends NE. Numerous small isls. dot the sound. Fishing centers are Ucluelet and Kildonan; there are fish-reduction plants at small settlements of Ecoole, Sechart, San Mateo, Toquart. Bamfield, transpacific cable terminal, is on S shore.

Barkly East, Afrikaans *Barkly-Oos* (bär′klē-ōs′), town (pop. 2,484), E Cape Prov., U. of So. Afr., in Drakensberg range, 55 mi. ESE of Aliwal North;

alt. 5,990 ft.; rail terminus; wool-production center; dairying. Airport.

Barkly Tableland (□ c.30,000), extends c.350 mi. SE from Newcastle Waters, N central Northern Territory, Australia, to Camooweal, Queensland; alt. 600–1,000 ft.; grassy, with some trees; cattle.

Barkly West, Afrikaans *Barkly-Wes* (bär'klē-vĕs'), town (pop. 2,683), N Cape Prov., near Orange Free State border, U. of So. Afr., in Griqualand West, on Vaal R. (bridge) and 20 mi. NW of Kimberley, on edge of Kaap Plateau; diamond-mining center; stock, fruit. Airfield.

Barkol or **Barkul** (bär'kōl'), Chinese *Chensi* or *Chen-hsi* (both: jŭn'shē'), town, ⊙ Barkol co. (pop. 19,097), E Sinkiang prov., China, in easternmost Tien Shan, on branch of Silk Road and 60 mi. NW of Hami, near the lake Bar Kol; wool textiles; millet, corn, medicinal plants.

Bark River, SE Wis., rises in small lake in Washington co., flows c.40 mi. SW through a lake region, past Hartland, to Scuppernong R. 4 mi. N of Whitewater.

Barksdale. 1 Village (pop. c.200), Edwards co., SW Texas, on Edwards Plateau, on Nueces R., c.40 mi. NNW of Uvalde; trading point in ranching area (goats, sheep, cattle). **2** Village, Bayfield co., extreme N Wis., on SW shore of Chequamegon Bay, 4 mi. NW of Ashland; produces chemicals and explosives.

Barksdale Air Force Base, La.: see SHREVEPORT.

Barkuhi, India: see CHHINDWARA, town, Chhindwara dist., Madhya Pradesh.

Barkul, China: see BARKOL.

Barlad (bûr'läd), Rum. *Bârlad*, town (1948 pop. 24,035), ⊙ Barlad prov., E Rumania, in Moldavia, on Barlad R. and 140 mi. NE of Bucharest; rail junction and trading center (corn, livestock, hides, wool, lumber), with annual fairs; flour milling, tobacco and food processing, mfg. of soap, ice, textiles. Has 18th-cent. church. Dates from 11th cent. Occupied (1944) by USSR troops. Formerly sometimes spelled Berlad.

Barla Dag (bärlä' dä), Turkish *Barla Dağ*, peak (8,970 ft.), W central Turkey, 14 mi. NNE of Egridir.

Barlad River (bûr'läd), Rum. *Bârlad*, E Rumania, in Moldavia, rises 10 mi. E of Roman, flows in a broad curve S past Vaslui, Barlad, and Tecuci, to Siret R. 3 mi. below Ivesti; c.110 mi. long.

Barlaston, village and parish (pop. 1,202), N central Stafford, England, near Trent R., 4 mi. S of Stoke-on-Trent; pottery.

Barlborough, town and parish (pop. 1,980), NE Derby, England, 10 mi. SE of Sheffield; coal mining. Has 13th-cent. church and, near by, 16th-cent. Barlborough Hall.

Barleben (bär'lā"bŭn), residential village (pop. 6,372), in former Prussian Saxony prov., central Germany, after 1945 in Saxony-Anhalt, 5 mi. N of Magdeburg; electrical-equipment mfg.

Bar-le-Duc (bär-lü-dük'), town (pop. 14,015), ⊙ Meuse dept., NE France, on Ornain R. and Marne-Rhine Canal, and 50 mi. W of Nancy; mfg. (cotton textiles, fruit preserves and jellies, beer, sparkling wines), founding, printing. In picturesque winegrowing valley, it has many 16th–18th-cent. houses, and a 15th–16th-cent. church (containing sculpture by Richier). Was ⊙ of medieval county, later duchy, of Bar. Connected by "Sacred Road" with besieged Verdun during First World War, it was important road center.

Barlee, Lake (bär'lē'), (□ 550), SW central Western Australia, 250 mi. NE of Perth; 70 mi. long; usually dry.

Barle River, W Somerset, England, rises on Exmoor, flows 20 mi. SE, past Dulverton, to Exe R. 2 mi. SE of Dulverton.

Barletta (bärlĕt'tä), city (pop. 51,597), Bari prov., Apulia, S Italy, port on the Adriatic, 33 mi. WNW of Bari. Industrial and commercial center; wine, alcohol, canned foods, candy, chemicals, pharmaceuticals, soap, cement; tannery, foundry. Exports wine, chemicals, cement. Archbishopric. Has cathedral (12th–15th cent.), church of San Sepolcro with 12th-cent. frescoes, medieval castle, and 14-ft.-high bronze statue of a Byzantine emperor.

Barlin (bärlē'), town (pop. 8,479), Pas-de-Calais dept., N France, 5 mi. S of Béthune; coal-mining center. Lime and cement works.

Barlinek (bärlē'nĕk), Ger. *Berlinchen* (bĕrlēn'khŭn), town (1939 pop. 7,595; 1946 pop. 2,686) in Brandenburg, after 1945 in Szczecin prov., NW Poland, on small lake, 18 mi. N of Landsberg (Gorzow Wielkopolski); mfg. (furniture, agr. implements). Founded 1278. After 1945, briefly called Berlinek.

Barliyar, India: see COONOOR.

Barlovento (bärlōvĕn'tō), town (pop. 279), Palma, Canary Isls., 9 mi. N of Santa Cruz de la Palma; cereals, potatoes, bananas, onions; timber. Charcoal burning, tile mfg.

Barlow (–lō), agr. village and parish (pop. 967), N Derby, England, 4 mi. NW of Chesterfield; abandoned coal mines. Has 14th-cent. church.

Barlow. 1 Town (pop. 657), Ballard co., SW Ky., 25 mi. W of Paducah, in agr. area; canned vegetables, lumber. Fishing (small lakes), hunting near by. **2** City (pop. 75), Clackamas co., NW Oregon, 9 mi. SW of Oregon City.

Barmbeck (bärm'bĕk), NE residential district of Hamburg, Germany, adjoining Eilbeck (S) and Wandsbek (SE); site of insane asylum.

Barmedman (bär'mĭdmŭn), village (pop. 535), S central New South Wales, Australia, 130 mi. NW of Canberra; rail junction; tin-mining center.

Barmen (bär'mŭn), E section (1925 pop. 187,099) of WUPPERTAL, W Germany, on the Wupper; textile-mfg. center (since 18th cent.); metal working. Chartered 1808. Interurban suspension tramway opened here in 1903. Inc. (1929) with Elberfeld (just W) and other neighboring towns to form city of Wuppertal.

Barmer (bŭrmār'), town (pop. 12,051), W Rajasthan, India, on railroad and 110 mi. WSW of Jodhpur, on Thar Desert; trade center for wool, camels, sheep, salt; handicraft making of millstones, camel fittings, leather bags. Fuller's earth quarried near by.

Barmera (bär'mŭrŭ), village (pop. 933), SE South Australia, 125 mi. NE of Adelaide; rail terminus; orchards.

Barmouth (bär'mŭth), Welsh *Abermawddach* (ăbŭr-mou'dhäkh), urban district (1931 pop. 2,489; 1951 census 2,466), W Merioneth, Wales, on Cardigan Bay of Irish Sea, at mouth of Mawddach R., 7 mi. W of Dolgelley; seaside resort; manganese mining. On Cardigan Bay, 2 mi. NNE, is agr. village and parish of Llanaber (lănä'bŭr) (pop. 600), with early 13th-cent. church.

Barmstedt (bärm'shtĕt), town (pop. 8,489), in Schleswig-Holstein, NW Germany, 5 mi. NE of Elmshorn; mfg. of shoes; leather, tobacco, wax products; furniture. Meat canning. Tree nurseries and horticulture (roses) in vicinity.

Bärn, Czechoslovakia: see MORAVSKY BEROUN.

Barnabus (bär'nŭbŭs), village (pop. 3,073, with adjoining Omar), Logan co., SW W.Va., 8 mi. S of Logan, in coal-mining region.

Barnaby Island (3 mi. long), E Que., in the St. Lawrence, just off Rimouski.

Barnacre with Bonds, agr. parish (pop. 1,346), NW Lancashire, England, just E of Garstang; cattle raising, dairying. Has cotton mill and paper mill.

Barnagar (bŭr'nŭgŭr), town (pop. 11,985), W Madhya Bharat, India, 26 mi. WSW of Ujjain; trades in wheat, cotton, opium; cotton ginning, hand-loom weaving.

Barnala (bŭrnä'lŭ), town (pop. 12,341), central Patiala and East Punjab States Union, India, 50 mi. W of Patiala; agr. market (wheat, gram, millet, cotton); cotton ginning, hand-loom weaving; steel-rolling mill.

Barnard. 1 (bär'nŭrd) City (pop. 242), Lincoln co., N central Kansas, on small affluent of Solomon R. and 32 mi. NW of Salina; livestock, grain. **2** (bär'-nŭrd) Plantation (pop. 66), Piscataquis co., central Maine, 10 mi. NE of Dover-Foxcroft. **3** (bärnärd') Town (pop. 275), Nodaway co., NW Mo., on One Hundred and Two R. and 12 mi. S of Maryville. **4** (bär'nŭrd) Town (pop. 439), Windsor co., central Vt., 20 mi. NE of Rutland; summer resort; lumber.

Barnard, Mount (14,003 ft.), E Calif., in the Sierra Nevada, c.4 mi. NNW of Mt. Whitney and on E boundary of Sequoia Natl. Park.

Barnard Castle (bär'nŭrd), urban district (1931 pop. 3,884; 1951 census 4,433), SW Durham, England, on Tees R. and 15 mi. W of Darlington; woolen milling; agr. market. Has art mus. and remains of castle built (1112–32) by Barnard Baliol. Rokeby is SSE, in Yorkshire.

Bärnau (bĕr'nou), town (pop. 2,086), Upper Palatinate, NE Bavaria, Germany, in the Bohemian Forest, 6 mi. SE of Tirschenreuth, near Czechoslovak border; rail terminus; mfg. of textiles, mother-of-pearl buttons; woodworking. Chartered 1343.

Barnaul (bŭrnŭōōl'), city (1926 pop. 73,858; 1939 pop. 148,129; 1947 pop. estimate 200,000), ⊙ Altai Territory, Russian SFSR, in SW Siberia, on left bank of Ob R., at mouth of short Barnaulka R., and 120 mi. SSE of Novosibirsk; 53°21'N 83°48'E. Industrial and transportation center at junction of Turksib and S.Siberian RRs; ship repair and freight yards; cotton milling (Central Asian raw cotton), mfg. (clothing, shoes, sheepskins, machines, lathes, boilers); food processing (flour, dairy products, meat, sugar); growing chemical industry (based on Kulunda Steppe soda). Site of agr., agr. machinery, and teachers colleges, meteorological observatory, geological mus., mining school. Founded 1738 as gold- and silver-refining center; became, after 1900, center of important newly-settled agr. area. Its development as industrial and rail center dates from 1930s.

Bärnbach (bĕrn'bäkh), town (pop. 3,687), Styria, S Austria, 14 mi. W of Graz; wheat, potatoes, cattle.

Barn Bluff, peak (5,114 ft.), W central Tasmania, near Cradle Mtn. in natl. park.

Barnby Dun with Kirk Sandall, England: see KIRK SANDALL.

Barnegat (bär'nŭgăt), village (1940 pop. 881), Ocean co., E N.J., 2 mi. inland from Barnegat Bay, 13 mi. S of Toms River; mfg. (hosiery, shingles, boats).

Barnegat Bay, E N.J., arm of the Atlantic extending c.30 mi. along coast; protected by Island Beach peninsula and Long Beach isl., sites of many resorts. Entered from ocean through Barnegat Inlet, N of Barnegat Light borough, site of famous old Barnegat Lighthouse. Bay is link in N.J. sec. of Intracoastal Waterway, which enters N end through Bayhead-Manasquan Canal at Bay Head village, and continues S into Manahawkin Bay.

Barnegat Light, borough (pop. 227), Ocean co., E N.J., at N end of Long Beach isl., on Barnegat Inlet (entrance to Barnegat Bay) and 14 mi. SSE of Toms River; fishing. Site of abandoned Barnegat Lighthouse (1855), replaced (1930) by lightship. Formerly Barnegat City.

Barnes, residential municipal borough (1931 pop. 42,440; 1951 census 40,558), N Surrey, England, on the Thames and 6 mi. WSW of London. In the borough (W) is MORTLAKE.

Barnes (bärnz), county (□ 1,486; pop. 16,884), SE N.Dak.; ⊙ Valley City. Agr. area drained by Sheyenne R. Wheat, oats, barley, potatoes; flour milling, dairy products. Formed 1871.

Barnes, city (pop. 308), Washington co., N Kansas, 36 mi. NNW of Manhattan; grain; dairying.

Barnesboro, borough (pop. 3,442), Cambria co., SW central Pa., 25 mi. NNE of Johnstown and on West Branch of Susquehanna R.; bituminous coal; clothing, beverages; crushed stone. Laid out 1891, inc. 1893.

Barnes City, town (pop. 326), on Mahaska-Poweshiek co. line, S central Iowa, near South Fork English R., 17 mi. NNE of Oskaloosa.

Barneston, village (pop. 208), Gage co., SE Nebr., 17 mi. SSE of Beatrice and on Big Blue R., near Kansas line. Post office name formerly Barnston.

Barnesville. 1 City (pop. 4,185), ⊙ Lamar co., W central Ga., 13 mi. SSE of Griffin; trade and processing center for agr. and timber area; mfg. (clothing, tire fabric, furniture, lumber). Gordon Military (jr.) Col. Settled c.1825, inc. 1854. **2** Town (pop. 130), Montgomery co., central Md., 30 mi. NW of Washington; dairying. **3** City (pop. 1,593), Clay co., W Minn., 24 mi. SE of Fargo, N. Dak., in Red R. valley; shipping point for grain, potatoes, livestock; dairy products, poultry. Railroad shops. **4** City (pop. 4,665), Belmont co., E Ohio, 26 mi. WSW of Wheeling, W.Va.; mfg. (machinery, textiles, clothing, glass, cigars, dairy products).

Barnet (bär'nĭt), village, SW B.C., on Burrard Inlet, just E of Vancouver; lumber-shipping port.

Barnet, residential urban district (1931 pop. 14,726; 1951 census 25,017), S Hertford, England, 11 mi. NNW of London; electrical equipment, leather. Obelisk marks spot where Warwick was killed in battle (1471) bet. Lancastrians and Yorkists. Has 15th-cent. church. Urban dist. includes residential dists. of South Mimms (3 mi. N), Chipping Barnet (SW), and Arkley (W).

Barnet (bär'nĭt), town (pop. 1,425), Caledonia co., NE Vt., on the Connecticut (site of Fifteen-Mile Falls Dam, with large power plant) and 8 mi. S of St. Johnsbury. Includes villages of West Barnet (pop. 88; resort on Harvey Pond), East Barnet (wood products), and Passumpsic, on Passumpsic R. Settled 1770.

Barnett, town (pop. 200), Morgan co., central Mo., near L. of the Ozarks, 10 mi. ESE of Versailles.

Barnett Shoals, town (1940 pop. 18), Oconee co., NE central Ga., 9 mi. SSE of Athens and on Oconee R.

Barneveld (bär'nŭvĕlt), town (pop. 5,748), Gelderland prov., central Netherlands, 17 mi. WSW of Apeldoorn; poultry-raising center, egg market; leather goods, bicycle parts, wood products; beekeeping. Old church tower.

Barneveld (bär'nŭvĕld). **1** Village, N.Y.: see TRENTON. **2** Village (pop. 373), Iowa co., S Wis., 26 mi. WSW of Madison, in dairying region.

Barnevelt Islands, small rocky group in Tierra del Fuego, Chile, 20 mi. NE of Cape Horn; 55°50'S 66°50'W.

Barneville or **Barneville-sur-Mer** (bärnvēl'-sür-mâr'), village (pop. 660), Manche dept., NW France, on the Channel, on W coast of Cotentin Peninsula, 18 mi. SSW of Cherbourg; mfg. of building materials; horse raising, dairying in area. Bathing beach 1 mi. SW.

Barney, town (pop. 157), Brooks co., S Ga., 18 mi. NW of Valdosta.

Barney, Mount, Australia: see MCPHERSON RANGE.

Barnhart, village (pop. c.250), Irion co., W Texas, 50 mi. SW of San Angelo; livestock-shipping point.

Barnhart Island, St. Lawrence co., N N.Y., in the St. Lawrence, at Ont. line, 5 mi. NE of Massena; c.3 mi. long, ½–1½ mi. wide.

Barnhill, village (pop. 392), Tuscarawas co., E Ohio, 5 mi. ESE of New Philadelphia.

Barnihat (bŭr'nĭhät), village, Khasi and Jaintia Hills dist., W Assam, India, in Jaintia Hills, 32 mi. N of Shillong; rice, sesamum. Citrus fruit research station.

Barnoldswick (bärnōldz'wĭk, bär'lĭk), urban district (1931 pop. 11,914; 1951 census 10,282), West Riding, W Yorkshire, England, 8 mi. WSW of Skipton; cotton milling. Has old church (1524).

Barnsdall (bärnz'dôl), city (pop. 1,708), Osage co., N Okla., 12 mi. SE of Pawhuska, and on Bird Creek, in oil-producing and stock-raising area. Oil refineries; bleach mfg. Called Bigheart until 1921.

Barnsley, county borough (1931 pop. 71,522; 1951 census 75,625), West Riding, S Yorkshire, England, on Dearne R. and 12 mi. N of Sheffield; rail and industrial center; coal mining, linen milling, mfg. of machinery, clothing, paper, chemicals. In county borough (NE) is residential town of Monk Bretton, with chemical works and remains of Cluniac priory founded 1157.

Barns Ness, cape on North Sea, E East Lothian, Scotland, 3 mi. ESE of Dunbar; lighthouse (55°59'N 2°26'W).

Barnstable (bärn'stŭbŭl), county (□ 399; pop. 46,805), SE Mass., coextensive with CAPE COD; ⊙ Barnstable. Summer resort area with many fine beaches; its small winter population is swelled by a great influx of summer visitors and residents. Some agr., mostly in S; large quantities of cranberries are grown. Its oysters are famous; some fishing, particularly at Provincetown. In early 19th cent. a shipbuilding, shipping, and whaling center. Business center, Hyannis. Formed 1685.

Barnstable, town (pop. 10,480), ⊙ Barnstable co., SE Mass., extending across central Cape Cod, 25 mi. SE of Plymouth; summer resort; cranberries, truck, oysters. Has several 18th-cent. buildings. Grew as fishing, farming, shipping center; became resort in 20th cent. State game farm, hatchery. Includes resort villages of Barnstable (⊙ Barnstable co.), HYANNIS, Hyannis Port, Cotuit (kŭtū'ĭt) (noted for oysters), Santuit (săntū'ĭt), Centerville (1940 pop. 522), Osterville (pop. 1,003), West Barnstable (1940 pop. 556), Wianno (wēä'nō), Craigville, Marstons Mills. Settled 1639.

Barnstaple (bärn'stŭpŭl) or **Barum** (bâ'rŭm), port and municipal borough (1931 pop. 14,700; 1951 census 16,302), N Devon, England, on Taw R. estuary and 35 mi. NW of Exeter; 51°4'N 4°3'W. Mfg. of pottery ("Barum ware"), shoes, gloves, lace, clothing; metal- and woodworking, tanning; agr. market and resort. Food and clay products are exported. Has 13th-cent. bridge, 14th-cent. church, and Elizabethan school attended by John Gay. Annual Barnstaple Fair is centuries old.

Barnstaple Bay or **Bideford Bay** (bĭ'dŭfŭrd), N Devon, England, inlet of Bristol Channel bet. Hartland Point (SW) and Baggy Point (NE); 15 mi. wide, 7 mi. long. Receives Taw R. and Torridge R.

Barnstead, town (pop. 846), Belknap co., central N.H., on Suncook R. and 17 mi. NE of Concord; small mfg.; summer colony.

Barnston, Nebr.: see BARNESTON.

Barnstone, England: see LANGAR CUM BARNSTONE.

Barntrup (bärn'trōōp), town (pop. 3,514), in former Lippe, NW Germany, after 1945 in North Rhine-Westphalia, 6 mi. W of Bad Pyrmont; woodworking. Has Renaissance castle.

Barnum, village (1939 pop. 27), SW Alaska, near Kuskokwim Bay, 20 mi. NE of Platinum; platinum mining.

Barnum. 1 Town (pop. 193), Webster co., central Iowa, 9 mi. W of Fort Dodge; livestock, grain. **2** Village (pop. 344), Carlton co., E Minn., on branch of Kettle R. and 33 mi. SW of Duluth; egg-producing center in livestock, poultry, potato area; dairy products.

Barnwell, county (□ 553; pop. 17,266), W S.C.; ⊙ Barnwell. Bounded W by Savannah R., NE by South Fork of Edisto R. Includes most of U.S. Atomic Energy Commission installation along Savannah R. Agr. area (asparagus, melons, cucumbers, cotton); lumber; naval stores. Formed 1785.

Barnwell, town (pop. 2,005), ⊙ Barnwell co., W S.C., 33 mi. SW of Orangeburg, in agr. area; turpentine, lumber; cotton gins. Settled 1798, inc. 1842.

Barnwood, town and parish (pop. 1,829), N central Gloucester, England, 2 mi. E of Gloucester; concrete works. Site of 2 large mental hospitals. Has 15th-cent. church.

Baro (bä'rō), town (pop. 217), Niger prov., Northern Provinces, W central Nigeria, port on Niger R. and 70 mi. S of Minna (linked by rail spur); sheanut processing, wine, sackmaking; roofing timber; cotton, cassava, yams, durra.

Baroda (bŭrō'dŭ), former princely state (□ 8,236; pop. 2,855,010), W India; ⊙ was Baroda. Comprised several detached areas geographically within N Bombay and on Kathiawar peninsula; major subdivisions were Baroda, Mehsana, Navsari, Amreli. Upon breakup of Mogul empire in 18th cent., state rose to importance as independent Mahratta kingdom under successive Gaikwars; made treaty 1805 with British. In 1944, merged with Western India and Gujarat states to form 1 large agency under govt. of India. Merged 1948 with Bombay; in 1949, divided into 3 newly-created dists. of Baroda, Mehsana, and Amreli, while other parts were inc. into Surat and Kaira dists. Former state was also called the Gaikwar's (Gaekwar's) Dominions.

Baroda, district (created 1949), N Bombay, India; ⊙ Baroda. Bounded S by Narbada R., NW by Mahi R. Agr. (rice, cotton, millet); cotton ginning, handloom weaving. Manganese mined in NE section. Baroda city is large cotton-milling center; other centers include Dabhoi (rail junction), Padra, and Sankheda. Dist. comprises most of Baroda div. of former Baroda state, former Gujarat state of Chota Udaipur, and numerous former petty states (NW, S).

Baroda. 1 City (pop., including NW cantonment area, 153,301), ⊙ Baroda dist., N Bombay, India, 230 mi. N of Bombay, in Gujarat; road and rail junction; cotton-milling center; agr. market (cotton, millet, rice); mfg. of chemicals, matches, handicraft cloth, rubber goods, machinery, furniture, hosiery, soap, cigarettes; calico printing, dyeing, woolen milling; enamel factory, liquor distillery, flour mills, ordnance factory and depot. Col., mus., technical and commercial schools. Was ⊙ former princely state of Baroda. Goya Gate (S) has cotton mill, metalworks, and soap factory. **2** Village, N Madhya Bharat, India, 12 mi. S of Sheopur; millet, wheat, gram; wood carving.

Baroda (bŭrō'dŭ), village (pop. 344), Berrien co., extreme SW Mich., 10 mi. S of St. Joseph, near L. Michigan, in orchard and farm area.

Baroghil Pass (bŭrōgēl', bŭrō'gĭl) (alt. 12,460 ft.), in E Hindu Kush, on Afghanistan-Pakistan (Chitral) line; 36°54'N 73°23'E. Links upper Kunar and Wakhan river valleys. Also spelled Broghil.

Barolli, India: see BHAINSRORGARH.

Baron, village, Adair co., E Okla., 8 mi. N of Stilwell, near Ark. line; vegetable canning, charcoal burning; fishing.

Baron Bluff, headland on N St. Croix Isl., U.S. Virgin Isls., 5½ mi. NW of Christiansted; 17°47'N 64°47'W; rises to 395 ft.

Baronissi (bärōnēs'sē), town (pop. 2,697), Salerno prov., Campania, S Italy, 5 mi. N of Salerno; tomato canning, macaroni mfg.

Baronnies (bärônē'), hilly region in Dauphiné Pre-Alps, Drôme dept., SE France, around Nyons. Cattle raising, fruit and winegrowing. Poor communications. In process of depopulation.

Barons, village (pop. 270), S Alta., 24 mi. NNW of Lethbridge; wheat, dairying.

Baronsk, Russian SFSR: see MARKS.

Baro River (bä'rō), SW Ethiopia, rises in highlands 10 mi. S of Gore, flows c.190 mi. W, joining Pibor R. at Anglo-Egyptian Sudan border to form SOBAT RIVER. Navigable (May-Oct.) to GAMBELA for boats drawing less than 3 ft. Receives Birbir R. Its valley, malarial and infested by tsetse fly in lower part, has gold and platinum deposits.

Barot, Rumania: see BARAOLT.

Barotac Nuevo (bärōtäk' nwä'vō), town (1939 pop. 1,979; 1948 municipality pop. 21,860), Iloilo prov., E Panay isl., Philippines, 16 mi. NE of Iloilo; agr. center (sugar cane, rice); sugar milling.

Barotac Viejo (vyä'hō), town (1939 pop. 1,688; 1948 municipality pop. 16,732), Iloilo prov., E Panay isl., Philippines, 31 mi. NE of Iloilo; rice-growing center.

Barotse or **Barotseland** (bŭrŏt'sŭlănd), province (□ 63,000; pop. 260,000) of W Northern Rhodesia; ⊙ Mongu. Bounded W by Angola, S by Caprivi Strip of South-West Africa; drained by Zambezi R.; mainly savanna grasslands. Livestock (cattle, sheep, goats) and agr. (corn, millet) region. Hardwood (teak, mahogany) lumbering; fishing. Main centers: Mongu, Sesheke. The prov. is a native reserve, with hq. at Lealui, 8 mi. W of Mongu.

Barouéli (bärwĕlē'), village, S Fr. Sudan, Fr. West Africa, 80 mi. ENE of Bamako; peanuts, cotton, millet, shea nuts; livestock. Dispensary.

Barouk, Lebanon: see BARUK, EL.

Barpeta (bŭrpā'tŭ), town (pop. 18,466), Kamrup dist., W Assam, India, in Brahmaputra valley, 47 mi. W of Gauhati; trades in rice, mustard, jute, cotton. Has Vishnuite col. (founded 15th cent.).

Barqa, Libya: see CYRENAICA; BARCE.

Barquisimeto (bärkēsēmā'tō), city (1941 pop. 54,176; 1950 census 105,080), ⊙ Lara State, NW Venezuela, on headstream of Cojedes R. bet. coastal range and great Andean spur Sierra Nevada de Mérida, at S edge of arid Segovia Highlands, on Pan American Highway and 165 mi. WSW of Caracas; 10°4'N 69°18'W; alt. 1,857 ft. Terminus of railroad from Tucacas and Puerto Cabello on the Caribbean. Third largest city of Venezuela; commercial and industrial center in agr. region producing cattle, coffee, cacao, sugar cane, sisal, cereals, tobacco, goats, hides, which are exported. Mfg. (fiber sandals, hammocks, bags, tobacco goods, vegetable oil, soap, candles, ceramics, cement, leather products); flour and sugar milling, tanning, sawmilling. Airport. Bishopric. Has educational institutions, theater, fine parks and bldgs. Founded 1552, near present location, as Nueva Segovia. Career of infamous Lope de Aguirre ended here (1561). The city was destroyed by an earthquake in 1812.

Barquisimeto River, Venezuela: see COJEDES RIVER.

Barquito (bärkē'tō), village (1930 pop. 666), Atacama prov., N Chile, on small Pacific bay, and 3 mi. SW of Chañaral; 26°24'S. Rail terminus and base for inland copper mines. Its steam-generating plant supplies power to Potrerillos mines, 75 mi. inland.

Barr (bär), town (pop. 4,316), Bas-Rhin dept., E France, at E foot of the Vosges, 11 mi. N of Sélestat; a leading tanning and leather-mfg. center of France. Also makes chairs, footwear; wool spinning, winegrowing. Has many old houses. Resort.

Barr, agr. village and parish (pop. 494), S Ayrshire, Scotland, on Stinchar R. and 6 mi. ESE of Girvan; angling resort.

Barra (bä'rŭ), city (pop. 4,065), NW Bahia, Brazil, on left bank of São Francisco R. at influx of the Rio Grande, and 200 mi. SW of Juàzeiro; river trade center (navigation on both streams); ships cotton, cattle, fruit, maniçoba rubber, carnauba wax. Also called Barra do Rio Grande.

Barra (bä'rä), village (pop. 366), Western Div., Gambia, on the Atlantic, at mouth of Gambia R., opposite Bathurst (2½ mi. SW; ferry); police post.

Barra (bär'rä), town (pop. 16,689), Napoli prov., Campania, S Italy, 3 mi. E of Naples.

Barra (bă'rŭ), island (pop. 2,001), S Outer Hebrides, Inverness, Scotland, 5 mi. S of South Uist across the Sound of Barra; 8 mi. long, 5 mi. wide. Highest alt., 1,260 ft. Castlebay, chief town, in S part of isl., is herring-fishing center, with ruins of 15th-cent. Kisamul Castle. Barra, with a number of near-by smaller isls. (including Bernera, Mingulay, Vatersay, and Sandray), forms a parish (□ 34.7; pop. 2,250).

Barra, La, Mexico: see LA BARRA.

Barraba (bă'rŭbŭ), municipality (pop. 1,461), E New South Wales, Australia, 190 mi. NNW of Newcastle; terminus of railroad from Tamworth; gold-mining center.

Barra Bonita (bä'rŭ bōōnē'tŭ). **1** City, Paraná, Brazil: see IBAITI. **2** City (pop. 2,689), central São Paulo, Brazil, on Tietê R., on railroad and 15 mi. S of Jaú; mfg. of tile; dairy products, coffee, grain.

Barraca Concepción, Bolivia: see CONCEPCIÓN, Beni dept.

Barracas al Sud, Argentina: see AVELLANEDA, city, Buenos Aires prov.

Barrackpore (băr'ŭkpôr), Bengali *Chanak*, town (pop. 59,717), 24-Parganas dist., S West Bengal, India, on Hooghly R. and 14 mi. N of Calcutta city center; comprises North Barrackpore (pop. 26,966), Barrackpore (pop. 21,773), and former cantonment area (pop. 10,978). Jute and rice milling, sawmilling, hosiery mfg. Agr. Inst. Former residence of Viceroy of India. Figured in Sepoy rebellions of 1824 and 1857.

Barraco (bärä'kō), town (pop. 2,451), Ávila prov., central Spain, 13 mi. S of Ávila; wheat, rye, barley, carobs, chick-peas, potatoes, grapes, livestock. Lumbering, flour milling.

Barracón, Argentina: see BERNARDO DE IRIGOYEN, Misiones natl. territory.

Barra da Estiva (bä'rŭ dä ĭstē'vŭ), city (pop. 756), central Bahia, Brazil, in Serra do Sincorá, 60 mi. S of Andaraí; diamond mining and gold mining are carried on.

Barra de Aguán, Honduras: see AGUÁN.

Barra de Colorado (bä'rä dā kōlōrä'dō), village, Limón prov., NE Costa Rica, minor port on Caribbean Sea, at mouth of the Río Colorado (a branch of San Juan R. delta), 40 mi. NNE of Guápiles. Fishing, lumbering. Exports bananas, coconuts, turtles. Sometimes called Colorado.

Barra de Limón, Honduras: see LIMÓN.

Barra de Río Grande, Nicaragua: see RÍO GRANDE, village.

Barra de Santiago (bä'rä dā säntyä'gō), village (pop. estimate 200), Ahuachapán dept., W Salvador, on the Pacific, at mouth of short Santiago R., 18 mi. WNW of Acajutla; beach resort; fisheries.

Barra de São Francisco (bärŭ dĭ sä'ō frăsē'skōō), city, NW Espírito Santo, Brazil, claimed as **Mantena** by Minas Gerais, in disputed Serra dos Aimorés region, 50 mi. W of São Mateus; coffee, bananas, manioc.

Barra do Ariranha, Minas Gerais, Brazil: see AMETISTA, Espírito Santo.

Barra do Bugres (bä'rŭ dōō bōō'grĭs), city (pop. 571), W central Mato Grosso, Brazil, on upper Paraguay R. and 80 mi. WNW of Cuiabá; ipecac roots collected and shipped from here.

Barra do Corda (kôr'dŭ), city (pop. 2,079), central Maranhão, Brazil, on upper Mearim R. (navigable) and 140 mi. SW of Caxias; cattle, hides, resins. Roads to Coroatá and Carolina. Gypsum deposits in area.

Barra do Dande (dăn'dĭ), village, Congo prov., NW Angola, on the Atlantic at mouth of short Dande R., 25 mi. NNE of Luanda; palm oil, cotton, manioc.

Barra do Garças (gär'sŭs), city (pop. 281), E Mato Grosso, Brazil, on left bank of Araguaia R. (Goiás border) at influx of Garças R., and 250 mi. E of Cuiabá. Base for exploratory expeditions into the interior of Goiás and Mato Grosso. Site of Aragarças airfield.

Barra do Piraí (pērăē'), city (1950 pop. 20,254), W Rio de Janeiro state, Brazil, on Paraíba R., 50 mi. NW of Rio; important rail junction; chemical- and metalworks; textile and match mfg., distilling, dairying. Paper mill, meat-packing plant at Mendes (7 mi. SE). Formerly spelled Barra do Pirahy.

Barra do Quaraí (kwŭrăē'), town (pop. 811), southwesternmost Rio Grande do Sul, Brazil, on Quaraí R. (Uruguay border; international bridge) near its influx into Uruguay R., frontier station on railroad, and 40 mi. SW of Uruguaiana, just NE of Cuareim and Bella Unión (Uruguay). Railroad station. Also called Quaraím (old spelling, Quarahim).

Barra do Ribeiro (rēbä'rōō), town (pop. 1,995), E Rio Grande do Sul, Brazil, 20 mi. SSW of Pôrto Alegre, on opposite bank of Guaíba R.; grain, cattle.

Barra do Rio de Contas, Brazil: see ITACARÉ.

Barra do Rio Grande, Brazil: see BARRA.

Barrafranca (bär"räfräng'kä), town (pop. 13,111), Enna prov., S central Sicily, 11 mi. SE of Caltanissetta. Sulphur mines (SE).

Barrage de la Gileppe (bäräzh' dü lä zhēlĕp'), reservoir (200 acres), Liége prov., E Belgium, on Gileppe R. (small S branch of Vesdre R.) and 4 mi. SW of Eupen; supplies Verviers. Dam is 771 ft. long, 48 ft. wide, 154 ft. high; completed 1878.

Barrage de la Warche (wärsh'), hydroelectric power station, Liége prov., E Belgium, on Warche R. and 5 mi. ENE of Malmédy. Just N is village of Robertville (pop. 1,718).

Barra Head, Scotland: see BERNERA.

Barral (bäräl'), village (pop. 791), Constantine dept., NE Algeria, on the Oued Seybouse, on railroad and 18 mi. S of Bône; olive-oil milling, cork gathering.

Barra Mansa (bä'rü mã'sü), city (1950 pop. 21,344), W Rio de Janeiro, Brazil, on right bank of Paraíba R. and 65 mi. WNW of Rio; rail junction with spurs to Angra dos Reis and Bananal (São Paulo). Industrial center with metalworks (plumbing fixtures, tin sheets), flour and textile (cotton and silk) mills; dairying, lard processing, distilling. Volta Redonda steel mill 5 mi. ENE.

Barranca (bäräng'kä), village, Puntarenas prov., W Costa Rica, on the Pacific, near base of Puntarenas peninsula, rail junction (spur to Esparta) at mouth of Barranca R. (small coastal stream), 6 mi. E of Puntarenas. Seaside resort.

Barranca. 1 Town (pop. 3,873), Lima dept., W central Peru, on coastal plain, on Pan-American Highway and 27 mi. NNW of Huacho. Terminus of railroad from Supe, in cotton-growing area; cotton ginning, cotton-seed milling; railroad shops. **2** Town (pop. 192), Loreto dept., N central Peru, landing on Marañón R. and 80 mi. NW of Yurimaguas; 4°52'S 76°40'W; sugar cane, bananas; liquor distilling.

Barrancabermeja (bäräng"kābĕrmā'hä), town (pop. 9,307), Santander dept., N central Colombia, river port on E bank of the Magdalena, in Mares oil concession, 50 mi. W of Bucaramanga and on highway to Bogotá. Major petroleum-drilling and -refining center; mfg. of gasoline, asphalt, lubricants, and other petroleum products. A pipe line runs to Cartagena on the Caribbean, and a short rail line extends to Infantas, 15 mi. SSE, serving oil wells of El Centro in Infantas field. Sometimes Barranca Bermeja.

Barranca de Oblatos (bäräng'kä dā ōblä'tōs), gorge of Santiago R., Jalisco, central Mexico, near Guadalajara; c.2,000 ft. deep; tourist site.

Barrancas (bäräng'käs). **1** Village, Mendoza prov., Argentina: see LAS BARRANCAS. **2** Town (pop. estimate 2,000), S central Santa Fe prov., Argentina, 55 mi. NNW of Rosario; agr. and livestock center; flour milling, processing of flax fibers; grain elevators.

Barrancas, town (pop. 1,810), Santiago prov., central Chile, 5 mi. W of Santiago; residential suburb.

Barrancas, town (pop. 1,542), Magdalena dept., N Colombia, on Ranchería R. and 40 mi. S of Ríohacha; rice, livestock.

Barrancas. 1 Town (pop. 583), Barinas state, W Venezuela, 12 mi. NE of Barinas; cattle raising. **2** Town (pop. 1,276), Monagas state, NE Venezuela, landing on lower Orinoco R. (at head of delta), and 27 mi. SSW of Tucupita, in cattle-raising region.

Barrancas, Las, Argentina: see LAS BARRANCAS.

Barrancas River, W Argentina, on Mendoza-Neuquén border, rises in the Andes near Chile line, flows c.75 mi. SE to join the Río Grande, forming the Río Colorado.

Barranco (bäräng'kō), S section (pop. 18,625) of Lima, Lima dept., W central Peru, beach resort on the Pacific, just N of Chorrillos; favorite residence of foreigners. Wine festival in March. Destroyed 1881 by Chileans. The dist. is called San José de Surco. Inc. 1940 into Lima proper.

Barrancos (bäräng'kōōsh), town (pop. 3,467), Beja dist., S Portugal, 27 mi. E of Moura, at Sp. border; flour milling, cheese mfg.

Barrandov, Czechoslovakia: see SMICHOV.

Barranqueras (bärängkā'räs), town (1947 pop. 12,846), SE Chaco natl. territory, Argentina, port (with floating dock) on Paraná R., on railroad and 4 mi. SE of Resistencia, opposite Corrientes. Mfg. and agr. center. Ships hardwood and cotton from interior. Cotton ginning, meat packing, lumbering, sand quarrying; citriculture. A low isl., 3 mi. long, is in the river.

Barranquilla (bä"rūn-kē'ü, Sp. bärängkē'yä), city (pop. 150,395) and Caribbean seaport, ⊙ Atlántico dept., N Colombia, on left bank of Magdalena R., 8 mi. inland, and 65 mi. NE of Cartagena, 450 mi. N of Bogotá; 10°58'N 74°46'W. Colombia's leading port (river, sea, and air), it also rivals Medellín and Bogotá as an industrial and commercial center. A clearing point for Magdalena valley, it handles more than half of the country's foreign trade. Industries include cotton and rayon thread and textile mills, cementworks, steel plant, cigar factories, sawmills, foundries, breweries, shipyard; also produces hats, shoes, glassware, paper, building materials, chemicals and pharmaceuticals, vegetable oil, chocolate. Large-scale fishing. Products of the bordering agr. area are cotton, sugar cane, corn, rice, yucca, tropical fruit; cattle, hides. Thriving, modern city with many fine parks, plazas, bldgs., especially in the newer residential suburb of El Prado. Founded 1629, Barranquilla was a sleepy town until mid-19th cent., when it became a terminus for Magdalena steamship lines, navigating the river as far as Honda. When it was connected with Puerto Colombia (10 mi. W) by rail and highway, and when the mouth of the Magdalena (Bocas de Ceniza) was dredged (in 1930s), Barranquilla came into its own as a trans-oceanic port; it can now be reached by 10,000-ton vessels.

Barranquitas (bärängkē'täs), town (pop. 4,268), central Puerto Rico, summer resort in Cordillera Central, 18 mi. WSW of Caguas; alt. c.2,000 ft.

Barraqa Islands, Aden: see BARAQA ISLANDS.

Barras (bä'rüs), city (pop. 2,326), N Piauí, Brazil, 70 mi. NNE of Teresina; cotton, carnauba wax, oilseed. Formerly called Barras do Maratahoan.

Barras River, Bolivia: see COIPASA, LAKE.

Barra Strait, narrow passage (3 mi. long) bet. Bras d'Or Lake and Great Bras d'Or, NE N.S., in central Cape Breton Isl., 10 mi. SSW of Baddeck.

Barraute (bärōt'), village (pop. estimate 600), W Que., 24 mi. ESE of Amos; gold mining, lumbering, woodworking.

Barrâx (bäräks'), town (pop. 2,573), Albacete prov., SE central Spain, 19 mi. WNW of Albacete; cereals, saffron, wine, sheep.

Barre or **Barre-des-Cévennes** (bär-dā-sāvĕn') village (pop. 188), Lozère dept., S France, in the Cévennes, 6 mi. SSE of Florac; sericulture.

Barre (bă'rē). **1** Town (pop. 3,406), Worcester co., central Mass., near Ware R., and 18 mi. NW of Worcester; machine shop, dyeing, bleaching, mfg. (doors, screens); dairying. Has fine old houses. Settled c.1720, inc. 1774. Includes villages of White Valley and South Barre (1940 pop. 1,237). **2** Industrial city (pop. 10,922), Washington co., central Vt., just SE of Montpelier; granite center; mfg. (tools, machinery, wood products), dairy products; winter sports. Quarries, developed after War of 1812, supplied granite for state capitol (1836). Statue of Robert Burns (1899) by J. Massey Rhind; war memorial by C. P. Jennewein. Jr. col. for girls here. Inc. 1894. In surrounding Barre town (pop. 4,145; organized 1793) are granite-producing villages of EAST BARRE, Websterville, and Graniteville.

Barreal (bäräal'), town (pop. estimate 1,000), ⊙ Barreal dept. (formed c.1945), SW San Juan prov., Argentina, on the Río de los Patos (affluent of San Juan R.) and 55 mi. WSW of San Juan. Alfalfa, corn, wheat, potatoes, livestock. Iron, aluminum, manganese deposits near by.

Barreda (bärā'dhä), suburb (pop. 1,377) of Torrelavega, Santander prov., N Spain; chemical works.

Barre-des-Cévennes, France: see BARRE.

Barre des Écrins (bär dāzākrē'), or **Les Écrins** (lāzākrē'), highest peak (13,461 ft.) of the Massif du Pelvoux and of Dauphiné Alps in SE France, on Isère–Hautes-Alpes dept. border, 14 mi. W of Briançon. First climbed in 1864. Superb Alpine panorama. Also called Pic des Écrins.

Barreiras (bärā'rüs), city (pop. 4,144), W Bahia, Brazil, head of navigation on the Rio Grande and 430 mi. W of Salvador, near Goiás border; 12°16'S 45°1'W. Ships mangabeira rubber, cattle, alcohol, lumber. Airfield on Belém–Rio de Janeiro route.

Barreirinha (bärārē'nyü), city (pop. 326), E Amazonas, Brazil, landing on Furo de Ramos (right branch of Amazon R.) and 140 mi. WSW of Santarém; rubber, cereals, dried fish, guarana.

Barreirinhas (-nyüs), city (pop. 1,290), NE Maranhão, Brazil, near the Atlantic, 100 mi. E of São Luís; rice, beans, babassu nuts, carnauba wax.

Barreiro (bärā'rōō), city (pop. 872), extreme SE São Paulo, Brazil, on Rio de Janeiro border, 25 mi. E of Cruzeiro; grain, fruit.

Barreiro, town (pop. 19,846), Setúbal dist., S central Portugal, fishing port on S bank of Tagus estuary, opposite (5 mi. SSE of) Lisbon, of which it is an industrial suburb; rail terminus (ferry service to Lisbon); cork processing, mfg. (soap, chemical fertilizer, livestock feed, cordage, toys, rugs), codfish drying.

Barreiros (-rōōs), city (pop. 6,055), E Pernambuco, NE Brazil, near the Atlantic, 55 mi. SSW of Recife; terminus of rail spur from Ribeirão. Sugar-growing center; also ships coconuts, coffee, and cereals. Airfield.

Barrel of Butter or **Carlin Skerry,** islet of the Orkneys, Scotland, in Scapa Flow just S of Pomona.

Barrême (bärĕm'), village (pop. 388), Basses-Alpes dept., SE France, on the Asse and 12 mi. SSE of Digne, in Provence Alps; alt. 2,362. Lavender essence distilling.

Barren, county (□ 486; pop. 28,461), S Ky.; ⊙ Glasgow. Bounded SW by Barren R.; drained by several creeks. Agr. area (livestock, burley tobacco, grain, dairy products, fruit); oil and gas wells, hardwood timber, stone quarries. Some mfg. (especially clothing) at Glasgow. Part of MAMMOTH CAVE NATIONAL PARK and other limestone caves in NW. Formed 1798.

Barren Grounds or **Barren Lands,** arctic prairie region of N Canada, N of 59°N, including N part of the Prairie Provinces and SE part of the Northwest Territories; extends W from Hudson Bay to Great Bear and Great Slave lakes. A rolling plain, geologically part of the Laurentian Plateau, region has maximum elevation of c.600 ft. It is covered with innumerable lakes (Nueltin, Dubawnt, Yathkyed, Garry, Pelly, Aberdeen, Schultz, Baker, Kamiluk, Kaminuriak, Naturawit, Maguse, Lac de Gras, Aylmer, Clinton-Colden, and Artillery are the largest). Largest streams are Coppermine, Back, Thelon, Kazan rivers, and Chesterfield Inlet of Hudson Bay. Region includes Yellowknife Game Preserve (□ 70,000) and Thelon Game Sanctuary (□ 15,000); here are large herds of musk oxen and other arctic fauna (caribou, wolverines, lemmings). Vegetation consists largely of short grass or lichens, sedge, saxifrage, and, along river banks, stunted larch and spruce. Fish abound in the streams and lakes. Winter temperatures are below those of Hudson Bay and Mackenzie R. basin regions; ground is permanently frozen to within a few inches of the surface; during short summer thaw region is swampy. Only a few inland Eskimos live here. 1st crossed (1770-71) by Samuel Hearne, region was later explored by Sir John Franklin, Sir George Back, John Rae, and Joseph Tyrrell.

Barren Island, tiny volcanic rock in Andaman Sea, 65 mi. E of main Andaman Isls.; 12°16'N 93°50'E; rises to 1,160 ft.

Barren Island, Tasmania: see HUNTER ISLANDS.

Barren Islands, Fr. *Îles Stériles* (ēl' stärēl'), group of 4 islets, dependency of Madagascar, in Mozambique Channel of Indian Ocean, just off W coast of Madagascar; 18°30'S 43°50'E.

Barren Islands, group of 6 small islands, S Alaska, in NW part of Gulf of Alaska, bet. Kenai Peninsula (N) and Afognak Isl. (S), at mouth of Cook Inlet; 58°57'N 152°9'W. Largest is Ushgat Isl. (7 mi. long); rises to 1,965 ft.

Barren Lands, Northwest Territories: see BARREN GROUNDS.

Barren Mountains, Calif.: see CHOCOLATE MOUNTAINS.

Barren River, S Ky., formed near Fountain Run, Monroe co., by junction of small streams rising in Macon co., N Tenn.; flows 130 mi. generally NW past Bowling Green to Green R. just E of Woodbury. Navigable (by means of a lock) to Bowling Green.

Barrero Grande, Paraguay: see EUSEBIO AYALA.

Barretos (bärā'tōōs), city (1950 pop. 23,683), N São Paulo, Brazil, on railroad and 65 mi. NW of Ribeirão Prêto; major livestock center with meat-packing and -canning plants; also has dairies, sugar mills, and animal by-products plants. Ramie plantation near by.

Barrett, village (pop. 402), Grant co., W Minn., on small lake and 7 mi. SE of Elbow lake village; dairy products.

Barrett Dam, Calif.: see COTTONWOOD CREEK.

Barrhead, village (pop. 739), central Alta., on Paddle R., near its mouth on Pembina R., and 50 mi. NW of Edmonton; lumber and flour milling, oil drilling, dairying, mixed farming.

Barrhead, burgh (1931 pop. 12,308; 1951 census 12,971), E Renfrew, Scotland, 7 mi. SW of Glasgow; cotton milling, bleaching and printing, iron and brass founding, mfg. of machinery, soap, and sewing cotton.

Barrhill, Scotland: see COLMONELL.

Barrie, town (pop. 9,725), ⊙ Simcoe co., S Ont., on Kempenfelt Bay, arm of L. Simcoe, 50 mi. NNW of Toronto; tanning, meat packing, dairying, flour milling, lumbering, mfg. of shoes, stockings; resort.

Barrie Island (8 mi. long, 5 mi. wide; pop. 760), S central Ont., one of the Manitoulin Isls., in North Channel of L. Huron, just off N shore of Manitoulin Isl., 5 mi. W of Gore Bay; dairying, mixed farming.

Barrier Reef, Australia: see GREAT BARRIER REEF.

Barrigada (bä'rēgä'dü), village (pop. 1,665) and municipality (pop. 11,532), NE Guam; coconut plantations.

Barrington. 1 Village (pop. 4,209), on Cook-Lake co. line, NE Ill., 32 mi. NW of Chicago; mfg. of clothing, furniture, tableware, vases, surgical supplies; coffee and tea packing. Sand, gravel pits. Inc. 1865. **2** Town (pop. 1,052), Strafford co., SE N.H., 9 mi. WNW of Dover. **3** Borough (pop. 2,651), Camden co., SW N.J., 4 mi. SE of Camden. Laid out c.1890, inc. 1917. **4** Residential and resort town (pop. 8,246), Bristol co., E R.I., bet. Narragansett Bay and Mass. line, on Warren and Barrington rivers and 7 mi. SE of Providence, in agr. area; mfg. (yarns, lace, brick, rubber goods); shipbuilding; shellfishing. Has a jr. col. Includes villages of Barrington Center, West Barrington, and Nayatt (summer resort). Settled c.1670, included in Mass. until 1746, inc. 1770.

Barrington Island, Galápagos: see SANTA FE ISLAND.
Barrington River, Mass. and R.I., rises in Seekonk town, SE Mass.; flows 15 mi. S and SSW, through East Providence, R.I., to Warren R. opposite Warren; small craft anchorage; boatyards near mouth.
Barrios, Los (lōs bä'ryōs), town (pop. 4,972), Cádiz prov., SW Spain, near Algeciras Bay, 8 mi. NW of Gibraltar, 50 mi. ESE of Cádiz; agr. center (wheat, corn, vegetables, cork, livestock). Flour milling, liquor distilling.
Barrios, Puerto, Guatemala: see PUERTO BARRIOS.
Barrios de Luna, Los (lōs bä'ryōs dhā lōō'nä), village (pop. 149), Leon prov., NW Spain, 21 mi. NW of Leon; hydroelectric plant on Luna R. (affluent of the Órbigo).
Bar River, Ardennes dept., N France, rises near Buzancy, flows c.30 mi. N to the Meuse just below Donchery. Paralleled through most of its course by Ardennes Canal.
Barro Colorado Island (bä'rō kōlōrä'dō, –rä'dō), islet (c.3½ by 2 mi.) in Gatun L., Panama Canal Zone, 24 mi. NW of Panama city; rises to 537 ft. Wild-life sanctuary established 1924.
Barron, county (□ 866; pop. 34,703), NW Wis.; ⊙ Barron. Drained by Red Cedar and Hay rivers; contains many lakes. Dairying (principal industry), stock raising, agr. (potatoes, truck). Formed 1859.
Barron, city (pop. 2,355), ⊙ Barron co., NW Wis., at confluence of Yellow R. and small Vermillion R., 45 mi. NNW of Eau Claire; commercial center for farming and dairying area; canning, mfg. of woolen goods, woodworking. Has poultry hatcheries and large cooperative creamery. Building stone is quarried near by. Founded before 1878; inc. 1887.
Barrón Escandón, Mexico: see APIZACO.
Barrouallie (bärwäyē'), town (pop. 1,178), W St. Vincent, B.W.I., 6 mi. NW of Kingstown; cotton, arrowroot, sugar cane; fishing.
Barrow, village (pop. 1,397), N Alaska, on Arctic Ocean, near Point Barrow, N extremity of Alaska; hunting and trapping center and supply base; center of oil-bearing region (Naval Oil Reserve No. 4); trading point for N Alaska. Has Presbyterian mission, hosp., school; airfield, radio and meteorological stations. Near by is naval base, established 1944. SW, 12 mi., is monument (1938) to Will Rogers and Wiley Post, who lost their lives here in airplane crash (1935).
Barrow, England: see WENLOCK.
Barrow, county (□ 171; pop. 13,115), NE central Ga.; ⊙ Winder. Bounded S by Apalachee R. Piedmont agr. area (cotton, corn, hay, sweet potatoes, fruit); textile mfg. Formed 1914.
Barrow, Mount (4,644 ft.), NE Tasmania, 15 mi. E of Launceston; popular tourist drive on slopes.
Barrow, Point, northernmost point of Alaska, on Arctic Ocean 9 mi. NE of Barrow; 71°23'N 156°30'W. Discovered 1826 by F. W. Beechey and named for Sir John Barrow. Has played important part in Arctic exploration and aviation; starting point of Sir Hubert Wilkins' flight (1928) across North Pole. Naval base was established (1944) 6 mi. S of point. Near the cape is Point Barrow Eskimo village. U.S. meteorological station set up here during 1st International Polar Year, 1882–83.
Barrow Creek, settlement, S central Northern Territory, Australia, 145 mi. N of Alice Springs; cattle.
Barrowford, urban district (1931 pop. 5,299; 1951 census 4,765), NE Lancashire, England, 2 mi. W of Colne; cotton milling. Has many 17th-cent. houses.
Barrow-in-Furness (fûr'nĭs), county borough (1931 pop. 66,202; 1951 census 67,473), NW Lancashire, England, on SW coast of FURNESS peninsula, sheltered from Irish Sea by WALNEY ISLAND (connected by bridge), 18 mi. W of Lancaster; steel and shipbuilding center (blast furnaces, rolling mills), near iron mines; mfg. of armaments and chemicals. Near by are ruins of Furness Abbey, founded for Benedictines in 1127.
Barrow Island, Australia: see MONTE BELLO ISLANDS.
Barrow-on-Soar, town and parish (pop. 2,661), N Leicester, England, on Soar R. and 9 mi. N of Leicester; hosiery knitting. Has 14th-cent. church; site of Roman fort.
Barrow River, Ireland, rises in Slieve Bloom mts. in W Co. Laoighis, flows E past Portarlington to Co. Kildare line, then along borders of cos. Laoighis, Kildare, Carlow, Kilkenny, Wexford, and Waterford, past Athy, Carlow, Muine Bhead, and New Ross, to Waterford Harbour; 119 mi. long. Navigable below Athy. Receives Nore R.
Barrow Strait, central Franklin Dist., Northwest Territories, arm (150 mi. long, 40–70 mi. wide) of the Arctic Ocean, in 74°–75°N 90°–100°W; separates Bathurst, Cornwallis, and Devon isls. (N) and Prince of Wales and Somerset isls. (S); links Viscount Melville Sound (W) and Lancaster Sound (E). Peel Sound extends S, McDougall Sound and Wellington Channel extend N. Navigable only under favorable circumstances of weather, it is link in E-W route through the Arctic Archipelago. In strait are several isls.
Barruelo de Santullán (bärwā'lō dhā säntōōlyän'), mining village (pop. 4,991), Palencia prov., N central Spain, on S slopes of Cantabrian Mts., 45 mi. SW of Santander; sawmills. Anthracite and bituminous coal mines in area.
Barry, agr. village, S Angus, Scotland, 2 mi. W of Carnoustie.
Barry. 1 County (□ 549; pop. 26,183), SW Mich.; ⊙ Hastings. Drained by Thornapple R. Farm area: livestock, dairy products, poultry, grain, potatoes, beans, corn. Mfg. at Hastings. Lake resorts. Gun L. is W. State game area in co. Organized 1839. **2** County (□ 800; pop. 21,755), SW Mo., in the Ozarks; ⊙ Cassville. Drained by White R. Agr. (berries, apples, tomatoes), cattle, poultry, dairy products; hardwood timber; coal, zinc, lead. Part of Mark Twain Natl. Forest is here. Formed 1835.
Barry. 1 City (pop. 1,529), Pike co., W Ill., 24 mi. SE of Quincy; trade center of dairying and agr. area (corn, wheat, hay, apples); marble, granite works. Founded 1836, inc. 1859. **2** Village (pop. 74), Big Stone co., W Minn., near S.Dak. line, 19 mi. NNW of Ortonville in grain area.
Barry, municipal borough (1931 pop. 38,891; 1951 census 40,979), SE Glamorgan, Wales, on Bristol Channel, 8 mi. SW of Cardiff; 51°24'N 3°15'W; major coal and tinplate shipping port, with flour mills and paint works. Extensive docks were built 1844–99. Just S, in Bristol Channel, is small Barry Isl., with bathing beach. In the borough (NE) is Cadoxton (pop. 6,548).
Barry, Fort, Calif.: see SAUSALITO.
Barrydale, village (pop, 1,034), SW Cape Prov., U. of So. Afr., 18 mi. ENE of Swellendam; in Langeberg range; wheat, fruit, feed crops, viticulture.
Barry Links, Scotland: see BUDDON NESS.
Barry Mountains, Australia: see AUSTRALIAN ALPS.
Barry's Bay, village (pop. 1,198), SE Ont., at N end of Kamaniskeg L., 35 mi. SW of Pembroke, in lumbering region. Supply center for E part of Algonquin Provincial Park.
Barryton, village (pop. 445), Mecosta co., central Mich., on Chippewa R. and 17 mi. ENE of Big Rapids, in agr. area; poultry hatchery, creamery.
Barsac (bärsäk'), village (pop. 1,125), Gironde dept., SW France, on left bank of Garonne R. and 20 mi. SE of Bordeaux; noted for its white wines. Barrelmaking.
Barsana (bŭrsä'nŭ), village, Muttra dist., W Uttar Pradesh, India, 21 mi. WNW of Muttra; pilgrimage center; prosperous in 18th cent.; declined after being plundered (1774) by Mogul troops. Large Hindu pavilion.
Barsc, Poland: see ZASIEKI.
Barsha, El, or **Al-Barsha** (both: ĕl bärshä'), village (pop. 6,573), Asyut prov., central Upper Egypt, on E bank of the Nile, 3 mi. E of Mellawi; cereals, dates, sugar cane.
Barsi (bär'sē), town (pop., including suburban area, 36,870), Sholapur dist., E Bombay, India, 42 mi. NNW of Sholapur; cotton-milling center; agr. market; dal and oilseed milling, hand-loom weaving, biri mfg.
Barsinghausen (bär"zĭng-hou'zŭn), village (pop. 9,180), in former Prussian prov. of Hanover, W Germany, after 1945 in Lower Saxony, at N foot of the Deister, 13 mi. WSW of Hanover (linked by tramway); coal mining, sandstone quarrying. Summer resort. Has 13th-cent. church.
Barsi Takli or **Barsi-Takli** (bär'sē täk'lē), town (pop. 5,479), Akola dist., W Madhya Pradesh, India, 10 mi. SSE of Akola; trades in cotton, millet, oilseeds.
Barssel (bär'sŭl), village (commune pop. 10,450), in Oldenburg, NW Germany, after 1945 Lower Saxony, 14 mi. ESE of Leer, in peat region.
Barstow (bär'stō). **1** City (pop. 6,135), San Bernardino co., S Calif., in the Mojave Desert, on dry Mojave R. and 55 mi. N of San Bernardino; railroad division point; irrigated agr. (alfalfa), dairying, mining (silver, salt, borax) in region. Inc. 1947. **2** Town (pop. 683), Ward co., extreme W Texas, 7 mi. E of Pecos, near Pecos R.; trading center in irrigated fruit, truck area.
Barsuki (bŭrsōōkē'), two sandy desert areas in S Aktyubinsk oblast, Kazakh SSR, N of Aral Sea. The Greater Barsuki extend 125 mi. SW from Chelkar. Lesser Barsuki, 60 mi. E of Greater Barsuki, are 60 mi. long.
Bar-sur-Aube (bär-sür-ōb'), town (pop. 3,859), Aube dept., NE central France, on Aube R. and 30 mi. ESE of Troyes; woodworking (furniture, crates); forges, distilleries. Has two 12th-15th-cent. churches. Was site of medieval fairs.
Bar-sur-Loup, Le, France: see BAR, LE.
Bar-sur-Seine (–sür-sĕn'), village (pop. 1,875), Aube dept., NE central France, on Seine R. and 19 mi. SE of Troyes; agr. market; paper milling, brewing. Has 16th-17th-cent. Gothic and Renaissance church.
Bartang (bŭrtän-k'), village, NW Gorno-Badakhshan Autonomous Oblast, Tadzhik SSR, in the Pamir, on Bartang R. and 45 mi. NNE of Khorog; cattle, horses. Until c.1935, Siponzh or Sipondzh.
Bartang River, Tadzhik SSR, rises in W SAREZ LAKE, in the Pamir; flows c.75 mi. WSW, past Bartang, to Panj R. near Rushan.
Bartelso (bärtĕl'zō), village (pop. 304), Clinton co., S Ill., 18 mi. W of Centralia, in agr., bituminous-coal-mining, oil-producing area.
Bartensleben (bär'tŭnslā"bŭn), village (pop. 784), in former Prussian Saxony prov., central Germany, after 1945 in Saxony-Anhalt, 6 mi. E of Helmstedt; potash mining.
Bartenstein (bär'tŭn-shtīn"), town (pop. 842), N Württemberg, Germany, after 1945 in Württemberg-Baden, 10 mi. SSE of Mergentheim; grain.
Bartenstein, Poland: see BARTOSZYCE.
Barter Island (5 mi. long, 3 mi. wide), NE Alaska, in Arctic Ocean, just off mainland; 70°10'N 143°40'W; radio station; Eskimo summer trading camp.
Barter Island, Lincoln co., S Maine, isl., 3.5 mi. long, in Sheepscot R. just E of Boothbay; bridge to mainland.
Bartfa, Czechoslovakia: see BARDEJOV.
Bartfeld, Czechoslovakia: see BARDEJOV.
Barth (bärt), town (pop. 13,794), in former Prussian Pomerania prov., N Germany, after 1945 in Mecklenburg, on an inlet of the Baltic, at mouth of small Barthe R., 15 mi. WNW of Stralsund; fishing port; fish curing, sugar refining, jute milling; mfg. of agr. machinery, furniture. Has Gothic church. Formerly important trading center.
Barthe-de-Neste, La (lä bärt'-dŭ-nĕst'), village (pop. 635), Hautes-Pyrénées dept., SW France, on the Neste and 12 mi. E of Bagnères-de-Bigorre; agr. (corn, potatoes, cattle), slaked-lime kilns.
Bartholomäussee, Germany: see KÖNIGSSEE.
Bartholomew (bärthŏ'lŭmū), county (□ 402; pop. 36,108), S central Ind.; ⊙ Columbus. Drained by East Fork of White R. and tributaries. Farming (grain, corn, tomatoes), stock raising, dairying; timber. Mfg. at Columbus. Formed 1821.
Bartholomew, Bayou (bī'ō), river in Ark. and La., rises near Pine Bluff in Ark., flows generally S, into Morehouse parish of La., to Ouachita R. 10 mi. SW of Bastrop; c.300 mi. long.
Bartica (bärtē'kŭ), town (pop. 2,352), ⊙ Mazaruni-Potaro dist. Essequibo co., N Br. Guiana, head of navigation of Essequibo R. (here joined by Mazaruni and Cuyuni rivers), 40 mi. SW of Georgetown. Chief town of Essequibo, trading post and point of departure for near-by gold and diamond fields and the interior; linked by road and trail with famous Kaieteur Falls (100 mi. SW). Stone quarries in vicinity. Across the Essequibo R., a U.S. naval base was established 1940.
Bartin (bärtĭn'), Turkish *Bartın*, town (pop. 8,740), Zonguldak prov., N Turkey, 31 mi. ENE of Zonguldak; coal mines; grain, flax, hemp.
Bartle Frere, Mount, highest peak (5,438 ft.) of Queensland, Australia, in Bellenden-Ker Range, on NE coast, 20 mi. SSE of Cairns.
Bartles, Mount, peak (10,047 ft.) in West Tavaputs Plateau, E Utah, 23 mi. ENE of Price.
Bartlesville (bär'tŭlzvĭl), city (pop. 19,228), ⊙ Washington co., NE Okla., c.40 mi. N of Tulsa, and on Caney R.; trade and distribution center for agr. and oil-producing area. Has hq. for oil firms. Oil refining, zinc smelting; mfg. of oil-field equipment, seismographs, ventilators, sulphuric acid, metal products, leather. Seat of Bartlesville Jr. Col. Has U.S. Bureau of Mines experiment station. Near by are Hulah Dam and a state park. Founded c.1877 on site of trading post; inc. 1897.
Bartlett. 1 Village, Inyo co., E Calif., on W shore of Owens L., in Owens Valley, 7 mi. S of Lone Pine; alkali works. **2** Village (pop. 716), Cook co., NE Ill., NW suburb of Chicago, 4 mi. SE of Elgin. **3** City (pop. 143), Labette co., extreme SE Kansas, 20 mi. E of Coffeyville, near Okla. line, in dairying and agr. region. **4** Village (pop. 145), ⊙ Wheeler co., NE central Nebr., 60 mi. WSW of Norfolk; livestock, grain. **5** Town (pop. 1,074), Carroll co., E central N.H., on the Saco and 10 mi. NE of Conway; resort in White Mts. Includes Glen village. Settled after 1769, inc. 1790. **6** Village (pop. 61), Ramsey co., NE central N.Dak., 20 mi. ESE of Devils Lake. **7** Town (pop. 489), Shelby co., SW Tenn., 8 mi. NE of Memphis. **8** City (pop. 1,727), Williamson and Bell counties, central Texas, c.40 mi. NNE of Austin; trade center in cotton, corn, truck area. Settled 1882, inc. 1902.
Bartlett Colony, village (pop. 1,515), Fresno co., central Calif.
Bartlett Dam, central Ariz., on Verde R. and 35 mi. NE of Phoenix; final unit in Salt R. valley reclamation project. Multiple-arch type (287 ft. high, 1,063 ft. long; completed 1939); used for irrigation, flood control. Capacity, 65,000,000 gal.
Bartlett's Ferry Dam, Ga. and Ala.: see CHATTAHOOCHEE RIVER.
Bartlett Trough, broad-floored depression in Caribbean Sea, bet. Jamaica and Cayman Isls.; 22,788 ft. deep. Sometimes called Cayman Deep.
Bartley. 1 Village (pop. 399), Red Willow co., S Nebr., 15 mi. ENE of McCook and on Republican R.; livestock, grain. **2** Village (pop. 1,275), McDowell co., S W.Va., on Dry Fork, and 10 mi. WSW of Welch, in coal-mining and agr. region.
Bartolo, Bolivia: see BETANZOS.
Bartolomé Mitre, district, Argentina: see ARRECIFES.
Bartolomé Mitre (bärtōlōmā' mē'trā), residential town (pop. estimate 4,000) in Greater Buenos

Aires, Argentina, W suburb of Olivos, 10 mi. NW of Buenos Aires.

Bartolomeu Dias (bŭrtōōlōōmā'ōō dē'ŭsh), village, Sul do Save prov., S central Mozambique, on Mozambique Channel, 90 mi. S of Beira; ships rubber, bark, wax.

Barton, agr. village and parish (pop. 575), North Riding, N Yorkshire, England, 5 mi. SW of Darlington. Near by are limestone quarries.

Barton. 1 County (□ 892; pop. 29,909), central Kansas; ⊙ Great Bend. Sloping plain, drained (S) by Arkansas R. Wheat, livestock. Extensive oil fields. Formed 1872. **2** County (□ 594; pop. 12,678), SW Mo.; ⊙ Lamar. Drained by a branch of Spring R. and by affluents of the Osage. Agr. (wheat, corn, hay, livestock); coal. Formed 1855.

Barton. 1 Town (pop. 695), Allegany co., W Md., in the Alleghenies and 17 mi. WSW of Cumberland, in bituminous-coal-mining area. **2** Village (pop. 102), Pierce co., N central N.Dak., 12 mi. NW of Rugby. **3** Village (1940 pop. 1,275), Belmont co., E Ohio, 8 mi. NW of Bellaire, and on small Wheeling Creek, in coal-mining area. **4** Town (pop. 3,298), including Barton village (pop. 1,267), Orleans co., N Vt., 13 mi. S of Newport and on Barton R.; furniture, lumber, dairy and maple products. Winter sports. Includes Crystal L. (resort) and Willoughby and ORLEANS villages. Granted 1781, settled 1795. **5** Village (pop. 1,039), Washington co., E Wis., N suburb of West Bend, on branch of Milwaukee R.; mfg. (auto accessories, electrical-transmission equipment).

Barton-in-Fabis, agr. village and parish (pop. 261), S Nottingham, England, 6 mi. SW of Nottingham; cementworks. Has late 14th-cent. church.

Barton Island, Knox co., S Maine, just W of and bridged to Vinalhaven Isl.; ¾ mi. long.

Barton River, N Vt., rises in Crystal L. in Barton town, flows c.15 mi. N to L. Memphremagog at Newport.

Bartons, village, St. Catherine parish, S Jamaica, 12 mi. W of Spanish Town; mfg. of cassava starch.

Barton-under-Needwood, agr. village and parish (pop. 1,486), E Stafford, England, 3 mi. SW of Burton-on-Trent; cement mfg. Has 16th-cent. church.

Barton-upon-Humber, urban district (1931 pop. 6,332; 1951 census 6,235), Parts of Lindsey, N Lincolnshire, England, on Humber R. and 6 mi. SW of Hull; brick- and tileworks, metalworks. Has church dating from 10th cent., with one of earliest Saxon towers in England.

Barton-upon-Irwell (ûr'wŭl), town in Worsley urban dist., SE Lancashire, England, on Irwell R. and 6 mi. W of Manchester; cotton milling, petroleum refining. Manchester Ship Canal here crosses Irwell R. on a swing bridge.

Bartonville, village (pop. 2,437), Peoria co., central Ill., near junction of Illinois R. and Kickapoo Creek, just SSW of Peoria, in agr. and bituminous-coal-mining area; steel-fabricating plant. A state hosp. for the insane is here. Inc. 1903.

Bartoszyce (bärtô-shĭ'tsĕ), Ger. *Bartenstein* (bär'-tŭn-shtīn), town (1939 pop. 12,912; 1946 pop. 3,449) in East Prussia, after 1945 in Olsztyn prov., NE Poland, on Lyna (Alle) R. and 35 mi. SSE of Kaliningrad; frontier station near USSR border, 12 mi. SE of Bagrationovsk; grain and cattle market. Treaty of Bartenstein bet. Prussia and Russia signed here, 1807. In First World War, for some time Hindenburg's hq. In Second World War, c.90% destroyed.

Bartow (bär'tō), county (□ 476; pop. 27,370), NW Ga.; ⊙ Cartersville. Valley and ridge area drained by Etowah R., containing Allatoona Dam in E. Farming (cotton, hay, sweet potatoes, corn, fruit, livestock), mining (barite, ocher, manganese, iron, marble, limestone), and mfg. (textiles, lumber). Formed 1832.

Bartow. 1 City (pop. 8,694), ⊙ Polk co., central Fla., on Peace R. and 38 mi. E of Tampa, near L. Hancock; processing and shipping center for citrus fruit and phosphate (from near-by mines). Has packing houses, canneries, fertilizer plants, cigar factory, lumber mill; also makes fishing tackle. Settled 1851; inc. 1893, reinc. 1905. **2** Town (pop. 347), Jefferson co., E Ga., 9 mi. SSW of Louisville, in farm area.

Bartringen, Luxembourg: see BERTRANGE.

Bartschin, Poland: see BARCIN.

Bartsch River, Poland: see BARYCZ RIVER.

Barú (bärōō'), former territory (Sp. *comarca*) of W Panama; ⊙ was Puerto Armuelles. Formed (1938) out of Chiriquí prov.; returned to prov. in 1945.

Barú, volcano, Panama: see CHIRIQUÍ, volcano.

Barugaza, India: see BROACH, city.

Barugh, England: see DARTON.

Barugo (bärōō'gō), town (1939 pop. 3,797; 1948 municipality pop. 21,073), N Leyte, Philippines, on Carigara Bay, 19 mi. WNW of Tacloban; agr. center (coconuts, rice, sugar cane).

Baruipur (bär'wĭpōōr), town (pop. 7,130), 24-Parganas dist., SE West Bengal, India, 16 mi. SSE of Calcutta city center; rice, pulse, betel leaves, coconuts.

Barú Island (bärōō'), on Caribbean coast of Bolívar dept., N Colombia, forming S shore of Bay of Cartagena, 10 mi. S of Cartagena; 17 mi. long, ¼ mi. wide. Barú Point is at SW tip; 10°7'N 75°41'W.

Baruk, El, or **Al-Baruk** (both: ĕl bä'rōōk), Fr. *Barouk,* village, central Lebanon, 16 mi. SE of Beirut; alt. 3,700 ft.; sericulture, cereals, oranges. Summer resort.

Barul (bä'rōōl), village, Burdwan dist., W West Bengal, India, 9 mi. ENE of Asansol. Hematite and limonite deposits near by.

Barum, England: see BARNSTAPLE.

Barumbu (bärōōm'bōō), village, Eastern Prov., N Belgian Congo, on left bank of Congo R. opposite Basoko, and 125 mi. WNW of Stanleyville; agr. center with model cattle-raising farm, experimental coffee, cacao, and rubber plantations; palm milling.

Barumini (bärōō'mēnē), village (pop. 1,415), Cagliari prov., central Sardinia, near Flumini Mannu R., 34 mi. N of Cagliari.

Barun Bogdo, Mongolia: see IKHE BOGDO.

Baruni, India: see BARAUNI.

Barun Urt (bä'rōōn ōōrt') or **Baruun Urta** (ōōr'tä), town, ⊙ Sukhe Bator aimak, E Mongolian People's Republic, on road and 110 mi. SSW of Choibalsan.

Ba'rur, Umm al-, Iraq: see SHAMIYA, ASH.

Baruta (bärōō'tä), town (pop. 956), Miranda state, N Venezuela, in coastal range, 5 mi. SSE of Caracas; coffee, cacao, sugar cane.

Baruth (bä'rōōt), town (pop. 2,232), Brandenburg, E Germany, 15 mi. E of Luckenwalde; forestry; glass mfg.

Baruun Bogdo, Mongolia: see IKHE BOGDO.

Baruun Urta, Mongolia: see BARUN URT.

Baruva (bä'rōōvŭ), town (pop. 8,724), Vizagapatam dist., NE Madras, India, on Bay of Bengal, 95 mi. NE of Vizianagaram; copra, coir. Casuarina plantation on coast.

Barvas (bär'vŭs), agr. village, N Lewis with Harris, Outer Hebrides, in Ross and Cromarty, Scotland, 11 mi. NW of Stornoway.

Barvenkovo (bŭrvyĭn-kô'vŭ), city (1926 pop. 13,348), SE Kharkov oblast, Ukrainian SSR, 31 mi. E of Lozovaya; flour-milling center; distillery, machinery works.

Barwaha (bŭrvä'hŭ), town (pop. 7,302), S Madhya Bharat, India, near Narbada R., 33 mi. SSE of Indore; market center for wheat, cotton, millet, oilseeds; cotton ginning; distillery.

Bärwalde, Poland: see BARWICE.

Barwani (bŭrvä'nē), town (pop. 12,569), SW Madhya Bharat, India, 50 mi. WNW of Khargon; trades in cotton, wheat, timber, rice; cotton ginning. Bawangaja (Bawangaz) hill (c.2,110 ft.), 4 mi. SW, in Satpura Range, is Jain pilgrimage site. Town was ⊙ former princely state of Barwani (□ 1,189; pop. 176,666) of Central India agency, which was founded c.14th cent. by Sesodia Rajputs and in 1948 merged with Madhya Bharat.

Barwa Sagar (bŭr'vŭ sä'gŭr), town (pop. 6,620), Jhansi dist., S Uttar Pradesh, India, on small lake, 11 mi. SE of Jhansi; jowar, oilseeds, wheat, gram, rice. Near by are 11th-cent. Chandel Rajput remains. Also written Barwasagar.

Barwell, town and parish (pop. 3,869), SW Leicester, England, 2 mi. NE of Hinckley; shoe mfg. Has 14th-cent. church.

Barwice (bärvē'tsĕ). **1** Ger. *Bärwalde* or *Bärwalde in Pommern* (bär'väl"dŭ ĭn pô'mŭrn), town (1939 pop. 3,009; 1946 pop. 1,819) in Pomerania, after 1945 in Koszalin prov., NW Poland, 14 mi. W of Szczecinek; dairying; grain and cattle market. Until 1938, in former Prussian prov. of Grenzmark Posen-Westpreussen. **2** Ger. *Bärwalde* or *Bärwalde in Neumark* (ĭn noi'märk), town (1939 pop. 3,434; 1946 pop. 1,429) in Brandenburg, after 1945 in Szczecin prov., NW Poland, 15 mi. NNW of Küstrin (Kostrzyn); tanning; vegetable market.

Barwick, town (pop. 436), Thomas and Brooks counties, S Ga., 16 mi. ENE of Thomasville.

Barwon River, Australia: see DARLING RIVER.

Baryatino (bŭryä'tyĭnŭ), village (1926 pop. 381), W Kaluga oblast, Russian SFSR, 17 mi. NNE of Kirov; vegetable drying.

Barycz River (bä'rĭch), Ger. *Bartsch* (bärch), in Lower Silesia, after 1945 in SW Poland, rises SW of Kalisz, flows 102 mi. generally WNW, past Milicz and Wasosz, to the Oder 6 mi. E of Glogau (Glogow).

Barysh (bŭrĭsh'). **1** Town (1939 pop. over 2,000), W central Ulyanovsk oblast, Russian SFSR, on Barysh R. (right tributary of Sura R.) and 34 mi. ESE of Inza; tanning, food processing; sawmilling; tripoli quarrying, peat digging. Woolen mills near by, at Guryevka, Izmailovo, and Staro-Timoshkino. **2** Pol. *Barysz* (bä'rĭsh), town (1931 pop. 6,022), SW Ternopol oblast, Ukrainian SSR, 5 mi. WSW of Buchach; agr. center; flour milling, brick mfg.

Baryshevka (bŭrĭ'shĭfkŭ, bŭrĭshôf'kŭ), village (1926 pop. 2,661), E Kiev oblast, Ukrainian SSR, 35 mi. ESE of Kiev; truck produce.

Barysz, Ukrainian SSR: see BARYSH, Ternopol oblast.

Bârzana, Spain: see QUIRÓS.

Barzas (bŭrzäs'), town (1939 pop. over 2,000), N Kemerovo oblast, Russian SFSR, on railroad and 27 mi. N of Kemerovo, in Kuznetsk Basin; coal.

Bas (bä) or **Bas-en-Basset** (bäzã-bäsā'), village (pop. 976), Haute-Loire dept., S central France, on the Loire and 21 mi. NE of Le Puy; makes silk ribbon, lace; ships potatoes, lumber.

Basail (bäsäēl'), town (pop. estimate 500), S Chaco natl. territory, Argentina, on railroad and 35 mi. SSW of Resistencia; cotton, corn, livestock; lumbering.

Basalt. 1 (bŭsôlt') Town (pop. 173), Eagle co., W central Colo., on Roaring Fork R., just N of Elk Mts., and 22 mi. SSW of Eagle; alt. 6,600 ft.; agr. **2** (bă'sôlt, bă'-) Village (pop. 227), Bingham co., SE Idaho, 10 mi. SW of Idaho Falls and on Snake R.; alt. 4,572 ft. Potatoes, sugar beets, grain, livestock.

Basaltic Peak, Colo.: see BLACK MOUNTAIN, Jackson co.

Basankusu (bäsängkōō'sōō), town (1946 pop. c. 2,300), Equator Prov., W Belgian Congo, on left bank of Lubonga R. at confluence of Lopori and Maringa rivers, and 125 mi. NE of Coquilhatville; steamboat landing and center of copal and palm-oil trade; palm-oil milling. Has R.C. missions and schools, hosp. for Europeans. Founded 1889.

Basarabeasca, Moldavian SSR: see ROMANOVKA.

Basarabi (bäsäräb'), village (pop. 1,888), Constanta prov., SE Rumania, on railroad and 12 mi. W of Constanta; viticultural center; limestone quarrying, chalk mfg. Former Turkish Murfatlar.

Basarabia, region, USSR: see BESSARABIA.

Basargechar (bŭsŭrgyĭchär'), village (1932 pop. estimate 3,950), E Armenian SSR, near SE shore of L. Sevan, 65 mi. E of Erivan; wheat; rugmaking. Airfield.

Basarh, India: see LALGANJ, Muzaffarpur dist., Bihar.

Basauri (bäsou'rē), suburban commune (pop. 10,605), S of Bilbao, Vizcaya prov., N Spain, in the Basque Provs.; steel mills and metallurgical plants (tin plate, rivets, chains, kitchen utensils, auto accessories); also makes rubber tires, paints and varnishes, and toys. Iron mines. Arizgoiti (pop. 2,809) is seat of commune.

Basavilbaso (bäsävēlbä'sō), town (1947 census pop. 6,338), SE central Entre Ríos prov., Argentina, 40 mi. WNW of Concepción del Uruguay; rail junction, grain center; mfg. of paper bags and sweets, flour milling.

Basbeck (bäs'bĕk), village (pop. 2,976), in former Prussian prov. of Hanover, NW Germany, after 1945 in Lower Saxony, on the Oste and 13 mi. NW of Stade; weaving; flour products.

Bascharage (bäshäräzh'), Ger. *Niederkerschen* (nē'dŭrkĕr"shŭn), village (pop. 1,027), SW Luxembourg, 5 mi. NW of Esch-sur-Alzette; beer brewing; agr.

Basco, Philippines: see BATAN ISLAND, Batanes prov.

Basco, village (pop. 220), Hancock co., W Ill., 11 mi. ESE of Keokuk (Iowa), in agr. and bituminous-coal area.

Bascoup (bäskōō'), town, Hainaut prov., SW Belgium, 9 mi. WNW of Charleroi; coal mining.

Basel (bä'zŭl) or **Basle** (bäl), Fr. *Bâle* (bäl), city (1950 pop. 183,742), ⊙ and virtually coextensive with Basel-Stadt half-canton, N Switzerland, at Fr. and Ger. borders, on the Rhine (here becomes navigable), at mouths of Birs and Wiese rivers; 47°34'N 7°36'E. Founded by the Romans (anc. *Basilia,* later *Basilea*); became an episcopal see (7th cent.) and a free imperial city (11th cent.); joined Swiss Confederation in 1501. One of oldest intellectual centers of Europe. Seat of Bank for International Settlements and of Swiss Industries Fair, Basel is also an important economic center and chief railway junction in Switzerland. Mfg. (chemicals, metal products, foodstuffs, silk textiles); printing, woodworking. The Rhine divides city into Greater Basel (left bank, on 2 hills separated by the Birsig valley) and Lesser Basel. Klein Hüningen harbor, on the Rhine, is N of city; 5 Rhine bridges. Cathedral (consecrated 1019; Erasmus buried here), univ. (opened 1460), 3 rich museums (science and ethnological, historical, art; last with fine Holbein collection), town hall (16th cent.; Burgundian late Gothic), city hall (rococo; seat of municipal council), botanic and zoological gardens. City retains some old architecture in its churches (Clara, St. Leonard, Martin, St. Alban's convent), gates (notably Spalen-Tor), and guild houses. The celebrated Council of Basel sat here 1431–49.

Baselaugst, Switzerland: see AUGST.

Baselice (bäzä'lēchē), town (pop. 3,117), Benevento prov., Campania, S Italy, 20 mi. SE of Campobasso.

Basel-Land (bä'zŭl-länt"), Fr. *Bâle-Campagne* (bälkăpä'nyŭ), half-canton (□ 165; 1950 pop. 107,393), N Switzerland, forming with Basel-Stadt half-canton a full canton; ⊙ Liestal. Has forests, meadows, and fertile fields (cereals); some orchards, gardens, and pastures. Produces metal products, watches, textiles. Salt mines and hydroelectric plants on the Rhine. Pop. German speaking and Protestant.

Basel-Stadt (bä'zŭl-shtät'), Fr. *Bâle-Ville* (bälvēl'), half-canton (□ 14; 1950 pop. 196,658), N Switzerland, on Fr., Ger. borders. Smallest of Swiss half-cantons, virtually coextensive with city of Basel, and forming with Basel-Land half-canton a full canton; ⊙ Basel. Some forests and cultivated fields (notably maize); industry concentrated in Basel. Pop. German speaking and Protestant.

Bas-en-Basset, France: see BAS.

Basento River (bäzĕn'tô), anc. *Casuentus*, in Basilicata, S Italy, rises in the Apennines 11 mi. SSW of Potenza, flows 93 mi. N and ESE to Gulf of Taranto 15 mi. ESE of Pisticci.

Base Station, N.H.: see MARSH-FIELD.

Baset Dag (bä-shĕt' dä), Turkish *Başet Dağ*, peak (12,300 ft.), E Turkey, 24 mi. SE of Van.

Basey (bäsā'), town (1939 pop. 4,473; 1948 municipality pop. 35,523), SW Samar isl., Philippines, on San Pedro Bay, 5 mi. NE of Tacloban; agr. center (coconuts, hemp).

Basford (bās'fŭrd), N suburb of Nottingham, S Nottinghamshire, England; textile printing, mfg. of textile machinery, lace, chemicals, soap.

Bashahr (bŭsh'ŭhŭr), former princely state (including dependencies, □ 3,651; pop. 116,305) of Punjab Hill States, India; ⊙ was Rampur. Since 1948, merged with Himachal Pradesh. Sometimes spelled Bussahir.

Bashanta (bŭshŭntä'), town (1939 pop. over 500), S Rostov oblast, Russian SFSR, 35 mi. SE of Salsk; wheat, sunflowers, livestock. Until 1943, in Kalmyk Autonomous SSR.

Bashaw (bă'shô), village (pop. 511), S central Alberta, on small Valley L., near Buffalo L., 40 mi. NE of Red Deer; grain elevators, flour mills, dairying, mixed farming.

Bash Bish Falls, SW Mass., scenic waterfall in Bash Bish State Forest, 3 mi. E of Copake, N.Y.; trout fishing.

Bashi Channel (bä'shē), northernmost part of Luzon Strait, bet. Formosa (N) and Batan Isls. (S) off N Luzon, Philippines. Sometimes Bachi.

Bashi Islands, Philippines: see BATAN ISLANDS, Batanes prov.

Bashkaus River, Russian SFSR: see TELETSKOYE LAKE.

Bashkicheti or **Bashkichety**, Georgian SSR: see DMANISI.

Bashkir Autonomous Soviet Socialist Republic (băshkēr', băsh'kĕr, Rus. bŭshkēr'), administrative division (□ 55,400; 1939 pop. 3,144,713) of E European Russian SFSR; ⊙ Ufa. In W foothills of the Urals; includes the S Urals (SE); drained by Belaya R. and its tributaries and by Sakmara R. (SE). Humid continental climate (short summers). Mining region: metallic ores in the S Urals include iron (Komarovo-Zigazinski dist.), copper (Baimak), manganese, magnesite, gold, chromium, lead, bauxite, and barite; petroleum (Tuimazy, Ishimbai; pipe lines to Chernikovsk), lignite (Babai basin), peat (NW), talc, asbestos, jasper, rock crystal (S Urals), gypsum, limestone, and quartz sand (Belaya and Ufa river valleys). Wheat (SE, SW), rye, oats, potatoes (W, NW), truck (around Ufa); industrial agr. (recently introduced) includes sugar beets, ambary hemp, balloon flowers, castor beans, and *kok-sagyz* (rubber-bearing plant); livestock raising in Belaya R. valley and forested E. Industries are based on mining (ferrous and nonferrous metallurgy, oil cracking), quarrying (mfg. of building materials, glassworking), timber (paper and sawmilling, woodworking, wood distilling, veneering match mfg.), and agr. (food processing and preserving, distilling, tanning, woolen and flour milling). Machine mfg. (airplanes, combines, mining and oil-drilling tools, boilers, typewriters), and light mfg. (textiles, chemicals, leather and rubber goods) in main urban centers (Ufa, Sterlitamak, Chernikovsk, Beloretsk). Served by Trans-Siberian and S.Siberian RRs. Navigation on lower Belaya and Ufa rivers (steel, copper, petroleum, timber, and agr. exports). Pop. 40% Russians, 24% Bashkirs, 17% Tatars, 5% Mishars (related to Tatars); and Chuvash and Mari. The Bashkirs are Turkic nomadic steppe people (now settled) of Moslem religion; known in 10th cent.; dominated by Golden Horde (13th-15th cent.); colonized by Russians in 16th cent. Republic formed largely out of Ufa govt. in 1919.

Bashmakovo (bŭshmŭkô'vŭ), village (1926 pop. 812), W Penza oblast, Russian SFSR, on railroad and 22 mi. NW of Belinski; meat packing.

Bashtanka (bŭshtän'kŭ), village (1926 pop. 6,008), central Nikolayev oblast, Ukrainian SSR, 35 mi. NE of Nikolayev; metalworks. Until c.1930, called Poltavka.

Basi (bŭs'ē). **1** Town (pop. 14,400), E central Patiala and East Punjab States Union, India, 24 mi. N of Patiala; local market for wheat, corn, cotton, pepper; handicraft cloth weaving, mfg. of sewing-machine parts. Sometimes spelled Bassi. **2** Town (pop. 5,070), E Patiala and East Punjab States Union, India, 32 mi. NE of Patiala; wheat, gram, millet. Sometimes called Dera Bassi.

Basiawan or **Basiauan** (both: bäsyä'wän), town (1939 pop. 4,222), Davao prov., S Mindanao, Philippines, near Davao Gulf, 40 mi. SSW of Davao; abacá, coconuts.

Basil (bă'zŭl), former village, Fairfield co., central Ohio, annexed 1945 by BALTIMORE.

Basilan Island (bäsē'län) (□ 494; 1948 pop. c.50,000), Zamboanga prov., Philippines, off SW tip of Mindanao, 10 mi. S of Zamboanga across Basilan Strait; 35 mi. long, 22 mi. wide. Lamitan is on NE coast, and Isabela, formerly Isabela de Basilan, on N coast. Mountainous, rising to 3,317 ft. in Basilan Peak. Heavily forested. Rubber plantation. Coconuts, rice, corn, cattle. Fishing. Inhabited by Moros. Offshore are a number of islets which, with Basilan, comprise Basilan Isls. The Basilan Isls., forming part of Zamboanga city, were constituted (late 1940s) as Basilan City (1948 pop. 110,297).

Basildon, town (1951 pop. 24,566), S Essex, England, 10 mi. SSW of Chelmsford, in agr. area. Designated after Second World War as model residential community, including part of Billericay urban dist.

Basile (bäsē'lā), village (pop. 622), Fernando Po isl., Sp. Guinea, on N slope of Santa Isabel Peak, 4 mi. SSE of Santa Isabel; alt. c.2,000 ft. Hill station and governor's summer residence.

Basile (băzēl'), village (pop. 1,572), Evangeline parish, S central La., 40 mi. NE of Lake Charles city, in agr. area (truck, cotton, strawberries, melons, potatoes, livestock); lumber milling, cotton ginning. Oil and gas fields near by. Founded 1905.

Basilea or **Basilia**, Switzerland: see BASEL.

Basiliano (bäzēlyä'nô), village (pop. 1,160), Udine prov., Friuli-Venezia Giulia, NE Italy, 7 mi. SW of Udine. Called Pasian Schiavonesco until 1923.

Basilicata (bäzēlēkä'tä), anc. *Lucania*, region (□ 3,856; pop. 543,262), S Italy, at instep of Ital. boot; ⊙ Potenza. Bordered by regions of Apulia (N, E), Campania (W), and Calabria (S). Comprises provs. of POTENZA and MATERA. Largely mountainous and hilly; traversed by the Apennines, which descend abruptly in SW to Gulf of Policastro (Tyrrhenian Sea) and gradually in SE to coastal plain bordering Gulf of Taranto (Ionian Sea). Area c.15% forested. Watered by Agri, Basento, Bradano, and Sinni rivers. Mainly agr. (cereals, grapes, olives, fruit, potatoes) and stock raising (sheep, goats). Hindered by hot, dry summers (rainfall chiefly from Oct. to Dec.), malaria, and difficult communications. Region is also subject to earthquakes and landslides (*frana*). Mfg. and commerce are limited. Conquered by Romans in 3d cent. B.C.; later passed to Lombards, Byzantines, and in 11th cent. to Normans. In 13th cent. included in kingdom of Naples. Present backward conditions are being alleviated by reclamation works and agrarian reforms, in progress since beginning of 20th cent. Until 1927, when Matera prov. was established, region was coextensive with Potenza prov.

Basílio (bŭzē'lyŏŏ), town (pop. 213), S Rio Grande do Sul, Brazil, 40 mi. WSW of Pelotas; rail junction; cattle raising.

Basim (bä'sĭm), town (pop. 17,928), Akola dist., W Madhya Pradesh, India, in Ajanta Hills, 45 mi. SSE of Akola; road center; trades in millet, wheat, timber (teak); cotton ginning, oilseed milling. Has col. of arts.

Basin. 1 Village (pop. c.300), Jefferson co., SW Mont., 25 mi. SSW of Helena and on Boulder R.; gold, silver mines. **2** Town (pop. 1,220), ⊙ Big Horn co., N Wyo., on Bighorn R., just W of Bighorn Mts., and 60 mi. SW of Sheridan; beans, sugar beets, livestock. State tuberculosis sanitarium near by.

Basin and Range: see GREAT BASIN.

Basing, agr. village and parish (pop. 1,673), NE Hampshire, England, 2 mi. E of Basingstoke. Site of 16th-cent. Basing House, which, in Civil War, held out against Parliamentary forces for 4 years, surrendering 1645 to Cromwell personally.

Basingstoke (bā'zĭng–), municipal borough (1931 pop. 13,865; 1951 census 16,979), N Hampshire, England, 17 mi. NE of Winchester; agr. market, with mfg. of agr. machinery, leather, clothing. Has 16th-cent. church and ruins of Holy Ghost Chapel (1525). Near by, prehistoric remains have been found.

Basin Harbor, Vt.: see FERRISBURG.

Basirhat (bŭsēr'hät), town (pop. 26,348), 24-Parganas dist., SE West Bengal, India, on upper Jamuna (Ichamati) R. and 33 mi. E of Calcutta; sugar milling, metalware mfg.; trades in rice, jute, pulse, mustard, dates, potatoes.

Basit, Cape (băsēt'), Arabic *Ras el Basit* or *Ras al-Basit* (both: räs' ĕl-băsēt'), Fr. *Bassit*, W Syria, on the Mediterranean, 24 mi. N of Latakia.

Baska (bä'shkä), Serbo-Croatian *Baška*, Ital. *Marina di Besca* (mä'rēnä dē bĕ'skä), village, NW Croatia, Yugoslavia, on Krk Isl., on Adriatic Sea, 9 mi. SE of Krk; picturesque seaside resort. Also known as Nova Baska or Baskanova, Ital. *Bescanuova*.

Baskahegan Lake (băskŭhē'gŭn), Washington co., E Maine, in hunting, fishing area near Brookton, 32 mi. NW of Calais; 5 mi. long. Source of **Baskahegan Stream**, flowing c.20 mi. N and NW to Mattawamkeag R. near Bancroft.

Baskale (bäshkälĕ'), Turkish *Başkale*, village (pop. 1,647), Van prov., SE Turkey, 50 mi. SE of Van, near Iran line; wheat, barley.

Baskanova, Yugoslavia: see BASKA.

Baskatong Lake (bă'skŭtŏng) (27 mi. long, 20 mi. wide), SW Que., in the Laurentians, 90 mi. N of Ottawa, at foot of Mt. Sir Wilfrid; alt. 732 ft. Fed and drained by Gatineau R. At outlet of Gatineau R. is Mercier Dam.

Baskaya, Russian SFSR: see GREMYACHINSK.

Baskemolla (bäs"kŭmŭ'lä), Swedish *Baskemölla*, fishing village (pop. 392), Kristianstad co., S Sweden, on the Baltic 3 mi. N of Simrishamn.

Basket Dome, Calif.: see YOSEMITE NATIONAL PARK.

Baskil (bäskĭl'), village (pop. 1,066), Elazig prov., E central Turkey, on railroad and 24 mi. W of Elazig; grain, legumes, fruit.

Baskin, village (pop. 117), Franklin parish, NE La., 27 mi. SE of Monroe, in agr. area; wood products.

Basking Ridge, village (pop. 1,899), Somerset co., N central N.J., 7 mi. SW of Morristown, near Passaic R. At White's Tavern, here, Gen. Charles Lee was captured by British, 1776. Settled early 18th cent.

Baskovskaya, Russian SFSR: see BAZKOVSKAYA.

Baskunchak, Lake (bŭskŏŏnchäk'), salt lake (□ 42) in Caspian Lowland, in NE Astrakhan oblast, Russian SFSR, 130 mi. NNW of Astrakhan; 12 mi. long, 6 mi. wide. Major salt-producing center; extraction works on left shore (Nizhni Baskunchak), connected by rail with Verkhni Baskunchak (distribution point) and Vladimirovka (river- and rail-transshipment point; saltworks). Has supplied Astrakhan fish industry since late-18th cent.

Basle, Switzerland: see BASEL.

Baslow and Bubnell, former urban district (1931 pop. 854), N central Derby, England. Includes agr. market villages of Baslow (-lō), on Derwent R. and 3 mi. NE of Bakewell, with 14th-cent. church, and just N, Bubnell.

Basmat or **Basmath** (bŭs'mŭt), town (pop. 13,796), Parbhani dist., India, 25 mi. E of Parbhani; trade center for cotton, millet, wheat, peanuts. Also called Basmathnagar.

Basmoen (bôs'mōŭn) Nor. *Båsmoen*, village (pop. 356) in Nord-Rana canton (pop. 6,122), Nordland co., N central Norway, on Ran Fjord, 2 mi. NW of Mo. Pyrite mine, worked intermittently since 1897. Formerly spelled Bossmo or Baasmoen.

Basoda (bä'sōdŭ), town (pop. 6,862), SE Madhya Bharat, India, 24 mi. NNE of Bhilsa; agr. market (wheat, millet, gram); flour milling; glassworks.

Bas-Oha (bäz-ōhä'), village (pop. 1,312), Liége prov., E central Belgium, on Meuse R. and 2 mi. W of Huy; Portland-cement mfg.

Basoko (bäsō'kō), town, Eastern Prov., N Belgian Congo, on right bank of Congo R. opposite Elisabetha and Barumbu, at mouth of Aruwimi R. and 120 mi. WNW of Stanleyville; river port; transshipment of rice and palm products. Has R.C. mission, leprosarium, airfield. Basoko was the hq. of Congo Free State troops during the Arab campaign (1890–94) and still preserves part of old fortifications.

Basoli or **Basohli** (bŭsō'lē), town (pop. 2,383), Kathua dist., SW Kashmir, on Ravi R. and 19 mi. NE of Kathua; wheat, rice, corn, bajra. Large palace ruins. Seat of anc. rajaship.

Basongo (bäsông'gō), village, Kasai prov., central Belgian Congo, on left bank of Kasai R. opposite influx of the Sankuru, and 100 mi. NW of Luebo; steamboat landing, native trade center; palm products.

Basque Provinces (băsk), Sp. *Vascongadas* (bäskông-gä'dhäs), N Spain, comprises the provinces of ÁLAVA, GUIPÚZCOA, and VIZCAYA (combined: □ 2,803; pop. 955,764), on Bay of Biscay, bordering NE on France, and bounded W and SW by New Castile, E and SE by Navarre. (In a wider sense the name also applies to other territories largely inhabited by Basques: Sp. NAVARRE; and Fr. regions of Labourd, Soule, and Lower Navarre, all in Basses-Pyrénées dept.). BILBAO, ⊙ Vizcaya prov., is largest city and one of chief industrial centers of Spain. Other cities include SAN SEBASTIÁN (⊙ Guipúzcoa), VITORIA (⊙ Álava), and historic GUERNICA. Area includes S slopes of W Pyrenees and E spurs of Cantabrian Mts.; the Ebro forms most of SW boundary. The short, swift rivers include the Urumea, Deva, and Nervión, flowing to Bay of Biscay. The densely populated coastal provs. of Vizcaya and Guipúzcoa are highly industrialized, with important mining (iron, lead, copper, zinc), metalworking, shipbuilding, and fishing industries. Minerals are exported mainly to England. Álava is essentially agr. (chiefly corn; also sugar beets, wine—the sour wine *chacolí*—apple cider). Also extensive forests, and cattle and sheep pastures. The Basques, the majority of whom have preserved their ancient language, which is unrelated to any other tongue, have jealously guarded their ancient customs and traditions. Primarily a people of free peasants, shepherds, fishermen, navigators, miners, and metalworkers, they also have produced such figures as St. Ignatius of Loyola, St. Francis Xavier, and Francisco de Vitoria. The Basques may be descendants of Cro-Magnon Man; they almost certainly are the oldest surviving racial group in Europe, and they antedate the ancient Iberian tribes of Spain, with which they have been erroneously identified. Before Roman times, the Basque tribes extended further to the N and S than now, but the core of the Basque country was only nominally subject to Roman rule. Christianity was slow in penetrating (3d–5th cent.). Once converted, the Basques have remained fervent Catholics, but they retained a certain tradition of independence from the hierarchies of Spain and France. Both hardy and wily as warriors, the Basques withstood domination by the Visigoths and Franks. Late in the 6th cent. they expanded northward, occupying present GASCONY (Latin *Vasconia*), to which they gave their name. Early in 9th cent. they concentrated in their present habitat and in 824 founded, at Pamplona, the kingdom of Navarre, which under Sancho III (1000–35) united almost all the Basques. Although Castile acquired Guipúzcoa (1200), Álava (1332), and Vizcaya (1370), the Castilian kings had to acknowledge the wide democratic rights enjoyed by the Basques. With the conquest (1512) of Navarre by Ferdinand the Catholic, the Basques lost their last independent stronghold. After the 16th cent., Basque prosperity declined and emigration became widespread, especially in the 19th cent. Basque privileges remained in force until 1873, when they were abolished because of the Basques' pro-Carlist stand in the Carlist wars. To regain autonomy, the Basques in Spain supported nearly every political movement directed against the central authority. In the civil war of 1936–39 they wholeheartedly supported the Loyalist govt., which in 1936 granted them an autonomy which they fiercely defended against the Insurgents until their subjugation in 1937.

Basra or **Basrah** (băz′rŭ, bŭs′rŭ, bäs′rä), province (□ 4,758; pop. 352,039), extreme SE Iraq, bet. Iran (E) and Kuwait (W), at head of the Persian Gulf; ⊙ Basra. In spite of its large swamps, it is an extremely productive region, growing dates, rice, corn, millet. Through it flows (NW–SE) the Shatt al Arab (the stream formed by the union of the Tigris and the Euphrates), with the important port of Basra. In NW is part of the lake Hor al Hammar.

Basra or **Basrah,** city (pop. 93,889; with environs 206,302), ⊙ Basra prov., SE Iraq, on the Shatt al Arab (lower course of the combined Tigris and Euphrates), near Iran border, 75 mi. upstream from the Persian Gulf, and 280 mi. SE of Baghdad; 30°30′N 47°50′E. The principal port of Iraq and a major communication and trade center of the Near East, connected by rail with Baghdad, Iran, and Kuwait. The hub of a rich flood-land agr. region (dates, rice, corn, millet, barley, wheat), it has distilleries (whiskey, arrack, cordials) and exports agr. produce, wool, cotton, hides, livestock, and oil. It is a busy livestock market (sheep, goats, camels). Its modern port is Ma'qil, 5 mi. N, at head of navigation for ocean-going ships; its old port and commercial center is 'Ashar, NE. An airport and seaplane base were completed 1937. Founded originally at near-by Al Zubair in A.D. 636 by the caliph Omar, Basra grew as a commercial center on the great trade routes using the Persian Gulf. A cultural center under Harun-al-Rashid (late 8th cent.), it declined with the decay of the Abbasid caliphate, and was long contested by the Persians and Turks. With the opening of the rail connection to Baghdad, it regained commercial importance. Its modern port was begun in First World War by the British during the Mesopotamia campaign, and in Second World War it handled large quantities of oil and military supplies for transshipment to Russia. The city figures in the *Thousand and One Nights* and is sometimes spelled Bassora, Bassorah, Bussora, and Busra.

Bas-Rhin (bä-rē′) [Fr.,=lower Rhine], department (□ 1,848; pop. 673,281), in Alsace, E France; ⊙ Strasbourg. Bounded by Germany (border formed E by the Rhine, N by the Lauter), and by the N Vosges (W); occupies N part of Alsatian lowland. Drained W–E by tributaries of the Rhine (Bruche, Zorn, Moder, Sauer and Lauter). A rich agr. area: cereals, hops (Haguenau dist.), sugar beets, tobacco, potatoes, cabbage (for sauerkraut), onions, lettuce, fruit (cherries, peaches, prunes). Winegrowing along E Vosges slopes. Petroleum wells at Merkwiller-Péchelbronn. Metallurgy is chief industry; auto mfg. at Molsheim and Strasbourg; machine building at Strasbourg, Saverne, Mutzig, and Niederbronn; cables and springs at Reichshoffen; locomotives at Illkirch-Graffenstaden. Other industries are tanning (especially at Barr) and leatherworking (Dettwiller, Lingolsheim, Benfeld), textile milling and food processing (well-known *pâté de foie gras*). STRASBOURG is regional commercial center with fine rail and river (autonomous port on the Rhine) facilities. Access to Paris Basin principally through Saverne Gap across the N Vosges. As part of Alsace-Lorraine, dept. was under Ger. administration 1871–1918 and 1940–44.

Bassac, province, Laos: see PAKSE.

Bassac (bä′säk′), town (1941 pop. 3,117), Champassak prov., S Laos, on right bank of Mekong R. (port) and 14 mi. S of Pakse. In Thailand, 1941–46.

Bassac River, delta arm of Mekong R. in Cambodia and S Vietnam, branches off from Mekong R. at Pnompenh in QUATRE BRAS confluence, flows 200 mi. SE, past Chaudoc, Longxuyen, and Cantho, to South China Sea E of Soctrang.

Bassam, Fr. West Africa: see GRAND-BASSAM.

Bassano (bŭsä′nō, bŭsă′nô), town (pop. 590), S Alta., near Bow R., 70 mi. ESE of Calgary; coal mining, dairying. Near by, on Bow R., is the Bassano or Horseshoe Bend irrigation dam, one of longest in the world.

Bassano or **Bassano del Grappa** (bäsä′nô dĕl gräp′pä), town (pop. 11,774), Vicenza prov., Veneto, N Italy, at S foot of Monte Grappa, on Brenta R. and 18 mi. NNE of Vicenza. Rail junction; industrial center; ironworks, bell foundry, tanneries, mfg. (automobile chassis, agr. machinery, stoves, pottery, glass, wax, pens), alcohol distillery, sawmills. Has 10th-cent. cathedral (frequently remodeled), 13th-cent. Romanesque-Gothic church, anc. palaces, villas. Art mus. (war damaged, restored) contains works of Da Ponte family, surnamed Bassano, which headed school of painting here in 16th cent. Famous in 17th and 18th cent. for its printing plant. Under Venetian rule 1402–1796. Near here, in 1796, Napoleon defeated Austrians. Bombed (1945) in Second World War.

Bassano di Sutri (bäsä′nô dē sōō′trē), town (pop. 3,084), Viterbo prov., Latium, central Italy, 15 mi. SSE of Viterbo; mfg. of explosives. Has palace with frescoes by Domenichino.

Bassari (bäsä′rē), town (pop. 5,563), Fr. Togoland, 30 mi. NW of Sokodé; cotton, peanuts, corn, sheanuts; cattle, sheep, and goat raising. R.C. mission.

Bassas-de-India (bä′sŭs-dĕn′dyŭ), volcanic rock and reefs, outlying dependency of Madagascar in Mozambique Channel of Indian Ocean; 21°30′S 39°50′E. Sometimes called Baixo-da-Judia.

Bassas de Pedro (bä′säs dā pā′drō), bank of the Laccadives, India, in Arabian Sea, bet. 12°–14°N and 72°–73°E. Also called Padua Bank.

Basse (bä′sā), town (pop. 690), ⊙ Upper River div., E Gambia, on left bank of Gambia R. (wharf and ferry) and 160 mi. E of Bathurst; peanuts, beeswax; hides and skins. R.C. mission school at Mansajang, just S.

Bassée, La (lä bäsā′), town (pop. 4,619), Nord dept., N France, on Aire–La Bassée Canal, and 7 mi. E of Béthune; chemical works (fertilizer, soap), flour mills; textile weaving, furniture and shirt mfg. Captured by Germans in 1914, it became one of the most contested and best fortified points along the Br. front during First World War.

Bassein (bəsēn′, –sān′), Burmese *Pathein*, district (□ 4,149; 1941 pop. 664,727), Irrawaddy div., Lower Burma; ⊙ Bassein. In Irrawaddy delta, bet. Bay of Bengal and Bassein R.; flat except for southernmost spur (1,325 ft.) of Arakan Yoma. Intensive rice cultivation, fisheries. Pop. 70% Burmese, 20% Karen.

Bassein, town (pop. 45,662), ⊙ Irrawaddy div. and Bassein dist., Lower Burma, port on left bank of Bassein R. and 70 mi. above its mouth; 16°47′N 94°44′E. Rice-milling center reached by railroad from Henzada and by Irrawaddy delta steamers. Airport. Mfg. of pottery, sunshades. Early Br. factory (1757) and Br. fort (1852).

Bassein, town (pop. 13,969), Thana dist., W Bombay, India, on Arabian Sea, at mouth of Ulhas R. (Bassein Creek), 26 mi. N of Bombay, in the Konkan; fish-curing center (pomfrets, jewfish, Bombay duck); betel farming, salt panning, pottery mfg., rice, plantain, and sugar-cane growing. Has col. Town ceded 1534 to Portuguese; later became a prosperous port; captured 1739 by Mahrattas, 1780 by British.

Basse-Indre, La, France: see INDRE.

Bassein River, westernmost mouth of Irrawaddy R. delta, Lower Burma, branches off main stream N of Henzada, flows 200 mi. SSW, past Umyethwa, Ngathainggyaung, Thabaung, and Bassein, to Andaman Sea. Called Ngawun R. (ŭngŭwōōn′) in upper course.

Bassendean (bă′sŭndēn), town (pop. 5,243), SW Western Australia, 6 mi. NE of Perth; superphosphate works. Formerly West Guildford.

Bassens (bäsä′), NE suburb (pop. 405) of Bordeaux, Gironde dept., SW France, and part of its port on the Garonne; freight yards, refrigerated warehouses, fertilizer factories. Original harbor installations built by U.S. Army during First World War.

Bassenthwaite Lake, W Cumberland, England, on Derwent R., 5 mi. E of Cockermouth; 4 mi. long, 1 mi. wide; resort.

Basse-Pointe (bäs-pwĕt′), town (pop. 576), N Martinique, on the Atlantic, 13 mi. NNW of Fort-de-France, in sugar-growing region; sugar milling, rum distilling, mfg. of soap.

Basses-Alpes (bäs′zälp′) [Fr.,=lower Alps], department (□ 2,698; pop. 83,354), in Provence, SE France; ⊙ Digne. Borders on Italy (NE). Lies wholly within Provence Alps. Drained by upper Durance R. and its tributaries (Ubaye, Buëch, Bléone, Asse, Verdon). Generally infertile, agr. (mulberry and olive trees, fruits, wine) concentrated in alluvial river valleys. Lavender is widely processed. Magnesium is produced at Saint-Auban electrochemical works. Principal communication arteries: Durance valley (N–S); and Ubaye valley (W–E), which provides access to Italy via Maddalena Pass. Chief towns: Digne, Manosque, Sisteron, Barcelonnette.

Basses-Pyrénées (bäs-pērānā′) [Fr.,=lower Pyrenees], department (□ 2,978; pop. 415,797), in Béarn and part of Gascony, SW France, ⊙ Pau. Bounded by the Bay of Biscay and the crest of the PYRENEES (Sp. border). Very accidented terrain, drained by left tributaries (Gave d'Oloron, Gave de Pau, Nive) of the Adour. Agr. (corn, wheat, fruits, wine) in foothills and near Atlantic coast. Extensive sheep and cattle pastures in uplands. Horse breeding, hog raising. Saltworks and marble quarries. Mountain streams used for hydroelectric power. Main industries are food processing (meat preserving, chocolate and cheese mfg.), textile milling (woolens, table linen, handkerchiefs), and footwear mfg. Dept. has many popular spas and health resorts along the Bay of Biscay (Biarritz, Saint-Jean-de-Luz, Hendaye), in the foothills (Pau, Salies), and in the mountain valleys (Les Eaux-Bonnes, Les Eaux-Chaudes, Cambo-les-Bains). Chief towns are Pau, Bayonne (port and metallurgical center), Biarritz, and Oloron-Sainte-Marie (textiles). Pop. is largely Basque. Communication with Spain via Hendaye (rail), Roncesvalles and Pourtalet passes (road), and Somport pass (road and railroad).

Basse-sur-le-Rupt (bäs-sür-lŭ-rüpt′), village (pop. 132), Vosges dept., E France, in the Vosges, 9 mi. ESE of Remiremont; granite quarrying.

Basse-Terre (bäs-târ′), city (commune pop. 10,086), ⊙ GUADELOUPE dept., Fr. West Indies, port on SW coast of Basse-Terre isl. (W part of Guadeloupe isl.), 105 mi. NNW of Fort-de-France, Martinique, and 330 mi. ESE of San Juan, Puerto Rico; 16°N 61°42′W. Center of a rich agr. region (coffee, cacao, vanilla, bay leaves), whose products it ships; vessels anchor offshore. A picturesque city towered over by rugged mts. Has fine promenades, botanic garden, Notre Dame Cathedral. Dating from Fr. settlement (1643), Basse-Terre lost in late 18th cent. its commercial leadership to Pointe-à-Pitre (on Grande-Terre), center of the sugar industry. There are thermal springs in the vicinity.

Basse-Terre island (□ 364; pop. 103,772), the W half of Guadeloupe, is separated from Grande-Terre by narrow Rivière Salée channel. It is rocky and mountainous, rising in dormant volcano Soufrière to 4,869 ft. Chief products grown along the coast are cacao, coffee, vanilla, bananas, bay leaves, sugar cane. The isl. is sometimes referred to as Guadeloupe isl. proper.

Basseterre, town (pop. 12,194), ⊙ St. Kitts-Nevis presidency and St. Kitts isl., Leeward Isls., B.W.I., port on SW coast of St. Kitts, 60 mi. W of St. John's, Antigua; 17°18′N 62°43′W. Distributing center for neighboring isls. On open roadstead, it trades in sugar, molasses, cotton, salt, fruit; sugar milling. Rebuilt after 1867 fire, Basseterre has R.C. cathedral, St. George's Church, Govt. House, botanic station (established 1899), international cable station, and near-by airport. Old Brimstone Hill fort and former garrison is 7 mi. NW.

Basse Terre, village (pop. 1,376), S Trinidad, B.W.I., 15 mi. SE of San Fernando, in cacao-growing region.

Bassett, England: see SOUTHAMPTON.

Bassett. 1 Town (pop. 125), Chickasaw co., NE Iowa, near Little Cedar R., 8 mi. E of Charles City. **2** City (pop. 117), Allen co., SE Kansas, on Neosho R., just S of Iola. **3** Village (pop. 1,066), ⊙ Rock co., N Nebr., 115 mi. WNW of Norfolk; trading, shipping point; dairy products, grain. **4** or **Bassetts,** industrial village (pop. 3,421), Henry co., S Va., on Smith R. and 35 mi. WNW of Danville, in agr. area; furniture-mfg. center; also veneer, mirrors, knit goods.

Bassett Peak (7,650 ft.), SE Ariz., highest point in Galiuro Mts., c.45 mi. ENE of Tucson.

Bassetts, Va.: see BASSETT.

Basse-Yutz (bäs-yüts′), Ger. *Nieder Jeutz* (nē′dŭr yoits′), E suburb (pop. 7,381) of Thionville, Moselle dept., NE France, on right bank of the Moselle; steel milling, brewing.

Bassfield (băs′fēld), town (pop. 320), Jefferson Davis co., S central Miss., 30 mi. WNW of Hattiesburg; hosiery mill.

Bassi, India: see BASI.

Bassignana (bäsēnyä′nä), village (pop. 1,667), Alessandria prov., Piedmont, N Italy, near confluence of Po and Tanaro rivers, 8 mi. NE of Alessandria.

Bassigny (bäsēnyē′), old region of NE France, now chiefly in Haute-Marne dept., N of Plateau of Langres; ⊙ Chaumont. Long known for its artisan cutlery making.

Bassila (bäsē′lä), village, W central Dahomey, Fr. West Africa, near Togoland border, on road and 80 mi. NNW of Savalou; cotton, corn, millet. Customhouse.

Bassin, U.S. Virgin Isls.: see CHRISTIANSTED.

Bassin-Bleu (bäsē-blû′), town, Nord-Ouest dept., N Haiti, on Les Trois Rivières and 11 mi. S of Port-de-Paix, in fertile agr. region (coffee, cacao, cotton).

Bassingbourn, agr. village and parish (pop. 1,048), S Cambridge, England, 3 mi. NW of Royston. Has 13th–15th-cent. church.

Bass Islands, N Ohio, in L. Erie c.35 mi. W of Toledo; group includes North Bass (1¼ mi. long; site of Isle St. George village), Middle Bass (c.3 mi. long; site of Middle Bass village), and South Bass (c.3½ mi. long), site of PUT-IN-BAY village and natl. monument commemorating Perry's victory in battle of L. Erie. Isls. are noted summer resorts, produce much wine, and have lake fisheries. With neighboring isls., sometimes called Wine Isls.

Bass Isles or **Marotiri** (mä′rōtē′rē), small, uninhabited islet, Fr. Oceania, S Pacific, 50 mi. SE of Rapa; governed by Tubuai Isls. Also called Morotiri.

Bassit, Cape, Syria: see BASIT, CAPE.

Bass Lake. 1 In Calif.: see CRANE VALLEY LAKE. **2** In Itasca co., N central Minn., 5 mi. NW of Grand Rapids; 6.5 mi. long, 1 mi. wide. Drains into Mississippi R.

Bassopiano Occidentale, Eritrea: see AGORDAT.

Bassopiano Orientale, Eritrea: see MASSAWA.

Bassorah, Iraq: see BASRA.

Bassou (bäsōō′), village (pop. 550), Yonne dept., N central France, on Yonne R. at mouth of the Serein, and 9 mi. NNW of Auxerre; snail preserving.

Bass River, village, Mass.: see YARMOUTH.

Bass River (băs), SE N.J., rises in SE Burlington co., flows c.10 mi. generally S, through Bass R. State Forest, to Mullica R. near its mouth on Great Bay.

Bass Rock, rocky islet (1 mi. in circumference; 350 ft. high) at mouth of Firth of Forth, East Lothian, Scotland, 4 mi. ENE of North Berwick; nesting place of sea fowl. Formerly used as prison. Lighthouse (56°4′N 2°38′W).

Bass Rocks, Mass.: see GLOUCESTER.

Bass Strait, large channel (□ 30,000; mean depth 230 ft.) bet. the coasts of Victoria, Australia (N), and Tasmania (S); merges W with Indian Ocean and E with Tasman Sea (to which Banks Strait is SE opening); 80–150 mi. wide. Contains King Isl., Furneaux and Hunter isls. Discovered 1798 by George Bass.

Bassum (bä′sŏŏm), town (pop. 6,987), in former Prussian prov. of Hanover, NW Germany, after 1945 in Lower Saxony, 24 mi. NW of Nienburg; grain, cattle. Has 9th–14th-cent. church.

Basswood Lake, in chain of lakes on international line bet. Lake co., NE Minn., and W Ont., and 15 mi. NE of Ely, Minn.; length, including W arm, 10 mi.; max. width 4 mi. Includes several small isls. and is partly in Superior Natl. Forest. Has fishing resorts.

Bastad (bō′städ″), Swedish *Båstad*, town (pop. 2,206), Kristianstad co., SW Sweden, on Laholm Bay (5 mi. wide) of the Kattegat, 8 mi. S of Halmstad; fashionable seaside resort; noted for flowers and fruit grown here. Scene of annual tennis and golf championships. Has 15th-cent. church. Town chartered 1664.

Bastak (bästäk′), town (1945 pop. estimate 7,500), Seventh Prov., in Laristan, S Iran, 34 mi. S of Lar; tobacco, dates, cotton.

Bastam, Iran: see BUSTAM.

Bastar (bŭstŭr′), former princely state (□ 13,701; pop. 633,888) in Chhattisgarh States of Eastern States agency, India; ⊙ was Jagdalpur. Since 1948, inc. into Bastar dist. of Madhya Pradesh.

Bastar, district (□ 15,114; pop. 783,359), SE Madhya Pradesh, India, on Deccan Plateau; ⊙ Jagdalpur. Consists mainly of W outliers (average alt. 2,500 ft.) of Eastern Ghats, with central ridge (N–S) rising to over 4,000 ft.; drained mainly by Indravati R. and (N) by the Mahanadi. Mostly dense jungle (sal, bamboo, teak, myrobalan, tanning bark; lac growing); also exports rice, oilseeds, cattle. Dispersed hematite deposits; mica and corundum deposits (E, S). Dist. created 1948 by merger of former Chhattisgarh States of Bastar and Kanker. Pop. 75% tribal (mainly Gond), 25% Hindu.

Bastar, village, India: see JAGDALPUR.

Bastei (bästī′), small massif, Saxony, E central Germany, in Saxonian Switzerland, 2 mi. W of Wehlen, 6 mi. W of Pirna, overlooking the Elbe; rises to 1,040 ft. Popular tourist resort. Near by are noted rock formations.

Bastelica (bästĕlēkä′, It. bästä′lēkä), town (pop. 3,268), central Corsica, 17 mi. ENE of Ajaccio; alt. 2,523 ft. Chestnuts. Sampiero d'Ornano, who expelled the Genoese from Corsica in 1557, b. near by.

Bastenaken, Belgium: see BASTOGNE.

Basti (bŭs′tē), district (□ 2,822; pop. 2,185,641), NE Uttar Pradesh, India; ⊙ Basti. Bounded N by Nepal, S by the Gogra; fertile alluvial plain drained by Rapti R. Agr. (rice, wheat, barley, gram, mustard, sugar cane, corn); mango, bamboo, and mahua groves; hand-loom cotton weaving. Main towns: Basti, Mehndawal. Tomb of the Moslem and Hindu saint Kabir is at Maghar.

Basti, town (pop. 23,893), ⊙ Basti dist., NE Uttar Pradesh, India, 37 mi. E of Fyzabad; road center; rice milling; trades in rice, wheat, barley, gram, mustard, sugar cane. Sugar processing at village of Walterganj (4 mi. N) and Munderwa (10 mi. W).

Basti, Spain: see BAZA.

Bastia (bästyä′, It. bä′styä), city (pop. 37,122), N Corsica, on Tyrrhenian Sea, at E base of Cape Corse peninsula, 65 mi. NE of Ajaccio and 75 mi. SSW of Livorno (Italy); 42°42′N 9°25′E. Fortified port and island's chief city, with exports of liqueurs, olive oil, hides, citrus fruit, cork, tanning extracts. Mfg.: cigarettes, cutlery, brier pipes, flour products. Coral and anchovy fisheries. Old town (17th–18th cent.) S of modern city and port is dominated by 16th–17th-cent. citadel which replaced Genoese *bastiglia* built in 1380. Founded 14th cent. by Genoese, Bastia was ⊙ Corsica until 1791. Heavily bombed and its harbor gutted in Second World War; liberated by Allies in 1943.

Bastia (bä′styä), town (pop. 1,380), Perugia prov., Umbria, central Italy, 3 mi. W of Assisi; canned tomatoes, macaroni, soap, cement.

Bastian (băs′chŭn), lumber-milling village (1940 pop. 684), Bland co., SW Va., in the Alleghenies, 9 mi. SSE of Bluefield.

Bastide-de-Sérou, La (lä bästēd′-dü-särōō′), village (pop. 681), Ariège dept., S France, on the Arize and 10 mi. WNW of Foix; cheese making. Bauxite and iron mines near by.

Bastide-sur-l'Hers, La (-sür-lār′), village (pop. 653), Ariège dept., S France, in Plantaurel range, on the Hers and 15 mi. E of Foix; woolen milling, comb mfg.

Bastiglia (bästē′lyä), village (pop. 666), Modena prov., Emilia-Romagna, N central Italy, near Secchia R., 6 mi. NNE of Modena; sausage factory.

Bastimentos (bästēmĕn′tōs), village (pop. 349), Bocas del Toro prov., W Panama, on Bastimentos Isl., 2 mi. ENE of Bocas del Toro; stock raising and lumbering.

Basto, Norway: see BASTOY.

Bastogne (bästô′nyü), Flemish *Bastenaken* (bäs′-tünäkün), town (pop. 4,991), Luxembourg prov., SE Belgium, in the Ardennes, on Wiltz R. and 23 mi. N of Arlon; rail junction and road center; agr. market town; horse and cattle markets. During the German counteroffensive of Dec., 1944 (known as the Battle of the Bulge), elements of the 101st U.S. Airborne Division and of other units, all under Gen. Anthony McAuliffe, held (Dec. 20–26) encircled Bastogne until relieved by the U.S. Third Army. Invited by the Germans to surrender, McAuliffe supposedly replied with the word "Nuts!" The town was nearly destroyed in the battle.

Bastonnais River, Que.: see BOSTONNAIS RIVER.

Bastos (bä′stōōs), city (pop. 2,673), W São Paulo, Brazil, 55 mi. WNW of Marília, in pioneer settlement zone; cotton, coffee, tobacco, potatoes, wheat.

Bastoy (bäst′üü), Nor. *Bastøy*, island (□ c.1) in Oslo Fjord, SE Norway, 4 mi. SE of Horten; site of boarding school for homeless children, founded 1898. Formerly spelled Basto, Nor. *Bastø*.

Bastrop (bă′strŏp), county (□ 885; pop. 19,622), S central Texas; ⊙ Bastrop. Drained by Colorado R. Agr. (cotton, corn, truck, peanuts, grain sorghums); eggs, poultry shipped; dairying, livestock (cattle, hogs). Clay, lignite mining; oil, natural-gas wells; lumbering. Formed 1836.

Bastrop. 1 Industrial town (pop. 12,769), ⊙ Morehouse parish, NE La., 22 mi. NNE of Monroe; paper and pulp milling; mfg. of carbon black, brick, chemicals, glass, varnish, printer's ink; lumber milling. Diversified agr. (cotton, peaches, truck). Founded c.1845. Boomed after discovery of natural gas in 1916. **2** City (pop. 3,176), ⊙ Bastrop co., S central Texas, on Colorado R. and 23 mi. ESE of Austin; trade, shipping center of agr. (corn, pecans, poultry, cotton), lignite, lumber area; cedar-chest mfg. State park near by. Settled 1827, inc. 1837.

Bastutrask (bäs′tütrĕsk″), Swedish *Bastuträsk*, village (pop. 631), Vasterbotten co., N Sweden, 30 mi. W of Skelleftea; rail junction; woodworking. Limestone deposits.

Basutoland (bŭsōō′tōlănd), British protectorate (□ 11,716; 1946 pop. 553,827; with absent laborers 624,605) administered directly by the Crown, in S Africa, surrounded by provinces of U. of So. Afr. (Natal, E; Cape Prov., S; Orange Free State, W and N); ⊙ Maseru. W part of territory consists of high plateau (c.5,000 ft.), the center of population. E part of country is mountainous, crossed by Maluti Mts. (rising to over 10,000 ft.), part of Drakensberg range, which forms E border of territory. Orange R. crosses Basutoland; part of N border is formed by Caledon R. Climate is dry, with temp. range from 11°F. to 93°F.; average annual rainfall 20–30 in. Stock raising (cattle, sheep, goats, horses, mules); wool, mohair, hide, skin production; and grain growing (wheat, corn, Kaffir corn, beans, barley, oats) are main occupations. Numerous Basutos work in the Witwatersrand gold mines in the Transvaal. Chief villages: Leribe, Mafeteng, Mohales Hoek, Mokhtlong, Qachas Nek, Quthing, and Teyateyaneng. Various Basuto tribes were united bet. 1815 and 1831 by Chief Moshesh who, after defeating the Matabele, made his hq. at Thaba Bosiu. From 1835 onward there was constant friction with advancing Boers; British expedition (1852) resulted in short-lived peace. By 1867 the Basuto were almost totally defeated by Boers and requested to be taken under British protection. British sovereignty established March 12, 1868. Basutoland, Bechuanaland Protectorate, and Swaziland constitute the High Commission Territories.

Baswa (bŭs′vŭ). **1** Town (pop. 5,500), E Rajasthan, India, 50 mi. ENE of Jaipur; millet, wheat; handicraft pottery making. **2** Village, Birbhum dist., W West Bengal, India, 27 mi. NE of Suri; silk-weaving center; rice, wheat, gram, corn, sugar cane. Also spelled Basoa.

Basyanovski or **Bas'yanovskiy** (bŭsyä′nŭfskē), town (1938 pop. over 500), central Sverdlovsk oblast, Russian SFSR, 15 mi. N of Nizhnyaya Salda; peat. Gold placers near by.

Basyun (băsyōōn′), village (pop. 11,952), Gharbiya prov., Lower Egypt, on Rosetta branch of the Nile, and 16 mi. NW of Tanta; cotton, cereals, rice, fruits. Site of anc. Sais is 5 mi. NW.

Bata (bä′tŏ), Hung. *Báta*, town (pop. 3,674), Tolna co., S Hungary, on arm of the Danube and 11 mi. NNE of Mohacs; wheat, honey; dairy farming.

Bata (bä′tä), chief town (pop. 848) of continental Sp. Guinea (or Río Muni), on the Gulf of Guinea, 150 mi. SSE of Santa Isabel (⊙ Sp. Guinea, on Fernando Po isl.), and 100 mi. N of Libreville (Gabon, Fr. Equatorial Africa); 1°50′N 9°47′E. Offshore anchorage. Coffee export center. Also ships cacao, cabinetwoods, yucca, copra, palm oil, palm kernels. Airfield. Residence of sub-governor administering continental Sp. Guinea. R.C. mission.

Bataan (bŏŏtăn′, bätä-än′), province (□ 517; 1948 pop. 92,901), S Luzon, Philippines, occupying the whole of Bataan Peninsula; ⊙ BALANGA. Chief products: sugar cane, rice.

Bataan, Mount (4,700 ft.), highest peak on Bataan Peninsula, S Luzon, Philippines, 6 mi. NNW of Mariveles.

Bataan Peninsula, mountainous peninsula, coextensive with Bataan prov., S Luzon, Philippines, sheltering Manila Bay from S.China Sea; 30 mi. long, 20 mi. wide; rises to 4,700 ft. in Mt. Bataan in S central area. Subic Bay indents NW part of peninsula; Mariveles Harbor is in S. Largely jungle, with pop. centers concentrated on E coast. Isl. of Corregidor is off S tip. In Second World War, U.S. and Philippine forces withdrew to Bataan after fall of Manila (Jan. 2, 1942) and fought a fierce delaying action until they surrendered April 9, 1942; Gen. Wainwright, who had succeeded Gen. MacArthur, fought on from Corregidor.

Batabanó (bätäbänō′), town (pop. 3,177), Havana prov., W Cuba, on railroad and 29 mi. S of Havana, in agr. region (sugar cane, fruit, vegetables). Its port Surgidero de Batabanó (2½ mi. S) is point of embarkation for Isle of Pines; sponge-fishing.

Batabanó, Gulf of, inlet, SW Cuba, bounded S by Isle of Pines and NE by Zapata Peninsula, and 30 mi. S of Havana; shallow sea dotted by numerous keys. Important sponge-fishing area. Its NE section is also called Gulf of Matamanó or Ensenada de la Broa.

Batac (bä′täk), town (1939 pop. 6,819; 1948 municipality pop. 22,587), Ilocos Norte prov., NW Luzon, Philippines, 10 mi. SSW of Laoag; rice-growing center.

Batagai or **Batagay** (bŭtŭgī′), town (1946 pop. over 500), N Yakut Autonomous SSR, Russian SFSR, near Verkhoyansk.

Batagai-Alyta or **Batagay-Alyta** (-ŭlĭtä′), village (1948 pop. over 500), N Yakut Autonomous SSR, Russian SFSR, N of Arctic Circle, on tributary of Yana R. and 80 mi. W of Verkhoyansk.

Batag Island (bätäg′) (□ 12; 1939 pop. 2,646), Samar prov., Philippines, in Philippine Sea, just off NE coast of Samar isl., near Laoang Isl.; 6 mi. long, 3.5 mi. wide. Coconut growing.

Bataisk or **Bataysk** (bŭtīsk′), city (1926 pop. 22,891), SW Rostov oblast, Russian SFSR, 6 mi. S of Rostov, across marshy Don R. valley; rail center (freight yards); metalworking, aircraft mfg.; grain and livestock trade. Became city in 1938. During Second World War, held (1942–43) by Germans.

Batak (bätäk′), village (pop. 5,794), Plovdiv dist., S Bulgaria, summer resort in W Rhodope Mts., on branch of Maritsa R. and 8 mi. SSW of Peshtera; sawmill and lumber center in coniferous woodland; livestock. Has woodworking school, old church. Burned by Turks during Bulg. uprising in 1876.

Bataklik, Lake (bätäklŭk′), Turkish *Bataklık* (□ 70), S central Turkey, 33 mi. SE of Konya; 13 mi. long, 7 mi. wide.

Batala (bŭtä′lŭ), town (pop. 44,458), Gurdaspur dist., NW Punjab, India, 18 mi. SW of Gurdaspur; rail junction; trade center (grain, sugar cane); mfg. of woolen goods, machine tools, agr. implements, leather goods, enamel, soap; cotton ginning, hand-loom weaving, sugar refining; metalware. Has col.

Batalha (bŭtä′lyŭ). **1** City (pop. 492), central Alagoas, NE Brazil, landing on left bank of lower São Francisco R. and 55 mi. NW of Penedo. Until 1949, called Belo Monte. **2** City (pop. 1,080), N Piauí, Brazil, 90 mi. NNE of Teresina; cattle, carnauba wax. Amethysts found in area.

Batalha, town (pop. 506), Leiria dist., W central Portugal, on railroad and 6 mi. S of Leiria. Here is the magnificent Dominican monastery and church (Santa Maria da Vitória), built by John I of Portugal to commemorate his victory (1385) over John I of Castile at near-by Aljubarrota. The monastery, now a natl. mus., is a masterpiece of architecture.

Batalhão, Brazil: see TAPEROÁ, PARAÍBA.

Batalpashinsk, RSFSR: see CHERKESSK, city.

Batam (bätäm′), island (□c.180; 17 mi. long, 13 mi. wide), Riouw Archipelago, Indonesia, in the S.China Sea, at entrance to Strait of Malacca, 12 mi. SE of Singapore; 1°5′N 104°1′E. Hilly on SE coast. Produces timber, gambier, pepper, copra.

Batamshinski or **Batamshinskiy** (bŭtŭmshēn′skē), town (1945 pop. over 500), N Aktyubinsk oblast, Kazakh SSR, on railroad and 50 mi. NE of Aktyubinsk; nickel-mining center. Until 1945, Kimpersaiski or Kimpersayskiy mines.

Batan (bätän′), town (1939 pop. 977; 1948 municipality pop. 14,714), Capiz prov., N Panay isl., Philippines, port on small inlet of Sibuyan Sea, 18 mi. W of Capiz; ships copra, rice, hemp.

Batanagar, India: see BUDGE-BUDGE.

Batanes, province, Philippines: see BATAN ISLANDS.

Batang, China: see PAAN.

Batang (bätäng′), town (pop. 28,655), central Java, Indonesia, near Java Sea, 4 mi. ESE of Pekalongan; 6°54′S 109°44′E; trade center in agr. area (rice, sugar, rubber, tobacco); textile mills.

Batangafo (bätäng-gäfō′), village, N central Ubangi-Shari, Fr. Equatorial Africa, on the Bahr Sara and 80 mi. NE of Bossangoa; cotton ginning.

Batangan, Cape (bätängän′), central Vietnam, on South China Sea, 130 mi. SE of Hue; 15°15′N 108°56′E. Poulo Canton isl. lies 15 mi. NE.

Batangas (bŏotäng′gŭs, Sp. bätäng′gäs), province (□ 1,192; 1948 pop. 510,224), S Luzon, Philippines, bounded W by S.China Sea, S by Balayan and Batangas bays, E by Tayabas Bay; ⊙ Batangas. Includes MARICABAN ISLAND and VERDE ISLAND. In center of prov. is L. Taal, containing Volcano Isl. Generally mountainous and forested terrain, drained by many small streams. Fishing, agr. (rice, sugar cane, corn, coconuts), lumbering. LIPA city is in, but independent of, the prov.

Batangas, town (1939 pop. 6,711; 1948 municipality pop. 59,582), ⊙ Batangas prov., S Luzon, Philippines, port for interisland shipping near mouth of small Calumpan R., on Batangas Bay, 28 mi. SW of San Pablo; rail terminus. Trade center for agr. area (rice, sugar cane, corn, coconuts); fisheries. At near-by village of Santa Rita (1939 pop. 1,518) are lumber-finishing mills.

Batangas Bay, inlet, S Luzon, Philippines, connected with S.China Sea by Verde Isl. Passage, separated from Balayan Bay by narrow peninsula S of L. Taal; 10 mi. long, 10 mi. wide. Maricaban Isl. is at W side of entrance.

Batan Island (bätän′). **1** Island (□ 35; 1939 pop. 8,150), Albay prov., Philippines, off SE Luzon, bet. Lagonoy Gulf (N) and Albay Gulf (S), and bet. Cagraray and Rapu-Rapu isls.; 8 mi. long, 4½ mi. wide; rises to 1,300 ft. at Mt. Vizcaya. Important coal mines. **2** Island (□ 27; 1948 pop. 5,603), Batanes prov., Batan Isls., N Philippines, N of Luzon, in Luzon Strait, 18 mi. SE of Itbayat Isl.; 11½ mi. long, ½–3½ mi. wide; hilly. Corn, rice. Chief town is Basco (bä′skō) (1939 pop. 2,782), ⊙ Batanes prov., on NW coast.

Batan Islands, group (□ 76; 1948 pop. 10,705), constituting Batanes prov. (bätä′näs), Philippines, c.190 mi. N of Luzon, in Luzon Strait, separated from Formosa (N) by Bashi Channel and from Babuyan Isls. (S) by Balintang Channel; 20°N 121°53′E. Comprises N–S chain of 14 isls., the principal ones being ITBAYAT ISLAND (largest), Batan Isl., and SABTANG ISLAND. Isls. are generally flat. Rice and corn are grown. Coal is mined. Basco on Batan Isl. is ⊙ prov. Group was formerly called Bashi Isls. (bä′shē).

Batanovtsi (bätä′nôftsē), village (pop. 2,544), Sofia oblast, W Bulgaria, on Struma R. and 4 mi. W of Dimitrovo; grain, hemp, fruit, truck; cement mfg.

Batanta (bätän′tä), island belonging to Netherlands New Guinea, in Dampier Strait, just NW of Salawati; c.30 mi. long, 5 mi. wide; mountainous, wooded.

Batanun, El, or **Al-Batanun** (both: ĕl bătä′nōōn), town (pop. 18,925), Minufiya prov., Lower Egypt, on railroad and 5 mi. NNW of Shibin el Kom; flax, cotton, cereals.

Bataszek (bä′tŏsäk), Hung. *Bátaszék,* town (pop. 7,153), Tolna co., S Hungary, 11 mi. W of Baja; rail and market center; sawmills. Wheat, potatoes, honey, paprika; dairy farming. Large Ger. pop.

Batatais (bŏotŭtīs′), city (pop. 8,372), NE São Paulo, Brazil, on railroad and 25 mi. NE of Ribeirão Prêto, in cattle-raising region; mfg. (hats, textiles, wax); agr. (coffee, rice, tobacco). Formerly spelled Batataes.

Batatal (bätätäl′), thermal springs in Miranda state, N Venezuela, 75 mi. ESE of Caracas.

Batatal, El, Venezuela: see EL BATATAL.

Batavia, city, Indonesia: see JAKARTA.

Batavia. 1 (bŭtā′vēŭ, bŭtă′vēŭ) Industrial city (pop. 5,838), Kane co., NE Ill., on Fox R. (bridged here) and 34 mi. W of Chicago, in dairying and stock-raising area; mfg. (engines, pumps, tanks, truck bodies, agr. implements, windmills, wood products, metal specialties, pharmaceuticals, cosmetics and toilet preparations). Limestone quarries. Bellevue Sanatorium is here. Founded 1834; inc. as village in 1856, as city in 1891. Near by is Mooseheart, large residential and educational community supported by the Loyal Order of the Moose. **2** (bŭtā′vēŭ) Town (pop. 524), Jefferson co., SE Iowa, 13 mi. E of Ottumwa; concrete blocks. **3** (bŭtā′vēŭ) City (pop. 17,799), ⊙ Genesee co., W N.Y., on Tonawanda Creek and 30 mi. WSW of Rochester, in agr. area; mfg. (shoes, paper and metal products, machinery, farm tools, clothing); timber; sand and gravel pits, gypsum quarries. Co. fair held here. Site of monument to William Morgan; and birthplace of Albert Brisbane, whose home now serves as the city hall. Settled 1801 by Joseph Ellicott for the Holland Land Company, whose hq. bldg. (1804) is now a mus.; inc. as city in 1914. **4** (bŭtā′vēŭ) Village (pop. 1,445), ⊙ Clermont co., SW Ohio, 19 mi. E of Cincinnati, and on East Fork of Little Miami R., in agr. area; tools, machinery, grain products. Settled c.1797, laid out 1814, inc. 1842.

Batavian Republic (bŭtā′vēŭn), set up 1795 by the French during French Revolutionary wars in present-day Netherlands; changed 1806 into Kingdom of Holland by Napoleon. Named for anc. Batavia, a land bet. arms of the Rhine and North Sea peopled by Germanic Batavi.

Batavia River (bŭtā′vēŭ), N Queensland, Australia, rises in Great Dividing Range on Cape York Peninsula, SW of Cape Direction; flows 160 mi. generally NW to Gulf of Carpentaria at Port Musgrave (small inlet). Navigable 25 mi. by small craft below aboriginal reservation.

Bataysk, Russian SFSR: see BATAISK.

Batbakkara, Kazakh SSR: see AMANGELDY.

Batchawana, Mount (băchŭwä′nŭ) (2,100 ft.), central Ont., near L. Superior, 40 mi. N of Sault Ste Marie.

Batchtown, village (pop. 237), Calhoun co., W Ill., near the Mississippi, 27 mi. WNW of Alton, in applegrowing area.

Batea (bätā′ä), town (pop. 2,466), Tarragona prov., NE Spain, 7 mi. WNW of Gandesa; soap mfg., olive-oil and wine processing; agr. trade (cereals, almonds, fruit, vegetables).

Bateman's Bay, village (pop. 875), SE New South Wales, Australia, on Bateman's Bay (5 mi. long, 4 mi. wide) of Tasman Sea, 65 mi. ESE of Canberra; summer resort; oysters.

Batenburg (bä′tŭnbŭrkh), anc. *Oppidum Batavorum,* town (pop. 568), Gelderland prov., central Netherlands, on Maas R. and 10 mi. W of Nijmegen. Site of Slot Batenburg, castle burned by French in 1795.

Batère, France: see ARLES-SUR-TECH.

Baterno (bätĕr′nō), town (pop. 584), Badajoz prov., W Spain, 18 mi. E of Puebla de Alcocer; olives, cereals, grapes.

Bates, county (□ 841; pop. 17,534), W Mo.; ⊙ Butler. Drained by Marais des Cygnes and South Grand rivers. Agr. (corn, wheat, oats), livestock; coal, oil. Formed 1841.

Bates, town (pop. 130), Scott co., W Ark., 18 mi. W of Waldron, near Okla. line.

Batesar, India: see BAH.

Batesburg, town (pop. 3,169), Lexington and Saluda counties, W central S.C., 30 mi. WSW of Columbia; textiles, caskets, boxes; asparagus, peaches.

Bates City, town (pop. 87), Lafayette co., W central Mo., near Missouri R., 28 mi. E of Kansas City.

Batesville. 1 City (pop. 6,414), ⊙ Independence co., NE central Ark., c.80 mi. NNE of Little Rock and on White R. (head of navigation), in foothills of the Ozarks. Processing center for agr. area (fruit, cotton, corn, hay, livestock, poultry). Mfg. of shoes, dairy and wood products; cotton ginning, grist- and sawmilling. Manganese mining; marble and limestone quarrying and processing. Seat of Ark. Col.; has state Masonic orphans' home. Near by are experiment station of Univ. of Ark. and White R. dam. Settled c.1810, inc. 1841. **2** City (pop. 3,194), Ripley co., SE Ind., 40 mi. SSW of Richmond, in agr. area; meat packing, lumber milling; mfg. of hospital equipment, furniture, metal products, caskets, flour, tile, mirrors. **3** Town (pop. 2,463), a ⊙ Panola co., NW Miss., near Tallahatchie R., 55 mi. S of Memphis, Tenn.; trade center for agr. (cotton, corn; dairy products) and timber area; cotton gins, hosiery and lumber mills; sand and gravel. Founded 1855. **4** Village (pop. 149), Noble co., E Ohio, 17 mi. ESE of Cambridge. **5** Village (pop. c.200), Zavala co., SW Texas, 24 mi. NE of Crystal City; trade point in cattle-ranching area.

Batetski or **Batetskiy** (bŭtyĕt′skē), town (1939 pop. over 500), W Novgorod oblast, Russian SFSR, 35 mi. W of Novgorod; rail junction. Limestone near by. Formerly Batetskaya.

Batevo (bŭtyô′vŭ), Czech *Bat'ovo,* Hung. *Bátyú,* village (1941 pop. 1,898), W Transcarpathian Oblast, Ukrainian SSR, 10 mi. ESE of Chop; rail junction.

Bat Galim (bät′gälēm′), NW residential suburb of Haifa, NW Israel, on the Mediterranean, just E of Cape Carmel, at N foot of Mt. Carmel. Has large hosp.

Bath. 1 Village (pop. estimate c.400), W N.B., on St. John R. and 25 mi. N of Woodstock; potato growing, salmon fishing. **2** Village (pop. 303), SE Ont., on North Channel of L. Ontario, opposite Amherst Isl., 14 mi. W of Kingston; dairying, fruit-growing. Established 1784 by United Empire Loyalists.

Bath, county borough (1931 pop. 68,815; 1951 census 79,275) and city, NE Somerset, England, on the Avon and 11 mi. ESE of Bristol; residential and resort city, with metalworking, limestone quarrying, and mfg. of electrical equipment, paint, soap, biscuits. In 1st cent. A.D. the Romans discovered the warm springs here; there are remains (1st excavated 1755) of Roman watering place of *Aquae Solis* (or *Aquae Sulis*) or *Aquae Calidae,* destroyed by Saxons in 577. In 676 a convent was founded, and in 10th cent. a Benedictine abbey was built here; it was destroyed in 1090 and later rebuilt. The new abbey, completed in early 17th cent., was restored in 1873. In Chaucer's time Bath was woolen-milling and marketing town; in 18th cent. it became fashionable resort, of which Beau or Richard Nash was the social arbiter. The noted Royal Crescent, Circus, Assembly Rooms (destroyed in 1942 air raids) and other features were built by John Wood and his son, John Wood the Younger. There are many literary associations with the works of Chaucer, Smollett, Fielding, Jane Austen, Thackeray, Macaulay, and Dickens.

Bath, town (pop. 1,800), St. Thomas parish, E Jamaica, on Plantain Garden R. and 30 mi. E of Kingston; spa with sulphuric thermal springs. Trades in coconuts and copra.

Bath. 1 County (□ 287; pop. 10,410), NE Ky.; ⊙ Owingsville. Bounded NE by Licking R. Rolling upland agr. area, partly in outer Bluegrass region; burley tobacco, corn, potatoes; timber. Includes part of Cumberland Natl. Forest. Has once-famous mineral baths (Olympian Springs, others) which gave co. its name. Formed 1811. **2** County (□ 540; pop. 6,296), W Va.; ⊙ Warm Springs. In the Alleghenies; bounded W by W.Va.; drained by Jackson and Cowpasture rivers. Famous resort area, with noted medicinal springs at Hot Springs, Warm Springs, Healing Springs, and other places. Livestock raising (especially sheep), horse breeding, agr.; timber; hunting, fishing. Formed 1791.

Bath. 1 Village (pop. 423), Mason co., central Ill., on Illinois R. and 36 mi. NW of Springfield, in agr. area. **2** City (pop. 10,644), ⊙ Sagadahoc co., SW Maine, on W bank of Kennebec R. (here spanned, 1927, by Carlton Bridge) and 12 mi. from the Atlantic; shipbuilding center since 1762. Port of entry. Ships lumber, granite. With a good harbor, its shipbuilding industry developed after the Civil War, boomed during First World War, declined for 2 decades, and boomed again during Second World War. Settled c.1670, town inc. 1781, city 1847. Includes Winnegance village. **3** Town (pop. 706), Grafton co., NW N.H., on Connecticut and Ammonoosuc rivers and c.45 mi. SW of Berlin, at mouth of the Wild Ammonoosuc, in agr. region; paperboard mill. **4** Village (pop. 5,416), ⊙ Steuben co., S N.Y., on Cohocton R. and 30 mi. NW of Elmira, in rich agr. area (dairy products, potatoes); summer resort. Mfg. (flour, machinery, wood and metal products, aircraft parts). Site of a U.S. Veterans' Administration Center (opened 1878). Settled 1793, inc. 1816. **5** Town (pop. 381), Beaufort co., E N.C., on Pamlico R. estuary and 14 mi. ESE of Washington, in commercial fishing and agr. area. Oldest town in state; was ⊙ prov. of N.C. First public library in state started here in 1700. Settled c.1690 on site of an Indian village. **6** Borough (pop. 1,824), Northampton co., E Pa., 8 mi. N of Bethlehem; cement, clothing; slate. Laid out 1816, inc. 1856. **7** Village (pop. 3,696, with near-by Langley), Aiken co., W S.C., 10 mi. WSW of Aiken; textile milling, kaolin refining. **8** Town, W.Va.: see BERKELEY SPRINGS.

Batha, region, Fr. Equatorial Africa: see WADAI, state.

Batha River (bätä′), intermittent tributary of L. Fittri in central Chad territory, Fr. Equatorial Africa, rises near Anglo-Egyptian Sudan 30 mi. WSW of Adré, flows in wide curves generally W past Oum-Hadjer and Ati to L. Fittri at its NE extremity; c.325 mi. long.

Bath Beach, SE N.Y., a residential and shore-resort section of SW Brooklyn borough of New York city, on Gravesend Bay. U.S. Fort Hamilton is W.

Bathcay (bätkā′), town, Kompong Cham prov., S Cambodia, 30 mi. N of Pnompenh.

Batheaston, agr. village and parish (pop. 1,513), NE Somerset, England, on the Avon and 3 mi. NE of Bath. Has 13th-cent. church.

Bathelémont-lès-Bauzemont (bätlāmō′-lā-bōzmō′), village (pop. 88), Meurthe-et-Moselles dept., NE France, 7 mi. N of Lunéville. Here first 3 American soldiers of the A.E.F. were killed, 1917.

Bathgate, burgh (1931 pop. 10,097; 1951 census 11,290), S central West Lothian, Scotland, 18 mi. WSW of Edinburgh; coal and shale-oil mining and refining, steel milling, chemical mfg.

Bathgate, city (pop. 209), Pembina co., NE N.Dak., 10 mi. NE of Cavalier and on Tongue R. State school for the blind.

Bâthie, La (lä bätē′), village (pop. 484), Savoie dept., SE France, in Alpine Tarentaise valley, near the Isère, 5 mi. SE of Albertville; electrochemical works (carborundum).

Bathmen or **Batmen** (both: bät′mŭn), village (pop. 797), Overijssel prov., E Netherlands, 6 mi. E of Deventer; meat packing.

Bathsheba (băth′shēbŭ, băthshē′bŭ), village, E Barbados, B.W.I., 9 mi. NE of Bridgetown; popular seaside resort. Flying-fish fleet stationed here. Potteries are near by.

Bathurst (bă′thŭrst, bă′thûrst″), municipality (pop. 11,871), E central New South Wales, Australia, on Macquarie R. and 100 mi. WNW of Sydney; gold-mining center; silver, lead, zinc; dairy products, wheat. Has R.C. and Anglican cathedrals. First settlement (1815) on W side of Blue Mts. Gold discovered (1851) in vicinity.

Bathurst, town (pop. 3,554), ⊙ Gloucester co., NE N.B., on Nipisiguit Bay of Chaleur Bay, at mouth of Nipisiguit R., 110 mi. NNW of Moncton; seaside resort; pulp and newsprint-milling center; lumber mills; smelt, cod, mackerel, salmon, lobster fishing; tourist resort. Manganese and copper mines near by. Founded 1818 on site of earlier settlement (destroyed 1776); originally named St. Peters; renamed Bathurst 1826; inc. 1912.

Bathurst, town (1944 pop. 21,152), ⊙ British colony and protectorate of GAMBIA, Atlantic port on E half of St. Mary's Isl., at mouth of Gambia R., 120 mi. SE of Dakar; 13°27'N 16°34'W. Trade and administrative center; exports peanuts, beeswax, palm kernels, hides, skins; tomato processing, fish curing. Seaplane base. Site of Victoria Hosp., Methodist and R.C. secondary schools, and School of Science. Extensive drainage and sanitation work was begun after Second World War. Founded 1816 by the British as slave-suppression control post. Yundum airport is 12 mi. SW.

Bathurst, Cape, N Mackenzie Dist., Northwest Territories, on Beaufort Sea of the Arctic Ocean; 70°32'N 128°25'W; northernmost point of Canadian mainland. Just S is Baillie trading post; 4 mi. WNW are the 2 Baillie Isls.

Bathurst Inlet, trading post, NE Mackenzie Dist., Northwest Territories, on Bathurst Inlet (150 mi. long, 3–65 mi. wide) of Coronation Gulf; 66°51'N 108°1'W; radio station; site of R.C. mission.

Bathurst Island (□ 786), in Timor Sea, 40 mi. off NW coast of Northern Territory, Australia, just W of Melville Isl. across narrow Apsley Strait; triangular, 45 mi. wide at base. Aboriginal reservation. Mangrove forests.

Bathurst Island (□ 7,272), Parry Isls., central Franklin Dist., Northwest Territories, in the Arctic Ocean; 75°–76°41'N 97°35'–105°20'W; separated from Prince of Wales Isl. (S) by Barrow Strait, from Melville Isl. (W) by Byam Martin Channel, from Devon Isl. (E) by Queens Channel, and from Cornwallis Isl. (SE) by Crozier Strait and McDougall Sound. It is 160 mi. long, 50–100 mi. wide; irregular coastline is mostly hilly and is deeply indented (N) by Erskine and May inlets.

Batie (bä'tyä), village, Wallo prov., NE Ethiopia, on road and 25 mi. E of Dessye. Trade center (salt, livestock, cereals).

Batié (bä'tyā), village (pop. c.1,100), SW Upper Volta, Fr. West Africa, near Gold Coast and Ivory Coast borders, 40 mi. SSE of Gaoua, in agr. region (peanuts, shea nuts, millet; livestock). Customhouse, sleeping-sickness clinic.

Bâtie-Neuve, La (lä bätē-nûv'), village (pop. 239), Hautes-Alpes dept., SE France, at S foot of Dauphiné Alps, 6 mi. E of Gap; stone quarries.

Batignolles (bätēnyôl'), a NW quarter of Paris, France, comprised in 17th *arrondissement*, adjoining Montmartre. Has freight yards and shops of Saint-Lazare station.

Batiki, Fiji: see MBATIKI.

Batil, Gunong, mountain, Malaya: see LAWIT, GUNONG.

Batina or **Batinah** (bä'tĭnä), fertile, populous coastal district of N Oman, on Gulf of Oman, at the foot of the Western Hajar hills; extends 150 mi. from Khor Kalba (border of Fujaira sheikdom; NW) to Muscat dist. (SE); chief town, Sohar. Major date-growing region, noted for its fine dates, which ripen earlier than the Basra dates; fruit cultivation.

Batina or **Batina Skela** (bä'tĭnä skĕ'lä), Hung. *Kiskőszeg* (kĭsh'kûsĕg), village, NE Croatia, Yugoslavia, on the Danube (Serbia border) and 22 mi. NNE of Osijek, in the Baranja, near Hung. line. Trade center; rail terminus. Has Orthodox Eastern church and monument commemorating fighting here in Nov., 1944.

Batiscan (bätēskä'), village (pop. estimate 750), ⊙ Champlain co., S central Que., on the St. Lawrence, at mouth of Batiscan R., and 18 mi. NE of Trois Rivières; lumbering, dairying.

Batiscan River, S Que., issues from L. Batiscan (8 mi. long), in Laurentides Park, flows W, then generally S, past Lac aux Sables, to the St. Lawrence at Batiscan; 110 mi. long.

Batiste, Haiti: see BELLADÈRE.

Batizovce (bä'tyĭzôftsĕ), Hung. *Batizfalva* (bä'tĭsfŏl"vŏ), village (pop. 1,090), N Slovakia, Czechoslovakia, on S slope of the High Tatra, 6 mi. WNW of Poprad; rayon industry at SVIT, just S.

Batjan, Indonesia: see BACHAN.

Batkanu (bätkä'nōō), town (pop. 548), Northern Prov., NW Sierra Leone, on Mabole R. (affluent of Little Scarcies R.) and 28 mi. NW of Makeni, on road; palm oil and kernels, piassava, kola nuts. Hq. Karene dist.

Batken (bŭtkyĕn'), village (1939 pop. over 500), W Osh oblast, Kirghiz SSR, in Fergana Valley, 35 mi. S of Kokand; wheat. Until 1945, Batken-Buzhum.

Batlagundu (bŭtlŭgōōn'dē), town (pop. 7,871), Madura dist., S Madras, India, 30 mi. NW of Madura, on road to Kodaikanal; rice, tobacco, coconut palms. Formerly spelled Vattalkundu.

Batley, municipal borough (1931 pop. 34,573; 1951 census 40,192), West Riding, SW central Yorkshire, England, 7 mi. SSW of Leeds; coal mining, woolen and cotton milling, carpet weaving; textile machinery, chemical, pharmaceutical, soap, and metalworking plants. Mfg. of shoddy was invented here.

Batlle y Ordóñez, Uruguay: see JOSÉ BATLLE Y ORDÓÑEZ.

Batman River (bätmän'), SE Turkey, rises in Bitlis Mts. 12 mi. E of Genc, flows 83 mi. SE and S to Tigris R. 18 mi. ESE of Bismil.

Batmen, Netherlands: see BATHMEN.

Batmonostor (bät'mônôshtôr), Hung. *Bátmonostor,* town (pop. 2,513), Bacs-Bodrog co., S Hungary, 5 mi. SSW of Baja; grain, tobacco, cattle, hogs.

Batna (bätnä'), town (pop. 10,622), Constantine dept., NE Algeria, at S edge of the High Plateaus, guarding entrance into the Aurès massif, on railroad to Biskra and 60 mi. SSW of Constantine; alt. 3,415 ft. Trade center (wheat, horses, sheep, wool, skins, forest products); flour milling, mfg. of building materials. On slopes of the Djebel Touggour (6,900 ft.) is Algeria's largest cedar forest. Of numerous Roman ruins in area, those of Lambèse (7 mi. SE) and Timgad (17 mi. ESE) are most noteworthy. Batna was founded 1848 as a Fr. military outpost.

Bato (bätō'), town (pop. 10,439), Tochigi prefecture, central Honshu, Japan, 20 mi. NE of Utsunomiya; agr. center (rice, wheat, tobacco).

Bato (bätō'). **1** Town (1939 pop. 1,337; 1948 municipality pop. 14,816), Camarines Sur prov., SE Luzon, Philippines, on railroad and 29 mi. WNW of Legaspi, on N shore of L. Bato; fishing, agr. (rice, corn, abacá). **2** Town (1939 pop. 2,846; 1948 municipality pop. 18,716), S Catanduanes isl., Philippines, 5 mi. ENE of Virac; agr. center (coconuts, hemp). **3** Town (1939 pop. 3,060; 1948 municipality pop. 16,406), SW Leyte, Philippines, on Canigao Channel, 65 mi. SSW of Tacloban; agr. center (coconuts, rice, corn).

Bato, Lake (□ 15), SE Luzon, Philippines, in Camarines Sur and Albay provs., 26 mi. NW of Legaspi; 4 mi. in diameter. Outlet is Bicol R.

Batoche (bătōsh'), village (pop. estimate 200), central Sask., on South Saskatchewan R. and 40 mi. SSW of Prince Albert; dairying, mixed farming. Site of hq. of Louis Riel during Riel Rebellion; here rebels were defeated by Gen. Middleton's militia force, May 11, 1885.

Batoe Belat, Cape, Borneo: see BATU BELAT, CAPE.

Batoedaka, Indonesia: see TOGIAN ISLANDS.

Batoe Islands, Indonesia: see BATU ISLANDS.

Batoekaoe, Mount, Indonesia: see BATUKAU, MOUNT.

Batoeradja, Indonesia: see BATURAJA.

Batoka, former province, Northern Rhodesia; see LIVINGSTONE.

Batoka (bätō'kä), township (pop. 74), Southern Prov., Northern Rhodesia, on railroad and 20 mi. E of Choma; tobacco, wheat, corn; livestock.

Baton Rouge (bă'tŭn rōōzh"), city (1940 pop. 34,719; 1950 pop. 125,629), ⊙ La. and East Baton Rouge parish, SE central La., along bluffs on E bank of the Mississippi, c.70 mi. NW of New Orleans; 30°27'N 91°11'W. It is an important rail center, deepwater river and ocean port, and port of entry; ships rice, cotton, lumber, petroleum; bauxite is among its imports. Processing, trade, and distribution center for wide agr. and stock-raising region; cottonseed, lumber, and sugar mills; shipyards; important oil refineries (including one of world's largest), and chemical plants. Mfg. also of wood and concrete articles, synthetic rubber, machine-shop and foundry products, optical glass, foodstuffs. There is a Mississippi R. ferry here; and a highway bridge spans the river c.5 mi. N. Seat of La. State Univ. and Agr. and Mechanical Col., of state schools for the deaf and blind, and of a state agr. experiment station. Has natl. cemetery. The old state capitol (1882) and new capitol (1st occupied 1932) are here. Southern Univ. and Agr. and Mechanical Col. is at near-by Scotlandville. Established as a French fort in 1719, Baton Rouge was inc. in 1817, and made ⊙ La. in 1849. Taken by Farragut in Civil War (May, 1862); Confederate attempt at recapture failed (Aug., 1862). Seat of govt., removed during war, returned in 1882 to Baton Rouge upon completion of new capitol. City became a major distribution and commercial center in railroad boom following Civil War. Annexed adjacent areas (which had 1940 pop. of c.80,000) bet. 1940 and 1950.

Batopilas (bätōpē'läs), mining settlement (pop. 738), Chihuahua, N Mexico, in Sierra Madre Occidental, on affluent of Río Verde and 145 mi. SW of Chihuahua; alt. 1,824 ft.; gold, copper, silver mining.

Batouri (bätōō'rē), town, ⊙ Lom et Kadéï region, E Fr. Cameroons, on Kadéï R., near Fr. Equatorial border and 210 mi. ENE of Yaoundé; center of trade, communications point. Has meteorological station, airfield.

Batovany, Czechoslovakia: see PARTIZANSKE.

Bat'ovo, Ukrainian SSR: see BATEVO.

Batra or **Batrah** (bät'rŭ), village (pop. 6,721), Gharbiya prov., Lower Egypt, on railroad and 9 mi. NNE of Talkha; cotton.

Batraki, Russian SFSR: see SYZRAN.

Batrokar (bät'rōkär'), town, Takeo prov., SW Cambodia, 30 mi. S of Pnompenh; rice, lac.

Batroun, Lebanon: see BATRUN.

Batrun (băt'rōōn), Fr. *Batroun,* anc. *Botrys,* town (pop. 3,292), N Lebanon, on Mediterranean Sea 16 mi. SW of Tripoli; cotton, sericulture, cereals, oranges. Anc. Botrys was founded by the Phoenicians in 11th cent. B.C.

Bat Shlomo (bät' shlōmō'), settlement (pop. 100), NW Israel, at foot of Hills of Ephraim, 3 mi. ENE of Zikhron Ya'aqov; mixed farming, viticulture. Founded 1889. Also spelled Bat Shelomo.

Batskarsnas (bōt'shârs"nĕs"), Swedish *Båtskärsnäs,* village (pop. 867), Norrbotten co., NE Sweden, on Gulf of Bothnia, 20 mi. WSW of Haparanda; sawmills.

Batsto (băt'stō), village, Burlington co., SE N.J., on small Batsto R. (dammed here) and 9 mi. E of Hammonton, in pine-barrens area. Ironworks here (built 1765) made Revolutionary munitions.

Batsto River, SE N.J., rises in S Burlington co., flows c.10 mi. SSE, through pine barrens, to Mullica R. just below Batsto.

Battaglia Terme (bät-tä'lyä tĕr'mĕ), town (pop. 2,086), Padova prov., Veneto, N Italy, at E foot of Euganean Hills, 9 mi. SW of Padua. Noted for its hot mineral springs (140°–169°F.) and mud baths. Has castle built 1648.

Battambang (bät'täm'băng'), town (1941 pop. 23,567), ⊙ Battambang prov. (□ 7,800; 1948 pop. 357,968), W Cambodia, on Pnompenh-Bangkok RR and 160 mi. NW of Pnompenh, on Battambang R. (affluent of lake Tonle Sap; navigable at high water); major rice-growing center; cacao, betel nuts, fruit, salt fish, cardamom. Phosphate plant. An anc. Khmer town (10th-cent. ruins), it belonged to Siam, 1794–1907 and 1941–46.

Battel (bä'tŭl), village, Antwerp prov., N central Belgium, 2 mi. NW of Mechlin; agr. (peas, asparagus, cauliflower, chicory, early potatoes).

Battenberg (bă'tŭnbûrg, Ger. bä'tŭnbĕrk), town (pop. 1,851), in former Prussian prov. of Hesse-Nassau, W Germany, after 1945 in Hesse, on the Eder and 15 mi. NNW of Marburg; ruins of ancestral castle of princes of Battenberg.

Batten Kill (bă'tŭnkĭl), river (c.60 mi. long), Vt. and N.Y.; rises near Dorset, SW Vt.; flows SW and W, past Manchester, Vt., and Greenwich, N.Y., to the Hudson opposite Schuylerville.

Batterbee, Cape, most northerly headland of Enderby Land, Antarctica, on Indian Ocean; 65°50'S 53°47'E. Discovered 1930 by Sir Douglas Mawson.

Battersea (bă'tŭrsē), metropolitan borough (1931 pop. 159,552; 1951 census 117,130) of London, England, on S bank of the Thames (here crossed by Chelsea, Albert, and Battersea bridges), 3 mi. SW of Charing Cross; workers' residential dist. Battersea Park (c.200 acres) extends along river. Borough is site of London's largest electric power station; district suffered much damage in air raids (1940–41). Formerly noted for Battersea enamel.

Batticaloa (bătĭkälō'ŭ), Singhalese *Mudde Kalapuwa* [=muddy lagoon], town (pop. 12,948), ⊙ Batticaloa dist. (□ 2,872; pop., including estate pop., 203,095), Eastern Prov., Ceylon, mainly on isl. in lagoon (c.30 mi. long NNW–SSE) near E coast, 65 mi. SSE of Trincomalee. Rail terminus; connected with mainland by bridge, causeway, and ferry; coconut-palm and rice plantations, vegetable gardens. Meteorological observatory. Ruins of fort (commenced 1627 by Portuguese). Captured 1622 by Portuguese; taken 1638 by Dutch; ceded by Dutch to English in 1796. Known for natural phenomenon called the singing fish, musical sounds emanating at night from bottom of lagoon and attributed to a species of shellfish.

Battice (bätēs'), town (pop. 3,395), Liége prov., E Belgium, 4 mi. NNW of Verviers; dairying center.

Battie, Mount, Maine: see CAMDEN HILLS.

Battipaglia (bät"tēpä'lyä), town (pop. 5,817), Salerno prov., Campania, S Italy, 13 mi. ESE of Salerno; rail junction; tomato canning, paper milling, soap mfg. Badly damaged in Second World War, during Salerno landings (1943).

Battir, Israel: see BETHER.

Battle, former urban district (1931 pop. 3,491), E Sussex, England, 6 mi. NW of Hastings; agr. market; tanning and leather mfg. Scene of battle of Hastings (October 14, 1066) in which Harold was killed, resulting in William the Conqueror becoming king of England. Has ruins of Battle Abbey, founded by William to commemorate his victory. The actual site of the battle is called Battle Hill or Senlac Hill. There is a 13th-cent. church containing tomb of Edmund Cartwright.

Battleboro (bă'tŭlbŭrō), town (pop. 329), Nash and Edgecombe counties, E central N.C., 8 mi. NNE of Rocky Mount.

Battle Creek. **1** Town (pop. 873), Ida co., W Iowa, on Maple R. and 7 mi. WSW of Ida Grove; box mfg. **2** City (pop. 48,666), Calhoun co., S Mich., 20 mi. ENE of Kalamazoo, at confluence of Kalamazoo R. and the Battle Creek. Farm trade center. Health resort. Noted for mfg. of cereal foods; mfg. also of auto parts, farm equipment, steam pumps, stoves, printing presses, paper, ink. The Battle Creek Sanitarium, an army general hosp., Kellogg and Post products factories, and hq. of W. K. Kellogg Foundation are here; also the Kingman Memorial Mus. of natural history, in the

Leila Arboretum. Near by is the Kellogg Bird Sanctuary. U.S. Veterans Administration center and a convalescent hosp. are at near-by Fort Custer. Settled 1831; inc. as village 1850, as city 1859. **3** Village (pop. 630), Madison co., NE central Nebr., 10 mi. W of Norfolk and on Elkhorn R.; dairy, poultry produce; livestock, grain.

Battle Creek, stream in S central Mich., rises in small Duck L. (c.2 mi. long) in NE Calhoun co., flows N almost to Charlotte, then SW, past Bellevue, to Kalamazoo R. at Battle Creek city; c.50 mi. long.

Battlefield, residential village and parish (pop. 204), central Shropshire, England, 3 mi. NNE of Shrewsbury. Scene of battle (1403) in which Henry IV defeated Henry Percy (Hotspur). Church was founded by Henry IV to commemorate battle.

Battlefields, village, Salisbury prov., central Southern Rhodesia, in Mashonaland, on railroad and 20 mi. SSW of Gatooma; alt. 3,664 ft. Tobacco, cotton, peanuts, dairy products, citrus fruit. Gold mining.

Battleford, town (pop. 1,336), W Sask., on North Saskatchewan R. at mouth of Battle R., opposite North Battleford; grain elevators, flour mills. It was ⊙ Northwest Territories, 1876–83, and played important part in Riel rebellion, 1885. Formerly business center, Battleford has been superseded by North Battleford.

Battle Ground, town (pop. 634), Tippecanoe co., W central Ind., 7 mi. N of Lafayette, in agr. area. A memorial park marks scene of battle of Tippecanoe (1811), bet. Indians and troops under Gen. W. H. Harrison.

Battle Harbour, village (pop. 105), ⊙ Labrador, on small isl. just off SE coast, 25 mi. NW of Misery Point, Belle Isle; 52°16'N 55°36'W; fishing port. Has hosp. established 1892 by Sir Wilfred Grenfell.

Battle Lake, resort village (pop. 714), Otter Tail co., W Minn., on Battle L. and 17 mi. E of Fergus Falls, in grain, livestock, poultry area; dairy products. Battle here (1795) bet. Chippewa and Sioux Indians.

Battle Lake (□ 9), Otter Tail co., W Minn., near Otter Tail L., 17 mi. E of Fergus Falls; 6 mi. long, 2 mi. wide; sometimes referred to as West Battle L. Has E outlet into East Battle L. (□ 3.8).

Battle Mountain, village (1940 pop. 767), Lander co., N Nev., near Humboldt R., c.65 mi. WSW of Elko; alt. 4,511 ft.; supply center for mining (gold, lead, copper, silver) and ranching area.

Battle Mountain, peak, N Nev., S of Humboldt R., c.15 mi. W of Battle Mountain town. Antler Peak (8,265 ft.) and North Peak (8,577 ft.) are its highest spurs.

Battonya (bŏt'tônyŏ), town (pop. 13,297), Csanad co., SE Hungary, on Szaraz R. and 25 mi. E of Mako; market center; brickworks; extensive onion cultivation.

Batu (bä'tōō), village (pop. 509), central Selangor, Malaya, on railroad and 4 mi. NNW of Kuala Lumpur; rice, rubber. Batu limestone caves (2 mi. N) are visited by tourists.

Batu Anam (bä'tōō änäm'), village (pop. 633), NW Johore, Malaya, on railroad and 9 mi. NW of Segamat, near Negri-Sembilan line; rubber.

Batu Arang (bä'tōō äräng'), town (pop. 11,543), central Selangor, Malaya, on railroad and 20 mi. NW of Kuala Lumpur; major coal-mining center; brickworks, plywood mill.

Batu Belat, Cape, or **Cape Batoe Belat** (both: bä'tōō bĕ'lät), westernmost point of Borneo, in S.China Sea, SW of Singkawang; 0°49'N 108°52'E.

Batuc (bätōōk'), town (pop. 1,112), Sonora, NW Mexico, on Moctezuma R. and 75 mi. E of Hermosillo; livestock, wheat, corn, beans.

Batuco, Lake (bätōō'kō), Santiago prov., central Chile, 18 mi. NW of Santiago; 3 mi. long.

Batudaka, Indonesia: see TOGIAN ISLANDS.

Batu Gajah (bä'tōō gä'jä), town (pop. 7,480), central Perak, Malaya, at foot of Kledang Range, on railroad and Kinta R., 8 mi. SSW of Ipoh; a tin-mining center of Kinta Valley.

Batu Islands or **Batoe Islands** (both: bä'tōō), group (□ 463; pop. 12,619), Indonesia, off W coast of Sumatra, in Indian Ocean, bet. Nias and Mentawei Isls.; 0°26'S 98°26'E. Comprise 3 large isls. (TANAHMASA, Tanahbala, Pini) surrounded by many islets. Pulautelo, chief port of group, is on the islet of TELO. Group is generally low and forested. Chief products: copra, resin, fish.

Batukau, Mount, or **Mount Batoekaoe** (both: bä"tōōkou'), volcanic peak (7,467 ft.), central Bali, Indonesia, 15 mi. S of Singaraja.

Batu Kurau (bä'tōō kōōrou'), village (pop. 934), NW Perak, Malaya, 10 mi. NE of Taiping; rubber.

Batum (bätōōm', Rus. bŭtōōm'), Georgian *Batumi* (bŭtōō'mē), city (1939 pop. 70,807), ⊙ Adzhar Autonomous SSR, Georgian SSR, on deep, sheltered SE bay of Black Sea, near Turkish frontier, 160 mi. W of Tiflis, N of Chorokh R. mouth; 41°39'N 41°37'E. One of largest and best Black Sea ports, with elaborate petroleum, manganese, and coastal shipping facilities; connected by rail with Tiflis, by oil and kerosene pipe lines with Baku. Major oil-refining center; ship and locomotive repair shops, iron foundry; mfg. of tea-picking machinery, metal cans, tobacco, glass, paper textiles; food processing. Botanical garden (N) has flora of humid subtropical zone. Chakva, one of largest USSR tea farms, is 8 mi. NE; tobacco and citrus-fruit plantations near by. A subtropical resort and naval base, Batum has steamer connections with principal Black Sea ports; exports petroleum and refined products, manganese, timber, raw silk and silk cocoons, wool, cotton, fruit, oilseeds, and oil cakes. Teachers col. Known as Batum since 17th cent.; ceded by Turkey to Russia in 1878. Since 1936 officially Batumi.

Batu Pahat, Malaya: see BANDAR PENGGARAM.

Baturaja, Baturadja, or **Batoeradja** (all: bä"tōōrä'jä), town (pop. 2,955), S Sumatra, Indonesia, 90 mi. SW of Palembang, on Palembang-Telukbetung RR; trade center for agr. area (rubber, tea, coffee).

Baturin (bŭtōō'rĭn), village (1926 pop. 3,836), E Chernigov oblast, Ukrainian SSR, on Seim R. and 11 mi. NE of Bakhmach; hemp retting.

Baturino (bŭtōō'rēnŭ). **1** Village (1926 pop. 1,738), NW Kurgan oblast, Russian SFSR, 15 mi. S of Shadrinsk, in agr. area (wheat, livestock). **2** Town (1948 pop. over 2,000), E Tomsk oblast, Russian SFSR, on Chulym R. and 85 mi. NNE of Tomsk.

Baturité (bŏŏtōōrētā'), city (pop. 5,247), N Ceará, Brazil, on Fortaleza-Crato RR and 50 mi. SSW of Fortaleza; coffeegrowing and -processing center; cotton ginning, soap mfg. Ships coffee, sugar, tobacco, cotton, vegetable oil, lumber. Just W the Baturité range (40 mi. long) rises to 2,400 ft.

Bat Yam (bät' yäm'), residential settlement (pop. 4,000), W Israel, in Plain of Sharon, on Mediterranean, just S of Jaffa, 4 mi. SSW of Tel Aviv; seaside resort; metalworking, concrete mfg., brewing. Founded 1926. Heavily attacked by Arabs, 1948.

Batylinski or **Batylinskiy** (bŭtĭlyēn'skē), town (1940 pop. over 500), SE Yakut Autonomous SSR, Russian SFSR, on Allakh-Yun R. (right tributary of Aldan R.) and 15 mi. S of Allakh-Yun; gold mining.

Batyr Depression or **Batyr' Depression** (bŭtĭr') (427 ft. below sea level), S Guryev oblast, Kazakh SSR, near Caspian Sea, 100 mi. SE of Fort Shevchenko. Also called Karagiye Sink.

Batyrevo (–yĭvŭ), village (1926 pop. 2,417), SE Chuvash Autonomous SSR, Russian SFSR, on left tributary of Sviyaga R. and 32 mi. S of Kanash; wheat. Phosphorite deposits near by (S). Until c.1937, Bolshoye Batyrevo.

Batyu, Ukrainian SSR: see BATEVO.

Batz (bäts), island (pop. 1,150) in English Channel, 1 mi. N of Roscoff, Finistère dept., W France; 3 mi. long, 1.5 mi. wide. Grows early fruits and vegetables. Resort of Batz on S coast.

Batz-sur-Mer (bäts-sür-mâr'), village (pop. 1,655), Loire-Inférieure dept., W France, on Bay of Biscay, 13 mi. W of Saint-Nazaire; saltworks, oyster beds. Has 15th-16th-cent. church of Saint-Guénolé with fine steeple. Until 1931, Batz; sometimes Le Bourg-de-Batz.

Bau (bou'), town (pop. 1,019), SW Sarawak, in W Borneo, on tributary of Sarawak R. and 16 mi. SW of Kuching; agr. (rice, sago), stock raising, fishing.

Bau, Fiji: see MBAU.

Bauan (bä'wän), town (1939 pop. 3,242; 1948 municipality pop. 40,168), Batangas prov., S Luzon, Philippines, on Batangas Bay, 29 mi. SW of San Pablo; fishing and agr. center (rice, sugar cane, corn, coconuts). Includes MARICABAN ISLAND.

Bauang (bä'wäng), town (1939 pop. 2,628; 1948 municipality pop. 22,441), La Union prov., N central Luzon, Philippines, on small inlet of Lingayen Gulf, on railroad and 6 mi. S of San Fernando; rice-growing center.

Baubau or **Baoebaoe** (both: boubou'), chief town (pop. 2,493) and port of Buton isl., Indonesia, on SW coast, 5°28'S 122°38'E; exports asphalt, timber, cajuput oil, coffee, hides, tortoise shell, trepang.

Baucau, Portuguese Timor: see VILA SALAZAR.

Bauchi (bou'chē), province (□ 25,977; pop. 984,757), Northern Provinces, NE central Nigeria; ⊙ Bauchi. Drained by upper Gongola R.; includes savanna lowland and Bauchi Plateau (W; rises to 4,500 ft.). Major tin-mining region with centers on plateau at Bauchi, Burra, Toro, Lemmi, and Leri. Agr.: cassava, millet, durra (S); cotton and peanuts (N). Major towns: Bauchi, Azare, Gombe. Dominant tribe is Fulah. Bauchi was a 19th-cent. kingdom under Fulah rule until subdued (1902) by British.

Bauchi, town (pop. 10,629), ⊙ Bauchi prov., Northern Provinces, E central Nigeria, 145 mi. SE of Kano and 65 mi. NE of Jos; 10°20'N 9°50'E. Major tin-mining center. Has hosp., Moslem teachers col. Founded 1809. Formerly called Yakoba.

Bauchi Plateau, Northern Provinces, central Nigeria; 250 mi. long, 100 mi. wide; rises to 6,000 ft.; steep scarps rise above surrounding lowlands, especially in W and S. Africa's major tin-mining region, with chief centers at Jos, Naraguta, Bukuru, Bauchi, and Pankshin. Tin is shipped by rail to ports of Lagos and Port Harcourt. Sometimes known as Jos Plateau.

Baucina (bouchē'nä), village (pop. 3,154), Palermo prov., N Sicily, 10 mi. SW of Termini Imerese; macaroni.

Bauco, Italy: see BOVILLE ERNICA.

Baud (bō), village (pop. 1,863), Morbihan dept., W France, 17 mi. ENE of Lorient; beekeeping, woodworking.

Baudenbach (bou'dŭnbäkh), village (pop. 569), Middle Franconia, W Bavaria, Germany, 5 mi. NW of Neustadt; brewing, flour milling; grain, potatoes, hops, sheep. Chartered 1748.

Baudens (bōdãs'), village (pop. 862), Oran dept., NW Algeria, on railroad and 11 mi. E of Sidi-bel-Abbès; winegrowing, quarrying.

Baudette (bôdĕt'), village (pop. 929), ⊙ Lake of the Woods co., N Minn., on Rainy R. (at Ont. line) and c.55 mi. W of International Falls; summer resort, port of entry; farm trading point in grain and dairying area; lumber. Hq. of U.S. forest and game reservation. Lake of the Woods is 10 mi. N.

Baudh (boud), district (□ 1,956; pop. 232,954), central Orissa, India; ⊙ Baudh Raj. At N end of Eastern Ghats; bounded N by Mahanadi R. Rice, oilseeds; timber forests. S section inhabited by Khond tribes. Created 1949 by merging of former princely state of Baudh (□ 1,156; pop. 146,175) of Orissa States and NW subdivision (□ 800; pop. 86,779) of original Ganjam dist. Also spelled Baud or Bod.

Baudh Raj (boud' räj'), town (pop. 5,740), ⊙ Baudh dist., central Orissa, India, on Mahanadi R. and 100 mi. WNW of Cuttack; trades in rice, oilseeds, timber; metal handicrafts. Several old temples. Sometimes called Baudh or Baudgarh.

Baudó (boudō'), village (pop. 789), Chocó dept., W Colombia, 50 mi. SW of Quibdó, 10 mi. E of coast town of Pizarro.

Baudó, Serranía de (sĕrănē'ä dā), low range, W Colombia, extending S from Panama c.250 mi. along the Pacific coast of Chocó; rugged, eroded formation, rising to 5,938 ft. Forms W watershed of Atrato and San Juan rivers. Sometimes called Cordillera del Chocó.

Baudó River, Chocó dept., W Colombia, flows c.100 mi. S, paralleling the coast, then W to the Pacific at Pizarro; waters rich, rubber-producing forest region.

Baudouinville (bōdwĕvēl'), village, Katanga prov., SE Belgian Congo, on W shore of L. Tanganyika, 80 mi. SSE of Albertville; noted R.C. missionary center, established c.1882. Steamboat landing; cattle raising, farming. Seat of vicar apostolic of Tanganyika dist. Has large seminary, convent for native nuns, trade schools for Africans.

Baudour (bōdōōr'), town (pop. 4,937), Hainaut prov., SW Belgium, 6 mi. WNW of Mons; refractory bricks, ceramics, china, insulators.

Bauerbach (bou'ûrbäkh), village (pop. 416), Thuringia, central Germany, 5 mi. SSW of Meiningen. Schiller here wrote (1782–83) *Cabal and Love.*

Bauerwitz, Poland: see BABOROW.

Baugé (bōzhā'), town (pop. 3,007), Maine-et-Loire dept., W France, 19 mi. N of Saumur; road and market center; agr. processing (vegetable oils, cider, dairy produce), woodworking, brick mfg. Has 15th-cent. castle (now town hall). Damaged in Second World War.

Bauges (bōzh), Jurassic limestone massif of Savoy Alps, in Haute-Savoie and Savoie depts., SE France, bounded by Lac du Bourget and Chambéry trough (W), L. of Annecy (N) and Isère R. valley (S). Drained by Chéran R. Average alt. 3,300 ft. Rises to 7,415 ft. at the Dent du Pécloz. Dairying, woodworking. Le Châtelard (resort) in central valley. Also spelled Beauges.

Baugy (bō-zhē'), village (pop. 516), Cher dept., central France, on the Yèvre and 16 mi. E of Bourges; wool spinning.

Baúl, El, Latin America: see EL BAÚL.

Bauld, Cape (bôld), on Quirpon Isl., NE N.F., just off N extremity of the Great Northern Peninsula; 51°39'N 55°26'W.

Baule (bōl), village (pop. 913), Loiret dept., N central France, near right bank of the Loire, 12 mi. SW of Orléans; produces telephone equipment. Winegrowing.

Baule, La, or **La Baule-sur-Mer** (lä bōl'-sür-mâr'), resort (pop. 13,266), Loire-Inférieure dept., W France, on Bay of Biscay and 8 mi. W of Saint-Nazaire; one of France's finest resorts, with 5-mi.-long semi-circular beach lined with hotels and villas; E section amidst pine forests called La Baule-les-Pins. Damaged in Second World War.

Baulkham Hills (bôl'kŭm, bō'–), town (pop. 1,983), E New South Wales, Australia, 14 mi. NW of Sydney; coal-mining center.

Bauma (bou'mä), town (pop. 2,686), Zurich canton, NE Switzerland, on Töss R. and 16 mi. E of Zurich; cotton and silk textiles, metalworking.

Bauman, Uzbek SSR: see SHAFRIKAN.

Baumanabad, Tadzhik SSR: see KIROVABAD, Stalinabad oblast.

Baumannshöhle (bou'mäns-hû"lŭ), large stalactite cave, central Germany, in the lower Harz, just W of Rübeland. Discovered in 17th cent.; fossil remains found here.

Baume (bōm), village (pop. 255), Jura dept., E France, on the Seille and 5 mi. NE of Lons-le-Saunier; has 12th-16th-cent. abbey church. Stalactite caverns near by. Also called Baume-les-Messieurs.

Baume-les-Dames (bōm'-lä-däm'), village (pop. 1,921), Doubs dept., E France, near Doubs R. and Rhone-Rhine Canal, 18 mi. NE of Besançon; cotton milling, pipe mfg. Livestock market. Heavily damaged during Second World War.

Baume-les-Messieurs, France: see BAUME.

Baumholder (boum'hôl"dûr), town (pop. 2,873), in former Prussian Rhine Prov., W Germany, after 1945 in Rhineland-Palatinate, 6 mi. S of Idar-Oberstein; wine.

Baunei (bounā'), village (pop. 3,193), Nuoro prov., E Sardinia, 27 mi. SE of Nuoro, near coast. Nuraghe near by.

Baures (bou'rĕs), town (pop. c.1,800), Beni dept., NE Bolivia, on Río Negro and 42 mi. SE of Magdalena, in llanos; rice, cotton, rubber.

Baures River, Bolivia: see BLANCO, Río; SAN MARTÍN RIVER.

Baurtregaum, mountain (2,796 ft.), W central Co. Kerry, Ireland, 7 mi. SW of Tralee; highest in Slieve Mish mts.

Bauru (bourōō'), city (1950 pop. 53,126), São Paulo, Brazil, 175 mi. NW of São Paulo; important railroad and commercial center for W São Paulo's pioneer settlement areas. Ships cotton, coffee, citrus fruit, and dairy produce to São Paulo and Santos. Has food- (preserves, vinegar, butter, sausages) and staple-processing plants, tanneries, and a growing textile and woodworking industry. Airfield. City owes its rapid growth to recent westward spread of agr. colonies.

Bauschleiden, Luxembourg: see BOULAIDE.

Bauska (bou'skä), Ger. *Bauske*, Rus. (until 1917) *Bausk*, city (pop. 4,904), S Latvia, in Zemgale, on the Lielupe (here formed by junction of Memele and Musa rivers), and 23 mi. SE of Jelgava, on rail spur. Agr. market (grain, fodder, sugar beets); commercial center; mfg. of leather, knitwear, cement ware, bricks; machine shops, sawmilling, brewing. Castle ruins. Chartered 1511 by Livonian Knights.

Bauta (bou'tä), town (pop. 7,291), Havana prov., W Cuba, on Central Highway, on railroad and 15 mi. SW of Havana; cigar factories, cotton mill. Grows tobacco, sugar cane, pineapples, vegetables.

Bautzen (bou'tsûn), town (pop. 38,524), Saxony, E central Germany, in Upper Lusatia, on the Spree and 25 mi. W of Görlitz, 30 mi. ENE of Dresden; rail junction; mfg. of railroad cars, machinery, automobile bodies, Diesel engines, glass, chemicals, lacquer, musical instruments; paper and textile (wool, linen, jute) milling, printing. Center of kaolin-quarrying region. Seat (since 1921) of R.C. bishops of MEISSEN. Has noted 13th-cent. cathedral, used by both Protestants and Roman Catholics; 15th-cent. Ortenburg castle; anc. town walls. Originally the Slav fortress of *Budissin*, town became German and was chartered in 11th cent. Contested among Poland, Bohemia, Meissen, and Brandenburg; passed 1320 to Bohemia. Was member of Lusatian League. Burned down (1634) in Thirty Years War; went to Saxony in 1635. Near by Napoleon defeated (May, 1813) Russo-Prussian army under Blücher.

Bauvin (bōvē'), town (pop. 3,746), Nord dept., N France, on the Deûle (canalized) and 11 mi. SW of Lille, in irrigated agr. area; clothing mfg.

Baux, Les (lā bō'), ruined medieval town (pop. 55), Bouches-du-Rhône dept., SE France, in rocky heights of the Alpines, 6 mi. NE of Arles; alt. c.900 ft. Once the seat of a powerful feudal family, it is now a tourist curiosity. Bauxite, first discovered here, was named after Les Baux, and is still mined in vicinity.

Bauxite (bôk'sīt), village (pop. 2,459), Saline co., central Ark., near short Hurricane Creek, 17 mi. SW of Little Rock, in major U.S. bauxite-mining area. Bauxite-reduction (alumina) plant at near-by Hurricane Creek village.

Bauya (bou'yä), village (pop. 1,000), South-Western Prov., W Sierra Leone, 50 mi. ESE of Freetown; rail junction; palm oil and kernels, piassava, rice.

Bavai, France: see BAVAY.

Bavanat, Iran: see BAWANAT.

Bavandpur, Iran: see GILAN, town.

Bavani, India: see BHAVANI.

Bavaniste or **Bavanishte** (both: bä'vänĭshtĕ), Serbo-Croatian *Bavanište*, Hung. *Homokbálványos* (hô'-môkbälvä"nyôsh), village (pop. 5,899), Vojvodina, NE Serbia, Yugoslavia, 12 mi. ESE of Pancevo, in the Banat.

Bavaria (bûvâ'rēû), Ger. *Bayern* (bī'ûrn), state (without LINDAU and the RHENISH PALATINATE, □ 27,119; 1946 pop. 8,789,650, including displaced persons 9,029,090; 1950 pop. 9,118,635), S Germany; ⊙ Munich. Divided into 7 administrative dists. [Ger. *Regierungsbezirke*]: UPPER BAVARIA, LOWER BAVARIA, UPPER PALATINATE, UPPER FRANCONIA, MIDDLE FRANCONIA, LOWER FRANCONIA, and SWABIA. Bordered E by Czechoslovakia, SE and S by Austria, W by Württemberg-Hohenzollern and Württemberg-Baden, NW by Hesse, N by Thuringia, and NE by Saxony. Located at N foot of the central Alps, it is a hilly region traversed in center by FRANCONIAN JURA plateau (SW-NE). Major mtn. ranges, located on its periphery, are: ALLGÄU ALPS; BAVARIAN ALPS, with the Zugspitze, Germany's highest mtn. (S); BOHEMIAN FOREST; and the FICHTELGEBIRGE (E). Also includes (N) the FRANCONIAN FOREST, outliers of the Rhön Mts., and The SPESSART. Major portion of country is drained (by Iller, Lech, Isar, Inn, and Altmühl rivers) towards the Danube, which at Regensburg (head of navigation) reaches its northernmost point; NW is drained by the Main, in whose valley (below Aschaffenburg) is the lowest elevation (c.300 ft.) of Bavaria; LUDWIG CANAL connects the Danube and the Rhine via the Main. Agr. region: rye (main, staple), wheat (in Lower and Upper Bavaria, S of the Danube), spelt, potatoes; intensive hop growing in Landshut and Nuremberg region; wine in valley of the Main and its tributaries. Cattle (especially in S) and hogs are principal stock; dairying in Swabia (Kempten region) and Alpine foothills. Industries centered at MUNICH, NUREMBERG, FÜRTH (mirrors), AUGSBURG and HOF (textiles), ERLANGEN, WÜRZBURG (machine tools), and SCHWEINFURT (dyes); glass and porcelain mfg. in Upper Palatinate and NE Upper Franconia; Bavarian beer is world-renowned. Lignite mined in Amberg, Schwandorf, and Sulzbach-Rosenberg region, and on N slope of Bavarian Alps (Hausham, Peissenberg, Peiting, Penzberg); graphite mines at Pfaffenreuth; large salt deposits at Berchtesgaden and Bad Reichenhall; some iron ore in Upper Palatinate; kaolin quarries near Pegnitz, Schnaittenbach, and Tirschenreuth. Bavarian Alps and lakes S of Munich are features of favorite tourist region (GARMISCH-PARTENKIRCHEN, OBERAMMERGAU, BAD REICHENHALL; AMMERSEE, CHIEMSEE, KÖNIGSSEE); ROTHENBURG and DINKELSBÜHL are shrines of medieval architecture; BAYREUTH is noted cultural center. There are 3 universities: Erlangen (Protestant), Munich, and Würzburg. Originally inhabited by Celts, and conquered by Drusus and Tiberius in 15 B.C., region was invaded by the Germanic Bajuoarii in early 6th cent. and became one of the stem duchies of Germany. Christianized by St. Boniface in 8th cent., duchy was inc. (788) by Charlemagne into his empire. In 911 the duchy (then comprising, roughly, Bavaria proper, present Austria, and part of Upper Palatinate) came under native rulers. Frequent Magyar raids were halted (955) by Emperor Otto I. After nearly 3 centuries of turbulent history, marked by constant quarrels of Bavaria's dukes (since 1070 of the Guelph dynasty) with the emperor, the duchy, now constituting only Upper and Lower Bavaria, passed (1180) to Wittelsbach family, which ruled it until 1918. In 1214 the Rhenish Palatinate was added to the duchy. Emperor Louis IV (1314–47) united all the Wittelsbach holdings, and in 1329 he constituted Upper and Rhenish PALATINATE under the senior Wittelsbach line. Bavaria remained under the junior line; frequent subdivisions among the several branches of the family prevented a powerful duchy. Duke Albert IV of Bavaria-Munich united Bavaria proper, and introduced (1506) primogeniture. At the time of the Reformation, Bavaria remained firm in its Roman Catholicism. Country was ravaged by Protestant forces in Thirty Years War. Duke Maximilian I headed the Catholic League and was rewarded with the rank of elector and the Upper Palatinate. Its agr. wealth and strategic position made Bavaria a coveted prize, and it was frequently overrun by foreign armies in the wars of the 17th and 18th cent. In 1777 the Bavarian line of Wittelsbachs died out; duchy fell to Palatine line, and in 1799 Elector Maximilian of Zweibrücken united all Wittelsbach lands. Allying himself with Napoleon (1801), Maximilian became (1806) king of Bavaria. In 1813 he joined the Allies, and Bavaria emerged from the Congress of Vienna with virtually its present size, including the Rhenish Palatinate. In 1818 a liberal constitution was proclaimed, lasting exactly 100 years. Bavaria viewed the rise of Prussia with alarm, and sided with Austria in the Austro-Prussian War (1866), but was nevertheless forced to join the German Empire in 1871. In 1918 Bavaria became a republic; it joined the Weimar Republic even though its royalist sentiments remained strong. Although Munich soon became the center of National Socialism, Catholic and separatist Bavaria resisted the movement until Hitler's accession; Bavarian autonomy was lost under the Third Reich. Conquered (spring, 1945) by American troops; the Potsdam Conference placed Bavaria in the U.S. zone of occupation, with the exception of the Rhenish Palatinate and the town and rural dist. of Lindau, which fell to the French zone. A new constitution was drawn up in 1946. Bavaria joined (1949) the German Federal Republic.

Bavarian Alps (bûvâ'rēûn), Ger. *Bayrische Alpen*, northeasternmost division of Central Alps along Austro-Ger. border; extends c.70 mi. WSW-ENE from Lechtal Alps at headwaters of Loisach R. to the Inn at Kufstein. Highest peak, ZUGSPITZE (9,721 ft.). Subsidiary ranges are the Wettersteingebirge, Karwendelgebirge, and Nordkette (overlooking Innsbruck). S slopes (in Austria) form steep wall of Inn valley. Gentle N slopes provide excellent cattle pastures. Crossed by railroad at Scharnitz Pass., by road at Achen Pass. Lignite mines (at Grossweil, Peissenberg, Penzberg); petroleum deposits (at Bad Tölz and Tegernsee). Chief resort: Garmisch-Partenkirchen. In Austria also called Tyrol Alps or North Tyrol Alps.

Bavarian Forest, Germany: see BOHEMIAN FOREST.

Bavarian Palatinate, Germany: see RHENISH PALATINATE.

Bavay or **Bavai** (bävĕ'), anc. *Bagacum*, (pop. 2,214), Nord dept., N France, near Belg. border, 10 mi. ESE of Valenciennes; road center. Important Roman town and anc. ⊙ Nervii. Severely damaged in Second World War.

Bavda (bäv'dŭ), village, Kolhapur dist., S Bombay, India, 29 mi. WSW of Kolhapur, in Western Ghats; sugar milling. Teak, sandalwood, and blackwood in near-by forests. Sometimes spelled Bavada.

Baveno (bävā'nō), village (pop. 921), Novara prov., Piedmont, N Italy, port on W shore of Lago Maggiore, 18 mi. SE of Domodossola; health resort (mineral waters). Excursions to near-by Borromean Isls. Cotton mills, bottling works, mfg. of textile machinery. Granite quarries 1 mi. W.

Bavent (bävä'), village (pop. 336), Calvados dept., NW France, 9 mi. ENE of Caen; varnished tile mfg. Damaged in Normandy campaign of Second World War.

Baviácora (bävyä'kōrä), town (pop. 1,287), Sonora, NW Mexico, on Sonora R. (irrigation) and 65 mi. NE of Hermosillo; wheat, corn, beans, sugar, cattle.

Bavispe (bävē'spā), town (pop. 887), Sonora, NW Mexico, on Bavispe R., and 80 mi. SE of Douglas, Ariz.; corn, wheat, vegetables, sugar, livestock.

Bavispe River, Sonora, NW Mexico, rises in W outliers of Sierra Madre Occidental SW of Bacerac, flows N, encircling a mtn. mass, turns S, past Oputo, Huásabas, Granados, to the Yaqui (of which it is a principal headstream) 12 mi. N of Sahuaripa; c.200 mi. long.

Bavly (bŭvlē'), village (1926 pop. 2,047), SE Tatar Autonomous SSR, Russian SFSR, near Ik R., 22 mi. ESE of Bugulma; center of petroleum area; distilling; wheat, livestock.

Bawal (bä'vŭl), town (pop. 5,709), S Patiala and East Punjab States Union, India, 10 mi. S of Rewari; millet.

Bawan, Indonesia: see BAWEAN.

Bawan (bŭvŭn'), town (pop. 3,487), Anantnag dist., SW central Kashmir, in Vale of Kashmir, 4 mi. NE of Anantnag; rice, corn, oilseeds, wheat. Has sacred springs. At Bumazuv, 1 mi. N, is only important group of artificial caves in Kashmir; 10th-cent. Hindu temple ruins near by. Also called Machha Bhawan.

Bawanat or **Bavanat** (bävänät'), village (1945 pop. estimate 1,700), Seventh Prov., in Fars, S Iran, 90 mi. NE of Shiraz; center of rich agr. area; grain, opium, cotton; rugmaking.

Bawangaja, hill, India: see BARWANI, town.

Bawdwin (bôdwĭn'), village, Tawngpeng state, Northern Shan State, Upper Burma, on spur of Mandalay-Lashio RR and 30 mi. WNW of Lashio. Major silver- and lead-mining center, producing, as by-products, zinc, copper, nickel, iron, and gold. Worked by Chinese in early 15th cent.; modern development began 1891.

Bawean (bä"vāän'), volcanic island (□ 77; pop. 29,862), Indonesia, in Java Sea, 100 mi. N of Surabaya, Java; 5°48'S 112°39'E; roughly circular, 11 mi. in diameter; rises to 2,247 ft. (volcanic peak). Agr. (rice, corn), fishing, weaving. Chief town and port is Sangkapura or Sankapura (both: säng"käpōō'rä) on S coast. Also called Bawan.

Bawiti, El, or **Al-Bawiti** (both: ĕl bä'wētē), village (pop. 2,039), in Bahariya oasis, Western Desert prov., central Egypt, 200 mi. SSW of Alexandria; dates.

Bawku (bô'kōō), town, Northern Territories, NE Gold Coast, near White Volta R. (Fr. West Africa border), 40 mi. NNE of Gambaga; road junction; ropemaking; millet, durra, yams; cattle, skins.

Bawlake (bô'lūkĕ'), former Karenni state (□ 568; pop. 13,782) of Upper Burma; ⊙ was Bawlake, village on the Nam Pawn and 35 mi. SSE of Loikaw. Hilly jungle. Pop.: Red Karens. Since 1947, part of the Karenni State.

Bawlf, village (pop. 231), central Alta., 17 mi. ESE of Camrose; dairying, mixed farming.

Bawli Bazar, village, Akyab dist., Lower Burma, in Arakan, 18 mi. NW of Maungdaw, near E Pakistan border, on route to Cox's Bazar.

Baworow, Poland: see BABOROW.

Bawtry, town and parish (pop. 1,460), West Riding, S Yorkshire, England, 8 mi. SE of Doncaster; agr. market.

Baxar, India: see BUXAR.

Baxat (bä'sät'), town, Laokay prov., N Vietnam, on Red R. (China frontier) and 8 mi. NW of Laokay; market center; customs post.

Baxenden, England: see ACCRINGTON.

Baxley, city (pop. 3,409), ⊙ Appling co., SE central Ga., 38 mi. N of Waycross; tobacco market; mfg. (naval stores, boxes, lumber). Inc. 1875.

Baxter, county (□ 571; pop. 11,638), N Ark.; ⊙ Mountain Home. Bounded N by Mo. line, S and SE by White R. (site of Bull Shoals Dam); drained by the North Fork (site of Norfolk Dam). Situated in Ozark region. Agr. (cotton, truck, hay, corn, livestock). Cotton ginning, grist milling at Mountain Home. Resorts; fishing. Formed 1873.

Baxter. **1** Town (pop. 618), Jasper co., central Iowa, 28 mi. NE of Des Moines; livestock, grain. **2** Village (1940 pop. 704), Harlan co., SE Ky., in the Cumberlands, at junction of Poor and Clover forks to form Cumberland R., 2 mi. N of Harlan; bituminous coal, lumber. **3** Village (pop. 507), Crow Wing co., central Minn., near Mississippi R., 4 mi. W of Brainerd, in grain area. Inc. 1939. **4** Town (pop. 861), Putnam co., central Tenn., 5 mi. W of Cookeville; lumber, insecticides. Seat of Baxter Seminary, a preparatory school. **5** Village (1940 pop. 1,017), Marion co., N W.Va., 4 mi. N of Fairmont; bituminous coal.

Baxter Estates, residential village (pop. 862), Nassau co., SE N.Y., on Manhasset Neck, W Long Isl., overlooking Manhasset Bay (W) and just N of Port Washington.

Baxter Springs, city (pop. 4,647), Cherokee co., extreme SE Kansas, on Spring R., near Okla. line, and 13 mi. WSW of Joplin, Mo.; rail center for mining and agr. area; mining supplies. Lead, zinc, tripoli, and chat mines in vicinity. Settled c.1850, inc. 1868. Grew as cattle town in 1860s and 1870s. Near-by monument commemorates Baxter Springs Massacre (1863), in which 87 Union soldiers were killed by guerrilla band under William Quantrill.

Bay-, in Rus. names: see BAI-.

Bay. **1** County (□ 753; pop. 42,689), NW Fla., bounded S by Gulf of Mexico; ⊙ Panama City. Flatwoods area, with swampy coast indented by St. Andrew Bay. Cattle raising, forestry (paper and pulp, naval stores), fishing, and some agr. (cotton, peanuts, sugar cane). Formed 1913. **2** County (□ 446; pop. 88,461), E Mich.; ⊙ Bay City. Bounded E by Saginaw Bay; drained by Saginaw R. and short Kawkawlin R. Agr. area (sugar beets, beans, chicory, dairy products). Mfg. at Bay City. Commercial fishing, soft-coal mining. Resorts; small-game hunting and fishing. State park. Organized 1858.

Bay. **1** Town (pop. 500), Craighead co., NE Ark., 10 mi. SE of Jonesboro. **2** Village, Calif.: see BODEGA BAY. **3** City, Ohio: see BAY VILLAGE.

Bay, Laguna de (lägōō'nä dā bī'), largest lake (□ 344) of the Philippines, S Luzon, Philippines, 8 mi. SE of Manila; c.30 mi. long, c.25 mi. wide, broken in N by 2 peninsulas. Talim Isl. is largest of many isls. dotting the lake. Outlet: Pasig R.

Baya, Sierra, Argentina: see SIERRAS BAYAS.

Bayadiya, El, or **Al-Bayadiyah** (both: ĕl bŭyădē'yŭ), village (pop. 5,262), Asyut prov., central Upper Egypt, on W bank of the Nile and 23 mi. SSE of Minya; cereals, dates, sugar cane.

Bayaguana (bīägwä'nä), town (1935 pop. 1,240; 1950 pop. 1,357), Trujillo prov., E central Dominican Republic, 25 mi. NE of Ciudad Trujillo; rice-growing center. Founded 1606.

Bayambang (bäyämbäng'), town (1939 pop. 2,960; 1948 municipality pop. 35,171), Pangasinan prov., central Luzon, Philippines, on Agno R., on railroad and 17 mi. SSE of Dagupan; agr. center (rice, copra, corn).

Bayamo (bīä'mō), town (pop. 16,161), Oriente prov., E Cuba, on small Bayamo R., on Central Highway and 60 mi. WNW of Santiago de Cuba. Rail junction and stock-raising center, hq. of Cuban dairy industry. Produces also tobacco, coffee, cacao, sugar cane. Tanning, tobacco processing, mfg. of tiles. Has airfield; natl. monuments. Sugar centrals, manganese and copper mines in vicinity. Founded as San Salvador de Bayamo in 1513, it was one of Cuba's leading towns in Colonial era. Played an important part in the natl. history. Here broke out the Ten Years War (1868–78) and the successful 1895 revolt. The revolutionists Céspedes and Estrada Palma were b. in Bayamo. Near by General García received the famous message. Sometimes spelled Bayamó.

Bayamón (bīāmōn'), town (pop. 20,171), N Puerto Rico, on Bayamón R., on railroad and 5 mi. SSW of San Juan. Gateway to the interior; processing and trading center in agr. region (sugar, tropical fruit, tobacco, vegetables); sugar milling, tobacco stripping; mfg. of leatherware, rayon, alcohol, liquor, clothing, cigars. Radio station. Juanita sugar mill is just N. Fort Buchanan, adjoined by ruins of the old colonial settlement Caparra, is 2 mi. E. Limestone quarries near by.

Bayamón River, E central and NE Puerto Rico, rises N of Cayey, flows c.25 mi. N, past Bayamón, to the Atlantic 2½ mi. WNW of Cataño.

Bayana (bŭyä'nŭ), town (pop. 8,662), E Rajasthan, India, 24 mi. SSW of Bharatpur, near Banganga R.; rail junction; local market center (millet, gram, wheat, barley). Formerly also spelled Biana.

Bayan-Aul (bŭyän"ŭōōl'), village (1948 pop. over 2,000), SW Pavlodar oblast, Russian SFSR, 115 mi. SW of Pavlodar. Barite and copper deposits near by.

Bayandai or **Bayanday** (bŭyŭndī'), village (1948 pop. over 500), E Ust-Orda Buryat-Mongol Natl. Okrug, Irkutsk oblast, Russian SFSR, on Irkutsk-Kachuga highway and 75 mi. NE of Irkutsk; agr.

Bayan Kara Mountains (bäyän' kärä'), W spur of the Kunlun system, S central Tsinghai prov., China, forming divide bet. upper Yangtze and Yellow rivers; mts. rise to over 15,000 ft.

Bayan Khongor, Bain Khongor, or **Bayan Hongor** (all: bä'yän không'gôr, bīn'), aimak (□ 45,800; pop. 55,000), SW central Mongolian People's Republic; ⊙ Bayan Khongor. Bounded S by China's Ningsia prov., it extends from the Khangai Mts. (N) across the Gobi Altai (center) into the Gobi desert (S). Aridity increases toward S. Sparsely populated by Khalkha Mongols.

Bayan Khongor, Bain Khongor, or **Bayan Hongor,** town, ⊙ Bayan Khongor aimak, W central Mongolian People's Republic, 330 mi. WSW of Ulan Bator, at S foot of Khangai Mts. Established in 1930s.

Bayan Lepas (bī'än lā'päs), village (pop. 1,589) on Penang isl., NW Malaya, 10 mi. SSW of George Town; rubber, coconuts, fruit. Airport.

Bayano (bīä'nō), village (pop. 215), Los Santos prov., S central Panama, in Pacific lowland, 7 mi. SSW of Las Tablas; sugar cane, coffee; stock.

Bayano River, Panama: see CHEPO RIVER.

Bayan Tumen, Mongolia: see CHOIBALSAN, city.

Bayan Ulegei, Bain Ulegei, or **Bayan Ölögey** (all: ŭ'lŭgā), aimak (□ 18,200; pop. 40,000) of W Mongolian People's Republic; ⊙ Ulegei. Bounded SW by China's Sinkiang prov. and NW by Gorno-Altai Autonomous Oblast of Russian SFSR, it lies in the Mongolian Altai and the adjoining wooded steppe, drained by upper Kobdo R. Hunting and rudimentary agr. are the main occupations. Pop. is primarily Kazakh, with Tuvinians and West Mongols.

Bayard, town, France: see LANEUVEVILLE-À-BAYARD.

Bayard. **1** (bā'ûrd) Town (pop. 634), Guthrie co., W central Iowa, 23 mi. W of Perry, in agr. area. **2** (bā'ûrd) City (pop. 1,869), Morrill co., W Nebr., 20 mi. ESE of Scotts Bluff and on N.Platte R.; beet sugar, livestock, dairy produce, grain. Chimney Rock, landmark on Oregon Trail, is near by. Founded c.1887. **3** (bī'ûrd, bä'–) Village, N.Mex.: see FORT BAYARD. **4** (bârd) Town (pop. 589), Grant co., W.Va., in Eastern Panhandle, on North Branch of the Potomac and 24 mi. SW of Keyser at the Md. line.

Bayard, Col (kôl bäyär'), pass (alt. 4,088 ft.), in Dauphiné Alps, Hautes-Alpes dept., SE France, 4 mi. N of Gap, connecting upper Drac R. (Champsaur valley) and Durance R. valley. Crossed by Grenoble-Gap road.

Bayaz (bäyäz'), village, Eighth Prov., in Kerman, SE Iran, 100 mi. NW of Kerman and on highway to Yezd.

Bayazit, province, Turkey: see AGRI.

Bayazit or **Bayazid,** village, Turkey: see DOGUBAYAZIT.

Baybay (bī"bī'), town (1939 pop. 5,943; 1948 municipality pop. 50,725), W Leyte, Philippines, on Camotes Sea, 40 mi. SSW of Tacloban; agr. center (coconuts, rice, corn). Manganese deposits.

Bayboro (bā'bŭrō), town (pop. 453), ⊙ Pamlico co., E N.C., 16 mi. E of New Bern, at head of Bay R. (inlet of Pamlico Sound); fishing, sawmilling.

Bayburt (bībōōrt'), town (pop. 9,473), Gumusane prov., NE Turkey, on Coruh R. and 45 mi. ESE of Gumusane; wheat, barley; lignite; carpets. Also spelled Baiburt.

Baychester (bā'chĕ"stûr), SE N.Y., a residential section of NE Bronx borough of New York city, on Eastchester Bay. Pelham Bay Park is here.

Baychunas, Kazakh SSR: see BAICHUNAS.

Bay City. **1** City (pop. 52,523), ⊙ Bay co., E Mich., deepwater harbor on Saginaw R. near its mouth on Saginaw Bay, and c.100 mi. NNW of Detroit. Port for Great Lakes and ocean shipping; shipbuilding; fishing fleet. Port of entry. Mfg. of auto parts, heavy machinery, metal products, chemicals, cement, clothing, beet sugar; oil refining. Summer resort. Has jr. col. Bituminous coal mines near by. State park and fish hatchery in vicinity. City was a thriving lumber center in 1890s. Settled c.1831; inc. as village 1859, as city 1865. **2** Town (pop. 761), Tillamook co., NW Oregon, 5 mi. NNW of Tillamook and on Tillamook Bay; salmon canneries. **3** Town (pop. 9,427), ⊙ Matagorda co., S Texas, c.65 mi. SW of Houston, near Colorado R., 20 mi. N of Matagorda Bay; shipping, processing center of agr. area (rice, livestock, poultry); oil and sulphur production; oil refining; rice, flour, lumber mills; cotton gins; creamery; hatchery. Inc. 1902. **4** Fishing village (pop. 326), Pierce co., W Wis., 4 mi. ENE of Red Wing (Minn.), across L. Pepin.

Bayda, Yemen: see BEIDHA.

Baydag Bogdo, Mongolia: see BAITAK BOGDO.

Baydarag Gol, Mongolia: see BAIDARIK RIVER.

Baydarata Bay, Russian SFSR: see BAIDARATA BAY.

Baydarik River, Mongolia: see BAIDARIK RIVER.

Baydary, Russian SFSR: see BAIDARY.

Baydzhansay, Kazakh SSR: see BAIDZHANSAI.

Bayel (bäyĕl'), village (pop. 1,133), Aube dept., NE central France, on Aube R. and 4 mi. SE of Bar-sur-Aube; crystal.

Bayenga (bäyĕng'gä), village, Eastern Prov., NE Belgian Congo, 135 mi. WNW of Irumu; gold-mining and processing center, employing c.5,500 workers; also cotton ginning. Sometimes called Matetete. Babeyru (bäbā'rōō) gold mines are 4 mi. SSE.

Bayern, Germany: see BAVARIA.

Bayeux (bäyû'), medieval Latin *Baiocasses*, town (pop. 8,744), Calvados dept., NW France, 5 mi. S of Channel coast, 17 mi. WNW of Caen, on the Aure; road center; dairying, mfg. (stained-glass windows, lace, biscuits, cement pipes). Has fine Gothic cathedral (chiefly 13th cent.) with sections of earlier Romanesque church (burned 1105 by Henry I of England). The archaeological mus. contains famous Bayeux Tapestry probably made by Matilda, queen of William the Conqueror. Chief town of Gallic Baiocasses tribe; medieval ⊙ of Bessin dist. First larger Fr. town liberated from Ger. occupation by British troops (June 8, 1944) in Second World War.

Bayevo (bī'ŭvŭ), village (1926 pop. 2,506), W Altai Territory, Russian SFSR, on Kulunda R. and 40 mi. SW of Kamen; dairy farming.

Bay Farm Island, Calif.: see ALAMEDA, city.

Bayfield, village (pop. 321), S Ont., on L. Huron, at mouth of Bayfield R., 12 mi. S of Goderich; dairying, mixed farming.

Bayfield, county (□ 1,474; pop. 13,760), extreme N Wis., bounded N by L. Superior, E by Chequamegon Bay; ⊙ Washburn. A large portion of co. is on a wide peninsula. Drained by Namekagon R.; and generally wooded, with some cutover farm land. There are several resort lakes. Dairying, lumbering, fishing, some agr. and mfg. W end of Gogebic iron range is in co. Red Cliff Indian Reservation and a section of Chequamegon Natl. Forest are here. Formed 1845.

Bayfield. **1** Town (pop. 335), La Plata co., SW Colo., on Los Pinos R., in foothills of San Juan Mts., and 15 mi. E of Durango; alt. 6,500 ft. **2** City (pop. 1,153), Bayfield co., extreme N Wis., on L. Superior, opposite Madeline Isl., 16 mi. N of Ashland; fishing resort, fruitgrowing center. Mfg.: fishhooks, woodwork. Apostle Isls. are reached from here. Settled 1856, inc. 1913.

Bayhan, Aden: see BEIHAN.

Bay Harbor, village (pop. 1,676), Bay co., NW Fla., suburb of Panama City.

Bay Harbor Islands, town (pop. 296), Dade co., S Fla.

Bay Head (bā' hĕd"), resort borough (pop. 808), Ocean co., E N.J., 12 mi. S of Asbury Park, at N end of Barnegat Bay, here entered by Bayhead-Manasquan Canal (part of Intracoastal Waterway; connects NW with Manasquan R.); yachting center; boatbuilding.

Bayina Bashta, Yugoslavia: see BAJINA BASTA.

Bayindir (bīŭndŭr'), Turkish *Bayındır*, town (pop. 9,931), Smyrna prov., W Turkey, near Kucuk Menderes R., on railroad, and 30 mi. ESE of Smyrna; olives, figs, grain, tobacco. Sometimes Baindir.

Bayir (bäyēr'), village, E Jordan, in desert area 70 mi. NE of Ma'an; junction of desert trails; airfield, police post. Sheep, goats, and camels raised.

Bay Islands, Sp. *Islas de la Bahía* (ē'släs dā lä bäē'ä), archipelago and dept. (□ 144; 1950 pop. 8,863) of Honduras; ⊙ Roatán. In Bay of Honduras of Caribbean Sea off N Honduras coast, comprise ROATÁN ISLAND, GUANAJA ISLAND, UTILA ISLAND, BARBARETA ISLAND, SANTA ELENA ISLAND, MORAT ISLAND, and HOG ISLANDS. Agr. (coconuts, sugar cane, plantains, pineapples); lumbering. Coconut processing, fishing, and shipbuilding are principal industries. Pop. (English-speaking, Protestant) descends from Negroes and Caribs brought here (end of 18th cent.) by British from the West Indies, white English immigrants, and mestizos. Caribs were deported. Main centers: Roatán, Guanaja, Utila. Guanaja Isl. was sighted (1502) by Columbus. Group was ceded (1859) by British to Honduras.

Baykadam, Kazakh SSR: see BAIKADAM.

Baykaim, Russian SFSR: see BAIKAIM.

Baykal, Russian SFSR: see BAIKAL.

Baykalovo, Russian SFSR: see BAIKALOVO.

Baykan (bīkän'), village (pop. 1,023), Siirt prov., SE Turkey, 21 mi. NW of Siirt; wheat. Also called Siyanis.

Bay-Khak, Russian SFSR: see BAI-KHAK.

Baykibashevo, Russian SFSR: see BAIKIBASHEVO.

Baykit, Russian SFSR: see BAIKIT.

Baykonur, Kazakh SSR: see BAIKONUR.

Baykovo, Russian SFSR: see BAIKOVO.

Baylen, Spain: see BAILÉN.

Baylis, village (pop. 307), Pike co., W Ill., 30 mi. SE of Quincy; grain, livestock, poultry; dairy products.

Baylor (bā'lŭr), county (□ 857; pop. 6,875), N Texas; ⊙ Seymour. Prairie region, drained by Wichita R. (here dammed into Kemp and Diversion lakes), and Salt Fork of the Brazos. Livestock raising (beef, dairy cattle; some hogs, poultry); agr. (cotton, wheat, oats, grain sorghums). Oil, natural-gas wells. Formed 1858.

Baymak, Russian SFSR: see BAIMAK.

Baymakliya, Moldavian SSR: see BAIMAKLIYA.

Bay Meadows, Calif.: see SAN MATEO, city.

Bay Mills, village, Chippewa co., E Upper Peninsula, Mich., on St. Marys R., near Whitefish Bay, and 11 mi. SW of Sault Ste. Marie. Site of Chippewa tribal land reserve. Fishing.

Bay Minette (mĭnĕt'), town (pop. 3,732), ⊙ Baldwin co., SW Ala., 22 mi. NE of Mobile, in farming, hunting, and fishing area; naval stores, lumber and wood products. Founded c.1861.

Baymok, Yugoslavia: see BAJMOK.

Bay of Islands, N.F.: see ISLANDS, BAY OF.

Bay of Islands, county, New Zealand: see KAWAKAWA.

Bay of Whales, Antarctica: see WHALES, BAY OF.

Bayombong (bīŭmbŏng', Sp. bäyōmbōng'), town (1939 pop. 5,876; 1948 municipality pop. 14,078), ⊙ NUEVA VIZCAYA prov., central Luzon, Philippines, on Magat R. and 32 mi. E of Baguio; 12°20'N 121°10'E. Trade center for agr. area (rice, corn).

Bayon (bäyõ'), village (pop. 1,048), Meurthe-et-Moselle dept., NE France, on Moselle R. and Canal de l'Est, and 12 mi. SW of Lunéville; chicory mfg., flour milling, winegrowing. Ger. invasion was checked here, 1914.

Bayona (bīō'nä), town (pop. 1,852), Pontevedra prov., NW Spain, Atlantic fishing port on Vigo Bay, 10 mi. SW of Vigo; fish processing, boatbuilding. Sea-bathing resort. Has 12th-cent. Romanesque church and 16th-cent. castle.

Bayoneisu-iwa, Japan: see BAYONNAISE ROCKS.

Bayonnaise Rocks (bäyônĕz'), uninhabited rocks of isl. group Izu-shichito, Greater Tokyo, Japan, in Philippine Sea, 75 mi. S of Hachijo-jima; barren. Sometimes called Bayoneisu-iwa.

Bayonne (bäyôn'), anc. *Lapurdum,* town (pop. 28,110), Basses-Pyrénées dept., SW France, port on Adour R. (at mouth of Nive R.), near Bay of Biscay, 100 mi. SSW of Bordeaux; 43°30'N 1°28'W; commercial and road center for Pyrenees hinterland; shipbuilding, distilling, tanning, mfg. of chocolates, paints, linen goods. Metallurgical industries at BOUCAU. Exports hams, lumber, cork, resinous products, brandy. Accessible to ships drawing 21 ft. Heavy swells and shifting sandbar off Adour R. mouth render entrance hazardous. Has 13th-cent. cathedral; citadel (built by Vauban); mus. of Basque folklore; noted fine arts mus. French, Spanish, and Basque spoken here. Bayonne was chief port of Roman Novempopulana. Here Napoleon I forced Charles IV and Ferdinand VII of Spain to abdicate (1808). During ensuing Peninsular War, the town resisted an English siege until 1814. Cardinal Lavigerie and the painter Bonnat b. here.

Bayonne (bāyōn'), city (pop. 77,203), Hudson co., NE N.J., on 3-mi. peninsula S of Jersey City, bet. Upper New York Bay and Newark Bay. A 1,675-ft. bridge (1931) connects with Staten Isl. across Kill Van Kull. Has large oil refineries (since 1875; connected by pipe line to oil fields of the Southwest), several mi. of waterfront with docks, and U.S. navy dry dock and supply depot. Mfg. (chemicals, clothing, textiles, machinery, metal products, paint, food products, cottonseed oil, cork, radiators, motors, generators, condensers); boatbuilding. Has a jr. col. Settled by Dutch traders c.1650, British gained possession in 1664, inc. 1869.

Bayo Point (bä'yō), southernmost point of Panay isl., Philippines, at N side of entrance to Panay Gulf; 10°26'N 121°54'E.

Bayou (bī'ō), for names beginning thus and not found here: see under following part of the name; e.g., for Bayou Teche, see TECHE, BAYOU.

Bayou Cane, village (pop. 2,212), Terrebonne parish, SE La.

Bayou Goula (gōō'lŭ), village (pop. c.1,000), Iberville parish, SE central La., 16 mi. S of Baton Rouge, and on W bank of the Mississippi, in sugarcane area; sugar milling.

Bayou La Batre (bī'ōō lŭ bă"trē, bī'ō, bī' lŭ bă'trē), village (pop. 2,196), Mobile co., extreme SW Ala., 21 mi. SSW of Mobile, near Mississippi Sound of Gulf of Mexico; packing (chiefly seafood) and canning.

Bayou Pierre Lake, La.: see PIERRE, BAYOU.

Bayovar (bīōvär'), abandoned Pacific port, Piura dept., NW Peru, on Sechura Bay, 24 mi. SW of Sechura, at N end of Cerro Illesca; former shipping center for the old sulphur mines of Reventazón (rāvĕntäsōn'), at S end of Cerro Illesca, connected by railroad.

Baypore River, India: see BEYPORE RIVER.

Bay Port, village (1940 pop. 588), Huron co., E Mich., on Saginaw Bay, and 31 mi. NE of Bay City; commercial fishing. Resort.

Bayport. 1 Village (pop. 2,502), Washington co., E Minn., at N end of St. Croix L. (in St. Croix R.) and 16 mi. E of St. Paul, in resort area; ice cream, wood products. State prison here. **2** Village (pop. 1,463), Suffolk co., SE N.Y., on S Long Isl., on Great South Bay, just E of Sayville, in shore-resort area.

Bayport Park, village (pop. 1,209, with adjacent Lakeside), Genesee co., SE central Mich.

Bayrakdar, Turkey: see KARAYAZI.

Bayram-Ali, Turkmen SSR: see BAIRAM-ALI.

Bayramic (bīrămĭch'), Turkish *Bayramiç,* village (pop. 4,291), Canakkale prov., NW Turkey, on Kucuk Menderes R. and 26 mi. SSE of Canakkale; cereals, beans, vetch.

Bayreuth (bīroit'), city (1950 pop. 58,630), ⊙ Upper Franconia, NE Bavaria, Germany, on the Red Main and 41 mi. NE of Nuremberg; 49°57'N 11°34'E. Cultural center known for its annual music festivals. Rail junction; mfg. of machinery, textiles, chemicals, pianos, porcelain, jewelry, glassware; paper milling, brewing. Severe Second World War damage included destruction of 18th-cent. castle and "Villa Wahnfried," Wagner's residence. The noted 18th-cent. opera and 19th-cent. Festspielhaus, where Wagner's operas are performed during festivals, were preserved. Bayreuth was founded 1194. Belonged to Hohenzollern family 1248–1807. Residence of numerous artists during 19th cent. Captured by U.S. troops in April, 1945. Wagner, Franz Liszt, and poet Jean Paul are buried here. Sometimes spelled Baireuth.

Bay Ridge. 1 Summer resort, Anne Arundel co., central Md., on Chesapeake Bay at S side of Severn R. mouth, 4 mi. SE of Annapolis. **2** A residential section of SW Brooklyn borough of New York city, along the Narrows N of Fort Hamilton.

Bayrische Alpen, Europe: see BAVARIAN ALPS.

Bayrisch Eisenstein, Germany: see EISENSTEIN.

Bayrische Pfalz, Germany: see RHENISH PALATINATE.

Bayrischer Wald, Germany: see BOHEMIAN FOREST.

Bay River, E N.C., an irregular W inlet (c.15 mi. long) of Pamlico Sound, with Bayboro at its head; Intracoastal Waterway crosses its mouth.

Bay Roberts, village (pop. 1,281), SE N.F., on Conception Bay, 8 mi. S of Harbour Grace; woodworking, mfg. of furniture, hardware, nails, bricks. Formerly the base for a great fleet of schooners that fished the Labrador banks. Site of transatlantic cable station.

Bayrut, Lebanon: see BEIRUT.

Bays, Lake of (13 mi. long, 6 mi. wide), S Ont., in Muskoka lake region, 50 mi. E of Parry Sound. Drained by Muskoka R.

Bay Saint Louis (lōō'ĭs), resort city (pop. 4,621), ⊙ Hancock co., SE Miss., on Mississippi Sound, at entrance to St. Louis Bay, 15 mi. WSW of Gulfport; sea-food packing and canning, lumber milling. Inc. 1854.

Bay Shore, residential village and resort (pop. 9,665), Suffolk co., SE N.Y., on S shore of W Long Isl., on Great South Bay, 5 mi. E of Babylon, in dairying and truck-farming area; fishing, duck-hunting center. Mfg. of clothing, awnings, machinery, signs, paving materials, greeting cards, aircraft parts; barge building. Ferry to Fire Isl.

Bayside. 1 A section of NE Queens borough of New York city, SE N.Y., on Little Neck Bay; mainly residential; mfg. (electrical equipment, wood products, aircraft parts). U.S. Fort Totten is near by. **2** Resort village, Refugio co., S Texas, on Copano Bay, 15 mi. S of Refugio.

Bays Mountain, NE Tenn., forested ridge in Great Appalachian Valley, E of Holston R.; from Knoxville area extends c.75 mi. NE to vicinity of Va. line; highest point (3,118 ft.) is 12 mi. SW of Kingsport.

Bay Springs, town (pop. 1,302), a ⊙ Jasper co., E central Miss., 22 mi. NNW of Laurel, in agr. and timber area; hosiery mfg., lumber milling. Settled 1896, inc. 1904.

Baysun, Uzbek SSR: see BAISUN, BAISUN-TAU.

Bayswater. 1 Town (pop. 1,472), S Victoria, Australia, 15 mi. E of Melbourne, in fruitgrowing area. **2** Town (pop. 4,651), SW Western Australia, NE residential suburb of Perth.

Bay-Syut, Russian SFSR: see BAI-SYUT.

Bayt al-Falaj, Oman: see BAIT AL FALAJ.

Bayt al-Faqih, Yemen: see BAIT AL FAQIH.

Bayt Miri, Lebanon: see BEIT MIRI.

Baytown, industrial city (pop. 22,983), Harris co., S Texas, at head of Galveston Bay, 20 mi. E of Houston, in oil-producing area; petroleum port (part of Houston port area), oil-pipeline terminus; oil refining, synthetic rubber and chemical mfg., lumber milling. Producing salt dome near by. Seat of Lee Col. Formed 1947 by consolidation of 3 cities, Goose Creek, Pelly, and Baytown.

Bayuca, Spain: see ARTEIJO.

Bay View. 1 or **Bayview,** village (pop. 1,420), Jefferson co., N central Ala., 10 mi. NW of Birmingham. **2** Village, Mass.: see GLOUCESTER. **3** Resort village, Emmet co., NW Mich., on Little Traverse Bay, just NE of Petoskey. Religious and educational program and a music festival conducted here each summer by Methodist Church.

Bayview. 1 Village, Ala.: see BAY VIEW. **2** Village, Humboldt co., NW Calif., just S of Eureka. **3** Summer resort, Beaufort co., E N.C., 17 mi. ESE of Washington, on Pamlico R. estuary mouth.

Bay Village or **Bay,** city (pop. 6,917), Cuyahoga co., N Ohio, on L. Erie, c.10 mi. W of downtown Cleveland.

Bayville, resort village (pop. 1,981), Nassau co., SE N.Y., on N shore of W Long Isl., at base of Centre Isl. peninsula, c.3 mi. NNW of Oyster Bay village. Inc. 1919.

Baza (bä'thä), anc. *Basti,* city (pop. 14,330), Granada prov., S Spain, in Andalusia, at foot of Sierra de Baza, 52 mi. ENE of Granada; mfg. of cement, pottery, soap, canvas; esparto and olive-oil processing, flour and sugar milling. Cattle, cereals, wine, fruit, hemp in area. Summer resort with mineral springs. Has Gothic collegiate church on site of anc. Visigothic church, later a mosque; and ruins of Moorish fort or *alcazaba.* Belonged to Romans and Moors; liberated 1489 by the Catholic Kings. Cave dwellings on hill near by. Copper, iron, sulphur, and lead mining in dist.

Bazaikha (bŭzī'ūkhŭ), suburb of Krasnoyarsk, Krasnoyarsk Territory, Russian SFSR.

Bazaliya (bŭzä'lyēŭ), village (1926 pop. 3,020), W Kamenets-Podolski oblast, Ukrainian SSR, on upper Sluch R. and 30 mi. NW of Proskurov; wheat, sugar beets.

Bazar (bŭzär'), town (1926 pop. 2,293), NE Zhitomir oblast, Ukrainian SSR, 29 mi. ENE of Korosten; dairy plant.

Bazar-Dyuzi (bŭzär"-dyōōzē'), peak (c.14,720 ft.) in the SE Greater Caucasus, on Azerbaijan-Dagestan border, 35 mi. E of Nakha.

Bazargic, or **Bazarjik,** Bulgaria: see TOLBUKHIN.

Bazar-Kurgan (bŭzär"-kōōrgän'), village (1939 pop. over 2,000), SW Dzhalal-Abad oblast, Kirghiz SSR, 15 mi. NW of Dzhalal-Abad; walnuts.

Bazarnye Mataki or **Bazarnyye Mataki** (–nēŭ mŭtŭkē'), village (1926 pop. 2,196), S Tatar Autonomous SSR, Russian SFSR, 23 mi. ESE of Kuibyshev; wheat, livestock.

Bazarny Karabulak or **Bazarnyy Karabulak** (bŭzär'-nē kŭrŭ"bōōlăk'), town (1926 pop. 10,843), N Saratov oblast, Russian SFSR, 45 mi. WNW of Volsk; flour milling; wheat, sunflowers.

Bazarny Syzgan or **Bazarnyy Syzgan** (sĭzgän'), town (1926 pop. 3,539), W Ulyanovsk oblast, on railroad (Bazarnaya station) and 15 mi. WNW of Barysh; paper mfg.

Bazaruto Islands (bäzärōō'tō), in Indian Ocean just off Mozambique, 150 mi. N of Inhambane; 21°40'S 35°30'E.

Bazar-Yaipan or **Bazar-Yaypan** (bŭzär"-yīpän'), village (1939 pop. over 2,000), W Fergana oblast, Uzbek SSR, 12 mi. SW of Kokand; cotton. Until c.1940, Yaipan.

Bazas (bäzäs'), town (pop. 2,042), Gironde dept., SW France, 19 mi. WSW of Marmande; agr. market (dairy products, potatoes, poultry); winegrowing, horse breeding, porcelain mfg. Has 13th-17th-cent. church (cathedral until 1790) and parts of 13th-cent. ramparts. Former ⊙ Vasates (a Gallic tribe) and important city of Roman Novempopulana.

Bazeilles (bäzā'), village (pop. 1,038), Ardennes dept., N France, 2 mi. SE of Sedan; scene of heroic Fr. stand (1870) in Franco-Prussian War.

Bazel (bä'zŭl), agr. village (pop. 4,030), East Flanders prov., N Belgium, 7 mi. E of St-Nicolas, near Scheldt R.

Bazet (bäzā'), village (pop. 638), Hautes-Pyrénées dept., SW France, on the Adour and 4 mi. N of Tarbes; large insulator factory.

Bazhenovo (bŭzhĕ'nŭvŭ), village (1939 pop. over 500), S Sverdlovsk oblast, Russian SFSR, on Trans-Siberian RR and 30 mi. ESE of Sverdlovsk; junction of rail spur to Asbest; mfg. of building materials; flour milling, truck gardening.

Bazile Mills (bŭzēl'), village (pop. 46), Knox co., NE Nebr., 40 mi. NW of Norfolk and on Bazile Creek.

Bazine (bŭzēn'), city (pop. 456), Ness co., W central Kansas, on Walnut Creek and 12 mi. E of Ness City; grain, livestock.

Bazkovskaya (bŭskôf'skīŭ), village (1939 pop. over 500), NE Rostov oblast, Russian SFSR, on right bank of Don R. and 28 mi. ESE of Kazanskaya; wheat, sunflowers; cattle raising. Pop. largely Cossack. Until c.1940, spelled Baskovskaya.

Bazna (bäz'nä), Hung. *Bázna* (bäz'nŏ), village (pop. 1,838), Sibiu prov., central Rumania, 14 mi. E of Blaj; health resort with radioactive iodine springs and mud baths. Also methane-production center; extensive vineyards, hog raising in vicinity. Has 15th-cent. fortified church.

Bazoche-Gouët, La (lä bäzôsh'-gwā'), village (pop. 816), Eure-et-Loir dept., NW central France, 14 mi. SE of Nogent-le-Rotrou; peat extracting.

Bazoches-sur-Hoëne (bäzôsh'-sür-ōĕn'), village (pop. 228), Orne dept., NW France, 4 mi. NW of Mortagne; sawmilling.

Bazzano (bätsä'nô), town (pop. 2,869), Bologna prov., Emilia-Romagna, N central Italy, 13 mi. W of Bologna, on branch of Reno R.; hardware, boxes, marmalade, beet sugar.

B. Boeto, Bolivia: see VILLA SERRANO.

Bcharreh, Lebanon: see BSHERRI.

Beach. 1 Town (pop. 62), Ware co., SE Ga., 17 mi. NNW of Waycross. **2** City (pop. 1,461), ⊙ Golden Valley co., W N.Dak., near Mont. line, 58 mi. W of Dickinson; grain-shipping point; wheat, barley, oats. Inc. 1910.

Beach Arlington, N.J.: see SHIP BOTTOM.

Beach Bluff, Mass.: see SWAMPSCOTT.

Beachburg, village (pop. estimate 500), SE Ont., 15 mi. ESE of Pembroke; dairying, mixed farming.

Beach City, village (pop. 940), Stark co., E central Ohio, 14 mi. SW of Canton and on Sugar Creek (a tributary of Tuscarawas R.). Flood-control dam (completed 1937) near by.

Beach Haven, resort borough (pop. 1,050), Ocean co., E N.J., on Long Beach isl. and 17 mi. NE of Atlantic City; fishing. Just S is **Beach Haven Inlet,** passage from the Atlantic leading into Intracoastal Waterway and channels to Little Egg Harbor (NW) and Great Bay (W).

Beach Island, Maine: see DEER ISLAND, Hancock co.

Beachport, village (pop. 293), SE South Australia, 195 mi. SSE of Adelaide on Indian Ocean; rail terminus; dairy products, livestock.

Beachville, village (pop. estimate 750), S Ont., on Thames R. and 5 mi. SW of Woodstock; lime quarrying, dairying, mixed farming.

Beachwood. 1 Resort borough (pop. 1,251), Ocean co., E N.J., on Toms R. opposite Toms River village, near Barnegat Bay. **2** Village (pop. 1,073), Cuyahoga co., N Ohio, an E suburb of Cleveland.

Beachy Head, high (565 ft.) chalk promontory, S Sussex, England, on the Channel, 3 mi. SW of Eastbourne. Site of lighthouse (50°44′N 0°15′E), and scene of naval battle (1690) in which French under Tourville defeated English and Dutch under Torrington.

Beacon. 1 Town (pop. 371), Mahaska co., S central Iowa, 2 mi. SW of Oskaloosa, in coal-mining area. **2** City (pop. 14,012), Dutchess co., SE N.Y., on E bank of the Hudson (ferry), opposite Newburgh; trade center in summer-resort area. Mfg.: hats, rubber goods, clothing, textiles, furniture, brick, chemicals, paint, paper products. Incline railway ascends Mt. Beacon (1,602 ft.), just SE. Matteawan State Hosp. for insane criminals is here, and a tuberculosis hosp. for veterans is at near-by Castle Point. Formed and inc. in 1913 with union of Fishkill Landing and Matteawan (mă'tùwăn″) villages.

Beacon, Mount, N.Y.: see BEACON.

Beacon Falls, town (pop. 2,067), New Haven co., SW Conn., on Naugatuck R. and 8 mi. S of Waterbury; hardware. State forest here. Settled c.1678, inc. 1871.

Beaconsfield (bē'kŭnz–), residential town (pop. 706), S Que., on S shore of Montreal Isl., on L. St. Louis, 15 mi. SW of Montreal.

Beaconsfield (bĕ'kŭnzfēld, bē'kŭnz–), residential urban district (1931 pop. 4,846; 1951 census 7,909), S Buckingham, England, 5 mi. ESE of High Wycombe. Home of Edmund Waller and Edmund Burke, both buried here. Disraeli became earl of Beaconsfield in 1876.

Beaconsfield (bē'kŭnzfēld), town (pop. 722), N Tasmania, 25 mi. NW of Launceston; gold, iron. Asbestos in near-by Asbestos Range.

Beaconsfield (bē'kŭnz–), town (pop. 104), Ringgold co., S Iowa, 24 mi. SE of Creston, in agr. area.

Beadle (bē'dŭl), county (□ 1,261; pop. 21,082), E central S.Dak.; ⊙ Huron. Agr. area drained by James R. Dairy products, poultry, grain, livestock; mfg. at Huron. Formed 1873.

Beagle Channel, strait in Tierra del Fuego, separating the main isl. (N) from other isls. of the archipelago, notably Hoste and Navarino isls.; c.150 mi. long (E-W). 3-8 mi. wide. At its Atlantic entrance are the isls. of Pictón, Lennox, and Nueva (all disputed by Chile and Argentina); on the Pacific side, it splits into 2 arms which encircle Gordon Isl. and enter Cook Bay. Main port: Ushuaia, ⊙ Argentine part of Tierra del Fuego. Named for Fitzroy's exploring ship *Beagle,* on which Darwin was the naturalist.

Bealanana (bĕälänä'nŭ), town, Majunga prov., N Madagascar, at foot of Tsaratanana Massif, 180 mi. NE of Majunga; coffee-trading and stock-raising center; also rice. Airfield.

Beale, Camp, Calif.: see MARYSVILLE.

Beallsville. 1 (bĕlz'vĭl) Village (pop. 410), Monroe co., E Ohio, 12 mi. SE of Barnesville, in agr. area; sawmilling. **2** (bĕlz'–) Borough (pop. 598), Washington co., SW Pa., 13 mi. SE of Washington.

Beals (bēlz), town (pop. 590), Washington co., E Maine, 30 mi. ENE of Bar Harbor. Comprises Beals Isl. and village of Beals; summer resort, fishing port. Set off from Jonesport 1925.

Beals Creek, W Texas, formed W of Big Spring by headstreams rising on Llano Estacado, flows c.55 mi. generally E to the Colorado 15 mi. S of Colorado City.

Bealwood, village (1940 pop. 4,793), Muscogee co., W Ga., residential suburb of Columbus.

Beaman, town (pop. 191), Grundy co., central Iowa, on Wolf Creek and 31 mi. SW of Waterloo.

Beaminster (bĕ'–, bĕ'–), town and parish (pop. 1,612), W Dorset, England, on Brit. R. and 5 mi. N of Bridport; agr. market in dairying region; shoe mfg., milk canning, cheese making. Has 15th-cent. church.

Beamsville, village (pop. 1,309), S Ont., near L. Ontario, 12 mi. W of St. Catharines; fruit and vegetables canning, woodworking; mfg. of chemicals, pottery, cement.

Bean City, village (1940 pop. 602), Palm Beach co., SE Fla., on S shore of L. Okeechobee, near Belle Glade, in truck-farming region.

Beann Éadair, Ireland: see HOWTH.

Bear, Cape, at SE extremity of P.E.I., 13 mi. SSE of Georgetown; 46°N 62°27′W.

Béar, Cape (bäär'), headland on Gulf of Lion, in Pyrénées-Orientales dept., S France, formed by spur of the Monts Albères; 42°31′N 3°8′E. Its old fort and lighthouse overlook Port-Vendres (NE).

Bear, Mount (14,850 ft.), S Alaska, in St. Elias Mts., 130 mi. NNW of Yakutat; 61°18′N 141°8′W.

Bear Camp River, Carroll co., E central N.H., rises N of Squam L., flows 15 mi. E to Ossipee L.

Bear Creek. 1 Town (pop. 223), Marion co., NW Ala., 31 mi. S of Tuscumbia. **2** Village (pop. 476), Outagamie co., E Wis., 25 mi. NW of Appleton; dairying, farming.

Bearcreek, town (pop. 162), Carbon co., S Mont., near Wyo. line, 5 mi. ESE of Red Lodge.

Bear Creek. 1 In W Ill., rises near Carthage in Hancock co., flows c.55 mi. SW and S to Mississippi R. at Quincy. **2** In W central Ky., rises in Grayson co., flows 40 mi. SSW to Green R. 9 mi. WSW of Brownsville. Navigable for 8 mi. above mouth.

Bearden (bēr'dŭn). **1** Town (pop. 1,300), Ouachita co., S Ark., 15 mi. NE of Camden, in agr. area; lumbering. Founded 1882, inc. 1892. **2** Village (1940 pop. 1,280), Knox co., E Tenn., residential suburb just WSW of Knoxville, near the Tennessee.

Beardmore (bērd'môr), village (pop. estimate 450), W central Ont., 100 mi. NE of Port Arthur near L. Nipigon; 1,009 ft.; gold mining.

Beardmore Glacier, one of world's largest known valley glaciers (100 naut. mi. long, 12 naut. mi. wide), Antarctica, in 83°30′S 173°E; descends from South Polar Plateau to Ross Shelf Ice. Discovered 1908 by Sir Ernest Shackleton.

Beardsley (bērdz'lē), village (pop. 435), Big Stone co., W Minn., near Big Stone L., 22 mi. NW of Ortonville in grain, poultry, livestock area; dairy products.

Beardstown, city (pop. 6,080), Cass co., W central Ill., on Illinois R. (bridged) and c.45 mi. WNW of Springfield; trade and shipping center in agr. area; mfg. of flour, gloves, cigars, feed; railroad shops; commercial fisheries. Treadway L. is just NE. Old city hall and courthouse (1845), in which Lincoln won the Armstrong murder case, is preserved. Indian mounds near by. Settled 1819 as ferry crossing; platted 1827, inc. 1837.

Beargrass, town (pop. 128), Martin co., E N.C., 7 mi. SSW of Williamston.

Bearhaven, Ireland: see CASTLETOWN BERE.

Bear Head, southernmost point of Cape Breton Isl., E N.S., on the Atlantic, at entrance to Canso Strait, 5 mi. SE of Port Hawkesbury; 45°33′N 61°17′W.

Bear Island or **Bere Island** (both: bâr) (4,381 acres), in Bantry Bay, SW Co. Cork, Ireland; 6 mi. long, 2 mi. wide.

Bear Island, Nor. *Bjørnøya* (byûrn'ûyä), island (□ 69; pop. 5) in the Norwegian possession Svalbard, in Arctic Ocean, bet. West Spitsbergen (N) and Norway (SSE), 450 mi. NNW of Hammerfest; 74°26′N 19°5′E. Isl. is 12 mi. long (N-S), 2-10 mi. wide; rises to 1,759 ft. (E). Site of meteorological station; whaling.

Bear Island Lake, St. Louis co., NE Minn., in Superior Natl. Forest, 9 mi. SSW of Ely; 3.5 mi. long, 2 mi. wide. Resorts. Connected by small stream with near-by White Iron L.

Bear Islands, Rus. *Medvezhi Ostrova* (myĭdvyĕ'zhē ŭstrŭvä'), in E.Siberian Sea, bet. mouths of Alazeya and Kolyma rivers, NE Siberia Russian SFSR; 71°N 162°E. Consist of Krestovski (largest and highest), Pushkarev, Leontyev, and Lysov isls., and Chetyrekhstolbovoi Isl., site of govt. arctic station. Form part of Chukchi Natl. Okrug, Khabarovsk Territory.

Bear Lake (26 mi. long, 4 mi. wide), N central Man.; 55°13′N 96°W; drains into Hayes R.

Bear Lake, county (□ 988; pop. 6,834), SE Idaho; ⊙ Paris. Mtn. area bordering on Wyo. and Utah. Agr. (hay, grain, livestock, turkeys) near Bear L. and in valley of Bear R. Includes parts of Cache and Caribou natl. forests. Formed 1875.

Bear Lake. 1 Village (pop. 364), Manistee co., NW Mich., on Bear L. (c.2 mi. long, 1 mi. wide) and 15 mi. NNE of Manistee. Trade and shipping center for resort and farm area (apples, cherries, berries). **2** Borough (pop. 239), Warren co., NW Pa., 8 mi. NE of Corry, near N.Y. line.

Bear Lake, lake (□ 109), N Utah and SE Idaho, near Wasatch Range; c.20 mi. long, 7 mi. wide; alt. 5,924 ft.; used for irrigation. Drains into Bear R. through canal completed 1915.

Bear Mountain. 1 Highest peak (2,355 ft.) in Conn., in Taconic Mts., near Mass. and N.Y. borders, NW of Salisbury village. **2** Peak (1,314 ft.), SE N.Y., overlooking the Hudson, 13 mi. S of Newburgh. Bear Mtn.–Harriman section (c.41,000 acres) of Palisades Interstate Park here has summer- and winter-sports facilities, a section of Appalachian Trail, mus. bldgs., an inn, and remains of Fort Clinton (Revolutionary War). Popular outing resort for residents of New York city (rail, boat, highway connections). The Hudson is spanned here by Bear Mountain Bridge (suspension type; 2,257 ft. long; opened 1924; acquired by state in 1940).

Béarn (bäärn'), village (pop. estimate 300), W Que., near L. Timiskaming, 18 mi. SE of Haileybury; gold mining.

Béarn (bäär', bäärn'), region and former province, SW France, in W Pyrenees along Spanish border, now included in Basses-Pyrénées dept.; ⊙ Orthez (until 1460), succeeded by Pau. Agr. in fertile mountain valleys; cattle, sheep, horse raising. Has popular spas (Pau, Les Eaux-Bonnes, Les Eaux-Chaudes). Part of pop. is Basque. The medieval viscounty of Béarn passed (13th cent.) to counts of Foix. Became Protestant stronghold under Jeanne d'Albret (16th cent.). Her son, Henry IV, united it with France in 1620. Together with Lower Navarre it became a prov. Inc. into present dept. in 1790.

Bearpark (bĕr″pärk'), town and parish (pop. 1,912), central Durham, England, 2 mi. W of Durham; coal mining. In parish (SW) is coal-mining town of Ushaw Moor (ŭ'shù, ŭ'shô), site of St. Cuthbert's R.C. Col.

Bear Pond Mountains, NW Md. and S Pa., part of the Appalachians, in Franklin co., Pa., and Washington co., Md.; alt. c.1,000–2,000 ft.; form NW boundary of Hagerstown Valley.

Bear River, village (pop. estimate 1,000), NW N.S., on Bear R., near its mouth on Annapolis Basin, and 7 mi. SE of Digby; cherry center; lumber, pulpwood.

Bear River, in W N.S., flows 25 mi. NW to Annapolis Basin 4 mi. E of Digby.

Bear River, city, Utah: see BEAR RIVER CITY.

Bear River. 1 In E central Calif., rises in N Placer co., flows c.75 mi. SW and W, forming Placer-Nevada co. line, to Feather R. 15 mi. S of Marysville. Site of projected Rollins Dam and reservoir of CENTRAL VALLEY project. **2** In W Maine, rises in W Oxford co., flows c.12 mi. SE to the Androscoggin at Newry. Screw Auger Falls in Grafton Notch is scenic feature. **3** In Utah, Wyo., and Idaho, rises near Hayden Peak in Uinta Mts., NE Utah, flows N and NW in long loop through SW Wyo. and SE Idaho, passing around N end of Wasatch Range and continuing S to Bear River Bay of Great Salt L. 13 mi. W of Brigham City; c.350 mi. long; not navigable. Used to irrigate c.50,000 acres in Utah and Idaho; drains Bear L. (on state line bet. Utah and Idaho) through canal completed 1915. Around mouth is U.S. migratory waterfowl refuge (c.64,000 acres), established 1928.

Bear River Bay, Utah: see GREAT SALT LAKE.

Bear River City or **Bear River,** city (pop. 438), Box Elder co., N Utah, 10 mi. NW of Brigham City and on Bear R.; alt. 4,253 ft.; sugar beets. Utah dry farming begun here 1863.

Bearsden (bârzdĕn') or **New Kilpatrick,** residential town in New Kilpatrick parish, SE Dumbarton, Scotland, 5 mi. NW of Glasgow.

Beartooth Range, S Mont., NW Wyo., NE spur of ABSAROKA RANGE, bet. Stillwater R. (W) and Clark Fork of Yellowstone R. (E and S), NE of Yellowstone Natl. Park; includes GRANITE PEAK (12,850 ft.), highest point in Mont. Range includes parts of Custer and Shoshone natl. forests. Sometimes known in W half as Snowy Range. NW extension is Granite Range, rising to 12,661 ft. in Mt. Wood.

Bear Town, village (pop. 2,002), Pike co., S Miss.

Beartown Mountain (1,865 ft.), SW Mass., in Beartown State Forest (8,004 acres), 5 mi. NE of Great Barrington, in the Berkshires. A winter-sports center; picnicking and campgrounds.

Bearwood, England: see SMETHWICK.

Beas (bä'äs), town (pop. 3,000), Huelva prov., SW Spain, 14 mi. NE of Huelva, in agr. region (olives, chick-peas, almonds, oranges, grapes, cereals, corn, livestock). Has olive industry and flour mills; mfg. of artificial flowers. Trades in wool. Mineral springs near by.

Beasaín (bääsäēn'), town (pop. 3,553), Guipúzcoa prov., N Spain, 6 mi. SW of Tolosa; mfg. of railroad engines and rolling stock.

Beas de Segura (bä'äs dhā sägōō'rä), town (pop. 8,891), Jaén prov., S Spain, 15 mi. NE of Villacarrillo; agr. trade center. Olive-oil processing, soap mfg., wool and cotton spinning, flour- and sawmilling. Dam and hydroelectric power plant on Guadalquivir R. 7 mi. SE.

Beas River (bē'äs), anc. *Hyphasis,* NW India, one of 5 rivers of the Punjab. Rises in SE Pir Panjal Range of Punjab Himalayas, near Rohtang Pass, at alt. c.13.000 ft.; flows S through fertile Kulu valley, generally W through N central Himachal Pradesh, past Mandi, and again into Indian Punjab, breaking through Siwalik Range, and SSW to Sutlej R. 13 mi. WSW of Sultanpur; total length, c.285 mi. Marked E limit (somewhere in present Gurdaspur dist.) of Alexander the Great's invasion in 326 B.C. Receives Uhl R. (right). Sometimes spelled Bias.

Beata, Cape (bää'tä), Caribbean headland of SW Dominican Republic, southernmost point of Hispaniola isl., 45 mi. SSW of Barahona; 17°36′N 71°27′W. Beata Isl. is 3 mi. SW.

Beata Island (c.5 mi. long, 5 mi. wide), in the Caribbean, just off SW coast of Dominican Republic, 50 mi. SW of Barahona; 17°35′N 71°30′W.

Beatenberg (bää'tŭnbĕrk″), village (pop. 1,190), Bern canton, central Switzerland, near L. of Thun, 3 mi. W of Interlaken; resort (alt. 3,773 ft.) noted for winter sports.

Beath, parish (pop. 21,523, including COWDENBEATH burgh), S Fifeshire, Scotland.

Beatia, Spain: see BAEZA.

Beatitudes, Mount of, Palestine: see CAPERNAUM.

Beatrice, township (pop. 192), Salisbury prov., E central Southern Rhodesia, in Mashonaland, on Umfuli R. and 30 mi. SSW of Salisbury; gold-mining center.

Beatrice (bēă'trĭs). **1** Town (pop. 375), Monroe co., SW central Ala., 48 mi. SSW of Selma; lumber. **2** City (pop. 11,813), ⊙ Gage co., SE Nebr., 40 mi. S of Lincoln and on Big Blue R. Trade, railroad, and industrial center for grain, dairy, and livestock region; farm implements, wood and hardware products; plant seeds, dairy and poultry produce, grain. Has state home for feeble-minded. Founded 1857 on Oregon Trail, inc. as town 1871, as city 1873. Near by is Homestead Natl. Monument of America (162.7 acres; established 1939), on site of 1st land claim under Homestead Act of 1862; commemorates opening of land in public domain for settlement and development.

Beattie (bā'tē), city (pop. 321), Marshall co., NE Kansas, 12 mi. E of Marysville, in grain area.

Beattock Summit, mountain pass (1,014 ft.) in Lowther Hills, Scotland, on Lanark-Dumfries border, 6 mi. NW of Moffat; highest point on main London-Glasgow railroad and road.

Beattyville (bā'tēvĭl), town (pop. 1,042), ⊙ Lee co., E central Ky., in the Cumberlands, on Kentucky R., at its South Fork mouth, and 40 mi. SE of Winchester, in farm (corn, potatoes, hay, livestock), coal-mine, oil-well, hardwood timber region. Cumberland Natl. Forest near by.

Beau Bassin (bō' bäsē'), residential town (pop. 14,774), W central Mauritius, in central plateau, on railroad and 5 mi. SSW of Port Louis. Has hosp., insane asylum, prison. Contiguous with ROSE HILL.

Beaucaire (bōkâr'), town (pop. 6,996), Gard dept., S France, on right bank of Rhone R., opposite Tarascon, at N end of Rhone-Sète Canal, and 9 mi. N of Arles; chemical, cement, hosiery factories; brewery, boat yard. Has medieval castle and 17th-cent. town hall. Known, since 13th cent., for its annual (July) fair.

Beaucamps-le-Vieux (bōkā'-lŭ-vyû'), village (pop. 1,240), Somme dept., N France, 19 mi. S of Abbeville; drugget and furniture mfg.

Beauce (bōs), county (□ 1,128; pop. 48,073), S Que., on Maine border and on Chaudière R.; ⊙ Beauceville East.

Beauce, fertile limestone tableland (average alt. 450 ft.) of NW France, SW of Paris, bet. Seine and upper Loir rivers, comprised in Eure-et-Loir, Loiret, and Loir-et-Cher depts. Covered by extensive wheat fields ("the granary of France"). Commercial center: Chartres. **Little Beauce,** Fr. *Petite Beauce,* W of Orléans, bet. great bend of the Loire and Loir R., is also a cereal-growing dist. Its markets are Vendôme and Châteaudun.

Beaucens (bōsã'), village (pop. 153), Hautes-Pyrénées dept., SW France, on Gave de Pau R. and 3 mi. SE of Argelès-Gazost; small spa. Lead mining.

Beauceville (bōs'vĭl), town (pop. 899), S Que., on Chaudière R. and 50 mi. SSE of Quebec, opposite Beauceville East; lumbering, shoe mfg.; in dairying, pig-raising region. Some gold has been found near by.

Beauceville East, town (pop. 1,251), ⊙ Beauce co., S Que., on Chaudière R. and 50 mi. SSE of Quebec, opposite Beauceville; lumbering; market in dairying, pig-raising region.

Beauchamp (bō-shã'), town (pop. 3,907), Seine-et-Oise dept., N central France, 6 mi. SE of Pontoise; mfg. (railroad equipment, springs, buttons, baby shoes).

Beauchene Island (bōshān'), rocky islet in the South Atlantic, 40 mi. S of East Falkland Isl.

Beaucoup Creek (bŭ'kōō), S Ill., rises SW of Nashville, flows c.65 mi. SE and S, past Pinckneyville, to Big Muddy R. E of Murphysboro.

Beaucourt (bōkōōr'), town (pop. 3,745), Territory of Belfort, E France, 6 mi. ESE of Montbéliard; electrical equipment and hardware factories.

Beaudesert (bō'dĕzûrt), town (pop. 1,548), SE Queensland, Australia, 37 mi. S of Brisbane in agr. area (corn, sugar cane, alfalfa).

Beaufort (bō'fûrt), town (pop. 1,049), S central Victoria, Australia, 85 mi. WNW of Melbourne; livestock center.

Beaufort, town (pop. 2,000, including environs), W Br. North Borneo, 50 mi. SSW of Jesselton, on railroad; ⊙ Interior and Labuan residency; shipping center for rubber- and sago-producing area.

Beaufort, town (pop. 4,033) in Ebbw Vale urban dist., NW Monmouth, England, 2 mi. W of Brynmawr; coal mining.

Beaufort (bōfôr'). **1** or **Beaufort-du-Jura** (–dü-zhürä'), village (pop. 512), Jura dept., E France, 9 mi. SW of Lons-le-Saunier; winegrowing. Stone quarries. **2** Village, Maine-et-Loire dept., France: see BEAUFORT-EN-VALLÉE. **3** Village (pop. 581), Savoie dept., SE France, on the Doron de Beaufort and 9 mi. NE of Albertville; alt. 2,487 ft. Tourist and winter sports center of Beaufortin (Savoy Alps); gruyère cheese mfg. Large dam and hydroelectric station inaugurated here in 1949.

Beaufort (bōfôr'), **Befort** (bā'fôrt), or **Bofort** (bō'fôrt), village (pop. 751), E Luxembourg, 6 mi. ESE of Diekirch, near Sûre R.; liquor distilling; agr. Ruins of 11th-cent. castle.

Beaufort. 1 (bō'fûrt) County (□ 831; pop. 37,134), E N.C., on the Atlantic coast; ⊙ Washington. Tidewater area indented by Pamlico and Pungo river estuaries. Fishing, lumbering, and farming (tobacco, corn) region; resorts along coast. Formed 1705. **2** (bū'fûrt) County (□ 672; pop. 26,993), extreme S S.C.; ⊙ Beaufort. Extends along Atlantic coast from Savannah R. (S) to St. Helena Sound (NE) and Combahee R. (N.) Includes several of SEA ISLANDS, notably PORT ROYAL ISLAND (site of Beaufort), Parris Isl., St. Helena Isl., Hilton Head Isl. Intracoastal Waterway passes along coast. Formerly a region of great plantations; now winter-resort area, with fishing, canning, agr. (truck, corn, hogs), lumbering. Formed 1785.

Beaufort. 1 (bō'fûrt) Town (pop. 3,212), ⊙ Carteret co., E N.C., 35 mi. SE of New Bern, opposite Morehead City on Beaufort Harbor (bridged; connected with the Atlantic by Beaufort Inlet), here entered by short Newport R. Fishing center; resort; port of entry; mfg. of fish meal and oil; lumber milling, boatbuilding. Fort Macon State Park near by. Laid out 1722. **2** (bū'fûrt) City (pop. 5,081), ⊙ Beaufort co., S S.C., 50 mi. SW of Charleston, on PORT ROYAL ISLAND, one of SEA ISLANDS. Year-round resort and tourist center; canning, processing, and shipping point for truck, shrimping, oystering, and lumbering area, with good harbor. Second-oldest town in S.C.; founded 1711. Held by Union forces from Nov., 1861, to end of Civil War. Has many fine old buildings, including Episcopal church (built 1724; remodeled), natl. cemetery, arsenal (1795).

Beaufort-du-Jura, Jura dept., France: see BEAUFORT.

Beaufort-en-Vallée (bōfôr"tã-vălā'), village (pop. 1,788), Maine-et-Loire dept., W France, 16 mi. ESE of Angers; dairying; truck gardening, winegrowing. Has ruins of 14th-cent. castle and a 15th-cent. church. Formerly Beaufort.

Beaufortin (bōfôrtē'), mountainous district of N Savoie dept., SE France, bounded by Mont Blanc massif (NE), Tarentaise valley (S) and Arly R. (W). Drained by Doron de Beaufort R. Chief resort: Beaufort.

Beaufort Sea (bō'fûrt), part of the Arctic Ocean, bet. N Alaska and the Arctic Archipelago of Canada. Unlike the Siberian shelf seas, Beaufort Sea is part of the deep Arctic basin (more than 10,000 ft. deep) and contains no isls. Has not been fully explored, but its ice was crossed by Stefansson (1915) and by Storkersen (1918).

Beaufort West (bō'fûrt), Afrikaans *Beaufort-Wes* (vĕs'), town (pop. 10,908), S Cape Prov., U. of So. Afr., on the Great Karroo, at foot of Nieuwveld Range, on upper Gamka R. and 260 mi. ENE of Cape Town; 32°21'S 22°34'E. Center of sheep-raising (wool, karakul, mutton), grain- and fruit-growing region; railroad workshops. Airport, radio station. Founded 1818.

Beaugency (bōzhãsē'), town (pop. 2,927), Loiret dept., N central France, on right bank of Loire R. and 15 mi. SW of Orléans; mattress-mfg. center. Building materials, sparkling wines. Has a 16th-cent. Renaissance town hall and 11th-cent. rectangular keep. Damaged in Second World War.

Beauges, France: see BAUGES.

Beauharnois (bōhär'nwä, Fr. bōärnwä'), county (□ 147; pop. 30,269), SW Que., on the St. Lawrence; ⊙ Beauharnois.

Beauharnois, town (pop. 3,550), SW Que. ⊙ Beauharnois co., on S shore of L. St. Louis, 20 mi. SW of Montreal, at NE end of Beauharnois Canal; steel and paper milling, furniture mfg.; hydroelectric station; market in fruitgrowing region.

Beauharnois Canal, SW Que., extends 15 mi. bet. L. St. Francis (W) and L. St. Louis (NE), on S side of the St. Lawrence, bypassing rapids. First canal, opened 1843, soon became obsolete and was superseded (1899) by Soulanges Canal, on N side of the St. Lawrence. New Beauharnois Canal was begun 1930, has fall of 83 ft., and has important hydroelectric power station. Project was subject of political scandal.

Beaujeu (bōzhû'), village (pop. 1,414), E central France, bet. Monts du Beaujolais (W) and Monts du Mâconnais (N), 13 mi. NNW of Villefranche; winegrowing. Has 12th-cent. church. Was earliest ⊙ Beaujolais.

Beaujolais (bōzhôlā'), region of E central France, in N Rhône dept., traversed by the Monts du Beaujolais, and bounded by the Saône (E). Its noted wines are marketed at Belleville. During Middle Ages it was ruled by the lords of Beaujeu. Beaujeu was its early capital, Villefranche its later. Annexed to the crown in 1531, it became part of Lyonnais prov.

Beaujolais, Monts du (mõ'-dü–), range of the Massif Central, E central France, on Loire-Rhône dept. border, bet. the Loire (W) and Saône (E) valleys. Rises to 3,320 ft. Continued by the Monts du Lyonnais (S) and the Monts du Charolais (N). Poor grazing area with vineyards on valley slopes. Widespread handicraft weaving. Chief towns are the cotton- and silk-milling centers of Tarare, Cours, and Thizy.

Beau Lake (bō), Maine and Que., narrow lake on international line and 23 mi. NW of Fort Kent, Maine; 5 mi. long.

Beaulieu, Que.: see SAINTE PÉTRONILLE.

Beaulieu (bū'lē), town and parish (pop. 1,201), S Hampshire, England, in New Forest on Beaulieu R., and 6 mi. SSW of Southampton; agr. market. Has ruins of Cistercian abbey founded 1204 by King John. The 13th-cent. refectory is now parish church. In 1471 Margaret of Anjou, wife of Henry VI, took refuge here with Prince Edward after battle of Barnet. Perkin Warbeck also fled here in 1497.

Beaulieu (bōlyû'), town (pop. 2,649), Doubs dept., E France, on the Doubs and 5 mi. SSE of Montbéliard; bicycle factory.

Beaulieu-sur-Dordogne (bōlyû'-sür-dôrdô'nyù), village (pop. 1,706), Corrèze dept., S central France, on the Dordogne and 19 mi. SE of Brive-la-Gaillarde; fruit and vegetable growing; sawmilling. Has 12th–13th-cent. Benedictine church. Formerly called Beaulieu.

Beaulieu-sur-Mer (–mâr'), town (pop. 2,095), Alpes-Maritimes dept., SE France, 4 mi. ENE of Nice, at E base of Cape Ferrat peninsula on the Mediterranean; well-known health resort of Fr. Riviera noted for its mild winter climate, and frequented by foreigners. Backed by high cliffs, it lies amidst lush subtropical vegetation. Slightly damaged in Second World War.

Beauly (bū'lē), village, N Inverness, Scotland, at head of Beauly Firth, at mouth of Beauly R., 9 mi. W of Inverness; agr. market. Has ruins of Cistercian priory founded 1230.

Beauly Firth, W continuation (7 mi. long, 2½ mi. wide) of Moray Firth, with which it is connected by a narrow strait at Inverness, bet. N Inverness and SE Ross and Cromarty, Scotland; receives Beauly R. at its head.

Beauly River, Inverness, Scotland, formed by confluence of Farrar R. (28 mi. long) and Glass R. (12 mi. long) 9 mi. WSW of Beauly, flows 10 mi. NE, past Beauly, to Beauly Firth.

Beaumaris (bōmä'rĭs, –mă'rĭs), municipal borough (1931 pop. 1,710; 1951 census 2,128), E Anglesey, Wales, at NE end of Menai Strait, 3 mi. NNE of Bangor; seaside resort. Has ruins of castle, built 1295 by Edward I. Church dates from 14th cent.

Beaumes or **Beaumes-de-Venise** (bōm-dù-vùnēz'), village (pop. 784), Vaucluse dept., SE France, 5 mi. N of Carpentras; noted muscatel wines; apricot preserving, olive-oil mfg.

Beaumesnil (bōmānēl'), agr. village (pop. 381), Eure dept., NW France, 8 mi. SE of Bernay; sanatorium.

Beaumetz-lès-Loges (bōmĕts'-lā-lôzh'), agr. village (pop. 581), Pas-de-Calais dept., N France, 6 mi. SW of Arras.

Beaumont (bōmõ'), village (pop. 1,601), Hainaut prov., S Belgium, 8 mi. SSW of Thuin, near Fr. border; dairying.

Beaumont (bōmõ'). **1** or **Beaumont-du-Périgord** (–dü-pārēgôr'), village (pop. 469), Dordogne dept., SW France, 15 mi. ESE of Bergerac; road junction; flour milling. Mineral springs near by. **2** or **Beaumont-Hague** (–äg'), village (pop. 296), Manche dept., NW France, near NW tip of Cotentin Peninsula, 10 mi. W of Cherbourg; dairying. Cape La Hague is 6 mi. NW. **3** S residential suburb (pop. 3,720) of Clermont-Ferrand, Puy-de-Dôme dept., central France; lingerie mfg., alcohol distilling; winegrowing.

Beaumont (bō'mŏnt). **1** City (pop. 3,152), Riverside co., S Calif., 15 mi. SE of Redlands, at summit of San Gorgonio Pass; fruitgrowing (mainly cherries). Settled in mid-19th cent.; inc. 1912. **2** City (pop. 94,014), ⊙ Jefferson co., SE Texas, c.75 mi. ENE of Houston; important oil port, on deep-water channel in Neches R. (an arm of SABINE-NECHES WATERWAY to Gulf of Mexico). Also ships lumber, rice, cotton; port of entry. Oil-refining center. Transportation (rail, air, road), distribution, and industrial center for large petroleum-producing, agr., lumbering, cattle-raising region of Gulf Coast. Synthetic rubber plant, shipyards, lumber, paper, rice mills, creosoting plants, meat-packing plants; mfg. of chemicals, paints, varnishes, oil-field equipment, metal products. Seat of Lamar Jr. Col. South Texas State Fair held here. Settled before 1835, laid out 1837, inc. 1881. Lumbering, rice growing supplanted in importance by oil after near-by Spindletop field (still producing) came in, 1901. Completion of deep-water river channel (1916) made it an important port.

Beaumont-de-Lomagne (bōmõ'-dù-lōmä'nyù), town (pop. 2,335), Tarn-et-Garonne dept., SW France, on the Gimone and 12 mi. SSW of Castelsarrasin; agr. market (cereals, grapes, vegetables, poultry); horse breeding, brick mfg.

Beaumont-du-Périgord, France: see BEAUMONT, Dordogne dept.

Beaumont-en-Argonne (–ãnärgôn'), village (pop. 378), Ardennes dept., N France, near the Meuse, 12 mi. SSE of Sedan; distilling. Scene of Fr. defeat (1870) and of American breakthrough (1918).

Beaumont-Hague, France: see BEAUMONT, Manche dept.

Beaumont-Hamel (–ämĕl'), village (pop. 115), Somme dept., N France, 6 mi. N of Albert, commanding Ancre R. valley. Carried by British (1916) in First World War.

Beaumont-le-Roger (–lù-rô-zhā'), village (pop. (1,463), Eure dept., NW France, on the Risle and

8 mi. E of Bernay; tanning, belt mfg., lumbering. Its 14th–16th-cent. church was destroyed in 1943.

Beaumont-Port Arthur Canal, Texas: see SABINE-NECHES WATERWAY.

Beaumont-sur-Oise (–sür-wäz′), town (pop. 5,354), Seine-et-Oise dept., N central France, on left bank of Oise R., opposite Persan, and 20 mi. N of Paris; Portland cement; mfg. (clocks, corsets), tanning.

Beaumont-sur-Sarthe (–särt′), village (pop. 1,449), Sarthe dept., W France, on Sarthe R. and 15 mi. N of Le Mans; grain and dairy market; hemp.

Beaune (bōn), town (pop. 11,022), Côte-d'Or dept., E central France, on SE slope of the Côte d'Or, 22 mi. SSW of Dijon; noted center for finest Burgundy wines. Produces winegrowing equipment. Has remarkable 15th-cent. hosp. (Hôtel-Dieu), containing mus. (celebrated polyptych of Roger van der Weyden); 12th-cent. Romanesque church with 15th-cent. Flemish tapestries; and bastioned 16th-cent. ramparts. It flourished in 13th–14th cent. under dukes of Burgundy.

Beaune-la-Rolande (–lä-rôläd′), agr. village (pop. 1,173), Loiret dept., N central France, 11 mi. SE of Pithiviers; distilling.

Beauport (bōpôr′), residential town (pop. 3,725), ⊙ Quebec co., S central Que., on the St. Lawrence opposite SW end of Île d'Orleans, 5 mi. NE of Quebec. One of the oldest towns in Canada, settled 1634. French here repulsed Wolfe's attacks, necessitating landing (1759) below the Plains of Abraham. Beauport East (pop. 587) is just E.

Beaupréau (bōprāō′), town (pop. 2,524), Maine-et-Loire dept., W France, 11 mi. WNW of Cholet; mfg. (textiles, footwear), winegrowing. Has 15th–16th-cent. castle partially burned (1793) during the Vendée war which raged in the vicinity.

Beauregard (bō′rĭgärd), parish (□ 1,184; pop. 17,766), W La.; ⊙ De Ridder. Bounded W by Sabine R., here forming Texas line. Diversified lumber and agr. area (cotton, corn, cattle, sheep, peanuts, hay, sweet potatoes, citrus fruit, truck). Petroleum, natural gas. Farm-products processing; also naval stores, creosoted products. Formed 1906.

Beauregard, village (pop. 231), Copiah co., SW Miss., c.40 mi. SSW of Jackson.

Beaurepaire (bōrůpâr′). **1** Town (pop. 2,308), Isère dept., SE France, 16 mi. SE of Vienne; tanning; tobacco growing. **2** Agr. village (pop. 224), Saône-et-Loire dept., E central France, 7 mi. W of Lons-le-Saunier.

Beaurivage (bōrēväzh′), village (pop. 224), S Que., 28 mi. S of Quebec; dairying; pigs, cattle.

Beauséjour (bō′säzhŏŏr′, bōsäzhŏŏr′), town (pop. 1,181), SE Man., near Brokenhead R., 30 mi. ENE of Winnipeg; lumber and flour milling, dairying. Glass-sand quarries near by.

Beauséjour, Fort, national park in SE N.B., at head of Cumberland Basin, 4 mi. WNW of Amherst, on N.S.-N.B. border. Built 1751 by the French to guard Isthmus of Chignecto, it was captured (1755) by British and American troops under General Monckton, renamed Fort Cumberland, and abandoned after War of 1812. Site of mus.

Beausoleil (bōsôlā′), town (pop. 10,861), Alpes-Maritimes dept., SE France, adjoining Monte-Carlo (S), and 9 mi. ENE of Nice; resort on Fr. Riviera, sometimes referred to as "upper Monte-Carlo."

Beausset, Le (lů bōsā′), village (pop. 1,410), Var dept., SE France, 9 mi. NW of Toulon; olives, wine; truck.

Beautor (bōtôr′), village (pop. 1,763), Aisne dept., N France, on the Oise and Oise-Sambre Canal, and 14 mi. SSE of Saint-Quentin; metal- and woodworking.

Beauty, Ky.: see HIMLERVILLE.

Beauty Point, village (pop. 294), N Tasmania, 26 mi. NW of Launceston and on W shore of Tamar R. estuary; fruit canneries.

Beauvais (bōvā′), anc. *Caesaromagus,* later *Bellovacum* or *Belvacum,* city (pop. 20,910), ⊙ Oise dept., N France, on the Thérain and 40 mi. NNW of Paris, surrounded by wooded hills; commercial and road center formerly known for its state manufactures of tapestries (founded 1664 by Colbert; bldgs. partially destroyed in Second World War; industry transferred to Gobelin workshops in Paris). Mfg. (tiles and miscellaneous building materials, buttons, brushes, cartons, rayon, and pharmaceuticals), cider distilling. Of Roman origin and an early episcopal see. Became ⊙ Beauvaisis countship (9th cent.). Later ruled by its bishops. Center of the Jacquerie (1358). Successfully withstood a siege (1472) by Burgundians under Charles the Bold. Jeanne Hachette's prowess in the town's defense is still commemorated by a yearly celebration. Central part of Beauvais (containing numerous old buildings) was bombed and set afire by Germans in 1940. The famous cathedral of St. Pierre (also damaged) was begun in 1227 and never completed, still lacking a nave. Its choir vault (154 ft.), highest of all Gothic vaults, was reinforced after collapsing twice during 13th cent. Transept was completed in 1548.

Beauval (bōväl′), town (pop. 2,231), Somme dept., N France, 15 mi. N of Amiens; phosphate mining center.

Beau Vallon, Mauritius; see MAHÉBOURG.

Beauville (bōvēl′), village (pop. 292), Lot-et-Garonne dept., SW France, 12 mi. SE of Villeneuve-sur-Lot; small grains, poultry, eggs.

Beauvoir or **Beauvoir-sur-Mer** (bōvwär′-sür-mâr′), village (pop. 807), Vendée dept., W France, near Bay of Bourgneuf of the Atlantic, 30 mi. SW of Nantes; saltworks, oyster beds. A fishing port before silting of bay. A causeway, usable only at low tide, connects mainland here with the Île de Noirmoutier.

Beauvoir, Palestine: see BELVOIR.

Beauvoir-sur-Mer, France: see BEAUVOIR.

Beauvoir-sur-Niort (–nyôr′), village (pop. 519), Deux-Sèvres dept., W France, 10 mi. S of Niort; footwear mfg., dairying.

Beauvois or **Beauvois-en-Cambrésis** (bōvwä′-ä-käbräsē′), town (pop. 2,468), Nord dept., N France, 7 mi. ESE of Cambrai, in sugar-beet dist.; wool industry.

Beaver, village (pop. 100), N central Alaska, on Yukon R. and 110 mi. N of Fairbanks, near Arctic Circle; supply base for trappers and prospectors.

Beaver. 1 County (□ 1,793; pop. 7,411), extreme NW Okla.; ⊙ Beaver. High plains (alt. c.2,500 ft.) at base of Panhandle; bounded N by Kansas, S by Texas; intersected by North Canadian and Cimarron rivers and by Crooked Creek. Winter wheat, barley, sorghums, livestock. Silica deposits. Formed 1890. **2** County (□ 441; pop. 175,192), W Pa.; ⊙ Beaver. Mining and mfg. area; drained by Ohio and Beaver rivers; bounded W by Ohio. Gen. Anthony Wayne established (1792–93) one of 1st army training camps here. Metal products, glass, chemicals; bituminous coal, sandstone, clay, oil, gas; dairy products. Formed 1800. **3** County (□ 2,587; pop. 4,856), SW Utah; ⊙ Beaver. Mtn. area drained by Beaver R. and bordering on Nev. Some agr. and ranching in valleys. Part of Fishlake Natl. Forest in W. Livestock, alfalfa; lead, sulphur. Formed 1856.

Beaver. 1 Town (pop. 114), Boone co., central Iowa, on Beaver Creek and 13 mi. W of Boone. **2** Village (pop. 285), Pike co., S Ohio, 20 mi. NNE of Portsmouth and on small Beaver Creek; sawmills. **3** or **Beaver City,** town (pop. 1,495), ⊙ Beaver co., extreme NW Okla., on high plains of the Panhandle, on North Canadian R. and c.70 mi. NW of Woodward; shipping center for wheat and cattle area; dairy products; poultry. First settled by squatters c.1880; in 1887 became capital of short-lived Territory of Cimarron. **4** Residential borough (pop. 6,360), ⊙ Beaver co., W Pa., on Ohio R.. near mouth of Beaver R., and 24 mi. NW of Pittsburgh, in mineral region. Beverages, monuments, novelties; sand. Site of Fort McIntosh (1778). Laid out 1791, inc. 1802. **5** City (pop. 1,685), ⊙ Beaver co., SW Utah, on Beaver R. and c.45 mi. NE of Cedar City, W of Tushar Mts.; alt. 5,970 ft.; resort and processing point for livestock and irrigated agr. area; dairy products, powdered milk. Settled 1856 by Mormons. Had mining boom in 19th cent.

Beaver Bay, village, Lake co., NE Minn., on L. Superior and c.50 mi. NE of Duluth; low-grade iron ore (taconite) concentration plant.

Beaver City. 1 City (pop. 913), ⊙ Furnas co., S Nebr., 80 mi. WSW of Hastings and on Beaver Creek, near Kansas line; dairy produce, grain. **2** Town, Okla.: see BEAVER, town.

Beaver Creek, district (pop. 17), central Alaska, 40 mi. N of Fairbanks; placer gold mining.

Beaver Creek. 1 Village (pop. c.250), Washington co., W Md., on small Beaver Creek (water power) and 6 mi. SE of Hagerstown; cannery, grain mills. Near by are Mt. Aetna Caverns, a tourist attraction. **2** Village (pop. 245), Rock co., extreme SW Minn., on small tributary of Big Sioux R. and 19 mi. ENE of Sioux Falls, S.Dak., in corn, oat, and barley area.

Beaver Creek. 1 In Colo., Kansas, and Nebr., rises in E Colo., flows ENE through NW Kansas into S Nebr., past Beaver City, to Republican R. near Orleans; 152 mi. long. **2** In central Iowa, rises 20 mi. S of Fort Dodge, flows c.65 mi. S and SE to Des Moines R. just N of Des Moines. **3** In E Mont., rises in Fallon co., flows c.100 mi. N, past Wibaux, thence NE to Little Missouri R. in W N.Dak. **4** In NE central Nebr., rises in Wheeler co., flows 84 mi. SE, past Albion and St. Edward, to Loup R. near Genoa **5** In SW Okla., rises in NE Comanche co., flows c.65 mi. generally S, through oil-producing area, past Waurika, Sugden, and Ryan, to Red R. just below Ryan.

Beaver Crossing, village (pop. 425), Seward co., SE Nebr., 30 mi. W of Lincoln and on W.Fork of Big Blue R.; glue; grain.

Beaverdale, village (pop. 2,560, with adjacent Lloydell), Cambria co., W central Pa., 11 mi. E of Johnstown.

Beaver Dam, locality, S Ont., 7 mi. S of St. Catharines; battle (June 24, 1813) in War of 1812.

Beaver Dam. 1 City (pop. 1,349), Ohio co., W Ky., 29 mi. SSE of Owensboro; trade and mining center in bituminous-coal, agr. (grain, burley tobacco, hay, strawberries) area; lumbering, flour and feed milling. Holds annual (June) strawberry festival. **2** City (pop. 11,867), Dodge co., S central Wis., at SE end of Beaverdam L. (c.8 mi. long, 3 mi. wide), 30 mi. SW of Fond du Lac; shipping center for agr. area (dairy products; barley, hemp, peas); mfg. (shoes, stoves, iron castings, refrigerators, dairy equipment, canned foods, cheese, beer). Seat of Wayland Jr. Col. and Acad. Settled 1841, inc. 1856.

Beaverdam, village (pop. 450), Allen co., W Ohio, 10 mi. NE of Lima, in stock-raising area.

Beaver Dam Creek, Va.: see MECHANICSVILLE.

Beaverdam Lake. 1 In Dodge co., Wis.: see BEAVER DAM. **2** In Barron co., NW Wis., 13 mi. WNW of Rice Lake; 4 mi. long, c.½ mi. wide; drained by Hay R. Cumberland is on S shore, on what was formerly an isl.

Beaverdell, village (pop. estimate 100), S B.C., on Westkettle R. and 23 mi. E of Penticton; silver and lead mining.

Beaver Falls. 1 Village (1940 pop. 639), Lewis co., N central N.Y., on Beaver R. and 25 mi. ESE of Watertown; paper and textile milling. **2** City (pop. 17,375), Beaver co., W Pa., 28 mi. NW of Pittsburgh and on Beaver R.; industrial and trading center; metal products, chinaware, cork products, paint, lumber, bricks, textiles; bituminous coal, clay; agr. Geneva Col. here. Founded on Indian trail, later a pioneer road. Settled c.1793, laid out 1806, inc. as borough 1868, as city 1930.

Beaverhead, county (□ 5,556; pop. 6,671), SW Mont.; ⊙ Dillon. Mtn. region bordering on Idaho; bounded N by Big Hole R.; crossed by Big Hole and Beaverhead rivers in Jefferson R. system and by Upper and Lower Red Rock lakes. Livestock. Sections of Beaverhead Natl. Forest and Bitterroot Range in W. Big Hole Battlefield Natl. Monument in NW. Formed 1865.

Beaverhead Mountains, Idaho and Mont.: see BITTERROOT RANGE.

Beaverhead River, Mont.: see JEFFERSON RIVER.

Beaverhill Lake (□ 80), central Alta., 35 mi. E of Edmonton. Drains N into North Saskatchewan R. through Beaverhill Creek.

Beaver Island. 1 or **Big Beaver Island,** Mich., largest isl. of BEAVER ISLANDS archipelago in NE L. Michigan, 25 mi. NW of Charlevoix (ferry, plane connections); c.13 mi. long, c.6 mi. wide; part of Charlevoix co. Several lakes, and beaches, wildlife, and woodland attract summer visitors. Lumbering, commercial fishing, some farming. At N tip is St. James (pop. 350), only village of the archipelago, a trade center with harbor. Nomad (resort colony) is on SE shore. James J. Strang established a Mormon settlement here in 1847; made king in 1850, he was killed by rebellious subjects in 1856, after which the colony was dispersed. **2** In N.Y.: see GRAND ISLAND.

Beaver Islands, Mich., archipelago (c.70 mi. long) in NE L. Michigan; extends SW-NE, from 20 mi. W of Leelanau peninsula to c.30 mi. W of Straits of Mackinac. Part of Charlevoix co. Includes MANITOU ISLANDS, FOX ISLANDS, and BEAVER ISLAND (c.13 mi. long, largest of group). NW and N of Beaver Isl. are Garden Isl. (5 mi. long, 2½ mi. wide; Indian burial grounds); High Isl. (3½ mi. long, 2 mi. wide); Hog Isl. (3 mi. long, 1½ mi. wide; bass fishing); Gull Isl. (1½ mi. long, ½ mi. wide).

Beaver Kill, stream in SE N.Y., rises in the Catskills in W Ulster co., flows c.35 mi. generally W to East Branch of Delaware R. 8 mi. E of Hancock. Trout fishing; state park on upper course.

Beaverlodge, village (pop. 443), W Alta., near B.C. border and near Beaverlodge R., 26 mi. W of Grande Prairie; coal mining, lumbering, mixed farming, wheat.

Beaverlodge Lake or **Beaver Lodge Lake,** in northernmost Sask., N of L. Athabaska; 59°30′N 108°25′E; 8 mi. long, 1 mi. wide. Development of uranium deposits begun here, 1951.

Beaver Meadows, borough (pop. 1,723), Carbon co., E Pa., 3 mi. SE of Hazleton; anthracite mines; textiles. Settled 1787.

Beaver River. 1 In Alta. and Sask., issues from Beaver L. (11 mi. long) in Alta. just S of Lac la Biche, flows E into Sask. and near Doré L. turns N to Churchill R. at W end of Lac la Plonge; 305 mi. long. **2** In the SE Yukon, flowing c.150 mi. SE to the Liard in B.C. W of Nelson Forks.

Beaver River, resort village, Herkimer co., N central N.Y., in the Adirondacks, c.60 mi. NNE of Utica. Many lakes near by.

Beaver River. 1 In N central N.Y., rises in small lakes in Hamilton co., flows c.50 mi. W to Black R. 7 mi. N of Lowville. In upper course, it widens into Beaver River Flow (c.9 mi. long, c.1 mi. wide). **2** In Okla.: see NORTH CANADIAN RIVER. **3** In W Pa., formed by junction of Mahoning and Shenango rivers at New Castle; flows 21 mi. S, past Beaver Falls and Brighton, to Ohio R. at Rochester. **4** In Utah, rises in Tushar Mts., SW Utah, flows W, past Beaver and Minersville, then N, past Milford, terminating in dry area in SE corner of Millard co.; c.80 mi. long; intermittent. Dammed 5 mi. E of Minersville; used for irrigation.

Beaverton, village (pop. 934), S Ont., on L. Simcoe, at mouth of Beaverton R., 22 mi. W of Lindsay; mfg. of toys, bricks; lumbering. Resort.

Beaverton. 1 Town (pop. 192), Lamar co., W Ala., 43 mi. WNW of Jasper. **2** City (pop. 794), Gladwin co., E central Mich., on Tobacco R. and 36 mi. NW of Bay City, in farm area (livestock, grain, seed); mfg. of flour, feed. **3** City (pop. 2,512), Washington co., NW Oregon, 7 mi. W of Portland in agr. area. Founded 1868, inc. 1893. Has 2 orphanages (R.C.), one for boys, one for girls.

Beavertown, borough (pop. 700), Snyder co., central Pa., 20 mi. WSW of Sunbury; bricks, shirts; silk and planing mills.

Beaverville, village (pop. 383), Iroquois co., E Ill., 15 mi. SE of Kankakee, in rich agr. area.

Beawar (bëä'vŭr), town (pop. 36,720), W Ajmer state, India, 31 mi. SW of Ajmer; agr. market center (cotton, corn, millet, wheat); cotton ginning and milling, hosiery mfg., hand-loom weaving, wood carving. Formerly also called Nayanagar.

Beazley, town (pop. estimate 500), W San Luis prov., Argentina, on railroad and 40 mi. SW of San Luis; lumbering.

Beba, Egypt: see BIBA.

Bebedero (bābādā'rō), village, Guanacaste prov., NW Costa Rica, on Bebedero R. (40 mi. long; left affluent of the Tempisque) and 6 mi. SW of Cañas, in livestock region. Lumber port, exporting hardwood, grain.

Bebedero, Lake, shallow salt lake (□ 33) in W central San Luis prov., Argentina, 20 mi. SW of San Luis, in Desaguadero-Salado basin; c.10 mi. long, 3 mi. wide. Saltworks.

Bebedouro (bĭbĭdō'rōō). **1** City, Pernambuco, Brazil: see AGRESTINA. **2** City (pop. 11,632), N São Paulo, Brazil, 45 mi. WNW of Ribeirão Prêto; rail junction and agr. trade center in stock-raising and coffee zone; mfg. of dairy products, soap, manioc flour, alcohol, tiles, soft beverages, textiles; coffee and rice processing.

Bebeji (bābäjē'), town (pop. 5,812), Kano prov., Northern Provinces, N Nigeria, 30 mi. SSW of Kano; cotton, peanuts, millet; cattle, skins.

Bebelsheim (bā'bŭls-hīm), village (pop. 544), SE Saar, near Fr. border, 6 mi. NE of Sarreguemines; stock, grain.

Bebenhausen (bā″bŭnhou'zŭn), village (pop. 306), S Württemberg, Germany, after 1945 in Württemberg-Hohenzollern, 2.5 mi. N of Tübingen; site of noted former Cistercian monastery (founded c.1190), after 1807 a royal hunting castle. William II, last king of Württemberg, died here (1921).

Bebhamburh, England: see BAMBURGH.

Bebie, Alpi, Yugoslavia: see VELEBIT MOUNTAINS.

Bebington (bĕ'-), formerly Bebington and Bromborough, municipal borough (1931 pop. 26,740; 1951 census 47,742), on Wirral peninsula, NW Cheshire, England. Includes contiguous towns of Higher Bebington and Lower Bebington, on Mersey R. and 4 mi. S of Liverpool (across the river); mfg. of soap and feed cakes. Lower Bebington has church with Norman nave and 14th-cent. tower. Bromborough has chemical industry and is site of the docks of PORT SUNLIGHT. Near by is 14th-cent. chapel.

Bebra (bā'brä), town (pop. 6,922), in former Prussian prov. of Hesse-Nassau, W Germany, after 1945 in Hesse, near the Fulda, 8 mi. NNE of Hersfeld; rail junction; textiles; woodworking.

Bèbre River, France: see BESBRE.

Bebside, England: see BLYTH.

Bec Abbey, France: see BRIONNE.

Becal (bākäl'), town (pop. 2,539), Campeche, SE Mexico, in W Yucatan Peninsula, 45 mi. SW of Mérida; corn, sugar, henequen, chicle, fruit, livestock.

Bécancour (bākäkōōr'), village (pop. 276), ⊙ Nicolet co., S Que., on Becancour R., near its mouth on the St. Lawrence, and 5 mi. E of Trois Rivières; dairying, pig raising.

Becancour River or **Bécancour River,** S Que., rises near Thetford Mines, flows WSW, then NW, past Daveyluyville and Bécancour, to the St. Lawrence 5 mi. ENE of Trois Rivières; 75 mi. long.

Becca d'Audon, Switzerland: see OLDENHORN.

Beccar (bākär'), town (pop. estimate 6,000) in Greater Buenos Aires, Argentina, 14 mi. NW of Buenos Aires; mfg. (food preserves, paper, cardboard, chemicals).

Beccavole, India: see BIKKAVOLU.

Beccles (bĕ'kŭlz), municipal borough (1931 pop. 6,545; 1951 census 6,869), NE Suffolk, England, on Waveney R. and 8 mi. WSW of Lowestoft; agr. market; flour mills, printworks. Has 15th-cent. church. Noted for crayfish caught here.

Bec d'Ambès, France: see AMBÈS.

Bec de l'Aigle, France: see AIGLE, CAP DE L'.

Becedas (bā-thā'dhäs), town (pop. 1,215), Ávila prov., central Spain, 38 mi. S of Salamanca; cereals, apples, pears, nuts, vegetables, sheep, cattle; lumbering, flour milling.

Beceite (bā-thā'tā), town (pop. 1,073), Teruel prov., E Spain, 18 mi. W of Tortosa; paper mfg. (playing cards, filters); olive-oil processing, flour- and sawmilling. Has a few Roman remains.

Becej, Bechei, or **Bechey** (all: bĕ'chā), Serbo-Croatian *Bečej*, Hung. *Becse* (bĕ'chĕ), village (pop. 22,923), Vojvodina, N Serbia, Yugoslavia, port on Tisa R. and 27 mi. NNE of Novi Sad, in the Backa. Rail junction; E terminus of Danube-Tisa Canal; flour milling. Natural-gas wells in vicinity. Until c.1947, Stari Becej, Hung. *Óbecse.*

Becerril de Campos (bā-thĕrēl' dhā käm'pōs), town (pop. 2,073), Palencia prov., N central Spain, on Tierra de Campos branch of Canal of Castile, and 9 mi. NW of Palencia; woolen mills; cereals, wine, vegetables. The *communeros* were routed here by troops of Charles V.

Becerril de la Sierra (lä syĕ'rä), town (pop. 684), Madrid prov., central Spain, on E slopes of the Sierra de Guadarrama, 27 mi. NW of Madrid; goats, cattle. Ships milk.

Bech (bĕsh). **1** Village (pop. 267), SE Luxembourg, on Moselle R. and 11 mi. SE of Luxembourg city, on Ger. border; grape-growing center. **2** Village (pop. 345), E Luxembourg, 5 mi. SSW of Echternach.

Becharof Lake (bŭshâr'ŭf) (40 mi. long, 12 mi. wide), SW Alaska, 130 mi. W of Kodiak; 57°55'N 156°21'W.

Béchateur (bāshätûr'), village, Bizerte dist., N Tunisia, near the Mediterranean, 7 mi. WNW of Bizerte; lead and zinc mines.

Bechei, Yugoslavia: see BECEJ.

Bec-Hellouin, Le, France: see BRIONNE.

Bécherel (bāshrĕl'), village (pop. 687), Ille-et-Vilaine dept., W France, 17 mi. NW of Rennes; horse raising.

Bechhofen (bĕkh'hō″fŭn), village (pop. 3,058), Middle Franconia, W Bavaria, Germany, 10 mi. S of Ansbach; wood- and metalworking. Potatoes, rye, oats, cattle, sheep.

Bechí (bächē'), town (pop. 2,241), Castellón de la Plana prov., E Spain, 10 mi. SW of Castellón de la Plana; oranges, wine, flax; sericulture.

Beching, Czechoslovakia: see BECHYNE.

Bechtelsville (bĕk'tŭlzvĭl), borough (pop. 603), Berks co., SE Pa., 15 mi. E of Reading. Founded 1852, inc. 1890.

Bechtheim (bĕkht'hīm), village (pop. 1,805), Rhenish Hesse, W Germany, 7 mi. NNW of Worms; wine.

Bechuanaland (bĕ″chŭwä'nŭlănd″), commonly called **British Bechuanaland,** district (□ 52,393; pop. 222,687), N Cape Prov., U. of So. Afr., bounded by Griqualand West (S), Orange R. (SW), South-West Africa (W), Molopo R., Bechuanaland Proctectorate border (N), and Transvaal Prov. (E); ⊙ Vryburg. Other towns are Mafeking, Taungs, Kuruman. Stock raising, dairying are chief occupations. Generally high plateau region; S part of dist. forms part of Kaap Plateau. Dist. is bisected by Kuruman Hills and Kuruman R. Vryburg region was proclaimed republic of Stellaland 1883; entire dist. became crown colony 1885; annexed to Cape Colony 1895. In NW part of dist. is Kalahari Natl. Park.

Bechuanaland Protectorate, British protectorate (□ c.275,000; pop. 296,883), S Africa, bounded by U. of So. Afr. (S and SE), South-West Africa (W and N), and Southern Rhodesia (NE); extraterritorial ⊙ is Mafeking, in British Bechuanaland. Plateau area, generally over 3,000 ft. high; chief rivers are the Okovanggo, Limpopo (SE border) and Molopo (S border). Kalahari Desert covers entire S part of territory. In N part of territory are several sandy depressions or pans, formerly sites of lakes; largest is Makarikari. L. Ngami and Okovanggo Basin (NW) are marsh regions. Climate is subtropical, with average annual rainfall of 18–25 in. Some grains are grown on irrigated tracts; stock raising (cattle, sheep, goats) is main occupation. Gold and silver are mined in Tati dist., near Francistown; asbestos mined near Kanye. Center of pop. is in E and SE part of territory, where there are some European farm blocks and Tati dist. mining concession; apart from these, entire territory is native reserve. Mafeking-Bulawayo RR (1896–97) traverses SE and E part of territory. Towns include Serowe, Francistown, Maun, Mahalapye, Gaberones, Mochudi, Molopolole, Kanye, Lobasti, Tshabong, and Ghanzi. British protectorate established 1885 after period of hostilities bet. the Bechuana and South African Republic. Boundaries defined 1891; generally the territory was treated as part of crown colony of British Bechuanaland until latter was annexed to Cape Colony in 1895, when administration of territory (apart from some native reserves) was transferred to British South Africa Co.; administration reassumed by British govt. 1896. All land, apart from native reserves and European farm blocks, was vested in the crown, 1910. Bechuanaland, Basutoland, and Swaziland constitute the High Commission Territories.

Bechyne (bĕ'khĭnyĕ), Czech *Bechyně*, Ger. *Beching* (bĕ'khĭng), town (pop. 2,251), S Bohemia, Czechoslovakia, 12 mi. SW of Tabor, in fire-clay dist.; rail terminus; ceramic mfg. center; distilling. Health resort (ferruginous springs, peat baths). Has school of ceramics, 16th-cent. Franciscan abbey, 16th-cent. castle.

Beckemeyer (bĕ'kŭmī″ŭr), village (pop. 1,045), Clinton co., S Ill., 16 mi. WNW of Centralia, in agr., bituminous-coal-mining, and oil-producing area; metal products.

Beckenham (bĕ'kŭnŭm), residential municipal borough (1931 pop. 43,832; 1951 census 74,834), NW Kent, England, just S of London; also has tanneries, cable works.

Beckenried (bĕ'kŭnrēt″), village (pop. 1,817), Nidwalden half-canton, central Switzerland, on L. of Lucerne, 5 mi. E of Stans; resort; cement products, woodworking.

Becker, county (□ 1,315; pop. 24,836), W Minn.; ⊙ Detroit Lakes. Agr. area watered by numerous lakes, including White Earth L., in N, and Detroit L. and Cormorant L., in SW. Dairy products, livestock, grain; deposits of marl and peat. Wildlife refuge and part of White Earth Indian Reservation in N. Co. formed 1858.

Becker, village (pop. 264), Sherburne co., central Minn., on Elk R. and c.40 mi. NW of Minneapolis; dairy products.

Beckerich (bĕ'kŭrĭkh), village (pop. 648), W Luxembourg, 14 mi. NW of Luxembourg city, near Belg. border; sawmills, lumbering; agr. (potatoes, wheat, oats).

Beckermet Saint Bridget (bĭkûr'mŭt), village and parish (pop. 647), W Cumberland, England, 8 mi. SSE of Whitehaven; dairy farming. Has Norman church and remains of Norman graves. Just W is **Beckermet Saint John,** a dairying village and parish (pop. 1,076).

Becket, town (pop. 755), Berkshire co., W Mass., on W.Branch of Westfield R. and 12 mi. SE of Pittsfield; baskets.

Beckham (bĕ'kŭm), county (□ 898; pop. 21,627), W Okla.; ⊙ Sayre. Rolling plains, bounded W by Texas line; intersected by North Fork of Red R. and by Elk Creek. Agr. (cotton, wheat, sorghums). Mfg. at Elk City, Erick, and Sayre. Oil and natural-gas wells. Formed 1907.

Beckingen bĕ'kĭng-ŭn), town (pop. 3,167), W Saar, on Saar R. and 7 mi. NNW of Saarlouis; metalworking.

Beckley, city (pop. 19,397), ⊙ Raleigh co., S W.Va., 40 mi. N of Bluefield. Center of rich semibituminous-coal and agr. (truck, dairy, livestock, fruit, tobacco) region; mfg. of machine-shop and foundry products, mining supplies. Jr. col., state tuberculosis sanatorium. Chartered 1858.

Beckov (bĕts'kôf), Hung. *Beckó* (bĕts'kō), village (pop. 1,477), W Slovakia, Czechoslovakia, near Vah R., 9 mi. SW of Trencin; barley, wheat. Noted for ruins of 13th-cent. castle; has 15th-cent. church, 17th-cent. monastery.

Beckum (bĕ'kōōm), town (pop. 16,065), in former Prussian prov. of Westphalia, NW Germany, after 1945 in North Rhine-Westphalia, 6 mi. E of Ahlen; mfg. of machinery; cement works. Has Gothic church and town hall.

Beckville, town (pop. 550), Panola co., E Texas, near the Sabine, 22 mi. SSW of Marshall, in agr., lumber area.

Beckwourth Pass (bĕk'wûrth), Plumas co., NE Calif., rail and highway pass (alt. c.5,250 ft.) across the Sierra Nevada E of Sierra Valley and c.30 mi. NW of Reno, Nev. Was route of an emigrant trail in 1850s. Beckwourth village and Beckwourth Peak (c.7,250 ft.) are W. Formerly spelled Beckwith.

Beclean (bĕklä'än), Hung. *Betlen* (bĕt'lĕn), village (pop. 3,439), Rodna prov., N Rumania, on Great Somes R., on railroad and 13 mi. ENE of Dej; flour milling, mfg. of edible oils and knitwear. Has 18th-cent. Greek-Catholic church. In Hungary, 1940–45.

Bécon-les-Granits (bākō'-lā-gränē'), village (pop. 880), Maine-et-Loire dept., W France, 11 mi. WNW of Angers; granite quarries.

Becov or **Becov nad Teplou** (bĕ'chôf nät'tĕ″plō), Czech *Bečov*, Ger. *Petschau* (pĕ'chou), town (pop. 887), W Bohemia, Czechoslovakia, on railroad and 7 mi. N of Tepla.

Becse, Yugoslavia: see BECEJ.

Becsehely (bĕ'chĕhĕĭ), town (pop. 2,829), Zala co., W Hungary, 10 mi. W of Nagykanizsa; wheat, corn, hogs.

Bective, agr. village (district pop. 502), S central Co. Meath, Ireland, on the Boyne and 4 mi. NE of Trim; site of ruins of 1146 abbey. Hugh de Lacy is buried here.

Becva River (bĕch'vä), Czech *Bečva*, E Moravia, Czechoslovakia, formed at Valasske Mezirici by junction of Horni Becva (Czech *Horní Bečva*) and Dolni Becva (Czech *Dolní Bečva*) rivers, both rising in the Beskids; flows in a curve W, across the Moravian Gate, past Lipnik nad Becou, to Morava R. just N of Kromeriz; 74 mi. long.

Bedale (bē'dŭl, –dāl), town and parish (pop. 1,043), North Riding, N Yorkshire, England, 11 mi. N of Ripon; agr. market. Has church dating mainly from 16th cent.

Beda Littoria (bā'dä lēt-tô'rēä), Arabic *Sidi Rafa*, village (pop. 1,280), W Cyrenaica, Libya, 10 mi. SW of Cyrene, on the plateau Gebel el Akhdar; agr. settlement (wheat, grapes, olives, almonds; livestock) founded 1933 by the Italians. Has power station.

Bédar (bä'dhär), town (pop. 507), Almería prov., S Spain, 36 mi. NE of Almería; iron and lead mining. Terminus of mining railroad from Mediterranean port of Garrucha.

Bédarieux (bādärēû'), town (pop. 6,488), Hérault dept., S France, in the Monts Garrigues, on Orb R. and 19 mi. N of Béziers; industrial center; textile mills, tanneries, tile- and cementworks; biscuit, candy, paint, and dye factories. Has 15th-16th-cent. church.

Bédarrides (bādärēd'), village (pop. 828), Vaucluse dept., SE France, at junction of Ouvèze and Sorgue rivers, and 8 mi. NNE of Avignon; wine-growing, mfg. (fertilizer, flour products).

Bedburg (bät'bŏŏrk), town (pop. 7,460), in former Prussian Rhine Prov., W Germany, after 1945 in North Rhine-Westphalia, on the Erft and 16 mi. WNW of Cologne; rail junction; coal mining.

Beddgelert (bādh-gĕ'lûrt), agr. village and parish (pop. 913), S central Caernarvon, Wales, 6 mi. N of Portmadoc; tourist resort. According to legend Llewelyn ap Iorweth here killed his dog Gelert (given him by King John), believing he had killed Llewelyn's child. Church dates from 13th cent.

Beddington, town (pop. 26), Washington co., E Maine, on Beddington L. and 32 mi. NW of Machias; diatomaceous earth.

Beddington and Wallington (wô'lĭngtŭn), residential municipal borough (1931 pop. 26,251; 1951 census 32,751), NE Surrey, England, just WSW of Croydon. Includes towns of Beddington, with 14th-cent. church, and Wallington, with leather, printing, and food-products industries.

Bede, Point (bēd), S Alaska, SW tip of Kenai Peninsula, at E side of entrance to Cook Inlet; 59°19'N 152°W.

Bedeau (bŭdō'), village, Oran dept., NW Algeria, on S slope of the Tell Atlas, overlooking the High Plateaus, on railroad and 50 mi. SSW of Sidi-bel-Abbès; road junction; cereals, sheep, esparto. Also called Bedeau-les-Pins.

Bedel Pass (bĕdĕl') (alt. 14,016 ft.), in Kokshaal-Tau section of Tien Shan system, on USSR-China border, on Aksu-Przhevalsk trade route.

Bedeque Bay (bŭdĕk'), inlet (8 mi. long, 12 mi. wide at entrance) of Northumberland Strait, SW P.E.I. At head of bay is Summerside.

Bederkesa (bā'dûrkä"zä), village (pop. 2,967), in former Prussian prov. of Hanover, NW Germany, after 1945 in Lower Saxony, on W shore of small L. Bederkesa, 12 mi. ENE of Bremerhaven; food processing.

Bedessa (bĕdĕ'sä), village (pop. 500), Harar prov., E central Ethiopia, in Chercher Mts., 15 mi. SW of Asba Tafari; coffee growing.

Bedeyeva Polyana (byĭdyā'ŭvŭ pŭlyä'nŭ), village, central Bashkir Autonomous SSR, Russian SFSR, near Ufa R., 60 mi. NNE of Ufa; rye, oats, livestock. Until c.1940, Bedeyevo.

Bedford. 1 Village (pop. estimate 1,000), S N.S., on Bedford Basin, N part of Halifax Harbour, 7 mi. NNW of Halifax; woolen milling. Site of Dominion rifle range. **2** Town (pop. 1,697), ⊙ Missisquoi co., S Que., near N.Y. border, on Pike R. and 18 mi. SW of St. Jean, in oats, hay, cattle region; lumbering, needle mfg. Inc. 1890.

Bedford or **Bedfordshire** (-shĭr), county (□ 473.3; 1931 pop. 220,525; 1951 census 311,844), S central England; ⊙ Bedford. Bounded by Buckingham (W), Northampton (NW), Huntingdon (NE), Cambridge (E), and Hertford (SE and S). Drained by Ouse R. and Ivel R. Level country, rising in S to a spur of the Chilterns. Wheat cultivation, truck gardening. Chief industries: automobile mfg. (Luton), agr. machinery, straw-plaiting, hat mfg. (Luton). Other important towns: Dunstable, Leighton Buzzard, and Biggleswade. Much of co. is associated with travels of John Bunyan, b. at Elstow. Shortened form, Beds.

Bedford, municipal borough (1931 pop. 40,554; 1951 census 53,065), ⊙ Bedfordshire, England, in W center of co., on Ouse R. and 50 mi. NNW of London; 52°8'N 0°28'W; agr. market, with some light industries (agr. implements, boilers, electrical equipment, chocolate products). The town is associated with John Bunyan and John Howard. There is a Bunyan Meeting House and chapel on site of bldg. where he preached. The town's schools are well known, and were founded by Sir William Harper in 1556. Bedford School, founded 1552, is one of England's largest public schools. St. Peter's church incorporates Saxon and Norman parts. The churches of St. Mary and St. John date mainly from 14th cent. There are also earthwork remains of anc. castle. In 6th cent. Bedford was a battle-field for Saxons and Britons.

Bedford, town (pop. 3,117), SE Cape Prov., U. of So. Afr., at foot of Winterberg mts., 50 mi. NNW of Grahamstown; stock raising (cattle, goats, horses), dairying. Airfield.

Bedford. 1 County (□ 1,018; pop. 40,775), S Pa.; ⊙ Bedford. Mountainous agr. and mineral-producing area; drained by Raystown Branch of Juniata R.; bounded S by Md., E by Sideling Hill. Allegheny Mts. lie along NW border, Wills Mtn. is in SW part. Bituminous coal, limestone, sand; lumber; grain, livestock, fertilizer. Formed 1771. **2** County (□ 482; pop. 23,627), central Tenn.; ⊙ Shelbyville. In state's central basin; drained by Duck R.; livestock raising (especially the noted Tenn. "walking horse"), dairying, agr. (corn, grain). Mfg. at Shelbyville. Formed 1807. **3** County (□ 744; pop. 29,627), SW central Va.; ⊙ Bedford. Partly in the piedmont, with Blue Ridge in NW; Peaks of Otter are on Botetourt co. line. Bounded SW by Roanoke R., NE by James R.; drained by short Otter R. Includes part of Jefferson Natl. Forest. Crossed by Appalachian Trail. Agr. (tobacco, wheat, tomatoes), dairying, mfg. (especially textiles, pulp and paper products); lumbering; feldspar mining. Formed 1754.

Bedford. 1 City (pop. 12,562), ⊙ Lawrence co., S Ind., 22 mi. S of Bloomington; a center of limestone-quarrying industry; mfg. (work clothing, stone-working machinery, tools, excelsior). Laid out 1826. **2** Town (pop. 533), ⊙ Trimble co., N Ky., 35 mi. NE of Louisville, in outer Bluegrass region; lumber, grain. **3** City (pop. 2,000), ⊙ Taylor co., SW Iowa, near Mo. line, 33 mi. SW of Creston; dairy products, packed poultry; stoneworks. Bedford State Park, with fish hatchery and small lake, is near by. Inc. 1885. **4** Town (pop. 5,234), including Bedford village (pop. 1,407), Middlesex co., E Mass., 15 mi. NW of Boston, near Concord R.; pharmaceuticals, textiles; truck, poultry, fruit, dairying. Settled c.1640, inc. 1729. U.S. veterans hosp. **5** Agr. town (pop. 2,176), Hillsboro co., S N.H., just SW of Manchester. Settled 1737, inc. 1750. **6** A residential section of N Brooklyn borough of New York city, SE N.Y. Site of Pratt Inst. Settled 1662 by Dutch. **7** or **Bedford Village,** village (1940 pop. 893), Westchester co., SE N.Y., E of Mount Kisco; feldspar powder, sand, gravel. State reformatory for women is at near-by Bedford Hills village (1940 pop. 1,407). **8** City (pop. 9,105), Cuyahoga co., N Ohio, 11 mi. SE of downtown Cleveland; residential, with some mfg. (chinaware, chairs, metal products, electrical goods, rubber products). Settled c.1813, inc. 1931. **9** Agr. borough (pop. 3,521), ⊙ Bedford co., S Pa., 32 mi. S of Altoona and on Raystown Branch of Juniata R.; wood products, flour, feed, toys; timber; apple orchards, dairying. Colonial fort (built c.1757) was Washington's hq. in Whisky Rebellion in 1794. Settled c.1750, laid out 1766, inc. 1795. **10** Town (pop. 4,061), ⊙ Bedford co., SW central Va., in the piedmont, and 20 mi. W of Lynchburg, in agr. area. An important tobacco market; mfg. of textiles, tin cans, rubber goods, furniture, printed labels; flour milling, feldspar mining and processing. Lumbering near by. Elks Natl. Home here. "Poplar Forest" (1806–09), country home of Jefferson, is 12 mi. E; Peaks of Otter are just NW. Inc. 1890; re-inc. 1912. **11** Village, Lincoln co., W Wyo., near Salt R. and Idaho line, 12 mi. N of Afton; alt. 5,620 ft. Dairy products, grain, livestock. Salt River Range just E.

Bedford Basin, N part of HALIFAX HARBOUR, N.S.

Bedford Hills, N.Y.: see BEDFORD.

Bedford Level, flat marshy region (□ c.700), SE England, comprising great part of The FENS and including parts of Isle of Ely, Huntingdon, Norfolk, Northampton, Suffolk, and Lincoln; 60 mi. N–S, 35 mi. E–W. Romans built large embankment here; in 17th cent. drainage was carried out by Vermuyden under patronage of duke of Bedford, after whom region is named. It is now fertile agr. area, growing vegetables, fruit, flowers; there is much wild game.

Bedford Park, town (pop. 651), Cook co., NE Ill., just W of Chicago.

Bedfordshire, England: see BEDFORD, county.

Bedford Springs, resort village, Bedford co., S Pa., just S of Bedford; mineral springs.

Bedford Village, N.Y.: see BEDFORD.

Bedhampton, agr. village and parish (pop. 1,411), SE Hampshire, England, near Langstone Harbour, 6 mi. NE of Portsmouth.

Bedi (bā'dē), village, W Saurashtra, India, port on Gulf of Cutch, 4 mi. NW of Jamnagar; wharves and rail terminus lie just W, at head of tidal creek; exports peanuts, wool, cotton; imports sugar, food-grains, hardware. Pearl fishery offshore (N).

Bedjoebang or **Bedjubang**, Indonesia: see BEJUBANG.

Bedlingtonshire, urban district (1931 pop. 27,461; 1951 census 28,836), SE Northumberland, England. Includes coal-mining towns of Bedlington (pop. 7,148), 11 mi. N of Newcastle-upon-Tyne, with steel foundries; Choppington (NW); Netherton (W); and West Sleekburn (NE). Bedlington is famous for its terrier kennels.

Bedloe's Island (area c.10 acres), SE N.Y., in Upper New York Bay off S tip of Manhattan; site of the Statue of Liberty, it is under jurisdiction of Natl. Park Service. New York city's 1st quarantine station was here; later U.S. Fort Wood (abandoned 1937) was built. The statue, 152 ft. high, was designed by F. A. Bartholdi; presented to the U.S. in 1884 and dedicated in 1886.

Bedmar (bĕdhmär'), town (pop. 4,477), Jaén prov., S Spain, 21 mi. ENE of Jaén; olive-oil center. Flour mills; sericulture. Cereals, truck, esparto, livestock.

Bedminster, SW district (pop. 46,588) of Bristol, SW Gloucester, England; tanneries, boilerworks; tobacco processing.

Bedminster, village, Somerset co., N central N.J., on North Branch of Raritan R. and 8 mi. N of Somerville, opposite Far Hills, in country-estate area.

Bednodemyanovsk or **Bednodem'yanovsk** (byĕd"nŭdyĭmyä'nŭfsk), city (1926 pop. 6,889), NW Penza oblast, Russian SFSR, 90 mi. NW of Penza; road center in grain and potato area; hemp, legumes; orchards. Chartered 1627; called Spassk until renamed (1923) for Soviet poet Demyan Bedny.

Bednur, India: see NAGAR, Shimoga dist., Mysore.

Bédoin (bādwē'), village (pop. 750), Vaucluse dept., SE France, at foot of Mont Ventoux, 8 mi. NE of Carpentras; wine, fruits, asparagus, olives.

Bedok (bĕdôk'), village (pop. 1,348) of Singapore isl., on SE coast, 7 mi. ENE of Singapore; fisheries, coconuts, rubber.

Bedong (bĕdŏŏng'), village (pop. 1,349) W central Kedah, Malaya, on railroad and 6 mi. N of Sungei Patani; rubber plantations.

Bedonia (bĕdô'nyä), town (pop. 1,194), Parma prov., Emilia-Romagna, N central Italy, near Taro R., 40 mi. SW of Parma.

Bed-Pak-Dala, Kazakh SSR: see BET-PAK-DALA.

Bedra, Germany: see BRAUNSBEDRA.

Bedrashen, Egypt: see BADRASHEIN, EL.

Bedretto, Val (väl'bĕdrĕt'tō), valley of Ticino canton, S Switzerland, along Ticino R. from its source to Airolo.

Beds, England: see BEDFORD, county.

Bedum (bā'dŭm), town (pop. 3,196), Groningen prov., N Netherlands, 6 mi. NNE of Groningen; grain-trade center; mfg. (bicycles, agr. machinery, bricks, drainage pipes), vegetable canning, flax spinning; dairying.

Bedwas and Machen (bĕd'wäs, mäkh'ĕn), urban district (1931 pop. 9,192; 1951 census 8,712), SW Monmouth, England. Includes steel-milling towns of Bedwas (pop. 2,887), on Rhymney R. and 8 mi. N of Cardiff, and (3 mi. E, on Rhymney R.) Machen (pop. 1,945). Also in urban dist. (4 mi. N of Bedwas, on Rhymney R.) is coal-mining town (pop. 1,483) of Maesycwmmer (mīsŭkŏŏ'mûr).

Bedwellty (bĕdwĕl'tē, bādwĕ'thŭltē), urban district (1931 pop. 30,074; 1951 census 28,826), W Monmouth, England, on Sirhowy R. and 6 mi. SSE of Tredegar; coal mines, metal foundries. In urban dist. are coal-mining towns of Argoed (ärgoid') (S; pop. 4,433), Aberbargoed (ăbûrbärgoid') (W, on Rhymney R.; pop. 5,215), Blackwood (S; pop. 6,330) with shoe factories, Pengam (SW; pop. 3,630), Cwmsyfiog (kŏŏmsĭv'yôg) (NW, on Rhymney R.; pop. 2,568), and New Tredegar (trĕdē'gûr) (NW, on Rhymney R.; pop. 2,519).

Bedworth, urban district (1931 pop. 12,055; 1951 census 24,866), N central Warwick, England, 5 mi. NNE of Coventry; coal-mining center. Has 15th-cent. church.

Bedzin (bĕ'jēn), Pol. *Będzin*, Ger. *Bendzin* (bĕn'tsĭn), Rus. *Bendin* (bĕn'dyĭn), city (1946 pop. 27,754), Katowice prov., S Poland, on the Czarna Przemsza and 7 mi. NE of Katowice; coal mining, quarrying; zinc rolling, mfg. of metalware, chemicals, bricks; food processing. Unlike other near-by cities, Bedzin is an old settlement (founded 14th cent.) at foot of a castle once guarding the river crossing. Passed (1795) to Prussia and (1815) to Russia; returned 1919 to Poland. Developed in 1890s (1890 pop. 9,000; 1897 pop. 23,757; 1937 pop. 51,549). Before Second World War, pop. was 50% Jewish; during war, under Ger. rule, called Bendsburg.

Bee, county (□ 842; pop. 18,174), S Texas; ⊙ Beeville. Drained by Aransas R. Oil, natural-gas wells; agr. (corn, grain sorghums, cotton, broom-corn, peanuts); hogs, poultry; cattle, sheep ranching. Formed 1857.

Bee, village (pop. 160), Seward co., SE Nebr., 22 mi. NW of Lincoln.

Beebe (bē'bē). **1** Town (pop. 1,192), White co., central Ark., 32 mi. NE of Little Rock; shipping point in agr. area (cotton, strawberries); cotton ginning, sawmilling (hardwoods). Seat of state jr. agr. col. **2** Village, in Logan county, W.Va.: see HOLDEN.

Beebe Plain (bē'bē), village (pop. 1,024), S Que., near L. Memphremagog, 32 mi. SSW of Sherbrooke, at Vt. boundary; dairying.

Bee Branch, town (pop. 137), Van Buren co., N central Ark., 25 mi. N of Conway.

Beechbottom or **Beech Bottom**, steel-making village (1940 pop. 1,128), Brooke co., NW W.Va., in Northern Panhandle, on Ohio R. and 10 mi. N of Wheeling; coal mining.

Beech Creek. 1 Mining village (1940 pop. 1,477), Muhlenberg co., W central Ky., 32 mi. NE of Hopkinsville; bituminous coal. **2** Borough (pop. 574), Clinton co., central Pa., 8 mi. SW of Lock Haven.

Beecher, village (pop. 956), Will co., NE Ill., near Ind. line, 35 mi. S of Chicago; farming.

Beecher City, farming village (pop. 437), Effingham co., SE central Ill., 14 mi. WNW of Effingham.

Beecher Falls, Vt.: see CANAAN.

Beechey, Cape, NE Ellesmere Isl., NE Franklin Dist., Northwest Territories, on Robeson Channel, near N entrance of Lady Franklin Bay; 81°52'N 63°W.

Beechey Island, islet, E central Franklin Dist., Northwest Territories, in Erebus Bay, inlet of Barrow Strait, at S end of Wellington Channel, just off SW Devon Isl.; 74°43'N 92°56'W; rises to c.650 ft. Franklin wintered here, 1845–46; later isl. was base of Arctic explorers and searchers for Franklin's expedition.

Beechey Islands, Jap. *Chichi-jima-retto,* volcanic group, Bonin Isls., W Pacific, 525 mi. S of Yokohama; 27°6'N 142°12'E; comprises CHICHI-JIMA (largest isl.), Ani-jima (□ 3.1), Ototo-jima (□ 2), and many smaller isls.

Beechey Point, Eskimo village (pop. 12), N Alaska, on Arctic Ocean, 185 mi. ESE of Barrow; 70°28'N 149°2'W; trading post. Airfield.

Beech Fork, stream, central Ky., rises in Boyle co., flows c.125 mi. NNW and generally W to Rolling Fork 10 mi. NE of Elizabethtown.

Beech Grove. 1 City (pop. 5,685), Marion co., central Ind., just SE of Indianapolis; railroad shops. Settled 1902, inc. 1906. **2** Town (pop. 162), McLean co., W Ky., 21 mi. NNE of Madisonville.

Beechwood. 1 Village (pop. 1,567, with adjacent Oaklawn), Ottawa co., SW Mich. **2** Village, Pa.: see HAVERFORD.

Beechworth, town (pop. 2,936), NE Victoria, Australia, 140 mi. NE of Melbourne; sheep, agr. center; wool, wine. Tin and gold mines at near-by Eldorado.

Beecroft, town (pop. 2,292), E New South Wales, Australia, 11 mi. NW of Sydney; coal-mining center.

Beedenbostel (bā'dŭnbō"stŭl), village (pop. 1,067), in former Prussian prov. of Hanover, NW Germany, after 1945 in Lower Saxony, 7 mi. E of Celle; canned goods. Rock-salt and potash mining in vicinity.

Beef Island, islet (c.2½ mi. long), Br. Virgin Isls., just E of Tortola isl., on Sir Francis Drake's Channel; 18°27'N 64°31'W.

Beek (bāk), village (pop. 5,537), Limburg prov., SE Netherlands, 2 mi. W of Juliana Canal, 8 mi. NNE of Maastricht; cigars, syrup. Near by is site of chief camp of 9th-cent. Viking invaders.

Beekbergen (bāk'bĕrkhŭn), village (pop. c.1,000), Gelderland prov., E central Netherlands, 4 mi. S of Apeldoorn; sandstone quarrying.

Beelitz (bā'lĭts), town (pop. 5,895), Brandenburg, E Germany, 12 mi. SSW of Potsdam; market gardening, asparagus growing. Has Gothic church. Radio station; tuberculosis sanitariums.

Beemer, village (pop. 613), Cuming co., NE Nebr., 8 mi. NNW of West Point and on Elkhorn R.; grain.

Beemster Polder (bām'stŭr pōl'dŭr), reclaimed area (□ 27.7) of the Ijsselmeer, North Holland prov., NW Netherlands, N of Amsterdam; c.6 mi. long, 7 mi. wide; cattle raising. Chief town, Purmerend (on SE edge). One of oldest polder areas in the Netherlands; drained in 1612. Village of Beemster (pop. 3,727) lies in its center, 12 mi. N of Amsterdam.

Beenleigh, village (pop. 975), SE Queensland, Australia, 21 mi. SE of Brisbane; corn, sugar cane.

Beenoskee, mountain (2,713 ft.), W Co. Kerry, Ireland, 10 mi. ENE of Dingle.

Beer, village and parish (pop. 1,266), E Devon, England, on the Channel just WSW of Seaton; fishing port, with lace mfg.; tourist resort. Lace industry was introduced from Flanders in 17th cent.

Beerberg or **Grosser Beerberg** (grō"sŭr bâr'bĕrk), highest peak (3,222 ft.) of the Thuringian Forest, central Germany, 4 mi. E of Zella-Mehlis.

Beerenberg, in Norwegian Arctic: see JAN MAYEN.

Beeri (bĕ-ērē'), settlement (pop. 150), SW Israel, in NW part of the Negev, near border of Egyptian-held Palestine, 5 mi. S of Gaza; sulphur quarrying, mixed farming. Founded 1946.

Beeringen, Belgium: see BERINGEN.

Beernem (bār'nŭm), town (pop. 5,378), West Flanders prov., NW Belgium, 7 mi. SE of Bruges; agr. market. Agr. col.

Beerot Yitzhak or **Beerot Yits-haq** (both: bĕ-ĕrōt' yĕts-häk'), settlement (pop. 150), SW Israel, in NW part of the Negev, on border of Egyptian-held Palestine, 3 mi. SSE of Gaza; mixed farming. Founded 1943; suffered heavily during Arab invasion, 1948.

Beerse (bār'sŭ), town (pop. 6,712), Antwerp prov., N Belgium, 4 mi. W of Turnhout; antimony processing; Portland cement, bricks. Formerly spelled Beersse.

Beersheba (bērshē'bŭ, bĭr'shĭbŭ, bĕrshĕ'bä), town (1946 pop. estimate 6,490), S Israel, in the Negev, 45 mi. SW of Jerusalem, 55 mi. S of Tel Aviv; commercial and transportation center for the Negev; light industries. Has large hosp. Evacuated by Arab pop., 1948; became Egyptian base during invasion of Israel; captured by Israeli forces, Oct., 1948. In biblical history Beersheba was S extremity of Israelite territory (N extremity at Dan); connected with biblical stories of Abraham, Hagar, Isaac, and Elijah. In First World War 1st Palestinian town captured (Oct., 1917) by British forces.

Beersheba Springs, resort village, Grundy co., SE central Tenn., 35 mi. NNW of Chattanooga, in the Cumberlands; chalybeate spring.

Beersse, Belgium: see BEERSE.

Beerta (bār'tä), town (pop. 2,013), Groningen prov., NE Netherlands, 4 mi. NE of Winschoten; iron industry, mfg. (agr. machinery, acetylene apparatus), building stone.

Beer Tuvya or **Beer Tuvia** (both: bĕ-ĕr' tōōvyä'), settlement (pop. 750), W Israel, in Judaean Plain, 12 mi. SSW of Rehovot; dairying, mixed farming. Founded 1896; destroyed (1929) in Arab riots; rebuilt 1930. Bombed by Arabs, 1948. Also spelled Beer Tuviya.

Beer Yaakov or **Beer Ya'aqov** (both: bĕ-ĕr' yä-äkōv'), settlement (pop. 400), W Israel, in Judaean Plain, on railroad and 2 mi. SE of Rishon le Zion; mixed farming. Founded 1907. Scene of fighting during Arab invasion (1948), when settlement was temporarily evacuated.

Beeskow (bā'skō), town (pop. 7,571), Brandenburg, E Germany, on the Spree and 18 mi. SW of Frankfurt; mfg. (chemical equipment, containers, starch). Has late-Gothic church, medieval town walls. Passed to Brandenburg in 1575.

Beeston. 1 Former urban district (1931 pop. 16,017) now in Beeston and Stapleford urban dist. (1951 census pop. 49,849), S Nottingham, England, 4 mi. SW of Nottingham; pharmaceutical center, with mfg. also of hosiery, lace, bicycles, machinery, glassware; textile printing. **2** Town (pop. 15,220) in Leeds county borough, West Riding, S central Yorkshire, England, just SSW of Leeds; woolen mills, chemical works.

Beetham (bē'thŭm), village and parish (pop. 246), S Westmorland, England, near Kent R. estuary 8 mi. S of Kendal; paper mfg.; limestone quarrying. Has church with 12th-cent. tower and ruins of 14th-cent. mansion.

Beeton, village (pop. 594), S Ont., 35 mi. NW of Toronto, in grain-growing region; grain elevators, flour mills.

Beeville, city (pop. 9,348), ⊙ Bee co., S Texas, c.50 mi. NW of Corpus Christi; market, trade center for agr. (cotton, grain), cattle-ranching, dairying, oil-producing area; mfg. (oil-field equipment, brooms, boots, saddles, cottonseed oil, mattresses). Former cow town; settled in 1830s, laid out 1878, inc. 1908.

Beez (bāz), village (pop. 1,051), Namur prov., S central Belgium, on Meuse R. and 3 mi. E of Namur; barge building; grain market.

Befale (bĕfä'lā), village, Equator Prov., NW Belgian Congo, near Maringa R., 175 mi. ENE of Coquilhatville, in palm and rubber region.

Befandriana (bĕfändrē'nŭ). **1** Town, Majunga prov., N Madagascar, 150 mi. ENE of Majunga; native market; rice, cattle. **2** Village, Tuléar prov., SW Madagascar, 90 mi. N of Tuléar; cattle raising.

Beffes (bĕf), village (pop. 249), Cher dept., central France, on Loire Lateral Canal and 10 mi. NW of Nevers; cementworks.

Befori (bĕfō'rē), village, Equator Prov., NW Belgian Congo, on right bank of Maringa R. and 275 mi. E of Coquilhatville; terminus of navigation, agr. center (palm products, rubber).

Befort, Luxembourg: see BEAUFORT.

Befu (bā'fōō), town (pop. 5,956), Hyogo prefecture, S Honshu, Japan, on Harima Sea, 11 mi. NE of Himeji, in agr. area (rice, wheat, market produce, flowers, poultry); leather goods, woodworking, medicine, paper milling.

Bega (bē'gŭ), municipality (pop. 2,856), SE New South Wales, Australia, 105 mi. SSE of Canberra; dairying center; granite.

Begalkot, India: see BAGALKOT.

Begamabad (bā"gŭmäbäd'), village, Meerut dist., NW Uttar Pradesh, India, 13 mi. SW of Meerut; oilseed refining. Sugar and vegetable-ghee processing, oilseed milling, biscuit mfg. near by.

Begamganj (bā'gŭmgŭnj), town (pop. 4,382), E Bhopal state, India, 60 mi. ENE of Bhopal; millet, gram. Sometimes spelled Begumganj.

Begampett, India: see HYDERABAD, city.

Bégard (bāgär'), village (pop. 886), Côtes-du-Nord dept., W France, 8 mi. NW of Guingamp; dairying, tanning.

Bega River (bä'gä), Hung. *Béga* (bā'gŏ), Serbo-Croatian *Begej* (bā'gā), in W Rumania and NE Yugoslavia, rises in Poiana Rusca Mts. 20 mi. E of Lugoj, flows c.130 mi. W and SW, past Faget and through Timisoara, to Tisa R. at Knicanin. Its lower course (also called *Novi Begej*) is canalized for c.45 mi. bet. Timisoara and Zrenjanin.

Begej River, Yugoslavia and Rumania: see BEGA RIVER.

Begemdir (bĕgĕm'dĭr) or **Begemeder** (bĕgĕ'mŭdŭr), province (□ c.30,000), NW Ethiopia; ⊙ Gondar. Borders on Eritrea (N) and Anglo-Egyptian Sudan (W). Largely mountainous, it consists of highland region (over 6,000 ft.) in E and plateau (1,500–3,000 ft.) in W. Contains highest range, Simen Mts. (c.15,150 ft.), and most of largest lake, TANA (□ c.1,400), in Ethiopia. Includes DEMBEA dist. Situated bet. Takkaze, Blue Nile, and Dinder rivers; drained by Atbara, Angareb, and Rahad rivers. Pop. largely Amharic- and Tigrinya-speaking. Agr. (cereals, coffee, honey, legumes) and stock raising (cattle, sheep, horses, mules). Trade centers: GONDAR, Debra Tabor, Metamma, Chilga. Crossed by main road (N–S). Formerly part of Amhara prov.

Beggen (bĕ'gŭn), village, S Luxembourg, just N of Luxembourg city; metal foundries; mfg. of synthetic fertilizer.

Beggs, city (pop. 1,214), Okmulgee co., E central Okla., 10 mi. NW of Okmulgee; supply center for oil area. Mfg. of petroleum products, feed; cotton ginning. Inc. 1902.

Begíjar (bāhē'här), town (pop. 4,257), Jaén prov., S Spain, 8 mi. SE of Linares; agr. trade center (olive oil, wheat, barley, sheep).

Bègles (bĕ'glŭ), S industrial suburb (pop. 22,289) of Bordeaux, Gironde dept., SW France, on the Garonne; has petroleum storage tanks and codfish-processing plants; important chemical industry (fertilizer, soap, varnish, resinous products); metalworks, crating and carton mills. Cabinetmaking from imported hardwoods.

Beglezh (bĕglĕsh'), village (pop. 3,386), Pleven dist., N Bulgaria, 14 mi. SSW of Pleven; wheat, corn, legumes.

Begna River (bĕng'nä), S Norway, rises in 2 headstreams on S slope of Jotunheim Mts., flows c.150 mi. generally SE, past Fagernes, through the lake Sperillen, then past Honefoss, to Tyri Fjord 5 mi. SSW of Honefoss. Below Honefoss it is also called Adal R. (Nor. *Ådal*), sometimes spelled Aadal.

Begoml or **Begoml'** (byĭgô'mŭl), town (1948 pop. over 2,000), N Minsk oblast, Belorussian SSR, 60 mi. NNE of Minsk; flour mill. Formerly Begomlya.

Begoro (bĕgō'rō), town, Eastern Prov., central Gold Coast colony, 21 mi. NNW of Koforidua; road head; cacao, cassava, corn.

Begovat (byĕgŭvät'), city (1949 pop. over 10,000), S Tashkent oblast, Uzbek SSR, on the Syr Darya (rapids), on railroad (Khilkovo station) and 75 mi. S of Tashkent, near Mogol-Tau iron deposits; metallurgical center (iron and steel mills); cement mfg., cotton ginning. Site of Farkhad dam and hydroelectric plant (construction begun 1943) on the Syr Darya; feeds irrigation canals of S part of Golodnaya Step and high-voltage line to Tashkent. Originally an agr. village; became (c.1935) a town; boomed following start (1943) of building of steel plant for scrap conversion Second World War.

Begram, Afghanistan: see BAGRAM.

Begshehr, Lake, Turkey: see BEYSEHIR, LAKE.

Begtrup Bay, Denmark: see MOLS.

Beguildy (bŭgĭl'dē), agr. village and parish (pop. 691), NE Radnor, Wales, on Teme R. and 9 mi. SE of Newtown.

Begumganj, India: see BEGAMGANJ.

Begumpet, India: see HYDERABAD, city.

Begun (bā'gōōn), town (pop. 4,831), S Rajasthan, India, 25 mi. ENE of Chitor; local agr. market (millet, gram, wheat).

Begusarai (bā'gōōsŭrī), town (pop. 12,803), Monghyr dist., N central Bihar, India, near the Ganges, 21 mi. W of Monghyr; rice, wheat, corn, gram, barley, oilseeds; mango groves.

Béhague, Point (bāäg'), on Atlantic coast of NE Fr. Guiana, 38 mi. SE of Cayenne; 4°33'N 51°56'W.

Behala, India: see SOUTH SUBURBAN.

Behar, India: see BIHAR, state.

Behara (bähä'rŭ), village, Tuléar prov., S Madagascar, on highway and 40 mi. WNW of Fort-Dauphin; hardwood lumbering, cattle raising. R.C. and Lutheran missions.

Behat (bä'hŭt), town (pop. 4,538), Saharanpur dist., N Uttar Pradesh, India, on Eastern Jumna Canal and 14 mi. N of Saharanpur; wheat, rice, rape, mustard, gram, sugar cane.

Behbahan, Iran: see BEHBEHAN.

Behbehan or **Behbahan** (both: bĕbähän'), town (1940 pop. 22,610), Sixth Prov., in Khuzistan, SW Iran, 120 mi. E of Abadan, in oil- and gas-producing region; trades in grain, rice, dates, oranges. Near by are AGHA JARI and GACH SARAN oil fields and PAZANUN gas field.

Behbit el Hagara, Egypt: see BAHBIT EL HIGARA.

Beheira (bŭhā'rŭ), **El Beheira,** or **Al-Buhayrah** (both: ĕl bŭhā'rŭ), province (□ 1,785, land only; pop. 1,245,943), Lower Egypt; ⊙ Damanhur. Bounded N by Mediterranean Sea and Alexandria Governorate, E by Rosetta branch of the Nile, S and W by Libyan Desert. L. Maryut (soda production), L. Idku, and Abukir Bay, on N coast, are fishing grounds. Cotton ginning, rice husking, straw-mat making. Agr.: cotton, rice, cereals. Served by main Cairo-Alexandria RR, the Nile, Raiyah Beheira, and Mahmudiya Canal. Near ROSETTA was found the famous Rosetta stone. Near Teh el Barud are ruins of anc. NAUCRATIS.

Beheira, Raiyah, or **Rayah Buhayrah** (rä'yŭ), navigable canal of the Nile delta, Lower Egypt, extends c.50 mi. from the Delta Barrage to Kafr Bulin regulator. Irrigates Beheira prov. and part of Giza prov.

Behen, ruins, Anglo-Egyptian Sudan: see WADI HALFA.

Beheya, India: see ARRAH.

Behisni, Turkey: see BESNI.

Behistun (bā"hĭstōōn', Persian bähĕstōōn'), **Bisutun,** or **Bisotun** (both: bēsōtōōn'), village, Fifth Prov., in Kermanshah, W Iran, on road and 20 mi. E of Kermanshah. Near it is a mountainous rock which bears on its face, c.300 ft. above ground, a bas-relief depicting Darius I with a group of captive chiefs, together with a record of the reign of Darius in Old Persian, in Susian (Elamitic), and Assyrian. The rock was not unknown, but it was not until 1835 that Sir Henry Rawlinson scaled the rock, copied the inscriptions, and thus made it possible to decipher the Assyrian text and provide a key for study of anc. Mesopotamia. Also spelled Bisitun and Bisetun.

Behm Canal (bēm), SE Alaska, natural channel (120 mi. long) almost circling Revillagigedo Isl., which it separates from the mainland (E) and from Cleveland Peninsula (N and NW). In it is Bell Isl.

Behnesa, Egypt: see OXYRHYNCUS.

Behringersdorf (bā'rĭng-ŭrsdôrf"), village (pop. 2,696), Middle Franconia, N central Bavaria, Germany, on the Pegnitz and 6 mi. ENE of Nuremberg; mfg. (textiles, chemicals). Hops, horseradish, hogs.

Behror (bā'rōr), town (pop. 4,514), E Rajasthan, India, 29 mi. NW of Alwar; local market for millet, oilseeds, cotton, gram; hand-loom weaving. Sometimes spelled Bahror.

Behshahr (bĕ"shä'hŭr), town (1941 pop. estimate 8,000), Second Prov., in E Mazanderan, N Iran, on Gurgan Lagoon of Caspian Sea, 45 mi. ENE of Babul, and on railroad; has large cotton-textile factory. Founded in 17th cent. by Abbas the Great, it was called Ashraf until mid-1930s.

Beida, Yemen: see BEIDHA.

Beidha, Beida, or **Bayda** (all: bā'dhŭ), district in SE Yemen, on Aden "Status Quo Line," occupying the Dahr plateau N of the Kaur range. Its capital Al Beidha (pop. 1,000), 44 mi. NNW of Shuqra and 135 mi. SE of Sana, was formerly known as Beihan Umm Rusas. Considered part of Aden hinterland until 1934 treaty left it under Yemen suzerainty.

Beierland, Netherlands: see BEIJERLAND.

Beiersfeld (bī'ŭrsfĕlt"), village (pop. 5,034), Saxony, E central Germany, in the Erzgebirge, 4 mi. ESE of Aue, near Czechoslovak border, in uranium-mining region; metal- and woodworking.

Beiertheim (bī'ŭrt-hīm), SW suburb of Karlsruhe, Germany.

Beighton (bā'-, bī'-), town and parish (pop. 5,553), NE Derby, England, 6 mi. SE of Sheffield; coal-mining center. Has 15th-cent. church.

Beigua, Monte (môn'tĕ bā'gwä), peak (4,222 ft.) in Ligurian Apennines, N Italy, 18 mi. WNW of Genoa.

Beihan, Baihan, or **Bayhan** (bähän'), tribal area (pop. 13,000) of Western Aden Protectorate, on Yemen "Status Quo Line"; ⊙ Nuqub. Situated along the Wadi Beihan, which rises near Beidha and flows 100 mi. N to the Rub' al Khali; agr. and pastoral pop. ruled by a sherif (sharif). Protectorate treaty was concluded in 1903 and an adviser agreement in 1944.

Beihan ad Daula or **Bayhan al-Dawlah** (both: ăd dou'lŭ), town, Beihan tribal area, Western Aden Protectorate, 70 mi. N of Shuqra, near Yemen "Status Quo Line"; 14°22'N 45°42'E. Also spelled Beihan ad Dola.

Beihan al Qasab or **Bayhan al-Qasab** (ăl käsäb'), town, Beihan tribal area, Western Aden Protectorate, 100 mi. N of Shuqra, near Yemen "Status Quo Line"; 14°48'N 45°43'E. Center of agr. area (grain, sesame, indigo). Airfield; radio station. Sometimes spelled Beihan el Jezab.

Beihan Umm Rusas, Yemen: see BEIDHA.

Beijerland or **Beierland** (both: bī'ŭrlänt), island, South Holland prov., SW Netherlands, S of Rotterdam; bounded by Hollandschdiep (S), Dortsche Kil R. (E), Old Maas R. (N), Spui R. (NW); 16 mi. long, 9 mi. wide. Agr. (flax, sugar beets, vegetables). Chief villages: Oud Beijerland, Nieuw Beijerland. Sometimes spelled Beyerland; also called Hoeksche Waard.

Beijós (bāzhôsh'), village (pop. 1,002), Viseu dist., N central Portugal, 11 mi. S of Viseu; corn, rye, wine, olives.

Beilan Pass, Turkey: see BELEN.

Beilen (bī'lŭn), town (pop. 2,828), Drenthe prov., NE Netherlands, 10 mi. S of Assen; cattle and bee market; dairying. Sanitarium for nervous diseases.

Beilinson (bā'lĭnsōn), **Shkhunat Beilinson,** or **Shchunat Beilinson** (both: shkhōōnät'), residential settlement (pop. 450), W Israel, in Plain of Sharon, just E of Petah Tiqva, 9 mi. E of Tel Aviv. Has large hosp. Founded 1938; shelled by Arabs, 1948.

Beilngries (bī'lŭn-grēs), town (pop. 3,509), Upper Palatinate, central Bavaria, Germany, bet. Altmühl R. and Ludwig Canal, 16 mi. NE of Eichstätt; brewing, paper milling, woodworking. Has late-15th-cent. walls. Chartered 1485.

Beilstein (bīl'shtīn), town (pop. 1,760), Württemberg, Germany, after 1945 in Württemberg-Baden, 8 mi. SE of Heilbronn; wine. Has ruined castle.

Beilul (bālōōl'), village (pop. 350), Assab div., SE Eritrea, fishing port on Red Sea, 25 mi. WNW of Assab.

Beine (bĕn), agr. village (pop. 396), Marne dept., N France, 9 mi. E of Rheims.

Beinn a'Bheitir, Scotland: see BALLACHULISH.

Beinn-an-Oir, Scotland: see PAPS OF JURA.

Beinwil am See (bīn'vēl äm zā'), town (pop. 2,099), Aargau canton, N Switzerland, on the Hallwilersee, 9 mi. SE of Aarau; tobacco, cotton textiles.

Beira (bā'rŭ), former province (□ 9,216; 1940 pop. 1,900,946), N central Portugal; ⊙ Coimbra. It contained Aveiro, Castelo Branco, Coimbra, Guarda, and Viseu dists. Bounded by the Douro (N), Spain (E), the Tagus (SSE), and the Atlantic (W). A hilly region, it is traversed by the Serra da Estrêla, Portugal's highest range. The chief feature of its low, marshy coastline is the Aveiro lagoon, formed by mouth of Vouga R. Other rivers draining region are the Mondego and the Zêzere. The arable land yields wheat, corn, and vegetables, and there are vineyards (especially near the Douro) and olive groves. Sheep raised in hills supply wool industry (Covilhã). Area had been reconquered from the Moors even before Portugal was formed, but Moorish attacks continued into 13th cent. Later Beira was contested in the incessant Portuguese-Castilian wars. In 1936, Beira was divided into 3 new provs. (Beira Alta, Beira Baixa, Beira Litoral), which together slightly exceed area of old prov.

Beira, city (1950 commune pop. 42,549), ⊙ Manica and Sofala prov., central Mozambique, port on Mozambique Channel of Indian Ocean, at mouth of Buzi and Pungùe rivers, 450 mi. NNE of Lourenço Marques and 280 mi. SE of Salisbury (Southern Rhodesia); 19°50'S 34°50'E. Second-largest city of Mozambique and its chief shipping center; ocean terminus of Beira RR (to the Rhodesias and U. of So. Afr.; links with Angola's Benguela RR in Belgian Congo's Katanga prov.) and of Trans-Zambezia RR (serving Nyasaland). Through its deep and sheltered harbor (accommodates, since 1927, ships drawing 30 ft.; improved 1950) it exports cotton, sugar, corn, tobacco, sisal, vegetable oil, minerals (chromite, copper, coal, lead, asbestos, gold). Processing industries; new cotton mill. Relatively healthful climate (mean annual rainfall 63 in.). City, situated on sandspit, was founded 1891 as seat of Mozambique Company. Administration taken over by Mozambique govt. 1942. Also ⊙ Beira dist. (□ 49,506; 1950 pop. 710,052).

Beira Alta (bā'räl'tŭ), province (□ 3,682; 1940 pop. 662,616), N central Portugal, formed 1936 from old Beira prov.; ⊙ Viseu. It contains major portion of Viseu and Guarda dists. and small section of Coimbra dist. Cities: Viseu, Guarda, Pinhel.

Beira Baixa (bā'rŭ bī'shŭ), province (□ 2,897; 1940 pop. 334,788), N central Portugal, formed 1936 from old Beira prov.; ⊙ Castelo Branco. It contains Castelo Branco dist. and small sections of Coimbra and Santarém dists. Cities: Castelo Branco, Covilhã.

Beira Litoral (lētōōräl'), province (□ 2,908; 1940 pop. 896,719), N central Portugal, formed 1936 from old Beira prov. and from N part of old Estremadura prov.; ⊙ Coimbra. It contains major portion of Aveiro and Coimbra dists. and smaller sections of Leiria and Santarém dists. Cities: Coimbra, Aveiro, Leiria, Figueira da Foz.

Beiron, Formosa: see HWALIEN.

Beirut or **Beyrouth** (both: bārōōt'), anc. *Berytus,* city (1946 pop. 181,271), ⊙ Lebanon, seaport on the Mediterranean, at foot of the Lebanon mts., 60 mi. NNE of Haifa and 50 mi. WNW of Damascus (connected by rail); 33°53'N 35°30'E. With few industries (canneries, mfg. of confections, beer, ice), it is principally an administrative, commercial, and transit center for this region of the Levant, having gradually eclipsed the declining ports of Tyre and Saida (Sidon). An old Phoenician city of the 2d millenium B.C., it flourished under later Phoenician rule, as it did under its successive conquerors—the Seleucids, Romans, Byzantines. In 3d cent. A.D. it had a famous school of Roman law. Declined after earthquake in 551. Captured by Arabs in 635. The Crusaders under Baldwin I took it in 1110, and it was part of the Latin Kingdom of Jerusalem until 1291, despite a siege by Saladin and the Egyptians in 1182. The Druses gained control and held it under Ottoman Empire. In 19th cent. it was one of the storm centers of the revolt of Mohammed Ali of Egypt. Ibrahim Pasha took it, but in 1840 the British and French bombarded and captured the city. Taken by Allied troops in the First World War; under French mandate, capital of Syria and Lebanon. With the proclamation (1941) of the independence of Lebanon, its importance was enhanced. Beirut is the seat of a coeducational American university which has been of importance in the Middle East since the 1860s. Sometimes also spelled Bayrut.

Beisan (bāsän'), Hebrew *Bet Shan* or *Beith-Shean,* town (1946 pop. estimate 5,540), NE Israel, in Jordan valley, at SE end of Plain of Jezreel, 19 mi. SE of Nazareth; 322 ft. below sea level. Abandoned by Arabs, 1948. Modern town on site of important anc. fortress on trade route from Egypt to Damascus and Mesopotamia. The biblical *Beth-shan* or *Beth-shean,* it was Canaanite city-state; connected with story of Saul. In time of Pompey called *Scythopolis,* ⊙ the Decapolis. Called Bessan during Crusades, it was seat of a seigneurie. After First World War, excavations yielded important finds dating back to 1500 B.C., among them ruins of a temple. Sometimes spelled Baisan.

Beiseker (bī'sŭkŭr), village (pop. 272), S Alta., 35 mi. NE of Calgary; wheat.

Beishehr, Lake, Turkey: see BEYSEHIR, LAKE.

Beisso, Uruguay: see PIÑERA.

Beisug River or **Beysug River** (byăsōōk'), in Krasnodar Territory, Russian SFSR, rises NW of Kropotkin, flows c.110 mi. NW, through steppe, past Novo-Malorossiskaya and Bryukhovetskaya, to Beisug Liman, a lagoon (20 mi. long, 5 mi. wide) of Sea of Azov, NE of Primorsko-Akhtarskaya. Frequently dry in lower course.

Beit Alfa or **Beit Alpha** (both: bĕt' älfä'), settlement (pop. 550), NE Israel, at SE end of Plain of Jezreel, at N foot of Mts. of Gilboa, 4 mi. WNW of Beisan; agr. (viticulture; fruit, grain, feed crops, vegetables, poultry); dairying; fish ponds. Modern village founded 1922 on site of anc. locality of same name; remains of synagogue (6th cent. A.D.) excavated here. Also spelled Bet Alfa or Bet Alpha.

Beit Bridge, Northern Rhodesia: see LUANGWA RIVER.

Beitbridge or **Beit Bridge** (bīt'brĭj'), township (pop. 156), Bulawayo prov., S Southern Rhodesia, in Matabeleland, on left bank of Limpopo R. (road and rail bridge) and 170 mi. SE of Bulawayo; alt. 1,523 ft. Rail terminus (line from Pretoria) on Transvaal border opposite Messina. Cattle raising; corn. Hq. of native commissioner; police post.

Beit ed Din, Beit el Din, or **Bayt al-Din** (all: bāt' ĕd-dēn'), Fr. *Beit ed Dine,* village (pop. 827), central Lebanon, 12 mi. SSE of Beirut; alt. 3,300 ft. The huge and elaborate castle here, begun in late 18th cent. and completed in early 19th cent., is one of the most striking examples of Arab architecture.

Beit el Faqih, Yemen: see BAIT AL FAQIH.

Beit el Felej, Oman: see BAIT AL FALAJ.

Beit Eshel or **Bet Eshel** (both: bĕt' ĕ'shĕl), settlement (pop. 100), S Israel, in the Negev, just SE of Beersheba; dairying; poultry, vegetables. Founded 1943; destroyed 1948 by Arabs; later rebuilt.

Beit Gan or **Bet Gan** (both: bĕt' gän'), agr. settlement (pop. 200), Lower Galilee, NE Israel, 6 mi. SSW of Tiberias; mixed farming. Founded 1904.

Beit Guvrin, Israel: see BEIT JIBRIN.

Beith (bēth), town and parish (pop. 5,977), N Ayrshire, Scotland, 10 mi. N of Irvine, just W of Kilbirnie Loch; mfg. of leather, linen thread, furniture.

Beit Hanan or **Bet Hanan** (both: bĕt' hänän'), settlement (pop. 450), W Israel, in Judaean Plain, 2 mi. SW of Rishon le Zion; mixed farming, citriculture. Founded 1930.

Beithar, Palestine: see BETHER.

Beit ha Shitta, Beit hash Shitta, or **Bet Hashitta** (all: bĕt' häshĕtä'), settlement (pop. 900), NE Israel, in E part of Plain of Jezreel, on railroad and 5 mi. NW of Beisan; textile knitting; mixed farming; vehicle and agr.-machinery repair shop. Founded 1935. Also spelled Bet Hashita.

Beit Hillel or **Bet Hillel** (both: bĕt' hĕlĕl'), settlement (pop. 100), Upper Galilee, NE Israel, near Lebanese and Syrian borders, at S foot of Lebanon range, 18 mi. NNE of Safad; dairying center; mixed farming. Founded 1940.

Beith-Shean, Israel: see BEISAN.

Beit Itzhak, Israel: see BEIT YITS-HAQ.

Beit Jala (bāt' jă'lă), village (1946 pop. estimate 3,740) of Palestine, after 1948 in W Jordan, in Judaean Hills, just NW of Bethlehem.

Beit Jann (bāt' jăn') or **Bet Jann** (bĕt' yän'), agr. settlement, Upper Galilee, N Israel, bet. Mt. Heidar (SSW) and Mt. Jarmaq (NE), 7 mi. W of Safad.

Beit Jibrin (bāt' jĭbrēn'), Hebrew *Beit Guvrin* or *Bet Guvrin* (both: bĕt gōōvrĕn'), village, E Israel, in Judaean Hills, 20 mi. WSW of Jerusalem. Site of noted caves, reputedly inhabited since pre-Israelite times. In Roman times site of fortress of *Betogabri,* later called *Eleutheropolis;* there are remains of Roman *Columbarium,* and of Crusaders' fortress of Beth Gibelin. Sometimes spelled Beth Jibrin. Just SSE is biblical locality of *Mareshah.*

Beit Keshet, Israel: see BEIT QESHET.

Beit Lahm, Jordan: see BETHLEHEM.

Beit Meri or **Bayt Miri** (bāt' mĕrē'), Fr. *Beit Méri* or *Beit Mery,* village (pop. 1,970), central Lebanon, 6 mi. ESE of Beirut; alt. 2,500 ft.; resort; sericulture, cotton, cereals, fruits. Has abbey on site of anc. temple.

Beit Oren or **Bet Oren** (both: bĕt' ō'rĕn), settlement (pop. 300), NW Israel, on SW slope of Mt. Carmel, 6 mi. S of Haifa; horticulture, plums, apples. Health resort. Founded 1939.

Beit Oved or **Bet Oved** (both: bĕt' ōvĕd'), settlement (pop. 200), W Israel, in Judaean Plain, 3 mi. SW of Rishon le Zion; mixed farming, citriculture. Founded 1933.

Beit Qeshet or **Beit Keshet** (both: bĕt' kĕ'shĕt), settlement (pop. 100), Lower Galilee, N Israel, at N foot of Mt. Tabor, 6 mi. E of Nazareth; mixed farming. Founded 1944; scene (1948) of heavy fighting during Arab invasion. Also spelled Bet Qeshet or Bet Keshet.

Beit Shearim or **Bet Shearim** (both: bĕt' shŭ-ärēm'), settlement (pop. 350), NW Israel, at N end of Plain of Jezreel, 13 mi. ESE of Haifa; mixed farming. Modern village founded 1936 on site of anc. town of same name, a Jewish center and seat of Sanhedrin in early Christian era.

Beit Shemesh, Palestine: see BETH-SHEMESH.

Beitstad (bāt'stä), village and canton (pop. 2,602), Nord-Trondelag co., central Norway, on an inlet of Beitstad Fjord (an extension of Trondheim Fjord), 8 mi. NW of Steinkjer; lumber milling.

Beit Yannai or **Beit Yanai** (both: bĕt' yänī'), settlement (pop. 100), W Israel, in Plain of Sharon, on Mediterranean, 3 mi. NNW of Natanya; mixed farming. Founded 1933. Also spelled Bet Yannai or Bet Yanai.

Beit Yehuda Halevi or **Bet Yehuda Halevi** (both: bĕt′ yĕhōōdä′ hälĕvē′), settlement (pop. 160), W Israel, in Plain of Sharon, 4 mi. ENE of Natanya; mixed farming. Founded 1945.

Beit Yits-haq or **Beit Yitzhak** (both: bĕt′ yēts-häk′), settlement (pop. 300), W Israel, in Plain of Sharon, 2 mi. E of Natanya; poultry; mixed farming; cheese mfg. Founded 1940. Also spelled Bet Yits-haq, Bet Yitzhak, Beit Itzhak, or Bet Itzhak.

Beit Yosef or **Beit Yoseph** (both: bĕt′ yōsĕf′), settlement (pop. 200), Lower Galilee, NE Israel, near right bank of the Jordan, on railroad and 5 mi. NE of Beisan; mixed farming. Founded 1937. Also spelled Bet Yosef or Bet Yoseph.

Beit Zera, Israel: see KFAR NATHAN.

Beius (bä′yōōsh), Rum. *Beiuş*, Hung. *Belényes* (bĕ′lānyĕsh), town (1948 pop. 5,807), Bihor prov., W Rumania, on Black Körös R., on railroad and 33 mi. SE of Oradea, in viticultural dist.; mfg. of alcohol, bricks; coal mining, sawmilling. Base for excursions into Bihor Mts. Has 17th-cent. monastery. Former gold- and silver-processing center. Most of inhabitants are Magyars.

Beja (bā′zhù), district (□ 3,968; pop. 275,441), in Baixo Alentejo prov., S Portugal; ⊙ Beja. Bounded by the Atlantic (SW) and by Spain (E), part of the latter frontier being formed by Chanza R. The Guadiana traverses E part of dist., and the Mira drains SW. Grain is extensively grown. Cork-oak forests. Copper mines at Aljustrel and Mina de São Domingos.

Beja, anc. *Pax Julia*, city (pop. 12,516), ⊙ Beja dist. and Baixo Alentejo prov., S Portugal, on railroad and 85 mi. SE of Lisbon; 38°3′N 7°49′W. Major commercial center with trade in grain, olive oil, wine, fruits and vegetables; mfg. (cheese, textiles, leather, pottery). Copper mined at Aljustrel (19 mi. SW). Episcopal see. Has a 14th-cent. citadel, an old monastery and church. Founded by Romans, Beja was used as a fortress city by Moors and, after its reconquest (1162), by the Portuguese as a stronghold against the Moors.

Béja (bāzhä′), anc. *Vaga* or *Vacca*, city (pop. 22,208), ⊙ Béja dist. (□ 553; pop. 101,909), N Tunisia, 55 mi. W of Tunis; center of Medjerda valley wheat-growing region; flour milling and mfg. of flour products. Copper, lead, and zinc mined in area. Experimental agr. station. The *casbah* tower was part of a Roman citadel. City was important agr. market in 1st cent. B.C. Occupied by Arabs c.1000 A.D. Scene of fighting in last stages (April, 1943) of battle of Tunisia during Second World War. Also spelled Béjà.

Bejaburi, Thailand: see PHETBURI.

Bejaburn, Thailand: see PHETCHABUN.

Béjar (bā′här), city (pop. 10,474), Salamanca prov., W Spain, in Leon, 40 mi. SSW of Salamanca; summer resort (alt. 3,077 ft.) encircled by mts. Noted center of the wool industry. Other mfg.: candy, soap, buttons, meat processing, tanning, flour- and sawmilling. Cereals, wine, livestock in area. Has remains of anc. walls, some notable churches, and castle of dukes of Béjar. Mineral springs near by.

Bejestan, Iran: see BIJISTAN.

Beji River, W Pakistan: see NARI RIVER.

Bejou (bù-zhōō′), village (pop. 173), Mahnomen co., NW Minn., on small affluent of Wild Rice R., in White Earth Indian Reservation, and 9 mi. N of Mahnomen, in grain area.

Bejrburi, Thailand: see PHETBURI.

Bejrburn, Thailand: see PHETCHABUN.

Bejubang, Bedjubang, or **Bedjoebang** (all: bùjōō′-băng), village, SE Sumatra, Indonesia, 25 mi. ESE of Jambi; oil-production center, linked by pipe line with Plaju.

Bejucal (bāhōōkäl′), town (pop. 8,319), Havana prov., W Cuba, on railroad and 13 mi. S of Havana; cigar factories. Grows tobacco, sugar cane, fruit; cattle raising.

Bejucal, officially Bejucal de Ocampo, town (pop. 353), Chiapas, S Mexico, in Sierra Madre, 7 mi. NE of Motozintla; fruit.

Bejuco (bāhōō′kō), village (pop. 867), Panama prov., central Panama, in Pacific lowland, on Inter-American Highway and 34 mi. SW of Panama city; coffee center; coconuts, livestock.

Bejuma (bāhōō′mä), town (pop. 2,927), Carabobo state, N Venezuela, 18 mi. W of Valencia; agr. center (coffee, cacao, corn, sugar cane, fruit, livestock).

Bekaa, El Bekaa, El Bika, El Beqa‘, or **Al-Biqa‘** (all: bĕkä′, bĭkä′, ĕl), anc. *Coele-Syria* [hollow, or concave, Syria], elevated valley (alt. c.3,000 ft.) in central Lebanon, bet. the Lebanon and Anti-Lebanon mts.; c.75 mi. long, 5–9 mi. wide. Watered by Litani R. (anc. Leontes), it is richest agr. area of Lebanon: vegetables, corn, apples, oranges, pears, grapes, cotton, wheat, barley; sericulture. Arrack is distilled. Main towns: Baalbek (notable ruins here), Zahle, Jedita, Mureijat, Rasheiya, Meshghara. Bekaa constitutes a province (□ 1,634; pop. 162,147) of Lebanon.

Bekalta (bĕkältä′), village, Mahdia dist., E Tunisia, near the Mediterranean, 24 mi. SE of Sousse; olive-oil pressing; grows cereals, grapes, figs, tomatoes, melons, pimentos. Saltworks near by.

Bekasmegyer (bā′kăsh-mĕdyĕr), Hung. *Békásmegyer*, town (pop. 13,089), Pest-Pilis-Solt-Kiskun co., N central Hungary, near the Danube, 7 mi. N of Budapest; bricks, tiles, roof slates; flax weaving; bottles mineral water. Csillaghegy, popular summer resort is near by.

Bek-Budi, Uzbek SSR: see KARSHI.

Bek-Dash, Turkmen SSR: see SARTAS.

Bekes (bā′kăsh), Hung. *Békés*, county (□ 1,356; pop. 295,897), SE Hungary; ⊙ Gyula. Level agr. region, drained by Körös R. Grain, tobacco, clover; cattle, hogs, sheep. Processing centers at Bekes, Gyula, BEKESCSABA, Oroshaza.

Bekes, Hung. *Békés*, town (pop. 29,283), Bekes co., SE Hungary, on the White Körös and 6 mi. NNE of Bekescsaba; agr. and market center; rail terminus. Mfg. (reed furniture, textiles, baskets, bricks, flour); agr. (grain, clover, sugar beets), poultry.

Bekescsaba (bā′kăsh-chŏbŏ), Hung. *Békéscsaba*, city (1941 pop. 52,404) in, but independent of, Bekes co., SE Hungary, 53 mi. NE of Szeged; rail, agr., market center. Mfg. of machines, furniture, shoes, boxes, textiles (silk, wool, rugs, stockings); flour mills, brickworks, tobacco warehouses. Large Slovak pop. near by; agr. (grain, tobacco), dairy farming. Sometimes called Csaba. City lost much of its surrounding area in 1950.

Bekessamson (bā′kăsh-shämshôn), Hung. *Békéssámson*, town (pop. 4,470), Bekes co., SE Hungary, 13 mi. E of Hodmezövasarhely; grain, tobacco.

Bekesszentandras (bā′kăsh-sĕntŏndräsh), Hung. *Békésszentandrás*, town (pop. 6,396), Bekes co., SE Hungary, 11 mi. SW of Mezötur; flour mills; grain, camomile, poultry.

Bekily (bĕkē′lē), town, Tulear prov., S Madagascar, 120 mi. SE of Tuléar; cattle raising. R.C. and Lutheran missions.

Bekkelaget (bĕk′kùlägù), residential suburb (pop. 6,581) of Oslo, SE Norway, at head of Oslo Fjord, 3 mi. S of city center. Until 1948, in Akershus co.

Bekok (bĕkôk′), village (pop. 950), central Johore, Malaya, on railroad and 70 mi. NW of Johore Bharu; rubber plantations.

Bekovo (byĕ′kùvŭ), village (1926 pop. 2,374), SW Penza oblast, Russian SFSR, in Khoper R. valley, on rail spur and 17 mi. NNW of Rtishchevo, in wheat and sugar-beet area; flour milling, metalworking. Peat bogs near by.

Bekwai (bĕkwī′), town (pop. 4,499), Ashanti, S central Gold Coast, on railroad and 15 mi. S of Kumasi; road junction; cacao center; cassava, corn. Has Seventh-Day Adventist col. Gold, diamond, and manganese deposits near by.

Bel, Rumania: see BELIU.

Bela, Bulgaria: see BYALA.

Bela or **Bela Partabgarh** (bä′lù pŭrtäb′gŭr), town (pop. 12,829), ⊙ Partabgarh dist., SE Uttar Pradesh, India, on Sai R. and 34 mi. NNE of Allahabad; rail and road junction; trades in rice, barley, gram, mustard. Founded 1802 as a cantonment.

Bela (bä′lù), town (pop. 3,905), ⊙ Las Bela state, SE Baluchistan, W Pakistan, near Porali R., 105 mi. NNW of Karachi; trades in oilseeds, millet, wool, rice, ghee; crocheting, woolen-carpet weaving. An 8th-cent. Buddhist center; in Middle Ages, lay on important Arab trade route from Persia to Sind. Formerly called Las Bela or Lus Bela.

Bela, Poland: see BIALA, town, Lublin province.

Bela Aliança, Brazil: see RIO DO SUL.

Bélâbre (bālä′brù), village (pop. 839), Indre dept., central France, 8 mi. SE of Le Blanc; shirt mfg., woodworking, distilling, linen weaving.

Bela Crkva or **Bela Tsrkva** (both: bĕ′lä tsŭrk′vä) [Serbo-Croatian,=white church], Hung. *Fehértemplom* (fĕ′hārtĕm″plôm), Ger. *Weisskirchen* (vīs′kĭrkh″ùn), village (pop. 9,373), Vojvodina, E Serbia, Yugoslavia, on railroad and 45 mi. E of Belgrade, in the Banat, near Rum. border; noted for carnivals and agr. exhibitions. Winegrowing; curative baths near by.

Belagach or **Bel'agach** (bĕlùgäch′), town (1944 pop. over 500), N Semipalatinsk oblast, Kazakh SSR, on Turksib RR and 25 mi. NE of Semipalatinsk, near Russian SFSR border; textile milling; gypsum quarrying. Also called Belagachski.

Belagola, India: see MYSORE, city.

Bel Air (bĕlâr′), village (pop. 1,604), E Mauritius, on railroad and 5 mi. SSE of Flacq; sugar cane.

Bel Air (bĕl″ âr′, bĕl′ âr″). **1** W residential section of LOS ANGELES city, Los Angeles co., S Calif., in foothill canyons of Santa Monica Mts., just W of Beverly Hills. **2** Town (pop. 2,578), ⊙ Harford co. (since 1782), NE Md., 22 mi. NE of Baltimore; trade center for horse-breeding and agr. area (dairy products, poultry, grain); vegetable cannery, clothing factory. Tudor Hall (built 1822 by Junius Brutus Booth), birthplace of Edwin and John Wilkes Booth, is near by. Settled c.1782, inc. 1901.

Belakavadi (bĕlŭkŭvä′dē), town (pop. 4,250), Mandya dist., S Mysore, India, near Cauvery R., 25 mi. SE of Mandya, in sugar-cane and silk-growing area. Hydroelectric plant on Sivasamudram isl., 3 mi. E.

Belalcázar (bälälkä′sär). **1** Town (pop. 2,499), Caldas dept., W central Colombia, in Cauca valley, 20 mi. WSW of Manizales; alt. 5,345 ft.; coffee, livestock. Its railroad station is 4 mi. SE. **2** or **Páez** (pīs), village (pop. 408), Cauca dept., SW Colombia, in Cordillera Central, 45 mi. ENE of Popayán; gold and platinum mining.

Belalcázar (bälälkä′thär), town (pop. 9,297), Córdoba prov., S Spain, agr. trade center 6 mi. N of Hinojosa del Duque; olive-oil and cheese processing, footwear mfg.; stock raising; cereals, fruit, vegetables. Lead mining near by. Has ruins of Moorish fort.

Belalp, Switzerland: see ALETSCH GLACIER.

Bel Alton (bĕl″ ôl′tùn), village (pop. c.250), Charles co., S Md., 30 mi. S of Washington. Near by are St. Ignatius Church and St. Thomas Manor House, both built in 18th cent.

Belampalli (bälŭmpŭl′lē), town (pop. 6,294), Adilabad dist., NE Hyderabad state, India, 75 mi. SE of Adilabad; chemical fertilizer. Coal mining 7 mi. NNW, at village of Tandur. Sometimes spelled Bellampalli.

Belanganj, India: see AGRA, city.

Belanovica or **Belanovitsa** (both: bĕ′länôvĭtsä), village, central Serbia, Yugoslavia, 39 mi. S of Belgrade, in the Sumadija.

Bela Palanka (bĕ′lä pä′län-kä), village (pop. 3,428), SE Serbia, Yugoslavia, on Nisava R., on railroad and 22 mi. ESE of Nis.

Bela Partabgarh, India: see BELA, Uttar Pradesh.

Bela pod Bezdezem (byĕ′lä pôd′ bĕz″dyĕzĕm), Czech *Bělá pod Bezdězem*, Ger. *Weisswasser* (vīs′vä″sûr), town (pop. 3,623), N Bohemia, Czechoslovakia, on railroad and 21 mi. SSW of Liberec; paper mills. On near-by Bezdez Mtn. (1,984 ft.), 4 mi. NW, are remains of 12th-cent. castle.

Belapur (bä′läpōōr), town (pop., including suburb of Ainatpur, 6,303), Ahmadnagar dist., E Bombay, India, on Pravara R. and 33 mi. N of Ahmadnagar; trade center for millet, gur, wheat; sugar milling, gur and oilseed pressing.

Belas (bä′lùsh), village (pop. 1,209), Lisboa dist., central Portugal, 8 mi. NW of Lisbon; resort.

Belasica or **Belasitsa** (both: bĕläsē′tsù), Greek *Kerkine* or *Kerkini* (both: kĕrkē′nē), mountain range in Macedonia, at junction of Greek, Bulgarian, and Yugoslav frontiers; extends c.35 mi. W-E, bet. Vardar and Struma rivers, S of Strumica R.; rises to 6,660 ft. in RADOMIR peak. Granite formations. Climatic border bet. Mediterranean and humid continental regions. Deciduous woodland; chestnut and wine groves on N slopes.

Bela Slatina, Bulgaria: see BYALA SLATINA.

Bela Tsrkva, Yugoslavia: see BELA CRKVA.

Bela Vista (bĕ′lù vēsh′tù), town (pop. 999), Benguela prov., W central Angola, on Benguela RR and 50 mi. WSW of Nova Lisboa.

Bela Vista. **1** City, Goiás, Brazil: see SUÇUAPARÁ. **2** City (pop. 5,641), S Mato Grosso, Brazil, on right bank of Apa R., opposite Bella Vista (Paraguay), and 160 mi. SW of Campo Grande; cattle-shipping center. Old military post. Formerly spelled Bella Vista. In Ponta Porã territory, 1943–46. **3** City, São Paulo, Brazil: see ECHAPORÃ.

Bela Vista, village, Sul do Save prov., S Mozambique, on Maputo R. and 28 mi. S of Lourenço Marques; corn, beans; cattle raising.

Belawan (bùlä′wän), town, NE Sumatra, Indonesia, on Strait of Malacca, at mouth of Deli R., 15 mi. N of Medan, near Labuan Deli; port for Medan. Ships rubber, tobacco, tea, fibers, palm oil, spices, copra, gambir. Also called Belawan Deli.

Belaya [Rus.,=white], in Rus. names: see also BELO- [Rus. combining form], BELOYE, BELY, BELYE.

Belaya Berezka (byĕ′līŭ bĭryôs′kŭ), town (1940 pop. over 500), S Bryansk oblast, Russian SFSR, on Desna R. and 15 mi. SW of Trubchevsk; sawmilling.

Belaya Glina (glyē′nŭ), village (1926 pop. 21,330), NE Krasnodar Territory, Russian SFSR, on railroad and 38 mi. NE of Tikhoretsk, in agr. area; flour milling, metalworking.

Belaya Kalitva (kŭlyĕt′vŭ), town (1939 pop. over 2,000), W central Rostov oblast, Russian SFSR, on Northern Donets R., at mouth of the Kalitva, on railroad and 25 mi. ESE of Kamensk. Center of Bogurayev coal dist. (main mines at KOKSOVY and SINEGORSKI); limestone, glassworks. Known as Ust-Belokalitvenskaya until c.1935; also called Belokalitvenskaya in late 1930s.

Belaya Krinitsa (krĭnyē′tsŭ), town (1939 pop. over 500), E Zhitomir oblast, Ukrainian SSR, on Teterev R. and 12 mi. NE of Radomyshl; ceramics.

Belaya River (byĕ′līŭ). **1** In Bashkir Autonomous SSR, Russian SFSR, rises in the S Urals E of Iremel mtn., flows SW through forested area, past Beloretsk, W, N past Meleuz, Ishimbai, Sterlitamak (head of navigation), Ufa, and Chernikovsk, and generally NW past Blagoveshchensk and Birsk, to Kama R. just N of Derbeshkinski; 882 mi. long. Receives Sim, Ufa, and Bystry Tanyl (right) and Sterlya, Dema, Chermasin, and Syun (left) rivers. Navigation important for iron ore, grain, and lumber exports. Limestone, gypsum (central valley), and peat (lower valley) deposits. **2** In Buryat-Mongol Autonomous SSR and Irkutsk oblast, Russian SFSR, rises in Eastern Sayan Mts., flows 166 mi. E to Angara R. N of Usolye. Non-navigable. **3** In Krasnodar Territory, Russian SFSR, rises in the W Greater Caucasus on Fisht peak, flows N, past Maikop, and NNW, past Belorechenskaya, to Kuban R. E of Krasnodar; 125 mi. long. Forms reservoir (10 mi. long, 3 mi. wide) near its mouth.

Belaya Tserkov or **Belaya Tserkov'** (tsĕr'kŭf), city (1926 pop. 42,974), W Kiev oblast, Ukrainian SSR, on Ros R., on railroad and 45 mi. SSW of Kiev. Road junction; flour-milling center; metalworks, leather products, mfg. (clothing, furniture). Agr. col. Short-lived peace bet. Poland and Boldan Chmielnicki (Bogdan Khmelnitski) signed here (1651). Passed (1793) to Russia. Scene of Decembrist revolt (1825–26). In Second World War, held (1941–43) by Germans.

Belaya Zemlya (zĭmlyä') [Rus.,=white land], Norwegian *Hvidtland*, northeasternmost group (5 isls.) of Franz Josef Land, Russian SFSR, in Arctic Ocean; 81°45'N 63°E. Discovered 1894–95 by Fridtjof Nansen.

Belbasovka (byĕlbä'sŭfkŭ), town (1939 pop. over 500), N Stalino oblast, Ukrainian SSR, in the Donbas, 5 mi. W of Slavyansk.

Belbeis, Egypt: see BILBEIS.

Belbek River or **Bel'bek River** (byĕlbyĕk'), S Crimea, Russian SFSR, rises in the Ai-Petri section of Crimean Mts., flows c.35 mi. WNW, past Kuibyshevo, and W to Black Sea 3 mi. N of Sevastopol.

Belbo River (bĕl'bô), NW Italy, rises in Ligurian Alps 5 mi. ESE of Ceva, flows 55 mi. NE, past Canelli and Nizza Monferrato, to Tanaro R. 5 mi. W of Alessandria.

Belcaire (bĕlkâr'), village (pop. 572), Aude dept., S France, 21 mi. SW of Limoux; livestock raising.

Belcamp (bĕl'kămp), village, Harford co., NE Md., on Bush R. and 23 mi. ENE of Baltimore; model industrial town, developed around shoe factory established here 1939.

Belcesti-cu-Tansa (bĕl-chĕsh'tĭ-kōō-tän'sä), Rum. *Belceşti-cu-Tansa*, village (pop. 4,449), Jassy prov., NE Rumania, on railroad and 7 mi. NE of Targu-Frumos; agr. center with agr. school.

Belchatow (bĕōō-khä'tōōf), Pol. *Bełchatów*, Rus. *Belkhatov* (bĕl-khä'tŭf), town (pop. 4,780), Lodz prov., central Poland, 28 mi. S of Lodz; mfg. of textiles, cement ware; tanning, sawmilling.

Belchen (bĕl'khŭn), mountain (4,639 ft.) in Black Forest, S Germany, 9 mi. E of Müllheim. Sometimes called Herzogenhorn.

Belcher, village (1940 pop. 591), Pike co., E Ky., in the Cumberlands, on Russell Fork and 12 mi. SE of Pikeville, in bituminous-coal area.

Belcher Channel, N Franklin Dist., Northwest Territories, arm (70 mi. long, 30–40 mi. wide) of the Arctic Ocean, bet. Cornwall Isl. (N) and Grinnell Peninsula of Devon Isl. (S).

Belcher Islands, SE Keewatin Dist., Northwest Territories, group of isls. (□ 1,096) in E part of Hudson Bay, off W Ungava Peninsula, Que.; 55°40'–57°N 78°38'–80°6'W; covers area c.90 mi. long and 60 mi. wide. Flaherty Isl. is largest. On W coast of Tukarak Isl. is Hudson's Bay Co. trading post; 56°13'N 78°52'W. Group supports small Eskimo population. First seen by Henry Hudson, 1610, isls. were not explored and mapped until 1915. N and S of this group are other groups of islets.

Belchertown, town (pop. 4,487), Hampshire co., W central Mass., 15 mi. NE of Springfield, near Quabbin Reservoir; poultry, dairying, apples. Settled 1731, inc. 1761. Includes village of Dwight.

Belcherville, town (pop. 31), Montague co., N Texas, near Red R., 38 mi. E of Wichita Falls, in agr. area.

Belchite (bĕlchē'tā), town (pop. 3,214), Saragossa prov., NE Spain, 26 mi. SSE of Saragossa; agr. trade center (cereals, olive oil, wine, fruit, saffron). Airport 2 mi. E. Town was rebuilt after destruction in Sp. civil war (1938). Here, June 16–19, 1809, the French under Suchet defeated the Spaniards under Blake.

Belcourt, village (pop. c.200), Rolette co., N N.Dak., 7 mi. W of Rolla and at SE end of Turtle Mts. Agency hq. for Turtle Mtn. Indian Reservation are here.

Beldanga (bāldäng'gŭ), town (pop. 6,002), Murshidabad dist., E West Bengal, India, in Ganges Delta, 11 mi. S of Berhampore; silk weaving, sugar milling; trades in rice, gram, oilseeds, jute, barley.

Belden, village (pop. 192), Cedar co., NE Nebr., 15 mi. S of Hartington.

Beldenville, village, Pierce co., W Wis., 17 mi. E of Hastings, Minn.; dairying, stock raising, limestone quarrying.

Belding, city (pop. 4,436), Ionia co., S central Mich., on Flat R. and 24 mi. NE of Grand Rapids, in agr. area (apples, beans, potatoes). Mfg. of castings, paint, varnish, baskets, silk. Settled c.1855; inc. 1893.

Belebei or **Belebey** (bĕlyĭbyā'), city (1926 pop. 11,320), W Bashkir Autonomous SSR, Russian SFSR, 85 mi. SW of Ufa, on rail spur; grain-exporting center; flour milling, distilling. Founded 1781.

Belebelka (bĕlyĭbyĕl'kŭ), village, SW Novgorod oblast, Russian SFSR, on Polist R. and 33 mi. SSW of Staraya Russa; flax; lumbering.

Belecke (bĕlĕ'kŭ), town (pop. 3,176), in former Prussian prov. of Westphalia, W Germany, after 1945 in North Rhine-Westphalia, on the Möhne and 13 mi. S of Lippstadt; grain.

Beled, Iraq: see BALAD.

Belém (bŭlĕm'). **1** or **Pará** (pŭrä'), city (1950 pop. 230,181), ⊙ Pará, N Brazil, in Amazon delta at confluence of Guajará and Guamá rivers here entering Pará R., 90 mi. from the open Atlantic, 1,500 mi. NNW of Rio de Janeiro; 1°27'S 48°30'W. Seaport, hub of air communications, and leading commercial center of the Amazon basin, which includes states of Pará and Amazonas (Brazil), and E Peru and N Bolivia. The following products of the interior are exported through Belém: rubber, Brazil nuts, cacao, vegetable ivory, manioc meal, tagua nuts, tobacco, jute, medicinal plants and roots, miscellaneous fibers, tropical hardwood, and water-buffalo hides. Industries: sawmills, machine shops, shipyards, brick- and tileworks; biscuit, soap, and candle factories. Belém has humid tropical climate (average temp. 80°F., with small diurnal range; heavy, almost daily, rainfall). Terminus of railroad to Bragança and of several short roads. City is attractively laid out with shaded avenues and squares, and with numerous luxuriant parks with exotic flora. Public bldgs. include govt. palace (built 1762), early 18th-cent. cathedral in Port. colonial style, 17th-cent. Jesuit church of St. Alexander, fashionable modern church of Our Lady of Nazareth, and episcopal palace. Belém also has noted Goeldi mus. containing varied Amazonian exhibits, botanical garden, 2 libraries, a theater and opera house, agr. inst.; schools of law, medicine, fine arts, dentistry, and pharmacy; and a modern leprosarium. Health conditions were much improved by drainage program in Second World War. Founded c.1615 as Santa Maria de Belém do Grão Pará; its official Brazilian name is now Belém, though it has traditionally been known as Pará to foreigners. **2** City, Pernambuco, Brazil: see JATINÃ. **3** City, Piauí, Brazil: see PALMEIRAIS.

Belém, suburb of Lisbon, W central Portugal, on right bank of Tagus estuary, 4 mi. WSW of city center. It is now within city limits. A noted monastery (Mosteiro dos Jerónimos) in exuberant Manueline style was built here (begun in 1502) to commemorate Vasco da Gama's voyage to India. Its church contains tombs of Vasco da Gama, Camões, and of several Port. kings. It is one of Portugal's great shrines. The Belém palace (also called Quinta de Baixo) is official residence of president of Portugal; one wing contains natl. coach mus. Just W is the famous Tôrre de Belém, a 16th-cent. white tower in Manueline style (with Moorish decorations), whose distinctive outline has become a natl. emblem.

Belén (bĕlān'). **1** Town, Buenos Aires prov., Argentina: see ESCOBAR. **2** Town (pop. 4,301), ⊙ Belén dept. (□ 6,100; pop. 14,085), central Catamarca prov., Argentina, on Belén R. and 95 mi. NW of Catamarca; alt. c.4,000 ft. Road and agr. center (alfalfa, grain, aniseed, cuminseed, livestock; viticulture); flour and textile milling, limestone quarry.

Belén, village (pop. 359), Tarapacá prov., N Chile, in the Andes, at foot of Cerro de Belén, 55 mi. E of Arica; stock raising (llamas, alpacas).

Belén, village (pop. 985), Boyacá dept., central Colombia, on Pan-American Highway, in Cordillera Oriental, 45 mi. NE of Tunja; alt. 8,842 ft.; cereals, sugar cane, silk, stock.

Belén, village (1950 pop. 1,912), Guanacaste prov., NW Costa Rica, 4 mi. W of Filadelfia; sugar cane, livestock.

Belén, town (1950 pop. 1,500), Rivas dept., SW Nicaragua, 6 mi. NW of Rivas, on Inter-American Highway; livestock; cacao.

Belén, town (dist. pop. 6,700), Concepción dept., central Paraguay, on Ypané R. and 12 mi. SE of Concepción; maté and lumber center. Founded 1770 by Jesuits.

Belen (bĕlĕn'), village (pop. 1,238), Hatay prov., S Turkey, 8 mi. S of Iskenderun (Alexandretta), in a pass (2,395 ft.) of the Amanos Mts., bet. Aleppo (Syria) and the anc. region of Cilicia. Here the Egyptians defeated the Turks in 1832. The pass (formerly also spelled Beilan and Bailan) has been identified with the anc. Syrian Gates (*Portae Syriae*).

Belen (bŭlĕn'). **1** Village (1940 pop. 90), Quitman co., NW Miss., 5 mi. W of Marks, in cotton-growing area. **2** Village (pop. 4,495), Valencia co., W central N.Mex., on Rio Grande and 30 mi. S of Albuquerque; alt. 4,801 ft. Trade and shipping point in irrigated grain, livestock, fruit region; flour mill, railroad yards and repair shops.

Belén (bĕlān'), town (pop. 1,500), Salto dept., NW Uruguay, in W foothills of the Cuchilla de Belén, on Uruguay R., on highway, and 45 mi. N of Salto; cereals, livestock.

Belén, town (pop. 899), Carabobo state, N Venezuela, 26 mi. SE of Valencia; coffee, corn, sugar, fruit, stock.

Belén, Cerro de (sĕ'rō dā), Andean peak (17,135 ft.), N Chile, 60 mi. E of Arica; 18°29'S.

Belén, Cuchilla de (kōōchē'yä dā), hill range on Artigas-Salto dept. border, NW Uruguay, extends c.100 mi. from Brazil border W to Belén. Rises to 1,000 ft.

Belén, Llanos de (yä'nōs dā), subandean plains in S Catamarca prov., Argentina, extend 50 mi. S from Belén bet. the Sierra de Fiambalá (W) and the Salar de Pipanaco (E).

Belén, San Antonio de, Costa Rica: see SAN ANTONIO, Heredia prov.

Belene (bĕ'lĕnĕ), village (pop. 6,867), Pleven dist., N Bulgaria, port and rail terminus on swampy branch of the Danube, 11 mi. WNW of Svishtov, in agr. area (grain, livestock). Belene L. (W; □ 4) has fisheries. Irrigation development.

Belenikhino (bĕlyĭnyē'khĭnŭ), village (1939 pop. over 500), S central Kursk oblast, Russian SFSR, 22 mi. N of Belgorod; sugar beets.

Belenkoye or **Belen'koye** (bâ'lyĭnkŭyŭ), town (1939 pop. over 500), N Stalino oblast, Ukrainian SSR, in the Donbas, 5 mi. NE of Kramatorsk.

Belén River (bĕlān'), central Catamarca prov., Argentina, formed by 2 branches rising in Sierra Changoreal at c.10,000 ft., flows c.85 mi. S and SE, past Belén, to the Salar de Pipanaco. Called San Fernando R. in upper course.

Belenyes, Rumania: see BEIUS.

Belep Islands (bālĕp'), small inhabited coral group, SW Pacific, 7 mi. NW of New Caledonia, of which it is a dependency; largest isl. is c.10 mi. long, c.3 mi. wide.

Beles, Luxembourg: see BELVAUX.

Belesa (bĕlĕ'sä), village (pop. 300), Asmara div., central Eritrea, 6 mi. N of Asmara. Has hydroelectric plant which furnishes power to Asmara.

Bélesta (bālŭstä'), village (pop. 1,009), Ariège dept., S France, on Hers R. and 17 mi. ESE of Foix; comb mfg., lumbering, sawmilling. Building materials quarried near by.

Belet Uen (bälĕt' wĕn'), town (pop. 1,500), in the Mudugh, central Ital. Somaliland, on the Webi Shebeli and 180 mi. N of Mogadishu, in durra-growing region; 4°44'N 45°13'E; trade center.

Belev (bĭlyôf'), city (1926 pop. 13,560), SW Tula oblast, Russian SFSR, on Oka R. and 65 mi. SW of Tula; flour milling, dairying, distilling, metalworking. Art mus. Dates from 12th cent.; chartered 1396.

Belevo, Lake (bĕ'lĕvô) (□ 1.5), in Stalin dist., E Bulgaria, on Provadiya R. and 10 mi. W of Stalin. Seaplane base.

Belfast, Australia: see PORT FAIRY.

Belfast (bĕl'făst, bĕlfăst'), county borough (1937 pop. 438,086; 1951 census 443,670), ⊙ Northern Ireland, mainly in S part of Co. Antrim (of which it is ⊙) and partly in N Co. Down, on Belfast Lough, an inlet of the North Channel, at mouth of Lagan R., 90 mi. N of Dublin; 54°36'N 5°56'W. Seaport and industrial city, with major shipyards, including those of Harland and Wolff Co. (the *Titanic*, *Olympic*, and many other large liners were built here), center of Irish linen industry (spinning, weaving, bleaching). Other industries include tobacco processing, flour milling, food canning, alcohol distilling, brewing, iron founding, marine and railroad engineering, jute and woolen milling, mfg. of rope, cables, chemicals, soap, textile machinery, agr. implements, clothing, shirts, shoes. Port, begun in 17th cent., is 8½ mi. long and has extensive quays and several drydocks. Among Belfast's features are City Hall, with 175-ft.-high dome; Queen's Univ., founded 1845, inc. as Univ. of Belfast in 1909; Presbyterian Training Col. (1853); Mus. and Art Gall.; Protestant Cathedral of St. Anne, begun 1899; Col. of Technology; Academical Institution (1810), where Sheridan and Knowles taught; and Albert Memorial Clock Tower. In 1177 John de Courcy established castle on site of Belfast; in 1315 it was taken by Edward Bruce. After revocation of Edict of Nantes, influx of French Huguenots considerably stimulated growth of town's linen industry. In 1888 Belfast became city and, 1920, ⊙ Northern Ireland. Following Orange Day celebrations in 1935 city was scene of serious religious riots. In April and May, 1941, city and surroundings were subjected to heavy German air raids, causing considerable casualties and damage to homes, hospitals, churches, and industrial plants. Among chief suburbs are Sydenham (E), site of Belfast airport, and Stormont (E), site of Parliament House of Northern Ireland, completed 1932.

Belfast, village (pop. 3,074), E Transvaal, U. of So. Afr., 55 mi. ENE of Witbank; alt. 6,463 ft.; rail junction; coal mining. Resort.

Belfast (bĕl'făst). **1** City (pop. 5,960), ⊙ Waldo co., S Maine; resort on Penobscot Bay opposite Castine and 30 mi. SSE of Bangor. Mfg. (shoes, hardware, wood products). Port of entry. Shipping and shipbuilding center in mid-19th cent. Settled 1770; sacked twice by British (1779, 1814); inc. town 1773, city 1853. **2** Village (1940 pop. 646), Allegany co., W N.Y., on Genesee R. and 23 mi. W of Hornell, in dairying and poultry area.

Belfast Lough (lŏkh), inlet (12 mi. long, 3 to 7 mi. wide) of the North Channel, Northern Ireland, bet. Cos. Antrim (N) and Down (S); natural harbor, providing excellent anchorage. At head of lough, at mouth of Lagan R., is Belfast city. Other towns on it are Carrickfergus, Bangor, and Whitehead.

Belfield, village (pop. 147), Demerara co., N Br. Guiana, near Atlantic coast, on Georgetown-Rosignol RR and 15 mi. ESE of Georgetown; rice, sugar cane, fruit, stock.

Belfield, city (pop. 1,051), Stark co., W N.Dak., 20 mi. W of Dickinson and on tributary of Heart R. Soap plant is here.

Belfiore (bĕlfyô′rĕ), village (pop. 918), Verona prov., Veneto, N Italy, near Adige R., 11 mi. ESE of Verona; matches, ceramics, lime, cement.

Belfodio (bĕlfō′dyō), village, Wallaga prov., W central Ethiopia, near Anglo-Egyptian Sudan border, 40 mi. NE of Asosa.

Belford, town and parish (pop. 684), N Northumberland, England, 14 mi. NNW of Alnwick.

Belford, village (pop. 1,832), Monmouth co., E N.J., near Sandy Hook Bay, 5 mi. N of Red Bank.

Belford, Mount (14,052 ft.), in Rocky Mts., Chaffee co., central Colo.

Belford Roxo (bĕlfôr′ rō′shōō), town (pop. 4,051), S Rio de Janeiro state, Brazil, on railroad and 15 mi. NW of center of Rio, in orange-growing region.

Belfort (bāfôr′, bĕlfôr′), town (pop. 35,952), ⊙ Territory of Belfort, E France, 25 mi. WSW of Mulhouse; important transport and industrial center, commanding the BELFORT GAP, thus dominating the roads bet. France, Switzerland, and Germany. Has large cotton mills and metalworks (rolling stock, engines, turbines). Also builds smoke stacks, industrial ovens, cables, cement pipe. An Austrian possession, it passed (1648) to France and was fortified by Vauban. In Franco-Prussian War (1870–71), its garrison withstood a 108-day siege (commemorated by a statue of the *Lion of Belfort*, 36 ft. high, 72 ft. long), surrendering only on orders of Fr. govt. When Alsace was annexed to Germany in 1871, Belfort with its surrounding territory remained with France. Of great strategic value, it was successfully defended by the French in First World War. In 1940, by swinging around the Maginot Line, the Germans captured it from the rear. Belfort was easily taken by Allies in Nov., 1944.

Belfort, Territory of (bāfôr′, bĕlfôr′), department (□ 235; pop. 86,648), in former Alsace prov., E France; ⊙ Belfort. Bounded by the Vosges (N) and Switzerland (S). Lies athwart BELFORT GAP; traversed by major rail lines and Rhone-Rhine Canal. Grows cereals, vegetables, hops, and hemp. Important mfg. dist. (continuation of Montbéliard industrial area) with metallurgical factories (machines, electrical equipment, hardware) and textile mills. Dept. was created in 1871 from only section of Alsace then left to France.

Belforte del Chienti (bĕlfôr′tĕ dĕl kyĕn′tē), village (pop. 182), Macerata prov., The Marches, central Italy, on Chienti R. and 4 mi. SW of Tolentino; cementworks.

Belfort Gap (bāfôr′, bĕlfôr′) or **Burgundy Gate,** Fr. *Trouée de Belfort* (trōōā′ dü) or *Porte de Bourgogne* (pôrt′ dü bōōrgô′nyü), in E France, bet. the Vosges (N) and the Jura (S), c.15 mi. wide. Lies chiefly in Territory of Belfort. A strategic passageway from Rhine R. valley to Paris Basin, it is commanded by the stronghold of BELFORT. Traversed by international railroad lines and by Rhone-Rhine Canal. Heavily industrialized bet. Belfort and Montbéliard.

Belfry, mining village (pop. 1,315), Pike co., E Ky., in the Cumberlands, 3 mi. S of Williamson, W.Va.; bituminous coal.

Belgard, Poland: see BIALOGARD.

Belgaum (bāl′goum), district, S Bombay, India; ⊙ Belgaum. Bordered W by Western Ghats and Kolhapur dist., N by Satara South dist.; drained by Kistna R. (N) and Ghatprabha R. Agr. (millet, cotton, rice, tobacco, wheat); several bauxite deposits. Handicraft cloth weaving, dyeing, tanning, wood carving. Chief towns and trade centers: Athni, Belgaum, Gokak, Nipani (tobacco). Under sultans of Bijapur in 17th cent.; later passed to Mahrattas. Original dist. (□ 4,527; 1941 pop. 1,225,428) enlarged by inc. (1949) of parts of former Deccan states of Sangli, Jamkhandi, Kolhapur, Kurandvad Senior, Kurandvad Junior, Miraj Senior, Miraj Junior, Ramdurg, Jath, and Wadi Estate. Pop. 86% Hindu, 8% Moslem, 1% Christian.

Belgaum, city (pop. 58,319; including suburban and SW cantonment areas, 75,482), ⊙ Belgaum dist., S Bombay, India, 250 mi. SSE of Bombay. Military station; road center; trades in rice, ghee, jaggery, timber; rice and oilseed milling, truck-body building, tanning, mfg. of handicraft cloth, furniture, matches, chemicals, cameras, biscuits. Has arts and law cols.

Belgentier (bĕl-zhätyā′), village (pop. 468), Var dept., SE France, 9 mi. NNE of Toulon; tanning, fruit and flower shipping.

Belgern (bĕl′gürn), town (pop. 3,845), in former Prussian Saxony prov., central Germany, after 1945 in Saxony-Anhalt, on the Elbe and 8 mi. SE of Torgau; agr. market (grain, sugar beets, potatoes, livestock); potteries. Has 15th-cent. church; remains of anc. Cistercian monastery.

Belgian Congo (bĕl′jŭn kŏng′-gō), Fr. *Congo belge*, Flemish *Belgisch Congo*, only colony (□ 904,754; 1948 pop. 10,962,799) of Belgium, in heart of central Africa, administered by a governor-general under direction of Belgian Ministry of Colonies; ⊙ Leopoldville. Lying astride the equator, bet. 5°N and 12°S, it is bordered W and N by a long frontier with Fr. Equatorial Africa along Congo, Ubangi, and Bomu rivers; in E it shares the divide of great African lakes with Uganda, Tanganyika, and Northern Rhodesia. Northern Rhodesia also borders the SE, the Anglo-Egyptian Sudan border is NE, and Angola S and SW, while the Cabinda (an exclave of Angola on N bank of Congo R. estuary) constricts the narrow outlet to the Atlantic to a coast 25 mi. wide. Colony covers ⅔ of Congo basin, a vast flat depression of the African plateau, encircled by highlands broken only by lower Congo R. gorge (Livingstone Falls) across Crystal Mts. Lowest portion is in NW center, in the basin of a former Jurassic lake; the last vestiges of this inland sea are L. Leopold II, L. Tumba, and the extensive swamps at confluence of the Congo with the Ubangi. E highlands (6–7,000 ft.), on W edge of Albertine Rift, culminate in the snow-clad Ruwenzori (16,795 ft.) and the intermittently active Virunga volcanoes (11,400 ft.). In SE lies the highly mineralized Katanga plateau. Great tributaries of CONGO RIVER converge fan-wise on the main stream. Chief components of Congo-Lualaba system are: Ubangi, Kasai, Uele, Kwango, Sankuru, Lomami, Aruwimi-Ituri, Ruki-Busira, Luapula-Luvua. Fimi-Lukenie, Itimbiri; L. Tanganyika, L. Kivu, and L. Moero. A few rivers (Rutshuru, Semliki) and L. Albert and L. Edward drain to Nile basin. Shiloango R. alone flows directly to the Atlantic. Climate is hot, always close to 80°F. The zone astride the equator receives abundant and constant precipitation (60–80 in.), mostly afternoon thunderstorms; northwards and southwards of equatorial belt copious rains fall 7–9 months of the year; midwinter is dry. By contrast the climate of E and SE highlands is fairly invigorating and European settlers find here (Kivu, Marungu, High Katanga) a favorable zone of colonization. Most of N half of colony is densely covered with tropical rain forest, though a strip of grasslands fringes northernmost boundary. S half is mainly savanna country with frequent forest galleries along the streams. Congo's fauna is noted for abundance of game, now preserved in several natl. parks, particularly ALBERT NATIONAL PARK; rare species include white rhinoceros, okapi, dwarf elephant, Derby eland, gorilla, Congo peacock. The insects are often carriers of disease (tsetse fly, tick, anopheles mosquito). African elephants are domesticated at Gangala na Bodio. Chief agr. exports of Congo are palm oil, palm kernels, cotton (Ubangi-Uele), coffee (Kivu), cacao(Mayumbe),cinchona,fibers,tea,essentialoils, hides. Pyrethrum, tobacco, sugar cane, rice, peanuts, also grown. Native farming: manioc, corn, plantain, sweet potatoes, pulse, sorghum, sesame. Stock raising is limited by tsetse fly to Kivu, Lomami, E Kasai regions. Extremely varied mineral resources have laid foundation for mining and mineral processing industry of Katanga. Belgian Congo is world's leading producer of industrial diamonds (Tshikapa, Bushimaie R.), uranium (Shinkolobwe), and cobalt, and ranks high as supplier of gold (Kilo, Moto) and tin (Manono). Manganese, zinc, tantalum, wolfram, platinoids, low-grade coal (Luena) are mined as well. Industry also includes textile mills (Leopoldville, Albertville), palm-oil mills, cotton gins; mfg. of chemicals, explosives, construction materials, insecticides, soap, sugar, beer, flour. Main centers are Leopoldville, Elisabethville, Stanleyville, Jadotville, Costermansville, Albertville, Boma, Coquilhatville, Thysville, Lusambo, Luluabourg. Matadi is Congo's main seaport and outlet of colony's produce. Navigable rivers are many; steamers ply most lakes. Railroad development was chiefly prompted by need of circumventing numerous rapids. Principal tracks are Matadi-Leopoldville, Stanleyville-Ponthierville, Kindu-Albertville, Port-Francqui-Bukama (known as B.C.K.) which connects with Northern Rhodesia via Elisabethville, and with Angola via Tenke-Dilolo. Secondary tracks run from Aketi to Mungbere (branch to Bondo and Titule), Boma to Tschela, Manono to Muyumba, Charlesville to Makumbi, Uvira to Kamaniola. Roads are only of local importance, except for Congo-Nile highway (Bumba-Juba). Air traffic is fairly well developed; Leopoldville is a well-known hub. Administratively Belgian Congo is divided into 6 provs.: LEOPOLDVILLE, EQUATOR PROVINCE, EASTERN PROVINCE, KIVU, KASAI, and KATANGA; it also administers the U.N. trust territory of RUANDA-URUNDI. Native pop. consists of many Bantu tribes (Bacongo, Bateke, Waregga, Baluba, Batetela, Bayaka), Nilotics, Sudanese (Azande, Mangbettu), and remnants of aboriginal Pygmies. Over 200 dialects are spoken, Swahili (Kingwana), Luba, Kongo, and Ngala being the 4 lingua franca. Despite vigorous missionary activity, over 60% of natives still remain fetishists. Europeans number c.48,000 (72% Belgians). Diogo Cão visited the mouth of Congo R., 1482. Various explorers attempted to push inland from E and W—Lacerda (1798) in Katanga, J. K. Tuckey (1816) in lower Congo, Schweinfurth (1870) in Uele, Livingstone (1866–71) at sources of Lualaba—but penetration was defeated by dense vegetation and the difficult terrain. The "International Association for Exploration and Civilization of Central Africa" was founded, 1876, under chairmanship of Leopold II of Belgium; soon its attention was attracted by H. M. Stanley's progress down Congo R. At his return to Europe, 1878, Stanley was commissioned by the Belgian king on behalf of *Comité d'Etudes du Haut-Congo* (later changed to International Association of Congo, 1883–85) to continue exploration and procure submission of native chiefs. Congo Free State was formally proclaimed after Conference of Berlin (1884–85) with Leopold II as monarch and chief stockholder. Campaigns were waged against Arab slave-traders 1886–94, Katanga chief M'siri 1891, and the Mahdists 1894. In 1894 Great Britain granted to Leopold II an extension of Free State to NE and a lease on Bahr-el-Ghazal region. Fr. pressure led to the return of LADO enclave to Anglo-Egyptian Sudan (1910) but W shore of L. Albert remained in Congo. Increasing mercantilism of Free State govt., and the policy of large concessions and merciless treatment of natives provoked violent international reaction. A less personal regime was demanded, and Belgium assumed (1908) sovereignty over the Congo, which became a colony. Ruanda-Urundi (League of Nations mandate) was awarded (1923) to Belgium in recognition of participation of Congo troops in expeditions against German East Africa (1915) and the Cameroons. Convention of 1927 bet. Portugal and Belgium exchanged territory in SW Katanga and Matadi area. During Second World War, Congo troops fought in Ethiopia (1941) and Egypt (1943).

Belgica (bĕl′jĭkü), anc. Roman prov. of N Gaul, comprising most of present-day N France and Belgium. Was inhabited by the Celtic Belgae.

Belgioioso (bĕljôyô′zô), town (pop. 3,990), Pavia prov., Lombardy, N Italy, 8 mi. ESE of Pavia, in irrigated region. Agr. (cheese, cereals, swine) and commercial center; silk mills, foundry. Has medieval castle (rebuilt 18th cent.).

Belgique (bĕlzhēk′, bĕljēk′), town (pop. 66), Perry co., E Mo., on Mississippi R. and 9 mi. NNE of Perryville.

Belgium (bĕl′jüm), Flemish *België* (bĕl′khēü), Fr. *Belgique* (bĕlzhēk′), kingdom (□ 11,779; 1947 pop. estimate 8,512,195), NW Europe; ⊙ BRUSSELS. A constitutional monarchy, divided into 9 provs., which enjoy a large measure of self-govt.—ANTWERP, BRABANT, EAST FLANDERS, WEST FLANDERS, HAINAUT, LIÉGE, LIMBURG, LUXEMBOURG, and NAMUR. Has 42-mi. coast line on North Sea; borders N on the Netherlands, E on Germany, SE on grand duchy of Luxembourg, S and SW on France; approximately bet. 49°30′–51°30′N and 2°35′–6°25′E. Its greatest length (Ostende-Arlon) is 175 mi. One of the Low Countries, long disputed among European powers, Belgium serves as an entrepôt for the continent. On the SCHELDT RIVER estuary lies the great port of ANTWERP, which handles c.90% of Belgium's foreign trade. The North Sea coast is almost straight and lined by dunes; on it are fashionable beach resorts (OSTENDE, KNOKKE) and the minor port ZEEBRUGGE. Apart from the Scheldt, the country is drained by MEUSE RIVER, which is joined by SAMBRE RIVER at NAMUR. Both the Scheldt and the Meuse, which rise in France, are of good navigability and feed a network of canals. Topographically, Belgium may be divided into 3 sections: the low, sandy regions of Belgian Flanders and CAMPINE in N; the central, slightly elevated plain of fertile loess soil bet. Meuse and Scheldt rivers, centered on Brussels (in Brabant prov.); and, in E, the rugged plateau of the ARDENNES mts., which reach into Germany, France, and Luxembourg, and rise here in the Botrange to 2,283 ft. The climate is distinctly maritime, somewhat similar to England's, i.e., mild winters, cool summers, frequent fogs. Only the Ardennes, because of their greater distance from the sea and higher alt., display more rigorous, continental conditions. Annual mean temp. for entire country is c.50°F. Belgium is one of the most densely populated (712 persons per sq. mi.) and highly industrialized nations of Europe, but agr. also plays a prominent part in its economy; local crops have, however, to be supplemented by imports, chiefly cereals. There is intensive cultivation, even in the Ardennes, a backward section still largely wooded (c.20% of the area is forest). Main crops are oats, rye, wheat, potatoes, barley, sugar beets, tobacco, flax, grapes, forage; truck gardens and orchards. Cattle raising, dairying, breeding of heavy horses are important. Belgium's industry is almost completely based on its rich coal fields. About 200,000 people alone are employed in the mines. Principal deposits have long been the bituminous beds in the Borinage of Hainaut, at W foot of the Ardennes near MONS and CHARLEROI. Though these resources are becoming depleted, a new, even richer basin has been discovered in the Campine region (Limburg prov.) E of Antwerp. There are minor iron deposits in SE corner adjoining the Lorraine basin of France; however, practically all the ore for Belgium's siderurgical industry, among the world's greatest, is imported from France. Other minerals extracted include copper, silver, zinc, lead, tin, phosphates—chiefly from the uplands. The metallurgical and engineering industries furnish most exports. A string of industrial towns in the Sambre-Meuse Valley (Mons, Charleroi, Namur, and, foremost,

LIÉGE) turns out iron, steel, machinery, and appliances; there are also refining of copper and zinc, and mfg. of rubber, soap, electrical articles, paper, chemicals. Brussels, the splendid metropolis remindful of Paris, produces railroad equipment, textiles, clothing, leather and metal goods, foodstuffs, chemicals, paper. Antwerp, one of Europe's great ports and the country's 2d city, has shipyards and varied consumer industries, besides being a diamond-cutting center rivalling Amsterdam. Next to metallurgy, textiles are Belgium's leading manufacture, for which the once-flourishing towns of Flanders attained great fame. Historic BRUGES and GHENT, veritable treasure-houses of medieval and northern Renaissance architecture, manufacture celebrated lace, as do COURTRAI, Brussels, and MALINES (seat of R.C. primate). Ghent, though it has lost its front rank in trade and industry, is still a busy port and Belgium's chief center for cotton and linen goods. The woolen industry has its center at VERVIERS in the Ardennes. Carpet weaving, tanning, cement milling at TOURNAI (W). Other industrial products: beet sugar, alcohol, beer, pharmaceuticals, fertilizers, matches, leatherware, ceramics, glassware, crystal, bricks. Large fishing fleets are based on the coast. Belgium's communications are commensurate with its industry and large transit trade. There is a dense railroad net (3,080 mi.) consisting of a standard-gauge railroad which connects with all parts of Europe, besides narrow-gauge lines for interurban traffic. An intricate pattern of canals totaling c.1,100 mi., is woven across the plains. Among these are the ALBERT CANAL linking Liége with Antwerp, the Ghent-Terneuzen Canal (partly in the Netherlands), and the Willebroek Canal, which renders Brussels an inland port for vessels drawing up to 18 ft.; also, the canals from Brussels to Charleroi, and from Zeebrugge on North Sea to Bruges. Belgium's great art treasures, fine beaches, and resorts (e.g., SPA in HOHE VENN) bring it numerous tourists. Here, European oil-painting began at least as early as in Italy. The universities of LOUVAIN (founded 1426), Brussels, Ghent, and Liége are great Western centers of learning. The Belgians are almost evenly divided into 2 language groups by a line running roughly E-W below Brussels. N of this line the prevailing language is Flemish (a Low German dialect akin to Dutch); S of the line the prevailing language is French, the inhabitants speaking Walloon, a Fr. dialect; though Brussels is predominantly a Walloon-speaking enclave, it can generally be said to be bilingual. German is spoken in the E parts of Liége prov. Both Flemish and French are official languages. The R.C. church embraces virtually the entire pop. Belgium takes its name (in general use only since late 18th cent.) from the Belgae, a Celtic people of anc. Gaul mentioned by Julius Caesar. The Roman prov. Belgica was much larger than modern Belgium. The region was conquered (3d cent.) by the Franks. After the divisions (9th cent.) of Charlemagne's empire, Belgium was comprised in Lotharingia and later in the duchy of Lower Lorraine, which disintegrated in 12th cent. History of medieval Belgium is largely that of feudal states like the duchies of Brabant and Luxembourg, Flanders, Hainaut, Limburg, and the bishopric of Liége. It was then that such trading and textile cities as Ghent, Bruges, and YPRES rose, achieving virtual independence. In 15th cent. all present Belgium passed to duchy of Burgundy, which was soon absorbed by the Hapsburgs. Treaty of Campo Formio (1797) transferred Belgium from Austria to France; Treaty of Paris (1815) gave it to the Netherlands. After a revolt in 1830 Belgian independence was declared, and in 1831 Leopold I of Saxe-Coburg-Gotha became king of the Belgians. Final Dutch-Belgian peace treaty signed in 1839. Belgium received part of Limburg and Luxembourg, and had its perpetual neutrality guaranteed. King Leopold II assumed (1885) personal possession of the BELGIAN CONGO, which passed to Belgian administration as a colony in 1907. Germany invaded the country in both World Wars. After the First World War Belgium obtained MORESNET, EUPEN, and MALMÉDY, and, as a mandate of League of Nations, RUANDA-URUNDI, in Africa. It was again overrun in May, 1940; Leopold III surrendered unconditionally, but his cabinet continued in London. Liberation by Allied troops was effected in Sept., 1944. The unsuccessful German counteroffensive (Dec., 1944–Jan., 1945) in the Battle of the Bulge near Bastogne caused much destruction in addition to the damage wrought by Allied air raids. However, Belgian economy recovered far more rapidly than the rest of Europe, mainly on account of the contribution of the Belgian Congo during the war. Politically, the controversy over the return of Leopold was resolved when he abdicated in favor of his eldest son, Prince Baudouin. Belgium joined with the Netherlands and Luxembourg to form a customs union. This bloc, known as Benelux, signed (1948) with England and France a Five-Power Pact, participated in the European Recovery Program, and became (1949) partner to the North Atlantic Treaty. Also a member of the U.N. For further information see separate articles on provs., cities, towns, and physical features.

Belgium. 1 Village (pop. 493), Vermilion co., E Ill., 3 mi. S of Danville, in agr. and bituminous-coal-mining area. **2** Village (pop. 460), Ozaukee co., E Wis., 32 mi. N of Milwaukee; shoe mfg., vegetable canning.

Belgodère (bělgôdâr'), village (pop. 545), NW Corsica, 13 mi. ENE of Calvi; mispickel quarrying.

Belgorai, Poland: see BILGORAJ.

Belgorod (byěl'gŭrŭt), city (1926 pop. 31,036), S Kursk oblast, Russian SFSR, on the upper Northern Donets and 45 mi. NNW of Kharkov; rail junction; agr. center; fruit canning, flour milling, meat packing; brewery, metalworks; extensive chalk quarries. Founded 1593 as S outpost of Moscow domain. During Second World War, held (1941–43) by Germans.

Belgorod-Dnestrovski or **Belgorod-Dnestrovskiy** (–ŭdnyĭstrôf'skē), Rum. *Cetatea-Albă* (chĕtä'tyä-äl'bă) [=white city], former Rus. and Turkish *Akkerman* (ŭkyĭrmän'), anc. *Tyras*, city (1930 pop. 20,907; 1941 pop. 7,766), E Izmail oblast, Ukrainian SSR, in Bessarabia, on Dniester Liman and 25 mi. SW of Odessa; 46°12'N 30°22'E. Commercial center; fish canning, saltworking, agr. processing (meat, flour, fruit, wine, vegetable oils, vinegar). Has teachers col., archaeological mus., 14th-cent. Armenian church, and remains of 15th-cent. Genoese-Moldavian fortress (restored 1928). Founded (7th cent. B.C.) as anc. Milesian colony of Tyras; taken (4th cent. B.C.) by Macedonians and (A.D. c.50) by Romans. Abandoned during Barbarian invasions; settled (13th cent.) by Tatars; developed as a trading center with Armenian and Gr. pop.; became (14th cent.) a Genoese colony. Under Moldavian princes in 15th cent.; passed (1484) to Turks, who named it Akkerman, and (1812) to Russians. While in Rumania (1918–40; 1941–44), it was ⊙ Cetatea-Alba dept. (□ 2,932; 1930 pop. 341,176). Renamed Belgorod-Dnestrovski (1944), following Rus. recapture.

Belgrade (běl'grād). **1** Resort town (pop. 1,099), Kennebec co., S Maine, 13 mi. SW of Waterville; includes Belgrade Lakes and North Belgrade villages. Hq. for BELGRADE LAKES resort area. Settled 1774, inc. 1796. **2** Village (pop. 659), Stearns co., central Minn., c.40 mi. WSW of St. Cloud; livestock, grain, poultry area; dairy products, flour. **3** Town (pop. 663), Gallatin co., SW Mont., near Gallatin R., 10 mi. NW of Bozeman; flour; stock, dairy and poultry products. **4** Village (pop. 284), Nance co., E central Nebr., 10 mi. NNW of Fullerton and on Cedar R.; dairy produce, grain, livestock.

Belgrade (běl'grād, bělgrād'), Serbo-Croatian *Beograd* (bāô'grät) [=white town], anc. *Singidunum*, city (pop. 388,246), ⊙ Yugoslavia and Serbia, port on the Danube, at Sava R. mouth, on Paris-Istanbul RR and on internatl. highway; 44°48'N 20°28'E. Called, because of its strategic position, the key to the Balkans. Rail and road junction; E terminus of highway of Ljubljana (begun 1947, completed 1950); airport. Industrial center; mfg. of agr. machinery, electrical equipment, heavy machine tools (at ZELEZNIK), automobiles and aircraft (at RAKOVICA), shoes, woolen textiles, paper; sugar milling (dried beet pulp, molasses, confections, spodium), flour milling, meat packing, distilling, brewing; fish trade. Truck gardening in vicinity. Seat of univ. (founded 1863), R.C. archbishop, Orthodox Eastern patriarch. Has 19th-cent. palaces (one with art gall.), ethnographical mus. Kalemegdan [Turkish, =battlefield] Park has anc. and medieval remains and a military mus. In Topcider Park is country palace of Prince Milosh Obrenovich I; now hunter's mus. Near by is a monastery (at RAKOVICA) and memorial to Unknown Soldier on AVALA mtn. A bridge (nearly 1 mi. long) over the Danube links city with PANCEVO. Belgrade grew around fortifications built by Celts, Illyrians, and Romans; Decius b. (A.D. 201) and proclaimed emperor here. In early Middle Ages, Belgrade alternated bet. Bulgars, Byzantines, and Hungarians. In 14th cent., it passed to Serbia and became its capital. John Hunyadi and St. John Capistran repulsed a Turkish attack in 1456, but in 1521 Belgrade fell to the Turks, who made it their chief fortress in Europe. Austrians stormed it repeatedly (1688, 1717, 1789), but were able to keep it only for short periods, the longest from 1718 to 1739. Belgrade was scene (early-19th cent.) of Serbian insurrections, which led to final withdrawal (1867) of Turkish garrison. In First World War, Belgrade was occupied (1914, 1915–18) by Austrians. During Second World War, Belgrade was under Ger. occupation (1941–44) and suffered widespread damage, but it was quickly rebuilt. After the war, ZEMUN was joined with Belgrade and construction of Novi Beograd [Serbo-Croatian, =new Belgrade], a section bet. Zemun and city center, began; this section was former site of Ger. concentration camp and future site of government and univ. bldgs.

Belgrade Lakes, S Maine, group of stream-linked lakes in NW Kennebec co., at center of recreational area noted for canoeing, fishing. Include Great Pond (6 mi. long, 2–4 mi. wide), Long Pond (7 mi. long, c.1 mi. wide), Messalonskee L. (mě"sŭlŏn'skē) (10 mi. long, c.1 mi. wide), and smaller East, North, Ellis, and McGrath ponds.

Belgrano, for Argentine names not found here: see under GENERAL BELGRANO.

Belgrano. 1 Department, San Luis prov., Argentina: see VILLA GENERAL ROCA. **2** Department, Santa Fe prov., Argentina: see LAS ROSAS. **3** Department, Santiago del Estero prov., Argentina: see BANDERA.

Belgrano (bělgrä'nō), NW residential section of Buenos Aires, Argentina; favorite resort of foreign residents; parks, recreation grounds.

Belgrano, Cerro (sě'rō), Andean peak (7,800 ft.) in NW Santa Cruz natl. territory, Argentina, at S end of L. Pueyrredón; 47°42'S.

Belgrano, Lake (□ 26; alt. 2,323 ft.), in the Patagonian Andes, NW Santa Cruz natl. territory, Argentina, at 47°50'S, near Chile border; 9 mi. long.

Belgravia (bělgrā'vēŭ), fashionable residential district of London, England, 2 mi. SW of Charing Cross, bounded by Hyde Park (N), Buckingham Palace Gardens (E), Victoria Station (S), and Brompton (W).

Belgres, Belorussian SSR: see OREKHOVSK.

Belhaf, Aden: see BALHAF.

Belhaven (běl"hā'vŭn), town (pop. 2,528), Beaufort co., E N.C., 24 mi. E of Washington, on NW shore of Pungo R. estuary; fishing, fish canning, sawmilling.

Belhelvie (bělhěl'vē), agr. village and parish (pop. 1,514), E Aberdeen, Scotland, 7 mi. N of Aberdeen.

Belianes (bālyä'něs), village (pop. 1,047), Lérida prov., NE Spain, 13 mi. SW of Cervera; olive oil, cereals, almonds.

Beliatta, Ceylon: see TANGALLA.

Belice, Br. Honduras: see BELIZE.

Belice River (bělē'chě), anc. *Hypsas*, W Sicily, rises S of Piana dei Greci in 2 branches (each c.27 mi. long) joining E of Salaparuta, flows 19 mi. SW to the Mediterranean E of Marinella. Dam on upper right branch forms L. PIANA DEI GRECI.

Belich, Poland: see BIELSKO.

Belichi (byĭlyē'chē), W suburb (1939 pop. over 2,000) of Kiev, Ukrainian SSR, just N of Svyatoshino; summer resort. Rail settlement of Belichi at rail station (N).

Beli Drim River, Yugoslavia-Albania: see WHITE DRIN RIVER.

Bélignat (bālēnyä'), village (pop. 516), Ain dept., E France, in the Jura, 6 mi. N of Nantua; celluloid mfg. for OYONNAX plastics industry.

Beli Lom River, Bulgaria: see RUSENSKI LOM RIVER.

Beli Manastir (bě'lē mä'nästĭr), Hung. *Pélmonostor* (pāl'mônôshtôr), village (pop. 3,530), NE Croatia, Yugoslavia, 15 mi. N of Osijek, in the Baranja, near Hung. border; rail junction; trade center; meat packing, sugar milling (sugar, molasses, dried beet pulp), brick mfg.

Belin (bŭlē'), village (pop. 752), Gironde dept., SW France, on the Leyre and 26 mi. SSW of Bordeaux; woodworking, mfg. of resinous products.

Belinchón (bālēnchōn'), town (pop. 1,120), Cuenca prov., central Spain, on Madrid-Valencia highway and 40 mi. SE of Madrid, in agr. region (cereals, almonds, grapes, olives, sheep, goats). Has saltworks and medicinal springs.

Belington (bē'lĭngtŭn), city (pop. 1,699), Barbour co., N W.Va., on Tygart R. and 8 mi. NNW of Elkins, in agr., coal-mining, timber area; lumber milling and shipping. Inc. 1905. Civil War battle was fought on LAUREL RIDGE (E).

Belingwe (bělĭng'gwä), township (pop. 115), Gwelo prov., S central Southern Rhodesia, in Matabeleland, 90 mi. ESE of Bulawayo; livestock center (cattle, sheep, goats); corn. Gold deposits. Important asbestos mines in dist.

Belinskaya Kamenka, Russian SFSR: see KAMENKA, Penza oblast.

Belinski or **Belinskiy** (byĭlyēn'skē), city (1926 pop. 5,869), W Penza oblast, Russian SFSR, 65 mi. WSW of Penza; road center in grain-growing region; hemp, legumes; orchards. Mineral pigment and phosphorite deposits near by. Chartered 1780 and named Chembar; renamed 1948 for 19th-cent. Rus. critic b. here.

Beli Osam River, Bulgaria: see OSAM RIVER.

Belisce (bě'lĭshtyě), Serbo-Croatian *Belišće*, village, NE Croatia, Yugoslavia, on the Drava, on railroad and 13 mi. NW of Osijek, in Slavonia, near Hung. border; lumbering, tannin mfg., wood cracking. Fish ponds in vicinity.

Beli Timok River (bě'lē tē'môk) [Serbo-Croatian, = white Timok], E Serbia, Yugoslavia, formed by junction of 2 headstreams, Svrljiski Timok and Trgoviski Timok, just N of Knjazevac; flows c.30 mi. N, parallel to Bulg. border, joining the Crna Reka just NNE of Zajecar to form TIMOK RIVER.

Belitoeng or, **Belitong,** Indonesia: see BILLITON.

Belitsa (bělē'tsä), village (pop. 3,446), Gorna Dzhumaya dist., SW Bulgaria, on SE slope of Rila Mts., 7 mi. NE of Razlog; lumbering, flour milling; stock raising.

Belitung, Indonesia: see BILLITON.

Beliu (bělē'ōō), Hung. *Bél* (bāl), village (pop. 2,258), Arad prov., W Rumania, 38 mi. S of Oradea; has oldest glass factory in Rumania.

Belize (bŭlēz′), Sp. *Belice* (bälē′sä), district (□ 1,623, including 140 sq. mi. of cays; pop. 26,781) of central Br. Honduras; ⊙ Belize. Mostly level, it reaches to Maya Mts. (SW), and is drained by Belize and Sibun rivers. Dist. includes several lagoons and Corker, Ambergris, and Turneffe cays. Agr. (bananas, coconuts, rice, citrus fruit); mahogany lumbering; fisheries. Sawmilling at Belize.

Belize, Sp. *Belice,* town (pop. 21,884), ⊙ Br. Honduras and Belize dist., port on Caribbean Sea, at mouth of Belize R., and 860 mi. S of New Orleans; 17°29′N 88°12′W. Trading center for chicle, lumber, coconuts, rice, bananas, livestock (cattle, hogs); fisheries. Sawmilling, rice hulling; electric power plant. Site of Saint John Col., park, radio station, lighthouse, and customhouse; airport 10 mi. W. The region was settled, perhaps in mid-17th cent., by Englishmen who exploited the logwood (used in making dyes) found here. By early 18th cent. Belize was chief port of region. Fort George, on tip of a small peninsula, was built 1803.

Belize River, Sp. *Belice,* in Guatemala and Br. Honduras, rises as Mopán R. near Dolores (Guatemala), flows 180 mi. NE, past Benque Viejo, to Caribbean Sea at Belize. Navigable for small craft; carries lumber and chicle. Also called Old R. in Br. Honduras.

Belje (bĕ′lyĕ) or **Bilje** (bĭ′lyĕ), Hung. *Bellye* (bĕl′yĕ), village, NE Croatia, Yugoslavia, near Drava R., 4 mi. NE of Osijek, in the Baranja; dairy products.

Belkhatov, Poland: see BELCHATOW.

Belknap (bĕl′năp″), county (□ 401; pop. 26,632), central N.H.; ⊙ Laconia. Recreational and agr. area, with summer and winter resorts on L. Winnipesaukee; agr., mfg. (textiles, hosiery, wood products, mill machinery). Drained by Pemigewasset, Winnipesaukee, and Suncook rivers. Formed 1840.

Belknap, village (pop. 247), Johnson co., S Ill., near Cache R., 26 mi. NE of Cairo, in rich agr. area.

Belknap, Fort, Texas: see NEWCASTLE.

Belknap, Mount, peak (12,139 ft.) in Tushar Mts., SW central Utah, 30 mi. SW of Richfield.

Belknap Mountains, Belknap co., central N.H., small range in recreational area SW of L. Winnipesaukee; Belknap Mtn. (2,378 ft.) is highest peak.

Belkofski or **Belkofsky** (bĕlkŏf′skē), village (pop. 119), SW Alaska, near tip of Alaska Peninsula; 55°5′N 162°2′W; fur farming and trapping. Natives work at near-by fish canneries during summer.

Belkovski Island, Russian SFSR: see NEW SIBERIAN ISLANDS.

Bell. 1 County (□ 370; pop. 47,602), extreme SE Ky., in the Cumberlands; ⊙ Pineville. Bounded S by Tenn., SE by Va.; drained by Cumberland R. and its tributaries. Includes Pine Mtn. State Park, Pinnacle Mtn., Kentucky Ridge Forest, and parts of Cumberland Gap, Cudjo's Cave, and Fern L. Bituminous-coal-mining area, with limestone quarries, iron deposits, and some farms (dairy products, livestock, poultry, tobacco, fruit); some mfg. (chiefly at Middlesboro). Formed 1867 as Josh Bell co.; renamed bet. 1870 and 1880. **2** County (□ 1,079; pop. 73,824), central Texas; ⊙ Belton. Drained by Little, Leon, Lampasas rivers. Rich blacklands agr. area (cotton, corn, oats, grain sorghums, hay, broomcorn, pecans, fruit, truck); livestock (cattle, hogs, poultry); extensive dairying. Hunting, fishing. Chalk rock quarrying. Processing, mfg. at Temple, Belton. Includes part of U.S. Camp Hood. Co. formed 1850.

Bell. 1 Residential city (pop. 15,430), Los Angeles co., S Calif., 6 mi. SSE of downtown Los Angeles, in mfg. area; steel- and ironworking plants; mfg. of automobile and aircraft parts. Inc. 1927. **2** Town (pop. 108), Gilchrist co., N Fla., 33 mi. WNW of Gainesville.

Bella (bĕl′lä), town (pop. 3,915), Potenza prov., Basilicata, S Italy, 17 mi. WNW of Potenza; woolen mill.

Bella Bella, village, W B.C., on NW Denny Isl., on inlet of Hecate Strait, 170 mi. SSE of Prince Rupert; 52°9′N 128°8′W; fish canning, lumbering.

Bellac (bĕlăk′), town (pop. 3,455), Haute-Vienne dept., W central France, 22 mi. NNW of Limoges; road center; tanning and shoe mfg., wool spinning, cider making. Has 12th-14th-cent. church.

Bellaco (bĕyä′kō), village, Río Negro dept., W central Uruguay, on railroad and 38 mi. NE of Fray Bentos; wheat, corn, cattle, sheep.

Belladère (bĕlädĕr′), town (1950 census pop. 1,294), Ouest dept., E Haiti, near Dominican Republic border, 11 mi. ENE of Lascahobas; logwood, cattle. A model town with new agr. colony, Batiste, near by.

Bella Flor (bĕ′yä flōr′), village, Pando dept., NW Bolivia, on Tahuamanu R. and 12 mi. WSW of Puerto Rico, on road; rubber.

Bellagio (bĕl-lä′jō), village (pop. 864), Como prov., Lombardy, N Italy, port on N tip of promontory dividing L. Como into its 2 S arms, 15 mi. NNE of Como. Popular resort, with many villas and gardens, and 12th-cent. Romanesque church. Has artisan olivewood-carving industry.

Bellaire. 1 (bĕl″âr′) Village (pop. 693), ⊙ Antrim co., NW Mich., 25 mi. NE of Traverse City, near Bellaire L. (c.4 mi. long, 1½ mi. wide), in farm area (fruit, potatoes, vegetables); resort. **2** (bĕl″âr′) Residential section of E Queens borough of New York city, SE N.Y.; mfg. of conveyors. Belmont Park Race Track is near by. **3** (bĕl″âr′) City (pop. 12,573), Belmont co., E Ohio, 6 mi. SSW of Wheeling, W.Va., across Ohio R. (bridged); mfg. (glass products, enamelware, stoves, clay products, food products, caskets); coal mining. Settled c.1802. **4** (bŭlâr′) Suburb, Harris co., S Texas, SW residential section (pop. 10,178) of Houston, absorbed 1948 by Houston.

Bellaire Lake, Mich.: see BELLAIRE.

Bellamar Caves (bĕyämär′), large subterranean caverns, Matanzas prov., W Cuba, 1½ mi. SE of Matanzas, with an entrance at Matanzas Bay. Their extent is still unknown. Famed for their beautiful limestone stalactites and stalagmites. Best-known cavern is the Gothic Temple, 250 ft. long, 80 ft. wide.

Bellampalli, India: see BELAMPALLI.

Bellamy (bĕ′lŭmē), village (1940 pop. 539), Sumter co., W Ala., 18 mi. WSW of Demopolis; lumber.

Bellamy River, SE N.H., rises in Strafford co. W of Dover, flows SE c.15 mi., past Dover, to Great Bay.

Bellananagh, Ireland: see BALLINAGH.

Bellano (bĕl-lä′nō), village (pop. 2,381), Como prov., Lombardy, N Italy, port on E shore of L. Como, 14 mi. NNW of Lecco. Resort; silk and cotton mills, nail factory. Tommaso Grossi b. here.

Bellaria (bĕl-lä′rēä), town (pop. 3,584), Forlì prov., Emilia-Romagna, N central Italy, on the Adriatic, 8 mi. NNW of Rimini; bathing resort.

Bellarthur or **Bell Arthur,** town (pop. 190), Pitt co., E N.C., 6 mi. W of Greenville. Formerly Arthur.

Bellary (bĕ′lŭrē), district (□ 5,872; pop. 1,067,049), NW Madras, India; ⊙ Bellary. On Deccan Plateau; drained by Hagari R. Agr.: millet, cotton, oilseeds (extensive peanut growing). Fibers, bamboo, and gum arabic in dispersed forests. Important manganese mines near Sandur. Main towns: Bellary, Adoni, Hospet. Dam and power plant under construction on Tungabhadra R., near Hospet. Famous ruins of anc. city of Vijayanagar at village of Hampi. Original dist. (□ 5,714; pop. 1,051,235) enlarged 1949 by inc. of former Madras State of Sandur.

Bellary, city (pop. 56,148), ⊙ Bellary dist., NW Madras, India, 265 mi. NW of Madras. Rail junction (spur to Rayadrug); road and trade center in cotton-growing area; cotton, silk, and woolen goods; oilseed milling; tannery, distillery. Col., industrial school. Hq. of regional malaria control. Anc. fort (in city center) figured in 18th-cent. struggle bet. Deccan sultans and English. Experimental farm 9 mi. E, at village of Hagari.

Bella Tola (bĕl′lä tō′lä), mountain (9,935 ft.) in Valaisian Alps, S Switzerland, 5 mi. S of Leuk. Bella Tola Glacier and Pas de Boeuf lie near by.

Bella Unión (bĕ′yä ōōnyōn′), town (pop. 3,000), Artigas dept., NW Uruguay, on Uruguay R., opposite Monte Caseros (Argentina), and just SW of Cuareim (Brazil border), on railroad and highway, and 80 mi. NNE of Salto. Trade center; cereals, sugar cane, cattle, horses. Airport, customhouse. Until 1930s, Santa Rosa.

Bella Villa, town (pop. 557), St. Louis co., E Mo.

Bella Vista (bĕ″yä vē′stä). **1** Town (pop. 9,062), NE Buenos Aires prov., Argentina, 2 mi. SE of San Miguel; industrial center; alcohol distilling, brewing, mfg. of tires, carpets, textiles. Also called Teniente General Pablo Riccheri. **2** Town (pop. 8,197), ⊙ Bella Vista dept. (□ c.600; pop. 23,681), W Corrientes prov., Argentina, port on Paraná R., on railroad and 70 mi. S of Corrientes. Commercial and agr. center; ships tobacco, citrus fruit. Mfg. (agr.-equipment works, sawmills); agr. (oranges, corn, cotton, tobacco, manioc, livestock). **3** Town (1947 pop. 8,475), central Tucumán prov., Argentina, 15 mi. SSW of Tucumán; rail junction, agr. center (sugar cane, oranges, corn, alfalfa, livestock); sugar refineries.

Bella Vista, Brazil: see BELA VISTA.

Bellavista, village (1930 pop. 879), Concepción prov., S central Chile, 14 mi. NNE of Concepción; woolens.

Bella Vista, town (pop. 498), Chiapas, S Mexico, in Sierra Madre, 19 mi. N of Motozintla; sugar, fruit. San Pedro Remate until 1934.

Bellavista, processing center (pop. 1,366), Nayarit, W Mexico, N suburb of Tepic, in rich agr. region.

Bella Vista, town (dist. pop. 5,774), Amambay dept., E Paraguay, on Apa R., opposite Bela Vista (Brazil), and 50 mi. NW of Pedro Juan Caballero. Cattle-raising center. Airport. Founded 1902.

Bellavista. 1 Village (pop. 140), Cajamarca dept., NW Peru, at E slopes of Cordillera Occidental, on Marañón R. and 8 mi. ENE of Jaén; wheat, corn, sugar cane; cattle raising. **2** Town (pop. 8,273), Callao constitutional prov., W central Peru, residential suburb on the Pacific, just SE of Callao. Has large Anglo-Amer. colony. La Perla bathing resort and the president's residence are near by (S). **3** Town (pop. 1,650), San Martín dept., N central Peru, landing on Huallaga R. and 18 mi. ESE of Saposoa; sugar cane, cotton, coca, rice, tobacco are grown.

Bella Vista (bĕ′lŭ vĭ′stŭ), resort village, Benton co., extreme NW Ark., 4 mi. N of Bentonville, in the Ozarks; mineral springs.

Bellbird, town (pop. 1,502), E New South Wales, Australia, 27 mi. W of Newcastle; coal mining.

Bellbrook, village (pop. 425), Greene co., S central Ohio, 10 mi. SE of Dayton, near Little Miami R.

Bell Buckle, town (pop. 341), Bedford co., central Tenn., 10 mi. NE of Shelbyville, in rich farm area. Seat of Webb School.

Bellcaire de Urgel (bălkī′rä dhä ōōrhĕl′), village (pop. 1,255), Lérida prov., NE Spain, 6 mi. SE of Balaguer, near the Urgel Canal; olive-oil processing; trades in wine, sugar beets, alfalfa.

Bell Center, village (pop. 195), Crawford co., SW Wis., near Kickapoo R., 23 mi. NE of Prairie du Chien; stock raising, dairying.

Bell City, city (pop. 482), Stoddard co., SE Mo., in Mississippi flood plain, 10 mi. SW of Oran.

Belle. 1 Town (pop. 906), Maries co., central Mo., in the Ozarks, near Gasconade R., 32 mi. SE of Jefferson City; agr.; fire clay, iron mines. **2** Village (1940 pop. 1,993), Kanawha co., W W.Va., on Kanawha R. and 10 mi. SE of Charleston; makes ammonia, nylon, and other coal- and salt-derived chemical products.

Belleair (bĕlâr′), town (pop. 961), Pinellas co., W Fla., a S suburb of Clearwater.

Belle-Alliance, La, Belgium: see WATERLOO.

Belleau Wood (bĕ′lō, Fr. bĕlō′), Aisne dept., N France, 5 mi. WNW of Château-Thierry; captured by American forces (June, 1918) in First World War. Renamed *Bois de la Brigade de Marine* by the French in honor of a brigade of Marines fighting with U.S. 2d Div. In 1923 it was dedicated as permanent memorial to American war dead; it is owned by U.S. Government. Aisne-Marne American Cemetery (just S of Belleau village) has 2,288 graves.

Belle Ayr Mountain, Ulster co., SE N.Y., peak (c.3,300 ft.) of the Catskills, near Pine Hill and NW of Kingston; skiing center, with chair ski-lift.

Belle Bay, NE arm of FORTUNE BAY, S N.F.

Belle Center, village (pop. 889), Logan co., W central Ohio, 10 mi. N of Bellefontaine; butter, cheese; limestone.

Bellechasse (bĕlshăs′), county (□ 653; pop. 23,676), SE Que., on Maine border, on the St. Lawrence; ⊙ St. Raphael.

Belledonne (bĕldôn′), mountain range of Dauphiné Alps, in Isère and Savoie depts., SE France, extending c.40 mi. SSW from Maurienne valley to lower Romanche R. valley, paralleled E by the Grandes-Rousses range and W by low Grésivaudan valley. Rises to 9,781 ft. at the Grand-Pic de Belledonne. Average alt. 8,000 ft., with no low passes. Hydroelectric and metallurgical plants near Allevard. Spa of Uriage on SW slopes.

Belleek (bŭlēk′), town (pop. 781), NW Co. Fermanagh, Northern Ireland, on Erne R. and 12 mi. S of Donegal; frontier station on Irish border; pottery-mfg. center, famous for Belleek ware; trout fishing.

Belleflower, village (pop. 413), McLean co., E central Ill., 25 mi. ESE of Bloomington, in rich agr. area.

Bellefontaine, Algeria: see MÉNERVILLE.

Bellefontaine. 1 (bĕlfŏn′tĭn) Village (1940 pop. 144), Webster co., central Miss., 50 mi. E of Greenwood. **2** (bĕlfoun′tĭn, –fŏn′–) City (pop. 10,232), ⊙ Logan co., W central Ohio, 30 mi. N of Springfield; trade and railroad center for agr. area; motor vehicles, printed matter, heating apparatus, furniture, food products. Laid out 1820. Campbell Hill (1,550 ft.), highest point in Ohio, is just E.

Bellefonte (bĕl″fŏnt′). **1** Residential town (pop. 1,472), New Castle co., N Del., just NE of Wilmington on Delaware R. Inc. 1915. **2** Borough (pop. 5,651), ⊙ Centre co., central Pa., 44 mi. SW of Williamsport; mtn. resort; limestone quarries; brass, metal products, matches, flour, feed; agr. Laid out 1795, inc. 1806.

Belle Fourche (bĕl′ fōōsh′), city (pop. 3,540), ⊙ Butte co., W S.Dak., 50 mi. NW of Rapid City, at confluence of Redwater Creek and Belle Fourche R., near Orman (Belle Fourche) dam. Shipping center for cattle and sheep; flour, wool, beet sugar, dairy products, bricks and tiles, bentonite; wheat, alfalfa. Black Hills Round-up takes place here annually. Settled 1878, inc. 1903.

Belle Fourche Reservoir, W S.Dak., N of Black Hills; 10 mi. long, 3 mi. wide; irrigates c.75,000 acres. Formed by Belle Fourche Dam (6,262 ft. long, 112 ft. high; earth fill; completed 1911), on small Owl Creek, which holds flood waters (received via canal) of **Belle Fourche River.** River rises in Campbell co., NE Wyo.; flows c.290 mi. NE and E, past Belle Fourche, to Cheyenne R.

Bellegarde (bĕlgärd′). **1** or **Bellegarde-sur-Valserine** (–sür-välsürēn′), town (pop. 5,345), Ain dept., E France, on the Rhone (at mouth of small Valserine R.) and 17 mi. SW of Geneva, in the Jura; railroad custom station. Diversified industrial center with chemical and light metallurgical plants, paper and cotton mills, and tanneries. Produces pharmaceuticals, straw hats, and lithographic work. Has 2 hydroelectric plants. The former Perte du Rhône (narrow chasm in which the river all but disappeared) has been engulfed by a reservoir which has drowned the valley above GÉNISSIAT dam (3 mi. S). **2** Town (pop. 2,026), Gard dept., S France, on Rhone-Sète Canal and 9 mi. SE of Nîmes; winegrowing center. Cementworks. **3** or **Bellegarde-du-Loiret** (–dü-lwärā'), village (pop. 1,131), Loiret dept., N central France, 13 mi. W of Montargis; refractories. Has Romanesque church.

Bellegarde-du-Loiret, France: see BELLEGARDE, Loiret dept.

Bellegarde-en-Marche (–ā-märsh'), village (pop. 409), Creuse dept., central France, 6 mi. ENE of Aubusson; cattle and sheep raising.

Bellegarde-sur-Valserine, France: see BELLEGARDE, Ain dept.

Bellegem (bĕ'lŭkhĕm), agr. village (pop. 3,294), West Flanders prov., W Belgium, 4 mi. S of Courtrai; flax growing. Formerly spelled Belleghem.

Belleghem, Belgium: see BELLEGEM.

Belle Glade, town (pop. 7,219), Palm Beach co., SE Fla., 39 mi. W of West Palm Beach, near S tip of L. Okeechobee; trade and shipping center for large truck-farming region; canning, ramie processing. In 1928 a hurricane devastated the town. Near by are the Everglades Experiment Station and the state prison farm. Founded c.1925, inc. 1928.

Belle Glade-Chosen, Fla.: see CHOSEN.

Belle Harbor, SE N.Y., a residential section of S Queens borough of New York city, on Rockaway Peninsula, in shore-resort area.

Belle Haven or **Bellehaven,** town (pop. 453), Accomack co., E Va., on Eastern Shore, 37 mi. SSW of Pocomoke City, Md.

Belle-Île or **Belle-Île-en-Mer** (bĕl-ēl'-ā-mâr'), Breton *Enez ar Gerveur,* island (□ 32; pop. 4,670) in N Bay of Biscay, off coast of Brittany, W France, 8 mi. S of Quiberon Peninsula; administratively part of Morbihan dept.; 11 mi. long, 6 mi. wide. Fishing and sardine canning. Resort area noted for spectacular marine cliffs and caves. Chief villages are Le Palais (port) and Sauzon on N shore. Sarah Bernhardt's residence near NW tip. Privately owned until 1718. Held by English 1761–63, then exchanged in peace treaty for Nova Scotia. Sometimes spelled Belle-Isle.

Belle Isle (bĕlīl') (□ 20; inhabited in fishing season only), off N N.F., at N entrance of the Strait of Belle Isle, 30 mi. ENE of Cape Norman; 10 mi. long, 3 mi. wide; rises to 660 ft. At N extremity is Misery Point lighthouse (52°1'N 55°17'W).

Belle-Isle, France: see BELLE-ÎLE.

Belle Isle (bĕl" īl'), town (1940 pop. 178), Orange co., central Fla., suburb of Orlando.

Belle Isle. 1 Island, one of the Five Isls., in St. Mary parish, S La., a salt dome (alt. c.130 ft.) rising above sea marshes on N shore of Atchafalaya Bay, c.40 mi. SE of New Iberia. Oil and natural-gas wells near by. **2** Island, SE Mich., in Detroit R. at Detroit; c.2 mi. long, 1 mi. wide. Recreation park (bathing, boating, riding); symphony shell, zoological gardens, aquarium, rose gardens. **3** Island, Va.: see RICHMOND.

Belle Isle, Strait of, N entrance to Gulf of St. Lawrence, bet. N.F. and Labrador; 60 mi. long, 10–15 mi. wide. Has strong tidal current and is free of rocks and shoals. During winter months ice forms here; in summer icebergs drift through strait.

Belle-Isle-en-Terre (bĕl-ēl-ā-târ'), village (pop. 949), Côtes-du-Nord dept., W France, 11 mi. W of Guincamp; paper and cider milling.

Bellem (bĕ'lŭm), agr. village (pop. 1,580), East Flanders prov., NW Belgium, 10 mi. WNW of Ghent.

Bellême (bĕlĕm'), village (pop. 1,515), Orne dept., NW France, 10 mi. S of Mortagne, in the wooded Perche hills; road junction; agr. equipment mfg., sawmilling. Anc. stronghold of counts of Alençon.

Belle Meade, city (pop. 2,831), Davidson co., N central Tenn., residential suburb SW of Nashville.

Bellencombre (bĕlākō'brŭ), village (pop. 357), Seine-Inférieure dept., N France, 16 mi. SSE of Dieppe; sawmilling.

Bellenden-Ker Range (bĕ'lŭndŭn-kûr'), NE Queensland, Australia, extends c.40 mi. NE from Nerada to Pacific coast near Cairns. Mt. Bartle Frere, highest peak (5,438 ft.) of state, here.

Belle Plaine. 1 City (pop. 3,056), Benton co., E central Iowa, near Iowa R., 32 mi. WSW of Cedar Rapids; railroad division point; corn canning, cement-block mfg. Platted 1861, inc. 1863. **2** City (pop. 971), Sumner co., S Kansas, near Arkansas R., 22 mi. S of Wichita, in wheat region; cottonwood timber. **3** Borough (pop. 1,708), Scott co., S Minn., on Minnesota R. and 35 mi. SW of Minneapolis, in livestock, grain, poultry region; dairy products, flour. Platted 1853.

Belle Prairie, town (pop. 82), Hamilton co., SE Ill., 38 mi. SE of Centralia, in rich agr. area.

Bellerium, England: see LAND'S END.

Bellerive (bĕlrēv'), town (pop. 2,350), SE Tasmania, 2 mi. E of Hobart across Derwent R. estuary; sawmills.

Belle Rive (bĕl rēv'), village (pop. 313), Jefferson co., S Ill., 10 mi. SE of Mount Vernon, in agr. area.

Bellerive, town (pop. 180), St. Louis co., E Mo., near Mississippi R., 10 mi. W of St. Louis.

Belle River, village (pop. 999), S Ont., on S shore of L. St. Clair, 15 mi. E of Windsor; dairying, mixed farming.

Belle River, E Mich., rises near Imlay City in Lapeer co., flows c.65 mi. SE, past Memphis, to St. Clair R. at Marine City.

Bellerive-sur-Allier (bĕlrēv'-sür-älyā'), W suburb (pop. 3,246) of Vichy, on left bank of Allier R., Allier dept., central France; has mineral springs and an intermittent geyser.

Bellerose (bĕl'rōz), village (pop. 1,134), Nassau co., SE N.Y., on W Long Isl., just W of Floral Park; mfg. (screens, shades, wood products). Belmont Park Race Track is near by. Settled 1908, inc. 1924.

Belle Terre (bĕl" târ'), summer-resort village (pop. 120), Suffolk co., SE N.Y., on N shore of Long Isl., overlooking Port Jefferson Harbor and just N of Port Jefferson.

Belle Valley, village (pop. 458), Noble co., E Ohio, 17 mi. S of Cambridge, and on small Duck Creek, in livestock area; coal mining.

Belle Vernon or **Bellevernon** (bĕlvûr'nŭn), borough (pop. 2,271), Fayette co., SW Pa., 23 mi. S of Pittsburgh and on Monongahela R.; glass; bituminous coal. Laid out 1813, inc. 1863.

Belleview, town (pop. 595), Marion co., N central Fla., 10 mi. SSE of Ocala; packing houses (citrus fruit, truck), citrus-fruit cannery.

Belleville, city (pop. 15,710), ⊙ Hastings co., SE Ont., on Bay of Quinte of L. Ontario, at mouth of Moira R., 45 mi. W of Kingston; meat packing, dairying, mfg. of machinery, optical equipment, locks, cement, industrial alcohol, radios. Airport. Site of Albert Col. (founded 1854, chartered 1857), affiliated with Univ. of Toronto.

Belleville (bĕlvēl'). **1** An E quarter of Paris, France, comprised in 20th *arrondissement.* **2** Village (pop. 922), Meurthe-et-Moselle dept., NE France, on left bank of Moselle R. and 10 mi. NNW of Nancy; foundries. **3** or **Belleville-sur-Saône** (–sür-sōn), town (pop. 2,663), Rhône dept., E central France, near the Saône, 8 mi. N of Villefranche; noted winegrowing and trading center; produces tools and sprayers for vineyards; barrel making. Has 12th-cent. Romanesque church.

Belleville (bĕl'vĭl). **1** Town (pop. 372), Yell co., W central Ark., 22 mi. SW of Russellville, near Petit Jean R. **2** City (pop. 32,721), ⊙ St. Clair co., SW Ill., just SE of East St. Louis; industrial and railroad center within St. Louis metropolitan area. Mfg.: stoves; clay, metal, and enamel products; clothing, food products, shoes, brick, concrete blocks, chemicals, mining machinery, drinking fountains, beverages, office equipment, leather products. Bituminous-coal mines, clay, sand deposits near by. Has a jr. col. Scott Air Force Base is in vicinity. Platted 1815, inc. 1819. **3** City (pop. 2,858), ⊙ Republic co., N Kansas, 18 mi. N of Concordia; trade center for corn, wheat, and livestock area; also dairy products, poultry. Annual state fair is held here in fall. Founded 1869, inc. 1878. **4** City (pop. 1,722), Wayne co., SE Mich., on Huron R. and 24 mi. SW of Detroit, in diversified agr. area; resort. Settled 1826; inc. as village 1905, as city 1946. **5** Town (pop. 32,019), Essex co., NE N.J., on Passaic R. just N of Newark; mfg. (leather, machinery, electrical equipment, tools, rubberized materials, chemicals, food products). Steam engine built here (1798) for John Stevens' steamboat, which ran bet. Passaic and New York. Settled c.1680, set off from Newark 1839, inc. 1910. **6** Village (pop. 1,304), Mifflin co., central Pa., 8 mi. W of Lewistown, in rich agr. area. **7** Village (pop. 735), Dane and Green cos., S Wis., on Sugar R. and 17 mi. SSW of Madison, in farm area; processes dairy products.

Belleville-sur-Meuse (bĕlvĕl'-sür-mûz'), N suburb (pop. 2,199) of Verdun, Meuse dept., NE France; limekilns, quarries. Formed part of Verdun fortifications in First World War.

Belleville-sur-Saône, France: see BELLEVILLE, Rhône dept.

Bellevue (bĕlvü'), village (pop. 1,199), Oran dept., NW Algeria, on the Chéliff and 14 mi. NE of Mostaganem; winegrowing.

Bellevue (bĕl'vū). **1** City (pop. 528), Blaine co., S central Idaho, 5 mi. SE of Hailey and on Big Wood R.; alt. 5,175 ft. Agr., livestock. **2** Village (pop. 1,529), Peoria co., N central Ill., just W of Peoria. Inc. 1941. **3** Town (pop. 1,932), Jackson co., E Iowa, on Mississippi R. (lock and dam here) and 21 mi. SE of Dubuque; mfg. (hydrotherapy equipment, washing machines). Clay pits and limestone quarry near by. Bellevue State Park and U.S. fish hatchery are here. Settled 1830s, inc. 1844. **4** City (pop. 9,040), Campbell co., N Ky., on left bank (levee) of the Ohio opposite Cincinnati, bet. Newport and Dayton, Ky.; mfg. of metal cabinets, auto lamps, sheet metal, plastic products, roofing, watch crystals. **5** Fishing village (pop. c.150), Talbot co., E Md., 11 mi. NNW of Cambridge and on Tred Avon R. (ferry to Oxford); cans vegetables, fruit, seafood. **6** Village (pop. 1,168), Eaton co., S central Mich., on the Battle Creek and 12 mi. NE of Battle Creek city, in farm area (grain, corn, beans); cement mfg.; grain elevator. Settled 1830; inc. 1867. **7** Village (pop. 3,858), Sarpy co., E Nebr., 10 mi. S of Omaha and on Missouri R. Oldest town in state; once seat of territorial govt., site of Presbyterian Mission completed 1848. Cemetery and church, here, oldest in Nebr. Established as trading post c.1823, inc. 1855. **8** City (pop. 6,906), on Huron-Sandusky co. line, N Ohio, 13 mi. SW of Sandusky; railroad junction (with repair shops) in agr. area (cherries, grain, livestock); electrical products, auto accessories, machinery, food products. Limestone quarries. Seneca Caverns are near by. Named Bellevue in 1839. **9** Residential borough (pop. 11,604), Allegheny co., SW Pa., on Ohio R. just NW of Pittsburgh. Settled 1802, inc. 1867. **10** Town (pop. 418), Clay co., N Texas, 33 mi. SE of Wichita Falls; market, trade point in agr. area (cotton, grain, peanuts).

Bellevue Mountain, peak (12,350 ft.) in Rocky Mts., Gunnison co., W central Colo.

Belley (bĕlā'), town (pop. 3,762), Ain dept., E France, in the S Jura, near the Rhone, 17 mi. NW of Chambéry; produces gaskets and pipe joints; cotton weaving, tanning, wine trading. Seat of a bishop.

Bellflower. 1 Town (1940 pop. 11,425), Los Angeles co., S Calif., 14 mi. SE of downtown Los Angeles; truck, flowers, dairy products. **2** Town (pop. 226), Montgomery co., E central Mo., near West Fork of Cuivre R., 8 mi. E of Montgomery City.

Bell Gardens, suburb (1940 pop. 6,879), Los Angeles co., S Calif., in industrial dist. SE of downtown Los Angeles, near Bell.

Bellglade Camp, village (pop. 1,497), Palm Beach co., SE Fla.

Bellheim (bĕl'hīm), village (pop. 4,490), Rhenish Palatinate, W Germany, 7 mi. E of Landau; woodworking, brewing. Grain, sugar beets, tobacco.

Bellicourt (bĕlēkōōr'), agr. village (pop. 527), Aisne dept., N France, 8 mi. NNW of Saint-Quentin. Captured by Americans Sept.,1918. Near-by memorial commemorates American soldiers who fought with the British in First World War. Bellicourt Tunnel (4 mi. long) of Saint-Quentin Canal was Ger. stronghold in Hindenburg Line.

Bellingen (bĕ'lĭnjŭn), town (pop. 1,248), E New South Wales, Australia, 180 mi. NNE of Newcastle; dairying center. Arsenic ore mined near by.

Bellingham (bĕ'lĭnjŭm), town and parish (pop. 1,287), central Northumberland, England, on North Tyne R. and 14 mi. NW of Hexham; coal mining.

Bellingham (bĕ'lĭng-hăm"). **1** Town (pop. 4,100), Norfolk co., S Mass., 20 mi. SE of Worcester; woolens. Settled c.1713, inc. 1719. Includes South Bellingham village (pop. 1,919). **2** Village (pop. 388), Lac qui Parle co., SW Minn., near S.Dak. line, 10 mi. NNW of Madison, in grain area; dairy products. **3** Port city (pop. 34,112), ⊙ Whatcom co., NW Wash., on Bellingham Bay and 80 mi. N of Seattle. Shipping, processing, and industrial center for region producing fruit, truck, poultry, dairy products, lumber, paper, coal, fish. Port of entry. Gateway to Mt. Baker Natl. Forest recreational area (E). Seat of state teachers col. L. Whatcom (9 mi. long) is just SE; Lummi Indian Reservation is near by. Settled 1852 as Whatcom, merged (1903) with 3 other towns and became Bellingham.

Bellingshausen Island (bĕ'lĭngs-hou"zŭn) or **Motu One** (mō'tōō ō'nā), uninhabited atoll, Leeward group, Society Isls., Fr. Oceania, S Pacific, 150 mi. W of Bora-Bora; owned by Fr. copra company.

Bellingshausen Sea, part of the South Pacific bordering Antarctica, W of base of Palmer Peninsula bet. Alexander I Isl. and Thurston Peninsula. Named for Thaddeus von Bellingshausen, commander of Russian expedition of 1819–21 which discovered Alexander I Isl.

Bellingwolde (bĕ'lĭng-vôldŭ), village (pop. 1,913), Groningen prov., NE Netherlands, 5 mi. ESE of Winschoten; potato-flour milling; peat production.

Bellinzago Novarese (bĕlēnzä'gô nôvärä'zĕ), village (pop. 4,722), Novara prov., Piedmont, N Italy, 8 mi. N of Novara.

Bellinzona (bĕl'lĕnzō'nä), town (1950 pop. 12,073), ⊙ Ticino canton, S Switzerland, on Ticino R., 7 mi. ENE of E shore of Lago Maggiore, 6 mi. from Ital. border. Roads lead N to St. Gotthard, Lukmanier, and San Bernardino passes. Metal- and woodworking, printing; beer, cement products, hats. Has three 15th-cent. castles of dukes of Milan, two 16th-cent. churches, and remains of Murata wall which barred (c.1500) the Ticino valley. Possibly a Roman settlement, Bellinzona belonged at times to Lombardy, Como, Milan, France, and the Four Forest Cantons.

Bell Island (8 mi. long, 2–3 mi. wide), SE Alaska, in Alexander Archipelago, in Behm Canal, N of Revillagigedo Isl., 40 mi. N of Ketchikan; 55°57'N 131°29'W; has hot-springs health resort.

Bell Island (□ 11; pop. 8,167), SE N.F., in Conception Bay, 13 mi. WNW of St. John's, 3 mi. off Avalon Peninsula; 6 mi. long, 3 mi. wide, with rocky coastline and high cliffs. Here are large iron-ore deposits; mine levels run out under the sea. Ore is shipped from village of Bell Island (pop. 7,020), on NW coast of isl., to Sydney, N.S., and to England. Fishing and subsistence agr. are carried on. Another Bell Isl. is off N N.F.: see GREY ISLANDS.

Belliso Solfare (bĕl-lē'zô sôlfä'rĕ), village (pop. 1,326), Ancona prov., The Marches, central Italy, 7 mi. NNW of Sassoferrato. Sulphur mines near.

Bell-Lloch (bāl-lôk,-yôk), village (pop. 1,577), Lérida prov., NE Spain, 8 mi. E of Lérida; olive-oil processing, linen mfg.; livestock, cereals.

Bellmawr (bĕl″mär′), residential borough (pop. 5,213), Camden co., SW N.J., 5 mi. S of Camden. Inc. 1926.

Bellmont, village (pop. 368), Wabash co., SE Ill., 8 mi. W of Mount Carmel, in agr. area.

Bellmore, residential village (1940 pop. 6,793), Nassau co., SE N.Y., near S shore of Long Isl., 8 mi. SE of Mineola; mfg. (clothing, chemicals, scientific instruments, celluloid, wood and metal products, boats). Summer resort.

Bello (bĕ′yō), town (pop. 8,180), Antioquia dept., NW central Colombia, on Porce R., on railroad and 6 mi. N of Medellín, in agr. region (sugar cane, coffee, corn, yucca, cattle); alt. 4,987 ft. Textile-milling center; mfg. of brushes.

Bello (bā′lyō), village (pop. 1,299), Teruel prov., E Spain, 14 mi. SSW of Daroca; cereals, wine, saffron, sheep.

Bello Horizonte, Brazil: see BELO HORIZONTE.

Bello Jardim, Brazil: see BELO JARDIM.

Bellot (bĕlō′), village (pop. 323), Seine-et-Marne dept., N central France, on the Petit-Morin and 14 mi. SSW of Château-Thierry; horse breeding.

Bellot Strait, arctic channel (30 mi. long, 2–8 mi. wide), S Franklin Dist., Northwest Territories, bet. Boothia Peninsula (S) and Somerset Isl. (N); 72°N 94°30′W. Connects Gulf of Boothia and Prince Regent Inlet (E) with Peel Sound and Franklin Strait (W). N shore rises steeply to c.1,500 ft., S shore to c.2,500 ft. Fort Ross trading post, on N shore, was established 1937. Bellot Strait is keystone of the Northwest Passage; it was discovered (1852) by Lt. Joseph Réné Bellot while searching for the Franklin expedition. First crossed from W by Hudson's Bay Co. ship *Aklavik* in 1937.

Bellovacum, France: see BEAUVAIS.

Bellows Falls, industrial village (pop. 3,881) of Rockingham town, Windham co., SE Vt., on terraces above the Connecticut (2 bridges) and 20 mi. N of Brattleboro. Makes paper (industry begun 1802), farm machinery, shoes, wood products; railroad center; ships dairy products. Navigation canal, said to have been 1st begun (1792) in U.S., was completed 1802 around 50-ft. falls here; used for some time after arrival of railroad (1849; 1st in Vt.) and rebuilt (1926–28) as part of hydro-electric power development. First bridge over Connecticut R. here (1785).

Bellport, summer-resort village (pop. 1,449), Suffolk co., SE N.Y., on S shore of Long Isl., on Bellport Bay (inlet of Great South Bay), 4 mi. ESE of Patchogue.

Bellpuig (bālpōōch′), town (pop. 2,566), Lérida prov., NE Spain, 14 mi. WSW of Cervera, near Urgel Canal; olive-oil and wine processing; in well-irrigated agr. area (livestock, cereals, almonds, sugar beets, alfalfa). Has old castle of Anglesolas and a 12th-cent. convent (completely restored) with 16th-cent. cloisters. In church is monument (1525) of Ramón de Cardona.

Bellreguart (bālrĕgwärt′), village (pop. 2,879), Valencia prov., E Spain, 2 mi. SSE of Gandía; mfg. (bonnets, tiles); truck products; mulberry trees.

Bell Rock or **Inchcape Rock,** sandstone reef in North Sea, off coast of Angus, Scotland, 12 mi. SE of Arbroath; site of lighthouse (56°26′N 2°23′W) built 1807–11 by Robert Stevenson. According to legend the abbot of Arbroath had 120-ft. tower built here, with bell rung by motion of the water; bell was stolen by the pirate Ralph the Rover, who was later wrecked and drowned here, as related in Southey's *Ballad of Inchcape Rock.*

Bells. 1 Town (pop. 1,225), Crockett co., W Tenn., on South Fork of Forked Deer R. and 16 mi. WNW of Jackson; rail junction; shipping point for cotton, strawberries, tomatoes. **2** Town (pop. 614), Grayson co., N Texas, 11 mi. E of Sherman, in agr. area.

Bellshill (bĕlz-hĭl′), town in Old Monkland parish, N Lanark, Scotland, 9 mi. ESE of Glasgow; coal mining, mfg. of electrical switchgear. Near by are red sandstone quarries.

Bell Sound, Nor. *Bellsund,* inlet (15 mi. long, 10 mi. wide) of Arctic Ocean, SW West Spitsbergen, Spitsbergen group; 77°40′N 14°25′E. Extends several arms: VAN MIJEN FJORD (E), Van Keulen Fjord (SE), and Recherche Fjord (S). Receives several glaciers.

Bellton, town (pop. 266), Hall and Banks cos., NE Ga., 12 mi. NE of Gainesville.

Belluno (bĕl-lōō′nō), province (□ 1,423; pop. 216,333), Veneto, N Italy, bordering Austria on NE; ⊙ Belluno. Consists largely of E Dolomites and W Carnic Alps. Drained by Piave, Cordevole, Boite, and Cismon rivers. Stock raising (cattle, sheep) and forestry predominate. Agr. (corn, potatoes, beans, fruit) chiefly around Belluno and Feltre. Tourist resorts (Cortina d'Ampezzo, Auronzo) in the Dolomites. Hydroelectric plants near Lago di Santa Croce. Copper mining at Agordo. Mfg. at Feltre and Belluno.

Belluno, town (pop. 10,083), ⊙ Belluno prov., Veneto, N Italy, on Piave R. and 50 mi. N of Venice; 46°9′N 12°13′E. Tourist center near resort area of the Dolomites. Mfg. (electrical apparatus, furniture, liquor, soap). Bishopric. Has 16th-cent. cathedral, early Renaissance palace, and mus. Ruled by Venice from 1420 to 1797. Occupied (1917–18) by Austrians in First World War.

Bell Ville (bĕl vēl′), city (pop. 16,130), ⊙ Unión dept. (□ c.5,300; pop. 88,303), E Córdoba prov., Argentina, on the Río Tercero and 120 mi. SE of Córdoba. Agr., processing, and educational center. Cement products, frozen meat, dairy products, malt extracts, soap. Handles wheat, corn, oats, flax, livestock. Has professional and agr. schools.

Bellville, town (pop. 9,963), SW Cape Prov., U. of So. Afr., 10 mi. E of Cape Town, in wheat-growing region; metalworking; mfg. of machinery, fertilizer.

Bellville. 1 Village (pop. 1,355), Richland co., N central Ohio, 10 mi. S of Mansfield, and on Clear Fork of Mohican R., in agr. area (grain, fruit, potatoes, dairy products); greenhouses. Settled 1809, platted 1815, inc. 1841. **2** City (pop. 2,112), ⊙ Austin co., S Texas, c.55 mi. WNW of Houston; trade, shipping point in farm area; cotton ginning, poultry packing and hatching, dairying; machine shops. Oil field near. Settled 1847, inc. 1927.

Bellvís (bālvēs′), town (pop. 2,332), Lérida prov., NE Spain, 14 mi. ENE of Lérida; agr. trade (cereals, sugar beets, olive oil, wine); sheep raising.

Bellwood. 1 Town (pop. 263), Geneva co., SE Ala., near Choctawhatchee R., 24 mi. WSW of Dothan. **2** Village (pop. 8,746), Cook co., NE Ill., W suburb of Chicago, in agr. area (grain, truck, livestock; dairy products); mfg. (radio parts, metal products, electrical appliances, wood products). Stone quarries. Inc. 1900. **3** Village (pop. 389), Butler co., E Nebr., 45 mi. NW of Lincoln, near Platte R. **4** Borough (pop. 2,559), Blair co., central Pa., 8 mi. NNE of Altoona and on Little Juniata R.; metal products, flour; bituminous coal; agr.

Bellye, Yugoslavia: see BELJE.

Belly River, N Mont. and S Alta., rises in Mont. at foot of Mt. Merrit, flows 150 mi. NNE, crossing into Alta. at SE edge of Waterton Lakes Natl. Park, to Oldman R. 10 mi. NW of Lethbridge.

Belmar (bĕl′mär), resort borough (pop. 4,636), Monmouth co., E N.J., on the coast, near Shark R. mouth, and 4 mi. S of Asbury Park; fishing, yachting; mfg. (awnings, boats). Inc. 1890.

Belmeken, Bulgaria: see KOLAROV PEAK.

Bélmez (bĕl′mĕth), town (pop. 8,088), Córdoba prov., S Spain, on Guadiato R. and 35 mi. NW of Córdoba; center of mining basin (bituminous coal and anthracite). Olive-oil processing, mfg. of willow articles and tiles. Cereals, vegetables, livestock. Hill here is crowned by Moorish castle.

Bélmez de la Moraleda (dhā lä mōrälā′dhä), town (pop. 1,756), Jaén prov., S Spain, 23 mi. ESE of Jaén; olive-oil processing; cereals, esparto, fruit.

Belmond, town (pop. 2,169), Wright co., N central Iowa, near Iowa R., 30 mi. SW of Mason City; soybean-processing plant; dairy products, feed, hybrid seed corn; inc. 1881.

Belmont. 1 Town (pop. 4,786), E New South Wales, Australia, 65 mi. N of Sydney; rail terminus; coal-mining center. **2** Town (pop. 2,159), SW Western Australia, E suburb of Perth; tile, brick; horse racing.

Belmont, village (pop. estimate 500), S Ont., on Kettle Creek and 10 mi. SE of London; dairying, mixed farming.

Belmont, Lancashire, England: see TURTON.

Belmont, Loire dept., France: see BELMONT-DE-LA-LOIRE.

Belmont, NE residential suburb of Port of Spain, NW Trinidad, B.W.I.

Belmont, county (□ 539; pop. 87,740), E Ohio; ⊙ St. Clairsville. Bounded E by Ohio R., here forming W.Va. line; also drained by small Captina, Wheeling, and McMahon creeks. Includes Piedmont Reservoir. Coal mining; mfg. at Bellaire, Martins Ferry, and Bridgeport; agr. (truck, fruit, tobacco, grain; dairy products); limestone quarries. Formed 1801.

Belmont. 1 City (pop. 5,567), San Mateo co., W Calif., 19 mi. SSE of San Francisco, just SE of San Mateo; ships flowers. Col. of Notre Dame is here. Inc. 1926. **2** Village (pop. 1,933, with adjacent Highland Park), Pinellas co., W Fla. There is also a Belmont in Hamilton co., N Fla., near Jasper. **3** Agr. town (pop. 258), Waldo co., S Maine, just SW of Belfast; has resorts on Tilden Pond. **4** Residential town (pop. 27,381), Middlesex co., E Mass., 6 mi. NW of Boston. Settled 1636, inc. 1859. Includes village of Waverley. **5** Town (pop. 814), Tishomingo co., extreme NE Miss., 34 mi. ENE of Tupelo, in timber and agr. area. **6** Ghost mining town, Nye co., central Nev., c.40 mi. NNE of Tonopah; silver mines discovered 1863 yielded until 1885. **7** Town (pop. 1,611), Belknap co., central N.H., 6 mi S of Laconia; hosiery mills. Inc. as Upper Gilmanton 1859, renamed 1869. **8** Village (pop. 1,211), ⊙ Allegany co., W N.Y., on Genesee R. and 21 mi. WSW of Hornell, in dairying area; makes handles, machinery. Inc. 1871. **9** Town (pop. 5,330), Gaston co., S N.C., 12 mi. W of Charlotte, near Catawba R.; textile mfg. (cotton yarn, hosiery, fabrics), dyeing, and finishing. Seat of Belmont Abbey Col. and Sacred Heart Jr. Col. and Acad. **10** Village (pop. 638), Belmont co., E Ohio, 15 mi. W of Bellaire, in coal-mining area. **11** Town (pop. 215), Pleasants co., NW W.Va., on Ohio R. and 4 mi. W of St. Marys. **12** Village (pop. 474), Lafayette co., SW Wis., 25 mi. NE of Dubuque (Iowa); makes cheese. First Capitol State Park and Platte Mounds are near by.

Belmont-de-la-Loire (bĕlmō′-dù-lä-lwär′), village (pop. 631), Loire dept., SE central France, in Monts du Beaujolais, 16 mi. NE of Roanne; cotton milling. Until 1936, Belmont.

Belmonte (bĕlmōn′tĭ). **1** City (pop. 6,137), SE Bahia, Brazil, on the Atlantic at mouth of Jequitinhonha R., and 70 mi. S of Ilhéus; ships cacao, piassava, coconuts, lumber. Pink-marble quarrying, gold panning. Arifield. **2** City, Pernambuco, Brazil: see MANISSOBAL.

Belmonte, town (pop. 1,497), Castelo Branco dist., central Portugal, on railroad and 10 mi. NE of Covilhã; olives, wine, grain, corn; cheese making. Has ruins of anc. granitic castle (restored in 13th cent.) and a 14th-cent. church. Roman ruins near by. Tin and radium deposits in vicinity.

Belmonte (bĕlmōn′tā), town (pop. 3,413), Cuenca prov., E central Spain, in La Mancha region of New Castile, 45 mi. SW of Cuenca. Historic town, a spa and agr. center (cereals, grapes, saffron, sheep). Lumbering, flour milling, dairying, gypsum quarrying. Has old castle (built 1299) and Gothic church of San Bartolomé.

Belmonte de Tajo (bĕlmōn′tā dhā tä′hō), town (pop. 1,455), Madrid prov., central Spain, 26 mi. SE of Madrid; grain- and winegrowing.

Belmontejo (bĕlmōntā′hō), town (pop. 774), Cuenca prov., central Spain, 20 mi. SSW of Cuenca; saffron, wheat, grapes, truck, sheep; lumbering.

Belmonte Messagno (bĕlmôn′tĕ mĕsä′nyô), village (pop. 4,718), Palermo prov., N Sicily, 5 mi. S of Palermo, in cereal- and grape-growing region.

Belmont Junction, N.C.: see NORTH BELMONT.

Belmont Lake, SE N.Y., small lake on S Long Isl., just NW of Babylon. State park (348 acres) here: water sports, picnicking; hiking and bridle paths.

Belmont Park, N.Y.: see NASSAU, county.

Belmont-sur-Rance (bĕlmō′-sür-rãs′), village (pop. 541), Aveyron dept., S France, 25 mi. SW of Millau; sheep raising; cheese.

Belmore, village (pop. 216), Putnam co., NW Ohio, 17 mi. WNW of Findlay, in agr. region.

Belmullet (bĕlmŭ′lĭt), Gaelic *Béal an Mhurthid,* town (pop. 691), NW Co. Mayo, Ireland, at head of Blacksod Bay, on isthmus connecting Mullet Peninsula with mainland, 31 mi. W of Killala; fishing port.

Bel-Nor, town (pop. 1,290), St. Louis co., E Mo., near Mississippi R., 10 mi. W of St. Louis. Inc. 1937.

Belo- [Rus. combining form, =white], in Rus. names: see also BELAYA, BELOYE, BELY, BELYE.

Belo or **Belo sur Tsiribihina** (bĕ′lōō sür tsērēbēhē′-nù), town (1948 pop. 3,278), Tuléar prov., W Madagascar, at head of Tsiribihina R. estuary, 260 mi. NNE of Tuléar; small inland port and trading center; mfg. of edible oils; growing of tobacco, peas, beans. R.C. and Lutheran missions.

Belobozhnitsa (byĕlŭbôzh′nyĭtsŭ), Pol. *Białobożnica,* village (1931 pop. 1,300), S Ternopol oblast, Ukrainian SSR, 5 mi. WNW of Chortkov; distilling; grain, tobacco.

Beloeil (bùlû′ē), town (pop. 2,304), Hainaut prov., SW Belgium, 12 mi. NW of Mons; blast furnaces. Has 15th-cent. castle.

Beloeil, town (pop. 2,008), S Que., on Richelieu R. and 18 mi. ENE of Montreal; mfg. of explosives; market in dairying, fruitgrowing, potato-growing, cattle region.

Beloglazovo (byĕlŭglä′zùvŭ), village (1926 pop. 1,698), SW Altai Territory, Russian SFSR, on Charysh R. (head of navigation) and 25 mi. SSW of Aleisk, in agr. area.

Belogorsk (byĕlŭgôrsk′), city (1939 pop. over 10,000), central Crimea, Russian SFSR, at N foot of Crimean Mts., 12 mi. ENE of Simferopol; road and market center in wine- and fruitgrowing dist.; leather and canned goods. Agr. school. Has ruins of Tatar fortress, old caravansary. Pop. included Tatars and Crimean Jews until Second World War. City was for a time ⊙ Crimean khanate and major trade and caravan center (pop. up to 100,000) on Crimea-Caucasus route. Sacked 1737 by Russians. Until 1944, called Karasubazar.

Belogorye or **Belogor'ye** (byĕlŭgôr′yĭ). **1** Village, S Khanty-Mansi Natl. Okrug, Tyumen oblast, Russian SFSR, on left bank of Ob R. (landing) and 20 mi. W of Khanty-Mansisk; sawmilling. **2** Village (1926 pop. 6,493), S Voronezh oblast, Russian SFSR, on Don R. and 28 mi. NE of Rossosh; wheat, sunflowers. **3** Town (1926 pop. 1,581), NW Kamenets-Podolski oblast, Ukrainian SSR, on Goryn R. and 30 mi. SW of Shepetovka; metalworks. Until 1946, Lyakhovtsy.

Belogradchik (bĕ″lôgrächēk′), city (pop. 2,042), Vidin dist., NW Bulgaria, in W Balkan Mts., 28 mi. SSW of Vidin; grain, sheep. Anthracite mined near by. Has ruins of old fortress. Rock formations and caves (prehistoric relics) attract tourists. Linked with Pirot (Yugoslavia) by road through Sveti Nikola Pass. *Belogradchik Pass* (alt. 1,902 ft.) is on Bulg.-Yugoslav border, bet. Babin-nos

Mts. (N) and Sveti Nikola Mts. (S); links Belogradchik (9 mi. E) with Knjazevac (Yugoslavia). Formerly Kada-boaz Pass.

Belogradets (bĕ'lôgrä"dĕts), village (pop. 3,949), Kolarovgrad dist., E Bulgaria, 7 mi. E of Novi Pazar; wheat, corn, livestock. Formerly Tyurk-Arnautlar.

Beloha (bĕlōō'hŭ), village, Tuléar prov., S Madagascar, on road and 120 mi. WSW of Fort-Dauphin; castor beans. R. C. and Lutheran missions.

Belo Horizonte (bā"lôrēzōn'tĭ), city (1950 pop. 346,207), ⊙ Minas Gerais, E Brazil, on plateau (2,900 ft. high) just W of the Serra do Espinhaço, 210 mi. NNW of Rio de Janeiro; 19°55'S 43°56'W. Brazil's 2d largest inland city (after São Paulo), noted for its healthful upland climate (average temp. 67°F.). Center of country's most highly mineralized region yielding high-grade iron ore (at Itabira, Itabirito), manganese (Conselheiro Lafaiete), gold (Nova Lima). Situated at edge of cattle-raising interior (*sertão*). Linked to coast by 2 trunk rail lines (Rio Doce valley railroad shipping iron to Vitória (Espírito Santo); also on railroad to Rio across the Serra da Mantiqueira and on modern highway to Rio de Janeiro city. Belo Horizonte is a new, planned city. Laid out in regular pattern (based on that of Washington, D.C.); construction was begun in 1895. Seat of state govt. was transferred here in 1897 from OURO PRÊTO, after all public bldgs. and utilities had been completed. Most conspicuous in city plan are broad, tree-lined avenues (Avenida Afonso Pena is main concourse) and central square (Praça da Liberdade) with governor's palace and administrative bldgs. Recreation area was laid out in NW around artificial Pampulha lake, near airport. City has univ. (founded 1929), veterinary school (transferred here from Viçosa in 1941). Cheap local hydroelectric power has encouraged rapid industrialization: has textile mills (using São Francisco valley cotton); furniture, footwear, and pottery factories; light-metal works; diamond cutting. Heavy industry concentrated along railroad E of city, notably at Sabará, Caeté, Barão de Cocais, Rio Acima. Originally named Cidade de Minas. Formerly spelled Bello Horizonte.

Belohrad, Czechoslovakia: see LAZNE BELOHRAD.

Beloit (bŭloit'). **1** City (pop. 4,085), ⊙ Mitchell co., N Kansas, on Solomon R. and 50 mi. NNW of Salina, in grain and livestock area; flour milling; poultry hatcheries. State reform school for girls is here. Settled 1868, inc. 1872. **2** Village (pop. 778), Mahoning co., E Ohio, 22 mi. SW of Youngstown; fire-clay mines; dairy and grain products. **3** City (pop. 29,590), Rock co., S Wis., on Ill. line, at junction of Rock R. and Turtle Creek, 42 mi. SSE of Madison, in dairying area; mfg. (papermaking and woodworking machinery, Diesel engines, auto parts, knit goods, boxboard, shoes, refrigerators, scales, home appliances, farm implements). Noted for winter sports. Seat of Beloit Col. (1847). Founded c.1837, inc. 1857. Roy Chapman Andrews b. here.

Belo Jardim (bā'lōō zhärdēm'), city (pop. 4,489), E central Pernambuco, NE Brazil, on railroad and 30 mi. W of Cauaru, in coffee- and cotton-growing area; also ships corn, livestock. Formerly spelled Bello Jardim.

Belokalitvenskaya, Russian SFSR: see BELAYA KALITVA.

Belokany (byĕlŭkä'nē), village (1926 pop. 9,524), N Azerbaijan SSR, at S foot of the Greater Caucasus, on road and 55 mi. NW of Nukha, near Georgian border; nut woods, tobacco; sericulture.

Belokholunitski or **Belokholunitskiy** (–khŭlōōnyēt'skē), town (1926 pop. 3,038), N central Kirov oblast, Russian SFSR, 45 mi. ENE of Kirov; metalworking center; iron foundry; agr. implements. Dates from 1764.

Belokurakino (–kōōrä'kĭnŭ), village (1926 pop. 8,101), N Voroshilovgrad oblast, Ukrainian SSR, 20 mi. NNW of Starobelsk; wheat, sunflowers.

Belokurikha (byĕ"lŭkōōrē'khŭ), village (1949 pop. over 2,000), SE Altai Territory, Russian SFSR, at foot of Altai Mts., 50 mi. SW of Bisk; health resort (baths).

Belolutsk (–lōōtsk'), village (1926 pop. 5,826), N Voroshilovgrad oblast, Ukrainian SSR, on Aidar R. and 29 mi. N of Starobelsk; wheat, sunflowers. Until 1937, Belolutskaya.

Belomestnaya (–myĕst'nĭŭ), village (1939 pop. over 500), S Orel oblast, Russian SFSR, just S of Livny; metalworks, machine shops.

Belo Monte, Brazil: see BATALHA, Alagoas.

Belomorsk (byĕlŭmôrsk'), city (1939 pop. over 10,000), E Karelo-Finnish SSR, port on White Sea, at N end of White Sea–Baltic Canal, on Murmansk RR and 190 mi. N of Petrozavodsk; lumber milling, fish canning, shipbuilding. Until 1933, Soroka, Finnish *Sorokka*, Developed rapidly after completion (1932) of canal.

Belonia (bālōn'yŭ), village, Tripura, NE India, 41 mi. SSE of Agartala; rail spur terminus; rice, cotton, tea, mustard, jute.

Beloomut (byĕlŭ-ō'mōōt), town (1939 pop. over 2,000), SE Moscow oblast, Russian SFSR, on Oka R. and 23 mi. SE of Kolomna; mfg. of men's garments.

Belopolye or **Belopol'ye** (–pô'lyĭ), city (1926 pop. 17,940), E Sumy oblast, Ukrainian SSR, 25 mi. NW of Sumy; metalworking center; flour milling, sugar refining.

Belorado (bālōrä'dhō), town (pop. 2,468), Burgos prov., N Spain, on Tirón R., on Burgos-Logroño highway and 27 mi. ENE of Burgos; agr. center (cereals, vegetables, fruit, truck); sawmilling, plaster mfg.

Belorechenskaya (byĕlŭrĕ'chĭnskĭŭ), village (1926 pop. 14,958), S central Krasnodar Territory, Russian SFSR, on Belaya R. and 45 mi. ESE of Krasnodar; agr. center; sunflower-oil press, flour mill, metalworks. Junction of branch line to Maikop.

Belorechka (–rĕch'kŭ), town (1939 pop. over 2,000), SW central Sverdlovsk oblast, Russian SFSR, 7 mi. S (under jurisdiction) of Kirovgrad; rail spur terminus; copper- and zinc-mining center, supplying Kirovgrad refinery.

Beloretsk (–rĕtsk'), city (1932 pop. estimate 31,680), E Bashkir Autonomous SSR, Russian SFSR, in the S Urals, on Belaya R., on S. Siberian RR and 115 mi. ESE of Ufa. Rail junction; major metallurgical center (steel, pig iron), based on Komarovo-Zigazinski iron-mining dist. and partly on local charcoal production; mfg. (wire, nails, building materials), wood cracking, fruit canning. Pyrite (mined), copper, manganese, and magnesite deposits. Developed in 2d half of 18th cent.; became city in 1923. Formerly called Beloretski Zavod.

Belorussia, Belorussiya, or **Byelorussia** (bĕlōrōō'sēä, byĕlō–) or **Belorussian Soviet Republic** (bĕlōrŭ'shŭn, –rōō'sēŭn), constituent republic (□ 80,150; 1947 pop. estimate 7,220,000) of W European USSR; ⊙ Minsk. Borders on Poland (W), Lithuania and Latvia (NW), Russian SFSR (E), and the Ukraine (S). Largely a lowland, it lies bet. Lithuanian-Belorussian Upland (N) and Pripet Marshes (S). Principal rivers, the Dnieper (E), its affluents (Sozh, Berezina, Pripet rivers), the Western Dvina (N), and the Neman (E), are used for timber floating; linked across low watersheds by Dnieper-Bug, Oginski, and Berezina canals. Moderate humid continental climate; mean temp., 20°F. (January), 65°F. (July); yearly precipitation, 20–24 in. Soils are generally turfy or sandy in type, although drained swamp soils prove quite fertile. Mixed forests cover over ¼ of total area, chiefly in N Pripet Marshes and in NW. Peat (main power source), building materials (limestone, quartz sand, pottery clays), phosphorite, and common salt are chief mineral resources. Pop. consists of Belorussians (80%; a Slavic group influenced by Pol. culture, and of R.C. and Greek Orthodox religion), Russians, Jews, Ukrainians (S), and Poles (W). Administratively divided into govts., *uyezds*, and volosts until 1924, then (1924–38) into okrugs and *raions* (*rayons*). Since 1944, Belorussia comprises 12 oblasts: BARANOVICHI, BOBRUISK, BREST, GOMEL, GRODNO, MINSK, MOGILEV, MOLODECHNO, PINSK, POLESYE, POLOTSK, VITEBSK. Agr. conditions improved in recent times through swamp drainage, plant rotation with forages (clover, vetch, lupine), root and industrial crops, and use of peat and phosphate fertilizers. Leading crops are potatoes (⅓ of sown area; connected with hog raising) and fiber flax (N; linked with dairy farming); hemp and *kok-sagyz* (a rubber-bearing plant) prosper on drained swamp soils (S) rich in nitrous and phosphorous matter. Rye, oats, and wheat also grown. Peat is chief mineral raw material, used in power stations (*Belgres* plant at Orekhovsk) and in chemical industry (briquettes, tar, gas, coke). Other industries are lumber milling (sawn timber, veneers, paper, matches, furniture), textile milling (linen, hemp, and cotton goods, knitwear), and machine mfg. (autos, tractors, bicycles, agr. and peat-cutting implements, hydroturbines). Chief industrial centers (Minsk, Gomel, Mogilev, Vitebsk, Grodno, Brest) are served by dense rail network (including direct Moscow-Warsaw RR) and Moscow-Minsk highway. After 9th cent. ruled by Kievan Russia, later by Rus. principalities; Belorussian area fell (14th cent.) under Lith. (later Pol.) rule until it passed (18th cent.) to Russia in Pol. partitions. Modern Belorussian SSR was originally formed (1919; confirmed 1920) out of Minsk govt.; joined (1922) the USSR; considerably enlarged (1924, 1926) through cession of additional territory (Mogilev, Gomel, Vitebsk) by Russian SFSR. Following Pol. partition of 1939, the republic's area and pop. nearly doubled by occupation of NE Poland (Bialystok, Grodno, Brest, Pinsk, Baranovichi, Molodechno). Vilna area was briefly held and transferred (1939) to Lithuania, which also gained additional ethnic territory from Belorussian SSR in 1940. After Second World War, when Belorussia was held (1941–44) by Germans and suffered great devastation, the border with Poland was adjusted (1944–45) along the Curzon line, resulting in the retrocession of Bialystok.

Beloslav (bĕ'lôsläf"), village (pop. 3,221), Stalin dist., E Bulgaria, on Belevo L. and 10 mi. W of Stalin (Varna); glassworks; fisheries (crabs); winegrowing, truck gardening. Interesting stone formations and caves near by. Formerly Belevo.

Belostok, Poland: see BIALYSTOK, city.

Belostok (byĕlŭstôk'), former oblast of W Belorussian SSR; ⊙ was Bialystok, Rus. *Belostok*. Formed 1939 out of Pol. Bialystok prov., following Soviet occupation of E Poland. Held by Germany (1941–44). W part reverted (1944) to Poland; E part became GRODNO oblast.

Belotsarsk, Russian SFSR: see KYZYL, city.

Belousovka (byĕlŭōō'sŭfkŭ), town (1948 pop. over 2,000), N East Kazakhstan oblast, Kazakh SSR, 15 mi. N of Ust-Kamenogorsk; mining (lead-zinc).

Belovar, Yugoslavia: see BJELOVAR.

Beloves, Czechoslovakia: see NACHOD.

Belovezhskaya Pushcha, Belorussian SSR: see BIALOWIESA FOREST.

Belovo (bĕlyô'vô). **1** or **Gara Belovo** (gä'rä) [Bulg., =Belovo station], village (pop. 1,295), Plovdiv dist., W central Bulgaria, on E slope of W Rhodope Mts., on Maritsa R. and 16 mi. W of Pazardzhik; furniture, cardboard, and paper mfg. Villages of Golyamo [great] Belovo (pop. 2,066) and Malko [little] Belovo (pop. 1,130), just SW, have marble quarries and lumber mills. **2** Village Sofia dist., Bulgaria: see ZEMEN.

Belovo (byĕ'lŭvŭ), city (1932 pop. estimate 17,000), W central Kemerovo oblast, Russian SFSR, on branch of Trans-Siberian RR and 65 mi. S of Kemerovo, in Kuznetsk Basin. Rail junction; zinc metallurgical plant (linked by rail with Salair mines); steel milling, mfg. (radios, movie apparatus, building materials). Coal mining (S). Developed in 1930s.

Belovodsk (byĕlŭvôtsk'), village (1926 pop. 13,739), NE Voroshilovgrad oblast, Ukrainian SSR, 30 mi. E of Starobelsk; metalworks; wheat, sunflowers. Until 1937, Belovodskoye.

Belovodskoye, Kirghiz SSR: see STALINSKOYE, Frunze oblast.

Beloyarskoye (–yär'skŭyŭ), village (1926 pop. 1,265), S Sverdlovsk oblast, Russian SFSR, on Pyshma R. and 28 mi. ESE of Sverdlovsk, near Bazhenovo; lumbering; livestock.

Beloye [Rus.,=white], in Rus. names: see also BELAYA, BELO- [Rus. combining form], BELY, BELYE.

Beloye (byĕ'lŭyŭ). **1** Village (1926 pop. 5,431), S Kursk oblast, Russian SFSR, near Psel R., 26 mi. WSW of Oboyan; sugar beets. **2** Town (1939 pop. over 2,000), S central Voroshilovgrad oblast, Ukrainian SSR, in the Donbas, 11 mi. WSW of Voroshilovgrad; coal mines, marlpits.

Beloye Ozero (–ô'zyĭrŭ) [Rus.,=white lake], lake (□ 463) in Vologda oblast, Russian SFSR, NW of Vologda; 27 mi. long, 20 mi. wide, up to 66 ft. deep; nearly circular in shape, with sandy bottom. Frozen Nov.–Apr.; abounds in fish. Receives Kovzha R. (W), which is linked with Sheksna R. (outlet, E) by BELOZERSK CANAL, part of Mariinsk canal system. Belozersk city lies on S shore.

Beloyevo (–vŭ), village (1939 pop. over 500), S Komi-Permyak Natl. Okrug, Molotov oblast, Russian SFSR, 10 mi. NW of Kudymkar; wheat, livestock.

Belozem (bĕlôzĕm'), village (pop. 4,421), Plovdiv dist., S central Bulgaria, 17 mi. ENE of Plovdiv; rice, fruit, truck. Formerly Giren.

Belozerka (byĕlŭzyôr'kŭ, –zyĕr'kŭ), village (1939 pop. over 500), SW Kherson oblast, Ukrainian SSR, on small lake (Beloye Ozero), 6 mi. W of Kherson; metalworks.

Belozersk (–zyôrsk', –zyĕrsk'), city (1926 pop. 6,990), W central Vologda oblast, Russian SFSR, on S shore of lake Beloye Ozero, on Belozersk Canal and 90 mi. NW of Vologda; distilling, metalworking, flour milling. One of oldest cities of USSR; founded 862. Became ⊙ principality (13th cent.); passed (1362–89) to Muscovy. **Belozersk Canal** (42 mi. long; built 1846) parallels W and S shores of BELOYE OZERO, linking Kovzha R. (inlet) and Sheksna R. (outlet) and forming part of Mariinsk canal system.

Belozerskoye (–zyôr'skŭyŭ, –zyĕr'–), village (1948 pop. over 2,000), N Kurgan oblast, Russian SFSR, on Tobol R. and 25 mi. N of Kurgan; dairy plant, metalworks.

Belp (bĕlp), town (pop. 3,593), Bern canton, W Switzerland, on Gürbe Canal and 5 mi. SE of Bern; bakery products, woodworking. Old castle 2 mi. S of town.

Belpasso (bĕlpäs'sō), town (pop. 9,482), Catania prov., E Sicily, on S slope of Mt. Etna, 8 mi. NW of Catania, in agr. region (cereals, vineyards, citrus fruit); soap mfg.

Belpech (bĕlpĕsh'), village (pop. 633), Aude dept., S France, near Hers R., 9 mi. NE of Pamiers; flour milling, dairying, poultry raising. Ruins of 14th-cent. castle.

Belper, urban district (1931 pop. 13,204; 1951 census 15,716), central Derby, England, on Derwent R. and 7 mi. N of Derby; cotton and hosiery mills, foundries, coal mines, limestone quarries. The cotton-milling and knitting industry was introduced here (mid-19th cent.) by Jedediah Strutt (inventor of a knitting machine), buried here.

Belpre. **1** (bĕl'prē) City (pop. 231), Edwards co., S central Kansas, 17 mi. E of Kinsley; wheat. **2** (bĕl'prā) Village (pop. 2,451), Washington co., SE Ohio, on the Ohio (bridged), opposite Parkersburg (W.Va.), in fruit and truck area. Settled 1789, laid out 1852, inc. 1902. Near by is Blennerhassett Isl.

Belqas, Egypt: see BILQAS.
Bel-Ridge, town (pop. 1,116), St. Louis co., E Mo., just NW of St. Louis.
Belsele (bĕl'sūlū), town (pop. 4,582), East Flanders prov., N Belgium, 9 mi. N of Dendermonde; agr. market (grain, stock). Has Gothic church, partly dating from 17th cent., and 18th-cent. castle.
Belsen (bĕl'zŭn), village (pop. 222), in former Prussian prov. of Hanover, NW Germany, after 1945 in Lower Saxony, 12 mi. NW of Celle. With nearby Bergen it was site of large and infamous concentration camp during Hitler regime.
Belsk, Poland: see BIELSK.
Belt, city (pop. 702), Cascade co., central Mont., on small branch of Missouri R. and 18 mi. SE of Great Falls; dairy and poultry products, livestock, grain; coal.
Belt, Great, and Little Belt, Denmark: see GREAT BELT and LITTLE BELT.
Beltana, settlement (pop. 136), E central South Australia, 150 mi. N of Port Pirie and on Port Pirie–Alice Springs RR; wool, livestock.
Belterra (bĕltĕ'rŭ), rubber plantation in W Pará, Brazil, on right bank of Tapajós R. and c.30 mi. SSW of Santarém. A self-contained project with modern hosp., power plant, water reservoir, workers' homes, community bldgs., roads, docks, and airfield. Concession (□ 1,072) acquired 1934 by Ford in exchange for section of older Fordlândia (c.70 mi. S). Reverted to Brazilian ownership after Second World War.
Belton. 1 City (pop. 1,233), Cass co., W Mo., 15 mi. S of Kansas City; agr.; garment factory. **2** Village, Mont.: see WEST GLACIER. **3** Town (pop. 3,371), Anderson co., NW S.C., 10 mi. E of Anderson; textiles, clothing, bagging; cotton, grain. **4** City (pop. 6,246), ⊙ Bell co., central Texas, 7 mi. W of Temple and on small Nolan Creek and Leon R.; trade, market center in rich agr. area (cotton, corn, grain, pecans); mfg. (furniture, machinery). Seat of Mary Hardin-Baylor Col. Founded 1850, renamed 1851, inc. 1884.
Beltrami (bĕltră'mē), county (□ 2,517; pop. 24,962), NW Minn.; ⊙ Bemidji. Agr. and resort area drained by Upper and Lower Red lakes and, in S, by headwaters of Mississippi R. Dairy products, potatoes, grain, livestock; peat. Includes most of Red Lake Indian Reservation. Co. formed 1866.
Beltrami, village (pop. 199), Polk co., NW Minn., on small tributary of Red R. and 16 mi. SSE of Crookston, in grain and potato area; dairy products.
Beltrán (bĕltrăn'), town (pop. estimate 1,000), W central Santiago del Estero prov., Argentina, on railroad and 13 mi. SE of Santiago del Estero; wheat, alfalfa, cotton, livestock.
Beltrán, village (pop. 695), Cundinamarca dept., central Colombia, landing on Magdalena R., opposite Ambalema, connected by rail with Ibagué and La Dorada, 45 mi. WNW of Bogotá.
Beltsville, village (1940 pop. 909), Prince Georges co., central Md., 12 mi. NNE of Washington; has airport. Near by are U.S. Dept. of Agr. research center (c.14,000 acres) and Patuxent wildlife research refuge of Dept. of the Interior.
Beltsy or **Bel'tsy** (byĕl'tsē), Rum. *Bălţi* (bûlts), city (1930 pop. 34,760; 1941 pop. 18,236), N central Moldavian SSR, in Bessarabia, on right bank of Reut R. and 65 mi. NW of Kishinev; rail and agr.-processing center for Beltsy steppe (sugar beets, fruit, wine, corn, wheat, oilseeds); sugar refining, flour and oilseed milling, meat packing, brewing, distilling, mfg. of Diesel motors, lacquers, dyes, sheepskins; woodworking. Teachers col. Bishopric. While in Rumania (1918–40, 1941–44), it was ⊙ Balti dept. (□ 2,032; 1941 pop. 410,248).
Belturbet (bĕltûr'bĭt), Gaelic *Béal Tairbeirt*, urban district (pop. 1,179), N Co. Cavan, Ireland, on Erne R. and 8 mi. NNW of Cavan; agr. market (cattle, pigs; potatoes); mfg. of stains, inks, waxes. Slight remains of anc. round tower and fort.
Beluchistan, W Pakistan: see BALUCHISTAN.
Belukha (byĭlōō'khŭ), highest summit (15,157 ft.) of Altai Mts., in Katun Alps, S Siberia, on Russian SFSR–Kazakh SSR border; rises in 2 peaks; gives rise to 16 glaciers (4–6 mi. long).
Belupur, India: see BENARES, city.
Belur (bā'lōōr). **1** Town (pop. 3,703), Hassan dist., W Mysore, India, 20 mi. NW of Hassan. Large 12th-cent. polygonal temple to Vishnu here; more extensive ruins of same period at Halebid (or Halebidu) village, 8 mi. ENE; their richly-carved façades, friezes, and stone screens are considered the most typical masterpieces of Chalukyan architecture and sculpture in India. Halebid was ⊙ a S Indian dynasty, 11th–14th cent.; then called Dorasamudra or Dwarasamudra. **2** Village, Howrah dist., S West Bengal, India, near the Hooghly, 3 mi. NNE of Howrah city center; jute and cotton milling, glass mfg.; iron and steel rolling works. Hq. of Ramakrishna Mission.
Belusa (bĕ'lōōshä), Slovak *Beluša*, Hung. *Bellus* (bĕl'lōōsh), village (pop. 3,213), W Slovakia, Czechoslovakia, on Vah R., on railroad and 22 mi. SW of Zilina; health resort with mineral springs.
Belushya Guba (byĭlōō'shyŭ gōōbä') or **Belushye** (byĭlōō'shyĭ), settlement on W coast of S isl. of Novaya Zemlya, Russian SFSR; 71°33'N 50°20'E. Administrative hq. of Novaya Zemlya.
Belushye, Russian SFSR: see BELUSHYA GUBA.
Belval (bĕlväl'), Ger. *Ernshof* (ĕrns'hōf), town, S Luxembourg, just W of Esch-sur-Alzette; steel center (blast furnaces, rolling mills); iron mining; mfg. (bricks, synthetic fertilizer, oxygen).
Belvandi (bāl'vŭndē), village (pop. 3,504), Ahmadnagar dist., E central Bombay, India, 27 mi. SSW of Ahmadnagar; sugar milling. Also called Belvandi Budrukh.
Belvaux (bĕlvō'), Ger. *Beles* (bā'lŭs), town (pop. 2,562), S Luxembourg, 2 mi. WNW of Esch-sur-Alzette, near Fr. border; silicon mining.
Belvedere, England: see ERITH.
Belvedere (bĕl'vŭdēr", bĕl"vŭdēr', Ger. bĕl"vādā'-rŭ), hunting lodge, Thuringia, central Germany, 2 mi. SSE of Weimar, in suburb of Ehringsdorf. Built in 18th cent., it is now mus. Has open-air theater; many associations with Goethe
Belvedere. 1 Urban residential township (1940 pop. 37,192), Los Angeles co., S Calif., bet. E Los Angeles and Monterey Park; truck gardening. Unincorporated Belvedere Gardens (1940 pop. 33,502) is adjacent. **2** Residential town (pop. 800), Marin co., W Calif., on San Francisco Bay, 7 mi. N of San Francisco.
Belvedere Gardens, Calif.: see BELVEDERE, Los Angeles co.
Belvedere Marittimo (bĕlvĕdā'rĕ märēt'tēmō), village (pop. 1,824), Cosenza prov., Calabria, S Italy, near Tyrrhenian Sea, 14 mi. S of Scalea, in fruit- and olive-growing region.
Belver (bĕlvăr'), village (pop. 1,634), Huesca prov., NE Spain, near Cinca R., 14 mi. NW of Fraga, in irrigated agr. area (olives, wine, cherries, figs).
Belver de los Montes (bĕlvăr' dhā lōs mōn'tĕs), town (pop. 1,299), Zamora prov., NW Spain, 22 mi. NE of Zamora; flour mills; cereals, chick-peas, wine.
Belvès (bĕlvĕs'), village (pop. 1,129), Dordogne dept., SW France, 13 mi. SW of Sarlat; mushrooms; flour milling, woodworking. Has 15th-cent. belfry.
Belvidere (bĕl'vĭdēr", bĕlvĭdēr'). **1** City (pop. 9,422), ⊙ Boone co., N Ill., on Kishwaukee R. (bridged here) and 12 mi. E of Rockford; trade and shipping center in grain, livestock, and dairy area. Mfg. (dairy and grain products, sewing machines, canned foods, scales, machine parts, clothing, hardware, polish). Founded 1836, inc. 1852. **2** Village (pop. 1,886, with adjoining Crestlawn), Madison co., central Ind. **3** Village (pop. 274), Thayer co., SE Nebr., 5 mi. N of Hebron and on branch of Little Blue R.; dairy and poultry produce, livestock, grain. **4** Town (pop. 2,406), ⊙ Warren co., NW N.J., on Delaware R., at mouth of Pequest R., and 11 mi. NNE of Phillipsburg; mfg. (building blocks, felt, hosiery); dairy products. Settled 1759, laid out 1799, inc. 1845. **5** Town (pop. 172), Jackson co., S central S.Dak., 11 mi. E of Kadoka; cattle-shipping point; wheat, oats. **6** Town (pop. 207), Lamoille co., N Vt., on North Branch Lamoille R. and 26 mi. SW of Newport, in Green Mts.; asbestos.
Belview, village (pop. 381), Redwood co., SW Minn., near Minnesota R., 11 mi. WNW of Redwood Falls, in livestock, grain, and poultry area; dairy products, granite.
Belvis de la Jara (bĕlvēs' dhā lä hä'rä), village (pop. 4,361), Toledo prov., central Spain, 15 mi. SSW of Talavera de la Reina, in agr. region (cereals, vegetables, olives, grapes, sheep, goats, hogs). Sulphurous springs.
Belvoir (bē'vŭr), agr. village and parish (pop. 80), NE Leicester, England, 10 mi. NNE of Melton Mowbray; site of Belvoir Castle, seat of duke of Rutland, and dating from Norman times. The Belvoir Hunt was founded in mid-18th cent.
Belvoir (bĕlvwär'), **Beauvoir** (bōvwär'), or **Coquet** (kōkā'), Crusaders' castle, Lower Galilee, NE Palestine, overlooking Jordan valley, 7 mi. N of Beisan. Established (1140) by King Fulke, captured (1188) by Saladin. Ruins extant.
Belvoir, Fort (bĕl'vôr), U.S. military installation, Fairfax co., E Va., on peninsula extending into Potomac R., 18 mi. SSW of Washington, D.C.; a permanent post of Corps of Engineers. Ruins of "Belvoir" (1741), Lord Fairfax's estate, here. U.S. fish hatchery near by. Formerly Fort Humphreys.
Belvue, city (pop. 193), Pottawatomie co., NE Kansas, on Kansas R. and 27 mi. WNW of Topeka.
Bely or **Belyy** [Rus.,=white], in Rus. names: see also BELAYA, BELO- [Rus. combining form], BELOYE, BELYE.
Bely or **Belyy** (byĕ'lē), city (1926 pop. 6,882), SE Velikiye Luki oblast, Russian SFSR, 50 mi. NNE of Yartsevo; road center; dairying, flax retting. Dates from 13th cent.; chartered 1359; fought over by Poland and Russia; annexed (1667) by Moscow. During Second World War, held (1941–42) by Germans.
Belyasuvar (bĕlyäsōōvär'), village, SE Azerbaijan SSR, on Iran border, 35 mi. WSW of Salyany, and on highway to Tabriz, Iran; Soviet customs post. Adjoins small Iranian frontier station of Pilesavar, Pileh Savar, or Bileh Savar (W).
Belyayevka (bĭlyī'ŭfkŭ). **1** Village (1948 pop. over 2,000), central Chkalov oblast, Russian SFSR, on left bank of Ural R. and 60 mi. ESE of Chkalov; wheat, livestock. **2** Village (1926 pop. 6,949), SW Odessa oblast, Ukrainian SSR, on the Dniester and 22 mi. W of Odessa; limestone works. Water filtration plant (Odessa water-supply system).
Bely Bychek, Russian SFSR: see CHAGODA.
Belye or **Belyye** [Rus.,=white], in Rus. names: see also BELAYA, BELO- [Rus. combining form], BELOYE, BELY.
Belye Berega or **Belyye Berega** (byĕ'lēŭ bĕrĭgä'), town (1939 pop. over 2,000), NE Bryansk oblast, Russian SFSR, 12 mi. E of Bryansk; peat-working center. Peat-fed power plant.
Belye Kresty, Russian SFSR: see SAZONOVO.
Belye Vody or **Belyye Vody** (byĕ'lēŭ vô'dē), village (1939 pop. over 500), SE South Kazakhstan oblast, Kazakh SSR, on Turksib RR (Mankent station) and 12 mi. NE of Chimkent; cotton; metalworks.
Bely Island or **Belyy Island** (byĕ'lē), in Kara Sea, just N of Yamal Peninsula, in Tyumen oblast, Russian SFSR; 73°N 71°E; 40 mi. long, 28 mi. wide. Separated from mainland by 7-mi.-wide Malygin Strait. Site of arctic observation post (on NW coast).
Bely Kamen or **Belyy Kamen'** (byĕ'lē kä'mĭnyŭ), Pol. *Biały Kamień*, town (1931 pop. 1,950), E Lvov oblast, Ukrainian SSR, on Bug R. and 6 mi. NNW of Zolochev; tanning, distilling, flour milling.
Bely Kolodez or **Belyy Kolodez'** (-kŭlô'dyĭs), town (1926 pop. 4,134), NE Kharkov oblast, Ukrainian SSR, 40 mi. ENE of Kharkov; sugar refining.
Belynichi (byĕlĭnyē'chē), town (1926 pop. 2,429), W Mogilev oblast, Belorussian SSR, on Drut R. and 27 mi. WNW of Mogilev; clothing and shoe mfg., wood distilling.
Bely Yar or **Belyy Yar** (byĕ'lē yär"). **1** Village, E Tomsk oblast, Russian SFSR, near Ket R., 75 mi. E of Kolpashevo; agr. **2** Village (1926 pop. 4 991), E Ulyanovsk oblast, Russian SFSR, port on left arm of Volga R., 6 mi. E of Sengilei; grain orchards, livestock. Has old fortress.
Belz (bĕlz), village (pop. 684), Morbihan dept., W France, on Étel R. and 10 mi. ESE of Lorient; oyster beds. Megalithic monuments near by.
Belz (byĕlz), village, N Lvov oblast, Ukrainian SSR, on railroad and 19 mi. ENE of Rava-Russkaya. Until 1951 in Poland.
Belzec (bĕ'ōō-zhĕts), Pol. *Bełżec*, Rus. *Belzhets* (bĕl'zhĭts), village, Lublin prov., SE Poland, on railroad and 5 mi. S of Tomaszow Lubelski. Ger. extermination camp here in Second World War.
Belzig (bĕl'tsĭkh), town (pop. 7,597), Brandenburg, E Germany, 19 mi. S of Brandenburg; agr. market (grain, potatoes, stock); woolen milling. Has 16th-cent. Eisenhart castle.
Belzoni (bĕlzō'nē), city (pop. 4,071), ⊙ Humphreys co., W Miss., on Yazoo R. and 29 mi. SW of Greenwood; cottonseed products, lumber. Prehistoric Indian artifacts found near here, 1951. Founded c.1827.
Bembe (bĕm'bā), village, Congo prov., NW Angola, 150 mi. NE of Luanda; copper deposits.
Bembesi (bĕmbĕ'sē), village, Bulawayo prov., SW central Southern Rhodesia, in Matabeleland, on railroad and 24 mi. NE of Bulawayo; alt. 4,482 ft. Tobacco, corn, peanuts; livestock. Gold deposits.
Bembibre (bĕmbē'vrā), town (pop. 1,946), Leon prov., NW Spain, 10 mi. NE of Ponferrada; brandy distilling; chestnuts, wine, potatoes, livestock. Has ruined medieval castle and 15th-cent. church (formerly a synagogue). Anthracite mines near by.
Bembridge, town and parish (pop. 1,749), on Isle of Wight, Hampshire, England, on the Spithead 4 mi. SE of Ryde; seaside resort. Site of Bembridge School, a public school.
Bement (bĕmĕnt'), village (pop. 1,459), Piatt co., central Ill., 19 mi. ENE of Decatur, in grain and soybean area. Inc. 1874.
Bemersyde or **Bemerside** (bē'mûrsīd), locality in Mertoun parish, SE Berwick, Scotland, near the Tweed, 3 mi. E of Melrose; ancestral seat of earls Haig since 12th cent. Presented to Field Marshal Earl Haig by nation in 1921.
Bemerton (bĕ'mûrtŭn), agr. village and parish (pop. 418), SE Wiltshire, England, on Wylye R. just WNW of Salisbury. Has 14th-cent. church. George Herbert lived here.
Bemetara (bāmā'tŭrŭ), village, Drug dist., E central Madhya Pradesh, India, 40 mi. NNE of Drug; rice, oilseeds, wheat.
Bemidji (bŭmĭ'jē), city (pop. 10,001), ⊙ Beltrami co., NW central Minn., on Bemidji L. and c.140 mi. WNW of Duluth. Resort and trade center in lake and forest area; dairy products, poultry; mfg. (wood products, wool, bricks, beverages). State teachers col. and 18-ft. statue of Paul Bunyan are here; Greater Leech Lake Indian Reservation is near by. Settled c.1892, inc. as village 1896, as city 1905. Grew as lumber center.
Bemidji Lake (□ 11; 5 mi. long, c.2 mi. wide), Beltrami co., NW central Minn., at Bemidji. Fed and drained by Mississippi R. Boating, fishing, and bathing resorts. State park is on NE shore.
Bemis (bĕ'mĭs), village (pop. 3,248), Madison co., W Tenn., 3 mi. S of Jackson; a company-owned cotton-mill community.
Bemis Heights (bē'mŭs), village, Saratoga co., E N.Y., on the Hudson and 11 mi. SE of Saratoga Springs. American Revolution battles (Sept. 19

and Oct. 7, 1777) fought near here are commemorated by natl. historical park 9 mi. SE of SARATOGA SPRINGS.

Bemiston, village (pop. 1,007), Talladega co., E central Ala., just SW of Talladega.

Bemus Point (bē'mŭs), resort village (pop. 424), Chautauqua co., extreme W N.Y., on Chautauqua L., 9 mi. WNW of Jamestown.

Bemyzh (byĭmĭsh'), village (1939 pop. over 2,000), SW Udmurt Autonomous SSR, Russian SFSR, 24 mi. SW of Mozhga; wheat, rye, oats, livestock.

Bena (bē'nŭ), village (pop. 331), Cass co., N central Minn., on Winnibigoshish L., in Greater Leech Lake Indian Reservation, and 33 mi. ESE of Bemidji; grain, potatoes.

Benab, village, Berbice co., NE Br. Guiana, in Atlantic coastland, 33 mi. SE of New Amsterdam; sugar cane, rice.

Benabarre (bānävä'rā), town (pop. 1,213), Huesca prov., NE Spain, 20 mi. ENE of Barbastro; olive-oil processing. Livestock, wine, hemp, almonds in area. Some coal mines near by. Chief town of Ribagorza dist., with medieval castle.

Benacazón (bānäkä-thōn'), town (pop. 3,426), Seville prov., SW Spain, 11 mi. W of Seville, in agr. region (olives, cereals, grapes, livestock, timber); olive-oil pressing.

Benaco, Lago di, Italy: see GARDA, LAGO DI.

Benacre, agr. village and parish (pop. 206), NE Suffolk, England, near North Sea, 6 mi. SSW of Lowestoft. Just E, on North Sea, is promontory of Benacre Ness. North Sea cables from Zandvoort, Netherlands, terminate here.

Benacus, Lacus, Italy: see GARDA, LAGO DI.

Benadalid (bānä-dhälēdh'), town (pop. 503), Málaga prov., S Spain, on Guadiaro R. and 13 mi. SW of Ronda; chestnuts, apples, raisins, olives, cereals.

Bena Dibele (bĕ'nä dĕbĕ'lā), village, Kasai prov., central Belgian Congo, on Sankuru R. and 70 mi. NW of Lusambo; steamboat landing; cotton ginning, rice processing. Has R.C. mission.

Benadir (bĕnädĕr'), coastal region of Ital. Somaliland, on Indian Ocean, bounded SW by Kenya. Hot, arid lowland with sand dunes along coast; many offshore islets S of Kismayu. Agr. (durra, corn, sesame, cotton, bananas) along Juba and Webi Shebeli rivers; pastoralism (cattle, goats, sheep, camels). Fishing; mother of pearl, trochus, tunny. Chief centers: Mogadishu, Kismayu, Merca, Brava, Villabruzzi, Genale. Sultan of Zanzibar held strongholds along Benadir coast until end of 19th cent.

Benagalbón (bānägälvōn'), town (pop. 894), Málaga prov., S Spain, near the coast, 9 mi. E of Malaga; olive oil, lemons, truck, cereals.

Benaguacil (bānägwä-thēl'), town (pop. 7,849), Valencia prov., E Spain, 14 mi. NW of Valencia; agr. trade center (vegetables, cereals, wine, cattle); flour milling, wood turning. Gypsum and kaolin quarries. Has some Moorish remains.

Benahavís (bānä-ävēs'), town (pop. 244), Málaga prov., S Spain, at SE slopes of the Sierra Bermeja (Cordillera Penibética), near the Mediterranean, 30 mi. NE of Gibraltar; timber, carob beans, charcoal. Has unexploited silver and iron deposits.

Benahmed or **Ben Ahmed** (bĕnämĕd'), town (pop. 5,800), Casablanca region, W Fr. Morocco, 45 mi. SE of Casablanca; agr. trade center.

Bena Kamba (bĕ'nä käm'bä), village, Kivu prov., central Belgian Congo, on Lomami R. and 175 mi. NW of Kasongo; terminus of steam navigation; fiber-growing area.

Benalauría (bānälourē'ä), town (pop. 656), Málaga prov., S Spain, 11 mi. SSW of Ronda; chestnuts, acorns, fruit, cork, hogs. Antimony mines near by.

Ben Alder (bĕn ôl'dŭr), mountain (3,757 ft.), S Inverness, Scotland, 15 mi. ESE of Spean Bridge, overlooking Loch Ericht.

Benalla (bĕnă'lŭ), town (pop. 4,949), N central Victoria, Australia, 105 mi. NNE of Melbourne; rail junction in agr., sheep-raising area.

Benalmádena (bänälmä'dhänä), town (pop. 915), Málaga prov., S Spain, in coastal hills, 11 mi. SW of Málaga; cereals, olives, truck. Has paper mill and hydroelectric plant.

Benalúa de Guadix (bānäloo'ä dhä gwädĕks'), village (pop. 4,134), Granada prov., S Spain, 4 mi. NNW of Guadix; sugar- and sawmilling, brandy distilling. Cereals, wine, olive oil, fruit; lumbering.

Benalúa de las Villas (läs vē'lyäs), town (pop. 1,583), Granada prov., S Spain, 18 mi. NNW of Granada; cereals, vegetables, wine, aniseed.

Benamargosa (bānämärgō'sä), town (pop. 2,033), Málaga prov., S Spain, 16 mi. NE of Málaga; olives, grapes, raisins, figs, lemons, goats, hogs.

Benamaurel (bānämourĕl'), town (pop. 1,359), Granada prov., S Spain, 10 mi. NE of Baza; olive-oil processing, wool spinning. Cereals, vegetables, wine. Sulphur mines near by.

Benamejí (bānämähē'), town (pop. 5,667), Córdoba prov., S Spain, near Genil R., 11 mi. SSW of Lucena; olive-oil presses, flour mills, mat and soap factories. Ships aniseed. Cereals, hemp, beans, melons in area.

Benamocarra (bānämōkä'rä), town (pop. 1,782), Málaga prov., S Spain, 16 mi. ENE of Málaga; olive growing and processing.

Benaocaz (bänoukäth'), town (pop. 680), Cádiz prov., SW Spain, in spur of the Cordillera Penibética, 15 mi. W of Ronda; fruit, cereals, livestock. Coal deposits near by.

Benaoján (bānouhän'), town (pop. 1,867), Málaga prov., S Spain, in Sierra de Ronda, 5 mi. SW of Ronda, in agr. region (wheat, oats, chick-peas, tubers, peas, olives, grapes, fruit); timber; livestock. Mfg. of flour, olive oil, meat products.

Benares (bŭnärz', bŭnä'rŭs) or **Banaras** (bŭnä'rŭs), former princely state (□ 866; pop. 451,428), N India; ⊙ was Ramnagar. Consisted of 3 separate enclaves: 1 in Mirzapur dist., 1 in Benares dist., 1 bet. Benares and Allahabad dists. Created as princely state in 1911; Ramnagar town added 1918; joined Gwalior Residency in 1936. Merged 1949 with Benares dist. Main towns were Ramnagar, Bhadohi, Gopiganj, Gyanpur, and Chakia.

Benares, since 1948 officially **Banaras,** district (□ 1,960; pop. 1,670,057), SE Uttar Pradesh, India; ⊙ Benares. On Ganges Plain, along the Ganges. Agr.: rice, barley, gram, wheat, sugar cane, oilseeds, millets, corn. Main centers: Benares, Ramnagar, Mughul Sarai, Gopiganj. Extensive Buddhist remains at SARNATH. Original dist. (□ 1,094; pop. 1,218,629) was enlarged 1949 by inc. of former princely state of Benares.

Benares, since 1948 officially **Banaras,** anc. *Varanasi*, city (pop., including cantonment and Benares Hindu Univ. area, 263,100), ⊙ Benares dist., SE Uttar Pradesh, India, on the Ganges and 75 mi. E of Allahabad. Rail (workshops) and road junction; trade center; has famous hand-loom textile (silk saries, brocade, kincob) and engraved brassware and jewelry industries; cotton and oilseed milling, mfg. of glass, chemicals, shoes, carpets, fountain pens; iron- and steel-rolling mill; tobacco factory. Hosiery mfg. in Belupur (S suburb). Benares Hindu Univ. (extreme S area; opened 1921), Queens Col. (NW; noted Sanskrit dept.), soil survey laboratory. One of 7 most sacred Hindu centers in India. Regarded as Siva's capital while on earth, built at point where the Ganges has obtained its greatest sanctity. Also sacred to Buddhists and Jains. Annually over 1,000,000 pilgrims visit city's many ghats and shrines. Ghats stretch for 4 mi. along left bank of river and include (S to N) Asi Ghat (one of 5 special pilgrimage sites of city), Tulsi Ghat (sacred to 17th-cent. Hindu poet Tulsi Das), Sivala Ghat (assigned to Gosain sect), Smashan (Harish Chandra) Ghat (oldest crematorium in city), Kedar Ghat (with Sivaite temple), Dasaswamedh Ghat (here Brahma made the 10-horse sacrifice; near by is famous anc. observatory), the great Manikarnika Ghat (considered the most sacred cremation ghat), and Trilochan Ghat (with 2 turrets in river). Temples and mosques include the Golden Temple (built 1777; dedicated to Siva; a great pilgrimage center, with near-by sacred well), Durga temple (also called Monkey Temple from the great swarms of monkeys found there), 17th-cent. Aurangzeb's mosque, and Jain temples. A flourishing Hindu city as early as 6th cent. B.C.; raided in 1033 by Afghans; later, Moslems destroyed all the early temples, building mosques from the materials. Under Moslem rule until late-18th cent.; ceded to British in 1775. From anc. times city was also called Kasi (name of present rail junction).

Benarrabá (bānärävä'), town (pop. 1,130), Málaga prov., S Spain, 14 mi. SSW of Ronda; cork, olives, grapes, fruit, timber, livestock.

Benas, Ras, or **Ra's Banas** (both: räs' bĕnăs'), headland, E Egypt, on W coast of the Red Sea at N entrance to Foul Bay, 180 mi. SE of Kosseir, 20 mi. E of the ruins of BERENICE; 23°53'N 35°47'E.

Benasal (bänäsäl'), town (pop. 1,544), Castellón de la Plana prov., E Spain, 28 mi. NNW of Castellón de la Plana; cement and knitwear mfg.; olive oil, cereals, potatoes, wine. Mineral springs at Fuente En Segures near by.

Benasque (bänä'skä), village (pop. 620), Huesca prov., NE Spain, in central Pyrenees at foot of Maladetta massif, on Esera R. and 45 mi. NNE of Barbastro; customs station. Has mineral springs; and 16th-cent. castle near by.

Benasque, pass, France and Spain: see VÉNASQUE.

Bénat, Cape (bānä'), rocky headland of Var dept., SE France, on the Mediterranean, 12 mi. ESE of Hyères, opposite Îles d'Hyères. Formed by S spur of Monts des Maures. Bounds Rade d'Hyères (W). Lighthouse (43°7'N 6°22'E).

Benatky nad Jizerou (bĕ'nätkĭ näd' yĭ"zĕrō), Czech *Benátky nad Jizerou*, Ger. *Benatek* (bä'nätĕk), town (commune pop. 4,266), central Bohemia, Czechoslovakia, on Jizera R., on railroad and 23 mi. NE of Prague; carborundum production. Has old castle, once an observatory of Tycho Brahe. Formerly known as Nove Benatky, Czech *Nové Benátky*.

Ben Attow, Scotland: see KINTAIL.

Benavente (bänävän'tĭ), town (pop. 3,922), Santarém dist., central Portugal, on Sorraia R. near its influx into the Tagus, and 25 mi. NE of Lisbon; agr. center (rice, wheat, corn, livestock). Mfg. (flour products, cheese, pottery).

Benavente (bänävĕn'tä), city (pop. 7,713), Zamora prov., NW Spain, in Leon, bet. Esla and Órbigo rivers, 35 mi. N of Zamora; road center; mfg. of candy, burlap, ceramics, flour products; tanning, cotton spinning, flour milling; trades in livestock, lumber, cereals, wine. Has 12th-cent. Romanesque collegiate church, Gothic church of Santa María (12th–13th cent.). Castle of counts of Benavente on hill near by.

Benavides (bänävē'dhĕs), town (pop. 1,871), Leon prov., NW Spain, 9 mi. ENE of Astorga; flour milling, candy and wax mfg., lumbering, stock raising; cereals, sugar beets, wine.

Benavides (bĕnŭvĭ'dŭs, -vē'dŭs), city (pop. 3,016), Duval co., S Texas, c.60 mi. WSW of Corpus Christi; rail, trade center in area producing oil, salt (piped as brine to Corpus Christi chemical works), cotton, cattle. Inc. 1936.

Ben Avon (bĕn än'), peak (3,843 ft.) of Grampian Mts., Scotland, on Aberdeen-Banffshire border, 7 mi. N of Braemar.

Ben Avon (bĕn ā'vŭn), residential borough (pop. 2,465), Allegheny co., SW Pa., NW suburb of Pittsburgh, on Ohio R. Inc. 1891.

Ben Avon Heights, borough (pop. 394), Allegheny co., SW Pa., NW suburb of Pittsburgh.

Benaya, Israel: see BARCAI.

Ben-Bachir (bĕn-bäshēr'), village, Souk-el-Arba dist., NW Tunisia, on Medjerda R., on Tunis-Algiers RR, and 21 mi. WSW of Béja, in wheat-growing region. Also spelled Béni-Béchir.

Benbane Head (bĕnbăn'), promontory on the North Channel, N Co. Antrim, Northern Ireland, 11 mi. NE of Coleraine; 55°15'N 6°29'W; ENE end of GIANT'S CAUSEWAY. Just E is Bengore Head.

Benbaun (bĕnbôn'), mountain (2,395 ft.), highest point of Benna Beola mts., Connemara dist., NW Co. Galway, Ireland, 8 mi. ENE of Clifden.

Benbecula (bĕnbĕ'kūlŭ), island (pop. 961), Outer Hebrides, Inverness, Scotland, bet. North Uist and South Uist, 16 mi. W of Skye across the Little Minch; 7 mi. long, 6 mi. wide; rises to 409 ft. Soil is mainly barren and unproductive; fishing is chief industry. On S coast are fishing villages of Creagorry (krēgō'rē) and Gramisdale. Balivanich (bă"lĭvă'nĭkh) (NW) has airfield.

Benbow (bĕn'bō"), summer resort, Humboldt co., NW Calif., on South Fork Eel R. and c.55 mi. SSE of Eureka, in the redwood country.

Benbrook, town (pop. 617), Tarrant co., N Texas, just SW of Fort Worth.

Benbrook Reservoir, Texas: see TRINITY RIVER.

Benburb (bĕnbûrb'), agr. village (district pop. 1,229), SE Co. Tyrone, Northern Ireland, on Blackwater R. and 5 mi. NW of Armagh; flax, potatoes, oats; cattle. Has ruins of castle of the O'Neills. Owen O'Neill here defeated (1646) the English under General Monroe.

Bencat (bän'kät'), village, Thudaumot prov., S Vietnam, 27 mi. NNW of Saigon; rubber-plantation center.

Bencatel (bāng-kätĕl'), village (pop. 1,485), Évora dist., S central Portugal, 28 mi. ENE of Évora; oil, wine, wheat.

Ben Cleuch, Scotland: see OCHIL HILLS.

Bencoolen, Indonesia: see BENKULEN.

Ben Cruachan (bĕn krookh'ŭn, kroo'ŭhŭn), mountain (3,689 ft.), NW Argyll, Scotland, bet. lochs Etive and Awe, 13 mi. E of Oban.

Bend, city (pop. 11,409), ⊙ Deschutes co., central Oregon, on Deschutes R., in E foothills of Cascade Range, and 20 mi. E of the Three Sisters; alt. 3,623 ft.; trade and tourist center in lumbering and irrigated agr. area; lumber milling, dairying. Hq. of near-by Deschutes Natl. Forest here. Laid out and inc. 1905.

Ben Davis, village (1940 pop. 1,292), Marion co., central Ind., suburb 7 mi. W of downtown Indianapolis.

Bende (bĕndā), town, Oweri prov., Eastern Provinces, S Nigeria, 40 mi. ENE of Owerri; palm oil and kernels, kola nuts. Lignite deposits. Has hosp.

Ben Dearg (bĕn dûrg'), mountain (3,547 ft.), N central Ross and Cromarty, Scotland, 12 mi. SE of Ullapool.

Bendemeer (bĕn'dŭmēr), village (pop. 369), E New South Wales, Australia, 145 mi. NNW of Newcastle; tin mines.

Bender, Moldavian SSR: see BENDERY.

Bender Beila (bĕndĕr' bā'lä), village (pop. 250), in the Mijirtein, N Ital. Somaliland, on Indian Ocean, 70 mi. SSW of Hafun.

Bender Kassim or **Bender Cassim** (bĕndĕr' käsēm'), town (pop. 3,000), in the Mijirtein, N Ital. Somaliland, near Br. Somaliland border, port on Gulf of Aden, 120 mi. N of Gardo; 11°18'N 49°11'E. Terminus of road (922 mi. long) to Mogadishu. Commercial center and customs station; exports tunny, frankincense. Has warehouses, airfield, hosp.

Bendersville, borough (pop. 409), Adams co., S Pa., 10 mi. N of Gettysburg.

Bendery (bĭndyĕ'rē), Rum. *Tighina* (tēgē'nä), city (1930 pop. 31,384; 1941 pop. 15,075), SE Moldavian SSR, in Bessarabia, 32 mi. SE of Kishinev, on high right bank of Dniester R., W of Tiraspol and on railroad; major wine- and fruitgrowing center; canning of grape and fruit juices, flour milling, brewing, soap mfg. Remains of 15th-cent. Moldavian fortress. City developed (14th cent.) near former Genoese colony as Moldavian Tigin (Tighin); under Turkish rule (1538–1812), renamed Bender and flourished as fortified Dniester R. crossing. Charles XII of Sweden sought refuge (1709–13) at its port of Varnitsa (just N), following his defeat at Poltava. Prosperity continued under Rus. rule (1812–1918), when Bendery (with Varnitsa) developed into an important river-rail transfer point. City declined while in Rumania (1918–40; 1941–44), when it was ⊙ Tighina dept. (□ 3,345; 1914 pop. 290,835).

Bender Ziada (bĕndĕr' zyä'dä), village (pop. 400), in the Mijirtein, N Ital. Somaliland, on Br. Somaliland border, 15 mi. W of Bender Kassim; frontier station. Has native forts and mosques.

Bendigo (bĕn'dĭgō), city (pop. 26,739; metropolitan Bendigo 30,779), central Victoria, Australia, 80 mi. NNW of Melbourne; rail junction; commercial center for wheat-growing area; flour mills. School of mines, R.C. cathedral. Gold mines near by. Founded 1851 with gold rush; formerly important mining town popularly called Sandhurst. Includes NW suburb of Eaglehawk (pop. 4,040).

Bendin, Poland: see BEDZIN.

Bendix, N.J.: see TETERBORO.

Bendorf (bĕn'dôrf), town (pop. 10,540), in former Prussian Rhine Prov., W Germany, after 1945 in Rhineland-Palatinate, on right bank of the Rhine and 4 mi. N of Coblenz; mfg. of ceramics.

Bendsburg, Poland: see BEDZIN.

Bendzin, Poland: see BEDZIN.

Bene-berak, Palestine: see BNEI BRAQ.

Beneden Merwede River, Netherlands: see LOWER MERWEDE RIVER.

Benedict. **1** City (pop. 176), Wilson co., SE Kansas, on Verdigris R. and 16 mi. WSW of Chanute; livestock, poultry, grain; dairying. **2** Summer resort and fishing village, Charles co., S Md., on Patuxent R. (bridged) and 33 mi. SE of Washington. British disembarked here in 1814 to march on Washington. **3** Village (pop. 206), York co., SE central Nebr., 11 mi. N of York. **4** Village (pop. 127), McLean co., central N.Dak., 38 mi. N of Washburn. **5** Village (pop. 1,486, with near-by Leona Mines), Lee co., extreme SW Va., 13 mi. W of Big Stone Gap, in bituminous-coal region.

Benedicta (bĕnŭdĭk'tŭ), agr. town (pop. 225), Aroostook co., E central Maine, 18 mi. NE of Millinocket, in lumbering, recreational area.

Benedict Field, airfield, St. Croix Isl., U.S. Virgin Isls., 7 mi. WSW of Christiansted; built during Second World War, deactivated 1947.

Benediktbeuern (bā'nădĭktboi"ŭrn), village (pop. 2,200), Upper Bavaria, Germany, on N slope of the Bavarian Alps, 8 mi. WSW of Bad Tölz; lumber milling, woodworking. Former Benedictine monastery (founded mid-8th cent.) has late-17th-cent. Renaissance bldgs. and baroque church.

Beneditinos (bĭnĭdētē'nŏŏs), city (pop. 639), N central Piauí, Brazil, on Poti R. and 40 mi. SE of Teresina; cotton, babassu nuts. Until 1944, called São Benedito.

Benedito Leite (bĭnĭdē'tŏŏ lā'tĭ), city (pop. 342), SE Maranhão, Brazil, on left bank of Parnaíba R. at influx of Balsas R., opposite Uruçuí (Piauí) and 100 mi. ENE of Balsas. Airfield. Formerly spelled Benedicto Leite.

Benefactor (bānāfäktōr'), interior province (□ 1,344; 1935 pop. 73,018; 1950 pop. 107,060), W Dominican Republic; ⊙ San Juan. Comprises fertile, irrigated San Juan valley; bounded by Cordillera Central (N) and Sierra de Neiba (S), watered by the Yaque del Sur. Main crops: rice, corn, coffee, bananas, potatoes, chick-peas, sugar cane. Lumbering. Prov., formerly part of Azua prov., was set up 1938. From it was separated San Rafael prov. in 1942.

Benei Beraq, Israel: see BNEI BRAQ.

Benejama (bānāhä'mä), town (pop. 1,805), Alicante prov., E Spain, 15 mi. W of Alcoy; olive-oil processing, brandy and liqueur distilling, flour milling; fruit, cereals, wine. Ships olives.

Benejúzar (bānāhōō'thär), town (pop. 2,424), Alicante prov., E Spain, on Segura R. and 16 mi. SW of Elche; hemp, cereals, oranges, pepper.

Benelux (bĕ'nŭlŭx), abbreviative term for Belgium, Netherlands, and Luxembourg, coined in 1947 to designate political and economic alliance of the 3 countries.

Beneraird (bĕnŭrârd'), peak (1,435 ft.) of Carrick Mts., S Ayrshire, Scotland, 5 mi. SE of Ballantrae.

Benesov (bĕ'nĕshôf), Czech *Benešov*, Ger. *Beneschau* (bā'nŭshou), town (pop. 8,241), S central Bohemia, Czechoslovakia, 24 mi. SSE of Prague; rail junction; agr. center (barley, oats); noted for its horse fairs. Has 13th-cent. Gothic church, remains of 13th-cent. monastery. Castle of Konopiste (Czech. *Konopiště*, Ger. *Konopischt*), former seat of Archduke Francis Ferdinand (1863–1914), is 2 mi. W; famous for its rose gardens.

Benesov nad Ploucnici (bĕ'nĕshôf nät' plōch"nyĭtsē), Czech *Benešov nad Ploučnicí*, Ger. *Bensen* (bĕn'sŭn), town (pop. 2,823), N Bohemia, Czechoslovakia, 13 mi. NE of Usti nad Labem; rail junction.

Benest (bŭnā'), agr. village (pop. 296), Charente dept., W France, 10 mi. W of Confolens.

Benestare (bĕnĕstä'rĕ), village (pop. 1,816), Reggio di Calabria prov., Calabria, S Italy, SW of Locri.

Bénestroff (bānŭstrôf'), Ger. *Bensdorf* (bĕns'dôrf), village (pop. 431), Moselle dept., NE France, 18 mi. NW of Sarrebourg; rail junction.

Benetúser (bānātōō'sär), S suburb (pop. 3,436) of Valencia, Valencia prov., E Spain; brandy and liqueur distilling, rice milling, meat processing, tanning; mfg. of furniture, tiles, dairy products.

Bene Vagienna (bā'nĕ väjĕn'nä), village (pop. 1,239), Cuneo prov., Piedmont, NW Italy, 11 mi. S of Bra, in sericulture region; silk factories. Gypsum quarries in vicinity. Near by are scanty remains of fortifications, temple, theater of anc. Augusta Bagiennorum. Also written Benevagienna.

Bénévent-l'Abbaye (bānāvā'-läbā'), agr. village (pop. 1,086), Creuse dept., central France, 12 mi. WSW of Guéret. Has 12th-cent. Romanesque church.

Benevento (bĕnĕvĕn'tô), province (□ 796; pop. 303,235), Campania, S Italy; ⊙ Benevento. Hill and mtn. terrain, watered by Calore R. Agr. (cereals, grapes, olives, legumes, tobacco), stock raising. Mfg. at Benevento. In 1945 part of territory (□ 202; pop. 46,472) in W passed to Caserta prov.

Benevento, anc. *Beneventum*, town (pop. 26,692), ⊙ Benevento prov., Campania, S Italy, on Calore R. and 33 mi. NE of Naples; 41°8'N 14°47'E. Produces candy (*torrone*), liquor, matches, macaroni, wine, olive oil, agr. machinery. Archbishopric. Has well-preserved arch of Trajan, remains of Roman theater, and 8th-cent. church of Santa Sofia with 12th-cent. cloister. A town of the Samnites, it became under the Romans an important commercial center on the Appian Way. From 6th to 11th cent., seat of powerful Lombard duchy extending over much of S Italy. Near by in 1266 Charles of Anjou defeated Manfred, king of Sicily. Chiefly under papal rule from 11th cent. to 1860. In Second World War the lower town, including its fine cathedral, was severely damaged.

Benevolence, town (pop. 157), Randolph co., SW Ga., 8 mi. NNE of Cuthbert.

Benewah (bĕ'nŭwä, –wô), county (□ 791; pop. 6,173), N Idaho; ⊙ St. Maries. Rolling, hilly area drained by St. Joe and St. Maries rivers and bordering on Wash. Lumber, hay, flax, wheat, livestock. Formed 1915.

Benfeld (bĕfĕld', Ger. bĕn'fĕlt), town (pop. 2,554), Bas-Rhin dept., E France, on the Ill and 10 mi. NE of Sélestat; fruit shipping, tanning, shoe and bandage mfg. Has 16th-cent. town hall.

Ben Fhada, Scotland: see KINTAIL.

Benfieldside (bĕn'fēldsīd), former urban district (1931 pop. 9,193), N Durham, England, on Derwent R. and 13 mi. SW of Newcastle-upon-Tyne; coal mining. Inc. 1937 in Consett.

Benfleet, residential urban district (1931 pop. 12,091; 1951 census 19,881), S Essex, England, 5 mi. W of Southend. Includes town of South Benfleet (pop. 4,170), on short Benfleet Creek (bridge), which separates Canvey Isl. from mainland. In urban dist. are towns of Hadleigh (E; pop. 3,713) and Thundersley (NE; pop. 2,043). Hadleigh has Norman church and ruins of 13th-cent. castle.

Benga (bĕng'gä), village, Manica and Sofala prov., W Mozambique, on left bank of Zambezi R. and 5 mi. ESE of Tete; transshipment point and railhead for Moatize coal mine (10 mi. NE).

Bengal (bĕng-gôl'), Hindi *Bangala* (bŭng'gŭlŭ), region of NE India and E Pakistan, during 1937–47 an autonomous province (in 1941: □ 77,442; pop. 60,306,525; ⊙ Calcutta) of Br. India; divided 1947 into Indian state of West Bengal and Pakistani prov. of East Bengal. Mainly in the common delta of BRAHMAPUTRA RIVER and GANGES RIVER, it extends N bet. Orissa and Bihar (W) and Burma and Assam (E) from the Bay of Bengal to Sikkim and Bhutan in the E HIMALAYAS. Alluvial rice- and jute-producing Ganges-Brahmaputra delta, with the half-reclaimed mangrove swamps and tidal creeks of the SUNDERBANS in its S area, is interlaced by numerous distributaries, navigable on their main courses by steamer and on their lesser ones by coracle. In N, plains rise to sal forests of the Himalayan foothills (peaks over 8,000 ft.). Chittagong Hills (in SE part of region) are 600–3,000 ft. high. Fertile lower Damodar Valley lies SW. Overall climate is monsoon tropical, with annual rainfall averaging 75 in. (100 in. in E Sundarbans and 90–120 in. in Himalayan foothills), mean temp. ranging from 65°F. in Jan. to 83°F. in May (max. in hot weather is 110°–115°F.). Although the above definition represents the usual geographical and cultural concept of Bengal, Bengal's political boundaries have fluctuated widely throughout history. After becoming successively the NE wing of the Mauryan, Asokan, and Gupta empires (4th cent. B.C.–6th cent. A.D.), the delta developed indigenous Buddhist Pal and Hindu Sen dynasties, which expanded W over Bihar in 9th cent.; in early 13th cent. their domains came under Delhi sultanate, which disintegrated in mid-14th cent. into warring Moslem states; these were conquered (1576) by the Moguls and organized into a prov. of the Mogul empire, with governors (nawabs) appointed by the emperor at Delhi. With the rise of the Mahrattas in 17th cent., the Mogul empire declined, and the nawabs of Bengal became virtually independent of Delhi's control. In 1700, Br. East India Co. (1st Br. settlement in delta at Hooghly, 1651) established nucleus of Bengal presidency at Fort William (Calcutta). Robert Clive's defeat of nawab of Bengal at PLASSEY (1757) and the Br. victory at BUXAR (1764) brought most of the Ganges plain, including Mogul AGRA PROVINCE (later became Br. Agra presidency; roughly equivalent to greater part of present UTTAR PRADESH) under Bengal presidency. The French, except for brief periods, retained their settlement of Chandernagore (founded 1673) until 1950; the Portuguese and the Dutch had early settlements at Hooghly and Chinsura. In 1774, Bengal was given supremacy over Bombay and Madras presidencies; acquired Orissa in 1803 and Assam in 1826; CALCUTTA became ⊙ India in 1833 (⊙ India removed 1912 to Delhi). During 19th cent., term Bengal was loosely used to denote all spheres of Br. military control in N India, including the Punjab, as distinct from those of Br. Bombay and Madras armies. Agra presidency was detached in 1833 and Assam in 1874. In 1905, E dists. were transferred to Assam, creating a new prov. called Eastern Bengal and Assam; in 1912, these dists. were rejoined to Bengal, and Bihar and Orissa were severed, leaving the Bengali-speaking core, which was created an autonomous prov. in 1937. The prov. represented a racial admixture of Caucasian, Dravidian, and Mongolian stock and achieved a cultural homogeneity that transcended Hindu-Moslem distinctions to a remarkable degree. Bengal produced such world-renowned men as the spiritual leaders Ramakrishna, Vivekananda, and Aurobindo, the botanist Jagadis Chandra Bose, the social and religious reformer Ram Mohan Roy, and the poet Rabindranath Tagore, and was known for its leadership in India's independence movement. In 1941, pop. (density 778 per sq. mi.) comprised Hindus (42%), Moslems (54%), and tribes (partly Animist, partly Christianized; 4%). Bengali was spoken by over 90% of pop., Tibeto-Burman and Munda dialects by the tribes; overall pop. was 16% literate. Floods and a hurricane precipitated a famine in 1943 which took a toll of almost 2,000,000 lives. In 1947, upon creation of independent dominions of India and Pakistan, the larger, Moslem-majority area (E) was assigned to Pakistan (along with most of the Assam dist. of Sylhet) as East Bengal and the W, Hindu-majority area to India as West Bengal. Adjacent Bengal States (total □ 9,404; pop. 2,144,829)—Cooch Behar (N), Mayurbhanj (SW), and Tripura (SE)—were inc. into India (1949–50) as a dist. of West Bengal, a dist. of Orissa, and a chief commissioner's state, respectively. **East Bengal** is a province (□ 54,501; 1951 pop. 42,119,000) of Pakistan, coextensive with E Pakistan, separated from rest of Pakistan by c.900 mi. of Indian territory; ⊙ Dacca. Bordered on its land side by Indian states of West Bengal (W and N), Bihar (NW), and Assam and Tripura (E), and by Burma (SE). Mainly in low-lying deltaic tract (mostly less than 300 ft. above sea level), formed (E–W) by MEGHNA RIVER (lower course of SURMA RIVER), JAMUNA RIVER (now main lower channel of the Brahmaputra), PADMA RIVER (main lower bed of the Ganges), and their numerous distributaries, which, with the tidal creeks of the Sundarbans, form an intricate network of waterways. Dists. N of the delta are drained by the Tista. Sylhet dist. (E) is in W Surma Valley. SE of the delta, Chittagong dist. (backed by CHITTAGONG HILLS) extends c.150 mi. along Bay of Bengal's NE coast. Although East Bengal inherited almost all the jute-growing delta of undivided Bengal and produces 85% of whole subcontinent's and 75–80% of world's jute, prov. is barely self-sufficient in food crops; rice is the main staple; some rape and mustard, barley, sugar cane, tobacco, and chillies are grown; tea—in Surma Valley and Chittagong dist.—is important. Coconut and areca palms, mangoes, and bananas are abundant in the delta. Chief forest products are bamboo and resin (in Chittagong Hills and the Sundarbans), sal (mainly in N dists.), and silkworms (mainly in Rajshahi dist.; W). Prov. is rich in fresh water and estuarine fish resources (hilsa, prawn, shrimp). Much wild life (tigers, leopards, wild hogs, snakes) is found in the Sundarbans. Some sheep and goat raising. Mineral resources are insignificant; small coal deposits in Chittagong dist.; salt is obtained from sea water. Partition left all Bengal's jute-weaving mills in West Bengal, along with most of the major industries. East Bengal's industry is mainly connected with agr. processing—jute (pressing), rice, tobacco, cotton, sugar, tea. There is some mfg. of leather goods, soap, matches, chemicals, bricks, and glass; also general and electrical engineering. Industries are mainly located in the textile centers of DACCA (main airport), KUSHTIA, NARAYANGANJ, and PABNA. Other important towns include BARISAL, COMILLA, Dinajpur, Khulna (trade center for the Sundarbans), MYMENSINGH, RANGPUR, and SYLHET. In 1951, construction of jute mills was begun in Dacca-Narayanganj area, and hydroelectric projects in the Chittagong Hills were planned to develop jute milling and other industries in prov.'s SE section. CHITTAGONG handles bulk of E Pakistan's exports (jute, tea, tobacco, hides) and imports (metals, machinery, coal, sugar, textiles); after 1950, new port of Port Jinnah or Chalna Anchorage became the main jute port. Handicraft industries are important, especially cotton weaving; others include making of silver filigree, ivory carving, pottery mfg., and mat weaving; the once famous Dacca muslin is now made in small quantities there. Roads and railways (major workshops at Saidpur) are adequate, and the network of delta waterways is important for internal rice and jute traffic. Has Dacca Univ. (with many affiliated colleges), Surma Valley Technical Inst. (at Sylhet), and rice research station (at Habiganj). Extensive Buddhist archaeological remains at Paharpur. East Bengal's pop. (c.95% rural) is greatly overcrowded (density averages 780 per sq. mi. and is over 1,000 in central dists.); comprises Moslems (70%), Hindus (20%), and Tibeto-Burman tribes (10%); these computations, based on 1941 census figures for area, do not include changes due to migrations following partition. Comprises 17 dists.: Bakarganj, Bogra, Chittagong, Chittagong Hill Tracts, Dacca, Dinajpur, Faridpur, Jessore, Khulna, Kushtia, Mymensingh, Noakhali, Pabna, Rajshahi, Rangpur, Sylhet, Tippera. **West Bengal** is (since 1950) a constituent state (□ 29,476; 1951 pop. 24,786,683) of republic of India; ⊙ Calcutta. Major portion (S) is bordered SW by Orissa, W by Bihar, N and E by East Bengal (Pakistan); N dists. of Cooch Behar, Darjeeling, and Jalpaiguri are separated from main body of state by a strip (c.150 mi. wide) consisting of East Bengal and Bihar; this detached section is bordered W by Nepal, N by Sikkim and Bhutan, and E by Assam. S portion is drained by the Ganges, which bifurcates into Padma R. and BHAGIRATHI RIVER (called HOOGHLY RIVER in lower course; forms W demarcation of Ganges Delta) and by main tributaries of the Bhagirathi (Mor, Damodar, and Rupnarayan); E part of area's coast on Bay of Bengal is in the Sundarbans; mainly alluvial soil, merging (SW) with lateritic E outliers of Chota Nagpur Plateau. N dists., drained by Tista and Mahananda rivers, have marshy Terai region in S, Western Duars and spurs of SE Nepal Himalayas and SW Assam Himalayas in N. Rice, millet, jute, rape and mustard, sugar cane, chillies, and barley are grown in most areas of entire state. N section has important tea and tobacco tracts; extensive forests (sal, teak, oak, bamboo, silver fir, cinchona); orange orchards. Dispersed mango and palm trees grow on plains. Extensive lac cultivation in Bankura dist. (W). Considerable raising of cattle (primarily as draft animals), especially in SW. Noted wild game (elephants, tigers, leopards, rhinoceroses) in Himalayan foothills. Silk growing in W Murshidabad dist. Fishing (hilsa, prawn, shrimp) is mainly confined to the Sundarbans. Coal field around RANIGANJ, in central Damodar Valley, produces almost ⅓ of India's coking coal; supplies fuel for major locomotive shops at ASANSOL and large iron- and steelworks at BURNPUR and KULTI. Important industrial concentration along HOOGHLY R., with center at CALCUTTA, owes its development largely to the coal, iron, and other minerals of Bihar and Orissa; industries here include jute, cotton, rice, oilseed, paper, and sugar milling, mfg. of chemicals, cement, leather and rubber goods, matches, glass, shellac, and soap; and engineering (railroad shops, iron- and steelworks); centers are at BARANAGAR, BARRACKPORE, BUDGE-BUDGE, GARDEN REACH, HOWRAH, SERAMPORE, and TOLLYGUNGE. Rail junction of Kharagpur (in SW) has large railroad shops. Rice and jute milling is important throughout state, as are small-scale pottery and cutlery industries. Bishnupur and Murshidabad are silk-weaving centers. Hand-loom cotton weaving is widespread. Calcutta (on intercontinental air route), India's major commercial port, is linked by rail with all major cities of India; in 1950, a link was built in N section of state to provide connection bet. Calcutta and trading centers of upper Assam without crossing Pakistan territory. Kalimpong, 13 mi. E of DARJEELING (rail terminus; famous hill resort), is on major India-Tibet trade route (through Chumbi Valley). River traffic is important throughout state. A navigation canal, connecting coal fields of Bihar–West Bengal border with Calcutta, is part of multipurpose DAMODAR VALLEY development project. In Calcutta are Univ. of Calcutta (has affiliated colleges elsewhere in state), School of Tropical Medicine, and several other leading Indian research institutes. Visva Bharati, univ. founded by Rabindranath Tagore is at Santiniketan; Bengal Silk Technological Inst. at Berhampore; hq. of Ramakrishna Mission at Belur. Noted remains of Islamic architecture at Gaur. West Bengal is predominantly rural, and, except for Calcutta-Howrah conurbation, slightly less densely populated than East Bengal. Pop. consists of Hindus (70%), Moslems (25%) and several aboriginal tribes (mainly Mundas and Santals; 5%); these computations, based on 1941 census figures for area, do not include changes due to migrations following partition. State comprises 15 dists.: Bankura, Birbhum, Burdwan, Calcutta, Cooch Behar, Darjeeling, Hooghly, Howrah, Jalpaiguri, Malda, Midnapore, Murshidabad, Nadia, Twenty-Four Parganas, West Dinajpur.

Bengal, Bay of, broad arm of Indian Ocean, on S coast of Asia, bet. India and Ceylon (W) and Andaman and Nicobar isls. (E), which separate it from Andaman Sea; 1,000 mi. wide. It receives the Kistna and Godavari rivers and the combined Ganges-Brahmaputra delta (N). Main ports are: Madras, Vizagapatnam, and Calcutta (India); Chittagong (Pakistan); and Akyab (Burma).

Bengal Duars, India: see WESTERN DUARS.

Bengal States, subordinate agency (□ 9,404; pop. 2,144,829) of former Eastern States agency, India; hq. were at Calcutta. Comprised princely states of Cooch Behar (merged 1950 with West Bengal), Mayurbhanj (merged 1949 with Orissa), and Tripura (placed 1949 under chief commissioner).

Ben-Gardane (bĕn-gärdän'), town and oasis (pop. 1,687), Southern Territories, SE Tunisia, near the Mediterranean and Libyan border, 45 mi. ESE of Médenine. Olives, cereals; sheep raising, fish trade.

Bengasi, Cyrenaica: see BENGHAZI.

Bengawan River, Indonesia: see SOLO RIVER.

Bengazi, Cyrenaica: see BENGHAZI.

Benghazi, Bengasi, Bengazi, or Benghasi, (all: bĕn-gä'zē), anc. *Berenice*, city (1950 pop. 56,325), ⊙ Cyrenaica, Libya, port and bathing resort at E end of Gulf of Sidra, 400 mi. E of Tripoli, in a plain (15 mi. wide); 30°7'N 20°3'E. Commercial, communications (road and rail hub), and tourist center; saltworks, flour mills, olive-oil refinery, food cannery, tanneries, liquor distilleries, brewery, ice factory, foundries, construction industry (cement, brick, asphalt); sponge and tunny fishing. Consists of old Arab quarter and modern European section around the harbor. Has mosques, cathedral, synagogue, hosp., archaeological mus., and airport. Chief port of Cyrenaica; exports sponges, hides, wool. Anciently a Greek colony. Ruled by Turks (16th cent.–1911) and by Italians (1911–42) under whom it became a center of colonization. In Second World War, damaged by bombing and fighting; changed hands several times (1941–42) in seesaw battle bet. Axis and British, who finally took it in 1942. The ruler of the Senusi, who resides here, was proclaimed (1950) king of Libya. After Libyan independence (Jan., 1952), Benghazi was to be one of the 2 capitals (Tripoli is the other) of Libya.

Bengies (bĕn'jēz), suburban village (1940 pop. 829), Baltimore co., central Md., 12 mi. ENE of downtown Baltimore.

Bengkalis (bŭngkä'lēs), island (42 mi. long, 12 mi. wide), Indonesia, in Strait of Malacca, just off E coast of Sumatra, 120 mi. W of Singapore; 1°30'N 102°15'E. Swampy and low. At W end of isl. is port of Bengkalis (pop. 3,291), shipping timber, rubber, resin, tobacco from Sumatra.

Bengkulu, Indonesia: see BENKULEN.

Bengoi Bay (bān'goi'), inlet (c.15 mi. wide, 15 mi. long) of South China Sea in S central Vietnam, separated from sea by a peninsula (20 mi. long, 1–5 mi. wide). Tubong and Vangia are on NW shore; Honecohe on SW shore. Russian fleet sailed from here before defeat of Tsushima (1905).

Bengore Head (bĕn-gôr'), promontory on the North Channel, N Co. Antrim, Northern Island, just E of the Giant's Causeway.

Bengouanou (bĕng-gwä'nōō), village (pop. c.2,200), S central Ivory Coast, Fr. West Africa, 90 mi. N of Abidjan; coffee, cacao, palm kernels.

Bengough (bĕn-gôf',-gôf'), village (pop. 337), S Sask., 40 mi. ESE of Assiniboia; wheat; in coal-mining region.

Bengower (bĕn-gou'ûr), mountain (2,184 ft.), NW Co. Galway, Ireland, in Benna Beola mts., 8 mi. E of Clifden.

Bengtsfors (bĕngts"fôrs', -fôsh'), town (pop. 2,543), Alvsborg co., SW Sweden, 17 mi. W of Amal; lumber, paper, and pulp mills, furniture factories. Power station.

Benguela (bĕng-gĕ'lù), province (□51,000; pop. 1,100,104), W Angola, on the Atlantic; ⊙ Benguela. From narrow coastal plain rises escarpment (Serra Upanda), beyond which extends central Angola's Bié Plateau (highest point, 8,270 ft.). Drained by Cuanza R. (N). Fertile upland areas settled along Benguela RR from Lobito. Chief crops: coffee, cotton, sisal, corn, sugar (in Benguela area). Lobito is Angola's best port; lesser ports are Benguela, Novo Redondo, and Pôrto Amboim. Nova Lisboa, on central plateau, was originally planned as colonial ⊙. Prov. is divided into 3 dists.: Cuanza-Sul, Benguela, and Huambo.

Benguela, city (pop. 14,243), ⊙ Benguela prov., W Angola, on the Atlantic, on Benguela RR and 18 mi. S of Lobito; 12°35'S 13°25'E. Open roadstead. Exports corn, beeswax, hides and skins, but near-by Lobito handles most of foreign trade. Sugar milling, fish drying; mfg. of soap, tools, pottery; sawmilling. Airfield. Fort built here 1587. Town founded 1617. The Benguela RR (which now has its ocean terminus at Lobito) was built in 1920s to tap the central plateau of Angola and copper-rich Katanga prov. of Belgian Congo; it links up with Belgian Congo rail system at Tenke; gauge 3 ft. 6 in. Section (838 mi.) crossing Angola to Dilolo-Gare (border station) opened 1929: section in Belgian Congo opened 1931. Formerly spelled Benguella.

Benguela Current, cold current of S Atlantic Ocean moving northward along W coast of Africa S of the Gulf of Guinea. Like the Peru Current off W South America, it brings desert-like aridity to adjacent coastal area.

Benguérir (bĕn-gārēr'), town (pop. 1,198), Marrakesh region, W Fr. Morocco, 40 mi. N of Marrakesh; rail junction on Casablanca-Marrakesh line (spur to Louis Gentil and Safi). Also spelled Ben Guerir.

Benguet, Philippines: see MOUNTAIN PROVINCE.

Bengut, Cape (bĕngüt'), headland in Alger dept., N central Algeria, on the Mediterranean coast of Great Kabylia, bet. the mouth of the Oued Lebaon (W) and the port of Dellys (E); 36°55'N 3°54'E; lighthouse. Also spelled Benngut.

Benha or **Banha** (both: bĕn'hä, bĕnhä'), town (pop. 35,245; with suburbs, 36,295), ⊙ Qalyubiya prov., Lower Egypt, on Raiyah Taufiqi and 28 mi. NNW of Cairo; 30°27'N 31°11'E. Rail and trade center; cotton ginning, wool spinning; cereals, cotton, flax.

Benham (bĕ'nŭm), mining village (pop. 7,952, with adjacent Lynch), Harlan co., SE Ky., in the Cumberlands, near Poor Fork of Cumberland R. 22 mi. ENE of Harlan; bituminous coal, timber. Big Black Mtn. is SE.

Ben Hill, county (□ 255; pop. 14,879), S central Ga.; ⊙ Fitzgerald. Bounded NE by Ocmulgee R., W by Alapaha R. Coastal plain agr. (cotton, corn, tobacco, peanuts, livestock) and timber area. Formed 1906.

Benholm (bĕn'hōm), agr. village and parish (pop. 1,092), SE Kincardine, Scotland, near North Sea, 3 mi. SW of Inverbervie. Has remains of anc. Benholm Castle.

Beni (bĕ'nē), village, Kivu prov., E Belgian Congo, 110 mi. NNE of Costermansville; trading and tourist center near W border of Albert Natl. Park, base for excursions to the Ruwenzori. Seat of vicar apostolic. Has R.C. mission, leprosarium, hosp. for Europeans. In vicinity live Pygmy tribes.

Beni (bā'nē), department (□ 80,302; 1949 pop. estimate 73,900), N Bolivia; ⊙ Trinidad. Bounded by Brazil (NE; along Guaporé and lower Mamoré rivers) and by Beni R. (W and NW). Consists of extensive tropical lowlands (llanos; S), which change to dense forests, principally along the rivers, in its N and NE sections. Drained by the Mamoré and its affluents. Served by Bolivia's main river transportation network. Sparsely inhabited; dept. is one of chief Bolivian rubber areas; also cattle raising, tropical agr. (sugar cane, bananas, cacao) in llanos, rubber and quinine-bark collecting in forests. Brazil nuts are important export item. Chief centers: Trinidad, Riberalta, Magdalena, Santa Ana.

Béni-Abbès (bā'nē-ābĕs'), village (pop. 3,268) and Saharan oasis, Aïn-Sefra territory, W Algeria, 100 mi. S of Colomb-Béchar, on projected extension of trans-Saharan RR; 30°8'N 2°10'W. Date palms; coal deposits. Mfg. of esparto products. Irrigated by waters from intermittent Oued Saoura. Has modern experiment station for Saharan agr.

Beni 'Adi or **Bani 'Adi** (both: bĕ'nē ădē'), 2 villages, Beni 'Adi el Bahariya (N; pop. 9,680) and Beni 'Adi el Qibliya (S; pop. 6,927), Asyut prov., Upper Egypt, 5 mi. SW of Manfalut; pottery making; cereals, dates, sugar cane. Battle (1798) bet. Fr. troops and the Arabs.

Beni Ahmad or **Bani Ahmad** (both: bĕ'nē ä'măd), village (pop. 7,870), Minya prov., Upper Egypt, on railroad and 4 mi. S of Minya; cotton, cereals, sugar.

Beniarjó (bānyärhō'), village (pop. 1,434), Valencia prov., E Spain, 3 mi. SSW of Gandía; ships oranges; sericulture.

Beniarrés (bānyärās'), town (pop. 1,865), Alicante prov., E Spain, 15 mi. SW of Gandía; olive-oil and wine processing, flour milling.

Beni-Bahdel Dam, Algeria: see TAFNA, OUED.

Béni-Béchir, Tunisia: see BEN-BACHIR.

Beni bu Ifrur (bā'nē bōō ēfrōōr'), mining area in Kert territory, E Sp. Morocco, just S of Segangan; Sp. Morocco's leading iron deposits. Ore is shipped by rail to Melilla (11 mi. NE) for export. Lead deposits. Also spelled Beni Buifrur.

Benicarló (bānēkärlō'), city (pop. 9,001), Castellón de la Plana prov., E Spain, in Valencia, port on the Mediterranean, and 40 mi. NE of Castellón de la Plana; exports wine, brandy, fruit. Fishing, boatbuilding, alcohol and brandy distilling, olive-oil and almond processing; mfg. of cement, chocolate, soap, hats, furniture. Cereals, wine, fruit, hogs in area. Has old castle, parochial church with tiled dome.

Benicasim (bānēkäsēm'), town (pop. 1,577), Castellón de la Plana prov., E Spain, on the Mediterranean, and 7 mi. NE of Castellón de la Plana; olive-oil processing, liqueur distilling; grapes, beans, sheep. Popular bathing resort. Carmelite convent of Desierto de las Palmas 2 mi. NW.

Benicia (bŭnē'shŭ), city (pop. 7,284), Solano co., W Calif., port on Carquinez Strait, 25 mi. NE of San Francisco, near Vallejo (NW). U.S. arsenal here was established as army post in 1849. Mfg.

of dredges; canneries. Has many mid-19th-cent. landmarks. Founded 1847, inc. 1850.

Benidorm (bānēdôrm'), town (pop. 2,164), Alicante prov., E Spain, on the Mediterranean, and 24 mi. NE of Alicante; dried-fish processing, olive pressing, wool-cloth mfg.; wine, almonds, raisins. Bathing resort.

Beniel (bänyĕl'), town (pop. 1,850), Murcia prov., SE Spain, on the Segura and 9 mi. NE of Murcia; mfg. of insecticides. Citrus and other fruit, cereals, pepper, hemp; sericulture.

Benifairó de Valldigna (bānēfīrō' dhā välydē'nyä), village (pop. 1,435), Valencia prov., E Spain, 10 mi. NW of Gandía; truck produce, olive oil.

Benifallet (bānēfäyĕt'), town (pop. 1,348), Tarragona prov., NE Spain, on the Ebro and 7 mi. SE of Gandesa; olive-oil processing; ships carob beans, almonds. Mineral springs near by.

Benifayó (bānēfīō'), town (pop. 7,030), Valencia prov., E Spain, 13 mi. SSW of Valencia; rice milling, olive-oil processing; mfg. of willow baskets, sausage, cheese. Truck produce, wine, cereals, sheep. Stone quarries. Moorish tower near by.

Benigánim (bānēgä'nēm), town (pop. 3,594), Valencia prov., E Spain, 6 mi. SE of Játiva; cement works; mfg. of candy, alcohol, soap, tiles. Olive oil, cereals, wine, truck produce.

Beniganj (bä'nēgŭnj), town (pop. 2,048), Hardoi dist., central Uttar Pradesh, India, 20 mi. ESE of Hardoi; wheat, gram, barley, pearl millet.

Beni Haram or **Bani Haram** (both: bĕ'nē häräm'), village (pop. 11,707), Asyut prov., central Upper Egypt, 4 mi. NNW of Dairut; cereals, dates, sugar.

Beni Hassan or **Bani Hassan** (both: bĕ'nē hăs'săn, hä'sän), village (pop. 4,879), Minya prov., Upper Egypt, on E bank of the Nile and 14 mi. SSE of Minya. Here are remarkable anc. rock tombs and a fine XIIth dynasty group (2500–2200 B.C.) representing the earliest known columns of Egyptian architecture. Also spelled Beni Hasan.

Beni 'Ibeid or **Bani 'Ibayd** (both: bĕ'nē ībād'). **1** Village (pop. 9,223), Daqahliya prov., Lower Egypt, 15 mi. E of Mansura; cotton, cereals. **2** Village (pop. 7,575), Minya prov., Upper Egypt, near the Nile, 15 mi. S of Minya; cotton, cereals, sugar cane.

Béni-Isguen (bā'nē-ēsgĕn'), Saharan village, Ghardaïa territory, central Algeria, one of the Mzab oases, just SE of Ghardaïa; date palms. It is the Mzabites' holy city.

Béni-Khiar (bā'nē-khyär'), village, Grombalia dist., NE Tunisia, on Cape Bon Peninsula, near Gulf of Hammamet, 3 mi. NE of Nabeul; olive-oil pressing; mfg. of wool blankets.

Benimaclet (bānēmäklĕt'), E suburb (pop. 5,421) of Valencia, Valencia prov., E Spain.

Benimamet (bānēmämĕt'), suburb (pop. 6,717) of Valencia, Valencia prov., E Spain.

Béni-Mansour (bā'nē-mänsōōr'), village, Alger dept., N central Algeria, near the Oued Sahel at N foot of the Biban Range, 40 mi. NE of Aumale; important junction on Algiers-Constantine RR (spur to Bougie).

Beni Mazar or **Bani Mazar** (both: bĕ'nē măzär'), town (pop. 21,615; with suburbs, 23,118), Minya prov. Upper Egypt, on W bank of the Nile, on Ibrahimiya Canal, on railroad, and 28 mi. NNE of Minya; cotton ginning, woolen and sugar milling; cotton, cereals, sugar cane.

Béni Mellal (bā'nē mĕl-läl'), town (pop. 17,456), Casablanca region, W central Fr. Morocco, at foot of the Middle Atlas, 110 mi. SE of Casablanca; center of rich agr. area noted for its fruit orchards, olive and mulberry trees; trade in wool, livestock, hand-woven cloth. Fruit preserving (apricots, figs, carobs), palm-fiber processing, olive-oil pressing. Kasba Zidania Dam on Oum er Rbia is 11 mi. N.

Béni-Méred (bā'nē-mārĕd'), village (pop. 476), Alger dept., N central Algeria, in the Mitidja plain, 4 mi. NE of Blida; sulphur refining, distilling of essential oils; winegrowing.

Benimodo (bānēmō'dhō), village (pop. 1,394), Valencia prov., E Spain, 6 mi. NW of Alcira, in rice-growing area. Olive-oil processing; wheat, wine.

Beni Muhammadiyat or **Bani Muhammadiyat** (both: bĕ'nē mōōhăm'mădīyăt), village group (pop. 14,564), Asyut prov., central Upper Egypt, on E bank of the Nile and 10 mi. NW of Asyut; cereals, dates, sugar cane.

Benin (bĕnēn', bĕnē'), province (□ 8,627; pop. 459,906), Western Provinces, S Nigeria, in equatorial forest belt; ⊙ Benin City. Mainly rain forest, with deciduous woods and savanna (N and NE), mangrove swamps (SW). Major products: hardwood, rubber, palm oil and kernels, cacao, kola nuts, cotton; cotton weaving, brassworking, wood carving. Main food crops: yams, cassava, plantains. Lignite deposits. Pop. largely Beni. Chief centers: Benin City, Ubiaja, Agbor, Ogwashi Uku. A powerful state long before arrival of Europeans, it maintained its importance until middle of 19th cent., participating in European slave trade; came under Br. domination by 1899.

Benin, Bight of (bĕnēn', bŭnĭn'), Atlantic bay of the Gulf of Guinea, on coast of W central Africa, just W of Niger delta, extending roughly bet. 1° and 5°E. Washes shores of the Gold Coast, Togoland, Dahomey, SW Nigeria. Receives Benin R.

Benin City, city (pop. 8,530), ⊙ Benin prov., Western Provinces, S Nigeria, on branch of Benin R. and 150 mi. E of Lagos; alt. 275 ft.; 6°10'N 5°38'E. Major road and trade center; hardwood and rubber industry, wood carving; palm oil and kernels, kola nuts, cacao. Airfield. Formerly (with its port GWATO) a notorious slave-trade center, and the site of human sacrifices. Known for its brass casting and ivory carving until late 19th cent. Stormed by British in 1897.

Benin River, S Nigeria, formed 30 mi. S of Benin City by junction of Ethiope (right) and Jamieson (left) rivers, flows 60 mi. W, past Sapele and Koko, to Gulf of Guinea at Fishtown. Navigable below Sapele. Connected (left) with Niger R. delta.

Beniopa (bänyō'pä), agr. village (pop. 2,568), Valencia prov., E Spain, 2 mi. NW of Gandía.

Béni-Ounif (bā'nē-ōōnēf'), village (pop. 940), Aïn-Sefra territory, NW central Algeria, on Oran–Colomb-Béchar RR and 70 mi. NE of Colomb-Béchar, at Fr. Morocco border; date palms; leatherworking.

Benipeixcar (bānēpāshkär'), SW suburb (pop. 1,230) of Gandía, Valencia prov., E Spain; brandy distilling; truck produce, wheat, olive oil.

Beni Rafi' or **Bani Rafi'** (both: bĕ'nē rä'fē), village (pop. 8,691), Asyut prov., central Upper Egypt, 6 mi. NW of Manfalut; cereals, dates, sugar.

Beni River (bā'nē), NW Bolivia, formed by confluence of BOPI RIVER and SANTA ELENA RIVER at Huachi (La Paz dept.); flows c.600 mi. NW, N, and NE, through llanos and forests, past Puerto Pando, Rurrenabaque, Concepción, and Riberalta, joining the Mamoré at Villa Bella to form MADEIRA RIVER. Receives Kaka, Tuichi, Madidi, Madre de Dios, and Orton rivers (left), and small Río Negro, only outlet of L. Rogagua (right). Forms part of La Paz–Beni border in middle course and Beni–Pando border in lower course. Rubber and quinine bark found in dense forests along its lower course, below mouth of the Madidi. Navigable bet. Cachuela Esperanza and Puerto Pando, a distance of c.500 mi. One of Bolivia's most important streams, forming with its affluents an extensive river transportation network.

Beni Rizah or **Bani Rizah** (both: bĕ'nē rīză'), village (pop. 13,879), Asyut prov., central Upper Egypt, 6 mi. NNW of Asyut; pottery making, wood and ivory carving; cereals, dates, sugar.

Benisa (bānē'sä), town (pop. 3,505), Alicante prov., E Spain, near the Mediterranean, 20 mi. SE of Gandía; olive-oil processing, linen mfg.; ships muscat grapes, raisins, almonds. Also wine, cereals, vegetables in area. Ophite quarries.

Béni-Saf (bā'nē-säf'), town (pop. 6,516), Oran dept., NW Algeria, port on the Mediterranean, 30 mi. N of Tlemcen; iron-mining and shipping center; also exports agr. products of Tlemcen area (with which it has been linked by rail since 1925), esparto, bristles. Fish salting, smoking, and canning; cord mfg. Harbor built 1881 by mining interests.

Benisalem, Balearic Isls.: see BINISALEM.

Benisanet (bānēsänĕt'), town (pop. 1,176), Tarragona prov., NE Spain, on the Ebro and 11 mi. E of Gandesa; olive-oil processing, sawmilling; agr. trade (sheep and hogs, wine, almonds).

Benisanó (bānēsänō'), village (pop. 1,267), Valencia prov., E Spain, 15 mi. NW of Valencia; olive-oil processing. Francis I of France was briefly imprisoned (1525) in medieval castle here.

Beni Shangul (bĕ'nē shäng'gōōl), district (□ c.4,600; pop. c.50,000), in NW corner of Wallaga prov., W central Ethiopia, bet. Anglo-Egyptian Sudan (W) and the Blue Nile (E). Plateau region (1,500–3,000 ft. high) noted for its gold placers. Chief center, Asosa. Detached (1898) from the Sudan by Menelik II. Slavery flourished here until recently.

Beni Shiqeir or **Bani Shiqayr** (both: bĕ'nē shĭkār') village (pop. 8,055), Asyut prov., central Upper Egypt, on railroad and 4 mi. NNW of Manfalut; cereals, dates, sugar cane.

Beni Suef or **Bani Suwayf** (both: bĕ'nē swāf'), province (□ 423; pop. 613,365), Upper Egypt, in Nile valley; ⊙ Beni Suef. Bounded S by Minya prov., E by Arabian Desert, N by Giza prov., W by Libyan Desert. Cotton ginning, woolen and sugar milling; agr. (cotton, cereals, sugar cane). Main urban centers, besides Beni Suef, are Bush and Biba. Served by railway along W bank of the Nile, with a junction at El Wasta to Faiyum prov.

Beni Suef or **Bani Suwayf,** city (pop. 56,356; with suburbs, 57,464), ⊙ Beni Suef prov., Upper Egypt, on W bank of the Nile, on Ibrahimiya Canal, on railroad, and 68 mi. SSW of Cairo; 29°5'N 31°5'E. Important mfg. and trading center: woolen and sugar milling, cotton ginning, shoe making, mfg. of cigarettes; building stone. Agr.: cotton, cereals, sugar cane.

Benitachell (bānētächāl'), village (pop. 1,494), Alicante prov., E Spain, near the Mediterranean, 25 mi. SE of Gandía; straw-hat mfg. Olive oil, fruit, wine, raisins in area.

Béni Tadjit (bā'nē täjĕt'), village, Meknès region, SE Fr. Morocco, on E slope of the High Atlas, 30 mi. NNE of Boudenib; 32°18'N 3°28'W. Here are Bou Dahar lead and zinc mines.

Benítez, Argentina: see COLONIA BENÍTEZ.

Benítez, Campo (käm'pō bānē'tĕs), oil field in Zulia state, NW Venezuela, on NE shore of L. Maracaibo, 6 mi. S of Cabimas; extends c.8 mi. into lake.

Benito (bŭnē'tō), village (pop. 328), W Man., 18 mi. SW of Swan River; mixed farming; wheat.

Benito, town, Sp. Guinea: see RÍO BENITO.

Benito Juárez (bānē'tō hwä'rĕs). **1** Town (pop. 791), Michoacán, central Mexico, 13 mi. SSW of Zitácuaro; alt. 6,506 ft.; cereals, livestock. **2** Town (pop. 242), Veracruz, E Mexico, 50 mi. WNW of Tuxpan; corn, fruit.

Benito River, continental Sp. Guinea, rises as the Woleu in Gabon (Fr. Equatorial Africa) SE of Oyem, flows c.200 mi. generally W to the Gulf of Guinea at Río Benito town. Interrupted by rapids. Also called San Benito R.

Beni Ulid (bĕ'nē ōōlĕd'), town (pop. 13,630), central Tripolitania, Libya, on secondary road and 65 mi. SSW of Homs, in agr. (olives, dates, figs, barley) and livestock (sheep, goats, camels) area; alt. 755 ft.; domestic weaving (rugs, bags) and grindstone mfg. Roman and Byzantine ruins (cisterns, mausoleums) in region.

Benjamin, town (pop. 530), ⊙ Knox co., N Texas, c.75 mi. WSW of Wichita Falls; trade, shipping point in grain and cattle area.

Benjamín Aceval (bĕnhämēn' äsäväl'), town (dist. pop. 5,176), Presidente Hayes dept., central Paraguay, in Chaco region, near Paraguay R., 7 mi. N of Villa Hayes. Agr. center (tobacco, sugar cane, alfalfa, cotton, cattle, horses); alcohol distilling, sugar milling.

Benjamín Aráoz (ärous'), town (pop. estimate 500), NE Tucumán prov., Argentina, 5 mi. SW of Burruyacú, in stock-raising and lumbering area.

Benjamin Constant (bĕnzhämēn' kōstä'), city (pop. 999), W Amazonas, Brazil, on right bank of Javari R. at its influx into the Amazon (Peru border), and 14 mi. SSW of Leticia (Colombia), 700 mi. WSW of Manaus. Steamboat and hydroplane landing. Name Benjamin Constant was applied until 1939 to Remate de Males (40 mi. W); present Benjamin Constant was formerly called Esperança.

Benjamin Harrison, Fort, Ind.: see INDIANAPOLIS.

Benjamin Island, Chile: see CHONOS ARCHIPELAGO.

Benjamín Larroudé (bĕnhämēn' lärōōdā') or **Larroudé,** town (pop. estimate 1,200), NE La Pampa natl. territory, Argentina, on railroad and 45 mi. NNE of General Pico; wheat, corn, alfalfa, livestock; dairying.

Benkelman, village (pop. 1,512), ⊙ Dundy co., S Nebr., 50 mi. WSW of McCook and on Republican R., near Kansas line; farm trade center in Great Plains region; livestock, grain, dairy and poultry produce. Fish hatchery. Settled 1880.

Benkoelen, Indonesia: see BENKULEN.

Benkovac (bĕn'kôväts), Ger. *Benkovatz*, Ital. *Bencovazzo*, village (pop. 2,411), W Croatia, Yugoslavia, 20 mi. SE of Zadar, in Dalmatia; local trade center of the Ravni Kotari.

Benkulen or **Benkoelen** (both: bŭng-kōō'lŭn), Indonesian *Bengkulu*, town (pop. 13,418), SW Sumatra, Indonesia, port on Indian Ocean, 180 mi. WSW of Palembang; 3°47'S 102°15'E. Trade center for mining, agr., and cattle-raising area. Exports gold, silver, coffee, pepper, corn, cinchona bark. Here is Fort Marlborough, built c.1710 by the British. In early 17th cent. the Dutch began trading here; control over area passed 1685 to the British, who kept it until 1824, when the Dutch won it by treaty. Also spelled Bencoolen.

Ben Laoigh, Scotland: see BEN LUI.

Ben Lawers (bĕn lô'ŭrz), mountain (3,984 ft.) in W central Perthshire, Scotland, 7 mi. NE of Killin, overlooking Loch Tay; noted for alpine flora and fine view.

Benld (bĕnĕld', –ĕl'), city (pop. 2,093), Macoupin co., SW Ill., 25 mi. ENE of Alton, in agr. and bituminous-coal-mining area. Inc. 1904; reincorporated 1930 as city.

Ben Ledi (bĕn lĕ'dē), mountain (2,873 ft.) in SW Perthshire, Scotland, 4 mi. WNW of Callander, overlooking Loch Katrine.

Benlloch (bĕnyôk'), town (pop. 1,192), Castellón de la Plana prov., E Spain, 16 mi. NNE of Castellón de la Plana; olive-oil processing; cereals.

Ben Lomond, Australia: see NEW ENGLAND RANGE.

Ben Lomond (bĕn lō'mŭnd), mountain (3,192 ft.), NW Stirling, Scotland, overlooking Loch Lomond (W), 27 mi. WNW of Stirling.

Ben Lomond, highest mountain range in Tasmania; extends 10 mi. S from upper course of N.Esk R. to middle course of S.Esk R., on plateau with hills and small lakes; rises to Legge Tor (5,160 ft.). Coal, granite; winter sports.

Ben Lomond. 1 Town (pop. 284), Sevier co., SW Ark., 20 mi. SE of De Queen, near Little River. **2** Resort village (pop. c.450), Santa Cruz co., W Calif., in Santa Cruz Mts., 9 mi. NNW of Santa Cruz. Redwood groves near by.

Ben Lui or **Ben Laoigh** (both: bĕn lōō'ē), mountain (3,708 ft.) in W Perthshire, Scotland, on Argyll border, 7 mi. E of Dalmally. Dochart R., headstream of the Tay, rises here.

Ben Macdhui or **Ben Muich-Dhui** (both: bĕn mŭkdōō'ē), mountain (4,296 ft.) in Cairngorm Mts., SW Aberdeen, Scotland, 12 mi. WNW of Braemar; 2d-highest peak in Scotland (Ben Nevis is higher). The Dee rises here.

Benmore (bĕnmôr') or **Fair Head,** picturesque promontory on N coast of Co. Antrim, Northern Ireland, 5 mi. ENE of Ballycastle; 55°14'N 6°9'W; 636 ft. high, with sheer cliffs of basaltic rock.

Ben More (bĕn môr'). **1** Mountain (3,169 ft.), highest on Mull isl., Argyll, Scotland, in SW part of isl., 7 mi. SSW of Salen. **2** Mountain (3,843 ft.), SW Perthshire, Scotland, 7 mi. WNW of Balquhidder.

Ben More Assynt, Scotland: see ASSYNT.

Ben Muich-Dhui, Scotland: see BEN MACDHUI.

Benna Beola, Bennebeola (both: bĕ"nùbē'ùlù), **Bunnabeola** (bŭ'-), **The Twelve Bens,** or **The Twelve Pins,** mountain range, Ireland, extending 10 mi. E-W in Connemara district, NW Co. Galway. Highest peak is Benbaun (2,395 ft.), 8 mi. ENE of Clifden.

Benneckenstein (bĕnĕ'kŭn-shtīn"), town (pop. 4,040), in former Prussian Saxony prov., central Germany, after 1945 in Thuringia, in the lower Harz, 12 mi. NNW of Nordhausen; climatic health resort; woodworking.

Bennet or **Bennett,** village (pop. 396), Lancaster co., SE Nebr., 10 mi. SE of Lincoln; livestock, grain, dairy, poultry.

Bennett, county (□ 1,187; pop. 3,396), S S.Dak., on Nebr. line; ⊙ Martin. Farming area drained by South Fork White R. and several creeks. Wheat, flax, livestock. La Creek Teal and Migratory Fowl Refuge in S. Formed 1909.

Bennett. 1 Town (pop. 272), Adams co., N central Colo., 30 mi. E of Denver; alt. 5,485 ft. **2** Town (pop. 357), Cedar co., E Iowa, 25 mi. NW of Davenport, in agr. area. **3** Village, Nebr.: see BENNET. **4** Town (pop. 236), Chatham co., central N.C., 18 mi. ESE of Asheboro.

Bennett Island, Rus. *Ostrov Bennet,* largest (□ 75) of De Long Isls., in E. Siberian Sea, 290 mi. off N Yakut Autonomous SSR, Russian SFSR; 76°40'N 149°E. Discovered 1881 by De Long.

Bennettsville (bĕ'nĭtsvĭl), town (pop. 5,140), ⊙ Marlboro co., NE S.C., 30 mi. N of Florence; mfg. (cotton products, furniture, mattresses, textiles), lumber, tobacco, vegetables. Laid out 1818.

Ben Nevis (bĕn nĕ'vĭs, nē'vĭs), highest peak (4,406 ft.) in Great Britain, SW Inverness, Scotland, 5 mi. ESE of Fort William; 56°48'N 5°W. Overlooks Glen Nevis, the picturesque valley of the Water of Nevis, river flowing 12 mi. NW to Loch Linnhe at Fort William. On summit of Ben Nevis are ruins of an observatory. There is an impressive view, especially on NE side, where there is a precipice of c.1,450 ft.

Benning, Fort, Ga.: see COLUMBUS.

Bennington, county (□ 672; pop. 24,115), SW Vt., on Mass. and N.Y. lines, in Green Mts.; ⊙ Bennington and Manchester. Mfg. (textiles, paper, wood products); dairying; resorts. Includes Mt. Equinox, part of Green Mtn. Natl. Forest. Drained by Batten Kill and Deerfield, Hoosic, Walloomsac, and Mettawee rivers. Organized 1779.

Bennington. 1 City (pop. 325), Ottawa co., N central Kansas, near Solomon R., 13 mi. N of Salina, in livestock and grain region. **2** Village (pop. 315), Douglas co., E Nebr., 10 mi. NW of Omaha, near Missouri R. **3** Town (pop. 593), Hillsboro co., S N.H., on the Contoocook (water power) and 24 mi. W of Manchester; paper mills. **4** Town (pop. 361), Bryan co., S Okla., 20 mi. E of Durant; trade center for rich agr. and stock-raising area. **5** Resort town (pop. 12,411), a ⊙ Bennington co., SW Vt., on Walloomsac R. and 34 mi. NE of Albany, N.Y. Mfg. (textiles, paper, clothing, ceramics, plastic and wood products, mill machinery); fruit, dairy products. Includes industrial Bennington village (pop. 8,002), historic Old Bennington (pop. 198), and NORTH BENNINGTON, seat of Bennington Col. Bennington Battle Monument (over 300 ft. high) commemorates victory (Aug. 16, 1777) by Colonials (led by John Stark) over Br. forces; the battlefield itself is just over the line in N.Y. Ethan Allen, Seth Warner, and Green Mountain Boys made Old Bennington their hq., meeting at Catamount Tavern (site marked). Other points of interest: Walloomsac Inn (1764), Old First Church (1806; restored 1937 as state monument), hist. mus., old frame house (1763), sites of 1st schoolhouse in Vt. and of William Lloyd Garrison's printing shop. Pottery made in Bennington for cent. from late 1700s is prized by collectors. Chartered 1749 as a N.H. town, 1st W of the Connecticut; settled 1761.

Bennington Battlefield, Rensselaer co., E N.Y., near state line, just NW of Bennington town, Vt. State park here (171 acres) is on field of American Revolution battle of Bennington (Aug. 16, 1777), in which Continentals defeated British forces.

Bennisch, Czechoslovakia: see HORNI BENESOV.

Benns Church, hamlet, Isle of Wight co., SE Va., near the James (bridged near by), 5 mi. SE of Smithfield. St. Lukes Church (or Old Brick Church), one of oldest Protestant churches in America, now restored, said to have been built in 1632.

Bénodet (bānôdā'), village (pop. 1,066), Finistère dept., W France, near mouth of Odet R. on Bay of Biscay, and 8 mi. S of Quimper; bathing and yachting resort noted for its mild climate.

Benoit (bùnoit'), town (pop. 444), Bolivar co., NW Miss., 18 mi. N of Greenville, in cotton-growing area.

Benoni (bùnō'nē), town (pop. 74,238), S Transvaal, U. of So. Afr., on Witwatersrand, 16 mi. E of Johannesburg; alt. 5,419 ft.; gold-mining center; iron, brass foundries, jute mills, electrical-equipment works. Airfield. Municipality set up 1907.

Benoué (bĕn'wā, bān'wā, bānwā'), administrative region (□ 23,440; 1950 pop. 255,729), N Fr. Cameroons; ⊙ Garoua. Bordered W by Nigeria and Br. Cameroons, E by Fr. Equatorial Africa. Drained by Benue R. Open savanna plain, with occasional shrub forests. Livestock, millet, peanuts. Pop. composed of Fulahs and Hausas, mostly Moslem. Region formerly part of Adamawa native Kingdom.

Benoué River, Nigeria and Fr. Cameroons: see BENUE RIVER.

Bénouville (bānōōvēl'), village (pop. 512), Calvados dept., NW France, on Caen maritime canal and 6 mi. NE of Caen. Captured (June 6, 1944) by Allied airborne troops shortly before landings on Normandy beaches.

Benquerencia de la Serena (bĕng-kārĕn'syä dhā lä sărā'nä), town (pop. 1,168), Badajoz prov., W Spain, 3 mi. ESE of Castuera; cereals, olives, chick-peas, livestock. Has ruined castle.

Benque Viejo (bĕng'kā vyā'hō), town (pop. 1,264), Cayo dist., central Br. Honduras, on Belize R. and 8 mi. SW of Cayo, on Guatemala border; chicle, lumber. Pop. mostly Maya Indians.

Benrath (bĕn'rät), district (since 1929) of Düsseldorf, W Germany, on right bank of the Rhine (harbor) and 6 mi. SE of city center; mfg. of chemicals and machinery. Has rococo castle.

Ben Rinnes (bĕn rĭ'nĭz), mountain (2,755 ft.), central Banffshire, Scotland, 5 mi. SW of Dufftown.

Bensberg (bĕns'bĕrk), town (pop. 21,059), in former Prussian Rhine Prov., W Germany, after 1945 in North Rhine-Westphalia, 9 mi. E of Cologne; lead and zinc mining; furniture mfg., leatherworking. Has 11th-cent. church; 18th-cent. castle; R.C. seminary.

Bensdorf, France: see BÉNESTROFF.

Ben Sekka, Ras (räs' bĕn sĕk-kä'), cape on the Mediterranean coast of N Tunisia, 8 mi. NW of Bizerte; 37°21'N 9°45'E. Lighthouse. Northernmost point of Africa.

Bensen, Czechoslovakia: see BENESOV NAD PLOUCNICI.

Bensenville (bĕn'sùnvĭl), village (pop. 3,754), Du Page co., NE Ill., WNW of Chicago and 17 mi. ESE of Elgin, in truck-farming area; poultry, dairy products; railroad shops. Inc. 1894.

Bensheim (bĕns'hīm), town (pop. 20,207), S Hesse, W Germany, in former Starkenburg prov., on the Bergstrasse, at W foot of the Odenwald, 13 mi. S of Darmstadt; rail junction; produces aluminum household goods, fire extinguishers, metal tubes, clothing, furniture, paper. Stone cutting. Vineyards. Chartered 1320. After belonging successively to several neighboring rulers, it came to Hesse in 1803.

Ben Shemen (bĕn' shĕ'mĕn), settlement (pop. 1,000), W Israel, in Plain of Sharon, adjoining Kfar Vitkin; agr.-training school for children. Founded 1927 near Lydda; moved (1948) to present site.

Benson, agr. village and parish (pop. 1,264), S Oxfordshire, England, on the Thames and 2 mi. NNE of Wallingford. Site of an anc. Br. settlement. Here was a defeat (777) of the West Saxons by Mercia. Has 13th-cent. church.

Benson, county (□ 1,412; pop. 10,675), N central N.Dak.; ⊙ Minnewaukan. Agr. area watered by Sheyenne R. Devils L. is on E border. Dairy products, grain, livestock, poultry. Formed 1883.

Benson. 1 Town (pop. 1,440), Cochise co., SE Ariz., on left bank of San Pedro R. and 44 mi. SE of Tucson; explosives; livestock, poultry, dairy products. Copper mines in Dragoon Mts. (E). **2** Village (pop. 387), Woodford co., central Ill., 26 mi. ENE of Peoria, in agr. and bituminous-coal area. **3** City (pop. 3,398), ⊙ Swift co., W Minn., on Chippewa R. and 30 mi. NW of Willmar; shipping point for grain, dairy products, and livestock; beverages, ice cream. Platted 1870, inc. as village 1877, as city 1908. **4** W suburb (pop. 1,892, with adjacent West Dodge) of Omaha, Douglas co., E Nebr. **5** Town (pop. 2,102), Johnston co., central N.C., 30 mi. S of Raleigh, in farm area (cotton, tobacco, corn); mfg. of clothing, cottonseed oil; lumber milling. Settled 1779; inc. 1887. **6** Borough (pop. 377), Somerset co., SW Pa., 6 mi. S of Johnstown. **7** Town (pop. 573), Rutland co., W Vt., on L. Champlain and 18 mi. NW of Rutland; lumber.

Bensonhurst, SE N.Y., a residential section of SW Brooklyn borough of New York city.

Bent, county (□ 1,533; pop. 8,775), SE Colo.; ⊙ Las Animas. Irrigated agr. area, drained by Purgatoire and Arkansas rivers. Has John Martin Reservoir. Livestock, sugar beets, feed. Formed 1870.

Bentham (-thùm), parish (pop. 2,452), West Riding, W Yorkshire, England. Includes silk-milling towns of Lower Bentham, 12 mi. ENE of Lancaster, and, just E, High Bentham.

Bentheim (bĕnt'hīm), town (pop. 5,797), in former Prussian prov. of Hanover, NW Germany, after 1945 in Lower Saxony, 12 mi. WNW of Rheine; customs station near Dutch border; rail junction; textile mfg. Resort with sulphur spring and mud baths. Natural-gas fields in vicinity. Has 15th–16th-cent. castle. Was residence of princes of Bentheim.

Benthuy (bān'twē'), town, Nghean prov., N central Vietnam, South China Sea port on left bank of the Song Ca and on railroad, 2 mi. SE of Vinh, which it serves as port (13-ft. draught); timber center; sawmilling, match mfg., food canning; railroad shops. Trades in cattle, rice, corn.

Bentinck Island, Australia: see WELLESLEY ISLANDS.

Bentinck Island (bĕn'tĭngk), in central Mergui Archipelago, Lower Burma, in Andaman Sea, 60 mi. SW of Mergui town; 15 mi. long, 5 mi. wide.

Bentley, village (pop. 362), S central Alta., near Gull L., on Blindman R. and 18 mi. NW of Red Deer; dairying, mixed farming.

Bentley, town (pop. 88), Hancock co., W Ill., 15 mi. ESE of Keokuk (Iowa), in agr and bituminous-coal area.

Bentley Priory, mansion in Harrow-on-the-Hill urban dist., central Middlesex, England, just N of Harrow; now Royal Air Force depot.

Bentleyville. 1 Village (pop. 152), Cuyahoga co., N Ohio, a SE suburb of Cleveland. **2** Borough (pop. 3,295), Washington co., SW Pa., 22 mi. S of Pittsburgh. Laid out 1816, inc. 1868.

Bentley with Arksey, urban district (1931 pop. 16,458; 1951 census 19,826), West Riding, S Yorkshire, England. Includes Arksey, NE suburb of Doncaster, near Don R. Has church of Norman origin, restored in 19th cent. by Sir Gilbert Scott.

Bento Gonçalves (bĕn'tōō gōsäl'vĭs), city (pop. 4,166), NE Rio Grande do Sul, Brazil, 60 mi. NNW of Pôrto Alegre; rail-spur terminus in fertile agr. region (winegrowing) settled by Italians in late 19th cent.

Benton. 1 County (□ 886; pop. 38,076), extreme NW Ark.; ⊙ Bentonville. Bounded W by Okla. line, N by Mo. line; drained by White and Illinois rivers; situated in Ozark region. Agr. (fruit, truck, grain, poultry, livestock); dairy products; timber. Mfg. at Bentonville and Rogers. Poultry hatcheries, nurseries. Mineral springs (resorts). Formed 1830. **2** County (□ 409; pop. 11,462), W Ind., bounded W by Ill. line; ⊙ Fowler. Agr. (corn, wheat, hay, soybeans, poultry, livestock); canneries, poultry hatcheries. Drained by small Sugar and Big Pine creeks. Formed 1840. **3** County (□ 718; pop. 22,656), E central Iowa; ⊙ Vinton. Prairie agr. area (hogs, cattle, poultry, corn, oats, wheat) drained by Cedar R.; limestone quarries. Formed 1837. **4** County (□ 404; pop. 15,911), central Minn.; ⊙ Foley. Agr. area bounded W by Mississippi R. Dairy products, livestock, grain; deposits of marl in NW. Formed 1849. **5** County (□ 412; pop. 8,793), N Miss., bounded N by Tenn. line; ⊙ Ashland. Drained by Wolf R. and small Tippah Creek. Agr. (cotton, corn, hay, sweet potatoes); lumbering. Includes part of Holly Springs Natl. Forest. Formed 1870. **6** County (□ 742; pop. 9,080), central Mo., in Ozark region; ⊙ Warsaw. Drained by Osage, South Grand, and Pomme de Terre rivers; crossed by L. of the Ozarks. Hunting, fishing; lumber; barite. Formed 1835. **7** County (□ 647; pop. 31,570), W Oregon; ⊙ Corvallis. Coast Range is in W, Willamette R. valley in E. Dairying, agr. (fruit, truck, grain, seeds, hay). Formed 1847. Small portion of Lincoln co. (W) was added (1949) to SW corner of Benton co. **8** County (□ 430; pop. 11,495), W Tenn.; ⊙ Camden. Bounded E and NW by arms of Kentucky Reservoir (Tennessee R.); traversed by Big Sandy R., here entering an arm of reservoir. Dairying, livestock and poultry raising, agr. (corn, cotton, soybeans, peanuts, sorghum). Gravel pits. Formed 1835. **9** County (□ 1,738; pop. 51,370), S Wash., on Oregon line; ⊙ Prosser. Bisected by Yakima R., which joins Columbia R. above Kennewick. Fruit, grain, nuts; sheep. Formed 1905.

Benton. 1 City (pop. 6,277), ⊙ Saline co., central Ark., 21 mi. SW of Little Rock, near Saline R., in bauxite-mining area. Hurricane Creek bauxite-reduction plant (near Bauxite) is near. Mfg. (wood products, furniture, pottery). State hosp. for nervous diseases near by. **2** Village (pop. c.100), Mono co., E Calif., 32 mi. N of Bishop; alt. c.5,000 ft. Mining, stock raising. **3** City (pop. 7,848), ⊙ Franklin co., S Ill., 22 mi. S of Mount Vernon; trade center for coal-mining and agr. area; mfg. (flour, electrical machinery, metal products, leather goods). Livestock, poultry, dairy products, grain. Inc. 1841. **4** Town (pop. 128), Ringgold co., S Iowa, on Grand R. and 25 mi. S of Creston. **5** City (pop. 269), Butler co., S Kansas, 13 mi. ENE of Wichita, in grain and stock area. **6** Town (pop. 1,980), ⊙ Marshall co., SW Ky., near East Fork Clarks R. and Kentucky Reservoir, 21 mi. SE of Paducah; ships strawberries; makes cigars, hosiery, concrete products; lumber mills. Annual (May) Southern Harmony Singing Festival (since 1884). **7** Village (pop. 741), ⊙ Bossier parish, NW La., near Red R., 12 mi. N of Shreveport, in agr. area; cotton ginning; pine timber. **8** Town (pop. 1,421), Kennebec co., S Maine, just N of Waterville, bet. the Kennebec and the Sebasticook; fibreboard mfg. Settled c.1775, inc. 1842 as Sebasticook, renamed 1850. **9** Town (pop. 546), ⊙ Scott co., SE Mo., near Mississippi R., 14 mi. S of Cape Girardeau; cotton, corn, wheat. **10** Town (pop. 247), Grafton co., NW N.H., 12 mi. SW of Franconia, in White Mtn. Natl. Forest recreational area. **11** Borough (pop. 890), Columbia co., NE central Pa., 27 mi. W of Wilkes-Barre; flour, lumber, clothing; agr. **12** Village (1940 pop. 668), ⊙ Polk co., SE Tenn., near Hiwassee R., 38 mi. ENE of Chattanooga, in timber and farm area; woodworking. **13** Village (pop. 842), Lafayette co., SW Wis., on Galena R. and 15 mi. ENE of Dubuque (Iowa), in dairy and livestock area. Formerly a lead- and zinc-mining center.

Benton, Lake, Lincoln county, SW Minn., at Lake Benton village; 5 mi. long. Almost dry.

Benton City. 1 Town (pop. 141), Audrain co., NE central Mo., near West Fork of Cuivre R., 7 mi. SE of Mexico. **2** Town (pop. 863), Benton co., S Wash., on Yakima R. and 10 mi. W of Richland.

Bentong (bĕntŏŏng'), town (pop. 7,087), W Pahang, Malaya, in central Malayan range, 30 mi. NE of Kuala Lumpur; tin-mining center.

Benton Harbor, city (pop. 18,769), Berrien co., extreme SW Mich., on L. Michigan at mouth of St. Joseph R., opposite St. Joseph, in a rich fruitgrowing and -marketing area (peaches, pears, plums, apples, cherries, grapes, melons). Resort with beaches, mineral springs. Mfg. of canned goods, hardware, tools, machinery, boats, wood and paper products, furniture, lamp shades, electrical supplies. The House of David, a religious colony founded here in 1903, has acquired business and farm interests; near by is rival, the Israelite City of David. The municipal fruit market, said to be the nation's largest, is here. Its Blossom Festival, held jointly with St. Joseph each year, takes place in co. Settled c.1840; inc. as village 1869, as city 1891.

Benton Heights. 1 Village (pop. 6,160) Berrien co., SW Mich. **2** Town (1940 pop. 768), Union co., S N.C., just NW of Monroe.

Bentonia, town (pop. 496), Yazoo co., W central Miss., 15 mi. S of Yazoo City, near Big Black R.

Benton Ridge, village (pop. 337), Hancock co., NW Ohio, 7 mi. WSW of Findlay.

Bentonville. 1 City (pop. 2,942), ⊙ Benton co., extreme NW Ark., 22 mi. N of Fayetteville, in the Ozarks. Ships dairy products, poultry, apples, grapes, berries. Canning of fruits and vegetables; feed, lumber milling. Mineral springs and Bella Vista (resort) near by. Settled 1837. **2** Village, Johnston co., central N.C., 17 mi. W of Goldsboro. Near here Union army under Sherman defeated (March, 1865) Josesph E. Johnston's Army of Tenn. in one of last major engagements of Civil War. Battlefield has been preserved; Confederate monument here.

Bentota (bĕntō'tŭ), anc. *Bhimatittha*, village, Southern Prov., Ceylon, seaside resort on SW coast, at mouth of the small Bentota Ganga, 36 mi. SSE of Colombo; vegetables, rice. Thorium deposits; oyster beds. Anc. Buddhist monasteries near by.

Bentranh (bān'trä'nyŭ), town, Mytho prov., S Vietnam, 4 mi. N of Mytho; rice.

Bentre (bān'trā'), town (1936 pop. 6,113), ⊙ Bentre prov. (□ 600; 1943 pop. 347,200), S Vietnam, in Mekong delta, 45 mi. SSW of Saigon; rice, fruit, copra, betel nuts, poultry raising; coconut-oil extraction, sericulture. R.C. and Protestant missions.

Bentschen, Poland: see ZBASZYN.

Bent's Fort, Colo.: see LA JUNTA.

Benty (bĕntē'), village (pop. c.750), SW Fr. Guinea, Fr. West Africa, on the Atlantic, near Sierra Leone border, 40 mi. SE of Conakry; ships bananas; also palm oil, palm kernels. Agr. station; seaplane base; customhouse.

Benue (bān'wā, bĕnōō'ĕ), province (□ 29,318; 1931 pop. 986,525), Northern Provinces, central Nigeria; ⊙ Makurdi. Prov. includes part (□ 1,236; 1931 pop. 5,766; 1948 pop. estimate 10,300) of Br. Cameroons. Located S of Bauchi Plateau; drained by Benue R.; savanna vegetation. Mining: tin (Nasarawa), lignite (Lafia), galena (Akwana). Agr. (shea nuts, sesame, cassava, durra, yams). Chief centers: Makurdi, Nasarawa, Oturkpo, Wukari. Pop. largely Tiv.

Benue River, Fr. *Benoué* (bānwā'), chief tributary of Niger R., rises in Fr. Cameroons N of N'Gaoundéré, flows N to Garoua, then generally WSW across E and S central Nigeria, past Yola, Ibi, and Makurdi, to the Niger at Lokoja. Length, c.870 mi. Receives Gongola (right), Katsina Ala and Donga (left) rivers. Navigable below Garoua for barges (used for peanut and cotton shipments) during flood season.

Benut (bĕnōōt'), town (pop. 1,738), SW Johore, Malaya, on Strait of Malacca, 25 mi. SSE of Bandar Penggaram; coconuts, rubber; fisheries.

Ben Venue (bĕn vŭnū'), mountain (2,393 ft.), SW Perthshire, Scotland, on S shore of Loch Katrine, 10 mi. WSW of Callander.

Ben Vorlich (bĕn vôr'lĭkh, -lĭk), mountain (3,224 ft.), S central Perthshire, Scotland, 7 mi. N of Callander, overlooking Loch Earn.

Benwee Head (bĕnwē'), promontory (829 ft. high) at NW extremity of Co. Mayo, Ireland, 11 mi. NE of Belmullet; 54°21'N 9°48'W.

Benwell, England: see NEWCASTLE-UPON-TYNE.

Benwood, city (pop. 3,485), Marshall co., NW W. Va., in Northern Panhandle, on the Ohio and 5 mi. S of Wheeling; bituminous-coal mining, steel mfg. Chartered 1853.

Ben Wyvis (bĕn wī'vĭs, wĭ'vĭs), mountain (3,429 ft.), E central Ross and Cromarty, Scotland, 8 mi. NW of Dingwall. On slopes is large deer forest.

Benyamina, Israel: see BINYAMINA.

Bény-Bocage, Le (lü bānē'-bôkăzh'), village (pop. 285), Calvados dept., NW France, in Normandy Hills, 7 mi. N of Vire.

Benzdorp (bĕns'dôrp), village (pop. 239), E Du. Guiana, on Lawa or Aoua R. and 5 mi. NW of Maripasoula (Fr. Guiana); 3°42'N 54°5'W. Gold placers. Police station.

Benzie (bĕn'zē), county (□316; pop. 8,306), NW Mich.; ⊙ Beulah. Bounded W by L. Michigan; drained by Betsie R. and small Platte R. Agr. (fruit, especially apples, cherries; also grain, truck, potatoes, beans); dairy products; fisheries. Resorts. Includes Crystal, Platte, and other small lakes, and a state park and state forest. Organized 1869.

Benzonia (bĕnzō'nēŭ), village (pop. 407), Benzie co. NW Mich., on Crystal L., 26 mi. SW of Traverse City, in agr. area (potatoes, corn, beans); lumber mill.

Beocin or **Beochin** (both: bāô'chĭn), Serbo-Croatian *Beočin*, village, Vojvodina, NW Serbia, Yugoslavia, near the Danube, 6 mi. WSW of Novi Sad, on N slope of Fruska Gora, in the Srem; rail terminus; cement plant. Coal mine near by. Monastery with church (restored 1732–40) noted for its fine iconostasis.

Beodra, Yugoslavia: see MILOSEVO.

Beograd, Yugoslavia: see BELGRADE.

Beposo (bĕpō'sō), town, Western Prov., S Gold Coast colony, on Pra R. (suspension bridge) and 13 mi. NE of Sekondi, on main coastal road; cacao, palm oil and kernels, cassava.

Beppu (băp'pōō), city (1940 pop. 64,724; 1947 pop. 96,685), Oita prefecture, NE Kyushu, Japan, 7 mi. WNW of Oita, on W shore of Beppu Bay. Noted health resort; alkaline, sulphide, ferruginous, and carbonated hot springs. Seat of Hot Springs Cure Inst. of Kyushu Imperial Univ.

Beppu Bay, Jap. *Beppu-wan*, inlet of Hoyo Strait, Oita prefecture, NE Kyushu, Japan; 12 mi. E-W, 9 mi. N-S. Oita is on S, Beppu (hot-springs center) on SW shore.

Beqa, Fiji: see MBENGGA.

Beqa', El, Lebanon: see BEKAA.

Bequia (bŭkē'ŭ), islet (□ 7; pop. 2,482), N Grenadines, dependency of St. Vincent, B.W.I., 8 mi. S of Kingstown; 13°N 61°15'W; 6 mi. long, up to 2 mi. wide. Cotton growing.

Bequimão (bĭkĕmā'ō), city (pop. 627), N Maranhão, Brazil, 30 mi. WNW of São Luís; cotton, sugar, babassu nuts. Until 1939, Santo Antonio e Almas.

Bera (bā'rŭ), village, Pabna dist., central East Bengal, E Pakistan, on Atrai R. and 25 mi. ENE of Pabna; trades in rice, jute, rape and mustard.

Berabevú (bārābāvōō'), town (pop. estimate 1,500), S Santa Fe prov., Argentina, 75 mi. WSW of Rosario; agr. center (wheat, flax, corn, hogs, cattle).

Beranang (bŭränäng'), village (pop. 721), SE Selangor, Malaya, on Negri Sembilan line, 10 mi. SE of Kajang; rice, rubber.

Berane, Yugoslavia: see IVANGRAD.

Berar (bārär'), SW division (□ 17,809; pop. 3,604,-866) of Madhya Pradesh, India, on Deccan Plateau; ⊙ Amraoti. Comprises 4 dists: AKOLA, AMRAOTI, BULDANA, YEOTMAL. Bordered N by central Satpura Range, E by Wardha R., S mostly by Penganga R. Broad valley of Purna R. (tributary of the Tapti) bet. N hill area and Ajanta Hills (S) forms one of richest and most extensive cotton-growing tracts in India (cotton represents over 50% of sown area in Amraoti dist.); also produces millet, wheat, oilseeds. Industry mainly based on agr., with cotton-textile centers at Akola, Badnera, Ellichpur. Amraoti, Yeotmal, and Akola are main cotton-trade centers. Area under successive Deccan dynasties and sultans of Delhi from 3d cent. A.D., until it became part of a prov. of Mogul empire in 1636. Although nominally part of Hyderabad dominions after 1724, sections of the area were frequently besieged and held by Mahrattas during 18th cent. Administered by Br. govt. from 1853 to 1903, when it became an administrative div. of Central Psovs. and Berar (renamed Madhya Pradesh in 1950). Pop. 84% Hindu, 9% Moslem, 7% tribal.

Bérard (bārär'), village (pop. 459), Alger dept., N central Algeria, on the Mediterranean, 15 mi. NW of Blida; fishing port. Winegrowing.

Bérarde, La, France: see SAINT-CHRISTOPHE-EN-OISANS.

Berasia (bā'rŭsyŭ), town (pop. 4,152), N Bhopal state, India, 25 mi. N of Bhopal; local market for millet, wheat, oilseeds.

Berastagi, Indonesia: see BRASTAGI.

Berat (bĕ'rät) or **Berati** (bĕ'rätē), city (1945 pop. 11,872), S central Albania, on Osum R., 30 mi. NE of Valona and 45 mi. S of Tirana, at foot of the Tomorr (ascended from here); commercial center; agr. (corn, tobacco, fruit, wine, olives). Consists of upper town or citadel (rebuilt by Byzantines in 13th cent.) which contains many old churches, a lower left-bank town with a 15th-cent. mosque, and the modern right-bank town. Probably built on site of anc. Antipatrea, taken (200 B.C.) by Romans, it was known as Pulcheriopolis under Theodosius II (408–450). Became bishopric in 10th cent. Captured 1345 by Serbs and called Beligrad (whence its modern name); fell 1440 to Turks. The autocephalic Albanian Orthodox Church was proclaimed here (1922).

Beratzhausen (bä"räts-hou'zŭn), village (pop. 2,841), Upper Palatinate, central Bavaria, Germany, on small Schwarze Laber R. and 14 mi. NW of Regensburg; bronze mfg., brewing.

Beraun, Czechoslovakia: see BEROUN.

Berau Peninsula, New Guinea: see VOGELKOP.

Berazategui (bārāsätā'gē), residential city (pop. 21,187) in Greater Buenos Aires, Argentina, near the Río de la Plata, 13 mi. SE of Buenos Aires. Mfg. of machinery, glass. Fresh-water fishing (shad) in Río de la Plata; bathing beaches.

Berber (bûr'bŭr), town (pop. 16,100), Northern Prov., Anglo-Egyptian Sudan, on right bank of the Nile, on railroad, and 20 mi. N of Atbara; caravan center; mfg. of leather and cotton goods; trade in cotton, wheat, barley, corn, fruits, and livestock (camels). Destroyed during Mahdist rebellion; later rebuilt just N of former site. Berber prov. (⊙ Ed Damer) became part (1930s) of Northern Prov.

Berbera (bur'bŭrŭ), town (pop. estimates are from 15,000 to 30,000), N Br. Somaliland, port on Gulf of Aden, 140 mi. SE of Djibouti, 150 mi. S of Aden; 10°27'N 45°1'E. Exports sheep, hides and skins, ghee and gums (frankincense, myrrh). Fisheries. Has an abattoir. Hq. Berbera dist. About half of town's pop. moves to interior uplands during hot season. Winter ⊙ of Br. Somaliland until 1941, when it was succeeded by Hargeisa.

Berbérati (bĕrbărătē'), town, ⊙ Haute-Sangha region (□ 16,100; 1950 pop. 93,300), SW Ubangi-Shari, Fr. Equatorial Africa, 195 mi. W of Bangui; gold- and diamond-mining center. Has military camp, airfield, R.C. and Protestant missions.

Berbice (bûrbēs'), county (□ 16,920; pop. 96,623), E Br. Guiana, on the Atlantic; ⊙ New Amsterdam. Bounded by Du. Guiana (E) and Brazil (S). Drained by Berbice and Courantyne rivers. Agr. settlements along coast produce rice, sugar cane, tropical fruit, cattle. In interior are large bauxite and kaolin deposits. Tropical forests yield balata and greenheart hardwood. First settled 1627 by the Dutch, it formed (after 1732) a separate colony until it joined (1831) the united colonies of Essequibo and Demerara to form Br. Guiana. The co. (mainly of historical importance) is divided into Berbice administrative dist. (N of 4°N; □ 8,377) and Rupununi dist. (S).

Berbice River, E Br. Guiana, rises in densely forested interior at 3°11'N 57°57'W, flows c.350 mi. NNE to the Atlantic near New Amsterdam, its main port. Navigable for small vessels to Paradise (100 mi. upstream). Along the river, forest products (greenheart, balata), diamonds, and, especially, bauxite are worked. Sugar cane, rice, tropical fruit are cultivated in lower reaches. Main tributary, Canje R.

Berbinzana (bĕrbēn-thä'nä), town (pop. 1,037), Navarre prov., N Spain, on Arga R. and 22 mi. SW of Pamplona; wine, cereals, fruit.

Bercel (bĕr'tsĕl), town (pop. 2,277), Nograd-Hont co., N Hungary, 15 mi. SSE of Balassagyarmat; flour mills; wheat, potatoes, sheep, hogs.

Berceto (bĕrchā'tô), village (pop. 1,078), Parma prov., Emilia-Romagna, N central Italy, 11 mi. NE of Pontremoli; canned foods. Has Romanesque church.

Berchem (bĕr'khŭm). **1** SE industrial suburb (pop. 45,954) of Antwerp, N Belgium; metallurgy; mfg. (textiles, clothing, food products); important railroad switching yards. Scene of battle (1830) early in Belg. war of independence. **2** Village (pop. 2,346), East Flanders prov., W central Belgium, on Scheldt R. and 6 mi. SW of Oudenaarde; agr., cattle. Has 14th-cent. Gothic church.

Berchem (bĕr'khŭm), village (pop. 231), S Luxembourg, on Alzette R. and 5 mi. S of Luxembourg city; mfg. (agr. machinery, lighting appliances).

Berchem-Sainte-Agathe (bĕr-khĕm'-sĕt-ägät'), Flemish *Sint-Agatha-Berchem* (sĭnt-ä'gätä-bĕr'-khŭm), residential town (pop. 11,061), Brabant prov., central Belgium, W suburb of Brussels.

Berchidda (bĕrkēd'dä), village (pop. 2,261), Sassari prov., N Sardinia, 32 mi. E of Sassari.

Berching (bĕr'khĭng), town (pop. 3,108), Upper Palatinate, central Bavaria, Germany, on Ludwig Canal and 19 mi. NE of Eichstätt; textile and jewelry mfg. Surrounded by walls from 2d half of 15th cent.; has late-Romanesque church (renovated in late-17th cent.), and Gothic church. Chartered before 1015. Limestone and dolomite quarried in area.

Berchogur (byĕrchŭgōōr'), town (1942 pop. over 500), central Akhyubinsk oblast, Kazakh SSR, in Mugodzhar Hills (near peak, Ber-Chogur), on Trans-Caspian RR and 60 mi. NW of Chelkar; coal mining.

Berchtesgaden (bĕrkh'tŭsgä"dŭn), village (pop. 5,752), Upper Bavaria, Germany, in Salzburg Alps, at confluence of several mtn. streams, near the Königssee, 8 mi. SE of Bad Reichenhall, surrounded by mts. of great scenic beauty. Popular summer and winter resort (alt. 1,880 ft.). Salt-mining center since 12th cent.; wood carving. Has churches of 11th, 12th, and 14th cent. Abbots of Augustinian abbey (founded 12th cent.) here were rulers of independent ecclesiastic state until 1803. At foot of near-by Obersalzberg is the Berghof, Hitler's residence; atop mtn., connected with Berghof by elevator, was his private retreat.

Bérchules (bĕr'chōōlĕs), village (pop. 1,785), Granada prov., S Spain, 27 mi. SE of Granada; olive-oil processing, flour milling, lumbering. Nuts, chestnuts, truck produce. Summer resort with mineral springs. Iron and sulphur mines.

Berck or **Berck-sur-Mer** (bârk-sür-mâr'), town (pop. 10,059), Pas-de-Calais dept., N France, 9 mi. SW of Montreuil; consists of **Berck-Plage** (bathing and health resort on channel coast) and **Berck-Ville** (1.5 mi. inland); fisheries. Numerous hospitals and sanatoria, particularly for bone ailments. Beach (9 mi. long) extends from mouth of the Authie (S) to Canche R. estuary (N). Heavily damaged in Second World War.

Bercy (bĕrsē'), a SE quarter of Paris, France, on right bank of the Seine, contained in 12th *arrondissement*. Has large freight yards of Paris-Lyons-Marseilles RR, and bonded warehouses.

Berd (byĕrt), village (1932 pop. estimate 3,180), NE Armenian SSR, 13 mi. SW of Tauz (Azerbaijan SSR); wheat, tobacco; rug weaving. Formerly called Tauzkala.

Berdell Hills, town (pop. 583), St. Louis co., E Mo.

Berdichev (byĭrdyĕ'chĭf), city (1939 pop. 66,306), S Zhitomir oblast, Ukrainian SSR, 24 mi. S of Zhitomir; sugar-refining, tanning center; machine shops, brickworks; flour milling, woodworking. Teachers col. Founded 1482; passed 1569 to Poland, 1793 to Russia; became flourishing trade center. Pop. over 50% Jewish until Second World War, when it was held (1941–43) by Germans.

Berdigyastyakh (byĭrdyĕ"gyŭstyäkh'), village (1948 pop. over 500), central Yakut Autonomous SSR, Russian SFSR, 85 mi. W of Yakutsk, in agr. area. Formerly Berdigistyakh.

Berdsk (byĕrtsk), city (1939 pop. over 10,000), SE Novosibirsk oblast, Russian SFSR, on Ob R., on Turksib RR and 10 mi. S of Novosibirsk; flour-milling center; radio mfg. Industrialized after c.1935.

Berdyansk, Ukrainian SSR: see OSIPENKO.

Berdyaush (byĕrdyŭōōsh'), town (1948 pop. over 2,000), W Chelyabinsk oblast, Russian SFSR, in the S Urals, 10 mi. NE of Satka; rail junction; iron mining.

Berdyuzhye or **Berdyuzh'ye** (byĭrdyōō'zhyĭ), village (1948 pop. over 2,000), S Tyumen oblast, Russian SFSR, 45 mi. SW of Ishim; grain, livestock.

Berea, Greece: see VEROIA.

Berea, Syria: see ALEPPO.

Berea (bürē'ŭ), chief residential section of Durban, E Natal, U. of So. Afr., on hill rising to c.500 ft. above city.

Berea (bürē'ŭ). **1** Town (pop. 3,372), Madison co., central Ky., near the Cumberlands, 36 mi. SSE of Lexington; summer resort in agr. area. Seat of Berea Col. (1853), oldest and largest Ky. mtn. school. Churchill Weavers, noted for their hand-woven products, are here. Near by are anc. Indian fortifications. **2** City (pop. 12,051), Cuyahoga co., N Ohio, 10 mi. SW of downtown Cleveland; stone quarries; makes brick, tile, metal products, farm implements. Seat of Baldwin-Wallace Col. Settled 1809, inc. 1850.

Bereda (bĕrĕ'dä), village (pop. 700), in the Mijirtein, N Ital. Somaliland, port on Indian Ocean, near Cape Guardafui, 22 mi. ESE of Alula; fishing; mother of pearl, tunny.

Beregovo (byĕ'rĭgŭvŭ), Czech *Berehovo* (bĕ'rĕhôvô), Hung. *Beregszász* (bĕ'rĕksäs), city (1941 pop. 19,373), SW Transcarpathian Oblast, Ukrainian SSR., near Hung. border, 17 mi. SSW of Mukachevo; rail junction; wine and tobacco trade center; furniture mfg.; kaolin quarrying. Extensive vineyards in vicinity (mostly Tokay-type grapes). A town of Austria-Hungary which passed 1920 to Czechoslovakia, 1938 to Hungary, and 1945 to USSR.

Bereguardo (bĕrĕgwär'dô), village (pop. 1,114), Pavia prov., Lombardy, N Italy, near Ticino R., 9 mi. NNW of Pavia.

Berehaven, Ireland: see CASTLETOWN BERE.

Berehovo, Ukrainian SSR; see BEREGOVO.

Bere Island, Ireland: see BEAR ISLAND.

Berekböszörmeny (bĕ'rĕkbû'sûrmănyû), Hung. *Berekböszörmény*, town (pop. 3,168), Bihar co., E Hungary, 32 mi. S of Debrecen, near Rumanian line; corn, wheat, hogs, poultry.

Bereldange (bĕrŭldäzh'), town (pop. 880), S central Luxembourg, on Alzette R. and 3 mi. N of Luxembourg city; molybdenum and tungsten processing; mfg. of brushes.

Berelyakh (byŭryŭlyäkh'), town (1942 pop. over 500), N Khabarovsk Territory, Russian SFSR, at S end of Cherski Range, on Berelyakh R. (head-stream of Kolyma R.) just NE of Susuman, and 225 mi. NW of Magadan; 62°88'N 148°12'E. Gold-mining center.

Beremend (bĕ'rĕmĕnd), town (pop. 3,022), Baranya co., S Hungary, 22 mi. SSE of Pecs; flour mill.

Berende, Bulgaria: see KALOTINA.

Berendeyevo (byĕrĭndyā'ŭvŭ), town (1944 pop. over 500), S Yaroslavl oblast, Russian SFSR, 11 mi. SE of Pereslavl-Zalesski; peat.

Berendrecht (bā'rŭn-drĕkht), village (pop. 2,539), Antwerp prov., N Belgium, 10 mi. NNW of Antwerp; beet sugar.

Berenguela (bārĕnggā'lä), village, Cochabamba dept., central Bolivia, on NE slopes of Cordillera de Azanaques, 6 mi. S of Arque, with which it is connected by road; alt. 12,155 ft.; tin mining.

Berenguela, Peru: see SANTA LUCÍA.

Berenice, Cyrenaica: see BENGHAZI, city.

Berenice (bĕ"rŭnī'sē), anc. city of SE Egypt, on the Red Sea, 20 mi. W of the cape Ras Benas, 170 mi. SSE of Kosseir. Founded by Ptolemy II, it was the major port for Indian trade. Ruins.

Berent, Poland: see KOSCIERZYNA.

Bere Regis (bēr rē'jĭs), town and parish (pop. 1,027), S central Dorset, England, 7 mi. NW of Wareham; agr. market. Has 15th-cent. church.

Beresford (bĕrz'fŭrd, bĕr'ĭz–), city (pop. 1,686), Union and Lincoln counties, SE S.Dak., 30 mi. S of Sioux Falls. Trade center for corn-raising region; farm implements; dairy products, livestock, cattle. Children's home and Lutheran home for aged and infirm are here.

Berestechko (bĕrĭstyĕch'kŭ), Pol. *Beresteczko* (bĕrĕstĕch'kô), city (1931 pop. 6,314), SE Volyn oblast, Ukrainian SSR, on Styr R. and 28 mi. SSW of Lutsk; tanning, flour milling, pitch processing, hat-making, brick mfg. Founded 1547; site of defeat (1651) of Cossacks and Tatars by Pol. king John II Casimir. Passed from Poland to Russia (1795); reverted to Poland (1921); ceded to USSR in 1945.

Beresti-Targ (bĕrĕsh'tĭ-tûrg'), Rum. *Bereşti-Târg*, agr. village (pop. 2,962), Putna prov., E Rumania, 45 mi. NNW of Galati.

Berettyo River (bĕ'rĕt-tyō), Hung. *Berettyó*, Rum. *Beretau* (bĕ'rĕtou), W Rumania and E Hungary, rises in Rumania 15 mi. SW of Zalau, flows c.115 mi. W and SW, past Marghita and Berettyoujfalu, to the Rapid Körös SW of Szeghalom. Berettyo Canal starts near Zsaka, flows c.20 mi. W; joined by Hortobagy R. E of Kisujszallas, thence flows c.35 mi. S as another Berettyo R. to the Körös below Mezötur.

Berettyoujfalu (bĕ'rĕt-tyō-ōōĭ"fŏlōō), Hung. *Berettyóújfalu*, market town (pop. 11,781), ⊙ Bihar co., E Hungary, on Berettyo R. and 21 mi. S of Debrecen; flour mills. Large Rumanian pop.

Berevo (bĕrĕ'vōō), village, Tuléar prov., W Madagascar, on Tsiribihina R. and 27 mi. ESE of Belo; native market in rice region. R.C. and Protestant missions.

Bereza or **Bereza Kartuskaya** (bĭryô'zŭ kŭrtōō'skīŭ), Pol. *Bereza Kartuska* (bĕrĕ'zä kärtōō'skä), city (1931 pop. 4,521), E Brest oblast, Belorussian SSR, on Yaselda R. and 60 mi. NE of Brest; mfg. (concrete blocks, bricks, cloth), flour milling, saw-milling. Has 17th-cent. monastery and church. Passed (1795) from Poland to Russia; reverted (1921) to Poland. Site of Pol. prison camp until 1939; ceded to USSR in 1945.

Berezaika or **Berezayka** (byĕrĭzī'kŭ), town (1926 pop. 1,278), NW Kalinin oblast, Russian SFSR, 9 mi. NW of Bologoye; glassworking center; peat works, sand quarry.

Berezan or **Berezan'** (byĕrĭzän'yŭ), village (1926 pop. 7,604), E Kiev oblast, Ukrainian SSR, 40 mi. ESE of Kiev; peat cutting, metalworking.

Berezdov (byĕrĭzdôf'), town (1939 pop. over 500), N Kamenets-Podolski oblast, Ukrainian SSR, 19 mi. N of Shepetovka; wheat.

Berezhany (byĕrĭzhä'nē), Pol. *Brzeżany* (bzhĕzhä'-nē), city (1931 pop. 11,721), W Ternopol oblast, Ukrainian SSR, on Zolotaya Lipa R. (here forms artificial lake) and 32 mi. WSW of Ternopol; agr. center; flour milling, brick mfg.; auto repair shops. Has technical school, old churches and synagogues, and ruins of 16th-cent. castle. Old Pol. town, frequently assaulted (16th–17th cent.) by Tatars; chartered and fortified in 1530. Passed to Austria (1772); scene of Ger. break-through of Rus. front during First World War; reverted to Poland (1919); ceded to USSR in 1945.

Berezichi, Russian SFSR: see KOZELSK.

Berezina River (bĭrĕ'zēnŭ, bĕrĭzē'nŭ), Belorussian SSR, rises near Dokshitsy in Lithuanian-Belorussian Upland, flows 365 mi. S, past Borisov (near point of Napoleon's crossing in 1812), Berezino, and Bobruisk, to Dnieper R. 14 mi. NNW of Rechitsa. Navigable for 330 mi. **Berezina Canal** (built 1798–1805) links upper course with Ulla R., an affluent of the Western Dvina, forming navigable Black Sea–Baltic Sea route.

Berezino (bĭrĕ'zēnŭ), town (1926 pop. 2,970), E Minsk oblast, Belorussian SSR, on Berezina R. and 60 mi. E of Minsk; agr. products, distilling.

Berezna (byĕrĭznä'), agr. town (1926 pop. 9,860), N central Chernigov oblast, Ukrainian SSR, 20 mi. ENE of Chernigov; grain, flax, buckwheat. Formerly also Bereznoye.

Berezne, Ukrainian SSR: see BEREZNO.

Bereznegovatoye (bĭryĕz"nyĭgŭvä'tŭyŭ), village (1926 pop. 7,830), E Nikolayev oblast, Ukrainian SSR, 45 mi. NE of Nikolayev; metalworks.

Berezniki (bĭryĕznyĭkē'), city (1939 pop. 63,575), central Molotov oblast, Russian SFSR, port on left bank of Kama R., opposite Usolye, on railroad (Usolskaya station) and 90 mi. NNE of Molotov. Leading center of Soviet chemical industry, processing local common salt and Solikamsk potash (carnallite, silvinite) deposits, Kizel coal, and upper Kama (Rudnichny, Kirov oblast) phosphorites. Produces potassium, nitrate, and phosphate fertilizers, aniline dyes, sulphuric acid, soda, and ammonia; light mfg., food processing. Developing around giant chemical works constructed in early 1930s, Berezniki was formed (1932) when old salt-processing center of Usolye or Usolye-Solikamskoye (on right Kama R. bank) amalgamated with left-bank satellite towns of Lenva (1926 pop. 3,789), Dedyukhino (1926 pop. 3,607), Veretiya (1926 pop. 1,465), Ust-Zyryanka (1926 pop. 679), and Churtan (1926 pop. 1,230). The original USOLYE was again separated from Berezniki in 1940.

Berezno (bĭryôz'nŭ), Pol. *Bereźne* (bĕrĕzh'nĕ), village (1931 pop. 2,857), central Rovno oblast, Ukrainian SSR, on Sluch R. and 32 mi. NE of Rovno; agr. (cereals, vegetables, hops) processing, tanning, sawmilling.

Berezovka (bĭryô'zŭfkŭ). **1** Village, S Krasnoyarsk Territory, Russian SFSR, 13 mi. ENE of Krasnoyarsk; metalworks. **2** Village (1926 pop. 923), SE Molotov oblast, Russian SFSR, 20 mi. NE of Kungur; food processing; wheat, clover, livestock. **3** Village (1939 pop. over 500), SW Ryazan oblast, Russian SFSR, 16 mi. NW of Dankov; coarse grain, rubber-bearing plants. **4** Village (1939 pop. over 500), N Saratov oblast, Russian SFSR, on Medveditsa R. and 16 mi. NNE of Atkarsk; wheat, sunflowers. **5** Town (1939 pop. over 500), N central Kharkov oblast, Ukrainian SSR, 9 mi. SW of Kharkov city center, just NE of Yuzhny. **6** Town (1926 pop. 7,561), E Odessa oblast, Ukrainian SSR, 50 mi. NNE of Odessa; metalworks, flour, leather products. Kolosovka rail junction (line E to Nikolayev) is 5 mi. N.

Berezovo (bĭryô'zŭvŭ), village (1946 pop. over 4,000), NW Khanty-Mansi Natl. Okrug, Tyumen oblast, Russian SFSR, on (Northern) Sosva R. and 230 mi. NNW of Khanty-Mansisk; fur- and fish-marketing center; fish canning, glassworking; airport. Founded 1593 as fortress against Ostyak tribes; flourished in early colonization of Siberia. Menshikov exiled here (18th cent.). Called Berezov until 1926, when it lost city status.

Berezovskaya (byĕrĭzôf'skīŭ), village (1926 pop. 2,854), N central Stalingrad oblast, Russian SFSR, on Medveditsa R. and 34 mi. NE of Mikhailovka; metalworks; wheat, sunflowers.

Berezovski or **Berezovskiy** (–skē), city (1932 pop. estimate 16,500), S Sverdlovsk oblast, Russian SFSR, on SE slope of the central Urals, 8 mi. NE of Sverdlovsk; center of gold-mining dist.; mfg. of building materials. Developed in 18th cent.; became city in 1938. Formerly Berezovski Zavod.

Berezovskoye (–skŭyŭ). **1** Village (1939 pop. under 500), SE Chita oblast, Russian SFSR, 6 mi. S of Nerchinski Zavod; iron-ore deposits; metalworks. **2** Village (1939 pop. over 2,000), SW Krasnoyarsk Territory, Russian SFSR, 45 mi. SW of Achinsk; metalworks.

Berg (bĕrk), village (pop. 2,164), N Upper Austria, adjacent to Rohrbach, 23 mi. NW of Linz, near Czechoslovak line; rye, potatoes.

Berg, former duchy, W Germany, extending along right bank of the Rhine bet. Ruhr and Sieg rivers. After a stormy history, it finally passed (1815) to Prussia.

Berg. 1 Village (pop. 1,848), Upper Bavaria, Germany, on E shore of the Starnberger See, 2.5 mi. S of Starnberg; metalworking. Has small mid-17th-cent. castle, renovated 1851. Louis II of Bavaria drowned here (1886). **2** Village (pop. 1,148), Rhenish Palatinate, W Germany, on the Lauter, diagonally opposite Lauterbourg, France; wine, tobacco products; woodworking. **3** NE suburb of Stuttgart, N. Württemberg, Germany, on left bank of the Neckar; mineral baths on isl. in river.

Berg, Luxembourg: see COLMAR.

Berg, Norway: see SENJEHOPEN.

Berg, Den, Netherlands: see GEERTRUIDENBERG.

Berga or **Berga an der Elster** (bĕr'gä än dĕr ĕl'stür), town (pop. 2,580), Thuringia, central Germany, on the White Elster and 7 mi. N of Greiz; woolen and silk milling.

Berga (bĕr'gä), city (pop. 5,605), Barcelona prov., NE Spain, on S slopes of the central Pyrenees, on Llobregat R. and 24 mi. NW of Vich; cotton spinning and weaving, meat processing, mfg. of chemicals and cement; sericulture. Lumber, livestock, cereals, fruit in area. Lignite deposits near by. One of oldest places in Catalonia.

Berga (bĕr'gä), village (pop. 775), Kalmar co., SE Sweden, near Em R., 18 mi. W of Oskarshamn; rail junction; stone quarrying; mfg. of furniture, bricks.

Bergama (bĕr'gämä"), town (1950 pop. 16,509), Smyrna prov., W Turkey, 50 mi. N of Smyrna, in the valley of the Bakir; mfg. of carpets; iron, copper, and silver deposits; trade in tobacco, olives, valonia, wheat, barley, millet, legumes, cotton. It is on site of anc. PERGAMUM, of which there are extensive remains.

Bergamasque Alps (bûr'gůmăsk, Fr. bĕrgämäsk'), Ital. *Alpi Bergamasche*, Lombardy, N Italy, S outliers of Rhaetian Alps, extend from the Valtellina S to Po plain at Bergamo, bet. Val Camonica (E) and L. Como (W). Highest peaks, Pizzo di Coca (10,013 ft.) and Pizzo Redorta (9,964 ft.), in NE. Pizzo dei Tre Signori (8,379 ft.) is in NW. Contains a few small glaciers. Source of Serio and Brembo rivers.

Bergamo (bĕr'gämô), province (1,065; pop. 605,810), Lombardy, N Italy; ⊙ Bergamo. Consists of Bergamasque Alps (N) and Po plain (S). Watered by Adda, Oglio, Serio, and Brembo rivers. Forestry (fir, larch, chestnut) and hydroelectric plants (Serio, Brembo rivers) in N. Agr. (corn, wheat, raw silk) in S. Stock raising (cattle, horses, swine) widespread. Mfg. at Bergamo, Treviglio.

Bergamo, anc. *Bergomum*, city (pop. 73,534), ⊙ Bergamo prov., Lombardy, N Italy, at S foot of Bergamasque Alps, bet. Serio and Brembo rivers, 28 mi. NE of Milan; 45°42'N 9°42'E. Industrial center; foundries, aluminum works, textile mills, tanneries, furniture factories, alcohol distillery, brewery; mfg. (automobile chassis, textile machinery, refrigerators, cement, glass, soap, wax, macaroni). Has art acad. (1795) with picture gall., agr. and trade schools. Bishopric. In upper old town are Romanesque cathedral and Renaissance Colleoni chapel (1470–76). Anciently a Gallic town. Ruled by Visconti (1329–1427) and by Venice until 1797, when it was included in Cisalpine Republic. Gaetano Donizetti b. here.

Bergantín (bĕrgäntēn'), town (pop. 493), Anzoátegui state, NE Venezuela, on slopes of coastal range, 23 mi. ESE of Barcelona; coffee plantations.

Bergantino (bĕrgäntē'nô), village (pop. 1,342), Rovigo prov., Veneto, N Italy, on Po R. and 6 mi. E of Ostiglia.

Bergedorf (bĕr'gůdôrf), suburb (1933 pop. 19,564) of Hamburg, NW Germany, on the Bille and 10 mi. ESE of Hamburg city center; mfg. of machinery, chemicals, glass; hand weaving. Has 15th–16th-cent. church. Site of Hamburg observatory (1912). Chartered 1275. Property of both Hamburg and Lübeck from 1420 until 1867, when Hamburg bought Lübeck's portion. Inc. 1938 into Hamburg.

Bergeggi (bĕrjĕd'jē), village (pop. 539), Savona prov., Liguria, NW Italy, port on Gulf of Genoa and 4 mi. SSW of Savona; quartz mining. Rocky islet of Bergeggi is 1 mi. S, has ruins of Roman bath and monastery.

Bergeik, Netherlands: see BERGEYK.

Bergel (bĕr'gůl), village (pop. 1,522), Middle Franconia, W Bavaria, Germany, 5 mi. SSW of Windsheim; oats, wheat, sheep.

Bergen, Belgium: see MONS.

Bergen (bĕr'gůn). **1** Village (pop. 4,132), in former Prussian prov. of Hanover, NW Germany, after 1945 in Lower Saxony, 13 mi. NW of Celle; building materials; sawmilling. With near-by Belsen it was site of notorious concentration camp during Hitler regime. **2** or **Bergen auf Rügen** (ouf rü' gůn), town (pop. 8,745), in former Prussian Pomerania prov., N Germany, after 1945 in Mecklenburg, on central Rügen isl., 16 mi. ENE of Stralsund; rail junction; agr. center (grain, sugar beets, potatoes, stock). Has 13th-cent. church.

Bergen (bĕr'khůn), town (pop. 7,091), North Holland prov., NW Netherlands, 3 mi. NNW of Alkmaar; cattle raising, dairying. Bergen aan Zee (pop. 221), on North Sea coast, 3 mi. W, is a growing tourist resort.

Bergen (bûr'gůn, Nor. băr'gůn), city (pop. 110,424), ⊙ Hordaland co. and a co. in itself, SW Norway, port on Vagen or Vaagen [Nor. *Vågen*,=the bay] and on Pudde Fjord (2 inlets of a sound of the North Sea), 190 mi. WNW of Oslo; 60°20'N 5°20'E. Second largest city in Norway and chief shipping center, with a large mercantile fleet. The city, built on a high promontory, is protected by Bergenhus and Sverresborg fortresses (N of Vagen) and Fredriksberg (S of Vagen). It has a mild but wet climate. The metropolis of W Norway, at the terminus of a rail line from Oslo, Bergen is a trade, fishing, commercial, and industrial center. Shipbuilding; processing of iron and aluminum; mfg. of paper, wood products, furniture, pianos, electrical appliances, glassware, pottery, leather goods, textiles, rope, fishing equipment, silver filigree, tobacco products, fish and canned foodstuffs, beer. At its suburb of Minde (SSE) are steel production (plates, beams, turbines), textile milling. Bergen is also a cultural center: Bergen Univ., commercial col., marine acad., music acad.; museums of natural history, fishery, and industrial arts; art galleries, meteorological observatory, geographical institute, marine biological station, theater. It is also a tourist center, with Haakon's Hall, a 12th-cent. palace (restored after 1944 damage); 12th-cent. Maria Church; 13th-cent. cathedral and Cross Church. The formerly walled Hanseatic quarter, with German Quay, is guarded by Rosenkrantz Tower (16th cent.; restored). Founded 1070 as Bjorgvin (Nor. *Bjørgvin*) by Olaf Kyrre (Olaf III), Bergen soon prospered as an export center (chiefly of codfish) and became largest city of medieval Norway. The Norwegian kings made it their main residence; as an episcopal see and as seat of numerous monasteries, it had cultural as well as economic importance. Foreign, especially German, merchants acquired (13th and 14th cent.) increasing trading privileges, and the Hanseatic League created (c.1350) one of its 4 great foreign establishments at Bergen. The Hansa merchants, enjoying extra-territorial privileges, imposed their unpopular rules on the city until 1560. In 1395 Bergen was sacked by pirates. During the disturbances accompanying the Reformation most of the anc. churches and monasteries were destroyed. Scene (1665) of Dutch naval victory over the British. Central part of city was rebuilt after severe fire in 1916; heavily damaged in bombings of German installations in Second World War. Grieg was b. here.

Bergen (bûr'gůn), county (□ 233; pop. 539,139), extreme NE N.J., bounded E by Palisades of Hudson R. and N by N.Y. line; ⊙ Hackensack. Industrial and residential area; mfg. (metal products, textiles, chemicals, embroideries, food products, paper goods, concrete products); agr. (fruit, truck, poultry, dairy products). Includes part of Palisades Interstate Park and Oradell Reservoir. Drained by Ramapo, Saddle, Passaic, and Hackensack rivers. Formed 1675.

Bergen. **1** (bûr'gůn) Village, N.J.: see JERSEY CITY. **2** (bûr'jůn, bůrjĕn') Village (pop. 786), Genesee co., W N.Y., 15 mi. WSW of Rochester; vegetable canning. Bergen Swamps near by. **3** (bûr'gůn) Village (pop. 51), McHenry co., central N.Dak., 31 mi. ESE of Minot.

Bergen aan Zee, Netherlands: see BERGEN.

Bergen auf Rügen, Germany: see BERGEN, Pomerania.

Berg en dal (bĕrkh' ĕn däl'), village (pop. 148), Surinam dist., N Du. Guiana, on Surinam R. and 48 mi. S of Paramaribo; coffee, rice.

Bergen-Enkheim (bĕr'gůn-ĕngk'hīm''), village (pop. 7,219), in former Prussian prov. of Hesse-Nassau, W Germany, after 1945 in Hesse, 4 mi. ENE of Frankfurt; mfg. (machinery, leather goods).

Bergenfield (bûr'gůnfēld), residential borough (pop. 17,647), Bergen co., NE N.J., 4 mi. NNE of Hackensack; mfg. (machinery, cutlery, knitwear, wood products, ice cream). Old South Church here was built 1799. Inc. 1894.

Bergenhus, Norway: see BERGEN.

Bergen op Zoom (bĕr'khůn ôp sōm'), town (pop. 26,642; commune pop. 28,464), North Brabant prov., SW Netherlands, on the Eastern Scheldt and 23 mi. WSW of Breda; shipping; fishing; oyster culture; sugar and potash refining; iron foundries, machine shops, distilleries; mfg. (cigars, ceramics); salt production; fish and vegetable canning. Has 14th-cent. town hall (*Stadhuis*), 15th-cent. church (*Groote Kerk*) and Markiezenhof (palace of marquises). Once a strong fortress, frequently besieged by Spaniards (bet. 1581 and 1622), by French (1747, 1795), and by British (1814).

Berger (bûr'gůr), town (pop. 210), Franklin co., E central Mo., in Ozark region, near Missouri R., 20 mi. WNW of Washington.

Bergerac (bûr'zhůrăk, Fr. bĕrzhräk'), town (pop. 17,014), Dordogne dept., SW France, at head of navigation on Dordogne R. and 26 mi. SSW of Périgueux; commercial center noted for its white and red wines, and for its chestnuts. Industries: distilling, food processing (*pâté de foie gras* and truffles), tanning, metalworking, mfg. (clothing, felt slippers). Held and fortified by English in 14th cent. With large Huguenot pop., town suffered from revocation of Edict of Nantes.

Bergerville (bûr'gůrvĭl), SW suburb (pop. estimate 500) of Quebec, on the St. Lawrence; airport, radio station.

Bergeshövede (bĕr''gůs-hů'vůdů), village, in former Prussian prov. of Westphalia, NW Germany, after 1945 in North Rhine-Westphalia, in Teutoburg Forest, on Dortmund-Ems Canal 1 mi. SE of its junction (lock) with Ems-Weser Canal, and 4 mi. W of Ibbenbüren.

Bergeyk or **Bergeik** (bĕr'khīk), village (commune pop. 4,503), North Brabant prov., S Netherlands, 10 mi. SSW of Eindhoven; condensed milk, cigars, methylated spirits; dairying.

Berggiesshübel (bĕrk''gēs'hü''bůl), town (pop. 2,102), Saxony, E central Germany, in Saxonian Switzerland, 6 mi. S of Pirna, near Czechoslovak border; iron mining and smelting. Spa. Scene (Aug., 1813) of defeat of Napoleon's forces under Saint-Cyr by Allied army.

Berghausen (bĕrk''hou'zůn). **1** Village (pop. 3,493), N Baden, Germany, after 1945 in Württemberg-Baden, on the Pfinz and 5 mi. E of Karlsruhe; paper milling. **2** Village (pop. 1,770), Rhenish Palatinate, W Germany, 2 mi. SW of Speyer; wine; also tobacco, corn, sugar beets.

Bergheim (bĕrg''ĕm', Ger. bĕrk'hīm), village (pop. 1,670), Haut-Rhin dept., E France, at E foot of the Vosges, 2 mi. ENE of Ribeauvillé; wines.

Bergheim (bĕrk'hīm), town (pop. 5,734), in former Prussian Rhine Prov., W Germany, after 1945 in North Rhine-Westphalia, on the Erft and 13 mi. W of Cologne, in lignite-mining region; rail junction.

Bergholz (bûr'gōlz), village (pop. 1,035), Jefferson co., E Ohio, 17 mi. NW of Steubenville, and on small Yellow Creek, in coal-mining area; lumber, metal stampings. Settled 1885, inc. 1906.

Bergisch Gladbach (bĕr'gĭsh glät'bäkh''), town (pop. 30,230), in former Prussian Rhine Prov., W Germany, after 1945 in North Rhine-Westphalia, 9 mi. ENE of Cologne; 50°59'N 7°9'E. Iron foundry (machine tools); mfg. of paper, glass wool. Has 12th-cent. church. Chartered 1856.

Bergisch-Neukirchen (–noi'kĭr''khůn), town (pop. 3,766), in former Prussian Rhine Prov., W Germany, after 1945 in North Rhine-Westphalia, 1.5 mi. ENE of Opladen.

Bergkamen (bĕrk'kä''můn), town (pop. 6,563), in former Prussian prov. of Westphalia, W Germany, after 1945 in North Rhine-Westphalia, in the Ruhr, 2 mi. NNW of Kamen; coal mining.

Bergkvara (bĕr''yůkvä'rä), fishing village (pop. 732), Kalmar co., SE Sweden, on Kalmar Sound of the Baltic, 20 mi. SSW of Kalmar; sawmilling, woodworking.

Berglistock (bĕrg'lĕshtôk''), peak (12,004 ft.) in Bernese Alps, S central Switzerland, 5 mi. E of Grindelwald.

Bergneustadt (bĕrk''noi'shtät), village (pop. 6,039), in former Prussian Rhine Prov., W Germany, after 1945 in North Rhine-Westphalia, 4 mi. E of Gummersbach; cattle. Formerly also called Neustadt.

Bergomum, Italy: see BERGAMO, city.

Bergreichenstein, Czechoslovakia: see KASPERSKE HORY.

Bergsche Maas River (bĕrk'sů mäs'), W Netherlands, navigable offshoot of Maas R.; leaves main stream 7 mi. NW of 's Hertogenbosch, at Heusden; flows 22 mi. W, joining New Merwede R. 6 mi. SSE of Dordrecht to form the HOLLANDSCHDIEP. Its lower course is also called the Amer; forms S boundary of the Biesbosch.

Bergsjo (bĕr'yů-shû''), Swedish *Bergsjö*, village (pop. 507), Gavleborg co., E Sweden, 18 mi. N of Hudiksvall; berry-growing center; grain, flax, potatoes, stock.

Bergslag, Swedish *Bergslagen* (bĕr'yůslä''gůn), region of central Sweden, in Varmland, Kopparberg, Vastmanland, and Orebro cos. Noted for its rich iron mines, some of which have been in operation since 13th cent. Copper, lead, zinc, and other metals are also mined. Chief centers are Grangesberg, Fagersta, Avesta, Hedemora, Ludvika, and Filipstad.

Bergstadt, Poland: see LESNICA.

Bergstadt Platten, Czechoslovakia: see HORNI BLATNA.

Bergstrasse (bĕrk'shträ''sů) [Ger.,=mountain street], name applied to W slope of the Odenwald, W Germany; rises to 1,696 ft. in the Malchen. Fruit; vineyards. Since Roman times an important trade route has led along W foot.

Bergstrom Air Force Base, Texas: see AUSTIN.

Berguent (bârgĕnt'), town (pop. 1,198), Oujda region, NE Morocco, on railroad and 45 mi. S of Oujda, near Algerian border; sheep and wool market. Alfa shipping.

Bergues (bârg), town (pop. 3,155), Nord dept., N France, 6 mi. SSE of Dunkirk; agr. trade center; metalworking, canning. Laid out by Vauban (17th cent.) as a frontier fortress, its walls are protected by a moat formed by junction of 3 canals. Preserving a strong 18th-cent. Flemish character, it was severely damaged in Second World War.

Bergulae, Turkey: see LULEBURGAZ.

Bergum (bĕr'khům), town (pop. 2,791), Friesland prov., N Netherlands, on the Wijde Ee and 8 mi. E of Leeuwarden, near Bergum L.; truck gardens, tree nurseries.

Bergum Lake, Du. *Bergumermeer* (bĕr'gůmůrmär''), Friesland prov., N Netherlands, 10 mi. E of Leeuwarden; 1 mi. long, 2 mi. wide. KOLONELSDIEP and WIJDE EE canals join here.

Bergün (bĕrgün'), Romansh *Bravuogn* (brůwō'nyů), village (pop. 653), Grisons canton, E Switzerland, on Albula R. and 10 mi. NNW of St. Moritz; summer resort (alt. c.4,500 ft.), winter sports center. Old church.

Bergville, village (pop. 788), W Natal, U. of So. Afr., in Drakensberg range, on Tugela R. and 30 mi. WSW of Ladysmith; alt. 3,737 ft.; rail terminus; tourist center for Drakensberg resorts.

Bergzabern (bĕrk''tsä'bůrn), town (pop. 3,447), Rhenish Palatinate, W Germany, at E foot of Hardt Mts., 8 mi. SW of Landau; wine; health resort. Almonds, chestnuts. Has 16th-cent. castle. Of Roman origin, it was chartered 1286. Limestone quarries in area.

Berhala Strait (bĕrhä'lä), channel (20–60 mi. wide) of S. China Sea, Indonesia, bet. E coast of Sumatra and Singkep isl. of Lingga Archipelago.

Berhampore (bûr'ůmpōr), town (pop. 41,558), ⊙ Murshidabad dist., E West Bengal, India, in Ganges Delta, on Bhagirathi R. and 105 mi. N of Calcutta; trade center (rice, gram, oilseeds, jute, wheat, barley); mfg. of silk cloth, matches; rice and oilseed milling. Has Bengal Silk Technological Inst., Krishnanath Col., sericulture research station. Scene of 1st overt act of Sepoy Rebellion in 1857. Irish sailor who became raja of Hansi buried here. Former cantonment. Also spelled Bahrampur. Hindu ruins 7 mi. SW, at village of Rangamati (anc. *Karna Suvarna;* 7th cent. A.D.).

Berhampur (bär'hŭmpŏŏr), town (pop. 43,536), Ganjam dist., SE Orissa, India, 105 mi. SW of Cuttack; trade center for rice, oilseeds, cloth fabrics, turmeric, sugar cane; silk weaving, rice milling, mfg. of turmeric polish, vegetable ghee; distillery. Col., midwifery training school.

Berhida (bĕr'hĭdō), town (pop. 3,831), Veszprem co., NW central Hungary, on Sed R. and 11 mi. E of Veszprem; corn, wheat, flax; dairy farming.

Berhomet, Ukrainian SSR: see BERKHOMET.

Beri (bā'rē), former petty state (□ 32; pop. 5,092) of Central India agency; in 1948 merged with Vindhya Pradesh; in 1950 transferred to Uttar Pradesh.

Beri, town (pop. 9,785), Rohtak dist., SE Punjab, India, 13 mi. S of Rohtak; millet, gram, cotton, oilseeds; hand-loom weaving. Sometimes called Beri Khas.

Berici, Monti (môn'tē bā'rēchē), range of volcanic hills, N Italy, SW of Vicenza; 12 mi. long NE-SW; rise to 1,457 ft. in Monte Alto (E). Quarries (basalt, limestone, marble).

Berikulski or **Berikul'skiy** (byĕrĭkŏŏl'skē), town (1939 pop. over 10,000), NE Kemerovo oblast, Russian SFSR, near Kiya R., 45 mi. SSW of Tyazhin; gold mines.

Beringel (bĭrēn-zhĕl'), town (pop. 2,374), Beja dist., S Portugal, 7 mi. WNW of Beja; pottery making, grain, olives, sheep.

Beringen (bā'rĭng-ŭn), town (pop. 3,274), Limburg prov., NE Belgium, 9 mi. NNW of Hasselt, near Albert Canal; coal mining. Formerly spelled Beeringen.

Bering Glacier (bĕr'ĭng, bâ'rĭng, bē'–), S Alaska, in St. Elias Range glacier system, W and NW of Cape Yakataga; 60°15'N 143°30'W; c.45 mi. long, 20 mi. wide; drains into Gulf of Alaska.

Bering Island, in SW Bering Sea, largest of KOMANDORSKI ISLANDS, off Kamchatka Peninsula, Russian SFSR, 330 mi. NE of Petropavlovsk; 54 mi. long, 22 mi. wide. Chief village, Nikolskoye. Named for 18th-cent. Rus. navigator, who died here in 1741.

Bering Sea, Rus. *Beringovo More,* N part of Pacific Ocean, bet. NE Siberia and Alaska; bounded S by Aleutian and Komandorski isls.; connected N through Bering Strait with Chukchi Sea of Arctic Ocean; 930 mi. N–S, 1,240 mi. E–W, □ 878,000. Receives Anadyr and Yukon rivers; forms large gulfs (Anadyr, Bristol, Norton); contains several large isls. (St. Lawrence, St. Matthew, Nunivak) and Pribilof Isls. Shallow N and W, its deepest point (13,422 ft.) is at W end of Aleutian Isls. Its severe climate is little influenced by warm Japan Current; N section frozen Oct.-June. Main ports: Anadyr, Provideniya, Nome. International Date Line passes through the sea, NE–SW. Fishing, whaling, and fur-seal hunting are important. Discovered 1648 by Dezhnev; named for Bering, who sailed through it in 1728. Formerly called Sea of Kamchatka.

Bering Strait separates Chukchi Peninsula of NE Siberia (W) and Seward Peninsula of Alaska (E), joining Bering and Chukchi seas; 55 mi. wide bet. Cape Dezhnev and Cape Prince of Wales; max. depth 170 ft. Frozen Oct.–June. International Date Line passes through Diomede Isls. in center of strait. Discovered 1648 by Dezhnev; named for Bering, who sailed into it in 1728.

Beris (bĕ'rĭs) or **Baris** (bä'rĭs), village (pop. 1,886) in Kharga oasis, S central Egypt, 52 mi. S of Kharga; dates, cotton. Near by (S) are the ruins of an anc. Roman temple.

Berislav (byĕrĭsläf'), city (1926 pop. 7,529), central Kherson oblast, Ukrainian SSR, on Dnieper R. (landing), opposite Kakhovka, and 40 mi. NE of Kherson; metalworks; dairying. Founded c. 1450 as Turkish fort of Kizi-Kermen; passed 1774 to Russia.

Berisso (bārē'sō), town (pop. 19,852), NE Buenos Aires prov., Argentina, 5 mi. NE of La Plata, on the Río de la Plata; meat-packing and fishing center; sawmilling.

Berit Dag (bĕrĭt'dä), Turkish *Berit Dağ,* peak (9,888 ft.), S central Turkey, in the Anti-Taurus, 20 mi. E of Goksun.

Beriya, Imeni (ē'mĭnyē byĕ'rēŭ), town (1945 pop. over 500), W central Armenian SSR, at SE foot of Mt. Aragats, 6 mi. NW of Erivan (on road to Ashtarak), in irrigated area; vineyards, cotton, wheat. Built in Second World War, in former desert area.

Berja (bĕr'hä), city (pop. 7,291), Almería prov., S Spain, near the Sierra de Gádor, 27 mi. W of Almería; lead-mining, -processing, and -shipping center. Mfg. of brandy and soap; olive-oil processing, wool spinning. Exports grapes and other fruit. Cereals, vegetables, livestock in area.

Berka (bĕr'kä). **1** or **Berka an der Werra** (än dĕr vĕ'rä), town (pop. 1,807), Thuringia, central Germany, on the Werra and 12 mi. W of Eisenach, opposite Obersuhl, in potash-mining region. **2** or **Bad Berka** town, Thuringia, Germany, on the Ilm see: BAD BERKA.

Berkane (bârkän'), town (pop. 8,235), Oujda region, northeasternmost Fr. Morocco, 29 mi. NW of Oujda, near Sp. Morocco border; agr. trade center, shipping wine, citrus fruit, early vegetables, wheat, barley; flour milling.

Berkeley (bärk'lē, bûrk'lē), town and parish (pop. 664), SW Gloucester, England, near Severn R., 15 mi. SW of Gloucester; agr. market in dairying region. Has 14th-cent. castle, enclosing Norman keep; here Edward II was murdered (1327). The church dates from 14th–15th cent. Dr. Edward Jenner b. here.

Berkeley (bûr'klē). **1** County (□ 1,214; pop. 30,251), SE S.C.; ⊙ Moncks Corner. Bounded N by Santee R.; Santee-Cooper irrigation and power development centers in N sec., with dams on Cooper and Santee rivers forming lakes Marion and Moultrie. Includes part of Francis Marion Natl. Forest. Cotton, dairy products, poultry, truck, timber. Formed 1882. **2** County (□ 316; pop. 30,359), W.Va., in Eastern Panhandle; ⊙ MARTINSBURG. Bounded NE by Potomac R., and SW by Va.; Mtn. ridges; partly in Great Appalachian Valley; drained by Opequon and Black creeks, short tributaries of the Potomac. Agr. (livestock, dairy products, fruit); limestone quarrying. Mfg. at Martinsburg. Formed 1772.

Berkeley. 1 City (pop. 113,805), Alameda co., W Calif., just N of Oakland, rises into Berkeley Hills from E shore of San Francisco Bay. Seat of Univ. of Calif., Armstrong Col., 4 divinity schools, state schools for deaf and blind. Largely residential, with industrial water front (industrial gases, soap, paint, food products, chemicals, metal products, machinery, vehicles). Yacht harbor and aquatic park (1937). Founded 1853, inc. 1878. **2** Village (pop. 1,882), Cook co., NE Ill., W suburb of Chicago. **3** City (pop. 5,268), St. Louis co., E Mo., 12 mi. WNW of St. Louis. Inc. 1937. **4** Village, N.J.: see SEASIDE PARK. **5** Village, R.I.: see CUMBERLAND.

Berkeley, Cape, N extremity of Prince of Wales Isl., central Franklin Dist., Northwest Territories, on Barrow Strait and Viscount Melville Sound; 73°59'N 100°25'W.

Berkeley Heights, village (1940 pop. 1,146), Union co., NE N.J., on Passaic R. and 14 mi. W of Newark; mfg. (chemicals, pottery, metal products).

Berkeley Hills, W Calif., NW–SE range (c.1,000–2,000 ft.) rising E of S San Francisco Bay; suburbs of Berkeley and Oakland extend up W slopes.

Berkeley Point, W extremity of Victoria Isl., SW Franklin Dist., Northwest Territories, on Prince of Wales Strait; 70°39'N 119°5'W.

Berkeley Sound (bär'klē), inlet (c.10 mi. long, 2–3 mi. wide), East Falkland Isl., just N of Stanley; 51°35'S 57°56'W.

Berkeley Springs (bûr'klē), town (pop. 1,213), ⊙ Morgan co., W.Va., in Eastern Panhandle, 18 mi. NW of Martinsburg. Health resort (since colonial days) with mineral springs, within a state park; glass-sand pits; mfg. of beverages, canned foods, hosiery; lumbering. Sanatorium. Chartered 1776 as Bath, still its official name.

Berkel River (bĕr'kŭl), in NW Germany and E Netherlands, rises 2 mi. SE of Billerbeck, flows 60 mi. W and NW, past Coesfeld, crossing into Netherlands 2 mi. NW of Ammeloe, and continuing past Eibergen, Borculo, and Lochem, to the Ijssel at Zutphen.

Berkey (bûr'kē), village (pop. 239), Lucas co., NW Ohio, 15 mi. WNW of Toledo, near Mich. line.

Berkhampsted, England: see GREAT BERKHAMPSTEAD.

Berkhomet (byĕrkhŭmyĕt'), Rum. *Berhomet* (bĕrhômĕt'), village (1941 pop. 6,046), W Chernovtsy oblast, Ukrainian SSR, in N Bukovina, on Sereth R. and 30 mi. WSW of Chernovtsy, in Carpathian foothills; rail terminus.

Berkley. 1 Town (pop. 71), Boone co., central Iowa, on Beaver Creek and 7 mi. N of Perry, in livestock and grain area. **2** Rural town (pop. 1,284), Bristol co., SE Mass., at mouth of Taunton R., 4 mi. S of Taunton. Settled 1638, inc. 1755. Includes Assonet Neck, site of Dighton Rock, whose mysterious inscriptions are probably Indian in origin. **3** City (pop. 17,931), Oakland co., SE Mich., NW suburb of Detroit. Inc. as village 1924, as city 1932.

Berkovets, Ukraine: see KOTSYUBINSKOGO, IMENI.

Berkovitsa (bĕrkô'vētsä), city (pop. 6,870), Vratsa dist., NW Bulgaria, on N slope of Berkovitsa Mts., at N end of road through Petrokhan Pass, and 38 mi. NNW of Sofia. Rail terminus; summer resort in chestnut and fruitgrowing dist.; furniture mfg., fruit preserving, wine making (raspberry); exports lumber. Has ruins of medieval fortress.

Berkovitsa Mountains, part of W Balkan Mts., just S of Berkovitsa, extend 15 mi. bet. Chiporov Mts. (NW) and Vratsa Mts. (SE); rise to 6,613 ft. in Kom peak. Crossed by Petrokhan Pass.

Berks, England: see BERKSHIRE.

Berks, county (□ 864; pop. 255,740), SE central Pa.; ⊙ Reading. Agr. and industrial area, drained by Schuylkill R.; bounded NW by Blue Mtn. First settled by Swedes. Daniel Boone b. near Reading. Machinery, textiles, food products; railroad shops. Formed 1752.

Berkshire (bärk'shĭr, –shûr), county (□ 724.7; 1931 pop. 311,453; 1951 census 402,939), S England; ⊙ Reading. Bounded by Wiltshire (W), Gloucester (NW), Oxford and Buckingham (N), Surrey (SE), and Hampshire (S). Drained by Thames, Kennet, Loddon, and Blackwater rivers. Dairying; sheep and hog raising. Fertile soil, especially in Valley of the White Horse and in Kennet R. valley. Berkshire is underlain by chalk, and a tract of downs extends through its center. Industrialization was spurred by Second World War; there are aircraft works at Reading and Newbury; other light industries are at Reading. Other important towns: Newbury, Hungerford, Wantage (associations with Alfred the Great), Abingdon, Wallingford, Windsor (site of royal castle), and Sandhurst (Royal Military Col.). Shortened form, Berks (bärks).

Berkshire (bûrk'shĕr, –shûr), county (□ 942; pop. 132,966), W Mass., bordering Vt., N.Y., and Conn.; ⊙ Pittsfield. Embraces most of the Berkshire Hills; popular summer and winter resort area, with mfg. towns. Mt. Greylock (3,505 ft.), highest point in Mass., is near North Adams. Rivers include Housatonic, Hoosic, and Farmington. In N, Hoosac Tunnel pierces the Hoosac Range. Appalachian Trail traverses co. (N-S). Formed 1761.

Berkshire. 1 Village, Mass.: see LANESBORO. **2** Village (pop. c.350), Tioga co., S N.Y., on Owego Creek and 20 mi. NW of Binghamton; furniture, crates. **3** Town (pop. 1,063), Franklin co., N Vt., 19 mi. NE of St. Albans and on Missisquoi R., at Que. line; mfg. (threshers, wagons, sleds); dairy products. Settled 1792, inc. 1795 or 1796.

Berkshire Hills, W Mass., wooded region embracing most of Berkshire co., from Vt. to Conn. lines. Name is generally applied to all highlands (part of Appalachian system) of W Mass., including HOOSAC RANGE, a S extension of Green Mts., but is sometimes restricted to that part of TACONIC MOUNTAINS in Mass. and sometimes to highlands lying E of main range of the Taconics. S extension of the Berkshires is known in Conn. as LITCHFIELD HILLS. Mt. Greylock (3,505 ft.), highest point in state, is in area; there are many lakes and streams, state parks and forests, and summer and winter resorts; Appalachian Trail traverses region N-S. Among Berkshire towns are North Adams, Pittsfield, Great Barrington, Lenox, and Stockbridge. Housatonic, Westfield, Hoosic, and other rivers drain region and supply water power to mfg. towns.

Berlaar (bĕr'lär), town (pop. 8,376), Antwerp prov., N Belgium, on Grande Nèthe R. and 4 mi. E of Lierre; woodworking; agr. market. Has 13th-cent. church. Formerly spelled Berlaer.

Berlad, Rumania: see BARLAD.

Berlaer, Belgium: see BERLAAR.

Berlaimont (bĕrlāmō'), town (pop. 2,671), Nord dept., N France, port on the Sambre and 7 mi. NW of Avesnes.

Berlanga (bĕrläng'gä). **1** Town (pop. 5,976), Badajoz. prov., W Spain, 10 mi. ENE of Llerena; lead mining. Agr. (olives, cereals, livestock). **2** or **Berlanga de Duero** (dhä dhwä'rō), town (pop. 2,055), Soria prov., N central Spain, near the Duero, 30 mi. SW of Soria; cereals, sweet potatoes, grapes, fruit, livestock; apiculture. Flour milling, hosiery mfg. Hydroelectric plant. Has noted collegiate church.

Berlare (bĕrlä'rŭ), town (pop. 5,482), East Flanders prov., N Belgium, near Scheldt R., 5 mi. W of Dendermonde; agr. market (fruit, vegetables, poultry); textile milling. Has 13th-cent. chapel and 17th-cent. castle.

Berleburg (bĕr'lŭbŏŏrk), town (pop. 5,646), in former Prussian prov. of Westphalia, W Germany, after 1945 in North Rhine-Westphalia, 24 mi. NW of Marburg; forestry. Has 18th-cent. castle.

Berlenga Island (bĭrläng'gŭ), in the Atlantic, off Peniche peninsula (5 mi. NW) of W central Portugal. Of irregular shape (c.1 mi. long), it rises to 280 ft. in nearly perpendicular cliffs. On it are a fort, a 16th-cent. monastery, and a lighthouse (39°25'N 9°30'W).

Berlengas, Brazil: see VALENÇA DO PIAUÍ.

Berlichingen (bĕr'lĭ-khĭng"ŭn), village (pop. 824), N Württemberg, Germany, after 1945 in Württemberg-Baden, on the Jagst and 16 mi. SW of Mergentheim; wine. Ancestral seat of Berlichingen family.

Berlicum (bĕr'lēkŭm), village (pop. 1,799), North Brabant prov., S Netherlands, on the Zuid-Willemsvaart and 4 mi. E of 's Hertogenbosch; cigar mfg.; cattle raising, agr.

Berlik (byĕr'lyĭk), town (1948 pop. over 500), E Dzhambul oblast, Kazakh SSR, on Turksib RR and 20 mi. NE of Chu; S terminus of N–S Trans-Kazakhstan RR; railroad shops. Berlik village is on edge of Muyun-Kum desert, 40 mi N of Chu.

Berlikum (bĕr'lēkŭm), village (pop. 2,302), Friesland prov., N Netherlands, 7 mi. WNW of Leeuwarden; fruit growing, dairying, agr.

Berlin, Ont.: see KITCHENER.

Berlin (bûr"lĭn', bûrlĭn', Ger. bĕrlēn'), largest city (□ 344; 1939 pop. 4,338,756; 1946 pop. 3,187,470, with displaced persons 3,199,938) and former ⊙ Germany and Prussia, in Brandenburg (from which it is administratively separate), N Germany, 100 mi. from Baltic Sea, 150 mi. ESE of Hamburg, 300 mi. W of Warsaw; 52°31′N 13°25′E. Situated on a flat, sandy, lake-studded plain, it is traversed SE–NW by the Spree, which joins the Havel at Spandau dist. Until its virtual destruction in the Second World War, Berlin was 2d largest city in continental Europe (2d only to Moscow) and one of the 5 largest cities in the world. With 8 large railroad stations, extensive harbor facilities, and several airports (the most important at Tempelhof, others at Gatow and Johannisthal), it was a busy inland port and the transportation center of N central Europe. Even after the war, Berlin's place as the political, cultural, and commercial center of the country made its ruins the center of the ideological struggle for post-war Germany. Berlin produces quantities of electrical equipment and appliances (mostly in the dists. of Siemensstadt and Treptow), and also locomotives, machinery, clothing, chemicals, pharmaceuticals, food and tobacco products; printing, textile milling. Teltow and Berlin-Spandau canals link the Spree and the Havel, by-passing the city center. A suburban railroad system is supplemented by an underground railroad system. Berlin is seat of Berlin Univ. (founded 1810 by Karl Wilhelm von Humboldt and by Fichte), Free Univ. of Berlin (founded after 1945 in Dahlem section, SW), technical col., and numerous other higher educational institutions. The noted Kaiser Wilhelm Inst. was dissolved after 1945, but its divisions survived independently. Other scientific institutions include the Ger. Acad. of Sciences, and a medico-biological institute. Seat of Lutheran and R.C. bishops. Before the war, the city presented architecturally a scene of heavy Prussian splendor and of purely functional design. Almost all noted bldgs. were destroyed or very heavily damaged; these include most museums, among them the Kaiser Friedrich Mus. and the Natl. Gall., the imperial palace (built 1699–1706 by Schlüter; razed after 1950), the cathedral, the state and univ. libraries, and many other public bldgs., including the Chancellery, where Hitler presumably committed suicide. The Reichstag bldg. has remained gutted since the historic fire in 1933. The art treasures of the various museums were evacuated during Second World War; although some have survived undamaged, only a few have been returned to Berlin, and they were housed in 18th-cent. Zeughaus (rebuilt after 1945). The noted Pergamon Altar has disappeared. The State Opera and City Opera and many theaters survived with little or no damage. Among Berlin's many splendid streets, Unter den Linden (deriving its name from the linden trees lining it) was world-renowned. The imposing Brandenburg Gate (1793), at its W end, remained intact, but in 1950 the Quadriga statue which crowned it was removed by East Berlin authorities. The Wilhelmstrasse was center of govt. offices; the Kurfürstendamm and Tauentzienstrasse were fashionable shopping centers. The Tiergartenstrasse was known as the diplomatic quarter, and the Bendlerstrasse was synonymous with the war ministry, located here. On the Alexanderplatz (Soviet sector) was Berlin's general police hq.; city's best-known prison was in Moabit (French sector). Industry and workers' residences are located in E, SE, S, and NW (Spandau). Elegant residential quarters (Tiergarten, with large park; Wilmersdorf; Zehlendorf) are W and SW of the central dist. called Mitte. Except for its inner core, which developed from the 13th-cent. Wendish villages of Berlin and Kölln (merged 1307), the metropolis is of very recent origin. Became residence of electors of Brandenburg (after 1701 kings of Prussia) in late-15th cent. It was occupied (1757 and 1760) in Seven Years War by Austrians and Russians, and in Napoleonic Wars by the French. Berlin emerged into the early-19th cent. as focal point of Ger. natl. aspirations and as an increasingly serious rival of Vienna. The city's spectacular growth began when it became (1871) ⊙ German Empire; its pop. increased by almost a million bet. 1875 and 1900. The extensive building program necessitated by this phenomenon resulted in erection of numerous huge, bleak tenements, which long were an outstanding feature of Berlin. Because of rapid expansion in area, incorporation of neighboring towns and suburbs began in 1912 and continued after First World War. The Ger. collapse of 1918 brought on a period of political and social unrest. City was scene of communist Spartacus party rising (Jan., 1919) and of right-wing Kapp *Putsch* (March, 1920). Inflation and unemployment in the early 1920s made Berlin a seat of profiteering speculators; the city's low moral tone became notorious. During the brief recovery before the crisis years of 1929, Berlin was an *avant-garde* center of the arts, literature, and music. The murder (1930) of Nazi storm trooper Horst Wessel inaugurated a long series of street battles bet. Nazis and Communists. City was scene in 1936 of the Olympic Games. In the Second World War Berlin suffered not only from aerial bombardment but also from heavy artillery fire (April–May, 1945) when the Russians took the city. After the war, Berlin came under joint rule (July, 1945) of American, British, French, and Soviet occupation authorities, governing through the Allied *Kommandatura*. The 20 administrative dists. of Berlin, each of which is headed by a mayor, were thereupon grouped to form 4 zones of occupation: CHARLOTTENBURG, SPANDAU, TIERGARTEN, and WILMERSDORF formed the British sector (W; □ 64; pop. 605,287); REINICKENDORF and WEDDING the French sector (NW; □ 43; pop. 427,755); KREUZBERG, NEUKÖLLN, SCHÖNEBERG, STEGLITZ, TEMPELHOF, and ZEHLENDORF the U.S. sector (SW; □ 81; pop. 979,846); and FRIEDRICHSHAIN, KÖPENICK, LICHTENBERG, Mitte, PANKOW, PRENZLAUER BERG, TREPTOW, and WEISSENSEE the Soviet sector (□ 156; pop. 1,174,582), also called East Berlin. West Berlin (the Br., Fr., and U.S. zones) totaled □ 188; pop. 2,012,888. Political friction bet. Russia and the 3 Western nations soon split the city into 2 distinct administrations. After imposing (April 1, 1948) stringent restrictions on rail and highway traffic into Berlin from the West, the Russians left the *Kommandatura* on June 15 and on June 24 stopped all rail and highway traffic from the West. The Allies countered with a tremendous air-supply operation (mostly U.S. operated) until the blockade was lifted late in 1949. When the Russian-occupied zone of Germany was organized (1949) as the "German Democratic Republic," Berlin—or, practically, East Berlin—was made its capital; West Berlin became (1951) one of the states of the "German Federal Republic" (the West German state).

Berlín (bĕrlēn′), city (pop. 5,118), Usulután dept., E central Salvador, on W slope of volcano Tecapa, 12 mi. NW of Usulután; coffee, sugar cane. Founded 1855.

Berlin (bûrlĭn′), village (pop. 1,656), SE Cape Prov., U. of So. Afr., 11 mi. E of Kingwilliamstown; stock, grain; lumbering. Resort.

Berlin (bûr′lĭn). **1** Industrial town (pop. 7,470), Hartford co., central Conn., 10 mi. SSW of Hartford; metal products, machinery, tools, lacquer, fishing tackle, bricks, wood and paper products; dairying. Includes mfg. villages of East Berlin (1940 pop. 531) and Kensington. Hanging Hills are S. Settled 1686, inc. 1785. **2** Town (pop. 309), Colquitt co., S Ga., 11 mi. SE of Moultrie, in farm area. **3** Village (pop. 218), Sangamon co., central Ill., 14 mi. W of Springfield, in agr. and bituminous-coal-mining area. **4** Town (pop. 2,001), Worcester co., SE Md., 21 mi. E of Salisbury, in agr. (truck, potatoes, wheat, corn) and timber area. Poultry packing, mfg. of clothing, wood products, flour; vegetable canneries, large fruit-tree nurseries. Birthplace of Stephen Decatur. Near by is a thoroughbred farm. **5** Town (pop. 1,349), Worcester co., E central Mass., 12 mi. NE of Worcester, near Wachusett Reservoir; fruit, dairying. Settled 1665, inc. 1784. **6** City (pop. 16,615), Coos co., NE N.H., at falls of the Androscoggin at N edge of White Mts., 18 mi. E of Lancaster; pulp and paper mills, foundries. In heavily forested country, it early became lumber and milling center. Winter sports resort; has 1st ski club organized in U.S. Settled 1821 on Maynesborough grant, town inc. 1829, city 1897. **7** Borough (pop. 2,339), Camden co., SW N.J., 15 mi. SE of Camden; mfg. (hosiery, fruit pressers); truck farming. Inc. 1927. **8** Village (pop. c.800), Rensselaer co., E N.Y., on Hoosic R. and 16 mi. E of Troy; woodworking; rose growing. **9** Village (pop. 124), La Moure co., SE central N.Dak., 10 mi. W of La Moure. **10** Agr. borough (pop. 1,507), Somerset co., SW Pa., 9 mi. SE of Somerset; highest borough (alt. 2,322 ft.) in Pa.; maple sugar. Settled c.1769 by Germans, laid out 1784, inc. 1833. **11** Town (pop. 1,158), Washington co., central Vt., just S of Montpelier. **12** City (pop. 4,693), Green Lake and Waushara cos., central Wis., on Fox R. and 20 mi. WSW of Oshkosh, in dairy and farm area; mfg. (leather garments, fur coats, canning machinery, dairy products, beer). Inc. 1857.

Berlinchen, Poland: see BARLINEK.

Berlin Dam, Ohio: see MAHONING RIVER.

Berlinek, Poland: see BARLINEK.

Berlin Heights (bûr′lĭn), village (pop. 613), Erie co., N Ohio, 14 mi. SE of Sandusky, in fruit- and potato-growing area.

Berlin Reservoir, Ohio: see MAHONING RIVER.

Berlin-Spandau Canal (–shpän′dou), Ger. *Berlin-Spandauer Schiffahrtskanal*, Berlin, Germany, extends 9 mi. NW-SE bet. the Spree at NE end of Tiergarten dist. and the Havel in Spandau dist.; serves NW part of city.

Berlin-Stettin Canal (shtĕtēn′), Ger. *Berlin-Stettiner Gross-Schiffahrtsweg*, canal system, E Germany, extending c.110 mi. bet. Berlin and Stettin; links Havel (W) and Oder (E) rivers. Consists of HOHENZOLLERN CANAL, linked at Hohensaaten with the canalized West Oder arm and at Oranienburg with the canalized Havel; 8 locks; navigable for ships up to 600 tons. Completed 1914.

Bermamyt (byĕrmŭmōōt′), peak (c.8,660 ft.) in N front range of the central Greater Caucasus, on Russian SFSR–Georgian SSR border, 22 mi. SW of Kislovodsk.

Bermeja, Sierra (syĕ′rä bĕrmä′hä), Andalusia, S Spain, spur of the Cordillera Penibética in Málaga prov., running parallel (S) to Sierra de Ronda for c.20 mi. near Mediterranean coast; rises to 4,829 ft.

Bermejal, dam, Spain: see SAN JUAN DEL PUERTO.

Bermejillo (bĕrmähē′yō), town (pop. 2,003), Durango, N Mexico, at NW edge of irrigated dist., 27 mi. NNW of Torreón. Rail junction; grain, cotton, fruit.

Bermejo, department, Argentina: see SAN CAMILO.

Bermejo (bĕrmä′hō), town (pop. estimate 600), N Mendoza prov., Argentina, on railroad (Lagunita station) and 4 mi. NW of Mendoza; wine making, fruit canning.

Bermejo, town (pop. c.1,500), Tarija dept., S Bolivia, at confluence of Bermejo and Santa Victoria rivers, 45 mi. S of Tarija, on Argentina border; airport. Bermejo oil fields 40 mi. SSE, on Bermejo R.

Bermejo Island (□ 18), in the Bahía Blanca (bay), SW Buenos Aires prov., Argentina, 20 mi. SE of Bahía Blanca.

Bermejo Pass, Chile-Argentina: see USPALLATA PASS.

Bermejo River. **1** In N Argentina, rises near Tarija (Bolivia) at c.6,500 ft., flows c.650 mi. SE into Argentina, past Bermejo, Embarcación, San Camilo, El Pintado, and Kilómetro 642, along border of Chaco and Formosa natl. territories, to Paraguay R. 10 mi. NE of Puerto Bermejo and opposite Pilar (Paraguay). Its central course is usually called the Teuco (tĕ′ōōkō). Navigable for small craft. The old course of the Bermejo paralleled the central part of its present course 20 mi. to the S. **2** In La Rioja and San Juan provs., Argentina, the upper course of the Río Salado; rises in the subandean mts. of N La Rioja prov., flows c.250 mi. S to the HUANACACHE lakes 75 mi. SE of San Juan, where it becomes the Desaguadero and, finally, the Río SALADO.

Bermeo (bĕrmā′ō), town (pop. 10,235), Vizcaya prov., N Spain, in the Basque Provs., fishing port on Bay of Biscay, 15 mi. NE of Bilbao; fish processing, boatbuilding, mfg. of marine motors. Has nautical school. Trades in *chacolí* wine.

Bermillo de Sayago (bĕrmē′lyō dhā sīä′gō), town (pop. 965), Zamora prov., NW Spain, 22 mi. WSW of Zamora; flour milling, blanket mfg.

Bermius, Greece: see VERMION.

Bermo (bär′mō), town (pop. 5,674), Hazaribagh dist., central Bihar, India, on Damodar R. and 40 mi. ESE of Hazaribagh; coal-mining center in Bokaro coal field; trades in rice, rape and mustard, oilseeds, corn, sugar cane, barley.

Bermondsey (bûr′mŭndzē), residential and industrial metropolitan borough (1931 pop. 111,542; 1951 census 60,661) of London, England, on S bank of the Thames, 3 mi. ESE of Charing Cross. There are docks, wool warehouses, tanneries.

Bermuda (bûrmū′dŭ, bûr–), British crown colony (□ 21; 1949 pop. estimate 35,560) in the W Atlantic; 580 nautical mi. ESE of Cape Hatteras (N.C.), c.670 nautical mi. SE of New York city; 32°15′N 64°51′W. Comprising a group of over 300 coral isls. (c.20 of which are inhabited), the Bermudas (also long known as Somers or Somers' Isls.) form an irregular, open oval c.22 mi. long; the isls. are from ¼ to 2 mi. wide. Generally flat and rocky; highest point, Gibb's Hill (240 ft.). In the center of the chain is Main Isl. or Bermuda Isl. (14 mi. long), on which is HAMILTON, ⊙ Bermuda. The larger isls. of the chain, just off either end of Bermuda Isl., are joined by causeway and road. In W are Somerset, Boaz, and Ireland isls.; in E, St. George's and St. David's isls. Sheltered lagoons (Great Sound, Harrington Sound, Castle Harbour, St. George's Harbour) indent the coast. The charm, luxuriant tropical vegetation, and climate (mean monthly temp. 71.4°F., ranging from 63°F. in winter to 79°F. in summer; rainfall 60–70 inches, evenly distributed) have made Bermuda a popular tourist resort, by far its main activity (over 60,000 visitors in 1949). Lily bulbs, bananas, cut flowers, vegetables are exported. Fishing off coast. A Br. naval base is on Ireland Isl., and in 1941 the U.S. leased for 99 years bases on St. David's Isl. and on a peninsula at W tip of Bermuda Isl. St. George town (founded 1612), on St. George's Isl., was long ⊙ Bermuda before it was superseded (1815) by Hamilton. The colony, divided into 9 parishes, is governed by a governor assisted by a Legislative Council and a House of Assembly. The pop. is 60% colored. Isls. were discovered 1515 by Juan de Bermúdez, a Spaniard, but remained uninhabited until a group of colonists under George Somers was wrecked here in 1609. Isls. were acquired (1684) by the Crown. In 1767 they became a base for the Br. fleet. The tourist industry developed in late 19th cent. Since the Second World War, automobiles are permitted in the isls.

Bermuda Hundred, fishing village, Chesterfield co., E central Va., on peninsula in James R., at mouth of the Appomattox, 11 mi. NE of Petersburg. Founded 1613. In Civil War, Union Army of the James was bottled up here after its defeat, May 16, 1864, at Drewrys Bluff.

Bern or **Berne** (bûrn, Ger. bĕrn), canton (□ 2,658; 1950 pop. 798,264), W central Switzerland, most populous and 2d largest of Swiss cantons; ⊙ Bern. Pop. largely Protestant and —except in the Jura—German speaking. Physiographically it is in 3 sections: the Oberland (Ger.,=highland) (S), including lakes of Thun and Brienz, and consisting of pastures, high peaks, and glaciers of Bernese Alps, with forests and meadows in the valleys; the Mittelland (Ger.,=midland) (center), including valley of lower Aar R., the EMMENTAL, and city of Bern, and comprising an area of fertile fields (cereals, sugar beets), meadows, forests, some gardens and orchards; the Seeland (Ger.,=lake region) (N), including area N of lakes of Biel and Neuchâtel and Bernese JURA, and consisting of fertile fields (cereals), meadows, forests, some pastures. Many resorts and winter sports centers in the Oberland (Interlaken, largest); hydroelectric developments include Oberhasli works. Mfg. of watches (N), metal products, textiles, foodstuffs, clothes; woodworking (S).

Bern or **Berne**, city (1950 pop. 145,740), ⊙ Switzerland and Bern canton, on Aar R.; 46°57'N 7°28'E; alt. 1,781 ft. Founded 1191 as a military post by Berchtold V of Zähringen; was made (1218) a free imperial city by Emperor Frederick II. In 1353 Bern joined Swiss Confederation, in 1848 became its ⊙. Seat of bureaus of Universal Postal Union, International Telecommunication Union, and International Copyright Union. Old section of Bern was built on a ridge surrounded on 3 sides by the Aar, which flows 115–130 ft. below; modern section is on its right bank. Bern retains much medieval architecture in its fountains, towers, and arcades. A large tourist center, it is noted for cathedral (late Gothic), city hall (Burgundian late Gothic), Federal Palace (Florentine Renaissance) with the parliament and governmental offices, Univ. of Bern (1834), Swiss Alpine Mus., Bern Historical Mus., Natural History Mus., Art Mus., Swiss Natl. Library, Bears' Dens (the bear is Bern's official mascot), and medieval Clock Tower (Bern's traditional landmark). Produces metal goods (telephone equipment, electrical apparatus, printing presses, pianos), knit goods, textiles (woolen, cotton, linen), canned goods, flour, chocolate, beer, biscuits; printing, woodworking.

Bern (bûrn), city (pop. 216), Nemaha co., NE Kansas, near Nebr. line, 10 mi. NNE of Seneca, in livestock and grain region.

Bernal (běrnäl'), city (pop. 30,740) in Greater Buenos Aires, Argentina, 7 mi. SE of Buenos Aires; seaside resort on the Río de la Plata; residential, industrial. Mfg. of china, textiles, paper goods, linseed oil, citric acid, cement articles.

Bernal, town (pop. 1,192), Querétaro, central Mexico, 32 mi. NE of Querétaro; alt. 6,768 ft.; corn, wheat, beans, sugar, fruit, maguey, livestock.

Bernal, town (pop. 969), Piura dept., NW Peru, on coastal plain, on lower Piura R. and 20 mi. SSW of Piura, in irrigated cotton area.

Bernalda (běrnäl'dä), town (pop. 7,735), Matera prov., Basilicata, S Italy, near Basento R., 7 mi. ENE of Pisticci; olive oil, wine, cheese.

Bernalillo (bûrnùlē'ō), county (□ 1,163; pop. 145,673), central N.Mex.; ⊙ Albuquerque. Livestock and agr. area; drained by Rio Grande. Coal. Part of Cibola Natl. Forest, Sandia Mts. and Manzano Range in E, Pueblo Indian area in S. Formed 1852.

Bernalillo, village (pop. 1,922), ⊙ Sandoval co., central N.Mex., on Rio Grande, just NW of Sandia Mts., and 18 mi. NNE of Albuquerque; alt. 5,048 ft. Trade and shipping point in livestock, fruit, truck region; dairy and lumber products, grain. Located in Sandia Pueblo land grant. Part of Cibola Natl. Forest near by. Coronado State Monument, just N, includes ruins of pueblos once used (1540–42) by Coronado as hq. Village settled 1698 by Spaniards.

Bernam River (bùrnäm'), W Malaya, on Selangor-Perak line, rises in central Malayan range on Pahang border, flows 100 mi. along state line, past Tanjong Malim and Hutan Melintang, to Strait of Malacca S of Bagan Datoh. Receives Slim R.

Bernard (bùrnärd'), town (pop. 149), Dubuque co., E Iowa, 15 mi. SSW of Dubuque, in agr. area.

Bernardino de Campos (běrnärdē'nŏŏ dĭ käm'pŏŏs), city (pop. 3,158), SW central São Paulo, Brazil, 24 mi. E of Ourinhos; rail junction (spur to Santa Cruz do Rio Pardo); mfg. of candies, furniture, leather goods; distilling.

Bernardino Pass, Switzerland: see SAN BERNARDINO PASS.

Bernardo de Irigoyen (běrnär'dō dā ērēgoi'ěn). **1** Village (pop. estimate 600), ⊙ Frontera dept. (1947 census 1,705), N Misiones natl. territory, Argentina, on Pepirí Guazú R. (Brazil border), at NE foot of Sierra de Misiones, and 150 mi. NE of Posadas; agr. center (corn, livestock); lumbering. Easternmost point in Argentina. Formerly called Barracón. Adjoins Brazilian town of Dionísio Cerqueira. **2** Town (pop. estimate 1,000), S central Santa Fe prov., Argentina, 60 mi. NNW of Rosario; rail junction (Irigoyen station) and agr. center (corn, flax, sunflowers, wheat, livestock, poultry); grain elevators.

Bernardos (běrnär'dōs), town (pop. 1,521), Segovia prov., central Spain, 18 mi. NW of Segovia; cereals, carobs, livestock; mfg. of woolen goods.

Bernardston (bûr'nùrdstùn), agr. town (pop. 1,117), Franklin co., N Mass., on short Falls R. and 6 mi. N of Greenfield, near Vt. line; dairying. Permanently settled 1738, inc. 1762.

Bernardsville (bûr'nùrdzvĭl), residential borough (pop. 3,956), Somerset co., N central N.J., 7 mi. SW of Morristown, in agr., resort area; dairy products; flour milling. Settled early 18th cent., inc. 1924.

Bernartice (běr'närtyĭtsě), village (pop. 1,318), N Silesia, Czechoslovakia, 13 mi. NNW of Jesenik; rail junction; mfg. of smokers' supplies.

Bernasconi (běrnäskō'nē), town (pop. estimate 1,500), ⊙ Hucal dept. (pop. 11,386), SE La Pampa prov., Argentina, on railroad and 60 mi. SE of General Acha; lumbering and farming center (wheat, oats, livestock); salt mining.

Bernati or **Bernaty** (běr'nätē), Lettish *Bernāti*, Ger. *Bernathen*, beach resort, W Latvia, on Baltic Sea, 10 mi. S of Liepaja.

Bernau (běr'nou), town (pop. 12,984), Brandenburg, E Germany, 13 mi. NE of Berlin; cotton and silk milling, glove mfg. Formerly noted for beer brewed here. Has 16th-cent. church and 15th-cent. town walls. Chartered 1232.

Bernaville (běrnävēl'), village (pop. 732), Somme dept., N France, 17 mi. NNW of Amiens; mother-of-pearl button mfg.

Bernay (běrnē'), town (pop. 6,483), Eure dept., NW France, 26 mi. WNW of Évreux; ribbon-mfg. and dairying center. Also makes clothing, caps. Cider distilling, soap mfg. Noted for its annual horse fair. Has two 15th-cent. churches and a town hall which occupies 17th-cent. bldgs. of an abbey (founded early 11th cent.).

Bernburg (běrn'bŏŏrk), city (pop. 53,367), in former Anhalt State, central Germany, after 1945 in Saxony-Anhalt, on the Saxonian Saale, at mouth of the Wipper, and 25 mi. S of Magdeburg; 51°47' N 11°45'E. Rail junction; mining center (potash and rock salt), with large Solvay soda plant. Sugar refining; mfg. of machinery, leather goods, bricks, pottery, chocolate. Overlooked by 14th-cent. castle. Was ⊙ (1244–1468; 1603–1863) duchy of Anhalt-Bernburg. Just SE is suburb of Solvayhall; potash mining.

Berncastel, Germany: see BERNKASTEL-KUES.

Berndorf (běrn'dôrf), town (pop. 9,226), E Lower Austria, on Triesting R. and 7 mi. SW of Baden; ironworks, copper refinery, machine mfg. Coal mined near by.

Berne (běr'nù), village (commune pop. 13,425), in Oldenburg, NW Germany, after 1945 Lower Saxony, bet. Weser and Hunte rivers, 15 mi. NW of Bremen; mfg. of cigars and pipe tobacco. Commune is called Stedingen (shtā'dĭng-ùn).

Berne, Switzerland: see BERN.

Berne (bûrn). **1** Town (pop. 2,277), Adams co., E Ind., 31 mi. SSE of Fort Wayne, in agr. area; poultry hatcheries; mfg. of dairy products, cedar chests, boxes, furniture, work clothes; printing and publishing. Settled 1840 by Swiss; inc. 1887. **2** Village, Albany co., E N.Y., 19 mi. W of Albany; summer resort, with small lakes near by.

Berneck (běr'něk). **1** or **Berneck im Fichtelgebirge** (ĭm fĭkh'tùlgùbĭr"gù), town (pop. 3,449), Upper Franconia, NE Bavaria, Germany, on W slope of the Fichtelgebirge, 9 mi. NE of Bayreuth; mfg. of chemicals, textiles, costume jewelry; lumber milling, brewing. Summer resort. Ruins of medieval castle, destroyed in 1431 by Hussites, on near-by hill. **2** Town (pop. 496), S Württemberg, Germany, after 1945 in Württemberg-Hohenzollern, in Black Forest, 6 mi. NW of Nagold; summer resort (alt. 1,495 ft.). Has 19th-cent. castle.

Berneck, town (pop. 2,225), St. Gall canton, NE Switzerland, 10 mi. E of St. Gall; embroideries, woodworking.

Bernera (bûr'nùrù, bûr'nùrā). **1** Island (1 mi. long) just off SW coast of Lismore isl., Argyll, Scotland. **2** or **Berneray**, island (pop. 331), Outer Hebrides, Inverness, Scotland, just N of North Uist isl., separated from Harris by the Sound of Harris; 4 mi. long, 2 mi. wide, rises to 281 ft. **3** or **Berneray**, southernmost island (pop. 6) of the Outer Hebrides, Inverness, Scotland, 13 mi. SSW of Barra; 2 mi. long, 1 mi. wide. At S end is Barra Head, cape 683 ft. high. At SW extremity is lighthouse (56°47'N 7°38'W).

Bernera, Great, Scotland: see GREAT BERNERA.

Berneray, Scotland: see BERNERA.

Bernese Alps (bûrnēz', It. běrnā'zě) or **Bernese Oberland** (ō'bùrlänt), Ger. *Berner Alpen* or *Berner Oberland*, Fr. *Alpes Bernoises*, N division of central Alps, in Bern and Valais cantons, SW central Switzerland; extend from L. Geneva and Rhone R. bend at Martigny-Ville (WSW) to Grimsel Pass and Hasletal (ENE). Bounded by upper Rhone valley (S) and by lakes of Brienz and Thun (N). Highest peaks, Finsteraarhorn (14,032 ft.), Aletschhorn (13,774 ft.), Jungfrau (13,653 ft.). Many glaciers, including Aletsch Glacier (largest in Alps). Numerous tourists attracted by superb Alpine scenery. Interlaken, Grindelwald, Kandersteg, Leukerbad, Gstaad are but a few of region's resorts. Bernese Alps are crossed by Lötschen Pass and Lötschberg Tunnel (railroad), Col du Pillon, Gemmi and Jaun passes.

Bernesga River (běrnäz'gä), Leon prov., NW Spain, rises in Cantabrian Mts. near Pajares Pass, flows 52 mi. SSE, past Leon, to the Esla 10 mi. S of the city. Coal mines in upper valley.

Bernesq, France: see LITTRY.

Bernhards Bay (bûrn'härdz), resort village, Oswego co., N central N.Y., on N shore of Oneida L., 22 mi. W of Rome.

Bernhausen (běrn"hou'zùn), village (pop. 3,546), N Württemberg, Germany, after 1945 in Württemberg-Baden, 7 mi. S of Stuttgart; wine.

Bernice (bûrnēs'). **1** Town (pop. 1,524), Union parish, N La., 20 mi. N of Ruston; farming; cotton gins, sawmills. Settled 1841, inc. 1889. **2** Town (pop. 91), Delaware co., NE Okla., 12 mi. E of Vinita, near L. of the Cherokees (just E).

Bernicia (bûrnĭ'shù), Anglian kingdom. Established 547, it later extended from the Tees to the Forth. In late 6th cent. it was united with Deira to form NORTHUMBRIA.

Bernie, city (pop. 1,308), Stoddard co., SE Mo., in Mississippi flood plain, 9 mi. S of Dexter; cotton ginning. Inc. as city 1908.

Bernières-sur-Mer (běrnyâr'-sür-mâr'), village (pop. 783), Calvados dept., NW France, resort on English Channel, 11 mi. NNW of Caen. Has 12th–14th-cent. Gothic church (damaged). In Second World War, Canadians landed here (June 6, 1944) in Normandy invasion.

Bernier Island (bûrn'yùr), uninhabited island (□ 25) in Indian Ocean, 26 mi. off W coast of Western Australia; forms S end of Geographe Channel and W shore of Shark Bay; 16 mi. long, 1.5 mi. wide. Limestone; sand dunes.

Bernierville, Que.: see SAINT FERDINAND.

Bernina, Piz (pēts běrnē'nä), peak (13,304 ft.) in the Alps, SE Switzerland, 9 mi. SSE of St. Moritz, on Ital. border; 1st ascended in 1850. Highest of **Bernina Alps**, part of Rhaetian Alps. About 10 mi. SE of St. Moritz, near Bernina Hospice, is **Bernina Pass** (7,645 ft.), crossed by Bernina Road and Bernina RR, which lead from Upper Engadine through Val Poschiavo into Italy.

Bernissart (běrnēsär'), town (pop. 2,621), Hainaut prov., SW Belgium, 12 mi. SSW of Ath; coal-mining center.

Bernkastel-Kues (běrn'kä"stùl-kōō'ùs), town (pop. 5,239), in former Prussian Rhine Prov., W Germany, after 1945 in Rhineland-Palatinate, on the Mosel and 22 mi. NE of Trier; noted for its wine. Formerly separate towns, spelled Berncastel, Cues.

Bernoises, Alpes, Switzerland: see BERNESE ALPS.

Bernsbach (běrns'bäkh), village (pop. 5,812), Saxony, E central Germany, in the Erzgebirge, 3.5 mi. ESE of Aue, near Czechoslovak border, in uranium-mining region; metal- and woodworking, paper milling.

Bernsdorf (běrns'dôrf), town (pop. 5,082), in former Prussian Lower Silesia prov., E central Germany, after 1945 in Saxony, 7 mi. NNW of Kamenz, in Upper Lusatia; lignite; metalworking, glass mfg.

Bernstadt (běrn'shtät), town (pop. 1,994), Saxony, E central Germany, in Upper Lusatia, 10 mi. SW of Görlitz, near Neisse R; paper milling, glass mfg.

Bernstadt, Poland: see BIERUTOW.

Bernstadt (bûrn'stăt), village (pop. c.400), Laurel co., SE central Ky., in Cumberland foothills, 24 mi. ENE of Somerset; makes cheese. Settled 1881; was largest of several Swiss colonies in this area.

Bernstein, Poland: see PELCZYCE.

Bernterode (běrn"tùrō'dù), village (pop. 2,104), in former Prussian Saxony prov., central Germany, after 1945 in Thuringia, on Wipper R. and 13 mi. N of Mühlhausen; potash and salt mining. In near-by salt mine, U.S. troops found (April, 1945) many important art treasures and historic relics; also found were sarcophagi of Frederick the Great, Frederick William I, and Hindenburg (all subsequently reburied at Marburg, Hesse).

Bernville, borough (pop. 363), Berks co., SE central Pa., 12 mi. WNW of Reading. Founded 1819, inc. 1851.

Beroea, Greece: see VERROIA.

Beroea, Syria: see ALEPPO, city.

Berón de Astrada (bārōn' dā ästrä'dä), village (pop. estimate 500), ⊙ Berón de Astrada dept. (□ c.250; pop. 2,094), N Corrientes prov., Argentina, 80 mi. E of Corrientes; mixed-farming zone. Another village of Berón de Astrada, usually called COLONIA BERÓN DE ASTRADA, is in extreme SW Corrientes.

Beroroha (běrōōrōō'hù), town, Tuléar prov., W central Madagascar, on Mangoky R. (head of navigation) and 150 mi. NE of Tuléar; climatic resort and trading center; pulse, cattle.

Beroun (bě'rōn), Ger. *Beraun* (bě'roun), town (pop. 12,345), SW central Bohemia, Czechoslovakia, on Berounka R. and 18 mi. SW of Prague; rail junction; mfg. (textiles, asbestos, cement, tiles), sugar milling. Has 14th-cent. town hall, castle ruins. Iron and coal mines, ironworks (largest at KRALUV DVUR), limestone quarries, lime kilns in vicinity. Near by is 14th-cent. castle founded by Charles IV.

Berounka River (bě'rōn-kä), W central Bohemia, Czechoslovakia, formed by junction of Mze and Radbuza rivers at Pilsen; flows c.70 mi. NE and E, past Beroun and Karlstejn, to Vltava R. at S outskirts of Prague.

Berovo (bě'rôvô), village (pop. 3,524), Macedonia, Yugoslavia, 21 mi. NNE of Strumica, near Bulg. border; trade center for tobacco-growing, cattle-raising region; homemade candles, tar.

Berra (bĕr'rä), village (pop. 1,774), Ferrara prov., Emilia-Romagna, N central Italy, on Po R. and 6 mi. SSW of Adria.

Berre, Étang de (ātā' dů bâr'), lagoon of the Mediterranean, in Bouches-du-Rhône dept., SE France, enclosed by low limestone hills except for narrow outlet (Caronte canal, 4 mi. long, bet. Martigues and Port-de-Bouc) to the Gulf of Fos; 13 mi. long, 3–8 mi. wide. A link in the Rhone-Marseilles canal, it is connected with Marseilles bay by the ROVE Tunnel. Receives Arc R. Fisheries. Its shores are lined with orchards, olive groves, and saltworks. Chief towns: Istres (naval flying school), Berre-l'Étang, Martigues.

Berrechid (bâr-rĕshēd'), town (pop. 1,922), Casablanca region, NW Fr. Morocco, on railroad and 23 mi. S of Casablanca, in wheat-growing area. Insane asylum; seismic observatory. Also spelled Ber Rechid.

Berre-l'Étang (bâr-lātā'), town (pop. 4,115), Bouches-du-Rhône dept., SE France, seaport on N shore of Étang de Berre, 16 mi. NW of Marseilles; industrial center (petroleum refinery, aircraft plant) with large saltworks.

Berri (bĕ'rē), town (pop. 1,931), SE South Australia, on Murray R. and 125 mi. ENE of Adelaide, near Victoria border; wine center; fruit.

Berri, France: see BERRY.

Berrian or **Berriane** (bâryän'), Saharan village, Ghardaïa territory, central Algeria, one of the Mzab oases, 24 mi. N of Ghardaïa, on road to Laghouat.

Berriane, Algeria: see BERRIAN.

Berrien (bĕ'rēun). **1** County (□ 466; pop. 13,966), S Ga.; ⊙ Nashville. Coastal plain agr. (cotton, corn, tobacco, peanuts, livestock) and forestry (naval stores, lumber) area drained by Alapaha and Withlacoochee rivers. Formed 1856. **2** County (□ 580; pop. 115,702), extreme SW Mich.; ⊙ St. Joseph. Bounded S by Ind. line, W by L. Michigan; drained by St. Joseph and Paw Paw rivers and small Galien R. Fruitgrowing region (peaches, apples, pears, plums, grapes, cherries, strawberries, melons); also grain, truck, livestock, dairy products. Mfg. at Benton Harbor, Niles, and St. Joseph. Commercial fisheries. Lake and health resorts. Includes state park. Organized 1831.

Berrien Springs, village (pop. 1,761), Berrien co., extreme SW Mich., on St. Joseph R. and 12 mi. SE of Benton Harbor, in fruit and dairy area. Mfg. of auto parts, tools, baskets, brooms, fruit products. Clam fisheries. Has medicinal springs, resorts. Seat of Emmanuel Missionary Col. Platted 1830, inc. 1867.

Berriew (be'rū), agr. village and parish (pop. 1,357), E Montgomery, Wales, near Severn R., 5 mi. SSW of Welshpool.

Berriozabal (bĕryōsäbäl'), town (pop. 2,382), Chiapas, S Mexico, in Chiapas Valley, 10 mi. W of Tuxtla; cereals, sugar, tobacco, fruit, livestock.

Berrocal (bĕrōkäl'), town (pop. 670), Huelva prov., SW Spain, 32 mi. NE of Huelva (linked by rail); cork and hog center. Also grain growing, lumbering, hunting. Its rail station is 1 mi. S.

Berrocalejo (bĕrōkälā'hō), village (pop. 1,023), Cáceres prov., W Spain, 30 mi. WSW of Talavera de la Reina; olive-oil processing, stock raising; cereals, wine.

Berrotarán (bĕrōtärän'), town (pop. estimate 1,200), W Córdoba prov., Argentina, 47 mi. N of Río Cuarto; grain, flax, sunflowers, peanuts, cattle, hogs.

Berrouaghia (bârwägyä'), town (pop. 3,673), Alger dept., N central Algeria, in the Tell Atlas, on railroad and 24 mi. SSE of Blida; road junction. Agr. trade (essential oils, wine, wheat).

Berry, municipality (pop. 2,777), E New South Wales, Australia, 65 mi. S of Sydney; dairying center; tourist resort.

Berry or **Berri** (bĕrē'), region and former province of central France, now forming Indre, Cher, and parts of adjoining depts.; ⊙ Bourges. A generally barren area used for stock raising, with fertile agr. strips along the Cher and the Indre. Chief towns: Bourges and Châteauroux. A part of the Roman prov. of Aquitania, Berry was conquered (5th cent.) by the Visigoths and (507) by the Franks. It became a county (8th cent.) and was purchased by Fr. crown c.1100. In 1360 it was made a duchy and was given in appanage to various princes of the blood. Berry was broken up into present depts. in 1790. The country and its people (Berrichons) are described in the novels of George Sand, who lived and died here.

Berry. 1 Town (pop. 715), Fayette co., W Ala., 22 mi. SW of Jasper; pine and hardwood lumber. **2** Town (pop. 312), Harrison co., N Ky., on South Fork of Licking R. and 10 mi. NNW of Cynthiana, in Bluegrass region.

Berry-au-Bac (bĕrē'-ō-bäk'), village (pop. 435), Aisne dept., N France, on the Aisne at junction of Aisne-Marne Canal, and 12 mi. NNW of Rheims; agr. equipment. Scene of heavy fighting in First World War.

Berry Canal (bĕrē'), in Allier, Cher, and Loir-et-Cher depts., central France, connects coal-mining dist. of Montluçon with industrial centers of Bourges and Vierzon. Its N branch ends at Noyers on the Cher, its E branch at Marseilles-les-Aubigny on Loire Lateral Canal (14 mi. below Nevers); c.155 mi. long, 16 ft. wide, 5 ft. deep. Barges drawn by mules transport coal, building materials.

Berry Head, England: see BRIXHAM.

Berry Hill, town (pop. 1,248), Davidson co., N Tenn., near Nashville.

Berry Islands, archipelago and district (□ 14; pop. 403), NW Bahama Isls.; group of numerous cays on NE edge of the Great Bahama Bank, N of Andros Isl., 140 mi. E of Miami, Fla., and 35 mi. NW of Nassau, extending in large curve c.50 mi. bet. 25°20'N and 25°50'N. Some agr. (coconuts, sisal; stock). Surrounding waters teem with fish.

Berry Pomeroy (pŏ'mŭroi), agr. village and parish (pop. 381), S Devon, England, 2 mi. ENE of Totnes. Has 13th-cent. castle, 16th-cent. church.

Berrysburg, borough (pop. 386), Dauphin co., S central Pa., 18 mi. S of Sunbury.

Berryville. 1 Town (pop. 1,753), a ⊙ Carroll co., NW Ark., 39 mi. NE of Fayetteville, in the Ozarks, in fruit, dairy, and truck area; lumber milling, canning, cheese factories. Resort area (fishing). Laid out 1850. **2** Town (pop. 1,401), ⊙ Clarke co., N Va., in Shenandoah Valley, 10 mi. E of Winchester; agr. (apples, grain); horse breeding; flour milling; canned foods, baskets. Annual horse show. Laid out 1798; inc. 1870.

Berseba (bĕrsĕ'bä), town, S South-West Africa, in Great Namaqualand, c.150 mi. ENE of Lüderitz; center of Hottentot reserves.

Bersenbrück (bĕr"sŭnbrük'), village (pop. 3,140), in former Prussian prov. of Hanover, NW Germany, after 1945 in Lower Saxony, on the Haase and 19 mi. N of Osnabrück; grain, cattle.

Bershad or **Bershad'** (byĭrshät'yŭ), town (1926 pop. 11,847), SE Vinnitsa oblast, Ukrainian SSR, 90 mi. SE of Vinnitsa; sugar refining, distilling, fruit canning, flour milling.

Bersham, town and parish (pop. 5,348), E Denbigh, Wales, just SW of Wrexham; coal mining, paper milling.

Bersimis River (bĕrsēmē') or **Betsiamites River** (bĕtsyämēt'), SE central Que., rises S of Pletipi L., on St. Lawrence-Hudson Bay watershed, flows S and SE to the St. Lawrence 30 mi. SE of Baie Comeau; 250 mi. long. Navigable for 35 mi. above its mouth. Property of the Montagnais Indians. Fisheries.

Bert (bâr), village (pop. 246), Allier dept., central France, 6 mi. NE of Lapalisse; coal mining.

Berta, Cyrenaica: see GUBBA.

Bertha, village (pop. 577), Todd co., W central Minn., 22 mi. NNW of Long Prairie, in grain, livestock, and potato area; dairy products.

Bertha, Mount (10,182 ft.), SE Alaska, in Fairweather Range, 100 mi. WNW of Juneau, in Glacier Bay Natl. Monument; 58°41'N 137°1'W.

Bertha Island, in Congo R., central Belgian Congo, 20 mi. W of Stanleyville; c.3 mi. long, 1–2 mi. wide. Palm plantations; palm-oil milling.

Berthecourt (bĕrtŭkōōr'), village (pop. 669), Oise dept., N France, 8 mi. SE of Beauvais.

Berthier (bĕrtyā'), county (□ 1,816; pop. 21,233), S Que., extending NW from the St. Lawrence; ⊙ Berthierville.

Berthierville (bĕr'tyāvĭl) or **Berthier** (bĕrtyā'), town (pop. 2,634), ⊙ Berthier co., S Que., on the St. Lawrence and 45 mi. NNE of Montreal; textile milling, knitting, lumbering, distilling, match mfg.; market in dairying, cattle-raising, grain-growing region. Site of ruins of 1st Protestant church built (1786) after British conquest of Canada.

Berthold (bûr'thōld), city (pop. 459), Ward co., NW central N.Dak., 20 mi. W of Minot; wheat, potatoes, cattle.

Bertholène (bĕrtôlĕn'), village (pop. 452), Aveyron dept., S France, near Aveyron R., 11 mi. ENE of Rodez; quarrying.

Berthoud, Switzerland: see BURGDORF.

Berthoud (bûr'thŭd), town (pop. 867), Larimer co., N Colo., 40 mi. N of Denver, in lake region; alt. 5,240 ft. Sugar beets, potatoes, grain. Oil field near by.

Berthoud Pass (11,314 ft.), in Front Range, N central Colo., c.40 mi. W of Denver. Crossed by highway. Skiing facilities.

Bertie (bûr'tē), county (□ 693; pop. 26,439), NE N.C.; ⊙ Windsor. On coastal plain; bounded S and SW by Roanoke R., E by Chowan R. and Albemarle Sound; drained by Cashie R. Agr. (peanuts, tobacco, corn, cotton); sawmilling; fishing. Timber (gum, pine). Formed 1722.

Bertie, town (pop. 259), Bertie co., NE N.C., adjacent to Windsor; residential.

Bertincourt (bĕrtĕkōōr'), village (pop. 776), Pas-de-Calais dept., N France, 11 mi. N of Péronne; beet-sugar refining.

Bertinoro (bĕrtēnō'rō), town (pop. 1,580), Forlì prov., Emilia-Romagna, N central Italy, 7 mi. SE of Forlì; noted for its wine. Bishopric. Near by are 9th-cent. church (restored), ruined 11th-cent. castle, mineral springs.

Bertolínia (bĕrtōōlē'nyŭ), city (pop. 359), W central Piauí, Brazil, 55 mi. SW of Floriano, in cattle area; carnauba wax. Until 1944, called Aparecida; formerly spelled Apparecida.

Bertona (bĕrtō'nä), village, Lom et Kadéï region, E Fr. Cameroons, 55 mi. WNW of Batouri; mfg. of peanut oil; coffee plantations. Sawmills in vicinity.

Bertram. 1 Town (pop. 128), Linn co., E Iowa, 7 mi. E of Cedar Rapids. Limestone quarries near by. **2** Village (1940 pop. 582), Burnet co. central Texas, 38 mi. NNE of Austin, in cotton, wheat, corn area.

Bertrand. 1 Town (pop. 390), Mississippi co., extreme SE Mo., in Mississippi flood plain, 6 mi. W of Charleston. **2** Village (pop. 584), Phelps co., S Nebr., 15 mi. WNW of Holdrege; livestock, grain, dairy and poultry produce.

Bertrand, Cerro (sĕ'rō bĕrträn'), peak (10,730 ft.) in Patagonian Andes, on Argentina-Chile border, on NW shore of L. Argentino; westernmost point of Argentina; 49°57'S 73°29'30"W.

Bertrand, Lake, Chile: see BUENOS AIRES, LAKE.

Bertrange (bĕrtrãzh'), Ger. *Bartringen* (bär'trĭng-ŭn), village (pop. 1,088), S Luxembourg, 3 mi. W of Luxembourg city; mfg. of tar products; agr. (potatoes, wheat, oats).

Bertrich, Bad, Germany: see BAD BERTRICH.

Bertrix (bĕrtrē'), town (pop. 3,939), Luxembourg prov., SE Belgium, in the Ardennes, 8 mi. W of Neufchâteau; rail junction and market center; mfg. of wood chemicals (acetates, creosote); tourist resort.

Bertry (bĕrtrē'), town (pop. 2,640), Nord dept., N France, 11 mi. SE of Cambrai; scarves, embroidered cloth; metalworking. On battlefield of Le Cateau (1914) in First World War.

Bertys, Kazakh SSR: see BALKHASH.

Beru (bĕrōō'), village, Kaffa prov., SW Ethiopia, near Anglo-Egyptian Sudan border, 20 mi. WNW of Maji, in cereal- and coffee-growing region.

Beru (bā'rōō), atoll (□ 8; pop. 2,231), Kingsmill Group, S Gilbert Isls., W central Pacific; 1°19'S 176°E. Site of hq. of London Missionary Society. Also spelled Peru.

Berun, Poland: see BIERUN.

Beruni, India: see BARAUNI.

Beruri (bĭrōōrē'), town (pop. 180), E central Amazonas, Brazil, on Purus R. above its influx into the Amazon, and 105 mi. SW of Manaus. Formerly spelled Berury.

Beruwala (bā'rōōvŭlŭ), town (pop. 11,547), Western Prov., Ceylon, on SW coast, 32 mi. S of Colombo; fishing; vegetables, rice, coconuts, rubber. Regarded as original settlement of Ceylonese Moors. Lighthouse just off coast. Sometimes called Barberyn.

Bervie, Scotland: see INVERBERVIE.

Bervie Water (bûr'vē), river, Kincardine, Scotland, rises 5 mi. NW of Glenbervie, flows 20 mi. S and ESE, past Glenbervie, to North Sea at Inverbervie.

Berwick, town (pop. 962), NW N.S., near Cornwallis R., 12 mi. W of Kentville; fruitgrowing and packing center.

Berwick or **Berwickshire** (bĕ'rĭk,–shĭr), county (□ 457; 1931 pop. 26,612; 1951 census 25,060), SE Scotland; ⊙ Duns. Bordering SE on England (Northumberland), it is bounded by Roxburgh (S), Midlothian (W), East Lothian (N), the North Sea (E). Drained by the Tweed, Eye, Leader Water, Whiteadder Water, and Blackadder Water rivers. Surface is flat in S, rising to Lammermuir Hills (N) and Lauderdale (W); coastline is high and rocky. Fishing (in the North Sea and the Tweed) is important; sheep are raised in NW uplands. Industries include limestone and sandstone quarrying, woolen, linen, paper milling. Besides Duns, other towns are Coldstream, Eyemouth, Lauder. There are many associations with border warfare. Lauderdale attracts many anglers.

Berwick (bûr'wĭk). **1** Town (pop. 2,619), St. Mary parish, S La., on Berwick Bay of Atchafalaya R., opposite Morgan City (just E; connected by bridge); mfg. of canned sea food, oyster-shell products; lumber milling; boat yards. **2** Town (pop. 2,166), including Berwick village (pop. 1,326), York co., SW Maine, on Salmon Falls R. opposite Somersworth, N.H. and 5 mi. N of Dover; textiles. Settled c.1627. SOUTH BERWICK and NORTH BERWICK set off from Berwick in early 19th cent. **3** Village (pop. 71), McHenry co., N central N.Dak., 8 mi. E of Towner. **4** Borough (pop. 14,010), Columbia co., E central Pa., on Susquehanna R. and 23 mi. SW of Wilkes-Barre; silk mills; mfg. (railway cars, clothing, potato chips); agr. Settled 1783, inc. 1818.

Berwickshire, Scotland: see BERWICK.

Berwick-upon-Tweed or **Berwick-on-Tweed** (bĕ'rĭk), municipal borough (1931 pop. 12,299; 1951 census 12,550) and self-governing county, N Northumberland, England, on North Sea, at mouth of the Tweed, 60 mi. NNW of Newcastle-upon-Tyne. An important town on the English-Scottish border, it was involved in border wars and disputes for many centuries until it was inc. into Northumberland in 1885. It has Elizabethan walls, considered forerunners of defenses later built on the Continent by Vauban. The Tweed is crossed by a modern road bridge, a railroad bridge built (1847) by Robert Stephenson, and a bridge dating from 1624. Has 17th-cent. church and town hall built 1757. Chief industries are herring and salmon fishing, metal casting, chemical mfg. Site of lighthouse (55°46'N 1°59'W). In municipal borough are Spittal (S), with chemical industry, and Tweedmouth (S), with coal mines.

Berwind (bûr'wĭnd), mining village (pop. 1,354), McDowell co., S W.Va., on Dry Fork and 11 mi. SSW of Welch, in semibituminous-coal field.

Berwyn, village (pop. 308), W Alberta, near Peace R., 19 mi. WSW of Peace River; lumbering, mixed farming, wheat.

Berwyn (bûr'wĭn). **1** Residential city (pop. 51,280), Cook co., NE Ill., W suburb of Chicago; some mfg. (electrical equipment, machine tools; clay, leather, and tobacco products). Dairying, horticulture in area. Founded 1890; inc. as village in 1891, as city in 1908. **2** Village (pop. c.1,500), Prince Georges co., central Md., a NE suburb of Washington. **3** Village (pop. 138), Custer co., central Nebr., 8 mi. SE of Broken Bow and on Mud Creek. **4** Town, Okla.: see GENE AUTRY. **5** Village (pop. c.2,000), Chester co., SE Pa., 16 mi. WNW of Philadelphia.

Berwyn Heights, town (pop. 674), Prince Georges co., central Md., NE suburb of Washington, adjacent to Berwyn (W).

Berwyn Mountains, Wales, on borders of Merioneth, Montgomery, and Denbigh. Highest point (2,713 ft.) is Moel Sych (moil sĭkh'), 7 mi. S of Corwen.

Berytus, Lebanon: see BEIRUT.

Berzée (bĕrzā'), town (pop. 717), Namur prov., S Belgium, 10 mi. S of Charleroi; foundries; metal utensils.

Berzence (bĕr'zĕntsĕ), town (pop. 4,185), Somogy co., SW Hungary, on branch of the Drava and 18 mi. SE of Nagykanizsa; wheat. Before 1918, Berzencze.

Berzocana (bĕr-thōkä'nä), town (pop. 1,880), Cáceres prov., W Spain, 22 mi. E of Trujillo; stock raising, meat processing; cereals, chestnuts, wine.

Besadalar (bĕ-shä'dälär"), Turkish *Beşadalar*, tiny isls. just off S tip of Cape Gelidonya, SW Asia Minor, at W entrance to Gulf of Antalya (Adalia).

Besalampy (bĕsäläm'pē), town, Majunga prov., W Madagascar, near W coast, on road and 110 mi. SW of Majunga; native market; cattle raising.

Besalú (bāsäloō'), town (pop. 1,116), Gerona prov., NE Spain, 16 mi. NNW of Gerona; livestock; lumber. Has early Romanesque churches.

Besana Brianza (bĕzä'nä brēän'tsä), village (pop. 1,919), Milano prov., Lombardy, N Italy, 8 mi. N of Monza; mfg. (macaroni, sausage, ribbon).

Besançon (bůzäsō'), anc. *Vesontio*, city (pop. 51,939), ⊙ Doubs dept., E France, in loop of Doubs R. and 45 mi. E of Dijon, at foot of the Jura; center of E France's clock- and watchmaking industry; produces also artificial silk, pottery, chocolates and candies, rubber fabrics, leather goods, paper. Trade in cattle, cheese, salt, wines. Brine baths. Chief points of interest: 12th–16th-cent. cathedral; the 16th-cent. Palais Granvelle (housing mus.), one of many fine bldgs. in Sp. Renaissance style; and the numerous forts and ramparts surrounding the city. A citadel on a rock (387 ft. high) commands the neck of the Doubs bend which nearly encloses the old city. Besançon is seat of a univ. (founded 1422 in Dôle, transferred here in 1691), a natl. watchmaking institute, and a meteorological observatory. It was an important Roman military post and an early archiepiscopal see. It passed in turn to Burgundy and Franche-Comté kingdoms, and became a free imperial city under Emperor Frederick I in 1184. It preserved its independence until 1648 when, through reincorporation into Franche-Comté, it passed under Sp. rule. In 1674, Besançon was retaken by Louis XIV and succeeded Dôle (1676) as ⊙ Franche-Comté prov. Suffered some damage in Second World War. Fourier, Proudhon, and Victor Hugo b. here.

Besar, Indonesia: see PENIDA.

Besaya River (bāsī'ä), Santander prov., N Spain, rises in Cantabrian Mts. 2 mi. N of Reinosa, flows 22 mi. N, past Torrelavega, to Bay of Biscay at Suances. Hydroelectric plants.

Besbre River or **Bèbre River** (both: bĕ'brů), Allier dept., central France, rises in the Bois Noirs near Laprugne, flows 60 mi. N, past Lapalisse, to the Loire 3 mi. below Dompierre-sur-Besbre.

Bescanuova, Yugoslavia: see BASKA.

Besedino (bĭsyĕ'dyĭnŭ), village (1926 pop. 2,561), N central Kursk oblast, Russian SFSR, 10 mi. E of Kursk; sugar beets.

Besenyszög (bĕ'shĕnyůsůg), town (pop. 5,708), Jasz-Nagykun-Szolnok co., E central Hungary, 6 mi. SE of Jaszladany; wheat, corn.

Beserah (bůsĭrä'), village (pop. 1,297), NE Pahang, Malaya, fishing port on South China Sea, 4 mi. NE of Kuantan.

Besh-Aryk, Uzbek SSR: see KIROVO, Fergana.

Beshchady Mountains (byĭshchä'dē), Pol. *Bieszczady* (byĕshchä'dē), section of the Carpathians on Pol.-Czechoslovak border and in SW Ukrainian SSR, bet. Lupkow Pass (NW) and Veretski Pass (SE); 60 mi. long; rise to 4,792 ft. Beech forests; agr. Crossed by Uzhok Pass (Lvov-Uzhgorod RR). Latoritsa R. rises on S, San R. on N slope.

Beshenkovichi (byĕshĭnkô'vēchē), town (1926 pop. 2,690), W central Vitebsk oblast, Belorussian SSR, on Western Dvina R. and 31 mi. WSW of Vitebsk; flax processing.

Beshkent (byĭshkyĕnt'), village (1926 pop. 2,698), W Kashka-Darya oblast, Uzbek SSR, 8 mi. W of Karshi; wheat.

Beshkubur (byĕshkŏŏbōōr'), village, S South Kazakhstan oblast, Kazakh SSR, 10 mi. NW of Yangi-Yul; cotton.

Beshnagar, India: see BHILSA.

Besh-Tau (byĕsh-tou'), volcanic mountain (4,590 ft.) of the N Caucasus foothills, Russian SFSR; rises in 5 peaks just NW of Pyatigorsk, in resort area. Climbed from Zheleznovodsk, at N foot; offers fine views of the main Caucasus range (S).

Beshtaunit (–tounyĕt'), town (1946 pop. over 500), S Stavropol Territory, Russian SFSR, at foot of the Besh-Tau, 5 mi. S of Mineralnye Vody; quartz porphyry quarry.

Besigheim (bā'zĭkh-hīm"), town (pop. 4,807), N Württemberg, Germany, after 1945 in Württemberg-Baden, on the Neckar at mouth of Enz R., and 7 mi. NNW of Ludwigsburg; mfg. of chemicals, textiles, ceramics, shoes; food processing. Brick and gravel works. Has 15th-cent. town hall. Chartered in 13th cent.

Besike Bay (bĕshĭkĕ'), Turkish *Beşike*, on NW coast of Anatolia, Turkey, on the Aegean opposite isl. of Bozcaada (Tenedos), S of the Dardanelles. Sometimes spelled Besika.

Besikion Lake, Greece: see VOLVE, LAKE.

Besiktas (bĕ-shĭktäsh'), Turkish *Beşiktaş*, NE section (pop. 63,611) of Istanbul, Turkey in Europe, on the Bosporus.

Besiri (bĕ-shĭrē'), Turkish *Beşiri*, village (pop. 1,169), Siirt prov., SE Turkey, 36 mi. W of Siirt; grain. Formerly Kabin.

Beskids or **Beskid Mountains** (bĕs'kĭdz, –kĭd), Czech and Slovak *Beskydy* (bĕ'skĭdĭ), Pol. *Beskidy* (bĕskē'dē), mountain group of the Carpathians (c.200 mi. long), along Czechoslovak-Pol. border, bet. Moravian Gate (W) and Lupkow Pass (E); rise to 5,658 ft. in Babia Gora. In 2 parts, the West Beskids (the W part of which is sometimes called Moravian-Silesian Beskids) and the East Beskids (sometimes called Slovak Beskids). Traversed by several well-known passes, notably Jablunkov and Dukla. Covered by deep and extensive forests; numerous tourist attractions and winter-sports facilities, mostly centered around Radhost mtn. (W). The once-abundant iron deposits in NW foothills led to establishment of iron- and steelworks of Ostrava area; important coal basin of Ostrava-Karvina lies just NW. E ridges, lower in height (2,500–3,000 ft.) are famous as scene of severe fighting bet. Austro-Hungarian and Russian armies in winter of 1915. Becva, Ostravice, and Olse rivers rise on W, Ondava and Laborec rivers on SE slopes.

Beskudnikovo (byĭskŏŏd'yĭkůvů), town (1939 pop. over 500), central Moscow oblast, Russian SFSR, suburb at N city limits of Moscow; 8 mi. NNW of city center; rail junction; chemical plant; bricks.

Beslan (byĭslän'), town (1939 pop. over 2,000), central North Ossetian Autonomous SSR, Russian SFSR, on Terek R., near Beslan station (rail junction; freight yards), and 15 mi. NW of Dzaudzhikau; large corn-processing works (starch, syrup), chemical plant.

Beslinac, Yugoslavia: see NOVI, Bosnia.

Besna Kobila (bĕ'snä kô'bĭlä), mountain (6,304 ft.) in SE Serbia, Yugoslavia, 17 mi. E of Vranje, near Bulg. line.

Besnard Lake (bĕz'närd) (28 mi. long, 6 mi. wide), N central Sask., 150 mi. N of Prince Albert. Drains NE into Churchill R.

Besni (bĕsnĕ'), town (pop. 9,154), Malatya prov., S central Turkey, 50 mi. SSW of Malatya; wheat, pistachios. Formerly Behisni.

Besós River (bāsōs'), Barcelona prov., NE Spain, rises in several headstreams in coastal range of Catalonia N of Granollers, flows c.25 mi. S and SE to the Mediterranean N of Barcelona.

Besozzo (bĕzô'tsô), village (pop. 2,926), Varese prov., Lombardy, N Italy, 8 mi. WNW of Varese; silk and cotton textiles, flour, paper, matches.

Bess, Mount (10,550 ft.), on Alta.-B.C. line, in Rocky Mts. at NW edge of Jasper Natl. Park, 65 mi. WNW of Jasper; 53°22'N 119°22'W.

Bessan (bĕsā'), town (pop. 2,253), Hérault dept., S France, on the Hérault and 11 mi. E of Béziers; known for its white and rosé wines. Basalt quarries.

Bessan, Palestine: see BEISAN.

Bessarabia (bĕsůrā'bēů), Rum. *Basarabia* (bäsärä'-byä), region (□ c.18,000) of SW European USSR, bet. the Dniester (E and N), the Prut (W), and the Danube and Black Sea (S); consists largely of Beltsy (N) and Budzhak (S) steppes, separated by Kodry hills. Corn, wheat, tobacco, wine, wool are chief products; Kishinev, Beltsy, and Bendery the principal centers. Pop. includes Moldavians, Ukrainians, Russians, Jews, Bulgarians. Always a marsh country, the region changed hands often. In Roman times, it was a Barbarian region separated from Lower Moesia by Trajan's Wall; invaded by successive waves of migrations (Goths, Bulgars, Petchenegs, Cumans, Mongols); conquered (14th cent.) by princes of MOLDAVIA. The name Bessarabia is derived from that of Bassarab, a princely family of Walachia, which extended its rule briefly (14th cent.) into Budzhak steppe. By end of 15th cent., the Turks and their vassals, the Crimean Tatars, conquered Bessarabia; ceded (1812) to Russia by treaty of Bucharest and made (1818) a Rus. govt. (□ 17,143; 1897 pop. 1,935,412; ⊙ Kishinev). In 1829, Russia extended its rule S over the Danube delta, but was forced (1856) to return the delta to Turkey and S Bessarabia (including Kiliya, Izmail, Kagul) to Moldavia. Congress of Berlin (1878) returned S Bessarabia to Russia. In 1918, all Bessarabia was annexed by Rumania, where it constituted a historical prov. (□ 18,035; 1941 pop. 2,526,671). The Soviet govt. which never recognized its loss of the prov., presented (1940) an ultimatum to Rumania demanding the return of Bessarabia and N Bukovina, and obtained them. In 1941, Rumania, having joined Germany in its war on Russia, reoccupied Bessarabia, which was recovered by Rus. troops in 1944. The Rum. peace treaty of 1947 confirmed Bessarabia as part of the USSR. Larger (central) part was inc. (1940) into Moldavian SSR; extreme N (Khotin) and S sections, with predominantly Ukrainian-speaking pop., were added to Ukrainian SSR, forming Chernovtsy and Izmail oblasts.

Bessarabskaya, Moldavian SSR: see ROMANOVKA.

Bessastadir or **Bessastadhir** (bĕ'sästä"dhĭr), Icelandic *Bessastaðir*, locality, Gullbringu og Kjosar co., SW Iceland, on Reykjanes Peninsula, on Faxa Bay, 3 mi. SW of Reykjavik. In anc. times seat of Icelandic govt.; now official residence of president of Iceland.

Bessbrook, town (pop. 2,355), SE Co. Armagh, Northern Ireland, 5 mi. WNW of Newry; linen milling.

Besse (bĕs). **1** or **Besse-en-Chandesse** (–ā-chädĕs'), village (pop. 555), Puy-de-Dôme dept., central France, in Monts Dore, 15 mi. W of Issoire; alt. 3,400 ft. Winter sports. Mfg. (skis, knitwear). Has 12th–17th-cent. church. **2** or **Besse-sur-Issole** (–sür-ēsôl'), village (pop. 719), Var dept., SE France, in Lower Provence Alps, 20 mi. NE of Toulon; olive and winegrowing.

Bessèges (bĕsĕzh'), town (pop. 5,483), Gard dept., S France, at foot of the Cévennes on Cèze R. and 12 mi. N of Alès; coal-mining and industrial center with blast furnaces, steel mills (rails and tubes), and silk-spinning plants.

Bessemer. **1** (bĕ'sůmůr) City (pop. 28,445), Jefferson co., central Ala., on branch of Black Warrior R. just SW of Birmingham. Metalworking center in iron and coal area. Manufactures steel and steel products (railroad cars, bridges, ship parts), cast-iron soil pipe and pipe fittings, furniture, chemicals. Has bottling works and meat-packing plant. Limestone quarries are near by. Founded 1887 as steel town. **2** (bĕ'sůmůr, bĕ'zůmůr) City (pop. 3,509), ⊙ Gogebic co., W Upper Peninsula, Mich., 6 mi. NE of Ironwood, in Gogebic iron-mining region. Agr. (potatoes, hay, grain); lumber and flour milling. Only place in state where copper and iron lodes meet. Inc. as village 1887, as city 1889. **3** (bĕ'sůmůr) E suburb (1940 pop. 2,351) of Greensboro, Guilford co., N central N.C. **4** (bĕ'-sůmůr) Borough (pop. 1,461), Lawrence co., W Pa., 8 mi. WSW of New Castle; cement mfg. Inc. c.1910.

Bessemer City, town (pop. 3,961), Gaston co., SW N.C., 6 mi. WNW of Gastonia; cotton textiles, foundry products.

Bessé-sur-Braye (bĕsā'-sür-brĕ'), village (pop. 1,748), Sarthe dept., W France, 15 mi. W of Vendôme; paper and cotton mills.

Besse-sur-Issole, Var Dept., France: see BESSE.

Besshi (bās'shē), copper field (□ c.10), Ehime prefecture, N Shikoku, Japan, just S of Niihama (mining center). Some gold and silver also mined. Discovered 1690.

Bessie, town (pop. 205), Washita co., W Okla., 10 mi. S of Clinton, in agr. area; cotton ginning.

Bessines-sur-Gartempe (bĕsēn'-sür-gärtăp'), village (pop. 589), Haute-Vienne dept., W central France, near Gartempe R., 16 mi. E of Bellac; lime kilns.

Bessiré, Syria: see BUSEIRE.

Bessmay, village (1940 pop. 1,042), Jasper co., E Texas, 28 mi. NNE of Beaumont; lumber milling.

Bessonovka (byĭsô'nůfků), village (1926 pop. 11,289), central Penza oblast, Russian SFSR, on Sura R. and 8 mi. N of Penza; grain, potatoes; orchards.

Best, village (pop. 2,088), North Brabant prov., S Netherlands, 6 mi. NW of Eindhoven; leather tanning, shoe mfg.

Bestobe (byĕstŭbyĕ'), town (1941 pop. over 500), NE Akmolinsk oblast, Kazakh SSR, 115 mi. E of Makinsk.

Bestun (bĕs'tōōn), suburb (pop. 4,641) of Oslo, SE Norway, at head of Oslo Fjord, 3 mi. W of city center. Until 1948, in Akershus co.

Besut, Malaya: see KUALA BESUT.

Beswan (bā'svän), town (pop. 2,707), Aligarh dist., W Uttar Pradesh, India, 11 mi. WNW of Hathras; wheat, barley, pearl millet, gram, corn, cotton. Also spelled Baiswan.

Beszterce, Rumania: see BISTRITA.

Besztercebanya, Czechoslovakia: see BANSKA BYSTRICA.

Bet, India: see BEYT.

Bet, for names in Israel beginning thus: see BEIT.

Betafo (bĕtä'fōō), town, Tananarive prov., central Madagascar, 80 mi. SSW of Tananarive; alt. 4,493 ft. Trading center; rice processing; also beans, corn, potatoes, coffee. R.C. and Protestant missions, hosp.

Betaghstown, Ireland: see BETTYSTOWN.

Betamcherla, India: see DHONE.

Betancuria (bätäng-kōō'ryä), town (pop. 221), Fuerteventura, Canary Isls., 12 mi. SW of Puerto de Cabras; cereals, corn, tomatoes, grapes, potatoes, onions, alfalfa, goats, sheep. Cheese processing, granite quarrying. In its parochial church is preserved Sp. banner of Jean de Béthencourt, founder (1410) of the town.

Betania (bätä'nyä), town (pop. estimate 700), central Salta prov., Argentina, on railroad and 17 mi. NE of Salta; lumbering and agr. center (citrus fruit, wine, sugar cane, alfalfa, stock).

Betanzos (bätän'sōs), town (pop. c.4,100), ⊙ Cornelio Saavedra prov., Potosí dept., S central Bolivia, 21 mi. E of Potosí, on road and on Potosí-Sucre RR; alt. 11,178 ft.; local trade (barley, fruit, potatoes, timber). Until 1900s, Bartolo.

Betanzos (bätän'thōs), city (pop. 6,908), La Coruña prov., NW Spain, in Galicia, on hill near head of Betanzos Bay (inlet of Atlantic Ocean: 8 mi. long, 2–6 mi. wide), 12 mi. SE of La Coruña; mfg. (linen cloth, leather, glass); fishing, lumbering, cattle raising. Cereals, potatoes, wine, fruit in area. One of oldest towns of Galicia; has ruins of Moorish castle, 13th–14th-cent. churches, and Franciscan convent.

Betar, Palestine: see BETHER.

Bétaré-Oya (bĕtä'rā-ō'yä), village, Lom et Kadéï region, E Fr. Cameroons, on Lom R. and 85 mi. NNW of Batouri; brick mfg.; gold mining near by. Has hydroelectric power plant, airfield.

Betawad (bā'tŭvŭd), town (pop. 4,549), West Khandesh dist., NE Bombay, India, on Panjhra R. and 20 mi. NNE of Dhulia; local market center for cotton, millet, peanuts; cotton ginning. Also spelled Betavad.

Betchworth, residential town and parish (pop. 2,399), central Surrey, England, on Mole R. and 3 mi. W of Reigate. Church dates from Norman times.

Bétera (bā'tārä), town (pop. 4,742), Valencia prov., E Spain, 10 mi. NW of Valencia; olive-oil processing, flour milling; cereals, oranges, wine, vegetables. Limestone and gypsum quarries. Has remains of Moorish castle. Abbey of Portacoeli (founded in 13th cent.) is 5 mi. N.

Beterverwagting (bā"tŭrvŭrväkh'tĭng), village (pop., including adjoining Triumph, 4,703), Demerara co., N Br. Guiana, in fertile Atlantic lowland, on railroad and 6 mi. E of Georgetown; sugar, rice.

Beth, for names in Israel beinning thus: see BEIT.

Beth, Oued (wĕd' bĕt'), stream in NW Fr. Morocco, rises in the Middle Atlas near Azrou, flows c.120 mi. generally NNW, past Sidi Slimane, across the marshy Rharb lowland, to the Sebou 15 mi. NE of Port-Lyautey. El Kansera Dam (167 ft. high; 15 mi. S of Sidi Slimane; completed 1934) irrigates citrus- and cotton-growing region W of Petitjean. Hydroelectric plant.

Bethal (bĕ'thŭl), town (pop. 5,666), SE Transvaal, U. of So. Afr., 40 mi. SSE of Witbank; alt. 5,680 ft.; agr. center (stock, corn, potatoes). Grain elevator.

Bethalto (bŭ-thŏl'tō), village (pop. 2,115), Madison co., SW Ill., 8 mi. E of Alton, in bituminous-coal and agr. area (corn, wheat, poultry, livestock; dairy products). Inc. 1869.

Bethanga (bŭthăng'gŭ), village (pop. 131), NE Victoria, Australia, 165 mi. NE of Melbourne, near Hume Reservoir; copper mines.

Bethanie (bĕ'thŭnē), town (pop. 554), S South-West Africa, on Konkiep R. and 60 mi. W of Keetmanshoop; sheep raising. Near by is reserve of Bethanie Hottentots.

Bethany (bĕ'thŭnē), village (pop. estimate 300), S Ont., 15 mi. SW of Peterborough; dairying, mixed farming.

Bethany. **1** Town (pop. 1,318), New Haven co., S Conn., 8 mi. NW of New Haven, in hilly agr. region; dairy products. Has fine Episcopal church (1809) and Beecher House. **2** Village (pop. 850), Moultrie co., central Ill., 16 mi. SE of Decatur; corn, wheat, soybeans, livestock, poultry; dairy products. **3** Village, Caddo parish, extreme NW La., on Texas line, 19 mi. SW of Shreveport, in natural-gas area; cotton ginning, lumber milling. **4** City (pop. 2,714), ⊙ Harrison co., NW Mo., 55 mi. NE of St. Joseph; agr. (corn, wheat, oats), livestock; limestone quarry. Founded 1845, inc. 1858. **5** City (pop. 5,705), Oklahoma co., central Okla., 7 mi. W of Oklahoma City, in cotton- and alfalfa-growing area; feed and flour milling, cotton ginning. Seat of Bethany-Peniel Col. Inc. 1931. **6** Borough (pop. 148), Wayne co., NE Pa., 3 mi. NW of Honesdale. **7** Town (pop. 1,063), Brooke co., W.Va., in Northern Panhandle, 12 mi. NE of Wheeling. Seat of Bethany Col. (coeducational).

Bethany Beach, resort town (pop. 190), Sussex co., SE Del., on Atlantic coast and 20 mi. SE of Georgetown; fishing.

Bethel (bĕ'thŭl), village (pop. 643), SW Alaska, on lower Kuskokwim R. and 270 mi. SSE of Nome; 60°48'N 161°45'W; center of placer gold-mining region; fur farming; supply point for trappers and prospectors. Hosp.; airport. Established 1885 as Moravian mission.

Bethel (bĕ'thŭl), anc. town of Palestine, 10 mi. N of Jerusalem; the Biblical Luz. Here Jacob dreamed of a ladder reaching from heaven to earth (Gen. 28.19). On its site is small Jordanian village of Beitin.

Bethel (bĕ'thŭl), village (pop. 1,271), SW Tobago, B.W.I., 3½ mi. NW of Scarborough; coconuts.

Bethel. **1** Town (pop. 5,104), including Bethel village (pop. 4,145), Fairfield co., SW Conn., just SE of Danbury; hat mfg. (since c.1800), leather and wood products. P. T. Barnum b. here. Settled c.1700, inc. 1855. **2** Town (pop. 271), Sussex co., SW Del., 3 mi. W of Laurel and on Laurel R. (oysters), in agr. area. **3** Town (pop. 2,367), including Bethel village (pop. 1,067), Oxford co., W Maine, 15 mi. SW of Rumford and on Androscoggin R., in resort area at foot of White Mts.; winter-sports center; wood products. **4** Village (pop. 250), Anoka co., E Minn., near Rum R., 30 mi. N of Minneapolis, in agr. area; dairy products. **5** Town (pop. 194), Shelby co., NE Mo., on North R. and 5 mi. N of Shelbyville. Founded 1844 by William Keil as a communistic enterprise. **6** Resort village, Sullivan co., SE N.Y., 9 mi. W of Monticello, near White L. (E). **7** Town (pop. 1,402), Pitt co., E central N.C., 15 mi. N of Greenville; sawmilling. **8** Village (pop. 1,932), Clermont co., SW Ohio, 25 mi. ESE of Cincinnati, in agr. area; makes shoes, clothing; nurseries. Settled 1797. **9** Borough (pop. 11,324), Allegheny co., SW Pa., 8 mi. S of downtown Pittsburgh. Inc. 1949. **10** Town (pop. 1,534), Windsor co., central Vt., on White R. and 30 mi. S of Montpelier; lumber, sports equipment; dairy and maple products. Granite quarries closed 1925. Chartered 1778.

Bethel Springs, town (pop. 623), McNairy co., SW Tenn., 29 mi. SSE of Jackson, in pine-timber and cotton region.

Bethel Town (bĕ'thŭl, bĕ'thĕl), town (pop. 4,150), Westmoreland parish, W Jamaica, 13 mi. S of Montego Bay; marketing center in agr. region (sugar cane, rice, coffee, cacao, spices, breadfruit, livestock).

Béthencourt-sur-Mer (bātăkōōr'-sür-mâr'), village (pop. 1,120), Somme dept., N France, 15 mi. W of Abbeville; copper and bronze founding; padlocks.

Bether (bē'thŭr) or **Betar** (bētär'), anc. locality, central Palestine, in Judaean Hills, 6 mi. SW of Jerusalem; on site is modern village of Battir or Bittir. Scene (A.D. 135) of Simon Bar Kochba's last stand against Romans. Sometimes spelled Beithar.

Bethesda (bŭ-thĕz'dŭ). **1** Residential town, Montgomery co., central Md., a NW suburb of Washington, adjacent to D.C. line. Seat of Naval Medical Center (1942), Natl. Institutes of Health, Natl. Cancer Inst. research center (1939). Has a jr. col. (coed.). **2** Village (pop. 1,158), Belmont co., E Ohio, 17 mi. W of Bellaire; makes wooden containers, cigars; mills lumber.

Bethesda (bĕ-thĕz'dŭ), urban district (1931 pop. 4,480; 1951 census 4,436), N Caernarvon, Wales, 5 mi. SE of Bangor; slate-quarrying center. Includes districts of Gerlan (E; pop. 1,305), Ogwen (S; pop. 1,922), and Rachub (N; pop. 1,253).

Beth Gibelin, Palestine: see BEIT JIBRIN.

Béthisy-Saint-Pierre (bātēzē'-sē-pyâr'), village (pop. 1,696), Oise dept., N France, at S edge of Forest of Compiègne, 8 mi. S of Compiègne; woodworking (brushes, furniture, barrels).

Beth Jerah, Palestine: see DEGANIYA.

Bethlehem (bĕth'lēŭm, bĕth'lĭhĕm), Arabic *Beit Lahm*, anc. also *Ephrata*, town (1946 pop. estimate 9,140) of Palestine, after 1948 in W Jordan, in Judaean Hills, 5 mi. SSW of Jerusalem; alt. 2,250 ft. As birthplace of Jesus, it is one of Christianity's principal shrines. Here is Church of the Nativity, on site of basilica built (A.D. 330) by Emperor Constantine; under it is grotto, traditional site of the manger. There are several monasteries and convents, and numerous shrines. In Old Testament history town is connected with story of David. St. Jerome lived here for 30 years while translating the Bible. During Crusades it was captured (1099) by Godfrey of Bouillon; Baldwin I crowned here (1101). It became episcopal see in 1110. Town has predominantly Christian pop. Just N is Rachel's Tomb.

Bethlehem, town (pop. 13,530), SE Orange Free State, U. of So. Afr., 110 mi. SE of Vereeniging; alt. 5,368 ft.; rail junction with workshops; grain elevator, cold-storage plants; flour milling, dairying, malting; furniture mfg. Center of stock-raising region. Airfield.

Bethlehem. **1** Town (pop. 1,015), Litchfield co., W Conn., on Pomperaug R. and 10 mi. NW of Waterbury, in hilly agr. region. One of country's 1st theological seminaries conducted here by Rev. Joseph Bellamy in mid-18th cent. Inc. 1787. **2** Town (pop. 240), Barrow co., NE central Ga., 20 mi. W of Athens. **3** Village, Caroline co., E Md., 15 mi. NNE of Cambridge; cannery. **4** Resort town (pop. 882), Grafton co., NW N.H., on Ammonoosuc R. and 28 mi. SW of Berlin; partly in White Mtn. Natl. Forest. One of state's highest towns (alt. 1,440); health resort; winter sports. Includes Maplewood and Pierce Bridge villages. **5** City (pop. 66,340), Northampton and Lehigh counties, E Pa., 45 mi. NNW of Philadelphia and on Lehigh R. Mfg. center (steel, textiles, clothing, electrical equipment, metal products, coke, furniture, cement, chemical products); site of Bethlehem Steel Corp. Seat of Lehigh Univ., Moravian Col. (men), Moravian Col. for Women. Annual music festival (May), with famous Bach Choir. Points of interest: Central Moravian Church (c.1803), Schnitz House (1749), Moravian Buildings. Settled 1740–41 by Moravians; inc. as borough 1845, as city 1917. **6** Town (pop. 1,146), Ohio co., W.Va., in the Northern Panhandle just SE of Wheeling. Inc. after 1940.

Bethlehem, village, central St. Croix Isl., U.S. Virgin Isls., 5 mi. W of Cristiansted; sugar mill.

Bethnal Green (bĕth'nŭl), metropolitan borough (1931 pop. 108,194; 1951 census 58,374) of London, England, N of the Thames, 4 mi. NE of Charing Cross. Industrial and workers' residential dist., it was once noted for silk weaving. Bethnal Green Mus. is branch of Victoria and Albert Mus. East London Col. here is part of Univ. of London. Severely damaged by air raids, 1940–41.

Bethpage (bĕth"päj'), residential village (1940 pop. 2,590), Nassau co., SE N.Y., 3 mi. SE of Hicksville; mfg. (brick, machinery, glassware, aircraft, upholstery). Called Central Park, 1841–1936. Bethpage State Park (1,390 acres) is just E; has sports stadium, and facilities for golf, tennis, picnicking, polo, horseback riding, winter sports.

Beth-shan (bĕth-shăn') or **Beth-shean** (bĕth-shē'ŭn), biblical locality, NE Palestine, on site of modern BEISAN.

Beth-shemesh, Egypt: see HELIOPOLIS.

Beth-shemesh (bĕth-shē'mĕsh), biblical locality, central Palestine, in Judaean Hills, 15 mi. W of Jerusalem. Ark of God was returned here by Philistines; scene of several other events in later biblical history. Also spelled Beit Shemesh or Beth Shemesh.

Bethulie (bĭtōō'lē), town (pop. 3,165), SW Orange Free State, U. of So. Afr., near Cape Prov. border, near Orange R. (bridges), 45 mi. WNW of Aliwal North; alt. 4,291 ft.; sheep raising, fruitgrowing.

Béthune (bātün'), town (pop. 20,521), Pas-de-Calais dept., N France, at junction of Lawe R. and Aire–La Bassée Canal, 20 mi. WSW of Lille; commercial center in important coal-mining basin (mines at Bruay-en-Artois, Barlin, Labourse, Beuvry, Noeux-les-Mines) and fertile agr. area (wheat, sugar beets, potatoes, peas, beans, tobacco). Footwear and clock mfg., metalworking, brewing, sugar-beet distilling. Just behind Br. front lines in First World War, it was heavily damaged during Ger. offensive of April, 1918. Near by were battlefields of La Bassée (7 mi. E), of Loos and Lens (SE). Severely hit in Second World War.

Bethune. **1** (bŭthōōn', bŭthūn') Town (pop. 71), Kit Carson co., E Colo., 8 mi. W of Burlington, near Kansas line; alt. 4,000 ft. **2** (bŭ-thūn') Town (pop. 639), Kershaw co., N central S.C., 20 mi. NE of Camden; pottery; sawmill.

Béthune River (bātün'), Seine-Inférieure dept., N France, rises NE of Forges-les-Eaux, flows 28 mi. NW, past Neufchâtel, to Arques-la-Bataille, where, with 2 other streams, it forms the Arques.

Beth-yerah, Palestine: see DEGANIYA.

Bética, Cordillera, Spain: see SIERRA MORENA.

Betigeri, India: see GADAG.

Betijoque (bātēhō'kā), town (pop. 3,419), Trujillo state, W Venezuela, in Andean foothills, 20 mi. W of Trujillo; sugar cane, corn, tobacco, cacao. Petroleum wells near by.

Betio, Gilbert Isls.: see TARAWA.

Betioky (bĕtēōō'kē), town, Tuléar prov., SW Madagascar, 50 mi. SE of Tuléar; agr. center (cattle, beans) with experimental station.

Betlen, Rumania: see BECLEAN.

Betlitsa (byĕt'lyĭtsŭ), village (1939 pop. over 500), SW Kaluga oblast, Russian SFSR, 18 mi. WSW of Kirov; potatoes.

Betogabri, Palestine: see BEIT JIBRIN.

Betong (bŭtŏŏng'), town (pop. 1,543), S Sarawak, in NW Borneo, on Lupar R. and 12 mi. NNE of Simanggang; agr. (rice, sago), stock raising, fishing are carried on.

Betong (bĕ'tông'), village (1937 pop. 6,989), Yala prov., S Thailand, in Malay Peninsula, 60 mi. S of Yala, in Kalakhiri Range (Malaya border); border-control point on road to Kroh (Perak); tin mining.

Bet-Pak-Dala (byĕt-päk-dŭlä'), Rus. *Golodnaya Step'* (gŭlôd'nīŭ styĕp') [=hunger steppe], desert steppe in S central Kazakh SSR, W of L. Balkhash, bet. the Sary-Su (N) and Chu R. (S). Clay plateau (alt. near Chu R., 425 ft.) with some sandy areas, rising toward N; site of semi-nomadic spring grazing (sheep). N of Chu R. is Kagashik, desert meteorological station. Desert crossed by Trans-Kazakhstan RR in extreme E, near L. Balkhash. Abounds in mineral resources (coal, copper, tin, tungsten, molybdenum, gypsum, quartz, salt). Formerly spelled Bed-Pak-Dala.

Betroka (bĕtrōō'kŭ), town, Tuléar prov., S Madagascar, on highway, on Onilahy R., and 135 mi. NNW of Fort-Dauphin; mica-mining center and climatic resort. R.C. and Protestant missions.
Betsiamites River, Que.: see BERSIMIS RIVER.
Betsiboka River (bĕtsĕbōō'kŭ, –bō'kŭ), main river of Madagascar, in N central and NW sections of the isl., rises just N of Tananarive, flows c.325 mi. NNW, past Ambato-Boéni, Madirovalo, and Marovoay, to Mozambique Channel of Indian Ocean. Its estuary expands into Bombetoka Bay. Navigable for medium-sized craft for c.70 mi. above Marovoay. Receives Ikopa R. Valley has gold placers. Lower Betsiboka is noted for extensive rice fields.
Betsie River, NW Mich., rises in small Grass L. in SE Benzie co., flows SW, past Thompsonville, then NW to L. Michigan at Frankfort; c.35 mi. long.
Betsimitatra (bĕt"sĕmētä'trä), fertile, alluvial plain in central Madagascar, at W foot of Tananarive, drained by Ikopa R. One of the leading rice-producing regions of Madagascar.
Betsy Layne, mining village (1940 pop. 664), Floyd co., E Ky., in Cumberland foothills, on Levisa Fork and 9 mi. NW of Pikeville; bituminous coal.
Bettborn, Luxembourg: see PLATEN.
Bettembourg (bĕtäbōōr'), town (pop. 4,445), S Luxembourg, on Alzette R. and 7 mi. S of Luxembourg city; frontier station on Fr. border; dairying center; mfg. of construction equipment, slide fasteners, bricks, tiles, ceramics, ethyl alcohol.
Bettendorf (bĕ'tŭndôrf), village (pop. 486), E Luxembourg, on Sûre R. and 3 mi. E of Diekirch; farinaceous food products; liquor distilling.
Bettendorf, city (pop. 5,132), Scott co., E Iowa, industrial E suburb of Davenport, on Mississippi R. (bridged near by); mfg. (industrial gases, farm and bakery machinery, foundry and dairy products). Settled c.1840; inc. 1902 as town, 1922 as city.
Bettenhausen (bĕ"tŭnhou'zŭn), SE suburb (pop. 11,314) of Kassel, W Germany.
Betteravia (bĕtŭrā'vēŭ), village (pop. c.375), Santa Barbara co., SW Calif., 5 mi. WSW of Santa Maria; large beet-sugar refinery.
Betterton (bĕ'tŭrtŭn), fishing and resort town (pop. 314), Kent co., E Md., 13 mi. S of Havre de Grace and on Sassafras R. Pears, apples, peaches grown near by.
Bettiah (bä'tyŭ), town (pop. 30,309), Champaran dist., NW Bihar, India, 29 mi. WNW of Motihari; road center; trades in rice, wheat, barley, corn, oilseeds. Noted Asoka stone column and Vedic monuments 19 mi. NNW, at Lauriya Nandangarh.
Bettigeri, India: see GADAG.
Bettles, village (pop. 50), N central Alaska, on upper Koyukuk R. and 120 mi. N of Tanana; 66°54'N 151°50'W; supply center for rich gold-placer workings. Airstrip; radio.
Bettola (bĕt'tôlä), village (pop. 630), Piacenza prov., Emilia-Romagna, N central Italy, on Nure R. and 20 mi. SSW of Piacenza; rail terminus; agr. tools.
Bettolle (bĕt-tôl'lĕ), village (pop. 1,065), Siena prov., Tuscany, central Italy, 3 mi. E of Sinalunga; mfg. (motorcycles, bicycles).
Bettona (bĕt-tô'nä), village (pop. 493), Perugia prov., Umbria, central Italy, 8 mi. SE of Perugia. Has ruins of Etruscan and medieval walls, town hall with works of Perugino.
Bettsville, village (pop. 687), Seneca co., N Ohio, 9 mi. NNW of Tiffin, in agr. area; dolomite products.
Bettws (bĕ'tōōs), parish (pop. 1,055), SE Carmarthen, Wales, 2 mi. WSW of Ammanford; coal.
Bettws and Pontyrhyl (pôntŭrĭl'), parish (pop. 3,073) in Ogmore and Garw urban dist., central Glamorgan, Wales. Includes coal-mining towns of Bettws and Pontyrhyl.
Bettws-y-Coed (–ŭ-koid'), urban district (1931 pop. 912; 1951 census 776), E Caernarvon, Wales, on tributary of Conway R. (15th-cent. bridge) and 16 mi. SE of Bangor; tourist resort in beautiful wooded area; fishing.
Bettyhill, Scotland: see FARR.
Bettystown or **Betaghstown,** Gaelic *Baile an Bhiadhtaigh*, resort village, E Co. Meath, Ireland, on the Irish Sea, 4 mi. ESE of Drogheda.
Betul (bā'tōōl), district (□ 3,885; pop. 438,342), W Madhya Pradesh, India, on Deccan Plateau; ⊙ Betul. On central plateau of Satpura Range (average alt. 2,000 ft.), with encircling forested peaks rising to 3,658 ft. (SW) and 2,923 ft. (N); drained mainly by Tapti R. Wheat, millet, oilseeds (chiefly peanuts), cotton, sugar cane grown on open central plateau. Timber (teak, sal) and myrobalan in hills; cattle raising, lac growing. Sawmilling, essential-oil (*rosha* or Andropogon) extraction and distilling; silk growing. Betul is road and agr. trade center; graphite workings near by. Coal deposits in N hill area. Dist. ⊙ moved in mid-19th cent. from present-day Betul Bazar (then called Betul) to present-day Betul (then called Badnur). Pop. 59% Hindu, 38% tribal (mainly Gond), 2% Moslem.
Betul, town (pop. 11,841), ⊙ Betul dist., W Madhya Pradesh, India, 90 mi. NW of Nagpur; road and agr. trade center (wheat, millet, sugar); sawmilling, oilseed milling, essential-oil (*rosha* or Andropogon) distilling; silk growing. Graphite workings 3 mi. N, at village of Maramjhiri. Ruined 14th-cent. fortress of Kherla, 3 mi. NE, was seat of a major Gond dynasty. Formerly called Badnur.
Betul, village, S Goa dist., Portuguese India, on Arabian Sea, 27 mi. SSE of Pangim; betel farming, fishing; coir work.
Betul Bazar (bŭzär'), town (pop. 5,384), Betul dist., W. Madhya Pradesh, India, 4 mi. SE of Betul; sugar milling, pottery; wheat, millet, oilseeds. Was ⊙ dist. until mid-19th cent. Formerly called Betul.
Betuwe (bā'tüvŭ), fertile lowland region of Gelderland prov., central Netherlands, bet. Lek R. (N), the Lower Rhine (N and E), and Waal R. (S). Fruit and vegetable growing; mfg. (jam, syrups). Chief towns: Tiel, Culemborg, Geldermalsen.
Betwa River (bā'tvŭ), central India, rises in Vindhya Range in Bhopal, c.15 mi. N of Hoshangabad; flows generally NNE into Madhya Bharat, NE through S Uttar Pradesh and W Vindhya Pradesh, and E to Jumna R. 4 mi. SE of Hamirpur; c.380 mi. long. Not navigable. Betwa Canal leaves left bank (dam) 13 mi. ENE of Jhansi; irrigates area S of the Jumna, bet. Sind and Betwa river mouths, via numerous distributaries. Betwa R. dammed at Dukwan village, 18 mi. S of Jhansi, to form Dukwan Reservoir (irrigation project); hydroelectric plant. Another storage dam is 8 mi. SSE of Deogarh (Jhansi dist.).
Between, town (pop. 120), Walton co., N central Ga., 6 mi. WNW of Monroe.
Betz (bĕ), agr. village (pop. 430), Oise dept., N France, 14 mi. NNE of Meaux. Suffered in First World War.
Betzdorf (bĕts'dôrf), village (pop. 8,055), in former Prussian Rhine Prov., W Germany, after 1945 in Rhineland-Palatinate, on the Sieg and 8 mi. SW of Siegen; rail junction.
Betzenstein (bĕ'tsŭn-shtīn), town (pop. 849), Upper Franconia, N Bavaria, Germany, 8 mi. SW of Pegnitz; rye, barley, cattle. Chartered 1359.
Beuel (boi'ŭl), town (pop. 21,330), in former Prussian Rhine Prov., W Germany, after 1945 in North Rhine-Westphalia, on right bank of the Rhine, opposite Bonn; mfg. of machinery, chemicals, tar, abrasives, furniture, wallpaper; jute spinning and weaving, food processing. Cement works. Second World War destruction (c.40%) includes Rhine bridge to Bonn, and noted 11th-cent. Romanesque church in Vilich section (NE) of town. Has 13th-cent. church and castle. First mentioned in 12th cent. Passed to Prussia in 1815. Industrial development began after 1870.
Beulah (bū'lŭ). **1** Village (pop. c.300), Pueblo co., S central Colo., in E foothills of Wet Mts., 25 mi. SW of Pueblo; alt. 6,205 ft. Soda springs here. Large marble deposits near by. **2** Resort village (pop. 458), ⊙ Benzie co., NW Mich., on E end of Crystal L. and 25 mi. SW of Traverse City; cherries, apples, poultry. Annual smelt run festival held on small Cold Creek here. **3** Town (pop. 342), Bolivar co., NW Miss., 5 mi. SSE of Rosedale, on L. Beulah (c.6 mi. long), an oxbow lake of the Mississippi. **4** Village (pop. 1,501), Mercer co., W central N.Dak., 55 mi. NW of Bismarck and on Knife R. Lignite mines; livestock, dairy produce, poultry, wheat, corn. **5** Village, Crook co., NE Wyo., just N of Black Hills, near S.Dak. line, 17 mi. NE of Sundance; farm trading point.
Beulah, Lake, Wis.: see LAKE BEULAH.
Beulah Heights, village (1940 pop. 462), Saline co., SE Ill., 6 mi. NE of Harrisburg, in bituminous-coal-mining and agr. area.
Beulah Reservoir, Oregon: see NORTH FORK.
Beulaville (bū'lŭvĭl), town (pop. 724), Duplin co., SE N.C., 25 mi. SSW of Kinston, in farm area.
Beusichem (bŭ'zĭ-khŭm), village (pop. 1,628), Gelderland prov., central Netherlands, 7 mi. NW of Tiel; horse and cattle market; agr.
Beuthen (boi'tŭn) or **Bytom** (bĭ'tôm), large mining city (1939 pop. 101,084; 1946 pop. 93,179; 1950 pop. estimate 120,700) in Upper Silesia, after 1945 in Katowice prov., S Poland, 8 mi. NW of Katowice; 50°50'N 18°53'E. Rail junction; coal, zinc, and lead-mining center; machinery mfg. Chartered 1254, when it was already known for its metal mines. For a long time property of local counts; passed 1742 to Prussia. Former town of Rossberg (E) inc. 1927. Until 1939, Ger. frontier station on Pol. border, opposite Chorzow. Heavily damaged in Second World War. Pop. now entirely Polish.
Beuthen an der Oder, Poland: see BYTOM ODRZANSKI.
Beuvrages (bûvräzh'), N suburb (pop. 2,918) of Valenciennes, Nord dept., N France; galvanizing plant; mfg. of enameled household articles.
Beuvray, Mont (mō bûvrā'), summit (2,657 ft.) of the Morvan, E central France, on Nièvre-Saône-et-Loire dept. border, 13 mi. WSW of Autun. Site of anc. Gallic stronghold of BIBRACTE.
Beuvron River (bûvrō'), Loir-et-Cher dept., N central France, rises 9 mi. WSW of Gien, flows 80 mi. W across the Sologne, past Lamotte-Beuvron, and Bracieux, joining the Cosson 1 mi. before emptying into the Loire 7 mi. below Blois.
Beuvry (bûvrē'), outer E suburb (pop. 2,752) of Béthune, Pas-de-Calais dept., N France; coal.
Beuzeville (bûzvēl'), village (pop. 1,520), Eure dept., NW France, 15 mi. SE of Le Havre, in apple-growing area; Calvados distilling, cement mfg.
Bevagna (bĕvä'nyä), anc. *Mevania*, town (pop. 2,052), Perugia prov., Umbria, central Italy, 16 mi. SE of Perugia. Has Gothic palace (c.1270) and 2 Romanesque churches of 12th–13th cent.
Beveland, North, Netherlands: see NORTH BEVELAND.
Beveland, South, Netherlands: see SOUTH BEVELAND.
Bevelle (bŭvĕl'), village (1940 pop. 1,051), Tallapoosa co., E Ala., 37 mi. SSE of Talladega, near Martin L.
Bevensen (bā'vŭnzŭn), town (pop. 5,062), in former Prussian prov. of Hanover, NW Germany, after 1945 in Lower Saxony, on the Ilmenau and 14 mi. SE of Lüneburg; metal- and woodworking, flour milling, distilling.
Bever (bā'vŭr), Fr. *Biévène* (byāvĕn'), agr. village (pop. 1,888), Hainaut prov., SW central Belgium, 5 mi. E of Lessines.
Bever, Germany: see HÜCKESWAGEN.
Beveren (bā'vŭrŭn), town (pop. 13,614), East Flanders prov., N Belgium, 7 mi. W of Antwerp; agr., cattle market. Has 15th-cent. castle, 15th-cent. Gothic church.
Bevergern (bā'vŭrgĕrn), town (pop. 2,038), in former Prussian prov. of Westphalia, NW Germany, after 1945 in North Rhine-Westphalia, at NW tip of Teutoburg Forest, near junction of Dortmund-Ems and Ems-Weser canals, 5.5 mi. E of Rheine.
Beverley, town (pop. 757), SW Western Australia, 65 mi. ESE of Perth and on Avon R.; agr. center; wheat.
Beverley, municipal borough (1931 pop. 14,012; 1951 census 15,499), ⊙ East Riding, SE Yorkshire, England, 7 mi. NNW of Hull; leather-tanning industry; mfg. of agr. machinery; agr. market. Has famous 13th-cent. Gothic minster (334 ft. long) on site of monastery founded by St. John of Beverly (d. 721); a 17th-cent. guildhall; St. Mary's church (14th cent.); and early 15th-cent. town gate.
Beverley Beach, resort, Anne Arundel co., central Md., on Chesapeake Bay 7 mi. S of Annapolis.
Beverloo (bā'vŭrlō"), village (pop. 4,557), Limburg prov., NE Belgium, 11 mi. NNW of Hasselt; agr., cattle raising.
Beverly, town (pop. 1,171), central Alta., E suburb of Edmonton.
Beverly. 1 Town (1940 pop. 132), Elbert co., NE Ga., 8 mi. E of Elberton. **2** City (pop. 255), Lincoln co., N central Kansas, on Saline R. and 22 mi. WNW of Salina; livestock, grain. **3** Residential city (pop. 28,884), Essex co., NE Mass., on coast just N of Salem; mfg. (shoes, shoe machinery, clothing, canvas products). Formerly shipping center. Had New England's 1st successful cotton-weaving mill (1789). Settled before 1630, inc. as town 1668, as city 1894. Includes resort villages of Beverly Farms (where Oliver Wendell Holmes and later his son the Associate Justice lived) and Prides Crossing. **4** City (pop. 3,084), Burlington co., W N.J., on Delaware R. and 4 mi. W of Burlington; mfg. (rayon textiles, rope, wallpaper, underwear); truck, fruit. Site of Civil War camp and hosp., and of a natl. cemetery. Inc. 1857. **5** Village (pop. 723), Washington co., SE Ohio, on Muskingum R. and 13 mi. NW of Marietta; large nursery; timber. Summer camps. **6** Town (pop. 515), Randolph co., E W.Va., on Tygart R. and 6 mi. S of Elkins. Civil War battle of Rich Mtn. (1861), a Union victory, was fought near by.
Beverly Farms, Mass.: see BEVERLY.
Beverly Hills. 1 Residential city (pop. 29,032), Los Angeles co., S Calif., completely surrounded by Los Angeles, and extending (N) up slopes of Santa Monica Mts. Home of many motion-picture stars; has fine shopping dist., hotels, restaurants. Developed after 1906, inc. 1914. **2** Town (pop. 938), St. Louis co., E Mo., near Mississippi R., 10 mi. W of St. Louis. **3** Village (pop. 701), McLennan co., E central Texas, S suburb of Waco.
Beverly Park, village, Snohomish co., NW Wash., 5 mi. S of Everett.
Beverly Shores, town (pop. 488), Porter co., NW Ind., on L. Michigan, 5 mi. SW of Michigan City.
Bevern (bā'vŭrn), village (pop. 2,861), in former Prussian prov. of Hanover, NW Germany, after 1945 in Lower Saxony, near right bank of the Weser, 3 mi. NE of Holzminden; metalworking, flour milling. Has 17th-cent. former castle, seat (1666–1735) of dukes of Brunswick-Bevern. Until 1941 in Brunswick.
Beverungen (bā'vŭrōōng"ŭn), town (pop. 4,420), in former Prussian prov. of Westphalia, NW Germany, after 1945 in North Rhine-Westphalia, on left bank of the Weser and 7 mi. S of Höxter; forestry.
Beverwijk (bā'vŭrvīk), town (pop. 24,009), North Holland prov., W Netherlands, 3 mi. NE of Ijmuiden; resort; extensive strawberry growing; motor-oil plant, canneries (vegetables, fruit, jam), mfg. (machinery, cigars, carpets). Sometimes spelled Beverwyk.
Bevier (bŭvēr'). **1** Mining village (1940 pop. 571), Muhlenberg co., W Ky., 24 mi. ESE of Madisonville; bituminous coal. **2** City (pop. 838), Macon

co., N central Mo., in valley of Chariton R., 5 mi. W of Macon; coal.

Bevington, town (pop. 48), on Madison-Warren co. line, S central Iowa, 17 mi. SSW of Des Moines.

Bewar (bā'vŭr), town (pop. 3,466), Mainpuri dist., W Uttar Pradesh, India, on distributary (Bewar Branch) of Lower Ganges Canal and 17 mi. E of Mainpuri; road center; wheat, gram, pearl millet, corn, barley.

Bewar Branch, canal, India: see Ganges Canals.

Bewcastle (bū'–), village and parish (pop. 533), N Cumberland, England, 16 mi. NE of Carlisle; sheep raising. A military post in Roman times. The churchyard contains the Bewcastle Cross, dating from 7th or 8th cent. Just N and NE is **Bewcastle Fells,** a range of hills rising to 1,702 ft.

Bewdley, municipal borough (1931 pop. 2,868; 1951 census 4,914), N Worcester, England, on Severn R. and 3 mi. W of Kidderminster; agr. market, with many 17th-cent. bldgs. Just W, along the Severn, is the large Wyre Forest.

Bex (bā), town (pop. 4,264), Vaud canton, SW Switzerland, on short Avançon R., near its confluence with the Rhone, and 26 mi. SE of Lausanne; health resort noted for iodized brine and lye baths. Salt mining; calcium carbide, chemicals, flour.

Bexar (bâr), county (□ 1,247; pop. 500,460), SW central Texas; ⊙ San Antonio. Balcones Escarpment crosses co. SW-NE, dividing hills (in NW) from prairies; co. alt. c.600–1,200 ft. Drained by Medina and San Antonio rivers. Agr. (corn, grain sorghums, peanuts, potatoes, pecans, truck); beef and dairy cattle, sheep, goats (wool and mohair marketed); poultry raising, beekeeping. Oil, natural-gas wells; also clay, limestone, gravel. Formed 1836.

Bexhill (bĕks'hĭl'), municipal borough (1931 pop. 21,229; 1951 census 25,668), SE Sussex, England, on the Channel 5 mi. WSW of Hastings; seaside resort. Has church originally built by Saxons, rebuilt in Norman times and later.

Bexley (bĕks'lē), municipality (pop. 26,862), E New South Wales, Australia, 8 mi. SW of Sydney, in metropolitan area; mfg. center; knitting mills, shoe and furniture factories.

Bexley, residential municipal borough (1931 pop. 32,949; 1951 census 88,767), NW Kent, England, on Cray R., near London, 3 mi. W of Dartford; metalworking and electrical industries. Has 13th-cent. church (damaged in Second World War) and Hall Place, mansion dating from 1320. In the Red House here, William Morris lived for several years.

Bexley, residential city (pop. 12,378), Franklin co., central Ohio, within but politically independent of Columbus. Capital Univ. is here. Inc. 1908.

Beya (byä'ŭ), village (1939 pop. over 2,000), E Khakass Autonomous Oblast, Krasnoyarsk Territory, Russian SFSR, 45 mi. SW of Abakan, in cattle-raising area; metalworks.

Bey Dag (bā' dä), Turkish *Bey Dağ.* **1** Highest peak (10,020 ft.) of Tahtali Mts., S central Turkey, 45 mi. SE of Kayseri. **2** Highest peak (9,160 ft.) of Tecer Mts., central Turkey, 17 mi. SSE of Zara.

Beyenburg (bī'ŭnbŏŏrk), SE section of Wuppertal, W Germany, 6 mi. SE of Barmen; textile mfg., paper milling. Inc. 1929 with neighboring towns to form city of Wuppertal.

Beyerland, Netherlands: see Beijerland.

Beyin, Gold Coast: see Atuabo.

Beykoz (bākôz'), city (pop. 25,611), Istanbul prov., NW Turkey in Asia, on E shore of the Bosporus, 11 mi. NE of Istanbul, included in Istanbul metropolitan area; shoes and other leather products; furs.

Beyla (bālä'), town (pop. c.3,700), SE Fr. Guinea, Fr. West Africa, in interior highlands, 125 mi. SSE of Kankan, linked by road to Fr. Ivory Coast. Rice- and tobacco-growing center; cattle and sheep raising. Some diamond and iron mining in dist.

Bey Mountains (bā), SW Turkey, extend 35 mi. SSW-NNE parallel to W shore of Gulf of Antalya; rise to 10,125 ft. in Ak Dag.

Beynat (bĕnä'), village (pop. 422), Corrèze dept., S central France, 10 mi. ESE of Brive-la-Gaillarde; fruit and vegetable preserving.

Beyne-Heusay (bān-ûzā'), town (pop. 6,222), Liége prov., E Belgium, 4 mi. ESE of Liége; coal mining. Beyne and Heusay are contiguous towns.

Beyoglu (bā"ōlōō'), Turkish *Beyoğlu,* N section (pop. 253,588) of Istanbul, Turkey in Europe, on the Golden Horn.

Beypazari (bāpä'zärŭ"), Turkish *Beypazarı,* town (pop. 5,357), Ankara prov., central Turkey, 52 mi. WNW of Ankara; mohair goats.

Beypore, India: see Feroke.

Beypore River (bā'pŏŏr), SW Madras, India, rises in the Wynaad in 2 headstreams joining NE of Nilambur, flows c.90 mi. generally WSW, past Nilambur (teak plantations), to Arabian Sea 6 mi. SSE of Calicut. Navigable in lower course; logging. Sometimes spelled Baypore.

Beyrède-Jumet (bârĕd'-zhümā'), village (pop. 94), Hautes-Pyrénées dept., SW France, on the Neste (hydroelectric station) and 14 mi. SE of Bagnères-de-Bigorre. Produces aluminum, potassium chlorate, silico-manganese, Portland cement.

Beyrouth, Lebanon: see Beirut.

Beysehir (bā-shĕhĭr'), Turkish *Beyşehir,* village (pop. 2,894), Konya prov., W central Turkey, at SE corner of L. Beysehir, 45 mi. WSW of Konya; wheat, barley, vetch.

Beysehir, Lake, anc. *Karalis,* Turkish *Beyşehir,* lake (□ 251) in W central Turkey, 45 mi. W of Konya; 28 mi. long, 15 mi. wide; alt. 3,660 ft. Drains SE via Beysehir R. to L. Sugla. Beysehir on SE shore, Kireli on E. Formerly also Beishehr, Beyshehr, or Begshehr.

Beysug River, Russian SFSR: see Beisug River.

Beyt (bāt), town (pop. 4,036), Amreli dist., NW Bombay, India, on small Beyt isl. in Gulf of Cutch, 2 mi. E of Okha; fishing. Isl., sometimes called Beyt Shankhodhar, is sacred place to Hindus; has Vishnuite temple. Also spelled Bet.

Beyt el Fekih, Yemen: see Bait al Faqih.

Beytussebap (bātüsh'shĕbäp"), Turkish *Beytüşşebap,* village (pop. 746), Hakari prov., SE Turkey, 32 mi. W of Hakari; millet. Also spelled Beytusebap and Beytisebap. Formerly Elki.

Beyü, China: see Paiyü.

Bezdan, Hung. *Bezdán* (both: bĕz'dän), village (pop. 6,350), Vojvodina, NW Serbia, Yugoslavia, port on the Danube, on railroad and 10 mi. NW of Sombor, in the Backa, near Hung. border; W terminus of Danube-Tisa Canal; fishing.

Bezdez Mountain, Czechoslovakia: see Bela pod Bezdezem.

Bezdrev, Czechoslovakia: see Hluboka nad Vltavou.

Bezdruzice (bĕz'drŏŏzhĭtsĕ), Czech *Bezdružice,* Ger. *Weseritz* (vā'zürĭts), town (pop. 618), W Bohemia, Czechoslovakia, 21 mi. WNW of Pilsen; rail terminus; rye, oats, potatoes. Health resort of Konstantinovy Lazne (kôn'stäntĭnôvĭ läz'nyĕ), Czech *Konstantinovy Lázně* (alt. 1,765 ft.), is 2 mi. S.

Bèze (bĕz), village (pop. 577), Côte-d'Or dept., E central France, 15 mi. NE of Dijon; woodworking, hop growing. Has remains of 7th-cent. abbey.

Bezenchuk (byĕzĭnchŏŏk'), village (1939 pop. over 2,000), W central Kuibyshev oblast, Russian SFSR, on railroad and 10 mi. W of Chapayevsk; metalworking, mfg. of building materials; wheat, sunflowers. Has noted agr. experimental station.

Bezerros (bĭzĕ'rŏŏs), city (pop. 6,772), E Pernambuco, NE Brazil, on railroad and 15 mi. ENE of Caruaru; ships sugar, coffee, tobacco to Recife.

Bezhanitsy (byĕ'zhŭnyētsē), village (1926 pop. 409), N Velikiye Luki oblast, Russian SFSR, 50 mi. NNW of Velikiye Luki, in flax area; distilling. **Bezhanitsy Upland,** a lake-studded hill area (SSW), rises to 915 ft.

Bezhanovo (bĕzhä'nôvô), village (pop. 4,344), Pleven dist., N Bulgaria, on branch of Vit R. and 12 mi. E of Lukovit; flour milling; livestock raising.

Bezhetsk (byĕ'zhĭtsk), city (pop. 12,817), E Kalinin oblast, Russian SFSR, on Mologa R. and 70 mi. NNE of Kalinin; produces flax-processing machinery; linen milling, distilling, tanning. Dates from 1137; belonged formerly to Novgorod; annexed (early 15th cent.) by Moscow.

Bezhitsa (byĕ'zhĭtsŭ), city (1926 pop. 36,040; 1939 pop. 82,331), NE Bryansk oblast, Russian SFSR, on Desna R. and 5 mi. NW of Bryansk; mfg. of machinery (locomotives, railway cars, steam-generating equipment, agr. implements); oxygen plant; power station. Has engineering col. (rolling-stock mfg.). Became city in 1925; called (c.1935–43) Ordzhonikidzegrad. During Second World War, held (1941–43) by Germans.

Béziers (bāzyā'), city (pop. 59,894), Hérault dept., S France, on Orb R., on the Canal du Midi, and 38 mi. SW of Montpellier; leading wine and alcohol trade center. Produces fertilizer, winegrowing equipment, rubber, biscuits, candy. Metalworking, distilling, petroleum refining. Has 13th–14th-cent. church of Saint-Nazaire. Its lively main thoroughfare is named after Paul Riquet (b. here), who built the Canal du Midi. An important Roman colony, it became a stronghold of the viscounts of Carcassonne (12th cent.). During the Albigensian Crusade Béziers was taken (1209) by Simon de Montfort and its inhabitants massacred. Episcopal see 4th cent. to 1802. Its pop. increased rapidly after 1870.

Bezlyudovka (byĭzlyŏŏ'dŭfkŭ), town (1926 pop. 5,654), N central Kharkov oblast, Ukrainian SSR, 8 mi. SSE of Kharkov.

Bezmein (byĕzmāēn'), village, S Ashkhabad oblast, Turkmen SSR, on Trans-Caspian RR and 14 mi. NW of Ashkhabad, in orchard area; wine making; rug weaving; cementworks.

Bezmer (bĕzmĕr'), village (pop. 1,859), Yambol dist., SE central Bulgaria, 7 mi. W of Yambol; grain, rice, tobacco, vineyards. Formerly Khamzoren or Hamzoren.

Bezons (bŭzō'), town (pop. 12,676), Seine-et-Oise dept., N central France, a NW suburb of Paris, 8 mi. from Notre Dame Cathedral, on right bank of the Seine, adjoining Argenteuil (NE); metallurgical (aircraft, elevators, cables) and chemical works (photographic equipment, synthetic resins); mfg. of rayon, shoe polish, dyes and varnishes. Damaged in Second World War.

Bezwada (bāzvä'dŭ), since 1949 officially **Vijayavada** or **Vijayawada** (vĭjä'yŭvädŭ), city (pop. 86,184), Kistna dist., NE Madras, India, on left bank of Kistna R. (rail bridge) and 155 mi. ESE of Hyderabad; road, rail, and trade center; headworks of Kistna navigable irrigation-canal system; cement, engineering, iron- and steelworks; rice and oilseed milling, tobacco curing; pharmaceuticals; hand-made paper and fiberboard. Col. (affiliated with Andhra Univ.). Mus. Site of duodecennial Hindu bathing festival. A Buddhist religious center; visited by Hsüan-tsang in A.D. 645. Brahmanic cave temples (7th-cent. Dravidian) just SW, across river, at village of Undavalle.

Bezymyannaya (byĕzĭmyä'nīŭ), village (1939 pop. over 500), central Saratov oblast, Russian SFSR, on railroad and 17 mi. ESE of Engels; wheat, tobacco, cattle.

Bhabar, region, India and Nepal: see Terai.

Bhabra (bä'brŭ), village, SW Madhya Bharat, India, 15 mi. N of Alirajpur, in W Vindhya Range; local grain and timber trade.

Bhabua (bŭb'wŭ), town (pop. 7,164), Shahabad dist., W Bihar, India, on tributary of the Ganges and 75 mi. SW of Arrah; road center; rice, wheat, gram, oilseeds, barley, sugar cane. Anc. Hindu temple near by. Rail station at Bhabua Road, 9 mi. N.

Bhachau (bŭchou'), town (pop. 3,814), S Cutch, India, 43 mi. E of Bhuj; rail spur terminus; trades in salt and cotton handicrafts.

Bhadar River (bŭdŭr'), Saurashtra, India, rises in hills on central Kathiawar peninsula, NE of Jasdan; flows c.125 mi. WSW, past Jetput and Kutiyana, to Arabian Sea at Navibandar.

Bhadarsa (bŭdär'sŭ), town (pop. 4,173), Fyzabad dist., E central Uttar Pradesh, India, 10 mi. S of Fyzabad; rice, wheat, gram, sugar. Moslem shrine.

Bhadarwah (bä'dŭrvŭ), town (pop. 2,989), Doda dist., SW Kashmir, in S Punjab Himalayas, on tributary of the Chenab and 35 mi. ENE of Udhampur; corn, wheat, barley, rice, fruit. Fort was former stronghold of Mian Rajputs. Also spelled Bhadrawah.

Bhadaur (bŭdour'), town (pop. 7,862), central Patiala and East Punjab States Union, India, 65 mi. WNW of Patiala; wheat, gram, cotton; metalware.

Bhadgaon (bŭd'goun), town (pop. 8,921), East Khandesh dist., E Bombay, India, on Girna R. and 32 mi. SW of Jalgaon; cotton ginning, handicraft cloth weaving; trades in peanuts, millet, cloth.

Bhadgaon or **Bhatgaon** (both: bŭd'goun), city (1920 pop., with environs, 93,176), central Nepal, in Nepal Valley, on small Hanuman R. and 7 mi. ESE of Katmandu city center; barley, rice, wheat, millet, vegetables, fruit. Nepalese military post. Many well-preserved, intricately carved temples and other buildings, including palace with famous Golden Door (built 1697) and Nyatpola Deval pagoda (temple of 5 stages; built 1703). Founded c.865, it was a petty kingdom, ruled by Newars of Malla dynasty, and for 2 centuries the chief power in Nepal Valley until its division (1480) into principalities. Captured 1769 by Gurkha leader Prithwi Narayan. Damaged by earthquake, 1934. Pop. mainly Newar. Hindu pilgrimage center 3 mi. N, with elaborately carved Vishnuite temple of Changu Narayan; considered finest example of Newar religious architecture; inscribed pillar dates from A.D. 496.

Bhadohi (bŭdō'hē), town (pop. 2,038), Benares dist., SE Uttar Pradesh, India, 20 mi. WNW of Benares; carpet mfg.; rice, barley, gram, wheat.

Bhadra (bä'drŭ), town (pop. 4,750), N Rajasthan, India, 135 mi. NE of Bikaner; local market for millet, gram, wool, cattle; hand-loom weaving; leather products.

Bhadrachalam (bŭdrä'chŭlŭm), village, East Godavari dist., NE Madras, India, on left bank of Godavari R. and 75 mi. NW of Rajahmundry; Hindu pilgrimage center, served by ferry from Borgampad (just SW, across river, in Hyderabad). Experimental silk-growing farm; rice, oilseeds. Graphite workings near by.

Bhadrachellam Road, India: see Kottagudem.

Bhadrakh (bŭd'rŭk), town (pop. 19,550), Balasore dist., NE Orissa, India, 40 mi. SW of Balasore; market center for rice, salt, cattle, hides; hand-loom weaving, palm-mat making. Has col. Sometimes spelled Bhadrak.

Bhadran (bä'drŭn), town (pop. 5,977), Kaira dist., N Bombay, India, 30 mi. SSE of Kaira; trades in tobacco, millet, rice; handicraft cloth weaving (saris, dhotis).

Bhadra River (bä'drŭ), right headstream of the Tungabhadra, in NW Mysore, India, rises in Western Ghats near Mysore-Madras border, flows c.110 mi. generally NNE, past Bhadravati, joining Tunga R. at Kudali (7 mi. NE of Shimoga) to form Tungabhadra R.

Bhadravati (bŭdrä'vŭtē), town (pop. 19,585), Shimoga dist., NW Mysore, India, on Bhadra R. (headstream of the Tungabhadra) and 10 mi. SE of Shimoga; industrial center. Large iron- and steel-milling plant produces charcoal, pig iron, industrial and domestic steel products; auxiliary works produce cement, refractory bricks, wood alcohol, formaldehyde, ferrochrome. Plant is supplied with iron ore from Baba Budan Range (S) and manganese from workings at Shimoga and Kumsi. Other industries include paper milling, sandalwood-oil processing. Construction of large chemical plant (chiefly fertilizers) begun 1949.

Bhadrawah, Kashmir: see BHADARWAH.

Bhadreswar (bŭdrās'vŭr), town (pop. 27,673), Hooghly dist., S central West Bengal, India, on Hooghly R. and 6 mi. SSW of Hooghly; rice trade center; jute milling.

Bhag (bäg), village, Kalat state, E Baluchistan, W Pakistan, on Nari R. and 34 mi. S of Sibi, on Kachhi plain; local market for millet, wheat, cattle; hand-loom weaving, embroidering; cattle raising.

Bhagalpur (bä'gŭlpo͝or), district (□ 4,248; pop. 2,408,879), NE Bihar, India, on Ganges Plain; ⊙ Bhagalpur. Bounded N by Nepal, E by Kosi R.; crossed by the Ganges; irrigated by the Kosi. Alluvial soil; rice, wheat, corn, barley, oilseeds, sugar cane. Rice and sugar milling, silk and woolen weaving. Bhagalpur is transportation and trade center; Gupta temple and cave sculptures near by.

Bhagalpur, city (pop. 93,254), ⊙ Bhagalpur dist., NE Bihar, India, on Ganges R. and 120 mi. ESE of Patna; rail and road junction; trade center (rice, wheat, corn, barley, oilseeds, sugar cane); hemp-narcotics distribution; rice and sugar milling, silk and woolen weaving. Silk-growing institute, agr. research station. Rail spur to Mandar Hill, 29 mi. S. Gupta temple at Sultanganj, 5 mi. W; cave sculptures near by.

Bhagamandala (bä"gŭmŭn'dŭlŭ), village (pop. 1,026), N Coorg, India, on Cauvery R. and 14 mi. W of Mercara, at E foot of Brahmagiri hill (source of the Cauvery). Experimental cardamom farm. Hindu pilgrimage temple.

Bhaga River, India: see CHENAB RIVER.

Bhagirathi River (bägē'rŭtē). **1** Headstream of the Ganges, in N Uttar Pradesh, India; rises in cave in Gangotri glacier in W Kumaun Himalayas, 10 mi. SE of Gangotri, at 30°55'N 79°7'E; flows W past Gangotri, and generally S past Tehri, joining Alaknanda R. at Devaprayag to form Ganges R.; c.120 mi. long. Traditionally considered the source of the Ganges, it is one of the most sacred rivers of India. **2** In West Bengal, India, leaves the Ganges 5 mi. NE of Jangipur, flows c.120 mi. S, past Jangipur, Azimganj, Berhampore, and Katwa, joining Jalangi R. at Nabadwip to form HOOGHLY RIVER. Forms W boundary of Ganges Delta. Until c.16th cent., part of original bed of the Ganges; then main waters of the Ganges shifted to the Padma. To Hindus, Bhagirathi is the sacred stream, not the Padma.

Bhagur (bä'go͝or), town (pop. 5,489), Nasik dist., central Bombay, India, 8 mi. SSE of Nasik; market center for millet, wheat, cotton.

Bhagwantnagar (bŭg'vŭntnŭg"ŭr), town (pop. 3,089), Unao dist., central Uttar Pradesh, India, 27 mi. SSE of Unao; metalware mfg.; wheat, barley, rice, gram.

Bhainsa or **Bhaisa** (bīn'sŭ, bī'sŭ), town (pop. 8,207), Nander dist., N Hyderabad state, India, 40 mi. E of Nander; cotton ginning; agr. market (chiefly millet, wheat).

Bhainsdehi (bīns'dāhē), village, Betul dist., W Madhya Pradesh, India, 25 mi. SW of Betul; cattle raising; wheat, millet, oilseeds.

Bhainsrorgarh (bīns'rōrgŭr), Rajput fort, SE Rajasthan, India, on Chambal R. and 60 mi. E of Chitor. Captured c.1303 by Ala-ud-din; withstood Mahratta attack in late-18th cent. Beautifully carved Barolli temples (9th or 10th cent.) 3 mi. E.

Bhairab Bazar (bī'rŭb bŭzär'), town (pop. 7,695), Mymensingh dist., E East Bengal, E Pakistan, on Meghna R. (rail ferry to Ashuganj), at mouth of the old Brahmaputra, and 55 mi. SSE of Mymensingh; rail junction; trade center (rice, jute, oilseeds, salt); cattle market; jute pressing.

Bhairwa, Nepal: see BUTWAL.

Bhaisa, India: see BHAINSA.

Bhaisaunda (bīsoun'dŭ), former petty state (□ 32; pop. 5,147) of Central India agency, NW of Karwi, one of the CHAUBE JAGIRS. In 1948, merged with Vindhya Pradesh.

Bhajji (bŭj'jē), former princely state (□ 94; pop. 16,474) of Punjab Hill States, India, N of Simla; ⊙ was Seoni. Since 1948, merged with Himachal Pradesh.

Bhakkar (bŭk'kŭr), town (pop. 9,006), Mianwali dist., W Punjab, W Pakistan, 70 mi. SSW of Mianwali; wheat, gram, dates, mangoes; local trade in hides, wool.

Bhakra (bä'krŭ), W Bilaspur state, India, 19 mi. WNW of Bilaspur, in outer W Himalayas. Near by is site of proposed dam across Sutlej R. to impound large reservoir for irrigation and hydroelectric development.

Bhalil, El, Fr. Morocco: see BAHLIL, EL.

Bhalki (bäl'kē), town (pop. 7,878), Bidar dist., W central Hyderabad state, India, 23 mi. WNW of Bidar; millet, cotton, rice, tobacco. Sheep raising.

Bhalwal (bŭl'vŭl), town (pop. 5,954), Shahpur dist., central Punjab, W Pakistan, 18 mi. NE of Sargodha; local market for wheat, cotton, millet; cotton ginning, dairy farming, soap mfg.

Bhamdun or **Bahamdun** (both: bŭhäm'do͞on), Fr. *Bhamdoun,* village (pop. 426), central Lebanon, on Beirut-Damascus RR and 10 mi. SE of Beirut; alt. 3,800 ft.; resort; sericulture, cereals, oranges.

Bhamo (bä'mō), Burmese *Bamaw* (bŭmô'), district (□ 4,148; 1941 pop. 129,302) of Kachin State, Upper Burma; ⊙ Bhamo. Bounded E by Chinese Yunnan prov., S by Shan State, it is drained by Irrawaddy R.; rises to over 7,000 ft. (SE). Agr.: rice, corn, tobacco; teak forests. Served by Irrawaddy steamers and branch of Burma Road. Pop. is 30% Thai, 25% Burmese, and 15% Kachin. Until 1947 in Sagaing div.

Bhamo, town (pop. 7,827), ⊙ Bhamo dist., Kachin State, Upper Burma, on left bank of Irrawaddy R. and 80 mi. S of Myitkyina, near China border; 24°15'N 97°14'E. Served by Irrawaddy steamers, on branch of Burma Road, and on road to Tengchung (Yunnan prov.), it has intensive trade with China in cotton, jade, finished goods. In Second World War captured (1944) by Chinese forces.

Bhandak, India: see CHANDA, town.

Bhandara (bŭndä'rŭ), district (□ 3,580; pop. 963,225), central Madhya Pradesh, India, on Deccan Plateau; ⊙ Bhandara. In broad Wainganga valley; contains isolated outliers of E Satpura Range. Rice, wheat, oilseeds (chiefly flax), mangoes, and millet in alluvial lowland (numerous irrigation tanks); sal, bamboo, lac, myrobalan in densely forested hills (corundum deposits, marble quarries; game hunting). An important source of India's manganese (mines N of Tumsar). Rice and oilseed milling, cotton and silk weaving, biri mfg. Gondia is trade and mfg. center. Pop. 86% Hindu, 12% tribal (mainly Gond), 2% Moslem.

Bhandara, town (pop. 19,708), ⊙ Bhandara dist., central Madhya Pradesh, India, on Wainganga R. and 37 mi. E of Nagpur; rice milling, biri mfg.; brass vessels. Bhandara Road (rail station) is 5 mi. N.

Bhander (bän'dār), town (pop. 4,793), NE Madhya Bharat, India, 50 mi. SE of Lashkar; market center for gram, millet, wheat, cotton; handicraft cloth.

Bhanga (bŭng'gŭ), village, Faridpur dist., S central East Bengal, E Pakistan, on river arm of Ganges Delta and 20 mi. NW of Madaripur; road terminus; rice, jute, oilseeds, sugar cane.

Bhangir, India: see BHONGIR.

Bhangnga, Thailand: see PHANGNGA.

Bhankri, India: see DAOSA.

Bhanpura (bän'po͝orŭ), town (pop. 5,865), NW Madhya Bharat, India, 55 mi. E of Nimach; markets millet, corn, wheat; hand-loom weaving. Jaswant Rao Holkar died here in 1811.

Bhanupratappur, India: see SAMBALPUR, Madhya Pradesh.

Bhanwar (bŭn'vŭr), town (pop. 8,378), W Saurashtra, India, 40 mi. SSW of Jamnagar; local market for millet, oilseeds, cotton; flour and oilseed milling, hand-loom weaving. Also spelled Bhanwad.

Bharat: see INDIA.

Bharatganj (bŭr'ŭtgŭnj), town (pop. 4,306), Allahabad dist., SE Uttar Pradesh, India, 35 mi. SE of Allahabad; gram, rice, barley, wheat, oilseeds.

Bharat Khali (bŭrŭt' kŭl'ē), village, Rangpur dist., N East Bengal, E Pakistan, on Jamuna R. (main course of the Brahmaputra; rail ferry) opposite Bahadurabad Ghat and 10 mi. SSE of Gaibanda; rail spur terminus.

Bharatpur (bŭrŭt'po͝or), former princely state (□ 1,978; pop. 575,625) in Rajputana States, India; ⊙ was Bharatpur. Area settled by Jats in late-17th and early-18th cent.; state firmly established under noted leader, Suraj Mal (died 1763). Mahratta invasions soon followed; treaty with British in 1803. In 1949, joined union of Rajasthan. Sometimes spelled Bhurtpore.

Bharatpur. 1 Village, Surguja dist., E Madhya Pradesh, India, 100 mi. WNW of Ambikapur, in dense sal forest; lac cultivation. Was ⊙ former princely state of Changbhakar, one of Chhattisgarh States. Prehistoric rock excavations 8 mi. NNW, at village of Harchoka. **2** City (pop. 35,541), E Rajasthan, India, 105 mi. ENE of Jaipur; rail junction; trade center (grain, oilseeds, cotton); oilseed milling, dal mfg.; handicrafts include chowries with ivory or sandalwood handles, cotton cloth, fibre fans, and earthenware goods. Col. Founded 1733 by Jat chieftain, Suraj Mal; unsuccessfully besieged 1805 by Br. General Lake. Was ⊙ former Rajputana state of Bharatpur. Sometimes spelled Bhurtpore. It is ⊙ Bharatpur dist.

Bharhut, India: see SATNA.

Bharthana (bŭr'tŭnŭ), town (pop. 4,553), Etawah dist., W Uttar Pradesh, India, 12 mi. E of Etawah; wheat, pearl millet, barley, corn, gram, oilseeds.

Bharuch, India: see BROACH.

Bharwari, India: see MANJHANPUR.

Bharwa Sumerpur, India: see SUMERPUR.

Bhasawar or **Bhusawar** (both: bŭsä'vŭr), town (pop. 6,699), E Rajasthan, India, 29 mi. WSW of Bharatpur; millet, wheat, gram.

Bhatapara (bätäpä'rŭ), town (pop. 9,974), Raipur dist., E Madhya Pradesh, India, 40 mi. NNE of Raipur; rice, oilseed, flour, and dal milling.

Bhatgaon, Nepal: see BHADGAON.

Bhatiapara Ghat, E Pakistan: see KALUKHALI.

Bhatinda (bŭtĭn'dŭ), town (pop. 24,833), W Patiala and East Punjab States Union, India, 85 mi. WSW of Patiala, near branch of Sirhind Canal; major rail junction; trades in agr. produce of surrounding area (wheat, millet, gram, oilseeds, sugar cane, rice); hand-loom weaving, flour milling. Col.

Bhatkal (bŭt'kŭl), town (pop. 10,718), Kanara dist., S Bombay, India, on Arabian Sea, 63 mi. SSE of Karwar; fish curing (mackerel, sardines), betel farming; rice, coconuts. Taken 1505 by Portuguese; became (14th-16th cent.) important port and commercial center.

Bhatnair, India: see HANUMANGARH.

Bhatpara (bätpä'rŭ), city (pop. 117,044), 24-Parganas dist., SE West Bengal, India, on Hooghly R. and 21 mi. N of Calcutta city center; jute, cotton, and paper milling. Anc. seat of Sanskrit learning.

Bhattiana (bŭt-tyä'nŭ), level tract in SW Punjab and N Rajasthan, India; from Ghaggar R. in Hissar dist. extends roughly NW and W into S Ferozepore dist. Inhabited (14th-18th cent.) by independent Moslem tribes.

Bhattiprolu (bŭtĭprō'lo͞o), town (pop. 11,667), Guntur dist., NE Madras, India, in Kistna R. delta, on rail spur and 26 mi. SE of Guntur; rice and oilseed milling; tobacco. Has ruined Buddhist stupa; caskets of jewels, discovered 1892, now in Central Mus., Madras. Sometimes spelled Bhattiprole.

Bhaun (boun), town (pop. 6,608), Jhelum dist., N Punjab, W Pakistan, 55 mi. W of Jhelum; rail terminus; agr. market (wheat, millet); hand-loom weaving.

Bhaunagar or **Bhavnagar** (bou'nŭgŭr), former princely state (□ 2,961; pop. 618,429) of Western India States agency, on Kathiawar peninsula, India; ⊙ was Bhaunagar. Founded by Gohel Rajputs, who 1st settled in country in mid-13th cent. Since 1948, merged with Saurashtra.

Bhaunagar or **Bhavnagar,** city (pop. 102,851), ⊙ Gohilwad dist., E Saurashtra, India, port on Gulf of Cambay, 90 mi. SSW of Ahmadabad. Rail terminus; airport; trades in cotton, grain, timber, cloth fabrics, hardware; mfg. of cotton and silk textiles, bakelite and rubber goods, vegetable oil, bone fertilizer, bricks, tiles, musical instruments, sugar candy, ice; metalworks, ordnance factory, sawmills. Handicrafts include cotton cloth, woodwork, and metalware. Col., mus. Port installations are just N. Chemical works 5 mi. SW, at Vartej. City founded 1723; was ⊙ former Bhaunagar state.

Bhavani (bŭvä'nē), town (pop. 9,090), Coimbatore dist., S central Madras, India, on Cauvery R., at Bhavani R. mouth, and 60 mi. NE of Coimbatore; rice; peanut-oil extraction. Steatite quarried near by. Place of pilgrimage (Sivaite and Vishnuite temples). Sometimes spelled Bavani.

Bhavani River, SW Madras, India, rises in Western Ghats in several headstreams NW of Coimbatore, flows generally ENE, past Satyamangalam, to Cauvery R. at Bhavani; c.110 mi. long. Receives MOYAR RIVER (irrigation works near confluence) 10 mi. WSW of Satyamangalam. Also spelled Bavani.

Bhavnagar, India: see BHAUNAGAR.

Bhawalpur, W Pakistan: see BAHAWALPUR, state.

Bhawani Mandi (bŭvä'nē mŭn'dē), village, SE Rajasthan, India, on railroad and 24 mi. SW of Brijnagar; cotton milling.

Bhawanipatna (bŭvä'nēpŭtnŭ), town (pop. 10,863), ⊙ Kalahandi dist., SW Orissa, India, 175 mi. WSW of Cuttack; trade center for timber, rice, hides; handicraft cloth weaving. Sometimes written Bhawani Patna.

Bhawanipur (bŭvä'nēpo͝or), suburban ward (pop. 97,464) in Calcutta municipality, SE West Bengal, India, 2.5 mi. S of city center; general engineering works; chemical mfg. Col. Also spelled Bhowanipur.

Bhayavadar (bäyä'vŭdŭr), town (pop. 8,805), W central Saurashtra, India, 45 mi. SW of Rajkot; peanut milling, cotton ginning, hand-loom weaving. Building stone quarried near by. Sometimes spelled Bhayavdar.

Bhelsa, India: see BHILSA.

Bhera (bā'rŭ), town (pop. 20,219), Shahpur dist., central Punjab, W Pakistan, near Jhelum R., on rail spur and 30 mi. NNE of Sargodha; wheat, millet; handicrafts (felts, cutlery, wood carvings, jade work). Near by is site of old town sacked in 11th cent. by Mahmud of Ghazni, in 13th cent. by armies of Genghis Khan.

Bheraghat, India: see MARBLE ROCKS.

Bheri River, Nepal: see GOGRA RIVER.

Bhikhna Thori, rail station, India: see NARKATIAGANJ.

Bhikhna Thori (bĭk'nŭ tō'rē), town, S Nepal, in the Terai, on India border, 38 mi. NNE of Bettiah (India); trades in rice, oilseeds, corn, hides, millet. Rail terminus of Bhikhna Thori is just inside India border.

Bhilai, India: see DRUG, town.

Bhilsa (bēl'sŭ), town (pop. 14,472), SE Madhya Bharat, India, near Betwa R., 135 mi. ENE of Indore; trades in wheat, millet, gram, cotton; flour milling, hand-loom weaving. Many near-by remains of Buddhist stupas (commonly called Bhilsa Topes), dating from 3d cent. B.C. to 1st cent. A.D.; most famous lie 5 mi. SW, at SANCHI. Just N is anc. site of Beshnagar with 2d-cent. B.C. Hindu pillar; on Udayagiri hill, 2 mi. NW, are Brahmanic cave temples of A.D. c.400–600. Town sacked by Altamsh in 1235, by Ala-ud-Din c.1290, and by Bahadur Shah of Gujarat in 1532. Formerly in princely state of Gwalior. Often spelled Bhelsa.

Bhilwara (bēlvä'rŭ), town (pop. 15,169), S central Rajasthan, India, 80 mi. NE of Udaipur; trades in cotton, millet, wheat, oilseeds, mica; cotton ginning and milling, hand-loom weaving; metalware.

Bhima River (bē'mä), in central Bombay and SW Hyderabad, India, rises in Western Ghats 35 mi. NNW of Poona, flows c.450 mi. generally SE, past Dhond and Pandharpur, to Kistna R. 14 mi. NNW of Raichur. Main tributaries: Mutha Mula and Nira (right), Sina and Kagna (left) rivers.

Bhimavaram (bē'mŭvŭrŭm), town (pop. 21,049), West Godavari dist., NE Madras, India, in Godavari R. delta, 30 mi. ESE of Ellore. Rail junction (spur to Narasapur, 13 mi. SE); rice and oilseed milling; coir products (rope, mats); tobacco, sugar cane. Col. (affiliated with Andhra Univ.).

Bhimbar (bĭm'bŭr), town (pop. 2,194), Mirpur dist., SW Kashmir, 20 mi. E of Jhelum; wheat, bajra, corn, pulse. Residence of former Moslem Rajput rajas. Occupied 1948 by Pakistan. Bentonite mines N. Sometimes spelled Bhimber.

Bhimphedi (bēmpā'dē), town, central Nepal, 15 mi. SW of Katmandu. Dharsing (or Dhursing) is 2 mi. W; S terminus of 14-mi.-long aerial ropeway to Kisipidi (N terminus) in Nepal Valley; proposed extension to Katmandu.

Bhind (bĭnd), town (pop. 13,244), NE Madhya Bharat, India, 45 mi. NNE of Lashkar; rail terminus; market center (grain, cotton); cotton ginning, hand-loom weaving; brassware.

Bhindar (bēn'dŭr), town (pop. 6,443), S Rajasthan, India, 32 mi. ESE of Udaipur; market for corn, millet, wheat; hand-loom weaving.

Bhinga (bĭng'gŭ), town (pop. 7,654), Bahraich dist., N Uttar Pradesh, India, near the Rapti, 22 mi. ENE of Bahraich; trades in rice, wheat, barley, corn, timber. Founded 16th cent.

Bhinmal (bēn'mäl), town (pop. 7,503), SW Rajasthan, India, 32 mi. SW of Jalor; millet, wheat, oilseeds; handicrafts (metal utensils).

Bhir, India: see BIR.

Bhira (bē'rŭ), section of Patnus village (pop. 1,692), Kolaba dist., W Bombay, India, in foothills of Western Ghats, 50 mi. SE of Bombay. Hydroelectric plant (93,000 kw.; in operation since 1927) is supplied by reservoir 5 mi. E, on Mula R (headstream of Mutha Mula R.); powers, via Panvel, industries and railroads in Bombay city and suburban areas.

Bhita (bē'tŭ), anc. ruined city, Allahabad dist., SE Uttar Pradesh, India, on the Jumna and 9 mi. SSW of Allahabad city center. Settlement from c.7th cent. B.C. to after A.D. 400. Fortified city during Mauryan and Gupta era, after which it was deserted. Antiquities include neolithic implements, bronze, ivory, and clay seals, terra-cotta statues, copper vessels, and goldsmith's utensils. Site of 1st example of complete domestic habitations excavated in India.

Bhitargarh (bĭtŭr'gŭr), ruined city, Jalpaiguri dist., N West Bengal, India, on tributary of the upper Atrai (Karatoya) R. and 9 mi. SW of Jalpaiguri, within moats (3¼ mi. long, 2 mi. wide) leading to river. Built c.9th cent. A.D.

Bhitri, India: see SAIDPUR, Uttar Pradesh.

Bhitsanulok, Thailand: see PHITSANULOK.

Bhivpuri (bēv'pŏŏrē), village (pop. 500), Kolaba dist., W Bombay, India, in foothills of Western Ghats, 40 mi. E of Bombay; rail terminus. Dam across upper Andhra R. (14 mi. SE) supplies 72,000-kw. power plant of Andhra valley hydroelectric scheme (in operation since 1922); powers industries and railroads in Bombay and suburban areas. Substation at Kalyan, 30 mi. NW.

Bhiwandi (bĭvŭn'dē), town (pop. 18,776), Thana dist., W Bombay, India, 6 mi. NW of Kalyan; trade center for rice, cloth fabrics, glass, timber; handicraft cloth weaving, rice milling, mfg. of machinery, agr. implements, bricks, ice.

Bhiwani (bĭvä'nē), town (pop. 43,921), Hissar dist., S Punjab, India, 35 mi. SE of Hissar; trade center (grain, cotton, salt, iron, oilseeds, piece goods); cotton ginning and milling, handloom weaving, copper and brass utensils, mfg. of bobbins. Col.

Bhognipur Branch, India: see GANGES CANALS.

Bhogriwala, India: see TAJEWALA.

Bhojpur (bōj'pŏŏr), village, central Bhopal state, India, on Betwa R. and 15 mi. SE of Bhopal. Remains of richly-carved, 12th- or 13th-cent. Sivaite temple. Just W are ruins of old dams.

Bhojpur, town, E Nepal, 110 mi. ESE of Katmandu; Nepalese military station.

Bhokardan (bō'kŭrdŭn), village (pop. 3,937), Aurangabad dist., NW Hyderabad state, India, 38 mi. NE of Aurangabad; cotton, millet, wheat, oilseeds. Village of Assaye, 8 mi. E, was scene of Br. victory over Mahratta forces in 1803.

Bhola, India: see SARDHANA.

Bhola (bō'lŭ), town (pop. 7,501), Bakarganj dist., S East Bengal, E Pakistan, on NW Dakhin Shahbazpur Isl., 18 mi. E of Barisal; rice, jute, sugar cane, oilseeds.

Bholath (bō'lŭt), village, N Patiala and East Punjab States Union, India, 13 mi. NNE of Kapurthala; wheat, gram.

Bhongaon (bōn'goun), town (pop. 5,844), Mainpuri dist., W Uttar Pradesh, India, 10 mi. ENE of Mainpuri; road junction; wheat, gram, pearl millet, corn, barley, cotton.

Bhongir (bōn'gēr), town (pop. 12,170), Nalgonda dist., central Hyderabad state, India, 23 mi. ENE of Hyderabad; agr. trade center; rice and castor-bean milling; ceramics. Sometimes spelled Bhangir.

Bhongra (bōng'grŭ), village, S Rajasthan, India, 10 mi. NNE of Banswara, near Mahi R.; corn, rice.

Bhopal (bō'päl), chief commissioner's state (□ 6,921; 1951 pop. 838,107), central India; ⊙ Bhopal. Lies largely on SE Malwa plateau; bounded S by Narbada R., NW by Parbati R., S and E by Madhya Pradesh, N and W by Madhya Bharat; crossed E-W by Vindhya Range, from which streams flow S to Narbada R. and N to Betwa and Dhasan rivers. Consists largely of rolling downs and thickly forested hills; annual rainfall, 30–50 in. Predominantly agr. (wheat, gram, millet, oilseeds, cotton, sugar cane); exports grain, teak, cotton, opium. Bhopal and Sehore are chief trade centers; at Sanchi are famous Buddhist monuments, including large 3d-cent. B.C. stupa. State founded by an Afghan in early-18th cent.; ruled 1844–1926 by begums of Bhopal; acceded to India in 1947; centrally administered since 1949. Chief language is Hindustani.

Bhopal, city (pop. 75,228), ⊙ Bhopal state, India, 105 mi. ENE of Indore, on N shores of 2 artificial lakes. Rail junction, airport; trade center (grain, cotton, opium, timber, cloth fabrics); cotton and flour milling, mfg. of matches, strawboard, ice, ghee, sealing wax, sporting goods; handicraft cloth weaving and painting, jewelry making. Has old fort (built 1728) and several mosques, including large Taj-ul-Masajid.

Bhopal Agency, subdivision (□ 10,086; pop. 1,331,-732) of former CENTRAL INDIA agency; hq. were at Bhopal. Comprised former princely states of Bhopal, Dewas (Senior and Junior branches), Khilchipur, Korwai, Makrai, Muhammadgarh, Narsinghgarh, Pathari, Rajgarh. Created 1818.

Bhor (bōr), town (pop. 6,335), Poona dist., central Bombay, India, 26 mi. S of Poona; rice, millet; cotton milling, hand-loom weaving. Was ⊙ former princely state of Bhor (□ 910; pop. 155,961) in Deccan States, Bombay, which was inc. 1949 into dists. of Poona, Kolaba, and Satara North.

Bhowali (bō'vŭlē), town (pop. 1,018), Naini Tal dist., N Uttar Pradesh, India, 3 mi. E of Naini Tal, in Siwalik Range; rice, wheat, mustard.

Bhowanipur, India: see BHAWANIPUR.

Bhuban (bŏŏb'ŭn), town (pop. 7,231), Dhenkanal dist., E Orissa, India, near Brahmani R., 22 mi. NE of Dhenkanal; rice, oilseeds; handicraft metalwork.

Bhubaneswar (bŏŏbŭnā'svŭr), town, ⊙ Orissa, Puri dist., India, 30 mi. N of Puri; since 1948, being developed as model administrative center; airport; rice market. Noted for group of Sivaite temples (6th-12th cent.), which exhibit every phase of Orissan art; outstanding is Lingaraj temple (mid-7th cent.) with elaborately carved, 180-ft.-high tower. Flourished (5th–10th cent.) as ⊙ Hindu dynasty and a center of Sivaism; long a pilgrimage site. Asokan rock edict 5 mi. SW, at Dhauli. Also spelled Bhubaneshwar, Bhuvanesvar, Bhuvaneswar.

Bhucho Mandi (bŏŏch'ō mŭn'dē), village, Ferozepore dist., W Punjab, India, in enclave in Patiala and East Punjab States Union, 9 mi. E of Bhatinda; gram, wheat; cotton ginning, oilseed and flour milling; sawmill. Sometimes spelled Bhuchhu Mandi.

Bhudgaon, India: see BUDHGAON.

Bhuj (bŏŏj), town (pop. 23,282; including suburban area, 26,331), ⊙ Cutch, India, 190 mi. W of Ahmadabad; rail terminus; airport; trades in wheat, barley, cattle, cotton, salt; handicrafts (cotton cloth, silver products).

Bhuket, Thailand: see PHUKET.

Bhulua, E Pakistan: see NOAKHALI, district.

Bhupalsagar (bōō"pälsä'gŭr), village, S Rajasthan, India, 39 mi. ENE of Udaipur; sugar and oilseed milling. Also called Karera.

Bhurtpore, India: see BHARATPUR, Rajasthan.

Bhusawal (bŏŏsä'vŭl), town (pop. 36,352), East Khandesh dist., NE Bombay, India, near Tapti R., 14 mi. E of Jalgaon; rail junction (large workshops); trade center; markets wheat, millet, oilseeds; cotton ginning, hand-loom weaving, tanning, ice mfg. Also spelled Bhusaval.

Bhusawar, India: see BHASAWAR.

Bhutan (bōōtän'), Bhutanese *Druk-yul*, protectorate (□ c.18,000; pop. c. 300,000) of India, in W Assam Himalayas, S Central Asia; ⊙ Punakha. Bounded NW and N by Tibet, E, S, and SW by India; 190 mi. long E-W, up to 90 mi. wide; lies bet. 26°43'–28°N and 88°45'–92°E. Drained by Manas, Sankosh, Raidak, Torsa, and Tongsa rivers. W Assam Himalayas along undefined N border; peaks include Kula Kangri (28,780 ft.), Kangri (28,740 ft.), and Chomo Lhari (23,997 ft.); in center is Black Mtn. Range, a S spur. Agr. mainly confined to S area; rice, corn, millet, wheat, mustard, potatoes, cardamom, oranges; dispersed lac cultivation; raising of local breed of sturdy ponies. Also in S are valuable forests (including sal) with extensive wild life (leopards, tigers, deer, hogs, a few rhinoceros, large herds of elephants). Copper mines near Chamarchi. Noted for its metalware (silver, brass, copper); mfg. of muzzle-loading rifles and swords of well-tempered steel, musk and wax processing, some hand-weaving of cloth. Principal access routes (mainly in W) are from Sikkim and Tibet (through Chumbi Valley) and from India (through Sinchula Pass). Principal *dzongs* (fortress or castle; also applied to administrative divisions) are Punakha, Paro, Tongsa, Tashi Chho (containing main lamasery of Bhutan), Wangdu Phodrang, Byakar, Ha, and Dukye. S area settled by Nepalese (including Limbus, Rais) and Lepchas; principal areas are CHAMARCHI (W) and CHIRANG (trade center at Sarbhang; E). In mid-8th cent. A.D., Bhutan was converted to Buddhism by Indian Buddhist saint Padma Sambhava. In 9th cent., original inhabitants (Tephus) were conquered by Tibetan soldiers who intermingled with them to form the present Bhotias. First Br. relations with Bhutan in 1772, when Bhotias invaded Cooch Behar. In 1864, British occupied DUARS region, then a part of S Bhutan, resulting (1865) in Bhutan War which ended in same year at Sinchula; in 1866, the Duars was formally annexed by British. From mid-16th cent. to 1907, under dual control of a spiritual (*dharma raja*) and a temporal (*deb raja*) ruler; in 1907, the governor of Tongsa, Sir Ugyen Wangchuk, became 1st hereditary maharaja. In 1910 a treaty was concluded bet. British and Bhutan whereby an annual subsidy was given to Bhutan and the British were to direct the foreign affairs of Bhutan without interfering with the internal administration. In Aug., 1949, a treaty with India returned Dewangiri area to Bhutan; India assumed former role of British in subsidizing state and directing its external affairs. In 1897, an earthquake created widespread destruction. Religion professed by the dominant race (Bhotias) is the Dukpa (Red Cap) sect of Lamaism.

Bhuvanagiri (bŏŏvŭnŭg'ĭrē), town (pop. 8,882), South Arcot dist., SE Madras, India, on Vellar R. (road bridge) and 5 mi. NW of Chidambaram; rice, cassava, sugar cane; cotton and silk weaving.

Bhuvanesvar, India: see BHUBANESWAR.

Bia (bĭ'ŏ), town (pop. 3,820), Pest-Pilis-Solt-Kiskun co., N central Hungary, 13 mi. WSW of Budapest; grain, cattle, truck farming (poultry, grapes, honey).

Biabanak (bēābänäk'), village (1940 pop. estimate 6,000), Tenth Prov., in Yezd, central Iran, 105 mi. NNE of Yezd, in the desert Dasht-i Kavir; barley, gums; camel breeding. Also called Baiazeh.

Biache-Saint-Vaast (byäsh-sē-väst'), town (pop. 2,483), Pas-de-Calais dept., N France, on canalized Scarpe R. and 8 mi. ENE of Arras; rolling mill, Portland cement works.

Biafo Glacier (byä'fō), a great glacier in Karakoram mtn. system, N Kashmir, bet. main range (E) and Kailas-Karakoram Range (W); c.35 mi. long (NW-SE), bet. c.36°N 75°33'E and c.35°40'N 75°54'E. Height of snout, 10,360 ft.

Biafra, Bight of (bēä'frŭ), inlet of the Atlantic on W coast of Africa, the innermost bay of Gulf of Guinea, bet. Niger delta (NW) and Cape Lopez (S); 370 mi. wide, 200 mi. long. Nigeria, the Cameroons, Sp. Guinea, and Gabon border it. Contains Sp. isl. of Fernando Po. Receives Río Muni and Niger R.

Biak (bē'ăk, –äk, bĭ'–), largest island (pop. 21,382) of SCHOUTEN ISLANDS, Netherlands New Guinea, at entrance to Geelvink Bay, just E of Supiori; 1°5'S 136°5'E; c.50 mi. long, 25 mi. wide. Generally hilly, rising to 1,936 ft. Agr., fishing. Has airport; chief town is Bosnek or Bosnik. In Second World War Biak was an important Jap. base; was regained (May–June, 1944) by U.S. forces. Also called Wiak.

Biaka, Bhutan: see BYAKAR.

Biala (byä'wä), Pol. *Biała*. **1** or **Biala Krakowska** (kräkôf'skä), town (pop. 19,564), Katowica prov., S Poland, on Biala R. (small right tributary of the Vistula) opposite Bielsko, and 45 mi. WSW of Cracow. Rail junction; center of textile industry; mfg. of woolens, hats, chemicals, brushes, soap; tanning, flour milling, sawmilling; metal- and brickworks; stone quarry, lime kiln. Fish hatching, dating from 13th cent., in vicinity. Sometimes called Biala Malopolska (mäwôpôl'skä), Pol. *Biała Małopolska*. Until 1951 in Krakow prov. **2** or **Biala Podlaska** (pôdlä'skä), Rus. *Bela* (byĕ'lŭ), town (pop. 15,007), Lublin prov., E Poland, on Krzna R. and 60 mi. NNE of Lublin. Rail junction; trade center (grain, livestock); mfg. of aircraft and construction materials (cement, shingles, etc.), flour milling, sawmilling, tanning. In Rus. Poland, 1815–1921. Before Second World War, pop. over 50% Jewish. **3** or **Biala Piska** (pē'skä), Ger. *Bialla* (byä'lä), after 1938 *Gehlenburg* (gā'lŭnbŏŏrk), town (1939 pop. 2,623; 1946 pop. 1,137) in East Prussia, after 1945 in Olsztyn prov., NE Poland, 30 mi. N of Lomza; stone quarrying. Chartered 1722. **4** Ger. *Zülz* (tsülts), town (1939 pop. 3,786; 1946 pop. 3,367) in Upper Silesia, after 1945 in Opole prov., SW Poland, 25 mi. SSW of Oppeln (Opole); agr. market (grain, sugar beets, potatoes, livestock). **5** or **Biala Rawska** (räf'skä), town (pop. 2,088), Lodz prov., central Poland, 10 mi. ENE of Rawa Mazowiecka; rail spur terminus; flour milling, mfg. of sirup, cereals.

Biala Przemsza River (byä'wä pshĕm'shä), Pol. *Biała Przemsza* [white Przemsza], S Poland, rises

W of Wolbrom, flows 35 mi. generally WSW, past Szczakowa, joining the Czarna Przemsza just SE of Myslowice to form Przemsza R.

Biala River, Pol. *Biała Rzeka* (zhĕ'kä) [white river]. **1** In S Poland, rises on Czechoslovak border 7 mi. E of Krynica, flows c.60 mi. N, past Grybow, Tuchow, and Tarnow, to Dunajec R. 4 mi. WNW of Tarnow. In upper course, forms parts of Krakow-Rzeszow prov. border; course followed by railroad N of Brybow. **2** In S Poland, rises S of Bielsko, flows 20 mi. N, past Bielsko and Biala Krakowska, to the Vistula 5 mi. SSE of Pszczyna. **3** In NE Poland: see Suprasl River.

Bialet Massé (byälĕt' mäsā'), village (pop. estimate 500), W central Córdoba prov., Argentina, 18 mi. WNW of Córdoba; health resort in the Sierra de Córdoba; granite quarrying, chalk mfg.

Bialla, Poland: see Biala, Olsztyn prov.

Bialoboznica, Ukrainian SSR: see Belobozhnitsa.

Bialobrzezie, Poland: see Bytom Odrzanski.

Bialogard (byäwô'gärt), Pol. *Białogard*, Ger. *Belgard* (bĕl'gärt), town (1939 pop. 16,456; 1946 pop. 12,211) in Pomerania, after 1945 in Koszalin prov., NW Poland, on Prosnica R. and 70 mi. ENE of Stettin, 15 mi. SW of Köslin (Koszalin), in sugar-beet and fruitgrowing region. Rail junction; furniture mfg.; linen and flour mills, tanning. Power station. First mentioned as town in 12th cent. Has Gothic church and town gate. Ger. pop. evacuated after Second World War.

Bialowieza Forest (byäwôvyĕ'zhä), Pol. *Puszcza Białowieska* (pōōsh'chä byäwôvyĕ'skä), Rus. *Belovezhskaya Pushcha* (byĭlŭvĭzh-skī'ŭ pōōsh'chŭ) (□ c.450), E Poland and W Belorussian SSR, extends c.30 mi. E-W across international border, S of Narew R., 40 mi. SE of Bialystok; average alt. 550 ft. Varied trees (pine, elm, oak, plane, lime, red fir, birch, ash); extensive swamps. One of principal Pol. hunting grounds; abundant game includes boar, aurochs, deer. Towns on edge of forest are Bielsk (Poland) and Shereshevo (Belorussian SSR). Once property and favorite hunting preserve of Pol. kings and later of Rus. tsars. Lumbering begun in 18th cent., intensified (1915–18) under Ger. occupation. First Pol. natl. park (□ 18) established 1921 in center of forest.

Bialy Bor (byä'wĭ bōōr'), Pol. *Biały Bór*, Ger. *Baldenburg* (bäl'dŭnbōōrk), town (1939 pop. 2,292; 1946 pop. 1,077) in Pomerania, after 1945 in Koszalin prov., NW Poland, on small lake, 14 mi. NNE of Szczecinek; dairying; grain, livestock. Until 1938, in former Prussian prov. of Grenzmark Posen-Westpreussen. Sometimes written Bialybor, Pol. *Białybór*.

Bialy Dunajec River, Poland: see Dunajec River.

Bialy Kamien (kä'myĕnyŭ), Pol. *Biały Kamień*, Ger. *Weiss-stein* (vīs'shtīn), town (1939 pop. 17,348; 1946 pop. 18,717) in Lower Silesia, after 1945 in Wroclaw prov., SW Poland, 2 mi. NW of Waldenburg (Walbrzych), near Czechoslovak border; coal mining; leather and shoe mfg. Chartered after 1945.

Bialy Kamien, Ukrainian SSR: see Bely Kamen.

Bialystok (byäwĭ'stôk), Pol. *Białystok*, province [Pol. *województwo*] (□ 8,696; 1946 pop. 917,563), NE Poland; ⊙ Bialystok. Borders N and E on USSR, NE on Lithuania. Agr. region of low rolling hills; heavily forested. Drained by Narew, Bug, and tributaries of the Neman. Principal crops: rye, oats, potatoes, flax. Industries are concentrated in Bialystok city; other towns are Augustow, Bielsk Podlaski, Grajewo, Elk, and Ciechanowiec. Boundaries of pre-Second World War prov. (□ 12,525; 1931 pop. 1,643,844) are considerably altered, with post-war prov. losing its E section to USSR and gaining part of East Prussia in N.

Bialystok, Pol *Białystok*, Rus. *Belostok* (byĕlŭstôk'), important industrial city (1946 pop. 56,759; 1950 pop. estimate 65,800), ⊙ Bialystok prov., NE Poland, 105 mi. NE of Warsaw. Rail junction (2 stations); major center of textile industry (woolen goods, cloth, artificial woolens, velvet, ribbons, knit goods; spinning, weaving, finishing). Iron foundry; mfg. of agr. machinery, tools, tiles, cutlery, soap, chemicals, tobacco; food processing (beer, flour, vinegar, liqueur, candy), sawmilling, woodworking. Founded 1310; passed (1795) to Prussia and (1807) to Russia; returned to Poland in 1921. Developed into a large industrial city (majority of pop. Jewish) in 2d half of 19th cent.; in 1937, pop. was 100,101. In Second World War, under administration of East Prussia; suffered heavy damage. The large Jewish pop. was forced out of the city.

Biana, India: see Bayana.

Biancavilla (byäng"kävēl'lä), town (pop. 16,076), Catania prov., E Sicily, on SW slope of Mt. Etna, 15 mi. NW of Catania, in cereal and citrus-fruit region; soap mfg.

Bianchi (byäng'kē), village (1950 pop. 4,000), W Tripolitania, Libya, on road and 20 mi. SW of Tripoli, in the Gefara plain. Agr. settlement (grain, olives, almonds, citrus fruit, grapes) founded by Italians in 1935. Has tree nursery.

Bianco (byäng'kô), town (pop. 3,127), Reggio di Calabria prov., Calabria, S Italy, port on Ionian Sea, 12 mi. SSW of Locri; wine making.

Bianco, Cape, point on SW coast of Sicily, near mouth of Platani R.; 37°23'N 13°17'E. Tunny fisheries. Site of ruins of Eraclea or Eraclea Minoa, anc. *Heracleia Minoa*, founded by Gr. colonists from Selinus (29 mi. NW) at end of 6th cent. B.C.; theater, necropolis, town wall.

Biano (byä'nō), village, Katanga prov., SE Belgian Congo, on railroad and 70 mi. NW of Jadotville; alt. 5,248 ft.; center of cattle-raising region. Also a climatic resort.

Bianzè (byändzā'), village (pop. 1,990), Vercelli prov., Piedmont, N Italy, 15 mi. W of Vercelli.

Biao (byä'ō, bēou'), town (1939 pop. 5,061) in Davao city, Davao prov., S central Mindanao, Philippines, 17 mi. NW of Davao proper; abacá, coconuts.

Biaora (byou'rŭ), town (pop. 7,214), N Madhya Bharat, India, 18 mi. NW of Narsinghgarh; market center for wheat, millet, corn, opium; cotton ginning, hand-loom weaving.

Biar (byär), town (pop. 2,600), Alicante prov., E Spain, 17 mi. WSW of Alcoy; olive-oil and wine processing; mfg. of footwear, porcelain, nougat candy. Cereals, wine, fruit, lumber; ships olives. Iron and copper deposits.

Biar, El- (ĕl-byär'), town (pop. 12,689), Alger dept., N central Algeria, a W residential suburb of Algiers; essential-oil distilling.

Biards, Les, France: see Saint-Yrieix-la-Perche.

Bia River (byä, bē'ä), W Africa, rises W of Sunyani, Gold Coast, flows c.160 mi. S to Aby Lagoon (Atlantic inlet) in Ivory Coast, Fr. West Africa.

Biaro (byä'rō), village, Eastern Prov., E Belgian Congo, on railroad and 19 mi. SSE of Stanleyville; agr. center with coffee and rubber plantations.

Biaro (bēä'rō), island (7 mi. long, 3 mi. wide), Sangi Isls., Indonesia, bet. Celebes Sea and Molucca Passage, 30 mi. NNE of Celebes; mountainous, forested. Lumbering, agr., fishing.

Biarritz (bēŭrĭts', byärēts'), town (pop. 20,447), Basses-Pyrénées dept., SW France, on the Bay of Biscay, 4 mi. W of Bayonne, one of France's most fashionable and frequented resorts, noted for its mild climate and sandy beaches (7 mi. long). Favorite residence of Napoleon III and Empress Eugenie. Visits by Queen Victoria, Edward VII of England, and Alfonso XIII of Spain gave Biarritz its international reputation. Native pop. is Basque.

Bias Bay, China: see Taya Bay.

Biasca (bēä'skä), town (pop. 2,586), Ticino canton, S Switzerland, near confluence of Brenno R. with the Ticino, 12 mi. N of Bellinzona, in the Riviera, a valley of Lepontine Alps. Granite quarries; cotton textiles. Romanesque church.

Biaschina (byäskē'nä), ravine of Ticino R., Ticino canton, S Switzerland, 7 mi. NW of Biasca; spiral railway tunnels, Biaschina hydroelectric plant.

Bias River, India: see Beas River.

Biassono (byäs'sônô), village (pop. 3,634), Milano prov., Lombardy, N Italy, 3 mi. N of Monza; sausage factory.

Biba or **Beba** (both: bĭbă'), town (pop. 15,971), Beni Suef prov., Upper Egypt, on W bank of the Nile, on Ibrahimiya Canal, on railroad, and 12 mi. SW of Beni Suef; cotton ginning, woolen and sugar milling; cotton, cereals, sugar cane.

Bibai (bēbī'), town (pop. 72,222), W central Hokkaido, Japan, 32 mi. NE of Sapporo; coal-mining and agr. center.

Biban or **Bibans** (both: bēbän'), range of the Tell Atlas, in NE Algeria, paralleling the Oued Sahel valley on S, bet. Aumale and Bordj-bou-Arréridj. Rises to 5,550 ft. Crossed (N-S) by a deep gorge (*Portes de Fer*) followed by Algiers-Constantine road and railroad.

Bibb. 1 County (□ 625; pop. 17,987), central Ala.; ⊙ Centreville. Mining and agr. area crossed (N-S) by Cahaba R. and (SE-NW) by fall line. Coal deposits in N, hog raising in plateau region (SE), cotton in Black Belt (SW). Formed 1818. Part of Talladega Natl. Forest in S. **2** County (□ 251; pop. 114,079), central Ga.; ⊙ Macon. Mfg. area (textiles, clay and wood products) drained by Ocmulgee R. and intersected by the fall line; agr. (corn, truck, cattle); clay mining. Contains Ocmulgee Natl. Monument. Formed 1822.

Bibb City, town (pop. 1,452), Muscogee co., W Ga., N suburb of Columbus; mfg. (textiles, yarns, tire cord).

Bibbiano (bēb-byä'nô), town (pop. 1,386), Reggio nell'Emilia prov., Emilia-Romagna, N central Italy, 8 mi. WSW of Reggio nell'Emilia; sausage mfg.

Bibbiena (bēbyä'nä), town (pop. 2,320), Arezzo prov., Tuscany, central Italy, near the Arno, 16 mi. N of Arezzo; mfg. (cement, woolen textiles, tanning extracts, electrical equipment). Has church with terra cottas by G. della Robbia.

Bibbona (bēbō'nä), village (pop. 1,052), Livorno prov., Tuscany, central Italy, 5 mi. SE of Cecina, in grape- and olive-growing region.

Biberach (bē'bürākh). **1** Village (pop. 1,615), S Baden, Germany, in Black Forest, on the Kinzig and 9 mi. SSE of Offenburg; metal- and woodworking. **2** or **Biberach an der Riss** (än dĕr rĭs'), town (pop. 13,291), S Württemberg, Germany, after 1945 in Württemberg-Hohenzollern, 22 mi. SW of Ulm; mfg. (machinery, precision instruments, pharmaceuticals, textiles). Has 14th–15th-cent. church, 16th-cent. town hall. Was free imperial city until 1803. Wieland b. near by.

Biberist (bē'bŭrĭst), town (pop. 4,774), Solothurn canton, NW Switzerland, on Emme R. and 2 mi. S of Solothurn; paper, metal products, tobacco.

Bibiani (bēbyä'nē), town (pop. 7,189), Western Prov., W Gold Coast colony, 50 mi. NW of Dunkwa, on road; gold-mining center.

Bibi-Eibat or **Bibi-Eybat** (bēbē"-ābät'), suburb (1939 pop. over 2,000) in Stalin dist. of Greater Baku, Azerbaijan SSR, on Apsheron Peninsula, 3 mi. S of Baku, on Ilich Bay of Caspian Sea; oil wells (developed 1884).

Bibile (bĭb'ĭlā), town (pop. 141), Uva Prov., SE central Ceylon, near the Gal Oya, 16 mi. NE of Badulla; rice, rubber. Hot springs near by. Sometimes Bibila.

Bibiyana River (bĭbĭyä'nŭ), E Pakistan, W arm of Kusiyara R. arm of Surma R. system; 25 mi. long.

Biblián (bēblēän'), town (1950 pop. 2,029), Cañar prov., S central Ecuador, in the Andes, on rail and highway, and 3 mi. NW of Azogues, in fertile valley (corn, potatoes, fruit, stock). Visited by pilgrims for its near-by church and shrine. Also has coal mines.

Biblis (bĭ'blĭs), village (pop. 4,571), Rhenish Hesse, W Germany, after 1945 in Hesse, 5 mi. NE of Worms; rail junction; wine.

Bibosi, Bolivia: see General Saavedra.

Bibra, Bad, Germany: see Bad Bibra.

Bibracte (bĭbrăk'tē), former stronghold of Gaul occupying site atop Mont Beuvray (2,657 ft.), in central France, on Nièvre-Saône-et-Loire dept. border, 13 mi. WSW of Autun. Scene of defeat of the Helvetii by Caesar in 58 B.C. Pop. of Bibracte was removed to Augustodunum (now Autun) by Augustus.

Bibundi (bēbōōn'dē), village (pop. 300), S Br. Cameroons, administered as part of Eastern Provinces of Nigeria, on Gulf of Guinea, 20 mi. NW of Victoria; cacao, bananas, palm oil and kernels. A Ger. trading station in 19th cent.

Bic (bĕk), village (pop. 1,117), SE Que., on the St. Lawrence and 10 mi. SW of Rimouski; resort; woodworking, woolen milling. Near by is Bic Isl.

Bica de Pedra, Brazil: see Itapuí.

Bicaj (bēt'sī) or **Bicajt** (bēt'sīt), village (1930 pop. 1,587), N Albania, near Yugoslav border, 7 mi. S of Kukës, on road to Peshkopi.

Bicas (bē'kŭs), city (pop. 4,166), S Minas Gerais, Brazil, on railroad and 18 mi. E of Juiz de Fora; coffee, sugar, dairy products. Kaolin, mica.

Bicaz (bē'käz), village (pop. 834), Bacau prov., NE Rumania, on E slopes of the Moldavian Carpathians, on Bistrita R. and 14 mi. W of Piatra-Neamt; lumbering center and base for excursions to near-by Ceahlau mts. and the wild gorges of Bicaz R. Former summer residence of Rumanian royal family. Hydroelectric project.

Biccari (bēk'kärē), village (pop. 4,383), Foggia prov., Apulia, S Italy, 10 mi. SW of Lucera; wine, olive oil, cheese; cement.

Biccavol, India: see Bikkavolu.

Bicester (bĭ'stür), urban district (1931 pop. 3,110; 1951 census 4,171), E Oxfordshire, England, 11 mi. NNE of Oxford; agr. market. Has church of Norman origin and remains of 12th-cent. priory. It is a hunting center.

Bicêtre, France: see Kremlin-Bicêtre.

Biche, Lac la (läk lä bēsh'), lake (20 mi. long, 10 mi. wide), E Alta., 40 mi. ENE of Athabaska. On S shore is Lac la Biche village. Drained W by La Biche R. into Athabaska R.

Bicheno, town and port (pop. 121), E Tasmania, 85 mi. NE of Hobart and on Tasman Sea; livestock.

Bichini (bē'chēnē), town (pop. 293), Zaria prov., Northern Provinces, central Nigeria, 65 mi. S of Kaduna; tin mining. Sometimes spelled Bishini.

Bichitr, Thailand: see Phichit.

Bichura (bēchōō'rŭ), village (1939 pop. over 2,000), S Buryat-Mongol Autonomous SSR, Russian SFSR, 85 mi. S of Ulan-Ude; near Khilok R., in agr. area (wheat, livestock).

Bic Island (bĭk) or **Île de Bic** (ēl dŭ bĕk'), island (3 mi. long) in the St. Lawrence, SE Que., 15 mi. WSW of Rimouski. Formerly a St. Lawrence pilot station, now a resort.

Bickendorf (bĭ'kŭndôrf), NW suburb of Cologne, W Germany; airport.

Bickensohl (bĭ'kŭnzōl), village (pop. 391), S Baden, Germany, in the Kaiserstuhl, 11 mi. NW of Freiburg; known for its wine.

Bickerstaffe, village and parish (pop. 1,429), SW Lancashire, England, 3 mi. SE of Ormskirk; coal mining; truck gardening.

Bickerton Island, in Gulf of Carpentaria, 6 mi. off NE coast of Northern Territory, Australia, W of Groote Eylandt; 12 mi. long, 10 mi. wide; rocky, wooded. Aboriginal reservation.

Bickett Knob (3,300 ft.), a summit of the Alleghenies, Monroe co., S W.Va., 7 mi. SSE of Alderson.

Bicknell (bĭknĕl'). **1** Mining city (pop. 4,572), Knox co., SW Ind., 13 mi. NE of Vincennes, in bituminous-coal area; makes concrete products; grain, fruit farms. Mine rescue station here. City grew after opening of 1st coal mine, in 1875. **2** Town (pop. 373), Wayne co., S central Utah, 7 mi. SE of Loa, near Fremont R.; alt. 7,125 ft.

Bicocca, La (lä bēkôk'kä), former village, now a N suburb of Milan, Lombardy, N Italy. Here forces of Charles V defeated the French and the Swiss in 1522.

Bicol River (bē'kōl), SE Luzon, Philippines, rises in L. Bato, flows c.60 mi. NW, past Bula and Naga, to San Miguel Bay 8 mi. NW of Naga.

Bic River (bēch), Serbo-Croatian *Bič*, N Croatia, Yugoslavia, in Slavonia; rises 12 mi. E of Slavonski Brod, flows c.35 mi. E to Bosut R. 9 mi. SW of Vinkovci. Partly canalized; partly marshy.

Bicsad, Rumania: see NEGRESTI.

Bicske (bĭch'kĕ), market town (pop. 8,319), Fejer co., N central Hungary, 19 mi. W of Budapest; rail center; distilleries, flour mills. Ger. pop. in area raises wheat, corn, cattle.

Bida (bēdä'), town (pop. 25,231), Niger prov., Northern Provinces, W central Nigeria, 55 mi. SW of Minna, E of Kaduna R.; agr. trade center; copperworking, shea-nut processing, twine, sack-making; roofing timber; cotton, peanuts, cassava, durra, yams. Drainage and irrigation development. Airfield. Former ⊙ 19th-cent. Nupe kingdom.

Bida, Qatar: see DOHA.

Bidache (bēdäsh'), village (pop. 467), Basses-Pyrénées dept., SW France, 17 mi. E of Bayonne; dairying.

Bidar (bē'dŭr), district (□ 4,825); pop. 1,023,482), W central Hyderabad state, India, on Deccan Plateau; ⊙ Bidar. Mainly lowland, drained by Manjra R. Largely red lateritic soil, with black soil in river valleys; millet, cotton, oilseeds (chiefly peanuts), wheat, rice, sugar cane, tobacco. Cotton ginning, rice and oilseed milling, tanning; cattle raising. Main towns: Bidar (trade center; noted bidri handicraft), Udgir (road center). Became part of Hyderabad during state's formation in 18th cent. Pop. 80% Hindu, 17% Moslem, 1% Christian.

Bidar, town (pop. 20,514), ⊙ Bidar dist., W central Hyderabad state, India, 70 mi. NW of Hyderabad; agr. trade center (chiefly millet, cotton, peanuts, rice); since 14th cent., center of noted bidri handicraft. Industrial school (carpentry, bidri). Architectural relics include 15th-cent. Bahmani col. and fort. Rail station called Mohamadabad-Bidar.

Bidaruhalli, India: see NAGAR, Shimaga dist., Mysore.

Bidasar (bĭdä'sär), town (pop. 8,094), N central Rajasthan, India, 60 mi. ESE of Bikaner; local trade in salt, hides, leather goods.

Bidassoa River (bēdŭsō'ŭ), Sp. *Bidasoa* (bē-dhä-sō'ä), N Spain and SW France, rises in Spain on S slopes of W Pyrenees in Navarre, flows 35 mi. NNW into the Bay of Biscay bet. Fuenterrabía and Hendaye. Forms international border for over 10 mi. of its lower course. On small, neutral Pheasant Isl. (Fr. *Île de Faisans*) in midstream 2 mi. above Hendaye, Treaty of the Pyrenees was concluded (1659) bet. France and Spain.

Biddeford (bĭd'ĭfŭrd), city (pop. 20,836), York co., SW Maine, at falls of the Saco (water power) opposite Saco and 15 mi. SW of Portland. Mfg. (textiles, textile machinery, lumber products, shoes). Settled 1630 by Richard Vines, who 1st visited area in 1616; town inc. 1718, city 1855. **Biddeford Pool,** resort village, is at mouth of Saco R.

Biddle, village (pop. 1,234, with adjacent Westmoreland City), Westmoreland co., SW Pa., 10 mi. E of McKeesport.

Biddulph (bĭ'dŭlf), urban district (1931 pop. 8,346; 1951 census 10,898), N Stafford, England, 8 mi. N of Stoke-on-Trent; metalworking; agr. market. Has hosp. for crippled children.

Bideford (bĭ'dŭfŭrd), port and municipal borough (1931 pop. 8,778; 1951 census 10,100), N Devon, England, on Torridge R. estuary (crossed by 16th-cent. 22-arch bridge), near Bristol Channel, and 8 mi. SW of Barnstaple. Mfg. of leather goods, textiles, pottery; also ironware, ship fixtures, food; market center; tourist resort. A great English port in Elizabethan times, it was starting point for expeditions of Grenville, Drake, and Raleigh. Grenville b. here. Near by is WESTWARD Ho, named after Kingsley's novel, written in Bideford.

Bideford Bay, England: see BARNSTAPLE BAY.

Bidente River, Italy: see RONCO RIVER.

Bidh, India: see BIR.

Bidhuna (bĭdōō'nŭ), village, Etawah dist., W Uttar Pradesh, India, on tributary of the Jumna and 30 mi. E of Etawah; pearl millet, wheat, barley, corn.

Bidon V, Algeria: see POSTE CORTIER.

Bidor (bēdôr'), town (pop. 2,331), S central Perak, Malaya, 35 mi. SSE of Ipoh and on railroad; tin mining, rubber.

Bidwell Bar Dam, Calif.: see FEATHER RIVER.

Bidzhan River (bējän'), Jewish Autonomous Oblast, Khabarovsk Territory, Russian SFSR, rises in S Bureya Range, flows 100 mi. S to Amur R. below Stalinsk. Lumbering along banks.

Bié (byĕ), province (□ c.175,800; pop. 700,400), central and SE Angola; ⊙ Silva Pôrto. Bounded NE by Belgian Congo, E by Northern Rhodesia, S by South-West Africa. Drained by the Okovanggo (forming S border), the Kwando (forming SE border), and several right tributaries of the Zambezi, all rising in Angola's central plateau, in NW part of prov. Mostly savanna. Sparsely populated. Commercial agr. found only along Benguela RR, in N; on it are chief towns, Silva Pôrto, Vila General Machado, Vila Luso, Teixeira de Sousa. Since 1946, Bié prov. is subdivided into 3 dists.: Bié (⊙ Silva Pôrto), Moxico (⊙ Vila Luso), and Cuando-Cubango (⊙ Serpa Pinto). Formerly spelled Bihé.

Bieber (bē'bŭr), N suburb (pop. 6,051) of Offenbach, W Germany, on left bank of canalized Main. Inc. 1938 into Offenbach.

Bieber (bē'bŭr), village (pop. c.300), Lassen co., NE Calif., on Pit R. and c.55 mi. NNW of Susanville; trade center for stock-raising and farming region.

Biebesheim (bē'bŭs-hīm), village (pop. 3,673), S Hesse, W Germany, in former Starkenburg prov., near the Rhine, 10 mi. SW of Darmstadt; wine.

Biebrich (bē'brĭkh), S suburb (pop. 27,995) of Wiesbaden, W Germany, on right bank of the Rhine (landing), 2.5 mi. S of city center. Has noted baroque castle, formerly residence of dukes of Nassau.

Biebrza River (byĕb'zhä), NE Poland, rises W of Grodno, flows 112 mi. generally SW, past Goniadz, to Narew R. 14 mi. E of Lomza. Navigable in lower course, below Augustow Canal, which links it with the Czarna Hancza. Also called Bobr.

Biecz (byĕch), town (pop. 3,745), Rzeszow prov., SE Poland, on railroad and 26 mi. ENE of Nowy Sacz; petroleum wells; sawmills; flour milling, mfg. of cement ware.

Bieda (byā'dä), village (pop. 2,722), Viterbo prov., Latium, central Italy, 11 mi. SSW of Viterbo.

Biedenkopf (bē'dŭn-kôpf), town (pop. 6,001), in former Prussian prov. of Hesse-Nassau, W Germany, after 1945 in Hesse, in the Westerwald, on the Lahn and 13 mi. NW of Marburg; mfg. (wire; iron, steel, and other metal goods). Has 13th–14th-cent. castle.

Biederitz (bē'dŭrĭts), village (pop. 4,169), in former Prussian Saxony prov., central Germany, after 1945 in Saxony-Anhalt, near the Elbe, 4 mi. ENE of Magdeburg; rail junction; sugar beets, grain, potatoes.

Biedma, Argentina: see PUERTO MADRYN.

Biei (bēā'), town (pop. 18,363), W central Hokkaido, Japan, 14 mi. SSE of Asahigawa; agr. (sugar beets, soybeans, pyrethrum), dairying, livestock raising.

Biel (bēl) or **Bienne** (byĕn), town (1950 pop. 48,401), Bern canton, W Switzerland, on NE shore of L. Biel, on Schüss R., near Aar Canal, 17 mi. NW of Bern. Watch-making center; mfg. (automobiles, radios, pianos, soap, flour); canning, printing. Modern section is at mouth of Schüss R.; medieval town was built on slopes of the Jura. Has town hall (Gothic), town church (late Gothic), West Swiss Technical Inst., Schwab Mus. (archaeological). Cable railways connect Biel with Macolin (Ger. *Magglingen*, alt. 2,885 ft.) and Evilard (Ger. *Leubringen*, alt. 2,310 ft.), health resorts W and NW of town.

Biel-, for Russian names beginning thus: see BEL-.

Biel, Lake, or **Lake of Bienne,** Ger. *Bielersee* (bē'-lŭrzā"), Fr. *Lac de Bienne* (läk dü byĕn'), W Switzerland, bordering on cantons of Bern and Neuchâtel; 10 mi. long, □ 15, alt. 1,407 ft., max. depth 243 ft.; the Jura rise on W shore. Aar R. flows into lake (E shore) through Hagneck Canal and leaves it at Nidau (NE shore), rejoining its old bed (at Büren) by means of Aar Canal. Thièle (or Zihl) Canal connects lake with L. of Neuchâtel. Schüss R. flows into lake at Biel. Strip of SE bank was reclaimed in 19th cent. and numerous lake dwellings discovered there. The Île SAINT-PIERRE is connected by a peninsula with S shore. Biel is main town on lake.

Biela, Bulgaria: see BYALA.

Bielawa (byĕlä'vä), Ger. *Langenbielau* (läng'ŭnbē'-lou), town (1939 pop. 20,116; 1946 pop. 17,269) in Lower Silesia, after 1945 in Wroclaw prov., SW Poland, at NW foot of the Eulengebirge, 35 mi. SSW of Breslau (Wroclaw); cotton-milling center; clothing mfg.

Bieldside (bēl'sīd), agr. village in Peterculter parish, SE Aberdeen, Scotland, on the Dee and 4 mi. SW of Aberdeen. Site of Blairs Col., founded 1827.

Bielefeld (bē'lŭfĕlt), city (1946 pop. 132,276; 1950 pop. 153,111), in former Prussian prov. of Westphalia, NW Germany, after 1945 in North Rhine-Westphalia, on N slope of Teutoburg Forest, 55 mi. WSW of Hanover; 52°2'N 8°32'E. Center of noted Westphalian linen industry; mfg. of machinery, machine tools, sewing machines, bicycles, pharmaceuticals, cosmetics, garments, shirts; woodworking. Has early- and late-Gothic churches; and 13th-cent. fortress, rebuilt after fire of 1877. Chartered 1214. Fell to Jülich (1346); passed to Brandenburg (1647). Second World War destruction was 30–40%.

Biele Karpaty, Czechoslovakia: see WHITE CARPATHIAN MOUNTAINS.

Bielersee, Switzerland: see BIEL, LAKE.

Bielitz, Poland: see BIELSKO.

Biella (byĕl'lä), town (pop. 24,328), Vercelli prov., Piedmont, N Italy, 24 mi. NW of Vercelli, in cereal- and vegetable-growing region; rail terminus. Chief center of Ital. woolen industry; also cotton and linen textiles, hats, furniture, soap, leather goods, beer, dyes, textile machinery, automobile parts, cash registers. Bishopric. Has 9th-cent. baptistery adjoining Gothic cathedral (1402; later remodeled), Renaissance churches, including San Sebastiano (1504), and palaces. Has industrial and commercial institutes. Near by are Santuario di Graglia (5 mi. W), a pilgrimage church of 17th–18th-cent., and Santuario di Oropa (6 mi. NNW), most frequented pilgrim resort in Piedmont (200,000 visitors annually), founded in late 4th cent.

Bielsk or **Bielsk Podlaski** (byĕlsk pôdlä'skē), Rus. *Belsk* or *Bel'sk* (both: byĕlsk), town (pop. 6,203), Bialystok prov., NE Poland, on railroad and 25 mi. S of Bialystok; mfg. of cement, non-mineral oil, stockings, liqueur; flour milling. Before Second World War, pop. over 50% Jewish; during war, under administration of East Prussia.

Bielsko (byĕl'skô), Ger. *Bielitz* (bē'lĭts), city (pop. 25,725), Katowice prov., S Poland, on Biala R. (small right tributary of the Vistula) opposite Biala Krakowska, and 30 mi. S of Katowice. Noted for its textile industry, which dates from Middle Ages; rail junction; trade center; iron foundries; mfg (machines, munitions, bricks, paper, wood products, boarding, beer, soap), food processing. Health resorts near by. Passed (1772) to Austria; returned (1919) to Poland. Joined (1950) with Biala to form a single city, Biala-Bielsko.

Biely Vah River, Czechoslovakia: see VAH RIVER.

Bienfait (bĕn'fāt), village (pop. 715), SE Sask., 9 mi. E of Estevan, near N.Dak. border; coal mining.

Bienhoa, lake, Cambodia: see TONLE SAP.

Bienhoa (byĕn'hwä'), town, ⊙ Bienhoa prov. (□ 4,300; 1943 pop. 202,000), S Vietnam, in Cochin China, on Dongnai R. and Saigon-Hanoi RR, 20 mi. NE of Saigon; timber and rubber center; oil palms, fruit orchards; mfg. (tiles, pottery). Ceramics school Granite quarries near by. Airport (military base). One of oldest cities of S Vietnam; captured 1861 by French in conquest of Indochina.

Bienne, Switzerland: see BIEL.

Bienne, Lake of, Switzerland: see BIEL, LAKE.

Bienne River (byĕn), Jura dept., E France, rises near Les Rousses in the Jura, flows 34 mi. SW, past Morez and Saint-Claude, to the Ain 2 mi. SSE of Vescles. Clockmaking and optical industry in its gorge-like upper valley. Harnessed for hydroelectric power.

Bienno (byĕn'nô), village (pop. 2,174), Brescia prov., Lombardy, N Italy, 28 mi. N of Brescia, in Val Camonica; iron mining; mfg. (agr. machinery, kitchen utensils, hosiery).

Bienservida (byĕnsĕrvē'dhä), town (pop. 2,334), Albacete prov., SE central Spain, 55 mi. SW of Albacete; olive-oil processing, flour milling; cereals, truck, wine, livestock.

Bientina (byĕn'tēnä), village (pop. 1,644), Pisa prov., Tuscany, central Italy, 11 mi. E of Pisa; macaroni factory.

Bien Unido (byān' ōōnē'dhō), town (1939 pop. 3,057), N Bohol isl., Philippines, on Camotes Sea, 50 mi. NE of Tagbilaran; agr. center (rice, corn).

Bienvenida (byĕnvānē'dhä), town (pop. 5,913), Badajoz prov., W Spain, 6 mi. ENE of Fuente de Cantos; processing of cereals, olives, grapes; stock raising. Its rail station is 3 mi. NE.

Bienvenido (byĕnvānē'dō), town (pop. 606), Puebla, central Mexico, 22 mi. E of Huauchinango; sugar, coffee, fruit.

Bienville (bēĕn'vĭl), parish (□ 826; pop. 19,105), NW La.; ⊙ Arcadia. Bounded partly W by L. Bistineau; drained by several tributaries of Red R. Driskill Mtn. (NE) is highest point (535 ft.) in state. Agr. (cotton, corn, sweet potatoes, truck), and cattle raising. Petroleum, natural gas, clay. Cotton ginning, lumber milling; mfg. of clay and cottonseed products. Formed 1848.

Bienville, village (pop. 445), Bienville parish, NW La., 50 mi. ESE of Shreveport, in agr. area. Natural-gas fields, and Driskill Mtn. are near by.

Bienville, Lake (byĕvēl') (□ 392), N Que.; 55°25'N 72°30'W; 54 mi. long, 12 mi. wide; drained by Great Whale R.

Bié Plateau (byĕ), highest section of central Angola plateau, in Benguela and Bié provs., N of Benguela RR. Rises to 8,270 ft. W of Nova Lisboa. Average alt. 5–6,000 ft. Healthful climate. European agr. settlement.

Biere (bē'rŭ), village (pop. 3,269), in former Prussian Saxony prov., central Germany, after 1945 in Saxony-Anhalt, 5 mi. SW of Schönebeck; lignite.

Bière, Mont de (mõ dü byâr'), peak (5,000 ft.) in the Jura, W Switzerland, 11 mi. WNW of Morges, near Bière village.

Bierghes-lez-Hal (byĕrzh-lāzäl'), Flemish *Bierk* (bĕrk), village (pop. 1,040), Brabant prov., central Belgium, 5 mi. SW of Hal; porphyry quarrying.

Bierk, Belgium: see BIERGHES-LEZ-HAL.

Bierné (byĕrnā'), village (pop. 341), Mayenne dept., W France, 21 mi. SSE of Laval; cattle raising.

Bierset (byĕrsā'), town (pop. 1,000), Liége prov., E Belgium, 5 mi. WNW of Liége; steel rolling mills. Just N is town of Awans (pop. 2,181).

Bierstadt (bēr'shtät), residential suburb (pop. 5,453) of Wiesbaden, W Germany, 2 mi. E of city center.

Bierstadt, Mount (bēr'stăt) (14,048 ft.), N central Colo., in Front Range, 1½ mi. SW of Mt. Evans, 9 mi. S of Georgetown.

Bierum (bē'rŭm), agr. village (pop. 585), Groningen prov., NE Netherlands, 6 mi. NNW of Delfzijl. One of oldest villages of Groningen prov.

Bierun or **Bierun Stary** (byĕ'rōōnyŭ stä'rĭ), Pol. *Bieruń Stary*, Ger. *Berun* or *Alt-Berun* (ält'-bā'-

rōōn), town (pop. 3,702), Katowice prov., S Poland, 12 mi. SSE of Katowice; mfg. of explosives.

Bierutow (byĕrōō'tōōf), Pol. *Bierutów*, Ger. *Bernstadt* or *Bernstadt in Schlesien* (bĕrn'shtät ĭn shlā'zēŭn), town (1939 pop. 4,858; 1946 pop. 1,471) in Lower Silesia, after 1945 in Wroclaw prov., SW Poland, 20 mi. E of Breslau (Wroclaw); cattle market.

Biervliet (bēr'vlēt), agr. village (pop. 993), Zeeland prov., SW Netherlands, on Flanders mainland, 7 mi. W of Terneuzen. Founded 1183.

Bierzo (byĕr'thō), district of Leon prov., NW Spain, on S slopes of Cantabrian Mts., consisting of fertile valleys of upper Sil R. and its affluents. Coal and iron mines.

Biesbosch (bēs'bôs), reclaimed fenland area (□ 55; pop. 1,517), North Brabant prov., SW Netherlands, SSE of Dordrecht; 6 mi. long, 4.5 mi. wide; bounded by Amer sec. of Bergsche Maas R. (S), by New Merwede R. (N and NW). Drained by electric pumping station; has beet-sugar refinery 8 mi. E of Dordrecht; cattle raising, dairying, truck gardening. Before reclamation, it was a lake formed (1421) by an inundation.

Biescas (byā'skäs), town (pop. 1,093), Huesca prov., NE Spain, on Gállego R. and 13 mi. ENE of Jaca; lumbering, stock raising, trout fishing. Hydroelectric plant near by.

Biesenthal (bē'zŭntäl), town (pop. 4,212), Brandenburg, E Germany, 20 mi. NE of Berlin; market gardening.

Bieshorn (bēs'hôrn), peak (13,652 ft.) in Pennine Alps, S Switzerland, 7 mi. N of Zermatt.

Biesles (byĕl'), village (pop. 918), Haute-Marne dept., NE France, 8 mi. ESE of Chaumont; cutlery workshops.

Bieszczady, Ukrainian SSR: see Beshchady Mountains.

Bietigheim (bē'tĭkh-hīm"). **1** Village (pop. 3,319), S Baden, Germany, 9 mi. SW of Karlsruhe. **2** Town (pop. 10,523), N Württemberg, Germany, after 1945 in Württemberg-Baden, on the Enz and 5 mi. NNW of Ludwigsburg; rail junction; mfg. (linoleum, furniture, wool). Has 17th-cent. town hall. Chartered in 14th cent.

Bietschhorn (bēch'hôrn), peak (12,918 ft.) in Bernese Alps, S Switzerland, 7 mi. N of Visp.

Biévène, Belgium: see Bever.

Biezelinge, Netherlands: see Kapelle.

Biferno River (bēfĕr'nô), anc. *Tifernus*, S central Italy, formed N of Boiano by junction of several headstreams; flows 52 mi. NE to the Adriatic 2 mi. SE of Termoli.

Bifuka, Japan: see Piuka.

Biga (bēgä'), town (pop. 8,182), Canakkale prov., NW Turkey, on Kocabas R. and 45 mi E of Canakkale; manganese, zinc, lead; lignite; rich agr. area (wheat, barley, rye, broad beans, vetch, corn, tobacco). Sometimes Bigha.

Bigach, Russian SFSR: see Akhtuba River.

Big Ada, Gold Coast: see Ada.

Bigadic (bēgädĭch'), Turkish *Bigadiç*, village (pop. 3,354), Balikesir prov., NW Turkey, 22 mi. SE of Balikesir; cereals, beans.

Bigand (bēgän'), town (pop. estimate 2,500), S Santa Fe prov., Argentina, 45 mi. SW of Rosario; corn, wheat, flax, alfalfa, potatoes, poultry.

Big Annemessex River (ănŭmĕ'sĭks), SE Md., tidal estuary (c.15 mi. long) entering Tangier Sound of Chesapeake Bay, c.4 mi. N of Crisfield. Fishing, oystering.

Bigastro (bēgä'strō), village (pop. 2,633), Alicante prov., E Spain, 4 mi. SE of Orihuela; plaster mfg., olive-oil processing; citrus, hemp, cereals.

Big Bald, peak, N.C. and Tenn.: see Bald Mountains.

Big Basin, valley in Santa Cruz Mts., Santa Cruz co., W Calif., c.20 mi. NNW of Santa Cruz; here in Big Basin Redwoods State Park (c.10,000 acres) are groves of giant redwoods, some 300 ft. high and 5,000 years old. Campgrounds, lodgings; sports facilities.

Big Bay, village (1940 pop. 541), Marquette co., NW Upper Peninsula, Mich., on L. Independence, near L. Superior, and 26 mi. NW of Marquette.

Big Bay De Noc (dŭ nŏk'), a N arm of Green Bay, Upper Peninsula, Mich., penetrating c.20 mi. into Delta co. Separated from L. Michigan (E) by Garden Peninsula, from Little Bay De Noc (W) by peninsula terminating in Peninsula Point.

Big Bear Lake, San Bernardino co., S Calif., man-made lake in Bear Valley in San Bernardino Mts., 21 mi ENE of San Bernardino; c.7 mi. long; alt. c.6,750 ft. Center of year-round resort region; winter sports. Big Bear City (pop. 1,434) is on E shore.

Big Beaver, village (1940 pop. 928), Oakland co., SE Mich., 9 mi. SE of Pontiac.

Big Beaver Island, Mich.: see Beaver Island.

Big Belt Mountains, range of Rocky Mts. in W central Mont., E of Missouri R.; extend c.80 mi. N–S. Rise to alt. of 9,478 ft. in S tip.

Big Bend. 1 City (pop. 207), McLean co., central N.Dak., near Missouri R., 20 mi. NW of Washburn. **2** Village (pop. 480), Waukesha co., SE Wis., on Fox R. and 19 mi. SW of Milwaukee, in farm and lake area.

Big Bend National Park (□ 1,081.7; established 1944), Brewster co., extreme W Texas, in wide angle (Big Bend) of the Rio Grande, here forming Mex. border. Region of deserts, mtn. ranges, and canyons formed by long process of uplift, volcanic activity, and erosion. Includes Chisos Mts. (up to 7,835 ft.) in S, and parts of Santiago Mts. and Sierra del Carmen (both forested at higher alt.) in E. Rio Grande bounds park on SW, S, SE, and E, passing through spectacular Santa Elena Canyon (săn'tŭ ùlē'nŭ) (15 mi. long, 1,500–1,800 ft. deep; sometimes called Grand Canyon of Santa Helena), on SW boundary; through Mariscal Canyon (c.1,900 ft. deep) on S boundary; and through Boquillas Canyon (bōkē'yùs) (c.1,600 ft. deep), on SE boundary. Area long occupied by prehistoric Indians, who have left numerous remains of their civilization; later inhabited by Apaches and visited by Sp. conquistadors and missionaries. There are camping facilities and trails and interesting variety of plant and animal life. Projected Big Bend Internatl. Park will include Mex. territory across the Rio Grande in states of Chihuahua and Coahuila.

Big Bethel, Va.: see Hilton Village.

Big Black Mountain (4,150 ft.), SE Ky., highest peak in the state, in Big Black Mts. (a short range of the Cumberlands) just S of Lynch and near Va. line.

Big Black River, central and W Miss., rises in Webster co., flows c.330 mi. SW to the Mississippi 23 mi. SSW of Vicksburg.

Big Blue River. 1 In central Ind., rises in Henry co., flows c.75 mi. generally SW, past New Castle and Shelbyville, to East Fork of White R. near Edinburg. Also called Blue R. **2** In Nebr. and Kansas, rises in several branches in SE Nebr., flows c.250 mi. S, past Beatrice, Nebr., to Kansas R. near Manhattan, Kansas. Receives Little Blue R. at Blue Rapids, Kansas.

Big Bone Lick, Ky.: see Burlington.

Big Bromley, Vt.: see Manchester.

Big Bureau Creek, Ill.: see Bureau Creek.

Big Burro Mountains, SW N.Mex., extend N–S in Grant co.; lie within part of Gila Natl. Forest. Highest at Big Burro Peak (8,081 ft.), 6 mi. SW of Tyrone. Sometimes called Burro Mts. Little Burro Mts. are NE extension.

Big Butt, peak, N.C. and Tenn.: see Bald Mountains.

Big Cabin, town (pop. 210), Craig co., NE Okla., 8 mi. SSW of Vinita, in agr. area; poultry raising.

Big Creek, village (pop. 147), Calhoun co., N central Miss., 23 mi. ENE of Grenada.

Big Creek. 1 In SW Ala. and SE Miss., rises in NW Mobile co., Ala., flows c.40 mi. S, joining Escatawpa R. in SE Jackson co., Miss., 13 mi. NE of Pascagoula. **2** In SE Ind., rises in Ripley co., flows generally SW, joining small Graham Creek to form Muscatatuck R. in W Jefferson co.; c.40 mi. long. **3** In SW Ind., rises N of Evansville in Vanderburgh co., flows c. 40 mi. NW and SW to the Wabash c.6 mi. NW of Mount Vernon. **4** In W central Kansas, rises in Gove co., flows 124 mi. E, past Ellis and Hays, to Smoky Hill R. 7 mi. SSW of Russell. **5** In NE La., rises in West Carroll parish, flows c.75 mi. SW to Boeuf R. 11 mi. W of Winnsboro. Big Creek oil field is situated along stream c.15 mi. N of Winnsboro.

Big Cypress Bayou, Texas: see Cypress Bayou.

Big Cypress Swamp. 1 In Del. and Md.: see Great Pocomoke Swamp. **2** In S Fla., large forest morass mainly in Collier co.; borders on the Everglades (E). Lumbering; oil wells at Sunniland. Contains Seminole Indian Reservation.

Big Darby Creek, Ohio: see Darby Creek.

Big Delta or McCarty, village (pop. 120), E Alaska, on Tanana R. at mouth of Delta R., and 75 mi. SE of Fairbanks, on Alaska Highway; trading post, supply point for upper Tanana Valley. Big Delta air base 11 mi. SSE, on Alaska Highway at junction with Richardson Highway; 64°N 145°43'W.

Big Diomede Island, Russian SFSR: see Ratmanov Island.

Big Eau Pleine Reservoir, Wis.: see Eau Pleine River.

Bigelow (bĭ'gūlō). **1** Town (pop. 292), Perry co., central Ark., 27 mi. NW of Little Rock, near Arkansas R. **2** Village (pop. 238), Nobles co., SW Minn., on Iowa line, 9 mi. SW of Worthington; grain area. **3** Town (pop. 132), Holt co., NW Mo., near Tarkio R., 33 mi. NW of St. Joseph.

Bigelow Mountain (4,150 ft.), on Franklin-Somerset co. line, W Maine, c.35 mi. NW of Farmington.

Big Falls. 1 Village (pop. 441), Koochiching co., N Minn., on Big Fork R., in state-forest area, and 35 mi. SW of International Falls; logging point; grain, livestock, potatoes. **2** Village (pop. 146), Waupaca co., central Wis., on Little Wolf R. (tributary of the Wolf) and 18 mi. NNE of Waupaca, in dairy and farm area.

Bigflat, town (pop. 197), Baxter co., N Ark., c.40 mi. SE of Harrison.

Big Flats, village (1940 pop. 523), Chemung co., S N.Y., near Chemung R., 7 mi. WNW of Elmira; mfg. of fertilizers.

Bigfork, village (pop. 463), Itasca co., N Minn., at head of Big Fork R., 35 mi. N of Grand Rapids; logging point; also grain, potatoes, dairy products. Near by are state forest and Scenic State Park, including wooded lake region.

Big Fork River, N Minn., formed by confluence of small fork with Bowstring R. at village of Bigfork, flows 160 mi. generally N, past Big Falls, to Rainy R. on Ont. line, 16 mi. WSW of International Falls.

Bigga, islet of the Shetlands, Scotland, bet. Mainland and Yell isls.; c.1 mi. long; rises to 108 ft.

Biggar, town (pop. 1,799), W Sask., 50 mi. SSE of North Battleford; railroad junction; grain elevators, lumbering.

Biggar, burgh (1931 pop. 1,323; 1951 census 1,437), E Lanark, Scotland, 11 mi. ESE of Lanark; agr. market. Has 16th-cent. church. Near by are remains of Boghall Castle.

Bigge Island (bĭg), in Timor Sea, at NE entrance to York Sound, NE Western Australia; 14 mi. long, 7 mi. wide; rises to 470 ft. Composed of quartzite; rugged, barren.

Biggers, town (pop. 333), Randolph co., NE Ark., 11 mi. NE of Pocahontas, bet. Current and Black rivers.

Big Geysers, Calif.: see Geyserville.

Biggin Hill, England: see Orpington.

Biggleswade (bĭ'gŭlzwād), urban district (1931 pop. 5,844; 1951 census 7,280), E Bedford, England, at head of navigation of Ivel R. and 9 mi. ESE of Bedford; agr. market, with flour mills and chocolate works. Has 15th-cent. church.

Biggs, city (pop. 784), Butte co., N central Calif., just N of Gridley; ships fruit, nuts, rice.

Biggs Air Force Base, Texas: see El Paso, city.

Biggsville, village (pop. 379), Henderson co., W Ill., 13 mi. ENE of Burlington (Iowa), in agr. area.

Bigha, Turkey: see Biga.

Bigheart, Okla.: see Barnsdall.

Big Hole Battlefield National Monument (200 acres; established 1910), SW Mont., 60 mi. SW of Butte. Field of battle (Aug. 9, 1877) on which U.S. troops under Gen. John Gibbon defeated band of Nez Percé Indians who had refused to be confined to a reservation.

Big Hole River, SW Mont., rises in several branches in Beaverhead Range of Bitterroot Range, flows N and generally E, around Pioneer Mts., joining Jefferson R. just N of Twin Bridges; drains livestock region. Length, 142 mi.

Big Horn. 1 County (□ 5,033; pop. 9,824), S Mont.; ⊙ Hardin. Irrigated region bordering on Wyo.; drained by Bighorn and Little Bighorn rivers. Livestock, sugar beets, beans. Part of Crow Indian Reservation and Bighorn Mts. in S, Custer Battlefield Natl. Monument in center. Formed 1913. **2** County (□ 3,176; pop. 13,176), N Wyo.; ⊙ Basin. Irrigated agr., oil, and coal region bordering on Mont.; watered by Bighorn R. Sugar beets, beans, grain, livestock. Part of Bighorn Natl. Forest and Bighorn Mts. in NE. Formed 1890.

Bighorn, village, Treasure co., S central Mont., on Yellowstone R., near mouth of Bighorn R., and 55 mi. NE of Billings.

Big Horn, village (pop. c.150), Sheridan co., N Wyo., on Little Goose Creek, just E of Bighorn Mts., and 9 mi. S of Sheridan; alt. 4,059 ft.; livestock, fruit.

Bighorn Basin, Wyo.: see Bighorn River.

Big Horn Mountains, W Ariz., E of Harquahala Mts., W of Hassayampa R.; rise to c.3,000 ft.

Bighorn Mountains, range of Rocky Mts. in S Mont. and N Wyo.; rise just E of Bighorn R. in Mont., extend c.120 mi. SE into Wyo., along E side of Bighorn Basin. Highest peaks are in Wyo.: include Cloud Peak (13,165 ft.), Mather Peak (12,410 ft.), Hazelton Peak (10,545 ft.). Drained by branches of Bighorn and Powder rivers. Livestock grazing, irrigated agr. in foothills. Bighorn Natl. Forest, in Wyo. part of range, contains extensive stands of pine, fir, and spruce.

Bighorn River, N Wyo. and S Mont., formed at Riverton, central Wyo., by confluence of Popo Agie and Wind rivers; flows 461 mi. N, bet. Absaroka Range and Bighorn Mts., past Worland and Basin, Wyo., to Yellowstone R. at Bighorn, Mont. Drains livestock area in foothills of Absaroka Range, and oil-producing and agr. Bighorn Basin (c.100 mi. N-S, 60 mi. E-W). Tributaries: Shoshone R., Greybull R., Wyo.; Little Bighorn R., Mont. Plan for development of Missouri R. basin provides for 2 projects on Bighorn R.: Boysen project, including Boysen Dam (now under construction), c.20 mi. NE of Riverton, Wyo.; Hardin project, with Kane and Yellowtail dams S of Hardin, Mont. Projects now in operation in Bighorn Basin are Riverton (on Wind R. at town of Riverton) and Shoshone (on Shoshone River at Cody).

Big Indian, resort village, Ulster co., SE N.Y., in the Catskills, on Esopus Creek and 25 mi. WNW of Kingston. Big Indian Mtn. (3,721 ft.) is 5 mi. S.

Big Indian Lake, Somerset co., central Maine, near St. Albans, 18 mi. NE of Skowhegan; 3.5 mi. long.

Big Indian River, Upper Peninsula, Mich.: see Indian River, stream.

Big Island. 1 Island (36 mi. long, 3–16 mi. wide), SE Franklin Dist., Northwest Territories, in Hudson Strait, off S Baffin Isl.; 62°40'N 70°45'W. **2** Island (12 mi. long, 7 mi. wide), W Ont., in S part of L. of the Woods, bet. Aulneau Peninsula and Minn. line, 40 mi. S of Kenora. Just S is Bigsby Isl.

Big Island, mill village (1940 pop. 551), Bedford co., SW central Va., on James R. and 13 mi. NW of Lynchburg; pulp and paperboard products.

Big Lake. 1 Village (pop. 480), Sherburne co., S central Minn., near Elk R., 35 mi. NW of Minneapolis; lake resort. **2** Town (pop. 2,152), ⊙ Reagan co., W Texas, in rough prairie, c.60 mi. WSW of San Angelo; market, shipping point for oil and ranching area (sheep, cattle).

Big Lake. 1 Lake, NE Ark., 11 mi. W of Blytheville; c.10 mi. long, 1 mi. wide; fishing. Migratory bird refuges. **2** Lake, Ill.: see BANNER. **3** Lake, Washington co., E Maine, 30 mi. NNW of Machias; 8 mi. long; resorts. **4** Lake, S Mont., in Stillwater co., 25 mi. WNW of Billings; 5 mi. long; average width 1 mi. **5** Lake, N.Y.: see TULLY.

Biglerville (bĭ'glŭrvĭl), borough (pop. 870), Adams co., S Pa., 7 mi. N of Gettysburg; apples, cherries.

Big Lost River, central Idaho, rises in Pioneer Mts. N of Hyndman Peak, flow NE then SE, past Mackay and Arco, and disappears into a depression in E part of Butte co.; c.120 mi. long. Dam in upper course (4 mi. NW of Mackay) forms Mackay Reservoir.

Big Manitou Falls, Wis.: see BLACK RIVER.

Big Monon Creek (mō'nŏn"), NW Ind., rises in NW Pulaski co., flows c.35 mi. generally SSE to Shafer L.

Big Moose, resort village, Herkimer co., N central N.Y., in the Adirondacks, c.50 mi. NNE of Utica. Big Moose L. (□ c.2) is just E.

Big Muddy Creek, Sask. and Mont., rises in Canada, just across international line; flows 191 mi. S, past Plentywood and Medicine Lake, to Missouri R. just W of Culbertson.

Big Muddy River, S Ill., rises in Jefferson co., flows c.135 mi. S and SW, past Murphysboro, to the Mississippi S of Grand Tower.

Bignona (bēnyō'nä), town (pop. c.2,450), SW Senegal, Fr. West Africa, in Casamance region, 15 mi. N of Ziguinchor; peanuts, timber. Military post.

Bigny-Vallenay (bēnyē'-välnā'), village, Cher dept., central France, 7 mi. NW of Saint-Amand-Montrond; wire mill.

Big Oak Flat, village (pop. c.325), Tuolumne co., central Calif., in mining and resort region of the Sierra Nevada, c.60 mi. ESE of Stockton. Yosemite Natl. Park is E.

Bigolino (bēgôlē'nô), village (pop. 1,249), Treviso prov., Veneto, N Italy, on Piave R. and 18 mi. NNW of Treviso; lime and cement works.

Bigonville (bēgōvēl'), Ger. *Bondorf* (bôn'dôrf), village (pop. 421), W Luxembourg, 10 mi. SSW of Wiltz; sawmills, lumbering; potatoes, wheat, oats.

Bigoritis, Lake, Greece: see VEGORITIS, LAKE.

Bigorre (bēgôr'), region in Hautes-Pyrénées dept., SW France, roughly co-extensive with the upper Adour valley; center is Tarbes. Formerly a division of Gascony.

Big Pigeon River, N.C. and Tenn.: see PIGEON RIVER.

Big Pine, village (1940 pop. 556), Inyo co., E Calif., in Owens Valley, 15 mi. S of Bishop. Palisades Peaks of the Sierra Nevada are W.

Big Pine Key, Fla.: see FLORIDA KEYS.

Big Pine Lake, Minn.: see PINE LAKE.

Big Pine Mountain, Calif.: see SAN RAFAEL MOUNTAINS.

Big Piney, town (pop. 206), Sublette co., W Wyo., near Green R., 25 mi. SSW of Pinedale; alt. 6,780 ft.; livestock.

Big Port Walter, Alaska: see PORT WALTER.

Big Raccoon Creek, Ind.: see RACCOON CREEK.

Big Rapids, city (pop. 6,736), ⊙ Mecosta co., central Mich., on Muskegon R. rapids and c.50 mi. NNE of Grand Rapids. Agr. (fruit, grain, potatoes); dairy products; mfg. of machinery, tools, flooring. Resort. Its large gas field supplies a wide area. Seat of Ferris Inst. A state fish hatchery is near by. Settled 1854, inc. as city 1869.

Big Rice Lake, Minn.: see RICE LAKE.

Big River, village (pop. 502), central Sask., on Cowan L., 70 mi. NW of Prince Albert; lumbering mixed farming. Resort.

Big River, stream, Que.: see FORT GEORGE RIVER

Big River. 1 In NW Calif., rises in SE Mendocino co., flows c.40 mi. W to the Pacific at Mendocino. **2** In E central Mo., rises in Washington co., meanders N c.130 mi., through Jefferson co., to the Meramec 25 mi. WSW of St. Louis.

Big Run, borough (pop. 896), Jefferson co., W central Pa., 5 mi. ENE of Punxsutawney.

Big Sable River, W Mich., rises in W Lake co., flows W, widening into Hamlin L. (c.10 mi. long, 2 mi. wide) near its mouth, and enters L. Michigan just N of Ludington; c.30 mi. long. Ludington State Park is bet. Hamlin L. and L. Michigan.

Big Saline Bayou (sùlēn' bī'ō), river in E central La., flows c.30 mi. SE from its source in Catahoula L., widens into Saline L. (c.5 mi. long), and reaches Red R. 10 mi. NNE of Marksville.

Big Sandy. 1 Town (pop. 743), Chouteau co., N Mont., on branch of Milk R. and 70 mi. NE of Great Falls; coal, natural gas; timber, livestock, dairy and poultry products, grain. **2** Town (pop. 621), Benton co., NW Tenn., on arm of Kentucky Reservoir, near mouth of Big Sandy R., and 14 mi. ESE of Paris, in dairying, livestock area. **3** Town (pop. 689), Upshur co., NE Texas, 14 mi. SW of Gilmer; trade point in cotton, corn, oil, lumber area; oil refining.

Big Sandy Creek, central and E Colo., rises in N El Paso co., flows ENE to Limon, then SE, past Hugo, to Arkansas R. E of Lamar; 193 mi. long.

Big Sandy Lake, Minn.: see SANDY LAKE.

Big Sandy River. 1 In Ariz., formed by confluence of 3 forks near Hualpai Peak, W Ariz., flows c.80 mi. S, past Hualpai Mts., and joins Santa Maria R near S tip of range to form Bill Williams R.; intermittent. **2** In NE Ky. and W W.Va., formed at Louisa, Ky. (dam near here) by junction of TUG FORK and LEVISA FORK; flows 27 mi. generally N partly along Ky.-W.Va. border, past Fort Gay and Kenova, W.Va., to Ohio R. at Catlettsburg, Ky., where Ky., W.Va., and Ohio meet. Navigable by means of locks and dams. Picturesque Breaks of Sandy (gorge and rapids) are on RUSSELL FORK. **3** In W Tenn., rises N of Lexington in Henderson co., flows c.65 mi. N, past Bruceton, to Kentucky Reservoir (Tennessee R.) c.15 mi. N of Big Sandy, near Ky. line; lower course, chiefly below Big Sandy town, forms arm of reservoir.

Big Savage Mountain, NW Md. and SW Pa., ridge of the Alleghenies, rising to 3,000 ft. W of Barton, Md. N extension of Backbone Mtn., it runs c.30 mi. NE from Savage R. W of Westernport, to point WNW of Hyndman, Pa.

Bigsby Island (7 mi. long, 6 mi. wide), W Ont., in S part of L. of the Woods, bet. Big Isl. and Minn. line, 50 mi. S of Kenora.

Big Sioux River (sōō), S.Dak., rises N of Watertown, flows 420 mi. S, past Sioux Falls, to Missouri R. near Sioux City, Iowa; forms part of boundary bet. S.Dak. and Iowa. Not navigable.

Big Slide Mountain (4,255 ft.), Essex co., NE N.Y., in the Adirondacks, c.4 mi. NE of Mt. Marcy and 9 mi. SSE of Lake Placid village.

Big South Fork, Tenn. and Ky.: see SOUTH FORK CUMBERLAND RIVER.

Big Spring, city (pop. 17,286), ⊙ Howard co., W Texas, c.60 mi. WSW of Sweetwater; shipping, distributing, processing center of oil, cattle, farm region; oil refineries, railroad shops, cotton gins; mfg. of oil-field supplies, cottonseed and clay products, mattresses; dairying, meat and poultry packing. Has jr. col., state hosp.; state park near by. Founded with coming of railroad, 1881; inc. 1907. Industrial growth came after oil discovery near by, 1928.

Big Springs, village (pop. 527), Deuel co., W Nebr., 20 mi. E of Chappell and on S.Platte R.; grain, sugar beets.

Big Spruce Knob (4,695 ft.), Pocahontas co., E W.Va., 7 mi. NW of Marlinton; highest summit of Gauley Mtn., a N-S ridge (14 mi. long) of the Alleghenies. Sometimes called Spruce Mtn. SPRUCE KNOB (c.45 mi. NE) is highest point in state.

Big Squaw Mountain (3,262 ft.), Piscataquis co., central Maine, W of Moosehead L., 7 mi. NW of Greenville, in recreational area. Big Squaw Mountain village (1940 pop. 30) is on the lake.

Big Stone, county (□ 510; pop. 9,607), W Minn.; ⊙ Ortonville. Agr. area bordering S.Dak. and bounded W by Big Stone L. Grain, livestock. Formed 1862.

Big Stone City, city (pop. 829), Grant co., NE S.Dak., 10 mi. NE of Milbank and on Big Stone L., at Minn. line; resort; granite, cans, bricks; dairy products, grain.

Big Stone Gap, town (pop. 5,173), Wise co., SW Va., on Powell R., at its gap through the Cumberlands near Ky. line, and 30 mi. E of Harlan, Ky. Mtn. resort (alt. c.1,400 ft.); dairy products; bituminous coal mines. Southwest Va. Mus. (founded 1935), with regional historical and cultural collections, here. Natural Tunnel is 12 mi. S. Inc. 1888.

Big Stone Lake (25 mi. long, average width 1 mi.), NE S.Dak. and W Minn., on state boundary; source of Minnesota R. Was once part of S outlet of glacial L. Agassiz. Cities of Big Stone, S.Dak., and Ortonville, Minn., are at S end. Dam on Minnesota R. near Ortonville and dike on Whetstone Creek have raised level of lake and are units in water-conservation project. Lake is lowest point (962 ft.) in S.Dak.

Big Stone Mountain, Va.: see CUMBERLAND PLATEAU.

Big Sunflower River, Miss.: see SUNFLOWER RIVER.

Big Sur (sûr, sōōr), resort, Monterey co., W Calif., near the coast 25 mi. S of Monterey, and on Big Sur R., a short stream in Santa Lucia Range. Situated in Pfeiffer State Redwood Park (fī'fûr) (c.700 acres), with recreational facilities. Beach near by.

Big Thompson River, N Colo., rises in Continental Divide N of Longs Peak in Rocky Mtn. Natl. Park, flows 78 mi. E, past Estes Park and Loveland, to South Platte R. 6 mi. SE of Greeley. Receives water from Colorado R. (via ALVA B. ADAMS TUNNEL and temporary pipe line). Olympus Dam (60 ft. high, 1,880 ft. long; constructed 1947–49 as unit in Colorado–Big Thompson project) is just E of Estes Park; forms small reservoir; hydroelectric power.

Big Timber, city (pop. 1,679), ⊙ Sweet Grass co., S Mont., on Yellowstone R. and 70 mi. W of Billings; livestock-shipping point in rich agr., sheep-raising area; grain. Fish hatchery here. Dude ranches near by. Inc. 1902.

Big Timber Creek, SW N.J., rises NE of Glassboro, flows c.20 mi. generally NNW, forming part of Gloucester-Camden co. line, to Delaware R. at Westville. Lower 8 mi. navigable.

Big Trout Lake (28 mi. long, 20 mi. wide), NW Ont., in NW Patricia dist.; 53°45'N 90°W; alt. 770 ft. Drains N into Severn R.

Big Tujunga Canyon; Big Tujunga Creek; Big Tujunga No. 1 Dam, Calif.: see TUJUNGA CREEK.

Big Tupper Lake, N.Y.: see TUPPER LAKE.

Biguaçu (bēgwäsōō'), city (pop. 2,478), E Santa Catarina, Brazil, on the Atlantic, opposite Santa Catarina Isl., 10 mi. NW of Florianópolis; hogs, corn, sugar cane. Formerly spelled Biguassú.

Big Valley, village (pop. 209), S central Alta., on Big Valley Creek and 40 mi. N of Drumheller; coal mining, mixed farming.

Big Wells, city (pop. 1,077), Dimmit co., SW Texas, 17 mi. SE of Crystal City, near the Nueces; rail point in irrigated truck-growing area. Inc. 1933.

Big Wichita River, Texas: see WICHITA RIVER.

Big Wills Creek, Ala.: see WILLS CREEK.

Big Wood River, rises in Sawtooth Mts., S central Idaho, flows S, past Ketchum and Hailey, then W to Snake R. 10 mi. SW of Gooding; c.120 mi. long. Magic Dam (129 ft. high, 700 ft. long; completed 1907) is 19 mi. S of Hailey; forms Magic Reservoir (11 mi. long, 2 mi. wide). Used for irrigation.

Bihac or **Bihach** (both: bē'häch), Serbo-Croatian *Bihać*, town (pop. 8,330), NW Bosnia, Yugoslavia, on Una R. and 65 mi. W of Banja Luka; rail terminus; local trade center; hydroelectric plant. Orthodox Eastern bishopric. Has former Turkish castle. Formerly Turkish *Behke*.

Bihar (bĭ'hŏr), county (□ 1,070; pop. 183,531), E Hungary; ⊙ Berettyoujfalu. Level region in E part of the Alföld; drained by Rapid Körös and Berettyo rivers. Agr. (grain, corn, hemp, tobacco), dairy farming, hogs, poultry. Extensive irrigation.

Bihar (bēhär'), constituent state (□ 70,368; 1951 census pop. 40,218,916), NE India; ⊙ Patna. Bordered N by Nepal, E by West Bengal (India) and East Bengal (E Pakistan), S by Orissa, SW by Madhya Pradesh, W by Uttar Pradesh. N half of state lies in middle GANGES RIVER basin, while S half comprises major portion of CHOTA NAGPUR PLATEAU; E end of Kaimur Hills (E extension of Vindhya Range) is in W section. From the swampy Terai along N boundary the land slopes gently S through a fertile, alluvial plain to the Ganges, which crosses state from W to E; area intersected by numerous streams—chiefly GANDAK RIVER, Burhi Gandak R., and KOSI RIVER—all flowing S in several channels from S slopes of the Himalayas to the Ganges. S of the Ganges, plain is broken by N outliers of Chota Nagpur Plateau and drained mainly by Son R. (W). Extensive plateau region (2,000–3,500 ft.), in S, consists of wild hill tracts and narrow valleys, drained by Damodar, Subarnarekha, South Koel, and North Koel rivers; upland descends abruptly to Bengal plain on E; Rajmahal Hills are NE spur. Overall climate is tropical savanna, with annual rainfall in plains averaging 40–70 in. (W–E) and mean temp. ranging from 60°F. in Jan. to 95°F. in May; S plateau is cooler and slightly wetter. Bihar has total pop. density of 521 persons per sq. mi., but bulk of people live in the Ganges valley where density is over 1,000. Rich N plain also has most of state's agr. land; rice is dominant crop; corn, oilseeds, gram, barley, and wheat are also raised; sugar cane, jute (mostly in Purnea dist.), and tobacco are important cash crops. Only major irrigation work is SON CANALS system (W); projects on Kosi R. and in DAMODAR VALLEY to provide additional irrigation and hydroelectric power. Partly-forested (mainly sal) Chota Nagpur Plateau is major lac-producing area; dispersed mango and palm trees grow on plains. State has some 16,000,000 head of cattle, used primarily as draft animals; best grazing in Chota Nagpur grasslands and Kaimur Hills. Bihar contains major portion of India's mineral wealth, producing about half of the iron ore, 75–85% of the mica (India produces c.60% of the world's output), over 50% of the coal, and almost all of the copper ore, as well as lesser amounts of chromite, manganese, bauxite, cyanite, and asbestos. Rich coal fields of Jharia (Manbhum dist.), Bokaro, and Giridih (Hazaribagh dist.) are chief sources of Indian coking coal; mica is worked in Hazaribagh, Manbhum, and Gaya dists.; iron (hematite) and copper ores are mined in Singhbhum dist. The Tata iron and steel plant at JAMSHEDPUR is largest in country; aluminum works at Muri. Cement is manufactured in places, utilizing local limestone deposits. Other industries include sugar milling and refining, rice, oilseed, and jute milling, shellac and hemp-narcotics mfg.; cigarette factory at Monghyr; railway workshops at Jamalpur. Handicrafts include silk and cotton cloth, metalware, pottery, stonework. Principal cities are PATNA, Jamshedpur, Gaya, MONGHYR, Bhagalpur, Darbhanga, RANCHI, Chapra, Bihar, Muzaffarpur, and Arrah. Two E-W railroads traverse state just N and S of the Ganges;

in N, Raxaul is Indian frontier point for only railway into Nepal; in S, major mining centers have rail connections with main lines crossing Chota Nagpur Plateau; small steamers ply the Ganges; Patna and Gaya linked by air with Calcutta and Delhi. State's pop. comprises Hindus (73%), Moslems (12%), and several aboriginal tribes (14%)—mostly Santals, Oraons, Mundas, and Hos. Chief language, Bihari. Leading educational institutions are Patna Univ. and Indian School of Mines and Applied Geology (at Dhanbad). Literacy is low (9%). State derives name from city of Bihar, once the site of noted Buddhist monastery (Sanskrit *vihara*). NW part of region was in old Aryan kingdom of Mithila (or Videha), which flourished as early as 10th cent. B.C. At beginning of 6th cent. B.C., 1st of great Magadha dynasties rose to importance, with heart of its dominions in central Bihar; ⊙ was *Pataliputra* (modern Patna). In this period Gautama Buddha achieved enlightenment and preached at BUDDH GAYA, and Vardhamana Mahavira organized the Jain sect. Magadha fell, c.320 B.C., to Chandragupta Maurya; under Asokan empire (250 B.C.) Buddhism spread throughout E Asia; from 4th to 6th cent. A.D. kingdom flourished under Guptas. In 9th cent., Bihar was annexed by Pal dynasty of Bengal; then followed long period of various degrees of Moslem control, exercised by Delhi sultans (13th–14th cent.), a Bengal dynasty, Afghans under Sher Shah (mid-16th cent.), and Mogul empire (17th cent.); on Chota Nagpur Plateau tribes generally maintained semi-independence under local chiefs. After English defeated a Moslem confederacy at BUXAR in 1764, East India Co. administered Bihar as part of Bengal presidency. Formed N part of Bihar and Orissa prov. from 1912 until 1937, when it was separated from Orissa and made an autonomous prov. N dists. suffered severe earthquake in 1934. In 1941 Bihar was smaller (□ 69,745; pop. 36,340,151); it was enlarged 1948 by inc. of former Orissa states (□ 623; 1941 pop. 205,424) of Saraikela and Kharsawan; became constituent state of Indian republic in 1950. Comprises 16 dists.: Bhagalpur, Champaran, Darbhanga, Gaya, Hazaribagh, Manbhum, Monghyr, Muzaffarpur, Palamau, Patna, Purnea, Ranchi, Santal Parganas, Saran, Shahabad, and Singhbhum. Sometimes spelled Behar.

Bihar, city (pop. 54,551), Patna dist., N central Bihar, India, on tributary of the Ganges and 38 mi. SE of Patna, near railroad (Biharshariff station); road center; trades in rice, gram, wheat, oilseeds, barley, corn. Silica mining just W. Buddhist, Hindu, and Mogul ruins near by. Station also written Bihar Sharif.

Biharamulo (bēhärämōō'lō), town, Lake Prov., NW Tanganyika, 95 mi. SSW of Bukoba, on road; tobacco center. Wheat, corn, livestock.

Bihar and Orissa, former prov., India: see BIHAR, state; ORISSA, state.

Bihar-Dioszeg, Rumania: see DIOSIG.

Bihardobrosd, Rumania: see DOBRESTI.

Biharkeresztes (bĭ'hôrkĕ"rĕstĕsh), town (pop. 4,007), Bihar co., E Hungary, 28 mi. S of Debrecen; wheat, corn, tobacco, poultry.

Biharnagybajom (bĭ'hôrnŏ"dyŭbŏyôm), town (pop. 4,725), Bihar co., E Hungary, 16 mi. ESE of Karcag; wine.

Biharpüspoki, Rumania: see EPISCOPIA-BIHORULUI.

Biharshariff, India: see BIHAR, city.

Biharugra (bĭ'hôrōōgrŏ), town (pop. 2,139), Bihar co., E Hungary, 17 mi. S of Berettyoujfalu; tobacco, corn, cattle.

Bihat (bē'hŭt), former petty state (□ 16; pop. 4,365) of Central India agency. In 1948 merged with Vindhya Pradesh; in 1950 inc. into Hamirpur dist. of Uttar Pradesh.

Bihbit al-Hajarah, Egypt: see BAHBIT EL HIGARA.

Bihé, Angola: see BIÉ.

Bihen (bēhĕn'), locality, SE Br. Somaliland, on Ital. Somaliland border (just NW of Garoe), on road and 75 mi. E of Las Anod.

Bihiya, India: see ARRAH.

Bihor, province, Rumania: see ORADEA.

Bihorel or **Bihorel-les-Rouen** (bēôrĕl'-lā-rōōä'), NNE suburb (pop. 3,830) of Rouen, Seine-Inférieure dept., N France; agr. machinery mfg.

Bihor Mountains, Rumania: see APUSENI MOUNTAINS.

Bihoro (bēhō'rō), town (pop. 19,820), E Hokkaido, Japan, 15 mi. SW of Abashiri; agr. center (grain, sugar beets, potatoes, hemp); livestock raising.

Bihor Peak (bē-khôr), highest peak (6,071 ft.) in Apuseni Mts., W central Rumania, on Crisana-Transylvania border, 10 mi. ESE of Vascau. Also called Bihor-Cucurbeta. Black Körös R. rises here on W, Aries R. on E slopes.

Bihta, India: see KHAGAUL.

Biisk, Russian SFSR: see BISK.

Bija (bĭj'ŭ), former princely state (□ 5; pop. 1,058) of Punjab Hill States, India, SW of Simla. Since 1948, merged with Himachal Pradesh.

Bijagós Islands (bēzhŭgôsh') or **Bissagos Islands** (bĭsä'gŭs), small archipelago (□ c.600; pop. 15,867) in the E Atlantic, just off Port. Guinea (to which it belongs), opposite mouths of Geba R. and the Rio Grande. Consists of c.15 large isls. and numerous islets bet. 11°N and 11°40'N, and bet. 15°30'W and 16°30'W. Largest isls. are Orango, Formosa, Caravela, Roxa. Chief settlement is Bubaque. Bolama (on isl. of same name less than 2 mi. from mainland) is administratively part of mainland Guinea. Isls. are low and unhealthful. Chief products are coconuts, rice, tropical fruit; cattle and pigs are raised. Formerly spelled Bijagoz.

Bijaigarh (bĭjī'gŭr), town (pop. 2,580), Aligarh dist., W Uttar Pradesh, India, near Upper Ganges Canal, 14 mi. SE of Aligarh; wheat, barley, millet, gram, corn, cotton. Formerly also called Gambhira.

Bijainagar (bĭjī'nŭgŭr), village, S Ajmer state, India, on railroad and 37 mi. S of Ajmer; sugar and cotton milling.

Bijaipur (bĭjī'pōōr). **1** Village, N Madhya Bharat, India, 50 mi. WSW of Lashkar; trades in timber and grain. Marble deposits 5 mi. N. **2** Village, Madhye Pradesh, India: see BIJAPUR.

Bijapur (bĭjä'pōōr), district, S Bombay, India; ⊙ Bijapur. Bordered E and SE by Hyderabad, N by Bhima R.; drained by Kistna and Ghatpragha rivers. Agr. (millet, cotton, wheat, oilseeds); handicraft cloth weaving, oilseed pressing, dyeing. Sandstone, slate, and limestone quarried near Kaladgi. Bagalkot, Bijapur, and Guledgarh are agr. markets. In late-15th cent., independent Deccan sultanate of Bijapur was founded by 1st of Adil Shahi kings; overcome by Aurangzeb in 1686. Territory later passed to Mahrattas. Original dist. (□ 5,704; 1941 pop. 975,982) was enlarged by inc. (1949) of former Deccan states of Mudhol and (parts of) Jamkhandi, Ramdurg, Aundh, Sangli, and Kurandvad Senior. Pop. 87% Hindu, 12% Moslem.

Bijapur. 1 Town (pop. 48,968), ⊙ Bijapur dist., S Bombay, India, 245 mi. SE of Bombay; road junction; trade center (cotton, millet, wheat); cotton ginning, oilseed milling, mfg. of soap, chemicals, dyes, biscuits; iron and copper products. Col. In 16th–17th cent., was ⊙ Deccan kingdom of Bijapur under Adil Shahi sultans, who built many outstanding bldgs. Most celebrated tomb is Gol Gumbaz with great dome (124 ft. in diameter); also Jami Masjid, and several mosques, palaces, and pavilions. Town captured 1686 by Aurangzeb. Formerly called *Vijayapur* (city of victory). **2** Village, Bastar dist., SE Madhya Pradesh, India, 80 mi. WSW of Jagdalpur, in forest area (sal, teak, myrobalan). Also spelled Bijaipur.

Bijar (bējär'), town (1940 pop. 12,928), Fourth Prov., in Garus, NW Iran, in the Kurd country, 130 mi. SE of Maragheh and 50 mi. NE of Sanandaj; grain, tobacco, fruit; sheep raising.

Bijawar (bĭjä'vŭr), town (pop. 6,163), SW Vindhya Pradesh, India, 21 mi. SSW of Chhatarpur; markets millet, gram, wheat, cloth fabrics. Was ⊙ former princely state of Bijawar (□ 980; pop. 120,990) of Central India agency, since 1948 merged with Vindhya Pradesh.

Bijbihara or **Bijbiara** (both: bijbyä'rŭ), town (pop. 4,532), Anantnag dist., SW central Kashmir, in Vale of Kashmir, on tributary of upper Jhelum R. and 5 mi. NNW of Anantnag; rice, corn, oilseeds, wheat. Also spelled Bijbehara.

Bijela Lisica, Yugoslavia: see VELIKA KAPELA.

Bijeljina or **Biyelyina** (both: bēyĕ'lyĭnä), town (pop. 13,830), NE Bosnia, Yugoslavia, near the Drina (Serbia border), on railroad and 30 mi. NE of Tuzla; trades in cereals, cattle.

Bijelo Polje or **Biyelo Polye** (both: bēyĕ'lô pô'lyĕ), town (pop. 3,587), E Montenegro, Yugoslavia, on Lim R. and 45 mi. NE of Titograd; local trade center. Medieval seat of Serbian bishops; has monastery (c.1198). Under Turkish rule (until 1878), called Akyale.

Bijistan or **Bejestan** (both: bĕjĕstän'), village, Ninth Prov., in Khurasan, NE Iran, 35 mi. N of Firdaus, near salt desert; grain, cotton. Hand-made woolen textiles, embroidery; rugmaking.

Bijna (bĭj'nŭ), former petty state (□ 7; pop. 1,742) of Central India agency. In 1948 merged with Vindhya Pradesh; in 1950 inc. into Jhansi dist. of Uttar Pradesh.

Bijnor (bĭj'nōr), district (□ 1,869; pop. 910,223), Rohilkhand div., N Uttar Pradesh, India; ⊙ Bijnor. Bounded W by the Ganges; W Kumaun Himalaya foothills in NE; drained by the Ramnagar. Agr. (rice, wheat, gram, barley, sugar cane, oilseeds, pearl millet, cotton); sal forest (N); a major Indian sugar-processing dist. Main towns: Najibabad, Nagina, Bijnor, Chandpur. Also spelled Bijnaur.

Bijnor, town (pop. 27,900), ⊙ Bijnor dist., N Uttar Pradesh, India, near the Ganges, 75 mi. NE of Delhi; road junction; trades in grains, sugar cane; mfg. of Brahmanic thread (*janeo*). Was 17th-cent. Jat stronghold. Also spelled Bijnaur.

Bijou Creek, NE central Colo., formed by confluence of 2 headstreams in Arapahoe co.; flows N to S.-Platte R. near Fort Morgan; length, including longer fork, 114 mi. Flow is intermittent.

Bijoutier Island, Seychelles: see ALPHONSE ISLAND.

Bika, El, Lebanon: see BEKAA.

Bikaner (bĭkŭnĕr' bē'kŭnär), former princely state (□ 23,181; pop. 1,292,938) in Rajputana States, India; ⊙ was Bikaner. Established in 15th cent. by a Rajput clan; in 18th cent., saw constant struggle with Jodhpur; treaty made with British in 1818. In 1949, joined union of Rajasthan.

Bikaner, city (pop., including suburban area, 127,226), N Rajasthan, India, on Thar Desert, 170 mi. NW of Jaipur; rail junction (workshops); trade center (wool, hides, building stone, salt, grain); mfg. of woolen goods (notably carpets, shawls, blankets), chemicals, shoes, candy, cigarettes, ice, rubber stamps, soap, hair oil, toiletries; glass- and pottery works, electrical and mechanical engineering. Noted handicrafts include woolen fabrics, ivory products, lacquerware, leather goods, and jewelry. Has several fine bldgs., including Maharaja's palace (just N of walled city proper). Cols. Founded 1488 by Rajput chieftain; was ⊙ former Rajputana state of Bikaner.

Bikaner Canal, India: see GANG CANAL.

Bikapur (bē'käpōōr), village, Fyzabad dist., E central Uttar Pradesh, India, 13 mi. S of Fyzabad; rice, wheat, gram, sugar cane.

Bikar (bē'kär), uninhabited atoll, Ratak Chain, Marshall Isls., W central Pacific, 250 mi. NE of Kwajalein; 5 mi. long; guano.

Bikfeiya or **Bikfaya** (both: bĭkfä'yä), village (pop. 2,864), central Lebanon, 9 mi. ENE of Beirut; alt. 3,000 ft.; health resort known for its mineral waters; sericulture, peaches, apples, tobacco, lemons.

Bikin (bĭkēn'), city (1948 pop. over 10,000), S Khabarovsk Territory, Russian SFSR, on Trans-Siberian RR and 120 mi. S of Khabarovsk, on Bikin R. (right tributary of Ussuri R.), near its mouth; sawmilling center.

Bikini (bĭkē'nē), uninhabited atoll (□ 2), Ralik Chain, Marshall Isls., W central Pacific, 225 mi. NW of Kwajalein; 11°35'N 165°25'E; 36 islets on reef 25 mi. long. After its inhabitants were removed to RONGERIK, Bikini was scene (1946) of U.S. tests of the atom bomb. In 1949 the Bikini natives were on KILI. Formerly Escholtz Isls.

Bikita (bēkē'tä), village, Victoria prov., SE Southern Rhodesia, in Mashonaland, 50 mi. E of Fort Victoria; cattle, sheep, goats. Hq. of native commissioner for Bikita dist. Police post.

Bikkavolu (bĭkŭvō'lōō), town (pop. 6,273), East Godavari dist., NE Madras, India, 12 mi. W of Cocanada, on irrigation canal; rice milling; sugar cane, oilseeds. Also spelled Biccavol or Beccavole. Tobacco curing 6 mi. W, at village of Anaparti.

Bikoro (bēkō'rō), village, Equator Prov., W Belgian Congo, on E shore of L. Tumba, 55 mi. S of Coquilhatville; trading and agr. center, steamboat landing. Has R.C. missions and schools. Baptist mission at Tondo, 3 mi. S.

Bikschote (bĭk'skō"tŭ), village (pop. 813), West Flanders prov., W Belgium, 5 mi. N of Ypres. Scene during First World War of 1st German gas attack (1915). Formerly spelled Bixschoote.

Bikszed, Rumania: see NEGRESTI.

Bikuni (bēkōō'nē), town (pop. 4,491), W Hokkaido, Japan, on Ishikari Bay, 12 mi. NW of Yoichi; fishing, agr., livestock. Sometimes spelled Mikuni.

Bilac (bĕläk'), city (pop. 1,383), NW São Paulo, Brazil, 13 mi. S of Araçatuba; coffee, rice, grain, timber, cattle.

Bila Hora, Czechoslovakia: see WHITE MOUNTAIN.

Bilara (bĭlä'rŭ), town (pop. 8,864), central Rajasthan, India, 42 mi. ESE of Jodhpur; rail spur terminus; markets millet, wheat, cotton, gram. Canal headworks on Luni R., just N.

Bilari (bĭlä'rē), town (pop. 6,121), Moradabad dist., N central Uttar Pradesh, India, 15 mi. S of Moradabad; wheat, rice, pearl millet, sugar cane. Sugar research station.

Bilasipara (bĭlä'sĭpärŭ), village, Goalpara dist., W Assam, India, on Brahmaputra R. and 21 mi. NE of Dhubri; sal timber center; rice, mustard, jute. Also spelled Bilashipara.

Bilaspur (bĭläs'pōōr), chief commissioner's state (□ 453; 1951 pop. 127,566), NW India; ⊙ Bilaspur. In W Himalayas; drained by Sutlej R.; bordered E by Himachal Pradesh, S by detached E area of Patiala and East Punjab States Union, W and N by Indian Punjab. Chief crops are wheat, corn, rice, ginger; hand-loom weaving; timber forests. Projected dam across the Sutlej at Bhakra and weir near Nangal will serve irrigation canals and hydroelectric plants. Formerly one of Punjab Hill States; since 1948, centrally administered as a chief commissioner's state. Also called Kahlur.

Bilaspur, district (□ 7,513; pop. 1,549,509), E central Madhya Pradesh, India, on Deccan Plateau; ⊙ Bilaspur. Bordered S by Mahanadi R. and its tributary, the Seonath. Mainly plains; forested hills (NW, E) rise to over 3,200 ft.; drained by tributaries of the Mahanadi. Rice, oilseeds (chiefly flax), wheat, corn, and cotton in plains area; sal, bamboo, myrobalan in hills (lac growing; coal mining; mica and manganese deposits). Rice, flour, and oilseed milling, sawmilling. Bilaspur (rail junction; shellac mfg.) is trade center. Archaeological remains at Ratanpur. Pop. 80% Hindu, 18% tribal (mainly Gond), 1% Moslem.

Bilaspur. 1 Town (pop. 2,873), ⊙ Bilaspur state, India, on Sutlej R. and 29 mi. NW of Simla; local trade in grain, tobacco, spices. **2** Town (pop. 37,460), ⊙ Bilaspur dist., E central Madhya Pradesh, India, 205 mi. ENE of Nagpur, in Chhattisgarh Plain; rail junction (workshops); trade center; rice and flour milling, shellac mfg., sawmilling. Experimental silk-growing farm. Has col. of arts.

Village of Ratanpur, 15 mi. N, was ⊙ anc. Hindu kingdom; has noted ruins, several dating from 8th cent. **3** Town (pop. 2,990), Bulandshahr dist., W Uttar Pradesh, India, 14 mi. W of Bulandshahr; wheat, oilseeds, cotton, barley, corn. **4** Town (pop. 5,345), Rampur dist., N central Uttar Pradesh, India, 15 mi. ENE of Rampur; corn, wheat, rice, gram, millet, sugar cane.

Bilatan Island (bēlä'tän) (□ 6.7; 1939 pop. 241), in Tawitawi Group, Sulu prov., Philippines, in Sulu Archipelago, off S coast of Tawitawi.

Bilati, Belgian Congo: see LUTUNGURU.

Bilauri (bĭlou'rē) or **Kanchanpur** (kŭn'chŭnpŏŏr), town, SW Nepal, in the Terai, on India border, 32 mi. ENE of Pilibhit (India); rice, jute, oilseeds, sabai grass, vegetables.

Bilbao (bĭlbou', Sp. bēlbä'ō), city (pop. 183,200), ⊙ Vizcaya prov., N Spain, in the Basque Provs., one of leading Sp. ports, 200 mi. NNE of Madrid, finely situated amidst wooded hills on both banks of Nervión R., c.8 mi. above its mouth on Bilbao Bay, an inlet of Bay of Biscay; 43°16'N 2°56'W. The rich iron mines near by have made Bilbao—with its outlying industrial suburbs (Baracaldo, Sestao, Alzaga, Portugalete) reaching to the sea—one of the chief industrial areas of Spain; its greatest development has occurred since 19th cent. The canalized river and modern improvements permit large freighters to reach the inner harbor at Bilbao; shipping docks line the river from the city to Bilbao Bay, where the outer harbor is protected by 2 breakwaters. Containing large shipyards, it has a heavy trade with N Europe (mainly England) and with North and South America; it exports iron ore, lead, oil, wine. Bilbao is the foremost iron and steel center in Spain, mfg. rolling stock, motors, wire and cables, and machinery. Also has chemical works (dyes, explosives, fertilizers, pharmaceuticals); oil refinery; mfg. of cement, paper, electrical equipment, glass, canned fish, flour products. The old town, on right bank crowded bet. hills and river, has 2 Gothic churches (14th and 15th cent.), baroque town hall, and fine Arenal promenade. Several bridges connect it with large modern town (left bank), which has wide squares and fine bldgs. Has univ. (in Deusto suburb), nautical and engineering schools. Airport in Sondica suburb. Founded c.1300, Bilbao early received privileges from Castilian kings and has been noted since Middle Ages for its iron and steel. It was sacked (1808) by the French in the Peninsular War, and in the Carlist Wars resisted 3 sieges (1834, 1836, 1873). In the Sp. civil war, it was seat of short-lived Basque autonomous govt. (1936–37) until its capture (1937) by the Nationalists after a heroic defense of 9 months.

Bilbeis or **Bilbays** (both: bĭl'bās), town (pop. 23,694), Sharqiya prov., Lower Egypt, on Ismailia Canal, on railroad, and 12 mi. SSE of Zagazig, 32 mi. NE of Cairo; flax industry; cotton, cereals, dates. Lies on the old caravan route bet. Cairo and the East. Sometimes spelled Belbeis,Belbes.

Bilbilis, Spain: see CALATAYUD.

Bilciuresti (bēl-chōōrĕsht'), Rum. *Bilciureşti*, village (pop. 985), Bucharest prov., S central Rumania, 22 mi. SE of Targoviste; wheat.

Bilderlingshof, Latvia: see RIGAS JURMALA.

Bildeston, agr. village and parish (pop. 656), S central Suffolk, England, 11 mi. WNW of Ipswich. Has 14th–15th-cent. church.

Bildt, Het, or **'t Bildt,** Netherlands: see 'T BILDT.

Bildudalur (bēl'tüdä"lür), Icelandic *Bíldudalur*, fishing village (pop. 389), Bardastrandar co., NW Iceland, on Vestfjarda Peninsula, 30 mi. SSW of Isafjordur, on Arnar Fjord (25-mi. inlet of Denmark Strait); fish processing, canning.

Bileca or **Bilecha** (both: bē'lĕchä), Serbo-Croatian *Bileća*, town (pop. 1,215), S Herzegovina, Yugoslavia, on railroad and 45 mi. SE of Mostar, near Montenegro border. First mentioned in 1388; in Middle Ages, an important station on Dubrovnik-Nis road; from 1878 to 1918 an important Austro-Hungarian fortress.

Bilecik (bĭ"lĕjĭk'), province (□ 2,030; 1950 pop. 136,844), NW Turkey; ⊙ Bilecik. On S are Ulu Mts.; drained by Sakarya R. Sugar beets, wheat, tobacco. Coal at Bozuyuk. Sometimes spelled Bilejik.

Bilecik, village (1950 pop. 4,886), ⊙ Bilecik prov., NW Turkey, on railroad and 80 mi. SE of Istanbul; cereals, tobacco.

Bileh Savar, Iran: see BELYASUVAR.

Bile Karpaty, Czechoslovakia: see WHITE CARPATHIAN MOUNTAINS.

Bilgi (bĭl'gē), town (pop. 4,657), Bijapur dist., S Bombay, India, 13 mi. NNW of Bagalkot; millet, peanuts, cotton, wheat. Granite deposits near by.

Bilgoraj (bēōōgô'rī), Pol. *Biłgoraj*, Rus. *Belgorai* or *Belgoray* (both: byĕlgōrī'), town (pop. 4,745), Lublin prov., E Poland, 27 mi. WSW of Zamosc; rail spur terminus; mfg. of sieves, vegetable oil; flour milling, sawmilling.

Bilgram (bĭl'gräm), town (pop. 10,292), Hardoi dist., central Uttar Pradesh, India, 16 mi. SSW of Hardoi; mfg. of brassware, shoes, pottery, cotton cloth; wheat, gram, barley, pearl millet, oilseeds. Anc. Hindu remains, 13th-cent. mosques.

Bilgya or **Bil'gya** (bĭlgyä'), town (1939 pop. over 500) in Mashtagi dist. of Greater Baku, Azerbaijan SSR, on N shore of Apsheron Peninsula, 18 mi. NE of Baku; resort; vineyards, subtropical agr.

Bilhaur (bĭlour'), town (pop. 5,321), Cawnpore dist., S Uttar Pradesh, India, near the Ganges, 31 mi. NNW of Cawnpore; gram, wheat, jowar, barley, mustard. Makanpur village, 7 mi. NW, is pilgrimage center, with shrine of Moslem saint.

Bili (bē'lē), village, Eastern Prov., N Belgian Congo, on Bili R., a tributary of Bomu R., and 100 mi. NNE of Buta; mission center in cotton area; cotton ginning. Former local chief Bili waged a protracted war (until 1896) against govt. of Congo Free State.

Bilikul, lake, USSR; see ASSA RIVER, Kazakh SSR.

Bilimbai or **Bilimbay** (bēlyĭmbī'), town (1926 pop. 4,435), SW Sverdlovsk oblast, Russian SFSR, in the central Urals, on Chusovaya R. and 30 mi. WNW of Sverdlovsk, near railroad; metallurgical center (steel, pig iron, pipes); silicate mfg., charcoal burning. Developed in 18th cent. Until 1929, Bilimbayevski Zavod.

Bilimora (bĭlĭmō'rŭ), town (pop. 15,460), Surat dist., N Bombay, India, 30 mi. SSE of Surat; rail junction; trade center (cotton, millet, molasses, timber, fish); cotton, rice, and vegetable-oil (castor, rapeseed) milling, sandalwood and ivory carving, mfg of chemicals, matches, chocolates, candles, bobbins, bricks, barrels.

Bilin (bē'lĭn"), village, Thaton dist., Lower Burma, 60 mi. NNW of Moulmein, on Bilin R. (coastal stream of Gulf of Martaban); road junction.

Bilina (bē'lĭnä), Czech *Bílina*, Ger. *Bilin* (bĭ'lĭn), town (pop. 7,915), NW Bohemia, Czechoslovakia, 40 mi. NW of Prague. Rail junction; summer health resort with mineral springs and baths; exports bottled mineral waters; glassworks. Has 17th-cent. castle.

Biliran Island (bēlē'rän) (□ 192; 1948 pop. 55,104), Leyte prov., Philippines, in Samar Sea, just off NW coast of Leyte isl. across Biliran Strait (1–5 mi. wide); 20 mi. long, 12 mi. wide. Mountainous, rising to 4,230 ft. Agr. (coconuts, rice, corn), sulphur mining, fishing. Shale oil in SW area. Chief centers: Caibiran (kībē'rän, kībērän') (1939 pop. 4,306; 1948 municipality pop. 21,511) on E coast, and Naval (näväl') (1939 pop. 3,049; 1948 municipality pop. 12,506) on W coast.

Bilisht (bē'lēsht) or **Bilishti** (bē'lēshtē), town (1945 pop. 2,827), SE Albania, near Gr. border, 10 mi. ENE of Koritsa, on Devoll R. just S of L. Prespa.

Bilje, Yugoslavia: see BELJE.

Bilke, Ukrainian SSR: see BILKI.

Bilkha (bĭl'kŭ), former Western Kathiawar state (□ 135; pop. 31,790) of Western India States agency. Merged 1948 with Saurashtra.

Bilkha, town (pop. 5,422), S Saurashtra, India, 10 mi. SE of Junagarh; agr. market (millet, peanuts, cotton).

Bilki (bēl'kē), Czech *Bilky* (bēl'kē), Hung. *Bilké* (bēl'kā), village (1941 pop. 6,252), S central Transcarpathian Oblast, Ukrainian SSR, on railroad and 12 mi. NW of Khust; viticulture center.

Bilky, Ukrainian SSR: see BILKI.

Billate River (bĭlä'tä), S Ethiopia, rises in Gurage mts. 45 mi. NE of Hosseina, flows c.120 mi. S, through Great Rift Valley to L. Abaya.

Billenkamp, Germany: see AUMÜHLE-BILLENKAMP.

Billerbeck (bĭ'lûrbĕk"), town (pop. 4,016), in former Prussian prov. of Westphalia, NW Germany, after 1945 in North Rhine-Westphalia, on Berkel R. and 6 mi. ENE of Coesfeld; dairying. Has noted 13th-cent. parish church.

Billère (bēyâr'), NW suburb (pop. 2,276) of Pau, Basses-Pyrénées dept., SW France; pharmaceuticals; cooperage.

Billerica (bĭl'rĭkŭ), town (pop. 11,101), Middlesex co., NE Mass., on Concord R. and 7 mi. S of Lowell; residential; mfg. (woolens, building supplies); agr. (truck, apples, strawberries). Railroad shops. Settled 1637, inc. 1655. Includes villages of North Billerica (1940 pop. 1,571) and Pinehurst (1950 pop. 2,905).

Billericay (bĭ"lŭrĭ'kē), urban district (1951 census 43,352), S central Essex, England, 8 mi. SSW of Chelmsford; agr. market. The chantry hall where Pilgrim Fathers assembled before sailing is now mus., called Mayflower Hall. S half of Billericay was made part of model community of Basildon after Second World War.

Bille River (bĭ'lŭ), NW Germany, rises 4 mi. NE of Trittau, flows c.35 mi. W, past Bergedorf, to the Elbe at SE edge of Hamburg city center (lock).

Billesholm (bĭ"lŭs-hôlm'), village (pop. 1,294), Malmohus co., S Sweden, 11 mi. E of Halsingborg; coal mining, glass mfg.: clay quarrying.

Billigheim (bĭ'lĭkh-hīm"), village (pop. 1,186), Rhenish Palatinate, W Germany, 4 mi. S of Landau; winegrowing and -distilling. Chartered 1453.

Billingborough, agr. village and parish (pop. 996), Parts of Kesteven, S central Lincolnshire, England, 13 mi. E of Grantham; synthetic-fertilizer works. Has remains of Norman abbey and church with 150-ft. 14th-cent. tower.

Billinge and Winstanley (bĭl'ĭnj, wĭn'stŭnlē), urban district (1931 pop. 5,111; 1951 census 6,157), SW Lancashire, England. Includes agr. market of Billinge, 5 mi. SW of Wigan, and coal-mining town of Great Moss, 4 mi. WSW of Wigan. Winstanley is a country seat 3 mi. SW of Wigan.

Billingham (bĭ'lĭng-ŭm), urban district (1931 pop. 17,972; 1951 census pop. 23,944), SE Durham, England, 3 mi. NNE of Stockton-on-Tees; chemical-mfg. center; coal hydrogenation plant. Has church with 10th-cent. tower. In urban dist., on Tees R. estuary opposite, Middlesbrough (bridge), is Port Clarence, with foundries, saltworks.

Billinghurst, town (pop. estimate 2,400) in Greater Buenos Aires, Argentina, 12 mi. WNW of Buenos Aires; horticulture, poultry; mfg. (textiles, tile).

Billings, county (□ 1,139; pop. 1,777), W N.Dak.; ⊙ Medora. Agr. area watered by Little Missouri R. and rich in lignite; livestock, grain. Section of Theodore Roosevelt Natl. Memorial Park is here. Formed 1879.

Billings. 1 City (pop. 597), Christian co., SW Mo., in the Ozarks, 18 mi. SW of Springfield; dairying; poultry, strawberries. **2** City (pop. 31,834), ⊙ Yellowstone co., S Mont., on Yellowstone R. and 180 mi. ESE of Helena; 45°47'N 108°30'W. Third largest city in state; trade and shipping point of wool, livestock, alfalfa, and dairy products in extensively irrigated region; beet sugar, flour, meat products, vegetables; oil refinery; electrical equipment, farm implements. Eastern Mont. Col. of Education, Rocky Mtn. Col., airport, and one of largest sugar refineries in world here. Near by is Inscription Cave, containing anc. Indian writing on walls (found 1937). Founded 1882 by Northern Pacific RR, inc. 1885. **3** Town (pop. 620), Noble co., N Okla., 26 mi. ENE of Enid, in grain and livestock area. Oil and gas wells. Oil refining; mfg. of oil-field equipment, concrete and canvas products.

Billings Bridge, village (pop. estimate 650), SE Ont., suburb of Ottawa.

Billingsfors (bĭ"lĭngsfôrs', –fôsh'), village (pop. 980), Alvsborg co , SW Sweden, on Lax L., Swedish *Laxsjön* (läk'shûn") (7 mi. long, ½ mi. wide), on Dalsland Canal, and 16 mi. W of Amal; paper and pulp mills.

Billingsgate (–gĭt), district and site of former city gate of London, England, on N bank of the Thames, 1.5 mi. E of Charing Cross. Here are London's main fish market and fish wharves.

Billingshurst, town and parish (pop. 1,880), W central Sussex, England, near Arun R., 6 mi. WSW of Horsham; agr. market, with mfg. of agr. implements and pharmaceuticals. Has 12th-cent. church.

Billingsley, village and parish (pop. 142), SE Shropshire, England, 10 mi. NW of Kidderminster; brickworks. Has 13th-14th-cent. church. Near by are coal mines.

Billingsley, town (pop. 158), Autauga co., central Ala., 20 mi. NW of Prattville; lumber.

Billington, village and parish (pop. 2,471), central Lancashire, England, on Calder R. and 6 mi. NNE of Blackburn; cotton milling, dairy farming.

Billiton, Du. Guiana: see ONVERDACHT.

Billiton (bēlētôn'; also bē'–, bĭlē'–), **Belitung,** or **Belitoeng** (both: bĕlē"tōōng'), island (□ 1,866; pop. 73,429, including offshore islets), Indonesia, bet. S.China Sea (N) and Java Sea (S), bet. Bangka (W) and SW Borneo (E); 2°55'S 104°55'E; almost square in shape, 50 mi. long; generally low. Isl. has important tin mines, worked by Chinese labor. Other products: copra, resin, pepper, spices, trepang. Chief town and port is TANJUNGPANDAN. Isl. was opened to trade by Du. East India Co. in early 17th cent. Occupied 1812 by the British who ceded isl. 1814 to the Dutch. Tin was discovered 1851; exploitation began in 1860. Also spelled Belitong.

Billnas (bĭl'nĕs"), Swedish *Billnäs*, Finnish *Pinjainen* (pĭn'yĭnĕn), village in Pojo commune (pop. 6,507), Uusimaa co., SW Finland, 2 mi. W of Karis; metalworking (office furniture, tools).

Bill of Portland, England: see PORTLAND.

Billom (bēyō'), town (pop. 2,918), Puy-de-Dôme dept., central France, in Limagne, 13 mi. ESE of Clermont-Ferrand; livestock market; mfg. (brushes and baskets, felt hats); woodworking.

Bill Quay, England: see FELLING.

Bill Williams Mountain (9,264 ft.), Coconino co., N central Ariz., 3 mi. S of Williams.

Bill Williams River or **Williams River,** W Ariz., formed byconfluence of Big Sandy and Santa Maria rivers near S tip of Hualpai Mts., flows c.40 mi. W to HAVASU LAKE in Colorado R. on Calif. line.

Billy-Montigny (bēyē'-mōtēnyē'), town (pop. 9,622), Pas-de-Calais dept., N France, 4 mi. E of Lens; coal mines.

Bilma (bĭl'mä), town (pop. c.1,100), E Niger territory, Fr West Africa, oasis and road junction in the Sahara, 440 mi. NE of Zinder; 18°41'N 13°22'E. Exports salt and dates. Also produces peanuts, wheat, alfalfa, livestock. Airfield; meteorological station. Several smaller oases (Fachi 95 mi. WSW, Djado 175 mi. N) are in the dist.

Bilo Gora (bē'lô gô'rä), mountain range, N Croatia, Yugoslavia, in Slavonia; extends c.45 mi. NW-SE, along right bank of the Drava; rises to 966 ft. at extreme NW section, 15 mi. N of Bjelovar.

Biloli (bĭlō'lē), village (pop. 3,169), Nander dist., N Hyderabad state, India, 4 mi. SW of Kondalwadi; millet, rice.

Bilovec (bē'lôvěts), Czech *Bílovec*, Ger. *Wagstadt* (väk'shtät"), town (pop. 3,085), central Silesia, Czechoslovakia, 13 mi. WSW of Ostrava, in sugar-beet area; rail terminus; mfg. of sewing supplies and metal articles.

Biloxi (bĭlŭk'sē, -lŏk'-), city (pop. 37,425), Harrison co., SE Miss., 12 mi. E of Gulfport, on peninsula bet. Mississippi Sound (S) and Biloxi Bay (N, E); summer and winter resort; important fishing port (oysters, shrimp), and canning and packing center; boatbuilding, lumber milling; mfg. of fertilizer, machine-shop products. Coast guard air base. Near by are a U.S. military air base (Keesler Field), a U.S. veterans hosp.; and "Beauvoir," last home of Jefferson Davis, now a state Confederate veterans home. First white settlement in lower Mississippi valley was established in 1699 across bay at Old Biloxi (now Ocean Springs) by the French under Iberville; the present Biloxi was founded in 1719 and was seat of La. govt. until 1722. Inc. as town in 1838, as city in 1896.

Biloxi Bay, S Miss., arm of Mississippi Sound (c.17 mi. long, 1–3 mi. wide), partly sheltered by peninsula with Biloxi at its tip. Bridged 1930 bet. Biloxi and Ocean Springs. Receives Biloxi R. (45 mi. long) from NW.

Bilqas (bĭl'käs), town (pop. 22,205; with suburbs, 38,780), Gharbiya prov., Lower Egypt, canal center, on railroad and 30 mi. SW of Damietta; cotton ginning. Also spelled Belqas.

Bilram (bĭlräm'), town (pop. 5,101), Etah dist., W Uttar Pradesh, India, 4 mi. W of Kasganj; wheat, pearl millet, barley, corn, jowar, oilseeds.

Bilsanda (bĭlsŭn'dŭ), town (pop. 2,680), Pilibhit dist., N Uttar Pradesh, India, 10 mi. ESE of Bisalpur; rice, wheat, gram, sugar cane, oilseeds.

Bilsen, Belgium: see BILZEN.

Bilsi (bĭl'sē), town (pop. 6,236), Budaun dist., central Uttar Pradesh, India, 14 mi. WNW of Budaun; wheat, pearl millet, mustard, barley, gram. Founded 18th cent.

Bilsthorpe, town and parish (pop. 1,972), central Nottingham, England, 7 mi. E of Mansfield; coal mining. Has church dating from 14th cent.

Bilston, municipal borough (1931 pop. 31,255; 1951 census 33,464), S Stafford, England, 3 mi. SE of Wolverhampton; coal mining, pottery making, steel casting, chemical engineering, bacon and ham curing and packing, mfg. of electrical equipment. Includes (W) town of Ettingshall (pop 5,393) with metalworking industry, mfg. of tar products.

Bilt or **De Bilt,** town (pop. 7,837), Utrecht prov., W central Netherlands, 3 mi. E of Utrecht; mfg. (electric heaters, precision instruments, weighing and meat-cutting machines). Royal Netherlands meteorological station.

Bilt, Het, or **'t Bilt,** Netherlands: see 'T BILDT.

Bilthoven (bĭlt'hōvŭn), residential village (pop. 10,223), Utrecht prov., central Netherlands, 5 mi. NE of Utrecht. Tuberculosis sanatorium.

Biltine (bēltēn'), village, E Chad territory, Fr. Equatorial Africa, 50 mi. N of Abéché; native trade center and military outpost on caravan road to the Ennedi and Libya.

Biltmore or **Biltmore Forest,** town (pop. 657), Buncombe co., W N.C., just S of Asheville. Large Vanderbilt estate here.

Bilugyun Island (bŭlōō'jōōn") (□ 107), Amherst dist., Lower Burma, off Moulmein; separated from mainland by N and S mouths of Salween R. Main village is Chaungzon.

Bilwaskarma (bēlwäskär'mä), village, Cabo Gracias a Dios territory, Zelaya dept., NE Nicaragua, on Coco R. and 60 mi. NW of Puerto Cabezas; lumbering. Has airfield, Moravian mission, hosp.

Bilyarsk (bēlyärsk'), village (1926 pop. 5,640), S central Tatar Autonomous SSR, Russian SFSR, 28 mi. SSW of Chistopol; wheat, livestock. Built on site of anc. city of Blyumer, ⊙ Volga Bulgars in 10th cent.

Bilzen (bĭl'zŭn), town (pop. 5,155), Limburg prov., NE Belgium, 9 mi. SE of Hasselt; market center for fruitgrowing area (apples, cherries, plums). Formerly spelled Bilsen.

Bim, village (pop. 1,631, with adjacent Wharton), Boone co., SW W.Va., 12 mi. SE of Madison.

Bimban (bĭm'băn), village (pop. 6,619), Aswan prov., S Egypt, on W bank of the Nile and 24 mi. N of Aswan; cereals, dates. Consists of Bimban Bahari (N; pop. 3,433) and Bimban Qibli (S; pop. 3,186).

Bimbéréké (bēmbĕrĕ'kā), village, N central Dahomey, Fr. West Africa, on road and 55 mi. N of Parakou; cotton, peanuts, shea nuts, livestock.

Bimbia River (bēm'byä), Br. Cameroons, a W arm of Cameroon R., on Gulf of Guinea. On right bank are port of Tiko and (at mouth) Bimbia village on Cape Nachtigal (3°55'N 9°16'E).

Bimbo (bēmbō'), village, S Ubangi-Shari, Fr. Equatorial Africa, on Ubangi R. (Belgian Congo border) and 13 mi. SW of Bangui.

Bimini Islands (bĭ'mĭnē, bŭmē'nē) or **Biminis** (-ēz), islands and district (□ 8.5; pop. 718), NW Bahama Isls., on the Straits of Florida, 55 mi. E of Miami (Fla.), 110 mi. W of Nassau. Consist of a string of cays extending 45 mi. N-S. The largest, North and South Bimini, are at N end, adjoined S by the Cat Cays, among them Gun Cay. Products: sponge, fish, sisal, coconuts, corn. Chief settlements, Alice Town and Bailey's Town, both on North Bimini. The Lerner Marine Laboratory is just N of Bailey's Town. Increasingly popular as a tourist resort within easy reach of Florida. The legendary Fountain of Youth which Ponce de Leon searched for was supposed to have been situated here.

Bimlipatam (bĭm'lēpŭtŭm), since 1949 officially **Bimlipatnam** (-pŭtnŭm), city (pop. 9,914), Vizagapatam dist., NE Madras, India, port (roadstead) on Bay of Bengal, 16 mi. NNE of Vizagapatam; exports sunn hemp (jute substitute) and jute products (cordage, gunny bags), myrobalan, oilseeds; saltworks; Casuarina plantations. Ceded to English 1825 by Dutch. Sometimes called Bimly. Jute mills 3 mi. NNW, at suburb of Chittivalsa or Chittavalsa.

Bina (bē'nŭ), town (1939 pop. over 500) in Azizbekov dist. of Greater Baku, Azerbaijan SSR, on E Apsheron Peninsula, 14 mi. ENE of Baku, on electric railroad; vineyards. Airfield.

Binab, Iran: see BUNAB.

Binaced (bēnä-thādh'), village (pop. 1,561), Huesca prov., NE Spain, 26 mi. NW of Lérida, in irrigated agr. area (wine, sugar beets, alfalfa); olive-oil processing, sawmilling.

Binacka Morava, river, Yugoslavia: see SOUTHERN MORAVA RIVER.

Bina-Etawa, India: see ETAWA, town, Madhya Pradesh.

Binagady (bē"nŭgŭdē'), town (1926 pop. 1,170) in Kirov dist. of Greater Baku, Azerbaijan SSR, on W Apsheron Peninsula, 7 mi. N of Baku; oil wells (developed 1903).

Binalbagan (bēnälbä'gän), town (1939 pop. 11,057; 1948 municipality pop. 19,748), Negros Occidental prov., W Negros isl., Philippines, on Panay Gulf, 34 mi. SSW of Bacolod; trade center for agr. area (rice, sugar cane). Sugar mill, distillery.

Binalonan (bēnälō'nän), town (1939 pop. 2,610; 1948 municipality pop. 23,361), Pangasinan prov., central Luzon, Philippines, 17 mi. E of Dagupan; road center; agr. (rice, corn, copra).

Binalud Range (bēnälōōd'), Persian *Kuh-i-Binalud* (kōō'hē-), one of the Turkmen-Khurasan ranges in NE Iran, rising to 10,000 ft. 40 mi. W of Meshed. Kashaf R. flows at N foot. Range is continued NW by the Ala Dagh.

Biñan (bēnyän'), town (1939 pop. 1,619; 1948 municipality pop. 20,794), Laguna prov., S Luzon, Philippines, on Laguna de Bay, 20 mi. SSE of Manila; agr. center (rice, coconuts, sugar cane).

Binangonan (bēnäng-ō'nän), town (1939 pop. 3,673; 1948 municipality pop. 20,422), Rizal prov., S Luzon, Philippines, on peninsula in Laguna de Bay, 15 mi. SE of Manila; agr. center (rice, fruit); cement factory.

Binarville (bēnärvēl'), village (pop. 214), Marne dept., N France, on W slope of the Argonne, 11 mi. N of Sainte-Menehould. The "Lost Battalion" fought 1.5 mi. NE of here (Oct., 1918).

Binasco (bēnä'skō), village (pop. 2,740), Milano prov., Lombardy, N Italy, 10 mi. SSW of Milan; benzine; sausage.

Binatang (bē'nätäng), town (pop. 1,840), W Sarawak, port on Rajang R. and 100 mi. ENE of Kuching.

Binboga Mountains (bĭnbôä'), Turkish *Binboğa*, S central Turkey, part of the Anti-Taurus, extend 25 mi. NNE from Goksun; rise to 9,285 ft. in Binboga Dag.

Binbrook, agr. village and parish (pop. 738), Parts of Lindsey, N Lincolnshire, England, 9 mi. NW of Louth.

Binche (bēsh), town (pop. 10,716), Hainaut prov., S Belgium, 10 mi. ESE of Mons; mfg. (clothing, lace). Has carnival (started in 16th cent.) to celebrate conquest of Peru by Spaniards.

Binchester, agr. village and parish (pop. 60), central Durham, England, on Wear R. and 2 mi. NE of Bishop Auckland. Site of Roman station of *Vinovia*. Near by is 7th-cent. church.

Bindalseidet (bĭn'näls-ā"dŭ), village in Bindal canton (pop. 2,866), Nordland co., central Norway, on inlet of North Sea, 50 mi. NNE of Namsos; agr., cattle raising, lumbering; sawmilling, boatbuilding. At Terrak (tĕr'rôk) (Nor. *Terråk*) village (pop. 213), 3 mi. SE: mfg. of lumber, wood pulp, wood products.

Bindar (bĭn'där), village (pop. 12,985), Girga prov., central Upper Egypt, on railroad and 4 mi. NW of Girga; cotton, cereals, dates, sugar.

Bindhachal, India: see MIRZAPUR, city.

Bindjai, Indonesia: see BINJAI.

Bindki (bĭnd'kē), town (pop. 10,454), Fatehpur dist., S Uttar Pradesh, India, 16 mi. NW of Fatehpur; road junction; trade center (gram, barley, rice, jowar, wheat, ghee, cattle).

Bindloe Island, Galápagos: see MARCHENA ISLAND.

Bindraban, India: see BRINDABAN.

Bindura (bēndōō'rä), town (pop. 659), Salisbury prov., NE Southern Rhodesia, in Mashonaland, on railroad and 40 mi. NNE of Salisbury; alt. 3,737 ft. Major gold-mining and agr. center; tobacco, cotton, peanuts, corn, citrus fruit; dairy products. Just W is Phoenix Prince (or Prince of Wales) mine township (pop. 1,301).

Binéfar (bēnā'fär), town (pop. 3,395), Huesca prov., NE Spain, 24 mi. NW of Lérida; hardware mfg., vegetable canning, olive-oil processing, flour milling. Agr. trade (livestock, sugar beets, wine, grain).

Bin el Ouidane, Fr. Morocco: see ABID, OUED EL.

Binfield, agr. village and parish (pop. 2,104), E Berkshire, England, 3 mi. NE of Wokingham. Has 14th–15th-cent. church. Pope spent his boyhood here.

Binford, village (pop. 309), Griggs co., E central N.Dak., 13 mi. NW of Cooperstown.

Binga (bĭng'gä), village, Equator Prov., NW Belgian Congo, on left bank of Mongala R. and 75 mi. WNW of Lisala; agr. and trading center; coffee processing, palm-oil milling. R.C. mission at Busu Baya, 15 mi. W.

Bingara (bĭng-gă'rŭ), town (pop. 1,511), N New South Wales, Australia, on Gwydir R. and 220 mi. NNW of Newcastle; gold-mining center.

Bingemma Hills (bĭnjĕm'mä), low limestone ridge in W Malta, extends c.5 mi. SW from Mosta to the coast, rising over 700 ft. Has Phoenician vaults.

Bingen (bĭng'ŭn), town (pop. 15,373), Rhenish Hesse, W Germany, port on left bank of the Rhine (rail bridge), just above whirlpool known as Binger Loch, at mouth of Nahe R. (rail bridge), 8 mi. N of Bad Kreuznach; rail junction; cigar mfg.; noted wine. Active river trade (coal, wood, fertilizer, wine). Has 15th-cent. church. Medieval castle of Klopp (renovated in 19th cent.) towers above town. Bingen was important Roman fortress. Joined Hanseatic League in 1254. Came to archbishops of Mainz in 1281, to Hesse in 1803. Below Bingen, on a rock in the Rhine, is the well-known Mäuseturm [Mouse Tower], where, according to legend, Archbishop Hatto of Mainz was devoured by mice for wronging his subjects.

Bingen (bĭn'jŭn), town (pop. 736), Klickitat co., S Wash., 3 mi. across Columbia R. NE of Hood River, Oregon, and 55 mi. E of Vancouver. Sawmills; apples, pears, dairy products, truck.

Binger (bĭng'ŭr), town (pop. 773), in Caddo co., W central Okla., 17 mi. NNW of Anadarko, in agr. area (wheat, cotton, corn); oil wells; cotton ginning.

Bingerville (bĕzhāvēl'), town (pop. c.650), SE Ivory Coast, Fr. West Africa, near Ebrié Lagoon (Atlantic inlet), 7 mi. E of Abidjan. Former ⊙ Ivory Coast (1900–35), it is still seat of govt. offices of agr. and education. Has school of agr. and forestry; experiment station (chiefly cacao and coffee). Region produces coffee and palm kernels.

Bingham, town and parish (pop. 1,587), S Nottingham, England, 8 mi. E of Nottingham; agr. market in dairying region. Has 15th-cent. church.

Bingham, county (□ 2,072; pop. 23,271), SE Idaho; ⊙ Blackfoot. Irrigated agr. area drained by Snake and Blackfoot rivers and American Falls Reservoir. Part of Snake River Plain in W and of Fort Hall Indian Reservation in S. Potatoes, dry beans, sugar beets, livestock. Formed 1885.

Bingham. 1 Village (pop. 170), Fayette co., S central Ill., 11 mi. NNW of Vandalia, in agr. area. **2** Town (pop. 1,354), Somerset co., central Maine, on the Kennebec and 22 mi. NNW of Skowhegan, in resort area; wood products. Wyman Dam (for hydroelectric power) impounds Wyman L. here. Settled 1780, inc. 1812. **3** Town (pop. 169), Dillon co., NE S.C., 20 mi. NE of Florence. **4** Town, Utah: see BINGHAM CANYON.

Bingham Canyon or **Bingham,** mining town (pop. 2,569), Salt Lake co., N central Utah, 22 mi. SW of Salt Lake City, in Oquirrh Mts.; alt. 6,100 ft. Area produces lead, zinc, gold, silver, and, especially, copper. Settled 1848 by Mormons. Grew as mining point. Mtn. tunnel (6,988 ft. long; for automobiles and pedestrians) extends to Upper Bingham, where there is a large, open-pit copper mine.

Bingham Lake, village (pop. 229), Cottonwood co., SW Minn., on small lake, near Des Moines R., 4 mi. ENE of Windom, in corn, oat, barley area.

Binghamstown, Gaelic *Sáilín*, agr. village (district pop. 2,894), on Mullet Peninsula, NW Co. Mayo, Ireland, near Blacksod Bay, 3 mi. SW of Belmullet; cattle, pigs; potatoes, oats. Near by are remains of anc. Cross Abbey. Islet of Inishglora is off coast.

Binghamton (bĭng'ŭmtŭn), industrial city (pop. 80,674), ⊙ Broome co., S N.Y., at junction of Chenango and Susquehanna rivers, near Pa. line, c.65 mi. S of Syracuse; with neighboring Endicott and Johnson City, comprises the Triple Cities, known for shoe mfg. Shipping center for agr. and industrial products; also mfg. of photographic supplies, textiles, flour, furniture, clothing, airplanes, refrigerators, machinery, metal and wire products, cosmetics, patent medicines; printing. Seat of a state institute of applied arts and sciences and a state mental hosp. Chenango Valley State Park is near by. Laid out 1800; inc. as village in 1813, as city in 1867. Grew after opening of Chenango Canal to Utica (1837) and coming of Erie RR (1848).

Bingley (bĭng'lē), urban district (1931 pop. 20,553; 1951 census 21,566), West Riding, W central Yorkshire, England, on Aire R. and 5 mi. NW of Bradford; woolen and silk milling, leather tanning and mfg.; also produces paper, machine tools, paint.

The church contains an 8th-cent. stone with Runic inscriptions. In urban dist. are suburbs of Harden (WSW) with leatherworks, East Morton (N) with woolen and paper mills, and Wilsden (SW) with woolen mills.

Bingo (bĭng'gō), former province in SW Honshu, Japan; now part of Hiroshima prefecture.

Bingol (bĭngûl'), Turkish *Bingöl*, province (□ 3,307; 1950 pop. 97,225), E central Turkey; ⊙ Bingol. On S are Bitlis Mts.; drained by Murat and Peri rivers; mountainous and unproductive. Formerly Genc.

Bingol, Turkish *Bingöl*, village (1950 pop. 3,728), ⊙ Bingol prov., E central Turkey, 80 mi. SW of Erzurum; wheat. Formerly Capakcur.

Bingol Dag (bĭngûl' dä), Turkish *Bingöl Dağ*, peak (11,975 ft.), E central Turkey, 14 mi. WSW of Hinis.

Bingo Sea, Japan: see HIUCHI SEA.

Binhdinh, province, Vietnam: see QUINHON.

Binhdinh (bĭng'dĭng'), town, Binhdinh prov., central Vietnam, 10 mi. NW of Quinhon; old Annamese prov. capital. Succeeded anc. Cham capital of Chaban (3 mi. NW), of which ruins remain.

Binhphuoc (bĭng'fwŭk'), village, Tanan prov., S Vietnam, on West Vaico R. and 25 mi. SSW of Saigon; rice.

Binhthuan, province, Vietnam: see PHANTHIET.

Binhthuan, town, Vietnam: see PHANRI.

Binisalem (bēnēsälĕm'), town (pop. 4,076), Majorca, Balearic Isls., on railroad and 11 mi. NE of Palma; agr. center (grapes, figs, almonds, olives, apricots). Liquor distilling, sawmilling, shoe and pulp mfg. Lignite mines. Sometimes Benisalem.

Binjai or **Bindjai** (both: bĭnjī'), town (pop. 9,176), NE Sumatra, Indonesia, 12 mi. W of Medan, in Deli region, on Medan-Kutaraja RR; trade center for agr. area (tea, rubber, palm oil, fibers, tobacco). Also spelled Binjei or Bindjei.

Binka (bĭng'kŭ), town (pop. 3,825), Bolangir dist., W Orissa, India, on Mahanadi R. and 30 mi. NE of Bolangir; local trade in rice, oilseeds.

Binkos (bĕn'kôs), village (pop. 551), Yambol dist., E central Bulgaria, on Tundzha R., on railroad (Chumerna station), and 11 mi. W of Sliven; sheep raising. Lignite mining on slopes of central Balkan Mts. (N). Chumerna peak is 8 mi. NW.

Binley, town and parish (pop. 3,189), E central Warwick, England, 3 mi. E of Coventry; coal mining. Near by is Combe Abbey, dating from 12th cent.

Binmaley (bēnmälā'), town (1939 pop. 1,635; 1948 municipality pop. 26,501), Pangasinan prov., central Luzon, Philippines, near S shore of Lingayen Gulf, on Agno delta, just E of Lingayen; copra, rice, corn.

Binnenalster, Germany: see ALSTER RIVER.

Binnental (bĭ'nüntäl), valley of upper Valais canton, S Switzerland, NE of Brig.

Binningen (bĭ'nĭng-ün), town (pop. 6,724), Basel-Land half-canton, N Switzerland, on Birsig R., adjacent to and SSW of Basel; metal products (notably aluminumware).

Bin of Cullen, Scotland: see CULLEN.

Binongko (bēnŏŏng'kō), island (□ 36; pop. 13,849), Tukangbesi Isls., Indonesia, bet. Flores and Molucca seas, 45 mi. SE of Wangiwangi; 5°55'S 124°2'E; 12 mi. long, 4 mi. wide; generally low. Fishing, agr. (coconuts, sago).

Binscarth, village (pop. 384), W Man., on Silver Creek and 65 mi. NW of Brandon; wheat.

Binsdorf (bĭns'dôrf), town (pop. 678), S Württemberg, Germany, after 1945 in Württemberg-Hohenzollern, 5 mi. NW of Balingen; cattle.

Binta, Port. Guinea: see FARIM.

Bintan or **Bintang** (bĭntäng'), largest island (□ 415; 30 mi. long, 30 mi. wide) of RIOUW ARCHIPELAGO, Indonesia, in the S.China Sea, at entrance to Strait of Malacca, 30 mi. SE of Singapore; 1°N 104°28'E; roughly triangular, c.30 mi. wide at base; hilly. Bauxite and tin are mined. Principal products: timber, rubber, gambier, pepper, copra, fish. TANJUNGPINANG on SW coast is chief town of Riouw Archipelago.

Bintang (bĭntäng'), residential area of Cameron Highlands, NW Pahang, Malaya, on road and 23 mi. NNE of Tapah (Perak), just N of hill station Tanah Rata (alt. 4,500 ft.); hotel, golf course.

Bintang, Gunong (gōō'nŏŏng), peak (6,103 ft.) on Kedah-Perak line, NW Malaya, 35 mi. E of George Town.

Bintimane or **Bintimani** (bĕntēmä'nē), highest peak (6,390 ft.) of Sierra Leone, in Loma Mts., 40 mi. N of Sefadu; 9°13'N 11°7'W.

Bintree, agr. village and parish (pop. 688), N central Norfolk, England, 7 mi. SE of Fakenham; flour milling. Has 14th-cent. church.

Bintulu (bĭntōō'lōō), coast town (pop. 3,957), central Sarawak, W Borneo, at mouth of Kemena R. and 105 mi. SW of Miri; agr. (sago, rice), fishing, stock raising.

Binyamina (bĭnyämē'nä), settlement (pop. 2,000), W Israel, in Plain of Sharon, on railroad and 20 mi. S of Haifa; citrus-growing center; flour milling, limestone quarrying; mfg. of essential oils. Founded 1922. Sometimes spelled Benyamina. Large immigrants' reception camp near by.

Binz (bĭnts), village (pop. 4,678), in former Prussian Pomerania prov., N Germany, after 1945 in Mecklenburg, on E Rügen isl., on the Baltic, 8 mi. E of Bergen; popular seaside resort.

Bío-Bío (bē'ō-bē'ō), province (□ 4,343; 1940 pop. 127,312, 1949 estimate 129,310), S central Chile; ⊙ Los Angeles. An inland area along the Bío-Bío valley, bordered E by the Andes. L. Laja, at foot of Antuco Volcano, is in E. Copahue Volcano is on Argentina border. Has temperate climate. Wholly agr. area: wheat, rye, peas, fruit, wine. Flour milling, wine making, lumbering. Centers: Los Angeles, Mulchén. Formed 1875 from Arauco prov.

Bío-Bío River, S central Chile, rises in Andean lakes near Argentina border 75 mi. E of Temuco (Cautín prov.), flows c.240 mi. NW through Cautín, Bío-Bío, and Concepción provs., past Coihüe, San Rosendo, Hualqui, Chiguayante, and Concepción, to the Pacific (Arauco Gulf) 6 mi. W of Concepción. Receives Laja R One of Chile's largest rivers, it is navigable only for flat-bottomed boats operating from Concepción near its mouth.

Biograd or **Biograd na Moru** (bēō'grät nä mô'rōō) [Serbo-Croatian,=Biograd on the sea], Ital. *Zaravecchia* (tsärävĕk'kyä), village, W Croatia, Yugoslavia, port on Adriatic Sea, 16 mi. SSE of Zadar, in Dalmatia; resort. Ruins of 11th-cent. cathedral. Scene of coronations of Croatian kings (11th cent.) and of Hung. king Coloman I (1102). Declined in 13th cent.

Biokovo Mountains (bē'ôkôvô), in Dinaric Alps, S Croatia, Yugoslavia, in Dalmatia; extend c.15 mi. NW-SE, along Adriatic coast. Highest peak (5,689 ft.) is 4 mi. N of Makarska.

Biola Junction, village (pop. 1,002), Fresno co., central Calif., 7 mi. NW of Fresno.

Biorka (bēôr'kŭ), village (1939 pop. 20), SW Alaska, on Sedanka Isl. (10 mi. long, 4 mi. wide), Aleutian Isls., 15 mi. E of Unalaska; 53°50'N 166°13'W.

Biot, Le (lü byō'), village (pop. 91), Haute-Savoie dept., SE France, on Dranse R. and 11 mi. SE of Thonon-les-Bains, in the Chablais.

Biota (byō'tä), town (pop. 1,340), Saragossa prov., NE Spain, 26 mi. NE of Tudela; sheep raising; wheat, wine.

Bioul (byōōl), village (pop. 1,527), Namur prov., S central Belgium, 8 mi. NNW of Dinant; marble quarrying.

Biqa', Al-, Lebanon: see BEKAA.

Bir (bēr), district (□ 4,132; pop. 713,630), NW Hyderabad state, India, on Deccan Plateau; ⊙ Bir. Bordered N by Godavari R., S by Manjra R.; highland (SW); lowland (NE). In black-soil area; cotton, wheat, millet, oilseeds (chiefly peanuts, flax). Cotton ginning, flour and oilseed milling; cattle raising. Main trade center, Parli. Dist. became part of Hyderabad during state's formation in 18th cent. Pop. 88% Hindu, 10% Moslem. Sometimes spelled Bidh; formerly spelled Bhir.

Bir, town (pop. 15,222), ⊙ Bir dist., NW Hyderabad state, India, 70 mi. SSE of Aurangabad; road center; millet, wheat, oilseeds; cotton ginning, noted leather handicraft. Sometimes spelled Bidh; formerly spelled Bhir.

Bir, Turkey: see BIRECIK.

Bira (bē'rŭ), town (1926 pop. 2,092), N Jewish Autonomous Oblast, Khabarovsk Territory, Russian SFSR, on Bira R., on Trans-Siberian RR and 26 mi. WNW of Birobidzhan; coal mines, sawmills, metalworks.

Birac (bēräk'), town (1939 pop. 15,258) in Itogon municipality, Benguet sub-prov., Mountain Prov., N Luzon, Philippines, 4 mi. SE of Baguio; trade center for lumbering and rice-growing area.

Bir Ahmad or **Bir Ahmed** (bĭr' ämĕd'), town, ⊙ Aqrabi tribal area, Western Aden Protectorate, 11 mi. NW of Aden and on the Wadi Tiban; irrigated agr. Sultan's residence with conspicuous tower.

Biraimi, Oman: see BARAIMI.

Birakan (bērŭkän'), town (1939 pop. over 2,000), NW Jewish Autonomous Oblast, Khabarovsk Territory, Russian SFSR, on Trans-Siberian RR and 60 mi. W of Birobidzhan; sawmills, cement plant.

Bira Kapra (bē'rä kä'prä), village, Mosul prov., N Iraq, near Turkish frontier, on Great Zab R. and 60 mi. NE of Mosul; wheat, barley, fruits.

Bir Ali or **Bir 'Ali** (bĭr' älē'), Wahidi sultanate (□ 500; pop. 3,000) of Eastern Aden Protectorate, on Gulf of Aden and on right (W) bank of the Wadi Hajr. Includes guano-yielding Baraqa Isls. off coast. Protectorate treaty concluded in 1888 and an adviser agreement in 1944. The capital Bir Ali (pop. 250), on the coast 60 mi. SW of Mukalla, has shark fisheries. Airfield at Majdaha (E).

Birao (bērou'), town, ⊙ Birao autonomous dist. (□ 19,300; 1950 pop. 7,400), NE Ubangi-Shari, Fr. Equatorial Africa, in vast swampy region near Anglo-Egyptian Sudan border, 500 mi. NE of Bangui; native trade center on caravan road to Darfur; customs station; sheep, goats.

Bira River or **Bolshaya Bira River** (bŭlshī'ŭ bērä', bē'rŭ), Jewish Autonomous Oblast, Khabarovsk Territory, Russian SFSR, rises in Bureya Range, flows 155 mi. E, past Bira, and SE, past Birobidzhan, to Amur R. below Leninskoye. Lumbering, gold mining along upper course; farming above mouth.

Bir Asakir or **Bir 'Asakir** (bēr' äsä'kĭr), desert outpost, Eastern Aden Protectorate, 80 mi. WSW of Shibam, on caravan route to Upper Aulaqi country; 15°37'N 47°29'E. Radio station; airfield.

Bir 'Asluj, Israel: see HALUTSA.

Biratnagar (bĭrät'nŭgŭr), town, SE Nepal, in the Terai, 5 mi. N of Jogbani, India; jute, sugar, and cotton milling; hand-loom cotton weaving.

Birba, El, or **Al-Birba** (both: ĕl bĭr'bă), village (pop. 5,149), Girga prov., Upper Egypt, 3 mi. WNW of Girga; cotton, cereals, dates, sugar.

Bir Beida or **Bi'r Baydah** (both: bēr' bā'dŭ), town, Red Sea prov., E Egypt, 10 mi. W of Kosseir; phosphate mining.

Birbhum (bēr'bōōm), district (□ 1,743; pop. 1,048,317). W West Bengal, India; ⊙ Suri. Bounded W by Bihar, S by Ajay R.; drained by MOR RIVER (barrage near Suri) and by tributaries of Padma and Bhagirathi rivers. Undulating plain; rice, gram, wheat, sugar cane, corn, mangoes; forests in W contain sal, piar (*Buchanania latifolia*), mahua. Coal and iron deposits (W). Cotton weaving, oilseed and rice milling (center at Bolpur), silk weaving (center at Baswa), metalware and pottery mfg. Visva Bharati, univ. founded by Rabindranath Tagore, at Santiniketan. Dist. was Dacoit stronghold in 18th cent.

Birbir River (bĭr'bĭr), Wallaga prov., W central Ethiopia, rises in highlands 25 mi. NW of Gimbi, flows c.110 mi. SW to Baro R. 25 mi. E of Gambela. Its valley, infested by the tsetse fly in lower part, has gold and platinum deposits mined in Yubdo area.

Bir-bou-Rekba (bēr'-bōō-rĕkbä'), village, Grombalia dist., NE Tunisia, near Gulf of Hammamet, 3 mi. NW of Hammamet; rail junction; wine.

Birch Creek or **Twelve Mile House**, village (1939 pop. 32), E Alaska, on Birch Creek (200 mi. long, flows N to the Yukon), on Steese Highway and 115 mi. ENE of Fairbanks, 12 mi. SW of Circle; trapping.

Birchenough Bridge (bûrch'ŭnŭf), E Southern Rhodesia, on Sabi R. and 100 mi. E of Fort Victoria, on Fort Victoria-Chipinga road.

Birch Hills, village (pop. 396), central Sask., 20 mi. SE of Prince Albert; flour milling.

Birchington, town and parish (pop. 3,756), NE Kent, England, on Isle of Thanet, on Thames estuary, 3 mi. W of Margate; bathing resort. Has 13th-cent. church; churchyard has tomb of Dante Gabriel Rossetti.

Birchip, town (pop. 740), N central Victoria, Australia, 170 mi. NW of Melbourne; agr. center (wheat, oats).

Birchircara, Malta: see BIRKIRKARA.

Birchis (bĕr'kēsh), Rum. *Birchiş*, Hung. *Marosberkes* (mŏ'rôsh-bĕr"kĕsh), village (pop. 1,140), Arad prov., W Rumania, near Mures R., 23 mi. NE of Lugoj; agr. center.

Birch Island, SW Maine, resort isl. in Casco Bay just W of Harpswell; c.1.5 mi. long.

Birch Lake (□ 9), St. Louis and Lake counties, NE Minn., 12 mi. S of Ely in Superior Natl. Forest; 15 mi. long, 1 mi. wide. Fishing resorts. Lake is fed and drained by South Kawishiwi R.

Birch Mountains, NE Alta., W of Athabaska R., near S edge of Wood Buffalo Natl. Park; extend c.150 mi. NE–SW; rise to 2,689 ft. at 57°23'N 112°39'W.

Birch Point, Maine: see WEST BATH.

Birch Run, village (1940 pop. 519), Saginaw co., E central Mich., 14 mi. SSE of Saginaw, in bean and oil-producing area.

Birch Tree, city (pop. 409), Shannon co., S Mo., in the Ozarks, 27 mi. NE of West Plains; lumber mills.

Birch Vale, England: see HAYFIELD.

Birchwood. **1** Village (pop. 312), Washington co., E Minn., on White Bear L. and 10 mi. NNE of St. Paul; grain, livestock. **2** Village (pop. 502), Washburn co., NW Wis., 13 mi. NE of Rice Lake, in lake-resort area; wood products.

Bird, Cape, S extremity of Somerset Isl., S Franklin Dist., Northwest Territories; 72°N 95°10'W.

Bird City, city (pop. 784), Cheyenne co., extreme NW Kansas, 27 mi. W of Atwood, in agr. area (grain and dairy farms; cattle).

Bird Creek, river in NE Okla., rises in Osage co., flows c.100 mi. SE, past Nelagoney, Barnsdall, Avant, and Skiatook, to Verdigris R. just N of Catoosa.

Bird Island, T.H.: see NIHOA.

Bird Island or **Sea Cow Island**, northernmost (160 acres; pop. 25) of the Seychelles, in Indian Ocean, 70 mi. NNW of Victoria; 3°43'S 55°13'E; granite formation. Copra; fisheries.

Bird Island, village (pop. 1,333), Renville co., S Minn., 5 mi. E of Olivia, in agr. area; dairy products.

Bird Island, Venezuela: see AVES ISLAND.

Bird of Paradise Island, B.W.I.: see LITTLE TOBAGO ISLAND.

Bird Rocks, islet in the Gulf of St. Lawrence, E Que., NE of the Magdalen Isls.; 47°50'N 61°9'W; lighthouse.

Birds, village (pop. 234), Lawrence co., SE Ill., 7 mi. N of Lawrenceville, in agr. area.

Birdsboro, borough (pop. 3,158), Berks co., SE Pa., on Schuylkill R. and 8 mi. SE of Reading; steel milling. Settled 1740, inc. 1872. Just SE is HOPEWELL VILLAGE NATIONAL HISTORIC SITE.

Birdseye, town (pop. 354), Dubois co., SW Ind., 14 mi. ESE of Jasper, in agr. and bituminous-coal area.

Birdsville, village, SW Queensland, Australia, on Diamantina R. and 365 mi. SSW of Cloncurry, near South Australia border; cattle.

Birdum (bûr'dŭm), settlement, N central Northern Territory, Australia, 265 mi. SE of Darwin; terminus of railroad from Darwin; airport; cattle.

Birdwood, Mount (10,160 ft.), on Alta.–B.C. line, in Rocky Mts. near S edge of Banff Natl. Park, 30 mi. SSE of Banff; 50°47'N 115°21'W.

Birecik (bĭrĕjĭk'), anc. *Birtha*, town (1950 pop. 11,214), Urfa, S Turkey, on Euphrates R., 45 mi. WSW of Urfa; wheat, barley, millet, lentils, vetch, onions. At a crossing of the Euphrates, it was long important on the Aleppo-Baghdad route. Sometimes Birejik, Birijik, or simply Bir.

Bir el 'Abd or **Bi'r al-'Abd** (both: bēr' ĕl ăbd'), village (pop. 1,001), Sinai prov., NE Egypt, on Cairo-Haifa RR, near the coast, 45 mi. ESE of Port Said.

Bir Fadhl (bĭr' fä'dhŭl), village, Aden Colony, just W of Sheikh Othman; civil airfield.

Bir Gandus (bēr' gän'dōōs), Saharan outpost and oasis, SW Río de Oro, Sp. West Africa, 65 mi. NE of Port-Étienne in Fr. West Africa; 21°42'N 16°25'W. Also spelled Bir Ganduz, Bir Guenduz.

Birganj (bēr'gŭnj), town, S Nepal, in the Terai, near India border, on railroad, on main India-Katmandu road and 55 mi. SSW of Katmandu; rice, wheat, barley, corn, oilseeds, jute. Sometimes spelled Birgunj.

Birghorn (bĭrk'hôrn), peak (10,650 ft.) in Bernese Alps, S central Switzerland, 6 mi. SE of Kandersteg.

Birgu, Malta: see VITTORIOSA.

Bir Hacheim or **Bir Hakeim** (bēr' häkām'), village, E Cyrenaica, Libya, 45 mi. SW of Tobruk; caravan center. Scene of heavy fighting (1942) bet. Axis and Free French troops in Second World War.

Birhan (bĭrhän'), highest peak (13,625 ft.) in Choke Mts., NW Ethiopia, 30 mi. NNE of Debra Markos; 10°40'N 37°55'E.

Biria, Israel: see BIRIYA.

Birigui (bērēgē'), city (pop. 8,284), NW São Paulo, Brazil, on railroad and 9 mi. ESE of Araçatuba; coffeegrowing center; cotton and rice processing, textile and tile mfg., sawmilling.

Biri Island (bē"rē') (□ 6; 1939 pop. 2,066), Samar prov., Philippines, just off NW coast of Samar isl., bet. San Bernardino Strait (W) and Philippine Sea (E); 12°40'N 124°22'E; 5 mi. long, 2 mi. wide. Coconut growing.

Birijik, Turkey: see BIRECIK.

Birilyussy (bĭrēlyōō'sē), village (1948 pop. over 2,000), SW Krasnoyarsk Territory, Russian SFSR, on Chulym R., on Achinsk-Yeniseisk highway and 60 mi. N of Achinsk; dairy farming.

Birimbal el Qadima or **Birimbal al-Qadimah** (bĭrĭm'băl ĕl kädē'mŭ), village (pop. 9,679), Daqahliya prov., Lower Egypt, on El Bahr el Saghir, a delta canal, and 23 mi. ENE of Mansura; cotton, cereals.

Birim River (bērēm'), S Gold Coast, rises SW of Kibi, flows c.100 mi. SW, past Kade and Oda, to Pra R. 14 mi. W of Oda. Drains rich cacao and oil-palm area.

Biriya or **Biria** (both: bēr'yä), agr. settlement (pop. 150), N Israel, Upper Galilee, just NNE of Safad. Founded 1945. In Middle Ages site of Jewish village where Rabbi Joseph Caro completed the *Shulhan Aruk*.

Birjand (bērjänd'), town (1939 pop. 23,488), Ninth Prov., in Khurasan, NE Iran, in oasis, 230 mi. S of Meshed, and on road to Zahidan; alt. 4,800 ft.; road and trade center; mfg. (carpets, felt, woolen fabrics, matches). Saffron cultivation. Copper and lead mining near by. A dependency of Herat from early-18th cent. to 1871, it later largely supplanted Qain as center of Qainat dist.

Birk, Saudi Arabia: see BIRQ.

Birkadem (bērkädĕm'), village (pop. 3,865), Alger dept., N central Algeria, 5 mi. S of Algiers; mfg. of irrigation equipment; truck, wine.

Birkby. 1 Village, Cumberland, England: see CROSSCANONBY. **2** Suburb, Yorkshire, England: see HUDDERSFIELD.

Birkdale, resort, S suburb of Southport, W Lancashire, England, on Irish Sea; golf course.

Birkeland (bĭr'kùlän), village (pop. 392) in Birkenes canton (pop. 1,826), Aust-Agder co., S Norway, on Tovdal R. at Flak L., and 15 mi. NE of Kristiansand. Burial mounds near by.

Birkelane (bērkùlän'), village, W Senegal, Fr. West Africa, on Saloum R., on Dakar-Niger RR, and 21 mi. E of Kaolack; peanut growing. Airfield.

Birkenau (bĭr'kùnou), village (pop. 3,845), S Hesse, W Germany, in former Starkenburg prov., in the Odenwald, just ENE of Weinheim; woodworking.

Birkenau, Poland: see OSWIECIM.

Birkenberg, Czechoslovakia: see BREZOVE HORY.

Birkendorf (bĭr'kùndôrf), village (pop. 537), S Baden, Germany, on S slope of Black Forest, 10 mi. NNE of Waldshut; silk mfg.

Birkenes, Norway: see BIRKELAND.

Birkenfeld (bĭr'kùnfĕlt). **1** Town (pop. 3,802), in former Prussian Rhine Prov., W Germany, after 1945 in Rhineland-Palatinate, 8 mi. WSW of Idar-Oberstein; brickkilns, sawmills. Roman artifacts found here. Was ⊙ Birkenfeld principality (1569–1733), ruled by a branch of the line Pfalz-Zweibrücken. Principality came (1776) to Baden, then (1797) to France; passed (1815) to OLDENBURG, forming an exclave (□ 194; 1933 pop. 58,543). Annexed 1937 by Prussia. **2** Village (pop. 4,237), S Württemberg, Germany, after 1945 in Württemberg-Hohenzollern, on N slope of Black Forest, on the Enz 3 mi. WSW of Pforzheim; furniture mfg.

Birkenhead (bûr'kùnhĕd), county borough (1931 pop. 147,803; 1951 census 142,392), on Wirral peninsula, NW Cheshire, England, on Mersey R. opposite Liverpool, with which it is linked by a tunnel (road and rail); 53°23'N 3°1'W; shipping, shipbuilding, flour milling, steel mfg. (mfg. of ship machinery, railroad rolling stock, boilers; steel mills). Exports coal, flour, machinery and other metal products; imports grain, cattle. Has ruins of 12th-cent. abbey, a mus., and an art gall. Its modern industrial foundation was laid with the building of the 1st shipyard in 1824. The docks were opened in 1847 and now form part of port of Liverpool. In Second World War Birkenhead sustained much damage by bombing (1941). Just SE on Mersey R. is residential and resort suburb of Rock Ferry, with metal industry as well.

Birkenhead, borough (pop. 3,806), N N.Isl., New Zealand, NW suburb of Auckland, on Waitemata Harbour; orchards.

Birkenshaw, England: see SPENBOROUGH.

Birkenwerder (bĭr"kùnvĕr'dùr), village (pop. 7,023), Brandenburg, E Germany, near the Havel, 13 mi. NNW of Berlin; brick mfg.; market gardening. Excursion resort.

Birkesdorf (bĭr'kùsdôrf), village (pop. 5,563), in former Prussian Rhine Prov., W Germany, after 1945 in North Rhine-Westphalia, on the Rur and 2 mi. NW of Düren; mfg. of paper products.

Birket Ghitas or **Birkit Ghitas** (bĭr'kĭt gĭtäs'), village (pop. 9,371), Beheira prov., Lower Egypt, on Mahmudiya Canal and 13 mi. WNW of Damanhur; cotton ginning.

Birket Karun or **Birkit Qarun** (kä'rōōn), shallow inland lake (□ 90), Faiyum prov., Upper Egypt, 50 mi. SW of Cairo; 25 mi. long, 4 mi. wide; 150 ft. below sea level. Occupies the basin of anc. L. Moeris (mē'rĭs), an artificial lake of anc. Egypt. Valuable archaeological finds made in the area.

Birket Lut, Palestine: see DEAD SEA.

Birkigt, Germany: see FREITAL.

Birkirkara (bĭrkĭrkä'rä), town (pop. 16,070), central Malta, 2½ mi. W of Valletta; mfg. of lace, bricks, tiles, pottery; fish canning. Citrus-fruit and flower growing. Only slightly damaged in Second World War. Bldgs. include several 16th-cent. houses, 2 fortified towers, ruined Renaissance Church of the Annunciation, baroque parish church of St. Helen (1727), and 17th-cent. church of the Assumption. Sometimes spelled Birchircara.

Birkit Ghitas, Egypt: see BIRKET GHITAS.

Birkit Qarun, Egypt: see BIRKET KARUN.

Birkkar (bērk-kär'), highest peak (9,042 ft.) in Karwendelgebirge of Bavarian Alps, in Tyrol, W Austria, 10 mi. N of Innsbruck.

Birlenbach (bĭr'lùnbäkh), village (commune pop., including Fachingen, 1,067), in former Prussian prov. of Hesse-Nassau, W Germany, after 1945 in Rhineland-Palatinate, 1 mi. S of Diez. On the Lahn and 1 mi. WNW, is Fachingen (1939 pop. 245), with mineral waters.

Birma (bĭr'mä), village (pop. 10,874), Gharbiya prov., Lower Egypt, 7 mi. NW of Tanta; cotton.

Birmandreïs (bērmändrās'), village (pop. 3,534), Alger dept., N central Algeria, a residential S suburb of Algiers.

Bir-M'Cherga or **Bir-Mcherga** (bērmshârgä'), village, Zaghouan dist., N central Tunisia, 23 mi. SSW of Tunis; European agr. settlement. Cereals, livestock.

Birmingham (bûr'mĭng-ùm), county borough (1931 pop. 1,002,603; 1951 census 1,112,340) and city, NW Warwick, England, 110 mi. NW of London, in the industrial Black Country; 52°29'N 1°53'W; 2d-largest city in England and major industrial center. With iron and coal in the vicinity, it has metal and brass foundries and mfg. of automobiles, railroad rolling-stock, machinery, munitions, machine tools, chemicals, plastics, soap, leather goods. Most of Britain's brass and bronze coins minted here. Has univ. (1898), 13th-cent. church of St. Martin's, R.C. and Anglican cathedrals, important library and art gall. Utilities and a bank are city owned, and Birmingham has a well-known city orchestra. Noted citizens have included Joseph Priestley, John Baskerville, James Watt (founder of the Soho ironworks in Handsworth), Joseph Chamberlain, and Edward Burne-Jones. The annual British Industries Fair is held here (at CASTLE BROMWICH). Before 13th cent. Birmingham was a market town. A metal-mfg. town since 16th cent., Birmingham was taken and partly destroyed by Prince Rupert (1643), and was severely affected by the Great Plague (1665). The Reform Act of 1832 enfranchised the city, and the Greater Birmingham scheme of 1911 extended its area to 80 sq. mi. Suffered severe air raids in Second World War, resulting in heavy damage. Among the most important industrial suburbs are Yardley, Selly Oak, Edgbaston, Erdington, and Soho. Fort Dunlop (NE) is an important tire-mfg. center. County borough also includes town of BOURNVILLE.

Birmingham (bûr'mĭng-hăm"). **1** City (pop. 326,037), ⊙ Jefferson co., N central Ala., c.140 mi. W of Atlanta, near S tip of Appalachian Mts.; 33°31'N 86°52'W; alt. 600 ft. Largest city in state, leading iron and steel center of South, well situated in coal, iron-ore, and limestone area supplying raw materials for its mills and foundries. Noted for mfg. of pig iron and cast-iron pipe; also iron and steel products including cotton gins, Diesel engines, auto parts, lathes, stoves and ranges, industrial drills, tool castings, and milling, mining, and electrical equipment. Other industrial products are cotton textiles, women's hats, and work clothes, coal and coke, chemicals and explosives, furniture, and construction materials (Portland cement, insulation, roofing, paving). There are meat-packing plants, flour and feed mills, wholesale bakeries, and creameries. Important air and rail terminus, with municipal airport (Air Force base) and railroad repair shops. Port of entry. Founded and inc. 1871. Grew with development of iron and steel industry. Seat of Birmingham-Southern Col. (affiliated 1940 with Birmingham Conservatory of Music), Howard Col., and Miles Col.; state industrial school for boys and state training school for girls are near by. A huge iron statue of Vulcan is on crest of Red Mtn., overlooking city. **2** Town, Calif.: see VAN NUYS. **3** Town (pop. 643), Van Buren co., SE Iowa, 9 mi. S of Fairfield, in agr. and bituminous-coal-mining area. **4** City (pop. 15,467), Oakland co., SE Mich., bet. Detroit and Pontiac, on River Rouge; NW residential suburb of Detroit. Mfg. of trailer parts, electrical equipment; dairy and truck farming. Settled 1819; inc. as village 1864, as city 1933. **5** Town (pop. 236), Clay co., W Mo., 10 mi. NE of Kansas City. **6** Borough (pop. 178), Huntingdon co., central Pa., 2 mi. SE of Tyrone and on Little Juniata R.

Birmitrapur (bĭrmĭt'rŭpŏŏr), village, Sundargarh dist., N Orissa, India, on rail spur and 50 mi. ENE of Sundargarh. Limestone quarried near by.

Birnagar (bēr'nŭgŭr), town (pop. 1,813), Nadia dist., E West Bengal, India, 12 mi. SSE of Krishnagar; rice, jute, linseed, sugar cane. Formerly called Ula.

Birnam (bûr'nùm), agr. village in Little Dunkeld parish, E central Perthshire, Scotland, on the Tay, just SSE of Dunkeld. Just S of village is Birnam Hill (1,324 ft.), once forested with the Birnam Wood of the march on DUNSINANE in *Macbeth*.

Birnamwood, village (pop. 561), Shawano co., E central Wis., 21 mi. E of Wausau, in dairying and farming area (potatoes, corn); sawmilling, cheese making, flour and feed milling.

Birnbaum, Poland: see MIEDZYCHOD.

Birnie Island, uninhabited coral islet (44 acres), smallest and most central of Phoenix Isls., S Pacific, 45 mi. S of Canton Isl. Discovered 1823 by Americans, included 1937 in Br. colony of Gilbert and Ellice Isls.

Birnin Gwari (bĭrn'ĭn gwä'rē), town (pop. 1,695), Zaria prov., Northern Provinces, N central Nigeria, 60 mi. W of Zaria; cotton, ginger, peanuts. Gold mining.

Birnin Kebbi (kĕ'bē), town (pop. 7,461), Sokoto prov., Northern Provinces, NW Nigeria, near Kebbi R., 80 mi. SW of Sokoto; agr. trade center (cotton, millet, rice); timber; cattle and skins. Has hosp. Limestone deposits near by.

Birni-N'Konni or **Birni-N'Koni** (bĭr"nĭng kō'nē), town (pop. c.6,000), S Niger territory, Fr. West Africa, on Nigeria border (opposite Kalmalo), 50 mi. N of Sokoto, 110 mi. E of Niamey. Exports hides and meat. Region also produces millet, corn, manioc, beans, peanuts; livestock. Airfield; meteorological and veterinary stations.

Bir Nzaran (bēr' nŭthä'rän), Saharan outpost and well, central Río de Oro, Sp. West Africa, 100 mi. ENE of Villa Cisneros; 23°49'N 14°27'W.

Birobidzhan (bĭr"ōbĭjän', Rus. bērŭbējän'), city (1939 pop. 29,654), ⊙ Jewish Autonomous Oblast, Khabarovsk Territory, Russian SFSR, on Bira R., on Trans-Siberian RR and 100 mi. W of Khabarovsk; 48°45'N 132°55'E. Sawmills, woodworking shops (prefabricated houses, furniture); clothing and shoe mfg., brick and lime plants. Name also applied to JEWISH AUTONOMOUS OBLAST. Formerly called Tikhonkaya; variant spellings are Birobidjan, Birobijan.

Biron (bī'rŭn), village (pop. 528), Wood co., central Wis., on Wisconsin R. and 3 mi. NE of Wisconsin Rapids; paper, pulp, and sulphite milling.

Birpur Katra (bēr'pŏŏr kŭt'rŭ) or **Katra,** town (pop. 2,220), Gonda dist., NE Uttar Pradesh, India, on tributary of the Gogra and 8 mi. NE of Colonelganj; rice, wheat, corn, gram.

Birq (bĭrk), village, S Hejaz, Saudi Arabia, minor Red Sea port 70 mi. SSE of Qunfidha; dates, wheat, vegetables, fruit; fishing. Formerly in Asir. Sometimes spelled Birk.

Birr (bûr), Gaelic *Biorra*, urban district (pop. 3,224), W Co. Offaly, Ireland, on Brosna R. and 22 mi. SW of Tullamore; malting center and agr. market (hops, barley, potatoes; cattle), with shoe mfg. In anc. times town and its castle were hq. of the O'Carrols; in 1620 land was granted to

Lawrence Parsons by James I. The 3d earl of Rosse, descendant of Parsons, installed noted telescope in castle. Has modern R.C cathedral. Formerly called Parsonstown.

Birr (bĭr), village (pop. 549), Aargau canton, N Switzerland, 3 mi. S of Brugg. Here, in 1768, Pestalozzi initiated his system of education.

Birrens (bûr'ŭns), hamlet in S Dumfries, Scotland, just NE of Ecclefechan; site of remains of Roman station.

Birse River, Switzerland: see BIRS RIVER.

Birsfelden (bĭrs'fĕldŭn), town (pop. 5,703), Basel-Land half-canton, N Switzerland, at confluence of Birs R. with the Rhine, adjacent to and E of Basel; metal- and woodworking; foodstuffs.

Birshtonas, Lithuania: see BIRSTONAS.

Birsilpur (bĭr'sĭlpŏŏr), village, W Rajasthan, India, 65 mi. WNW of Bikaner, in Thar Desert; caravan center; trades in cattle, hides, wool, millet. Allegedly founded c.2d cent. A.D.

Birsinghpur (bĕr'sĭngpŏŏr), village, SE Vindhya Pradesh, India, on railroad and 80 mi. SSW of Rewa; cement factory.

Birsk (bērsk), city (1932 pop. estimate 17,500), NW Bashkir Autonomous SSR, Russian SFSR, on Belaya R. and 50 mi. NNW of Ufa; river port (grain exports); food-processing (flour, meat, fruit, vegetables) center; canning (jams, marmalade), distilling. Has teachers col., Bashkir mus. Founded 1663.

Birs Nimrud, Iraq: see BORSIPPA.

Birs River or **Birse River** (both: bĭrs), NW Switzerland, rises near Tavannes, flows 45 mi. NE to the Rhine at Basel.

Birstall (bûr'stôl). **1** Residential town and parish (pop. 3,131), central Leicester, England, on Soar R. and 3 mi. N of Leicester; leather industry. Has 13th-cent. church. **2** Former urban district (1931 pop. 7,204), West Riding, S central Yorkshire, England, 7 mi. SW of Leeds; woolen milling, coal mining, textile printing, soap mfg. Inc. 1937 in Batley.

Birstonas or **Birshtonas** (bērshtō'näs), Lith. *Birštonas,* town (1925 pop. 270), S central Lithuania, on right bank of Neman R. and 20 mi. S of Kaunas; noted health resort; mineral springs, mud baths, sanatorium. Sawmilling.

Birta (bûr'tŭ), town (pop. 78), Yell co., W central Ark., c.50 mi. WNW of Little Rock.

Birtha, Turkey: see BIRECIK.

Birthday Mine, Southern Rhodesia: see SHABANI.

Birtle, town (pop. 677), SW Man., on Birdtail R. and 50 mi. NW of Brandon; mixed farming. Indian training school.

Birtle-cum-Bamford, parish (pop. 1,619), SE Lancashire, England. Includes: village of Birtle (textile bleaching), 2 mi. NE of Bury; and town of Bamford, 2 mi. W of Rochdale, with textile industry (cotton and wool).

Birtley, town and parish (pop. 12,297), NE Durham, England, 4 mi. S of Gateshead; coal mines; chemicals, electrical goods.

Biruaca (bērwä'kä), town (pop. 226), Apure state, W central Venezuela, in llanos, 4 mi. SW of San Fernando; cattle.

Birur (bĭrōōr'), town (pop. 6,679), Kadur dist., W central Mysore, India, 23 mi. NE of Chikmagalur; rail junction (branch to Talguppa, near hydroelectric works at Jog); trade in rice, grain, betel nuts, coconuts.

Biryakovo (bēryä'kŭvŭ), village (1939 pop. over 500), S Vologda oblast, Russian SFSR, 60 mi. ENE of Vologda; flax, wheat.

Biryuch, Russian SFSR: see BUDENNOYE.

Biryulevo (bēryŏŏlyô'vŭ), town (1926 pop. 2,018), central Moscow oblast, Russian SFSR, S suburb of Moscow, 2 mi. S of Lenino; freight yards.

Biryusa River (bēryōō'sŭ), in SW Irkutsk oblast and S Krasnoyarsk Territory, Russian SFSR, rises in 2 headstreams in Eastern Sayan Mts., flows N, past Taishet, and NW, joining Chuna R. to form Taseyeva R.; 468 mi. long. Also called Ona R.

Birzai, Birzhai, or **Birzhay** (bēr'zhī), Lith. *Biržai,* Ger. *Birsen,* Rus. *Birzhi,* city (pop. 8,281), N Lithuania, on small lake, 36 mi. NNE of Panevezys, near Latvian border; rail terminus; road center; linen and jute weaving, wool spinning, tanning, sawmilling, flour milling; mfg. of furniture, rope. Regional mus. City dates from 1415; in Rus. Kovno govt. until 1920.

Birzebbuga (bērdzĕb-bōō'jä) or **Birzebbugia** (–bōō'-jä), Maltese *Birżebbuġa,* village (parish pop. 5,339), SE Malta, summer resort on Marsaxlokk Bay, 5 mi. SSE of Valletta. Fishing. Has seaplane anchorage and petroleum tanks; fortifications. Several churches. Environs (N) are rich in prehistoric remains, notably the cave of Ghar Dalam and a temple and acropolis at Borg-in-Nadur.

Birzhai or **Birzhi,** Lithuania: see BIRZAI.

Birzula, Ukrainian SSR: see KOTOVSK, Odessa oblast.

Bisaccia (bēzät'chä), town (pop. 6,546), Avellino prov., Campania, S Italy, 31 mi. ENE of Avellino.

Bisacquino (bēzäkwē'nô), town (pop. 8,060), Palermo prov., SW central Sicily, 8 mi. S of Corleone, in cereal- and legume-growing region; woolens, soap.

Bisalpur (bē'sŭlpŏŏr), town (pop. 12,862), Pilibhit dist., N Uttar Pradesh, India, 23 mi. S of Pilibhit; trades in rice, wheat, gram, sugar cane; hand-loom silk weaving; sugar refining. Rohilla fort ruins. Founded 16th cent.

Bisaltia or **Visaltia** (both: vĭsŭltē'ŭ), region of Greek Macedonia, in Serrai nome, on Aegean Sea, bet. lower Struma R. and the Vertiskon; main town, Nigrita.

Bisanthe, Turkey: see TEKIRDAG.

Bisauli (bĭsou'lē), town (pop. 7,217), Budaun dist., N central Uttar Pradesh, India, 21 mi. NW of Budaun; wheat, pearl millet, mustard, barley, gram. Rohilla fort (built 1750) ruins, tomb of a Rohilla leader.

Bisayas, Philippines: see VISAYAN ISLANDS.

Bisbal, La (lä bēsväl'), city (pop. 4,134), Gerona prov., NE Spain, 11 mi. E of Gerona; cork, wine, and olive-oil processing; tanning, pottery mfg.

Bisbal del Panadés (bēsväl' dhĕl pänä-dhās'), town (pop. 1,231), Tarragona prov., NE Spain, 5 mi. NW of Vendrell; olive-oil processing, almond shipping, lumbering, sheep raising; cereals, wine.

Bisbee (bĭz'bē). **1** City (pop. 3,801), ⊙ Cochise co., SE Ariz., in Mule Mts., near Mex. line 23 mi. WNW of Douglas; alt. 5,300 ft. Copper-producing center. Copper, gold, silver mines near by. Dude ranches in vicinity. Founded c.1880 after discovery (c.1876) of copper here, inc. 1900. **2** Village (pop. 365), Towner co., N N.Dak., 11 mi. NW of Cando.

Biscari, Sicily: see ACATE.

Biscay, province, Spain: see VIZCAYA.

Biscay, village (pop. 90), McLeod co., S central Minn., 6 mi. SE of Hutchinson; dairying.

Biscay, Bay of, anc. *Aquitanicus Sinus,* wide inlet of the Atlantic indenting the coast of W Europe from Ushant isl. off Brittany, France, to Cape Ortegal, NW Spain. Receives the Vilaine, Loire, Charente, Gironde (estuary of the Garonne), and Adour, all in France. Chief isls., all off Fr. coast, are Belle-Île, Île de Noirmoutier, Île d'Yeu, Île de Ré, Île d'Oléron. Principal ports on the bay or on its inlets are Brest, Saint-Nazaire, La Rochelle, Rochefort, Arcachon and Bayonne in France; Pasajes, San Sebastián, Bilbao, and Santander on N coast of Spain. Nantes and Bordeaux, at head of Loire and Garonne estuaries, are also reached by ocean-going ships. Well-known resorts along Fr. coast are La Baule, Les Sables-d'Olonne, Royan, Biarritz, and Saint-Jean-de-Luz. The N (Breton) and S (Cantabrian) shores are rocky and irregular, with many natural harbors, while the central section, bet. the Gironde and the Adour estuary, is straight and lined with sand dunes (see LANDES). The bay is noted for its sudden severe storms caused by NW winds. The tidal range (up to 40 ft.) is among the highest in the world. The Sp. term *Mar Cantábrico* (Cantabrian Sea) and the Fr. term *Golfe de Gascogne* (Gulf of Gascony) refer to sections of the bay; the former is limited to the waters off the N coast of Spain, whereas the latter is usually applied to the head of the bay bounded by the Landes and the Basque coasts which form a right angle near Fr.-Sp. border. The name Biscay is a form of Vizcayan (Basque).

Biscayne Bay (bĭskān'), shallow arm of the Atlantic in S Fla., sheltered by the Florida Keys and MIAMI BEACH isl.; c.40 mi. long, 2–10 mi. wide. Connects with the Atlantic chiefly through Safety Valve Entrance and with Florida Bay (SW) through small sounds. Forms part of Intracoastal Waterway.

Biscayne Park, village (pop. 2,009), Dade co., S Fla., a N suburb of Miami. Inc. 1932.

Bisceglie (bēshā'lyĕ), town (pop. 32,552), Bari prov., Apulia, S Italy, port on the Adriatic, 20 mi. WNW of Bari; wine, olive oil, macaroni. Exports olives, grapes, cherries. Bishopric. Has ruins of medieval castle, Romanesque-Apulian cathedral, and other 11th- and 12th-cent. churches. Flourished in Middle Ages.

Bischheim (bē-shĕm', Ger. bĭsh'hīm), outer N suburb (pop. 10,513) of Strasbourg, Bas-Rhin dept., E France, on Marne-Rhine Canal; furniture and porcelain mfg.

Bischoflack, Yugoslavia: see SKOFJA LOKA.

Bischofsburg, Poland: see BISKUPIEC.

Bischofsgrün (bĭ'shôfsgrün"), village (pop. 2,308), Upper Franconia, NE Bavaria, Germany, at N foot of Ochsenkopf mtn., near source of the White Main, 14 mi. NE of Bayreuth; textile mfg.; glassworks, paper mills. Winter and health resort.

Bischofsheim (bĭ'shôfs-hīm"), former suburb (pop. 7,056) of MAINZ, after 1945 in Hesse, W Germany, bet. the Rhine and the canalized Main, 4 mi. E of Mainz; rail junction.

Bischofshofen (bĭsh'ôfs-hōf"ŭn), town (pop. 7,924), Salzburg, W central Austria, on the Salzach and 28 mi. SSE of Hallein; rail junction. Copper mined at near-by Mitterberg.

Bischofstal, Poland: see UJAZD.

Bischofstein, Poland: see BISZTYNEK.

Bischofswerda (bĭ"shôfsvĕr'dä), town (pop. 10,835), Saxony, E central Germany, in Upper Lusatia, 20 mi. ENE of Dresden; rail junction; textile milling (cotton, wool, linen, jute); mfg. of machinery, glass, leather goods. Granite quarrying.

Bischofswerder, Poland: see BISKUPIEC.

Bischofswiesen (bĭ'shôfsvē"zŭn), village (pop. 6,779), Upper Bavaria, Germany, at S foot of the Untersberg, 6 mi. SSE of Bad Reichenhall; dairying; marble quarries.

Bischofszell (bĭsh'ôfs-tsĕl"), town (pop. 3,000), Thurgau canton, NE Switzerland, at confluence of the Sitter with the Thur, 8 mi. NW of St. Gall; rubber products, canned goods, flour. Medieval church.

Bischofteinitz, Czechoslovakia: see HORSOVSKY TYN.

Bischwiller (bēsh-vēlâr'), Ger. *Bischweiler* (bĭsh'-vīlŭr), town (pop. 7,018), Bas-Rhin dept., E France, on the Moder and 5 mi. SE of Haguenau; textile center (jute, hemp, wool); paper milling, mfg. (building materials, shoes). Hops grown.

Biscioftiu, Ethiopia: see BISHOFTU.

Biscoe (bĭ'skō). **1** or **Fredonia** (frēdō'nēŭ), town (pop. 406), Prairie co., E central Ark., 12 mi. WSW of Brinkley. **2** Town (pop. 1,034), Montgomery co., central N.C., 24 mi. S of Asheboro, in peach-raising area; cotton milling.

Biscoe Islands (bĭ'skō), group of small isls. of Antarctica, just off W shore of Palmer Peninsula, in the South Pacific, bet. Anvers Isl. (N) and Adelaide Isl. (S); center at 66°S 66°W. Discovered 1832 by John Biscoe, Br. sealer.

Biscucuy (bēskōōkwē'), town (pop. 1,627), Portuguesa state, W Venezuela, on upper Guanare R., on Trujillo–Barquisimeto highway, and 22 mi. NW of Guanare; cotton, coffee, corn, sugar cane.

Bisenti (bēzĕn'tē), town (pop. 1,111), Teramo prov., Abruzzi e Molise, S central Italy, 11 mi. SE of Teramo, in agr. region (grapes, olives, fruit).

Bisenz, Czechoslovakia: see BZENEC.

Biser (bē'syĭr), town (1926 pop. 1,479), E Molotov oblast, Russian SFSR, on Koiva R. and 39 mi. ENE (under jurisdiction) of Chusovoi; charcoal-fed ironworks; manganese and hematite deposits. Until 1928, called Biserski Zavod. Biser rail station (7 mi. N; 1926 pop. 1,031) serves Sarany chromite mines.

Biserovo (bē'syĭrŭvŭ), village (1939 pop. over 2,000), NE Kirov oblast, Russian SFSR, on Kama R. and 50 mi. NE of Omutninsk; coarse grain, flax.

Bisert or **Bisert'** (bēsyĕrt'yŭ), town (1926 pop. 8,080), SW Sverdlovsk oblast, Russian SFSR, on Bisert R. (right tributary of Ufa R.), on railroad and 55 mi. W of Sverdlovsk; agr.-machinery mfg. Until 1942, Bisertski Zavod.

Bisetun, Iran: see BEHISTUN.

Bisevo Island (bē'shĕvô), Serbo-Croatian *Biševo,* Ital. *Busi* (bōō'zē), Dalmatian island in Adriatic Sea, S Croatia Yugoslavia, c.40 mi. SSW of Split; 3 mi. long, 1 mi. wide. Sometimes spelled Bishevo.

Bisha (bē'shä), Ital. *Biscia,* village, Agordat div., W Eritrea, 20 mi. W of Agordat; terminus of railroad from Massawa; senna, fruit, grain, dom nuts; cattle. Mica mine near by.

Bisha or **Bishah** (bē'shŭ), town and oasis in Asir hinterland, Saudi Arabia, on the interior Wadi Bisha and 140 mi. ENE of Qunfidha, and on caravan route to the Wadi Dawasir; noted date-growing center. Briefly held in 1834 by Egyptians.

Bisharri, Lebanon: see BSHERRI.

Bishenpur (bĭshän'pŏŏr). **1** Village, Manipur, NE India, 17 mi. SW of Imphal; rice, mustard, sugar cane. Figured in Jap. invasion of India in 1944. **2** Town, West Bengal, India: see BISHNUPUR.

Bishevo Island, Yugoslavia: see BISEVO ISLAND.

Bishini, Nigeria: see BICHINI.

Bishkhali River, E Pakistan: see ARIAL KHAN RIVER.

Bishla (bĭsh'lă), village (pop. 8,020), Daqahliya prov., Lower Egypt, 4 mi. N of Mit Ghamr; cotton, cereals.

Bishnupur (bĭsh'nōōpŏŏr), town (pop. 24,961), Bankura dist., W central West Bengal, India, on Rupnarayan R. and 19 mi. SE of Bankura: silk-weaving center; rice and oilseed milling, cotton weaving; general engineering works. Has col. Was ⊙ Hindu kingdom founded 8th cent. A.D.; surrounded by 7 mi. of fortification ruins. Formerly spelled Bishenpur.

Bishoftu (bĭshō'too), Ital. *Biscioftu,* village, Shoa prov., central Ethiopia, on railroad and 25 mi. SE of Addis Ababa. Emperor's summer residence. Agr. settlement (cereals, vegetables, fruit) founded here (1937) by Italians.

Bishop. 1 Town (pop. 2,891), Inyo co., E Calif., in Owens Valley, at E base of the Sierra Nevada, c.50 mi. SE of Mono L.; alt. 4,145 ft. Its railroad station is Laws (4 mi. NE). Resort in stock-raising and mining region (tungsten, gold, silver). Hq. of Inyo Natl. Forest. In Bishop Creek Canyon (SW) is a power plant. Paiute Indian reservation near by. Settled 1861, inc. 1903. **2** Town (pop. 253), Oconee co., NE central Ga., 10 mi. SSW of Athens. **3** Town (pop. 2,731), Nueces co., S Texas, 29 mi. SW of Corpus Christi; trade, processing center in oil, cotton area; cotton ginning, feed milling; large plant near by produces chemicals from natural gas.

Bishop and Clerk, Tasmania: see MACQUARIE ISLAND.

Bishop and Clerks (–klärks), group of small rocky islands in St. George's Channel, off Pembrokeshire, Wales. South Bishop, Welsh *Em-sger,* has lighthouse (51°51'N 5°26'W).

Bishop Auckland (ô'klŭnd), urban district (1931 pop. 12,277; 1951 census 36,350), central Durham, England, on Wear R. and 9 mi. SSW of Durham; coal mining, machine shops. Seat of bishops of Durham since c.1300; Auckland Castle dates mainly from 16th cent. and has late 12th-cent. chapel.

Bishopbriggs, town in Cadder parish, N Lanark, Scotland, 4 mi. NNE of Glasgow; coal mining, soap mfg.

Bishop Hill, village (pop. 202), Henry co., NW Ill., 20 mi. NE of Galesburg, in agr. and bituminous-coal area. Founded 1846 as a religious communal venture by Swedish immigrants led by Erik Janson, who is buried here.

Bishopric, village, S Sask., on Johnstone L., 28 mi. SSW of Moose Jaw; sodium-sulphate production.

Bishop Rock, islet of Scilly Isls., Cornwall, England, in the Atlantic 7 mi. WSW of Hugh Town; site of lighthouse (49°52'N 6°27'W), major navigational landmark.

Bishop's Castle, municipal borough (1931 pop. 1,352; 1951 census pop. 1,291), SW Shropshire, England, 15 mi. NW of Ludlow; agr. market. The town arose about the Norman castle of the bishops of Hereford; there are remains of the castle.

Bishop's Falls, village (pop. 2,521), central N.F., on Exploits R. and 8 mi. NE of Grand Falls; pulp-milling and lumbering center. Pulp is pumped to Grand Falls paper mills.

Bishop's Hatfield, England: see HATFIELD.

Bishops Head, fishing village (pop. c.250), Dorchester co., E Md., on the Eastern Shore 22 mi. S of Cambridge, and on Honga R.

Bishop's Lydeard (lĭd'yŭrd), town and parish (pop. 2,309), W central Somerset, England, 5 mi. NW of Taunton; agr. market; sandstone quarries. Site of mental hosp. Has 15th-cent. church.

Bishop's Stortford (stôr'fŭrd), residential urban district (1931 pop. 9,510; 1951 census 12,772), E Hertford, England, on Stort R. and 12 mi. ENE of Hertford; electrical-equipment mfg. Has 14th-cent. church and remains of Norman castle, formerly property of bishops of London. Cecil Rhodes b. here.

Bishopsteignton (–tān'tŭn), agr. village and parish (pop. 1,176), S Devon, England, 2 mi. W of Teignmouth. Has 15th-cent. church.

Bishopstoke, England: see EASTLEIGH.

Bishopston, agr. village and parish (pop. 1,504), SW Glamorgan, Wales, 6 mi. SW of Swansea.

Bishop's Waltham (wôl'tŭm, –thŭm), town and parish (pop. 2,782), S central Hampshire, England, 9 mi. ENE of Southampton; agr. market. Has 15th-cent. church and ruins of 12th-cent. palace of bishops of Winchester.

Bishopsworth, residential town and parish (pop. 1,866), N Somerset, England, 3 mi. SSW of Bristol. Has Norman church.

Bishopthorpe, agr. village and parish (pop. 779), West Riding, central Yorkshire, England, on Ouse R. and 3 mi. S of York. Palace of Archbishop of York, here, dates mainly from late 18th cent.

Bishopton, Scotland: see ERSKINE.

Bishopville, town (pop. 3,076), ⊙ Lee co., NE central S.C., 20 mi. NNE of Sumter, in agr. area; lumber, grain, cottonseed oil. Lee State Park is E, along Lynches R.

Bishopwearmouth, Durham, England, part of SUNDERLAND.

Bisignano (bēzēnyä'nô), town (pop. 5,483), Cosenza prov., Calabria, S Italy, near Crati R., 16 mi. N of Cosenza; agr. center (wine, olive oil, figs), livestock; anc. ceramic industry. Bishopric. Has cathedral and remains of castle. Damaged by several earthquakes.

Bisingen (bē'zĭng-ŭn), village (pop. 2,588), Hohenzollern, S Germany, after 1945 in Württemberg-Hohenzollern, in Swabian Jura, 3.5 mi. SW of Hechingen; knitwear and shoe mfg.

Bisitun, Iran: see BEHISTUN.

Bisk, Biisk, or **Biysk** (bēsk), city (1939 pop. 80,190), central Altai Territory, Russian SFSR, on Biya R. (head of navigation), near its confluence with Katun R., and 80 mi. SE of Barnaul. Terminus of branch of Turksib RR; center of dairy-farming area; meat plant, linen mills, sugar refinery, distillery. Trade with Mongolia via Chuya highway. Teachers col. Founded 1709; a Rus. frontier stronghold in 18th cent.

Biskotasi Lake (bĭ'skōtă"sē) (27 mi. long, 2 mi. wide), SE central Ont., 75 mi. NW of Sudbury; drained S by Spanish R.

Biskra (bēskrä', bĭs'krŭ), anc. *Vescera*, town and oasis (pop. 36,347), in Constantine dept., NE Algeria, at border of Southern Territories, 115 mi. SSW of Constantine (linked by rail) and 120 mi. N of Touggourt (narrow-gauge railroad); 34°52'N 5°44'E. Date-shipping center of the semi-arid, oasis-dotted Ziban region, and well-known health resort (large hotels) noted for its dry and cool winter climate (Jan. temp. average 52°F; almost no rainfall). Oasis is irrigated by intermittent streams from S slopes of the Saharan Atlas (Zab Mts., Aurès) and by artesian wells. Olives and Mediterranean fruit are grown in addition to date palms. Has govt. agr. experiment station. Airfield. Modern Biskra was founded 1844 as Fr. military post; its garrison was massacred by Arabs. Reinforced, the French withstood the insurrection of 1849. Among smaller near-by oases are Sidi-Okba (mosque), Ourlal, Chetma, and Tolga (rail spur).

Biskupiec (bēskōō'pyĕts). **1** Ger. *Bischofsburg* (bĭ'shôfsbŏŏrk"), town (1939 pop. 8,463; 1946 pop. 2,422) in East Prussia, after 1945 in Olsztyn prov., NE Poland, in Masurian Lakes region, 20 mi. ENE of Allenstein (Olsztyn); grain and cattle market; woodworking, brewing; power station. In Second World War, c.55% destroyed. **2** Ger. *Bischofswerder* (bĭ"shôfsvĕr'dŭr), town (1939 pop. 1,828; 1946 pop. 1,463) in East Prussia, after 1945 in Olsztyn prov., NE Poland, 8 mi. SSE of Kisielice; grain and cattle market. Until 1939, Ger. frontier station on Pol. border.

Bisley (bĭz'lē), agr. village and parish (pop. 1,151), W Surrey, England, 4 mi. W of Woking; site of ranges of Natl. Rifle Association and scene of annual competition.

Bisley with Lypiatt, agr. parish (pop. 1,782), central Gloucester, England. Includes agr. village of Bisley, 3 mi. E of Stroud, with anc. Saxon cross and church dating partly from 13th cent. Just W is village of Lypiatt Park, with mansion.

Bislig (bĭs'lĭg, Sp. bēslēg'), town (1939 pop. 2,814; 1948 municipality pop. 5,019), Surigao prov., E Mindanao, Philippines, 15 mi. S of San Juan; copra.

Bismarck (bĭz'märk). **1** City (pop. 1,244), St. Francois co., E Mo., in the St. Francois Mts., 8 mi. SE of Flat River; agr.; lumber products. Laid out 1868. **2** City (pop. 18,640), ⊙ N.Dak. and Burleigh co., on Missouri R. and 190 mi. W of Fargo; 46°48'N 100°45'W; alt. 1,670 ft. Coal mines; railroad junction; shipping of dairy products, wool, honey, corn; mfg. (optical equipment, concrete products, farm machinery, brick and tile); farm produce (spring wheat, livestock, dairy goods, poultry). Has a jr. col. Became railroad center and supply point for Black Hills gold mines in 1874 and territorial ⊙ in 1883. The capitol is a skyscraper built in 1932. State penitentiary is near by. Settled 1871–72, inc. 1877.

Bismarck, Cape (bĭz'märk), NE Greenland, on Greenland Sea, opposite N ends of Great Koldewey and Little Koldewey isls.; 76°42'N 18°40'W.

Bismarck Archipelago, volcanic group (□ 19,200), Territory of New Guinea (see NEW GUINEA, TERRITORY OF), SW Pacific; includes NEW BRITAIN (largest isl.), NEW IRELAND, LAVONGAI, ADMIRALTY ISLANDS, DUKE OF YORK ISLANDS, MUSSAU, VITU ISLANDS. Mountainous, with several active volcanoes; dense vegetation. Several good harbors; best in Blanche Bay, New Britain, site of Rabaul (former ⊙ Territory of New Guinea). Produces copra, pearls, cacao, some copper and gold. Group became German protectorate 1884. Occupied 1914 in First World War by Australian forces; became 1920 Australian mandated territory. In Second World War, site of Jap. naval and air bases (Rabaul being chief stronghold) which were neutralized 1943–44. U.N. approved (1947) Australian trusteeship of group.

Bismarckburg, Tanganyika: see KASANGA.

Bismarckhütte, Poland: see CHORZOW.

Bismarck Mountains, NE New Guinea, SW of upper course of Ramu R. Highest peaks: Mt. Wilhelm (14,107 ft.), Mt. Herbert (13,123 ft.).

Bismarck Sea, SW arm of Pacific Ocean, NE of New Guinea and NW of New Britain. In Second World War, scene (1943) of destruction of Jap naval force by U.S. aircraft.

Bismark (bĭz'märk, Ger. bĭs'märk), town (pop. 3,412), in former Prussian Saxony prov., central Germany, after 1945 in Saxony-Anhalt, 13 mi. WNW of Stendal; agr. market (grain, potatoes, livestock); mfg. of incubators, bricks. Has 13th-cent. church; remains of ancestral castle of Bismarck family.

Bismil (bĭsmĭl'), village (pop. 2,049), Diyarbakir prov., E Turkey, on railroad, on Tigris R., and 25 mi. E of Diyarbakir; wheat, barley, millet, chickpeas, lentils.

Bisnulok, Thailand: see PHITSANULOK.

Bison (bī'sŭn). **1** City (pop. 326), Rush co., central Kansas, 6 mi. E of La Crosse, in wheat and stock area. **2** Town (pop. 457), ⊙ Perkins co., NW S.Dak., 110 mi. NNE of Rapid City; trade center for cattle and grain area; lignite mines.

Bison Peak (12,427 ft.), in Tarryall Mts., central Colo., c.40 mi. SSW of Denver.

Bisotun, Iran: see BEHISTUN.

Bispfors (bĭsp"fôrs', –fôsh'), village (pop. 434), Jamtland co., N central Sweden, on Indal R. (falls) and 20 mi. WSW of Solleftea; hydroelectric station; dairying.

Bispgarden (bĭsp'gôr"dŭn), Swedish *Bispgården*, village (pop. 403), Jamtland co., N central Sweden, on Indal R. and 20 mi. WSW of Solleftea; resort.

Bispingen (bĭs'pĭng-ŭn), village (pop. 2,327), in former Prussian prov. of Hanover, NW Germany, after 1945 in Lower Saxony, 9 mi. NE of Soltau; rope mfg., sawmilling.

Bisra (bĭs'rŭ), village, Sundargarh dist., N Orissa, India, 60 mi. E of Sundargarh. Limestone quarries near by.

Bisrampur, India: see AMBIKAPUR.

Bissagos Islands, Port. Guinea: see BIJAGÓS ISLANDS.

Bissau (bĭs'sou), town (pop. 8,472), N Rajasthan, India, 21 mi. WNW of Jhunjhunu; local market for cattle, wool; camel breeding.

Bissau (bēsou'), city (pop. 3,362), ⊙ Portuguese Guinea, seaport on Bissau isl. in Geba R. estuary, 250 mi. SSE of Dakar (Fr. West Africa); 11°52'N 15°37'W. Exports tropical hardwoods, peanuts, copra, palm oil, palm kernels, rubber, cattle, hides and skins; rice milling, pottery mfg. Transshipping point (new pier) for river navigation to the interior. Airfield 3 mi. W. Radio transmitter. Its recently completed public bldgs. include governor's mansion, cathedral, mus., hosp. Established as a fortified post and slave-trading center end of 17th cent. A free port since 1869. Capital was transferred here in 1941 from Bolama.

Bissegem (bĭ'sŭ-khŭm), town (pop. 4,222), West Flanders prov., NW Belgium, on Lys R., WSW suburb of Courtrai.

Bissen (bĭ'sŭn), village (pop. 1,040), central Luxembourg, 12 mi. N of Luxembourg city; nail mfg.; agr., fruit growing (apples, pears).

Bissikrima (bēsēkrē'mä), village, central Fr. Guinea, Fr. West Africa, on Conakry-Kankan RR and 12 mi. ENE of Dabola; rice, peanuts, rubber, honey, beeswax, cattle.

Bissingen or **Bissingen an der Enz** (bĭ'sĭng-ŭn än dĕr ĕnts'), village (pop. 3,945), N. Württemberg, Germany, after 1945 in Württemberg-Baden, on the Enz and 1.5 mi. SW of Bietigheim; wine, hops.

Bisten (bē'stŭn), village (pop. 508), SW Saar, on Fr. border, on Bist R. and 5 mi. SSW of Saarlouis; flour milling; grain, stock. Just S is Überherrn, frontier station opposite town of Hargarten-Falck, France.

Bistineau, Lake (bĭ'stĕnō), NW La., c.20 mi. SE of Shreveport; c.16 mi. long; fishing. Inlet is Bayou Dorcheat; drains through outlet to Red R.

Bist Jullundur Doab (bĭst' jōōl-lōōn'dōōr dō'äb), tract in Punjab, India, bet. Sutlej R. (S) and Beas R. (N, W); comprises Jullundur dist., Kapurthala (Patiala and East Punjab States Union), and most of Hoshiarpur dist.

Bistra Mountains (bē'strä), in the Pindus system, W Macedonia, Yugoslavia; highest point (6,426 ft.) is 11 mi. NW of Kicevo.

Bistrica (bē'strĭtsä). **1** or **Ilirska Bistrica** (ēlēr'skä), Ital. *Villa del Nevoso* (vēl'lä dĕl nävō'zō), village (pop. 3,470), SW Slovenia, Yugoslavia, on the Reka, on railroad and 17 mi. NNW of Rijeka, at W foot of Sneznik mtn.; woodworking; timber trade. Until 1947, in Italy. **2** or **Slovenska Bistrica** (slô'vĕnskä), Ger. *Windisch-Feistritz* (vĭn'dĭsh-fī'strĭts), village, NE Slovenia, Yugoslavia, 12 mi SSW of Maribor, in brown-coal area; vineyards. Terminus of branch of Vienna-Zagreb RR. Has old church, castle. Until 1918, in Carniola.

Bistrita or **Bistritsa** (bē'strētsä), Rum. *Bistrița*, Ger. *Bistritz*, Hung. *Beszterce* (bĕ'stĕrchĕ), town (1948 pop. 15,801), ⊙ Rodna prov., N central Rumania, in Transylvania, on railroad and 180 mi. NNW of Bucharest; commercial center, trading mainly in lumber and agr. produce; cabinetmaking, brewing, tanning, food processing; mfg. of footwear, painting brushes, stoves, earthenware, soap, vinegar, alcohol. High-quality wine is produced by the near-by vineyards. One of the original 7 towns founded in Transylvania by Ger. colonists (12th-13th cent.), it still preserves many medieval houses and some remains of fortifications built by Janos Hunyadi. Notable landmarks are 13th-cent. Greek-Catholic church, with old frescoes; Gothic Evangelical church with 235-ft. tower; arcaded market-place. Former royal free town, it fell in 13th cent. under Tatar domination and was later governed by Moldavian voivodes (14th cent.). The well-known skill of its stone-carvers was much in demand during Middle Ages. About 25% pop. are Germans and Magyars (Szeklers). In Hungary, 1940–45.

Bistrita, Rumania: see HOREZU.

Bistrita River, Rum. *Bistrița*, Ger. *Bistritz*, Hung. *Beszterce*. **1** In E and NE Rumania, in Bukovina and Moldavia, rises on E slopes of the Carpathians at Prislop Pass, 30 mi. W of Campulung, flows SE through the Moldavian Carpathians and past Vatra-Dornei, Piatra-Neamt, and Bacau to Siret R. 4 mi. below Domnita-Maria; c.175 mi. long. Forms many rapids and is extensively used for logging. Has regular summer schedule for navigation by rafts below Vatra-Dornei. Lower valley is noted as site of many hydroelectric plants and picturesque Moldavian monasteries. **2** In Transylvania, Rumania, rises on W slopes of the Carpathians SW of Vatra-Dornei, flows 50 mi. W, past Bistrita, to a tributary of Somes R.

Bistritsa River, Greece: see ALIAKMON RIVER.

Bisutun, Iran: see BEHISTUN.

Biswan (bĭsvän'), town (pop. 10,549), Sitapur dist., central Uttar Pradesh, India, 20 mi. ESE of Sitapur; road junction; sugar processing, mfg. (cotton prints, pottery, tabuts). Founded c.1350. Has 11th-cent. Moslem tombs, 17th-18th-cent. mosques.

Bisztynek (bēsh-tĭ'nĕk), Ger. *Bischofstein* (bĭ'shôfshtīn"), town (1939 pop. 3,163; 1946 pop. 1,178) in East Prussia, after 1945 in Olsztyn prov., NE Poland, 30 mi. NNE of Allenstein (Olsztyn); grain, cattle market; sawmilling, limestone quarrying.

Bitam (bētäm′), village, N Gabon, Fr. Equatorial Africa, 40 mi. NNW of Oyem, near Sp. Guinea and Fr. Cameroons border; customs station; cacao.

Bitburg (bĭt′bŏŏrk), town (pop. 3,864), in former Prussian Rhine Prov., W Germany, after 1945 in Rhineland-Palatinate, in the Eifel, 16 mi. N of Trier. Was Roman settlement.

Bitche (bēch), Ger. *Bitsch* (bĭch), town (pop. 3,241), Moselle dept., NE France, in the N Vosges, 17 mi. ESE of Sarreguemines; road center; mfg. (shoes, porcelain). Fort atop hill (c.250 ft. high) overlooking town was besieged in 1793 and again in 1870. During Second World War Germans resisted Allied advance in winter of 1944–45.

Bitchu (bēchōō′), former province in SW Honshu, Japan; now part of Okayama prefecture.

Bitetto (bētĕt′tō), town (pop. 5,991), Bari prov., Apulia, S Italy, 8 mi. SSW of Bari. Has cathedral (begun 1335).

Bithlo, town (pop. 50), Orange co., central Fla., 17 mi. E of Orlando.

Bithur (bĭtōōr′), town (pop. 2,543), Cawnpore dist., central Uttar Pradesh, India, on the Ganges and 11 mi. NNW of Cawnpore; gram, wheat, jowar, barley. Mahratta temple. Mahratta palaces here destroyed during Sepoy Rebellion of 1857. Large annual bathing festival, connected with Brahma legend. Reputedly the site where original Sanskrit version of the Ramayana was composed. First recorded implement (harpoon) of the Copper Age in India discovered here, 1821.

Bithynia (bĭ-thĭ′nēŭ), anc. country of NW Asia Minor, in present Turkey, bordering on Black Sea and Sea of Marmara. It was an independent kingdom and later an important prov. of Rome, taken from Byzantine Empire by the Seljuks in 11th cent. Cities included Nicaea, Nicomedia, Prusa, Chalcedon, Heraclea Pontica. Mysia was to SW, Phrygia to S, Galatia to SE, Paphlagonia to E.

Bitkow, Ukrainian SSR: see BYTKOV.

Bitlis (bĭtlĭs′), prov. (□ 2,679; 1950 pop. 88,422), SE Turkey; ⊙ Bitlis. Borders E on L. Van. Mountainous; produces some grain, tobacco, potatoes. Pop. largely Kurd.

Bitlis, town (1950 pop. 11,152), ⊙ Bitlis, SE Turkey, 105 mi. ENE of Diyarbakir, 12 mi. SW of L. Van; alt. 4,600 ft. Tobacco factory for local crops; potatoes, arsenic and mineral springs near by. Old town in Kurd and Armenian area. Has mosques and convent of whirling dervishes.

Bitlis Mountains, E central Turkey, part of Taurus Mts., extend 90 mi. W from Bitlis; rise to 9,735 ft. in Sasun Dag. Lignite, copper, silver in W.

Bitolj, Bitol, or **Bitol'** (all: bē′tôl, bē′tôlyŭ), Macedonian *Bitola* (bē′tôlä), Turkish *Monastir*, city (pop. 31,131), ⊙ Bitolj oblast (formed 1949), Macedonia, Yugoslavia, on railroad and 65 mi. S of Skoplje. Center of fertile Pelagonija valley and of Bitolj Plain (noted for homemade reed and rush mats); homemade ropes. Has many mosques, covered Turkish market; teachers col. Ruins of Heraclea Lyncestis, a Roman city, near by. First mentioned in 1014; became bishopric (11th cent.); surpassed Skoplje in Turkish period (1382–1913); heavily damaged in First World War. Formerly also spelled Bitolia or Bitolya.

Bitonto (bētōn′tō), anc. *Butuntum*, town (pop. 27,341), Bari prov., Apulia, S Italy, 9 mi. WSW of Bari. Agr. center; wine, olive oil, macaroni, cement, wax products, musical instruments; foundry. Bishopric. Noted for its Romanesque-Apulian cathedral.

Bitov, Czechoslovakia: see VRANOV.

Bitovnja Mountains or **Bitovnya Mountains** (both: bē′tôvnyä), in Dinaric Alps, N Herzegovina, Yugoslavia; c.3 mi. long Highest point (5,776 ft.) is 11 mi. N of Konjic.

Bitragunta, India: see ALLUR.

Bitritto (bētrēt′tō), town (pop. 5,072), Bari prov., Apulia, S Italy, 6 mi. S of Bari; wine, olive oil.

Bitsch, France: see BITCHE.

Bitschwiller-lès-Thann (bēchvēlâr′-lā-tän′), Ger. *Bitschweiler* (bĭch′vīlŭr), village (pop. 1,737), Haut-Rhin dept., E France, on the Thur and 2 mi. NW of Thann, in the SE Vosges; thermostats, pressure gauges, furniture. Until 1938, Bitschwiller.

Bitter Creek, SW Wyo., rises in Rocky Mts. in SE Sweetwater co., flows c.80 mi. NW and W, past Rock Springs, to Green R. near Green River town.

Bitterfeld (bĭ′tŭrfĕlt), town (pop. 32,833), in former Prussian Saxony prov., central Germany, after 1945 in Saxony-Anhalt, on the Mulde and 18 mi. NE of Halle; rail junction. Industrial center. metallurgy (light metals, steel, alloys), mfg. of basic chemicals, dyes, pottery, glass; textile milling. Center of important lignite-mining region. Power station. Founded in 12th cent. by Flemish settlers.

Bitter Lake, Day co., NE S.Dak., 25 mi. NNW of Watertown; 4 mi. long, 2 mi. wide.

Bitter Lakes, 2 lakes, now joined, NE Egypt, N of Suez, and traversed by the SUEZ CANAL. Great Bitter Lake (N), 14 mi. long, 8 mi. wide, is 7 mi. S of L. Timsah; Little Bitter Lake (S), 8 mi. long, 2 mi wide, is 13 mi. N of Suez. When the canal was built the lakes were nearly dry.

Bitterley, agr. village and parish (pop. 985), S Shropshire, England, 4 mi. NE of Ludlow; granite quarrying. Has church dating from 13th cent.

Bitterne, England: see SOUTHAMPTON.

Bittern Lake, village (pop. 38), central Alta., on Bittern L. (8 mi. long, 5 mi. wide), 10 mi. W of Camrose; coal mining.

Bitterroot Range, in Rocky Mts., extends S along Idaho-Mont. line, from the Clark Fork to Monida in SW Mont.; bounded NE and E by the Clark Fork, E by Bitterroot R. Part of Bitterroot Natl. Forest in center. Crossed W of Missoula by Lolo Pass (5,187 ft.), used by Lewis and Clark in 1805 and 1806. Prominent peaks: Lolo Peak (9,075 ft.), El Capitan (9,936 ft.), Trapper Peak (10,175 ft.). S part of range is also known as Beaverhead Mts.; extending SE from Nez Perce Pass (on Idaho line, c.25 mi. SW of Darby, Mont.) to Monida, the Beaverhead section contains Ajax Mtn. (10,900 ft.) and Garfield Mtn. (10,961 ft.; highest point in range).

Bitterroot River, W Mont., rises at S tip of Ravalli co., flows c.120 mi. N, past Darby and Hamilton, bet. Bitterroot Range and Sapphire Mts., to the Clark Fork just W of Missoula; irrigates rich agr. region.

Bitti (bēt′tē), town (pop. 5,224), Nuoro prov., NE central Sardinia, 12 mi. N of Nuoro. Dolmen near by.

Bittir, Israel: see BETHER.

Bitton, town and parish (pop. 3,359), SW Gloucester, England, 6 mi. ESE of Bristol; shoes, paper. Has 14th-cent. church.

Bityug River (bētyōōk′), S central European Russian SFSR, rises NE of Tokarevka (in Tambov), flows 220 mi. W and S, past Bobrov, to Don R. 14 mi. NW of Pavlovsk. Horse-breeding farms along banks.

Biu (byōō), town (pop. 4,127), Bornu prov., Northern Provinces, NE Nigeria, 110 mi. SW of Maiduguri; agr. trade center; cattle, skins; gum arabic, peanuts, cassava, millet. Limestone deposits.

Biumba (byōōm′bä), village, N Ruanda-Urundi, in Ruanda, 24 mi. N of Kigali; alt. 7,544 ft.; center of native trade in grazing and coffee-growing region; dairying, brick making.

Bivalve (bī′vălv). **1** Village (pop. c.300), Wicomico co., SE Md., 17 mi. WSW of Salisbury and on Nanticoke R.; fishing, oystering, muskrat trapping. **2** Village (pop. c.350), Cumberland co., S N.J., on Maurice R., near Delaware Bay, and 11 mi. S of Millville; oysters, oyster-shell products.

Biver, Luxembourg: see WECKER.

Biviere di Lentini, Sicily: see LENTINI, LAKE.

Bivolari (bēvôlä′rē), agr. village (pop. 3,226), Jassy prov., NE Rumania, on Prut R. (USSR border) and 25 mi. NNW of Jassy.

Bivona (bēvô′nä), village (pop. 5,222), Agrigento prov., SW central Sicily, near Magazzolo R., 23 mi. NNW of Agrigento. Has 12th-cent. church.

Bivongi (bēvôn′jē), village (pop. 3,823), Reggio di Calabria prov., Calabria, S Italy, 17 mi. NE of Siderno Marina; wine, olive oil, raw silk.

Biwa, Lake (bē′wä), Jap. *Biwa-ko*, largest lake (□ 261) of Japan, in Shiga prefecture, S Honshu, 5 mi. NE of Kyoto; 40 mi. long, 2–12 mi. wide, 315 ft. deep; contains many small isls. Its only outlet is Seta R. (upper course of Yodo R.) at S end. Canal (7.5 mi. long) connects lake with Kyoto; supplies city with hydroelectric power. Excursion steamers. Lake contains many species of fish, including trout, carp, sheatfish.

Biwabik (bĭwä′bĭk, bĭ–), village (pop. 1,245), St. Louis co., NE Minn., in Mesabi iron range, in lake region, 10 mi. E of Virginia; iron mines. Superior Natl. Forest near by.

Bixby, town (pop. 1,517), Tulsa co., NE Okla., on Arkansas R. and 16 mi. SSE of Tulsa, in agr. area (grain, truck, pecans); food canning, pecan shelling, cotton ginning; oil wells; also gasoline and naphtha mfg. Founded 1893, inc. 1907.

Bixby Dam, S.Dak.: see MOREAU RIVER.

Bixschoote, Belgium: see BIKSCHOTE.

Biyala or **Biyalah** (bĭ′yălŭ), village (pop. 17,731; with suburbs, 20,622), Gharbiya prov., Lower Egypt, on railroad and 15 mi. NNE of El Mahalla el Kubra; cotton.

Biya River (bē′ŭ), E Altai Territory, Russian SFSR, right headstream of Ob R.; rises in TELETSKOYE LAKE of Altai Mts.; flows NW, past Turochak, and W, past Bisk (head of navigation), joining Katun R. at Katun to form Ob R.; 147 mi. long. Upper course has rapids.

Biyelo Polye, Yugoslavia: see BIJELO POLJE.

Biyelyina, Yugoslavia: see BIJELJINA.

Biy-Khem, Russian SFSR: see YENISEI RIVER.

Biysk, Russian SFSR: see BISK.

Biyuk-Onlar, Russian SFSR: see OKTYABRSKOYE, Crimea.

Bizanet (bēzänā′), village (pop. 1,112), Aude dept., S France, 7 mi. WSW of Narbonne; distilling, winegrowing. Near by is 12th-13th-cent. Benedictine abbey of Fontfroide.

Bizanos (bēzänō′), SW suburb (pop. 2,761) of Pau, Basses-Pyrénées dept., SW France, on the Gave de Pau; mfg. of berets, furniture, candies.

Bizard, Île (ēl bēzär′), island (4 mi. long, 3 mi. wide; pop. 783), S Que., in L. of the Two Mountains, just W of Montreal Isl.

Bizcocho, Cuchilla del (kōōchē′yä dĕl bēskō′chō), hill range, Soriano dept., SW Uruguay, NW continuation of the Cuchilla Grande Inferior, extends NW from Cardona, c.50 mi. to area of Mercedes; rises 570 ft. Crossed by Montevideo-Mercedes RR.

Bize-Minervois (bēz-mēnĕrvwä′), village (pop. 1,067), Aude dept., S France, 11 mi. NW of Narbonne; winegrowing. Coal mining.

Bizen (bē′zān), former province in SW Honshu, Japan; now part of Okayama prefecture.

Bizerte (bĭzûr′tŭ, Fr. bēzârt′) or **Bizerta** (bĭzûr′tŭ), anc. *Hippo Zarytus*, city (pop. 39,327), ⊙ Bizerte dist. (□ 1,360; pop. 238,284), N Tunisia, important port and naval base strategically located near narrowest part of the Mediterranean, 37 mi. NNW of Tunis; northernmost city of Africa; 37°16′N 9°53′E. Situated on N bank of outlet (Fr. *goulet*) of L. of Bizerte to the sea, city has a 3-fold harbor: the outer basin (directly on the Mediterranean), protected by 2 converging jetties and a breakwater; the inner harbor along entrance channel to the lake and in Sebra Bay (a widening of the *goulet* about midway bet. the lake and the sea); and the naval base of Sidi Abdallah, with adjacent military installations at Ferryville, on S shore of L. of Bizerte, 9 mi. from city proper. In addition to metalworks connected with the Ferryville arsenal, Bizerte has olive-oil and flour mills, brick- and tileworks, fish-processing plants. Marble quarries near by. Airport. Little remains of the old Arab quarter surrounding the *casbah* and of anc. port dist. on the Mediterranean. Modern European city has arisen further S, directly on the canalized section of the *goulet*. Anciently a colony of Tyre, Bizerte had a checkered career under Romans, Vandals, Arabs, Moors, Spaniards (1534–72), and Barbary pirates. Occupied by French in 1881. Its port, which had fallen into disuse, was rebuilt and reopened in 1895. Heavily bombed by Allies during Tunisian campaign of 1943, when it was a German base, city was almost leveled by the time it was finally captured May 7–9, 1943. Reconstruction proceeded rapidly after Second World War.

Bizerte, Cape, headland on coast of Tunisia, 4 mi. N of Bizerte; 37°19′N 9°52′E.

Bizerte, Lake of, circular lagoon (□ 42) in N Tunisia, linked with the Mediterranean by an outlet (Fr. *goulet*) c.4 mi. long, 650 ft. to 1 mi. wide. City of Bizerte is at canalized N end of outlet. Over ⅓ of lake has depth of 33 ft. On its S shore, 9 mi. from Bizerte, is naval base of Sidi Abdallah and adjacent military installation of Ferryville. Just N is outlet from near-by L. Achkel.

Bizhbulyak (bēzhbŏŏlyäk′), village (1948 pop. over 2,000), W Bashkir Autonomous SSR, Russian SFSR, 70 mi. WNW of Sterlitamak; wheat, rye.

Bizot (bēzō′), village (pop. 1,164), Constantine dept., NE Algeria, on railroad and 6 mi. N of Constantine; brickworks; wheat growing.

Bjarkoy (byärk′ûü), Nor. *Bjarkøy*, island (□ 5.6; pop. 717) in Norwegian Sea, in Vesteralen group N of Hinnoy, Troms co., N Norway, 12 mi. N of Harstad; 69°N. It is 4 mi. long. Bjarkoy village is in NE. Iron mines; fishing.

Bjarna, Finland: see PERNIÖ.

Bjarnum (byâr′nŭm″), Swedish *Bjärnum*, village (pop. 1,589), Kristianstad co., S Sweden, 9 mi. N of Hassleholm; furniture mfg.

Bjarred (byâ′răd″), Swedish *Bjärred*, residential village (pop. 1,147), Malmohus co., S Sweden, on Oresund, 7 mi. N of Malmo; seaside resort.

Bjasta (byĕ′stä″), Swedish *Bjästa*, village (pop. 500), Vasternorrland co., NE Sweden, near Gulf of Bothnia, 9 mi. SW of Ornskoldsvik; lumber and pulp mills.

Bjelasica or **Byelasitsa** (both: byĕ′läsĭtsä), mountain in Dinaric Alps, E Montenegro, Yugoslavia, bet. Tara and Lim rivers; highest point (6,940 ft.) is 8 mi. E of Kolasin.

Bjelasnica or **Byelashnitsa** (both: byĕ′läshnĭtsä), Serbo-Croatian *Bjelašnica*. **1** Mountain in Dinaric Alps, Yugoslavia, on Bosnia-Herzegovina line. Highest point (6,780 ft.) is 15 mi. E of Konjic. **2** Mountain (4,579 ft.) in Dinaric Alps, S Herzegovina, Yugoslavia, 7 mi. SSE of Ljubinje, along right bank of Trebisnica R.

Bjelopavlici or **Byelopavlichi** (both: byĕ′lôpäv″lĭchē), Serbo-Croatian *Bjelopavlići*, plain in Dinaric Alps, S central Montenegro, Yugoslavia; extends c.15 mi. along Zeta R., in area of Danilov Grad.

Bjelovar (byĕ′lôvär), Hung. *Belovár* (bĕl′ôvär), town (pop. 13,147), ⊙ Bjelovar oblast (formed 1949), N Croatia, Yugoslavia, in Slavonia, 40 mi. E of Zagreb, at S foot of Bilo Gora; rail junction; trade center; meat packing, mfg. of agr. tools. Orthodox Eastern cathedral.

Bjelovo, Bulgaria: see ZEMEN.

Bjerringbro (byĕ′rĭngbrō), town (pop. 2,337), Viborg amt, N central Jutland, Denmark, 10 mi. SE of Viborg; meat packing, mfg. (furniture, cement, electrical materials).

Bjolvefoss (byûl′vŭfôs), Nor. *Bjølvefoss*, falls on short Bjolve R. at its influx into Hardanger Fjord, in Hordaland co., SW Norway, near Alvik and 37 mi. E of Bergen; site of hydroelectric plant and carbide factory.

Bjorbo (byûr′bōō″), Swedish *Björbo*, village (pop. 931), Kopparberg co., central Sweden, on West Dal R. and 20 mi. W of Borlange; rail junction; woodworking.

Bjorgvin, Norway: see BERGEN.
Bjorkasen, Sweden: see GRANGESBERG.
Bjorkboda (byûrk'bōō"dä), Swedish *Björkboda*, village in DRAGSFJARD commune (pop. 4,645), Turku-Pori co., SW Finland, 20 mi. NW of Hango; metalworking.
Bjorko (byûrk'û"), Swedish *Björkö*, fishing village (pop. 721), Goteborg och Bohus co., SW Sweden, on Bjorkon, Swedish *Björkön*, islet in the Skagerrak, 10 mi. WNW of Goteborg.
Björkö, Russian SFSR: see PRIMORSK.
Bjorna Fjord (byûr'nä), Nor. *Bjørnafjord* (formerly *Bjørnefjord*), inlet of the North Sea in Hordaland co., SW Norway; c.15 mi. long, c.6 mi. wide. Entrance is sheltered by many isls.
Bjorneborg, Finland: see PORI.
Bjorneborg (byûr"nùbôr'yù), Swedish *Björneborg*, village (pop. 1,339), Varmland co., W Sweden, 6 mi. SE of Kristinehamn; ironworks.
Bjornefjord, Norway: see BJORNA FJORD.
Bjornerod (byûr'nûrûd"), Swedish *Björneröd*, village (pop. 626), Goteborg och Bohus co., SW Sweden, on Ide Fjord, 10 mi. ENE of Stromstad; customs point on Norwegian border, 8 mi. S of Halden. Includes Kroken (krōō'kùn) village.
Bjornevatn, Norway: see SOR-VARANGER.
Bjornor (byûr'nûr), Nor. *Bjørnør*, former canton in Sor-Trondelag co., central Norway, since 1892 divided into Roan, Osen, and Stoksund cantons.
Bjornoya, Svalbard: see BEAR ISLAND.
Bjornskinn (byûrn'shĭn), Nor. *Bjørnskinn*, village (pop. 153; canton pop. 1,951), Nordland co., N Norway, on SE shore of Andoy in the Vesteralen group, 30 mi. NW of Harstad. Risoyhamn (rēs'ûühäm) (Nor. *Risøyhamn*) village (pop. 124), 2 mi. S, is port and traffic center. Fishing; harvesting of wild mulberries on surrounding moorland.
Bjugn (byōōg'ùn), village and canton (pop. 1,284), Sor-Trondelag co., central Norway, port on an inlet of North Sea, 30 mi. NW of Trondheim; fishing and lobstering center; canneries, herring-oil factories.
Bjurholm (byür"hôlm'), village (pop. 675), Vasterbotten co., N Sweden, 35 mi. W of Umea; road junction; stock; dairying.
Bjurliden, Sweden: see BOLIDEN.
Bjuv (byüv), town (pop. 2,747), Malmohus co., S Sweden, 9 mi. ENE of Halsingborg; rail junction; coal mining, brick making, food canning.
Blaauwberg Strand (blō'bĕrkh), village (pop. 127), SW Cape Prov., U. of So. Afr., on the Atlantic, 10 mi. N of Cape Town; fishing; resort. British forces landed (Jan., 1806) near by prior to their 2d capture of the Cape; defeated Dutch at battle of Blaauwberg. Robben Isl. offshore.
Blaby, town and parish (pop. 2,329), central Leicester, England, 5 mi. SSW of Leicester; hosiery, shoes. Has 13th-cent. church.
Blace or **Blatse** (both: blä'tsĕ), village, S central Serbia, Yugoslavia, 18 mi. S of Krusevac.
Blachownia or **Blachownia Slaska** (bläkh-ôv'nyä shlō'skä), Pol. *Blachownia Śląska*, Ger. *Blechhammer* (blĕkh'hä"mùr), commune (1939 pop. 1,124; 1946 pop. 5,469) in Upper Silesia, after 1945 in Opole prov., S Poland, on Klodnica R. (Gliwice Canal) and 16 mi. WNW of Gleiwitz (Gliwice); synthetic-oil plant; mfg. of chemicals. In Second World War, site, until 1945, of notorious Ger. concentration camp.
Black, native village (1939 pop. 15), W Alaska, on Bering Sea, 30 mi. SW of Akulurak; 62°20'N 165°19'W; trapping; trading post.
Black, town (pop. 239), Geneva co., SE Ala., 26 mi. SW of Dothan, near Fla. line.
Black, Cape, NE extremity of Ellesmere Isl., NE Franklin Dist., Northwest Territories, on Lincoln Sea of the Arctic Ocean, at N entrance of Robeson Channel; 82°23'N 61°W. Peary here landed a supply cache, 1908.
Blackadder Water, river, Berwick, Scotland, rises in Lammermuir Hills 7 mi. NE of Lauder, flows 20 mi. SE and NE to Whiteadder Water 5 mi. E of Duns.
Blackall, town (pop. 1,747), central Queensland, Australia, on Barcoo R. and 145 mi. NNW of Charleville; livestock.
Black Bay, inlet (40 mi. long, 11 mi. wide) of L. Superior, W central Ont., 24 mi. E of Port Arthur, adjoining Thunder Bay. Receives Black Sturgeon R.
Black Bayou (bī'ō) or **Bayou Black,** SE La., waterway extending c.45 mi. generally W from vicinity of Houma, past Houma, and through marshy coastal region, to Atchafalaya R. near Morgan City. Partly followed by Gulf Intracoastal Waterway.
Black Bear Creek, N Okla., rises E of Enid, flows c.100 mi. E, through Noble co., past Pawnee, to Arkansas R. c.40 mi. NW of Tulsa.
Black Belt, SE U.S., region (25–50 mi. wide) of rich, black, limestone-derived soils, curving westward across inner part of Gulf Coast plain from Ga.-Ala. line across central Ala. into W Miss. Drained by Alabama, Black Warrior, and Tombigbee rivers. Pop. of much of region is predominantly Negro. Cotton, long the chief crop, has been replaced in importance by diversified farming (including peanut growing) and livestock raising. Name is also applied generally and more loosely to any region in the South in which the Negro pop. is larger than the white, and in which a plantation-type economy has survived to a certain extent.
Black Bottom, mining village, Harlan co., SE Ky., ENE of Harlan and near Louellen and Closplint; bituminous coal.
Blackburn, county borough (1931 pop. 122,697; 1951 census 111,217), central Lancashire, England, on Leeds-Liverpool Canal and 21 mi. NNW of Manchester; 53°45'N 2°28'W; one of the great cotton-weaving centers of the world, noted especially for calicoes; mfg. also of textile chemicals, pharmaceuticals, paper, light metals; coal mining, engineering A textile center since 17th cent., its importance dates from the invention of the spinning jenny (1764) by James Hargreaves, a native of Blackburn. John Morley b. here. Has art gall. with large collection of English paintings. In the borough is cotton-milling town of Guide.
Blackburn. 1 Town (pop. 306), Saline co., central Mo., 15 mi. W of Marshall. **2** Town (pop. 135), Pawnee co., N Okla., 37 mi. WNW of Tulsa, and on Arkansas R.
Blackburn, Mount (16,140 ft.), S Alaska, in Wrangell Mts., 100 mi. ENE of Valdez; 61°44'N 143°27'W.
Black Butte (būt). **1** Summit (7,450 ft.) of the Coast Ranges, N central Calif., 35 mi. W of Orland. **2** In Mont.: see GRAVELLY RANGE. **3** In Slope co., SW N.Dak., highest point in N.Dak.; alt. 3,468 ft.
Black Butte Reservoir, Calif.: see STONY CREEK.
Black Canyon, gorge cut by Colorado R. bet. NW Ariz. and SE Nev.; extends 21 mi. S from HOOVER DAM.
Black Canyon Dam, SW Idaho, on Payette R. and 5 mi. NE of Emmett. Concrete gravity dam (c.180 ft. high, more than 1,000 ft. long) completed 1924. Unit in Payette div. of Boise irrigation project. Power plant supplies electricity to Minidoka and Owyhee projects.
Black Canyon of the Gunnison National Monument (□ 20.5; established 1933), SW Colo., NE of Montrose. Includes 10-mi. section of Black Canyon, deep (up to 2,425 ft.) narrow gorge of Gunnison R. Noted for sheerness of walls, variety of rock formations, and sombre hues.
Black Cart Water, river, Renfrew, Scotland, rises in Castle Semple Loch, flows 9 mi. NE, past Johnstone, to White Cart Water at Inchinnan.
Black Cheremosh River, Ukrainian SSR: see CHEREMOSH RIVER.
Black Country, highly industrialized region of England, mainly in S Stafford and partly in N Worcester and NW Warwick. Has extensive coal mines, steel mills, iron foundries, and blast furnaces. Includes cities of Birmingham, Wolverhampton, Walsall, Tipton, West Bromwich, Wednesbury, Rowley Regis, Oldbury.
Blackcraig Hill (2,298 ft.), E Ayrshire, Scotland, 5 mi. SE of New Cumnock.
Black Creek. 1 Town (pop. 316), Wilson co., E central N.C., 7 mi. S of Wilson. **2** Village (pop. 650), Outagamie co., E Wis., 15 mi. N of Appleton; dairying, farming.
Black Creek. 1 In S Miss., rises WNW of Hattiesburg, flows c.120 mi. SE to Pascagoula R. in N Jackson co. **2** In NE S.C., rises in Chesterfield co. near N.C. line, flows c.80 mi. generally SE, past Hartsville, to Pee Dee R. 11 mi. NE of Florence.
Black Diamond, village (pop. 1,380), S Alta., at foot of Rocky Mts., on Sheep R. and 25 mi. SSW of Calgary, on E edge of Turner Valley oil field; coal mining.
Black Diamond, mining village (pop. c.1,000), King co., W central Wash., 30 mi. SE of Seattle; coal.
Black Dome, peak (3,990 ft.) of the Catskills, in Greene co., SE N.Y., 13 mi. WNW of Catskill.
Black Down or **Blackdown,** mountain (1,068 ft.), NE Somerset, England, highest point of Mendip Hills, 4 mi. ENE of Axbridge.
Black Down Hills or **Blackdown Hills,** range in W England, extending 8 mi. along Devon-Somerset border just S of Wellington and Taunton; rises to c.900 ft.
Black Drin River (drēn), Serbo-Croatin *Crni Drim* or *Tsrni Drim*, Albanian *Drin i zi* or *Drini i zi*, Ital. *Drin Nero*, left headstream of Drin R., in W Macedonia (Yugoslavia) and N Albania, rises in L. Ochrida at Struga, flows c.80 mi. NNW into Albania, joining the White Drin at Kukës to form the Drin.
Blackduck, resort village (pop. 732), Beltrami co., N Minn., near Blackduck L., 23 mi. NE of Bemidji, in grain and potato region; dairy and lumber products.
Blackduck Lake, Beltrami co., N Minn., 22 mi. NE of Bemidji, in state forest; 3 mi. long, 2 mi. wide. Fishing resorts. Site of prehistoric village on S shore.
Black Eagle, village (pop. 1,449), Cascade co., W central Mont., N suburb of Great Falls, across Missouri R.; electrolytic refining of copper and zinc.
Black Earth, village (pop. 655), Dane co., S Wis., 19 mi. W of Madison, in agr. area; makes cheese.
Black Elster River, Germany: see ELSTER RIVER.
Blackey (blă'kē), town (pop. 393), Letcher co., SE Ky., in the Cumberlands, on North Fork Kentucky R. and 15 mi. ESE of Hazard; sawmill, meat-packing plant.
Blackfalds, village (pop. 119), S central Alta., near Red Deer R., 8 mi. N of Red Deer; mixed farming, dairying, wheat.
Blackfoot, city (pop. 5,180), ⊙ Bingham co., SE Idaho, bet. Snake R. and Blackfoot R. just above their confluence, 22 mi. N of Pocatello in irrigated agr. area (sugar beets, potatoes, grain); beet sugar. Alt. 4,500 ft. Eastern Idaho Fair takes place here annually. Founded 1878, inc. 1907. Seat of state hosp. for insane.
Blackfoot River. 1 In SE Idaho, formed by confluence of 2 forks in Caribou co., flows NW, through Blackfoot Reservoir (14 mi. long; stores water for irrigation), and W to Snake R. 10 mi. NE of American Falls Reservoir; 100 mi. long. **2** In W Mont., rises in Lewis and Clark co., flows c.85 mi. W to the Clark Fork 4 mi. E of Missoula.
Blackford, town and parish (pop. 1,399), S Perthshire, Scotland, 8 mi. SSE of Crieff; shoe mfg. Just SW are remains of anc. Ogilvie Castle.
Blackford, county (□ 167; pop. 14,026), E Ind.; ⊙ Hartford City. Livestock, dairy products, soybeans, grain. Gas and oil wells; stone quarries. Mfg. at Hartford City and Montpelier. Drained by Salamonie R. and small Lick Creek. Formed 1838.
Blackford, town (pop. 165), Webster co., W Ky., on Tradewater R. and 26 mi. WNW of Madisonville.
Black Forest, Ger. *Schwarzwald* (shvärts'vält"), mountain range in S Germany, extends 90 mi. NE from the Rhine (Ger.-Swiss border); rises to 4,898 ft. in the Feldberg. Divided by valley of Kinzig R. into Lower (N) and Upper (S) Black Forest. N section rises to 3,819 ft. in the Hornisgrinde. Heavily forested slopes, which give name to the range, drop abruptly toward Rhine plain (W), but descend gently toward valleys of the Neckar and the Nagold (E), almost merging (SE) with the Swabian Jura. The Danube, the Neckar, and numerous smaller rivers rise here. Excellent wine is grown on lower W slopes (Markgräfler Land, Breisgau). Mfg. of world-renowned cuckoo clocks, music boxes, and other mechanical toys is centered in S section. Extensive lumbering and woodworking. Active year-round tourist trade; numerous health resorts (Baden-Baden, Wildbad, Triberg, Villingen, Sankt Blasien).
Blackfork, village (1940 pop. 597), Lawrence co., S Ohio, 15 mi. S of Jackson; clay products; coal mining.
Black Fork, E W.Va., stream formed in S Tucker co. by junction of Glady (W), Laurel (central), and Dry (E) forks; flows 15 mi. NW, joining Shavers Fork at Parsons to form Cheat R. Sometimes called Dry Fork.
Black Hawk, county (□ 567; pop. 100,448), E central Iowa; ⊙ Waterloo. Prairie agr. area (hogs, cattle, poultry, corn, oats, soybeans) drained by Cedar R.; limestone quarries, sand pits. Industry at Waterloo and Cedar Falls. Formed 1853.
Black Hawk, city (pop. 166), Gilpin co., N central Colo., on N fork of Clear Creek, in Front Range, and 25 mi. W of Denver; alt. 8,032 ft. Gold mines. Near by is site of 1st gold lode discovery (1859) in Colo.
Black Hawk Lake (2 mi. long), W Iowa, 8 mi. S of Sac City. State park is here.
Black Hawk State Park, Ill.: see ROCK ISLAND, city.
Black Head, cape on Galway Bay, NW Co. Clare, Ireland, 13 mi. SW of Galway, culminating in Doughbraneen mtn. (1,045 ft.); 53°9'N 9°16'W.
Black Head, promontory on North Channel, at mouth of Belfast Lough, Co. Antrim, Northern Ireland, just NE of Whitehead, at SE end of Island Magee; lighthouse (54°46'N 5°41'W).
Black Head, promontory on W coast of the Rhinns of Galloway, W Wigtown, Scotland, 6 mi. WSW of Stranraer; lighthouse (54°53'N 5°8'W).
Blackhead Peak (12,500 ft.), in San Juan Mts., Archuleta co., SW Colo.
Blackheath, municipality (pop. 2,349), E New South Wales, Australia, 55 mi. WNW of Sydney; alt. 3,495 ft.; tourist resort; cattle-raising center.
Blackheath, common (267 acres) and district in Lewisham and Greenwich metropolitan boroughs, London, England, S of the Thames, 6 mi. ESE of Charing Cross. It was meeting place of highwaymen, and also of followers of Wat Tyler and Jack Cade. Henry V was welcomed here by Londoners on his return from Agincourt. Prehistoric subterranean caves were converted into air-raid shelters in 1939.
Black Heath, town (pop. 6,695) in Rowley Regis municipal borough, S Stafford, England; mfg. of machinery, metalworking.
Black Hills. 1 Range in Yavapai co., central Ariz., just W of Jerome. Rises 7,720 ft. in MINGUS MOUNTAIN. Copper is mined. **2** Mountain region (□ c.6,000) of SW S.Dak. and NE Wyo., lying largely within Black Hills and Harney natl. forests; enclosed by Belle Fourche R. and Cheyenne R. Rises c.2,000 ft. above near-by plains, which are c.3,250 ft. above sea level; highest at Harney Peak (7,242 ft.). Chief products are livestock, dairy goods, sugar, flour, bricks, cement, timber, petroleum; gold, silver, coal, tungsten, quartz, tin, granite, mica are mined. History of region begins with discovery of gold near Custer, 1874, and par-

allels development of mineral deposits at Custer, Lead, Deadwood, Rapid City, Spearfish. Places of interest are Custer State Park, Wind Cave Natl. Park, Fossil Cycad and Jewel Cave natl. monuments, and Mt. Rushmore Natl. Memorial.

Blackhope Scar, Scotland: see Moorfoot Hills.

Blackie, village (pop. 222), S Alta., 35 mi. SSE of Calgary; wheat.

Blackinton, Mass.: see North Adams.

Black Irtysh River (ĭrtĭsh'), Rus. *Cherny Irtysh* (chôr'nē ĭrtĭsh'), Uigur *Kara Irtis* (kärä' ĕrtĭsh'), name applied to upper Irtysh River in northernmost Sinkiang prov., China, and in USSR above L. Zaisan; flows 300 mi. W, past Burchun, forming a delta on E shore of L. Zaisan.

Black Island (2 mi. long, 1 mi. wide), E N.F., in E part of Notre Dame Bay, 3 mi. W of New World Isl. and 6 mi. SSE of Twillingate. On E coast is settlement of Black Island (pop. 20).

Black Island, Maine: see Long Island, plantation.

Black Isle, peninsular district in SE Ross and Cromarty, Scotland, projecting into Moray Firth, bounded in N by Cromarty Firth; 18 mi. long, up to 9 mi. wide. Chief towns: Cromarty, Fortrose, Rosemarkie.

Black Körös River, Hungary and Rumania: see Körös River.

Black Lake, town (pop. 2,276), S Que., on Black L. (2 mi. long), 5 mi. SW of Thetford Mines; asbestos-mining center.

Black Lake (35 mi. long, 2–11 mi. wide), N Sask., E of L. Athabaska; 59°10'N 105°20'W. Drained through Wollaston L. into Churchill R. by Fond du Lac R.

Black Lake. 1 In Natchitoches parish, NW La., c.50 mi. SE of Shreveport, in fish- and game-preserve (camping) area; c.14 mi. long. Receives Black L. Bayou in NW; drains SE through outlet to Saline Bayou. **2** In Cheboygan and Presque Isle counties, N Mich.: see Black River. **3** In Ottawa co., SW Mich.: see Black River. **4** In St. Lawrence co., N N.Y., narrow lake (c.16 mi. long) lying parallel to St. Lawrence R., c.5 mi. S of Ogdensburg; resorts. Receives Indian R. in S; discharges N through a short outlet to the Oswegatchie R.

Black Lake Bayou (bī'ō), NW La., rises S of Homer, flows c.60 mi. S into Black L. (c.50 mi. SE of Shreveport).

Black Lane, England: see Radcliffe.

Blacklead Island, islet, SE Franklin Dist., Northwest Territories, in Cumberland Sound, off Baffin Isl.; 64°59'N 66°11'W; former Hudson's Bay Co. post and Br. whaling station.

Blackley, N suburb of Manchester, SE Lancashire, England; textile printing, leather tanning; mfg. of chemicals for textile and tanning industry, cables, steel and copper wire, paint, soap, lubricating oil.

Blacklog Mountain, central Pa., NE–SW ridge (1,800–2,000 ft.), runs from SE Huntingdon co. c.35 mi. NE, forming part of border bet. Juniata and Mifflin counties.

Blackman Bay, triangular inlet of Tasman Sea, E Tasmania; S and E shores are formed by N Forestier Peninsula; 6 mi. long, 5 mi. wide. Dunalley on SW shore; Tasman monument near entrance. Tasman landed here 1642 and took possession of isl. Sometimes called Blackman's Bay.

Black Mesa (mā'sŭ). **1** Tableland (7,000 ft.), NE Ariz., located chiefly in Hopi Indian Reservation, Apache, Coconino, and Navajo counties. Bituminous coal deposits. Ruins of anc. Pueblo Indian fort found here. Hopi Indian pueblos in SW. Yale Point (8,050 ft.) on E flank, is highest elevation. **2** Tableland in Yavapai co., NW central Ariz., N of Prescott. Rises to 6,800 ft. Lies in natl. forest. **3** In Cimarron co., extreme NW Okla., volcanic plateau (alt. 4,978 ft.) in the Panhandle, NW of Kenton and near N.Mex. and Colo. lines; highest point in state.

Blackmore, Mount, Mont.: see Gallatin Range.

Black Mountain, resort town (pop. 1,174), Buncombe co., W N.C., in the Blue Ridge, 13 mi. E of Asheville; hosiery mfg., lumber milling. Black Mountain Col. (1933; experimental school), Montreat Jr. Col. for girls, Y.M.C.A. and Presbyterian assembly areas are near by.

Black Mountain. 1 Peak (10,760 ft.), in Rocky Mts., Jackson co., N Colo. Also known as Basaltic Peak. **2** Peak (11,656 ft.), in Rocky Mts., Park co., central Colo., 32 mi. NW of Canon City. **3** Peak, N.C.: see Balsam Mountain.

Black Mountain or **Fforest Fawr** (fô'rĕst vour'), mountain range, SE Carmarthen and S Brecknock, Wales, extends 30 mi. E–W. Highest point is Fan Fawr (vän) (2,409 ft.), 7 mi. SW of Brecknock. Also in range is Gareg Lwyd (gä'rĕg lo͝o'ĭd) (2,026 ft.), highest point of Carmarthen, 8 mi. ENE of Ammanford. At E edge of range are Brecon Beacons.

Black Mountain Range, S spur of W Assam Himalayas, central Bhutan, bet. Sankosh R. (W) and Tongsa R. (E), S of Kula Kangri peak; highest point (16,130 ft.), Black Mtn., is 17 mi. SSW of Tongsa. Pele La is main pass.

Black Mountains, range in E Brecknock, Wales, N Monmouth and SW Hereford, England, extends 15 mi. NNW–SSE bet. Abergavenny and Hay; 12 mi. wide. Highest peaks: Waun Fach (wĭn väkh') (2,660 ft.), 5 mi. SE of Talgarth, and Pen-y-Gader Fawr (pĕn-ŭ-gä'dĕr vour') (2,624 ft.), 6 mi. SE of Talgarth. Sometimes called Cradle Mts.

Black Mountains. 1 In W Ariz., extend c.90 mi. along Colorado R., S from L. Mead. Hoover Dam is in Black Canyon. Mt. Wilson (5,750 ft.) is highest point in range. Gold and silver are mined. **2** In Calif.: see Amargosa Range. **3** In W N.C. highest range in the Appalachians and a spur of the Blue Ridge, in Yancey and Buncombe counties. From Burnsville extend 20 mi. S; rise to 6,684 ft. in Mt. Mitchell, highest point E of the Mississippi. Other peaks include Balsam Cone (6,645 ft.) and Cattail Peak (6,593 ft.). Included in Pisgah Natl. Forest.

Black Oak, town (pop. 261), Craighead co., NE Ark., 27 mi. WSW of Blytheville.

Black Peak (9,020 ft.), SW N.Mex., in Pinos Altos Mts., 12 mi. NE of Silver City.

Black Pond, Piscataquis co., N central Maine, narrow lake (6 mi. long) NW of Chesuncook L., 45 mi. NNE of Greenville, in wilderness recreational area.

Blackpool, county borough (1931 pop. 101,553; 1951 census 147,131), W Lancashire, England, on Irish Sea and 15 mi. WNW of Preston; popular seaside resort and amusement center. Has beaches, piers, many mechanical amusements, and a tower (520 ft. high) modeled on the Eiffel Tower in Paris.

Black Range, SW N.Mex., extends N–S through parts of Grant and Sierra counties; lies largely within Gila Natl. Forest. Prominent point, Reeds Peak (10,011 ft.).

Black Rapids Glacier (25 mi. long, 2 mi. wide), E Alaska, Alaska Range, at foot of Mt. Hayes; 63°28'N 146°W; 400 ft. high at face. In 1936, due to undetermined disturbance, glacier moved forward 5 mi. in 6 months.

Black Regen River (rā'gŭn), Ger. *Schwarzer Regen* (shvär'tsŭr), Bavaria, Germany, rises 11 mi. N of Zwiesel across the Czechoslovak border, flows 47 mi. SSW and NW, past Zwiesel, joining White Regen R. SW of Kötzting to form Regen River.

Black River, E Alaska, rises in two headstreams in the Yukon, flows c.200 mi. W to Porcupine R. 12 mi. E of Fort Yukon. Gold placer mining. District pop. in 1939 was 22.

Black River, town (pop. 1,263), ⊙ St. Elizabeth parish, SW Jamaica, port at mouth of Black R., 70 mi. W of Kingston; 18°2'N 77°51'W. Exports logwood, coffee, sugar, ginger, citrus fruit, honey. Base for river and deep-sea fishing.

Black River, St. Elizabeth parish, SW Jamaica, longest river (44 mi. long) of the isl., rises in S outliers of the Cockpit Country just W of Balaclava, flows SW to coast at town of Black River. Navigable for small vessels for c.25 mi. Used for irrigation.

Black River, village (pop. 412), SW Mauritius, on Indian Ocean at mouth of Black River, 15 mi. SSW of Port Louis; sugar. Salt pans on coast near by.

Black River, Annamese *Song Bo* (shông' bô'), Chinese *Hei Chiang* (hā' jyäng'), Fr. *Rivière Noire*, in Tonkin (N Vietnam), rises 50 mi. S of lake Ehr Hai in China's Yunnan prov. at alt. of c.4,000 ft., flows over 500 mi. SE, parallel to Red R. and in deep canyons, past Laichau (head of junk navigation), to Red R. 5 mi. E of Viettri.

Black River, village (pop. 1,062), Jefferson co., N N.Y., on Black R. and 6 mi. ENE of Watertown.

Black River. 1 In E Ariz., rises SE of White Mts. in S part of Apache co., flows SW then NW to White R., forming Salt R. c.40 mi. NE of Globe; c.130 mi. long. **2** In La., name given to section (57 mi. long) of Ouachita River bet. influx of Tensas R. and its mouth. **3** In SW Mich., rises in SE Ottawa co., flows c.20 mi. W to Holland, widening into Black L. or L. Macatawa (c.8 mi. long) W of Holland, then W through short passage into L. Michigan. **4** In SW Mich., rises in N Van Buren co., flows c.25 mi. W, past Bloomingdale, Breedsville, and Bangor, to L. Michigan at South Haven. Receives North Fork (c.15 mi. long), Middle Fork (c.20 mi. long). **5** In N Mich., formed in NW Montmorency co. by branches rising in Otsego and Montmorency counties, flows N through forested region to Black L. (c.6 mi. long, 3 mi. wide) SE of Cheboygan, then NW to Cheboygan R. c.4 mi. above its mouth; c.65 mi. long. State park (camping, fishing) is on lake. **6** In E Mich., rises N of Sandusky in Sanilac co., flows c.60 mi. SSE, past Applegate and Croswell, to St. Clair R. at Port Huron. **7** In SE Mo. and NE Ark., rises in Reynolds co., Mo., meanders c.300 mi. SE and SW, through the Ozarks, past Poplar Bluff, to White R. near Newport, Ark. Navigable from mouth of Current R., near Pocahontas, Ark., to White R. junction. Clearwater Dam (143 ft. high, 4,425 ft. long; for flood control) was completed 1948, 6 mi. SW of Piedmont, Mo. **8** In N N.Y., rises in Herkimer co. in small lakes of the Adirondacks, flows c.120 mi. SW, NNW, and again SW, past Deferiet, Carthage, and Watertown, to Black River Bay (5 mi. long, 1–2 mi. wide), an inlet of L. Ontario 7 mi. W of Watertown. Black River Canal (abandoned 1926) connected it with the Erie Canal at Rome after 1836. Falls along its course supply power to paper mills and other industries. **9** In SE N.C., rises ESE of Dunn, flows c.75 mi. SSE to Cape Fear R. 10 mi. NW of Wilmington. Receives South R. **10** In N Ohio, formed by East and West branches at Elyria, flows c.12 mi. N to L. Erie at Lorain, where navigable lower section (c.4 mi. long) is part of harbor of Lorain. East Branch rises in Medina co., flows generally N, past Lodi and Grafton. West Branch rises near New London, flows NE c.30 mi., past Rochester. **11** In E S.C., rises in Lee co., flows 135 mi. SE, past Kingstree, to Pee Dee R. just above its mouth on Winyah Bay, near Georgetown; partly navigable. **12** In N Vt., rises near Craftsbury, flows c.30 mi. N to L. Memphremagog at Newport. **13** In S central Vt., rises near Plymouth, flows c.40 mi. S and SE, through small Amherst, Echo, and Rescue lakes, past Proctorsville and Cavendish, to the Connecticut near Springfield. Supplies water power. **14** In Douglas co., extreme NW Wis., rises in small lake near Minn. border, flows c.25 mi. generally NNE, through Pattison State Park, to Nemadji R. 9 mi. S of Superior. Big Manitou or Manitou Falls (mă'nĭto͞o), 165 ft. high, in Pattison State Park, 12 mi. S of Superior, are highest in Wis. **15** In W central Wis., rises in lake region in Taylor co., flows S, past Greenwood and Neillsville (hydroelectric plant), then SW, past Black River Falls, to the Mississippi at La Crosse; c.160 mi. long. Formerly important in lumbering industry.

Black River Bay, N.Y.: see Black River, stream.

Black River Canal, N.Y.: see Black River, stream.

Black River Falls, city (pop. 2,824), ⊙ Jackson co., W central Wis., on both banks of Black R. and c.45 mi. SE of Eau Claire; trade center in timber and farm area; boxes, beverages, dairy products, lumber, packed poultry. Settled before 1840; inc. 1883.

Black River Range, SW Mauritius, rises to 2,711 ft. in the Black River Peak, 6 mi. S of Tamarin.

Blackrock, Gaelic *Carraig Dhubh*. **1** Town (pop. 1,914), SE central Co. Cork, Ireland, on Lee R. estuary, 3 mi. E of Cork; agr. market (dairying; potatoes, oats, beets). **2** Residential suburb, E Co. Dublin, Ireland, on Dublin Bay, 5 mi. SE of Dublin. Blackrock Col. is large boys' school.

Black Rock, town (pop. 662), Lawrence co., NE Ark., 27 mi. NW of Jonesboro and on Black R.; sawmills, button factory.

Black Rock Desert, NW Nev., arid region of lava beds and alkali flats stretching c.70 mi. NE from Gerlach. The section in NW corner of Pershing co. is sometimes known as Granite Creek Desert. SW extension is Smoke Creek Desert.

Blackrod, urban district (1931 pop. 3,599; 1951 census 3,151), S central Lancashire, England, 4 mi. NNE of Wigan; cotton spinning and weaving; agr. market for dairy-farming, potato-growing region.

Blacksburg. 1 Town (pop. 2,056), Cherokee co., N S.C., 8 mi. ENE of Gaffney, bet. N.C. line and Broad R., in agr. area; textiles, chemicals. **2** College town (pop. 3,358), Montgomery co., SW Va., 26 mi. W of Roanoke. Seat of Va. Polytechnic Institute. Mountain L. is NW. Settled 1745; inc. 1871.

Black Sea, former government of Russia, on Black Sea coast of the Caucasus; ⊙ was Novorossisk. It was merged (1920) with Kuban oblast to form the Kuban-Black Sea oblast.

Black Sea, sometimes **Euxine Sea** (ūk'sĭn, –sēn), anc. *Pontus Euxinus*, Bulg. *Cherno More*, Rum. *Marea Neagră*, Rus. *Chernoye More*, Turkish *Karadeniz*, large inland sea (□ 159,000; including the Sea of Azov it is □ 173,000) bet. Europe and Asia, connected SW with the Mediterranean via the Bosporus, Sea of Marmara, and the Dardanelles; bounded N and NE by the USSR (Ukrainian SSR, Russian SFSR, Georgian SSR), S by Turkey, and W by Bulgaria and Rumania; 750 mi. long (W-E), 350 mi. wide; maximum depth c.7,360 ft. Coast is generally rocky and steep in S (Asia Minor) and NE (Caucasus), low, sandy, and dissected in N and NW, where shore is marked by characteristic limans (flooded river mouths). Here the Crimean Peninsula separates the Karkinit Gulf and the Sea of Azov (connected with the Black Sea by Kerch Strait). The principal tributaries are the Danube (large delta by-passed by Danube-Black Sea Canal), Dniester, Southern Bug, Dnieper rivers (limans), Rion, Coruh, Kizil Irmak, and Sakarya rivers. The Don and Kuban rivers flow into the Sea of Azov. The Black Sea contains 2 layers of water of different density: a top layer of low salinity (17–18%), subject to seasonal temperature fluctuations, and a denser, more saline layer (below 600 ft.), contaminated by hydrogen sulphide and devoid of marine life. A surface flow out through the Bosporus is compensated by a submarine inward current of denser saline water. No perceptible tides reach the Black Sea, which is, however, subjected to severe winter storms. Fisheries (important chiefly in shallow N reaches) yield herring, mackerel, pike, perch, bream, and, at Danube R. delta, sturgeon. Porpoises are also hunted. Ice-free all year round, except for thin ice cover in NW, the Black Sea is an important navigation route, linking the ports of Odessa, Nikolayev, Kherson, Sevastopol (Soviet naval base), Novorossisk, Poti, and Batum (in USSR); Trebizond, Giresun, Samsun, and Zonguldak (in Turkey); Burgas and Stalin (in Bulgaria); and Midia and Constanta (in Rumania). The predominant freight is grain, timber, petroleum, cement, and manganese. The Soviet Black Sea resorts along the S Crimean coast (Yalta) and the W Caucasus (Sochi) are well known Originally linked with the Caspian Sea by the Manych Depression, the Black Sea became separated in the late Tertiary period. At the same time the link with the Mediterranean was effected through the formation of the Turkish straits. The Black Sea shore was colonized (8th–6th cent. B.C.) by Greeks and later (3d–1st cent. B.C.) by Romans. Following the Barbarian migrations, the Genoese established colonies in 13th cent. and from 15th to 18th cent. the Black Sea was a Turkish lake. Russia became a riparian nation with the annexation (1783) of the Crimean khanate and later, following the fall of the Ottoman Empire, became the dominant Black Sea power. Following the Second World War, the USSR unsuccessfully proposed control of the Black Sea by the riparian nations and revision of the status of the Turkish straits.

Black Sea Lowland, Rus. *Prichernomorskaya Nizmennost*, littoral plain, S Ukrainian SSR, extending along Black Sea shore from Dniester R. to Sea of Azov; dry steppe; rich agr. region (wheat, cotton). Principal rivers (Dniester, Southern Bug, Dnieper) form lagoonlike mouths (limans) nearly closed off by sandspits from open sea. Numerous dry river valleys and burial mounds.

Blacks Fork, NE Utah and SW Wyo., rises near Tokewanna Peak in Uinta Mts., Utah; flows NE, past Fort Bridger and Granger, Wyo., and SE to Green R. 20 mi. N of Utah line; c.120 mi. long.

Blacks Harbour, village (pop. estimate c.600), SW N.B., on the Bay of Fundy, 38 mi. WSW of St. John; hake, cod, sardine, lobster fishing; sardine- and lobster-canning center.

Blackshear, city (pop. 2,271), ⊙ Pierce co., SE Ga., 9 mi. NE of Waycross; tobacco market; mfg. (lumber, fertilizer, shoes). Inc. 1859.

Blacksod Bay, inlet (10 mi. long, 5 mi. wide) of the Atlantic, NW Co. Mayo, Ireland, separating S part of Mullet Peninsula from mainland, and sheltered S by Achill Isl. At head of bay is Belmullet.

Black Springs, town (pop. 90), Montgomery co., W Ark., 38 mi. W of Hot Springs.

Black Squirrel Creek, E central Colo., rises in N El Paso co., flows c.60 mi. S to Arkansas R. 13 mi. E of Pueblo.

Blackstairs Mountains, range, Ireland, extending c.15 mi. NNE–SSW along border of Co. Carlow and Co. Wexford; rises to 2,610 ft. on Mt. Leinster, 12 mi. NW of Enniscorthy. Blackstairs Mtn. (2,409 ft.) is 10 mi. WNW of Enniscorthy.

Blackstock, town (1940 pop. 175), Chester and Fairfield counties, N S.C., 11 mi. S of Chester; lumber.

Blackstone. 1 Residential town (pop. 4,968), including Blackstone village (pop. 1,815), Worcester co., S Mass., on Blackstone R. and 22 mi. SSE of Worcester, at R.I. line. Settled 1662, inc. 1845. **2** Town (pop. 3,536), Nottoway co., central Va., 34 mi. WSW of Petersburg; tobacco market; trade center for agr., livestock, dairying, timber area; tobacco stemming, mfg. of fertilizer, textiles. Girls' jr. col. U.S. Camp Pickett near by. Inc. 1888; reinc. 1914.

Blackstone River, in Mass. and R.I., rises near Worcester, Mass.; flows c.50 mi. generally SSE, past Worcester and Northbridge, Mass., and Woonsocket, Central Falls, and Pawtucket (Pawtucket Falls here), furnishing power to highly industrialized valley, to head of Providence R. at Providence. River below Pawtucket (head of navigation) now called Seekonk R.; formerly Pawtucket R.

Black Sturgeon Lake (12 mi. long, 3 mi. wide), W central Ont., 60 mi. NNE of Port Arthur, S of L. Nipigon; alt. 829 ft. Drains S into Black Bay of L. Superior by Black Sturgeon R., 45 mi. long.

Black Sugar Loaf, The, mountain (4,901 ft.), E New South Wales, Australia, in Great Dividing Range ESE of Tamworth.

Blacksville, town (pop. 241), Monongalia co., N W.Va., at Pa. line, 16 mi. NW of Morgantown.

Black Tom Island, N.J.: see JERSEY CITY.

Blackville, town (pop. 1,294), Barnwell co., W S.C., 25 mi. WSW of Orangeburg; ships melons and cucumbers. Near by is experiment station of Clemson Agr. Col.

Black Volta River (vŏl'tŭ), rises in Upper Volta (Fr. West Africa) near Bobo-Dioulasso, flows c.500 mi. S and E into Gold Coast, past Lawra and Bamboi, joining the White Volta 38 mi. NW of Yeji to form VOLTA RIVER. Forms part of boundary bet. Ivory Coast and Gold Coast and, in Gold Coast, bet. Northern Territories and Ashanti.

Blackwall, district of Poplar, London, England, on N bank of the Thames, 6 mi. E of Charing Cross; has shipyards, the East India docks, and N terminus of Blackwall Tunnel to Greenwich.

Black Warrior River, W Ala., formed by Locust and Mulberry forks c.20 mi. W of Birmingham; flows 178 mi. SW to Tombigbee R. near Demopolis. Locks above Tuscaloosa make it navigable for barges to Birmingham area. With TOMBIGBEE RIVER forms important inland waterway for trade bet. Mobile and Birmingham. Sometimes known, bet. Demopolis and Tuscaloosa, as Warrior R.

Blackwater, Gaelic *Baile na gCloch*, town (pop. 160), SE Co. Wexford, Ireland, near St. George's Channel, 10 mi. ESE of Enniscorthy; agr. market (dairying; wheat, barley, potatoes, beets).

Blackwater, Ross and Cromarty, Scotland: see GARVE WATER.

Blackwater, town (pop. 313), Cooper co., central Mo., on Blackwater R., near the Missouri, and 13 mi. W of Boonville.

Blackwater Bay, NW Fla., NE arm of Pensacola Bay, opening S into the East Bay arm; receives Blackwater and Yellow rivers.

Blackwater Falls State Park (c.450 acres), N W.Va., in the Alleghenies just SW of Davis. Scenic area surrounds Blackwater Falls (63-ft. drop) in Blackwater R., a short E tributary of Black Fork of Cheat R.; below falls is Blackwater Canyon, a gorge with 1,000-ft. walls.

Blackwater Lake (30 mi. long, 2–8 mi. wide), W Mackenzie Dist., Northwest Territories, E of Franklin Mts.; 64°N 123°5'W. Drains W into Mackenzie R. by short Blackwater R.

Blackwater National Wildlife Refuge, Md.: see BLACKWATER RIVER.

Blackwater River, S central B.C., rises in Coast Mts. W of Quesnel, flows 140 mi. E to Fraser R. 25 mi. NW of Quesnel. Sometimes called West Road R.

Blackwater River. 1 Anc. *Idumania*, in Essex, England, rises 3 mi. SE of Saffron Walden as Pant R., flows SE to Kelvedon, thence S to Maldon (where it receives Chelmer R.), and E in estuarine course to North Sea S of Mersea Isl.; 40 mi. long. **2** In Hampshire and Berkshire, England, rises just SE of Aldershot, flows 20 mi. NW, forming boundary bet. Hampshire and Berkshire, to Loddon R. at Swallowfield.

Blackwater River. 1 In cos. Cavan and Meath, Ireland, rises 9 mi. NW of Virginia, flows 40 mi. SE, through Lough Ramor, to the Boyne at An Uaimh. **2** Rises E of Castleisland, Co. Kerry, Ireland, flows E through Co. Cork, past Mallow and Fermoy, into Co. Waterford, turning S at Cappoquin and flowing to the Atlantic at Youghal Harbour; c.100 mi. long.

Blackwater River, Co. Tyrone, Northern Ireland, rises 3 mi. NNW of Fivemiletown, flows 50 mi. E and N, past Clogher, Augher, Caledon, and Benburb, to SW end of Lough Neagh. Forms SE border bet. Co. Tyrone and cos. Monaghan and Armagh.

Blackwater River. 1 In Ala. and Fla., rises 15 mi. SW of Andalusia in S Ala., flows c.55 mi. SW, across NW Fla., into BLACKWATER BAY near Bagdad. **2** In E Md., on the Eastern Shore, rises in W Dorchester co., winds c.35 mi. SE through marshes (muskrat trapping) to Fishing Bay. Bordered by Blackwater Natl. Wildlife Refuge (c.9,000 acres), established 1931 for research on fur-bearing animals and for waterfowl preservation. **3** In W Mo., rises in Johnson co., flows c.55 mi. NE to Lamine R. in Cooper co. **4** In S central N.H., rises NW of Andover, flows SE, forming reservoir near Salisbury, to the Contoocook 8 mi. NW of Concord; c.35 mi. long. **5** In E Va., rises in Prince George co. near Petersburg, flows 80 mi. SE and S, past Franklin (head of 12-ft. navigation channel), joining Nottoway R. at N.C. line to form Chowan R. **6** In S Va., rises in the Blue Ridge SW of Roanoke, flows c.50 mi. SE and E, across Franklin co., to Roanoke R. 25 mi. SE of Roanoke.

Blackwatertown, agr. village, NW Co. Armagh, Northern Ireland, on Blackwater R. and 5 mi. NNW of Armagh; potatoes, flax, oats; cattle.

Blackwell, town and parish (pop. 4,857), E Derby, England, 3 mi. NE of Alfreton; coal mining.

Blackwell. 1 City (pop. 9,199), Kay co., N Okla., 12 mi. WNW of Ponca City, and on Chikaskia R.; market and shipping center for agr. (wheat, grain, livestock, poultry) and oil-producing area. Oil refining, glassmaking, zinc smelting, meat packing; mfg. of oil tanks, brick, tile, flour, feed, dairy products. Founded and inc. 1893. **2** Village (pop. c.500), Nolan co., W Texas, 26 mi. S of Sweetwater; market point in farm and cattle-ranching area.

Blackwells Island, N.Y.: see WELFARE ISLAND.

Blackwood, England: see BEDWELLTY.

Blackwood, village (pop. 1,344), Camden co., SW N.J., on Big Timber Creek and 10 mi S of Camden; clothing mfg.; poultry, truck, dairy products. Near by are co. institutions. Settled 1701.

Blackwood River, SW Western Australia, rises in hills near Narrogin, flows 190 mi. generally SW, past Bridgetown, to Flinders Bay of Indian Ocean at Augusta.

Bladen (blā'dŭn), county (□ 879; pop. 29,703), SE N.C.; ⊙ Elizabethtown. On coastal plain; bounded E by South R.; crossed by Cape Fear R.; several small lakes (resorts). Agr. (tobacco, corn, peanuts, cotton); timber (pine, gum, cypress); sawmilling. Formed 1734.

Bladen, village (pop. 282), Webster co., S Nebr., 20 mi. SSW of Hastings and on Little Blue R.

Bladenboro (blā'dŭnbŭrŭ), town (pop. 796), Bladen co., SE N.C., 14 mi. SE of Lumberton; cotton milling.

Bladensburg (blā'dŭnzbûrg), town (pop. 2,899), Prince Georges co., central Md., ENE suburb of Washington, on Anacostia R. Makes industrial gases. Here James Barren mortally wounded Stephen Decatur in a duel. Near by is site of battle (Aug. 24, 1814) of War of 1812, in which British under Gen. Robert Ross defeated Americans under Gen. W. H. Winder before entering Washington. Chartered 1742. Was terminus of railroads to Washington until 1835.

Blades, town (pop. 789), Sussex co., SW Del., on Nanticoke R. opposite Seaford; oyster packing.

Bladnoch (blăd'nŏkh, –nŏk), village in Wigtown parish, E Wigtown, Scotland; whisky distilling, dairying. Near by are remains of Baldoon Castle.

Blad-Touaria (blăd'-twäryä'), village (pop. 854), Oran dept., NW Algeria, 10 mi. SE of Mostaganem; winegrowing, distilling.

Blaenau-Ffestiniog or **Blaenau-Festiniog** (blī'nī-fĕstĭn'yôg), town in Ffestiniog urban district, NW Merioneth, Wales, 9 mi. NE of Portmadoc; woolen milling; slate-quarrying center.

Blaenavon (blĭnä'vŭn), urban district (1931 pop. 11,076; 1951 census 9,777), W central Monmouth, England, on Cwm Avon R. and 5 mi. E of Ebbw Vale; iron and steel milling, coal mining.

Blaengarw (blīn-gä'rōō), town (pop. 3,435) in Ogmore and Garw urban dist., central Glamorgan, Wales, on Garw R.; coal mining.

Blaengwawr (blīn-gour'), town (pop. 8,123) in Aberdare urban dist., NE Glamorgan, Wales; coal mining, stone quarrying.

Blaengwynfi, Wales: see ABERGWYNFI AND BLAENGWYNFI.

Blaenhonddan, Wales: see CILFREW.

Blagnac (blänyäk'), NW suburb (pop. 2,540) of Toulouse, Haute-Garonne dept., S France, on left bank of Garonne R. Airplane factory.

Blagodarnoye (blŭgŭdär'nŭyŭ), village (1926 pop. 12,209), central Stavropol Territory, Russian SFSR, on Stavropol Plateau, 70 mi. E of Stavropol (linked by rail); rail terminus in wheat and cotton area; flour mill, metalworks.

Blagodat or **Blagodat'** (blŭgŭdät'yŭ), mountain (1,164 ft.) of the central Urals, W Sverdlovsk oblast, Russian SFSR, just NE of Kushva, 3 mi. NE of Goroblagodatskaya rail junction; magnetite deposits, mined since 1735; limestone crushing. Supplies metallurgical plants of Kushva.

Blagodatnoye (–nŭyŭ), village (1948 pop. over 2,000), E Akmolinsk oblast, Kazakh SSR, 55 mi. E of Akmolinsk; grain, cattle. **2** Town (1939 pop. over 500), central Stalino oblast, Ukrainian SSR, in the Donbas, 28 mi. SW of Stalino.

Blagojev Kamen, Yugoslavia: see MAJDAN PEK.

Blagoveshchenka (blŭgŭvyĕsh'chĭn-kŭ), village (1948 pop. over 2,000), W Altai Territory, Russian SFSR, on Kulunda L., 50 mi. ESE of Slavgorod; dairy farming.

Blagoveshchensk (–chĭnsk). **1** City (pop. 58,761), ⊙ Amur oblast, Russian SFSR, on Amur R., at mouth of Zeya R., opposite Aigun (Manchuria), and 360 mi. WNW of Khabarovsk, on spur of Trans-Siberian RR; 50°16'N 127°32'E. Industrial and agr. center; shipbuilding (for Amur R. traffic), mfg. of agr. and gold-mining machinery, leather and felt boots, matches; food processing (flour, biscuits, sunflower-seed oil), lumber milling. Supply point for Zeya R. gold-mining basin; river port. Teachers col., regional mus. Founded 1856 as Rus. military post of Ust-Zeisk; named Blagoveshchensk in 1858. Suffered severe Amur R. flood (1872). Flourished during settlement (1880s) of fertile Zeya-Bureya Plain and development of Zeya gold mines. Growth stunted when city was by-passed (1910) by Trans-Siberian RR. **2** City (1939 pop. over 10,000), N central Bashkir Autonomous SSR, Russian SFSR, on Belaya R. and 20 mi. N of Ufa; metalworking center; mfg. (lathes, agr. machinery). Gypsum deposits near by. Until 1942, Blagoveshchenski Zavod.

Blagoyevgrad, Bulgaria: see GORNA DZHUMAYA.

Blain (blẽ), village (pop. 1,963), Loire-Inférieure dept., W France, on Brest-Nantes Canal and 21 mi. NNW of Nantes; dairying, cider making, sawmilling. Has ruined castle with 13th–14th-cent. drawbridge and towers.

Blain, borough (pop. 315), Perry co., S central Pa., 35 mi. W of Harrisburg.

Blaina, England: see NANTYGLO AND BLAINA.

Blaine. 1 County (□ 2,649; pop. 5,384), S central Idaho; ⊙ Hailey. Winter resort area. Livestock grazing. Mining of silver, lead, gold, zinc, copper. Sawtooth Natl. Forest, in N and NW, includes parts of Pioneer and Sawtooth mts. Formed 1895. **2** County (□ 4,267; pop. 8,516), N Mont.; ⊙ Chinook. Agr. region bordering on Sask.; drained by Milk R. Livestock, wheat, sugar beets. Fort Belknap Indian Reservation in SE. Formed 1912. **3** County (□ 711; pop. 1,203), central Nebr.; ⊙ Brewster. Agr. region drained by N.Loup and Middle Loup rivers; part of Halsey Div. of Nebr. Natl. Forest in SW. Livestock, grain. Formed 1885. **4** County (□ 925; pop. 15,049), W central Okla.; ⊙ Watonga. Intersected by North Canadian, Canadian, and Cimarron rivers. Agr. (cotton, wheat, corn, oats, livestock; dairy products). Shipping, processing of farm products at Watonga. Gypsum mining and processing. Has state park. Includes Seger and Cantonment Indian reservations. Formed 1891.

Blaine. **1** Town (1940 pop. 124), Lawrence co., NE Ky., 34 mi. SSW of Ashland, in mtn. agr. and coal area. **2** Agr. town (pop. 1,118), Aroostook co., NE Maine, 14 mi. SSE of Presque Isle, near N.B. line. Inc. 1874. **3** Coal-mining village (pop. c.800), Belmont co., E Ohio, 4 mi. ESE of St. Clairsville. **4** City (pop. 1,693), Whatcom co., NW Wash., on Georgia Strait, at British Columbia line, and 20 mi. NW of Bellingham, in agr. region. Tourist and farm trade center; port of entry. The Peace Arch is on international line. Platted c.1884.

Blaine Lake, village (pop. 514), central Sask., 50 mi. N of Saskatoon, near 2 small Blaine Lakes; grain elevators, flour mills.

Blainville (blĕvēl'), village (pop. 1,573), Calvados dept., NW France, on Caen maritime canal and 4 mi. NE of Caen; shipbuilding, horse raising. Also called Blainville-sur-Orne.

Blainville-sur-l'Eau (blĕvēl'-sür-lō'), town (pop. 2,980), Meurthe-et-Moselle dept., NE France, on left bank of Meurthe R. and 5 mi. WSW of Lunéville; rail junction; jute bags, work clothing.

Blair, county (□ 530; pop. 139,514), central Pa.; ⊙ Hollidaysburg. Mountainous agr. and industrial area; drained by Frankstown Branch of Juniata R. and by Little Juniata R. Allegheny Mts. form W border, Tussey Mtn. E border; part of Bald Eagle Mtn. in N part. Most of lead used by Washington's armies in Revolution mined here. Mfg. (metal products, railroad rolling stock, paper, textiles); limestone, sandstone, clay, shale, bituminous coal; agr. (dairy products, fruit, grain). Formed 1846.

Blair. **1** City (pop. 3,815), ⊙ Washington co., E Nebr., 20 mi. NNW of Omaha and on Missouri R.; farm trade center; horse collars, lumber, flour; livestock, grain, dairy and poultry produce. Dana Col. here. Founded 1869. **2** Town (pop. 700), Jackson co., SW Okla., 10 mi. N of Altus, in agr. and stock-raising area; glass mfg., cotton ginning. **3** City (pop. 873), Trempealeau co., W Wis., on Trempealeau R. (water power) and 33 mi. N of La Crosse; ships livestock; processes dairy products, lumber, canned vegetables.

Blair-Atholl (blâr-ă'thŭl), town and parish (pop. 1,557), N Perthshire, Scotland, on Garry R., a tributary of the Tay, and 7 mi. NW of Pitlochry; agr. market; whisky distilling. Blair Castle (13th cent.; restored), seat of duke of Atholl, figured in 17th-cent. conflicts.

Blairgowrie and Rattray (blârgou'rē, ră'trā), burgh (1931 pop. 4,676; 1951 census 5,383), E Perthshire, Scotland. Includes Blairgowrie (pop. 2,970), on Ericht R. and 14 mi. NNE of Perth; agr. market in fruitgrowing region, with linen and jute mills, mfg. of agr. machinery and fertilizer, and curing of bacon and ham. Just E of Blairgowrie is Rattray (pop. 1,706), agr. market. N of Blairgowrie, 2 mi., is mansion of Craighall Rattray, dating from c.1100.

Blairlogie (blârlō'gē), resort village, NE Stirling, Scotland, 4 mi. NE of Stirling.

Blairmont, village (pop. 2,327), Berbice co., NE Br. Guiana, at mouth of Berbice R., opposite New Amsterdam, just S of Rosignol; rice, sugar, coconuts.

Blairmore, town (pop. 1,767), S Alta., near B.C. border, in Rocky Mts., on Crowsnest R. and 100 mi. SSW of Calgary; alt. 4,235 ft.; distributing center for Crowsnest coal-mining region; also lumbering, lime kilns, foundries.

Blairsburg, town (pop. 257), Hamilton co., central Iowa, 10 mi. E of Webster City.

Blairsden (blârz'dŭn), resort village, Plumas co., NE Calif., in the Sierra Nevada, on Middle Fork Feather R. and 21 mi. SE of Quincy. Mohawk Valley (W; hot springs), Gold L. (S), and winter-sports areas are near by.

Blairstown. **1** Town (pop. 523), Benton co., E central Iowa, 22 mi. WSW of Cedar Rapids; feed milling. **2** Town (pop. 199), Henry co., W central Mo., on Big Creek of South Grand R. and 16 mi. NW of Clinton; agr. **3** Resort village (1940 pop. 603), Warren co., NW N.J., on Paulins Kill and 12 mi. SW of Newton, in hilly region; fruit, poultry, dairy products; makes airplane parts. Blair Acad. for boys (1848) here.

Blairsville. **1** Town (pop. 430), ⊙ Union co , N Ga., 24 mi. N of Dahlonega, in the Blue Ridge, near Nottely Reservoir. State agr. experiment station near by. **2** Borough (pop. 5,000), Indiana co., SW central Pa., 35 mi. E of Pittsburgh and on Conemaugh R.; mfg. (metal products, cement products, chemicals); bituminous coal, stone quarries; railroad shops; agr. Canal and turnpike center (c.1830). Settled c.1792, laid out c.1819, inc. 1825.

Blaise River (blāz), Haute-Marne dept., NE France, rises above Juzennecourt, flows c.60 mi. NNW, past Wassy, to the Marne 10 mi. W of Saint-Dizier.

Blaj (blăzh), Ger. *Blasendorf* (blä'zŭndôrf), Hung. *Balázsfalva* (bŏ'läsh-fŏl"vŏ), town (1948 pop. 6,641), Mures prov., central Rumania, in Transylvania, 165 mi. NW of Bucharest, 40 mi. SSE of Cluj; rail junction and cultural center; mfg. of alcohol, bricks, tiles; clay quarrying. Seat (since 1738) of Greek-Catholic Archbishop of Alba-Iulia and Fagaras. Has a large theological seminary, major library (founded in 1747), 2 teachers' colleges, and several other educational institutions. Notable are 18th-cent. cathedral with fine frescoes, and 16th-cent. archiepiscopal palace restored in 19th cent. Founded in 13th cent. and formerly residence of Transylvanian princes. Treaty of Blaj recognized suzerainty of Leopold I of Hapsburgs over Transylvania (1687). Assembly of Rumanians of Transylvania confirmed here (1848) their loyalty to the Hapsburgs and proclaimed themselves against reannexation to Hungary.

Blakang Mati (blä'käng mä'tē), fortified island (pop. 6,329) in Singapore Strait, just S of Singapore isl., across Keppel Harbor; 1°15'N 103°50'E; 2 mi. long, 1 mi. wide. Military station.

Blake Deep, ocean depth (27,365 ft.) in North Atlantic Ocean, N of Puerto Rico. Discovered 1882 by the *U.S.S. Blake,* it was then the deepest sounding in the Atlantic.

Blakely. **1** City (pop. 3,234), ⊙ Early co., SW Ga., 37 mi. NW of Bainbrige, near Ala. line; peanut market and processing center; mfg. of hosiery, wood products. Indian mounds near by. Founded 1821. **2** Residential borough (pop. 6,828), Lackawanna co., NE Pa., 6 mi. NNE of Scranton and on Lackawanna R. Inc. 1867.

Blakely Dam, Ark.: see OUACHITA RIVER.

Blake Mere, England: see ELLESMERE.

Blakeney (blăk'nē), town and parish (pop. 641), N Norfolk, England, on an inlet of the North Sea, 7 mi. E of Wells. Formerly an important seaport, but silting has made its harbor accessible to small craft only. Has 15th-cent. church. On the seaward salt marshes is bird sanctuary of Blakeney Point.

Blakesburg, town (pop. 401), Wapello co., SE Iowa, 12 mi. WSW of Ottumwa, in agr. and coal-mining area.

Blakeslee, village (pop. 142), Williams co., extreme NW Ohio, 10 mi. WNW of Bryan.

Blakiston Island (blā'kĭstŭn), St. Marys co., S Md., in Potomac R. 8 mi. SW of Leonardtown; less than 1 mi. long. Large cross here commemorates 1st mass celebrated (1634) by colonists brought by the Calverts. Also known as St. Clements Isl.

Blama (blä'mä), town (pop. 653), South-Eastern Prov., SE Sierra Leone, on railroad and 10 mi. W of Kenema; road and trade center; palm oil and kernels, cacao, coffee.

Blamannsisen, Norway and Sweden: see SULITJELMA.

Blâmont (blämõ'), village (pop. 1,062), Meurthe-et-Moselle dept., NE France, on the Vezouze and 16 mi. E of Lunéville; cotton and flour milling.

Blanc, Cap (käp blã), Sp. *Cabo Blanco* (kä'bō bläng'kō), promontory on the Atlantic, W Africa, at S tip of Cap Blanc Peninsula; 20°47'N 17°4'W; lighthouse. Border bet. Río de Oro (Sp. West Africa) and Mauritania (Fr. West Africa) bisects peninsula (30 mi. long, 2–6 mi. wide) to the cape. Settlements are Port-Étienne (Fr.) on E shore, La Agüera (Sp.) on W shore. Excellent trawl fisheries offshore.

Blanc, Cap, or **Cape Blanc** (blăngk, Fr. blã), on the Mediterranean, N Tunisia, 5 mi. NNW of Bizerte; 37°20'N 9°51'E; lighthouse. Although often considered the northernmost point of Africa, near-by Ras ben Sekka actually reaches 37°21'N lat.

Blanc, Lac, Haut-Rhin dept., France: see ORBEY.

Blanc, Le (lŭ blã'), town (pop. 5,198), Indre dept., central France, on the Creuse and 32 mi. WSW of Châteauroux; road and rail center; livestock market; tanning, mfg. of agr. machinery. Fortified in Middle Ages.

Blanc, Mont, France: see MONT BLANC.

Blanca (bläng'kä), town (pop. 2,367), Murcia prov., SE Spain, on the Segura and 5 mi. SE of Cieza; agr. processing (esparto, fruit conserves); hose mfg., sawmilling. Citrus, cereals, olive oil; sericulture.

Blanca (blăng'kŭ), town (pop. 376), Costilla co., S Colo., in San Luis Valley just W of Sangre de Cristo Mts., 10 mi. S of Blanca Peak, 19 mi. E of Alamosa; alt. 7,870 ft.; vegetables.

Blanca, Cordillera (kôrdĭyā'rä bläng'kä), E section of Cordillera Occidental of the Andes, in Ancash dept., W central Peru, bet. Marañón R. and Callejón de Huaylas; extends 110 mi. SSE from area of Sihuas to area of Chiquián. Rises to 22,205 ft. in the Huascarán, highest in Peru. Contains silver, lead, and copper deposits at Chacas, Huari, and Pomabamba.

Blanca, La, Mexico: see LA BLANCA.

Blanca, Laguna (lägōō'nä). **1** Patagonian lake (14 mi. long, 4–7 mi. wide) in Magallanes prov., S Chile, 45 mi. NNW of Punta Arenas; village on N shore. **2** Andean lake (alt. 13,875 ft.) on Peru-Chile border, at NE foot of Cerro de Tacora; c.5 mi. long, 1–2 mi. wide.

Blanca Peak (blăng'kŭ), S Colo., highest point (14,363 ft.) in Sierra Blanca of Sangre de Cristo Mts., just SW of Old Baldy, 22 mi. ENE of Alamosa.

Blanchard (blăn'chŭrd). **1** Town (pop. 214), Page co., SW Iowa, on Mo. line, near Tarkio R., 15 mi. SE of Shenandoah, in agr. area. **2** Town (pop. 75), Piscataquis co., central Maine, on the Piscataquis and 19 mi. WNW of Dover-Foxcroft. **3** Town (pop. 1,311), McClain co., central Okla., 17 mi. ENE of Chickasha, in agr. area; cotton ginning; grain elevators; mfg. of feed, cement blocks. Settled 1906, inc. 1907.

Blanchard River, NW Ohio, rises N of Kenton in Hardin co., flows N, past Mount Blanchard, then W, past Findlay and Ottawa, to Auglaize R. at Dupont; c.95 mi. long.

Blanchardstown, Gaelic *Baile Luindín,* NW suburb of Dublin, Co. Dublin, Ireland, on the Liffey; site of Dunsink Observatory (founded 1782) of Trinity Col.; 53°23'N 6°20'W.

Blanchardville, village (pop. 707), Lafayette co., S Wis., on East Branch of Pecatonica R. and 30 mi. SW of Madison, in dairy, livestock, and poultry area; cheese factories.

Blanchart, Raz, Channel Isls.: see ALDERNEY, RACE OF.

Blanche, village (1940 pop. 502), Bell co., SE Ky., in the Cumberlands, 15 mi. N of Middlesboro; bituminous-coal mining.

Blanche, Montagne de la (mõtā'nyŭ dŭ lä blãsh'), range in Provence Alps, Basses-Alpes dept., SE France, c.10 mi. SW of Barcelonnette. Rises to 9,603 ft. at the Pic des Trois-Évêchés (glacier).

Blanche Bay (blănch), NE New Britain, Bismarck Archipelago, SW Pacific, opens on St. George Channel; 4 mi. wide, 6 mi. long. Rabaul is on Simpson Harbour in N corner of bay.

Blanchester (blăn'chĕ"stŭr), village (pop. 2,109), Clinton co., SW Ohio, 31 mi. ENE of Cincinnati, in stock-raising and farming area; mfg. of pumps, clothing, canned foods.

Blanchetown, village (pop. 113), SE South Australia, 70 mi. NE of Adelaide and on Murray R.; some livestock.

Blanchisseuse (blăn"shĭsŏz', blăn"shĭsōōz'), village on N Trinidad coast, B.W.I., 17 mi. NE of Port of Spain; coconuts, cacao. Situated on fine bay with noted surf. Fishing.

Blanchland, agr. village in parish of Shotland High Quarter (pop. 207), S Northumberland, England, on Derwent R. and 9 mi. S of Hexham; picturesque resort. Church includes remains of Blanchland Abbey, built 1165.

Blanc-Mesnil, Le (lŭ blã-mānĕl'), town (pop. 18,172), Seine-et-Oise dept., N central France, a NE suburb of Paris, just W of Aulnay-sous-Bois, 7 mi. from Notre Dame Cathedral; metalworks (rolling stock), boilerworks; food processing. Large chemical laboratories. Railroad yards.

Blanc-Misseron, France: see QUIÉVRECHAIN.

Blanc Mont Ridge, France: see SOMMEPY.

Blanc-Nez, Cape, France: see WISSANT.

Blanco, town, Dominican Republic: see LUPERÓN.

Blanco (blăng'kō), county (□ 719; pop. 3,780), S central Texas; ⊙ Johnson City. In hill country of Edwards Plateau; alt. c.750–1,600 ft.; drained by Pedernales and Blanco rivers. Ranching (cattle, sheep, goats); mohair, wool marketed; agr. (cotton, corn, oats, grain sorghums, truck, fruit, pecans). Good hunting, fishing. Formed 1858.

Blanco, town (pop. 718), Blanco co., S central Texas, c.45 mi. N of San Antonio and on Blanco R., in ranching, farm area. State park near by (camping, bathing, fishing).

Blanco, Cabo, W Africa: see BLANC, CAP.

Blanco, Cabo (kä'bō bläng'kō), Patagonian cape on the Atlantic, SE Comodoro Rivadavia military zone, Argentina, at S edge of Gulf of San Jorge; 47°12'S 65°46'W.

Blanco, Cabo, S extremity of Nicoya Peninsula, on the Pacific, W Costa Rica; 9°33'N 85°14'W; lighthouse.

Blanco, Cabo, Peru: see CABO BLANCO.

Blanco, Cape, on S coast of Majorca, Balearic Isls., 16 mi. SSW of Palma; 39°22'N 2°48'W.

Blanco, Cape (blăng'kō), promontory, westernmost point of Oregon, 65 mi. WSW of Roseburg; 42°50'N 124°34'W.

Blanco, Río, Argentina: see ZANJÓN RIVER.

Blanco, Río (rē'ō bläng'kō), Santa Cruz and Beni depts., NE Bolivia; rises near Yotaú, flows 330 mi. N to Guaporé R. on Brazil border, 10 mi. SE of Forte Príncipe da Beira (Brazil). Receives Río Negro and San Martín rivers (right). Navigable below mouth of Río Negro for c.100 mi. Lower course, below mouth of the San Martín, is also known as Baures R.

Blanco, Río, river in Esmeraldas and Pichincha provs., N Ecuador, rises near the equator in Andean foothills W of Quito, flows c.50 mi. NW to join Guaillabamba R., forming the Esmeraldas at 0°28'N 79°25'W.

Blanco, Río, Peru: see TAPICHE RIVER.

Blanco, Río, small river in E Puerto Rico, flows c.10 mi. to the ocean S of Naguabo. Near its source are waterfalls and the Río Blanco hydroelectric plant. Isl.'s main rice-growing region.

Blanco River (blăng'kō), S central Texas, rises in springs on Edwards Plateau in Kendall co., flows c.70 mi. E and SE to the San Marcos just S of San Marcos. Blanco State Park in Blanco co. is recreation area (camping, fishing, swimming, boating).

Bland, county (□ 369; pop. 6,436), SW Va.; ⊙ Bland. Scenic mtn. region of the Alleghenies; bounded N by W.Va. Entire co. lies within Jefferson Natl. Forest. Drained by tributaries of New R. Livestock, timber, agr. (corn, wheat, hay); lumber milling; manganese deposits. Formed 1861.

Bland. 1 Town (pop. 596), Gasconade co., E central Mo., in the Ozarks, 35 mi. SE of Jefferson City; shoe factory. **2** Agr. village (pop. c.250), ⊙ Bland co., SW Va., 12 mi. SSE of Bluefield; hosiery, lumber mills.

Blanda (blän'tä), river, NW Iceland, rises on Hofsjokull, flows 80 mi. NNW to Huna Bay at Blonduos.

Blandain (blãdē'), town (pop. 2,582), Hainaut prov., SW Belgium, 4 mi. WNW of Tournai; frontier station on Fr. border; market center for tobacco-growing area.

Blandburg, village (1940 pop. 797), Cambria co., central Pa., 12 mi. N of Altoona; ceramic refractories.

Blandford, officially **Blandford Forum,** municipal borough (1931 pop. 3,370; 1951 census 3,663), E central Dorset, England, on Stour R. and 13 mi. NW of Poole; agr. market in dairying and sheep-raising region. Has 17th-cent. almshouses. Site of Bryanston School, a public school.

Blandford (blăn'fůrd), agr. town (pop. 597), Hampden co., SW Mass., 19 mi. WNW of Springfield.

Blanding, town (pop. 1,177), San Juan co., SE Utah, just S of Abajo Mts., 19 mi. SW of Monticello, in irrigated stock-raising area; alt. 6,105 ft. Settled 1905 as Grayson, renamed 1915. Hovenweep and Natural Bridges natl. monuments near by.

Blandinsville, village (pop. 918), McDonough co., W Ill., 12 mi. WNW of Macomb; corn, wheat, oats, livestock, poultry; dairy products.

Blandville, town (pop. 124), Ballard co., SW Ky., near Mayfield Creek, 23 mi. WSW of Paducah.

Blanefield, town in Strathblane parish, S Stirling, Scotland, 3 mi. N of Milngavie; textile printing.

Blanes (blä'nĕs), city (pop. 5,898), Gerona prov., NE Spain, port on the Mediterranean, and 21 mi. S of Gerona; rayon mfg.; cork, wine, and leather processing; fishing.

Blaney, town (pop. 183), Kershaw co., central S.C., 18 mi. NE of Columbia.

Blaney Park, resort, Schoolcraft co., S Upper Peninsula, Mich., c.20 mi. NE of Manistique; fishing. Has lumbering mus. Game sanctuary here.

Blangy or **Blangy-sur-Bresle** (blãzhē'-sür-brāl'), village (pop. 1,515), Seine-Inférieure dept., N France, on the Bresle and 15 mi. SW of Abbeville; glassworks, foundry. Damaged in Second World War.

Blangy-le-Château (-lü-shätō'), village (pop. 241), Calvados dept., NW France, 7 mi. NNE of Lisieux.

Blankenberge (bläng'kůnbĕrgů), town (pop. 9,024), West Flanders prov., NW Belgium, on North Sea, 8 mi. NNW of Bruges; seaside resort. Formerly spelled Blankenberghe.

Blankenburg (bläng'kůnbŏŏrk). **1** or **Blankenburg am Harz** (äm härts'), town (pop. 18,445), in former Brunswick exclave, central Germany, after 1945 in Saxony-Anhalt, at N foot of the lower Harz, 9 mi. SW of Halberstadt; iron mining; foundries, tileworks, sawmills; tree and seed nurseries. Climatic health resort. Ocher and marble worked near by. Has early-18th-cent. former ducal castle, residence (1796–98) of Louis XVIII of France. First mentioned 1123, town was destroyed (1182) by Emperor Frederick I. County of Blankenburg passed to duchy of Brunswick-Wolfenbüttel in 1599. On near-by Bode R., 4 mi. SSW, is the Bodetalsperre (dam), with hydroelectric power station. **2** or **Bad Blankenburg,** town, Thuringia, Germany: see Bad Blankenburg.

Blankenese (blängkůnā'zů), residential district (1925 pop. 13,692) of Hamburg, NW Germany, on steep right bank of Elbe R. estuary, 8 mi. W of Hamburg city center; hq. of deep-sea fishing fleet. Inc. 1929 into Hamburg. The Elbchaussee, a scenic road, leads to Altona, 5 mi. E.

Blankenfelde (bläng'kůnfĕl"dů), village (pop. 6,667), Brandenburg, E Germany, 13 mi. S of Berlin; market gardening.

Blankenhain (bläng'kůnhīn"), town (pop. 4,637), Thuringia, central Germany, 9 mi. S of Weimar; china mfg. Resort. Insane asylum in former castle.

Blankenloch (bläng'kůnlôkh"), village (pop. 3,401), N Baden, Germany, after 1945 in Württemberg-Baden, on the Pfinz and 5 mi. NNE of Karlsruhe; tobacco, fruit.

Blankenstein (bläng'kůn-shtīn"), town (pop. 2,011), in former Prussian prov. of Westphalia, W Germany, after 1945 in North Rhine-Westphalia, on the Ruhr and 2 mi. E of Hattingen. Has ruins of noted 13th-cent. castle.

Blanket, town (pop. 361), Brown co., central Texas, 14 mi. NE of Brownwood, in farm area.

Blanquefort (blãkfôr'), village (pop. 1,263), Gironde dept., SW France, in Médoc, 6 mi. NNW of Bordeaux; red wines, truck.

Blanquilla (blängkē'yä), Caribbean island (6 mi. long) and a federal dependency of Venezuela, NNW of Margarita Isl., 180 mi. NE of Caracas; uninhabited. Los Hermanos isls. are E.

Blansko (blän'skô), Ger. *Blanz* (blänts), town (pop. 5,416), W central Moravia, on Svitava R., on railroad and 11 mi. N of Brno; large iron foundries; mfg. of agr. machinery, surveying equipment, ceramics. Summer resort and point of departure for excursions into Moravian Karst. Former iron-mining place. Adamov (ä'dämôf), Ger. *Adamsthal* (ä'dämstäl"), ironworks are 4 mi. S. Pipes and smokers' articles made at village of Prosec (prô'sĕch), Czech *Proseč*, 7 mi. SE.

Blantyre (blăntīr'), town (pop. 6,443), ⊙ Southern Prov. (□ 12,114; pop. 1,007,671), Nyasaland, in Shire Highlands, on railroad and 37 mi. SW of Zomba; 15°48'S 35°2'E; alt. 3,400 ft. Commercial and agr. center; tobacco, tung, corn, wheat, coffee. Has Church of Scotland mission (founded 1876), Anglican and R.C. cathedrals, technical schools. Airport at Chileka (7 mi. N). One of oldest settlements of Nyasaland; became Br. consular post in 1883, township in 1895. Named after Livingstone's birthplace in Scotland. Mpemba (ůmpĕm'bä), c.6 mi. SW, is artisan and agr. training center.

Blantyre or **High Blantyre,** town and parish (pop. 17,015, including part of Hamilton burgh), N Lanark, Scotland, 8 mi. SE of Glasgow, in coal-mining region, machinery and chemical works, cotton mills. David Livingstone b. here; there is a mus. with Livingstone relics. Near by are slight remains of Blantyre Priory (13th cent.).

Blanz, Czechoslovakia: see Blansko.

Blanzac (blãzäk'), village (pop. 651), Charente dept., W France, 13 mi. SSW of Angoulême; brandy distilling.

Blanzy (blãzē'), NE suburb (pop. 2,169) of Montceau-les-Mines, Saône-et-Loire dept., E central France, in Le Creusot industrial dist., on Canal du Centre; coal mining.

Blao (blou), village, Haut-Donnai prov., S central Vietnam, in Moi Plateaus, 35 mi. WSW of Djiring, on Saigon-Dalat highway, at Blao Pass (2,790 ft.).

Blaricum or **Blarikum** (blä'rēkům), village (pop. 4,646), North Holland prov., W central Netherlands, 5 mi. NE of Hilversum, in farming area, on clay deposited by the IJsselmeer; fabric weaving.

Blarney, Gaelic *Blárna* (blär'nä), village (pop. 885), central Co. Cork, Ireland, near Lee R., 4 mi. NW of Cork; woolen milling (tweed). The 15th-cent. Blarney Castle has celebrated *Blarney Stone,* which, when kissed, reputedly endows one with power of invincible eloquence.

Blasdell (bläz'důl), village (pop. 3,127), Erie co., W N.Y., near L. Erie, 6 mi. S of Buffalo; metal products, abrasives, chemicals; truck farming. Inc. 1898.

Blasendorf, Rumania: see Blaj.

Blasewitz (blä'zůvĭts), E suburb of Dresden, Saxony, E central Germany, on the Elbe; climatic health resort.

Blashki, Poland: see Blaszki.

Blasket Islands, group of rocky isls. of Co. Kerry, Ireland, in the Atlantic, just W of Slea Head, at entrance to Dingle Bay. Great Blasket Isl. (1,132 acres; 4 mi. long; rises to 937 ft.), the only inhabited isl. of the group, is 3 mi. W of Slea Head. It was site of castle of Piaras Ferriter, last Irish chieftain to surrender to Cromwell. Chief industry is fishing; pop. is decreasing. Isl. is westernmost inhabited point of Europe, apart from Iceland. Tearaght Isl. (chä'rät), 9 mi. W of Slea Head, has lighthouse (52°5'N 10°40'W).

Blaszki (bwäsh'kē), Pol. *Błaszki,* Rus. *Blashki* (bläsh'kē), town (pop. 3,030), Poznan prov., central Poland, 16 mi. ESE of Kalisz; agr. market.

Blatna (blät'nä), Czech *Blatná,* town (pop. 3,209), S Bohemia, Czechoslovakia, 14 mi. NW of Pisek; rail junction, summer resort; rose gardens, nurseries. Has 11th-cent. castle with large deer park. Carp breeding in near-by lakes.

Blatna Horni, Czechoslovakia: see Horni Blatna.

Blatnica or **Blatnitsa** (both: blät'nĭtsä), village (pop. 5,476), N central Bosnia, Yugoslavia, near Usora R., 11 mi. SSW of Teslic; lumbering.

Blatnice (blät'nyĭtsĕ), village (pop. 2,112), SE Moravia, Czechoslovakia, on railroad and 21 mi. SSW of Gottwaldov; noted for picturesque regional summer fairs.

Blato (blä'tô), village (pop. 5,433), on W Korcula Isl., S Croatia, Yugoslavia, 18 mi. W of Korcula.

Blaton (blätõ'), agr. village (pop. 3,857), Hainaut prov., SW Belgium, 13 mi. WNW of Mons.

Blatse, Yugoslavia: see Blace.

Blaubeuren (blou"boi'rŭn), town (pop. 6,951), N Württemberg, Germany, after 1945 in Württemberg-Baden, 9 mi. W of Ulm; mfg. of machinery, pharmaceuticals, textiles, clothing, portland cement; metal- and woodworking, brewing. Has former Benedictine monastery with late-Gothic church; 16th-cent. town hall. Chartered in 13th cent.

Blauvelt (blô'vĕlt), village (1940 pop. 716), Rockland co., SE N.Y., near W bank of the Hudson, 3 mi. SW of Nyack. Blauvelt section of Palisades Interstate Park is here.

Blavet River (blävĕ'), Morbihan dept., W France, rises in Armorican Massif 8 mi. SW of Guingamp, flows 80 mi. S to the Atlantic, forming a common estuary with Scorff R. below Hennebont. In its middle course, bet. Gouarec and Pontivy, it constitutes a section of Brest-Nantes Canal.

Blawnox, industrial borough (pop. 2,165), Allegheny co., SW Pa., opposite N Pittsburgh on Allegheny R.; steel, iron alloys. Settled 1867.

Blaydon (blā'dŭn), urban district (1931 pop. 32,263; 1951 census 30,791), N Durham, England, on Tyne R. and 4 mi. W of Newcastle-upon-Tyne; coal-mining center, producing steel, metal products, brick, bottles, coal by-products. In urban dist. (W) is town of Stella, with coal mines and chemical works, and (E) steel-milling town of Derwenthaugh (dûr'wĕnt-häf), on Tyne R. at mouth of Derwent R.

Blaye-et-Sainte-Luce (bläē'-ā-sēt-lüs'), town (pop. 3,127), Gironde dept., SW France, on E shore of the Gironde, 20 mi. NNW of Bordeaux; port for Bordeaux, handling coal, oil, pit props. Wine-growing, flour milling. Has citadel built 1685 by Vauban.

Blaye-les-Mines (blĕ-lā-mēn'), village (pop. 649), Tarn dept., S France, 7 mi. N of Albi; coal mines.

Blayney (blā'nē), town (pop. 1,592), E central New South Wales, Australia, 115 mi. WNW of Sydney; rail junction; mining center (copper, iron).

Blaze, Point, NW Northern Territory, Australia, at E end of Joseph Bonaparte Gulf; 12°52'S 130°11'E.

Blazowa (bwä-zhô'vä), Pol. *Błażowa,* town (pop. 4,002), Rzeszow prov., SE Poland, 11 mi. SSE of Rzeszow; flour milling, sawmilling; brickworks.

Blázquez, Los (lōs bläth'kĕth), town (pop. 1,569), Córdoba prov., S Spain, 11 mi NW of Peñarroya-Pueblonuevo; cereals, olive oil, livestock, lumber.

Blechhammer, Poland: see Blachownia.

Bleckede (blĕ'kůdů), town (pop. 3,976), in former Prussian prov. of Hanover, NW Germany, after 1945 in Lower Saxony, on left bank of the Elbe and 13 mi. ENE of Lüneburg; metalworking, weaving, sawmilling.

Bleckley, county (□ 219; pop. 9,218), central Ga.; ⊙ Cochran. Bounded W by Ocmulgee R.; drained by Little Ocmulgee R. Coastal plain agr. (corn, peanuts, truck, fruit, livestock) and timber area. Formed 1912.

Bled-el-Djerid (blĕd'-ĕl-jĕrēd') [Arabic, =date country], region in SW Tunisia, near Algerian border, bet. Chott el Rharsa (NW) and Chott Djerid (SE); includes Nefta, Tozeur, El-Oudiane, and El Hamma-Djerid oases; ⊙ Tozeur. Forms transition bet. steppe and desert country. Dates are exported. Area was settled by Romans and reached comparative prosperity in 14th cent. Point of departure for trans-Saharan caravans. Also called Djerid.

Bled Lake (blĕt), Ger. *Veldeser See* (fĕl'dŭzůr zā'), NW Slovenia, Yugoslavia, 30 mi. NW of Ljubljana, in Julian Alps; 1½ mi. long, 1 mi. wide; alt. 1,560 ft. Bathing in summer, skating in winter. Medieval castle (alt. 1,980 ft.) on N shore, former royal villa on S shore, railroad station on W shore; church on islet. Bled, Ger. *Veldes,* village, on N shore, is mtn. and bathing resort (alt. 1,715 ft.). Until 1918, in Carniola.

Bledsoe (blĕd'sō), county (□ 404; pop. 8,561), central Tenn.; ⊙ Pikeville. On Cumberland Plateau, here cut by fertile Sequatchie R. valley. Timber, dairying, livestock raising, fruitgrowing. Formed 1807.

Bleiberg or **Bleiberg ob Villach** (blī'bĕrk ôp fĭ'läkh), town (pop. 3,606), Carinthia, S Austria, on N slope of Villach Alp and 8 mi. W of Villach; lead, zinc mines.

Bleiburg (blī'bŏŏrk), village (pop. 1,264), Carinthia, S Austria, 23 mi. E of Klagenfurt; lead, zinc mined near by.

Bleicherode (blī"khůrō'dů), town (pop. 7,923), in former Prussian Saxony prov., central Germany, after 1945 in Thuringia, near Wipper R., 11 mi. WSW of Nordhausen; cotton and linen milling; potash mining. Power station. Geographer Petermann b. here.

Bleik, Norway: see Andenes.

Bleiksoy, Norway: see Andenes.

Bleilochsperre (blī'lôkh"shpĕ'rů) or **Saaletalsperre** (zä'lůtäl"shpĕ'rů), irrigation dam and reservoir (□ 3.5), Thuringia, central Germany, on the Thuringian Saale and 15 mi. NW of Hof; hydroelectric power station. Built 1925–32; dam is 213 ft. high. On E shore of reservoir is Saalburg.

Blekinge (blā'kĭng-ů), county [Swedish *län*] (□ 1,173; 1950 pop. 145,909), S Sweden, on the Baltic; ⊙ Karlskrona. Low and undulating, drained by Morrum, Ronneby, and several smaller rivers. Intensively cultivated, it is called the "garden of Sweden." Industries include steel and textile milling, stone quarrying; mfg. of industrial and home equipment. Cities are Karlskrona (main Swedish naval base), Karlshamn, Ronneby, and Solvesborg. The county is coextensive with the historical province [Swedish *landskap*] of Blekinge, conquered from Denmark by Charles X of Sweden in 1658.

Blencathara, England: see Saddleback.

Blencoe (blĕn'kō), town (pop. 328), Monona co., W Iowa, near Missouri R., 7 mi. S of Onawa; farm trade center.

Blendecques (blãdĕk'), town (pop. 3,505), Pas-de-Calais dept., N France, on the Aa and 3 mi. SE of Saint-Omer; paper milling, brewing, tanning, lime mfg.

Bléneau (blānō') agr. village (pop. 1,216), Yonne dept., N central France, 15 mi. E of Gien; cattle.

Blenheim (blĕ'nŭm), town (pop. 1,952), S Ont., 10 mi. ESE of Chatham; mfg. of hardware, gloves; resort; agr. (corn, vegetable, fruit).

Blenheim (blĕ'nŭm), Ger. *Blindheim* (blĭnt'hīm), village (pop. 969), Swabia, W Bavaria, Germany, near the Danube, 10 mi. SW of Donauwörth. Bet. here and near-by Höchstädt, on Aug. 13, 1704, took place one of the most important battles of the War of the Spanish Succession, Marlborough and Eugene of Savoy defeating the French and Bavarians under Marshal Tallard.

Blenheim (blĕ'nŭm), borough (pop. 5,780), ⊙ Marlborough co. (□ 1,920; pop. 7,856), NE S.Isl., New Zealand, near Cloudy Bay, 155 mi. NNE of Christchurch. Flour and flax mills, brewery. Two airfields near by. Picton, its port, is 15 mi. NNE.

Blenheim, town (pop. 153), Marlboro co., NE S.C., 22 mi. N of Florence.

Blenheim Park, estate and parish (pop. 109), central Oxfordshire, England, on lake formed by the small Glyme R. just W of Woodstock; seat of the duke of Marlborough. The castle (built by Vanbrugh) and estate were voted by Parliament as a grant to the victor of the battle of Blenheim.

Blenio (blā'nyō), district (pop. 5,672), Ticino canton, S Switzerland; Val Blenio, valley, extends from W of Adula mts. to N of Biasca and is watered by Brenno R.

Blenky Islands, group of islets, S Franklin Dist., Northwest Territories, in James Ross Strait, bet. Boothia Peninsula (NE) and King William and Matty isls. (SW); 69°33'N 95°17'W.

Blennerhassett Island (blĕnŭrhă'sĭt) (c.500 acres), in the Ohio 2½ mi. below Parkersburg, NW W.Va. Site of mansion (now in ruins) of Harman Blennerhassett, who plotted here (1805–6) with Aaron Burr to seize an empire in the West.

Blennerville (blĕ'nŭrvĭl), fishing village, W Co. Kerry, Ireland, on Tralee Bay, just SW of Tralee; terminus of short ship canal linking Tralee with the sea.

Blénod-lès-Pont-à-Mousson (blānō'-lā-pō-ä-mōōsō'), S suburb (pop. 2,248) of Pont-à-Mousson, Meurthe-et-Moselle dept., NE France, on the Moselle; slag blocks, cartons.

Blénod-lès-Toul (–lā-tōōl'), village (pop. 821), Meurthe-et-Moselle dept., NE France, 6 mi. SSW of Toul; woodworking, winegrowing. Has 16th-cent. Gothic church.

Bléone River (blāôn'), Basses-Alpes dept., SE France, rises in Provence Alps (at foot of Pic des Trois-Évêchés), flows 40 mi. SW, past Digne, to the Durance above Les Mées.

Blérancourt (blārăkōōr'), village (pop. 858), Aisne dept., N France, 12 mi. NW of Soissons; glass mfg. A mus. commemorates historic Franco-American cooperation.

Bléré (blārā'), town (pop. 1,848), Indre-et-Loire dept., W central France, on Cher R. and 15 mi. ESE of Tours; iron founding, sawmilling, mfg. of explosives. Has 12th-15th-cent. church. Chenonceaux castle near by.

Blerick or **Blerik** (blĕ'rĭk), town (pop. 10,211), Limburg prov., SE Netherlands, 1 mi. WSW of Venlo, across Maas R.; railroad shops; wire mfg.

Blesle (blĕl), village (pop. 609), Haute-Loire dept., S central France, near the Alagnon, 10 mi. W of Brioude; antimony works. Has a 13th-cent. keep.

Blessington, Gaelic *Cros Bhaile Coimín,* town (pop. 382), NW Co. Wicklow, Ireland, on the Liffey and 17 mi. SW of Dublin; agr. market (dairying; cattle, sheep; potatoes). Has 1669 church.

Bletchingley, residential town and parish (pop. 2,365), E Surrey, England, 5 mi. E of Reigate. Has 12th–15th-cent. church, remains of castle.

Bletchley, urban district (1931 pop. 6,170; 1951 census 10,916), NE Buckingham, England, on Ouzel R. and 13 mi. NNE of Aylesbury; agr. market, with chemical works. Has 13th-15th-cent. church. In urban dist. (NE) is market town of Fenny Stratford (pop. 4,411).

Bletterans (blĕtŭrä'), agr. village (pop. 963), Jura dept., E France, on the Seille and 7 mi. NW of Lons-le-Saunier; dairying, poultry raising.

Bléville (blāvēl'), outer NW suburb (pop. 3,346) of Le Havre, Seine-Inférieure dept., N France, near Cape La Hève; pottery mfg., cider distilling.

Blevins (blĕ'vĭnz), town (pop. 271), Hempstead co., SW Ark., 14 mi. N of Hope.

Blewett, village, Uvalde co., SW Texas, 14 mi. W of Uvalde; asphalt mining.

Blewett Falls Lake, S N.C., formed by hydroelectric dam in Pee Dee R., 6 mi. WNW of Rockingham; c.10 mi. long.

Bleymard, Le (lŭ blāmär'), village (pop. 356), Lozère dept., S France, on N slope of Mont Lozère, near the Lot, 11 mi. E of Mende; lead mine near by.

Blgarka, Bulgaria: see BALGARKA.

Blickling, agr. village and parish (pop. 264), N Norfolk, England, just NW of Aylsham. The noted Jacobean hall, in 600-acre park, contains some famous paintings and library of early books. Anne Boleyn spent part of her childhood here. There is a 15th-cent. church. Near by is site of palace of the Saxon king Harold.

Blida (blēdä'), city (pop. 30,170), Alger dept., N central Algeria, 25 mi. SW of Algiers, beautifully located on S edge of the Mitidja plain at foot of the Tell Atlas, amidst citrus and olive groves, vineyards, and rose gardens; commercial center (oranges, wine, truck produce, essential oils, tobacco, cereals); mfg. of flour products, olive-oil, soap, building materials; printing, canning, vulcanizing. Airfield at Joinville (just NW). Excursions to Chiffa gorge (5 mi. SW), Abd-el-Kader peak (5,344 ft.) overlooking city on S, and the resort of Chréa (5 mi. SE). Blida dates from 16th cent. A noted recreation center under Turkish rule. Destroyed by earthquake in 1825. Occupied by French in 1839. Again damaged by earthquake in 1867.

Blidworth (blĭd'ŭrth,–wŭrth), town and parish (pop. 5,316), central Nottingham, England, 5 mi. SE of Mansfield; coal. Church has 15th-cent. tower.

Bliek, Netherlands: see AMELAND.

Blieskastel (blēs'kästĕl"), city (pop. 4,731), SE Saar, near Ger. border, on Blies R. and 5 mi. W of Zweibrücken; mfg. (shoes, tobacco products). Has remains of castle (c.1700). In early Middle Ages, it was ⊙ Bliesgau, dist. of Trier electorate.

Bliesmengen-Bolchen (blēs'mĕng"ŭn-bôl'khŭn), village (pop. 1,194), S Saar, on Fr. border, on Blies R. and 3.5 mi. NE of Sarreguemines; construction industry; stock, grain.

Blies River (blēs), E Saar, rises 6 mi. WNW of St. Wendel, flows generally S, past St. Wendel, Ottweiler, Neunkirchen, and Blieskastel, to Fr. border at Reinheim, where it turns W and flows in winding course, forming border bet. Saar and France, to Saar R. at Sarreguemines; 52 mi. long.

Bligh Sound (blī), inlet of Tasman Sea, Fiordland Natl. Park, SW S.Isl., New Zealand; c.12 mi. long, 1.5 mi. wide; formerly visited by whalers.

Bligny-sur-Ouche (blēnyē'-sür-ōōsh'), village (pop. 621), Côte-d'Or dept., E central France, on W slope of the Côte d'Or, 10 mi. NW of Beaune; cattle, sheep.

Blijke, Netherlands: see AMELAND.

Blind Bay, New Zealand: see TASMAN BAY.

Blindheim, Germany: see BLENHEIM.

Blind River, town (pop. 2,619), S central Ont., on L. Huron, 70 mi. ESE of Sault Ste. Marie; port and lumbering center.

Blinman, settlement, E central South Australia, 140 mi. NNE of Port Pirie; wool, livestock.

Bliss. 1 Town (pop. 126), Gooding co., S Idaho, on Snake R. and 35 mi. NW of Twin Falls. **2** Village (pop. c.400), Wyoming co., W N.Y., 13 mi. SSW of Warsaw; makes rulers; farming, dairying.

Bliss, Fort, Texas: see EL PASO, city.

Blissfield, village (pop. 2,365), Lenawee co., SE Mich., on Raisin R. and 9 mi. SE of Adrian, in agr. area (corn, truck, wheat, sugar beets, livestock). Mfg. of fur goods; beet-sugar refining, food canning. Settled 1824; inc. 1875.

Blisworth (blĭz'wŭrth), agr. village and parish (pop. 792), S central Northampton, England, 5 mi. SSW of Northampton; bacon and ham processing. Has 14th-cent. church.

Blitar (blētär'), town (pop. 27,846), SE Java, Indonesia, 70 mi. SSW of Surabaya; 8°6'S 112°10'E; alt. 528 ft.; trade center for agr. area (coffee, rice, sugar, rubber, peanuts, cassava).

Blitta (blē'tä), village, central Fr. Togoland, 40 mi. NNW of Atakpamé; terminus of railroad from Lomé; cacao, palm oil and kernels, cotton.

Bliznetsy (blyĕznĭ'tsē), village (1932 pop. estimate 550), S Kharkov oblast, Ukrainian SSR, 12 mi. E of Lozovaya; flour milling, metalworking.

Block Island, Newport co., S R.I., bet. Block Isl. Sound and the Atlantic, 14 mi. ENE of Montauk Point, Long Isl., and 10 mi. S of Point Judith, R.I.; 7 mi. long, 1.5–3.5 mi. wide; coextensive with New Shoreham (shô'rŭm) town (pop. 732). Popular summer resort, with New Harbor (formed 1900 by artificial channel to Great Salt Pond), one of more than 300 ponds on isl.; yatching; fishing fleet; some agr. (potatoes, vegetables); peat deposits. Has 2 lighthouses (S light is at 41°9'N 71°33'W), coast guard station, U.S. weather station. Isl., known to Indians as Manisees, was visited by Adriaen Block in 1614, settled 1661 from Mass. New Shoreham town inc. 1672.

Block Island Sound, R.I., arm of the Atlantic bet. Block Isl. and R.I., E of Long Isl. Sound and NE of Montauk Point, Long Isl.; c.10 mi. wide.

Blockley, agr. village and parish (pop. 1,784), NE Gloucester, England, 10 mi. SE of Evesham. The Norman church was extended in 14th–15th cent.

Blocksberg, Germany: see BROCKEN.

Blocksberg, Hungary: see GELLERT, MOUNT.

Blockton, town (pop. 407), Taylor co., SW Iowa, near Mo. line, on Little Platte R. and 31 mi. SSW of Creston; wood products.

Blodgett. 1 Town (pop. 5), Jones co., SE Miss., 18 mi. SSE of Laurel. **2** Town (pop. 218), Scott co., SE Mo., in Mississippi flood plain, 20 mi. S of Cape Girardeau.

Bloedel (blōdĕl'), village, SW B.C., on E central Vancouver Isl., on Discovery Passage 35 mi. NNW of Courtenay; lumbering.

Bloemendaal (blōō'mŭndäl), residential town (pop. 6,684), North Holland prov., W Netherlands, 2 mi. N of Haarlem, in bulb fields; mfg. (wire products, metal castings, chemicals). Testing laboratory for canned foods.

Bloemfontein (blōōmfŏntān'), city (pop. 67,196; including suburbs 83,226), ⊙ Orange Free State, U. of So. Afr., in W part of prov., 100 mi. ESE of Kimberley, 230 mi. SW of Johannesburg; 29°8'S 26°13'E; alt. 4,568 ft. Judicial ⊙ U. of So. Afr., seat of Appellate Division of the Supreme Court. Site of Univ. Col. of the Orange Free State, founded 1855 as Grey Col., affiliated (1910) with Univ. of South Africa; also has technical col. There are large railroad workshops; industries include metalworking, meat canning, mfg. of furniture, glassware. Among notable features are Natl. Mus. (1877), War Mus. (1931), Anglican cathedral, Old Fort (1848), several parks. The Old Raadzaal (council chamber; 1849), seat of govt. (1849–57) of Orange River Sovereignty and of Orange Free State Republic, is now natl. monument. On NAVAL HILL (N) is Lamont-Hussey Observatory of Univ. of Michigan; at MAZELSPOORT (ENE) is Boyden Station observatory of Harvard. Airport at Bloemspruit. Town grew around site chosen 1846 for establishment of fort; became ⊙ Orange River Sovereignty 1849 and Orange Free State Republic 1854. Failure of Bloemfontein conference (1899) bet. Sir Alfred Milner and President Kruger led to outbreak of South African War (Oct. 11, 1899); city was taken (March 13, 1900) by Lord Roberts.

Bloemspruit (blōōm'sproit), residential town (pop. 1,357), W Orange Free State, U. of So. Afr., 7 mi. ENE of Bloemfontein; alt. 4,424 ft.; site of Bloemfontein airport (29°5'S 26°19'E).

Blois (blwä), anc. *Blæsum* or *Blesum,* town (pop. 21,666), ⊙ Loir-et-Cher dept., N central France, on Loire R. and 32 mi. ENE of Tours; commercial center; has ironworks, chocolate, biscuit, vinegar, and footwear factories; woodworking. Commerce in wines and brandies. Tourist trade. Noted for its historical 13th-17th-cent. Renaissance château built largely by Louis XII, Francis I, and Gaston d'Orléans, with 17th-cent. additions designed by Mansart. The early counts of Blois were the most powerful feudal lords of France (10th cent.). In 1397 the last count sold his fief to Louis, duc d'Orléans, whose grandson, Louis XII of France, incorporated it into the royal domain in 1498 as part of Orléanais. The castle (birthplace of Louis XII) became the residence of several kings and queens of France, including Mary Queen of Scots and Catherine de Medici. Henri, duc de Guise, was assassinated in the château during the States-General of 1588. Denis Papin, Augustin Thierry b. in Blois. Damaged in Second World War.

Blokzijl (blôkzīl'), town (pop. 1,231), Overijssel prov., N central Netherlands, at E edge of North East Polder, 10 mi. WNW of Meppel; mfg. (boxes, crates, barrels), mat weaving, dairying. Former port of the IJsselmeer, founded in 16th cent. Sometimes spelled Blokzyl.

Blomberg (blôm'bĕrk), town (pop. 6,470), in former Lippe, NW Germany, after 1945 in North Rhine-Westphalia, 9 mi. E of Detmold; furniture mfg.

Blomidon, Cape (blŏ'mĭdŭn), promontory (alt. 670 ft.), on N coast of N.S., S of Parrsboro, on E side of peninsula separating Minas Channel and Minas Basin, and at NE end of North Mts.; 45°18'N 64°19'W.

Blomidon Range, coast range in W Newfoundland, on S shore of the Bay of Islands; part of the Lewis Hills; rises to 2,502 ft. 18 mi. W of Corner Brook.

Blomstermala (blōōm'stûrmō"lä), Swedish *Blomstermåla,* village (pop. 1,019), Kalmar co., SE Sweden, near Alster R., 20 mi. N of Kalmar; metal- and woodworking.

Blond, Monts de (mō dŭ blō'), hills in Haute-Vienne dept., W central France, S of Bellac, with tin and tungsten deposits.

Blonduos (blŭn'tüōs"), Icelandic *Blönduós,* town (pop. 457), ⊙ Hunavatn co., NW Iceland, commercial center of Huna Bay region, at mouth of the Blanda, 60 mi. W of Akureyri; fishing port.

Blonie (bwô'nyĕ), Pol. *Błonie,* Rus. *Blone* (blô'nyĕ), town (pop. 6,416), Warszawa prov., E central Poland, on railroad and 17 mi. W of Warsaw; mfg. of matches, nails, screws, bricks, flour; sawmilling.

Blood River, locality, Zululand, central Natal, U. of So. Afr., on short Blood R. (tributary of Buffalo R.) and 20 mi. E of Dundee; scene of battle (Dec. 16, 1838) in which Afrikaners under Andries Pretorius defeated Zulu forces under chief Dingaan in retribution for DINGAANS KRAAL massacre. Dingaan's Day, anniversary, is one of chief So. Afr. holidays.

Bloodsworth Island, low marshy isl. (c.5 mi. long, 4 mi. wide), Dorchester co., E Md., in Chesapeake Bay; on E is Tangier Sound, on N is Hooper Strait; South Marsh Isl. lies just S.

Bloody Foreland, promontory on the Atlantic, NW Co. Donegal, Ireland, 14 mi. N of Dungloe; 55°8'N 8°18'W.

Bloomburg, town (pop. 477), Cass co., NE Texas, 20 mi. S of Texarkana, near Ark. line, in agr. area.

Bloomdale, village (pop. 592), Wood co., NW Ohio, on South Branch of Portage R. and 7 mi. W of Fostoria; food products, farm equipment.

Bloomer, city (pop. 2,556), Chippewa co., W central Wis., on tributary of Chippewa R. and 13 mi. NNW of Chippewa Falls, in dairying area; brewing, canning. Settled before 1850; inc. 1920.

Bloomfield, village (pop. 647), SE Ont., near L. Ontario, 15 mi. SSE of Belleville; flour, lumber.

Bloomfield. **1** Farming town (pop. 5,746), including Bloomfield village (pop. 1,205), Hartford co., N central Conn., just NW of Hartford; tobacco. R.C. seminary here. Settled c.1660, inc. 1835. **2** Town (pop. 2,086), ⊙ Greene co., SW Ind., near West Fork of White R., c.40 mi. SE of Terre Haute, in agr. area; mfg. (furniture, metal products, silos, brick). **3** City (pop. 2,688), ⊙ Davis co., SE Iowa, near Fox R., 18 mi. S of Ottumwa, in sheep-raising area; mfg. (wood products, poultry-processing machinery). Has James B. Weaver homestead. Lake Wapello State Park is near by. Inc. 1863. **4** Town (pop. 666), Nelson co., central Ky., 34 mi. SE of Louisville, in outer Bluegrass agr. region; flour and feed mills. **5** City (pop. 1,382), ⊙ Stoddard co., SE Mo., near Castor R., 19 mi. W of Sikeston; farm, dairy, lumber center. Settled 1824. **6** City (pop. 1,455), Knox co., NE Nebr., 65 mi. W of Sioux City, Iowa; livestock, dairy and poultry produce, grain. Settled 1890. **7** Town (pop. 49,307), Essex co., NE N.J., just NW of Newark; residential; mfg. (metal products, electrical appliances, chemicals, cosmetics, pharmaceuticals, woolens, porcelains); automobile assembling. Has Presbyterian col. and seminary (1810), 18th-cent. Presbyterian church. Inc. 1900. **8** Village (pop. 619), San Juan co., NW N.Mex., on San Juan R., near Colo. line, 8 mi. S of Aztec; alt. 5,400 ft. Trade center for irrigated grain and bean region; oil refinery. Aztec Ruins Natl. Monument is 9 mi. N, Navajo Indian Reservation 15 mi. W, Chaco Canyon Natl. Monument c.40 mi. S. **9** Village, Jefferson co., Ohio: see BLOOMINGDALE. **10** Agr. borough (pop. 1,098), ⊙ Perry co., central Pa., 20 mi. NW of Harrisburg; planing and hosiery mills. Laid out c.1824. Post office is New Bloomfield. **11** Town (pop. 291), Essex co., NE Vt., on Connecticut R., at mouth of Nulhegan R., and 30 mi. ESE of Newport; lumber, wood products.

Bloomfield Hills, city (pop. 1,468), Oakland co., SE Mich., NW suburb of Detroit. The Cranbrook Foundation (including private schools, science institute, art acad.) is here. Settled c.1819; inc. as village 1926, as city 1932.

Bloomingburg. **1** or **Bloomingburgh,** village (pop. 263), Sullivan co., SE N.Y., at base of the Shawangunk range, on Shawangunk Kill and 10 mi. N of Middletown, in resort area. **2** Village (pop. 623), Fayette co., S central Ohio, 5 mi. NNE of Washington Court House.

Bloomingdale. **1** Village (pop. 339), Du Page co., NE Ill., WNW of Chicago and 11 mi. SE of Elgin, in agr. area; dairy products. **2** Town (pop. 434), Parke co., W Ind., 28 mi. NNE of Terre Haute, in agr. and bituminous-coal area. **3** Village (pop. 465), Van Buren co., SW Mich., on Black R. and 20 mi. WNW of Kalamazoo. **4** Borough (pop. 3,251), Passaic co., N N.J., on Pequannock R. and 10 mi. NW of Paterson; mfg. (carbonated beverages, clothing); poultry, truck. Inc. 1918. **5** Village (pop. 476), Essex co., NE N.Y., in the Adirondacks, 6 mi. NNE of Saranac Lake village. **6** Village (pop. 324), Jefferson co., E Ohio, 10 mi. W of Steubenville, in coal-mining area. Laid out 1816. Also called Bloomfield.

Blooming Grove, town (pop. 736), Navarro co., E central Texas, 14 mi. W of Corsicana; market point in agr. area.

Blooming Prairie, village (pop. 1,442), Steele co., SE Minn., 17 mi. SSE of Owatonna; shipping point for butter and eggs; grain, livestock, poultry area; ice cream.

Bloomington. **1** Village (1940 pop. 2,726), San Bernardino co., S Calif., 6 mi. SW of San Bernardino; citrus fruit, vegetables. **2** Village (pop. 302), Bear Lake co., SE Idaho, near Bear L., 5 mi. S of Paris; alt. 5,985 ft.; agr., livestock. **3** City (pop. 34,163), ⊙ McLean co., central Ill., c.35 mi. ESE of Peoria; rail, commercial, and industrial center in a rich agr., stock-raising, and bituminous-coal area; has large railroad shops; mfg. of heaters, air-conditioning and ventilating equipment, household appliances, food products. Near by is L. Bloomington (500 acres; resort; reservoir), impounded by dam on small Money Creek. Presents annual Passion play. Settled 1822, inc. 1839. The establishment of Ill. Wesleyan Univ. (1851), coming of railroad (1854), and founding of Ill. State Normal Univ. (1857) at adjacent Normal, all stimulated city's growth. In 1856, Lincoln made his famous "lost speech" here to the 1st Republican state convention. Elbert Hubbard b. here. **4** Industrial city (pop. 28,163), ⊙ Monroe co., S central Ind., c.45 mi. SSW of Indianapolis, in farming and dairying area, with large limestone quarries near by; mfg. (furniture, flour, limestone and glass products, wax, gloves, creosoted products). Seat of Indiana Univ. Settled 1818. **5** Village (pop. 293), Franklin co., S. Nebr., 5 mi. W of Franklin and on Republican R., near Kansas line; livestock, grain, poultry produce. **6** Resort village, Ulster co., SE N.Y., on Rondout Creek and 4 mi. SW of Kingston. **7** Village (pop. c.750), Victoria co., S Texas, near Guadalupe R., 13 mi. SSE of Victoria; trade center in oil-producing, agr. area. **8** Village (pop. 631), Grant co., extreme SW Wis., on branch of small Grant R. and 16 mi. SE of Prairie du Chien, in farm area; cement blocks, dairy products.

Bloomington, Lake, Ill.: see BLOOMINGTON.

Blooming Valley, borough (pop. 256), Crawford co., NW Pa., 6 mi. ENE of Meadville.

Bloomsburg, town (pop. 10,633), ⊙ Columbia co., E central Pa., 35 mi. WSW of Wilkes-Barre and on Susquehanna R., in agr. area; mfg. (carpets, clothing, rayon). State teachers col. here. Settled 1772, laid out 1802, inc. 1870. Only inc. "town" in Pa.

Bloomsbury, residential and academic district of Holborn and Saint Pancras metropolitan boroughs, London, England, N of the Thames, 1.5 mi. N of Charing Cross. Here are Univ. of London, London School of Economics, Univ. Hosp., British Medical Association, and the British Museum. Contains several squares and gardens (Bedford, Tavistock, Bloomsbury, Russell squares), laid out on Bedford estate in 18th cent. Many artists, writers, and students live in the district, which has reputation of an intellectual center.

Bloomsbury, borough (pop. 722), Hunterdon co., W N.J., on Musconetcong R. and 6 mi. ESE of Phillipsburg; makes pencils. Iron, limestone, ocher, and mica deposits here.

Bloomville, village (pop. 759), Seneca co., N Ohio, 9 mi. ESE of Tiffin, in agr. area; flour and feed mills; limestone quarry.

Blora (blō'rŭ), town (pop. 18,451), central Java, Indonesia, 90 mi. W of Surabaya; 6°58'S 110°14'E; oil-production center. Teak forests near by.

Blore Heath, locality, NE Shropshire, England, 2 mi. ENE of Market Drayton. Scene of battle bet. Yorkists and Lancastrians (1459).

Blosdorf, Czechoslovakia: see MORAVSKA TREBOVA.

Blossburg, borough (pop. 1,954), Tioga co., N Pa., 30 mi. N of Williamsport and on Tioga R.; bituminous coal; mfg. (pipe fittings). Settled c.1802.

Blosseville-Bonsecours (blôsvēl'-bōsŏokōor'), SE suburban commune (pop. 2,685) of Rouen, Seine-Inférieure dept., N France, on Seine R.; metal-working, brick mfg. At Bonsecours is 19th-cent. basilica and monument to Joan of Arc.

Blosseville Coast (blŏs'vĭl), region, SE Greenland, on Denmark Strait, extending c.300 mi. NE-SW bet. Scoresby Sound and Kangerdlugssuak inlet; 68°–70°10'N 22°–30°W. Indented by many small bays and fjords; inland icecap here slopes steeply to the sea from altitudes ranging bet. 4,000 ft. and 7,824 ft. (on Mt. Riguy); numerous glaciers discharge icebergs into Denmark Strait. Charted (1833) by Jules de Blosseville. Near coast is Mt. Gunnbjorn, highest known peak of Greenland.

Blossom, town (pop. 780), Lamar co., NE Texas, 10 mi. E of Paris; trade center in agr. area (cotton, corn, alfalfa).

Blotzheim (blôtsĕm', Ger. blôts'hīm), town (pop. 1,896), Haut-Rhin dept., E France, near Swiss border, 6 mi. NW of Basel; fish hatchery near by.

Bloudane, Syria: see BLUDAN.

Blount (blŭnt). **1** County (□ 640; pop. 28,975), N central Ala.; ⊙ Oneonta. Hilly region drained by Mulberry and Locust forks of Black Warrior R. Cotton, corn, poultry; coal, iron, limestone. Formed 1818. **2** County (□ 584; pop. 54,691), E Tenn.; ⊙ Maryville. Bounded SE by N.C., SW by Little Tennessee R., NW by Fort Loudoun Reservoir (Holston R.). Great Smoky Mts. in E and SE. Includes part of Great Smoky Mts. Natl. Park. Lumbering, marble quarrying, livestock raising, dairying, agr. (corn, tobacco, hay). Industry at Alcoa (aluminum reduction), Maryville. Formed 1795.

Blount Hills, village (pop. 3,503, with Eagleton Village), Blount co., E Tenn.

Blountstown (blŭnts'toun), city (pop. 2,118), ⊙ Calhoun co., NW Fla., 45 mi. W of Tallahassee, near Apalachicola R.; lumber and naval-stores center. Founded c.1823, inc. 1925.

Blountsville. **1** (blŭnts'vĭl) Trading town (pop. 695), Blount co., N central Ala., 15 mi. SE of Cullman; meat processing. **2** (blounts'vĭl) Town (pop. 229), Henry co., E Ind., 12 mi. SE of Muncie, in agr. area.

Blountville (blŭnt'vĭl), village, ⊙ Sullivan co., NE Tenn., in Great Appalachian Valley, 15 mi. N of Johnson City.

Blovice (blô'vĭtsĕ), Ger. *Blowitz* (blō'vĭts), town (pop. 2,388), SW Bohemia, Czechoslovakia, on Uslava R., on railroad, and 13 mi. SSE of Pilsen; brickmaking, sugar milling. Health resort of Letiny (lĕ'tyĭnĭ), with alkaline springs and peat baths, is 5 mi. SW.

Blowing Rock, resort town (pop. 661), Watauga and Caldwell counties, NW N.C., in the Blue Ridge, 16 mi. NNW of Lenoir, on Blue Ridge Parkway. Summer school of English held here annually.

Blowitz, Czechoslovakia: see BLOVICE.

Bloxham (blŏk'sŭm), agr. village and parish (pop. 1,080), N Oxfordshire, England, 3 mi. SW of Banbury. Has 13th–14th-cent. church.

Bloxwich, England: see WALSALL.

Blubber Bay, village, SW B.C., at N tip of Texada Isl., on the Strait of Georgia 80 mi. NW of Vancouver; lime-shipping port; limestone quarrying, copper mining, lumbering.

Bludan or **Baludan** (both: blōō'dăn), Fr. *Bloudane,* village, Damascus prov., SW Syria, 18 mi. NW of Damascus, in the Anti-Lebanon mts.; alt. 4,900 ft.; popular summer and health resort. Also grows grapes, apricots, walnuts, olives. Roman ruins.

Bludenz (blōō'dĕnts), town (pop. 9,790), Vorarlberg, W Austria, on Ill R. and 12 mi. ESE of Feldkirch; tourist center (alt. 1,920 ft.); cotton mills, weaving, watch mfg., food processing.

Bludov (blōō'dôf), village (pop. 2,418), N Moravia, Czechoslovakia, 3 mi. SW of Sumperk; rail junction; health resort (radioactive and sulphur springs) in foothills of the Jeseniky.

Blue, Mount. **1** Peak (3,187 ft.), Franklin co., W central Maine, center of Mt. Blue State Park, 4 mi. NE of Weld. **2** Peak (4,530 ft.) of White Mts., Grafton co., NW N.H., W of Franconia Notch.

Blue Ash, village (1940 pop. 1,266), Hamilton co., extreme SW Ohio, 11 mi. NE of Cincinnati.

Blue Ball, Pa.: see WEST DECATUR.

Blue Bank, resort village, Lake co., extreme NW Tenn., on Reelfoot L., 20 mi. N of Dyersburg. Edgewater Beach (swimming) near by.

Blue Basin, waterfalls, N Trinidad, B.W.I., 5 mi. N of Port of Spain, in valley of small Diego Martin R. Tourist site.

Blue Bell Knoll, highest peak (11,253 ft.) in Aquarius Plateau, S central Utah, 27 mi. NNE of Escalante.

Blue Diamond, mining village (pop. 2,336, with adjacent Harveyton), Perry co., SE Ky., in Cumberland foothills, 5 mi. N of Hazard; bituminous coal.

Blue Earth, county (□ 740; pop. 38,327), S Minn.; ⊙ Mankato. Agr. area bounded N by Minnesota R. and drained by Blue Earth R. Corn, oats, barley, livestock, dairy products, poultry. Food processing and mfg. at Mankato. Formed 1853.

Blue Earth, city (pop. 3,843), ⊙ Faribault co., S Minn., on Blue Earth R., near Iowa line, and 37 mi. S of Mankato; trade center for diversified-farming area (grain, livestock, truck products, and sugar beets); food processing (canned corn and peas, dairy products). Platted 1856, inc. 1874.

Blue Earth River, rises in Kossuth co., N Iowa, flows 130 mi. generally N into S Minn., past Blue Earth city, to Minnesota R. at Mankato. Tributaries: Watonwan and Le Sueur rivers.

Bluefield, city (pop. 21,506), Mercer co., S W.Va., in the Alleghenies, 70 mi. W of Roanoke, Va., contiguous to Bluefield town (pop. 4,212), Tazewell co., SW Va.; alt. c.2,600 ft. Administratively separate but an economic unit, the Bluefields are semibituminous-coal-mining, rail shipping, and distribution center of Pocahontas coal field; rail junction; lumber, textile and flour milling, mfg. of mine equipment and supplies, mattresses, beverages; silica, limestone produced. State teachers col. in W.Va. city; in Va. is Bluefield Col. (jr. col.). Pinnacle Rock State Park (W.Va.), is 5 mi. NW. Settled 1777; coal shipping began 1883. In 1921, Bluefield, Va., was renamed from Graham.

Bluefields, minor port, SW Jamaica, 7 mi. ESE of Savanna-la-Mar; ships logwood.

Bluefields, department, Nicaragua: see ZELAYA.

Bluefields, city (1950 pop. 7,463), ⊙ Zelaya dept., E Nicaragua, port on Bluefields Bay of Caribbean Sea, at mouth of Escondido R., 175 mi. E of Managua; 12°1'N 83°46'W. Commercial center; light mfg. Exports bananas, coconuts, lumber, alligator skins. Its outer port is EL BLUFF.

Bluefields River, Nicaragua: see ESCONDIDO RIVER.

Blue Grass, town (pop. 337), Scott co., E Iowa, 10 mi. W of Davenport; livestock, grain.

Bluegrass, The, N and central Ky., physiographic region (□ c.8,000) with Lexington at its heart; bounded NW, N, and NE by Ohio R., on other sides by semicircle of hills (the Knobs) extending SE from vicinity of Louisville in curve enclosing Bardstown, Danville, and Richmond, then swinging NE to the Ohio in vicinity of Maysville. A gently rolling plain (alt. c.1,000 ft.) of exceptionally rich phosphatic limestone soil; watered by Kentucky R. and Licking R. and its forks. Inner Bluegrass (□ c.2,400), the richest part, centers on Lexington; here especially are the famed Ky. thoroughbred horse farms. Around it is a less fertile shale belt, in turn surrounded by the Outer Bluegrass, with soils similar to the inner region. Besides saddle and race horses, cattle, mules, sheep, and other stock, region produces bluegrass seed, burley tobacco, forage crops, corn, grains.

Blue Hill. **1** Resort town (pop. 1,308), Hancock co., S Maine, on W shore of Blue Hill Bay opposite Mt. Desert Isl. Pottery made here. Hill for which it is named is 940 ft. high. Copper, diatomaceous earth, and other minerals have been found here. Settled 1762, inc. 1789. **2** Village (pop. 574), Webster co., S Nebr., 20 mi. S of Hastings; shipping point for grain, livestock.

Blue Hill Bay, Hancock co., S Maine, inlet of the Atlantic extending inland 20 mi. from entrance W of Mt. Desert Isl.

Blue Hills or **Providenciales** (prŏ″vĭdĕn″sēä'lĭs), island (□ 41.6; 17 mi. long, 12 mi. wide; pop. 804), Turks and Caicos Isls., dependency of Jamaica, bet. North Caicos isl. (NE) and West Caicos isl. (SSW), on Caicos Passage; 21°45'N 72°15'W. Sponge fishing.

Blue Hills, E Mass., low wooded hills just S of Boston, just S of Milton; hiking, bridle trails. On Great Blue Hill (635 ft.) is Harvard observatory.

Blue Hole Spring, Ohio: see CASTALIA.

Blue Island, residential and industrial city (pop. 17,622), Cook co., NE Ill., on Calumet Sag Channel (lock here), just S of Chicago, in dairying and truck-farming area. Mfg. of wire, steel and iron products, brick, tile, lumber, barrels, boiler compounds; oil refining; food-packing and -canning plants, railroad shops. Settled 1835, inc. 1843.

Bluejacket or **Blue Jacket,** town (pop. 274), Craig co., NE Okla., 11 mi. NNE of Vinita, in farm area.

Blue Lake, city (pop. 824), Humboldt co., NW Calif., 12 mi. NE of Eureka; dairy, truck, and fruit farming; lumber milling.

Blue Lake, oxbow lake (c.8 mi. long) in Monona co., W Iowa, near Missouri R., 1 mi. W of Onawa. Lewis and Clark State Park here.

Blue Lakes. 1 In E Calif., 2 small lakes (East Blue, West Blue) in Alpine co., in the Sierra Nevada, c.10 mi. SW of Markleeville; fishing. **2** In NW Calif., 2 small lakes in Lake co., in the Coast Ranges, 9 mi. NW of Lakeport; resorts.

Blue Licks Springs or **Blue Lick Springs,** village, Nicholas co., N Ky., on Licking R. and 40 mi. NE of Lexington, in Bluegrass region. Former resort with mineral springs. Blue Licks Battlefield State Park, commemorating a Revolutionary battle (August 19, 1782), is here. A mus. houses fossil mammals found in vicinity.

Blue Mound. 1 Village (pop. 886), Macon co., central Ill., 12 mi. SW of Decatur; wheat, corn, oats, soybeans. **2** City (pop. 424), Linn co., E Kansas, 24 mi. NW of Fort Scott, in agr. area.

Blue Mounds, village (pop. 207), Dane co., S Wis., 23 mi. W of Madison, at foot of Blue Mounds (alt. 1,716 ft.).

Blue Mountain (2,085 ft.), in Long Range Mts., NW N.F., 24 mi. SE of Point Riche.

Blue Mountain. 1 Town (pop. 529), Calhoun co., E Ala.; N suburb of Anniston; cotton milling. Fort McClellan is near by. **2** Town (pop. 122), Logan co., W Ark., 11 mi. E of Booneville. **3** Town (pop. 875), Tippah co., N Miss., 25 mi. ESE of Holly Springs. Seat of Blue Mountain Col. (Baptist; for women; 1873).

Blue Mountain. 1 In W Ark., one of 2 highest peaks in state, 13 mi. NE of Mena, in Ouachita Mts.; alt. c.2,850 ft. **2** In N.Y.: see BLUE MOUNTAIN LAKE. **3** In E Pa., NE-SW ridge (1,300–2,000 ft.) of the Appalachians; runs from N Franklin co. c.150 mi. NE to Northampton co., where it joins Kittatinny Mtn. Traversed by Appalachian Trail. Slate, limestone.

Blue Mountain Dam, Ark.: see PETIT JEAN RIVER.

Blue Mountain Lake, resort village (pop. c.350), Hamilton co., NE central N.Y., in the Adirondacks, at E end of Blue Mountain L. (c.2½ mi. long, c.1 mi. wide), 26 mi. S of Tupper Lake village, in summer- and winter-resort area. Blue Mtn. (3,759 ft.) is just N.

Blue Mountain Peak (7,520 ft.), E Jamaica, in the Blue Mts., highest peak of the isl., 15 mi. ENE of Kingston; 18°2′N 76°33′W. Hostel near its summit. Known for its view. Coffee grown on slopes.

Blue Mountains, E New South Wales, Australia, E spur of Great Dividing Range, c.40 mi. W of Sydney; actually sandstone plateau rising to 4,000 ft.; traversed by railroad; summer resorts. Site of Jenolan Caves, near Oberon. Bathurst was 1st settlement (1815) on W side of plateau.

Blue Mountains, range in E Jamaica, highest of the isl., extending c.30 mi. E-W from Stony Hill (8 mi. N of Kingston). Popular tourist area, known for its dense vegetation and fine scenery. Coffee is grown on slopes of mts. Rises in Blue Mountain Peak (15 mi. ENE of Kingston) to 7,520 ft. There are many other high peaks.

Blue Mountains, NE Oregon–SE Wash., a rolling range (c. 6,500 ft.), including all the mts. of NE Oregon (except Wallowa Mts.) and extending to bend of Snake R. in Wash. Strawberry Mts. and Elkhorn Ridge are parts of Blue Mts. Heavily forested; gold mines; stock grazing, agr. (mainly feed crops) in valleys; foothills have large acreages of peas for canning.

Blue Mud Bay, W inlet of Gulf of Carpentaria, NE Northern Territory, Australia, bet. Groote Eylandt and Cape Shield; Bickerton Isl. forms S shore; 30 mi. long, 24 mi. wide; broken into small inlets. Woodah Isl. largest of several isls. in bay.

Blue Nile, province (□ 54,775; 1948 estimated pop. 1,721,190), E central Anglo-Egyptian Sudan; ⊙ Wad Medani. Bounded by Ethiopia (SE). Drained by the Blue and White Niles. Intensive agr. in the irrigated GEZIRA, fed by SENNAR dam. Chief crops: cotton, wheat, barley, corn, fruits, durra; livestock (cattle, sheep, goats). Main centers are Wad Medani, Kosti, Dueim, Singa. Formerly called Gezira prov. Enlarged 1930s by inc. of former Fung and White Nile provs.

Blue Nile, Arabic *Bahr el Azraq* (bä′hŭr ĕl ăz′räk), Amharic *Abbai*, right headstream of the main Nile in E central Anglo-Egyptian Sudan, rises in SE end of L. Tana (alt. c.6,000 ft.), NW Ethiopia, flows SE and W, around Choke Mts., then NW, past Roseires (head of navigation), Singa, Suki, Sennar (dam), Wad Medani, and Hasiheisa, joining the White Nile at Khartoum to form Nile R. proper; total length, 1,000 mi. Navigable June–Dec. bet. Suki (rail-steamer transfer point) and Roseires (below rapids). A dam is planned at its outlet from L. Tana. Upper course has rocky bed and flows through rugged country. Contributing 68% of main Nile flow in high flood, but only 17% at low water, the Blue Nile is characterized by a very irregular regime. Following the spring rains on the Ethiopian plateau, the river begins to rise in mid-May and reaches its peak at end of Aug. Only 10% of flood water stems from the right affluents (Rahad and Dinder), which later dry up to series of pools. Receives (left) Dadessa and Dabus rivers.

Blue Point, shore-resort village (pop. 1,613), Suffolk co., SE N.Y., near S shore of Long Isl., near Great South Bay, 2 mi. WSW of Patchogue; vegetable oils, fertilizer. Blue-point oysters take their name from this place.

Blue Range, Greenlee co., E Ariz., W of Blue R., N of Morenci. Chief peaks are MITCHELL PEAK (7,947 ft.) and ROSE PEAK (8,787 ft.), highest point in range. Lies in section of Crook Natl. Forest.

Blue Rapids, city (pop. 1,430), Marshall co., NE Kansas, on Big Blue R. near mouth of Little Blue R., and 32 mi. N of Manhattan; flour and lumber milling, gypsum processing, bottling; stone quarries, sand pits. Laid out 1869, inc. 1872.

Blue Ridge. 1 Resort city (pop. 1,718), ⊙ Fannin co., N Ga., 38 mi. ENE of Dalton, in the Blue Ridge and Chattahoochee Natl. Forest; mfg. (bedspreads, clothing, lumber). Blue Ridge dam and lake near by. Inc. 1887. **2** Town (pop. 27), Harrison co., NW Mo., 16 mi. SE of Bethany. **3** Resort village, Essex co., NE N.Y., in the Adirondacks, 17 mi. WSW of Port Henry. **4** Village, Buncombe co., W N.C., 15 mi. E of Asheville, in the Blue Ridge; conference center for Y.M.C.A. and Y.W.C.A. **5** Town (pop. 306), Collin co., N Texas, 25 mi. SSE of Sherman, in cotton, truck area. **6** Resort village, Botetourt co., W Va., in the Blue Ridge, 11 mi. NNE of Roanoke.

Blue Ridge, the, or **Blue Ridge Mountains,** SE U.S., southwesternmost portion of the Older APPALACHIAN MOUNTAINS, extends NE-SW for c.650 mi., from S Pa. to Mt. Oglethorpe in N Ga., and lies bet. the Piedmont (E) and the Great Appalachian Valley (W). Beginning near Carlisle, Pa., as SOUTH MOUNTAIN (its name in Pa. and Md.), the Blue Ridge traverses parts of Md., Va. (where the Shenandoah Valley lies at W base), N.C., S.C., and Ga. N of Roanoke R., the Blue Ridge is generally a narrow (10–15 mi.) linear ridge in form; S of the river, name is sometimes applied to entire E Appalachian chain but is often restricted to ridge-like E front range of complex mtn. zone widening to c.70 mi. in W N.C., and including BLACK MOUNTAINS (where Mt. Mitchell, 6,684 ft., is highest peak E of the Mississippi), GREAT SMOKY MOUNTAINS, UNAKA MOUNTAINS, and many lesser ranges. In geology and physiography, the Blue Ridge province, composed of some of the most ancient rocks (strongly folded pre-Cambrian metamorphic rocks, with igneous intrusions) of the Appalachians, embraces the entire mtn. belt E of Great Appalachian Valley from South Mtn. southward, as well as the Piedmont transitional zone bet. the mts. and coastal plain. The Blue Ridge proper (E front range), whose general alt. is c.2,000–4,000 ft., contains highest points in Ga. (Brasstown Bald, 4,784 ft.), Va. (Mt. Rogers, 5,720 ft., in Iron Mts., a W outlier), and S.C. (Sassafras Mtn., 3,560 ft.); other high summits are Grandfather Mtn., N.C. (5,964 ft.), and Stony Man (4,010 ft.) and Hawks Bill (4,049 ft.), both in Va. The Potomac (at Harpers Ferry), the Roanoke (at Roanoke), and the James (near Lynchburg) have cut transverse gaps through the ridge; S of the Roanoke, the E escarpment is the E-W drainage divide. Famous for its scenery, the region has many resorts. In Va., SHENANDOAH NATIONAL PARK is traversed by the Skyline Drive, which connects with Blue Ridge Parkway (c.500 mi. long; established 1933), continuing S to Great Smoky Mts. Natl. Park. Appalachian Trail follows much of range. Forests, chiefly of mixed hardwoods, are chief resource; few minerals have been found. Remote Blue Ridge valleys, particularly in the S, shelter mountain people who have preserved many old ways of life and speech.

Blue Ridge Dam, N Ga., in Toccoa R. (known in Tenn., as Ocoee R.), 3 mi. E of Blue Ridge city. Privately built power dam (167 ft. high, 1,000 ft. long; completed 1931) now owned by TVA. Forms irregularly-shaped L. Toccoa (□ 5; 10 mi. long, max. width 3 mi.; capacity 200,800 acre-ft.; also called Blue Ridge L.). Swimming, boating, hunting. Chattahoochee Natl. Forest here.

Blue Ridge Mountains, U.S.: see BLUE RIDGE, THE.

Blue Ridge Parkway, Va. and N.C.: see BLUE RIDGE, THE.

Blue Ridge Summit, resort village, Franklin co., S Pa., on South Mtn. at Md. line, 6 mi. ESE of Waynesboro. U.S. Camp Ritchie near by (in Md.) was active in Second World War.

Blue River, village (pop. estimate 500), SE B.C., at foot of Rocky Mts., on North Thompson R. and 75 mi. SW of Jasper; lumbering.

Blue River, China: see YANGTZE RIVER.

Blue River, village (pop. 425), Grant co., SW Wis., on Wisconsin R. and Small Blue R., and 30 mi. E of Prairie du Chien; makes cheese.

Blue River. 1 In E Ariz., rises near N.Mex. line, flows c.65 mi. generally S to San Francisco R. 12 mi. NE of Clifton. **2** In N central Colo., rises in Park Range near Quandary Peak, flows c.75 mi. NNE, past Gore Range (W), to Colorado R. opposite Kremmling. Green Mtn. Dam (309 ft. high, 1,060 ft. long; completed 1943 as unit in Colorado–Big Thompson project) is 13 mi. SSE of Kremmling. Green Mtn. Reservoir, formed by dam, has capacity of 154,645 acre-ft.; stores water for generation of power and irrigation. **3** In S Ind., rises in NE Washington co., flows c.50 mi. SW and S, past Salem, to Ohio R. just SE of Leavenworth. **4** In central Ind.: see BIG BLUE RIVER. **5** In S Okla., rises in SW Pontotoc co., flows c.95 mi. SE, past Milburn, to Red R. 16 mi. W of Hugo.

Blue River Peak, Colo.: see GORE RANGE.

Blue Springs. 1 Town (pop. 111), Barbour co., SE Ala., 27 mi. SW of Eufaula. **2** Village (pop. 125), Union co., N Miss., 10 mi. SE of New Albany, in agr. and dairying area. **3** City (pop. 1,068), Jackson co., W Mo., 18 mi. E of Kansas City; wheat, corn, oats, dairy farms; creamery. **4** Village (pop. 581), Gage co., SE Nebr., 10 mi. SSE of Beatrice and on Big Blue R.; poultry products, grain.

Blue Stack, peak (2,219 ft.), S Co. Donegal, Ireland, 7 mi. N of Donegal, highest of the CROAGHGORM or Blue Stack Mts.

Bluestone Dam, S W.Va., in New R. just S of Hinton; 165 ft. high, 2,062 ft. long; for flood control, power; completed 1948. Bluestone Reservoir (capacity 631,000 acre-ft.) extends c.36 mi. up New R.; a W arm extends c.8 mi. up Bluestone R.

Bluestone River, in Va. and W.Va., rises near Va.–W.Va. line in Tazewell co., SW Va., W of Bluefield, flows 77 mi. generally NE into W.Va., to New R. (Bluestone Reservoir) 4 mi. S of Hinton, W.Va.

Bluewater, village (pop. c.300), Valencia co., W N.Mex., on San Jose R., just E of Zuni Mts., and 45 mi. ESE of Gallup; alt. 6,627 ft.; railroad loading point. Bluewater State Park and Reservoir and Cibola Natl. Forest near by.

Bluff, village (1939 pop.14), W Alaska, on S Seward Peninsula, on N shore of Norton Sound, 50 mi. E of Nome; gold placers, gold quartz, and cinnabar.

Bluff, borough (pop. 2,059) and port, S S.Isl., New Zealand, 12 mi. S of Invercargill and on Foveaux Strait; rail terminus. Exports oysters, fish, granite, quartz. Harbor is ½ mi. wide across mouth, 4 mi. long. Formerly Port Macquarie.

Bluff, El, Nicaragua: see EL BLUFF.

Bluff City. 1 City (pop. 172), Harper co., S Kansas, on small affluent of Chikaskia R. and 10 mi. SE of Anthony, near Okla. line; grain, livestock. **2** Town (pop. 1,074), Sullivan co., NE Tenn., on South Fork of Holston R. and 12 mi. NNE of Johnson City, in hilly agr. area. Cherokee Natl. Forest near by.

Bluff Dale, village (pop.c.500), Erath co., N central Texas, c.45 mi. SW of Fort Worth; rail point in agr. area.

Bluff Knoll, Australia: see STIRLING RANGE.

Bluffs, village (pop. 784), Scott co., W central Ill., near Illinois R., 16 mi. W of Jacksonville, in agr. area.

Bluffton. 1 Town (pop. 244), Clay co., SW Ga., 17 mi. SSW of Cuthbert, in farm area. **2** City (pop. 6,076), ⊙ Wells co., E Ind., on the Wabash and 24 mi. S of Fort Wayne; farming and dairying center; mfg. (furniture, pianos, windmills, pumps, machinery, gloves); limestone quarrying. Has a large arboretum. Settled 1829, inc. 1858. **3** Village (pop. 239), Otter Tail co., W Minn., on Leaf R. and c.40 mi. ENE of Fergus Falls, in agr. area; dairy products. **4** Village (pop. 2,423), Allen co., W Ohio, 15 mi. NE of Lima; rail junction; limestone quarrying and crushing; mfg. of electrical apparatus, clothing, food and dairy products. Seat of Bluffton Col., a Mennonite institution. Founded 1833, inc. 1861. **5** Town (pop. 474), Beaufort co., S S.C., on tidewater inlet and 17 mi. NE of Savannah, Ga.; fishing, bathing resort.

Bluford (bloo͞′fŭrd), village (pop. 477), Jefferson co., S Ill., 8 mi. E of Mount Vernon, in agr. area.

Bluie West 1, Greenland: see NARSARSSUAK.

Bluie West 8, Greenland: see SONDRE STROM FJORD.

Blum (blŭm), town (pop. 368), Hill co., N central Texas, 13 mi. NW of Hillsboro, in farm area.

Blumau (bloo͞′mou), village (pop. 292), Styria, SE Austria, 29 mi. E of Graz, N of Fürstenfeld; mfg. of explosives.

Blumberg (bloo͞m′bĕrk), village (pop. 3,540), S Baden, Germany, in Black Forest, 15 mi. SSE of Villingen; mfg. (chemicals, vehicles).

Blumenau (bloo͞mŭnou′), city (1950 pop. 22,919), E Santa Catarina, Brazil, 60 mi. NW of Florianópolis; head of navigation to Itajaí (Atlantic port) on lower Itajaí Açu R., and terminus of railroad serving upper river valley. Chief processing and distributing center of fertile region cultivated by small farmers with modern agr. methods. Principal crops are cereals, corn, sugar cane, rice, tobacco, manioc, and European-type vegetables and fruit. Region's surplus dairy products are shipped to Rio de Janeiro. Industries include textile and sugar milling, brewing; and mfg. of furniture, cigarettes, soap, and footwear. Hydroelectric plant. Airport. City has picturesque, Old World appearance. Founded 1850 by German pioneer immigrants from Pomerania. Later settlers included Austrians, Swiss, and Italians, but Ger. culture is dominant.

Blümlisalp (blüm'lĭs-älp) or **Frau** (frou), mountain in Bernese Alps, S central Switzerland, SW of Jungfrau. The Blümlisalphorn, its highest peak (12,032 ft.), is 7 mi. SW of Mürren. Other peaks include Weisse Frau (11,992 ft.), Morgenhorn (11,864 ft.), Oeschinenhorn (11,448 ft.), Rothorn (10,828 ft.), Wilde Frau (10,705 ft.), Blümlisalpstock (10,560 ft.). The Blümlisalp Hut (9,125 ft.) is on N slope.

Blunham (blŭ'nŭm), town and parish (pop. 590), central Bedford, England, on Ivel R. and 7 mi. E of Bedford; leather industry; truck gardening. The church is of Norman origin; John Donne was rector here for last 10 years of his life.

Blunt, city (pop. 423), Hughes co., central S.Dak., 20 mi. NE of Pierre and on Medicine Knoll Creek; farm trading point.

Bluntisham (blŭn'tĭshŭm, –sŭm), agr. village in parish of Bluntisham cum Earith (pop. 1,008), E Huntingdon, England, 4 mi. ENE of St. Ives; agr. equipment. Has 14th-15th-cent. church, 16th-cent. inn. Just E, on Ouse R., is agr. village of Earith (ûr'ĭth).

Blyava, Russian SFSR: see Mednogorsk.

Blying Sound, S Alaska, NW arm of Gulf of Alaska, washes Kenai Peninsula S of Seward.

Blyth (blīth, blīdh), village (pop. 611), S Ont., 15 mi. E of Goderich; flour milling, lumbering, dairying.

Blyth (blīdh), municipal borough (1931 pop. 31,680; 1951 census 34,742) and seaport, SE Northumberland, England, on North Sea, at mouth of Blyth R., 12 mi. NNE of Newcastle-upon-Tyne; coal-mining center, with shipbuilding and fishing industries. Exports coal, imports timber (pit props). Site of nautical col. In municipal borough are coal-mining towns of Bebside (W), Delaval (SW), Newsham (SW), and Cowpen (W).

Blythe. 1 (blīth) City (pop. 4,089), Riverside co., SE Calif., in irrigated Palo Verde Valley, near Colorado R., c.60 mi. N of Yuma, Ariz.; cotton, alfalfa, melons. Laid out 1910, inc. 1916. **2** (blīdh) Town (pop. 268), Richmond and Burke counties, E Ga., 16 mi. SW of Augusta.

Blythedale (blīdh'–), town (pop. 238), Harrison co., NW Mo., 16 mi. NNE of Bethany.

Blytheville (blīdh'vŭl, –vĭl), city (pop. 16,234), a ⊙ Mississippi co., NE Ark., c.55 mi. N of Memphis (Tenn.), near the Mississippi. Industrial center and market for state's richest cotton area, which also produces soybeans, feed, vegetables. Cotton ginning and compressing, cottonseed-oil milling, grist- and sawmilling; mfg. of cotton clothing, awnings, dairy products, lumber. U.S. bird refuge near by. Settled c.1853, inc. 1891.

Blyth River. 1 In Northumberland, England, rises in several branches in the Cheviot Hills, 12 mi. W of Blyth, flows 20 mi. E to North Sea at Blyth. **2** In Suffolk, England, rises 5 mi. N of Framlingham, flows 15 mi. NE and E, past Halesworth, to North Sea at Southwold. Navigable below Halesworth.

Blyukherovo, Russian SFSR: see Leninskoye, Khabarovsk Territory.

Blyukherovsk, Russian SFSR: see Srednyaya Nyukzha.

Bnaya, Israel: see Barcai.

Bne Beraq, Palestine: see Bnei Braq.

Bnei Braq or **Bnei Brak** (both: bŭnā' bräk'), settlement (pop. 12,000), W Israel, in Plain of Sharon, on the Yarkon and 3 mi. NE of Tel Aviv; industrial center; woolen mills; mfg. of aluminum tubes and containers, textile machinery, wire, glass, plastics, soaps, dyes, tobacco products, sausages, chocolate; citriculture. Has theological seminary. Modern village founded 1924. Also spelled Benei Beraq or Benei Berak. Site of the biblical *Bene-berak* or *Bne Braq* is 4 mi. ESE of Tel Aviv; traditional form of celebrating Passover had its inception here.

Bo (bû), Nor. *Bø*, village and canton (pop. 5,828), Nordland co., N Norway, on SW tip of Langoy in the Vesteralen group, 25 mi. N of Svolvaer; fishing port and trade center for numerous W shore fisheries, notably at Hovden (hôv'dŭn) village, 15 mi. N, at N tip of isl.

Bo (bō), town (pop. 7,853), ⊙ Sierra Leone protectorate and 2d-largest town of Sierra Leone, on railroad and road, 110 mi. ESE of Freetown; 7°57'N 11°40'W. Administrative and trade center; palm oil and kernels, cacao, coffee. Has teachers col., United Methodist mission. Airfield. Also ⊙ South-Western Prov. (□ 7,789; pop. 659,231) and hq. Bo dist.

Bo, Song, Vietnam: see Black River.

Boa (bō'ŭ), island (1,321 acres; 5 mi. long, 1 mi. wide) in Lough Erne, Co. Fermanagh, Northern Ireland, near Irish border, 2 mi. S of Pettigo; connected with mainland by causeways.

Boac (bō'äk), town (1939 pop. 2,958; 1948 municipality pop. 19,687), ⊙ Marinduque prov., Philippines, on W coast of Marinduque isl.; 13°27'N 121°50'E. Trade center for agr. area (coconuts, rice, abacá).

Boaco (bwä'kō), department (□ 2,085; 1950 pop. 50,151), S central Nicaragua; ⊙ Boaco. Bounded N by Río Grande, SW by L. Nicaragua, SE by Huapi Mts. Mainly a livestock-raising region; some agr. (coffee, sugar cane, corn, beans, fodder grasses). Lumbering (E); rubber and chicle extraction. Mfg. of Panama hats (Camoapa); dairying. Main centers: Boaco, Camoapa. Formed 1935 out of Chontales dept.

Boaco, city (1950 pop. 3,078), ⊙ Boaco dept., S central Nicaragua, 45 mi. NE of Managua; agr. and commercial center in livestock area; dairying, processing of livestock products; mfg. (Panama hats, soap, bricks, mineral water); sawmilling.

Boa Esperança (bō'ŭ ĭspĭrä'sŭ). **1** City (pop. 3,531), SW Minas Gerais, Brazil, near the Rio Grande, 22 mi. SW of Campo Belo; coffee, sugar. Until 1940, called Dores da Boa Esperança. **2** City, Piauí, Brazil: see Esperantina. **3** City, São Paulo, Brazil: see Boa Esperança do Sul.

Boa Esperança do Sul (dŏŏ sōōl'), city (pop. 1,208), central São Paulo, Brazil, on railroad and 20 mi. SW of Araraquara; dairying, distilling, mfg. of mattresses; coffee, sugar, tobacco. Sericulture. Until 1944, Boa Esperança.

Boal (bōäl'), town (pop. 1,011), Oviedo prov., NW Spain, 12 mi. SE of Ribadeo; cereals, wine.

Boalsburg, village (1940 pop. 535), Centre co., central Pa., 4 mi. E of State College. Laid out 1810; was important stagecoach stop.

Boanamary, Madagascar: see Majunga, town.

Boano (bōä'nō), island (□ 57; pop. 1,677), S Moluccas, Indonesia, in Ceram Sea, just W of Ceram; 2°59'S 127°55'E; 13 mi. long, 6 mi. wide. Level in N, rises to 2,034 ft. near S coast. Chief products: chalk, timber.

Boa Nova (bō'ŭ nô'vŭ), city (pop. 1,420), E Bahia, Brazil, in the Serra do Periperi, 50 mi. SSW of Jiquié; coffee, cacao, tobacco. Gold deposits in area.

Boara Pisani (bôä'rä pēsä'nē), village (pop. 1,184), Padova prov., Veneto, N Italy, 3 mi. N of Rovigo, in sugar-beet and cereal region; sausage mfg.

Boara Polesine (pôlä'zēnĕ), village (pop. 1,745), Rovigo prov., Veneto, N Italy, on Adige R. and 2 mi. N of Rovigo.

Boardman, town (pop. 120), Morrow co., N Oregon, 50 mi. W of Pendleton and on Columbia R.

Boardman River, NW Mich., rises NE of Kalkaska in Kalkaska co., flows SW and N, past Kalkaska and through forest region, to West Arm of Grand Traverse Bay at Traverse City; c.45 mi. long. Trout fishing.

Boar Island, N.F.: see Burgeo Islands.

Boat Basin, village, SW B.C., on W central Vancouver Isl., on Clayoquot Sound, 32 mi. NW of Tofino; gold mining.

Boath or **Both** (both: bōt), village (pop. 2,173), Adilabad dist., NE Hyderabad state, India, 27 mi. SSW of Adilabad; millet, oilseeds, rice.

Boat-of-Garten, Scotland: see Duthil and Rothiemurchus.

Boa Viagem (bō'ŭ vyä'zhĕn), city (pop. 719), central Ceará, Brazil, 30 mi. WNW of Quixeramobim; cotton, cattle, hides.

Boa Vista (bō'ŭ vēsh'tŭ). **1** Town, Amazonas, Brazil: see Santa Rita do Weil. **2** City, Goiás, Brazil: see Tocantinópolis. **3** City, Pernambuco, Brazil: see Coripós. **4** City (1950 pop. 5,125), ⊙ Rio Branco territory, northernmost Brazil, on right bank of the Rio Branco and 400 mi. N of Manaus, near Br. Guiana border; 2°50'N 60°45'W. Center of cattle-raising area. Ships tobacco, rubber, Brazil nuts. Some gold and diamond mining in Cotinga R. basin (N). Airport. Sometimes called Boa Vista do Rio Branco.

Boa Vista, Morro da, Brazil: see Bocaina, Serra da.

Boa Vista do Erechim, Brazil: see Erechim.

Boa Vista Island (□ 239; 1940 pop. 2,653; 1950 pop. 2,902), easternmost of Cape Verde Isls., in Windward group, bet. Sal (25 mi. N) and Maio (50 mi. SSW) isls., in the Atlantic, 300 mi. WNW of Cape Vert (Fr. West Africa). Sal-Rei (16°11'N 22°57'W), its chief town, is on NW shore. Isl. is roughly circular (diameter 15 mi.), with a hilly interior reaching 1,270 ft., and sandy shores. Produces salt and archil. Originally called São Christovão.

Boavita (bōävē'tä), town (pop. 1,209), Boyacá dept., central Colombia, in Cordillera Oriental, 10 mi. SW of El Cocuy; alt. 7,228 ft. Wheat, cotton, silk, sheep; mfg. (textile goods, mineral water). Coal and gypsum deposits near by.

Boaz (bō'ăz). **1** Town (pop. 3,078), Marshall co., NE Ala., 15 mi. NW of Gadsden, in cotton area; textiles, twine; cheese, beverages. Jr. col. here. Settled 1878, inc. 1891. **2** Village (pop. 188), Richland co., S central Wis., on Mill Creek (tributary of the Wisconsin) and 7 mi. W of Richland Center, in dairy and livestock region.

Boaz Island (bō'ăz), small island (½ mi. long, ⅕ mi. wide) of W Bermuda, just NE of Somerset Isl., 4.5 mi. W of Hamilton; inhabited. Road connects SW with Somerset Isl., NE with Ireland Isl.

Bobadilla (bōvä-dhē'lyä). **1** Village (pop. 3,774), Jaén prov., S Spain, 19 mi. WSW of Jaén; olive oil, cereals, fruit, lumber. **2** Village (pop. 574), Málaga prov., S Spain, 7 mi. W of Antequera; olives, cereals, fruit, livestock. Bobadilla station (pop. 1,194), 1½ mi. W, is where the Málaga-Córdoba and Granada-Algeciras rail lines meet.

Bobandana (bōbändä'nä), village, Kivu prov., E Belgian Congo, on W shore of L. Kivu, 30 mi. N of Costermansville; agr. center; extensive coffee plantations. Has R.C. mission. Also known as Saint-Joseph-de-Pelichy.

Bobare (bōbä'rā), town (pop. 616), Lara state, NW Venezuela, in Segovia Highlands, 17 mi. NNE of Barquisimeto; corn, goats.

Bobbili (bŏ'bĭlē), town (pop. 22,090), Vizagapatam dist., NE Madras, India, 32 mi. N of Vizianagaram; rail junction; trade center in agr. area; sugar, oilseed, and rice milling; brass and bell-metal works. Rail spur to Salur, 10 mi. SW.

Bobbio (bôb'byô), town (pop. 1,787), Piacenza prov., Emilia-Romagna, N central Italy, on Trebbia R. and 24 mi. SW of Piacenza. Bishopric. St. Columban founded here, 612, the oldest monastery (rebuilt 15th and 17th cent.) of N Italy. Center of European religious and cultural life from 9th to 12th cent. The codes and MSS of its rich library were dispersed in 15th and 16th cent.

Bobcaygeon (–kā'jŭn), village (pop. 1,002), S Ont., on small isl. bet. Sturgeon L. (W) and Pigeon L. (E), 20 mi. NW of Peterborough; center for Kawartha lakes resorts; boatbuilding, dairying. Former lumber center.

Bobenheim or **Bobenheim am Rhein** (bō'bŭnhīm äm rīn'), village (pop. 2,764), Rhenish Palatinate, W Germany, on oxbow lake of the Rhine and 4 mi. N of Frankenthal; wine; grain, sugar beets.

Bober River, Poland: see Bobrawa River.

Bobí, Paraguay: see General Artigas.

Bobigny (bôbēnyē'), town (pop. 16,547), Seine dept., N central France, a NE suburb of Paris, 5.5 mi. from Notre Dame Cathedral, on Ourcq Canal opposite Noisy-le-Sec; boilerworks, forges, brewery; mfg. of toys, carbonic acid, soap, celluloid, hosiery.

Bobingen (bō'bĭng-ŭn), village (pop. 6,001), Swabia, SW Bavaria, Germany, in the Lechfeld, 7 mi. SSW of Augsburg; viscose-silk mfg.

Böblingen (bû'blĭng-ŭn), town (pop. 10,809), Württemberg, Germany, after 1945 in Württemberg-Baden, 9 mi. SE of Stuttgart; rail junction; foundry, auto repair shops; textiles, shoes, furniture. Site (until 1945) of Stuttgart airport, Böblingen was heavily damaged in Second World War.

Boboci (bôbôch'), health resort, Buzau prov., SE central Rumania, 8 mi. ENE of Buzau; iodine, saline, and sulphurous springs.

Bobo-Dioulasso (bō'bō-dyōōlä'sō), town (pop. c.37,750), SW Upper Volta, Fr. West Africa, on wooded plateau, on railroad from Abidjan (Ivory Coast) and 200 mi. WSW of Ouagadougou, linked by motor road; trading and agr. center (peanuts, shea nuts, sesame, sisal; livestock). Mfg. of vegetable oil, soap, bricks. Has airfield, R.C. and Protestant missions, medical services, climatological station.

Bobonaro (bōbōnä'rōō), town (pop. 467), ⊙ Bobonaro dist. (□ 565; pop. 49,168), Portuguese Timor, in central Timor, 33 mi. SW of Dili; trade center for coffee-growing, lumbering area (sandalwood).

Bobonaza River (bōbōnä'sä), Napo-Pastaza prov., E Ecuador, rises at E slopes of the Andes E of Puyo, flows c.110 mi. SE to Pastaza R. at Peru border.

Boboshevo (bô'bôshĕvô), village (pop. 3,219), Sofia dist., W Bulgaria, on Struma R. and 8 mi. SW of Marek; wine making; fruit, tobacco, poppies.

Bobota (bôbô'tä), Hung. *Nagyderzsida* (nŏ'dyŭdĕr″-zhĕdŏ), village (pop. 1,736), Bihar prov., NW Rumania, 11 mi. N of Simleul-Silvaniei; lignite mining; mfg. of edible oils. In Hungary, 1940–45.

Bobov-dol (bôbôv'-dôl'), village (pop. 2,627), Sofia dist., W Bulgaria, in Konovo Mts., 9 mi. NNW of Marek; rail terminus; lignite-mining center.

Bobr. 1 River in NE Poland: see Biebrza River. **2** River in SW Poland: see Bobrawa River.

Bobr (bô'bŭr), town (1926 pop. 2,477), NE Minsk oblast, Belorussian SSR, 31 mi. ENE of Borisov; peat digging, lumbering.

Bobrawa River (bôbrä'vä), Ger. *Bober* (bō'bŭr), in Lower Silesia, after 1945 in SW Poland, rises at SE foot of the Riesengebirge SW of Lubawka, flows NNE past Lubawka and Kamienna Gora, WNW past Hirschberg (Jelenia Gora), and generally NNW past Lwowek Slaskie, Boleslawiec, Szprotawa, and Sagan (Zagan), to Oder R. just W of Krosno Ordzanskie; 166 mi. long. Sometimes called Bobr R. Receives Kwisa R. (left).

Bobrek or **Bobrek Karb** (bô'brĕk kärp'), Ger. *Bobrek-Karf* (bō'brĕk-kärf'), commune (1941 pop. 22,095; 1946 pop. 17,993) in Upper Silesia, after 1945 in Katowice prov., S Poland, 3 mi. WSW of Beuthen (Bytom); coal, zinc, and lead mining, steel milling, chemical mfg. Includes Karb, Ger. *Karf*, rail junction, 2 mi. W of Beuthen.

Bobrik-Donskoi, Russian SFSR: see Donskoi.

Bobriki, Russian SFSR: see Stalinogorsk.

Bobrinets (bô'brēnyĭts, bŭbrē'nyĭts), city (1926 pop. 11,079), S Kirovograd oblast, Ukrainian SSR, on road and 32 mi. S of Kirovograd; metalworks, dairy plant, flour mill.

Bobrka (bô'bŭrkŭ), Pol. *Bóbrka* (bōō'bŭrkä), city (1931 pop. 5,441), S Lvov oblast, Ukrainian SSR, 17 mi. SE of Lvov; agr. processing (grain, flax).

Bobrov (bŭbrôf'), city (1926 pop. 17,404), central Voronezh oblast, Russian SFSR, on Bityug R. and 50 mi. SE of Voronezh; flour-milling center; sunflower-oil extraction. Poultry farming, horse breeding near by. Dates from 17th cent.; chartered 1779.

Bobrovitsa or **Bobrovitsy** (bŭbrô'vētsŭ, –tsē). 1 Town (1926 pop. 7,018), SW Chernigov oblast, Ukrainian SSR, 30 mi. SW of Nezhin; sugar refining. 2 Village (1926 pop. 1,230), W Chernigov oblast, Ukrainian SSR, 4 mi. NE of Chernigov; truck produce.

Bobrovo-Dvorskoye (–vŭ-dvôr'skŭyŭ), village (1926 pop. 332), E central Kursk oblast, Russian SFSR, 19 mi. WSW of Stary Oskol; wheat, sunflowers, essential oils. Formerly called Bobrovskiye Dvory.

Bobr River. 1 In NE Poland: see BIEBRZA RIVER. 2 In SW Poland: see BOBRAWA RIVER.

Bobruisk or **Bobruysk** (bŭbrōō'ēsk), oblast (□ 7,600; 1946 pop. estimate 800,000), central Belorussian SSR; ⊙ Bobruisk. In N Pripet Marshes; drained by Berezina, Ptich, and Sluch rivers. Agr. (potatoes, rye, oats, barley) and livestock (pigs, some dairy cattle) area; truck gardens and orchards near Bobruisk; flax (NE). Lumbering is important (sawmills, wood distilleries, woodworking plants). Peat works (chiefly NW of Bobruisk). Phosphorite deposits. Industry centered at Bobruisk and Slutsk. Formed 1944.

Bobruisk or **Bobruysk**, city (1939 pop. 84,107), ⊙ Bobruisk oblast, Belorussian SSR, on Berezina R. and 85 mi. SE of Minsk; 53°8'N 29°12'E. Road, rail junction; lumber center (plywood, furniture); food processing, mfg. of clothing, shoes; metalworks. Site of anc. fortress. Pop. 40% Jewish until Second World War, when city was held (1941–44) by Germans.

Bobryshevo (bŭbrĭ'shĭvŭ), village (1939 pop. over 2,000), central Kursk oblast, Russian SFSR, 8 mi. E of Oboyan; sugar beets.

Bobtown, village (pop. 1,553), Greene co., SW Pa., 13 mi. SE of Waynesburg, near W.Va. line.

Bobures (bōbōō'rēs), town (pop. 1,420), Zulia state, NW Venezuela, on SE shore of L. Maracaibo, 50 mi. WSW of Trujillo; sugar-growing and -milling center.

Boca, La, Argentina: see LA BOCA.

Boca, La, Chile: see LA BOCA.

Boca, La, Panama Canal Zone: see LA BOCA.

Boca Araguao, Venezuela: see ARAGUAO, BOCA.

Boca Bío-Bío, Chile: see LA BOCA, Concepción prov.

Boca Chica, Colombia: see CARTAGENA, BAY OF.

Boca Chica (bō'kä chē'kä), town (1935 pop. 1,290), S Dominican Republic, beach resort on a small Caribbean bay, 19 mi. E of Ciudad Trujillo; sugar milling and refining.

Boca Chica, village (pop. 116), Chiriquí prov., W Panama, 6 mi. SSW of Horconcitos, minor port on Chiriquí Gulf of the Pacific; livestock, vegetables.

Boca Chica, Texas: see BRAZOS ISLAND.

Boca Chica Key, Fla.: see FLORIDA KEYS.

Boca Ciega (bō'kŭ syā'gŭ), town (pop.159), Pinellas co., W Fla., near St. Petersburg.

Boca Dam, Calif.: see LITTLE TRUCKEE RIVER.

Boca de Cangrejos (bō'kä dā käng-grā'hōs), beach and fishing resort, NE Puerto Rico, 4 mi. E of San Juan. Known for its submarine gardens.

Boca de Cupe (bō'kä dā kōō'pā), village (pop. 389), Darién prov., E Panama, on Tuira R. and 10 mi. SE of El Real; corn, rice, beans; stock raising, lumbering.

Boca de la Sierpe, Venezuela–Trinidad: see SERPENT'S MOUTH.

Boca del Monte (dĕl mōn'tā), village (pop. 435), Chiriquí prov., W Panama, in Pacific lowland, 22 mi. E of David, on Inter-American Highway. Stock-raising center; vegetables.

Boca del Punkire, Peru: see INAMBARI.

Boca del Río (rē'ō), town (pop. 727), Veracruz, E Mexico, on Gulf of Mexico, on railroad and 6 mi. S of Veracruz; beach resort, with adjoining Mocambo beaches.

Boca de Maipo, Chile: see LA BOCA, Santiago prov.

Boca de Navíos, Venezuela: see GRANDE, BOCA.

Bôca do Acre (bō'kŭ dōō ä'krĭ), city (pop. 1,099), SW Amazonas, Brazil, on Purus R. at influx of Acre R. (both navigable), and 90 mi. NNE of Rio Branco.

Bôca do Jari (zhärē'), town, S Amapá territory, N Brazil, on left bank of Jari R. near its influx into the Amazon delta, and 110 mi. SE of Macapá.

Bôca do Tapauá (täpou-ä'), town (pop. 399), S central Amazonas, Brazil, on Purus R. and 340 mi. SW of Manaus; rubber.

Boca Grande, Colombia: see CARTAGENA, BAY OF.

Boca Grande, Fla.: see GASPARILLA ISLAND.

Boca Grande, Venezuela: see GRANDE, BOCA.

Bocaína (bōōkī'nŭ), city (pop. 2,234), central São Paulo, Brazil, on railroad and 10 mi. NNE of Jaú; macaroni processing, tanning, agr. (coffee, corn, beans). Until 1938, São João da Bocaina.

Bocaina, La, channel, Canary Isls.: see BOCAYNA, LA.

Bocaina, Serra da (sĕ'rŭ dä), range in extreme SE São Paulo, Brazil, a section of the Serra do Mar W of Bananal and S of Paraíba R. Rises to 6,791 ft. in the peak Morro da Boa Vista.

Bocairente (bōkīrĕn'tä), town (pop. 2,497), Valencia prov., E Spain, 8 mi. NW of Alcoy; mfg. of woolen textiles, burlap; olive-oil processing; lumber, sheep, cereals, wine, fruit. Stone quarries.

Bocaiúva (bōkīōō'vŭ). 1 City (pop. 3,005), N central Minas Gerais, Brazil, in the Serra do Espinhaço, on railroad and 30 mi. S of Montes Claros; rock crystals, lumber, cotton. Airfield. Eclipse of the sun (1947) observed from here. Formerly spelled Bocayuva. 2 City, São Paulo, Brazil: see MACATUBA.

Bocaiúva do Sul (dōō sōōl'), city (pop. 325), E Paraná, Brazil, 18 mi. NNE of Curitiba; galena mining; maté processing. Until 1944, called Bocaiúva (old spelling, Bocayuva); and, 1944–48, Imbuial.

Bocapán (bōkäpän'), village (pop. 249), Tumbes dept., NW Peru, minor port on the Pacific, on Pan American Highway and 4 mi. SW of Zorritos, at periphery of Zorritos oil fields.

Bocaranga (bōkäräng-gä'), village, NW Ubangi-Shari, Fr. Equatorial Africa, 195 mi. NW of Bozoum; cotton.

Boca Raton (bō'kŭ rŭtōn'), resort town (pop. 992), Palm Beach co., SE Fla., 25 mi. S of West Palm Beach.

Bocas de Ceniza (bō'käs dā sānē'sä), mouth of Magdalena R. on Caribbean Sea, N Colombia, on Atlántico–Magdalena dept. border. Dredged and canalized in 1930s, it accommodates ocean vessels up to 10,000 tons, which dock at Barranquilla c.11 mi. SE by waterway.

Bocas del Dragón, Venezuela-Trinidad: see DRAGON'S MOUTH.

Bocas del Toro (bō'käs dĕl tō'rō), province (□ 3,508; 1950 pop. 22,077; 40% Indians) of W Panama, on Caribbean coast; ⊙ Bocas del Toro. Bounded W by Costa Rica (in part along Sixaola R.), it includes Bocas del Toro Archipelago. Agr. mainly in Changuinola R. lowland: bananas (once important plantations; abandoned in 1929), cacao, abacá, coconuts, tobacco; stock raising, lumbering. Main centers are Bocas del Toro and Almirante. Formed 1903 out of Colón prov.

Bocas del Toro, town (1950 pop. 2,910), ⊙ Bocas del Toro prov., W Panama, Caribbean port at S tip of Colón Isl., 200 mi. WNW of Panama city. Important commercial center, exporting plantains, cacao, coconuts to Colón. Has Park de Bolívar, cathedral (Nuestra Señora del Carmen). Founded by Negro immigrants (early 19th cent.); destroyed by fire in 1904 and 1907.

Bocas del Toro Archipelago, island group in Caribbean Sea, Bocas del Toro prov., W Panama, off Almirante Bay and Chiriquí Lagoon. Includes Colón Isl. (with town of Bocas del Toro), Bastimentos Isl. (with village of Bastimentos), Popa and San Cristóbal isls., and Cayo de Agua.

Boca Tigris (bō'kŭ tē'grĭs) or **The Bogue** (bōg'), Cantonese *Fu Mun*, Mandarin *Hu Men* [mouth of the tiger], mouth of Canton R. at head of its estuary, in Kwangtung prov., China, bet. Taikoktow isl. (W) and Anunghoi isl. (E), 35 mi. SE of Canton. In its center are the islets of North Wantong and South Wantong, site of the Bogue Forts established in mid-19th cent. and captured by British (1841, 1856). The name Boca Tigris is sometimes restricted to E channel bet. Wantong isls. and Anunghoi isl. Formerly spelled Bocca Tigris.

Bocaue (bōkä'wä), town (1939 pop. 2,279; 1948 municipality pop. 16,537), Bulacan prov., S central Luzon, Philippines, 14 mi. NNW of Manila, near railroad; agr. center (rice, sugar, corn).

Bocay (bōkī'), village, Jinotega dept., N Nicaragua, on Coco R., at mouth of Bocay R., and 105 mi. NE of Jinotega; lumbering; gold placers.

Bocayna, La, or **La Bocaina** (both: lä bōkī'nä), Atlantic channel bet. Lanzarote (N) and Fuerteventura (S), Canary Isls.; c.6 mi. wide, 15 mi. long. The Isla de Lobos is in SE section.

Bocay River (bōkī'), N Nicaragua, rises in Cordillera Isabelia 20 mi. NE of Peña Blanca peak, flows c.80 mi. NE to Coco R. at Bocay.

Bocayuva, Brazil: see BOCAIÚVA, Minas Gerais.

Bocca Serriola (bôk'kä sĕr-rēô'lä), pass (alt. 2,395 ft.), central Italy, at SE end of Etruscan Apennines, 7 mi. NE of Città di Castello. Crossed by road bet. Città di Castello and Fossombrone.

Bocca Tigris, China: see BOCA TIGRIS.

Bocca Trabaria (bôk'kä träbärē'ä), pass (alt. 3,425 ft.) in SE Etruscan Apennines, central Italy, 5 mi. ENE of Sansepolcro. Crossed by road bet. Sansepolcro and Urbino.

Bocche di Cattaro, Yugoslavia: see KOTOR, GULF OF.

Boccheggiano (bôk-kĕd-jä'nô), village (pop. 914), Grosseto prov., Tuscany, central Italy, 8 mi. ENE of Massa Marittima; iron-pyrites mining.

Bocchetta (bôk-kĕt'tä), pass (alt. 2,533 ft.) in Ligurian Apennines, N Italy, W of Giovi Pass, 11 mi. NNW of Genoa. Crossed by road bet. Genoa and Novi Ligure.

Bocchigliero (bôk-kēlyā'rô), village (pop. 3,746), Cosenza prov., Calabria, S Italy, 13 mi. SSE of Rossano; lumbering, domestic weaving.

Bochalema (bōchälā'mä), town (pop. 1,454), Norte de Santander dept., N Colombia, in valley of Cordillera Oriental, on Pamplonita R. and 21 mi. SSW of Cúcuta; alt. 3,838 ft. Coffee, cacao, corn.

Bochil (bōchēl'), town (pop. 1,337), Chiapas, S Mexico, in N spur of Sierra Madre, 23 mi. NE of Tuxtla; alt. 3,609 ft.; cereals, tobacco, sugar, fruit.

Bochkarevo, Russian SFSR: see KUIBYSHEVKA.

Bochnia (bôkh'nyä), town (pop. 10,072), Krakow prov., S Poland, on railroad and 22 mi. ESE of Cracow, near Raba R. Rock-salt (deposits estimated at 50,000,000 tons) and gypsum mining; mfg. of cement products, flour, bricks. Founded 12th cent. During Second World War, under Ger. rule, called Salzberg.

Bocholt (bô'khôlt), city (1950 pop. 37,662), in former Prussian prov. of Westphalia, NW Germany, after 1945 in North Rhine-Westphalia, 28 mi. N of Duisburg; rail junction; textile center (cotton, linen, garments); foundries. Extensive Second World War damage includes Gothic church of St. George and noted Renaissance town hall. Chartered 1222. Heavy fighting in vicinity (March, 1945).

Bochov (bô'khôf), Ger. *Buchau* (bōō'khou), town (pop. 1,084), W Bohemia, Czechoslovakia, 8 mi. SE of Carlsbad; rail terminus.

Bochum (bō'khōōm), city (□ 47; 1939 pop. 305,485; 1946 pop. 246,477; 1950 pop. 290,406), in former Prussian prov. of Westphalia, W Germany, after 1945 in North Rhine-Westphalia, extends to the Ruhr (S), adjoins (E) Dortmund; 51°29'N 7°11'E. Rail junction; coal-mining center; bell foundries; mfg. of coke and coal-tar products, structural forms, railroad and mining equipment, vehicles, cigars, cigarettes. Brewing. Became glassworking center after Second World War. Has 11th- and 12th-cent. churches, 13th-cent. castle; also school of economics and management, and silicose-research institute. First mentioned in 9th cent. Chartered 1298 and 1324. Passed to duchy of Cleves in 1461, to Brandenburg in early-17th cent. Second World War destruction c.65%.

Bock, village (pop. 96), Mille Lacs co., E Minn., on branch of Rum R. and 34 mi. NE of St. Cloud, in agr. area; dairy products.

Bockau (bô'kou), village (pop. 4,415), Saxony, E central Germany, in the Erzgebirge, 3.5 mi. S of Aue, near Czechoslovak border, in uranium-mining region; woodworking, distilling.

Bockenem (bô'kŭnŭm), town (pop. 4,393), in former Prussian prov. of Hanover, NW Germany, after 1945 in Lower Saxony, 12 mi. SE of Hildesheim; food processing (flour products, canned goods, sugar, beer); mfg. of chemicals.

Bockenheim (bô'kŭnhīm), NW industrial district (pop. 22,867) of Frankfurt, W Germany.

Bockfliess (bôk'flēs), village (pop. 1,462), E Lower Austria, 15 mi. NE of Vienna; corn, vineyards.

Bockhorn (bôk'hôrn''), village (commune pop. 16,973), in Oldenburg, NW Germany, after 1945 in Lower Saxony, 5 mi. W of Varel, in East Friesland; cotton mfg., brewing. Brickworks. Commune is called Friesische Wehde (frē''zĭshŭ vā'dŭ).

Bocking, England: see BRAINTREE AND BOCKING.

Böckingen (bû'kĭng-ŭn), SW suburb of HEILBRONN, Germany.

Böckstein (bûk'shtīn), village, Salzburg, W central Austria, near N exit of Tauern Tunnel, 23 mi. SSW of Bischofshofen. Has 18th-cent. church.

Bockum-Hövel (bô'kōōm-hû'vŭl), town (pop. 19,168), in former Prussian prov. of Westphalia, NW Germany, after 1945 in North Rhine-Westphalia, near the Lippe, 3 mi. NW of Hamm; coal mining. Formed 1939 through incorporation of Bockum and Hövel.

Bockwitz (bôk'vĭts), village (pop. 6,782), in former Prussian Saxony prov., central Germany, after 1945 in Saxony-Anhalt, 11 mi. W of Senftenberg; lignite mining.

Boconó (bōkōnō'), town (pop. 4,181), Trujillo state, W Venezuela, in Andean spur, on Boconó R., on transandine highway and 15 mi. SE of Trujillo; alt. 3,920 ft. Agr. center (coffee, corn, wheat, sugar cane, potatoes).

Boconó River, W Venezuela, rises in Andean spur E of Trujillo, flows c.80 mi. SE, along Barinas–Portuguesa border, to Guanare R. 25 mi. SSE of Guanare.

Bocoyna (bōkoi'nä), town (pop. 510), Chihuahua, N Mexico, in Sierra Madre Occidental, on railroad and 110 mi. WSW of Chihuahua; alt. 7,290 ft.; grain, beans, fruit, cattle.

Bocsa-Montana (bōk'shä-môntä'nŭ), Rum. *Bocşa-Montană*, Hung. *Boksánbánya* (bôk'shämbä''nyŏ), village (pop. 3,300), Severin prov., SW Rumania, on railroad and 25 mi. NNE of Oravita; iron, copper, and manganese mining, tanning, mfg. of gloves. Also a climatic resort with noted sanatorium. Near-by Bocsa-Romana (pop. 3,132) produces agr. machinery, Vasiova (pop. 1,443) has sawmills.

Bocsarlapujtö (bô'chärlŏpōōĭtû), Hung. *Bocsárlapujtő*, town (pop. 2,367), Nograd-Hont co., N Hungary, 5 mi. NW of Salgotarjan; rye, potatoes, sheep.

Bocsa-Romana, Rumania: see BOCSA-MONTANA.

Bod, India: see BAUDH.

Bod (bōd), Hung. *Botfalu* (bôt'fōlōō), village (pop. 2,538), Stalin prov., central Rumania, on Olt R. and 9 mi. NNE of Stalin (Brasov); large sugar mills.

Boda (bōdä'), village, S Ubangi-Shari, Fr. Equatorial Africa, 80 mi. W of Bangui; coffee center; cotton ginning, lumbering.

Bodafors (bōō"däfôrs', -fôsh'), town (pop. 2,173), Jonkoping co., S Sweden, on Em R. and 9 mi. S of Nassjo; furniture mfg.

Bodaibo or **Bodaybo** (bŭdībô'), city (1939 pop. over 10,000), NE Irkutsk oblast, Russian SFSR, on Vitim R. (head of navigation), at mouth of short Bodaibo R., and 550 mi. NE of Irkutsk, 225 mi. NE of L. Baikal. Center of Lena-Vitim gold-mining dist.; river port; sawmilling, tanning, distilling; machine shops. Narrow-gauge railroad extends to principal mines at Andreyevsk, Aprelsk, Artemovski, Kropotkin, Svetly.

Bodalla (bŏdă'lŭ), village (pop. 239), SE New South Wales, Australia, 75 mi. SE of Canberra; gold-mining center; dairy products.

Bodaybo, Russian SFSR: see BODAIBO.

Bodcau Bayou (bŏd'kô bī'ō) river in Ark. and La., rises S of Hope in SW Ark., flows c.125 mi. generally S, past Stamps, into NW La., to Red R. just S of L. Bistineau. Dam 35 mi. NE of Shreveport is a unit of Red R. flood-control system. In Ark., called Bodcau Creek.

Boddam, fishing village, NE Aberdeen, Scotland, on North Sea, 3 mi. S of Peterhead. Near by are pink-granite quarries. Remains of Boddam Castle date from 14th cent. Just E is small promontory of Buchan Ness (bŭkh'ŭn), with lighthouse (57°28'N 1°46'W).

Bodden (bô'dŭn), Baltic strait, N Germany, separating Rügen isl. from mainland; 18 mi. long; crossed at Stralsund by Rügen Dam.

Bodden Town, town (pop. 618) in Cayman Isls., dependency of Jamaica, on S central coast of Grand Cayman isl., 8 mi. E of Georgetown. Collects turtle shells, sharkskins, timber.

Boddhnath (bŏd'nät) or **Boudh** (bōd), village, central Nepal, in Nepal Valley, near the Baghmati, 3 mi. NE of Katmandu city center. Buddhist pilgrimage center; large, well-preserved stupa (built 1st cent. B.C.). Also spelled Bodhnath.

Bode (bōd), town (pop. 492), Humboldt co., N central Iowa, 26 mi. NNW of Fort Dodge; dairy products.

Bodedern (bōdĕ'dŭrn), village and parish (pop. 857), W Anglesey, Wales, 6 mi. ESE of Holyhead; woolen milling.

Bodega Bay (bōdā'gŭ, bŭ-), W Calif., shallow, sand choked inlet of Pacific Ocean, 20 mi. W of Santa Rosa; sheltered on W by peninsula terminating at Bodega Head. On E shore is Bodega Bay village (fishing), formerly called Bay. A Russian fur post was established here c.1811. Was an active harbor until 1870s.

Bodega Central (bōdā'gä sĕnträl'), town (pop. 443), Bolívar dept., N Colombia, on Magdalena R. at mouth of Lebrija R., and 28 mi. WSW of Ocaña.

Bodegraven (bō'dŭgrävŭn), town (pop. 4,829), South Holland prov., W Netherlands, on the Old Rhine and 12 mi. ESE of Leiden; linseed oil pressing; mfg. (soap, dairy machinery, bicycles, cement); cheese processing; cheese market. Destroyed (1673) by French.

Bodélé or **Bodeli** (bōdĕlē'), large alluvial depression (alt. 300-400 ft.) in N Chad territory, Fr. Equatorial Africa, in SE part of the Sahara, NE of L. Chad and near Fr. West Africa border. Here converge the wadis descending from Tibesti Massif and Ennedi Plateau.

Bodeli (bōdā'lē), town (pop. 2,890), Baroda dist., N Bombay, India, 32 mi. E of Baroda; market center for cotton, millet, rice; cotton ginning. Granite deposits near by.

Bödeli (bû'dŭlē), lowland in Bern canton, central Switzerland, bet. lakes of Thun and Brienz. Interlaken is on it.

Boden (bōō'dŭn), city (1950 pop. 11,458), Norrbotten co., N Sweden on Lule R. and 20 mi. NW of Lulea; important rail junction on line from Stockholm to Narvik, Lulea, and Haparanda; site of Sweden's strongest modern fortress. Shoe mfg., sawmilling, woodworking. Inc. as city in 1918. Airfield (N) is hq. of flying ambulance services for Lapland.

Bodenbach, Czechoslovakia: see PODMOKLY.

Bodenburg (bō'dŭnbŏŏrk), village (pop. 2,419), in former Prussian prov. of Hanover, NW Germany, after 1945 in Lower Saxony, 9 mi. SSE of Hildesheim; brewing. A Brunswick exclave until 1941.

Bodenfelde (bō"dŭnfĕl'dŭ), village (pop. 3,641), in former Prussian prov. of Hanover, W Germany, after 1945 in Lower Saxony, on right bank of the Weser and 18 mi. NW of Göttingen; woodworking.

Bodenheim (bō'dŭnhīm), village (pop. 3,694), Rhenish Hesse, W Germany, 4 mi. SSE of Mainz; brickworks. Vineyards.

Bodenmais (bō'dŭnmīs"), village (pop. 3,792), Lower Bavaria, Germany, in Bohemian Forest, 7 mi. WNW of Zwiesel; woodworking; summer resort. Mining center since Middle Ages; former silver mines now produce rose quartz and pyrites.

Bodensee, Austria, Germany, and Switzerland: see CONSTANCE, LAKE OF.

Bodenwerder (bō"dŭnvĕr'dŭr), town (pop. 3,056), in former Prussian prov. of Hanover, NW Germany, after 1945 in Lower Saxony, on left bank of the Weser and 10 mi. NNE of Holzminden; mfg. (transportation equipment, furniture, apparel). Baron Munchausen (Ger. *Münchhausen*) b. here; his house is now a museum.

Bode River (bō'dŭ), central Germany, rises in 2 headstreams at foot of the Brocken in the upper Harz, flows c.100 mi. E, NE, and SE, past Thale, Quedlinburg, Oschersleben, and Stassfurt, to the Saxonian Saale at Nienburg. Dammed SSW of Blankenburg.

Bodetalsperre, Germany: see BLANKENBURG.

Bodhan (bō'dŭn), town (pop. 19,443), Nizamabad dist., N central Hyderabad state, India, 13 mi. W of Nizamabad; sugar factory and distillery, served by rail branch from Jankampet (11 mi. ENE). Experimental farm (sugar cane) 5 mi. S, at village of Rudrur.

Bodh Gaya, India: see BUDDH GAYA.

Bodhnath, Nepal: see BODDHNATH.

Bodicote, agr. village and parish (pop. 638), N Oxfordshire, England, 2 mi. S of Banbury; flour milling. Church dates from 13th cent.

Bodie, village (pop. c.100), Mono co., E Calif., in the Sierra Nevada, c.65 mi. NNW of Bishop; gold mining. In 1870s, was gold boom town, with pop. of c.12,000.

Bodie Island, E N.C., name given to stretch of the Outer Banks N of Oregon Inlet, and just E of Roanoke Isl.; lighthouse at 35°49'N 75°34'W.

Bodinayakkanur or **Bodinayakanur** (both: bōdĭnä'-yŭkŭnōōr"), city (pop. 28,435), Madura dist., S Madras, India, 55 mi. W of Madura; rail spur terminus; trade center for products (teak, sandalwood, bamboo) of N Cardamom Hills (W) and of Kambam Valley. Road leads through hills to Travancore, serving cardamom, tea, and coffee plantations.

Bodjonegoro, Indonesia: see BOJONEGORO.

Bodkin Point (bŏd'kĭn), low headland, Anne Arundel co., central Md., at S side of mouth of Patapsco R. on Chesapeake Bay, and 15 mi. SE of downtown Baltimore. Baltimore lighthouse stands just offshore.

Bodmin (bŏd'mĭn), municipal borough (1931 pop. 5,526; 1951 census 6,058), ⊙ Cornwall, England, in center of co., 27 mi. WNW of Plymouth; 50°28'N 4°41'W. Market center (cattle, sheep, dairy products). Has 15th-cent. church, 17th-cent. guildhall, mus.

Bodmin Moor, wild tract in E Cornwall, England, bet. Bodmin and Launceston; has many prehistoric remains. Brown Willy, 4 mi. SE of Camelford, is highest peak (1,375 ft.) in Cornwall. Dozmary Pool, 7 mi. NW of Liskeard, is legendary site of The Lady of the Lake in Arthurian legend.

Bodo (bōd'ŭ), Nor. *Bodø*, city (pop. 6,344), ⊙ Nordland co., N Norway, port on North Sea at mouth of Salt Fjord, 110 mi. SW of Narvik; 67°17'N 14°26'E. Base for Lofoten fisheries; has ship-repair yards, brewery. Tourist center; seaplane base. Ships metals from Sulitjelma village and marble and slate from Fauske; trading center. In Second World War, about 60% destroyed (1940) by German air and ground action. Proposed terminus of railroad under construction from Trondheim.

Bodoc (bô'dôk), Hung. *Sepsibodok* (shĕp'shēbō"-dôk), village (pop. 1,147), Stalin prov., central Rumania, on railroad, on Olt R. and 8 mi. ENE of Sfantu-Gheorghe; summer resort (alt. 1,801 ft.) noted for its bottled mineral waters. In Hungary, 1940-45.

Bodocó (bŏŏdŏŏkô'), city (pop. 1,363), W Pernambuco, NE Brazil, on S slope of Serra do Araripe, 50 mi. SW of Crato (Ceará); manioc, coffee, livestock.

Bodón, El (ĕl bō-dhōn'), town (pop. 1,181), Salamanca prov., W Spain, 8 mi. SSW of Ciudad Rodrigo; cereals, lumber, livestock.

Bodonal de la Sierra (bō-dhōnäl' dhā lä syĕ'rä), town (pop. 2,857), Badajoz prov., W Spain, in the Sierra Morena, 17 mi. SE of Jerez de los Caballeros; hog raising; also processes grapes, olives.

Bodoquena, Serra da (sĕ'rŭ dä bōdōkä'nŭ), low range in SW Mato Grosso, Brazil, at E edge of Paraguay flood plain, SW of Miranda. Has colored marble deposits.

Bodrogkeresztur (bôd'rôk-kĕ"rĕstōōr), Hung. *Bodrogkeresztúr*, town (pop. 2,248), Zemplen co., NE Hungary, on Bodrog R. and 3 mi. NW of Tokaj; flour mills, brickworks; vineyards. Bronze Age remains near by.

Bodrogköz (bôd'rôk-kûz), section of NE ALFÖLD, in NE Hungary and E Czechoslovakia, bounded by Latoritsa (N), Tisza (E), and Bodrog (W) rivers. Grain, tobacco, potatoes, plums, apples, pears; cattle, hogs.

Bodrog River (bô'drôg), E Czechoslovakia and NE Hungary; formed 8 mi. NE of Satoraljaujhely by junction of Ondava and Latoritsa rivers; meanders 40 mi. SW, past Sarospatak, to the Tisza at Tokaj.

Bodrum (bōdrōōm'), anc. *Halicarnassus* (hă"lĭ-kärnă'sŭs), village (pop. 4,963), Mugla prov., SW Turkey, Aegean port on peninsula N of Gulf of Kos opposite Kos isl., 55 mi. WSW of Mugla, 95 mi. S of Smyrna; tobacco, grain, beans. Sometimes spelled Budrum and Budrun. See HALICARNASSUS.

Bodvad (bōd'vŭd), town (pop. 7,630), East Khandesh dist., NE Bombay, India, 28 mi. ESE of Jalgaon; trades in cotton, oilseeds, millet.

Bodva River (bôd'vä), Hung. *Bódva* (bōd'vŏ), E Czechoslovakia and NE Hungary, rises on SE slopes of Slovak Ore Mts., 10 mi. E of Roznava; flows c.60 mi. S, past Szendrö and Edeleny, to Sajo R. 6 mi. N of Miskolc.

Bodyul: see TIBET.

Bodzafordulo, Rumania: see INTORSATURA-BUZAULUI.

Boechout (bōōkhout'), residential town (pop. 6,553), Antwerp prov., N Belgium, 5 mi. SE of Antwerp. Has 17th-cent. castle.

Boëge (bôĕzh'), village (pop. 442), Haute-Savoie dept., SE France, on E slope of the Voirons, 12 mi. E of Geneva.

Boekelo (bōōk'ŭlō), town (pop. 932), Overijssel prov., E Netherlands, 5 mi. S of Hengelo; rock-salt-mining center; chemicals (chlorine, soda). Sometimes spelled Boekeloo.

Boekittinggi, Indonesia: see BUKITTINGGI.

Boela, Indonesia: see BULA.

Boelan, Indonesia: see BULAN.

Boele (bō'lŭ), N district (since 1929) of Hagen, W Germany.

Boeleleng, Indonesia: see BULELENG.

Boelus (bō'lŭs), village (pop. 167), Howard co., SE central Nebr., on Middle Loup R. and 16 mi. SW of St. Paul. Near-by dam, on Loup R., is part of power project. Inc. as Howard City, by which name it is sometimes called.

Boemiajoe, Indonesia: see BUMIAYU.

Boemitsa, Greece: see AXIOUPOLIS.

Boën or **Boën-sur-Lignon** (bôĕ'-sür-lēnyō'), town (pop. 2,479), Loire dept., SE central France, in Forez Plain, on the Lignon, and 10 mi. NNW of Montbrison; agr. market; metalworking, mfg. of hosiery, velvet ribbons, footwear, tiles. Has 18th-cent. castle.

Boende (bwĕn'dā), town, ⊙ Tshuapa dist. (□ 88,812; 1948 pop. c.680,000), Equator Prov., W Belgian Congo, port on left bank of Tshuapa R. near confluence of Tshuapa and Lomela rivers, 170 mi. ESE of Coquilhatville; commercial and agr. center; river and land communications hub. Rubber growing and copal gathering in vicinity. Has R.C. mission, hosp. for Europeans, medical school for natives. Inganda, 8 mi. N, has palm-oil mills.

Boengoeran, Indonesia: see GREAT NATUNA.

Boën-sur-Lignon, France: see BOËN.

Boeo, Cape (bôä'ô), westernmost point of Sicily; 37°48'N 12°25'E. Site of MARSALA. Formerly called Cape Lilibeo.

Boeotia (bēō'shŭ), Gr. *Voiotia*, nome (□ 1,300; pop. 105,162), E central Greece; ⊙ Levadia. Situated on Attica peninsula, it is bounded SE by Attica, S by Gulf of Corinth, W by Phocis, N by Locris section of Phthiotis, and E by the Euripus and Gulf of Euboea, separating it from Euboea. Consists of Cephisus R. valley (with drained L. Copais), rimmed by Parnassus (W) and Helicon (S) massifs. Agr.: wheat, cotton, tobacco, wine, olives; livestock raising. Tourist trade. Textile milling at Levadia and Thebes, the leading centers, on Athens-Salonika RR. The Boeotians came from Thessaly before the Dorian invasion and their cities, led by Thebes, joined in the Boeotian League (c.600 B.C.). Other important centers were Orchomenus, Plataea, and Thespiae. In connection with the changing power of Thebes, several important battles were fought on Boeotian soil—Plataea, Leuctra, Coronea, and Chaeronea. Dominated briefly (457-447 B.C.) by Athens, Boeotia's history was associated with Theban hegemony (379-362 B.C.). Hesiod and Pindar were natives of Boeotia. In Middle Ages, the region became part of the duchy of Athens and passed 1458 to the Turks.

Boerne (bûr'nē), city (pop. 1,802), ⊙ Kendall co., S central Texas, on Edwards Plateau, 30 mi. NNW of San Antonio, on Cibolo Creek; trade center, vacation and health resort in hilly sheep- and cattle-ranching region. Cascade Caverns are near. Founded c.1850 by Germans, inc. 1909.

Boeroe, Indonesia: see BURU.

Boetoeng, Indonesia: see BUTON.

Boeton, Indonesia: see BUTON.

Boeuf River (bĕf), in Ark. and La., rises in SE Ark. near Pine Bluff, flows c.230 mi. SW, through NE La., to Ouachita R. c.6 mi. NNE of Harrisonburg. Partly navigable.

Bofete (bŏŏfĕ'tĭ), city (pop. 892), S central São Paulo, Brazil, 20 mi. SE of Botucatu; sugar milling; coffee, rice, and macaroni processing.

Boffa (bô'fä), village (pop. c.600), W Fr. Guinea, Fr. West Africa, landing on Atlantic inlet (Rio Pongo), 50 mi. NNW of Conakry. Exports peanuts, palm oil, palm kernels, rice, rubber, sesame, honey, beeswax, kola nuts. R.C. mission.

Bofferdange (bôfŭrdäzh'), village (pop. 191), S central Luxembourg, on Alzette R. and 6 mi. N of Luxembourg city.

Boffzen (bôf'tsŭn), village (pop. 3,503), in former Prussian prov. of Hanover, NW Germany, after 1945 in Lower Saxony, on right bank of the Weser and 6 mi. SW of Holzminden; woodworking. Until 1941 in Brunswick.

Bofors (bō'fôrs, Swed. bōō"fôrs', -fôsh'), industrial E suburb of Karlskoga, Orebro co., S central Sweden, at N end of L. Mockel; site of Sweden's largest armament works; steel milling; mfg. of aircraft, automobiles.

Bofort, Luxembourg: see BEAUFORT.

Bofu (bō'fōō) or **Hofu** (hō'–), city (1940 pop. 58,890; 1947 pop. 67,182), Yamaguchi prefecture, SW Honshu, Japan, 10 mi. SE of Yamaguchi, adjacent to Tokuyama, and on Suo Sea; mfg. center (rubber goods, rayon textiles, sake, soy sauce). Rice, sweet potatoes, oranges, livestock produced in suburbs.

Bogachevka River, Russian SFSR: see KRONOTSKAYA RIVER.

Bogachiel River (bō'gů-chēl, bōgů-shēl'), NW Wash., rises NW of Mt. Olympus, flows c.50 mi. NW through recreational area to junction with Soleduck R., forming Quillayute R. E of Lapush.

Bogale (bōgůlě'), town (pop. 8,074), Pyapon dist., Lower Burma, 60 mi. SE of Bassein, on Bogale R. (arm of Irrawaddy delta).

Bogalusa (bōgůlōō'sů), city (pop. 17,798), Washington parish, SE La., 60 mi. NNE of New Orleans, near Pearl R., in lumbering region; paper-milling and wood-products-mfg. center; also tung oil, creosoted products, naval stores, auto parts. Pine nurseries. La. State Univ. forestry camp is here. Founded 1906, inc. 1914.

Bogan River (bō'gůn), central New South Wales, Australia, rises in hills N of Parkes, flows 451 mi. NNW, past Peak Hill and Nyngan, to Darling or Barwon R. 25 mi. NE of Bourke.

Bogard, town (pop. 285), Carroll co., NW central Mo., 7 mi. N of Carrollton.

Bogarra (bōgä'rä), town (pop. 1,841), Albacete prov., SE central Spain, 28 mi. WNW of Hellín; stock raising, lumbering; olive oil, wine.

Bogart (bō'gärt), town (pop. 459), Oconee and Clarke counties, NE central Ga., 9 mi. W of Athens.

Bogart, Mount (10,315 ft.), SW Alta., near B.C. border, near SE edge of Banff Natl. Park, 23 mi. SE of Banff.

Bogata (bōgä'tů), town (pop. 936), Red River co., NE Texas, 24 mi. SE of Paris, near Sulphur R., in agr. area.

Bogatic or **Bogatich** (both: bô'gätĭch), Serbo-Croatian *Bogatić*, village (pop. 5,513), Macva co., W Serbia, Yugoslavia, 11 mi. SW of Mitrovica.

Bogatoye, Russian SFSR: see PAVLOVKA, Kuibyshev oblast.

Bogatye Saby or **Bogatyye Saby** (bŭgä'tēů sŭbē'), village (1948 pop. over 2,000), NW Tatar Autonomous SSR, Russian SFSR, 22 mi. ESE of Arsk; grain, legumes, livestock. In late 1930s, Saby.

Bogatynia (bôgätĭ'nyä), Ger. *Reichenau* (rī'khůnou), town (1939 pop. 6,782; 1946 pop. 2,851) in Saxony, after 1945 in Wroclaw prov., SW Poland, near Germany and Czechoslovak borders, in Upper Lusatia, 7 mi. E of Zittau, in lignite-mining region; cotton milling, metalworking, jam making. Chartered after 1945 and briefly called Rychwald. Ger. pop. evacuated after Second World War.

Bogazkale, Turkey: see BOGAZKOY.

Bogazkopru (bôäz'kûprü"), Turkish *Boğazköprü*, rail junction, Kayseri prov., central Turkey, 9 mi. WNW of Kayseri.

Bogazkoy (bôäzkû'ē), Turkish *Boğazköy*, village (pop. 929), Corum prov., N central Turkey, 17 mi. NW of Yozgat, 95 mi. E of Ankara. Remarkable for remains of Hittite architecture and sculpture and for important Hittite inscriptions. In anc. times the center of Khatti territory, then the Hittite ⊙ Khattusas. It was later, according to tradition, site of Pteria, the Cappadocian city where Cyrus defeated Croesus (546 B.C.). Also spelled Boghazkeui, Bogazkale.

Bogazliyan (bôäz'lŭyän"), Turkish *Boğazlıyan*, village (pop. 3,641), Yozgat prov., central Turkey, 50 mi. SSE of Yozgat; grain, potatoes, mohair goats.

Bogdan (bôgdän'), central Bulgaria, highest peak (5,061 ft.) in central Sredna Gora, 17 mi. W of Karlovo.

Bogdanovich (bŭgdŭnô'vĭch), city (1939 pop. over 2,000), S Sverdlovsk oblast, Russian SFSR, 50 mi. E of Sverdlovsk; rail junction; metalworking, food processing. Became city in 1947. Troitskoye (1939 pop. over 2,000) is 4 mi. S; refractory-clay quarrying, fireproof-brick mfg.

Bogdanovka (bŭgdä'nůfků). **1** Village (1939 pop. over 500), S Georgian SSR, on Akhalkalaki-Leninakan highway and 70 mi. SW of Tiflis; livestock, potatoes. **2** Village (1948 pop. over 2,000), SW Chkalov oblast, Russian SFSR, 28 mi. SW of Sorochinsk; wheat, cattle, sheep.

Bogdarin, Russian SFSR: see BAGDARIN.

Bogdo Ola (bōgdō' ōlä') or **Bogdo Ula** (ōōlä') [Mongol,=holy mountain], mountain massif in the E Tien Shan, Sinkiang prov., China, N of the Turfan depression; extends over 150 mi. E from Urumchi, rising to 17,946 ft. Sacred to Kalmucks (Mongols).

Bogen (bō'gůn), village (pop. 2,458), Lower Bavaria, Germany, on the Danube and 6 mi. ENE of Straubing; metal- and woodworking, tanning; gravel quarrying. Chartered 1341. On near-by Bogenberg (1,417 ft.) is late-Gothic pilgrimage church.

Bogen (bō'gůn), village (pop. 128) in Evenes canton (pop. 2,526), Nordland co., N Norway, on N shore of Ofot Fjord, 12 mi. NW of Narvik; iron mines.

Bogense (bôkh'ůnsů), city (pop. 3,029) and port, Odense amt, Denmark, on N Fyn isl. and 17 mi. NW of Odense, on the Kattegat; meat canning, mfg. of agr. machinery, tanning.

Boger City (bō'jůr) or **Goodsonville,** textile-mill village (pop. 1,733), Lincoln co., W central N.C., 2 mi. E of Lincolnton.

Bogestrom (bō'wů-strôm), strait, Denmark, bet. S Zealand and Nyord isl. and bet. Stege Bay and Praesto Bay; joins SMAALANDSFARVAND strait with Baltic Sea via the Ulvsund.

Bogetici or **Bogetichi** (both: bô'gĕtĭchē), Serbo-Croatian *Bogetići*, village (pop. 5,183), W central Montenegro, Yugoslavia, 6 mi. S of Niksic.

Boggy Creek, Okla.: see CLEAR BOGGY CREEK.

Boggy Peak (1,329 ft.), SW Antigua, B.W.I., 5 mi. S of St. John's.

Boghari (bôgärē'), town (pop. 8,852), Alger dept., N central Algeria, on railroad to Djelfa and 40 mi. S of Blida at N edge of the High Plateaus where the Chéliff cuts its valley across the Tell Atlas; trade center (sheep, wool, skins, cereals, esparto grass) for nomads of the interior. Tobacco and wine-growing at near-by European colony of Boghar.

Boghazkeui, Turkey: see BOGAZKOY.

Boghé (bō'gā), village (pop. c.1,200), SW Mauritania, Fr. West Africa, on right bank of Senegal R. and 150 mi. ENE of Saint-Louis, Senegal; millet, gum; livestock. Fishing.

Boghni (bôgnē'), village (pop. 1,645), Alger dept., N central Algeria, in Great Kabylia, on branch railroad and 13 mi. SSW of Tizi-Ouzou; olive-oil pressing.

Boghra Canal (bō'grů), irrigation canal in Kandahar prov., S Afghanistan, in Helmand R. valley; fed by Girishk dam; completed 1949. Irrigated area W of Helmand R. yields grain and pasture land.

Bognanco Terme (bônyäng'kô tĕr'mĕ), village (pop. 126), Novara prov., Piedmont, N Italy, 6 mi. W of Domodossola; resort (alt. 2,175 ft.) famed for mineral springs.

Bognor Regis (bŏg'nůr rē'jĭs), urban district (1931 pop. 13,521; 1951 census 25,624), SW Sussex, England, on the Channel, 6 mi. SE of Chichester; seaside resort, with some shoe mfg. Several gardens and a large park. FELPHAM is just ENE.

Bogo (bô'wů), Dan. *Bogø*, island (□ 5; pop. 1,189), Denmark, in E Smaalandsfarvand strait, bet. Falster and Moen isls., 2 mi. off S Zealand; grain farming, fishing. Formerly also spelled BAAGO, the name of another Danish isl. in the Little Belt.

Bogo (bōgō'), town (1939 pop. 5,039; 1948 municipality pop. 26,132), N Cebu isl., Philippines, on inlet of Visayan Sea, 50 mi. N of Cebu city; agr. center (corn, coconuts).

Bogodukhov (bŭgůdōō'khůf), city (1926 pop. 16,020), NW Kharkov oblast, Ukrainian SSR, 33 mi. WNW of Kharkov; flour milling, fruit canning; metalworks, clothing mill.

Bogodukhovka, Kazakh SSR: see CHKALOVO, Kokchetav oblast.

Bogolyubovo (bŭgůlyōō'bůvů). **1** Village (1948 pop. over 2,000), central North Kazakhstan oblast, Kazakh SSR, on Ishim R. and 22 mi. SW of Petropavlovsk; wheat, cattle; metalworks. **2** Village (1939 pop. over 500), N Smolensk oblast, Russian SFSR, 33 mi. N of Yartsevo; flax. **3** Village (1926 pop. 1,600), central Vladimir oblast, Russian SFSR, on Klyazma R. and 6 mi. NE of Vladimir. Remains of 12th-cent. palace. Founded (12th cent.) by Prince Andrei Bogolyubski of Vladimir.

Bogomdarovanny, Russian SFSR: see KOMMUNAR.

Bogong, Mount (bō'gông, –gŏng), highest peak (6,508 ft.) of Victoria, Australia, in Australian Alps, 150 mi. NE of Melbourne; snow-capped (May-Sept.).

Bogor (bō"gōr'), formerly **Buitenzorg** (boi'tůnzôrkh), town (pop. 65,431), W Java, Indonesia, 30 mi. S of Jakarta, in foothills of Mt. Gedeh and Mt. Salak; 6°36'S 106°48'E. Health resort with summer homes of wealthy residents of Jakarta. Town is known primarily for magnificent botanical gardens (laid out 1817). Has palace formerly occupied by Du. governor-general of Du. East Indies. Some mfg. of automobile tires, machinery, textiles. Indonesian Institute for Rubber Research is here. Tea is grown in surrounding highlands. Founded 1745.

Bogoro, Belgian Congo: see KASENYI.

Bogorodchany (bŭgůrô'chŭnē), Pol. *Bohorodczany* (bôhôrôchä'nē), town (1931 pop. 3,151), central Stanislav oblast, Ukrainian SSR, on Bystritsa Solotvinskaya R. and 12 mi. SW of Stanislav, in petroleum and ozocerite area; flour and sawmilling. Has old church and monastery.

Bogoroditsk (bŭgůrô'dyĭtsk), city (1939 pop. over 10,000), E Tula oblast, Russian SFSR, 35 mi. SE of Tula; lignite-mining center in Moscow Basin; iron mines; flour milling, clothing mfg. Chartered 1777. During Second World War, held (1941) by Germans in Moscow campaign.

Bogorodsk (bŭgůrôtsk'). **1** City (1926 pop. 14,931), W Gorki oblast, Russian SFSR, 25 mi. SW of Gorki; leather center; tanneries, shoe factories. Became city in 1925. **2** City, Moscow oblast, Russian SFSR: see NOGINSK, city. **3** Town, Tatar Autonomous SSR, Russian SFSR: see KAMSKOYE USTYE.

Bogorodskoye (bŭgůrôt'skůyů). **1** Village (1926 pop. 400), E Kirov oblast, Russian SFSR, 45 mi. SSW of Zuyevka; flax processing. **2** Village (1948 pop. over 2,000), SE Lower Amur oblast, Khabarovsk Territory, Russian SFSR, on lower Amur R. and 50 mi. S of Nikolayevsk; fish cannery. Pop. largely Olchi (Ulchi).

Bogoslof Island (bō'gůslôf), volcanic islet, SW Alaska, Aleutian Isls., in Bering Sea, 27 mi. N of Umnak Isl.; 53°56'N 168°2'W. Of recent formation, its recorded eruptions, changing isl.'s shape in each case, were in 1796 (when it 1st appeared), 1883, 1906, 1910, and 1923–27. Useful landfall for navigators to Bering Sea.

Bogoslovsk, Russian SFSR: see KARPINSK.

Bogoso (bōgō'sō), town, Western Prov., SW Gold Coast colony, 19 mi. N of Tarkwa, on road; gold-mining center.

Bogos Range (bô'gůs), N spur of the E Greater Caucasus in W Dagestan Autonomous SSR, Russian SFSR; extends 35 mi. N bet. Avar Koisu (E) and Andi Koisu (W) rivers; rises to 13,570 ft.

Bogotá (bōgōtä'), city (pop. 325,658), ⊙ Colombia and Cundinamarca dept., central Colombia, on high Andean plateau in Cordillera Oriental, 450 mi. S of Barranquilla; 4°36'N 74°5'W; alt. 8,660 ft. The largest city of Colombia, it is political, social, financial, and cultural center of the country, though its commerce and industry are surpassed by Barranquilla and Medellín. Has a mild, pleasant climate (mean annual temp. 58°F). From the city radiate highways and railroads which overcome the difficult accessibility of the terrain and link it through combined land, river, and air communication with the Magdalena and Cauca valleys, and with the Pacific and Caribbean coasts. Situated in a fertile agr. region (corn, wheat, potatoes, fruit, livestock). Its main products are: tobacco products, textile goods, glassware, chemicals, perfumes, caustic soda, paint, cement, bricks, matches, leather articles, beer, chocolate, biscuits, refined sugar. It serves as distribution point for the great tableland. Bogotá has been known for its great cultural activity since early colonial days. A center for the arts and sciences, it possesses a natl. col., several universities (natl. univ., Universidad Libre, Universidad Javeriana), Acad. of Languages, Colombian-American center, a conservatory, natl. library, natl. mus., and archaeological, historical, and scientific collections. The city is outstanding for its colonial and modernistic architecture, including churches, administrative bldgs., attractive office bldgs. and apartment houses. Broad avenues cut across narrow colonial streets. In the oldest section is Plaza de Bolívar, the palace of San Carlos (residence of Bolívar and now Ministry of Foreign Affairs), the churches of Santa Inés, San Ignacio, San Agustín, and San Francisco, the observatory (oldest in South America), the Capitol (built on noble classical lines), municipal palace, the mint, the impressive cathedral (begun 1572, rebuilt 1807) containing many colonial relics and fine pictures, and the 17th-cent. chapel El Sagrario. The modern university city is in N. A funicular railway ascends the Monserrate peak in E outskirts, on summit of which is a noted chapel and shrine; the Quinta de Bolívar is located at its foot. W of the city limits are the Madrid and Techo (near Fontibón) airports. Bogotá was founded by Jiménez de Quesada on Aug. 6, 1538, as Santa Fé de Bogotá, a name derived from the Chibcha chief Bacatá. It served as the capital of Sp. viceroyalty of New Granada. By the late 16th cent. the city had become a cultural center of the New World; its univ. was founded 1572. Bogotá maintained its cultural tradition. In 1810 a junta was formed here to prepare the ground for final independence. Bolívar took the city in 1815; forced to abandon it 11 months later, he reentered it on Aug. 10, 1819, after the decisive victory of Boyacá. In April, 1948, Ninth International Conference of American States convened here.

Bogota (bůgō'tů), residential borough (pop. 7,662), Bergen co., NE N.J., on Hackensack R., just SE of Hackensack; mfg. (paper products, neckwear, metal products). Inc. 1894.

Bogotá, Sabana de (säbä'nä dā bōgōtä'), plateau (mean alt. 8,500 ft.), Cundinamarca dept., central Colombia, a broadening of Cordillera Oriental, c.55 mi. long NE-SW, 25 mi. wide. Bogotá is in its center. The most densely populated area of Colombia, it enjoys a temperate climate; wheat, corn, and fruit are grown, and cattle raised.

Bogotá River or **Funza River** (fōōn'sä), Cundinamarca dept., central Colombia, rises N of Chocontá, flows c.120 mi. SW, past Chocontá, Charquito, and Tocaima, to the Magdalena E of Girardot. On it, W of Charquito, are famed TEQUENDAMA FALLS.

Bogotol (bŭgŭtôl'), city (1939 pop. over 10,000), SW Krasnoyarsk Territory, Russian SFSR, on Trans-Siberian RR, on Chulym R. and 35 mi. W of Achinsk; grain and livestock exporting center; tanning, flour milling. Chartered 1911.

Bogovarovo (bŭgůvä'růvů), village, NE Kostroma oblast, Russian SFSR, 10 mi. ENE of Vokhma; flax.

Bogoyavlensk, Ukrainian SSR: see OKTYABRSKOYE, Nikolayev oblast.

Bogoyavlenskoye (bŭgůyůvlyĕn'skůyů), village (1939 pop. over 500), NW Tambov oblast, Russian SFSR, 25 mi. NNW of Michurinsk; rail junction (Bogoyavlensk station); grain, potatoes.

Bogra (bō'grŭ), dist. (□ 1,931; 1951 pop. 1,283,000), central East Bengal, E Pakistan; ⊙ Bogra. Bounded E by the Jamuna (main course of Brahmaputra R.), W by West Bengal, India; drained by tributaries of Atrai and Jamuna rivers. Alluvial soil (pipal and sal trees in forest area); rice, jute (major jute-growing area), rape and mustard, sugar cane, wheat, corn. Main industrial center, Bogra; rice milling at Jaipurhat; textile, silk-weaving, and slate factories; rail workshops at Santahar. Silk growing (research station at Bogra). Extensive archaeological ruins at Bogra. Part of Pal kingdom (9th-11th cent. A.D.); conquered by Sen kingdom; passed 1199 to independent Moslem rulers. Sherpur was 15th-cent. Mogul frontier post. Ceded to English by Moguls in 1765. Present dist. formed 1859. Part of former Br. Bengal prov. until inc. (1947) into new Pakistan prov. of East Bengal; original dist. altered to include S portion of original Dinajpur dist. Pop. 84% Moslem, 14% Hindu. Formerly called Bagura.

Bogra, town (pop. 21,681), ⊙ Bogra dist., N central East Bengal, E Pakistan, on Karatoya R. (tributary of the Atrai) and 65 mi. W of Mymensingh; road and trade (rice, jute, rape and mustard, sugar cane, wheat) center; rice, atta, and oilseed milling, mfg. of matches, hosiery, candles, soap. Sericulture (research station). Was ⊙ anc. Hindu kingdom from 3d cent. B.C. to 11th cent. A.D.; extensive archaeological excavations, including Brahmi inscription. Large Mogul fort ruins at Mahastan, 8 mi. NNW. Formerly called Bagura.

Boguchany (bŭgŏŏchä'nē), village (1948 pop. over 2,000), SE Krasnoyarsk Territory, Russian SFSR, on Angara R. and 160 mi. NNE of Kansk; lumbering.

Boguchar (–chär'), city (1926 pop. 7,958), S Voronezh oblast, Russian SFSR, near Don R., 130 mi. SSE of Voronezh; metalworks, flour mills, soap factory. Dates from 1716; chartered 1779.

Bogucice, Poland: see KATOWICE, city.

Bogue (bōg), city (pop. 211), Graham co., NW Kansas, on South Fork Solomon R. and 8 mi. E of Hill City; grain.

Bogue, The, China: see BOCA TIGRIS.

Bogue Chitto (bō"gŭ chĭ'tŭ), town (1940 pop. 384), Lincoln co., SW Miss., 10 mi. S of Brookhaven and on the Bogue Chitto.

Bogue Chitto, stream in Miss. and La., rises in SW Miss., flows c.105 mi. SE, past Johnstons Station (Miss.) and Franklinton (La.), to Pearl R. c.24 mi. S of Bogalusa.

Bogue Falia (fŭlī'ŭ), stream in SE La., rises in Washington parish, flows generally SSE c.23 mi., past Covington, to Tchefuncta R. c.10 mi. above its mouth.

Bogue Forts, China: see BOCA TIGRIS.

Bogue Island or **Bogue Banks** (bōg), narrow barrier beach (c.25 mi. long), Carteret co., E N.C., bet. Onslow Bay (S) and Bogue Sound. On E end are ATLANTIC BEACH and Fort Macon State Park (500 acres; recreational facilities; old fort begun in 1820s, restored 1936).

Bogue Islands (bōg), group of small coral atolls of Jamaica, just off Montego Bay, St. James parish; known for oyster beds and marine gardens.

Bogue Sound, E N.C., waterway sheltered from the Atlantic by Bogue Isl.; c.30 mi. long E-W, 2 mi. wide, it is connected with ocean by Bogue Inlet at W end, Beaufort Inlet at E end. Bridged (E) bet. Morehead City and Atlantic Beach.

Bogunai or **Bogunay** (bŭgŏŏnī'), town (1939 pop. over 500), SE Krasnoyarsk Territory, Russian SFSR, 45 mi. W of Kansk, in lignite-mining area.

Bogurayev (bŭgŏŏrī'ŭf), village (1939 pop. over 2,000), W central Rostov oblast, Russian SFSR, 7 mi. W of BELAYA KALITVA, in coal-mining dist.; glassworks; limestone quarries.

Bogushevsk (–shĕfsk'), agr. town (1948 pop. over 2,000), E Vitebsk oblast, Belorussian SSR, 25 mi. S of Vitebsk; furniture mfg.

Boguslav (–släf'), city (1926 pop. 12,111), S central Kiev oblast, Ukrainian SSR, on Ros R. and 60 mi. SSE of Kiev; woolen-milling center; cotton and flour mills; tanning.

Boguszow (bôgôō'shōōf), Pol. *Boguszów*, Ger. *Gottesberg* (gô'tŭsbĕrk"), town (1939 pop. 11,011; 1946 pop. 10,862) in Lower Silesia, after 1945 in Wroclaw prov., SW Poland, in N foothills of the Sudetes, 4 mi. WSW of Waldenburg (Walbrzych); mining (coal, galena, barite, tetrahedrite). After 1945, briefly called Boza Gora, Pol. *Boża Góra*.

Bogutschütz, Poland: see KATOWICE, city.

Bog Walk, town (pop. 2,100), St. Catherine parish, central Jamaica, on gorge of Cobre R. (irrigation), on railroad and 9 mi. NNW of Spanish Town; grows coconuts and bananas. Condensed-milk plant (opened 1940). Hydroelectric station.

Bogyiszlo (bô'dyĭslō), Hung. *Bogyiszló*, town (pop. 2,930), Tolna co., S Hungary, on isl. in the Danube and 6 mi. ENE of Szekszard; wheat, potatoes, honey.

Bohain (bōē'), town (pop. 5,582), Aisne dept., N France, 12 mi. NE of Saint-Quentin; cloth-weaving center (for lingerie, embroidery, and upholstering). Electric cable mfg. Also called Bohain-en-Vermandois (–ā-vârmădwä').

Bohdanec (bô'dänĕch), Czech *Bohdaneč*, village (pop. 1,992), E Bohemia, Czechoslovakia, 5 mi. NW of Pardubice; health resort with peat baths and ferruginous springs. Old town hall.

Bohea Hills (bōhē'), Chinese *Wui Shan* or *Wuyi Shan* (both: wōō'yē shän'), on Kiangsi-Fukien prov. border, China; rise to over 3,000 ft. in Bohea Hill, NW of Chungan. One of China's leading tea-growing regions, for which the bohea tea is named.

Böheimkirchen (bû'hīmkĭr"khŭn), town (pop. 3,038), central Lower Austria, on short Perschling R. and 6 mi. E of Sankt Pölten; truck farming (vegetables, fruit).

Bohemia (bōhē'mēŭ, –myŭ), Czech *Čechy* (chĕ'khĭ), Ger. *Böhmen* (bû'mŭn), historic province (□ 20,102; 1947 pop. 5,490,000) of Czechoslovakia, bounded by Austria (SE), Germany (SW, W, NW), Poland (N, NE); adjoins Moravia and Silesia (E). A dissected quadrangular plateau (500–2,000 ft.), its natural boundaries are Bohemian Forest, Erzgebirge, Sudetes mtn. system, and rolling Bohemian-Moravian Heights. Mtn. ridges are covered with dense forests. Continental climate (mean annual temp. 45°-50°F.). Drained by Elbe R. (rising in NE) and its main tributary, the Vltava (Moldau). Most rivers flow S to N. There are no important lakes, but in the numerous artificial ponds (SE) there is an intensive carp-breeding industry. Soils are especially fertile along the upper Elbe and around Prague. Principal crops: wheat, sugar beets, barley, oats, potatoes, flax, rape-seed; truck gardening N of Prague. Bohemian hops (Zatec) are unexcelled. Extensive orchards (including apricots and peaches) in NW; northernmost vineyards of central Europe are near Litomerice. Cattle, goats, swine, poultry, geese are raised. Main wealth is mineral: coal is basis of local metallurgical industry; lignite is important in synthetic fuel production (Most) and feeding of power plants; large peat marshes in SE; iron mined mostly in Kladno-Beroun area and in foothills of the Erzgebirge. Pitchblende deposits at Jachymov are among foremost sources of uranium ore on the continent. Other underground resources: graphite, kaolin, silver, gold, tin, lead, vanadium, bismuth, semi-precious stones (agates, amethysts). An important heavy industry belt stretches along S slopes of the Erzgebirge, another from Prague to Pilsen. Characteristic light industries include mfg. of Bohemian cut glass, textiles, musical instruments, toys, and porcelain (Carlsbad), brewing (Pilsen), smoked meats (Prague). Well-developed network of communications connects main cities: Prague, Pilsen, Budweis, Liberec, Usti nad Labem, Pardubice, Hradec Kralove. NW Bohemia is famous for its mineral springs and much-frequented water resorts of Carlsbad, Marienbad, and Teplice. Since expulsion in 1945 of most of Ger. minority, pop. is predominantly Czech; Czech language is spoken. Elbe and Eger river valleys show evidence of thick settlement since Bronze Age. Original historical pop. of Boii (probably Celts) was displaced (after 1st cent. A.D.) by Marcomanni and Quadi (Teutons), and later (5th cent.) by Slavonic settlers. First Bohemian dynasty, the Premyslides, is of legendary foundation. Christianity developed through efforts of Cyril and Methodius from Moravia (9th cent.). In 9th cent., territory was part of Great Moravian Empire. After its disruption by the Magyars (10th cent.), it became heart of a Czech state (duchy) within the Holy Roman Empire and was overwhelmingly under Western influence; its dominions included Moravia, much of Hungary, Silesia, and Poland. St. Wenceslaus (920–929) was 1st great Bohemian ruler. Bishopric of Prague was founded in 973. Ger. settlement (12th cent.) in the border dists. and further penetration inland were encouraged by Ottocar I, who obtained from Ger. emperor the hereditary title of King of Bohemia. Luxemburg dynasty came to power in 1310 and consolidated Bohemian territories. "Golden Age" was attained under Charles IV (1336–1378), with Prague established as cultural center of Central Europe. Hussite Reform movement and resulting Hussite Wars (1420–36) weakened power of the crown and structure of state. Georges of Podebrad (1458–1471), only Hussite king of Bohemia, attempted to form a League of Christian Princes for preservation of peace in Europe. After brief rule by Jagellon dynasty (1471–1526), Ferdinand I of Hapsburg was elected to thrones of Bohemia and Hungary. From 1526 to 1918, during which time Bohemia was under Hapsburg domination, Bohemia was gradually deprived of self-rule. Germans were appointed to key posts and Jesuits introduced to reconvert country to Roman Catholicism. Revolt of Bohemian Diet and Second Defenestration of Prague (1618) set spark to growing tension between Catholics and Protestants throughout Western Europe, ushering in the Thirty Years War. After defeat (1620) of Protestant armies at the White Mtn., Bohemia was laid waste and reduced to a Hapsburg crownland (1627). Forcible Germanization reached peak under Maria Theresa (who lost most of Silesia to Frederick II of Prussia) and under Joseph II. The 19th-cent. movement for an independent Czechoslovak state centered in Prague; it reached its goal in 1918, under T. G. Masaryk, founder of Czechoslovakia. Bohemia became prov. of the new republic (1918–39); stripped of borderland dists. (Sudetenland) by Munich Pact and proclaimed part of Ger. protectorate of Bohemia and Moravia in 1939. Liberated in 1945 by U.S. and Soviet troops, it recovered its status of prov. and its pre-war territory until administrative reforms of Dec., 1948, when it was divided into provs. (Czech *Kraj*) of Praha, Karlovy Vary, Usti nad Labem, Liberec, Plzen, Hradec Kralove, Pardubice, and Ceske Budejovice, and W part of Jihlava prov. With Moravia and Silesia, Bohemia forms (since 1949) one of the 2 constituent states of Czechoslovakia; Slovakia constitutes the other.

Bohemia, village (1940 pop. 765), Suffolk co., SE N.Y., in central Long Isl., 5 mi. WNW of Patchogue; mfg. (handbags, cigars).

Bohemian Forest, Ger. *Böhmerwald* (bû'mŭrvält'), Czech *Český Les* (chĕs'kē lĕs') and *Šumava* (shōō'-mävä), forested mountain range along Czechoslovak-German border, with foothills extending into Austria; consists of main range, divided by Furth pass (1,540 ft.) into low NW section and higher SE massif, and a parallel (S) subsidiary range, the Bavarian Forest; total length, 150 mi. The NW portion [Ger. *Oberpfälzer Wald* (ō"bŭrpfĕl'tsŭr vält'), Czech *Český Les*] extends bet. the Fichtelgebirge and Furth (railroad) pass, rises to 3,408 ft. in the Cerchov; low average elevation; agr. (rye, oats, potatoes) and cattle raising. High SE portion, the Bohemian Forest proper [Czech *Šumava*, Ger. *Hoher Böhmerwald*] extends 80 mi. E from Furth pass, rising to 4,780 ft. in the Great Arber. Largely covered by primeval forest (BOUBIN region), it has marshes, swamps, and peat bogs. Pastures; agr., because of harsh climate, is negligible. Some coal, lignite, and graphite deposits; industrial stone quarries. The Bavarian Forest [Ger. *Bayrischer Wald* (bī'rĭshŭr vält')], bet. the Bohemian Forest proper and the Danube, rises to 3,704 ft. in the Einödriegel; agr. (grain, potatoes), cattle raising; granite and kaolin quarries. The entire Bohemian Forest area is known for its glass industry; also woodworking, lumber and paper milling. Numerous resorts on Czechoslovak slopes. Vltava, Regen, and Ilz rivers rise here.

Bohemian-Moravian Heights, Czech *Česko-Moravska Vysočina* or *Vrchovina* (chĕ'skō-mô'räfskä vĭ'sōchĭnä, vŭr'khôvĭnä), rolling uplands along S part of Bohemia-Moravia border, Czechoslovakia; extend c.75 mi. bet. Jindrichuv Hradec (SSW) and Svitavy (NE); rise to 2,738 ft. in Javorice peak, to 2,745 ft. in Devet Skal mtn. Iron, lead, zinc, graphite deposits, manganese mines (at Chvaletice). Net-making trades, starch, distilling, and mother-of-pearl industries characterize area. Many artificially-stocked ponds (Rozmberk, Bezdrev), located in SSE foothills, are noted for carp breeding and fishing, mainly for export. Main towns: Jihlava, Jindrichuv Hradec.

Bohemian Paradise, Czech *Český Ráj* (chĕ'skē rī'), picturesque region of peculiar rocky formations (mostly sandstone) at SE extremity of Lusatian Mts., bet. Turnov and Jicin; rises to 2,440 ft. Among its notable sights are Prachov Rocks near Jicin, 14th-cent. ruins of castle of Trosky, 6 mi. SE of Turnov, and ruins of Waldstein castle, ancestral seat of Wallenstein.

Bohicon (bōhēkōn'), village, S Dahomey, Fr. West Africa, rail junction 60 mi. NW of Porto-Novo, in agr. region (peanuts, palm kernels, palm oil, cotton, corn). Cotton gin and research station. R.C. and Protestant missions; mosque.

Bohinj Lake (bô'hĭnyŭ), Ger. *Wocheiner See* (vô'-khīnŭr zā'), NW Slovenia, Yugoslavia, c.35 mi. NW of Ljubljana, in Julian Alps; c.2 mi. long, c.1 mi. wide; alt. 1,715 ft. Situated in cheese-producing and tourist region noted for its mtn. climate and scenic beauty; bathing, boating, trout fishing. Triglav peak is 6 mi. N. Receives Sava Bohinjka R. Resort of Bohinjska Bistrica, Ger. *Feistritz*, on the Sava Bohinjka, on railroad and 3 mi. E of lake, is a local trade center; fishing school, fish hatchery; ironworking. Until 1918, in Carniola.

Böhl (bûl), village (pop. 3,064), Rhenish Palatinate, W Germany, 8 mi. NW of Speyer; metalworking. Grain, tobacco.

Böhlen (bû'lŭn), town (pop. 6,424), Saxony, E central Germany, on the Pleisse and 10 mi. S of Leipzig; industrial center; lignite mining; steel milling. Synthetic-oil plant; power station.

Böhlitz-Ehrenberg (bû'lĭts-ā'rŭnbĕrk), town (pop. 10,453), Saxony, E central Germany, 6 mi. W of Leipzig city center; foundries; mfg. of ball and roller bearings; pianos.

Böhmen, Czechoslovakia: see BOHEMIA.

Böhmerwald, Europe: see BOHEMIAN FOREST.

Böhmisch-Aichel, Czechoslovakia: see CESKY DUB.

Böhmisch-Brod, Czechoslovakia: see CESKY BROD.

Böhmisch-Eisenstein, Czechoslovakia: see ZELEZNA RUDA.

Böhmisch-Kamnitz, Czechoslovakia: see CESKA KAMENICE.

Böhmisch-Leipa, Czechoslovakia: see CESKA LIPA.

Böhmisch-Skalitz, Czechoslovakia: see CESKA SKALICE.

Böhmisch-Trübau, Czechoslovakia: see CESKA TREBOVA.

Bohodle, Br. Somaliland: see BOHOTLEH.
Bohol (bôhôl'), island (□ 1,491; 1939 pop. 449,549), S central Philippines, one of the Visayan Isls., SW of Leyte across Canigao Channel, bet. Camotes Sea (N) and Mindanao Sea (S), separated from Cebu isl. (W) by Bohol Strait; 9°36'–10°10'N 123°47'–124°35'E. The isl. is c.55 mi. long, 39 mi. wide, with a regular coast line. Mountainous, it rises to 2,630 ft. in central area. Agr. (rice, coconuts, hemp, corn); manganese mining; buri-palm hats. Bohol province (□ 1,575; 1948 pop. 553,407) comprises Bohol isl. and offshore isls., including PANGLAO ISLAND and LAPININ ISLAND; ⊙ TAGBILARAN.
Bohol Strait (12–25 mi. wide), Philippines, bet. Bohol isl. (E) and Cebu (W), leading S from Camotes Sea to Mindanao Sea.
Bohom (bōm), town (pop. 442), Chiapas, S Mexico, in Sierra de Hueytepec, 5 mi. NW of San Cristóbal de las Casas; cereals, fruit. Indian village with market, picturesque fiestas. Formerly Chamula.
Bohonal de Ibor (bōnäl' dhä ēvōr'), town (pop. 1,477), Cáceres prov., W Spain, near the Tagus, 32 mi. NE of Trujillo; olive oil, cereals, livestock.
Böhönye (bû'hûnyĕ), town (pop. 3,388), Somogy co., SW Hungary, 20 mi. W of Kaposvar; wheat, corn.
Bohorodczany, Ukrainian SSR: see BOGORODCHANY.
Bohosudov (bô'hôsōōdôf), Ger. *Mariaschein* (märē'-äshīn), village (pop. 2,339), N Bohemia, Czechoslovakia, on railroad and 7 mi. E of Usti nad Labem. Has pilgrimage church, Jesuit monastery.
Bohotleh (bōhōt'lā), village, SE Br. Somaliland, on Ethiopian border, on road and 70 mi. WSW of Las Anod; stock raising. Sometimes Bohodle.
Bohoyo (bō-oi'ō), town (pop. 857), Ávila prov., central Spain, on Tormes R. and 17 mi. ESE of Béjar; potatoes, fruit, forage, livestock.
Bohumin, Czechoslovakia: see NOVY BOHUMIN.
Bohus (bōō'hüs"), village (pop. 759), Alvsborg co., SW Sweden, on Gota R. and 2 mi. E of Kungalv; mfg. of chemicals; shipbuilding. Remains of anc. Bohus Castle are at Kungalv.
Bohuslan (bōō'hüslĕn"), Swedish *Bohuslän*, province [Swedish *landskap*] (□ 1,778; pop. 153,655), SW Sweden, on the Skagerrak and on Norwegian border. Included in N part of Goteborg och Bohus co. In old times called Viken. Its coastal region belonged to Denmark until 1658. Reputed to be country of Beowulf.
Bohutin, Czechoslovakia: see PRIBRAM.
Boiana River, Albania-Yugoslavia: see BOJANA RIVER.
Boiano (bôyä'nô), town (pop. 3,885), Campobasso prov., Abruzzi e Molise, S central Italy, near upper Biferno R., 11 mi. SW of Campobasso, in tobacco-growing region; cutlery, nails, woolen textiles. Bishopric. Formerly also Bojano.
Boiceville (bois'vĭl), resort village, Ulster co., SE N.Y., in the Catskills, on Esopus Creek and 15 mi. WNW of Kingston, near Ashokan Reservoir.
Boichinovtsi or **Boychinovtsi** (boi'chĭnôftsē), village (1946 pop. 1,427; 1949 estimate 5,000), Vratsa dist., NW Bulgaria, on Ogosta R. and 8 mi. NE of Mikhailovgrad; rail junction; vegetable canning, flour products (macaroni).
Boiestown (boiz'toun), village (pop. estimate 250), central N.B., on Southwest Miramichi R. and 40 mi. NNW of Fredericton; lumbering, salmon fishing.
Boigu (boi'gōō), island (pop. 143) in Torres Strait, 95 mi. N of Cape York Peninsula, N Queensland, Australia, near S coast of New Guinea; 9 mi. long, 4.5 mi. wide. Low, swampy; fishing.
Boilefoss, Norway: see BOYLEFOSS.
Boiling Lake, S Dominica, B.W.I., 6 mi. ENE of Roseau; really a geyser of boiling sulphur, about 300 ft. by 200 ft.
Boiling Springs. 1 Town (pop. 1,145), Cleveland co., S N.C., 7 mi. WSW of Shelby; hosiery mfg. Seat of Gardner-Webb Jr. Col. **2** Village (1940 pop. 738), Cumberland co., S Pa., 15 mi. WSW of Harrisburg; railroad shops.
Boinik, Yugoslavia: see BOJNIK.
Boinitsa or **Boynitsa** (boinē'tsä), village (pop. 3,562), Vidin dist., NW Bulgaria, 6 mi. N of Kula; grain, livestock, truck.
Boinu River (boinōō'), left headstream of Kaladan R., on India-Burma border, rises SW of Falam in Chin Hills, flows over 100 mi. in U-shaped course to international line where it joins Tyao R. to form Kaladan R. 23 mi. ESE of Lungleh.
Bois [Fr.,=forest], for names beginning thus and not found here: see under following part of the name.
Bois, Lac des (läk dā bwä'), lake (30 mi. long, 12 mi. wide), NW Mackenzie Dist., Northwest Territories, NW of Great Bear L.; 66°50'N 125°10'W. Drains N into Anderson R.
Bois Blanc Island (bwä blã') (1½ mi. long), S Ont., in Detroit R., opposite Amherstburg, at Mich. line, just E of Grosse Île; lighthouse.
Bois Blanc Island (bäb'lō", boi" blăngk'), Mackinac co., N Mich., in the Straits of Mackinac, 6 mi. N of Cheboygan; c.12 mi. long, 4 mi. wide; resort.
Bois Brule River (boi" brōōl'), NW Wis., rises in central Douglas co., flows c.35 mi. NE and N, through Brule River State Forest, to L. Superior 23 mi. E of Superior; trout fishing. Sometimes called Brule R.
Bois-Colombes (bwä-kôlōb'), town (pop. 25,698), Seine dept., N central France, NW of Paris, 6 mi. from Notre Dame Cathedral, within N bend of the Seine, adjoining Asnières (SE) and Colombes (SW); mfg. (auto and bicycle parts, radio sets, perfumes).
Boisdale, Loch, Scotland: see LOCHBOISDALE.
Bois-d'Amont (–dämō'), village (pop. 1,068), Jura dept., E France, on Swiss border, 16 mi. NE of Saint-Claude, in the E Jura; mfg. of wooden boxes and chests; Gruyère cheese.
Bois de Boulogne (dù bōōlô'nyù), park (area 2,095 acres) of Paris, France, forming part of the 16th *arrondissement*, and bounded by Neuilly-sur-Seine (N), Boulogne-Billancourt (S), and the Seine (W). A favorite pleasure ground and resort of fashion, it contains the racecourses of Auteuil and Longchamp, and the Jardin d'Acclimatation.
Bois-de-Cise, France: see AULT.
Bois de la Chaize, France: see NOIRMOUTIER, ÎLE DE.
Bois-de-Lessines (–dù-lĕsēn'), Flemish *Lessenbosch* (lĕ'sùnbōs), village (pop. 1,613), Hainaut prov., SW central Belgium, 3 mi. ESE of Lessines; agr.; stone quarrying.
Bois-de-Nèfles (–nĕf'lù), village (pop. 5,408), NW Réunion isl., 3 mi. ENE of Saint-Paul; tobacco, grain.
Bois de Sioux River (boi" dù sōō'), rises in L. Traverse, NE S.Dak., flows N 30 mi. and joins Otter Tail R. at Wahpeton, N.Dak. (opposite Breckenridge, Minn.), to form Red River of the North.
Bois de Vincennes (vēsĕn'), park (area 2,270 acres) of Paris, France, at city's ESE edge, bounded by suburbs of Vincennes (N), Nogent-sur-Marne and Joinville-le-Pont (E), Charenton-le-Pont and Saint-Maurice (SW), and by the Marne (S). Divided into 2 sections by a drill ground and adjoining race track. Rivalling the more fashionable Bois de Boulogne in appearance, it is the place of popular weekend outings. At its N edge are the château and fort of Vincennes. Site of Fr. colonial exhibition of 1931. Has new zoological garden.
Bois d'Haine (bwä dĕn'), town (pop. 4,136), Hainaut prov., S central Belgium, 12 mi. WNW of Charleroi; mfg. of railroad rolling stock; glass blowing.
Bois-d'Oingt, Le (lù bwä-dwē'), agr. village (pop. 655), Rhône dept., E central France, 8 mi. SW of Villefranche.
Bois-du-Roi (bwä-dü-rwä'), highest summit (2,959 ft.) of the Morvan, E central France, in Saône-et-Loire dept., 13 mi. WNW of Autun.
Boise (boi'sē, –zē), county (□ 1,913; pop. 1,776), W Idaho; ⊙ Idaho City. Mtn. area cut by canyons of Payette R. and its branches. Arrowrock Dam and Reservoir on Boise R. at S boundary. Gold, silver, lead; lumber, cattle. Boise Natl. Forest extends throughout. Co. formed 1864.
Boise, city (pop. 34,393), ⊙ Idaho and Ada co., in SW part of state, on Boise R. and c.290 mi. SSE of Spokane, Wash.; 43°36'N 116°14'W; alt. 2,740 ft. Largest city in state. Trade, rail, and distribution center for gold-mining and agr. area served by Boise irrigation project. Food processing (dairy and meat products, flour, feed, candy, fruit) is important. Also mfg. of furniture, electrical equipment, foundry and wood products, rugs, mattresses. Has municipal airport, veterans' hosp., and state penitentiary. Points of interest are state capitol (housing mus. of state historical society), Julia Davis Park, and art mus. Near-by hot springs supply hot mineral water for heating some of the homes and for use in municipal natatorium. City founded 1863 after discovery of gold in vicinity and establishment of military post near present site of city, inc. 1864, made capital of Idaho Territory in same year. Grew as trading point for miners. Following construction of ARROWROCK DAM (1911–15; 14 mi. E) became commercial center for agr. area in Boise irrigation project.
Boise City (boi'zā), town (pop. 1,902), ⊙ Cimarron co., extreme NW Okla., on high plains of the Panhandle, c.110 mi. NW of Amarillo (Texas); alt. 4,165 ft. In wheat and broomcorn area. Has creamery, grain elevator. Inc. 1925.
Boise River (boi'sē, –zē), SW Idaho, formed by confluence of Middle Fork (c.45 mi. long) and North Fork (c.40 mi. long) SE of Idaho City, flows 95 mi. W, through Arrowrock Reservoir and past Boise, to Snake R. at Oregon line W of Parma. Longest tributary is South Fork, rising in Camas co. and flowing c.100 mi. generally W to Arrowrock Reservoir. River is used in Boise irrigation project, serving 400,000 acres in SW Idaho and in small part of E Oregon. Arrowrock div. (area bet. Boise and Snake rivers) is served by ARROWROCK DAM on Boise R., by diversion dam on Boise R. 7 mi. SE of Boise, by ANDERSON RANCH DAM on South Fork, and by DEER FLAT RESERVOIR (also known as L. Lowell). Notus div. is N of Boise R., bet. Caldwell and Notus. The Payette div., bet. Boise and Payette rivers, E of Snake R., is served by BLACK CANYON DAM on Payette R., by DEADWOOD DAM on Deadwood River, and by CASCADE DAM on North Fork of Payette R. Grain, livestock, fruit, vegetables, potatoes, and sugar beets are raised in project area. Boise and Nampa are principal cities.
Bois-Grenier (bwä-grùnyā'), agr. village (pop. 305), Nord dept., N France, 3 mi. S of Armentières. Here Germans attacked British, April, 1918, in First World War.
Bois-Guillaume (–gēyōm'), N residential suburb (pop. 5,833) of Rouen, Seine-Inférieure dept., N France. Has Br. cemetery of First World War.
Bois Island (bwä) (9 mi. long, 3 mi. wide), S N.F., in Bay d'Espoir; 47°45'N 55°57'W.
Bois-le-Duc, Netherlands: see 's HERTOGENBOSCH.
Bois-le-Roi (–lù-rwä'), town (pop. 2,272), Seine-et-Marne dept., N central France, near left bank of the Seine, 5 mi. SSE of Melun, resort at N edge of forest of Fontainebleau; sawmilling.
Bois Noirs (nwär'), wooded upland in Massif Central, central France, on border of Allier, Loire, and Puy-de-Dôme depts; forms a N outlier of the Monts du FOREZ; rises to 4,239 ft.
Boissevain (boi'sùvān), town (pop. 836), SW Man., 45 mi. S of Brandon; wheat. International Peace Gardens are 15 mi. S, on U.S. border.
Boissevain (bwä'sùvān, boi'sùvān), village (pop. 1,197), Tazewell co., SW Va., near W.Va. line, 7 mi. NW of Bluefield.
Boissezon (bwäsùzō'), village (pop. 450), Tarn dept., S France, 7 mi. ESE of Castres; woolen mills.
Boissy-le-Châtel (bwäsē'-lù-shätĕl'), village (pop. 406), Seine-et-Marne dept., N central France, on the Grand-Morin and 15 mi. SE of Meaux; paper milling, cheese mfg.
Boissy-Saint-Léger (–sē-lāzhā'), town (pop. 2,624), Seine-et-Oise dept., N central France, an outer SE suburb of Paris, 10 mi. from Notre Dame Cathedral; mfg. of telephone equipment. Near-by 17th-cent. château of Gros-Bois contains fine Empire furniture and 17th-cent. frescoes.
Boite River (bôē'tē), N Italy, rises in the Dolomites 3 mi. W of Croda Rossa, flows 25 mi. SE, past Cortina d'Ampezzo, to Piave R. 2 mi. S of Pieve di Cadore.
Boitsfort, Belgium: see WATERMAEL-BOITSFORT.
Boituva (boitōō'vù), city (pop. 1,267), S São Paulo, Brazil, 20 mi. NW of Sorocaba; rail junction (spur to Pôrto Feliz); pineapple- and winegrowing; textile milling, rum distilling.
Boius, Greece: see VOION.
Boizenburg or **Boizenburg an der Elbe** (boi'tsùnbōōrk än dĕr ĕl'bù), town (pop. 10,609), Mecklenburg, N Germany, on the Elbe and 16 mi. NE of Lüneburg; shipbuilding, sawmilling; mfg. of building materials, hosp. equipment. Has Gothic church. In Middle Ages, was fortified customs station and a center of trade with E Europe.
Bojador, Cape (bŏjùdôr', Sp. bōhädôr'), Arabic *Ras bu Yeidur*, headland of Sp. West Africa on the Atlantic, near border of Saguia el Hamra and Río de Oro; 26°7'N 14°29'W. False capes Bojador North and South are 30 mi. and 13 mi. NE respectively.
Bojana River or **Boyana River** (both: bōyä'nä), Albanian *Buenë* or *Buena*, also *Bunë* or *Buna*, Ital. *Boiana*, navigable outlet of L. Scutari, on Albanian-Yugoslav (Montenegrin) border, flows from L. Scutari at Scutari 25 mi. S in tortuous course to the Adriatic. Receives (since 1858–59) the Drinassa (arm of Drin R.) just S of Scutari.
Bojanowo (bôyänô'vô), town (1946 pop. 1,944), Poznan prov., W Poland, 12 mi. SSE of Leszno; rail junction; brick mfg.
Bojeador, Cape (bōhäädhôr'), Ilocos Norte prov., NW Luzon, Philippines, in S.China Sea; 18°30'N 120°35'E.
Bojkovice (boi'kôvĭtsĕ), Ger. *Bojkowitz* (boi'kō-vĭts), town (pop. 2,448), E Moravia, Czechoslovakia, on railroad and 14 mi. SSE of Gottwaldov; lumbering; oat growing.
Bojnice (boi'nyĭtsĕ), Hung. *Bajmóc* (boi'mōts), village (pop. 1,800), W central Slovakia, Czechoslovakia, near Nitra R., 26 mi. ESE of Trencin; health resort (alt. 917 ft.) with alkaline cold springs, sulphurous warm springs (102°–105°F.), peat baths.
Bojnik, Boinik, or **Boynik** (all: boi'nĭk), village, S Serbia, Yugoslavia, 11 mi. W of Leskovac.
Bojnurd, Iran: see BUJNURD.
Bojolali, Indonesia: see BOYOLALI.
Bojonegoro or **Bodjonegoro** (both: bōjōnĕgō'rō), town (pop. 19,784), N Java, Indonesia, on Solo R. and 60 mi. W of Surabaya; trade center for forested and agr. area (teak, tobacco, rice, corn). Until 1827 called Radjegwesi.
Boka (bô'kä), Hung. *Bóka* (bō'kō), village, Vojvodina, NE Serbia, Yugoslavia, on Tamis R. and 21 mi. E of Zrenjanin, in the Banat; rail junction.
Boka Kotorska, Yugoslavia: see KOTOR, GULF OF.
Bokaro (bōkä'rō), coal field in Hazaribagh dist., central Bihar, India, N of Damodar R., just W of Jaria coal field; Bermo is mining center.
Bokaro River, India: see DAMODAR RIVER.
Bokchito (bōk-chē'tù), town (pop. 643), Bryan co., S Okla., 14 mi. E of Durant, in agr. area (cotton, corn, peanuts); cotton ginning.
Boké (bōkā'), town (pop. 3,550), W Fr. Guinea, Fr. West Africa, landing on the Rio Nunez, near coast, 100 mi. NNW of Conakry; palm kernels, sesame, honey, beeswax, gum, rice, peanuts. Cattle raising. R. C. mission.
Bokhan (bùkhän'), village (1948 pop. over 2,000), S Ust-Orda Buryat-Mongol Natl. Okrug, Irkutsk oblast, Russian SFSR, 30 mi. E of Cheremkhovo; dairy farming.

Bokhara, Uzbek SSR: see BUKHARA, city.
Bokkeveld, U. of So. Afr.: see COLD BOKKEVELD.
Bokkor, Cambodia: see BOKOR.
Bokla Mordovskaya, Russian SFSR: see MORDOVSKAYA BOKLA.
Bo Klua (bô'klŭ'ä), village (1937 pop. 3,072), Nan prov., N Thailand, in Luang Prabang Range (Laos border), 35 mi. NE of Nan; salt extraction from brine wells.
Bokn Fjord (bô'kŭn), Nor. *Boknfjord* or *Boknafjord*, inlet of the North Sea, Rogaland co., SW Norway, bet. Karmoy (N) and Stavanger (S); 13 mi. wide at mouth, c.35 mi. long. Branches into fjords of Skjold and Sandeid (N), Sand and Josen (NE), Lyse and Hogs (SE), and Gands (S). Contains many isls., including Bokn isl. (□ 14; pop. 590) at N side of its mouth, and Ombo at its head. Formerly spelled Bukken, Bukn, and Boken.
Boko (bōkō'), village, SE Middle Congo territory, Fr. Equatorial Africa, near Congo R. (Belgian Congo border), 60 mi. SW of Brazzaville; woodworking. R.C. mission.
Boko (bō'kō), village, Kamrup dist., W Assam, India, at N foot of Khasi Hills, on tributary of the Brahmaputra and 25 mi. WSW of Gauhati; rice, mustard, jute.
Bokobá (bōkōbä'), town (pop. 791), Yucatan, SE Mexico, 29 mi. E of Mérida; henequen.
Bokod (bōkōdh'), town (1939 pop. 2,024; 1948 municipality pop. 5,503), Benguet sub-prov., Mountain Prov., N Luzon, Philippines, 17 mi. ENE of Baguio; sawmilling.
Bokol (bōkōl'), highest peak (c.7,150 ft.) in Gurafarda mts., SW Ethiopia, 50 mi. NW of Maji.
Bokombayevskoye (bŭkŭmbī'ŭfskŭyŭ), village (1948 pop. over 2,000), W Issyk-Kul oblast, Kirghiz SSR, near S shore of Issyk-Kul (lake), 75 mi. WSW of Przhevalsk; wheat, opium.
Bököny (bû'kûnyŭ), town (pop. 3,441), Szabolcs co., NE Hungary, 15 mi. S of Nyiregyhaza; brickworks; wheat, corn, cattle.
Bokor (bōkôr'), town, Kampot prov., SW Cambodia, in S Elephant Range, 9 mi. W of Kampot; hill station (alt. 3,378 ft.); big-game hunting in forested hills. Agr. station at near-by Emerald Valley. Also spelled Bokkor.
Boko-retto, Formosa: see PESCADORES.
Bokoro (bōkōrō'), agr. village, W central Chad territory, Fr. Equatorial Africa, 140 mi. E of Fort-Lamy.
Bokoshe (bŭkō'shē), town (pop. 589), Le Flore co., E Okla., 25 mi. WSW of Fort Smith (Ark.), in farm area.
Boko-to, Pescadores: see PENGHU ISLAND.
Bokovo-Antratsit (bô"kŭvŭ-äntrŭtsēt'), city (1939 pop. over 5,000), SW Voroshilovgrad oblast, Ukrainian SSR, in the Donbas, 6 mi. ESE of Krasny Luch; anthracite-mining center.
Bokovo-Platovo (bô'kŭvŭ-plä'tŭvŭ), town (1939 pop. over 500), S Voroshilovgrad oblast, Ukrainian SSR, in the Donbas, 3 mi. WNW of Bokovo-Antratsit; anthracite mines.
Bokovskaya (bô'kŭfskīŭ), village (1939 pop. over 500), NE Rostov oblast, Russian SFSR, on Chir R. and 70 mi. ENE of Millerovo; flour mill, metalworks; wheat, sunflowers, cattle. Pop. largely Cossack.
Bokpyin (bŏk'pyĭn), village, Mergui dist., Lower Burma, in Tenasserim, on Andaman Sea, 80 mi. S of Mergui.
Boksanbanya, Rumania: see BOCSA-MONTANA.
Boksburg (bôks'bûrkh), town (pop. 53,432), S Transvaal, U. of So. Afr., on Witwatersrand, 13 mi. E of Johannesburg; alt. 5,348 ft.; gold- and coal-mining center. Coal discovered here 1887.
Boksitogorsk (bŭksēt"ŭgôrsk'), town (1939 pop. over 2,000), SE Leningrad oblast, Russian SFSR, on rail spur and 18 mi. SE of Tikhvin; major bauxite-mining center; metalworks.
Boksity (bŭksē'tē) [Rus.,=bauxite], rail junction, N Sverdlovsk oblast, Russian SFSR, on right tributary of Sosva R. and 4 mi. SSW of Severouralsk. Serves Severouralsk and other bauxite mines supplying Krasnoturinsk aluminum works.
Boksmeer, Netherlands: see BOXMEER.
Bokstel, Netherlands: see BOXTEL.
Bokuma (bōkōō'mä), village, Equator Prov., W Belgian Congo, on Ruki R. and 30 mi. E of Coquilhatville; R.C. missions center with seminary and schools.
Bokungu (bōkōōng'gōō), village, Equator Prov., central Belgian Congo, on Tshuapa R. and 100 mi. ESE of Boende; steamboat landing and trading center; bananas, manioc, palm products.
Bokushi, Formosa: see PUTZE.
Bokwankusu (bōkwängkōō'sōō), village, Equator Prov., central Belgian Congo, on Lomela R. and 170 mi. SE from Boende; steamboat landing and trading post in rice-growing region.
Bol (bôl), village, W Chad territory, Fr. Equatorial Africa, on E shore of L. Chad, 120 mi. WSW of Moussoro; natron extracting, fishing.
Bol, Yugoslavia: see BRAC ISLAND.
Bolahun or **Masambolahun** (mäsämbō'lähōōn), town, Western Prov., NW Liberia, 7 mi. SW of Kolahun; palm oil and kernels, cotton, cassava, rice; cattle. Has hosp.
Bolama (bōlä'mä, bōōlä'mŭ), city, SW Port. Guinea, seaport on Bolama isl. in the Bijagós group, facing estuary of the Rio Grande, 20 mi. SSE of Bissau; 11°35'N 15°30'W. Trade in almonds, rice, copra, palm oil; cattle raising. Seaplane landing. Hosp. Radio transmitter. Claimed and temporarily occupied by England in 18th cent. Capital of Port. Guinea until 1941, when seat of govt. was transferred to Bissau. Formerly spelled Bulama.
Bolan (bō'län), subdivision (□ 407; pop. 6,009), N central Baluchistan, W Pakistan; ⊙ Mach. Includes BOLAN PASS in Central Brahui Range. Agr. (wheat, millet); some cattle raising (SE). Ceded 1879 to British by khan of Kalat. Pop. 80% Moslem, 16% Hindu, 3% Sikh.
Bolangir (bōläng'gĭr), district (□ c.3,000; pop. c.700,000), W Orissa, India; ⊙ Bolangir. Bounded NE by Mahanadi R., SE by Tel R. (right affluent of the Mahanadi), N by Sambalpur dist. Mainly open country, broken by isolated peaks and hills. Agr. (rice, oilseeds); handicraft cloth and metalware mfg.; graphite deposits worked. Chief towns: Bolangir, Sonepur, Titlagarh. Created 1949 by merger of former princely states of PATNA and part of Sonepur.
Bolangir, town (pop. 11,105), ⊙ Bolangir dist., W Orissa, India, 150 mi. W of Cuttack; agr. market (rice, oilseeds); handicraft mfg. (metal implements, gold and silver ornaments). Has col. Was ⊙ former princely state of Patna.
Bolaños (bōlä'nyōs), town (pop. 647), Jalisco, W Mexico, on affluent of Santiago R. and 75 mi. NNW of Guadalajara; grain, vegetables, livestock. The region near by was formerly known for silver mines.
Bolaños or **Bolaños de Calatrava** (dhā kälä-trä'vä), town (pop. 7,045), Ciudad Real prov., S central Spain, in New Castile, 15 mi. E of Ciudad Real; agr. center on La Mancha plain; olives, potatoes, cereals, grapes, anise, saffron. Processes olive oil, flour, cheese, alcohol; woolwashing, sawmilling.
Bolaños River, Jalisco, W Mexico, formed by Mezquitic and Colotlán rivers 40 mi. SW of Colotlán near Zacatecas border, flows c.80 mi. S, past Bolaños and San Martín de Bolaños, to Santiago R.
Bolan Pass (bō'län), gap in Central Brahui Range, NE central Baluchistan, W Pakistan, bet. Rindli and Kolpur; c.55 mi. long. Highest point (c.5,880 ft.) just NE of Kolpur. Used by railroad and highway bet. Sibi and Quetta. Historically an important "gateway" to India for invaders, traders, and nomad tribes.
Bolan River, E Baluchistan, W Pakistan, rises S of Kolpur in Central Brahui Range, flows SE, through Bolan Pass, and S, through Kachhi plain, to North Western Canal of Sukkur Barrage system c.20 mi. SW of Garhi Khairo; c.195 mi. long. Intermittent.
Bolans (bō'lŭnz), village (pop. 1,357), SW Antigua, B.W.I., 5 mi. SSW of St. John's; sugar central.
Bolarque Falls (bōlär'kā), New Castile, central Spain, at confluence of Guadiela and Tagus rivers, on Guadalajara-Cuenca prov. border, 4 mi. W of Buendía. Site of hydroelectric plant.
Bolarum, India: see SECUNDERABAD.
Bolbaite (bōlvī'tā), village (pop. 1,440), Valencia prov., E Spain, 10 mi. NW of Játiva; olive-oil processing, flour milling.
Bolbe, Lake, Greece: see VOLVE, LAKE.
Bolbec (bôlbĕk'), town (pop. 10,238), Seine-Inférieure dept., N France, 17 mi. ENE of Le Havre; textile center (cotton yarn and fabrics; dyeing and printing); mfg. of spinning and weaving equipment, tanning, sugar refining.
Bolbitinic, branch of the Nile: see ROSETTA.
Bolchen, France: see BOULAY.
Bolchen, Saar: see BLIESMENGEN-BOLCHEN.
Bolckow (bŏl'kou, bŏl'kō), town (pop. 250), Andrew co., NW Mo., on One Hundred and Two R. and 25 mi. N of St. Joseph.
Bölcske (bûlch'kĕ), town (pop. 4,040), Tolna co., W central Hungary, on the Danube and 5 mi. SSE of Dunaföldvar; honey, paprika, wheat, corn.
Bold, parish (pop. 2,066), SW Lancashire, England. Includes agr. village of Bold Heath, 2 mi. NNE of Widnes.
Bolderaa, town, Latvia: see BOLDERAJA.
Bolderaa, river, Latvia: see LIELUPE RIVER.
Bolderaja or **Bolderaya** (bŏl'dĕrīä), Lettish *Bolderāja*, Ger. *Bolderaa*, outer timber port of Riga, Latvia, on left bank of the Western Dvina, at mouth of Lielupe R. (opposite Daugavgriva), and 6 mi. NNW of Riga city center; sawmilling.
Boldesti (bôldĕsht'), Rum. *Boldeşti*, village (pop. 1,707), Prahova prov., S central Rumania, on railroad and 6 mi. N of Ploesti; oil, natural gas.
Boldon Colliery or **Boldon** (bōl'dŭn), urban district (1951 census 16,692), NE Durham, England, 4 mi. NW of Sunderland; coal mining. Just SE are adjacent residential towns of West Boldon and East Boldon (with paint works).
Boldovo (bôl'dŭvŭ), village (1926 pop. 3,520), S Mordvinian Autonomous SSR, Russian SFSR, on Insar R. and 13 mi. WSW of Ruzayevka; hemp, legumes.
Boldre (bōl'dŭr), agr. village and parish (pop. 1,736), SW Hampshire, England, in New Forest, on Lymington R. just N of Lymington. Has Norman 13th-cent. church.
Boldu (bôl'dōō), village (pop. 3,083), Buzau prov., E central Rumania, 10 mi. SE of Ramnicu-Sarat.
Boldzhuan or **Bol'dzhuan** (bŭljōōän'), village (1932 pop. estimate 420), W Kulyab oblast, Tadzhik SSR, on the Kyzyl-Su and 28 mi. NNW of Kulyab; wheat, cattle. Until c.1940, spelled Baldzhuan.
Bole (bō'lā), town, Northern Territories, W Gold Coast, 110 mi. WSW of Tamale; millet, durra grown in area.
Bolea (bōlā'ä), town (pop. 1,380), Huesca prov., NE Spain, 10 mi. NW of Huesca; lumbering, stock raising; agr. trade (olive oil, wine, cereals).
Bolechow, Ukrainian SSR: see BOLEKHOV.
Bolehall, England: see GLASCOTE.
Bolekhov (bŭlyĕ'khŭf), Pol. *Bolechów* (bôlĕ'khōōf), city (1931 pop. 10,744), W Stanislav oblast, Ukrainian SSR, at N foot of E Beskids, on right tributary of the Dniester and 13 mi. S of Stry; summer resort; mfg. center; petroleum refining (gasoline), chemicals, leather, woodworking (furniture, lumber), food processing (cereals, fruit); saltworks. Passed from Poland to Austria (1772); reverted to Poland (1919); ceded to USSR in 1945.
Bolenge (bōlĕng'gā), village, Equator Prov., W Belgian Congo, on Congo R. and 6 mi. SSW of Coquilhatville. Its Protestant mission has a printing shop and industrial school.
Bolerium, England: see LAND'S END.
Boleslaw, Poland: see OLKUSZ.
Boleslawiec (bôlĕswä'vyĕts), Pol. *Bolesławiec*, Ger. *Bunzlau* (bōōnts'lou), town (1939 pop. 22,455; 1946 pop. 3,145) in Lower Silesia, after 1945 in Wroclaw prov., SW Poland, on Bobrawa R. and 30 mi. ENE of Görlitz; center of copper-mining, quartzite, fireclay, and marble-quarrying region; cement mfg. Suffered heavy damage in Second World War (c.80% destroyed). Formerly noted for its pottery. Poet Opitz b. here.
Boleszkowice (bôlĕsh-kôvē'tsĕ), Ger. *Fürstenfelde* (fŭr"stŭnfĕl'dŭ), town (1939 pop. 1,531; 1946 pop. 630) in Brandenburg, after 1945 in Szczecin prov., NW Poland, 10 mi. NNW of Küstrin (Kostrzyn); grain, potatoes, vegetables; livestock.
Boletice nad Labem (bô'lĕtyĭtsĕ näd' lä"bĕm), village (pop. 2,029), N Bohemia, Czechoslovakia, on Elbe R. and 3 mi. SSW of Decin; mfg. of roller bearings.
Boley (bō'lē), city (pop. 646), Okfuskee co., E central Okla., 30 mi. WSW of Okmulgee, in farming area.
Bolgarka, Bulgaria: see BALGARKA.
Bolgary (bŭlgä'rē), village (1939 pop. over 500), SW Tatar Autonomous SSR, Russian SFSR, near Volga R., 13 mi. WSW of Kuibyshev; grain, livestock. Formerly called Uspenskoye. Site of extinct city of Bolgar or Bulgar, ⊙ Volga Bulgars (10th–13th cent.), on trade route bet. Muscovy and the Orient; captured (1236) by Tatars. Excavations begun in 18th cent.
Bolgatanga (bōlgätäng'gä), town, Northern Territories, N Gold Coast, 95 mi. N of Tamale; road junction; shea nuts, durra, yams; cattle, skins. Future hq. Mamprusi dist.
Bolgrad (bŭlgrät'), city (1941 pop. 10,713), SW Izmail oblast, Ukrainian SSR, in Bessarabia, on railroad and 25 mi. NNW of Izmail, at N tip of Yalpug Lagoon (fisheries), at mouth of Yalpug R.; agr. center; flour milling, tanning; brickworks, handicrafts (silk and linen goods, rugs, embroidery). Pop. largely Bulgarian. Has cathedral and former bishop's palace.
Boli, Turkey: see BOLU, town.
Boliden (bōō'lē"dŭn), village (pop. 2,380), Vasterbotten co., N Sweden, near Skellefte R., 18 mi. WNW of Skelleftea; mining center (gold, arsenic, copper, sulphur) since 1925. Includes Stromfors (strŭm"fôrs', -fôsh), Swedish *Strömfors*, and Bjurliden (byŭr'lē"dŭn), mining villages. Ores shipped to smelters at Ronnskar; also ships ores brought by 60-mi.-long cable railroad from Kristineberg.
Boligee (bōlĭjē'), farming town (pop. 168), Greene co., W Ala., 40 mi. SW of Tuscaloosa, near Tombigbee R.
Bolinao (bōlēnä'ō,-nou'), town (1939 pop. 1,349; 1948 municipality pop. 19,391), Pangasinan prov., central Luzon, Philippines, at N tip of Cape Bolinao peninsula, at W side of entrance to Lingayen Gulf, 37 mi. NW of Dagupan; fishing, agr. (rice, copra).
Bolinao, Cape, central Luzon, Philippines, in S. China Sea, at W side of entrance to Lingayen Gulf, at tip of W peninsula of Pangasinan prov.; 16°21'N 119°49'E.
Bolinas (bōlē'nŭs), village (pop. c.200), Marin co., W Calif., 10 mi. WSW of San Rafael, on Bolinas Bay at entrance to Bolinas Lagoon (c.3½ mi. long); resort; fishing. Coast guard lifesaving station here.
Boling (bō'lĭng), village (1940 pop. 1,141), Wharton co., S Texas, c.45 mi. SW of Houston; rail, trade point in agr., sulphur-producing area.
Bolingbroke (bŏ'lĭngbrōōk), agr. village and parish (pop. 275), Parts of Lindsey, E central Lincolnshire, England, 3 mi. W of Spilsby. Has remains of Norman castle dismantled after capture (1643) by Parliamentary troops. Henry IV b. here.
Bolingbroke (bō'lĭngbrŏk), town (pop. 87), Monroe co., central Ga., 12 mi. NW of Macon.
Bolintin-Vale (bôlēntēn-vä'lā), village (pop. 4,460), Bucharest prov., S Rumania, 17 mi. W of Bucharest; agr. center, dairying. Formerly spelled Bolintineanu.

Bolívar (bōlē'vär), city (pop. 13,773), ⊙ Bolívar dist. (□ 1,932; pop. 38,649), central Buenos Aires prov., Argentina, 75 mi. NW of Azul; flour milling, dairying, meat packing; mfg. of cement articles, soap, tile, textiles. Has natl. col. Founded 1878 as San Carlos.

Bolívar. 1 Town (pop. c.4,800), Cochabamba dept., central Bolivia, in the Cordillera de Cochabamba, 9 mi. S of Tacopaya; corn, vegetables. **2** Village, Pando dept., NW Bolivia, on Sena R. and 100 mi. WSW of Riberalta; rubber.

Bolívar, department (□ 22,996; 1938 pop. 765,194; 1950 estimate 1,047,320), N Colombia, on Caribbean Sea; ⊙ CARTAGENA. Bounded by Magdalena R. (E), it is watered by its affluents, the San Jorge, Cauca, and Sinú. Except for some low ranges, outliers of Cordillera Occidental, it consists mainly of alluvial, forested lowlands and savannas. Has a humid, tropical climate, slightly relieved by trade winds on coast during winter months; rainy season, April–Oct. Mineral resources include petroleum (Montería), gold, coal, lime. Forests yield fine cabinet woods, tagua nuts, vanilla, gums, tolu balsam and other medicinal plants. On the great pasturelands cattle are raised on large scale. Main crops are sugar cane, tobacco, cotton, corn, rice, beans, bananas, cacao, coconuts. Cartagena, linked by rail and Canal del Dique with the Magdalena, is its trading, shipping, and mfg. center. Carmen is a tobacco center and Sincelejo a sugar-refining center.

Bolívar. 1 Town (pop. 4,213), Antioquia dept., NW central Colombia, 40 mi. SW of Medellín; alt. 3,688 ft.; agr. center (coffee, sugar cane, tobacco, cacao, livestock); textile and processing industries. Founded 1853. **2** Town (pop. 2,495), Cauca dept., SW Colombia, in Cordillera Central, 50 mi. SSW of Popayán; alt. 5,830 ft. Sugar cane, tobacco, coffee, cereals, stock. Gold and copper deposits near by. **3** Town (pop. 1,934), Valle del Cauca dept., W Colombia, in Cauca valley, 17 mi. N of Tuluá; sugar cane, tobacco, corn, bananas, coffee, yucca, livestock.

Bolívar, province (□ 1,252; 1950 pop. 104,872), central Ecuador, in the Andes; ⊙ Guaranda. Mtn. region bounded by the Chimborazo (E) and the Cordillera de Guaranda (W). Has a semitropical to temperate climate, with main rains Dec.–April. Watered by Chimbo R. Its forests yield fine timber and cinchona. Agr. crops include corn, barley, wheat, sugar cane, oranges, bananas, tobacco, coffee, vegetables. Cattle and sheep raising. Some mercury and salt deposits. The prov. was set up 1884, after having formed a part of Los Ríos.

Bolívar, town (pop. 918), ⊙ Bolívar prov. (□ 774; pop. 6,421), Libertad dept., NW central Peru, on W slopes of Cordillera Central, near Marañón R., 70 mi. ENE of Trujillo; alt. 10,492 ft. Barley, potatoes; sheep raising. Until 1925 called Cajamarquilla.

Bolivar (bŏ'lĭvůr, -lů-), county (□ 917; pop. 63,004), W Miss., bounded W by the Mississippi, here forming Ark. line; ⊙ Rosedale and Cleveland. In rich agr. region (cotton, corn, alfalfa); lumbering; cotton and lumber processing. Drained by Sunflower R. Formed 1836.

Bolivar. 1 City (pop. 3,482), ⊙ Polk co., SW central Mo., in the Ozarks, bet. Pomme de Terre R. and Little Sac R., 29 mi. N of Springfield; dairy, grain center. Seat of Southwest Baptist Col. Statue of Simón Bolívar dedicated here (1948) by president of Venezuela. **2** Village (pop. 1,490), Allegany co., W N.Y., 14 mi. E of Olean; summer resort. Oil refinery; mfg. of nitroglycerin, machinery; dairy farms. Inc. 1882. **3** Village (pop. 776), Tuscarawas co., E Ohio, 11 mi. N of New Philadelphia and on Tuscarawas R. Near here on a tributary (Sandy Creek) is Bolivar Dam (6,300 ft. long, 87 ft. high; completed 1937 for flood control), impounding reservoir of 149,600 acre-ft. capacity. Fort Laurens State Park is near by. **4** Borough (pop. 828), Westmoreland co., SW central Pa., 14 mi. NW of Johnstown and on Conemaugh R. **5** Town (pop. 2,429), ⊙ Hardeman co., SW Tenn., 27 mi. SSW of Jackson, in cotton, corn, livestock area; lumbering. State hosp. for insane near by. Founded 1824. **6** Town (pop. 637), Jefferson co., W.Va., in Eastern Panhandle just SW of Harpers Ferry.

Bolívar (bōlē'vär), state (□ 91,890; 1941 pop. 94,522; 1950 census 122,114), S and SE Venezuela; ⊙ Ciudad Bolívar. Bordered by Br. Guiana (E) and Brazil (SE). Largest state of Venezuela. Largely covered by little-explored GUIANA HIGHLANDS. Watered by navigable Orinoco R. (N boundary), and its many affluents, including Caroní and Caura rivers. Generally extremely hot and tropical climate; rainy season (May–Oct.). Mineral resources include gold (El Callao, Tumeremo, Guasipati), mica (El Palmar), iron (El Pao), and diamonds. In N lowlands of Orinoco R. basin cattle and horses are raised, and some rice, sugar cane, corn, tobacco, yuca, and fruit are grown. Vast semi-deciduous forests of highlands are largely unexploited; yield fine cabinet woods, cedar, mahogany, rubber, balata, chicle, vanilla, divi-divi, oil-bearing and medicinal plants. Ciudad Bolívar is an important port on the Orinoco and the leading commercial center of S Venezuela.

Bolívar, peak, Venezuela: see COLUMNA, LA.

Bolívar, Cerro (sĕ'rō), mountain (2,018 ft.) in Bolívar state, E Venezuela, 50 mi. S of Ciudad Bolívar; iron mining (exploitation begun c.1950). Until 1948 called La Parida.

Bolívar, Ciudad, Venezuela: see CIUDAD BOLÍVAR.

Bolivar Peninsula (bŏ'lĭvůr), S Texas, NE of Galveston, extends to SW bet. Galveston and East bays (NW and N) and the Gulf (S); c.23 mi. long. Port Bolivar, on Galveston Bay entrance, is at tip; High Island oil field is near base; resort beaches along Gulf shore. Gulf Intracoastal Waterway follows land cut extending full length of peninsula.

Bolivia (bůlĭ'vēů, bō-, Sp. bōlē'vyä), republic (□ 412,777; 1950 pop. estimate 3,990,200), W central South America; though SUCRE is constitutional ⊙ and seat of judiciary, LA PAZ is the de facto ⊙ and leading city. One of the 2 South American countries without a coast line (Paraguay is the other), it borders NW on Peru, with which it shares L. TITICACA, the world's highest (alt. 12,507 ft.) deep-water body plied by large vessels. Chile, to which it lost its maritime section, the nitrate-rich ATACAMA DESERT, lies SW beyond the volcanic crest of the Andes. In N and E it borders Brazil, partly along ABUNÁ RIVER, MAMORÉ RIVER, and GUAPORÉ RIVER, headstreams of the MADEIRA RIVER, part of the Amazon system. Paraguay, on SE, now owns most of the long-disputed CHACO region. Its S boundary with Argentina runs just above the Tropic of Capricorn. Though Bolivia is an Andean country, with all important activities carried on high up in the mts., ¾ of Bolivian territory is nevertheless made up of vast, tropical lowlands dissected by a network of mostly navigable rivers, through which it can communicate with the distant Atlantic via the Amazon and Río de la Plata. Among these streams are the PARAGUAY RIVER, the Guaporé (Iténez), and BENI RIVER. Accessible to smaller craft are the PILCOMAYO RIVER, Mamoré, MADRE DE DIOS, Itonamas rivers. The plains are covered by dense forests (*selvas*) of the Amazon basin, yielding in SE to the savannas and scrub growth of the more arid Chaco. Sparsely populated and underdeveloped, though potentially a fertile agr. region, tropical Bolivia has only one large city, SANTA CRUZ. Some sugar cane, rice, tobacco, and cotton are grown. There is extensive cattle raising in the grasslands. Rubber (caoutchouc, hevea) is gathered for export, as are Brazil nuts and cinchona bark. But the vast resources of fine timber are practically untapped. The lowlands merge W with the subtropical Andean piedmont generally called YUNGAS. Farther westward, in the highlands, headstreams of Amazon and Chaco basins have carved deep gorges and long, fingerlike valleys, which have become Bolivia's garden spots. With an excellent, salubrious climate, this potentially productive region has suffered from relative seclusion and large landholdings. Chief crops are coca, coffee, cacao, tobacco, citrus fruit, grapes, wheat; the subsistence crops barley and potatoes grow in higher sections. The center for the region is COCHABAMBA, the republic's 2d largest city. Other such garden spots are Sucre and remote TARIJA in S. The Andes reach their greatest width (c.400 mi.) in Bolivia and rise to some of the loftiest peaks of this formidable continental divide—the snow-capped twin peaks ILLAMPÚ (21,275 ft.) and ANCOHUMA (21,490 ft.) and ILLIMANI (21,185 ft.), situated in the higher Eastern Cordillera or Cordillera Oriental, which—partly or in its entirety—is frequently called Cordillera Real. The Western Cordillera or Cordillera Occidental, along the international line, falling abruptly toward the Pacific, is towered over by the inactive volcano SAJAMA (21,390 ft.). Bet. the 2 ranges curving SSE from S Peru to the Argentine border is the ALTIPLANO, a high (average altitude c.12,000 ft.) intermontane plateau about 450 mi. long, 80 mi. wide. Upon this, one of the world's most elevated settled areas, depends the Bolivian economy. In it live the bulk of the people. Most of the area is, however, bleak and wind bitten, especially toward the S with its great salt flats, Salar de UYUNI and Salar de COIPASA. In the N, L. Titicaca exercises a moderating influence. The large lake, together with salty L. POOPÓ (linked by Desaguadero R.), is the center of the Altiplano's interior drainage system, which is without outlet to the sea. The climate—conditioned rather by altitude than geographic latitude—is rigorous, with great variations. La Paz, the globe's highest metropolis (11,909 ft.), nestling in a steep gorge, has an annual mean temp. of about 50°F. Rainfall is scant, 17.2 inches at La Paz and decreasing southward. The forbidding heights of the barren, tundra-like *puna* are even more inhospitable, but it is here where most of the nation's enormous mineral wealth is located. Tin is by far the leading product, constituting alone about 75% (81% in 1947) of all exports, and putting Bolivia in 3d place among the world's producers of tin. Altogether, minerals amount to c.90% of all exports. Principal tin mines center around ORURO (where some tin is now smelted) and POTOSÍ (e.g., CARACOLES, UNCIA, CATAVÍ). Other minerals mined include silver (for which Potosí ranked for centuries as richest known source), native copper (COROCORO), tungsten (Kami); also lead, zinc, antimony, bismuth, gold, sulphur, fluorine, asbestos. Saltworks at Salar de Uyuni. Petroleum, supplying most of the country's requirements, is drilled for and refined in the S at SANANDITA and CAMIRI, near Argentine border. From the latter a pipe line leads to Sucre and Cochabamba, which have topping plants. Further extensive oil deposits, said to be among the continent's richest, have been reported. There are also petroleum seepages in tropical lowland of Santa Cruz dept. Despite the economic importance of the mines, only about 7% of the people gain their livelihood from them. The majority eke out a precarious existence from agr., employing primitive methods. Potatoes, wheat, corn, and barley are most widely grown. Sheep, llamas, alpacas, vicuñas, and chinchillas are raised. Industries, lacking in skilled labor, are few, apart from mining, and of those about 80% are concentrated in La Paz. Because of absence of fuel, metallurgy has made little strides. Principal consumer goods turned out are textiles (woolen, cotton, rayon), shoes, cement, glassware, cigarettes, vegetable oils, flour, canned food, beer, liquor (*chicha*). Sawmilling in Yungas. Leading imports are: wheat, sugar, coal, iron and steel products, mining equipment, vehicles, textiles. Transportation is a paramount problem in Bolivian affairs. The foreign trade passes through the Pacific ports MOLLENDO and Matarani (Peru), ARICA and ANTOFAGASTA (Chile). All these are linked by railroads radiating from VIACHA (SW of La Paz), the line with Peru being interrupted by a shipping route across L. Titicaca (GUAQUI-Puno). The mining center Oruro is the major rail hub, connected with Cochabamba, Potosí, and Sucre. A S branch to Jujuy (N Argentina) establishes direct link with Buenos Aires. A feeder line to Brazil (Maporé-Madeira RR) in extreme NE circumvents Madeira R. rapids; while a new line from Santa Cruz to Corumbá (Brazil) was begun in 1950. Since land communication is difficult and good roads are scarce, air lines play an increasingly important part. Among the most backward of Latin American republics, Bolivia has also the highest amount of illiteracy, c.80%. However, the San Francisco Xavier Univ. of Sucre (founded 1624) is one of the oldest on the continent. The people are overwhelmingly R.C. Official language is Spanish, spoken by the whites (c.13%) and the *cholos* mestizos (c.32%). The predominantly rural Indians (c.55%), of Aymará and Quechua stock, still speak their own languages, for the most part. In L. Titicaca basin flourished a high pre-Inca civilization, to which testify imposing ruins near TIAHUNACO. The Incas extended their domain into Bolivia long before Sp. conquest. Upper or Alto Peru—as it was called in colonial period—fell to Gonzalo and Hernando Pizarro in 1538. Discovery of enormous silver deposits brought influx of Spaniards, who ruthlessly forced the Indians to work in the mines. Potosí (silver discovered here 1545) rose to be one of the hemisphere's earliest and most fabulous boom towns. In 1559 Upper Peru became the *audiencia* of Charcas, attached to viceroyalty of Peru until 1776, when it was transferred to viceroyalty of La Plata (Buenos Aires). An uprising (1809) at Sucre was unsuccessful. The country won liberty through expeditions of San Martín and Bolívar, sealed by 1824 victory at Ayacucho (Peru). Independence was proclaimed 1825, and the new republic adopted name of Bolivia and installed Gen. Sucre as 1st president. There was a short-lived (1836–39) confederation with Peru. Ensuing history was disturbed by corrupt government, an autocratic oligarchy, and disastrous military adventures. The War of the Pacific (1879–83) led to loss of Pacific littoral to Chile. Brazilian revolt (1899) severed Acre; another huge section was ceded (1903) to Brazil in Treaty of Petropolis. Costliest of all campaigns was the Chaco War (1932–35) with Paraguay, which exhausted both countries and resulted in Bolivia being stripped of most of the Chaco area she claimed. Bolivia is still the prey of its mineral wealth and the few men who own it. An ill-balanced economy depending on world market for tin, and considerable political, social, and ethnic differences remain disruptive forces. For further information see individual articles on towns, cities, regions, physical features, and the following 9 depts.: BENI, COCHABAMBA, CHUQUISACA, LA PAZ, ORURO, PANDO, POTOSÍ, SANTA CRUZ, TARIJA.

Bolivia, town (pop. 215), Brunswick co., SE N.C., 18 mi. SW of Wilmington; sawmilling.

Bolivia (bolē'vyä), town (pop. 531), Trujillo state, W Venezuela, in Andean spur, 16 mi. NNE of Trujillo; alt. 4,426 ft.; coffee, grain.

Bolivia, Ciudad, Barinas state, Venezuela: see CIUDAD BOLIVIA.

Boljevac or **Bolyevats** (both: bô'lyĕväts), village (pop. 1,538), E Serbia, Yugoslavia, on railroad and 16 mi. W of Zajecar. The RTANJ rises 5 mi. SW.

Boljoon (bōlhō'ōn, bōlhōn'), town (1939 pop. 1,707; 1948 municipality pop. 11,299), S Cebu isl., Philippines, 27 mi. W of Tagbilaran across Bohol Strait; agr. center (corn, coconuts, hemp).

Bolkar Mountains (bôlkär'), S Turkey, part of the great Taurus Mts. (Turkish *Toros*), S of Eregli, extend c. 70 mi. WSW-ENE. Highest peak (11,762 ft.) is Medetsiz Dag or Mededsiz Dag in a small E section called *Toros Dağı*, 13 mi. SE of Ulukisla. Formerly also spelled Bulgar or Bulghar; also called Bozoglan. Lead, silver, gold.

Bolkenhain, Poland: see BOLKOW.

Bolkhov (bŭlkhôf'), city (1926 pop. 17,535), NW Orel oblast, Russian SFSR, 32 mi. N of Orel; agr. center in grain and hemp area; mfg. (clothing, knit goods), hemp milling, vegetable and fruit canning. Dates from 13th cent.; chartered 1556.

Bolkow (bôl'kōōf), Pol. *Bolków*, Ger. *Bolkenhain* (bôl'kunhīn), town (1939 pop. 4,589; 1946 pop. 2,818) in Lower Silesia, after 1945 in Wroclaw prov., SW Poland, 13 mi. NW of Waldenburg (Walbrzych); linen milling, tanning. Overlooked by 13th-cent. castle.

Boll (bôl), village (pop. 2,211), N Württemberg, Germany, after 1945 in Württemberg-Baden, 4.5 mi. SSW of Göppingen; resort with sulphur baths.

Bollate (bôl-lä'tĕ), town (pop. 4,994), Milano prov., Lombardy, N Italy, 6 mi. NNW of Milan; toys, glue, rubber shoes.

Bollebygd (bô'lübügd"), village (pop. 818) Alvsborg co., SW Sweden, 12 mi. W of Boras; grain, stock. Includes Gronkullen (grûn'kŭ"lun), Swedish *Grönkullen*, village.

Bollène (bôlĕn'), town (pop. 1,700), Vaucluse dept., SE France, on the Lez and 10 mi. NNW of Orange; refractory brick, tile, and pottery mfg. center. Winegrowing.

Bolligen (bô'lĭgun), residential town (pop. 8,434), Bern canton, W Switzerland, 3 mi. NE of Bern.

Bolling Air Force Base, D.C.: see WASHINGTON, D.C.

Bollinger (bōō'lĭng-ur, bō'-, bŏ'lĭnjur), county (□ 621; pop. 11,019), SE Mo.; ⊙ Marble Hill. Crossed by Castor and Whitewater rivers; drainage canals in SE. Corn, wheat, livestock. Formed 1851.

Bollington (bŏ'lĭng-tun), urban district (1931 pop. 5,027; 1951 census 5,313), E Cheshire, England, 3 mi. NNE of Macclesfield; silk and cotton milling; metallurgy; mfg. of paper and paint.

Bollnas (bôl'nĕs"), Swedish *Bollnäs*, city (pop. 4,742), Gavleborg co., E Sweden, on Ljusna R. and 50 mi. NNW of Gavle; rail junction; metal- and woodworking, sawmilling, chocolate mfg., fruit-juice processing. Has biological mus.

Bollsta (bôl'stä"), village (pop. 1,331), Vasternorrland co., NE Sweden, on Angerman R. estuary, 18 mi. SE of Solleftea; sawmilling, woodworking.

Bollullos de la Mitación (bōlū'lyōs dhā lä mētä-thyōn'), town (pop. 2,646), Seville prov., SW Spain, 8 mi. WSW of Seville; grapes, olives, eucalyptus, timber, sheep, goats.

Bollullos par del Condado (pär dhĕl kōndä'dhō), town (pop. 9,493), Huelva prov., SW Spain, 23 mi. ENE of Huelva; linked by narrow-gauge railroad with La Palma 4 mi. N. Viticultural center (alcohol, vinegar, wine, cognac, vermouth); also corn, fruit, cork, livestock. Mfg. of textiles.

Bollwiller (bôlvēlär'), Ger. *Bollweiler* (bôl'vīlur), town (pop. 2,282), Haut-Rhin dept., E France, near SE foot of the Vosges, 9 mi. NNW of Mulhouse; potash mining and processing. Tree nurseries.

Bolm Lake, Swedish *Bolmen* (bôl'mun) (□ 71), S Sweden, 11 mi. SW of Varnamo; 20 mi. long (N-S), 5 mi. wide; drained (S) into Laga R. Contains Bolmso (bôlms'û"), Swedish *Bolmsö*, isl. (9 mi. long, 1–2 mi. wide).

Bolnes (bôl'nus), town (pop. 3,763), South Holland prov., W Netherlands, on Ijsselmonde isl., on New Maas R. and 5 mi. E of Rotterdam; shipbuilding; mfg. (ship machinery, rubber products).

Bolnisi (bŭlnyē'sē), town (1926 pop. 5,658), S Georgian SSR, 20 mi. SW of Tiflis; wineries. Formerly Yekaterinofeld; renamed Lyuksemburg and (1936–43) Lyuksemburgi.

Bolobo (bōlō'bō), village (1946 pop. c.5,700), Leopoldville prov., W Belgian Congo, on left bank of Congo R. (Fr. Equatorial Africa border) and 150 mi. WSW of Inongo; customs station, steamboat landing, and center of native trade; ivory working, basket weaving, brick making, palm products. Has Baptist mission, industrial school. One of the oldest trading posts in Congo, founded 1881.

Bologna (bôlô'nyä), province (□ 1,429; pop. 714,705), Emilia-Romagna, N central Italy; ⊙ Bologna. Consists of fertile, irrigated Po plain (N) and Etruscan Apennines (S). Watered by Reno, Santerno, Idice, and Sillaro rivers. Agr. (wheat, rice, hemp, sugar beets, vegetables). Cattle raising. Mfg. at Bologna, Imola, and Casalecchio di Reno.

Bologna, anc. *Felsina* or *Bononia*, city (pop. 226,771), ⊙ Emilia-Romagna and Bologna prov., N central Italy, at foot of Etruscan Apennines, on the Aemilian Way, 50 mi. N of Florence; 44°30'N 11°21'E. Industrial, commercial, and transportation center; produces automobile chassis, motorcycles, refrigerators, agr. machinery, precision tools, aluminum, plastics, furniture, glassware, shoes, pharmaceuticals; macaroni, sausage, canned foods; hemp products, paper, asphalt, fertilizer. An important agr. market. Archbishopric. City has retained a medieval aspect with its many arcaded streets and anc. buildings, including town hall (13th–16th cent.), 13th-cent. palace of King Enzo, Podestà palace (13th–15th cent.), the Archiginnasio (1562–63; severely damaged; former seat of university), 2 medieval leaning towers, and many fine 13th- and 14th-cent. churches, including San Francesco (1236–63; severely damaged). On near-by hills are Renaissance church of San Michele in Bosco, with frescoes by A. Carracci, and the Certosa, a former Carthusian monastery. Has municipal mus., observatory, and art gall. in which the Bolognese school (notably Francia, Carracci, and Guido Reni) is best represented. Of pre-Roman origin, came under Byzantine rule (6th cent.) and under the papacy (8th cent.). A strong, free commune in 12th cent.; added to its power by defeating Frederick II at Fossalta in 1249. Ranked among greatest centers of learning in medieval Europe, famous for its anc. university (late 11th cent.) and its traditional printing and publishing industries. Suffered from rivalry bet. Guelphs and Ghibellines. Returned in 1506 to papal rule, which continued with a brief interruption (1797–1815) until 1860. As a vital railroad center and a key to Ger. line of resistance, city suffered heavy air and artillery bombing (1944–45) in Second World War.

Bolognano (bôlônyä'nô), village (pop. 655), Pescara prov., Abruzzi e Molise, S central Italy, 14 mi. SW of Chieti; mfg. (cement, chemicals).

Bologne (bôlô'nyù), village (pop. 683), Haute-Marne dept., NE France, on Marne R. and Marne-Saône Canal, and 7 mi. N of Chaumont; metal founding and stamping for cutlery mfg. Sometimes called Bologne-sur-Marne.

Bolognesi, Peru: see CHIQUIÁN.

Bologovo (bŭlŭgô'vù), village (1939 pop. over 500), N Velikiye Luki oblast, Russian SFSR, 28 mi. NW of Andreapol; flax.

Bologoye (bŭlŭgoi'ù), city (1926 pop. 10,863), NW Kalinin oblast, Russian SFSR, on small L. Bologoye (fisheries), 95 mi. NW of Kalinin; rail junction; railroad shops; woodworking, food processing.

Bolokhovo (bŭlŭkhô'vù), city (1939 pop. over 2,000), E Tula oblast, Russian SFSR, 13 mi. SE of Tula, in Moscow Basin; lignite mining; refractory clays. Became city in 1943.

Bolola River, Port. Guinea: see GRANDE, RIO.

Bolon or **Bolon'** (bô'lŭnyù), town (1948 pop. over 500), S Khabarovsk Territory, Russian SFSR, on branch of Trans-Siberian RR and 45 mi. SW of Komsomolsk; sawmilling. Fish cannery of Bolon is 15 mi. SE, on L. Bolon (left arm of Amur R.).

Bolonchenticul (bōlōnchĕntēkōōl'), town (pop. 1,242), Campeche, SE Mexico, on Yucatan Peninsula, 50 mi. ENE of Campeche; timber, sugar cane, henequen, chicle, tropical fruit. Famous water caves with a number of picturesque caverns and pools are near by.

Bolondrón (bōlōndrōn'), town (pop. 3,168), Matanzas prov., W Cuba, on railroad and 20 mi. SSE of Matanzas; agr. center (sugar cane, fruit, honey); stone quarrying, lumbering.

Bolor Tagh, China: see MUZTAGH ATA RANGE.

Bolotana (bôlô'tänä), village (pop. 4,165), Nuoro prov., central Sardinia, 20 mi. W of Nuoro. Has 16th-cent. church. Numerous nuraghi in vicinity.

Bolotino (bŭlô'tyĭnŭ), Rum. *Balotina* (bälō'tēnä), village (1941 pop. 2,845), NW Moldavian SSR, near Prut R. (Rum. border), 26 mi. W of Beltsy; corn, wheat, oilseeds.

Bolotnoye (bŭlôt'nŭyù), city (1939 pop. over 10,000), NE Novosibirsk oblast, Russian SFSR, on Trans-Siberian RR, on highway to Tomsk and 70 mi. NE of Novosibirsk; metalworks. Industrialized in 1930s.

Boloven Plateau (bŭlō'vĕn), S Laos, extends bet. Mekong R. (E) and the Se Khong (W); c.60 mi. wide, 50 mi. long, it rises to 4,100 ft. toward the Se Khong. Of basaltic formation, it is wooded and inhabited by Khas (indigenous aborigines). Agr.: tea, coffee, cinchona, kapok, cardamoms. Pakse is distributing center.

Bolozon (bôlôzō'), village (pop. 113), Ain dept., E France, on the Ain and 7 mi. WNW of Nantua; Cize-Bolozon dam and hydroelectric plant near by.

Bolpebra (bōlpā'brä), village, northwesternmost point of Bolivia, in Pando dept., port on Acre R. and 55 mi. W of Cobija, at junction of Bolivia-Brazil-Peru border; customs station. Iñapari (Peru) adjoins W.

Bolpur (bōl'pōōr), town (pop. 13,856), Birbhum dist., W West Bengal, India, 14 mi. SSE of Suri; trade center (rice, gram, wheat, sugar cane, potatoes); rice and oilseed milling, cotton weaving. Visva Bharati (univ.) is at Santiniketan, 1 mi. NNW.

Bolsena (bôlsā'nä), town (pop. 3,063), Viterbo prov., Latium, central Italy, on L. Bolsena, 8 mi. SW of Orvieto, in grape- and olive-growing region; fishing; wine making. Has 11th-cent. church, 12th-cent. castle, and medieval bldgs. According to tradition, a priest witnessed (c.1265) the miracle of transubstantiation here while celebrating the mass. The *Mass of Bolsena* is the subject of a famous fresco by Raphael in the Stanze at the Vatican. Near by is site of the second Volsinii of Etruscan origin.

Bolsena, Lake (□ 44), anc. *Lacus Volsiniensis*, crater lake, Latium, central Italy, 11 mi. NW of Viterbo; 8 mi. long, 7 mi. wide, alt. 1,000 ft., max. depth 479 ft. Abounds in fish; contains (S) rocky islets of Bisentina and Martana. Has S outlet (Marta R.). On its shores, used for growing grapes and olives, are Bolsena, Capodimonte, and Marta.

Bolshakovo or **Bol'shakovo** (bŭlshŭkô'vù), village (1939 pop. 2,256), N central Kaliningrad oblast, Russian SFSR, 17 mi. NNW of Chernyakhovsk; agr. market; road center. Until 1945, in East Prussia, where it was called Gross Skaisgirren (grōs skīs'gĭ"rùn) and, later (1938–45), Kreuzingen (kroit'sĭngùn).

Bolshaya or **Bol'shaya** [Rus.,=GREAT, GREATER, LARGE, BIG], in Rus. names: see also BOLSHE- [Rus. combining form], BOLSHIYE, BOLSHOI, BOLSHOYE.

Bolshaya Aleksandrovka or **Bol'shaya Aleksandrovka** (bŭlshī'ŭ ŭlyĭksän'drŭfkŭ), village (1926 pop. 6,194), NW Kherson oblast, Ukrainian SSR, on Ingulets R. 55 mi. NNE of Kherson; metalworks.

Bolshaya Atnya or **Bol'shaya Atnya** (ŭtnyä'), village (1926 pop. 3,429), NW Tatar Autonomous SSR, Russian SFSR, 34 mi. NNE of Kazan; woodworking; grain.

Bolshaya Belozerka or **Bol'shaya Belozerka** (byĕlŭzyĕr'kŭ), village (1926 pop. 16,477), W Zaporozhe oblast, Ukrainian SSR, 40 mi. NW of Melitopol; cotton, wheat, castor beans.

Bolshaya Berestovitsa or **Bol'shaya Berestovitsa** (byĕrĭstô'vētsŭ), Pol. *Brzostowica Wielka*, town (1937 pop. 2,000), W Grodno oblast, Belorussian SSR, 35 mi. S of Grodno, on Pol. border; flour milling, dairying.

Bolshaya Bira River, Russian SFSR: see BIRA RIVER.

Bolshaya Chernigovka or **Bol'shaya Chernigovka** (chĭrnyē'gŭfkŭ), village (1948 pop. over 2,000), SE Kuibyshev oblast, Russian SFSR, in Obshchi Syrt hills, on headstream of Greater Irgiz R. and 26 mi. SE of Bolshaya Glushitsa; dairying; wheat.

Bolshaya Churakovka or **Bol'shaya Churakovka** (chōōrä'kŭfkŭ), village (1939 pop. over 500), N Kustanai oblast, Kazakh SSR, 30 mi. ESE of Kustanai; wheat, cattle.

Bolshaya Garmanda, Russian SFSR: see EVENSK.

Bolshaya Glushitsa or **Bol'shaya Glushitsa** (glōōshē'-tsŭ), village (1926 pop. 8,079), SE Kuibyshev oblast, Russian SFSR, in Obshchi Syrt hills, on Greater Irgiz R. and 55 mi. SSE of Kuibyshev; metalworking, flour milling; wheat, cattle, sheep.

Bolshaya Gribanovka or **Bol'shaya Gribanovka** (grēbä'nŭfkŭ), village (1926 pop. 11,078), E Voronezh oblast, Russian SFSR, 7 mi. NW of Borisoglebsk; sugar refining, woodworking.

Bolshaya Izhora or **Bol'shaya Izhora** (ēzhô'rŭ), town (1939 pop. over 500), W Leningrad oblast, Russian SFSR, on Gulf of Finland, 8 mi. W of Lomonosov; brickworks.

Bolshaya Kandala, Russian SFSR: see MALAYA KANDALA.

Bolshaya Kudara, Russian SFSR: see KUDARA-SOMON.

Bolshaya Lepetikha or **Bol'shaya Lepetikha** (lyĕpĭtyē'khŭ), village (1926 pop. 11,929), N Kherson oblast, Ukrainian SSR, on Dnieper R. (landing) and 70 mi. NE of Kherson; flour; metalworks, lumber mill.

Bolshaya Markha or **Bol'shaya Markha** (mär'khŭ), village (1948 pop. over 500), central Yakut Autonomous SSR, Russian SFSR, on Lena R. and 5 mi. N of Yakutsk, in agr. area.

Bolshaya Martynovka or **Bol'shaya Martynovka** (mŭrtĭ'nŭfkŭ), village (1926 pop. 3,398), S central Rostov oblast, Russian SFSR, on Sal R. and 55 mi. N of Salsk; flour mill, metalworks; wheat, cotton, livestock. Until c.1944, Martynovka or Martynovskoye.

Bolshaya Murta or **Bol'shaya Murta** (mōōr'tŭ), village (1948 pop. over 2,000), S Krasnoyarsk Territory, Russian SFSR, 60 mi. NNE of Krasnoyarsk on Krasnoyarsk-Yeniseisk highway; metalworks.

Bolshaya Novoselka or **Bol'shaya Novoselka** (nŭvŭsyôl'kŭ), village (1939 pop. over 2,000), W Stalino oblast, Ukrainian SSR, 45 mi. WSW of Stalino; flour milling. Until 1946, Bolshoi Yanisol.

Bolshaya Pisarevka or **Bol'shaya Pisarevka** (pē'sŭryĭfkŭ), village (1926 pop. 8,366), SE Sumy oblast, Ukrainian SSR, on Vorskla R. and 26 mi. ENE of Akhtyrka; flour milling.

Bolshaya Rechka or **Bol'shaya Rechka** (ryĕch'kŭ), town (1943 pop. over 500), S Irkutsk oblast, Russian SFSR, on Angara R. and 30 mi. SE of Irkutsk.

Bolshaya River or **Bol'shaya River** (bŭlshī'ŭ). **1** In SW Kamchatka Peninsula, Russian SFSR, rises in central mtn. range, flows 125 mi. SW, past Bolsheretsk (here receiving Bystraya R.), to form a 14-mi.-long lagoon, which opens into Sea of Okhotsk at Ust-Bolsheretsk. Hot springs abound along banks. **2** or **Onemen River** (ŭnyĭmyĕn'), in NE Siberian Russian SFSR, rises in Koryak Range in SE Chukchi Natl. Okrug, flows 185 mi. NE, through tundra, to Anadyr R. just W of Anadyr, here forming Onemen Gulf, a W section of Anadyr Bay.

Bolshaya Sosnova or **Bol'shaya Sosnova** (sŭsnô'vŭ), village (1926 pop. 2,445), SW Molotov oblast, Russian SFSR, 27 mi. WSW of Okhansk; food processing; rye, oats, livestock. Formerly called Bolshe-Sosnovo.

Bolshaya Ucha or **Bol'shaya Ucha** (ōō'chŭ), village (1926 pop. 1,085), SW Udmurt Autonomous SSR,

Russian SFSR, 13 mi. NNW of Mozhga; wheat, rye, flax, livestock.

Bolshaya Usa or **Bol'shaya Usa** (ŏŏ'sŭ), village (1948 pop. over 2,000), SW Molotov oblast, Russian SFSR, 41 mi. SSW of Osa; flax processing, lumbering; livestock.

Bolshaya Vishera or **Bol'shaya Vishera** (vē'shĭrŭ), town (1948 pop. over 10,000), N Novgorod oblast, Russian SFSR, on right headstream of Vishera R. and 5 mi. NW of Malaya Vishera; glassworking.

Bolshaya Viska or **Bol'shaya Viska** (vē'skŭ), village (1926 pop. 6,884), central Kirovograd oblast, Ukrainian SSR, 18 mi. W of Kirovograd; flour mill.

Bolshaya Vradiyevka or **Bol'shaya Vradiyevka** (vrä'-dyēüfkŭ), village (1926 pop. 7,973), N central Odessa oblast, Ukrainian SSR, 18 mi. SW of Pervomaisk; metalworks. Formerly called Vradiyevka.

Bolshaya Yelan or **Bol'shaya Yelan'** (yĭlän'yŭ), village (1926 pop. 2,049), central Penza oblast, Russian SFSR, 16 mi. SW of Penza; wheat, legumes, truck produce. Sometimes called Yelan.

Bolshaya Zapadnaya Litsa, Russian SFSR: see ZAPADNAYA LITSA, BOLSHAYA.

Bolshe- or **Bol'she-** [Rus. combining form, =GREAT, GREATER, LARGE, BIG], in Rus. names: see also BOLSHAYA, BOLSHIYE, BOLSHOI, BOLSHOYE.

Bolshe-Krepinskaya or **Bol'she-Krepinskaya** (bŭl″-shĭ-kryĕ'pĭnskĭŭ), village (1926 pop. 3,443), SW Rostov oblast, Russian SFSR, 30 mi. NW of Rostov; flour mill, metalworks; wheat, sunflowers, cattle. Formerly also called Bolshe-Krepkaya.

Bolsherechye or **Bol'sherech'ye** (bŭlshĭrĕch'yĭ), village (1926 pop. 781), E central Omsk oblast, Russian SFSR, on Irtysh R. (landing) and 90 mi. NE of Omsk; dairy farming.

Bolsheretsk or **Bol'sheretsk** (bŭlshĭrĕtsk'), village, Kamchatka oblast, Khabarovsk Territory, Russian SFSR, on S Kamchatka Peninsula, at confluence of Bolshaya and Bystraya rivers, 90 mi. W of Petropavlovsk. A Rus. fort, Bolsheretsk was founded (1700) here or at site of near-by Ust-Bolsheretsk.

Bolshe-Troitskoye or **Bol'she-Troitskoye** (bŭl″shĭ-trô'yĭtskŭyŭ), village (1926 pop. 4,405), SE Kursk oblast, Russian SFSR, 30 mi. E of Belgorod; fruit and vegetable processing, flour milling.

Bolsheuki, Russian SFSR: see BOLSHIYE UKI.

Bolshe-Ustikinskoye or **Bol'she-Ust'ikinskoye** (bôl″-shĭ-ŏŏstyĭkēn'skŭyŭ), village (1926 pop. 2,388), NE Bashkir Autonomous SSR, Russian SFSR, on Ai R. and 120 mi. NE of Ufa; rye, oats livestock. Gypsum deposits 4 mi. W, at Alegazovo (1939 pop. under 2,000).

Bolshevik Island or **Bol'shevik Island** (bōl'shŭvĭk, bŏl'–; Rus. bŭlshĭvēk'), S island (□ 4,450) of Severnaya Zemlya archipelago, in Arctic Ocean, in Krasnoyarsk Territory, Russian SFSR; separated by Boris Vilkitski Strait from N Taimyr Peninsula; 20% glacier-covered.

Bolshevo, Russian SFSR: see STALINSKI, Moscow oblast.

Bolshezemelskaya Tundra or **Bol'shezemel'skaya Tundra** (bŭl″shĭzĭmĕl'skĭŭ) [Rus., =great land], in Nenets Natl. Okrug, Archangel oblast, Russian SFSR; extends from lower Pechora R. c.250 mi. E to outliers of the N Urals and from Barents Sea coast c.50 mi. S; reindeer raising.

Bolshiye or **Bol'shiye** [Rus., =GREAT, GREATER, LARGE, BIG], in Rus. names: see also BOLSHAYA, BOLSHE- [Rus. combining form], BOLSHOI, BOLSHOYE.

Bolshiye Arabuzy, Russian SFSR: see PERVOMAISKOYE, Chuvash Autonomous SSR.

Bolshiye Berezniki or **Bol'shiye Berezniki** (bŭlshē'ŭ bĭryĕz'nĭkē), village (1926 pop. 4,772), SE Mordvinian Autonomous SSR, Russian SFSR, on Sura R. (head of navigation) and 31 mi. E of Saransk; hemp, wheat, potatoes; carpet weaving.

Bolshiye Chapurniki or **Bol'shiye Chapurniki** (chŭpŏŏr'nyĭkē), village (1926 pop. 2,463), SE Stalingrad oblast, Russian SFSR, in Sarpa Lakes valley, near railroad (Chapurniki station), 20 mi. SSE of central Stalingrad; truck produce, fruit; quarries. Larger village, including Malye Chapurniki (just N; 1926 pop. 2,107), is sometimes called Chapurniki.

Bolshiye Dvory or **Bol'shiye Dvory** (dvŭrē'), NE suburb of Pavlovski Posad, Moscow, oblast, Russian SFSR; cotton milling. Inc. into city c.1940.

Bolshiye Kaibitsy or **Bol'shiye Kaybitsy** (kībē'tsē), village (1939 pop. over 500), W Tatar Autonomous SSR, Russian SFSR, 29 mi. ESE of Kanash; grain, livestock. Also called Kaibitsy.

Bolshiye Klyuchishchi or **Bol'shiye Klyuchishchi** (klyŏŏ'chĭshchē), village (1926 pop. 5,498), N Ulyanovsk oblast, Russian SFSR, on Sviyaga R. and 13 mi. SSW of Ulyanovsk; fruit, truck. Formerly called Klyuchishchi.

Bolshiye Soli, Russian SFSR: see NEKRASOVSKOYE.

Bolshiye Tarkhany or **Bol'shiye Tarkhany** (tŭrkhä'-nē), village (1926 pop. 2,713), SW Tatar Autonomous SSR, Russian SFSR, near Volga R., 29 mi. NNE of Ulyanovsk; grain, livestock. Oil-shale and phosphorite deposits near by (S).

Bolshiye Uki or **Bol'shiye Uki** (ŏŏ'kē), village (1939 pop. over 500), N Omsk oblast, Russian SFSR, on Ishim Steppe, 105 mi. NNE of Novo-Nazyvayevka; dairy farming. Formerly also Bolsheuki.

Bolshoi or **Bol'shoy** [Rus., =GREAT, GREATER, LARGE, BIG], in Rus. names: see also BOLSHAYA, BOLSHE- [Rus. combining form], BOLSHIYE, BOLSHOYE.

Bolshoi Istok or **Bol'shoy Istok** (bŭlshoi″ēstôk'), town (1926 pop. 2,010), S Sverdlovsk oblast, Russian SFSR, on Iset R., just NW of Aramil, on rail spur; pig-iron production; machine mfg. Developed before First World War.

Bolshoi Koshelei, Russian SFSR: see KOMSOMOLSKOYE, Chuvash Autonomous SSR.

Bolshoi Log or **Bol'shoy Log** (lôk″), town (1939 pop. over 500), S Voroshilovgrad oblast, Ukrainian SSR, in the Donbas, 17 mi. W of Krasnodon; coal.

Bolshoi Lyakhov Island or **Bol'shoy Lyakhov Island** (lyä'khŭf) [Rus., =great Lyakhov], largest of Lyakhov Isls., bet. Laptev and E. Siberian seas of Arctic Ocean; separated from mainland of N Yakut Autonomous SSR, Russian SFSR, by 30-mi.-wide Dmitri Laptev Strait; 73°30'N 142°E. Site of arctic observation posts.

Bolshoi Never, Russian SFSR: see NEVER.

Bolshoi Sundyr or **Bol'shoy Sundyr'** (sŏŏndĭr'), village (1939 pop. over 2,000), NW Chuvash Autonomous SSR, Russian SFSR, 20 mi. W of Cheboksary; wheat, rye, oats.

Bolshoi Tokmak or **Bol'shoy Tokmak** (tŭkmäk'), city (1939 pop. over 10,000), central Zaporozhe oblast, Ukrainian SSR, on Molochnaya R. and 40 mi. SE of Zaporozhe, on rail spur; machinery plant.

Bolshoi Ului or **Bol'shoy Uluy** (ŏŏlŏŏ'ē), village (1926 pop. 1,520), SW Krasnoyarsk Territory, Russian SFSR, on Chulym R., on Achinsk-Yeniseisk highway 25 mi. N of Achinsk, in agr. area.

Bolshoi Vyass or **Bol'shoy V'yass** (vyäs'), village (1926 pop. 4,015), NE Penza oblast, Russian SFSR, 28 mi. SSE of Saransk, in hemp area.

Bolshoi Yanisol, Ukrainian SSR: see BOLSHAYA NOVOSELKA.

Bolshoi Yenisei River, Russian SFSR: see YENISEI RIVER.

Bolshovtsy or **Bol'shovtsy** (bŭlshôf'tsē), Pol. *Bolszowce* (bô″ŏŏshôf'tsĕ), town (1931 pop. 3,697), N Stanislav oblast, Ukrainian SSR, on Gnilaya Lipa R. and 17 mi. N of Stanislav; grain, potatoes, livestock.

Bolshoye or **Bol'shoye** [Rus., =GREAT, GREATER, LARGE, BIG], in Rus. names: see also BOLSHAYA, BOLSHE- [Rus. combining form], BOLSHIYE, BOLSHOI.

Bolshoye Batyrevo, Russian SFSR: see BATYREVO.

Bolshoye Boldino or **Bol'shoye Boldino** (bŭlshoi″ŭ bôl'dyĭnŭ), village (1939 pop. over 2,000), SE Gorki oblast, Russian SFSR, 32 mi. E of Lukoyanov; hemp, wheat. Pushkin lived and worked here; mus.

Bolshoye Ignatovo or **Bol'shoye Ignatovo** (ēgnä'-tŭvŭ), village (1939 pop. over 500), NE Mordvinian Autonomous SSR, Russian SFSR, 30 mi. WNW of Ardatov; grain, hemp. Until c.1940, Ignatovo.

Bolshoye Korovino or **Bol'shoye Korovino** (kŭrô'-vēnŭ), village (1926 pop. 1,151), W Ryazan oblast, Russian SFSR, 18 mi. N of Mikhailov; wheat.

Bolshoye Kozino or **Bol'shoye Kozino** (kô'zēnŭ), town (1939 pop. over 2,000), W Gorki oblast, Russian SFSR, on Volga R. and 7 mi. SE of Balakhna; truck produce.

Bolshoye Kushalino or **Bol'shoye Kushalino** (kŏŏ'-shŭlyēnŭ), village (1926 pop. 1,323), S central Kalinin oblast, Russian SFSR, 18 mi. NNE of Kalinin; flax. Also called Kushalino.

Bolshoye Maresyevo or **Bol'shoye Mares'yevo** (mŭrĭsyĕ'vŭ), village (1926 pop. 2,435), SE Gorki oblast, Russian SFSR, 17 mi. E of Lukoyanov; hemp, wheat.

Bolshoye Murashkino or **Bol'shoye Murashkino** (mŏŏräsh'kēnŭ), village (1926 pop. 5,323), S central Gorki oblast, Russian SFSR, 21 mi. SW of Lyskovo; tanning center.

Bolshoye Nagatkino or **Bol'shoye Nagatkino** (nŭgät'-kēnŭ), village (1939 pop. over 2,000), N Ulyanovsk oblast, Russian SFSR, 22 mi. NW of Ulyanovsk; grain, potatoes, orchards.

Bolshoye Narymskoye or **Bol'shoye Narymskoye** (nŭrĭm'skŭyŭ), village (1948 pop. over 2,000), central East Kazakhstan oblast, Kazakh SSR, en Narym R. and 100 mi. SE of Ust-Kamenogorsk; grain, cattle.

Bolshoye Podberezye or **Bol'shoye Podberez'ye** (pŭdbĭryĕ'zyĭ), village (1939 pop. over 500), W Tatar Autonomous SSR, Russian SFSR, 22 mi. SE of Kanash; grain, livestock.

Bolshoye Polpino or **Bol'shoye Polpino** (pôl'pēnŭ), town (1939 pop. over 2,000), NE Bryansk oblast, Russian SFSR; E suburb of Bryansk; superphosphate works.

Bolshoye Selo or **Bol'shoye Selo** (syĭlô'), village (1926 pop. 439), central Yaroslavl oblast, Russian SFSR, 33 mi. WNW of Yaroslavl; linen mill.

Bolshoye Sheremetyevo or **Bol'shoye Sheremet'-yevo** (shĕrĭmă'tyĭvŭ), village (1926 pop. 4,206), NE Tambov oblast, Russian SFSR, 30 mi. SE of Morshansk; grain.

Bolshoye Soldatskoye or **Bol'shoye Soldatskoye** (sŭldät'skŭyŭ), village (1926 pop. 2,738), SW Kursk oblast, Russian SFSR, 38 mi. SW of Kursk; sugar beets.

Bolshoye Sorokino or **Bol'shoye Sorokino** (sŭrô'-kēnŭ), village (1948 pop. over 2,000), SE Tyumen oblast, Russian SFSR, 37 mi. NNE of Ishim; dairy farming. Formerly Sorokino.

Bolsón (bōlsōn'), village (dist. pop. 2,467), Guanacaste prov., NW Costa Rica, port (head of navigation) on Tempisque R., opposite Ballena, and 13 mi. N of Nicoya; trading center; livestock, grain. Connected by road with Santa Cruz and Filadelfia.

Bolsón, El, Argentina: see EL BOLSÓN.

Bolsón de los Lipanos, Mexico: see LIPANOS, BOLSÓN DE LOS.

Bolsón de Mapimí, Mexico: see MAPIMÍ, BOLSÓN DE.

Bolsover (bōl'zōvŭr), urban district (1931 pop. 11,811; 1951 census 10,815), NE Derby, England, 6 mi. E of Chesterfield; coal-mining center; production of smokeless fuel; limestone quarrying. Has remains of Norman castle with early 17th-cent. additions.

Bolsward (bōls'värt), town (pop. 7,389), Friesland prov., N Netherlands, 15 mi. SW of Leeuwarden; dairy center; mfg. (linseed cakes, bricks) Has 15th-cent. church, 17th-cent. Renaissance town hall. Member of Hanseatic League in Middle Ages.

Bolszowce, Ukrainian SSR: see BOLSHOVTSY.

Boltaña (bōltä'nyä), town (pop. 899), Huesca prov., NE Spain, in the central Pyrenees, 32 mi. NE of Huesca; chief center of historic dist. of SOBRARBE. Agr. trade. Has mineral springs.

Boltenhagen or **Ostseebad Boltenhagen** (ôst'zā″bät' bôl'tŭnhä'gŭn), village (pop. 2,437), Mecklenburg, N Germany, on W shore of Wismar Bay of the Baltic, 13 mi. NW of Wismar; seaside resort.

Bolton, village (pop. 578), S Ont., on Humber R. and 22 mi. NW of Toronto; woolen and flour milling, metal casting, dairying. Resort.

Bolton. 1 or **Bolton-le-Moors** (bōl'tŭn-lŭ-mŏŏrz'), county borough (1931 pop. 177,250; 1951 census 167,162), S central Lancashire, England, 11 mi. NW of Manchester; 53°35'N 2°26'W; major textile center (cotton, wool, and rayon spinning, weaving, and printing, especially of calicoes and muslins); coal mining, leather tanning, steel milling; electrical, chemical, and textile engineering. Very early Bolton became known for textile making (woolen weaving was introduced by the Flemings in 14th cent.), but the modern industry dates from late 18th cent., when spinning factories were built and a canal (1791) put through to Manchester. The inventions of spinning machinery by Arkwright and Crompton, who were b. here, spurred its development. In borough (E) is cotton-milling suburb (pop. 13,502) of Tonge (tŏng). **2** Town, Yorkshire, England: see BRADFORD.

Bolton (bōl'tŭn, Sp. bōl'tōn), town (1939 pop. 4,154), Davao prov., S Mindanao, Philippines, on an inlet of Davao Gulf, 28 mi. SSW of Davao; abacá, coconuts.

Bolton, village, Salisbury prov., E Southern Rhodesia, in Mashonaland, 25 mi. SSW of Marandellas; tobacco, peanuts, citrus fruit, dairy products.

Bolton (bōl'tŭn). **1** Town (pop. 1,279), Tolland co., central Conn., 13 mi. E of Hartford, in agr. area. Has state park and small lakes at scenic Bolton Notch. Settled 1718, inc. 1720. **2** Village, on Saline-Williamson co. line, Ill.: see STONEFORT. **3** Agr. town (pop. 956), Worcester co., E central Mass., 15 mi. NNE of Worcester. **4** Town (pop. 741), Hinds co., W Miss., 25 mi. E of Vicksburg. **5** City (pop. 606), Columbus co., SE N.C., 26 mi. WNW of Wilmington; lumber milling. **6** Town (pop. 301), Chittenden co., NW Vt., on Winooski R. and 18 mi. E of Burlington, in Green Mts.; winter sports.

Bolton Abbey, agr. village and parish (pop. 193), West Riding, W central Yorkshire, England, on Wharfe R. and 5 mi. ENE of Skipton; site of ruins of Cistercian abbey founded 1153.

Bolton Landing, summer-resort village (1940 pop. 619), Warren co., E N.Y., on W shore of L. George, 17 mi. N of Glens Falls.

Bolton-le-Moors, England: see BOLTON.

Bolton-le-Sands, village and parish (pop. 1,153), N Lancashire, England, on Morecambe Bay 4 mi. N of Lancaster; cattle, agr. (wheat, barley, potatoes). Has 15th-cent. church tower.

Bolton-upon-Dearne (–dûrn), former urban district (1931 pop. 14,245), West Riding, S Yorkshire, England, on Dearne R. and 7 mi. N of Rotherham; coal mining; agr. market. Inc. 1937 in Dearne.

Bolu (bôlŏŏ'), prov. (□ 4,433; 1950 pop. 302,805), NW Turkey, on Black Sea; ⊙ Bolu. Bordered N by Bolu Mts., S by Koroglu Mts.; drained by Devrek, Soganli, and Aladag rivers. Heavily forested. Some copper near Duzce. Agr. products include grain (wheat, barley, corn, spelt), flax, tobacco, opium; mohair goats.

Bolu, town (1950 pop. 7,927), ⊙ Bolu, NW Turkey, on Devrek R. and 85 mi. NW of Ankara; agr. center (grain, flax, mohair goats); timber, mineral springs; leather goods. Sometimes spelled Boli.

Bolu Mountains (bôlŏŏ'), NW Turkey, extend 90 mi. E from lower Sakarya R., rise to 6,411 ft. in Ciledorugu. Town of Duzce on N slope. Zinc, copper, and lead in W; coal, manganese, and asbestos in E.

Bolungarvik (bô'lüng-gärvēk"), Icelandic *Bolungarvík*, town (pop. 689), Isafjardar co., NW Iceland, on Vestfjarda Peninsula, on the Isafjardardjup, 6 mi. NW of Isafjordur; fishing port.

Bolus Head (bō'lŭs), cape, SW Co. Kerry, Ireland, bet. St. Finan's Bay and Ballinskelligs Bay, 33 mi. W of Kenmare; 51°47'N 10°20'W; rises to 940 ft. Offshore are The Skelligs.

Bolvadin (bôlvädĭn'), anc. *Polybotus*, town (1950 pop. 11,083), Afyonkarahisar prov., W central Turkey, 28 mi. E of Afyonkarahisar; wheat, barley, vetch, potatoes; opium; mohair.

Bolwa, Latvia: see BALVI.

Bolyevats, Yugoslavia: see BOLJEVAC.

Bolzaneto (bôltsänā'tô), town (pop. 7,035), Genova prov., Liguria, N Italy, 3 mi. NNW of Genoa, within Greater Genoa; iron- and steelworks, stone cutting (marble, granite).

Bolzano (bôltsä'nô), province (□ c.3,090; pop. c.300,000), TRENTINO-ALTO ADIGE, N Italy; ⊙ Bolzano. Bounded N by Austria and Switzerland. Corresponds to physical dist. called Alto Adige. Alpine terrain with high mtn. ranges (Dolomites, Ortlers) and picturesque valleys (Val Venosta, Val Gardena, Pustertal). Drained by Isarco, Rienza, and upper Adige rivers. Agr. (cereals, apples, pears, grapes, potatoes); cattle and horse raising. Forestry. Hydroelectric power extensively developed, with major plants at Bressanone, Cardano, and Ponte Gardena. Marble quarries in Val Venosta; porphyry quarries at Brunico, Bronzolo, Laives; lead mines at Terlano; iron and zinc deposits. Noted tourist center, with many resorts, including Bolzano, Bressanone, Merano, Brunico, and Dobbiaco. Mfg. at Bolzano and Merano. Important international highways via Brenner, Stelvio, and Resia passes. Formerly part of Austrian Tyrol; pop. is predominantly German. After First World War passed to Italy; became a prov. in 1927. In 1948 enlarged by addition of German-speaking communes (□ c.355; pop. c.22,280) from Trento prov. (S).

Bolzano, Ger. *Bozen* (bō'tsŭn), city (pop. 41,722), ⊙ Bolzano prov., Trentino-Alto Adige, N Italy, on Isarco R., near its confluence with Adige R., and 31 mi. NNE of Trent, 35 mi. SSW of Brenner Pass; 46°30'N 11°22'E. Rail junction; tourist resort; industrial center; steelworks, foundry, alcohol distillery, fruit cannery, piano factory, woolen and cotton mills; mfg. of wine, wax, insecticides, candy, marmalade, sausage. Major hydroelectric plant at near-by Cardano. A trade center since the Middle Ages; still commercially important. Has Gothic cathedral (13th-15th cent.; severe war damage being restored) with tall campanile (1501–19), monastery (badly damaged), convent (largely destroyed), anc. Dominican church (severe damage being repaired), castle, mus., and picturesque Renaissance and Gothic houses. Belonged to bishops of Trent from 9th cent. Ruled by Austria, with exception of 2 brief periods, from 1513 to 1919, when it passed to Italy. Suffered heavy bomb damage (1943–45) in Second World War because of its position on strategic Brenner railroad. It is center of German-speaking population of S Tyrol.

Boma (bō'mä, bômä'), town (1948 pop. 11,084), ⊙ Lower Congo dist. (□ 15,217; 1948 pop. c.576,000), Leopoldville prov., W Belgian Congo, on N side of the mouth of Congo R. c.60 mi. inland from the Atlantic coast and 175 mi. SW of Leopoldville; commercial center and main port of the Mayumbe region, exporting chiefly tropical hardwoods, palm kernels, bananas, coffee, and cacao. Also head of railroad to Tshela. Mfg. (soap, ice, soft drinks, edible oil, pharmaceuticals), fisheries. Has hospitals for Europeans and natives, R.C. and Protestant missions, several business and trade schools for Africans; seat of vicar apostolic. Airport. Just W of town is the fort of Shinkakasa, built for the defense of Congo estuary. One of the oldest European trading settlements in central Africa, Boma was already known in 18th cent., 1st as Lombi, later as Embomma, for its flourishing slave trade. After the passing of various acts abolishing this trade (1807–36), it exported palm oil, ivory, copal, rubber, and groundnuts. Henry Stanley reached Boma in 1877, at the end of his epic journey on Congo R. Boma succeeded Vivi in 1886 as ⊙ Congo Free State; later became ⊙ Belgian Congo and was itself succeeded by Leopoldville in 1926.

Bomarsund (bōō"märsŭnd'), locality on E shore of Aland isl., SW Finland, 14 mi. NE of Mariehamn. Formerly site of major Russian fortress (1830), destroyed (1854) in Crimean War by Anglo-French fleet.

Bomarton (bō'–), village (pop. c.500), Baylor co., N Texas, 11 mi. SW of Seymour; rail point in cattle area.

Bomba (bôm'bä), town (pop. 2,255), Chieti prov., Abruzzi e Molise, S central Italy, near Sangro R., 14 mi. S of Lanciano; cementworks.

Bombal (bômbäl'), agr. town (pop. estimate 1,500), S Santa Fe prov., Argentina, 55 mi. SW of Rosario; corn, potatoes, flax, wheat, alfalfa.

Bombala (bŏmbä'lŭ), municipality (pop. 1,111), SE New South Wales, Australia, 110 mi. S of Canberra; rail terminus; sheep center; potatoes, oats. Copper mines near by.

Bombali, Sierra Leone: see MAKENI.

Bombarai (bōmbärī'), peninsula in Netherlands New Guinea, 15 mi. S of Vogelkop peninsula across McCluer Gulf; c.110 mi. N-S, c.90 mi. E-W, with W projection (50 mi. long), site of Fakfak; largely marshy.

Bombardopolis (bōbärdōpōlē'), agr. town (1950 census pop. 600), Nord-Ouest dept., NW Haiti, 38 mi. WSW of Port-de-Paix; cotton growing.

Bombarral (bōmbäräl'), town (pop. 3,111), Leiria dist., W central Portugal, on railroad, 10 mi. S of Caldas da Rainha, in winegrowing dist.; distilling, metalworking, pottery mfg.

Bombay (bŏmbā'), constituent state (□ c.115,570; 1951 pop. 35,943,559), W India; ⊙ Bombay. Bounded W by Arabian Sea, Saurashtra, Cutch, N by Rajasthan, E by Madhya Bharat, Madhya Pradesh, and Hyderabad, S by Madras and Mysore; borders Portuguese coastal possessions of Goa and Damão. S of Narbada R. state rises from rock-bound coastal strip (KONKAN) through Western GHATS (average alt. 3–4,000 ft.) onto DECCAN PLATEAU. Section N of the Narbada, which includes GUJARAT plain, encloses N end of Gulf of Cambay, and is bordered by Rann of Cutch (NW) and S Aravalli Range (NE); has enclaves (Amreli dist.) in Saurashtra on Kathiawar peninsula (W). Along its coast Bombay has a monsoon tropical climate characterized by year-round hot weather and a heavy seasonal (June–Sept.) rainfall, known as SW or Bombay monsoon; Konkan has annual precipitation of c.100 in., while Western Ghats receive 120–200 in. On Deccan tableland and in N parts of state climate is semi-arid tropical, with a long, dry, hot season and short period of rainfall (20–25 in.). State is drained by Godavari, Bhima, and Kistna rivers which rise in Western Ghats and flow SE to Bay of Bengal, and, in N section, by lower courses of Narbada, Mahi, and Sabarmati rivers which all empty into Gulf of Cambay. Majority (c.60%) of pop. engaged in agr. Rice, coconuts, mangoes, betel and cashew nuts cultivated along coast, while millet, cotton, oilseeds, wheat, and sugar cane are chief crops of upland and N regions, where irrigation tanks and canals supplement meagre rainfall. Over 10,000,000 head of cattle are raised throughout state, primarily as draft animals. Hill forests yield teak, blackwood, sandalwood, and bamboo. Manganese mining in Baroda, Panch Mahals, and Kanara dists.; salt mfg. (solar evaporation) along coast. Bombay is India's leading commercial and industrial state, with major concentration of industry (chiefly textile) in BOMBAY city area; other important centers are Ahmadabad, Sholapur, and Baroda (cotton-milling cities), and Surat, Poona (large military station; summer hq. of state govt.), Kolhapur, Ahmadnagar, Broach, Satara, Sangli, and Hubli. Besides textiles, industries include oilseed, sugar, and rice milling, tanning, paper and soap mfg.; handicrafts (cloth goods and embroideries, wood products, pottery, gold and silver thread, carpets, metal utensils) are widespread. Mackerel, sardines, pomfrets, seerfish, and sharks are caught in coastal waters; fishing ports at Okha, Bombay, Ratnagiri, Malvan, and Karwar. There are popular hill resorts at Abu (with its Jain temples), Mahabaleshwar, and Matheran, sacred Hindu pilgrimage centers at Dwarka and Nasik, and noted cave-temples on Elephanta and Salsette isls. and at Karli. In 3d cent. B.C., area formed part of Mauryan empire, but after its decline it fell under rule of independent dynasties until 7th cent. A.D., when early Chalukyas established themselves S of the Narbada. In 11th cent., Mahmud of Ghazni raided Gujarat, but not until 14th cent. did Moslem power appear in S parts; soon independent Deccan sultanates arose at Ahmadnagar and Bijapur. By 1600, N section was annexed to Mogul empire by Akbar, but in late-17th cent. Mahrattas, under Sivaji, became dominant and, under the peshwas (18th cent.), controlled all of W India. Meanwhile, Portuguese had captured Goa in 1510 and settled at other coastal places. British set up trading posts (1st at Surat) in 17th cent., acquired (1661) and developed port of Bombay, and in early-19th cent. conquered Mahrattas in decisive battles near Poona. To newly-established Bombay presidency most of Gujarat and some S Mahratta kingdoms were soon annexed. Later additions included Aden (1839) and Sind (1843). Aden was detached 1932; in 1937 Sind became a separate autonomous prov., and rest of Bombay presidency an autonomous prov. Those adjacent princely states not inc. into Br. India were grouped into political agencies under Bombay and, later, Indian govts. Bombay was center (early-20th cent.) of Indian nationalist movement, and for many years Gandhi made Ahmadabad his hq. Prov. (1941 □ 76,443; pop. 20,849,840) was enlarged 1948–49 by merger of former princely states of DECCAN STATES, GUJARAT STATES, BARODA, Kolhapur, some WESTERN INDIA STATES, and Palanpur and Danta of Rajputana States. In 1950, Bombay became a constituent state of republic of India; inc. part of SIROHI; exchanged enclaves with Hyderabad and Saurashtra. Chief languages: Marathi, Gujarati (N), Kanarese (S), Hindi. Pop. 80% Hindu, 9% Moslem, 8% tribal, 1% Christian. Literacy (26%) is highest in India. Comprises 28 dists.: Ahmadabad, Ahmadnagar, Amreli, Banas Kantha, Baroda, Belgaum, Bijapur, Bombay Suburban, Broach, Dangs, Dharwar, East Khandesh, Kaira, Kanara, Kolaba, Kolhapur, Mehsana, Nasik, Panch Mahals, Poona, Ratnagiri, Sabar Kantha, Satara North, Satara South, Sholapur, Surat, Thana, and West Khandesh.

Bombay, city (□ 30; pop. 1,489,883), ⊙ Bombay state, W India, port on Arabian Sea, at S end of Salsette Isl., 740 mi. SSW of New Delhi, 1,020 mi. WSW of Calcutta; 18°56'N 72°50'E. Major commercial, industrial, and financial center; rail hub; airport at suburb of Santa Cruz (N). City's large and picturesque Bombay Harbour (E) is best in India, accommodating large numbers of both ocean-going and coastal vessels. Bombay rivals Calcutta in amount of total trade and shipping; exports cotton, oilseeds, rice, wheat, manganese ore, raw wool, hides; imports textiles, fabricated iron and steel, machinery, railway equipment, automobiles, sugar, coal. Chief center of cotton-milling industry in India; main market for raw cotton from Gujarat, Khandesh, and Dharwar areas. Other industries include engineering and metalworking, shipbuilding, mfg. of chemicals, agr. machinery, matches, confectioneries, paper, soap, leather goods, carpets; fishing; automobile assembly plant, motion picture studios, printing presses, sawmills, distilleries. Bombay has hot, humid climate; mean temp. ranges from 91°F. in May to 67°F. in Jan.; annual rainfall, 71 in. City area, which in 17th cent. consisted of 7 isls. and is now often called Bombay Isl., has been converted into a peninsula of Salsette Isl. by drainage and reclamation projects. At SE end of city, in Colaba and Fort sections, are govt. and business offices, shopping dist., and naval dockyard. Along Mahatma Gandhi (formerly Esplanade) Road and Mayo Road are rows of fine bldgs., including Elphinstone Col., Univ. Library (with Rajabai Tower), Science Inst., and High Court. Near by are noted Taj Mahal hotel and Gateway of India, a large arch in 16th-cent. Gujarat style built to commemorate visit (1911) of George V and Queen Mary. Hornby Road runs N past elaborate Victoria rail terminus and Crawford Market (vegetables, fish) into a crowded bazaar area, where jewelers, smiths, wood and ivory carvers, weavers, and others ply their wares. Along E side of city, on BOMBAY HARBOUR, are extensive docks, oil installations, timber yards, and storage facilities for cotton, grain, coal and manganese ore. On W side, facing sea, are residential dists. of Cumbala Hill (with Breach Candy and Mahalakshmi Temple) and Malabar Hill (with Govt. House and Parsi Towers of Silence). Bet. S promontories of Malabar Hill and Colaba is shallow inlet of Back Bay. In N part of city—in Byculla and Parel sections—lies industrial zone with its cotton mills, railway workshops, and other factories, for which power is supplied by hydroelectric plants at Khopoli, Bhivpuri, and Bhira in Kolaba dist. Mahim, Dharavi, and Matunga sections in extreme N have tanneries, flour and cotton mills, and tenement dwellings. Large salt pans on NE lowland. Bombay Univ. (founded 1857) is mainly an examining body; also has teaching facilities and numerous affiliated cols. throughout W India. Other educational and cultural institutions include Prince of Wales Mus., Bombay Asiatic Society, Haffkine Inst., Victoria and Albert Mus., several technical cols. and research societies. Bombay was acquired in 1530s from a Gujarat sultan by Portuguese, who used it as a mission center and subsidiary trading post to their main ports of Surat and Goa. Ceded (1661) to England by marriage treaty bet. Charles II of Great Britain and the Infanta Catherine of Portugal. Trade increased gradually, but establishment of textile industry at time of American Civil War as well as opening of rail communications in India greatly enhanced city's importance. Industrial expansion and pop. growth have led to suburbanization of SALSETTE ISLAND; projected Greater Bombay scheme will relieve congestion in present city area. Pop. 69% Hindu, 17% Moslem, 7% Christian; includes important Parsi community (pop. 59,813).

Bombay Harbour, inlet of Arabian Sea, W India, bet. Salsette Isl. (W) and mainland of Bombay state (E); c.10 mi. long (N-S), 6–8 mi. wide. Along city waterfront (W) are 2 dry docks, 3 wet docks, with c.50 berths, and numerous open wharves, accommodating large number of overseas and coastal vessels. Elephanta Isl. (noted cave-temples) and Butcher Isl. lie in harbor. Receives (NE) Thana Creek, distributary of Ulhas R.

Bombay Hook Island, Kent co., E Del., in Delaware Bay, 6 mi. E of Smyrna, separated from mainland by creek (W) and Leipsic R. (S); 8.5 mi. long. Woodland Beach, near N end, is resort; bridge to mainland near here.

Bombay Suburban, district (□ 153; pop. 251,147), W Bombay, India, on SALSETTE ISLAND; ⊙ Bandra. Bounded W by Arabian Sea, E by Thana Creek and Bombay Harbour. Agr. (rice, coconuts); fishing along coasts. Suburban towns of Bandra, Kurla, Ghatkopar, and Andheri have local industries. Large airport for Bombay city near Santa Cruz. Pop. 64% Hindu, 15% Christian, 12% Moslem, 6% tribal.

Bombetoka Bay, Madagascar: see BETSIBOKA RIVER.

Bombimba (bōmbēm'bä), village, Equator Prov., W Belgian Congo, on Ikelemba R. and 70 mi. NE of Coquilhatville; steamboat terminus and trading post in copal-gathering area; rubber plantations in vicinity.

Bombo, Uganda: see NAMALIGA.

Bomboli (bōmbō'lē), village, NW Fr. Guinea, Fr. West Africa, in Fouta Djallon mts., 45 mi. NNW of Mamou. Coffee experiment station.

Bomboma (bōmbō'mä), village, Equator Prov., NW Belgian Congo, on a tributary of Giri R. and 170 mi. WNW of Lisala; trading center; cotton ginning; palm groves. Makengo, 5 mi. E, has palm-oil mills.

Bombon, Lake, Philippines: see TAAL, LAKE.

Bombure, Ceylon: see TELDENIYA.

Bom Conselho (bō kō sä'lyōō), city (pop. 5,257), E central Pernambuco, NE Brazil, near Alagoas border, 24 mi. SW of Garanhuns; coffee, cotton, corn.

Bom Despacho (bō dĭspä'shōō), city (pop. 5,577), central Minas Gerais, Brazil, on railroad and 80 mi. W of Belo Horizonte; agr. trade center (cereals, cattle, dairy products); cobalt deposits.

Bömelö, Norway: see BOMLO.

Bomfim. 1 City, Bahia, Brazil: see SENHOR DO BONFIM. **2** City, Goiás, Brazil: see SILVÂNIA.

Bomi Hills (bō'mē), Western Prov., Liberia, 40 mi. N of Monrovia (linked by railroad); major iron-mining dist. (since 1950).

Bom Jardim (bō zhärdēm'). **1** Town, Bahia, Brazil: see CATUIÇARA. **2** City (pop. 2,409), E Pernambuco, NE Brazil, on S slope of Serra dos Cariris Velhos, 10 mi. NW of Limoeiro; terminus of rail spur. Ships cotton, coffee, corn, livestock. **3** City (pop. 1,096), central Rio de Janeiro, Brazil, in the Serra do Mar, on railroad and 11 mi. NE of Nova Friburgo; brandy distilling, coffee- and orange-growing. Called Vergel, 1944–48.

Bom Jardim de Minas (dĭ mē'nŭs), city (pop. 1,268), S Minas Gerais, Brazil, on N slope of the Serra da Mantiqueira, 45 mi. NNW of Barra do Piraí (Rio de Janeiro); rail junction; rutile mining; peat works. Until 1944, called Bom Jardim.

Bom Jesus (bō' zhä'zōōsh), village, Congo prov., NW Angola, on lower Cuanza R. and 10 mi. WSW of Catete; cotton, sugar.

Bom Jesus. 1 City (pop. 1,068), S Piauí, Brazil, on Gurgueia R. and 180 mi. SSW of Floriano; hides, maniçoba rubber. **2** City, Rio Grande do Sul, Brazil: see APARADOS DA SERRA.

Bom Jesus da Lapa (dä lä'pŭ), city (pop. 2,330), W central Bahia, Brazil, on right bank of São Francisco R. (navigable) and 150 mi. S of Barra; cotton, rice, corn, skins. Important airfield. Formerly called Lapa.

Bom Jesus do Galho (dōō gä'lyōō), city (pop. 1,691), E Minas Gerais, Brazil, near railroad, 15 mi. W of Caratinga; nickel deposits.

Bom Jesus do Itabapoana (ētäbäpwä'nŭ), city (pop. 3,688), NE Rio de Janeiro state, Brazil, on Itabapoana R. (Espírito Santo border) and 45 mi. NNW of Campos; rice and corn processing, dairying.

Bom Jesus do Norte (nôr'tĭ), town (pop. 2,200), S Espírito Santo, Brazil, on Rio de Janeiro state border, 35 mi. SW of Cachoeiro de Itapemirim; rail-spur terminus; coffeegrowing.

Bom Jesus dos Meiras, Brazil: see BRUMADO.

Bom Jesus do Triunfo (trēōōm'fōō), city (pop. 1,954), E Rio Grande do Sul, Brazil, on Jacuí R. opposite São Jerônimo, at mouth of Taquari R., and 30 mi. W of Pôrto Alegre; ships iron, timber. Has 18th-cent. church. Until 1944, Triunfo or Triumpho.

Bomlo (bûm'lô), Nor. *Bømlo,* island (□ 69; pop. 5,393) in North Sea, Hordaland co., SW Norway, 11 mi. N of Haugesund; 21 mi. long, 7 mi. wide. Its central isthmus is crossed by a canal. At SE tip is MOSTERHAMN; on NE shore, RUBBESTADNESET. Formerly spelled Bömelö and Bömmelö. Includes Bomlo canton (pop. 1,355).

Bommel, Netherlands: see ZALTBOMMEL.

Bömmelö, Norway: see BOMLO.

Bommelwaard (bô'mŭlvärt), island (□ 45), Gelderland prov., central Netherlands, N of 's Hertogenbosch; bounded by Waal R. (N) and by Maas R. (S, SW, and SE); 15 mi. long, 5 mi. wide. Chief places: Zaltbommel and Hedel. At NW end, at confluence of Waal and Maas R., 2 mi. SE of Gorinchem, is castle of Loevestein, site of imprisonment (1619–20) of Grotius.

Bommes (bôm), village (pop. 76), Gironde dept., SW France, on the Ciron and 23 mi. SSE of Bordeaux; sauternes.

Bomnak (bŭmnäk'), village (1948 pop. over 500), N Amur oblast, Russian SFSR, 200 mi. ENE of Skovorodino and on upper Zeya R. (head of navigation), in gold-mining dist.

Bomokandi River (bōmōkän'dē), in NE and N Belgian Congo, rises 40 mi. SSE of Watsa, flows c.300 mi. NW and W, past Gombari, Rungu, and Poko, to Uele R. opposite Bambili. Drains cotton-growing area; rapids in middle course. First explored 1871.

Bomoseen, Lake (bŏ"mūzēn', bŏ'mūzēn"), W Vt., resort lake 10 mi. W of Rutland; c.8 mi. long. Bomoseen village, at S end, is in Castleton town.

Bompata (bōmpä'tä), town, Ashanti, S central Gold Coast, 50 mi. E of Kumasi; cacao, cassava, corn. Gold deposits.

Bompland, Venezuela: see CORONA, LA.

Bom Retiro (bō rĭtē'rōō). **1** Town, Rio Grande do Sul, Brazil: see INHANDAVA. **2** City (pop. 623), central Santa Catarina, Brazil, in the Serra do Mar, 60 mi. WSW of Florianópolis; hog and stock raising.

Bomst, Poland: see BABIMOST.

Bom Successo, Brazil: see BOM SUCESSO.

Bom Sucesso (bō sōōsä'sōō), city (pop. 3,384), S Minas Gerais, Brazil, on railroad and 35 mi. WNW of São João del Rei; alt. 3,085 ft. Ships cattle, dairy products, tobacco, cereals. Founded 1720. Formerly spelled Bom Successo.

Bomu River (bō'mōō), **M'bomu River,** or **M'Bomou River** (mŭbō'mōō, mŭbōmōō'), right headstream of the Ubangi in N central Africa, forming Belgian Congo–Fr. Equatorial Africa border; rises in N Belgian Congo near Anglo-Egyptian Sudan frontier, 25 mi. NW of Doruma, flows c.450 mi. W in wide curves through savannas, past Bangassou, to join Uele R., forming the Ubangi. Rapids in lower course.

Bon, Cape (bŏn, Fr. bō), Arabic *Ras Addar* (räs' ăd-där'), headland on the Mediterranean coast of NE Tunisia, 50 mi. ENE of Tunis and 90 mi. SW of westernmost tip of Sicily; lighthouse; 37°5'N 11°2'E. It is at tip of **Cape Bon Peninsula,** c.20 mi. wide and jutting 50 mi. into the Mediterranean, forming E margin of Gulf of Tunis. Administratively, peninsula forms Grombalia dist. (also called Cape Bon dist.; □ 1,115; 1946 pop. 211,434). Of great fertility, it has vineyards, orchards, citrus groves, and tobacco plantations (especially near its base). Lignite deposits (Oum-Douil). Tuna fisheries (Sidi-Daoud). Chief towns are Grombalia, Nabeul, Hammamet, Soliman, and Kélibia. Here the German forces in North Africa surrendered to the Allies in May, 1943.

Bona, Algeria: see BÔNE.

Bona, Mount (bō'nŭ) (16,420 ft.), S Alaska, in St. Elias Mts., 150 mi. ENE of Cordova; 61°23'N 141°45'W.

Bonab, Iran: see BUNAB.

Bonaberi (bōnäbĕ'rē), suburb of Douala, Wouri region, SW Fr. Cameroons, on right shore of Wouri R. estuary, just N of city's center; banana-shipping point, railhead to N'Kongsamba; soap mfg.

Bonacca Island, Honduras: see GUANAJA ISLAND.

Bon Accord (bŏnäkôr'), village (pop. estimate 150), central Alta., 20 mi. N of Edmonton; oil production.

Bonai (bō'nī), former princely state (□ 1,280; pop. 92,537) in Orissa States, India; ⊙ was Bonaigarh. Inc. 1949 into newly-created dist. of Sundargarh, Orissa.

Bonaigarh (bō'nīgŭr), village, Sundargarh dist., N Orissa, India, on Brahmani R. and 70 mi. ENE of Sambalpur; local market for rice, timber, lac, oilseeds; hand-loom weaving, metalware working. Was ⊙ former princely state of Bonai.

Bon Air. 1 Town (pop. 360), Talladega co., E central Ala., 18 mi. SW of Talladega, near Coosa R.; yarn. **2** Village (pop. c.300), White co., central Tenn., 5 mi. E of Sparta. Surveying camp of Vanderbilt Univ. School of Engineering near by.

Bonaire (bônâr'), island (including Little Bonaire, □ 98.45; 1948 pop. estimate 5,000), Du. West Indies, 30 mi. E of Curaçao isl.; 22 mi. long, up to 6 mi. wide; bet. 12°3'–12°19'N and 68°11'–68°25'W. Chief town, Kralendijk. Has tropical, semiarid climate, relieved by trade winds. Main products are salt, divi-divi, goat manure, exported through Kralendijk. Salt panning. Sometimes Buen Ayre.

Bonanza or **La Bonanza** (lä bōnän'sä), village, Zelaya dept., E Nicaragua, in Pis Pis Mts. (E outlier of Cordillera Isabelia), 75 mi. W of Puerto Cabezas; gold-mining center for Neptune mines. Airfield.

Bonanza (bōnän'thä), village (pop. 577), Cádiz prov., SW Spain, wine-shipping port for Sanlúcar de Barrameda (2 mi. S) on the Guadalquivir, 18 mi. N of Cádiz. Linked by rail with Jerez. The Levante saltworks are 2 mi. N.

Bonanza (bŭnăn'zŭ, bō–). **1** Town (pop. 361), Sebastian co., W Ark., 10 mi. S of Fort Smith, near Okla. line. **2** Town (pop. 51), Saguache co., S central Colo., in S tip of Sawatch Mts., 5 mi. SE of Ouray Peak and 14 mi. N of Saguache; alt. 9,444 ft. **3** Town (pop. 259), Klamath co., S Oregon, on Lost R. and 17 mi. E of Klamath Falls; dairy.

Bonanza Creek (bŭnăn'zŭ), river, W Yukon, rises S of Dawson, flows 20 mi. NNW to Klondike R. just SE of Dawson. Its valley was scene (Aug. 17, 1896) of 1st gold strike in Yukon.

Bonao, Dominican Republic: see MONSEÑOR NOUEL.

Bonaparte, island in Indian Ocean: see RÉUNION.

Bonaparte (bō'nŭpärt), town (pop. 642), Van Buren co., SE Iowa, on Des Moines R. and 30 mi. NW of Keokuk; produces gloves, feed, agr. lime.

Bonaparte, Lake, Lewis co., N central N.Y., 28 mi. ENE of Watertown, in W foothills of the Adirondacks; c.2 mi. long. Bonaparte or Lake Bonaparte, a resort community, is on S shore.

Bon Aqua (bŏn ă'kwŭ), resort village, Hickman co., Tenn., 33 mi. SW of Nashville; mineral springs.

Bonar (bōnyär'), town (pop. 1,414), Leon prov., NW Spain, 23 mi. NE of Leon; cereals, lumber, livestock. Mineral springs. Coal mines near by.

Bonar Bridge (bŏ'nŭr), agr. village, SE Sutherland, Scotland, at head of Dornoch Firth, at mouth of Oykell R., 12 mi. W of Dornoch.

Bonarcado (bōnär'kädō), village (pop. 1,638), Cagliari prov., W Sardinia, 14 mi. N of Oristano. Site of Santa Maria church (consecrated 1147) and 13th-cent. chapel.

Bonares (bōnä'rĕs), town (pop. 4,865), Huelva prov., SW Spain, 15 mi. E of Huelva; agr. center (cereals, olives, almonds, oranges, grapes, truck produce, sheep); sawmilling, vegetable canning.

Bonaset (bōō'nĕ"sŭt), Swedish *Bonäset,* village (pop. 522), Vasternorrland co., NE Sweden, on small inlet of Gulf of Bothnia, 2 mi. SE of Ornskoldsvik; sawmills.

Bonasse (bŭnăs'), village (pop. 799), SW Trinidad, B.W.I., on Cedros Bay, 45 mi. SW of Port of Spain.

Bonaventure (bŏ"nŭvĕn'chŭr), county (□ 3,464; pop. 39,196), E Que., in S part of Gaspé Peninsula, on Chaleur Bay; ⊙ New Carlisle.

Bonaventure, village (pop. estimate 500), E Que., on SE Gaspé Peninsula, on Chaleur Bay, at mouth of Bonaventure R., 7 mi. WNW of New Carlisle; lumbering, dairying.

Bonaventure Island (2½ mi. long), E Que., in the Gulf of St. Lawrence, at end of Gaspé Peninsula, 2 mi. E of Percé. Granted to Captain Duval, a privateer, by George III, it is still inhabited by Duval's descendants. Site of large bird sanctuary.

Bonaventure River, E Que., on Gaspé Peninsula, rises in the Shickshock Mts., flows 75 mi. S to Chaleur Bay at Bonaventure. Trout, salmon.

Bonavista (bŏ'nŭvĭ"stŭ), town (pop. 1,399), E N.F., on E shore of Bonavista Bay, near Cape Bonavista, on railroad and 80 mi. NNW of St. John's; 48°38'N 53°7'W; fishing center, with fish-filleting, cold-storage plants. Site of govt. bait depot, lighthouse, radio station. Near by is a mink farm.

Bonavista, Cape, promontory, E N.F., at SE limit of Bonavista Bay, 4 mi. NNE of Bonavista; 48°41'N 53°5'W. Reputed landfall of John Cabot, discoverer of Newfoundland, in 1497.

Bonavista Bay (40 mi. long, 40 mi. wide at mouth), E N.F.; 49°N 53°30'W. Bounded S by Bonavista Peninsula, ending in Cape Bonavista. Has deeply indented coastline; contains numerous isls., including Cottle, Pittsound, Greenspond, Swale isls.; receives Terra Nova R. Several fishing villages, largest (Bonavista) on SE side of bay.

Bonawe (bŏnô'), village, N central Argyll, Scotland, on Awe R. near its mouth on Lock Etive, and 10 mi. E of Oban; slate-quarrying center.

Bonbon (bōbō'), town (1950 pop. 545), Sud dept., SW Haiti, on NW tip of Tiburon Peninsula, 17 mi. W of Jérémie; coffee, cacao.

Bonchurch, England: see VENTNOR.

Bonclarken, N.C.: see FLAT ROCK.

Bond, county (□ 383; pop. 14,157), SW central Ill.; ⊙ Greenville. Drained by Kaskaskia R. and Shoal Creek. Agr. area (corn, wheat, poultry, livestock), with bituminous-coal mines, natural-gas wells. Mfg. (dairy products, evaporated milk, clothing, steel products). Formed 1817.

Bond. 1 Village (pop. 4,611, with adjacent South City), Leon co., N Fla. **2** or **Bondtown,** town (pop. 240), Wise co., SW Va., in coal-mining area of the Allegheniés, 17 mi. ENE of Big Stone Gap.

Bondari (bŏn'dŭrē), village (1926 pop. 4,863), E central Tambov oblast, Russian SFSR, 23 mi. NE of Tambov; metalworks; wheat.

Bondeno (bōndā'nō), town (pop. 3,463), Ferrara prov., Emilia-Romagna, N central Italy, on Panaro R. and 10 mi. WNW of Ferrara; tomato cannery, foundry.

Bondo (bŏn'dō). **1** Town, Eastern Prov., N Belgian Congo, on Uele R. and 95 mi. NW of Buta; rail terminus in gold-mining and cotton-producing area; cotton ginning; palm products. Has R.C. and Baptist missions and schools, hosp. for Europeans. **2** Village, Equator Prov., W Belgian Congo, on Tshuapa R. and 215 mi. SE of Boende; steamboat landing and trading post in copal-gathering region.

Bondoc Peninsula (bōndōk'), Quezon prov., S Luzon, Philippines, bet. Mompog Pass (W) and Ragay Gulf (E), with its S tip (Bondoc Point) projecting into Sibuyan Sea; c.35 mi. long, 12 mi. wide. Rugged terrain rises to 1,456 ft. in central part of peninsula. Oil is found here.

Bondoc Point, southernmost point of Bondoc Peninsula, Quezon prov., S Luzon, Philippines, in Sibuyan Sea; 13°9'N 122°35'E.

Bondorf, Luxembourg: see BIGONVILLE.

Bondoukou or **Bonduku** (bŏndōō'kōō), town (pop. c.5,400), E Ivory Coast, Fr. West Africa, near Gold Coast border, 200 mi. NNE of Abidjan. Trading center for fertile region yielding coffee, cacao, shea nuts, castor nuts, tobacco, rubber.

Bondowoso (bōndōwō'sō), town (pop. 18,751), E Java, Indonesia, 90 mi. ESE of Surabaya; trade center for agr. area (rice, sugar, peanut, corn).

Bondsville, Mass.: see PALMER.

Bondtown, Va.: see BOND.

Bonduel (bŏndōōĕl'), village (pop. 742), Shawano co., NE Wis., 26 mi. NW of Green Bay, in dairying and poultry-raising area; dairy products.

Bondues (bōdü′), WSW suburb (pop. 784) of Tourcoing, Nord dept., N France, 5 mi. NNE of Lille; oleomargerine mfg.

Bonduku, Fr. West Africa: see BONDOUKOU.

Bondurant (bŏn′dŭrănt″), town (pop. 328), Polk co., central Iowa, 10 mi. NE of Des Moines, in bituminous-coal-mining and agr. area.

Bondville, Vt.: see WINHALL.

Bondy (bōdē′), residential town (pop. 19,473), Seine dept., N central France, a NE suburb of Paris, 7 mi. from Notre Dame Cathedral, on Ourcq Canal; metalworks; mfg. (chemicals, biscuits, custom jewelry). The forest of Bondy (E) formerly sheltered highwaymen.

Bondyuzhski or **Bondyuzhskiy** (bŭndyōō′zhŭskē), town (1926 pop. 5,124), NE Tatar Autonomous SSR, Russian SFSR, 15 mi. NE of Yelabuga; mfg. of explosives. Until c.1940, Bondyuzhski Zavod. Tikhiye Gory, village (1939 pop. under 500), is just S, on right bank of Kama R.; mfg. of building materials; limestone quarrying.

Bône (bōn), city (pop. 77,675), Constantine dept., NE Algeria, on the Mediterranean, 260 mi. E of Algiers, near Tunisia border; 36°53′N 7°45′E. Algeria's 3d seaport and its principal mineral-exporting center, with modern harbor installations for loading phosphates from Tebessa area and iron ore from the Djebel Ouenza. Also ships small quantities of zinc, lead, and antimony; cork from Kabylia's cork-oak forests; wines, cereals, tobacco, citrus fruit, and truck produce from the coastal lowland and the Oued Seybouse valley (just S); sheep and esparto grass from the semi-arid interior. Chief industrial plants are chemical works (fertilizer, sulphuric acid), tobacco factory, briquette factory, and railroad shops. Other plants produce building materials, paint and varnish, brooms and brushes, olive oil, and flour paste. Reached by rail from Constantine (75 mi. SW) and Tebessa (via Souk-Ahras), Bône is also an important commercial center of the N Tell region. Airport is 6 mi. SE. Beautifully situated at E foot of the wooded Edough range, Bône has an old Moslem quarter, dominated by the *casbah* (citadel), and large European dists. The port consists of an outer harbor and of 2 inner loading basins. Just S of Bône are the ruins of anc. *Hippo*, founded as a Carthaginian colony and later ⊙ of the Numidian kings. It flourished under Romans (who called it *Hippo Regius* or *Hippone*), and was a center of early Christianity, the episcopal see (A.D. 396–430) of St. Augustine (for whom a modern basilica has been erected here). Sacked (430–31) by the Vandals, it was refounded (7th cent.) by Arabs on present site of Bône; it became an early center of piracy, and was the target of Pisane and Genoese punitive expeditions (1034). It attained renewed commercial importance in 17th-18th cent. but had declined to a pop. of c.2,000 when occupied by French in 1832. In addition to a large French pop., Bône has an important element of Italian and Maltese origin. Formerly spelled Bona.

Bone, Gulf of (bōnē′), large inlet of Flores Sea, Indonesia, indenting S coast of Celebes, separating SW peninsula from SE peninsula of isl.; 150 mi. N–S, 30–90 mi. E–W. Also spelled Boni.

Bonefro (bônä′frô), town (pop. 4,870), Campobasso prov., Abruzzi e Molise, S central Italy, 7 mi. S of Larino.

Bone Gap, village (pop. 327), Edwards co., SE Ill., 12 mi. WNW of Mount Carmel, in agr. area.

Boneng (bŭnĕng′), village, Khammouane prov., central Laos, on the small Nam Patene and 25 mi. N of Pak Hin Boun; tin-mining center (founded 1933).

Bonerate (bōnĕră′tä), coral island (pop. 3,909; 7 mi. long, 6 mi. wide), Indonesia, in Flores Sea, 70 mi. N of Flores, near Kalao; 7°22′S 121°7′E.

Bo'ness, Scotland: see BORROWSTOUNNESS.

Bonesteel, city (pop. 485), Gregory co., S S.Dak., 20 mi. ESE of Burke; corn, rye, oats.

Bonete (bōnā′tā), town (pop. 1,879), Albacete prov., SE central Spain, 14 mi. W of Almansa; wine, cereals, saffron.

Bonfield, town (pop. 497), SE central Ont., on L. Nosbonsing, 16 mi. ESE of North Bay in dairying, mica-mining region.

Bonfield (bŏn′fēld), village (pop. 143), Kankakee co., NE Ill., 10 mi. W of Kankakee, in agr. area.

Bonfim. 1 City, Bahia, Brazil: see SENHOR DO BONFIM. **2** City, Goiás, Brazil: see SILVÂNIA.

Bong, Wash.: see SPOKANE, city.

Bonga (bōng′gä), town (pop. 3,000), Kaffa prov., SW Ethiopia, on a hill, 50 mi. SW of Jimma; 7°12′N 36°17′E; alt. 5,660 ft. Commercial center (coffee, hides, wax, corn, tea). Former ⊙ Kaffa kingdom.

Bongabon (bōng-ä′bōn, –gä′bōn), town (1939 pop. 3,259; 1948 municipality pop. 14,958), Nueva Ecija prov., central Luzon, Philippines, 15 mi. NE of Cabanatuan, near Pampanga R.; agr. (rice, corn).

Bongabong (–bōng), town (1939 pop. 1,320; 1948 municipality pop. 17,800), on E coast of Mindoro isl., Philippines, on Tablas Strait, 50 mi. SSE of Calapan; rice-growing center.

Bongandanga (bông-gändäng′gä), village, Equator Prov., NW Belgian Congo, on Lopori R. and 200 mi. NE of Coquilhatville; trading center in copal-gathering and palm-oil region; rubber plantations near by. Protestant mission.

Bongao Island (bŏng′gou, bŏng′ou) (□ 4.2; 1939 pop. 974), Tawitawi Group, Sulu prov., Philippines, in Sulu Archipelago, off SW Tawitawi Isl. It is in Bonggaw or Bongaw municipality (bŏng′gô″) (1948 pop. 5,626), which includes Sanga Sanga Isl. and offshore islets.

Bongaon, India: see BANGAON.

Bongará, Peru: see JUMBILLA.

Bongaw, Philippines: see BONGAO ISLAND.

Bonggaw, Philippines: see BONGAO ISLAND.

Bongmieu (bông′myō′), village, Quangnam prov., central Vietnam, at foot of Annamese Cordillera, 45 mi. SSE of Tourane; gold mines.

Bongo Island (bŏng′ō, –gō, Sp. bōng′gō) (1939 pop. 1,262), Cotabato prov., Philippines, off W central coast of Mindanao, in Moro Gulf opposite Cotabato; 6 mi. long.

Bongong, India: see BANGAON.

Bongor (bông-gôr′), town, ⊙ Mayo-Kebbi region (□ 12,700; 1950 pop. 297,800), SW Chad territory, Fr. Equatorial Africa, on Logone R. (Fr. Cameroons border) and 130 mi. S of Fort-Lamy; customs station; cotton ginning, fishing; millet, livestock. Important school for natives. Founded 1910 by Germans.

Bongson (bông′shûn′), town, Binhdinh prov., central Vietnam, on railroad and 45 mi. NNW of Quinhon; coconut-processing center; coconut-oil extraction; rope making; silk spinning, distilling.

Bonham (bŏ′nŭm), city (pop. 7,049), ⊙ Fannin co., NE Texas, near Red R., 25 mi. E of Sherman; trade, shipping center of dairy, cotton, truck area; cotton ginning, cheese making, mfg. of textiles, pumps, mattresses, furniture. A state park and a replica of old Fort Inglish are near by. Platted 1837.

Bonheiden (bônhā′dŭn), town (pop. 4,895), Antwerp prov., N Belgium, 3 mi. E of Mechlin; agr. market (vegetables, potatoes).

Bonhill (bŏnhĭl′), town and parish (pop. 15,565), S central Dumbarton, Scotland, on Leven R. and 3 mi. N of Dumbarton; textile printing.

Bon Homme (bŏ′nŭm), county (□ 580; pop. 9,440), SE S.Dak., on Neb. line, bounded S by Missouri R.; ⊙ Tyndall. Diversified farming; dairy products, grain. Formed 1862.

Bonhomme, Col du (kôl dü bônôm′). **1** Alpine pass on S slopes of Mont Blanc massif, SE France, on main watershed bet. Arve and Isère river basins, and on Haute-Savoie–Savoie border. Its highest point (8,147 ft.) is called Col de la Croix du Bonhomme. **2** Pass (alt. 3,113 ft.) in the central Vosges, E France, on Vosges–Haut-Rhin dept. border and on Saint-Dié–Colmar road, 9 mi. SE of Saint-Dié. Franco-German border, 1871–1919.

Boni, Gulf of, Indonesia: see BONE, GULF OF.

Boniface, Que.: see SAINT BONIFACE DE SHAWINIGAN.

Bonifacio (bōnēfäsyō′, It. bônēfä′chô), town (pop. 1,755), southernmost Corsica, port on Strait of Bonifacio (7.5 mi. wide) facing N tip of Sardinia, 45 mi. SE of Ajaccio; cork and olive oil mfg. Oyster trade. Old town, situated on narrow peninsula which encloses port, has 12th-13th-cent. church in Pisan style, and 16th-cent. ramparts. Oldest Corsican town, founded c.828 on site of a citadel built by Boniface I, count of Tuscany. Sea caves near port entrance.

Bonifacio, Strait of (bônēfä′chô), bet. Point Falcone (Sardinia) and Cape Pertusato (Corsica); joins Tyrrhenian and Mediterranean seas; 7.5 mi. wide. Chief ports: Santa Teresa Gallura (Sardinia), Bonifacio (Corsica).

Bonifati (bônēfä′tē), village (pop. 1,932), Cosenza prov., Calabria, S Italy, near Tyrrhenian Sea, 28 mi NW of Cosenza, in olive- and fig-growing region.

Bonifay (bŏnĭfā′), town (pop. 2,252), ⊙ Holmes co., NW Fla., c.45 mi. N of Panama City, in stock-raising and agr. area.

Bonillo, El (ĕl bōnē′lyō), town (pop. 4,643), Albacete prov., SE central Spain, 22 mi. SSE of Villarrobledo; agr. trade center. Chocolate mfg., tanning, flour milling. Saltworks 9 mi. SSW.

Bonin Islands (bō′nĭn, bōnēn′), Jap. *Ogasawara-gunto*, volcanic group (□ 40; 1940 pop. 7,361), W Pacific, 535 naut. mi. S of Tokyo; 27°45′N 140°E. Comprise 3 main groups: BAILEY ISLANDS, BEECHEY ISLANDS, PARRY ISLANDS. Largest and most important isl. is CHICHI-JIMA, site of the chief harbor. Bananas, betel nut, breadfruit; fruit bats, rats; many species of birds. Mean annual temp. 73°F., rainfall 62.5 in. Produce sugar cane, coca, ornamental coral. Inhabitants: Japanese, Koreans, Formosans. Discovered 1543 by Spaniards; claimed 1875 by Japan, placed 1880 under Tokyo prefecture. After the group was surrendered (1945) to the U.S. with Jap. defeat in Second World War, it was occupied by U.S. forces.

Bonita (bŭnē′tŭ), village (pop. 504), Morehouse parish, NE La., 18 mi. NE of Bastrop, near Ark. line; agr., lumbering; cotton ginning; wood products.

Bonita, Point (bōnē′tŭ, bŭ–), promontory, Marin co., W Calif., on N shore of the Golden Gate at its Pacific entrance, opposite San Francisco; radio beacon station, lighthouse (established 1855).

Bonitas, Las, Venezuela: see LAS BONITAS.

Bonita Springs (bŭnē′tŭ), town (1940 pop. 356), Lee co., SW Fla., 22 mi. S of Fort Myers, on Gulf Coast; mfg. of shell novelties; fishing.

Bonito (bōnē′tōō), city (pop. 3,180), E Pernambuco, NE Brazil, 65 mi. SW of Recife; sugar, coffee, cotton.

Bonito (bônē′tô), village (pop. 1,753), Avellino prov., Campania, S Italy, 6 mi. SW of Ariano Irpino.

Bonito de Santa Fé (bōnē′tōō dĭ sän′tŭ fĕ′), city (pop. 1,171), W Paraíba, NE Brazil, on Ceará border, 30 mi. S of Cajàzeiras; cotton, beans, tobacco. Until 1944, called Bonito.

Bonmahon, Ireland: see BUNMAHON.

Bonn (bŏn, Ger. bôn), city (1946 pop. 94,694; 1950 pop. 111,287), in former Prussian Rhine Prov., W Germany, after 1945 in North Rhine-Westphalia, harbor on left bank of the Rhine (which here enters lower Rhine plain) and 15 mi. SSE of Cologne; 50°44′N 7°4′E. Rail junction; airport (at Hangelar, 3 mi. ENE). Cultural center with noted univ. Well-known stoneware and office-equipment (writing materials, office furniture) industries; also mfg. of light metals, radiators, magnets, pharmaceuticals, dyes, lacquer, porcelain, cardboard. Printing. Romanesque basilica (11th cent.) was restored in 19th cent. The house where Beethoven was born was converted into a mus., and contains numerous manuscripts, letters, and portraits of the composer and his family. Univ., housed in former electoral palace (17th-18th cent.) and at POPPELSDORF, was established 1784, suppressed 1797, and reconstituted 1818. Seat of Old Catholic bishop. Bonn (anc. *Bonna* or *Castra Bonnensia*) was founded by Drusus in c.10 B.C. and soon became hq. of several legions. Of little importance in Middle Ages until fortified c.1240. Residence of archbishops-electors of Cologne from 1263 until captured 1794 by France, by whom it was annexed in 1801. Passed to Prussia in 1815. Occupied by Br., later Fr. troops (1918–26). Heavily bombed during Second World War (destruction about 45%), it was captured (March, 1945) by U.S. troops. In 1948 a constitutional assembly for Western Germany (the parts occupied by U.S., France, and Great Britain) met here, and in 1949 Bonn became ⊙ newly formed German Federal Republic.

Bonnat (bônä′), village (pop. 571), Creuse dept., central France, 11 mi. N of Guéret; stock raising.

Bonndorf (bôn′dôrf), village (pop. 1,885), S Baden, Germany, in Black Forest, 9 mi. SE of Neustadt; rail terminus; lumber milling. Climatic health resort and skiing center (alt. 2,772 ft.).

Bonneau (bŏ′nō), town (pop. 408), Berkeley co., E S.C., 37 mi. N of Charleston, near L. Moultrie.

Bonne Bay (bŏn), inlet (15 mi. long, 4 mi. wide at mouth) of Gulf of St. Lawrence, W N.F., 40 mi. N of Corner Brook, at foot of Gros Morne mtn. On shores are numerous fishing settlements, with salmon and cod canneries.

Bonnechère River (bōnshâr′), SE Ont., rises in Algonquin Provincial Park, flows 120 mi. E, through several lakes, past Renfrew, to Ottawa R. 10 mi. ENE of Renfrew.

Bonner, county (□ 1,736; pop. 14,853), N Idaho; ⊙ Sandpoint. Mtn. area bordering on Mont. and Wash., drained by Priest and Pend Oreille rivers and Clark Fork. Includes Priest L. and part of Kaniksu Natl. Forest in NW, most of Pend Oreille L. in SE. Silver, lead, copper; dairy products, lumber. Formed 1907.

Bonner, town (pop. c.500), Missoula co., W Mont., on the Clark Fork and 5 mi. E of Missoula. Largest sawmill in Mont., producing laths, shingles, and timber for use in mines, here.

Bonne River (bôn), Isère dept., SE France, rises in the Massif du Pelvoux, flows c.20 mi. W through Alpine gorges, past Valbonnais, to the Drac 2 mi. S of La Mure.

Bonners Ferry, village (pop. 1,776), ⊙ Boundary co., N Idaho, on Kootenai R. and 20 mi. from Can. line, 90 mi. NE of Spokane, Wash.; trade center for irrigated agr. area; lumbering. Inc. 1894. Floods on the Kootenai caused much damage May, 1948.

Bonner Springs, city (pop. 2,277), Wyandotte co., NE Kansas, on Kansas R. and 14 mi. W of Kansas City (Kansas), in wheat, potato, and livestock region; mfg. (cement, milling equipment). Small gas wells near by. Inc. 1898.

Bonnet, Lac du (läk dü bônā′), lake (20 mi. long, 1–4 mi. wide), SE Man., 55 mi. NE of Winnipeg; expansion of Winnipeg R. At N end are McArthur and Great Falls, hydroelectric stations; at S end is Lac du Bonnet village.

Bonnétable (bônātä′blü), town (pop. 2,409), Sarthe dept., W France, 17 mi. NE of Le Mans; agr. market (hemp, apples, potatoes), furniture mfg. Has restored 15th-cent. château.

Bonnet Carre Floodway (bŏ′nā kără′), SE La., emergency flood-control spillway bet. left bank of the Mississippi, c.25 mi. above New Orleans, and L. Pontchartrain; c.7 mi. long; completed 1935.

Bonne Terre (bŏn târ′, bŏ′nē târ), city (pop. 3,533), St. Francois co., E Mo., in the St. Francois Mts. near Big R., 5 mi. N of Flat River; lead-mining and railroad-shipping center. Grain; clothing, cooperages; limestone quarrying, cobalt, nickel, zinc mining. Inc. 1864.

Bonnet Mountain (10,615 ft.), SW Alta., near B.C. border, in Rocky Mts., in Banff Natl. Park, 24 mi. NW of Banff; 51°26′N 115°53′W.

Bonneuil-Matours (bônû'ē-mätōōr'), village (pop. 651), Vienne dept., W central France, on Vienne R. and 9 mi. S of Châtellerault; mfg. of clothing. Hydroelectric plant.

Bonneuil-sur-Marne (-sür-märn'), town (pop. 2,446), Seine dept., N central France, a SE suburb of Paris, 8 mi. from Notre Dame Cathedral; port on left bank of the Marne opposite Saint-Maur-des-Fossés; cement and flour products.

Bonneval (bônväl'), town (pop. 2,364), Eure-et-Loir dept., NW central France, on the Loir and 19 mi. SSW of Chartres; metalworking, basketmaking, cider distilling, poultry shipping. Its old Benedictine abbey houses insane asylum. Damaged in Second World War.

Bonneville (bônvēl'), village (pop. 1,496), Haute-Savoie dept., SE France, on the Arve and 15 mi. SE of Geneva; trade center of FAUCIGNY valley; cheese mfg. Hydroelectric plants near by.

Bonneville (bŏ'nùvĭl, bŏ'nē–, bŏn'vĭl), county (□ 1,846; pop. 30,210), SE Idaho; ⊙ Idaho Falls. Mtn. area bordering on Wyo. Irrigated Snake R. valley extends through NW; parts of Targhee and Caribou natl. forests are in E. Sugar beets, seed peas, beans, potatoes, rye, livestock. Formed 1911.

Bonneville, La (lä bônvēl'), village (pop. 967), Eure dept., NW France, on the Iton and 6 mi. WSW of Évreux; brass mfg.

Bonneville, Lake (bŏ'nùvĭl, bŏ'nē–, bŏn'vĭl), enormous, prehistoric body of water that once covered much of what is now Utah and extended into Nev. and Idaho. Thought to have lasted 25,000 years and to have been 350 mi. long, 150 mi. wide. Its various levels are indicated by wide terraces formed by action of its waves on mountains (Wasatch Range) near Great Salt and Utah lakes (remnants of L. Bonneville). Estimated height above sea level 5,200 ft., max. depth more than 1,000 ft. Delta deposits formed by its tributaries account for fertility of soil in river valleys near Salt Lake City. Lake was named after Benjamin de Bonneville, American explorer.

Bonneville Dam, in Columbia R. (144 mi. above its mouth), bet. Oregon and Wash., c.40 mi. E of Portland. Built 1933–37; designed to supply power and aid navigation. Spillway (over-all length 1,450 ft., average height 170 ft.) extends S from Wash. shore to small Bradford Isl., in midstream. Powerhouse is in stream bet. isl. and Oregon shore; has 10 generators (installed 1938–43) with total rated capacity of 518,400 kw. Navigation lock (76 ft. wide, 500 ft. long, 24 ft. deep; vertical lift 30–70 ft.) is at S end of powerhouse, adjoining Oregon shore; permits passage of vessels up to 8,000 tons. Ladder and lock at N end of spillway assist fish migration.

Bonneville Salt Flats, Utah: see GREAT SALT LAKE DESERT.

Bonnevoie (bônvwä'), Ger. *Bonneweg* (bô'nùvāk), S suburb of Luxembourg city, S Luxembourg; copper, bronze, and aluminum casting.

Bonneweg, Luxembourg: see BONNEVOIE.

Bonney, Mount (10,194 ft.), SE B.C., in Selkirk Mts., in Glacier Natl. Park, 30 mi. ENE of Revelstoke; 51°12'N 117°32'W.

Bonney Lake, town (pop. 275), Pierce co., W central Wash., 15 mi. ESE of Tacoma.

Bonnie, village (pop. 257), Jefferson co., S Ill., 7 mi. S of Mount Vernon, in agr. area.

Bonnie Blue, Va.: see BONNY BLUE.

Bonnières-sur-Seine (bônyâr'-sür-sĕn'), village (pop. 1,542), Seine-et-Oise dept., N central France, on left bank of the Seine and 7 mi. WNW of Mantes-Gassicourt; forges; assembling of sewing machines, petroleum refining.

Bonnieux (bônyû'), village (pop. 535), Vaucluse dept., SE France, on N slope of Montagne du Lubéron, 6 mi. SW of Apt; almonds, cherries, wine. Stone quarries near by.

Bonnievale, village (pop. 1,553), SE Cape Prov., U. of So. Afr., on Breede R. and 20 mi. WNW of Swellendam; grain, feed crops, fruit.

Bönnigheim (bû'nĭkh-hīm), town (pop. 3,537), N Württemberg, Germany, after 1945 in Württemberg-Baden, 6 mi. NNW of Bietigheim; wine.

Bonny, town (pop. 8,690), Owerri prov., Eastern Provinces, S Nigeria, minor port and river pilot station on Gulf of Guinea, at mouth of Bonny R. (an arm of Niger R. delta), and 25 mi. SSE of Port Harcourt; fisheries; palm oil and kernels, hardwood, rubber. Flourished (15th-19th cent.) in European slave trade.

Bonny Blue or **Bonnie Blue,** coal-mining village (1940 pop. 2,387), Lee co., SW Va., in the Cumberlands at Ky. line, 16 mi. W of Big Stone Gap.

Bonnybridge, town in Falkirk parish, SE Stirling, Scotland; coal mining, refractory-brick making.

Bonnyman (bŏ'nēmăn), mining village (1940 pop. 687), Perry co., SE Ky., in Cumberland foothills, 4 mi. NW of Hazard; bituminous coal.

Bonnyrigg and Lasswade (–wād'), burgh (1931 pop. 4,481; 1951 census 5,434), E central Midlothian, Scotland. Includes Bonnyrigg (pop. 3,593), 7 mi. SE of Edinburgh, with carpet factory and cement-works. Just NW of Bonnyrigg, on North Esk R., is Lasswade (pop. 888), with paper mills. For some years it was residence of Sir Walter Scott. There are remains of Norman church, with grave of William Drummond. Just S of Bonnyrigg is Hawthornden, on North Esk R., birthplace and longtime residence of William Drummond.

Bonny-sur-Loire (bônē'-sür-lwär'), village (pop. 1,060), Loiret dept., N central France, on right bank of Loire R. and 11 mi. NNW of Cosne; pottery mfg. Captured (1429) from English by Joan of Arc.

Bonnyville, village (pop. 730), E Alta., near Sask. border, on small lake, 65 mi. N of Vermilion; lumber and flour milling, dairying.

Bono (bô'nô), village (pop. 4,518), Sassari prov., N central Sardinia, at SE foot of Monte Rasu, 33 mi. SE of Sassari.

Bono (bō'nō), town (pop. 352), Craighead co., NE Ark., 8 mi. NW of Jonesboro.

Bononia, France: see BOULOGNE.

Bononia, Italy: see BOLOGNA, city.

Bonorva (bônôr'vä), town (pop. 7,076), Sassari prov., NW Sardinia, 25 mi. SSE of Sassari, in agr. area. Numerous nuraghi and Roman ruins near by.

Bonpas Creek (bŏn'păs"), SE Ill., rises E of Olney, flows c.40 mi. S to Wabash R. at Grayville.

Bon-Port, France: see PONT-DE-L'ARCHE.

Bonsall, town and parish (pop. 1,173), central Derby, England, 2 mi. SW of Matlock; agr. market; produces cement. Formerly a lead-mining center. Has 14th-cent. church, and 17th-cent. inn.

Bon Secour (bŏn" sùkōōr'), village (pop. c.500), Baldwin co., SW Ala.; fishing resort on inlet (crossed by Intracoastal Waterway) of Bon Secour Bay (SE arm of Mobile Bay) and 32 mi. SE of Mobile.

Bon Secours, Que.: see L'ISLET, village.

Bonsecours, France: see BLOSSEVILLE-BONSECOURS.

Bon Success, Br. Guiana: see LETHEM.

Bontebok National Park (bŏn'tĭbŏk") (□ 2.8), SW Cape Prov., U. of So. Afr., near Cape Agulhas; reserve for bontebok; established 1938.

Bonthain (bōntīn'), town (pop. 6,711), SW Celebes, Indonesia, port on Flores Sea, 55 mi. SE of Macassar, at foot of Mt. Lompobatang; fisheries; ships copra and kapok. Also called Bantaeng.

Bonthain Peak, Indonesia: see LOMPOBATANG, MOUNT.

Bonthe (bŏn'tē), town, Sierra Leone colony, on E shore of Sherbro Isl., on Sherbro R. (inlet of the Atlantic; ferry) and 85 mi. SE of Freetown. Commercial center and 2d port of Sierra Leone; exports palm oil and kernels, piassava, cacao. Has R.C. and United Brethren in Christ missions. Together with York Isl. and other islets, Bonthe constitutes Sherbro Judicial District (□ 12.5; pop. 7,612), a separate administrative entity within the colony. Town is also hq. of Bonthe dist. (□ 1,350; pop. 100,350), which includes all of Sherbro Isl. and adjacent mainland and forms part of South-Western Prov., Sierra Leone protectorate.

Bontoc, sub-province, Philippines: see MOUNTAIN PROVINCE.

Bontoc (bŏntŏk', Sp. bōntōk'), town (1939 pop. 3,875; 1948 municipality pop. 15,005), Bontoc subprov., Mountain Prov., N Luzon, Philippines, on Chico R. and 55 mi. NNE of Baguio; ⊙ Mountain Prov. Sulphur mining, lumbering, rice growing.

Bon Tsagan Nor or **Böön Tsagaan Nuur** (both: bûn' tsä'gän nôr', nōōr'), salt lake (□ 90) of SW central Mongolian People's Republic, in Gobi desert, 180 mi. SE of Uliassutai; 15 mi. long, 10 mi. wide; alt. 4,383 ft. Receives right arm of Baidarik R.

Bony (bônē'), village (pop. 91), Aisne dept., N France, 10 mi. NNW of Saint-Quentin. Here Americans broke through Hindenburg Line in Sept., 1918. U.S. donated a new town hall to Bony after First World War. Just SW is Somme American cemetery with 1,833 graves.

Bonyha, Rumania: see BAHNEA.

Bonyhad (bô'nyùhäd), Hung. *Bonyhád,* town (pop. 8,333), Tolna co., S Hungary, 9 mi. SW of Szekszard; vegetable oil, cognac, flour. Ger. pop. in vicinity engaged in agr.

Bönyretalap (bû'nyù-rätŏlŏp), Hung. *Bőnyrétalap,* town (pop. 3,015), Györ-Moson co., NW Hungary, 10 mi. E of Györ; grain, honey; cattle, hogs, horses.

Bóo (bō), village (pop. 1,076), Oviedo prov., NW Spain, on Aller R. and 17 mi. SE of Oviedo; coal.

Booischot (bōĭs'hôt), town (pop. 4,510), Antwerp prov., N Belgium, 9 mi. E of Mechlin; agr. market (vegetables, potatoes).

Book Cliffs, E Utah and W Colo., rugged escarpment (c.1,500 ft. high) N of Colorado R., extending through parts of Carbon and Grand counties, Utah, and Mesa and Garfield counties, Colo. Form S limit of East Tavaputs Plateau in E Utah and of Roan Plateau in W Colo. Remnants of Basket-Maker culture have been found near cliffs in Carbon co. Roan or Brown Cliffs are parallel escarpment (just N) extending NE into Colo.

Booker, town (pop. 619), on Lipscomb-Ochiltree co. line, extreme N Texas, in high plains of the Panhandle, c.70 mi. W of Woodward, Okla.; grain elevator, cold-storage plant.

Boolaroo (bōōlùrōō'), town (pop. 1,478), E New South Wales, Australia, 10 mi. WSW of Newcastle; sulphide works.

Boolburra, village, E Queensland, Australia, on Dawson R. and 55 mi. WSW of Rockhampton; cotton.

Booleroo Centre (bōō'lùrōō'), village (pop. 551), S South Australia, 29 mi. NE of Port Pirie; wool, wheat.

Boom (bōm), town (pop. 19,596), Antwerp prov., N Belgium, on Rupel R. and 9 mi. S of Antwerp; bricks, glassworks.

Boom, El, Nicaragua: see EL BOOM.

Boomer, village (pop. 2,096, with adjacent Harewood), Fayette co., S central W.Va., on Kanawha R. and 22 mi. SE of Charleston, in coal-mining and industrial area.

Boom Gorge (bŭōm'), Rus. *Boomskoye Ushchel'ye,* defile along Chu R., in Kirghiz SSR, bet. Kirghiz Range (W) and the Kungei Ala-Tau (E), 15 mi. W of Rybachye; traversed by road and railroad. Site of ORTO-TOKOI reservoir. Also spelled Buam Gorge.

Boomkensdiep (bōm'kùnzdēp), strait (3.5 mi. wide) of North Sea, NW Netherlands, bet. Vlieland isl. (SW) and Terschelling isl. (NE); leads from North Sea to the Waddenzee.

Boomplaats (bōm'pläts"), hill (3,838 ft.), NE Cape Prov., U. of So. Afr., near Orange R., 19 mi. S of Hopetown. Scene (July 29, 1848) of important battle in which Voortrekkers under Andries Pretorius defeated troops of Sir Harry Smith, governor of Cape Colony.

Boonah (bōō'nù), town (pop. 1,323), SE Queensland, Australia, 29 mi. SW of Brisbane; agr. center (corn, sugar, bananas).

Boone. 1 County (□ 602; pop. 16,260), N Ark.; ⊙ Harrison. Bounded N by Mo. line; drained by small tributaries of White R.; situated in Ozark region. Agr. (fruit, cotton, truck, livestock); timber. Mfg. at Harrison. Lead and zinc mines, marble deposits, glass sand. Formed 1869. **2** County (□ 283; pop. 17,070), N Ill., on Wis. line (N); ⊙ Belvidere. Drained by Kishwaukee R. Agr. (livestock, corn, wheat, oats, truck, poultry). Mfg. (dairy and grain products, canned foods, sewing machines, scales, machine parts, clothing, hardware). Formed 1837. **3** County (□ 427; pop. 23,993), central Ind.; ⊙ Lebanon. Diversified mfg. at Lebanon; agr. (grain, livestock, truck; dairy products). Drained by Sugar and Raccoon creeks and Eel R. Formed 1830. **4** County (□ 573; pop. 28,139), central Iowa; ⊙ Boone. Prairie agr. area (hogs, cattle, poultry, corn, oats, soybeans) drained by Des Moines R. and Beaver Creek; bituminous-coal deposits mined in central region. Has state parks. Formed 1846. **5** County (□ 252; pop. 13,015), N Ky.; ⊙ Burlington. Bounded N and W by Ohio R., separating co. from Ohio (N) and Ind. (W); drained by several creeks. Gently rolling agr. area (burley tobacco, corn, livestock, poultry, dairy products, fruit) in outer Bluegrass region. Includes Big Bone Lick near Burlington. Formed 1798. **6** County (□ 683; pop. 48,432), central Mo., on Missouri R.; ⊙ Columbia. Corn, wheat, oats, hay, livestock; lumber, coal; mfg. at Columbia and Centralia. Formed 1820. **7** County (□ 683; pop. 10,721), E central Nebr.; ⊙ Albion. Agr. region drained by Cedar R. and Beaver Creek. Livestock, grain, dairy and poultry produce. Formed 1875. **8** County (□ 501; pop. 33,173), SW W.Va.; ⊙ Madison. On Allegheny Plateau; drained by Coal and Mud rivers and tributaries. Bituminous-coal-mining region; natural-gas and oil fields; some agr. (livestock, fruit, tobacco); timber. Formed 1847.

Boone. 1 City (pop. 12,164), ⊙ Boone co., central Iowa, near Des Moines R., 35 mi. NNW of Des Moines; trade, railroad, and mining center, with repair shops, ironworks, and deposits of bituminous coal, clay, and gravel. Has a jr. col. Ledges State Park near by. Laid out 1865 by the railroad, it annexed in 1887 the near-by rival town of Boonesboro (founded 1851). **2** Town (pop. 2,973), ⊙ Watauga co., NW N.C., 22 mi. NNW of Lenoir, near the Blue Ridge Parkway; burley tobacco market and cattle center; mtn. resort; hosiery mfg., sawmilling, food canning. Seat of Appalachian State Teachers Col. Settled in 18th cent., it is in territory once occupied by Watauga Association.

Boone Mill, Va.: see BOONES MILL.

Boone River, N central Iowa, rises in Hancock co., flows 100 mi. S, past Webster City, to Des Moines R. 17 mi. N of Boone.

Boonesboro, village, Clark co., central Ky., on Kentucky R. and 8 mi. SW of Winchester; small resort, with bathing beach. Monument here to Daniel Boone is on site of Fort Boonesboro, established 1775 at end of Boone's Trace (an offshoot of Wilderness Road) by Boone and a company of N.C. men under sponsorship of Transylvania Company. Fort was seat of govt. of Transylvania for several years; frequently attacked by Indians.

Boones Mill or **Boone Mill,** town (pop. 335), Franklin co., S Va., in Blue Ridge foothills, 10 mi. S of Roanoke; wood products.

Booneville. 1 City (pop. 2,433), a ⊙ Logan co., W Ark., 32 mi. SE of Fort Smith and on Petit Jean R. Market for agr. area (fruit, cotton, truck, livestock, poultry); dairy products; sawmilling, cotton ginning; railroad yards. Hq. for fishermen and hunters. Near by is state tuberculosis sanatorium. **2** Town (pop. 165), ⊙ Owsley co., E central Ky., on South Fork Kentucky R. and 32 mi. WNW of Hazard, in the Cumberlands. **3** Town (pop. 3,295),

⊙ Prentiss co., NE Miss., 20 mi. S of Corinth, in agr. and lumbering area; cotton, corn, hay. Mfg. of brick, tile, shirts; lumber milling; cotton gins. Settled 1859, inc. 1869. In Civil War, scene of a Union victory won by Gen. P. H. Sheridan (1862).

Boon Island, off SW Maine, small lighthouse isl. 10 mi. E of York Harbor.

Boonsboro, town (pop. 1,071), Washington co., W Md., at W base of South Mtn. and 11 mi. SSE of Hagerstown. Scenic Crystal Grottoes attract tourists. Near by is Washington Monument State Park.

Boonton (bōōn'tun), town (pop. 7,163), Morris co., N N.J., on Rockaway R. and 9 mi. NNE of Morristown; mfg. (plastics, electrical and radio equipment, hosiery, bronze powder), agr. (dairy products, livestock, truck). Parsippany Reservoir (just S) is impounded by Boonton Dam (114 ft. high, 3,100 ft. long; completed 1905) in Rockaway R. Boonton was iron center in mid-19th cent. First bakelite factory here. Settled 1760, inc. 1867.

Böön Tsagaan Nuur, Mongolia: see BON TSAGAN NOR.

Boonville. 1 Village (pop. c.750), Mendocino co., NW Calif., in Anderson Valley (apple orchards), in the Coast Ranges, 12 mi. SW of Ukiah. **2** City (pop. 5,092), ⊙ Warrick co., SW Ind., 18 mi. ENE of Evansville; trade center for bituminous-coal-mining and agr. area (grain, soybeans, fruit, tomatoes); mfg. (underwear, food and dairy products, tile, brick). Scales Lake State Forest is near by. Platted 1818. **3** City (pop. 6,686), ⊙ Cooper co., central Mo., on Missouri R. and 23 mi. W of Columbia; agr.; mfg. (corncob pipes, shoes, flour, dairy products). Kemper Military School (a jr. col.); state park and training school for boys near by. Platted 1817. Union forces won a Civil War battle near here in 1861. **4** Village (pop. 2,329), Oneida co., central N.Y., 20 mi. NNE of Rome; trade center for dairying region; resort; mfg. (athletic equipment, furniture, machinery); timber. Walter D. Edmonds b. here. Settled c.1791, inc. 1855. **5** Town (pop. 502), Yadkin co., N N.C., 8 mi. E of Elkin; mfg. of baskets, wood and grain products.

Boort (bōōrt), village (pop. 711), N central Victoria, Australia, 140 mi. NW of Melbourne, near Loddon R.; livestock.

Boos (bō), village (pop. 433), Seine-Inférieure dept., N France, 6 mi. SE of Rouen; truck gardening.

Boothbay (bōōth'bā'), town (pop. 1,559), Lincoln co., S Maine, on peninsula S of Wiscasset; resort, boatbuilding, fishing center; sea food canned. Settled as Newagen 1630, inc. 1764. **Boothbay Harbor** (bōōth'bā), town (pop. 2,290), also a resort, was set off in 1889. Has summer theater (1934), U.S. fish hatchery (1903).

Boothia, Gulf of (bōō'thēu), Northwest Territories, inlet (250 mi. long) of the Arctic Ocean, bet. Boothia Peninsula (W) and Baffin Isl. and Melville Peninsula (E); 67°10'–70°N 85°30'–92°W. Up to 130 mi. wide.

Boothia Peninsula, Franklin Dist., Northwest Territories, extends 190 mi. N into Arctic Ocean from Keewatin Dist. mainland; 69°26'–71°59'N 91°15'–96°40'W. Up to 130 mi. wide, connected S with mainland by 20-mi.-wide Boothia Isthmus; separated from King William Isl. (SW) by James Ross Strait, from Prince of Wales Isl. (NW) by Franklin Strait, and from Somerset Isl. (N) by Bellot Strait. Hilly and rugged E coast is washed by the Gulf of Boothia. Formerly called Boothia Felix, it was discovered and explored (1829–33) by Sir James Ross, who in 1831 established the position of the magnetic north pole here at 70°50'N 96°46'W; later explored by Sir John Franklin (1847–48) and by Roald Amundsen (1903–05), who relocated the magnetic pole at 70°30'N 95°30'W; in 1948 the magnetic pole was on Prince of Wales Isl., at 73°N 100°W. N part of peninsula is sometimes called Cockburn Land.

Booth Point, S King William Isl., Franklin Dist., Northwest Territories, on Simpson Strait, opposite Adelaide Peninsula; 68°29'N 96°28'W.

Boothroyd, England: see DEWSBURY.

Boothstown, England: see TYLDESLEY.

Boothville, village (1940 pop. 538), Plaquemines parish, extreme SE La., on W bank (levee) of the Mississippi and 50 mi. SE of New Orleans; fishing, fur trapping; oysters.

Bootle (bōō'tul). **1** Village and parish (pop. 684), SW Cumberland, England, 5 mi. SSE of Ravenglass; cattle raising, dairying. Has church containing 15th-cent. font. **2** County borough (1931 pop. 76,770; 1951 census 74,302), SW Lancashire, England, on Mersey R. just NNW of Liverpool; major port (with extensive docks and warehouses), integrated into Liverpool port system; leather tanning, flour milling, engineering, tin smelting; mfg. of chemicals, soap, oleomargarine, paint, cables; lumberyards.

Booué (bōwā'), town, ⊙ Ogooué-Ivindo region (□ 23,550; pop. 35,900), NE Gabon, Fr. Equatorial Africa, on Ogooué R. and 170 mi. ESE of Libreville; gold mining. Protestant mission.

Bopa (bō'pä), village, S Dahomey, Fr. West Africa, on N shore of L. Ahémé, 45 mi. WNW of Porto-Novo; palm kernels, palm oil. R.C. and Protestant missions.

Bopfingen (bôp'fĭng-un), town (pop. 2,812), N Württemberg, Germany, after 1945 in Württemberg-Baden, 12 mi. E of Aalen; grain. Has early-Gothic church. Created free imperial city in 1384.

Bo Phloi (bô' ploi'), village (1937 pop. 1,421), Kanchanaburi prov., S Thailand, 20 mi. N of Kanchanaburi; ruby and sapphire mining.

Bopi River (bō'pē), La Paz dept., W Bolivia; formed by confluence of La Paz and Tamampaya rivers 20 mi. ENE of Chulumani; flows c.50 mi. N, joining Santa Elena R. at Huachi to form BENI RIVER. Sometimes name Bopi is applied to 70-mi. length of Beni R. above mouth of Kaka R.

Boppard (bô'pärt), town (pop. 7,189), in former Prussian Rhine Prov., W Germany, after 1945 in Rhineland-Palatinate, on left bank of the Rhine (landing) and 8 mi. S of Coblenz; rail junction; wine. Has remains of Roman fort; late-Romanesque church; Gothic church. Of Celtic origin; fortified by Romans. Free imperial city from 12th cent. until 1312, when it came to electors of Trier.

Boquerón (bōkärōn'), minor port of Guantánamo, Oriente prov., E Cuba, on Guantánamo Bay, opposite Caimanera, and just N of U.S. naval reserve.

Boquerón, village (pop. 452), Chiriquí prov., W Panama, on lower slopes of the volcano Chiriquí, near Inter-American Highway, 11 mi. WNW of David; coffee, cacao, livestock, lumber.

Boquerón, department (□ 64,876; pop. 38,937), N Paraguay, in the Chaco; ⊙ Mariscal Estigarribia. Bounded by Bolivia (N and W), Brazil (SE, Paraguay R.), Argentina (SW, Pilcomayo R.), and the Río Verde (S). Consists of low grasslands, marshes, dense jungles, and scattered forests. Has humid, tropical climate; however, there is a scarcity of drinking water. Among its mineral resources are iron ores on Paraguay R. and some petroleum deposits (N). Produces primarily quebracho and other hardwood. Along Paraguay R. are cattle-raising establishments. The Mennonite settlements (S) grow mainly cotton. Puerto Sastre, Puerto Casado, and Puerto Pinasco (SE) are lumbering and stock-raising centers. The area, heavily disputed in Chaco War (1932–35) by Bolivia and Paraguay, was awarded to Paraguay in 1938. Boquerón dept. was set up 1944.

Boquerón, village, SW Puerto Rico, on Mona Passage, on railroad and 12 mi. S of Mayagüez; saltworks.

Boquerón Abad (bōkärōn' äbädh') or **El Boquerón,** narrow gorge on Huánuco-Loreto dept. border, N central Peru, in Cordillera Azul, gateway to Amazon R. basin. Crossed by bridges. Through it passes trans-Andean highway to Pucallpa. Sometimes Boquerón Padre Abad.

Boquete (bōkā'tā), town (pop. 1,426), Chiriquí prov., W Panama, on Caldera R. and 22 mi. N of David, railhead at E foot of Chiriquí volcano. Resort (hotels); agr. (coffee, potatoes), lumbering. Also called Bajo Boquete.

Boquillas Canyon, Texas: see BIG BEND NATIONAL PARK.

Boquiñeni (bōkēnyā'nē), village (pop. 1,079), Saragossa prov., NE Spain, on the Ebro and 23 mi. NW of Saragossa; sugar beets, olive oil, wine, cereals.

Bor (bōr), town, Upper Nile prov., S Anglo-Egyptian Sudan, on right bank of the Bahr el Jebel (White Nile) and 230 mi. S of Malakal; 6°12'N 31°34'E; livestock raising. Airfield. Military post. Area inhabited by Dinka tribes.

Bor or **Bor u Tachova** (bôr' ōō' täkhôvä), Ger. *Haid* (hīt), village (pop. 958), W Bohemia, Czechoslovakia, 8 mi. SE of Tachov; rail junction; noted for making of wooden puppets.

Bor (bôr), town (pop. 10,665), Nigde prov., S central Turkey, on railroad and 9 mi. SW of Nigde; rye, wheat, barley.

Bor (bôr), city (1939 pop. over 10,000), W Gorki oblast, Russian SFSR, port on Volga R., opposite Gorki (ferry); metalworks, flour mills, glassworks. Became city in 1938. Shipyards (6 mi. SE) at Imeni V. M. MOLOTOVA.

Bor (bôr), town (pop. 12,261), E Serbia, Yugoslavia, on narrow-gauge railroad and 16 mi. NNW of Zajecar. Copper-mining center (largest in Yugoslavia and one of largest in Europe), in operation since 1906; copper-concentrating plant, smelter, refinery. Gold and silver produced as by-products.

Bora-Bora (bō'rä bō'rä), volcanic island (□ 15; pop. 1,683), Leeward group, SOCIETY ISLANDS, Fr. Oceania, S Pacific, 25 mi. NW of Raiatea; 4 mi. long, 2.5 mi. wide. Mountainous, with Mt. Taimanu, highest peak (2,379 ft.). Large lagoon surrounded by coral islets; good harbor. Produces copra, oranges, vanilla, tobacco. Chief town, Vaitape. Sometimes spelled Porapora.

Borabu (bô'räbōō'), village (1937 pop. 13,797), Mahasarakham prov., E Thailand, in Korat Plateau, 20 mi. SW of Mahasarakham; rice.

Boradli, Ras (räs' böräd'lē), cape on SW shore of Aden peninsula; 12°46'30"N 44°59'E. Site of telegraph station.

Bora Holm, Scotland: see BORAY HOLM.

Borah Peak (12,655 ft.), in Lost River Range, S central Idaho, c.50 mi. NE of Hailey. Highest point in state.

Borama (bōrä'mä), town, W Br. Somaliland, on Ethiopian border, in plateau, 65 mi. WNW of Hargeisa; stock-raising center (camels, sheep, and goats); sorghum, corn, beans. Customs station. Hq. Borama-Zeila dist. Formerly spelled Buramo.

Boras (bōōrōs'), Swedish *Borås*, city (1950 pop. 58,076), Alvsborg co., SW Sweden, on Viska R. 35 mi. E of Goteborg; 57°43'N 12°57'E; rail junction; textile-milling center, with dyeing, printing, and hosiery-knitting works. Site of textile tradeschools. Has 17th-cent. church, crafts mus. Town chartered 1622.

Boraure (bōrou'rā), town (pop. 846), Yaracuy state, N Venezuela, 7 mi. SSW of San Felipe; sugar, cacao, corn, fruit.

Boray Holm or **Bora Holm** (both: bô'rù), islet of the Orkneys, Scotland, just S of Gairsay isl.

Borazjan (bōräzjän'), town (1940 pop. 8,543), Seventh Prov., in Fars, S Iran, 30 mi. NE of Bushire and on road to Shiraz; grain, dates. Surrounding area was formerly known as Dashtistan, inhabited by seminomads known for their patriotism and their stand against British troops prior to First World War.

Borba (bôr'bù), city (pop. 1,272), E Amazonas, Brazil, steamer and hydroplane landing on right bank of Madeira R., and 95 mi. SSE of Manaus; rubber, guarana.

Borba, town (pop. 3,639), Évora dist., S central Portugal, on railroad and 7 mi. SE of Estremoz; road junction; winegrowing center, also noted for its white-marble quarries; olive-oil pressing, soap and earthenware mfg. Has a 16th-cent. church and convent. Emeralds formerly found in area.

Borbeck (bôr'bĕk), industrial district (since 1913) of ESSEN, W Germany, near Rhine-Herne Canal, 3 mi. NW of city center; ironworking center; coal mining. Has 14th-cent. castle.

Borbollón, El, Argentina: see EL BORBOLLÓN.

Borbon (bôrbōn'), town (1939 pop. 2,450; 1948 municipality pop. 18,333), N Cebu isl., Philippines, on Camotes Sea, 29 mi. NNE of Cebu city; agr. center (corn, coconuts).

Borborema (bôrbōrā'mù), city (pop. 2,763), central São Paulo, Brazil, on railroad and 45 mi. N of Bauru; pottery mfg., distilling; coffee, cotton, cattle.

Borborema Plateau, tableland of NE Brazil, extends across central Paraíba and S Rio Grande do Norte states, and forms E outlier of NE Brazilian highlands. Average alt., 1,700 ft. Steep escarpment (E) overlooks coastal lowland. A highly mineralized area, recent surveys of which have revealed important copper, tin ore, tungsten, columbite, tantalite, and beryl deposits. Picuí is chief mining center. Inadequate communications.

Borburata (bôrbōōrä'tä), town (pop. 578), Carabobo state, N Venezuela, near Caribbean coast, 4 mi. SE of Puerto Cabello; coconuts, cacao, corn.

Borby (bôr'bē), N suburb of ECKERNFÖRDE, NW Germany.

Borca (bôr'kä), village (pop. 760), Jassy prov., NE Rumania, on Bistrita R. and 45 mi. E of Piatra-Neamt; health resort (alt. 1,968 ft.) on E slopes of the Moldavian Carpathians; mineral springs; lumbering.

Borchalo, Georgian SSR: see MARNEULI.

Borcka (bôrchkä'), Turkish *Borçka*, village (pop. 2,071), Coruh prov., NE Turkey, on Coruh R. and 15 mi. NNW of Coruh, near USSR line; grain. Formerly Yenikol.

Borculo or **Borkelo** (both: bôr'külō), town (pop. 2,596), Gelderland prov., E Netherlands, on the Berkel, 16 mi. SW of Enschede; parchment-paper industry, bleaching plants, cigar mfg. Also spelled Borkeloo.

Borda da Mata (bôr'dù dä mä'tù), city (pop. 2,763), SW Minas Gerais, Brazil, on railroad and 15 mi. WSW of Pouso Alegre; dairying.

Bor Dag (bôr'dä), Turkish *Bor Dağ*, peak (7,943 ft.), SW Turkey, in Mentese Mts., 12 mi. SW of Acipayam.

Bord-de-Mer-Jean-Rabel, Haiti: see JEAN-RABEL.

Bordeaux (bôrdō'), anc. *Burdigala*, city (pop. 238,653), ⊙ Gironde dept., on Garonne R. and 300 mi. SSW of Paris; 44°50'N 0°34'W; leading port and chief economic and educational center of SW France; principally known for its trade in superfine wines (MÉDOC, Sauternes, GRAVES, Saint-Émilion), it also engages in processing the produce of a rich agr. hinterland (cereals, cattle, tobacco, vegetables). Has copper and iron foundries, metalworks (naval construction, electrical and refrigeration equipment, precision instruments), distilleries, chemical and rubber mfg. plants. Produces bottles, corrugated cartons and crating for wine exports, hosiery, footwear, and a variety of foods. Imported colonial hardwoods are worked and petroleum is refined. The harbor, undamaged during Second World War, carries on much trade formerly cleared through Le Havre and Marseilles. Bordeaux has a univ. (founded 1441), commercial and technical schools, and a hydrographic institute. The Place des Quinconces (with statues of Montaigne and Montesquieu) is the center of the city. Chief sites are the Gothic 12th-15th-cent. cathedral of St. André; the 18th-cent. theater; and the numerous fine 18th-cent. bldgs. which have made Bordeaux attractive. There are several excellent art museums. As ⊙ Aquitaine, Bordeaux has prospered since Roman times. Archiepiscopal see since 4th cent. After several centuries of Visigothic and Frankish domination, it recovered as the seat (11th cent.) of the dukes of Aquitaine. Assumed commercial importance while in English hands (1154–1453). Restored to France, it became ⊙ Guienne prov. under Louis XI, who established the powerful *parlement* of Bordeaux and granted privileges to the univ. The city's prosperity in 18th cent. was marked by architectural improvements. Bordeaux was center of the Girondists in the Fr. Revolution and site of Natl. Assembly of 1871 which established the Third Republic. In 1914 and again in 1940 it became temporary capital of Fr. govt. Suffered some damage in Second World War. Bordeaux is surrounded by a belt of populous suburbs, including Le Bouscat and Caudéran (NW), Talence and Bègles (S), Mérignac and Pessac (W), Cenon and Floirac (E; on right bank of the Garonne).

Bordeaux Mountain (bôrdō'), highest peak (1,277 ft.) of St. John Isl., U.S. Virgin Isls., 13 mi. E of Charlotte Amalie; 18°20'N 64°44'W.

Bordelais (bôrdůlā'), region in Gironde dept., SW France, identified with the winegrowing area surrounding Bordeaux; it includes the MÉDOC, GRAVES, and ENTRE-DEUX-MERS dists., and the country around Libourne and Blaye-et-Sainte-Luce.

Borden, village (pop. 205), S central Sask., near North Saskatchewan R., 30 mi. NW of Saskatoon; wheat, mixed farming.

Borden, county (□ 914; pop. 1,106), NW Texas; ⊙ Gail. E-facing Cap Rock escarpment of Llano Estacado runs N-S through center; co. alt. 2,000–3,000 ft. Drained by Colorado R. Cattle ranching, some agr. (cotton, grain sorghums, some fruit and truck), some sheep raising. Formed 1876.

Borden Islands, 2 isls. (□ c.4,000), formerly thought to be a single isl., NW Franklin Dist., Northwest Territories, in the Arctic Ocean; 77°21'–78°39'N 108°40'–113°10'W; separated from Prince Patrick Isl. (SW) by Ballantyne Strait, from Melville Isl. (S) by Hazen Strait, and from Ellef Ringnes and Lougheed isls. (E) by Prince Gustav Adolph Sea. Consists of North Borden Isl. (65 mi. long, 30 mi. wide) and South Borden Isl. (55 mi. long, 40 mi. wide), separated by Wilkins Sound. Plateau on South Borden Isl. rises to over 1,000 ft. Off South Borden Isl. is Brock Isl.

Borden Peninsula, N Baffin Isl., SE Franklin Dist., Northwest Territories, extends 140 mi. N into Lancaster Sound; 71°52'–73°50'N 80°40'–85°40'W; 40–105 mi. wide. Coastal cliffs rise to c.1,500 ft. (NE); interior of peninsula consists of mountainous country rising to over 3,000 ft.

Bordentown, city (pop. 5,497), Burlington co., W N.J., on Delaware R. and 5 mi. S of Trenton; mfg. (box-making machinery, clothing, brick, dyes), printing; grain, dairy products. Damaged by British in Revolution. Clara Barton's school (built 1739; now a Red Cross memorial) and state industrial school for boys here. Joseph Bonaparte lived here 1816–39. Settled 1682; inc. as borough 1825, as city 1867.

Bordères-Louron (bôrdâr'-lōōrō'), village (pop. 200), Hautes-Pyrénées dept., SW France, in central Pyrenees, 11 mi. WNW of Bagnères-de-Luchon; livestock raising. Slate quarries and manganese mines near by. Hydroelectric station.

Bordertown, town (pop. 985), SE South Australia, 160 mi. SE of Adelaide, near Victoria border; wheat.

Bordesholm (bôr'dŭs-hôlm"), village (pop. 7,098), in Schleswig-Holstein, NW Germany, 10 mi. SW of Kiel, on a small lake; furniture mfg. Was site of Augustinian chapter which was changed (1566) into an acad. and became (1665) nucleus of Kiel Univ. Has Gothic church.

Bordighera (bôrdēgâ'rä), town (pop. 5,978), Imperia prov., Liguria, NW Italy, port on Gulf of Genoa and 6 mi. WSW of San Remo. A leading winter resort (mean winter temp. 54°F.) of Riviera di Ponente, with many fine villas and gardens. Noted for floriculture, olive oil, palms. Exports over 100,000 palm branches annually for religious ceremonies. Has Inst. of Ligurian Studies (formerly Bicknell Mus.).

Bordj-bou-Arréridj (bôrj'-bōō-ärärēj'), town (pop. 5,492), Constantine dept., NE Algeria, on railroad and 36 mi. WSW of Sétif; road center on N slope of Hodna Mts., in barley- and wheat-growing region. Phosphate mines at the Djebel M'Zaïta near Tocqueville (SE). Here began the Kabylian insurrection of 1871.

Bordj-le-Boeuf (–lü-bûf'), Saharan outpost, Southern Territories, S Tunisia, 55 mi. SSW of Foum-Tatahouine, on caravan route and desert track; 32°12'N 10°2'E.

Bordj-Ménaïel (–mānäyĕl'), town (pop. 6,392), Alger dept., N central Algeria, on the Oued Isser, on railroad and 36 mi. E of Algiers; agr. trade center (wine, cereals, tobacco).

Bordj-Redir (–rĕdēr'), village, Constantine dept., NE Algeria, on N slope of Hodna Mts., 15 mi. SSE of Bordj-bou-Arréridj; phosphate mining.

Bordo (bôrdh"ů'), Dan. *Bordø*, Faeroese *Borðoy*, island (□ 37; pop. 2,611) of the NE Faeroe Isls.; c.14 mi. long, 6 mi. wide. Mountainous terrain; highest point is Lokken (2,476 ft.). Klaksvig is chief town. Fishing, sheep raising.

Bordon Camp, England: see WHITEHILL.

Boreas Mountain (bô'rēůs) (3,815 ft.), Essex co., NE N.Y., in the Adirondacks, 9 mi. SSE of Mt. Marcy and 13 mi. NW of Schroon Lake village.

Borego Desert State Park, Calif.: see ANZA DESERT STATE PARK.

Borehamwood, England: see ELSTREE.

Borek (bô'rĕk), town (1946 pop. 1,833), Poznan prov., W central Poland, 36 mi. SSE of Poznan; machine mfg., sawmilling, flour milling.

Borensberg (bōō"rŭnsbĕr'yů), village (pop. 1,115), Ostergotland co., S Sweden, on L. Bor, Swedish *Boren* (7 mi. long, 1–2 mi. wide), on Gota Canal, and 8 mi. E of Motala; mfg. of glass, concrete; sawmilling.

Boreray. 1 Island (pop. 8), Outer Hebrides, Inverness, Scotland, just off N coast of North Uist; 1½ mi. long, 1 mi. wide. **2** Island, Outer Hebrides, Inverness, Scotland, 4 mi. NE of St. Kilda; 1 mi. long, ½ mi. wide.

Borga (bôr'gō), Swedish *Borgå*, Finnish *Porvoo* (pōr'vō), city (pop. 8,478), Uusimaa co., S Finland, at mouth of small river on bay of Gulf of Finland, 30 mi. ENE of Helsinki; port, shipping timber products; rail terminus. Lumber, pulp, cellulose, and plywood mills, machine shops, ceramics works, printing plants. Seat of Lutheran bishop since 1723. Has 15th-cent. Gothic cathedral, and many picturesque medieval streets and houses. Pop. is predominantly Swedish-speaking. A cultural center, it was for some time home of the poet Runeberg. Trade center since c.1300, it is one of Finland's oldest cities; inc. c.1350. In 1809 Finnish diet here swore allegiance to Alexander I of Russia.

Borgampad (bōr'gůmpäd) or **Borgampahad** (–pŭhäd), town (pop. c.5,500), Warangal dist., SE Hyderabad state, India, on Godavari R. and 17 mi. NE of coal-mining center of Kottagudem; rice, oilseeds. Ferry to pilgrimage town of Bhadrachalam (just across river), in Madras. Also called Borgam Pahar.

Borgarfjardar or **Borgarjardhar** (bôr'kärfyär"dhär), Icelandic *Borgarfjarðar*, county [Icelandic *sýsla*] (pop. 1,328), SW Iceland; ⊙ Borgarnes. Extends NE from Faxa Bay to SW edge of Langjokull; includes Ok glacier. Drained by the Hvita. Mountainous. Sheep and cattle raising, fishing. Akranes city is in but independent of co. Reykholt was home of Snorri Sturluson.

Borgar Fjord, Iceland: see FAXA BAY.

Borgarnes (bôr'kärnĕs"), town (pop. 716), ⊙ Myra co. and Borgarfjardar co., W Iceland, on Borgar Fjord, arm of Faxa Bay, 25 mi. N of Reykjavik; communications center (road terminus, shipping services to Reykjavik) and fishing port.

Borge, canton, Norway: see SARPSBORG.

Borge (bôr'hā), town (pop. 958), Málaga prov., S Spain, 10 mi. NE of Málaga; olives, raisins, vegetables, lemons, figs, almonds, cereals, stock.

Borgefjell (bûr'yůfyĕl), Nor. *Børgefjell*, mountains in Nord-Trondelag and Nordland counties, N central Norway, S of Ros L. and Vefsna R. valley, near Swedish border; rise to 5,587 ft. at Kvigtind, 45 mi. SSE of Mosjoen. Also called Store Borgefjell.

Borgentreich (bôr'gůntrīkh), town (pop. 2,002), in former Prussian prov. of Westphalia, NW Germany, after 1945 in North Rhine-Westphalia, 7 mi. NE of Warburg; grain.

Borger (bôr'gůr), oil city (pop. 18,059), Hutchinson co., extreme N Texas, in high plains of the Panhandle near Canadian R., 40 mi. NE of Amarillo; a center of rich Panhandle oil and natural-gas region; oil refineries, carbon-black and synthetic rubber plants; mfg. of tanks, torpedoes, metal products; agr. in area (grain, livestock). Grew after discovery of oil, 1925; inc. 1926.

Borgerhout (bôr'gůrhout), E suburb (pop. 51,645) of Antwerp, N Belgium; mfg. (food products, chemicals, clothing, leather, tobacco); diamond polishing and cutting. Has 19th-cent. church, 1st in neo-Gothic style built in Belgium.

Borges (bōr'hĕs), residential town (pop. estimate 8,000) in Greater Buenos Aires, Argentina, 11 mi. NW of Buenos Aires.

Borgestad (bôr'gůstä), village (pop. 1,798) in Gjerpen canton (pop. 11,100), Telemark co., S Norway, 4 mi. SSE of Skien; cellulose and brick mfg. Large ironworks at Fossum, near by, were founded 1543.

Borgetto (bôrjĕt'tô), town (pop. 6,216), Palermo prov., NW Sicily, 13 mi. WSW of Palermo, in citrus-fruit and grape region.

Borghetto Lodigiano (bôrgĕt'tô lôdējä'nô), town (pop. 2,200), Milano prov., Lombardy, N Italy, near Lambro R., 7 mi. S of Lodi; silk mill.

Borghi (bôr'gē), town (pop. estimate 500), SE Santa Fe prov., Argentina, 12 mi. NNW of Rosario; grain center. Its adjoining port (E) on Paraná R. is called Puerto Borghi.

Borgholm (bôr'yůhôlm"), city (pop. 2,024), ⊙ Oland isl. and prov., Kalmar co., SE Sweden, on W coast of isl., on Kalmar Sound of the Baltic, 19 mi. NE of Kalmar; 56°53'N 16°40'E; seaside resort; port, shipping grain, stock, chalk. Has remains of 16th-cent. castle, on site of old fortress 1st mentioned 1281. Town chartered 1816.

Borgholzhausen (bôrk"hōlts-hou'zůn), town (pop. 1,975), in former Prussian prov. of Westphalia, NW Germany, after 1945 in North Rhine-Westphalia, in Teutoburg Forest, 12 mi. NW of Bielefeld; woodworking. Has ruined 9th-cent. castle.

Borghorst (bôrk'hôrst), village (pop. 13,163), in former Prussian prov. of Westphalia, NW Germany, after 1945 in North Rhine-Westphalia, 10 mi. SSW of Rheine; linen weaving.

Borgia (bôr'jä), town (pop. 4,728), Catanzaro prov., Calabria, S Italy, 7 mi. SW of Catanzaro; wine, olive oil, dried fruit.

Borgloon (bôrkh'lōn) or **Looz** (lōz), town (pop. 3,199), Limburg prov., NE Belgium, 5 mi. WNW of Tongres; market for fruitgrowing area (apples, cherries, plums).

Borgne, Lake (bôrn), salt-water bay (c.27 mi. long) in SE La., 15 mi. E of New Orleans; a W arm of the Mississippi Sound and a link bet. the Gulf of Mexico (through Mississippi Sound) and L. Pontchartrain (NW), to which it is connected by navigable Rigolets and Chef Menteur passes. Lake Borgne Canal links bay with Mississippi R. at Violet.

Borgne, Le (lů bôr'nyů), town (1950 census pop. 1,365), Nord dept., N Haiti, on the Atlantic, 21 mi. WNW of Cap-Haïtien; bananas, coffee, cacao.

Borgne River (bôr'nyů), S Switzerland, rises near Arolla, flows 18 mi. N to the Rhone just E of Sion. Bramois hydroelectric plant is on it. It drains Val d'Hérens.

Borgo (bôrgō', It. bôr'gô), village (pop. 538), N Corsica, 10 mi. S of Bastia; winegrowing.

Borgo or **Borgo Valsugana** (bôr'gô välsōōgä'nä), town (pop. 4,056), Trento prov., Trentino–Alto Adige, N Italy, on Brenta R. and 16 mi. E of Trent; mfg. (agr. machinery, cutlery, shoes, silk textiles). Chief center of the Valsugana. Has ruins of castle. Largely rebuilt since First World War.

Borgo a Buggiano (ä bōōd-jä'nô), village (pop. 1,542), Pistoia prov., Tuscany, central Italy, 10 mi. WSW of Pistoia; mfg. of sulphur oils.

Borgo a Mozzano (ä môtsä'nô), village (pop. 1,079), Lucca prov., Tuscany, central Italy, on Serchio R. and 10 mi. NNE of Lucca; agr. tool factories, paper mill.

Borgo d'Ale (dä'lĕ), village (pop. 3,119), Vercelli prov., Piedmont, N Italy, 18 mi. W of Vercelli.

Borgo di Tossignano (dē tôs-sēnyä'nô), village (pop. 1,035), Bologna prov., Emilia-Romagna, N central Italy, on Santerno R. and 8 mi. SW of Imola; cement, bricks, pencils.

Borgofranco d'Ivrea (bôr"gôfräng'kô dēvrä'ä), village (pop. 1,068), Torino prov., Piedmont, NW Italy, near Dora Baltea R., 3 mi. N of Ivrea; aluminum industry, cheddite factory, brewery. Bauxite, quartz mines near by.

Borgo Lavezzaro (bôr'gô lävĕt-tsä'rô), village (pop. 2,142), Novara prov., Piedmont, N Italy, 9 mi. SSE of Novara, in rice-growing region.

Borgomanero (bôr"gômänâ'rô), town (pop. 7,669), Novara prov., Piedmont, N Italy, on Agogna R. and 19 mi. NNW of Novara, in sericulture region; rail junction; commercial center; textiles, majolica, sausage; foundries. Kaolin quarries near by. Has anc. palace.

Borgonovo Val Tidone (bôr"gô'nô'vô väl tēdō'nĕ), town (pop. 3,135), Piacenza prov., Emilia-Romagna, N central Italy, 12 mi. WSW of Piacenza; flour and lumber mills, brick- and cementworks; trade in cereals, cheese, fruit.

Borgo Panigale (bôr'gô pänēgä'lĕ), W suburb (pop. 3,123) of Bologna, Emilia-Romagna, N central Italy, on Reno R.; rail junction; toys, liquor. Damaged (1944–45) in Second World War.

Borgoprund, Rumania: see PRUNDUL-BARGAULUI.

Borgoricco (bôrgôrēk'kô), village (pop. 596), Padova prov., Veneto, N Italy, 10 mi. NNE of Padua; broom factories.

Borgo San Dalmazzo (bôr'gô sän dälmä'tsô), village (pop. 3,017), Cuneo prov., Piedmont, NW Italy, 5 mi. SW of Cuneo; jute, bricks, pottery. Limestone quarries near by.

Borgo San Donnino, Italy: see FIDENZA.

Borgo San Giacomo (sän jä'kômô), village (pop. 2,917), Brescia prov., Lombardy, N Italy, near Oglio R., 18 mi. SW of Brescia; macaroni mfg.

Borgo San Lorenzo (sän lôrĕn'tsô), town (pop. 5,555), Firenze prov., Tuscany, central Italy, on Sieve R. and 14 mi. NNE of Florence; rail junction; mfg. (straw hats, gloves, majolica, glass). Chief center of the MUGELLO. Severely damaged by bombing (1944) in Second World War.

Borgo San Sepolcro, Italy: see SANSEPOLCRO.

Borgosatollo (bôr"gôsätôl'lô), village (pop. 2,948), Brescia prov., Lombardy, N Italy, 4 mi. S of Brescia.

Borgosesia (bôr"gôsâ'zyä), town (pop. 5,788), Vercelli prov., Piedmont, N Italy, on Sesia R. and 15 mi. NE of Biella; woolen, cotton, and paper mills, foundries; shoe factory, cork industry.

Borgotaro, Italy: see BORGO VAL DI TARO.

Borgou, Dahomey and Nigeria: see BORGU.

Borgo Val di Taro (väl dē tä'rô), town (pop. 3,655), Parma prov., Emilia-Romagna, N central Italy, on Taro R. and 10 mi. NW of Pontremoli. Chief center of Taro R. valley; cheese, flour, lumber, chemicals, lime and cement. Talc mine near by. Called Borgotaro until c.1930.

Borgo Valsugana, Italy: see BORGO.

Borgo Vercelli (vĕrchĕl'lē), village (pop. 2,212), Vercelli prov., Piedmont, N Italy, 3 mi. NE of Vercelli.

Borgu (bôr'gōō), Fr. *Borgou*, former kingdom of W Africa, W of Niger R.; now part of DAHOMEY of Fr. West Africa and ILORIN prov. of Northern Provinces of Nigeria. Extends from 9° to 11°N, from 2° to 5°E. Subject of Br.-Fr. territorial dispute (1894–98) which determined present division.

Borgue (bôrg), agr. village and parish (pop. 990), S Kirkcudbright, Scotland, 4 mi. SW of Kirkcudbright.

Borgund. 1 Village and canton, More og Romsdal co., Norway: see SPJELKAVIK. **2** Canton, Sogn og Fjordane co., Norway: see MARISTOVA.

Borgworm, Belgium: see WAREMME.

Boriane or **Boriani**, Greece: see HAGIOS ATHANASIOS.

Boril (bô'rēl), village (pop. 2,039), Vratsa dist., NW Bulgaria, on the Danube, at mouth of Iskar R., and 23 mi. E of Oryakhovo; vineyards; fisheries. Ruins of Roman town of Oescus near by. Formerly Beshlii.

Borinage (bôrēnäzh'), region in S Hainaut prov., SW Belgium, surrounding Mons and extending W to Fr. border; important coal-mining and glass-mfg. area.

Borinquén (bōrĭng-kĕn'), locality, Puerto Rico, site of airfield N of AGUADILLA. Borinquén was an old native name for PUERTO RICO.

Borinskoye (bô'rĭnskŭyŭ), village (1939 pop. over 2,000), NW Voronezh oblast, Russian SFSR, 13 mi. SW of Lipetsk; sugar refinery.

Borinya (bô'rĭnyŭ), Pol. *Borynia*, village (1939 pop. over 500), SW Drogobych oblast, Ukrainian SSR, in E Beskids, 6 mi. S of Turka; sheep; lumbering.

Boriquén, old native name of PUERTO RICO.

Boris Gleb (bō'rĭs glĕp'), village in Sor-Varanger canton, Finnmark co., NE Norway, on USSR border, on Pasvik R. and 6 mi. SSE of Kirkenes, 25 mi. W of Pechenga. Has remains of 16th-cent. monastery. Near by is settlement of Greek-Orthodox Lapps.

Borislav (bŭrēsläf'), Pol. *Boryslaw* (bôrĭ'släf), city (1931 pop. 41,683), central Drogobych oblast, Ukrainian SSR, at N foot of E Beskids, 6 mi. SW of Drogobych; rail terminus; major petroleum, natural-gas, and ozocerite extracting center (linked by gas pipe lines with Dashava and Drogobych); petroleum refining (gasoline, benzine, paraffin, lubrication oil), iron casting, mfg. (drilling machinery, tools, candles). Several mining settlements adjoin city. Developed in 18th cent. as 1st petroleum-producing center of Austria-Hungary. Passed to Poland in 1919; ceded to USSR in 1945.

Borisoglebsk (bŭrē"sŭglyĕpsk'), city (1926 pop. 21,031; 1948 pop. over 50,000), E Voronezh oblast, Russian SFSR, on Khoper R., at mouth of the Vorona, and 120 mi. ESE of Voronezh; grain center; railroad shops; meat packing, flour milling, distilling. Poultry farming near by. Teachers col. Founded 1645 as fortress against Tatars.

Borisoglebskiye Slobody (–glyĕp'skēŭ slô'bŭdē), village (1926 pop. 1,346), SE central Yaroslavl oblast, Russian SFSR, 11 mi. WNW of Rostov; tobacco, potatoes.

Borisov (bŭrē'sŭf), city (1926 pop. 25,842), N central Minsk oblast, Belorussian SSR, on Berezina R. and 45 mi. NE of Minsk; match-making center; wood distilling, glassworking; musical instruments, enamelware, food products. In 1812, Napoleon I crossed Berezina R. at Studenki, 9 mi. NNW. Pop. 40% Jewish until Second World War, when city was held (1941–44) by Germans.

Borisovgrad, Bulgaria: see PARVOMAI.

Borisovka (bŭrē'sŭfkŭ). **1** Town (1939 pop. over 10,000), central South Kazakhstan oblast, Kazakh SSR, former suburb (4 mi. SW) of Turkestan, on Trans-Caspian RR (Turkestan station); railroad shops, metalworks, orchards. Developed at rail depot following construction of railroad. **2** Village (1926 pop. 20,655), S Kursk oblast, Russian SFSR, on Vorskla R. and 23 mi. W of Belgorod; flour milling, sugar refining.

Borisovo-Sudskoye (–sŭvŭ-sōōt'skŭyŭ), village (1926 pop. 378), W Vologda oblast, Russian SFSR, on Suda R. and 36 mi. N of Babayevo; flax, wheat; limestone quarries.

Borisovski or **Borisovskiy** (bŭrē'sŭfskē), town (1939 pop. over 2,000), SW Omsk oblast, Russian SFSR, 8 mi. E of Sherbakul; metalworks.

Borispol or **Borispol'** (bŭrēs'pŭl), town (1926 pop. 11,578), E Kiev oblast, Ukrainian SSR, 20 mi. ESE of Kiev; flour, clothing; metalworking.

Boris Vilkitski Strait or **Boris Vil'kitskiy Strait** (bŭrēs" vĭlkēt'skē), joins Kara and Laptev seas of Arctic Ocean at c.78°N; separates Severnaya Zemlya archipelago from Taimyr Peninsula, Krasnoyarsk Territory, Russian SFSR; 80 mi. long, 35–50 mi. wide. Named for 20th-cent. Rus. navigator. Also called Vilkitski Strait.

Borivli (bō'rĭvlē), village, Bombay Suburban dist., W Bombay, India, on Salsette Isl., 20 mi. N of Bombay city center; hosiery mills. Kanheri caves, 4 mi. SE, have many 2d-9th-cent. A.D. Buddhist temples; 8th-cent. Brahmanic caves are 1 mi. N.

Borja (bôr'hä), town (dist. pop. 7,124), Guairá dept., S Paraguay, 12 mi. S of Villarrica; rail junction in agr. area (sugar cane, cotton, fruit, stock).

Borja, village (pop. 241), Loreto dept., N Peru, landing on Marañón R. just below the Pongo de Manseriche; 4°25'S 77°31'W; rice, sugar cane.

Borja, city (pop. 4,905), Saragossa prov., NE Spain, 36 mi. WNW of Saragossa; agr. trade center (sugar beets, wine, hemp, alfalfa); mfg. of soap, brandy, glue, chocolate; olive-oil processing, flour- and sawmilling. Has ancestral palace of Borgia family. Cistercian monastery is 8 mi. WSW.

Borjas Blancas (bôr'häs bläng'käs), city (pop. 4,240), Lérida prov., NE Spain, on Urgel Canal, and 14 mi. SE of Lérida; olive-oil processing and shipping; mfg. of soap, flour products, rubber soles; agr. trade (cattle, cereals, almonds, wine).

Borjas del Campo (dhĕl käm'pō), town (pop. 1,073), Tarragona prov., NE Spain, 5 mi. W of Reus; olive oil, wine, filbert nuts, vegetables.

Bork (bôrk), village (pop. 5,080), in former Prussian prov. of Westphalia, NW Germany, after 1945 in North Rhine-Westphalia, 4 mi. NW of Lünen; grain, cattle, hogs.

Borkelo, Netherlands: see BORCULO.

Borken (bôr'kŭn). **1** Town (pop. 3,464), in former Prussian prov. of Hesse-Nassau, W Germany, after 1945 in Hesse, 5 mi. WNW of Homberg; lignite mining. **2** Town (pop. 7,547), in former Prussian prov. of Westphalia, NW Germany, after 1945 in North Rhine-Westphalia, 10 mi. E of Bocholt; rail junction; textile mfg.

Borkhaya Bay, Russian SFSR: see BUOR-KHAYA BAY.

Borki (bŭrkē'), town (1926 pop. 2,561), W central Kharkov oblast, Ukrainian SSR, 20 mi. SSW of Kharkov; metalworks.

Borki Wielkie, Ukrainian SSR: see VELIKIYE BORKI.

Borkou or **Borku** (bôrkōō', bôr'kōō), country and former sultanate of N central Africa, roughly coextensive with present Borkou dist. (1950 pop. 17,800) of Borkou-Ennedi-Tibesti region, N Chad territory, Fr. Equatorial Africa, in SE part of the Sahara; ⊙ Largeau (Faya). Bounded N by the Tibesti, E by the Ennedi Plateau. Largely a sandy desert (part of L. Chad depression). Dates, barley, vegetables grown in the oases; camels, asses, goats. Its nomadic and semi-nomadic Tibbus, Arabs, and Berbers (*Ouled-Slimans*) are still fervent Senussites. A former vassal state of Wadai, it was ceded to France by Anglo-French agreement (1899), but Fr. troops occupied it only in 1907.

Borkou-Ennedi-Tibesti, Fr. Equatorial Africa: see LARGEAU.

Borku, Fr. Equatorial Africa: see BORKOU.

Borkum (bôr'kōōm), easternmost German North Sea island (□ 14; pop. 5,876) of East Frisian group, off Ems estuary, 24 mi. NW of Emden (steamer connection), near Dutch border; 6 mi. long (E-W), 2-3 mi. wide (N-S). Grazing. Nordseebad Borkum (W) is popular seaside resort.

Borlange (bôr'lĕng"ŭ), Swed. *Borlänge*, city (1950 pop. 21,614), Kopparberg co., central Sweden, in Bergslag region, on Dal R. and 10 mi. SW of Falun; rail junction; iron- and steel-milling center; paper and lumber mills. Inc. as city, 1944, when it absorbed village of Domnarvet (dômnär'vĕt), just N, with large iron- and steelworks.

Bormes (bôrm), village (pop. 964), Var dept., SE France, near the Mediterranean, 21 mi. E of Toulon, at foot of Monts des Maures; health resort on Fr. Riviera. Iron mine near by. Also called Bormes-les-Mimosas.

Bormida River (bôr'mēdä), Piedmont, N Italy, formed 6 mi. W of Acqui by confluence of the Bormida di Millesimo (left branch; 50 mi. long) and the Bormida di Spigno (right branch; 35 mi. long) rising in E Ligurian Alps N of Albenga; flows 33 mi. generally NNE, past Acqui, to Tanaro R. just E of Alessandria. Chief affluent, Orba R. (right).

Bormio (bôr'myô), town (pop. 2,276), Sondrio prov., Lombardy, N Italy, in upper Valtellina, on Stelvio Pass road, 32 mi. NE of Sondrio; hydroelectric plant. Winter resort (alt. 4,019 ft.), with near-by mineral baths. Its iron mines and marble, gypsum, and limestone quarries are largely abandoned.

Bormla, Malta: see COSPICUA.

Bormujos (bôrmōō'hōs), town (2,317), Seville prov., SW Spain, 4 mi. W of Seville, in agr. region (grapes, olives, cereals, vegetables, fruit, livestock); lumber.

Born (bôrn), village (pop. 259), E Luxembourg, on Sûre R. and 20 mi. NE of Luxembourg city, on Ger. border; stone quarrying; tree nurseries, fruit-growing (apples, plums).

Born (bôrn), town (pop. 1,449), Limburg prov., SE Netherlands, 4 mi. NW of Sittard. Near by, on Juliana Canal, is coal-loading point for Limburg coal mines.

Borna (bôr'nä). **1** Town (pop. 18,425), Saxony, E central Germany, 15 mi. SSE of Leipzig, in market-gardening region; lignite-mining center; machinery and shoe mfg. Chartered 1264. **2** NW suburb of Chemnitz, Saxony, E central Germany; hosiery knitting, steel milling; mfg. of pianos, organs, clothing.

Borndiep (bôrn'dēp), strait (2 mi. wide) of North Sea, NW Netherlands, bet. Terschelling isl. (W) and Ameland isl. (E); leads from North Sea to the Waddensee. Also called Amelander Gat.

Borne (bôr'nŭ), town (pop. 8,121), Overijssel prov., E Netherlands, 3 mi. NW of Hengelo; textile center (cotton spinning and weaving, damask weaving).

Börnecke, Preussisch, Germany: see PREUSSISCH BÖRNECKE.

Bornel (bôrnĕl'), village (pop. 1,338), Oise dept., N France, 17 mi. SSE of Beauvais; founding of non-ferrous metals.

Bornem (bôr'nŭm), town (pop. 9,118), Antwerp prov., N Belgium, on Scheldt R. and 12 mi. SW of Antwerp; textile milling, brewing. Formerly spelled Bornhem.

Borneo (bôr'nēō), third largest island (□ 286,969; pop. c.3,080,000, including offshore isls.) of the world (after Greenland and New Guinea), largest of Greater Sundas and Malay Archipelago, bet. Sulu Sea (N) and Java Sea (S), and bet. S.China Sea (W) and Macassar Strait (E); 7°2'N–4°10'S 108°52'–119°16'E; 800 mi. long, 160-690 mi. wide. Largely jungle, with swampy lowlands in S and SW coastal areas. Mountainous interior rises to 13,455 ft. at Mt. Kinabalu in N. Many rivers are navigable, the largest being the Kapuas, Barito, and Rajang. Climate is hot and humid with annual rainfall of more than 100 in. There is a prolonged monsoon season. Densely forested in interior with valuable woods (sandalwood, camphor), there are also large tracts of sago palm, coconut, and mangrove. Fauna roughly resembles that of Sumatra; includes elephants, rhinoceroses, tapirs, deer, orangutans, gibbons, and lemurs. The Dyaks (principal native group) live mostly in interior; some of them still practice headhunting. In coastal areas are the Malays, Javanese, and Chinese. Major products are rubber, rice, copra, resin. Borneo has rich mineral resources. There are large oil fields; iron, copper, diamonds, and coal are mined. Also deposits of gold, silver, lead, and antimony. Isl. was visited 1521 by the Portuguese, followed by the Dutch in 1600 and the English in 1665. In Second World War, isl. was seized Dec., 1941–Feb., 1942, by the Japanese who occupied it for almost duration of war. Borneo is divided politically into 4 sections: the Br. crown colonies of NORTH BORNEO and SARAWAK, the Br. protectorate of BRUNEI, and the Indonesian section which occupies roughly three-quarters of the isl. **Indonesian Borneo** (Indonesian *Kalimantan*), formerly **Dutch Borneo** (□ 208,285; pop. 2,168,661), is part of republic of INDONESIA; bounded N by Br. North Borneo, S by Java Sea, E by Celebes Sea and Macassar Strait, and W by Sarawak and S.China Sea; 4°22'N–4°10'S 108°52'–119°16'E. Chief centers are BANJERMASIN, PONTIANAK, BALIKPAPAN, and SAMARINDA. Du. influence was established in W part in early 19th cent., and was gradually extended S and E. After 1907, area was divided into 2 Du. residencies (West Borneo and South and East Borneo) as part of Netherlands East Indies. After Second World War, it was briefly divided into the autonomous states of West Borneo, Great Dayak, East Borneo, Southeast Borneo, and Banjar. In 1950 all Indonesian Borneo became part of the republic of Indonesia.

Bornes (bôrn), limestone massif of Savoy Alps, in Haute-Savoie dept., SE France, bounded by Faucigny valley (N), Arly R. (SE), and L. of Annecy (SW). Rises to 9,029 ft. (Pointe-Percée peak) in the Chaîne du Reposoir, its E escarpment, which extends 13 mi. from Col des Aravis (SSW) to Cluses (N).

Bornes, Serra de (sĕ'rŭ dĭ bôr'nĭsh), range in Bragança dist., N Portugal, S of Macedo de Cavaleiros; rises to 3,937 ft.

Bornheim (bôrnhīm). **1** NE district (pop. 27,503) of Frankfurt, Hesse, W Germany. **2** Village (pop. 11,051), in former Prussian Rhine Prov., W Germany, after 1945 in North Rhine-Westphalia, 4 mi. WNW of Bonn, in lignite-mining region.

Bornhem, Belgium: see BORNEM.

Bornholm (bôrn'hôlm), amt (□ 227; pop. 47,337), Denmark, comprises BORNHOLM isl. and 8 small adjacent isls. (total □ less than 1); ⊙ Ronne.

Bornholm, isl. (□ 227; 1950 pop. 48,134), Denmark in Baltic Sea, 105 mi. ESE of Copenhagen and 24 mi. off Swedish coast; 23 mi. long, 18 mi. wide. N and central areas are granite (highest point, at center of isl., 531 ft.); N and W coasts are rocky and high. Agr., fishing, granite quarrying, pottery making, seafaring. Ronne, chief port. In 1645 isl. seized by Sweden; returned to Denmark in 1660.

Bornhöved (bôrnhû'fŭt), village (pop. 2,705), in Schleswig-Holstein, NW Germany, 10 mi. E of Neumünster; woodworking. Scene (1227) of decisive victory over the Danes by count of Holstein and other Ger. princes.

Borno (bôr'nô), village (pop. 1,895), Brescia prov., Lombardy, N Italy, 29 mi. N of Brescia, in Val Camonica; iron mining. Has tuberculosis sanitarium.

Bor Nor (bôr'nōr') or **Buir Nor** (bwēr), lake (□ 235) on Manchuria-Mongolia line, 125 mi. SW of Hailar; 25 mi. long, 12 mi. wide, 30 ft. deep; alt. 1,900 ft.

Fisheries. Receives Khalka R. (SE). Its outlet, Orchun R., empties into the lake Hulun Nor.

Bornos (bôr'nōs), town (pop. 6,025), Cádiz prov., SW Spain, in hills near Guadalete R., 37 mi. NE of Cádiz. Spa and agr. center (cereals, vegetables, olive oil, fruit, cattle). Liquor and olive-oil distilling, dairying.

Bornova (bôr"nôvä'), town (pop. 17,887), Smyrna prov., W Turkey, 4 mi. NE of Smyrna, for which it is a summer resort. Formerly also Burunabat, Burnabat, or Bournabat.

Bornu (bôr'nōō), province (□ 45,900; 1931 pop. 1,044,632), Northern Provinces, NE Nigeria; ⊙ Maiduguri. The prov. includes a part (□ 5,149; 1931 pop. 185,481; 1948 pop. estimate 228,100) of Br. Cameroons. Bounded N by Fr. West Africa, NE by L. Chad, and E by Fr. Cameroons; includes savanna (S), steppe (N), and marshy salt flats near L. Chad. Mainly agr. (cotton, peanuts, indigo, gum arabic, millet, durra); cattle raising, game hunting. Diatomite and limestone deposits (S). Major centers: Maiduguri, Potiskum, Nguru (rail terminus), and, in Br. Cameroons, Dikwa. Pop. largely Kanuri, Fulah, and Shuwa Arab. A powerful Mohammedan state since 11th cent., Bornu formerly extended from 11°N to 15°N and from 10°E to 15°E, including areas now in Fr. West Africa. Attained the height of its power, when, after absorbing Kanem, it extended beyond L. Chad to edges of the Sahara. At end of 19th cent. it was divided into Br., Fr., and Ger. spheres of influence. Largest part came under Nigeria in 1902; the Ger. portion went to Great Britain in 1922 as part of Br. Cameroons mandate. Kukawa was its former capital (until 1908).

Boroa (bōrō'ä), village (pop. 1,117), Cautín prov., S central Chile, 16 mi. WSW of Temuco; wheat, oats, livestock. Indian reservation. Its railroad station is 4 mi. N, on Imperial R.

Boroaia (bôrwä'yä), village (pop. 2,427), Suceava prov., NE Rumania, 7 mi. S of Falticeni; woodworking.

Borobia (bōrō'vyä), town (pop. 801), Soria prov., N central Spain, 30 mi. E of Soria; cereals, timber, livestock. Plaster mfg.

Boroboedoer, Indonesia: see BOROBUDUR.

Borobudur or **Boroboedoer** (both: bōrōbōōdōōr'), ruins of vast Buddhist monument in central Java, Indonesia, near Magelang, 17 mi. NNW of Jogjakarta. It is a truncated pyramid covered with intricately carved blocks of stone. The seated Buddha within may be seen from 3 platforms above the many terraces encircling the pyramid. Built in either 8th or 9th cent.

Borodino (bŭrŭdyĭnô'). **1** Town (pop. over 500), S Krasnoyarsk Territory, Russian SFSR, near Zaozerny, in Kansk lignite basin. **2** Village, W Moscow oblast, Russian SFSR, on Kolocha R. (right affluent of Moskva R.) and 7 mi. W of Mozhaisk. Scene, in 1812 of hard-won Fr. victory over Russians. **3** Village (1930 pop. 2,585; 1941 pop. 796), N Izmail oblast, Ukrainian SSR, 55 mi. WNW of Belgorod-Dnestrovski. Founded, after 1812, as Ger. agr. colony; Ger. pop. repatriated in 1940.

Borodulikha (bŭrŭdōō'lyĭkhŭ), village (1939 pop. over 500), N Semipalatinsk oblast, Kazakh SSR, 35 mi. NE of Semipalatinsk; grain; metalworks.

Borodulino, Russian SFSR: see VERESHCHAGINO.

Borodyanka (bŭrŭdyän'kŭ), village (1926 pop. 3,896), N central Kiev oblast, Ukrainian SSR, 28 mi. NW of Kiev; wheat, truck.

Borogontsy (bŭrŭgôn'tsē), village (1948 pop. over 500), SW Yakut Autonomous SSR, Russian SFSR, 70 mi. NE of Yakutsk, in agr. area.

Borohoto or **Borokhoto**, Manchuria: see LINTUNG.

Borokhoro Range (bōrō'khōrō'), branch of the Tien Shan, NW Sinkiang prov., China, forming right-bank divide of upper Ili R.; rises to c.10,000 ft.

Boromo (bōrō'mō), village, W central Upper Volta, Fr. West Africa, on motor road half way (110 mi.) bet. Ouagadougou (ENE) and Bobo-Dioulasso (WSW), in agr. region (shea nuts, peanuts, millet, rice; livestock). Shea-nut butter processing. Landing field.

Boro Myoda (bō'ro myō'dä), Ital. *Borumieda*, village, Wallo prov., NE Ethiopia, 8 mi. N of Dessye. Salt market with church.

Boron (bô'rŏn"), village (pop. c.900), Kern co., S central Calif., near Muroc Dry L., c.30 mi. E of Mojave; borax works.

Borongan (bōrōng'än), town (1939 pop. 2,853; 1948 municipality pop. 25,638), E Samar isl., Philippines, port on small inlet of Philippine Sea, 39 mi. ESE of Catbalogan; agr. center (coconuts, rice, corn).

Borore (bô'rôrĕ), village (pop. 2,488), Nuoro prov., central Sardinia, 28 mi. WSW of Nuoro.

Borosjenö, Rumania: see INEU.

Borossebes, Rumania: see SEBIS.

Borota (bô'rôtŏ), town (pop. 4,049), Bacs-Bodrog co., S Hungary, 20 mi. NE of Baja; wheat, corn, cattle, horses.

Boroughbridge, town and parish (pop. 862), West Riding, central Yorkshire, England, on Ure R. and 6 mi. ESE of Ripon; agr. market. Here Edward II defeated (1322) the earl of Lancaster. Site of 3 monoliths, called Devil's Arrows. Near by are remains of Roman camp.

Borough Green, England: see IGHTHAM.

Borough Hill, England: see DAVENTRY.

Borough Park, SE N.Y., a residential section of SW Brooklyn borough of New York city. Prospect Park is near by.

Borouj, El (ĕl bôrōōj'), agr. village, Casablanca region, W central Fr. Morocco, 45 mi. SE of Settat; sheep raising.

Borovan (bôrôvän'), village (pop. 5,905), Vratsa dist., NW Bulgaria, 10 mi. WSW of Byala Slatina; grain, livestock.

Borovaya (bŭrŭvī'ŭ), village (1926 pop. 3,055), E Kharkov oblast, Ukrainian SSR, near Oskol R., 19 mi. NE of Izyum; wheat, sunflowers.

Borovichi (bŭrŭvē'chē), city (1926 pop. 18,785), E Novgorod oblast, Russian SFSR, on Msta R. and 95 mi. E of Novgorod; rail-spur terminus; road center; mfg. of refractory and acid-resistant products (bricks, pipes) and prefabricated houses; metalworking, distilling, cotton spinning. Teachers col. Knitting and weaving handicrafts in vicinity. Lignite mines at Komarovo and Zarubino (NW). Chartered 1770.

Borovlyanka (bŭrŭvlyän'kŭ), town (1939 pop. over 500), central Altai Territory, Russian SFSR, on rail spur (Sokolinskaya station) and 45 mi. WNW of Bisk; sawmilling.

Borovo (bô'rôvô), village, NE Croatia, Yugoslavia, on the Danube (Serbia border) and 4 mi. N of Vukovar, in Slavonia; rail junction; airfield; footwear mfg.

Borovoye (–voi'ŭ). **1** Town (1939 pop. over 2,000), S Kokchetav oblast, Kazakh SSR, 10 mi. NNE of Shchuchinsk, in wooded area. Noted health resort with tuberculosis sanatorium, climatic and kumiss cures. **2** Village (1926 pop. 5,641), N Kustanai oblast, Kazakh SSR, 45 mi. NNE of Kustanai; wheat, cattle.

Borovsk (bô'rŭfsk). **1** City (1939 pop. over 10,000), N Kaluga oblast, Russian SFSR, on Protva R. and 45 mi. NNE of Kaluga; woolen-milling center; metalworking, tanning. Cotton mill at Balabanovo (E). Dates from 13th cent.; chartered 1356, when it passed to Moscow. During Second World War, briefly held (1941–42) by Germans in Moscow campaign. **2** City (1949 pop. over 10,000), N central Molotov oblast, Russian SFSR, port on left bank of Kama R., at mouth of short Borovaya R., and 4 mi. NNW of Solikamsk; shipbuilding; chemical works. Originally called Ust-Borovaya; inc. (c.1930) into Solikamsk suburbs; became a separate city in 1949.

Borovskoye (bô'rŭfskŭyŭ), town (1926 pop. 5,149), W Voroshilovgrad oblast, Ukrainian SSR, in the Donbas, 7 mi. SE of Lisichansk, across the Northern Donets; coal mines.

Borox (bōrōks'), town (pop. 1,771), Toledo prov., central Spain, 24 mi. S of Madrid; cereals, olives, sugar beets, fruit. Gypsum quarrying; plaster.

Bor Peak (9,073 ft.), SE B.C., in Selkirk Mts., 30 mi. NW of Nelson; 49°50'N 117°45'W.

Borracha Island (bôrä'chä), in the Caribbean, off coast of Anzoátegui state, NE Venezuela, 10 mi. NNW of Barcelona; c.3 mi. long, 2 mi. wide; 10° 17'N 64°45'W.

Borracho, El, Uruguay: see EL BORRACHO.

Borrby (bôr'bü"), village (pop. 1,098), Kristianstad co., S Sweden, 9 mi. SW of Simrishamn; mechanical industries.

Borre (bôr'rŭ), village and canton (pop. 4,517), Vestfold co., SE Norway, 3 mi. SSW of Horten. In canton are iron foundry and machine shop, and mills processing textiles, lumber, flour, and peat. Nykirke is the rail station.

Borregaard, Norway: see SARPSBORG.

Borregard, Norway: see SARPSBORG.

Borriol (bôryōl'), town (pop. 2,540), Castellón de la Plana prov., E Spain, 4 mi. NNW of Castellón de la Plana; olive-oil processing, sawmilling; ships beans and oranges. Limestone quarries.

Borris or **Borris Idrone** (bŏ'rĭs ĭ'drōn), Gaelic *Buirgheas Ó nDróna*, town (pop. 482), SE Co. Carlow, Ireland, near Barrow R., 15 mi. ESE of Kilkenny; agr. market (wheat, potatoes, beets; sheep, cattle).

Borris-in-Ossory (ŏ'sŭrē), Gaelic *Buirgheas Mór Osraighe*, town (pop. 203), W Co. Laoighis, Ireland, on the Nore and 16 mi. WSW of Port Laoighise; agr. market (wheat, barley, potatoes, beets). Has remains of anc. castle of the Fitzpatricks, once of great strategic importance.

Borrisoleigh, Gaelic *Buirgheas Uí Luighdheach*, town (pop. 482), N Co. Tipperary, Ireland, 6 mi. SW of Templemore; agr. market (dairying, cattle raising; potatoes, beets).

Borrodale (bŏ'rōdāl), locality, W Inverness, Scotland, on the Sound of Arisaig, 3 mi. ESE of Arisaig. Prince Charles Edward, the Young Pretender, landed here 1745 from France; and embarked here 1746 after failure of his uprising.

Borroloola (bŏ"rŭlōō'lŭ), settlement (dist. pop. 73), NE Northern Territory, Australia, 435 mi. SE of Darwin and on McArthur R.; cattle. Airport.

Borromean Islands (bŏrōmē'ŭn), group of 4 islets (49 acres; pop. 250) in Lago Maggiore, N Italy, bet. Pallanza (N) and Stresa (S). Isola Bella (ē'zōlä bĕl'lä), most famous islet (1,050 ft. by 590 ft.), formerly barren, was transformed (1650–71) by Count Vitaliano Borromeo into a garden, rising 92 ft. in 10 terraces, enclosing a palace with paintings and statues. Here the Conference of Stresa, among Italy, France, and England, was held in 1935. Isola Madre (ē'zōlä mä'drĕ), largest islet (1,082 ft. by 722 ft.), is covered with citrus trees and gardens of rare plants. Isola San Giovanni (sän jôvän'nē) or Isolina (ēzōlē'nä), smallest and northernmost islet, also has gardens. Isola Superiore (sōōpĕrēō'rĕ) or Isola dei Pescatori (dā pĕskätō'rē) (984 ft. by 328 ft.) is site of picturesque fishing village.

Borrowash, England: see DRAYCOTT.

Borrowdale (bŏ'rō–), picturesque valley in the Lake District, S Cumberland, England, 6 mi. S of Keswick, frequented by tourists. Site of plumbago mines, now exhausted.

Borrowstounness (bōnĕs', bŏ"rōstŭn-nĕs') or **Bo'ness** (bōnĕs'), burgh (1931 pop. 10,095; 1951 census 9,949), NW West Lothian, Scotland, on Firth of Forth, 3 mi. N of Linlithgow, 15 mi. WNW of Edinburgh; coal mining, mfg. of pottery, synthetic fertilizer; iron founding, whisky distilling; coal-shipping port. Just S are traces of Wall of Antoninus (Graham's Dyke).

Borsa (bûr'sä), Nor. *Børsa*, village and canton (pop. 1,556), Sor-Trondelag co., central Norway, on an inlet of Trondheim Fjord, 12 mi. SW of Trondheim; agr., cattle raising. Has medieval parish church. Formerly called Borsen (Nor. *Børsen*).

Borsa (bôr'shä), Rum. *Borşa*, Hung. *Kolozsborsa* (kô'lôzh-bôr"shŏ). **1** Village (pop. 3,083), Cluj prov., W central Rumania, 11 mi. NNE of Cluj; agr. center. In Hungary, 1940–45. **2** Village (pop. 12,294), Rodna prov., NW Rumania, on W slopes of the Carpathians, 38 mi. SE of Sighet; rail terminus and lumbering center; also summer resort (alt. 2,182 ft.); mineral springs. In Hungary, 1940–45.

Borsad (bōr'sŭd), town (pop. 16,937), Kaira dist., N Bombay, India, 27 mi. SSE of Kaira; market center for rice, millet, cotton, tobacco; hand-loom weaving. Has 18th-cent. Mahratta fortress.

Borsec (bôr'sĕk), Hung. *Borszék* (bôr'säk), village (pop. 2,247), Mures prov., central Rumania, in Transylvania, in the Moldavian Carpathians, 45 mi. NE of Targu-Mures; well-known health resort (alt. 2,887 ft.) with carbonic springs and mud baths; also winter-sports center, notably for skiing. Bottles and exports mineral waters. Lignite mining. In Hungary, 1940–45.

Borsen, Norway: see BORSA.

Borshchev (bôr'shchĭf), Pol. *Borszczów* (bôr'-shchōōf), city (1931 pop. 6,073), SE Ternopol oblast, Ukrainian SSR, 18 mi. SE of Chortkov; livestock-trading and agr.-processing (grain, vegetable oils, tobacco) center. Has ruins of old castle. Passed from Poland to Austria (1772); reverted to Poland (1919); ceded to USSR in 1945.

Borshchovochny Range or **Borshchovochnyy Range** (bŭrshchô'vŭchnē), S Chita oblast, Russian SFSR, extends from Mongolian frontier 375 mi. NE to confluence of Shilka and Argun rivers. Highest peak, SOKHONDO. Abounds in precious stones.

Borsippa (bôrsĭ'pŭ), anc. Babylonian city near Babylon; its site is thought to be the ruins at the mound Birs Nimrud, central Iraq, in Hilla prov., 12 mi. S of site of Babylon, near the Euphrates. A large square temple (ziggurat) here is sometimes mentioned as possible site of Tower of Babel.

Borskoye (bôr'skŭyŭ), village (1926 pop. 5,271), E Kuibyshev oblast, Russian SFSR, on Samara R., on railroad and 65 mi. ESE of Kuibyshev; flour milling; wheat, sunflowers.

Borsod-Gömör (bôr'shôd-gû'mûr), county (□1,407; pop. 276,812), NE Hungary; ⊙ Miskolc. Predominantly forested mts.; level in SE; includes Bükk Mts. (center); drained by Tisza, Sajo, and Bodva rivers. Lignite mined in lower Sajo valley. Steel and iron mills at MISKOLC, Diosgyör, and Ozd. Some agr. (grain, tobacco, lentils), livestock (cattle, hogs) in SE; agr. center is MEZÖKÖVESD.

Borsodnadasd (bôr'shôdnädŏzhd), Hung. *Borsodnádasd*, town (pop. 3,269), Borsod-Gömör co., NE Hungary, 7 mi. S of Ozd; sheet-metal works.

Börssum (bûr'sōōm), village (pop. 2,516), in Brunswick, NW Germany, after 1945 Lower Saxony, 7 mi. SSE of Wolfenbüttel, in sugar-beet region; rail junction.

Borstal, village, Kent, England, just SW of Rochester. At Borstal Institution originated (1902) the system whereby for the indiscriminate punishment of young offenders was substituted a work-rehabilitation program.

Borszczow, Ukrainian SSR: see BORSHCHEV.

Borszek, Rumania: see BORSEC.

Borth, small seaside resort in Llancynfelyn (lăn-kĭnvĕ'lĭn) parish (pop. 552), N Cardigan, Wales, on Cardigan Bay of Irish Sea, 5 mi. N of Aberystwyth. Agr. village of Llancynfelyn is 3 mi. ENE of Borth.

Borthwick (bôrth'wĭk), agr. village and parish (pop. 3,169), E Midlothian, Scotland, 12 mi. SE of Edinburgh. Near by is 15th-cent. Borthwick Castle, retreat of Mary Queen of Scots and Bothwell after their marriage. It was shelled (1650) by Cromwell.

Bortigali (bôrtēgä'lē), village (pop. 2,601), Nuoro prov., central Sardinia, 26 mi. W of Nuoro.

Bort-les-Orgues (bôr-lāzôrg′), town (pop. 4,365), Corrèze dept., S central France, in a widening of Dordogne R. gorge and 14 mi. SE of Ussel; commercial and industrial center with textile mills (work clothes, silk), tanneries, and flour mills. Near-by organ-shaped basalt columns (280 ft. high) are a tourist attraction. Marmontel b. here. Formerly called Bort.

Bor u Ceske Lipy, Czechoslovakia: see NOVY BOR.

Borujan or **Brujan** (both: brōōjän′), village, Tenth Prov., in Isfahan, central Iran, 30 mi. W of Shahriza.

Borujerd, Iran: see BURUJIRD.

Borumieda, Ethiopia: see BORO MYODA.

Borup (bō′rōōp), town (pop. 659), Copenhagen amt, Zealand, Denmark, 25 mi. SW of Copenhagen; chemicals.

Bor u Tachova, Czechoslovakia: see BOR.

Borynia, Ukrainian SSR: see BORINYA.

Boryslaw, Ukrainian SSR: see BORISLAV.

Borysthenes, USSR: see DNIEPER RIVER.

Borzhomi (bŭrzhô′mē), city (1939 pop. over 10,000), central Georgian SSR, on Kura R., on railroad and 70 mi. W of Tiflis; alt. 2,660 ft. Subalpine health resort in picturesque location; mineral (alkaline-carbonic) springs; mineral-water bottling, sawmilling. Linked by narrow-gauge railroad with resorts of Tsagveri and Bakuriani. Until 1936, Borzhom.

Borzna (bŭrznä′), town (1926 pop. 10,903), E central Chernigov oblast, Ukrainian SSR, 15 mi. WNW of Bakhmach; food processing, clothing mfg.

Borzonasca (bôrtsônä′skä), village (pop. 906), Genova prov., Liguria, N Italy, 8 mi. NNE of Chiavari; cotton mills; charcoal trade; hydroelectric plant. Abbey, founded 1184, near by.

Börzsöny Mountains (bûr′zhûnyû), N Hungary, extend c.20 mi. bet. the Danube and the Ipoly, rising to 3,080 ft. in Mt. Csovanyos; forested slopes; quarries.

Borzya (bŭrzyä′), town (1948 pop. over 10,000), SE Chita oblast, Russian SFSR, on branch of Trans-Siberian RR and 175 mi. SE of Chita, in livestock-raising area; meat-packing. Junction for railroad to Choybalsan, Mongolia.

Bosa (bô′zä), town (pop. 6,828), Nuoro prov., W Sardinia, port on Mediterranean coast, 15 mi. WNW of Macomer; rail terminus; tunny fishing; tanning; olive oil, Malmsey wine; domestic embroidery and netting. Bishopric has cathedral and church of San Pietro (built 1173). Ruins of Serravalle (12th-cent. castle), nuraghi near by.

Bosanska, Bosanski, Bosansko [Serbo-Croatian, =Bosnian], for Yugoslav names beginning thus: see under following part of the name.

Bösarkany (bû′shärkänyû), Hung. *Bősárkány*, town (pop. 2,388), Sopron co., W Hungary, 18 mi. W of Györ; wheat, corn, cattle.

Bosau (bō′zou), village (pop. 5,875), in Schleswig-Holstein, NW Germany, on E shore of Plön L., 8 mi. WSW of Eutin; summer resort. Has 12th-cent. church. Until 1937 in Oldenburg.

Boscastle (bŏs′kă″sŭl), village, NE Cornwall, England, on the Atlantic and 15 mi. WNW of Launceston. Tourist resort; fishing port.

Boscawen (bŏs′kwĭn, -kûwĭn), town (pop. 1,857), Merrimack co., S central N.H., on the Merrimack just above Concord; wood products. Site of Daniel Webster's 1st law office (1805). W. P. Fessenden b. here. Town includes part of PENACOOK village. Settled 1734, inc. 1760.

Boscawen Island, Tonga: see TAFAHI.

Bosch, Den, Netherlands: see 's HERTOGENBOSCH.

Boschplaat (bŏs′plät), uninhabited island, Groningen prov., N Netherlands, bet. North Sea and the Waddenzee, 11 mi. N of Warffum; 1.5 mi. long, 1 mi. wide.

Boschvoorde, Belgium: see WATERMAEL-BOITSFORT.

Boscobel (bŏ′skōbĕl), agr. hamlet and parish (pop. 17), E Shropshire, England, 5 mi. ENE of Shifnal. After the battle of Worcester (1651), Boscobel Manor here was refuge of Charles II, who hid also in a near-by oak tree.

Boscobel (bŏ′skûbĕl, bŏskûbĕl′), city (pop. 2,347), Grant co., extreme SW Wis., on Wisconsin R. and 23 mi. ENE of Prairie du Chien, in dairy and farm area; beer, lumber, garage equipment, metal products. Gideons Bible society founded here, 1898. Inc. 1873.

Bosco Marengo (bôs′kô märĕng′gô), village (pop. 1,907), Alessandria prov., Piedmont, N Italy, 7 mi. SSE of Alessandria; sausage.

Boscombe, England: see BOURNEMOUTH.

Boscoreale (bôs″kôrĕä′lĕ), town (pop. 7,972), Napoli prov., Campania, S Italy, at S foot of Vesuvius, adjacent to Boscotrecase; macaroni, Lachryma Christi wine. A famous collection of silverwork (1st cent. A.D.), consisting mostly of plates and cups with relief ornamentation, was unearthed here in 1895 and is now in the Louvre, Paris.

Boscotrecase (bôs″kôtrĕkä′zĕ), town (pop. 11,259), Napoli prov., Campania, S Italy, at S foot of Vesuvius, adjacent to Boscoreale, 1 mi. N of Torre Annunziata. Produces Lachryma Christi wine. Destroyed 1631, damaged 1906 by lava flow. Start of road ascending Vesuvius.

Bosdorf (bûs′dôrf), village (pop. 1,474), Saxony, E central Germany, on the White Elster and 8 mi. SW of Leipzig; synthetic-oil plant.

Bosham (bŏ′zŭm), town and parish (pop. 1,744), W Sussex, England, on Bosham Channel, an inlet of Chichester Harbour, 4 mi. W of Chichester; agr. market, with flour mills; fishing port and yachting center. Town is associated with Canute, whose daughter is reputedly buried in 11th-cent. church, which appears on Bayeux Tapestry.

Boshchekul or **Boshchekul'** (bŭshchĭkōōl′), village, W Pavlodar oblast, Kazakh SSR, near S.Siberian RR, 110 mi. W of Pavlodar; extensive copper deposits.

Boshippo, Korea: see TAEJONG.

Boshnyakovo (bŭshnyä′kûvû), town (1947 pop. over 500), on W coast of S Sakhalin, Russian SFSR, 18 mi. N of Lesogorsk; coal mining. Under Jap. rule (1905–45), called Nishi-shakutan.

Boshof (bôs′hôf), town (pop. 2,641), W Orange Free State, U. of So. Afr., 30 mi. ENE of Kimberley; stock, grain.

Boshruyeh, Iran: see BUSHRUYEH.

Bo'si, Aden: see YAFA.

Bosiljgrad, Bosilgrad, or **Bosil'grad** (all: bô′sĭlgrät), Bulg. *Bosilegrad*, village (pop. 2,111), SE Serbia, Yugoslavia, 23 mi. E of Vranje, near Bulg. border. In Bulgaria, 1913–19.

Boskoop (bŏs′kōp), town (pop. 8,571), South Holland prov., W Netherlands, 5 mi. NNW of Gouda; tree and flower nursery center (roses, rhododendrons, azaleas), fruit, strawberry growing; shipbuilding machine shops, mfg. of crates, boxes.

Boskovice (bô′skôvĭtsĕ), Ger. *Boskowitz* (bôs′kōvĭts), town (pop. 6,396), W central Moravia, Czechoslovakia, on railroad and 20 mi. NNE of Brno; textile mfg.; coal mining, quarrying. Has 16th-cent. Gothic church, 17th-cent. town hall and synagogue, large castle.

Bosmoreau-les-Mines (bōsmôrō′-lā-mēn′), village (pop. 206), Creuse dept., central France, on Taurion R. and 13 mi. SW of Guéret; anthracite.

Bosna i Hercegovina, Yugoslavia: see BOSNIA AND HERZEGOVINA.

Bosna River (bôs′nä), E Bosnia, Yugoslavia, rises at NE foot of the Treskavica, 12 mi. S of Sarajevo; flows 191 mi. N, past Visoko, Zenica, Maglaj, and Doboj, to Sava R. at Samac. Navigable for 96 mi. Receives Miljacka, Krivaja, Usora, and Spreca rivers. Trout-breeding station near Sarajevo. Its valley, through which passes Sarajevo-Samac RR (opened 1947) is site of growing metallurgical industry.

Bosna-Saraï, Yugoslavia: see SARAJEVO.

Bosnia and Herzegovina (bŏz′nēû, hĕrtsûgōvē′nû), Serbo-Croatian *Bosna i Hercegovina* (bôs′nä ē hĕr′tsĕgôvĭnä), constituent republic (□ 19,909; pop. 2,561,961), central Yugoslavia; ⊙ Sarajevo. Bounded by Croatia (W, N), Serbia (E), and Montenegro (SE). Consists of 2 regions: Bosnia, Turk. *Bosna*, Ger. *Bosnien*, in N; smaller HERZEGOVINA (S), which approximately corresponds to basin of Neretva R. The republic reaches the Adriatic Sea near NEUM and nearly extends to Gulf of Kotor, but its coastline lacks harbor facilities. Lies entirely in DINARIC ALPS; drained by Sava and Neretva rivers and their tributaries. Area is 50% forested, 25% cultivated, 25% meadows and pastures. Agr. is most developed in Sava and Drina valleys; chief crops are grain (mostly corn, wheat, oats, barley); vegetables (mostly potatoes) and industrial crops (sugar beets, rape, flax, tobacco) are also grown. Fruit (chiefly plums) raised in central and N Bosnia; winegrowing in Herzegovina (notably near MOSTAR and STOLAC). Forestry and stock raising (mostly sheep) are also important. Minerals include coal (near SARAJEVO and MOSTAR), lignite (near TUZLA), iron (VARES, LJUBIJA), copper (GORNJI VAKUF), manganese (CEVLJANOVICI), lead, mercury, and silver (SREBRENICA), and salt (TUZLA). Hydroelectric power at JAJCE, mineral waters at ILIDZA, TESLIC, and SREBRENICA. Well-developed home industry and handicrafts, producing a variety of metal, leather, and textile products. Industry is limited chiefly to lumber milling, iron- and steelworking (at ZENICA), mfg. of tobacco and leather, brewing, sugar milling, and plum processing. Transportation facilities are poor. Roads are insufficient and nearly all railroads are of narrow gauge. Besides Sarajevo, chief towns are Banja Luka, Tuzla, Mostar, Zenica, and Bijeljina. Pop. mainly agr., consists of Serbs and Croats, divided among Moslem, R.C., and Orthodox Eastern religions. Bosnia was settled by Croatians and Serbs in 7th cent.; by 12th cent. was an independent country ruled by bans who acknowledged kings of Hungary as suzerains. Became (1376) a kingdom; fell to Turks in 1463. Herzegovina (intermittently ruled by Bosnia after 1325) was finally inc. into Bosnia under Turkish rule. Frequent Christian insurrections (notably 1850, 1875). Congress of Berlin (1878) placed Bosnia and Herzegovina under Austro-Hungarian administration and occupation, while recognizing theoretical sovereignty of the sultan. Bosnia and Herzegovina was fully annexed to Austria-Hungary in 1908; this aroused Serbian nationalism, and the assassination (1914) by a Serbian nationalist of Archduke Francis Ferdinand at Sarajevo precipitated the First World War. Bosnia and Herzegovina were annexed to Serbia in 1918 as part of Yugoslavia. In 1929, they were divided into the banovinas of Primorje, Vrbas, Drina, and Zeta; in 1941, became part of Croatia. In 1946 Bosnia and Herzegovina became one of the 6 Yugoslav people's republics and includes (since 1949) oblasts of Banja Luka, Mostar, Sarajevo, and Tuzla.

Bosobolo (bōsōbō′lō), village, Equator Prov., NW Belgian Congo, 175 mi. NW of Lisala, in cotton-growing area; trading center; cotton ginning.

Bosohli, Kashmir: see BASOLI.

Boso Peninsula, Japan: see CHIBA PENINSULA.

Bosoteni (bôshôtän′), Rum. *Boşoteni*, village (pop. 438), Dolj prov., S Rumania, 12 mi. NW of Caracal.

Bosphorus, Eastern, strait, Russian SFSR: see EASTERN BOSPHORUS.

Bosporus (bŏs′pûrûs) [Gr.,=ox ford, in reference to its crossing by Io in the form of a cow], Turkish *Karadeniz Boğazı*, strait (17 mi. long, ½–1½ mi. wide), separating European from Asiatic Turkey and joining the Black Sea with the Sea of Marmara. The Bosporus and DARDANELLES, leading to the Mediterranean, have long been of great strategic importance. ISTANBUL (Constantinople) is on the Bosporus, which is lined with villas and old castles. On it is the narrow inlet, the Golden Horn, forming the harbor of Istanbul. The strait has been refortified by Turkey after the Montreux Convention of 1936. Formerly sometimes Bosphorus.

Bosporus Cimmerius, USSR: see KERCH STRAIT.

Bosque (bŏ′skē), county (□ 1,003; pop. 11,836), central Texas; ⊙ Meridian. Hilly in W, bounded NE and E by Brazos R., drained by Bosque R. Agr. (oats, corn, grain sorghums, peanuts, cotton, wheat, pecans, legumes); livestock (cattle, sheep, goats, hogs); wool, mohair, poultry, eggs marketed. Limestone quarrying; timber (mainly cedar). Formed 1854.

Bosque, El, Mexico: see EL BOSQUE.

Bosque, El (ĕl bō′skā), town (pop. 1,184), Cádiz prov., SW Spain, in spur of the Cordillera Penibética, 17 mi. E of Arcos de la Frontera; cereals, olives, fruit, timber. Has saltworks and mineral springs. Jasper, coal, sulphur, and gypsum deposits near by.

Bosque River (bŏ′skē), central Texas, rises as intermittent stream (sometimes called North Bosque R.) in Erath co., flows c.100 mi. generally SE, past Stephenville, to the Brazos just NW of Waco. Near mouth, dam (1923) impounds L. Waco (39,000 acre-ft.; recreational area). Lake receives Middle Bosque R. (c.35 mi. long) from W, South Bosque R. (c.20 mi. long) from S.

Bosquet (bôskā′), village (pop. 1,109), Oran dept., NW Algeria, 17 mi. NE of Mostaganem; wine.

Bosra, Syria: see BUSRA.

Bosra Eski Sham, Syria: see BUSRA.

Bossaga (bŭsûgä′), village, SE Chardzhou oblast, Turkmen SSR, on the Amu Darya and 35 mi. SE of Kerki; frontier station on Afghan border. Has canal installations at head of Kara-Kum Canal.

Bossangoa (bōsäng-gwä′), town, ⊙ Ouham region (□ 19,300; 1950 pop. 123,100), N central Ubangi-Shari, Fr. Equatorial Africa, on left bank of Ouham R. and 170 mi. NW of Bangui; cotton center; also millet growing.

Bossekop (bôs′sûkōp), fishing village (pop. 914) in Alta canton, Finnmark co., N Norway, on Alta Fjord, just N of Alta, 50 mi. SSW of Hammerfest. Scene of Lapp fairs and reindeer markets.

Bossembélé (bōsĕmbĕlā′), village, S Ubangi-Shari, Fr. Equatorial Africa, 85 mi. NW of Bangui.

Bossier (bō′zhûr), parish (□ 841; pop. 40,139), NW La.; ⊙ Benton. Situated on Ark. line (N); bounded W by Red R., SE by L. Bistineau; drained by the Bodcau Bayou. Agr. area (cotton, corn, hay, fruit, sweet potatoes, peanuts), with oil and natural-gas fields, refineries, pipelines; timber. Industry at Bossier City; also cotton ginning, lumber milling in parish. Shipping on Red R. Formed 1843.

Bossier City, town (pop. 15,470), Bossier parish, NW La., on Red R. (bridged here), opposite Shreveport; oil refineries, railroad shops; cotton and cottonseed processing; mfg. of fertilizer, wood and metal products, machinery, chemicals, mattresses, concrete and creosoted products. Ruins of Confederate Fort Smith were made a memorial park in 1936. Inc. as village in 1907, as town in 1923.

Bossmo, Norway: see BASMOEN.

Bosso (bō′sō), village, SE Niger territory, Fr. West Africa, at mouth of Komadugu-Yobe R., on L. Chad, and on Nigeria border; millet, livestock.

Bossons, Les (lā bôsô′), Alpine village of Haute-Savoie dept., SE France, resort in Chamonix valley, 2 mi. SW of Chamonix; alt. 3,320 ft. Bossons glacier (3 mi. long) descends from Aiguille du Midi (SE) to within 1 mi. of village.

Bostam, Iran: see BUSTAM.

Bostan, Iran: see BUSTAN.

Bostan (bō′stän), village, Quetta-Pishin dist., NE Baluchistan, W Pakistan, 13 mi. N of Quetta; rail junction; market center (wheat, carpets).

Bostanabad, Iran: see BUSTANABAD.

Bostic (bŏ′stĭk), town (pop. 227), Rutherford co., SW N.C., 17 mi. WNW of Shelby.

Boston or **Central Boston** (sĕnträl′), sugar-mill village (pop. 945), Oriente prov., E Cuba, on Banes Bay, and 4 mi. S of Banes.

Boston, municipal borough (1931 pop. 16,600; 1951 census 24,453), Parts of Holland, SE Lincolnshire, England, on Witham R. 4 mi. NW of its mouth on The Wash, and 28 mi. SE of Lincoln; once an important port, now a fishing center and agr. market center, with agr.-machinery works. The 14th-cent. St. Botolph's Church, with blunt 290-ft. tower (called the Stump), is on site of 7th-cent. monastery founded by St. Botolph. In the old Guildhall some of the Pilgrim Fathers were tried (1607) and imprisoned for trying to leave the country. The settlers of Boston, Mass., under John Cotton sailed from here in 1633. In early 13th cent. Boston was the 2d-largest port of England.

Boston. 1 Town (pop. 700), Marion co., NW Ala., 31 mi. NW of Jasper. 2 City (pop. 1,035), Thomas co., S Ga., 12 mi. ESE of Thomasville, in farm, livestock, and lumber area. Inc. 1870. 3 Town (pop. 257), Wayne co., E Ind., near Ohio line, 7 mi. S of Richmond. 4 City (□ 65.9; 1940 pop. 770,816; 1950 pop. 801,444), ⊙ Mass. and Suffolk co., E Mass., on an arm (Boston Bay) of Massachusetts Bay and c.180 mi. NE of New York; 42°21′N 71°3′W; alt. sea level to 330 ft. Largest city of New England and 10th largest of U.S., Boston is focus of a metropolitan region containing c.½ of pop. of Mass. and extending into S N.H., and is the commercial, industrial, financial, and cultural center of New England; it is a large seaport and port of entry, its historical shrines attract tourists, and it is an important market for wool and fish (leads U.S.) and leather. Industries produce textiles (cotton, woolen), shoes, leather, machinery, food products (packed meat, frozen and canned fish, bakery goods, refined sugar, confectionery), rubber goods, petroleum products, soap, chemicals, medicines, electrical equipment, furniture, pianos; has shipbuilding and repair yards, printing and publishing plants. Port, which ranks high in U.S. in value of imports, receives fish, hides, wool, rubber, fertilizer, sugar, coffee, fruit, ores, petroleum, coal, wood pulp, lumber, cotton, flax, hemp, and sisal; ships textiles, leather, grain products, wood products, cordage, machinery, and other manufactured goods. Served by 3 railroads, many foreign and coast-wise steamship lines, several airlines; Logan Internatl. Airport is in E.Boston. Its educational institutions include Harvard Univ. and Mass. Inst. of Technology (both in near-by CAMBRIDGE), New England Medical Center and Harvard Medical School, Simmons Col., Emmanuel Col., Boston Univ., Boston Col. (mainly at CHESTNUT HILL), Tufts Col. (at near-by Medford), Northeastern Univ., Mass. Col. of Pharmacy, New England Conservatory of Music (founded 1867), Wentworth Inst., Franklin Technical Inst. Noted Mass. General Hosp. (founded 1811) is here. Military and naval air bases, Boston Army Base, and several forts are in city and on isls. in Boston Bay. Boston was settled 1630 by the elder John Winthrop as main colony of Massachusetts Bay Company. A center of American Puritanism, with notable ministers and statesmen, Boston (whose ships and fisheries early made it the colonies' commercial leader), soon provided for its intellectual life. Boston Public Latin School (one of 1st free public schools in the country) was est. 1635, Harvard Univ. in 1636; a public library was started in 1653; the 1st newspaper in the colonies (the *News Letter*) appeared in 1704. At approach of the Revolution, Boston workers and merchants joined to oppose the British and conservative Loyalists; the Boston Massacre (1770) and the Boston Tea Party (1773) were pre-Revolutionary incidents which aroused great patriotic feeling. After the actions at Lexington and Concord, the British retreated to Boston, where the 1st large-scale battle of the Revolution was fought at Bunker Hill (in CHARLESTOWN) on June 17, 1775; the British finally withdrew in March, 1776. At close of the war began the period of prosperity based on world-girdling ships and on fortunes yielded by shoe and textile mills on New England rivers which continued until middle of 19th cent., when industrial expansion in the Boston area attracted many immigrants and modified city's predominantly commercial character. The cultural traditions of the "Athens of America," where learning, arts, and letters flourished, survived, however, despite economic change and influx of newcomers from many lands; such men as Emerson, Hawthorne, Longfellow, Whittier, Lowell, Oliver Wendell Holmes, and Thoreau contributed to its intellectual leadership; and, despite Boston's general conservatism, Abolitionists, such as William Lloyd Garrison, Wendell Phillips, and Charles Sumner, were strongly backed. Today, among cherished landmarks and monuments of the past in Boston are the 17th-cent. Paul Revere house, city's oldest; Faneuil Hall (fă'nŭl) (built 1742), where Revolutionary patriots met; Christ (Old North) Church, in whose tower lanterns signaled start of Paul Revere's ride; Old South Meetinghouse, a Revolutionary rallying place; old statehouse (now a mus.), near which occurred the Boston Massacre; Boston Common (with the Old Granary burial ground, containing graves of John Hancock, Samuel Adams, Paul Revere, Peter Faneuil, Robert Treat Payne), and the Public Gardens; the golden-domed statehouse, with its "front" designed by Bulfinch; the old houses of Beacon Hill, Louisburg Square, and Back Bay; King's Chapel (1754), birthplace (1785) of American Unitarianism, with a graveyard in which Governor Winthrop, John Cotton, and John Davenport are buried. Also in Boston are the Mother Church of Christian Science; Trinity Church (built 1872–77), designed by H. H. Richardson and decorated by John La Farge; the Public Library (founded 1852; oldest free municipal library in U.S.); the Mus. of Fine Arts; the Athenaeum (ă"thūnē'ŭm); the Mass. Historical Society; and the Isabella Stewart Gardner Mus. of Art. The famous Boston Symphony Orchestra (founded 1881) performs in Symphony Hall (1900). Expansion of Boston's limits (it became a city in 1822) to meet Brookline on the W, Dedham on the SW, and Quincy on the SE, took in cities and towns, some with traditions as long as Boston's: Roxbury and West Roxbury (with Roxbury Latin School, Forest Hills Cemetery, and Brook Farm, which flourished 1841–47 as a noted experiment in group living), Dorchester (dôr'chĕ"stŭr, dôr'-chĭstŭr), Charlestown (site of Boston Navy Yard), Brighton, Hyde Park, Allston (ôl'stŭn), Roslindale, Neponset (nĭpŏn'sĭt), Mattapan (mă'tŭpăn"), Jamaica Plain, East Boston (on isl. to NE, across the harbor: ferry and tunnel connections; site of Logan Internatl. Airport), and South Boston. Settlement's location on a NE-pointing peninsula (called by early settlers the Neck) bet. Charles R. (N) and an inlet of Boston Bay (dividing it from South Boston) has dictated the modern city's crowded and irregular street pattern as well as the concentration of historical, commercial, and cultural points of interest within this limited area. Tip of Boston peninsula has wheel-like street layout, with streets radiating irregularly from its center and others running in roughly concentric circles. Wharves and docks line the NE and E shores (the harbor dist. also extends into South Boston); on N (Charles R.) shore opposite Cambridge extends the Charles R. Embankment, where, along the Esplanade, the Boston Symphony has performed its annual summer "Pops" concerts since 1929; near by are the Common and the Public Gardens, from whose vicinity Beacon St. and Commonwealth Ave., among city's finest residential streets, extend W to the Back Bay dist., also exclusively residential. Beyond to SW lie Roxbury, West Roxbury, and Hyde Park; to S extend South Boston, Dorchester, and Neponset. City's nickname, "the Hub of the Universe," is derived from its 19th cent. position of intellectual, political, and commercial leadership. 5 Village, Erie co., W N.Y., 20 mi. SSE of Buffalo; canned foods. 6 Village (1940 pop. 1,367), Allegheny co., SW Pa., on Youghiogheny R. and 4 mi. SE of McKeesport. 7 Village (pop. c.100), ⊙ Bowie co., NE Texas, near Red R., 22 mi. W of Texarkana, just S of NEW BOSTON, in agr. area.

Boston Bay, inlet of Spencer Gulf, S South Australia, on SE Eyre Peninsula, bet. Boston Point (N) and Point Kirton (S); 6 mi. long, 3 mi. wide. Sheltered (E) by Boston Isl. (4 mi. long, 1.5 mi. wide). Port Lincoln on SW shore.

Boston Bay, Mass., inner portion (13 mi. long NW–SE) of Massachusetts Bay of the Atlantic; its entrance is bet. S tip of Deer Isl. (N) and Allerton Point (S). Boston is at head of N arm (Boston Harbor), which is entered by Mystic and Charles rivers in N and by Neponset R. in S (Dorchester Bay); Quincy Bay is the portion lying off Quincy (on SW shore); SE arm, sheltered on E by Nantasket Peninsula, is called Hingham Bay (hĭng'ŭm). Has deepwater anchorages, dredged channels, and extensive port facilities in its bordering cities. Largest of its isls. are Thompson, Spectacle, Long, and Peddocks. Name Boston Harbor is sometimes applied to entire bay.

Boston Heights, village (pop. 646), Summit co., NE Ohio, 11 mi. N of Akron.

Bostonia, village (1940 pop. 1,398), San Diego co., S Calif., 15 mi. E of San Diego, in vineyard and orchard region (citrus fruit, avocados).

Boston Island, Australia: see BOSTON BAY.

Boston Island, Marshall Isls.: see EBON.

Boston Mountains, in Okla. and Ark., most rugged section (c.200 mi. long, 35 mi. wide) of the Ozarks, bounded S by Arkansas R., and extending E from Illinois R. (E Okla.) to White R. (E central Ark.); rise to c.2,345 ft. NW of Fort Smith. White R. has its source here. Include Devil's Den State Park and part of Ozark Natl. Forest.

Bostonnais River (bôstônā'), S central Que., issues from Grand Lac Bostonnais (8 mi. long), 40 mi. S of L. St. John, flows 70 mi. SW to St. Maurice R. just N of La Tuque. There are several falls. Also called Bastonnais R.

Boston Point, S South Australia, in Spencer Gulf; forms N end of Boston Bay of SE Eyre Peninsula; 34°39′S 135°56′E.

Boston Spa, resort town and parish (pop. 1,433), West Riding, central Yorkshire, England, on Wharfe R. and 12 mi. WSW of York; medicinal springs. Near by is Wharfedale Col..

Bostra, Syria: see BUSRA.

Bostwick (bŏst'wĭk), town (pop. 287), Morgan co., N central Ga., 17 mi. SSW of Athens.

Bosumtwi, Lake (bōsōōm'twē), largest (□ 18.4) of Gold Coast, in S Ashanti, 17 mi. SE of Kumasi; 233 ft. deep. Probably volcanic in origin; lies in circular depression (5 mi. in diameter) surrounded by steep hills rising 1,400 ft. above lake level. No surface outlet.

Bosut River (bô'sōōt), in Slavonia and the Srem, Yugoslavia, rises 6 mi. N of Samac (Croatia), flows 115 mi. ESE, past Vinkovci, to Sava R. 12 mi. W of Sremska Mitrovica. Navigable for 25 mi.

Bosvoorde, Belgium: see WATERMAEL-BOITSFORT.

Boswell (bŏz'wĕl). 1 Town (pop. 963), Benton co., W Ind., 26 mi. WNW of Lafayette, in grain area; poultry hatchery. 2 Town (pop. 875), Choctaw co., SE Okla., 21 mi. W of Hugo, in agr. area (livestock, grain, cotton); lumber milling. 3 Borough (pop. 1,679), Somerset co., SW Pa., 11 mi. SW of Johnstown; coal, coke; lumber; clothing. Inc. 1904.

Boswell Reservoir, Okla.: see CLEAR BOGGY CREEK.

Bosworth (bŏz'wûrth), city (pop. 503), Carroll co., NW central Mo., near Grand R., 13 mi. NE of Carrollton; grain.

Bosworth Field, England: see MARKET BOSWORTH.

Bot (bôt), village (pop. 1,348), Tarragona prov., NE Spain, 4 mi. SW of Gandesa; olive-oil processing, almond shipping; wine, cereals.

Bota (bō'tä), village (pop. 342), central Perak, Malaya, on Perak R. and 22 mi. SW of Ipoh; rice.

Botad (bō'täd), town (pop. 15,842), E Saurashtra, India, 40 mi. NW of Bhaunagar; rail junction; trade center (grain, cotton, salt, oilseeds); cotton ginning, hand-loom weaving; metalware.

Botafogo (bôtŭfō'gōō), old residential district of Rio de Janeiro, Brazil, on Botafogo Bay (semi-circular inlet of Guanabara Bay) skirted by palm-lined Avenida Beira Mar. It is overlooked by CORCOVADO peak.

Botan River, Turkey: see BUHTAN RIVER.

Botany, municipality (pop. 9,462), E New South Wales, Australia, on NE shore of Botany Bay, 6 mi. S of Sydney, in metropolitan area; mfg. center (chemicals, soap, shoes, gelatin, cereal foods); iron foundries, tanneries.

Botany Bay, inlet of Pacific Ocean, E New South Wales, Australia, just S of Sydney, bet. Cape Banks and Cape Solander; roughly circular; 1 mi. wide at mouth, 5 mi. in diameter. Visited 1770 by Capt. Cook, who proclaimed Br. sovereignty over E coast of Australia; site of landing marked by monument on Inscription Point on S shore. Botany on NE shore. Although the landing site is often considered site of Australia's 1st penal colony, it was actually SYDNEY, 5 mi. N on Port Jackson.

Boteke (bōtĕ'kä) or **Flandria** (flăndrēä'), village, Equator Prov., W Belgian Congo, on Momboyo R. just SW of Ingende; center of palm-oil industry. Has R.C. mission and trade schools.

Botelhos (bōtā'lyōōs), city (pop. 2,477), SW Minas Gerais, Brazil, near São Paulo border, 15 mi. NE of Poços de Caldas; alt. 3,150 ft. Coffee, dairy products, cereals.

Botel Tobago, Formosa: see HUNGTOW ISLAND.

Boteni (bôtăn'), village (pop. 2,105), Arges prov., S central Rumania, 10 mi. SSE of Campulung; lignite mines.

Botesdale, agr. village and parish (pop. 402), N Suffolk, England, 13 mi. NE of Bury St. Edmunds. Important stage point in coaching days.

Botetourt (bŏ'tŭtŏt), county (□ 549; pop. 15,766), W Va.; ⊙ Fincastle. Mainly in Great Appalachian Valley, traversed by ridges; Blue Ridge is along SE boundary. Drained by James R. and Craig Creek. Includes part of Jefferson Natl. Forest. Agr. (especially tomatoes, grain, potatoes, fruit); dairying, lumbering; limestone quarrying, lime burning. Mtn. resorts. Formed 1770.

Botevgrad (bô'tĕvgrät), city (pop. 5,925), Sofia dist., W Bulgaria, at N end of Botevgrad Pass, 27 mi. NE of Sofia; agr. center in Botevgrad Basin (□ 57; average alt. 1,000 ft.; cattle, hogs, fruit, vegetables); dairying, woodworking. Site of battles during Russo-Turkish war in 1877 (commemorated by monuments). Until 1934, Orkhaniye; sometimes spelled Orchanie.

Botevgrad Pass (alt. 3,123 ft.), W Bulgaria, just S of Botevgrad, on highway to Sofia (SW); separates central and W Balkan Mts. Formerly Arabo Konak Pass.

Botev Peak (bô'tĕf), highest peak (7,793 ft.) in Kalofer and Balkan mts., central Bulgaria, 7 mi. NE of Karlovo. Tundzha R. rises at E foot. Formerly called Ferdinandov-vrakh and, until 1950, Yumrukchal.

Botfalu, Rumania: see BOD.

Both, India: see BOATH.

Botha (bŏ'thŭ), village (pop. 112), S central Alta., 8 mi. E of Stettler; dairying, wheat.

Bothaville (bō'tăvĭl), town (pop. 2,967), N Orange Free State, U. of So. Afr., near Transvaal border, on Valsch R., near its mouth on Vaal R., and 35 mi. S of Klerksdorp; alt. 4,236 ft.; agr. center (corn, sheep, stock); grain elevator.

Bothel and Threapland (bōōl-thrĕp'lŭnd), parish (pop. 364), W Cumberland, England. Includes granite-quarrying village of Bothel, 6 mi. NE of

Cockermouth, and cattle- and sheep-raising village of Threapland, 6 mi. NNE of Cockermouth.

Bothell (bŏ'thŭl, bä'–), town (pop. 1,019), King co., W central Wash., 12 mi. NNE of Seattle, near L. Washington; wood and dairy products, stock feed.

Bothnia, Gulf of (bŏth'nēŭ), N arm of Baltic Sea, bet. Sweden and Finland and closed off by Aland Isls.; 400 mi. long, 50–150 mi. wide. Of very low salinity, this shallow arm freezes over for 3–5 months in winter. It receives the Angerman, Ume, Lule, Torne, Kemi, and Oulu rivers. Chief ports are Pori, Vaasa, and Oulu, in Finland; Lulea, Harnosand, Sundsvall, and Gavle, in Sweden. Named for former riparian region of Bothnia (Swedish *Botten*), whose name remains in Norrbotten and Vasterbotten, 2 Swedish counties on NW shore.

Bothwell, town (pop. 677), S Ont., near Thames R., 23 mi. NE of Chatham; oil production; in dairying, mixed-farming region. Its oil industry has declined.

Bothwell (bŏth'wŭl), town and parish (pop. 60,660, including part of Motherwell and Wishaw burgh), N Lanark, Scotland, on the Clyde and 8 mi. ESE of Glasgow; residential district for Glasgow, in coal-mining region. Bothwell Bridge (or Brig) was scene (1649) of defeat of Covenanters by Royalists under Monmouth and Claverhouse, described in Scott's *Old Mortality*. Just NW of town are remains of noted 13th-cent. Bothwell Castle. Joanna Baillie b. in Bothwell.

Bothwell, town (pop. 241), SE central Tasmania, 37 mi. NNW of Hobart; livestock, wheat, oats.

Bothwell, town (pop. 317), Box Elder co., N Utah, 18 mi. NW of Brigham.

Boticas (bōtē'kŭsh), town (pop. 626), Vila Real dist., N Portugal, 12 mi. WSW of Chaves; candle making.

Botkins, village (pop. 608), Shelby co., W Ohio, 13 mi. N of Sidney; grain products.

Botlek, Netherlands: see BRIELSCHE MAAS RIVER.

Botley, town and parish (pop. 1,099), S Hampshire, England, on Hamble R. and 6 mi. E of Southampton; agr. market, with flour mills.

Botlikh (bôt'lyĭkh), village (1926 pop. 1,253), W Dagestan Autonomous SSR, Russian SFSR, on left bank of the Andi Koisu and 45 mi. WSW of Buinaksk; terminus of road from Grozny across Andi Range; fruit canning; orchards, grain. Pop. largely Andi.

Botnang (bōt'näng), residential W suburb of Stuttgart, Germany.

Botna River (bôt'nŭ), Moldavian SSR, rises W of Strasheny, flows 80 mi. SE and ENE, past Kainary and Kaushany, to marshy Dniester R. bank S of Tiraspol.

Botne (bôt'nù), village and canton (pop. 3,020), Vestfold co., SE Norway, 2 mi. W of Holmestrand; dairy plant. Rail junction at Hillestad, 4 mi. NW.

Botoma River (bŭtŭmä'), S Yakut Autonomous SSR, Russian SFSR, rises on NW Aldan Plateau, flows 300 mi. NNE to Lena R. above Pokrovsk. Iron deposits in lower course.

Botosani (bōtōshän'), Rum. *Botoşani*, town (1948 pop. 29,145), ⊙ Botosani prov., NE Rumania, in Moldavia, 60 mi. NW of Jassy; rail terminus and trading center (notably for grain and livestock). Mfg. of underwear, ribbons, earthenware, paper, soap, candles, toys, confectionery; tanning, flour milling, brewing. Founded in 14th cent., it has 15th- and 18th-cent. churches, and 15th-cent. monastery with old frescoes. About ⅓ of pop. are Jews. Sometimes spelled Botoshani.

Botrange (bōträzh'), highest mountain (2,283 ft.) in Belgium, in the Hohe Venn (N section of the Ardennes), 5 mi. NNE of Malmédy.

Botrys, Lebanon: see BATRUN.

Botte Donato (bôt'tĕ dônä'tô), highest peak (6,329 ft.) in La Sila mts., S Italy, 11 mi. E of Cosenza.

Bottineau (bŏtĭnō'), county (□ 1,699; pop. 12,140), N N.Dak., on Can. line; ⊙ Bottineau. Agr. area watered by Souris R., with Turtle Mts. in NE. Timber, diversified farming, dairy produce, livestock, wheat. Formed 1873.

Bottineau, city (pop. 2,268), ⊙ Bottineau co., N N.Dak., 57 mi. NE of Minot and on branch of Souris R., near Turtle Mts. Resort; diversified farming; timber; dairy products, wheat, potatoes, corn. Seat of N.Dak. School of Forestry. Inc. 1904.

Bottom, principal settlement of Saba, Du. West Indies, in the Leewards, 30 mi. NW of St. Kitts; 17°38'N 63°15'W. Built within extinct crater, and reached from ocean through steps ("The Ladder") cut into rock. Inhabitants engage in fishing, shipbuilding, mfg. of laces.

Bottom Creek, W.Va.: see VIVIAN.

Bottrighe (bôt-trē'gĕ), village (pop. 3,234), Rovigo prov., Veneto, N Italy, on Po R. and 2 mi. SSE of Adria.

Bottrop (bôt'rôp), city (1950 pop. 91,892), in former Prussian prov. of Westphalia, W Germany, after 1945 in North Rhine-Westphalia, in the Ruhr, on Rhine-Herne Canal, adjoining (N) Essen; coal-mining center; extraction of coal-tar products. Was peasant community with c.4,000 inhabitants in 1860. Opening of coal mines fostered rapid development. Chartered 1921.

Botucatu (bōōtōōkätōō'), city (1950 pop. 23,692), S São Paulo, Brazil, in the Serra de Botucatu, 90 mi. W of Campinas; rail junction and commercial center; mfg. (agr. machinery, footwear, clothing, flour products). Has experimental agr. station. Airfield.

Botucatu, Serra de (sĕ'rŭ dĭ), E escarpment of the Paraná plateau in central São Paulo, Brazil, extending c.50 mi. SW-NE from Paranapanema R. to Tietê R., just E of Botucatu.

Botwood, town (pop. 2,744), NE central N.F., at head of the Bay of Exploits, near mouth of Exploits R., 160 mi. NW of St. John's; 49°9'N 55°21' W. Port for Grand Falls newsprint mills and Buchans copper, lead, zinc, gold, silver output; site of fish-smoking plant. Lumbering is carried on in region. Port is closed during winter months. Botwood is site of seaplane base; experiments in transatlantic transport flights were made from here, 1937–38. In 1939 it became fuelling point for 1st transatlantic flying-boat service bet. New York and Southampton; later superseded by Gander. In Second World War Botwood was base of North Atlantic air patrols.

Bouaflé (bwä'flā), village (pop. c.800), central Ivory Coast, Fr. West Africa, on Bandama R. and 65 mi. SW of Bouaké; cacao, coffee, palm kernels. Gold placers near by.

Bouaké (bwä'kā, bwäkā'), town (pop. c.22,200), central Ivory Coast, Fr. West Africa, on railroad and 180 mi. NNW of Abidjan. Road junction, and processing and commercial center for productive interior region (coffee, cacao, tobacco, palm kernels, yams, rice, sisal, cotton). Cotton ginning, sisal processing; mfg. of textiles. Govt. veterinary dept.; livestock station, school of forestry. Airport. R.C. and Protestant missions. Gold and manganese deposits in vicinity.

Bou Anane (bōō änän'), Saharan outpost in Meknès region, SE Fr. Morocco, on Ksar-es-Souk–Bou Arfa road; 32°2'N 3°3'W.

Bouar (bwär'), village, NW Ubangi-Shari, Fr. Equatorial Africa, 70 mi. WSW of Bozoum; cotton gin. Has R.C. and Protestant missions, military camp.

Bou-Arada (bōō-ärädä'), town (pop. 1,820), Medjez-el-Bab dist., N central Tunisia, 22 mi. ESE of Teboursouk; wheat, barley, olive, and livestock trade. Silos. Scene of fighting (1943) during Second World War.

Bou Arfa (bōō ärfä'), village, Oujda region, E Fr. Morocco, on trans-Saharan RR (completed from Nemours to Colomb-Béchar, Algeria, and traversing Morocco territory) and 150 mi. S of Oujda; 32°38'N 1°55'W. Manganese-mining center worked since 1919. Beneficiation plant. Ore exported mostly through Nemours (Algeria). Also spelled Bouarfa.

Bouaye (bōōī'), village (pop. 428), Loire-Inférieure dept., W France, near N shore of L. of Grand-Lieu, 8 mi. SW of Nantes; truck gardening.

Bou Azzer (bōō äz-zĕr'), locality, Marrakesh region, SW Fr. Morocco, in E spur of the Anti-Atlas, 27 mi. S of Ouarzazate, at N edge of the Sahara; 30°32'N 6°57'W. Here is one of the world's leading cobalt mines, exploited since 1933. Nickel, gold, and asbestos also occur. Output shipped by road to Safi or Agadir.

Bou Beker (bōō bĕkĕr'), village, Oujda region, NE Fr. Morocco, near Algerian border, in W spurs of Tlemcen Mts., 14 mi. SSE of Oujda; important lead-mining center (expanded 1950) with smelter at Oued el Haïmer (5 mi. SW on railroad to Oujda).

Boubin (bō'bēn), Czech *Boubín*, mountain (4,467 ft.) in the Bohemian Forest, SW Bohemia, Czechoslovakia, 4 mi. SSW of Vimperk. Site of a forest reservation, under govt. protection (116 acres).

Bouble River (bōō'blù), Allier dept., central France, rises in Combrailles dist. 5 mi. W of Menat (Puy-de-Dôme dept.), flows 35 mi. NE, past Saint-Éloy-les-Mines and Chantelle, to the Sioule 2 mi. above Saint-Pourçain-sur-Sioule. Its slopes are lined with vineyards.

Bouca or **Bouka** (bōōkä'), village, central Ubangi-Shari, Fr. Equatorial Africa, 70 mi. E of Bossangoa; road communications point in cotton region; cotton ginning. Has a colony for trypanosomatic patients.

Bou-Caïd, Algeria: see ORLÉANSVILLE.

Boucau (bōōkō'), town (pop. 4,287), Basses-Pyrénées dept., SW France, port on right bank of Adour R. near its mouth on Bay of Biscay, and 2.5 mi. NNW of Bayonne; metallurgical center, with blast furnaces and forges; chemical factory (phosphate and pyrite processing); lumber mills (mfg. of pit-props). Handles bulky cargoes.

Bouchain (bōōshē'), town (pop. 1,937), Nord dept., N France, on the Escaut and 9 mi. NNE of Cambrai; mfg. (chicory, metal boxes, chemicals, cement). Formerly fortified.

Bou-Chebka (bōō-shĕbkä'), village, Kasserine dist., W Tunisia, on Algerian border, 21 mi. W of Kasserine. Customhouse. Pine woods. Roman ruins.

Boucheron (bōōshrō'), town (pop. 2,874), Casablanca region, NW Fr. Morocco, 30 mi. SE of Casablanca; agr. market (wheat, barley, cattle).

Boucherville (bōō'shŭrvĭl), village (pop. 1,047), S Que., on the St. Lawrence and 10 mi. NE of Montreal; food canning, clothing mfg. Founded 1668 by Pierre Boucher; manor house built by him still stands near by, now owned by Jesuits.

Bouches-du-Rhône (bōōsh-dü-rōn') [Fr.,=mouths of the Rhone], department (□ 2,026; pop. 976,241), in Provence, SE France; ⊙ Marseilles. Bounded by the Gulf of Lion (S), the Rhone and its delta (W), the lower Durance (N). E part mountainous, with limestone hills reaching the Mediterranean on both sides of Marseilles. The Étang de Berre (a lagoon with an outlet into the Gulf of Fos) lies in center. W part occupied by the stony CRAU lowland, dominated (N) by the Alpines hill range, and by the deltaic isl. of CAMARGUE. Though agr. is important only in Rhone and Durance valleys, dept. has large olive (for Marseilles soap factories), wine, fruit, and almond yields. Livestock raised in the Camargue. Here are France's leading lignite mines (near Fuveau) and saltworks (Berre-l'Étang, Fos-sur-Mer, Martigues). Commercial and industrial activity concentrated at MARSEILLES, chief Fr. Mediterranean port, linked to Arles on the Rhone by a shipping canal (Rove Tunnel, Étang de Berre, Arles–Port-de-Bouc Canal). Other towns are the spa of Aix-en-Provence, and Arles, rich in Roman remains.

Bouchoux, Les (lā bōōshōō'), village (pop. 138), Jura dept., E France, in the central Jura, 7 mi. SSW of Saint-Claude; alt. 3,150 ft. Cheese mfg.

Bou Dahar, Fr. Morocco: see BÉNI TADJIT.

Boudenib (bōōdĕnēb'), town (pop. 3,111), Meknès region, SE Fr. Morocco, oasis on the Oued Guir, 50 mi. E of Ksar-es-Souk; 35°27'N 3°36'W. Dates, figs, cereals. Trade in wool, leather, esparto. Lead and zinc deposits at the Djebel bou Dahar, 30 mi. NE. Also spelled Bou Denib.

Boudk, Nepal: see BODDHNATH.

Boudry (bōōdrē'), town (pop. 2,467), Neuchâtel canton, W Switzerland, on Areuse R., near L. of Neuchâtel, and 5 mi. SW of Neuchâtel; metal products. Marat b. here.

Boué (bōōā'), village (pop. 1,003), Aisne dept., N France, on the Sambre and 13 mi. SW of Avesnes; mfg. (cottons, jams, flour products).

Bouère (bōōār'), village (pop. 543), Mayenne dept., W France, 20 mi. SE of Laval; apiculture. Pink-marble quarries.

Boufarik (bōōfärēk'), town (pop. 11,447), Alger dept., N central Algeria, in the Mitidja plain, 17 mi. SW of Algiers, amidst vineyards and citrus groves; other products of fertile region are cereals, perfume plants (lavender, geraniums), artichokes, tobacco, and forage crops. Town has winemaking and alcohol distilling cooperatives, essential-oil distilleries, perfume factory, chemical laboratories (pharmaceuticals, anticryptogamic products), and a large tree-nursery. Among exports are oranges, tangerines, early fruits and vegetables.

Bouffioulx (bōōfēōō'), town (pop. 4,856), Hainaut prov., S central Belgium, 4 mi. ESE of Charleroi; ceramics, pottery.

Bou-Ficha (bōō-fēshä'), village, Sousse dist., NE Tunisia, on Gulf of Hammamet, 33 mi. NNW of Sousse; produces muscatel, olives, cereals.

Bougainville (bōō'gŭnvĭl, bō'–, Fr. bōōgĕvēl'), volcanic island (□ 3,880; pop. c.40,000), largest of Solomon Isls., SW Pacific, 300 mi. NW of Guadalcanal; 6°12'S 155°15'E; c.110 mi. long. Emperor Range in N, with Mt. Balbi (10,170 ft.) highest peak; Mt. Bagana, in Crown Prince Range, in S. Best harbors: Kieta on SE coast, Empress Augusta Bay on S coast. Exports copra, ivory nuts, some tortoise shell. Discovered 1768 by Bougainville; became 1884 German possession; occupied 1914 by Australia; included 1920 in Australian mandated Territory of NEW GUINEA; under U.N. trusteeship (1947) held by Australia. In Second World War, isl. (site of Jap. air base) was last major Jap. stronghold in Solomons; fighting continued until end of war. Bougainville and Buka isls. form Bougainville (until 1950, Kieta) dist. (⊙ Sohano) of Territory of New Guinea.

Bougainville, Cape, NE Western Australia, in Timor Sea; N extremity of peninsula bet. Admiralty Gulf (W) and Vansittart Bay (E); 13°54'S 126°6'E.

Bougainville Channel, New Hebrides: see MALEKULA.

Bougainville Strait, Solomon Isls., SW Pacific, separates Bougainville (W) and Choiseul (E), joining Coral Sea and Pacific Ocean; 30 mi. wide.

Bougaroun, Cape (bōōgärōōn'), anc. *Metagonium Promontorium*, headland of Constantine dept., NE Algeria, bounding Gulf of Philippeville on W, 28 mi. NW of Philippeville; 37°5'N 6°28'E. Lighthouse. Northernmost point of Algeria.

Boughton (bōō'tŭn, bou'–), town and parish (pop. 1,318), central Nottingham, England, on Maun R. and 9 mi. NE of Mansfield; coal mining.

Bougie (bōōzhē'), anc. *Saldae*, city (pop. 21,011), Constantine dept., NE Algeria, beautifully situated on W shore of Gulf of Bougie (Mediterranean Sea), at mouth of Oued Soummam valley, 110 mi. E of Algiers; 36°45'N 5°6'E. Well-sheltered chief port for KABYLIA, exporting agr. products (olive oil, cork, figs, cereals, wool) and minerals (phosphates, iron, zinc, antimony) of the Tell hinterland; rail terminus. Located in Algeria's main olive-growing dist., city has given its name to the wax-candle (bougie), 1st shipped to Europe from here. Industries include mfg. of corks, tobacco products, and liqueurs, and fish preserving. City is built in shape of an amphitheater along slope of the Djebel Gouraya (2,165 ft.), which shelters harbor from N and W winds. Because it receives some of N Africa's heaviest rainfall (annual average 40 in.), Bougie is surrounded by luxuriant subtropical vegetation. The modern commercial section lies S of the old quarter, along the inner harbor (under development). Founded as a veterans' colony by Augustus. A minor port until Genseric made it capital of the Vandals. In 11th cent., chief city of a powerful Berber dynasty. After Spanish occupation (1509–55), it was taken by Turks and declined until French occupation, beginning in 1833. Development of near-by mines and of port facilities has brought prosperity in 20th cent. Large Kabylian pop.

Bougie, Gulf of, semi-circular bay of the Mediterranean, off Constantine dept., NE Algeria, extending from Cape Carbon (W) to Cape Cavallo (E); 27 mi. wide, 10 mi. deep. On its W shore, near mouth of the Oued Soummam is port of Bougie. Bay is skirted by Babor range of Little Kabylia.

Bougival (bo͞o-zhēväl'), town (pop. 3,370), Seine-et-Oise dept., N central France, a W suburb of Paris, 9 mi. from Notre Dame Cathedral, port on left bank of Seine R.; mfg. (paints, dyes, flags, thread).

Bouglon (bo͞oglō'), village (pop. 110), Lot-et-Garonne dept., SW France, 8 mi. SSW of Marmande; food canning, sawmilling.

Bougouni (bo͞ogo͞o'nē), town (pop. c.2,250), S Fr. Sudan, Fr. West Africa, 90 mi. SSE of Bamako; trade in shea nuts and peanuts. Cotton gin. Region also produces millet, rice, corn, peanuts, manioc, potatoes, beans; livestock. Gold deposits in vicinity. R.C. and Protestant missions.

Bou Grara, Gulf of (bo͞o grärä'), inlet of the central Mediterranean, off SE Tunisia. Its entrance is blocked by Djerba isl., leaving only 2 passages to the open sea, off Adjim (NW; 1 mi. wide) and off El-Kantara (NE; 4.5 mi. wide).

Bouguirat (bo͞ogērät'), village (pop. 588), Oran dept., NW Algeria, 15 mi. SE of Mostaganem; winegrowing.

Bou-Hanifia, spa, Algeria: see AÏN-FEKAN.

Bou-Hanifia Dam, Algeria: see HAMMAM, OUED.

Bou-Haroun (bo͞o-häro͞on'), village (pop. 1,564), Alger dept., N central Algeria, small fishing port on the Mediterranean, 14 mi. NW of Blida; sardine canning; truck-gardening.

Bou Iblane, Djebel (jĕ'bĕl bo͞o ēblän'), peak (10,466 ft.) of the Middle Atlas, N central Fr. Morocco, 45 mi. ESE of Sefrou; 33°43'N 4°3'W.

Bouillante (bo͞oyät'), town (commune pop. 5,147), W Basse-Terre, Guadeloupe, 10 mi. NNW of Basse-Terre; mfg. of alcohol; trading. Thermal springs near by.

Bouille, La (lä bo͞o'yů), village (pop. 591), Seine-Inférieure dept., N France, on left bank of the Seine and 10 mi. SW of Rouen; picturesque excursion resort.

Bouillon (bo͞oyō'), town (pop. 2,830), Luxembourg prov., SE Belgium, on Semois R. and 17 mi. WSW of Neufchâteau, in the Ardennes; tourist resort; mfg. of metal products. Its old castle belonged to Godfrey of Bouillon, who sold (1095) the town to the bishop of Liége. Strategically situated, Bouillon often changed hands. Nominally under the suzerainty of the prince-bishops of Liége, the town and environs passed (15th cent.) to William de la Marck, whose descendants assumed titles duke of Bouillon and prince of Sedan. Bouillon was annexed to France from 1678 to 1815. The ducal title lapsed in 1732.

Bouillon, village (pop. 74), Manche dept., NW France, 5 mi. SSE of Granville; bathing resorts of Jullouville (1 mi. W) and Carolles (2 mi. S) on Channel coast.

Bouillonville (bo͞oyōvēl'), village (pop. 84), Meurthe-et-Moselle dept., NE France, 10 mi. WNW of Pont-à-Mousson.

Bouilly (bo͞oyē'). **1** Agr. village (pop. 557), Aube dept., NE central France, 8 mi. SSW of Troyes. **2** Village (pop. 67), Marne dept., N France, 8 mi. SW of Rheims; winegrowing (champagne).

Bouin (bo͞oē'), former island in the Bay of Bourgneuf of the Atlantic, Vendée dept., W France, 25 mi. SW of Nantes, now embedded in the coastal salt marshes. The village of Bouin (pop. 968) is at the center of the Marais BRETON.

Bouïnan (bo͞oēnän'), village (pop. 767), Alger dept., N central Algeria, in the Mitidja plain, 18 mi. SSW of Algiers; wine, citrus fruit, truck, essential oils.

Bouïra (bwērä'), town (pop. 5,231), Alger dept., N central Algeria, in the Tell at S foot of Djurdjura range, 55 mi. SE of Algiers; rail junction (spur to Aumale); agr. trade center of upper Oued Sahel valley (wine, cereals, olives); distilling. Also spelled Bouira.

Bou Izakarn (bo͞o ēzäkärn'), Saharan military outpost, Agadir frontier region, southwesternmost Fr. Morocco, at SW foot of the Anti-Atlas, 36 mi. S of Tiznit, near Ifni enclave (Spanish); 29°10'N 9°44'W.

Bou Jaber, Djebel, Tunisia: see KALAAT-ES-SENAM.

Boujad (bo͞ozhäd'), town (pop. 13,181), Casablanca region, W central Fr. Morocco, 90 mi. SE of Casablanca; Moslem religious center; grain market. Founded in 16th cent.

Boujniba, Fr. Morocco: see KHOURIBGA.

Bouka, Fr. Equatorial Africa: see BOUCA.

Bou Kadra, Djebel, Algeria: see OUENZA, DJEBEL.

Boukanéfis (bo͝okänāfēs'), village (pop. 1,306), Oran dept., NW Algeria, on the Mékerra, on railroad and 10 mi. SSW of Sidi-bel-Abbès; winegrowing; flour milling. Also spelled Bou-Khanéfis.

Boukia, Greece: see PARANESTION.

Boulaide (bo͞olĕd'), Ger. *Bauschleiden* (boush'līdůn), village (pop. 437), W Luxembourg, in the Ardennes, 8 mi. SW of Wiltz, near Belg. border; mfg. of tanning fluid; agr.

Boularderie Island (bo͞olärdůrē') (25 mi. long, 2–6 mi. wide), NE N.S., off Cape Breton Isl., bet. Great Bras d'Or and St. Andrew Channel, NW of Sydney; coal is mined in N.

Boulay or **Boulay-Moselle** (bo͞olā'-mōzĕl'), Ger. *Bolchen* (bôl'khůn), town (pop. 2,095), Moselle dept., NE France, 15 mi. ENE of Metz, mfg. (organs, cigarette paper, flour products), wool spinning.

Boulboul, Syria: see BULBUL.

Boulder, Australia: see KALGOORLIE AND BOULDER.

Boulder (bōl'důr), county (□ 753; pop. 48,296), N central Colo.; ⊙ Boulder. Irrigated agr. and livestock region. Sugar beets, beans, fruit, grain. Mining (coal, gold). Part of Rocky Mtn. Natl. Park in NW and of Front Range in W. Formed 1861.

Boulder. 1 City (pop. 19,999), ⊙ Boulder co., N central Colo., on Boulder Creek, just E of Front Range, and 25 mi. NW of Denver; alt. 5,350 ft. Health resort, with mild, dry climate; seat of Univ. of Colo.; rail, trade center for mining, stock-raising, and agr. region; mfg. (cutlery, bricks, tile, beverages). U.S. Bureau of Standards radiological laboratory here; U.S. Atomic Energy Commission production plant was begun 1951 at Rocky Flats (8 mi. S). Gold, silver, lead, tungsten, copper, and coal mines in vicinity. Laid out 1859, inc. 1871; grew with arrival of railroad (1873) and opening (1877) of the university. Chautauqua Park (community center) and site of 1st schoolhouse in Colo. (1860) are here. Near-by points of interest: Boulder Canyon, Rocky Mtn. Natl. Park, Gold Hill and Sunshine (early gold-mining camps), and Arapaho Glacier (source of city's water supply) on Arapaho Peak. **2** Town (pop. 1,017), ⊙ Jefferson co., SW central Mont., on Boulder R. and 25 mi. S of Helena; resort; gold, silver, lead, zinc mines; livestock. School for feeble-minded here. Inc. 1865. **3** Village, Nev.: see BOULDER CITY.

Boulder City, Australia: see KALGOORLIE AND BOULDER.

Boulder City or **Boulder,** village (pop. 3,903), Clark co., SE Nev., near Hoover Dam, 20 mi. SE of Las Vegas. Built and owned by U.S. for workers on Hoover Dam. Dist. hq. for Reclamation and Natl. Park Service; year-round tourist center.

Boulder Creek, resort village (pop. 1,497), Santa Cruz co., W Calif., in Santa Cruz Mts., 13 mi. NNW of Santa Cruz. Gateway to Big Basin Redwoods State Park (NW).

Boulder Creek, N central Colo., rises in several branches in N Front Range, near Arapaho Peak; flows 55 mi. E and NE, past Boulder, to St. Vrain Creek just E of Longmont. On its middle fork, near Nederland, is hydroelectric plant.

Boulder Dam, Nev. and Ariz.: see HOOVER DAM.

Boulder River, SW Mont., rises in Jefferson co., flows 71 mi. SE and S, past Boulder, to Jefferson R. near Whitehall.

Boulge (bo͞olj, bōlj), agr. village and parish (pop. 68), SE Suffolk, England, 7 mi. ENE of Ipswich, near Woodbridge. Edward Fitzgerald buried here.

Boulhaut (bo͞olō'), town (pop. 5,372), Casablanca region, NW Fr. Morocco, 28 mi. E of Casablanca; palm-fiber and esparto processing, essential-oil distilling. Near-by iron deposits mined on small scale before Second World War.

Bouligny (bo͞olēnyē'), commune (pop. 4,816), Meuse dept., NE France, 10 mi. WNW of Briey; iron mines.

Boulogne (bo͞olô'nyů), town (pop. estimate 3,000), in Greater Buenos Aires, Argentina, 13 mi. NW of Buenos Aires; railroad shops; horticulture, floriculture center; mfg. of chinaware.

Boulogne (bo͞olô'nyů). **1** or **Boulogne-sur-Gesse** (–sür-zhĕs'), village (pop. 935), Haute-Garonne dept., S France, on Lannemezan Plateau, 13 mi. NNW of Saint-Gaudens; dairying, woodworking. Was a medieval fortress. **2** or **Boulogne-sur-Mer** (–sür-mâr'), anc. *Gesoriacum,* later *Bononia,* city (1946 pop. 34,389; 1936 pop. 51,011), Pas-de-Calais dept., N France, at mouth of small Liane R. on English Channel, 135 mi. NNW of Paris and 30 mi. SE of Folkestone (steamer connection); 50°44' N 1°36'E. Until 1940, France's leading fishing port; industrial center and bathing resort. Destruction of harbor facilities and of major part of lower city has reduced economic activity. Boulogne still has fish-salting and canning plants, boatbuilding yards, well-known pen and pencil factories, and Portland cement works. Other mfg.: fishing equipment, waterproof raincoats, fireclay goods. In old upper town (still enclosed by medieval ramparts) is 19th-cent. Basilica of Notre Dame (heavily damaged), which contains replica of famous wooden statue (burned 1793) of Our Lady of Boulogne (pilgrimage shrine). Two mi. N of Boulogne stands a marble column (174 ft. high; damaged in Second World War) commemorating Napoleon's intended invasion of England. From here Romans sailed (A.D. 43) to conquer Britain. Chief city of a medieval county, it was incorporated into royal domain by Louis XI. Occupied by British, 1544–50. Became major Br. army base in First World War. During Second World War it suffered almost 400 aerial bombings. Godfrey of Bouillon and Saint-Beuve b. here.

Boulogne, Bois de, France: see BOIS DE BOULOGNE.

Boulogne-Billancourt (bo͞olô'nyů-bēyäko͞or'), city (pop. 78,925), Seine dept., N central France, just WSW of Paris, 5 mi. from Notre Dame Cathedral, within S bend (on right bank) of Seine R., and at S edge of Bois de Boulogne; automobile, aircraft, and bicycle plants; other mfg.: plumbing fixtures, rubber articles, hosiery, cosmetics, fruit preserves. Until 1925, commune named Boulogne-sur-Seine.

Boulogne-sur-Gesse, France: see BOULOGNE, Haute-Garonne dept.

Boulogne-sur-Mer, France: see BOULOGNE, Pas-de-Calais dept.

Bouloire (bo͞olwär'), village (pop. 638), Sarthe dept., W France, 17 mi. E of Le Mans; textile mill.

Boulonnais (bo͞olônā'), old district of N France, in Pas-de-Calais dept., surrounding Boulogne. Stock raising.

Boulou, Le (lů bo͞olo͞o'), town (pop. 2,006), Pyrénées-Orientales dept., S France, at foot of Monts Albères, on Tech R. and 12 mi. SSW of Perpignan, on road to Perthus pass (Sp. frontier); watering place and cork-mfg. center.

Boulouparis (bo͞olo͞opärē'), village (dist. pop. 588), New Caledonia, on W coast, 40 mi. NW of Nouméa; agr. products, livestock. Sometimes spelled Bouloupari.

Boulton, England: see ALVASTON AND BOULTON.

Boumalne or **Boumalne du Dadès** (bo͞omäln' dü dädĕs'), village (pop. 433), Marrakesh region, S Fr. Morocco, bet. the High Atlas (N) and the Djebel Sagho (S), on road and 100 mi. SW of Ksar es Souk; 31°22'N 5°59'W. Sheep raising.

Bou-Medfa (bo͞o-mĕdfä'), village (pop. 572), Alger dept., N central Algeria, on railroad and 15 mi. ENE of Miliana; winegrowing.

Bouna (bo͞o'nä), town (pop. c.2,600), E Ivory Coast, Fr. West Africa, near Gold Coast border, 80 mi. N of Boundoukou; coffee, cacao, lumber. Mfg. of plaited goods. Customhouse.

Bou Naceur, Djebel (jĕ'bĕl bo͞o näsûr'), highest peak (10,794 ft.) of the Middle Atlas, in N central Fr. Morocco, overlooking the Moulouya valley, 60 mi. SE of Sefrou; 33°33'N 3°53'W.

Bound, Scotland: see OUT SKERRIES.

Boundary, county (□ 1,275; pop. 5,908), N Idaho; ⊙ Bonners Ferry. Mtn. area drained by Kootenai R. and bordering on British Columbia, Wash., and Mont. Dairying, stock raising, lumbering, mining (lead, zinc, silver, molybdenum). Kaniksu Natl. Forest extends throughout much of co. Formed 1884.

Boundary Peak. 1 Mountain (12,800 ft.), in Sangre de Cristo Mts., Costillo co., S Colo. **2** Mountain (13,145 ft.), SW Nev., in N White Mts., near Calif. line, 65 mi. WSW of Tonopah; highest point in Nev.

Bound Brook, borough (pop. 8,374), Somerset co., NE N.J., on Raritan R. and 6 mi. NW of New Brunswick; mfg. (paint, chemicals, textiles, clothing, metal products, roofing material); hothouse flowers, truck. Cornwallis defeated colonial force here, 1777. Settled 1681, inc. 1891.

Boundiali (bo͞ondyä'lē), village (pop. c.2,200), N Ivory Coast, Fr. West Africa, 60 mi. W of Korhogo; kapok, sisal; sheep, goats. Livestock fair.

Bountiful, city (pop. 6,004), Davis co., N Utah, near Great Salt L., 8 mi. N of Salt Lake City in irrigated agr. area; alt. 4,408 ft.; fruit; turkeys. Early Mormon chapel (built 1857–63) here. U.S. wildlife refuge near by. Bountiful Peak (9,482 ft.) is 5 mi. NNE, in Wasatch Range. Settled 1847, inc. 1855.

Bounty Islands, uninhabited group (□ c.1) of some 15 islets in S Pacific, one of outlying isl. groups of New Zealand, 415 mi. ESE of Dunedin; 47°43'S 179°E.

Bouquet River (bůkĕt', bō–), NE N.Y., rises in the Adirondacks in E central Essex co., flows c.40 mi. NE and N, past Elizabethtown, to L. Champlain 2 mi. below Willsboro. Receives North Branch above Willsboro.

Bourail (bo͞orī'), village (dist. pop. 1,974), W New Caledonia, 80 mi. NW of Nouméa; commercial center of livestock, agr. area; cheese.

Bourbeuse River (bûr'bůs), central Mo., rises NE of Rolla, meanders 138 mi. NE to Meramec R. in Franklin co.

Bourbince River (bo͞orbēs'), Saône-et-Loire dept., E central France, rises near Le Creusot, flows c.40 mi. SW, past Montceau-les-Mines and Paray-le-Monial, to the Arroux just N of Digoin. Paralleled by Canal du Centre.

Bourbon, island in Indian Ocean: see RÉUNION.

Bourbon. 1 (bûr'bůn, bo͝or'bůn) County (□ 639; pop. 19,153), SE Kansas; ⊙ Fort Scott. Rolling plains, bordered E by Mo.; watered by Marmaton and Little Osage rivers. Stock raising, dairying, general agr. Coal deposits; scattered oil and gas fields. Formed 1855. **2** (bûr'bŭn) County (□ 300; pop. 17,752), N central Ky.; ⊙ PARIS. Drained by South Fork of Licking R. Gently rolling agr. area (burley tobacco, livestock, dairy products, poultry), in Bluegrass region; limestone quarries. Some mfg. at Paris; at Paris was one of the earliest (1790) distilleries in the state; whisky from the region was 1st called bourbon after the county. Co. formed 1785.

Bourbon (bûr'bŭn). **1** Town (pop. 1,404), Marshall co., N Ind., 26 mi. SSW of South Bend; trading center in agr. area (livestock, grain, poultry); feed milling. **2** Town (pop. 543), Crawford co., E central Mo., in the Ozarks, near Meramec R., 6 mi. SW of Sullivan; grain, livestock. U.S. fish hatchery here.

Bourbon-Lancy (bōōrbō'-lãsē'), town (pop. 2,968), Saône-et-Loire dept., E central France, near the Loire, 21 mi. E of Moulins; noted health resort with mineral springs.

Bourbon-l'Archambault (–lärshãbō'), village (pop. 1,917), Allier dept., central France, 13 mi. W of Moulins; health resort with state-owned mineral springs for rheumatic ailments. Has ruined 13th-cent. castle of dukes of Bourbon. Romans built baths here.

Bourbonnais (bōōrbônā'), old province of central France now forming Allier and part of Cher depts.; ⊙ Moulins. It includes the N spurs of the Massif Central (Combrailles, Montagnes de la Madeleine), N section of the LIMAGNE and the SOLOGNE BOURBONNAISE. Drained by the Cher (W), Allier (center), and Loire (E). Uplands are arid, but the Limagne grows cereals, vegetables, fruits, and wine and raises high-grade cattle. Area is traversed by a coal seam mined chiefly near Commentry. Chief towns: Moulins, Montluçon (heavy industry), Vichy (health resort). The counts, later dukes, of Bourbon, ancestors of the French royal family, held Bourbonnais as an appanage until 1527, when it was united with the crown by Francis I. Prov. divided into present depts. in 1790.

Bourbonnais (bōōrbōnā', bûrbō'nĭs), village (pop. 1,598), Kankakee co., NE Ill., near Kankakee R., 3 mi. NNW of Kankakee, in agr. area. Settled by French. Seat of Olivet Nazarene Col.

Bourbonne-les-Bains (bōōrbôn'-lā-bē'), anc. *Aquae Borvonis*, town (pop. 2,662), Haute-Marne dept., NE France, 20 mi. ENE of Langres; watering station with hot saline springs. Known since Roman times. National thermal baths; military hosp.

Bourbon-Vendée, France: see ROCHE-SUR-YON, LA.

Bourboule, La (lä bōōrbōōl'), town (pop. 2,821), Puy-de-Dôme dept., central France, in the Monts Dore, on Dordogne R. and 21 mi. SW of Clermont-Ferrand; well-known thermal station frequented since Roman times for high arsenic content of its hot springs. Funicular railway to Charlannes (alt. 4,000 ft.; winter sports).

Bourbourg (bōōrbōōr'), town (pop. 3,924), Nord dept., N France, 10 mi. SW of Dunkirk; agr. market (cereals, flax; dairying). Beet-sugar refining, flour milling, vegetable canning, wire and chicory mfg. Until 1945, called Bourbourg-Ville.

Bourbre River (bōōr'brü), Isère dept., SE France, rises in the Pre-Alps above La Tour-du-Pin, flows 40 mi. generally NW, past Bourgoin, to the Rhone near Chavanoz.

Bourbriac (bōōrbrēäk'), village (pop. 875), Côtes-du-Nord dept., W France, 6 mi. SSW of Guingamp; horse raising; dairying.

Bourdeaux (bōōrdō'), agr. village (pop. 450), Drôme dept., SE France, on Roubion R. and 16 mi. SW of Die; hog raising.

Bourdonnais, La, Madagascar: see BRICKAVILLE.

Bou Regreg, Oued (wĕd' bōō rĕgrĕg'), river of Rabat region, NW Fr. Morocco, rises in foothills of the Middle Atlas near Oulmès, flows 110 mi. NW to the Atlantic, which it enters bet. Rabat (left bank) and Salé (right bank). Navigable in estuary for shallow-draft vessels.

Bourem (bōōrĕm'), village (pop. c.1,700), E Fr. Sudan, Fr. West Africa, market place on left bank of the Niger, 170 mi. E of Timbuktu. Medical post; fishing. Phosphate deposits c.40 mi. NE.

Bouresches (bōōrĕsh'), village (pop. 187), Aisne dept., N France, 4 mi. W of Château-Thierry. Captured by Americans (June, 1918) in fighting for Belleau Wood (just W).

Bourg. 1 or **Bourg-en-Bresse** (bōōrk', bōōrgãbrĕs'), town (pop. 21,169), ⊙ Ain dept., E France, 36 mi. NNE of Lyons; transportation and commercial center; important poultry and grain market. Produces pottery, plastics, furniture, and hardware; wire- and watchmaking. Has noted 15th-cent. late-Gothic church of Brou. Bourg was ⊙ of BRESSE, which passed from Savoy to France in 1601. **2** or **Bourg-sur-Gironde** (bōōr'-sür-zhērōd'), village (pop. 1,091), Gironde dept., SW France, on right bank of Dordogne R. near its junction with the Garonne, and 14 mi. N of Bordeaux; wine trade; stone cutting, barrelmaking.

Bourganeuf (bōōrgänûf'), town (pop. 2,881), Creuse dept., central France, on Taurion R. and 16 mi. SSW of Guéret; industrial center (carpets, porcelain, hats, electrical equipment). Its 15th-cent.-tower belonged to a priory founded by Knights of Malta. Dam and hydroelectric plant at Châtelus-le-Marcheix on Taurion R., 8 mi. WNW.

Bourg-Argental (bōōrg-ärzhätäl'), town (pop. 2,400), Loire dept., SE central France, on S slope of Mont Pilat, 13 mi. SE of Saint Étienne; silk-milling center; tanning.

Bourg-de-Batz, Le, France: see BATZ-SUR-MER.

Bourg-de-Péage (bōōr'-dŭ-pāäzh'), town (pop. 5,764), Drôme dept., SE France, on left bank of Isère R., opposite Romans-sur-Isère, and 11 mi. NE of Valence; felt-hat mfg. Woodworking, footwear mfg. Damaged in Second World War.

Bourg-de-Thizy (–dŭ-tēzē'), town (pop. 2,214), Rhône dept., E central France, adjoining Thizy, 11 mi. E of Roanne; cotton weaving and printing. Silk-veil mfg.

Bourg-de-Visa (–dŭ-vēzä'), village (pop. 301), Tarn-et-Garonne dept., SW France, 16 mi. SE of Villeneuve-sur-Lot; plum growing, dairying.

Bourg-d'Oisans, Le (lŭ bōōr-dwäzã'), village (pop. 1,495), Isère dept., SE France, on the Romanche and 18 mi. SE of Grenoble; center of Alpine OISANS valley; resort and excursion center for Dauphiné Alps; silk spinning. Anthracite mines and talc quarries in area. Hydroelectric plants near by.

Bourg-en-Bresse, France: see BOURG, Ain dept.

Bourges (bōōrzh), anc. *Avaricum*, city (pop. 41,597), ⊙ Cher dept., central France, on Berry Canal, at marshy confluence of the Yèvre and the Auron, and 122 mi. S of Paris; 47°5'N 2°23'E. Industrial and transportation center; has important military installations (artillery arsenal, cannon foundries, workshops of aviation and pyrotechnics, service schools), forges and machine shops, railroad yards. Produces woolens, pianos, linoleum, metal shutters, porcelain, fertilizer, biscuits. Grain, poultry, wine trade. Its remarkable 13th–16th-cent. Gothic cathedral is noted for the absence of transepts. Also has fine Gothic houses of Jacques Coeur (b. here), and the Renaissance Berry mus. As seat of the Bituriges, a powerful Gallic tribe, Bourges withstood a siege by Caesar (52 B.C.). Augustus made it ⊙ of N Aquitania; early archiepiscopal see and ⊙ of Berry. Charles VII ("King of Bourges") resided here while most of France was in English hands. In 1438 he promulgated the Pragmatic Sanction of Bourges. Louis XI (b. here) founded (1463) the univ. which was abolished in Fr. Revolution.

Bourget, Lac du (läk dü bōōr-zhā'), scenic Alpine lake (□ 16) in Savoie dept., SE France, filling N part of Chambéry trough; 11 mi. long, 2 mi. wide, c.500 ft. deep; its S end is 6 mi. NNW of Chambéry. Outlet (2.5 mi. long) at N end drains into the Rhone. Mont du Chat rises abruptly just W. Aix-les-Bains, near E shore, is center of resort area. Abbey of Hautecombe (founded 12th cent., restored 19th cent.) on W shore. Lake celebrated by Lamartine.

Bourget, Le (lŭ bōōr-zhā'). **1** or **Le Bourget-du-Lac** (–dü-läk'), village (pop. 506), Savoie dept., SE France, at S end of Lac du Bourget, 6 mi. NNW of Chambéry, at E foot of Mont du Chat; resort. Paper mill. **2** Town (pop. 7,327), Seine dept., N central France, an outer NNE suburb of Paris, 7 mi. from Notre Dame Cathedral, with chief metropolitan airport. Metallurgical and chemical works. Monument commemorates Fr. defendants of Paris (1870). Here Charles Lindbergh landed (May, 1927) after his transatlantic flight.

Bourget-du-Lac, Le, France: see BOURGET, LE, Savoie dept.

Bourgfelden (bōōrfĕldĕn'), Ger. *Burgfelden* (bōōrk'-fĕldŭn), village (pop. 1,400), Haut-Rhin dept., France, on Swiss border, 2 mi. NW of Basel; custom house.

Bourg-la-Reine (bōōr-lä-rĕn'), town (pop. 10,137), Seine dept., N central France, an outer S suburb of Paris, 6 mi. from Notre Dame Cathedral, just E of Sceaux; truck and flower gardens; mfg. (candles, cider, surgical instruments).

Bourg-Lastic (–lästēk'), village (pop. 669), Puy-de-Dôme dept., central France, in Auvergne Mts., 14 mi. NE of Ussel; cattle, sheep.

Bourg-Léopold (bōōr-läôpôld'), Flemish *Leopoldsburg* (lĕôpôldzbōōrk'), town (pop. 7,667), Limburg prov., NE Belgium, 14 mi. NNW of Hasselt; glass and explosives mfg. Scene of fighting (1944–45) in Second World War.

Bourg-lès-Valence (–lā-väläs'), N suburb (pop. 5,503) of Valence, Drôme dept., SE France; mfg. (ammunition, jewelry), woodworking.

Bourg-Madame (–mädäm'), village (pop. 399), Pyrénées-Orientales dept., S France, in Cerdagne, on Sègre R. and 1 mi. E of Puigcerdá; alt. 3,707 ft. Custom station on Sp. border. Grazing; rye and wheat growing.

Bourgneuf, Bay of (bōōrnûf'), on Bay of Biscay off Loire-Inférieure and Vendée depts., W France, bet. Pointe de Saint-Gildas (N) and Île de Noirmoutier (SW); 12 mi. long, 16 mi. wide. SE part is in the process of silting up and is lined by salt marshes. Several bathing resorts (Pornic, Préfailles, La Bernerie) on NE shore.

Bourgneuf-en-Retz (–ã-rĕz'), village (pop. 624), Loire-Inférieure dept., W France, near Bay of Bourgneuf of the Atlantic, 22 mi. WSW of Nantes; saltworks, fisheries.

Bourgogne, province, France: see BURGUNDY.

Bourgogne (bōōrgô'nyŭ), village (pop. 541), Marne dept., N France, 7 mi. N of Rheims; sheep.

Bourgogne, Canal de, France: see BURGUNDY CANAL.

Bourgoin (bōōrgwē'), town (pop. 6,488), Isère dept., SE France, on the Bourbre, adjoining Jallieu (N), and 25 mi. SE of Lyons; industrial center specializing in engraving for textile prints; silk weaving, flour milling, mfg. of batteries, brushes, hosiery, chemicals; foundries, textile machinery workshops. Peat bogs near by.

Bourg-Saint-Andéol (bōōr'-sĕtãdāôl'), town (pop. 2,277), Ardèche dept., S France, on right bank of Rhone R. and 14 mi. SSW of Montélimar; wine commerce. Pottery and tile mfg. Damaged during Second World War.

Bourg-Saint-Maurice (–sē-mōrēs'), village (pop. 1,450), Savoie dept., SE France, railhead in upper TARENTAISE valley (Savoy Alps), 19 mi. ESE of Albertville, at foot of Little Saint Bernard Pass; alt. 2,668 ft. Resort. Roads to Col de l'Iseran (20 mi. SE) and Lanslebourg.

Bourg-sur-Gironde, France: see BOURG, Gironde dept.

Bourgtheroulde (bōōrtārōōd'), village (pop. 467), Eure dept., NW France, 14 mi. SW of Rouen; cider distilling.

Bourguébus (bōōrgābüs'), village (pop. 125), Calvados dept., NW France, 5 mi. SE of Caen.

Bourgueil (bōōrgû'ē), village (pop. 1,571), Indre-et-Loire dept., W central France, 12 mi. E of Saumur; noted for its red wines.

Bourke (bûrk), municipality (pop. 2,205), N New South Wales, Australia, on Darling R. and 410 mi. NW of Sydney; rail terminus; sheep center.

Bourlamaque (bōōr"lŭmäk'), town (pop. 1,545), W Que., 60 mi. ESE of Rouyn, just S of Val d'Or; mining (gold, copper, molybdenum, zinc, lead) and agr. (grain, potatoes, dairying) center. Inc. 1934.

Bourlon (bōōrlō'), village (pop. 1,118), Pas-de-Calais dept., N France, 5 mi. W of Cambrai. Near-by Bourlon Wood was scene of heavy fighting, 1917, in First World War.

Bourmont (bōōrmō'), agr. village (pop. 456), Haute-Marne dept., NE France, on Meuse R. and 12 mi. SSW of Neufchâteau; winegrowing.

Bournabat, Turkey: see BORNOVA.

Bourne (bûrn, bōōrn), urban district (1931 pop. 4,889; 1951 census 5,100), Parts of Kesteven, S Lincolnshire, England, 15 mi. SE of Grantham; agr. market, with fertilizer plant and brickworks. Mineral springs. Hereward the Wake and Robert Mannyng (or Manning) lived here. Lord Burghley b. here.

Bourne (bôrn). **1** Town (pop. 4,720), Barnstable co., SE Mass., on Buzzards Bay, at base of Cape Cod, 19 mi. ENE of New Bedford; summer resort; agr. center (cranberries, dairy products, truck). Includes resort villages of Buzzards Bay (pop. 1,459; business and rail center), Cataumet (kŭtô'mŭt), Monument Beach, Pocasset (pōkă'sĭt, pŭ–), Sagamore (1940 pop. 938), Sagamore Beach, and Bournedale. Bourne village has replica (1930) of Aptucxet trading post (1627). Cape Cod Canal (bridged 1935) crosses town (N). Settled c.1640, set off from Sandwich 1884. **2** Town (1940 pop. 19), Baker co., NE Oregon, 18 mi. W of Baker.

Bournedale, Mass.: see BOURNE.

Bourne End, England: see WOOBURN.

Bourne Field (bôrn), naval base, S St. Thomas Isl., U.S. Virgin Isls., 2½ mi. W of Charlotte Amalie. Built during Second World War for submarines and for Marine Corps air facilities; deactivated 1947. Part of the U.S. Army chemical installations were moved here in 1948 from Panama.

Bournemouth (bôrn'mŭth), county borough (1931 pop. 116,797; 1951 census 144,726), SW Hampshire, England, on Poole Bay of the Channel, 25 mi. WSW of Southampton; 50°43'N 1°52'W; fashionable seaside resort and fine-arts center, with mild climate, in the sheltered valley of the Bourne. There are many parks, a sandy beach, pine woods, and numerous entertainment facilities. Mfg. includes metal products, electrical appliances, pharmaceuticals. Since mid-19th cent., when it was a small fishing village, the town's growth has been rapid. Robert Louis Stevenson lived here for some time, and Mary Shelley is buried here, with her father, William Godwin, and his wife, Mary Wollstonecraft. Resort suburbs include Boscombe (E; pop. 18,072), Westbourne (W; pop. 6,484), Winton (N; pop. 12,818), and Pokesdown (E).

Bournemouth Bath, Jamaica: see ROCK FORT.

Bourne River (bōōrn), Isère dept., SE France, rises in the Vercors, flows c.25 mi. SW through Pre-Alps, to the Isère 6 mi. below Pont-en-Royans.

Bournville (bôrn–), town in Birmingham county borough, NE Worcester, England, 4 mi. SW of Birmingham; built as a garden city for workers employed in chocolate and cocoa factories.

Bourré (bōōrā'), village (pop. 343), Loir-et-Cher dept., N central France, on Cher R. and 17 mi. SSW of Blois; truck gardening, mushroom growing. Stone quarried here was used in construction of several châteaux in Loire valley.

Bourscheid, Luxembourg: see GOEBELSMÜHLE.

Bous (bōōs), village (pop. 406) SE Luxembourg, 10 mi. ESE of Luxembourg city, near Moselle R.; gypsum and alabaster quarrying.

Bous (bōōs), town (pop. 5,470), SW Saar, near Fr. border, on Saar R. and 9 mi. WNW of Saarbrücken; rail junction; coal and salt mining; steel and metallurgical industry; mfg. of machinery, chemicals, tobacco products. Called Buss, 1936–45.

Bou-Saâda (bōō-sä-ädä'), town (pop. 11,637), Alger dept., N central Algeria, in the Saharan Atlas at edge of the Hodna depression, 125 mi. SE of Algiers and 90 mi. WNW of Biskra. Northernmost Saharan oasis at S terminus of road from Algiers; tourist resort; ships dates, wool, esparto; flourmilling. Handicraft. Picturesque native village.

Bousbecque (bōōzbĕk'), village (pop. 1,734), Nord dept., N France. on the Lys (Belg. border) and 5 mi. NW of Tourcoing; paper milling, flax processing, glycerine mfg.

Bouscat, Le (lü bōōskä'), NW suburb (pop. 17,809) of Bordeaux, Gironde dept., SW France; mfg. of dyes, varnishes, paper, crates; canning.

Bou Sellam, Oued (wĕd' bōō sĕläm'), stream in Constantine dept., NE Algeria, rises in the Tell Atlas (Babor range) just N of Sétif, flows generally NW across Little Kabylia to the Oued Soummam at Akbou; 170 mi. long.

Bou-Sfer (bōō-sfâr'), village (pop. 2,209), Oran dept., NW Algeria, 10 mi. W of Oran; truck gardens, vineyards.

Bousov, Czechoslovakia: see LOSTICE.

Bousquet (bōōskä'), village, W Que., on small L. Bousquet, 22 mi. E of Rouyn; copper mining.

Bousquet-d'Orb, Le (lü bōōskā'-dôrb'), town (pop. 2,132), Hérault dept., S France, on NE slope of Monts de l'Espinouse, on Orb R. and 8 mi. WSW of Lodève; coal mines, glassworks.

Boussa, Nigeria: see BUSSA.

Boussac (bōōsäk'), village (pop. 1,386), Creuse dept., central France, on Petite Creuse R. and 18 mi. W of Montluçon; livestock market. Tin deposits 4 mi. E. Has 15th-16th-cent. castle and small 12th-cent. church.

Boussens (bōōsã'), village (pop. 352), Haute-Garonne dept., S France, on the Garonne and 13 mi. ENE of Saint-Gaudens; electrochemical factory, petroleum refinery.

Boussières (bōōsyâr'), village (pop. 330), Doubs dept., E France, near Doubs R. and Rhone-Rhine Canal, 8 mi. SW of Besançon; paper milling.

Bousso (bōōsō'), village, W Chad territory, Fr. Equatorial Africa, on Shari R. and 150 mi. SE of Fort-Lamy; millet, livestock. Airfield. Sometimes called Fort-Bretonnet (fôr-brütônā').

Boussois (bōōswä'), town (pop. 2,242), Nord dept., N France, on the Sambre and 4 mi. ENE of Maubeuge, near Belg. border; glassworks.

Boussole Strait (bōōsôl', bōōsōl'), Rus. *Proliv Bussol*, Jap. *Kita-uruppu-suido*, widest strait of the Kuriles, Russian SFSR, in central section; separates Simushir Isl. (N) from Brouton Isl. and Chernye Bratya isls. (S); 40 mi. wide.

Boussu (bōōsü'), town (pop. 12,371), Hainaut prov., SW Belgium, on Haine R. and 7 mi. WSW of Mons; heavy-engineering industry; coke plants; glass blowing.

Bou-Thadi (bōō-tädē'), village, Sfax dist., E central Tunisia, 37 mi. NW of Sfax; olive-oil pressing, sheep raising. Roman ruins.

Boutilimit (bōōtēlēmēt'), village, SW Mauritania, Fr. West Africa, 155 mi. NE of Saint-Louis, Senegal. Produces gum arabic, hides, and salt for export; also millet, corn, beans, melons; livestock. Climatologic station.

Boutkovon, Greece: see KERKINE.

Bou-Tlelis (bōō-tlĕlēs'), village (pop. 1,549), Oran dept., NW Algeria, on railroad and 17 mi. SW of Oran, at NW edge of the Oran Sebkha; winegrowing.

Bouton, town (pop. 159), Dallas co., central Iowa, on Beaver Creek and 27 mi. NW of Des Moines, in agr. area.

Boutonne River (bōōtôn'), Deux-Sèvres and Charente-Maritime depts., W France, rises near Chef-Boutonne, flows 58 mi. SW, past Saint-Jean-d'Angély and Tonnay-Boutonne, to the Charente 5 mi. above Rochefort.

Bouverie, La (lä bōōvürē'), town (pop. 7,842), Hainaut prov., SW Belgium, 7 mi. SW of Mons; coal mining, metalworking.

Bouvesse-Quirieu (bōōvĕs-kērēû'), commune (pop. 912), Isère dept., SE France, near left bank of the Rhone, 16 mi. N of La Tour-du-Pin; lime- and cementworks.

Bouvet Island (bōōvā') (□ 22), in South Atlantic Ocean, c.1,500 mi. SW of S tip of Africa, c.1,000 mi. N of Princess Astrid Coast, Antarctica; 54°26'S 3°24'E. Discovered 1739 by French naval officer. Claimed 1927 by Norway, placed 1928 under Nor. sovereignty, made dependency 1930.

Bouvignes (bōōvē'nyü), village (pop. 1,012), Namur prov., S Belgium, on Meuse R., just NNW of Dinant; dairying center.

Bouvines (bōōvēn'), village (pop. 598), Nord dept., N France, 7 mi. SE of Lille. Here Philip II of France defeated (1214) joint forces of John of England, Emperor Otto IV, and count of Flanders.

Bouxwiller (bōōksvēlâr'), Ger. *Buchsweiler* (bōōkhs'-vīlür), town (pop. 2,607), Bas-Rhin dept., E France, 8 mi. NE of Saverne; woodworking (furniture, skis); glass blowing, dye mfg.

Bouzaréa (bōōzäräā'), village (pop. 2,959), Alger dept., N central Algeria, on hill (1,335 ft.; panorama) overlooking Algiers (2 mi. E). Has teachers col. and meteorological observatory.

Bouzas (bō'thäs), town (pop. 4,385), Pontevedra prov., NW Spain, on Vigo Bay of the Atlantic, 2 mi. WSW of Vigo; fishing and fish processing, boatbuilding; livestock, cereals, fruit.

Bouzigues (bōōzēg'), village (pop. 624), Hérault dept., S France, on NW shore of the Étang de Thau, 4 mi. NNW of Sète; winegrowing; oyster beds.

Bouznika (bōōznēkä'), village, Rabat region, NW Fr. Morocco, near the Atlantic, on Casablanca-Rabat road, 30 mi. NE of Casablanca; livestock raising, truck farming.

Bouzonville (bōōzõvēl'), Ger. *Busendorf* (bōō'zündôrf), village (pop. 1,637), Moselle dept., NE France, on the Nied and 17 mi. ESE of Thionville, near Saar border; metalworking, furniture mfg.

Bouzy (bōōzē'), village (pop. 821), Marne dept., N France, 9 mi. ENE of Épernay; winegrowing (champagne).

Bov (bôf), village (pop. 1,375), Sofia dist., W Bulgaria, in W Balkan Mts., just E of Iskar R. gorge, 24 mi. N of Sofia; zinc mining. Scattered copper and lead deposits E.

Bova (bô'vä), village (pop. 1,231), Reggio di Calabria prov., Calabria, S Italy, on S slope of the Aspromonte, 18 mi. ESE of Reggio di Calabria. Bishopric. Its port is **Bova Marina** (pop. 2,098), 5 mi. S, on Ionian Sea.

Bovalino Marina (bôvälē'nô märē'nä), town (pop. 3,176), Reggio di Calabria prov., Calabria, S Italy, port on Ionian Sea, 8 mi. SSW of Locri.

Bovallstrand (bōō"välstränd'), fishing village (pop. 501), Goteborg och Bohus co., SW Sweden, on the Skagerrak, 14 mi. NNW of Lysekil; seaside resort; stone quarries.

Bovec (bô'vĕts), Ger. *Flitsch* (flĭch), Ital. *Plezzo* (plĕt'tsō), village (1936 pop. 1,173), NW Slovenia, Yugoslavia, near Isonzo R., 50 mi. WNW of Ljubljana, at E foot of Mt. Canin, on road leading via Predil Pass to Tarvisio, Italy. Until 1947, in Italy.

Bóveda de Toro, La (lä bō'vā-dhä dhä tō'rō), town (pop. 1,924), Zamora prov., NW Spain, 21 mi. SE of Zamora; lumbering, horse breeding; cereals, wine.

Bovegno (bôvä'nyô), village (pop. 901), Brescia prov., Lombardy, N Italy, on Mella R. and 18 mi. N of Brescia; resort (alt. 2,234 ft.); lace mill. Chief center of upper Val Trompia.

Bovenden (bō'vündün), village (pop. 2,262), in former Prussian prov. of Hanover, W Germany, after 1945 in Lower Saxony, on the Leine and 5 mi. N of Göttingen; ceramics, shoes.

Bovenkarspel (bō'vünkär"spül), village (pop. 3,525), North Holland prov., NW Netherlands, 8 mi. ENE of Hoorn; vegetable market.

Boven Merwede River, Netherlands: see UPPER MERWEDE RIVER.

Boves (bôv), village (pop. 1,814), Somme dept., N France, on Avre R. and 5 mi. SE of Amiens; mfg. of flour products; truck gardening.

Boves (bô'vĕs), village (pop. 3,021), Cuneo prov., Piedmont, NW Italy, 4 mi. S of Cuneo, in cereal- and potato-growing region; silk, cotton, lime, bricks, starch, potato flour. Has meteorological observatory (1874).

Bovesse, Belgium: see SAINT-DENIS-LEZ-GEMBLOUX.

Bovey (bō'vē), village (pop. 1,320), Itasca co., N central Minn., in Mesabi iron range, 7 mi. NE of Grand Rapids in mining, dairying, and agr. area; beverages. Iron mines in vicinity. Ore-washing plant near by on Trout L. Inc. 1921.

Bovey Tracey (bŭ'vē trā'sē), town and parish (pop. 3,053), S central Devon, England, on Bovey R. and 11 mi. SW of Exeter; agr. market; lignite mines; mfg. (pottery, agr. equipment), woolen milling; clay quarrying. Has 15th-cent. church.

Bovill (bō'vĭl), village (pop. 437), Latah co., N Idaho, 30 mi. ENE of Moscow and on Potlatch R.; lumber.

Boville Ernica (bôvēl'lĕ ĕr'nēkä), village (pop. 738), Frosinone prov., Latium, S central Italy, 6 mi. E of Frosinone. Formerly Bauco.

Bovina (bŭvē'nŭ), town (pop. 612), Parmer co., W Texas, 75 mi. SW of Amarillo.

Bovingdon (bŏ'–, bō'–, bŭ'–), town and parish (pop. 1,722), SW Hertford, England, 7 mi. NW of Watford; agr. market. Large airport.

Bovino (bôvē'nô), anc. *Vibinum*, town (pop. 7,843), Foggia prov., Apulia, S Italy, near Cervaro R., 18 mi. SW of Foggia. Agr. trade center (livestock, cheese, wool, olive oil); soap mfg. Bishopric. Has 13th-cent. cathedral and ruins of medieval castle.

Bovolenta (bôvôlĕn'tä), village (pop. 1,047), Padova prov., Veneto, N Italy, 10 mi. SSE of Padua; soap factory.

Bovolone (bôvôlô'nĕ), village (pop. 1,598), Verona prov., Veneto, N Italy, 14 mi. SSE of Verona; canned foods, marmalade.

Bovril (bōvrēl'), town (pop. estimate 1,000), N central Entre Ríos prov., Argentina, on railroad and 75 mi. NE of Paraná; cattle, sheep raising; trading in meat and grain; flour milling.

Bow or **Stratford le Bow** (străt'fürd lü bō), workers' residential and industrial district of Poplar metropolitan borough, London, England, N of the Thames, 5 mi. ENE of Charing Cross; named from 12th-cent. arched bridge over Lea R. Has 15th-cent. church, on site of earlier chapel; there are also relics of Roman occupation. Near-by French convent is mentioned in Chaucer's *Prologue*. In 18th cent. Bow was noted for china mfg.

Bow, town (pop. 1,062), Merrimack co., S central N.H., on the Merrimack just S of Concord. Mary Baker Eddy b. here. Bow Mills village has state's oldest sawmill (c.1800).

Bowbells (bō–), city (pop. 806), ⊙ Burke co., NW N.Dak., 60 mi. NW of Minot; coal mines, dairy farms; livestock, poultry, wheat, grain, flax.

Bowden (bō'dŭn), village (pop. 273), S central Alta., 25 mi. SSW of Red Deer; mixed farming, dairying.

Bowden, town (pop. 1,210), St. Thomas parish, SE Jamaica, just E of Port Morant, 32 mi. ESE of Kingston; ships bananas. Served by narrow-gauge railroad.

Bowden Point, SW Devon Isl., E central Franklin Dist., Northwest Territories, on Wellington Channel; 75°2'N 92°15'W.

Bowdens (bou'dŭnz), town (pop. 239), Duplin co., E central N.C., 10 mi. SSW of Mt. Olive; lumber milling.

Bowditch Island: see FAKAOFO.

Bowdle (bou'dŭl), city (pop. 788), Edmunds co., N central S.Dak., 30 mi. W of Ipswich; dairy products, livestock, poultry, grain.

Bowdoin (bō'dŭn), town (pop. 638), Sagadahoc co., SW Maine, 12 mi. NW of Bath.

Bowdoin, Lake (bou'dŭn), NE Mont., in Phillips co., 8 mi. ENE of Malta; 7 mi. long, max. width 2 mi.; fed by Milk R. U.S. migratory waterfowl refuge here.

Bowdoinham (bō'dŭnhăm), town (pop. 1,039), Sagadahoc co., SW Maine, on the Kennebec and 8 mi. NW of Bath.

Bowdon (bō'dŭn), urban district (1931 pop. 3,285; 1951 census 3,529), N Cheshire, England, just SW of Altrincham.

Bowdon. 1 (bou'dŭn) Town (pop. 1,155), Carroll co., W Ga., 10 mi. WSW of Carrollton, near Ala. line in agr. area; mfg. of rubber goods. Settled 1830, inc. 1859. **2** (bō'dŭn) Village (pop. 348), Wells co., central N.Dak., 13 mi. S of Fessenden.

Bowen, town (pop. estimate 1,500), E central Mendoza prov., Argentina, on railroad and 55 mi. SE of San Rafael; tomatoes, wine, fruit, onions, grain; food canning.

Bowen (bō'ŭn), town and port (pop. 3,276), E Queensland, Australia, 110 mi. ESE of Townsville and on Port Denison (small NW inlet of Edgecumbe Bay); rail junction; coal-mining center; exports sugar, tobacco, coal. State coke works. Copper, silver, and graphite mines near by.

Bowen (bō'ĭn), village (pop. 573), Hancock co., W Ill., 27 mi. NE of Quincy, in agr. and bituminous-coal area.

Bowen Island (□ 10), SW B.C., in Howe Sound, 13 mi. NW of Vancouver; 5 mi. long, 3 mi. wide, rises to 2,479 ft.; resort; lumbering.

Bowen Mountains, Australia: see AUSTRALIAN ALPS.

Bower, agr. village and parish (pop. 1,059), NE Caithness, Scotland, 3 mi. SE of Castletown.

Bowerbank (bou'–), resort town (pop. 20), Piscataquis co., central Maine, on Sebec L. and 6 mi. N of Dover-Foxcroft.

Bowers or **Bowers Beach**, resort town (pop. 284), Kent co., E Del., on Delaware Bay and 10 mi. SE of Dover, at mouth of Murderkill R.; fishing; oysters.

Bowers Mill, town (pop. 29), Lawrence co., SW Mo., 18 mi. E of Carthage.

Bowerston, village (pop. 522), Harrison co., E Ohio, 14 mi. NW of Cadiz.

Bowersville. 1 Town (pop. 303), Hart co., NE Ga., 8 mi. W of Hartwell, in agr. area. **2** Village (pop. 362), Greene co., S central Ohio, 27 mi. ESE of Dayton, in agr. area.

Bowery, the (bou'ŭrē), SE N.Y., a section and street of lower Manhattan borough of New York city, E of Broadway, bet. Chatham Square and Astor Place. The Bowery area was 1st the country estate of Governor Stuyvesant (who is buried at St. Mark's-in-the-Bouwerie Church), later the site of fine theaters (in 1860s and 1870s), then a notorious section of saloons and dives, then the haunt of the city's derelicts, who patronize its cheap lodgings, restaurants, and pawnshops. It is also in part a commercial dist.

Bowes, village and parish (pop. 565), North Riding, NW Yorkshire, England, on Greta R. and 19 mi. W of Darlington; lead mining. Site of remains of Roman camp, of ruins of Bowes Castle, built 1187, and of church of Norman origin.

Bow Fell, mountain (2,960 ft.) of the Cumbrians, S Cumberland, England, at Westmorland line 8 mi. W of Ambleside.

Bowie (bōō'ē), county (□ 921; pop. 61,966), NE Texas; ⊙ Boston. In extreme NE corner of state, bounded W by Red R. (here the Okla. and Ark. lines), E by Ark. line, S by Sulphur R. Partly forested (pine, oak, gum); lumbering, agr. (cotton, corn, grains, peanuts, hay, fruit, truck, pecans);

cattle, sheep, poultry; dairying. Mfg., processing at TEXARKANA (partly in Ark.). Formed 1840.

Bowie. **1** Town (pop. 860), Prince Georges co., central Md., 15 mi. ENE of Washington, in truck-farm area. State teachers col. for Negroes. Near by are Bowie race track (established 1914) and "Belair" (built c.1745), an estate with noted grounds. **2** City (pop. 4,544), Montague co., N Texas, c.45 mi. SE of Wichita Falls; poultry-shipping center in agr. region (truck, grain, dairy products); makes cheese. Founded 1882, inc. 1892.

Bow Island, town (pop. 432), SE Alta., near South Saskatchewan R., 35 mi. WSW of Medicine Hat; natural-gas center; coal mining.

Bow Lake, N.H.: see STRAFFORD, town.

Bowland Forest (bō'lŭnd), wooded area, W Yorkshire and E Lancashire, England, 10 mi. NW of Clitheroe. Rises to c.1,500 ft.

Bowler, village (pop. 344), Shawano co., E central Wis., 33 mi. ESE of Wausau; lumbering.

Bowling Green. **1** City (pop. 884), Hardee co., central Fla., 6 mi. N of Wauchula; ships strawberries. **2** Town (pop. 235), Clay co., W Ind., on Eel R. and 21 mi. ESE of Terre Haute, in agr. and bituminous-coal area. **3** City (pop. 18,347), ⊙ Warren co., S Ky., on Barren R. (head of navigation) and 65 mi. NNE of Nashville, Tenn.; shipping, market center for agr. (dark tobacco, strawberries, corn, livestock, horses, poultry) area, with limestone and asphalt quarries, oil and gas wells. Mfg. of evaporated milk, packed meat, soft drinks, dairy products, foundry products, electric tubes, men's underwear, signs, building material, concrete products, air-conditioning equipment, water coolers; flour and feed mills, tobacco stemmeries, sawmills, oil and rock-asphalt processing plants, marble works; airport. Seat of Western Ky. State Teachers Col. (with Ky. Library of Folklore and mus. of Kentuckiana) and Bowling Green Col. of Commerce. Lost River Cave, hiding place of Gen. John Hunt Morgan, is near by; ruins of Shaker colony are SW; Mammoth Cave Natl. Park is NE. Occupied early in Civil War by Gen. S. B. Buckner's Confederate forces until Union advance under generals U. S. Grant and D. C. Buell forced retreat (1862). Founded 1780; inc. 1812. **4** City (pop. 2,396), ⊙ Pike co., E Mo., near Mississippi R., 26 mi. SSE of Hannibal. Agr.; mfg. (metal products, garments); limestone. U.S. nursery near by. Settled 1819. **5** City (pop. 12,005), ⊙ Wood co., NW Ohio, 19 mi. SSW of Toledo, in fertile agr. area (dairy products; livestock, grain); food products, packed meat, machine tools, motor vehicles, machinery, metal products, cut glass, burial vaults. Seat of Bowling Green State Univ. Settled 1833, inc. 1835. **6** Village, York co., N S.C., at N.C. line, 11 mi. N of York; textiles, twine. **7** Town (pop. 616), ⊙ Caroline co., E Va., 19 mi. SSE of Fredericksburg, in agr. area; makes baskets, excelsior. Rail station at Milford, 2 mi. SW. Hill Military Reservation is just E.

Bowling Green, Cape, E Queensland, Australia, in Coral Sea, 25 mi. E of Cape Cleveland; 19°18'S 147°25'E. Forms E side of entrance to Bowling Green Bay; lighthouse.

Bowlus (bō'lŭs), village (pop. 233), Morrison co., central Minn., near Mississippi R., 10 mi. S of Little Falls, in grain, livestock, and potato area; dairy products.

Bowman (bō'mŭn), county (□ 1,170; pop. 4,001), extreme SW N.Dak.; ⊙ Bowman. Agr. area watered by Little Missouri R. and Grand R. Lignite coal abundant; stock raising; dairy, grain, poultry farms; wheat, flax, vegetables. Formed 1883.

Bowman. **1** City (pop. 714), Elbert co., NE Ga., 11 mi. NW of Elberton, in farm area. **2** Village (pop. 1,382), ⊙ Bowman co., extreme SW N.Dak., 56 mi. SSW of Dickinson. Lignite mines; stock raising; dairy, poultry farms; grain, wheat, flax. Inc. 1908. **3** Town (pop. 857), Orangeburg co., S central S.C., 15 mi. SE of Orangeburg; lumber, pecans.

Bowman Field, Ky.: see LOUISVILLE.

Bowman Island (bō'mŭn), just off Antarctica, NW of Knox Coast, in Indian Ocean; 65°10'S 103°15'E; 11 naut. mi. long. Discovered 1931 by Sir Douglas Mawson.

Bowmans (bō'mŭnz), village, SE South Australia, 70 mi. S of Port Pirie; rail junction; agr. center.

Bowmanstown, borough (pop. 878), Carbon co., E Pa., on Lehigh R. just W of Palmerton.

Bowmansville, village (pop. c.500), Erie co., W N.Y., 10 mi. ENE of Buffalo; stone quarrying.

Bowmanville (bō'–), town (pop. 4,113), S Ont., on L. Ontario, 9 mi. E of Oshawa; port, with good natural harbor; mfg. of automobile parts, rubber products, cans, silver plate, pottery, bricks, furniture, gloves; textile knitting, flour milling; resort.

Bowmore, village on ISLAY, Hebrides, Scotland.

Bowness (bōnĕs', bō'nĕs), village and parish (pop. 1,024), NW Cumberland, England, on Solway Firth, 12 mi. WNW of Carlisle; dairy farming. Has Norman church. In Roman times it was the W pivot of Hadrian's Wall, traces of which are still visible.

Bowness-on-Windermere, England: see WINDERMERE.

Bowral (bou'rŭl, bä'–), municipality (pop. 3,660), E New South Wales, Australia, 60 mi. SW of Sydney; alt. 2,216 ft. Health resort; coal-mining center; syenite, bauxite.

Bowringpet (bou'rĭngpĕt), town (pop. 7,515), Kolar dist., E Mysore, India, 10 mi. SSE of Kolar; rail junction (spur to Kolar Gold Fields, SE); cigarette mfg.

Bow River (bō), in Alta., chief headstream of South Saskatchewan R., rises in Rocky Mts. at foot of Mt. Gordon, flows SE, through magnificent mtn. scenery of Banff Natl. Park, past Lake Louise, then generally E, past Banff, leaving the Rockies through the canyonlike Bow River Pass, to Calgary It then flows SE to confluence with the Oldman R. 45 mi. W of Medicine Hat, here forming South Saskatchewan R. Bow R. is 315 mi. long. Near Calgary it feeds extensive irrigation system, serving S Alta. Its valley from Calgary westward to near its head is route of chief transcontinental line of the Canadian Pacific RR. Bassano or Horshoe Bend irrigation dam, one of longest in the world, is 70 mi. ESE of Calgary.

Bowstring Lake (□ 15), Itasca co., N Minn., largely in Greater Leech Lake Indian Reservation, near Wabatawangang L., 25 mi. NW of Grand Rapids; 5.5 mi. long, 3.5 mi. wide. Fishing resorts. Fed and drained by Bowstring R. and surrounded by Chippewa Natl. Forest. Sometimes written Bow String.

Bowstring River, rises in small lake in Itasca co., N Minn., flows 60 mi. N, through Bowstring and Wabatawangang lakes, and E to Bigfork village, where it joins small stream to form Big Fork R.

Box, agr. village and parish (pop. 2,197), W Wiltshire, England, 5 mi. ENE of Bath. Has 15th-cent. church.

Boxberg (bôks'bĕrk″), town (pop. 1,099), N Baden, Germany, after 1945 in Württemberg-Baden, 6 mi. W of Mergentheim; mfg. of costume jewelry.

Boxboro or **Boxborough,** town (pop. 439), Middlesex co., NE central Mass., 21 mi. NE of Worcester; fruit, dairying.

Box Butte (būt), county (□ 1,066; pop. 12,279), NW Nebr.; ⊙ Alliance; agr. area; livestock, poultry products, grain, seed potatoes. Formed 1886.

Box Elder, county (□ 5,594; pop. 19,734), NW Utah; ⊙ Brigham City. Agr. area bordering on Nev. and Idaho. Great Salt L. (SE) is entered by Bear R. Great Salt Lake Desert is in SW. Mfg. and canning at Brigham City; sugar beets, peaches, livestock, grain. Formed 1856.

Box Elder, village (pop. c.200), Hill co., N Mont., on branch of Milk R. and 23 mi. SW of Havre, in livestock region. Hq. of Rocky Boy's Indian Reservation.

Boxford, rural town (pop. 926), Essex co., NE Mass., 9 mi. ESE of Lawrence.

Box Hill, municipality (pop. 21,373), S Victoria, Australia, 9 mi. E of Melbourne, in metropolitan area; fruitgrowing region.

Box Hill, England: see DORKING.

Boxholm (bôks'hôlm″), village (pop. 2,803), Ostergotland co., S Sweden, on Svart R. and 8 mi. S of Mjolby; foundry (established 1754), sawmills.

Boxholm (bŏks'hōm″), town (pop. 304), Boone co., central Iowa, 14 mi. NW of Boone.

Boxmeer or **Boksmeer** (bôks'mār), town (pop. 4,379), North Brabant prov., E Netherlands, near Maas R., 14 mi. SSE of Nijmegen; cigar mfg.; grain. Many monasteries in vicinity.

Boxmoor, England: see HEMEL HEMPSTEAD.

Boxtel or **Bokstel** (bôks'tŭl), town (pop. 8,595), North Brabant prov., S Netherlands, on Dommel R. and 10 mi. E of Tilburg; rail junction; linen, woodwork, strawboard, meat products; dairying.

Boyabat (bôyäbät'), village (pop. 3,996), Sinop prov., N Turkey, on Gok R. and 45 mi. SSW of Sinop; grain, onions, vetch, naphtha near by.

Boyacá (boiäkä'), department (□ 24,934; 1938 pop. 737,368; 1950 estimate 791,300), central and E Colombia; ⊙ Tunja. The Cordillera Oriental, with high massif Sierra Nevada de Cocuy (W), gives way E to vast llano area bet. Casanare (N) and Meta (S) rivers. Climate varies greatly from unhealthy tropical llanos to cool uplands. Rich mineral deposits include petroleum (Vásquez Territory, and along Meta R.), emeralds (Muzo), iron (Paz del Río), coal (Sogamoso), copper (Moniquirá, Santa Rosa). Dense forests on mtn. slopes yield fine wood, rubber, resins, balsam. Main crops are wheat, potatoes (in higher regions), corn, rice, sugar cane, cotton, cacao, coffee, fique, silk, tobacco, livestock. Cattle are also extensively raised in llanos. Processing and textile milling centers are Tunja, Sogamoso, Chiquinquirá, and Samacá. Paipa is a spa with notable thermal springs. Exports hides, coffee, wheat, emeralds, forest products. Region was settled in pre-Columbian times by Chibcha Indians of whose advanced culture there are many archaeological remains. Boyacá was a nucleus of the liberating forces in struggle for independence from Spain. Llanos section was separated (1950) to form Casanare intendancy.

Boyacá, village (pop. 370), Boyacá dept., central Colombia, in Cordillera Oriental, 5 mi. S of Tunja; alt. 7,746 ft.; cereals, cotton, silk, livestock. Founded 1556. Site of decisive patriot victory (Aug. 7, 1819) by Simón Bolívar and Santander over the Spanish, paving way for independence of Colombia and Venezuela.

Boyalik, Turkey: see CICEKDAGI.

Boyana (bôyä'nä), village (pop. 3,292), Sofia dist., W. Bulgaria, SSW suburb of Sofia, on N slope of Vitosha Mts.; livestock, truck produce. Has 12th-cent. church.

Boyana River, Albania-Yugoslavia: see BOJANA RIVER.

Boyange (bōyäng'gä) or **Budja-Saint-Paul** (bōōjä-sē-pōl'), village, Equator Prov., NW Belgian Congo, 20 mi. ENE of Lisala; has R.C. mission and several schools. Elaeis-palm growing in vicinity.

Boyanovka, Russian SFSR: see POKROVSK-URALSKI.

Boyanup (boi'ŭnŭp), town (pop. 454), SW Western Australia, 105 mi. S of Perth; rail junction; butter.

Boyarka-Budayevka (bŭyär'kŭ-bōōdī'ŭfkŭ), town (1926 pop. 4,396), central Kiev oblast, Ukrainian SSR, on railroad and 12 mi. SW of Kiev.

Boyce (bois). **1** Town (pop. 981), Rapides parish, central La., 15 mi. NW of Alexandria, near Red R.; farming; cotton ginning, lumber milling. **2** Town (pop. 372), Clarke co., N Va., in Shenandoah Valley, 9 mi. SE of Winchester.

Boyceville, village (pop. 645), Dunn co., W Wis., 12 mi. NNW of Menomonie, in dairy and grain area.

Boychinovtsi, Bulgaria: see BOICHINOVTSI.

Boyd. **1** County (□ 159; pop. 49,949), NE Ky.; ⊙ Catlettsburg. Bounded NE by the Ohio (Ohio line), E by Big Sandy R. (W.Va. line). Hilly industrial and mineral region; includes part of HUNTINGTON (W.Va.)–ASHLAND (Ky.) metropolitan dist., with extensive mfg. Bituminous-coal mines, oil and gas wells, clay pits, limestone and sandstone quarries, iron deposits; hardwood timber tracts; some farms (livestock, fruit, tobacco). Formed 1860. **2** County (□ 538; pop. 4,911), N Nebr.; ⊙ Butte. Agr. area bounded N by S.Dak., S by Niobrara R., NE by Missouri R.; drained by Keya Paha R. and Ponca Creek. Livestock, grain. Formed 1891.

Boyd. **1** Village (pop. 496), Lac qui Parle co., SW Minn., on small tributary of Minnesota R. and 18 mi. SE of Madison, in livestock, grain, and poultry area; dairy products. **2** Village, Carbon co., S Mont., on Red Lodge Creek and 35 mi. SW of Billings; livestock, sugar beets, grain, vegetables, honey. **3** Town (pop. 550), Wise co., N Texas, 27 mi. NW of Fort Worth, near West Fork of Trinity R., in agr. area. **4** Village (pop. 619), Chippewa co., W central Wis., 17 mi. E of Chippewa Falls; lumbering, dairying, flour milling.

Boyden, town (pop. 541), Sioux co., NW Iowa, near source of West Branch Floyd R., 7 mi. W of Sheldon; dairy products, feed.

Boydton, town (pop. 501), ⊙ Mecklenburg co., S Va., 65 mi. SW of Petersburg, in agr. area (tobacco); sawmilling. Randolph-Macon Col. here, 1832–68, was moved to Ashland.

Boyer, village, SE Tasmania, 12 mi. NNW of Hobart and on Derwent R.; newsprint mills.

Boyer River, W Iowa, rises near Storm Lake city, flows 139 mi. S and SW, past Denison, Logan, and Missouri Valley, to Missouri R. 13 mi. N of Council Bluffs.

Boyertown (boi'ŭrtoun), borough (pop. 4,074), Berks co., SE Pa., 15 mi. E of Reading; metal and leather products, shoes, caskets, clothing. Founded c.1835, inc. 1866.

Boyes Springs or **Boyes Hot Springs,** village (pop. 2,391, with near-by Fetters Springs), Sonoma co., W Calif., 16 mi. SE of Santa Rosa.

Boyevo, Bulgaria: see ZLATOGRAD.

Boyevo, Russian SFSR: see BAGARYAK.

Boykin, town (pop. 120), Miller co., SW Ga., 16 mi. NNW of Bainbridge.

Boykins, town (pop. 811), Southampton co., SE Va., 35 mi. WSW of Suffolk, near N.C. line; peanut processing. Raids of Nat Turner's slave insurrection (1831) began here.

Boy Lake, Cass co., N central Minn., in Greater Leech Lake Indian Reservation and Chippewa Natl. Forest, 29 mi. WSW of Grand Rapids; 4 mi. long, 1.5 mi. wide. Resorts. Drains through small stream into Leech L. just W.

Boyle, village (pop. estimate 1,000), central Alta., 20 mi. ESE of Athabaska; wheat, livestock.

Boyle, Gaelic *Mainistir na Búille,* town (pop. 2,071), N Co. Roscommon, Ireland, on Boyle R. and 22 mi. SSE of Sligo; agr. market (cattle, sheep; potatoes). Has remains of Cistercian abbey founded 1161. Near by are Curlew Mts. and Lough Key.

Boyle, county (□ 181; pop. 20,532), central Ky.; ⊙ Danville. Bounded E by Dix R. (Herrington L.) drained by Salt R. and Beech Fork. Gently rolling and partly hilly upland, partly in outer Bluegrass agr. area; burley tobacco, wheat, livestock, berries; stone quarries. Mfg. at Danville. Includes Perryville Battlefield State Park near Perryville and Weisiger Memorial and Dr. Ephraim McDowell state shrines at Danville. Formed 1842.

Boyle, town (pop. 799), Bolivar co., NW Miss., 3 mi. S of Cleveland, in agr. area.

Boylefoss (bû'ülůfôs), Nor. *Bøylefoss,* falls on Nid R., in Aust-Agder co., S Norway, 12 mi. N of Arendal; hydroelectric plant. Sometimes spelled Boilefoss, Nor. *Bøilefoss.*

Boylston, residential town (pop. 1,700), Worcester co., central Mass., just E of Wachusett Reservoir, 7 mi. NNE of Worcester. Settled 1705, inc. 1786. Includes village of Morningdale.

Boyndie, agr. village and parish (pop. 2,014), N Banffshire, Scotland, near Moray Firth, 3 mi. W of Banff; site of co. insane asylum.

Boyne City, city (pop. 3,028), Charlevoix co., NW Mich., on L.Charlevoix at mouth of small Boyne R., and 12 mi. SSW of Petoskey, in area producing cherries, apples, potatoes; leather tanning; greenhouse. Resort. Smelt festival held here each spring. Inc. as village 1885, as city 1907.

Boyne Falls, village (pop. 236), Charlevoix co., NW Mich., on short Boyne R. and 14 mi. S of Petoskey; mfg. of lumber, wood novelties. Resort; fishing.

Boyne River, Ireland, in Leinster, rises in the Bog of Allen near Carbury, Kildare, flows 70 mi. NE, through Co. Meath, passing Trim, An Uaimh, Slane, and Drogheda, to the Irish Sea 4 mi. E of Drogheda. The battle of the Boyne was fought at OLDBRIDGE, near Drogheda.

Boynik, Yugoslavia: see BOJNIK.

Boynitsa, Bulgaria: see BOINITSA.

Boynton, town (pop. 718), Muskogee co., E Okla., 18 mi. WSW of Muskogee, in agr. area; cotton ginning; oil wells.

Boynton Beach, city (pop. 2,542), Palm Beach co., SE Fla., 13 mi. S of West Palm Beach; resort; vegetable-shipping point. Inc. 1920 as Boynton. For a time, the adjacent town of Ocean Ridge was also called Boynton Beach.

Boyolali or **Bojolali** (both: bōyōlä'lē), town (pop. 10,261), central Java, Indonesia, 25 mi. NE of Jogjakarta at foot of Mt. Merapi; alt. 1,380 ft.; trade center in agr. region (tobacco, rice, cassava, peanut). Has healthful climate.

Boy River, resort village (pop. 82), Cass co., N central Minn., near Leech L., and Greater Leech Lake Indian Reservation, c.40 mi. ESE of Bemidji; grain, potatoes.

Boys Town, village (pop. 975), Douglas co., E Nebr., 10 mi. W of Omaha, near Missouri R.; developed from refuge for homeless boys established in 1917 by Father Edward J. Flanagan in Omaha. Located on 320 acres of farm land, governed by boys, supported by private contribution. Inc. as village 1936.

Boyuibe (boiwē'bā), village (pop. c.850), Santa Cruz dept., SE Bolivia, 60 mi. SE of Lagunillas.

Boz, Cape (bôz), NW Turkey, on Sea of Marmara, 12 mi. NNW of Mudanya, at mouth of Gulf of Gemlik.

Boza (bō'sä), village (pop. 799), Lima dept., W central Peru, near the Pacific, 30 mi. N of Lima; spa with thermal springs.

Boza Gora, Poland: see BOGUSZOW.

Bozanonu (bôzä'nünü"), Turkish *Bozanönü*, village (pop. 463), Isparta prov., W central Turkey, 8 mi. N of Isparta; rail junction.

Bözberg Tunnel (bŭts'bĕrk) (2 mi. long), Aargau canton, N Switzerland, 6 mi. NE of Aarau; used by Basel-Baden railway.

Bozburun Dag (bôzbŏŏrŏŏn' dä), Turkish *Bozburun Dağ*, peak (8,215 ft.), S Turkey, in Taurus Mts., 34 mi. NE of Antalya.

Bozcaada or **Bozca Island,** Turkey: see TENEDOS.

Boz Dag or **Boz Dagh,** Greece: see PHALAKRON.

Boz Dag or **Boz Dagh** (bôz' dä), Turkish *Boz Dağ*. **1** Peak (7,077 ft.), anc. *Tmolus* (tŭmō'lŭs), W Turkey, 50 mi. E of Smyrna, in Boz Mts., which extend 75 mi. E-W bet. the Kucuk Menderes (anc. Cayster) and Gediz (anc. Hermus) rivers; lignite. Anc. city of Sardis, ⊙ Lydia, lay at its N foot. **2** Peak (5,065 ft.), central Turkey, 29 mi. NE of Konya.

Bozdogan (bôzdôän'), Turkish *Bozdoğan*, village (pop. 3,842), Aydin prov., W Turkey, near Ak R., 28 mi. ESE of Aydin; figs, cotton.

Bozeat (bō'zŭt), town and parish (pop. 1,175), E Northampton, England, 6 mi. S of Wellingborough; shoe mfg.

Bozel (bô'zĕl'), village (pop. 694), Savoie dept., SE France, Alpine resort on the Doron de Bozel and 6 mi. SE of Moutiers in the Massif de la Vanoise; alt. 2,870 ft. Chemicals.

Bozeman (bōz'mŭn), city (pop. 11,325), ⊙ Gallatin co., SW Mont., 75 mi. ESE of Butte, near Gallatin R., just S of Bridger Range. Tourist stop on route to Yellowstone Natl. Park, shipping point for grain and livestock; coal; canned vegetables. Mont. State Col., agr. experiment station here. Near by is site of Fort Ellis, former army post and outfitting point. City founded 1864, inc. 1883.

Bozen, Italy: see BOLZANO, city.

Bozhedarovka, Ukrainian SSR: see SHCHORSK.

Bozhidar (bô"zhēdär'). **1** Village (pop. 817), Kolarovgrad dist., NE Bulgaria, in SW Dobruja, 19 mi. N of Novi Pazar; rail terminus; porcelain mfg. Kaolin quarried near by (E). Formerly Shumnubokhchalav. **2** Village (pop. 2,396), Plovdiv dist., central Bulgaria, on Strema R. and 5 mi. E of Klisura; rose-growing center in Karlovo Basin; vineyards. Formerly Rakhmanlare.

Bozhurishte (bôzhŏŏ'rēshtĕ), village (pop. 1,116), Sofia dist., W Bulgaria, 8 mi. NW of Sofia; military stud farm; airport. Manganese deposits in near-by Pozharevo (pop. 751).

Bozi Dar (bô'zhĭdär"), Czech *Boži Dar*, Ger. *Gottesgab* (gŭ'tŭsgäp"), town (pop. 189), W Bohemia, Czechoslovakia, in the Erzgebirge, 3 mi. N of Jachymov; highest town (alt. 3,411 ft.) in Czechoslovakia; former mining community.

Bozkir (bôzkŭr'), Turkish *Bozkır*, village (pop. 1,499), Konya prov., SW central Turkey, 50 mi. SSW of Konya; potatoes, barley, wheat, onions. Formerly Silistat.

Bozoglan Mountains, Turkey: see BOLKAR MOUNTAINS.

Bozouls (bôzŏŏl'), village (pop. 477), Aveyron dept., S France, 11 mi. NE of Rodez; sheep raising.

Bozoum (bōzŏŏm'), town, ⊙ Ouham-Pendé region (□ 23,550; 1950 pop. 201,000), NW Ubangi-Shari, Fr. Equatorial Africa, on Ouham R. and 200 mi. NW of Bangui; trading center and road communications point; cotton ginning. Also gold mining.

Bozova (bô'zôvä"), village (pop. 1,605), Urfa prov., S Turkey, 29 mi. NW of Urfa; barley, wheat. Formerly Yaylak, Huvek, or Hevenk.

Bozovici (bōzōvēch'), Hung. *Bozovics* (bô'zôvēch), village (pop. 3,431), Severin prov., SW Rumania, in SW foothills of the Transylvanian Alps, 15 mi. SE of Oravita; coal mining, lumbering, cheese making. Founded in 14th cent.

Bozrah (bŏz'rŭ). Two biblical cities of unknown location, one in Edom (Gen. 36.33), the other in Moab (Jer. 48.24). The Edomite Bozrah is sometimes identified with the Jordanian village of El Buseira, 25 mi. SSE of S end of Dead Sea. Bozrah should not be confused with BUSRA (Bosra).

Bozrah, town (pop. 1,154), New London co., SE Conn., on Yantic R. and 5 mi. W of Norwich; mfg. (textiles, bedding) at villages of Gilman and Fitchville; agr. Resorts on Gardner L. (S). Settled in late 17th cent., inc. 1786.

Bozuyuk (bôzüyük'), Turkish *Bozüyük*. **1** Town (pop. 7,582), Bilecik prov., NW Turkey, on railroad and 17 mi. S of Bilecik; coal deposits; grain, vetch. **2** Village, Mugla prov., Turkey: see YATAGAN.

Bozzolo (bô'tsôlô), town (pop. 3,947), Mantova prov., Lombardy, N Italy, near Oglio R., 16 mi. WSW of Mantua; agr. center (cereals, raw silk, grapes); mfg. (macaroni, pottery, pumps, leather goods). Has old castle.

Bra (brä), town (pop. 11,651), Cuneo prov., Piedmont, NW Italy, 27 mi. SSE of Turin; rail junction; industrial center; tanneries, distilleries, mfg. of flour, textiles, machinery, automobile chassis, fertilizers.

Braamspunt (bräms'pŭnt), island and cape on Atlantic coast of N Du. Guiana, guarding mouth of Surinam R., 8 mi. NNW of Paramaribo; 5°56'N 55°15'W. Valsch Braamspunt (cape) is 9 mi. NE.

Braas (brä'ōs"), Swedish *Braås*, village (pop. 505), Kronoberg co., S Sweden, at S end of L. Ork, Swedish *Örken* (ûr'kŭn) (9 mi. long, 1 mi. wide), 15 mi. NE of Vaxjo; lumbering, sawmilling.

Braband (brä'bän), town (pop. 2,499), Aarhus amt, E Jutland, Denmark, 4 mi. W of Aarhus; truck produce.

Brabant (brŭbănt', bră'bŭnt, Flemish brä'bänt), province (□ 1,268; pop. 1,811,330), central Belgium; ⊙ Brussels. Bounded by Antwerp prov. (N), Limburg and Liége provs. (E), Namur and Hainaut provs. (S), East Flanders prov. (W). Fertile soil, watered by Dyle, Senne, and Demer rivers; crossed by Charleroi-Brussels and Willebroek canals; vegetable, chicory, grape, and sugarbeet growing. Machine mfg. (Brussels, Tubize), textile, clothing, and leather industries (Brussels). Important towns: Brussels, Louvain, Hal, Tubize, Nivelles, Tirlemont. Except for S part, prov. is largely Flemish-speaking, while Brussels is bilingual (French, Flemish). Brabant was formerly part of old duchy of Brabant, which was ruled from late 12th cent. by dukes of Brabant and from 15th cent. by dukes of Burgundy. After Belg. independence was won in 1830, part of old duchy passed to the Netherlands as North Brabant prov., Belg. part became provs. of Brabant and Antwerp.

Brabanta (bräbäntä'), village, Kasai prov., central Belgian Congo, on left bank of Kasai R. and 100 mi. NW of Luebo; palm-products center; steamboat landing; palm-oil milling. Has R.C. mission and trade schools. Also known as Mobendi.

Brabant Island (33 naut. mi. long, 20 naut. mi. wide), 2d largest of Palmer Archipelago, Antarctica, in South Pacific just off NW coast of Palmer Peninsula, NE of Anvers Isl.; 64°15'S 62°20'W. Rises to 6,260 ft. Discovered 1898 by Adrien de Gerlache, Belgian explorer.

Brabova (bräbô'vä), agr. village (pop. 1,092), Dolj prov., S Rumania, 18 mi. WNW of Craiova.

Bracara Augusta, Portugal: see BRAGA, city.

Bracciano, Lake (brät-chä'nô), crater lake (□ 22), Latium, central Italy, 18 mi. NW of Rome; 5.5 mi. in diameter, max. depth 525 ft. Its outlet (Arrone R.; SE) flows S to Tyrrhenian Sea. On W shore is town of Bracciano (pop. 4,129), with 15th-cent. walls and castle.

Bracebridge, town (pop. 2,341), ⊙ Muskoka dist., S Ont., on Muskoka R., near L. Muskoka, and 70 mi. NW of Peterborough; woolen and lumber milling, boat building, mfg. of leather, casting. Tourist center for Muskoka dist. Airport.

Braceville, village (pop. 384), Grundy co., NE Ill., 23 mi. SSW of Joliet, in agr. and bituminous-coal-mining area.

Brach or **Brak** (both: bräk'), town (pop. 730), central Fezzan, Libya, 35 mi. NNW of Sebha, in an oasis near SE edge of the Hammada el Hamra region of the Sahara; road junction; dates, cereals; sheep, camels, poultry. Has mosque, forts.

Brachami, Greece: see HAGIOS DEMETRIOS.

Brach Island, Yugoslavia: see BRAC ISLAND.

Bracieux (bräsyû'), village (pop. 837), Loir-et-Cher dept., N central France, on the Beuvron and 10 mi. ESE of Blois; hog market; woodworking. Has 16th-cent. château of Villesavin.

Bracigliano (brächēlyä'nô), village (pop. 2,532), Salerno prov., Campania, S Italy, 10 mi. NNW of Salerno.

Bracigovo, Bulgaria: see BRATSIGOVO.

Brac Island (bräch), Serbo-Croatian *Brač*, Ital. *Brazza* (brät'tsä), largest (□ 152) of Dalmatian islands in Adriatic Sea, S Croatia, Yugoslavia, SE of Split, N of Hvar Isl.; rises to 2,552 ft. Marble and asphalt deposits; fishing and fish canning; tourist center. Chief village (pop. 1,707) is Supetar, Ital. *San Pietro*, on N coast; wine-trade center. Other villages: Sutivan, Ital. *San Giovanni*, on N coast; Sumartin, Ital. *San Martino*, on E coast; Bol, on S coast; Milna, on W coast; Nerezisce, Serbo-Croatian *Nerežišće*, Ital. *Neresi*, inland. Sometimes spelled Brach.

Bracke (brĕ'kŭ), Swedish *Bräcke*, village (pop. 1,044), Jamtland co., N central Sweden, on Revsund L., Swedish *Revsundsjön* (räv'sŭnd"shûn") (15 mi. long, 1-6 mi. wide), 40 mi. SE of Ostersund; important rail junction on main lines from Stockholm to Narvik and Trondheim; sawmilling, woodworking.

Bracken, county (□ 206; pop. 8,424), N Ky.; ⊙ Brooksville. Bounded N by Ohio R. (Ohio line), S by North Fork of Licking R. Gently rolling upland agr. area (burley tobacco, corn, wheat, dairy products), in outer Bluegrass region; shipping, some mfg. at Augusta. Formed 1796.

Brackenheim (brä'kŭnhīm), town (pop. 2,447), N Württemberg, Germany, after 1945 in Württemberg-Baden, 8 mi. SW of Heilbronn; wine. Has late-Romanesque church, and Renaissance castle.

Brackenridge, industrial borough (pop. 6,178), Allegheny co., W central Pa., 17 mi. NE of Pittsburgh and on Allegheny R.; bituminous coal; coke, stainless steel, glass; brewery. Inc. 1901.

Brackettville (bră'kĭtvĭl), city (pop. 1,858), ⊙ Kinney co., SW Texas, 29 mi. E of Del Rio; trading center for ranching region (sheep, cattle, goats). Here are large Las Moras Springs and old U.S. Fort Clark (founded 1852, deactivated 1946). Inc. 1928.

Brackley, municipal borough (1931 pop. 2,181; 1951 census 2,525), S Northampton, England, 7 mi. WNW of Buckingham; agr. market; flour milling. Has remains of old castle, scene of meeting (1215) that eventually led to granting of Magna Carta. Has school founded as a hospital in 13th cent., and church dating from same period.

Bracknell, town (1951 census 5,142), E Berkshire, England, 9 mi. E of Reading; residential town in agr. area. Became, after Second World War, nucleus of model community of c.25,000.

Brackwede (bräk'vädŭ), town (pop. 18,702), in former Prussian prov. of Westphalia, NW Germany, after 1945 in North Rhine-Westphalia, on S slope of Teutoburg Forest, 2 mi. SW of Bielefeld; rail junction; transshipment point. Steel plants; mfg. of turbines, boilers, linen, garments.

Bracquegnies, Belgium: see STRÉPY.

Brad (bräd), Hung. *Brád* (brät), town (1948 pop. 6,210), Hunedoara prov., W central Rumania, in Transylvania, on White Körös R. and 17 mi. NNW of Deva; rail terminus and center of a gold-mining dist.; also mines lignite, produces silk textiles, peppermint oil; trades in livestock, nuts, fruit, lumber. Has power station. Noted for its geological and mineralogical mus.

Bradano River (brädä'nô), in Basilicata, S Italy, rises in the Apennines 13 mi. N of Potenza, flows 73 mi. SE to Gulf of Taranto 16 mi. E of Pisticci. Receives Basentello (32 mi. long) and Gravina (22 mi. long) rivers (left).

Bradbury Heights, village (1940 pop. 991), Prince Georges co., central Md., suburb just SE of Washington.

Bradbury Island, Maine: see DEER ISLAND, Hancock co.

Bradbury Park, village (1940 pop. 525), Prince Georges co., central Md., suburb SE of Washington.

Bradda Head, Isle of Man: see PORT ERIN.

Braddock (bră'dŭk). **1** Village (pop. 175), Emmons co., S N.Dak., 36 mi. ESE of Bismarck. **2** Industrial borough (pop. 16,488), Allegheny co., SW Pa., SE suburb of Pittsburgh on Monongahela R.; steel products, machinery, gasoline, wall paper. Braddock defeated (1755) near here by French and Indians. A center of Whisky Rebellion, 1794. Iron mills established in early 1870s. Settled 1742, inc. 1867.

Braddock Heights, summer resort, Frederick co., W Md., on crest of Catoctin Mtn. (alt. here c.1,000 ft.) and 5 mi. W of Frederick. Near by is Gambrill State Park.

Braddock Hills, borough (pop. 1,965), Allegheny co., SW Pa., E suburb of Pittsburgh, just N of Braddock. Inc. 1946.
Braddyville, town (pop. 249), Page co., SW Iowa, on Mo. line, on Nodaway R. and 10 mi. S of Clarinda.
Bradenton (brā'dŭntŭn), city (pop. 13,604), ⊙ Manatee co., SW Fla., fishing port on Manatee R. (bridged here) near its mouth on Tampa Bay, and 11 mi. N of Sarasota; winter resort, and shipping center for citrus fruit, truck, and gladioli; packing houses, citrus-fruit canneries; mfg. of concrete products. Quarrying (dolomite, limestone). Has agr. experiment station. Near by are De Soto Natl. Memorial (5 mi. W, on Tampa Bay; 24.18 acres; authorized 1948), commemorating De Soto's landing (May, 1539), probably in this region; ruins of Braden Castle (1850); and the Gamble Mansion, a state monument. Founded 1878, inc. 1903.
Bradenville, village, Westmoreland co., SW Pa., 2 mi. E of Latrobe.
Bradet (brŭdĕt'), Rum. *Brădet,* village, Arges prov., S Rumania, on S slopes of Transylvanian Alps, 12 mi. NNE of Curtea-de-Arges; health resort.
Bradfield. 1 Agr. village and parish (pop. 1,336), S central Berkshire, England, 7 mi. W of Reading. Bradfield Col., a public school, is noted for Greek plays performed in amphitheater in old chalk pit. **2** Residential town and parish (pop. 9,887), West Riding, S Yorkshire, England, 7 mi. NW of Sheffield; site of Sheffield water reservoirs. Near by are extensive grouse moors.
Bradford, village (pop. 1,033), S Ont., on Schomberg R. and 35 mi. NNW of Toronto; woodworking, lumbering.
Bradford, county borough (1931 pop. 298,041; 1951 census 292,394), West Riding, SW Yorkshire, England, 9 mi. W of Leeds and on a small tributary of the Aire; 53°48'N 1°45'W; important woolen- and worsted-milling center (1st mill was built 1798); has chemical, automobile, machinery, leather-tanning works. Near by are coal and iron mines and stone quarries. Has St. Peter's church (1485; now cathedral of Bradford diocese), Gothic town hall (built 1873; has 200-ft. campanile), 17th-cent. grammar school, and a memorial hall (with art gall.) dedicated to Edmund Cartwright, inventor of the power loom. Frederick Delius b. here. In county borough are woolen-milling suburbs of Allerton (pop. 16,239), Bolton (pop. 11,379), Eccleshill (pop. 14,722), Great Horton (pop. 23,652), Little Horton (pop. 14,632), Idle (pop. 9,518), Thornton (pop. 6,226), Manningham (pop. 20,907), Clayton (pop. 5,491), Tong (pop. 6,568).
Bradford, village (pop. 420), South-Western Prov., W Sierra Leone, on railroad and 36 mi. ESE of Freetown; palm oil and kernels, piassava, rice.
Bradford. 1 County (□ 293; pop. 11,457), N Fla., bounded S by Santa Fe R.; ⊙ Starke. Flatwoods area dotted with lakes. Agr. (corn, strawberries, vegetables, tobacco, pecans), stock raising, and forestry. Formed 1858. **2** County (□1,147; pop. 51,722), NE Pa.; ⊙ Towanda. Hilly agr. and industrial region, drained by Susquehanna R. Settled 1763 by Moravian missionaries. Refuge for French nobles founded 1793 at Asylum; flourished until Napoleon's grant of amnesty 1802. Agr. (buckwheat, hay, honey); dairying; mfg. (textiles, clothing, metal products). Formed 1812.
Bradford. 1 Village (pop. 1,325, with adjacent Dixiana), Jefferson co., N central Ala., 17 mi. NNE of Birmingham. **2** Town (pop. 720), White co., central Ark., 26 mi. SW of Newport; ships pecans, strawberries, cotton. **3** Village (pop. 952), Stark co., N central Ill., 14 mi. ESE of Kewanee, in agr. and bituminous-coal area; mfg. of horse collars. **4** Village (pop. c.100), Chickasaw co., NE Iowa, 11 mi. SE of Charles City. Site of "The Little Brown Church in the Vale" (erected 1862), familiarized in the song by W. S. Pitts. **5** Agr. town (pop. 793), Penobscot co., central Maine, 17 mi. NW of Old Town; wood products. **6** Town (pop. 606), Merrimack co., S central N.H., 22 mi. W of Concord; summer resort. **7** Village (pop. 2,055), on Miami-Darke co. line, W Ohio, 10 mi. W of Piqua, in agr. area; baskets; canned tomatoes; tobacco warehouse. **8** City (pop. 17,354), McKean co., N Pa., 65 mi. SSE of Buffalo, N.Y., oil wells and refining; metal products, bricks and tiles, chemicals, explosives; railroad shops. Oil discovered c.1871. Settled c.1823, inc. as borough 1873, as city 1879. **9** Village (pop. 1,024) in Westerly town, Washington co., SW R.I., on Pawcatuck R. (bridged here) and 4 mi. E of Westerly village; textile dyeing, bleaching; granite quarrying. **10** Town (pop. 599), Gibson co., NW Tenn., 10 mi. NE of Trenton, in farm area. **11** Town (pop. 1,551), including Bradford village (pop. 725), Orange co., E Vt., on the Connecticut and 23 mi. SE of Barre, at mouth of Waits R.; wood and dairy products, maple sugar. Winter sports. C. E. Clark b. here. First geographical globes in U.S. said to have been made here (c.1814) by James Wilson. Settled 1765.
Bradford-on-Avon (–ā'vŭn, ă'–), urban district (1931 pop. 4,768; 1951 census 5,627), W Wiltshire, England, on the Avon and 6 mi. ESE of Bath; agr. market in dairying region; woolen milling, mfg. of rubber products. Has 8th-cent. Saxon church, also 11th-cent. parish church, 13th-cent. bridge, 14th-cent. tithe barn.
Bradfordwoods, borough (pop. 458), Allegheny co., W Pa., 14 mi. NNW of Pittsburgh.
Bradgate, town (pop. 188), Humboldt co., N central Iowa, on Des Moines R. and 24 mi. NNW of Fort Dodge; livestock, grain.
Bradgate Park, England: see GROBY.
Bradiceni (brŭdēchān'), Rum. *Brădiceni,* agr. village (pop. 845), Gorj prov., SW Rumania, 10 mi. W of Targu-Jiu.
Brading (brā'–), town and parish (pop. 1,775), on Isle of Wight, Hampshire, England, 2 mi. NNE of Sandown; agr. market; cement works. Has Norman 13th-cent. church and remains of Roman villa.
Bradley, England: see HUDDERSFIELD.
Bradley. 1 County (□ 649; pop. 15,987), S Ark.; ⊙ Warren. Bounded W by Moro Creek, SW by Ouachita R., and E by Saline R. Agr. (cotton, potatoes, truck); timber. Mfg. of wood products, cotton ginning, cottonseed-oil milling at Warren. Formed 1840. **2** County (□ 338; pop. 32,338), SE Tenn., ⊙ Cleveland. Bounded S by Ga., N by Hiwassee R. Timber, corn, cotton, hay, fruit, livestock; mfg. at Cleveland. Includes part of Cherokee Natl. Forest. Formed 1835.
Bradley. 1 Town (pop. 444), Lafayette co., SW Ark., 26 mi. WSW of Magnolia, near La. line. **2** Town (pop. 422), Polk co., central Fla., 17 mi. S of Lakeland; phosphate mines. Formerly Bradley Junction. **3** Village (pop. 5,699), Kankakee co., NE Ill., near Kankakee R., just N of Kankakee, in agr. area; mfg. (agr. implements, furniture, wood products). Organized as North Kankakee in 1892; inc. and renamed in 1896. **4** Town (pop. 786), Penobscot co., S central Maine, on the Penobscot and 11 mi. above Brewer. **5** Town (pop. 248), Grady co., central Okla., 18 mi. SE of Chickasha, and on Washita R.; cotton ginning. Inc. 1938. **6** Town (pop. 226), Clark co., NE S.Dak., 15 mi. NNE of Clark.
Bradley Beach, resort borough (pop. 3,911), Monmouth co., E N.J., on the coast 2 mi. S of Asbury Park; fisheries. Settled c.1858, inc. 1893.
Bradley Junction, Fla.: see BRADLEY.
Bradley Quarters, village (pop. 2,880), Bradley co., S Ark., adjacent to Warren; company town for lumber mill.
Bradleyville, town (pop. 69), Taney co., S Mo., in the Ozarks, 20 mi. NE of Branson.
Bradlo, mountain, Czechoslovakia: see LITTLE CARPATHIAN MOUNTAINS.
Bradner, village (pop. 924), Wood co., NW Ohio, 12 mi. ESE of Bowling Green, in agr. area; mfg. of oil-well machinery, feed milling; stone quarries; poultry hatcheries.
Bradninch (brăd'nĭnch), town and parish (pop. 1,592), E Devon, England, 9 mi. NNE of Exeter; old agr. market town. Has Elizabethan manor house and 15th-cent. church.
Bradshaw, England: see TURTON.
Bradshaw. 1 Village, Baltimore co., central Md., 15 mi. ENE of downtown Baltimore; holds annual tilting tournament. **2** Village (pop. 352), York co., SE central Nebr., 10 mi. W of York; livestock, dairy and poultry produce. **3** Mining village (pop. 1,062), McDowell co., S W.Va., on Dry Fork and 12 mi. WSW of Welch; semibituminous coal.
Bradshaw Mountains, Yavapai co., central Ariz., S of Prescott. Rises to 7,600 ft. in TOWERS MOUNTAIN. Large quantities of gold have been mined.
Bradstowe, England: see BROADSTAIRS.
Bradwell. 1 Agr. village and parish (pop. 421), N Buckingham, England, just SE of Wolverton. Has 14th-cent. church. **2** Town and parish (pop. 1,313), N Derby, England, 9 mi. NE of Buxton; lead mining. Site of a stalactite cavern.
Bradwell-on-Sea, bathing resort and parish (pop. 657), E Essex, England, bet. North Sea and Blackwater R. estuary, 9 mi. E of Maldon. Has 14th-cent. church. On North Sea, 2 mi. NE, is St. Peter's Chapel, probably built in 7th cent.
Brady. 1 Village, Pondera co., NW Mont., 10 mi. SSE of Conrad, in irrigated region; grain-shipping point. **2** Village (pop. 320), Lincoln co., S central Nebr., 22 mi. ESE of North Platte city and on Platte R. **3** City (pop. 5,944), ⊙ McCulloch co., central Texas, on Brady Creek and c.70 mi. ESE of San Angelo; trade, shipping, processing center of agr., ranching region; ships turkeys, wool, mohair, cotton; cottonseed-oil milling, dairying, mfg. of mattresses. Settled c.1876, inc. 1906.
Brady, Fort, Mich.: see SAULT SAINTE MARIE.
Brady Creek, W central Texas, rises near Eden on edge of Edwards Plateau, flows c.60 mi. generally E to the San Saba 21 mi. E of Brady.
Brady Glacier, SE Alaska, in Fairweather Range; 58°38'N 136°50'W; flows in 2 branches, one to Glacier Bay (N), the other 40 mi. S to Cross Sound.
Brady Lake, village (pop. 444), Portage co., NE Ohio, 12 mi. NE of Akron, on Brady L. (c.4 mi. long), a reservoir supplying water to Akron.
Brady Mountains, Texas: see MCCULLOCH county.
Braedstrup, Denmark: see BRAESTRUP.
Braeholm, village (pop. 2,386, with adjacent Accoville), Logan co., SW W.Va., c.10 mi. SE of Logan, in coal-mining region.
Braemar (brāmär'), officially Castleton of Braemar, resort village in Crathie and Braemar parish, SW Aberdeen, Scotland, on the Dee and 14 mi. W of Ballater. There are remains of 11th-cent. castle. Braemar is site of meteorological observatory (57°N 3°24'W). In August village is scene of the Braemar Gathering, with highland games and folk dancing. It is also center of Braemar district, extending 25 mi. along upper course of the Dee, including BALMORAL CASTLE. The dist. is a scenic tourist area of hilly, wooded country.
Braeriach, Scotland: see CAIRNGORM MOUNTAINS.
Braeside (brā'sīd), village (pop. 505), SE Ont., on L. des Chats, 3 mi. NW of Arnprior; lumbering.
Braestrup or **Braedstrup** (both: brĕ'strŏop), town (pop. 1,445), Skanderborg amt, E Jutland, Denmark, 13 mi. WSW of Skanderborg; pottery, margarine, dairy products.
Braga (brä'gŭ), district (□ 1,054; pop. 482,914), Minho prov., N Portugal; ⊙ Braga. Borders on the Atlantic (W) and Spain (NE). Drained by Ave and Cávado rivers. Hilly in W. Chief towns: Braga, Guimarãis, Barcelos.
Braga, anc. *Bracara Augusta,* city (pop. 29,875), ⊙ Minho prov. and Braga dist., N Portugal, 30 mi. NNE of Oporto; rail-spur terminus; agr. trade center with minor industries (felt hats, shoes, scales, cutlery, leather goods, chocolate); sugar refining, soap and candle mfg., bookbinding. The cathedral (built c.1100; rebuilt in 16th cent.) contains tomb of Henry of Burgundy. Probably founded by Carthaginians in 296 B.C., city was later chief Roman station in N Lusitania. Occupied by Moors, 730–1040. Important in Middle Ages as see of powerful bishop of Braga. As seat of Portugal's titular primate, it remains a religious center. Atop Monte Espinho (1,850 ft.) is pilgrimage church of Bom Jesus do Monte, reached by funicular railway. Ruins of anc. Citánia 5 mi. SE.
Bragado (brägä'dō), city (pop. 16,532), ⊙ Bragado dist. (□ 854; pop. 36,138), N central Buenos Aires prov., Argentina, near The Río Salado, 32 mi. SW of Chivilcoy, in agr. region (corn, wheat, cattle); dairy industry. Has natl. col.
Bragança (brägä'sù). **1** City (pop. 3,752), easternmost Pará, Brazil, near the Atlantic, 120 mi. ENE of Belém (linked by railroad); cotton, tobacco, manioc, corn, rice, and sugar-cane growing in agr. colonies. Limekilns. Airfield. **2** City, São Paulo, Brazil: see BRAGANÇA PAULISTA.
Bragança or **Braganza,** district (□ 2,527; pop. 213,233), in Trás-os-Montes e Alto Douro prov., N Portugal; ⊙ Bragança. Bounded by Spain (N and E), and Douro R. (S and SE). Mountainous. Drained by Tua and Sabôr rivers. Sparsely populated.
Bragança or **Braganza,** Celtic *Brigantia,* Roman *Juliobriga,* city (pop 6,977), ⊙ Bragança dist., N Portugal, 110 mi. NE of Oporto, in Trás-os-Montes e Alto Douro prov.; rail terminus; agr. trade center (grain, olive-oil, wine, livestock); mfg. (textiles, hats, chocolates). Episcopal see. Airfield. Its feudal castle (built 1187) was seat of Braganza family, long the kings of Portugal.
Bragança, Paulista (poulē'stù), city (pop. 12,757), E São Paulo, Brazil, on W slope of Serra da Mantiqueira, on railroad and 40 mi. N of São Paulo; mfg. (textiles, tiles, lard); coffee and rice processing; also ships livestock, citrus fruit, tobacco, sugar, potatoes, grain. Until 1944, called Bragança.
Bragernes, Norway: see DRAMMEN.
Bragg, Fort, N.C.: see FAYETTEVILLE.
Bragg City, town (pop. 294), Pemiscot co., extreme SE Mo., in Mississippi flood plain, 15 mi. WNW of Caruthersville.
Braggs, town (pop. 374), Muskogee co., E Okla., 11 mi. SE of Muskogee, in agr. area.
Bragin (brä'gĭn), town (1926 pop. 4,883), SE Polesye oblast, Belorussian SSR, 40 mi. ESE of Mozyr; agr. processing, shoe mfg.; brickworks.
Braham (brā'ŭm), village (pop. 697), Isanti co., E Minn., 11 mi. NNE of Cambridge, in livestock and potato area; food processing (dairy products, flour); woolen goods.
Brahea, Finland: see PANKAKOSKI.
Brahe River, Poland: see BRDA RIVER.
Brahestad, Finland: see RAAHE.
Brahmagiri (brä'mŭgĭrē), peak (4,447 ft.), in Western Ghats, N Coorg, India, 17 mi. W of Mercara; gives rise to Cauvery R. (E). Anc. temple is site of annual pilgrimage. The Brahmagiris is term applied to a section of Western Ghats on S border of state.
Brahmanbaria (brä"mŭnbär'yŭ), town (pop. 35,887), Tippera dist., E East Bengal, E Pakistan, on arm of Meghna R. and 36 mi. N of Comilla; rice, jute, oilseeds; mfg. of bricks, brassware; fertilizer factory.
Brahmani River (brä'mŭnē). **1** In NE Orissa, India, formed 14 mi. E of Raj Gangpur by confluence of 2 headstreams (Sankh R., South Koel R.) rising on Chota Nagpur Plateau in S Bihar; flows SSE past Bonaigarh and Talcher, and E forming 12-mi.-long joint outlet with Baitarani R., to Bay of Bengal at Palmyras Point; c.300 mi. long. **2** In Bihar and West Bengal, India, rises in S Rajmahal Hills, flows c.60 mi. E and SE to Dwarka R. 16 mi. WNW of Berhampore.

Brahmapuri, India: see BRAMHAPURI.

Brahmaputra River (brä″mŭpōō′trŭ) [Sanskrit,=son of Brahma]. **1** Great river of S Asia (c.1,800 mi. long; drains □c. 361,200) flowing E across Tibet and into SW China, S in Assam (India), WSW across Assam and into E Pakistan, and S to Bay of Bengal, forming with Ganges and Meghna rivers a vast delta mouth. River is formed in SW Tibet by 3 headstreams (Kubi Tsangpo, Chemyundung Chu, Mayun Chu) joining 70 mi. ESE of Tokchen, on S slope of Kailas Range, at 30°20′N 82°50′E; it is here known as the Tsangpo or Matsang Tsangpo. Flows c.900 mi. E, across Tibet (at alt. c.12,000 ft.), near Shigatse (on the Nyang Chu), where it is generally known as the Tsangpo (navigable by yak-hide coracles for c.400 mi.); at 95°E, at extreme E end of the Himalayas and here known as the Dihang, it bends S, cutting an 8,000-ft.-deep gorge near the Namcha Barwa, and flows S for 200 mi. into NE Assam (India). Near Sadiya it is joined by Dibang and Luhit rivers and below this point the name Brahmaputra begins; flows c.500 mi. WSW, through extensive tea-garden, rice, and sugar-cane area, past Dibrugarh, Texpur, Gauhati, Goalpara, and Dhubri. Turning S around W flank of Garo Hills, river flows into E Pakistan, through major jute area of the world; near Bahadurabad Ghat it divides into the Brahmaputra proper (old bed) and JAMUNA RIVER, which now carries bulk of water. Continuing S, the Jamuna joins PADMA RIVER and MEGHNA RIVER arms of GANGES DELTA before emptying into Bay of Bengal. In Assam and E Pakistan, the Brahmaputra drains S slopes of Assam Himalayas, receiving as its principal tributaries Subansiri, Manas, Sankosh, Raidak, Torsa, Jaldhaka, and Tista rivers. An important artery of commerce, navigable for 800 mi. by river steamer, up to Dibrugarh. Its identity with the Tsangpo was established in 1884; Dihang section 1st explored in 1913. In Tibet, the Brahmaputra at one time flowed in opposite direction from its present course, although retaining the same bed, as evidenced by its principal affluents (including Kyi Chu and Nyang Chu rivers), which flow contrary to the main stream. Earthquake in 1950 disrupted river traffic and caused great damage, especially in Luhit R. confluence area. Called Dyardanes and Oedanes by anc. Greek geographers. **2** Old course of the Brahmaputra, which leaves present main stream (Jamuna R.) N of Bahadurabad Ghat and flows c.180 mi. S, past Jamalpur and Mymensingh, bifurcating in its lower course, with 1 stream flowing to Meghna R. at Bhairab Bazar, the other to Dhaleswari R. E of Narayanganj. In late-18th cent., became silted and JAMUNA RIVER, once a small stream, became the Brahmaputra's main channel.

Brahmaur (brä′mour), village, N Himachal Pradesh, India, 25 mi. ESE of Chamba, near upper Ravi R.; exports corn, rice, timber.

Brahui Range, Central (brä′hōōē), in N central Baluchistan, W Pakistan, from S bend of Mula R. extends N to just N of Quetta and thence SE, enclosing N end of Kachhi plain, to central Sibi dist. (here offshoots join S Sulaiman Range); c.240 mi. long, 60 mi. wide. Generally above 6,000 ft.; rises to c.11,740 ft. in peak E of Quetta; Khalifat Mtn. (11,434 ft.) and Takatu Mtn. (11,340 ft.) are in N section. Watered by seasonal streams, including Nari R. (NE) and Bolan R. (center). Railroad and highway bet. Sibi and Quetta cross range via Bolan Pass. Limestone ridges are partly forested (juniper); rice grown on lower slopes. Coal mined near Mach, Quetta, Khost, and Shahrig; gypsum deposits (NE). S area inhabited by Brahui tribes; Ziarat (N) is summer hq. of Baluchistan govt.

Braich-y-Pwll (brīkh-ŭ-pōōl′), promontory at SW extremity of Lleyn Peninsula, SW Caernarvon, Wales, at N end of Cardigan Bay, 16 mi. WSW of Pwllheli; 52°48′N 4°46′W.

Braidwood, town (pop. 1,065), SE New South Wales, Australia, 40 mi. ESE of Canberra; gold-mining center.

Braidwood, city (pop. 1,485), Will co., NE Ill., 19 mi. SSW of Joliet; trade center in agr. and bituminous-coal-mining area; mfg. (clothing, beverages, macaroni). Inc. 1873. City has been a center for mine-labor organization. John Mitchell b. here.

Braila (brŭē′lä), Rum. *Brăila*, former Turkish *Ibraila*, city (1948 pop., including suburbs, 95,514), Galati prov., SE Rumania, in Walachia, on W bank of the Danube opposite its confluence with the Dunarea Veche arm, on railroad and 105 mi. NE of Bucharest; 45°16′N 27°58′E. Major inland grain-shipping port; also fishing, commercial, and industrial center. Has large locomotive repair shops and shipyards, steel-rolling mills, grain-processing plants, flour mills, lumber yards. Manufactures cement, enamel paints, wire products, hardware, rugs, furniture, leather goods, food products. Noted for its important Orthodox cathedral and its 18th-cent. church with valuable archives. Probably dating from Greek times, it was chartered in 14th cent.; burned by the Turks (1462) and by Stephen the Great of Moldavia (1470); occupied by the Turks (1544–1828). Modern layout dates from 1830 and temporary period of Russian occupation. Metropolitan Braila includes suburbs of Brailita, Nedelcu P. Chercea, and Radu Negru. Bathing resort of Lacu-Sarat is 6 mi. SW.

Brailita (brŭēlē′tsä), Rum. *Brăilița*, NNE suburb (1941 pop. 7,340) of Braila, Galati prov., SE Rumania; mfg. of rolling-stock parts.

Brainard, village (pop. 373), Butler co., E Nebr., 30 mi. NNW of Lincoln; dairy and poultry produce, livestock, grain.

Braine (brĕn), village (pop. 1,147), Aisne dept., N France, on the Vesle and 10 mi. ESE of Soissons; sugar milling. Has remains of 12th-cent. abbey church.

Braine-l'Alleud (brĕn-lälŭ′), Flemish *Eigenbrakel* (ī′gŭn-bräkŭl), town (pop. 12,121), Brabant prov., central Belgium, 12 mi. S of Brussels; wool, cotton weaving, spinning; agr. market.

Braine-l'Alleud Saint-Joseph (sē-zhôsĕf′), village, Katanga prov., E Belgian Congo, on railroad and 185 mi. WNW of Albertville; rice, cotton. Has noted R.C. mission and schools, including special school for mulattoes. Also called Lubunda.

Braine-le-Château (–lŭ-shätō′), Flemish *Kasteelbrakel* (kä′stălbräkŭl), town (pop. 4,108), Brabant prov., central Belgium, 4 mi. SSE of Hal; cotton weaving.

Braine-le-Comte (–kōt′), Flemish *'s Gravenbrakel* (skrä′vŭnbräkŭl), town (pop. 10,174), Hainaut prov., S central Belgium, 13 mi. NNE of Mons; rail center, mfg. of railroad rolling stock, machines; cotton weaving. Has 14th-cent. church.

Brainerd (brā′nŭrd), city (pop. 12,637), ⊙ Crow Wing co., central Minn., on Mississippi R., near Cuyuna iron range, and 60 mi. N of St. Cloud in resort region of lakes and woods. Shipping point and industrial and commercial center with railroad repair shops; dairy products, beverages; mfg. (wood, paper, and foundry products, clothing). Junior col. is here. Paul Bunyan carnival takes place annually in June. Settled 1870, inc. 1881. Grew as lumbering point.

Braintree, England: see BRAINTREE AND BOCKING.

Braintree. 1 Residential town (pop. 23,161), Norfolk co., E Mass., on arm of Hingham Bay, 11 mi. SSE of Boston; mfg. (shoes, abrasives, petroleum and rubber products, paper boxes), bleaching. Settled 1634, inc. 1640. Includes suburban and industrial villages of South Braintree (scene of murders, 1920, for which Sacco and Vanzetti were executed) and East Braintree. **2** Town (pop. 626), Orange co., central Vt., 21 mi. SSW of Montpelier and on Third Branch of White R.; lumber.

Braintree and Bocking, urban district (1951 census 17,480), N central Essex, England, on Blackwater R. and 15 mi. W of Colchester; silk and artificial-silk mills, metal foundries. Braintree has 13th-cent. church; Bocking church dates from 1006. Formerly separate towns, Braintree urban dist. (1931 pop. 8,912) and Bocking parish (1931 pop. 4,274).

Braithwaite, England: see ABOVE DERWENT.

Brajrajnagar, India: see JHARSUGUDA.

Brak, Fezzan: see BRACH.

Brake (brä′kŭ), town (pop. 13,819), in Oldenburg, NW Germany, after 1945 Lower Saxony, port on left bank of the Weser and 21 mi. below Bremen; rail junction; shipbuilding; mfg. of textiles (wool, jute; sails), stearine, wax. Before development of Bremen's port facilities, it was that city's deep-sea harbor.

Brakel (brä′kŭl), town (pop. 6,216), in former Prussian prov. of Westphalia, NW Germany, after 1945 in North Rhine-Westphalia, 9 mi. SW of Höxter; forestry. Has 12th-cent. church. Mineral spring near by.

Brakne-Hoby (brĕk′nŭ-hōō′bü″), Swedish *Bräkne-Hoby*, village (pop. 1,182), Blekinge co., S Sweden, 10 mi. ENE of Karlshamn; sawmilling.

Brakpan (brăk′păn, Afrikaans bräkpän′), town (pop. 83,456), S Transvaal, U. of So. Afr., on E Witwatersrand, 20 mi. E of Johannesburg; alt. 5,372 ft.; gold- and coal-mining center; ironworks. Technical col. Municipality founded 1919, formerly part of Benoni.

Bralanda (brō′län″dä), Swedish *Brålanda*, village (pop. 715), Alvsborg co., SW Sweden, near SW shore of L. Vaner, 12 mi. N of Vanersborg; grain, stock.

Bralorne (brā′lôrn), village (pop. estimate 500), SW B.C., in Coast Mts., 110 mi. N of Vancouver; gold and silver mining.

Bram (brã), village (pop. 1,827), Aude dept., S France, near the Canal du Midi, 9 mi. SE of Castelnaudary; grain market and storage depot; brick and fertilizer mfg.

Braman (brā′mŭn), town (pop. 392), Kay co., N Okla., near Kansas line, 21 mi. NW of Ponca City, in agr. area.

Brambach or **Radiumbad Brambach** (rä′dyōōmbät″ bräm′bäkh), village (pop. 2,706), Saxony, E central Germany, in the Erzgebirge, 20 mi. SSE of Plauen, in uranium-mining region; frontier station near Czechoslovak border, opposite Vojtanov; spa with radioactive springs. Mfg. of musical instruments.

Bramber, agr. village and parish (pop. 270), central Sussex, England, on Adur R. and 9 mi. WNW of Brighton. Has remains of Bramber Castle (Saxon and Norman), destroyed in Civil War.

Bramford, town and parish (pop. 2,197), S central Suffolk, England, on Gipping R. and 3 mi. NW of Ipswich; agr. market. Has 14th-cent. church.

Bramhall, England: see HAZEL GROVE AND BRAMHALL.

Bramhapuri or **Brahmapuri** (both: brä′mŭpōōrē), town (pop. 6,337), Chanda dist., S Madhya Pradesh, India, near Wainganga R., 60 mi. NE of Chanda; rice milling; oilseeds, millet. Rail junction of Nagbhir is 10 mi. W. Hematite deposits near by.

Bramhope, town and parish (pop. 670), West Riding, central Yorkshire, England, 3 mi. ESE of Otley; mfg. of electrical equipment.

Bramley. 1 Residential town and parish (pop. 2,023), W central Surrey, England, 3 mi. S of Guildford; agr. market. Has 12th-13th-cent. church. **2** Town (pop. 17,631) in Leeds county borough, West Riding, S central Yorkshire, England, on Aire R. and just W of Leeds; woolen milling; also produces leather goods, chemicals, paint, soap, asbestos, metal products.

Bramminge (brä′mĭng-ŭ), town (pop. 2,588), Ribe amt, SW Jutland, Denmark, 9 mi. E of Esbjerg; rail junction; mfg. (candy, baby carriages).

Bramois (brämwä′), village (pop. 882), Valais canton, SW Switzerland, on Borgne R., near its confluence with the Rhone, and 2 mi. E of Sion; hydroelectric plant.

Brampton, town (pop. 6,020), ⊙ Peel co., S Ont., 16 mi. W of Toronto; flower-growing center; tanneries, lumber mills.

Brampton. 1 Agr. market town and parish (pop. 2,526), NE Cumberland, England, 9 mi. ENE of Carlisle. Near Hadrian's Wall, it has excavations of Roman relics. **2** Agr. village and parish (pop. 1,031), central Huntingdon, England, on Ouse R. and 2 mi. SW of Huntingdon. Has 15th-cent. church with 17th-cent tower.

Brampton and Walton, former urban district (1931 pop. 2,323), N central Derby, England. Includes towns of Brampton, just SW of Chesterfield, with metal foundries, and Walton, 2 mi. SW of Chesterfield, with slate quarries.

Brampton Bierlow, town and parish (pop. 3,437), West Riding, S Yorkshire, England, 6 mi. N of Rotherham; coal mining.

Bramsche (bräm′shŭ), town (pop. 7,486), in former Prussian prov. of Hanover, NW Germany, after 1945 in Lower Saxony, on the Haase and 9 mi. N of Osnabrück; textile mfg.

Bramshott, town and parish (pop. 3,183), E Hampshire, England, 8 mi. NE of Petersfield; agr. market. Has 13th-cent. church. Sanitarium. Just S, in parish, is market town of Liphook.

Bramstedt, Bad, Germany: see BAD BRAMSTEDT.

Bramwell, town (pop. 1,587), Mercer co., S W.Va., on Bluestone R. at Va. line, 6 mi. NW of Bluefield, in coal-mining area. Inc. 1888.

Bran or **Bran-Poarta** (brän-pwär′tŭ), Rum. *Bran-Poartă*, Ger. *Törzburg* (tûrts′bōōrk), village (pop. 1,913), Stalin prov., central Rumania, at N end of the Bran Pass, 14 mi. SW of Stalin (Brasov); climatic resort (alt. 2,625 ft.) in the Transylvanian Alps; lumbering, wool spinning, flour milling. Site of noted 13th-cent. castle of Teutonic Knights restored in 17th cent. and later summer residence of Queen Marie.

Branca (bräng′kä), village, Perugia prov., Umbria, central Italy, 6 mi. NW of Gualdo Tadino; coal mining.

Brancavarâ (bränkävärä′), town (pop. 5,902), Diu dist., Portuguese India, 7 mi. W of Diu; cocoanuts, millet; cattle raising. Fishing in Arabian Sea.

Branch, county (□ 506; pop. 30,202), S Mich.; ⊙ Coldwater. Bounded S by Ind. line; drained by St. Joseph and Coldwater rivers. Agr. (fruit, grain, corn, livestock); dairy products. Mfg. at Coldwater. Marl and clay deposits. Many small lakes (resorts). Organized 1833.

Branch, town (pop. 308), Franklin co., W Ark., 25 mi. ESE of Fort Smith.

Branch Lake, Hancock co., S Maine, NW of Ellsworth in hunting, fishing area; 5.5 mi. long; drains SE into Union R.

Branch River, N R.I., formed near Oakland by junction of Pascoag and Chepachet rivers; flows 10 mi. NE, furnishing water power at Oakland, Glendale, Nasonville, and Forestdale, to Blackstone R. at Mass. line, just NW of Woonsocket; dam at Slatersville forms Slatersville Reservoir (c.3 mi. long).

Branchville. 1 Borough (pop. 810), Sussex co., NW N.J., near Paulins Kill, 6 mi. N of Newton, in hilly agr. region. Annual livestock show held here. **2** Town (pop. 1,353), Orangeburg co., S central S.C., 17 mi. S of Orangeburg; rail junction; lumber, ice. **3** Town (pop. 169), Southampton co., SE Va., near N.C. line 38 mi. WSW of Suffolk.

Branco, Cabo (kä′bōō brä′kōō, brăng′kōō), headland of Paraíba state, NE Brazil, on the Atlantic, and 5 mi. SE of João Pessoa; together with Pedras Point (32 mi. S), it is considered easternmost point of South America (7°9′S 34°47′W), although it barely stands out from coast line.

Branco, Rio (rē′ōō), river in Rio Branco territory, northernmost Brazil, formed by several headstreams (Uraricoera, Tacutú, Cotinga) rising on S slopes of Serra Pacaraima, flows 350 mi. S, past Boa Vista and Caracaraí (head of navigation), to the Rio Negro above Moura. Diamond, gold, and diatomite deposits in upper course.

Branco Island (□ 1), one of Cape Verde Isls., in Windward Group, 5 mi. SSE of Santa Luzia Isl., in the Atlantic; 16°39'N 24°41'W; 2.5 mi. long, 1,073 ft. high. Uninhabited and barren.

Brand (bränt), village (pop. 7,328), in former Prussian Rhine Prov., W Germany, after 1945 in North Rhine-Westphalia, 4 mi. ESE of Aachen; reservoir; race track.

Brandberg (bränt'bĕrkh), mountain (8,550 ft.), W South-West Africa, 100 mi. N of Swakopmund; 21°8'S 14°33'E; highest peak of South-West Africa, in Kaokoveld Mts., on W edge of inland plateau.

Brande (brän'nù), town (pop. 3,449), Vejle amt, central Jutland, Denmark, 23 mi. NW of Vejle; machinery mfg., margarine, meat packing.

Brandeis an der Elbe, Czechoslovakia: see BRANDYS NAD LABEM.

Brandenburg (brăn'dùnbûrg, Ger. brän'dùnbŏŏrk), state (□ 10,416; 1946 pop. 2,527,492), E Germany; ⊙ POTSDAM. Bordered by Saxony (S), Saxony-Anhalt (W), Lower Saxony (NW), Mecklenburg (N), and Polish-administered Germany (E); Berlin, located within its borders, is separate administrative entity. Situated partly in N German lowlands, it is a level region of which about ½ is covered by pine forests. Drained by Havel and Spree rivers (which flow towards the Elbe in W) and by the Oder (E); crisscrossed by network of canals (HOHENZOLLERN CANAL, ODER-SPREE CANAL), which connects with the great Mittelland Canal system via the Elbe. Sandy soil yields large crops of potatoes, some grain and sugar beets; vegetables and fruit grown along middle course of the Havel and in SPREE FOREST. Major lignite deposits in SPREMBERG-SENFTENBERG region. Industry is centered in Berlin area and at BRANDENBURG city (machinery), COTTBUS (textiles), EBERSWALDE (railroad workshops), FORST (textiles), FRANKFURT an der Oder, RATHENOW (optical and precision instruments), and WITTENBERGE. Slavic inhabitants of region were subdued (12th cent.) by Albert the Bear, whose descendants, the Ascanians, ruled Brandenburg until their extinction in 1320. For one century it was held by different dynasties until, in 1415, Emperor Sigismund gave Brandenburg, which had been raised to an electorate by Emperor Charles IV, to Frederick I of Hohenzollern. Primogeniture was introduced in 1473. The expansion of Brandenburg began in 17th cent.; the duchy of Cleves and other W German territories were acquired in 1614, duchy of Prussia (roughly, the later EAST PRUSSIA) in 1618. Though devastated in Thirty Years War, Brandenburg emerged as a military power under Frederick William, the Great Elector, who received Halberstadt, Magdeburg, and Minden at Peace of Westphalia (1648), acquired E Pomerania, and freed Prussia from Polish suzerainty. In 1701 his son, Elector Frederick III, took the title king of Prussia as Frederick I. The later history of Brandenburg is that of PRUSSIA. In the Second World War, Brandenberg was captured by Soviet troops in April–May, 1945. At the Potsdam Conference of 1945, the parts of Brandenburg E of the Oder and the Neisse were placed under Polish administration. After the formal dissolution of Prussia (Feb. 1947), the Prussian Brandenburg province (□ 14,779; 1939 pop. 3,007,933) was reconstituted as a state in the Soviet occupation zone. Became (1949) one of the states of the German Democratic Republic (the Soviet zone).

Brandenburg or **Brandenburg an der Havel** (än dĕr hä'fùl), city (1939 pop. 83,726; 1946 pop. 70,632), Brandenburg, E Germany, port on the Havel and 40 mi. W of Berlin; 52°25'N 12°33'E. Rail junction; mfg. of steel products, trucks, tractors, bicycles, baby carriages, machinery, machine tools, lubricants, textiles (wool, silk), leather goods, pharmaceuticals. Power station. Built on several isls. formed by arms of the Havel, city has 12th-cent. cathedral, two 15th-cent. churches, 14th- and 15th-cent. town halls, and several medieval town gates. Slav settlement of Brennabor or Brennaburg was conquered (928–29) by King Henry I, retaken (983) by Slavs. Conquered c.1150 by Albert the Bear, who transferred its name to margraviate and later to electorate of Brandenburg, and established bishopric here (dissolved in 16th cent.).

Brandenburg, town (pop. 755), ⊙ Meade co., NW Ky., port on Ohio R. and 28 mi. SW of Louisville, in agr. area; makes cement.

Brand-Erbisdorf (bränt'-ĕr'bĭsdôrf), town (pop. 6,494), Saxony, E central Germany, in the Erzgebirge, 4 mi. SSW of Freiberg; lead and silver mining. Mfg. of hosiery, glass, plastics; metal- and woodworking.

Branderburgh, Scotland: see LOSSIEMOUTH.

Brandfort, town (pop. 3,601), W central Orange Free State, U. of So. Afr., 35 mi. NE of Bloemfontein; alt. 4,617 ft.; cattle, sheep, goats.

Brandis (brän'dĭs), town (pop. 5,883), Saxony, E central Germany, 10 mi. E of Leipzig; lignite mining. Brickworks.

Brandizzo (brändē'tsô), village (pop. 2,461), Torino prov., Piedmont, NW Italy, near Po R., 10 mi. NE of Turin.

Brandon, city (pop. 17,551), SW Man., on Assiniboine R. and 130 mi. W of Winnipeg; distributing center for W Man. grain region; tanning, woolen milling, oil refining, meat packing; mfg. of steel and sheet-metal products, farm implements. Site of Brandon Col., established 1899 and affiliated with Univ. of Manitoba; Indian industrial school; and prov. mental hosp. Dominion experimental farm (842 acres), 3 mi. NW, was established 1888. Brandon is scene of annual Provincial Exhibition and of Manitoba Winter Fair. Airport. City is named after Hudson's Bay Co. post of Brandon House, established 1794, 17 mi. SW of present site, abandoned 1814.

Brandon, town and parish (pop. 2,427), NW Suffolk, England, on Little Ouse R. and 5 mi. WNW of Thetford; agr. market. Has 13th-cent. church. Flint-knapping has long been an industry here. Near by are flint quarries, where neolithic implements and drawings have been found.

Brandon, **1** Town (pop. 319), Buchanan co., E Iowa, 29 mi. NW of Cedar Rapids; limestone quarries. **2** Village (pop. 319), Douglas co., W Minn., 13 mi. WNW of Alexandria, in grain and livestock region; dairy products. **3** Town (pop. 1,827), ⊙ Rankin co., central Miss., 13 mi. E of Jackson, in agr. (cotton, corn, sweet potatoes, truck) and timber area. A state hosp. for the insane is near by. Natural-gas field in vicinity. **4** or **Branwood,** village (pop. 11,008, with near-by Judson), Greenville co., NW S.C., just SW of Greenville. **5** Village and township (pop. 672), Minnehaha co., SE S.-Dak., 5 mi. ENE of Sioux Falls. **6** Town (pop. 180), Hill co., N central Texas, 9 mi. E of Hillsboro, in farm area. **7** Town (pop. 3,304), including Brandon village (pop. 1,673), Rutland co., W Vt., on Otter Creek and 15 mi. NNW of Rutland, in resort area; wood and dairy products; marble; poultry. Stephen A. Douglas's birthplace is preserved. From bog iron discovered here, 1810, John Conant made stoves after 1820. State school for feeble-minded, natl. hq. of Ayrshire cattle breeders' assn. here. Town chartered 1761 as Neshobe, renamed 1784. **8** Hamlet, Prince George co., E Va., near James R., 16 mi. E of Hopewell. Near by are historic Brandon and Upper Brandon estates, with 18th-cent. houses and famous gardens. **9** Village (pop. 728), Fond du Lac co., E central Wis., 16 mi. WSW of Fond du Lac, in agr. area (dairy products; peas, hemp); textiles, canned vegetables.

Brandon, Mount, mountain (1,694 ft.), E Co. Kilkenny, Ireland, 8 mi. N of New Ross.

Brandon and Byshottles (bī'–), urban district (1931 pop. 17,116; 1951 census 19,751), central Durham, England. Includes coal-mining towns of Brandon, 3 mi. WSW of Durham, and New Brancepeth.

Brandon Bay, inlet (5 mi. long, 4 mi. wide) of the Atlantic, W Co. Kerry, Ireland, 10 mi. NE of Dingle. On W side of entrance is Brandon Point.

Brandon Mountain (3,127 ft.) in W Co. Kerry, Ireland, near the Atlantic, 7 mi. NNE of Dingle.

Brandon Point, cape, W Co. Kerry, Ireland, on W side of entrance to Brandon Bay, 12 mi. NNE of Dingle; 52°16'N 10°8'W.

Brandonville, town (pop. 100), Preston co., N W.Va., 14 mi. NNE of Kingwood.

Brandsen, Argentina: see CORONEL BRANDSEN.

Brandsville, city (pop. 204), Howell co., S Mo., in the Ozarks, 10 mi. SE of West Plains; agr.

Brandt, town (pop. 211), Deuel co., E S.Dak., 7 mi. SSE of Clear Lake.

Brandy or **Brandy Station,** village, Culpeper co., N Va., 6 mi. ENE of Culpeper. In Civil War, scene (June 9, 1863) of war's greatest cavalry engagement (also called battle of Fleetwood Hill), an indecisive encounter bet. Union troops under Pleasanton and Confederates commanded by Jeb Stuart; 1st clash of Gettysburg campaign.

Brandypot, group of 3 islets, E Que., in the St. Lawrence just E of Hare Isl., opposite Rivière du Loup.

Brandys nad Labem (brän'dēs näd' lä"bĕm), Czech *Brandýs nad Labem*, Ger. *Brandeis an der Elbe* (brän'dĭs än dĕr ĕl'bù), town (pop. 6,904), N central Bohemia, Czechoslovakia, on Elbe R. opposite Stara Boleslav, on railroad and 12 mi. NE of Prague, in wheat and sugar-beet region. Agr.-machinery mfg., flour milling.

Brandys nad Orlici (ôr"lĭtsĭ), Czech *Brandýs nad Orlicí*, Ger. *Brandeis an der Adler* (äd'lùr), village (pop. 1,534), E Bohemia, Czechoslovakia, on Ticha Orlice R., on railroad and 6 mi. ENE of Vysoke Myto; mfg. of brass articles. Was once hq. of Bohemian Moravian Church.

Brandy Station, Va.: see BRANDY.

Brandywine Creek, in SE Pa. and N Del., rises in small E and W branches in Chester co., Pa., joining 10 mi. SE of Coatsville; flows c.20 mi. SE, past Chadds Ford, through N Delaware, to Christina R. just above its mouth on the Delaware at Wilmington. On its banks, near Chadds Ford, Howe defeated Washington Sept. 11, 1777.

Branford. **1** Town (pop. 10,944), including Branford borough (pop. 2,552), New Haven co., S Conn., on Long Isl. Sound at mouth of Branford R. (c.10 mi. long), and 7 mi. ESE of New Haven; agr., mfg. (electrical appliances, toy trains, wire, boats, metal products, clothing). Includes shore resort villages of Pine Orchard, Stony Creek (oysters), and Short Beach. Some pre-Revolutionary houses remain. Branford was settled 1644. **2** Town (pop. 753), Suwannee co., N Fla., on Suwannee R. and 23 mi. S of Live Oak.

Brani, Pulau (pōōlou' brä'nē), island (pop. 2,556) in Keppel Harbor, bet. Singapore isl. and Blakang Mati; 1°16'N 103°50'E; 1 mi. long, ½ mi. wide. Site of large Singapore tin smelters, dealing with bulk of Malayan production.

Braniewo (brănyĕ'vô), Ger. *Braunsberg* (brouns'-bĕrk), town (1939 pop. 21,142; 1946 pop. 1,373) in East Prussia, after 1945 in Olsztyn prov., NE Poland, on Pasleka R., near its mouth on Vistula Lagoon, and 25 mi. NE of Elbing, 35 mi. SW of Kaliningrad; frontier station near USSR border, 7 mi. SW of Mamonovo. Chief town of Ermland; fishing port; sawmilling; power station. Castle established here (1241) by Teutonic Knights; town chartered 1284 by bishops of Ermland, who originally had seat here; joined Hanseatic League in same year. Passed 1466 to Poland; held 1626–35 by Swedes. Heavily damaged in Swedish-Polish wars in 17th and 18th cent.; passed 1772 to Prussia. Jesuit col. established in late-16th cent. After Second World War (during which town was c.80% destroyed) it was evacuated by Ger. pop.

Branksome, England: see POOLE.

Branksome, Scotland: see HAWICK.

Branne (brän), village (pop. 473), Gironde dept., SW France, on the Dordogne and 6 mi. SSE of Libourne; winegrowing.

Bran Pass (brän) (alt. 4,166 ft.), in the Transylvanian Alps, SE central Rumania, bet. the Piatra-Craiului and Bucegi Mts., 12 mi. WNW of Sinaia; highway corridor, formerly a major trade and communications channel bet. Transylvania and Walachia. Bran is at its N end.

Bran-Poarta, Rumania: see BRAN.

Bransfield Strait, channel (c.200 naut. mi. long, 60 naut. mi. wide) in the South Pacific, separating the South Shetlands from Palmer Peninsula of Antarctica, in 63°S 59°W. Named 1820 by James Weddell.

Bransk (brä'nyùsk), Pol. *Brańsk*, Rus. *Bryansk* (brēänsk'), town (pop. 2,542), Bialystok prov., NE Poland, on Nurzec R. and 30 mi. SSW of Bialystok; brewing, flour milling.

Branson. **1** Town (pop. 157), Las Animas co., S Colo., 36 mi. ESE of Trinidad, near N.Mex. line; alt. 6,000 ft. **2** Resort city (pop. 1,314), Taney co., S Mo., in the Ozarks, on L. Taneycomo (formed by White R.) and 40 mi. S of Springfield; wood products; rock quarries.

Brant, county (□ 421; pop. 56,695), S Ont., on Grand R.; ⊙ Brantford.

Brantas River (brän'tùs), E Java, Indonesia, rises in mts. near SE coast of isl., 70 mi. WSW of Bondowoso, flows W, then N and E in wide arc, past Kediri, Kertosono, and Mojokerto, thence through its delta to Madura Strait, 20 mi. S of Surabaya; 160 mi. long. Near Mojokerto are extensive irrigation works (in use since 1836). Surabaya is near the mouth of KALI MAS RIVER, the most important stream in Brantas delta.

Brantevik (brän"tùvēk'), fishing village (pop. 792), Kristianstad co., S Sweden, on the Baltic, 3 mi. S of Simrishamn; limestone quarries.

Brantford, city (pop. 31,948), ⊙ Brant co., S Ont., on Grand R. and 60 mi. SW of Toronto; railroad center; paper milling, lumbering; mfg. of electrical equipment, refrigerators, machinery, stoves, radiators, furniture, stockings, gloves, agr. implements, paper boxes, chemicals, wax polish. Airport. Named for Joseph Brant, Mohawk chief, who brought Iroquois nations here after American Revolution, Brantford became site (1785) of 1st church in Ont. Until 1830 center of Indian reservation, city remains hq. of the Six Nations and is site of Indian Institute. At suburb of Tutela Heights, Alexander Graham Bell made his 1st successful experiment which led to invention of the telephone.

Brantingham (brăn'tĭng-hăm"), resort village, Lewis co., N central N.Y., 40 mi. N of Utica, on **Brantingham Lake** (c.1½ mi. long).

Brant Lake, summer-resort village (1940 pop. 585), Warren co., E N.Y., in the Adirondacks, at S end of Brant L. (c.5 mi. long), 26 mi. N of Glens Falls. Sometimes called Horicon.

Brantley, county (□ 447; pop. 6,387), SE Ga.; ⊙ Nahunta. Bounded N and E by Satilla R. Coastal plain agr. (tobacco, corn, melons, sweet potatoes) and timber (lumber, naval stores) area. Formed 1920.

Brantley, town (pop. 1,102), Crenshaw co., S Ala., on Conecuh R. and 55 mi. S of Montgomery; lumber, work clothes. Inc. 1895.

Brantôme (brătōm'), village (pop. 1,126), Dordogne dept., SW France, on Dronne R. and 13 mi. NNW of Périgueux; food processing, footwear mfg. Has 13th-15th cent. abbatial church; an isolated belfry; and a curved bridge.

Brantovka, Russian SFSR: see OKTYABRSKI, Kostroma oblast.

Brant Rock, Mass.: see MARSHFIELD.
Brantwood, England: see CONISTON.
Branwood, S.C.: see BRANDON.
Branxholm, Scotland: see HAWICK.
Branxholm (brăngk'sŭm), village (pop. 335), NE Tasmania, 36 mi. NE of Launceston and on Ringarooma R., in tin-mining area, wheat.
Branxton, town (pop. 1,107), E New South Wales, Australia, 27 mi. NW of Newcastle; coal-mining center.
Branzoll, Italy: see BRONZOLO.
Bras d'Or Lake (brä" dôr'), tidal salt-water lake (□ 360; 44 mi. long, up to 20 mi. wide) in central Cape Breton Isl., NE N.S. It opens on the sea by means of Great Bras d'Or channel (N) and the Grand Narrows channel (S). Its shore, surrounded by low hills, is deeply indented by several bays. Lake contains several small isls.; coal is mined on shores. The Great Bras d'Or section (32 mi. long, 2–6 mi. wide) of the lake opens NE on the Atlantic, forming NW side of Boularderie Isl. Great Bras d'Or has 2 long, narrow inlets: St. Patrick Channel, extending 20 mi. SW from Baddeck; St. Andrew Channel, extending 22 mi. NE from S end of Boularderie Isl. Baddeck is chief village on Great Bras d'Or. The district was the scene of important experiments in the early history of aviation. In 1907 Dr. Alexander Graham Bell founded at Baddeck the Aerial Experiment Association, and on Feb. 23, 1909, J. A. D. McCurdy piloted his airplane, the "Silver Dart," a distance of half a mile.
Braselton (brä'zŭltŭn), town (pop. 165), Jackson co., NE central Ga., 23 mi. WNW of Athens.
Brashear (brŭshēr', brä'shēr), town (pop. 119), Adair co., N Mo., on Salt R. and 10 mi. ESE of Kirksville.
Brasher, town (pop. 152), Pemiscot co., extreme SE Mo., on Mississippi R.and 9 mi. S of Caruthersville.
Brasher Falls, village (1940 pop. 565), St. Lawrence co., N N.Y., on St. Regis R. and 10 mi. SSE of Massena; mfg. of machinery.
Brasiléia (bräzĕlĕ'yŭ), city (pop. 1,469), S Acre territory, westernmost Brazil, on Bolivia border, on Acre R., opposite Cobija (Bolivia), and 90 mi. SW of Rio Branco; rubber. Airport. Until 1944, spelled Brasília or Brasilea.
Brasília (bräzē'lyŭ). **1** City, Acre territory, Brazil: see BRASILÉIA. **2** City (pop. 1,696), N Minas Gerais, Brazil, 50 mi. NW of Montes Claros; cotton. Formerly spelled Brazilia.
Braslav (brŭsläf'), Pol. *Brasław* (brä'swäf), city (1948 pop. over 2,000), W Polotsk oblast, Belorussian SSR, on L. Drivyaty, 70 mi. WNW of Polotsk; agr. processing (hides, grain, flax), mfg. (cardboard, bricks). Has old castle, ruins of 12th-cent. church. Passed (1795) from Poland to Russia; reverted (1921) to Poland; ceded to USSR in 1945.
Brasov, Rumania: see STALIN.
Brasovo, Russian SFSR: see LOKOT, Bryansk oblast.
Bras-Panon (brä'-pänō'), town and commune (pop. 3,506), near NE coast of Réunion isl., on railroad and 16 mi. ESE of Saint-Denis; sugar milling, rum distilling.
Brass (bräs), town, Owerri prov., Eastern Provinces, S Nigeria, minor port on Gulf of Guinea, at mouth of Brass R. (an arm of Niger R. delta), 60 mi. WSW of Port Harcourt; fisheries; palm oil and kernels, hardwood, rubber. In late 19th cent., a major port and Br. consular hq.
Brassac (bräsäk'), village (pop. 1,117), Tarn dept., S France, in the Monts de Lacaune, on Agout R. and 13 mi. E of Castres; woolen milling.
Brassac-les-Mines (-lā-mēn'), village (pop. 1,755), Puy-de-Dôme dept., central France, on the Allier and 9 mi. NNW of Brioude; coal-mining center; mfg. (electrical equipment, lace).
Brasschaat (bräs'ät), town (pop. 16,573), Antwerp prov., N Belgium, 6 mi. NNE of Antwerp; residential dist. with many large estates. Formerly spelled Brasschaet.
Brassington, village and parish (pop. 645), central Derby, England, 6 mi. SW of Matlock; barite mining. Abandoned lead mines. Norman church has 14th- and 15th-cent. additions.
Brass Islands, 2 uninhabited islets known as Outer Brass (108 acres) and Inner Brass (128 acres), NW U.S. Virgin Isls., just off N coast of St. Thomas Isl., 4 mi. NW of Charlotte Amalie; 18°23'N 64°57'W.
Brasso, Rumania: see STALIN (Brasov), city.
Brasstown Bald or **Mount Enotah** (ē"nō'tŭ), highest peak (4,784 ft.) in Ga., in the Blue Ridge, on Towns and Union co. line, 8 mi. E of Blairsville. U.S. Forest Service lookout tower at summit.
Brassua Lake (brä'sōōŭ), Somerset co., W central Maine, 16 mi. E of Jackman and just W of Moosehead L., in hunting, fishing area; irregularly shaped, 6 mi. max. width.
Brassus, Le, Switzerland: see CHENIT, LE.
Brastagi or **Berastagi** (both: bŭrästä'gē), town, N Sumatra, Indonesia, 30 mi. SSW of Medan, near Mt. Sibayak; alt. 4,600 ft.; mtn. resort. Airfield.
Braswell (bräz'wŭl), town (pop. 25), Paulding co., NW Ga., 37 mi. NW of Atlanta, in farm area.
Bratan (brätän'), central Bulgaria, highest peak (4,344 ft.) in Sirnena Gora (E part of Sredna Gora), 14 mi. WSW of Kazanlak.
Bratca (brät'kä), Hung. *Barátka* (bŏ'rät-kŏ), village (pop. 1,786), Bihor prov., W Rumania, on Rapid Körös R., on railroad and 32 mi. E. of Oradea. Titanium and aluminum mining.
Brat Chirpoyev Island, Russian SFSR: see CHERNYE BRATYA.
Bratenahl (brä'tŭnôl), village (pop. 1,240), Cuyahoga co., N Ohio, a NE suburb surrounded on 3 sides by Cleveland, and bordered N by L. Erie.
Brates, Lake (brä'tĕsh), Rum. *Brateş*, lake (□ 29.7; 5 mi. long, 7 mi. wide), Galati prov., E Rumania, near confluence of the Prut and the Danube, just NE of Galati; noted fishing grounds.
Bratislava (brä'tyĭslä"vä), Ger. *Pressburg* (prĕs'bōōrk), Hung. *Pozsony* (pô'zhônyŭ), city (pop. 132,509; metropolitan area pop. 165,134), ⊙ Slovakia and Bratislava prov. (□ 2,903; pop. 838,134), SW Slovakia, Czechoslovakia, at S base of the Little Carpathians, on Danube R. and 175 mi. SE of Prague, 35 mi. ESE of Vienna; 48°9'N 17°7'E. Industrial, shipping, railroad, and cultural center, strategically important because of its location on international waterway, near meeting point of Czechoslovak, Austrian, and Hung. borders. Seat of Supreme Court and Slovak Natl. Council; R. C. and Protestant bishops' sees. Mfg. of textiles (notably rayon), chemicals, paints, paper, leather and metal goods, cables, electrical goods, agr. machinery, cement, tires, soap, candles; food and tobacco processing, brewing, shipbuilding, woodworking, printing. Has large oil refinery, modern airports at VAJNORY and IVANKA, broadcasting station. Extensive harbor installations on left bank (SE). During Second World War, oil pipe line laid by Germans from here to Melnik on the Elbe. Chief imports: E European raw materials (oil, minerals, textile fibers), foodstuffs (wheat, corn, flour, fruit), tobacco. Main exports: manufactured products of W Czechoslovakia (ironware, glass, chemicals, paper) and Slovak malt. Core of city lies in flatlands along left bank of the Danube; residential dists. compete with vineyards on surrounding hills. Notable historic buildings: Gothic St. Martin's Cathedral (dating from 13th cent.), with 14th-15th cent. dome, site of coronation of Hung. kings; 4-towered castle (founded in 9th cent.; several times rebuilt); old town hall on Masaryk square (originally 13th cent.; now municipal mus.); St. John's Chapel (1380) with noted spire; 15th-cent. Michael's Gate (part of medieval fortifications); 16th-cent. Roland's Fountain; 18th-cent. baroque archbishop's palace (now the new town hall), site of signature of treaty of Pressburg (1805; bet. Napoleon I and Emperor Francis II), and hq. of Hung. revolutionaries (1848–49). Oldest city structure is 13th-cent. Franciscan convent and church, rebuilt in 16th-18th cent. Has Comenius Univ., Catholic and Evangelical theological faculties, technical and commercial colleges. Originally a Roman settlement, Bratislava was chartered in 1291; seat (1526–1848) of Hungarian Diet and ⊙ Hungary from 1536 to 1683. Modern growth dates from late-19th cent., when it became center of Slovak natl. liberation movement. Proclaimed ⊙ Slovakia in 1918, and later (1938–45) of short-lived Slovakian republic. Captured by Soviet troops in 1945; harbor facilities were seriously damaged during Second World War. Post-war expulsion of Germans (formerly ⅓ of inhabitants) led to some decrease in pop.
Bratlandsdal, Norway: see BRATTLANDSDAL.
Bratocea Pass (brätô'chä) (alt. 4,159 ft.), SE central Rumania, on SW slopes of Buzau Mts., 15 mi. SE of Stalin (Brasov); highway pass bet. Transylvania and Muntenia.
Bratsberg, county, Norway: see TELEMARK.
Bratsi, Greece: see TANAGRA.
Bratsigovo (brä'tsēgôvô), city (pop. 3,364), Plovdiv dist., S central Bulgaria, on N slope of W Rhodope Mts., 3 mi. E of Peshtera; wine and tobacco growing, fruit, horticulture; sawmilling, cloth fulleries. Has technical school. Sometimes spelled Bracigovo.
Bratsk (brätsk), village (1948 pop. over 2,000), W central Irkutsk oblast, Russian SFSR, on Angara R., at mouth of Oka R., and 115 mi. NNE of Tulun. Site of Angara R. rapids, at downstream end of navigation; ship repair yards; lumber milling. Extensive iron-ore deposits found near by. Founded 1631 as Rus. fortress on Siberian colonization route.
Bratskoye (brät'skŭyŭ), village (1926 pop. 3,246), NW Nikolayev oblast, Ukrainian SSR, 22 mi. NNE of Voznesensk; metalworks.
Bratslav (brŭtsläf'), agr. town (1926 pop. 7,842), central Vinnitsa oblast, Ukrainian SSR, in Podolia, on the Southern Bug and 34 mi. SE of Vinnitsa; road junction; metalworks. Flourished as administrative center in 17th and 18th cents.
Brattahlid, Greenland: see JULIANEHAAB.
Brattlandsdal (brät'länsdäl), narrow, wild valley in SW Norway, overhung with rocks, at E extremity of the Haukelifjell; begins at Roldal in Hordaland co. and extends S, along foot of Breidfonn glacier, to Nesflaten on Suldal L. (Rogaland co.); traversed by a torrent abounding in salmon. A scenic highway follows the valley. Popular tourist dist. Sometimes spelled Bratlandsdal.
Brattleboro, town (pop. 11,522), including Brattleboro village (pop. 9,606), Windham co., SE Vt., on the Connecticut, at mouth of West R., and 32 mi. E of Bennington. Mfg. (wood products, textiles, pipe organs, optical goods, paints, flour and feed), printing; winter-sports center in agr. area (apples, maple and dairy products). Hq. Holstein-Friesian cattle breeders' assn., school for deaf, hosp. for insane here. W. M. Hunt, R. M. Hunt b. here. "Naulahka," N of village, was home of Rudyard Kipling, who married a Brattleboro girl in 1892. Settled around Fort Dummer (established 1724), chartered 1753.
Brattvaer (brät'văr), village (pop. 109; canton pop. 1,634), More og Romsdal co., W Norway, on W shore of Smola isl., 21 mi. N of Kristiansund; fishing center. Sometimes spelled Bratvaer.
Brattvag (brät'vôg), Nor. *Brattvåg*, village (pop. 695) in Haram canton, More og Romsdal co., W Norway, on North Sea, 13 mi. NE of Alesund; mfg. of deck machinery.
Bratunac or **Bratunats** (brä'tōōnäts), village (pop. 5,033), E Bosnia, Yugoslavia, 5 mi. NNE of Srebrenica.
Bratuseni, Moldavian SSR: see BRATUSHANY.
Bratushany (brŭtōōshä'nē), Rum. *Brătuşeni* (brŭtōōshĕm'), village (1941 pop. 3,842), N Moldavian SSR, 33 mi. NW of Beltsy; flour milling.
Bratvaer, Norway: see BRATTVAER.
Brätz, Poland: see BROJCE.
Braubach (brou'bäkh), town (pop. 3,399), in former Prussian prov. of Hesse-Nassau, W Germany, after 1945 in Rhineland-Palatinate, on right bank of the Rhine and 3 mi. SE of Oberlahnstein; lead refining. Has 16th-cent. church. Anc. fortress of Marksburg towers above town.
Braunau or **Braunau am Inn** (brou'nou äm ĭn'), city (pop. 11,744), W Upper Austria, on the Inn (Ger. border), 31 mi. N of Salzburg; rail junction; breweries, tanneries. Adolf Hitler b. here. Ranshofen, with one of Austria's largest aluminum plants, became part of Braunau after 1938.
Braunau, Czechoslovakia: see BROUMOV.
Braunfels (broun'fĕls"), town (pop. 3,337), in former Prussian prov. of Hesse-Nassau, W Germany, after 1945 in Hesse, 5 mi. SW of Wetzlar; resort. Has castle rebuilt in 19th cent. in Gothic style.
Braunlage (broun'lä"gŭ), town (pop. 7,625), in Brunswick, NW Germany, after 1945 Lower Saxony, in the upper Harz, 9 mi. NE of Bad Lauterberg; climatic health resort and winter-sports center (alt. 1,970 ft.). Paper- and sawmilling, brewing.
Bräunlingen (broin'lĭng-ŭn), village (pop. 2,087), S Baden, Germany, in Black Forest, on the Breg and 9 mi. S of Villingen; silk mfg., woodworking, lumber milling.
Braunsbedra (brouns"bā'drä), village (pop. 3,563), in former Prussian Saxony prov., central Germany, after 1945 in Saxony-Anhalt, 7 mi. SW of Merseburg; lignite mining. Power station. Created after 1945 through incorporation of Braunsdorf (brouns'dôrf) and Bedra (bā'drä).
Braunsberg, Poland: see BRANIEWO.
Braunschweig, Germany: see BRUNSWICK.
Braunsdorf, Germany: see BRAUNSBEDRA.
Braunstone, residential town and parish (pop. 6,997), central Leicester, England, just SW of Leicester. Has medieval church.
Braunton (brăn'tŭn), town and parish (pop. 3,019), N Devon, England, near mouth of Taw R., 6 mi. WNW of Barnstaple; agr. market, with agr.-implement works. Has 13th-cent. church.
Braunwald (broun'vält), village (pop. 327), Glarus canton, E central Switzerland, 7 mi. SSW of Glarus; health resort (alt. 4,115 ft.); winter sports.
Braus, Col de (kôl dŭ brōs'), pass (alt. 3,287 ft.), of Maritime Alps, in Alpes-Maritimes dept., SE France, on Nice-Turin road, 14 mi. NNE of Nice. Rail tunnel (3¾ mi. long, longest in France) under pass completed 1928.
Braux (brō), village (pop. 1,803), Ardennes dept., N France, on left bank of Meuse R. (canalized) and 6 mi. NNE of Mézières, in the Ardennes; nut and bolt factories.
Brava (brä'vŭ), southernmost island (□ 25; 1940 pop. 8,510; 1950 pop. 7,904), of the Cape Verde Isls., in Leeward group, 12 mi. WSW of Fogo isl., in the Atlantic. Nova Sintra (14°52'N 24°42'W), near center, is chief town; Furna, the only port. Isl. is roughly circular (diameter 5 mi.) and mountainous, rising to 3,202 ft. at Fontaínhas peak. Some agr. (beans, corn). Fishing.
Brava (brä'vä), town (pop. 9,000), in the Benadir, S Ital. Somaliland, port on Indian Ocean, 105 mi. SW of Mogadishu; 1°6'N 44°2'E. Commercial center (hides, livestock, corn, durra, sesame); leather factory (sandals, handbags, cushions), sawmill. In 16th cent. under Portuguese and then Turkish control. Passed (17th cent.) to Zanzibar; leased (1892) and then sold (1905) to Italy.
Brava, Laguna (lägōō'nä brä'vä), salt lake (□ 20; alt. c.11,000 ft.) in NW La Rioja prov., Argentina, NW of Vinchina; c.12 mi. long.
Brava Point (brä'vä), cape, Montevideo dept., S Uruguay, on the Río de la Plata, at southernmost point of Montevideo city; 34°57'S 56°8'W.
Bravard (brävärd'), Andean peak (18,865 ft.), W Mendoza prov., Argentina, near Chile line just S

of Tupungato peak. Tupungatito peak (18,500 ft.), just NW, is sometimes called Bravard.

Bravard, Sierra de (syĕ'rä dā), hill range in SW Buenos Aires prov., Argentina, N of the Sierra de la Ventana, extends c.25 mi. SE-NW, in area S of Coronel Suárez.

Bravicha (brä'vēchŭ), Rum. *Bravicea* (brä'vēchä), village (1941 pop. 4,407), central Moldavian SSR, 17 mi. W of Orgeyev; fruit- and winegrowing.

Bravo, Río, U.S. and Mexico: see Rio Grande.

Bravo del Norte, Río, U.S. and Mexico: see Rio Grande.

Brawley, city (pop. 11,922), Imperial co., S Calif., c.20 mi. SE of Salton Sea; largest city in Imperial Valley and one of state's largest shippers of fruit and truck. Anza Desert State Park is W. Inc. 1908.

Braxton, county (□ 517; pop.18,082), central W.Va.; ⊙ Sutton. On Allegheny Plateau; drained by Elk and Little Kanawha rivers. Agr. (livestock, fruit, tobacco); oil and natural-gas wells, coal mines, granite quarries; timber. Some industry at Sutton and Gassaway. Formed 1836.

Braxton, village (pop. 206), Simpson co., S central Miss., 22 mi. SSE of Jackson; lumber.

Bray (brĕ), town (pop. 3,784), Hainaut prov., S Belgium, 7 mi. ESE of Mons; coal mining.

Bray (brā), town and parish (pop. 4,141), E Berkshire, England, on the Thames just SE of Maidenhead; agr. market. Famous for ballad about the vicar of Bray, who changed his religion according to that of the reigning monarch; traditionally ascribed to time of George I, but reputed to refer to Simon Aleyn, vicar of Bray probably 1540–88. Has 13th-15th-cent. church and Jesus Hosp. (built 1616).

Bray (brĕ), small region of Normandy, N France, included in NE Seine-Inférieure dept. Good cattle- and horse-raising area. Market center: Neufchâtel.

Bray or **Bray-sur-Somme** (brĕ-sür-sôm'), agr. village (pop. 1,033), Somme dept., N France, on the Somme and 10 mi. W of Péronne. Heavily damaged in First World War.

Bray (brā), Gaelic *Bri Chuallan,* urban district (pop. 11,085), NE Co. Wicklow, Ireland, on the Irish Sea, 12 mi. SE of Dublin; fishing center and seaport; popular bathing resort, especially for Dublin. Near by is cape of Bray Head.

Bray-Dunes (brĕ-dün'), town (pop. 1,959), Nord dept., N France, resort on North Sea, near Belg. border, 7 mi. ENE of Dunkirk; customhouse.

Braye-en-Laonnois (brā-ā-läônwä'), village (pop. 195), Aisne dept., N France, at foot of the Chemin des Dames, 9 mi. S of Laon.

Bray Head, cape on the Irish Sea, NE Co. Wicklow, Ireland, just SE of Bray; 53°11'N 6°4'W.

Braymer, city (pop. 955), Caldwell co., NW Mo., 19 mi. SW of Chillicothe; agr., dairy products, feed mill.

Bray-sur-Seine (brĕ-sür-sĕn'), village (pop. 1,328), Seine-et-Marne dept., N central France, on left bank of Seine R. and 10 mi. SSW of Provins; grain market; produces chemicals (for tanning, dyeing); sugar-beet distilling, fertilizer mfg.

Bray-sur-Somme, Somme dept., France: see Bray.

Brayton, town (pop. 239), Audubon co., W central Iowa, near East Nishnabotna R., 11 mi. NNE of Atlantic; concrete products. Sand pit near by.

Brazatortas (brä"thätôr'täs), town (pop. 1,669), Ciudad Real prov., S central Spain, on N slopes of the Sierra Morena, 30 mi. SW of Ciudad Real; cereals, olives, honey, timber, livestock. Lead mines near by.

Brazeau, Alta.: see Nordegg.

Brazeau, Mount (bră'zō), (11,386 ft.), W Alta., near B.C. border, in Rocky Mts., in Jasper Natl. Park, 40 mi. SE of Jasper; 52°33'N 117°21'W.

Brazey-en-Plaine (bräzā'-ā-plĕn'), village (pop. 1,429), Côte-d'Or dept., E central France, on Burgundy Canal and 15 mi. SE of Dijon; cotton milling, cement-pipe mfg.

Brazi or **Brazii** (bräz), village (pop. 1,530), Prahova prov., S central Rumania, on railroad and 5 mi. S of Ploesti; oil-refining center; mfg. of glass and clay products.

Brazil (brŭzĭl'), Portuguese *Brasil* (bräzēl'), called in full the United States of Brazil, Portuguese *Estados Unidos do Brasil,* federal republic (□ 3,287,842, including interior waters; 1950 pop. 52,645,479; 1940 pop. 41,236,315), E South America, largest and most populous of the Latin American nations, with 48% of the continent's area and pop.; ⊙ Rio de Janeiro. A massive triangular block extending 2,683 mi. N–S and 2,688 mi. E–W, Brazil is larger than continental U.S.; only the USSR, China, and Canada are larger. With over 9,750 mi. of land frontier, Brazil borders on all South American countries except Ecuador and Chile; these are: N–S, the Guianas (French, Dutch, and British), Venezuela, Colombia, Peru, Bolivia (longest common frontier), Paraguay, Argentina, and Uruguay. Its Atlantic coast line is 4,600 mi. long. Though traversed by the equator (the mouth of the Amazon is bisected by it) and reaching its northernmost point at 4°21'N (Cape Orange), the Bulk of Brazil lies in the Southern Hemisphere, tapering off to a narrower coastal strip S of the Tropic of Capricorn; its southernmost tip is at 33°45'S. Despite its great width (maximum near 7°S), all of Brazil is E of the longitude of New York. Its easternmost point (Cabo Branco, also Point Pedras, 34°47'W) is but 1,850 mi. from Africa. Brazil has 26 constituent political units (20 states, 5 federal territories, and the federal district). The states of Amazonas and Pará, the territories of Acre, Guaporé, Rio Branco, and Amapá, roughly coextensive with the Amazon basin (Amazonia), form the N region; Maranhão, Piauí, Ceará, and the 4 small states of the "bulge" (Rio Grande do Norte, Paraíba, Pernambuco, Alagoas) constitute the NE; Bahia, Sergipe, Minas Gerais, Espírito Santo, Rio de Janeiro state, and the federal dist. are in E Brazil; Mato Grosso and Goiás form the W central region; São Paulo (the economic heartland), Paraná, Santa Catarina, and Rio Grande do Sul are in the S. Brazil's isl. possessions include Fernando de Noronha (a federal territory) and the distant Atlantic islets of Trindade, Martim Vaz, and Saint Paul Rocks. Physiographically, Brazil consists of a vast central plateau bordered by lowlands which range in size from the sprawling Amazon flood plain in N to a narrow coastal strip in E and SE. The absence of a wide coastal plain with easy access to the interior (as found in North America) has been a major obstacle to the nation's economic development. Brazil's other lowlands are the poorly drained flood plain (*pantanal*) of the Paraguay R. (in SW Mato Grosso along Bolivian border) and S part of Rio Grande do Sul where the plateau merges with the Uruguayan and Argentine pampa. The rolling topography of the central plateau is interrupted by a few mtn. ranges which rise to 7–9,000 ft. Though in NE Brazil the rise from the coastal plain to the interior is gradual, bet. Bahia and Rio Grande do Sul the steep mountain-like Great Escarpment (known for much of its length by the collective name of Serra do Mar) is a formidable obstacle to transportation; in one section, called Serra do Caparaó, along the Minas Gerais–Espírito Santo border, the escarpment rises to 9,462 ft. (Pico da Bandeira), Brazil's loftiest peak. Only the outermost piedmont slopes of the Andes penetrate NW Brazil, along Peruvian border. In N Brazil, the Guiana Highlands form the border ranges (Tumuc-Humac, Acaraí, Pacaraima) and send several low spurs southward. In Mato Grosso, the divide bet. South America's 2 major drainage systems, the Amazon and the Río de la Plata, the Amazon (navigable for ocean-going vessels throughout its Brazilian course) receives its principal tributaries. All of the Río de la Plata's headstreams rise in Brazil, the Paraguay R. draining W Mato Grosso and forming part of Brazil–Bolivia frontier, the Paraná R. flowing SSW across the central plateau. Where the Paraná forms the Brazil–Paraguay border it drops from the central upland over Guaíra Falls; further S, one of its tributaries forms the spectacular Iguassú Falls. Uruguay R. forms the border bet. Rio Grande do Sul and Argentina. São Francisco R. reaches the Atlantic just below the bulge. Brazil's long coast line has few natural harbors; principal inlets, aside from Amazon delta, are Rio's famed Guanabara Bay, Bahia's Todos os Santos Bay, and the bay of Santos (São Paulo). Lagoa dos Patos, a coastal lagoon in Rio Grande do Sul, is country's largest lake. Amazonia is the world's largest region of rainy tropical climate, noted for its year-round rainfall (which everywhere exceeds 60 in.) and uniformly high temperatures. The coastal areas flanking the Amazon delta, as well as a narrow strip along the Bahia, Espírito Santo, and Rio de Janeiro coasts, have a similar climate, slightly modified by the trade winds. Much of the interior N of the Tropic of Capricorn has a tropical savanna climate with alternating wet (summer) and dry seasons. A region in the NE (especially in Ceará and the interior of Pernambuco) situated in the lee of the SE trades has a tropical steppe climate. The southern states constitute Brazil's only humid subtropical region. Vegetation ranges from Amazonia's rain forest (*selva*) of mixed evergreens to the scrub forest (*coatinga*) and bunch grass of the arid NE. While the E coastal ranges as far S as São Paulo as well as the slopes of the Paraná R. valley are clad with semideciduous trees, most of Brazil's interior is covered with a mixture of long and short grass savanna, park savanna, and scrub forest. S of São Paulo are 2 types of mid-latitude vegetation: the Araucaria pine forests of Paraná and the tall grass prairies of Rio Grande do Sul. Although but 2% of its area is under cultivation, Brazil is essentially agr., with 65% of its labor force engaged in farming, and large tracts in the interior given to grazing. Leading crops (by acreage) are corn, coffee, cotton, rice, beans, manioc, and sugar cane. Coffee is Brazil's principal export product; in many years it constitutes ½ of total value of exports; Brazil usually supplies about ½ of the world's coffee. Coffee plantations (*fazendas*) are concentrated on the upland slopes of central and W São Paulo (state produces almost ½ total crop), S Minas Gerais, Espírito Santo, and N Paraná. The fertile *terra roxa* (purple soil derived from diabase) is especially suited to the cultivation of coffee. Brazil is also an important cotton producer; about ⅔ of the crop is grown in São Paulo. A perennial upland cotton plant grown in the NE supplies Pernambuco's textile mills. Cacao, concentrated in the humid tropical coastal strip of Bahia (bet. Salvador and Ilhéus), is also a leading export item. Rice, primarily a subsistence crop, is grown in São Paulo, Rio de Janeiro, Rio Grande do Sul, Minas Gerais, and Goiás. Wheat, in which Brazil is deficient, is limited to the 3 southern states, chiefly Rio Grande do Sul. Brazil is self-sufficient in sugar-cane production; the cane has been grown for 4 centuries in the coastal dists. bet. Paraíba and Bahia; more recently emphasis has shifted to the lower Paraíba R. valley around Campos (Rio de Janeiro), the Piracicaba area of São Paulo, and several centers in Minas Gerais. Coastal São Paulo and Rio de Janeiro specialize in bananas; these same states grow most of Brazil's citrus fruit. Tobacco from the dists. of Salvador (Bahia) and Santa Cruz do Sul (Rio Grande do Sul) satisfies the natl. demand as well as a small export market. The mamona plant, cultivated in Ceará, São Paulo, and Bahia, yields the castor bean, of which Brazil is the world's leading producer. Important forest products of the N and NE include carnauba wax, oiticica oil, caroa fiber (a jute substitute), medicinal plants and roots (copaiba, ipecac), Brazil and babassu nuts—all exported. Wild rubber collected in Amazonia is now a minor commercial product; cultivation of rubber trees is limited to the experimental plantations (Belterra, Fordlândia) established since 1927. Maté comes from the forests of W Paraná and S Mato Grosso. Truck gardens (mostly under Japanese ownership) have grown up near the largest cities, while mixed farming is assuming importance in the pioneer areas of W São Paulo and N Paraná, and in S Brazil's agr. dists. settled by European immigrants during last century. Except in Rio Grande do Sul, Brazil's cattle (totalling 40,000,000 head) is of an inferior grade, due to climate and inadequate cross-breeding. Grazing is extensive throughout the *sertão* ("back country"), notably in the Triângulo Mineiro of Minas Gerais and in São Paulo; Goiás, Bahia, and Mato Grosso have large herds. Hog raising is concentrated in the 4 southern states and in Minas Gerais, where the North American corn-hog economy is practiced; Rio Grande do Sul is the leading sheep-raising state. Brazil has the large estates, absentee ownership, and widespread tenancy characteristic of the coffee and sugar economy, but in the pioneer "frontier" areas and in S Brazil small farm ownership is spreading. Brazil's rich mineral resources are in the initial stages of exploitation. Its high-grade iron ore reserves are said to be the largest in the world; mined at Itabira in Minas Gerais (the leading mining state), iron now feeds Brazil's steel mills and is also exported to the U.S. Large manganese deposits have been blocked out in Mato Grosso and in Amapá territory; it is mined in S Minas Gerais. Minas Gerais also leads in the mining of bauxite and zirconium, commercial quartz crystals, gold, semiprecious stones, mica, arsenic, rutile, graphite, and chromite. Industrial diamonds are found in Bahia and Minas Gerais. The Borborema Plateau of NE Brazil contains deposits of copper, tin, beryl, and columbite. Salt is panned along the coast of Rio Grande do Norte and Rio de Janeiro. Brazil is poorly supplied with energy resources; coal (non-coking) is mined in Rio Grande do Sul and Santa Catarina and in small quantities in Paraná and São Paulo but does not satisfy industrial needs. Petroleum was discovered 1939 in the Recôncavo of Bahia, but yields are low. Despite Brazil's huge hydroelectric potential, less than 10% is harnessed for power: the Cubatão plant serves São Paulo and Santos, and the new plant at the Paulo Afonso Falls is designed to supply factories in the NE. Charcoal (from extensively planted eucalyptus forests) remains the chief industrial fuel. Modern mfg. is undergoing rapid development, with the basic steel industry given greatest prominence. The ambitious national steel mill at Volta Redonda (in Paraíba R. valley bet. Rio and São Paulo), in operation since 1947, and smaller private plants in Minas Gerais (Sabará, Monlevade), including a new special steel mill at Coronel Fabriciano, have considerably reduced Brazil's dependence on imports. Metalworking is growing in Rio and São Paulo. Here, too, are most of country's cement mills. Cotton spinning and weaving employs c.25% of all industrial workers; São Paulo state, with ½ of the mills, is followed by Minas Gerais, Pernambuco, and the federal dist. Rio Grande do Sul leads in meat packing and Pernambuco in alcohol distilling, but São Paulo, leading Brazil in agr. output, is also the first industrial state, its dynamic capital having outdistanced Rio, the nearest rival. Aside from these 2 metropolises (each with pop. exceeding 2,000,000 in 1950), Brazil's largest cities are Recife (⊙ Pernambuco), the economic center of the bulge; Salvador (⊙ Bahia), the old ⊙ Brazil; Pôrto Alegre (⊙ Rio Grande do Sul); modern Belo Horizonte (⊙ Minas Gerais); Santos, the great coffee port for São Paulo; Belém (⊙ Pará) at the mouth of the Amazon; Manaus

(⊙ Amazonas), the city of the short-lived rubber boom, 1,000 mi. upstream; NATAL (⊙ Rio Grande do Norte); FORTALEZA (⊙ Ceará); GOIÂNIA, newly laid out ⊙ Goiás; the old gold-rush city of CUIABÁ, ⊙ Mato Grosso; NITEROI, ⊙ Rio de Janeiro state; summer resorts of PETRÓPOLIS and TERESÓPOLIS, overlooking Guanabara Bay; CURITIBA and Londrina in Paraná. A tentative site for the future federal ⊙ has been selected in E central Goiás. Brazil's leading exports (in order of value) are coffee, raw cotton, cacao, hides and skins, pine lumber, cotton textiles, carnauba wax, castor beans, and tobacco. Brazil's railroads are for the most part inefficient and antiquated; the 22,000 mi. of track operate on 5 different gauges. Only in São Paulo is there an integrated rail net linking the coffeegrowing hinterland with the capital, and across the escarpment with Santos. The line connecting Rio with São Paulo continues S to the Uruguayan border. Among the principal railroads tapping the interior of Brazil are the line across São Paulo and S Mato Grosso to Corumbá (on Paraguay R.), which is being continued W into Bolivia; and rail spurs leading to N Paraná, central Goiás (Anápolis), and the headwaters of the São Francisco at Pirapora (Minas Gerais). In NE Brazil, rail tentacles penetrate the hinterland from the chief port cities, but their interconnection is far from completion. The Madeira-Mamoré RR was built during the rubber boom of the early 1900s in deepest Amazonia around the rapids of the Madeira. Highway construction is growing. Inland waterways totalling 20,000 mi. include navigation on the Amazon and its tributaries, the Paraguay, long sections on the São Francisco, and short stretches on the Alto Paraná. Brazil is of ethnic diversity, combining Indian, Negro, and European strains. In 1940, over 60% of pop. was officially classified as white, 15% as Negro, and over 20% as mulatto. Only in the most remote interior have isolated Indian tribes (mostly of the Guaraní-Tupí language group) resisted European penetration. The Negro element, descending from African slaves employed on sugar plantations, is still concentrated in the NE and on the Bahia coast. Large-scale European immigration, dating from 1820s, has totalled almost 5,000,000. Most Italian, German, and Slavic immigrants have settled in the S states and have maintained their natl. customs and language, especially in agr. areas. Japanese immigrants (c.200,000) have settled chiefly in São Paulo and in a few agr. colonies in Amazonia. Portuguese is the official language. Most of the pop. is at least nominally Roman Catholic. While early records of Port. discoveries in Brazil remain uncertain, it is known that the coast was visited by the Sp. mariner Vicente Yáñez Pinzón before the Portuguese under Pedro Alvares Cabral claimed the land (in 1500) as coming within the Port. sphere defined by the Treaty of Tordesillas (1494). Not until 1532, however, was the 1st permanent settlement (São Vicente on São Paulo coast) established. About the same time, the NE was opened under Martin Afonso de Sousa, the 1st royal governor, and 12 captaincies extending inland from the coast were created. Soon Port. claims were challenged by the French, who occupied Villegaignon isl. in Rio de Janeiro Bay (but were dislodged by Mem de Sá in 1567), and by the Dutch, who under the able administration of Maurice of Nassau held most of the NE, 1632–54. Sugar, cultivated with the help of imported slaves, early became Brazil's great export crop, creating a one-crop plantation economy in the NE. This dependence on sugar was somewhat lightened by the discovery of gold (late 17th cent.) in Minas and gold and diamonds (early 18th cent.) in Mato Grosso. Though enterprising groups (*bandeirantes*) of *paulistas* soon penetrated the interior in search of Indian slaves and precious minerals, agr. frontier development did not also take place. With the growth of early mining centers (especially OURO PRÊTO, São João del Rei, Diamantina), Rio de Janeiro became the chief outlet for shipments to Portugal, and in 1763 supplanted Bahia (now Salvador) as ⊙. Early attempts at achieving independence (notably in Minas Gerais under the leadership of Tiradentes) failed, but with the Napoleonic invasion of Portugal, its King John VI, fled (1807–8) to Brazil, and Rio de Janeiro became (1808) ⊙ Portuguese Empire. When John returned to Portugal, his son Pedro remained behind and in 1822 became emperor of Brazil, having uttered the "cry" of independence on the banks of the Ipiranga (or Ypiranga) outside of São Paulo. In 1831, Pedro I was forced to abdicate in favor of his son Pedro II, the dashing and popular monarch who during his long reign laid the foundations of modern Brazil. In his ambition for territorial expansion he involved the country in a war against Argentina's dictator Juan Manuel de Rosas, and again in the War of the Triple Alliance against Paraguay. Of greater importance to Brazil, however, was the beginning (in mid-19th cent.) of large-scale European immigration to supplant slave labor (slave trade was abolished 1850, complete abolition of slavery was achieved 1888) and work on the expanding coffee plantations of São Paulo. While the NE declined, the S and SE became the heart of economic development. The empire was overthrown in 1889 in a bloodless revolution, and Deodoro da Fonseca became 1st president of the federal republic. Unrest continued, however, in the form of clashes bet. states and the federal army. The expanding coffee market and the short-lived wild rubber boom brought great wealth to Brazil around 1900 (when Acre territory was acquired from Bolivia), but the danger of dependence on one or two export products was brought home when rubber plantations developed in the Far East. In 1917 Brazil joined the Allies in First World War, shared in peace settlement, but withdrew (1926) from the League of Nations. The flood of immigration reached its crest in early 1920s, and coffee once more boomed before the world-wide economic collapse. A revolution (1930) placed Getulio Vargas in power, and 15 years of benevolent dictatorial rule followed. Brazil once again prospered during the Second World War, supplying the U.S. with strategic minerals and raw materials. It joined the Allies in 1942; during the war, most of the frontier areas became federal territories (for purposes of defense), while elsewhere assimilation of immigrant communities was speeded. Iguaçu and Ponta Pora federal territories were dissolved in 1946. For further details see articles on states, territories, cities, towns, and physical features.

Brazil (brůzĭl'), city (pop. 8,434), ⊙ Clay co., W Ind., on small Birch Creek and 16 mi. ENE of Terre Haute; railroad center in agr. area (livestock, grain); mfg. (floor wax, sewer pipes, brick, tile, cigars, roofing, building blocks). Clay pits, bituminous-coal mines.

Brazil Current, warm ocean current of South Atlantic Ocean, a branch of South Equatorial Current, flowing S along E coast of South America; meets cold Falkland Current at c.30°S.

Brazo de Loba (brä'sō dā lō'bä), left arm of Magdalena R., Bolívar dept., N Colombia; with the Brazo Seco de Mompós, it encloses large Margarita Isl. It is c.100 mi. long from El Banco (SE) to point 12 mi. N of Magangué. Receives San Jorge and Cauca rivers. Navigable, with main inland port at Magangué.

Brazópolis (bräzō'pōōlēs), city (pop. 3,175), SW Minas Gerais, Brazil, on N slope of the Serra da Mantiqueira, near São Paulo border, 10 mi. WSW of Itajubá; sugar, coffee, cereals.

Brazoria (brůzôr'ēů), county (□ 1,441; pop. 46,549), S Texas; ⊙ Angleton. On Gulf of Mexico; drained by Brazos and San Bernard rivers; Gulf Intracoastal Waterway passes along coast; Freeport (center of BRAZOSPORT industrial area) is deepwater port (ships sulphur, chemicals). Large oil, sulphur, natural gas, salt production; magnesium extracted from sea water; extensive chemical industry. Agr. (rice, wheat, truck, fruit; also corn, cotton); livestock raising, dairying. Fishing, bathing on coast. Formed 1836.

Brazoria, town (pop. 776), Brazoria co., S Texas, near Brazos R., c.50 mi. SSW of Houston, in agr. area. Original town (Old Brazoria, c.½ mi. away), founded in 1820s, was a port for Austin's colony, later a cotton center; it was abandoned when town moved to site on railroad.

Brazos (bră'zůs), county (□ 583; pop. 38,390), E central Texas; ⊙ Bryan. Bounded E by Navasota R., W and SW by Brazos R. Rich agr. area (cotton, corn, grain, alfalfa, peanuts, fruit, truck); extensive dairying, livestock ranching (cattle, poultry, hogs, goats, sheep). Fuller's earth mining. Mfg., processing at Bryan. Formed 1841.

Brazo Seco de Mompós (brä'zō sā'kō dā mōmpōs'), right arm of Magdalena R. on Bolívar-Magdalena dept. border, N Colombia; with the Brazo de Loba, it encloses large Margarita Isl. It is c.75 mi. long from El Banco to a point 12 mi. N of Magangué. Mompós is on it.

Brazos Island (bră'zůs), extreme S Texas, 3 mi. SE of Port Isabel; a barrier beach c. 4 mi. long, bet. Laguna Madre and Gulf of Mexico; bridged to mainland. Here is Del Mar (resort), sometimes called Boca Chica (bō'kŭ chē'kŭ) after beach region (bathing, fishing) of which isl. is a part, extending c.8 mi. S from Brazos Santiago Pass to mouth of the Rio Grande. In Mexican War, Gen. Zachary Taylor established a supply base at port of Brazos Santiago (since destroyed) on Brazos Isl.

Brazosport (bră'zůs-pôrt"), Brazoria co., S Texas, industrial area (pop. c.25,000) at mouth of Brazos R. of Gulf of Mexico, on Gulf Intracoastal Waterway; centered on FREEPORT (deepwater port), it also includes VELASCO, LAKE JACKSON, CLUTE, and other communities. Sulphur production, processing, shipping; chemical mfg. (especially extraction of magnesium and bromine from sea water.)

Brazos River, Texas, formed in Stonewall co. by its Double Mtn. and Salt forks, flows generally SE across state, past Waco, to Gulf of Mexico at Freeport; total length more than 800 mi.; drains □ 44,500. Clear Fork (c.220 mi. long) enters from S in Young co. Salt Fork (c.100 mi. long) heads in intermittent streams on edge of Llano Estacado SW of Lubbock, flows generally E; Double Mtn. Fork rises in intermittent streams in E N.Mex. and Bailey co., NW Texas, flows c.270 mi. SE and NE. River and tributaries feed many municipal reservoirs. POSSUM KINGDOM DAM is chief flood-control, power, irrigation project. WHITNEY DAM was begun 1946.

Brazos Santiago Pass (bră'zůs săntēä'gō), extreme S Texas, channel connecting Gulf of Mexico and Laguna Madre; passes bet. Padre and Brazos isls., 3 mi. E of Port Isabel; its deepwater channel connects with Gulf Intracoastal Waterway near Port Isabel and continues W through land cut to port of Brownsville.

Brazza, island, Yugoslavia: see BRAC ISLAND.

Brazzaville (bră'zůvĭl, Fr. bräzävēl'), city (1950 pop. 83,400), ⊙ Fr. Equatorial Africa, SE Middle Congo territory, on right bank of Stanley Pool opposite Leopoldville (Belgian Congo) and Bamu isl., 240 mi. ENE of Pointe-Noire; 4°15'S 15°20'E. Largest town of Fr. Equatorial Africa, commercial center and river port. Terminus of railroad from Pointe-Noire and head of navigation on Congo-Ubangi river system. Railroad repair shops, shipyards, foundries. Mfg. of shoes, soap, matches, cigarettes, furniture, bricks, tiles, food products; gold smelting. Near by are experimental plantations and stock farms, and hydroelectric power station. Has school for native administrators, technical school for foremen, 2 teachers' colleges, Pasteur Institute (since 1908), large hosp., military camp, R.C. and Protestant missions. Seat of vicar apostolic of Middle Congo. Known for its powerful short-wave radio station. Municipal airport is at Maya-Maya, just NNE. Brazzaville was long a straggling, neglected settlement which relied for most of its supplies and services on rival Leopoldville. Its strategic location and its radio station brought it prominence in Second World War (when it was hq. of Free French forces in Africa), and in 1948 its development was accelerated. Was founded in 1880 by Savorgnan de Brazza and thus became the base for Fr. claims in lower Congo area.

Brcko or **Brchko** (both: bůrch'kô), Serbo-Croatian *Brčko*, town (pop. 9,305), NE Bosnia, Yugoslavia, on Sava R. (Croatia border), on railroad and 23 mi. N of Tuzla; trade center (plums); canning. Brown-coal deposits near by.

Brda (bůr'dä), E section of MONTENEGRO, Yugoslavia, in Dinaric Alps; separated from Montenegro proper by valley of Zeta R. Large forests, rich pastures; sheep and goat raising. Under Turkish rule until 1878.

Brda River (bůrdä'), Ger. *Brahe* (brä'ů), NW Poland, rises 4 mi. ENE of Miastko, flows S and E through several lakes, S past Koronowo, and E past Bydgoszcz (here canalized) to Vistula R. 5 mi. E of Bydgoszcz; 121 mi. long. Navigable bet. Bydgoszcz and the Vistula; linked with Notec R. (W) via Bydgoszcz Canal.

Brdy (bůr'dĭ), mountain range, SW central Bohemia, Czechoslovakia, extending c.60 mi. NE-SW, bet. Klatovy and S outskirts of Prague; rises to 2,827 ft. in Tok mtn. Extensively forested; formerly had great mineral resources; silver and lead mining is still carried on in Pribram dist. Industrial basin of Pilsen, with metallurgical industry and iron and coal deposits, lies below its W foothills.

Brea (brā'ů), city (pop. 3,208), Orange co., S Calif., 10 mi. N of Anaheim; oil-field center; citrus fruit. Inc. 1917.

Brea, Cordón de la (kōrdōn' dā lä brā'ä), Andean range in W La Rioja prov., Argentina, near Chile border, E of Cerro del Potro; extends c.40 mi. NNE-SSW; rises to over 14,000 ft.

Brea, La, in Latin America: see LA BREA.

Breadalbane (brĕdôl'bůn), barren mountainous district of the Grampians, NW Perthshire, Scotland, extending bet. Strathearn (S) and Loch Rannoch (N); c.35 mi. long, 30 mi. wide. Chief town, Aberfeldy.

Brea de Aragón (brā'ä dhā ärägōn'), town (pop. 1,832), Saragossa prov., NE Spain, 12 mi. NNE of Calatayud; shoe mfg., tanning; olive oil, cereals, sheep.

Brea de Tajo (tä'hō), town (pop. 994), Madrid prov., central Spain, 33 mi. ESE of Madrid; olives, cereals, grapes, livestock. Vegetable-oil extracting, wine making.

Bread Loaf, village in RIPTON town, Addison co., W central Vt., 10 mi. ESE of Middlebury. Here is **Bread Loaf Mountain** (3,823 ft.), in forest area belonging to Middlebury Col., which here holds summer session in writing and languages.

Breage (brĕg), town and parish (pop. 2,202), W Cornwall, England, 3 mi. W of Helston; agr. market in dairying region. Has 15th-cent. church.

Breaksea Sound, inlet of Tasman Sea, Fiordland Natl. Park, SW S.Isl., New Zealand; 20 mi. long, 2 mi wide; contains several islets.

Breaksea Spit, dangerous shoal in Pacific Ocean off SE coast of Queensland, Australia; extends 17 mi. NW from Sandy Cape on Fraser Isl.

Breaks of Sandy, Ky. and Va.: see RUSSELL FORK.

Brea Pozo (brā'ä pō'sō), village (pop. estimate 500), central Santiago del Estero prov., Argentina, on railroad and 17 mi. ENE of Loreto; wheat, alfalfa; lumbering. Formerly called Kilómetro 485.

Breasta (brēä'stä), village (pop. 837), Dolj prov., S Rumania, near Jiu R., 6 mi. W of Craiova; agr. center; known for rug weaving.

Breathitt (brĕ'thĭt), county (□ 494; pop. 19,964), E central Ky., in the Cumberlands; ⊙ Jackson. Drained by North and Middle forks of Kentucky R., small Troublesome Creek, and several other creeks. Mtn. agr. area (poultry, cattle, apples, sweet and Irish potatoes, tobacco, soybeans for feed, corn, truck); bituminous-coal mines, timber. Has been called "Bloody Breathitt" because of mtn. feuds which occurred here. Formed 1839.

Bréauté (brāōtā'), village (pop. 469), Seine-Inférieure dept., N France, 16 mi. NE of Le Havre. Rail junction (spur to Fécamp) at Bréauté-Beuzeville (2 mi. SE).

Breaux Bridge (brō' brĭj), town (pop. 2,492), St. Martin parish, S central La., 45 mi. WSW of Baton Rouge, and on navigable Bayou Teche, in agr. area (sugar cane, cotton, vegetables). Sugar, rice, and lumber milling; cotton ginning; mfg. of sugar-cane machinery, trailers, wagons. Inc. 1871. A state park is near by.

Brebach (brā'bäkh), town (pop. 24,125), S Saar, on Saar R. and 2.5 mi. ESE of Saarbrücken; steel industry; coke ovens; machinery mfg., woodworking.

Brebes (brĕ'bĕs), town (pop. 13,707), central Java, Indonesia, near Java Sea, 35 mi. ESE of Cheribon; trade center for agr. area (rice, sugar, peanuts).

Brécey (brāsā'), village (pop. 815), Manche dept., NW France, on the Sée and 9 mi. ENE of Avranches; cider distilling, sawmilling.

Brèche-de-Roland (brĕsh'-dū-rôlā'), narrow defile of central Pyrenees, bet. France and Spain, leading into Cirque de GAVARNIE, 21 mi. S of Argelès-Gazost; alt. 9,200 ft. According to legend Roland opened the breach with his sword.

Brechin (brēkh'ĭn), burgh (1931 pop. 6,840; 1951 census 7,264), E central Angus, Scotland, on South Esk R. and 11 mi. NE of Forfar; agr. market, with jute, linen, and paper mills, and whisky distilleries. Cathedral, now parish church, partly dates from its foundation by David I in 1150 and has 10th- or 11th-cent. round tower. Brechin Castle, seat of Maule family, was taken (1303) by Edward I after 3-week siege.

Brechou (brūkōō'), Fr. *Brecqhou* (brĕkōō'), island (74 acres), one of the Channel Isls., just off W coast of Sark.

Brecht (brĕkht), town (pop. 5,657), Antwerp prov., N Belgium, near Antwerp-Turnhout Canal, 14 mi. NE of Antwerp; mfg. (bricks, tiles); agr. market. Has 15th-cent. Gothic church.

Breckenridge. **1** Town (pop. 296), ⊙ Summit co., central Colo., on Blue R., just S of Gore Range, and 60 mi. WSW of Denver; alt. 9,579 ft. Gold, silver mines; livestock. Once a trade center, with pop. of c.8,000, for group of gold-mining camps. Quandary Peak and Mt. Lincoln are in the vicinity. **2** Village (pop. 985), Gratiot co., central Mich., 27 mi. W of Saginaw, in farm area (livestock, dairy products, grain, beans, sugar beets, seed); grain elevator, flour mill. **3** City (pop. 3,623), ⊙ Wilkin co., W Minn., just E of Wahpeton, N.Dak., at point where Otter Tail and Bois de Sioux rivers join to form Red River of the North, 25 mi. W of Fergus Falls. Rail center, trade and shipping point for agr. area (grain, livestock, potatoes, poultry); food processing (dairy and poultry products). Laid out 1857, inc. 1908. **4** City (pop. 617), Caldwell co., NW Mo., 13 mi. W of Chillicothe; agr.; lumber mill, coal mines. **5** Town (pop. 67), Garfield co., N Okla., 8 mi. ENE of Enid, in agr. area. **6** City (pop. 6,610), ⊙ Stephens co., N central Texas, c.90 mi. W of Fort Worth and on small Gonzales Creek; trade, shipping center for cattle, agr., oil-producing area; mfg. (gasoline, oil-well equipment, carbon black, farm tools, chemicals, machine-shop products). Settled 1876, inc. 1919.

Breckenridge Hills, town (pop. 4,063), St. Louis co., E Mo., just W of St. Louis.

Breckerfeld (brĕ'kŭrfĕlt"), town (pop. 5,578), in former Prussian prov. of Westphalia, W Germany, after 1945 in North Rhine-Westphalia, in the Ruhr, 12 mi. E of Wuppertal; textile mfg.

Breckinridge, county (□ 566; pop. 15,528), NW Ky.; ⊙ Hardinsburg. Bounded NW by the Ohio (Ind. line), S by Rough R.; drained by South Fork Panther Creek and small Sinking Creek. Rolling agr. area (burley tobacco, corn, wheat, hay, livestock, cotton); timber tracts, limestone quarries, asphalt deposits; some mfg. (especially quilted articles, textiles) at Hardinsburg and Cloverport. Formed 1799.

Breckinridge, Camp, Ky.: see MORGANFIELD.

Brecknock or **Brecknockshire** (brĕk'nŏk, –shĭr), county (□ 733.2; 1931 pop. 57,775; 1951 census 56,484), SE Wales; ⊙ Brecknock. Bounded by Carmarthen and Cardigan (W), Radnor (N), Hereford (E), Monmouth (SE), and Glamorgan (S). Drained by Usk, Wye, and Loughor rivers. Mountainous country, crossed by ranges of Mynydd Eppynt (N), Black Mtn., and Brecon Beacons (S; rise to 2,906 ft.). Industries include farming, grazing, coal mining, woolen milling, leather and shoe mfg., metalworking, limestone quarrying. Besides Brecknock, other towns are Brynmawr, Builth Wells, Hay, Llanwrtyd. Also called Brecon or Breconshire.

Brecknock or **Brecon** (brĕ'kŭn), Welsh *Aberhonddu* (ăbĕrhôn'dhē), municipal borough (1931 pop. 5,332; 1951 census 6,466), ⊙ Brecknockshire, Wales, in center of co., amid hills on Usk R. at mouth of Honddu R., and 35 mi. NNW of Cardiff; agr. market with woolen and flannel mills. Has remains of 11th-cent. castle. Priory Church of St. John, belonging to former 11th-cent. Benedictine priory, became cathedral in 1923. Just SW is suburb of Llanfaes (lănvīs'), site of Christ's Col., a public school founded 1541 by Henry VIII.

Brecknock Beacons, Wales: see BRECON BEACONS.

Brecknock Peninsula, W part of main isl. of Tierra del Fuego, Chile, 90 mi. S of Punta Arenas; c.40 mi. long. Irregular, with numerous sounds. Uninhabited.

Brecknockshire, Wales: see BRECKNOCK, county.

Brecknock Van, Welsh *Banau Brycheiniog* (bä'nī brĭkh-īn'yôg), mountain (2,632 ft.), W Brecknock, Wales, 9 mi. SSE of Llandovery. Just W is peak of CARMARTHEN VAN.

Brecksville, village (pop. 2,664), Cuyahoga co., N Ohio, 12 mi. SSE of downtown Cleveland. Settled c.1811, inc. 1921.

Breclav (bûrzhĕ'tsläf), Czech *Břeclav*, Ger. *Lundenburg* (lōōn'dŭnbōōrk), town (10,371), S Moravia, Czechoslovakia, on Dyje R. and 33 mi. SSE of Brno; rail junction; agr. center; large sugar and flour mills; mfg. of malt, agr. machinery, wood products, ceramics. Has milling-trade school, 14th-cent. castle. Known since 11th cent.

Brecon, city, Wales: see BRECKNOCK.

Brecon Beacons (brĕ'kŭn) or **Brecknock Beacons,** range, central Brecknock, Wales, at E end of BLACK MOUNTAIN, extending 2 mi. E-W, 5 mi. SW of Brecknock; includes peaks of Corn Du (kôrn dē') (2,863 ft.) and Pen-y Fan (pĕn-ū-văn') (2,906 ft.).

Brecqhou, Channel Isls.: see BRECHOU.

Breda (brādä'), town (pop. 81,873; commune pop. 85,294), North Brabant prov., SW Netherlands, on Mark R. and 27 mi. SSE of Rotterdam; machine shops, foundries; preserves, canned goods; mfg. of artificial silk, machine tools, weaving machinery, leather, shoes, industrial belting, paints, lacquers; beet-sugar refining; egg, vegetable, and fruit market. Has 13th-cent. Gothic church (*Groote Kerk*). Royal military acad.; see of R.C. bishop. Site (1566) of Compromise of Breda, a union of Dutch nobles against their Spanish rulers. Captured (1581) by Spaniards; in Dutch hands (1590–1625); retaken by Spain and finally taken (1637) by Prince Frederick Henry. Residence of English King Charles II who here (1660) issued Declaration of Breda, announcing terms on which he would ascend English throne. The Peace of Breda (1667) awarded colonies of New York and New Jersey to the English. Breda captured by French under Dumouriez (1793) and under Pichegru (1795); held until 1813.

Breda or **San Salvador de Breda** (sän' sälvädhōr' dhā brā'dhä), town (pop. 1,193), Gerona prov., NE Spain, 20 mi. SW of Gerona; cattle raising.

Breda (brē'dū), town (pop. 506), Carroll co., W central Iowa, 10 mi. NNW of Carroll; dairy products, feed.

Bréda River (brādä'), Isère dept., SE France, rises in the Belledonne range, flows N, then W, in narrow Alpine gorge, past Allevard, to the Isère below Pontcharra; 20 mi. long. Hydroelectric plants and electrometallurgical works.

Bredasdorp (brā'däsdôrp"), town (pop. 3,375), SW Cape Prov., U. of So. Afr., 100 mi. ESE of Cape Town; southernmost town of Africa. Center of sheep-raising, wool-producing, grain-growing region; limestone quarrying, lime mfg. Airfield. Bredasdorp Natl. Park (□ 17), 17 mi. S, was established 1931; reserve for bontebok, species threatened with extinction.

Bredbury and Romiley (brĕd'bŭrē, rŏ'mĭlē), urban district (1931 pop. 10,876; 1951 census 17,810), NE Cheshire, England. Includes town of Bredbury, 3 mi. NE of Stockport, with coal mining, cotton spinning, steel mfg.; and town of Romiley, 3 mi. E of Stockport, with cotton industry and electrical engineering.

Bredbyn (brād'bün"), village (pop. 421), Västernorrland co., NE Sweden, on 5-mi.-long Anund L., Swedish *Anundsjö* (ä'nŭnd-shû"), 20 mi. NW of Ornskoldsvik; shoe mfg., sawmilling.

Bredenborn (brā'dŭnbôrn"), town (pop. 1,529), in former Prussian prov. of Westphalia, NW Germany, after 1945 in North Rhine-Westphalia, 8 mi. WNW of Höxter; forestry.

Bredenbury, agr. town (pop. 365), SE Sask., near Man. border, 26 mi. SE of Yorkton.

Bredene (brā'dŭnŭ), town (pop. 7,401), West Flanders prov., NW Belgium, near North Sea, E suburb of Ostend. Formerly spelled Breedene.

Bredeney (brā'dŭnī), residential district (since 1915) of Essen, W Germany, near the Ruhr, 3 mi. SSW of city center.

Bredevoort or **Breedevoort** (both: brā'dŭvōrt), town (pop. 1,425), Gelderland prov., E Netherlands, 4 mi. WSW of Winterswijk; weaving and dyeing center; also mfg. of shoes, strawboard; chicory growing.

Bredfield, agr. village and parish (pop. 372), SE Suffolk, England, 2 mi. N of Woodbridge. Edward Fitzgerald b. here.

Bredfond, Norway: see BREIDFONN.

Bredstedt (brĕt'shtĕt"), town (pop. 5,530), in Schleswig-Holstein, NW Germany, near the North Sea, 10 mi. N of Husum; a center of North Friesland, with grain and cattle market. Tobacco products. Agr. school. First mentioned 1231. Developed in 18th cent. in connection with reclamation of coastal polders. Chartered 1910.

Bredvads River, Denmark: see GUDEN RIVER.

Bredy (bryĕ'dē), town (1939 pop. over 2,000), S Chelyabinsk oblast, Russian SFSR, on left tributary of Tobol R., on railroad and 45 mi. SSW of Kartaly; anthracite mining; metalworking. Gold mining along railroad (N); gold placers (E); chromite deposits (S).

Bree (brā), town (pop. 5,879), Limburg prov., NE Belgium, near the Zuid-Willemsvaart, 9 mi. WNW of Maaseik; mfg. (cigars, clay pipes). Has 15th-cent. Gothic church.

Breedene, Belgium: see BREDENE.

Breede River (brē'dū), SW Cape Prov., U. of So. Afr., rises NNW of Worcester, flows 200 mi. SE, past Ceres, Robertson, and Bonnievale, to the Indian Ocean 35 mi. SE of Swellendam.

Breedevoort, Netherlands: see BREDEVOORT.

Breed's Hill, Mass.: see CHARLESTOWN.

Breedsville, village (pop. 239), Van Buren co., SW Mich., on Black R. and 25 mi. W of Kalamazoo.

Breendonk or **Breendonck** (brān'dŏngk), town (pop. 2,779), Antwerp prov., N central Belgium, 2 mi. SW of Willebroek; agr. market. In Second World War, site of infamous Ger. concentration camp.

Breese (brēz), city (pop. 2,181), Clinton co., SW Ill., 34 mi. E of East St. Louis, in agr. and bituminous-coal-mining area; corn, wheat, fruit, poultry, livestock, dairy products; makes harvest hats. Inc. 1905.

Brefet (brĕ'fĕt), village (pop. 180), Western Div., Gambia, on left bank of Gambia R. and 20 mi. SE of Bathurst; coconuts, cassava, corn. It is part of Gambia colony but is administered under the protectorate.

Bregaglia (brāgä'lyä), circle (pop. 1,564), Maloja dist., Grisons canton, SE Switzerland. Val Bregaglia, Ger. *Bergell*, valley traversed by Mera R., extends into Italy. Protestant and Italian-speaking pop.

Bregalnica River or **Bregalnitsa River** (both: brĕgäl'nĭtsä), Macedonia, Yugoslavia, rises at foot of the Ilov-vrakh on Bulg. border, 9 mi. E of Berovo; flows N past Berovo and Carevo Selo, and SW past Stip, to Vardar R. 11 mi. SSE of Titov Veles; 130 mi. long. Receives Zletovo R. Its valley, through which runs Titov Veles–Kocane RR produces rice (near Kocane), poppies and plums (upper valley).

Breganze (brĕgän'tsĕ), village (pop. 1,262), Vicenza prov., Veneto, N Italy, near Astico R., 11 mi. N of Vicenza; mfg. (agr. machinery, wine presses, pumps, silk textiles), wine making.

Bregava River (brĕ'gävä), SW Herzegovina, Yugoslavia, rises 4 mi. E of Stolac, flows c.20 mi. W, past Stolac, to Neretva R. SE of Capljina.

Bregenz (brā'gĕnts), anc. *Brigantium*, city (pop. 20,720), ⊙ Vorarlberg, W Austria, harbor on E shore of L. of Constance, 80 mi. WNW of Innsbruck; rail and tourist center with winter and summer sports. Large hydroelectric plant. Mfg. (cotton, silk, electrical supplies, chemicals, machines, shoes, canned goods), ironworks, sugar refineries. Regional mus. with Celtic and Roman collections. Suspension railway to Mt. Pfänder (3,490 ft.), with excellent view.

Bregenzer Ache (brā'gĕntsŭr ä'khū) or **Ache,** river, W Austria, rises near Schröcken, flows c.35 mi. W, through the Bregenzerwald, to L. of Constance 2 mi. W of Bregenz. Hydroelectric works at Andelsbuch.

Bregenzerwald (brā'gĕntsŭrvält), forested mountain range in W Austria, part of Allgäu Alps, rising to 7,314 ft.; traversed by river Bregenzer Ache. Pastures, dairy farming; tourist trade.

Brege River, Germany: see BREG RIVER.

Bregovo, Bulgaria: see BRYAGOVO.

Breg River (brāk) or **Brege River** (brā'gū), right headstream of the Danube, S Baden, Germany, rises in the Black Forest 4 mi. NNW of Furtwangen, flows 25 mi. SE, joining BRIGACH RIVER just below Donaueschingen to form the Danube.

Bréhal (brāäl'), village (pop. 736), Manche dept., NW France, near English Channel, 11 mi. SSW of Coutances.

Bréhat (brāä'), island (pop. 855) in English Channel, off Côtes-du-Nord dept., W France, 5 mi. NNE of Paimpol; 2 mi. long, 1 mi. wide; difficult of access amidst rocky shoals. Produces early potatoes; lobster fishing. Village of Bréhat (pop. 154), near center of isl., attracts tourists.

Brehna (brā'nä), town (pop. 4,102), in former Prussian Saxony prov., central Germany, after 1945 in Saxony-Anhalt, 6 mi. SW of Bitterfeld, in lignite-mining region.

Breich (brēkh), village in West Calder parish, SW Midlothian, Scotland; shale-oil mining.

Breidfonn (brād'fôn, brā'fôn), glacier in Hordaland co., SW Norway, at E extremity of the Haukelifjell, 6 mi. NNE of Nesflaten. Rising over 4,000 ft., it dominates the Brattlandsdal. Sometimes spelled Breifonn. Formerly Bredfond.

Breidi Fjord or **Breida Fjord,** Icelandic *Breiðifjörður* (brā'dhĕfyûr"dhür) or *Breiðafjörður* (brā'dhä–), inlet (80 mi. long, 40 mi. wide at mouth) of Denmark Strait, W Iceland, bet. Vestfjarda (N) and Snaefellsnes (S) peninsulas; 65°15'N 23°15'W. Gils Fjord, Icelandic *Gilsfjörður*, and Hvamm Fjord, Icelandic *Hvammsjörður*, are E arms. Fjord contains numerous islets, among them Flatey. Chief fishing ports: Sandur, Olafsvik, Stykkisholmur. Also spelled Breidhi Fjord or Breidha Fjord.

Breifonn, Norway: see BREIDFONN.

Breil-sur-Roya (brā-sür-rwäyä'), Ital. *Breglio*, village (pop. 1,223), Alpes-Maritimes dept., SE France, in Maritime Alps, on Roya R. and 21 mi. NE of Nice, on Nice-Turin road and railroad; custom house near Ital. border (road to Ventimiglia); flour milling, olive oil processing. Dairy and hydroelectric plant near-by. Territories of Tende and La Brigue (acquired in Fr.-Ital. treaty of 1947) have temporarily come under administration of Breil-sur-Roya.

Breisach (brī'zäkh), town (pop. 2,093), S Baden, Germany, on right bank of the Rhine (rail bridge), opposite NEUF-BRISACH (France), and 12 mi. WNW of Freiburg; sparkling-wine and paper mfg. Fortified since Roman times. Came to Hapsburgs shortly after it was created (1275) imperial city. Its location in strategic position resulted in repeated capture by France. Passed to Baden in 1805; fortifications razed shortly thereafter. Second World War destruction (about 50%) includes heavy damage of noted Romanesque-Gothic church of St. Stephen. Sometimes called Altbreisach or Alt-Breisach (ält'brī'zäkh).

Breisgau (brīs'gou), region, S Baden, Germany, extends S of the Elz to Swiss border, includes the Rhine plain and W slopes of Black Forest; wine and fruit. Originally belonging to house of Zähringen, it came to the Hapsburgs in 1368. Ceded to Baden in 1805. Chief city: Freiburg.

Breitenau (brī'tūnou), town (pop. 2,274), Styria, SE central Austria, 16 mi. E of Leoben; processes magnesite.

Breitenbach, Czechoslovakia: see POTUCKY.

Breitenbrunn (brī'tünbrōōn"), village (pop. 2,035), Upper Palatinate, central Bavaria, Germany, 15 mi. SSE of Neumarkt; brewing, flour and lumber milling. Has early-18th-cent. church.

Breitenfeld (brī'tünfĕlt"), district (since 1913) of Lindenthal, E central Germany, NW of Leipzig. During Thirty Years War, scene of victory in 1631 of Gustavus Adolphus over Imperials under Tilly and Pappenheim, and in 1642 of Swedes under Torstensson over Imperials commanded by Piccolomini.

Breitenlee (brī'tünlā), town (pop. 2,499), after 1938 in Grossenzersdorf dist. of Vienna, Austria, 6 mi. ENE of city center; truck farming (vegetables, poultry).

Breitfurt (brīt'fōort), village (pop. 1,057), SE Saar, near Ger. border, on Blies R. and 7 mi. WSW of Zweibrücken; stock, grain; flour milling.

Breithorn (brīt'hôrn). **1** Peak (12,419 ft.) in Bernese Alps, S central Switzerland, 6 mi. S of Mürren. **2** Peak (Lötschentaler Breithorn) (12,428 ft.) in Bernese Alps, S Switzerland, 9 mi. N of Visp. **3** Peak (13,684 ft.) in Pennine Alps, on Swiss-Ital. border S of Zermatt, bet. Matterhorn and Monte Rosa.

Breitingen, Germany: see REGIS-BREITINGEN.

Breitovo or **Breytovo** (brā'tùvŭ), village (1926 pop. 597), NW Yaroslavl oblast, Russian SFSR, on Rybinsk Reservoir, 40 mi. NW of Shcherbakov; boatbuilding, metalworking.

Breitungen or **Breitungen an der Werra** (brī'tōōng-ùn än dĕr vĕ'rä), commune (pop. 4,108), Thuringia, central Germany, at W foot of Thuringian Forest, on the Werra and 6 mi. NW of Schmalkalden; tobacco growing. Power station. Has 12th-cent. former Benedictine monastery, converted into palace in 15th cent. Includes villages of Herrenbreitungen, Altenbreitungen, Frauenbreitungen.

Brejinho das Ametistas (brĭzhē'nyōō däs ämĭtē'stùs), town (pop. 396), S central Bahia, Brazil, 15 mi. SW of Caetité; amethysts found here.

Brejo (brā'zhōō), city (pop. 2,911), NE Maranhão, Brazil, near left bank of Parnaíba R. (Piauí border), 80 mi. SW of Parnaíba; commercial center shipping cotton, cereals, carnauba wax, sugar, babassu nuts, and cattle. Roads to Itapecuru Mirim and to Repartição (5 mi. E); airport and river landing on the Parnaíba.

Brejo da Madre de Deus (dä mä'drĭ dĭ dā'ōōs), city (pop. 1,554), E Pernambuco, NE Brazil, 30 mi. WNW of Caruaru; cotton, corn, coffee. Called Madre de Deus, 1939–48.

Brejo do Cruz (dōō krōōs'), city (pop. 784), W Paraíba, NE Brazil, 45 mi. NNW of Patos; cotton, sugar, beans.

Brejo Santo (sän'tōō), city (pop. 1,754), SE Ceará, Brazil, near Pernambuco and Paraíba borders, 40 mi. SE of Crato; sugar, cotton. On route of projected Fortaleza-Salvador RR. Formerly called Brejo dos Santos.

Brekhov Islands (bryĭkhôf'), in NW Krasnoyarsk Territory, Russian SFSR, in S section of Yenisei Bay; separated by arms of Yenisei R. mouth; tundra; fishing.

Brelsford, Lake, Texas: see LEON RIVER.

Brelsford Caves, Ky.: see CADIZ.

Bremanger or **Bremangerland** (brä'mäng-ùrlän"), island (□ 59; pop. 1,836) in North Sea, Sogn og Fjordane co., W Norway, at entrance to Nord Fjord, separated from mainland by narrow strait, 13 mi. N of Floro; 15 mi. long, 10 mi. wide. At E shore is 2,800-ft.-high Hornelen rock, which plunges vertically to sea. Isl. is in Bremanger canton (pop. 3,148), whose industrial village is SVELGEN, on the mainland.

Bremberg (brĕm'bĕrk) or **Zarek** (zhä'rĕk), Pol. *Żarek*, village in Lower Silesia, after 1945 in Wroclaw prov., SW Poland, near the Katzbach, 9 mi. S of Liegnitz (Legnica). Scene (Aug., 1813) of battle of the Katzbach; here Prussians under Blücher defeated French under Macdonald.

Brembio (brĕm'byô), village (pop. 2,014), Milano prov., Lombardy, N Italy, 7 mi. SSE of Lodi; fertilizer factory.

Brembo River (brĕm'bô), Lombardy, N Italy, rises in Bergamasque Alps in 2 headstreams joining 7 mi. N of San Pellegrino, flows 45 mi. S to Adda R. 10 mi. SW of Bergamo. Used for hydroelectric power in upper course.

Bremen (brā'mùn, brĕ'–, Ger. brā'mùn), Ger. officially *Freie Hansestadt Bremen* (frī'ù hän'zù-shtät") [=free Hansa city of Bremen], state (□ 156; 1946 pop. 486,539; 1950 pop. 568,335), N Germany. It consists of 2 separate cities, Bremen and BREMERHAVEN—33 mi. apart, along the lower Weser—which form enclaves in what was the prov. of Hanover and after 1945 became the state of Lower Saxony. **Bremen** (□ 125; 1939 pop. 424,137; 1946 pop. 386,266; 1950 pop. 455,999), 60 mi. SW of Hamburg, is on the Weser 40 mi. SSE of its mouth on the North Sea; 53°5'N 8°43'E. It is Germany's 2d largest port, whose trade and passenger traffic has for a century been oriented primarily towards the U.S. Leading imports: cotton, wool, jute, tobacco, grain, rice, coffee, timber, petroleum, and petroleum products; exports coal, fertilizer, scrap metal, building materials. Industrial center, known for its tobacco factories (cigars, cigarettes, pipe and chewing tobacco); marine equipment, cars, trucks, machinery, chemicals, silverware; wool-carding, and jute-spinning and -weaving mills. Also food processing (grain, oil, and rice milling; coffee roasting, fish canning, brewing); petroleum refining. In the Old Town, on right bank of the Weser (3 bridges), are Romanesque-Gothic St. Petri cathedral; noted Gothic town hall with Renaissance façade, faced by the Roland statue (1404), landmark of Bremen. Heavy Second World War destruction (about 50%) included numerous medieval bldgs. (weighhouse, corn house, guildhall). Two noted churches, the Liebfrauenkirche (13th cent.) and the Johanniskirche (14th cent.), were damaged. Harbor installations are concentrated in NW, in basins off the Weser. Suburbs surround Old Town in large semicircle; the New Town (founded 1627) is on left bank of river. Bremen, Germany's oldest port city, was created an archbishopric in 845. The archbishops ruled a vast territory bet. Weser and Elbe rivers, and in 11th cent. the archdiocese included all Scandinavia, Iceland, and Greenland. Bremen city, steadily growing in commercial importance, was virtually independent of the archbishops. It became a member of Hanseatic League in 13th cent., was expelled, and later rejoined (1358) as a leading member. Accepted Reformation; was created (1646) free imperial city. At Peace of Westphalia (1648), archbishopric (but not the city) of Bremen passed to Sweden, which ceded it to Hanover in 1719. For a while overshadowed by near-by Hamburg, Bremen city (despite its relatively small hinterland) again became an important continental port in 19th cent. With its outer port of Bremerhaven (founded 1827), it was Europe's leading emigration port; the establishment (1857) of North German Lloyd shipping company greatly furthered overseas trade. Channel of the Weser was enlarged 1883–94; free harbor was opened 1888. As "Republic and Free Hansa City," Bremen was member of German Empire and, after First World War, of Weimar Republic. Until Second World War, when it was one of the hardest-hit targets of Allied bombing, it was one of the world's leading cotton and tobacco entrepôts. Bremerhaven, which in 1939 had been detached from Bremen to become part of the Hanoverian city of Wesermünde, was returned in 1947 with additional area and Bremen became a state in U.S. occupation zone; it joined (1949) the West German govt. formed under the Bonn constitution as the German Federal Republic.

Bremen (brē'mùn). **1** City (pop. 2,299), Haralson co., NW Ga., c.45 mi. W of Atlanta, near Ala. line, in agr. area; clothing mfg. Inc. 1883. **2** Town (pop. 2,664), Marshall co., N Ind., 15 mi. SSE of South Bend; extraction of spearmint and peppermint oil; mfg. of feed, flour, building materials, clothing. **3** Town (pop. 410), Muhlenberg co., W Ky., 16 mi. E of Madisonville, in bituminous-coal-mining, agr. area; lumber. **4** Town (pop. 409), Lincoln co., S Maine, on Muscongus Bay and 21 mi. NE of Bath. Includes village of Medomak. **5** Village (pop. 1,187), Fairfield co., central Ohio, 9 mi. E of Lancaster, and on small Rush Creek, in agr. area; mfg. of glass products, building materials, cheese; lumber milling. Oil wells, molding-sand pits; timber.

Bremer (brē'mùr), county (□ 439; pop. 18,884), NE Iowa; ⊙ Waverly. Rolling prairie agr. area (hogs, cows, poultry, corn, oats) drained by Cedar, Wapsipinicon, and Shell Rock rivers. Limestone quarries, sand and gravel pits. Formed 1851.

Bremerhaven (brā"mùrhä'fùn), constituent city (□ 31; 1946 pop. 99,208; 1950 pop. 112,336) of BREMEN state, N Germany, 33 mi. N of city of Bremen, for which it is the port; 53°33'N 8°35'E. Germany's largest passenger, deep-sea, and coastal fishing port, at head of Weser R. estuary. Has extensive shipyards. Industry is based primarily on fishing (fish processing; mfg. of barrels, cans, cables, nets); also has foundries. Founded (1827) in Hanover by Mayor Johann Schmidt of Bremen as transatlantic port for Bremen, Bremerhaven developed rapidly after 1857 as hq. of the North German Lloyd shipping company. Before First World War it was the continent's chief cotton entrepôt. The municipal history of the town is a little complex. In 1857 the govt. of Hanover founded the rival town of Geestemünde (gā"stùmün'dù) just S of Bremerhaven, and it, too, developed rapidly as a passenger and fishing port. In 1924 Geestemünde and the residential town of Lehe (lā'hù), just NE of Bremerhaven, were combined to form the Hanoverian city of Wesermünde (vā"zùrmün'dù). Wesermünde, in turn, absorbed Bremerhaven in 1939 (when the combined pop. was 112,831), but in 1947 the whole municipality was renamed Bremerhaven and returned to the state of Bremen. During Second World War (destruction of city about 50%), the liner *Bremen* was sunk here.

Bremer River, Australia: see BRISBANE RIVER.

Bremersdorp (brĕ'mùrsdôrp), village, ⊙ Central Dist., central Swaziland, on main E-W road and 19 mi. SE of Mbabane. Until 1902 it was ⊙ Swaziland. Near by is hq. of paramount chief of territory.

Bremerton (brĕ'mùrtùn), port city (pop. 27,678), Kitsap co., W central Wash., on an arm of Puget Sound and 15 mi. W of Seattle. Lumber, dairy products; shipbuilding. Has a jr. col. Pop. trebled in Second World War because of work in great Puget Sound Navy Yard here. Founded 1891, inc. 1901.

Bremervörde (brā"mùrfûr'dù), town (pop. 7,498), in former Prussian prov. of Hanover, NW Germany, after 1945 in Lower Saxony, on the Oste and 15 mi. SW of Stade; rail junction; mfg. of textiles and of leather, paper and wood products; food processing, sawmilling.

Bremgarten (brĕm'gärtùn), town (pop. 3,190), Aargau canton, N Switzerland, on Reuss R. and 9 mi. W of Zurich; silk textiles, clothes, rubber and metal products; woodworking. Has 16th-cent. castle.

Bremnes, canton, Norway: see RUBBESTADNESET.

Bremo Bluff (brē'mō), village, Fluvanna co., central Va., on James R. (bridged) and 25 mi. SSE of Charlottesville; hydroelectric plant; sand, gravel. Slate quarrying near by. "Bremo" estate (just W), with mansion (begun 1815) designed by Thomas Jefferson, attracts tourists.

Bremond (brĭmŏnd'), city (pop. 1,141), Robertson co., E central Texas, c.40 mi. SE of Waco; trade center in cotton, corn, truck area. Inc. 1938.

Bremsnaes, Norway: see BREMSNES.

Bremsnes (brĕms'nās), village and canton (pop. 5,210), More og Romsdal co., SW Norway, on NE tip of Averoy, 4 mi. SW of Kristiansund; fishing; sawmilling. Has agr. school. Mtn. caves attract tourists. Formerly spelled Bremsnaes.

Breña Alta (brā'nyä äl'tä), town (pop. 349), Palma, Canary Isls., 1½ mi. SSW of Santa Cruz de la Palma; cereals, fruit, wine, tobacco.

Breña Baja (brā'nyä bä'hä) or **San José** (sän' hōsā'), village (pop. 78), Palma, Canary Isls., 3 mi. S of Santa Cruz de la Palma; onions, tobacco, sweet potatoes, grapes, wine, livestock.

Breñas, Las, Argentina: see LAS BREÑAS.

Brenchley, England: see PADDOCK WOOD.

Brendon Hills, ridge, W Somerset, England, extends 10 mi. ESE from Exmoor; rises to 1,391 ft. Once noted for iron mines.

Brenes (brā'nĕs), town (pop. 4,333), Seville prov., SW Spain, on the Guadalquivir, on railroad and 12 mi. NNE of Seville; agr. center (grain, oranges, olives). Fisheries.

Brenet, Lac, Switzerland: see JOUX, LAC DE.

Brenets, Lake of (brùnā'), or **Lake of Chaillexon** (shīyĕksō'), natural reservoir on Franco-Swiss border, in the E Jura, formed by Doubs R. 3 mi. WNW of Le Locle, bet. Neuchâtel canton (E) and Doubs dept. (W); alt. 2,470 ft.; 2.5 mi. long, c.200 yds. wide, terminating (N) in falls (88 ft. high) known as the Saut du Doubs. Tourist area.

Brenham (brĕ'nùm), city (pop. 6,941), ⊙ Washington co., S central Texas, c.70 mi. WNW of Houston; trade, shipping, processing center in rich Brazos valley agr. area; cotton ginning, cottonseed-oil milling, dairying, mfg. of canned foods, brooms, foundry products, beverages; hatchery. Oil wells near. Seat of Blinn Col. Brenham was founded in 1844.

Brenitsa (brĕnē'tsä), village (pop. 6,022), Vratsa dist., N Bulgaria, 11 mi. ESE of Byala Slatina; flour milling; grain, legumes, livestock.

Brennbergbanya (brĕn'bĕrgbänyŏ), Hung. *Brennbergbánya*, town (pop. 1,940), Sopron co., W Hungary, 4 mi. SW of Sopron; rail terminal; lignite mined near by.

Brenne (brĕn), poorly drained district (□ 400) of Indre dept., central France, bet. Indre and Creuse rivers and c.20 mi. W of Châteauroux; region comparable to the SOLOGNE, studded with lakes, sparsely populated, and recently afforested. Le Blanc (SW) is regional market center.

Brenner, village, Italy: see BRENNERO.

Brenne River (brĕn), Côte-d'Or dept., E central France, rises W of Sombernon, flows c.30 mi. NNW, past Vitteaux, to the Armançon 3 mi. below Montbard. Accompanied in its lower course by section of Burgundy Canal.

Brennero (brĕn'nĕrō), Ger. *Brenner*, village (pop. 483), Bolzano prov., Trentino-Alto Adige, N Italy, in Brenner Pass, 9 mi. NNE of Vipiteno; customs station. Hot mineral baths at near-by Terme del Brennero.

Brenner Pass (brĕ'nŭr), Ital. *Passo Brennero*, lowest (4,495 ft.) of main Alpine passes, forming divide bet. Ötztal group of Central Alps and Zillertal group of Eastern Alps, connects Innsbruck, Austria, with Bolzano, Italy. Crossed by Romans and by Teutonic invaders of Italy. Carriage road over pass built 1772. Railroad (with 22 tunnels and numerous bridges) built 1864–67. Scene (1940–41) of meetings bet. Hitler and Mussolini.

Brenno River (brĕn'nō), S Switzerland, rises near Lukmanier Pass, flows 21 mi. SSE to the Ticino near Biasca. It waters Val Blenio.

Breno (brā'nō), village (pop. 1,757), Brescia prov., Lombardy, N Italy, on Oglio R. and 29 mi. N of Brescia. Chief center of Val Camonica; ironworks, nail factory, silk mill. Iron mine near by.

Brénod (brānō'), village (pop. 438), Ain dept., E France, in the Jura, 6 mi. S of Nantua; cheese mfg.

Brent. 1 Town (pop. 1,100), Bibb co., central Ala., near Cahaba R., opposite Centerville; lumber. **2** Village, Escambia co., extreme NW Fla., near Pensacola.

Brenta River (brĕn'tä), N Italy, rises in Alpine lakes of Caldonazzo and Levico SE of Trent, flows E, through the Valsugana, past Borgo, S, past Bassano, and SSE through Venetian plain, past Stra, to the Adriatic 3 mi. SE of Chioggia; total length, 100 mi. Canalized below Stra; here joined by a distributary canal, Naviglio di Brenta, which flows 15 mi. E, past Dolo and Mira, to Lagoon of Venice 3 mi. SW of Venice. Prior to 1896, when its mouth was shifted, the Brenta flowed into the lagoon. Used for irrigation. Receives Cismon R. (left).

Brentford, town (pop. 132), Spink co., NE central S.Dak., 22 mi. SSE of Aberdeen.

Brentford and Chiswick (chĭ'zĭk), residential municipal borough (1931 pop. 62,618; 1951 census 59,354), ⊙ Middlesex, England, W suburb of London. Includes town of Brentford, on the Thames, at mouth of the Brent, and 9 mi. W of London; terminal of Grand Junction Canal. Shipping; mfg. (machinery, electrical equipment, tires, pharmaceuticals); market gardening. Scene (1016) of defeat of Danes by Edmund Ironside, and (1642) victory of Royalists over Parliamentarians. Just E, on the Thames, is residential town of Chiswick, site of Chiswick House, seat of dukes of Devonshire. Has church with 15th-cent. tower. William Hogarth buried here. Chiswick was residence of William Morris. Also in borough (E) is Gunnersbury (pop. 5,655), with large park.

Brentford Bay, N Boothia Peninsula, SE Franklin Dist., Northwest Territories, small inlet of Prince Regent Inlet, opposite Fort Ross; 71°55'N 94°20'W.

Brentonico (brĕntō'nēkō), village (pop. 960), Trento prov., Trentino–Alto Adige, N Italy, on NE slope of Monte Baldo, 6 mi. SW of Rovereto; sausage factory. Marble quarries near by.

Brent River, Hertford and Middlesex, England, rises as Dollis Brook just S of Barnet, flows 20 mi. SW, through Brent Reservoir, just S of Hendon, to the Thames at Brentford.

Brentwood, residential urban district (1931 pop. 7,208; 1951 census 29,898), SW Essex, England, 20 mi. NE of London. Has grammar school founded 1557 and remains of 1221 chapel. Formerly a staging post on important forest road.

Brentwood. 1 City (pop. 1,729), Contra Costa co., W Calif., 11 mi. SE of Pittsburg; shipping center for irrigated agr. area (fruit, nuts, vegetables). Inc. 1948. **2** W residential section of LOS ANGELES city, Los Angeles co., S Calif., extending into foothills of Santa Monica Mts., just NE of Santa Monica. **3** Town (pop. 3,523), Prince Georges co., central Md., suburb just NE of Washington, near Anacostia R. Inc. 1922. **4** City (pop. 7,504), St. Louis co., E Mo., suburb W of St. Louis. Inc. 1929. **5** Town (pop. 819), Rockingham co., SE N.H., on Exeter R. and 15 mi. WSW of Portsmouth; wood products. **6** Resort village (pop. 2,803), Suffolk co., SE N.Y., on central Long Isl., 4 mi. N of Bay Shore; mfg. of clothing; truck, dairy products, vegetables. **7** Residential borough (pop. 12,535), Allegheny co., SW Pa., SE suburb of Pittsburgh.

Brescello (brĕshĕl'lō), anc. *Brixellum*, town (pop. 1,430), Reggio nell'Emilia prov., Emilia-Romagna, N central Italy, on Po R. and 11 mi. NW of Parma; fertilizer, packing boxes, candy. Here, in 69 A.D., defeated Roman emperor Otho committed suicide.

Brescia (brā'shä), province (□ 1,834; pop. 744,571), Lombardy, N Italy; ⊙ Brescia. Bet. lakes Garda (E) and Iseo (W); mountainous in N, culminating in glacier-covered Monte Adamello (11,660 ft.); fertile, irrigated Po plain in S. Watered by Oglio, Mella, and Chiese rivers. Forestry, cattle raising, iron mining, and many major hydroelectric plants in N (CAMONICA and TROMPIA valleys). Agr. (fodder, wheat, corn, raw silk, flax) in S. Exports fodder to Switzerland. Mts. at Brescia, Chiari, Darfo, Lumezzane, Palazzolo sull'Oglio, and Rovato.

Brescia, anc. *Brixia*, city (pop. 92,583; pop. metropolitan area 123,332) ⊙ Brescia prov., Lombardy, N Italy, at foot of Alps, on Garza R. (branch of Mella R.) and 52 mi. ESE of Milan; 45°33'N 10°15'E. Transportation and industrial center; iron and steel mills, aluminum works, hosiery factories, tanneries, distilleries; mfg. of firearms, automobile chassis, agr. and textile machinery, cutlery, furniture, hats, glassware, macaroni. Bishopric. Has Roman ruins, including temple (now mus. of antiquities) erected A.D. 72 by Vespasian; also old cathedral (11th-12th cent.), new cathedral (begun 1604), 14th-cent. castle, town hall (1492–1574), many baroque churches and palaces, public library (1747) containing Dante MS, picture gall., acad. of science, arts, and letters (1802), and technical, commercial, and agr. schools. A Gallic town, it became a Roman stronghold and, later, seat of Lombard duchy. In 16th cent. had flourishing school of painting. Held by Venice, France, and Austria prior to its union with Italy in 1860. In Second World War heavily bombed (1944–45); many monumental bldgs. destroyed.

Breskens (brĕs'kŭns), town (pop. 2,193), Zeeland prov., SW Netherlands, on Flanders mainland and 3 mi. S of Flushing (ferry across the Western Scheldt); fishing port; candy mfg., woodworking, quarrying, sugar refining, flax spinning. Taken (1631) by Dutch from Spaniards.

Breslau (brĕs'lou) or **Wroclaw** (vrôts'wäf), Pol. *Wrocław*, large industrial city (1939 pop. 629,565; 1946 pop. 170,656; 1950 estimate 341,500) in Lower Silesia, after 1945 ⊙ Wroclaw prov., SW Poland, on the Oder, at Olawa R. mouth, and 180 mi. ESE of Berlin, 190 mi. WSW of Warsaw; 51°7'N 17°2'E. Rail junction; river port; airport (W). Industrial center; railroad shops; mfg. of machinery, machine tools, pumps, water meters, insulating materials, cement, chemicals, pottery, food products, cigarettes; woolen, rayon, and paper milling, metalworking and refining. R.C. archbishopric. Univ., technical col. In Second World War, c.65% destroyed; 13th-cent. cathedral and 14th–15th-cent. town hall (both restored), and several Gothic churches remain, as well as old inner part of city. Undamaged portions of 18th-cent. univ. bldgs. house Pol. univ. (1945), staffed by faculties of former universities of Lvov and Vilna. First mentioned c.1000 as episcopal see; became (1163) ⊙ duchy of Silesia under branch of Pol. Piast dynasty. After destruction (1241) by Mongols, city was rebuilt by Ger. settlers; rapidly rose in commercial importance. Passed 1335 to Bohemia; was member (1368–1474) of Hanseatic League. Accepted Reformation in 1523; passed 1526 to the Hapsburgs. Captured 1741 by Frederick the Great; ceded to Prussia in 1742 under peace treaty signed here. In Seven Years War, Prussians here repulsed Austrians; besieged (1806–07) by French. Univ. founded 1811, when it absorbed Breslau Jesuit Col. (founded 1702) and univ. of Frankfurt an der Oder; associated with Mommsen and Freytag. In 1813, city was temporary seat of Prussian govt.; from here Frederick William III initiated rising against French. Until 1945, was ⊙ former Prussian Lower Silesia prov.; captured (May 9, 1945) by Soviet forces after prolonged siege. After Second World War, remaining Ger. inhabitants were expelled and Poles, chiefly from Lvov and Vilna, settled here.

Bresle River (brĕl), N France, rises N of Formerie (Oise dept.), flows 45 mi. NW, forming Somme–Seine-Inférieure dept. border, past Aumale, Blangy, and Eu, to the English Channel at Le Tréport. Picturesque valley with glassworks.

Bresles (brĕl), town (pop. 2,113), Oise dept., N France, 8 mi. E of Beauvais; mfg. of sugar, agr. tools, dairy products.

Bressanone (brĕs-sänō'nĕ), Ger. *Brixen*, town (pop. 6,520), Bolzano prov., Trentino–Alto Adige, N Italy, on Isarco R. at mouth of Rienza R., and 20 mi. NE of Bolzano, on Brenner railroad. Health resort (alt. 1,834 ft.); produces wax, marmalade, liquor, beer. Major hydroelectric plant. Bishopric since 992. Has 11th-cent. baptistery, cloister with Romanesque columns (13th cent.), baroque cathedral (1745–54), mus. Prince-bishops ruled Bressanone and surrounding territory from 11th cent. Property of their powerful vassals, the counts of Tyrol; passed to Hapsburgs in 1363. After secularization (1803) bishopric came to Austria as part of Tyrol. Passed from Austria to Italy in 1919.

Bressay (brĕ'sā, brĕ'sŭ), island (□ 11.6, including Noss isl.; pop. 448) of the Shetlands, Scotland, just off E coast of Mainland isl. across Bressay Sound, opposite Lerwick; 6 mi. long, up to 3 mi. wide; rises to 743 ft. Crofting and pony breeding are main occupations.

Bresse (brĕs), region of E France, in Ain, Jura, and Saône-et-Loire depts., bet. the Revermont (E) and Saône R. (W); ⊙ Bourg. Anc. lake bottom; fertile agr. dist. noted for its chickens. Grows cereals, corn, rapeseed, potatoes; dairying. Together with BUGEY and the GEX territory, Bresse was ceded to France by the dukes of Savoy in 1601. It remained part of Burgundy prov. until 1790.

Bresse, La, commune (pop. 3,020), Vosges dept., E France, on Moselotte R. and 13 mi. E of Remiremont; cotton milling, granite working. La Bresse village (pop. 604) was seriously damaged in Second World War during fighting in the Vosges (fall, 1944).

Bressoux (brĕsōō'), town (pop. 15,568), Liége prov., E Belgium, NE suburb of Liége; coal mining.

Bressuire (brĕswēr'), town (pop. 5,535), Deux-Sèvres dept., W France, 17 mi. NW of Parthenay; road and railroad center; livestock market and meat-processing center; petroleum refining. Has ruins of 11th–13th-cent. castle. Burned down 3 times: in 1214 for adhering to the Plantagenet cause; by the Protestants in 1598; and by the Republicans in the Vendée rebellion (1794).

Brest- in Bulg. names: see BRYAST-.

Brest, (brĕst), city (pop. 62,707), Finistère dept., W France, on N shore of Brest Roads, 315 mi. W of Paris; 48°22'N 4°32'W. Seaport and chief Fr. naval station on the Atlantic, with a fortified land-locked harbor. Exports pit-props, fruits, and early vegetables to England. Mfg. (explosives, brushes, footwear, textiles); food preserving, brewing. Military port, arsenal, and naval schools form heart of city at mouth of Penfeld R. and separate old town and commercial harbor (E) from W dist. named Recouvrance. Before Second World War, Brest was France's first and finest naval base. Built (1631) by Richelieu and fortified by Vauban. In 1694, the French here repulsed the English; in 1794, the English under Lord Howe defeated French fleet. Important debarkation point of American troops and supplies in First World War. During Second World War, Brest became a German submarine base and was severely damaged by Allied bombing. Ger. garrison surrendered to Allies in Sept., 1944, after a brief but costly siege.

Brest, Poland: see BRZESC.

Brest (bryĕst), oblast (□ 5,200; 1946 pop. estimate 700,000), W Belorussian SSR; ⊙ Brest. In lowland extending E into Pripet Marshes; bounded W by Bug R. (Pol. border); drained by Mukhavets and Lesna rivers. Humid continental climate (short summers). Heavily forested. Agr. (rye, oats, barley, potatoes, flax); livestock; fisheries. Industries based on agr. (flour milling, tanning, food processing and preserving, distilling, brewing) and timber (sawmilling, woodworking); mfg. of metalware (Brest), concrete blocks, (Bereza), bricks. Main centers: Brest, Pruzhany, Kobrin. Well-developed rail and road net. Navigation on Bug and Mukhavets rivers and on Dnieper-Bug Canal (chiefly lumber and grain shipments). Formed (1939) out of W part of Pol. Polesie prov., following Soviet occupation of E Poland. Held by Germany (1941–44); ceded to USSR in 1945.

Brest, Pol. *Brześć nad Bugiem* (bŭzhĕshch'näd bōō'gyĕm), fortified city (1931 pop. 48,435), ⊙ Brest oblast, Belorussian SSR, on Bug R. opposite Terespol (Poland), at mouth of Mukhavets R. (W end of Dnieper-Bug waterway), and 225 mi. SW of Minsk; 52°7'N 23°41'E. Rail junction; river transportation center; agr. processing (hides, wool, grain, flaxseed, vegetables, hops, tobacco), mfg. (metalware, bricks, musical instruments), cotton spinning, woodworking, sawmilling. Has teachers col., 15th-cent. church, and old synagogues. Founded in 11th cent.; successively under Lithuania and Poland; frequently assaulted by Tatars and Teutonic Knights. Union of Pol. Orthodox and R.C. churches signed here, 1596. Sacked (1657) by Swedes; captured (1794) by Rus. general Suvorov; passed (1795) to Russia and strongly fortified in 1830s. Developed as livestock-trading center. Russo-German peace treaty signed here, 1918. Reverted (1921) to Poland; ceded to USSR in 1945. Jewish pop. largely exterminated during Second World War. Until 1921, Brest-Litovsk (brĕst'-lĭtôfsk'), Pol. *Brześć Litewski* (lyĭtĕf'skē).

Brest-Litovsk, Belorussian SSR: see BREST, city.

Brest-Nantes Canal (brĕst-nänts, Fr.–nāt), in Brittany, W France, traverses Finistère, Morbihan, Ille-et-Vilaine and Loire-Inférieure depts., using channels of several rivers (Aulne, Blavet, Oust, Vilaine, and Erdre) and 219 locks. It is 225 mi. long and navigable for barges, drawing 5 ft., which carry iron ore and building materials. Passes Châteaulin, Pontivy, Redon. Canal completed 1838.

Brestovac or **Brestovats** (both: brĕ'stôväts). **1** Village (pop. 5,095), S central Serbia, Yugoslavia, on railroad and 12 mi. S of Nis. **2** or **Backi Brestovac** or **Bachki Brestovats** (both: bäch'kē), Serbo-Croatian *Bački Brestovac*, Hung. *Szilberek* (shĭl'bĕrĕk), village (pop. 5,671), Vojvodina, NW Serbia, Yugoslavia, 13 mi. SE of Sombor, in the Backa.

Brestovacka Banja or **Brestovachka Banya** (both: brĕ'stôvächkä bä'nyä), Serbo-Croatian *Brestovačka Banja*, village, E Serbia, Yugoslavia, 3 mi. WSW of Bor; health resort.

Brest Roads, Fr. *Rade de Brest* (räd-dů-brĕst'), bay on Atlantic Ocean, off Finistère dept., W France; 14 mi. long, 7 mi. wide; landlocked but for a channel (the Goulet) 1.5 mi. wide. Receives Aulne and Elorn rivers. City and military port of Brest are on N shore.

Bretagne, France: see BRITTANY.

Bretenoux (brĕtnōō'), village (pop. 676), Lot dept., SW France, on the Cère, near its influx into the Dordogne, and 22 mi. SE of Brive-la-Gaillarde; food canning, barite mining

Breteuil (brůtů'ē). **1** Village (pop. 1,536), Eure dept., NW France, on the Iton and 17 mi. SW of Évreux; woodworking, cider distilling. Sometimes called Breteuil-sur-Iton. Just W is Forest of Breteuil. **2** Village (pop. 1,736), Oise dept., N France, 12 mi. W of Montdidier; road center. Mfg. (religious articles, furniture, phosphate of lime). Heavily damaged in Second World War. Also called Breteuil-sur-Noye.

Brétigny (brātēnyē'), hamlet of Eure-et-Loir dept., N central France, 4 mi. SE of Chartres. Important treaty signed here (1360) bet. France and England.

Brétigny-sur-Orge (-sür-ôrzh'), town (pop. 3,133), Seine-et-Oise dept., N central France, 8 mi. W of Corbeil; grain market; metalworks.

Breton (brĕ'tůn), village (pop. estimate 300), S central Alta., 50 mi. SW of Edmonton; mixed farming, dairying.

Breton, Cape (brĕ'tůn), E extremity of Cape Breton Isl., E N.S., 23 mi. SE of Sydney; 45°56'N 59°48'W.

Breton, Marais (märĕ' brůtõ'), marshy coastal area of Vendée dept., W France, on the Bay of Biscay opposite Île de Noirmoutier; c.15 mi. long, 5 mi. wide. Now an artificially drained and fertile region with cattle raising and truck farming; saltworks, oyster beds. Has villages of Beauvoir, Bouin.

Breton, Pertuis (pĕrtwē' brůtõ'), inlet of Bay of Biscay, off coast of W France, bet. mainland (Vendée dept. N, Charente-Maritime dept. E) and Île de Ré (S); 17 mi. long, 10 mi. wide; connected with Pertuis d' Antioche by strait 2 mi. wide Marshy Aiguillon Bay (E; mussel beds) merges with the Marais POITEVIN.

Breton Island (brĕtŏn'), SE La., hook-shaped island (c.6 mi. long) in Gulf of Mexico, E of Mississippi R. delta and c.60 mi. SE of New Orleans; with near-by isls., comprises Breton Isl. bird reservation. To NW is **Breton Sound** (c.20 mi. wide), an arm of the Gulf of Mexico lying bet. La. coast (W) and Breton Isl. (SE); Chandeleur Sound adjoins on E.

Breton Woods (brĕ'tůn), village (pop. 1,619, with near-by Osbornsville), Ocean co., E N.J., 8 mi. NNE of Toms River.

Bretten (brĕ'tůn), town (pop. 8,447), N Baden, Germany, after 1945 in Württemberg-Baden, on the Saalbach and 8 mi. SE of Bruchsal; rail junction; foundries. Mfg. of stoves, textiles, Bakelite; lumber milling, wood inlaying. Melanchthon b. here.

Bretteville-sur-Laize (brĕtvēl'-sür-lāz'), village (pop. 257), Calvados dept., NW France, 10 mi. S of Caen; stone quarries in area.

Bretton Woods, N.H.: see CARROLL, town.

Bretzenheim (brĕ'tsůnhīm), SW suburb of Mainz, W Germany.

Breuches (brůsh), village (pop. 670), Haute-Saône dept., E France, 11 mi. NW of Lure; lace mfg.

Breuëh, Indonesia: see BRUE.

Breukelen (brů'kůlůn), town (pop. c.4,000), Utrecht prov., W central Netherlands, on Vecht R. and 7 mi. NW of Utrecht, on Merwede Canal; rail junction; machine shops; mfg. (cement, furniture, leather products); building stone; dairying, truck gardening, honey making. Brooklyn, N.Y., was named for this town.

Brevard (brĭvärd'), county (□ 1,032; pop. 23,653), central Fla., on the Atlantic (E); ⊙ Titusville. Lowland region bordered by barrier beaches enclosing Indian R. and Banana R. lagoons, and Merritt Isl.; W part is a marshy peat area drained by St. Johns R., which forms several lakes here. Included in Indian River dist., which is noted for its citrus fruit (especially oranges). Co. also has truck, tourist, and fishing industries. Formed 1844.

Brevard, resort town (pop. 3,908), ⊙ Transylvania co., SW N.C., near French Broad R., 27 mi. SSW of Asheville, in the Blue Ridge, at edge of Pisgah Natl. Forest; agr. trade center. Brevard Col. (jr.; coeducational) here. Many picturesque waterfalls in vicinity. Inc. 1867.

Brévenne River (brävĕn'), Rhône dept., E central France, rises NW of Saint-Symphorien-sur-Coise, flows 20 mi. NE, bet. the Monts du Beaujolais (N) and the Monts du Lyonnais (S), to the Azergues 3 mi. below L'Arbresle.

Brévent, Mont, France: see CHAMONIX.

Breves (brā'vĭs), city (pop. 557), E Pará, Brazil, on SW shore of Marajó isl. in Amazon delta, 140 mi. W of Belém; rubber, cacao.

Breviglieri (brĕvēlyā'rē), village (1950 pop. 2,567), central Tripolitania, Libya, on the plateau Gebel Nefusa, on main road and 33 mi. WSW of Homs; alt. c.1,300 ft. Agr. settlement (cereals, olives, almonds, livestock) founded by Italians 1938–39. Has Roman ruins.

Brevik (brā'vĭk, -vēk), city (pop. 2,160), Telemark co., S Norway, at tip of peninsula on Langesund Fjord, 10 mi. SSE of Skien; 59°3'N 9°41'E; rail terminus; mfg. and seafaring town, with lumber trade and production of hardware, wood pulp, cement.

Brévilly (brāvēyē'), village (pop. 335), Ardennes dept., N France, on Chiers R. and 7 mi. ESE of Sedan; steel-wire mfg.

Brevoort Island. 1 Island (25 mi. long, 5 mi. wide), SE Franklin Dist., Northwest Territories, in the Atlantic, off Hall Peninsula, SE Baffin Isl.; 63°30'N 64°20'W. **2** Islet, NE Franklin Dist., Northwest Territories, off E Ellesmere Isl., in Smith Sound, just S of Cape Sabine (Pim Isl.); 78°48'N 74°50'W.

Brevoort Lake (brĕ'vôrt), Mackinac co., SE Upper Peninsula, Mich., 12 mi. NW of St. Ignace, in Marquette Natl. Forest; c.5 mi. long, 2 mi. wide; fishing, camping.

Brewarrina (brůwŏ'růnů), municipality (pop. 841), N New South Wales, Australia, on Darling or Barwon R. and 360 mi. NW of Newcastle; rail terminus; sheep center.

Brewer, industrial city (pop. 6,862), Penobscot co., S Maine, on E bank of the Penobscot opposite Bangor; pulp and paper mills, quarries. Settled 1770, town inc. 1812, city 1889.

Brewer, Mount, peak (13,577 ft.) of the Sierra Nevada, E Calif., in Kings Canyon Natl. Park, 17 mi. WSW of Independence.

Brewers Lagoon, Honduras: see BRUS LAGOON.

Brewerton, village (1940 pop. 562), Onondaga co., central N.Y., at W end of Oneida L., 13 mi. N of Syracuse; summer resort. Here are remains of Fort Brewerton (1759), now in state reservation.

Brewood (brōōd), village and parish (pop. 2,718), SW Stafford, England, 6 mi. NNW of Wolverhampton; agr. market. In parish is village of Four Ashes, with chemical industry.

Brewster, county (□ 6,208; pop. 7,309), extreme W Texas; ⊙ Alpine. State's largest co.; rugged mtn. area (alt. c.1,700–7,000 ft.) within Big Bend of the Rio Grande (here forming Mex. border); much of most scenic wild area in S (including Chisos Mts. and Santa Elena, Mariscal, and Boquillas canyons) is included in BIG BEND NATIONAL PARK. Santiago Mts. are in central part, Glass Mts. partly in NE. Large-scale cattle, sheep, goat, horse ranching; tourist trade, dude ranches; some irrigated agr.; beekeeping. Quicksilver mines (now inactive); copper, sulphur deposits. Formed 1887.

Brewster. 1 Village (1940 pop.744), Polk co., central Fla., 20 mi. S of Lakeland; processes phosphate from near-by mines. **2** City (pop. 467), Thomas co., NW Kansas, 18 mi. W of Colby, in grain and poultry region. **3** Town (pop. 987), Barnstable co., SE Mass., 12 mi. ENE of Barnstable, on Cape Cod Bay; summer resort. Was shipping center in sailing-ship days. Includes villages of East and West Brewster. Settled 1656, inc. 1803. **4** Village (pop. 478), Nobles co., SW Minn., near Iowa line, 9 mi. NE of Worthington, in grain, livestock, and poultry area; dairy products. **5** Village (pop. 69), ⊙ Blaine co., central Nebr., 100 mi. NW of Grand Island and on N.Loup R.; livestock, grain. **6** Village (pop. 1,810), Putnam co., SE N.Y., 9 mi. W of Danbury, Conn.; trade center for farming, dairying, summer-resort area; mfg. (wood products, leather and cloth bags). Peach L. (resort) and several New York city water-supply reservoirs are near by. James Kent b. near by. Settled 1850, inc. 1894. **7** Village (pop. 1,618), Stark co., E central Ohio, 13 mi. WSW of Canton and on small Sugar Creek; dairy products. **8** Town (pop. 851), Okanogan co., N Wash., 20 mi. SSW of Okanogan, at confluence of Okanogan and Columbia rivers; lumber, fruit.

Brewster, Cape, E Greenland, on S side of mouth of Scoresby Sound; 70°9'N 22°3'W.

Brewster Islands, E Mass., group of isls. lying in entrance to Boston Bay from Massachusetts Bay, N of Point Allerton. Boston Lighthouse (102 ft. above water) is on Little Brewster (Lighthouse) Isl. Others in group include Great Brewster, Middle Brewster, Outer Brewster, and Calf isls.

Brewton. 1 City (pop. 5,146), ⊙ Escambia co., S Ala., near Fla. line and Conecuh R., 50 mi. NE of Mobile, in cotton and livestock area; lumber and lumber products, textiles, clothing, naval stores. Fort Crawford established here 1818. **2** Town (1940 pop. 109), Laurens co., central Ga., 7 mi. ENE of Dublin.

Breydon Water, tidal lake, SE Norfolk, England, formed by confluence of Yare R. and Waveney R. 4 mi. WSW of Yarmouth, extends ENE to W outskirts of Yarmouth, where it is joined by Bure R.; linked with North Sea by 3-mi. narrow channel. Up to 1 mi. wide; lined by wide mud flats.

Breyell (brīĕl'), village (pop. 6,779), in former Prussian Rhine Prov., W Germany, after 1945 in North Rhine-Westphalia, 5.5 mi. WNW of Süchteln; cattle.

Breyten (brā'tůn), town (pop. 2,196), SE Transvaal, U. of So. Afr., 15 mi. N of Ermelo; alt. 5,886 ft.; rail junction; stock, corn, potatoes. Collieries under development.

Breytovo, Russian SFSR: see BREITOVO.

Breza (brĕ'zä), village, S Bosnia, Yugoslavia, 3 mi. NE of Visoko, on rail branch; brown-coal mine.

Brezhani (brĕzhä'nē), village (pop. 3,283), Gorna Dzhumaya dist., SW Bulgaria, on W slope of Pirin Mts., 11 mi. SSE of Gorna Dzhumaya; lignite-mining center; vineyards, tobacco, truck. Formerly Sarbinovo.

Brezice (brĕ'zhĭtsĕ), Slovenian *Brežice*, Ger. *Rann* (rän), village, S Slovenia, Yugoslavia, on the Sava, opposite Krka R. mouth, on railroad and 20 mi. WNW of Zagreb, near Croatia border; local trade center. First mentioned in 1241; has old castle. Until 1918, in Styria.

Breziny, Poland: see BRZEZINY.

Breznice (bůrzhĕz'nyĭtsĕ), Czech *Březnice*, town (pop. 2,384), S Bohemia, Czechoslovakia, 9 mi. SSW of Pribram; trade center for rye-growing area; rail junction.

Breznik (brĕznĕk'), city (pop. 2,780), Sofia dist., W Bulgaria, in Breznik Basin (□ 23; bet. Kraishte highlands and Struma R. valley), 20 mi. W of Sofia; market and dairying center; butter and cheese exports. Has school of dairying; mineral springs. Iron-ore deposits just S.

Brezno or **Brezno nad Hronom** (brĕz'nô nät' hrô"nôm), Hung. *Breznóbánya* (brĕz'nōbä"nyŏ), town (pop. 5,649), central Slovakia, Czechoslovakia, in the Low Tatra, on Hron R. and 23 mi. ENE of Banska Bystrica; rail junction; lumbering, ewe-cheese making. Former gold- and silver-mining center. Many picturesque villages in vicinity (E) noted for lace making and colorful folkways Podbrezova, 5 mi. W, produces machine tools; tanneries.

Brezolles (brůzôl'), agr. village (pop. 820), Eure-et-Loir dept., NW central France, 14 mi. WSW of Dreux.

Brezova nad Bradlom (brĕ'zôvä nät' brädlôm), Slovak *Brezová nad Bradlom*, Hung. *Berezó* (bĕ'rĕzō), village (pop. 2,846), W Slovakia, Czechoslovakia, in the Little Carpathians, at SW foot of Bradlo mtn., 23 mi. SE of Hodonin; leather industry.

Brezove Hory (bůrzhĕ'zôvä hô'rĭ), Czech *Březové Hory*, Ger. *Birkenberg* (bĭr'kůnbĕrk), village (pop. 2,225), S Bohemia, Czechoslovakia, on SW outskirts of Pribram; silver and lead mining; mfg. of wooden toys.

Brezovo (brĕ'zôvô), village (pop. 3,595), Plovdiv dist., S central Bulgaria, on tributary of the Maritsa and 23 mi. NE of Plovdiv; rye, potatoes, livestock. Formerly Abrashlare.

Bria (brēä'), village, central Ubangi-Shari, Fr. Equatorial Africa, on Kotto R. and 110 mi. NE of Bambari; trading and diamond-mining center; also cotton ginning.

Briance River (brēãs'), Haute-Vienne dept., W central France, rises in Monts du Limousin near St.-Germain-les-Belles, flows 26 mi. NW, past Pierre-Buffière, to the Vienne 4 mi. below Limoges.

Briançon (brēãsõ'), anc. *Brigantium*, Alpine town (pop. 3,483), Hautes-Alpes dept., SE France, in valley of upper Durance R. at mouth of the Guisane, and 37 mi. NE of Gap; tourist center and winter-sport resort bet. Massif du Pelvoux (W) and Cottian Alps (E), at junction of roads to Grenoble (via Col du Lautaret), to Italy (via Montgenèvre Pass, 5 mi. ENE), and to Gap; rail terminus. Lumber trade; mfg. (furniture, cheese); chalk quarries and anthracite mines near by. Consists of modern Sainte-Catherine dist. near railroad station (alt. 3,950 ft.), and of old town (alt. 4,350 ft.) strongly fortified by Vauban in 17th–18th cent. Outlying forts command road to Italy. Briançon suffered some damage in Second World War. Serre-Chevalier (W; road and cable car) is noted for winter sports.

Brian Head, peak (11,315 ft.), on W rim of Markagunt Plateau, SW Utah, 13 mi. E of Cedar City.

Briansk, Russian SFSR: see BRYANSK.

Briarcliff Manor, residential village (pop. 2,494), Westchester co., SE N.Y., 2 mi. SE of Ossining. Briarcliff Jr. Col. and Edgewood Park School for girls are here. Settled 1896, inc. 1902.

Briar Creek, borough (pop. 348), Columbia co., E central Pa., on Susquehanna R. just below Berwick.

Briare (brēär'), town (pop. 3,360), Loiret dept., N central France, on right bank of the Loire and 6 mi SE of Gien, port at N terminus of LOIRE LATERAL CANAL (aqueduct over the Loire) and at S end of Briare Canal; transshipping center. Known for its manufactures of beads, buttons, and mosaics. Also makes building materials.

Briare Canal, Loiret dept., N central France, one of waterways connecting Loire and Seine rivers, bet. Briare (at N end of LOIRE LATERAL CANAL) and Montargis (beyond which it is continued by LOING CANAL). Bet. Rogny and Montargis it parallels course of upper Loing R. Total length, 35 mi. Built 1604–42.

Briatico (brēä'tēkô), village (pop. 1,318), Catanzaro prov., Calabria, S Italy, on Gulf of Sant'Eufemia, 5 mi. WNW of Vibo Valentia; bathing resort; wine, olive oil. Lignite mines near by.

Bribano (brēbä'nō), village (pop. 817), Belluno prov., Veneto, N Italy, near Piave R., 7 mi. SW of Belluno; rail junction; mfg. (paper, doors).

Bribie Island (brī'bē) (□ 59), in Pacific Ocean just off SE coast of Queensland, Australia; forms W side of entrance to Moreton Bay; 18 mi. long, 4 mi. wide. Low, wooded; timber.

Bribiesca, Spain: see BRIVIESCA.

Bricelyn (brī'slĭn), village (pop. 639), Faribault co., S Minn., near Iowa line, 16 mi. ESE of Blue Earth, in corn, oat, barley, livestock area; dairy products, canned corn.

Brices Cross Roads National Battlefield Site, Miss.: see BALDWYN.

Briceville, village (1940 pop. 1,978), Anderson co., E Tenn., 20 mi. NW of Knoxville, at foot of Cross Mtn.; coal mining.

Brichany (brēchä'nē), Rum. *Briceni* (brēchĕn'), town (1941 pop. 3,525), N Moldavian SSR, 55 mi. E of Chernovtsy; road and agr. center; flour and oilseed milling. Until Second World War, pop. largely Jewish.

Bricherasio (brēkĕrä'zyō), village (pop. 811), Torino prov., Piedmont, NW Italy, 4 mi. SW of Pinerolo; rail junction; alcohol distillery. Graphite mines near by.

Brickaville (brēkävēl'), town (1948 pop. 4,830), Tamatave prov., E Madagascar, river port on Canal des Pangalanes, near the coast, on railroad and 45 mi. SSW of Tamatave; agr. and trading center; mfg. of rum, alcohol, fruit preserves, carbonated drinks, coffee, citrus, and cacao plantations, stone quarrying. Agr. fairs held here. Near-by La Bourdonnais (4 mi. WNW) has sugar mills.

Brickeys (brĭ'kēz), town (pop. 62), Lee co., E Ark., 12 mi. ENE of Marianna.

Bricquebec (brēkbĕk'), village (pop. 1,611), Manche dept., NW France, on Cotentin Peninsula, 12 mi. S of Cherbourg; dairying center. Has a 14th-cent. castle. Near-by Trappist monastery produces cheese.

Bridal Veil, Norway: see GEIRANGER FJORD.

Bridalveil Fall, Calif.: see YOSEMITE NATIONAL PARK.

Bride River. 1 In Co. Cork, Ireland, rises 5 mi. NE of Dunmanway, flows 14 mi. NE to Lee R. 7 mi. W of Cork. **2** In cos. Cork and Waterford, Ireland, rises in Nagle Mts., flows 35 mi. E to Blackwater R. 8 mi. N of Youghal.

Brides-les-Bains (brēd-lā-bē), village (pop. 253), Savoie dept., SE France, on the Doron de Bozel and 3 mi. SE of Moutiers, in the Massif de la Vanoise; Alpine spa with mineral springs.

Bridgeburg, S Ont., N suburb of Fort Erie, on Niagara R., opposite Buffalo, at W end of International Bridge. Merged 1932 with Fort Erie.

Bridgehampton, shore-resort village (1940 pop. 1,462), Suffolk co., SE N.Y., on SE Long Isl., 6 mi. ENE of Southampton, in dairying, and truck- and potato-growing area.

Bridgend. 1 Village on ISLAY, Hebrides, Scotland. **2** Village, Perthshire, Scotland: see PERTH, burgh.

Bridgend (brĭjĕnd'), urban district (1931 pop. 10,029; 1951 census 13,646), S Glamorgan, Wales, on Ogwr R. and 18 mi. W of Cardiff; mfg. of electrical equipment, pharmaceuticals; agr. market. Has 12th-cent. fortified church, remains of Norman castle, and a 15th-cent. bldg. reputed to have been Hospice of Knights Hospitallers of St. John.

Bridgenorth, England: see BRIDGNORTH.

Bridge of Allan, burgh (1931 pop. 2,897; 1951 census 3,173), NE Stirling, Scotland, on Allan Water and 3 mi. N of Stirling; resort with mineral springs; paper milling, bacon and ham curing.

Bridge of Cally, village, E Perthshire, Scotland, on Ericht R. and 5 mi. NNW of Blairgowrie; woolen milling.

Bridge of Earn, town in Dunbarney parish, SE Perthshire, Scotland, on Earn R. (anc. bridge) and 3 mi. S of Perth; agr. market and resort, with near-by mineral springs.

Bridge of Marnoch (mär'nŭkh), agr. village, NE Banffshire, Scotland, on Deveron R. and 2 mi. SW of Aberchirder.

Bridge of Weir (wēr), town in Kilbarchan parish, central Renfrew, Scotland, 12 mi. W of Glasgow; tanning and leather mfg. center. Site of Ranfurly Castle, seat of ancestors of John Knox. Near by are large Quarrier Orphan Homes.

Bridgeport, village (pop. estimate 500), NE N.S., on NE coast of Cape Breton Isl., 10 mi. NE of Sydney; coal mining. Mine shafts extend under the sea.

Bridgeport. 1 City (pop. 2,386), Jackson co., extreme NE Ala., on Tennessee R., near Tenn. line, and 50 mi. NE of Huntsville; hosiery, stoves, ranges. Settled in early-19th cent. **2** Village (pop. c.200), ⊙ Mono co., E Calif., 75 mi. NW of Bishop, near Nev. line; mining, stock raising; resort area. Bridgeport Reservoir is just N. **3** Industrial city (pop. 158,709), coextensive with Bridgeport town, a ⊙ Fairfield co., SW Conn., on harbor on Long Isl. Sound, at mouth of Poquonock R., and 15 mi. SW of New Haven. State's chief mfg. city (electrical equipment, firearms, ammunition, sewing machines, typewriters, tools, machinery, hardware, clothing, textiles, aluminum, brass, steel and asbestos products); port of entry. Univ. of Bridgeport, Bridgeport Engineering Inst., and a teacher training school are here. Privateering port in Revolution; early shipping center; grew rapidly after coming of railroad (1836). First Socialist mayor and board of aldermen in Conn. elected here (1933). P. T. Barnum lived here; gave city Seaside Park (Barnum statue here), Barnum Inst. of Science and History. "General Tom Thumb" (Charles S. Stratton) b. here. Settled 1639; inc. as town 1821, as city 1836. **4** City (pop. 2,358), Lawrence co., SE Ill., 4 mi. W of Lawrenceville, in oil, natural-gas, and agr. area; oil refineries, pumping station; makes electronic equipment. Inc. 1865. **5** Village (pop. c.350), Saginaw co., E central Mich., on Cass R. and 5 mi. SSE of Saginaw, in farm area. **6** City (pop. 1,631), ⊙ Morrill co., W Nebr., 30 mi. ESE of Scotts Bluff and on N.Platte R.; trade center for irrigated grazing, alfalfa, sugar-beet area. Near-by buttes, Courthouse Rock and Jail Rock, are points of interest. **7** Village (pop. 4,309), Belmont co., E Ohio, on the Ohio (bridged), opposite Wheeling, W.Va.; makes steel bearings, dairy products. Laid out 1806. **8** City (pop. 199), Caddo co., W central Okla., on Canadian R. and 22 mi. W of El Reno, in agr. area; cotton ginning. **9** Borough (pop. 5,827), Montgomery co., SE Pa., on Schuylkill R. opposite Norristown; coke, iron, textiles. Dolomite mined here. Settled 1829, inc. 1851. **10** City (pop. 2,049), Wise co., N Texas, c.40 mi. NW of Fort Worth and on West Fork of Trinity R., dammed just W into L. Bridgeport; agr. (grain, cotton, corn); mfg. (brick, mattresses, brooms); hatcheries; limestone processing. Settled 1873, inc. 1913. Formerly had coal mining. **11** Town (pop. 802; 1951 special census pop. 1,340), Douglas co., central Wash., 50 mi. NE of Wenatchee and on Columbia R., here crossed by bridge. **12** Town (pop. 2,414), Harrison co., N W.Va., 5 mi. E of Clarksburg; ships cattle. Chartered 1816.

Bridgeport, Lake, N Texas, in West Fork of Trinity River, c.40 mi. NW of Fort Worth; □ 18; capacity 784,000 acre-ft. Impounded by Bridgeport Dam (earth fill; 153 ft. high, 1,750 ft. long), completed 1931; for flood control, irrigation, and water supply to Fort Worth.

Bridgeport Dam, Texas: see BRIDGEPORT, LAKE.

Bridgeport Reservoir, Calif.: see EAST WALKER RIVER.

Bridger, town (pop. 854), Carbon co., S Mont., on Clarks Fork Yellowstone R. and 40 mi. SW of Billings; coal mines; oil, gas; beets, grain, livestock, timber.

Bridger Peak (11,007 ft.), in Sierra Madre, S Wyo., 12 mi. WSW of Encampment.

Bridger Range, in Rocky Mts., S Mont., rises just NE of Bozeman; extends c.25 mi. N. Bridger Peak (9,106 ft.), highest.

Bridger's Pass (7,300 ft.), in Sierra Madre of Continental Divide, Carbon co., S Wyo., c.25 mi. SSW of Rawlins. Discovered by Jim Bridger, famous Indian scout and guide; used in 1860s by Pony Express; was part of Overland Route.

Bridgeton, SE industrial suburb (pop. 52,286) of Glasgow, Lanark, Scotland; tanneries, woolen and cotton mills, chemical works.

Bridgeton. 1 Town (pop. 202), St. Louis co., E Mo., 12 mi. NW of St. Louis. **2** City (pop. 18,378), ⊙ Cumberland co., SW N.J., on Cohansey Creek and 36 mi. S of Philadelphia; shipping center for agr. region; dairy products, canned foods; mfg. (glassware, baskets, metal products, underwear). Has 18th-cent. Presbyterian church and Tumbling Dam Park, with dam built 1814. Seabrook (4 mi. N; pop. 2,284) is hq. for huge vegetable farm (packing, freezing plants). Bridgeton settled 1686, inc. 1864, adopted commission govt. 1907. **3** Town (pop. 805), Craven co., E N.C., on Neuse R. (bridged here), opposite New Bern; sawmilling. **4** Village, Providence co., R.I.: see BURRILLVILLE.

Bridgeton Terrace, town (pop. 578), St. Louis co., E Mo.

Bridgetown, town (pop. 1,351), SW Western Australia, 140 mi. S of Perth and on Blackwood R.; butter factory; orchards.

Bridgetown, city (pop. 13,340, with suburbs 68,924), ⊙ BARBADOS, B.W.I., chief town and port, on isl.'s SW shore, on open Carlisle Bay, 210 mi. NE of Port of Spain; 13°6'N 59°36'W. Coal- and oil-fueling station, and port of call for ocean vessels, which anchor offshore; smaller ships of up to 14 ft. draught dock alongside the inner Careenage harbor. Bridgetown ships the isl.'s main products —sugar cane, molasses, rum, cotton, soap, margarine, tamarinds—which are mainly processed here. A handsome city and tourist resort, favored for its equable climate and fine beaches. Among its bldgs. are St. Mary's Church, Anglican St. Michael's Cathedral, town hall, public bldgs. on Trafalgar Square, where a Nelson monument has been erected. George Washington's House, residence of the American statesman on a visit (1751) with his brother, is near by. Govt. House is in E outskirts. Among outlying residential suburbs and beach resorts are, adjoining SE: Hastings, Worthing, and St. Lawrence. Codrington agr. station is just NE, while noted Codrington Col. (founded 1710 and affiliated with Durham Univ.) is 10 mi. ENE.

Bridgetown, town (pop. 1,020), ⊙ Annapolis co., W N.S., on Annapolis R. and 12 mi. ENE of Annapolis Royal; woodworking, lumbering. First settled c.1650 by the French.

Bridgetown, town (pop. 16), Caroline co., E Md., on Tuckahoe Creek and 21 mi. WSW of Dover, Del.

Bridgeview, village (pop. 1,393) Cook co., NE Ill., SW suburb of Chicago. Inc. 1947.

Bridgeville. 1 Town (pop. 1,468), Sussex co., SW Del., 8 mi. N of Seaford; canning, shipping center in fruitgrowing, agr. region. Inc. 1871. **2** Industrial borough (pop. 5,650), Allegheny co., SW Pa., 8 mi. SW of Pittsburgh; metal products, bituminous coal, chemicals, beverages, light bulbs, glass, paint, bricks, lumber; agr. Inc. 1901.

Bridgewater. 1 Town (pop. 888), SE South Australia, 12 mi. SE of Adelaide; dairy products, livestock. **2** Village (pop. 333), N central Victoria, Australia, on Loddon R. and 100 mi. NW of Melbourne; flour mill.

Bridgewater, town (pop. 3,445), SW N.S., on La-have R. and 50 mi. WSW of Halifax; lumber-shipping port; sawmilling. Founded 1810.

Bridgewater. 1 Resort town (pop. 639), Litchfield co., W Conn., on Housatonic R. and 11 mi. NNE of Danbury, in hilly agr. region. Early 19th-cent. church and houses. **2** Town (pop. 296), Adair co., SW Iowa, 20 mi. NW of Creston; livestock shipping. **3** Rural town (pop. 1,279), Aroostook co., E Maine, 21 mi. N of Houlton, near N.B. line; ships potatoes; lumber. Port of entry. Inc. 1858. **4** Town (pop. 9,512), including Bridgewater village (pop. 3,445), Plymouth co., E Mass., on Taunton R. and 27 mi. S of Boston; bricks, foundry products, shoes; grain feed, truck, poultry, dairying. State teachers col. Settled 1650, inc. 1656. **5** Town (pop. 222), Grafton co., central N.H., on Newfound L. and Pemigewasset R. and 15 mi. NNW of Franklin; music colony; resort; winter sports. **6** Village (pop. 309), Oneida co., central N.Y., 15 mi. S of Utica. **7** Residential borough (pop. 1,316), Beaver co., W Pa., 25 mi. NW of Pittsburgh, opposite Rochester and on Ohio R., at mouth of Beaver R. Was 19th-cent. river port. Inc. 1835. **8** City (pop. 748), McCook co., SE S.Dak., 28 mi. ESE of Mitchell; trade center for diversified farming region; dairy products, livestock, poultry, corn, wheat, rye. **9** Town (pop. 903), Windsor co., S central Vt., on Ottauquechee R. and 15 mi. E of Rutland; textiles, lumber, wood products. **10** Town (pop. 1,537), Rockingham co., NW Va., on North R. and 17 mi. NNE of Staunton, in Shenandoah Valley; mfg. of furniture, clothing, rayon textiles. Seat of Bridgewater Col. Inc. 1835.

Bridgewater, Cape, extreme SW Victoria, Australia, in Indian Ocean, SW tip of peninsula forming E shore of Discovery Bay; 38°24'S 141°25'E; rises to 440 ft.

Bridgman, village (pop. 977), Berrien co., extreme SW Mich., on L. Michigan and 13 mi. SW of Benton Harbor, in fruitgrowing and truck-farming area; nurseries. Mfg. of auto parts, stoves, compressors, pumps. Resort. State park near by.

Bridgnorth (brĭj'nôrth), municipal borough (1931 pop. 5,151; 1951 census 6,244), SE Shropshire, England, on the Severn and 13 mi. W of Wolverhampton; carpet-weaving center. The town rises in tiers on a sandstone hill, the higher part being reached by a funicular railroad. Has ruins of castle built 1101; a royalist stronghold in Civil War, destroyed 1646 by Parliamentary troops. The church was built by Thomas Telford. Thomas Percy b. here; Richard Baxter was curate in the town. Town formerly also spelled Bridgenorth. Just S is residential village and parish (pop. 270) of Oldbury, former site of a Saxon castle.

Bridgton, town (pop. 2,950), including Bridgton village (pop. 1,866), Cumberland co., SW Maine, bet. Highland L. and Long L., 35 mi. NW of Portland. Mfg. (textiles, wood products, toys); resort center. Settled 1770, inc. 1794. At North Bridgton village is Bridgton Acad.

Bridgwater (brĭj'wôtŭr), municipal borough (1931 pop. 17,139; 1951 census 22,221), central Somerset, England, on Parrett R. and 9 mi. NE of Taunton; agr. market and small port; mfg. of bricks (*Bath bricks*), dry batteries, paint; bacon and ham curing. Has 15th-cent. church, remains of 13th-cent. castle. Admiral Blake b. here. Near by is site of battle (1685) of SEDGEMOOR. Duke of Monmouth proclaimed king in Bridgwater in 1685.

Bridgwater Bay, inlet of Bristol Channel, NW Somerset, England, extends WSW from Weston-super-Mare; 20 mi. wide, 7 mi. long. Receives Brue R. and Parrett R.

Bridlington (brĭd'lĭng-tŭn, bûr'–), municipal borough (1931 pop. 19,705; 1951 census 24,767), East Riding, E Yorkshire, England, on Bridlington Bay of North Sea, 17 mi. SE of Scarborough; well-protected port and seaside resort with mineral springs; agr. market. Has remains of Augustinian priory founded 1113, including a 14th-cent. gate; and a 13th–15th-cent. church, restored by Sir Gilbert Scott. Bridlington Quay, 1 mi. SE, is a popular resort, with mineral springs.

Bridoire, La (lä brēdwär'), village (pop. 399), Savoie dept., SE France, 9 mi. SW of Chambéry; mfg. (synthetic rubber, hardware).

Bridport (brĭd'pôrt), municipal borough (1931 pop. 5,917; 1951 census 6,273), W Dorset, England, on Brit R., near the Channel, and 14 mi. W of Dorchester; agr. market; mfg. of rope, cordage, and thread for textile and leather industries. Has 15th-cent. church. Just S, on the Channel, is seaside resort of West Bay, with fishing port at mouth of the Brit.

Bridport, village (pop. 330), N Tasmania, on Anderson Bay of Bass Strait and 31 mi. NNE of Launceston; agr. center; sheep.

Bridport, town (pop. 663), Addison co., W Vt., on L. Champlain and 7 mi. W of Middlebury; agr., sheep; wood products.

Brie (brē), natural region of N central France, lying chiefly in Seine-et-Marne dept., bet. the Seine (S) and the Marne (N), E of Paris. A fertile wheat-growing area, second only to the Beauce, noted for its soft white cheese. Former ⊙ and principal commercial center: Meaux. Former countship of Meaux (E Brie) was combined (11th cent.) with that of Troyes, to form county, later prov., of Champagne and Brie. W Brie became part of Île-de-France.

Briec (brēĕk'), town (pop. 1,208), Finistère dept., W France, 9 mi. NE of Quimper; flour milling, horse breeding.

Brie-Comte-Robert (brē-kōt-rôbâr'), town (pop. 2,968), Seine-et-Marne dept., N central France, 16 mi. SE of Paris; mfg. (hardware, test tubes). Flower gardens in area. Has fine 13th-cent. Gothic church (restored 15th–16th cent.).

Brieg (brēk) or **Brzeg** (bzhĕk), town (1939 pop. 31,419; 1946 pop. 7,744) in Lower Silesia, after 1945 in Opole prov., SW Poland, port on the Oder and 25 mi. SE of Breslau (Wroclaw); rail junction; tanning and food-processing center; mfg. of chemicals, sugar refining. Heavy damage in Second World War included 13th-cent. castle (rebuilt 16th cent.) and church and 16th-cent. town hall. Has remains of 13th-cent. Franciscan monastery. Chartered 1250; was (1311-1675) ⊙ duchy under branch of Pol. Piast dynasty; passed 1675 to Hapsburgs. In near-by battle in Thirty Years War, imperial forces under Piccolomini and Archduke Leopold defeated (1642) Swedes under Torstensson. After Second World War the Germans were expelled.

Brielle (brē'lŭ) or **The Brill,** town (pop. 3,536), South Holland prov., SW Netherlands, on NE coast of Voorne isl , at mouth of Brielsche Maas R., and 13 mi. W of Rotterdam; limekilns, sandstone quarries; woodworking. First town taken from Spaniards (1572) by Beggars of the Sea. Also called Den Briel.

Brielle (brēĕl'), resort borough (pop. 1,328), Monmouth co., E N.J., near mouth of Manasquan R., 8 mi. S of Asbury Park; fishing; mfg. (boats, belt fasteners).

Brielsche Maas River (brēl'sŭ mäs'), SW Netherlands, formed by junction of OLD MAAS RIVER and NEW MAAS RIVER 7 mi. WSW of Rotterdam; flows 13 mi. WNW, past Brielle, forming NW boundary of Putten isl. and N boundary of Voorne isl., to North Sea. Its E part also known as the Botlek, its estuary as Brielsche Gat. Sometimes also called New Maas R.

Brienne-le-Château (brēĕn'-lŭ-shätō'), village (pop. 1,468), Aube dept., NE central France, near Aube R., 14 mi. NW of Bar-sur-Aube; agr.-machine mfg., flour milling; tree nurseries. Had military school attended (1779–84) by Napoleon. At Brienne-la-Vieille (1 mi. S) is 12th-cent. church.

Brienon-sur-Armançon (brēnō'-sür-ärmäsō'), town (pop. 2,268), Yonne dept., N central France, on Armançon R. and Burgundy Canal, and 14 mi. N of Auxerre; sugar and flour milling; fruit and vegetable shipping; fuse mfg.

Brienz (brēĕnts'), town (pop. 2,637, Bern canton, central Switzerland, on NE shore of L. of Brienz and 31 mi. SE of Bern; year-round resort; a center of Swiss woodworking industry.

Brienz, Lake of, Ger. *Brienzersee* (brēĕnts'ürzā'), Bern canton, central Switzerland, in Bernese Alps; 9 mi. long, 1.5 mi. wide, □ 11, alt. 1,850 ft., max. depth 856 ft. Hilly, wooded shores. Aar R. enters lake at NE, leaves at SW, connecting it with L. of Thun (lakes were once one); Lütschine R. enters at SW. Brienz is main town on lake.

Brienza (brēĕn'tsä), town (pop. 3,893), Potenza prov., Basilicata, S Italy, 15 mi. SW of Potenza; woolen mill.

Brienzer Rothorn (brēĕnts'ür rōt'hôrn), peak (7,720 ft.) in the Bernese Alps, central Switzerland, 2 mi. NNE of Brienz; ascended by Brienzergrat, a ridge, extends WSW.

Brienzersee, Switzerland: see BRIENZ, LAKE OF.

Briercliffe (brī'ür–), parish (pop. 2,752), E Lancashire, England. Contains cotton-milling village of Haggate, 3 mi. NE of Burnley.

Brier Creek (brī'ür), E Ga., rises near Warrenton, flows c.75 mi. SE, past Keysville, to Savannah R. 12 mi. E of Sylvania. Sometimes written Briar Creek.

Brierfield (brī'ür–), urban district (1931 pop. 7,696; 1951 census 7,005), E Lancashire, England, 3 mi. N of Burnley; cotton weaving; mfg. of textile machinery.

Brier Island (brī'ür) (4 mi. long, 2 mi. wide), W N.S., at entrance to Bay of Fundy, 30 mi. NNW of Yarmouth and just SW of Long Isl.; 44°15'N 66°22'W. On W coast is fishing village of Westport (pop. c.400).

Brierley, town and parish (pop. 6,723), West Riding, S Yorkshire, England, 5 mi. NE of Barnsley; coal.

Brierley Hill, urban district (1931 pop. 14,347; 1951 census 48,943), S Stafford, England, 7 mi. S of Wolverhampton; steel mills, blast furnaces; mfg. of machinery, pottery, glass.

Brieselang (brē'zŭläng), village (pop. 4,977), Brandenburg, E Germany, 18 mi. N of Potsdam; laboratory-equipment mfg.

Briesen, Poland: see WABRZEZNO.

Brieskow-Finkenheerd (brēs'kō-fĭng'kŭnhârt), village (pop. 3,022), Brandenburg, E Germany, on Friedrich-Wilhelm Canal, near the Oder, 7 mi. S of Frankfurt; lignite mining; power station.

Brieulles-sur-Meuse (brēûl'-sür-mûz'), village (pop. 443), Meuse dept., NE France, on left bank of the Meuse and 15 mi. NW of Verdun. Monument to American crossing of the Meuse (1918) in First World War.

Briey (brēā'), town (pop. 2,539), Meurthe-et-Moselle dept., NE France, 14 mi. NW of Metz; center of Briey iron-mining basin; cementworks.

Brig (brēk), Fr. *Brigue* (brēg), town (pop. 3,278), Valais canton, S Switzerland, on the Rhone and 26 mi. S of Interlaken, in a valley (alt. 2,234 ft.) among Alpine peaks, at N end of Simplon Pass. Junction of Simplon, Lötschberg, and Furka railroads. Printing, flour. Stockalper Palace (17th cent.) here. Several hydroelectric plants near by.

Briga, France: see BRIGUE, LA.

Brigach River (brē'gäkh), left headstream of the Danube, S Baden, Germany, rises in the Black Forest 1 mi. S of Sankt Georgen, flows 25 mi. generally SSE, past Villingen, joining BREG RIVER just below Donaueschingen to form the Danube.

Briga Marittima, France: see BRIGUE, LA.

Brigantia, Portugal: see BRAGANÇA, city.

Brigantine (brĭ'gŭntēn), resort city (pop. 1,267), Atlantic co., SE N.J., on Brigantine Isl. and 3 mi. NE of Atlantic City.

Brigantine Island (6 mi. long), off N.J. coast, just NE of Atlantic City, with which it is connected by bridge across Absecon Inlet. Brigantine, resort city, on E coast.

Brigden, village (pop. estimate 500), S Ont., on Bear Creek and 12 mi. SSE of Sarnia; dairying, fruitgrowing; in oil-producing region.

Brigg, urban district (1931 pop. 4,019; 1951 census 4,508), Parts of Lindsey, Lincolnshire, England, 16 mi. NE of Gainsborough; agr. market, producing beet sugar and agr. machinery.

Briggsdale, village (pop. c.200), Weld co., N Colo., on Crow Creek and 24 mi. NE of Greeley; alt. 4,950 ft. Trading point; grain, livestock.

Briggsville, Mass.: see CLARKSBURG.

Brigham (brĭ'gŭm), village and parish (pop. 750), W Cumberland, England, 2 mi. W of Cockermouth; granite quarrying, dairy farming. Has medieval church.

Brigham City, city (pop. 6,790), ⊙ Box Elder co., N Utah, near Bear R. and Bear River Bay (in Great Salt Lake), 20 mi. N of Ogden, at foot of Wasatch Range; alt. 4,310 ft. Woolen-mfg. and food-processing center (flour, beet sugar, canned goods, dairy products). Peach culture (begun 1855) is extensive in surrounding region, which is served by Ogden R. irrigation project. U.S. bird refuge near by. City settled 1851 by Mormons. Formerly Brigham.

Brighouse (brĭg'hous), municipal borough (1931 pop. 19,756; 1951 census 30,587), West Riding, SW Yorkshire, England, on Calder R. and 4 mi. N of Huddersfield; woolen-, cotton-, and silk-milling center; also produces carpets, leather, textile machinery, aniline dyes, paint, soap, asbestos, metal products. Near by are stone quarries. Just SSE is woolen-milling suburb of Rastrick.

Bright, village (pop. 740), NE central Victoria, Australia, on Ovens R. and 130 mi. ENE of Melbourne, in Australian Alps; rail terminus; winter resort. Mt. Feathertop, Mt. Buffalo, and Mt. Hotham near by. Gold mines in vicinity.

Brighthelmstone, England: see BRIGHTON.

Brightlingsea (brīt'lĭng-sē), urban district (1931 pop. 4,147; 1951 census 4,501), E Essex, England, on Colne R. estuary and 8 mi. SE of Colchester; noted oyster-fishing and yachting port, and resort. Has 15th-cent. church.

Brighton. 1 Town (pop. 7,507), SE South Australia, on Gulf St. Vincent and 8 mi. SW of Adelaide; agr.; Portland cement. **2** Municipality (pop. 39,769), S Victoria, Australia, 8 mi. SSE of Melbourne, on NE shore of Port Phillip Bay, in metropolitan area; seaside resort.

Brighton, village (pop. 1,651), S Ont., near L. Ontario, 20 mi. WSW of Belleville; fruit and vegetable canning, metalworking, mfg. of clothing, chemicals; corn, vegetable, fruit market. E is L. Ontario end of Murray Canal, from Bay of Quinte.

Brighton (brī'tŭn), county borough (1931 pop. 147,427; 1951 census 156,440), S Sussex, England, on the Channel 50 mi. S of London; 50°49'N 0°8'W; important seaside resort, backed by South Downs. Until c.1750 it was fishing village spelled Brighthelmstone. Patronage of George IV (as Prince of Wales) made it a fashionable resort, with an ornate Royal Pavilion (bought by town in 1850). Other features are sea-front promenade, piers, the Dome (formerly royal stables, now an assembly room), and aquarium. Fishing is carried on; industries include mfg. of shoes, asbestos, electrical appliances, and food products. Contiguous with Brighton (W) is town of HOVE. In county borough are residential dists. of Rottingdean, Preston, Moulescomb, and Patcham.

Brighton, village (pop. 1,275, including adjoining New Jersey), SW Trinidad, B.W.I., on the Gulf of Paria, at famous Pitch Lake, and 11 mi. WSW of San Fernando; works and ships asphalt. Also loading of petroleum.

Brighton. 1 Town (pop. 1,689), Jefferson co., central Ala.; N suburb of Bessemer. **2** City (pop. 4,336), ⊙ Adams co., N central Colo., on South Platte R. and 20 mi. NNE of Denver; alt. 4,979 ft. Shipping and processing point in grain and sugar-beet region; canned vegetables, pickles, dairy products. Inc. 1887. **3** Village (pop. 934), on Jersey-Macoupin co. line, W Ill., 10 mi. N of Alton; agr., bituminous-coal mining. **4** Town (pop. 705), Washington co., SE Iowa, 10 mi. SW of Washington; food cannery. **5** Plantation (pop. 106), Somerset co., W central Maine, 18 mi. N of Skowhegan. **6** District of BOSTON, Mass. **7** City (pop. 1,861), Livingston co., SE Mich., 18 mi. N of Ann Arbor, in rich agr. area; timber; mfg. of export boxes, metal stampings. Summer resort. State park near by. Settled 1832; inc. as village 1867, as city 1928. **8** Town (pop. 306), Tipton co., W Tenn., 28 mi. NE of Memphis, in cotton area. **9** Year-round resort, Salt Lake co., N central Utah, in a basin of Wasatch Mts. near Alta, c.17 mi. SE of Salt Lake City; alt. 8,730 ft. Skiing, skating, hiking, fishing, swimming. Small Silver L. is here. **10** Town (pop. 1,671), Essex co., NE Vt., 20 mi. SE of Newport and on Nulhegan R.; its center is Island Pond village (pop. 1,252), port of entry on scenic Island Pond. Lumber, dairy products, feed, truck; cannery. Chartered 1781, settled 1820.

Brighton Beach, N.Y.: see CONEY ISLAND.

Brightwaters, village (pop. 2,336), Suffolk co., SE N.Y., on S shore of W Long Isl., on Great South Bay, just W of Bay Shore, in summer-resort area. Laid out 1907, inc. 1916.

Brigittenau (brĭgĭ'tŭnou), district (□ 2; pop. 69,635) of Vienna, Austria, on isl. formed by the Danube and Danube Canal, just N of city center; mfg of machines.

Brignano Gera d'Adda (brēnyä'nô jä'rä däd'dä), village (pop. 3,024), Bergamo prov., Lombardy, N Italy, 10 mi. S of Bergamo; agr. center.

Brignoles (brēnyôl'), town (pop. 4,671), Var dept., SE France, in Lower Provence Alps, 20 mi. NNE of Toulon; bauxite-mining center (alumina processing); marble working, wine shipping and distilling, footwear mfg. Has 15th–16th-cent. church containing 2d-cent. sarcophagus.

Brignoud (brēnyōō'), N industrial suburb (pop. 1,001) of Villard-Bonnot, Isère dept., SE France, port on Isère R. and 10 mi. NE of Grenoble, in GRÉSIVANDAN valley; mfg. (rolling stock, electric ranges and heaters, calcium carbide), paper milling.

Brigue, Switzerland: see BRIG.

Brigue, La (lä brēg'), Ital. *Briga* or *Briga Marittima* (brē'gä märēt'tēmä), village (1936 pop. 1,047), Alpes-Maritimes dept., SE France, in Maritime Alps, 30 mi. NE of Nice and 7 mi. S of Tenda Pass (Ital. border); alt. 2,510 ft. Resort. Has 15th-cent. church. Part of Italy until 1947.

Brigus (brĭ'gŭs), village (pop. 885), SE N.F., on N coast of Avalon Peninsula, at head of Conception Bay, on railroad and 25 mi. W of St. John's; fishing port; woolen and sawmilling.

Brihuega (brēwā'gä), town (pop. 2,010), Guadalajara prov., central Spain, in New Castile, on Tajuña R. (affluent of the Henares) and 18 mi. NE of Guadalajara; trading and processing center; paper and textile milling, chocolate mfg.; stock raising, apiculture. Has notable bldgs., such as Romanesque-Gothic church of Virgin of Peña, San Felipe parochial church, Piedra Bermeja castle, and Puente de Cozajón gate. The duke of Vendôme here defeated (1710) Lord Stanhope, taking c.5,000 prisoners. The famed civil war battle of Guadalajara (March, 1937), in which Italian contingents were crushingly defeated by the Loyalists, thus arresting the advance on Madrid, was fought in the vicinity of Brihuega.

Brijnagar (brĭj'nŭgŭr), town (pop. 11,549), SE Rajasthan, India, near Kali Sindh R., 160 mi. SSE of Jaipur; market center for cotton, millet, wheat; hand-loom weaving. Has col. Was ⊙ former Rajputana state of Jhalawar; is now ⊙ Jhalawar dist. Formerly called Jhalrapatan Chhaoni. Town of Jhalrapatan is 4 mi. S.

Brijoni Islands (brēô'nē), Ital. *Brioni* (brēō'nē), in N Adriatic Sea, NW Croatia, Yugoslavia, off SW coast of Istria. On largest isl. (1705 acres; 1936 pop. 310) is health resort of Brijoni, 7 mi. NW of Pula. Until 1947, in Italy.

Brikama (brēkä'mä), town (pop. 1,788), ⊙ Western Div., Gambia, 13 mi. S of Bathurst (linked by road); cassava, corn. School; police post.

Brilhante, Rio, Brazil: see IVINHEMA RIVER.

Brill, The, Netherlands: see BRIELLE.

Brillanne, La (lä brēyän′), village (pop. 383), Basses-Alpes dept., SE France, on the Durance and 8 mi. NE of Manosque; hydroelectric plant near by.

Brilliant, village (pop. estimate 700), S B.C., on Columbia R. at mouth of Kootenay R., and 16 mi. NNE of Trail, in mining (gold, silver, lead, zinc) and lumbering region.

Brilliant, village (pop. 2,066), Jefferson co., E Ohio, 6 mi. S of Steubenville and on the Ohio.

Brillion (brĭl′yŭn), city (pop. 1,390), Calumet co., E Wis., 17 mi. ESE of Appleton; trade center for agr. area (peas, oats, clover seed); mfg. (lime, machinery, ironware, cheese). Settled 1850; inc. as village in 1885, as city in 1944.

Brillon-en-Barrois (brēyō′-ā-bärwä′), village (pop. 432), Meuse dept., NE France, 5 mi. SW of Bar-le-Duc; kirsch distilling.

Brilon (brē′lōn), town (pop. 10,134), in former Prussian prov. of Westphalia, W Germany, after 1945 in North Rhine-Westphalia, 21 mi. SE of Lippstadt; rail junction; metalworking. Has 13th–14th-cent. church. Was member of Hanseatic League.

Brimfield. 1 Village (pop. 648), Peoria co., central Ill., 17 mi. WNW of Peoria, in agr. and bituminous-coal area. Jubilee Col. State Park is near by. **2** Rural town (pop. 1,182), Hampden co., S Mass., 19 mi. E of Springfield. Settled c.1706, inc. 1731.

Brimington, town and parish (pop. 5,073), NE Derby, England, 3 mi. NE of Chesterfield; coal.

Brimley, village (pop. c.450), Chippewa co., E Upper Peninsula, Mich., on Whitefish Bay, 12 mi. SW of Sault Ste. Marie; agr., lumbering, commercial fishing; hunting. Has state park.

Brimson, town (pop. 139), Grundy co., N Mo., on Thompson R. and 8 mi. NW of Trenton.

Brinches (brĕn′shĭsh), village (pop. 2,682), Beja dist., S Portugal, near the Guadiana, 14 mi. ENE of Beja; pottery and cheese mfg.

Brindaban (brĭndä′bŭn), since 1948 officially **Vrindaban** (vrĭn–), town (pop. 20,718), Muttra dist., W Uttar Pradesh, India, on the Jumna and 6 mi. N of Muttra; rail spur terminus; pilgrimage center. Has c.1,000 Hindu shrines and temples, notably the red Govind Deva (built 1590). Traditionally associated with youth of Krishna. Sometimes spelled Bindraban or Bindrabund.

Brindakit (brēndŏŏkēt′), town (1947 pop. over 500), SE Yakut Autonomous SSR, Russian SFSR, on Allakh-Yun R. (right tributary of Aldan R.) and 75 mi. SSW of Allakh-Yun; gold mining.

Brindavan Gardens, India: see KRISHNARAJASAGARA.

Brindisi (brĭn′dĭzē, It. brēn′dēzē), province (□ 710; pop. 254,062), Apulia, S Italy, bordering on the Adriatic; ⊙ Brindisi. Situated on the "heel" of the Ital. peninsula; consists of low hilly region enclosing flat coastal plain; watered by a few small streams. Agr. (grapes, olives, figs, almonds, vegetables), stock raising, fishing. Industry at Brindisi. Formed 1927 from Lecce prov.

Brindisi, anc. *Brundisium,* town (pop. 35,984), ⊙ Brindisi prov., Apulia, S Italy, port on the Adriatic, at head of small bay, 39 mi. ENE of Taranto; 40°38′N 17°56′E. Fishing; food canning, flour milling; wine, olive oil, sulphur oils. Exports wine, olive oil, fruit. Noted since anc. times for its trade with the Levant. Archbishopric. Has 2 Romanesque churches, fine cloister, castle built by Emperor Frederick II, and a column marking end of the Appian Way. Its excellent port was a Roman naval station, the chief embarkation point for the Crusades, and an important Ital. naval base in First World War. Capital of prov. since 1927. Vergil died here in 19 B.C.

Brindle, village and parish (pop. 1,050), W central Lancashire, England, 5 mi. SE of Preston; dairy farming, agr.

Brinje (brē′nyĕ), village (pop. 1,957), W Croatia, Yugoslavia, 11 mi. W of Senj; local trade center.

Brinkley, city (pop. 4,173), Monroe co., E central Ark., c.60 mi. ENE of Little Rock; cotton ginning, lumber milling, mfg. of buttons; locomotive works. Laid out c.1872.

Brinkman, town (pop. 102), Greer co., SW Okla., 9 mi. N of Mangum; ships wheat; cotton ginning.

Brinkmann (brĭngk′män), town (pop. estimate 1,500), NE Córdoba prov., Argentina, 40 mi. N of San Francisco; agr. center (wheat, flour, oats); frozen meat, milk products.

Brinkworth, village (pop. 218), S South Australia, 40 mi. SE of Port Pirie; rail junction; agr. center.

Brinon-sur-Beuvron (brēnō′-sür-bûvrō′), village (pop. 262), Nièvre dept., central France, in the Nivernais Hills, 12 mi. S of Clamecy; cattle, hogs.

Brinsmade, village (pop. 136), Benson co., NE central N.Dak., 22 mi. WNW of Devils Lake.

Brinson, town (pop. 248), Decatur co., SW Ga., 11 mi. WNW of Bainbridge, in farm area.

Briones (brēō′nĕs), town (pop. 1,744), Logroño prov., N Spain, on hill overlooking Ebro R., 18 mi WNW of Logroño; asphalt production; wine, cereals, fruit, sugar beets, lumber. Has 16th-cent. church, remains of anc. walls and castle.

Brioni, islands, Yugoslavia: see BRIJONI ISLANDS.

Brion Island (brēō′) (4 mi. long, 1 mi. wide) in the Gulf of St. Lawrence, E Que., northernmost of the Magdalen Isls., 30 mi. NE of Grindstone Isl.; 47°48′N 61°28′W.

Brionne (brēôn′), town (pop. 2,326), Eure dept., NW France, on the Risle and 9 mi. NE of Bernay; mfg. (radio equipment, cotton wadding, springs). Its 14th-15th-cent. church damaged in 1944. At Le Bec-Hallouin (3 mi. N) are ruins of Bec Abbey (founded 11th cent.), a medieval seat of learning.

Brioude (brēōōd′), town (pop. 5,113), Haute-Loire dept., S central France, on the Allier and 36 mi. SSE of Clermont-Ferrand; agr. market and center of artisan industry; copper smelting, bead- and lacemaking. Antimony mined near by. Has 12th–13th-cent. church.

Brioux-sur-Boutonne (brēōō′-sür-bōōtôn′), village (pop. 684), Deux-Sèvres dept., W France, near Boutonne R., 17 mi. SE of Niort; dairying, sawmilling.

Briouze (brēōōz′), village (pop. 858), Orne dept., NW France, 16 mi. WSW of Argentan; livestock market; alcohol distilling, pump mfg. Damaged during battle of Argentan-Falaise pocket (Aug., 1944) in Second World War.

Brisbane (brĭz′bŭn), city and port (pop. 21,391; metropolitan Brisbane 402,030), ⊙ Queensland, Australia, on N shore of Brisbane R. and 14 mi. from its mouth on Moreton Bay; 27°28′S 153°2′E. Principal port of Queensland; cultural and mfg. center; govt. munitions plant, steel and textile mills, automobile plants, railway workshops, shipyards, abattoir. Produces furniture, pottery, shoes, glass products, electrical appliances. Exports livestock, wool, gold, tin, copper, sugar, coal. Seat of Univ. of Queensland (1909), mus. (1871), natl. art gall. (1895), Anglican and R.C. cathedrals. Victoria Park separates city from NW suburbs. Principal suburbs: SOUTH BRISBANE, NORTH BRISBANE, EAST BRISBANE, ENOGGERA, KELVIN GROVE, SANDGATE, WYNNUM, REDCLIFFE, ASCOT, BALD HILLS, BANYO. Coastal area around Redcliffe settled 1824 as penal colony; named for Sir Thomas Macdougall Brisbane, governor of New South Wales.

Brisbane (brĭz′bān), residential suburb (1940 pop. 1,902), San Mateo co., W Calif., on San Francisco Bay, just S of San Francisco.

Brisbane River (brĭz′bŭn), SE Queensland, Australia, rises in Great Dividing Range near Nanango, flows SSE and ENE, past Brisbane and South Brisbane, to Moreton Bay; 200 mi. long. Navigable 14 mi. by steamer below Brisbane, 50 mi. by small craft below Ipswich.

Brisbin (brĭz′bĭn), borough (pop. 463), Clearfield co., central Pa., 14 mi. SSE of Clearfield.

Briscoe, county (□ 887; pop. 3,528), NW Texas; ⊙Silverton. SW part in Llano Estacado, bounded by E-facing Cap Rock escarpment; co. alt. 2,100–3,300 ft. Drained by Tule Creek and Prairie Dog Town Fork of Red R. Agr., cattle ranching; wheat, grain sorghums, barley, oats, alfalfa, cotton, winter peas, some fruit, truck, dairy products; sheep, poultry. Clay products, fuller's earth. Formed 1876.

Brisée Verdière (brēzā′ vĕrdyâr′), village (pop. 1,491), E Mauritius, 4 mi. W of Flacq; sugar cane.

Brisighella (brēzēgĕl′lä), town (pop. 2,397), Ravenna prov., Emilia-Romagna, N central Italy, near Lamone R., 7 mi. SW of Faenza; lime, cement, ink. Gypsum quarries;mineral springs. Near by is 9th-cent. Romanesque church.

Brissac (brēsäk′), village (pop. 849), Maine-et-Loire dept., W France, 9 mi. SE of Angers; truck gardening, winegrowing. Feudal castle rebuilt in 17th cent.

Brissago (brēs-sä′gô), village (pop. 1,762), Ticino canton, S Switzerland, on Lago Maggiore and 5 mi. SW of Locarno, near Ital. border; resort; tobacco.

Bristenstock (brĭ′stŭnshtôk″), peak (10,091 ft.) in Glarus Alps, central Switzerland, 8 mi. WNW of Disentis.

Bristol (brĭ′stŭl), county borough (1931 pop. 397,012; 1951 census 442,281) and city, SW Gloucester, England, on the Avon at mouth of the Frome, and 110 mi. W of London; 51°27′N 2°35′W; commercial, industrial, and shipping center of West of England. Its port has extensive North and Central American trade, and its docks are supplemented by the adjacent ports of AVONMOUTH and PORTISHEAD. Chief imports: grain, sugar, fruit, tobacco, hides, cattle, crude oil; chief exports: chemicals, cotton, tin, salt, machinery, petroleum products, chocolate, glass, pottery (Bristol ware), soap, and leather goods. The city's main industries are shipbuilding, and mfg. of shoes and leather, chocolate, tobacco products, aircraft, and tires. It is an important flour-milling center; there are coal mines near by. One of the 1st transatlantic steamships, the *Great Western,* was built here by Brunel in 1838. Among the city's features are Bristol Univ. (formerly Univ. Col.); a 16th-cent. grammar school; the Cathedral, originally church of 12th-cent. Augustinian abbey, enlarged in 14th cent. and later; 13th-cent. church of St. Mary Redcliffe; technical col. of the Merchant Venturers' Association; and George Muller orphanage. There is a municipal mus. and art gall. The city was probably founded in 6th cent. B.C. In 1141 King Stephen was held prisoner here for 3 months. By 12th cent. it had become a major port; later it became a slave-trading center. In 1497 John and Sebastian Cabot sailed from Bristol on 1st voyage to American mainland; the city was associated with colonization of Newfoundland. In Civil War it was important Royal stronghold, until captured (1645) by Fairfax. It has many literary associations; Thomas Chatterton and Robert Southey were b. here, Macaulay lived in Bristol for a time, and here Defoe met or heard the story of Alexander Selkirk; it is also birthplace of Sir Thomas Lawrence. In 1940–41 Bristol suffered heavy air raids, which destroyed or heavily damaged numerous bldgs., including 15th-cent. church of St. Mary-le-Port, St. Peter's Hospital (1610), the Merchant Venturers' almshouses, and the Guildhall. Among the chief suburbs are Avonmouth, Clifton, St. George, Horfield, and Bedminster.

Bristol. 1 County (□ 556; pop. 381,569), SE Mass.; ⊙ Fall River, New Bedford, and Taunton. On Buzzards Bay and the Atlantic; intersected by Taunton R. Its early activities of whaling and shipping gave way to textile milling after mid-19th cent., with centers at Fall River, New Bedford, Taunton. Resort activities on coast. Formed 1685. **2** County (□ 25; pop. 29,079), E R.I., bounded by Narragansett Bay (SW), Mass. line (NE), and Mt. Hope Bay (SE); ⊙ Bristol. Resorts; fishing; mfg. (yarns, lace, textiles, dresses, rubber goods, saddles, brick, food products, machinery, slide fasteners); shipbuilding; agr. (dairy products, poultry, truck). Drained by Barrington, Warren, and Kickamuit rivers. Inc. 1747.

Bristol. 1 City (pop. 35,961), coextensive with Bristol town, Hartford co., central Conn., on Pequabuck R. and 14 mi. SW of Hartford; mfg. (ball bearings, clocks and timing devices, electrical and sports equipment, tools, textiles, cutlery, metal products, bicycle brakes, concrete products, paints); nursery. Clockmaking began here 1790. Includes Forestville, mfg. village. Settled 1727; inc. as town 1785, as city 1911. **2** Village (1940 pop. 521), ⊙ Liberty co., NW Fla., on Apalachicola R. and c.40 mi. W of Tallahassee; lumber, naval stores. **3** Town (pop. 137), Pierce co., SE Ga., 18 mi. NNE of Waycross. **4** Village (pop. 541), Kendall co., NE Ill., on Fox R. (bridged here) and 7 mi. SW of Aurora, in agr. area. **5** Town (pop. 738), Elkhart co., N Ind., on St. Joseph R. and 9 mi. ENE of Elkhart, near Mich. line; mfg. (canned vegetables, electrical pumps). **6** Resort and fishing town (pop. 1,476), Lincoln co., S Maine, 16 mi. E of Bath, on the coast and Damariscotta R. This area, Pemaquid (pĕm′ŭkwĭd), was visited by early explorers and traders; settled c.1626; became a well-known trading post. Several forts were built here, and area was subject to Indian and French attacks in 17th and 18th cents. Includes villages of Round Pond and New Harbor. MONHEGAN ISLAND is off the coast. **7** Town (pop. 1,586), Grafton co., central N.H., on the Pemigewasset and 30 mi. NNW of Concord; textiles, mica, wood products, agr., dairy products. Surrounded by hills and lakes, notably Newfound L. (N). Winter sports. Inc. 1819. **8** Borough (pop. 12,710), Bucks co., SE Pa., 20 mi. NE of Philadelphia and on Delaware R. (bridged here); rugs, textiles, metal and chemical products, paper. Settled c.1681, laid out 1697, inc. 1720. **9** Town (pop. 12,320), including Bristol village (pop. 10,335), ⊙ Bristol co., E R.I., on peninsula bet. Mt. Hope Bay and Narragansett Bay, 12 mi. SE of Providence. Mt. Hope Bridge connects with Bristol Ferry village in Portsmouth town (S). Mfg. (textiles, dresses, lace, yarns, saddles, rubber products, food products, machinery); shipbuilding; agr. (dairy products, poultry, truck); fishing; yachting at Bristol Harbor, arm of Narragansett Bay. Inc. 1681; originally in Plymouth colony; passed to R.I. in 1746. Monument near Mt. Hope marks spot where King Philip fell; mus. with Indian relics here. Herreshoff boat works, noted for racing yachts, established 1863. Many pre-Revolutionary bldgs. survive. The 1938 hurricane caused heavy damage. **10** City (pop. 647), Day co., NE S.Dak., 11 mi. W of Webster; dairy products, livestock, poultry, grain. **11** City (pop. in Tenn. 16,771, in Va. 15,954), on Tenn.-Va. line, in Great Appalachian Valley, 23 mi. NNE of Johnson City, Tenn.; politically separate (Tenn. city in Sullivan co.; Va. city in but independent of Washington co.), but economically a unit. Rail and highway junction for farm, coal, timber region; shipping center (livestock, farm produce); mfg. of textiles, paper and pulp, lumber and wood products, furniture, structural steel, mine equipment, knit-goods, butter, cheese. Seat of King Col., 2 jr. colleges (Virginia Intermont, Sullins) for women. Settled 1749 as Sapling Grove; inc. as towns (Va. town as Goodson, Tenn. town as Bristol) 1856, as Bristol city 1890. **12** Town (pop. 1,988), including Bristol village (pop. 1,308), Addison co., W Vt., 10 mi. NNE of Middlebury and on New Haven R. (water power), in Green Mts.; wood products, timber; dairy products, truck. Chartered 1762, settled 1786. **13** Village (pop. c.500), Kenosha co., extreme SE Wis., 11 mi. W of Kenosha, in dairy and livestock region.

Bristol Avon River, England: see AVON RIVER.

Bristol Bay, arm (250 mi. long, 180 mi. wide at mouth) of Bering Sea, bet. SW Alaskan mainland (N) and Alaska Peninsula (S and E); 57°–59°N 157°20′–162°W. Receives Togiak, Nushagak, and Kvichak rivers. Important salmon-fishing region, with many cannery villages. Shallow; navigation hazardous for larger vessels.

Bristol Channel, inlet of Atlantic, separating Wales and SW England, extends 85 mi. E from line bet. Hartland Point (Devon) and St. Ann's Head (Pembroke) to mouth of the Severn bet. Cardiff and Weston-super-Mare; 5 to 43 mi. wide. Chief inlets: Milford Haven, Carmarthen Bay, Barnstaple or Bideford Bay, Swansea Bay, and Bridgwater Bay. Receives the Severn, Usk, Rhymney, Taff, Tawe, Loughor, Towy, Avon, Parrett, Taw, and Torridge rivers. Chief riparian cities and ports: Cardiff, Barry, Swansea, Pembroke, Minehead, Ilfracombe, Barnstaple, and Bideford; also forms approach to Severn ports of Newport, Avonmouth, Bristol, and Gloucester. Has highest tidal rise in England, producing sudden tidal wave or "bore" in mouths of tributary rivers. Bristol Channel contains isls. of Lundy, Flat Holme, and Steep Holme. Navigational channels are marked by several lightships; at W entrance is a lightship, 7 mi SW of St. Govan's Head.

Bristol Ferry, village in Portsmouth town, Newport co., E R.I., at N end of Rhode Isl., 16 mi. SSE of Providence. Mt. Hope Bridge (1929) leads to Bristol, on mainland.

Bristol Lake, S Calif., intermittently dry bed (c.10 mi. long) in Mojave Desert, just S of Amboy.

Bristow (brĭ′stō). **1** Town (pop. 313), Butler co., N central Iowa, 30 mi. SSE of Mason City, in agr. area. **2** Village (pop. 146), Boyd co., N Nebr., 15 mi. ESE of Butte bet. the Niobrara and the Missouri. **3** City (pop. 5,400), Creek co., central Okla., 32 mi. SW of Tulsa, in diversified agr. and oil-producing area; oil refineries. Mfg. of oil-field machinery, cottonseed oil, dairy products, clothing, furniture, metal products, toys; cotton ginning. Settled c.1898.

Britain: see GREAT BRITAIN.

Britannia, Mauritius: see RIVIÈRE DRAGON.

British Baluchistan: see BALUCHISTAN, W Pakistan.

British Bechuanaland, U. of So. Afr.: see BECHUANALAND, district.

British Bundelkhand, India: see BUNDELKHAND.

British Cameroons: see CAMEROONS.

British Central Africa: see NYASALAND.

British Channel, Rus. *Britanskiy Kanal*, strait of Arctic Ocean E of George Land, Franz Josef Land, Russian SFSR; c.52°E. Also called British Sound.

British Columbia, most westerly province (land area □ 359,279, total □ 366,255; 1941 pop. 817,861; 1948 estimate 1,082,000) of Canada; ⊙ Victoria. Bounded by Mont. and Wash. (S), the Pacific (W), Alaska (NW), the Yukon and Mackenzie Dist. (N), and Alta. (E). Almost wholly mountainous, prov. is bordered E by the Rockies, continued W by a series of ranges, including Selkirk Mts. The Coast Mts. extend along Pacific coast. Ranges are cut by fertile valleys of the Fraser, Kootenay, Thompson, and Columbia rivers and their tributaries. NE portion of B.C. forms part of the Great Plain and consists of basins of Peace and Liard rivers. NW part of prov. is drained by the Taku, Stikine, Iskut, Nass, and Skeena rivers. Of the numerous lakes, Atlin, Teslin, Dease, Talsa, Cross, Babine, Stuart, François, Quesnel, Chilko, Harrison, Okanagan, Kootenay, and the Arrow Lakes are the largest. The coastline is deeply indented by numerous inlets. Offshore are Vancouver Isl., the Queen Charlotte Isls., Porcher, Banks, Pitt, Princess Royal, Aristazabal, and many smaller isls. Mean coastal temp. ranges are: (Prince Rupert) from 35°F. (Jan.) to 58°F. (Aug.), with average annual rainfall of 97.9 inches; (Victoria) 39°F. (Jan.) to 60°F. (July-Aug.), with rainfall of 27 inches. Fruit and vegetable growing and dairying are carried on extensively in the river valleys (S), wheat is grown in NE of prov. Lumbering is major industry. There are extensive mineral deposits; coal, gold, silver, copper, lead, zinc, tungsten, and some uranium are mined. Industries include shipbuilding, woodworking, metal smelting, food processing, fish canning. On the coast salmon and herring fisheries are important. Vancouver is largest city and chief port of prov. Other important towns are Victoria, New Westminster, Prince George, Prince Rupert, Port Alberni, Chilliwack, Kamloops, Revelstoke, Cranbrook, Fernie. Trail, Nelson, Rossland, Nanaimo, North Vancouver, Kelowna, Vernon, and Kimberley. Prov. attracts many tourists; it contains Yoho, Mt. Revelstoke, Glacier, and Kootenay natl. parks, and Hamber, Wells Gray, Garibaldi, Strathcona, Mt. Robson, Mt. Assiniboine, and Kokanee Glacier provincial parks. Coast of B.C. was 1st seen (1774) by Juan Pérez, and was visited by the Heceta and Quadra expeditions. Capt. James Cook discovered Nootka Sound in 1778. Trade with the region began at end of 18th cent.; Capt. John Meares was one of 1st traders. He came in conflict with the Spaniards, who claimed the territory, but under the Nootka Convention (1790) Spain relinquished her claim to England. In the following years the coast was charted by Capt. George Vancouver, and in 1795 the last colony at Nootka was abandoned by Spain. Alexander Mackenzie, of the North West Co., reached the Pacific coast by land, 1793. Fort McLeod was founded (1805) by Simon Fraser; this was followed by forts St. James, Fraser, and George. Further trading posts were established after Hudson's Bay Co. had absorbed the North West Co. in 1821. Nootka Convention did not clarify sovereignty of the territory; S boundary of Alaska was defined in 1825, its E boundary in 1903. Treaty of Washington (1846), the Oregon Treaty, fixed the U.S.–British border at the 49th parallel, with a deviation to include Vancouver Isl. in British territory. This isl. was then granted to Hudson's Bay Co., with provision that a colony be established here; in 1849 isl. became a crown colony. Following the Fraser R. gold rush of 1858 the mainland colony of British Columbia was established. The Cariboo gold rush (1862) led to further population influx. The San Juan Isls. came under joint U.S.–British occupation in 1859 and were awarded to the United States by arbitration decision in 1872. Vancouver Isl. and the mainland colony were united under the name of British Columbia by Act of Parliament of 1866; colony joined Canada in 1871. Discontent over non-completion of transcontinental railroad led to a secession movement; this failed, and in 1885 the Canadian Pacific RR reached Vancouver.

British Commonwealth of Nations, a loose confederation of independent nations, including the UNITED KINGDOM OF GREAT BRITAIN AND NORTHERN IRELAND, to whose crown the members pay nominal allegiance. All the constituent members of the commonwealth are self-governing countries which were formerly in various degrees of subordination to Great Britain and gradually acquired dominion status—Canada (1867), Australia (1901), New Zealand (1907), Union of South Africa (1910), India (1947), Pakistan (1947), and Ceylon (1948). In 1949 India became a republic within the commonwealth. Ireland, made a dominion in 1921, became a republic and left the commonwealth in 1949. Burma, separated from India in 1937, became a republic in 1948 and left the commonwealth. The British Commonwealth of Nations, formally changing the relationship among the independent parts of the British Empire, was established by the Statute of Westminster (1931), which expressed the sentiment of the Imperial Conference of 1926 (dominions were defined as "autonomous Communities within the British Empire, equal in status, in no way subordinate one to another in any aspect of their domestic or foreign affairs"). Actually, this measure belatedly recognized the status achieved by the dominions since the First World War. After the Second World War the term *dominion* tended to be more and more avoided among the members of the commonwealth. The Statute of Westminster seems not to have affected the status of the members of the British Empire subordinate to the United Kingdom; for a list of these members and for the history of the empire, see the article BRITISH EMPIRE.

British East Africa, name given to 4 British possessions in E Africa: KENYA, TANGANYIKA, UGANDA, and ZANZIBAR. Since 1948 the technical services (railroads, mail, customs, statistical services, etc.) of Kenya, Uganda, and Tanganyika have been coordinated under an administrative body called the East Africa High Commission, composed of the governors of the 3 territories, with administrative hq. at Nairobi, Kenya.

British Empire, the United Kingdom of Great Britain and Northern Ireland, the other nations of the British Commonwealth, and the dependencies of the United Kingdom and of the Commonwealth members. The nations of the BRITISH COMMONWEALTH OF NATIONS (see that article) are of equal rank, while the other parts of the empire are controlled mostly by Great Britain. These parts of the empire, under varying degrees of control, are classed as crown colonies, dependencies of crown colonies, protectorates, trust territories under the U.N. (former mandates under the League of Nations), condominiums, and several other special categories. It was, at its height in late 19th cent. and early 20th cent., the greatest empire of the ancient or modern world in area, population, and resources. Even in 1950, after some parts had severed connection with the empire, the totals of all the dominions and the areas of the world in some way attached to them or to the United Kingdom was ¼ of the earth's surface and ⅕ of the world's pop.: □ c.13,015,000 [not including Antarctic claims], pop. c.600,000,000. Less the figures for the Commonwealth nations the area is □ c.3,915,000, pop. c.80,250,000. Most of the dependencies of the United Kingdom are administered through the colonial office: in the Mediterranean —the colonies CYPRUS, GIBRALTAR, and MALTA, the last with internal self-govt.; in Africa—the colonies and protectorates GOLD COAST, GAMBIA, KENYA, NIGERIA, and SIERRA LEONE, the protectorates NYASALAND, NORTHERN RHODESIA, BRITISH SOMALILAND, UGANDA, and ZANZIBAR (with PEMBA), and the trust territories CAMEROONS, TANGANYIKA, and TOGOLAND; in the Far East—the colonies HONG KONG, SINGAPORE, CHRISTMAS AND COCOS ISLANDS, NORTH BORNEO, and SARAWAK, the "protected state" BRUNEI, and, in the Federation of Malaya, the settlements MALACCA and PENANG, as well as the 9 "protected states" which make up the rest of the Federation; in the W Pacific—the colonies FIJI, GILBERT AND ELLICE ISLANDS, and PITCAIRN ISLAND, the protectorate British SOLOMON ISLANDS, and the "protected state" TONGA; in the Indian Ocean—the colonies MAURITIUS and SEYCHELLES, the "protected state" MALDIVE ISLANDS, and the colony and protectorate ADEN; in the mid-Atlantic—the colony SAINT HELENA (with ASCENSION ISLAND and TRISTAN DA CUNHA); in the W Atlantic—the colonies BERMUDA, the British West Indies (BAHAMA ISLANDS, BARBADOS, JAMAICA, LEEWARD ISLANDS, WINDWARD ISLANDS, TRINIDAD AND TOBAGO), British GUIANA, and BRITISH HONDURAS; and in the S Atlantic—the colony FALKLAND ISLANDS and its dependencies. SOUTHERN RHODESIA is in a separate category, a self-governing territory virtually with dominion status. The commonwealth relations office administers 3 high-commission territories in S Africa—BASUTOLAND, SWAZILAND, and BECHUANALAND PROTECTORATE. Britain also shares 3 condominiums: ANGLO-EGYPTIAN SUDAN (with Egypt), CANTON ISLAND and ENDERBURY ISLAND (with U.S.), and NEW HEBRIDES (with France). In addition, Great Britain has claims in ANTARCTICA, as do Australia and New Zealand. Dependencies of commonwealth countries include: for Australia—PAPUA and NORFOLK ISLAND and the trust territories of NAURU and Territory of NEW GUINEA; New Zealand—TOKELAU, KERMADEC ISLANDS, CHATHAM ISLANDS, and COOK ISLANDS, and the trust territory Western SAMOA; U. of So. Afr.—SOUTH-WEST AFRICA. England acquired its 1st colony, Newfoundland, in 1583. But the foundations of the empire were not started until early 17th cent., with the chartering of the East India Co. and the consequent strife with Dutch and Portuguese colonies in the East. English settlements were also made in North America and the West Indies. Though the Thirteen Colonies were lost in the American Revolution, the Canadian and Indian provs. conquered from the French in the Seven Years War remained. Gibraltar was taken 1704, and in French and Napoleonic wars Br. sea power was strengthened by such conquests as Ceylon and Malta and the Dutch settlement at Cape of Good Hope. In late 18th cent. British power in Malaya grew. By 1829 all Australia was a Br. dependency and New Zealand was being rapidly settled. Aden was taken 1839 and Hong Kong in 1841. Its African territories were obtained in the 19th-cent. partition of the continent and, after First World War, in mandated former German territory. In the early stages of the growth of the empire, the English parliament made laws and imposed taxes enforced by royal governors in the colonies. It was some time after the American Revolution before Lord Durham made his report (1839) and the rigid colonial system was substantially changed. The same movement which resulted in the Reform Bill of 1832 extending the English franchise was reflected in the desire to make the colonies ever more self-governing members of the empire. The slave trade was abolished in 1833, and free trade became English policy in 1842–46, giving the colonies freedom to develop economically. Canada set the pattern of self-govt. by taking over direction of Canadian foreign policy in 1859 and became a dominion in 1867. In 1858 the long history of the East India Co. ended, and India came to be ruled by Parliament and crown. In 1877 Queen Victoria was proclaimed empress of INDIA, and in 1885 BURMA was added to India. In the European race for colonies in the last 20 years of the 19th cent., Great Britain not only increased British holdings in Africa immensely but also gained power in Egypt and acquired Malaya, Borneo, and over 100 isls. in the Pacific, and part of New Guinea. New dominions were created from the old colonies—Australia (1907), New Zealand (1907), Newfoundland (1907; joined Canada, 1949), and the Union of South Africa (1910). Through the Imperial Conference, begun in 1887, this loose association was held together with the United Kingdom and met the test of the First World War successfully. In the stress of war Egypt was declared a protectorate, and in the settlement after the war England received mandates over Tanganyika, PALESTINE (surrendered 1948), and IRAQ (surrendered 1932); Egypt regained independence in 1923, with the British reserving control of the Suez Canal (which it has held since 1875), and dominion status was granted to the Irish Free State in 1921. For the current organization of the self-governing dominions, see the article BRITISH COMMONWEALTH OF NATIONS.

British Guiana: see GUIANA, BRITISH.

British Honduras (hŏndōō′rŭs), formerly called *Belize* or *Balize*, Sp. *Belice*, British crown colony (□ 8,867, including 159 sq. mi. of coastal keys; pop. 59,220), Central America; ⊙ BELIZE, the chief port. On Caribbean coast and at SE base of YUCATAN PENINSULA, it is bounded N, along Río Hondo, by Mexican territory of Quintana Roo, and W (disputed boundary) and S (Sarstoon R.) by Guatemala, which claims all of Br. Honduras. The Gulf of Honduras flanks it SE. Within 300 mi. of Jamaica and 800 mi. S of New Orleans, the colony is bet. 18°29′–15°54′N and 88°10′–89°9′W. About 175 mi. long N–S, 70 mi. wide. The indented, swampy coast, stretching S from CHETUMAL BAY, is lined by lagoons and fringed by numerous keys (or cays) and reefs, among them AMBERGRIS CAY, and TURNEFFE ISLAND. The tropical land, covered by vast jungles, is largely low and flat, bisected by many short, turbulent rivers, such as NEW RIVER, BELIZE RIVER, and SIBUN RIVER. Inland (S) rise the MAYA MOUNTAINS, which reach 3,681 ft. in Victoria Peak of COCKSCOMB MOUNTAINS. W of those forested ridges are fine grasslands (savannas), The climate, tempered by NE tradewinds, varies bet. 90°F. and 60°F., while rainfall (annual mean 81.48 inches) increases considerably in S. Dry season lasts from mid-Feb. to mid-May. Hurricanes have frequently caused heavy damage. The fauna (reptiles, wild fowl, jaguars, tapirs, armadillos) is picturesque, and fish are plentiful in coastal waters. Country's entire economy depends on its ample forest products, chiefly mahogany, cedar, pine—shipped as logs and lumber—calaba or Santa Maria tree (timber and oil), rosewood, chicle, and sapodilla gum. Commercial crops, raised principally on coastal strip, include coconuts, bananas (decreasing because of plant disease), citrus fruit, sugar cane, cohune kernels, plantains. Grazing of cattle, hogs, and sheep. Alligator skins are a minor export. Br. Honduras also handles transit trade in mahogany and chicle from Petén (Guatemala). Imported are cotton goods, petroleum, hardware, clothing, shoes, liquor, tobacco. Bulk of foreign trade is with the U.S. Industries are almost exclusively devoted to lumbering and sawmilling; some rice hulling and extracting of fruit juices. The colony's communications are mostly by sea and air (Stanley Field, 10 mi. W of Belize). A small railroad from STANN CREEK (E) serves the banana plantations. Next to Belize rank the minor towns of COROZAL, ORANGE WALK, Stann Creek, PUNTA GORDA, CAYO, BENQUE VIEJO. The people are racially of very different components; about 38% Negro, 17% Indian (partly Maya), 7% Carib, c.2½% Asian, and 4% European. The rest are of mixed mulatto and mestizo stock. English is the official language, though Spanish is widely used; several Indian languages survive. Br. Honduras was part of the Maya civilization, to which testify remarkable ruins. It was probably entered by Cortés on his march to Honduras (1524–25), but the Spanish made no efforts at colonization. Instead, Br. bucanneers operated from the keys, founding Belize perhaps in mid-17th cent. First proper settlements were undertaken (about mid-17th cent.) by English woodcutters from Jamaica, who exploited the logwood (used in making dyes) found here. Spanish continued to contest the Br. possession until the battle of SAINT GEORGE'S CAY in 1798. With independence (1821) of Central American nations, Guatemala claimed the area, but abrogated (1859) its sovereignty in return for Br. promise to build road from Belize to Petén (N Guatemala). Since the project has so far not been carried out, Guatemala recently (1940s) renewed its claims. The dispute was brought (1946) to attention of the United Nations. Br. Honduras became a dependency of Jamaica in 1882, and an independent colony in 1884. It is headed by a governor assisted by an executive and legislative council. Divided administratively into 5 districts: BELIZE, CAYO, NORTHERN DISTRICT, STANN CREEK, and TOLEDO.

British India, name applied to that part of the former Br. INDIAN EMPIRE under direct Br. administration, in contradistinction to the INDIAN (or Native) STATES; ⊙ was New Delhi. From 1937, when Burma was separated from India and Aden became a crown colony, to 1947, when independent India and Pakistan were created, Br. India—in accordance with Govt. of India Act of 1935—comprised 11 governor's provs. (Assam, Bengal, Bihar, Bombay, Central Provs. and Berar, Madras, North-West Frontier Prov., Orissa, Punjab, Sind, United Provs.) and 6 chief commissioner's provs. (Ajmer-Merwara, Andaman and Nicobar Isls., Br. Baluchistan, Coorg, Delhi, Panth Piploda). In 1941: □ 865,446; including non-tabulated Assam tribal areas, □ 893,634; pop. 295,808,722.

British Isles: see GREAT BRITAIN and IRELAND.

British Kaffraria, U. of So. Afr.: see KAFFRARIA.

British Kombo, Gambia: see KOMBO SAINT MARY.

British Malaya: see MALAYA.

British New Guinea: see PAPUA, TERRITORY OF.

British North Borneo: see NORTH BORNEO.

British Somaliland (sōmä'lēlănd), officially **Somaliland Protectorate,** Br. protectorate (□ 68,000; pop. c.500,000) in E Africa, on Gulf of Aden; ⊙ Hargeisa. Bounded E by Ital. Somaliland, S and SW by Ethiopia, NW by Fr. Somaliland. Consists of a torrid coastal plain (Guban) in NE; the steep Ogo escarpment (rising to 7,900 ft.), NW of Hargeisa, which runs generally ENE, approaching coast E of Berbera; and the arid Haud plateau (nomadic grazing) in S. Extremely hot and dry. Rainfall (only in April, May) is adequate only near the escarpment. Stock raising (sheep, goats, camels) is chief occupation; some agr. (millet, corn, beans) in NW. Saltworks. Berbera, the chief port and former capital, exports sheep, hides and skins, gums (frankincense, myrrh). Coastal trade by dhow with Aden and S Arabian ports. Other pop. centers are Zeila (2d port), Hargeisa, Burao, Erigavo, Borama, and Las Anod. There are no railroads or interior waterways, but c.2,000 mi. of gravel roads. Airfields at Berbera and Hargeisa. The native Somali pop. (Moslem) is predominantly nomadic; the language possesses no written alphabet. Part of a powerful sultanate in Middle Ages. Under Br. influence throughout 19th cent., but nominally under Egypt until 1884, when Br. protectorate over Somali Coast was established. Was 1st administered by resident at Aden as a dependency of India. Bet. 1901 and 1910, British were harassed by native insurrections led by the "Mad Mullah," a self-proclaimed messiah. During Second World War, occupied by Italians (Aug., 1940–March, 1941). Hargeisa became permanent ⊙ after Br. reconquest.

British Sound, Madagascar: see DIÉGO-SUAREZ.

British Togoland: see TOGOLAND.

British West Indies: see WEST INDIES.

Brito (brē'tō), village, Rivas dept., SW Nicaragua, small port on the Pacific, 10 mi. SW of Rivas; 11°20′N 85°59′W. Terminus of one of routes of long-proposed Nicaragua Canal.

Briton Ferry, town (pop. 9,383) in Neath municipal borough, W Glamorgan, Wales, on inlet of Swansea Bay of Bristol Channel, at mouth of Neath R., 2 mi. SSW of Neath; coal and tinplate shipping port; tinplate, steel, and machinery works.

Brit River, Dorset, England, rises just N of Beaminster, flows 9 mi. S, past Beaminster and Bridport, to Lyme Bay of the Channel at West Bay, just S of Bridport.

Brits (brĭts), town (pop. 3,691), SW central Transvaal, U. of So. Afr., on Limpopo R. and 25 mi. W of Pretoria; rail junction; agr. center in Hartebeestpoort Irrigation Scheme region (wheat, tobacco, stock); site of agr. school and experimental farm.

Britt, town (pop. 1,908), Hancock co., N Iowa, near West Branch Iowa R., 30 mi. W of Mason City; processing of dairy products, tankage; mfg. of cabinets. A state park is NE. Inc. 1887.

Brittania Beach, town (pop. estimate 1,500), SW B.C., on E shore of Howe Sound, 26 mi. N of Vancouver; copper-mining center; by-products are gold and silver. Hydroelectric plant.

Brittany (brĭ'tunē), Breton *Breiz* (brĕz), Fr. *Bretagne* (brŭtä'nyŭ), region and former province of W France occupying a peninsula (175 mi. long, 125 mi. wide) bet. the English Channel (N) and the Bay of Biscay (S). It is now administratively divided into Finistère, Côtes-du-Nord, Ille-et-Vilaine, Morbihan, and Loire-Inférieure depts. Traditionally divided into *Armor* (densely pop. coastal region with numerous inlets, drowned rivers, headlands, and off-shore isls.) and *Argoat* (interior traversed by W ranges of Armorican Massif; cattle pastures). Breton language is still spoken by rural pop. in W Brittany. Extensive coastwise and deep-sea fishing is carried on from Saint-Malo (which sends its fleet to Newfoundland and Iceland), Saint-Brieuc, Douarnenez, Quimper, Quimperlé, Lorient, and the isls. of Belle-Île and Groix. Early vegetables, cultivated in the small coastal plains, are exported to England from Morlaix, Roscoff, Lannion. E Brittany, of gentler relief, near base of the peninsula, is drained by the Vilaine, the region's only noteworthy stream. In the Rennes basin agr. (including apple growing) and cattle raising are carried on. The Loire estuary, forming Brittany's S border, is the site of W France's major industrial area centered on Nantes and Saint-Nazaire. Though Nantes is the largest city and commercial center of Brittany, Rennes, its historical ⊙, has remained its intellectual center, where the Breton language is kept alive. Brest, Lorient, and Saint-Nazaire (all heavily damaged during Second World War) are important naval stations. The barren and rugged countryside, the numerous megalithic monuments (notably at Carnac and Locmariaquer), the colorful fishing ports, the remarkable architectural sites (churches, calvaries) and local traditions (old-fashioned dress, pilgrimages) of its inhabitants have made Brittany an outstanding tourist attraction. As part of anc. Armorica, it was conquered by Caesar during Gallic Wars. Settled (c.500) by refugees of Celtic origin from Britain (who gave Brittany its modern name), it went through a long struggle for independence, first from the Franks (5th–9th cent.), then from the counts of Anjou, and later from the kings of England. Unconquered by arms during the Hundred Years War, Brittany was joined to France by the marriage of Anne of Brittany to Charles VIII (1491) and Louis XII (1498), and of her daughter to Francis I (1514). During the French Revolution it became a royalist stronghold and sparked the Chouans and Vendée rebellion. Breton nationalism increased during the 19th cent. However, during Second World War the autonomous movement resisted collaboration with the Germans. Brittany was liberated by U.S. troops in Aug.–Sept., 1944, except for two pockets of resistance (Lorient and Saint-Nazaire) which held out until May, 1945. Damage to works of art was considerable.

Brittnau (brĭt'nou), town (pop. 2,791), Aargau canton, N Switzerland, on Wigger R. and 7 mi. SSE of Olten; shoes.

Britton. 1 Village (pop. 517), Lenawee co., SE Mich., 12 mi. NE of Adrian, in agr. area. **2** or **Britton City,** city (1940 pop. 2,239), Oklahoma co., central Okla., 5 mi. N of Oklahoma City, in oil-producing, agr., and dairying area. Mfg. of aluminum awnings, wood products, drilling supplies. Inc. as town 1909, as city 1933. **3** City (pop. 1,430), ⊙ Marshall co., NE S.Dak., 42 mi. NE of Aberdeen, near N.Dak. line; farming and cattle center; dairy products, livestock, poultry, wheat, corn. Municipal hosp. is here.

Brive Basin (brēv), Corrèze dept., S central France, extends c.40 mi. NW–SE from Lubersac to Beaulieu-sur-Dordogne, bet. Massif Central and Aquitaine Basin. Its vegetables and fruits are shipped to Paris from Brive-la-Gaillarde.

Brive-la-Gaillarde (–lä-gäyärd'), town (pop. 30,000), Corrèze dept., S central France, on Corrèze R. and 14 mi. ESE of Tulle; major communication and agr. trade center, shipping fruits (pears, melons, cherries, peaches) and vegetables (peas, asparagus, beans, tomatoes) to Paris area. Also trades in cattle, wool, poultry, truffles, chestnuts. Forges. Mfg.: footwear, tin cans, clothing and hosiery, paper, ink, accordions. Canning, brewing, distilling. Old town, clustered around 11th-13th-cent. church of St. Martin, surrounded by belt of boulevards. Many medieval bldgs. are preserved. Locally called Brive.

Brives-Charensac (brēv'-shärăsäk'), village (pop. 1,138), Haute-Loire dept., S central France, on the Loire and 2 mi. E of Le Puy; agr. market (grows and ships lentils); lacemaking.

Briviesca (brēvyä'skä), city (pop. 3,379), Burgos prov., N Spain, on Burgos-Vitoria highway, on railroad and 24 mi. NE of Burgos, and on fertile plain (La Bureba) watered by small Oca R. and abounding in fruit, cereals, nuts, livestock, timber. Flour milling, lumbering, tanning; mfg. of soap, chocolate, woolen goods, meat products. Old town of Roman origin. Here the Cortes met (1388) to create title of prince of Asturias for Castilian heir to throne. Parochial church and Santa Clara monastery. Sometimes spelled Bribiesca.

Brivio (brē'vyô), village (pop. 1,111), Como prov., Lombardy, N Italy, on Adda R. and 8 mi. SSE of Lecco, in cereal and raw silk region. Has anc. castle and many villas.

Brixellum, Italy: see BRESCELLO.

Brixen, Italy: see BRESSANONE.

Brixham (brĭk'sŭm), urban district (1931 pop. 8,145; 1951 census 8,761), S Devon, England, on Tor Bay of the Channel and 23 mi. S of Exeter; 50°24′N 3°30′W. Port, fishing center, and tourist resort, with paint works and limestone quarries. William of Orange landed here 1688. On near-by Windmill Hill is Bone Cavern, containing prehistoric remains. On the Channel, 2 mi. E, is promontory of Berry Head, with lighthouse (50°24′N 3°29′W).

Brixia, Italy: see BRESCIA, city.

Brixlegg (brēks'lĕk), town (pop. 1,862), Tyrol, W Austria, on the Inn and 17 mi. SW of Kufstein; smelters (lead, copper); summer resort. Copper pyrites mines, sulphur springs near by.

Brixton, workers' residential district of Lambeth, London, England, S of the Thames, 3 mi. SSE of Charing Cross. Here is one of London's largest prisons.

Brixworth, town and parish (pop. 1,173), central Northampton, England, 6 mi. N of Northampton; ironstone quarrying. Has church, built c.675, one of the oldest in England.

Brize Norton (brīz), village, SW Oxford, England, 13 mi. W of Oxford; large air base.

Brno (bûr'nô), Ger. *Brünn* (brün), city (pop. 133,637), ⊙ Brno prov. (□ 2,876; pop. 934,437), S Moravia, Czechoslovakia, just above confluence of Svitava R. with the Svratka, 115 mi. SE of Prague; 42°12′N 16°37′E. Second-largest city in Czechoslovakia; long ⊙ of Moravia and still seat of supreme court of Czechoslovakia. Trade, cultural, and communications center; hq. of cloth and woolen-textiles mfg.; terminus of gas pipe line from Podivin; mfg. of automobiles, wagons, arms (notably the Bren gun), machinery, electrical goods, clothing, leather goods, furniture, soap, candles, confectionery; brewing, sugar refining, food-, fur-, and rubber-processing industries. Greater Brno (pop. 213,127) includes 23 surrounding villages (e.g., KRALOVO POLE, LISEN, Husovice); airports at Cernovice and Turany. Old Town, with narrow streets, is enclosed by belt of boulevards and formerly had medieval fortifications; residential and mfg. suburbs date from 19th cent. Fortress of Spilberk (Czech *Špilberk*; Ger. *Spielberg*), once residence of margraves of Moravia and later (1621–1857) an Austrian political prison, dominates city from hill to W; Franz von der Trenck and Silvio Pellico were jailed here. Notable architectural features include 14th-cent. churches, 15th-cent. St. Peter and Paul cathedral, 16th-cent. old town hall with late-Gothic portal and Renaissance arcade, new town hall (formerly Guild Hall), 18th-cent. Plague column. Has major educational institutions: Mazaryk Univ. (1919), Benes technical college (1899), veterinary school, agr. and forestry institute, acad. of music, various trade schools. Local museums contain extensive prehistoric and folklore collections. R.C. bishopric. Founded in 9th cent., Brno's charter was confirmed (1229) by Ottocar I of Bohemia; inc. as city in 1243; ⊙ Moravia under Luxemburg rule (14th cent.), alternating with Olomouc, and from 1640 to 1948, when administrative divisions of Czechoslovakia were altered. Besieged (1645) for 16 weeks by Swedes under Torstensson: hq. (1805) of Napoleon's armies before battle of Austerlitz. Developed from agr. to industrial center after 1815. Formerly predominantly German, it now has all-Czech pop., particularly after Second World War, when Germans were expelled. War destroyed many residential parts and much of its industry; captured by Soviet troops in 1945. J. G. Mendel was abbot of Augustine monastery here. Some of most noted remains of Cro-Magnon man were found in alluvial deposits near Brno.

Broa, Ensenada de la, Cuba: see MATAMANÓ, GULF OF.

Broach (brōch), district, N Bombay, India; ⊙ Broach. Bounded W by Gulf of Cambay, NW by Mahi R., NE by Narbada R.; W end of Satpura Range is in E section. Agr. (cotton, millet, rice, wheat); timber forests (E); salt pans along coast. Chief towns: Broach, Anklesvar, Jambusar, Rajpipla. In 1930s, temporarily merged with Panch Mahals dist. Sometimes spelled Bharuch (bŭr′ŏŏch). Original Broach dist. (□ 1,468; pop. 397,201) was enlarged by inc. (1949) of former Gujarat state of Rajpipla.

Broach, anc. *Barugaza,* city (pop. 55,810), ⊙ Broach dist., N Bombay, India, port on Narbada R. and 185 mi. N of Bombay; rail junction; trade center; exports cotton, wheat, tiles, dal, firewood; cotton milling, hand-loom weaving, ink and glass mfg. An important port under Mauryan dynasty; taken 1573 by Akbar; had English and Dutch trading posts in early-17th cent. Sometimes Bharuch.

Broadalbin (brôdăl′bĭn, brôdôl′bĭn), village (pop. 1,400), Fulton co., E central N.Y., 8 mi. N of Amsterdam; summer resort, on Sacandaga Reservoir. Makes leather gloves. Settled 1770, inc. 1924.

Broad Bay or **Loch A Tuath** (lŏkh-ä tōō′ŭth), inlet of The Minch on E coast of Lewis with Harris, Outer Hebrides, Scotland, shielded E by Eye Peninsula; 8 mi. long, 4 mi. wide.

Broadbottom, England: see MOTTRAM IN LONGENDALE.

Broad Brook, Conn.: see EAST WINDSOR.

Broad Clyst (klĭst), town and parish (pop. 1,904), E central Devon, England, 5 mi. NE of Exeter; agr. market. Has 15th-cent. church.

Broad Creek, Del.: see LAUREL RIVER.

Broadford, town (pop. 1,101), central Victoria, Australia, 43 mi. N of Melbourne, in forested area; paper mills.

Broad Haven, inlet (7 mi. long, up to 5 mi. wide) of the Atlantic, NW Co. Mayo, Ireland, separating N part of Mullet Peninsula from mainland.

Broadhaven, small seaside resort in Walton West parish (pop. 328), W Pembroke, Wales, on St. Brides Bay of Irish Channel, 6 mi. WSW of Haverfordwest.

Broadheath, N suburb of urban dist. of Altrincham, N Cheshire, England, 8 mi. SW of Manchester; metal casting; mfg. of machine tools and chemicals.

Broadkill River, SE Del., rises W of Milton, flows c.15 mi. E, past Milton (head of navigation), to Delaware Bay c.4 mi. NW of Lewes. One of N entrances to Lewes and Rehoboth Canal is just inside its mouth.

Broadland (brôd′lŭnd), town (pop. 74), Beadle co., E central S.Dak., 10 mi. NNW of Huron.

Broadlands, village (pop. 333), Champaign co., E Ill., 19 mi. SE of Champaign, in agr. area.

Broad Law, Scotland: see MOFFAT HILLS.

Broadmoor, SW suburb (pop. 1,585) of Colorado Springs, El Paso co., central Colo.

Broad Pass, village (1939 pop. 10), S central Alaska, 90 mi. S of Nenana, on Alaska RR; supply point for gold-mining dist.

Broad Peak, peak (26,400 ft.), in main range of Karakoram mtn. system, N Kashmir, SE of K² peak, at 35°49′N 76°34′E. Up to 1950, not attempted by climbers.

Broad River. 1 In NE Ga., rises in the Blue Ridge, near Toccoa, flows c.90 mi. SE to Savannah R. 21 mi. SE of Elberton. **2** In N.C. and S.C., rises on E slope of the Blue Ridge SE of Asheville, flows SE into S.C., then S to Columbia, joining Saluda R. to form Congaree R.; 143 mi. long. Extensively used for hydroelectric power; has dams near Lake Lure town, N.C., and Pomaria, S.C. (Parr Shoals Dam). **3** In S S.C., tidal channel, c.18 mi. long, bet. mainland (W) and Port Royal and Parris isls. (E). Receives Coosawhatchie R. at N head; joins Coosaw R. channel on NE; continued S by Port Royal Sound.

Broads, The, region of shallow lakes and lagoons on E coast of England bet. Yarmouth (Norfolk) and Lowestoft (Suffolk), surrounded by marshland, and connected by the rivers Bure, Waveney, Yare, and others. It is a yachting and vacation center. There is an abundance of waterfowl. Also called Norfolk Broads.

Broad Sound, inlet of Coral Sea, E Queensland, Australia, bounded E by peninsula N of Rockhampton, just W of Shoalwater Bay; 35 mi. long, 30 mi. wide.

Broadstairs, resort town in urban dist. of Broadstairs and St. Peter's (1931 pop. 12,745; 1951 census 15,082), NE Kent, England, on the Channel, 2 mi. NNE of Ramsgate. Residence of Dickens here is now called Bleak House. York Gate (16th cent.) remains from town's former defenses. Town is sometimes called Bradstowe. Just W is village of St. Peter's (pop. 3,205).

Broad Top City, borough (pop. 483), Huntingdon co., S central Pa., 21 mi. SSW of Huntingdon, on Broad Top Mtn.; bituminous coal.

Broad Top Mountain, S Pa., plateaulike mtn.(c.2,000 ft.) of the Appalachian system, c.30 mi. SE of Altoona; rich bituminous coal beds.

Broadus (brô′dŭs), town (pop. 517), ⊙ Powder River co., SE Mont., on Powder R. and 70 mi. SSE of Miles City; trading point for agr. region; coal mines; livestock, grain, wool.

Broadview, town (pop. 634), SE Sask., 90 mi. E of Regina; grain elevators, lumbering.

Broadview. 1 Residential village (pop. 5,196), Cook co., NE Ill., W suburb of Chicago, in dairying and horticultural area. Veterans hosp. near by. Inc. 1913. **2** Village (pop. 1,630), Monroe co., S central Ind. **3** Town (pop. 164), Yellowstone co., S Mont., 27 mi. NW of Billings.

Broadview Heights, village (pop. 2,279), Cuyahoga co., N Ohio, a suburb 13 mi. S of downtown Cleveland. Inc. 1926.

Broadwater, village (pop. 614), NE New South Wales, Australia, on Richmond R. and 110 mi. SSE of Brisbane; sugar mill.

Broadwater, England: see WORTHING.

Broadwater, county (□ 1,243; pop. 2,922), W central Mont.; ⊙ Townsend. Agr. and mining region, drained by Missouri R. Livestock, grain; gold. Sections of Helena Natl. Forest in W and E. Formed 1897.

Broadwater, city (pop. 300), Morrill co., W Nebr., 15 mi. ESE of Bridgeport and on N.Platte R.; trout fishing; grain. Relics of prehistoric man near by.

Broadway, town and parish (pop. 2,138), SE Worcester, England, 5 mi. SE of Evesham; agr. market. Picturesque village, frequented by artists. Has 14th-cent. house, once belonging to abbots of Pershore, and 14th-cent. church.

Broadway. 1 Town (pop. 469), Lee co., central N.C., 7 mi. ESE of Sanford. **2** Town (pop. 561), Rockingham co., NW Va., in Shenandoah Valley, 12 mi. NNE of Harrisonburg; poultry-packing center.

Broadwell, village (pop. 149), Logan co., central Ill., 20 mi. NNE of Springfield, in agr. and bituminous-coal area.

Broager (brwä′yûr), town (pop. 1,158), Aabenraa-Sonderborg amt, S Jutland, Denmark, 4 mi. SW of Sonderborg; pottery, bricks.

Broby (brōō′bü″), village (pop. 817), Kristianstad co., S Sweden, on Helge R. and 16 mi. NNW of Kristianstad; grain, potatoes, sugar beets, stock. Sanitarium (just W).

Broc (brôk), Ger. *Bruck* (brŏŏk), village (pop. 1,553), Fribourg canton, W Switzerland, on Sarine R. and 14 mi. S of Fribourg; hydroelectric plant.

Brocéliande, France: see PAIMPONT, FOREST OF.

Broceni or **Brotseny** (brŏt′sānē), Lettish *Broceni,* town, W Latvia, in Kurzeme, on railroad and 3 mi. NNE of Saldus; cement plant.

Brochon (brôshõ′), village (pop. 349), Côte-d'Or dept., E central France, on E slope of the Côte d'Or, 7 mi. SSW of Dijon; Burgundy wines.

Brochow (brô′khōōf), Pol. *Brochów,* Ger. *Brockau* (brôk′ou), town (1939 pop. 8,689; 1946 pop. 3,150) in Lower Silesia, after 1945 in Wroclaw prov., SW Poland, 4 mi. SE of Breslau (Wroclaw) city center. Chartered after 1938.

Brock, village (pop. 283), Nemaha co., SE Nebr., 10 mi. NW of Auburn and on Little Nemaha R.; dairy and poultry produce, grain.

Brocken (brô′kŭn) or **Blocksberg** (blôks′bĕrk″), highest peak (3,747 ft.) of the Harz, central Germany, 8 mi. WSW of Wernigerode; 51°47′N 10°37′E. Site of meteorological observatory. "Specter of the Brocken" is magnified shadow of the spectator, reflected in foggy weather by the setting sun. In popular legend, mtn. is associated with Walpurgis Night or Witches' Sabbath. A scene in Goethe's *Faust* is laid here.

Brockenhurst, town and parish (pop. 2,482), SW Hampshire, England, in New Forest, 10 mi. SW of Southampton; agr. market. Norman church.

Brocket, England: see WELWYN GARDEN CITY.

Brocket, village (pop. 212), Ramsey co., NE central N.Dak., 24 mi. ENE of Devils Lake.

Brock Island (□ 414), NW Franklin Dist., Northwest Territories, in Arctic Ocean, off Borden Isls.; 77°55′N 114°W; 25 mi. long, 20 mi. wide.

Brockman, Mount (3,654 ft.), NW Western Australia, S of Hamersley Range.

Brockport, village (pop. 4,748), Monroe co., W N.Y., on the Barge Canal and 15 mi. W of Rochester, in agr. area; mfg. of canned foods, paper boxes, buttons, machinery; cold-storage plants; nurseries. Seat of a state teachers col. Inc. 1829.

Brock's Creek, settlement (dist. pop. 42), NW Northern Territory, Australia, 80 mi. SSE of Darwin; gold.

Brockton, industrial city (pop. 62,860), Plymouth co., E Mass., 20 mi. S of Boston. Formerly shoe capital of America and still 1 of the great centers (over 50 firms); mfg. (clothing, shoe machinery, leather, paper boxes, bakery products, beverages), printing. Settled c.1700, set off from Bridgewater 1821, inc. as city 1881.

Brockville, town (pop. 11,342), ⊙ Leeds and Grenville cos., SE Ont., river port on the St. Lawrence and 60 mi. S of Ottawa; dairying center; milk canning, meat packing, lumbering; mfg. of electrical equipment, hardware, castings, chemicals, hats. Also summer resort, near Thousand Isls.

Brockway. 1 Village (pop. c.150), McCone co., E Mont., on Redwater Creek and 10 mi. SW of Circle, in grain and livestock region. **2** Borough (pop. 2,650), Jefferson co., W central Pa., 8 mi. N of Du Bois; glass bottles, tiles, lumber, machinery, pigments; coal, gas; potatoes. Settled 1822, inc. 1883.

Brocton. 1 Village (pop. 406), Edgar co., E Ill., 14 mi. WNW of Paris; ships grain. **2** Village (pop. 1,380), Chautauqua co., extreme W N.Y., near L. Erie, 9 mi. SW of Dunkirk, in grape-growing area; mfg. (wine, preserved foods, plywood, machinery, furniture, veneer); agr. (poultry, truck). Annual grape festival held here. A short-lived community of the Brotherhood of the New Life was founded here in 1867 by Thomas Lake Harris. Inc. 1894.

Brod (brôt). **1** or **Bosanski Brod** (bô′sänskē), village (pop. 4,789), N Bosnia, Yugoslavia, on Sava R. (Croatia border), on railroad and 50 mi. NE of Banja Luka, opposite Slavonski Brod. Petroleum refinery (fuel oil, gasoline, kerosene); rail repair shops; lumber mills; plum trading. **2** or **Brod Makedonski** (măkĕdôn′skē), town (pop. 1,172), Macedonia, Yugoslavia, on Treska R. and 36 mi. SSW of Skoplje; market center for fruitgrowing region. Until c.1945, called Juzni Brod or Yuzhni Brod, Serbo-Croatian *Južni Brod.* **3** or **Brod Moravice** (mô′rävētsĕ), village, NW Croatia, Yugoslavia, on railroad and 18 mi. NW of Ogulin, near Slovenia border. **4** or **Brod na Kupi** (nä kōō′pē), village, NW Croatia, Yugoslavia, on Kupa R. and 23 mi. NE of Rijeka (Fiume), on Slovenia border. **5** or **Slavonski Brod** (slä′vônskē), Hung. *Bród* (brōd), anc. *Marsonia,* town (pop. 15,176), N Croatia, Yugoslavia, on Sava R. (Bosnia border) and 110 mi. ESE of Zagreb, at S foot of the Dilj, in Slavonia. Major river port; rail junction; trade and industrial center in wine- and plum-growing region; mfg. (railroad cars, locomotives, steam rollers, steam shovels, boilers), woodworking; fishing. Linked with Bosanski Brod, across the Sava, by one of largest bridges in Yugoslavia. Heavily damaged in Second World War.

Broderick, village (1940 pop. 1,721), Yolo co., central Calif., on Sacramento R., opposite Sacramento; river port in fruit growing and dairying area.

Broderick Falls, village, Nyanza prov., W Kenya, on railroad and 22 mi. N of Kakamega; cotton, peanuts, sesame, corn.

Brodeur Peninsula (brōdûr′), NW Baffin Isl., Northwest Territories, extends 200 mi. N into Lancaster Sound, bet. Prince Regent Inlet and the Gulf of Boothia (W) and Admiralty Inlet (E); 71°–73°52′N 83°58′–90°10′W; 45–90 mi. wide. It is connected with rest of Baffin Isl. by narrow isthmus. Coastal cliffs rise to c.1,000 ft.

Brodhead (brŏd′hĕd″). **1** Town (pop. 808), Rockcastle co., central Ky., on Dix R. and 26 mi. SE of Danville, in agr. area; flour and feed mills. **2** City (pop. 2,016), Green co., S Wis., near Sugar R., 20 mi. NW of Beloit, in dairying area; makes cheese, butter, buttons. Inc. 1891.

Brodheadsville, village (pop. c.600), Monroe co., E Pa., 11 mi. SW of Stroudsburg, in agr. and resort area.

Brodick (brŏ′dĭk), chief village of ARRAN isl., Buteshire, Scotland, on Arran's E coast; fishing port and resort.

Brod Makedonski, Yugoslavia: see BROD, Macedonia.

Brod Moravice, Yugoslavia: see BROD, NW Croatia.

Brod na Kupi, Yugoslavia: see BROD, NW Croatia.

Brodnax (brŏd′năks), town (pop. 499), Brunswick and Mecklenburg counties, S Va., 50 mi. SW of Petersburg, in agr. area (cotton, tobacco); cotton milling.

Brodnica (brôdnē′tsä), Ger. *Strasburg* (shträs′bŏŏrk), town (pop. 10,665), Bydgoszcz prov., N central Poland, on Drweca R. and 33 mi. ENE of Torun. Rail junction; mfg. of bricks, agr. machinery, furniture; tanning, flour milling, distilling. Castle ruins.

Brodokalmak (brŭdŭkŭlmäk'), village (1926 pop. 3,225), NE Chelyabinsk oblast, Russian SFSR, 37 mi. NE of Chelyabinsk; dairying; grain, livestock.

Brodósqui (brōdō'skē), city (pop. 1,959), NE São Paulo, Brazil, on railroad and 17 mi. NE of Ribeirão Prêto; coffee, sugar cane, grain. Formerly Brodowski.

Brody (brô'dē), city (1931 pop. 12,401), E Lvov oblast, Ukrainian SSR, 50 mi. ENE of Lvov; agr.-processing center (cereals, hops); cement mfg., sawmilling. Has ruins of 14th-cent. castle, old synagogue. Founded 1584; chartered 1684; developed as border station on Rus. frontier and commercial center (silk, hides, furs) under Austrian rule (1772–1918). In First World War, scene of military operations (1916). Reverted to Poland in 1919; ceded to USSR in 1945. Pop. largely Jewish prior to Second World War.

Bröe, Indonesia: see BRUE.

Broek or **Broek in Waterland** (brōōk' ĭn vä'tŭrlänt), village (pop. 1,148), North Holland prov., NW Netherlands, 6 mi. NE of Amsterdam; vegetable market.

Broga (brō'gä), village (pop. 578), NW Negri Sembilan, Malaya, on Selangor border, 14 mi. N of Seremban; tin mining.

Broghil Pass, Afghanistan and Pakistan: see BAROGHIL PASS.

Broglie (brôlyē'), village (pop. 805), Eure dept., NW France, 6 mi. SSW of Bernay; ribbon weaving, fruit preserving. Has partly Romanesque 12th-16th-cent. church.

Broich (broikh), industrial suburb of MÜLHEIM, W Germany, on left bank of the Ruhr, just opposite Mülheim city center.

Broichweiden (broikh'vī"dŭn), village (pop. 7,088), in former Prussian Rhine Prov., W Germany, after 1945 in North Rhine-Westphalia, 5 mi. NE of Aachen; leatherworking. Formed 1935 through unification of Broich and Weiden.

Brojce (brōō'ētsĕ), Pol. *Brójce*, Ger. *Brätz* (brĕts), town (1939 pop. 1,053; 1946 pop. 807) in Brandenburg, after 1945 in Zielona Gora prov., W Poland, 8 mi. NE of Swiebodzin; agr. market (grain, potatoes, livestock).

Brok (brôk), town (pop. 2,351), Warszawa prov., E central Poland, on Bug R. and 7 mi. S of Ostrow Mazowiecka; cement mfg., flour and groat milling.

Brokaw (brō'kô), village (pop. 380), Marathon co., central Wis., on Wisconsin R. and 4 mi. above Wausau; paper milling.

Broken Arrow, city (pop. 3,262), Tulsa co., NE Okla., 13 mi. SE of Tulsa, in agr. area (cotton, grain, fruit); cotton ginning, canning; mfg. of mattresses, flour, feed. Strip coal mining. Founded 1903.

Broken Bay, inlet of Pacific Ocean, E New South Wales, Australia, 25 mi. N of Sydney; 3 mi. wide across mouth; broken into small inlets. Receives Hawkesbury R. Kuring-gai Chase (large natl. park) on S shore. Woy Woy on N inlet and Palm Beach on S inlet, resort towns.

Broken Bow (bō). **1** City (pop. 3,396), ⊙ Custer co., central Nebr., 75 mi. NW of Grand Island and on Mud Creek; shipping point for livestock and grain. Settled 1880, inc. as city 1888. **2** Town (pop. 1,838), McCurtain co., extreme SE Okla., 45 mi. E of Hugo, in agr. (truck, grain, fruit, cotton) and timber area. Lumber milling, cotton ginning; mfg. of wood products, machine-shop products, novelties. A state park is c.8 mi. N. Settled 1910, inc. 1912.

Broken Hill, municipality (pop. 27,054), W New South Wales, Australia, near South Australia border, 220 mi. NE of its port, Port Pirie; 31°52'S 141°28'E. Principal silver-lead mining center of state; zinc, tin. Has steel and tin-plate mills. Mines began operating 1884.

Broken Hill, township (pop. 4,058), ⊙ Central Prov. (□ 47,000; pop. 200,000), Northern Rhodesia, on railroad and 70 mi. N of Lusaka; 14°28'S 28°25'E. Mining center (lead, zinc, vanadium); sulphide-ore treating plant. Airport. Broken Hill Mine township (pop. 4,543) adjoins W. Mine is noted for discovery (1921) of skull of prehistoric *Homo Rhodesiensis*. Mulungushi dam and power station for Broken Hill mine is 32 mi. SE. Broken Hill was ⊙ former Luangwa prov.

Brombach (brôm'bäkh), village (pop. 2,726), S Baden, Germany, on S slope of Black Forest, 1.5 mi. NNE of Lörrach; mfg. (cotton, machinery). Has ruined castle.

Bromberg, Poland: see BYDGOSZCZ, city.

Bromberger Kanal, Poland: see BYDGOSZCZ CANAL.

Bromborough, England: see BEBINGTON.

Brome, county (□ 488; pop. 12,485), S Que., on Vt. border; ⊙ Knowlton.

Brome, village (pop. 216), S Que., 16 mi. SE of Granby; dairying.

Bromham (brō'mŭm), agr. village and parish (pop. 1,296), central Wiltshire, England, 4 mi. NW of Devizes. Has 15th-cent. church where Thomas Moore is buried.

Bromide, town (pop. 258), on Coal-Johnston co. line, S Okla., 27 mi. SSE of Ada, in farm area; produces agr. lime.

Bromley (brŭm'lē), residential municipal borough (1931 pop. 45,374; 1951 census 64,178), NW Kent, England, 10 mi. SE of London; electrical and shoe industries. The 15th-cent. parish church, containing tomb of Dr. Johnson's wife, was destroyed by bombs in Second World War. There is home for widows of clergymen, founded 1666.

Bromley, village, Salisbury prov., E central Southern Rhodesia, in Mashonaland, 28 mi. SE of Salisbury; alt. 5,128 ft. Tobacco, corn, citrus fruit, dairy products.

Bromley (brŏm'–), town (pop. 980), Kenton co., N Ky., on left bank (levee) of the Ohio adjacent to LUDLOW; makes truck bodies.

Bromley Cross, England: see TURTON.

Bromley Mountain, Vt.: see MANCHESTER.

Bromma (brô'mä"), district (pop. 81,516) in W part of Stockholm city, Sweden, on L. Malar, 6 mi. W of city center; 59°21'N 17°57'E; has large airport.

Brommat (brômä'), village (pop. 106), Aveyron dept., S France, 13 mi. SE of Aurillac; has underground hydroelectric plant (completed 1934) on the Truyère. Sarrans plant (finished 1932) is 5 mi. upstream. Potential output: 270,000 kw.

Bromolla (brōō'mŭ"lä), Swedish *Bromölla*, town (pop. 2,833), Kristianstad co., S Sweden, on SE shore of Ivo L., 12 mi. E of Kristianstad; mfg. of bricks, cement, china, pottery.

Brompton, England: see GILLINGHAM, Kent.

Bromptonville, town (pop. 1,672), S Que., on St. Francis R. and 5 mi. NNW of Sherbrooke; lumbering, metalworking. Hydroelectric plant.

Bromsgrove (brŏmz'grōv), urban district (1931 pop. 9,520; 1951 census 27,924), N Worcester, England, 12 mi. NNE of Worcester; railroad shops, iron and bronze foundries, mfg. of nails, buttons, textiles. Has an old grammar school with late 17th-cent. bldgs., and 13th–15th-cent. church. Near by is the Birmingham sanatorium. Includes industrial former urban dist. of North Bromsgrove (1931 pop. 10,981).

Bromsten (brōm'stăn"), residential village (pop. 2,247), Stockholm co., E Sweden, 6 mi. NW of Stockholm city center.

Bromwich, England: see WEST BROMWICH.

Bromyard, urban district (1931 pop. 1,570; 1951 census 1,695), NE Hereford, England, on Frome R. and 13 mi. NE of Hereford; agr. market, with agr.-implement works. Church is of Norman origin. Grammar school was founded by Elizabeth.

Bron (brō), SE suburb (pop. 10,399) of Lyons, Rhône dept., E central France; aluminum and copper smelters. Produces household articles, hosiery, adding machines, construction materials, cartons, perfumes. Site of Lyons airport.

Bronaugh (brŭnô'), town (pop. 214), Vernon co., W Mo., 12 mi. SW of Nevada; agr.; coal mines.

Broncoed, Wales: see MOLD.

Bronderslev (brŭ'nŭrslĕv), Dan. *Brønderslev*, city (pop. 7,275), Hjorring amt, N Jutland, Denmark, 13 mi. S of Hjorring; machine shops, meat canneries, brewery.

Brondesbury Park, England: see WILLESDEN.

Broni (brô'nē), town (pop. 5,474), Pavia prov., Lombardy, N Italy, 10 mi. SE of Pavia; rail junction; wine, alcohol, canned foods, sausage. Mineral springs near by.

Bronitskaya Guta (brô'nyĭtskīŭ gōō'tŭ), town (1939 pop. over 500), W Zhitomir oblast, Ukrainian SSR, 27 mi. NW of Novograd-Volynski; refractory-clay quarries, peat bogs.

Bronkhorstspruit (brôngk'hôrst-sproit"), town (pop. 1,062), S central Transvaal, U. of So. Afr., on Bronkhorst Spruit R. and 35 mi. E of Pretoria; alt. 4,679 ft.; wheat, tobacco, potatoes. Scene (Dec., 1880) of opening action of Transvaal revolt; British defeated here.

Bronnitsy (–nyĭtsē), city (1926 pop. 3,797), central Moscow oblast, Russian SFSR, on Moskva R. and 35 mi. SE of Moscow; sawmilling, food processing, clothing mfg.; orchards. Chartered 1781.

Bronson. 1 Town (pop. 624), ⊙ Levy co., N Fla., 23 mi. SW of Gainesville; lumber, naval stores. **2** Town (pop. 247), Randolph co., E Ind., 16 mi. SE of Muncie, in agr. area. **3** City (pop. 415), Bourbon co., SE Kansas, 18 mi. W of Fort Scott; grain, livestock, poultry; dairying. **4** City (pop. 2,106), Branch co., S Mich., 11 mi. SW of Coldwater; shipping point for agr. area; mfg. of metal products, electrical equipment, fishing tackle, neon signs. Inc. as village 1866, as city 1934. **5** or **Lake Bronson,** village (pop. 438), Kittson co., NW Minn., on S fork of Two Rivers and 13 mi. ESE of Hallock, in grain, livestock, and potato area; dairy products. State park near by.

Bronte (brôn'tĕ), town (pop. 17,673), Catania prov., E Sicily, at W foot of Mt. Etna, 24 mi. NW of Catania; agr. center (cereals, fruit, almonds); wine, olive oil. Bombed (1943) in Second World War.

Bronte (brŏnt), town (pop. 1,020), Coke co., W Texas, 30 mi. N of San Angelo; farm market, processing and shipping point. Old Fort Chadbourne is c.7 mi. N.

Bronwood, town (pop. 337), Terrell co., SW Ga., 6 mi. NE of Dawson.

Bronx, the, northernmost borough (□ 41; pop. 1,451,277) of NEW YORK city, SE N.Y., bet. Manhattan and Westchester co.; bounded by water on 3 sides: Hudson R. (W), Spuyten Duyvil Creek and Harlem R. (SW), East R. (S), Long Isl. Sound (E); coextensive with Bronx co., formed 1914. Connected with Manhattan by subway tunnels, rail and vehicular bridges; with Manhattan and Queens by Triborough Bridge; with Queens by Hell Gate railroad bridge and Bronx-Whitestone Bridge. Generally hilly in center and W, lower in SE and E along East R. and Long Isl. Sound; includes City and Harts isls. in the sound, Rikers and North Brother isls. in East R. Small Bronx and Hutchinson rivers (paralleled by landscaped highways) and Westchester Creek flow generally S through borough. Main highways bet. New York city and upstate and New England points pass through borough: Henry Hudson Parkway (becoming Saw Mill River Parkway in Van Cortlandt Park), Broadway (becoming Albany Post Road in Westchester), the Grand Concourse (leading into Bronx River Parkway near Bronx Park), Boston Post Road, and Hutchinson River Parkway, which is connected (via Bronx-Whitestone Bridge) with Long Isl. highways. Served by subways, bus and trolley lines, and the N.Y., New Haven and Hartford and the N.Y. Central railroads. Mainly residential; its best-known sections are Jerome Park, Riverdale, University Heights, Westchester Heights, Williamsbridge (site of N.Y. Inst. for the Education of the Blind), and Woodlawn. Industries are mainly in SW and S, along Harlem R. (shipping); here are railroad yards, a barge terminal, factories, coal- and lumberyards, and Bronx Terminal Market (wholesale produce). Mfg. of clothing, textiles, food products, chemicals, machinery, musical instruments, furniture; and wood, paper, and stone products. Among its large parks are Bronx Park (□ c.1), with noted zoo (N.Y. Zoological Park) and N.Y. Botanical Garden, and Van Cortlandt and Pelham Bay parks, with extensive recreational facilities. Here are Fordham Univ., Manhattan Col., Col. of Mount St. Vincent, N.Y. State Maritime Col. (at Fort Schuyler), divisions of New York Univ. (with Hall of Fame), and divisions of Hunter Col. Other points of interest: Yankee Stadium, home of N.Y. Yankees baseball team; Bronx Co. Bldg.; cottage occupied (1846–49) by Edgar Allen Poe; and the Van Cortlandt House (1748) in Van Cortlandt Park. Region 1st settled (1641) for Dutch West India Company by Jonas Bronck. Remained part of Westchester co. until its W townships were annexed (1874) by New York city; other townships followed in 1895, and the Bronx subsequently became (1898) a borough of New York city and (1914) a co. of N.Y. state.

Bronx River, SE N.Y., small river issuing from S end of Kensico Reservoir in S Westchester co., flows c.20 mi. SSW, past many residential communities and through Bronx borough of New York city, to bay on N shore of East R. Navigable in lower 2¼ mi.; has shipping terminals. Part of its course is followed by Bronx River Parkway, one of 1st landscaped super-highways in New York city area.

Bronxville, residential village (pop. 6,778), Westchester co., SE N.Y., a N suburb of New York city, bet. Mount Vernon (S) and Tuckahoe (N); part of Eastchester town. Seat of Sarah Lawrence Col., Concordia Collegiate Inst., and a school for girls. Settled 1664, inc. 1898.

Bronx-Whitestone Bridge, SE N.Y., vehicular suspension bridge across East R. bet. SE Bronx borough and Whitestone section of Queens borough of New York city; link bet. New England and Long Isl. highways. Completed 1939; 3,770 ft. long, with 2,300-ft. center span 135 ft. above water.

Bronzani Majdan, Bronzani Maidan, or **Bronzani Maydan** (all: brôn'zänē mī'dän), village (pop. 5,126), NW Bosnia, Yugoslavia, 12 mi. W of Banja Luka.

Bronzolo (brôn'tsôlô), Ger. *Branzoll*, Bolzano prov., Trentino–Alto Adige, N Italy, near Isarco R., 7 mi. S of Bolzano; porphyry quarries.

Brook, town (pop. 915), Newton co., NW Ind., near Iroquois R., c.40 mi. NW of Lafayette, in agr. area; mfg. of cosmetics.

Brookdale, resort village, Santa Cruz co., W Calif., in Santa Cruz Mts., 12 mi. NNW of Santa Cruz. Redwood groves near by.

Brooke, county (□ 89; pop. 26,904), W.Va., in industrial Northern Panhandle; ⊙ Wellsburg. Bounded W by Ohio R. (Ohio line), E by Pa. Mfg. (especially iron, steel, chemicals, glass, paper products) at Wellsburg, Follansbee. Coal mines, natural-gas and oil wells. Some agr. (fruit, grain, sheep, poultry). Formed 1797.

Brooker, town (pop. 277), Bradford co., N Fla., 15 mi. N of Gainesville.

Brooke's Point, town (1939 pop. 1,180; 1948 municipality pop. 28,476), on SE coast of Palawan isl., Philippines, 90 mi. SW of Puerto Princesa, at foot of Mt. Mantalingajan; 8°46'N 117°50'E.

Brooketon, Brunei, Borneo: see MUARA.

Brookeville, town (pop. 117), Montgomery co., central Md., 20 mi. N of Washington; truck, dairy products.

Brook Farm, Mass.: see BOSTON.

Brookfield. 1 Resort town (pop. 1,688), Fairfield co., SW Conn., bet. L. Candlewood and the Housatonic, on Still R. and 6 mi. NNE of Danbury; metalworking. Inc. 1788. **2** Residential village (pop. 15,472), Cook co., NE Ill., W suburb of Chicago. Chicago Zoological Park, or Brookfield Zoo, is near by. Inc. 1893. **3** Town (pop. 1,567), including Brookfield village (pop. 1,017), Worcester co., S central Mass., 15 mi. WSW of Worcester; resort (Quaboag Pond); mfg. (wire, cables, gummed paper); dairying. Settled 1664, inc. 1718. **4** City (pop. 5,810), Linn co., N central Mo., 40 mi. SW of Kirksville; ships grain; some mfg.; railroad shops; coal. Pershing State Park at near-by Laclede. Founded 1859. **5** Town (pop. 159), Carroll co., E N.H., 20 mi. ENE of Laconia, in recreational area. **6** Town (pop. 762), Orange co., central Vt., in Green Mts., 16 mi. S of Montpelier and on Second Branch of White R. Allis State Forest near by.

Brookford, town (pop. 768), Catawba co., W central N.C., 2 mi. S of Hickory; mfg. of cotton goods.

Brookgreen, former plantation, Georgetown co., E S.C., bet. Waccamaw R. and the Atlantic, 15 mi. NE of Georgetown. Brookgreen Gardens (4,000 acres), created from parts of 4 old estates, attract tourists.

Brookhaven. 1 City (pop. 7,801), ⊙ Lincoln co., SW Miss., c.50 mi. SSW of Jackson; trade and processing center for dairying, agr., and timber area; work clothes, cottonseed oil, dairy products, furniture, brick, lumber. Has a jr. col. Founded 1851. **2** Summer-resort village (1940 pop. 518), Suffolk co., SE N.Y., on S shore of Long Isl., on Bellport Bay (inlet of Great South Bay), 5 mi. ENE of Patchogue. Brookhaven Natl. Laboratory for atomic research is c.7 mi. N. **3** Borough (pop. 1,042), Delaware co., SE Pa., 10 mi. SW of downtown Philadelphia. Inc. 1945.

Brookings, county (□ 801; pop. 17,851), E S.Dak., on Minn. line; ⊙ Brookings. Agr. area drained by Big Sioux R. Dairy products, livestock, poultry, corn. Formed 1862.

Brookings. 1 Village (pop. c.400), Curry co., SW Oregon, on the Pacific, c.55 mi. SW of Grants Pass, in dairying area; lumber milling. **2** City (pop. 7,764), ⊙ Brookings co., E S.Dak., 50 mi. N of Sioux Falls; trade center for farming area; flour, dairy products, livestock, poultry, corn, oats, barley. Hq. of Cooperative Wool Growers Assn. S.Dak. State Col. of Agr., Mechanic Arts here. Col. has bell tower equipped with beacon light that serves local airport. Platted 1879.

Brookland. 1 Town (pop. 334), Craighead co., NE Ark., 8 mi. NW of Jonesboro. **2** Town, Lexington co., S.C.: see WEST COLUMBIA.

Brooklands, village (pop. 2,728), SE Man., suburb of Winnipeg.

Brooklands, England: see WALTON AND WEYBRIDGE.

Brookland Terrace, residential village (1940 pop. 874), New Castle co., N Del., just W of Wilmington. Reform school for boys near by.

Brooklawn, residential borough (pop. 2,262), Camden co., SW N.J., on Delaware R. just below Camden. Built in First World War to house shipyard workers; inc. 1924.

Brooklet, town (pop. 536), Bulloch co., E Ga., 8 mi. SE of Statesboro; lumber, feed.

Brookley Air Force Base, Ala.: see MOBILE, city.

Brooklin, town (pop. 546), Hancock co., S Maine, 25 mi. SW of Belfast, in agr., recreational area; cannery here.

Brookline (brŏŏk'līn). **1** Town (pop. 57,589), in exclave of Norfolk co. (bet. Suffolk and Middlesex counties), E Mass.; a beautiful residential W suburb of Boston, with some small mfg. Included in Boston as "Muddy River" until separately inc. in 1705. Includes part of CHESTNUT HILL. **2** Village (pop. 1,504), Jackson co., S Mich. **3** Agr. town (pop. 671), Hillsboro co., S N.H., on Mass. line and 10 mi. WSW of Nashua; lumbering, granite quarrying; winter sports. **4** Village, Delaware co., Pa.: see HAVERFORD. **5** Town (pop. 132), Windham co., SE Vt., 13 mi. N of Brattleboro.

Brooklyn, village (pop. estimate 400), SW N.S., on Liverpool Harbour, at mouth of Mersey R., opposite Liverpool; paper milling.

Brooklyn (brŏŏk'lĭn). **1** Town (pop. 2,652), Windham co., E Conn., on Quinebaug R. and 14 mi. ENE of Willimantic, in agr. area; electrical products, yarn. Includes East Brooklyn village (pop. 1,062). Has 18th-cent. houses, monument to Gen. Israel Putnam, whose farm and tavern are here. Settled c.1703, inc. 1786. **2** Village (pop. 2,568), St. Clair co., SW Ill., on the Mississippi just above East St. Louis, within St. Louis metropolitan dist.; all-Negro community. Also called Lovejoy. Inc. 1873. **3** Town (pop. 592), Morgan co., central Ind., on Whitelick R. and 20 mi. SW of Indianapolis, in agr. area; brick, tile. **4** Town (pop. 1,323), Poweshiek co., central Iowa, 14 mi. E of Grinnell, in livestock and grain area. Inc. 1869. **5** Village (pop. 862), Jackson co., S Mich., 13 mi. SE of Jackson; packs popcorn. **6** Borough (□ 71; pop. 2,738,175) of NEW YORK city, SE N.Y., on extreme W Long Isl. SE of downtown Manhattan, from which it is separated by East R.; coextensive with Kings co. Bounded N and NE by Newtown Creek, by Queens borough line (E), Jamaica Bay (SE), Lower New York Bay (S and SW), the Narrows (separating borough from Staten Isl.) and Upper New York Bay (W). Connected with Manhattan by Brooklyn, Manhattan, and Williamsburg bridges, by subway tunnels, and Brooklyn-Battery vehicular tunnel (completed 1950). Ferries connect with Staten Isl., which will eventually be linked to Brooklyn by bridge across the Narrows. A belt highway system (Shore Parkway) runs around SW, S, and SE shores to join Southern Parkway in Queens. Although most of borough is residential (it is often called "City of Homes"), Brooklyn's extensive water front on the Upper Bay is an important port area handling much foreign and domestic commerce; chief products of the adjacent industrial dist. are machinery, textiles, clothing, shoes, paint, beer, paper and chemical goods, and processed foods, especially coffee and sugar. Here are huge Bush Terminal (docks and warehouses), Erie and Atlantic shipping basins, N.Y. State Barge Canal Terminal, Brooklyn Army Base, grain elevators, shipyards, and miles of piers. On Wallabout Bay (wŏ'lŭbout) (inlet of East R.) is N.Y. Naval Shipyard (established 1801), commonly called Brooklyn Navy Yard. Heart of downtown Brooklyn is at Borough Hall (1849), not far from Brooklyn Bridge; here are courthouses, co. and borough govt. bldgs., and chief business, shopping, and entertainment dist. To W is old Brooklyn Heights (once most exclusive residential area of New York city), overlooking the Upper Bay; to NE is Navy Yard dist.; beyond is residential Williamsburg, site of Wallabout Market (public) and a naval hosp.; and at N tip of borough is Greenpoint, at junction of Newtown Creek with East R. To SW and S of Borough Hall are port and industrial dists. (SOUTH BROOKLYN, Gowanus, Red Hook, Bush Terminal) centering on Gowanus Bay (gŭwä'nŭs). Along the Narrows and Gravesend Bay (an arm of Lower Bay) in SW are residential Sunset Park, Bay Ridge, Fort Hamilton (U.S. Fort Hamilton here), Dyker Beach Park (golfing). In S, on Lower Bay near the Atlantic, are CONEY ISLAND, famed amusement resort, and adjacent shore communities. Floyd Bennett Field (naval air station) and Marine Park are on Jamaica Bay in SE. Points of interest in Brooklyn: Prospect Park (c.500 acres), with notable Brooklyn Botanic Garden, a zoo, a lake, and recreational facilities; Brooklyn Mus., Children's Mus., the borough's central library, Grand Army Plaza, Long Island Historical Society, Ebbets Field (home of the Brooklyn Dodgers), Lefferts Homestead (1777). Brooklyn neighborhoods (some the survivals of earlier independent villages) include Bushwick, Bedford, Bensonhurst, Ridgewood, Flatbush, Sheepshead Bay, Flatlands, Canarsie, Brownsville, East New York. Seat of Brooklyn Col., Polytechnic Inst. of Brooklyn, Pratt Inst., St. John's Univ., St. Joseph's Col. for Women, Long Isl. Univ., Long Isl. Col. of Medicine, St. Francis Col., Brooklyn Law School, Cathedral Col. of the Immaculate Conception, the jr. col. of the Packer Collegiate Inst., and a state institute of applied arts and sciences. Brooklyn Inst. of Arts and Sciences directs the noted Brooklyn Acad. of Music, the museums, and the Botanic Garden. Among the many churches are Reformed Protestant Dutch Church of Flatbush (built 1654; present bldg. dates from 1796), St. Ann's Episcopal Church (established 1784), and Plymouth Church, where Henry Ward Beecher preached. Hollanders and Walloons settled about Gowanus and Wallabout bays in 1636–37; c.1645, Dutch farmers founded the hamlet of Breuckelen, near present Borough Hall. Area became known as Brooklyn under the English; inc. as village of Brooklyn Ferry in 1816, chartered as Brooklyn city in 1834. Williamsburg was absorbed in 1855, and Brooklyn became 3d-largest city in U.S. During its growth, it absorbed many early settlements (Flatbush, New Utrecht, Gravesend, and others) until it included all of Kings co. (established 1683). Completion of Brooklyn Bridge (1883) as 1st crossing over East R. gave impetus to movement for consolidation with New York city; in 1898, with pop. of c.1,000,000, Brooklyn became a borough of greater New York. Battle of Long Island (1776), a Colonial defeat in the Revolution, was fought here. Walt Whitman was editor (1846–47) of its noted newspaper, the Brooklyn *Daily Eagle* (begun 1841). In Brooklyn's long past as a separate municipality, its educational and cultural institutions arose independently of those in neighboring New York and contributed greatly to the spirit of individuality which characterizes the borough. Its citizens' fervid local patriotism and alleged characteristic speech ("Brooklynese") have inspired countless amiable jokes. **7** City (pop. 6,317), Cuyahoga co., N Ohio, a S suburb of Cleveland. Inc. 1927. **8** Village (pop. 479), on Green-Dane co. line, S Wis., 15 mi. S of Madison; dairy, stock, poultry farms; makes condensed milk.

Brooklyn Bridge, SE N.Y., first-built (1869–83) and southernmost of the bridges across East R., bet. lower Manhattan and Brooklyn; a suspension bridge, with a 1,595-ft. span.

Brooklyn Center, village (pop. 4,284), N suburb of Minneapolis, Hennepin co., E Minn., on Mississippi R. Inc. 1911.

Brooklyn Heights. 1 A residential section of NW Brooklyn borough of New York city, SE N.Y. **2** Village (pop. 931), Cuyahoga co., N Ohio, a S suburb of Cleveland.

Brookneal, town (pop. 883), Campbell co., SW central Va., on Roanoke R. and 27 mi. SE of Lynchburg; tobacco market; makes agr. machinery. Grave and former estate ("Red Hill") of Patrick Henry near by.

Brook Park. 1 Village (pop. 148), Pine co., E Minn., 10 mi. NW of Pine City; dairy products. **2** Village (pop. 2,606), Cuyahoga co., N Ohio, a SW suburb of Cleveland; municipal airport is here. Inc. 1914.

Brookport, city (pop. 1,119), Massac co., extreme S Ill., on Ohio R. (bridged here), opposite Paducah, Ky.; trade center for agr. area (wheat, corn, hay); mfg. (buttons, railroad ties). Large U.S. wicket dam (1926) is near by. Inc. 1888.

Brooks, town (pop. 1,091), S Alta., near L. Newell (10 mi. long, 5 mi. wide), 65 mi. NNW of Medicine Hat, in irrigated region; natural-gas production, alfalfa-seed processing, ranching.

Brooks. 1 County (□ 492; pop. 18,169), S Ga.; ⊙ Quitman. Bounded S by Fla. line, E by Little and Withlacoochee rivers. Coastal plain agr. (tobacco, cotton, corn, melons, peanuts, livestock) and timber (lumber, naval stores) area. Formed 1858. **2** County (□ 908; pop. 9,195), S Texas; ⊙ Falfurrias. Diversified irrigated agr.: citrus, truck, fruit, cotton; beef cattle; dairying, poultry raising, beekeeping. Oil and natural-gas fields; gypsum, clay, slate. Formed 1911.

Brooks. 1 Town (pop. 136), Fayette co., W central Ga., 12 mi. WNW of Griffin, in agr. area. **2** Town (pop. 747), Waldo co., S Maine, 10 mi. NNW of Belfast, in recreational area.

Brooks Air Force Base, Texas: see SAN ANTONIO.

Brooksburg, town (pop. 132), Jefferson co., SE Ind., near Ohio R., 8 mi. E of Madison, in agr. area.

Brookshire (brŏŏk'shĭr), town (pop. 1,015), Waller co., S Texas, 35 mi. W of Houston, in cotton, rice, truck area; cotton gins. Inc. after 1940.

Brookside. 1 Town (pop. 733), Jefferson co., central Ala., 11 mi. NW of Birmingham. Coal mines in vicinity. **2** Town (pop. 175), Fremont co., S central Colo., near Arkansas R., 4 mi. SE of Canon City; alt. 5,240 ft. **3** Mining village (pop., with adjacent Ages, 1,190), Harlan co., SE Ky., in the Cumberlands, on Clover Fork of Cumberland R. and 4 mi. E of Harlan; bituminous coal. **4** Village (pop. 845), Belmont co., E Ohio, 4 mi. N of Bellaire, and on small Wheeling Creek, in coal-mining area.

Brooks Mount (11,910 ft.), S central Alaska, in Alaska Range, in Mt. McKinley Natl. Park, 140 mi. N of Anchorage; 63°11′N 150°39′W.

Brooks Peninsula, SW B.C., on NW Vancouver Isl., forming Brooks Bay (NW) and Checleset Bay (SE); 12 mi. long, 6 mi. wide. W extremity is Cape Cook (50°7′N 127°55′W).

Brooks Range, N Alaska, northernmost part of Rocky Mts., extends c.600 mi. W-E in lat. 68°N from Chukchi Sea to Yukon border, bet. Yukon R. and Arctic Ocean. Includes Baird, Davidson, De Long, Endicott mts. Highest peak, Mt. Michelson (9,239 ft.), in E part of range; rises over 7,000 ft. in W part. S foothills forested; sparsely populated, with some gold-mining villages on S slope. Named for A. H. Brooks, geologist.

Brookston. 1 Town (pop. 1,014), White co., NW central Ind., 13 mi. N of Lafayette, in agr. area. **2** Village (pop. 180), St. Louis co., E Minn., on St. Louis R. near mouth of Cloquet R., in Fond du Lac Indian Reservation, and 23 mi. W of Duluth; grain, potatoes.

Brooksville. 1 City (pop. 1,818), ⊙ Hernando co., W central Fla., c.40 mi. N of Tampa; rail junction; shipping center for citrus fruit and limestone area; packing houses, cannery, concrete plant, sawmill. Near by are Devil's Punch Bowl, an arid sink, and Weekiwachee Spring, which forms a river flowing 12 mi. to Gulf of Mexico. Inc. 1925. **2** Town (pop. 622), ⊙ Bracken co., N Ky., 24 mi. NNE of Cynthiana, in agr. area (burley tobacco, corn, wheat, dairy products). **3** Town (pop. 751), Hancock co., S Maine, 18 mi. SW of Belfast, in agr., recreational area. **4** Town (pop. 819), Noxubee co., E Miss., 20 mi. SSW of Columbus, in agr., dairy, and timber area; cheese plant. Post office name formerly Brookville.

Brookton, town (pop. 206), Washington co., E Maine, on Baskahegan L. and 35 mi. NW of Calais, in hunting, fishing area.

Brookvale, town (pop. 1,988), E New South Wales, Australia, 8 mi. NNE of Sydney; coal mining.

Brookville. 1 Town (pop. 2,538), ⊙ Franklin co., SE Ind., on Whitewater R. at influx of its East Fork, and 29 mi. SSW of Richmond; trading center in agr. area (grain, tobacco); mfg. (furniture, feed, fiber boxes). Settled 1804, platted 1808. Lew Wallace b. here. **2** City (pop. 213), Saline co., central Kansas, 15 mi. WSW of Salina, in wheat and livestock region. 3 Town, Noxubee co., Miss.: see BROOKSVILLE. **4** Village (pop. 337), Nassau co., SE N.Y., on W Long Isl., 7 mi. NE of Mineola, in potato- and cabbage-growing area. **5** Village (pop. 1,908), Montgomery co., W Ohio, 14 mi. WNW of

Dayton, and on small Wolf Creek, in agr. area (tobacco, grain); furniture, transportation equipment, grain and dairy products. 6 Borough (pop. 4,274), ⊙ Jefferson co., W central Pa., on Redbank Creek and 38 mi. SE of Oil City. Bituminous coal, oil, gas; metal and clay products, glass; railroad shops; peas. Settled 1801, laid out 1830, inc. 1843. Cook Forest State Park is NNW.

Brookwood, England: see WOKING.

Broom, Loch (lŏkh), sea inlet in NW Ross and Cromarty, Scotland; 15 mi. long, 5 mi. wide at mouth. On E shore is ULLAPOOL. In its mouth are the SUMMER ISLES. Little Loch Broom (9 mi. long) is S.

Broome, town and port (pop. 793), N Western Australia, 700 mi. SW of Darwin and on N shore of Roebuck Bay; 17°58'S 122°14'E. Pearling center; exports pearls, pearl shell, hides, livestock, wool. Airport.

Broome, county (□ 710; pop. 184,698, S N.Y., bounded by Pa. line (S); ⊙ Binghamton. Drained by Susquehanna, Chenango, Tioughnioga, West Branch of the Delaware, and Otselic rivers. Includes Chenango Valley State Park. Dairying area, with extensive mfg., especially at shoe-mfg. centers of Binghamton, Endicott, and Johnson City; agr. (grain, truck, poultry, livestock, potatoes); produces maple sugar and syrup. Formed 1806.

Broome, Mount, Australia: see King LEOPOLD RANGES.

Broomes Island, village, Calvert co., S Md., on narrow point in Patuxent R. and 9 mi. SSW of Prince Frederick; sport fishing.

Broomfield, town and parish (pop. 1,646), central Essex, England, on Chelmer R. and 3 mi. N of Chelmsford; agr. market.

Broomhill, town in parish of East Chevington (pop. 3,237), E Northumberland, England, 8 mi. SSE of Alnwick; coal mining.

Broons (brõ), village (pop. 917), Côtes-du-Nord dept., W France, on Arguenon R. and 14 mi. SW of Dinan; cider making. Birthplace of Bertrand Du Guesclin.

Broos, Rumania: see ORASTIE.

Brooten (brōō'tĭn), village (pop. 669), Stearns co., central Minn., c.45 mi. W of St. Cloud, in agr. area; dairy products.

Brora (brô'rů), town, SE Sutherland, Scotland, on coast at mouth of Brora R., 11 mi. NNE of Dornoch; seaside resort; woolen milling. Clynekirkton village, 2 mi. NNW, has distillery.

Brora River, Sutherland, Scotland, rises 9 mi. N of Lairg, flows 26 mi. SE to Moray Firth at Brora. On lower course is Loch Brora, 4 mi. long, with salmon hatchery.

Brorup (brů'rŏŏp), Dan. *Brørup,* town (pop. 1,650), Ribe amt, S central Jutland, Denmark, 22 mi. E of Esbjerg; furniture mfg. Agr. school.

Broseley, England: see WENLOCK.

Broshnev-Osada (brôsh'nyĭf-ŭsä'dů), Pol. *Brosz-niów,* town (1939 pop. over 500), W Stanislav oblast, Ukrainian SSR, 9 mi. ENE of Dolina, in salt and potash area.

Brosna River, cos. Westmeath and Offaly, Ireland, issues from Lough Ennell, flows 30 mi. SW, past Clara and Ferbane, to the Shannon at Shannon Harbour.

Bross, Mount (14,169 ft.), central Colo., in Park Range, 12 mi. NE of Leadville.

Brossac (brôsäk'), agr. village (pop. 321), Charente dept., W France, 11 mi. SSE of Barbezieux.

Brossasco (brôs-sä'skô), village (pop. 455), Cuneo prov., Piedmont, NW Italy, on Varaita R. and 8 mi. SW of Saluzzo; hydroelectric plant.

Brosso (brôs'sô), village (pop. 559), Torino prov., Piedmont, NW Italy, 4 mi. NW of Ivrea. Pyrite mine near by.

Brosteni (brôshtān'), Rum. *Broşteni.* **1** Agr. village (pop. 106), Gorj prov., SW Rumania, 15 mi. NE of Turnu-Severin. **2** Village (pop. 715), Jassy prov., NE Rumania, on Bistrita R. and 40 mi. NW of Piatra-Neamt; climatic resort in the Moldavian Carpathians; lumbering center.

Broszniow, Ukrainian SSR: see BROSHNEV-OSADA.

Brotas (brô'tŭs). **1** City, Bahia, Brazil: see BROTAS DE MACAÚBAS. **2** City (pop. 2,686), central São Paulo, Brazil, on railroad and 37 mi. WNW of Rio Claro; coffee, cotton, sugar cane, cattle, poultry.

Brotas de Macaúbas (dĭ mäkäōō'bůs), city (pop. 922), central Bahia, Brazil, 90 mi. NW of Andaraí; diamond and gold mining. Until 1944, Brotas.

Brothers, The, two small islands in Indian Ocean, c.30 mi. SW of Socotra isl., of which they are a dependency, and 150 mi. E of Cape Guardafui; fisheries.

Brothertown, village (pop. c.150), Calumet co., E Wis., on E shore of L. Winnebago and 15 mi. NNE of Fond du Lac, in agr. region. Settled 1832 by Brothertown Indians.

Brotseny, Latvia: see BROCENI.

Brotterode (brô"tŭrō'dů), town (pop. 4,632), formerly in an exclave of former Prussian prov. of Hesse-Nassau, central Germany, after 1945 in Thuringia, in Thuringian Forest, at S foot of the Inselsberg, 7 mi. N of Schmalkalden; metalworking; climatic health and winter-sports resort. Destroyed by fire in 1895.

Brotton, England: see SKELTON AND BROTTON.

Brou (brōō), town (pop. 2,507), Eure-et-Loir dept., NW central France, 12 mi. NW of Châteaudun; agr. market (cereals, poultry, dairy produce) in horse-raising area. Agr. equipment mfg.

Brouage, France: see HIERS-BROUAGE.

Brough (brŭf). **1** Town and parish (pop. 596), E Westmorland, England, 8 mi. ESE of Appleby; agr. market. Has ruins of castle built c.1170 on site of Roman station, and restored in 17th cent. Near-by Brough Hill is scene of annual fair. **2** Town, Yorkshire, England: see ELLOUGHTON WITH BROUGH.

Brougham (brōōm), agr. village and parish (pop. 243), N Westmorland, England, 2 mi. SE of Penrith. Has ruins of Brougham Castle, built 1170. Was site of Roman station.

Broughshane, town (pop. 1,585), central Co. Antrim, Northern Ireland, on Braid R. and 4 mi. NE of Ballymena; woolen milling.

Broughton (brô'tůn). **1** Parish (pop. 1,211), W Cumberland, England. Includes coal-mining village of Great Broughton, on Derwent R. and 3 mi. W of Cockermouth, and dairying village of Little Broughton, 3 mi. WNW of Cockermouth. **2** NW suburb of Manchester, SE Lancashire, England, included in Salford borough; cotton milling, mfg. of chemicals, paint. **3** Town and parish (pop. 1,959), Parts of Lindsey, NW Lincolnshire, England, 3 mi. NW of Brigg; agr. market. Has church of Saxon origin, with 11th-cent. tower.

Broughton, village, W Peebles, Scotland, 5 mi. E of Biggar; mfg. of light metals.

Broughton. **1** (brō'tůn) Village (pop. 324), Hamilton co., SE Ill., 14 mi. NNE of Harrisburg, in agr. area. **2** (brou'tůn) Village (pop. 128), Paulding co., NW Ohio, 16 mi. SW of Defiance.

Broughton (brô'tůn), parish (pop. 7,756), E Denbigh, Wales, 4 mi. NW of Wrexham; coal mining.

Broughton Bay, Korea: see EAST KOREA BAY.

Broughton-in-Furness (fûr'nĭs), town and parish (pop. 963), N Lancashire, England, on Furness peninsula, near Duddon R., 12 mi. N of Barrow-in-Furness; agr. market for region raising barley, oats, potatoes, cattle. Has 14th-cent. Broughton Tower and church of Norman origin, now part of newer church.

Broughton Island (□ 49), SW B.C., in NE Queen Charlotte Strait, 15 mi. NNE of Alert Bay; 17 mi. long, 1–5 mi. wide. Just off NW coast is North Broughton Isl. (□ 16), 8 mi. long, 1–3 mi. wide.

Broughton Island, Russian SFSR: see BROUTON ISLAND.

Broughton Moor, village and parish (pop. 823), W Cumberland, England, 2 mi. SE of Maryport; coal mining.

Broughton Vale, municipality (pop. 184), E New South Wales, Australia, 60 mi. SSW of Sydney, near coast; dairying center.

Broughty Ferry, Scotland: see DUNDEE.

Broummana, Lebanon: see BRUMMANA.

Broumov (brō'môf), Ger. *Braunau* (brou'nou), town (pop. 4,557), NE Bohemia, Czechoslovakia, in the Sudetes, on railroad and 25 mi. ENE of Dvur Kralove; textile mills (notably cotton). Has Benedictine abbey with large library.

Broussa, Turkey: see BURSA, city.

Broussard (brōō'särd), village (pop. 1,237), Lafayette parish, S La., 6 mi. SE of Lafayette; sugar and molasses, cement blocks, wood products.

Brouton Island or **Broughton Island,** Jap. *Buroton-to,* islet of S main Kurile Isls. chain, Russian SFSR; separated from Simushir Isl. (N) by Boussole Strait; 46°43'N 150°45'E; 7 mi. in circumference; rises to 2,628 ft.

Brouvelieures (brōōvůlyûr'), village (pop. 336), Vosges dept., E France, 11 mi. WSW of Saint-Dié; lumbering.

Brouwershaven (brou'ůrs-hävůn), town (pop. 1,211) and port, Zeeland prov., SW Netherlands, on N coast of Schouwen isl., 6 mi. N of Zierikzee; shrimp fishing and packing; ships sugar beets; wheat growing.

Brovary (brŭvä'rē), town (1926 pop. 5,279), E Kiev oblast, Ukrainian SSR, 10 mi. ENE of Kiev; hemp, lumber, chemicals.

Brovst (broust), town (pop. 1,411), Hjorring amt, N Jutland, Denmark, 30 mi. SSW of Hjorring; cement, machinery.

Broward (brou'ůrd), county (□ 1,218; pop. 83,933), S Fla., on the Atlantic (E) coast; ⊙ Fort Lauderdale. Coastal fringe is a tourist, truck and dairy area, with some citrus-fruit growing and limestone quarrying. Interior lies in the Everglades, which are underlaid by peat deposits and here crossed by drainage canals bet. L. Okeechobee (NW) and coast. Contains Seminole Indian reservations. Formed 1915.

Browder (brou'důr), village (1940 pop. 717), Muhlenberg co., W Ky., 25 mi. ESE of Madisonville, in bituminous-coal and agr. area.

Brower, Eskimo trading village (1939 pop. 18), N Alaska, 55 mi. SE of Barrow, SW of Smith Bay.

Browerville, village (pop. 735), Todd co., central Minn., on Long Prairie R. and 8 mi. N of Long Prairie, in livestock and poultry area; dairy products, grain, potatoes.

Brown. **1** County (□ 307; pop. 7,132), W Ill.; ⊙ Mount Sterling. Bounded by Illinois R. (SE) and La Moine R. (NE); drained by small McKee Creek. Agr. (livestock, corn, wheat, oats, poultry); mfg. (butter, cheese, brick); bituminous-coal mining. Formed 1839. **2** County (□ 324; pop. 6,209), S central Ind.; ⊙ Nashville. Drained by small Bean Blossom Creek, and by Salt Creek and its north fork. Agr. (grain, tobacco, fruit, livestock); timber. Formed 1836. **3** County (□ 578; pop. 14,651), NE Kansas; ⊙ Hiawatha. Gently rolling corn-belt region bordered N by Nebr.; watered by headstreams of Delaware R. Kickapoo Indian Reservation is in SW. Grain, livestock, poultry. Formed 1855. **4** County (□ 613; pop. 25,895), S Minn.; ⊙ New Ulm. Agr. area bounded N by Minnesota R. and drained by Cottonwood R. Corn, oats, barley, livestock, dairy products, poultry. L. Hanska in SE. Co. formed 1855. **5** County (□ 1,218; pop. 5,164), N Nebr.; ⊙ Ainsworth. Agr. region bounded N by Niobrara R.; drained in S by Calamus R. Livestock. Formed 1883. **6** County (□ 491; pop. 22,221), SW Ohio; ⊙ Georgetown. Bounded S by Ohio R., here forming Ky. line; drained by Little Miami R. and small White Oak Creek. Agr. (livestock, tobacco, grain, poultry; dairy products); mfg. at Georgetown. Includes Grant Memorial State Park. Formed 1817. **7** County (□ 1,677; pop. 32,617), NE S.Dak., on N.Dak. line; ⊙ Aberdeen. Agr. area drained by James R. and numerous creeks. Mfg. at Aberdeen; dairy products, livestock, wheat, corn. Formed 1879. **8** County (□ 949; pop. 28,607), central Texas; ⊙ BROWNWOOD. Bounded S by Colorado R.; drained by Pecan Bayou (dam impounds L. Brownwood). Agr. (peanuts, oats, grain sorghums, cotton, wheat, pecans, fruit, truck), livestock (beef and dairy cattle, sheep, goats, hogs, poultry); wool, mohair, eggs, milk marketed. Oil, natural gas, clay, glass sand. Fishing in L. Brownwood (state park here). Formed 1856. **9** County (□ 525; pop. 98,314), E Wis., bounded N by Green Bay of L. Michigan; ⊙ Green Bay. Partly on Door Peninsula; drained by Fox R. Primarily a dairying and lumbering region, with mfg. at Green Bay and De Pere. Formed 1818.

Brown, mill village (pop. 4,802, with adjacent Norcott Mills), Cabarrus co., S central N.C., just W of Concord; textiles.

Brown, Fort, Texas: see BROWNSVILLE.

Brown Atoll, Marshall Isls.: see ENIWETOK.

Brown City, city (pop. 878), Sanilac co., E Mich., 32 mi. NW of Port Huron, in agr. area (grain, sugar beets, beans).

Brown Clee Hill, England: see CLEE HILLS.

Brown Cliffs, Utah and Colo.: see BOOK CLIFFS.

Brownell, city (pop. 211), Ness co., W central Kansas, 16 mi. NE of Ness City; grain, livestock.

Brownfield. **1** Town (pop. 612), Oxford co., W Maine, on the Saco and 36 mi. WSW of Auburn; wood products. Severely damaged (1947) by forest fire. **2** Town (pop. 6,161), ⊙ Terry co., NW Texas, on Llano Estacado, 35 mi. SW of Lubbock, near Sulphur Draw (intermittent stream); trade, shipping, processing point for cattle, mineral, agr. (cotton, corn, grain sorghums) region. Mfg. (sodium sulphate, cottonseed oil, feed, mattresses, ice); cotton compress, chick hatcheries. Inc. 1926.

Brownhills, urban district (1931 pop. 18,368; 1951 census 21,482), S Stafford, England, 9 mi. ENE of Wolverhampton; coal mining, metalworking. Has remains of Roman earthworks.

Browning. **1** Village (pop. 324), Schuyler co., W central Ill., on Illinois R. and 27 mi. SE of Macomb, in agr. and bituminous-coal area. **2** City (pop. 492), Linn and Sullivan counties, N Mo., 18 mi. NNW of Brookfield; grain, livestock. **3** Town (pop. 1,691), Glacier co., N Mont., on headstream of Marias R. and 32 mi. WSW of Cut Bank, near Glacier Natl. Park; trade point and hq. for Blackfeet Indian Reservation; grain, livestock, dairy products; oil wells. Inc. 1920.

Brownington. **1** Town (pop. 179), Henry co., W central Mo., near South Grand R., 9 mi. S of Clinton. **2** Town (pop. 673), Orleans co., N Vt., on Willoughby R. and 8 mi. S of Newport; whetstones; agr.

Brownlee Park, village (pop. 4,171, with adjacent Englewood Park), Calhoun co., S Mich.

Brownlow Point, NE Alaska, cape on Beaufort Sea, on W side of Camden Bay; 70°9'N 145°50'W. Eskimo settlement (1939 pop. 27) here is barter center for trappers.

Browns, village (pop. 336), Edwards co., SE Ill., on Bonpas Creek and 12 mi. WSW of Mount Carmel.

Brownsboro, city (pop. 518), Henderson co., E Texas, 19 mi. W of Tyler, in agr. area.

Brownsburg, village (pop. 3,105), S Que., 4 mi. WNW of Lachute; explosives and cartridge mfg.; also dairying center.

Brownsburg, town (pop. 1,578), Hendricks co., central Ind., 14 mi. WNW of Indianapolis, in agr. area; vegetable canning.

Brownsdale, village (pop. 493), Mower co., SE Minn., near Iowa line, 8 mi. NE of Austin, in agr. area; dairy products.

Brownsea Island, at E end of Poole Harbour, SE Dorset, England; 2 mi. long, 1 mi. wide. Scene of 1st camp (1907) of Br. Boy Scout movement.

Browns Mills, village (1940 pop. 563), Burlington co., central N.J., on Rancocas Creek and 11 mi. E of Mt. Holly; health resort. Mirror L. (c.2 mi. long) just E.

Brownson Deep, Atlantic Ocean: see PUERTO RICO TRENCH.

Brown's Point, Tobago, B.W.I.: see CROWN POINT.

Browns River, NW Vt., rises near Mt. Mansfield, flows c.30 mi. W and N to Lamoille R. at Fairfax.

Brown's Town, town (pop. 2,663), St. Ann parish, N Jamaica, 10 mi. WSW of St. Ann's Bay; road and market center in agr. region (fruit, grain, livestock). Germans settled here 1836–42.

Brownstown. 1 Village (pop. 649), Fayette co., S central Ill., 8 mi. E of Vandalia, in agr. and oil-producing area. **2** Town (pop. 1,998), ⊙ Jackson co., S Ind., near East Fork of White R., 24 mi. E of Bedford, in agr. area (truck, poultry, grain); mfg. of flour, silverware, brick; lumber, paper milling; canned goods. A state forest is near by. Laid out 1816. **3** Borough (pop. 1,508), Cambria co., SW central Pa., just W of Johnstown.

Brownstown Head, cape, SE Co. Waterford, Ireland, 9 mi. S of Waterford; 52°8′N 7°7′W.

Browns Valley, village (pop. 1,117), Traverse co., W Minn., on S.Dak. line, bet. Big Stone L. and L. Traverse, 22 mi. SW of Wheaton, in grain, livestock, and poultry area; dairy products. Remains of Browns Valley man, associated by some anthropologists with Folsom culture, found here 1934.

Brownsville. 1 Village, Escambia co., Fla.: see WEST PENSACOLA. **2** Town (pop. 447), ⊙ Edmonson co., central Ky., near Green R. just W of MAMMOTH CAVE NATIONAL PARK, 18 mi. NE of Bowling Green, in agr. area. Game refuge near by. Many Indian artifacts have been found in vicinity. **3** Village (pop. 2,207), Ouachita Parish, N La., just SW of Monroe. **4** Village (pop. 330), Houston co., extreme SE Minn., on Mississippi R. and 8 mi. S of La Crosse, Wis., in corn, oat, barley, and potato area. **5** A residential section of E Brooklyn borough of New York city, SE N.Y. **6** City (pop. 1,175), Linn co., W Oregon, 17 mi. SSE of Albany and on Calapooya R. in dairying and grain area; lumber, wool. **7** Industrial borough (pop. 7,643), Fayette co., SW Pa., 29 mi. S of Pittsburgh and on Monongahela R.; distillery, railroad shops, machine shops; coal, coke. Pioneers on Cumberland Road transferred here to water travel on Mississippi R. system. Laid out 1785, inc. 1815; consolidated 1933 with South Brownsville. **8** City (pop. 4,711), ⊙ Haywood co., W Tenn., 24 mi. W of Jackson, in timber and cotton area; packed meat, gloves; lumbering, cotton ginning. Settled c.1810; inc. 1823. **9** City (pop. 36,066), ⊙ Cameron co., extreme S Texas, on the Rio Grande (bridged) opposite Matamoros, Mexico, and c.130 mi. S of Corpus Christi; internatl. air, rail, highway focus, and port of entry; deepwater port on land-cut channel (completed 1936) to Gulf of Mexico; SW terminus of Gulf Intracoastal Waterway (opened to Brownsville 1949). Winter resort and tourist gateway bet. NE Mexico and U.S. Metropolis of rich irrigated lower valley of the Rio Grande, handling its petroleum, citrus, truck, and cotton, and cotton and metals (especially lead) from Mexico; packing plants, cotton-processing plants, chemical industries based on oil and natural gas; mfg. of brick, tile, oil-well equipment, clothing, hats, bags; fisheries. Seat of a jr. col. Old Fort Brown (inactive since 1944) is here. City holds annual pre-Lenten Charro Days festival. Laid out 1848 around Fort Taylor, established here 1846 by Gen. Zachary Taylor; inc. 1850. Besieged at beginning of Mex. War, fort was relieved (1846) by Gen. Taylor after battles of Palo Alto (pă″lō ăl′tō) (c.9 mi. NNE), and Resaca de la Palma (rĭză′kŭ dā lä päl′mŭ) (c.4 mi. N); fort renamed Fort Brown for its defender. In Civil War, despite a period of Union occupation, town was a principal port of the Confederacy; on May 12–13, 1865, a skirmish (called "last battle of Civil War") was fought near by. First telephone cable bet. U.S. and Mexico laid across Rio Grande here to Matamoros, c.1880.

Brownton, village (pop. 696), McLeod co., S Minn., 20 mi. WSW of Glencoe, in agr. area; dairy products.

Browntown, village (pop. 279), Green co., S Wis., 8 mi. W of Monroe and on Pecatonica R.; dairy products.

Brownvale, village (pop. estimate 200), W Alta., 25 mi. WSW of Peace River; lumbering, mixed farming, wheat.

Brownville. 1 Town (pop. 1,964), including Brownville Junction village (pop. 1,086), Piscataquis co., central Maine, on Pleasant R. and 35 mi. NNW of Bangor, bet. Sebec and Schoodic lakes; wood products, machine parts. Old slate quarries here. Inc. 1824. **2** City (pop. 357), Nemaha co., SE Nebr., 10 mi. E of Auburn and on Missouri R.; trade center in fruit region. Was busy river port in 1850s. **3** Village (pop. 1,013), Jefferson co., N N.Y., on Black R. and 4 mi. NW of Watertown; paper mfg.

Brown Willy, England: see BODMIN MOOR.

Brownwood. 1 City (pop. 20,181), ⊙ Brown co., central Texas, on Pecan Bayou and c.85 mi. ENE of San Angelo; industrial, shipping, distribution center for agr. region (grain, cotton, peanuts, livestock), with oil, natural-gas wells. Mfg. of petroleum products, brick, clothing, glass, food products; cotton ginning, cottonseed-oil milling, peanut shelling; railroad shops. Seat of Howard Payne Col. and Daniel Baker Col. (a branch of Southern Methodist Univ.). L. Brownwood (recreation) is c.7 mi. NW. Military camp here in Second World War. **2** Village (pop. 1,241, with adjacent Oakland), Orange co., SE Texas.

Brownwood, Lake, Texas: see PECAN BAYOU.

Broxburn, town in Uphall parish, E West Lothian, Scotland, 10 mi. W of Edinburgh; coal and shale-oil mining, fertilizer mfg.

Broxton, village and parish (pop. 507), SW Cheshire, England, 9 mi. SE of Chester; dairy farming, cheese mfg.

Broxton, city (pop. 890), Coffee co., S central Ga., 7 mi. NNW of Douglas; sawmilling.

Broye River (brwä), W Switzerland, rises 5 mi. SW of Bulle, flows 53 mi. N to L. of Neuchâtel. L. of Morat is on it.

Brozas (brō′thäs), town (pop. 5,786), Cáceres prov., W Spain, 24 mi. NW of Cáceres; wool-trade center; flour- and sawmilling, stock raising; cereals, olive oil, wine. Mineral springs.

Brozzi (brô′tsē), village (pop. 3,556), Firenze prov., Tuscany, central Italy, near the Arno, 4 mi. WNW of Florence; mfg. (hats, brooms).

Brtonigla, Trieste: see VERTENEGLIO.

Bruar River (brōō′ŭr), Perthshire, Scotland, rises in the Grampians 10 mi. NW of Blair Atholl, flows 10 mi. S to Garry R. 3 mi. W of Blair Atholl. Near its mouth are the Falls of Bruar, largest of which falls 200 ft.

Bruas (brōō′äs), village (pop. 1,225), W Perak, Malaya, 25 mi. S of Taiping; rubber.

Bruay-en-Artois (brüā′-änärtwä′), town (pop. 31,664), Pas-de-Calais dept., N France, on the Lawe and 6 mi. SW of Béthune; major coal-mining center.

Bruay-sur-l'Escaut (–sür-lĕskō′), outer N suburb (pop. 8,642) of Valenciennes, Nord dept., N France, on left bank of the Escaut; iron foundries; mfg. (malt, plastics).

Bruce, county (□ 1,650; pop. 41,680), S Ont., on L. Huron; ⊙ Walkerton.

Bruce, New Zealand: see MILTON.

Bruce. 1 Town (pop. 1,719), Calhoun co., N central Miss., 30 mi. ENE of Grenada and on Skuna R.; hardwood, pine lumber; furniture. Inc. 1927. **2** City (pop. 305), Brookings co., E S.Dak., 10 mi. NNW of Brookings, and on Big Sioux R. **3** Village (pop. 867), Rusk co., NW Wis., 45 mi. N of Eau Claire; dairy products, livestock, lumber.

Bruce, Mount, highest peak (4,024 ft.) of Western Australia, S of Hamersley Range.

Bruce Coast, part of coast of Coats Land, Antarctica, on the South Atlantic, bet. 16°30′ and 23°W. Discovered 1904 by W. S. Bruce, Scottish explorer.

Bruce Mines, town (pop. 362), S central Ont., on L. Huron, 30 mi. SE of Sault Ste. Marie; copper and traprock mining, dairying.

Bruceton, town (pop. 1,204), Carroll co., NW Tenn., on Big Sandy R. and 10 mi. E of Huntingdon, in agr. area; railroad shops. Settled 1920; inc. 1925.

Bruceton Mills or **Bruceton,** town (pop. 165), Preston co., N W.Va., 15 mi. E of Morgantown.

Bruceville, village (1940 pop. 706), Knox co., SW Ind., 8 mi. NE of Vincennes, in agr. area; formerly mined bituminous coal.

Bruche River (brüsh), Bas-Rhin dept., E France, rises near crest of the Vosges at Saales, flows c.40 mi. NE, through picturesque Bruche valley, past Fouday and Schirmeck, into Alsatian lowland at Molsheim, to the Ill just above Strasbourg. Lower course canalized. Followed by Strasbourg–Saint-Dié RR. Upper valley, called Ban-de-la-Roche, Ger. *Steinthal,* was made famous by Oberlin.

Bruchmühlbach (brōōkh′mül′bäkh), village (pop. 1,385), Rhenish Palatinate, W Germany, on Saar border, 6 mi. NE of Homburg; leatherworking.

Bruchsal (brōōkh′zäl), town (pop. 14,089), N Baden, Germany, after 1945 in Württemberg-Baden, on the Saalbach and 12 mi. NE of Karlsruhe. Communications and industrial center; metal (railroad signals, machinery, stoves) and tobacco (cigars, cigarettes) industries. Other mfg.: chemicals, paper, textiles; food processing, woodworking. Trades in tobacco and cattle. Small oil wells in vicinity. Severe Second World War damage included completely destroyed 18th-cent. residence, one of S Germany's most noted rococo castles. Bruchsal was property (from 1056) and residence (from 1720) of prince bishops of Speyer until 1802.

Bruck (brōōk). **1** or **Bruck an der Grossglocknerstrasse** (än dĕr grōsglôk′nürshträsŭ), town (pop. 3,099), Salzburg, W central Austria, on the Salzach and 20 mi. WSW of Bischofshofen; summer resort (alt. 2,486 ft.), with radioactive springs. **2** or **Bruck an der Leitha** (lī′tä), town (pop. 8,284), E Lower Austria, 22 mi. ESE of Vienna and on Leitha R.; sugar refinery; market center for fruit and wine area. Old town with castle. **3** or **Bruck an der Mur** (mōōr′), city (pop. 14,467), Styria, SE central Austria, at confluence of Mur and Mürz rivers, 24 mi. NNW of Graz; rail junction; metallurgical industry (steel, copper); paper mills. Has 15th-cent. Gothic church; ruins of fortress on near-by hill.

Bruck or **Bruck in der Oberpfalz** (brōōk′ ĭn dĕr ō′bürpfälts″), village (pop. 3,273), Upper Palatinate, E Bavaria, Germany, in Bohemian Forest, 11 mi. SE of Schwandorf; woodworking.

Brück (brük), town (pop. 2,583), Brandenburg, E Germany, 17 mi. SE of Brandenburg; grain, flax, potatoes.

Bruck, Switzerland: see BROC.

Brücken (brü′kŭn), village (pop. 1,984), Rhenish Palatinate, W Germany, 18 mi. W of Kaiserslautern; diamond grinding.

Brückenau (brü′kŭnou), town (pop. 5,615), Lower Franconia, NW Bavaria, Germany, at SW foot of the Hohe Rhön, on Sinn R. and 17 mi. SSE of Fulda; textile mfg., flour and lumber milling, brewing. Has 18th-cent. church. Includes Bad Brückenau (W), with mineral springs.

Bruck in der Oberpfalz, Germany: see BRUCK.

Brückl (brü′kŭl), town (pop. 2,445), Carinthia, S Austria, on Gurk R. and 13 mi. NE of Klagenfurt; summer resort (alt. 1,633 ft.); mfg. of chemicals.

Bruckmühl (brōōk′mül″), village (pop. 2,467; commune pop. 6,430), Upper Bavaria, Germany, 10 mi. WNW of Rosenheim; mfg. of textiles, chemicals; metal- and woodworking, lumber and paper milling. Commune was called Kirchdorf am Haunpold until 1948.

Brudeslor, Norway: see GEIRANGER FJORD.

Brudvik, Norway: see BRUVIK.

Brue, Bröe, or **Breuëh** (brōō, brû′ĕ), island (pop. 1,260), Indonesia, in Indian Ocean, off NW tip of Sumatra, 15 mi. NW of Kutaraja; 9 mi. long, 5 mi. wide. Hilly, rising to 2,300 ft. At N end of isl. is important lighthouse (5°45′N 95°3′E). Coconut growing, fishing. Sometimes called Lampuyang, Lam Poejang, or Pulau Bras.

Bruederheim (brōō′dürhīm), village (pop. 232), central Alta., 30 mi. NE of Edmonton; mixed farming, dairying.

Brüel (brü′ŭl), town (pop. 3,177), Mecklenburg, N Germany, 15 mi. ENE of Schwerin; agr. market (grain, sugar beets, potatoes, stock).

Bruère-Allichamps (brüâr′-älēshä′), village (pop. 639), Cher dept., central France, on the Cher and 5 mi. WNW of Saint-Amand-Montrond; porcelain mfg.

Brue River, central Somerset, England, rises 4 mi. ENE of Bruton, flows 30 mi. W and NW, past Bruton and Glastonbury, to Bridgwater Bay just S of Burnham-on-Sea.

Bruff, Gaelic *Brugh na nDéise,* town (pop. 317), E central Co. Limerick, Ireland, 13 mi. SSE of Limerick; agr. market (grain, potatoes; dairying).

Brugelette (brüzhŭlĕt′), village (pop. 1,637), Hainaut prov., SW Belgium, on Dender R. and 4 mi. SE of Ath; beet-sugar refining.

Bruges (brōōzh, Fr. brüzh), Flemish *Brugge* (brû′khŭ) [Flemish,=bridge], city (pop. 52,984), ⊙ West Flanders prov., NW Belgium, 55 mi. WNW of Brussels; 51°13′N 3°13′E. Rail and canal junction (Bruges-Zeebrugge, Bruges-Ostend, and Bruges-Ghent canals); lace-mfg. center; tourist trade; metal industry; mfg. of yeast, brushes, furniture, concrete; brewing, printing. See of R.C. bishop. Episcopal col., 13th-cent. market hall with famous belfry and 47-bell carillon, 14th-cent. Gothic town hall, church of Notre Dame (containing tombs of Charles the Bold and Mary of Burgundy), mus. of anc. pictures with early Flemish paintings, several small museums, many old buildings. Over 50 bridges cross its canals. Jan van Eyck lived here; Caxton 1st learned his printing trade here. Founded in 865 on North Sea inlet, Bruges rapidly developed as a port and trade center. Annexed by France in 1301 but revolted a year later. Under rule of dukes of Burgundy later in 14th cent.; became leading member of Hanseatic League, reaching its commercial zenith in 15th cent.; at same time its tapestry and weaving industries developed rapidly. Silting up of North Sea inlet in 16th cent. led to its decline; superseded by Antwerp and Ghent. In 1895 extensive harbor works were begun in an attempt to revive trade, and a new port, ZEEBRUGGE, was built up on North Sea and connected with Bruges by canal. City is mainly Flemish-speaking.

Bruges-Zeebrugge Canal (–zā′brû″khŭ), NW Belgium, runs 7.4 mi. N–S bet. Bruges and North Sea at Zeebrugge; navigable for small sea-going ships. Built 1895 to give Bruges direct access to sea.

Brugg (brōōk), town (pop. 4,778), Aargau canton, N Switzerland, on the Aar and 9 mi. NE of Aarau; metal products, chemicals; printing, woodworking. Mus. with finds from Vindonissa camp (see WINDISCH), Romanesque tower, late-Gothic church. HABSBURG castle is SW of town.

Brugge, Belgium: see BRUGES.

Brugherio (brōōgā′rēō), village (pop. 3,457), Milano prov., Lombardy, N Italy, 8 mi. NE of Milan; mfg. (silk textiles, woodworking machinery).

Brugnato (brōōnyä′tō), village (pop. 621), La Spezia prov., Liguria, N Italy, near Vara R., 11 mi. NNW of Spezia. Bishopric. Has noted abbey founded by the Longobardi.

Bruhimi, Aden: see BARHIMI.

Brühl (brül). **1** Village (pop. 5,108), N Baden, Germany, after 1945 in Württemberg-Baden, 1.5 mi. WNW of Schwetzingen; metal- and woodworking.

2 Town (pop. 25,974), in former Prussian Rhine Prov., W Germany, after 1945 in North Rhine-Westphalia, 7 mi. S of Cologne; 50°50'N 6°54'E. Rail junction; lignite-mining center; metal construction; mfg. of briquettes, railroad cars, machinery, broilers; sugar refining. Has 18th-cent. castle Augustusburg. Founded 1285 by an archbishop of Cologne. Passed to France in 1801, to Prussia in 1814.

Bruin, borough (pop. 717), Butler co., W Pa., 15 mi. NE of Butler.

Bruin, Lake, Tensas parish, E La., oxbow lake (c.12 mi. long) formed by a cutoff of the Mississippi, 3 mi. N of St. Joseph; fishing, boating; fish hatchery.

Bruinisse (broi'nĭsŭ), town (pop. 1,952), Zeeland prov., SW Netherlands, on E coast of Duiveland isl. and 7.5 mi. E of Zierikzee, on the Krammer; oyster beds, mussel fishing; agr. (wheat, potatoes, beans, flax); ship and machinery building.

Bruinkruis (broin'krois), agr. village, Antwerp prov., N central Belgium, just N of Mechlin.

Bruin Peak (brōō'ĭn) (10,285 ft.), in West Tavaputs Plateau, E Utah, 25 mi. E of Price.

Brujan, Iran: see BORUJAN.

Bruja Point (brōō'hä), SW cape of Panama Canal Zone, on the Pacific 5 mi. SW of Panama city; 8°53'N 79°35'W.

Brule (brōōl, brōō'lā), county (□ 829; pop. 6,076), S central S.Dak.; ⊙ Chamberlain. Agr. area bounded W by Missouri R. Diversified farming; dairy products. Formed 1875.

Brule (brōōl). **1** Village (pop. 330), Keith co., SW central Nebr., 10 mi. W of Ogallala and on S.Platte R. **2** Resort village, Douglas co., NW Wis., on Bois Brule R. and 26 mi. ESE of Superior; fishing. Has govt. fish hatchery. Near by are Brule River State Forest and Wisconsin Cooperative Park.

Brûlé, Le (lŭ brülā'), village (pop. 702), N Réunion isl., 2 mi. S of Saint-Denis; hill resort.

Brûlé, Mont (mõ brülā'), peak (8,448 ft.) in Pennine Alps, SW Switzerland, 13 mi. SSE of Martigny-Ville.

Brûlé Lake (8 mi. long, 1 mi. wide), expansion of Athabaska R., W Alta., in Rocky Mts., on E edge of Jasper Natl. Park, 26 mi. NNE of Jasper; alt. 3,228 ft. Jasper House, Hudson's Bay Co. trading post, was established 1799 at outlet of lake; moved 1801 to Jasper L. and abandoned 1875.

Brule Lake (brōōl), Cook co., NE Minn., in Superior Natl. Forest, 20 mi. NW of Grand Marais; 7 mi. long, 2 mi. wide.

Brule River. 1 In SW Upper Peninsula, Mich., rises in small lake in SW Iron co., flows c.50 mi. SE, forming part of Mich.-Wis. line, to the Michigamme in SE Iron co., forming Menominee R. **2** In Wis.: see BOIS BRULE RIVER.

Brûlon (brülõ'), village (pop. 943), Sarthe dept., W France, 20 mi. W of Le Mans; cereals, poultry. Birthplace of Claude Chappe.

Brumado (brōōmä'dōō), city (pop. 1,045), S Bahia, Brazil, near Brumado R., 75 mi. NW of Vitória da Conquista; rail terminus. Large magnesite deposits. Precious and semiprecious stones (aquamarines, beryls, emeralds) and asbestos also found here. Formerly called Bom Jesus dos Meiras.

Brumado River, central Bahia, Brazil, right tributary (50 mi. long) of the Rio de Contas, rises NW of Rio de Contas city. Gold placers exploited since early 18th cent.

Brumath (brümät'), town (pop. 4,856), Bas-Rhin dept., E France, on the Zorn and 11 mi. NNW of Strasbourg; metalworking, sawmilling, mfg. of building materials; hop and tobacco growing. Insane asylum.

Brumley, town (pop. 78), Miller co., central Mo., near Osage R., 19 mi. SSE of Eldon.

Brummana or **Burummana** (both: brŏŏm-mă'nă), Fr. *Broumana* or *Broummana*, village (pop. 1,917), central Lebanon, 8 mi. E of Beirut; alt. 2,400 ft.; summer resort; sericulture, cotton, cereals, fruits.

Brummen (brŭ'mŭn), residential village (pop. 2,221), Gelderland prov., E Netherlands, 13 mi. NE of Arnhem, near Ijssel R.; stone quarries; laundries.

Brumunddal (brōō'mŏŏndäl), village (pop. 2,729) in Furnes canton (pop. 6,368), partly also in Ringsaker canton, Hedmark co., SE Norway, on E shore of L. Mjosa, on railroad and 9 mi. NW of Hamar; lumber industry (sawmills, wallboard and fiberboard plants); fruit canning, agr.-tool mfg.

Brunai, Borneo: see BRUNEI.

Brunate (brōōnä'tĕ), village (pop. 845), Como prov., Lombardy, N Italy, 1 mi. NE of Como. Resort (alt. 2,349 ft.), with fine view of the Alps.

Brundidge (brŭn'dĭj), town (pop. 2,605), Pike co., SE Ala., 10 mi. SE of Troy; lumber and lumber products, peanut butter.

Brundisium, Italy: see BRINDISI, town.

Bruneau River (brōōnō'), SW Idaho, formed by confluence of East Fork (50 mi. long) and West Fork (100 mi. long) in Owyhee co., flows 40 mi. N, through picturesque canyon, to Snake R. 18 mi. SW of Mountain Home. West Fork rises in Elko co., NE Nev., flows generally N. Used for irrigation.

Bruneck, Italy: see BRUNICO.

Brunei (brōōnī'), sultanate and British protectorate (□ 2,226; pop. 40,657) in NW Borneo, bordering on S.China Sea, consisting of 2 parts surrounded (except for coast) by Br. colony of Sarawak, c.750 naut. mi. ENE of Singapore; 4°2'–5°3'N 114°4'–115°22'E; ⊙ Brunei. A strip of Sarawak territory (5–20 mi. wide) divides Brunei in 2 parts: W section is c.55 mi. wide, E section 7–15 mi. wide. Terrain is generally low and drained by many small streams. Climate is tropical with high humidity and mean annual temp. of 80°F. Rainfall ranges from 100 in. in coastal areas to 200 in. in interior; Oct.-Jan. is period of NW monsoon. Agr.: rice, sago, cassava, sugar cane, pineapples, bananas. Stock raising (buffaloes, cattle, hogs), fishing, lumbering. Principal exports are oil and rubber. Pop. consists mainly of several Malayan groups culturally different from each other; among foreigners the Chinese are the most numerous. Islam is predominant faith. Chief centers: Brunei, KUALA BELAIT. Brunei was formerly (16th to early 19th cent.) a powerful state which had control over all Borneo and near-by isls., including Sulu Archipelago. The Portuguese visited Brunei in 1526; Port. trading post and R.C. mission were established in early 17th cent. Subsequently the Spaniards, English, and Dutch came for brief periods. In 1841 the sultan ceded Sarawak to Sir James Brooke. Gr. Brit. acquired Labuan isl. in 1846 and all of N Borneo in 1877. Brunei became (1888) a Br. protectorate and in 1906 was placed under rule of Br. resident. In Second World War, invaded (Dec., 1941) by the Japanese; liberated June, 1945. Formerly sometimes spelled Brunai.

Brunei, town (pop. 10,619), ⊙ sultanate of Brunei, NW Borneo, in W section of the state, near Brunei Bay on Brunei R. (15 mi. long) and 750 naut. mi. ENE of Singapore; 5°51'N 114°52'E; trade center for agr., stock-raising, and rubber-growing area. Until 1910 all the houses here were built on piles in mud flats in the river; subsequently some have been built on banks. Severely damaged during Second World War. Also called Daru'l Salam and sometimes spelled Bruni.

Brunei Bay, inlet (16 mi. long, 8 mi. wide) of S.China Sea in NW Borneo, forming chief coastal feature of sultanate of Brunei. Contains several isls.; Labuan isl. is at entrance. Parts of Sarawak and Br. North Borneo also touch the bay.

Brunete (brōōnā'tā), town (pop. 678), Madrid prov., central Spain, 16 mi. W of Madrid; cereals, chickpeas, sheep. Bitterly disputed during Sp. civil war (1936–39), the town has been rebuilt.

Brunette Downs (brōōnĕt'), settlement, E central Northern Territory, Australia, 370 mi. NNE of Alice Springs; airport; sheep.

Brunette Island (□ 9; pop. 202), S N.F., in Fortune Bay, 12 mi. NW of Grand Bank; 47°17'N 55°55'W; 5 mi. long, 3 mi. wide. Has lighthouse and radio station. Fishing.

Brunflo (brün'flōō"), village (pop. 710), Jamtland co., N central Sweden, at SE end of Stor L., 8 mi. SE of Ostersund; rail junction; limestone and marble quarrying. Has medieval church.

Brunheiro (brōōnyā'rōō), village (pop. 3,687), Aveiro dist., N central Portugal, near Aveiro Lagoon, 9 mi. N of Aveiro; dairying, fruitgrowing. Also spelled Bunheiro.

Bruni, Borneo: see BRUNEI, town.

Brunico (brōōnē'kô), Ger. *Bruneck*, town (pop. 3,730), Bolzano prov., Trentino–Alto Adige, N Italy, on Rienza R. and 14 mi. ENE of Bressanone. Rail junction; resort (alt. 2,756 ft.); lumber, flax, and woolen mills, pottery works, agr. machinery factory. Has castle (1251; restored) and agr. school. Porphyry quarries near by.

Brünig Pass (brü'nĭkh) (3,315 ft.), old route in Bernese Alps, central Switzerland, 5 mi. E of Brienz; crossed by road and railway which lead from the Forest Cantons to the Bernese Oberland.

Bruning, village (pop. 246), Thayer co., SE Nebr., 10 mi. N of Hebron; flour; dairy, poultry produce.

Bruniquel (brünēkĕl'), village (pop. 264), Tarn-et-Garonne dept., SW France, on the Aveyron and 15 mi. E of Montauban; brickworks.

Brünn, Czechoslovakia: see BRNO.

Brunn am Gebirge (brŏŏn' äm gŭbĭr'gŭ), town (pop. 5,510), after 1938 in Mödling dist. of Vienna, Austria, 8 mi. SW of city center; brewing. Vineyards.

Brunndöbra (brŏŏn'dû'brä), village (pop. 3,684), Saxony, E central Germany, in the Erzgebirge, 18 mi. ESE of Plauen, near Czechoslovak border; mfg. of musical instruments.

Brunne, Sweden: see LIMSTA.

Brunnen (brōō'nŭn), resort village, Schwyz canton, central Switzerland, on L. of Lucerne and 3 mi SW of Schwyz. Rack-and-pinion railway leads S to Morschach.

Brunner (brŭ'nŭr), borough (pop. 1,038), W S.Isl., New Zealand, 5 mi. E of Greymouth and on Grey R.; coal-mining center.

Brunner, Lake (□ 16), W S.Isl., New Zealand, 15 mi. SE of Greymouth; 5 mi. long, 4 mi. wide.

Bruno, village (pop. 527), S central Sask., 18 mi. WNW of Humboldt; grain elevators; dairying, brick making.

Bruno. 1 Village (pop. 193), Pine co., E Minn., c.45 mi. SW of Duluth, in agr. area; dairy products. **2** Village (pop. 155), Butler co., E Nebr., 35 mi. NNW of Lincoln, S of Platte R.

Brunoy (brünwä'), town (pop. 9,745), Seine-et-Oise dept., N central France, on the Yères and 13 mi. SSE of Paris; toy mfg. Just S (bet. Seine and Yères rivers) is Forest of Sénart (□ 10), a favorite excursion center.

Brunsbüttel (brōōns'bü"tŭl), village (pop. 2,677), in Schleswig-Holstein, NW Germany, on the Elbe estuary, 17 mi. W of Itzehoe, in the S Dithmarschen; knitwear; woodworking. Was completely rebuilt after flood of 1676.

Brunsbüttelkoog (brōōns'bü"tŭlkōk'), town (pop. 9,088), in Schleswig-Holstein, NW Germany, port on both sides of mouth of Kiel Canal on Elbe estuary, 40 mi. NW of Hamburg, in the S Dithmarschen; potash plant; mineral-oil processing. Mfg. of structural forms, baking machinery, steel furniture, concrete goods, shoes, textiles, nets, barrels; fish canning. Outer and inner (canal) harbors connected by double locks. Developed in 1930s as industrial center. Chartered 1949.

Brunshaupten, Germany: see KÜHLUNGSBORN.

Brunson, town (pop. 607), Hampton co., SW S.C., 11 mi. SE of Allendale; naval stores.

Brunssum or **Brunsum** (brûn'sŭm), town (pop. 18,776), Limburg prov., SE Netherlands, 4 mi. N of Heerlen. Hendrick coal mine here.

Brunstatt (brünstät', Ger. brōōn'shtät), SSW suburb (pop. 3,886) of Mulhouse, Haut-Rhin dept., E France, on the Ill and on Rhone-Rhine Canal; brewing, metalworking.

Brunsum, Netherlands: see BRUNSSUM.

Brunsville (brōōnz'vĭl), town (pop. 112), Plymouth co., NW Iowa, 5 mi. W of Le Mars; livestock, grain.

Brunswick (brŭnz'wĭk), municipality (pop. 57,529), S Victoria, Australia; N suburb of Melbourne; mfg. (hosiery, confectioneries), brickyards.

Brunswick (brŭnz'wĭk), Ger. *Braunschweig* (broun'-shvīk), former state (□ 1,379; 1939 pop. 602,873), N central Germany, after 1945 included (except for several exclaves placed in Russian-occupied Saxony-Anhalt) as an administrative division [Ger. *Verwaltungsbezirk*] (□ 1,182; 1946 pop. 782,950) in British-occupied Lower Saxony; ⊙ Brunswick. Was surrounded by former Prussian provs. of Hanover, Saxony, and Westphalia. Situated in N German lowlands and the upper Harz (S), where silver, copper, lead, and iron are mined. Drained by Leine and Oker rivers. Grain, sugar beets, and potatoes are main crops. Duchy of Brunswick was homeland and, after 1180, only remaining property of the Guelphs. Two major lines, Brunswick-Lüneburg and Brunswick-Wolfenbüttel emerged. Duke of Brunswick-Lüneburg became (1692) elector of Hanover. Brunswick-Wolfenbüttel line ruled Brunswick, of which, until 1753, Wolfenbüttel was capital. Duchy was part (1807–13) of Napoleonic kingdom of Westphalia. Line became extinct in 1884, and Brunswick then was ruled by regents until Ernest Augustus, grandson of King George V of Hanover, was made duke. A member of North German Confederation after 1866, and of German Empire after 1871, duchy became republic in 1918 and joined Weimar Republic.

Brunswick, Ger. *Braunschweig*, city (1946 pop. 181,375; 1950 pop. 223,263), ⊙ Brunswick, N central Germany, after 1945 in Lower Saxony, on the Oker and 34 mi. ESE of Hanover, near Weser-Elbe Canal; 52°15'N 10°30'E. Rail junction. Food-processing and -transshipment center noted for its sausages, asparagus, and honey cakes; also one of Germany's leading sugar markets; canned and dried fruit and vegetables, meat and flour products, beer. Other mfg.: automobiles, bicycles, railroad equipment, calculating machines, radios, metalware, quinine, furniture, pianos; jute spinning, printing. Moated old city, with its historic bldgs. and many painted, timbered houses, was about 90% destroyed in Second World War. Romanesque-Gothic basilica, founded 1173 by Henry the Lion and containing his tomb, was only slightly damaged. Heavily damaged were Romanesque-Gothic churches of St. Martin and St. Andrew, Gothic churches of St. Ulric and St. Catherine, and Till Eulenspiegel fountain. Gutted were the 12th-cent. castle (rebuilt in 19th cent.), 14th-cent. old town hall. Art mus., now housed in 17th-cent. château, has paintings by Rembrandt, Rubens, Vermeer, and Lucas van Leyden. Lessing's grave is in small Magni cemetery (E). Industry centered in sections W of the Oker (about 50% destroyed). City has institute of technology, teachers col. Founded in 9th cent. and chartered in 12th cent. by Henry the Lion. Was flourishing member of Hanseatic League. In 1753, residence of dukes of Brunswick-Wolfenbüttel was shifted here. Became ⊙ free state of Brunswick in 1918. Captured by American troops in April, 1945.

Brunswick (brŭnz'wĭk, brŭn'zĭk). **1** County (□ 873, pop. 19,238), SE N.C., ⊙ Southport. Bounded E by Cape Fear R., S by the Atlantic, SW by S.C., W by Waccamaw R. Forested and swampy tidewater area; includes Smith Isl. Farming (tobacco, corn, sweet potatoes, livestock), fishing, sawmilling. Resorts along coast. Formed 1764. **2** County (□ 579; pop. 20,136), S Va.; ⊙ Lawrenceville. Bounded S by N.C., N by Nottoway R.; drained by

Meherrin R. and short Fontaine Creek. Agr. (especially tobacco; also grain, cotton, hay, sweet potatoes, peanuts), some dairying, livestock (cattle, hogs, poultry). Lumber milling; mfg., processing of farm products at Lawrenceville. Formed 1732.

Brunswick. 1 City (pop. 17,954), ⊙ Glynn co., SE Ga., c.65 mi. SSW of Savannah, on St. Simons Sound of Atlantic Ocean. Industrial and shipping center with shrimp and crab processing plants (packing, canning, freezing), shipyards, creosoting works; mfg. of naval stores, lumber, boxes, pulp, plywood, clothing, paint. Port of entry with natl. quarantine station. Sea Islands, offshore, are popular resorts. Fort Frederica Natl. Monument near by. Founded 1771–72, inc. 1856. **2** Town (pop. 10,996), including Brunswick village (pop. 7,342), Cumberland co., SW Maine, at falls on the Androscoggin (here dammed), c.25 mi. NE of Portland. Textile and paper mills; canned foods; trade center for resort area. Seat of Bowdoin Col. (1794), with Walker Art Gall. Begun as trading post (1628) at what was called Pejepscot, inc. 1739. **3** Town (pop. 3,752), Frederick co., W Md., on the Potomac (bridged here to Va.) in Middletown Valley (grain, dairying), and 15 mi. WSW of Frederick; railroad shops (established 1890). Railroad and Chesapeake and Ohio Canal (now abandoned) arrived here c.1834. Laid out 1787 as Berlin; renamed 1890. **4** City (pop. 1,653), Chariton co., N central Mo., on Grand R., near the Missouri, and 25 mi. S of Brookfield; grain, livestock; meat storage plant. Site of Fr. Fort Orleans (1723) is near. Laid out c.1837. **5** Village (pop. 260), Antelope co., NE Nebr., 15 mi. N of Neligh. **6** Town (pop. 190), Columbus co., S N.C., 4 mi. S of Whiteville; lumber milling. **7** Town (pop. 73), Essex co., NE Vt., on the Connecticut and 32 mi. SE of Newport; mineral springs.

Brunswick Peninsula, southernmost part of South American mainland, Magallanes prov., S Chile, bounded E and S by Strait of Magellan and NW by Otway Sound; c.70 mi. long. The most populated area of the prov., with the city of PUNTA ARENAS on its NE coast. Predominantly sheep raising and lumbering, with some coal mining at Loreto, 4 mi. NW of Punta Arenas. Froward Cape (S) is the southernmost point (53°54'S 71°18'W) of Amer. mainland; rises abruptly to 1,200 ft. In W, peninsula rises to 3,900 ft. (Mt. Muela).

Bruntal (brōōn'täl), Czech *Bruntál*, Ger. *Freudenthal* (froi'dŏŏntäl), town (pop. 6,348), W Silesia, Czechoslovakia, in the Jeseniky, 28 mi. NNE of Olomouc; rail junction; linen and broadcloth mfg., woodworking, lace making. Has old castle of Teutonic Knights. Former mining town.

Bruny (brōō'nē), island (□ 142; pop. 679) in Tasman Sea, separated from SE coast of Tasmania by D'Entrecasteaux Channel; narrow isthmus (3 mi. long) joins South Bruny with North Bruny; 32 mi. long, 10 mi. wide; irregular coast line. Adventure Bay on E side of isthmus. North Bruny more fertile and populous than South Bruny. Sheep raising, dairying; penguins. Allonah, on South Bruny, chief town.

Bruray, Scotland: see OUT SKERRIES.

Bruree (brōōrē'), Gaelic *Brugh Riogh*, town (pop. 284), S Co. Limerick, Ireland, on Maigue R. and 17 mi. S of Limerick; agr. market (grain, potatoes; dairying). Has remains of anc. fort of the de Laceys and of castle of the Knights Templars. Until 1746 the Irish bards held semi-annual meetings here.

Brus (brōōs), village (pop. 3,515), S central Serbia, Yugoslavia, on Rasina R. and 15 mi. SW of Krusevac.

Brusa, Turkey: see BURSA.

Brusartsi (brōōsär'tsē), village (pop. 2,061), Vidin dist., NW Bulgaria, 12 mi. SSW of Lom; rail junction; grain, legumes.

Brush, town (pop. 2,431), Morgan co., NE Colo., near South Platte R., 9 mi. E of Fort Morgan; alt. 4,280 ft. Shipping point in grain, sugar-beet, livestock region; cheese, beet sugar. Annual rodeo and fiesta here. Inc. 1884.

Brushton, village (pop. 516), Franklin co., N N.Y., on small Little Salmon R. and 11 mi. W of Malone, in farming and dairying area; makes footwear.

Brusilov (brōōsē'lŭf), town (1926 pop. 5,100), SE Zhitomir oblast, Ukrainian SSR, 37 mi. E of Zhitomir; dairy plant, flour mill, metalworks.

Brusio (brōō'zyô), village and circle (pop. 1,470), Grisons canton, SE Switzerland, on Poschiavino R. and 5 mi. SSE of Poschiavo. Its hydroelectric works (water supplied by L. of Poschiavo, power produced at Campocologno) extend to Italy (2 mi. S of village).

Brus Lagoon (brōōs) or **Brewers Lagoon**, on Mosquitia coast of E Honduras, 35 mi. ESE of Iriona; 15 mi. long, 4–6 mi. wide. Separated from Caribbean Sea by narrow sandspit (coconuts). Receives Tom-Tom (or Toom-Toom) Creek, left arm of lower Patuca R. Sometimes called Cartina Lagoon.

Brus Laguna (brōōs' lägōō'nä), village, Colón dept., E Honduras, in Mosquitia, on S shore of Brus Lagoon, 45 mi. ESE of Iriona; sawmilling; coconuts, livestock.

Brusly or **Brusly Landing** (brŭs'lē), village (pop. 493), West Baton Rouge parish, SE central La., 6 mi. SSW of Baton Rouge and on W bank of the Mississippi. Just N is Cinclare, with large sugar plantation and refinery.

Brusno, Czechoslovakia: see SLOVENSKA LUPCA.

Brusovo (brōō'sŭvŭ), village (1926 pop. 296), N Kalinin oblast, Russian SFSR, 50 mi. E of Bologoye; flax processing.

Brusque (brōō'skĭ), city (pop. 5,968), E Santa Catarina, Brazil, 15 mi. SE of Blumenau; industrial center (textile mills); dairying; sugar cane, tobacco, coffee grown in region. Founded 1860 by German immigrants.

Brus River, Costa Rica: see DIQUÍS RIVER.

Brussa, Turkey: see BURSA.

Brussels (brŭ'sŭlz), Flemish *Brussel* (brŭ'sŭl), Fr. *Bruxelles* (brüsĕl'), city (pop. 185,112; with suburbs 960,740), ⊙ Belgium and Brabant prov., on Senne R., at junction of Charleroi-Brussels and Willebroek canals, and 26 mi. S of Antwerp; 50°50'N 4°20'E. Rail junction; airports at HAREN and MELSBROEK; cultural, commercial, and industrial city. Lace-mfg. center; motorcycles, tools, cutlery, chemicals, pharmaceuticals, textiles, clothing, leather, shoes; food processing, beer brewing. City's expansion followed plan laid down in 14th cent.; has series of peripheral boulevards with diagonal avenues and streets in all but oldest quarters. Center of city is *Grand' Place*, site of original 10th-cent. settlement of Brussels; here is town hall (*Hôtel de Ville*, begun in 14th cent., completed in 17th cent) and medieval guildhalls. Univ. (founded 1834), academies of arts, sciences, and medicine (in 19th-cent. *Palais des Academies*), mus. of natural history, mus. of decorative and industrial arts (in *Palais du Cinquantenaire* which, with triumphal arch, commemorates 50th anniversary of Belg. revolution of 1830), Royal Gallery of painting and sculpture, mus. of modern painting, large botanical garden. Has large church of Ste-Gudule (founded in 11th cent.; burned down in 1072; rebuilt after 1225, additions being made until 17th cent.); 15th–16th-cent. church of Notre-Dame-du-Sablon; 18th-cent. royal palace, rebuilt 1904–12; *Palais de Justice* (a major landmark; begun in 1866). Congressional column (*Colonne du Congrès*), built 1850–59, commemorates Belgium's independence. Parliament is housed in *Palais de la Nation*. Founded in 10th cent. as a military post, Brussels grew as a market center and, later, became a center of wool industry. By 13th cent. it had achieved considerable economic importance and in 15th cent. became the capital for Philip the Good of Burgundy. During Middle Ages Brussels was renowned for luxury and gaiety of its life, as well as for its manufacture of carpets, tapestries, and lace. By 1450 its population had reached 46,000. With completion of Willebroek Canal in 1561 Brussels received direct connection with the sea. Center of city was destroyed (1695) by bombardment, in war bet. Louis XIV and the Augsburg League. In 1819 Brussels became, with The Hague, an alternate meeting place of parliament of United Netherlands; became ⊙ new country with establishment of independent Belgium in 1830. Brussels was occupied by the Germans from 1914 until the armistice of 1918, and from 1940 until its liberation (Sept., 1944) by British troops. In both World Wars it was cruelly oppressed by the occupation forces. Memorable is the heroic stand of Cardinal Mercier and the help extended by American minister, Brand Whitlock. Physically, Brussels suffered no damage in either war. Brussels is officially bilingual (French, Flemish).

Brussels, village (pop. 825), S Ont., on Middle Maitland R. and 23 mi. E of Goderich; dairying, lumbering.

Brussels. 1 Village (pop. 205), Calhoun co., W Ill., near the Mississippi, 24 mi. W of Alton, in apple-growing area. **2** Village (pop. c.200), Door co., NE Wis., on Door Peninsula, 14 mi. SW of Sturgeon Bay; dairying, farming. Settled 1854 by Belgians.

Brusson (brüsō'), village (pop. 516), Val d'Aosta region, NW Italy, 20 mi. E of Aosta. Gold mine near by.

Brüssow (brüs'ō), town (pop. 2,431), Brandenburg, E Germany, 13 mi. ENE of Prenzlau; agr. market (potatoes, grain, stock); potato-flour milling.

Brustem (brŭ'stŭm), agr. village (pop. 1,963), Limburg prov., NE Belgium, 2 mi. ESE of St-Trond. Here Charles the Bold defeated (1467) the Liégeois. Has ruins of 12th-cent. castle. Formerly spelled Brusthem.

Bruton (brōō'tŭn), town and parish (pop. 1,553), E Somerset, England, on Brue R. and 7 mi. SE of Shepton Mallet; agr. market in dairying region. Has 15th-cent. church, 16th-cent. grammar school, 17th-cent. Sexey Hosp.

Bruttium, Italy: see CALABRIA.

Bruvik (brōō'vĭk, -vēk), village and canton (pop. 5,152), Hordaland co., SW Norway, on SE shore of Osteroy, 14 mi. NE of Bergen; woolen mills. Formerly called Brudvik.

Brüx, Czechoslovakia: see MOST.

Bruxelles, Belgium: see BRUSSELS.

Bruyères (brüyâr'), resort town (pop. 2,953), Vosges dept., E France, in the W Vosges, 13 mi. ENE of Épinal; embroidering, beret mfg., woodworking.

Bruzual (brōōswäl'), town (pop. 271), Apure state, W central Venezuela, port on S bank of Apure R. opposite Puerto de Nutrias and 130 mi. WNW of San Fernando, in cattle region.

Bruzual, Villa, Venezuela: see VILLA BRUZUAL.

Bryagovo (bryä'gôvô). **1** Village (pop. 3,098), Plovdiv dist., S central Bulgaria, at N foot of E Rhodope Mts., 9 mi. S of Parvomai; tobacco, vineyards, fruit, truck. Formerly Kara-alan. **2** Village (pop. 5,271), Vidin dist., NW Bulgaria, on Timok R. (Yugoslav border) and 14 mi. NW of Vidin; flour milling; winegrowing, truck, livestock. Sometimes spelled Bregovo.

Bryan. 1 County (□ 439; pop. 5,965), SE Ga.; ⊙ Pembroke. Bounded SE by the Atlantic, NE by Ogeechee R.; drained by Canoochee R. Includes Ossabaw Isl. coastal plain agr. (corn, truck, sugar cane, livestock), forestry (naval stores, lumber), and fishing area. Formed 1793. **2** County (□ 913; pop. 28,999), S Okla.; ⊙ Durant. Bounded S by Red R., and W by L. Texoma, which is impounded by Denison Dam (in SW); drained by Blue R. Agr. (cotton, corn, oats, peanuts, livestock; dairy products). Mfg. at Durant. Stone quarrying. Timber. Formed 1907.

Bryan. 1 City (pop. 6,365), ⊙ Williams co., extreme NW Ohio, 16 mi. NW of Defiance; trade center for agr. area; mfg. (furniture, lubricating equipment, automobile accessories, advertising novelties, wood and metal products). Laid out 1840; inc. as village in 1841, as city in 1941. **2** City (pop. 18,102), ⊙ Brazos co., E central Texas, c.75 mi. SE of Waco; commercial, shipping center of agr. (cotton, alfalfa, truck), dairying, poultry area; cotton ginning, lumber and cottonseed-oil milling, mfg. of insecticides, furniture, fertilizer, food products. Seat of Allen Acad.; Texas Agr. and Mechanical Col. is at near-by COLLEGE STATION. Founded 1865.

Bryan, Mount, Australia: see MOUNT LOFTY RANGES.

Bryansk, Poland: see BRANSK.

Bryansk (brēänsk'), oblast (□ 13,400; 1946 pop. estimate 1,800,000) in W European Russian SFSR; ⊙ Bryansk. In mixed forest zone; drained by Desna R.; sandy soils. Basic crops: hemp (E), coarse grain and potatoes (W); also sugar beets (Komarichi), buckwheat, tobacco; truck produce in Bryansk industrial dist. Hog raising widespread. Lumber industries are important: sawmilling along rail lines, paper milling (Surazh), match mfg. (Novozybkov, Zlynka). Agr. products form basis of hemp processing and milling, distilling, starch, and tobacco industries. Chief mineral resources: peat (used in electric power plants), phosphorites (phosphate fertilizers), quartzite (glassworking at Dyatkovo). Heavy industry (machine mfg.) centered at Bryansk and Bezhitsa; large cement works at Tsementny. Formed 1944 from part of Orel oblast. Also spelled Briansk.

Bryansk, city (1926 pop. 45,962; 1939 pop. 87,473), ⊙ Bryansk oblast, Russian SFSR, port on Desna R. and 210 mi. SW of Moscow; 34°23'N 53°14'E. Rail hub; center of Bryansk-BEZHITSA industrial dist. Foundry and ironworks, mfg. of road-making machinery; sawmills, rope mill, brickworks, cement, artificial-slate works. Lumber trade school, regional mus. Has 17th-cent. cathedral and monastery. City founded (1146) on high right bank of Desna R.; originally named Debryansk; became ⊙ principality. Later under Lithuania; annexed (1503) to Moscow. Shipbuilding site in 17th cent. Was ⊙ Bryansk govt. (1920–29). During Second World War, held (1941–43) by Germans. Modern Bryansk includes low left-bank section, site of several rail junctions and industrial suburbs of Uritski (ironworks), Imeni Volodarskogo (cement), Imeni Tolstogo, and Imeni Fokina (sawmills). Superphosphate works in outer E suburb of Bolshoye Polpino; large peat-fed power plant at Belye Berega (E). Also spelled Briansk.

Bryanski or **Bryanskiy** (brēän'skē), town (1939 pop. over 10,000), SW Voroshilovgrad oblast, Ukrainian SSR, in the Donbas, 4 mi. SSE of Kadiyevka; coal-mining center; chemicals. Formerly Bryanski Rudnik.

Bryan Station, locality, Fayette co., central Ky. just NE of Lexington; site of historic fort. Unsuccessful attack made here by British and Indians (Aug., 1782) immediately preceded Revolutionary battle of Blue Licks at BLUE LICKS SPRINGS.

Bryant. 1 Town (pop. 387), Saline co., central Ark., 15 mi. SW of Little Rock, in bauxite-mining region. **2** Village (pop. 396), Fulton co., central Ill., 7 mi. SSW of Canton, in agr. and bituminous-coal area. **3** Town (pop. 339), Jay co., E Ind., 34 mi. NE of Muncie, in agr. area. **4** Town (pop. 88), Okmulgee co., E central Okla., 5 mi. SW of Henryetta. **5** City (pop. 624), Hamlin co., E S.Dak., 30 mi. SW of Watertown; dairy products, livestock, poultry, grain.

Bryant Mountain (3,002 ft.), NW S.C., in the Blue Ridge, c.20 mi. NNE of Greenville.

Bryant Pond, Maine: see WOODSTOCK.

Bryast (bryäst), village (pop. 6,079), Pleven dist., N Bulgaria, 17 mi. WSW of Nikopol; flour milling; livestock, fruit, truck.

Bryastovene (bryä'stôvĕnĕ), village (pop. 4,271), Ruse dist., NE Bulgaria, 16 mi. NNE of Razgrad; grain, sunflowers, and legumes. Formerly called Karaach.

Bryastovitsa (bryä″stôvē′tsä), village (pop. 4,985), Plovdiv dist., S central Bulgaria, at N foot of W Rhodope Mts., 9 mi. SW of Plovdiv; rice, tobacco, fruit, truck.

Bryce, Mount (11,507 ft.), SE B.C., near Alta. border, in Rocky Mts., in Hamber Provincial Park, 65 mi. SSE of Jasper; 52°2′N 117°20′W.

Bryce Canyon National Park (□ 56.2; established 1928), SW Utah, 20 mi. SE of Panguitch. Intricately dissected and vividly colored area of wide canyons in the Pink Cliffs (sandstone), the SE escarpment of Paunsaugunt Plateau. Bryce Canyon (c.1,000 ft. deep, 3 mi. long, 2 mi. wide) is enormous amphitheater enclosing multicolor-striped myriad of towering domes, spires, and pinnacles. Excellent views are obtainable from Bryce Point (8,294 ft.), S of canyon, and Inspiration Point (8,316 ft.), SW. Other features of interest are Fairyland Canyon (in N) and Natural Bridge, the Promontory (9,091 ft.), and Rainbow Point (9,105 ft.) in S. Cedar Breaks Natl. Monument is c.40 mi. W; Zion Natl. Park is c.50 mi. SW.

Bryceland, village (pop. 123), Bienville parish, NW La., 45 mi. E of Shreveport, in farming area.

Bryher, island (353 acres; pop. 64) of SCILLY ISLANDS, Cornwall, England, 3 mi. NW of St. Mary's; resort.

Brymbo (brĭm′bō), town and parish (pop. 4,268), E Denbigh, Wales, 4 mi. NW of Wrexham; coal mining, steel milling, mfg. of synthetic fertilizer.

Bryn, England: see INCE-IN-MAKERFIELD.

Bryn Athyn (brĭn″ ă′thĭn), residential borough (pop. 913), Montgomery co., SE Pa., N suburb of Philadelphia.

Bryn Bras, Wales: see LLANRUG.

Brynford (brĭn′fûrd), agr. village and parish (pop. 1,011), Flint, Wales, just SW of Holywell.

Bryn Mawr (brĭn″ mär′), residential village (1940 pop. 4,777), partly in LOWER MERION township, Montgomery co., SE Pa., W suburb of Philadelphia. Seat of Bryn Mawr Col. and Harcum Jr. Col. Settled c.1800.

Brynmawr (brĭnmôr′, –mour′), urban district (1931 pop. 7,247; 1951 census 6,524), SE Brecknock, Wales, 3 mi. NE of Ebbw Vale; coal mining, steel milling, shoe mfg. Exceptionally hard hit by depression of 1930s, it became scene of experiment in alternative employment for coal miners, initiated by Society of Friends.

Bryn Siencyn or **Brynsiencyn** (brĭn shĕn′kĭn), agr. village in Llanidan (lănē′dŭn) parish (pop. 1,065), S Anglesey, Wales, near Menai Strait, 3 mi. N of Caernarvon.

Bryson, village (pop. 264), SW Que., on Ottawa R. and 60 mi. NW of Ottawa; dairying; cattle, pigs.

Bryson, town (pop. 588), Jack co., N Texas, 12 mi. E of Graham; trade point in agr., oil-producing area; oil refining.

Bryson City, town (pop. 1,499), ⊙ Swain co., W N.C., on Tuckasegee R., near its mouth in Fontana Reservoir, and 50 mi. WSW of Asheville; resort center bet. Great Smoky Mts. Natl. Park and Nantahala Natl. Forest and near a Cherokee Indian reservation; wood and textile products.

Bry-sur-Marne (brē-sür-märn′), town (pop. 4,699), Seine dept., N central France, an outer E suburb of Paris, 8 mi. from Notre Dame Cathedral, on left bank of Marne R.; truck gardens.

Bryte (brīt), village (1940 pop. 1,370), Yolo co., central Calif., W suburb of Sacramento, across Sacramento R.

Bryukhovetskaya (bryōō′khŭvyĭtskīŭ), village (1926 pop. 12,433), W central Krasnodar Territory, Russian SFSR, on small lake formed by Beisug R., 55 mi. N of Krasnodar, in agr. area (wheat, sunflowers, castor beans, southern hemp); flour milling, metalworking, bast-fiber processing.

Bryukhovichi (bryōō′khŭvēchē), Pol. *Brzuchowice*, town (1931 pop. 1,110), central Lvov oblast, Ukrainian SSR, 4 mi. NNW of Lvov; summer resort; flour milling.

Brza Palanka (bŭr′zä pä′länkä), village, E Serbia, Yugoslavia, on the Danube (Rum. border) and 17 mi. N of Negotin; fish trade.

Brzeg, town, Opole prov., Poland: see BRIEG.

Brzeg Dolny (bzhĕk′ dôl′nĭ), Ger. *Dyhernfurth* (dü′hĕrn″fŏŏrt″), town (1939 pop. 2,013; 1946 pop. 1,363) in Lower Silesia, after 1945 in Wroclaw prov., SW Poland, on the Oder and 17 mi. NW of Breslau (Wroclaw); chemical mfg. Has 18th-cent. castle.

Brzesc Kujawski (bzhĕshch′ kōōyäf′skē), Pol. *Brześć Kujawski*, Rus. *Brest Kuyavsk* (brĕst′ kōōyäfsk′), town (pop. 4,973), Bydgoszcz prov., central Poland, 8 mi. WSW of Wloclawek; rail spur terminus; beet-sugar milling, chicory drying, brick mfg. Chief town of the Kujawy. Has old walls and ramparts, church (built 1240).

Brzesc-Litewski, Belorussian SSR: see BREST, city.

Brzesc nad Bugiem, Belorussian SSR: see BREST, city.

Brzesko (bzhĕ′skô), town (pop. 2,684), Krakow prov., S Poland, 30 mi. ESE of Cracow; food processing.

Brzezany, Ukrainian SSR: see BEREZHANY.

Brzezinka, Poland: see OSWIECIM.

Brzeziny (bzhĕzē′nĭ), Rus. *Breziny* (brĕzē′nē), town (pop. 6,008), Lodz prov., central Poland, 12 mi. E of Lodz city center; mfg. of textiles, cement, bricks, flour. Before Second World War, pop. 50% Jewish; during war, under Ger. rule, called Löwenstadt.

Brzostowica Wielka, Belorussian SSR: see BOLSHAYA BERESTOVITSA.

Brzozow (bzhô′zōōf), Pol. *Brzozów*, town (pop. 3,725), Rzeszow prov., SE Poland, 23 mi. S of Rzeszow; petroleum wells; cementworks, tannery.

Brzuchowice, Ukrainian SSR: see BRYUKHOVICHI.

Bsherri or **Bisharri** (bĭshär′rē), Fr. *Bcharreh*, village (pop. 5,204), N Lebanon, near the Cedars of Lebanon, 16 mi. SE of Tripoli; alt. 4,600 ft.; summer resort; cereals, walnuts, figs, mulberries. In vicinity are a series of cascades. Old town, dating from Phoenician times.

Bua, island, Yugoslavia: see TROGIR.

Buad Island (bwäd′) (□ 14; 1939 pop. 3,922), Samar prov., Philippines, in Samar Sea, just off W coast of Samar isl., 6 mi. S of Catbalogan; 11°39′N 124°51′E; 5 mi. long. Hilly, rising to 1,174 ft. Rice, coconuts. Chief center is Zumarraga (sōōmä′rägä) (1939 pop. 2,782; 1948 municipality pop. 30,593, including near-by Daram Isl.).

Buam Gorge, Kirghiz SSR: see BOOM GORGE.

Buarbrae or **Buarbre,** Norway: see FOLGEFONN.

Buarcos (bwär′kōōsh), town (pop. 2,402), Coimbra dist., N central Portugal, fishing port and bathing resort on the Atlantic 2 mi. NW of Figueira da Foz and SE of Cape Mondego; sardine canning, fertilizer mfg. A prosperous shipping center in 17th-18th cent. Just N are the Buarcos hills with coal deposits.

Bua River (bōō′ä), central Nyasaland, rises near Fort Manning, flows c.150 mi. NE to L. Nyasa 15 mi. NNW of Kota Kota.

Bua Yai (bōō′ŭ yī′), village (1937 pop. 13,649), Nakhon Ratchasima prov., E Thailand, in Korat Plateau, on railroad and 55 mi. SSW of Khonkaen; rice. Road to Chaiyaphum.

Buayan (bwä′yän), town (1939 pop. 3,931; 1948 municipality pop. 32,019), Cotabato prov., Philippines, S Mindanao, on Sarangani Bay of Celebes Sea, 70 mi. SSW of Davao; rice, coconuts.

Buba (bōō′bä), village, SW Port. Guinea, at head of the Rio Grande, 32 mi. E of Bolama. Former slave-trading center.

Bubak (bōōbäk′), village, Dadu dist., W Sind, W Pakistan, near Manchhar L., 19 mi. S of Dadu; wheat, rice, millet; handicraft carpet mfg.; local fish trade.

Bubaque (bōōbä′kä), village, W Port. Guinea, on Bubaque isl. (one of Bijagós Isls.), 30 mi. SW of Bolama; palm-oil processing.

Bubastis (būbăs′tĭs), anc. city of NE Egypt, just SE of modern Zagazig, at Tell Basta; ⊙ Egypt in XXII and XXIII dynasties. Reached its full glory under Sheshonk I. Declined rapidly after 2d Persian conquest (343 B.C.). Was center of worship of lion-headed (or cat-headed) goddess Bast. In the bible it appears as Pibeseth.

Bubi, district, Southern Rhodesia: see INYATI.

Bubiyan Island (bōōbīyăn′), uninhabited island at head of Persian Gulf, adjoining delta of the Shatt al Arab and belonging to Kuwait; 25 mi. long, 15 mi. wide. Remains of Turkish fort (1902) on SE shore. Summer fisheries.

Bubnell, England: see BASLOW AND BUBNELL.

Bubye River (bōō′byä), S Southern Rhodesia, rises in middle veld NE of West Nicholson, flows 175 mi. SE to Limpopo R. 75 mi. E of Beitbridge.

Buçaco or **Bussaco** (bōōsä′kōō), resort, Aveiro dist., N central Portugal, 13 mi. NNE of Coimbra, adjacent to Luso; fashionable hotel surrounded by forest (noted for its Lebanese cedars). Was a monastery in 17th cent., and a royal summer residence in 19th cent. Here, in 1810, Portuguese and British stopped French march on Lisbon in Peninsular War. Formerly also spelled Busaco.

Bucak (bōōjäk′), village (pop. 4,786), Burdur prov., SW Turkey, 24 mi. SE of Burdur; wheat, barley.

Bucaramanga (bōōkärämäng′gä), city (pop. 41,714), ⊙ Santander dept., N central Colombia, in a W valley of Cordillera Oriental, on Pan American Highway (from Bogotá to Caracas), linked by roads with Barrancabermeja and by railroad with Puerto Wilches (both on Magdalena R.), 190 mi. NNE of Bogotá; 7°7′N 73°8′W; alt. 3,340 ft. Trading, communication, and industrial center in fertile agr. region (coffee, cacao, tobacco, sugar cane, cotton, silk, fruit, livestock). Mfg.: cement, tobacco products, straw hats; silk, woolen, and cotton goods; soap, chemicals, matches, canned pineapples, chocolate, beverages. Flour mills, foundries, tanneries. Airport. Its railroad station is 4 mi. NW. Gold mines near by. A beautiful colonial city, founded 1622–23, it developed after 1880 as a coffee center. Has fine parks and bldgs., cathedral, sericultural institute.

Bucas Grande Island (bōōkäs′ grän′dā) (□ 50; 1939 pop. 2,556), Surigao prov., Philippines, just off NE tip of Mindanao, just SW of Siargao Isl.; 13 mi. long. Coconuts. Offshore are Middle Bucas Isl. (□ 5) and East Bucas Isl. (□7; 1939 pop. 2,370).

Bucatunna Creek, E Miss., rises SE of Meridian near Ala. line, flows c.90 mi. generally S to Chickasawhay R., 13 mi. SE of Waynesboro.

Bucay (bōōkī′) or **General Elizalde** (hānārāl′ ālēsäl′dā), village, Guayas prov., S Ecuador, on W slopes of the Andes, 50 mi. E of Guayaquil. It is on railroad to Quito, which enters here into mtn. terrain of deep gorges. Near by are bridges across small Chanchán R., an affluent of the Guayas.

Buccaneer Archipelago, in Indian Ocean, at NE entrance to King Sound, N Western Australia; 16°10′S 123°30′E. Comprises Macleay Isl. (largest; 2.3 mi. long), KOOLAN ISLAND, and many small isls. and rocks connected by coral reefs.

Buccari, Yugoslavia: see BAKAR.

Buccheri (bŏŏk-kā′rē), village (pop. 4,614), Siracusa prov., SE Sicily, on Monte Lauro and 15 mi. NNE of Ragusa.

Bucchianico (bōōkyä′nēkô), village (pop. 1,308), Chieti prov., Abruzzi e Molise, S central Italy, 3 mi. S of Chieti; macaroni mfg.

Buccino (bōōt-chē′nô), town (pop. 5,594), Salerno prov., Campania, S Italy, in the Apennines, 16 mi. E of Eboli; resort (alt. 2,129 ft.); olive oil, wine; irrigation pumps. Has medieval castle. Marble quarries near by.

Buccleugh (bŭklōō′), locality, seat of castle of dukes of Buccleugh, S Selkirk, Scotland, 4 mi. E of Ettrick.

Buccoo Reef (bŭ′kōō), off SW Tobago, B.W.I., 6 mi. E of Scarborough; 11°11′N 60°50′W. Has submarine gardens. Lobster fishing.

Bucecea (bōōchā′chä), village (pop. 3,050), Botosani prov., NE Rumania, on railroad and 11 mi. WNW of Botosani; agr. center. Includes Bucecea-Sat and Bucecea Targ. Also called Bucegea.

Bucegi Mountains (bōōchăj′), horseshoe-shaped group of the Transylvanian Alps, in S central Rumania, partly in Transylvania, partly in Muntenia, just W of Sinaia; rise to 8,236 ft. in Omu Peak. Their steep slopes are mostly bare. Alpinism, skiing, scenic caverns (S). Ialomita R. rises on S.

Bucelas (bōōsä′lŭsh), village (pop. 1,213), Lisboa dist., central Portugal, 12 mi. N of Lisbon, in winegrowing dist.

Bucephala, W Pakistan: see JALALPUR.

Buch (bōōkh), section of Pankow dist., N Berlin, Germany, 10 mi. NE of city center. Has medico-biological institute. Bronze Age village excavated here in 1910. After 1945 in Soviet sector.

Bucha (bōōchä′), town (1926 pop. 1,254), N central Kiev oblast, Ukrainian SSR, on railroad and 15 mi. NW of Kiev; glass, chemicals.

Buchach (bōōchäch′), Pol. *Buczacz* (bōō′chäch), city (1931 pop. 10,265), SW Ternopol oblast, Ukrainian SSR, on Strypa R. and 19 mi. WNW of Chortkov; horse-raising and grain-trading center; tapestry and carpet mfg., stone quarrying, brick-working, distilling, flour milling. Technical school. Has ruins of medieval castle, rococo town hall, and old churches. Pol.-Turkish peace treaty concluded here (1672), by which Poland ceded Ukraine to Cossacks. Passed from Poland to Austria (1772); reverted to Poland (1919); ceded to USSR in 1945.

Buchan (bŭ′kŭn), village (pop. 213), SE Victoria, Australia, 180 mi. E of Melbourne, in forested region; tourist resort; cattle. Limestone caves near by.

Buchan (bŭ′khŭn, –kŭn), district of NE Aberdeen and E Banff, Scotland, extending bet. Ythan R. (SE) and Deveron R. (NW), with rocky coastline along the North Sea, and including towns of Peterhead, Fraserburgh, and Old Deer. Buchan Ness, on the North Sea, 3 mi. S of Peterhead, is easternmost promontory of Scotland (57°28′N 1°46′W). The Bullers (boilers) of Buchan, on the North Sea, 5 mi. SSW of Peterhead, are a large hollow rock formation, c.200 ft. deep and 50 ft. in diameter, into which the ocean rushes at high tide; a near-by fishing village is named for them.

Buchanan (būkă′nŭn), village (pop. 448), SE Sask., 15 mi. WNW of Canora; mixed farming.

Buchanan or **Lower Buchanan,** town, ⊙ Grand Bassa co., S Liberia, port on Atlantic Ocean, on Grand Bassa Point, 60 mi. ESE of Monrovia; 5°53′N 10°4′W. Palm oil and kernels, cassava, rice. Formerly called Grand Bassa. Village of Upper Buchanan is 2 mi. NNW, at mouth of St. John R.

Buchanan (būkă′nŭn, bŭ–). **1** County (□ 569; pop. 21,927), E Iowa; ⊙ Independence. Prairie agr. area (cattle, hogs, poultry, corn, oats) drained by Wapsipinicon R. and Buffalo Creek. Many sand and gravel pits, some limestone quarries. Formed 1837. **2** County (□ 411; pop. 96,826), NW Mo.; ⊙ St. Joseph. Bounded W by Missouri R.; drained by the Little Platte. Stock raising, agr. (corn, oats, wheat, hay, apples); mfg. centered at St. Joseph. Formed 1838. **3** County (□ 508; pop. 35,748), SW Va.; ⊙ Grundy. In the Alleghenies; bounded NW by Ky., NE by W.Va.; drained by Levisa Fork of the Big Sandy. Bituminous-coal mining, lumbering; agr. (apples, soybeans, hay, potatoes, sweet potatoes, corn, oats), poultry, livestock. Formed 1858.

Buchanan. **1** City (pop. 651), ⊙ Haralson co., NW Ga., 15 mi. S of Cedartown, near Ala. line; clothing mfg. **2** City (pop. 5,224), Berrien co., extreme SW Mich., on St. Joseph R. and 12 mi. NW of South Bend, Ind. Mfg. of auto parts, insulation materials; railroad shops. Resort. Indian village sites and mounds near by. Platted 1837; inc. as village 1863, as city 1929. **3** Village (pop. 1,820), Westchester co., SE N.Y., just S of Peekskill, near

E bank of the Hudson; mfg. of oilcloth, rain-wear fabric. Inc. 1928. **4** Town (pop. 1,300), Botetourt co., W Va., on James R., in the Blue Ridge, and 22 mi. NNE of Roanoke; makes buttons; limestone quarrying and processing. Peaks of Otter are SE.

Buchanan, Lake, salt lake (□ 50), E central Queensland, Australia, 160 mi. SSW of Townsville; 15 mi. long, 4.5 mi. wide.

Buchanan, Lake, Texas: see BUCHANAN DAM.

Buchanan Bay, E Ellesmere Isl., NE Franklin Dist., Northwest Territories, arm (40 mi. long, 12–20 mi. wide) of Kane Basin, on S side of Bache Peninsula; 78°40′–79°3′N 74°30′–77°30′W. On N shore of bay was site of BACHE PENINSULA post and meteorological station.

Buchanan Dam. 1 In Calif.: see CHOWCHILLA RIVER. **2** In S central Texas, in Colorado R. c.12 mi. W of Burnet; concrete dam 155 ft. high, 11,000 ft. long; for power, flood control, irrigation; completed 1937. Formerly Hamilton Dam. Impounds L. Buchanan (□ 32; capacity 1,000,000 acre-ft.). Buchanan Dam village (pop. c.250) is on S shore.

Buchanhaven, Scotland: see PETERHEAD.

Buchan Ness, Scotland: see BUCHAN.

Buchans (bŭ′kŭnz), town (pop. 1,399), W central N.F., on railroad and 50 mi. E of Corner Brook, near S shore of small Buchans L. (3 mi. long, 1 mi. wide); mining center (copper, lead, zinc, gold, silver). Power from Deer Lake hydroelectric plant.

Bucharest (bōōkŭrĕst′, bū–), Rum. *București* (bōōkōōrĕsht′), city (1948 pop. 886,110; with suburbs 1,041,807), ⊙ Rumania and Bucharest prov., in central Walachia, on Dambovita R. (tributary of the Danube) and 575 mi. SE of Vienna, 180 mi. NNW of Istanbul; 44°25′N 26°6′E. Largest city of Rumania, and a leading industrial, commercial, cultural, and communications center (7 rail lines; highways, airlines). Seat of govt. and of patriarch of Rumanian Orthodox church. Notable among its diversified mfg. are the making of aircraft, automobile bodies, electrical products, munitions, machinery, radios, construction materials, textiles, clothing, leather and rubber goods, plastics, pharmaceuticals, chemicals, liquor, beer, tobacco, oriental sweetmeats, and various kinds of food products. It has major railroad repair and construction shops (at GRIVITA), large printing shops, and glassworks. A substantial transit trade in petroleum (pipe line from Ploesti), lumber, and agr. produce passes through city's markets. Until Sept. 1, 1950, Bucharest proper was divided into 4 administrative sections, *Galben* (=yellow), *Negru* (=black), *Albastru* (=white), *Roșu* (=red), which include the suburbs of Crangasi, Serban Voda, Tudor Vladimirescu I, and Herastrau. The municipal area (□ 13.88) includes, in addition, 7 outer urban suburbs and 6 outer rural suburbs circumscribed by a belt railroad. Climate is continental with warm summers (mean temp. 72.9°F.) and cold, windy winters (mean temp. 9.2°F.). Municipal airport is at Baneasa. Dambovita R., traversing city W–E, is bordered by high quays and spanned by number of bridges; in the heart of the capital it is covered by a large square, on which are the palace of justice and the richly carved 18th-cent. Domnita Baleasa church. On an eminence (S) is the Metropolitan church (1656–65), adjoining the palace of the patriarch; just SSW is the 17th-cent. St. Antim church together with palace of St. Synod. *Calea Victoriei* (Victory Street), principal thoroughfare, laid originally by Constantine Brancovan as road to his summer residence at Mogosoaia, begins at left bank of the Dambovita and crosses city NNW. Along it are the natl. theater, former royal palace (erected 1935–37, now called Palace of the Republic), *Biserica Alba* (=white basilica) known for its murals and icons, the Acad. of Sciences, and various govt. edifices. Its continuation after *Piața Victoriei*, the plaza where military parades are held, is the Kisseleff Road, the pleasure-grounds of Bucharest. On it are the huge Arc of Triumph, the city's largest stadium, the public artificial beach and swimming pool, and the race course of Baneasa. Near by is a large park with open-air ethnological mus. Other noteworthy landmarks of Bucharest are: 17th-cent. St. George church with sepulcher of Constantine Brancovan; 17th-cent. Zlatari, Radu Voda, and Stavropoleos churches; 18th-cent. church of Spiridon the New; the Athenaeum, devoted to music and arts; Targul Mosilor, popular amusement park; and the traditional peasant market of Obor. Bucharest is known for its fine parks, libraries, and museums, notably Natl. Mus. of Antiquities (founded 1864 by Cuza) and museums of natural hist. and natl. art. Educational institutions include the univ. (1864), polytechnic and agr. institutes, and schools of mines, architecture, textiles (1946), drama, music, fine arts, and commerce; also military acad. Bucharest's foundation is attributed to a legendary shepherd Bucur, also said to be founder of the primitive *Biserica* (=church) *Bucur* (in SSW part of city), now a historic monument. As *Cetatea Dambovitei* it gained in importance in medieval times, changed its name to Bucharest (15th cent.), and became ⊙ of Walachia under Constantine Brancovan, replacing Targoviste. The Phanariots of Constantinople introduced into the primitive town the Byzantine spirit and luxury. In 18th–19th cent. it was visited by plague and earthquakes Peace of Bucharest (1812) bet. Russia and Turkey advanced Russia's frontier to Prut R. An accord bet. Serbia and Bulgaria was also signed here. City was repeatedly occupied by Russians and Austrians (19th cent.). Made ⊙ Rumania in 1861. Treaty of Bucharest (1913) stripped Bulgaria of conquests made during Balkan Wars. In First World War Germans entered the city without resistance in spite of strong fortifications, and remained there, 1916–18. In the interwar years, pop. greatly increased and industrial quarters sprang up. It fell again under Ger. control (1940–44) and was liberated by Soviet troops (Aug., 1944). Subsequent Ger. air raids did considerable damage. In 1948 the hq. of the Cominform were moved from Belgrade to Bucharest. Long known as the city of contrasts because of palatial buildings standing side by side with slum hovels, it is now undergoing intensive reconstruction, especially in the workers' districts.

Buchau, Czechoslovakia: see BOCHOV.

Buchau (bōō′khou), town (pop. 2,383), S Württemberg, Germany, after 1945 in Württemberg-Hohenzollern, near the Federsee, 8 mi. WSW of Biberach; peat baths.

Buchchireddipalem, India: see BUCHIREDDIPALEM.

Bu Chemmasc, Tripolitania: see PISIDA.

Buchen (bōō′khŭn), town (pop. 3,975), N Baden, Germany, after 1945 in Württemberg-Baden, on S slope of the Odenwald, 29 mi. ENE of Heidelberg; mfg. (furniture, costume jewelry). Climatic resort (alt. 1,115 ft.). Has late-Gothic church, baroque town hall. First mentioned 733; chartered 1216.

Büchen (bü′khŭn), village (pop. 2,824), in Schleswig-Holstein, NW Germany, on Elbe-Trave Canal and 8 mi. NNE of Lauenburg, 4 mi. NW of Schwanheide (Mecklenburg); rail junction; woodworking. After 1945, traffic check point bet. East and West Germany.

Buchenberg (bōō′khŭnbĕrk″), village (pop. 2,361), Swabia, SW Bavaria, Germany, in the Allgäu, 4 mi. WSW of Kempten; dairying; cattle. Has late-18th-cent. church. Chartered 1485.

Buchenwald (bōō′khŭnvält″), locality, Thuringia, central Germany, on the Grosser Ettersberg, 5 mi. NW of Weimar. Site (1937–45) of notorious concentration camp under Hitler regime.

Buchholz (bōōkh′hôlts). **1** Village (pop. 5,917), in former Prussian prov. of Hanover, NW Germany, after 1945 in Lower Saxony, 15 mi. SW of Hamburg; rail junction; sawmilling. **2** Town (pop. 8,067), Saxony, E central Germany, in the Erzgebirge, 18 mi. S of Chemnitz, in mining region (uranium, bismuth, cobalt, tin, silver); mfg.: ribbons, silk, lace, machinery, cardboard. Has 16th-cent. church. Chartered 1501.

Buchireddipalem (bōōchĭrĕ′dĭpä″lĕm), town (pop. 5,720), Nellore dist., E Madras, India, 10 mi. NW of Nellore; millet, rice, cashew. Experimental farm (rice research). Also spelled Buchchireddipalem.

Buchkirchen (bōōkh′kĭrkhŭn), town (pop. 3,003), central Upper Austria, 4 mi. N of Wels; wheat, cattle.

Buchloe (bōōkh′lō), village (pop. 4,951), Swabia, SW Bavaria, Germany, 12 mi. NNE of Kaufbeuren; rail junction; pottery mfg., dairying, tanning. Chartered 1354.

Buchlovice (bōōkh′lôvĭtsĕ), Ger. *Buchlowitz* (bōōkh′lōvĭts), village (pop. 1,925), E Moravia, Czechoslovakia, 5 mi. W of Uherske Hradiste; sugar beets, barley, wheat. Has 13th-cent. castle.

Buchon, Point (bŭ-shŏn′), SW Calif., coastal promontory at SW extremity of Estero Bay, just S of Morro Bay village.

Buchs (bōōks). **1** Town (pop. 3,255), Aargau canton, N Switzerland, on Suhr R. and 1 mi. E of Aarau; cotton textiles, foodstuffs; woodworking. **2** Town (pop. 4,776), St. Gall canton, NE Switzerland, on the Rhine, at Liechtenstein border, and 3 mi. NW of Vaduz, Liechtenstein; woolen textiles, embroideries, beer, flour; printing.

Buchsweiler, France: see BOUXWILLER.

Buchtel (bōōk′tŭl), village (pop. 569), Athens co., SE Ohio, 10 mi. NNW of Athens, in coal-mining area.

Buchupureo (bōōchōōpōōrā′ō), village (1930 pop. 408), Ñuble prov., S central Chile, on the coast, 50 mi. NW of Chillán; resort.

Buchy (büshē′), agr. village (pop. 734), Seine-Inférieure dept., N France, 15 mi. NE of Rouen.

Bucine (bōō′chēnĕ), village (pop. 500), Arezzo prov., Tuscany, central Italy, 13 mi. W of Arezzo.

Buciumi or **Bucium** (both: bōōchōōm′). **1** Hung. *Vármező* (vär′mĕzû), village (pop. 2,127), Cluj prov., NW Rumania, 8 mi. S of Zalau; mfg. of edible oils. In Hungary, 1940–45. **2** Suburb (pop. 500) of Jassy, NE Rumania, 4 mi. SSE of city center. Has 16th- and 17th-cent. churches.

Buckau (bōō′kou), S industrial suburb of Magdeburg, Saxony-Anhalt, central Germany, on the Elbe; electrical-equipment mfg.

Buckden, town and parish (pop. 1,037), S central Huntingdon, England, 4 mi. SW of Huntingdon; hosiery knitting; agr. market. Has 15th-cent. church, where Laurence Sterne was ordained. Near by is Buckden Palace (14th cent.), former episcopal mansion of bishops of Lincoln.

Bückeburg (bü′kŭbōōrk), town (pop. 10,496), ⊙ former Schaumburg-Lippe, W Germany, after 1945 in Lower Saxony, 6 mi. ESE of Minden; mfg. of machinery and machine tools. Airport. Lutheran bishopric. Has 2 castles, baroque church.

Buckeye. 1 Town (pop. 1,932), Maricopa co., SW central Ariz., near Gila R., 30 mi. W of Phoenix in agr. area (cotton, grain). Inc. 1929. **2** Town (pop. 192), Hardin co., central Iowa, 9 mi. SW of Iowa Falls, in agr. area.

Buckeye Lake, village (pop. 1,401), Licking co., central Ohio, 9 mi. SSW of Newark and on Buckeye L. (c.7 mi. long). State park (c.4,000 acres) here; camping, recreational facilities.

Buckeystown (bŭ′kēztoun), village (pop. c.300), Frederick co., W Md., near Monocacy R., 6 mi. SSW of Frederick; canned vegetables, bricks. Near by is site of plant (1785) where John Frederick Amelung produced some of finest early American glass.

Buckfastleigh (bŭkfŭst′lē), urban district (1931 pop. 2,410; 1951 census 2,592), S Devon, England, on Dart R. and 5 mi. NW of Totnes; woolen milling, stone quarrying, paper milling. Has 13th-cent. church. Near by is Buckfast Abbey, medieval Cistercian monastery restored in early 20th cent. by Benedictine monks from France.

Buckfield, town (pop. 899), Oxford co., W Maine, on Nezinscot R. and 15 mi. NNW of Auburn, in farming, recreational area; wood products.

Buck Grove, town (pop. 67), Crawford co., W Iowa, 7 mi. S of Denison.

Buckhannon (bŭk″hă′nŭn), city (pop. 6,016), ⊙ Upshur co., central W.Va., on Buckhannon R. and 21 mi. SSE of Clarksburg, in region known for its agr. (especially strawberries; also livestock, tobacco). Mfg. of building materials, clothing, beverages, dairy products; lumber milling; coal mines, gas wells, timber. West Va. Wesleyan Col. here. Settled 1770.

Buckhannon River, central W.Va., formed in SW Randolph co. by junction of short Right and Left forks; flows c.45 mi. generally N to Tygart R. 6 mi. S of Philippi.

Buckhaven and Methil (bŭk-hā′vŭn, mĕ′thĭl), burgh (1931 pop. 17,643; 1951 census 20,154), central Fifeshire, Scotland. Includes coal-mining towns and coal-shipping ports of Methil, on the Firth of Forth, just SW of Leven; and Buckhaven, on the Firth of Forth, 3 mi. SW of Leven, with anc. castle ruin known as Macduff's Castle.

Buckhead, town (pop. 220), Morgan co., N central Ga., 7 mi. ESE of Madison.

Buck Hill Falls, resort village, Monroe co., NE Pa., in Pocono Mts., 14 mi. N of Stroudsburg; summer and winter sports, hunting, fishing.

Buckholts (bŭk′hōlts), village (pop. c.900), Milam co., central Texas, c.55 mi. NE of Austin, in cotton, cattle, corn area.

Buckhorn Island, N.Y.: see GRAND ISLAND.

Buckhorn Lake (9 mi. long, 1–3 mi. wide), Kawartha Lakes, S Ont., 11 mi. NNW of Peterborough. Drained E by Trent Canal.

Buckhurst Hill, residential former urban district (1931 pop. 5,486), SW Essex, England, on Roding R. and 12 mi. NE of London, near Epping Forest; makes electrical equipment. Inc. 1933 in Chigwell.

Buckie (bŭ′kē), burgh (1931 pop. 8,689; 1951 census 7,705), NW Banffshire, Scotland, on Moray Firth, 17 mi. W of Banff; herring-fishing center, with good harbor. Burgh includes fishing ports of Ianstown and Portessie.

Buckingham, town (pop. 4,516), SW Que., on Lièvre R. near its mouth on Ottawa R., and 17 mi. NE of Ottawa; paper milling, lumbering, mining (feldspar, silica, phosphate rock); mfg. of chemicals; dairying.

Buckingham or **Buckinghamshire** (bŭ′kĭng-ŭm, –shĭr), county (□ 749; 1931 pop. 271,586; 1951 census 386,164), S England; ⊙ Aylesbury. Bounded by Oxford (W), Northampton (NW), Bedford, Hertford, and Middlesex (E), and Berkshire (S). Drained by Thames, Thame, Wye, and Ouse rivers. Undulating land (with the fertile Aylesbury Vale) intersected by the Chiltern Hills. Arable land in N, growing wheat and beans, grazing land in S. Largely a residential area for London. Industries include furniture (High Wycombe), paper, leather, and railroad rolling stock (Wolverton). Other important towns: Slough, Bletchley, Amersham, Chesham. There are many large country seats, and literary and historical associations. Shortened form, Bucks.

Buckingham, municipal borough (1931 pop. 3,083; 1951 census 3,944), NW Buckingham, England, on Ouse R. and 15 mi. NW of Aylesbury; agr. market. Has Norman chantry and 16th-cent. Castle House. NNW 3 mi. is noted Stowe House, former residence of the dukes of Buckingham; site of Stowe School, a well-known public school.

Buckingham (bŭ′kĭng-hăm″), county (□ 576; pop. 12,288), central Va.; ⊙ Buckingham. Bounded NW and N by James R., S by Appomattox R.; drained by small Slate and Willis rivers. Includes part of a state forest. Agr. (mainly tobacco; also grain, fruit), livestock, dairying. Extensive lumbering, slate quarrying. Power plant on the James. Formed 1761.

Buckingham. 1 Village (pop. 140), Kankakee co., NE Ill., 16 mi. WSW of Kankakee, in agr. area. 2 Town (pop. 264), ⊙ Buckingham co., central Va., 34 mi. ENE of Lynchburg. Also called Buckingham Court House.

Buckingham Bay (bŭ'kĭng-ŭm), inlet of Arafura Sea, Arnhem Land, N Northern Territory, Australia, bet. Napier Peninsula (NW) and Flinders Point peninsula (SE), NW of Arnhem Bay; 14 mi. long, 8 mi. wide.

Buckingham Canal, navigation canal along E coast of Madras, India; from Merkanam extends c.260 mi. N, past Mahabalipuram, Madras, and Pulicat L., to Pedda Ganjam, 15 mi. NE of Ongole, here joining navigable irrigation-canal system of Kistna R. delta. Links numerous lagoons (locks; saltworks). Constructed piecemeal, 1806–83. Although its value as a trade artery was greatly decreased by construction of railroads, it is still largely used for shipping salt, firewood (Casuarina), and stone.

Buckingham Court House, Va.: see BUCKINGHAM, town.

Buckingham Palace, in Westminster, LONDON, England.

Buckinghamshire, England: see BUCKINGHAM, county.

Buck Island. 1 Islet (41.55 acres), U.S. Virgin Isls., off SE St. Thomas Isl., 5 mi. SSE of Charlotte Amalie; 18°16'N 64°54'W; lighthouse. 2 Islet (17.64 acres), U.S. Virgin Isls., off NE St. Croix Isl., 6 mi. NE of Christiansted; 17°48'N 64°37'W.

Buckland, village (1939 pop. 115), NW Alaska, on NE Seward Peninsula, on Buckland R. and 10 mi. SE of Kotzebue; fur-trading point for Eskimo trappers.

Buckland. 1 Town (pop. 1,605), Franklin co., NW Mass., in hills, 10 mi. W of Greenfield; apple orchards, dairying. Deerfield R. bounds township on N. Inc. 1779. Includes part of SHELBURNE FALLS village. 2 Village (pop. 274), Auglaize co., W Ohio, 12 mi. SW of Lima, and on Auglaize R., in agr. area.

Buckland Monachorum (bŭ'klŭnd mŭnă'kŭrŭm), agr. village and parish (pop. 2,617), SW Devon, England, 4 mi. S of Tavistock. Site of Buckland Abbey, Sir Francis Drake's home. Has 15th-cent. church.

Buckland River, NW Alaska, at base of Seward Peninsula, rises near 65°25'N 159°30'W, flows 120 mi. NW, past Buckland, to Eschscholtz Bay, 15 mi. N of Buckland.

Buckleboo, village (pop. 129), S South Australia, on central Eyre Peninsula, 125 mi. NNE of Port Lincoln; rail terminus; wheat, wool.

Bucklebury, village and parish (pop. 1,392), central Berkshire, England, 6 mi. ENE of Newbury; old wood-turning industry.

Buckley, urban district (1931 pop. 6,899; 1951 census 7,699), Flint, Wales, 6 mi. SSE of Flint; coal mining, brick mfg. Just S remains of Offa's Dyke are visible. Urban dist. includes coal-mining dists. of Ewloe (pop. 2,033) and Pentrobin (pop. 961).

Buckley. 1 Village (pop. 554), Iroquois co., E Ill., 37 mi. SSW of Kankakee, in agr. area. 2 Village (pop. 194), Wexford co., NW Mich., 18 mi. S of Traverse City, in agr. area. 3 Town (pop. 2,705), Pierce co., W central Wash., 20 mi. ESE of Tacoma and on White R., near foothills of Cascade Range. Lumber, fruit, truck, hops; hunting, mining, logging in region. Settled 1888, inc. 1890.

Bucklin. 1 City (pop. 824), Ford co., SW Kansas, 25 mi. SE of Dodge City; grain, livestock. 2 City (pop. 783), Linn co., N central Mo., 10 mi. E of Brookfield; grain, coal.

Buckman, village (pop. 173), Morrison co., central Minn., 15 mi. ESE of Little Falls, in agr. area; dairy products.

Buckminster, village and parish (pop. 265), NE Leicester, England, 8 mi. ENE of Melton Mowbray; ironstone quarrying. Has 14th-15th-cent. church.

Buckner. 1 Town (pop. 335), Lafayette co., SW Ark., 34 mi. E of Texarkana. 2 Village (pop. 783), Franklin co., S Ill., 12 mi. N of Herrin, in bituminous-coal-mining and agr. area. 3 City (pop. 639), Jackson co., W Mo., 22 mi. E of Kansas City; ships wheat, livestock.

Buckner Bay, inlet of Philippine Sea, in SE Okinawa, Okinawa Isls., in the Ryukyus. It is 12 mi. long, 5 mi. wide; best harbor of isl. Was major Jap. naval and seaplane base in Second World War. Called Nakagusuku Bay by Japanese; renamed (1945) Buckner Bay by U.S. for Gen. Simon Bolivar Buckner. Formerly sometimes called Mathews.

Buckow (bŏŏ'kō), town (pop. 2,344), Brandenburg, E Germany, 30 mi. E of Berlin; excursion resort, surrounded by many small lakes.

Buckroe Beach, Va.: see PHOEBUS.

Bucks, England: see BUCKINGHAM, county.

Bucks, county (□ 617; pop. 144,620), SE Pa.; ⊙ Doylestown. Agr. and residential area; bounded E and SE by Delaware R. Washington crossed the Delaware at WASHINGTON CROSSING. Mfg. (textiles, metal products); limestone, sandstone, granite quarrying. Formed 1682.

Bucksburn, town in Newhills parish (pop. 6,722), SE Aberdeen, Scotland, on Don R. and 4 mi. NW of Aberdeen; paper milling, cement mfg.

Buckskin, Mount, Colo.: see PARK RANGE.

Bucksport, town (pop. 3,120), including Bucksport village (pop. 2,094), Hancock co., S Maine, on the Penobscot and 16 mi. S of Bangor. Paper mill built 1930. Site of Jed Prouty Tavern (1804) and Waldo-Hancock bridge. Old Fort Knox (1846) is across river. Settled 1762, inc. 1792.

Buckton Vale, town in Stalybridge urban dist., NE Cheshire, England; textile printing. Near by are slate quarries. Has ruins of Buckton Castle.

Bucoda (bŭkō'dŭ), town (pop. 473), Thurston co., W Wash., 18 mi. S of Olympia, in agr. region.

Bucovice (bŏŏ'chôvĭtsĕ), Czech *Bučovice*, Ger. *Butschowitz* (bŏŏ'chōvĭts), town (pop. 3,384), S central Moravia, Czechoslovakia, on railroad and 18 mi. E of Brno; agr. market (wheat, barley, sugar beets); woodworking. Has 16th-cent. castle.

Bucovina, region, Europe: see BUKOVINA.

Bucquoy (bükwä'), village (pop. 1,322), Pas-de-Calais dept., N France, 11 mi. S of Arras; agr. tools.

Buctouche (bŭktōōsh'), village (pop. estimate c.800), E N.B., on Northumberland Strait, at mouth of Buctouche R. (30 mi. long), 20 mi. NNW of Shediac; fishing (oysters, cod, lobster, herring, smelt) and lumber port. Area settled by Acadians.

Buctzotz (bōōktsōts'), town (pop. 1,401), Yucatan, SE Mexico, 23 mi. NNE of Izamal; henequen.

Bucuresti, Rumania: see BUCHAREST.

Bucy-le-Long (büsē-lü-lõ'), village (pop. 640), Aisne dept., N France, 3 mi. ENE of Soissons; sugar distilling, fertilizer mfg.

Bucyrus (būsī'rŭs). 1 Village (pop. 111), Adams co., SW N.Dak., 8 mi. NW of Hettinger. 2 City (pop. 10,327), ⊙ Crawford co., N central Ohio, 23 mi. W of Mansfield and on Sandusky R.; industrial and rail center; machinery, metal products, rubber goods, tools, clothing, light bulbs, incubators, glass products. Settled 1819, laid out 1822.

Buczacz, Ukrainian SSR: see BUCHACH.

Bud, village (pop. 1,056, with adjoining Alpoca), Wyoming co., S W.Va., 13 mi. ENE of Welch; coal.

Buda, Hungary: see BUDAPEST.

Buda (bū'dŭ). 1 Village (pop. 761), Bureau co., N Ill., 13 mi. ENE of Kewanee; grain, livestock. 2 Village (pop. 483), Hays co., S central Texas, 15 mi. SSW of Austin; trade point in agr. area.

Budafok (bŏŏ'dŏfŏk), city (pop. 24,375), Pest-Pilis-Solt-Kiskun co., N central Hungary, on the Danube, just S of Budapest; rail center. Textiles, matches; extensive champagne and cognac mfg., distilleries, breweries; soap- and candleworks. Site of Roman settlement.

Buda Island (bōō'dhä), in Ebro R. delta, Tarragona prov., NE Spain, c.20 mi. ESE of Tortosa; 2 mi. long, 4 mi. wide.

Budakalasz (bŏŏ'dŏkŏläs), Hung. *Budakalász*, town (pop. 3,259), Pest-Pilis-Solt-Kiskun co., N central Hungary, 8 mi. N of Budapest; textiles (wool, linen); poultry, apples, grapes.

Budakeszi (bŏŏ'dŏkĕsē), town (pop. 7,322), Pest-Pilis-Solt-Kiskun co., N central Hungary, in Buda Mts., 7 mi. W of Budapest; mfg. of artificial marble. Several tuberculosis sanatoria in vicinity.

Buda-Koshelevo (bōō"dä-kŭshĭlyō'vŭ), town (1939 pop. over 2,000), central Gomel oblast, Belorussian SSR, 27 mi. NW of Gomel; lumber milling. Formerly Buda-Koshelevskaya.

Budalin (bōō'dŭlĭn), village, Lower Chindwin dist., Upper Burma, 65 mi. WNW of Mandalay, on railroad to Yeu; rice, wheat, cotton.

Buda Mountains (bŏŏ'dŏ), N central Hungary, extend 13 mi. W from the Danube, rising to 1,738 ft. in Mt. Janos (S range); beyond residential dist. of Hüvösvölgy N range rises to 1,627 ft. in Mt. Harmashatar. W slope forested; residential dists. of Buda on E slopes. Wine and champagne made at Budafok is stored in natural caves of Teteny Plateau (S). Thermal springs on Mt. Gellert, at Aquincum, and along the Danube (see BUDAPEST); lignite mines at Pilisvörösvar, Solymar.

Buda Nilkantha, Nepal: see KATMANDU.

Budanov (bōōdä'nŭf), Pol. *Budzanów* (bōōdzä'nōōf), village (1931 pop. 4,798), S central Ternopol oblast, Ukrainian SSR, on Seret R. and 10 mi. S of Terebovlya; flour milling, brickworking; grain, tobacco. Has ruins of old castle and convent.

Budaörs (bŏŏ'dŏ-ûrsh), town (pop. 9,814), Pest-Pilis-Solt-Kiskun co., N central Hungary, 7 mi. WSW of Budapest; champagne. Municipal airport. Open-air Passion plays.

Budapest (bōō'dŭpĕst, Hung. bŏŏ'dŏpĕsht'), city (1941 pop. 1,164,963), ⊙ Hungary and Pest-Pilis-Solt-Kiskun co., N central Hungary, on the Danube and 135 mi. SE of Vienna; 47°30'N 19°20'E; alt. 377 ft. Commercial, industrial, communications, and cultural center, and largest city of Hungary. Formed 1873 by unification of Buda (Ger. *Ofen*), Obuda (Hung. *Óbuda*, Ger. *Alt-Ofen*), and Pest. Buda, on right bank of the Danube, is much older than Pest. A grain market and wine center, Budapest has varied industries: iron and steel mfg., textile milling, food processing (flour mills, breweries, distilleries). Two-thirds of Hungary's industry centers in Greater Budapest (Budapest proper and 22 suburbs). Over 50% of the country's industrial workers are in the city and its environs. In its suburbs are: iron- and steelworks (CSEPEL, PESTSZENTLÖRINC), textile mills (KISPEST, ALBERTFALVA, RAKOSPALOTA, PESTSZENTERZSEBET), wineries (BUDAFOK, BUDAÖRS), chemicals, pharmaceuticals (UJPEST). Budapest is hub of railway network of the Carpathian basin; municipal airports at Budaörs and Matyasföld; a free port on CSEPEL ISLAND. Budapest is also a resort, with St. Gellert, Rudas, Csaszar, St. Emeric, Kiraly, and Szechenyi baths and thermal and mineral springs. Buda is residential dist.; slopes of mounts SVAB, JANOS, GELLERT, HARS, and HARMASHATAR built up with villas and modern apartment houses. Several bridges cross the Danube here; MARGARET ISLAND is joined to mainland. Roman colony of Aquincum (remains of amphitheater and baths still extant) became core of Obuda. After Tatar destruction (1241) of Obuda and Pest (which had developed on left side of Danube around another Roman settlement) Bela IV built a fortress, called Buda, on a hill near Mt. Gellert. A cent. later, Emperor Sigismund erected a palace there and Buda became residence of ruler, reaching its height as cultural center under Matthias Corvinus in 2d half of 15th cent. Occupied and devastated in 1541 by Turks, twin cities remained under Ottoman rule as seat of a pasha until 1686, when Charles of Lorraine conquered them for the Hapsburgs. The original population having almost disappeared, Pest was resettled with Serbs, Buda with Germans. Made a free royal town in 1703, Buda experienced a brief renaissance when Maria Theresa built the royal palace and when in 1777 she had the univ., founded in 1635 by Peter Pazmany at Nagyszombat, transferred here. In 1784, univ. was removed to Pest, which in 19th cent. developed rapidly as a commercial center. Buda became the residential sector. The ALFÖLD had recovered from destruction wrought by Turks and Pest subsequently developed rapidly as commercial and market center. After a devastating flood (1838), Pest was rebuilt on modern lines; its old bldgs. were renovated and many new ones added, including Hungarian Acad. of Sciences, National Theater, Basilica of St. Stephen with its 315-ft.-high dome, Opera (Ybl), and the imposing Parliament bldg. Industrial suburbs sprang up, and by 1917 Budapest was a grain and flour milling center 2d only to Minneapolis. After the First World War machines, chemicals, and textiles became the most important products. Famed for its beauty, its literary, theatrical, and musical life, its many places of entertainment, and its numerous mineral springs, Budapest also became an international tourist center. In the Second World War Budapest suffered severely from air raids and from a 14-week siege (1945) by Russian army. The 7 bridges connecting Buda and Pest, including the Szechenyi suspension bridge (built 1840–49), were destroyed. Almost 70% of Buda's bldgs., including royal palace, the Romanesque Coronation Church, and the Rudas and Emeric baths, were demolished or heavily damaged. In Pest the famous Corso (promenade) along the Danube, Calvin Square, and the art gall. in municipal park were destroyed; most museums were badly damaged and looted. Of the 200,000 Jews (almost half the Jews of Hungary) who lived in Budapest before the war, only c.116,000 remained. After the war the city absorbed certain suburban areas, and in 1949 its pop. was 1,600,000.

Budardalur or **Budhardalur** (bōō'dhärdä"lür), Icelandic *Búðardalur*, fishing village, ⊙ Dala co., W Iceland, at head of Hvamm Fjord, SE arm of Breidi Fjord; 65°6'N 21°46'W.

Budareyri or **Budareyri i Reydarfjordur** (bōō'dhä-rä"rē ē rä'dhärfyûr"dhür), Icelandic *Búðareyri í Reyðarfjörður*, fishing village (pop. 401), Sudur-Mula co., E Iceland, at head of Reydar Fjord, 16 mi. SSW of Seydisfjordur, in feldspar-quarrying region. Also spelled Budhareyri i Reydharfjordhur.

Budarino, Russian SFSR: see CHERKESOVSKI.

Budateteny (bŏŏ'dŏtā"tānyŭ), Hung. *Budatétény*, SW suburb (pop. 3,278) of Budapest, Pest-Pilis-Solt-Kiskun co., N central Hungary; poultry, grapes, mushrooms.

Budaun (bŏŏdoun'), district (□ 1,994; pop. 1,162,-322), Rohilkhand div., central Uttar Pradesh, India; ⊙ Budaun. On W Ganges Plain; bounded W by the Ganges. Agr. (wheat, pearl millet, mustard, barley, gram, jowar, corn, sugar cane, cotton, rice); mango groves and dhak jungle (N). Main centers: Budaun, Sahaswan, Ujhani, Kakrala. Also spelled Badayun.

Budaun, city (pop. 52,077), ⊙ Budaun dist., central Uttar Pradesh, India, near tributary of the Ganges, 28 mi. SW of Bareilly; road junction; mfg. of chemicals; trades in grains, mustard, sugar cane, cotton. Large mosque (Jama Masjid) built 1223 by Altamsh (Iltutmish), tomb of Ala-ud-din (Alam Shah), last Saiyid king of Delhi, who died here in 1453. Captured by Kutb-ud-Aibak in 1196, when last Hindu king was killed. Important under Afghan-Delhi empire. Early Moslem historian, Badayuni, b. here. Also spelled Badayun.

Budd Coast, mountainous part of coast of Wilkes Land, Antarctica, on Indian Ocean, bet. 110°30'E and 114°E. Discovered 1840 by Charles Wilkes, U.S. explorer.

Buddh Gaya (bŏŏd' gŭ'yŭ) or **Bodh Gaya** (bōd'), village, Gaya dist., central Bihar, India, on tributary of the Ganges and 7 mi. S of Gaya. Site of pipal (Bo) tree under which Prince Gautama Siddartha is said to have achieved enlightenment and become the Buddha. Present temple of Buddh Gaya (built over Asokan temple remains) maintained by Sivaite monks. Extensive Buddhist remains include stupas, temples, and monasteries. One of 8 great anc. Buddhist pilgrimage centers. Also known as Mahabodhi.

Budd Lake, resort village (pop. 1,032), Morris co., N N.J., on Budd L. (c.2 mi. long) and 14 mi. WNW or Morristown.

Buddon Ness, promontory on North Sea, at mouth of Firth of Tay, SE Angus, Scotland, 4 mi. ESE of Monifieth; site of 2 lighthouses (56°28′N 2°45′ W). Near by is Barry Links, principal military training ground in Scotland. In North Sea 2 mi. ESE of Buddon Ness is Abertay Lightship, marking entrance to the Firth of Tay.

Buddusò (bŏŏd-dōōzô′), village (pop. 3,860), Sassari prov., N central Sardinia, 38 mi. ESE of Sassari. Dolmens near by.

Bude, England: see BUDE-STRATTON.

Bude (būd), town (pop. 1,195), Franklin co., SW Miss., 32 mi. E of Natchez, and on Homochitto R., in agr. and timber area; lumber. Inc. 1912.

Budejovice, Czechoslovakia: see BUDWEIS.

Budel (bü′dŭl), town (pop. 1,806), North Brabant prov., SW Netherlands, 12 mi. SSE of Eindhoven, on Belg. border; zinc and sulphuric-acid mfg.

Büdelsdorf (bü′dŭlsdôrf), industrial N suburb (pop. 8,756) of Rendsburg, Schleswig-Holstein, NW Germany; foundry; woodworking.

Budenheim (bōō′dŭnhīm), village (pop. 4,085), Rhenish Hesse, W Germany, on left bank of the Rhine and 4 mi. WNW of Mainz; chemical mfg., metalworking. Limestone quarries.

Budennovka (bŏŏdyô′nŭfkŭ), town (pop. over 2,000), S Stalino oblast, Ukrainian SSR, on Sea of Azov, 25 mi. E of Zhdanov; metalworking, fish canning. Until c.1935, Novo-Nikolayevka.

Budennovsk (bŏŏdyô′nŭfsk), city (1926 pop. 15,776), E Stavropol Territory, Russian SFSR, on left bank of Kuma R. and 55 mi. NE of Georgiyevsk (linked by rail); rail terminus in wheat, cotton, and winegrowing dist.; flour milling, cotton ginning, wine making. Originally named Svyatoi Krest; called Prikumsk (1922–c.1935). Across Kuma R., 3 mi. SE, is wine center of Praskoveya.

Budennovski or **Budennovskiy** (-skē). **1** Town (1939 pop. over 500), SW Rostov oblast, Russian SFSR, 8 mi. W of Novocherkassk. **2** Town (1939 pop. over 500), NE Stalino oblast, Ukrainian SSR, in the Donbas, 4 mi. NNE of Artemovsk; salt mining.

Budennoye (bŏŏdyô′nŭyŭ), village (1926 pop. 2,032), SW Vornezh oblast, Russian SFSR, on Tikhaya Sosna R. and 32 mi. SW of Ostrogozhsk; fruit and vegetable processing, flour milling. Until early 1920s, called Biryuch.

Budenny or **Budennyy** (bŏŏdyô′nē), village (1939 pop. over 500), NE Talas oblast, Kirghiz SSR, on Talas R. and 18 mi. E of Talas; wheat. Until c.1937, Chatbazar.

Büderich (bü′dŭrĭkh), village (pop. 8,464), in former Prussian Rhine Prov., W Germany, after 1945 in North Rhine-Westphalia, near the Rhine, 4 mi. WNW of Düsseldorf; cheese mfg.

Budesti (bŏŏdĕsht′), Rum. *Budeşti*, village (pop. 2,927), Bucharest prov., S Rumania, on Arges R. at mouth of the Dambovita, on railroad and 23 mi. SE of Bucharest; wheat, corn, vegetables.

Bude-Stratton (būd′-), urban district (1931 pop. 3,836; 1951 census 5,230), NE Cornwall, England. Includes resort town of Bude (pop. 2,905), on the Atlantic, 15 mi. NNW of Launceston; and agr. market of Stratton (E; pop. 931), with 14th-cent. church. At near-by Stamford Hill royalist Cornish army defeated Parliamentarians in Civil War. Formerly called Stratton and Bude; inc. under new name in early 1930s.

Budge-Budge (bŭj′bŭj), town (pop. 32,394), 24-Parganas dist., SE West Bengal, India, on Hooghly R. and 12 mi. WSW of Calcutta city center; rail spur terminus; jute-milling center; large petroleum depots. Also spelled Baj-Baj. A major Indian boot and shoe factory is 3 mi. NE, at Batanagar.

Budhana (bŏŏdä′nŭ), town (pop. 6,030), Muzaffarnagar dist., N Uttar Pradesh, India, on tributary of the Jumna and 18 mi. SW of Muzaffarnagar; wheat, gram, sugar cane, oilseeds.

Budhardalur, Iceland: see BUDARDALUR.

Budhareyri, Iceland: see BUDAREYRI.

Budhgaon (bŏŏd′goun), town (pop. 4,464), Satara South dist., S central Bombay, India, 4 mi. NE of Sangli; agr. market (millet, sugar cane, peanuts); cotton ginning, hand-loom weaving. Sometimes spelled Bhudgaon. Was ⊙ former Deccan state of Miraj Junior.

Budhir, Iceland: See BUDIR.

Budhlada (bŏŏdlä′dŭ), town (pop. 5,364), S central Patiala and East Punjab States Union, India, 60 mi. SW of Patiala; local market center for millet, oilseeds, gram, cotton. Formerly in exclave of Hissar dist., Indian Punjab.

Budi, Laguna del (lägōō′nä dĕl bōō′dē), lagoon (□ 20) in Cautín prov., S central Chile, 37 mi. WSW of Temuco, connected with the Pacific by 8-mi.-long Budi R.; c.9 mi. long, 4 mi. wide. On its E bank is Puerto Domínguez. Includes a number of isls.; largest is GUAPI ISLAND. Resort.

Budia (bōōdh′yä), town (pop. 928), Guadalajara prov., central Spain, 22 mi. E of Guadalajara; cereals, grapes, olives, honey, sheep, goats; tanning, flour milling; lime quarrying.

Büdingen (bü′dĭng-ŭn), town (pop. 6,005), central Hesse, W Germany, in former Upper Hesse prov., 13 mi. NE of Hanau; lumber milling. Has Romanesque chapel, late-Gothic town hall. Chartered 1330.

Budir or **Budir i Faskrudsfirdi** (bōō′dhĭr ē fous′-krōōdhsfĭr″dhē), Icelandic *Búðir í Fáskrúðsfirði*, town (pop. 564), Sudur-Mula co., E Iceland, 15 mi. SSW of Seydisfjordur, on Faskrud Fjord (Icelandic *Fáskrúðsfjörður*), 10-mi.-long inlet; fishing port. Also spelled Budhir i Faskrudhsfirdhi.

Budjala (bōōjä′lä), village, Equator Prov., NW Belgian Congo, 125 mi. WNW of Lisala; trading center; cotton ginning.

Budja-Saint-Paul, Belgian Congo: see BOYANGE.

Budleigh Salterton (bŭd′lē sôl′-), urban district (1931 pop. 3,162; 1951 census 3,953), E Devon, England, on Lyme Bay of the Channel, at mouth of Otter R., 4 mi. ENE of Exmouth; fishing port and seaside resort.

Budnany, Czechoslovakia: see KARLSTEJN.

Budogoshch or **Budogoshch′** (bŏŏdŭgôshch′), town (1948 pop. over 2,000), SE Leningrad oblast, Russian SFSR, 45 mi. SW of Tikhvin; rail junction; brickworks. During Second World War, briefly held (1941) by Germans.

Budop (bōōdôp′), town, Thudaumot prov., S Vietnam, 17 mi. NE of Locninh (railhead), near Cambodia line; sheep-raising center.

Budrio (bōō′drēō), town (pop. 2,892), Bologna prov., Emilia-Romagna, N central Italy, near Idice R., 10 mi. ENE of Bologna; rail junction; agr. center; hemp mill. Has noted ocarina industry.

Budrum, Turkey: see BODRUM.

Büdszentmihaly (büt′sĕntmĭhī), Hung. *Büdszentmihály*, town (pop. 12,008), Szabolcs co., NE Hungary, 16 mi. W of Nyiregyhaza; mfg. of chemicals; flour mills; wheat, tobacco, corn; cattle, hogs, sheep.

Budua, Yugoslavia: see BUDVA.

Budva (bōōd′vä), Ital. *Budua* (bōō′dōōä), village, S Montenegro, Yugoslavia, port on the Adriatic, 25 mi. WSW of Titograd; summer bathing resort. Orthodox Eastern cathedral (1418), castle ruins. Originally (4th cent. B.C.) a Roman settlement. Until 1921, in Dalmatia.

Budweis (bŭd′wīs, Ger. bōōt′vīs), Czech *České Budějovice* (chĕ′skā bōō′dyĕyôvĭtsĕ), city (pop. 38,194), ⊙ Ceske Budejovice prov. (□ 3,462; pop. 493,730), S Bohemia, Czechoslova a, on Vltava R. (Moldau), at mouth of Malse R., and 75 mi. S of Prague; 48°58′N 14°28′E. Rail junction; industrial center noted for its Budweiser beer; mfg. of pencils (since 1790), enamelware, furniture, tobacco and food products; lumber trade. R.C. bishopric. Founded in 13th cent. Has preserved 13th-cent. convent and church, early Gothic Dominican abbey with cloisters, 14th–15th-cent. tower, 18th-cent. town hall, mus. Broadcasting station. Anthracite and lignite deposits in vicinity.

Budworth Mere, England: see GREAT BUDWORTH.

Budy (bōō′dē), town (1926 pop. 2,158), N central Kharkov oblast, Ukrainian SSR, 11 mi. SW of Kharkov; ceramics.

Budzanow, Ukrainian SSR: see BUDANOV.

Budzhak (bŏŏjäk′), Rum. *Bugeac* (bōōjäk′), dry steppe region of S Moldavian SSR and Izmail oblast of Ukrainian SSR, S of Kodry hills; wheat, corn, barley; karakul-sheep raising.

Bue, Monte (môn′tĕ bōō′ĕ), second highest peak (5,840 ft.) in Ligurian Apennines, N Italy, near Monte Maggiorasca.

Buea (bōōä′ü), town (pop. 1,265), S Br. Cameroons, on SE slopes of Cameroon Mtn., 10 mi. NNE of Victoria port (linked by road), 420 mi. ESE of Lagos; alt. over 3,000 ft.; 4°10′N 9°14′E. Administrative and trade center; seat of commissioner of Br. Cameroons; cacao, bananas, palm oil and kernels; hardwood, rubber. R.C. bishopric. Former ⊙ German Cameroons, it is hq. of Cameroons prov. (□ 16,581; 1948 pop. estimate 481,000) which is administered as part of Eastern Provs. of Nigeria.

Buechel (bü′chŭl), village (1940 pop. 875), Jefferson co., NW Ky., 7 mi. ESE of downtown Louisville, within Louisville metropolitan dist.; makes burial vaults, bricks, monuments.

Buëch River (bwĕsh′), Hautes-Alpes dept., SE France, formed just above Serres by 2 headstreams, the Grand Buëch and the Petit Buëch (both rising in the Dévoluy); flows SSE, past Larague, to the Durance just above Sisteron; 50 mi. long. Lumber floating.

Buell (bū′ŭl), town (pop. 69), Montgomery co., E central Mo., near West Fork of Cuivre R., 5 mi. NE of Montgomery City.

Buena, river, Albania-Yugoslavia: see BOJANA RIVER.

Buena (bū′nŭ), town (pop. 2,640), Atlantic co., S N.J., 6 mi. ENE of Vineland. Inc. after 1940.

Buenache de Alarcón (bwānä′chā dhā älärkōn′), town (pop. 2,099), Cuenca prov., E central Spain, 28 mi. S of Cuenca; olives, grapes, saffron, cereals, potatoes, vegetables, stock.

Buena Esperanza (bwā′nä ĕspärän′sä), town (pop. estimate 1,000), SE San Luis prov., Argentina, on railroad and 75 mi. S of Mercedes; agr. center (grain, livestock).

Buena Esperanza, Gran Banco de, Cuba: see GRAN BANCO DE BUENA ESPERANZA.

Buenamesón, hydroelectric plant, Spain: see VILLAMANRIQUE DE TAJO.

Buena Park (bwā′nŭ), village (pop. 5,483), Orange co., S Calif., just W of Fullerton. Oil fields, citrus-fruit groves, truck farms near by.

Buena River, Albania-Yugoslavia: see BOJANA RIVER.

Buenaventura (bwānävĕntōō′rä), city (pop. 14,515), Valle del Cauca dept., W Colombia, Pacific port on Chocó Bay, on small Cascajal Isl. (originally a swamp), 50 mi. NW of Cali (joined by rail and highway); 3°54′N 77°5′W. Colombia's main Pacific port, outlet for interior highlands, for fertile Cauca valley, and for Chocó mining region. Processing and trading center in mining (silver, gold, platinum) and agr. region (coffee, sugar cane, tobacco, cotton, bananas, cacao, rice, livestock). Main exports: gold, platinum, coffee, sugar, hides. Tanning, alcohol distilling. Has modern harbor installations, customhouse, airport. Founded 1540, it was destroyed by Indians late in 16th cent. Developed with opening of Panama Canal and completion (1914) of railroad to Cali. Climate is rainy and unhealthy.

Buenaventura, town (pop. 2,122), Chihuahua, N Mexico, in Sierra Madre Occidental, on Santa María R. and 120 mi. NW of Chihuahua; alt. 5,165 ft.; agr. center (cotton, corn, wheat, beans, tobacco, cattle). Formerly San Buenaventura.

Buenaventura, town (pop. 967), Toledo prov., central Spain, 15 mi. N of Talavera de la Reina; cereals, timber, livestock.

Buena Vista (bwā′nä vē′stä). **1** Village, Chuquisaca dept., Bolivia: see ÑANCORAINZA. **2** Town (pop. c.3,200), ⊙ Ichilo prov., Santa Cruz dept., central Bolivia, 40 mi. NW of Santa Cruz; sugar cane, rice, cacao.

Buenavista (bwānävē′stä), village (pop. 1,756), Tenerife, Canary Isls., on elevated plain 37 mi. WSW of Santa Cruz de Tenerife; bananas, oranges, apples, tomatoes, potatoes, wheat, grapes; cheese processing. Medicinal waters.

Buena Vista, village (pop. 279), Coahuila, N Mexico, 5 mi. SSW of Saltillo. A Mexican War battle (Feb. 22–23, 1847) bet. U.S. forces under Zachary Taylor and Mexicans under Santa Anna took place near by; after fierce fighting, Santa Anna withdrew.

Buena Vista, village, Carazo dept., SW Nicaragua, 5 mi. WSW of Diriamba, in coffee zone.

Buena Vista, town (dist. pop. 1,500), Caazapá dept., S Paraguay, 45 mi. SE of Villarrica; maté, fruit, livestock; lumbering.

Buena Vista (bū″nŭ vī′stŭ), county (□ 573; pop. 21,113), NW Iowa; ⊙ Storm Lake. Prairie agr. area (hogs, cattle, poultry, corn, oats, soybeans) drained by Little Sioux R. and by headstreams of Raccoon, Boyer, and Maple rivers; includes reclaimed swampland and has system of drainage ditches. Sand and gravel pits. Contains Storm Lake and Wanata state parks. Formed 1851.

Buena Vista. 1 Town (pop. 783), ⊙ Chaffee co., central Colo., on Arkansas R., in foothills of Sawatch Mts., and 22 mi. NNW of Salida; alt. 7,800 ft. Resort; trade and shipping point in agr. and silver-mining region; lettuce, potatoes, grain, livestock. State reformatory near by; Mt. Yale 9 mi. W. **2** City (pop. 1,428), ⊙ Marion co., W Ga., 29 mi. ESE of Columbus, in farm and timber area; box mfg. Settled 1830. **3** City (pop. 5,214), in but independent of Rockbridge co., W Va., in the Blue Ridge, on North R. and 25 mi. NNW of Lynchburg, on edge of George Washington Natl. Forest; mfg. of paper, silk textiles, bricks, leather goods. Jr. col. Natural Bridge is 12 mi. SW. Founded 1889; inc. 1891.

Buena Vista (bwā′nä vē′stä), village, Cerro Largo dept., NE Uruguay, on W slopes of the Cuchilla Grande Principal, on Melo-Aceguá highway, and 15 mi. N of Melo; grain, cattle, sheep.

Buena Vista, town (pop. 895), Falcón state, NW Venezuela, on Paraguaná Peninsula, 5 mi. S of Pueblo Nuevo; goat grazing.

Buena Vista Bay, shallow inlet of N coast of central Cuba, separated by keys from Old Bahama Channel, 10 mi. E of Caibarién; c.30 mi. E–W, 6 mi. wide.

Buenavista de Cuéllar (bwānävē′stä dā kwĕ′yär), town (pop. 2,358), Guerrero, SW Mexico, on railroad and 12 mi. NE of Iguala; alt. 3,596 ft.; cereals, sugar, fruit, forest products (resin, vanilla, rubber).

Buena Vista Lake, Calif.: see KERN RIVER.

Buenavista Tomatlán, Mexico: see TOMATLÁN, Michoacán.

Buen Ayre, Du. West Indies: see BONAIRE.

Buendía (bwāndē′ä), town (pop. 1,607), Cuenca prov., central Spain, in Tagus basin, 50 mi. E of Madrid; cereals, olives, cherries, sheep, goats. Olive-oil pressing, flour milling. Hydroelectric project. Ruins of Recópolis (founded in 6th cent. by Leovigild) are 4 mi. W at confluence of Guadiela and Tagus rivers.

Buenë River, Albania-Yugoslavia: see BOJANA RIVER.

Bueno, Río (rē'ō bwā'nō), river in S central Chile, rises in L. Ranco, flows c.75 mi. W along Valdivia-Osorno prov. border, past Río Bueno, to the Pacific 40 mi. SW of Valdivia. Navigable for c.40 mi.

Buenópolis (bwĭnô'pōōlēs), city (pop. 1,597), central Minas Gerais, Brazil, on railroad and 50 mi. NW of Diamantina. Rock-crystal and kaolin deposits near by.

Buenos Aires (bwā'nŭs ī'rēz, â'rēz, Sp. bwā'nōs ī'rēs), province (□ 116,322; pop. 4,272,337), E Argentina, on the Atlantic; ⊙ La Plata (since 1882). Located in the humid Pampa bet. Paraná R. and the Río de la Plata (N) and the Río Negro (S), it is drained by the Río Salado, and Quequén Grande, and Sauce Grande rivers and includes Sierra del Tandil and Sierra de la Ventana. Precipitation varies from 40 inches annually (NE) to 20 inches (SW). Major agr. and livestock region of Argentina, the prov. produces 50% of country's wheat (S and W), corn (40%) and flax (30%) in N and W; oats, rye, barley (W), sunflowers and potatoes (E). Cattle (50% of Argentine herds) are raised on alfalfa in E and NE, sheep (30%) in S, hogs on corn (NW). Fruits and vegetables are grown in NE coastal strip bet. La Plata and N of Buenos Aires. Fisheries along coast (centered at Mar del Plata). Quarrying (dolomite, limestone, quartzite, building stone) in the sierras. Rural industries: flour milling, meat packing, dairying, tanning. Mfg. concentrated in main centers and ports: Greater Buenos Aires, Zárate, La Plata, Mar del Plata, Bahía Blanca. Main resorts are Mar del Plata, Miramar, Necochea (on coast), and Carhué (on L. Epecuén). Dense rail network includes 35% of Argentine railroads. Prov. is divided into 110 dists. [Sp. *partidos*], not including federal dist. of Buenos Aires city (former prov. ⊙), separated from the prov. in 1880.

Buenos Aires, largest city (□ 77; pop. 2,982,680) of Latin America, a federal district and ⊙ Argentina, on right bank of the Río de la Plata (here 30 mi. wide), 150 mi. from the Atlantic; 34°40'S 58°30'W. Principal port and commercial, industrial, financial, and social center of Argentina, on E edge of the Pampa, whose rich agr. products are exported through the extensive port facilities principally along the Río de la Plata and also along the small Riachuelo R. (the lower course of the Matanzas, which bounds the city on S). Buenos Aires is also the outlet for the vast inland river system of Río de la Plata-Paraná-Paraguay-Uruguay, linking it with Uruguay, Paraguay, and Brazil. It is served by large airports at near-by Morón, General Pacheco, and Ezeiza. Main exports: beef, mutton, dairy products, hides, wheat, corn, oats, barley, flax (fibers and linseed oil), quebracho. Chief imports: coal, oil, timber, iron, and manufactured goods. Industries include food-processing plants (frozen meat; canned fish, meat, fruit, and vegetables; dairy products; liquor and beer), metalworks (aluminum, lead, copper), automobile factory, oil refineries, alcohol distilleries, paper mills, paint factories, sugar refineries, textile mills (cotton, wool, rayon), chemical works, tobacco factories, printing plants (newspapers, magazines, books). A city of great wealth, Buenos Aires is modern and well built, with spacious parks, attractive bldgs., and some fine streets, such as: Avenida de Mayo (the principal artery, with rows of trees), which begins at Plaza de Mayo (President's Palace, the Casa Rosada; the historic Cabildo; cathedral with archbishop's residence; govt. offices), leads to the classic bldgs. of the Natl. Congress, and continues, as the Calle Rivadavia, for miles into Buenos Aires prov.; Calle Corrientes (with banks, shipping offices, foreign trade firms; the upper part is the Argentine Broadway); Calle Florida (fashionable shopping dist.). Other notable places are the numerous educational and cultural institutions, including Univ. of Buenos Aires, Natl. Library, the Colón Theater, Natl. Gall., Natural History Mus. and other museums, and, besides the cathedral (completed 1804 on site of 1st church; has San Martín's tomb), the churches of San Ignacio de Loyola (1722) and La Merced (reconstructed 1732). A modern subway system augments the city's transportation lines. Buenos Aires was 1st founded 1536 by Pedro de Mendoza, but was abandoned 1541 because of Indian attacks, the colonists moving to Asunción. In 1580 Juan de Garay refounded the settlement, but it did not become important until after 1617, when it became seat of a provincial govt. During 17th cent. it ceased to be endangered by Indians, but was frequently raided by the French, Portuguese, and Danes. In 1776 it was selected as capital of the viceroyalty of the Río de la Plata and shortly afterward was made an open port. A Br. expeditionary force under Gen. Beresford took the town in 1806 but was quickly ousted by Liniers; a 2d assault in 1807 was repulsed. These invasions strengthened the self-confidence of the Argentinian patriots and made Buenos Aires a stronghold in the War of Independence. On May 25, 1810, a junta was formed which deposed the Sp. viceroy. The most important Argentine revolutionary leaders were Belgrano, Moreno, Pueyrredón, and San Martín. A long period of internal conflict (bet. federalist and unitarian forces, the latter demanding a dominant position for Buenos Aires) followed, until a constitutional govt. was adopted in 1853; because of political jealousies the capital was moved to Paraná. The dictator Juan Manuel Rosas and generals Urquiza, Mitre, and Sarmiento played an outstanding part. Finally, in 1880, a compromise was reached. The city was detached from Buenos Aires prov. and set up as a separate federal dist. Since then its ascent has been rapid; it has attracted immigrants and foreign capital on a large scale, and become dominant in its country's economy, politics, and culture. Within the limits of the federal dist. are the sections Palermo, Belgrano, Nuñez, Saavedra, Liniers, Nueva Chicago, Flores, La Boca. Around the federal dist., in Buenos Aires prov., cluster a number of towns which form, with Buenos Aires proper, **Greater Buenos Aires** (□ 660; pop. 4,644,499). These include: TIGRE, SAN FERNANDO, SAN ISIDRO, VICENTE LÓPEZ, SAN MARTÍN, MORÓN, SAN JUSTO, LOMAS DE ZAMORA, LANÚS, ADROGUÉ, AVELLANEDA, QUILMES.

Buenos Aires, town (dist. pop. 2,993), Puntarenas prov., S Costa Rica, 70 mi. SE of San José. Trading center for lower General R. valley; rice, corn, tobacco; poultry and stock raising.

Buenos Aires, town (1950 pop. 779), Rivas dept., SW Nicaragua, 2½ mi. N of Rivas; cacao, plantains; livestock.

Buenos Aires. 1 Village (pop. 389), Libertad dept., NW Peru, on the Pacific, 3 mi. WSW of Trujillo; beach resort. **2** Town (pop. 1,130), Piura dept., NW Peru, in irrigated Piura R. valley, 18 mi. SE of Chulucanas; rice, cattle.

Buenos Aires, Lake, large fresh-water lake (□ 865; alt. 705 ft.) in Patagonian Andes of Chile (Aysén prov.) and Argentina (Comodoro Rivadavia military zone) at 46°30'S; c.80 mi. long, up to 13 mi. wide. It is cut N-S by international line. Surrounded by forests and mts. Outlet: Baker R., rising in the SW arm of the lake, called L. Bertrand. On S shore are villages of Los Antiguos (Argentina) and Chile Chico (Chile).

Buen Suceso, Cape (bwān' sōōsā'sō), at SE tip of Tierra del Fuego natl. territory, Argentina, on Le Maire Strait opposite Staten Isl.; 54°48'S 65°13'W.

Buer (bōō'ŭr), suburb (1925 pop. 99,058) of Gelsenkirchen, W Germany, N of Lippe Lateral Canal, 5 mi. NNW of city center; mfg. of nitrogen compounds. Coal mining. Inc. 1928 into Gelsenkirchen.

Buersill (bûr'sĭl), town, SE Lancashire, England, in Rochdale borough; cotton milling.

Buesaco (bwāsä'kō), town (pop. 1,776), Nariño dept., SW Colombia, on Pasto-Popayán highway, in the Andes, and 15 mi. NE of Pasto; wheat, corn, potatoes, coffee, cacao, sugar cane, fruit, stock.

Buet, Le (lü bwā'), Alpine resort, Haute-Savoie dept., SE France, 7 mi. NNE of Chamonix. Mont Buet (10,200 ft.) is 3 mi. W.

Bueu (bwā'ōō), town (pop. 1,026), Pontevedra prov., NW Spain, fishing port on Pontevedra Bay, 10 mi. SW of Pontevedra; fish processing, boatbuilding. Sea-bathing resort.

Buey, Páramo del (pä'rämō dĕl bwā'), Andean massif (13,780 ft.), SW Colombia, in Cordillera Central, 32 mi. S of Popayán.

Buffalo. 1 County (□ 952; pop. 25,134), S central Nebr.; ⊙ Kearney. Agr. area drained by S.Loup and Wood rivers; bounded S by Platte R. Livestock, grain, potatoes. Formed 1870. **2** County (□ 494; pop. 1,615), central S.Dak.; ⊙ Gannvalley. Agr. area with Crow Creek Indian Reservation in W; bounded W by Missouri R. Diversified farming; wheat. Formed 1864. **3** County (□ 712; pop. 14,719), W Wis.; ⊙ Alma. Bounded NW by Chippewa R., W and SW by the Mississippi, SE by Trempealeau R.; drained by Buffalo R. Hilly dairy and livestock area; also produces poultry, clover, corn, oats; timber. Includes Merrick State Park. Formed 1853.

Buffalo. 1 Village (pop. 416), Sangamon co., central Ill., 12 mi. ENE of Springfield, in agr. and bituminous-coal-mining area. **2** Town (pop. 695), Scott co., E Iowa, on the Mississippi and 8 mi. WSW of Davenport; concrete blocks, clay products, pearl buttons. **3** City (pop. 437), Wilson co., SE Kansas, 12 mi. WNW of Chanute; livestock, poultry, grain; dairying. **4** Town (pop. 495), Larue co., central Ky., 16 mi. SE of Elizabethtown, in agr. area. **5** Resort village (pop. 1,914), ⊙ Wright co., E Minn., on small lake and 34 mi. WNW of Minneapolis, in livestock, grain, and poultry area; dairy and wood products. Settled c.1855, inc. 1887. **6** City (pop. 1,213), ⊙ Dallas co., SW central Mo., in the Ozarks, near Niangua R., 32 mi. NNE of Springfield; flour mill; poultry, dairying. Settled 1839, inc. 1854. **7** City (pop. 580,132), ⊙ Erie co., W N.Y., at E end of L. Erie at its Niagara R. outlet (here the U.S.-Canada border), 65 mi. WSW of Rochester; 42°43'N 78°52'W. State's 2d-largest city, a major Great Lakes port (also handling much Barge Canal shipping), railroad hub, and port of entry. A major U.S. industrial center, with huge plants producing steel, pig iron, flour, rubber, linseed oil, gypsum products; also makes airplanes, automobiles, plastics, electrical equipment, abrasives, lumber, furniture, machinery, lenses, wallboard, textiles; meat packing, oil refining, printing and publishing. Stone and gypsum quarries. Railroad shops (at adjacent East Buffalo). Here are Univ. of Buffalo, a state teachers col., Canisius Col., D'Youville Col., a Catholic teachers col., and a state institute of applied arts and sciences; Grosvenor Library, with extensive reference collection; Delaware Park, with Albright Art Gall., historical mus., and zoological gardens; Humboldt Park, with science mus. Other points of interest: Peace Bridge (1927) to Fort Erie, Ont.; City Hall (1932); the Prudential Bldg. designed by Louis Sullivan (1894), and the Larkin office bldg. designed by Frank Lloyd Wright. A state hosp. for mental diseases and a state institution for the study of malignant diseases are here. Laid out in 1803 by Joseph Ellicott, for the Holland Land Company; fired by the British in War of 1812. Inc. as village in 1816; and as city in 1832, after commercial and industrial expansion following completion of Erie Canal (1825). Became rail center in Civil War; harnessing of Niagara Falls at end of 19th cent. further stimulated growth of industry. In 1881, Grover Cleveland became mayor of Buffalo. In 1901, President McKinley was assassinated while attending the Pan-American Exposition here; and here Theodore Roosevelt took the presidential oath. Millard Fillmore lived in city. **8** Village (pop. 261), Cass co., E N.Dak., 36 mi. W of Fargo. **9** Town (pop. 1,544), ⊙ Harper co., NW Okla., 30 mi. NNW of Woodward in grain-growing, dairying, and stock-raising area; poultry, dairy products, packed meat. Gas wells. Founded 1907, inc. 1908. **10** Mill village (pop. 1,580), Union co., N S.C., 3 mi. W of Union; cotton textiles. **11** Town (pop. 380), ⊙ Harding co., NW S.Dak., 105 mi. N of Rapid City; trade center for sheep and cattle region. **12** Town (pop. 970), Leon co., E central Texas, 65 mi. E of Waco; trade point in cotton, truck, timber, natural-gas area. **13** Village (pop. 333), Putnam co., W W.Va., near the Kanawha, 25 mi. NW of Charleston. **14** City (pop. 319), Buffalo co., W Wis., on the Mississippi and 43 mi. NW of La Crosse. **15** City (pop. 2,674), ⊙ Johnson co., N Wyo., on Clear Creek and 37 mi. SSE of Sheridan, just E of Bighorn Mts. and Bighorn Natl. Forest; alt. 4,645 ft. Resort; shipping point in sheep and cattle region; sawmill; dairy products, sugar beets, grain. Soldiers' and sailors' home near by, at former Fort McKinney. L. De Smet 7 mi. N. Founded c.1880, inc. 1884.

Buffalo, Mount (5,645 ft.), E central Victoria, Australia, in Australian Alps, 120 mi. NE of Melbourne, near Bright; skiing (May-Sept.). Sometimes called the Horn.

Buffalo Bayou (bī'ō), S Texas, rises in creeks W of Houston, flows c.45 mi. E, through Houston, to San Jacinto R. near its mouth. Turning basin in bayou is port of Houston; deep-water HOUSTON SHIP CHANNEL to Gulf of Mexico follows bayou's lower course.

Buffalo Bill Dam, Wyo.: see SHOSHONE RIVER.

Buffalo Center, town (pop. 1,087), Winnebago co., N Iowa, c.40 mi. WNW of Mason City, in agr. area.

Buffalo Creek. 1 In E Iowa, rises E of Oelwein, flows c.50 mi. SE to Wapsipinicon R. at Anamosa. **2** In S central Minn., rises in marshy area of Renville co., flows 70 mi. generally E, past Glencoe, to South Fork Crow R. near New Germany.

Buffalo Gap. 1 Town (pop. 186), Custer co., SW S.Dak., 24 mi. SE of Custer and on branch of Cheyenne R.; trade center for ranching region. **2** Village, Texas: see ABILENE.

Buffalo Lake (□ 55), S central Alta., 35 mi. ENE of Red Deer. Drains S into Red Deer R.

Buffalo Lake, village (pop. 724), Renville co., S Minn., 18 mi. E of Olivia, in agr. area; dairy products.

Buffalo Lake. 1 In Texas: see TIERRA BLANCA CREEK. **2** In Marquette co., S central Wis., 11 mi. N of Portage; an expansion of Fox R., c.16 mi. long. Montello is at E end.

Buffalo Lithia Springs, Va.: see BUFFALO SPRINGS.

Buffalo Mineral Springs, Va.: see BUFFALO SPRINGS.

Buffalo National Park, former park (□ 197.5), E Alta., near Wainwright. Set aside (1908) for the Dominion govt. buffalo herd of over 5,000 head. In Second World War herd was transferred to Elk Island Natl. Park, and area was used by Dept. of Natl. Defense. In 1947 the park was abolished.

Buffalo Peak, Colo.: see TARRYALL MOUNTAINS.

Buffalo Peaks (13,541 ft.), in Rocky Mts., on Chaffee and Park border, central Colo.

Buffalo River. 1 In SE Cape Prov., U. of So. Afr., rises N of Kingwilliamstown, flows S to Kingwilliamstown, thence in winding course ESE, past Woodbrook, to the Indian Ocean at East London; 70 mi. long. **2** In N Natal, U. of So. Afr., rises in Transvaal, in Drakensberg range, just N of Volksrust, flows c.200 mi. generally SE, past Volksrust and Rorkesdrift, to Tugela R. 25 mi. N of Greytown. Lower course forms SW border of Zululand.

Buffalo River. 1 In N Ark., rises in Newton co., flows c.150 mi. ENE, through the Ozarks, past Gilbert, to White R. 14 mi. SE of Yellville. Flood-control dam near mouth. State park (recreational area) is along river in S Marion co. **2** In W Minn., rises in Becker co., flows 80 mi. generally W, past Hawley and Glyndon, to Red River of the North near Georgetown. **3** In W central Tenn., rises in N Lawrence co., flows W and N past Linden, to Duck R. 7 mi. SSW of Waverly; c.72 mi. long. **4** In W Wis., rises in Jackson co., flows W, past Osseo and Mondovi (hydroelectric plant), then turns SW, reaching the Mississippi near Alma; c.55 mi. long.

Buffalo Springs, health resort, Mecklenburg co., S Va., near junction of Dan and Roanoke rivers, 40 mi. E of Danville; mineral springs. Also called Buffalo Lithia Springs and Buffalo Mineral Springs.

Buff Bay, town (pop. 1,252), Portland parish, NE Jamaica, on coast, on railroad and 15 mi. WNW of Port Antonio; bananas, coconuts, cacao.

Buffington, village (pop. 2,131, with adjacent New Salem), Fayette co., SW Pa., 6 mi. W of Uniontown.

Buford (bū'fůrd), city (pop. 3,812), Gwinnett co., N central Ga., 33 mi. NE of Atlanta, in agr. area; mfg. of harnesses, saddles, shoes; lumber milling, tanning.

Buftea (bŏŏf'tyä), village (pop. 1,526), Bucharest prov., S Rumania, on railroad and 12 mi. NW of Bucharest; cotton growing; fruit and vegetable processing; mfg. of medical supplies. Motion-picture studios.

Bug, rivers, Ukrainian SSR and Poland: see BUG RIVER (Southern Bug, Western Bug).

Buga (bōō'gä), city (pop. 19,595), Valle del Cauca dept., W Colombia, in Cauca valley, on railroad and highway, in E foothills of the Cordillera Central, 35 mi. NNE of Cali. Trading and processing center in fertile agr. region (tobacco, sugar cane, coffee, cacao, cotton, rice, cattle). Old colonial city (founded 1650), with fine parks, a cathedral, and the shrine El Cristo Milagroso de Buga. Coal deposits near by.

Bugaba (bōōgä'bä), village (pop. 427), Chiriquí prov., W Panama, in Pacific lowland, 2 mi. S of Concepción; bananas, coffee, cacao; stock raising.

Bugac Steppe (bŏŏ'găts), section of the Alföld, S central Hungary, S of Kecskemet, bet. the Danube and the Tisza. One of the remaining *puszta* sections of the Hungarian plain, its saline soil is used mainly for cattle grazing.

Bugalagrande (bōōgälägrän'dā), town (pop. 1,768), Valle del Cauca dept., W Colombia, in Cauca valley, 10 mi. NE of Tuluá; coffee, cacao, tobacco, livestock; dairying. Silver, gold, and platinum mines near by.

Buganda (bōōgän'dä), kingdom and province (□ 25,631, including 8,320 sq. mi. of lakes; pop. 1,317,705), S Uganda; ⊙ Kampala. Bounded S by Tanganyika, it encompasses NW ¼ of L. Victoria, including the Sese Isls. Mainly elephant grasslands, with dense forests along rivers. Cotton is chief crop, cultivated exclusively by natives (called the Baganda). Coffee, sugar cane, bananas, corn, millet also grown. Livestock raising, lake fishing. Main towns are Entebbe (⊙ Uganda), Kampala (Uganda's chief commercial center), and Masaka. Mengo (suburb of Kampala) is seat of native administration headed by the Kabaka (king). John Speke 1st met the comparatively civilized Baganda in 1862. Br. protectorate over kingdom established 1894; native self-govt. under Uganda protectorate dates from 1900.

Bugarra (bōōgä'rä), village (pop. 1,226), Valencia prov., E Spain, on Turia R. and 22 mi. WNW of Valencia; soap mfg., olive-oil processing; wine, vegetables, lumber, livestock. Gypsum quarries.

Bugarura, Ruanda-Urundi: see LUGARAMA.

Bugasong (bōōgäsōng'), town (1939 pop. 2,681; 1948 municipality pop. 15,642), Antique prov., W Panay isl., Philippines, near Cuyo East Pass, 41 mi. NW of Iloilo; rice- and hemp-growing center.

Bugayevka (bōōgī'ůfků), town (1939 pop. over 500), SW Voroshilovgrad oblast, Ukrainian SSR, in the Donbas, 3 mi. SSE of Voroshilovsk; limestone quarries.

Bugaz (bōōgäs'), Rum. *Băile-Bugaz* (bů'ēlĕ-bōōgäz'), village, E Izmail oblast, Ukrainian SSR, on Black Sea, at mouth of Dniester Liman, 10 mi. SSE of Belgorod-Dnestrovski; rail terminus; seaside resort.

Bugbrooke, town and parish (pop. 826), S central Northampton, England, 6 mi. WSW of Northampton; shoe industry. Has 14th-cent. church.

Bugeac, Moldavian SSR: see BUDZHAK.

Bugeat (büzhä'), village (pop. 835), Corrèze dept., S central France, in Monts du Limousin, near the Vézère, 19 mi. WNW of Ussel.

Bugeaud (büzhō'), village (pop. 465), Constantine dept., NE Algeria, in coastal Edough range, 5 mi. W of Bône; alt. 2,950 ft. Summer resort amidst cork-oak forests.

Búger (bōō'här), town (pop. 1,080), Majorca, Balearic Isls., 22 mi. NE of Palma; cereals, grapes, almonds, figs, carobs, apricots, tobacco, hogs; mfg. of bells and wooden spoons.

Bugey (büzhā'), small region of E France, in the S Jura, bet Ain R. (W) and Rhone R. (S and W); ceded to France by Savoy in 1601, it is now in Ain dept.; ⊙ was Belley. Cattle raising, lumbering; artisan industries in valleys.

Buggenhout (bû'gůnhout), town (pop. 9,118), East Flanders prov., N Belgium, on Scheldt R. and 4 mi. E of Dendermonde; agr. market.

Buggerru (bōōd-jĕr'rōō), village (pop. 2,272), Cagliari prov., SW Sardinia, port on Mediterranean Sea and 9 mi. NW of Iglesias. Lead-zinc mine of Malfidano just S.

Buggingen (bŏŏ'gĭng-ůn), village (pop. 1,244), S Baden, Germany, 14 mi. SW of Freiburg; large potash mines.

Buggs Island Dam, N.C. and Va.: see ROANOKE RIVER.

Bughea (bōō'gyä), health resort and monastery, Arges prov., S central Rumania, just NW of Campulung.

Bugio, Madeira: see DESERTAS.

Buglas Island, Philippines: see NEGROS.

Buglawton (bŭglô'tůn), former urban district (1931 pop. 1,651), E Cheshire, England, just NE of Congleton; cotton spinning and weaving. Inc. 1936 in Congleton.

Bug Liman (bŏŏk' lyĭmän"), estuary of Southern Bug R., S Ukrainian SSR; 15 mi. long, 3 mi. wide; opens S into Dnieper Liman of Black Sea.

Bugojno, Bugoino, or **Bugoyno** (all: bōō'goinô), town (pop. 2,523), S central Bosnia, Yugoslavia, on Vrbas R., on railroad and 50 mi. WNW of Sarajevo; cattle and grain trade.

Bugondo (bōōgōn'dō), town, Eastern Prov., Uganda, port on L. Kyoga, 24 mi. WSW of Soroti; cotton, peanuts, sesame; livestock.

Bugrasi, India: see BAGRASI.

Bug River (bōōg, bŭg, Rus. bŏŏk). **1** or **Southern Bug River,** Rus. *Yuzhnyy Bug* (yŏŏzh'nē bŏŏk'), anc. *Hypanis,* in S Ukrainian SSR, rises NW of Proskurov in Volyn-Podolian Upland, flows 532 mi. SE, past Proskurov, Vinnitsa, Pervomaisk, and Voznesensk, to the BUG LIMAN below Nikolayev. Navigable March–Dec. for 65 mi. below Voznesensk, chiefly for grain. **2** or **Western Bug River,** Rus. *Zapadnyy Bug* (zä'půdnē bŏŏk'), in W Ukrainian SSR and NE Poland, rises 9 mi. ENE of Zoluchev, flows NNW past Busk, Kamenka-Bugskaya, and Sokal, N past Wlodawa and Brest, and generally W past Brok and Wyszkow to Narew R. opposite Serock; length, c.500 mi. Navigable below Brest, where its right tributary, Mukhanets R., joins it with Dnieper-Bug Canal. Since 1945, forms Poland–USSR border, originally established after First World War as the Curzon Line, for 200 mi. Main tributaries, Krzna and Liwiec (left), Mukhanets and Nurzec (right) rivers.

Bugsuk Island (bōōgsōōk') (□ 47; 1939 pop. 347), Palawan prov., Philippines, 5 mi. E of S tip of Palawan; heavily wooded. Coconuts.

Bugten, Norway: see BUKTA.

Bugue, Le (lů büg'), village (pop. 1,429), Dordogne dept., SW France, on the Vézère near its mouth into the Dordogne, and 14 mi. W of Sarlat; meat processing, mfg. (sabots, felt hats).

Bugui Point (bōō'gē), northernmost point of Masbate isl., Philippines, in Sibuyan Sea; 12°36'N 123°14'E.

Bugulma or **Bugul'ma** (bōōgōōlmä'), city (1939 pop. estimate 24,900), SE Tatar Autonomous SSR, Russian SFSR, on railroad and 165 mi. SE of Kazan; agr.-processing (grain, meat) and -trading (hides, wool) center; metal- and glassworking; handicraft industries (carriages, cloth, felt boots). Agr. experimental station. Chartered 1781.

Buguma (bōōgōō'mä), town, Owerri prov., Eastern Provinces, S Nigeria, on New Calabar R. in Niger R. delta, 10 mi. W of Port Harcourt; native market; palm oil and kernels, hardwood, rubber. Its trade has been absorbed by Port Harcourt.

Bugungu (bōōgōōng'gōō), town, Buganda prov., SE Uganda, port on L. Victoria, at efflux of the Victoria Nile, opposite Jinja (ferry service); cotton, coffee, sugar cane; cattle, sheep, goats; fishing.

Bugur or **Bugur Bazar** (bōōgōōr' bäzär'), Chinese *Luntai* or *Lun-t'ai* (lŏŏn'tī'), town and oasis (pop. 32,426), central Sinkiang prov., China, 95 mi. W of Kurla, and on highway S of the Tien Shan; sericulture; agr. products; cattle, sheep.

Buguruslan (bōōgōōrōōslän'), city (1926 pop. 17,646), NW Chkalov oblast, Russian SFSR, on Greater Kinel R., on railroad and 100 mi. NW of Kuibyshev; flour-milling, grain-trading center; petroleum extracting and refining (pipe line to Kuibyshev), food processing (butter, starch), brick mfg. Has teachers col., theater. Founded 1748; chartered 1781. Oil industry grew after Second World War.

Bugyi (bŏŏ'dyē), town (pop. 4,326), Pest-Pilis-Solt-Kiskun co., central Hungary, 19 mi. S of Budapest; distilleries; grain, potatoes; cattle, horses, hogs.

Buha, El, or **Al-Buha** (ĕl bōō'hä), village (pop. 5,651), Daqahliya prov., Lower Egypt, 5 mi. NE of Mit Ghamr; cotton, cereals.

Buhayrah, Al-, Egypt: see BEHEIRA.

Buhen, ruins, Anglo-Egyptian Sudan: see WADI HALFA.

Buhera (bōōhĕ'rä), village, Gwelo prov., E central Southern Rhodesia, in Mashonaland, 40 mi. SE of Enkeldoorn; tobacco, wheat, dairy products; livestock raising. Buhera dist. is a native reserve.

Buhi (bōō'hē, bōō'ē), town (1939 pop. 5,642; 1948 municipality pop. 25,057), Camarines Sur prov., SE Luzon, Philippines, on L. Buhi, 25 mi. NW of Legaspi; fishing and agr. center (rice, corn).

Buhi, Lake (□ 4), Camarines Sur prov., SE Luzon, Philippines, 29 mi. NW of Legaspi; 3 mi. long.

Buhl, Ger. *Bühl* (both: bül), town (pop. 2,403), Haut-Rhin dept., E France, in winegrowing valley of SE Vosges Mts., 2 mi. NW of Guebwiller; cotton milling, tie mfg.

Bühl (bül), town (pop. 7,027), S Baden, Germany, at W foot of Black Forest, 11 mi. SSW of Rastatt; rail junction; noted for its kirsch and plums. Mfg. of agr. machinery, chemicals, clothing; printing, woodworking, lumber milling.

Buhl (būl). **1** City (pop. 2,870), Twin Falls co., S Idaho, near the Snake (bridged near by), 15 mi. W of Twin Falls; shipping center for irrigated agr. area (beans, potatoes, sugar beets); dairy products. Has U.S. fish hatchery. Founded 1906, inc. 1909. **2** Village (pop. 1,462), Saint Louis co., NE Minn., in Mesabi iron range, 9 mi. ENE of Hibbing, in mining and agr. area. Open-pit and underground iron mines in vicinity. Superior Natl. Forest near by.

Buhler (bū'lůr), city (pop. 750), Reno co., S central Kansas, on small affluent of Arkansas R. and 10 mi. NE of Hutchinson; wheat.

Bühlertal (bü'lůrtäl), village (pop. 5,989), S Baden, Germany, on W slope of Black Forest, 2 mi. ESE of Bühl; noted for its red wine and fruit. Metal- and woodworking, lumber milling. Tobacco. Summer resort.

Buhtan River (bōōtän'), SE Turkey, rises in Hakari Mts. 20 mi. NW of Hakari, flows 140 mi. W, past Satak, Perveri, and Siirt, to Tigris R. 16 mi. SW of Siirt. Upper portion called Norduz R., lower called Botan R.

Buhusi (bōōhōōsh'), Rum. *Buhuşi,* town (1948 pop. 8,198), Bacau prov., E Rumania, on Bistrita R., on railroad and 20 mi. SE of Piatra-Neamt; woolen-textile mfg. center; oil refining; distilling; mfg. of candles, cheese.

Buhut (bōōhōōt'), village (pop. 9,190), Gharbiya prov., Lower Egypt, 9 mi. NNW of Talkha; cotton.

Bui or **Buy** (bōō'ē), city (1939 pop. over 10,000), W Kostroma oblast, Russian SFSR, on Kostroma R (landing) and 55 mi. NNE of Kostroma; rail junction; metalworking, sawmilling; food products, chemicals. Regional mus. Chartered 1536.

Buie (bōō'yā), Slovenian *Buje* (bōō'yä), town (pop. 2,885), S Free Territory of Trieste, 17 mi. SSW of Trieste; agr. center; wine, olives, wheat, fruit. Has 17th-cent. cathedral. Placed 1947 under Yugoslav administration.

Buie (bū'ē) or **Buies** (bū'ēz), town (1940 pop. 118), Robeson co., S N.C., 11 mi. NW of Lumberton.

Buies Creek, town (pop. 435), Harnett co., central N.C., near Cape Fear R., 26 mi. NNE of Fayetteville. Seat of Campbell Col. (jr.; coeducational). Settled 1746.

Buiko (bwē'kō), village, Tanga prov., NE Tanganyika, on Pangani R., on railroad, and 20 mi. NW of Lushoto; hardwood.

Buildwas, agr. village and parish (pop. 246), central Shropshire, England, on Severn R. and 4 mi. S of Wellington; has ruins of Cistercian abbey founded 1135.

Builth Wells (bĭlth' wĕlz"), urban district (1931 pop. 1,663; 1951 census 1,708), N Brecknock, Wales, on Wye R. and 14 mi. N of Brecknock; resort (with mineral springs) and agr. market, with shoe mfg. Remains of small Norman castle; Norman church.

Buin (bwēn), town (pop. 3,580), ⊙ Maipo dept. (□ 334; pop. 35,153), Santiago prov., central Chile, on railroad, on Maipo R. and 20 mi. S of Santiago; agr. center (alfalfa, wheat, fruit, tobacco, stock).

Buin (bōōēn'), town on S coast of Bougainville isl., N Solomons, in Territory of New Guinea; local govt. station.

Buin, Piz, Switzerland: see PIZ BUIN.

Buinaksk or **Buynaksk** (bōōēnäksk'), city (1926 pop. 10,923), central Dagestan Autonomous SSR, Russian SFSR, on road, on railroad and 20 mi. SW of Makhachkala, in agr. area (fruit, vegetables, wheat); fruit-canning center; tanning, fruit trade. Petroleum near by. Founded at end of 14th cent. on site of Tamerlane camp; made Rus. fortress in 1830s. Original ⊙ Dagestan until its removal (1922) to Makhachkala. Called Temir-Khan-Shura until 1922, when it was renamed for a Dagestan revolutionary.

Buinen (boi'nůn), town (pop. 900), Drenthe prov., NE Netherlands, 12 mi. ESE of Assen, on the Hondsrug; potato-flour milling, glassworking.

Buinsk (bōōēnsk'). **1** Town (1938 pop. over 500), S central Chuvash Autonomous SSR, Russian SFSR, on railroad and 30 mi. NNE of Alatyr; sawmilling. **2** City (1926 pop. 4,728), SW Tatar Autonomous SSR, Russian SFSR, on railroad and 45 mi. N of Ulyanovsk; lumber-trading center; flour milling, sawmilling. Oil-shale deposits near by. Founded in 17th cent.; chartered 1780.

Buíque (bwē'kĭ), city (pop. 1,219), central Pernambuco, NE Brazil, 32 mi. SW of Pesqueira; corn, livestock. Nitrate deposits.

Buir Nor, Manchuria and Mongolia: see BOR NOR.

Buiskoye or **Buyskoye** (bōō'ēskůyů), village (1939 pop. over 500), S Kirov oblast, Russian SFSR, 11 mi. WSW of Urzhum; wheat.

Buis-les-Baronnies (bwē-lā-bärônē'), village (pop. 1,139), Drôme dept., SE France, on the Ouvèze and 9 mi. SE of Nyons, in the Baronnies; sericulture; olives, lavender.

Buissière, La, Belgium: see LABUISSIÈRE.

Buisson, Le (lü bwēsõ'), village (pop. 1,000), Dordogne dept., SW France, on the Dordogne and 15 mi. WSW of Sarlat; rail junction; distilling.

Buitenpost (boi'tůnpōst), village (pop. 1,515), Friesland prov., N Netherlands, on the Kolonelsdiep and 15 mi. ENE of Leeuwarden; truck gardening; medicinal herbs; peat production. Part of commune (pop. 18,054) of Achtkarspelen.

Buitenzorg, Indonesia: see BOGOR.

Buitrago del Lozoya (bwēträ'gō dhĕl lō-thoi'ä), town (pop. 602), Madrid prov., central Spain, on Lozoya R. (with reservoir) and 40 mi. N of Madrid; potatoes, rye, sheep. Silver mines near by.

Buitrón, El (ĕl bwētrōn'), village (pop. 266), Huelva prov., SW Spain, 28 mi. NNE of Huelva (linked by rail); copper and iron mining.

Buittle, Scotland: see DALBEATTIE.

Buizingen (boi'zĭng-ůn), town (pop. 3,586), Brabant prov., central Belgium, just NE of Hal; cable mfg. Formerly spelled Buysinghen.

Buj (bŏŏ'ĭ), town (pop. 3,490), Szabolcs co., NE Hungary, 11 mi. NNW of Nyiregyhaza; corn, wheat, hogs.

Bujak (bŏŏ'yäk), Hung. *Buják,* town (pop. 2,487), Nograd-Hont co., N Hungary, 17 mi. SE of Balassagyarmat; honey, vineyards, sheep.

Bujalance (bōōhälän'thä), city (pop. 14,392), Córdoba prov., S Spain, agr. trade center 24 mi. E of Córdoba; mfg. of woolen cloth, soap, mats, sirups; olive-oil processing, flour- and sawmilling. Has ruined Moorish castle with towers, built 935 by caliph of Córdoba. Torquemada b. here.

Bujama (bōōhä'mä), village (pop. 30), Lima dept., W central Peru, small fishing port on the Pacific, and 5 mi. S of Mala. Nitrate deposits near by.

Bujanovac or **Buyanovats** (bōō'yänôväts), village (pop. 3,930), S Serbia, Yugoslavia, on railroad and 9 mi. SW of Vranje.

Bujaraloz (bōōhärälōth'), town (pop. 1,194), Saragossa prov., NE Spain, 20 mi. NNW of Caspe, and on arid plain yielding some cereals and vegetables. Airport.

Bujaru (bōōzhärōō'), city (pop. 390), E Pará, Brazil, 25 mi. SE of Belém.

Bujavica (bōō'yävĭtsä), petroleum and natural-gas field, N Croatia, Yugoslavia, 6 mi. NE of Novska, in Slavonia. Supplies natural gas to compressor plant producing bottled gas for motor fuel. Petroleum wells used by Austrians in First World War.

Buje, Free Territory of Trieste: see BUIE.

Buji (bōōjē'), town (pop. 2,248), Plateau Prov., Northern Provinces, central Nigeria, on Bauchi Plateau, on railroad and 12 mi. NNW of Jos; tin-mining center; cassava, millet, durra.

Bujnurd or **Bojnurd** (both: bōjnōōrd'), town (1941 pop. 15,293), Ninth Prov., in Khurasan, NE Iran, on road and 150 mi. NW of Meshed, near USSR border, in Atrek R. valley; wool, rugs. Agr.: wheat, opium, walnuts. Airfield.

Bujor-Targ (bōōzhôr-tûrg'), Rum. *Bujor-Târg,* agr. village (pop. 849), Galati prov., E Rumania, on railroad and 30 mi. NNW of Galati.

Bük (bük), town (pop. 2,447), Sopron co., W Hungary, on Repce R. and 22 mi. SSE of Sopron; sugar refinery.

Buk (bŏŏk), town (1946 pop. 3,213), Poznan prov., W Poland, 18 mi. W of Poznan; flour milling, distilling, mfg. of roofing materials.

Buka (bōō'kä), volcanic island (□ 190; pop. c.7,800), Solomon Isls., SW Pacific, 5 mi. NW of Bougainville, across Buka Passage; 30 mi. long, 5 mi. wide. Queen Carola Harbor on W coast. Copra plantations. Discovered 1767 by the British; became 1884 German possession; occupied 1914 by Australian forces; included 1920 in Australian mandated Territory of NEW GUINEA; under U.N. trusteeship (1947) held by Australia. In Second World War, site of Jap. air base.

Bukachacha (bŏŏkŭchä'chŭ), town (1948 pop. over 2,000), central Chita oblast, Russian SFSR, on spur of Trans-Siberian RR and 155 mi. ENE of Chita; coal-mining center; cement, clay deposits. Developed in 1930s.

Bukachevtsy (bŏŏkŭchĕf'tsē), Pol. *Bukaczowce,* town (1931 pop. 2,346), N Stanislav oblast, Ukrainian SSR, on left tributary of the Dniester and 25 mi. NNW of Stanislav; flour milling, distilling; brickworks.

Bukakata (bōōkäkä'tä), town, Buganda prov., S Uganda, port on NW shore of L. Victoria, opposite Bugala Isl. (largest of Sese Isls.), 20 mi. ENE of Masaka; cotton, coffee, bananas, corn, millet; fishing.

Bukama (bōōkä'mä), town, Katanga prov., SE Belgian Congo, on Lualaba R., on railroad, and 100 mi. SE of Kamina; rail-steamer transshipment point and trading center.

Bukan (bōōkän'), village, Fourth Prov., in Azerbaijan, NW Iran, in the Kurd country, on road and 20 mi. N of Saqqiz; sheep raising; grain, fruit, sugar beets.

Bukavu, Belgian Congo: see COSTERMANSVILLE.

Bukei, Kazakh SSR: see URDA.

Bukene (bōōkĕ'nä), village, Western Prov., W central Tanganyika, on railroad and 55 mi. N of Tabora; cotton, peanuts, corn; cattle, sheep, goats.

Bukhara (bŏŏkä'rŏŏ, Rus. bōōkhŭrä'), oblast (□ 49,600; 1946 pop. estimate 600,000), central Uzbek SSR; ⊙ Bukhara. Includes lower Zeravshan R. valley (Bukhara oasis) and large section of the Kyzyl-Kum (N). In irrigated river valley are cotton, sericulture, orchards; in desert are karakul sheep. Cotton ginning, karakul processing. Trans-Caspian RR crosses S section, with line to Stalinabad branching off at Kagan. Pop. chiefly Uzbeks (in Bukhara oasis), Kara-Kalpaks and Kazakhs (N desert). Formed 1938. Tamdy-Bulak dist. (□ c.25,000) transferred (1943) from Kara-Kalpak Autonomous SSR.

Bukhara, city (1939 pop. 50,382), ⊙ Bukhara oblast, Uzbek SSR, on oasis around Zeravshan R., on spur of Trans-Caspian RR and 270 mi. SW of Tashkent; 39°45'N 64°25'E. Karakul processing (Bokhara fur), silk spinning, clothing mfg. Bokhara rugs are named for the city. Has mosques, palaces, and other buildings (9th–17th cent.) of noted architectural style (majolica ornamentation). Teachers col. In late 19th cent., building of Trans-Caspian RR by-passed Bukhara at request of its emir. Around the station (8 mi. SE) grew Rus. city of Novaya Bukhara [Rus.,=new Bukhara]; until Novaya Bukhara was renamed (c.1935) Kagan, the old city was officially called Staraya Bukhara [Rus.,=old Bukhara]. Situated in anc. region of *Transoxiana* or *Sogdiana,* Bukhara (formerly spelled Bokhara) became a center of Islamic culture under Arab rule (7th–9th cent.); flourished (10th cent.) under Persian Samanid dynasty; dominated in 12th cent. by Turks, rulers of Khiva, and by Mongols (to 15th cent.). Fell to the Uzbeks in early 16th cent.; became ⊙ Bukhara emirate, which was conquered (1868) by Russians and made Rus. protectorate. After Bolshevik revolution, the emirate became (1920) a Soviet People's Republic and was divided (1924) bet. Uzbek, Tadzhik, and Turkmen SSRs.

Bukharino, Ukrainian SSR: see DOLGINTSEVO.

Bukhedu, Manchuria: see POKOTU.

Bukhta [Rus.,=bay], for names beginning thus and not found here: see under following part of the name.

Bukhtarma River (bōōkhtŭrmä'), in East Kazakhstan oblast, Kazakh SSR, rises in Bukhtarma Glacier of Altai Mts., on China border; flows 264 mi. W, through fertile valley, to Irtysh R. at Ust-Bukhtarma. Important for irrigation; extensive lead-zinc deposits along banks (Zyryanovsk). Valley colonized by Russians in 18th cent.

Bukhtarminsk, Kazakh SSR: see UST-BUKHTARMA.

Buki (bōō'kē). **1** Town (1926 pop. 3,028), S Kiev oblast, Ukrainian SSR, 25 mi. NNE of Uman; sugar refining. **2** Village (1926 pop. 2,518), S Tashkent oblast, Uzbek SSR, 32 mi. S of Tashkent; cotton. Formerly called Buka.

Bukidnon (bōōkĭd'nōn, Sp. bōōkēdh'nōn), province (□ 3,103; 1948 pop. 63,470), N central Mindanao, Philippines; ⊙ Malaybalay. Large pineapple plantations. Also abacá, corn, rice. Mts. in center rise to 7,804 ft.

Bukit (bōō'kĭt) [Malay,=hill]. For Malayan names beginning thus and not found here, see under following part of the name.

Bukit Besi, Kelantan, Malaya: see TEMANGAN.

Bukit Besi, Trengganu, Malaya: see KUALA DUNGUN.

Bukit Gambir (gämbĕr'), village (pop. 1,426), NW Johore, Malaya, near Muar R., 15 mi. NE of Bandar Maharani; rubber plantations.

Bukit Merah (mŭrä'), village (pop. 454), NW Perak, Malaya, on railroad and 14 mi. NNW of Taiping; site of Kurau R. irrigation headworks feeding Krian rice dist.

Bukit Mertajam (mŭrtä'jäm), town (pop. 12,345), Prov. Wellesley, Penang, NW Malaya, at W foot of hill Bukit Mertajam (1,787 ft.), 9 mi. ESE of George Town; rail junction on W coast railroad with spur to Prai railhead.

Bukit Panjang (pänjäng'), village (pop. 3,742) of Singapore isl., on railroad and 9 mi. NW of Singapore; rubber, pineapples. Pop. is Chinese.

Bukit Pasir (päsĕr'), village (pop. 693), NW Johore, Malaya, 6 mi. NE of Bandar Maharani; rubber plantations.

Bukit Timah (tēmä'), village (pop. 3,243) of Singapore isl., on railroad and 6 mi. NW of Singapore; rubber factory, motor assembly plant. Pop. is Chinese. Scene of Singapore surrender (Feb., 1942) in Second World War. Just N is hill Bukit Timah (581 ft.), highest point of Singapore isl.

Bukittinggi or **Boekittinggi** (both: bōōkĭt'tĭng'gē), formerly **Fort de Kock** (dů kôk'), town (pop. 14,657), W Sumatra, Indonesia, 45 mi. N of Padang, in Padang Highlands; alt. c.3,000 ft.; agr. center (rice, copra, tobacco, coffee). Has Du. fort, built 1825.

Bukken Fjord, Norway: see BOKN FJORD.

Bükk Mountains (bük), a S spur of the Carpathians, NE Hungary, extending 25 mi. from Eger R. to Miskolc; rise to 3,145 ft. at Mt. Istallosko. Heavily forested; lignite deposits on N slopes (at Ozd). Miskolc at E foot; resort of LILLAFÜRED in a valley.

Bukkur, W Pakistan: see SUKKUR, city.

Bukn Fjord, Norway: see BOKN FJORD.

Bukoba (bōōkō'bä), town (pop. c.3,000), NW Tanganyika, port on W shore of L. Victoria, 110 mi. NW of Mwanza, just S of Uganda border; coffee center in densely populated dist.; tobacco, sisal, corn; fisheries. Glass-sand deposits. Tin and tungsten mining in dist. 70 mi. W along Ruanda-Urundi border.

Bukoko (bōōkōkō'), village, SE Ubangi-Shari, Fr. Equatorial Africa, just NNW of Bangui; has experimental agr. station for coffee, rubber, fibers, hardwoods; school of agr.

Bukom, Pulau, Singapore: see BUKUM, PULAU.

Bukovina (bōōkůvē'nů), Ger. *Bukowina,* Rum. *Bucovina,* region (□ c.4,000) of E Europe, in NE Rumania and W Ukrainian SSR, bet. the Carpathians and the Dniester; drained by upper Prut and Siret (Sereth) rivers. Heavily forested (oak, beech) on mtn. slopes; grain, sugar beets, livestock. CHERNOVTSY in the Ukraine is chief center. Pop. is mixture of many nationalities, including Rumanians, Ukrainians, Russians, Jews, and Germans. Bukovina was historical nucleus of principality of MOLDAVIA, which had its first capital, Suceava, in Bukovina. Ceded (1775) by Ottoman Empire to Austria, it was made at first a dist. of Galicia, but in 1848 became autonomous crownland ranking as titular duchy (□ 4,031; 1910 pop. 800,098). Transferred to Rumania in 1918. By treaty of June, 1940, Rumania ceded, along with Bessarabia, N Bukovina (□ c.2,000; 1941 pop. 458,643) to Russia. From 1941 to 1944, Rum. troops again occupied all Bukovina, but the Rum. peace treaty of 1947 confirmed N Bukovina as part of the USSR. The remainder (□ c.2,000; 1941 pop. 336,215; 1948 pop. 300,751) forms one of the historical provs. of Rumania.

Bukovtsi or **Buk'ovtsi** (bōō'kyôftsē), village (pop. 5,042), Vratsa dist., NW Bulgaria, on Skat R. and 5 mi. SW of Oryakhovo; flour milling; winegrowing, truck gardening.

Bukrino (bōō'krĭnů), village (1939 pop. over 500), W central Ryazan oblast, Russian SFSR, 21 mi. SSE of Ryazan; truck produce, wheat, fruit.

Buksina, Russian SFSR: see VERKHNYAYA.

Buksnes, Norway: see BALLSTAD.

Bukta (bŏŏk'tä), fishing village (pop. 483) in Alta canton, Finmark co., N Norway, on Alta Fjord, 2 mi. E of Alta. Formerly Bugten.

Bukuka (bōōkōō'kŭ), town (1948 pop. over 2,000), SE Chita oblast, Russian SFSR, in Nerchinsk Range, 25 mi. NNE of Borzya; tungsten mine.

Bukum, Pulau, or **Pulau Bukum Besar** (pōōlou' bōō'kōōm bĕsär'), island (pop. 2,855) in Singapore Strait, off SW Singapore isl.; 1°14'N 103°46'E; 2 mi. long, ½ mi. wide. Site of Singapore oil-storage tanks and oiling station. Sometimes Pulau Bukom.

Bukuru (bōō'kōō'rōō'), town (pop. 14,707), Plateau Prov., Northern Provinces, central Nigeria, on Bauchi Plateau, on railroad and 10 mi. S of Jos; major tin-mining center; cassava, millet, durra.

Bula or **Boela** (both: bōō'lü), village on NE coast of Ceram, Indonesia, on the Ceram Sea, 70 mi. ESE of Wahai; oil center.

Bula (bōō'lä), town (1939 pop. 1,370; 1948 municipality pop. 11,952), Camarines Sur prov., SE Luzon, Philippines, on Bicol R. and 12 mi. SE of Naga; agr. center (rice, corn).

Bulacan (bōōläkän'), province (□ 1,021; 1948 pop. 411,382), S central Luzon, Philippines, bounded SW by Manila Bay; ⊙ MALOLOS. Generally mountainous terrain, drained by tributaries of Pampanga R. Iron and gold mining. Agr. (rice, sugar cane, corn). The prov. is known for buri-palm hats.

Bulacan, town (1939 pop. 833; 1948 municipality pop. 13,242), Bulacan prov., S central Luzon, Philippines, 15 mi. NW of Manila; rice, sugar cane, corn. Sometimes called San Jose.

Bülach (bü'läkh), town (pop. 3,877), Zurich canton, N Switzerland, 10 mi. N of Zurich; metal products, glass, cotton textiles.

Bulachauri (bōōlŭchōō'rē), village, E central Georgian SSR, on Aragva R. and c.30 mi. N of Tiflis. Site of waterworks supplying Tiflis and Rustavi.

Bulagan, Mongolia: see BULGAN.

Bulak or **Bulaq** (bōō'läk), NW suburb (pop. 232,602), of Cairo, NE Egypt, on the Nile. Founded in 15th cent. and served as a port; now a part of Cairo. It is connected (W) by a bridge (built 1909) to GEZIRA, an isl. in the Nile. Bulak, now a printing and paper-milling center, was formerly known for the great museum now in Cairo proper.

Bulalacao (bōōlälä'kou), town (1939 pop. 1,478; 1948 municipality pop. 3,597), on S coast of Mindoro isl., Philippines, 75 mi. S of Calapan; coal-mining center.

Bulan or **Boelan** (both: bōōlän'), island (□ c.35; 10 mi. long, 4 mi. wide), Riouw Archipelago, Indonesia, just SW of Batam, 20 mi. S of Singapore. Timber, copra, fish.

Bulan (bōō'län), town (1939 pop. 9,535; 1948 municipality pop. 37,231), Sorsogon prov., extreme SE Luzon, Philippines, port on Ticao Pass, 34 mi. SSE of Legaspi; agr. center; exports abacá and copra. Airfield.

Bulan (bū'lŭn), village (pop. 1,446), Perry co., SE Ky., in Cumberland foothills, 4 mi. NNE of Hazard, in bituminous-coal, oil, gas, and timber region.

Bulancak (bōōlänjäk'), village (pop. 4,709), Giresun prov., N Turkey, on Black Sea, 9 mi. W of Giresun; hazel nuts. Formerly Akkoy.

Bulandshahr (bŏŏlŭnd'shär), district (□ 1,889; pop. 1,317,223), W Uttar Pradesh, India; ⊙ Bulandshahr. In Ganges-Jumna Doab; agr. (wheat, oilseeds, barley, jowar, corn, cotton, sugar cane, gram). Main towns: Khurja, Bulandshahr, Sikandarabad, Dibai, Jahangirabad. Headworks of Lower Ganges Canal at Naraura. Dist. invaded by Mahmud of Ghazni in 1018.

Bulandshahr, town (pop. 29,701), ⊙ Bulandshahr dist., W Uttar Pradesh, India, on railroad and 40 mi. ESE of Delhi; road center; trades in wheat, barley, jowar, cotton, sugar cane. Has Buddhist remains of 5th–7th cent. A.D. Noted 14th-cent. Moslem historian, Zia-ud-din Barni, b. here. Formerly called Baran.

Bulanik (bōōlänŭk'), Turkish *Bulanık*. **1** Village (pop. 1,987), Mus prov., E Turkey, 50 mi. NE of Mus; wheat. Formerly Kop. **2** Village, Seyhan prov., Turkey: see BAHCE.

Bulanovo (bŏŏlä'nŭvŭ), village (1926 pop. 2,123), N Chkalov oblast, Russian SFSR, on right tributary of Sakmara R. and 45 mi. N of Chkalov; wheat, sunflowers, livestock.

Bulaq (bōō'läk). **1** Suburb of Cairo, Egypt: see BULAK. **2** Village (pop. 1,219) in Kharga oasis, S central Egypt, 16 mi. S of Kharga; dates, cotton.

Bulawayo (bōōläwä'yō), province (□ 46,324; pop. c.422,000), W and SW Southern Rhodesia; ⊙ Bulawayo. Largely in middle veld (2–4,000 ft.), except in Plumtree-Bulawayo high-veld ridge (above 4,000 ft.) followed by main railroad. S of Bulawayo the Matopo Hills rise to 5,091 ft. Tributaries of the Zambezi flow NW; tributaries of the Limpopo flow SE. Chief crops: corn, peanuts, tobacco, citrus fruit. Livestock raising (especially in Gwanda dist.). Teak forests in Nyamandhlovu dist. Prov. has diversified mineral deposits: gold (Antelope, Legion, Fred, Mayfair, Lonely, and Turk mines), coal (in Wankie basin), asbestos, copper. Chief centers: Bulawayo, Plumtree, Wankie, Victoria Falls (near falls on Zambezi R.). European pop. (1946), 23,983, concentrated in high veld. Prov. formed c.1948.

Bulawayo, city (pop. 42,792; including suburbs, 52,737), ⊙ Bulawayo prov., SW Southern Rhodesia, in Matabeleland, 230 mi. SW of Salisbury, and on Matsheumlope R. (a branch of Umguza R.); alt. 4,405 ft.; 20°10'S 28°35'E. Major commercial and industrial center of Southern Rhodesia; rail junction, linked with Mafeking and Capetown and with Victoria Falls, Salisbury, and Beira. Airport. Rail and engineering workshops, ironworks; wheat and corn milling, sugar refining, brewing, meat packing (cold-storage plant), mfg. of soap, clothing, paper articles. Cement mill at Cement, 7 mi. ENE. Gold mines in dist. Seat of Rhodesia mus. (founded 1901), public library, observatory, meteorological station, memorial hosp., school of mines, and govt. technical school. Its residential suburbs include Bellevue, Hillside, Queensdale, and Sauerstownship. Raylton (just S of Bulawayo station) is residential area for railway staff. Water supply from Khami Dam on upper Khami R. (near Khami Ruins; 10 mi. W) and from Matopos Dam (14 mi. SSW, on headstream of Tuli R.). Mean annual temp. 66°F.; yearly rainfall 23 in. Founded 1893, original settlement was 1st located 3 mi. N of present site; moved 1894 to permanent site. Sometimes spelled Buluwayo.

Bulayevo (bŏŏlī'ŭvŭ), town (1948 pop. over 2,000), NE North Kazakhstan oblast, Kazakh SSR, on Trans-Siberian RR and 50 mi. E of Petropavlovsk; wheat.

Bulboki or **Bul'boki** (bŏŏlbô'kē), Rum. *Bulboaca* (bŏŏlbŏŏä'kä), village (1941 pop. 1,852), SE Moldavian SSR, on Byk R., on railroad and 8 mi. NW of Bendery; white-wine-making center.

Bulbul (bŏŏl'bŏŏl), Fr. *Boulboul*, village, Aleppo prov., NW Syria, near Turkish border, 45 mi. NNW of Aleppo; cotton, cereals, pistachios.

Buldan (bŏŏldän'), town (pop. 9,761), Denizli prov., SW Turkey, 24 mi. NNW of Denizli; barley, vetch.

Buldana (bŏŏldä'nŭ), district (□ 3,763; pop. 820,862), Berar div., W Madhya Pradesh, India, on Deccan Plateau; ⊙ Buldana. Lowland (N), drained by Purna R. (tributary of the Tapti), and bordered N by central Satpura Range; Ajanta Hills (S), drained by Purna (tributary of the Godavari) and Penganga rivers. In major black-soil cotton-growing tract; also produces millet, wheat, oilseeds. Timber (teak) forests in Ajanta Hills (cattle raising); cotton ginning, oilseed milling. Sodium carbonate and salt extracted at lake 13 mi. S of Mehkar. Khamgaon is cotton-trade center. Pop. 90% Hindu, 10% Moslem.

Buldana, town (pop. 8,849), ⊙ Buldana dist., W Madhya Pradesh, India, in Ajanta Hills, 55 mi. WSW of Akola; road center; oilseed milling. Industrial school. Teak forests near by.

Buldibuyo (bŏŏldēbōō'yō), town (pop. 1,467), Libertad dept., N central Peru, in Cordillera Central, 12 mi. NW of Tayabamba; alt. 10,640 ft.; corn, wheat; goat raising.

Buldur, Turkey: see BURDUR.

Bulduri, Latvia: see RIGAS JURMALA.

Buleleng or **Boeleleng** (both: bŏŏlĕlŭng'), town, N Bali, Indonesia, on Java Sea; port for Singaraja (2 mi. S), exporting rice, coffee.

Bulford, town and parish (pop. 3,923), E Wiltshire, England, on the Avon and 9 mi. N of Salisbury; agr. market. Site of large military camp. Has 12th-cent. church.

Bulgan or **Bulagan** (bōōl'gän), aimak (□ 19,000; pop. 50,000), N Mongolian People's Republic; ⊙ Bulgan. Bounded N by Buryat-Mongol Autonomous SSR of USSR, it lies almost entirely on wooded steppe plateau traversed by Selenga and Orkhon rivers. Pop. includes Buryat and Chinese minorities; aimak has considerable agr. and high livestock density.

Bulgan or **Bulagan,** town, ⊙ Bulgan aimak, N Mongolian People's Republic, near Orkhon R., 170 mi. WNW of Ulan Bator.

Bulgar, Russian SFSR: see BOLGARY.

Bulgaria (bŭlgâ'rēŭ), Bulgarian *Bulgariya* or *Blgariya* (both: bŭlgä'rēyä), republic (□ 42,796; pop. 7,022,206), SE Europe; ⊙ SOFIA. Situated in E Balkan Peninsula along the Black Sea (E), it borders S on Greece, approaching within 20 mi. of the Aegean Sea. In N across the navigable lower Danube is Rumania. It is bounded W by Yugoslavia, SE by Turkey in Europe. Lies bet. 41°14'–44°12'N and 22°21'–28°37'E. The rugged country —roughly ⅔ mts.— is crossed E-W by the BALKAN MOUNTAINS, rising in Botev Peak to 7,793 ft. In SW are the even higher RHODOPE MOUNTAINS, which include PIRIN and KILA spurs, the latter attaining Bulgaria's highest elevation in STALIN PEAK or Musala Peak (9,596 ft.). These formidable, still partly wooded, and often snow-bound ranges are divided by numerous low passes—the SHIPKA PASS is the best known—into several subranges. They are furrowed by river valleys which facilitate communication. N to the Danube flows the Iskar R., in whose upper valley lies Sofia. The Struma and Mesta rivers run S to the Aegean Sea, an outlet to which has constantly been the aim of Bulgaria's political and military designs. Principal river next to the Danube is the MARITSA RIVER, watering the THRACIAN PLAIN that drives a wedge bet. the Balkan and Rhodope Mts. This fertile lowland, the N plain along the Danube merging with the DELIORMAN hills of the piedmont, and the valleys of the W are the principal agr. regions. In Bulgaria the Mediterranean exerts only a limited influence, mostly in S near Macedonian border. The climate is generally continental, with long cold winters and warm summers. The shielded valleys are milder and well watered, while the calcareous, windswept plateaus are more arid. Sofia, at an alt. of 1,820 ft., has a Jan. mean temp. of 29°F. and a July mean of 68.7°F. Though various minerals occur, only coal (DIMITROVO, BOBOV-DOL) has achieved major economic importance. Other deposits include copper (Meden-rudnik near Burgas), manganese (BYALA), graphite (at Botev Peak), oil shale (near Dimitrovo), salt (L. ATANASOVO). Also mined are lead, zinc, silver, iron, bauxite, kaolin, marble. The country abounds in mineral springs. Some of the larger cities, such as Sofia, Burgas, Sliven, have spas in their outskirts. There are extensive coniferous forests in the mts. Fisheries are maintained both on the Danube and the Black Sea. Bulgaria is, however, predominantly a peasant country, where about 80% of the people depend on agr. for their livelihood. It is traditionally a land of small landholdings, though ownership was further limited in 1945 to 20 hectares. Almost half of the land is under cultivation. Leading crops are wheat and corn, followed by barley, oats, rye, alfalfa. Tobacco is the principal export. Among commercial crops are grapes, sugar beets, cotton, rice, flax, hemp, sunflowers, soybeans, tomatoes. Deciduous fruit dists. are around KYUSTENDIL, a health resort, and PLOVDIV. From widely-grown plum trees *slivovits* (liquor) is distilled. Sericulture is prominent. Bulgaria takes a front rank in production of attar of roses (perfume essence), based on extensive flowerfields near KAZANLIK, though output has greatly decreased since 1930s. In the mts. livestock are grazed widely, foremost sheep, besides cattle, buffaloes, goats, horses, poultry. Industries are mainly devoted to processing, i.e., winemaking, flour milling, distilling, sugar refining, vegetable-oil extracting, canning, tanning, tobacco curing. Most of the larger towns have textile plants. The mfg. of rugs, embroidery, and delicate metalware is practiced by artisans. Sofia, the political and financial center, turns out chemicals, electrical equipment, furniture, and cigarettes. As a commercial and industrial hub it vies with Plovdiv, Bulgaria's 2d city, which is also a tobacco and livestock center. Heavy industries are now established at Gabrovo, Dimitrovo (formerly Pernik), and the fast-growing Dimitrovgrad (formerly Rakovski). Other trading and processing centers are PLEVEN, STARA ZAGORA, Sliven, KOLAROVGRAD (formerly Shumen), YAMBOL, and PAZARDZHIK. Principal Black Sea ports and resorts are STALIN (formerly Varna) and Burgas. On the Danube are RUSE and VIDIN. Through these ports passes the bulk of foreign trade. Exports are topped by tobacco (about ⅘ of entire volume in 1947), followed by lead concentrates, wine and spirits, iron ore, attar of roses, tomato pulp, hides. Among Bulgaria's imports are petroleum products, textiles, chemicals, machinery, vehicles. In 1948 more than half of all trade was with the USSR. Before the Second World War the country had 2,211 mi. of railroads. Through Sofia passes the Orient Express to Istanbul. The capital also has 2 airports. There are 9 universities and colleges, principally at Sofia, Stalin, and Plovdiv. Since primary education was made compulsory, the once high percentage of illiteracy is on the decrease. The pop. consists chiefly of Bulgars (88%) and Turks (8%). Nominally 85% belong to the Orthodox Eastern Church, and 13% are Moslems. Modern Bulgaria occupies sections of anc. THRACE and the Eastern Roman prov. of MOESIA. It was entered 2d half of the 7th cent. A.D. by the Bulgars, a Turkic tribe from central Asia, who were to adopt Slavic speech and culture. The Bulgars conquered (809) Sofia from the Byzantines and advanced to Constantinople. Boris I introduced (865) Christianity; his son Simeon I greatly expanded the Bulgarian domain. There followed a seesaw fight with the Byzantine Empire and, later, the Ottomans. In 1018 it was annexed by Byzantine Emperor, Basil II, but arose again as an agressive force towards the end of the 12th cent. under Ivan I. The height of Bulgar power was reached under Ivan II, whose rule extended over the whole Balkan Peninsula, except for Greece. In 1330 Bulgaria became tributary to the Serbs and fell (1395) to the Ottoman Empire. Remained a Turkish prov. until 1878; rebellions were put down ruthlessly. Through Russian pressure (Treaty of San Stefano) Bulgaria achieved virtual independence, somewhat curtailed by the Congress of Berlin (1878). N Bulgaria became an autonomous principality under Turkish suzerainty, while present-day S Bulgaria—then called EASTERN RUMELIA—and MACEDONIA remained under direct Turkish rule. In 1885 Eastern Rumelia was annexed. The ruling prince Ferdinand of Saxe-Coburg-Gotha proclaimed himself (1908) tsar of an independent Bulgaria. The *Drang* to the Aegean involved the country in the ultimately unsuccessful Balkan Wars of 1912–13. The S DOBRUJA was ceded (1913, confirmed 1919) to Rumania. Bulgaria fought the 2 World Wars on the German side. By the Treaty of Neuilly (1919) it lost its outlet to the Aegean and some territory to Yugoslavia. In 1940 Rumania was forced to restore the S Dobruja to Bulgaria. One year later Bulgaria became an active partner of the Axis. In 1944 the country passed from the German into the Russian orbit after obtaining an armistice with the Soviet Union. The 1947 peace treaty allowed Bulgaria to keep S Dobruja. The Communists took full control, the monarchy was abolished, and George Dimitrov became (1946) premier. By 1948 all industries were nationalized. Since 1949 Bulgaria is administratively divided—apart from Sofia urban zone—into the following 14 dists.: Burgas, Gorna Dzhumaya (Blagoyevgrad), Gorna Oryakhovitsa, Khaskovo, Kolarovgrad, Pleven, Plovdiv, Ruse, Sofia, Stalin (Varna), Stara Zagora, Vidin, Vratsa, Yambol.

Bulgar Mountains, Turkey: see BOLKAR MOUNTAINS.

Bulghar Mountains, Turkey: see BOLKAR MOUNTAINS.

Bulgnéville (bülnyāvēl'), agr. village (pop. 615), Vosges dept., E France, 12 mi. SSE of Neufchâteau.

Bulhar (bŏŏlhär'), town, N Br. Somaliland, minor port on Gulf of Aden, 45 mi. W of Berbera; fisheries; millet, ghee, gums.

Bulí or **San Miguel de Bulí** (sän mēgĕl' dā bōōlē'), town (pop. 1,132), Ñuble prov., S central Chile, 20 mi. NE of Chillán; agr. center (grain, wine, potatoes, vegetables, livestock); flour milling, dairying, lumbering.

Bulkington, former urban district (1931 pop. 2,474), NE Warwick, England, 6 mi. NE of Coventry.

Bulkley River, W central B.C., rises in Coast Mts. near W side of Babine L., flows a short distance W, then NW, past Telkwa and Smithers, to Skeena R. at Hazelton; 120 mi. long.

Bull, The, rocky islet in the Atlantic, off SW coast of Co. Cork, Ireland, 3 mi. W of Dursey Head; 51°35'N 10°18'W.

Bullaque River (bōōlyä'kā), Ciudad Real prov., S central Spain, rises in the Montes de Toledo, flows c.50 mi. S to the Guadiana at Luciana.

Bullard, village (pop. 317), Smith co., E Texas, 15 mi. S of Tyler, near the Neches; rail, trade point in agr. area.

Bullards Bar Dam, Calif.: see YUBA RIVER.

Bulla Regia, Tunisia: see SOUK-EL-ARBA.

Bullas (bōō'lyäs), town (pop. 6,981), Murcia prov., SE Spain, 21 mi. SW of Cieza; alcohol and brandy distilling, flour milling, cottonseed-oil processing. Agr. trade (wine, saffron, livestock).

Bull Bay, E S.C., inlet on coast, c.25 mi. NE of Charleston, bet. Bull Isl. (SW) and Raccoon Key (NE); c.9 mi. long. Intracoastal Waterway passes bet. W shore and swampy isls. in bay. Often called Bulls Bay.

Bulle (bül), Ger. *Boll* (bôl), town (pop. 4,644), Fribourg canton, W Switzerland, on Trême R. (affluent of the Sarine) and 14 mi. SSW of Fribourg; largest town in the GRUYÈRE. Ships cheese. Metal- and woodworking industries. Site of medieval castle.

Bullecourt (bülkōōr'), village (pop. 321), Pas-de-Calais dept., N France, 10 mi. SE of Arras; sugar-beet processing. Ravaged during First World War.

Bullen, Cape (bŏŏ'lŭn), S extremity of Devon Isl., E Franklin Dist., Northwest Territories, on Lancaster Sound; 74°22'N 85°12'W.

Bullen Bay (bŏŏ'lĭn), inlet of W Curaçao, Du. West Indies, 10 mi. NW of Willemstad, with which it is linked by pipe lines. Petroleum products are shipped from here.

Buller, New Zealand: see WESTPORT.

Buller, Mount (bŏŏ'lŭr) (5,911 ft.), E central Victoria, Australia, in Australian Alps, 95 mi. NE of Melbourne.

Buller River, NW S.Isl., New Zealand, rises in L. Rotoiti 45 mi. SSW of Nelson, flows 105 mi. SW to Tasman Sea at Westport.

Bullers of Buchan, Scotland: see BUCHAN.

Bullfinch, town (pop. 181), SW central Western Australia, 205 mi. ENE of Perth, near Southern Cross; gold-mining center.

Bulli (bŏŏ'lī), town (pop. 2,478), E New South Wales, Australia, 35 mi. S of Sydney, on coast; coal mines; tourist resort.

Bull Island, E S.C., on coast, c.20 mi. ENE of Charleston, just S of Bull Bay; c.6 mi. long. Often called Bulls Isl.

Bullitt, county (□ 300; pop. 11,349), NW Ky.; ⊙ Shepherdsville. Bounded W by Salt R., SW by Rolling Fork; drained by Floyds Fork. Rolling agr. area (livestock, grain, burley tobacco, dairy products). Some mfg. (especially whisky and food products). Formed 1796.

Bulloch (bŏŏ'lŭk), county (□ 684; pop. 24,740), E Ga.; ⊙ Statesboro. Bounded NE by Ogeechee R. Coastal plain agr. (cotton, tobacco, corn, peanuts, livestock) and forestry (lumber, naval stores) area. Formed 1796.

Bullock (bŏŏ'lŭk), county (□ 615; pop. 16,054), SE Ala.; ⊙ Union Springs. Rolling agr. area watered by headstreams of Conecuh and Pea rivers. Cotton, livestock. Formed 1866.

Bullock Creek, village (pop. 1,894), Midland co., central Mich.

Bull Run, battlefield in Prince William co., N Va., just NW of Manassas, c.30 mi. W of Washington, D.C. Named for near-by small stream (c.20 mi. long), on right bank of which were fought Civil War battles of Bull Run; officially known as Manassas Natl. Battlefield Park (1,604.57 acres; est. 1940). In 1st battle of Bull Run (July 21, 1861; 1st major engagement of the war; also called 1st battle of Manassas), unseasoned Union troops under McDowell were routed by Confederates under Beauregard and Jackson; Jackson's successful stand here earned him the nickname "Stonewall." The 2d battle of Bull Run (Aug. 29–30, 1862), also known as 2d battle of Manassas, was preceded (Aug. 9) by Jackson's defeat of Banks's corps at Cedar Mtn. and again ended in victory for the Confederates. Longstreet and Jackson, under Lee's command, forced Federals under Pope to retreat across Bull Run; Confederate victory led to Lee's 1st invasion of the North, in Antietam campaign.

Bull Run River, NW Oregon, rises in Cascade Range, flows c.30 mi. W to Sandy R. near Sandy. Bull Run Dam (200 ft. high, 935 ft. long; completed 1929 by city of Portland) is in lower course c.10 mi. upstream. Forms small reservoir (4 mi. long) supplying Portland.

Bulls, town (pop. 605), S N.Isl., New Zealand, on Rangitikei R. and 85 mi. NNE of Wellington; sawmills, dairy plant.

Bullsgap or **Bulls Gap,** village (1940 pop. 597), Hawkins co., NE Tenn., 50 mi. NE of Knoxville.

Bull Shoals Dam, Ark.: see WHITE RIVER, Ark. and Mo.

Bulltofta, airport, Sweden: see MALMO.

Bullychoop Mountains, Calif.: see KLAMATH MOUNTAINS.

Bully-les-Mines (bülē'-lā-mēn'), town (pop. 8,627), Pas-de-Calais dept., N France, 5 mi. WNW of Lens; coal mines.

Bulnes (bŏŏl'nĕs), town (pop. 4,961), Ñuble prov., S central Chile, on railroad and 15 mi. SW of Chillán. Agr. center (wheat, corn, oats, lentils, potatoes, stock); flour milling, dairying, lumbering.

Bulo Burti (bŏŏ'lō bŏŏr'tē), town (pop. 3,000), in the Mudugh, central Ital. Somaliland, on the Webi Shebeli and 120 mi. N of Mogadishu, in durra-growing region; 3°51'N 45°35'E. Trade center (livestock, hides); road junction.

Buloh Kasap (bōōlō' kä'säp), village (pop. 690), NW Johore, Malaya, on railroad and 4 mi. NW of Segamat, on Muar R.; rubber.

Bulolo (bōōlō'lō), gold-mining town in Territory of New Guinea, 15 mi. NW of Wau.

Bulpitt (bŏŏl'pĭt), village (pop. 376), Christian co., central Ill., 18 mi. SE of Springfield, in agr. and bituminous-coal-mining area.

Bulqizë (bōōlkyē'zŭ) or **Bulqiza** (bōōlkyē'zä), village, E central Albania, 15 mi. SW of Peshkopi; chrome mining.

Bulsar (bōōlsär'), town (pop., including suburban area, 23,251), Surat dist., N Bombay, India, port on Gulf of Cambay, 40 mi. S of Surat; exports timber, cotton and silk fabrics, millet, wheat, molasses, tiles; handicraft cloth weaving, dyeing, coach building, brick and pottery mfg.; castor-oil extraction, fruitgrowing; engineering workshops. Lighthouse 2 mi. W. Also spelled Balsar.

Bultfontein (bŭlt"fŏntän'). **1** Village, NE Cape Prov., U. of So. Afr., SSE suburb of Kimberley; important diamond mine. **2** Town (pop. 1,988), W central Orange Free State, U. of So. Afr., 60 mi. N of Bloemfontein; alt. 4,393 ft.; rail terminus; stock, wool, grain.

Buluan (bōōlōō'än), town (1939 pop. 915; 1948 municipality pop. 63,388), Cotabato prov., Philippines, S central Mindanao, 50 mi. SE of Cotabato, and on Pulangi R. near L. Buluan (□ 24). The municipality includes the Liguasan Marsh to N. Rice and coconut growing.

Buluarte River (bōōlwär'tā), Sinaloa, W Mexico, rises on Durango border, flows c.75 mi. SW through fertile coastal lowlands, past Rosario, to the Pacific 38 mi. SE of Mazatlán.

Bulun (bōōlōōn'), village (1948 pop. over 500), N Yakut Autonomous SSR, Russian SFSR, N of Arctic Circle, port on Lena River and 265 mi. NW of Verkhoyansk; trading post; reindeer raising, sealing, fishing. Coal deposits near by.

Bulungan River, Borneo: see KAJAN RIVER.

Bulungir River, China: see SHULEH RIVER.

Bulun Tokhoi (bōōlōōn' tōkhoi'), Chinese *Fuhai* (fōō'hī'), town, ⊙ Bulun Tokhoi co. (pop. 8,269), northernmost Sinkiang prov., China, in the Dzungaria, 70 mi. SW of Sharasume, near lake Ulyungur Nor; cattle raising; grain. Also Puluntohai.

Bulunzir River, China: see SHULEH RIVER.

Bulus, Tanjong, Malaya: see PIAI, TANJONG.

Bulusan (bōōlōō'sän), town (1939 pop. 3,424; 1948 municipality pop. 12,144), Sorsogon prov., extreme SE Luzon, Philippines, on San Bernardino Strait, near Mt. Bulusan, 17 mi. SE of Legaspi; agr. center (abacá, coconuts, rice).

Bulusan, Mount, active volcano (5,115 ft.), Sorsogon prov., extreme SE Luzon, Philippines, just W of Bulusan, 15 mi. SSE of Sorsogon. A crater lake is near the summit. Last erupted 1919.

Buluwayo, Southern Rhodesia: see BULAWAYO, city.

Bulwell (bŏŏl'-), NW suburb of Nottingham, S Nottingham, England; mfg. of hosiery, soap, pottery; textile printing.

Bumazuv, Kashmir: see BAWAN.

Bumba (bōōm'bä), town (1946 pop. c.4,650), Equator Prov., N Belgian Congo, on right bank of Congo R., 25 mi. W of mouth of Itimbiri R., and 65 mi. E of Lisala; important transshipment point for produce from Uele region and starting point of Congo-Nile highway; rice milling. Has airfield, R.C. mission.

Bumbesti-Jiu (bōōmbĕsh'tĭ-zhē'ōō), Rum. *Bumbeşti-Jiu*, village (pop. 2,114), Gorj prov., SW Rumania, on Jiu R. and 10 mi. NNE of Targu-Jiu; rail terminus; mfg. of munitions.

Bumbuna (bōōmbōō'nä), town (pop. 827), Northern Prov., N central Sierra Leone, on Rokel R. and 27 mi. NNE of Magburaka (linked by road), in gold-mining area; trade center.

Bumiaju, Indonesia: see BUMIAYU.

Bumiayu, Bumiaju, or **Boemiajoe** (all: bōōmēä'yōō), town (pop. 9,879), central Java, Indonesia, 50 mi. SE of Cheribon, at foot of Mt. Slamet; trade center in agr. area (rice, rubber, sugar, peanuts, cassava).

Bum Kittam River, Sierra Leone: see KITTAM RIVER.

Bum La (bōōm lä'), pass (alt. 14,210 ft.) in central Assam Himalayas, on undefined India-Tibet border, on important India-Tibet trade route, 12 mi. NNE of Towang (India).

Bum River, Sierra Leone: see SEWA RIVER.

Bumtang, Bhutan: see BYAKAR.

Buna, river, Albania-Yugoslavia: see BOJANA RIVER.

Buna (bōō'nä, bū'nŭ), town, Northern Div., Territory of Papua, SE New Guinea, 55 mi. E of Yodda goldfields, 100 mi. NE of Port Moresby; rubber, coffee. In Second World War, site of Jap. air base taken 1942 by Allied forces after a fierce struggle. Nearby Buna Mission (site of govt. station) was also taken 1943.

Bunab or **Bonab** (both: bōnäb'), town (1941 pop. estimate 14,000), Fourth Prov., in Azerbaijan, NW Iran, 10 mi. WSW of Maragheh, near L. Urmia; grain, fruit. Sometimes Binab.

Buna River, Albania-Yugoslavia: see BOJANA RIVER.

Bunawan (bōōnä'wän), town (1939 pop. 9,738) in Davao city, Davao prov., S central Mindanao, Philippines, 12 mi. N of Davao proper, just NW of Samal Isl.; abacá, coconuts.

Bunbury, municipality and port (pop. 6,240), SW Western Australia, 95 mi. S of Perth, at N end of Geographe Bay; superphosphate works, woolen and textile mills. Exports timber, wheat, wool, coal.

Bunce Island, W Sierra Leone, in Bunce R. (S arm of Sierra Leone R., along N side of Sierra Leone Peninsula), c.10 mi. SE of Freetown. An early Br. trading post (established c.1700); hq. of Br. possessions in Sierra Leone in 18th cent. Ceded to the Crown in 1824.

Bunceton city (pop. 556), Cooper co., central Mo., 13 mi. S of Boonville.

Buncombe (bŭng'kŭm), county (□ 646; pop. 124,403), W N.C.; ⊙ Asheville. In the Blue Ridge; Black Mts. in E, Pisgah Natl. Forest in E and SW; crossed by French Broad R. Farming (tobacco, corn, dairy products, cattle), lumbering, and tourist region; textile mfg. at Asheville and Enka. Formed 1791.

Buncombe, village (pop. 210), Johnson co., S Ill., 17 mi. S of Marion, in rich agr. area.

Buncrana (bŭnkră'nŭ), Gaelic *Bun Crannaighe*, urban district (pop. 2,729), NE Co. Donegal, Ireland, on E shore of Lough Swilly, 11 mi. NNW of Londonderry; fishing center; tobacco processing, shirt mfg.; seaside resort.

Bundaberg (bŭn'dŭbûrg), city and port (pop. 15,926), SE Queensland, Australia, on Burnett R., 10 mi. from its mouth, and 180 mi. NNW of Brisbane; sugar-producing center (sugar mills, refinery); rum, agr. implements.

Bunde (bōōn'dŭ), village (pop. 3,018), in former Prussian prov. of Hanover, NW Germany, after 1945 in Lower Saxony, 8 mi. SW of Leer, near Dutch border; food processing.

Bünde (bün'dŭ), town (pop. 7,782), in former Prussian prov. of Westphalia, NW Germany, after 1945 in North Rhine-Westphalia, 7 mi. NNW of Herford; rail junction; mfg. (machinery, cigars). Saline springs. Has Romanesque church.

Bundelkhand (bōōn'dŭlkhŭnd, bŭn'-), region of central India, S of Jumna R.; adjoins Baghelkhand (E); comprises W portion of Vindhya Pradesh and S dists. of Uttar Pradesh. Crossed by Vindhya Range; consists largely of hill ranges and jungle (S) and alluvial plain (N); drained by Betwa, Dhasan, and Ken rivers. Name derived from Bundela Rajputs, who settled here c.14th cent. Invaded by Moguls in 16th cent.; in 18th cent., under Mahratta control. Former British Bundelkhand included dists. of Jalaun, Jhansi, Hamirpur, Banda, and S Allahabad of United Provs. **Bundelkhand Agency,** a subdivision (□ 11,669; pop. 1,728,886) of former CENTRAL INDIA agency, comprised princely states of Ajaigarh, Baoni, Baraunda, Bijawar, Charkhari, Chhatarpur, Datia, Maihar, Nagod, Orchha, Panna, Samthar, Kothi, and Sohawal, and petty states of Alipura, Banka Pahari, Beri, Bihat, Bijna, Dhurwai, Garrauli, Gaurihar, Jaso, Jigni, Lugasi, Naigawan Rebai, Sarila, Tori Fatehpur, and CHAUBE JAGIRS. Originally created in 1802; absorbed BAGHELKHAND AGENCY in 1931; hq. were at Nowgong. In 1948–50, all states merged with Vindhya Pradesh and Uttar Pradesh.

Bündheim (bünt'hīm), village (pop. 5,674), in Brunswick, NW Germany, after 1945 in Lower Saxony, on N slope of the upper Harz, 1 mi. NW of Bad Harzburg; woodworking. Stud (established in 16th cent.).

Bundi (bōōn'dē), former princely state (□ 2,205; pop. 249,374) in Rajputana States, India; ⊙ was Bundi. Established in mid-14th cent. by Chauhan Rajputs and known as Harroti. In 1948, merged with union of Rajasthan.

Bundi, city (pop. 20,846), SE Rajasthan, India, 100 mi. S of Jaipur; trades locally in wheat, millet, cotton, oilseeds; cotton ginning, handloom weaving. Picturesquely situated in a gorge and surrounded by forested hills on which are several forts and palaces. Was ⊙ former Rajputana state of Bundi; is now ⊙ Bundi dist.

Bundi, mine, Malaya: see CHUKAI.

Bundoran (bŭndô'rŭn), Gaelic *Bun Dobhráin*, urban district (pop. 1,825), S Co. Donegal, Ireland, on Donegal Bay, 14 mi. SW of Donegal; fishing port, seaside resort.

Bundroes (bŭndrōz'), fishing village, N Co. Leitrim, Ireland, on Donegal Bay, just SW of Bundoran.

Bundu (bōōn'dōō), town (pop. 6,982), Ranchi dist., S Bihar, India, 22 mi. SE of Ranchi; trade center (rice, oilseeds, corn, cotton); shellac mfg.

Bunë River, Albania-Yugoslavia: see BOJANA RIVER.

Bungay (bŭng'gē), urban district (1931 pop. 3,100; 1951 census 3,531), NE Suffolk, England, on Waveney R. and 14 mi. W of Lowestoft; agr. market; printing industry, mfg. of agr. implements and shoes. Has remains of 12th-cent. castle. There is Norman church and anc. market cross. Near by are remains of a fortress, probably Saxon.

Bunge Land, Russian SFSR: see KOTELNY ISLAND.

Bungo (bōōng'gō), former province in E Kyushu, Japan; now part of Oita prefecture.

Bungoma (bōōng-gō'mä), village, Nyanza prov., W Kenya, on railroad and 22 mi. NNW of Kakamega; cotton, peanuts, sesame, corn.

Bungo Strait, Japan: see HOYO STRAIT.

Bunguran, Indonesia: see GREAT NATUNA.

Bunheiro, Portugal: see BRUNHEIRO.

Bunia (bōōn'yä), village (1948 pop. 3,419), Eastern Prov., NE Belgian Congo, 30 mi. ENE of Irumu, near W shore of L. Albert (Uganda border); trading center for gold-mining and cattle-raising region, also noted for number of white colonists; rice processing. Has R.C. mission with trade, agr., and business schools for natives. Mudzi Maria (mōōdzē märyä'), R.C. mission and seat of vicar apostolic, is just NNE. Only in Bunia region can still be encountered the Negro women noted for characteristic lip deformation made by the introduction of a large wooden disk.

Buniar, Kashmir: see RAMPUR, Muzaffarabad dist.

Bunji (bōōn'jē), village, ⊙ Astore dist., W Kashmir, in extreme N Punjab Himalayas, on the Indus (seasonal ferry) and 26 mi. SE of Gilgit; pulse, wheat, corn. Fort, built by Dogras.

Bunker Hill. **1** City (pop. 1,238), Macoupin co., SW central Ill., 15 mi. NE of Alton, in agr. area; bituminous-coal mining; ships grain; mfg. (condensed milk; burial vaults and monuments). Inc. 1857. A tornado in March, 1948, did much damage here. **2** Village (1940 pop. 792), Knox co., SW Ind., just S of Vincennes, in agr. and bituminous-coal area. **3** Town (pop. 659), Miami co., N central Ind., 8 mi. S of Peru, in livestock and grain area; dairy products. **4** or **Bunkerhill,** city (pop. 271), Russell co., central Kansas, 8 mi. E of Russell, near Smoky Hill R., in livestock and grain region. Oil fields in vicinity. **5** Village (pop. 1,409), Coos co., SW Oregon, on Coos Bay and 2 mi. S of Coos Bay city. **6** Village, Berkeley co., W.Va.: see MARTINSBURG.

Bunker Hill, height, Mass.: see CHARLESTOWN.

Bunkeya (bŏŏngkä'yä), village, Katanga prov., SE Belgian Congo, 45 mi. NNE of Jadotville; copper mining. R.C. and Protestant missions. Before establishment of Congo Free State and until 1891 Bunkeya was the noted ⊙ (pop. c.20,000) of a ruthless African potentate who ruled most of present Katanga prov. and carried on a brisk trade in ivory, slaves, copper, iron, and salt.

Bunkie, town (pop. 4,666), Avoyelles parish, E central La., 28 mi. SE of Alexandria, in agr. area (cotton, sugar cane, corn); cotton and cottonseed products, canned foods, sugar, Spanish moss, wood products. Founded 1882.

Bunlevel or **Bunnlevel,** town (pop. 177), Harnett co., central N.C., 17 mi. N of Fayetteville; lumber milling.

Bunmahon or **Bonmahon** (both: bŭn"mŭhōōn', –mŭhōn'), Gaelic *Bun Machan,* village, S Co. Waterford, Ireland, on the coast 11 mi. ENE of Dungarvan; fishing port and resort. Near by is copper-mining village of Knockmahon.

Bunn, town (pop. 255), Franklin co., N central N.C., 25 mi. ENE of Raleigh.

Bunnabeola, Ireland: see BENNA BEOLA.

Bunnell (bŭnĕl'), town (pop. 1,341), ⊙ Flagler co., NE Fla., 29 mi. S of St. Augustine; ships vegetables, citrus fruit.

Bunnlevel, N.C.: see BUNLEVEL.

Bun Nua (bōōn' nōōä'), town, Phongsaly prov., N Laos, 12 mi. WSW of Phongsaly.

Buñol (bōōnyōl'), town (pop. 5,709), Valencia prov., E Spain, 23 mi. WSW of Valencia; paper-mfg. center; cement works; olive-oil processing, flour milling, lumbering. Limestone and gypsum quarries near by. Has remains of Moorish castle. Was ⊙ county of Buñol in kingdom of Valencia.

Buñola (bōōnyō'lä), town (pop. 2,248), Majorca, Balearic Isls., on railroad and 9 mi. NNE of Palma, in agr. region. Stock raising, lumbering, olive-oil pressing, liquor distilling; mfg. of textiles, cement, metalwork.

Bunsen, Korea: see MUNCHON.

Bun Thai (bōōn' tī'), town, Phongsaly prov., N Laos, 22 mi. SSW of Phongsaly.

Buñuel (bōōnŭĕl'), town (pop. 2,533), Navarre prov., N Spain, on the Ebro and 10 mi. SE of Tudela; sugar beets, cereals, pepper, livestock.

Bunumbu (bōōnōōm'bōō), town (pop. 1,050), South-Eastern Prov., E Sierra Leone, 12 mi. WNW of Pendembu; palm oil and kernels, cacao, coffee. Wesleyan Methodist mission (teachers col.).

Bunyan (bünyän'), Turkish *Bünyan,* village (pop. 5,175), Kayseri prov., central Turkey, 22 mi. ENE of Kayseri; woolen mill; agr. (wheat, barley, rye).

Bunyoni, Lake, Uganda: see KABALE.

Bunyoro, district, Uganda: see HOIMA.

Bunzlau, Poland: see BOLESLAWIEC.

Buochs (bōō-ōks'), town (pop. 2,026), Nidwalden half-canton, central Switzerland, on S shore of L. of Lucerne, at mouth of Engelberger Aa; silk textiles, clothes; woodworking.

Buonabitacolo (bwô"näbētä'kôlô), village (pop. 2,555), Salerno prov., Campania, S Italy, 9 mi. S of Sala Consilina.

Buonalbergo (bwô"nälbĕr'gô), village (pop. 2,760), Benevento prov., Campania, S Italy, 12 mi. NE of Benevento.

Buona Vista (bwô'nä vē'stä), fishing village (pop. 1,995), Singapore isl., on S coast and 5 mi. W of Singapore.

Buonconvento (bwôn"kônvĕn'tô), village (pop. 1,336), Siena prov., Tuscany, central Italy, on Ombrone R. and 15 mi. SSE of Siena. Has 14th-cent. walls.

Buor-Khaya Bay (bōōôr"-khī'ŭ), inlet of E.Siberian Sea, in N Yakut Autonomous SSR, Russian SFSR, bet. Lena R. delta (W) and Cape Buor-Khaya (E; site of govt. observation post); 80 mi. wide. Tiksi Bay is inlet of its NW shore. Also spelled Borkhaya Bay.

Buqqa, Saudi Arabia: see ABQAIQ.

Buquim (bōō'kēm), city (pop. 2,851), S Sergipe, NE Brazil, on railroad and 12 mi. NW of Estância; has model farms growing sugar, cotton, coffee, tobacco. Mineral springs.

Bur, El (ĕl bōōr'), village (pop. 200), in the Mudugh, central Ital. Somaliland, on road and 95 mi. E of Belet Uen, in durra-growing region.

Bura (bōō'rä), village, Coast Prov., SE Kenya, on Tana R., on road and 110 mi. NNW of Kipini; rice, sugar cane.

Bur Acaba (bōōr äkä'bä), town (pop. 2,500), in the Upper Juba, Ital. Somaliland, on road and 100 mi. NW of Mogadishu; agr. center (durra, corn), livestock market.

Buraida, Buraidah, or **Buraydah** (bōōrī'dŭ), town and oasis (pop. 30,000), Qasim prov. of Nejd, Saudi Arabia, 16 mi. N of Anaiza and 210 mi. NW of Riyadh; 26°20'N 43°59'E. Caravan center, noted for its camel and cattle markets; exports ghee, dates, grain. Was former ⊙ Qasim.

Buraimi, Oman: see BARAIMI.

Buramo, Br. Somaliland: see BORAMA.

Buran (bōōrän'), locality, E Br. Somaliland, near Ital. Somaliland border, in Ogo highland, 100 mi. ESE of Erigavo; water well; camels, sheep, goats. Formerly spelled Baran.

Burannoye (bōōrä'nŭyŭ), village (1926 pop. 2,145), S Chkalov oblast, Russian SFSR, 25 mi. SW of Sol-Iletsk; wheat, livestock. Formerly Burannaya.

Burano (bōōrä'nô), town (pop. 5,678), Venezia prov., Veneto, N Italy, on 4 islets in Lagoon of Venice, 5 mi. NNE of Venice; fishing center. Noted for its lace industry since 15th cent. Has school of lacemaking, church with paintings by Tiepolo.

Burao (bōōrou'), town (pop. 10,000), central Br. Somaliland, in Ogo highland, on road and 105 mi. E of Hargeisa; stock-raising center; sorghum, corn, beans. Hq. Burao dist.

Buras (byōō'rŭs), village (1940 pop. 1,183), Plaquemines parish, extreme SE La., 55 mi. SE of New Orleans, and on W bank (levee) of the Mississippi, in the delta; citrus-fruit growing and shipping center; fish and shellfish; boat yard. Hunting, fur trapping near by.

Burauen (bōōrä'wān), town (1939 pop. 5,288; 1948 municipality pop. 37,252), central Leyte, Philippines, 20 mi. SW of Tacloban, at foot of Mt. Majunag (4,426 ft.); sulphur-mining and agr. center (rice, coconuts, sugar cane).

Buraydah, Saudi Arabia: see BURAIDA.

Burayevo (bōōrī'ŭvŭ), village (1926 pop. 2,599), NW Bashkir Autonomous SSR, Russian SFSR, 29 mi. NNE of Birsk; grain, livestock. Peat deposits.

Buraymi, Oman: see BARAIMI.

Burbach, Saar: see MALSTATT-BURBACH.

Burbage (bûr'bĭj). **1** Town and parish (pop. 3,570), SW Leicester, England, just SE of Hinckley; hosiery, shoes. Has church dating from 14th cent. **2** Agr. village and parish (pop. 1,057), E Wiltshire, England, 6 mi. SSE of Marlborough. Has 15th-cent. church.

Burbáguena (bōōrvä'gānä), village (pop. 1,274), Teruel prov., E Spain, on Jiloca R. and 8 mi. SE of Daroca; wine, sugar beets, hemp, cereals, fruit.

Burbank. **1** City (pop. 78,577), Los Angeles co., S Calif., N industrial and residential suburb 10 mi. NNW of downtown Los Angeles, in San Fernando Valley; motion-picture studio, aircraft plant; large airport. Founded 1887, inc. 1911. **2** Village (pop. 393), Wayne co., N central Ohio, 13 mi. NNW of Wooster, in agr. area. **3** Town (pop. 268), Osage co., N Okla., 22 mi. W of Pawhuska, in oil-producing area.

Burbure (bürbür'), residential town (pop. 3,245), Pas-de-Calais dept., N France, 8 mi. W of Béthune, in agr. area.

Burchard, village (pop. 201), Pawnee co., SE Nebr., 10 mi. W of Pawnee City.

Burcht (bûrkht), town (pop. 6,203), Antwerp prov., N Belgium, on Scheldt R. and 3 mi. W of Antwerp; aluminum-processing center; shipbuilding; Portland cement, synthetic fertilizer. Formerly spelled Burght.

Burchun (bōōrchōōn'), Chinese *Puerhtsin* (bōōr'jĭn') or *Pu-erh-ching* (jĭng'), town, ⊙ Burchun co. (pop. 15,276), northernmost Sinkiang prov., China, on the Black Irtysh and 60 mi. W of Sharasume, and on road to Zaisan (USSR); livestock, agr. products. Coal mines near by.

Burdalyk (bōōrdŭlĭk'), town (1932 pop. estimate 1,780), SE Chardzhou oblast, Turkmen SSR, near the Amu Darya, 60 mi. SE of Chardzhou; cotton.

Burdeau (bürdō'), village (pop. 2,144), Alger dept., N central Algeria, on the Sersou Plateau, 25 mi. ENE of Tiaret; European wheat-growing colony.

Burdekin River (bûr'dŭkĭn), E Queensland, Australia, rises in hills W of Ingham, flows SE and N, past Home Hill, to Upstart Bay of Pacific Ocean; 440 mi. long. Receives Suttor and Bowen rivers.

Burden, city (pop. 541), Cowley co., SE Kansas, 33 mi. SE of Wichita, in grain, cattle area; oil.

Burdett (bûrdĕt'), village (pop. 110), SE Alta., near South Saskatchewan R., 40 mi. WSW of Medicine Hat; ranching.

Burdett, village (pop. 432), Schuyler co., W central N.Y., in Finger Lakes region, near Seneca L., 3 mi. NE of Watkins Glen.

Burdette (bûrdĕt'), town (pop. 122), Mississippi co., NE Ark., 7 mi. S of Blytheville.

Burdiehouse, S suburb of Edinburgh, Midlothian, Scotland. Lime kilns; fossils have been found in limestone here.

Burdigala, France: see BORDEAUX.

Burduguz (bōōrdōōgōōs'), town (1946 pop. over 500), S Irkutsk oblast, Russian SFSR, on Angara R. and c.15 mi. SE of Irkutsk; lumbering center.

Burdujeni (bōōrdōōzhān'), village (pop. 5,347), Suceava prov., N Rumania, 3 mi. NE of Suceava; food canning, bacon curing, tanning; stone and sand quarries.

Burdur (bōōrdōōr'), province (□ 2,876; 1950 pop. 136,359), SW Turkey; ⊙ Burdur. Bordered SE by Elmali Mts., SW by Mentese Mts.; oak forests yield valonia. Opium, hemp, anise, wheat, potatoes. Formerly sometimes spelled Buldur.

Burdur, town (1950 pop. 14,901), ⊙ Burdur prov., SW Turkey, on railroad near shore of L. Burdur, and 120 mi. W of Konya; valonia, carpets, attar of roses; wheat, barley, hemp. Sometimes spelled Buldur.

Burdur, Lake (□ 68), SW Turkey, just W of Burdur; 22 mi. long, 5 mi. wide; alt. 2,770 ft.

Burdwan (bōōrdvän'), district (□ 2,705; pop. 1,890,732), W West Bengal, India; ⊙ Burdwan. Bounded N by Ajay R., E by Bhagirathi R., W by Bihar, SW by Damodar R.; dist. will benefit from Damodar Valley irrigation and flood-control project. Lateritic soil W (rice, pulse, sugar cane, wheat, corn); alluvial soil E (rice, gram, potatoes, sugar cane, wheat, corn). Raniganj coal field (W), with coal-mining center at Raniganj, coal-trade center at Asansol (major Indian locomotive workshop; aluminum extraction). Iron ore deposits near Barul. Iron- and steelworks (Kulti, Burnpur, Hirapur); large rail workshops at Andal; Siva lingam temples at Burdwan and Kalna. Under 7th-cent. Gupta empire and 12th-cent. Sen kingdom; figured (16th cent.) in Akbar's struggles in Bengal. In 18th cent., raided by Mahrattas; ceded 1760 to English. Present dist. formed 1885.

Burdwan, city (pop. 62,910), ⊙ Burdwan dist., central West Bengal, India, near the Damodar, 60 mi. NW of Calcutta; road center; rice and oilseed milling, hosiery mfg.; general engineering works; trades in rice, rape and mustard, sugar cane, jute, gram, potatoes. Col., medical school. Near by are 108 Siva lingam temples. Cutlery and tool mfg. in SW suburb of Kanchannagar.

Bure (bōō'rā) or **Burye** (bōōr'yä), town, Gojjam prov., NW Ethiopia, 55 mi. NW of Debra Markos; trade center (coffee, hides, honey).

Bure, Pic de, France: see DÉVOLUY.

Burea (bü'rāō"), Swedish *Bureå,* village (pop. 1,710), Vasterbotten co., N Sweden, on Gulf of Bothnia, 12 mi. SE of Skelleftea; seaport, shipping wood and wood products; sawmilling, woodworking, wood-drying plants. Has noted modern church (1920).

Bureau (byōō'rō), county (□ 868; pop. 37,711), N Ill.; ⊙ Princeton. Bounded SE by Illinois R.; drained by Green and Spoon rivers and Bureau Creek; includes L. Depue, a bayou of Illinois R. Crossed by old Illinois and Mississippi Canal. Agr. (corn, oats, wheat, fruit, livestock, poultry). Bituminous-coal mines, sand and gravel pits. Mfg. (cheese and other dairy products, furniture, brick, tile, vinegar, sealing wax, shale products, feed, clothing, cigars). Formed 1837.

Bureau, village (pop. 480), Bureau co., N Ill., on Bureau Creek, near Illinois R., and 14 mi. W of La Salle, in agr. and bituminous-coal area. Also called Bureau Junction.

Bureau Creek or **Big Bureau Creek,** N Ill., rises in Lee co., flows SW and S to Tiskilwa, thence generally E, past Bureau, to Illinois R. 3 mi. SW of Depue; c.65 mi. long.

Bureau Junction, Ill.: see BUREAU, village.

Bureba, La (lä bōōrā'vä), fertile tableland, Burgos prov., N Spain; Briviesca is its agr. center.

Burei (bōōrā'), town (pop. 3,000), Ilubabor prov., SW Ethiopia, near confluence of Birbir and Baro rivers, on road and 31 mi. WNW of Gore; trade center (coffee, hides, beeswax).

Bureika, Aden: see LITTLE ADEN.

Burela, Cape (bōōrā'lä), Lugo prov., N Spain, headland on Bay of Biscay 12 mi. E of Vivero; 43°41'N 7°20'W.

Büren (bü'rŭn), town (pop. 5,820), in former Prussian prov. of Westphalia, NW Germany, after 1945 in North Rhine-Westphalia, 12 mi. SE of Lippstadt; mfg. of machinery. Cement works.

Buren (bü'rŭn). **1** Village on AMELAND isl., Friesland prov., N Netherlands. **2** Village (pop. 961), Gelderland prov., central Netherlands, 4 mi. WNW of Tiel; brick mfg.; dairying, cattle raising. Has 12th-cent. town hall.

Bure River, Norfolk, England, rises 8 mi. W of Fakenham, flows 50 mi. SE, past Aylsham, to Breydon Water at Yarmouth. Navigable below Aylsham. Lower course passes through The BROADS.

Burewala (bōōrā'välŭ), town (pop. 7,318), Multan dist., S Punjab, W Pakistan, 70 mi. E of Multan; road center; agr. market (wheat, cotton, rice); cotton ginning. Also called Mandi Burewala.

Bureya (bōōrā'ŭ, –rāä'), town (1939 pop. over 2,000), SE Amur oblast, Russian SFSR, on Trans-Siberian RR, on Bureya R. and 105 mi. ESE of Blagoveshchensk; sawmills. Junction for railroad to Raichikhinsk.

Bureya Range, SW Khabarovsk Territory, Russian SFSR, extends from headstreams of Selemdzha R. SSW to the Amur, continuing into Manchuria as Lesser Khingan Mountains; forms E watershed of

Bureya R. basin. Rises to 7,267 ft. in N section (here known as Dusse-Alin and Yam-Alin). Gold (Sofisk), tungsten and molybdenum (Umaltinski) in N, coal in W central slopes; iron and tin in S (here also known as Lesser Khingan Mts.).

Bureya River, in SW Khabarovsk Territory and SE Amur oblast, Russian SFSR, rises in N Bureya Range, flows 445 mi. SSW, through Bureya coal basin, past Chekunda (head of navigation) and Bureya, to Amur R. 100 mi. below Blagoveshchensk. Navigable for 300 mi.; up to 660 yds. wide in lower course. Gold, molybdenum, tungsten in upper reaches.

Burford, village (pop. estimate 700), S Ont., 9 mi. WSW of Brantford; dairying, mixed farming.

Burford, town and parish (pop. 907), W Oxfordshire, England, 17 mi. WNW of Oxford; agr. market. Has many 15th–16th-cent. houses, and was once important for its leather, woolens, and paper. The church dates from Norman times. The grammar school was founded in 16th cent.

Burfordville, town (pop. 88), Cape Girardeau co., SE Mo., on Whitewater R. and 8 mi. W of Jackson.

Burg (bo͝ork'). **1** or **Burg an der Wupper** (än dĕr vo͞o'pûr), village (pop. 1,494), in former Prussian Rhine Prov., W Germany, after 1945 in North Rhine-Westphalia, on the Wupper and 2.5 mi. W of Wermelskirchen. Castle (built in 12th cent.; destroyed 1648; rebuilt after 1890) was a residence of counts of Berg. **2** or **Burg bei Magdeburg** (bī mäk'dùbo͝ork), city (pop. 27,088), in former Prussian Saxony prov., central Germany, after 1945 in Saxony-Anhalt, on Ihle Canal and 13 mi. NE of Magdeburg; 52°16'N 11°51'E. Woolen-milling center; mfg. of shoes, leather goods, machinery, chemicals, lacquer, furniture; metalworking. Has 12th-cent. church. **3** or **Burg auf Fehmarn** (ouf fā'märn), town (pop. 6,370), in Schleswig-Holstein, NW Germany, Baltic port on Fehmarn isl., 10 mi. NE of Heiligenhafen (on mainland); mfg. of chemicals; flour milling, brewing. Harbor is at Burgstaaken, c.1 mi. S. Has ruined castle. **4** or **Burg in Dithmarschen** (ĭn dĭt'mär"shùn), village (pop. 5,295), in Schleswig-Holstein, NW Germany, near Kiel Canal (rail bridge just N), 12 mi. NW of Itzehoe; textile mfg., metalworking. Resort.

Burg, Netherlands: see TEXEL.

Burg, El (ĕl bo͝org'), or **Al-Burj** (ĕl bo͝orj'), village (pop. 9,056), Gharbiya prov., Lower Egypt, on sandbank bet. Mediterranean Sea and L. Burullus, 7 mi. WNW of Baltim; fisheries.

Burgan or **Burghan** (bo͝orgăn'), major oil field in S Kuwait, linked by pipe line with AHMADI tank farm (10 mi. NE) and loading terminal of MENA AL AHMADI (12 mi. ENE). First test well drilled in 1937; large-scale production begun in 1946.

Burg an der Wupper, Germany: see BURG, Rhine Prov.

Bur Gao (bo͞or' gou'), village (pop. 237), in the Benadir, S Ital. Somaliland, fishing port on Indian Ocean, 75 mi. SW of Kismayu. Formerly in JUBALAND and called Port Durnford.

Burgas (bo͝orgäs'), city (pop. 43,684), ⊙ Burgas dist. (formed 1949), E Bulgaria, port (grain exports) and rail terminus on Gulf of Burgas of Black Sea, 215 mi. E of Sofia; 42°29'N 27°29'E. Commercial and mfg. center; fish market; produces agr. machinery, metalware, cotton textiles, pencils, soap; processes foodstuffs (flour, vegetable oil, sugar, chocolate); liquor distilling, sardine canning. Technical schools. Summer resort (hot mineral springs). Copper mining in Meden-rudnik (pop. 772), SE; formerly called Kara-bair. Atanasovo L. (N) has saltworks. Founded in 18th cent. on site of 14th-cent. fortified town of Pirgos. Was ⊙ former Burgas oblast (1934–47).

Burgas, Gulf of, westernmost inlet of Black Sea, in E Bulgaria; 6 mi. wide, 8 mi. long, 33–40 ft. deep. Burgas is on W shore; Pomoriye (N) and Sozopol (S) flank its entrance. Along shore lie salt lakes of Pomoriye, Atanasovo, Burgas, Mandra.

Burgas Lake, Bulgaria: see DOLNO YEZEROVO.

Burgau (bo͞or'gou), village (pop. 1,219), Styria, SE Austria, near Lafnitz R., 30 mi. E of Graz; wheat, cattle, vineyards.

Burgau, town (pop. 3,628), Swabia, W Bavaria, Germany, on the Mindel and 6 mi. ESE of Günzburg; mfg. (textiles, metal and leather products). Chartered c.1300; Austrian possession until 1805.

Burg auf Fehmarn, Germany: see BURG, Schleswig-Holstein.

Burgaw (bûr'gô), town (pop. 1,613), ⊙ Pender co., SE N.C., 22 mi. N of Wilmington, in strawberry-growing area; mfg. (of wooden containers).

Burgaya, El (ĕl bo͝orgä'yù), or **Al-Burjayah** (ĕl bo͝orjä'yù), village (pop. 6,796), Minya prov., Upper Egypt, on W bank of the Nile, on railroad, and 10 mi. SSE of Samalut; cotton, cereals, sugar cane.

Burgaz Island (bo͝orgäz') (pop. 2,823, including Kinali), one of Princes Isls., in Sea of Marmara, NW Turkey, 10 mi. SE of Istanbul, of which it is part, included in Adalar dist.; 1 mi. long.

Burg bei Magdeburg, Germany: see BURG, Saxony.

Burgbernheim (bo͝ork"bĕrn'hīm), village (pop. 2,641), Middle Franconia, W Bavaria, Germany, 6 mi. SW of Windsheim; mfg. of precision instruments, brewing, flour milling. Limestone quarries in area.

Burgbrohl (bo͝ork'brōl"), village (commune pop., including Bad Tönnisstein, 1,229), in former Prussian Rhine Prov., W Germany, after 1945 in Rhineland-Palatinate, in the Eifel, 6 mi. WNW of Andernach. E (1 mi.) is Bad Tönnisstein, with mineral springs.

Burgdorf (bo͝ork'dôrf"), town (pop. 10,192), in former Prussian prov. of Hanover, NW Germany, after 1945 in Lower Saxony, 17 mi. NW of Hanover; mfg. of costume jewelry, furniture; food processing (flour products, canned goods, sugar, beer), weaving, sawmilling.

Burgdorf, Fr. *Berthoud* (bĕrto͞o'), town (1950 pop. 11,524), Bern canton, NW Switzerland, on Emme R. and 11 mi. NE of Bern. Textiles (linen, woolen, cotton), metal products. Gothic church. It has a medieval castle in which Pestalozzi held his 1st school (1799–1804).

Bürgel (bür'gùl). **1** SE suburb (pop. 6,051) of Offenbach, S Hesse, W Germany, 2.5 mi. SE of city center. **2** Town (pop. 2,685), Thuringia, central Germany, 8 mi. E of Jena; pottery mfg., woodworking. Near by are remains of 12th-cent. Talbürgel Benedictine monastery.

Burg el Arab (bo͝org' ĕl ä'räb) or **Burj al-'Arab** (bo͝orj' ĕl), village (1937 pop. 1,190), Western Desert prov., Egypt, on coastal railroad and 30 mi. SW of Alexandria.

Burgenland (bo͝or'gùnlänt), autonomous province [Ger. *Bundesland*] (□ 1,526; 1951 pop. 275,911), E Austria, a narrow, hilly area bordering Hungary (E), Lower Austria and Styria (W); indented (NE) by Neusiedler L.; ⊙ Eisenstadt. Leitha Mts. (NW) have limestone quarries. Agr. (grain, sugar beets), livestock raising, extensive wine making and fruitgrowing (cherries, peaches). Antimony mined near Stadtschlaining, lignite near Tauchen. Some sugar refining and textile mfg. Territory was transferred from Hungary by treaties of Saint-Germain (1919) and Trianon (1920). SOPRON, its leading town, was returned to Hungary in 1921 after a plebiscite. Placed (1945) in Soviet occupation zone.

Bürgenstock (bür'gùnshtôk"), mountain (2,926 ft.) and resort area (6 mi. long, 1–2 mi. wide), Nidwalden half-canton, central Switzerland, on L. of Lucerne, c.5 mi. SSE of Lucerne.

Burgeo (bûr'gēō), coast village (pop. 750), SW N.F., 70 mi. E of Port aux Basques; 47°37'N 57°39'W; fishing port, with fish-filleting, freezing, cold-storage plants. Just SE are Burgeo Isls.

Burgeo Islands, group of 12 islets just off S N.F., 2 mi. SE of Burgeo. Principal isl. is Boar Isl., 2 mi. E of Burgeo; lighthouse (47°47'N 57° 36'W).

Burgess (bûr'jĭs), town (pop. 123), Barton co., SW Mo., 18 mi. W of Lamar.

Burgess Hill, urban district (1931 pop. 2,114; 1951 census 8,524), central Sussex, England, 9 mi. N of Brighton; agr. market, with tile works.

Burgettstown (bûr'jĭts-), borough (pop. 2,379), Washington co., SW Pa., 22 mi. WSW of Pittsburgh; bituminous coal; metals, beverages, machine shops; agr. Laid out 1795, inc. 1881.

Burgfelden, France: see BOURGFELDEN.

Burgh, Netherlands: see HAAMSTEDE.

Burghan, Kuwait: see BURGAN.

Burghausen (bo͝ork"hou'zùn), town (pop. 9,479), Upper Bavaria, Germany, on the Salzach and 22 mi. NNE of Traunstein, on Austrian border; rail terminus; chemical center; mfg. of carbide, chlorinated hydrocarbons, chlorine, fertilizer, gelatin, synthetic fiber; brewing. Has Gothic chapel; 13th–14th-cent. castle; 14th-cent. church and town hall. Chartered 1309.

Burgh-by-Sands (brŭf'-bī-săndz'), village and parish (pop. 741), NW Cumberland, England, 5 mi. WNW of Carlisle; dairy farming. Here died Edward I while on his way to crush the rebellion of Robert Bruce. A military post in Roman times.

Burgh Castle (bûrg), agr. village and parish (pop. 595), NE Suffolk, England, on Breydon Water and 3 mi. SW of Great Yarmouth. Site of ruins of Roman fortress.

Burghead (bûrg-hĕd'), burgh (1931 pop. 1,255; 1951 census 1,367), N Moray, Scotland, on Burghead Bay of Moray Firth, 8 mi. NW of Elgin; fishing port and seaside resort, on a promontory.

Burghersdorp (bûr'gùrsdôrp), town (pop. 5,428), E Cape Prov., U. of So. Afr., on small tributary of Orange R. and 30 mi. SW of Aliwal North; rail junction; agr. center (stock, wheat, dairying, wool).

Burghfield (bûr'fēld), agr. village and parish (pop. 1,283), S central Berkshire, England, 4 mi. SW of Reading.

Burghill, town and parish (pop. 1,553), central Hereford, England, 4 mi. NW of Hereford; agr. market. Has 13th-cent. church, co. mental hosp.

Burgh-le-Marsh (bûr'ù-lù-märsh'), town and parish (pop. 916), Parts of Lindsey, E Lincolnshire, England, 4 mi. W of Skegness; agr. market. Has 15th-cent. church.

Burght, Belgium: see BURCHT.

Burgi, Ethiopia: see BURJI.

Burgin (bûr'gĭn), town (pop. 777), Mercer co., central Ky., 26 mi. SW of Lexington, in Bluegrass region; whisky, flour, feed. Dix R. Dam is near by.

Burg in Dithmarschen, Germany: see BURG, Schleswig-Holstein.

Burgio (bo͞or'jô), village (pop. 5,569), Agrigento prov., SW Sicily, 13 mi. NE of Sciacca, in olive- and almond-growing region; rail terminus; foundry. Has anc. castle.

Burgkirchen (bo͝ork'kĭrkhùn), town (pop. 2,595), W Upper Austria, 5 mi. SE of Braunau; potatoes, rye, hogs.

Burgkunstadt (bo͝ork'ko͞on'shtät), town (pop. 3,611), Upper Franconia, N Bavaria, Germany, on the Main and 8 mi. E of Lichtenfels; leather- and metalworking, tanning, basket weaving. Has 17th-cent. town hall. Chartered c.1095.

Bürglen (bür'glùn), industrial town (pop. 2,527), Uri canton, central Switzerland, near Altdorf; alleged birthplace of William Tell. Has 16th-cent. chapel and mus.

Burglengenfeld (bo͝ork'lĕng'ùnfĕlt"), town (pop. 6,692), Upper Palatinate, E central Bavaria, Germany, on the Nab and 13 mi. N of Regensburg; mfg. of cement, precision instruments; brewing. Has 16th-cent. town hall, 18th-cent. church. Chartered 1442.

Burgo (bo͞or'gō), town (pop. 2,814), Málaga prov., S Spain, at NE slopes of the Sierra de Ronda, 29 mi. W of Málaga; cereals, almonds, esparto, olives, grapes, timber, livestock. Mfg. of olive oil and flour. Has mineral springs.

Burgo de Osma, El (ĕl bo͞or'gō dhā ōz'mä), town (pop. 3,349), Soria prov., N central Spain, in Old Castile, on affluent of the Duero, and 34 mi. WSW of Soria. Bishopric (since 6th cent.), with fine 13th-cent. cathedral. Also agr. center (cereals, sugar beets, pepper, fruit, truck, livestock). Flour milling; plaster works, limekilns. The anc. city of Osma is 1 mi. W.

Burgohondo (bo͞orgō-ōn'dō), town (pop. 1,586), Ávila prov., central Spain, near Alberche R., at N foot of the Sierra de Gredos, 19 mi. SSW of Ávila, in fertile region (cereals, vegetables, grapes, fruit). Livestock market.

Burgoon (bûrgo͞on'), village (pop. 223), Sandusky co., N Ohio, 9 mi. SW of Fremont, in agr. area.

Burgörner (bo͝orgûr'nùr), village (pop. 4,602), in former Prussian Saxony prov., central Germany, after 1945 in Saxony-Anhalt, at E foot of the lower Harz, on the Wipper, just S of Hettstedt; copper-slate mining and smelting.

Burgos (bo͞or'gōs), town (pop. 636), Tamaulipas, NE Mexico, 50 mi. ENE of Linares; cereals, sugar, cattle.

Burgos, province (□ 5,535; pop. 378,580), N Spain, in Old Castile; ⊙ Burgos. Borders N on Santander prov., NE on Vizcaya prov. and Álava prov. (with Condado de TREVIÑO enclave), E on Logroño and Soria provs., S on Segovia prov., W on Valladolid and Palencia provs. Outliers of the monotonous great central plateau (Meseta) extend northward to the Cantabrian Mts. Average alt. c.3,800 ft. The Ebro and Douro (Duero) rivers (both unnavigable) cross the prov., watering its N and S sections, respectively. Along those streams and its affluents are fertile plains (La Lora, La Bureba, etc.). The climate is of the continental type (cold winters, hot summers). Agr. is little developed in the sparsely populated, largely forested region. Among chief crops are cereals, grapes, chick-peas, potatoes, sugar beets, and fruit. Extensive sheep (merino) and goat grazing. Stock raising ranks with forest industry (timber, naval stores, paper, cellulose) as mainstay. Wool and flour are exported. Industries, almost entirely confined to processing (cheese, wine, meat products, etc.), are of secondary importance. Little-exploited mineral resources include iron, copper, manganese, lead, mica, gypsum, bituminous coal, lignite, salt, sodium sulphate, marble; medicinal springs. The rivers abound in fish. Chief center is Burgos. Other towns with some activity are: Miranda de Ebro, Lerma, Aranda de Duero. Originally a county, Burgos is the historic heartland of Castile. It became a prov. in 1833. The prov. was taken by the Nationalist forces early in the Sp. civil war (1936–39).

Burgos, city (pop. 51,177), ⊙ Burgos prov., N Spain, in Old Castile, on both banks of Arlanzón R. (affluent of the Douro or Duero), on interior plateau, and 80 mi. SW of Bilbao, 130 mi. N of Madrid; 42°20'N 3°42'W. One of the anc. capitals of Castile, situated in a fertile region (cereals, chick-peas, grapes, livestock) at alt. of c.2,800 ft., its older section nestling on San Miguel hill, which is topped by a ruined castle (once residence of counts of Castile). Has a rigorous climate, with long, cold winters and dry, hot summers. A communications and trading center of considerable importance, its industries include liquor distilling, flour and paper milling; mfg. of woolen and leather goods, cellulose, fertilizers, chocolate; iron foundries. Burgos is chiefly known, however, for its remarkable architecture and great historic tradition. Most outstanding structure is the Gothic cathedral, begun 1221 and among the finest in Europe; its lofty, 15th-cent. filigree spires dominate the city, though the 16th-cent. octagonal dome matches them in beauty; the ornate interior treasures many relics (burial place of the Cid). The cathedral is adjoined by the archbishop's palace. Other religious edifices include the churches of San Nicolás, San Estebán, and

Santa Agueda or Santa Gadea. Just as imposing are the civic bldgs., fortifications, and manorial palaces (Casa del Cordón, Casa de Miranda). The 12th-cent. Hospital del Rey, reconstructed along plateresque lines in 16th cent., was built as stopping place for pilgrims to Santiago or Santiago de Compostela. An archaeological mus. is housed in the Arco de Santa María, a 16th-cent. gateway which is also a military tower and municipal palace. Center of the city's life is the Plaza Mayor, surrounded by arcades. Beautiful promenades lead to the outskirts, the Charterhouse of Miraflores, San Pedro de Cardeña convent (former burial place of the Cid and Jimena), and the Huelgas monastery with graves of Alfonso VIII and his English wife. Burgos is believed to have been founded in 884. Originally dependent on the kings of Asturias, it became ⊙ united kingdoms of Leon and Castile until replaced by Toledo (1087), when it gradually lost some of its importance. As the birthplace of the Cid, the city takes great pride in his exploits, which personify the Sp. ideal of honor and valiancy. During the Sp. civil war (1936–39), Burgos was made by Franco the provisional ⊙ Spain.

Burgstaaken, Germany: see BURG, Schleswig-Holstein.

Bürgstadt (bürk'shtät″), village (pop. 2,606), Lower Franconia, W Bavaria, Germany, on the Main (canalized) and 1 mi. NNE of Miltenberg; woodworking, flour and lumber milling. Just W is 12th–13th-cent. Romanesque chapel. Sandstone quarries in area.

Burgstädt (bo͝ork'shtĕt″), town (pop. 19,453), Saxony, E central Germany, 8 mi. NW of Chemnitz; hosiery- and glove-knitting center; mfg. of textile machinery, sewing machines, needles. One of earliest Saxon textile-industry centers (cotton milling introduced 1750).

Burgstall (bo͝ork'shtäl), village (pop. 932), N Württemberg, Germany, after 1945 in Württemberg-Baden, 3 mi. SW of Backnang; furniture mfg.

Burg Stargard (bo͝ork' shtär'gärt), town (pop. 5,561), Mecklenburg, N Germany, 5 mi. SE of Neubrandenburg; sawmilling, furniture mfg.; agr. market (grain, sugar beets, potatoes, stock). Has remains of old fortification. Founded 1259 as fortified outpost by margraves of Brandenburg. Went to Mecklenburg in 1292. In Thirty Years War, Tilly's hq. (1631) during operations against Neubrandenburg. Was ⊙ lordship of Stargard until 1701, when it passed to newly created line of Mecklenburg-Strelitz. Formerly called Stargard, or Stargard in Mecklenburg.

Burgsteinfurt (bo͝ork'shtīn'fo͝ort″), town (pop. 10,729), in former Prussian prov. of Westphalia, NW Germany, after 1945 in North Rhine-Westphalia, 10 mi. SW of Rheine; rail junction; cotton spinning.

Burgsvik (bŭr'yüsvēk″), village (pop. 300), Gotland co., SE Sweden, on SW coast of Gotland isl., on small bay of the Baltic, 40 mi. S of Visby; seaside resort; grain, potatoes, sugar beets. Limestone quarries.

Burguillos (bo͝orgē'lyōs), town (pop. 1,149), Seville prov., SW Spain, 13 mi. N of Seville; cereals, livestock; processing of palm fibers.

Burguillos del Cerro (dhĕl sĕ'rō), town (pop. 5,492), Badajoz prov., W Spain, 10 mi. ENE of Jerez de los Caballeros; agr. center (chick-peas, wheat, barley, tubers, olives, grapes, stock). Iron mining, marble quarrying; mfg. of bottle corks, pottery.

Burgundy (bûr'gündē), Fr. *Bourgogne* (bo͝orgô'nyü), region and former prov. of E central and E France; historical ⊙ DIJON. Name applied to 2 successive kingdoms and to a duchy, all of which embraced larger territories than area of 17th–18th-cent. Burgundy prov. After 1790 it was administratively divided into Ain, Saône-et-Loire, and Côte-d'Or depts., and part of Yonne dept. Bounded by Loire R. (SW), Monts du Morvan (W), Plateau of Langres (NNE), the Jura (E), and Rhone R. above Lyons (S). Traversed N–S by Saône R. Of its many fertile lands, the winegrowing areas of the CÔTE D'OR, MÂCONNAIS, and Chablis are famous. Burgundy is traditionally a crossroad of transportation routes converging upon Dijon. The Burgundy Canal connects the Saône with the Yonne. Chief industrial dist. centered on Le CREUSOT. Other towns are Auxerre, Chalon-sur-Saône, Mâcon, Autun, and Bourg. Conquered by Julius Caesar during Gallic Wars, it was settled (5th cent.) by Burgundians, a Germanic tribe, who established First Kingdom of Burgundy. Partitioned throughout Merovingian and Carolingian era, it was reunited (933) in Second Kingdom of Burgundy (or Kingdom of Arles), comprising Cisjurane Burgundy (or Provence) (S) and Transjurane Burgundy (N). At same time a smaller duchy of Burgundy was created by Emperor Charles II and absorbed in Holy Roman Empire (1034). The duchy entered its golden age under Philip the Bold, and came to include most of present Netherlands, Belgium, and N, E, and E central France. During 15th cent. Burgundy was a leading commercial and industrial power with a brilliant court at Dijon. However, in 1477 Charles the Bold was defeated and killed by the Swiss at Nancy. The French part of duchy was then incorporated into French crownland by Louis XI, while other Burgundian possessions went to house of Hapsburg.

Burgundy, Free County of, France: see FRANCHE-COMTÉ.

Burgundy Canal, Fr. *Canal de Bourgogne* (känäl' dü bo͝orgô'nyü), in Côte-d'Or and Yonne depts., E central France. Joins the Saône at Saint-Jean-de-Losne to the Yonne at Laroche-Saint-Cydroine; 150 mi. long. Following valley of Ouche R., it passes by Dijon; crosses drainage divide in a tunnel (2 mi. long) near Pouilly-en-Auxois; touches Montbard, Tonnerre, and Saint-Florentin in valley of Brenne and Armançon rivers; and enters navigable Yonne R. above Joigny, thus establishing connection (by means of 189 locks) bet. Saône-Rhone valleys and Paris Basin. Carries chiefly construction materials.

Burgundy Gate, France: see BELFORT GAP.

Burha, India: see BALAGHAT, town.

Burhabalang River (bo͝orhŭbäläng'), tortuous stream in NE Orissa, India, rises in hills in central Mayurbhanj dist., flows c.145 mi. N and SSE, past Baripada and Balasore, to Bay of Bengal 8 mi. E of Balasore.

Burhanilkantha, Nepal: see KATMANDU.

Burhaniye (bo͝orhä'nĭyĕ″), town (pop. 6,802), Balikesir prov., NW Turkey, near Gulf of Edremit, 7 mi. SSW of Edremit; olive-growing center, cereals. Formerly Kemer.

Burhanpur (bo͝orhän'po͝or), town (pop. 53,987), Nimar dist., W Madhya Pradesh, India, on Tapti R. and 185 mi. W of Nagpur; cotton-textile and cotton-trade center; shellac mfg., oilseed milling. Founded c.1400; was Deccan hq. of Mogul empire, 1600–35; developed extensive trade (declined during 18th cent.) in its fine muslins and in gold and silver brocade and lace. Its famous handicraft gold- and silver-wire industry still continues on small scale. Has ruins of 16th-cent. palace and mosque. Strategic hill fortress of Asirgarh, 12 mi. N, dates from 13th cent.; was scene of several sieges by English, Mahratta, and Mogul forces during late-18th and early-19th cent.

Burhave, Germany: see BUTJADINGEN.

Burhi Dihing River (bo͝or'hē dēhĭng'), NE Assam, India, rises in Patkai Range on Burma border, flows 95 mi. W, through extensive tea gardens, past Ledo and Margherita, to Brahmaputra R. 20 mi. SW of Dibrugarh.

Burhi Gandak River (gŭn'dŭk), left affluent of the Ganges, in Bihar, India, formed by several headstreams, joining 11 mi. SE of Motihari; flows c.200 mi. SE, past Muzaffarpur, Samastipur, and Khagaria, to the Ganges 10 mi. ESE of Monghyr.

Burhi Ganga River, E Pakistan: see DHALESWARI RIVER.

Burhwal, India: see RAMNAGAR, Uttar Pradesh.

Buri (bo͝orē'), city (pop. 1,525), S São Paulo, Brazil, on railroad and 38 mi. WSW of Itapetininga; corn meal, beverages, dairy products, tiles and bricks. Formerly Bury.

Burial Island, islet in Irish Sea off Burr Point, Co. Down, Northern Ireland.

Buriasan (bo͝orēäsän'), village (1939 pop. 190), Lanao prov., NW Mindanao, 40 mi. WSW of Dansalan; site of agr. resettlement project.

Burias Island (bo͝or'yäs) (□ 164; 1939 pop. 4,573), Masbate prov., Philippines, 10 mi. NW of Masbate isl., separated from SE Luzon by Burias Pass; 42 mi. long, ½–10 mi. wide; generally low. Rice and coconut growing. Chief center is San Pascual (sän päskwäl') (1939 pop. 1,043; 1948 municipality pop. 6,960) on N coast.

Burias Pass, strait in the Philippines, bet. Burias Isl. and SE coast of Luzon, merges NW with Ragay Gulf, SE with Ticao Pass and Masbate Pass; c.40 mi. long, 8–20 mi. wide.

Buriat-Mongol, USSR: see BURYAT-MONGOL.

Buribai or **Buribay** (bo͝orĭbī'), town (1948 pop. over 2,000), SE Bashkir Autonomous SSR, Russian SFSR, in the S Urals, on Tanalyk R. and 45 mi. S of Baimak; mining center (bauxite, copper, and gold deposits). Until 1938, Buryubai.

Burica Peninsula (bo͝orē'kä), extends S into Pacific Ocean on Costa Rica–Panama border; 15 mi. long, 3–5 mi. wide. Terminates in Burica Point (8°2′N 82°54′W), off which lies small Burica Isl.

Burie (bürē'), village (pop. 522), Charente-Maritime dept., W France, 7 mi. NW of Cognac; cognac distilling, dairying.

Burin (byo͝or'ĭn, bûr'ĭn), village (pop. 611), S N.F., on inlet of Placentia Bay, on E coast of Burin Peninsula, 28 mi. E of Grand Bank; fishing port, with cold-storage plants, lobster and salmon canneries.

Burino (bo͞o'rĭnü), village (1926 pop. 661), NE Chelyabinsk oblast, Russian SFSR, 32 mi. S of Kamensk-Uralski, near railroad; grain, livestock. Peat digging near by (S).

Burin Peninsula (85 mi. long, 20 mi. wide), S N.F., bet. Fortune Bay and Placentia Bay. Mainly hilly, rising to 995 ft. Chief towns on peninsula are Grand Bank, Burin, Fortune. Lumbering.

Buriram (bo͝orē'rŭm), town (1947 pop. 6,581); ⊙ Buriram prov. (□ 3,708; 1947 pop. 339,480), E Thailand, in Korat Plateau, on railroad and 120 mi. WSW of Ubon; rice, corn. Pop. is largely Cambodian. Sometimes spelled Buriramya.

Buriti (bo͝orētē'), city (pop. 1,396), NE Maranhão, Brazil, near left bank of Parnaíba R. (Piauí border), 80 mi. N of Teresina; ships sugar, cotton, tobacco, babassu nuts. Formerly spelled Burity.

Buriti Alegre (ālā'grĭ), city (pop. 2,434), S Goiás, central Brazil, 60 mi. NW of Uberlândia (Minas Gerais); tobacco, corn, sugar, castor beans. Diamond deposits in area. Formerly spelled Burity Alegre.

Buriti Bravo (brä'vo͞o), city (pop. 1,026), E Maranhão, Brazil, on Itapecuru R. (navigable) and 65 mi. SW of Caxias; babassu nuts, cotton. Formerly spelled Burity Bravo.

Buriti dos Lopes (do͞os lō'pĭs), city (pop. 1,075), N Piauí, Brazil, near right bank of Parnaíba R. (Maranhão border), 18 mi. SSW of Parnaíba; tobacco, rice, cotton, carnauba wax. Formerly spelled Burity dos Lopes.

Buritizeiro, Brazil: see PIRAPORA.

Buriya (bo͝or'yŭ), town (pop. 3,857), Ambala dist., E Punjab, India, on Western Jumna Canal and 3 mi. E of Jagadhri; wheat, rice, sugar cane. Sometimes spelled Buria.

Burj, Al-, Egypt: see BURG, EL.

Burj al-'Arab, Egypt: see BURG EL ARAB.

Burjasot (bo͝orhäsōt'), NW suburb (pop. 11,235) of Valencia, Valencia prov., E Spain; mfg. (silk textiles, ceramics, burlap, auto accessories, celluloid articles, candy, brandy). Wine and truck produce in area. Has some 16th-cent. underground granaries in Moorish style.

Burji (bo͝or'jē), Ital. *Burgi*, town (pop. 3,000), Sidamo-Borana, S Ethiopia, 34 mi. SE of Gardula, in mts. S of L. Chamo; 5°23′N 37°55′N; trade center.

Burji La (bo͝orjē' lä'), pass (alt. 16,830 ft.) in Deosai Mts., W central Kashmir, 9 mi. SW of Skardu.

Burkburnett (bûrkbûrnĕt'), city (pop. 4,555), Wichita co., N Texas, near Red R. (Okla. line), 11 mi. N of Wichita Falls; center of oil field; gasoline plants, oil refinery. Ships cotton, cattle, wheat. Settled 1907, inc. 1913. Oil discovery (1918) brought a wild, rich, but temporary boom.

Burke. **1** County (□ 832; pop. 23,458), E Ga.; ⊙ Waynesboro. Bounded NE by S.C. line, formed here by Savannah R.; drained by Brier Creek. Coastal plain cotton region; also produces truck, melons, and pecans. Formed 1777. **2** County (□ 506; pop. 45,518), W central N.C.; ⊙ Morganton. Piedmont region; part of Pisgah Natl. Forest in N; drained by Catawba R. (forms L. James, Rhodhiss L.; hydroelectric plants). Dairying, poultry raising, farming (sweet potatoes, hay, corn, wheat); timber. Mfg. of textiles, furniture; lumber mills. Formed 1777. **3** County (□ 1,121; pop. 6,621), NW N.Dak.; ⊙ Bowbells; rich agr. area. Stock raising, mining; dairy produce, wheat, grain, vegetables. Formed 1910.

Burke. **1** Village (pop. 1,000), Shoshone co., N Idaho, near Mont. line, 7 mi. NE of Wallace. Lead, zinc, silver, copper mines. **2** Village (pop. 316), Franklin co., NE N.Y., 8 mi. NE of Malone, near Que. line, in dairying area. **3** City (pop. 602), ⊙ Gregory co., S S.Dak., 100 mi. SE of Pierre; trade center for farming and ranching region; livestock; dairy products, grain. **4** Town (pop. 1,042), Caledonia co., NE Vt., on Passumpsic R. and 12 mi. N of St. Johnsbury. Includes villages of West Burke (pop. 414) and East Burke, site of historical mus. Burke Mtn. (3,267 ft.) is in Darling State Forest here.

Burkes Garden, village (1940 pop. 677), Tazewell co., SW Va., 13 mi. SW of Bluefield, in Burkes Garden, a fertile mtn. basin (c.8 mi. long, 4.5 mi. wide; alt. c.3,000 ft.) of the Alleghenies. Livestock raising.

Burkesville, city (pop. 1,278), ⊙ Cumberland co., S Ky., in Cumberland foothills, on Cumberland R. and 34 mi. ESE of Glasgow; summer resort in agr. area (livestock, poultry, fruit, corn, hay, burley tobacco); makes wood products. One of earliest U.S. oil wells, accidentally tapped in 1829, was near by. Dale Hollow Reservoir is S. Inc. as town 1810, as city 1926.

Burket (bûr'kĭt), town (pop. 217), Kosciusko co., N Ind., c.40 mi. SSE of South Bend, in agr. area.

Burketown, village and port, N Queensland, Australia, on Albert R., 30 mi. from its mouth on Gulf of Carpentaria, and 215 mi. NNW of Cloncurry; exports meat, wool.

Burkett, Mount (8,001 ft.), on Alaska-B.C. border, in Coast Range, 40 mi. NE of Petersburg; 57°13′N 132°15′W.

Burkettsville (bûr'kĭtsvĭl), village (pop. 211), on Mercer-Darke co. line, W Ohio, 17 mi. N of Greenville; tile factory.

Burkeville, town (pop. 695), Nottoway co., central Va., c.45 mi. W of Petersburg; rail junction; veneer; granite.

Burkhalinski or **Burkhalinskiy** (bo͝orkhŭlyēn'skē), town (1940 pop. over 500), SE Yakut Autonomous SSR, Russian SFSR, 40 mi. N of Allakh-Yun; gold mining.

Burkhardtsdorf (bo͝ork'härtsdôrf″), village (pop. 5,853), Saxony, E central Germany, at N foot of the Erzgebirge, 7 mi. S of Chemnitz; hosiery knitting.

Burkittsville (bûr'kĭtsvĭl), town (pop. 190), Frederick co., W Md., at E base of South Mtn. and 12 mi. W of Frederick. Near by are a memorial (erected

1896) to Civil War correspondents and field of Civil War battle of South Mtn. (Sept. 14, 1862).

Burk's Falls or **Burks Falls,** village (pop. 710), SE central Ont., 45 mi. S of North Bay; lumbering.

Burla (bŏŏrlä'), village (1939 pop. over 500), W Altai Territory, Russian SFSR, on Burla R., on railroad and 25 mi. NNW of Slavgorod, in agr. area.

Burladingen (bŏŏr"lä'dĭng-ŭn), village (pop. 2,716), Hohenzollern, S Germany, after 1945 in Württemberg-Hohenzollern, in Swabian Jura, 8 mi. SE of Hechingen; knitwear mfg.

Burla River (bŏŏrlä'), W Altai Territory, Russian SFSR, rises at border, near Ob R.; flows c.175 mi. SW, past Khabary and Burla, to Topolnoye L. of Kulunda Steppe.

Burlatskoye, Russian SFSR: see SOTNIKOVSKOYE.

Burleigh (bûr'lē), county (□ 1,648; pop. 25,673), central N.Dak.; ⊙ Bismarck, the state capital. Agr. area drained by Apple Creek and bounded W by Missouri R. Coal mines; ships agr. products. Formed 1873.

Burleson (bûr'lŭsŭn), county (□ 679; pop. 13,000), S central Texas; ⊙ Caldwell. Bounded NE and E by Brazos R., S by Yegua Creek. Diversified agr. (cotton, corn, grain sorghums, peanuts, pecans), dairying, livestock (cattle, poultry, hogs, sheep, goats). Farm products processed at Caldwell, Somerville. Formed 1846.

Burleson, town (pop. 791), Johnson co., N central Texas, 15 mi. S of Fort Worth; trade point in cotton, corn, grain area.

Burley, town and parish (pop. 1,566), SW Hampshire, England, 7 mi. NE of Christchurch.

Burley, city (pop. 5,924), ⊙ Cassia co., S Idaho, on Snake R. and 35 mi. E of Twin Falls; alt. 4,240 ft. Shipping point for irrigated agr., dairy area; sugar-beet, alfalfa-meal, potato-flour mills. Hq. Minidoka Natl. Forest. Founded 1905, inc. 1906.

Burley-in-Wharfedale, former urban district (1931 pop. 3,961), West Riding, W central Yorkshire, England, on Wharfe R. and 8 mi. N of Bradford; woolen milling. Near by is early-17th-cent. mansion of Weston Hall. Inc. 1937 in Ilkley.

Burli (bŏŏrlyē'). **1** Village (1948 pop. over 500), NW Kustanai oblast, Kazakh SSR, near railroad, 35 mi. SSE of Troitsk; wheat, cattle. **2** Village (1948 pop. over 500), N West Kazakhstan oblast, Kazakh SSR, on Ural R. and 60 mi. NE of Uralsk; wheat, cattle.

Burlingame (bûr'lĭng-gām). **1** Residential city (pop. 19,886), San Mateo co., W Calif., suburb 15 mi. S of San Francisco, on the bay; flower growing. Founded 1868, inc. 1908. **2** City (pop. 1,065), Osage co., E Kansas, 22 mi. SSW of Topeka; trading and shipping point in livestock, poultry, and grain region. Coal mines near by. Founded 1855, inc. 1861.

Burlington, town (pop. 3,815), S Ont., on L. Ontario, 5 mi. N of Hamilton; fruitgrowing center, with fruit and vegetable canneries, chemical works, lumber mills; resort.

Burlington, county (□ 819; pop. 135,910), W and central N.J., bounded NW by Delaware R.; ⊙ Mt. Holly. Mfg. (textiles, shoes, clothing; metal, leather, and concrete products; canned goods, rope, bricks, dyes); agr. (truck, fruit, grain, dairy products). E and SE parts of co. are in pine barrens region, producing timber, cranberries, and huckleberries; several state forests here. Drained by Rancocas Creek and Bass, Wading, and Batsto rivers. Formed 1681.

Burlington. 1 Town (pop. 2,247), ⊙ Kit Carson co., E Colo., c.150 mi. ESE of Denver, near Kansas line; alt. 4,250 ft. Grain-shipping point. Inc. 1888. **2** Town (pop. 1,846), Hartford co., central Conn., on Farmington R. and 14 mi. W of Hartford; wood products. State trout hatchery, state forest here. Settled 1740, inc. 1806. **3** Village (pop. 263), Kane co., NE Ill., 13 mi. W of Elgin, in dairying and livestock area. **4** City (pop. 30,613), ⊙ Des Moines co., SE Iowa, c.85 mi. SSE of Cedar Rapids, on 4 hills overlooking the Mississippi (bridged here); mfg. and shipping center with railroad shops, docks, ironworks, and many factories producing baskets, desks, caskets, combines, poultry equipment, fertilizer, soap, clothes, gloves, buttons, paint, paper boxes, food products. Large munitions plant (scene of explosion in 1942) built here during Second World War. Has jr. col. City is site of annual Tri-State Fair. Flint Hills State Park near by. Platted 1833 on sites of Indian village (1820) and trading post (1829). Inc. as town in 1836, chartered as city in 1838. **5** City (pop. 2,304), ⊙ Coffey co., E Kansas, on Neosho R. and 27 mi. SE of Emporia; trade center for diversified-farming region; dairy products. Walnut, oak, and cottonwood timber in vicinity. Inc. 1870. **6** Village (pop. c.300), ⊙ Boone co., N Ky., 12 mi. WSW of Covington; farm trade center in outer Bluegrass region. Big Bone Lick, where many bones of prehistoric mammals have been removed, is S. **7** Town (pop. 425), Penobscot co., E central Maine, 35 mi. NE of Bangor, in hunting, fishing area. **8** Agr. town (pop. 3,250), Middlesex co., E Mass., 11 mi. NW of Boston; pork products. Settled 1641, inc. 1799. **9** Village (pop. 329), Calhoun co., S Mich., on St. Joseph R. and 15 mi. SSE of Battle Creek city, in agr. area. **10** City (pop. 12,051), Burlington co., W N.J., on Delaware R. (bridged here) opposite Bristol, Pa., and 15 mi. NE of Camden; mfg. (silk, textiles, shoes, typewriter ribbons, canned goods, metal products, clothing, novelties); shipping center for agr. region. Settled by Friends 1677, inc. 1733. Was ⊙ West Jersey (1681–1702); then alternate ⊙ N.J. for a time. Grew mainly as a port, ranking with Philadelphia in 18th cent. First colonial money printed here by Benjamin Franklin (1726), first N.J. newspaper printed here (1777). Has St. Mary's Church (1703) and other 18th-cent. buildings, and a girls' school (founded 1837). James Fenimore Cooper b. here. **11** City (pop. 24,560), Alamance co., N central N.C., near Haw R., 19 mi. E of Greensboro; important hosiery-mfg., textile-weaving, -dyeing, and -finishing center; mfg. of radio parts, foundry products, coffins, paper boxes; lumber mills; tobacco warehouses. Elon Col. (coeducational) is near by. Inc. 1887. **12** Town (pop. 181), Alfalfa co., N Okla., 15 mi. ENE of Alva, in grain-growing and stock-raising area. **13** Borough (pop. 148), Bradford co., NE Pa., 8 mi. W of Towanda. **14** City (pop. 33,155), ⊙ Chittenden co., NW Vt., on slopes above L. Champlain, just below mouth of Winooski R., and 35 mi. NW of Montpelier; 44°29'N 73°13'W. Largest city in state; industrial (maple sugar and other food products, textiles, wood and metal products, tools, electrical machinery, brush fibers, printing); granite and talc quarries; shipping center (rail, lake); port of entry; summer resort. Lake ferry to Port Kent, N.Y. Seat of Univ. of Vt. (with Fleming Mus.), Trinity Col., R.C. cathedral, grave of Ethan Allen. After Revolution, it flourished as lake port, shipping mainly lumber and potash. Chartered by N.H. 1763, settled 1773. **15** City (pop. 2,350), Skagit co., NW Wash., 20 mi. SSE of Bellingham; trade center for agr. region; strawberries, dairy products. Settled 1882, inc. 1902. **16** Resort village, Mineral co., W.Va., in Eastern Panhandle, on Patterson Creek and 7 mi. SSE of Keyser. Has restored tavern dating from c.1785. **17** City (pop. 4,780), Racine co., SE Wis., on Fox R. at mouth of small White R., and 31 mi. SSW of Milwaukee, in farm area; mfg. (textiles; iron, steel, and brass products; beer, dairy products, sauerkraut); lake resort. Seat of St. Francis Col. Site of Mormon colony (1844–49) near by. Settled 1835; inc. as village 1896, as city 1900. **18** Village (pop. c.150), Big Horn co., N Wyo., near Greybull R., 20 mi. WNW of Basin, in elevated grain-growing area known as Emblem Bench; alt. c.4,300 ft.

Burlington Junction, city (pop. 746), Nodaway co., NW Mo., on Nodaway R. and 12 mi. NW of Maryville.

Burlos, Lake, Egypt: see BURULLUS, LAKE.

Burlus, Lake, Egypt: see BURULLUS, LAKE.

Burlyu-Baital or **Burlyu-Baytal** (bŏŏrlyŏŏ"-bītäl'), village, NE Dzhambul oblast, Kazakh SSR, port at SW end of L. Balkhash, on railroad and 190 mi. NE of Dzhambul; fish canning.

Burlyu-Tobe (–tŭbyĕ'), town (1948 pop. over 2,000), N Taldy-Kurgan oblast, Kazakh SSR, port at E end of L. Balkhash, on spur of Turksib RR and 115 mi. NNE of Taldy-Kurgan, in desert area; fish cannery. Also known as Burlyu-Tyube.

Burma (bûr'mŭ), since 1948, officially **Union of Burma,** republic (□ 261,757; 1941 pop. 16,823,798), SE Asia, on Indochinese Peninsula; ⊙ Rangoon. Bounded W by Bay of Bengal, E Pakistan, and India, E by China's Yunnan prov., Laos (along the Mekong), and Thailand, and S by Andaman Sea; extends 1,200 mi. N-S bet. E Himalayas (28°N) and Isthmus of Kra (10°N) and bet. 92° and 102°E. On the landward side, Burma is cut off from its neighbors by a chain of high N-S mtn. ranges stemming from the Himalayan system and enveloping the country in the shape of a giant horseshoe, rising to nearly 20,000 ft. in the extreme north. The W prong is composed from N to S of the NAGA HILLS (rising to the PATKAI RANGE), MANIPUR HILLS, CHIN HILLS, and the ARAKAN YOMA; the E arc consists of the KAOLIKUNG MOUNTAINS, TANEN TAUNGGYI RANGE, and the TENASSERIM RANGE, fronted in part by Kachin hills, Shan plateau, and Karenni hills. Enclosed within this mountain barrier is the heart of Burma, with most of agr. land and pop., and consisting essentially of a central basin formed by the valleys of the IRRAWADDY RIVER (with its main tributary, the CHINDWIN RIVER) and the SITTANG RIVER, separated by the wooded hills of the PEGU YOMA. The SALWEEN RIVER, cutting deep gorges through E Burma's Shan plateau and Karenni hills, separates, S of its estuary, the narrow, 400-mi.-long Tenasserim coast from the central basin. A similar narrow coastal strip, the Arakan, lies in the W bet. the Bay of Bengal and the Arakan Yoma. Burma has essentially a rainy tropical climate, of the monsoon variety along the coasts (Arakan and Tenasserim receive 200 in. a year) and of the savanna type inland. Central Burma, situated in the lee of the Arakan Yoma, constitutes the dry zone with 25–45 in. of rain. The rainy SW monsoon occurs May-Oct.; during the other seasons, cool in Nov.-Feb. and hot in March-May, rain is extremely rare. Primarily an agr. country with 80% of pop. engaged in or dependent on farming, Burma is the world's leading rice exporter. Rice, concentrated in the alluvial lands of the Irrawaddy delta and in the valleys of the lower Chindwin and Sittang rivers, accounts for 70% of total sown acreage. Oilseeds (sesame, peanuts), second in importance, cotton, millet, and beans are grown under irrigated conditions in the dry zone of central Burma, where cattle breeding is also important. Sugar cane is grown in Myitkyina and Toungoo dists, with mills at Sahmaw and Zeyawaddy. Fruit, vegetables, tobacco are grown generally throughout the country, tea and tung trees in the Shan State, and rubber in Tenasserim. Coastal and inland fisheries (salt fish is a staple Burmese food item) and pearling grounds (Mergui Archipelago) are important. Burma is first among world's exporters of teak, which is found in the mixed deciduous forests of the inland hills; other hardwoods (such as pyengadu or acle) and dipterocarps are also floated to sawmills at Rangoon, Moulmein, and Toungoo. Mineral resources are restricted to non-ferrous metals (tin, tungsten, lead, silver), petroleum, gems, jade, and amber. Metallic mining activities are identified primarily with the major MAWCHI mines, producing 10% of world's tungsten with tin as by-product, and with the rich BAWDWIN mines, whose complex silver-lead ore furnishes zinc, copper, nickel, iron, and gold as by-products. Large tin mines are worked near Tavoy, gems at Mogok, jade at Lonkin, and amber in Hukawng Valley. Petroleum, the most valuable of Burma's mineral assets, is produced at Yenangyaung, Chauk, Lanywa, Yenangyat, and Minbu, with refineries at Chauk and Syriam. Industry, concerned primarily with processing of agr. products and timber, is centered in Rangoon, Mandalay, and Moulmein. There are mills for rice, timber (mainly teak), cotton (largest at Thamaing), and oilseeds. Other mfg. products are tobacco, rubber shoes, cement (Thayetmyo), and matches Burma's leading exports (rice, teak, petroleum) move through the ports of Rangoon (which handles 80% of the country's trade), Bassein, Akyab, Moulmein, Tavoy, and Mergui. Transportation relies on railroads (main lines from Rangoon to Mandalay, Myitkyina, and Lashio, to Prome and Bassein, and to Moulmein and Ye), internal waterways, and air routes (centered on Rangoon's Mingaladon airport). Aside from the leading ports, Mandalay, Prome, and Toungoo rank among the principal towns of Burma. The country's pop. is multinational, consisting of Burmese and related Arakanese, Tavoyans, and Merguese (65%), Karens (10%), Shans (Thai; 7%), Indians (6%), Chins, Mons (Talaings), Chinese, and Kachins. While the Burmese are concentrated in the central dry zone and in Lower Burma (mainly in Irrawaddy delta), the non-Burmese indigenous peoples are largely settled in the peripheral mountains. Pop. is 85% Buddhist, 5% Animist, 4% Hindu and Moslem, and 2.5% Christian (one-half being Karen Baptists). The Burmese, a Mongoloid race of the Tibeto-Burman group, of Buddhist religion, speaking a monosyllabic, agglutinative language and using an alphabet derived from the Pali script, moved from Tibet into central Burma before 9th cent. The petty Burmese states were welded into a unified kingdom (⊙ Pagan) by Anawratha (1044–97), who also extended his rule over the Irrawaddy delta and the Mon (Talaing) kingdom of Thaton, and introduced Hinayana Buddhism to Burma. Following the end of this dynasty, crushed 1287 by the Mongols under Kublai Khan, Burma split up once more into small states under the rule of the Shans (Thai), who owed allegiance to Peking. In early 16th cent., new Burmese dynasties arose, the chief having their seats at Ava, Pegu, and Toungoo. The Toungoo ruler, Tabinshweti (1531–50), again unified the country, but in 18th cent. the rising Mons of the Irrawaddy delta overran much of central Burma. Alaungpaya (1752–60), chief of the Shwebo area, rallied the Burmese, defeated the Mons, and founded Rangoon. European contacts, initiated by Portuguese in 16th cent., had brought Du., Br., and Fr. trade stations to Syriam, which were abandoned at this time. Under Alaungpaya's successors, 3 Anglo-Burmese Wars resulted in the piecemeal annexation of Burma by the British. The 1st Anglo-Burmese War (1824–26) resulted in the loss of Arakan and Tenasserim, the 2d (1852) in the loss of Pegu, the entire annexed territory being formed (1862) into the Indian prov. of Br. Burma, now known as Lower Burma. The rump Burmese kingdom (1852–1885) with its ⊙ at Amarapura, later at Mandalay, also passed to Britain after a brief campaign, and became known as Upper Burma. In 1886, all of Burma was constituted a prov. of India. With other Indian provs., it acquired prov. autonomy in 1923 and, in 1937, was separated from India and became a separate territory of quasi-dominion status under a separate Secretary of State for Burma. In Second World War, the country was occupied in early 1942 by the Japanese. An Allied (U.S., Br., Chinese) campaign from the north liberated Burma in 1944–45. After the war, Burma obtained complete independence from Britain under the 1947 constitution and was set up Jan. 4, 1948, as a sovereign republic. However, armed risings of various insurgent groups, such as Communists and Karens, created a confused political situation, which continued into 1951. According to the 1947 constitution, Burma falls into Lower Burma, with the administrative divisions of Arakan, Pegu, Irrawaddy, and Tenasserim, and Upper Burma, with the divisions of Magwe, Mandalay, Sagaing, the autonomous Chin Hills, and the constituent units known as the Shan, Kachin, and Karenni states.

Burmakino (bo͝ormä'kĭnŭ), town (1926 pop. 769), E Yaroslavl oblast, Russian SFSR, 20 mi. SE of Yaroslavl; metalworks.

Burma Road, in China and Burma, extends from Burmese railhead of Lashio to Kunming, Yunnan prov., China; c.700 mi. long. Construction started by the Chinese after outbreak of Sino-Japanese War in 1937; completed in 1938, it carried war supplies landed at Rangoon and shipped by railroad to Lashio. Its importance to China increased after the Japanese had taken effective control of the Chinese coast and Indochina and until the Jap. occupation (1942) of Burma. In 1944, during N Burma campaign, it served as a vital supply route and was connected with the Ledo (Stilwell) Road near Muse (Burma). The end of the war substantially reduced the importance of the road.

Burmerange (bo͝or'mûräzh), village (pop. 210), extreme SE Luxembourg, 12 mi. SE of Luxembourg city, near Fr. border; vineyards; mfg. (agr. machinery, pumps, presses).

Burnabat, Turkey: see Bornova.

Burnaby, E suburb of Vancouver, SW B.C.; asphalt mfg.

Burnas Lagoon (bo͝ornäs'), on Black Sea coast, E Izmail oblast, Ukrainian SSR, just NE of Alibei Lagoon; 5 mi. long, 2 mi. wide. Tuzly on N shore.

Burneside, England: see Strickland Ketel.

Burnet (bûr'nĭt), county (□ 1,003; pop. 10,356), central Texas; ⊙ Burnet. Bounded W by Colorado R., with large lakes (recreation) impounded by Buchanan and Roy Inks dams (power, flood control, irrigation). Part of L. Travis in SE. Mts. in W rise to c.1,600 ft. Ranching (goats, sheep, cattle); agr. (cotton, corn, grain sorghums, legumes); some dairying, hogs, poultry. Noted for granite, limestone quarries. Tourist trade (guest ranches, hunting, fishing); Longhorn Cavern is near Burnet. Formed 1852.

Burnet, town (pop. 2,394), ⊙ Burnet co., central Texas, near Colorado R., c.45 mi. NW of Austin, in agr., livestock region; ships wool, mohair, cattle; limestone quarrying. Tourist trade attracted by Longhorn Cavern (in state park 9 mi. SW) and lakes formed by Buchanan and Roy Inks dams in the Colorado (W); U.S. fish hatchery here. Grew around Fort Croghan (established 1849); inc. 1885.

Burnett (bûrnĕt'), county (□ 840; pop. 10,236), NW Wis.; ⊙ Grantsburg. St. Croix R. here (W) forms Minn. line; also drained by Namekagon R. Wooded terrain with numerous lakes. Dairying, lumbering. Formed 1856.

Burnettown, town (pop. 578), Aiken co., W S.C., 8 mi. WSW of Aiken.

Burnett River (bûrnĕt'), SE Queensland, Australia, rises in Auburn Range SSW of Gladstone, flows S, past Eidsvold, thence E and NE, past Gayndah and Bundaberg, to the Pacific at N end of Hervey Bay; 250 mi. long. Navigable 10 mi. below Bundaberg by small steamers carrying sugar. Auburn and Boyne rivers, main tributaries.

Burnettsville (bûr'nŭtsvĭl), town (pop. 457), White co., NW central Ind., 12 mi. W of Logansport.

Burney, village (pop. 1,513), Shasta co., N Calif., in an agr. valley of Cascade Range, c.45 mi. NE of Redding; lumber, grain, potatoes. McArthur-Burney Falls State Park (120-ft. waterfall; recreational, camping facilities) is N.

Burnham, England: see Slough.

Burnham (bûr'nŭm). **1** Village (pop. 1,331), Cook co., NE Ill., S suburb of Chicago, at Ind. line N of Calumet City; oil refining. **2** Town (pop. 706), Waldo co., S Maine, on the Sebasticook and 27 mi. NW of Belfast; furniture mfg. Includes Winnecook, resort village near Unity Pond. **3** Borough (pop. 2,954), Mifflin co., central Pa., 2 mi. N of Lewistown; metal products. Settled 1795, inc. 1911.

Burnham Market (bûr'nŭm), town and parish (pop. 1,131), N Norfolk, England, 9 mi. NW of Fakenham; agr. market. Has 15th-cent. church. Also called Burnham Westgate. Just SE is agr. village and parish (pop. 290) of Burnham Thorpe; Lord Nelson b. here.

Burnham-on-Crouch, urban district (1931 pop. 3,416; 1951 census 3,962), SE Essex, England, on Crouch R. estuary and 8 mi. NE of Southend-on-Sea; fishing and yachting port; oyster-cultivating center. Has 15th-cent. church.

Burnham-on-Sea, urban district (1931 pop. 5,120; 1951 census 9,136), central Somerset, England, on Bridgwater Bay of Bristol Channel, at mouth of Brue R. and 8 mi. N of Bridgwater; seaside resort; agr. market in dairying region. Has 15th-cent. church. In urban dist. (SE) is town of Highbridge; agr.-machinery mfg., bacon and ham curing, cheese making.

Burnham Thorpe, and **Burnham Westgate,** England: see Burnham Market.

Burnhaven, Scotland: see Peterhead.

Burnie, town and port (pop. 7,235), N Tasmania, 70 mi. WNW of Launceston and on Bass Strait; rail junction; agr., dairying center; paper mills, butter factories.

Burnley, county borough (1931 pop. 98,258; 1951 census 84,950), E Lancashire, England, on Calder R. and 22 mi. N of Manchester; textile and metal-working center. Cotton and rayon spinning, weaving, and printing; leather tanning and mfg., coal mining; mfg. of chemicals, soap, pharmaceuticals, machine tools, light metals; engineering works. Has 14th-cent. mansion containing an art collection and furniture which belonged to Lord Byron.

Burnmouth, fishing village in Ayton parish, E Berwick, Scotland, on North Sea, 2 mi. SSE of Eyemouth. Here were signed (1384 and 1497) treaties bet. England and Scotland.

Burnopfield, England: see Whickham.

Burnoye (bo͝or'nŭyŭ), village (1948 pop. over 2,000), SW Dzhambul oblast, Kazakh SSR, on Turksib RR and 30 mi. WSW of Dzhambul; cotton; metal-works. Until 1951, in South Kazakhstan oblast.

Burnpur (bûrn'po͝or), town (pop. 13,678), Burdwan dist., W West Bengal, India, in Damodar Valley, 2 mi. WSW of Asansol; iron-, steel-, and industrial-gas works; general-engineering factory; coal-fed power station. Iron- and steelworks 1 mi. SW, at Hirapur.

Burns. 1 City (pop. 294), Marion co., SE central Kansas, 36 mi. NE of Wichita, in grain and livestock area. Oil wells near by. **2** City (pop. 3,093), ⊙ Harney co., E central Oregon, on Silvies R. N of Malheur L. and Harney L.; alt. 4,148 ft.; livestock center and lumber-milling point. Seat of experiment station of Oregon State Col. Inc. 1899. **3** Town (pop. 216), Laramie co., SE Wyo., near Lodgepole Creek, 24 mi. E of Cheyenne; alt. 5,475 ft.

Burnside, town (pop. 27,942), SE South Australia, 4 mi. E of Adelaide, in metropolitan area; dairying center.

Burnside, village (pop. 335), Coronie dist., N Du. Guiana, near the coast, 40 mi. E of Nieuw Nickerie; coconut plantations.

Burnside. 1 Village, Hartford co., Conn.: see East Hartford. **2** Town (pop. 615), Pulaski co., S Ky., in Cumberland foothills, on Cumberland R. and 8 mi. S of Somerset; veneer mfg.; lumber and flour mills. **3** Agr. borough (pop. 400), Clearfield co., W central Pa., 10 mi. N of Barnesboro and on West Branch of Susquehanna R.

Burns Lake, village (pop. 218), central B.C., on Burns L. (16 mi. long), 130 mi. WNW of Prince George; cattle-raising and lumbering center; gold, silver, copper, and lead mining.

Burnsville. 1 Town (pop. 525), Tishomingo co., extreme NE Miss., 13 mi. ESE of Corinth, in timber and agr. area; lumber milling. **2** Resort town (pop. 1,341), ⊙ Yancey co., W N.C., at N end of Black Mts., 26 mi. NNE of Asheville; nylon plant. Cyanite plant near by. **3** Town (pop. 731), Braxton co., central W.Va., on Little Kanawha R. and 15 mi. SW of Weston, in agr. area.

Burnt Creek Camp, iron-mining center in W Labrador, on Quebec border; 54°50'N 67°35'W.

Burnt Island (1 mi. long, 1 mi. wide), E N.F., on W side of Bonavista Bay, 35 mi. WNW of Cape Bonavista; 48°50'N 53°50'W; fishing; cold-storage plants.

Burntisland (bûrntĭ'lŭnd), burgh (1931 pop. 5,389; 1951 census 5,668), S Fifeshire, Scotland, on the Firth of Forth opposite Edinburgh and 5 mi. SW of Kirkcaldy; coal-shipping port and resort; has aluminum works and limestone quarries. Rossend Castle (now hotel) incorporates remains of 15th-cent. castle, sometime residence of Mary Queen of Scots. Church dates from 1592.

Burnt Oak, England: see Hendon.

Burnt River, NE Oregon, rises in Blue Mts., flows c.75 mi. E to Snake R. near Huntington. A dam (83 ft. high, 675 ft. long; completed 1938) in upper course forms small reservoir.

Burntside Lake (□ 11), St. Louis co., NE Minn., near Vermilion L., in Superior Natl. Forest, 4 mi. NW of Ely; 9 mi. long, 3 mi. wide. Resorts. Has many small islands.

Burono, Greece: see Vourinos.

Buroton-to, Russian SFSR: see Brouton Island.

Burr, village (pop. 91), Otoe co., SE Nebr., 28 mi. SE of Lincoln and on branch of Little Nemaha R.

Burra (bûr'ŭ), town (pop. 1,520), S South Australia, 90 mi. N of Adelaide; marble, mineral pigments (barite, malachite); wool, wheat, dairy products. Formerly important copper-mining center (1844–78). Sometimes called Kooringa (ko͝orĭng'gŭ).

Burra (bo͝orä'), town (pop. 1,004), Bauchi prov., Northern Provinces, E central Nigeria, 80 mi. NW of Bauchi; tin-mining center.

Burra, island, Scotland: see West Burra.

Burradon, England: see Longbenton.

Burrard Inlet (bŭrärd'), SW B.C., arm (extends 23 mi. E, 1–4 mi. wide) of Strait of Georgia. On S shore is Vancouver city, and, opposite, North Vancouver. Near head are Ioco and Port Moody. Indian Arm (13 mi. long) extends N.

Burray (bûr'ā), island (pop. 379) of the Orkneys, Scotland, just N of South Ronaldsay; 4 mi. long.

Burrel (bo͞o'rĕl) or **Burreli** (bo͞o'rĕlē), town (1945 pop. 1,141), N central Albania, 23 mi. NNE of Tirana and on Mat R.; police training school.

Burren Junction (bûr'ŭn), village (pop. 275), N New South Wales, Australia, 260 mi. NW of Newcastle; rail junction in sheep-raising area.

Burrero, El, Venezuela: see El Burrero.

Burriana (bo͞oryä'nä), city (pop. 15,725), Castellón de la Plana prov., E Spain, in Valencia, 8 mi. SSW of Castellón de la Plana; important fruit market exporting principally oranges and melons from its new harbor on the Mediterranean (2 mi. SE). Mfg. of paper, scales, liqueurs, candy, flour products. Trades in cereals, olive oil, wine, rice.

Burrillville (bŭ'rŭlvĭl), town (pop. 8,774), Providence co., extreme NW R.I., on Mass. and Conn. lines, on Branch R. and 17 mi. NW of Providence; includes textile-milling villages of Nasonville, Glendale, Mapleville, Oakland, Bridgeton, Mt. Pleasant, Pascoag (pă'skōg), Harrisville (pop. 1,055; administrative center), and Wallum Lake (wô'lŭm) village on Wallum L. (c.3 mi. long; partly in Mass.; site of state tuberculosis sanatorium). Dairying, apple growing, granite quarrying; resorts. Includes Pascoag Reservoir. Set off from Glocester and inc. 1806.

Burrinjuck (bûr'ĭnjŭk), village (pop. 509), S New South Wales, Australia, on Murrumbidgee R. and 170 mi. SW of Sydney; rice, fruit, wine. Burrinjuck Dam (1936), here, is 765 ft. long, 250 ft. high; hydroelectric plant.

Burro, Isla del (ē'slä dĕl bo͞o'rō), island in Uruguay R., Río Negro dept., W Uruguay, 1 mi. W of Nuevo Berlín; 32°55'S 58°10'W; 5 mi. long, 1½ mi. wide.

Burr Oak. 1 City (pop. 505), Jewell co., N Kansas, on affluent of Republican R., 8 mi. NW of Mankato, in corn and wheat area; feed milling. **2** Village (pop. 814), St. Joseph co., SW Mich., on Prairie R. and 34 mi. SE of Kalamazoo, in diversified agr. area (wheat, potatoes, corn); mfg. of electric motors, farm equipment; poultry hatchery.

Burroak, village (pop. c.350), Winneshiek co., NE Iowa, near Minn. line, 12 mi. NNW of Decorah. Limestone quarries near by.

Burro Mountains, N.Mex.: see Big Burro Mountains.

Burrow Head, promontory, SE Wigtown, Scotland, on Solway Firth, bet. Luce Bay and Wigtown bay inlets, 14 mi. S of Wigtown; 54°41'N 4°23'W.

Burr Point, promontory on NE coast of Co. Down, Northern Ireland, on the Irish Sea, 13 mi. ESE of Newtownards; easternmost point of Ireland (54° 29'N 5°26'W). Just off coast is tiny Burial Isl.

Burrton, city (pop. 749), Harvey co., S central Kansas, 30 mi. NW of Wichita, in wheat, livestock, and dairying region. Oil wells near by.

Burrundie (bûrŭn'dē), settlement, NW Northern Territory, Australia, 95 mi. SE of Darwin, on Darwin-Birdum RR. Tin at near-by Mt. Wells.

Burruyacú (bo͞oro͞oyäko͞o'), village (pop. estimate 500), ⊙ Burruyacú dept. (□ c.1,800; 1947 pop. 31,691), NE Tucumán prov., Argentina, 36 mi. NE of Tucumán in stock-raising and lumbering area; sawmills.

Burrwood, village (pop. c.400), Plaquemines parish, extreme SE La., on Southwest Pass (a mouth of the Mississippi) near SW extremity of the delta, 80 mi. SE of New Orleans; hq. for channel-maintenance engineers. Southwest Pass lighthouse (28°58'N 89°23'W) is on opposite bank of pass.

Burry Port, urban district (1931 pop. 5,755; 1951 census 5,927), S Carmarthen, Wales, on Loughor R. estuary, near Carmarthen Bay of Bristol Channel, and 4 mi. W of Llanelly; 51°41'N 4°16'W; coal-shipping port and agr. market, with copperworks. In 1928 Amelia Earhart landed near by after Atlantic flight.

Bursa (bo͝orsä'), prov. (□ 3,845; 1950 pop. 541,987), NW Turkey; ⊙ Bursa. Bordered N by Sea of Marmara and Samanli Mts.; drained by Simav, Nilufer, and Kirmasti rivers. L. Iznik in N. Chromium in SW, copper and iron scattered, with some mercury, manganese, and lignite. Most of Turkey's Merino sheep are raised here. Hot springs, mineral waters. Chestnuts, tobacco, oats, rasins, rice, olives, silk; fresh-water fishing. Formerly also spelled Brusa, Brussa. Before the revision of the old vilayets in the 1920s, Bursa was much larger (comprising the regions of anc. Bithynia and Phrygia) and was usually called Khodavendikyar.

Bursa, anc. *Prusa,* city (1950 pop. 100,007), ⊙ Bursa, NW Turkey, 55 mi. S of Istanbul and 16 mi. SE of its port Mudanya on the Sea of Marmara, at N foot of the Ulu Dag (Mt. Olympus); 40°10'N 29°3'E. Rail terminus, trade center, and mfg. town, known for its textile industry (especially silk milling); also mfg. of woolens, carpets, tiles. Trades in Merinos, tobacco, anise, beans, rice, cereals. Mercury reserves. There are mineral springs, ruins of a citadel, and several fine mosques and tombs of early sultans. Founded by King Prusias, it became flourishing city of Bithynia. After its capture (1326) by Orkhan it was ⊙ Ottoman Turks until transfer (1423) of ⊙ to Adrianople (Edirne), Tamerlane sacked it in 1402. Formerly spelled Brusa, Brussa, and Broussa.

Burscheid (bo͝or'shīt), town (pop. 10,699), in former Prussian Rhine Prov., W Germany, after 1945 in North Rhine-Westphalia, 6 mi. S of Solingen; mfg. of boots, weaving, dyeing.

Burscough, England: see ORMSKIRK.

Burshtyn (bo͝or'shtĭn), Pol. *Bursztyn* (bo͝or'shtĭn), town (1931 pop. 4,326), N Stanislav oblast, Ukrainian SSR, on Gnilaya Lipa R. and 23 mi. N of Stanislav; alabaster quarrying; tile and brick mfg., agr. processing (grain, vegetable oils). Has old town hall, palace, and churches.

Bursledon (bûr'zŭldŭn), agr. village and parish (pop. 1,243), S Hampshire, England, on Hamble R. estuary and 4 mi. ESE of Southampton. Church is of Norman origin.

Burslem (bûrz'lŭm), town in the Potteries dist., NW Stafford, England, since 1910 part of STOKE-ON-TRENT. Josiah Wedgwood b. here. Site of Wedgwood Institute.

Bürstadt (bür'shtät), village (pop. 9,647), Rhenish Hesse, W Germany, after 1945 in Hesse, 5 mi. E of Worms; rail junction; wine.

Burstow (bûr'stō), town and parish (pop. 1,905), SE Surrey, England, 7 mi. SE of Reigate. Has 13th-cent. church.

Bursztyn, Ukrainian SSR: see BURSHTYN.

Bursztynowo, Poland: see PELCZYCE.

Burt, county (□ 474; pop. 11,536), E Nebr.; ⊙ Tekamah. Agr. area bounded E by Missouri R. and Iowa; drained by Logan Creek. Grain, livestock, dairy products. Formed 1854; annexed part of Monona co., Iowa, in 1943.

Burt. 1 Town (pop. 572), Kossuth co., N Iowa, near East Des Moines R., 9 mi. N of Algona. **2** Village (pop. c.300), Niagara co., W N.Y., 30 mi. NNE of Buffalo, near L. Ontario; fruit and vegetable canning, shipping.

Burtenbach (bo͝or'tŭnbäkh), village (pop. 1,958), Swabia, W Bavaria, Germany, on Mindel R. and 12 mi. SE of Günzburg; grain, cattle. Chartered 1471.

Burt Lake, Cheboygan co., N Mich., 14 mi. NE of Petoskey; c.10 mi. long, 4.5 mi. wide; joined by streams to Mullett L. (E), Crooked L. (W). Forested resort area (fishing, hunting, bathing). State park on S shore.

Burtnieki Lake (bo͝ort'nyĕkē) (□ 14), in N Latvia, 12 mi. NNW of Valmiera; 8 mi. long, 3.5 mi. wide. Outlet: Salaca R.

Burton, village (district pop. 1,336), ⊙ Sunbury co., central N.B., on St. John R. and 14 mi. ESE of Fredericton, in fruitgrowing and lumbering region.

Burton. 1 Village (pop. 2,381), Tulare co., S central Calif. **2** Town, Floyd co., Ky.: see BYPRO. **3** Village (pop. 45), Keya Paha co., N Nebr., 10 mi. NE of Springview, near Keya Paha R. and S.Dak. line. **4** Village (pop. 932), Geauga co., NE Ohio, 28 mi. E of Cleveland, and on Cuyahoga R., in agr. area (dairy products, potatoes); maple syrup. **5** Village, Beaufort co., S.C.: see PORT ROYAL ISLAND. **6** Village (pop. c.800), Washington co., S central Texas, 13 mi. W of Brenham; trade, shipping center in agr. area.

Burton Lake (c.5 mi. long), Rabun co., extreme NE Ga., formed in Tallulah R. by power dam 10 mi. SW of Clayton.

Burton Latimer, urban district (1931 pop. 3,587; 1951 census 4,112), central Northampton, England, near Ise R. 3 mi. SE of Kettering; mfg. of leather and shoes; also cereal foods, concrete. Church dates from 13th cent.; schoolhouse was built 1662.

Burton-on-Trent or **Burton-upon-Trent,** county borough (1931 pop. 49,486; 1951 census 49,169), E Stafford, England, on Trent R. and 10 mi. SW of Derby; noted for its breweries. Also has mfg. of shoes, chemicals, paint, yeast, machinery, biscuits, knitted textiles; bacon and ham curing and packing. Has ruins of Benedictine abbey founded 1002, and a 16th-cent. grammar school. The brewing industry became important in 18th cent.

Burton Pidsea, agr. village and parish (pop. 299), East Riding, SE Yorkshire, England, 10 mi. ENE of Hull; mfg. of agr. machinery. Has 14th-cent. church with 15th-cent. tower.

Burtonwood, residential village and parish (pop. 2,280), S Lancashire, England, 4 mi. NW of Warrington; coal mining, truck gardening. Site of air force supply depot in Second World War.

Burtrask (bür'trĕsk"), Swedish *Burträsk*, village (pop. 945), Vasterbotten co., N Sweden, on small lake, 18 mi. SSW of Skelleftea; agr. market (stock, dairy products).

Burtrum, village (pop. 194), Todd co., central Minn., 11 mi. SE of Long Prairie, in lake region; grain, livestock.

Burtscheid (bo͝ort'shīt), SE district (inc. 1897) of Aachen, W Germany; mfg. (cloth, needles). Many of its baths (thermal springs) were destroyed in Second World War.

Buru or **Boeroe** (both: bo͞oro͞o', bo͞o'ro͞o), island (□ 3,668; pop. 19,625), S Moluccas, Indonesia, bet. Ceram Sea (N) and Banda Sea (S), 45 mi. W of Ceram; 3°24'S 126°32'E; 85 mi. long, 55 mi. wide, surrounded by coral reefs. Generally wooded and mountainous, rising to 7,874 ft. Chief products: cajuput oil, resin, rattan, timber, sago. Chief town, Namlea, is on NE coast. Colonization of Buru was begun 1652 by the Dutch, who won complete control of isl. in 1658.

Buru, Lake, Greece: see VISTONIS, LAKE.

Burujird or **Borujerd** (both: bōro͞ojĕrd'), town (1940 pop. 45,710), Sixth Prov., in Luristan, SW Iran, on highway and 60 mi. S of Hamadan, and on the upper Ab-i-Diz; its station on Trans-Iranian RR is Durud. Major trade center in and former ⊙ Luristan; rug and textile weaving, metalworking. Agr. (grain, fruit, grapes).

Burujón (bo͞oro͞ohōn'), town (pop. 1,258), Toledo prov., central Spain, 14 mi. W of Toledo; cereals, grapes, olives, sheep.

Buruldai or **Burulday** (bo͞oro͞oldī'), agr. village (1939 pop. over 2,000), E Frunze oblast, Kirghiz SSR, on the Lesser Kemin and 60 mi. E of Frunze.

Burullus, Lake (bŭrŭ'lŭs), or **Lake Burlos** (bo͝or'lôs), salt lake (□ 227, not including marshes), in Nile delta, Gharbiya prov., Lower Egypt, E of Rosetta; 35 mi. long and 3 to 10 mi. wide; fisheries. Through it ran the anc. Sebennytic branch of the Nile. Villages of Baltim and El Burg on NE shore. Also spelled Borlos and Burlus.

Burum (bo͞oro͞om'), village, Quaiti state, Eastern Aden Protectorate, port on Mukalla Bay of Gulf of Aden, on road and 15 mi. SW of Mukalla, sheltered by the cape Ras Burum (S); handles Mukalla shipping during SW monsoon.

Burum (bü'rŭm), village (pop. 573), Friesland prov., N Netherlands, 10 mi. ESE of Dokkum; cattle raising, dairying.

Burummana, Lebanon: see BRUMMANA.

Burunabat, Turkey: see BORNOVA.

Buruncan Point (bo͞oro͞ong'kän), southernmost point of Mindoro isl., Philippines, in Sulu Sea; 12°12'N 121°14'E.

Burundai or **Burunday** (bo͞oro͞ondī'), town (1944 pop. over 500), SW Alma-Ata oblast, Kazakh SSR, on railroad and 10 mi. W of Alma-Ata; beet-sugar refinery.

Bururi (bo͞oro͞o'rē), village, SW Ruanda-Urundi, in Urundi, 41 mi. SW of Kitega; native trade center; coffee, cattle; mfg. of bricks and tiles.

Burutu (bo͞oro͞o'to͞o), town (pop. 7,105), Warri prov., Western Provinces, N Nigeria, port in Niger R. delta, on Forcados R. and 4 mi. E of Forcados; palm-oil processing; hardwood, rubber. Exports palm oil and kernels, peanuts, shea nuts, cotton, hides. Accessible to ocean-going ships.

Burwash (bûr'ĭsh), town and parish (pop. 2,078), E Sussex, England, 7 mi. NW of Battle; agr. market. Has 13th-cent. church with Norman tower. Rudyard Kipling lived here.

Burwash Landing, trading post, SW Yukon, near Alaska border, on Kluane L. at foot of St. Elias Mts., 140 mi. WNW of Whitehorse, and on Alaska Highway; 61°22'N 139°W. Radio station. Gold, discovered (1903) near by, resulted in a small rush.

Burwell (bûr'wŭl), town and parish (pop. 2,257), central Cambridge, England, 10 mi. NE of Cambridge; agr. market, with fertilizer works. Has 15th-cent. church.

Burwell, village (pop. 1,413), ⊙ Garfield co., central Nebr., 70 mi. NNW of Grand Island, at junction of N.Loup and Calamus rivers; trade center for cattle area; grain, dairy products. Annual rodeo. Platted 1883.

Burwood, municipality (pop. 21,734), E New South Wales, Australia, 7 mi. W of Sydney, in metropolitan area; paint, enamel, brick.

Bury, Brazil: see BURI.

Bury (bĕ'rē), county borough (1931 pop. 56,182; 1951 census 58,829), SE Lancashire, England, on Irwell R. and 9 mi. NNE of Manchester; textile center since time of Edward III. Cotton and wool spinning, weaving, and printing; mfg. of textile machinery; leather tanning; mfg. of textile and tanning chemicals, paint, soap, asbestos, paper; metallurgy, engineering. Birthplace of Sir Robert Peel and of John Kay, inventor of the flying shuttle. Has art gall. with paintings of English school and Wedgwood china. In the borough are cotton-milling towns of Edenfield, Elton, and Woolfold.

Buryat-Mongol Autonomous Soviet Socialist Republic (bo͝oryät'-mŏng'gōl, -gŭl), administrative division (□ 135,700; 1939 pop. 542,170) of Russian SFSR, S Siberia, on Mongolian border; ⊙ Ulan-Ude. Largely in Transbaikalia. Bounded W by L. Baikal, E by Yablonovy Range; extends SW to Eastern Sayan Mts.; drained by Selenga (SE) and Vitim (NE) rivers. Mountainous region, with Vitim Plateau and Barguzin Range (NE), Khamar-Daban Range (S); 75% forested. Over half of pop. (50% Russian, 50% Buryat-Mongol) is settled in lower Selenga R. valley, its principal agr. area (wheat, coarse grain, truck produce, dairying). Livestock raising (N, NE) in forested mtn. sections. Tungsten and molybdenum (mined at Gorodok); tin, mercury, gold, silver, and iron found. Trans-Siberian RR crosses S section (via Babushkin and Ulan-Ude), which is also linked by highway (via Kyakhta) with Mongolia. Naushki branch of Trans-Siberian RR reaches Mongolian border W of Kyakhta. Exports meat, wool, hides, skins, furs, lumber, tungsten. Formed 1923 by union of Buryat-Mongol and Mongol-Buryat autonomous oblasts with Baikal govt. of Far Eastern Oblast. In 1937, 2 small sections of the republic were separated and reconstituted as Ust-Orda Buryat-Mongol and Aga Buryat-Mongol natl. okrugs within Irkutsk and Chita oblasts. Sometimes spelled Buriat-Mongol.

Buryn or **Buryn'** (bo͞o'rĭnyŭ), town (1926 pop. 1,325), central Sumy oblast, Ukrainian SSR, 27 mi. E of Konotop; sugar-refining center. Near by is village of Buryn (1926 pop. 5,690).

Bury St. Edmunds, municipal borough (1931 pop. 16,708; 1951 census 20,045), W Suffolk, England, 22 mi. NW of Ipswich; agr. market; foundries, pharmaceutical works, sugar mills, breweries. There are remains of monastery, founded c.630, where King Edmund was buried (903); later became famous shrine and Benedictine abbey. Also has 15th-cent. church of St. James (now cathedral), a Norman belfry tower, and 15th-cent. St. Mary's church, with grave of Mary Tudor, sister of Henry VIII.

Buryubai, Russian SFSR: see BURIBAI.

Burzaco (bo͞orsä'kō), town (pop. estimate 6,000) in Greater Buenos Aires, Argentina, 14 mi. SSW of Buenos Aires; residential, mfg. (chemicals, paper boxes, canned food); cattle and poultry raising.

Burzet (bürzā'), village (pop. 414), Ardèche dept., S France, in the Monts du Vivarais, 11 mi. NW of Aubenas; silk throwing, sheep raising.

Burzil Pass (bo͞orzēl') (alt. 13,775 ft.), in main range of W Punjab Himalayas, W Kashmir, 35 mi. SSE of Astor, on main Srinagar-Gilgit road.

Busachi (bo͞ozä'kē), village (pop. 2,727), Cagliari prov., central Sardinia, 18 mi. NE of Oristano. Dolmen near by.

Busaco, Portugal: see BUÇACO.

Busalla (bo͞ozäl'lä), village (pop. 2,490), Genova prov., Liguria, N Italy, near Giovi Pass, on Scrivia R. and 12 mi. N of Genoa; resort and commercial center for upper Scrivia R. valley. Ironworks, brewery, cotton mill.

Busanga (bo͞osäng'gä), village, Katanga prov., SE Belgian Congo, on left bank of Lualaba R and 100 mi. NW of Jadotville; oldest tin mine in Belgian Congo. Wolfram is also mined near by (N).

Busayrah, Syria: see BUSEIRE.

Busby (bŭz'bē), town in Mearns parish, E Renfrew, Scotland, 5 mi. SSW of Glasgow; cotton milling.

Busca (bo͞o'skä), village (pop. 2,698), Cuneo prov., Piedmont, NW Italy, on Maira R. and 9 mi. NW of Cuneo; rail junction; silk, pottery. Roman ruins, including fortifications.

Buseire or **Busayrah** (both: bo͞osä'rŭ), Fr. *Bessiré*, town, Euphrates prov., E Syria, on left bank of Euphrates R. and 20 mi. SE of Deir ez Zor.

Busendorf, France: see BOUZONVILLE.

Busento River (bo͞ozĕn'tō), Calabria, S Italy, rises in the Apennines 4 mi. N of Grimaldi, flows 10 mi. N to Crati R. at Cosenza, where the Visigoth Alaric was supposedly buried in its bed.

Busetsu, Japan: see INABU.

Buseu, Rumania: see BUZAU.

Bush (bo͞osh), town (pop. 16,004, largely Coptic), Beni Suef prov., Upper Egypt, on the Nile, on railroad, and 5 mi. NNE of Beni Suef; cotton, cereals, sugar cane.

Bush, village (pop. 504), Williamson co., S Ill., 6 mi. WNW of Herrin, in bituminous-coal-mining and agr. area.

Bushbury, N suburb (pop. 15,072) in Wolverhampton, S Stafford, England; important automobile-tire and industrial rubber-products works, metal-working. Has 14th-cent. church and mansion of Moseley Old Hall, where Charles II hid in 1651 after the battle of Worcester.

Bushehr, Iran: see BUSHIRE.

Bushey (bo͝o'shē), residential urban district (1931 pop. 11,245; 1951 census 14,801), SW Hertford, England, 3 mi. SE of Watford. Has 13th-cent. church.

Bushey Park, England: see TEDDINGTON.

Bushimaie River (bo͞oshēmā'), left tributary of the Sankuru, in S Belgian Congo, rises 35 mi. NE of Sandoa, flows c.240 mi. N, past Bakwanga, to Sankuru R. 15 mi. N of Tshilenge. Bushimaie diamond fields, with center at BAKWANGA, are among the richest known diamond areas in the world.

Bushire (bo͞oshēr'), Persian *Bushehr* or *Bandar Bushehr* (bändär' bo͞oshä'hûr), city (1940 pop. 27,317), Seventh Prov., in Fars, S Iran, port on Persian Gulf, 115 mi. WSW of Shiraz; 28°59'N 50°50'E. Terminus of road from Shiraz via Kazerun; airfield; cotton spinning and weaving; fishing. Exports tobacco, wool, rugs, opium, nuts and gums. Situated at N point of 15-mi.-long peninsula, Bushire was founded in 1736 by Nadir Shah 5 mi. N of small medieval port of RISHAHR. It rapidly developed as the focus of Persian maritime trade and supplanted Bandar Abbas as the chief Persian Gulf port. Continued to flourish through 19th cent., but declined after First World War with the shift of trade to the Abadan oil-producing area. Its shallow harbor has been replaced by new deep-water outport of Rishahr. It was occupied by the British in 1856–57 and again in 1915. It was originally known as Abu Shehr or Bandar Abu Shehr.

Bush Key, Fla.: see DRY TORTUGAS.

Bushkill, village, Pike co., NE Pa., on the Delaware and 13 mi. NE of Stroudsburg, in resort region. Bushkill Falls near by.

Bushman's Bay, New Hebrides: see MALEKULA.

Bushmills, town (pop. 1,035), NW Co. Antrim, Northern Ireland, on Bush R. near its mouth on the North Channel and 8 mi. NE of Coleraine; bauxite mining, alcohol distilling, salmon and trout fishing.

Bush Mountain, Texas: see GUADALUPE MOUNTAINS.

Bushnell (bo͝osh'nŭl). **1** City (pop. 536), ⊙ Sumter co., central Fla., c.55 mi. NNE of Tampa; agr. shipping point. Dade Memorial Park near by commemorates massacre of Major Francis L. Dade and his men by Indians in 1835. **2** City (pop. 3,317), McDonough co., W Ill., 28 mi. S of Galesburg; rail and industrial center in agr. and bituminous-coal area; corn, wheat, livestock, poultry; stockyards; mfg. (candy, beverages, garden implements). Inc. 1865. **3** Village (pop. 225), Kimball co., W Nebr., 10 mi. W of Kimball and on Lodgepole Creek, near Wyo. and Colo. lines; potatoes, grain. **4** Town (pop. 96), Brookings co., E S.Dak., 7 mi. E of Brookings.

Bushnellsville (bo͝osh'nŭlzvĭl), resort village, Ulster co., SE N.Y., in the Catskills, near Esopus Creek and 25 mi. NW of Kingston.

Bushong (bo͞o-shông'), city (pop. 93), Lyon co., E central Kansas, 17 mi. NNW of Emporia, in cattle-grazing region.

Bush River, NE Md., estuary (c.12 mi. long) entering Chesapeake Bay in S Hartford co.; traverses Aberdeen Proving Ground.

Bushrod Island, Liberia: see SAINT PAUL RIVER.

Bushruyeh or **Boshru'iyeh** (both: bōshro͞oēyĕ'), village, Ninth Prov., in Khurasan, NE Iran, 35 mi. WSW of Firdaus, at edge of salt desert; handwoven woolen textiles. Also spelled Boshruyeh.

Bushtick, village, Bulawayo prov., SW Southern Rhodesia, in Matabeleland, 25 mi. ESE of Bulawayo; gold mining. Railroad station is 3 mi. W.

Bushton, city (pop. 532), Rice co., central Kansas, 40 mi. NW of Hutchinson, in wheat area. Oil wells near by.

Bushwick, SE N.Y., a residential section of N Brooklyn borough of New York city.

Busi, island, Yugoslavia: see BISEVO ISLAND.

Busia, town, Eastern Prov., SE Uganda, on road and 17 mi. SSW of Tororo; Kenya border post; cotton, coffee, bananas, corn. Gold deposits.

Busigny (büzēnyē'), town (pop. 2,890), Nord dept., N France, 14 mi. SE of Cambrai; rail junction; ironworks, shirt factory. Captured 1918 by Americans and British.

Businga (bo͞osĭng'gä), village, Equator Prov., NW Belgian Congo, on Mongala R. and 85 mi. NNW of Lisala; terminus of navigation; cotton ginning.

Büsingen (bü'zĭng-ŭn), village (pop. 910), S Baden, Germany, in small enclave surrounded by Swiss territory, on the Rhine and 2.5 mi. E of Schaffhausen; fruit.

Busintsi, Bulgaria: see TRIN.

Busira River (bo͞osē'rä, bo͞osērä'), W Belgian Congo, formed just W of Boende by union of Tshuapa and Lomela rivers, flows 170 mi. W to join Momboyo R. at Ingende, forming the Ruki. Navigable for steamboats in entire course. Receives Salonga R. from the left.

Busiris (bo͞osī'rĭs), anc. city of Lower Egypt, in Nile delta, c.30 mi. SW of Tanis; was seat of worship of Osiris.

Busi River, Mozambique: see BUZI RIVER.

Busk (bo͞osk), city (1931 pop. 7,010), central Lvov oblast, Ukrainian SSR, on Bug R. and 15 mi. NW of Zolochev; agr. processing (cereals, hops, flax), woodworking, pottery; fisheries. Old palaces. Chartered in 15th cent.; subjected to several Tatar assaults; under Austrian rule (1772–1918). Reverted to Poland (1919); ceded to USSR in 1945.

Buskerud (bo͞osk'ŭro͞o), county [Nor. *fylke*] (□ 5,700; pop. 149,948), SE Norway; ⊙ Drammen. Extends NW from Oslo Fjord to the Hardangervidda and the Hallingskarv mts., from which the fertile Numedal and Hallingdal extend SSE; SE part of co. is forested. Drained by Lagen, Drammen, Hallingdal, and Begna rivers. Drammen, Kongsberg, and Honefoss are industrial centers; chief industries are lumbering, and milling of paper, wood pulp, cellulose, textiles. Oats, barley, fruit, and vegetables are grown; stock raising. There are important hydroelectric plants.

Busko or **Busko Zdroj** (bo͞o'skô zdro͞o'ē), Pol. *Busko Zdrój*, Rus. *Busk* (bo͞osk), town (pop. 5,975), Kielce prov., SE Poland, 28 mi. S of Kielce; mineral baths (sulphur).

Busot (bo͞osôt'), village (pop. 694), Alicante prov., E Spain, 12 mi. N of Alicante; spa (medicinal springs) and resort, surrounded by pine forests. Known for its mild winter climate. Has tuberculosis sanatorium. In vicinity are the noted Canelones caverns.

Busquístar (bo͞oskē'stär), village (pop. 753), Granada prov., S Spain, on S slopes of Sierra Nevada, 24 mi. SE of Granada; iron mines.

Busra (bo͞os'rŭ) or **Bosra** (bŏz'rŭ), anc. *Bostra*, Turkish *Bosra Eski Sham*, town, Hauran prov., SW Syria, near Jordan border, on railroad and 23 mi. ESE of Der'a, 70 mi. S of Damascus, in agr. area (grain). Bostra was an important city in Roman times. There are numerous Greco-Roman and Arab ruins, including a temple, a cathedral (6th cent.), and a mosque (perhaps early 7th cent.).

Buss, Saar: see BOUS.

Bussa (bo͞osä', bo͞o'sä), Fr. *Boussa*, town (pop. 1,195), Ilorin prov., Northern Provinces, W Nigeria, on Niger R. and 50 mi. NE of Kaiama; gold-mining center; shea-nut processing, cotton weaving; cassava, millet, rice, durra. Mungo Park died here, 1806. Formerly an important town in native state of Borgu.

Bussaco, Portugal: see BUÇACO.

Bussahir, former princely state, India: see BASHAHR.

Bussang (büsã'), village (pop. 1,523), Vosges dept., E France, near source of Moselle R., 16 mi. N of Belfort in the central Vosges; alt. 2,037 ft. Winter resort and watering place. Metalworks. Épinal-Mulhouse road crosses Bussang pass (2 mi. E; alt. 2,398) in tunnel (820 ft. long) damaged in Second World War.

Busselton, municipality (pop. 1,008), SW Western Australia, 120 mi. SSW of Perth and on S shore of Geographe Bay; summer resort; potatoes, corn, butter.

Busseto (bo͞os-sā'tô), town (pop. 2,530), Parma prov., Emilia-Romagna, N central Italy, 11 mi. S of Cremona; food cannery, tannery, mfg. (soap, buttons). Has castle remodeled 16th cent.

Bussey (bŭ'sē), town (pop. 633), Marion co., S central Iowa, near Cedar Creek, 28 mi. WNW of Ottumwa, in bituminous-coal-mining and stock-raising area.

Busshozan (bo͞os'shōzä), town (pop. 6,090), Kagawa prefecture, N Shikoku, Japan, 4 mi. S of Takamatsu; commercial center in agr. area; noodles, edible frogs.

Bussière-Galant (büsyâr'-gälã'), village (pop. 299), Haute-Vienne dept., W central France, 17 mi. SW of Limoges; rail junction; woodworking.

Bussi sul Tirino (bo͞os'sē so͞ol tērē'nô), town (pop. 3,368), Pescara prov., Abruzzi e Molise, S central Italy, on left affluent of Pescara R. and 3 mi. N of Popoli. Hydroelectric plant furnishes power for its chemical (acids, ammonia, calcium carbide) and aluminum industries.

Bussolengo (bo͞os-sôlĕng'gô), village (pop. 3,089), Verona prov., Veneto, N Italy, on Adige R. and 7 mi. WNW of Verona; mfg. (castor oil, soap, silk textiles, agr. tools). Has hydroelectric plant and pumping station for irrigation.

Bussoleno (bo͞os-sôlā'nô), village (pop. 2,924), Torino prov., Piedmont, NW Italy, on Dora Riparia R. and 5 mi. E of Susa; rail junction; mfg. center (metallurgical plants, cotton mills); hydroelectric station. Green-marble quarries near by.

Bussum (bû'sŭm), town (pop. 33,432), North Holland prov., W central Netherlands, 13 mi. ESE of Amsterdam, near the Ijsselmeer. Pharmaceuticals, chemicals, dye industry, cocoa mfg.; tree nurseries.

Bust, Afghanistan: see QALA BIST.

Bustam or **Bostam** (both: bōstäm'), town (1941 pop. estimate 4,000), Second Prov., in Shahrud, NE Iran; wheat, cotton. Moslem pilgrimage center, visited because of tomb of 9th-cent. mystic Bayazid Bustami and adjoining "shaking" minaret. Also spelled Bastam.

Bustamante (bo͞ostämän'tā), village (1930 pop. 220), Ñuble prov., S central Chile, 15 mi. ENE of Chillán, in agr. area (grain, wine, fruit, vegetables, livestock).

Bustamante. 1 Town (pop. 2,606), Nuevo León, N Mexico, in N outliers of Sierra Madre Oriental, on railroad and 60 mi. N of Monterrey; grain, livestock. **2** Town (pop. 1,142), Tamaulipas, NE Mexico, in Sierra Madre Oriental, 45 mi. WSW of Ciudad Victoria; alt. 5,636 ft.; cereals, livestock.

Bustan or **Bostan** (both: bōstän'), town, Sixth Prov., in Khuzistan, SW Iran, near Iraq border, 50 mi. NW of Ahwaz, and on Karkheh R., in Arab tribal area.

Bustanabad or **Bostanabad** (both: bōstän"äbäd'), town, Third Prov., in Azerbaijan, NW Iran, on highway and 32 mi. SE of Tabriz; junction for Sarab and Mianeh.

Bustard Bay, bight of S Pacific, SE Queensland, Australia, bet. Bustard Head (NW) and Round Hill Head (SE); 10 mi. wide. Site of Cook's 1st landing (1770) in Queensland.

Bustard Head, SE Queensland, Australia, forms NW side of entrance to Bustard Bay; 24°1'S 151°46'E; lighthouse.

Bustarviejo (bo͞ostärvyā'hō), town (pop. 1,370), Madrid prov., central Spain, 30 mi. N of Madrid; beans, apples, potatoes; tile mfg.

Bustehrad (bo͞o'shtĕkhrät), Czech *Buštehrad*, village (pop. 3,076), W central Bohemia, Czechoslovakia, 4 mi. NE of Kladno; coal mining. Castle.

Bustenari (bo͞oshtĕnä'rē), Rum. *Buştenari*, village (pop. 1,291), Prahova prov., S central Rumania, 16 mi. NNW of Ploesti; oil, natural gas.

Busteni (bo͞oshtĕn'), Rum. *Buşteni*, town (1948 pop. 4,552), Prahova prov., S central Rumania, in Walachia, on railroad and 4 mi. N of Sinaia; popular summer and winter-sports resort (alt. 2,887 ft.) at E foot of the Bucegi Mts., with noted skiing facilities. Also woodworking (paper, cellulose, furniture), glucose mfg.

Bustillo, Bolivia: see UNCÍA.

Bustinza (bo͞ostĕn'sä), town (pop. estimate 1,500), S Santa Fe prov., Argentina, 40 mi. WNW of Rosario; grain and livestock center; dairying.

Busto Arsizio (bo͞o'stô ärsē'tsyô), city (pop. 32,820), Varese prov., Lombardy, N Italy, 19 mi. NW of Milan. Rail junction; a major cotton-milling center of Italy; iron- and steelworks, rayon mills, shoe factories, dyeworks; mfg. of textile machinery, glue, starch, wax, celluloid. Has church of Santa Maria in Piazza (1515–23; designed by Bramante).

Busto Garolfo (gärôl'fô), town (pop. 5,294), Milano prov., Lombardy, N Italy, 5 mi. S of Busto Arsizio; cotton milling center; sausage, soap, glue works.

Buston (bo͞ostôn'), village, S Bukhara oblast, Uzbek SSR, on Trans-Caspian RR, near Kzyl-Tepe station, and 8 mi. SE of Gizhduvan; metalworks.

Bustos (bo͞o'stōs), town (1939 pop. 1,450; 1948 municipality pop. 10,493), Bulacan prov., S central Luzon, Philippines, 25 mi. NNW of Manila, just E of Baliuag; rice, sugar cane, corn. Sometimes called Tanawan (tänä'wän).

Busuanga Island (bo͞oswäng'ä) (□ 344; 1948 pop. with surrounding isls. 13,166), largest (35 mi. long) of the Calamian Isls., Palawan prov., Philippines, bet. Mindoro (NE) and Palawan (SW); 12°10'N 120°E. Chief town, Coron (kōrōn') (1939 pop. 2,864), is on SE coast, opposite Coron Isl. (11 mi. long). Busuanga town (1939 pop. 675) is on W coast. Fertile area, rising to 1,302 ft. in N. Coconuts, rice. Fishing. Manganese mine.

Busu Baya, Belgian Congo: see BINGA.

Busu Djanoa (bo͞o'so͞o jänō'ä), village, Equator Prov., NW Belgian Congo, 30 mi. S of Lisala; trading post; palm products, sesame.

Büsum (bü'zo͞om), village (pop. 5,016), in Schleswig-Holstein, NW Germany, on the North Sea, 10 mi. WSW of Heide; fishing (especially crabs) harbor of the Dithmarschen; popular seaside resort; food processing (fish meal, canned fish and crabs). Site (since 1919) of zoological station for deep-sea research.

Busumbu (bo͞oso͞om'bo͞o), mining center, Eastern Prov., SE Uganda, 11 mi. NE of Tororo; apatite mining (shipped by rail via Magodes).

Busu Melo (bo͞o'so͞o mĕ'lō), village, Equator Prov., NW Belgian Congo, near left bank of Congo R. and 90 mi. SW of Lisala; palm-oil milling. Busu Modanda R.C. mission is 12 mi. W.

Busu Modanda, Belgian Congo: see BUSU MELO.

Buta (bo͞o'tä, bo͞otä'), town (1948 pop. 9,262), ⊙ Uele dist. (□ 76,939; 1948 pop. c.798,000), Eastern Prov., N Belgian Congo, on Congo-Nile highway, on Rubi R., on railroad, and 150 mi. NNW of Stanleyville; terminus of steam navigation, transshipment point and commercial center; cotton ginning, rice processing. Seat of vicar apostolic of W Uele. Has hosp. for Europeans, school for European children, and school for sons of native chiefs; Baptist mission. Buta R.C. mission is noted for its model farm (notably cattle-raising) employing tame elephants for hard labor; here are also broken in the okapis before being shipped to zoos of Europe.

Buta-Chauques Island, Chile: see CHAUQUES ISLANDS.

Butalcura (bo͞otälko͞o'rä), village (1930 pop. 135), Chiloé prov., S Chile, on Chiloé Isl., on railroad and 27 mi. S of Ancud; potatoes, wheat, livestock; lumbering.

Butan (bo͞otän'), village (pop. 4,620), Vratsa dist., NW Bulgaria, on Ogosta R. and 12 mi. SW of Oryakhovo; vineyards, grain, livestock.

Butanko, Formosa: see WUTANKENG.

Buta Ranquil (bo͞o'tä räng-kēl'), village (pop. estimate 700), ⊙ Pehuenches dept. (1947 census 2,141), N Neuquén natl. territory, Argentina, near the Río Colorado, 165 mi. NW of Neuquén, in wheat and alfalfa area.

Butare, Belgian Congo: see ASTRIDA.

Butaritari, Gilbert Isls.: see MAKIN.

Butauanan Island (bo͞otäwä'nän), (1939 pop. 196), Camarines Sur prov., off SE Luzon, Philippines, at E side of entrance to San Miguel Bay; 3 mi. long, 1 mi. wide; fishing.

Butawal, Nepal: see BUTWAL.

Butcher Island, India: see BOMBAY HARBOUR.

Bute or **Buteshire** (būt, būt'shĭr), insular county (□ 218.2; 1931 pop. 18,823; 1951 census 19,285), SW Scotland; ⊙ Rothesay. Consists of several isls. in the Firth of Clyde and Kilbrannan Sound, of which Bute, ARRAN, GREAT CUMBRAE, and LITTLE CUMBRAE are the most important. Rothesay is a popular seaside resort.

Bute, island (□ 46.8, including Inchmarnock isl.; pop. 12,122), Buteshire, Scotland, in the Firth of Clyde, just S of Cowal peninsula, Argyll, from which it is separated by the narrow Kyles of Bute; 15 mi. long, up to 5 mi. wide; rises to 911 ft. Coastline is indented by several bays. Chief town, ROTHESAY, on E coast. On SE coast is fishing and resort village of Kilchattan, 7 mi. S of Rothesay. Rocky and hilly in N; in center and S farming is carried on.

Buteha or **Butkha** (bo͞otkhä'), Mongolian league of Manchuria, in N Inner Mongolian Autonomous Region; inhabited by Nonni River Mongols; main town, Yalu (Chalantun). Situated on E slopes of the Great Khingan Mts., bounded N by the Ilkuri

Mts. and E by the Nonni valley, Buteha has been largely penetrated by Chinese colonization. There are also some Orochon, Solon, and Daur minorities engaged in hunting and trapping. The area is poorly developed, with some agr. (wheat, soybeans) and lumbering along Chinese Eastern RR. The main centers are Yalu and Pokotu. Buteha was constituted in Manchukuo as East Hsingan prov., which was inc. 1946 into Hsingan prov. Part of the Inner Mongolian Autonomous Region after 1949, it was joined with Barga to form the Huna league.

Bute Inlet (būt), SW B.C., arm (50 mi. long, 1–3 mi. wide) of Strait of Georgia, a fjord receiving Homathko R. Inlet was proposed (1862) as terminal of transcontinental railroad.

Butembo (bōōtĕm'bō), village, Kivu prov., E Belgian Congo, 95 mi. NNE of Costermansville; gold-mining center employing c.5,500 workers. Has R.C. mission, hosp. for Europeans.

Butera (bōōtä'rä), town (pop. 7,911), Caltanissetta prov., S Sicily, 9 mi. NNW of Gela. Sulphur mines near by.

Butere (bōōtĕ'rā), village, Nyanza prov., W Kenya, 29 mi. NW of Kisumu; railhead in gold-mining area. Cotton, peanuts, sesame, corn.

Buteshire, Scotland: see BUTE, county.

Butetown, Wales: see CARDIFF.

Butgenbach (büt'khünbäkh), Ger. *Bütgenbach*, village (pop. 2,320), Liége prov., E Belgium, on Warche R. and 8 mi. E of Malmédy; hydroelectric power station.

Butha Buthe (bōō'tä bōō'tä), village, ⊙ Butha Buthe dist. (pop. 35,279, with absent laborers 40,655), N Basutoland, on main N-S road and 60 mi. NE of Maseru.

Buthidaung (bōō'dhēdoung'), village, Akyab dist., Lower Burma, in Arakan, on Mayu R. (head of navigation) and 10 mi. NE of Maungdaw (linked by road). Chief bazaar in Mayu valley.

Buthrotum (bōōthrō'tüm), anc. city of N Epirus, in modern Albania, 8 mi. S of Sarandë, on coastal lagoon of Channel of Corfu. Dating probably from 6th cent. B.C. as a fortress covering approaches to Corfu, it became one of the leading centers of Epirus, located, under Roman rule, on one of their main roads. It declined (5th cent. A.D.) after the passage of the Visigoths, but rallied under Venetian rule (1386–1797). On its site is Albanian village of Butrint or Butrinti, Ital. *Butrinto*, where Ital. excavations (1930s) uncovered Greek, Roman, Byzantine, and Venetian remains, including theater (4th cent. B.C.), baptistery (4th cent. A.D.), Roman baths, Byzantine churches, and Venetian castle (now mus.).

Buti (bōō'tē), town (pop. 1,864), Pisa prov., Tuscany, central Italy, 9 mi. E of Pisa, in olive-growing region; paper milling, broom mfg.

Butiá (bōōtyä'), town (pop. 6,281), E Rio Grande do Sul, Brazil, 45 mi. WSW of Pôrto Alegre; mines coal which is taken by rail to Jacuí R. (15 mi. NE), thence by barge to Pôrto Alegre and seaports. Leão mines (5 mi. W) are also reached by rail spur.

Butiaba (bōōtyä'bä), town, Western Prov., Uganda, port on E shore of L. Albert, 28 mi. WNW of Masindi; road-steamer transfer point for navigation on the Albert Nile to Nimule and on L. Albert to Kasenyi (Belgian Congo). Cotton, tobacco, bananas, coffee, corn; fishing. Oil deposits near by.

Butjadingen (bōōt"yä'dĭng-ün), village (commune pop. 10,953), in Oldenburg, NW Germany, after 1945 Lower Saxony, on left bank of Weser estuary and 8 mi. NW of Nordenham; deep-sea fishing. Until 1936, called Burhave.

Butka (bōōt'kŭ), village (1939 pop. over 2,000), SE Sverdlovsk oblast, Russian SFSR, on rail spur and 42 mi. NNE of Shadrinsk; lumbering; livestock.

Butkha, Manchuria: see BUTEHA.

Butkhak (bōōtkhäk'), village, Kabul prov., E Afghanistan, 10 mi. E of Kabul and on highway from Khyber Pass.

Butkovon, Greece: see KERKINE.

Butler. **1** County (□ 773; pop. 29,228), S Ala.; ⊙ Greenville. Coastal plain drained by branches of Sepulga R. Cotton, peanuts; lumber milling. Formed 1819. **2** County (□ 582; pop. 17,394), N central Iowa; ⊙ Allison. Rolling prairie agr. area (hogs, cattle, poultry, corn, oats, soybeans) drained by Shell Rock R. Limestone quarries, sand and gravel pits. Has state parks. Formed 1851. **3** County (□ 1,445; pop. 31,001), SE Kansas; ⊙ El Dorado. Rolling plain, drained by Walnut R. Livestock, grain. Highly productive oil fields. Formed 1855. **4** County (□ 443; pop. 11,309), W central Ky.; ⊙ Morgantown. Drained by Green, Barren, and Mud rivers. Rolling agr. area (livestock, grain, burley tobacco); coal mines, stone quarries; timber. Formed 1810. **5** County (□ 716; pop. 37,707), SE Mo.; ⊙ Poplar Bluff. In Ozark region, bounded E by St. Francis R.; drained by Black R. Resort, agr. area (cotton, rice, corn), livestock; lumber; fire-clay, iron mines. Parts of Clark Natl. Forest and Wappapello Reservoir are here. Formed 1849. **6** County (□ 582; pop. 11,432), E Nebr.; ⊙ David City. Agr. area bounded N by Platte R.; drained in SW by Big Blue R. Livestock, dairy products, grain. Formed 1868. **7** County (□ 471; pop. 147,203), extreme SW Ohio; ⊙ HAMILTON. Bounded W by Ind. line; intersected by Great Miami R. and its small tributaries. Includes site of Fort Hamilton. Agr. area (livestock, dairy products, grain, poultry, tobacco); mfg. at Hamilton and Middletown; limestone quarries. Formed 1803. **8** County (□ 794; pop. 97,320), W Pa.; ⊙ Butler. Industrial area, drained by tributaries of Beaver R. Bituminous coal, oil, gas, limestone; iron and steel products, chemicals, plate glass, clay products; butter, grain. Formed 1800.

Butler. **1** Town (pop. 659), ⊙ Choctaw co., SW Ala., 35 mi. SE of Meridian, Miss., in cotton and corn area; lumber milling, cotton ginning. **2** Town (pop. 1,182), ⊙ Taylor co., W central Ga., 40 mi. SW of Macon, in agr. and timber region; sawmilling center; clay pits near by. Inc. 1854. **3** Village (pop. 283), Montgomery co., S central Ill., 6 mi. E of Litchfield, in agr. and bituminous-coal-mining area. **4** Town (pop. 1,914), De Kalb co., NE Ind., 29 mi. NNE of Fort Wayne, near Ohio line; trading center in agr. area (poultry, livestock, grain, soybeans; dairy products); mfg. (foundry products, pumps, tanks, windmills, clothing, condensed milk, flour). **5** Town (pop. 404), Pendleton co., N Ky., on Licking R. and 23 mi. SSE of Covington; canned tomatoes, clothing. **6** City (pop. 3,333), ⊙ Bates co., W Mo., near Marais des Cygnes R., 58 mi. S of Kansas City; livestock auctions, annual horse show. Founded 1850s. **7** Borough (pop. 4,050), Morris co., N N.J., 10 mi. NW of Paterson; mfg. (rubber, paper products). St. Anthony's Monastery (Franciscan) here. Settled 1695, inc. 1901. **8** Village (pop. 833), Richland co., N central Ohio, 12 mi. SSE of Mansfield, and on Clear Fork of Mohican R., in agr. area. **9** Town (pop. 351), Custer co., W Okla., 16 mi. WNW of Clinton, in wheat-, livestock-, and cotton-producing area; cotton ginning. **10** Industrial city (pop. 23,482), ⊙ Butler co., W Pa., 29 mi. N of Pittsburgh and on Connoquenessing Creek, in bituminous-coal, gas, limestone, and oil region. Railroad cars, glass, metal products, truck trailers, cement. Settled c.1800, inc. as borough 1803, as city 1917. **11** Town (pop. 109), Day co., NE S.Dak., 10 mi. WSW of Webster; agr. trade center. **12** Former town, Johnson co., extreme NE Tenn., 20 mi. E of Johnson City. Site evacuated in late 1940s because of construction of Watauga Dam; CARDERVIEW was established 3 mi. W. **13** Village (pop. 1,047), Waukesha co., SE Wis., on Menomonee R. and 8 mi. NW of Milwaukee, in dairy and farm area. Until 1930, called New Butler.

Butler, Lake, Pinellas co., W Fla., near Tarpon Springs; c.5 mi. long, 1 mi. wide.

Butlerville, village (pop. 152), Warren co., SW Ohio, 26 mi. ENE of Cincinnati, in agr. area.

Butlin (bŭt'lĭn), resort village, NW Bahama Isls., on Grand Bahama Isl., E of West End; opened 1950.

Buto (bū'tō), anc. city, ⊙ Lower Egypt in prehistoric times (before 3400 B.C.), in the Nile delta; precise location unknown. Had a temple dedicated to goddess Buto.

Buton or **Boeton** (both: bōō'tôn), island (□ 1,759; pop. 106,406), Indonesia, bet. Molucca and Flores seas, just off SE tip of Celebes across Buton Strait (5 mi. wide) and just E of Muna isl.; 4°22'–5°40'S 122°32'–123°12'E; 90 mi. long, 40 mi. wide. Irregular coastline is indented in E by Buton Bay (30 mi. long, 20 mi. wide). Generally mountainous, rises to 3,740 ft.; swamps in NE area. Chief product is asphalt. Agr. (coffee, sago, sugar, tobacco), fishing, lumbering. Chief town is BAUBAU. Du. East India Co. began trade here 1613. Sometimes called Butung or Boetoeng.

Bütow, Poland: see BYTOW.

Butri (bōō'trē), village, Western Prov., Gold Coast colony, on Gulf of Guinea, at mouth of short Butri R., 11 mi. WSW of Takoradi; palm-oil exports.

Butrint, Butrinti, or **Butrinto**, Albania: see BUTHROTUM.

Butschowitz, Czechoslovakia: see BUCOVICE.

Bütschwil (büch'vēl), town (pop. 3,352), St. Gall canton, NE Switzerland, on Thur R. and 16 mi. WSW of St. Gall; cotton textiles, beer; woodworking.

Buttahatchee River (bŭtŭhă'chē), in NW Ala. and NE Miss., rises in Winston co., Ala., flows c.75 mi. generally SW to Monroe co., Miss., joining Tombigbee R. 12 mi. NNW of Columbus, Miss.

Buttala (bōōt'tŭlŭ), village, Uva Prov., SE Ceylon, 20 mi. SE of Badulla; extensive rice plantations; vegetables.

Buttapietra (bōōt-täpyā'trä), village (pop. 639), Verona prov., Veneto, N Italy, 7 mi. S of Verona; cotton and silk mills.

Butte (būt). **1** County (□ 1,665; pop. 64,930), N central Calif.; ⊙ Oroville. Flatlands (W) of the Sacramento Valley rise in E to c.6,600 ft. in the Sierra Nevada. Drained by scenic Feather R. (here joined by its forks) and the Sacramento. Includes parts of Lassen and Plumas natl. forests. Agr. (rice, nuts, citrus fruit, olives, prunes, peaches, grain, alfalfa, grapes); livestock (beef and dairy cattle, sheep, hogs). Gold dredging (a leading placer-gold producing co. of Calif.). Extensive lumbering (pine, fir, cedar). Processing industries (lumber and rice milling, olive-oil extracting, fruit canning). Formed 1850. **2** County (□ 2,240; pop. 2,722), SE central Idaho; ⊙ Arco. Livestock-grazing area watered by Big Lost R. Includes Craters of the Moon Natl. Monument in SW and part of Lost River Range and Challis Natl. Forest in NW. Mineral resources: silver, zinc, tungsten. Formed 1917. **3** County (□ 2,251; pop. 8,161), W S.Dak.; ⊙ Belle Fourche. Agr. area, bounded W by Wyo. and Mont.; drained by Belle Fourche R. and Reservoir. Diversified farming; mfg. at Belle Fourche; dairy products, grain, wool, cattle. Formed 1881.

Butte. **1** City (pop. 33,251), ⊙ Silver Bow co., SW Mont., 50 mi. SSW of Helena, just W of Continental Divide, and on branch of the Clark Fork (here known as Silver Bow Creek), in mtn. region extremely rich in mineral resources; 46°N 112°30'W; alt. 5,775 ft. Second largest city in state and leading copper center, producing almost a third of copper mined in U.S. Copper, zinc, silver, manganese mines; by-products of smelting (lead, arsenic, fertilizer); mfg. (mining equipment, chemicals, bricks, conduits, optical and electrical apparatus). Mont. State School of Mines, mine offices of Anaconda Copper Mining Company here. City founded during gold rush of 1864, platted 1867, inc. 1879. Further development followed discovery of copper (1880) and paralleled growth of Anaconda Copper Mining Company. **2** Village (pop. 614), ⊙ Boyd co., N Nebr., 95 mi. NW of Norfolk, near S.Dak. line, bet. Niobrara R. and Ponca Creek. **3** Village (pop. 272), McLean co., central N.Dak., 40 mi. SE of Minot.

Butte City, village (pop. c.250), Glenn co., N central Calif., 19 mi. SW of Chico and on Sacramento R.; prunes.

Butte des Morts (byōō' dŭ mōr'), resort village (pop. c.200), Winnebago co., E central Wis., 7 mi. NW of Oshkosh, on L. Butte des Morts (c.6 mi. long, 2 mi. wide; a widening of Fox R.).

Butte Falls (būt), town (pop. 372), Jackson co., SW Oregon, 22 mi. NE of Medford.

Buttelstedt (bōō'tŭl-shtĕt"), town (pop. 1,398), Thuringia, central Germany, 7 mi. N of Weimar; grain, potatoes, sugar beets, stock.

Buttenheim (bōō'tŭnhīm), village (pop. 1,091), Upper Franconia, N Bavaria, Germany, near Ludwig Canal and Regnitz R., 9 mi. SE of Bamberg; lumber and paper milling. Has 18th-cent. church.

Butterfield. **1** Village (pop. 529), Watonwan co., S Minn., 8 mi. W of St. James, in grain and livestock area; dairy products. **2** Town (pop. 136), Barry co., SW Mo., in Ozark region, 5 mi. NNW of Cassville.

Butterfield Lake, Jefferson co., N N.Y., 7 mi. E of Alexandria Bay; c.4 mi. long, ½–¾ mi. wide. Resort; fishing.

Butter Island, Maine: see DEER ISLAND, Hancock co.

Butterley, England: see RIPLEY.

Buttermere, lake on Cocker R. in the Lake District, SW Cumberland, England, 7 mi. SW of Keswick; 1¼ mi. long, ½ mi. wide; connected with CRUMMOCK WATER (NNW).

Buttermilk Channel, N.Y.: see NEW YORK BAY.

Buttermilk Falls State Park, W central N.Y., near Cayuga L., c.2 mi. S of Ithaca, along gorge of small Buttermilk Creek. Has scenic glens, many waterfalls and rapids; camping, hiking, swimming.

Butternut, village (pop. 522), Ashland co., N Wis., near small Butternut L., 43 mi. SSE of Ashland; lumbering, dairying, poultry raising, woodworking.

Butterworth, chief town (pop. 21,255) of Prov. Wellesley, Penang, NW Malaya, on Penang Channel opposite (2 mi. E of) George Town (ferry service), and on right bank of Prai R. opposite Prai railhead; tin smelting; oil storage tanks. Airport.

Butterworth, town (pop. 1,542), ⊙ Transkei dist. of the Transkeian Territories, E Cape Prov., U. of So. Afr., on Gcuwa R., tributary of Great Kei R., 50 mi. NNE of East London; center for dairying, stock-raising, wool-producing region. Bawa Falls, 5 mi. S, have total drop of 600 ft.

Buttevant, Gaelic *Cillna Mullach*, village (pop. 793), N Co. Cork, Ireland, 7 mi. N of Mallow; agr. market (dairying; potatoes, oats). Has modernized Buttevant Castle, seat of Barry family, and ruins of 13th-cent. abbey.

Büttgen (büt'gŭn), village (pop. 5,628), in former Prussian Rhine Prov., W Germany, after 1945 in North Rhine-Westphalia, 3 mi. W of Neuss.

Buttington, Wales: see WELSHPOOL.

Büttlassen (büt'läsŭn), peak (10,483 ft.) in Bernese Alps, S central Switzerland, 5 mi. SW of Mürren.

Buttle Lake (□ 11), long narrow lake (18 mi. long, 1 mi. wide) in mts. of central Vancouver Isl., B.C., 24 mi. W of Courtenay; lumbering area. Drained N by Campbell R. S part is in Strathcona Park.

Butt of Lewis, Scotland: see LEWIS WITH HARRIS.

Buttonwillow, village (1940 pop. 685), Kern co., S central Calif., 25 mi. W of Bakersfield; natural-gas field, with pipelines.

Buttonwoods, R.I.: see WARWICK.

Buttrio (bōōt'trēô), village (pop. 1,030), Udine prov., Friuli–Venezia Giulia, NE Italy, 6 mi. SE of Udine; agr. tools.

Butts, county (□ 185; pop. 9,079), central Ga.; ⊙ Jackson. Bounded E by Ocmulgee R. (here forming Lloyd Shoals Reservoir). Piedmont agr. area (cotton, corn, truck, fruit). Formed 1825.

Buttstädt (bo͝ot'shtĕt″), town (pop. 5,304), Thuringia, central Germany, 10 mi. NNE of Weimar; metalworking.

Buttzville, village, Warren co., NW N.J., on Pequest R. and 24 mi. W of Dover, in hilly region; trout fishing.

Butuan (bo͞oto͞o'än), town (1939 pop. 5,343; 1948 municipality pop. 31,628), ⊙ Agusan prov., NE Mindanao, Philippines, port near mouth of Agusan R., 55 mi. S of Surigao; trades in abacá and copra. Gold mines near by. Here Sp. sovereignty over the Philippines was 1st proclaimed (1521) by Magellan.

Butuntum, Italy: see BITONTO.

Buturlino (bo͞oto͞or'lyĭnŭ), village (1926 pop. 1,350), SE Gorki oblast, Russian SFSR, on Pyana R. and 22 mi. W of Sergach; wheat.

Buturlinovka (–ŭfkŭ), city (1926 pop. 27,537), E central Voronezh oblast, Russian SFSR, 80 mi. SE of Voronezh; flour-milling center; sunflower-oil extraction, distilling, tanning, dairying. Chalk quarries, mineral springs near by. Chartered 1917.

Butwal or **Butawal** (both: bo͞ot'vŭl), town, S Nepal, in the Terai, on tributary of the Rapti and 20 mi. N of Nautanwa (India); trade center (corn, rice, wheat, millet, barley, vegetables, buckwheat, fruit); ghee processing and tinning; agr. (medicinal plants and shrubs). Important Nepalese military station. Bhairwa (or Bhairahawa) village, 2 mi. SW, is actual hq. of Butwal dist.

Butysh (bo͞otĭsh'), town (1942 pop. over 500), SE Udmurt Autonomous SSR, Russian SFSR, port on left bank of Kama R. and 3 mi. NNW of Kambarka; shipyards. Developed in Second World War.

Butzbach (bo͞ots'bäkh″), town (pop. 8,019), central Hesse, W Germany, in former Upper Hesse prov., 10 mi. S of Giessen; iron- and leatherworking. Has 16th-cent. town hall.

Bützfleth (büts'flāt″), village (pop. 3,891), in former Prussian prov. of Hanover, NW Germany, after 1945 in Lower Saxony, near Elbe estuary, 4 mi. N of Stade; pottery works.

Bützow (bü'tsō), town (pop. 8,905), Mecklenburg, N Germany, on the Warnow (head of navigation) and 9 mi. WNW of Güstrow; mfg. of chemicals, furniture, barometers; paper milling, basket weaving. Lumber and cattle market. From 1171 until 16th cent., property of bishops of Schwerin and for some time their residence. Huguenot community settled here in 1685. Univ. founded here c.1770 was absorbed 1788 into Rostock univ.

Buvaidy or **Buvaydy** (bo͞ovīdē'), village (1926 pop. 2,274), NW Fergana oblast, Uzbek SSR, 10 mi. NNE of Kokand; cotton; sericulture.

Buxa Duar (bŭk'sŭ dwär'), village, Jalpaiguri dist., N West Bengal, India, in W foothills of Assam Himalayas, 55 mi. ENE of Jalpaiguri; frontier trade center (rice, tobacco, ivory, wax, wool, musk, cotton cloth). Formerly a Br. cantonment established as a frontier post (1865) during Bhutan War. Commands Sinchula Pass (sĭn'cho͞olŭ) (alt. 5,700 ft.), 2 mi. N, on India-Bhutan border, one of main India-Bhutan trade routes. Copper-ore deposits just W. Rail station 4 mi. S, at Buxa Road.

Buxar (bŭksär'), town (pop. 14,879), Shahabad dist., W Bihar, India, on Ganges R. and 45 mi. W of Arrah; rice, gram, wheat, oilseeds, barley, sugar cane. Here, in 1764, decisive English victory over Nawab of Oudh secured English possession of Bengal. In 1539, Sher Shah defeated Humayun at Chausa, 7 mi. SW. Formerly also Baxar.

Buxières-les-Mines (büksyâr'-lā-mēn'), village (pop. 707), Allier dept., central France, 19 mi. ENE of Montluçon; coal mining.

Buxted (bŭk'stĭd), town and parish (pop. 1,913), E central Sussex, England, 2 mi. NE of Uckfield; agr. market. Has 13th-cent. church. It was once center of Sussex iron industry.

Buxtehude (bo͝ok″stŭho͞o'dŭ), town (pop. 12,781), in former Prussian prov. of Hanover, NW Germany, after 1945 in Lower Saxony, 13 mi. W of Hamburg city center; mfg. of machinery, transportation equipment, precision instruments, chemicals, leather and paper goods, sailcloth; food processing (flour products, canned goods, beer, spirits). Has Gothic church. Was member of Hanseatic League.

Buxton, village (pop., including adjoining Friendship, 5,164), Demerara co., N Br. Guiana, on the Atlantic, on railroad and 10 mi. ESE of Georgetown, in rice-growing region. A Negro settlement established after abolition (1833–38) of slavery.

Buxton. 1 Municipal borough (1931 pop. 15,349; 1951 census 19,556), in The Peak, NW Derby, England, on Wye R. and 20 mi. WSW of Sheffield; year-round resort, with mineral springs and baths, at alt. of 1,000 ft., the highest town in England. Site of Devonshire Hosp. Has chapel built 1625. Near by is Poole's Hole, a stalactite cave. Buxton is in an important limestone-quarrying area. In municipal borough (N) is town of Fairfield (pop. 4,529). **2** Agr. village and parish (pop. 490), NE Norfolk, England, on Bure R. and 9 mi. N of Norwich; flour milling.

Buxton. 1 Town (pop. 2,009), York co., SW Maine, near the Saco, 13 mi. W of Portland. Settled 1740, inc. 1772. **2** Resort village, Dare co., E N.C., just N of Cape Hatteras, on barrier beach (Hatteras Isl.) bet. Pamlico Sound and the Atlantic; fishing, bathing. **3** Village (pop. 387), Traill co., E N.Dak., 23 mi. S of Grand Forks.

Buxy (büksē'), village (pop. 933), Saône-et-Loire dept., E central France, 9 mi. SW of Chalon-sur-Saône; winegrowing; granite quarries.

Buy, Russian SFSR: see BUI.

Buyanovats, Yugoslavia: see BUJANOVAC.

Buynaksk, Russian SFSR: see BUINAKSK.

Buysinghen, Belgium: see BUIZINGEN.

Buyuk Agri Dagi, Turkey: see ARARAT, MOUNT.

Buyukcekmece (büyük'chĕmĕjĕ″), Turkish *Büyükçekmece*, lake (□ 4), Turkey in Europe, 19 mi. W of Istanbul; 5 mi. long, 2 mi. wide. Connected with Sea of Marmara.

Buyuk Cokeles (chûkĕlĕs'), Turkish *Büyük Çökeles*, peak (6,040 ft.), W Turkey, in Aydin Mts., 5 mi. S of Cal.

Buyukdere (–dĕrĕ″), Turkish *Büyükdere*, town, Turkey in Europe, residential suburb 11 mi. NNE of Istanbul, on W shore of the Bosporus.

Buyukdoganca, Turkey: see MERIC.

Buyukhasan, Turkey: see HASAN DAG.

Buyuk Island, Turkish *Büyük* (□ 2; pop. 7,017), largest of Princes Isls., in Sea of Marmara, NW Turkey, 14 mi. SE of Istanbul, of which it is part, included in Adalar dist.; 2 mi. long, 1 mi. wide. Resort. Formerly Prinkipo. Trotsky lived here early in his exile.

Buyukliman, Turkey: see VAKFIKEBIR.

Buyuk Menderes River (mĕndĕrĕs') or **Menderes River,** Turkish *Büyük Menderes* [=great Menderes], anc. *Maeander* (mēăn'dûr), SW Turkey, rises S and W of Afyonkarahisar, flows c.250 mi. generally W to the Aegean Sea S of Samos isl. Olives grown in its valley. Its winding course gave rise to the term meander.

Buyun-Uzun (bo͝oyo͞on″-o͞ozo͞on'), village, NE Chardzhou oblast, Turkmen SSR, near the Amu-Darya, 16 mi. NW of Chardzhou; cotton.

Buzachi Peninsula (bo͞ozä'chē), former peninsula in W Guryev oblast, Kazakh SSR; extended into Caspian Sea N of Mangyshlak Peninsula, bet. former Kaidak (E) and Sary-Tash (W) gulfs; desert area; camels. Owing to lowering of Caspian Sea level and subsequent drying-up of Kaidak arm, peninsula has become attached to mainland.

Buzan (bo͞ozän'), arm of Volga R. delta mouth, in Astrakhan oblast, Russian SFSR, leaves main stream c.30 mi. NNW of Astrakhan, flows 75 mi. SE, parallel to Akhtuba R., past Krasny Yar and Marfino, to Caspian Sea 50 mi. ESE of Astrakhan. Navigable; fisheries.

Buzançais (büzäsĕ'), town (pop. 3,150), Indre dept., central France, on Indre R. and 14 mi. WNW of Châteauroux; mfg. of linen and cotton goods, bricks and tile. Silica quarried near by.

Buzancy (büzäsē'), agr. village (pop. 513), Ardennes dept., N France, 12 mi. ENE of Vouziers. Captured by Americans Nov., 1918.

Buzau (bo͞ozû'o͞o) Rum. *Buzău*, town (1948 pop. 43,365), ⊙ Buzau prov., SE central Rumania, in Walachia, on Buzau R. and 60 mi. NE of Bucharest; rail and industrial center with brisk trade in grain, lumber, salt, petroleum, wine, and fruit. Oil refining, metalworking, flour milling, distilling, mfg. of knitwear. Old Orthodox bishopric. Has noted 17th-cent. cathedral, restored in 1740. Formerly sometimes spelled Buseu or Buzeu. Health resort of Boboci is 8 mi. ENE.

Buzau Mountains, Rum. *Buzău*, highest section of the Moldavian Carpathians, in SE central Rumania, partly in Transylvania, partly in Muntenia; extend c.30 mi. on both sides of the upper course of Buzau R.; rise to 6,425 ft. in Ciucas Peak and 5,822 ft. in Penteleu Peak. Important timbering area. Buzau R. rises on W slopes.

Buzau Pass, Rum. *Buzău*, pass (alt. 3,798 ft.), in Buzau Mts., SE central Rumania, 25 mi. ESE of Stalin (Brasov); highway corridor.

Buzau River, Rum. *Buzău*, SE central Rumania, rises in Buzau Mts. 16 mi. NW of Nehoiasu, flows N, thence SE across Buzau Mts., E past Buzau, and NE to Siret R. 14 mi. WSW of Galati; 125 mi. long.

Buz Dag (bo͞oz' dä), Turkish *Buz Dağ*, peak (9,091 ft.; also given as 11,850 ft.), S central Turkey, 25 mi. SSW of Malatya.

Buzdyak (bo͞ozdyäk'), village (1926 pop. 2,051), W Bashkir Autonomous SSR, Russian SFSR, on railroad and 60 mi. WSW of Ufa; meat packing; grain.

Buzen (bo͞o'zĕn), former province in N Kyushu, Japan; now part of Fukuoka and Oita prefectures.

Buzet (bo͞ozĕt'), Ital. *Pinguente* (pĕngwĕn'tĕ), village (pop. 2,924), NW Croatia, Yugoslavia, on Mirna R., on railroad and 19 mi. SSE of Trieste, in Istria.

Buzet-sur-Baïse (büzā'-sür-bäēz'), village (pop. 736), Lot-et-Garonne dept., SW France, 9 mi. N of Nérac; pencil factory; fruitgrowing.

Buzias (bo͞o'zyäsh), Rum. *Buziaș*, Hung. *Buziásfürdő* (bo͞o'zyäsh-für″dû), village (pop. 2,856), Timisoara prov., W Rumania, 18 mi. SE of Timisoara; rail junction and popular health resort, with mineral springs and mud baths.

Búzios, Cape (bo͞o'zyo͞os), headland on the Atlantic, E Rio de Janeiro state, Brazil, 12 mi. NE of Cabo Frio city; 22°45'S 41°53'W.

Buzi River (bo͞o'zē), central Mozambique, rises at Southern Rhodesia border W of Espungabera, flows c.200 mi. ENE, past Nova Lusitânia, to Mozambique Channel at Beira. Navigable in lower course. Sugar plantations near mouth. Also spelled Busi.

Buzovny (bo͞o'zŭvnē), town (1939 pop. over 2,000) in Mashtagi dist. of Greater Baku, Azerbaijan SSR, on NE shore of Apsheron Peninsula, 28 mi. NE of Baku, on electric railroad; oil wells (developed during Second World War). Seaside resort; vineyards.

Buzovyazy or **Buzov'yazy** (bo͞ozŭvyä'zē), village (1926 pop. 3,748), central Bashkir Autonomous SSR, Russian SFSR, 33 mi. S of Ufa; dairying; wheat, livestock.

Buzsak (bo͞o'zhäk), Hung. *Buzsák*, town (pop. 2,549), Somogy co., SW Hungary, 22 mi. NNW of Kaposvar; wheat.

Buzuluk (bo͞ozo͞olo͞ok'), city (1932 pop. estimate 30,400), W Chkalov oblast, Russian SFSR, on Samara R., at mouth of Buzuluk R., and 90 mi. ESE of Kuibyshev, on railroad; grain- and livestock-trading center; ironworks; mfg. of heavy and agr. machinery, flour milling, distilling, sheepskin processing. Founded 1736 as Rus. stronghold on site of old Tatar town; assaulted 1775 by peasant rebels under Yemelyan Pugachev; chartered 1781.

Buzuluk River. 1 In Chkalov oblast, Russian SFSR, rises 15 mi. ESE of Bogdanovka, flows W and NNE, past Andreyevka and Kurmaneyevka, to Samara R. at Buzuluk; 100 mi. long. **2** In Stalingrad oblast, Russian SFSR, rises NW of Danilovka, flows c.150 mi. NW and SE, past Novo-Annenski, to Khoper R. opposite Ust-Buzulukskaya.

Buzzard Roost Dam, S.C.: see SALUDA RIVER.

Buzzards Bay, inlet (30 mi. long, 5–10 mi. wide) of the Atlantic, SE Mass.; extends NE to base of Cape Cod peninsula, bet. coast and Cape; bounded SE by Elizabeth Isls. Cape Cod Canal (NE) connects it with Cape Cod Bay. New Bedford is at head of one of its larger inlets. Village of **Buzzards Bay** (pop. 1,459), the business center, and seat of Cape Cod Canal administration, is in BOURNE town; rail junction.

Bwagaoia (bwä'gŭ-oi'ŭ), chief town of Louisiade Archipelago, Territory of Papua, on SE coast of Misima isl.; gold-mining center.

Bwamanda (bwämän'dä), village, Equator Prov., NW Belgian Congo, 170 mi. NW of Lisala; mission center.

Bwana Mkubwa (bwä'nä ŭmko͞o'bwä), village (pop. 63), Western Prov., N Northern Rhodesia, on railroad, near Belgian Congo border, 5 mi. SE of Ndola. Copper-mining center in 1920s; abandoned 1930–31.

Bwedu (bwĕ'do͞o), town (pop. 809), South-Eastern Prov., E Sierra Leone, 14 mi. E of Kailahun (linked by road), near Liberian border; customs station opposite Liberian crossing point of Foya. Also spelled Buedu.

Byadgi (byäd'gē), town (pop. 8,783), Dharwar dist., S Bombay, India, 10 mi. NW of Ranibennur; agr. market for betel nuts, chili, rice, gur, black pepper, peanuts.

Byakar (byä'kär) or **Byaka** (byä'kä), fortified town [Bhutanese *dzong*], E central Bhutan, on left tributary of the Tongsa and 14 mi. ENE of Tongsa town. Near-by lamaseries include temple regarded as holiest spot in Bhutan; here an 8th-cent. A.D. Buddhist saint, who 1st introduced Buddhism into Bhutan, meditated. Hot spring 14 mi. NNW. Also called Bumtang; formerly spelled Biaka.

Byala (byä'lä). **1** City (pop. 6,367), Ruse dist., NE Bulgaria, on Yantra R. and 28 mi. SSW of Ruse; agr. center (grain, livestock). Has mus. Sometimes spelled Bela or Biela. **2** Village (pop. 2,429), Stalin dist., E Bulgaria, port on Black Sea, 21 mi. S of Varna; lumber exports. Manganese deposits near by (W). Bathing resort Obzor (pop. 1,460) is 5 mi. S.

Byala Cherkva (chĕrk'vä), village (pop. 3,728), Gorna Oryakhovitsa dist., N Bulgaria, on Rositsa R. and 16 mi. NE of Sevliyevo; vineyards, wheat, corn. Formerly Gorni Turcheta.

Byala Slatina (byä'lä slä'tĕnä), city (pop. 9,357), Vratsa dist., N Bulgaria, on Skat R. and 26 mi. NE of Vratsa; stock-trading center. Has technical school. Until c.1945, Bela Slatina or Byela Slatina.

Byalven, Sweden: see BY RIVER.

Byam Martin Channel (bī'ŭm), N central Franklin Dist., Northwest Territories, arm (150 mi. long, 30-65 mi. wide) of the Arctic Ocean, bet. Melville Isl. (W) and Bathurst Isl. (E); 76°N 105°W. Connects Prince Gustav Adolph Sea (N) with Viscount Melville Sound (S).

Byam Martin Island (30 mi. long, 20 mi. wide), central Franklin Dist., Northwest Territories, in Byam Martin Channel; 75°10'N 104°10'W.

Byam Martin's Island, Tuamotu Isls.: see AHUNUI.

Byandovan (byŭndŭvän'), town (1945 pop. over 500), E Azerbaijan SSR, on Caspian Sea, N of Cape Byandovan, 50 mi. SSW of Baku; fisheries; oil wells.

Byars (bī'ŭrz), town (pop. 284), McClain co., central Okla., 22 mi. WNW of Ada, near Canadian R., in agr. area.

Byasen, Norway: see SELSBAKK.

Byblos or **Byblus** (bĭb'lŭs), anc. city of Phoenicia, a Mediterranean port 17 mi. NNE of present-day Beirut, Lebanon. Principal city of Phoenicia in 2d millenium B.C., it retained its importance as a port under the Persians. It was chief center of worship of Adonis. Also, because of its papyri, it was source of Gr. word for book and, hence, of the name of the Bible. Its valuable ruins have been studied, especially after 1922. Its biblical name, Gebal, is preserved in the name of the modern town (pop. 3,175) on the site, Jebeil, Jubeil, Jebail, Jubayl, Jbail, Djébail, or Djoubeil.

Byculla, India: see BOMBAY, city.

Byczyna (bĭchĭ'nä), Ger. *Pitschen* (pĭ'chŭn), town (1939 pop. 3,021; 1946 pop. 1,383) in Upper Silesia, after 1945 in Opole prov., S Poland, 10 mi. N of Kluczbork; mfg. of roofing tiles, bricks; sawmilling.

Bydgoszcz (bĭd'gôshch), province (Pol. *województwo*] (□ 8,106; pop. 1,457,653), N central Poland; ⊙ Bydgoszcz. Low level surface, partly wooded; dotted with numerous small lakes; includes (S) NW section of fertile Kujawy dist. Drained by Vistula, Brda, and Notec (linked with the Vistula by Bydgoszcz Canal) rivers. Principal crops are rye, potatoes, oats, rape, flax, sugar beets; livestock. Chief industries: metal- and woodworking, sugar refining, textile milling, food processing, mfg. of leather goods, glass, chemicals, bricks, furniture, machinery. Minerals worked include salt and silica sands. Principal cities: Bydgoszcz, Torun, Wloclawek, Grudziadz, Inowroclaw. Until 1950, called Pomorze; prov. includes S part of pre-Second World War Pomorze prov. (□ 6,335; 1931 pop. 1,080,138) which extended to the Baltic and formed the Polish Corridor. Before 1919, territory of present-day prov. was divided bet. Kalish (Kalisz) govt. of Rus. Poland and Ger. West Prussia prov.

Bydgoszcz, Ger. *Bromberg* (brôm'bĕrk), city (pop. 134,614), ⊙ Bydgoszcz prov., N central Poland, on Brda R. (here canalized) at E end of Bydgoszcz Canal, and 140 mi. NW of Warsaw, at N end of the Kujawy. Its suburbs reach to the Vistula's left bank. Rail junction; airport; trade and transportation (especially of timber) center; metalworks, mfg. of machines, textiles, clothing, paper, electrical and leather goods, chemicals, chocolate, candy; printing, sawmilling; building materials. Salt domes, lignite deposits, and glassworks near by. Developed following building (1774) of Bydgoszcz Canal; its pop. (c.1,000 in late-18th cent.) grew rapidly, Germanizing the city. Became an important grain-trade center; subsequent railroad construction helped its industrial development. Included in Prussia in 1772, it remained (except for brief period, 1808–15) in Germany until 1919, when it was returned to Poland. During Second World War, when it was a battlefield (1939, 1945) and suffered damage, it was again in Germany.

Bydgoszcz Canal, Pol. *Kanał Bydgoski* (kä'nou bĭdgô'skē), Ger. *Bromberger-Kanal* (brôm'bĕrgûr-känäl'), Bydgoszcz prov., N central Poland, bet. Notec and Brda rivers; 17 mi. long, 64 ft. wide. Naklo lies at W, Bydgoszcz at E end. Has several locks. Planned in 1766 by Pol. geographer F. Czaki; in 1774, Frederick II began its construction, chiefly to divert Pol. water transportation from the lower Vistula to the Oder, thereby weakening Danzig economically and forcing it to submit to Prussia. Canal rebuilt in early-19th cent. Chief westward-moving products were, first, lumber and grain, later almost exclusively lumber; eastward-moving products were of lesser importance. After First World War, canal lost its nationwide significance when water transportation was again directed to Danzig.

Byel-, in Russian names see BEL-.

Byel-, in Yugoslav names: see BJEL-.

Byerkski, Russian SFSR: see KRASNOOSTROVSKI.

Byers (bī'ûrz). **1** City (pop. 83), Pratt co., S Kansas, 12 mi. NNW of Pratt, in wheat area. **2** City (pop. 542), Clay co., N Texas, near Red R., 20 mi. NE of Wichita Falls; trade point in cotton, cattle, grain area; pecan nursery.

Byers Peak, Colo.: see VASQUEZ MOUNTAINS.

Byesville (bīz'vĭl), village (pop. 2,236), Guernsey co., E Ohio, 5 mi. SSE of Cambridge, and on Wills Creek, in agr. area; coal mining; mfg. (plastics, pottery, toys).

Byfield, town and parish (pop. 868), W Northampton, England, 9 mi. NNE of Banbury; leather-goods industry. Has 14th-cent. church.

Byfield, Mass.: see NEWBURY.

Byfleet (bī'–), residential town and parish (pop. 4,819), NW Surrey, England, 3 mi. ENE of Woking. Has 14th-cent. church.

Byford (bī'fûrd), town (pop. 303), SW Western Australia, 21 mi. SSE of Perth; govt.-owned brickworks.

Bygdin (büg'dĭn), village in Oystre-Slidre (Nor. *Øystre-Slidre*) canton (pop. 2,898), Opland co., S central Norway, bet. Bygdin (W) and Vinsteren (E) lakes, at S foot of Jotunheim Mts., 60 mi. WNW of Lillehammer; alt. 3,494 ft. Tourist resort. Bygdin L., expansion (□ 18) of Vinstra R., is 15 mi. long; overlooked by Knutsholtind mtn.

Bygdoy (bügd'ûü), Nor. *Bygdøy*, small peninsula on Oslo Fjord, in WSW part of Oslo city, SE Norway. Popular seaside resort; site of permanent exhibitions showing viking ships (A.D. c.800) excavated at Oseberg and Gokstad, and the *Fram*, the vessel used by polar expeditions of Nansen, Sverdrup, and Amundsen. Norwegian Folk Mus. includes 12th-cent. stave church and reconstructions of old wooden bldgs. and of Ibsen's study. Here is also Nautical Mus.

Bygland (büg'län), village and canton (pop. 1,954), Aust-Agder co., S Norway, on Byglandsfjord, 50 mi. N of Kristiansand; excursion center in the Setesdal. Ose (formerly spelled Osa) village, 10 mi. NNE, is also an excursion center.

Byglandsfjord (büg'länsfyôr"), lake (□ 15) in Aust-Agder co., S Norway, on Otra R. and 36 mi. N of Kristiansand; 12 mi. long. Village (pop. 255) of Byglandsfjord, at S tip, is terminus of railroad from Kristiansand. Sanatorium for lung diseases.

Byhalia (bīhāl'yù), town (pop. 581), Marshall co., N Miss., 27 mi. SE of Memphis (Tenn.), in cotton-growing area.

Bykhov (bĭkhôf'), city (1939 pop. over 10,000), SW Mogilev oblast, Belorussian SSR, on Dnieper R. and 27 mi. S of Mogilev; wood distillation, food processing, dairying. Until c.1930, also called Stary Bykhov. Pop. 30% Jewish until Second World War.

Bykle (bük'lù), village and canton (pop. 703), Aust-Agder co., S Norway, on Otra R. and 90 mi. NNW of Kristiansand; tourist center in the Bykle Mts. Before highway was built, access was by steep stairway hewn in rock.

Bykle Mountains, Nor. *Bykleheiane* or *Byklefjell*, high plateau in Rogaland and Aust-Agder counties, SW Norway, at N end of the Setesdal. Covered with many small lakes; drained by Otra R. Rises to 4,961 ft. 6 mi. NW of Bykle village. There are molybdenum deposits. Wildlife and fish abound.

Bykov (bĭkôf'), town (1947 pop. over 500), S Sakhalin, Russian SFSR, on Naiba R. and 11 mi. WSW of Dolinsk; coal mining. Under Jap. rule (1905–45), called Naibuchi.

Bykovka (–kŭ), town (1939 pop. over 500), SW Zhitomir oblast, Ukrainian SSR, 6 mi. S of Dovbysh; ceramics; kaolin.

Bykovo (bĭkô'vù). **1** Village (1926 pop. 3,450), central Moscow oblast, Russian SFSR, 20 mi. SE of Moscow; cotton and woolen textiles. One of Moscow's civil airports here. Formerly Bykovo-Udelnoye. **2** Village (1929 pop. 7,535), E central Stalingrad oblast, Russian SFSR, on left bank of Volga R. (landing) and 27 mi. S of Kamyshin, in melon dist.; flour mill, metalworks; wheat, mustard, cattle.

Bykovski or **Bykovskiy** (bĭkôf'skē), town (1943 pop. over 500), N Yakut Autonomous SSR, Russian SFSR, port on Laptev Sea, on Bykov branch of Lena R. delta mouth, 25 mi. N of Tiksi, on Bykov Peninsula; fish canning. Formerly called Tumus.

Byk River (bĭk), Rum. *Bâcu* (bû'kōō), central Moldavian SSR, rises S of Korneshty, flows 80 mi. SE, past Kalarash and Kishinev, to the Dniester N of Bendery. Valley is followed by Bendery-Kishinev-Jassy RR.

Bylas (bī'lŭs), village (1940 pop. 636), Graham co., SE Ariz., in San Carlos Indian Reservation and on San Carlos Reservoir, 80 mi. NE of Tucson. Agr. trade center. Evangelical Lutheran mission for Apaches is here.

Bylot Island (□ 4,968), E Franklin Dist., Northwest Territories, in the Arctic Ocean, off N Baffin Isl.; 72°49'–73°53'N 76°20'–81°W; bounded E by Baffin Bay, separated from Baffin Isl. by Pond Inlet, Eclipse Sound, and Navy Board Inlet, and from Devon Isl. (NW) by Lancaster Sound. Isl. is 90 mi. long, 60–70 mi. wide; mainly an ice-covered plateau, rising to c.2,000 ft.; Mt. Thule (S) rises to c.6,600 ft. On S coast are several spring and summer Eskimo camps.

Bynaeset, or **Byneset,** Norway: see SPONGDAL.

Byng Inlet, village (pop. estimate 650), S central Ont., on Byng Inlet of Georgian Bay, at mouth of Magnetawan R., 40 mi. NW of Parry Sound; fishing, lumbering.

Bynum (bī'nŭm), village, Teton co., NW Mont., 13 mi. NNW of Choteau and on branch of Teton R., near Bynum Reservoir; shipping point in irrigated wheat region.

Byoritsu, Formosa: see MIAOLI.

Bypro (bī'prō") or **Burton,** town (pop. 257), Floyd co., SE Ky., in the Cumberlands, 13 mi. SW of Pikeville, in bituminous-coal, oil, gas area.

Byram River (bī'rŭm), in N.Y. and Conn., rises in Byram L. S of Mt. Kisco, N.Y.; flows c.20 mi. S, through Conn., forming 1.5 mi. of S state line, to Long Isl. Sound at Port Chester, N.Y. Diversion dam directs part of its flow into Kensico Reservoir.

Byrd Deep, ocean depth (28,152 ft.) in Antarctic Ocean, off Ross Sea, at 62°S and 180th meridian. Discovered during Byrd expedition (1928–30) to Little America.

Byrdstown, town (pop. 379), ⊙ Pickett co., N Tenn., near Ky. line and Dale Hollow Reservoir, 70 mi. NW of Knoxville.

By River, Swedish *Byälven* (bü'ĕl"vŭn), W Sweden, rises in E Norway, near Swedish border, E of Kongsvinger, flows 80 mi. generally S, through Glaf Fjord, past Saffle, to L. Vaner 3 mi. SSW of Saffle.

Byrka (bĭr'kŭ), village (1939 pop. over 2,000), SE Chita oblast, Russian SFSR, 90 mi. ENE of Borzya, in agr. area (dairy products, wheat).

Byrock (bī'rŏk), village (pop. 139), N central New South Wales, Australia, 370 mi. NW of Sydney; rail junction; copper-mining center.

Byromville (bī'rŭmvĭl), agr. town (pop. 288), Dooly co., central Ga., 10 mi. NW of Vienna; box mfg.

Byron, Greece: see VYRON.

Byron. 1 Town (pop. 379), Peach co., central Ga., 13 mi. SSW of Macon. **2** City (pop. 1,237), Ogle co., N Ill., on Rock R. (bridged here) and 12 mi. SW of Rockford, in rich agr. area; cheese factory. Founded 1835 by New Englanders; inc. 1904. **3** Town (pop. 96), Oxford co., W Maine, on Swift R. and c.13 mi. W of Rumford, in agr., resort area. **4** Village (pop. 439), Shiawassee co., S central Mich., on Shiawassee R. and 18 mi. SW of Flint; mfg. of plumbing supplies. **5** Village (pop. 385), Olmsted co., SE Minn., 10 mi. W of Rochester, in corn, oat, and livestock area; dairy products. **6** Village (pop. 159), Thayer co., S Nebr., 15 mi. SW of Hebron, at Kansas line. **7** Town (pop. 131), Alfalfa co., N Okla., 22 mi. ENE of Alva, near Kansas line, in grain and livestock area. **8** Town (pop. 350), Big Horn co., N Wyo., on Shoshone R., near Mont. line, and 7 mi. WSW of Lovell, in irrigated sugar-beet region; alt. 4,020 ft. Gas wells near by.

Byron, Cape, easternmost point of Australia, forms S end of Byron Bay, E New South Wales; 28°38'S 153°39'E. Lighthouse.

Byron Bay, town and port (pop. 2,036), NE New South Wales, Australia, 90 mi. SSE of Brisbane, on Byron Bay; agr. (bananas), dairy plant.

Byron Island, Chile: see GUAYANECO ISLANDS.

Byron Island, Gilbert Isls.: see NIKUNAU.

Byron Strait, Bismarck Archipelago: see LAVONGAI.

Byrranga Mountains (bĭrŭn-gä'), tundra-covered plateau on Taimyr Peninsula, NW Krasnoyarsk Territory, Russian SFSR; rise to 2,000 ft.; coal deposits. L. Taimyr is at S foot.

Byshev (bĭ'shĭf), village (1926 pop. 4,164), W Kiev oblast, Ukrainian SSR, 30 mi. WSW of Kiev; grain, potatoes.

Byske (büs'kù), village (pop. 1,088), Vasterbotten co., N Sweden, on Gulf of Bothnia, at mouth of Byske R., Swedish *Byskeälv* (120 mi. long), 14 mi. NNE of Skelleftea; lumber and cellulose mills.

Bystrice nad Pernstejnem (bĭ'stûrzhĭtsĕ nät' pĕrn"-shtänĕm), Czech *Bystřice nad Pernštejnem*, town (pop. 2,312), W Moravia, Czechoslovakia, on railroad and 27 mi. NNW of Brno; oats. Noted PERNSTEJN castle is 5 mi. SSE.

Bystrice pod Hostynem (pôd' hô"stēnĕm), Czech *Bystřice pod Hostýnem*, Ger. *Bistritz* (bĭ'strĭts), town (pop. 4,735), E central Moravia, Czechoslovakia, on railroad and 23 mi. SE of Olomouc. Summer resort at NW foot of Hostyn (hô'stēn), Czech *Hostýn*, mtn. (2,414 ft.); mfg. of furniture, religious articles. Has picturesque castle. On Hostyn mtn. is a much-frequented 18th-cent. pilgrimage shrine.

Bystritsa River (bĭstrē'tsŭ), Pol. *Bystrzyca* (bĭstzhĭ'-tsä), in W Ukrainian SSR, formed 3 mi. N of Stanislav by confluence of Bystritsa Solotvinskaya (40 mi. long) and Bystritsa Nadvornyanskaya (45 mi. long) rivers, rising in the Gorgany; flows c.10 mi. N in an arc, past Zhovten, to Dniester R. 6 mi. SE of Galich.

Bystrovka (bĭ'strŭfkŭ), village, E Frunze oblast, Kirghiz SSR, in Chu valley, on railroad and 55 mi. E of Frunze; orchards, truck produce. Rail terminus until extension (late 1940s) of line to Rybachye.

Bystry Istok or **Bystryy Istok** (bĭ'strē ēstôk'), village (1948 pop. over 500), central Altai Territory, Russian SFSR, on Ob R. and 37 mi. W of Bisk; flour milling, sugar refining.

Bystrzyca Klodzka (bĭs-chĭ'tsä kwôt'skä), Pol. *Bystrzyca Kłodzka*, Ger. *Habelschwerdt* (hä'bŭl-shvĕrt), town (1939 pop. 7,067; 1946 pop. 9,564) in Lower Silesia, after 1945 in Wroclaw prov., SW Poland, near Czechoslovak border, at E foot of Habelschwerdt Mts., on the Glatzer Neisse and 10 mi. S of Glatz (Klodzko); match mfg., woodworking. Has 13th-cent. church, remains of medieval fortifications.

Bystrzyca River. 1 Ger. *Weistritz* (vīs'trĭts), in Lower Silesia, after 1945 in SW Poland, rises in the Eulengebirge NW of Nowa Ruda, flows 55 mi. NNE, past Schweidnitz (Swidnica) and Lesnica, to Oder R. 7 mi. NW of Breslau (Wroclaw). Storage reservoir on middle course, near Maniow. **2** Rus. *Bystritsa*, Lublin prov., E Poland, rises 6 mi. E of Krasnik, flows 43 mi. NNE, past Lublin, to Wieprz R. 11 mi. NE of Lublin. Another Bystrzyca R. in Lublin prov. is right tributary of Tsmienica R.

Bystrzyca River, Ukrainian SSR: see BYSTRITSA RIVER.

Bystrzyckie, Gory, Poland: see HABELSCHWERDT MOUNTAINS.

Bytca (bĭ'chä), Slovak *Bytča*, town (pop. 4,528), NW Slovakia, Czechoslovakia, on Vah R., on railroad, and 8 mi. W of Zilina; woodworking (matches, barrels, packing cases, construction materials), mfg. (agr. equipment, baskets); formerly noted for wire mfg. Has picturesque 16th-cent. Renaissance castle. Present municipal area includes formerly independent communes of Velka Bytca (Slovak *Vel'ká Bytča*), Mala Bytca (Slovak *Malá Bytča*), and Hlinik nad Vahom (Slovak *Hliník nad Váhom*). Historic ruins of 13th-cent. Dolni Hricov castle are 3 mi. E, across Vah R.

Byten or **Byten'** (bĭ'tyĭnyŭ), Pol. *Byteń*, village (1931 pop. 1,280), S Baranovichi oblast, Belorussian SSR, on Shchara R. and 28 mi. SW of Baranovichi; tanning, flour milling, sawmilling.

Bytkov (bĭt'kŭf), Pol. *Bitków*, village (1931 pop. 2,330), central Stanislav oblast, Ukrainian SSR, on N slope of E Beskids, 3 mi. W of Nadvornaya; petroleum and natural-gas extracting; gasoline mfg., brewing.

Bytom, Katowice prov., Poland: see Beuthen, Upper Silesia.

Bytom Odrzanski (bĭ'tôm ôd-zhä'nyŭskē), Pol. *Bytom Odrzański*, Ger. *Beuthen an der Oder* (boi'tŭn än dĕr ō'dŭr), town (1939 pop. 3,176; 1946 pop. 1,181) in Lower Silesia, after 1945 in Zielona Gora prov., W Poland, port on the Oder and 20 mi. SSE of Grünberg (Zielona Gora); fruit and vegetable market; basket weaving. In Middle Ages a residence of Pol. Piast princes. After 1945, briefly called Bialobrzezie, Pol. *Białobrzezie*.

Bytosh or **Bytosh'** (bĭ'tŭsh), town (1926 pop. 3,753), N Bryansk oblast, Russian SFSR, 17 mi. NW of Dyatkovo; glassworking center (window glass); metalworks.

Bytow (bĭ'tōōf), Pol. *Bytów*, Ger. *Bütow* (bü'tō), town (1939 pop 10,045; 1946 pop. 3,810) in Pomerania, after 1945 in Koszalin prov., NW Poland, 30 mi. SE of Stolp (Slupsk); agr. market (grain, sugar beets, potatoes, livestock); sawmilling. Has 15th-cent. castle of Teutonic Knights. In Second World War, c.50% destroyed.

Bytown, Ont.: see Ottawa.

Byul-Byuly or **Byul'-Byuly** (byōōl'-byōō'lē), town (1939 pop. over 500) in Ordzhonikidze dist of Greater Baku, Azerbaijan SSR, on central Apsheron Peninsula, 8 mi. ENE of Baku, on electric railroad; clothing mfg.

Bywood, Pa.: see Upper Darby.

Byzantium (bĭzăn'tēŭm, –shŭm), anc. city, on site of present Istanbul, Turkey. Founded 658 B.C. by Greeks from Megara, it early rose to importance because of its position on the Bosporus. In the Peloponnesian War it was captured and recaptured In A.D. 196 it was taken by Roman Emperor Severus. Constantine I in A.D. 330 ordered a new city built here; this was Constantinople, later the ⊙ of the Byzantine Empire (also called the Greek or Eastern empire), successor state to the Roman Empire. In 395 the empire was permanently divided into the Eastern and Western empires. The empire endured until 1453.

Bzenec (bzĕ'nĕts), Ger. *Bisenz* (bē'zĕnts), village (pop. 3,930), S Moravia, Czechoslovakia, 25 mi. SW of Gottwaldov, in fertile agr. dist. (vegetables, vineyards); rail junction. Noted for its wine and its colorful folkways. Coal mining in vicinity.

Bzura River (bzōō'rä), central Poland, rises just E of Zgierz, flows E past Zgierz, N past Ozorkow and Leczyca, E past Lowicz, and N past Sochaczew, to Vistula R. opposite Wyszogrod; c.85 mi. long. Receives Rawka R. (right).

Bzyb River or **Bzyb' River** (ŭbzĭp'), Abkhaz Autonomous SSR, Georgian SSR, rises in main range of the W Greater Caucasus on peak Pshish, flows c.80 mi. W to Black Sea S of Gagry. Its left (S) watershed is **Bzyb Range,** a S spur of the Caucasus.

C

Ca, Song (shông' kä') [Annamese,=red river]. **1** River in N central Vietnam, rises in the Laos SW of Samneua, flows c.300 mi. SE, past Cuarao (head of navigation), to South China Sea below Benthuy (port of Vinh). **2** River in N Vietnam, in Tonkin: see Red River.

Caa-Catí, Argentina: see General Paz, village, Corrientes prov.

Caacupé (käkōōpā'), town (dist. pop. 12,580), ⊙ La Cordillera dept., S central Paraguay, in valley of Cordillera de los Altos, 35 mi. ESE of Asunción; 25°22'S 54°8'W. Resort in agr. area (oranges, tobacco, sugar cane); sugar refining, tile mfg. Shrine of Blue Virgin on central plaza is center of yearly pilgrimages and picturesque festivals. Founded 1770.

Caaguazú (kägwäsōō'), department (□ 8,345; pop. 75,910), SE Paraguay; ⊙ Coronel Oviedo. Bounded N by Sierra de Amambay (Brazil border). Largely low plateau, an outlier of central Brazilian highlands, intersected by small rivers and marshes. Has subtropical, humid climate with heavy vegetation and forests. Predominantly a lumbering and maté-producing area; also sugar cane, oranges, tobacco, livestock. Main centers are Coronel Oviedo, San José, Caaguazú, Carayaó, Curuguaty.

Caaguazú, town (dist. pop. 6,342), Caaguazú dept., S central Paraguay, 28 mi. E of Coronel Oviedo; lumber, maté.

Caala, Angola: see Vila Robert Williams.

Caapiranga (käpērăng'gŭ), town (pop. 97), E central Amazonas, Brazil, near left bank of the Amazon, 75 mi. WSW of Manaus.

Caapucú (käpōōkōō'), town (dist. pop. 6,774), Paraguarí dept., S Paraguay, 75 mi. SE of Asunción; cattle-raising center. The adjoining hills are rich in iron ore, largely unexploited. Founded 1787.

Caazapá (käsäpä'), department (□ 3,670; pop. 73,920), S Paraguay; ⊙ Caazapá. Bounded S by Tebicuary R. Marshy, fertile lowlands with some hills in E. Dense vegetation and forests in subtropical, humid climate. Lumbering and agr. (maté, oranges, petitgrain, sugar cane, cattle).

Caazapá, town (dist. pop. 19,309), ⊙ Caazapá dept., S Paraguay, 100 mi. SE of Asunción; 26°9'S 56°23' W; lumbering and agr. center (maté, oranges, petitgrain, cattle); tanning. Founded 1607.

Cabaceiras (käbăsā'rŭs), city (pop. 508), central Paraíba, NE Brazil, 35 mi. SW of Campina Grande; cotton, beans, corn.

Cabadbaran (käbäd'bärän), town (1939 pop. 3,242; 1948 municipality pop. 18,886), Agusan prov., NE Mindanao, Philippines, on Mindanao Sea, 11 mi. N of Butuan; copra. Gold mining near by.

Cabagan (käbägän'), town (1939 pop. 1,682; 1948 municipality pop. 21,651), Isabela prov., N Luzon, Philippines, on Cagayan R. and 13 mi. SSE of Tuguegarao; agr. center (rice, corn).

Cabaiguán (käbīgwän'), town (pop. 9,853), Las Villas prov., central Cuba, on Central Highway, on railroad and 37 mi. SE of Santa Clara; agr. center (tobacco, sugar cane, fruit, livestock); sugar milling.

Cabalasan, Mount (käbälä'sän), highest peak (3,324 ft.) of Cebu isl., Philippines, in central part of isl., 12 mi. NW of Cebu city.

Cabalete Island (käbälā'tā) (1939 pop. 499), Quezon prov., Philippines, in Lamon Bay, at entrance to Lopez Bay, just off S Luzon, 7 mi. NW of Alabat Isl.; 4 mi. long, 3 mi. wide. Fishing.

Cabalian (käbälē'än), town (1939 pop. 2,420; 1948 municipality pop. 17,922), SE Leyte, Philippines, on small inlet of Surigao Strait, 70 mi. SSE of Tacloban; agr. center (coconuts, rice, corn).

Caballeria, Cape (kävälyä'ryä), northernmost point of Minorca, Balearic Isls., 17 mi. NW of Mahón; 40°5'N 4°6'E.

Caballero (käbäyā'rō), town (dist. pop. 8,034), Paraguarí dept., S Paraguay, on railroad and 60 mi. ESE of Asunción; lumbering and agr. center (oranges, cattle); tanning, extracting of oil of petitgrain, honey processing. Founded 1902.

Caballo Blanco (käbä'yō bläng'kō), village (pop. 55), Retalhuleu dept., SW Guatemala, on coastal plain, on Tilapa R. and 10 mi. WSW of Retalhuleu, on railroad; corn, beans, rice.

Caballococha (käbäyōkō'chä), town (pop. 665), Loreto dept., NE Peru, landing on right bank of upper Amazon R., near Brazil border, and 200 mi. E of Iquitos, in tropical forest region; 3°54'S 70°25'W.

Caballo Dam (kŭbī'ō), SW N.Mex., a unit of Rio Grande reclamation project, 22 mi. downstream from Elephant Butte Dam and 16 mi. S of Hot Springs. Earthfill dam 97 ft. high, 4,590 ft. long; completed 1938. Used for irrigation and flood control. Forms Caballo Reservoir (14 mi. long, 1 mi. wide; capacity 346,000 acre-ft.).

Caballones, Canal de (kănäl' dā käbäyō'nĕs), shallow channel (c.2 mi. long) through the Doce Leguas keys, off Caribbean coast of E Cuba, 75 mi. WSW of Camagüey; 20°50'N 78°57'W.

Caballos, Punta (pōōn'tä käbä'yōs), cape on Gulf of Honduras, NW Honduras, N of Cortés Bay; 15°49' N 87°58'W; lighthouse. Puerto Cortés is on S shore.

Cabana (käbä'nä). **1** City (pop. 2,802), ⊙ Pallasca prov. (□ 972; pop. 40,223), Ancash dept., W central Peru, in Cordillera Occidental, 85 mi. NNW of Huarás; 8°24'S 78°1'W; alt. 10,679 ft. Trade in minerals; agr. products (barley, alfalfa); cattle and sheep raising. **2** Town (pop. 1,945), Ayacucho dept., S Peru, on E slopes of Cordillera Occidental, 36 mi. N of Puquio; corn, beans, alfalfa, livestock.

Cabanaconde (käbänäkōn'dā), town (pop. 2,278), Arequipa dept., S Peru, in Andean valley, at N foot of Nudo de Ampato, 30 mi. WSW of Chivay; alfalfa, grain, potatoes, fruit, stock. Opal deposits.

Cabañal, El, Spain: see Pueblo Nuevo del Mar.

Cabañas (käbä'nyäs, –vä'–), town (pop. 1,877), Pinar del Río prov., W Cuba, minor port on sheltered Cabañas Bay, 38 mi. WSW of Havana, in agr. region (sugar cane, fruit, livestock); fishing, lumbering. Seaplane anchorage. Sugar mills near by.

Cabañas, town (1950 pop. 1,434), Zacapa dept., E Guatemala, on Motagua R. and 17 mi. WSW of Zacapa, on railroad; sugar cane, corn, beans.

Cabañas, town (pop. 646), Copán dept., W Honduras, on W slope of Sierra del Gallinero, 4 mi. E of Copán; tobacco.

Cabanas (käbä'nŭsh), village (pop. 1,878), Viseu dist., N Portugal, 14 mi. SSW of Viseu, in Mondego R. valley; corn, rye, wine, olives.

Cabañas (käbä'nyäs, –vä'–), department (□ 316; pop. 95,327), N Salvador; ⊙ Sensuntepeque. On Honduras border (NE); bounded N and E by Lempa R.; generally hilly except for broad Lempa R. valley. Agr. (grain, sugar, indigo). Gold (San Isidro), emery, and limestone mines. Once an important indigo producer, dept. now specializes in pottery making (Ilobasco) and livestock raising (dairy products). Formed 1873.

Cabañas de Yepes (dhā yā'pĕs), town (pop. 875), Toledo prov., central Spain, 11 mi. SSE of Aranjuez; cereals, olives, grapes, sheep.

Cabanatuan (käbänätwän'), town (1939 pop. 8,834; 1948 municipality pop. 54,668), ⊙ Nueva Ecija prov., central Luzon, Philippines, on Pampanga R. and 60 mi. N of Manila; rail terminus; trade center for agr. area (rice, corn).

Cabanes (käbä'nĕs), town (pop. 2,429), Castellón de la Plana prov., E Spain, 13 mi. NNE of Castellón de la Plana; olive-oil processing; wine, almonds, oranges, figs, grapes. Has Roman triumphal arch.

Cabangan (käbäng'gän), town (1939 pop. 1,814; 1948 municipality pop. 5,519), Zambales prov., central Luzon, Philippines, near W coast, 45 mi. SW of Tarlac; rice growing. Asbestos deposits.

Cabanilla or **Cabanillas** (käbänē'yä, –yäs), village (pop. 342), Puno dept., SE Peru, on the Altiplano, on Juliaca–Arequipa RR and 26 mi. NW of Puno; alt. 12,746 ft. Silver and copper mining; potatoes, barley, livestock.

Cabanillas (käbänē'lyäs), town (pop. 1,417), Navarre prov., N Spain, on Tauste Canal and 5 mi. SE of Tudela; sugar beets, olive oil, pepper.

Cabannes (käbän'), town (pop. 2,000), Bouches-du-Rhône dept., SE France, near left bank of the Durance, 9 mi. SE of Avignon; fruits, flowers, wine.

Cabannes, Les (lā käbän'), village (pop. 419), Ariège dept., S France, on the Ariège and 13 mi. SSE of Foix; forges. Iron mines near by.

Cabano (kăbănō'), village (pop. 2,031), SE Que., on L. Temiscouata, 32 mi. ESE of Rivière du Loup; lumbering, dairying, truck gardening.

Cabar (chä'bär), Serbo-Croatian *Čabar*, village, NW Croatia, Yugoslavia, 20 mi. NNE of Rijeka (Fiume), on Slovenia border; local trade center. Castle.

Cabaret (käbärā'), town (1950 pop. 523), Ouest dept., W Haiti, on Gulf of Gonaïves, on railroad and 13 mi. NNW of Port-au-Prince; sugar cane, cotton.

Cabaritta River (kăbŭrĭ'tŭ), Westmoreland parish, W Jamaica, flows c.25 mi. S, W, and S, to coast just W of Savanna-la-Mar.

Cabarrus (kŭbă'rŭs), county (□ 360; pop. 63,783), S central N.C.; ⊙ Concord. In piedmont region; drained by Rocky R. Agr. (cotton, corn, wheat, hay, dairying, poultry); timber (pine, oak). Textile mfg., sawmilling. Formed 1792.

Cabarruyan Island (käbärōō'yän) (□ 30; 1948 pop. 11,213), Pangasinan prov., Philippines, in Lingayen Gulf, just off Cape Bolinao peninsula of central Luzon; 8 mi. long, 1½–5 mi. wide; rice growing. Chief town is Anda

Cabatuan (käbätōō'än), town (1939 pop. 1,683; 1948 municipality pop. 24,743), Iloilo prov., E central Panay isl., Philippines, 13 mi. NW of Iloilo; rice-growing center.

Cabazon (kă'bŭzŏn"), village (pop. c.200), Riverside co., S Calif., 35 mi. E of Riverside, on floor of San Gorgonio Pass. Cabazon Tunnel carries Colorado R. Aqueduct through San Jacinto Mts., here, to Los Angeles.

Cabeça Gorda (käbā'sŭ gôr'dŭ), village (pop. 2,580), Beja dist., S Portugal, 7 mi. SE of Beja; grain, sheep.

Cabeção (käbĭsä'ō), village (pop. 2,045), Évora dist., S central Portugal, near railroad, 30 mi. NNW of Évora; pines, cork oaks.

Cabeceiras de Basto (käbĭsā'rŭsh dĭ bä'shtōō), town (1,726), Braga dist., N Portugal, 23 mi. ESE of Braga; textiles, ceramics; cork oak and pine forests.

Cabeço de Vide (käbā'sōō dĭ vē'dĭ), village (pop. 2,412), Portalegre dist., central Portugal, 14 mi. SW of Portalegre; watering place with mineral springs. Produces cork, olive oil.

Cabedelo (käbĭdĕ'lōō), town (pop. 5,403), E Paraíba, NE Brazil, at mouth of Paraíba R. on the Atlantic, 11 mi. NNE of João Pessoa, for which it is the seaport; good anchorage, modern harbor installations. Exports cotton, agave fibers, and sugar, and also rare minerals mined in Borborema Plateau. Whale-oil mfg., fish and coconut processing. Seaplane base. Railroad and new highway to João Pessoa. Built on site of 16th-cent. fort. Formerly spelled Cabedello. Lighthouse at Ponta do Mato (headland just N), 6°58'S 34°48'W.

Cabell (kă'bŭl), county (□ 279; pop. 108,035), W W.Va.; ⊙ HUNTINGTON, state's largest city. Bounded NW by Ohio R. (Ohio line); drained by Guyandot and Mud rivers. Agr. (dairy products, livestock, poultry, corn, tobacco, fruit, truck, grain); natural-gas and oil wells, bituminous-coal mines. Industry at Huntington, Milton, Barboursville. Formed 1809.

Cabellos, Uruguay: see ISLA CABELLOS.

Cabery (kā'bûrē), village (pop. 290), on Ford-Kankakee co. line, E Ill., 20 mi. WSW of Kankakee, in rich agr. area; makes cheese.

Cabezabellosa (kävā"thäbälyō'sä), village (pop. 1,175), Cáceres prov., W Spain, 9 mi. NE of Plasencia; stock raising; olive oil, wine.

Cabeza del Buey (kävā'thä dhĕl bwā'), town (pop. 10,748), Badajoz prov., W Spain, on railroad, near Córdoba prov. border, and 70 mi. WSW of Ciudad Real; trading and agr. center (olives, sheep, hogs); tanning, mfg. of textile goods and ceramics. Has mineral springs.

Cabeza la Vaca (lä vä'kä), town (pop. 3,640), Badajoz prov., W Spain, in Sierra Morena, 25 mi. SE of Jerez de los Caballeros; olives, walnuts, chestnuts, cereals. Limekilns.

Cabezamesada (kävā"thämäsä'dhä), town (pop. 1,405), Toledo prov., central Spain, 30 mi. ESE of Aranjuez; cereals, grapes, potatoes, livestock.

Cabezarados (kävā-thärä'dhōs), town (pop. 933), Ciudad Real prov., S central Spain, 22 mi. WSW of Ciudad Real; olives, cereals, livestock.

Cabezarrubias del Puerto (kävā"thäroo'vyäs dhĕl pwĕr'tō), town (pop. 1,371), Ciudad Real prov., S central Spain, in N Sierra Morena, 29 mi. SW of Ciudad Real; cereals, olives, livestock. Lead mines near by.

Cabezas (kävā'säs), town (pop. c.900), Santa Cruz dept., E central Bolivia, at W edge of the Chaco, on Río Grande and 65 mi. NNE of Lagunillas; sugar cane, rice, corn; cattle.

Cabezas or **San Antonio de Cabezas** (sän äntō'nyō dä), town (pop. 2,191), Matanzas prov., W Cuba, on railroad and 15 mi. SSW of Matanzas, in agr. region (sugar cane, fruit, poultry, cattle). Stone quarries near by.

Cabezas del Villar (dhĕl vēlyär'), town (pop. 1,238), Ávila prov., central Spain, 28 mi. W of Ávila; cereals, livestock; lumbering.

Cabezas de San Juan, cape, Puerto Rico: see SAN JUAN, CAPE.

Cabezas de San Juan, Las (läs kävā'thäs dhä sän' hwän'), town (pop. 6,077), Seville prov., SW Spain, in Las Marismas lowland (lower Guadalquivir basin), 37 mi. S of Seville; olive industry. Has Moorish ruins. Customhouse.

Cabezas Rubias (roo'vyäs), town (pop. 1,292), Huelva prov., SW Spain, in Sierra Morena, 33 mi. NNW of Huelva; cereals, acorns, timber; hogs, sheep, goats. Mines iron-copper pyrite.

Cabezón (kävā-thōn'), town (pop. 1,048), Valladolid prov., N central Spain, on Pisuerga R. and 7 mi. NE of Valladolid; chemical-fertilizer mfg.; grain, wine.

Cabezón de la Sal (dhä lä säl'), town (pop. 2,307), Santander prov., N Spain, 9 mi. WSW of Torrelavega; flour mills; dairy products; fruit, vegetables, lumber, cattle. Rock-salt quarries near by.

Cabezuela (kävāthwā'lä). **1** or **Cabezuela del Valle** (dhĕl vä'lyä), town (pop. 2,670), Cáceres prov., W Spain, 20 mi. NE of Plasencia; hog raising, fruit (especially cherries), olive oil, wine. **2** Town (pop. 1,204), Segovia prov., central Spain, 22 mi. NE of Segovia; wheat growing; flour milling, resin mfg.

Cabiao (käbyä'ō, -you'), town (1939 pop. 2,760; 1948 municipality pop. 15,902), Nueva Ecija prov., central Luzon, Philippines, near Pampanga R., 18 mi. SSW of Cabanatuan; agr. center (rice, corn, tobacco).

Cabildo (käbēl'dō), town (pop. 2,005), SW Buenos Aires prov., Argentina, 26 mi. NE of Bahía Blanca; agr. center (wheat, oats, sheep, cattle); distilling. Sometimes Colonia Cabildo.

Cabildo, town (pop. 1,862), Aconcagua prov., central Chile, on Ligua R., on railroad and 11 mi. ENE of La Ligua, in agr. area (grain, potatoes, livestock). Copper deposits near by.

Cabillonum, France: see CHALON-SUR-SAÔNE.

Cabimas (käbē'mäs), town (pop. 11,222), Zulia state, NW Venezuela, on NE shore of L. Maracaibo and 19 mi. SSE of Maracaibo. Petroleum-producing and -refining center in Ambrosio oil field; linked by pipe line with Lagunillas. La Salina oil refinery is just S.

Cabincreek or **Cabin Creek,** village (pop., with adjacent Chelyan, 1,616), Kanawha co., W W.Va., at mouth of small Cabin Creek on Kanawha R. and 16 mi. SE of Charleston; power plant; oil refining.

Cabinda (kŭbĭn'dŭ, käbēn'dä), autonomous district (□ c.2,800; pop. 46,277) and exclave of Angola N of Congo R. estuary, on the Atlantic; ⊙ Cabinda. Bounded by Fr. Equatorial Africa (N), by Belgian Congo (E and S). Separated from Angola proper by a corridor (belonging to Belgian Congo) c.20 mi. wide along lower Congo R. Lies in tropical coastal lowland bet. 4°20'S and 5°45'S. Drained by Chiloango R. Cacao and palm oil are chief products. Formerly also spelled Kabinda.

Cabinda, town (pop. 1,554), ⊙ Cabinda dist. (an exclave of Angola), port on the Atlantic c.35 mi. N of Congo R. estuary and 65 mi. WNW of Boma (Belgian Congo); 5°35'S 12°12'E. Exports palm oil and kernels, cacao; fishing.

Cabinet Mountains, range of Rocky Mts. in NW Mont., rise just W of Libby; extend c.65 mi. S along the Clark Fork to Thompson Falls. Highest point, Snowshoe Peak (8,712 ft.). Include much of Cabinet Natl. Forest. Lead and silver mines.

Cabingaan Island (käbēng-gä'än) (□ 4; 1939 pop. 2,856), in Tapul Group, Sulu prov., Philippines, in Sulu Archipelago, just E of Tapul Isl., 10 mi. S of Jolo Isl.

Cabin John, village, Montgomery co., central Md., on the Potomac c.10 mi. above Washington. Near by are a naval boat-testing basin and a biological observation station (on small Plummer Isl.).

Cabira, Turkey: see SIVAS, city.

Cabixi River (käbē-shē'), W Brazil, right tributary of the Guaporé, rises in Serra dos Parecis, and throughout its course (70 mi.) forms Mato Grosso-Guaporé territory border. Airfield at its influx into the Guaporé (on Bolivia border).

Cable, resort village (pop. 250), Bayfield co., N Wis., on small Cable L., 32 mi. SW of Ashland; produces lumber, chemicals.

Cabo [Sp. and Port.,=cape], for names beginning thus and not found here: see under following part of the name.

Cabo (kä'boo), city (pop. 4,685), E Pernambuco, NE Brazil, on railroad and 18 mi. SW of Recife; sugar milling, alcohol distilling; coffee, coconuts.

Caboalles de Abajo, Spain: see VILLABLINO.

Cabo Blanco (kä'bō bläng'kō), village (pop. 417), Piura dept., NW Peru, port on the cape Cabo Blanco, 4°15'S 81°15'W, on the Pacific, just N of Restín, and 23 mi. N of Talara; oil wells. Petroleum is shipped from here and LOBITOS.

Cabo Cruz (kä'bō kroos') or **Cape Cruz,** sugar-mill village (pop. 876), Oriente prov., E Cuba, on the Caribbean, 95 mi. W of Santiago de Cuba, 17 mi. E of the Cape Cruz. Has airfield.

Cabo de Gracias a Dios, Nicaragua: see CABO GRACIAS A DIOS.

Cabo de las Vírgenes, Argentina: see VÍRGENES, CABO.

Cabo Delgado, district, Mozambique: see PÔRTO AMÉLIA.

Cabo de San Lucas, Mexico: see SAN LUCAS.

Cabo Frio (kä'boo frē'oo), city (pop. 5,647), S Rio de Janeiro state, Brazil, near Cabo FRIO (cape), fishing-port outlet of Araruama Lagoon on the Atlantic, and 75 mi. E of Rio. Center of important saltworking area, with new chemical works (mfg. of caustic soda, and of sodium carbonate by Solvay process). Airfield. Tourist resort. Oldest town in state, founded 1615; retains colonial appearance.

Cabo Gracias a Dios (kä'bō grä'syäs ä dyōs'), territory (□ 5,520; 1950 pop. 16,900), Zelaya dept., NE Nicaragua; ⊙ Cabo Gracias a Dios. Bounded N (along Cruta R.) by Honduras, E by Caribbean Sea; drained by Coco R. Cacao, bananas, sugar cane; livestock. Exports lumber (pine, mahogany) and coconuts. Sometimes Cabo de Gracias a Dios.

Cabo Gracias a Dios, cape and town (1950 pop. 590), ⊙ Cabo Gracias a Dios territory, NE Nicaragua, 70 mi. NNE of Puerto Cabezas, on isl. in Caribbean Sea, at mouth of Coco R.; mfg. (beverages, coconut oil). Customhouse. Sometimes Cabo de Gracias a Dios.

Cabo Juby, Sp. West Africa: for the village, see VILLA BENS; for the cape, see JUBY, CAPE.

Cabool (kŭbool'), city (pop. 1,245), Texas co., S central Mo., in the Ozarks, 31 mi. NNW of West Plains; alt. 1,264 ft. Dairy, lumber products. State poultry experiment station near by. Inc. 1906.

Caborana (kävōrä'nä), village (pop. 2,432), Oviedo prov., NW Spain, in Aller R. valley, 20 mi. SE of Oviedo; corn, lumber, livestock; apple orchards. Coal mines near by.

Caborca (käbôr'kä), city (pop. 5,850), Sonora, NW Mexico, on Magdalena R. (irrigation) and 80 mi. SW of Nogales; agr. center (wheat, corn, cotton, beans). Silver, copper deposits near by.

Cabo Rojo (kä'bō rō'hō), town (pop. 4,797), SW Puerto Rico, near the coast, 7 mi. S of Mayagüez; processing center in agr. region (tobacco, sugar, coffee); mfg. of cigars, alcohol, fruit preserves, clothing, leather products, furniture). Near by on the ocean are saltworks. Cape ROJO is 11 mi. SSW.

Cabot. 1 Town (pop. 1,147), Lonoke co., central Ark., 22 mi. NE of Little Rock, in agr. area; cotton ginning, sawmilling. **2** Town (pop. 826), including Cabot village (pop. 219), Washington co., N central Vt., 15 mi. NE of Montpelier; lumber, boxes. Chartered 1781.

Cabot, Mount (5,160 ft.), in White Mts., Coos co., N central N.H., E of Lancaster.

Cabourg (käboor'), town (pop. 3,171), Calvados dept., NW France, on English Channel at mouth of the Dives, opposite Dives-sur-Mer and 13 mi. NE of Caen; fashionable bathing resort. Damaged in Normandy campaign of Second World War.

Cabo Verde (kä'boo vĕr'dĭ), city (pop. 2,298), SW Minas Gerais, Brazil, near São Paulo border, 23 mi. SE of Guaxupé; coffee, cereals, cattle.

Cabo Verde, Ilhas do: see CAPE VERDE ISLANDS.

Cabo Vírgenes, Argentina: see VÍRGENES, CABO.

Cabo Yubi, Sp. West Africa: for the village, see VILLA BENS; for the cape, see JUBY, CAPE.

Cabra (käv'rä), city (pop. 15,172), Córdoba prov., S Spain, in Andalusia, in irrigated agr. area, 34 mi. SE of Córdoba; agr. trade center (cereals, vegetables, fruit, wine). Olive-oil processing, tanning, marble and stone cutting, brandy distilling, vegetable canning; mfg. of chemicals (carbon disulphide). Marble, limestone, and gypsum quarries near by. It was an old Roman town. Has fine, 14th-cent. Gothic church.

Cabrabassa Rapids, Mozambique: see QUEBRABASA RAPIDS.

Cabra del Santo Cristo (käv'rä dhĕl sän'tō krē'st… town (pop. 4,655), Jaén prov., S Spain, 28 mi. E… of Jaén; cement and soap mfg., olive-oil and e… parto processing, flour milling; sheep raising.

Cabra Island (kä'brä) (2.5 mi. long, 2 mi. wide; 1939 pop. 1,026), in Lubang Isls., Mindoro prov., Philippines, in S. China Sea, just NW of Lubang Isl.; rice growing. Lighthouse at NW end of isl.

Cabral (käbräl'), town (1950 pop. 2,223), Barahona prov., SW Dominican Republic, on the Yaque del Sur and 6 mi. W of Barahona; coffeegrowing center.

Cabral, Serra do (sĕ'rŭ doo käbräl'), range in central Minas Gerais, Brazil, a W outlier of the Serra do Espinhaço, extends 70 mi. N of Corinto, rises to 4,250 ft. Diamond washings.

Cabrália Paulista (käbrä'lyŭ poulē'stŭ), town (pop. 1,461), W central São Paulo, Brazil, on railroad and 14 mi. WSW of Piratininga; grain, cotton, coffee. Until 1944, called Cabrália, and, 1944–48, Pirajaí.

Cabramatta and Canley Vale (kă"brŭmă'tŭ), municipality (pop. 10,966), E New South Wales, Australia, includes Cabramatta, 16 mi. W of Sydney, and Canley Vale, 5 mi. N of Cabramatta; coal-mining center; plaster, cement; sawmill.

Cabras (kä'bräs), village (pop. 4,882), Cagliari prov., W Sardinia, on Stagno di Cabras, 4 mi. NW of Oristano; fishing. Roman cemeteries near by.

Cabras, Las, Chile: see LAS CABRAS.

Cabre, Col de (kôl dŭ kä'brŭ), pass (alt. 3,871 ft.) in Dauphiné Pre-Alps, on Drôme-Hautes-Alpes dept. border, SE France, on Die-Gap road.

Cabreira, Serra da (sĕ'rŭ dŭ kŭbrā'rŭ), hill range in Braga dist., N Portugal, E of Vieira do Minho; rises to 5,900 ft.

Cabrejas del Pinar (kävrā'häs dhĕl pēnär'), agr. town (pop. 756), Soria prov., N central Spain, on railroad and 21 mi. W of Soria.

Cabrera, Argentina: see GENERAL CABRERA.

Cabrera (kävrā'rä), town (1950 pop. 512), Samaná prov., NE Dominican Republic, on the Atlantic, 50 mi. E of Puerto Plata, in agr. region (coffee, cacao, bananas). Until 1891 called Tres Amarras.

Cabrera, Greece: see SCHIZA.

Cabrera Island, anc. *Capraria,* islet (□ c.7.5; pop. 13), Balearic Isls., in the Mediterranean, 3 mi. SW of Cape Salinas (Majorca); 39°8'N 2°58'W. Covered by pines; some cereals are grown around Cabreras village. Isl. was used 1808–13 as prison for Fr. soldiers captured in Napoleonic Wars. Fishing in adjacent waters.

Cabrero (kävrā'rō), town (pop. 1,849), Concepción prov., S central Chile, on railroad and 40 mi. ESE of Concepción; agr. center (wheat, corn, vegetables, livestock); flour milling.

Cabreúva (käbrĕoo'vŭ), city (pop. 668), S São Paulo, Brazil, near Tietê R., 25 mi. NE of Sorocaba; coffee and rice processing; cattle raising.

Cabri, town (pop. 407), SW Sask., 40 mi. NW of Swift Current; grain elevators.

Cabricán (käbrēkän'), town (1950 pop. 638), Quezaltenango dept., SW Guatemala, c.20 mi. NNW of Quezaltenango; alt. 8,241 ft. Corn, wheat, fodder grasses; livestock.

Cabriel River (kävryĕl'), E central Spain, rises near source of the Tagus at Teruel-Cuenca prov. border, flows c.125 mi. S and SE to Júcar R. 19 mi. S of Requena.

Cabrillas (kävrē'lyäs), town (pop. 1,168), Salamanca prov., W Spain, 32 mi. WSW of Salamanca; cereals, livestock.

Cabrillo Beach, Calif.: see SAN PEDRO.

Cabrillo National Monument, Calif.: see LOMA, POINT.

Cabrobó (käbroobō'), city (pop. 544), W Pernambuco, NE Brazil, on left bank of São Francisco R. (not navigable here) and 100 mi. NE of Juàzeiro (Bahia).

Cabrón, Cape (käbrōn'), NE headland of Dominican Republic, NE of Samaná.

Cabucan Island (käboo'kän) (□ 10; 1939 pop. 1,066), Sulu prov., Philippines, in Sulu Archipelago, just off NW coast of Jolo Isl.

Cabudare (käboodä'rä), town (pop. 1,527), Lara state, NW Venezuela, at S edge of Segovia Highlands, 4 mi. ESE of Barquisimeto; sugar cane, coffee, cacao, cereals, stock.

Cabugao (käboo'gou), town (1939 pop. 3,778; 1948 municipality pop. 14,823), Ilocos Sur prov., N Luzon, Philippines, 30 mi. SSW of Laoag, near W coast; rice-growing center.

Cabure (käboo'rä), town (pop. 1,599), Falcón state, NW Venezuela, 20 mi. SSE of Coro; coffee, cacao, livestock.

Caburgua, Lake (käbōōr'gwä) (□ 8), in Andean valley of Cautín prov., S central Chile, in N part of Chilean lake dist., 50 mi. SE of Temuco, near Pucón; c.12 mi. long, c.2 mi. wide. Bounded by mts. Vacation and fishing area.

Cabuyao (käbōōyä'ō, –you'), town (1939 pop. 1,857; 1948 municipality pop. 15,206), Laguna prov., S Luzon, Philippines, on railroad and 24 mi. SSE of Manila, near Laguna de Bay; agr. center (rice, coconuts, sugar cane).

Cacabelos (käkävā'lōs), town (pop. 2,515), Leon prov., NW Spain, 8 mi. NW of Ponferrada; flour and sawmills, brandy distilleries.

Caçador (käsädôr'), city (pop. 3,524), central Santa Catarina, Brazil, on interior plateau, on railroad and 36 mi. S of União da Vitória (Paraná); stock raising, lumbering. Agr. experiment station. Formerly called Rio Caçador.

Cacaguatique, Salvador: see CIUDAD BARRIOS.

Cacahoatán (käkäwätän'), town (pop. 1,961), Chiapas, S Mexico, at S foot of Tacaná volcano, near Guatemala border, 8 mi. NE of Tapachula; coffee growing.

Cacahuamilpa (käkäwämēl'pä), large caves in Guerrero, SW Mexico, 10 mi. NE of Taxco, discovered 1835.

Cacak or **Chachak** (both: chä'chäk), Serbo-Croatian *Čačak*, town (pop. 14,413), W central Serbia, Yugoslavia, on the Western Morava and 60 mi. S of Belgrade; rail junction; ships plums; paper mfg. Apple growing.

Cacalchén (käkälchĕn'), town (pop. 2,144), Yucatan, SE Mexico, 25 mi. E of Mérida; rail junction in henequen-growing region.

Cacalomacán (käkälōmäkän'), town (pop. 2,626), Mexico state, central Mexico, 4 mi. SSW of Toluca; cereals, livestock.

Cacalotán (käkälōtän'), town (pop. 1,318), Sinaloa, NW Mexico, in coastal lowland, 38 mi. ESE of Mazatlán; sugar, tobacco, cotton, chick-peas, vegetables, fruit.

Cacao, El, Costa Rica: see EL CACAO.

Cacaopera (käkoupä'rä), town (pop. 1,854), Morazán dept., E Salvador, 6 mi. NNE of San Francisco; henequen center; produces rope, hammocks, bags.

Caçapava (käsäpä'vů). **1** City, Rio Grande do Sul, Brazil: see CAÇAPAVA DO SUL. **2** City (pop. 7,548), SE São Paulo, Brazil, on Paraíba R., on railroad and 10 mi. SW of Taubaté; livestock center; meat packing, agr. processing (sugar, rice, coffee). Lignite deposits.

Caçapava do Sul (dōō sōōl'), city (pop. 3,309), S central Rio Grande do Sul, Brazil, 60 mi. SSE of Santa Maria; road center and livestock market; cattle slaughtering, fruitgrowing. Marble deposits. Copper mined in vicinity. Until 1944, called Caçapava.

Cacapon Mountain (kůkā'pŏn) (c.2,000 ft.), W.Va., a ridge of the Appalachians, in Eastern Panhandle; from point 8 mi. NNE of Capon Bridge extends c.16 mi. NNE to the Potomac SE of Great Cacapon. Rises to 2,650 ft. near S end, at Va. line; Cacapon R. runs along W foot. On mtn. is Cacapon State Park (c.5,800 acres), with bridle and foot trails, observation points, and facilities for swimming, fishing, camping and sports. **Cacapon River** rises in S Hardy co. as Lost R., which flows c.25 mi. NE before plunging underground and emerging just W of Wardensville as Cacapon R.; thence flows c.85 mi. NNE to the Potomac at Great Cacapon. On Lost R. is Lost R. State Park (c.3,800 acres), with camping, picnicking, and recreational facilities and mineral springs.

Cacatachi (käkätä'chē), town (pop. 662), San Martín dept., N central Peru, in E outliers of the Andes, 5 mi. W of Tarapoto; tobacco, sugar cane, cotton.

Cacba Island and **Cacba, La,** Vietnam: see CATBA ISLAND.

Caccamo (käk'kämô), town (pop. 6,408), Palermo prov., N Sicily, 4 mi. S of Termini Imerese, in grape- and almond-growing region.

Caccavone, Italy: see POGGIO SANNITA.

Caccia, Cape (kät'chä), westernmost point of Sardinia, WSW of Sassari; 40°34'N 8°10'E. Stalactite caverns of Grotta Verde and Grotta del Nettuno here.

Caccivio, Italy: see LURATE CACCIVIO.

Caccuri (käk-kōō'rē), village (pop. 1,747), Catanzaro prov., Calabria, S Italy, in La Sila mts., 5 mi. ESE of San Giovanni in Fiore.

Cacequi (käsĭkē'), city (pop. 4,409), SW central Rio Grande do Sul, Brazil, near Ibicuí R., 45 mi. NW of São Gabriel; rail junction; cattle raising. Formerly spelled Cacequy.

Cáceres (kä'sĭrĭs), city (pop. 4,695), W Mato Grosso, Brazil, head of seasonal navigation on upper Paraguay R. and 110 mi. WSW of Cuiabá. Cattle-shipping and meat-packing center (dried beef). Also exports ipecac roots, sarsaparilla, rubber. Gold placers. Airfield. Founded 1778, during gold rush, as Villa Maria. Until 1939, called São Luiz de Cáceres.

Cáceres (kä'sārĕs), town (pop. 665), Antioquia dept., NW central Colombia, inland port on Cauca R. and 45 mi. N of Yarumal, in agr. region (corn, rice, beans, yucca, bananas, cattle). Serves 200-ton ships in rainy season. Gold, copper, and coal deposits near by.

Cáceres (kä'thārĕs), province (□ 7,699; pop. 511,-377), W Spain; ⊙ Cáceres. It constitutes Upper ESTREMADURA. Bounded W by Portugal; divided by Tagus R. into mountainous region (N) covered by S slopes and spurs of the Sierra de Gata, and tableland (S) crossed by the Sierra de Guadalupe and other small ranges; drained by Tagus R. and its tributaries (Alagón, Tiétar, Almonte, Salor). Has some fertile valleys and large barren areas with scarce rainfall. Essentially agr.: cereals, olive oil, wine, fruit, pepper, tobacco, flax, cork. Stock raising (sheep, goats, hogs, cattle) is important; transhumance from Leon and Old Castile. Lumbering. Phosphate-rock, and some tungsten and lead mining. Few industries, mostly based on agr.: flour milling, food processing (olive oil, wine, meat, dairy products, honey); mfg. of woolen cloth and blankets, soap, chemical fertilizers. Woolen trade. Communications are very poor. Chief cities: Cáceres, Plasencia, Trujillo, Valencia de Alcántara.

Cáceres, anc. *Castra Caecilia*, city (pop. 27,463), ⊙ Cáceres prov., W Spain, in Estremadura, 150 mi. SW of Madrid; 39°29'N 6°27'W. Agr.-trade and road center. Mfg. of chemical fertilizers, tiles, footwear, cork stoppers; food processing (olive oil, sausage, dairy products, honey), flour milling, tanning. Livestock market. Cereals, wine, fruit, cork, and lumber in area. The old part of town, on top of hill and circled by anc. walls and towers, has some Roman and Moorish remains, 2 Gothic churches, episcopal palace, and some medieval houses and fine 16th-cent. mansions; new town lies on lower slopes of hill. Ruins of 2 Roman military camps in plain near by. An important Roman colony of Lusitania; fell to the Moors (8th cent.); after changing hands several times in 12th–13th cent., it was finally liberated (1229) by Alfonso IX. Military order of Santiago founded here. Phosphate-rock mines and limestone quarries near by.

Cáceres, Lake, Bolivia: see PUERTO SUÁREZ.

Cacha, Peru: see SAN PABLO, Cuzco dept.

Cachan (kä-shā'), town (pop. 14,417), Seine dept., N central France, a S suburb of Paris, 4 mi. from Notre Dame Cathedral; mfg. of electrical equipment, furniture, ceramics, ribbons. Trade schools.

Cachapoal, department, Chile: see PEUMO.

Cachapoal River (kächäpwäl'), O'Higgins prov., central Chile, rises from glaciers in the Andes at Argentina border, flows c.100 mi. W, past Rancagua and Peumo, to Rapel R. 3 mi. WSW of Las Cabras. Used for irrigation, hydroelectricity.

Cachar (kä'chär), district (□ 2,794; pop. 987,220), S central Assam, India; ⊙ Silchar. Largely in Surma Valley; bordered E by Manipur, W by E Pakistan, S by Lushai Hills; drained by Barak (Surma) R. and its tributaries. Agr. (rice, tea, cotton, rape and mustard, sugar cane, tobacco, jute); tea processing, lumbering, kerosene tinning, rice milling, tea-box mfg.; silk growing. Oil wells at Badarpur and Masimpur; trade center at Silchar. Original dist. (□ 3,862; pop. 641,181) altered by gain of small W section transferred from SYLHET dist. following creation (1950) of Pakistan in 1947 and by loss (1950) of newly constituted North Cachar Hills dist. Pop. 85% Hindu and Moslem, 15% tribal (Kacharis, Kukis). Also spelled Kachar.

Cacharí (kächärē'), town (pop. 2,495), central Buenos Aires prov., Argentina, 35 mi. NE of Azul; grain, livestock.

Cache (kăsh), county (□ 1,175; pop. 33,536), N Utah; ⊙ Logan. Irrigated agr. area bordering on Idaho and drained by Bear R. Includes fertile Cache Valley (extending N–S) and part of Cache Natl. Forest and Wasatch Range in E. Livestock, hay, sugar beets, fruit, truck products; mfg. at Logan. Formed 1856.

Cache, town (pop. 677), Comanche co., SW Okla., 13 mi. W of Lawton, just S of the Wichita Mts.

Cache Bay (kăsh), town (pop. 1,004), SE central Ont., on NW shore of L. Nipissing, 26 mi. W of North Bay; lumbering, fishing center.

Cache Creek. **1** In NW Calif., issues from Clear L. in Lake co., flows SE c.85 mi. to Sacramento R. in Yolo co. **2** In SW Okla., rises in SE Caddo co., flows NE, then S, for c.100 mi., past Apache, Fort Sill, and Lawton, to Red R. c.17 mi. S of Walters.

Cache la Poudre River (kăsh" lů pōō'drů), N Colo., rises in NW corner of Rocky Mtn. Natl. Park, flows 126 mi. N, E, and SE, past Fort Collins and Windsor, to S.Platte R. 5 mi. E of Greeley. Waters sugar-beet, livestock region. Receives water from Laramie R. through Laramie-Poudre (or Greeley-Poudre) Tunnel (c.2 mi. long; finished 1911), used to irrigate 125,000 acres in Larimer and Weld counties.

Cache River (kăsh). **1** In S Ill., rises in E Union co., flows c.55 mi. SE, W, and S, through rich agr. area, to Ohio R. c.5 mi. above Cairo. **2** In Mo. and Ark., rises in Butler co., SE Mo., flows SW into Ark., past Grubbs, to White R. at Clarendon; c.213 mi. long.

Cacheu (kůshā'ōō), village, NW Port. Guinea, on S bank of Cacheu R. estuary and 50 mi. NW of Bissau; palm oil, copra, almonds; stock raising. A slave-trading center since 1588, it preserves an old fort.

Cacheu River, NW Port. Guinea, rises c.30 mi. E of Farim, flows over 150 mi. W to the Atlantic below Cacheu. Binta is head of ocean navigation. Formerly spelled Cacheo.

Cacheuta (kächĕōō'tä), village (pop. estimate 500), N Mendoza prov., Argentina, at S foot of the Sierra de los Paramillos, on Mendoza R., on railroad, and 20 mi. WSW of Mendoza; health resort (radio-active warm waters). Oil wells, with pipe line to Mendoza; hydroelectric station supplying Mendoza city.

Cachi (kä'chē), village (pop. estimate 500), ⊙ Cachi dept. (□ 930; 1947 census 5,547), W central Salta prov., Argentina, on right bank of the Calchaquí (here also called Cachi R.) and 50 mi. SW of Salta; corn, sugar cane. Salt deposits near by.

Cachí (kächē'), village (dist. pop. 3,038), Cartago prov., central Costa Rica, on Reventazón R. and 5 mi. ESE of Paraíso; coffee, sugar, beans, tobacco.

Cachi, Sierra Nevado de (syĕ'rä nävä'dō dā kä'chē), Andean range in W Salta prov., Argentina, S of San Antonio de los Cobres; extends c.25 mi. N–S; rises to over 21,000 ft.

Cachicadán (kächēkädän'), town (pop. 1,511), Libertad dept., NW Peru, in Cordillera Occidental, 3 mi. NNE of Santiago de Chuco; barley, corn; thermal baths.

Cachimba (kächēm'bä) or **Conto** (kōn'tō), town (pop. 2,214), Valle del Cauca dept., W Colombia, in Cauca valley, 23 mi. N of Cali; sugar cane, tobacco, cattle.

Cachinal (kächēnäl'), mining settlement (1930 pop. 36), Antofagasta prov., N Chile, in the Atacama Desert, 70 mi. NE of Taltal; rail terminus; silver and gold mining.

Cachoeira (käshwā'rů). **1** City (pop. 10,374), E Bahia, Brazil, port and head of navigation on left bank of Paraguaçu R. near its mouth on Todos os Santos Bay, and 40 mi. NW of Salvador; mfg. of tobacco products. Ships sugar, manioc meal. Connected by railroad bridge with São Félix (opposite bank). **2** City, Ceará, Brazil: see SOLONÓPOLE. **3** City, Pará, Brazil: see ARARIÚNA. **4** City, Rio Grande do Sul, Brazil: see CACHOEIRA DO SUL. **5** City, São Paulo, Brazil: see CACHOEIRA PAULISTA.

Cachoeira do Sul (dōō sōōl'), city (1950 pop. 23,827), Rio Grande do Sul, Brazil, head of navigation on Jacuí R., on railroad and 100 mi. W of Pôrto Alegre; commercial center of fertile Jacuí valley; livestock slaughtering, meat packing, mfg. of jerked beef. Processes and ships wool, rice, grain, fruit. Molybdenum deposits near by. Airfield. Until 1944, called Cachoeira.

Cachoeira Paulista (poulē'stů), city (pop. 5,250), extreme SE São Paulo, Brazil, on Paraíba R., on railroad and 6 mi. SW of Cruzeiro; dairying center; distilling, meat packing; coffee, fruit. Until 1944, called Cachoeira, and, 1944–48, Valparaíba.

Cachoeira River, coastal stream in SE Bahia, Brazil, entering the Atlantic at Ilhéus; 100 mi. long. In intensive cacao-growing region.

Cachoeiras de Macacu (käshwā'růs dĭ mäkäkōō'), city (pop. 2,612), central Rio de Janeiro state, Brazil, on railroad and 12 mi. SW of Nova Friburgo; coffee grown largely by German settlers; distilling. Until 1943, called Cachoeiras.

Cachoeiro de Itapemirim (käshōā'rōō dĭ ētäpĭmērēm'), city (1950 pop. 24,611), S Espírito Santo, Brazil, on Itapemirim R., 60 mi. SW of Vitória; rail junction; industrial center mfg. cement, cotton goods, refined sugar, rum, furniture, dairy products. Exports coffee and monazitic sands.

Cachoeiro de Santa Leopoldina, Brazil: see SANTA LEOPOLDINA.

Cachtice (chäkh'tyĭtsĕ), Slovak *Čachtice*, Hung. *Csejte* (chā'tĕ), village (pop. 3,266), W Slovakia, Czechoslovakia, on railroad and 3 mi. SW of Nove Mesto nad Vahom. Has 14th-cent. church with Gothic catacombs, picturesque castle ruins.

Cachuela Esperanza (käch-wā'lä ĕspärän'sä), town (pop. c.1,600), Beni dept., N Bolivia, port on Beni R. and 43 mi. NE of Riberalta; rubber-collecting center and transfer point for river and road shipments (road leads to outlet port of Guayaramerín). Until 1900s, Esperanza.

Cachuma Dam, Calif.: see SANTA YNEZ RIVER.

Cacilhas (käsē'lyůsh), town (pop. 2,685), Setúbal dist., S central Portugal, on S bank of Tagus estuary, opposite (1.5 mi. S of) Lisbon (ferry); fish processing, truck gardening.

Cacimbinhas, Brazil: see PINHEIRO MACHADO.

Cacine (käsē'nā), village, SW Port. Guinea, near Fr. Guinea border, 40 mi. SE of Bolama. Former slave-trading center.

Caciulata, Rumania: see CALIMANESTI.

Cacolo (käkō'lō), town (pop. 284), Malange prov., N central Angola, 80 mi. SW of Vila Henrique de Carvalho; manioc, beans, almonds, rubber; pottery.

Caconda (käkōn'dä), town (pop. 4,851), Huíla prov., W central Angola, on road and 80 mi. SW of Nova Lisboa; alt. c.5,000 ft. Cattle-raising center; corn, wheat, beans. Airfield.

Caconde (käkōn'dĭ), city (pop. 2,594), E São Paulo, Brazil, near Minas Gerais border, 17 mi. ENE of São José do Rio Pardo; butter processing, tanning; coffee, cotton, grain.

Cacoso (käkō'zō), village, Malange prov., N central Angola, on railroad and 40 mi. W of Malange; sisal, corn.

Cacouna (kŭkōō'nŭ), village (pop. 590), SE Que., on the St. Lawrence and 6 mi. NNE of Rivière du Loup; dairying, lumbering; resort. Just N, in the St. Lawrence, is Cacouna Isl. (2 mi. long).

Cacuí, Argentina: see VICENTINI.

Cadalen (kädälä'), agr. village (pop. 1,256), Tarn dept., S France, 10 mi. SW of Albi.

Cadalso de los Vidrios (kä-dhäl'sō dhā lōs vēdh'-ryōs), town (pop. 2,200), Madrid prov., central Spain, 40 mi. WSW of Madrid; cereals, grapes, olives, livestock. Known for fine wines. Sawmilling, glass mfg.

Cadaqués (kä-dhäkās'), town (pop. 1,091), Gerona prov., NE Spain, 16 mi. ENE of Figueras; resort on the Mediterranean; fishing; olive-oil, wine.

Cadasa, Palestine: see KEDESH.

Cadaval (kädäväl'), town (pop. 1,054), Lisboa dist., central Portugal, 36 mi. N of Lisbon; alcohol distilling.

Cadca (chä'tsä), Slovak *Čadca*, Hung. *Csaca* (chŏ'-kŏ), town (pop. 8,619), NW Slovakia, Czechoslovakia, 15 mi. N of Zilina; rail junction; mfg. of woolen textiles, woodworking.

Cadder, parish (pop. 19,196), N Lanark, Scotland, just NE of Glasgow, in coal-mining region; includes STEPPS and MUIRHEAD.

Caddington, residential town and parish (pop. 1,785), S Bedford, England, 2 mi. SW of Luton. Church dates from 13th cent.

Caddo (kă'dō). **1** Parish (□ 900; pop. 176,547), extreme NW La., situated on Texas-Ark. lines (W), bounded E by Red R.; ⊙ SHREVEPORT. Includes Cross L. (resort), and part of Caddo L. Large oil production; natural-gas wells, oil and gas refineries, pipelines. Agr. (chiefly cotton; also corn, hay, peanuts); timber. Milling of cotton, cottonseed, lumber. Shipping on Red R. Formed 1838. **2** County (□ 1,275; pop. 34,913), W central Okla.; ⊙ Anadarko. Intersected by Washita R. Hilly agr. area (cotton, wheat, sorghums, peanuts, livestock; dairy products). Mfg. and farm-products processing at Anadarko, Apache, and Cement. Oil and natural-gas wells; oil refining. Formed 1907.

Caddo. 1 Town (pop. 895), Bryan co., S Okla., 11 mi. NE of Durant, in farm area (grain, cotton, peanuts; dairy products); cotton ginning; timber. **2** Village (pop. c.500), Stephens co., N central Texas, 14 mi. E of Breckenridge; trade point in agr. area (cotton, grain, cattle).

Caddoa Reservoir, Colo.: see JOHN MARTIN DAM.

Caddo Gap (kă'dō), village, Montgomery co., W Ark., 5 mi. SE of Norman and on Caddo R.; fishing resort.

Caddo Lake, Texas and La., 18 mi. NW of Shreveport, La.; c.12 mi. long; receives Cypress Bayou (from W), other streams. Center of oil field. Mooringsport, Oil City, and a state park are on its shores.

Caddo Mills, city (pop. 509), Hunt co., NE Texas, 9 mi. SW of Greenville, in agr. area.

Caddonfoot, agr. village and parish (pop. 628), NE Selkirk, Scotland, on the Tweed and 3 mi. WSW of Galashiels.

Caddo River (kă'dō), SW Ark., rises W of Norman, flows c.80 mi. SE to Ouachita R. 4 mi. N of Arkadelphia.

Cadeby (kād'bē), village and parish (pop. 136), West Riding, S Yorkshire, England, 4 mi. WSW of Doncaster; coal mining.

Cadell (kă'dŭl), village (pop. 330), SE South Australia, 90 mi. NE of Adelaide and on Murray R.; orchards.

Cadenabbia (kädĕnäb'byä), village (pop. 348), Como prov., Lombardy, N Italy, port on W shore of L. Como, opposite Bellagio; resort. Near by are famous villa and gardens of Villa Carlotta (completed 1747), with works by Thorwaldsen and Canova.

Cadenet (kädŭnā'), village (pop. 1,668), Vaucluse dept., SE France, near the Durance, 10 mi. S of Apt; ships asparagus, grapes, olive-oil, cherries. Basketmaking.

Cadeo (kädā'ô), village (pop. 292), Piacenza prov., Emilia-Romagna, N central Italy, 9 mi. SE of Piacenza; pump machinery.

Cadereyta (kädärā'tä), officially Cadereyta de Montes, city (pop. 1,249), Querétaro, central Mexico, on central plateau, 38 mi. ENE of Querétaro; alt. 6,755 ft. Agr. center (corn, wheat, sugar, vegetables, alfalfa, livestock).

Cadereyta Jiménez (hēmā'nĕs), city (pop. 4,179), Nuevo León, N Mexico, on railroad and 20 mi. ESE of Monterrey; agr. center (grain, chick-peas, cotton, stock).

Cader Idris (kă'dŭr ĭ'drĭs), mountain ridge, W Merioneth, Wales, extends 7 mi. E-W, SW of Dolgelley; includes peaks of Pen-y-Gader (pĕn-ŭ-gä'dŭr) (2,927 ft.), 3 mi. SSW of Dolgelley, and Mynydd Moel (mŭnĭdh moil') (2,804 ft.), 2 mi. S of Dolgelley.

Caderousse (kädŭrōōs'), village (pop. 812), Vaucluse dept., SE France, on the Rhone and 4 mi. SW of Orange; broom mfg.

Cadí, Sierra de (syĕ'rä dhā kä-dhē'), spur of the main chain of the E Pyrenees, NE Spain, extending ENE-WSW between upper Segre R. and upper Llobregat R. from Fr. border S of Puigcerdá to S of Seo de Urgel. Rises to 8,422 ft.

Cadia, village, E central New South Wales, Australia, 130 mi. WNW of Sydney; iron mines.

Cádiar (kädh'yär), town (pop. 1,981), Granada prov., S Spain, 28 mi. SE of Granada; olive-oil processing, brandy distilling; cereals, wine, lumber.

Cadibona Pass (kädēbô'nä) or **Altare Pass** (ältä'rĕ), Ital. *Colle di Cadibona* or *Colle di Altare* (alt. c.1,450 ft.), NW Italy, bet. Ligurian Alps (W) and Ligurian Apennines (E), 7 mi. WNW of Savona; crossed by road and railroad bet. Savona and Ceva.

Cadillac (kă'dĭlăk). **1** Village (pop. 989), W Que., 14 mi. WNW of Malartic; gold mining. **2** Village (pop. 226), S Sask., 40 mi. S of Swift Current; wheat.

Cadillac (kädēyäk'), village (pop. 1,416), Gironde dept., SW France, on right bank of Garonne R. and 19 mi. SE of Bordeaux; winegrowing. Has 14th-cent. ramparts, castle (1598), insane asylum.

Cadillac (kă'dĭlăk), city (pop. 10,425), ⊙ Wexford co., NW Mich., on E shore of L. Cadillac (c.3 mi. long) and 37 mi. SSE of Traverse City. Trade center for resort and agr. area (livestock, poultry; dairy products; grain, beans, potatoes). Mfg. of truck and auto parts, metal products, machinery, furniture, wood products, plumbing fixtures, leather goods, clothing, potato flour. Hq. for Manistee and Huron Natl. forests. Year-round resort with recreational facilities. Settled c.1871; inc. as village 1875, as city 1877.

Cadillac, Lake, Mich.: see CADILLAC, city.

Cadillac Mountain, Maine: see MOUNT DESERT ISLAND.

Cadillal, El, Argentina: see EL CADILLAL.

Cadishead, England: see IRLAM.

Cadiz (kä'dĭz, kŭdĭz', Sp. kä'dhēs), town (1939 pop. 7,593; 1948 municipality pop. 48,960), Negros Occidental prov., N Negros isl., Philippines, on Visayan Sea, 31 mi. NE of Bacolod; lumbering and agr. center (rice, sugar cane).

Cádiz (kā'dĭz, kŭdĭz', kă'dĭz, Sp. kä'dhĕth), province (□ 2,827; pop. 600,440), SW Spain, southernmost of Iberian Peninsula, in ANDALUSIA; ⊙ Cádiz. Bounded by the Atlantic (SW), the Mediterranean (SE), and the Strait of Gibraltar (S). Málaga prov. is E, Seville prov. N. Mouth of Guadalquivir R. is in NW. The prov. has a mountainous E section, crossed by wooded spurs of the Cordillera Penibética; and a low-level W section, well watered by the Guadalete, Majaceite, Barbate, and numerous small rivers. Along the coast are marshes, abounding in salt ponds, providing one of the prov.'s principal industries. Inlets with fine harbors are Algeciras Bay (on which is the Rock of Gibraltar) and the Bay of Cádiz, at whose entrance is the leading port and chief commercial city, Cádiz. Among other coastal landmarks is famous Cape Trafalgar and Point Marroquí, southernmost cape of Eur. mainland. Climate is subtropical with mild winters (attracting tourists), though summers in lowlands are excessively hot and subject to droughts. The fertile prov. is known for its sherry (named for Jerez). Besides grapes, chief agr. products are olives, cereals, oranges, vegetables, cattle, hogs, horses, goats. The forested ranges yield cork. Coastal fisheries are a major source of income. Processing industries: wine making, alcohol and cognac distilling, olive-oil pressing, flour milling, fish salting and canning, tanning. Some lumbering, quarrying (marble, lime, jasper), and mining (coal, sulphur). Mineral springs. Among main urban centers are Cádiz, Jerez, Sanlúcar de Barrameda, San Fernando, Medina-Sidonia, Algeciras, La Línea, Tarifa, San Roque, El Puerto, Arcos de la Frontera, Grazalema. Cádiz was one of the major battlegrounds during Moorish invasions. Prov. was set up in 1833. Administratively, Ceuta in Sp. North Africa belongs to Cádiz prov.

Cádiz, city (pop. 87,630), ⊙ Cádiz prov., SW Spain, major port on Atlantic coast (Gulf of Cádiz) of Andalusia, 60 mi. WNW of Gibraltar and 300 mi. SSW of Madrid; 36°32'N 6°18'W. Almost entirely surrounded by the sea, it is built on a NW spit of the small León or San Fernando Isl. just off the mainland and guarding entrance to Bay of Cádiz (E). It was the leading maritime city of the colonial era, and is now chiefly a port of call for transoceanic vessels (America, Africa, W Europe, Mediterranean), shipping large volume of salt and wine, besides olive oil, cork, fruit, fish, and minerals. Has a free port with fine harbor installations, shipyards, and dry dock. La Carraca naval base and arsenal 6 mi. E. City is commercial and processing center of the rich agr. prov.; has wineries, breweries, flour mills, fish canneries, machine shops, and foundries; mfg. of flour and tobacco products, cork, pharmaceuticals, engines, musical instruments. One of the most attractive cities of Spain, noted for its mild winters. Though most of its bldgs. are of relatively recent date, Cádiz is of great architectural interest. The clean, sun-baked white city, with all its straight streets leading to the sea, has fine palm-lined promenades and parks. Outstanding bldgs. include the old cathedral (built in 13th cent., reconstructed after 1596 siege), the imposing new cathedral (begun 1722), former Capuchin convent, San Sebastián and Santa Catalina castles, and the city's landmark, the Torre de Vigía (=watch tower). Famed paintings, especially by Sp. masters—such as Valdés Leal, Ribera, Murillo, El Greco, Alonso Cano, Zurbarán—are treasured at the Acad. of Fine Arts. The small Santa Catalina church contains Murillo's last work, *The Marriage of St. Catherine;* while painting it he fell from the scaffold. At the Oratorio de San Felipe, the Cortes met in 1812 to draw up a new, liberal constitution. City also has an archaeological mus., a medical faculty, school of business, naval institute, and theater. It is an archbishopric. Cádiz was founded c.1100 B.C. as Gadir by the Phoenicians; it was taken c.500 B.C. by the Carthaginians and in late 3d cent. B.C. passed to the Romans, under whom it flourished as Gades. The Barbarian and later Moorish invasions brought about its decline. It was reconquered in 1262 by Alfonso X of Castile, and the discovery of America revived its prosperity. From here Columbus sailed on his 2d voyage. Cádiz was attacked and burned in 1596 by the earl of Essex but recovered quickly until the loss of the American colonies caused a considerable setback. The city resisted attacks by Nelson and a Fr. siege (1810–12), raised by Wellington. In the Bay of Cádiz a squadron initiated the 1868 revolution which removed Isabel II from the Sp. throne. The inhabitants of Cádiz are commonly referred to as Gaditanos.

Cadiz. 1 (kŭdĭz', kā'dĭz) Town (pop. 222), Henry co., E central Ind., 7 mi. WNW of New Castle, in agr. area. **2** (kā'dĭz) City (pop. 1,280), ⊙ Trigg co., SW Ky., on Little R. and 21 mi. W of Hopkinsville; trade, shipping center for agr. area (dark tobacco, wheat, corn, livestock), with timber; mfg. of wood products, clothing; flour and feed mills. Brelsford Caves, Kentucky Woodlands Wildlife Refuge are near by. **3** (kă'dĭz, –dĭs) Village (pop. 3,020), ⊙ Harrison co., E Ohio, 20 mi. WSW of Steubenville; trade and marketing center in farming, coal-mining, and stock-raising area; coal cleaning, mfg. of tools, dairying, flour and feed milling. Laid out 1803–4, inc. 1818.

Cádiz, Bay of (kā'dĭz, kŭdĭz', kă'dĭz, Sp. kä'dhĕth), small Atlantic inlet (7 mi. long, up to 5 mi. wide), Cádiz prov., SW Spain, 18 mi. S of Guadalquivir R. mouth. Cádiz city, built on spit of León or San Fernando Isl., is at its NW entrance (36°32'N 6°18'W). Other cities on the deep, protected bay are San Fernando (S), Puerto Real (E), and El Puerto or El Puerto de Santa María (NE). On it, too, are the Carriaca arsenal, naval installations, and shipyards. There are many saltworks along its coast. Receives Guadalete R.

Cádiz, Gulf of, wide Atlantic inlet of SW Iberian Peninsula, generally considered to extend from Cape Saint Vincent (Portugal) c.200 mi. SE to Gibraltar. Apart from those rocky promontories, it is flanked by alluvial, frequently marshy, lowlands. Into it flow the Guadiana and Guadalquivir rivers. Bay of Cádiz opens off it.

Cadiz Lake (kā'dĭz), SE Calif., intermittently dry bed (c.12 mi. long) in Mojave Desert, 55 mi. SW of Needles.

Cadolzburg (kä'dôltsbŏŏrk"), village (pop. 3,160), Middle Franconia, N central Bavaria, Germany, 6 mi. W of Fürth; machine-tool mfg., brewing. Hops, horse-radish. Has late-15th-cent. castle and town hall. Sandstone quarries in area.

Cadomin (kă'dōmĭn), village (pop. estimate 400), W. Alta., in Rocky Mts., near E side of Jasper Natl. Park, at foot of Luscar Mtn. (8,534 ft.), 33 mi. ENE of Jasper; coal mining.

Cadoneghe (kädô'nĕgĕ), village (pop. 423), Padova prov., Veneto, N Italy, on Brenta R. and 3 mi. NE of Padua; machinery.

Cadorago (kädôrä'gô), village (pop. 1,639), Como prov., Lombardy, N Italy, 6 mi. SSW of Como; silk mills.

Cadosia (kŭdō'shŭ, kŭdō'zēŭ), village (1940 pop 641), Delaware co., S N.Y., 33 mi. ESE of Binghamton, near junction of East and West branches forming Delaware R.

Cadott (kŭdŏt'), village (pop. 791), Chippewa co., W central Wis., near Yellow R., 12 mi. E of Chippewa Falls, in lumbering, dairying, and stock-raising area; flour milling.

Cadouin (kädwĕ'), village (pop. 288), Dordogne dept., SW France, 19 mi. E of Bergerac; agr. school. Has 12th-cent. church and a Flamboyant early 16th-cent. cloister.

Cadours (kädōōr'), village (pop. 359), Haute-Garonne dept., S France, 22 mi. WNW of Toulouse; flour milling; agr.

Cadoxton, Wales: see BARRY.

Cadreita (kädhrā'tä), town (pop. 1,326), Navarre prov., N Spain, near the Ebro, 12 mi. NNW of Tudela; sugar beets, wine, cereals.

Caduruan Point (kä"dōōrōōän', Sp. kädhŏŏrwän'), southeasternmost point of Masbate isl., Philippines, on Visayan Sea; 11°43'N 124°4'E.

Cadwell, town (pop. 310), Laurens co., central Ga., 17 mi. SSW of Dublin.

Cadyville, village (1940 pop. 745), Clinton co., extreme NE N.Y., on Saranac R. and 9 mi. W of Plattsburg.

Caelian Hill (sē'lēŭn, sĕl'yŭn), one of the 7 hills of Rome.

Caen (kā), city (1946 pop. 47,835; 1936 pop. 54,364), ⊙ Calvados dept., NW France, port on the Orne at influx of Odon R. and 125 mi. WNW of Paris; 49°11'N 0°21'W. A commercial and cultural center of Normandy; mfg. (pottery, furniture, textiles, lace, mirrors, paints, briquettes, electrical equipment), sawmilling. Metalworks in suburban Mondeville and Colombelles (3 mi. NE) process iron ore mined in Orne R. valley and Normandy Hills (S). Floating basin is connected with English Channel at Ouistreham by ship-canal (9 mi. long, paralleling lower Orne R.). Caen exports region's dairy produce, Calvados apple brandy, colza oil, and building stone. City center, including most medieval buildings, was 90% destroyed (June–July, 1944) in Normandy campaign of Second World War. The church of Saint-Étienne (also called Abbaye aux Hommes), burial place of William the Conqueror who founded it, was preserved; so were the church of the Trinity (or Abbaye aux Dames), founded by Queen Matilda, and the church of St. Nicholas. All 3 are outstanding examples of 11th-cent. Norman architecture. The 13th–16th-cent. church of St. Peter lost its much imitated spire. The castle of William the Conqueror, the 17th-cent. town hall, and the buildings housing mus. of painting and sculpture, and univ. (founded 1432) were destroyed. Caen rose to importance under William the Conqueror. Became ⊙ Lower Normandy. Taken and pillaged by Edward III of England in 1346. Again captured by Henry V in 1417, remaining in English hands until 1450. Girondin stronghold in French Revolution. Occupied (July 8, 1944) by Field Marshal Montgomery after full-scale assault and heavy fighting at near-by Hill 112. Malherbe b. here.

Caene or **Caenepolis,** Egypt: see QENA, town.

Caerano di San Marco (kīrä'nô dē sän mär'kô), village (pop. 784), Treviso prov., Veneto, N Italy, at W foot of the Montello, 15 mi. NW of Treviso; mfg. of acids.

Caerau, Wales: see MAESTEG.

Caer Caradoc Hill, England: see CHURCH STRETTON.

Caere, Italy: see CERVETERI.

Caerfyrddin, Wales: see CARMARTHEN.

Caergwrle, Wales: see HOPE.

Caer Gybi, Wales: see HOLYHEAD.

Caerlaverock (kär"lă'vŭrŏk, –lăv'rŭk), agr. village and parish (pop. 681), S Dumfries, Scotland, on Solway Firth at mouth of Nith R., 7 mi. SSE of Dumfries. Near by is Caerlaverock Castle, ruined 13th-cent. seat of the Maxwells and the "Ellangowan" of Scott's *Guy Mannering*.

Caerleon (kärlē'ŭn), residential urban district (1931 pop. 2,327; 1951 census 4,711), S Monmouth, England, on the Usk and 3 mi. NE of Newport. Site of Roman *Isca*, of which there are extensive remains. Has church (Norman to 15th cent.) and mus. Town is connected with Arthurian legend and is sometimes identified with CAMELOT.

Caerlon, England: see CHESTER.

Caer Luel, England: see CARLISLE.

Caermarthen, Wales: see CARMARTHEN.

Caernarvon, Carnarvon (both: kŭrnär'vŭn, kär–), **Caernarvonshire,** or **Carnarvonshire** (–shĭr), county (□ 568.9; 1931 pop. 120,829; 1951 census 124,074), NW Wales; ⊙ Caernarvon. Bounded by Irish Sea and Menai Strait (N), Denbigh (E), Merioneth and Cardigan Bay of Irish Sea (S). Drained by Conway R. Mainly mountainous terrain, including Snowdon (3,560 ft.), highest peak of Great Britain S of Scotland, and several other peaks over 3,000 ft. high. Chief industry is slate quarrying; lead, zinc, and ocher are also mined. On Lleyn Peninsula are numerous tourist resorts. Besides Caernarvon, other towns are Bangor, Bethesda, Bettws-y-Coed (mountain resort), Conway, Criccieth, Llandudno (resort), Portmadoc, Pwllheli. Co. contains numerous historic remains.

Caernarvon or **Carnarvon,** municipal borough (1931 pop. 8,469; 1951 census 9,255), ⊙ Caernarvonshire, Wales, in N part of co., on Menai Strait, 8 mi. SW of Bangor; woolen milling, mfg. of chemicals and agr. machinery; slate-shipping port. Site of 13th-cent. Caernarvon Castle, built by Edward I, reputed birthplace of Edward II, 1st prince of Wales. The 13th-cent. town walls are almost intact. There are considerable Roman remains; site of anc. Segontium is near.

Caernarvon Bay, inlet of St. George's Channel, Wales, extending 35 mi. N–S bet. Holy Isl. (Anglesey) and Braich-y-Pwll (Caernarvon); 20 mi. wide. Menai Strait opens on it.

Caernarvonshire, Wales: see CAERNARVON, county.

Caerphilly (kärfĭ'lē), urban district (1931 pop. 35,768; 1951 census 35,194), E Glamorgan, Wales, near Rhymney R., 7 mi. NNW of Cardiff; coal-mining center and agr. market, with cheese mfg. Its 13th-cent. castle is largest in Wales.

Caer Went, Hampshire, England: see WINCHESTER.

Caerwent (kärwĕnt'), town and parish (pop. 470), SE Monmouth, England, 4 mi. SW of Chepstow. Site of Roman city of *Venta Silurum* of which walls, gates, and parts of amphitheater and temple remain. Has 13th–14th-cent. church.

Caerwys (kĭr'wĭs), agr. village and parish (pop. 708), Flint, Wales, 7 mi. W of Flint; leather mfg. Scene of medieval Eisteddfod celebrations.

Caesaraugusta, Spain: see SARAGOSSA, city.

Caesarea, Algeria: see CHERCHEL.

Caesarea, Channel Isls.; see JERSEY.

Caesarea, Caesarea Palestinae (sĕsŭrē'ŭ pălĭstĭ'nē, sēzŭ–, sēzŭ–), or **Caesarea Maritima** (mŭrĭ'tĭmŭ), anc. city in NW Palestine, on Mediterranean, at edge of Plain of Sharon, 22 mi. S of Haifa. Captured by Maccabeans under Alexander Jannaeus; later ⊙ Herod the Great. In A.D. 66, Jewish citizens were massacred by Romans. A center of Levantine Christianity in 4th cent. Restored to importance by Crusaders, who built ramparts (remains extant), it was destroyed (1291) by Moslems. Bosnian Moslems established (1878) village here. There are remains of Roman city walls, hippodrome, breakwater, and Tower of Drusus. Since 1940 site of SDOT YAM settlement.

Caesarea Augusta, Spain: see SARAGOSSA, city.

Caesarea Maritima, Palestine: see CAESAREA.

Caesarea Mazaca, Turkey: see KAYSERI, city.

Caesarea Palestinae, Palestine: see CAESAREA.

Caesarea Philippi, Palestine: see BANIYAS, Syria.

Caesarodunum, France: see TOURS.

Caesaromagus, France: see BEAUVAIS.

Caesars Head (sē'zŭrz), summit (3,217 ft.) in the Blue Ridge, on N.C.–S.C. line, c.25 mi. NNW of Greenville. Its S face is a precipice c.1,500 ft. high, with fine view. Resort village of Caesars Head near by.

Caeté (kītě'), city (pop. 4,686), S central Minas Gerais, Brazil, in the Serra do Espinhaço, on railroad and 18 mi. E of Belo Horizonte; industrial center (pig iron, metal pipes, ceramics), with gold mines (at Juca Vieira) and diversified mineral deposits (asbestos, kaolin, manganese, arsenic). Old spelling, Caethé.

Caetité (kītětě'), city (pop. 2,837), S central Bahia, Brazil, on N spur of Serra do Espinhaço, 120 mi. SW of Andaraí; precious and semiprecious stones (amethysts, topazes, emeralds) found here. Thermal springs near by.

Cafayate (käfīä'tä), town (pop. estimate 1,000), ⊙ Cafayate dept. (□695; 1947 pop. 4,676), S Salta prov., Argentina, 95 mi. SSW of Salta; lumbering and winegrowing center; hides.

Cafelândia (käfĭlăn'dyŭ), city (pop. 5,342), W central São Paulo, Brazil, on railroad and 15 mi. SE of Lins; coffeegrowing center; coffee, rice, cotton processing; tile and furniture mfg., sawmilling.

Cafetal, El, Bolivia: see PUERTO VILLAZÓN.

Caffa, Russian SFSR: see FEODOSIYA.

Caffagiolo (käf-fäd-jô'lô), village, Firenze prov., Tuscany, central Italy, on Sieve R. and 13 mi. N of Florence. In 15th and 16th cent. had flourishing majolica industry. Near by is villa built 1455 for Cosimo de' Medici.

Cafferata (käfärä'tä), town (pop. estimate 1,000), S Santa Fe prov., Argentina, 90 mi. SW of Rosario; wheat, corn, flax, alfalfa, livestock, poultry.

Cagayan (kăgī'ŭn, Sp. kägäyän'), province (□ 3,470; 1948 pop. 311,088), N Luzon, Philippines, bounded N by Babuyan Channel, E by Philippine Sea; ⊙ TUGUEGARAO. Its port is APARRI. Drained by the Cagayan and its tributary, Chico R. N coast is low and swampy; part of the Sierra Madre parallels the E coast, rising to 3,800 ft. at Mt. Cagua. Rice is grown in N, and tobacco in Chico R. valley. Babuyan Isls. are in the prov.

Cagayan, town (1939 pop. 9,073; 1948 municipality pop. 46,266), ⊙ MISAMIS ORIENTAL prov., N Mindanao, Philippines, on Macajalar Bay, on small Cagayan R. and 95 mi. NE of Pagadian; 8°28'N 124°38'E. Trade center for agr. area (corn, coconuts).

Cagayan Islands (□ 2.9; 1948 pop. 4,167), Palawan prov., Philippines, in Sulu Sea, 70 mi. SW of Panay, bet. Palawan (W) and Negros (E); 9°40'N 121°15'E.

Cagayan River or **Rio Grande de Cagayan** (rē'ō grän'dā dā kägäyän'), largest river of the Philippines, in N Luzon, rises in mts. in Nueva Vizcaya prov. c.35 mi. SSE of Bayombong, flows c.220 mi. generally N, past Ilagan and Tuguegarao, to Babuyan Channel at Aparri. Navigable 13 mi. by small steamers; navigable 150 mi. in wet season and 70 mi. in dry season by small native boats. No longer a vital transportation route because of highways paralleling river's course. Drainage basin is □ c.10,000. Receives Magat and Chico rivers.

Cagayan Sulu Island (kägäyän' sōō'lōō, kăgī'ŭn) (□ 26; 1948 pop. 8,824), Sulu prov., Philippines, in Sulu Sea, 150 mi. NW of Sulu Archipelago, 65 mi. from Borneo; 7°N 118°30'E. It is 7 mi. long, rises to 1,020 ft. The isl. and offshore islets comprise municipality of Kagayan or Tana' Mapun. On E coast is town of Mahalu (1939 pop. 822). Fertile soil. Isl., inadvertently omitted from 1898 treaty with Spain, was ceded (along with Sibutu Isl.) to U.S. in 1900.

Caggiano (käd-jä'nô), town (pop. 3,397), Salerno prov., Campania, S Italy, 17 mi. WSW of Potenza.

Cagli (kä'lyē), town (pop. 2,745), Pesaro e Urbino prov., The Marches, central Italy, 13 mi. S of Urbino; tannery. Bishopric. Has cathedral.

Cagliari (kălyä'rē, It. kä'lyärē), province (□ 3,590; pop. 507,201), S Sardinia; ⊙ Cagliari. Mtn. terrain (rising to 4,045 ft. at Monte Linas), divided by CAMPIDANO lowland in SW; forests in SE; drained by Flumini Mannu, Tirso, and Flumendosa rivers. Richest mineral region of isl.: lead, zinc, silver, lignite, iron, molybdenum, manganese, barite in SW; silver, lead, zinc, antimony in SE; kaolin near Furtei; also granite, white marble, limestone, trachyte. Major saltworks near Cagliari and Carloforte. Agr. chiefly in Campidano lowland; oranges and lemons along S coast; livestock raising (goats, sheep, cattle) widespread in S. Fisheries (tunny, lobster, coral, sea mussel, oyster) along W coast. Chief hydroelectric station of isl. at L. Tirso. Industry concentrated at Cagliari, Iglesias, Guspini, Oristano, Carloforte.

Cagliari, anc. *Caralis*, city (pop. 78,632; pop. metropolitan area, 103,670), Sardinia and Cagliari prov., port on Gulf of Cagliari and 260 mi. SW of Rome; 39°12'N 9°7'E. Surrounded by salt lagoons, including Stagno di Cagliari (W) and Stagno di Quartu (SE); leads Italy in production of marine salt. Transportation and industrial center; salt-making, flour milling, distilling (liquor, wine), fishing; tobacco products; clothing mills, sawmills, tanneries, tomato cannery, soap and candle works; Portland cement, superphosphates, ceramics, chemicals, bicycles, motorcycles, wrought-iron products; printing, shipbuilding; power plant. Exports salt, cereals, minerals, wine; imports coal. Passenger port (service to mainland cities and Tunisia). Archbishopric, with Pisan cathedral of Santa Cecilia (completed 1312, later modernized), Torre dell'Elefante (1307), Byzantine churches, ruined medieval castle, palaces. Site of university (founded 1596) with mineralogical and paleontological collections, Mus. of Antiquities, Zoological Mus., Punic necropolis and cistern, amphitheater (greatest Roman monument in Sardinia), anc. reservoirs. Founded by Phoenicians; later became chief Carthaginian center of isl.; occupied by Romans (238 B.C.). Long the military hq. of isl., with important naval and air bases; heavily bombed (1941–43) in Second World War.

Cagliari, Gulf of, S Sardinia, inlet of Mediterranean Sea, bet. capes Pula (W) and Carbonara (E), 28 mi. wide, 13 mi. deep; tunny fisheries. Chief port, Cagliari. Because of its safe anchorage, sometimes called Golfo degli Angeli.

Cagliari, Stagno di (stä'nyō dē), inlet of Gulf of Cagliari, S Sardinia, just W of Cagliari; 6 mi. wide, 5 mi. long; nearly closed off by La Plaia sandspit (site of highway). S portion used for salt and bromine extraction at near-by MACCHIAREDDU. Receives Flumini Mannu R.

Cagnac-les-Mines (känyäk'-lā-mēn'), village (pop. 1,156), Tarn dept., S France, 5 mi. N of Albi; coal mining. Large Polish pop.

Cagnano Varano (känyä'nô värä'nô), town (pop. 5,704), Foggia prov., Apulia, S Italy, on Gargano promontory, near Lago di Varano, 15 mi. NW of Manfredonia. Agr. (olives, grapes, cereals), sheep raising; fishing.

Cagnes-sur-Mer (kä'nyŭ-sür-mâr'), town (pop. 7,755), Alpes-Maritimes dept., SE France, near the Mediterranean, 7 mi. WSW of Nice; winter resort on Fr. Riviera; olive oil pressing, biscuit mfg. An old Provençal town dominated by 14th–17th-cent. Grimaldi castle. Its port, Cros-de-Cagnes (krō-dŭ-kä'nyŭ), 1 mi. SE amidst flower gardens, has fish canneries and a zoological station. Damaged in Allied landings (Aug., 1944) Second World War.

Cagraray Island (kägrärī') (□ 28; 1939 pop. 9,568), Albay prov., Philippines, off SE Luzon, bet. Lagonoy Gulf (N) and Albay Gulf (S), and bet. San Miguel and Batan isls.; 8 mi. long, 6 mi. wide; rises to 351 ft. Fishing; agr. Included in Bacacay municipality.

Cagua (kä'gwä), town (pop. 5,472), Aragua state, N Venezuela, on small Aragua R. and 10 mi. ESE of Maracay; agr. center (coffee, cacao, sugar cane, tobacco, fruit).

Cagua, Mount, active volcano (3,800 ft.), Cagayan prov., NE Luzon, Philippines, in N part of the Sierra Madre, 32 mi. ESE of Aparri.

Caguache Island (kägwä'chä) (□ 3.8; pop. 368), bet. Chiloé Isl. and mainland of S Chile; 42°29'S 73°20'W.

Caguán River (kägwän'), Caquetá commissary, S Colombia, rises in Cordillera Oriental S of Neiva, flows SSE c.250 mi., through dense tropical forests, to Caquetá R. at 0°10'S 74°17'W.

Caguas (kä'gwäs), town (pop. 33,759), E central Puerto Rico, in the Cordillera Central, on San Juan–Ponce highway, on railroad, and 17 mi. S of San Juan. Fourth largest town of isl., the leading inland town, and a communication, trading, dairying, and processing center for fertile Caguas valley (sugar cane, tobacco, fruit, cattle). Sugar refining, alcohol distilling; mfg. of cigars, leatherware, cravats, furniture, rum, candy. Has a modern housing development. Marble and lime deposits near by.

Cahaba (kŭhô'bŭ), village, Dallas co., W central Ala., at junction of Cahaba and Alabama rivers, 10 mi. SW of Selma. State capital, 1819–26.

Cahaba River, central Ala., rises NE of Birmingham, flows SW, past Centreville, then S to Alabama R. 8 mi. SSW of Selma; c.200 mi. long. Used in upper course as source of water for Birmingham.

Cahabón (kä-äbōn'), town (1950 pop. 1,552), Alta Verapaz dept., central Guatemala, in N highlands, on Cahabón R. (left affluent of the Polochic) and 30 mi. ENE of Cobán; coffee, livestock.

Caha Mountains, range on border of cos. Cork and Kerry, Ireland, N continuation of Slieve Miskish mts., extending 10 mi. NE–SW along peninsula bet. Bantry Bay and Kenmare R.; rise to 2,251 ft. in Hungry Hill, 6 mi. ENE of Castletown Bere.
Caher, town, Ireland: see CAHIR.
Caher (kâr), island (128 acres; 1 mi. long) off SW Co. Mayo, Ireland, 5 mi. W of mainland, 5 mi. S of Clare Isl.
Caherbarnagh (kârbär'nä), mountain (2,239 ft.), highest point of the Derrynasaggart Mts., W Co. Cork, Ireland, 5 mi. WSW of Millstreet.
Caherconree (kâr"kŏnrē'), mountain (2,713 ft.) in Slieve Mish mts., W central Co. Kerry, Ireland, 8 mi. SW of Tralee.
Cahersiveen, Ireland: see CAHIRCIVEEN.
Cahir or **Caher** (both: kâr), Gaelic *Cathair Dhúin Iasgaigh*, town (pop. 1,652), S Co. Tipperary, Ireland, on Suir R. and 10 mi. W of Clonmel; agr. market (dairying; potatoes, beets); salmon fishing, clothing mfg. On isl. in Suir R. is castle (restored), built 1142 by Conor O'Brien, earl of Thomond; besieged 1599, 1647, and by Cromwell in 1650.
Cahirciveen or **Cahersiveen** (kâr"sĭvēn'), Gaelic *Cathair Saidhbh in*, town (pop. 1,779), W Co. Kerry, Ireland, at head of Valentia Harbour, 32 mi. SW of Tralee; agr. market (grain, potatoes; dairying), fishing port. Daniel O'Connell b. here.
Cahokia (kuhō'kēu), village (pop. 794), St. Clair co., SW Ill., on the Mississippi, just S of East St. Louis and within St. Louis metropolitan area. French mission here (1699) was 1st permanent settlement in Ill.; later a fur-trading post also was founded here, and site became a chief center of French influence in upper Mississippi valley. Captured by British (1765) and by Americans under George Rogers Clark (1778). Has several bldgs. dating from 18th cent. Cahokia was inc. in 1927. Cahokia Mounds State Park (NE) contains some of largest prehistoric Indian earthworks in U.S.
Cahokia Creek, central and SW Ill., rises in Macoupin co., flows c.55 mi. generally SW, past Edwardsville, to the Mississippi above East St. Louis.
Cahokia Mounds, SW Ill., group of more than 85 Indian earthworks (now in a state park), c.5 mi. E of East St. Louis. Monks' Mound, 100 ft. high and with a base area of 17 acres, is one of largest in U.S. Park has a mus., camping and picnic grounds.
Cahore Point (kuhôr'), promontory on St. George's Channel, E Co. Wexford, Ireland, 17 mi. ENE of Enniscorthy; 52°33'N 6°11'W.
Cahors (käôr'), anc. *Divona*, town (pop. 12,706), ⊙ Lot dept., SW France, within bend of Lot R., 60 mi. N of Toulouse; regional commercial center; canning, distilling, cotton spinning. Active trade in wines, liquor, truffles, walnuts, prunes, tobacco. Has 12th–15th-cent. cathedral (recently restored), and the remarkable fortified Valentré bridge (1308) with 3 machicolated towers. Cahors produced linen cloth in Roman times. It early became an episcopal see and was ruled by its bishops until 14th cent. During Middle Ages its money lenders made it one of Europe's leading banking centers. The univ., founded by Pope John XXII (b. here), was united with univ. of Toulouse in 1751. Before 1790 Cahors was ⊙ QUERCY. Clément Marot and Gambetta b. here.
Cahuacán (kāwäkän'), officially Santa María Magdalena Cahuacán, town (pop. 2,206), Mexico state, central Mexico, 23 mi. NW of Mexico city; cereals, livestock.
Cahuita (käwē'tä), village, Limón prov., E Costa Rica, port on Cahuita Point (9°45'N 82°49'W) of Caribbean Sea, 23 mi. SE of Limón; bananas, cacao, coconuts; petroleum deposits.
Cahul, city, Moldavian SSR: see KAGUL.
Cahul Lagoon, Ukrainian SSR: see KAGUL LAGOON.
Cahumayhumayan (kuhōō"mīhōō"mī'un, kä"hōō-mī"hōōmäyän'), village (1939 pop. 1,694), in Danao municipality, central Cebu isl., Philippines, 20 mi. NNE of Cebu city; coal mining.
Cahus (käü'), village (pop. 45), Lot dept., SW France, near the Cère, 23 mi. SE of Brive-la-Gaillarde; marble quarries.
Cahy River, Brazil: see CAÍ RIVER.
Caí (kä-ē'), city (pop. 2,932), NE Rio Grande do Sul, Brazil, head of navigation on Caí R. and 32 mi. NNW of Pôrto Alegre; ships sugar, fruit, rice, dairy produce; livestock slaughtering. Until c.1938, called São Sebastião do Caí (old spelling, Cahy).
Caiapônia (kīäpō'nyu), city (pop. 1,276), SW Goiás, central Brazil, on N slope of the Serra do Caiapó, 90 mi. NW of Rio Verde; rice, tobacco, sugar. Airfield. Diamonds found in vicinity. Until 1944, called Rio Bonito.
Caiapó River (kīäpô'), SW Goiás, central Brazil, rises in the Serra do Caiapó, flows 100 mi. NNW to Araguaia R. above Araguaiana. Diamond washings.
Caiarí River, Colombia and Brazil: see UAUPÉS RIVER.
Caiazzo (käyä'tsô), town (pop. 2,097), Caserta prov., Campania, S Italy, near Volturno R., 7 mi. NNE of Caserta, in agr. region (olives, grapes, cereals). Bishopric.
Caibarién (kībäryĕn'), city (pop. 21,382), Las Villas prov., central Cuba, 32 mi. ENE of Santa Clara; distributing and shipping point for agr. region (sugar cane, tobacco, fruit). Its port is served by natl. and international lines. Also an important sponge-fishing center. Sawmilling, sugar refining (at Central Reforma, SW), fish canning. Seaplane anchorage.
Caibe (kī'bă'), town, Mytho prov., S Vietnam, on left bank of Mekong R. and 23 mi. W of Mytho.
Caibiran, Philippines: see BILIRAN ISLAND.
Caiçara (kīsä'ru). **1** Town, Amazonas, Brazil: see ALVARÃES. **2** City (pop. 952), E Paraíba, NE Brazil, near railroad, 55 mi. NW of João Pessoa; cotton, sugar, rice, agave fibers.
Caicara (kīkä'rä). **1** Town (pop. 1,142), Bolívar state, SE Venezuela, landing on right bank of Orinoco R. and 180 mi. WSW of Ciudad Bolívar; cattle raising, dairying. Airport. **2** Town (pop. 1,530), Monagas state, NE Venezuela, 30 mi. W of Maturín; cattle raising.
Caicedonia (kīsādō'nyä), town (pop. 5,239), Valle del Cauca dept., W Colombia, in Cauca valley, on railroad and 26 mi. S of Cartago; agr. center (coffee, tobacco, sugar cane, corn, rice, bananas, cacao, livestock).
Caicó (kīkô'), city (pop. 3,948), S Rio Grande do Norte, NE Brazil, 90 mi. S of Mossoró; livestock center (cattle, mules). Gypsum quarries. Airfield.
Caicos Islands (kī'kus, kī'kōs), W group of TURKS AND CAICOS ISLANDS, B.W.I., dependency of Jamaica, 140 mi. N of Cap-Haïtien (Haiti), separated from Turks Isls. (E) by Turks Island Passage and from Mayaguana isl. (Bahama Isls.) by Caicos Passage; bet. 21°10'–22°N and 71°25'–72°30'W. Among the many isls. which surround Caicos Bank, a shoal c.60 mi. in diameter, are East Caicos, South Caicos (pop. 826), Middle Caicos or Grand Caicos (pop. 717), North Caicos (pop. 1,703), Blue Hills or Providenciales (pop. 804), and West Caicos. Principal industry is salt panning. The isls. were settled by Loyalists from the U.S. after the Revolution; they planted cotton, but left the isls. after abolition of slavery (1834).
Caicos Passage, channel (c.40 mi. wide) in the Caribbean, separates Mayaguana isl. in SE Bahama Isls. (W) from Caicos Isls., dependency of Jamaica (E), at about 22°20'N 72°–72°40'W.
Caicus River, Turkey: see BAKIR RIVER.
Caieiras (kīā'rus), town (pop. 851), SE São Paulo, Brazil, on railroad and 15 mi. NNW of São Paulo; manganese deposits.
Caiffa, Palestine: see HAIFA.
Caiguanabo River, Cuba: see SAN DIEGO RIVER.
Cailay (kī'lī'), town, Mytho prov., S Vietnam, 17 mi. WNW of Mytho; rice.
Cailín Island (kīlēn') (□ 12.5; pop. 665), Chiloé prov., S Chile, off SE coast of Chiloé Isl., 50 mi. SE of Castro; 5 mi. long, 2–3 mi. wide.
Cailloma, province, Peru: see CHIVAY.
Cailloma (kīyō'mä), town (pop. 923), Arequipa dept., S Peru, high in the Andes, on NW slopes of Cordillera de Chilca, 29 mi. NW of Chivay. Grain, potatoes, alpacas, cattle; gold, silver mining. Petroleum and coal deposits near by. Damaged by 1917 earthquake. Was ⊙ Cailloma prov.
Caillou Bay (käyōō', kälōō'), SE La., arm of the Gulf of Mexico bet. marshy coast and Isles Dernieres, 35 mi. SSW of Houma; c.10 mi. long NW–SE, 2–6 mi. wide. Connected by navigable waterways with tidal **Caillou Lake** (c.5 mi. long, 3 mi. wide) in marshy coastal area, c.3 mi. inland from Caillou Bay. Small **Caillou Island,** center of underwater oil field operations, is c.20 mi. E of Caillou Bay, bet. Terrebonne Bay and Timbalier Bay.
Caima, Peru: see CAYMA.
Caimanera (kīmänā'rä), town (pop. 4,035), Oriente prov., E Cuba, port for Guantánamo (11 mi. N; linked by rail), on W shore of sheltered Guantánamo Bay, just N of the U.S. naval reserve. Ships chiefly sugar cane and coffee.
Caimari (kīmä'rē), village (pop. 1,008), Majorca, Balearic Isls., 19 mi. NE of Palma; olives, olive oil, charcoal; soap mfg.
Caimito or **Caimito del Guayabal** (kīmē'tō dĕl gwīäbäl'), town (pop. 2,477), Havana prov., W Cuba, on Central Highway, on railroad and 19 mi. SW of Havana; tobacco, vegetables, fruit. Sugar milled at the central Habana (4 mi. NNW). Asphalt deposits and sulphurous springs near by.
Caín, El, Argentina: see EL CAÍN.
Caina (kī'nä), town (pop. 1,138), Huánuco dept., central Peru, in Cordillera Central, 20 mi. SSW of Huánuco; barley, potatoes, sheep.
Cainari, Moldavian SSR: see KAINARY.
Caine River (kī'nä), Cochabamba dept., central Bolivia, rises as Rocha R. in the Cordillera de Cochabamba 20 mi. E of Cochabamba, flows 140 mi. W, S, and SE, past Sacaba, Cochabamba, and Capinota, joining Chayanta R. at Pucara to form the Río Grande.
Cainguás, Argentina: see PUERTO RICO.
Cainscross, town and parish (pop. 2,294), central Gloucester, England, on Frome R. just W of Stroud; woolen milling.
Cainsdorf (kīns'dôrf), village (pop. 5,784), Saxony, E central Germany, 3 mi. S of Zwickau; coal mining; steel milling.
Cains River, in central N.B., rises 30 mi. NE of Fredericton, flows c.70 mi. NE to the Southwest Miramichi 30 mi. SW of Newcastle.
Cainsville, village (pop. estimate 600), S Ont., on Grand R. and 3 mi. E of Brantford; dairying; fruit, vegetables.
Cainsville, city (pop. 618), Harrison co., NW Mo., 18 mi. NE of Bethany; agr. (corn, wheat); rock quarries. Sometimes Cainesville.
Caio, Wales: see CONWIL CAIO.
Caio, Monte (môn'tĕ kä'yô), peak (5,184 ft.) in Etruscan Apennines, N central Italy, 15 mi. NE of Pontremoli. Sometimes written Cajo.
Caiphas, Palestine: see HAIFA.
Cairang (kī'räng'), village, Cantho prov., S Vietnam, 3 mi. SW of Cantho; rice center; distillery.
Caird Coast (kârd), part of coast of Coats Land, Antarctica, on Weddell Sea, bet. Bruce and Luitpold coasts, bet. 23° and 29°W. Discovered 1915 by Sir Ernest Shackleton.
Caí River (kä-ē'), NE Rio Grande do Sul, Brazil, rises in the Serra Geral, flows c.100 mi. W and S, past Caí, joining the Jacuí just above Pôrto Alegre to form the Guaíba. Formerly spelled Cahy.
Cairnbrook, village (pop. 1,504), Somerset co., SW Pa., 8 mi. S of Windber.
Cairnbulg, Scotland: see INVERALLOCHY.
Cairngorm Mountains (kârn'gôrm'), range in SE Inverness, S Banffshire, and SW Aberdeen, Scotland, part of the Grampians, extending E–W bet. the upper Spey and Dee valleys. Highest point is BEN MACDHUI (4,296 ft.). Other peaks are Braeriach (brārī'ukh) (4,248 ft.), 12 mi. E of Kingussie (kĭng-ū'sē), Cairntoul (kârntōōl', –toul') (4,241 ft.), 13 mi. E of Kingussie, and Cairngorm or Cairn Gorm (4,084 ft.), 12 mi. NW of Braemar. Ornamental yellow or brown quartz found here is called "cairngorm."
Cairnie, agr. village and parish (pop. 1,017), N Aberdeen, Scotland, 4 mi. NW of Huntly.
Cairn Ryan or **Cairnryan,** village, W Wigtown, Scotland, small port on E shore of Loch Ryan (inlet of Irish Sea), 5 mi. N of Stranraer; ammunition was dumped here by ships after Second World War.
Cairns (kârnz), city and port (pop. 16,644), NE Queensland, Australia, 860 mi. NNW of Brisbane, on Trinity Bay; 16°55'S 145°47'E. Principal sugar port of Australia; exports sugar cane, timber, gold, tin, copper, dairy products, fruit; woodworking.
Cairntoul, Scotland: see CAIRNGORM MOUNTAINS.
Cairo or **El Cairo** (ĕl kī'rō), village (dist. pop. 1,545), Limón prov., E Costa Rica, on railroad and 3 mi. NW of Siquirres; corn, rubber, bananas, livestock. Pop. largely Jamaican Negro.
Cairo (kī'rō), Arabic *El Kahirah* or *Al-Qahirah* [the victorious], also *Masr* or *Misr* [capital], city (□ 83; pop. 2,100,506), coextensive with Cairo governorate, ⊙ Egypt and largest city of Africa, on the E bank of the Nile at the head of the delta, and 110 mi. SE of Alexandria, 80 mi. W of Suez 30°31'N 31°15'E. Commercial, trade, communications, and mfg. center of Egypt, with a busy Nile trade and connections by railroad and canal with Upper Egypt, Alexandria, Port Said, and Suez. Mfg. of cotton textiles, tricot, clothing, knit goods, shoes and other leather goods, tarbooshes, watches, beer, liquor, perfume, cigarettes, soap, furniture; dairying, cottonseed-oil pressing, corn milling; printing and publishing. Part of Cairo is a modern city laid out in wide streets, but it is in the older sections—Arab, Jewish, and Coptic—that the famed mosques, palaces, and city gates are found. The mosques of Amur (7th cent.), Ibn Tulun (9th cent.), Hasan (1356), and Kait Bey (15th cent., on Roda Isl.) are notable. The mosque of El Azhar houses the most important orthodox Moslem univ. in the world, founded 972 and now having some 10,000 students. In Cairo are the famous Mus. of Antiquities (moved here from Bulak), the Arab mus., and the valuable Royal Library. The great citadel was built c.1179 by Saladin. The Nilometer, a graduated column used for years to measure the Nile water level, is on Roda Isl., where the infant Moses is said to have been found in the bulrushes. On Gizira, off the BULAK section of the city, is a 19th-cent. palace. Cairo was founded near the site of the Roman fortress city of Babylon. Here in A.D. 641 or 642 the Arabs established El Fustat or Al-Fustat (also El Fostat), now in the city's SW part called Old Cairo or Masr al-Qadimah, opposite Roda Isl.; adjacent to this a new capital city was founded in 969 by the Fatimite general Jauhar. In 12th cent. it was unsuccessfully attacked by Crusaders. Cairo throve under the Mamelukes (13th to early 16th cent.), but the period (1517–1798) of Ottoman rule saw a decline. Napoleon occupied the city 1798–1801. In 19th cent. it grew in size and commercial importance. The British occupation began in 1882 and did not end until 1936, when Egypt was restored to full independence. The great treasures of Egyptian antiquity are within easy reach of Cairo. The site of HELIOPOLIS is just NE, the pyramids of GIZA are a few miles across the Nile, and the ruins of MEMPHIS are upstream, across the Nile. In Cairo are Fuad (or Fouad) I Univ. (1908; renamed 1942) and the American Univ. at Cairo (1919).
Cairo (kâ'rō, kā'rō). **1** City (pop. 5,577), ⊙ Grady co., SW Ga., 13 mi. WNW of Thomasville. Major market and shipping center for cane syrup and col-

lard seed; processes sugar cane, pecans, peanuts; has mills (lumber, veneer, pulp), food canneries, furniture and box factories. Settled 1866, inc. 1870. **2** City (pop. 12,123), ⊙ Alexander co., extreme S Ill., 125 mi. SE of St. Louis, on levee-protected tongue of land at confluence of Mississippi and Ohio rivers (both bridged here); shipping center (rail, highway, river) for cotton, fruit, corn, and dairy products, in a region popularly called Egypt because of rich soil and delta-like geographical similarity. Cottonseed and soybean processing; mfg. of shoes, wood products, drugs, beverages. Inc. 1818, followed by unsuccessful settlement; reincorporated 1837; city adopted commission govt. in 1913. Important Union military base in Civil War; MOUND CITY (N) was naval base. Ohio R. bridge (1938; 6,229 ft. long) connects with Ky.; Mississippi R. bridge (1929; 3,720 ft. long) connects with Mo. **3** Town (pop. 264), Randolph co., N central Mo., 6 mi. N of Moberly. **4** Village (pop. 422), Hall co., S central Nebr., 15 mi. WNW of Grand Island and on branch of Platte R.; shipping point for grain and livestock; potatoes. **5** Resort village (pop. c.600), Greene co., SE N.Y., 9 mi. NW of Catskill, in applegrowing region of the Catskills. **6** Village (pop. 505), Allen co., W Ohio, 6 mi. NNE of Lima. **7** Town (pop. 500), Ritchie co., W W.Va., 22 mi. ESE of Parkersburg.

Cairo Montenotte (kī'rô môntĕnôt'tē), town (pop. 3,177), Savona prov., Liguria, NW Italy, on Bormida di Spigno R. and 12 mi. NW of Savona; mfg. (photographic materials, cement); limekilns.

Cairu (kīrōō'), city (pop. 1,233), E Bahia, Brazil, on isl. just off mainland, 50 mi. SW of Salvador; ships piassava, coconuts, fruit. Formerly spelled Cayrú.

Caister-on-Sea (kā'stūr), town in parish of East Caister (pop. 2,108), E Norfolk, England, on North Sea, 3 mi. N of Yarmouth; seaside resort; site of marine radio station. There are ruins of 15th-cent. castle, built by Sir John Fastolf. Site of a Roman coastal camp. Just W is agr. village and parish (pop. 248) of West Caister.

Caister Saint Edmund or **Caistor,** England: see NORWICH.

Caistor (kā'stūr). **1** Town and parish (pop. 1,486), Parts of Lindsey, N Lincolnshire, England, 11 mi. WSW of Grimsby; agr. market. Site of a Roman station and an early British fort. Has church of Norman origin. **2** Town, Norfolk, England: see NORWICH.

Caithness or **Caithness-shire** (kăthnĕs', kăth'nĕs, -shĭr), county (□ 685.7; 1931 pop. 26,656; 1951 census 22,705), NE Scotland; ⊙ Wick. Most northerly co. of British mainland, bounded by Sutherland (W), the Atlantic and Pentland Firth (N), and Moray Firth and the North Sea (E and SE). Drained by Thurso and Wick rivers. N coastline is rocky and dangerous to navigation; SE is low and sandy. Extensive deer forests and moorland tracts. Flagstone quarrying and sea fisheries are important; farming and crofting are also carried on. Inhabitants, unlike other Highlanders, speak English only. Besides Wick, Thurso is only other burgh. Scrabster is port for the Orkneys; Dunbeath and Lybster are fishing ports. Dunnet Head promontory is N extremity of isl. of Britain; Duncansbay promontory is its NE extremity; and near by is John o'Groat's House. Norse invasion of co. in 10th-cent. is recalled by many place names, and by Danish barrows and other relics.

Caiuás, Brazil: see RIO BRILHANTE.

Caiundo (kāyōōn'dō), town, Bié prov., S Angola, on right bank of Okovanggo R., and 75 mi. SSW of Serpa Pinto.

Caiuti (kŭyōōts'), Rum. *Căiuţi,* village (pop. 988), Bacau prov., E central Rumania, on railroad and 25 mi. S of Bacau; lignite mining; lumbering.

Caivano (kīvä'nô), town (pop. 15,164), Napoli prov., Campania, S Italy, 7 mi. N of Naples; hosiery mfg.

Caiza (kī'sä). **1** Town, Tarija dept., Bolivia: see VILLA INGAVI. **2** Town (pop. c.3,800), Potosí dept., S central Bolivia, 30 mi. S of Potosí, on road; orchards. Resort for Potosí.

Cajabamba (kähäbäm'bä), town (1950 pop. 1,843), Chimborazo prov., central Ecuador, in a high Andean basin, on Quito-Guayaquil RR, on Pan American Highway and 8 mi. W of Riobamba. Agr. center (grain, potatoes, cattle) largely populated by Indians and run on cooperative basis. Riobamba was formerly on site of Cajabamba and adjoining Sicalpa. Heavily damaged by 1949 earthquake. Small, picturesque L. Colta is 2 mi. S.

Cajabamba, city (pop. 3,479), ⊙ Cajabamba prov. (□ 504; pop. 42,395), Cajamarca dept., NW Peru, in Cordillera Occidental of the Andes, 40 mi. SE of Cajamarca; alt. 9,131 ft. Corn, wheat.

Cajacay (kähäkī'), town (pop. 1,094), Ancash dept., W central Peru, in Cordillera Occidental, on road, and 45 mi. S of Huarás; cereals, corn, livestock.

Caja de Muertos, Puerto Rico: see MUERTOS ISLAND.

Cajalco Reservoir, Calif.: see MATHEWS, LAKE.

Cajamala (kähämä'lä), town (pop. 239), Ancash dept., W central Peru, in Cordillera Occidental, 9 mi. SSW of Cabana; bauxite mining.

Cajamarca (kähämär'kä), town (pop. 3,014), Tolima dept., W central Colombia, in Cordillera Central, 13 mi. W of Ibagué; alt. c.6,000 ft. Agr. center (corn, potatoes, bananas, coffee, sugar cane, vegetables, cattle, hogs).

Cajamarca, department (□ 12,541; enumerated pop. 538,118, plus estimated 30,000 Indians), NW Peru; ⊙ Cajamarca. Bordered N by Ecuador, E by Marañón R. Crossed by Cordillera Occidental N–S, it is mainly mountainous, drained by Huancabamba, Chancay, and Llaucán rivers. One of Peru's most important wheat-growing areas, it produces also corn, potatoes, cattle, sheep; and sugar cane and coca in lower valleys of slopes of the Cordillera Occidental. Silver and copper mined at Hualgayoc and Sayapullo; coal at Yanacancha. Dept. is served by road net centering in Cajamarca and connected with the coast by Pacasmayo–Chilete RR. Main centers: Cajamarca, Cajabamba, Cutervo.

Cajamarca, city (pop. 15,553), ⊙ Cajamarca dept. and Cajamarca prov. (□ 1,519; pop, 133,949), NW Peru, in Cordillera Occidental, 75 mi. ENE of its port Pacasmayo (Libertad dept.), 235 mi. NNW of Lima; 7°9'S 78°31'W; alt. 9,022 ft. Communication and commercial center for agr. and mining region; flour milling, mfg. (straw hats, leather goods), weaving of native textiles, metalworking; trade in agr. products (wheat, corn, potatoes). It is a diocese and site of colonial bldgs., 17th-cent. cathedral, and ruins of an Inca palace. Once an important Inca center, here Francisco Pizarro captured (1532) the last Inca ruler, Atahualpa, thus breaking the power of the Inca empire. Formerly also spelled Caxamarca. The Inca thermal baths are at JESÚS, 10 mi. SE.

Cajamarquilla (kähämärkē'yä). **1** Town (pop. 563), Ancash dept., W central Peru, in Cordillera Negra of the Andes, 16 mi. WSW of Huarás; cereals, potatoes, sheep. **2** Town (pop. 313), Ancash dept., W central Peru, in Cordillera Occidental of the Andes, 18 mi. SSW of Chiquián; barley, livestock. **3** Town, Libertad dept., Peru: see BOLÍVAR. **4** Ruined pre-Incan city, W central Peru, 10 mi. ENE of Lima; anc. religious center or burial place.

Cajapió (kăzhăpyô'), city (pop. 896), N Maranhão, Brazil, near head of São Marcos Bay, 37 mi. SSW of São Luís; saltworks. Airfield.

Cajarc (käzhärk'), village (pop. 970), Lot dept., SW France, on Lot R. and 12 mi. SW of Figeac; sawmilling, winegrowing.

Cajatambo (kähätäm'bō), city (pop. 2,625), ⊙ Cajatambo prov. (□ 1,862; pop. 23,640), Lima dept., W central Peru, in Cordillera Occidental of the Andes, 110 mi. NNE of Lima; alt. 10,991 ft. Grain, potatoes; cattle, sheep. Silver deposits in prov.

Cajàzeiras (käzhäzā'rŭs), city (pop. 8,146), W Paraíba, NE Brazil, 250 mi. W of João Pessoa; 6°53'S 38°33'W. Terminus of rail spur from Antenor Navarro (13 mi. NE). Ships cotton, sugar, oiticica oil, fruit. Irrigation reservoirs on Piranhas R. near by. Founded c.1700.

Cajeme, Mexico: see CIUDAD OBREGÓN.

Cajetina or **Chayetina** (both: chä'yĕtĭnä), Serbo-Croatian *Čajetina,* village (pop. 2,386), W Serbia, Yugoslavia, 10 mi. SW of Titovo Uzice; arsenic ore deposits.

Cajicá (kähēkä'), village (pop. 715), Cundinamarca dept., central Colombia, 23 mi. N of Bogotá; fruit, cereals, stock. Tabio thermal springs are 5 mi. W.

Cajidiocan, Philippines: see SIBUYAN ISLAND.

Cajititlán (kähētētlän'), town (pop. 1,617), Jalisco, central Mexico, on small L. Cajititlán 18 mi. S of Guadalajara; wheat, vegetables, livestock.

Cajnice, Chainiche, or **Chayniche** (all: chī'nĭchĕ), Serbo-Croatian *Čajniče,* village, SE Bosnia, Yugoslavia, near Serbia-Montenegro border, 38 mi. SE of Sarajevo; lumber milling, fruit preserving. Orthodox Eastern monastery here.

Cajobi (käzhōōbē'), city (pop. 1,009), N São Paulo, Brazil, near railroad, 36 mi. E of São José do Rio Prêto; coffee, cotton, grain. Formerly Cajoby.

Cajolá (kāhōlä'), town (1950 pop. 1,033), Quezaltenango dept., SW Guatemala, 8 mi. NW of Quezaltenango; alt. 8,500 ft.; corn, wheat, fodder grasses; livestock.

Cajón (kähōn'), village (1930 pop. 575), Cautín prov., S central Chile, on Cautín R. and 6 mi. NE of Temuco; rail junction in agr. area (wheat, oats, potatoes, peas, livestock); lumbering.

Cajón, Sierra del (syĕ'rä dĕl), or **Sierra de Quilmes** (dā kēl'mĕs), subandean range on Catamarca-Tucumán-Salta prov. border, Argentina, N of Andalgalá, extends 50 mi. bet. Calchaquí R. (N) and Cajón R.; rises to over 16,000 ft.

Cajon Pass (kŭhōn'), railroad and highway pass (alt. c.3,800 ft.), S Calif., bet. E end of San Gabriel Mts. and NW end of San Bernardino Mts., NW of San Bernardino; connects Mojave Desert (N) with Los Angeles basin.

Cajón River, Argentina: see SANTA MARÍA RIVER.

Cajuata (kähwä'tä), village (pop. c.1,200), La Paz dept., W Bolivia, at NE foot of the Cordillera de Tres Cruces, c.15 mi. NNW of Inquisivi; potatoes, grain.

Cajuru (käzhōōrōō'), city (pop. 2,730), NE São Paulo, Brazil, 33 mi. E of Ribeirão Prêto; rail-spur terminus; dairying, sugar milling.

Cakirgol Dag (chäkŭrgûl' dä), Turkish *Çakırgöl Dağ,* peak (10,049 ft.), NE Turkey, in Trebizond Mts., 31 mi. S of Trebizond.

Cakovec (chä'kôvĕts), Serbo-Croatian *Čakovec,* Ger. *Csakathurn* (chä'kätōōrn), Hung. *Csáktornya* (chäk'tôrnyŏ), town (pop. 7,209), N Croatia, Yugoslavia, 7 mi. NE of Varazdin; trade and rail center in winegrowing region. Chief town of the Medjumurje. Petroleum fields near by. First mentioned in 1267.

Cakovice (chä'kôvĭtsĕ), Czech *Čakovice,* village (pop. 3,902), central Bohemia, Czechoslovakia, on railroad and 6 mi. NNE of Prague. Aircraft mfg. at Letnany (lĕt'nyänĭ), Czech *Letňany,* just SSW.

Cal (chäl), Turkish *Çal,* village (pop. 2,410), Denizli prov., SW Turkey, on Buyuk Menderes R. and 28 mi. NE of Denizli; copper deposits; wheat, barley. Formerly Demircikoy.

Cala (kä'lä), town (pop. 2,513), Huelva prov., SW Spain, in the Sierra Morena, near Badajoz prov. border, 15 mi. ENE of Aracena, 45 mi. NNW of Seville; narrow-gauge railroad carries its iron and copper ores to San Juan de Aznalfarache, a suburb of Seville. Also produces cork, olives, acorns, timber, and livestock. Has limekilns.

Cala (kä'lŭ), town (pop. 1,597), E Cape Prov., U. of So. Afr., in Tembuland dist. of the Transkeian Territories, 55 mi. ENE of Queenstown; stock, grain.

Calabanga (käläbäng'gä), town (1939 pop. 675; 1948 municipality pop. 21,791), Camarines Sur prov., SE Luzon, Philippines, 7 mi. N of Naga.

Calabar (kă'lùbär), province (□ 6,331; pop. 900,285), Eastern Provinces, SE Nigeria, in forest belt; ⊙ Calabar. On Gulf of Guinea; bounded E by Br. Cameroons. Includes swamp and marsh forest (S), rain forest (N); drained by Kwa Ibo, Cross, and Calabar rivers. Main products: palm oil and kernels, hardwood, rubber, cacao, kola nuts. Chief food crops: yams, corn, plantains. Palm-nut processing, wood carving (production of toys). Monazite deposits (NE). Fisheries along coast. Pop. largely Ibibio and Efik.

Calabar, town (pop. 16,653), ⊙ Calabar prov., Eastern Provinces, SE Nigeria, on Calabar R. near its mouth, and 350 mi. ESE of Lagos; 4°58'N 8°19'E. Major port, exporting palm oil and kernels, cacao, rubber, and benniseed. Palm-oil processing, wood carving; fisheries. Airfield. Has Church of Scotland mission, hosp., insane asylum. Its native quarter is called Duke Town. In 19th cent. a Br. commercial station and ⊙ Oil Rivers Protectorate, later Niger Coast Protectorate. Until 1904 called Old Calabar.

Calabar River, SE Nigeria, in equatorial forest belt, rises in W Oban Hills, flows 70 mi. SW, past Uwet and Calabar, to Cross R. delta just below Calabar.

Calabazar (käläbäsär'). **1** Town (pop. 4,067), Havana prov., W Cuba, on Almendares R., on railroad and 7 mi. S of Havana; dairying, mfg. of cigars. **2** or **Calabazar de Sagua** (dā sä'gwä), town (pop. 3,051), Las Villas prov., central Cuba, on railroad and 16 mi. N of Santa Clara; sugar-growing center with several centrals in vicinity: Unidad (NW), Santa Lutgarda (W), Purio (NNE), Macagua (SW).

Calabogie (kălùbō'gē), village (pop. estimate 500), SE Ont., on Madawaska R. and on Calabogie L. (4 mi. long), 50 mi. E of Ottawa; dairying, mixed farming; in lead-mining region.

Calabouço Point, Brazil: see RIO DE JANEIRO, city.

Calabozo (käläbō'sō), town (pop. 3,720), Guárico state, central Venezuela, in llanos, on Guárico R. and 65 mi. S of San Juan de los Morros; communication, trading, and cattle-raising center. Bishopric. Founded 1695. State capital until 1934.

Calabria (kùlā'brēù, It. kälä'brēä), anc. *Bruttium,* region (□ 5,828; pop. 1,771,651), S Italy; ⊙ Reggio di Calabria. Bordered by Basilicata (N). Comprises 3 provs.: COSENZA (N), CATANZARO (central), REGGIO DI CALABRIA (S). A mountainous peninsula (160 mi. long, 60 mi. wide) bet. Ionian (E) and Tyrrhenian (W) seas; forms the "toe" of Italy; separated from Sicily (S) by Strait of Messina. At its narrowest part, bet. gulfs of Squillace and Sant'-Eufemia, it is only 20 mi. wide. Chief Apennine ranges are the POLLINO (N), LA SILA (central), and ASPROMONTE (S). Forests cover 26% of area. Rainfall scarce; mostly in winter (Nov. to April). Watered by Crati, Neto, Lao, Savuto, and Trionto rivers. Predominantly agr., (wheat, olives, citrus fruit, figs, chestnuts, raw silk). Stock raising (sheep, goats) is widespread. Lumbering and fishing (Pizzo, Reggio di Calabria, Palmi) also important. Mining at Lungro (chief rock salt mines in Italy) and Strongoli (sulphur). Has several major hydroelectric plants (near SAN GIOVANNI IN FIORE and COTRONEI) and reservoirs (on the AMPOLLINO and ARVO) in La Sila mts. Mfg. at Crotone, Reggio di Calabria, Gioia Tauro, Palmi, and Locri. Settled along the coast (Sybaris, Crotona) by Greek colonists in 8th cent. B.C. Conquered by Romans in 3d cent. B.C. Named Calabria in early Middle Ages. Taken by Robert Guiscard in 11th cent.; became part of Norman kingdom of Sicily and (after 1282) of kingdom of Naples. Conquered by Garibaldi in 1860. Social and economic progress has long been hindered by feudalism (prevalent until modern times), malaria, frequent earthquakes (worst occurred in 1783 and 1908), droughts, and poor communications. Reforms and public works have been in progress since beginning of 20th cent.

Calabritto (käläbrēt'tō), village (pop. 2,970), Avellino prov., Campania, S Italy, near Sele R., 24 mi. ESE of Avellino.

Calaburras Point (kälävōō'räs), Mediterranean cape, Málaga prov., S Spain, 20 mi. SW of Málaga; 36°30'N 4°38'W. Lighthouse.

Calaca (käläkä', kälä'kä), town (1939 pop. 1,496; 1948 municipality pop. 13,551), Batangas prov., S Luzon, Philippines, on Balayan Bay, 35 mi. WSW of San Pablo; fishing, agr. (rice, sugar cane, corn, coconuts).

Calacala (käläkä'lä), N suburb of Cochabamba, Cochabamba dept., central Bolivia, on S slopes of Cordillera de Cochabamba, on the Rocha; fruit, corn, wheat.

Calaceite (kälä-thä'tā), town (pop. 1,856), Teruel prov., E Spain, 17 mi. E of Alcañiz; olive-oil processing, brandy mfg.; almonds, wine, cereals.

Calacoto (käläkō'tō), town (pop. c.2,400), La Paz dept., W Bolivia, on Desaguadero R. and 15 mi. WSW of Corocoro, on Arica–La Paz RR; alt. 12,483 ft. Oil deposits near by.

Calacte, Sicily: see Caronia.

Calacuccia (käläkōōt'chä), village (pop. 410), central Corsica, on Golo R. and 7 mi. WNW of Corte; cheese mfg. Monte Cinto is 5 mi. NW.

Calaf (käläf'), town (pop. 1,705), Barcelona prov., NE Spain, 12 mi. NW of Igualada; cement, mfg., cotton milling. Wine, cereals, fruit in area. Lignite mines near by.

Calafat (käläfät'), town (1948 pop. 8,251), Dolj prov., S Rumania, in Walachia, on Danube R., opposite Vidin (Bulgaria), and 48 mi. SW of Craiova; rail terminus and inland port, trading in livestock and grain; flour milling, tanning, tobacco processing, brewing, brick making. Founded in 14th cent. by Genoese colonists. Battleground in Russo-Turkish wars (19th cent.).

Calafate, El, Argentina: see El Calafate.

Calafell (käläfāl'), village (pop. 1,124), Taragona prov., NE Spain, 2 mi. SE of Vendrell, near the Mediterranean; soap mfg.; trades in fish, olive oil, wine.

Calafquén, Lake (käläfkĕn') (□ 45), Valdivia prov., S central Chile, in Chilean lake dist., 55 mi. ENE of Valdivia, S of Villarrica; c.15 mi. long, 4 mi. wide. Surrounded by forests and Andean peaks (Villarrica Volcano is NE), it is a tourist resort and lumbering and fishing dist. Village of Calafquén is on SW shore. A small stream connects it with L. Panguipulli (S).

Calaggio River, Italy: see Carapelle River.

Calagua Islands (kälä'gwä), small low-lying group of Camarines Norte prov., Philippines, off SE coast of Luzon, 20 mi. NE of Jose Pañganiban; comprises Tinaga Isl. (tēnägä') (□ 5; c.5 mi. long, 2 mi. wide) and Guintinua Isl. (gēntē'nwä) (□ 3; 4 mi. long, 1 mi. wide), and several islets.

Calagurris, Spain: see Calahorra.

Calah (kā'lŭ) or **Kalakh** (kä'läkh), ancient city of Assyria, S of Nineveh; the mound representing its site is 20 mi. S of modern Mosul, N Iraq, near the influx of the Great Zab into the Tigris. It was long the Assyrian capital; it seems in very early times to have been superseded by Nineveh and was restored (c.880) to its old position by Ashurnasirpal III, whose great palace there has been excavated. It continued to be a royal residence even after Ashur and Nineveh became the political capitals. It contained inscriptions of Tiglath-pileser III and Esar-Haddon. Calah is mentioned in Genesis. The mound site is also called Nimrud.

Calahorra (käläō'rä), anc. *Calagurris*, city (pop. 12,647), Logroño prov., N Spain, in Old Castile, near Ebro R., 28 mi. SE of Logroño; agr. and industrial center, with important canneries (peppers, tomatoes, asparagus, artichokes, fruit); mfg. of canning equipment, cement, tiles, liqueurs, candy and marmalades; tanning, olive-oil processing, sugar milling. Irrigation reservoir near by. Episcopal see since 5th cent. Has some Roman ruins; bishop's palace; and Gothic cathedral (restored 15th cent.), whose Casa Santa is place of pilgrimage. As the refuge of the rebel Sertorius, was scene (76 B.C.) of Pompey's unsuccessful siege. Changed hands several times bet. Moors and Christians (9th–11th cent.) until taken (1054) by the king of Navarre. Quintilian b. here.

Calais (kă'lā, Fr. kälĕ'), city (1946 pop. 41,536; 1936 pop. 56,102), Pas-de-Calais dept., N France, on Strait of Dover (Fr. *Pas de Calais*), 145 mi. N of Paris and 27 mi. ESE of Dover; 50°57'N 1°51'E. Until 1940, a major commercial port (transit trade) and France's leading tulle and lace-mfg. center. Recovering from very heavy war damages, Calais also builds and equips vessels for cod, mackerel, and herring fishing. Produces telephone cables, artificial ice, biscuits, and pharmaceuticals. Train ferries to Dover and Folkestone. Connected with Aa R. and chief navigable arteries of N France by canal. Just S of harbor entrance is circular, formerly fortified old town, completely surrounded by boat basins and canals, and virtually leveled in Second World War. Industrial and commercial dist. of Saint-Pierre (modern town) suffered lesser damages. The monument (by Rodin) commemorating the famous sacrifice of the 6 burghers of Calais has been moved from old town to new townhall square. A fishing village until 10th cent.; fortified (13th cent.) by counts of Boulogne. In 1347, after 11-month siege, fell to Edward III of England. Recovered by French under François de Guise in 1558. Scene of heavy fighting (1940 and 1944) and target of aerial bombings in Second World War.

Calais (kă'lĭs). **1** City (pop. 4,589), Washington co., E Maine, on St. Croix R. (here crossed by International Bridge) opposite St. Stephen, N.B.; port of entry. Mfg. (wood products, bldg. materials); dairy products; blueberries canned. Milltown (W) is a suburb. Wildlife refuge near. Champlain and Sieur de Monts planted settlement (1604) on St. Croix Isl. in the St. Croix here. Calais settled 1779, town inc. 1809, city 1850. **2** Town (pop. 778), Washington co., central Vt., just NNE of Montpelier; granite, lumber.

Calaisis (kälāzē'), old district of N France, in Pas-de-Calais dept., surrounding Calais.

Calalaste, Sierra de (syĕ'rä dā kälälä'stā), subandean range of the Puna de Atacama, in Catamarca and Salta provs., Argentina, extends c.120 mi. bet. Cerro Negro Muerto (S) and Salar Pocitos (N), forming E divide of Salar de Antofalla; rises to 17,850 ft. at the Cerro Calalaste, 25 mi. NW of Antofagasta.

Calalzo (käläl'tsô), village (pop. 1,261), Belluno prov., Veneto, N Italy, near Piave R., 23 mi. NNE of Belluno. Resort (alt. 2,818 ft.); sawmills, toy and spectacle factories.

Calama (kälä'mŭ), town (pop. 77), N Guaporé territory, W Brazil, on Madeira R. at influx of Gi-Paraná R., near Amazonas border; rubber.

Calama (kälä'mä), town (pop. 4,967), ⊙ Loa dept. (□ 16,426; pop. 30,300), Antofagasta prov., N Chile, an oasis on railroad, on Loa R., on W slope of Andes (alt. 7,435 ft.), and 125 mi. NE of Antofagasta (linked by aqueduct). Makes explosives. Trades in wheat, corn, alfalfa, vegetables. Receiving station for cattle herded across Andes from Argentina. Marble deposits near by. Smithsonian Institution maintains solar observatory in adjoining mts.

Calamar (kälämär'). **1** Town (pop. 6,934), Bolívar dept., N Colombia, river port on W bank of Magdalena R., at mouth of Canal del Dique, and 50 mi. S of Barranquilla; terminus of railroad from Cartagena, with which it is also linked by Canal del Dique. Trading and shipping point in agr. region (cotton, rice, tobacco, balsam, cattle, lumber). **2** Village, Vaupés commissary, S central Colombia, in region of tropical forests, on headstream of Vaupés R. and 275 mi. SE of Bogotá; 1°57'N 72°31'W. Gathering of forest products (rubber, balata gum). Former ⊙ Vaupés commissary.

Calamarca (kälämär'kä), village (pop. c.8,300), La Paz dept., W Bolivia, in the Altiplano, 30 mi. S of La Paz, on La Paz–Oruro RR; alt. 13,714 ft.; barley, sheep.

Calamba (kälăm'bä, kälämbä'). **1** Town (1939 pop. 4,220; 1948 municipality pop. 36,586), Laguna prov., S Luzon, Philippines, 30 mi. SSE of Manila, near Laguna de Bay; agr. center (rice, coconuts, sugar cane); sugar milling. José Rizal b. here. **2** Town (1939 pop. 3,007; 1948 municipality pop. 8,332), Misamis Occidental prov., W Mindanao, Philippines, at W side of entrance to Iligan Bay; agr. center (corn, coconuts). Until 1940s, called Plaridel. **3** Town (1939 pop. 7,771) in Guihulñgan municipality, Negros Oriental prov., E Negros isl., Philippines, on Tañon Strait, 29 mi. E of Binalbagan; agr. center (corn, coconuts, tobacco).

Calamian Islands (kälämyän') or **Calamianes** (kälämyä'nās), group (□ c.600; 1948 pop. 16,445), Palawan prov., Philippines, bet. Palawan and Mindoro; 12°N 120°E. Includes Busuanga Island (largest), Culion Island (site of govt. leper colony), and Linapacan Island (S). Hilly (Busuanga rises to 1,302 ft., Culion to 1,560 ft.), but fertile (rice, coconuts). Fishing. Manganese is mined.

Calamine, La (lä kälämēn'), Flemish *Kalmis* (kälmēs'), town (pop. 4,212), Liége prov., E Belgium, near Ger. border, 6 mi. SW of Aachen, in lead, zinc-mining region.

Calamo, Greece: see Kalamos.

Calamocha (kälämō'chä), town (pop. 2,161), Teruel prov., E Spain, on the Jiloca and 15 mi. SE of Daroca, and on fertile plain (sugar beets, saffron, wine); mfg. of pottery and chocolate; wool spinning, flour milling. Iron and copper mines near by.

Calamonte (kälämōn'tā), town (pop. 3,818), Badajoz prov., W Spain, 2½ mi. SW of Mérida; agr. center; processes grain, olives, grapes; stock raising. Mfg. of tiles.

Calamotta, island, Yugoslavia: see Kolocep Island.

Calamuchita, Argentina: see San Agustín, Córdoba prov.

Calamus (kă'lŭmŭs), town (pop. 381), Clinton co., E Iowa, 29 mi. W of Clinton, in agr. area.

Calamus River, N Nebr., rises in small lake in Brown co., flows 76 mi. SE to N.Loup R. at Burwell.

Calamutang Island, Philippines: see Laoang Island.

Calana (kälä'nä), town (pop. 267), Tacna dept., S Peru, in foothills of Cordillera Occidental, 7 mi. NE of Tacna; fruit, cotton, sugar, stock.

Calañas (kälä'nyäs), town (pop. 4,116), Huelva prov., SW Spain, on railroad and 27 mi. N of Huelva; mining (manganese, copper, iron, copper-iron pyrites); jasper quarrying; also sulphur and coal deposits. Lumbering and stock raising. Adjoined N by mining suburbs of Los Silos and El Perrunal.

Calanca (kälăng'kä), circle (pop. 1,301) and valley, Moësa dist., Grisons canton, S Switzerland; watered by Calancasca R., which flows parallel to and into Moësa R.

Calancala River, Colombia: see Ranchería River.

Calanda (kälän'dä), town (pop. 3,132), Teruel prov., E Spain, 9 mi. SSW of Alcañiz, at SW end of partly irrigated desert; soap, plaster, carbon sulphide, wax, olive-oil. Almonds, nuts, cereals in area.

Calangianus (kälänjä'nōōs), village (pop. 2,634), Sassari prov., N Sardinia, 36 mi. ENE of Sassari; cork working.

Calangute (käläng-gōō'tā), town (pop. 7,622), N Goa dist., Portuguese India, 5 mi. NW of Pangim; market center for rice, coconuts, fish, mangoes, cashew nuts; sea resort.

Calapan (käläpän'), town (1939 pop. 4,373; 1948 municipality pop. 22,340), ⊙ Mindoro prov., Philippines, on N coast of Mindoro isl., on Verde Isl. Passage, 85 mi. SSE of Manila; 13°24'N 121°10'E. Port for inter-isl. shipping. Exports copra and abacá.

Calape (kälä'pā), town (1939 pop. 2,135; 1948 municipality pop. 21,383), W Bohol isl., Philippines, on Bohol Strait, 17 mi. N of Tagbilaran; agr. center (rice, coconuts).

Calapooya River (kălŭpōō'yŭ), W Oregon, rises in Cascade Range ENE of Eugene, flows c.70 mi. WNW, past Brownsville, to Willamette R. at Albany.

Calarasi (kŭlŭrăsh'), Rum. *Călăraşi*, town (1948 pop. 24,533), ⊙ Ialomita prov., SE Rumania, in Walachia, on L. Calarasi (□ 30.8), on left bank of the Borcea arm of the Danube and 65 mi. ESE of Bucharest; rail terminus and trading center (wheat, lumber, hemp, linseed); freshwater fishing; mfg. of vegetable oil, candles, hardware. Airport. Formerly also spelled Calarashi.

Calarasi, Moldavian SSR: see Kalarash.

Cala Ratjada (kä'lä rät-hä'dhä), seaside resort (pop. 489) on E coast of Majorca, Balearic Isls., 1½ mi. E of Capdepera, 45 mi. ENE of Palma. Fishing.

Calarcá (kälärkä'), town (pop. 7,453), Caldas dept., W central Colombia, on W slopes of Cordillera Central, 2½ mi. E of Armenia; alt. 7,546 ft. Coffee center, on road to Ibagué across Quindío Pass; also sugar cane, silk, cereals, stock.

Calascibetta (käläshēbĕt'tä), town (pop. 7,149), Enna prov., central Sicily, 2 mi. N of Enna. Has Norman castle. Major sulphur mines near by.

Calasetta (käläzĕt'tä), village (pop. 2,419) and port on NNW Sant'Antioco Isl., just off SW Sardinia and 16 mi. SSW of Iglesias; rail terminus; fisheries (coral, tunny); saltworks (SW).

Calasiao (käläsēou', –syä'ō), town (1939 pop. 1,035; 1948 municipality pop. 23,269), Pangasinan prov., central Luzon, Philippines, on railroad and 2 mi. SE of Dagupan; makes buri-palm hats.

Calasparra (käläspä'rä), town (pop. 7,973), Murcia prov., SE Spain, near the Segura, 16 mi. WSW of Cieza; rice and flour milling, esparto processing, brandy distilling, olive pressing; trades in wine and truck products. Has ruins of medieval castle. Mineral springs. Limestone, porphyry, gypsum quarries. Irrigation reservoir near by.

Calata (kŭlä'tä), Rum. *Călata*, Hung. *Nagykalota* (nŏ'dyŭkō"lôtō), village (pop. 1,077), Cluj prov., W central Rumania, 8 mi. SSE of Huedin; agr. center; noted peasant art.

Calatabiano (kälätäbyä'nô), village (pop. 4,287), Catania prov., E Sicily, near Alcantara R., 15 mi. N of Acireale.

Calatafimi (kälätäfē'mē), town (pop. 11,125), Trapani prov., W Sicily, 7 mi. SW of Alcamo; agr. center (cereals, grapes, olives, citrus fruit). Has castle and monument to Garibaldi's 1st victory over Bourbons, won near here May 15, 1860. Near by are ruins of anc. Segesta.

Calatagan (kälätägän'), town (1939 pop. 1,579; 1948 municipality pop. 9,620), Batangas prov., S Luzon, Philippines, 29 mi. WNW of Batangas town, on peninsula forming W shore of Balayan Bay; sugar milling.

Calatagirone, Sicily: see Caltagirone.

Calatañazor (kälätänyä-thōr'), town (pop. 211), Soria prov., N central Spain, 20 mi. WSW of Soria. Famed as site of victory (1002) of Alfonso V over Moors under Almanzor.

Calatayud (kälätīŭdh', –tīŭ'), city (pop. 15,116), Saragossa prov., NE Spain, in Aragon, on Jalón R. and 45 mi. SW of Saragossa; communications center in fertile agr. area (fruit, wine, cereals, sugar beets); hemp processing (yarn, rope), sugar milling; mfg. of sandals, soap, biscuits, chocolate and candy, plaster, tiles; livestock market. Mineral springs. Has 8th-cent. Moorish castle and collegiate church of Santo Sepulcro (once chief church of Knights Templars in Spain). Founded (8th cent.)

by Moors, freed (1120) by Alfonso I of Aragon. Cave dwellings in vicinity. Ruins of Roman town of *Bilbilis*, birthplace of Martial, are 2 mi. E.

Calatele (kulútsä'lä), Rum. *Călățele*, Hung. *Kiskalota* (kēsh'kŏ"lôtŏ), village (pop. 1,571), Cluj prov., W central Rumania, in N foothills of the Apuseni Mts., 28 mi. W of Cluj; rail terminus; trading center in region noted for its peasant handicrafts (weaving and embroideries).

Calatorao (kälätōrou'), town (pop. 3,234), Saragossa prov., NE Spain, near Jalón R., 26 mi. WSW of Saragossa; sugar and flour mills; agr. trade (sugar beets, cereals, lumber, livestock). Black-marble quarries in vicinity. On hill near by are ruins of Moorish castle on Roman foundations.

Calatrava (käläträ'vä), town (1939 pop. 2,732; 1948 municipality pop. 53,805), Negros Occidental prov., NE Negros isl., Philippines, on Tañon Strait, 37 mi. E of Bacolod; agr. center (rice, sugar cane). Sawmill.

Calatrava, Campo de (käm'pō dhä), region in Ciudad Real prov., S central Spain, in New Castile, NE of Ciudad Real and bet. Guadiana R. and N outliers of the Sierra Morena. An anc. territory of the Knights of Calatrava, of which Almagro was ⊙, though the ruined fortress of Calatrava la Vieja (lä vyä'hä), 8 mi. NE of Ciudad Real, was their 1st seat. The military order was founded in 1158 and played major part in the reconquest.

Calau (kä'lou), town (pop. 5,372), Brandenburg, E Germany, in Lower Lusatia, 16 mi. W of Cottbus; mfg.: machinery, electrical equipment, bricks, paving stones, earthenware, shoes. Sometimes spelled Kalau.

Calauag (käläwäg'), town (1939 pop. 5,089; 1948 municipality pop. 16,875), Quezon prov., S Luzon, Philippines, on Calauag Bay, 65 mi. E of San Pablo; fishing and agr. center (coconuts, rice).

Calauag Bay, S arm of Lamon Bay, Philippines, bet. Alabat Isl. (W) and S coast of Luzon; 21 mi. long, 4–11 mi. wide. Calauag is on S shore.

Calavà, Cape (kälävä'), point on NE coast of Sicily, at W end of Gulf of Patti; 38°12'N 14°55'E. Tunny fisheries.

Calaveras (kălúvâ'rús), county (□ 1,028; pop. 9,902), central Calif., in the Sierra Nevada; ⊙ San Andreas. Mokelumne R. forms the N, and Stanislaus R. the S, boundary. Calaveras R. rises in NW. Stanislaus Natl. Forest and Calaveras Big Trees State Park (redwoods) are here. Dams (Pardee, Calaveras, Melones) store water for power, water supply, and irrigation. Winter-sports area; also camping, hunting, fishing. Gold mining; lumbering; cement production. Stock grazing, some general farming, and fruitgrowing. ANGELS CAMP, the scene of some of Mark Twain's stories, and other old Mother Lode towns survive. Formed 1850.

Calaveras Big Trees State Park (c.2,000 acres), Calaveras co., E central Calif., on W slope of the Sierra Nevada, c.60 mi. ENE of Stockton. In 1852, the 1st grove of *Sequoia gigantea* discovered in the sierras was found here by a hunter. Includes many of the finest sequoias (some almost 300 ft. high) in Calif. Recreational area; summer and winter sports, camping.

Calaveras Dam, Calif.: see CALAVERAS RIVER.

Calaveras Reservoir. 1 Reservoir (c.8 mi. long), Calaveras co., central Calif., impounded in CALAVERAS RIVER W of San Andreas. **2** Water-supply reservoir (c.2 mi. long) for San Francisco, in Santa Clara and Alameda counties, W Calif., formed by dam in valley of the small Arroyo Hondo, 8 mi. NNE of San Jose.

Calaveras River, central Calif., rises in NW Calaveras co. as North Fork, flows c.25 mi. W and SW to junction with South Fork just W of San Andreas, then flows c.50 mi. SW to San Joaquin R. just W of Stockton. In W Calaveras co. is Calaveras Dam (220 ft. high, 1,200 ft. long) impounding Calaveras Reservoir (c.8 mi. long). The Calaveras is also site of projected New Hogan Reservoir of CENTRAL VALLEY project.

Calavino (kälävē'nô), village (pop. 761), Trento prov., Trentino–Alto Adige, N Italy, 7 mi. W of Trent; foundry.

Calavite, Cape (kälävē'tä), westernmost point of Mindoro isl., Philippines, on NW peninsula, in S.China Sea; 13°26'N 120°17'E; lighthouse.

Calavon River, France: see COULON RIVER.

Calayan Island (käläyän'), largest island (□ 73; 1939 pop. 1,911) of the Babuyan Isls., Cagayan prov., Philippines, in Luzon Strait, forming S boundary of Balintang Channel, 48 mi. N of Luzon; 19°20'N 121°25'E. It is 14 mi. long, 9 mi. wide. Mountainous, rising to 1,780 ft. Rice growing, fishing. Calayan town is on S coast.

Calbayog (kälbä'yōg), city (1939 pop. 3,563; 1948 metropolitan area pop. 79,503), W Samar isl., Philippines, on Samar Sea, 29 mi. NW of Catbalogan; agr. center (rice, corn); fisheries.

Calbe (käl'bù). **1** or **Calbe an der Saale** (än děr zä'lù), town (pop. 15,161), in former Prussian Saxony prov., central Germany, after 1945 in Saxony-Anhalt, on the Saxonian Saale and 17 mi. SSE of Magdeburg; rail junction; lignite mining; metalworking, woolen and paper milling, sugar refining; mfg. of machinery, chemicals. Vegetable-market center. Has Romanesque church; medieval former palace of archbishops of Magdeburg. **2** or **Calbe an der Milde**, town, Germany: see KALBE.

Calbuco (kälbōō'kō), town (pop. 2,049), ⊙ Calbuco dept. (□ 194; pop. 16,405), Llanquihue prov., S central Chile, on small Calbuco Isl. (□ 2.1) in Gulf of Ancud, just offshore, 25 mi. SW of Puerto Montt; 41°46'S 73°8'W. Minor port, trading and fishing center; fish canneries.

Calbuco Volcano, Andean peak (6,610 ft.), Llanquihue prov., S central Chile, on SE bank of L. Llanquihue, 20 mi. NE of Puerto Montt; 41°20'S 72°39'W. Last erupted 1928.

Calca (käl'kä), city (pop. 3,373), ⊙ Calca prov. (□ 1,306; pop. 37,517), Cuzco dept., S central Peru, in the Andes, on upper Urubamba R. and 15 mi. N of Cuzco; alt. 9,020 ft. Grain, fruit, vegetables; silver and copper mining. Archaeological remains.

Calcahualco (kälkäwäl'kō), town (pop. 508), Veracruz, E Mexico, in Sierra Madre Oriental, at NE foot of the Pico de Orizaba, 8 mi. WSW of Huatusco; fruit.

Calcar, Germany: see KALKAR.

Calcara, Malta: see KALKARA.

Calcaria, England: see TADCASTER.

Calcasieu (kăl'kusōō), parish (□ 1,104; pop. 89,635), extreme SW La.; ⊙ Lake Charles. Bounded W by Sabine R., here forming Texas line; Lake Charles city is deepwater port on Calcasieu R. Agr. (rice, corn, cotton, sweet potatoes), stock raising. Oil and natural-gas wells; sulphur mine; sand and gravel pits; lumbering. Diversified mfg. and processing of farm products, lumber, and petroleum products. Has small lakes (resorts; fishing). Gulf Intracoastal Waterway crosses parish. Formed 1840.

Calcasieu Lake, La.: see CALCASIEU RIVER.

Calcasieu River, W central and SW La., rises in Vernon parish, flows c.215 mi. generally S to Gulf of Mexico, c.35 mi. ESE of Port Arthur, Texas. It widens into L. Charles at Lake Charles city, and into Calcasieu L. (c.20 mi. long) 11 mi. S of L. Charles; and it issues into Gulf through Calcasieu Pass (c.7 mi. long). Receives West Fork (c.60 mi. long) 10 mi. N of L. Charles. There is a 30-ft. ship channel to port of Lake Charles city. Just above Calcasieu L., the river is intersected by the Gulf Intracoastal Waterway, whose deepwater section to W (Lake Charles Canal) links Calcasieu R. with Sabine-Neches Waterway.

Calceta (kälsä'tä), town (1950 pop. 3,680), Manabí prov., W Ecuador, in tropical lowlands, on railroad and 13 mi. S of Chone; agr. center in fertile region (cacao, sugar cane, coffee, rice, tagua nuts, balsa wood). Mfg. of Panama hats.

Calcha (käl'chä), town (pop. c.5,100), Potosí dept., S central Bolivia, on Vitichi R. (N branch of the Tumusla) and 9 mi. S of Vitichi; corn, potatoes.

Calchaquí (kälchäkē'), town (pop. estimate 2,000), N central Santa Fe prov., Argentina, on railroad and 125 mi. N of Santa Fe, in agr. (flax, corn, sunflowers, livestock) and lumbering area; sawmills.

Calchaquíes, Cumbres (kōōm'brěs kälchäkē'ěs), mountain range in NW Tucumán prov., Argentina, extends c.40 mi. N to Salta prov. border, forming divide bet. Santa María R. (W) and the Salí R. or Río Dulce (E); rises to c.10,000 ft.

Calchaquí River (kälchäkē'), headstream of the Río Salado in Salta prov., Argentina, flows c.120 mi. S and SE, past La Poma and Cachi, to join the Cajón or Santa María 10 mi. ENE of Cafayate, forming GUACHIPAS RIVER. Sometimes called Cachi R.

Calchi, Greece: see CHALKE.

Calchín (kälchēn'), town (pop. estimate 1,000), central Córdoba prov., Argentina, 60 mi. SE of Córdoba; grain, livestock.

Calci (käl'chē), village (pop. 1,395), Pisa prov., Tuscany, central Italy, at S foot of Monte Pisano, 6 mi. E of Pisa; paper and woolen mills, macaroni factory. Has late 11th-cent. church. Near by is Certosa di Pisa, founded 1366.

Calcinaia (kälchēnä'yä), village (pop. 1,226), Pisa prov., Tuscany, central Italy, on the Arno and 11 mi. E of Pisa.

Calcinate (kälchēnä'tě), village (pop. 1,810), Bergamo prov., Lombardy, N Italy, 8 mi. SE of Bergamo; button mfg.

Calcinato (kälchēnä'tô), village (pop. 2,696), Brescia prov., Lombardy, N Italy, on Chiese R. and 11 mi. SE of Brescia; silk mill.

Calcio (käl'chô), village (pop. 2,868), Bergamo prov., Lombardy, N Italy, near Oglio R., 16 mi. SE of Bergamo; mfg. (sausage, buttons).

Calcite, Mich.: see ROGERS CITY.

Calcken, Belgium: see KALKEN.

Calcutta (kălkŭ'tù), city (largest in India; □ 28.3; pop. 2,070,619) and district (□ 33.7; pop. 2,108,891), ⊙ West Bengal, India, in Ganges Delta, on left bank of Hooghly R. opposite HOWRAH (bridge) and c.70 mi. N of Bay of Bengal, 800 mi. SE of New Delhi; 22°30'N 88°20'E. Chief commercial port of India; important communications center (rail and highway hub; airport at Dumdum, NE). The major outlet for mineral resources of Chota Nagpur Plateau and Damodar Valley; exports pig iron and manganese. Although Calcutta is still world's leading exporter of raw and milled jute, its shipment of this item was lessened in 1947, when partition of Bengal assigned the great jute-growing area of the Brahmaputra valley to newly-created prov. of East Bengal (Pakistan), which began to develop its port of Chittagong as outlet for E Pakistan's raw jute. Calcutta also exports tea, shellac, and vegetable oil, imports rice, sugar, and manufactured goods. One of India's important industrial centers; has heaviest concentration of country's jute mills and presses; a leading center of textile (cotton, silk), printing, and bookbinding industries; mfg. of chemicals, glass, paper, cigarettes, paint, soap, pottery, cement, bricks, rubber goods, matches, hosiery, shoes and other leather goods; rice, oilseed, and flour milling, sawmilling; general and electric engineering works, rail workshops, iron and steel rolling works, tanneries; silver refinery; pilot fishing station with cold-storage plant. The Maidan, a park along the Hooghly, is bounded E for 2 mi. by Chowringhi Road (hotels, theaters, restaurants); contains present Fort William (W; completed 1773); in SE is large marble Victoria Memorial (pictures, statues, documents of Indian hist. and Victorian era). N of the Maidan is Govt. House (formerly executive mansion of India's viceroys and presently of governor of West Bengal). Near Govt. House is site of original Fort William (built 1696); contained guardroom known as the "black hole" of notorious legend. Along Chowringhi Road (N–S) is Indian Mus. (extensive geological, zoological, and archaeological collections), Bengal School of Art, and Bengal Asiatic Society (large library). To SE is city's main wealthy residential section. In S area is Kali Ghat, with noted Kali temple (pilgrimage center) and bazaars. The most extensive commercial and industrial area is NE of the Maidan; contains Univ. of Calcutta (founded 1857; medical, arts, and law schools; nuclear physics laboratory), Natl. (formerly Imperial) Library, Bose Research Inst., and noted Jain temple. Other institutions include School of Tropical Medicine, with one of largest leprosy research stations in the East, Inst. of Rubber Industry, Central Glass and Ceramics Inst. Calcutta was ⊙ India from 1833 until 1912, when ⊙ was moved to Delhi. Founded 1690 (when Hooghly settlement was abandoned) by Job Charnock of English East India Co. at former village of Sutanuti and nucleus of Bengal established 1700 at Fort William; named after former village of Kalikata. Captured 1756 by Siraj-ud-daula, nawab of Bengal, who stifled most of the garrison in the "black hole"; recaptured 1757 by Clive. Port proper extends from Konnagar (N) to Budge-Budge (S). Included within municipality are suburbs of KIDDERPORE (SW; extensive dockyards), ALIPORE (S; zoological gardens), BHAWANIPUR (S), BALLYGUNGE (SE), and COSSIPORE (N; gun and shell factories). Calcutta municipal area and extra-municipal areas of Fort William and Maidan, and port and canals section constitute Calcutta dist.

Calcutta and Eastern Canals, system of navigable channels (artificial canals and tidal creeks) in the Sundarbans, in 24-Parganas dist., India, and Khulna, Bakarganj, and Faridpur dists., E Pakistan; extend c.1,130 mi.; include Tolly's Nullah. Created to increase trade efficiency.

Caldarasani, Rumania: see SNAGOV.

Caldaro (käldä'rô), Ger. *Kaltern*, town (pop. 1,827), Bolzano prov., Trentino–Alto Adige, N Italy, 8 mi. SSW of Bolzano; rail spur terminus; wine.

Caldarola (käldärô'lä), village (pop. 1,170), Macerata prov., The Marches, central Italy, near Chienti R., 6 mi. SW of Tolentino; tannery.

Caldas (käl'dùs), city (pop. 2,736), SW Minas Gerais, Brazil, 15 mi. SE of Poços de Caldas; alt. 3,400 ft. Has hot sulphur springs. Wine making, dairying. Zirconium and bauxite mining. Called Parreiras, 1940–48.

Caldas (käl'däs), department (□ 5,162; 1938 pop. 769,968; 1950 estimate 1,100,350), central Colombia; ⊙ Manizales. Hilly, mountainous area along Cauca valley bet. Cordillera Occidental (W) and Cordillera Central (E), extending in N across Cordillera Central to Magdalena R. Includes snow-capped Nevado del Ruiz on Tolima dept. border. Climate ranges from tropical, along Cauca and Magdalena rivers, to temperate and cool in uplands, with 2 rainy seasons. Mineral resources include gold (Marmato, Supía), coal (Quinchía, Ríosucio), silver, lead, mercury, and salt. One of Colombia's main coffee-producing regions, it also grows corn, wheat, sugar cane, cacao, bananas, cotton, yucca. Considerable cattle raising and sericulture. Mfg. and trading centers at Manizales, Pereira, Armenia, Santa Rosa de Cabal, with textile, cordage (Panama hats, fique bags), and food-processing industries. Termales (or Ruiz), near Manizales, has well-known thermal springs. Served by river boats, highways, railroads, and several aerial tramways, the last radiating from Manizales. Caldas was developed during 19th cent. by settlers from Antioquia.

Caldas, town (pop. 2,847), Antioquia dept., NW central Colombia, on Porce R., on W slopes of Cordillera Central, on railroad and 12 mi. SSW of Medellín; alt. 5,896 ft. Resort in agr. region (coffee, corn, bananas, yucca, milch cows, forest products); mfg. of glass, ceramics, china; machine shop. White-clay and quartz deposits near by.

Caldas, Las (läs käl'däs), or **El Puente** (ĕl pwĕn'tā), village (pop. 2,556), Orense prov., NW Spain, 4 mi. NW of Orense; sawmills; agr. trade (cereals, wine, fruit, chestnuts). Warm sulphur springs.

Caldas da Rainha (käl'dŭsh dŭ rī'nyŭ) [Port.,= the queen's hot springs], city (pop. 8,159), Leiria dist., Estremadura, W central Portugal, on railroad and 50 mi. N of Leiria; fashionable watering place (warm sulphur springs) founded 1485 by the queen of John II. Town is also noted for its ceramics (Portugal's principal majolica factory here). Atlantic bathing beach at Foz do Arelho, 6 mi. NW.

Caldas de Monchique (käl'dŭsh dĭ mōshē'kĭ), village (pop. 122), Faro dist., S Portugal, in the Serra de Monchique, 3 mi. S of Monchique; watering place with sulphur springs (known to Romans).

Caldas de Montbuy or **Caldas de Mombuy** (both: käl'däs dhā mōmbwē'), town (pop. 4,123), Barcelona prov., NE Spain, in Catalonia, 17 mi. N of Barcelona; cotton spinning, flour milling, olive-oil processing; hog raising; wine, wheat, cherries. Health resort with hot mineral springs, noted since Roman times.

Caldas de Reyes (rā'ĕs), town (pop. 1,960), Pontevedra prov., NW Spain, 12 mi. N of Pontevedra; flour milling, tanning, furniture mfg. Vineyards, fruit in area. Warm sulphur springs. Silver and pyrite mining near by.

Caldas de Vizela (käl'dŭsh dĭ vēzä'lŭ), village (pop. 1,963), Braga dist., N Portugal, on Ave R. and branch railroad, 23 mi. NE of Oporto; spa with hot sulphur springs, known since Roman times; textile mills.

Caldas Novas (nô'vŭs), city (pop. 1,082), S Goiás, central Brazil, 80 mi. SE of Goiânia; hog raising. Has radioactive springs. Rutile deposits in area.

Caldeira de Santa Bárbara (kŭldā'rŭ dĭ săn'tŭ bär'-bŭrŭ), quiescent volcano (alt. 3,356 ft.), central Azores, highest peak of Terceira Isl., 8 mi. NW of Angra do Heroísmo. Lava flows.

Caldera or **La Caldera** (lä käldä'rä), village (pop. estimate 500), ⊙ Caldera dept. (□ 550; 1947 pop. 2,866), central Salta prov., Argentina, in Lerma Valley, 13 mi. N of Salta; corn, sugar cane, livestock.

Caldera, town (pop. 1,525), Atacama prov., N Chile, port on Pacific coast (on small, well-protected bay), 35 mi. NW of Copiapó; 27°4'S. Rail terminus; shipping and mfg. center. Copper smelting and refining; railroad shops. Outlet for the rich mining prov., exporting copper, gold, silver, nitrates, borax. Reputed to have the oldest railway line in South America, constructed in 1849 by William Wheelwright and leading to Copiapó. The port was opened 1884.

Caldera, village, Puntarenas prov., W Costa Rica, port on Gulf of Nicoya, on railroad and 8 mi. ESE of Puntarenas; coffee.

Caldera, village (pop. 235), Chiriquí prov., W Panama, on Caldera R. (small tributary of Chiriquí R.) and 9 mi. SSE of Boquete; coffee, cacao; stock raising, lumbering.

Calderas (käldä'räs), town (pop. 687), Barinas state, W Venezuela, in Andean foothills, 25 mi. NW of Barinas; coffee, corn, livestock.

Calderas Bay, small inlet of the Caribbean, S Dominican Republic, just SE of Ocoa Bay, 45 mi. WSW of Ciudad Trujillo. Saltworks.

Calderbank (kôldŭrbăngk'), town in Old Monkland parish, N Lanark, Scotland, 2 mi. S of Airdrie; coal mining.

Caldercruix (kôldŭrkrōōks'), town in New Monkland parish, N Lanark, Scotland, 4 mi. ENE of Airdrie; paper milling. Just E is Hillend Reservoir.

Calderón Bridge, Mexico: see GUADALAJARA.

Calder River (kôl'dŭr). **1** In Lancashire and Yorkshire, England, rises just S of Burnley, flows 45 mi. E, past Halifax, Elland, Brighouse, Mirfield, and Dewsbury, to Aire R. at Castleford. Receives Colne R. 3 mi. NE of Huddersfield. **2** In central Lancashire, England, rises just N of Colne, flows 15 mi. WNW, past Burnley and Padiham, to Ribble R. near Whalley.

Calderwood Dam, Blount and Monroe counties, E Tenn., near N.C. line, in Little Tennessee R. below Cheoah Dam, 35 mi. S of Knoxville; 230 ft. high, 897 ft. long; concrete, arch, overflow type; for power; completed 1930. Impounds Calderwood Reservoir, c.5 mi. long.

Calderwood Island, Knox co., S Maine, in Penobscot Bay just SE of North Haven Isl.; ¾ mi. long.

Caldicot (kôl'dĭkŭt), town and parish (pop. 1,599), SE Monmouth, England, near Severn R., 5 mi. SW of Chepstow; mfg. of aluminum products. Has 14th–15th-cent. church and castle with 13th-cent. keep.

Caldiero (käldyā'rô), village (pop. 1,330), Verona prov., Veneto, N Italy, 9 mi. E of Verona; sausage factory. Has thermal saline springs. Archduke Charles defeated Masséna here in 1805.

Caldonazzo (käldônä'tsô), village (pop. 1,633), Trento prov., Trentino–Alto Adige, N Italy, 8 mi. SE of Trent, in Valsugana, just S of Lago di Caldonazzo (□ 2; 2.5 mi. long, 1 mi. wide; a source of Brenta R.). Alcohol distillery, box factory.

Caldwell. **1** (kôwĕl') County (□ 357; pop. 13,199), W Ky.; ⊙ Princeton. Bounded NE by Tradewater R. Rolling agr. area (burley tobacco, livestock, grain); fluorspar and coal mines, timber tracts, stone quarries. Some mfg. at Princeton. Includes part of Pennyrile State Forest. Formed 1809. **2** (kôld'wŭl, –wĕl) Parish (□ 550; pop. 10,293), NE central La.; ⊙ Columbia. Bounded E by Boeuf R.; intersected by Ouachita R. and Bayou Castor. Farming (cotton, corn, sweet potatoes, livestock; hay) and lumbering area. Cotton ginning, lumber milling. Natural-gas wells. Formed 1838. **3** (kôld'-wŭl, –wĕl) County (□ 430; pop. 9,929), NW Mo.; ⊙ Kingston. Agr. (corn, wheat, oats); coal. Formed 1836. **4** (kôld'wŭl, –wĕl) County (□ 476; pop. 43,352), W central N.C.; ⊙ Lenoir. The Blue Ridge in NW; drained by Catawba (Rhodhiss Dam and hydroelectric plant) and Yadkin rivers. Agr. (tobacco, corn, wheat, hay, livestock, dairy products, poultry); timber (pine, oak). Textile mfg., sawmilling. Formed 1841. **5** (kôld'wŭl, –wĕl) County (□ 544; pop. 19,350), S central Texas; ⊙ Lockhart. Bounded SW by San Marcos R. Agr. (cotton, corn, grain sorghums, vegetables, watermelons, pecans, peanuts); livestock (cattle, hogs, poultry). Oil, natural-gas fields. Mfg., farm-products processing at Lockhart and Luling. Formed 1848.

Caldwell (kôld'wŭl, –wĕl). **1** City (pop. 10,487), ⊙ Canyon co., SW Idaho, on Boise R. and 25 mi. W of Boise. Trade, processing, shipping center for irrigated agr., livestock area; dairy products, flour, lumber; printing shops. Cooperatives well established. Col. of Idaho (1891), and an agr. experiment station here. Founded 1883 on Oregon Trail, inc. in 1889. **2** City (pop. 2,000), Sumner co., S Kansas, near Okla. line, 19 mi. SSW of Wellington, in wheat and livestock region; mfg. (flour, lawn mowers). Oil wells near by. Laid out 1871, inc. 1879. City grew as trading point on Chisholm Trail. **3** Borough (pop. 6,270), Essex co., in NE N.J., 8 mi. NW of Newark; mfg. (airplane propellers, clothing, plastic products, pharmaceuticals); nurseries; dairy products. Seat of Caldwell Col. for Women. Grover Cleveland's birthplace, now a mus., here. Settled before 1785, inc. 1892. **4** Village (pop. 1,767), ⊙ Noble co., E Ohio, 20 mi. SSE of Cambridge, and on small Duck Creek, in coal-mining and livestock area; oil wells, clay pits. Laid out 1857. **5** Town (pop. 2,109), ⊙ Burleson co., S central Texas, c.65 mi. ENE of Austin; trade, processing center for cotton, corn area; cotton gins, cotton-seed-oil mill.

Caldy (käl'dē), island (449 acres; pop. 93), in Carmarthen Bay of Bristol Channel, Pembroke, Wales, 2½ mi. S of Tenby; 1 mi. long, 1 mi. wide; separated from mainland by Caldy Sound, 1 mi. wide. Has some remains of 5th-cent. monastery. The abbey established here 1127 by Benedictines is now held by Cistercian monks from Belgium. Neolithic and Roman remains have been found on isl. Site of lighthouse (51°38'N 4°40'W). Off NW corner is small St. Margaret's Isl.

Caledon (kă'lŭdŭn), town (pop. 955), SE Co. Tyrone, Northern Ireland, on Blackwater R. and 8 mi. W of Armagh, near Irish border; agr. market (flax, potatoes, oats; cattle).

Caledon (kă'lŭdŭn), town (pop. 3,250), SW Cape Prov., U. of So. Afr., 60 mi. ESE of Cape Town; health resort, established 1713, with radioactive mineral springs. Has noted Wild Flower Park.

Caledonia (kă"lĭdō'nēŭ, kă"lĭdō'nyŭ), Roman name for that part of the isl. of Britain which lies N of the Firths of Clyde and Forth. The name occurs in the works of Lucan (1st cent. A.D.) and is still used rhetorically, usually to mean all of Scotland.

Caledonia, village (pop. 165), Northern Dist., Br. Honduras, on New R. and 7 mi. S of Corozal; sugar cane, corn, coconuts.

Caledonia, village (pop. 1,401), S Ont., on Grand R. and 14 mi. SSE of Hamilton; dairying, gypsum mining, natural-gas production; hydroelectric station.

Caledonia, county (□ 614; pop. 24,049), NE Vt., partly bounded E by Connecticut R.; ⊙ St. Johnsbury. Mfg. (scales, machinery, paper); dairying; lumber, granite. Drained by Passumpsic, Moose, Lamoille, and Wells rivers. Organized 1792.

Caledonia. **1** Village (pop. 619), Kent co., SW Mich., 14 mi. SE of Grand Rapids, in agr. area; dairying. **2** Village (pop. 2,243), ⊙ Houston co., extreme SE Minn., near Mississippi R. and Iowa line, 17 mi. SW of La Crosse, Wis., in grain, livestock, and poultry area; dairy products, lumber, flour, potatoes. Hq. of U.S. soil-conservation project here. State park near by. Settled c.1855. **3** Village (pop. 252), Lowndes co., E Miss., 14 mi. NNE of Columbus. **4** Town (pop. 143), Washington co., E central Mo., in the Ozarks, near Big R., 15 mi. WSW of Flat River. **5** Village (pop. 1,683), Livingston co., W central N.Y., 18 mi. SW of Rochester; mfg. (electrical and farm machinery, chemicals); gypsum and limestone quarries; agr. (dairy products; grain). Site of state fish hatchery. Inc. 1887. **6** Village and township (pop. 338), Traill co., E N.Dak., 10 mi. ENE of Hillsboro, near junction of Goose R. with Red River of the North. **7** Village (pop. 655), Marion co., central Ohio, 9 mi. ENE of Marion, and on Olentangy R., in agr. area.

Caledonia Mines, village, NE N.S., near NE coast of Cape Breton Isl., just SW of Glace Bay; coal-mining center.

Caledonian Canal, waterway across Scotland from Loch Linnhe to Moray Firth at Inverness, following the Great Glen of Scotland. It is 60½ mi. long, of which 23 mi. consist of artificial canal, linking lochs Ness, Oich, and Lochy. Begun 1803 by Telford, it was finally opened 1847. Owing to its small capacity, it is little used now.

Caledonia Springs, village (pop. estimate 100), SE Ont., 45 mi. E of Ottawa; resort, with medicinal springs.

Caledon River (kă'lŭdŭn), S Orange Free State, U. of So. Afr., and Basutoland, rises in Drakensberg range near NE extremity of Basutoland, flows c.300 mi. SW, forming border bet. Orange Free State and Basutoland, past Ficksburg and Maseru to Orange R. 6 mi. E of Bethulie.

Calella (kälā'lyä), city (pop. 7,939), Barcelona prov., NE Spain, on the Mediterranean, and 12 mi. NE of Mataró; a center of the knit-goods industry; dyes, flour products; trades in wine, olive oil, fruit.

Calenzana (kälĕnzänä', It. kälĕnzä'nä), town (pop. 1,952), NW Corsica, 7 mi. SE of Calvi; olive oil, honey. Silver-bearing lead deposits.

Calenzano (kälĕntsä'nô), village (pop. 598), Firenze prov., Tuscany, central Italy, 8 mi. NW of Florence; mfg. (cement, bricks, sulphur oils).

Calera (kälā'rä). **1** or **Calera de Tango** (dā täng'gō), village (1930 pop. 237), Santiago prov., central Chile, 15 mi. SSW of Santiago, in fruit- and grain-growing area; lime quarrying. **2** or **La Calera** (lä), town (pop. 8,426), Valparaiso prov., central Chile, on Aconcagua R. and 32 mi. NE of Valparaiso; rail junction; agr. center (wine, hemp, fruit, corn, beans). Cement, flour, and paper milling; brewing, tanning, hemp processing. Furnishes limestone for blast furnaces at Corral (Valdivia prov.). Phosphate production.

Calera, officially Calera Victor Rosales, town (pop. 4,092), Zacatecas, N central Mexico, on railroad and 15 mi. NNW of Zacatecas; alt. 7,336 ft. Agr. center (grain, alfalfa, vegetables, livestock).

Calera (kŭlĕr'ŭ). **1** Town (pop. 1,361), Shelby co., central Ala., 28 mi. S of Birmingham; lumber, lime products. Settled in mid-19th cent. **2** Town (pop. 643), Bryan co., S Okla., 5 mi. SW of Durant; agr. (oats, peanuts, corn); cotton ginning.

Calera, La, Argentina: see LA CALERA.

Calera, La, Colombia: see LA CALERA.

Calera de León (kälā'rä dhā lāōn'), town (pop. 2,196), Badajoz prov., W Spain, in the Sierra Morena, 28 mi. SE of Jerez de los Caballeros; olives, acorns, cereals, grapes, livestock. A sanctuary is on Tentudia mtn. 4 mi. S.

Calera y Chozas (ē chō'thäs), village (pop. 3,359), Toledo prov., central Spain, near the Tagus, on railroad and 10 mi. SW of Talavera de la Reina, in agr. region (olives, grapes, cereals, sheep). Olive-oil pressing, fishing, tile mfg.

Caleruela (kälĕrwā'lä), town (pop. 1,050), Toledo prov., central Spain, near Cáceres border, 24 mi. WSW of Talavera de la Reina; wheat, olives, livestock; olive-oil pressing.

Caleta, La (lä kälā'tä), village (pop. 84), Lanzarote, Canary Isls., on fine bay 10 mi. N of Arrecife.

Caleta, La, E residential suburb of Málaga, S Spain; cement milling.

Caleta Buena (bwā'nä), village (pop. 4), Tarapacá prov., N Chile, port on the Pacific, 23 mi. N of Iquique; former nitrate-shipping port. Nearly abandoned in 1930s.

Caleta Coloso, Chile: see COLOSO.

Caleta del Sebo (dhĕl sā'vō), fishing village (pop. 423), Lanzarote, Canary Isls., on fine sheltered bay of El Río, opposite Graciosa Isl., 18 mi. N of Arrecife.

Caleta Josefina (hōsāfē'nä), village (1930 pop. 196), Magallanes prov., S Chile, on Useless Bay of main isl. of Tierra del Fuego, 55 mi. ESE of Punta Arenas; sheep raising.

Caleta Olivia (ōlē'vyä), village (pop. estimate 300), E Comodoro Rivadavia military zone, Argentina, on Gulf of San Jorge, 40 mi. S of Comodoro Rivadavia; sheep-raising and oil-producing center. Until 1946 in Santa Cruz natl. territory.

Caleu-Caleu, Argentina: see RÍO COLORADO, La Pampa natl. territory.

Caleufú (kälā-ōōfōō'), town (pop. estimate 1,200), NE La Pampa natl. territory, Argentina, 45 mi. W of General Pico; rail terminus; grain-growing and horse-raising center; sawmills.

Calexico (kŭlĕk'sĭkō), city (pop. 6,433), Imperial co., S Calif., c.40 mi. S of Salton Sea and across border from Mexicali, Mexico. Trade and shipping center, and port of entry in IMPERIAL VALLEY. Inc. 1908.

Calf, The, peak (2,220 ft.) of the Pennines, on Yorkshire and Westmorland border, England, 4 mi. NNE of Sedbergh.

Calf Island, Mass.: see BREWSTER ISLANDS.

Calf of Eday, Scotland: see EDAY.

Calf of Man, island in Irish Sea, just off SW extremity of Isle of Man, England; 2 mi. long, 1 mi. wide; rises to 421 ft.; site of lighthouse (54°4'N

4°51'W). Just off SW point of isl. is Chicken Rock, with lighthouse (54°2'N 4°52'W).

Calfpasture River, W Va., rises in the Alleghenies in W Augusta co., flows c.40 mi. SSW, past Goshen, joining Maury R. SE of Goshen to form North R.

Calgal Dag (chälgäl' dä), Turkish *Çalgal Dağ*, peak (8,930 ft.), central Turkey, in Divrigi Mts., 20 mi. S of Divrigi.

Calgary (kăl'gùrē, kălgâ'rē), city (pop. 100,044), S Alta., on Bow R. at mouth of Elbow R., and 180 mi. S of Edmonton, near foothills of Rocky Mts.; alt. c.3,500 ft.; 51°3'N 114°5'W; railroad, trade, and industrial center for S Alta., in stock-raising region, near Turner Valley oilfields (connected by pipe lines). Oil refineries, meat-packing plants, grain elevators, knitting, lumber, steel-rolling mills, iron foundries, tanneries, breweries, dairies; mfg. of machinery, chemicals, soap, paint, cereal foods, biscuits, clothing. Center of large irrigation system and terminal of irrigation canal serving country E of Calgary. Has grain exchange and prov. institute of technology and art, public library and mus. City has had commission form of govt. since 1907. Fort Calgary of the Royal North West Mounted Police was founded 1875 on site of city; reached 1883 by Canadian Pacific RR, it rapidly developed into distributing center (1911 pop. 43,704; 1931 pop. 83,761).

Calhan (kăl'hăn", kă'lùhăn"), town (pop. 375), El Paso co., central Colo., 30 mi. NE of Colorado Springs; alt. 6,508 ft. Dairy and poultry products, livestock, grain.

Calheta (kälyĕ'tù), town (pop. 820), Angra do Heroísmo dist., central Azores, on S shore of São Jorge Isl., 12 mi. ESE of Velas; fishing, dairying.

Calheta, town (pop. 2,735), Madeira, on SW coast of Madeira isl., 16 mi. WNW of Funchal; mfg. of alcohol, pottery.

Calhoun (kăl"hōōn', kăl'hōōn"). **1** County (□ 610; pop. 79,539), E Ala.; ⊙ Anniston. Agr. area bounded on W by Coosa R. Cotton, poultry; textiles. Deposits of iron ore, limestone, bauxite, barites. Part of Talladega Natl. Forest in E. Formed 1832. **2** County (□ 628; pop. 7,132), S Ark.; ⊙ Hampton. Bounded E by Moro Creek, S by Ouachita R. Agr. area (cotton, corn, truck); timber; lumber milling, cotton ginning. Formed 1852. **3** County (□ 557; pop. 7,922), NW Fla.; ⊙ Blountstown. Lowland area drained by Chipola R. and bounded E by Apalachicola R.; contains N end of Dead L. Agr. (corn, peanuts, sugar cane, vegetables), stock raising (hogs, cattle), and forestry (lumber, naval stores); clay pits in E. Formed 1838. **4** County (□ 289; pop. 8,578), SW Ga.; ⊙ Morgan. Intersected by Ichawaynochaway Creek. Coastal plain agr. (cotton, corn, truck, peanuts, pecans) and timber area. Formed 1854. **5** County (□ 259; pop. 6,898), W Ill., bounded by Mississippi (W, S) and Illinois (E) rivers, which join at co.'s SE tip; ⊙ Hardin. Applegrowing region, producing also corn, wheat, livestock, dairy products, vinegar. Bartholomew Beach at Kampsville is resort. Formed 1835. **6** County (□ 572; pop. 16,925), central Iowa; ⊙ Rockwell City. Prairie agr. area (corn, oats, soybeans, hogs, cattle, poultry) drained by Raccoon R. Bituminous-coal deposits, sand and gravel pits. Formed 1851. **7** County (□ 709; pop. 120,813), S Mich.; ⊙ Marshall. Drained by Kalamazoo and St. Joseph rivers, and by Battle Creek. Agr. area (livestock, grain, hay, onions, corn, fruit; dairy products). Mfg. at BATTLE CREEK, Albion, and Marshall. Kellogg Bird Sanctuary is in co. Formed 1833. **8** County (□ 592; pop. 18,369), N central Miss.; ⊙ Pittsboro. Drained by Skuna and Yalobusha rivers. Agr. (cotton, corn, lespedeza), stock raising; timber; bauxite, lignite, clay deposits. Formed 1852. **9** County (□ 389; pop. 14,753), central S.C.; ⊙ St. Matthews. Bounded by Congaree R. (N) and L. Marion (NE). Agr. area (pecans, cotton, asparagus), cattle, hogs. Formed 1908. **10** County (□ 537; pop. 9,222), S Texas; ⊙ Port Lavaca. On Gulf of Mexico coast, here indented by San Antonio, Lavaca, and Matagorda bays, and protected by Matagorda Isl. Includes Green L. Fisheries; seafood packing; agr. (cotton, corn, sorghums, rice, truck, fruit, flax); livestock raising, dairying. Oil, natural-gas wells; refineries. Coast resorts. Formed 1846. **11** County (□ 281; pop. 10,259), W central W.Va.; ⊙ Grantsville. On Allegheny Plateau; drained by Little Kanawha R. Agr. (livestock, fruit, tobacco); oil and natural-gas wells; some coal, timber. Formed 1856.

Calhoun. 1 City (pop. 3,231), ⊙ Gordon co., NW Ga., 21 mi. NNE of Rome, near Oostanaula R. Textile mfg. center (bedspreads, bath mats, sheeting), sawmilling. Inc. 1852. Near by is New Echota Marker Natl. Memorial (.92 acres; established 1930), site of last capital of Cherokee Indians in Ga.; Indian newspaper was printed here in syllabary devised by Sequoyah. **2** Village (pop. 215), Richland co., SE Ill., 6 mi. SSE of Olney, in agr. area (corn, wheat, livestock, apples). **3** Town (pop. 746), ⊙ McLean co., W Ky., on Green R. (bridged) and 20 mi. NE of Madisonville, in agr., coal, and timber area; canned goods, feed. **4** Village (pop. c.550), Ouachita parish, NE central La., 14 mi. W of Monroe; cotton ginning, lumber milling. Agr. experiment station near by. **5** City (pop. 463), Henry co., W central Mo., 11 mi. NE of Clinton. **6** Former town, Pickens co., S.C.: see CLEMSON.

Calhoun, Lake, Ill.: see GALVA.

Calhoun City, town (pop. 1,319), Calhoun co., N central Miss., 28 mi. E of Grenada and on Yalobusha R.; rail point in cotton and timber area; sawmills, cotton gins; clothing mfg. Inc. 1905.

Calhoun Falls, town (pop. 2,396), Abbeville co., NW S.C., 26 mi. WSW of Greenwood, near Savannah R.; textiles.

Cali (kä'lē), city (pop. 88,366), ⊙ Valle del Cauca dept., W Colombia, in Cauca valley, in E foothills of Cordillera Occidental, 185 mi. SW of Bogotá; 3°27'N 76°30'W; alt. 3,140 ft. Connected by railroad with Buenaventura (NW), Popayán (S), Manizales (NE), and linked by railroad-highway routes with Bogotá and Quito. It is Colombia's 4th largest city and a major communication, trading, and mfg. center, located in fertile agr. region (sugar cane, coffee, tobacco, cotton, cacao, bananas, rice, corn, vegetables, cattle, hogs). Mfg.: textiles, clothing, footwear, pharmaceuticals, soap, perfumes, cement, bricks, furniture, tobacco products, beer and alcoholic beverages. Airport. Old colonial city, with fine parks and churches (e.g., San Pedro Cathedral; church and monastery of San Francisco; San Antonio chapel) and modern bldgs. Founded 1536 by Benalcázar. Developed rapidly with construction of railroad to Buenaventura (1914) and opening of Panama Canal. Its population is predominantly Negro and mulatto. Gold and coal mines are in vicinity.

Caliacra, department, Rumania: see TOLBUKHIN.

Caliacra, Cape, Bulgaria: see KALIAKRA, CAPE.

Calibogue Sound (kă"lùbō'gē), S S.C., inlet of the Atlantic, 15 mi. E of Savannah, Ga.; entered from ocean bet. Hilton Head and Daufuskie isls.; connected by channel to Port Royal Sound (NE). Traversed by Intracoastal Waterway.

Calicoan Island (kälēkō'än, -kōän') (□ 7; 1939 pop. 1,870), Samar prov., Philippines, bet. Leyte Gulf and Philippine Sea, just off narrow SE peninsula of Samar isl., near Guiuan; 8 mi. long, 1 mi. wide. Coconut growing.

Calico Mountains (c.3,000 ft.), small range in Mojave Desert, just N of Daggett; noted for brilliantly colored strata. Calico, a ghost silver-mining town of 1880s, is here.

Calico Rock, town (pop. 963), Izard co., N Ark., 36 mi. NW of Batesville and on White R., in agr. area.

Calicut (kăl'ĭkŭt), city (pop. 126,352), ⊙ Malabar dist., SW Madras, India, port on Arabian Sea, 330 mi. WSW of Madras. Exports coir, copra, and products (coffee, tea, pepper, ginger, rubber) of forested hills of the Wynaad; shark- and vegetable-oil processing; mfg. of soap, perfumes, cosmetics at noted Kerala Soap Inst. (botanical research). Kallayi or Kallai, just S (connected by canal system with rivers from inland teak and rosewood forests), is timber depot and has cotton milling, and mfg. of hosiery, plywood, coir rope and mats, tiles, electrical supplies. Marine fishery-research station in N suburban area of West Hill. City has polytechnic school (chemical and electrical engineering). Climate is mild but humid. Extensive jack and mango groves disguise city's growing industrial character. Handicraft calico industry, to which city gave its name, was famed in days of early European explorers; now almost extinct. A center of trade with Arabia in 13th cent. Visited 1498 by Vasco da Gama. Trading posts established 1511 by Portuguese (abandoned 1525), 1644 by English, 1698 by French, and 1752 by Danes. In 1792, English gained control of whole area and in 1819 allotted a small coastal plot (*loge*) to French; French returned it to India in 1947.

Caliente (kă"lē-ĕn'tē), town (pop. 970), Lincoln co., SE Nev., on Meadow Valley Wash and 22 mi. S of Pioche; alt. c.4,400 ft. Railroad shops; gold, silver, lead, zinc; stock farms.

Califon (kă'lĭfŏn), borough (pop. 623), Hunterdon co., W N.J., on South Branch of Raritan R. and 19 mi. WSW of Morristown; mfg. (small boats, sports equipment, baskets); fruit, truck, dairy products.

California, village (pop. 1,763), W Trinidad, B.W.I., on railroad and 17 mi. SSE of Port of Spain; sugar cane, coconuts.

California (kălĭfôr'nyù), state (land □ 156,803; with inland waters □ 158,693; 1950 pop. 10,586,223; 1940 pop. 6,907,387), W U.S., bounded W by Pacific Ocean, N by Oregon, E by Nevada, SE by Ariz., S by Lower Calif., Mexico; 2d in area, 2d in pop. (in 1940, 5th); admitted 1850 as 31st state; ⊙ SACRAMENTO. The "Golden State" or "El Dorado" measures 770 mi. N–S, 150–375 mi. E–W; its coast line is 1,200 mi. long. It has more diverse topography and climate than any other state: here are nation's highest point (Mt. Whitney, 14,495 ft.), lowest point (in Death Valley, 280 ft. below sea level), and only active volcano (Lassen Peak) in continental U.S. It has regions of extremely dry climate (2–5 in. annual rainfall in SE deserts), great snowfall (over 500 in. in the Sierra Nevada) and rain (more than 100 in. on N coast); it has recorded the highest temperature in N.America (134°F. in Death Valley) and nation's most equable climate (at San Diego; 55°F. Jan. average, 69°F. Aug. average). State's backbone (near E border) is the towering SIERRA NEVADA, extending S for 400 mi. from the Cascade Range on the N, and forming most of E wall of the CENTRAL VALLEY, an alluvial trough c.450 mi. long, walled on W by the COAST RANGES and closed on N by meeting of Klamath Mts. and the Cascades, on S by Tehachapi Mts. E of the Cascades and the Sierra Nevada lies the Great Basin region, represented in N by a high, arid lava plateau, farther S by such desert basins as Death Valley, barren mtn. ranges, and, in SE Calif., the Mojave and Colorado deserts, containing IMPERIAL VALLEY and SALTON SEA. A narrow coastal strip boarders the Coast Ranges, whose only major break is the great depression of San Francisco Bay. S of Tehachapi Mts. lies S Calif., whose populous and productive W part, a coastal plain, is separated by mtn. ranges (over 10,000 ft. high) from deserts to NE and E. Large rivers are few; COLORADO RIVER is the SE boundary; the Sacramento and the San Joaquin drain the Central Valley and receive most of the W slope drainage of the Sierra Nevada before entering San Francisco Bay; both are partly navigable. Only N of San Francisco are there perennial rivers in the Coast Ranges. Natural lakes (except for desert playas) are few; largest are L. TAHOE and Clear L. N Calif. lies in the path of the prevailing westerly winds which bring fogs and up to 100 in. of rainfall to the Coast Ranges, and heavy snows to the Sierra Nevada crest. The Central Valley enjoys the tempering effect of the ocean's nearness and is sheltered from continental cold by the Sierra Nevada; rainfall in its N part is c.20 in., c.10 in. in S. S Calif., lying in a calm high-pressure belt, has a sunny, typically mediterranean 2-season climate with rainfall (15–20 in. at Los Angeles) only in winter. Very little rain falls in the lee of the high mts. Jan. average temp. at Eureka (N) is 47°F., at Fresno (central) 40°F., at San Francisco 50°F., at Los Angeles 56°F.; hottest month averages are 56°F. at Eureka, 82°F. at Fresno, 62°F. at San Francisco, 71°F. at Los Angeles. The ample precipitation of the N supports heavy tree growth in the Coast Ranges and on the W Sierra and Cascade slopes. The redwoods, found only in Calif., grow in a coastal belt 10–30 mi. wide, extending from just N of San Francisco to the Oregon line, and containing tallest (364 ft.) known tree in world, near Dyerville; redwoods also grow in scattered groves on W slope of the Sierra Nevada. State's 18 natl. forests embrace c.25,000,000 acres. Commercially valuable timber stands (fir, pine, redwood) are mostly in the Sierra Nevada and Cascades; some hardwoods are cut in the Coast Ranges, and fir and pine grow at higher alts. in S Calif. Agr. has been Calif.'s basic industry since the 1870s, when bonanza wheat farms put state in 2d place in U.S. wheat production. Soon after, development of refrigerator cars and improved canning processes stimulated the change-over to today's intensive cultivation of irrigated land. With largest area (6,000,000 acres) under irrigation of any state, Calif. is generally 2d only to Iowa in crop value and leads U.S. in per-acre value of farm land. Its fruit crop ranks 1st in value nationally, its canneries produce ⅓ of U.S. pack of fruits and vegetables, and its wineries make c.90% of domestic wines and brandies. Leading crops are citrus (oranges, lemons, grapefruit, limes), grown principally in S Calif.; grapes (for table use, raisins, and wine) from the Central Valley, S Calif., and Napa, Livermore, and Sonoma valleys; vegetables and fruits (peaches, prunes, pears, plums, apricots, apples, olives, berries, cherries) from many dists., subtropical fruits (avocados, pomegranates, figs, loquats, guavas) and nuts from S Calif., field crops (cotton, flax, alfalfa, potatoes, lima beans, wheat, barley, oats, and other grains, sorghum, hops, sugar beets) from many regions; asparagus, other truck, and rice come from the Sacramento–San Joaquin delta, great lettuce crops from Salinas Valley, dates from Coachella Valley, flower seeds and such special crops as artichokes from foggy S coastal valleys. Dairying is important, especially in Los Angeles co., poultry and egg production is led by Sonoma co., and cattle, sheep (producing one of nation's leading wool yields) and some goats range the Coast Range and Sierra foothills. A characteristic is the big-business handling, mostly through co-operative associations, of growing, processing, and marketing problems. Much of the farm labor has long been done by migrants, of whom it is estimated that there are 200,000. About 60 kinds of commercially-produced minerals put Calif. among 1st 3 mining states; petroleum and natural gas, mainly produced in Kern, Los Angeles, and Orange counties, are most valuable; gold, silver, copper, lead, zinc, quicksilver, cement rock, stone, borates, soda, potash, salt, pumice, clay, gypsum, chromite, silica, diatomaceous earth, iron ore, manganese, molybdenum, platinum, tungsten, and magnesium are also produced. About 40% of U.S. commercial fish catch is landed in Calif. ports; San Diego and San Pedro (Los Angeles Harbor) supply most of nation's canned tuna, and Monterey supplies most of pilchard sardines. Other fishing ports are San Francisco, Sacramento, Eureka; other commercial catches are barracuda, cod, flounder, mackerel, rockfish, salmon (in N), sea bass, shad, shellfish (spiny lobster, clams, abalone), and whales. The most valuable industry has long been the processing (milling, canning, and packing) of farm produce; oil refining and production of petroleum-derived chemicals, processing of other minerals, and sawmilling (especially in N) continue to be important. Since the end of the Second World War, diversified and heavier industry has increased greatly; a steel mill has been built (at FONTANA), aircraft mfg. (mainly in Los Angeles region) has continued on a large scale, and metalworking, mfg. of machinery and electrical equipment, automobile assembling, and mfg. of lumber, furniture, and other wood products, rubber goods, paper, textiles, apparel, leather, and plastics are of chief importance. S Calif. continues its world leadership in motion-picture production. Largest cities and chief seaports and industrial centers are Los ANGELES (4th largest in U.S.), and SAN FRANCISCO (11th largest in U.S.); others are San Diego, Sacramento, Stockton, Oakland, Long Beach. Water supply to farms and cities has been from the beginning an acute Calif. problem. The huge Central Valley project (including SHASTA DAM, FRIANT DAM), the ALL-AMERICAN CANAL, Imperial and Parker dams in the Colorado, and the Los Angeles Aqueduct (233 mi. long) tapping OWENS RIVER and COLORADO RIVER AQUEDUCT (242 mi. long) are among the major projects. The Calif. climate brings winter residents, and enormous tourist traffic is attracted by the natl. parks—Yosemite, Sequoia, and Kings Canyon, in the Sierra Nevada, and Lassen Volcanic Natl. Park, in the Cascades—which embrace some of the continent's finest scenery, the natl. monuments (Death Valley, Channel Isls., Devil Postpile, Joshua Tree, Lava Beds, Muir Woods, Pinnacles), many state parks, the summer and winter resorts of the mts., and shore, desert (Palm Springs), and isl. (Santa Catalina Isl.) playgrounds, the redwood country, and the old missions. Among Calif. educational institutions are the Univ. of California (at Berkeley and Los Angeles), Univ. of Southern California and Occidental Col. (at Los Angeles), Stanford Univ. (at Palo Alto), California Inst. of Technology (at Pasadena), Mills Col. (at Oakland), Claremont, Pomona, and Scripps colleges (at Claremont), and Whittier Col. (at Whittier). First explorer to visit Alta California, as region came to be known, was Juan Rodríguez Cabrillo in 1542; Drake came in 1579, Sebastian Vizcaíno came in 1602, but more than 160 years passed before Sp. colonizers came to San Francisco Bay under Gaspar de Portolá in 1769. A presidio was built at San Francisco in 1776; meanwhile, Father Junípero Serra and other Franciscans had founded a string of missions (some of them now historic shrines) and begun gathering the Indians about them. Early Yankee traders were welcomed by the Californians, and the fur-hunting Russians came as far south as Fort Ross (1812). However, entry of Jedediah S. Smith and other fur traders into Calif. from the East aroused official disapproval. Other Americans began to come across the mts. in 1841; John Augustus Sutter, established in the Sacramento valley, did much to encourage overland immigrants. The Californians drove out the last Mex. governor in 1845; under influence of Frémont, the Americans set up the Bear Flag republic at Sonoma in 1846. After the Mexican War, the territory was formally ceded (1848) to U.S. by treaty of Guadalupe Hidalgo. In the same year gold was discovered near Coloma and the great westward rush of forty-niners was touched off. The MOTHER LODE country was developed, the roaring camps grew up, and San Francisco became a boom city. Battle for statehood was begun in 1849, and Calif. came into the Union as a free state under the Compromise of 1850. By 1854 the great bonanza had slackened, and the economy of the new state was shakily founded on cattle and wheat; the 1st transcontinental railroad was completed in 1869. Successive waves of immigration began with a railroad rate war of 1884; in the 1st decade of the 20th cent., the development of petroleum, irrigation, citrus fruit, hydroelectric power, and new industries brought more expansion; later newcomers were those attracted by the real-estate boom of the 1920s, the Dust Bowl emigrants (1936–38), and more than a million war workers and service personnel in the Second World War, many of them later settlers. Particularly as the result of the latter, Calif. showed the nation's highest rate (53%) of pop. increase bet. 1940 and 1950. See also articles on the cities, towns, geographic features, and the 58 counties: ALAMEDA, ALPINE, AMADOR, BUTTE, CALAVERAS, COLUSA, CONTRA COSTA, DEL NORTE, EL DORADO, FRESNO, GLENN, HUMBOLDT, IMPERIAL, INYO, KERN, KINGS, LAKE, LASSEN, LOS ANGELES, MADERA, MARIN, MARIPOSA, MENDOCINO, MERCED, MODOC, MONO, MONTEREY, NAPA, NEVADA, ORANGE, PLACER, PLUMAS, RIVERSIDE, SACRAMENTO, SAN BENITO, SAN BERNARDINO, SAN DIEGO, SAN FRANCISCO, SAN JOAQUIN, SAN LUIS OBISPO, SAN MATEO, SANTA BARBARA, SANTA CLARA, SANTA CRUZ, SHASTA, SIERRA, SISKIYOU, SOLANO, SONOMA, STANISLAUS, SUTTER, TEHAMA, TRINITY, TULARE, TUOLUMNE, VENTURA, YOLO, YUBA.

California. 1 Town (pop. 117), Campbell co., N Ky., on the Ohio and 21 mi. SE of downtown Cincinnati. 2 City (pop. 2,627), ⊙ Moniteau co., central Mo., 21 mi. W of Jefferson City; agr. (wheat), dairying, stock raising; mfg. (flour, paper, woolen goods). Founded 1845, inc. 1857. 3 Borough (pop. 2,831), Washington co., SW Pa., 26 mi. S of Pittsburgh and on Monongahela R.; bituminous coal; agr. State teachers col. Laid out c.1850, inc. c.1863.

California, Gulf of, arm of the Pacific in NW Mexico, bet. Lower California (W) and Sonora and Sinaloa (E). Extends c.700 mi. SE from mouth of Colorado R.; generally c.100 mi. wide, 150 mi. wide at its mouth, narrowing toward its head; □ 62,500; greatest depth 2,660 ft., mean depth 8,651 ft. Many small bays and isls. Isls. include Montague, Angel de la Guarda, Tiburón, San José, and Cerralvo. In addition to Colorado R., several rivers empty into it from Mex. mainland (Magdalena, Sonora, Yaqui, and Fuerte). Major ports are La Paz (Lower California), Guaymas (Sonora), and Mazatlán (Sinaloa). Noted for deep-sea fishing and pearl fishing along SW coast. Cortés sent (1539) an expedition up the gulf under the command of Francisco de Ulloa; Hernando de Alarcón ascended the river in 1540. First survey was made 1746 by Father Consac, after Jesuit missionaries had entered the peninsula in 1697. Pearl fisheries had been discovered 1632. Because the gulf has a large tidal bore and the winds are tricky, exploration and shipping have been risky. In Sp. colonial period the gulf was sometimes called Sea of Cortés, and later it was sometimes called Vermilion Sea.

California, Lower, Mexico: see LOWER CALIFORNIA.

California Current, cold ocean current of North Pacific Ocean, a branch of Aleutian Current, flowing S along W coast of North America from 48° to 23°N, where it joins the North Equatorial Current.

California Hollow, village (pop. 1,594), Columbiana co., E Ohio.

Cálig (kä'lēg), town (pop. 2,412), Castellón de la Plana prov., E Spain, 7 mi. WSW of Vinaroz; olive-oil processing; ships wine, beans, almonds. Has 14th-cent. church.

Calilegua (kälēlä'gwä), town (1947 pop. 2,741), E Jujuy prov., Argentina, 45 mi. NE of Jujuy, in irrigated San Francisco R. valley; sugar cane, tropical fruit, livestock.

Calimanesti (kŭlēmŭnĕsht'), Rum. *Călimănești*, town (1948 pop. 3,329), Valcea prov., S central Rumania, on Olt R., on railroad and 10 mi. N of Ramnicu-Valcea; popular summer and health resort (alt. 898 ft.) in S foothills of the Transylvanian Alps. Has sulphurous, iodine, and bromine springs (notably the Caciulata spring, just N); exports bottled mineral waters. Near-by Cozia monastery (2 mi. N), founded in 14th cent., is one of most important historical and architectural monuments of Rumania.

Calimaya (kälēmī'ä), officially Calimaya de Díaz González, town (pop. 3,700), Mexico state, central Mexico, 10 mi. SSE of Toluca; agr. center (cereals, vegetables, livestock); dairying.

Calimera (kälēmā'rä), town (pop. 5,413), Lecce prov., Apulia, S Italy, 9 mi. SSE of Lecce, in olive-, tobacco-, and fig-growing region.

Calimere, Point (kăl'ĭmēr), Tamil *Kallimed* (kŭl-lĭmād'), southernmost point of Coromandel Coast of Bay of Bengal, in Tanjore dist., SE Madras, India, 200 mi. S of Madras; separated by Palk Strait from Point Pedro (40 mi. SE, on N end of Ceylon); lighthouse; 10°18'N 79°51'E. Projected port of Point Calimere is just W. Sacred Hindu bathing place. Known to Ptolemy as Calligicum.

Calimete (kälēmā'tā), town (pop. 2,040), Matanzas prov., W Cuba, on railroad and 40 mi. SSE of Cárdenas; sugar cane, fruit, cattle.

Calingapatam, India: see CHICACOLE.

Calingasta, department, Argentina: see TAMBERÍAS.

Calingasta (kälĭng-gä'stä), village (pop. estimate 500), SW San Juan prov., Argentina, on the Río de los Patos (affluent of San Juan R.) and 50 mi. WNW of San Juan. Alfalfa, corn, wheat, apples, wine, livestock. Apiculture; silver-fox breeding. Cider mills, sawmills.

Calino, Greece: see KALYMNOS.

Calinog (kälēnōg'), town (1939 pop. 1,787; 1948 municipality pop. 25,484), Iloilo prov., central Panay isl., Philippines, 30 mi. N of Iloilo; agr. center (rice, hemp).

Calio (kă'lēō), village (pop. 102), Cavalier co., NE N.Dak., 35 mi. N of Devils Lake.

Calion (kăl'yŭn), town (pop. 536), Union co., S Ark., 10 mi. NE of El Dorado and on Ouachita R. (bridged); ships cotton.

Calipatria (kălĭpă'trēū), city (pop. 1,428), Imperial co., S Calif., 10 mi. SE of Salton Sea, in IMPERIAL VALLEY; ships early vegetables. Inc. 1919.

Calistoga (kălĭstō'gŭ), city (pop. 1,418), Napa co., W Calif., 13 mi. NE of Santa Rosa, near head of Napa R. valley. Geysers and hot springs (health resorts), Mt. St. Helena (N), and a petrified forest (SW) are near by. Wine grapes, prunes, walnuts. Founded 1859; inc. as town in 1886, as city in 1937.

Calitri (kälē'trē), town (pop. 7,950), Avellino prov., Campania, S Italy, near Ofanto R., 34 mi. E of Avellino; cement.

Calitzdorp (kä'lĭtsdôrp), town (pop. 1,933), S Cape Prov., U. of So. Afr., at foot of Swartberg range, on Gamka R. and 30 mi. W of Oudtshoorn; fruitgrowing center.

Calixtlahuaca (kälēsläwä'kä), town (pop. 1,853), Mexico state, central Mexico, 4 mi. NW of Toluca. Has archaeological remains of various pre-Columbian cultures, including temple of Quetzalcoatl, pyramid of Tlaloc, Tzompantli (House of Skulls).

Calizzano (kälētsä'nô), village (pop. 430), Savona prov., Liguria, NW Italy, on Bormida di Millesimo R. and 19 mi. WSW of Savona; resort; market for coal and wood.

Calkiní (kälkēnē'), city (pop. 4,491), Campeche, SE Mexico, in NW Yucatan Peninsula, on railroad and 50 mi. SW of Mérida; lumbering and agr. center (corn, rice, sugar, henequen, chicle, fruit).

Call, village (1940 pop. 924), Newton co., E Texas, 40 mi. NNE of Beaumont, near the Sabine; rail point in lumbering area.

Callac (käläk'), village (pop. 1,848), Côtes-du-Nord dept., W France, 15 mi. SW of Guingamp; cattle and horse raising; tanning.

Callafo (kä'läfō), town (pop. 1,500), Harar prov., SE Ethiopia, on the Webi Shebeli, on road and 185 mi. SSE of Dagahbur; agr. trade center.

Callahan (kă'lŭhăn), county (□ 857; pop. 9,087), central Texas; ⊙ Baird. Drained to N by tributaries of Brazos R., to S by Colorado R. tributaries. Ranching (cattle, sheep, goats), agr. (grain sorghums, corn, oats, peanuts, fruit, truck). Oil, natural-gas production and processing. Formed 1858.

Callahan, town (pop. 722), Nassau co., NE Fla., 19 mi. NW of Jacksonville; lumbering, farming.

Callahan, Mount, Nev.: see TOIYABE RANGE.

Callan (kă'lŭn), Gaelic *Callain*, town (pop. 1,545), W Co. Kilkenny, Ireland, 10 mi. SW of Kilkenny; hosiery mfg.; agr. market (cattle; barley, potatoes). Of anc. origin, it has 15th-cent. Augustine abbey and remains of castle destroyed 1650 by Cromwell.

Callander (kă'lŭndŭr), village (pop. estimate 750), SE central Ont., on Southeast Bay of L. Nipissing, 8 mi. SE of North Bay; dairying, lumbering.

Callander, burgh (1931 pop. 1,572; 1951 census 1,727), S Perthshire, Scotland, on Teith R., near the Trossachs, 17 mi. WSW of Crieff; tourist center for near-by lakes, especially Loch Katrine; woolen mills.

Callanish, Scotland: see CALLERNISH.

Callao (käyä'ō), city (pop. 71,217), W central Peru, major port on the Pacific (Callao Bay), sheltered by San Lorenzo Isl., situated at base of low peninsula, 7 mi. W of Lima (connected by several railroads and wide boulevards); 12°4'S 77°13'W. Has dry, semitropical climate. One of the finest harbors on the Pacific coast, and a prosperous modern city, it handles about 60% of Peru's foreign trade. Seat of customhouse, foreign commercial houses, shipping offices, and consulates. Has drydocks, large modern piers with concrete moles, a naval arsenal, and shipyard. Exports cotton, sugar cane, coca, wool, hides, copper, silver, lead, and vanadium. Also an important fishing and processing center. Among its industries are a meat-packing and refrigerating plant, flour mills, fish canneries, breweries; soap, cocaine, and candle factories; foundries, lumber mills, machine shops. The colonial San Felipe castle (1770–75) has been restored. Founded 1537 shortly after Lima, it was repeatedly attacked by Drake (1578) and other buccaneers. During colonial times it was the leading Pacific port, though a tidal wave almost completely destroyed it in 1746. Spain abandoned the port 1826; another attack by a Sp. squadron (1866) was repelled. The city was severely damaged by 1940 earthquake. Adjoining SW, at tip of the peninsula next to the Chucuito section, is La Punta, a fashionable bathing resort and seat of the naval acad. Bellavista residential suburb lies E. Callao city is ⊙ Callao constitutional prov. (□ 14.3; pop. 84,438), an enclave of Lima dept. which has the status of a dept. Set up 1836, obtaining departmental rights 1857.

Callao (kă'lēō), city (pop. 370), Macon co., N central Mo., near Chariton R., 8 mi. W of Macon.

Callao, El, Venezuela: see EL CALLAO.

Callapa (käyä'pä), town (pop. c.4,400), La Paz dept., W Bolivia, in the Altiplano, on Desaguadero R. and 24 mi. SSE of Corocoro; alpaca and sheep raising.

Callaqui Volcano (käyäkē') or **Callaquén Volcano** (käyäkĕn'), Andean peak (10,135 ft.) in Bío-Bío prov., S central Chile, near Argentina border, 60 mi. SE of Los Angeles.

Callas (käläs'), village (pop. 458), Var dept., SE France, in Provence Alps, 5 mi. NE of Draguignan; olives. Lignite mine.

Callaway (kă'lŭwā), county (□ 835; pop. 23,316), central Mo.; ⊙ Fulton. Bounded S by Missouri R. Agr. (corn, wheat, oats), livestock (especially mules and saddle horses); fire clay, coal, stone; mfg. at Fulton. Formed 1820.

Callaway. 1 Village (pop. 193), Becker co., W Minn., in White Earth Indian Reservation, 12 mi. NNW of Detroit Lakes city, in grain and potato area; dairy products. 2 Village (pop. 744), Custer co., central Nebr., 17 mi. SW of Broken Bow and on South Loup R.; dairy and poultry produce, grain, cattle.

Callayuc (käyäyo͞ok'), town (pop. 243), Cajamarca dept., NW Peru, in Cordillera Occidental, 20 mi. NW of Cutervo; wheat, sugar cane, coffee.

Calle, La (lä käl'), town (pop. 4,106), Constantine dept., NE Algeria, its easternmost seaport, 37 mi. E of Bône, near Tunisia border; rail-spur terminus; fish and vegetable preserving. Formerly known for its coral fisheries and for silverbearing lead and copper mines at Oum-Theboul (7 mi. E).

Calle-Calle River (kä'yä-kä'yä), Valdivia prov., S central Chile, rises as San Pedro R. in L. Riñihue, flows 60 mi. W to Valdivia, where it is joined (right) by Cruces R. and becomes Valdivia R., a wide estuary extending 11 mi. to the Pacific at Corral Bay. The entire stream is sometimes called Valdivia.

Callejón de Huaylas, Peru: see HUAYLAS, CALLEJÓN DE.

Calle Larga (kä'yä lär'gä), village (1930 pop. 1,498), Aconcagua prov., central Chile, 3 mi. SE of Los Andes; agr. center (fruit, wine, hemp, livestock).

Callender, town (pop. 387), Webster co., central Iowa, 11 mi. SSW of Fort Dodge; livestock, grain.

Callensburg, borough (pop. 261), Clarion co., W central Pa., 10 mi. SW of Clarion and on Clarion R.

Callernish (kă'lŭrnĭsh) or **Callanish** (kă'lŭnĭsh), fishing port on W coast of Lewis with Harris, Outer Hebrides, Ross and Cromarty, Scotland, at head of Loch Roag, 13 mi. W of Stornoway. Near by are the "Standing Stones," prehistoric monument of 39 stones in form of a cross, 2d only to Stonehenge in preservation and interest.

Callery (kă'lŭrē), borough (pop. 407), Butler co., W Pa., 21 mi. N of Pittsburgh.

Calleva Atrebatum, England: see SILCHESTER.

Calliano (käl-lyä'nô). **1** Village (pop. 1,518), Asti prov., Piedmont, NW Italy, 8 mi. NNE of Asti; cement. **2** Village (pop. 772), Trento prov., Trentino–Alto Adige, N Italy, on Adige R. and 9 mi. S of Trento. Ruins of castle on near-by hill.

Calliaqua (kălēä'kwü), town (pop. 507), S St. Vincent, B.W.I., 2 mi. SE of Kingstown; cotton, arrowroot, sugar cane.

Callicoon (kă"lŭko͞on'), resort village (1940 pop. 602), Sullivan co., SE N.Y., on the Delaware (here forming Pa. line) and 21 mi. WNW of Monticello. Seat of St. Joseph Seraphic Seminary.

Calliham, village (pop. c.300), McMullen co., S Texas, near Frio R., 10 mi. W of Three Rivers, in cattle, oil-field area.

Callingapatnam, India: see CHICACOLE.

Callington, former urban district (1931 pop. 1,801), E Cornwall, England, 10 mi. S of Launceston; former tin-mining center, now agr. market; granite quarries; paint works. Has 15th-cent. church. Just NE is Kit Hill (1,067 ft.).

Callipolis, Turkey: see GALLIPOLI.

Callis (kälēs), village, in the Mijirtein, N Ital. Somaliland, 40 mi. E of Garoe, in Nogal Valley; market (sheep, camels, dates).

Callnberg, Germany: see LICHTENSTEIN.

Calloo, Belgium: see KALLOO.

Callosa de Ensarriá (kälyō'sä dhä ĕnsärē'ä), town (pop. 3,868), Alicante prov., E Spain, 20 mi. ESE of Alcoy; mfg. of footwear, hemp cloth, olive oil. Ships almonds, oranges, wine.

Callosa de Segura (sāgo͞o'rä), city (pop. 7,833), Alicante prov., E Spain, in Valencia, 27 mi. SW of Alicante; hemp-growing, -processing, and -shipping center. Mfg. of footwear, cement, furniture; canning (fruit, meat); sawmilling. Cereals, truck produce, olive oil, wine in area. Clay quarries. Mineral springs. Has Moorish aspect; 15th-cent. Gothic church.

Calloway (kă'lüwä), county (□ 407; pop. 20,147), SW Ky.; ⊙ Murray. Bounded S by Tenn., E by Kentucky Reservoir (Tennessee R.); drained by East and West forks of Clarks R. and by Mayfield Creek. Gently rolling agr. area (dark tobacco, corn, wheat, dairy products, poultry, livestock); some mfg. at Murray. Includes Kentucky L. State Park. Formed 1821.

Calmar (kăl'mär), village (pop. estimate 350), central Alta., near North Saskatchewan R., 25 mi. SW of Edmonton; mixed farming, dairying.

Calmar, Sweden; see KALMAR.

Calmar (kăl'mŭr), town (pop. 937), Winneshiek co., NE Iowa, 9 mi. SSW of Decorah; ships hay, grain, flax; mfg. of wood products.

Calmbach (kälm'bäkh), village (pop. 3,083), S Württemberg, Germany, after 1945 in Württemberg-Hohenzollern, in Black Forest, on the Enz and 9 mi. SW of Pforzheim; photographic equipment. Summer resort.

Calmeca (kälmä'kä), town (pop. 1,539), Puebla, central Mexico, 12 mi. W of Matamoros; corn, sugar, livestock.

Calnali (kälnä'lē), town (pop. 2,127), Hidalgo, central Mexico, in Sierra Madre Oriental, 20 mi. SW of Huejutla; corn, rice, sugar, tobacco, fruit, livestock.

Calne (kän), municipal borough (1931 pop. 3,463; 1951 census 5,552), N central Wiltshire, England, 5 mi. ESE of Chippenham; agr. market, with sausage- and bacon-curing works. Has Norman church. Near by is CHERHILL, with large white horse figure cut into the cliffs.

Calo, Song (shông'kälō') delta arm of Red R., N Vietnam, connects Red R. below Sontay with the Song Cau above Bacminh; 40 mi. long.

Calobre (kälō'brä), village (pop. 337), Veraguas prov., W central Panama, 15 mi. NE of Santiago; coffee, sugar cane, livestock.

Calolbon (kälōlbōn'), town (1939 pop. 3,216; 1948 municipality pop. 17,370), S Catanduanes isl., Philippines, on Lagonoy Gulf, 9 mi. W of Virac; fishing and agr. center (coconuts, hemp).

Calolot (kälōlōt'), town (1939 pop. 5,354) in Tangub municipality, Misamis Occidental prov., W Mindanao, Philippines, 20 mi. NE of Pagadian; agr. center (corn, coconuts).

Calolziocorte (kälôl"tsyôkôr'tē), village (pop. 2,312), Bergamo prov., Lombardy, N Italy, near Adda R., 4 mi. SSE of Lecco; foundry.

Calonge (kälōn'hä), town (pop. 1,242), Gerona prov., NE Spain, 15 mi. SE of Gerona; cork, wine, and olive-oil processing.

Calonne-Ricouart (kälôn"-rēkwär'), town (pop. 11,136), Pas-de-Calais dept., N France, 8 mi. WSW of Béthune; coal mines, glassworks.

Caloocan (kälō-ō'kän), town (1939 pop. 7,232; 1948 municipality pop. 58,208), Rizal prov., S Luzon, Philippines, just NW of Manila; agr. center (rice, fruit).

Caloosa, Lake, Fla.: see CROOKED LAKE.

Caloosahatchee River (kŭlo͞o"sŭhă'chē), S Fla., rises in L. Hicpochee near Moore Haven, flows c.75 mi. WSW, past Fort Myers, into Gulf of Mexico through San Carlos Bay (an inlet sheltered by Sanibel Isl.); tidal below La Belle, river is c.1 mi. wide in lower 19 mi. L. Hicpochee (c.4 mi. long) is connected with L. Okeechobee (just NE) by short Caloosahatchee Canal, thus joining river to E part of OKEECHOBEE WATERWAY system.

Calore River (kälô'rĕ), in Campania, S Italy, rises in the Apennines 15 mi. NE of Salerno, flows 60 mi. N and W, past Benevento, to Volturno R. 10 mi. NE of Caserta.

Calotmul (kälōtmo͞ol'), town (pop. 1,569), Yucatan, SE Mexico, 23 mi. N of Valladolid; henequen, sugar, corn.

Caloto (kälō'tō), town (pop. 1,046), Cauca dept., SW Colombia, in Cauca valley, on W slopes of Cordillera Central, on highway to Popayán, 28 mi. SSE of Cali; alt. 3,560 ft. Cacao, sugar cane, tobacco, coffee, stock. Founded 1543.

Calovo (tsä'lôvô), town (pop. 4,536), SW Slovakia, Czechoslovakia, on railroad and 36 mi. SE of Bratislava; agr. center (wheat, rye, barley, corn). Until 1948, called Velky Meder, Slovak *Vel'ky Meder,* Hung. *Nagymegyer.*

Calow (kā'lō, kô'lō), town and parish (pop. 1,263), NE Derby, England, 2 mi. E of Chesterfield; coal mining.

Calpan (käl'pän), officially San Andrés Calpan, town (pop. 3,165), Puebla, central Mexico, 16 mi. WNW of Puebla; agr. center (cereals, vegetables, maguey, livestock).

Calpe: see GIBRALTAR.

Calpe (käl'pā), town (pop. 1,488), Alicante prov., E Spain, on the Mediterranean, and 29 mi. E of Alcoy; fishing and fish processing, boatbuilding. Ships almonds, raisins, beans, salt. Granite quarries. On near-by promontory is isolated rock of Ifach (over 1,000 ft. high).

Calpet (kăl'pĕt), village, Sublette co., W Wyo., near Green R., 75 mi. NW of Rock Springs; oil refining.

Calpulálpam (kälpo͞oläl'päm), city (pop. 3,948), Tlaxcala, central Mexico, on railroad and 38 mi. NE of Mexico city; alt. 8,474 ft.; maguey-growing and -processing center.

Calshot (kôl'shŏt), promontory at mouth of Southampton Water on The Solent, S Hampshire, England, 2 mi. SE of Fawley. Royal Air Force seaplane base. Site of castle built by Henry VIII as coastal defense. Just SE, in The Solent, is Calshot Spit lightship (50°48'30"N 1°17'30"W), an important navigational landmark.

Calstock (kôl'stŏk), town, SE Cornwall, England, on Tamar R. and 10 mi. N of Plymouth; tin-mining center. Has Tudor mansion and 15th-cent. church.

Caltabellotta (käl"täbĕl-lôt'tä), village (pop. 6,095), Agrigento prov., SW Sicily, 9 mi. NE of Sciacca; macaroni. Has Norman cathedral.

Caltagirone (kältäjērō'nĕ), town (pop. 31,028), Catania prov., SE central Sicily, at NW foot of Monti Iblei, 25 mi. NW of Ragusa; pottery (terracotta figures, majolica), cork and rope industries. Sulphur mining, stone quarrying. Bishopric. Has 17th-cent. cathedral, old castle, mus. containing pre-Hellenic antiquities, Greek vases, and local majolica. Near by are Siculian and Greek necropolises. Founded by Saracens. Largely rebuilt following earthquake of 1693. In Second World War, scene of heavy fighting (1943). Formerly also Calatagirone.

Caltanissetta (kältänēs-sĕt'tä), province (□ 813; pop. 256,687), central and S Sicily; ⊙ Caltanissetta. Hilly terrain, rising to 3,120 ft. in N; drained by Platain and Salso rivers. Chief sulphur-mining region of isl., with over 250 mines yielding 40% of total Sicilian production. Rock salt mines in N. Agr. (wheat, grapes, olives, almonds); cotton growing near Gela; cork plantations to NE; livestock (sheep, goats).

Caltanissetta city (pop. 37,463), ⊙ Caltanissetta prov., central Sicily, near Salso R., 55 mi. W of Catania; 37°29'N 14°4'E. Chief center of Sicilian sulphur industry; principal city of the interior. Produces cement, glass, soap, furniture, organs, metal products, macaroni. Power station. Many sulphur mines near by. Has school of mineralogy, technical inst., meteorological observatory, and mus. Bishopric. Has cathedral (consecrated 1622; damaged in Second World War). Palaces include unfinished baroque palace started 1635. Near by is Norman abbey (founded 1153; damaged in Second World War). Greek necropolis, SE. In Second World War, scene of heavy fighting (1943).

Caltavuturo (kältävo͞oto͞o'rô), town (pop. 6,693), Palermo prov., N Sicily, in Madonie Mts., 16 mi. SE of Termini Imerese. Ruins of Saracen fortress near by.

Caltepec (kältāpĕk'), town (pop. 365), Puebla, central Mexico, 20 mi. SSW of Tehuacán; corn, livestock.

Calti River (chältŭ'), Turkish *Çaltı,* N central Turkey, rises 28 mi. SE of Sivas, flows 73 mi. E, past Divrigi, to Euphrates R. 9 mi. NW of Kemaliye.

Calton (käl'tŭn), E industrial suburb (pop. 52,810) of Glasgow, Lanark, Scotland; tobacco, paint, and metal works.

Calubian (kälo͞o'byän, kälo͞obyän'), town (1939 pop. 2,563; 1948 municipality pop. 19,423), NW Leyte, Philippines, on narrow Biliran Strait, opposite Biliran Isl., 40 mi. WNW of Tacloban; agr. center (rice, coconuts, sugar cane).

Calugareni (kŭlo͞ogŭrän'), Rum. *Călugăreni,* village (pop. 1,266), Bucharest prov., S Rumania, 21 mi. N of Giurgiu. Site of historic 17th-cent. battle.

Caluire-et-Cuire (kälwēr'-ā-kwēr'), N suburb (pop. 16,848) of Lyons, Rhône dept., E central France, on left bank of Saône R. Chemical and silk-processing factories; metalworking, food processing, dye and rubber mfg.

Calulo (kälo͞o'lō), town (pop. 2,763), Benguela prov., W Angola, on road and 140 mi. SE of Luanda; agr. processing (manioc, cotton, tobacco).

Calumet (kălümĕt'), village (pop. 705), SW Que., on Ottawa R. and 15 mi. W of Lachute; dairying.

Calumet (kă'lyo͞omĕt), county (□ 315; pop. 18,840), E Wis.; ⊙ Chilton. Bounded W by L. Winnebago; drained by Manitowoc R. Dairying, farming (grain, peas, clover). Varied mfg. at Chilton, New Holstein, and Brillion. Formed 1836.

Calumet, region (□ c.70; pop. c.285,000), Lake co., extreme NW Ind., along S shore of L. Michigan, adjacent to SE Chicago, of whose metropolitan area it is a part. Has one of world's greatest concentrations of heavy industry (especially steel). Includes contiguous cities of GARY, HAMMOND, EAST CHICAGO, and Whiting, known as the Cities of the Calumet. Traversed by Grand Calumet and Little Calumet rivers, whose channels link region with CALUMET RIVER, CALUMET (South Chicago) HARBOR, and (via Calumet Sag Channel) the ILLINOIS WATERWAY system; there are also port facilities at East Chicago and Gary. Grew mainly after establishment (1905) of U.S. Steel Corporation plant at Gary.

Calumet. 1 Town (pop. 250), O'Brien co., NW Iowa, 13 mi. N of Cherokee, in agr. area. **2** Village (pop. 1,256), Houghton co., NW Upper Peninsula, Mich., 10 mi. NNE of Houghton, on Keweenaw Peninsula, in copper-mining region. Dairy, truck, and fruit farming; lumbering. Resort. State park near by. Village grew after development of Calumet and Hecla copper mine here in 1860s. Inc. 1875 as Red Jacket, renamed 1929. **3** Village (pop. 854), Itasca co., N central Minn., in Mesabi iron range, near Swan L., and 14 mi. ENE of Grand Rapids, in mining and agr. area. Electrified, openpit iron mine and ore-washing plant near by. **4** Town (pop. 339), Canadian co., central Okla., 10 mi. WNW of El Reno; cotton ginning. **5** Village (pop. 2,155, with adjacent Norvelt), Westmoreland co., SW Pa., 7 mi. SSE of Greensburg.

Calumet, Lake, NE Ill., within industrial S Chicago and near CALUMET heavy-industry region of NW Ind.; shipping channel connects with Calumet R. and thence extends to Calumet (South Chicago) Harbor on L. Michigan.

Calumet City, residential city (pop. 15,799), Cook co., NE Ill., S suburb of Chicago, on Ind. line adjacent to Hammond, Ind.; mfg. (chemicals, pickles, packed meat). Inc. 1911; name changed from West Hammond in 1924. L. Calumet is just N; CALUMET PARK village is 7 mi. NW.

Calumet Harbor or **South Chicago Harbor,** NE Ill., port dist. within industrial S Chicago; handles bulk of city's water-borne commerce. Calumet Harbor proper, sheltered by breakwater in L. Michigan, receives dock-lined Calumet R., extending inland to connect with waterways (Calumet Sag Channel, Grand Calumet and Little Calumet rivers) of ILLINOIS WATERWAY system, and with L. Calumet. With near-by Indiana Harbor at East Chicago, Ind., and port of Gary, Ind., it serves the heavy industries of Chicago and the important adjoining CALUMET region of NW Ind.

Incoming cargoes are chiefly iron ore, coal, and limestone; grain and iron and steel products are shipped.

Calumet Island (kăl'ūmĕt'), village, SW Que., on Ottawa R. and 25 mi. ESE of Pembroke; lead, zinc mining.

Calumet Park (kă'lyōōmĕt), suburban village (pop. 2,500), Cook co., NE Ill., just S of Chicago. Inc. 1912; name changed from Burr Oak in 1925. CALUMET CITY is 7 mi. SE.

Calumet River, NE Ill., short stream entirely within industrial S Chicago; an important unit of Calumet (South Chicago) Harbor, which serves Chicago and the heavily-industrialized CALUMET region of NW Ind., and part of ILLINOIS WATERWAY system. Formed just SE of L. Calumet by Little Calumet and Grand Calumet rivers; flows c.8 mi. N, through dredged and dock-lined channel, to L. Michigan at Calumet Harbor. Little Calumet and Grand Calumet rivers, rising generally E of Gary, Ind., flow generally W, in dredged channels; handle much shipping at Gary. Little Calumet R. is linked to Calumet Sag Channel, and thence with Sanitary and Ship Canal. Grand Calumet R. is connected by ship canal to Indiana Harbor at East Chicago, Ind.

Calumet Sag Channel, NE Ill., federally operated navigation and drainage canal (c.16 mi. long) leading generally W from Little Calumet R. near Calumet Park to Sanitary and Ship Canal near Lemont; part of ILLINOIS WATERWAY system. Has a lock at Blue Island.

Calumpit (kälōōmpēt'), town (1939 pop. 1,051; 1948 municipality pop. 21,788), Bulacan prov., S central Luzon, Philippines, on Pampanga R. and 25 mi. NW of Manila; sugar milling.

Caluso (kälōō'zô), village (pop. 3,046), Torino prov., Piedmont, NW Italy, 19 mi. NNE of Turin, in fruit- and cereal-growing region; cotton textiles, fertilizer, wine.

Caluya Island, Philippines: see SEMIRARA ISLANDS.

Caluyo (kälōō'yä), town (pop. c.4,000), La Paz dept., W Bolivia, on E slopes of the Eastern Cordillera of the Andes, 30 mi. SSE of Inquisivi; grain, potatoes, *oca*.

Calvados (kăl'vúdōs, Fr. kälvädôs'), department (□ 2,198; pop. 400,026), in Normandy, NW France; ⊙ Caen. Borders on English Channel (N) bet. Cotentin Peninsula (W) and Seine R. estuary (E). Traversed E-W by low Normandy Hills. Drained by numerous coastal streams (Orne, Dives, Touques, Seulles, Aure). Chiefly a stock-raising area (Normandy cattle and horses) with extensive dairying (Isigny butter, Camembert cheese). Known for its Calvados brandy made from locally-grown apples. Coal and lignite mined near Littry; building stone quarried near Caen and Vire. Iron mined in Orne R. valley (Saint-Rémy, May-sur-Orne, Soumont) is processed in large metalworks of Mondeville and Colombelles (near Caen). Copper smelting at Dives-sur-Mer. Calvados has important textile industry (Condé-sur-Noireau, Vire, Lisieux, Caen). Well-developed tourist industry with numerous bathing resorts, led by fashionable Deauville, Trouville, Houlgate, and Cabourg. Chief ports: Caen, Honfleur, Trouville, Dives-sur-Mer, Port-en-Bessin, Isigny. In Second World War Calvados was hard hit by Normandy campaign, which was initiated by Allied landings (June 6, 1944) at several points along its shore bet. Grandcamp-les-Bains and Ouistreham. Caen, Vire, Falaise, and Lisieux were heavily damaged.

Calvados, Plateau of, underwater rock ledge of English Channel, just off Fr. coast (Calvados), extending 13 mi. from a point off Arromanches-les-Bains (W) to Langrune (E). Several shoals, including Calvados Rock, are uncovered.

Calvario, El, Colombia: see EL CALVARIO.

Calvello (kälvĕl'lô), town (pop. 3,575), Potenza prov., Basilicata, S Italy, 12 mi. SSE of Potenza; meat and dairy products.

Calver (kä'vûr), village and parish (pop. 402), N Derby, England, 11 mi. SW of Sheffield; lead mining.

Calverley (kä'vûrlē, kôv'lē), former urban district (1931 pop. 3,655), West Riding, central Yorkshire, England, 6 mi. WNW of Leeds; woolen milling. Site of Bradford water reservoir. Has remains of anc. Br. camp. Calverley Hall dates from 16th cent. Inc. 1937 in Pudsey.

Calvert (kăl'vûrt), county (□ 219; pop. 12,100), S Md.; ⊙ Prince Frederick. Narrow tidewater peninsula bounded E by Chesapeake Bay, S and W by Patuxent R.; drained by many small creeks. Agr. area (tobacco, grain, truck, livestock); fisheries (oysters, crabs, fish); timber; some boat building. Resort area (fishing, hunting, and water sports, especially at Solomons, Broomes Island, Chesapeake Beach). Includes Cliffs of Calvert and many historic houses. Holds annual jousting tournaments, a 17th-cent. survival. Co. contained seat of Puritan govt. of Md. (1652–56), at Lusby. In region of earliest settlement in Md., it was formed 1654.

Calvert. 1 Village (1940 pop. 529), Mobile and Washington counties, SW Ala., 33 mi. N of Mobile, near Alabama R.; lumber, naval stores. **2** Historic hamlet (founded 1701), Cecil co., NE Md., 24 mi. W of Wilmington, Del. Friends' meeting house, built 1724, is still used. **3** City (pop. 2,548), Robertson co., E central Texas, c.50 mi. SSE of Waco, near the Brazos; trade, market center in cotton, grain, truck, dairying, livestock area; cottonseed-oil mills, gravel pits. Settled near by as Sterling, c.1840; moved to present site on railroad and renamed 1869; inc. 1896.

Calvert City, village (1940 pop. 706), Marshall co., SW Ky., near Tennessee R., 15 mi. ESE of Paducah, in agr. area. Kentucky Dam is near by.

Calvert Island (□ 100), SW B.C., in Queen Charlotte Sound; 51°35'N 128°W; 20 mi. long, 2-10 mi. wide. Rises to 3,430 ft. on Mt. Buxton (N); S and W coasts are thickly wooded. Just N is Hecate Isl. (□ 17), 5 mi. long, 5 mi. wide.

Calvert Islands, Marshall Isls.: see AUR.

Calverton (kăl'vûrtún, kä'–), town and parish (pop. 1,058), central Nottingham, England, 6 mi. NE of Nottingham; hosiery industry. Has Norman church, rebuilt in 14th cent.

Calverton, village (1940 pop. 590), Suffolk co., SE N.Y., on E Long Isl., on Peconic R. and 4 mi. W of Riverhead; potatoes, cauliflower.

Calverton Park, town (pop. 514), St. Louis co., E Mo., 12 mi. NW of St. Louis.

Calvi (kälvē', It. käl'vē), town (pop. 2,029), NW Corsica, port on the Mediterranean, 45 mi. N of Ajaccio, with shipping service to Nice, Toulon, and Marseilles. Commerce in wines, olive oil, almonds, citrus fruit, cork bark, goat skins. Tuna and lobster fishing. Granite and porphyry quarries. Has 16th-cent. cathedral. Founded 1268. Chief Genoese stronghold in Corsica during Middle Ages. During English bombardment of Calvi in 1794, Nelson lost his right eye.

Calviá (kälvyä'), town (pop. 1,376), Majorca, Balearic Isls., 7 mi. W of Palma; olives, carobs, almonds, cereals, timber, sheep, hogs. Gypsum quarrying, olive-oil pressing, sawmilling.

Calvi dell'Umbria (käl'vē dĕlōōm'brēä), village (pop. 930), Terni prov., Umbria, central Italy, 12 mi. SSW of Terni; cement works.

Calvillo (kälvē'yō), city (pop. 3,486), Aguascalientes, N central Mexico, on Calvillo R. and 28 mi. W of Aguascalientes; agr. center (cereals, beans, chickpeas, tobacco, sugar, wine, fruit, livestock).

Calvillo River, N central Mexico, rises in mts. of Aguascalientes near Zacatecas border, flows c.50 mi. SW, past Calvillo, to Juchipila R. at Jalpa; irrigates fertile fruitgrowing area.

Calvin. 1 Village (pop. 152), Cavalier co., NE N.Dak., 26 mi. WNW of Langdon. **2** Town (pop. 557), Hughes co., central Okla., 27 mi. W of McAlester, and on Canadian R., in stock-raising and agr. area.

Calvinia (kălvĭ'nēù), town (pop. 3,627), W Cape Prov., U. of So. Afr., 190 mi. NNE of Cape Town; agr. center (sheep, wheat); rail terminus.

Calvisano (kälvēsä'nô), village (pop. 1,604), Brescia prov., Lombardy, N Italy, 15 mi. SSE of Brescia; fertilizer mfg.

Calvizzano (kälvētsä'nô), town (pop. 3,588), Napoli prov., Campania, S Italy, 5 mi. S of Aversa.

Calvo, Monte (môn'tĕ käl'vô), highest point (3,465 ft.) of Gargano promontory, S Italy, 2.5 mi. ENE of San Giovanni Rotondo.

Calvörde (käl'fûr'dù), village (pop. 3,129), in former Brunswick exclave, central Germany, after 1945 in Saxony-Anhalt, on the Ohre and on Weser-Elbe Canal, 9 mi. NW of Haldensleben; food canning.

Calw (kälv), town (pop. 6,795), S Württemberg, Germany, after 1945 in Württemberg-Hohenzollern, in Black Forest, on the Nagold and 12 mi. S of Pforzheim; rail junction; textile (wool blankets) and machinery mfg. On bridge across Nagold R. is small Gothic chapel. Founded in 11th cent.; chartered c.1250. Was for long period industrial (wool, lumber) center of duchy of Württemberg. Writer Hesse b. here.

Calycadnus River, Turkey: see GOKSU.

Calydon (kă'lĭdún), anc. city of Aetolia, W central Greece, on Evenus R. and 6 mi. E of modern Missolonghi, near Gulf of Calydon (modern Gulf of Patras). Here, in Gr. legend, Meleager killed the Calydonian boar.

Calymna, Greece: see KALYMNOS.

Calypso, France: see SAINT-MARTIN-DE-LA-PORTE.

Calypso (kúlĭp'sō), town (pop. 688), Duplin co., E central N.C., 17 mi. SSW of Goldsboro; sawmilling.

Calzada (kälsä'dä), town (pop. 832), San Martín dept., N central Peru, in E outliers of the Andes, 4 mi. W of Moyobamba; sugar, coca, rice, corn.

Calzada de Calatrava, La (lä käl-thä'dhä dhä käläträ'vä), city (pop. 8,256), Ciudad Real prov., S central Spain, in New Castile, on railroad and 20 mi. SSE of Ciudad Real; agr. center (grapes, truck produce, cereals, olives, chestnuts, fruit, chickpeas, livestock). Olive-oil pressing, alcohol and cognac distilling, cheese processing; mfg. of sulphur, ink, tartaric acid, textile goods; limekilns. Mineral springs.

Calzada de Oropesa, La (dhä ōrōpā'sä), town (pop. 2,315), Toledo prov., central Spain, on railroad and highway to Cáceres, and 25 mi. W of Talavera de la Reina; wheat, oats, olives, grapes, livestock. Olive-oil pressing, flour milling.

Calzadilla (käl-thä-dhē'lyä), village (pop. 1,363), Cáceres prov., W Spain, 24 mi. WNW of Plasencia; flour mills; olive oil, cork, cereals.

Calzadilla de los Barros (dhä lōs bä'rōs), village (pop. 1,447), Badajoz prov., W Spain, 25 mi. E of Jerez de los Caballeros; olives, cereals, grapes, livestock.

Calzones, Cerro (sĕ'rō kälsō'nĕs), peak (9,777 ft.) in Guanajuato, central Mexico, 15 mi. N of Guanajuato.

Cam, town and parish (pop. 2,114), SW Gloucester, England, just N of Dursley; woolen milling, leatherworking. Has 14th-cent. church. William Tyndale reputedly b. here.

Cam, river, England: see CAM RIVER.

Camabatela (kämäbätĕ'lä), town (pop. 3,383), Congo prov., NW Angola, on road and 150 mi. ENE of Luanda, in coffee-growing region.

Camaçari, Brazil: see CAMASSARI.

Camacha (kùmä'shù), village, Madeira, near E coast of Madeira isl., 5 mi. NE of Funchal; alt. 2,346 ft. Popular summer resort. Wickerworking.

Camacho, province, Bolivia: see PUERTO ACOSTA.

Camacho (kämä'chō), town (pop. c.1,300), Tarija dept., S Bolivia, 10 mi. WSW of Padcaya; road center; corn, fruit, sheep.

Camacupa, Angola: see VILA GENERAL MACHADO.

Camaguán (kämägwän'), town (pop. 809), Guárico state, central Venezuela, landing on Portuguesa R. and 60 mi. SSW of Calabozo, 17 mi. NW of San Fernando; cattle raising.

Camagüey (kämägwā'), province (□ 10,172; pop. 487,701), E Cuba; ⊙ Camagüey. Second largest prov. of Cuba; bet. Las Villas prov. (W) and Oriente prov. (E), bounded by Old Bahama Channel (N) and the Caribbean (S). Generally low and level, well-watered by numerous rivers. Indented coast is marshy and lined by many coral reefs, such as Camagüey Archipelago in N (with Coco, Romano, and Sabinal keys) and Jardines de la Reina (S). Among its mineral deposits are iron (Sierra de Cubitas), copper and chromium (Minas, Morón), and marble. Considerable fishing in coastal waters. Lumbering (mahogany, cedar, ebony, etc.) is a major source of income. The prov.'s economy depends, however, chiefly on cattle raising and sugarcane growing. Other products include coffee, cacao, tobacco, sisal, citrus fruit, bananas, corn, beeswax, honey. Principal trading and processing centers are Camagüey, an old colonial city, Morón, and Ciego de Ávila. Chief port is Nuevitas on N coast. Prov. is crossed by several rail lines and the Central Highway. Formerly called Puerto Príncipe prov.

Camagüey, city (pop. 80,509), ⊙ Camagüey prov., E Cuba, largest inland city of the isl., on a fertile elevated plain, on Central Highway and 300 mi. ESE of Havana; 21°23'N 77°55'W. Important communications center served by railroads, natl. and international airlines; linked by rail with its port Nuevitas, 45 mi. ENE. Outlet for a rich cattle-raising region, which also produces sugar cane, molasses, fruit, and lumber (cedar, mahogany). Industries include dairying, tanning, distilling, sawmilling; mfg. of meat products and furniture. Sugar central in outskirts. A distinctly colonial city, it preserves its traditional Sp. character, having narrow streets overhung by balconies, squares, fine historic bldgs., and splendid churches, such as its cathedral (rebuilt 1617). Originally founded (1514) as Santa María de Puerto Príncipe on N coast, it was moved inland to site of anc. Indian village Camagüey in 1530. In 1889 the name Puerto Príncipe was changed to Camagüey. Airport is just NE. Iron, asphalt, chromium, and manganese deposits near by.

Camagüey Archipelago, coral reefs off N coast of E Cuba, E of the Sabana Archipelago, and forming S flank of Old Bahama Channel; extend c.150 mi. NW–SE. Among the larger keys are Coco, Romano, Sabinal. Sometimes also Jardines del Rey.

Camaiore (kämäyô'rĕ), town (pop. 2,588), Lucca prov., Tuscany, central Italy, in Apuane Alps, 12 mi. NW of Lucca; resort; mfg. (hosiery, rope, aluminum, explosives). Marble quarries near by.

Camajuaní (kämäwänē'), town (pop. 11,339), Las Villas prov., central Cuba, on railroad and 14 mi. E of Santa Clara; agr. center (sugar cane, tobacco, cattle) with processing industries; mfg. of jerked beef, soft drinks, cigars, agr. implements. The sugar central of Fe is SE.

Camak (kùmăk'), town (pop. 379), Warren co., E Ga., 37 mi. W of Augusta; granite quarrying.

Camalaniugan (kämälänyōō'gän), town (1939 pop. 2,525; 1948 municipality pop. 7,708), Cagayan prov., NE Luzon, Philippines, on Cagayan R. and 6 mi. SSE of Aparri; agr. center (tobacco, rice).

Camaldoli (kämäl'dôlē), monastery, S Italy, on hill (1,503 ft.) overlooking Phlegraean Fields, 4 mi. W of Naples. Founded 1585.

Camalig (kämä'lēg), town (1939 pop. 2,559; 1948 municipality pop. 25,045), Albay prov., SE Luzon, Philippines, on railroad and 6 mi. NW of Legaspi; agr. center (abacá, rice, coconuts).

Camalotal, Lake, Salvador: see OLOMEGA, LAKE.

Camamu (kämämōō'), city (pop. 1,904), E Bahia, Brazil, port on the Atlantic, 80 mi. SSW of Salvador; barite quarries.

Camaná (kämänä'), city (pop. 2,321), ⊙ Camaná prov. (□ 3,360; pop. 10,498), Arequipa dept., S Peru, minor Pacific port near mouth of Majes R. (irrigation), linked with Pan-American Highway, 80 mi. WSW of Arequipa; 16°38'S 72°43'W. Processing and agr. center (cotton, sugar cane, rice, corn, barley, alfalfa, olives, grapes, fruit, potatoes); cotton ginning, cottonseed-oil extracting, fruit canning. Airport. Coal deposits near by.

Camanche (kŭmănch'), town (pop. 1,212), Clinton co., E Iowa, on the Mississippi (forms Ill. line here) and 6 mi. SW of Clinton. Pecan grove near by.

Camandag Island (kämändäg') (□ 3.5; 1939 pop. 2,421), Samar prov., Philippines, in Samar Sea, bet. Masbate and Samar isls., just N of Santo Niño Isl.; c.2 mi. in diameter; hilly. Coconuts.

Cam and Motor Mine, Southern Rhodesia: see EIFFEL FLATS.

Camano Island (kŭmā'nō), Island co., NW Wash., isl. (15 mi. long) in Puget Sound, E of Whidbey Isl. and NW of Everett; bridged to mainland; summer and fishing resorts.

Camaquã (kämäkwä'), city (pop. 2,456), SE Rio Grande do Sul, Brazil, near the Lagoa dos Patos, 65 mi. SW of Pôrto Alegre; rice, fruit. Copper mined in area. Until 1938, called São João de Camaquã (old spelling, Camaquam).

Camaquã River, S Rio Grande do Sul, Brazil, rises N of Bagé, flows c.200 mi. E to the Lagoa dos Patos 50 mi. NE of Pelotas. Navigable to rapids c.80 mi. upstream. Formerly spelled Camaquam.

Câmara de Lôbos (kä'mŭrŭ dĭ lō'bōōsh), town (pop. 4,968), Madeira, on S shore of Madeira isl., 4 mi. W of Funchal; picturesque fishing port; alcohol distilling, embroidering, tanning. Ships fruit, vegetables, salted fish. Basalt quarries. Excellent wine grown in area.

Camarasa (kämärä'sä), town (pop. 1,263), Lérida prov., NE Spain, on the Segre and 7 mi. NNE of Balaguer; agr. trade (cereals, wine, olive oil); stock raising (sheep, hogs, goats); lumbering. Hydroelectric plant 3 mi. N at junction of Noguera Pallaresa and Segre rivers.

Camarat, Cape (kämärä'), on the Mediterranean, in Var dept., SE France, formed by a spur of Monts des Maures, 6 mi. SSE of Saint-Tropez; 43°12'N 6°41'E. Lighthouse.

Camaratuba, Brazil: see SÃO JOAQUIM DO MONTE.

Camarazal, Brazil: see MULUNGU.

Camarena (kämärā'nä), town (pop. 1,949), Toledo prov., central Spain, 17 mi. NNW of Toledo; grapes, grain, carrots, chick-peas, olives, tubers, sheep, hogs.

Camarès (kämärĕs', –rā'), village (pop. 1,100), Aveyron dept., S France, 21 mi. SSW of Milau, in agr. region (wheat, fruit, cattle).

Camaret-sur-Mer (kämärā'-sür-mâr'), town (pop. 2,326), Finistère dept., W France, lobster-fishing port and canning center on W tip of Crozon Peninsula 9 mi. SW of Brest; bathing resort.

Camargo (kämär'gō), town (pop. c.3,420), ⊙ Nor Cinti prov., Chuquisaca dept., S Bolivia, on Cinti R. and 110 mi. S of Sucre, on Sucre-Tarija road; major grape-growing center, agr. products.

Camargo or **Ciudad Camargo** (syōōdädh'). **1** City (pop. 7,705), Chihuahua, N Mexico, near confluence of Conchos and Florido rivers, 85 mi. SE of Chihuahua; alt. 4,025 ft. Rail junction; health resort; mining (silver, gold, lead, copper) and agr. center (cotton, wheat, corn, tobacco, cattle); cotton and wheat milling, lumbering. Airfield. Ojo Caliente spas are 3 mi. SW. **2** City (pop. 1,271), Tamaulipas, NE Mexico, on San Juan R. in the Rio Grande basin, on railroad and 7 mi. S of Rio Grande City, Texas. Agr. center (cotton, sugar, corn, cattle).

Camargo (kŭmär'gō). **1** Village (pop. 236), Douglas co., E central Ill., on Embarrass R. and 21 mi. S of Urbana, in agr. area. **2** Town (pop. 312), Dewey co., W Okla., 29 mi. S of Woodward, near Canadian R., in grain-growing and stock-raising area.

Camargue (kämärg'), alluvial island (□ c.215) in Rhone delta, Bouches-du-Rhône dept., SE France, bet. Grand Rhône (E), Petit Rhône (W), and Gulf of Lion (S). Near its N apex is Arles. Its lagoons (largest: Étang de Vaccarès) are closed off from the sea by narrow sand bars; 125 sq. mi. of marshes and grasslands have been reclaimed. Here bulls, sheep, and small white horses are raised in ranch-like style. Wine, wheat, and rice growing. Chief village: Saintes-Maries-de-la-Mer.

Camarillo (kămŭrē'ō), village (pop. c.300), Ventura co., S Calif., 8 mi. E of Oxnard; state mental hosp., and St. John's Seminary are here.

Camarina, Sicily: see SANTA CROCE CAMERINA.

Camariñas (kämärē'nyäs), town (pop. 1,188), La Coruña prov., NW Spain, fishing port on inlet of the Atlantic, 42 mi. WSW of La Coruña; fish processing, and mfg. of laces.

Camarines Norte (kämärē'nās nôr'tā), province (□ 829; 1948 pop. 103,702), SE Luzon, Philippines, bounded N by Philippine Sea, W by Basiad Bay, E by San Miguel Bay; ⊙ DAET. Includes several offshore isls.—CALAGUA ISLANDS, CANIMO ISLAND. Terrain is largely mountainous with valuable forests of lauan (Philippine mahogany). Agr. products: coconuts, rice, abacá. The prov. is a major mining area (iron, gold, precious stones). Chief centers are Daet and JOSE PAÑGANIBAN.

Camarines Sur (sōōr'), province (□ 2,060; 1948 pop. 553,691), SE Luzon, Philippines; ⊙ NAGA. Bounded N by San Miguel Bay and Philippine Sea, E by Lagonoy Gulf, W by Ragay Gulf. Includes LAHUY ISLAND and QUINALASAG ISLAND. Mountainous terrain, drained by numerous streams, many of which rise on Mt. Isarog, a volcanic peak in central area. Chief river is the Bicol, rising in L. Bato, largest of several lakes. Agr. (rice, abacá, corn), lumbering (lauan or Philippine mahogany), chrome-ore mining.

Camarles (kämär'lĕs), village (pop. 1,155), Tarragona prov., NE Spain, 8 mi. E of Tortosa, at edge of the Ebro delta; olive-oil processing.

Camarón, Mexico: see VILLA TEJEDA.

Camarón (kämärōn'), village (pop. 1,124), Chiriquí prov., W Panama, in Chiriquí Viejo R. valley, 5 mi. W of Concepción, on railroad; coffee, bananas, cacao, livestock.

Camarón, Cape (kämärōn'), broad, low, wooded headland on Mosquitia coast of E Honduras, on Caribbean Sea, 8 mi. NE of Iriona; 16°N 85°5'W.

Camarones (kämärō'nĕs), village, ⊙ Camarones dept. (pop. 689), NE Comodoro Rivadavia military zone, Argentina, port on Camarones Bay (22 mi. N–S, 10 mi. E–W) of the Atlantic, and 115 mi. NE of Comodoro Rivadavia; sheep-raising center. Until 1946, ⊙ Florentino Ameghino dept. of Chubut natl. territory.

Camarones River, N Chile, rises in the Andes SE of Arica, flows c.65 mi. W to the Pacific. In its lower irrigated reaches some cotton and subtropical fruit grown.

Camas (kä'mäs), town (pop. 6,643), Seville prov., SW Spain, 2 mi. W of Seville across the Guadalquivir; trades in cereals and olives. Mfg. of disinfectants, liquor distilling.

Camas (kă'mŭs), county (□ 1,057; pop. 1,079), S central Idaho; ⊙ Fairfield. Livestock-grazing and dry-farming area. Grain, timber; deposits of lead, silver, zinc, gold, copper. Ranges of Sawtooth Mts. are in N. Co. formed 1917.

Camas. 1 Village (pop. c.100), Sanders co., NW Mont., 60 mi. NW of Missoula; resort; lumber, grain. **2** City (pop. 4,725), Clark co., SW Wash., 13 mi. E of Vancouver and on Columbia R.; lumber, paper mills; salmon, fruit, poultry. Inc. 1908.

Camasca (kämä'skä), town (pop. 526), Intibucá dept., SW Honduras, 22 mi. S of La Esperanza; cotton milling, tanning.

Camassari or **Camaçari** (kämäsä'rē), city (pop. 1,419), E Bahia, Brazil, on railroad and 25 mi. NE of Salvador; kaolin and ocher quarries. Until 1939, called Montenegro.

Camatagua (kämätä'gwä), town (pop. 550), Aragua state, N Venezuela, on upper Guárico R. and 50 mi. S of Caracas; cattle and horse raising. Coal deposits near by (N).

Camataquí, Bolivia: see VILLA ABECIA.

Camatindi (kämätēn'dē), village, Chuquisaca dept., SE Bolivia, on E foot of Serranía de Aguaragüe and 20 mi. N of Villa Montes, on road; petroleum center. Oil fields 3 mi. W.

Camau (kä'mou'), town (1936 pop. 8,506), Baclieu prov., S Vietnam, on Camau Peninsula, in Cochin China, 150 mi. SW of Saigon, in swamp forest area; port on tidal stream; exports rice, salt fish; lumbering, charcoal mfg.; honey and wax; mat making, fishing (shrimp). Held after 1946 by the Vietminh.

Camau, Point, Cochin China, southernmost point of S Vietnam, bet. South China Sea and Gulf of Siam, at tip of Camau Peninsula; 8°35'N 104°42'E.

Camaxilo (kämäshē'lō), village, Malange prov., N Angola, near Belgian Congo border, 20 mi. NE of Caúngula. R.C. mission.

Cambados (kämbä'dhōs), town (pop. 3,318), Pontevedra prov., NW Spain, in Galicia, fishing port on Arosa Bay, 10 mi. NW of Pontevedra; fish processing (sardines), mfg. (linen cloth, soap, candy). Wine, fruit, cereals, livestock in area.

Cambaluc, China: see PEKING.

Cambará (kãmbärä'), city (pop. 4,898), NE Paraná, Brazil, on railroad and 70 mi. ENE of Londrina, in coffee zone near São Paulo border; sawmilling, agr. processing (coffee, rice, corn, cotton), pottery mfg.

Cambay (kămbā'), town (pop. 34,941), Kaira dist., N Bombay, India, on Gulf of Cambay, at mouth of Mahi R., 31 mi. S of Kaira; rail terminus; trades in cotton, grain, tobacco, carpets, cloth fabrics; cotton milling, hand-loom weaving, embroidering, mfg. of salt, matches; carnelian, agate, and onyx ornaments. A prosperous port (late-15th cent.) under Moslem kings of Gujarat; lost its importance later, when Gulf of Cambay silted up. Was ⊙ former princely state of Cambay (□ 392; pop. 96,592) in Gujarat States, Bombay; inc. 1949 into Kaira dist.

Cambay, Gulf of, inlet of Arabian Sea, India, bet. N Bombay (E) and Kathiawar peninsula (W); 15–120 mi. wide bet. Diu and Damão, 130 mi. long. Receives Sabarmati, Mahi, Narbada, and Tapti rivers. Ports with coastal trade include Diu, Bhaunagar, Cambay, Surat, and Damão. Fishing (pomfrets, jewfish, Bombay duck). Rivers have largely silted up N end.

Cambé (kãmbĕ'), city (pop. 2,988), N Paraná, Brazil, on roailroad and 8 mi. WNW of Londrina, in pioneer coffee zone. Until 1944, called Nova Dantzig.

Cambérène (kämbārĕn'), fishing village and beach, W Senegal, Fr. West Africa, on N shore of Cape Verde peninsula, 9 mi. N of Dakar.

Camberg (käm'bĕrk), town (pop. 3,956), in former Prussian prov. of Hesse-Nassau, W Germany, after 1945 in Hesse, 11 mi. SE of Limburg.

Camberley, residential town in urban dist. of Frimley and Camberley (1931 pop. 16,532; 1951 census 20,376), W Surrey, England, 6 mi. N of Aldershot; site of Royal Staff Col. Has mfg. of machine tools and plastics. Bret Harte buried here. Just S is residential town of Frimley.

Camberwell (kăm'bûrwŭl), municipality (pop. 76,125), S Victoria, Australia, 5 mi. E of Melbourne, in metropolitan area; fruitgrowing.

Camberwell (kăm'bûrwŭl), metropolitan borough (1931 pop. 251,294; 1951 census 179,729) of London, England, S of the Thames, 5 mi. SE of Charing Cross; residential section, with several parks; includes district of DULWICH. Here is the South London Art Gall.

Cambiago (kämbyä'gô), village (pop. 1,999), Milano prov., Lombardy, N Italy, 14 mi. WNW of Milan; silk mill.

Cambiano (kämbyä'nô), village (pop. 1,820), Torino prov., Piedmont, NW Italy, 8 mi. SSE of Turin.

Cambil (kämbēl'), town (pop. 4,040), Jaén prov., S Spain, 14 mi. SE of Jaén; soap, footwear mfg.; olive-oil processing, flour milling. Esparto and livestock. Iron mines near by.

Cambirela, Brazil: see SANTO AMARO DA IMPERATRIZ.

Camblaya River, Bolivia: see PILAYA RIVER.

Cambodia (kămbō'dēū), Fr. *Cambodge* (kãbôj'), kingdom (□ 69,900; 1948 pop. 3,748,328), SW Indochina, a state associated with France in the French Union; ⊙ Pnompenh. Bounded SW by Gulf of Siam, W and N by Thailand, NE by the Laos, and E and SE by Cochin China (S Vietnam), Cambodia consists primarily of a vast alluvial plain (a former marine gulf filled by the sediment of the Mekong) bet. the forest-clad Dangrek (N), Cardamom (SW), and Elephant (S) mts. and the Mekong (E). This plain, centered on the lake Tonle Sap (a natural storage basin of the Mekong) and situated in the rain shadow of the Cardamom Mts., does not receive full benefit of (only 25–40 in.) the SW rainy summer monsoon and relies on the summer floods (July-Nov.) of the Mekong for its moisture. Agr. is important in alluvial soils along the Mekong and near the Tonle Sap, rice, the principal crop, being grown chiefly in Battambang area. Tobacco, kapok, cotton, pepper (along Gulf of Siam), palm sugar, rubber (Kompong Cham) are also grown. Forestry (teak), cattle raising, and lake and sea fishing are important activities. Native industry produces dried and salt fish, silk and cotton goods, pottery (Kompong Chhang), matting, and jewelry. Rice and rice alcohol are processed in modern mills. Iron ore (Pnom Dek), limestone, phosphate (Kampot), and precious stones (Pailin) are found, but not exploited on large scale. Corn, rice, pepper, fish are the chief exports (90% via the Mekong). The large pop. centers of Pnompenh, Battambang, and Pursat are located on railroad and highways to Thailand, the chief transportation routes, besides the Mekong. Kep and Ream are the main ports on Gulf of Siam, having supplanted the older Kampot; Pnompenh is an important Mekong R. port. Pop. is 90% Cambodian or Khmer (a Buddhist people of uncertain ethnic origin speaking an Austroasiatic language of the Mon-Khmer group), 5% Annamese, and 4% Chinese. Anc. Cambodia formed, at different periods, the large Khmer empire comprising the Laos, Siam, and Cochin China. First mentioned (2d cent. A.D.) as the Funan state, it was known (after 6th cent.) as the Chen-la state, which flourished (10th–11th cent.) with its capital at Angkor. The Khmer empire declined following Thai inroads (13th–14th cent.), and was contested (17th–18th cent.) by Siam and Annam. The Fr. protectorate (dating from 1863) was recognized (1867) by Siam, which was also forced to cede (1904, 1907) the areas of Meloupreу, Siemreap, and Battambang to Cambodia, but reoccupied them temporarily (1941–46) during Second World War. Cambodia became (1947) a constitutional monarchy and joined (1948–50) the French Union as an associated state recognized by the U.S.

Cambodunum, Germany: see KEMPTEN.

Cambo-les-Bains (kãbō'-lā-bē'), village (pop. 1,342), Basses-Pyrénées dept., SW France, on Nive R. and 9 mi. SSE of Bayonne; health resort with numerous sanatoriums.

Camboritum, England: see CAMBRIDGE.

Camboriú (kämbōrēōō'), city (pop. 1,639), E Santa Catarina, Brazil, on the Atlantic, 10 mi. SSE of Itajaí; coffee, sugar cane, rice, timber. Marble quarries.

Camborne-Redruth (kăm'bôrn, –bûrn; rĕdrōōth', rĕ'drōōth), urban district (1931 pop. 24,064; 1951 census 35,829), W Cornwall, England. Includes town of Camborne, 12 mi. WSW of Truro; tin, copper, tungsten, and arsenic mining. Has 15th-cent. church. Just N is site of Dolcoath Mine, once largest in Cornwall; now idle. Also in urban dist., 3 mi. ENE of Camborne, is Redruth, with tin and copper mines. Has mus. of mineral specimens. John Wesley preached here, and in 1655 George Fox was imprisoned in King's Head Tavern. Both towns have mining schools. Formerly independent urban dists.; towns combined in early 1930s.

Cambrai (kămbrā', Fr. kābrā'), town (pop. 24,580), Nord dept., N France, on Escaut R. at end of Saint-Quentin Canal, and 22 mi. ESE of Arras; road and rail center; long known for its fine textiles (cambric, 1st made here, is named after Cambrai). Produces chicory, starch, soap, beer, candies. Cloth dyeing, bleaching, and printing; metal founding, flour milling. In sugar-beet-growing dist. Episcopal see since 4th cent. and archdiocese since 16th cent.; Fénelon was archbishop of Cambrai 1695–1715. Original cathedral was destroyed in 1793. Present bldg. was damaged in both world wars. Together with surrounding Cambrésis county, Cambrai was ruled by bishops under Holy Roman Empire. The League of Cambrai (1508) against Venetians formed here. Treaty of Cambrai (1529) bet. Charles V and Francis I signed here. Town seized by Spain (1595) and by France (1677). Two important battles (1917 and 1918) took place SW of Cambrai during First World War. In 1917 British here temporarily pierced Hindenburg Line by using large number of tanks for 1st time. Town center was wrecked during Ger. withdrawal in 1918. In Second World War heavy damage was again inflicted, especially on E section.

Cambremer (kābrümâr'), village (pop. 422), Calvados dept., NW France, 8 mi. W of Lisieux; cider distilling.

Cambria (kăm'brēü, kăm'–), county (□ 695; pop. 209,541), central Pa.; ⊙Ebensburg. Mountainous mfg. and coal-mining area; bounded SW by Laurel Hill, E by Allegheny Mts. Conemaugh R. drains S part; West Branch of Susquehanna R. rises in N. Settled by Welsh. Mfg. (metals and metal products, railroad equipment); bituminous coal, clay, limestone; agr. (pears, potatoes, honey). Formed 1804.

Cambria. **1** (kăm'brēü) Village (pop. c.500), San Luis Obispo co., SW Calif., near the coast, 30 mi. NW of San Luis Obispo; dairying, stock raising. **2** (kăm'brēü) Village (pop. 625), Williamson co., S Ill., 5 mi. W of Herrin, in bituminous-coal-mining and agr. area. **3** (kăm'brēü, kăm'–) Town (pop. 853), Montgomery co., SW Va., 8 mi. E of Radford. **4** (kăm'brēü) Village (pop. 633), Columbia co., S central Wis., 18 mi. E of Portage, in agr. area; makes butter, cheese; cans peas.

Cambrian Mountains, name sometimes given the mountain system of Wales.

Cambridge or **Cambridgeshire** (kām'brĭj, –shĭr), county (less Ely: □ 492.5; 1931 pop. 140,004; 1951 census 166,863; with Ely: □ 867.4; 1931 pop. 217,702; 1951 census 255,901), SE England; ⊙ Cambridge. Bounded by Bedford and Huntingdon (W), Northampton (NW), Lincolnshire (N), Norfolk and Suffolk (E), Essex and Hertford (S). Drained by Ouse, Nene, and Cam (or Granta) rivers. Fertile soil, fenland in N, mainly growing fruit and vegetables; dairying. Fenlands (see BEDFORD LEVEL) were drained by Vermuyden in 17th cent. Gogmagog Hills are in S. There are small industries in the towns, including food canning, malting, and brewing. Besides Cambridge, important towns are Ely, March, Wisbech. The co. shows traces of Roman and Saxon occupation; in N part Hereford the Wake held out against William the Conqueror for some time. ELY is an administrative county.

Cambridge, municipal borough (1931 pop. 66,789; 1951 census 81,463), ⊙ Cambridgeshire, England, in S part of co., on Cam (or Granta) R. and 50 mi. N of London; 52°12'N 0°7'E. Anc. market town, famous as site of Cambridge Univ. A fort in Roman times (*Camboritum*). For academic purposes its Latin name is *Cantabrigia*. In Norman times it was site of castle built by William the Conqueror. In 12th cent. monks from Ely established the nucleus of present univ. Of the many colleges, most famous are Trinity, King's, Queen's, Pembroke, Emmanuel (John Harvard's col.), St. John's, Trinity Hall, and Clare, and women's colleges of Newnham and Girton. There are many medieval bldgs., including 10th-cent. Saxon church of St. Benedict, 13th-cent. church of St. Edward (Latimer preached here), and Church of the Holy Sepulchre, one of the 4 round Norman churches in England. Well-known features of Cambridge are the "Backs," a stretch of river running along backs of several colleges; tall spires of King's Col. Chapel; and large modern univ. library, donated by Rockefeller Foundation. Town is a market center, with electrical and radio industries. It sustained some air-raid damage in 1940. A U.S. military cemetery is here. In municipal borough are residential suburbs of Romsey (E; pop. 9,271) and Chesterton (NE; pop. 15,359).

Cambridge, town (pop. 2,700), St. James parish, NW Jamaica, in fertile interior valley, on Kingston–Montego Bay RR and 11 mi. S of Montego Bay; banana growing. Caves near by.

Cambridge, borough (pop. 2,567), N N.Isl., New Zealand, on Waikato R. and 80 mi. SSE of Auckland; rail terminus; dairy products. Near-by Horahora has hydroelectric plant.

Cambridge, NW residential suburb of East London, SE Cape Prov., U. of So. Afr.

Cambridge. **1** Village (pop. 354), Washington co., W Idaho, 17 mi. SW of Council and on Weiser R.; agr., dairy, lumber. **2** Village (pop. 1,489), ⊙ Henry co., NW Ill., 21 mi. SE of Moline, in agr. and bituminous-coal area; makes furniture. Inc. 1861. **3** Town (pop. 573), Story co., central Iowa, on Skunk R. and 21 mi. NNE of Des Moines; corn cannery. **4** City (pop. 221), Cowley co., SE Kansas, 40 mi. SE of Wichita, in livestock and grain area. **5** Town (pop. 326), Somerset co., central Maine, 22 mi. NE of Skowhegan. **6** Town (pop. 10,351), ⊙ Dorchester co. (since 1687), E Md., on the Eastern Shore 30 mi. WNW of Salisbury, and on Choptank R. (bridged here 1935). Fishing and yachting port, and port of entry; ships oysters, crabs, diamond back terrapin, fish, muskrat pelts; steamer connections with Baltimore. Processing center for vegetables, seafood, lumber, flour; mfg. (clothing, boats, steel and copper wire products, tin cans, fertilizer). Near by are convalescent home for crippled children, Blackwater Natl. Wildlife Refuge, Old Trinity Church (built c.1680), Eastern Shore state hosp. (mental). Settled 1684 as haven for religious refugees; inc. 1745. **7** City (pop. 120,740), a ⊙ Middlesex co., E Mass., on the Charles just N of Boston; educational, residential, and industrial center. Produces soap, bakery products, rubber goods, confectioneries, foundry and machine-shop products, sheet-metal products, shoes, electrical machinery, furniture, clothing, building supplies, ink; printing and publishing. Seat of Harvard Univ., Radcliffe Col., Mass. Inst. of Technology. Many beautiful homes. James Russell Lowell b. here. Longfellow's home is a memorial. First printing press in America established here (c.1639) by Stephen Daye. Washington took command of American army here in 1775. In Mt. Auburn cemetery are buried many notable people. Cambridge settled 1630, inc. as town 1636, as city 1846. **8** or **Cambridge Junction,** village, Lenawee co., SE Mich., 20 mi. NW of Adrian, in agr. area. The Walker Tavern (built 1832) is now a pioneer mus. **9** Village (pop. 2,978), ⊙ Isanti co., E Minn., on Rum R. and c.40 mi. N of Minneapolis, in agr. area; dairy products, wool. Colony for epileptics opened here 1925. **10** Village (pop. 1,352), Furnas co., S Nebr., 25 mi. ENE of McCook and on Republican R., in agr. (grain) and cattle-raising region. Founded 1874. **11** Village (pop. 1,692), Washington co., E N.Y., near Vt. line, 27 mi. NE of Troy; farm trade center; mfg. (underwear, hinges, electrical equipment, machinery, wood products); ships seed. Small lakes near by. Its weekly *Washington County Post* was founded in 1787. Settled c.1761, inc. 1866. **12** City (pop. 14,739), ⊙ Guernsey co., E Ohio, on Wills Creek and 24 mi. ENE of Zanesville, in agr. region also producing coal, clay, and gas; glass, furniture, pottery, steel, plastics, feed, clothing, lumber; coal mining. Settled 1798, laid out 1806, inc. 1837. **13** Town (pop. 1,435), including Cambridge village (pop. 244), Lamoille co., NW Vt., on Lamoille R. and 20 mi. NE of Winooski, in Green Mts. foothills, just NW of Mt. Mansfield; lumber, maple sugar. Includes Jeffersonville village (pop. 387), lumbering center. Settled 1783. **14** Village (pop. 552), Dane co., S Wis., on small Koshkonong Creek and 19 mi. ESE of Madison, in agr. and lake-resort area; candy, dairy products. Mink ranch here.

Cambridge Bay, trading post, SE Victoria Isl., W Franklin Dist., Northwest Territories, on Cambridge Bay of Dease Strait; 69°7'N 104°47'W; U.S.-Canadian weather station. Radio station, Royal Canadian Mounted Police post; site of Anglican mission.

Cambridge City, town (pop. 2,559), Wayne co., E Ind., on Whitewater R. and 15 mi. W of Richmond, in grain and livestock area; mfg. (metal products, caskets, chairs, pottery, gloves, feed); timber. Prehistoric earthworks have been found here.

Cambridge Gulf, SW arm of Joseph Bonaparte Gulf of Timor Sea, NE Western Australia; 50 mi. long, 10 mi. wide; receives Ord R. Wyndham at head.

Cambridge Island, off coast of S Chile, at NW entrance of Nelson Strait; 30 mi. long, 3–7 mi. wide. Sometimes called Almagro Isl. At SW tip is Cape George (51°37'S 75°18'W).

Cambridge Junction, Mich.: see CAMBRIDGE.

Cambridgeshire, England: see CAMBRIDGE, county.

Cambridge Springs, borough (pop. 2,246), Crawford co., NW Pa., 22 mi. S of Erie and on French Creek; evaporated milk, canned goods, tools, burial vaults; oil refineries. Health resort. Alliance Col. here.

Cambridge Strait, in Arctic Ocean, separates Alexandra Land (NW) and George Land (SE) of W Franz Josef Land, Russian SFSR.

Cambrils (kāmbrēls'), town (pop. 1,606), Tarragona prov., NE Spain, near the coast, 11 mi. WSW of Tarragona; cotton spinning, olive-oil and wine processing; trades in fish, cereals, filberts.

Cambrin (kābrē'), village (pop. 686), Pas-de-Calais dept., N France, near Aire–La Bassée Canal, 5 mi. ESE of Béthune; sugar beets.

Cambuci (kămbōōsē'), city (pop. 1,421), NE Rio de Janeiro state, Brazil, on Paraíba R., on railroad and 40 mi. WNW of Campos; coffee, sugar cane, rice. Limekilns. Formerly spelled Cambucy.

Cambuí (kămbwē'). **1** City (pop. 1,870), southwesternmost Minas Gerais, Brazil, in the Serra da Mantiqueira, near São Paulo border, 40 mi. WSW of Itajubá; coffee, tobacco, cattle. Formerly spelled Cambuhy. **2** Locality, Paraná, Brazil: see CONGONHINHAS.

Cambunia, Greece: see KAMVOUNIA.

Cambuquira (kămbōōkē'rü), city (pop. 3,564), S Minas Gerais, Brazil, on railroad and 10 mi. S of Três Corações; modern mtn. resort (alt. 3,000 ft.) in N spur of the Serra da Mantiqueira, with mineral waters and sports facilities. Asbestos deposits.

Camburg (käm'bōōrk), town (pop. 3,962), Thuringia, central Germany, on the Thuringian Saale and 10 mi. NE of Jena; flour-milling center; sugar refining, brewing; cattle market. Towered over by ruins of anc. castle. Near by are remains of Romanesque church. Formerly also Kamburg.

Cambus (kăm'büs), town in Alloa parish, Clackmannan, Scotland, on the Forth, at mouth of Devon R., 2 mi. WNW of Alloa; coal mining, whisky distilling.

Cambuskenneth (kămbŭskĕ'nĭth), abbey in NE Stirling, Scotland, on the Forth, just E of Stirling. Founded 1147 by David I, it was one of the richest abbeys in Scotland. Scottish Natl. Parliament held several sessions here. It contains graves of James III and Margaret of Denmark, to whom Queen Victoria here erected a monument.

Cambuslang (kămbŭslăng'), town and parish (pop. 27,129), N Lanark, Scotland, on the Clyde and 5 mi. SE of Glasgow; steel-milling center, with coal mining, textile printing.

Cambusnethan (kămbŭsnĕ'thŭn), town and parish (pop. 36,596, including part of Motherwell and Wishaw burgh), N Lanark, Scotland; coal mining.

Cambuston (kābüstō'), village (pop. 513) near NE coast of Réunion, isl., on railroad and 2 mi. N of Saint-André; sugar milling.

Camden, municipality (pop. 2,935), E New South Wales, Australia, 35 mi. WSW of Sydney; coal-mining center.

Camden. **1** County (□ 656; pop. 7,322), extreme SE Ga.; ⊙ Woodbine. Bounded S by St. Marys R. at Fla. line, E by the Atlantic, N by Little Satilla R.; intersected by Satilla R.; includes Cumberland Isl. Coastal plain lumbering, fishing, and farming (livestock, corn, sugar cane, truck) area. Formed 1772. **2** County (□ 655; pop. 7,861), central Mo.; ⊙ Camdenton. In the Ozarks, crossed by L. of the Ozarks; drained by Niangua R. Resort, agr. region (corn, wheat, potatoes), livestock; oak, pine timber; lead, barite, calcite mines. Formed 1841. **3** County (□ 221; pop. 300,743), SW N.J., bounded NW by Delaware R.; ⊙ Camden. Shipbuilding, food processing, mfg. (phonographs, records, radio and television equipment, textiles, leather, clothing, pens, metal products, chemicals); railroad shops, marine terminals; agr. (fruit, truck, poultry, dairy products). Drained by Great Egg Harbor and Mullica rivers and Big Timber Creek. Formed 1844. **4** County (□ 239; pop. 5,223), NE N.C.; ⊙ Camden. Bounded N by Va., SE by North R. estuary, S by Albemarle Sound, SW by Pasquotank R.; tidewater area, partly in Dismal Swamp (N). Timber (pine, gum), agr. (corn, soybeans, cotton, truck). Duck hunting, fishing, lumbering. Formed 1777.

Camden. **1** Town (pop. 931), ⊙ Wilcox co., SW central Ala., near Alabama R., 33 mi. SW of Selma; lumber. **2** City (pop. 11,372), ⊙ Ouachita co., S Ark., 28 mi. NNW of El Dorado and on Ouachita R.; trade and shipping center for farm area (cotton, corn, poultry); paper milling, mfg. of wood products, furniture, pottery, fertilizer. Settled 1824, inc. 1847. **3** Town (pop. 606), Kent co., central Del., 3 mi. S of Dover, in fruitgrowing area. **4** Village (pop. 153), Schuyler co., W Ill., 21 mi. SSW of Macomb, in agr. and bituminous-coal area. **5** Town (pop. 600), Carroll co., W central Ind., on Deer Creek and 24 mi. NE of Lafayette, in agr. area. **6** Town (pop. 3,670), Knox co., S Maine, resort center in Camden Hills, on W shore of Penobscot Bay and 35 mi. ESE of Augusta; summer-stock productions in garden theater; yacht harbor; winter sports. Clothing mfg.; boatbuilding. Settled 1769, inc. 1791. **7** Village (pop. 380), Hillsdale co., S Mich., 13 mi. SSW of Hillsdale, near Ohio line, in dairying and agr. area. **8** City (pop. 383), Ray co., NW Mo., on Missouri R. and 6 mi. S of Richmond. **9** City (pop. 124,555), ⊙ Camden co., SW N.J., on Delaware R. opposite Philadelphia (connected by bridge, 1926). Mfg. (textiles, clothing, soap, canned soups and food products, chemicals, television and electronic products, phonographs, radios, pens); shipbuilding, oil refining, printing; railroad shops, marine terminals. Seat of Col. of South Jersey. Settled 1681, laid out 1773, inc. 1828. Grew as commercial, shipbuilding, and mfg.

center after coming of railroad, 1834. Homes of Walt Whitman and Joseph Cooper here. **10** Village (pop. 2,407), Oneida co., central N.Y., 17 mi. NW of Rome, in farming and dairying area; resort; mfg. (furniture, wire, glass, canned foods). Inc. 1834. **11** Village (pop. c.250), ⊙ Camden co., NE N.C., near Pasquotank R., 3 mi. ENE of Elizabeth City. **12** Village (pop. 1,084), Preble co., W Ohio, 25 mi. WSW of Dayton and on small Seven Mile Creek; machinery, food products. **13** City (pop. 6,986), ⊙ Kershaw co., N central S.C., near Wateree R., 28 mi. NE of Columbia, in the sandhills. Popular winter resort, known for polo and hunting; trade and processing center in agr. and lumber area. Textile, cottonseed-oil, and lumber mills, brass and iron foundry; bakery products, naval stores, printing. Synthetic-fiber factories are near by. Settled c.1735, inc. 1791. In Revolutionary War the battles of Camden (Aug. 16, 1780) and Hobkirks Hill (April 25, 1781) were fought near by. City burned May 8, 1781, by evacuating British. In Civil War it was again burned (Feb., 1865). **14** Town (pop. 2,029), ⊙ Benton co., NW Tenn., 19 mi. E of Huntingdon, in agr. area (sorghum, corn, cotton, peanuts); sawmill, sand and gravel pits. Nathan Bedford Forrest Park, with mus. of Civil War relics, is near. Laid out 1836. **15** Village (pop. 1,001), Polk co., E Texas, 29 mi. S of Lufkin; lumbering.

Camden Bay, shallow indentation, NE Alaska, on Beaufort Sea, bet. Brownlow Point (W) and Barter Isl. (E); 70°2′N 144°40′W; 45 mi. wide. Receives Canning R.

Camden Hills, Knox co., S Maine, in semicircle around Camden, include Mt. Battie (800 ft.), Mt. Megunticook (mŭgŭn′tĭko͝ok) (1,380 ft.), Bald Mtn. (1,272 ft.), and Ragged Mtn. (1,300 ft.). Center of Camden Hills Recreation Area (4,962 acres), noted for winter sports.

Camden on Gauley, town (pop. 373), Webster co., central W.Va., on Gauley R. and 13 mi. SW of Webster Springs.

Camden Point, town (pop. 147), Platte co., W Mo., near Platte R., 28 mi. NNW of Kansas City.

Camdenton, town (pop. 1,142), ⊙ Camden co., central Mo., in the Ozarks, near L. of the Ozarks, 50 mi. SW of Jefferson City; resort; lead, calcite mines. Inc. 1931.

Camden Town, residential district of St. Pancras, London, England, N of the Thames, 2.5 mi. NNW of Charing Cross, on E side of Regent's Park.

Camelback Mountain (2,700 ft.), central Ariz., in SE spur of Phoenix Mts., 5 mi. NE of Phoenix.

Camelberg, peak (1,192 ft.), St. John Isl., U.S. Virgin Isls.; 18°20′N 64°45′W.

Camelford, town and parish (pop. 1,277), N Cornwall, England, on Camel R. and 11 mi. NNE of Bodmin; agr. market. With several other places, it has been identified with CAMELOT of Arthurian legend.

Camelon (kă′mùlùn), W suburb of Falkirk, SE Stirling, Scotland; iron- and boilerworks.

Camelot (kă′mùlŏt), England, in Arthurian legend, seat of King Arthur. Variously identified with Winchester, Camelford, and Caerleon, and with a hill in Queen's Camel parish, Somerset, 5 mi. ENE of Ilchester.

Camel River, central Cornwall, England, rises in moorland near Davidstow, flows 30 mi. S and NW, past Camelford and Wadebridge, to the Atlantic 3 mi. N of Padstow.

Camel's Hump, India: see WYNAAD.

Camels Hump, peak (4,083 ft.), N central Vt., 1 of highest in Green Mts., 20 mi. SE of Burlington; state forest here.

Camembert (kămăbâr′), village (pop. 17), Orne dept., NW France, in Normandy, 13 mi. NE of Argentan; here famous Camembert cheese was 1st made.

Camerano (kämĕrä′nô), town (pop. 1,672), Ancona prov., The Marches, central Italy, 6 mi. SSE of Ancona; mfg. (harmoniums, harmonicas, agr. tools).

Camerata (kämĕrä′tä), village (pop. 227), Perugia prov., Umbria, central Italy, 6 mi. S of Todi; wrought-iron products.

Cameri (kä′mĕrē), village (pop. 4,903), Novara prov., Piedmont, N Italy, near Cavour Canal, 4 mi. NE of Novara.

Camerino (kämärē′nô), anc. *Camerinum,* town (pop. 4,269), Macerata prov., The Marches, central Italy, 16 mi. SSE of Fabriano; rail terminus; cementworks. Archbishopric. Has cathedral, small university (1727), and picture gall.

Camerlata (kämĕrlä′tä), village (pop. 1,924), Como prov., Lombardy, N Italy, adjacent to Como; toy mfg. Near by are ruins of Castello Baradello.

Camerón (kämärōn′), village (1930 pop. 258), Magallanes prov., S Chile, on W coast of main isl. of Tierra del Fuego, 55 mi. SE of Punta Arenas; sheep raising.

Cameron (kăm′rùn). **1** Parish (□ 1,444; pop. 6,244), extreme SW La.; ⊙ Cameron. Marshy coastal area, bounded W by Sabine L. and Sabine R., S by Gulf of Mexico. Stock raising, fishing, duck hunting, fur trapping; also produces poultry, vegetables, fruit. Petroleum and natural-gas wells. Navigable waterways include Calcasieu, Mermentau, and Sabine rivers, and Gulf Intracoastal Waterway, here following Lake Charles Canal. Includes Sabine Migratory Waterfowl Refuge and Calcasieu and Grand lakes. Formed 1820. **2** County (□ 401; pop. 7,023), N central Pa.; ⊙ Emporium. Mountainous area, once important for lumbering; drained by Sinnemahoning Creek. Recreation region; dairy products; mfg. (leather, electronic and surgical equipment, explosives); bituminous coal, sandstone, shale, natural gas. Formed 1860. **3** County (□ 883; pop. 125,170), extreme S Texas; ⊙ BROWNSVILLE, metropolis of lower Rio Grande valley. Bounded S by the Rio Grande (Mex. border), E by Laguna Madre, inlet of Gulf of Mexico. Rich irrigated year-round agr. area, processing and shipping citrus, truck, cotton; also dairy products, some livestock. Warm winter climate, nearness to Mexico, and Gulf beaches and fishing attract tourists. Ocean shipping from Brownsville (on deepwater channel to Gulf and the Intracoastal Waterway) and Port Isabel. Oil, natural-gas production and refining, clay mining. Formed 1848.

Cameron. **1** Village (1940 pop. 697), ⊙ Cameron parish, extreme SW La., on Calcasieu R. bet. L. Calcasieu and mouth of river on Gulf of Mexico, and 31 mi. S of Lake Charles city; shrimp fishing and canning, cotton ginning. Hunting near by. **2** City (pop. 3,570), De Kalb and Clinton counties, NW Mo., 32 mi. E of St. Joseph; rail, trade center for agr. area (corn, oats, hay); mfg. (clothing, dairy products). State park near by. Platted 1855. **3** Town (pop. 284), Moore co., central N.C., 12 mi. SSW of Sanford; ships dewberries. **4** Town (pop. 209), Le Flore co., SE Okla., 17 mi. SSW of Fort Smith (Ark.), in farm area. **5** (also kă′mùrùn) Town (pop. 630), Calhoun co., central S.C., 10 mi. NE of Orangeburg; mattresses, lumber. **6** City (pop. 5,052), ⊙ Milam co., central Texas, on Little R. and c.45 mi. SSE of Waco; market, shipping, processing center in agr. area (cotton, cattle, poultry, truck); cotton ginning, grain, cottonseed milling; poultry hatchery; dairying. Founded 1846, inc. 1888. **7** City (pop. 1,736), Marshall co., W.Va., in Northern Panhandle, 11 mi. SE of Moundsville; mfg. of glass, tools, pottery. Farms, timber, coal fields, natural-gas and oil wells in region. Settled 1788. **8** Village (pop. 963), Barron co., NW Wis., 7 mi. S of Rice Lake, in lake-resort area; dairying, farming (potatoes, corn).

Cameron, Mount, peak (14,233 ft.) in Park Range, central Colo., 11 mi. NE of Leadville.

Cameron Bridge, village, central Fifeshire, Scotland, on Leven R. and 2 mi. W of Markinch; whisky distilling.

Cameron Cone, peak (10,705 ft.) in Rocky Mts., El Paso co., central Colo.

Cameron Falls, village, W central Ont., on Nipigon R. (falls) and 65 mi. NE of Port Arthur; hydroelectric-power center, in lumbering, gold-mining region.

Cameron Highlands, district (□ 275; pop. 8,204), northwesternmost Pahang, Malaya, in central Malayan range, on border of Perak, by which it is administered. Linked by road with Tapah (Perak), it was developed in 1940s as one of leading hill resorts (alt. 4,500–5,000 ft.) of Malaya; market gardening; coffee, tea. Main residential areas are Ringlet, Tanah Rata, and Bintang.

Cameron Pass (10,285 ft.), highway pass in S tip of Medicine Bow Mts., N Colo., bet. Larimer and Jackson counties. Near by are Rocky Mtn. Natl. Park and Cameron Pass Primitive Area, set aside to be preserved in natural state.

Cameroon Mountain (kămùro͞on′, kă′–), volcanic massif in S Br. Cameroons; extends 14 mi. inland from Gulf of Guinea; rises to 13,350 ft.; 4°14′N 9°10′E. Highest mtn. group in W Africa; erupted last in 1922. Victoria is at S foot, Buea on SE slope. Bananas, rubber, cacao plantations on lower slopes. First ascended (1861) by Richard Burton.

Cameroon River, an estuarial inlet (□ 230; 20 mi. long, 30 mi. wide) of the Gulf of Guinea, in Br. and Fr. Cameroons coast; receives Mungo and Wouri rivers. At its head is the port of Douala. Has several isls., of which Cape Cameroons, Fr. *Cap Cameroun,* is the largest.

Cameroons (kămùro͞onz′, kă′–), Fr. *Cameroun,* Ger. *Kamerun,* former German colony (□ 200,725) of W equatorial Africa, on Gulf of Guinea and extending to L. Chad. Ger. penetration began 1884 and had reached L. Chad by 1902. After the Agadir incident (1911), colony was enlarged by portions of FRENCH EQUATORIAL AFRICA. Conquered (1914–16) by British, French, and Belgian forces during First World War, it was divided into Br. (W) and Fr. (E) spheres, whose boundaries were adjusted in 1919. In 1922 the 2 parts of Cameroons were placed by the League of Nations under Br. and Fr. mandates. In 1946 Cameroons was placed by the U.N. under Br. and Fr. trusteeship. **British Cameroons,** a territory (□ 34,081; 1931 pop. 778,352; 1948 pop. estimate 1,027,500) under Br. trusteeship, is administered (since 1923) as part of NIGERIA. Extends from Gulf of Guinea c.700 mi. NE to L. Chad, bet. Nigeria (W) and Fr. Cameroons (E); consists of 2 non-contiguous areas (N and S section) separated by E-W corridor (valley of Benue R.) where Nigeria and Fr. Cameroons meet. S section contains Cameroon Mtn. (13,350 ft.) near coast, Bamenda and Shebshi highlands further inland. N of Benue valley lie the Mandara Mts. and a savanna lowland reaching to L. Chad. S section is drained by upper Temba, Katsina Ala, and Cross rivers. Forest zone (S) yields cacao, bananas, palm oil and kernels, rubber, and hardwood. Peanuts and livestock are products of savanna belt. Subsistence food crops are cassava, corn, plantains (S), millet, durra (N). Pop. is largely Kanuri and Shuwa Arab in N, Fulah (center), and Bantu speaking in S. Main towns are Buea (seat of Br. commissioner); ports of Victoria and Tiko; Kumba and Gashaka (all in S section); and Dikwa in N. Plantations of S forest section served by roads. For administration, the S section (□ 27,192; 1948 pop. estimate 598,800) is divided into Cameroons prov. (□ 16,581; 1948 pop. estimate 481,000; governed as part of Eastern Provinces, Nigeria) and E portions of BENUE and ADAMAWA provinces (both governed as part of Northern Provinces, Nigeria). The N section (□ 6,889; 1948 pop. estimate 428,700) is administered as part of Adamawa and BORNU provinces (both also governed as part of Northern Provinces, Nigeria). **French Cameroons,** a territory (□ 166,-489; 1950 pop. c.3,003,200) under Fr. trusteeship, is administered by a Fr. high commissioner; ⊙ Yaoundé. It is 5 times as large as Br. Cameroons; shaped like a triangle, its apex touches L. Chad (N). Bounded by Fr. Equatorial Africa (E and S), continental Sp. Guinea (SW), Br. Cameroons and Nigeria (W and NW). Its frontage on Gulf of Guinea is c.150 mi. long. Densely wooded plateau in S adjoins low coastal strip; savanna in N and W; scrub and thorn region near L. Chad. Drained by Logone R. (in N, to L. Chad), Benue R. (flowing W to Niger) and by tributaries of the Gulf of Guinea (Sanaga, Nyong, Wouri, Mungo). Rainy tropical climate (constant high temp., short dry season Dec.-Feb.) in S forest zone; semi-arid tropical climate in N. Export products: coffee, cacao, bananas, palm oil and kernels, rubber, hardwood, kola nuts, ivory. Local food crops: cassava, sweet potatoes, plantains, millet, pulses. Livestock in N. Minor gold, tin, titanium, molybdenum deposits. Pop. consists of Shuwa Arabs in N, Fulahs (center), and Bantu-speaking Fangs and Bamilekés in S. European pop. c.6,000. Chief towns are Yaoundé, Douala (only good port), N'Gaoundéré, Edéa, Garoua, Maroua, Kribi. Dschang is a hill resort. Railroads link Douala with Yaoundé and Bonaberi (suburb of Douala) with N'Kongsamba. Roads lead to adjoining Ubangi-Shari and Chad territories of Fr. Equatorial Africa. For administration, Fr. Cameroons is divided into 14 regions: ADAMAWA (Adamaoua), BAMILEKÉ, BAMOUN, BENOUÉ, HAUT-NYONG, KRIBI, LOM ET KADÉÏ, M'BAM, MUNGO, NORD-CAMEROUN, N'TEM, NYONG ET SANAGA, SANAGA-MARITIME, WOURI.

Camerota (kämĕrô′tä), village (pop. 1,508), Salerno prov., Campania, S Italy, 15 mi. SSE of Vallo della Lucania.

Camerton (kă′–). **1** Village and parish (pop. 203), W Cumberland, England, 3 mi. NE of Workington; coal mining. **2** Town and parish (pop. 2,003), NE Somerset, England, 6 mi. SW of Bath; agr. market in dairying region; coal mining. Has 13th–15th-cent. church.

Cametá (kämĭtä′), city (pop. 2,959), E Pará, Brazil, port on left bank of the lower Tocantins and 90 mi. SW of Belém; commercial center shipping cacao, rubber, and manioc flour. Airfield. Founded 1635.

Cami, Lake, Chile-Argentina: see FAGNANO, LAKE.

Camiers (kămyā′), village (pop. 1,062), Pas-de-Calais dept., N France, 11 mi. S of Boulogne, near English Channel. Br. First World War military cemetery near by.

Camiguin Island (kämēgēn′). **1** Island (□ 63; 1939 pop. 585) of Babuyan Isls., Cagayan prov., Philippines, in Luzon Strait, forming N boundary of Babuyan Channel, 35 mi. N of Luzon; 14 mi. long, 2–8 mi. wide. Rice growing. Mountainous, rising to 2,742 ft. Mt. Camiguin (2,372 ft.), in S part, is active volcano, with fumarole and several hot springs near by. **2** Volcanic island (□ 96; 1948 pop. 60,099), Misamis Oriental prov., Philippines, in Mindanao Sea, just off N coast of Mindanao, near Macajalar and Gingoog bays; 9°12′N 124°42′E; 13 mi. long, 9 mi. wide. Mountainous, it rises to 5,619 ft. at Mt. Mambajao in center of isl. Sulphur mining, agr. (corn, coconuts, rice). Chief center is MAMBAJAO on NE coast. Mt. Camiguin (4,370 ft.), in center of isl., erupted violently (1948), forcing evacuation of isl.

Camiling (kämēlĕng′, kämē′lĕng), town (1939 pop. 6,006; 1948 municipality pop. 33,935), Tarlac prov., central Luzon, Philippines, 18 mi. NW of Tarlac; agr. center (coconuts, rice, sugar cane).

Camilla (kùmĭ′lù), city (pop. 3,745), ⊙ Mitchell co., SW Ga., 24 mi. S of Albany, in farm and timber area; peanut and pecan processing; mfg. of clothing, cottonseed oil; lumbering. Laid out 1857, inc. 1858.

Camillus (kùmĭ′lùs), village (pop. 1,225), Onondaga co., central N.Y., 8 mi. W of Syracuse, in dairy and grain area; makes cutlery. Inc. 1852.

Camilo Aldao (kämē'lō äldou'), town (pop. 2,926), SE Córdoba prov., Argentina, 26 mi. S of Marcos Juárez; wheat, corn, flax, barley, alfalfa.

Camiña, Quebrada de (käbrä'dä dā kämē'nyä), river in N Chile, rises in the Andes at N foot of Isluga Volcano, flows c.90 mi. WSW to the Pacific 3 mi. N of Pisagua. Sometimes called Quebrada de Tana.

Caminada Bay (kŏmĭnäd'), shallow bay (c.10 mi. long NW-SE, 6 mi. wide) in extreme SE La., c.45 mi. S of New Orleans; adjoins Barataria Bay (E); connected with Timbalier Bay (W) by Southwestern Louisiana Canal. Grand Isle shelters bay from Gulf of Mexico on SE.

Caminha (kämē'nyů), town (pop. 2,067), Viana do Castelo dist., northernmost Portugal, at mouth of Minho R. (Sp. border) on the Atlantic and 12 mi. N of Viana do Castelo; minor fishing port. Has fine 15th-cent. church.

Camino (kůmē'nō), lumber-milling village (pop. c.700), El Dorado co., E central Calif., in Sierra Nevada foothills, c.45 mi. ENE of Sacramento.

Caminreal (kämēnräāl'), village (pop. 1,505), Teruel prov., E Spain, on the Jiloca and 37 mi. NNW of Teruel; sugar beets, saffron, potatoes.

Camiri (kämē'rē), town (pop. c.3,700), Santa Cruz dept., SE Bolivia, near Parapetí R., in Serranía de Charagua, 35 mi. SSE of Lagunillas, on highway from Sucre; major oil center, petroleum refining. Airport. Linked by oil pipe line with Sucre and Cochabamba. A railroad to Sucre is planned.

Camirus (kůmī'růs), anc. city of Rhodes, Greece, one of the members of the Dorian Hexapolis, 18 mi. SW of modern Rhodes city.

Camisano Vicentino (kämēzä'nô vēchēntē'nô), village (pop. 1,082), Vicenza prov., Veneto, N Italy, 8 mi. ESE of Vicenza, in grape- and cereal-growing region.

Camlachie (kămlă'chē), E industrial suburb (pop. 56,747) of Glasgow, Lanark, Scotland; chemicals.

Camlaren (kămlâ'rĭn), village, S central Mackenzie Dist., Northwest Territories, on Gordon L. (28 mi. long, 2–5 mi. wide), 50 mi. NE of Yellowknife; gold mining.

Cammack Village or Cammack, town (pop. 987), Pulaski co., central Ark., 3 mi. NW of Little Rock.

Cammarata (käm-märä'tä), town (pop. 7,638), Agrigento prov., W central Sicily, near Monte Cammarata, 22 mi. N of Agrigento. Rock salt mines 4 mi. SW.

Cammarata, Monte (môn'tě), highest mountain (5,180 ft.) in Agrigento prov., W central Sicily, 21 mi. N of Agrigento.

Cammin, Poland: see KAMIEN, Szczecin prov.

Camminer Bodden, Poland: see KAMIEN LAGOON.

Cammon, province, Laos: see THAKHEK.

Camoapa (kämwä'pä), town (pop. 1,380), Boaco dept., central Nicaragua, 14 mi. E of Boaco; mfg. of Panama hats; coffee, henequen; livestock.

Camocim (kämōosēm'), city (pop. 7,645), N Ceará, Brazil, good port on the Atlantic, 160 mi. WNW of Fortaleza; 2°55'S 40°45'W. N terminus of railroad to Crateús. Ships cotton, tobacco, corn, hides; carnauba-wax processing, tanning. Airport.

Camocuautla (kämōkwout'lä), town (pop. 592), Puebla, central Mexico, in Sierra Madre Oriental, 20 mi. SE of Huauchinango; corn, sugar, fruit.

Camoghè, Monte, Switzerland, see PIZZO CAMOGHÈ.

Camogli (kämô'lyē), town (pop. 4,628), Genova prov., Liguria, N Italy, port on Gulf of Genoa and 12 mi. ESE of Genoa; fishing (tunny, lobster). Has naval inst., sailors' mus.

Camolin, Gaelic *Cam Eolaing*, town (pop. 250), N Co. Wexford, Ireland, on Bann R. and 10 mi. NE of Enniscorthy; agr. market (dairying, cattle raising; wheat, barley, potatoes, beets).

Camonica, Val (väl kämô'nēkä), valley of upper Oglio R., in Brescia prov., Lombardy, N Italy; extends 50 mi. NNE from Lago d'Iseo, bet. Adamello mtn. group (E) and Bergamasque Alps (W). Noted for its iron mines (Bienno, Borno, Edolo, Ono San Pietro), sawmills, and many major hydroelectric plants (Sonico, Cividate Camuno, Isola, Temù, Cedegolo, Darfo). Agr. (grapes, corn, raw silk, chestnuts) in center and S. Cattle raising and tourist industry (Edolo, Ponte di Legno) in N. Chief center, Breno. Formerly an important route bet. Lombard plain and Central Europe.

Camooweal (kă"mōowēl'), village (pop. 192), NW Queensland, Australia, near Northern Territory border, 160 mi. WNW of Cloncurry; livestock.

Camopi River (kämôpē'), S Fr. Guiana, rises in Tumuc-Humac Mts. on Brazil line, flows c.150 mi. NE, through tropical forests, to Oyapock (or Oiapoque) R. at 3°10'N 52°15'W. Rapids.

Camorta Island (kůmôr'tů), one of Nicobar Isls., in Bay of Bengal, 60 mi. NNW of Great Nicobar Isl.; 16 mi. long N–S, 2–4 mi. wide.

Camotes Islands (kämō'täs), group (□ 86; 1948 pop. 47,309), Cebu prov., Visayan Isls., Philippines, in Camotes Sea, bet. Cebu (W) and Leyte (E); 10°40'N 124°23'E. Includes PORO ISLAND (largest), PACIJAN ISLAND, and PONSON ISLAND. Isls. are generally low; coconut growing, fishing.

Camotes Sea, Philippines, bet. Leyte (E), Cebu (W), Bohol (S), leading N to Visayan Sea and S to Mindanao Sea; Camotes Isls. in center.

Camp, county (□ 190; pop. 8,740), NE Texas; ⊙ Pittsburg. Agr. area, known for sweet potatoes, black-eyed peas; also cotton, peanuts, fruit, truck, cattle, hogs, poultry. Extensive lumbering, lumber milling; oil wells. Founded 1874.

Campagna (kämpä'nyä), village (pop. 704), Salerno prov., Campania, S Italy, in the Apennines, 18 mi. E of Salerno. Bishopric.

Campagnac (käpänyäk'), village (pop. 404), Aveyron dept., S France, in the Causse de Sauveterre, 22 mi. N of Millau; cheese making. Coal deposits near by.

Campagna di Roma (kämpä'nyä dē rô'mä), undulating lowland (□ c.800 mi.) in Roma prov., Latium, central Italy, surrounding Rome and extending to Tyrrhenian Sea bet. Tolfa and Alban hills. Covered largely by volcanic sediments; traversed by lower course of the Tiber and by many small streams, mostly dry in summer. Once a fertile cultivated region, as shown by Roman remains (aqueducts, monuments, tombs); deteriorated because of over-heavy sheep grazing, malaria, and lack of water. Abandoned for centuries, until large-scale reclamation works of 19th and 20th cent. restored it. Agr. (cereals, fodder, fruit, vegetables); stock raising (sheep, cattle).

Campagnatico (kämpänyä'tēkō), village (pop. 856), Grosseto prov., Tuscany, central Italy, near Ombrone R., 12 mi. NE of Grosseto.

Campagne (käpä'nyů), village (pop. 228), Landes dept., SW France, 7 mi. W of Mont-de-Marsan; turpentine processing.

Campagne-lès-Hesdin (käpä'nyů-läzädē'), agr. village (pop. 867), Pas-de-Calais dept., N France, 7 mi. SE of Montreuil; limekilns.

Campagnolo Emilia (kämpänyô'lô ěmē'lyä), village (pop. 1,114), Reggio nell'Emilia, N central Italy, 12 mi. NE of Reggio nell'Emilia.

Campamento (kämpämĕn'tō), town (pop. 1,998), Antioquia dept., NW central Colombia, on E slopes of Cordillera Central, 7 mi. ESE of Yarumal; alt. 6,043 ft. Sugar cane, coffee, corn, bananas, yucca; mfg. (yarns and textiles). Gold, copper, iron, silver, salt, and lime deposits near by.

Campan (käpä'), village (pop. 470), Hautes-Pyrénées dept., SW France, on upper Adour R. and 4 mi. SSE of Bagnères-de-Bigorre; woodworking, flour milling. Marble quarries and hydroelectric plant near by. Picturesque Campan valley extends c.8 mi. SE to headwaters of Adour R.

Campana (kämpä'nä), city (pop. 14,409), ⊙ Campana dist. (□ 117; pop. 19,231), NE Buenos Aires prov., Argentina, port on Paraná de las Palmas (S) arm of the Paraná delta, 7 mi. SE of Zárate. Oil refining, paper milling, meat packing, soap mfg.; railroad workshops.

Campana (kämpä'nä), village (pop. 3,423), Cosenza prov., Calabria, S Italy, 16 mi. SE of Rossano; wine, cheese.

Campana, La, Panama: see LA CAMPANA.

Campana, La (lä kämpä'nä), town (pop. 5,350), Seville prov., SW Spain, 33 mi. ENE of Seville; agr. center (olives, cereals, livestock).

Campana Island, off coast of Aysén prov., S Chile, just NW of Wellington Isl., bet. 48°2'S and 48°40'S; c.50 mi. long, c.12 mi. wide.

Campanário (kämpänä'rēōō), town, S Mato Grosso, Brazil, 50 mi. ESE of Ponta Porã. Hq. of leading maté-shipping company. Airfield.

Campanario (kämpänä'ryō), town (pop. 8,958), Badajoz prov., W Spain, 40 mi. E of Mérida; processing and agr. center (cereals, tubers, potatoes, chick-peas, olives, livestock); olive-oil pressing, flour milling; mfg. of esparto, woolen goods, tiles.

Campanario, Cerro de (sě'rō dä), Andean peak (13,190 ft.) on Argentina-Chile border, 55 mi. SW of Malargüe (Argentina); 35°55'S. At N foot is a pass (c.10,000 ft.).

Campanella, Punta della (pōōn'tä děl-lä kämpänĕl'lä), rocky SW extremity of peninsula of Sorrento, bet. Bay of Naples (N) and Gulf of Salerno (S), opposite Capri; 40°34'N 14°19'E; lighthouse.

Campanet (kämpänĕt'), town (pop. 2,617), Majorca, Balearic Isls., 22 mi. NE of Palma; olives, figs, almonds, sheep, hogs; lumbering, pottery mfg.

Campanha (kämpä'nyů), city (pop. 4,455), S Minas Gerais, Brazil, on railroad and 12 mi. SW of Três Corações, in mtn. resort area N of the Serra da Mantiqueira; alt. 2,880 ft. Hot mineral springs in area (especially at near-by Cambuquira and Lambari). Gold deposits.

Campania (kämpä'nyä), region (□ 5,249; pop. 3,696,632), S Italy; ⊙ Naples. Bordered by Latium and Abruzzi e Molise (N), Basilicata (S), Apulia (E), and Tyrrhenian Sea (W). Comprises 5 provs.: AVELLINO, BENEVENTO, CASERTA, NAPOLI, SALERNO. Includes Pontine Isls. and Capri, Ischia, and Procida isls. Extends from Liri (Garigliano) R. SSE to Gulf of Policastro. Traversed by the Apennines; mtn. and hill terrain predominates, with coastal lowlands N of Naples and S of Salerno. Coast indented by Bay of Naples and gulfs of Salerno and Gaeta. Watered by Volturno, Tanagro, Sele, and Calore rivers. One of most fertile regions of Italy; a leading producer of fruit (oranges, lemons, peaches), vegetables (tomatoes), hemp, and tobacco. Cereals, grapes, and olives also widely grown. Livestock raising (c.70% of Italy's Indian buffaloes, cattle, sheep). Fishing. Quarrying (lava, pozzuolana) and sulphur mining (Avellino prov.). Chief industries, centered mostly about Naples and Salerno, include macaroni factories (largest output of Italy), tomato canneries, textile, paper, and lumber mills, tanneries, iron- and steelworks, and shipbuilding. Tourist industry is important along Bay of Naples. After the fall of Rome, occupied by Goths and Byzantines. Conquered by Normans in 11th cent.; in 12th cent. became part of kingdom of Sicily. After the Sicilian Vespers (1282), inc. in kingdom of Naples, which was united with Italy in 1861.

Campania Island (kămpăn'yů) (□ 49; 18 mi. long, 2–5 mi. wide), W B.C., in Hecate Strait just S of Pitt Isl. and W of Princess Royal Isl.; 53°5'N 129°35'W.

Campanquiz, Cerros de (sě'rōs dā kämpäng-kēs'), E Andean outlier, N Peru, extends c.140 mi. N–S bet. 3° and 5°S; rises over 3,500 ft. The Marañón crosses it in the steep gorge Pongo de Manseriche.

Campaspe River (kămpă'spē), central Victoria, Australia, rises in Great Dividing Range S of Kyneton, flows 100 mi. N, past Malmsbury (reservoir), Elmore, and Rochester, to Murray R. at Echuca; used for irrigation.

Campaspero (kämpäspä'rō), town (pop. 1,999), Valladolid prov., N central Spain, 29 mi. ESE of Valladolid; brewery, flour mills; cereals.

Camp Beird (bērd), military reservation (pop. 666), Cristobal dist., Panama Canal Zone, 1½ mi. S of Colón, on railroad, on E shore of the old Fr. canal.

Campbell, fishing village (1939 pop. 10), S Alaska, on N shore of Turnagain Arm, 7 mi. SW of Anchorage.

Campbell (kă'můl, kăm'bůl). **1** County (□ 151; pop. 76,196), N Ky.; ⊙ Alexandria and Newport. Bounded N and E by Ohio R. (Ohio line), W by Licking R. Gently rolling uplands in outer Bluegrass region. Chiefly industrial and residential; includes part of Cincinnati metropolitan dist. in N. Mfg. at Newport. Some farms (vegetables, corn, alfalfa, burley tobacco, dairy products, poultry, livestock). Formed 1794. **2** County (□ 763; pop. 4,046), N S.Dak., on N.Dak. line; ⊙ Mound City. Agr. area, with state game refuge extending along Missouri R., the W boundary. Dairy products, livestock, wheat, corn, barley. Formed 1873. **3** County (□ 447; pop. 34,369), NE Tenn.; ⊙ Jacksboro. Partly (NW) in the Cumberlands; bounded N by Ky., SE by Clinch R. Includes part of Norris Reservoir. Bituminous-coal mining, lumbering (hardwoods), some agr. (livestock, fruit, tobacco, corn, hay). Formed 1806. **4** County (□ 465; pop. 28,877), SW central Va.; ⊙ Rustburg. Bounded N by James R., S by Roanoke R. LYNCHBURG, mfg., transportation, and market center, is in but independent of co.; ALTAVISTA is in S. Agr. (tobacco, corn, hay, wheat), dairying, poultry raising. Formed 1782. **5** County (□ 4,755; pop. 4,839), NE Wyo.; ⊙ Gillette. Grain and livestock area bordering Mont.; watered by Little Powder and Belle Fourche rivers. Coal. Formed 1911.

Campbell. 1 Village (1940 pop. 2,032), Santa Clara co., W Calif., 5 mi. SW of San Jose; fruit packing, canning; poultry hatcheries, lumberyards. **2** Village (pop. 391), Wilkin co., W Minn., on affluent of Bois de Sioux R. and 14 mi. SE of Breckenridge; grain. **3** City (pop. 1,931), Dunklin co., extreme SE Mo., near St. Francis R., 18 mi. N of Kennett; cotton gins, sawmill. Inc. 1900. **4** Village (pop. 412), Franklin co., S Nebr., 25 mi. SW of Hastings and on Little Blue R.; livestock, grain, poultry. **5** City (pop. 12,882), Mahoning co., E Ohio, just SE of Youngstown and on Mahoning R.; steel mills. Until 1926, called East Youngstown. **6** Village (1940 pop. 428), Hunt co., NE Texas, 9 mi. E of Greenville, in agr. area.

Campbell, Cape, NE S.Isl., New Zealand, at E entrance to Cook Strait, 41°42'S 174°21'E; lighthouse.

Campbell, Fort, Ky.: see HOPKINSVILLE.

Campbell Air Force Base, Ky.: see HOPKINSVILLE.

Campbellford, town (pop. 3,018), S Ont., on Trent R. and 25 mi. E of Peterborough; woolen, paper, pulp, flour milling; dairying; lumbering; resort.

Campbell Hill, village (pop. 336), Jackson co., SW Ill., 30 mi. WNW of Herrin, in agr. region.

Campbell Hill (1,550 ft.), Logan co., W central Ohio, just E of Bellefontaine; highest point in state.

Campbell Island (□ 64), SW B.C., in NE Queen Charlotte Sound, just W of Bella Bella; 52°8'N 128°12'W; 14 mi. long, 2–6 mi. wide. Rises to 1,160 ft. Campbell Island village on NE coast.

Campbell Island, volcanic island (□ 44; pop. 9), S Pacific, one of outlying isl. groups of New Zealand, 450 mi. S of Invercargill; 52°30'S 169°E. Semicircular, c.30 mi. in circumference; large bay in NW is 5 mi. wide; fur seals.

Campbellpur or **Campbellpore** (both: kăm'bůlpōōr), town (pop., including cantonment area, 13,999), ⊙ Attock dist., NW Punjab, W Pakistan, 42 mi. WNW of Rawalpindi; rail junction (workshop); market center (wheat, millet, cloth fabrics); cotton ginning, ice mfg., hand-loom weaving. Col.

Campbell River, village (pop. estimate 2,100), SW B.C., E central Vancouver Isl., on Discovery Passage at mouth of Campbell R. (40 mi. long), 26 mi. NNW of Courtenay; lumbering, fishing port; resort. Site of John Hart hydroelectric project.

Campbell's Bay, village (pop. 900), SW Que., on Ottawa R. and 26 mi. ESE of Pembroke; dairying; cattle, pigs.

Campbellsburg. 1 (kăm'bŭlzbûrg") Town (pop. 637), Washington co., S Ind., 20 mi. SE of Bedford, in agr. area. 2 (kă'mŭlzbûrg") Town (pop. 361), Henry co., N Ky., 12 mi. S of Carrollton, in Bluegrass region.

Campbellsport (kăm'bŭlz–), village (pop. 1,254), Fond du Lac co., E Wis., near branch of Milwaukee R., 14 mi. SE of Fond du Lac, in farm area (dairy products; grain, peas, sugar beets); mfg. of brooms. Inc. 1902.

Campbellsville (kă'mŭlzvĭl"), city (pop. 3,477), ⊙ Taylor co., central Ky., 40 mi. SW of Danville, in agr. area (burley tobacco, corn, oats, hay, wheat); oak and walnut timber; limestone quarries. Mfg. of wood products, furniture, carbon black, gasoline, concrete blocks, cheese, soft drinks; flour and lumber mills. Has airport. Jr. col. (coeducational) here. Inc. 1817.

Campbellton, town (pop. 6,748), N N.B., on estuary of Restigouche R. and 11 mi. W of Dalhousie; port and lumbering center; woodworking, pulp and silk milling, iron founding, fishing. Govt. fish hatcheries near by. Settled 1793, inc. 1889.

Campbellton (kă'mŭltŭn). 1 Town (pop. 307), Jackson co., NW Fla., near Ala. line, 16 mi. NW of Marianna; lumber- and gristmills. 2 Town (pop. 368), Atascosa co., SW Texas, 45 mi. SSE of San Antonio.

Campbelltown (kăm'bŭltoun). 1 Municipality (pop. 3,725), E New South Wales, Australia, 27 mi. SW of Sydney; coal-mining center. Founded 1810. 2 Town (pop. 5,233), SE South Australia, 5 mi. NE of Adelaide, in metropolitan area; agr. center.

Campbelltown, Inverness, Scotland: see ARDERSIER.

Campbelltown, town (pop. 770), E central Tasmania, 38 mi. SSE of Launceston, near Macquarie R.; wheat, oats, sheep. Bauxite deposits.

Campbeltown, burgh (1931 pop. 6,309; 1951 census 7,169), S Argyll, Scotland, near S end of Kintyre peninsula, on E coast, at head of Campbeltown Loch (3-mi.-long inlet of Kilbrannan Sound); 55°24'N 5°35'W; port and fishing center, with whisky distilleries; seaside resort. Has old granite cross. Its good harbor early made it a port of importance.

Camp Berteaux (kã bârtō'), village, Oujda region, NE Fr. Morocco, on the Moulouya and 12 mi. NW of Taourirt; smectic clay quarry.

Camp Borden, locality in S Ont., 50 mi. NNW of Toronto; in Second World War, Canadian army training center.

Camp Connell, mountain resort, Calaveras co., E central Calif., in the Sierra Nevada, c.60 mi. ENE of Stockton, near Calaveras Big Trees State Park; winter sports.

Camp Crook, town (pop. 122), Harding co., NW S.Dak., 20 mi. W of Buffalo, on Little Missouri R., near Mont. line; trade center for ranching area.

Camp d'Ambre, Madagascar: see JOFFREVILLE.

Camp-de-la-Santé (kã-dŭ-lä-sãtā') or **Camp-des-Chênes** (–dā-shĕn'), village, Tabarka dist., NW Tunisia, in Medjerda Mts., 16 mi. S of Tabarka; resort amidst oak forests.

Camp-des-Chênes, Tunisia: see CAMP-DE-LA-SANTÉ.

Campdevánol (kämp"dhävä'nōl), village (pop. 1,376), Gerona prov., NE Spain, 2 mi. NW of Ripoll, in the E Pyrenees; mfg. of farm machinery, cement; stock raising.

Camp Douglas, village (pop. 556), Juneau co., central Wis., c.50 mi. E of La Crosse. U.S. Camp Williams military reservation is here.

Campeche (kămpē'chē, Sp. kämpā'chā), state (□ 19,672; 1940 pop. 90,460; 1950 pop. 121,411), on W Yucatan Peninsula, SE Mexico; ⊙ Campeche. Borders W on Gulf of Campeche, bounded by Yucatan (N), Quintana Roo (E), and Tabasco (SW) states, and by Guatemala (S). Consists of vast lowlands, made up of porous limestone. A long bar, Carmen Isl., separates the ocean from the Laguna de Términos, which is fed by subterranean drainage from interior and navigable Candelaria R. Climate is tropical and unhealthy, with heavy rains all year. Its S is densely forested, yielding logwood, lignum vitae, mahogany, cedar, chicle, medicinal plants, dyewood, shipped by river to Carmen, which exports them. Cattle grazing in N; also agr. products (corn, coconuts, bananas, sugar cane, cotton, tobacco, rice). Fishing along coast and in the Laguna de Términos. State is crossed by railroad from Tenosique (Tabasco), via Campeche city to Mérida (Yucatan). Rivers, however, serve as main lines of communication. Principal ports and processing centers: Carmen and Campeche. At site of present Campeche city the Spanish made (1517) one of their 1st landings on Mex. soil. State was set up 1862.

Campeche, city (pop. 23,277), ⊙ Campeche, SE Mexico, port on Gulf of Campeche, on SW Yucatan Peninsula, 95 mi. SW of Mérida (linked by railroad), c.600 mi. E of Mexico city; 19°50'N 90°32'W. Trading and processing center; rail junction and airport. Exports logwood, chicle, cotton, sugar cane, tobacco, cigars, hides. Mfg. of cigars, cigarettes, chocolate, coconut oil, cordage products, shoes, palm hats; sugar milling, alcohol and liquor distilling, tanning. Because of shallow harbor, vessels anchor offshore. An old colonial town (founded 1540) and a leading port under Sp. rule. To Campeche's former wealth testify surrounding walls with citadel, fine public bldgs. anc. churches, and sumptuous residences. The site of a pre-Columbian town (called Kimpech), it was visited (1517) by Hernández de Córdoba during one of 1st Sp. landings on Mex. soil. The city was frequently sacked by the British and buccaneers in 17th cent.

Campeche, Gulf of, inlet of the Gulf of Mexico, SE Mexico, bounded by Yucatan Peninsula (E), Isthmus of Tehuantepec (S), and S section of Veracruz state (W); roughly bet. 18°10'–21°N. Into it flows Papaloápam, Coatzacoalcos, Grijalva, and Candelaria (through Laguna de Términos) rivers. Main ports: Veracruz, Coatzacoalcos, Carmen. Campeche. The shoal N of Yucatan Peninsula and NW of Gulf of Campeche is called Campeche Bank.

Campechuela (kämpăchwä'lä), town (pop. 2,782), Oriente prov., E Cuba, on E shore of the Gulf of Guacanayabo, 13 mi. SW of Manzanillo, in agr. region (sugar cane, pineapples, coffee).

Campegine (kämpā'jĕnĕ), village (pop. 466), Reggio nell'Emilia prov., Emilia-Romagna, N central Italy, 8 mi. NW of Reggio nell'Emilia; wine.

Campello (kämpā'lyō), village (pop. 3,323), Alicante prov., E Spain, fishing port on the Mediterranean, 6 mi. NE of Alicante; almonds, wine, olive oil.

Campeni (kûm'pān), Rum. *Câmpeni*, Hung. *Topánfalva* (tô'pänfŏl"vŏ), village (pop. 3,620), Cluj prov., NW central Rumania, on Aries R., in the Apuseni Mts., on railroad and 35 mi. WSW of Turda; summer resort (alt. 1,804 ft.).

Camperdown (kăm'–), town (pop. 3,192), S Victoria, Australia, 105 mi. WSW of Melbourne; livestock; dairy plants.

Camperdown, Du. *Kamperduin* or *Camperduin* (käm'pŭrdoin") [=dunes of Kamp] or simply *Kamp*, village (pop. 193), North Holland prov., NW Netherlands, 8 mi. NW of Alkmaar, near North Sea. In 1797 British defeated Dutch offshore in a naval battle.

Campero, Bolivia: see AIQUILE.

Campestre, Brazil: see SÃO JOSÉ DO CAMPESTRE.

Campfèr (kämpfâr'), Romansh *Champfèr* (shŭmfâr'), resort village (alt. 6,000 ft.) in Upper Engadine of Grisons canton, SE Switzerland, suburb of St. Moritz, on **Lake of Campfèr**, Ger. *Campfersee*, small lake joined at S by narrow neck to **L.** of Silvaplana.

Campgaw, N.J.: see FRANKLIN LAKES.

Campha (käm'fä'), town, Quangyen prov., N Vietnam, on Gulf of Tonkin, opposite Faitsilong Archipelago, 45 mi. ENE of Haiphong; 21°1'N 107°19'E. Major coal-shipping and mining center; briquette- and coal-treating plant. Mines are just NW. Pop. Annamese and Chinese.

Camp Hill. 1 Town (pop. 1,296), Tallapoosa co., E Ala., 50 mi. NE of Montgomery; lumber, cotton products. Inc. 1907. 2 Residential borough (pop. 5,934), Cumberland co., S Pa., 3 mi. SW of Harrisburg, across the Susquehanna. Founded 1756.

Campia-Turzii (kûm'pyä-tōōr'zē), Rum. *Câmpia-Turzii*, Hung. *Aranyosgyéres* (ŏ'rŏnyôsh-dyā"rĕsh), village (pop. 5,759), Cluj prov., NW central Rumania, in Transylvania, on Aries R. and 5 mi. ESE of Turda; rail junction; metalworking (wire, nails, textile-industry equipment), flour milling, mfg. of bricks and tiles. Michael the Brave was killed (1601) and is buried here.

Campi Bisenzio (käm'pē bēzĕn'tsyô), town (pop. 5,776), Firenze prov., Tuscany, central Italy, 7 mi. WNW of Florence; agr. center; mfg. (straw hats, phosphates, irrigation pumps, musical instruments). Has palace and ruins of 15th-cent. citadel.

Campidano (kämpēdä'nô), lowland in Cagliari prov., SW Sardinia; extends 70 mi. from Gulf of Cagliari NW to Gulf of Oristano; watered by Flumini Mannu R. Most fertile, populous region of isl. Agr. (cereals, grapes, olives, almonds, herbs, vegetables, citrus fruit); livestock raising. Chief towns: Oristano, Villacidro, Terralba.

Campierganj, India: see PHARENDRA.

Campiglia Marittima (kämpē'lyä märēt'tēmä), town (pop. 2,566), Livorno prov., Tuscany, central Italy, 10 mi. NNE of Piombino, in olive-growing region; mfg. (agr. machinery, cement, soap, paper). Has 12th-cent. Romanesque church. Iron, copper, and tin mines; marble and limestone quarries near by.

Campillo, El (ĕl kämpē'lyō), town (pop. 3,338), Huelva prov., SW Spain, 35 mi. NE of Huelva (linked by rail), in Riotinto mining (copper, manganese) region; also cereals, timber, livestock.

Campillo de Altobuey (dhā ältōbwā'), town (pop. 3,529), Cuenca prov., E central Spain, 36 mi. SE of Cuenca; agr. center (saffron, cereals, olives, vegetables, grapes). Olive-oil pressing, liquor distilling, soap and chocolate mfg.

Campillo de Arenas (ärā'näs), town (pop. 3,400), Jaén prov., S Spain, 17 mi. SSE of Jaén; mfg. of chemical fertilizers, olive-oil processing, sawmilling. Cereals, livestock, lumber. Gypsum quarries.

Campillo de la Jara, El (lä hä'rä), village (pop. 1,435), Toledo prov., central Spain, 28 mi. SSW of Talavera de la Reina; olives, cereals, grapes, livestock.

Campillo de Llerena (lyārā'nä), town (pop. 4,324), Badajoz prov., W Spain, 22 mi. SE of Castuera; grain and livestock center.

Campillos (kämpē'lyōs), town (pop. 6,953), Málaga prov., S Spain, at SW foot of the Sierra de Yeguas, 32 mi. NW of Málaga; processing and agr. center. Cereals, olives, livestock; flour milling, olive-oil pressing, liquor distilling, mfg. of woolen goods. Notable parochial church.

Campina (kûm'pēnä), Rum. *Câmpina*, town (1948 pop. 16,963), Prahova prov., S central Rumania, in Walachia, on Prahova R., on railroad and 19 mi. NW of Ploesti; major petroleum-producing and refining center. Also foundries, sulphuric-acid plants; mfg. of oil-industry equipment, furniture, earthenware. Site of large power plant. Saltworks near by (SE). Also a summer resort (alt. 1,404 ft.).

Campina Grande (kãmpē'nŭ grän'dĭ), city (1940 pop. 33,818; 1950 pop. 73,835), E central Paraíba, NE Brazil, 70 mi. W of João Pessoa; W terminus of rail spur joining main Natal-Recife line at Itabaiana; cotton-growing and -shipping center. Other products: sugar, agave fibers, tobacco, potatoes, beans, manioc, and fruit (pineapples, oranges). Columbite and tantalite deposits in area. Airfield.

Campinas (–nŭs). 1 City, Santa Catarina, Brazil: see ARARANGUÁ. 2 City (1950 pop. 101,746), E São Paulo, Brazil, 50 mi. NNW of São Paulo; state's 3d largest city; rail and highway hub for surrounding agr. dist. (cotton, citrus fruit, coffee, sugar, grain, dairy produce), and processing center for produce of the interior of São Paulo. Has foundries, sugar refineries, textile mills (cotton, ramie, silk), citrus-packing and coffee-grading plants. Produces wine, cottonseed-oil and cake, brandy, artificial flowers, pencils, agr. equipment. The noted São Paulo agr. experiment station (Instituto Agronômico) located here has extensive laboratories and farms. There is also a faculty of pharmacy and dentistry. Founded in 18th cent., Campinas became the leading coffee center of state in 19th cent. As a result of soil exhaustion, chief coffee areas have since moved further inland and Campinas has lost out to São Paulo as center of state's agr. output. The musician Antônio Carlos Gomes was b. here.

Campina Verde (kãmpē'nŭ vĕr'dĭ), city (pop. 1,161), westernmost Minas Gerais, Brazil, in the Triângulo Mineiro, 90 mi. W of Uberaba; cattle raising.

Campine (kãpēn'), Flemish *Kempen* (kĕm'pŭn), heathland area in Limburg prov. and Antwerp prov., NE Belgium, and North Brabant prov., Netherlands. Coal mining; mfg. of nonferrous metals, chemicals, glass, bricks. Chief towns: Turnhout, Hasselt, Herentals, Mol. Once a marsh and moorland area, subsequently reclaimed.

Campi Raudii, Italy: see RAUDIAN FIELDS.

Campi Salentina (käm'pē sälĕntē'nä), town (pop. 8,777), Lecce prov., Apulia, Italy, 9 mi. WNW of Lecce; trade center (wine, tobacco, wool, cereals).

Campli (käm'plē), town (pop. 1,212), Teramo prov., Abruzzi e Molise, S central Italy, 5 mi. N of Teramo; mfg. (harmoniums, harmonicas, terra cotta, mill machinery). Has late 14th-cent. cathedral and medieval palace.

Camp Meeker, resort village, Sonoma co., W Calif., 14 mi. W of Santa Rosa, in redwood region.

Camp Nelson, village, Jessamine co., central Ky., on Kentucky R. near Herrington L., and 21 mi. SSW of Lexington, in Bluegrass region. In Civil War, site of important Federal military camp. Natl. cemetery (established 1866) is near. Chimney Rock, a 125-ft.-high limestone formation, and Kentucky R. Palisades in vicinity.

Campo (käm'pō), village, Kribi region, SW Fr. Cameroons, on Gulf of Guinea, at mouth of Campo R. (Sp. Guinea border), 45 mi. S of Kribi; lumber-shipping point, customs station; sawmilling; rubber and cacao plantations.

Campo (kăm'pō). 1 Village (pop. c.500), San Diego co., S Calif., near Mex. border, c.40 mi. ESE of San Diego; feldspar mining. Campo Indian Reservation near by. 2 Town (pop. 266), Baca co., SE Colo., near Okla. line, 22 mi. S of Springfield.

Campo, El (ĕl käm'pō), village (pop. 1,369), Cáceres prov., W Spain, 20 mi. SSE of Trujillo; cereals, olive oil, livestock.

Campo Alegre (kăm'pōō ălā'grĭ), city (pop. 689), NE Santa Catarina, Brazil, in the Serra do Mar, 30 mi. WNW of Joinvile; fruit, cattle, timber.

Campoalegre (kämpōälā'grä), town (pop. 3,922), Huila dept., S central Colombia, in upper Magdalena valley, in W foothills of Cordillera Oriental, 17 mi. S of Neiva; agr. center (rice, cacao, tobacco, coffee, stock). Gold-placer mines near by.

Campobasso (käm"pôbäs'sô), province (□ 1,718; pop. 388,268), ABRUZZI E MOLISE, S central Italy, bordering on the Adriatic; ⊙ Campobasso. Traversed by the Apennines; watered by Trigno, Biferno, and upper Volturno rivers. Agr. (cereals, grapes, olives, fruit); stock raising (cattle, sheep, swine). Fishing (Termoli). Mfg. at Campobasso, Isernia, Agnone. In 1945 part of territory (□ 67; pop. 10,887) in SW passed to Caserta prov.

Campobasso, town (pop. 17,043), ⊙ Campobasso prov., Abruzzi e Molise, S central Italy, 55 mi.

NNE of Naples; 41°34'N 14°39'E. Agr. center; mfg. (cutlery, macaroni, flour, cement, furniture, soap). Has medieval castle, archaeological mus., technical institute. In Second World War damaged (1943) by air bombing and fighting.

Campo Bello, Brazil: see CAMPO BELO, Minas Gerais.

Campobello, town (pop. 394), Spartanburg co., NW S.C., 17 mi. NW of Spartanburg; fertilizer.

Campobello di Licata (käm″pôbĕl′lô dē lĕkä′tä), town (pop. 11,401), Agrigento prov., S Sicily, 11 mi. N of Licata. Sulphur mines near by.

Campobello di Mazara (mätsä′rä), town (pop. 10,285), Trapani prov., W Sicily, 27 mi. SSW of Alcamo; wine. Near-by quarries provided stone for temples of Selinus (5 mi. SE).

Campobello Island (kăm″pōbĕ′lō) (pop. 1,181; 9 mi. long, 3 mi. wide), SW N.B., in Bay of Fundy at entrance to Passamaquoddy Bay opposite Eastport, Maine; 44°53′N 66°55′W. Summer resort and fishing base. On W coast is village of Campobello. In center is Welchpool, where Franklin D. Roosevelt spent many vacations, commemorated by monument (1946).

Campo Belo (kã̃m′pŏŏ bä′lŏŏ). **1** City (pop. 7,094), S Minas Gerais, Brazil, on railroad and 65 mi. WNW of São João del Rei; agr. processing center (coffee, cereals, cattle). Rock-crystal deposits. Formerly spelled Campo Bello. **2** Town, Rio de Janeiro, Brazil: see ITATIAIA.

Campo Bom (kã̃m′pŏŏ bō′), town (pop. 1,696), E Rio Grande do Sul, Brazil, on railroad and 7 mi. NE of São Leopoldo; tobacco, black acacia.

Campocologno, Switzerland: see BRUSIO.

Campodarsego (käm″pôdär′sĕgō), village (pop. 303), Padova prov., Veneto, N Italy, 7 mi. N of Padua; mfg. of bicycle parts.

Campo de Criptana (käm′pō dhā krēptä′nä), town (pop. 14,361), Ciudad Real prov., S central Spain, in New Castile, 50 mi. NE of Ciudad Real; processing and agr. center in La Mancha region, surrounded by vineyards; also cereals, olives, truck produce, fruit, sheep, mules. Alcohol, liquor, and sweet-wine distilling; flour milling, lumbering; mfg. of tartaric acid and plaster. Characteristic of the town are its windmills and whitewashed houses.

Campo de la Cruz (käm′pō dā lä krōōs′), town (pop. 5,458), Atlántico dept., N Colombia, in marshy Caribbean lowlands, on Magdalena R. and 40 mi. S of Barranquilla; agr. center (rice, yucca, corn, sugar cane, livestock).

Campo del Cielo, Argentina: see GENERAL CAPDEVILA.

Campo de Mayo (käm′pō dā mī′ō), village (pop. estimate 300), NE Buenos Aires prov., Argentina, on rail spur 2 mi. E of San Miguel. Has military hydroelectric power station using water of Las Conchas R. (a small tributary of Paraná delta).

Campo do Brito (kã̃m′pŏŏ dŏŏ brē′tŏŏ), city (pop. 2,113), central Sergipe, NE Brazil, 30 mi. WNW of Aracaju, in rice-growing region. Also ships cotton, castor beans, livestock.

Campo Elías (käm′pō ālē′äs), town (pop. 1,206), Yaracuy state, N Venezuela, 15 mi. SW of San Felipe; coffee, sugar cane, corn, cacao, livestock.

Campo Florido (kã̃m′pŏŏ flôrē′dŏŏ), city (pop. 1,120), westernmost Minas Gerais, Brazil, in the Triângulo Mineiro, 40 mi. W of Uberaba; cattle raising; chromite deposits. Until 1944, Campo Formoso.

Campo Florido (käm′pō flōrē′dō), town (pop. 2,484), Havana prov., W Cuba, on railroad and 14 mi. E of Havana; vegetables, livestock.

Campoformido (käm″pôfôr′mēdô), formerly **Campo Formio** (fôr′myō), village (pop. 1,146), Udine prov., Friuli-Venezia Giulia, NE Italy, 5 mi. SW of Udine; paper mills. Famous for Treaty of Campo Formio (1797) bet. France and Austria, whereby France received Belgium, Lombardy, and Venetian territories W of the Adige, while Austria acquired remainder of Republic of Venice.

Campo Formoso (kã̃m′pŏŏ fôrmō′zŏŏ). **1** City (pop. 2,325), N central Bahia, Brazil, 10 mi. WSW of Senhor do Bonfim (linked by rail spur); chromite- and manganese-mining center. Also exploits gold, rock crystals, amethysts. **2** City, Goiás, Brazil: see ORIZONA. **3** City, Minas Gerais, Brazil: see CAMPO FLORIDO.

Campofrío (kämpōfrē′ō), town (pop. 1,062), Huelva prov., SW Spain, on slopes of the Sierra Morena, 8 mi. S of Aracena; acorns, cork, livestock.

Campogalliano (käm″pôgäl-lyä′nô), village (pop. 1,157), Modena prov., Emilia-Romagna, N central Italy, 5 mi. NW of Modena; wine making.

Campo Gallo (käm′pō gä′yō), town (pop. estimate 1,000), ⊙ Alberdi dept. (□ 5,045; 1947 pop. 18,288), N Santiago del Estero prov., Argentina, on railroad and 30 mi. NNW of Tintina; stock-raising and lumbering center.

Campo Grande (kã̃m′pŏŏ grăn′dĭ). **1** City, Ceará, Brazil: see INHUÇU. **2** City (1950 pop. 32,848), S Mato Grosso, Brazil, in Serra de Amambaí, on São Paulo-Corumbá RR, 220 mi. SE of Corumbá. State's largest, most rapidly growing city, and chief commercial center, shipping livestock, dried and packed meat, hides and skins to São Paulo. Also exports maté and region's agr. produce. Has airfield; also rail spur to Maracaju.

Campo Imperatore, Italy: see CORNO, MONTE.

Campo Largo (käm′pō lär′gō), town (pop. estimate 800), S central Chaco natl. territory, Argentina, on railroad and 25 mi. W of Presidencia Roque Sáenz Peña; cotton, corn, livestock; meat packing, cotton ginning, lumbering.

Campo Largo (kã̃m′pŏŏ lär′gŏŏ). **1** City (pop. 2,195), SE Paraná, Brazil, 15 mi. W of Curitiba; porcelain mfg., grain milling, maté processing; winegrowing, hog and cattle raising. Gold and kaolin deposits near by. Mineral springs. **2** São Paulo, Brazil: see ARAÇOIABA DA SERRA.

Campolato, Cape (käm″pôlä′tô), point on E coast of Sicily, at S end of Gulf of Catania; 37°18′N 15°13′E.

Campo Ligure (käm′pô lē′gōōrĕ), town (pop. 2,586), Genova prov., Liguria, N Italy, near N end of Passo del Turchino tunnel, 15 mi. NW of Genoa; mfg. (cotton textiles, dyes, silverware, nails). Winter sports and summer resort (alt. 1,115 ft.).

Campo Los Andes (käm′pō lōs′ än′dĕs), town (pop. estimate 200), N central Mendoza prov., Argentina, on railroad, on Tunuyán R. and 60 mi. SSW of Mendoza; agr. center (alfalfa, wheat, potatoes, wine). Military airport.

Campo Maior (kã̃m′pŏŏ mäyôr′), city (pop. 3,689), N central Piauí, Brazil, 50 mi. ENE of Teresina; road junction and cattle-raising center; carnauba wax. Airfield. Picturesque old town.

Campo Maior, town (pop. 7,518), Portalegre dist., central Portugal, near Sp. border, 10 mi. NNE of Elvas; agr. trade center (olives, grain, cork, livestock); flour milling, fruit preserving, pottery mfg. Copper mine at Degolados (5 mi. NW). Fortified since Roman times. Resisted Fr. siege in 1811.

Campomarino (käm″pômärē′nô), village (pop. 1,557), Campobasso prov., Abruzzi e Molise, S central Italy, near the Adriatic, 4 mi. SSE of Termoli; mfg. of hydraulic pumps.

Campomorone (käm″pômôrô′nĕ), industrial village (pop. 2,025), Genova prov., Liguria, N Italy, 7 mi. NNW of Genoa; cotton textiles, machinery, macaroni. Quarries (gypsum, limestone, green marble) near by.

Campo Mourão (kã̃m′pŏŏ mōrã′ō), town, W Paraná, Brazil, 65 mi. NW of Pitanga; distilling.

Campona, Lake (kämpō′nä), Sucre state, NE Venezuela, at E base of Araya Peninsula, 20 mi. WSW of Carúpano; linked by small river with Gulf of Cariaco; roughly circular, 6 mi. in diameter.

Campo Quijano (käm′pō kēhä′nō), town (pop. estimate 500), central Salta prov., Argentina, on railroad and 17 mi. SW of Salta, in agr. area (corn, alfalfa, sugar cane). Until 1930s, Kilómetro 1172.

Campo Real (käm′pō räāl′), town (pop. 1,557), Madrid prov., central Spain, 17 mi. ESE of Madrid; cereals, olives, grapes, sheep. Mfg. of pottery and ceramics. Sometimes spelled Camporreal.

Camporeale (käm″pōrĕä′lĕ), village (pop. 6,096), Trapani prov., W Sicily, 9 mi. SE of Alcamo, in cereal- and grape-growing region.

Camporgiano (kämpôrjä′nô), village (pop. 575), Lucca prov., Tuscany, central Italy, near Serchio R., 13 mi. ENE of Carrara; paper mill, mushroom cannery.

Campo River (käm′pō), tributary of the Gulf of Guinea in N Gabon (Fr. Equatorial Africa) and along Fr. Cameroons-Sp. Guinea frontier. Known as N'Tem (ŭntĕm′) in its upper course, it rises 40 mi. SE of Minvoul and flows c.250 mi. NW and W to the Atlantic at Campo. Forms several large isls. in its middle and upper course.

Camporosso Pass (käm″pôrôs′sô) or **Tarvisio Pass** (tärvē′zyō), Ger. *Tarvis Pass* (alt. 2,657 ft.), in Udine prov., NE Italy, at SE foot of Carnic Alps just W of Tarvisio. Adriatic-Black Sea drainage divide. Crossed by road and railroad.

Camporreal, Spain; see CAMPO REAL.

Camporredondo (käm″pōrādōn′dō), town (pop. 944), Amazonas dept., N Peru, on Andean slopes, 38 mi. WNW of Chachapoyas; cacao, sugar cane, coffee, grain. Formerly Cocochillo.

Camporrobles (kämpōrō′blĕs), town (pop. 2,201), Valencia prov., E Spain, 20 mi. NW of Requena; sawmilling, sheep raising; cereals, wine, saffron.

Campos (kã̃m′pŏŏs). **1** City (1950 pop. 63,384), NE Rio de Janeiro, Brazil, near head of Paraíba R. delta (23 mi. above mouth on the Atlantic), 140 mi. NE of Rio; major industrial (sugar refining, alcohol distilling) and commercial center in state's richest agr. dist.; mfg. of fruit preserves, brandy, textiles, leather goods, soap, furniture, building materials; coffee and tobacco processing. New aluminum plant. Linked by rail with Rio de Janeiro, Vitória (Espírito Santo), and cities in Paraíba valley. Airfield. Ship canal to Macaé. Bishopric. Has law school. Founded 1634. Presents modern appearance. **2** City, Sergipe, Brazil; see TOBIAS BARRETO.

Camposampiero (käm″pôsämpyä′rô), town (pop. 1,910), Padova prov., Veneto, N Italy, 11 mi. NNE of Padua, in sericulture region; rail junction; agr. center.

Campo Santo (käm′pō sän′tō), town (pop. estimate 800), ⊙ Campo Santo dept. (□ 850; 1947 census 13,652), central Salta prov., Argentina, on railroad and 21 mi. NE of Salta. Cement factory, sugar refinery; fruit, livestock.

Camposanto (käm″pôsän′tô), village (pop. 1,104), Modena prov., Emilia-Romagna, N central Italy, on Panaro R. and 14 mi. NW of Modena.

Campos del Puerto (käm′pōs dhĕl pwĕr′tō), town (pop. 4,404), Majorca, Balearic Isls., on railroad and 22 mi. ESE of Palma; agr. center (cereals, almonds, capers, truck). Lime quarrying. San Juan de Campos springs near by.

Campos del Río (rē′ō), town (pop. 1,394), Murcia prov., SE Spain, 13 mi. WNW of Murcia; fruit-conserve mfg.; cereals, olive oil.

Campos do Jordão (käm′pŏŏs dŏŏ zhôrdã′ō), city (pop. 4,785), SE São Paulo, Brazil, rail terminus in the Serra da Mantiqueira, near Minas Gerais border, 22 mi N of Taubaté; alt. 5,500 ft. Noted health resort (especially for tuberculosis treatment), amidst apple, pear, and peach orchards.

Campos Elísios, Brazil: see AGULHAS NEGRAS.

Campos Gerais (kã̃m′pŏŏs zhĭrīs′), city (pop. 2,401), SW Minas Gerais, Brazil, 40 mi. SW of Campo Belo; coffee, cattle, cereals.

Campos Novos (kã̃m′pŏŏs nô′vŏŏs), city (pop. 1,340), central Santa Catarina, Brazil, 60 mi. WNW of Lajes; cattle, horses; maté, timber.

Campos Point (käm′pōs), on Pacific coast of Colima, W Mexico, at SE gate of Manzanillo Bay, just S of Manzanillo; 19°2′N 104°21′W.

Campos Sales (kã̃m′pŏŏs sä′lĭs), city (pop. 1,346), SW Ceará, Brazil, near Piauí border, 65 mi. WNW of Crato; cattle, cotton, tobacco. Airfield. Formerly spelled Campos Salles.

Campotéjar (kämpōtā′här), town (pop. 1,656), Granada prov., S Spain, 21 mi. N of Granada; cereals, sugar beets, olive oil; lumbering.

Campo Tencia (käm′pō tĕn′chä), peak (10,090 ft.) in Lepontine Alps, S Switzerland, 9 mi. SSE of Airolo.

Campotosto (käm″pôtô′stô), town (pop. 1,440), Aquila prov., Abruzzi e Molise, S central Italy, in the Apennines, near Gran Sasso d'Italia, 15 mi. N of Aquila. Situated on small upper branch of Vomano R., dammed here (1940–46) to form a reservoir; has major hydroelectric plant.

Campo Tures (käm′pô tōō′rĕs), Ger. *Sand in Taufers*, village (pop. 996), Bolzano prov., Trentino-Alto Adige, N Italy, on Aurino R. and 9 mi. N of Brunico; rail spur terminus; resort (alt. 2,844 ft.).

Camp Parole, Md.: see PAROLE.

Camp-Perrin (kã-pĕrē′), town (1950 pop. 1,447), Sud dept., SW Haiti, on Tiburon Peninsula, 13 mi. NW of Les Cayes; bananas, sugar cane. Lignite deposits near by.

Camp Point, village (pop. 969), Adams co., W Ill., 18 mi. ENE of Quincy, in agr. area; feed mill. Inc. 1857.

Camp Richardson, resort village, El Dorado co., E Calif., in the Sierra Nevada, on S shore of L. Tahoe.

Camprodón (kämprō-dhōn′), town (pop. 1,204), Gerona prov., NE Spain, 12 mi. NE of Ripoll; popular summer resort in E Pyrenees; alt. 3,775 ft. Near by is 9th-cent. monastery.

Camp-Servière, Tunisia: see FONDOUK-DJEDID.

Campsie, parish (pop. 5,296), S Stirling, Scotland. Includes LENNOXTOWN.

Campsie Fells, Scotland: see LENNOX HILLS.

Camp Springs, village (1940 pop. 928), Prince Georges co., central Md., SE suburb of Washington. Andrews Air Force Base is just E.

Campti (kămp′tē), village (pop. 1,014), Natchitoches parish, NW central La., on Red R., 14 mi. NNW of Natchitoches; cotton, lumber; fishing. Inc. 1903.

Campton. 1 Town (pop. 163), Walton co., N central Ga., 5 mi. N of Monroe. **2** Town (pop. 431), ⊙ Wolfe co., E central Ky., in the Cumberlands, 40 mi. ESE of Winchester. Cumberland Natl. Forest is near by. **3** Town (pop. 1,149), Grafton co., central N.H., in White Mts., in Pemigewasset valley, 8 mi. N of Plymouth; resort area; textiles, wood products. Settled c.1765.

Campulung (kûm″pōōlōōng′), Rum. *Câmpulung*. **1** Town (1948 pop. 18,174), Arges prov., S central Rumania, in Walachia, in S foothills of the Transylvanian Alps, 80 mi. NW of Bucharest; rail terminus, trading center, and summer resort (alt. 1,903 ft.), surrounded by extensive vineyards. Lignite mining, lumbering; textile mills, paper mills, limekilns; large power station. Has 14th-cent. church, restored in 17th and 18th cent., another old church built on a rock, and a 13th-cent. tower of a monastery of the Teutonic Knights. The town, founded by Ger. colonists in 12th cent., was the earliest ⊙ Walachia. Annual fairs, noted for display of regional costumes, held here. Sometimes spelled Kimpolung. Bughea health resort and monastery just NW. **2** or **Campulung-Moldovenesc** (–môldôvänĕsk′), Ger. *Kimpulung* (kĭm″-pōōlōōng′), town (1948 pop. 11,041), ⊙ Suceava prov., N Rumania, in Bukovina, on railroad, on Moldova R., and 100 mi. WNW of Jassy; popular summer resort (alt. 2,034 ft.) and trading center; mfg. of textile machinery, furniture, clay products, cement; tanning; food processing (cheese, flour, fish). Has 18th-cent. wooden church.

Campulung-pe-Tisa (–pā-tē′sä), Rum. *Câmpulung-pe-Tisa*, Hung. *Hosszúmező* (hôs′sōōmĕ″zû), village (pop. 3,073), Baia-Mare prov., NW Rumania, on Tisa R. (USSR border) and 7 mi. NW of Sighet, on railroad. In Hungary, 1940–45.

Campus, village (pop. 183), Livingston co., NE central Ill., 20 mi. NE of Pontiac, in agr. and bituminous-coal area.

Campus Stellae, Spain: see SANTIAGO.

Camp Verde. 1 (vûrd) Village, Yavapai co., central Ariz., on Verde R. and 35 mi. E of Prescott. Montezuma Castle Natl. Monument is just N. **2** (vûr'dē) Village, Kerr co., SW Texas, c.50 mi. NW of San Antonio. On site of old U.S. fort (1856), where pre-Civil War camel corps was organized.

Camp Wood, city (pop. 785), Real co., SW Texas, on Edwards Plateau 34 mi. NNW of Uvalde and on Nueces R.; shipping point for wool, mohair, timber, in ranching area (cattle, sheep, goats).

Camranh Bay (käm'räng'), T-shaped inlet of South China Sea, S central Vietnam; 11°53'N; 10 mi. long, 20 mi. wide, closed by a neck 1 mi. wide; Bangoi is main port and naval base. Russian fleet stopped here (1905) on way to Tsushima.

Cam River or **Granta River,** Cambridge, England, rises 3 mi. W of Thaxted, flows 40 mi. N, past Cambridge, to Ouse R. 3 mi. S of Ely. Navigable below Cambridge.

Camrose (kăm'rōz), town (pop. 2,967), central Alta., near Bittern L., 45 mi. SE of Edmonton; railroad center; coal mining, tanning, dairying, flour and cereal-food milling. Site of prov. normal school and a Scandinavian Lutheran col.

Camucia (kämōō'chä), village (pop. 385), Arezzo prov., Tuscany, central Italy, 1 mi. SE of Cortona; mfg. of irrigation pumps. Near by is an Etruscan sepulcher.

Camulodunum, England: see COLCHESTER.

Camuñas (kämōō'nyäs), town (pop. 2,388), Toledo prov., central Spain, 5 mi. SE of Madridejos; cereals, grapes, olives, saffron, livestock; lumbering, stone quarrying, olive-oil extracting, alcohol distilling, wine making, flour milling.

Camú River (kämōō'), central Dominican Republic, rises in the Cordillera Central S of La Vega city, flows c.50 mi. N and E, past La Vega, and through fertile La Vega Real valley, to Yuna R. just SE of Pimentel.

Camuy (kämwē'), town (pop. 2,285), NW Puerto Rico, on the coast, on railroad and 8 mi. W of Arecibo; sugar-refining center; coconut growing; alcohol distilling. Adjoining N is the large Río Llanos sugar mill.

Can (chän), Turkish *Çan,* village (pop. 1,385), Canakkale prov., NW Turkey, 35 mi. ESE of Canakkale; magnesite, lead; agr. center (cereals, beans). Formerly Canpazar.

Cana (kä'nä), village (pop. 627), Grosseto prov., Tuscany, central Italy, 16 mi. E of Grosseto; coal mining.

Cana or **Cana of Galilee** (kā'nů, gă'lĭlē), biblical locality, Lower Galilee, N Palestine, perhaps located 3 mi. NE of Nazareth, on site of modern village of Kafr Kanna. In biblical history scene of Jesus' 1st miracle. Kafr Kanna has chapel built on site of Crusaders' church, and remains of Byzantine church (3d or 4th cent. A.D.). Some sources locate the biblical Cana 10 mi. N of Nazareth.

Cana (kä'nä'), village, Ninhthuan prov., S central Vietnam, minor South China Sea port, 15 mi. SSW of Phanrang; 11°20'N; salines.

Canaan (kā'nůn), name given by the Hebrews to PALESTINE before they occupied it. It is the country lying bet. the Jordan, the Dead Sea, and the Mediterranean. It was the promised land of the Israelites, and after their delivery from E Egypt they subdued it.

Canaan (kā'nůn). **1** Town (pop. 708), Litchfield co., NW Conn., on the Housatonic and 14 mi. NW of Torrington, in Taconic Mts. Includes villages of South Canaan and Falls Village (gypsum, limestone products). State forests. CANAAN village is in North Canaan town (N). **2** Village (pop. 1,189) in North Canaan town, Litchfield co., NW Conn., in Taconic Mts., 17 mi. NW of Torrington; trade center, railroad station of resort area. Canaan town is S. **3** Village (pop. 1,830, with adjacent Midway), Seminole co., E central Fla., just E of Sanford. **4** Rural town (pop. 785), Somerset co., central Maine, 8 mi. E of Skowhegan; wood products. **5** Town (pop. 1,465), Grafton co., W central N.H., 13 mi. E of Lebanon; lumber mills, agr.; resort activities. Includes Canaan Street, resort village. Settled 1766, inc. 1770. **6** Village, Columbia co., SE N.Y., near Mass. line, 11 mi. WSW of Pittsfield, Mass. Berkshire Industrial School for boys is near by. **7** Town (pop. 969), Essex co., extreme NE Vt., on the Connecticut and 30 mi. E of Newport; lumber, furniture. Includes Beecher Falls village, port of entry on Que. line.

Canaan Street, N.H.: see CANAAN.

Canach (kä'näkh), village (pop. 547), SE Luxembourg, 9 mi. E of Luxembourg city; dairying, fruit-growing (cherries).

Canácona (känä'kōnů), town (pop. 1,721), S Goa dist., Portuguese India, 37 mi. SSE of Pangim; market center for timber (teak, blackwood in E forests), cashew and betel nuts, rice, mangoes; sawmills; cattle raising. Formerly called Chauddi.

Canada (kă'nůdů), nation (□ 3,845,144, including inland waters; 1950 pop. estimate 13,921,000), N North America, member of the British Commonwealth of Nations; ⊙ OTTAWA. In 1941, when it did not include Newfoundland and Labrador, its area was □ 3,690,410 (of which □ 3,462,103 was land area alone) and its pop. 11,506,655. Canada occupies all the continent N of the U.S. except for the U.S.-owned Alaska in the far NW and the tiny French isls. of St. Pierre and Miquelon in the Atlantic. It consists of 10 provs.—NEWFOUNDLAND (which joined Canada in 1949), NOVA SCOTIA, NEW BRUNSWICK, PRINCE EDWARD ISLAND, QUEBEC, ONTARIO, MANITOBA, SASKATCHEWAN, ALBERTA, and BRITISH COLUMBIA—and includes the NORTHWEST TERRITORIES and the territory of YUKON. Canada is an entirely autonomous political unit, although the nominal head of its govt. is the king of Great Britain and Northern Ireland; his official acts regarding Canada and those of his representative, the governor, are completely determined by the Canadian ministers, who are responsible to the Canadian Parliament. The govt. draws its authority from the British North America Act of 1867, which is the Canadian constitution. The nation has long been called the Dominion of Canada, but the title is not now official or even quite correct, and since the Statute of Westminster set up the BRITISH COMMONWEALTH OF NATIONS, the term *dominion* has tended to fall into disuse. The huge nation sprawls across the continent from the Atlantic (where it is deeply indented by the Gulf of St. Lawrence) to the Pacific, where the mts. run into the sea. In the S it is separated by a 3,986.8-mi-long border from the U.S., the line marked in part by the Great Lakes, but for most of its length a land border, much adjusted in the past. Canada fronts in N on the Arctic Ocean from the border (1,539.8 mi. long) of Alaska eastward. Its enormous coast line is 14,820 mi. long. BOOTHIA PENINSULA and the forbidding isls. of the Arctic Archipelago in FRANKLIN dist. thrust far into the Arctic. In the E, ELLESMERE ISLAND all but touches the coast of Greenland high in the ARCTIC REGIONS. The N coast is deeply cut by gigantic HUDSON BAY, ice-locked much of the year. The extreme NE edge of the continent is also very cold, where the Labrador Current sweeps down along the inhospitable shore of Labrador. Just to the S it meets and mingles with the warm Gulf Stream, giving birth to the incessant fogs about Newfoundland. The provs. about the Gulf of St. Lawrence and on the coast S to the international boundary with Maine—the Maritime Provs. of Nova Scotia (with Cape Breton Isl.), Prince Edward Isl., and New Brunswick—have the narrowing northern end of the Atlantic coastal plain of North America. Here in the mts. of New Brunswick and the GASPÉ PENINSULA (of Quebec prov.) the Appalachian Mts. end S of the St. Lawrence R. The Maritime Provs. with their forests, their deep-cut coves and the many rivers of a rainy land, offer entrancing scenery that attracts tourists. Fishing has long been the mainstay of the region, and it is possible that Europeans were coming to the Grand Banks of Newfoundland before Columbus reached America. Fishing was later supplemented by lumbering, and today the forest yields also the pulp for paper mills. The rivers have been harnessed for hydroelectric power, and projects have been advanced for using the phenomenally high tides of the Bay of Fundy (bet. Nova Scotia and New Brunswick) for practical purposes. HALIFAX is one of the great ports of the Atlantic seaboard, and SAINT JOHN, N.B., has been of some prominence particularly for shipbuilding. The minerals of the Maritime Provs. have also been put to some use, and farming has been productive in limited areas since 1st the French settled Acadia. The heart of Old Canada (or rather of New France) was, however, farther to the W in the present prov. of Quebec. Here the St. Lawrence river opens a way from the Atlantic to the huge North American central plains E of, and about, the Great Lakes that lie on the border with the U.S. Here are the 2 great cities of Quebec prov., QUEBEC itself and MONTREAL. Notable industries of Quebec prov. include vast iron deposits in UNGAVA region, on Labrador border (Burnt Creek Camp), linked by railroad (under construction) with St. Lawrence port of Sept Îles; the important Rouyn-Noranda gold fields; major aluminum and hydroelectric plant at Arvida, on the Saguenay; the asbestos mines at Thetford Mines; and ilmenite mines near Havre St. Pierre. Quebec is still the home and fortress of the French Canadians, while Ontario shows more the mark of the long British heritage. The cities of Ontario have also developed much industry. TORONTO, HAMILTON, LONDON, and WINDSOR, all in region of the E Great Lakes, are tied to the West by rail and road. Industries range from food processing to the manufacture of automobiles and heavy machinery Like S Quebec, SE Ontario also has much diversified agr., including orchards, tobacco fields, and dairy farms. At W end of the Great Lakes are the twin lake ports of PORT ARTHUR and FORT WILLIAM, for shipment of produce from the Western prairies. Settlement in the provs. of Quebec and Ontario is, however, concentrated in the S, for N of the St. Lawrence and its tributary, the Ottawa, rises the inhospitable LAURENTIAN PLATEAU (also called the Pre-Cambrian Shield or the Canadian Shield), a great barrier stretching from the Atlantic around Hudson Bay and its deeper indentation, James Bay, westward across Ontario and into Man. and Sask. It comes down to the St. Lawrence at the THOUSAND ISLANDS. The plateau is a land of rocks, small mtn. ranges, and rolling country reaching in N to the Barren Grounds. It is largely heavily forested and interrupted by many lakes and streams. In the N this country is still a land of the fur trader, and the old ports of RUPERT HOUSE, FORT ALBANY, YORK FACTORY, PORT NELSON, and CHURCHILL persist; in the S there are regions attracting the sportsman and the vacationer. Especially of late its mineral possibilities have been explored and mining (especially nickel, gold, silver, copper, and platinum) operations started, centered on Sudbury, Cochrane, Kirkland Lake, and N shores of lakes Huron and Superior. Its forests have yielded vast quantities of lumber. A strip of clay soil S of James Bay has proved of agr. value. To the W of the Great Lakes lie the Prairie Provs., Man., Sask., and Alta. They are one of the great wheat-growing regions of the world. The plains, separated from those of the U.S. only by an imaginary line, rise more or less rapidly to the Great Plains and then through foothills to the great barrier of the ROCKY MOUNTAINS, which separates Alta. from British Columbia. The provs. have many lakes and rivers. Those in the E, such as L. WINNIPEG, L. MANITOBA, and the others linked with them, the Red River of the North, the Saskatchewan, and the Hayes, Nelson, and Churchill rivers are connected with Hudson Bay; those of NW Alberta, notably the Athabaska and the Peace, are connected through L. Athabaska, the Slave R., and Great Slave L. with the N system of the Mackenzie. A few in the S are part of the Missouri drainage. The 1st agr. settlement in the Prairie Provs. was the Red River Settlement in the region where the metropolis WINNIPEG now stands. Real development came to this domain of the fur trader only after the arrival of the Canadian Pacific Railway. Cattle raising was superseded by wheat farming, which is still dominant, though the hard times of the droughts caused a recession in the 1920s and '30s and now there is more of a trend to diversified farming with some cattle raising. Settlement has been centered in the S—with the notable exception of the Peace R. valley—and the larger cities—besides Winnipeg, REGINA, SASKATOON, EDMONTON, and CALGARY—are in the S half. Agr. production in this "breadbasket of the world" is supplemented by other resources. Alberta has vast coal reserves (now being exploited) and booming oil fields. The cities in this part of the Canadian West have in recent years seen a tremendous increase in industrial plants devoted to food processing and oil refining, with some metal-working and machinery plants. The Rockies of Alberta are notable for majestic beauty and have much frequented resorts, notably BANFF and LAKE LOUISE, both in Banff Natl. Park, which is adjoined NW by Jasper Natl. Park. Across the mts. in S B.C. the mild climate has helped to draw many year-round residents. B.C. for the most part is a land of peaks and of tumbling mtn. rivers. The Rockies seam most of the E, and in the S the young Columbia R. loops around the Selkirk Mts. In the W the Coast Mts. come down to the sea in slopes of great beauty. Other systems have headwaters in B.C.—the Mackenzie (especially in the Peace) and the Yukon (in the Lewes), and there are various rivers running directly to the Pacific (among them the Fraser). Though most of the prov. is wooded wilderness, in the S and more particularly in the SW around the coast and on VANCOUVER ISLAND there is one of the heaviest concentrations of pop. in Canada. The Pacific fisheries, lumbering, agr. (notably fruit orchards), and mining have contributed to the wealth of the region. Its cities are VANCOUVER, VICTORIA, and NEW WESTMINSTER. In the N fur trappers still gather pelts and Indians lead their relatively undisturbed lives. This region is not unlike that of neighboring Yukon, which is still largely undeveloped mtn. country though its name has been world known since the Klondike gold strike of 1896. The few settlements are on the rivers, and transportation—as in most of the N country—depends on the airplane, though Yukon has one railroad (White Horse to Skagway), and is reached by the Alaska Highway. The Northwest Territories are seeing the long-delayed beginnings of development. The westernmost of its 3 dists., Mackenzie dist. (named for the great river that drains its western part) has oil wells and a refinery at Norman Wells and has pitchblende silver (pitchblende yields uranium) mines at Port Radium on Great Bear Lake, one of its 2 enormous lakes (the other is Great Slave Lake, where large gold mines at Yellowknife, on N shore, have recently come into operation). The region is, however, still not thoroughly explored. This is particularly true of the arctic tundra and the mts., although a trader, Samuel Hearne, had crossed overland to the Coppermine river as early as 1771. The situation is perhaps still more true of Keewatin dist. to the E and Franklin dist. to the N (the Arctic Archipelago). In all this frontier region the forces of law are represented by the Royal Canadian Mounted Police. The climate of Canada is varied, though because of the latitude the winters are generally cold: the central plains have a continental climate with very cold winters and very hot summers; the N belongs to the Arctic regions; and about the Great Lakes the winters are temperate. The peoples of Canada show considerably less variation. The Indians have had a considerably more potent effect on the culture in Canada than in the U.S., partly because the Canadian settlers were less ruthless in destroying native peoples than were the U.S. settlers. The natives of Canada varied greatly from the Algonquian-speaking peoples of E and central Canada (including the Micmac, the Abnaki, the Ottawa, the Ojibwa, the Cree, and other well-known tribes) to the Athapascan-speaking peoples of W Canada (including the Chipewyan among others) and the variegated tribes of the Pacific coast. In the N sections there are also many Eskimo. From the very beginning of the activities of the white man (if the somewhat shadowy activities of the vikings after A.D. 1000 are ignored), the signs of imperial rivalry appeared—a rivalry that was to dominate the history of Canada until 1760. The man who made the Canadian coast widely known to Europe was John Cabot who in British service reached the coast in 1497. In 1543 the Frenchman Jacques Cartier planted a cross on the Gaspé Peninsula. The 1st settlement founded was that at Port Royal (now ANNAPOLIS, N.S.) founded by the sieur de Monts and Samuel Champlain in 1604, and a little later Champlain founded (1608) Quebec. The French attempted to establish an enormous but thinly settled empire, as opposed to the relatively dense settlements of the British on the Atlantic coast to the S. Champlain's policy of supporting the Huron Indians against their traditional enemies, the Iroquois, almost brought the French colony to extinction when later in the 17th cent. the Iroquois demolished the Huron. Before that time, however, the English had moved to support their claims under Cabot's discoveries. Sir Samuel Argall had attacked the Port Royal (N.S.) settlement in 1614, and in 1629 the English captured Quebec and Champlain. Quebec was restored in 1632, and the French administration under the Company of One Hundred Associates (established 1627) sought to exploit the fur trade and establish settlements. Exploration went on, and Jesuit missionaries were martyred, but the firm foundation of the Church in Canada came only later when French settlement advanced. The unsuccessful rule of the Company of One Hundred Associates ended in 1663, and French royal govt. was established. The greatest of the colonial governors was Louis de Buade, comte de Frontenac. Missionaries such as Marquette and Hennepin and traders such as Radisson, Jolliet, Groseilliers, and Aco, widened the scope of French knowledge and influence. The greatest of all the empire builders in the West was Robert Cavalier, sieur de la Salle, who went to the mouth of the Mississippi and envisioned the great empire in the West that was made a reality by men like Duluth, Bienville, Iberville, and Cadillac and by the many *coureurs de bois* and diligent missionaries. New France with Louisiana was a vast colony. The British kept returning to claims on Acadia (the British Nova Scotia), and the Hudson's Bay Co. in 1670 began from its posts on Hudson Bay to vie for the lucrative fur trade of the West. When the long series of wars bet. Britain and France broke out in Europe it was paralleled in North America by the French and Indian Wars. The French settlers in Acadia with their diked lands and the French seigneuries on the St. Lawrence were constantly threatened. By the middle of the 18th cent. the St. Lawrence valley was well settled and was a prize for British conquerors. Knowledge of the lands to the W and the far N had been expanded by explorations like those of the French La Vérendrye family and Englishmen like Henry Kelsey, and many of its riches as well as its limitations were known. The imperial contest came to an end after Gen. James Wolfe defeated Montcalm on the Plains of Abraham, bringing about the fall of Quebec in 1759. Montreal fell the next year, and the Treaty of Paris in 1763 ended New France and established British rule. The resultant conflict bet. the settled and R.C. French Canadians and the newly come Protestant British was to leave a legacy of antagonism that has persisted in steadily diminishing force to the present day. In the American Revolution the Canadians remained loyal to the British crown, and the effort to take Canada by arms for the revolutionary cause failed dismally. Loyalists from the colonies in revolt fled to Canada and did much to advance the country—especially in the Maritime Provs. but also further to the W. The period was one of expansion marked by such signal events as the journey of Alexander Mackenzie to the Arctic Ocean and his epoch-making overland voyage to the Pacific in 1793. Mariners were also reaching the Pacific Northwest and such men as Capt. James Cook, John Meares, and George Vancouver secured for Britain a firm hold on what is now British Columbia. The rivalry of the North West Co. and the Hudson's Bay Co. for the Western fur trade grew, and the enterprising Nor'westers, exemplified in Simon Fraser, David Thompson, and Alexander Henry, came also into rivalry with the American John Jacob Astor's traders on the Pacific at ASTORIA and came off successful, partly because of the War of 1812. That war did not change the general situation but did permanently settle the U.S.-Canadian boundary about the Great Lakes. The N.B. boundary and the boundary to W of the Great Lakes were to be subjected to long dispute, but since the War of 1812, except for minor flurries, the long Canadian-U.S. border has been a line of peace. The internal struggle for control bet. the North West Co. and the Hudson's Bay Co. rose to bloodshed in the Red River Settlement and was settled by amalgamation of the companies in 1821. The Hudson's Bay Co. then held undisputed sway over the Canadian West until U.S. immigrants challenged the British hold over Oregon and obtained the present boundary line. In the E the Canada Act of 1791 had divided Lower Canada (present Quebec) from Upper Canada (present Ontario). The earl of Durham, sent to Canada in 1838, urged the granting of responsible govt. He also urged the union of the 2 Canadas for the express purpose of making the French Canadians a minority and Anglicizing them. Responsible govt. was not won effectively until 1849. There was, however, no nation, only a string of provs. in the E and the Hudson's Bay Co. domain (Rupert's Land, B.C., and Vancouver Isl.) in the W. The leaders of the 2 Canadas in 1864 agreed to seek confederation of the provs. which would allow local separation of the Canadas under a common dominion govt. Already the Maritime Provs. were seeking union among themselves. Their Charlottetown Conference of 1864 was broadened to admit delegates from the Canadas. Two more conferences were held, the Quebec Conference later in 1864 and the London Conference, held in 1866 in the mother country, before the British North America Act in 1867 made confederation a fact. The new nation gained Rupert's Land from the Hudson's Bay Co. in 1869, and in 1871 B.C. agreed to come into the Union largely on the promise of a transcontinental railroad. Manitoba was made a prov. in 1870 and the Northwest Territories passed to dominion control. Prince Edward Isl. entered confederation 1873. Newfoundland did not enter until 1949. The prairie agr. empire bloomed in late 19th cent. Sasketchewan and Alberta were made provs. in 1905. The Klondike discovery in 1896 loosed in 1897–98 one of the wildest gold rushes of all time. Other mines were opened also, notably in the Laurentian Plateau. Large-scale development of hydroelectric resources helped to forward the growth of industry and urbanization. Canada played an important rôle in the First World War. After the First World War the farmers developed huge cooperatives (very thorough-going in Nova Scotia, very large in scale in the Prairie Provs.) and also took to radical political means—notably Social Credit and the Socialistic Co-operative Commonwealth Federation. The nation was again of vital importance in the Second World War. Despite great difficulties, Canada emerged from the war with enhanced prestige as one of the major nations of the world, actively concerned in the affairs of the U.N.

Cañada, Córdoba prov., Argentina: see CAÑADA DE LUQUE.

Canadá, Bolivia: see CHORRILLOS.

Canada, village (1940 pop. 1,135), Pike co., E Ky., in the Cumberlands, 5 mi. SW of Williamson, W.Va., in bituminous-coal-mining and timber area.

Cañada, La, Santiago del Estero prov., Argentina: see LA CAÑADA.

Cañada, La, Mexico: see EL MARQUÉS.

Canada, Lower: see QUEBEC, city.

Canada, Upper: see ONTARIO.

Cañada de Calatrava (känyä'dhä dä käläträ'vä), town (pop. 430), Ciudad Real prov., S central Spain, on railroad and 10 mi. SSW of Ciudad Real; cereals, olives, grapes; cement mfg.

Cañada de Gómez (gō'mĕs), city (pop. estimate 10,000), ⊙ Iriondo dept. (□ 1,240; 1947 census 52,760), S Santa Fe prov., Argentina, 45 mi. WNW of Rosario; rail junction, mfg. and agr. center (wheat, flax, corn, livestock). Vegetable-oil refinery, tannery; mfg. of buttons, shoes, cardboard. Site of a civil war battle in 1861.

Cañada del Hoyo (dĕl oi'ō), town (pop. 1,046), Cuenca prov., E central Spain, in the Serranía de Cuenca, 14 mi. ESE of Cuenca; cereals, beans, potatoes, stock; flour milling.

Cañada de Luque (dā lōō'kā), town (pop. estimate 500), N Córdoba prov., Argentina, 45 mi. N of Córdoba; corn, wheat, livestock. Sometimes called Cañada.

Cañada Honda (ōn'dä). **1** Village (pop. estimate 300), S San Juan prov., Argentina, 32 mi. S of San Juan; rail junction; wine making, lime quarrying. **2** Village (pop. estimate 300), N San Luis prov., Argentina, at E foot of Sierra de San Luis, on a tributary of the Río Quinto and 33 mi. NE of San Luis; gold-washing center; stock raising.

Cañadajuncosa (känyä"dhähōōnkō'sä), town (pop. 848), Cuenca prov., E central Spain, 36 mi. S of Cuenca; saffron, cereals, grapes, sheep.

Canada Lake, resort village, Fulton co., E central N.Y., on Canada L. (c.3 mi. long), in the Adirondacks, 12 mi. NW of Gloversville.

Cañada Morelos, Mexico: see MORELOS, Puebla.

Canadarago Lake (kăn"dùrô'gō, kă"nùdù–), Otsego co., central N.Y., 23 mi. SSE of Utica; 4 mi. long, c.1 mi. wide; drains S through outlet to Susquehanna R. Richfield Springs (health resort) is near by.

Cañada Rosquín (rōskēn'), town (pop. estimate 2,000), S central Santa Fe prov., Argentina, 85 mi. NW of Rosario; agr. (wheat, flax, barley) and livestock center; dairy products.

Cañadas, Mexico: see VILLA OBREGÓN, Jalisco.

Cañada Seca (sā'kä), town (pop. estimate 600), central Mendoza prov., Argentina, on Atuel R. (irrigation area) and 18 mi. ESE of San Rafael; agr. center (barley, alfalfa, wine, fruit, livestock). Wine making, dried-fruit processing, food canning.

Cañada Verde, Argentina: see VILLA HUIDOBRO.

Canadensis (kănùdĕn'sĭs), resort village, Monroe co., NE Pa., in Pocono Mts., 14 mi. N of Stroudsburg.

Canadian (kùnā'dēùn), county (□ 885; pop. 25,644), central Okla.; ⊙ El Reno. Intersected by North Canadian and Canadian rivers. Stock raising, dairying, agr. (wheat, oats, barley, alfalfa, corn, sorghums). Industries at El Reno and Yukon. Oil field in NE. Includes U.S. Fort Reno, and a school for Cheyenne and Arapaho Indians. Formed 1890.

Canadian. 1 Town (pop. 277), Pittsburg co., SE Okla., 18 mi. NNE of McAlester, near Canadian R., in agr. area; cotton ginning. **2** Town (pop. 2,700), ⊙ Hemphill co., extreme N Texas, in high plains of the Panhandle, c.45 mi. NE of Pampa, and on Canadian R.; trade, shipping, railroad center for wheat and cattle region; feed mills, grain elevators, cotton gins. Settled 1887 as railroad town, inc. 1908.

Canadian River, SW central U.S., rises in NE N.-Mex. in Sangre de Cristo Mts. near Colo. line, flows S and E through N.Mex., generally E through Texas Panhandle and Okla., to Arkansas R. in E Okla., 26 mi. SE of Muskogee; 906 mi. long; not navigable; drains □ 29,700. Receives North Canadian R. 27 mi. NE of McAlester (E Okla.). In N.Mex., 29 mi. WNW of Tucumcari, CONCHAS DAM, impounding Conchas Reservoir, is flood-control and irrigation project. River's valley across the prairie and high plains was followed by the Fort Smith–Santa Fe trail in mid-19th cent. River sometimes known as South Canadian.

Canadice Lake (kă'nùdĭs), Ontario co., W central N.Y., one of the Finger Lakes, bet. Hemlock L. (W) and Honeoye L. (E); c.3 mi. long.

Cañadón Grande, Sierra (syĕ'rä känyädōn' grän'dä), subandean range in S Chubut natl. territory, Argentina, SE of José de San Martín; c.40 mi. N–S; rises to c.4,000 ft.

Cañadón León (lā-ōn'), village (pop. estimate 500), ⊙ Río Chico dept. (1947 pop. 2,437), central Santa Cruz natl. territory, Argentina, on the Río Chico, at S foot of the Gran Meseta Central, and 120 mi. NW of Santa Cruz. Alfalfa-growing, sheep-raising center. Agr. experiment station. Airport.

Canajoharie (kă"nùjōhă'rē, –hâ'rē), village (pop. 2,761), Montgomery co., E central N.Y., on Mohawk R. and the Barge Canal, and 20 mi. WSW of Amsterdam; food packing, mfg. of paper products. Here are Van Alstyne House (1749), with historical collections, and a library and art gall. Settled c.1730 by Dutch and Germans; inc. 1829.

Canakkale (chänäk'kälĕ"), Turkish *Çanakkale*, province (□ 3,645; 1950 pop. 288,813), NW Turkey, on both sides of the Dardanelles; ⊙ Canakkale, on the Asiatic side. The European portion comprises GALLIPOLI PENINSULA and isl. of IMBROS. Agr.: wheat, beans, oats, barley. Asiatic portion, bordered W by Aegean Sea, N by Dardanelles, NE by Sea of Marmara, is drained by Kocabas, Gonen, and Kucuk Menderes (Scamander) rivers. Minerals: copper, lead, manganese, zinc, magnesite; coal and valonia also produced. The site of anc. Troy is on Aegean coast.

Canakkale, Turkish *Çanakkale,* town (1950 pop. 11,633) and fort, ⊙ Canakkale prov., NW Turkey, on Asiatic side of the Dardanelles, at its narrowest point, 22 mi. SW of and across from Gallipoli, 150 mi. WSW of Istanbul. Town has long been known for its pottery. Trade in wheat, rye. Minerals near by include manganese, magnesite, gold, asbestos; valonia derived from extensive oak forests. At near-by Abydos, Xerxes I crossed into Greece on a bridge of boats. The fort was bombarded by the British in the attack on Gallipoli, 1915. It is sometimes spelled Chanakkale and, formerly, Chanak Kallessi or Tchanak Kalessi; also formerly Kale Sultaniye.

Canakkale Bogazi, Turkey: see DARDANELLES.

Canala (kä'nälä'), village (dist. pop. 2,760), E New Caledonia, 60 mi. NW of Nouméa; coffee, livestock.

Canal d'Embranchement (känäl' dābrāshmä'), N Belgium, runs 27 mi. generally N–S, bet. Antwerp-

Turnhout Canal (at Turnhout) and Albert Canal (2.5 mi. NE of Tessenderloo). Crossed by Scheldt-Meuse Junction Canal 4 mi. NE of Mol.

Canal du Centre (känäl' dü sätr'ů), SW Belgium, runs 17 mi. generally ENE-WSW, bet. W end of Condé-Mons Canal (at Mons) and Charleroi-Brussels Canal (1 mi. SW of Seneffe). Serves Obourg, Houdeng-Aimeries, and Houdeng-Goegnies.

Canale (känä'lĕ), village (pop. 3,237), Cuneo prov., Piedmont, NW Italy, 7 mi. N of Alba.

Canale, Yugoslavia: see Kanal.

Canalejas del Arroyo (känälā'häs dhĕl äroi'ō), town (pop. 1,114), Cuenca prov., E central Spain, 29 mi. NW of Cuenca; olives, cereals, grapes, livestock. Gypsum quarrying.

Canal Fulton (fōōl'tůn), village (pop. 1,258), Stark co., E central Ohio, 13 mi. WNW of Canton and on Tuscarawas R.; trade center for agr. area; makes furniture, sporting goods.

Canal Governorate (settled area □ 133; pop. 246,770), NE Egypt, on N section of Suez Canal; ⊙ Port Said. Includes Ismailia and Qantara.

Canalou (kůnă'lōō), city (pop. 438), New Madrid co., extreme SE Mo., in Mississippi flood plain, 15 mi. NW of New Madrid.

Canal Point, village (pop. 1,022), Palm Beach co., SE Fla., 37 mi. WNW of West Palm Beach, on E shore of L. Okeechobee; truck, sugar cane.

Canals (känäls'), town (pop. 5,532), SE Córdoba prov., Argentina, 80 mi. SSE of Villa María; agr. center (corn, wheat, rye, sunflowers, livestock); dairy products, cement articles, furniture.

Canals, town (pop. 5,148), Valencia prov., E Spain, 4 mi. SW of Játiva; tanning, olive-oil processing, flour milling; mfg. of hose, soap; ships oranges. Alfonso de Borja (Borgia), later Pope Calixtus III, b. here.

Canal Winchester, village (pop. 1,194), on Fairfield-Franklin co. line, central Ohio, 13 mi. SE of Columbus, and on Little Walnut Creek, in grain, dairy, and fruit area; glass products.

Canal Zone, see: Panama Canal Zone.

Cañamares (känyämä'rĕs), town (pop. 973), Cuenca prov., E central Spain, 27 mi. NNW of Priego; beans, hemp, timber, resins, livestock.

Cañamero (känyämā'rō), town (pop. 2,843), Cáceres prov., W Spain, 28 mi. ESE of Trujillo; stock raising, cheese and olive-oil processing, flour milling; cereals, fruit, wine, cork.

Canandaigua (kănůndā'gwů), city (pop. 8,332), ⊙ Ontario co., W central N.Y., in Finger Lakes region, at N end and outlet of Canandaigua L., 25 mi. SE of Rochester; resort and farm trade center; mfg. (flour, chemicals, condiments, textiles, clothing, soap); agr. (grain, truck). Pickering treaty with the Six Nations was signed here (1794). City's Historical Society Mus. contains valuable historical documents; the courthouse was scene of the trial (1873) of Susan B. Anthony for voting. Site of a U.S. veterans' hosp. Settled 1789, inc. 1913.

Canandaigua Lake, W central N.Y., one of the Finger Lakes, 27 mi. SE of Rochester; c.15 mi. long, ½-1½ mi. wide. Squaw Isl. near its N end is a state reservation. Drains N through Canandaigua Outlet, which flows c.31 mi. NE, E, and N, past Canandaigua, becoming Clyde R. at Lyons.

Cananea (känänā'ä), city (pop. 11,006), Sonora, NW Mexico, in spur of Sierra Madre Occidental, on railroad and 45 mi. ESE of Nogales, Ariz.; alt. c.5,200 ft. One of the world's leading copper-mining centers; copper smelting. Also silver, lead, zinc, and gold deposits. Cattle raising. Airport. Has large American population.

Cananéia (känänĕ'yů), city (pop. 1,209), southernmost São Paulo, Brazil, port on Cananéia Isl. (in a tidal inlet of the Atlantic), near Paraná border, 125 mi. SW of Santos; grows rice, tropical fruit, manioc, sugar. Pop. largely Japanese. Formerly spelled Cananea.

Cana Point (kä'nä), E headland of E Saona Isl., off SE Hispaniola isl., at SW gate of Mona Passage; 18°7'N 68°34'W.

Cañar (känyär'), province (□ 1,277; 1950 pop. 95,838), S central Ecuador; ⊙ Azogues. Entirely in the Andes; watered by Naranjal or Cañar R. Climate is semitropical to temperate in the more settled regions, where corn, barley, potatoes, fruit, cattle, and sheep are raised. Near Azogues are gold, silver, copper, and mercury deposits. Coal mining at Biblián. Mfg. of Panama hats is main industry. Several remarkable Inca remains.

Cañar, town (1950 pop. 4,230), Cañar prov., Ecuador, in the Andes, on Pan-American Highway, on railroad and 24 mi. NNE of Cuenca, in cool mtn. valley where potatoes, corn, barley, and sheep are raised. Mfg. of woolen goods. Near by are the Ingapirca ruins of anc. Inca palace or temple.

Canara, district, India: see Kanara; South Kanara.

Canari (känä'rē), village (pop. 462), N Corsica, on W shore of Cape Corse peninsula, 12 mi. NNW of Bastia; asbestos mining.

Canaries, village (pop. 910), W St. Lucia, B.W.I., 8 mi. SW of Castries; sugar, coconuts; fishing.

Canaries Current, cold ocean current in the Atlantic, off NW coast of Africa. Branching S from the N Atlantic Drift in lat. of the Azores, it sweeps SW along the Saharan coast of SW Morocco and Sp. West Africa, then veers W in lat. of Senegal toward the Cape Verde Isls. It is the N hemisphere counterpart of the Benguela Current off SW Africa.

Canaro (känä'rô), village (pop. 546), Rovigo prov., Veneto, N Italy, near Po R., 11 mi. SSW of Rovigo, in hemp-growing region; soap factory.

Canarreos, Los (lōs känärā'ōs), archipelago off SW Cuba, in the Gulf of Batabanó, a chain of numerous keys extending for c.60 mi. along N and E shores of the Isle of Pines.

Cañar River, Ecuador: see Naranjal River.

Canarsie (kůnär'sē), SE N.Y., a section of E Brooklyn borough of New York city, on Jamaica Bay.

Canary Islands (kůnâ'rē), Sp. *Islas Canarias* (ē'släs känä'ryäs), perhaps the anc. *Fortunatae Insulae*, archipelago (□ 2,808 or 2,912; pop. 680,-294) off NW Africa in the Atlantic, belonging to Spain and consisting of 7 major isls. divided into 2 provs.—Las Palmas prov. (the isls. of Lanzarote and adjacent islets, Fuerteventura, and Grand Canary) and Santa Cruz de Tenerife prov. (the isls. of Tenerife, Palma, Gomera, and Hierro). Alegranza Isl. (NE) is c.680 mi. SW of Cádiz; Fuerteventura (E) is 65 mi. W of Cape Juby (Yubi) on coast of Sp. Morocco. The archipelago extends c.300 mi. E-W and 120 mi. N-S, bet. 27°37'N 17°57'W (Restinga Point, Hierro) and 29°25'N 13°29'W (Point Delgada, Alegranza). Entirely of volcanic origin (geologically related to the Azores and Madeira), the isls. are mostly mountainous, having steep coasts and presenting a succession of elevated plains, luxuriant valleys, active and extinct craters, lava fields, and deserts. They rise in the Pico de Teide (c.12,200 ft.) to highest elevation on Sp. soil. Catastrophic eruptions have occurred frequently, as late as 1824-25. There are no rivers. The isls. have long been famed for their mild year-round climate, which has little seasonal change; mean temp. in Las Palmas is 80°F. in summer and 57°F. in winter. Rainy period Nov.-Feb., but water is scarce. The dry, hot winds blowing from Africa are a great menace to vegetation, and large tracts, especially in E section, are practically deserts. Fauna and flora are remindful of North Africa. In more moist areas, forests (pine, laurel, oak, cedar, dragon trees) abound. Their fine scenery and healthful climate have made the Canaries one of the most popular winter resorts for Europeans. Agr. products, chiefly tropical, are varied, among them bananas, sugar cane, tobacco, tomatoes, coffee, cochineal, walnuts, citrus fruit, winter vegetables, almonds, cotton, medicinal plants, potatoes, cereals, grapes. Wine, once a particular product of the isls., has long since declined, following a blight of the vines. Goats, sheep, and cattle are raised. Camels and mules are used as beasts of burden. The surrounding seas abound in fish, and fish salting and canning are among the chief industries. Also mfg. of silk, embroidery; processing of local produce. Mineral deposits include salt, sulphur, iron, pumice. The Canary Isls. are strategically situated on cross-roads of transatlantic shipping. The 2 major ports of Las Palmas (with Puerto de la Luz) and Santa Cruz de Tenerife are important fueling and communications centers, where pleasure cruisers call regularly. Other leading cities are the bishopric and univ. town of La Laguna, La Orotava, and Icod on Tenerife; Santa Cruz de la Palma on Palma; Arrecife on Lanzarote. Originally inhabited by the Guanches, believed to be of Berber stock, these isls. were known to the Phoenicians, Greeks, Carthaginians, Romans, and Moors. By the end of the 15th cent. Spain had acquired them. The Norman Jean de Béthencourt began (1407-17) their conquest for Spain. About 1480, Pedro de Vera occupied Grand Canary, and soon after Tenerife and Palma were taken by Alonso Fernández de Lugo. They later became part of the Sp. crown. French, Dutch, and British attempts to invade the isls. were repelled. During such an attempt (1797) Nelson lost his arm. In 1927 the Canaries were divided into 2 provs. The aboriginal pop. has been entirely absorbed by the dominant Sp. element, but interesting archaeological remains are preserved, among them as yet undeciphered inscriptions. The prime meridian was for a long time drawn through Hierro isl., then thought to be exactly 20° W of meridian of Paris.

Cañas (kä'nyäs), town (1950 pop. 1,459), Guanacaste prov., NW Costa Rica, on Inter-American Highway and 25 mi. SE of Liberia; commercial center; rice and lumber milling; grain, coffee, livestock.

Cañas, town (pop. 1,206), Pinar del Río prov., W Cuba, on railroad and 3 mi. E of Artemisa; tobacco, sugar cane, fruit.

Canas, province, Peru: see Yanaoca.

Cañas, Las, Argentina: see Las Cañas.

Cañas, Las, Chile: see Las Cañas.

Canas de Senhorim (kä'nůsh dĭ sĭnyô'rēm), village (pop. 1,761), Viseu dist., N central Portugal, on railroad and 11 mi. S of Viseu; wine, olives, corn, rye. The sulphur springs of Felgueira are just SE.

Cañas Dulces (kä'nyäs dōōl'sĕs), village (dist. pop. 2,424), Guanacaste prov., NW Costa Rica, 8 mi. NNW of Liberia; corn, beans, cacao, livestock.

Canaseraga (kănůsůrô'gů), village (pop. 693), Allegany co., W N.Y., on Canaseraga Creek and 11 mi. NNW of Hornell.

Canaseraga Creek, W central N.Y., rises SE of Nunda, flows generally SE, past Canaseraga, then generally N, past Dansville, to the Genesee NE of Mount Morris; c.45 mi. long.

Cañasgordas (känyäsgôr'däs), town (pop. 1,967), Antioquia dept., NW central Colombia, 20 mi. NW of Antioquia; alt. 4,245 ft. Coffeegrowing, lumbering. Gold placer mines near by; also silver, copper, iron, coal deposits. Founded 1782.

Canasí or **Arcos de Canasí** (är'kōs dā känäsē'), town (pop. 1,042), Matanzas prov., W Cuba, near coast, on railroad and 14 mi. W of Matanzas, in sugar- and fruitgrowing region. The Puerto sugar central is just E, and the refinery and central of Elena is 5 mi. SE.

Canasmoro (känäzmō'rō), town (pop. c.2,000), Tarija dept., S Bolivia, on road and 5 mi. NNW of San Lorenzo; vineyards, fruit, grain.

Canastota (kănůstō'tů), village (pop. 4,458), Madison co., central N.Y., 21 mi. E of Syracuse, in onion-growing area; makes silverware, bakelite, wool, and metal products, machinery, canned foods, fertilizers. Inc. 1835.

Canastra, Serra da (sĕ'rů dä känä'strů), range on central Brazilian plateau, W Minas Gerais, extending c.150 mi. N-S from Goiás border to the upper Rio Grande, separating the Triângulo Mineiro (W) from main part of Minas Gerais state, and forming watershed bet. headstreams of Paraná and São Francisco R. (which rises here). Rises to 5,900 ft. in S. Diamonds found here.

Canastraeum, Cape, Greece: see Kanastraion, Cape.

Canatlán (känätlän'), town (pop. 3,450), Durango, N Mexico, on interior plateau, on railroad and 35 mi. NNW of Durango; stock-raising and agr. center (cereals, alfalfa, fruit).

Cañaveral (känyäväräl'), village (pop. 2,619), Cáceres prov., W Spain, 22 mi. N of Cáceres; mfg. of wax, chocolate, flour products; olive-oil processing; cereals, fruit.

Canaveral, Cape (kůnă'vůrůl), E Fla., on the Atlantic, seaward extremity of a barrier isl. sheltering Banana R. lagoon, 15 mi. NE of Cocoa; site of lighthouse (28°28'N 80°33'W) and military proving ground for guided missiles.

Cañaveral de León (känyävärăl' dhā lāōn'), town (pop. 910), Huelva prov., Spain, in Sierra Morena, near Badajoz prov. border, 8 mi. N of Aracena; olives, acorns, cork, timber, livestock. Has lime quarries and kilns.

Cañaveras (känyävä'räs), town (pop. 1,310), Cuenca prov., E central Spain, 25 mi. NW of Cuenca; olives, cereals, saffron, pepper, livestock; flour.

Canavieiras (känävyā'růs), city (pop. 5,587), SE Bahia, Brazil, port on the Atlantic at mouth of the Rio Pardo, and 60 mi. S of Ilhéus, in piassava- and cacao-growing area. Exports diamonds (found in Salobro area, 40 mi. NW), marble, lumber. Has airport on Salvador-Rio de Janeiro route. Formerly spelled Cannavieiras.

Cañazas (känyä'säs), village (pop. 734), Veraguas prov., W central Panama, near San Pablo R., amid S outliers of continental divide, 23 mi. NW of Santiago. Coffee, livestock; gold mining. Dist. pop. is largely Guaymie Indian.

Canbelego (kănbŭlē'gō), town (pop. 115), central New South Wales, Australia, 325 mi. NW of Sydney; mining center (gold, copper).

Canberra (kăn'bůrů, kănbĕ'rů, kăm'-), city (pop. 15,156), ⊙ Commonwealth of Australia, in Australian Capital Territory, in SE part of New South Wales, Australia, 150 mi. SW of Sydney, 300 mi. NE of Melbourne, 85 mi. W of Jervis Bay, on wide plain surrounded by hills. Seat of Parliament House, Duntroon Military Col., Canberra Univ. Col. (1929), Natl. Mus. of Australian Zoology, Mt. Stromlo observatory. Site of city chosen 1908, founded 1913; ⊙ Commonwealth transferred 1927 from Melbourne to Canberra. Built on plans by Walter Burley Griffin of Chicago.

Canby. 1 City (pop. 2,173), Yellow Medicine co., SW Minn., near S.Dak. line and Lac qui Parle R. 36 mi. WSW of Granite Falls, in agr. area; trade center for farm cooperatives; dairy products. Platted 1876, inc. as village 1879, as city 1905. **2** City (pop. 1,671), Clackamas co., NW Oregon, 8 mi SW of Oregon City and on Willamette R.; poultry.

Canby Mountain, peak (13,466 ft.) in San Juan Mts., San Juan co., SW Colo., E of Silverton.

Cancale (käkäl'), town (pop. 3,116), Ille-et-Vilaine dept., W France, on English Channel and 8 mi. E of Saint-Malo; bathing resort known for its oysters Old town (atop cliff) overlooks port where oyster beds are exposed at low tide.

Cancañiri (kängkänyē'rē), tin-mining settlement (pop. c.5,500), Potosí dept., W central Bolivia, at E foot of Cordillera de Azanaques, adjoining Catavi.

Cancellara (känchĕl-lä'rä), village (pop. 2,645), Potenza prov., Basilicata, S Italy, 9 mi. NNE of Potenza; meat and dairy products, wine.

Cancello (känchĕl'lô), village (pop. 1,529), Caserta prov., Campania, S Italy, on Volturno R. and 20 mi. NW of Naples; macaroni mfg.

Canche River (kāsh), Pas-de-Calais dept., N France, rises in Artois hills SE of Saint-Pol, flows 60 mi. W, past Hesdin and Montreuil (head of navigation), to the English Channel below Étaples.

Canchis, province, Peru: see SICUANI.

Canchungo, Port. Guinea: see TEIXEIRA PINTO.

Cancon (kākō'), village (pop. 542), Lot-et-Garonne dept., SW France, 10 mi. NNW of Villeneuve-sur-Lot; fruit preserving; prune and plum trade.

Cancuén River, Guatemala: see PASIÓN RIVER.

Canda (kän'dä), village (pop. 1,463), Rovigo prov., Veneto, N Italy, on Tartaro R. and 14 mi. WSW of Rovigo.

Candaba (kändä'bä), town (1939 pop. 3,019; 1948 municipality pop. 16,036), Pampanga prov., central Luzon, Philippines, on Pampanga R. and 10 mi. NE of San Fernando; agr. center (sugar cane, rice); fishing.

Candal (kändäl'), SW suburb (pop. 2,373) of Oporto, Pôrto dist., N Portugal, on left bank of Douro R. just W of Vila Nova de Gaia.

Candala (kändä'lä), town (pop. 600), in the Mijirtein, N Ital. Somaliland, port on Gulf of Aden, 50 mi. ENE of Bender Kassim; trade center (frankincense, myrrh, gum arabic); tunny fishing.

Candarli (chändärlŭ'), Turkish *Çandarlı*, village (pop. 1,993), Smyrna prov., W Turkey, 38 mi. NNW of Smyrna, on Gulf of Candarli.

Candarli, Gulf of, Turkish *Çandarlı*, inlet of Aegean Sea, in W Turkey, 30 mi. NW of Manisa; 14 mi. wide, 15 mi. long. Receives Bakir R.

Candarve (kändär'vā), town (pop. 721), Tacna dept., S Peru, at S foot of Tutupaca Volcano, on Locumba R. and 50 mi. E of Moquegua; cattle, sheep, mules. Sulphur deposits.

Candás (kändäs'), town (pop. 3,346), Oviedo prov., NW Spain, fishing port on Bay of Biscay, 6 mi. NW of Gijón; fish processing, boatbuilding, cider and champagne distilling. Sugar beets, vegetables; lumber; cattle raising. Parochial church has shrine.

Candé (kädā'), village (pop. 1,871), Maine-et-Loire dept., W France, on the Erdre and 19 mi. ESE of Châteaubriant; road center; tanning, woodworking. Peace treaty (1800) ending revolt of the Chouans was signed here.

Candeias (kändā'ūs). **1** Village, E Bahia, Brazil, near Todos os Santos Bay, on railroad and 20 mi. N of Salvador; center of recently discovered oil field; petroleum refining. **2** City (pop. 2,373), S central Minas Gerais, Brazil, on railroad and 22 mi. SSE of Formiga; agr. trade.

Candela (kändā'lä), town (pop. 6,518), Foggia prov., Apulia, S Italy, 23 mi. S of Foggia; mfg. (agr. machinery, fertilizer, cement).

Candela (kändā'lä), city (pop. 2,334), Coahuila, N Mexico, in E foothills of Sierra Madre Oriental, 16 mi. SW of Lampazos (Nuevo León); cereals, livestock.

Candelaria (kändälär'yä). **1** Town (pop. estimate 600), ⊙ Candelaria dept. (1947 pop. 41,198), S Misiones natl. territory, Argentina, on Paraná R. (Paraguay border) and 10 mi. SE of Posadas; agr. (maté, corn, rice). **2** or **La Candelaria** (lä), village (pop. estimate 400), ⊙ Candelaria dept. (□ 480; 1947 pop. 2,611), S Salta prov., Argentina, at W foot of the Sierra Candelaria (a minor subandean mtn. range), 95 mi. SSE of Salta, in agr. area; livestock raising; tanning. **3** Town (pop. estimate 500), N San Luis prov., Argentina, on railroad and 90 mi. NNE of San Luis; agr. center (grain, peanuts, fruit, livestock).

Candelária (kändĭlä'rēū), city (pop. 1,522), central Rio Grande do Sul, Brazil, 60 mi. E of Santa Maria; tobacco-growing center.

Candelaria (kändālä'ryä), village (pop. 918), Tenerife, Canary Isls., 10 mi. SW of Santa Cruz de Tenerife; cereals, cochineal, fruit, wine, bananas, tomatoes, potatoes, onions, livestock.

Candelaria. 1 Town (pop. 2,218), Atlántico dept., N Colombia, in marshy Caribbean lowlands, on Magdalena R. and 38 mi. SSW of Barranquilla; rice growing. **2** Town (pop. 1,300), Valle del Cauca dept., W Colombia, in Cauca valley, 10 mi. E of Cali; coffee, sugar cane, tobacco, cattle.

Candelaria, town (pop. 3,461), Pinar del Río prov., W Cuba, on Central Highway, on railroad and 45 mi. SW of Havana, in agr. region (sugar cane, tobacco coffee, corn, pineapples, cattle); mfg. of cigars.

Candelaria, town (pop. 460), Lempira dept., W Honduras, in Sierra de Congolón, 30 mi. SSE of Gracias, near Lempa R. (Salvador border); trade center; indigo, livestock.

Candelaria. 1 Town (1939 pop. 2,971; 1948 municipality pop. 21,116), Quezon prov., S Luzon, Philippines, 12 mi. SE of San Pablo, near railroad; agr. (coconuts, rice), fishing. **2** Town (1939 pop. 998; 1948 municipality pop. 7,167), Zambales prov., central Luzon, Philippines, near W coast, 45 mi. WNW of Tarlac; guano, phosphate rock.

Candelaria River, Campeche, SE Mexico, rises in Guatemala near international border, flows c.130 mi. NW and N, through tropical forest country, to the Laguna de Términos 38 mi. E of Carmen. Navigable for c.45 mi.; used for logging.

Candelario (kändālä'ryō), town (pop. 1,468), Salamanca prov., W Spain, 2 mi. SSE of Béjar; meat processing, paper mfg.; livestock, chestnuts, flax, lumber.

Candelaro River (kändĕlä'rō), Foggia prov., S Italy, rises in Apennine hills 5 mi. E of Serracapriola, flows 45 mi. SE, along base of Gargano promontory, to Gulf of Manfredonia 2 mi. S of Manfredonia.

Candeleda (kändālā'dhä), town (pop. 5,874), Ávila prov., central Spain, in Old Castile, at S foot of the Sierra de Gredos, 26 mi. NW of Talavera de la Reina, in fertile valley (forage, olives, cereals, vegetables, pepper, chestnuts, figs, oranges, tobacco, cotton); stock raising, lumbering, flour milling. Has ruins of anc. castle of the counts of Miranda. Near by is shrine.

Candelo (kändā'lō), village (pop. 2,667), Vercelli prov., Piedmont, N Italy, 3 mi. SE of Biella. Has 13th–15th-cent. fortifications.

Candia (kăn'dēū), Gr. *Herakleion* or *Iraklion* (both: ērä'klēōn), Lat. *Heracleum* (hĕrūklē'ŭm), city (1951 pop. 53,541), ⊙ Herakleion nome, Crete, port on Gulf of Candia of Aegean Sea, 75 mi. E of Canea; 35°20'N 25°9'E. Largest city of Crete and one of leading ports of Greece; trades in raisins, carobs, silk, wine, locust beans, olive oil. Soap is manufactured and exported. Airport. Has mus. of Minoan antiquities collected from near-by CNOSSUS. Its massive fortifications, arsenal, cathedral (seat of Gr. metropolitan) date from Venetian times. The anc. port for Cnossus, it was refounded 9th cent. A.D. by the Saracens. Candia was conquered 961 by Byzantium, was held (1300–1669) under Venetian rule until it passed to the Turks after a long siege. Heavily damaged in Second World War. Formerly also called Megalokastron.

Candia, island, Greece: see CRETE.

Candia, town (pop. 1,243), Rockingham co., SE N.H., 11 mi. NE of Manchester. Settled c.1743, inc. 1763.

Candia, Sea of, or **Sea of Crete** (krēt), Gr. *Kretikon Pelagos* or *Kritikon Pelagos*, deepest section of Aegean Sea, bet. Cyclades (N) and Crete (S); over 6,000 ft. deep.

Candia Lomellina (kän'dyä lōmĕl-lē'nä), village (pop. 1,943), Pavia prov., Lombardy, N Italy, near Sesia R., 8 mi. SW of Mortara; rice growing.

Candidius, Lake, Formosa: see JIHYÜEH LAKE.

Cândido Mota (kăn'dēdōō mô'tū), city (pop. 2,248), W São Paulo, Brazil, on railroad and 35 mi. WNW of Ourinhos; sawmilling, saddle making; coffee, rice, sugar cane.

Candijay (kändēhī'), town (1939 pop. 1,502; 1948 municipality pop. 15,658), E Bohol isl., Philippines, 45 mi. NNE of Tagbilaran; agr. center (rice, coconuts, hemp).

Candle, village (pop. 103), NW Alaska, on N side of Seward Peninsula, on Kiwalik R., near its mouth on Kotzebue Sound, 70 mi. SSE of Kotzebue; placer gold mining; center of game-fishing and hunting region. Has airfield, radio station, school. Scene of gold rushes, 1901 and 1906.

Candle Lake (□ 150), central Sask., 45 mi. NNE of Prince Albert; 12 mi. long, 7 mi. wide. Adjoined S by Torch L. (5 mi. long, 2 mi. wide). Drains E into Saskatchewan R.

Candler (kăn'lŭr), county (□ 251; pop. 8,063), E central Ga.; ⊙ Metter. Coastal plain agr. (cotton, corn, truck, tobacco, livestock) and timber area drained by Canoochee R. Formed 1914.

Candler, resort village (pop. c.300), Buncombe co., W N.C., in the Blue Ridge, 8 mi. WSW of Asheville.

Candlewood, Lake, SW Conn., power reservoir formed (1926) by dam in small Rocky R., near its mouth on the Housatonic, whose waters are pumped into lake by hydraulic plant; 15 mi. long; covers 6,000 acres. Summer resort; fishing.

Cando (kăn'dōō), city (pop. 1,530), ⊙ Towner co., N N.Dak., 30 mi. NNW of Devils Lake; grain elevator, creamery, livestock, poultry. Named 1884, inc. 1901.

Candon (kändōn'), town (1939 pop. 3,201; 1948 municipality pop. 22,362), Ilocos Sur prov., N Luzon, Philippines, 22 mi. SSE of Vigan, near W coast; agr. center (rice, sugar); sugar milling.

Candor (kăn'dŭr). **1** Village (pop. 802), Tioga co., S N.Y., on Catatonk Creek and 18 mi. SE of Ithaca; makes gloves; agr. (dairy products; poultry, grain). **2** Town (pop. 617), Montgomery co., central N.C., 26 mi. ESE of Albemarle; market center for peach-raising region; rug mfg.

Canduoc (kän'dwŭk'), village, Cholon prov., S Vietnam, 20 mi. SSW of Saigon; rice.

Candy, Ceylon: see KANDY.

Canea (kūnē'ū), Gr. *Chania* or *Khania* (both: khänyä'), nome (□ 926; pop. 126,093), W Crete, W of Mt. Leuka; ⊙ Canea. Agr. (citrus fruits, olives, wheat, vegetables); livestock products (meat, milk, cheese). Copper, lignite, and iron deposits. Fisheries. Main port, Canea, is on N shore; Sphakia and Palaiochora on S shore.

Canea, Gr. *Chania* or *Khania*, anc. *Cydonia* (sĭdō'nēū), city (1951 pop. 33,837), ⊙ Crete and Canea nome, W Crete, on Gulf of Canea of Aegean Sea, 170 mi. S of Athens; 35°31'N 24°2'E. Economic and political center, 2d largest city of Crete; trades in citrus fruits, carobs, wine, olive oil; livestock products (milk, cheese); extensive soap industry. Copper, iron ore, and lignite deposits near by. Airport. Seat of Gr. metropolitan. It has remains of Venetian fortifications, arsenal, galley-vaults, and public gardens. The anc. Cydonia was a Samian colony, conquered (69 B.C.) by the Romans. The city was occupied 9th cent. by the Saracens, and rebuilt after 1252 by Venice. It was captured 1645 by the Turks. Capital was moved here (1840) from Candia. Heavily bombed in Second World War.

Caneadea (kănūdē'ū), resort village, Allegany co., W N.Y., on Genesee R. at mouth of small Caneadea Creek, and 22 mi. NNW of Wellsville. About 2 mi. W, dam on creek impounds L. Rushford (c.2 mi. long).

Canegrate (kānĕgrä'tĕ), village (pop. 3,911), Milano prov., Lombardy, N Italy, 2 mi. S of Legnano; shoe factories.

Cane Grove, village (pop. 1,632), Demerara co., N Br. Guiana, in fertile lowlands near the Atlantic, 22 mi. SE of Georgetown; rice, sugar cane, fruit.

Canela (kănā'lū), city (pop. 2,224), NE Rio Grande do Sul, Brazil, on S slope of Serra do Mar, 50 mi. NNE of Pôrto Alegre; rail-spur terminus; wine-growing. Formerly spelled Canella.

Canela Alta (kănā'lä äl'tä), village (1930 pop. 870), Coquimbo prov., N central Chile, 20 mi. NW of Illapel; fruit, livestock.

Canelas (kănā'läs), town (pop. 534), Durango, N Mexico, in Sierra Madre Occidental, 55 mi. ENE of Culiacán (Sinaloa); silver, gold, lead mining.

Canella, Brazil: see CANELA.

Canelli (kānĕl'lē), village (pop. 3,852), Asti prov., Piedmont, NW Italy, on Belbo R. and 13 mi. S of Asti: wine, alcohol, barrels, hardware.

Canelones (kănĕlō'nĕs), department (□ 1,835; pop. 200,308), S Uruguay, on the Río de la Plata mouth, just N of Montevideo; ⊙ Canelones. Bounded W and N by Santa Lucía R. Mostly lowland, along whose coast are a string of notable beaches, such as Atlántida and La Floresta. Canelones is, apart from Montevideo, the most populous dept. in Uruguay. Almost entirely stock raising (cattle, sheep) and agr. (wheat, corn, flax, wine, olives). Granite is quarried at La Paz. Dept. was set up 1816.

Canelones, city (pop. 27,000), ⊙ Canelones dept., S Uruguay, on railroad and 25 mi. N of Montevideo; 34°32'S 56°16'W. Trading center in agr. region (grain, vegetables, cattle, sheep); flour and paper mills. Has industrial school. City was founded near by in 1774; moved to present site in 1783. For a short while (1828) it was seat of the Uruguayan govt. Formerly sometimes called Guadalupe.

Canelos (kănā'lōs), village, Napo-Pastaza prov., E central Ecuador, at E foot of the Andes, 10 mi. E of Puyo. Dominican mission.

Canena (kănā'nä), town (pop. 2,268), Jaén prov., S Spain, 10 mi. ESE of Linares; olive oil, cereals. Mineral springs.

Canencia (kănĕn'thyä), town (pop. 737), Madrid prov., central Spain, 35 mi. N of Madrid; rye, potatoes, livestock; flour milling.

Cane River or **Cane River Lake,** W central La., former main channel (until 1834) of Red R. in Natchitoches parish; branches from main stream NE of Natchitoches city, rejoins it opposite Colfax; c.65 mi. long. Natchitoches is on W bank. Known for good fishing; game preserve in its valley.

Cane River Falls, St. Andrew parish, SE Jamaica, scenic spot on small Cane R., and 6 mi. E of Kingston. Formerly a hideout of notorious bandits.

Canet de Mar (kănĕt'dhā mär'), town (pop. 4,225), Barcelona prov., NE Spain, on the Mediterranean, 8 mi. NE of Mataró; a center of the knit-goods industry; also laces, sandals, sails; cotton spinning; trades in wine, oranges, cereals.

Cañete (kănyā'tä), town (pop. 3,137), ⊙ Cañete dept. (□ 937; pop. 23,675), Arauco prov., S central Chile, on railroad and 20 mi. SE of Lebu; agr. center (grain, peas, beans, livestock); lumbering. One of Chile's oldest towns, it was founded 1557 by García Hurtado de Mendoza. Scene of Indian wars. Pedro de Valdivia was killed near by.

Cañete or **San Vicente de Cañete** (sän vēsĕn'tā dā), city (pop. 4,915), ⊙ Cañete prov. (□ 2,548; pop. 48,344), Lima dept., W central Peru, on coastal plain, near Cañete R., on highway, and 80 mi. SE of Lima. Cotton ginning, cotton-seed milling, mfg. of soap, oil, oil cakes. Cotton and sugar-cane growing in surrounding area. Connected by highway with its port Cerro Azul. Also called San Vicente and Pueblo Nuevo.

Cañete, town (pop. 1,612), Cuenca prov., E central Spain, in Serranía de Cuenca, 26 mi. E of Cuenca, surrounded by pine forests (timber, resins) and fine pastures. Cereals, saffron, livestock. Sulphur springs.

Cañete de las Torres (dhā läs tô'rĕs), town (pop. 6,317), Córdoba prov., S Spain, agr. center 4 mi. SE of Bujalance; olive-oil processing, flour milling; wool trade. Cereals, honey, livestock in area. Has Moorish remains.

Cañete la Real (lä rääl'), town (pop. 3,928), Málaga prov., S Spain, in SW outliers of the Sierra de Yeguas, 16 mi. NNE of Ronda, in agr. region (cereals, olives, livestock); flour milling, olive-oil pressing; mfg. of plaster, tiles, knit goods. Has mineral springs.

Cañete River, Lima dept., W central Peru, rises in Cordillera Occidental of the Andes 17 mi. WNW of Matucana, flows 120 mi. S and SW, past area of Yauyos and Lunahuaná, to the Pacific 4 mi. SSW of Cañete. Used for irrigation in lower course.

Canet lo Roig (kănĕt′ lō roig′, rôch′), town (pop. 1,973), Castellón de la Plana prov., E Spain, 12 mi. WNW of Vinaroz; olive oil, wine, cereals.

Caneva (kä′nĕvä), village (pop. 924), Udine prov., Friuli-Venezia Giulia, NE Italy, 2 mi. WNW of Sacile; silk mill. Has castle whose walls enclose an 11th-cent. church. Formerly Caneva di Sacile.

Caney or **El Caney** (ĕl känā′), town (pop. 1,296), Oriente prov., E Cuba, 4 mi. NE of Santiago de Cuba. Has iron mines. Site of fort stormed (1898) by American forces during Spanish-American War. San Juan Hill is just S.

Caney (kā′nē). **1** City (pop. 2,876), Montgomery co., SE Kansas, on affluent of Caney R. and 17 mi. W of Coffeyville, at Okla. line; small mfg. center (bottles, iodine products) in grain and livestock area. Shale pits, oil and gas wells near by. Founded 1871, inc. 1887. **2** Town (pop. 252), Atoka co., SE Okla., 20 mi. NNE of Durant, in agr. area.

Caney Fork, central Tenn., rises in W Cumberland co., flows 144 mi. W and NW to Cumberland R. near Carthage. Contains CENTER HILL DAM and GREAT FALLS DAM.

Caney River, in Kansas and Okla., rises in SE Kansas, flows S and SE into Osage co. in Okla., past Bartlesville, to Verdigris R. just NE of Tulsa; c.165 mi. long. Hulah Dam (hū′lū) (94 ft. high, 6,315 ft. long, including dikes; begun 1946 for flood control, water supply) is c.13 mi. NNW of Bartlesville; impounds Hulah Reservoir (capacity 295,000 acre-ft.).

Caneyville, town (pop. 377), Grayson co., W central Ky., 31 mi. N of Bowling Green, in agr. area.

Canezza (känĕ′tsä), village (pop. 227), Trento prov., Trentino-Alto Adige, N Italy, 7 mi. E of Trent; sausage factory.

Canfield, village (pop. estimate 150), S Ont., 20 mi. SSE of Hamilton; fruit. Just SE is railroad junction of Canfield Junction.

Canfield, village (pop. 1,465), Mahoning co., E Ohio, 7 mi. SW of Youngstown, in timber, coal, sandstone, and fruit area. Surveyed 1798.

Canfranc (känfrän′, Fr. kãfrã′), town (pop. 303), Huesca prov., NE Spain, in upper Aragon R. valley, in the central Pyrenees, 10 mi. N of Jaca; customs station on trans-Pyrenean railroad near Somport pass to France.

Cangallo (käng-gä′yō), city (pop. 990), ⊙ Cangallo prov. (□ 1,389; pop. 70,868), Ayacucho dept., S central Peru, on Pampas R. and 33 mi. S of Ayacucho (connected by highway); grain, sugar cane, livestock.

Cangamba (käng-gäm′bä), town (pop. 269), Bié prov., S central Angola, on road and 130 mi. S of Vila Luso.

Cangas (käng′gäs), town (pop. 4,774), Pontevedra prov., NW Spain, in Galicia, seaport on Vigo Bay, 4 mi. NW of Vigo; important fishing industries; boatbuilding. Wine and corn in area.

Cangas del Narcea (dhĕl när-thā′ä), town (pop. 2,431), Oviedo prov., NW Spain, on Narcea R. and 38 mi. WSW of Oviedo; meat processing, sawmilling; produces cereals, wine, apples, lumber, stock. Mineral springs. Iron and coal mines near by.

Cangas de Onís (dhā ōnēs′), city (pop. 1,932), Oviedo prov., NW Spain, 35 mi. E of Oviedo; corn, apples, hazelnuts, chestnuts, livestock, lumber. Coal mines near by. Has 12th-cent. bridge. Was (8th cent.) 1st seat of kings of Asturias.

Cangioc (kän′zhŏk′), town, Cholon prov., S Vietnam, 10 mi. S of Saigon; road center. Rice.

Canglong, Vietnam: see ANTRUONG.

Cangó, Paraguay: see GENERAL ARTIGAS.

Cango Berg (käng′gō bĕrkh′), mountain (6,645 ft.), S Cape Prov., U. of So. Afr., 14 mi. NE of Calitzdorp; 33°23′S 21°51′E; highest peak of central part of Swartberg range.

Cango Caves, S Cape Prov., U. of So. Afr., in the Great Swartberg range, 15 mi. N of Oudtshoorn; noted stalactite caverns, discovered 1780.

Cangrejal (käng-grāhäl′), peak (5,415 ft.) in Cordillera Dariense, central Nicaragua, 5 mi. NE of Matiguás.

Canguaretama (käng-gwärĭtä′mŭ), city (pop. 3,028), E Rio Grande do Norte, NE Brazil, near the Atlantic, 38 mi. S of Natal; saltworks; sugar, manioc, cotton. Airfield.

Canguçu or **Cangussú** (käng-gōōsōō′), city (pop. 1,611), S Rio Grande do Sul, Brazil, in the Serra dos Tapes, 35 mi. NW of Pelotas; road center. Hides, tobacco.

Canhotinho (känyŏŏtē′nyŏŏ), city (pop. 2,426), E central Pernambuco, NE Brazil, on railroad and 20 mi. E of Garanhuns; coffee, sugar, corn, cattle.

Caniçado (kŭnēsä′dŏŏ), village, Sul do Save prov., S Mozambique, on left bank of Limpopo R. and 110 mi. N of Lourenço Marques; cotton, corn, beans; cattle raising. Agr. station. Guijá (on opposite bank) is railhead of line to Lourenço Marques.

Canicatti (känēkät′tē), town (pop. 28,275), Agrigento prov., S central Sicily, 15 mi. SW of Caltanissetta, in agr. area (cereals, almonds, olives); rail junction; cement, soap mfg. Sulphur mines near by.

Canicattini Bagni (känēkät-tē′nē bä′nyē), town (pop. 9,827), Siracusa prov., SE Sicily, 13 mi. WSW of Syracuse, in agr. area (fruit, wheat, olives); canned peppers, glass mfg.

Canigao Channel (känēgä′ō, -gou′), Philippines, bet. SW tip of Leyte and NE Bohol, leading S from Camotes Sea to Mindanao Sea; 8 mi. wide at narrowest point.

Canigou, Massif du (mäsēf′ dü känēgōō′), spur of the E Pyrenees, Pyrénées-Orientales dept., S France, extending SW-NE from Sp. border bet. VALLESPIR (SE) and CONFLENT (NW) valleys. Its highest peak, Mont Canigou (9,137 ft.), 25 mi. SW of Perpignan, commands a splendid view. Iron is mined on its slopes at Batère, Taurinya, Escaro.

Canik, Turkey: see SAMSUN, province.

Canik Mountains (chänĭk′), N Turkey, S and SE of Samsun, extend 110 mi. ESE of the lower Kizil Irmak bet. Black Sea (N) and Kelkit R. (S), crossed by the lower Yesil Irmak; rise to c.6,000 ft. Town of Kavak on N slope. Copper and zinc in E.

Caniles (känē′lĕs), town (pop. 4,740), Granada prov., S Spain, 5 mi. SE of Baza; pottery and knit goods; olive-oil processing, flour and sugar milling. Cereals, sugar beets, almonds, wine in area.

Canillas (känē′lyäs), town (pop. 1,784), Madrid prov., central Spain, 4 mi. NE of Madrid (linked by tramway); grain growing; meat packing, mfg. of tiles and ceramics.

Canillas de Aceituno (dhā ä-thātōō′nō), town (pop. 1,976), Málaga prov., S Spain, 22 mi. NE of Málaga; olives, figs, raisins, oranges, livestock.

Canillas de Albaida (älvī′dhä), town (pop. 1,021), Málaga prov., S Spain, in coastal hills, 25 mi. ENE of Málaga; raisins, oranges, olives, cork, goats.

Canillejas (känēlyä′häs), town (pop. 1,567), Madrid prov., central Spain, 3 mi. E of Madrid; mfg. of lacquer, ceramics, liquor. Region produces carobs, chick-peas, cereals. Airfield.

Canillo (känē′lyō), village (pop. c.700), Andorra, on headstream of Valira R. and 6 mi. NE of Andorra la Vella; grazing.

Canimo Island (känē′mō) (□ 1), Camarines Norte prov., Philippines, in Philippine Sea, at W side of entrance to San Miguel Bay, just off SE Luzon, 7 mi. E of Daet.

Canin, Mount (kä′nēn), Slovenian *Kanin*, peak (8,481 ft.), in Julian Alps, on Italo-Yugoslav border, 12 mi. SSW of Tarvisio, Italy.

Canindé (känēndĕ′), city (pop. 2,461), N central Ceará, Brazil, 70 mi. SW of Fortaleza; cattle-raising center; cotton, sugar, maniçoba rubber. Talc quarries. Has 18th-cent. Capuchin church.

Canindé River, Piauí, NE Brazil, rises in the Serra dos Dois Irmãos near Pernambuco border, flows c.200 mi. NW to the Parnaíba at Amarante. Receives Piauí R. (left). Not navigable. Carnauba palms in valley.

Canino (känē′nô), village (pop. 3,443), Viterbo prov., Latium, central Italy, 19 mi. WNW of Viterbo. Has Farnese palace.

Canisbay (kă′nĭsbā), parish (pop. 1,365), NE Caithness, Scotland. Includes JOHN O' GROAT'S HOUSE.

Canisteo (kănĭstē′ō), village (pop. 2,625), Steuben co., S N.Y., on Canisteo R. at mouth of small Bennett Creek, and 5 mi. SE of Hornell; mfg. (advertising signs, textiles, clothing, cheese); timber; dairy products, poultry. Settled before 1790, inc. 1873.

Canisteo River, S N.Y., rises in W central N.Y. in area NW of Hornell, flows c.55 mi. generally S and SE, past Hornell, to Tioga R. 5 mi. SW of Corning.

Canistota (kă″nĭstō′tŭ), city (pop. 687), McCook co., SE S.Dak., 10 mi. SSE of Salem; livestock, grain. Clinic for bone diseases is here.

Canisy (känēzē′), village (pop. 237), Manche dept., NW France, 5 mi. SW of Saint-Lô. Damaged (July, 1944) in Allied Saint-Lô offensive of Second World War.

Cañizal (känyē-thäl′), town (pop. 1,399), Zamora prov., NW Spain, 20 mi. NE of Salamanca; lumber, cereals, wine.

Cañizares (känyē-thä′rĕs), town (pop. 624), Cuenca prov., E central Spain, 30 mi. N of Cuenca; cereals, resins, timber, livestock. Electrochemical industry (calcium carbide). Medicinal springs.

Canjáyar (käng-hī′är), town (pop. 2,602), Almería prov., S Spain, 20 mi. NW of Almería: olive-oil processing, sawmilling; cereals, fruit, wine, esparto. Ships grapes. Mineral springs. Lead and iron mines near by.

Canje River, NE Br. Guiana, rises near Du. Guiana border at 5°6′N 57°37′W, flows N c.150 mi. through forests (balata) to Berbice R. mouth on the Atlantic just below New Amsterdam. Narrow, but deep, it is navigable for c.50 mi.

Canjilon (kănhĭlōn′), village (pop. c.900), Rio Arriba co., N N.Mex., in foothills of San Juan Mts., 16 mi. SSE of Tierra Amarilla; alt. 7,800 ft. Trading point in sheep and agr. region, in Carson Natl. Forest.

Cankaya (chänkäyä′), Turkish *Çankaya*, city (pop. c.50,000), Ankara prov., central Turkey, on railroad and Cubuk R.; part of Ankara; textiles, mohair goats, vetch. Formerly Yenisehir.

Cankiri (chänkŭrŭ′), Turkish *Çankırı*, province (□ 3,507; 1950 pop. 218,289), N central Turkey; ⊙ Cankiri. Bordered on N by Ilgaz Mts.; drained by Kizil Irmak and Devrez rivers. Well forested. Copper, lignite, rock salt. Apples, grain, vetch; mohair goats. Formerly spelled Kangri.

Cankiri, Turkish *Çankiri*, anc. *Gangra*, town (1950 pop. 14,161), ⊙ Cankiri prov., N central Turkey, on railroad and 60 mi. NE of Ankara; rock salt and copper near by; apples, grain, vetch; mohair goats. The anc. Gangra, a town of Paphlagonia, later became a Roman city in Galatia. It was an early seat of the Christian church; synod held here in 4th cent. Formerly spelled Kangri, Kankari, Changra.

Canlaon, Mount (känläōn′), or **Malaspina** (mäläspē′nä), active volcano (8,088 ft.), N central Negros isl., Philippines, in Negros Occidental prov., Just W of Quezon; highest peak of isl. Also spelled Malaespina. Last erupted 1933.

Canley Vale, Australia: see CABRAMATTA AND CANLEY VALE.

Canlubang (känlōōbäng′), town (1939 pop. 8,308) in Calamba municipality, Laguna prov., S Luzon, Philippines, 28 mi. SSE of Manila; sugar milling. Airfield.

Canmore (kăn′môr), village (pop. estimate 750), SW Alta., near B.C. border, in Rocky Mts., on Bow R. and 12 mi. SE of Banff; alt. 4,296 ft.; coal mining. Oil and natural-gas deposits near by.

Canna, island (pop. 40), Inner Hebrides, Inverness, Scotland, 4 mi. NW of Rum; 5 mi. long, 1½ mi. wide; rises to 690 ft. in SE. Sanday is just off SE coast. Along W coast are iron deposits, affecting compasses of passing ships.

Cannae (kă′nē), anc. town of Apulia, S Italy, near mouth of the Aufidus (Ofanto R.), c.5 mi. NE of Canusium (CANOSA DI PUGLIA). Scene of Hannibal's decisive victory over Romans in 216 B.C.

Cannanore (kănŭnôr′), city (pop. 34,649), Malabar dist., SW Madras, India, port on Arabian Sea, 50 mi. NNW of Calicut; cotton-textile center; hosiery mfg.; exports coir, copra, pepper. An important center of trade with Persia and Arabia in 12th and 13th cent.; came under Portuguese in 1501, Dutch in 1656, and English in 1790. Formerly spelled Kananur. Baliapatam or Valarpattanam, on railroad (Azhikal station) and 4 mi. N, is timber depot; sawmilling, mfg. of plywood, matches. Promontory of Mt. Delly, 15 mi. NW, was 1st land in India sighted (1498) by Vasco da Gama. Agr. research station 17 mi. N, at village of Taliparamba.

Cannanore Islands, India: see LACCADIVE ISLANDS.

Cannara (kän-nä′rä), village (pop. 1,011), Perugia prov., Umbria, central Italy, 13 mi. SE of Perugia; biscuits, liquor.

Cannavieiras, Brazil: see CANAVIEIRAS.

Cannelburg, town (pop. 128), Daviess co., SW Ind., 28 mi. E of Vincennes, in agr. area.

Cannel City (kă′nŭl), village (1940 pop. 599), Morgan co., E Ky., 40 mi. ESE of Mt. Sterling city, in coal-mining and agr. area.

Cannelton (kă′nŭltŭn). **1** City (pop. 2,027), ⊙ Perry co., S Ind., on Ohio R. (ferry to Hawesville, Ky.) and c.50 mi. E of Evansville; shipping, mining, and mfg. center, in agr., coal, and clay area; makes clay products, cotton cloth, furniture, toys, caskets. Sandstone quarrying. Founded 1837. **2** Village (pop. 1,211, with adjacent Carbondale), Fayette co., S central W.Va., c.20 mi. SE of Charleston.

Cannes (kăn, kănz, Fr. kän), town (pop. 36,647), Alpes-Maritimes dept., SE France, 16 mi. SW of Nice; fashionable winter resort and summer watering place of the Fr. Riviera. Sheltered from land winds by the Estérel range (W), it is famed for its mild and healthy Mediterranean climate (mean winter temperature 50°F.), and for its luxuriant subtropical vegetation. Essential oil distilling, fruit candying. Modern town, extending c.4 mi. along Golfe de la Napoule to Croisette Cape (E; summer casino), has wide boulevards and numerous hotels. Old Cannes, just W of port, is topped by 16th-17th-cent. church and a medieval tower. Large suburb of Le Cannet is 2 mi. N on slopes of Provence Alps. The Îles de Lérins are just offshore. Cannes is known for its lavish carnival (mardi-gras) season, particularly for traditional "battle of flowers." At near-by Golfe-Juan, Napoleon landed (1815) on his return from Elba.

Cannes, Bayou (bī′ō kăn′), or **Bayou des Cannes** (bīōō dā kăn′), stream in S La., rises in Evangeline parish, flows c.50 mi. S, joining Bayou Nezpique to form Mermentau R. just above Mermentau. Navigable for 8½ mi. of its lower course. Receives Bayou Plaquemine Brule (navigable) near mouth.

Cannet, Le (lŭ känā′), N suburb (pop. 9,784) of Cannes, Alpes-Maritimes dept., SE France, on slopes of Provence Alps, overlooking Golfe de la Napoule of the Mediterranean; resort on Fr. Riviera.

Cannet-des-Maures, Le (-dā-mōr′), village (pop. 325), Var dept., SE France, 11 mi. SSW of Draguignan; bauxite mining.

Canneto (kän-nā′tô), village (pop. 380), Pisa prov., Tuscany, central Italy, 14 mi. SE of Cecina; lignite.

Canneto, Lipari Isls.: see LIPARI, island.

Canneto di Bari (dē bä′rē), town (pop. 4,534), Bari prov., Apulia, S Italy, 9 mi. S of Bari; wine, olive oil.

Canneto sull'Oglio (sōōlô′lyô), town (pop. 3,423), Mantova prov., Lombardy, N. Italy, on Oglio R. and 20 mi. W of Mantua; silk mills, toy factories.

Cannifton (kă′nĭftŭn), village, SE Ont., on Moira R., N suburb of Belleville.

Canning, village (pop. estimate 800), W central N.S., near SW shore of Minas Basin, 9 mi. NE of Kentville; fruitgrowing and dairying center.

Canning, India: see PORT CANNING.

Canning River, NE Alaska, rises in N Brooks Range near 68°37'N 146°37'W, flows c.130 mi. N to Camden Bay of Arctic Ocean at 70°3'N 145°35'W.

Canning River, SW Western Australia, rises in Darling Range 15 mi. E of Armadale, flows c.50 mi. generally NW, past Araluen, to estuary of Swan R. Canning Dam (near Araluen) is 218 ft. high, with reservoir 24 mi. in circumference.

Cannington, village (pop. 763), S Ont., on Beaverton R. and 15 mi. W of Lindsay; dairying, lumber.

Cannisnia, Lake, La.: see PIERRE, BAYOU.

Cannitello (kän-nētĕl'lô), village (pop. 1,150), Reggio di Calabria prov., Calabria, S Italy, port on Strait of Messina, 8 mi. N of Reggio di Calabria; silk mills.

Cannobio (kän-nô'byô), village (pop. 1,597), Novara prov., Piedmont, N Italy, port on W shore of Lago Maggiore, 20 mi. ESE of Domodossola, near Swiss border; candy, marmalade. Has palace (1291; remodeled 17th cent.) and church with paintings by Gaudenzio Ferrari.

Cannock (kă'nŭk), urban district (1931 pop. 34,585; 1951 census 40,927), central Stafford, England, 8 mi. NNE of Wolverhampton; mining center for the Cannock Chase coal area, a moorland region just E.

Cannon, county (□ 270; pop. 9,174), central Tenn.; ⊙ Woodbury. Drained by small affluents of Cumberland and Stones rivers. Livestock raising, dairying, lumbering, truck farming. Formed 1836.

Cannonball River, rises in SW N.Dak., flows ESE past Mott, receives Cedar Creek, and turns NE to the Missouri; 295 mi. long.

Cannondale, Conn.: see WILTON.

Cannon Falls, city (pop. 1,831), Goodhue co., SE Minn., on Cannon R. and 30 mi. S of St. Paul; farm trading point in grain, livestock, poultry area; dairy products, potatoes.

Cannon Mountain, N.H.: see PROFILE MOUNTAIN.

Cannon River, rises in lake region of Rice co., SE Minn., flows W, S, and NE, past Faribault, Northfield, and Cannon Falls, to Mississippi R. near Red Wing; 100 mi. long. Drains small lakes in upper course. Straight R. is tributary.

Cannonville, town (pop. 205), Garfield co., S Utah, 28 mi. SE of Panguitch and on Paria R.; alt. 6,000 ft.; agr.

Cannosa, Yugoslavia: see TRSTENO.

Cannouan Island (kănōōän'), islet (□ 2.6; pop. 481), central Grenadines, dependency of St. Vincent, B.W.I., 30 mi. S of Kingstown; 13°43'N 61°19'W. Cotton growing.

Cannstatt, Bad, Germany: see BAD CANNSTATT.

Cano or **El Cano** (ĕl kä'nō), town (pop. 1,258), Havana prov., W Cuba, on railroad and 8 mi. SW of Havana; sugar cane, vegetables, livestock.

Cano (kä'nōō), village (pop. 2,309), Portalegre dist., central Portugal, 29 mi. SSW of Portalegre; grain, olives, cork.

Caño, El, Panama: see EL CAÑO.

Canoa (känō'ä), officially San Miguel Canoa, town (pop. 4,652), Puebla, central Mexico, on Tlaxcala border, at SW foot of the Malinche, 10 mi. NE of Puebla; agr. center (grain, maguey, livestock).

Canoa, La, Guatemala: see LA CANOA.

Canoabo (känōä'bō), town (pop. 1,065), Carabobo state, N Venezuela, 25 mi. WNW of Valencia; coffee, corn, sugar, fruit.

Canoas (känō'ŭs), city (pop. 11,463), E Rio Grande do Sul, Brazil, 10 mi. N of Pôrto Alegre (linked by railroad); meat-packing plants (hogs, cattle).

Canoas River, one of the headstreams of Uruguay R. in Santa Catarina, S Brazil, rises on W slope of the Serra do Mar, flows c.200 mi. W, joining the Pelotas SW of Campos Novos.

Canobie Lake (kă'nŭbē), SE N.H., resort lake near Salem, 5 mi. W of Haverhill, Mass.; 1.5 mi. long.

Canoe Lake (13 mi. long, 10 mi. wide), W Sask., 170 mi. N of North Battleford; 55°10'N 108°15'W. Drains into Churchill R.

Canoga Park (kŭnō'gŭ), suburban section of Los ANGELES city, Los Angeles co., S Calif., in San Fernando Valley, 11 mi. SW of San Fernando; residential; small farms. Has a school of agr.

Canoinhas (kä″nōē'nyŭs), city (pop. 3,800), N Santa Catarina, Brazil, near the Rio Negro (Paraná border), on rail spur, and 40 mi. W of Mafra; lumbering, hog raising, maté processing. Formerly called Ouro Verde.

Canomã River, Brazil: see CANUMÃ RIVER.

Canon (kă'nŭn), city (pop. 596), Franklin and Hart counties, NE Ga., 9 mi. W of Hartwell.

Canonbie, agr. village and parish (pop. 1,498), E Dumfries, Scotland, on Esk R. and 5 mi. SSE of Langholm. Near-by Holehouse Tower was stronghold of Johnny Armstrong of Gilnockie, notorious 16th-cent. highwayman and blackmailer.

Canonchet, R.I.: see HOPKINTON.

Canon City (kăn'yŭn), city (pop. 6,345), ⊙ Fremont co., S central Colo., on Arkansas R., at mouth of ROYAL GORGE, and 35 mi. WNW of Pueblo; alt. 5,333 ft. Trade center for fruit-growing and mining region; livestock, poultry, truck and dairy products; mfg. (beverages, cement); coal, gold, silica. Mus. and state penitentiary are here. Front Range is just N of city, Wet Mts. just S. Laid out 1859, inc. 1872. Grew as gold-mining point.

Canonja, La (lä känōn'hä), village (pop. 1,193), Tarragona prov., NE Spain, 4 mi. WNW of Tarragona; wine, olive oil, fruit.

Canonsburg (kă'nŭnz–), borough (pop. 12,072), Washington co., SW Pa., 20 mi. SW of Pittsburgh. Bituminous coal-mining center; tin plate, steel, metal products, pottery; gas, oil; fruit, grain, potatoes. Whisky Rebellion began here 1794. Settled 1773, laid out 1787, inc. 1802. Log Academy (1780), oldest school bldg. W of the Alleghenies, is here.

Canoochee (kŭnōō'chē), town (pop. 62), Emanuel co., E central Ga., 9 mi. ENE of Swainsboro.

Canoochee River, SE Ga., rises N of Swainsboro, flows c.100 mi. SE to Ogeechee R. 15 mi. WSW of Savannah.

Cano Peak, Cape Verde Isls.: see FOGO.

Canopus (kŭnō'pŭs), anc. city of Egypt, 10 mi. NE of Alexandria, on Abukir Point, W of Abukir Bay near mouth of what was the westernmost (Canopic) mouth of the Nile, long since silted up. Believed to have been built by the Spartans and named in honor of Canopus, one of their sea pilots, buried here on the return of Menelaus to Greece. In Ptolemaic and Roman times it was noted for resorts and Hellenistic temples.

Canora (kănô'rŭ), town (pop. 1,205), E Sask., near Whitesand R., 30 mi. N of Yorkton; lumber and flour milling, dairying.

Caños (kä'nyōs), SW suburb (pop. 1,902), of Vigo, Pontevedra prov., NW Spain; fish processing, boatbuilding, flour- and sawmilling.

Canosa di Puglia (känô'zä dē pōō'lyä), anc. *Canusium*, town (pop. 28,163), Bari prov., Apulia, S Italy, near Ofanto R., 13 mi SW of Barletta; wine, liquor, olive oil, cheese, pottery. Has 11th-cent. cathedral with fine bronze doors and tomb of Bohemond, and Roman remains (walls, amphitheater). Noted under Romans for its wool and its vases (found in near-by tombs). Roman army fled to Canusium after its disastrous defeat (216 B.C.) at near-by CANNAE.

Canossa (känôs'sä), village (pop. 50), Reggio nell'Emilia prov., Emilia-Romagna, N central Italy, 12 mi. SW of Reggio nell'Emilia. Has ruined castle where, in 1077, Emperor Henry IV performed penance before Pope Gregory VII.

Canourgue, La (lä känōōrg'), village (pop. 905), Lozère dept., S France, in the Causse de Sauveterre, 15 mi. WSW of Mende; wool spinning, cheese making, leatherworking.

Canova (kŭnō'vŭ), town (pop. 340), Miner co., E S.Dak., 9 mi. S of Howard, near branch of Vermillion R.; dairy products, livestock, grain.

Canóvanas, Puerto Rico: see LOÍZA.

Canow, Poland: see SIANOW.

Canowindra (kŭnoun'drŭ), town (pop. 2,271), SE central New South Wales, Australia, 150 mi. WNW of Sydney; dairying center; sheep, wheat, corn.

Canrobert (kărôbâr'), village (pop. 2,890), Constantine dept., NE Algeria, on railroad and 45 mi. SE of Constantine, near the Tarf depression; wheat growing.

Cansahcab (känsäkäb'), town (pop. 2,476), Yucatan, SE Mexico, on railroad and 35 mi. ENE of Mérida; henequen center.

Canso (kăn'sō), town (pop. 1,418), E N.S., on the Atlantic, 130 mi. ENE of Halifax, near entrance to Chedabucto Bay, near E extremity of Nova Scotia peninsula; 45°21'N 61°W. Fishing port and transatlantic-cable terminal. Settled in early 17th cent., it was fortified by the British c.1720. Inc. 1910.

Canso, Cape, promontory on islet of Andrew, just off E extremity of Nova Scotia peninsula, 5 mi. ESE of Canso; 45°18'N 60°56'W.

Canso, Strait of, or **Gut of Canso,** channel (17 mi. long, 2 mi. wide), separating Cape Breton Isl. from Nova Scotia mainland and leading from the Atlantic to Northumberland Strait. Port Hawkesbury and Mulgrave are chief towns on it.

Canta (kän'tä), town (pop. 1,624), ⊙ Canta prov. (□ 1,762; pop. 28,670), Lima dept., W central Peru, in Cordillera Occidental of the Andes, on highway, and 55 mi. NE of Lima. Wheat, corn, potatoes; cattle raising.

Cantabrian Mountains (kăntā'brēŭn), Sp. *Cordillera Cantábrica* (kôrdēlyä'rä käntä'brēkä), major mountain range in N Spain, extending c.300 mi. E-W from the Pyrenees along the Bay of Biscay to the GALICIAN MOUNTAINS (sometimes considered a spur of the Cantabrians). An imposing, largely forested wall, the mts. traverse the Basque Provs., Santander prov., and Asturias, and form a forbidding barrier bet. the sea and the great central plateau (Meseta). They rise in the Picos de Europa (massif), with the Torre (or Peña) de Cerredo, to 8,687 ft. Among other high peaks are the Peña Vieja (8,573 ft.) and Peña Labra (7,136 ft.). There are several parallel subranges and spurs, namely the Sierra de Roñadoiro (NW) and the Leon Mts. (SW). Difficult of accessibility, they are crossed by several high, often snowbound passes, such as PAJARES, Reinosa, and Orduña. Drained by Ebro R. (SE). The Cantabrians are rich in minerals, chiefly iron and coal, and supply hydroelectric power to the coastal region. On the lower slopes cereals and grapes are grown and livestock grazed. The range, though geologically of the same origin as the Pyrenees, is generally classified as a separate formation.

Cantabrian Sea, Spain: see BISCAY, BAY OF.

Cantábrica, Cordillera, Spain: see CANTABRIAN MOUNTAINS.

Cantábrico, Mar, Spain: see BISCAY, BAY OF.

Cantabrigia, England: see CAMBRIDGE.

Cantagalo (käntŏogä'lōō), city (pop. 2,396), E central Rio de Janeiro state, Brazil, on railroad and 25 mi. NE of Nova Friburgo; dairying center; ships coffee, cattle. Marble quarries. Formerly spelled Cantagallo.

Cantal (kätäl'), department (□ 2,231; pop. 186,843), in Auvergne, S central France; ⊙ Aurillac. A mountainous region occupied by the volcanic Massif du Cantal (rising to 6,096 ft. at the Plomb du Cantal), bounded by Monts de Cézallier (N), Planèze (W), Montagnes de la Margeride (SW), and Monts d'Aubrac (S), which form S part of Auvergne Mts. Drained by the Dordogne and its tributaries (Rhue, Maronne, Cère), the Alagnon (W), and the Truyère (S). Wheat, rye, potatoes, fruits cultivated in high valleys and around chief towns. Cattle raising and dairying (mfg. of blue cheese) carried on extensively. Coal mined near Champagnac-les-Mines. Dept. has hot springs (Chaudes-Aigues) and several mountain resorts (Le Lioran, Vic-sur-Cère). Chief towns: Aurillac, Saint-Flour. Pop. decreasing because of migration to industrial cities.

Cantal, Massif du (mäsēf' dü), in Massif Central, S central France, covering central portion of Cantal dept.; an extinct volcano (base diameter 35 mi.) considerably eroded by streams (Cère, Jordanne, Rhue, Alagnon) which form a radial drainage pattern. The highest points on the crater rim are Plomb du Cantal (6,096 ft.), 16 mi. W of Saint-Flour, and Puy Mary (5,863 ft.), 21 mi. WNW of Saint-Flour. Massif traversed SW–NE by road and railroad which pass through a tunnel near Le Lioran. On its slopes are several cheese-mfg. villages (Salers, Saint-Cernin, Thiézac), a spa (Vic-sur-Cère), and the towns of Aurillac (SW) and Murat (E). Massif forms part of Auvergne Mts.

Cantalapiedra (kän″täläpyādh'rä), town (pop. 2,334), Salamanca prov., W Spain, 27 mi. ENE of Salamanca; chocolate mfg.; livestock, cereals, vegetables, wine.

Cantalejo (käntälā'hō), city (pop. 3,520), Segovia prov., central Spain, 24 mi. NNE of Segovia; agr. center (cereals, hemp, grapes, livestock); lumbering, hunting, flour milling; mfg. of cement articles, naval stores, sieves.

Cantalpino (käntälpē'nō), town (pop. 1,823), Salamanca prov., W Spain, 19 mi. ENE of Salamanca; cereals, sugar beets, wine.

Cantamayec (käntämīĕk'), town (pop. 862), Yucatan, SE Mexico, 9 mi. SW of Sotuta; henequen, sugar cane, fruit.

Cantanhede (käntänyā'dĭ), town (pop. 3,126), Coimbra dist., N central Portugal, on railroad and 13 mi. NW of Coimbra; agr. trade (wine, livestock, cereals, lumber); pottery mfg.

Cantaura (käntou'rä), town (pop, 2,666), Anzoátegui state, NE Venezuela, 60 mi. SSE of Barcelona; agr. center (cotton, cacao, corn, sugar cane, cattle).

Cantavir or **Chantavir** (both: chän'tävēr), Serbo-Croatian *Čantavir*, Hung. *Csantavér* (chŏn'tŏvār), village (pop. 11,006), Vojvodina, N Serbia, Yugoslavia, 13 mi. SSE of Subotica, in the Backa; rail terminus.

Cantel (käntĕl'), town (1950 pop. 1,666), Quezaltenango dept., SW Guatemala, on Samalá R. and 5 mi. SE of Quezaltenango; alt. 7,890 ft. Cotton-milling center; flour milling.

Canteleu (kätŭlû'), W suburban commune (pop. 4,330) of Rouen, Seine-Inférieure dept., N France, on right bank of the Seine; includes residential Canteleu, industrial Bapeaume-lès-Rouen (cotton milling and dyeing), and Dieppedalle-Croisset (mfg. of dyes and tanning extracts, paper milling).

Canterbury, municipality (pop. 99,396), E New South Wales, Australia, 8 mi. WSW of Sydney, in metropolitan area; mfg. center (knit goods, shoes); brass foundries, brickyards.

Canterbury, Latin *Cantuaria*, county borough (1931 pop. 24,446; 1951 census 27,778), E Kent, England, at foot of the North Downs, on Great Stour R. and 55 mi. ESE of London; 51°16'N 1°6'E. Anc. spiritual center of Great Britain and seat of archbishopric of Canterbury. The Roman *Durovernum Cantiaciorum*, it became the Saxon *Cantwaraburh*, and was capital of anc. kingdom of Kent. In 597 St. Augustine arrived here from Rome to convert the English; he was consecrated at Arles as "Bishop of the English," and became 1st archbishop of Canterbury and primate of all England. The abbey he founded has been replaced by a later bldg., known as St. Augustine Abbey. The early cathedral was burned several times, and subsequently rebuilt; the present bldg. dates from 11th-15th cent. After murder of Thomas à Becket (1170), and the penance of Henry II, Canterbury became major pilgrimage center; stories of pilgrims are celebrated in Chaucer's *Canterbury Tales*. Notable names connected with building of present cathedral are Lanfranc, Anselm, and William of

Sens. The great 15th-cent. tower is 235 ft. high. The cathedral contains tombs of Henry IV and of Edward the Black Prince. A tablet commemorates spot of murder of Thomas à Becket. Surrounding bldgs., including a library, destroyed in severe Ger. air raids (1942), but the cathedral received only blast damage. There are remains of anc. city walls; St. Martin's church, the "Mother Church of England," established before arrival of St. Augustine; Hosp. of St. Thomas, an old pilgrims' hostel; and several old inns. Christopher Marlowe, b. here, attended King's School. Industries include tanning, flour milling, concrete mfg.

Canterbury, provincial district (□ 13,940; pop. 246,848), E S.Isl., New Zealand; chief city is Christchurch. Canterbury Plains occupy large area; Southern Alps, with forested slopes, in W. Principal wheat center of New Zealand; other products: frozen meat, wool, dairy foods. Chief port is Lyttelton. Area roughly corresponds to Canterbury land dist.

Canterbury. 1 Farming town (pop. 1,321), Windham co., E Conn., bet. Little and Quinebaug rivers, 13 mi. NNE of Norwich. Has early 19th-cent. house in which Prudence Crandall had school for Negro girls, 1833–34. Site of Moses Cleaveland's birthplace is marked. Settled c.1690, inc. 1703. **2** Town (pop. 627), Merrimack co., S central N.H., on the Merrimack just N of Concord. Once flourishing Shaker village established here, 1792.

Canterbury Bight, inlet (115 mi. wide) of S Pacific, E S.Isl., New Zealand; Banks Peninsula at NE end; Timaru on SW shore. Receives Rakaia R.

Cantho (kän'tŭ'), town (1936 pop. 16,500), ⊙ Cantho prov. (□ 900; 1943 pop. 441,000), Vietnam, in Cochin China, on Bassac R. (ferry) in Mekong delta, 80 mi. SW of Saigon; important rice-growing center; fruit and coconuts (oil extraction, soap factory), rice milling, sawmilling, cigarette mfg. Experimental rice-growing station. Airport. A former Khmer dist., occupied (18th cent.) by Annamese.

Cantiano (käntyä'nô), town (pop. 1,199), Pesaro e Urbino prov., The Marches, central Italy, 18 mi. S of Urbino; marmalade, sirup, millstones.

Cantigny (kätēnyē'), village (pop. 102), Somme dept., N France, 4 mi. WNW of Montdidier. Captured by Americans in May, 1918. Monument commemorates 1st offensive operation of an American division in First World War.

Cantilan (käntē'län), town (1939 pop. 7,129; 1948 municipality pop. 20,519), Surigao prov., on NE coast of Mindanao, Philippines, 45 mi. SE of Surigao; copra; mining.

Cantillana (käntēlyä'nä), town (pop. 5,491), Seville prov., SW Spain, on Guadalquivir R. and 17 mi. NE of Seville; agr. center (cereals, grapes, olives, beet sugar, cotton, timber, livestock). Sawmilling, flour milling.

Cantimpalos (käntēmpä'lōs), town (pop. 1,083), Segovia prov., central Spain, 9 mi. N of Segovia; cereals, carobs, cattle; meat packing.

Cantin, Cape (kätē'), headland of W Fr. Morocco, on the Atlantic, 17 mi. N of Safi; 32°33'N 9°17'W. Lighthouse.

Cantley, agr. village and parish (pop. 406), SE Norfolk, England, on Yare R. and 10 mi. ESE of Norwich; beet-sugar refining.

Canto do Buriti (kăn'tōō dōō bōōrētē'), city (pop. 697), S central Piauí, Brazil, 110 mi. S of Floriano.

Canton (kăn"tŏn', kăn'tŏn"), Chinese *Kwangchow* or *Kuang-chou* (both: gwäng'jō'), city and independent municipality (□ 98; pop. 1,413,460), ⊙ Kwangtung prov., S China, port on Canton R. at N edge of its delta, c.700 mi. SW of Nanking; 23°7'N 113°16'E. Main commercial and industrial city of S China; mfg. of steel, machinery, chemicals (sulphuric acid, soda), cement, cotton and silk textiles, sugar, matches, paper, furniture. Handicraft industries produce china-, copper-, and lacquer-ware, and jade and ivory engraving. A major transportation center, Canton is the terminus of important railroads—Wongsha station (in W suburbs) for Hankow, Tashatow station (in E suburbs) for Kowloon (Hong Kong), and Shekwaitong station (in Fati) for Samshui—and is a junction point of air lines and river routes. Extensive docks and shipyards line both banks of Canton R., accessible since 1949 for deep-draught ships. Main section of city, on left (N) bank, includes the old city (walled until 1921) with govt. offices and public bldgs., the adjoining (S) new city, and the commercial and residential suburbs of Saikwan (W), Namkwan (S), and Tungkwan (E). Across Canton R. are the industrial suburbs of HONAM (S) and FATI (SW), included in Canton municipality. Industries are also concentrated in NW suburb of Saitsun (sī'tsōōn'), Mandarin *Hsi-ts'un*. The former foreign residential and business concession of Shameen (shä'mēn'), Mandarin *Shamien*, is an isl. in Canton R. off W suburbs. After 1921, when the city walls were torn down, the city was rebuilt in modern fashion. Canton has several higher educational institutions, including Sun Yat-sen univ. and Lingnan univ., and a memorial hall to Sun Yat-sen. Part of China since 3d cent. B.C., Canton was originally named Nanhai [Chinese,=southern sea] and received its present name in 3d cent. A.D. After contacts with Hindu and Arab merchants in 10th cent., it became the 1st Chinese port regularly visited by European traders, who corrupted its name from Kwangtung to Canton. Portugal secured a trade monopoly in 1517, but factories were later also established by the British in 1684 and by the Dutch and French in 18th cent. It was the scene of Chinese-British incidents (1841, 1856) that led to the 1st and 2d Opium Wars. Following occupation (1856–61) by British and French, Canton granted the Shameen isl. concession to foreign business and trade. Its early commercial prosperity was, however, affected by the phenomenal growth of the deepwater port of Hong Kong during 2d half of 19th cent. Canton was an active revolutionary center in 1911 and produced the Kuomintang under the leadership of Sun Yat-sen. From here, the Nationalist armies advanced N in middle 1920s to establish a govt. in Nanking. The city gained considerably in importance following completion (1936) of Canton-Hankow RR. During Second World War, it was held 1938–45 by the Japanese. In 1949 it passed to Chinese Communist control. Canton became a municipality under provincial jurisdiction in 1930 and has been since 1947 directly under the central govt. It was officially called PUNYÜ, 1913–35.

Canton (kăn'tŭn). **1** Town (pop. 3,613), Hartford co., NW central Conn., on Farmington R. and 11 mi. NW of Hartford; agr. (tobacco, dairy products). Mfg. at Collinsville village (pop. 2,078), whose edge-tool and metal-products industry began 1826. Settled 1737, inc. 1806. **2** Town (pop. 2,716), ⊙ Cherokee co., NW Ga., 33 mi. N of Atlanta and on Etowah R., at end of Allatoona Reservoir; mfg. (overalls, chenille products, marble monuments); poultry processing. Inc. 1833. **3** City (pop. 11,927), Fulton co., W central Ill., 25 mi. WSW of Peoria; trade and industrial center for rich agr. region (corn, wheat, livestock, poultry; dairy products); bituminous-coal mines. Mfg. (farm machinery, wood products, overalls). Founded 1825, inc. 1849. **4** City (pop. 771), McPherson co., central Kansas, 13 mi. E of McPherson, in wheat, livestock, and oil area. **5** Town (pop. 746), Oxford co., W Maine, on the Androscoggin and 14 mi. SE of Rumford, in farming, recreational area; wood, leather products. **6** Town (pop. 7,465), including Canton village (pop. 4,739), Norfolk co., E Mass., on Neponset R. and 15 mi. SSW of Boston; woolens, rubberized fabrics, food products, machine parts, radio and electric apparatus. Inc. 1797. State hosp. school for physically handicapped. **7** Village (pop. 459), Fillmore co., SE Minn., near Iowa line, 12 mi. SE of Preston; corn, oats, barley, potatoes. **8** City (pop. 7,048), ⊙ Madison co., central Miss., 23 mi. NNE of Jackson; trade and processing center in agr., truck, and timber area; furniture, lumber. Has fine ante-bellum homes. Inc. 1836. **9** City (pop. 2,490), Lewis co., NE Mo., on Mississippi R. and 30 mi. N of Hannibal; agr. (grain, livestock); mfg. (buttons, brooms). Culver-Stockton Col. Settled 1827. **10** Village (pop. 4,379), ⊙ St. Lawrence co., N N.Y., on Grass R. and 16 mi. SE of Ogdensburg, in agr. area (dairy products, poultry, potatoes, hay); food processing; summer resort. Seat of St. Lawrence Univ., with a state agr. and technical school. Frederic Remington b. here. Settled 1799, inc. 1845. **11** Town (pop. 4,906), Haywood co., W N.C., 16 mi. WSW of Asheville and on Pigeon R., in lumber and farm area; pulp and paper mfg. center. **12** Village, Pembina co., N.Dak.: see HENSEL. **13** City (pop. 116,912), ⊙ Stark co., E central Ohio, 20 mi. SSE of Akron; important iron- and steel-processing center, with steelworks and rolling mills, and a large plant making roller bearings; oil refinery. Also produces Diesel and gas engines, electric cleaners, rubber products, brick, enamelware, meat products, clothing, chemicals, furniture. Fire-clay quarrying, coal mining. Was home of William McKinley, who is buried here. Laid out 1806; inc. as town in 1822, as city in 1854. **14** Town (pop. 959), Blaine co., W central Okla., 17 mi. NW of Watonga, in agr. area (grain, livestock); dairying, cotton ginning. Has Cantonment school for Indian children. Near by is Canton Reservoir on North Canadian R. **15** Borough (pop. 2,118), Bradford co., N Pa., 31 mi. NNE of Williamsport; paper boxes, clothes hangers. Settled c.1796, inc. 1864. **16** City (pop. 2,530), ⊙ Lincoln co., SE S.Dak., 18 mi. S of Sioux Falls and on Big Sioux R. and Iowa state line; blocks and tiles; dairy products, livestock, poultry, grain. Normal school is here. Annual winter-sports tournament. Founded 1860. **17** Town (pop. 881), ⊙ Van Zandt co., NE Texas, 35 mi. WNW of Tyler, in cotton, truck area; cottonseed oil; chick hatchery.

Canton, Wales: see CARDIFF.

Canton, Poulo (pōōlō' kätō'), Annamese *Culao Re*, Vietnam island (3 mi. long, 1 mi. wide) in South China Sea, off Cape Batangan; 15°23'N 109°7'E; lighthouse.

Canton Island, atoll (□ 3.5; pop. 81), largest of Phoenix Isls., S Pacific, 2,000 mi. SW of Hawaii; 2°49'S 171°40'W. American guano companies claimed Canton for U.S. under terms of the Guano Act (1856); in 1937 British also claimed it and built radio station here. Formally claimed (1938) by the U.S. and placed under Dept. of Interior; colonized (1938) by both British and Americans; placed (1939), along with Enderbury Isl., under condominium of the 2 nations for 50 years. It is used as transpacific air-line base.

Cantonment, village, Escambia co., NW Fla., 15 mi. NNW of Pensacola; vegetable packing.

Canton Reservoir, W central Okla., 3 mi. N of Canton; impounded by earth-fill dam (15,100 ft. long, 68 ft. high) on North Canadian R. For flood control and irrigation; capacity 390,000 acre-ft.

Canton River, Chinese *Yüeh Kiang* or *Yüeh Chiang* (both: yüĕ'jyäng'), or **Pearl River,** Chinese *Chu Kiang* or *Chu Chiang* (both: jōō'jyäng'), S Kwangtung prov., China, at E side of Canton River Delta; 110 mi. long. It is the main navigation channel linking Canton to Hong Kong and the sea. Formed at Canton by union of rivers rising N of the city and of waterways rising in West R.–North R. confluence at Samshui, it flows E and S, past Canton and Whampoa, to S.China Sea, forming large estuary (25 mi. wide) bet. Macao (W) and Hongkong (E). At head of estuary, the mouth of the river channel is called BOCA TIGRIS. Main ports on estuary are Tangkiakwan (Chungshankong) and Macao (W), Taiping and Namtow (E). Receives East R. (right), and the waters of North and West rivers through the network of streams and canals of Canton River Delta. The bar at Boca Tigris was dredged and the river opened in 1949 to ocean-going vessels.

Canton River Delta or **Canton Delta,** extensive alluvial area (□ c.2,890; pop. 8,983,487) of S Kwangtung prov., China, bet. Canton (N) and Macao (S), and bet. CANTON RIVER (E) and main West R. branch (W). It is formed at Samshui by junction of WEST RIVER and NORTH RIVER and is intersected by network of streams or canals flowing generally SE from West R. to Canton R. One of chief economic regions of S China, it has a pop. density of 3,100 per sq. mi. Mainly agr. (rice, tobacco, tea, fruit); sericulture. Chief industries are silk and cotton milling, and mfg. of paper, matting, fans, firecrackers. Main urban centers are Canton, Namhoi, Samshui, Punyü, Shuntak, Chungshan, Macau.

Cantoria (käntōr'yä), town (pop. 1,275), Almería prov., S Spain, on Almanzora R. and 40 mi. NE of Almería; knit-goods mfg., olive-oil processing, flour milling, marble cutting. Cereals, wine, livestock. Has anc. church.

Cantrall (kăn'trŭl), village (pop. 145), Sangamon co., central Ill., 9 mi. N of Springfield.

Cantril, town (pop. 353), Van Buren co., SE Iowa, near Mo. line, 32 mi. SE of Ottumwa.

Cantù (käntōō'), town (pop. 10,314), Como prov., Lombardy, N Italy, 5 mi. SSE of Como; furniture mfg. center; silk textiles, lace, hardware, sausage. Has woodworking school.

Cantuaria, England: see CANTERBURY.

Cantwaraburh, England: see CANTERBURY.

Cantwell, village (pop. 66), S central Alaska, E of Mt. McKinley Natl. Park, 30 mi. S of Nenana, on Alaska RR; gold mining; supply point for Valdez Creek placer dist.

Cantyre, Scotland: see KINTYRE.

Canudos (känōō'dōōs), town (pop. 438), N Bahia, Brazil, on Vasa Barris R. and 75 mi. NE of Senhor do Bonfim; silver-bearing lead deposits; sheep raising. Scene of Euclides da Cunha's *Os Sertões*.

Cañuelas (kä"nyŏōwä'läs), town (pop. 7,419), ⊙ Cañuelas dist. (□ 461; pop. 14,356), NE Buenos Aires prov., Argentina, 38 mi. SSW of Buenos Aires; agr. center (flax, rye, alfalfa, livestock); dairying (casein), flour milling.

Canumã River (känōōmä'), Amazonas, Brazil, a right tributary of the Madeira, rises on Mato Grosso border, flows c.350 mi. N to the Madeira near village of Canumã (80 mi. SE of Manaus). Its upper course is called Sucunduri. Sometimes spelled Canomã.

Canusium, Italy: see CANOSA DI PUGLIA.

Canutama (känōōtä'mŭ), city (pop. 580), S central Amazonas, Brazil, on Purus R. and 370 mi. SW of Manaus; rubber.

Canute (kŭnōōt'), town (pop. 355), Washita co., W Okla., 6 mi. E of Elk City, in agr. area; cotton ginning.

Canutillo (kănūtē'yō), village (pop. 1,326), El Paso co., extreme W Texas, on the Rio Grande and 12 mi. NNW of El Paso; shipping point in irrigated agr. area; packed meat, canned foods.

Canvey Island, in the Thames, S Essex, England, 4 mi. WSW of Southend and opposite South Benfleet across Benfleet Creek; 5 mi. long, 2 mi. wide. Isl. is a residential urban dist. (1931 pop. 3,532; 1951 census 11,255).

Canwood, village (pop. 248), central Sask., 35 mi. WNW of Prince Albert; grain elevators.

Cany-Barville (kănē'-bärvēl'), village (pop. 1,061), Seine-Inférieure dept., N France, 22 mi. SW of Dieppe; market; hosiery mfg. Has Renaissance church.

Canyon, county (□ 580; pop. 53,597), SW Idaho; ⊙ Caldwell. Agr. area bordering on Oregon, bounded S by Snake R., and drained by Boise R. Dairy products, livestock; hay, sugar beets, fruit, truck. Deer Flat Reservoir, 5 mi. W of Nampa, is unit in Boise irrigation project, which includes most of co. Formed 1891.

Canyon, city (pop. 4,364), ⊙ Randall co., extreme N Texas, in high plains of the Panhandle, 15 mi. S of Amarillo, near junction of Palo Duro Creek and Tierra Blanca Creek to form Prairie Dog Town Fork of Red R.; alt. 3,566 ft. Market, shipping center for cattle and wheat area; seat of West Texas State Col. and Panhandle-Plains Historical Society Mus. Near-by state park in Palo Duro Canyon attracts tourists. Buffalo L. (recreational center) is SW. Settled 1892, inc. 1906.

Canyon City, town (pop. 508), ⊙ Grant co., NE central Oregon, 55 mi. N of Burns, near John Day R. in livestock area; alt. 3,194 ft.; beverages. Strawberry Mts. E.

Canyon de Chelly National Monument (dŭ shā') (□ 131; established 1931), NE Ariz., in Navajo Indian Reservation, 65 mi. NW of Gallup, N.Mex. Pre-Columbian ruins of Basket-Maker and Pueblo Indian cliff dwellings, in steep-walled red sandstone canyons (up to 800 ft. deep). Area now occupied by Navajo Indians.

Canyón de Perote, Peru: see SANTA RIVER.

Canyon Diablo (dēä'blō), gorge (225 ft. deep, 500 ft. wide), NE central Ariz., 30 mi. E of Flagstaff; formed by tributary of Little Colorado R.

Canyon Ferry Dam, Mont.: see MISSOURI RIVER.

Canyonville, city (pop. 861), Douglas co., SW Oregon, 20 mi. S of Roseburg.

Canzo (kän'tsô), village (pop. 2,130), Como prov., Lombardy, N Italy, 10 mi. ENE of Como; cutlery and sausage factories.

Caobal, Pico de (pē'kō dā koubäl'), mountain (6,525 ft.), Carabobo state, N Venezuela, in coastal range, 12 mi. NNE of Valencia.

Caobang (kou'bäng'), town (1936 pop. 9,000), ⊙ Caobang prov. (□ 2,600; 1943 pop. 230,500), N Vietnam, in Tonkin, near China border, on the Song Banggiang (left headstream of Li R.) and 120 mi. NNE of Hanoi; carpet mfg. Lignite mining, tin smelting (ore from Tinhtuc).

Caolanh (kou'lä'nyŭ), town, Sadec prov., S Vietnam, on left bank of the Mekong and 14 mi. NW of Sadec; rice.

Caonillas River (kounē'yäs), W central Puerto Rico, small affluent (c.25 mi. long) of the Arecibo, rises in the Cordillera Central. On it are L. Caonillas (artificial) and hydroelectric plant, adjoined NW by Dos Bocas reservoir and hydroelectric project. Caonillas Dam was dedicated Jan. 3, 1949.

Caorle (kä'ôrlĕ), village (pop. 2,100), Venezia prov., Veneto, N Italy, on the Adriatic, 29 mi. NE of Venice, near mouth of Livenza R. Flourishing seaport in early Middle Ages; bishopric from 598 to 1818. Has Romanesque cathedral (1038).

Caorso (käôr'sô), village (pop. 1,427), Piacenza prov., Emilia-Romagna, N central Italy, on Chiavenna R. and 9 mi. E of Piacenza; canned tomatoes; lime- and cementworks.

Cap [Fr.,=cape], for names beginning thus and not found here: see under following part of the name.

Cap, Le, Haiti: see CAP-HAÏTIEN.

Capac (kā'păk"), village (pop. 1,104), St. Clair co., E Mich., 25 mi. W of Port Huron, in farm area (truck, sugar beets, grain); dairying, flour milling. Inc. 1873.

Capaccio (käpät'chô), town (pop. 2,555), Salerno prov., Campania, S Italy, 25 mi. SSE of Salerno. Bishopric. Near by are ruins of Paestum.

Capacmarca, Peru: see CCAPACMARCA.

Capac-Urcu, Ecuador: see ALTAR, CERRO.

Capakcur, Turkey: see BINGOL, village.

Cap à l'Aigle (käp ä lĕ'glŭ), village (pop. 492), ⊙ Charlevoix East co., SE central Que., on the St. Lawrence and 2 mi. ENE of La Malbaie; resort.

Capanaparo River (käpänäpä'rō), in Venezuela and Colombia, rises at E foot of Cordillera Oriental in NE Colombia at about 72°W, flows c.350 mi. E, through llanos of Apure state in Venezuela parallel and S of Arauca R., to Orinoco R. at 7°3'N 67°7'W.

Capanema (käpänä'mŭ), city (pop. 3,094), E Pará, Brazil, on Belém-Bragança RR and 90 mi. ENE of Belém, in pioneer farming area; rubber, Brazil nuts, lumber. Limestone deposits.

Capannelle, Passo (päs'sô käpänĕl'lĕ), pass (4,209 ft.), S central Italy, bet. Gran Sasso d'Italia and Monti della Laga, near source of Vomano R., 8 mi. N of Aquila. On road bet. Teramo and Aquila.

Capannoli (käpän'nôlē), village (pop. 882), Pisa prov., Tuscany, central Italy, on Era R. and 17 mi. SE of Pisa; macaroni factory.

Capannori (käpän'nôrē), village (pop. 644), Lucca prov., Tuscany, central Italy, 3 mi. E of Lucca; paper mills, button and paint factories.

Capão Bonito (käpã'ō bōnē'tōō), city (pop. 2,563), S São Paulo, Brazil, 35 mi. SW of Itapetininga; coffee, sugar cane, cotton.

Caparaó, Serra do (sĕ'rŭ dōō käpäräô'), mountain range of E Brazil, part of the great coastal escarpment, extends c.50 mi. along Minas Gerais–Espírito Santo border. Contains the highest peak in Brazil, the Pico da Bandeira (9,462 ft.).

Caparra (käpä'rä), ruins in N Puerto Rico, adjoining Fort Buchanan, 4 mi. S of San Juan; 1st European settlement in Puerto Rico, founded 1508 by Ponce de León, abandoned 1521.

Caparrapí (käpäräpē'), town (pop. 1,111), Cundinamarca dept., central Colombia, on W slopes of Cordillera Oriental, 19 mi. NE of Honda; alt. 4,170 ft.; sugar cane, coffee, fruit, stock.

Caparroso (käpärō'sō), town (pop. 2,502), Navarre prov., N Spain, on Aragon R. and 19 mi. N of Tudela; sugar beets, wine, olive oil.

Capas (kä'päs), town (1939 pop. 2,741; 1948 municipality pop. 16,398), Tarlac prov., central Luzon, Philippines, on railroad and 11 mi. S of Tarlac; coconuts, rice, sugar cane.

Capatárida (käpätä'rēdä), town (pop. 1,100), Falcón state, NW Venezuela, near Gulf of Venezuela, 65 mi. WSW of Coro, in goat-grazing region. Known for tobacco. Former ⊙ Falcón state.

Capaya (käpī'ä), town (pop. 511), Miranda state, N Venezuela, in Caribbean lowlands, 45 mi. E of Caracas; cacao growing.

Capayán, Argentina: see CHUMBICHA.

Capbreton (käbrŭtō'), town (pop. 2,813), Landes dept., SW France, port on Bay of Biscay, 11 mi. N of Bayonne; bathing and health resort; fish canning. Sandy beach 6 mi. long. Near-by Hossegor (on a tidal lake) has summer colonies and oyster beds. Capbreton was important seaport at estuary of Adour R. until 1579, when the river's lower course was shifted to Bayonne.

Cap Chat (käp shä'), village (pop. 1,329), E Que., on N Gaspé Peninsula, on the St. Lawrence and 40 mi. ENE of Matane; lumbering, dairying.

Capcir or **Capsir** (both: käpsēr'), valley of upper Aude R. in Pyrénées-Orientales dept., S France, N of Mont-Louis; lumbering, rye and potato growing.

Cap-d'Ail (käp-dī'), town (pop. 2,567), Alpes-Maritime dept., SE France, on the Mediterranean, 7 mi. ENE of Nice, and just SW of Monaco; health and bathing resort of Fr. Riviera. Also called Cap-d'Aggio.

Cap de la Madeleine (käp dŭ lä mädlĕn'), city (pop. 11,961), S Que., on the St. Lawrence, at mouth of St. Maurice R., opposite Trois Rivières; paper, silk milling; mfg. of aluminum foil, clothing; metal-working, lumbering, dairying. Has chapel (1720), on site of 1659 structure, with Shrine of Our Lady of the Cape, since 1939 natl. place of pilgrimage.

Capdella (käp-dhĕl'yä), hamlet (pop. 111), Lérida prov., NE Spain, in the central Pyrenees, 21 mi. NNE of Tremp; 2 hydroelectric plants just S on Flamisell R.

Capdenac (käpdŭnäk'), village (pop. 107), Lot dept., SW France, on the Lot, opposite Capdenac-Gare, and 2 mi. SE of Figeac.

Capdenac-Gare (gär'), town (pop. 4,597), Aveyron dept., S France, near Lot R., 3 mi. SE of Figeac; railroad center; food processing and canning.

Capdepera (käp-dhāpā'rä), town (pop. 2,223), Majorca, Balearic Isls., near E coast, 40 mi. ENE of Palma; almonds, vegetables, cereals, stock; lobster fishing. Ermita or Artá caves are 3 mi. S.

Capdevila (käpdāvē'lä), village (pop. estimate 400), N Mendoza prov., Argentina, on railroad and 10 mi. N of Mendoza; cement mill.

Cape Bald, lobster-fishing village, SE N.B., on Northumberland Strait, 12 mi. E of Shediac.

Cape Barren Island, second largest island (□ 172; pop. 164) of Furneaux Isls., 21 mi. off NE coast of Tasmania and S of Flinders Isl.; 26 mi. long, 14 mi. wide; mountainous. Tin mines. Cape Barren Island, on NW coast, largest village.

Cape Bon Peninsula, Tunisia: see BON, CAPE.

Cape Breton (brĕ'tŭn), county (□ 972; pop. 110,703), E N.S., on E part of Cape Breton Isl.; ⊙ Sydney. Coal mining.

Cape Breton Island (land area □ 3,975; pop. 150,157), NE N.S., separated from mainland by 2-mi.-wide Strait of Canso (SW), and bounded by the Atlantic (S and E), Cabot Strait (N), and the Gulf of St. Lawrence (W). It is 110 mi. long, up to 80 mi. wide, bet. 45°33'–47°3'N 59°48'–61°32'W. Its extremities are Cape St. Lawrence (N), Cape Linzee (W), Bear Head (S), and Cape Breton (E). Central part of isl. is covered by the large tidal salt-water BRAS D'OR LAKE. Center and W parts of isl. are hilly, rising to 1,747 ft. in the Cape Breton Highlands National Park (□ 390), 40 mi. NNW of Sydney and circled by the Cabot Trail, a motor road. Coastline is deeply indented by numerous bays. Of the adjacent isls., Madame Isl. is the largest. Cape Breton Isl. is drained by Mira, Margaree, and several smaller rivers. Fishing and lumbering are important; in NE part of isl. the extensive coal fields in the Sydney–Glace Bay region support the steel industry there. Gypsum is quarried at Dingwall (N). Rail lines run to Sydney and also parallel the W coast to Inverness. Important towns are Sydney, North Sydney, Sydney Mines, Dominion, Glace Bay, Inverness, Port Hawkesbury, Louisburg, and Port Hood. At Point Tupper train ferry connects isl. with Mulgrave, on mainland. In 16th cent. isl. became North American base for European fishermen, mainly from Brittany. In 17th cent. Scotsmen arrived here, but the 1713 Treaty of Utrecht assigned isl. to France. It was renamed Île Royale, and absorbed part of Acadian pop. of Nova Scotia, which had become British. LOUISBURG (E) was French military and naval base (apart from 1745–49 British interregnum) until its capture by the British in 1758. In 1763 isl., formally ceded, along with Canada, to Britain by Treaty of Paris, became part of Nova Scotia; in 1784 it was made into separate prov., with ⊙ at Sydney; and in 1820 it was reincorporated in Nova Scotia.

Cape Charles, village (pop. 90), SE Labrador, on the Atlantic, on Cape St. Charles, 22 mi. NW of Misery Point, Belle Isle; 52°13'N 55°40'W; fishing; lumber.

Cape Charles, town (pop. 2,427), Northampton co., E Va., near tip (Cape Charles) of Eastern Shore peninsula, on harbor on Chesapeake Bay, 33 mi. NE of Norfolk. Port of entry; rail terminus; ferries to Old Point Comfort and Norfolk. Ships and cans fruit, vegetables, seafood; mfg. of radio parts. Resort (fishing, bathing). Inc. 1886.

Cape Clear Island, Ireland: see CLEAR ISLAND.

Cape Coast, town (pop. 23,061), ⊙ Gold Coast colony (S portion of GOLD COAST), on Gulf of Guinea, 38 mi. ENE of Takoradi; 5°5'N 1°16'W. Fisheries; coconuts, cassava, corn. Exports cacao. Modern hosp. Here are St. Augustine's, Adisadel (Church of England), and Mfantsipim (Methodist) colleges. Site of old Cape Coast castle and several forts (including Fort William; now lighthouse). Originally a Swedish post, founded 1652; passed later to Dutch. Ceded (1667) to British and became ⊙ Br. possessions on Gold Coast. Formerly called Cape Coast Castle.

Cape Cod, sandy peninsula (65 mi. long, 1–20 mi. wide) of glacial origin, comprising BARNSTABLE co., SE Mass.; bounded by Cape Cod Bay (N and W), Buzzards Bay (SW), Vineyard and Nantucket sounds (S), and the Atlantic (E); N tip of peninsula (Race Point) is at 42°4'N 70°15'W. Sandy and low (seldom exceeding 200 ft.); produces huge quantities of cranberries and some asparagus. Known particularly for its summer resorts and fishing towns (with good beaches and fine old houses), including Provincetown, Chatham, Barnstable, Falmouth, Bourne, Dennis, Truro, and villages of Hyannis, Buzzards Bay, Woods Hole. CAPE COD CANAL crosses peninsula's base. The name Cape Cod is attributed to Gosnold, who visited these shores in 1602. The Pilgrims put in at site of Provincetown, 1620.

Cape Cod Bay, S arm of Massachusetts Bay on Atlantic coast, E Mass.; enclosed by Cape Cod peninsula; c.25 mi. wide.

Cape Cod Canal, SE Mass., crosses Bourne town at base of Cape Cod, connecting Buzzards Bay with Cape Cod Bay; c.8 mi. long. Handles ocean-going craft. Built 1909–14; improved 1927. Part of Intracoastal Waterway.

Cape Colony, U. of So. Afr.: see CAPE OF GOOD HOPE PROVINCE.

Cape Comorin, town, India: see COMORIN, CAPE.

Cape Cruz, sugar-mill village, Cuba: see CABO CRUZ.

Cape Dorset, trading post, SW Baffin Isl., SE Franklin Dist., Northwest Territories, on small isl. at S extremity of Foxe Peninsula, on Hudson Strait; 64°14'N 76°33'W; radio station. Site of R.C. mission.

Cape Elizabeth, agr. and resort town (pop. 3,816), Cumberland co., SW Maine, just S of Portland and on S shore of Casco Bay. Lighthouse at tip of Cape Elizabeth peninsula. Settled c.1630, set off from Falmouth 1765.

Cape Fear River, SE N.C., formed 26 mi. WSW of Raleigh by junction of Deep and Haw rivers; flows generally SE past Fayetteville (head of navigation), Elizabethtown, and Wilmington (estuary head), and S to the Atlantic at Southport, near Cape Fear; c.200 mi. long. S estuary forms part of Intracoastal Waterway.

Cape Florida, Fla.: see KEY BISCAYNE.

Cape Girardeau (jĭrä'dō, jĭrä'dŭ), county (□ 576; pop. 38,397), SE Mo.; ⊙ Jackson. Bounded E by Mississippi R., crossed by Whitewater R.; drainage canals in S. Corn, wheat, hay; lumber; mfg. at Cape Girardeau city. Formed 1812.

Cape Girardeau, city (pop. 21,578), Cape Girardeau co., SE Mo., on Mississippi R. (bridged) and 100 mi. SSE of St. Louis. River traffic; commercial center of SE Mo. (shoes, cement, wood and tobacco products). Southeast Mo. State Col. Fort during Civil War. Founded 1793.

Cape Halkett, Alaska: see HALKETT, CAPE.

Cape Henry, Va.: see HENRY, CAPE.

Cape Island, S.C.: see ROMAIN, CAPE.

Cape Johnson Deep: see MINDANAO TRENCH.

Cape Krusenstern (krōō'zŭnstûrn), trading post, N Mackenzie Dist., Northwest Territories, on Cape Krusenstern, on Coronation Gulf, at E end of Dolphin and Union Strait; 68°23'N 113°55'W.

Capel (kā'pŭl), town (pop. 393), SW Western Australia, 110 mi. S of Perth, near E shore of Geographe Bay; butter.

Capel, residential town and parish (pop. 1,782), S Surrey, England, 6 mi. S of Dorking. Has 13th-cent. church.

Capela (käpä'lŭ). **1** City (pop. 3,332), E Alagoas, NE Brazil, on railroad and 25 mi. NW of Maceió, in sugar- and cotton-growing valley; sugar refining. Called Conceição do Paraíba, 1944–48. **2** City (pop. 4,499), N Sergipe, NE Brazil, on spur of Aracaju-Propriá rail line, and 28 mi. N of Aracaju; sugar milling, distilling. Ships sugar, cotton, livestock. Formerly spelled Capella.

Capel Dewi, Wales: see LLANDYSSUL.
Capel Fell (kā'pŭl), mountain (2,223 ft.) on Selkirk and Dumfries border, Scotland, 5 mi. E of Moffat. Ettrick Water rises here.
Capelinha (kăpĭlē'nyŭ), city (pop. 1,652), NE central Minas Gerais, Brazil, 65 mi. W of Teófilo Otoni; semiprecious stones. Formerly spelled Capellinha.
Capel Island (kā'pŭl), islet at entrance to Youghal Harbour, SE Co. Cork, Ireland, 5 mi. S of Youghal.
Capella, Brazil: see CAPELA, Sergipe.
Capellades (käpälyä'dhĕs), town (pop. 2,265), Barcelona prov., NE Spain, 5 mi. SE of Igualada; paper-mfg. center; also meat processing; wine, cereals.
Capelle, La, or **La Capelle-en-Thiérache** (lä käpĕl-ā-tyārăsh'), village (pop. 1,536), Aisne dept., N France, 10 mi. N of Vervins; wool spinning, brush mfg. Here Ger. armistice emissaries crossed Allied lines (Nov. 7, 1918).
Capelle aan den Ijssel (käpĕ'lŭ än dŭn ī'sŭl), Du. *Capelle aan den IJssel,* town (pop. 1,876), South Holland prov., W Netherlands, on Hollandsche Ijssel R. and 5 mi. ENE of Rotterdam; mfg. of synthetic fertilizer, woven mats, cement; shipbuilding, boiler making. Also spelled Kapelle aan den Ijssel.
Capelle-au-Bois, Belgium: see KAPELLE-OP-DEN-BOSCH.
Capellen (käpĕ'lŭn), village (pop. 94), SW Luxembourg, 7 mi. WNW of Luxembourg city.
Capellen-lez-Anvers, Belgium: see KAPELLEN.
Capellinha, Brazil: see CAPELINHA.
Capelongo (kŭpĭlông'gōō), village, Huíla prov., SW Angola, on upper Cunene R. and 110 mi. E of Sá da Bandeira.
Capels, mining village (1940 pop. 1,189), McDowell co., S W.Va., just N of Welch; semibituminous coal.
Capelulo, Wales: see PENMAENMAWR.
Cape May, county (□ 267; pop. 37,131), S extremity of N.J., occupying Cape May Peninsula (c.20 mi. long), bet. Atlantic Ocean and Delaware Bay; ⊙ Cape May Court House. Resorts on indented, isl.-dotted coast have been popular since mid-19th cent. Fisheries; agr. (truck, dairy products, poultry, fruit); mfg. (clothing, hats, rubber and concrete products, fertilizer, food products). Co. includes Belleplain State Forest and Great Cedar Swamp. Navigation canal across tip of peninsula built (1942–43) as part of N.J. section of Intracoastal Waterway. N part of co. drained by Tuckahoe R. Lighthouse at Cape May Point. Formed 1692.
Cape May or **Cape May City,** resort city (pop. 3,607), Cape May co., S N.J., near Cape May Harbor, at S end of Cape May Peninsula, 40 mi. SW of Atlantic City; canned goods, boats, soft drinks; fisheries; truck, poultry, dairy farming. Settled in 17th cent., inc. 1869. Important whaling port in early 18th cent.; summer resort before 1800; became very popular after mid-19th cent.
Cape May Court House, village (pop. 1,093), ⊙ Cape May co., S N.J., 30 mi. SW of Atlantic City; hosiery, agr. products (dairy, poultry, truck). Historical mus. here. Laid out 1703.
Cape May Harbor, S N.J., artificially enlarged bay (3 mi. long, ½ mi. wide) on Atlantic coast of Cape May Peninsula, just NE of Cape May city. Intracoastal Waterway channel enters from Jarvis Sound (N), connects WNW with Delaware Bay through Cape May Canal (1942–43) across S tip of peninsula.
Cape May Point, resort borough (pop. 198), Cape May co., S N.J., at tip of Cape May Peninsula, W of Cape May city. Near by is a lighthouse (38°56'N 74°58'W).
Cape Mount, county, Liberia: see GRAND CAPE MOUNT.
Capendu (käpädü'), village (pop. 1,361), Aude dept., S France, near the Aude, 11 mi. E of Carcassonne; winegrowing.
Cape Negro Island, islet, SW N.S., at entrance of small Negro Harbour, 18 mi. S of Shelburne; 43°31'N 65°21'W.
Capens, Maine: see DEER ISLAND, Piscataquis co.
Cape of Good Hope Province, commonly called **Cape Province,** Afrikaans *Kaapland* (käp'länt), province (□ 277,169; pop. 4,053,848), S U. of So. Afr., bounded by the Atlantic (W), Indian Ocean (S and E), Natal, Basutoland, Orange Free State, and Transvaal (NE), Bechuanaland Protectorate (N), and South-West Africa (NW); ⊙ Cape Town. Terrain consists of narrow coastal strip of fertile plain, backed by mtn. ranges (notably the Langeberg, Outeniqua, and Drakensberg), which enclose extensive inland plateaus, the Little Karroo and the GREAT KARROO. N part of prov. consists of Northern Karroo and adjoins arid plateau of Kalahari Desert. Compass Berg (8,209 ft.), in the Sneeuwberg, is highest elevation. Principal streams draining prov. are Orange, Molopo, Vaal, Olifants, Gamka, Gouritz, Sundays, Great Fish, Great Kei, Umzimvubu rivers. Karroo regions, where irrigated, support large sheep-grazing industry. Grain (wheat, corn, kaffir corn), hops, citrus fruit, tobacco, stock, wool (including karakul), hides, wine are chief agr. products. Rock-lobster fisheries are important. Mine products include diamonds (Kimberley) and copper (O'Okiep); some coal is worked. Industries include: auto assembly, textile milling; mfg. of shoes, leather, tires; fruit and jam canning, diamond cutting and polishing. Major towns are Kimberley, Port Elizabeth, East London, Grahamstown, Uitenhage, Oudtshoorn, De Aar, Beaufort West, Stellenbosch, Graaff Reinet, Upington, Mafeking, and Simonstown (naval base). TRANSKEIAN TERRITORIES, native area under separate administration, are in E part of prov. Although Cape of Good Hope was 1st circumnavigated by Bartholomew Diaz (1488) and Vasco da Gama (1497), permanent settlement was not established until 1652, when Jan van Riebeeck founded Cape Town. Toward end of 17th cent. there was considerable Huguenot immigration. By arrangement with Stadtholder of Holland, British troops landed at the Cape (1795) to prevent capture by French. Dutch rule was restored 1803, but British captured the colony in 1806 and established Cape Colony. British settlers landed (1820) at Algoa Bay and founded Port Elizabeth. Other crown colonies (Kaffraria, Bechuanaland) were established, but merged with Cape Colony later in 19th cent. Parliamentary govt. was introduced 1852. During South African War (1899–1902), Mafeking and Kimberley were besieged by Boer forces; actions were fought at Modder River and Magersfontein. With founding (1910) of U. of So. Afr., Cape Colony became Cape of Good Hope Prov.; Cape Town became legislative ⊙ Union.
Cape Palmas, Liberia: see HARPER.
Cape Point, U. of So. Afr.: see GOOD HOPE, CAPE OF.
Cape Province, U. of So. Afr.: see CAPE OF GOOD HOPE PROVINCE.
Capernaum (kŭpûr'nāŭm), biblical locality, Lower Galilee, NE Palestine, on N shore of Sea of Galilee, 6 mi. NNE of Tiberias; closely associated with Jesus' ministry. Has remains of synagogue dating from 2d cent. A.D., now on grounds of Franciscan hospice. Near-by elevation is said to be site of Mount of Beatitudes, scene of Sermon on the Mount.
Capers Island. 1 Island, c.2 mi. long, Beaufort co., S S.C., near N side of entrance to Port Royal Sound, S of St. Helena Isl., 11 mi. SE of Beaufort. **2** Swampy island, c.3 mi. long, Charleston co., SE S.C., just SW of Bull Isl., 15 mi. ENE of Charleston.
Cape Sable Island (7 mi. long, 3 mi. wide), off SW N.S., separated from mainland by narrow Barrington Passage, and 25 mi. SW of Shelburne; 43°28'N 65°35'W. On W coast is town of Clarkes Harbour. Just S is an islet on which is Cape Sable, southernmost point of Nova Scotia; 43°23'N 65°37'W.
Cape Smith, trading post, SW Smith Isl. (13 mi. long, 1–3 mi. wide), E Keewatin Dist., Northwest Territories, in Hudson Bay, off NW Ungava Peninsula; 60°44'N 78°28'W; radio station.
Capestang (käpĕstā'), town (pop. 2,652), Hérault dept., S France, on the Canal du Midi and 9 mi. W of Béziers; winegrowing.
Capesterre (käpstâr'). **1** Town (commune pop. 12,352), SE Basse-Terre isl., Guadeloupe, 11 mi. ENE of Basse-Terre; trading; sugar milling, liquor distilling. Sometimes called La Capesterre. **2** Town (commune pop. 9,181), SE Marie-Galante isl., Guadeloupe, 34 mi. ESE of Basse-Terre, in sugar-growing region; rum distilling.
Capestrano (käpĕsträ'nô), town (pop. 2,346), Aquila prov., Abruzzi e Molise, S central Italy, 20 mi. ESE of Aquila.
Cape Tormentine, N.B.: see TORMENTINE, CAPE.
Cape Town or **Capetown,** Afrikaans *Kaapstad* (käp'stät), city (pop. 383,830; including suburbs 470,911), legislative ⊙ Union of South Africa and ⊙ Cape of Good Hope Prov., in SW part of prov., on Table Bay of the Atlantic, at foot of Table Mtn. (3,549 ft.); 33°55'S 18°27'E. Largest passenger port of the Union, commercial and cultural center, and a resort noted for scenic beauty of its location. Extensive dock facilities on Table Bay include Sturrock Graving Dock (1945), oil tanks, cold-storage plants, terminal grain elevators, and enclosed water area of c.400 acres. Serves rich agr. region (fruit, wine, vegetables, grain, wool) and fisheries in adjacent waters. Terminus of "Cape-to-Cairo RR" and airlines. Among city's features are Houses of Parliament (1886, enlarged 1910), public library, South African Mus. (1897), Municipal Botanical Gardens, Sea Point Aquarium, South African Natl. Gallery, Michaelis Gallery, castle (begun 1666), Anglican and R.C. cathedrals, South African Col. (1829), Hewat Training Col., and technical col. On S outskirts is Groote Schuur estate of Cecil Rhodes, now official residence of Union premier, also site of Univ. of Cape Town (1916); near estate are Kirstenbosch Natl. Botanical Gardens. On SSW outskirts of city is the Royal Observatory (33°56'S 18°29'E), established 1829. Average temp. ranges from 52°F. (July) to 68°F. (Feb.); average annual rainfall 25 in. Settlement on site of Cape Town was established 1652 by Jan van Riebeeck as victualing base on route to East Indies; interior was subsequently settled from here, especially after influx (1688) of Huguenot immigrants. Held by the British (1795–1802) to prevent capture by the French, it was taken by the British 1806. Proclaimed legislative ⊙ Union of South Africa 1910. Near-by Simonstown is Royal Navy base. Principal suburbs are Maitland, Newlands, Rondebosch, Wynburg; airport at Wingfield.
Cape Verde Islands (vûrd, vûr'dē), Port. *Ilhas do Cabo Verde* (ē'lyŭsh dōō kä'bōō vĕr'dĭ), archipelago and Portuguese colony (□ 1,557; 1940 pop. 181,286; 1950 pop. 147,097), in Atlantic Ocean, off W African bulge, 300–450 mi. W of Cape Verde (site of Dakar, Fr. West Africa); ⊙ Praia (on São Tiago Isl.). Consist of 9 inhabited isls. and several small uninhabited ones. The main isls. are SANTO ANTÃO ISLAND, SÃO VICENTE ISLAND, SÃO NICOLAU ISLAND, SAL, and BOA VISTA ISLAND, in the Windward (Port. *Barlavento*) group, and MAIO, SÃO TIAGO ISLAND, FOGO, and BRAVA in the Leeward (Port. *Sotavento*) group. Santa Luzia, Branco, and Razo isls., and Secos islets are deserted. The crescent-shaped archipelago extends c.170 mi. N–S and 180 mi. E–W, bet. 14°48'N and 17°12'N, and 22°52'W and 25°22'W. Of volcanic origin (though probably older than the Canaries and the Azores), the isls. are mostly mountainous (rising to 9,281 ft. in the archipelago's only active volcano, on Fogo isl.), and have a rugged, inhospitable coast. Only Sal and Maio isls. have some level land. Earthquakes, though not as frequent and as widespread as in other Atlantic isls., have been recorded. The last severe eruption was in 1847. The archipelago is directly in the path of the NE trade winds, but does not have a salubrious climate. Temperatures are high (yearly average 75°F.), rainfall inadequate (5 to 10 in. per year) and seasonal (July–Nov.), and there is considerable humidity (especially in Leeward group). Agr. is limited to small areas. Chief products are coffee, oranges, sugar cane, tobacco, castor beans, and subsistence crops (corn, beans). Salt and archil are recovered. Fish are important in diet of predominantly Negro and mixed pop. The Cape Verde Isls. are important as steppingstones on transatlantic route bet. Africa and South America. Mindêlo (on Pôrto Grande bay of São Vicente Isl.) is a coaling and cable station; Espargo airport (on Sal isl.) was opened 1949 for transatlantic flights. Archipelago may have been discovered in 1450s by Cadamosto or by António de Nola, both in the service of Prince Henry the Navigator. Settled by Portuguese who conducted prosperous slave trade along W African coast (now Port. Guinea, administered until 1879 from Cape Verde Isls.). Coveted by British in 17th–18th cent. Pop. is now decreasing because of emigration to Western Hemisphere.
Cape Vincent, resort village (pop. 812), Jefferson co., N N.Y., on L. Ontario at its outlet via St. Lawrence R., 23 mi. NW of Watertown; a center for the Thousand Isls. resort area. Has ferry connections to Wolfe Isl., Ont., and thence to Kingston, Ont. Port of entry. Mfg. of fishing equipment, boatbuilding. U.S. fish hatchery.
Cape York Peninsula, N Queensland, Australia, bet. Gulf of Carpentaria (W) and Coral Sea (E); projects into Torres Strait (N); 280 mi. N–S, 150 mi. E–W. It is largely tropical jungle and is sparsely populated.
Cap-Français, Haiti: see CAP-HAÏTIEN.
Cap-Haïtien (kăp-hā'shŭn, –hā'tēŭn, Fr. käp-äēsyē'), locally called **Le Cap** (lŭ käp'), city (1950 census pop. 24,957), ⊙ Nord dept. (□ c.1,580; 1950 pop. 540,196), port and 2d largest city of Haiti, on N coast, 85 mi. N of Port-au-Prince, 35 mi. W of Monte Cristi (Dominican Republic), and linked by railroad with Grande-Rivière-du-Nord 13 mi. SSE; 19°46'N 72°13'W. Trade center for the fertile Plaine du Nord (sugar cane, coffee, cacao, tobacco, bananas, pineapples, sisal, fine wood). City handles about 10% of the republic's exports, ocean vessels anchoring ½ mi. offshore. Picturesque city, founded 1670 by the French as Cap-Français near the point (today Petite-Anse) where Columbus's flagship struck a sand bar on Christmas Day, 1492, and where the navigator built La Navidad Fort. As the chief city of France's richest possession, it remained until 1770 ⊙ Saint-Domingue. Here occurred (1791) uprisings of Negro slaves, and at near-by Vertières was fought (1803) last decisive battle of struggle for independence. To the ill-fated invasion by Napoleon's Gen. Leclerc testify ruins of the Palace of Pauline Bonaparte, the general's wife. Cap-Haïtien was site of the Northern Kingdom (1811–20) of Henri Christophe, who built, 9 mi. S near Milot, the famous citadel La Ferrière and Sans Souci palace. The town was devastated by 1842 earthquake.
Capharsaba, Palestine: see KFAR SAVA.
Caphereus, Cape, Greece: see KAPHEREUS, CAPE.
Capiatá (käpyätä'), town (dist. pop. 16,127), Central dept., S Paraguay, on railroad and 15 mi. E of Asunción; lumbering, processing, and agr. center (cotton, sugar cane, cacao); liquor distilling, honey making. Has fine old church. Founded 1640.
Capiberibe River (kä"pĕbĭrē'bĭ), Pernambuco, NE Brazil, rises in the Serra dos Cariris Velhos on Paraíba border, flows c.150 mi. E to the Atlantic at Recife. Intermittent-flowing stream. Also spelled Capibaribe and Capiboribe.

Capileira (käpēlā′rä), village (pop. 1,402), Granada prov., S Spain, 20 mi. SE of Granada; flour mills; cereals, sheep.
Capilla (käpē′lyä), town (pop. 598), Badajoz prov., W Spain, 16 mi. SE of Puebla de Alcocer; grain, livestock. Lead deposits.
Capilla, La, Argentina: see LA CAPILLA.
Capilla, La, Peru: see LA CAPILLA.
Capilla, Pueblo de la, Uruguay: see SAUCE DEL YÍ.
Capilla de Farruco (käpē′yä dā färōō′kō), village, Durazno dept., central Uruguay, in Cuchilla Grande del Durazno, 3 mi. NNE of Sarandí del Yí; corn, wheat, sheep.
Capilla de Guadalupe (gwädälōō′pā), town (pop. 1,825), Jalisco, central Mexico, 13 mi. E of Tepatitlán de Morelos; corn, vegetables, livestock.
Capilla del Monte (dĕl mōn′tā), town (pop. 2,408), NW Córdoba prov., Argentina, 45 mi. NNW of Córdoba, on W slope of the Sierra Chica; alt. 3,000 ft. Tourist resort (mineral waters). Hunting in mts. near by. Livestock, agr.; granite quarrying.
Capilla del Señor (sānyōr′), town (pop. 3,522), ⊙ Exaltación de la Cruz dist. (□ 245; pop. 8,581), N Buenos Aires prov., Argentina, 15 mi. SSW of Zárate; road junction and agr. center (wheat, corn, livestock).
Capilla San Antonio, Argentina: see SAN ANTONIO DE LITIN.
Capillitas (käpĭyē′täs), village, E Catamarca prov., Argentina, in Sierra Atajo, 17 mi. NNW of Andalgalá; copper mining; tungsten deposits.
Capillitas, Sierra, Argentina: see ATAJO, SIERRA.
Capim (kä′pēm), city (pop. 236), E Pará, Brazil, at influx of Capim R. into Guamá R., 50 mi. ESE of Belém. Called São Domingos da Boa Vista until 1939, and São Domingos do Capim, 1939–43.
Capim River, E Pará, Brazil, rises near 5°S 49°W, flows c.275 mi. N to the Guamá at Capim. Not navigable.
Capinha (käpē′nyů), village (pop. 1,543), Castelo Branco dist., central Portugal, 9 mi. SE of Covilhã; wine, olives; sheep and goat raising.
Capinota (käpēnō′tä), town (pop. c.11,600), ⊙ Capinota prov., Cochabamba dept., central Bolivia, on S slopes of Cordillera de Cochabamba, on Caine R. and 23 mi. SSW of Cochabamba, on Oruro-Cochabamba RR, in winegrowing region; alt. 8,000 ft.; fruit; distilling.
Capira (käpē′rä), village (pop. 432), Panama prov., central Panama, in Pacific lowland, on Inter-American Highway and 15 mi. SW of Panama city; head of navigation (4 ft. draught) on small Capira R. Orange-growing center; stock raising.
Capirenda (käpērĕn′dä), village (pop. c.55), Tarija dept., S Bolivia, in the Chaco, 33 mi. ENE of Villa Montes.
Capiricual, Venezuela: see NARICUAL.
Capistrano, Calif.: see SAN JUAN CAPISTRANO.
Capistrello (käpēstrĕl′lô), town (pop. 3,730), Aquila prov., Abruzzi e Molise, S central Italy, on Liri R., at mouth of Lago Fucino outlet, and 5 mi. SSW of Avezzano. Has hydroelectric plant furnishing power to near-by carbide factory.
Capitan (kăpĭtăn′), village (pop. 575), Lincoln co., S central N.Mex., just NE of Sierra Blanca, 18 mi. ESE of Carrizozo; alt. c.6,400 ft. Health resort; trading point in agr., livestock, mining region. Capitan Mts. just NE; part of Lincoln Natl. Forest near by. Fort Stanton, 4 mi. SE, is U.S. marine hosp. reservation.
Capitán Bado (käpētän′ bä′dō), town (dist. pop. 4,120), Amambay dept., E Paraguay, in Sierra de Amambay, on Brazil border, 55 mi. S of Pedro Juan Caballero; alt. c.1,600 ft.; maté center.
Capitán Meza (mā′sä), town (dist. pop. 1,587), Itapúa dept., SE Paraguay, on upper Paraná R. and 45 mi. NE of Encarnación; maté; lumbering.
Capitán Montoya, Argentina: see LAS PAREDES.
Capitan Mountains (kăpĭtăn′), S central N.Mex., NE spur of Sacramento Mts., in Lincoln co. Prominent point is Capitan Peak (10,083 ft.); highest elevation in range is 10,205 ft. Lies within part of Lincoln Natl. Forest.
Capitán Pastene (käpētän′ pästā′nā), town (pop. 1,193), Malleco prov., S Chile, 32 mi. SSW of Angol; rail terminus; agr. center (grain, fruit, potatoes); flour milling, lumbering.
Capitán Sarmiento (särmyĕn′tō), town (pop. 3,074), N Buenos Aires prov., Argentina, 20 mi. ESE of Arrecifes; agr. center (corn, flax, wheat); flour milling.
Capitán Ustares, Cerro (sĕ′rō, ōōstä′rĕs), hill on Bolivia-Paraguay border, 95 mi. E of Charagua (Bolivia), in the Chaco; 19°42′S 61°48′W. Boundary marker established (1938) in Chaco Peace Conference.
Capitola (kăpĭtō′lů), resort city (pop. 1,848), Santa Cruz co., W Calif., on N shore of Monterey Bay, 4 mi. E of Santa Cruz; flower growing. Has state park. Inc. 1949.
Capitol Heights, town (pop. 2,729), Prince Georges co., central Md., E suburb of Washington.
Capitoline Hill (kă′pĭtōlīn, kůpĭ′tůlīn) or **Capitol,** highest of the 7 hills of anc. Rome and its historical and religious center.
Capitol Peak, Colo.: see ELK MOUNTAINS.
Capitol Reef National Monument (□ 51.6; established 1937), S central Utah, just E of Torrey. Brightly colored sandstone cliffs, monoliths, and pinnacles; Capitol Reef is ridge extending 20 mi. NW–SE, buttressed at base by white sandstone domes, and cut by deep, narrow canyons. Cliff walls exhibit petroglyphs and pictographs of pre-Columbian Indians.
Capivari (käpēvärē′). **1** City, Rio de Janeiro, Brazil: see SILVA JARDIM. **2** City (pop. 5,880), E central São Paulo, Brazil, 29 mi. WSW of Campinas, in region of diversified agr. (cotton, sugar, citrus fruit, livestock); cotton ginning, sugar milling. Formerly spelled Capivary.
Capiz (kä′pēs), province (□ 1,703; 1948 pop., 441,871), N Panay isl., Philippines, bounded N by Sibuyan Sea, W by Tablas Strait; ⊙ Capiz. Forested and mountainous terrain, drained by many small streams. Agr. (rice, corn, tobacco, sugar cane), fishing, copper mining.
Capiz, town (1939 pop. 10,204; 1948 municipality pop. 32,353), ⊙ Capiz prov., N Panay isl., Philippines, port at mouth of small Panay R. on small inlet of Jintotolo Channel, 235 mi. SSE of Manila; 11°35′N 122°45′E. Rail terminus; trade center for agr. area (rice, coconuts, tobacco, hemp). Govt.-owned fish canneries. Exports copra, canned fish.
Capizzi (käpē′tsē), village (pop. 5,187), Messina prov., N Sicily, in Nebrodi Mts., 8 mi. SE of Mistretta.
Capljina or **Chaplyina** (both: chäp′lyĭnä), Serbo-Croatian *Čapljina*, village (pop. 2,114), W Herzegovina, Yugoslavia, near Neretva R., on railroad and 17 mi. SSW of Mostar, near Dalmatian border; local trade center.
Cap-Martin, France: see ROQUEBRUNE.
Cap-Matifou, village, Algeria: see MATIFOU, CAPE.
Capnic, Rumania: see CAVNIC.
Capo [Ital.,=cape], for names beginning thus and not found here: see under following part of name.
Capodichino, Italy: see SECONDIGLIANO-CAPODICHINO.
Capodimonte (käpôdēmôn′tĕ), village (pop. 1,871), Viterbo prov., Latium, central Italy, on promontory in SW L. Bolsena, 14 mi. NW of Viterbo; fishing. Has octagonal palace designed by A. Sangallo the younger.
Capodistria (kăpůdĭ′strēů, Ital. käpōdē′strēä), Slovenian *Koper* (kô′pĕr), Serbo-Croatian *Kopar* (kô′pär), anc. *Capris*, Byzantine *Justinopolis*, town (pop. 7,105), S Free Territory of Trieste, 7 mi. SSW of Trieste, port on Capodistria Bay, an Adriatic inlet of Gulf of Trieste; fish canning, distilling, boat building. Situated on a small circular isl. connected to the mainland by a causeway, Capodistria is of typical Venetian appearance, with 15th-cent. cathedral and 13th-cent. campanile, Gothic loggia, and pinnacled town hall. Was ⊙ Istria (1278–1797) under Venetian rule. Placed 1947 under Yugoslav administration.
Capolago (käpôlä′gô), town (pop. 483), Ticino canton, S Switzerland, at SE tip of L. of Lugano, 2 mi. N of Mendrisio.
Capon Bridge (kā′půn), town (pop. 223), Hampshire co., W.Va., in Eastern Panhandle, 28 mi. WSW of Martinsburg.
Capon Springs, village, Hampshire co., W.Va., in Eastern Panhandle near Va. line, 15 mi. W of Winchester, Va.; mineral springs (waters shipped). Was a noted ante-bellum resort.
Caporetto (kăpůrĕ′tō, Ital. käpōrā′tō), Serbo-Croatian *Kobarid* (kô′bärĭt), Ger. *Karfreit* (kär′frīt), village (1936 pop. 844), NW Slovenia, Yugoslavia, on Isonzo R., on railroad and 45 mi. WNW of Ljubljana, near Ital. border. Until 1947, in Italy. Here in Oct., 1917, the Italians suffered a disastrous defeat by the Austrians.
Caposele (käpōzā′lĕ), village (pop. 2,954), Avellino prov., Campania, S Italy, on upper Sele R. and 24 mi. ENE of Avellino, in cereal-growing region.
Capoterra (käpôtĕr′rä), village (pop. 3,316), Cagliari prov., S Sardinia, 8 mi. WSW of Cagliari, in olive-growing area. Iron mine near by.
Cappadocia (kăpůdō′shů), ancient region of Asia Minor, watered by the Halys (modern Kizil Irmak), in present E central Asiatic Turkey. Name was applied at various times to territories of varying size. At its greatest extent it stretched from Halys valley E to the Euphrates, from Black (Euxine) Sea in N to the heights of the Taurus and Anti-Taurus ranges in S. Mostly a high plateau, interrupted by mts. and isolated in winter by snow in the mtn. passes, it was largely devoted to grazing and was famous for its horses and its fat-tailed sheep. Attained a good deal of independence. Conquered by the Persians; developed as an independent kingdom in 3d cent. B.C. PONTUS, which had been 1st cut off in Persian times, now became completely separated from Cappadocia. The kings had their ⊙ at Mazaca (later Caesarea Mazaca), now Kayseri; the only other important cities were Tyana and Melitene (modern Malatya), though Iconium (Konya) was at times in Cappadocia. Rome annexed the region in A.D. 17 as a province. Cappadocia became prosperous. Christianity was introduced early (1st cent.), and the name appears in the Bible, though its importance as a separate region was already declining and later disappeared. In anc. times Armenia was to E, Cilicia to S, Lycaonia and Galatia to W.
Cappaghwhite, Ireland: see CAPPAWHITE.
Cappawhite, Cappaghwhite, or **Cappagh White** (all: kă″pů-hwīt′), town (pop. 312), W Co. Tipperary, Ireland, 7 mi. N of Tipperary; agr. market (dairying; potatoes, beets).
Cappel, Switzerland: see KAPPEL AM ALBIS.
Cappoquin, Gaelic *Ceapach Chuinn*, town (pop. 912), W Co. Waterford, Ireland, on the Blackwater and 10 mi. WNW of Dungarvan; agr. market (dairying, cattle raising, potato growing). Near by is Mt. Melleray Trappist monastery.
Capracotta (käpräkôt′tä), town (pop. 3,150), Campobasso prov., Abruzzi e Molise, S central Italy, in the Apennines, 17 mi. N of Isernia; resort (alt. 4,662 ft.). Domestic woolen industry; sawmill; dairy and meat products.
Caprag (tsä′präk), town, N Croatia, Yugoslavia, on Sava R., near Kupa R. mouth, just S of Sisak; rail junction; industrial center; steel mill; petroleum refinery (fuel oil, kerosene, gasoline).
Capraia (käprä′yä), anc. *Capraria*, island (□ 7.5; pop. 341) in Tuscan Archipelago, in Tyrrhenian Sea, Italy, in Livorno prov., 21 mi. NW of Elba, 19 mi. E of Cape Corse, Corsica; 5 mi. long, 2.5 mi. wide; rises to 1,466 ft. (N). On NE coast is village and port of Capraia, with 15th-cent. fortress. From 1872, site of agr. penal colony occupying ⅓ of area.
Capranica (käprä′nēkä), village (pop. 3,051), Viterbo prov., Latium, central Italy, 12 mi. SSE of Viterbo.
Caprara, Point (käprä′rä), N end of Asinara Isl., off NW Sardinia; 41°6′N 8°21′E. Also called Point Scorno.
Capraria, Balearic Isls.: see CABRERA ISLAND.
Capraria, Italy: see CAPRAIA.
Caprarola (käprärô′lä), town (pop. 5,461), Viterbo prov., Latium, central Italy, near Lago di Vico, 9 mi. SSE of Viterbo, in grape-growing region. Has splendid Farnese palace designed by Vignola (1547–59).
Capreae, Italy: see CAPRI.
Capreol (kā′prēōl, kă′prēōl), town (pop. 1,641), S central Ont., near Wapitei L., 16 mi. NNW of Sudbury; distributing center in mining (nickel, copper) and lumbering region.
Caprera Island (käprā′rä) (□ 6; pop. 118), 1 mi. off NE Sardinia, in Sassari prov., in Tyrrhenian Sea; 5 mi. long, 2 mi. wide; rises to 695 ft. Residence of Garibaldi and site of his tomb. Connected by causeway (W) with Maddalena Isl.
Caprese Michelangelo (käprā′zĕ mē″kĕlän′jĕlô), village (pop. 94), Arezzo prov., Tuscany, central Italy, 14 mi. NE of Arezzo. Michelangelo b. here. Formerly Caprese.
Capri (kä′prē), anc. *Capreae*, small rocky island (□ 4; pop. 7,984), Napoli prov., Campania, S Italy, opposite peninsula of Sorrento, near SE entrance to Bay of Naples, 20 mi. S of Naples; 3¾ mi. long, ½–1¾ mi. wide; rises to 1,932 ft. in Monte Solaro (S). Famous for its picturesque scenery, delightful climate (mean winter temp. 50°F.), and luxurious vegetation, it attracts many tourists. Capri (pop. 3,353; cord-shoe mfg.) and Anacapri (W) are its 2 towns. Bet. them is a bird sanctuary established by Dr. Axel Munthe. The Blue Grotto (rediscovered 1826), on NW shore of isl., is the most famous of many wave-cut caves along its high, precipitous coast. It is 175 ft. long, 98 ft. wide, 50 ft. high; has 3-ft.-high narrow entrance. When the sun shines, the grotto is filled with a dazzling blue light. Isl. produces citrus fruit, olive oil, and excellent dry white wine; fishing is also carried on Has remains of fine villas built by Augustus and Tiberius.
Capriati a Volturno (käprēä′tē ä vôltōōr′nô), village (pop. 1,375), Caserta prov., Campania, S Italy, near Volturno R., 5 mi. E of Venafro.
Capricorn, Cape, Australia: see CURTIS ISLAND.
Capricorn Islands, coral group in Coral Sea, bet. Great Barrier Reef and Keppel Bay, off E coast of Queensland, Australia, on Tropic of Capricorn. Consist of 5 islets surrounded by reefs; largest, HERON ISLAND. Low, wooded; tourist trade.
Caprino, Monte (käprē′nô), mountain (3,732 ft.) in the Alps, S Switzerland, on L. of Lugano, opposite Lugano.
Caprino Veronese (vĕrônā′zĕ), village (pop. c.4,000), Verona prov., Veneto, N Italy, at S foot of Monte Baldo, 15 mi. NW of Verona; mfg. (irrigation pumps, insulators, agr. machinery, pottery). Marble quarries near by.
Capriolo (käprēô′lô), village (pop. 2,692), Brescia prov., Lombardy, N Italy, near S shore of Lago d'Iseo, 7 mi. N of Chiari; metal furniture.
Capriva di Cormons (käprē′vä dē kôr′môns), village (pop. 920), Gorizia prov., Friuli-Venezia Giulia, NE Italy, 5 mi. W of Gorizia; alcohol distillery.
Caprivi Zipfel (käprē′vē tsĭp′fůl), **Caprivi Strip,** or **Caprivi Concession,** narrow strip of territory (□ c.10,000; pop. 14,020) in NE South-West Africa, extending 280 mi. E bet. Angola and Northern Rhodesia on N and Bechuanaland Protectorate on S to the Zambezi at Southern Rhodesia border 40 mi. W of Livingstone. Only 20–60 mi. wide, it was ceded 1893 to Germany by Great Britain to afford German Southwest Africa an outlet to the Zambezi. Chief village is Schukmansburg, on Zambezi R. and 70 mi. WNW of Livingstone, 4 mi. SW of Sesheke (Northern Rhodesia frontier point). Greater

part (□ 7,479) of territory is set aside for natives; cattle raising is chief occupation. The area has been part of mandated South-West Africa, but in 1939 the U. of So. Afr. annexed the E portion of Caprivi Zipfel and administers it as Eastern Caprivi Zipfel dist., with hq. at Katima Mulilo.

Cap Rock, Texas: see LLANO ESTACADO.

Capron (kā'prŭn). **1** Village (pop. 572), Boone co., N Ill., 19 mi. ENE of Rockford, in agr. area; tile, brick. **2** Town (pop. 100), Woods co., NW Okla., 8 mi. NNE of Alva, in wheat and livestock area. **3** Town (pop. 281), Southampton co., SE Va., 34 mi. W of Suffolk, in agr. area.

Caprus, Iraq: see ZAB, LITTLE.

Caprycke, Belgium: see KAPRIJKE.

Capsa, Tunisia: see GAFSA.

Cap Saint Ignace (kăp sĕtēnyäs'), village (pop. estimate 1,000), SE Que., on the St. Lawrence and 6 mi. ENE of Montmagny, opposite the Île aux Grues; dairying, lumbering.

Cap Saint-Jacques (kăp'sē-zhäk'), town and commune (□ 230; 1943 pop. 8,900; 1948 pop. 12,910), S Vietnam, in Cochin China, on South China Sea, 40 mi. SE of Saigon, situated on Cape Saint-Jacques at extreme S end of Annamese Cordillera, on E side of Ganhrai Bay; fortified town (coastal batteries), site of pilot and quarantine station for Saigon approaches; seaside resort, with villas and fine promenades. Lighthouse. Airport.

Cap Santé (kăp sātā'), village (pop. estimate 500), ⊙ Portneuf co., S central Que., on the St. Lawrence and 30 mi. W of Quebec; dairying; cattle, pigs, poultry, fruit, vegetables.

Capsir, France: see CAPCIR.

Captainganj (kŭp'tĭngŭnj), town (pop. 4,157), Gorakhpur dist., E Uttar Pradesh, India, 30 mi. NE of Gorakhpur; rail junction; sugar milling; trades in rice, wheat, barley, oilseeds, sugar.

Captieux (käptyû'), village (pop. 812), Gironde dept., SW France, in the Landes, 25 mi. SW of Marmande; lumber trade; brick, turpentine, honey.

Captiva Island (kăptē'vŭ), SW Fla., narrow barrier island (c.7 mi. long) in Gulf of Mexico N of Sanibel Isl.; partly shelters Pine Island Sound (E). Site of Captiva, a fishing village and resort. Captiva Pass is an inlet c.5 mi. N of Captiva village and at S end of Lacosta Isl.

Capua (kă'pōōŭ, It. kä'pwä), anc. *Casilinum,* town (pop. 10,218), Caserta prov., Campania, S Italy, on Volturno R. and 18 mi. N of Naples; mfg. (agr. machinery, fireworks, macaroni); wine. Archbishopric. Has early Norman palace (now an arsenal). Anc. cathedral severely damaged and nearby Roman bridge destroyed in Second World War. Anciently occupied site 3 mi. SE (where Santa Maria Capua Vetere now stands); a strategic Roman town on the Appian Way. Taken (216 B.C.) by Hannibal and retaken by Romans; became chief center of S Italy. Remains include amphitheater and triumphal arch. After its destruction (841) by Arabs, inhabitants moved to Casilinum and founded modern Capua. Strongly fortified to defend Naples; suffered various sieges; in 1860 taken by Piedmontese.

Capual Island (käpwäl') (□ 7.4; 1939 pop. 427), Sulu prov., Philippines, in Sulu Archipelago, just off NE tip of Jolo Isl.

Capulhuac (käpōōlwäk'), officially Capulhuac de Mirafuentes, town (pop. 4,469), Mexico state, central Mexico, 28 mi. W of Mexico city; cereals, livestock.

Capulin Mountain National Monument (kŭpū'lĭn) (680.4 acres; established 1916), NE N.Mex., 27 mi. ESE of Raton, near Colo. line. Area of extinct volcanic craters; largest is Capulin Mtn. (8,215 ft.), huge cinder cone estimated to be less than 2,000 years old, with crater 1,450 ft. wide, 415 ft. deep.

Capul Island (käpōōl') (□ 14; 1939 pop. 5,087), Samar prov., Philippines, just off NW coast of Samar isl., near Dalupiri Isl., in Samar Sea, near entrance to San Bernardino Strait; 8 mi. long, 2 mi. wide. Flat, becoming hilly in SW. Coconuts.

Capurso (käpōōr'sô), town (pop. 5,165), Bari prov., Apulia, S Italy, 6 mi. SSE of Bari; wine, olive oil.

Capury River, Colombia and Brazil: see PAPURY RIVER.

Caputh (kä'pōōt), village (pop. 3,973), Brandenburg, E Germany, on the Havel and 4 mi. SW of Potsdam; market gardening; excursion resort. Sometimes spelled Kaputh.

Caputh (kă'pŭth), agr. village and parish (pop. 1,079), E Perthshire, Scotland, 4 mi. ESE of Dunkeld. Near by is co. insane asylum.

Caputitlán (käpōōtētlän'), town (pop. 2,751), Mexico state, central Mexico, 4 mi. S of Toluca; cereals, livestock.

Capuzzo (käpōōt'tsō), village, E Cyrenaica, Libya, on Egyptian border, S of Bardia, 6 mi. W of Salum. Was fortified base for Ital. advance into Egypt in 1940. Changed hands several times in seesaw desert battles of 1940–42.

Capvern or **Capvern-les-Bains** (käpvârn'-lā-bē'), village (pop. 705), Hautes-Pyrénées dept., SW France, 9 mi. ENE of Bagnères-de-Bigorre; mineral springs.

Caquetá (käkätä'), commissary (□ 39,764; 1938 pop. 20,914; 1950 estimate 21,140), S Colombia; ⊙ Florencia. Tropical forest region on the equator, bounded W by Cordillera Oriental, S by Caquetá R. Drained by Caguán and Yarí rivers, affluents of the Caquetá. Has tropical, humid climate. It is an undeveloped forest area, sparsely populated by primitive Indians. Its forests yield some rubber, balata gum, fine wood, medicinal plants, cacao, and resins; wild animals hunted for furs and hides.

Caquetá River, S Colombia, upper course of JAPURÁ RIVER. The largest Colombian river, it rises in the Andes S of Páramo del Buey (Cauca dept.), flows ESE along borders of Cauca, Putumayo, Caquetá, and Amazonas, through region of dense tropical forests across the equator, joining APAPORIS RIVER at the Brazil line, where it becomes the Japurá proper. Length, c.750 mi. Receives from left Orteguaza, Caguán, Yarí, and Miriti Paraná rivers. Not navigable.

Cáqueza (kä'käsä), town (pop. 2,419), Cudinamarca dept., central Colombia, on affluent of Guatiquía R., in Cordillera Oriental, and 17 mi. SSE of Bogotá; alt. 5,151 ft. Trading center in agr. region (corn, peas, potatoes, yucca, hogs).

Cara, island (pop. 3), S Argyll, Scotland, just S of Gigha isl. and separated from Kintyre peninsula by 3-mi.-wide Sound of Gigha; 1 mi. long.

Caraballeda (käräbäyä'dä), town (pop. 571), Federal Dist., N Venezuela, minor port on the Caribbean, 5 mi. E of La Guaira, in cacao and coffee region.

Caraballo (käräbä'yō), town (pop. 1,634), Havana prov., W Cuba, on railroad and 28 mi. E of Havana; sugar cane, vegetables.

Caraballo Mountains or **Caraballos** (–yōs), central range of Luzon, Philippines, largely in Nueva Vizcaya prov.; rise to 5,517 ft. The name was also formerly applied to the Sierra Madre and the Cordillera Central.

Carabaña (kärävä'nyä), town (pop. 2,294), Madrid prov., central Spain, on Tajuña R., on railroad and 26 mi ESE of Madrid; agr. center (cereals, beans, potatoes, hemp, sugar beets, grapes, olives, sheep, goats). Wine making, olive-oil extracting, flour milling. Medicinal springs.

Carabanchel Alto (kärävänchĕl' äl'tō), town (pop. 5,788), Madrid prov., central Spain, 4 mi. SW of Madrid; mfg. of airplanes, furniture, tile, ceramics, wine. Has airport, aviation school, garrison, insane asylum.

Carabanchel Bajo (bä'hō), town (pop. 17,327), Madrid prov., central Spain, 3 mi. SW of Madrid; industrial center. Sawmilling, liquor distilling, meat packing; mfg. of starch, chocolate, lard, soap, ceramics, buttons, bells, leather goods, cardboard boxes, matches, scales, pharmaceuticals.

Carabane (käräbän'), village and islet, SW Senegal, Fr. West Africa, in mouth of Casamance R., 30 mi. W of Ziguinchor. Customhouse, landing.

Carabao Island (käräbä'ō, –bou') (1939 pop. 1,317), Romblon prov., Philippines, bet. Tablas Strait and Sibuyan Sea, just off S coast of Tablas Isl.; 4 mi. in diameter. Rice, coconuts.

Carabaya, province, Peru: see MACUSANI.

Carabaya, Cordillera de (kôrdĭyä'rä dā käräbī'ä), SE section of Cordillera Oriental of the Andes, in Cuzco and Puno depts., SE Peru. A continuation of Nudo de Apolobamba, it extends c.190 mi. NW to 13°S, rising to 19,193 ft. at Nudo de Quenamari (14°10'S 70°23'W). Parallel to it (W) runs the Cordillera de Vilcanota, the 2 ranges being linked by the Cordillera de ASUNGATE. Madre de Dios R. rises on its E central slopes. Has rich silver and gold deposits.

Carabelas or **Las Carabelas** (läs käräbā'läs), town (pop. 3,476), N Buenos Aires prov., Argentina, 21 mi. SW of Pergamino; agr. center (corn, wheat, flax, sunflowers, livestock).

Carabobo (käräbō'bō), state (□ 1,795; 1941 pop. 191,442; 1950 census 243,159), N Venezuela, on the Caribbean; ⊙ Valencia. Mountainous region with narrow coastal lowlands (N and NW); crossed by coastal range; includes larger section (W) of L. Valencia. Hot, tropical climate along coast and in lake basin; somewhat cooler in uplands; rainy season (May-Sept.). Carabobo is one of Venezuela's leading agr. regions, producing principally cotton and sugar cane; also corn, cacao, tobacco, rice, yucca, bananas, coconuts; and coffee at higher altitudes. Cattle driven here from S llanos for fattening. Valencia and its port Puerto Cabello are the leading commercial and industrial centers (textile milling, tanning, meat packing, sawmilling, marble quarrying).

Carabobo, town (pop. 1,182), Carabobo state, N Venezuela, 15 mi. SW of Valencia, in agr. region (coffee, corn, sugar cane, fruit, livestock). Site of famous victory (June 24, 1821) gained by Bolívar and Páez, which ended Sp. rule in NW South America; elaborate monument commemorates battle.

Carabuco (käräbōō'kō), town (pop. c.6,900), La Paz dept., W Bolivia, port on L. Titicaca, 80 mi. NW of La Paz; alt. 12,533 ft. Zinc mines near by.

Caracal (käräkäl'), town (1948 pop. 17,892), Dolj prov., S Rumania, in Walachia, on railroad and 85 mi. SW of Bucharest; tanning, flour milling, mfg. of rugs, tiled stoves, furniture.

Caracaraí (käräkäräē'), town, Rio Branco territory, northernmost Brazil, head of navigation on right bank of the Rio Branco and 75 mi. SSW of Boa Vista. Portage around Rio Branco rapids just NE. Formerly spelled Caracarahy.

Caracas (kŭră'kŭs, kŭrä'–, Sp. kärä'käs), largest city (1941 pop. 269,030; 1950 estimate 376,111) and ⊙ Venezuela and Federal District (□ 745; 1941 pop. 380,099; 1950 census 700,149), on Guaire R., in coastal range near the Caribbean, towered over by mts.; 10°30'N 66°55'W; alt. c.3,000 ft. Has warm, but healthful and pleasant climate (dry season Dec.-April). Chief metropolis of the republic, dominating all cultural and economic life and one of the main trading and mfg. centers, situated in fertile agr. region (sugar cane, cacao, coffee, corn, rice, beans, potatoes, cattle). Mfg. includes cotton, rayon, and silk textiles, clothing, shoes, paper, tobacco products, glassware, soap, matches, perfumes, candles, caustic soda, pharmaceuticals, rubber goods, processed food, dairy products; auto-assembly plant, sugar refineries, meat-packing plants, breweries, tanneries, sawmills. Here are the chief wholesale and banking houses. Ranks as important communication hub; linked with its port La Guaira (7 mi. N) by railroad and highway over mts.; from it radiate railroads, highways, and air lines to W Venezuela and to Ciudad Bolívar in S. It is a handsome city, dotted with spacious plazas and intersected by shady avenues; old colonial architecture contrasts with modern edifices. Center of city is Plaza Bolívar (with fine monument to the Liberator), around which are grouped all important bldgs.: govt. palace, capitol, palace of justice, city hall, president's residence, and chapel and cathedral. Bolívar, b. near by, is buried in the Pantheon, a former church. Among city's other important features are univ., mus., School of Geology, several theaters, military acad., observatory, racecourse, bull ring. Founded 1567 by Diego de Losada as Santiago de León de Caracas; became a capital 1577. Assumed a leading role in early revolution, advocating independence in April, 1810, and formally declaring its independence in July, 1811. Its almost complete destruction by earthquake of March 26, 1812, materially affected end of revolution as led by Miranda. In Aug., 1813, Bolívar recaptured city, but had soon to abandon it; finally, after decisive victory of Carabobo (June 24, 1821) he made a triumphal entry. Became capital of a separate Venezuelan republic in 1829.

Caracas Bay, inlet of SW Curaçao, Du. West Indies, 5 mi. SE of Willemstad. Noted for its scenery and old Sp. fortress, it is now a petroleum-bunkering station, exporting fuel and diesel oil. Has 3 wharves, which accommodate large vessels. Formerly a quarantine station.

Caracas Valley, in Federal Dist. and Miranda state, N Venezuela, in coastal range, along middle course of Guaire R., with Caracas in center; extends c.15 mi. E-W. Healthy climate, rich vegetation; sugar cane, cacao, coffee, corn, rice, beans, milch cows.

Caracato (käräkä'tō), town (pop. c.2,100), La Paz dept., W Bolivia, in Luribay Valley, on Caracato R. (branch of Luribay R.) and 40 mi. SE of La Paz; orchards, vineyards; mineral springs.

Carache (kärä'chā), town (pop. 2,010), Trujillo state, W Venezuela, in Andean spur, 23 mi. NNE of Trujillo; in agr. region (coffee, cacao, sugar cane, tobacco, corn, fruit).

Caracol (käräkōl'), suburb (pop. 1,044) of Tomé, Concepción dept., S central Chile.

Caracol, village, Los Ríos prov., W central Ecuador, on affluent of Guayas R. and 8 mi. NE of Babahoyo; cacao plantations; also rice, pineapples, oranges, and other tropical produce.

Caracol (käräkôl'), agr. town (1950 census pop. 1,061), Nord dept., N Haiti, on the Atlantic, 11 mi. ESE of Cap-Haïtien; sugar cane, fruit.

Caracoles (käräkō'lĕs), village, La Paz dept., W Bolivia, in Cordillera de Tres Cruces, 15 mi. W of Inquisivi; alt. c.15,000 ft.; tin-mining center.

Caracoles, mining settlement (1930 pop. 8), Antofagasta prov., N Chile, in the Atacama Desert, 100 mi. NE of Antofagasta, 25 mi. E of the railroad, in silver- and copper-mining area. The rich deposits, discovered 1870, are now mostly abandoned.

Caracollo (käräkō'yō), town (pop. c.5,800), Oruro dept., W Bolivia, in the Altiplano, on road and 20 mi. NNW of Oruro; potatoes, barley, sheep.

Carácuaro (kärä'kwärō), officially Carácuaro de Morelos, town (pop. 770), Michoacán, central Mexico, 15 mi. NNW of Huetamo; coffee, sugar, fruit.

Caracuel or **Caracuel de Calatrava** (käräkwĕl' dhä käläträ'vä), town (pop. 488), Ciudad Real prov., S central Spain, 11 mi. SW of Ciudad Real; cereals, grapes, olives, stock.

Caraglio (kärä'lyô), village (pop. 2,455), Cuneo prov., Piedmont, NW Italy, 6 mi. WNW of Cuneo, in silk-growing area.

Caraguatá, Arroyo (äroi'ō kärägwätä'), river, N central Uruguay, rises in the Cuchilla del Hospital NW of Vichadero, flows 50 mi. SW across Tacuarembó dept. to Tacuarembó R.

Caraguatatuba (kärägwä"tätōō'bŭ), city (pop. 1,816), E São Paulo, Brazil, on the Atlantic, 60 mi. ENE of Santos; sugar, manioc, tobacco, rice, fruit. Has fine bathing beach.

Caraguatay, department, Paraguay: see LA CORDILLERA.

Caraguatay (kärägwätī'), town (dist. pop. 15,355), La Cordillera dept., S central Paraguay, 50 mi. E of Asunción; tobacco-growing and -processing center; stock raising. Founded 1770.

Caraguatay River, Argentina: see SALADILLO, Río, Santa Fe prov.

Carahue (kärä'wä), town (pop. 4,341), Cautín prov., S central Chile, on Imperial R. and 32 mi. W of Temuco; rail terminus, river port, agr. center (wheat, oats, potatoes, peas, livestock). Flour milling, dairying, tanning. Some gold washing. A settlement called Imperial was founded here 1551 by Pedro de Valdivia; was site of many clashes bet. Indians and Spaniards.

Caraibamba, Peru: see CARAYBAMBA.

Caralis, Sardinia: see CAGLIARI, city.

Caramagna Piemonte (kärämä'nyä pyĕmôn'tĕ), village (pop. 1,807), Cuneo prov., Piedmont, NW Italy, 20 mi. S of Turin.

Caraman (kärämä'), village (pop. 662), Haute-Garonne dept., S France, 16 mi. ESE of Toulouse; hosiery mfg., poultry raising.

Caraman, Turkey: see KARAMAN.

Caramanico (kärämä'nēkô), town (pop. 1,931), Pescara prov., Abruzzi e Molise, S central Italy, 17 mi. SSW of Chieti; resort (alt. 1,968 ft.) with hot mineral springs.

Caramanta (käräman'tä), town (pop. 4,218), Antioquia dept., NW central Colombia, on E slopes of Cordillera Occidental, 50 mi. S of Medellín; alt. 6,958 ft. Coffeegrowing center; sugar cane, potatoes, beans, stock. Founded 1836.

Caramoan (kärämō'än), town (1939 pop. 3,066; 1948 municipality pop. 26,836), Camarines Sur prov., SE Luzon, Philippines, 45 mi. NNE of Legaspi, on Rungus Point peninsula; agr. (rice, abacá, corn); mineral pigments, guano, phosphate rock.

Caramoran, Philippines: see PANDAN.

Carampangue (kärämpäng'gä), village (1930 pop. 1,229), Arauco prov., S central Chile, near SE coast of Arauco Gulf of the Pacific, 38 mi. NE of Lebu; rail junction (branch to Arauco) in agr. area (grain, legumes, livestock); lumbering.

Caramulo, Serra do (sĕ'rŭ dōō kärämōō'lōō), mtn. range in Viseu dist., N central Portugal, W of Viseu and S of Vouga R. Rises to 3,514 ft.

Caranavi (käränä'vē), village, La Paz dept., W Bolivia, on Coroico R. and 29 mi. NNE of Coroico; quina, sugar cane.

Carandaí (kärändäē'), city (pop. 1,256), S central Minas Gerais, Brazil, on railroad and 18 mi. N of Barbecena; dairying; limekilns. Old spelling, Carandahy.

Carangas, Bolivia: see CORQUE.

Carangola (käräng-gô'lū), city (pop. 8,758), SE Minas Gerais, Brazil, near Espírito Santo border, on railroad and 85 mi. NW of Campos (Rio de Janeiro); mica-mining center; sawmilling, tobacco and coffee processing; ships cereals. Beryl deposits.

Caranqui (käräng'kē), village, Imbabura prov., N Ecuador, in the Andes, just SW of Ibarra, in fertile agr. region (cotton, sugar cane, fruit, cereals, stock). Has anc. Inca ruins revered by natives as birthplace of Atahualpa.

Caransebes (käränsä'bĕsh), Rum. *Caransebeş,* Hung. *Karánsebes* (kŏ'ränshĕ"bĕsh), town (1948 pop. 10,106), ⊙ Severin prov., W Rumania, in Banat, on Timis R. and 25 mi. SE of Lugoj; rail junction and trading center; woodworking (furniture, flooring, boxes and barrels), brick making, flour milling; extensive plum orchards in vicinity. Seat of Theological Academy and Uniate bishopric. Garrison town. Has 17th- and 18th-cent. churches, 17th-cent. episcopal residence. Founded in 12th-13th cent.; first Banat rulers resided here. Recreation center of Teius is just SW.

Carantec (käräték'), village (pop. 1,800), Finistère dept., W France, on English Channel, 8 mi. NNW of Morlaix; bathing resort.

Cara-Omer, Rumania: see NEGRU-VODA.

Cara-Paraná River (kä'rä-päränä'), Amazonas commissary, SE Colombia, rises E of Caucayá, flows c.120 mi. SE, through densely forested lowlands, to Putumayo R. (Peru border) at 1°15'S 73°53'W.

Carapari (käräpärē'), town, Tarija dept., S Bolivia, 14 mi. NNW of Yacuiba; corn, fruit, sheep.

Carapciu, Ukrainian SSR: see KARAPCHU.

Carapebus, town (pop. 1,027), E Rio de Janeiro state, Brazil, on railroad and 15 mi. NE of Macaé; coffee, sugar cane, fruit.

Carapeguá (käräpägwä'), town (dist. pop. 21,312), Paraguarí dept., S Paraguay, 45 mi. SE of Asunción. Trading and agr. center (oranges, sugar cane, cotton, cattle); sugar refining, liquor distilling, tanning.

Carapelle River (käräpĕl'lĕ) or **Carapella River,** S Italy, rises in the Apennines 12 mi. SE of Ariano Irpino, flows 50 mi. NE to Gulf of Manfredonia 9 mi. S of Manfredonia. In upper course called Calaggio R.

Carapichaima (kä"rŭpŭchī'mŭ), village (pop. 2,100), W Trinidad, B.W.I., 12 mi. SE of Port of Spain; sugar estates.

Caraquet (kă'rŭkĕt), village (pop. estimate c.1,500), NE N.B., on Caraquet Bay, inlet of Chaleur Bay, near mouth of Caraquet R. (18 mi. long), 36 mi. ENE of Bathurst; fishing center (oysters, lobster, clams, smelt, mackerel). Founded c.1770 by Breton fishermen.

Caraquet Island (2 mi. long), NE N.B., in Chaleur Bay, at entrance of Caraquet Bay (6 mi. long, 3 mi. wide), 4 mi. NE of Caraquet; 47°49'N 64°54'W.

Caráquez Bay (kärä'kĕs), small inlet of the Pacific in Manabí prov., W Ecuador; 0°30'S. Seaport Bahía de Caraquez at head. Receives Chone R.

Carás or **Caraz** (both: käräs'), city (pop. 3,355), ⊙ Huaylas or Huailas prov. (□ 1,331; pop. 40,210), Ancash dept., W central Peru, in the Callejón de Huaylas, on Santa R. and 38 mi. NW of Huarás, in silver- and copper-mining area; alt. 7,556 ft. Subtropical fruit, sugar cane, coffee.

Carasaljo, Lake, N.J.: see LAKEWOOD.

Carasinho, Brazil: see CARÀZINHO.

Caras River (kä'räsh), Rum. *Caraş,* Serbo-Croatian *Karaš* or *Karash,* in SW Rumania and N Yugoslavia, rises in Transylvanian Alps 12 mi. NE of Oravita (Rumania), flows c.50 mi. N and SW to the Danube 7 mi. SW of Bela Crkva.

Caratasca (kärätä'skä), village (pop. 35), Colón dept., E Honduras, in Mosquitia, on Caribbean Sea, at mouth of Caratasca Lagoon, 105 mi. ESE of Iriona; coconuts, livestock.

Caratasca Lagoon, largest of Honduras, in Mosquitia region, c.35 mi. NW of Cape Gracias a Dios; 35 mi. long, 8 mi. wide. Connected with Caribbean Sea by 3-mi. channel past Caratasca village. Lumbering (mahogany, cedar), stock raising along shores.

Carate, El, Panama: see EL CARATE.

Carate Brianza (kärä'tĕ brēän'tsä), town (pop. 6,800), Milano prov., Lombardy, N Italy, 15 mi. N of Milan; mfg. (ribbon, cotton textiles, machinery).

Caratinga (kärätĕng'gŭ), city (pop. 4,791), E Minas Gerais, Brazil, terminus of railroad from Ponte Nova and 120 mi. ENE of Belo Horizonte; important coffeegrowing center. Beryl and nickel deposits. Bishopric.

Caratunk, plantation (pop. 96), Somerset co., central Maine, on the Kennebec and c.33 mi. above Madison in hunting, fishing area.

Carauari (kärou"ärē'), city (pop. 484), W central Amazonas, Brazil, on Juruá R. and 180 mi. SW of Tefé.

Caraúbas (käräōō'bŭs), city (pop. 1,119), W Rio Grande do Norte, NE Brazil, on railroad and 45 mi. SSW of Mossoró; sugar, cotton, cattle, carnauba. Aquamarines found in area.

Caravaca (käräva'kä), city (pop. 9,629), Murcia prov., SE Spain, 43 mi. WNW of Murcia; mfg. of sandals; processing of hemp, olive oil, wine, essential oils; also mfg. of woolen, cotton, and linen textiles, and of chocolate and brandy. Has 15th-cent. Gothic parochial church; church of La Santissima Cruz (1617), which once had miraculous Cross of Caravaca; and 15th-cent. castle. City belonged (13th cent.) to Knights Templars. Well-known stalagmite caves are near by.

Caravaggio (käräväd'jô), town (pop. 7,816), Bergamo prov., Lombardy, N Italy, 14 mi. S of Bergamo; metal products, hats, shoes, starch, candy. Sanctuary (1575) near by. Michelangelo Amerighi, surnamed Caravaggio, b. here.

Caravela, Port. Guinea: see BIJAGÓS ISLANDS.

Caravelas (käräva'lŭs), city (pop. 2,155), SE Bahia, Brazil, fishing port on tidal inlet of the Atlantic, 140 mi. E of Teófilo Otoni (Minas Gerais); vegetable and whale oil, coffee, manioc. Has airport on Salvador–Rio de Janeiro route. Ponta d'Areia (3 mi. SE on the Atlantic) is E terminus of rail line to Araçuaí (Minas Gerais). Formerly spelled Caravellas.

Caravelí (käräväle'), city (pop. 1,212), ⊙ Caravelí prov. (□ 3,183; pop. 12,700), Arequipa dept., S Peru, on W slopes of Cordillera Occidental, 70 mi. NW of Camaná, and linked by highway with its Pacific landing Atico, 33 mi. SSW; alt. 5,985 ft. Grain, cotton, fruit, stock. Airfield.

Caravellas, Brazil: see CARAVELAS.

Caraway (kă'rŭwā), town (pop. 970), Craighead co., NE Ark., 22 mi. ESE of Jonesboro.

Carayaca (kärīä'kä), town (pop. 675), Federal Dist., N Venezuela, 15 mi. W of Caracas; coffee, sugar, corn, cacao.

Carayaó (kärīäō'), town (dist. pop. 4,262), Caaguazú dept., S central Paraguay, 20 mi. N of Coronel Oviedo; lumbering and agr. center (oranges, sugar cane, livestock); sawmilling, processing of oil of petitgrain. Founded 1770.

Caraybamba or **Caraibamba** (kärībäm'bä), town (pop. 1,392), Apurímac dept., S central Peru, in the Andes, at N foot of Cordillera de Huanzo, 70 mi. SW of Abancay; sugar cane, grain, potatoes, sheep, cattle.

Caraz, Peru: see CARÁS.

Caraza, Bolivia: see SANTIVÁÑEZ.

Caràzinho or **Carasinho** (kärä"zē'nyŏŏ), city (pop. 7,692), N Rio Grande do Sul, Brazil, in the Serra Geral, on railroad and 20 mi. W of Passo Fundo; lumbering, maté processing, livestock slaughtering. Semiprecious stones found in area. Airfield.

Carazo (kärä'sō), department (□ 370; 1950 pop. 52,174), SW Nicaragua, on Pacific coast; ⊙ Jinotepe. On Pacific slope of coastal range; dry climate (artesian wells furnish water supply). Agr.: mainly coffee (in area of San Marcos, Jinotepe, and Diriamba), sugar cane (Santa Teresa, La Conquista), rice, sesame; livestock. Hardwood lumbering near coast. Limestone and salt production. Main centers (served by railroad and Inter-American Highway from Managua): Jinotepe, Diriamba, San Marcos. Formed 1891.

Carbajales de Alba (kärvähä'lĕs dhä äl'vä), town (pop. 1,368), Zamora prov., NW Spain, 17 mi. NW of Zamora; lumbering; cereals, livestock.

Carballino (kärvälyē'nō), town (pop. 2,469), Orense prov., NW Spain, 14 mi. NW of Orense; tanning, meat processing, cotton and linen mfg.; trades in cereals, wine, lumber, livestock. Tin mines in vicinity are now little exploited. Warm sulphur springs.

Carballo (kärvä'lyō), town (pop. 1,584), La Coruña prov., NW Spain, 18 mi. SW of La Coruña; dairy products; linen milling, tanning, lumbering, stock raising. Mineral springs.

Carberry, town (pop. 857), SW Man., 26 mi. E of Brandon; mixed farming, stock raising.

Carberry Hill, hill (c.500 ft.) and locality, NE Midlothian, Scotland, 3 mi. SE of Musselburgh. Mary Queen of Scots surrendered here (1567) to the rebel barons. Carberry Tower dates from 1597.

Carbet (kärbā'), town (commune pop. 5,020), NW Martinique, at W foot of the Pitons du Carbet (3,960 ft.; 3 pinnacles), 10 mi. NW of Fort-de-France; trading center; cacao growing, rum distilling. Sometimes called Le Carbet.

Carbon, village (pop. 369), S Alta., on Kneehill R. and 19 mi. W of Drumheller; coal mining.

Carbon. 1 County (□ 2,070; pop. 10,241), S Mont.; ⊙ Red Lodge. Irrigated agr. and mining region bordering on Wyo.; drained by Clarks Fork of Yellowstone R. Livestock, sugar beets, beans; coal, natural gas. Two sections of Custer Natl. Forest here, one in SE and the other in mtn. area of SW. Formed 1895. **2** County (□ 405; pop. 57,558), E Pa.; ⊙ Mauch Chunk. Mtn. region drained by Lehigh R., which forms part of NW border and flows S through co. Blue Mtn. on S border; E part on Pocono plateau, rest in anthracite region. Settled 1746 by Moravian missionaries. Mfg. (metal products, textiles); agr. Formed 1843. **3** County (□ 1,474; pop. 24,901), central Utah; ⊙ Price. Mining and agr. region drained by Green and Price rivers. Coal fields; sugar beets, hay, grain. Includes much of West Tavaputs Plateau. Formed 1894. **4** County (□ 7,965; pop. 15,742), S Wyo.; ⊙ Rawlins. Grain and livestock area bordering Colo.; watered by N.Platte and Medicine Bow rivers. Pathfinder Reservoir in N. Coal, oil. Parts of Medicine Bow Forest in SE and S; Sierra Madre in S; Medicine Bow Mts. in SE. Formed 1868.

Carbon. 1 Town (pop. 480), Clay co., W Ind., 19 mi. NE of Terre Haute, in agr. and bituminous-coal area. **2** Town (pop. 282), Adams co., SW Iowa, near Middle Nodaway R., 6 mi. NW of Corning, in coal-mining region. **3** Town (pop. 444), Eastland co., N central Texas, 38 mi. N of Brownwood; ships cotton, peanuts; oil wells.

Carbon, Cape (kärbō'). **1** Headland, Constantine dept., NE Algeria, on the Mediterranean, at W end of Gulf of Bougie, just N of Bougie city; 36°46'N 5°7'E. Lighthouse. **2** Headland, Oran dept., NW Algeria, on the Mediterranean, at W end of Gulf of Arzew, 5 mi. NNW of Arzew; 35°54'N 0°20'W.

Carbon, Mount (14,259 ft.), W central Colo., highest point in Elk Mts., 12 mi. NNE of Crested Butte. Also known as Castle Peak.

Carbonado (kärbŭnä'dō), town (pop. 412), Pierce co., W central Wash., 25 mi. SE of Tacoma.

Carbonara, Cape (kärbônä'rä), SE Sardinia, at E end of Gulf of Cagliari; 39°5'N 9°31'E. Tunny fishing; granite.

Carbonara di Bari (dē bä'rē), town (pop. 13,426), Bari prov., Apulia, S Italy, 4 mi. S of Bari, in fruit- and vegetable-growing region; macaroni mfg. Adjacent to it is Ceglie del Campo.

Carbon-Blanc (kärbō'-blä'), village (pop. 752), Gironde dept., SW France, near right bank of the Garonne, 5 mi. NE of Bordeaux; winegrowing.

Carbon Cliff, residential village (pop. 676), Rock Island co., NW Ill., on Rock R. (bridged) and 8 mi. E of Moline.

Carbondale. 1 Town (pop. 441), Garfield co., W central Colo., on Roaring Fork R., at mouth of Crystal R., just N of Elk Mts., and 11 mi. SSE of Glenwood Springs, in irrigated region producing potatoes and grain; alt. 6,000 ft. **2** City (pop. 10,921), Jackson co., SW Ill., 19 mi. WSW of West Frankfort; trade and rail center in bituminous-coal and agr. area; mfg. of clothing, lumber milling. Seat of Southern Ill. Univ. U.S. army's Ill. Ordnance Plant, Crab Orchard L., and Giant City State Park (c.1,300 acres in Ill. Ozarks) are near by. Founded 1852, inc. 1869. **3** City (pop. 453), Osage co., E Kansas, 16 mi. S of Topeka, in livestock and grain region. **4** Industrial city (pop. 16,296), Lackawanna co., NE Pa., 13 mi. NE of Scranton and on Lackawanna R.; anthracite mining; textiles, metal products. First underground anthracite mine in world opened 1831. Settled 1814, inc. 1851. **5** Village (pop. 1,211, with adjacent Cannelton), Fayette co., S central W.Va., c.20 mi. SE of Charleston.

Carbonear (kär″bŭnēr′), town (pop. 3,468), SE N.F., on Avalon Peninsula, on W shore of Conception Bay, 28 mi. WNW of St. John's; commercial center and fishing port; mfg. of furniture, bedding, mineral water. Just N, at Victoria, is hydroelectric station.

Carboneras (kärvōnä′räs), town (pop. 1,721), Almería prov., S Spain, on the Mediterranean, 33 mi. ENE of Almería; iron foundry. Cereals, esparto. Iron mines in vicinity.

Carboneras de Guadazaón (dhā gwä-dhä-thäōn′), village (pop. 1,572), Cuenca prov., E central Spain, in Serranía de Cuenca, 17 mi. SE of Cuenca; grain, livestock; lumbering, apiculture.

Carbonero el Mayor (kärvōnā′rō ĕl mīōr′), town (pop. 2,524), Segovia prov., central Spain, 13 mi. NW of Segovia, in fertile agr. region (wheat, barley, carobs, chick-peas, sheep); timber and naval stores. Flour milling, mfg. of ceramics and tiles; lime and kaolin quarrying.

Carbones River (kärvō′nĕs), Andalusia, SW Spain, rises in W Sierra de Yeguas 10 mi. ESE of Olvera, flows c.75 mi. NW, past La Puebla de Cazalla, to the Guadalquivir near Villanueva del Río. Used for irrigation.

Carbon Glow, mining village (1940 pop. 640), Letcher co., SE Ky., in the Cumberlands, 14 mi. ESE of Hazard; bituminous coal.

Carbon Hill. 1 City (pop. 2,179), Walker co., NW central Ala., 50 mi. NW of Birmingham; coal mining; cotton, lumber. Inc. 1891. **2** Village (pop. 158), Grundy co., NE Ill., 20 mi. SSW of Joliet, in agr. and bituminous-coal area.

Carbonia (kärbô′nyä), town (pop. 2,814), Cagliari prov., SW Sardinia, 10 mi. S of Iglesias; lignite-mining center; built 1937–38. Lignite and barite mines at Serbariu, 1 mi. E.

Carbonne (kärbôn′), village (pop. 1,533), Haute-Garonne dept., S France, on the Garonne and 23 mi. SSW of Toulouse; winegrowing, fruit and vegetable preserving.

Carbost, Scotland: see SKYE, ISLE OF.

Carbrook, NE suburb of Sheffield, West Riding, S Yorkshire, England; steel milling.

Carbunesti, Rumania: see TARGU-CARBUNESTI.

Carbury, village, Bottineau co., N N.Dak., port of entry near Can. line, 5 mi. NW of Bottineau.

Carcabat, Eritrea: see KARKABAT.

Carcabuey (kärkävwā′), town (pop. 4,370), Córdoba prov., S Spain, 10 mi. E of Lucena; olive-oil processing, flour milling, brandy distilling, soap mfg. Livestock and fruit in area. Gypsum quarries.

Carcagente (kärkähĕn′tā), city (pop. 14,917), Valencia prov., E Spain, near the Júcar, 3 mi. SSW of Alcira, in fertile plain irrigated by canal built (1654) by Philip II. Orange-processing and -shipping center (extracts, beverages, essential oils); mfg. of furniture, hardware, insecticides; vegetable and fruit canning, olive-oil processing, sawmilling. Sericulture; cereals, fruit, honey. Has fine parochial church, town hall, old palace.

Carcar (kär′kär), town (1939 pop. 5,004; 1948 municipality pop. 32,818), central Cebu isl., Philippines, on railroad and 22 mi. SW of Cebu city, on Bohol Strait; fishing and agr. center (corn, coconuts).

Cárcar (kär′kär), town (pop. 1,612), Navarre prov., N Spain, on Ega R. and 19 mi. SSE of Estella; vegetable canning; wine, olive oil, sugar beets.

Carcaraña (kärkärä′nyä), town (pop. estimate 2,000), S Sante Fe prov., Argentina, on Carcaraña R. and 30 mi. W of Rosario, in grain and livestock area; flour mills, liquor and soap factories.

Carcaraña River, in S Córdoba and Santa Fe provs., Argentina, formed by union of the Cuarto and Tercero at Saladillo (Córdoba prov.), flows c.125 mi. E, past Los Surgentes, Cruz Alta, Carcaraña, Lucio Vicente López, and Andino, to an arm of the Paraná 34 mi. NNW of Rosario. Hydroelectric stations at Andino and Lucio Vicente López.

Carcassonne (kärkäsôn′), city (pop. 31,752), ⊙ Aude dept., S France, on Aude R. and Canal du Midi, 50 mi. ESE of Toulouse; tourist and wine center; tanning, distilling, fruit preserving, metalworking, mfg. of hosiery and fertilizer. The *Cité*, one of France's architectural marvels, atop hill on left bank of the Aude, is a medieval walled city. Within its crenelated fortifications are enclosed a 12th-cent. castle and the Romanesque and Gothic church of Saint-Nazaire (11th-14th cent.). The commercial and residential dist., including the cathedral and the 14th-18th-cent. church of St. Vincent, is on opposite side of river. A stronghold of the Albigenses, it was taken by Simon de Montfort in 1209. During 19th cent. the ruined *Cité* was restored by Viollet-le-Duc.

Carcastillo (kärkästēl′yō), town (pop. 2,260), Navarre prov., N Spain, on Aragon R. and 24 mi. NNE of Tudela; chocolate mfg.; agr. trade (cereals, wine, sugar beets). Oliva monastery near by.

Carcavelos (kärkävā′lōōsh), village (pop. 1,788), Lisboa dist., central Portugal, on the Atlantic at mouth of Tagus R., 10 mi. W of Lisbon; noted for its wines. Has Portugal's overseas cable station.

Carcelén (kär-thālĕn′), town (pop. 1,540), Albacete prov., SE central Spain, 20 mi. NW of Almansa; olive-oil processing; saffron, almonds, fruit.

Cárcer (kär′thār), village (pop. 1,783), Valencia prov., E Spain, 7 mi. NNW of Játiva, in fertile area yielding truck products and rice; cattle.

Carcès (kärsĕs′), village (pop. 1,642), Var. dept., SE France, on the Argens and 15 mi. WSW of Draguignan; agr. market (olives, wine).

Carchá or **San Pedro Carchá** (sän pā′drō kärchä′), town (1950 pop. 7,539), Alta Verapaz dept., Guatemala, in N highlands, 3 mi. E of Cobán; alt. 4,200 ft. Market center; weaving, pottery making; coffee, livestock. Pop. largely Indian.

Carchelejo (kärchālā′hō), town (pop. 2,331), Jaén prov., S Spain, 13 mi. SE of Jaén; knit-goods mfg., flour milling, olive-oil processing. Cereals, wine, sheep. Gypsum and stone quarries.

Carchemish (kär′kĭmĭsh, käkē′–), anc. city on the Euphrates at site of modern village (pop. 883) of Karkamis (Turkish *Karkamış*), in S Turkey at Syrian line (opposite Jerablus), 38 mi. ESE of Gaziantep. It was important ⊙ of the Hittites. Here Nebuchadnezzar won a decisive victory over the Egyptian pharaoh Necho in 605 B.C. Sometimes Charchemish.

Carchi (kär′chē), prov. (□ 1,439; 1950 pop. 76,129), N Ecuador, in the Andes, bordering Colombia; ⊙ Tulcán. Has semitropical to temperate climate, depending on alt. Little-exploited mineral resources include saltpeter deposits. Mainly stock raising (cattle, sheep) and agr., producing corn, wheat, barley, potatoes, sugar cane, coffee, fruit. Dairying, flour milling, and mfg. of woolen native goods (rugs, ponchos) are its main industries; Tulcán, San Gabriel, and El Angel its centers. The region has been frequently subject to earthquakes.

Carchi River, Colombia, rises in the Andes at foot of Nevado de Chiles, flows a short distance E along Ecuador line, bet. Ipiales and Tulcán, then N to Patía R.; c.100 mi. long. Its mid course is called the Guaitará (gwītärä′).

Carcoar, village (pop. 452), E central New South Wales, Australia, 120 mi. WNW of Sydney; mining center (gold, iron); orchards.

Carcroft, England: see ADWICK-LE-STREET.

Carcross, village (pop. estimate 150), S Yukon, on L. Bennett, 40 mi. SSE of Whitehorse, on railroad; coal, gold mining; tourist center. Airfield.

Cardal (kärdäl′), town (pop. 1,200), Florida dept., S central Uruguay, on railroad and 17 mi. SSW of Florida; dairy center; wheat, corn, cattle; supplies Montevideo.

Cardale, village (pop. 3,026, with adjacent Republic), Fayette co., SW Pa., 8 mi. WNW of Uniontown.

Cardamom Hills (kär′dŭmŭm, –mŏm), N central range (□ c.900) of S section of Western Ghats, S India, S of ANAIMALAI HILLS, in NE Travancore-Cochin; rise to over 4,500 ft. in E ridges. Noted for large output of tea, coffee, teak, bamboo, turmeric, and for the numerous cardamom estates which gave it its name. Products shipped mainly via Kambam Valley (E). Term Cardamom Hills (or Travancore Hills) is sometimes applied to whole section of Western Ghats S of PALGHAT GAP, from Anaimalai Hills to Cape Comorin.

Cardamom Mountains, Thai *Banthat* (bän′tät′), on Thailand-Cambodia frontier, extend 100 mi. NW–SE parallel to Chanthaburi Range in Thailand; highest point, Tadet peak (3,667 ft.), S of Pailin. Thickly wooded and inhabited by primitive Dravidian tribes originally from Coromandel Coast. Cardamoms, semi-precious stones.

Cardamum Island (kär′dŭmŭm), coral island of Amin Divi group of Laccadive Isls., India, in Arabian Sea; 11°15′N 72°45′E. Administered by South Kanara dist., Madras; coconuts; coir mfg. Also spelled Cardamat or Kadmat.

Cardano (kärdä′nô), Ger. *Kardaun*, village (pop. 668), Bolzano prov., Trentino–Alto Adige, N Italy, on Isarco R. just E of Bolzano; hydroelectric plant.

Cardano al Campo (äl käm′pô), village (pop. 3,586), Varese prov., Lombardy, N Italy, 1 mi. SW of Gallarate; textiles, liquor.

Cardedeu (kärdhä-dhä′ōō), town (pop. 2,024), Barcelona prov., NE Spain, 4 mi. ENE of Granollers; biscuit mfg., lumbering. Wine, hemp in area.

Cardeña (kär-dhā′nyä), town (pop. 2,138), Córdoba prov., S Spain, 18 mi. NNE of Montoro; flour mill. Livestock market; cereals, vegetables, lumber.

Cárdenas (kär′dänäs), city (pop. 37,059), Matanzas prov., W Cuba, port at head of Cárdenas Bay (13 mi. E–W, 11 mi. N–S), on railroad and 23 mi. E of Matanzas; 23°3′N 81°13′W. Exports sugar cane and sisal, which are processed here. Larger vessels anchor offshore. One of Cuba's leading fishing centers (sharks, sponge, etc.). Industries include sugar refining, distilling, tanning, mfg. of rope. The well-laid-out city has old churches, municipal mus., city hall, monument to Columbus. Narciso López landed here on his filibustering expedition of 1850. Near by are saltworks (Hicacos Peninsula) and several sugar centrals (Progreso, Dos Rosas). Famous Varadero beach resort is 8 mi. NNW.

Cárdenas. 1 City (pop. 8,478), San Luis Potosí, N central Mexico, on interior plateau, on railroad and 85 mi. E of San Luis Potosí. Agr. center (grain, cotton, fruit, livestock). **2** City (pop. 2,891), Tabasco, SE Mexico, near Grijalva R. and Chiapas border, 30 mi. W of Villahermosa; agr. center (bananas, tobacco, coffee, rice).

Cárdenas, town (1950 pop. 581), Rivas dept., SW Nicaragua, on S shore of L. Nicaragua, near Costa Rica border, 29 mi. SE of Rivas; agr., livestock.

Cardenete (kär-dhänā′tā), town (pop. 1,781), Cuenca prov., E central Spain, 30 mi. SE of Cuenca; wheat, grapes, saffron, beans, sheep, goats; apiculture; lumbering, olive-oil pressing.

Cardeñosa (kär-dhänyō′sä), town (pop. 1,103), Ávila prov., central Spain, 7 mi. NNW of Ávila; cereals, grapes, sheep; flour. Granite quarrying.

Carderview, village (pop. c.300), Johnson co., extreme NE Tenn., on Watauga Reservoir, 13 mi. E of Elizabethtown. Established 1947–48 following evacuation of former town of Butler, 3 mi. E.

Cardeston, England: see ALBERBURY.

Cardiel, Lake (kärdyĕl′) (□ 177; alt. 1,043 ft.), in Patagonia, W central Santa Cruz natl. territory, Argentina; 18 mi. long, 14 mi. wide.

Cardiff (kär′dĭf), town (pop. 3,896), E New South Wales, Australia, 7 mi. WSW of Newcastle; coal-mining center.

Cardiff. 1 Town (pop. 204), Jefferson co., N central Ala., 12 mi. NW of Birmingham; coal mining. **2** Village (pop. c.500), Harford co., NE Md., at Pa. line and 33 mi. NNE of Baltimore; serpentine quarry; makes clothing, canning machinery.

Cardiff, county borough (1931 pop. 223,589; 1951 census 243,627) and city, ⊙ Glamorganshire, Wales, in SE part of co., on Taff R. 2 mi. from its mouth on Bristol Channel, and 130 mi. W of London; 51°29′N 3°10′W; one of world's greatest coal-shipping ports, also exporting iron and steel products; imports iron ore, timber, and grains; steel milling, shipbuilding, mfg. of chemicals and paper, flour milling. Extensive docks were built 1839 by 2d marquis of Bute. Cardiff Castle, now residence of marquis of Bute, was built 1090 by Robert Fitzhamon, on site of Roman fort; scene of imprisonment (1108–34) of Robert, duke of Normandy; partly destroyed (1404) by Owen Glendower. Other notable features are Welsh Natl. Mus., law courts, city hall, Univ. Col of South Wales and Monmouthshire, Univ. of Wales Registry, Glamorgan County Hall, and 13th–15th-cent. church of St. John. Considerable damage was inflicted by concentrated German air raids in 1941. Co. borough includes suburbs of Canton (W; pop. 17,273), Cathays (N; pop. 16,566), LLANDAFF (W; pop. 27,762), Grangetown (SW; pop. 15,403), Butetown (SW), and Roath (E; pop. 15,792).

Cardiff-by-the-Sea, village (1940 pop. 509), San Diego co., S Calif., on the coast, 20 mi. N of San Diego; flowers, citrus fruit, truck, avocados.

Cardigan (kär′dĭgŭn), village (pop. estimate 500), E P.E.I., on Cardigan R., near its mouth on the Gulf of St. Lawrence, 24 mi. E of Charlottetown; mixed farming, dairying, potatoes.

Cardigan or **Cardiganshire** (kär′dĭgŭn, –shĭr), county (□ 692.4; 1931 pop. 55,184; 1951 census 53,267), W Wales; ⊙ Cardigan. Bounded by Cardigan Bay of Irish Sea (W), Merioneth (N), Montgomery, Radnor, Brecknock (E), Carmarthen (S), Pembroke (SW). Drained by Teifi, Rheidol, and Ystwyth rivers. Broken plateau, rising to 2,468 ft. in NE (Plinlimmon), leveling toward coast. Industries include woolen milling, leather mfg., farming. Besides Cardigan, other towns are Aberystwyth, Lampeter, Aberayron, New Quay. There are several monastic remains, including Strata Florida, traces of Roman and anc. Br. occupation, castles at Cardigan and Aberystwyth.

Cardigan, municipal borough (1931 pop. 3,310; 1951 census 3,497), ⊙ Cardiganshire, Wales, on Teifi R. estuary, near Cardigan Bay of Irish Sea, and 22 mi. NW of Carmarthen; agr. market, with woolen mills and agr. machinery works. Has 13th–15th-cent. church, remains of 12th-cent. castle, and slight remains of 12th-cent. priory.

Cardigan, Mount, N.H.: see ORANGE.

Cardigan Bay, inlet (10 mi. long, 7 mi. wide at entrance) of Gulf of St. Lawrence, E P.E.I. On it is Georgetown.

Cardigan Bay, inlet of Irish Sea, W Wales, extending 65 mi. SSW–NNE bet. Braich-y-Pwll in Caernarvon (NNE) and St. David's Head in Pembroke (SSW); 35 mi. wide. Receives the rivers Dovey, Ystwyth, Mawddach, Teifi. Chief towns on it: Pwllheli, Portmadoc, Barmouth, Towyn, Aberystwyth, Fishguard.

Cardigan Island (35 acres), in Cardigan Bay of Irish Sea, Cardigan, Wales, at mouth of Teifi R., 4 mi. NNW of Cardigan; ½ mi. long, ¼ mi. wide.

Cardiganshire, Wales: see CARDIGAN, county.

Cardin, village, Ottawa co., extreme NE Okla., just SW of Picher, near Kansas line; smelting center in lead- and zinc-mining region.

Cardinal, village (pop. 1,645), SE Ont., on the St. Lawrence and 8 mi. NE of Prescott, opposite Galop Isl. and at foot of the Galops Rapids; dairying, starch mfg.

Cardinale (kärdēnä′lĕ), town (pop. 3,136), Catanzaro prov., Calabria, S Italy, 21 mi. SSW of Catanzaro; woolen mills.

Cardington, agr. village and parish (pop. 346), central Bedford, England, 3 mi. ESE of Bedford. An Eleanor Cross was here. Here was Royal Air Force lighter-than-air craft experimental station and base of the ill-fated airship *R101*.

Cardington, village (pop. 1,465), Morrow co., central Ohio, 14 mi. ESE of Marion, in agr. area; metal products, sporting goods. Founded 1822.

Cardito (kärdē'tô), village (pop. 5,401), Napoli prov., Campania, S Italy, 6 mi. N of Naples, in agr. region (hemp, grapes, flax).

Carditsa, Greece: see KARDITSA.

Cardona (kär-dhō'nä), town (pop. 3,661), Barcelona prov., NE Spain, on the Cardoner and 15 mi. NW of Manresa; cotton spinning, flour- and sawmilling. Trades in wine, olive oil, cereals, livestock. Near by are extensively worked rock-salt dome (alt. 250 ft.) and potassium-salt deposits.

Cardona, town (pop. 2,000), Soriano dept., SW Uruguay, on railroad and 57 mi. SE of Mercedes; shipping center in agr. region (wheat, oats, linseed, corn); cattle and sheep raising. Its railroad station is called La Lata.

Cardoner River (kär-dhōnär'), in Lérida and Barcelona provs., NE Spain, rises on S slopes of the E Pyrenees, flows c.55 mi. SSE to Llobregat R. 3 mi. below Manresa.

Cardoso, Uruguay: see CARDOZO.

Cardoso Island (kärdō'zŏŏ), off SE coast of Brazil, part of São Paulo state, separated from mainland by narrow channel, and just S of Cananéia; 15 mi. long, 6 mi. wide; rises to 2,690 ft. Lighthouse on Bom Abrigo islet just E (25°7'S 47°52'W).

Cardoso Moreira (kärdō'zŏŏ môrā'rŏŏ), town (pop. 2,123), NE Rio de Janeiro state, Brazil, on Muriaé R., on railroad and 28 mi. NW of Campos; sugar.

Cardozo or **Cardoso** (kärdō'sō), village, Tacuarembó dept., central Uruguay, on large artificial lake formed by the Río Negro, on railroad and 18 mi. NE of Paso de los Toros; wheat, corn, cattle, sheep.

Cardross (kär'drŏs, kärdrŏs'), agr. village and parish (pop. 11,106, including part of Dumbarton burgh), S Dumbarton, Scotland, on the Clyde and 4 mi. WNW of Dumbarton. Robert Bruce died (1329) at Cardross Castle (no longer extant).

Cardston, town (pop. 2,334), S Alta., near B.C. and Mont. borders, at foot of Rocky Mts., on Lee Creek and 40 mi. SW of Lethbridge, in coal-mining region; alt. 3,775 ft.; tanning, dairying, grain. Founded in mid-19th cent. by Mormons from Utah, led by Charles Ora Card, son-in-law of Brigham Young; site of chief Canadian Mormon temple.

Cardwell, village (pop. 335), E Queensland, Australia, on Rockingham Bay, 95 mi. S of Cairns; sugar cane.

Cardwell, city (pop. 952), Dunklin co., extreme SE Mo., near St. Francis R., 19 mi. SW of Kennett.

Care Alto, Monte, Italy: see ADAMELLO.

Carega, Cima (chē'mä kärā'gä), highest peak (7,424 ft.) of Monti Lessini, N Italy, 12 mi. SSE of Rovereto.

Careggi (kärĕd'jē), village, Firenze prov., Tuscany, central Italy, 2 mi. N of Florence. Has Medici villa (enlarged 1433) where, under Lorenzo the Magnificent, the arts of the period flourished.

Carei (kärā'), formerly *Carei-Mare* or *Careii-Mare* (kärā'-mä'rä), Hung. *Nagykaroly* (nŏ'dyûkŏ'roi), town (1948 pop. 15,425), Baia-Mare prov., NW Rumania, in Transylvania, near Hung. border, 45 mi. NW of Zalau; rail junction; agr.-equipment trade; mfg. of paper, machinery, knitwear, buttons, cordage, edible oils, soap, alcohol, chemicals, tiles, bricks. Has 15th-cent. castle (now a hospital), former seat of Karolyi family, repeatedly restored; a Piarist monastery; R.C. baroque church; characteristic medieval bldgs. around its marketplace. Over 50% of pop. are Magyars. After inc. into Rumania (1919), Carei was known for a time as Carei-Mare, because of its former location in Hung. county of Szatmar. Returned to Hungary briefly (1940–45).

Careiro (kärā'rŏŏ), town (pop. 418), E central Amazonas, Brazil, on isl. (30 mi. long, 10 mi. wide) in the Amazon, 30 mi. ESE of Manaus. Sometimes spelled Carrero.

Carelia, USSR: see KARELIA.

Carelmapu (kärĕlmä'pŏŏ), village (1930 pop. 155), Llanquihue prov., S central Chile, on Chacao Strait across from Chiloé Isl., 10 mi. NNE of Ancud. Resort in agr. area (wheat, potatoes, livestock); dairying, fishing.

Carenage (kärûnä'jē), village (pop. 2,013, including adjoining St. Pierre), NW Trinidad, B.W.I., just outside U.S. naval base (W) and 3 mi. WNW of Port of Spain; coconuts; fishing.

Carenas (kärä'näs), town (pop. 1,139), Saragossa prov., NE Spain, 10 mi. SW of Calatayud; lumber, sheep, wine.

Carencro (kâ'rĭn-krō), village (pop. 1,587), Lafayette parish, S La., 6 mi. N of Lafayette, in agr. area (cotton, cattle); cotton ginning.

Carentan (kärätä'), town (pop. 3,687), Manche dept., NW France, port on a canal 5 mi. from English Channel, 15 mi. NNW of Saint-Lô; important butter-mfg. and shipping center (exports to England). Horse breeding. In Second World War, a strategic point in Normandy invasion, it was captured (June 12, 1944) by U.S. troops, linking Utah and Omaha beachheads.

Caresana (käräzä'nä), village (pop. 2,312), Vercelli prov., Piedmont, N Italy, 8 mi. SSE of Vercelli.

Caretta, village (pop. 1,856), McDowell co., S W.Va., 12 mi. SSW of Welch. Sometimes Juno.

Carevo Selo or **Tsarevo Selo** (both: tsä'rĕvô sĕ'lô), village (pop. 3,036), Macedonia, Yugoslavia, on Bregalnica R. and 70 mi. E of Skoplje, near Bulg. border; local trade center.

Carey, village (pop. 3,260), Wyandot co., N central Ohio, 15 mi. ESE of Findlay; trade, shipping center for truck-farming and dairying area; porcelain products, rubber goods, chemicals, wood products; limestone quarries. Shrine of Our Lady of Consolation is here. Platted 1843, inc. 1858.

Carey, Lake (□ 350), central Western Australia, 115 mi. NNE of Kalgoorlie; 30 mi. long, 11 mi. wide; usually dry.

Careysburg, town, Montserrado co., W Liberia, 18 mi. ENE of Monrovia; road junction; palm oil and kernels, rubber, coffee. Mission station.

Cargados Carajos Shoals (kärgä'dōs kûrä'zhōs), island dependency (□ ½; pop. 93) of Mauritius, in Mascarene group of Indian Ocean, c.300 mi. NNE of Mauritius. Includes several small isls. bet. 16°15' and 16°50'S, 59°30' and 59°45'E. Exports dried and salted fish. Meteorological station. Also called Saint Brandon Isls., for principal isl.

Cargelligo, Lake, Australia: see LAKE CARGELLIGO.

Cargèse (kär-zhĕz'), Ital. *Carghese* (kärgā'zĕ), village (pop. 744), W Corsica, on Gulf of Sagone of the Mediterranean, 17 mi. NNW of Ajaccio; wines. Founded 1774 by Gr. refugees from Turkish rule, it has Gr. Orthodox church.

Cargill, agr. village and parish (pop. 1,257), E Perthshire, Scotland, 5 mi. WSW of Coupar-Angus.

Cargofleet, England: see MIDDLESBROUGH.

Cargo Muchacho Mountains (kär'gō mŏŏchä'chō), SE Calif., small desert range near Colorado R., c.10 mi. NW of Yuma, Ariz.; max. alt. 2,225 ft. Gold mines.

Carhaix (kärĕ'), Breton *Keraez,* town (pop. 3,849), Finistère dept., W France, 31 mi. NE of Quimper; road and rail center; tanning, woodworking; slate quarries near by. Old Roman settlement. La Tour d'Auvergne b. here.

Carhuamayo (kärwämī'ō), town (pop. 1,717), Junín dept., central Peru, in Cordillera Central of the Andes, near L. Junín, on railroad and 17 mi. NNW of Junín; barley, potatoes, livestock. Silver mining near by.

Carhuás or **Carhuaz** (both: kärwäs'), city (pop. 2,582), ⊙ Carhuás prov. (□ 9,653; pop. 28,069), Ancash dept., W central Peru, in the Callejón de Huaylas, on Santa R. and 18 mi. NNW of Huarás (connected by road); alt. 8,819 ft. Wheat, corn. Silver and copper mining near by.

Carhué (kärwā'), town (pop. 5,770), ⊙ Adolfo Alsina dist. (□ 2,270; pop. 25,104), W Buenos Aires prov., Argentina, on L. Epecuén, 110 mi. NNW of Bahía Blanca; rail junction; grain, sheep. Health resort of Lago Epecuén (warm baths) 5 mi. NW.

Caria (kâ'rēû), anc. region of SW Asia Minor bordering the Aegean and the Mediterranean and S of Maeander R. (modern Menderes), which separated it from Lydia; area is in present-day SW Turkey. Early Doric and Ionic colonies were combined in a kingdom which later became a Roman prov. in 125 B.C. Cities included Halicarnassus, Cnidus, and Miletus. Phrygia was to E, Lycia to SE.

Caria (kärē'û), town (pop. 1,822), Castelo Branco dist., central Portugal, on railroad and 8 mi. E of Covilhã; olive and almond oil; grain, corn, wine.

Cariacica (kärēûsē'kû), city (pop. 1,445), central Espírito Santo, Brazil, near Espírito Santo Bay, on railroad and 6 mi. NW of Vitória; meat processing (lard, sausages); bananas.

Cariaco (käryä'kō), town (pop. 2,016), Sucre state, NE Venezuela, port on Gulf of Cariaco, on Cumaná-Carúpano highway, and 34 mi. E of Cumaná; cacao, coconuts, sugar cane.

Cariaco, Gulf of, inlet of the Caribbean, Sucre state, NE Venezuela, S of Araya Peninsula; 40 mi. long (W–E), c.10 mi. wide. Cumaná is near its entrance (W), Cariaco near its head. Linked by small river with L. Campona (E). Good anchorage and fishing ground.

Cariamanga (käryämäng'gä), town (1950 pop. 3,376), Loja prov., S Ecuador, in the Andes, 45 mi. SW of Loja; agr. (cereals, coffee, sugar cane, fruit, cattle, sheep).

Cariati (kärēä'tē), town (pop. 1,608), Cosenza prov., Calabria, S Italy, on SW shore of Gulf of Taranto, 18 mi. ESE of Rossano; fishing; stove mfg. Bishopric.

Caribana Point (kärēbä'nä), on Caribbean coast, NW Colombia, at E gate of Gulf of Urabá; 8°37'N 76°53'W.

Caribbean National Forest (kărĭbē'ûn, kûrĭ'bēûn), national reserves in Puerto Rico, consisting of the Toro Negro unit (center) 25 mi. SW of San Juan, and Luquillo unit (NE) 10 mi. SE of San Juan. Highest interior mtn. regions of the Cordillera Central, with wild game and tropical flora. Reforestation program. Several hydroelectric projects. Summer resort area. Established 1935.

Caribbean Sea, Sp. *Mar Caribe,* part (□ c.750,000) of the Atlantic Ocean, bet. N coast of South America (S), the archipelago of the West Indies (N and E), and Central America (W). Yucatan Peninsula (Mexico) bounds it NW and is separated from Cuba by c.135-mi.-wide Yucatan Channel, which links the Caribbean with Gulf of Mexico. Numerous narrow straits in the Greater and Lesser ANTILLES connect it with the Atlantic. The Panama Canal joins it with the Pacific, making it one of the world's busiest shipping lanes. Bordering it are 11 Latin American republics, Br. Honduras, and the Br., Du., Fr., U.S., and Venezuelan isls. in the West Indies. Situated entirely in the tropics, approximately bet. 9°–22°N and 61°–88°W. Greatest length (E–W), c.1,800 m.; greatest width, c.900 mi.; average depth, 8,400 ft.; greatest depth measured so far, Bartlett Trough (22,788 ft.). Salinity is comparatively low; waters are of unusual transparency and of a beautiful bluish color. Its temp., over 75°F., varies only slightly during the year. Little encumbered with rocks or isls.; navigation is clear and open. However, a low shoal (the so-called Jamaica rise) of banks and cays bet. the Mosquito Coast of Central America practically divides it into 2 basins. The W basin, W of Cayman Isls., is sometimes called Cayman Sea. Part of the Gulf Stream is formed in the Caribbean by waters entering from the Equatorial Current and passing through Strait of Yucatan into the Gulf of Mexico. The area is influenced by tempering NE trade winds, but hurricanes and volcanic disturbances along its fringes are common. The coast is generally rocky, flanked by Andean ranges and outliers on South American N coast (where L. MARACAIBO is the major indentation). Principal tributary is the Magdalena, from Colombia. Caribbean ports include: in the West Indies—Santiago de Cuba, Kingston (Jamaica), Port-au-Prince (Haiti), Ciudad Trujillo (Dominican Republic), Mayaguez and Ponce (Puerto Rico), Basse-Terre (Guadeloupe), Fort-de-France (Martinique), and Willemstad (Curaçao); Venezuela—La Guaira and Maracaibo; Colombia—Santa Marta, Barranquilla, and Cartagena; Central America—Cristóbal and Colón (at entrance of the Panama Canal), Limón (Costa Rica), Puerto Barrios (Guatemala), Belize (Br. Honduras). Predominant freight from the Caribbean ports is petroleum, iron ore, sugar, coffee, cacao, bananas. There are also numerous resorts, particularly on the isls., which are increasingly visited during winter by tourists from the U.S. First European to sight this sea was Columbus on his 1st voyage (1492); he further explored it on his later voyages and in 1502–3 sailed along the Central American shore. The voyages of his contemporaries, Vespucci, Ojeda, Bastidas, and Balboa, contributed additional knowledge. From early colonial days the Caribbean came to be associated with pirates, buccaneers, and a flourishing smuggling trade. The Caribbean takes its name from the fierce aboriginal Caribs who inhabited parts of the area; now almost extinct, they held much of South America and had before the arrival of Columbus driven out the Arawak Indians from the Lesser Antilles.

Caribbees, West Indies: see ANTILLES.

Caribblanco (kärē'bläng-kō), village, Heredia prov., N Costa Rica, on Sarapiquí R. and 16 mi. NNW of Heredia; fruit, fodder crops, livestock.

Cariboo Gold Mines (kă'rĭbŏŏ), locality, central N.S., 27 mi. SE of Truro; gold-mining center.

Cariboo Mountains, range in S central and E B.C., extends 200 mi. NW and SE, bet. upper North Thompson R. and N apex of Fraser R., roughly parallel to Rocky Mts. main range, from which it is separated by the Rocky Mtn. trench, here occupied by Fraser R. Highest peak of range is believed to be Mt. Titan (c.11,750 ft.); highest surveyed peak is Mt. Spranger (9,920 ft.). In SE part of range is Wells Gray Provincial Park, containing Hobson, Azure, Clearwater, and Murtle lakes. Wells and Barkerville (N) are gold-mining centers. In W foothills is the Cariboo District, scene (1860) of the Cariboo gold rush. Up to 1866 gold to value of about $20,000,000 was mined here; industry later declined in importance and was superseded by farming, stock raising, and hunting. The Cariboo Road, built 1862–65 by the Royal Engineers from Yale, at head of navigation of the Fraser R., via Ashcroft, to Barkerville, a distance of c.500 mi., at cost of $1,250,000, facilitated settlement of the district. Prince George, Quesnel, and Williams Lake are trade centers of region.

Caribou (kă'rĭbŏŏ), county (□ 1,175; pop. 5,576), SE Idaho; ⊙ Soda Springs. Mtn. area bordering on Wyo. and crossed by Blackfoot R., passing through Blackfoot Reservoir in NW. Wheat, livestock, dairy products. Phosphate mines near Conda; part of Caribou Natl. Forest in E. Co. formed 1919.

Caribou, town (pop. 9,923), including Caribou village (pop. 4,500), Aroostook co., NE Maine, on the Aroostook and 13 mi. N of Presque Isle; potato-shipping center, mfg. (wood products, textiles, wagons), winter sports. Port of entry for planes. Inc. 1859.

Caribou Island (kă'rĭbŏŏ) (3 mi. long, 1 mi. wide), in Northumberland Strait, N N.S., 5 mi. N of Pictou; 45°45'N 62°44'W.

Caribou Lake, Piscataquis co., central Maine, 30 mi. NW of Millinocket in recreational area; 8 mi. long, 1 mi. wide. Joined at NE end to Chesuncook L.

Caribrod, Yugoslavia: see DIMITROVGRAD.

Carical, Fr. India: see KARIKAL.
Carice (kärēs'), village (1950 pop. 371), Nord dept., NE Haiti, in the Massif du Nord, 25 mi. SE of Cap-Haïtien; coffeegrowing.
Caridad, Philippines: see CAVITE, city.
Carife (kärē'fē), village (pop. 3,317), Avellino prov., Campania, S Italy, 11 mi. SSE of Ariano Irpino.
Carigara (kärēgä'rä), town (1939 pop. 5,851; 1948 municipality pop. 26,803), N Leyte, Philippines, on Carigara Bay, 22 mi. WNW of Tacloban; agr. center (coconuts, rice, sugar cane).
Carigara Bay, wide inlet of Samar Sea, N Leyte, Philippines, sheltered NW by Biliran Isl.; 20 mi. E–W, 9 mi. N–S.
Carignan (kärēnyä'), village (pop. 1,335), Ardennes dept., N France, on the Chiers and 11 mi. ESE of Sedan; forges; clothing mfg. Its 15th-cent. church was destroyed in Second World War.
Carignano (kärēnyä'nô), town (pop. 4,992), Torino prov., Piedmont, NW Italy, on Po R. and 11 mi. S of Turin, in cereal- and hemp-growing region; woolen and lumber mills, mfg. of matches, cheese. Former reigning house of Italy was that of Savoy-Carignano.
Carihuairazo, Cerro (sĕ'rō kärēwīrä'sō), extinct Andean volcano, Tungurahua prov., central Ecuador, just NE of the Chimborazo, 15 mi. SSW of Ambato. Has 4 peaks, the highest rising to 16,496 ft.
Carillon (kärēyō'), village (pop. 240), SW Que., on Ottawa R. and 7 mi. SSW of Lachute; dairying.
Cariñena (kärēnyā'nä), city (pop. 3,111), Saragossa prov., NE Spain, 30 mi. SW of Saragossa; noted for its sweet red wine; mfg. of brandy, alcohol, tartaric acid, soap; flour milling; cereals, olive oil. Has old walls and a cathedral. Terminus of branch railroad from Saragossa.
Carinhanha (kärēnyä'nyŭ), city (pop. 1,267), SW Bahia, Brazil, on left bank of São Francisco R. (navigable) and 65 mi. SSW of Bom Jesus da Lapa; cotton, vegetable fibers, hides and skins. Kaolin deposits.
Carinhanha River, E central Brazil, rises near 15°5'S 46°W, flows 175 mi. NE to the São Francisco just above Carinhanha city, forming Bahia–Minas Gerais border throughout its course.
Carini (kärē'nē), town (pop. 13,782), Palermo prov., NW Sicily, 10 mi. W of Palermo. Has medieval castle. Remains of paleolithic man found in near-by grotto. Ruins of Hyccara in vicinity.
Cariño (kärē'nyō), village (pop. 2,707), La Coruña prov., NW Spain, fishing port on inlet of Bay of Biscay, and 25 mi. NE of El Ferrol; boatbuilding. Summer resort. Asbestos, copper, iron, lignite mined near by.
Carinthia (kŭrĭn'thēŭ), Ger. *Kärnten* (kĕrn'tŭn), autonomous province [*Bundesland*] (□ 3,681; 1951 pop. 474,180), S Austria, bordering Salzburg (N), Styria (N, E), Yugoslavia and Italy (S), and East Tyrol (W); ⊙ Klagenfurt. Predominantly mountainous region, level in SE; includes part of the Hohe Tauern (site of the Grossglockner, highest peak in Austria) and Gurktal Alps (N), Carnic Alps and Karawanken (S), Saualpe and Koralpe (E). Many small resort lakes, e.g., Weissensee, Millstättersee, Ossiachersee, Wörthersee. Drained by Drau (largest), Möll, Gail, Gurk, and Lavant rivers. Mining (lead, zinc, iron, lignite), lumbering, agr. (wheat, rye, corn), fruitgrowing, stock raising (horses in E, cattle and sheep in mtn. pastures). Main industries (metals, chemicals, textiles) at industrial centers of Klagenfurt, Villach, Wolfsberg. Part of Roman prov. of Noricum, Carinthia, then including Istria and Carniola, was created an independent duchy in 976. Fell to Rudolf I of Hapsburg in 1276. Became Austrian crownland in 14th cent. Before 1919 Carinthia included territories now belonging to adjoining Italy and Yugoslavia. Placed (1945) in Br. occupation zone.
Caripe (kärē'pā), town (pop. 2,830), Monagas state, NE Venezuela, in coastal range, 50 mi. ESE of Cumaná; agr. center (tobacco, coffee, cacao, sugar cane, stock). Several caverns, the best known called Guácharo for birds which inhabit it, are near by (S).
Caripito (kärēpē'tō), town (pop. 9,612), Monagas state, NE Venezuela, near San Juan R., 27 mi. N of Maturín. Linked by short railroad with its landing on San Juan R. Major oil terminus, connected by pipe line with Quiriquire and Jusepín fields. Petroleum refinery installed 1931. Airfield.
Caripuyo (kärēpōō'yō), town (pop. c.4,400), Potosí dept., W central Bolivia, 45 mi. ESE of Oruro; potatoes, wheat.
Cariré (kärērē'), city (pop. 891), NW Ceará, Brazil, on Camocim-Crateús RR and 20 mi. SSW of Sobral; cotton, carnauba wax.
Caririaçu (kärērēäsōō'), city (pop. 1,134), S Ceará, Brazil, 15 mi. NE of Crato; cotton, tobacco. Until 1944, called São Pedro or São Pedro do Cariry.
Carirís Velhos, Serra dos (sĕ'rŭ dōōs kärērēs' vĕ'-lyōōs), hill range of NE Brazil, extends c.80 mi. WSW–ENE along Paraíba-Pernambuco border; rises to 2,500 ft. Xerophytic vegetation. Formerly spelled Serra dos Carirys Velhos.
Carisbrooke (kă'rĭzbrŏŏk), town and parish (pop. 5,232), on Isle of Wight, Hampshire, England, just S of Newport; shoe mfg., limestone quarrying. Site of ruins of 11th-cent. castle in which Charles I and his children were imprisoned. Vestiges of Roman settlement. Church dates from 12th cent.
Carite, Lake (kärē'tā), reservoir, SE Puerto Rico, in the Sierra de Cayey, on headstream of the La Plata, and 6 mi. N of Guayama. Water from the lake, diverted into small Guamaní R., operates 3 hydroelectric plants and, after traversing a 3,060-ft. tunnel, reaches S coast.
Cariubana (kärūbä'nä), town (pop. 1,200), Falcón state, NW Venezuela, on SW coast of Paraguaná Peninsula, 40 mi. WNW of Coro; fisheries. Airfield. Petroleum wells near by.
Cariús (kärēōōs'), town (pop. 1,694), S Ceará, Brazil, at terminus of rail spur, 18 mi. SW of Iguatu. Magnesite mining. Dam on Cariús R., a tributary of the Jaguaribe, is under construction for irrigation and flood control.
Carl, town (pop. 214), Barrow co., NE central Ga., 5 mi. W of Winder.
Carla-de-Roquefort (kärlä'-dŭ-rôkfôr'), village (pop. 105), Ariège dept., S France, in Plantaurel range, 8 mi. E of Foix; comb mfg.
Carl Blackwell, Lake, Okla.: see STILLWATER CREEK.
Carlentini (kärlĕntē'nē), town (pop. 8,870), Siracusa prov., E Sicily, 21 mi. NW of Syracuse; macaroni. Founded 1551 by Charles V.
Carle Place (kärl), residential village (1940 pop. 991), Nassau co., SE N.Y., on W Long Isl., just E of Mineola.
Carlet (kärlĕt'), city (pop. 7,534), Valencia prov., E Spain, 8 mi. NW of Alcira; agr. trade center in the midst of vineyards, mulberry and olive groves, fruit orchards. Mfg. of cement pipes, tiles; alcohol and brandy distilling, peanut-oil processing. Table wines produced in area.
Carleton. 1 County (□ 1,300; pop. 21,711), W N.B., on Maine border, intersected by St. John R.; ⊙ Woodstock. **2** County (□ 947; pop. 202,520), SE Ont., on Ottawa R. and on Que. border; ⊙ Ottawa.
Carleton, village (pop. estimate 350), E Que., S Gaspé Peninsula, on Chaleur Bay, 13 mi. ENE of Dalhousie; fishing port, resort.
Carleton. 1 Village, Cumberland, England: see SAINT CUTHBERT WITHOUT. **2** Agr. parish (pop. 1,508), W Lancashire, England. Contains villages of Carleton, 3 mi. NE of Blackpool, and Little Carleton, 2 mi. NE of Blackpool.
Carleton. 1 Village (pop. 1,039), Monroe co., extreme SE Mich., 10 mi. N of Monroe, in farm area (wheat, corn, livestock); flour milling. Inc. 1911. **2** Village (pop. 291), Thayer co., SE Nebr., 10 mi. NNW of Hebron and on branch of Little Blue R.
Carleton, Mount (2,690 ft.), N N.B., 50 mi. SW of Dalhousie; 47°22'N 66°52'W. Highest in prov.
Carleton Island, Jefferson co., N N.Y., one of the Thousand Isls., in the St. Lawrence, at Ont. line, 3 mi. NE of Cape Vincent; 2¼ mi. long, ½–1¼ mi. wide.
Carleton Place, town (pop. 4,305), SE Ont., on Mississippi R., at N end of Mississippi L., and 28 mi. SW of Ottawa; railroad shops; woolen milling, machinery mfg., dairying, lumbering.
Carlin, town (pop. 1,203), Elko co., N central Nev., on Humboldt R. and 20 mi. WSW of Elko; alt. 4,897 ft. Repair shops, icing plant for Southern Pacific RR. Settled 1868, inc. 1927.
Carling (kärlĕng'), Ger. *Karlingen* (kär'lĭng-ŭn), village (pop. 1,512), Moselle dept., NE France, on Saar border, 5 mi. N of Saint-Avold; building materials.
Carlingford, Gaelic *Cáirlinn,* town (pop. 465), NE Co. Louth, Ireland, on SW shore of Carlingford Lough, 9 mi. ENE of Dundalk; seaport and agr. market (wheat, barley, potatoes; cattle). Anc. border post of Anglo-Norman area of Ireland, it has numerous fortified houses. King John's Castle was built 1210. Dominican abbey was founded 1305. Just E is Carlingford Mountain (1,935 ft.).
Carlingford Lough (lôkh), inlet of the Irish Sea, bet. Co. Down, Northern Ireland, and Co. Louth, Ireland; extends 10 mi. inland; 2 mi. wide. Main towns on it: Greencastle, Warrenpoint, Rosstrevor, Carlingford, Greenore.
Carlin Skerry, Scotland: see BARREL OF BUTTER.
Carlinville, city (pop. 5,116), ⊙ Macoupin co., SW central Ill., near Macoupin Creek, 37 mi. SSW of Springfield; bituminous-coal mines, natural-gas wells, clay pits; agr. (corn, wheat, oats, livestock, poultry); mfg. (brick, gloves); nursery. Inc. 1837. Elaborate co. courthouse (built 1867–70), and Blackburn Col. are here.
Carlisle (–līl'), anc. *Caer Luel* (kärlē'ĕl) and *Luguvallum,* city and county borough (1931 pop. 57,304; 1951 census 67,894), ⊙ Cumberland, England, on Eden R., near mouth of Caldew and Petteril rivers, and 270 mi. NNW of London; 54°55'N 2°55'W. Railroad and industrial center. Metalworking and flour milling; mfg. of wool textiles, carpets, leather, pharmaceuticals, metal containers, agr. machinery, food products, beer. Has Carlisle Castle, originally built 1092 and scene of brief imprisonment of Mary Queen of Scots in 1568; 12th-cent. cathedral; 14th-cent. guildhall, and 18th-cent. church of St. Cuthbert. In Middle Ages Carlisle was an important fortress on the Scottish border; during the Civil War it was besieged for 9 months (1644–45); it was entered by the Young Pretender in 1745, but after a few weeks surrendered to the duke of Cumberland. Thomas Woodrow, grandfather of President Wilson, was pastor here (1820–35). In First World War the town's tavern came under state ownership ("Carlisle Experiment").
Carlisle (kärlīl', kär'līl), county (□ 196; pop. 6,206), SW Ky.; ⊙ Bardwell. Bounded W by the Mississippi (Mo. line), N by Mayfield Creek; drained by Obion Creek. Gently rolling agr. area, partly in Mississippi flood plain; dark tobacco, livestock, corn, cotton, dairy products. Formed 1886.
Carlisle. 1 Town (pop. 1,396), Lonoke co., central Ark., 30 mi. E of Little Rock; trade center for agr. area; rice milling, cotton ginning; mfg. of cheese, feed, lumber. Founded 1871. **2** Town (pop. 767), Sullivan co., SW Ind., 21 mi. NNE of Vincennes; lumber, canned goods, liniment. **3** Town (pop. 903), Warren co., S central Iowa, near Des Moines R., 9 mi. SE of Des Moines; brick and tile plant. **4** City (pop. 1,524), ⊙ Nicholas co., N Ky., 15 mi. ENE of Paris, in Bluegrass region; burley tobacco, grain; makes clothing; flour and feed mills. **5** Town (pop. 876), Middlesex co., NE central Mass., 8 mi. S of Lowell, near Concord R.; dairying, fruit, truck, poultry. **6** Borough (pop. 16,812), ⊙ Cumberland co., S Pa., in the Cumberland Valley 18 mi. WSW of Harrisburg; textiles, clothing, leather goods, rugs, metal products. Has Dickinson Col. and Dickinson School of Law; Army Medical Field Service School (at Carlisle Barracks). Frontier fort erected here 1750. Home of Molly Pitcher and James Wilson. Munitions center during Revolution; Washington's headquarters during Whisky Rebellion. Attacked 1863 by Confederates. Seat of Carlisle Indian School, 1879–1918. Pennsylvania Turnpike whose E terminus was for a while 2 mi. NE, was extended eastward in 1950. Laid out c.1751, inc. 1782. **7** Town (pop. 405), Union co., N S.C., 14 mi. SE of Union. **8** Village (1940 pop. 1,283), Rusk co., E Texas, 7 mi. W of Henderson, in East Texas oil field.
Carlisle Bay, open roadstead (½ mi. long, ½ mi. wide), SW Barbados, B.W.I., isl.'s only harbor of importance, on which Bridgetown is located. Larger vessels anchor here, while ships up to 14 ft. draught can dock alongside the inner Careenage harbor in the city.
Carlitte, Pic de (pēk' dŭ kärlĕt'), summit (9,583 ft.) of small massif in central Pyrenees, Pyrénées-Orientales dept., S France, 7 mi. E of L'Hospitalet-près-l'Andorre. Têt and Aude rivers rise here.
Carl Junction, city (pop. 1,006), Jasper co., SW Mo., near Spring R., 7 mi. N of Joplin; agr., especially dairying; mfg. (chemical, lumber products).
Carloforte (kär"lôfôr'tĕ), town (pop. 8,030) and port on San Pietro Isl., just off SW Sardinia, on E coast, 17 mi. SW of Iglesias; ore-transshipping center for lead, zinc, lignite, silver, and other minerals; exports wood, cheese, wool, fish. Extraction of salt (S); manganese-jasper-ochre and trachyte mining; shipyard. Fishing (tunny, lobster). Site of international latitude observatory (39°8'N).
Carlopago, Yugoslavia: see KARLOBAG.
Carlopoli (kärlô'pôlē), village (pop. 2,143), Catanzaro prov., Calabria, S Italy, 13 mi. NW of Catanzaro; woolen mill.
Carlópolis (kärlô'pōōlēs), city (pop. 1,098), NE Paraná, Brazil, near São Paulo border, 22 mi. SE of Jacarèzinho; sawmilling; coffee, tobacco, cotton, hogs.
Carlos (kär'lŭs), village (pop. 233), Douglas co., W Minn., 8 mi. NNE of Alexandria, in agr. area; dairy products. L. Carlos near by.
Carlos, Lake, Douglas co., W Minn., just N of Alexandria near L. Ida and L. Miltona; 5 mi. long, 1 mi. wide. Resorts. Lake is fed and drained by Long Prairie R.
Carlos A. Carillo (kär'lōs ä kärē'yō), village (pop. 511), Veracruz, SE Mexico, on Papaloápam R. and 5 mi. E of Cosamaloapan. Sugar refinery. Formerly San Cristóbal.
Carlos Barbosa (kär'lōōs bärbô'zŭ), town (pop. 732), NE Rio Grande do Sul, Brazil, on S slope of the Serra Geral, 3 mi. SE of Garibaldi; rail junction; winegrowing, hog raising.
Carlos Casares (kär'lōs käsä'rĕs), town (pop. 7,484), ⊙ Carlos Casares dist. (□ 994; pop. 23,490), N central Buenos Aires prov., Argentina, 33 mi. ENE of Pehuajó; agr. center (sunflowers, wheat, corn, livestock); dairying.
Carlos Chagas (kär'lōōs shä'gŭs), city (pop. 1,651), NE Minas Gerais, Brazil, on Mucuri R., on railroad and 50 mi. ENE of Teófilo Otoni; rice, lumber. Formerly called Urucú.
Carlos Pellegrini (kär'lōs pĕlägrē'nē), town (pop. estimate 2,500), S central Santa Fe prov., Argentina, 90 mi. NW of Rosario; agr. center (wheat, flax, alfalfa, livestock); grain elevator.
Carlos Reyles (rä'lĕs), town (pop. 940), Durazno dept., central Uruguay, in the Cuchilla Grande del Durazno, on railroad (Molles station) and 23 mi. N of Durazno; grain, cattle, sheep. Until c.1945 called Molles.
Carlos Rojas (rō'häs), town (pop. 1,618), Matanzas prov., W Cuba, on railroad and 12 mi. S of Cárdenas, in agr. region (sugar cane, fruit, sisal). The refineries and sugar centrals of Santa Amalia and Carolina are 6 mi. NW.

Carlos Tejedor (tāhādôr'), town (pop. 2,704), ⊙ Carlos Tejedor dist. (□ 1,510; pop. 16,894), NW Buenos Aires prov., Argentina, 43 mi. NW of Pehuajó, in agr. region (wheat, sheep, cattle).

Carlota, La, Argentina: see La Carlota.

Carlota, La (lä kärlō'tä), town (pop. 2,003), Córdoba prov., S Spain, 17 mi. SW of Córdoba; olive-oil processing, flour milling; stock raising.

Carlow (kär'lō), Gaelic *Cheatharlach*, county (□ 346; pop. 34,081), Leinster, SE Ireland; ⊙ Carlow. Bounded by cos. Kilkenny (W), Laoighis (NW), Kildare (N), Wicklow and Wexford (E). Drained by Barrow and Slaney rivers. Surface is generally flat, rising SE toward Blackstairs Mts. (highest point, Mt. Leinster, 2,610 ft.). Limestone, granite, marble are quarried. Dairying, sheep raising, growing of potatoes, wheat, beets. Industries include sugar refining, brewing, shoe mfg. Towns are Carlow, Muine Bheag, Tullow, Borris, Leighlinbridge. There are ecclesiastical remains, several castles, and cathedrals at Carlow and Old Leighlin.

Carlow, Gaelic *Ceatharlach*, urban district (pop. 7,466), ⊙ Co. Carlow, Ireland, in N part of co., on Barrow R. and 45 mi. SW of Dublin; agr. market in dairying region, with sugar refining, flour milling, brewing, mfg. of shoes, cattle feed. Has 12th-cent. castle, 19th-cent. R.C. cathedral of diocese of Kildare and Leighlin, St. Patrick's theological col. (1793), and remains of town walls, built 1361. Of early strategic importance, Carlow was burned 1405 and 1577. In 1798 insurgent United Irishmen fought fierce street battle here. Just W, across Barrow R., is suburb of Graigue, in Co. Laoighis.

Carloway, Scotland: see Lewis with Harris.

Carlow Island, Washington co., E Maine, bet. Cobscook and Passamaquoddy bays; linked to mainland and Moose Isl. by dams.

Carlsbad (kärlz'băd), Czech *Karlovy Vary* (kär'lôvĭ vä'rĭ), Ger. *Karlsbad* (kärls'bät), town (pop. 17,187; with suburbs 31,322), ⊙ Karlovy Vary prov. (□ 1,768; pop. 299,625), W Bohemia, Czechoslovakia, on Ohre R. and 70 mi. W of Prague; 50°13'N 12°54'E. One of most frequented health resorts in Europe, with many hot alkaline-sulphur springs whose waters are taken for digestive diseases. Rail junction; airport; porcelain center; glass, art work, footwear. Exports mineral waters. Kaolin mines in vicinity. Town founded 1349 by Emperor Charles IV. Lesser health resorts of Kysibl-Kyselka, Ger. *Giesshübel-Sauerbrunn* (alt. 2,357 ft.), and Krondorf-Kyselka (alt. 2,351 ft.), also on Ohre R., are NE. Carlsbad Decrees, formulated here (1819) by conference of ministers of Ger. states, established a close supervision of Ger. and Austrian universities and dissolved student organizations (Burschenschaften) following murder of Kotzebue.

Carlsbad. 1 Village (pop. 4,383), San Diego co., S Calif., 4 mi. SE of Oceanside; health resort, with mineral springs, beaches, state park; winter vegetables, citrus fruit, avocados. **2** City (pop. 17,975), ⊙ Eddy co., SE N.Mex., on Pecos R. and 70 mi. SSE of Roswell. Resort, trade, and potash-refining center in irrigated agr., livestock region; cotton, alfalfa, dairy products. Large deposits of potash (discovered 1931) and potash mines in vicinity. Carlsbad Caverns Natl. Park is 19 mi. SW; bird reservation and Avalon Reservoir (unit in Carlsbad irrigation project) are 6 mi. N. Settled 1888. Expanded greatly during Second World War. **3** Village, Tom Green co., W Texas, 25 mi. NW of San Angelo and on North Concho R. Texas state tuberculosis sanatorium is at adjacent Sanatorium village.

Carlsbad Caverns National Park (□ 71.1; established as natl. monument 1923, as natl. park 1930), SE N.Mex., in E foothills of Guadalupe Mts., 18 mi. SSW of Carlsbad, near Texas line. Among world's largest and most beautiful caves, they are a spectacular network of subterranean chambers (lowest explored level 1,100 ft. down) of unknown total extent, formed by water erosion of limestone. Of the known chambers, on 3 main levels, most impressive is Big Room (4,000 ft. long, 625 ft. wide, 285 ft. high), reached by elevator or trail, and including great variety of stalactites and stalagmites. Others are King's Palace, Queen's Chamber, and Bat Cave, inhabited by millions of bats. Caverns were first explored 1901.

Carlsborg, Sweden: see Karlsborg.

Carlscrona, Sweden: see Karlskrona.

Carlshafen, Germany: see Karlshafen.

Carlshamn, Sweden: see Karlshamn.

Carlsruhe, Germany: see Karlsruhe.

Carlstad, Sweden: see Karlstad.

Carlstadt (kärl'stăt), industrial borough (pop. 5,591), Bergen co., NE N.J., 8 mi. NNE of Newark; mfg. (chemicals, clothing, textiles, candles, brushes, embroideries, paints, food products, boats); truck, livestock. Inc. 1894.

Carlton, village (pop. estimate 100), S central Sask., near North Saskatchewan R., 40 mi. SW of Prince Albert; dairying, mixed farming. Indian Treaty Diamond Jubilee celebrated here, Aug., 1936.

Carlton, residential urban district (1931 pop. 22,325; 1951 census 34,248), S Nottingham, England, just E of Nottingham; brickworks. Carlton House, built 1709 by Lord Carlton and residence of George IV as Prince of Wales, was destroyed in early 19th cent. London's Conservative Carlton Club is named after it. In urban dist. (E) is cotton-milling town of Netherfield.

Carlton, county (□ 860; pop. 24,584), E Minn.; ⊙ Carlton. Agr. area bordering on Wis. and drained in NE by St. Louis R. Dairy products, potatoes, livestock, poultry; paper. Includes part of Fond du Lac Indian Reservation in N, state forests in NW and SE. Co. formed 1857.

Carlton. 1 Town (pop. 249), Madison co., NE Ga., 10 mi. WSW of Elberton; granite quarrying. **2** City (pop. 76), Dickinson co., central Kansas, 20 mi. SE of Salina, in wheat area. **3** Village (pop. 650), ⊙ Carlton co., E Minn., on St. Louis R., near Wis. line, and 17 mi. WSW of Duluth, in diversified-farming area; dairy products, flour. Jay Cook State Park and Fond du Lac Indian Reservation near by. **4** City (pop. 1,081), Yamhill co., NW Oregon, on North Yamhill R. and 30 mi. SW of Portland; lumber milling, dairying.

Carlton Hill, N.J.: see East Rutherford.

Carlton-in-Lindrick, town and parish (pop. 1,421), N Nottingham, England, 3 mi. N of Worksop; coal mining. Church dates from Norman times.

Carluke (kär'lo͝ok, kärlo͝ok'), town and parish (pop. 10,507), N Lanark, Scotland, 7 mi. SE of Motherwell; coal mining, machinery mfg., tile making, fruit packing, jam making.

Carlux (kärlüks'), village (pop. 190), Dordogne dept., SW France, near Dordogne R., 7 mi. E of Sarlat; fruit and truffle processing. Fénelon b. in near-by château.

Carlyle, town (pop. 529), SE Sask., at foot of Moose Mtn., 50 mi. NE of Estevan; grain elevators, lumbering, dairying.

Carlyle (kärlīl'), city (pop. 2,669), ⊙ Clinton co., S Ill., on Kaskaskia R. and 13 mi. WNW of Centralia; trade center of agr. area (corn, wheat, livestock, poultry; dairy products); mfg. (paper and glass containers, shoes). Bituminous-coal mines, oil wells. State fish hatchery is near by. Laid out 1818, inc. 1837.

Carmacks (kär'măks), Indian village, S Yukon, on Lewes R. and 100 mi. NNW of Whitehorse; 62°6'N 136°19'W. Coal formerly mined; gold was discovered 1945.

Carmagnola (kärmänyô'lä), town (pop. 3,982), Torino prov., Piedmont, NW Italy, near Po R., 15 mi. S of Turin, in irrigated region (cereals, hemp, sericulture); rail junction. Hemp, silk, woolen, and paper mills; canned vegetables, macaroni; cork; hemp-seed market. Noted for its fairs.

Carman (kär'mŭn), town (pop. 1,555), S Man., on Boyne R. and 50 mi. SW of Winnipeg; grain elevators, dairying, woodworking; hydroelectric power.

Carmana, Iran: see Kerman, city.

Carmangay (kär'mŭn-gā), village (pop. 229), S Alta., 35 mi. NNW of Lethbridge; coal mining; grain elevators, dairying.

Carmania, Iran: see Kerman, province.

Carmans River, Suffolk co., SE N.Y., rises in small lake in E central Long Isl., flows c.11 mi. generally S, past Yaphank, to Bellport Bay (inlet of Great South Bay) just E of Brookhaven.

Carmarthen, Caermarthen (both: kŭrmär'dhŭn), **Carmarthenshire,** or **Caermarthenshire** (–shĭr), county (□ 919.5; 1931 pop. 179,100; 1951 census 171,742), S Wales; ⊙ Carmarthen. Bounded by Pembroke (W), Cardigan (N), Brecknock (E), Glamorgan (SE), and Bristol Channel (S). Drained by Taf, Towy, and Teifi rivers. Hilly country (highest point, Carmarthen Van) with large wasteland areas, leveling toward S; sheep and cattle raising in uplands, farming in S. Coal mining and metallurgical industry in SE, centered on Llanelly; copper, iron, and lead are also mined. Woolen-milling industry is widely spread over interior of co. Limestone and slate are quarried. Besides Carmarthen, other important towns are Llanelly, Burry Port, Ammanford, Cwmamman, Llandilo, Llandovery, and Kidwelly. There are traces of Roman occupation; *Maridunum* (Carmarthen) was important road center. Co. was scene of Rebecca Riots (1843–44) in which toll gates were destroyed.

Carmarthen or **Caermarthen,** Welsh *Caerfyrddin* (kīrfĭr'dhĭn), anc. *Maridunum*, municipal borough (1931 pop. 10,310; 1951 census 12,121), ⊙ Carmarthenshire, Wales, in center of co., on Towy R. 8 mi. above its mouth on Carmarthen Bay, and 22 mi. NW of Swansea; agr. market with agr. machinery works, milk canneries, flour mills, cheese factories. There are remains of Norman castle, once of strategic importance and hq. of Welsh chieftains. Has 13th-cent. church; mus. contains Roman relics. Richard Steele b. here.

Carmarthen Bay, largest inlet of Bristol Channel, S Wales, bet. St. Gowan's Head (W) and Worms Head (E); 27 mi. long, 12 mi. wide. Riparian counties are Glamorgan, Carmarthen, and Pembroke. Receives Loughor R., Towy R., and Taf R.

Carmarthenshire, Wales: see Carmarthen, county.

Carmarthen Van, Welsh *Banau Sir Gaer* (bä'nī sĭr gīr'), mountain (2,460 ft.), E Carmarthen, Wales, highest point of Carmarthen. Just E, in Brecknock, is peak Brecknock Van.

Carmaux (kärmō'), town (pop. 9,648), Tarn dept., S France, on small Cérou R. and 9 mi. N of Albi; coal-mining center; coking plant, glass mill, fertilizer factories.

Carmel. 1 (kärmĕl') or **Carmel-by-the-Sea,** city (pop. 4,351), Monterey co., W Calif., on Carmel Bay, 3 mi. SW of Monterey; art, literary, and recreation center, with fine beach. San Carlos Borromeo Mission (Carmel Mission), where Father Junípero Serra is buried, is just S; it was moved here in 1771 from Monterey. Carmel Bay, sheltered N by Monterey Peninsula, was named (1602) by Spaniards. Receives Carmel R. (c.30 mi. long), which flows NW through the Coast Ranges. **2** (kär'mŭl) Town (pop. 1,009), Hamilton co., central Ind., 16 mi. N of Indianapolis, in agr. area. **3** (kär'mŭl) Agr. town (pop. 996), Penobscot co., S Maine, 13 mi. W of Bangor. **4** (kär'mŭl) Village (pop. 1,526), ⊙ Putnam co., SE N.Y., 13 mi. W of Danbury (Conn.), and on L. Glenida (glĕn"ĭ'dŭ) (c.¾ mi. long; part of New York city water-supply system); trade center for dairying and summer-resort area. L. Carmel and many reservoirs near by. Seat of Drew Seminary for girls.

Carmel, Cape (kär'mŭl), NW Israel, on the Mediterranean, at foot of Mt. Carmel, 2 mi. WNW of Haifa; 32°50'N 34°57'E.

Carmel, Lake, Putnam co., SE N.Y., resort lake (c.2 mi. long) 1½ mi. N of Carmel.

Carmel, Mount, short rocky mountain ridge, NW Israel, extending 13 mi. NW from the Plain of Jezreel to the Mediterranean at Haifa, where it ends in a promontory marking S limit of Bay of Acre. Forms S boundary of Zebulun Valley. Rising steeply from sea to 1,791 ft., 5 mi. SSE of Haifa, it is one of the most striking physical features of the country and was long an object of veneration. In biblical times it was associated with the lives of the prophets Elijah and Elisha. Many of its caves were inhabited by early Christian anchorites; traditionally Pythagoras had his retreat here in 2d cent. B.C. On slopes are extensive vineyards and olive groves. Here are a Bahaist garden shrine with the tombs of Bab ed Din and of Abdul Baha. Near summit is a monastery (1st founded 1156). Remains of Palestinian man, a Neanderthaloid type, were found (1931–32) in near-by caves.

Carmel, Mount. 1 In Calif.: see Santa Lucia Range. **2** In Conn.: see Hamden.

Carmel Bay, Calif.: see Carmel.

Carmel-by-the-Sea, Calif.: see Carmel.

Carmel Head, Welsh *Trwyn y Gader* (tro͞o'ĭn ŭ gä'dŭr), promontory on Irish Sea at NW tip of Anglesey, Wales, 7 mi. NNE of Holyhead; site of lighthouse (53°24'N 4°34'W). In Irish Sea, 2 mi. NW, are The Skerries.

Carmelita (kärmälē'tä), village (pop. 39), Petén dept., N Guatemala, c.40 mi. NNW of Flores; airfield for chicle shipments.

Carmelo (kärmä'lō), town (pop. 12,000), Colonia dept., SW Uruguay, landing on small arroyo near its mouth on lower Uruguay R., and 40 mi. NW of Colonia, 40 mi. N of Buenos Aires, to which it ships grain, sand, and stone. Fishing and boating resort. Has shipyard. Founded 1816 by Artigas. There are granite quarries and sand pits near by.

Carmelo, town (pop. 1,143), Zulia state, NW Venezuela, on NW shore of L. Maracaibo and 20 mi. SSW of Maracaibo; oil wells.

Carmel Point (kärmĕl'), village, Monterey co., W Calif.

Carmel River, Calif.: see Carmel.

Carmel Woods, village, Monterey co., W Calif., just S of Monterey.

Carmen (kär'mĕn), town (pop. estimate 2,000), S Santa Fe prov., Argentina, 85 mi. SW of Rosario; rail junction in grain and livestock dist.; poultry farming.

Carmen, village, Pando dept., NW Bolivia, on Madre de Dios R. and 45 mi. SSW of Puerto Rico; rubber.

Carmen. 1 or **Carmen de Viboral** (dā bēbōräl'), town (pop. 2,137), Antioquia dept., NW central Colombia, in Cordillera Central, 20 mi. SE of Medellín; alt. 7,234 ft. Dairying, lime quarrying, ceramics mfg.; agr. products (corn, beans, sugar cane, coffee, fruit, livestock). **2** or **El Carmen** (ĕl), town (pop. 8,228), Bolívar dept., N Colombia, 60 mi. SE of Cartagena; tobacco center. **3** or **El Carmen,** village (pop. 993), Chocó dept., W Colombia, in Cordillera Occidental, 35 mi. W of Quibdó; alt. 5,223 ft. Corn, sugar cane, coffee, potatoes, vegetables, livestock. Summer resort.

Carmen. 1 or **Ciudad del Carmen** (syo͞odädh' dĕl), city (pop. 7,687), Campeche, SE Mexico, port on W tip of Carmen Isl., at channel linking Gulf of Campeche with Laguna de Términos, 120 mi. SW of Campeche; 18°38'N 91°49'W. Trading in and shipping of chicle and timber; sawmilling. Airport. **2** Town (pop. 733), Nuevo León, N Mexico, on Salinas R. and 19 mi. NNW of Monterrey, in irrigated agr. region (cotton, corn, sugar, livestock).

Carmen, town (1939 pop. 1,314; 1948 municipality pop. 19,006), central Bohol isl., Philippines, 27 mi. ENE of Tagbilaran; agr. center (rice, coconuts).

Carmen (kär'mŭn), town (pop. 654), Alfalfa co., N Okla., 35 mi. WNW of Enid, in agr. area (grain, livestock, poultry; dairy products).

Carmen (kär'mĕn), town (pop. 4,600), Durazno dept., Uruguay, in the Cuchilla Grande del Durazno, on highway, and 30 mi. ENE of Durazno; road junction; local trade center; cattle fairs. Sometimes called Carmen del Durazno.
Carmen, El, in Latin America: see EL CARMEN.
Carmen, Lake, Bolivia: see ITONAMAS, LAKE.
Carmen, Sierra del (syĕ'rä dĕl), N spur of the Sierra Madre Oriental in Coahuila, N Mexico, extends c.80 mi. NW from approximately 28°30'N 102°W to the Rio Grande (Texas border) at Big Bend Natl. Park; continued by its Amer. section Sierra del Carmen or Carmen Mts. Rises to over 5,000 ft.
Carmen, Sierra del (sēē'rü dĕl kär'mĕn), or **Carmen Mountains** (kär'mün), Brewster co., extreme W Texas, in the Big Bend; a NW extension of Sierra del Carmen (part of the Sierra Madre Oriental) of Coahuila, Mexico, range is a group of ridges extending c.30 mi. SE from point c.55 mi. SE of Alpine, through BIG BEND NATIONAL PARK, to the Rio Grande (U.S.–Mex. border), where river's gorge (Boquillas Canyon) is a scenic feature. Sue Peaks (5,857 ft.) have highest alt. of U.S. portion. One of main ridges is Sierra del Caballo Muerto (käbä'yō mwĕr'tō) or Dead Horse Mts. (c.22 mi. long).
Carmena (kärmā'nä), town (pop. 1,658), Toledo prov., central Spain, 20 mi. WNW of Toledo; olives, cereals, grapes, chick-peas, hides, wool, livestock. Lumbering.
Carmen de Areco (kär'mĕn dā ärā'kō), town (pop. 4,388), ⊙ Carmen de Areco dist. (□ 410; pop. 9,532), N Buenos Aires prov., Argentina, 43 mi. WNW of Luján; agr. center (corn, alfalfa, wheat, livestock).
Carmen de las Flores, Argentina: see LAS FLORES, Buenos Aires prov.
Carmen del Durazno, Uruguay: see CARMEN.
Carmen del Paraná (dĕl päränä'), town (dist. pop. 13,033), Itapúa dept., SE Paraguay, near the Paraná, on railroad and 20 mi. NW of Encarnación; lumbering and agr. center (maté, tobacco, cotton, corn, rice); sawmilling, grain milling. Colonia Fram, a Czech agr. settlement, is N.
Carmen de Patagones (dā pätägō'nĕs) or **Patagones,** town (pop. 5,425), ⊙ Patagones dist. (□ 5,186; pop. 16,258), SW Buenos Aires prov., Argentina, port on the Río Negro opposite Viedma, and 150 mi. SSW of Bahía Blanca; agr. center: grain growing, stock raising (sheep), viticulture; exports hides and skins; saltworks.
Carmen de Viboral, Colombia: see CARMEN, Antioquia dept.
Carmen Island. 1 In Campeche, SE Mexico; 23 mi. long, c.2 mi. wide; forms narrow bar bet. the Laguna de Términos (S) and the Gulf of Campeche (N). On its W tip is the port of Carmen (18°38'N 91°49'W). **2** In Lower California, NW Mexico, in Gulf of California, off the peninsula's SE coast, 10 mi. E of Loreto; □ 59; 10 mi. long, 2–6 mi. wide. Barren, uninhabited.
Carmen Mountains, Texas: see CARMEN, SIERRA DEL.
Carmen River, Chihuahua, N Mexico, rises in Sierra Madre Occidental as Santa Clara R. 45 mi. NE of Guerrero, flows c.150 mi. N to lagoon 5 mi. NNE of Villa Ahumada. Often dry.
Carmensa (kärmĕn'sä), town (pop. estimate 500), E Mendoza prov., Argentina, near Atuel R. (irrigation area), 55 mi. SE of San Rafael; rail terminus; lumbering and agr. center (alfalfa, tomatoes, wine, fruit, livestock). Wine; tomato canning.
Carmen Silva, Sierra (syĕ'rä kär'mĕn sĕl'vä), Patagonian range in N central part of main isl. of Tierra del Fuego, Chile and Argentina, 40 mi. NW of Río Grande (Argentina); extends c.40 mi. SW from San Sebastián Bay (Argentina) to Useless Bay (Chile); rises to c.1,200 ft.
Carmen-Sylva or **Carmen-Silva** (kär'mĕn-sĕl'vä), town (1948 pop. 1,075), Constanta prov., SE Rumania, on the Black Sea, on railroad and 11 mi. S of Constanta; popular summer resort with beautiful beach and mud baths. Sometimes called Movila.
Carmi (kär'mī), city (pop. 5,574), ⊙ White co., SE Ill., on Little Wabash R. and 32 mi. NE of Harrisburg; trade and shipping center in agr. area (wheat, corn, livestock, fruit, poultry); mfg. of clothing. Platted 1816, inc. 1819.
Carmi, Lake (kär'mü), NW Vt., in Franklin town, 14 mi. NE of St. Albans; 3 mi. long.
Carmiano (kärmyä'nô), town (pop. 5,543), Lecce prov., Apulia, S Italy, 7 mi. W of Lecce; wine, olive oil.
Carmichael, Scotland: see PONFEIGH.
Carmichael (kär'mīkül), village (pop. 4,499), Sacramento co., central Calif., 10 mi. E of Sacramento.
Carmichaels (–külz), borough (pop. 895), Greene co., SW Pa., 11 mi. E of Waynesburg.
Carmignano (kärmēnyä'nô), village (pop. 815), Firenze prov., Tuscany, central Italy, 12 mi. WNW of Florence; mfg. (straw hats, brooms), wine making.
Carmignano di Brenta (dē brĕn'tä), village (pop. 1,703), Padova prov., Veneto, N Italy, near Brenta R., 9 mi. NE of Vicenza, in grape- and cereal-growing region; paper mill.
Carmo (kär'mŏŏ). **1** City (pop. 1,071), N central Rio de Janeiro state, Brazil, near Minas Gerais border, on railroad and 25 mi. N of Nova Friburgo; sugar, coffee. **2** City, Sergipe, Brazil: see CARMÓPOLIS.
Carmo, airfield, Rio Branco territory, Brazil: see CATRIMANI.
Carmo, Spain: see CARMONA.
Carmo da Mata (kär'mŏŏ dä mä'tů), city (pop. 3,114), S central Minas Gerais, Brazil, on railroad and 30 mi. S of Divinópolis; agr. trade.
Carmo do Paranaíba (dŏŏ pärănäē'bů), city (pop. 2,999), W Minas Gerais, Brazil, 30 mi. SSE of Patos de Minas; dairying. Platinum deposits. Formerly spelled Carmo do Paranahyba.
Carmo do Rio Claro (rē'ŏŏ klä'rŏŏ), city (pop. 3,193), SW Minas Gerais, Brazil, 36 mi. SE of Passos; coffeegrowing, dairying.
Carmona (kärmō'nä), anc. *Carmo* or *Carmonia*, city (pop. 21,037), Seville prov., SW Spain, in Andalusia, on Seville-Córdoba RR and 20 mi. E of Seville; processing and agr. center (cereals, olives, grapes, fruit, livestock). Sawmilling, flour milling, liquor distilling, tanning; mfg. of vegetable oils, meat products, boxes, canvas goods, woolen goods, hats, soap, ceramics, artificial flowers, baskets. Picturesque city built on an isolated hill and surrounded by walls with imposing gates. Fine bldgs. include ruins of the Moorish alcazar, Gothic Santa María church, churrigueresque San Pedro church with lofty minaret. Just W lies a Roman necropolis (discovered 1881). City was taken from the Moors by Ferdinand III of Castile in 1247.
Carmonita (kärmōnē'tä), town (pop. 1,087), Badajoz prov., W Spain, on railroad and 16 mi. N of Mérida; grapes, olives, cereals, livestock. Has mineral springs.
Carmópolis (kärmô'pŏŏlēs), city (pop. 1,351), NE Sergipe, NE Brazil, on railroad and 20 mi. N of Aracaju, in sugar-growing region. Until 1944, called Carmo.
Carmyle (kärmīl'), town in Cambuslang parish, N Lanark, Scotland, near the Clyde, 4 mi. ESE of Glasgow; coal mining, steel milling, textile bleaching.
Carnac (kärnäk'), village (pop. 1,754), Morbihan dept., W France, 16 mi. WSW of Vannes, near base of Quiberon Peninsula. Site of remarkable megalithic monuments (particularly menhirs) which (numbering over 2,700) extend c.2.5 mi. in 11 parallel rows along the coast. These monuments probably antedate the druids. Near by is an artificial mound (50 ft. high) surmounted by a chapel. Carnac-Plage (just SW) is a beach resort.
Carnaro, province, Italy: see RIJEKA.
Carnaro; Carnarolo, Yugoslavia: see KVARNER.
Carnarvon (kŭrnär'vŭn, kär–), municipality (pop. 979), W Western Australia, 510 mi. NNW of Perth, at mouth of Gascoyne R., on E shore of Shark Bay; sheep center; bananas, pineapples.
Carnarvon, town (pop. 2,895), central Cape Prov., U. of So. Afr., 100 mi. NNW of Beaufort West; agr. center (sheep, wool, grain).
Carnarvon, Wales: see CAERNARVON.
Carnarvon Range, plateau, SE central Queensland, Australia, part of Great Dividing Range W of Bundaberg; extends c.90 mi. E; alt. 2,000 ft.
Carnatic (kärnă'tĭk), historic region in SE Madras, India, comprising roughly the area bet. S Coromandel Coast of Bay of Bengal and Deccan Plateau; represents domains of the nawabs of the Carnatic, who governed the territory (16th to early-17th cent.) under the Deccan sultans and (late-17th to early-18th cent.) under the Mogul emperors. Term originally evolved from KANARA, the Kanarese-speaking S section of Deccan Plateau, ruled by Vijayanagar kings. When the Deccan sultans defeated them in 1565, they extended the term to include the country (plains SE of Deccan Plateau) to which the Vijayanagars retired. The English restricted the name to the plains area, which became the arena of their 18th-cent. struggle with the French for supremacy in India, but the name is sometimes used to include Malabar Coast, where in 15th cent. the Portuguese established earliest European settlements in India. Sometimes spelled Karnatic.
Carn Ban, Scotland: see MONADHLIATH MOUNTAINS.
Carndonagh (kärndŏ'nů), Gaelic *Carn Domhnach*, town (pop. 639), NE Co. Donegal, Ireland, 18 mi. N of Londonderry; agr. market (flax, oats, potatoes; sheep, cattle), lead mining, mfg. of potato alcohol.
Carnduff, town (pop. 476), SE Sask., 55 mi. E of Estevan, near N.Dak. border; grain elevators, dairying.
Carnedd Dafydd (kär″nĕdh dä'vĭdh), mountain (3,426 ft.), N central Caernarvon, Wales, 4 mi. SE of Bethesda.
Carnedd Llewelyn (lŭē'lĭn), mountain (3,484 ft.), N central Caernarvon, Wales, 4 mi. ESE of Bethesda.
Carnegie. 1 (kär'nùgē) Town (pop. 197), Randolph co., SW Ga., 9 mi. S of Cuthbert. **2** (kär'nùgē) Town (pop. 1,719), Caddo co., W central Okla., 20 mi. W of Anadarko, and on Washita R., in agr. area (cotton, wheat, corn). Cotton ginning, meat processing; mfg. of feed, saddles, harnesses, flour. Seat of Carnegie Jr. Col. **3** (kärnā'gē) Industrial borough (pop. 12,105), Allegheny co., SW Pa., SW suburb of Pittsburgh; steel, metal products, bituminous coal, bedding, Diesel engines, lubricants, food, beverages, toys; agr. Inc. 1894.
Carnegie, Lake (kärnĕ'gē) (□ 125), central Western Australia, 560 mi. NE of Perth; 50 mi. long, 2.5 mi. long; usually dry.
Carn Eige (kärn āg'), highest mountain (3,877 ft.) in Ross and Cromarty, Scotland, in SW part of co., 15 mi. E of Dornie, just N of Mam Soul.
Carnerillo (kärnārē'yō), town (pop. estimate 800), W Córdoba prov., Argentina, 27 mi. NE of Río Cuarto; grain, flax, alfalfa, hogs, cattle.
Carnes Mountain (10,000 ft.), SE B.C., in Selkirk Mts., E of Glacier Park, 24 mi. N of Revelstoke; 51°21'N 118°7'W.
Carnesville (kärnz'vĭl), city (pop. 349), ⊙ Franklin co., NE Ga., 15 mi. SSE of Toccoa.
Carnethy, Scotland: see PENTLAND HILLS.
Carnew, Gaelic *Carn Nua*, town (pop. 423), S Co. Wicklow, Ireland, 14 mi. N of Enniscorthy; agr. market (dairying; cattle, sheep; potatoes); slate quarrying.
Carney. 1 Village (pop. 1,523), Baltimore co., N Md., 8 mi. NE of downtown Baltimore. **2** Town (pop. 227), Lincoln co., central Okla., 21 mi. S of Stillwater, in agr. area.
Carneys Point, village (1940 pop. 2,372), Salem co., SW N.J., on Delaware R. just S of Penns Grove; oil refining, mfg. of explosives.
Carnforth, urban district (1931 pop. 3,192; 1951 census 3,388), N Lancashire, England, near Morecambe Bay 6 mi. N of Lancaster; granite quarrying; market for cattle-raising, dairying dist.
Carnic Alps (kär'nĭk), Ger. *Karnische Alpen*, Ital. *Alpi Carniche*, range of Eastern Alps along Austro-Ital. border; extend c.60 mi. from the Pustertal (W) to Gailitz R. valley (E). Highest peaks, Kellerwand (9,219 ft.), Monte Peralba (8,835 ft.). Crossed by Plöcken Pass. Gailtal Alps are lower parallel range just N, overlooking Drau valley. Carnic Alps are continued (E) by the Karawanken. In SE they merge with Julian Alps, in SW with the Dolomites.
Carnicerías (kärnēsārē'äs), town (pop. 1,514), Huila dept., S central Colombia, in upper Magdalena valley, 45 mi. SW of Neiva; rice, cacao, coffee.
Car Nicobar Island (kär' nĭkōbär', nĭ'kōbär), northernmost island (□ 49) of the Nicobars, in Bay of Bengal, 90 mi. S of Little Andaman Isl. (separated by Ten Degree Channel). Fairly flat coral isl. with numerous coconut palms; most populous of Nicobar Isls. Chief village is Mus, on N coast; during Second World War, Japanese used harbor (1942–45) as naval base.
Carnières (kärnyâr'), town (pop. 8,147), Hainaut prov., S central Belgium, 9 mi. W of Charleroi; coal mining; metallurgical industry.
Carnières, village (pop. 883), Nord dept., N France, 5 mi. E of Cambrai; refrigeration equipment mfg.
Carnifex Ferry State Park, W.Va.: see GAULEY RIVER.
Carniola (kärnēō'lů), Ger. *Krain* (krīn), Slovenian *Kranj* (krä'nyů), former crownland and titular duchy (□ 3,843; 1910 pop. 525,995) of Austria; ⊙ was Laibach (Ljubljana). Part of anc. Pannonia; settled (6th cent.) by Slovenes; passed (1335) under the Hapsburgs. Remained a duchy until 1849, when it became a crownland. In 1918–19, it was partitioned bet. Italy (□ 613) and Yugoslavia (□ 3,230); since 1947, it lies entirely within Slovenia, Yugoslavia.
Carn Mairg, Scotland: see MONADHLIATH MOUNTAINS.
Carnock (kär'nŏk), village and parish (pop. 1,443), SW Fifeshire, Scotland, 3 mi. WNW of Dunfermline; coal mining.
Carnot (kärnō'), village (pop. 1,156), Alger dept., N central Algeria, near the Chéliff, 21 mi. ENE of Orléansville; cereals.
Carnot, village, SW Ubangi-Shari, Fr. Equatorial Africa, on a headstream of Sanga R. and 50 mi. N of Berbérati; trade center; diamond fields, coffee plantations.
Carnot, Cape (kär'nůt), on S Eyre Peninsula, S South Australia; forms E end of Great Australian Bight; 34°57'S 135°37'E.
Carnotville (kärnōvēl), village, S central Dahomey, Fr. West Africa, on Ouémé R. and 40 mi. SW of Parakou; cotton growing.
Carnoustie (kärnŏŏ'stē), burgh (1931 pop. 4,806; 1951 census 5,195), S Angus, Scotland, on North Sea, 11 mi. ENE of Dundee, just N of Buddon Ness; seaside resort, with golf links; also shoe mfg.
Carnsore Point (kärn'sôr), SE extremity of Ireland, on St. George's Channel, 12 mi. SSE of Wexford; 52°10'N 6°22'W.
Carnuntum: see BAD DEUTSCH ALTENBURG, Austria.
Carnutum, France: see CHARTRES.
Carnwath (kärnwŏth'), town and parish (pop. 5,258), E Lanark, Scotland, at foot of Pentland Hills, 6 mi. ENE of Lanark; agr. market. Has remains of 15th-cent. church. Near by are ruins of 12th-cent. Cowthally Castle.
Caro (kâ'rō), village (pop. 3,464), ⊙ Tuscola co., E Mich., on Cass R. and 28 mi. ENE of Saginaw, in farm area (livestock, sugar beets, beans, potatoes, grain); dairying, food processing, beet-sugar refining. Settled 1867; inc. 1871.

Caroga Lake (kůrō'gů), resort village, Fulton co., E central N.Y., in the Adirondacks, 10 mi. NW of Gloversville. Small East Caroga and West Caroga lakes are here.

Caroleen (kă'růlēn''), textile village (pop. 3,494, with adjacent Henrietta and Avondale), Rutherford co., SW N.C., c.15 mi. W of Shelby.

Carolina (kärōlē'nä), village (pop. estimate 500), N central San Luis prov., Argentina, in Sierra de San Luis, 35 mi. NNE of San Luis, in grain and livestock area. Las Carolinas gold mines near by.

Carolina (kärôlē'nů), city (pop. 3,359), SW Maranhão, Brazil, river port on right bank of Tocantins R. (Goiás border) and 400 mi. SSE of Belém; 7°20'S 47°25'W. Ships leather, hides, nuts. Important airport. Road to Caxias. Diamonds found just S in Tocantins valley.

Carolina (kärōlē'nä), town (pop. 2,049), Antioquia dept., NW central Colombia, in E valley of Cordillera Central, 39 mi. NE of Medellín; alt. 6,020 ft. Coffee, corn, sugar cane, rice, cacao, beans, livestock. Guadalupe Falls, on Guadalupe R. (affluent of the Porce), are near by.

Carolina, village (pop. 150), Surinam dist., N Du. Guiana, on Surinam R. and 29 mi. SSE of Paramaribo; coffee, rice, sugar cane. Another Carolina village is 15 mi. WSW of Paramaribo.

Carolina, town (pop. 5,041), NE Puerto Rico, on railroad and 12 mi. ESE of San Juan; sugar and tobacco center; textile mill (blankets). The Victoria sugar mill is just W.

Carolina (kărůlī'nů), village (pop. 3,014), SE Transvaal, U. of So. Afr., 30 mi. N of Ermelo, in coal, gold, asbestos mining region; alt. 5,636 ft. Airfield.

Carolina, village (pop. c.300), in Charlestown and Richmond towns, Washington co., SW R.I., on Pawcatuck R. and 29 mi. SSW of Providence.

Carolina, La (lä kärōlē'nä), city (pop. 12,820), Jaén prov., S Spain, in Andalusia, in the Sierra Morena foothills, 13 mi. N of Linares; center of rich lead-mining dist. and terminus of mining railroad from Linares. Silver-lead ore processing. Produces also olive oil, brandy, soap. Cereals, fruit, livestock in area. Was colonized (18th cent.) under Charles III with German immigrants to combat the lawlessness of the region. Airfield 3 mi. SE.

Carolina Beach (kărůlī'nů), resort town (pop. 1,080), New Hanover co., SE N.C., 14 mi. S of Wilmington, on the Atlantic coast; commercial fishing.

Caroline (kă'růlīn). **1** County (□ 320; pop. 18,234), E Md.; ⊙ Denton. On the Eastern Shore; bounded E by Del. line, W by Choptank R. and Tuckahoe Creek; drained by Marshyhope Creek. Agr. area (truck, especially tomatoes; fruit, dairy products, corn, wheat, poultry, livestock), with some timber (hardwoods, evergreens); vegetable canneries, poultry-dressing plants. Formed 1773. **2** County (□ 544; pop. 12,471), E Va.; ⊙ Bowling Green. Bounded NE by Rappahannock R. (bridged at Port Royal), SW and S by North Anna and Pamunkey rivers; intersected by the Mattaponi. Includes Hill Military Reservation. Agr. (truck, tobacco, sweet and white potatoes), livestock raising, some lumbering. Processing industries (canned foods, pickles, excelsior, lumber). Formed 1728.

Caroline Island (kă'růlīn), atoll, Line Isls., central Pacific, 450 mi. NNW of Papeete, Tahiti; 9°58'S 150°13'W; circumference 13 mi. Discovered 1795 by British; leased 1872 to Br. guano company. Formerly Thornton Isl.

Caroline Islands, archipelago (□ 461; pop. 35,119), W Pacific, 3°1'–5°19'N 131°11'–162°59'E. KUSAIE and PONAPE are largest single volcanic isls., while PALAU, TRUK, YAP are most important isl. groups; in addition, there are c.30 atolls broken into numerous islets. Four dists.: Yap and Palau dists. in W Carolines; Truk and Ponape dists. in E Carolines. Mean annual temp. 80°F., rainfall 105 in.; NE trade winds, SW monsoons. Coconuts, sugar cane, taro, arrowroot; rats, lizards. Phosphate, bauxite, iron. Produce tapioca, copra, dried bonito. Natives are Micronesians, except for inhabitants of Kapingamarangi and Nukuoro, who are Polynesians. Discovered 1526 by Spaniards; Sp. rule 1886–99. Germany bought group in 1899. Occupied 1914 by Japan; Jap. mandated territory 1920–35. Sovereignty over isls. claimed 1935 by Japan. In Second World War, Japan established large naval and air bases at Palau (taken 1944 by U.S. forces), Truk, and Yap. Group was included (1947) in U.S. Territory of the Pacific Islands under U.N. trusteeship. Formerly called New Philippines.

Carolles (kärôl'), village (pop. 480), Manche dept., NW France, bathing resort on the Channel, 6 mi. SSE of Granville.

Caromb (kärō'), village (pop. 1,293), Vaucluse dept., SE France, at W foot of Mont Ventoux, 5 mi. NE of Carpentras; fruit preserving, winegrowing, slaked lime mfg.

Caron, town (pop. 150), S Sask., 15 mi. WNW of Moose Jaw; wheat.

Caroni (kůrō'nē), county (□ 214; pop. 61,739), W Trinidad, B.W.I., on the Gulf of Paria.

Caroni, village (pop. 1,409), NW Trinidad, B.W.I., on Caroni R., on railroad and 8 mi. ESE of Port of Spain; sugar-cane growing and milling. Has new housing development.

Caronia (kärônē'ä), anc. *Calacte*, village (pop. 4,636) Messina prov., N Sicily, near Tyrrhenian Sea, 8 mi. NW of Mistretta. Founded c.450 B.C.

Caronie, Monti, Sicily: see NEBRODI MOUNTAINS.

Caroni River (kůrō'nē), NW Trinidad, B.W.I., flows c.25 mi. W to the Gulf of Paria just S of Port of Spain (Caroni Swamps). Partly navigable for flatboats.

Caroní River (kärōnē'), Bolívar state, SE Venezuela, rises at Mt. Roraima in Guiana Highlands near Br. Guiana–Brazil border, flows 430 mi. W and N to Orinoco R. 4 mi. WSW of San Félix, c.60 mi. E of Ciudad Bolívar. Lower course is navigable, though obstructed by rapids near mouth. Receives Paragua R. High ANGEL FALL is on affluent.

Caron is Clawdd, Wales: see TREGARON.

Caronno Pertusella (kärôn'nô pĕrtōozĕl'lä), village (pop. 3,679), Varese prov., Lombardy, N Italy, 2 mi. S of Saronno; icebox mfg. Until c.1940 called Caronno Milanese.

Caron Uwch Clawdd, Wales: see STRATA FLORIDA.

Carora, Eritrea: see KARORA.

Carora (kärō'rä), town (pop. 8,214), Lara state, NW Venezuela, on transandine highway, on affluent of Tocuyo R., in fertile cattle plains of otherwise arid Segovia Highlands, and 55 mi. W of Barquisimeto; trading, distributing, agr. center (sugar cane, bananas, coffee, corn, stock); tanning. Old colonial town with several fine churches.

Carosina (kärôzē'nä), village (pop. 3,386), Ionia prov., Apulia, S Italy, 8 mi. E of Taranto.

Carouge (kärōozh'), town (pop. 7,972), Geneva canton, SW Switzerland, on Arve R., just S of Geneva; metal products, pastry, tobacco, cotton textiles.

Carovigno (kärôvē'nyô), town (pop. 7,252), Brindisi prov., Apulia, S Italy, 16 mi. WNW of Brindisi; wine, olive oil, cheese. Has anc. remains (walls, necropolis).

Carovilli (kärôvēl'lē), town (pop. 1,089), Campobasso prov., Abruzzi e Molise, S central Italy, 9 mi. NNE of Isernia; woolen mill.

Caroya, Argentina: see COLONIA CAROYA.

Carpaneto Piacentino (kärpänā'tô pyächĕntē'nô), town (pop. 1,249), Piacenza prov., Emilia-Romagna, N central Italy, 10 mi. SSE of Piacenza; canned tomatoes.

Carpas Peninsula, Cyprus: see KARPAS PENINSULA.

Carpathia, Ukrainian SSR: see TRANSCARPATHIAN OBLAST.

Carpathian Mountains (kärpā'thēůn), anc. *Carpates*, Czech, Pol., and Rus. *Karpaty*, Rum. *Carpații*, major forested mtn. system of central and E Europe, enclosing the Great Hungarian Plain. A part of the relatively young Alpine uplift, which constitutes the continental backbone, they form the connecting arm bet. the Alps—through outliers of the Eastern Alps in Vienna basin—and the Balkan Mts., with which they merge in the subranges of E Serbia. They extend in a semicircular sweep (c.900 mi. long) from Bratislava on the Danube northward through Slovakia, then E along Czechoslovakian-Polish border (where they reach their greatest width, c.160 mi.) and SE through Ruthenian section of the Ukrainian SSR into Rumania. N of Bucharest they turn abruptly W and in the Transylvanian Alps thrust bet. Transylvania and Walachia to the Iron Gate near Orsova on the Danube (Yugoslav border). Thus they are a watershed bet. the Dniester and Vistula rivers, which rise on its E slopes, and the Danube basin in W and S. At DUKLA PASS, where the Hungarian plain makes its deepest incursion, the Carpathians narrow to barely 20 mi., offering an easy passage bet. the 2 densely populated basins. In no respect a formidable barrier comparable to the Alps or the Pyrenees, the Carpathians are cut by numerous low passes—e.g., JABLUNKOV PASS, Lupkow Pass, YABLONITSA PASS, PREDEAL PASS, TURNU ROSU PASS—which are crossed by principal railroads and highways. Structurally a conglomerate of many separate ridges and blocks, their geologic make-up is just as complex. Only the picturesque TATRA or HighTatra, a popular resort region, is truly Alpine; here the Carpathians rise to highest elevation in the Stalin (or Gerlachovka) Peak (8,737 ft.) and Lomnice Peak (8,639 ft.). Here are 16 jagged summits exceeding 8,000 ft. With abundance of glacial forms, this crystalline ridge is remarkable for its cirques, moraines, arêtes, and mtn. lakes. The TRANSYLVANIAN ALPS in the S do not reach, despite their name, the scenic beauty of the Tatra; but there is plentiful proof of past glaciation and a few peaks—such as Negoi (8,361 ft.) and Moldoveanu (8,344 ft.) in the FAGARAS massif—are almost as high. Since the snow line runs at about 8,500 ft., permanent snowfields exist only in the Tatra. The outer edge of the vast mtn. arch consists of Tertiary folds made of sandstone or Flysch. In its discontinuous central zone crystalline masses, exposed in the lofty ranges (Tatra, Transylvanian Alps) are overlaid in the lower sections by Cretaceous sediments. Lesser isolated blocks of folded Paleozoic rock, such as the Bihor massif of the detached, highly mineralized APUSENI MOUNTAINS in W Transylvania, stand out. Though the Carpathians break into rather well-defined separate ranges, the nomenclature of the subdivisions varies; the Carpathians are sometimes divided into Western Carpathians and Eastern Carpathians; sometimes into Northern and Southern; and sometimes into Western, Central, Eastern, and Southern [the Transylvanian Alps are often called the Southern Carpathians]. The headstreams of the Tisza (Tisa or Theiss) define some of the boundaries. Among the principal ranges W-E are: the low LITTLE CARPATHIANS and WHITE CARPATHIANS along Moravian-Slovakian border; the c.200-mi.-long BESKIDS bet. Moravian Gate (W) and Lupkow Pass (E) and rising in the Babia Gora to 5,628 ft.; S of the Beskids lie several more or less parallel E-W ridges, among them the High Tatra, LOW TATRA, GREATER FATRA, LESSER FATRA, SLOVAK ORE MOUNTAINS, SLOVAKIAN KARST, and, in N Hungary, the MATRA MOUNTAINS, BÜKK MOUNTAINS, and TOKAJ-EPERJES MOUNTAINS (Hegyalja). Flanking the Podolian plain of the Ukrainian SSR (N) stretch the CHERNAGORA and GORGANY ranges, with the Yablonitsa Pass bet. them; both rise above 6,000 ft. They are in turn continued in Rumania by the RODNA MOUNTAINS and the c.185-mi.-long (c.35 mi. wide) Moldavian Carpathians, which form the natural boundary bet. Transylvania (W) and Moldavia (E), rising to 6,425 ft. in the Ciucas and to 6,245 ft. in Ceatslau. Near Stalin (formerly Brasov), on railroad across Predeal Pass to Bucharest, the Carpathians turn sharply W in the c.170-mi.-long Transylvanian Alps. On the whole, the Carpathians are economically of little importance, supporting a scant pop., though they are particularly rich in minerals. Most valuable are the petroleum deposits of the Prahova valley around Ploesti (Rumania) at SE piedmont of Transylvanian Alps and at Borislav (Ukrainian SSR) at N foot of the East Beskids. Among other minerals are high-grade iron ore, mercury, copper, and magnesite in the Slovak Ore Mts., bauxite and iron in the Apuseni Mts., lignite in upper Jiu valley of the Transylvanian Alps, precious stones in the Muntii Metalici (spur of the Apuseni Mts.); also pyrite, silver, gold, rock salt, natural gas. The mts. have many mineral spas and summer and winter resorts, of which the best-known are ZAKOPANE in Poland and SINAIA in Rumania. Climate is of the rigorous continental type with long, cold winters and hot summers; heavy summer rainfall. The Hegyalja heights are the home of the well-known Tokay wine. Apart from the highest massifs, the ranges are densely wooded up to the very summits (tree line at about 4,750 ft. in Tatra, higher in S). Beech and oak give way to conifers in higher altitudes. In remote regions survive wild beasts (wolf, bear, lynx). The chamois is characteristic of the Tatra. Decisive battles during the Turkish invasions, as well as in the First and Second World Wars, were fought in these strategically placed mts. For further information see separate articles on the above-mentioned subranges.

Carpathian Ruthenia, Ukrainian SSR: see TRANSCARPATHIAN OBLAST.

Carpatho-Ukraine, Ukrainian SSR: see TRANSCARPATHIAN OBLAST.

Carpathus, Greece: see KARPATHOS.

Carpatii Meridionali, Rumania: see TRANSYLVANIAN ALPS.

Carpegna (kärpā'nyä), village (pop. 350), Pesaro e Urbino prov., The Marches, central Italy, 16 mi. WNW of Urbino; cement.

Carpenedolo (kärpĕnā'dôlô), town (pop. 4,873), Brescia prov., Lombardy, N Italy, near Chiese R., 16 mi. SE of Brescia; silk mills, macaroni and brick factories.

Carpentaria, Gulf of (–tâ'rēů), large arm of Arafura Sea, indents N coast of Australia bet. Cape Wessel, Northern Territory (W), and Cape York, Queensland (E); connnected with Coral Sea (E) by Torres Strait; bounded W by Arnhem Land, NE by Cape York Peninsula; 305 mi. wide (E-W), 370 mi. deep (N-S). Contains Groote Eylandt, Sir Edward Pellew and Wellesley isls. Receives Roper, Limmen Bight, McArthur, Leichhardt, Albert, Flinders, Mitchell, and other rivers.

Carpenter, town (pop. 165), Mitchell co., N Iowa, near Cedar R., 20 mi. NE of Mason City. Limestone quarries, sand and gravel pits near by.

Carpenter Dam, Ark.: see OUACHITA RIVER.

Carpentersville, village (pop. 1,523), Kane co., NE Ill., on Fox R. and 38 mi. WNW of Chicago, in agr. area (grain, livestock; dairy products); mfg. (iron and steel products, plowshares). Settled 1834, platted 1851, inc. 1887.

Carpentras (kärpâträs'), town (pop. 11,044), Vaucluse dept., SE France, 14 mi. NE of Avignon; important agr. market (fruit and vegetable shipping and preserving) known for its sweetmeat manufactures. Also makes films, cigarette paper, tin cans, plastics. Active trade in almonds, honey, olive oil, tomatoes, strawberries, wine, perfume essences, and truffles. Has 15th-16th-cent. Gothic church (former cathedral), fine mus. and library, and 18th-cent. synagogue. Massive 18th-cent. aqueduct just NE. Episcopal see (3d cent.–1790), and ⊙ Comtat Venaissin (1229–1791). Scene of long Conclave which elected Pope John XXII.

Carpeto-Vetónica, Cordillera (kôr-dhělyä'rä kärpā'tō-vātō'nēkä), mountain system of Iberian Peninsula, extending c.350 mi. W-E from the Serra da

Estrêla in Portugal into central Spain. Part of it, the Sierra de Gata, separates Leon from Estremadura; and the Sierra de Gredos and Sierra de Guadarrama separate Old Castile from New Castile. Rises in the Peñalara to 7,972 ft.

Carpi (kär'pē). **1** Town (pop. 13,805), Modena prov., Emilia-Romagna, N central Italy, 9 mi. N of Modena; rail junction; wine, alcohol, hats, stoves, sausage. Bishopric. Has cathedral (begun c.1514), several churches including San Nicolò (1493–1522) and San Francesco (1681–1742), Romanesque campanile (1217–21), and castle (14th-16th cent.; houses mus.). **2** Village (pop. 1,192), Verona prov., Veneto, N Italy, on Adige R. and 5 mi. SE of Legnago. Here in 1701 the French were defeated by Prince Eugene.

Carpignano Sesia (kärpēnyä'nô sä'zyä), village (pop. 2,332), Novara prov., Piedmont, N Italy, near Sesia R., 12 mi. NW of Novara.

Carpina (kärpē'nů), city (pop. 9,756), E Pernambuco, NE Brazil, 30 mi. NW of Recife; rail junction (spur to Bom Jardim); sugar-growing and -processing center.

Carpineti (kärpēnā'tē), village (pop. 282), Reggio nell'Emilia prov., Emilia-Romagna, N central Italy, 18 mi. SSW of Reggio nell'Emilia. Has old castle, once a refuge of Hildebrand.

Carpineto della Nora (kärpēnā'tô dĕl-lä nô'rä), village (pop. 403), Pescara prov., Abruzzi e Molise, S central Italy, 16 mi. W of Chieti; cementworks.

Carpino (kärpē'nô), town (pop. 6,533), Foggia prov., Apulia, S Italy, on Gargano promontory, 15 mi. NNW of Manfredonia, in sheep-raising region; olive oil, wine, cheese.

Carpinone (kärpēnô'nĕ), town (pop. 2,378), Campobasso prov., Abruzzi e Molise, S central Italy, 5 mi. E of Isernia; rail junction.

Carpintería (kärpēntärē'ä), town (pop. estimate 500), S San Juan prov., Argentina, on railroad and 20 mi. S of San Juan; wine, alfalfa, wheat, onions, livestock; apiculture. Lime deposits, limekilns.

Carpinteria (kär"pĭntůrē'ů), residential and resort village (pop. 2,864), Santa Barbara co., SW Calif., on the coast, 15 mi. E of Santa Barbara; asphalt pits; ships citrus fruit, olives, walnuts. Established 1863 on site of Indian village visited by Portolá in 1769.

Carpio (kär'pyō), town (pop. 1,382), Valladolid prov., N central Spain, 13 mi. SW of Medina del Campo; cereals, vegetables, lumber; sheep and hog raising. Has old mansion of counts of Carpio.

Carpio, village (pop. 194), Ward co., NW central N.Dak., 24 mi. NW of Minot and on Des Lacs R.

Carpio, El (ĕl), town (pop. 4,834), Córdoba prov., S Spain, near the Guadalquivir, 7 mi. NW of Bujalance; olive-oil and cheese processing, flour milling, soap mfg. Agr. trade (cereals, vegetables, livestock). Has 14th-cent. Moorish tower, and palace of dukes of Berwick and Alba.

Carpio de Tajo, El (dā tä'hō), town (pop. 3,479), Toledo prov., central Spain, near the Tagus, 22 mi. W of Toledo; agr. center (cereals, fruit, vegetables, grapes, olives, sheep, goats); wool, pottery, tiles.

Carp Lake, N Mich., in Emmet and Cheboygan counties, resort lake c.6 mi. S of Mackinaw City; c.3 mi. long, 1 mi. wide; fishing.

Carp River, SE Upper Peninsula, Mich., rises in Trout L. in SW Chippewa co., flows c.25 mi. SE to St. Martin Bay of L. Huron.

Carquefou (kärkfōō'), village (pop. 592), Loire-Inférieure dept., W France, 6 mi. NNE of Nantes.

Carquinez Strait (kärkē'nĭs) (8 mi. long, c.1 mi. wide at narrowest point), W Calif., swift tidal strait connecting SUISUN BAY with N part (San Pablo Bay) of SAN FRANCISCO BAY. Just SE of Vallejo is Carquinez Bridge (4/5 mi. long, more than 300 ft. above water), completed 1927.

Carra, Lough (lŏkh kă'rů), lake (6 mi. long, 2 mi. wide), S Co. Mayo, Ireland, just NE of Lough Mask.

Carrabassett (kă'rūbă'sĭt), logging village, Franklin co., W Maine, on the Carrabassett and 27 mi. N of Farmington.

Carrabassett River, W central Maine, rises in Franklin co. E of Rangeley L., flows c.40 mi. NE then SE, past Kingfield (water power), to the Kennebec above Madison.

Carrabelle (kă'rūbĕl), city (pop. 970), Franklin co., NW Fla., c.45 mi. SSW of Tallahassee; port of entry on St. George Sound; resort and fishing center; exports lumber. Inc. as city in 1931.

Carrae, Turkey: see HARAN.

Carranglan (käräng-glän'), town (1939 pop. 1,460; 1948 municipality pop. 6,328), Nueva Ecija prov., central Luzon, Philippines, 33 mi. NNE of Cabanatuan; rice, corn. Manganese deposits.

Carranque (käräng'kā), town (pop. 795), Toledo prov., central Spain, 20 mi. SW of Madrid; wheat, olives, grapes, sheep, goats.

Carrantuohill, Carrauntuohil, or **Carrantual** (all: kă"rūntōō'ŭl), highest peak (3,414 ft.) of Ireland, in the Macgillycuddy's Reeks, central Co. Kerry, 12 mi. WSW of Killarney.

Carranza, Cape (kärän'sä), Pacific headland in Maule prov., S central Chile, 25 mi. SW of Constitución; 35°38'S 72°42'W.

Carrara (kůrä'rů, It. kär-rä'rä), city (pop. 25,259), Massa e Carrara prov., Tuscany, central Italy, near Ligurian Sea, 13 mi. ESE of Spezia, in foothills of APUANE ALPS. Rail terminus; center of Ital. marble industry. The famous Carrara marble is extensively quarried and processed in its environs, and exported via near-by Marina di Carrara and Avenza to the whole world. Has medieval cathedral (12th-14th cent.), marble-working schools, mus., acad. of fine arts (housed in former ducal palace). With near-by Massa, constituted duchy of Massa and Carrara. In Second World War badly damaged (1944–45) by air and artillery bombing.

Carrascalejo (käräskälā'hō), village (pop. 1,162), Cáceres prov., W Spain, 30 mi. SW of Talavera de la Reina; stock raising, olive-oil processing; cereals.

Carrascalejo, El, village (pop. 122), Badajoz prov., W Spain, 7 mi. N of Mérida; cereals, chick-peas; charcoal burning.

Carrasco, Bolivia: see TOTORA, Cochabamba dept.

Carrasco (kärä'skō), E section of Montevideo, S Uruguay; notable beach resort on the Río de la Plata. Site of Montevideo's airport.

Carrascosa del Campo (käräskō'sä dhĕl käm'pō), town (pop. 1,832), Cuenca prov., E central Spain, 32 mi. W of Cuenca; cereals, grapes, olives, livestock; olive-oil pressing, flour milling.

Carrasquilla, La, Panama: see LA CARRASQUILLA.

Carratraca (käräträ'kä), town (pop. 1,158), Málaga prov., S Spain, 24 mi. WNW of Málaga; noted spa in fruitgrowing region. Nickel and chromium are mined in vicinity and milled here.

Carrauntuohil, Ireland: see CARRANTUOHILL.

Carrazeda de Anciãis (kärăzā'dů dĭ ãsyā'ēsh), town (pop. 814), Bragança dist., N Portugal, near the Douro, 25 mi. ESE of Vila Real; winegrowing; rye, potatoes. Also spelled Carrazeda de Ansiãis. Formerly spelled Carrazeda de Anciães.

Carrboro (kär'bůrů), town (pop. 1,795), Orange co., N central N.C., 11 mi. SW of Durham; woolen-textile and lumber mills.

Carrbridge, agr. village, E Inverness, Scotland, on Dulnan R. and 9 mi. WSW of Grantown; resort.

Carr Brigs, Scotland: see FIFE NESS.

Carrefour (kärůfōōr'), village, Ouest dept., S Haiti, 5 mi. W of Port-au-Prince, in cotton- and coffee-growing region.

Carregal do Sal (kärĭgäl' dōō säl'), town (pop. 1,194), Viseu dist., N central Portugal, on railroad and 17 mi. SSW of Viseu; agr. center in Mondego R. valley.

Carrenleufú River, Chile-Argentina: see PALENA RIVER.

Carrera, La, Argentina: see LA CARRERA.

Carrera Island (kärā'rä, kůrâ'rů), islet (20 acres; pop. 363), off NW Trinidad, B.W.I., in the Gulf of Paria, 6 mi. W of Port of Spain. Convict depot. Sometimes called, together with small adjoining Cronstadt Isl., San Diego Isls.

Carreras (kärä'räs), town (pop. estimate 2,000), S Santa Fe prov., Argentina, 60 mi. SW of Rosario; agr. center (flax, potatoes, grain, livestock, poultry); dairying, tanning.

Carresse (kärĕs'), village (pop. 530), Basses-Pyrénées dept., SW France, on the Gave d'Oloron and 11 mi. W of Orthez; plaster works. Kaolin quarries.

Carrhae, Turkey: see HARAN.

Carriacou (kă"rēůkōō'), island (□ 13; pop. 6,769), S Grenadines, largest isl. of the group, dependency of Grenada in B.W.I., 30 mi. NE of St. George's, Grenada. The hilly, indented isl. is 7 mi. long, up to 3 mi. wide; rises to 980 ft. Grows cotton and limes. Main settlement is Hillsborough, on W coast.

Carriches (kärē'chĕs), town (pop. 881), Toledo prov., central Spain, 24 mi. WNW of Toledo; cereals, olives, grapes, livestock; lumbering.

Carrick (kă'rĭk), mountainous area of S Ayrshire, Scotland, bet. Doon R. and Water of Girvan (N) and Wigtown and Kirkcudbright border (S). Rises to Polmaddie Hill (1,802 ft.), 10 mi. ESE of Girvan.

Carrick-a-rede or **Carrick-a-raide** (both: -ů-rād'), basalt islet in the Atlantic just off N Co. Antrim, Northern Ireland, 5 mi. NW of Ballycastle, connected with mainland by rope bridge, used by salmon fishermen.

Carrickbeg (-bĕg'), village (district pop. 307), N Co. Waterford, Ireland, on Suir R. (bridges) opposite Carrick-on-Suir.

Carrickfergus (-fûr'gůs), municipal borough (1937 pop. 4,399; 1951 census 8,650), Co. Antrim, Northern Ireland, on N shore of Belfast Lough, 9 mi. NE of Belfast; linen and rayon milling, rock-salt mining; fishing port. Parts of its castle (built 1178) remain. The Elizabethan Church of St. Nicholas is noteworthy. The old North Gate (restored) is relic of former town walls. Carrickfergus, former assize town of Co. Antrim, was superseded by Belfast.

Carrickmacross (-můkrŏs'), Gaelic *Carraig Mhachaire Rois*, urban district (pop. 2,116), SE Co. Monaghan, Ireland, 13 mi. W of Dundalk; agr. market (flax, oats, potatoes), with mfg. of leather goods, shoes, lace, potato alcohol. There are fragmentary remains of castle. Convent of St. Louis is noted for lace made here since 1820.

Carrick-on-Shannon, Gaelic *Cara Droma Rúisg*, town (pop. 1,497), ⊙ Co. Leitrim, Ireland, in SW part of co., on the Shannon (bridged) and 85 mi. WNW of Dublin; agr. market in dairying, cattle-raising, potato-growing region; fishing center. Part of town is in Co. Roscommon.

Carrick-on-Suir (-shōōr'), Gaelic *Carraig na Siúre*, urban district (pop. 4,859), SE Co. Tipperary, Ireland, on Suir R. and 12 mi. E of Clonmel; agr. market (dairying; potatoes, beets); tanning, wicker-goods mfg., salmon fishing. Has castle (built 1309) of the Butlers, and remains of 14th-cent. abbey. Two bridges, one very old, connect town with S suburb of Carrickbeg, Co. Waterford.

Carrick Roads, England: see FAL RIVER.

Carrick's Ford, W.Va.: see PARSONS.

Carrières-sur-Seine (kărēâr'-sür-sĕn'), town (pop. 4,973), Seine-et-Oise dept., N central France, a WNW suburb of Paris, 9 mi. from Notre Dame Cathedral, on right bank of the Seine; truck.

Carrier Mills, mining village (pop. 2,252), Saline co., SE Ill., 6 mi. SW of Harrisburg, in bituminous-coal region; agr. (corn, wheat, livestock; dairy products). Inc. 1894.

Carrieton, village (pop. 124), S South Australia, 60 mi. NNE of Port Pirie; wheat, wool, dairy products.

Carrigaholt (kă"rĭgůhōlt'), Gaelic *Carraig an Chobhaltaigh*, fishing village, SW Co. Clare, Ireland, on the Shannon estuary, 10 mi. WSW of Kilrush. Site of Irish Col.

Carrigain, Mount (kă'rĭgĭn), peak (4,647 ft.) of White Mts., N central N.H., WNW of Bartlett.

Carrigaline (kă"rĭgůlīn'), Gaelic *Carraig Uí Laighean*, village (pop. 357), S Co. Cork, Ireland, on Owenboy R. and 7 mi. SE of Cork; china-clay mining. Has anc. castle. In near-by Drake's Pool Drake took refuge (1587) when beset by a Spanish fleet.

Carrigallen (kă"rĭgă'lůn), Gaelic *Carraig Álainn*, town (pop. 190), SE Co. Leitrim, Ireland, 12 mi. W of Cavan; dairying; cattle, potatoes.

Carrigtwohill or **Carrigtohill** (both: kă"rĭgtōō'ŭl), Gaelic *Carraig Tuathail*, village (pop. 399), SE Co. Cork, Ireland, 10 mi. E of Cork; agr. market (dairying, cattle raising; potatoes, oats, beets). Has anc. church and keep; near by are anc. subterranean chambers, probably of Danish origin.

Carril (kärēl'), town (pop. 1,704), Pontevedra prov., NW Spain, fishing port on Arosa Bay, and 12 mi. NNW of Pontevedra; fish processing (shellfish). Sea-bathing resort.

Carri Laufquén, Lake, or **Lake Carrilafquén** (both: kärēläfkĕn') (□ 30), SW Río Negro natl. territory, Argentina, 45 mi. WNW of Maquinchao; 9 mi. long, 2–5 mi. wide.

Carrillo, canton, Costa Rica: see FILADELFIA.

Carrillo (kärē'yō), village, San José prov., N central Costa Rica, at NW foot of the volcano Irazú, 20 mi. NNE of San José (linked by road across La Palma saddle of Central Cordillera); corn, livestock. Former railhead of line from Limón, now dismantled to Toro Amarillo because of river flood danger.

Carrilobo (kärēlō'bō), town (pop. estimate 800), central Córdoba prov., Argentina, 70 mi. SE of Córdoba; railroad terminus; wheat, livestock.

Carrington, NW suburb of Newcastle, E New South Wales, Australia, on W shore of Port Hunter opposite Stockton; floating docks.

Carrington, city (pop. 2,101), ⊙ Foster co., central N.Dak., 42 mi. NNW of Jamestown; dairy products, livestock, poultry, wheat. Platted 1882, inc. 1900.

Carrión de Calatrava (käryōn' dhā käläträ'vä), town (pop. 4,031), Ciudad Real prov., S central Spain, 6 mi. ENE of Ciudad Real; processing and agr. center (grapes, olives, potatoes, melons, livestock). Olive-oil extracting, alcohol distilling, flour milling, vegetable canning; gypsum quarrying. Medicinal springs near by.

Carrión de los Céspedes (lōs thā'spādhĕs), town (pop. 3,048), Seville prov., SW Spain, on railroad and 19 mi. W of Seville; olive- and winegrowing; lumbering.

Carrión de los Condes (kōn'dĕs), city (pop. 3,247), Palencia prov., N central Spain, on Carrión R. and 24 mi. NNW of Palencia; tanning, flour milling, soap and chocolate mfg.; trades in cereals, wine, fruit, livestock. Has remains of town walls, Romanesque church (11th cent.), and church of Santiago which belonged to Knights Templars. Feats of counts of Carrión are celebrated in chronicle of the Cid.

Carrión River (käryōn'), Palencia prov., N central Spain, rises in Cantabrian Mts. near Peña Prieta, flows 120 mi. generally SSE, past Palencia, to Pisuerga R. near Dueñas.

Carrizal (kärē-thäl'), village (pop. 2,242), Grand Canary, Canary Isls., 12 mi. S of Las Palmas; bananas, tomatoes, cereals, livestock.

Carrizal Alto (kärēsäl' äl'tō), village (1930 pop. 20), Atacama prov., N central Chile, on railroad and 15 mi. E of Carrizal Bajo; former copper-mining center, now almost abandoned.

Carrizal Bajo (bä'hō), village (1930 pop. 33), Atacama prov., N central Chile, minor port on Pacific coast, 27 mi. N of Huasco; rail terminus. Formerly important copper-smelting center; shipped ore from Carrizal Alto mine.

Carrizales (kärēsä'lĕs), town (pop. estimate 1,500), S Santa Fe prov., Argentina, 38 mi. NNW of Rosario, on railroad (Clarke station); agr. center (flax, corn, wheat, alfalfa).

Carrizal Point (kärēsäl'), headland on Pacific coast of Colima, W Mexico, 9 mi. W of Manzanillo; 19°5'N 104°27'W.

Carrizo de la Ribera (kärē'thō dhā lä rēvä'rä), town (pop. 1,141), Leon prov., NW Spain, 13 mi. W of Leon; livestock, potatoes, flax, sugar beets.

Carrizo Gorge (kûrē'zō), S Calif., spectacular canyon (c.11 mi. long, more than 1,000 ft. deep), at SE end of Laguna Mts., just N of Jacumba.

Carrizo Mountains, in NE corner of Ariz., in Navajo Indian Reservation; PASTORA PEAK (9,420 ft.) is highest point.

Carrizo Peak (kä'rĭzō) (9,656 ft.), in Sacramento Mts., S central N.Mex., 9 mi. ENE of Carrizozo.

Carrizosa (kärē-thō'sä), town (pop. 2,739), Ciudad Real prov., S central Spain, 23 mi. ESE of Manzanares; grapes, cereals; plaster mfg.

Carrizo Springs (kûrē'zō, -rĭ'zō), city (pop. 4,316), ⊙ Dimmit co., SW Texas, 11 mi. S of Crystal City; a rail, shipping and trade center of irrigated Winter Garden truck area; also cattle, fruit. Settled 1862, inc. 1910.

Carrizozo (kärĭzō'zō, -zō'sù), village (pop. 1,389), ⊙ Lincoln co., S central N.Mex., just NW of the Sierra Blanca, 50 mi. NNE of Alamogordo; alt. 5,425 ft. Mtn. resort; trade and cattle-shipping center. Iron and soft-coal deposits in vicinity. Carrizo Peak is 9 mi. ENE, Mal Pais (extensive lava stretch with deep crevasses and much-eroded hills) just W. Town laid out 1899 with coming of railroad.

Carro, El, Mexico: see VILLA GONZÁLEZ ORTEGA.

Carroll. 1 County (□ 634; pop. 13,244), NW Ark.; ⊙ Eureka Springs and Berryville. Bounded N by Mo. line; drained by White and Kings rivers and small Osage Creek; situated in Ozark region. Agr. (fruit, truck, grain, hay, livestock); dairy products; pine and oak timber. Mfg. at Berryville and Eureka Springs. Mineral springs, health resorts. U.S. soil-conservation project in co. Formed 1833. **2** County (□ 495; pop. 34,112), W Ga.; ⊙ Carrollton. Bounded W by Ala. line and SE by Chattahoochee R. Cotton-growing and textile-mfg. area drained by Little Tallapoosa R.; also stock raising and lumbering. Formed 1826. **3** County (□ 468; pop. 18,976), NW Ill.; ⊙ Mount Carroll. Bounded W by the Mississippi; drained by Plum R. and Elkhorn Creek. Includes Mississippi Palisades State Park. Livestock, corn, hay, wheat, oats, truck, poultry; dairy products. Formed 1839. **4** County (□ 374; pop. 16,010), NW central Ind.; ⊙ Delphi. Intersected by Wabash R.; drained by Tippecanoe R. and Wildcat and Deer creeks. Farming and dairying (grain, dairy products, livestock); meat and poultry packing, lumber milling, other mfg.; timber. Includes part of Freeman L. Formed 1828. **5** County (□ 574; pop. 23,065), W central Iowa; ⊙ Carroll. Prairie agr. area (cattle, hogs, poultry, corn, oats, wheat) drained by Raccoon, Middle Raccoon R., East and West Nishnabotna rivers. Bituminous-coal deposits. Has state park. Formed 1851. **6** County (□ 131; pop. 8,517), N Ky.; ⊙ Carrollton. Bounded N by Ohio R. (Ind. line), SE by Eagle Creek; drained by Kentucky R. Gently rolling upland agr. area in outer Bluegrass region; burley tobacco, livestock, grain, dairy products, poultry. Sand and gravel pits. Some mfg. at Carrollton. Includes Butler Memorial State Park. Formed 1838. **7** County (□ 456; pop. 44,907), N Md.; ⊙ Westminster. Bounded NW by Monocacy R., N by Pa. line; drained by branches of Patapsco R. and by Gunpowder Falls (stream), several creeks. Piedmont region; dairying, stock and poultry raising, agr. (corn, wheat, potatoes, truck, apples; wormseed); soapstone quarries; some mfg., vegetable canning. Formed 1836. **8** County (□ 638; pop. 15,499), central Miss.; ⊙ Carrollton and Vaiden. Drained by Big Black R. (SE boundary) and Yalobusha R. (NE boundary). Agr. (cotton, corn, hay); timber. Formed 1833. **9** County (□ 694; pop. 15,589), NW central Mo.; ⊙ Carrollton. Bet. Missouri R. (S) and Grand R. (E); agr. (wheat, corn, oats), livestock; coal. Formed 1833. **10** County (□ 938; pop. 15,868), E N.H., on Maine line; ⊙ Ossipee. Agr. and recreational region; summer and winter resorts in L. Winnipesaukee area in S, White Mtn. Natl. Forest area in N. Granite quarrying; some mfg. (wood products, machinery); dairy products, poultry. Drained by Saco, Ellis, and Ossipee rivers. Formed 1840. **11** County (□ 396; pop. 19,039), E Ohio; ⊙ Carrollton. Drained by small Sandy, Conotton, and Yellow creeks. Includes Atwood Reservoir. Agr. area (livestock, dairy products, grain); mfg. at Carrollton and Malvern; coal mines, fire-clay quarries. Formed 1832. **12** County (□ 596; pop. 26,553), NW Tenn.; ⊙ Huntingdon. Drained by Big Sandy R. and headstreams of the Obion. Agr. area (cotton, corn, livestock, sweet potatoes, truck). Formed 1821. **13** County (□ 496; pop. 26,695), SW Va.; ⊙ Hillsville. In the Blue Ridge; bounded S by N.C. Includes part of Jefferson Natl. Forest; traversed by Appalachian Trail and Blue Ridge Parkway. Drained by New R. Agr., livestock raising, dairying; fruit, clover, grain, cabbage; some mfg. (especially textiles and wood products) at Galax (partly in co.) and Hillsville; pyrrhotite mining. Formed 1842.

Carroll. 1 City (pop. 6,231), ⊙ Carroll co., W central Iowa, on Middle Raccoon R. and 50 mi. W of Boone; rail junction; mfg. (farm equipment, dairy products, feed, flour). Has Franciscan hosp. State park near by. Inc. 1869. **2** Plantation (pop. 288), Penobscot co., E central Maine, 38 mi. SE of Millinocket in hunting, fishing area. **3** Village (pop. 309), Wayne co., NE Nebr., 10 mi. WNW of Wayne. **4** Town (pop. 359), Coos co., N central N.H., on the Lower Ammonoosuc and 11 mi. E of Littleton, NW of Crawford Notch, in White Mts. Includes resorts of Twin Mountain, Fabyan House, and Bretton Woods (scene in 1944 of U.N. monetary conference). **5** Village (pop. 416), Fairfield co., central Ohio, 19 mi. SE of Columbus, in agr. area; makes tools.

Carroll Inlet, long, narrow inlet of Bellingshausen Sea, in Antarctica, extending SE for 35 naut. mi. into George Bryan Coast, W of Cape Smiley, in 73°15'S 79°W.

Carrollton (kă'rûltûn). **1** Town (pop. 710), ⊙ Pickens co., W Ala., 30 mi. W of Tuscaloosa; lumber milling, cotton ginning. **2** City (pop. 7,753), ⊙ Carroll co., W Ga., c.40 mi. WSW of Atlanta, near Little Tallapoosa R. Mfg. center; clothing, yarn, chenille products, braid, shoes, lumber, pencils, fertilizer, marble monuments. State jr. col. near by. Inc. 1856. **3** City (pop. 2,437), ⊙ Greene co., W Ill., 30 mi. NNW of Alton; trade center of agr. area; ships grain; livestock, dairy products, poultry; tile- and brickworks. Settled 1818, laid out 1821, inc. 1861. **4** City (pop. 3,226), ⊙ Carroll co., N Ky., on left bank (levee) of the Ohio, at Kentucky R. mouth, and 45 mi. NE of Louisville, in agr. area (livestock, poultry, dairy products, grain, burley tobacco); canned vegetables, packed meat; mfg. of beverages, radio cabinets, millwork, clothing; distillery; tobacco warehouses. Butler Memorial State Park is near by. Inc. 1794 as Port William; renamed Carrollton 1838. **5** Village (1940 pop. 2,984), Saginaw co., E central Mich., on Saginaw R., just N of Saginaw; beet-sugar refining. **6** Town (pop. 475), a ⊙ Carroll co., central Miss., 15 mi. E of Greenwood; lumber milling, cotton ginning. **7** City (pop. 4,380), ⊙ Carroll co., NW central Mo., near Missouri R., 30 mi. S of Chillicothe; agr. trading center. State children's home near by. Settled 1818, inc. 1833. **8** Village (pop. c.100), Cattaraugus co., W N.Y., on Allegheny R. and 10 mi. WNW of Olean, in Allegany Indian Reservation; oil wells. **9** Village (pop. 2,658), ⊙ Carroll co., E Ohio, 21 mi. SE of Canton, in agr. area (grain, wool); rubber goods, heating apparatus, chinaware, brick, dairy products; coal mining. Laid out 1815. **10** Town (pop. 1,610), Dallas co., N Texas, near West Fork of Trinity R., 14 mi. NW of Dallas, in agr. area (cotton, corn); feed milling, cotton ginning.

Carrolltown, borough (pop. 1,452), Cambria co., SW central Pa., 23 mi. NNE of Johnstown; potatoes, cabbages; bituminous coal. Laid out 1840, inc. 1858.

Carrollville, village (pop. 1,240), Milwaukee co., SE Wis., near L. Michigan, 12 mi. S of Milwaukee; mfg. (tar, glue, fertilizers).

Carron (kă'rûn). **1** Town in Larbert parish, E Stirling, Scotland, on Carron R. and 2 mi. N of Falkirk; iron foundries (established 1760) and electrical equipment works. Town gives its name to carronade naval gun and to carron oil, 1st used at ironworks here. **2** Village, Moray, Scotland: see KNOCKANDO.

Carron, Loch, Scotland: see LOCHCARRON.

Carronbridge, Scotland: see THORNHILL.

Carron River, Stirling, Scotland, rises in Lennox Hills, flows 20 mi. E, past Denny and Carron, to the Forth estuary at Grangemouth.

Carrot River, village (pop. 223), E Sask., 35 mi. NE of Tisdale; dairying, wheat.

Carrot River, E Sask. and W Man., issues from Wakaw L. (12 mi. long, 1 mi. wide), 35 mi. SSE of Prince Albert, flows 250 mi. ENE, parallel to Saskatchewan R., crossing into Man. to Saskatchewan R. 6 mi. W of The Pas. Valley is one of richest agr. regions of prov.; here the Chevalier de la Corne introduced (1754) 1st grain in the Prairies.

Carrouges (kärōōzh'), village (pop. 599), Orne dept., NW France, on a hilltop, 15 mi. NW of Alençon; stock raising.

Carrowmore (kă"rōmôr'), locality in NE Co. Sligo, Ireland, 2 mi. SW of Sligo. On low hill here is largest group of megalithic stone monuments in British Isles.

Carrowmore, Lough (lŏkh), lake (1 mi. long), central Co. Mayo, Ireland, 5 mi. E of Castlebar.

Carrsville, town (pop. 205), Livingston co., SW Ky., on left bank of the Ohio and 26 mi. NNE of Paducah.

Carrù (kär-rōō'), village (pop. 2,237), Cuneo prov., Piedmont, NW Italy, near Tanaro R., 7 mi. NNE of Mondovì; cotton textiles, macaroni.

Carrville, town (pop. 760), Tallapoosa co., E central Ala., on Tallapoosa R. and 28 mi. WSW of Opelika. Yates Dam is just NW.

Carry Ponds, Somerset co., W central Maine, c.11 mi. NW of Bingham; 3 lakes ranging from 1 to 2 mi. in length.

Carsa (kär'sä), village (pop. 800), Harar prov., E central Ethiopia, in highlands 21 mi. WNW of Harar; coffee growing.

Carsamba (chärshämbä'), Turkish *Çarşamba*. **1** Village, Kastamonu prov., Turkey: see AZDAVAY. **2** Town (pop. 8,010), Samsun prov., N Turkey, on Yesil R. and 22 mi. ESE of Samsun; rail terminus and agr. center (corn, tobacco).

Carshalton (kûshôl'tûn, käs-hō'tûn), residential urban district (1931 pop. 28,763; 1951 census 62,804), NE Surrey, England, 3 mi. W of Croydon; chemical and paint works.

Carso, Yugoslavia: see KARST.

Carsoli (kärsô'lē), town (pop. 2,148), Aquila prov., Abruzzi e Molise, S central Italy, 18 mi. WNW of Avezzano. Partly destroyed (1944) in Second World War, with loss of 14th-cent. Orsini palace and many medieval houses.

Carson, county (□ 899; pop. 6,852), extreme N Texas; ⊙ Panhandle. In high plains of the Panhandle; alt. 3,300–3,500 ft. Drained by McClellan Creek, forks of Red R., and small tributaries of Canadian R. Cattle-ranching and grain region, underlaid by Panhandle natural-gas and oil field, one of world's largest, with gas pipe lines to several U.S. cities; carbon-black plants. Formed 1876.

Carson. 1 Town (pop. 596), Pottawattamie co., SW Iowa, 23 mi. E of Council Bluffs; shipping point for livestock and farm produce. **2** Village (pop. 493), ⊙ Grant co., S N.Dak., 45 mi. SW of Bismarck; flour mills, coal mines, dairy farms; poultry, wheat, corn.

Carson, Camp, Colo.: see COLORADO SPRINGS.

Carson City. 1 Village (pop. 1,168), Montcalm co., central Mich., on Fish Creek and 35 mi. NNW of Lansing, in agr. area (grain, beans, sugar beets, livestock, poultry; dairy products). Oil refining, flour and feed milling. Settled 1854; inc. 1887. **2** City (pop. 3,082), ⊙ Nevada and Ormsby co., W Nev., near Calif. line and Carson R., just E of L. Tahoe and Carson Range, 24 mi. S of Reno; 39°10'N 119°46'W; alt. 4,660 ft. Rail and trade center, and resort in silver-mining and agr. area; cattle slaughtering, brewing. Seat of state capitol (built 1870–72), old U.S. mint (now state mus.), Supreme Court and State Library Bldg. (1936), and state penitentiary. U.S. Indian school and Indian reservation hq. are near by, at Stewart. Named for Kit Carson and laid out (1858) on site of trading post established (1851) as Eagle Station. Served as supply point for mining region. Growth stimulated by discovery of Comstock Lode (1859; chiefly silver) and by construction of Virginia and Truckee RR for removal of ore. Became territorial ⊙ 1861, state ⊙ 1864, inc. 1875.

Carson Lake, W Nev., intermittent body of water S of Carson Sink, 10 mi. SSE of Fallon; 9 mi. long, 6 mi. wide.

Carson Pass or **Kit Carson Pass,** E Calif., highway pass (alt. 8,600 ft.) across the Sierra Nevada, in Alpine co., c.50 mi. ENE of Jackson and c.30 mi. SW of Carson City, Nev. Discovered by Kit Carson when he guided Frémont's expedition into Calif. in 1843–44; it was later crossed by an emigrant trail.

Carson Range, W Nev., E spur of Sierra Nevada, extending N-S along E shore of L. Tahoe. Rises to 10,800 ft. in Mt. Rose, 14 mi. SSW of Reno.

Carson River, W Nev., formed by confluence, near L. Tahoe, of East Carson and West Carson rivers, which rise in the Sierra Nevada in Alpine co., Calif.; flows c.125 mi. NE, past Fallon, and disappears in Carson Sink. Lahontan Dam (129 ft. high, 1,400 ft. long; completed 1915) is in lower course, 15 mi. W of Fallon; used for hydroelectric power and irrigation; forms Lahontan Reservoir (max. capacity 290,000 acre-ft.). Part of Newlands irrigation project, which includes TRUCKEE RIVER. Agr. (alfalfa, wheat, barley, corn, potatoes, truck, small fruits), livestock and poultry raising, and dairying are important.

Carson Sink, W Nev., intermittently dry lake bed (remnant of anc. L. Lahontan) in Churchill co., NE of Fallon; 20 mi. long, 15 mi. wide. Swampy area in S is catch basin for Carson R.

Carsonville, village (pop. 487), Sanilac co., E Mich., 33 mi. NNW of Port Huron, in agr. area (wheat, corn, sugar beets).

Carstairs, village (pop. 385), S central Alta., 35 mi. N of Calgary; grain elevators, lumbering, clay mining, mixed farming.

Carstairs, town and parish (pop. 2,291), E Lanark, Scotland, near the Clyde, 5 mi. E of Lanark; rail junction; market.

Carstensz, Mount (kär'stûnz), highest peak (c.16,400 ft.) of New Guinea, in Nassau Range, W central New Guinea; highest isl. peak in the world. Mt. Carstensz and adjacent peaks are often collectively called Carstensz Mts.

Carswell, village (pop. 1,428), McDowell co., S W.Va., 3 mi. E of Welch.

Carswell Air Force Base, Texas: see FORT WORTH.

Cartagena (kärtähä'nä), town (pop. 2,384), Santiago prov., central Chile, on the Pacific, and just N of San Antonio; rail terminus; popular beach resort.

Cartagena (kärtûjē'nù, Sp. kärtähä'nä), city (pop. 73,190), ⊙ Bolívar dept., N Colombia, seaport on Bay of Cartagena of Caribbean Sea, protected by reefs and sandbanks, 65 mi. SW of Barranquilla

415 mi. NNW of Bogotá; 10°25'N 75°31'W. With a rail line to Calamar, a pipe line to the oil fields of Barrancabermeja, and a natural waterway (Canal del Dique) to Magdalena R., it is a principal outlet for NW Colombia. Shipping, fishing, trading, and mfg. center for a large agr. area (sugar cane, rice, corn, tobacco, tagua nuts, tropical fruit, livestock, hides). Mfg.: tobacco products, cotton goods, soap, leather goods, perfumes, pharmaceuticals, candles, furniture, rubber goods, lead, biscuits, chocolate, beer, sugar, canned fish. Besides agr. products and oil, it exports gold and platinum. Has a humid, tropical climate. One of the oldest cities in the Western Hemisphere, it was founded 1533 by Pedro de Heredia and soon became the treasure city of the Spanish Main, where precious stones and minerals brought down the rivers awaited transshipment to Spain. The harbor was guarded by 29 stone forts (surviving forts include San José, San Fernando, and Drake's Spit) and the city encircled by a high wall of coral. It was sacked by buccaneers in 16th cent. and by Drake in 1586; it withstood (1741) a 3-month siege by Admiral Vernon during war bet. England and Spain. Cartagena is revered for its part in the War of Independence, when it was the 1st city of New Granada to proclaim independence from Spain (Nov. 11, 1811); it fell, however, to royalist forces under Pablo Morillo in 1815, after a 106-day magnificent defense, and was recaptured 1821. Through continuous revolutionary struggles Cartagena lost its supremacy to Barranquilla. Its lifeline, the Canal del Dique, silted up; but this has recently been dredged, and Cartagena has regained some of its importance, especially as terminus of the oil pipe line from Barrancabermeja, which terminates at its petroleum port Mamonal, immediately S. Its fine bldgs. include the archbishop's palace, municipal palace, cathedral (begun 1538), church and monastery of San Pedro Claver, church and convent of Santa Teresa de Jesús, Palace of Inquisition, La Popa castle, Univ. of Cartagena, naval school, customhouse, railroad station. Main residential sections outside the walled city, on peninsulas and islets, are La Manga (S) and El Cabrero (N); the Marbella beach resort is NE. Its maritime port is La Machina. The airport Manzanillo is located S on Manzanillo Isl.

Cartagena, town (pop. 1,267), Las Villas prov., central Cuba, 19 mi. N of Cienfuegos; sugar cane, cattle.

Cartagena, anc. *Carthago Nova,* city (pop. 43,104), Murcia prov., SE Spain, fortified naval base on small bay in the Mediterranean, 28 mi. SSE of Murcia; 37°36'N 0°58'W. Entrance to safe natural harbor (protected by breakwaters) is defended on each side by fort crowning rocky hill; military installations include naval arsenal for warship repairs and submarine school. Exports lead, iron, some zinc, mined in surrounding hills, and agr. products. Boatbuilding, metalworking, lead and iron smelting, wood turning; chemical works (explosives, fertilizers, paints, soap); makes also bicycles, storage batteries, tiles, brandy. Truck produce, wine, livestock in area. One of the sees of the bishop of Cartagena-Murcia. Has anc. cathedral (13th cent.; largely restored); 18th-cent. church of Santa María de Gracia; and ruins of Castillo de la Concepción (Roman foundations; rebuilt 12th cent.) on rocky hill near harbor. Founded c.225 B.C. by Hasdrubal on site of Iberian settlement, the town became chief Carthaginian base in Spain. After its capture (209 B.C.) by Scipio Africanus Major, it continued to flourish under the Romans as thriving port and outlet for silver (now practically exhausted) and lead mined in hinterland. Fell to Moors (8th cent.); definitely liberated by Christians (13th cent.). Sacked 1585 by Drake. Philip II made it great military port; figured in Peninsular and Carlist wars. Has numerous thriving suburbs. Military airport is near Mar Menor salt lagoon, 10 mi. NE.

Cartagena, Bay of, inlet of Caribbean Sea, Bolívar dept., N Colombia, just S of Cartagena, for which it forms a fine harbor. Bounded by Barú Isl. (S) and Tierra Bomba Isl. (W). Its entrances from the ocean are 2 narrow straits: Boca Grande (NW) and Boca Chica (SW). A channel (S) bet. Barú Isl. and mainland connects with Canal del Dique.

Cartago (kär'tägō), city (pop. 14,750), Valle del Cauca dept., W Colombia, in Cauca valley, on railroad and 36 mi. SW of Manizales; trading center in fertile agr. region (tobacco, sugar cane, coffee, cacao, bananas, corn, cattle); sericulture. Airport. Old colonial city, founded 1540. Has anc. viceregal residence.

Cartago, province (□ 1,000; 1950 pop. 100,725), central Costa Rica; ⊙ Cartago. Located entirely on Caribbean slopes of Andean divide (Cordillera de Talamanca), it is drained by Reventazón R.; contains volcanoes Irazú and Turrialba and Guarco Valley (site of Cartago). Agr.: coffee, sugar cane, corn, beans, potatoes; fruit orchards; stock raising, dairying (butter, cheese). Served by railroad (San José–Limón) and Inter-American Highway. Main centers are Cartago, Turrialba, Paraíso, and Tejar.

Cartago, city (1950 pop. 12,944), ⊙ Cartago prov., central Costa Rica, at foot of Irazú volcano, on Inter-American Highway, on railroad and 12 mi. ESE of San José; 9°53'N 83°56'W; alt. 5,622 ft. Commercial center; home industries; processing of food products, sawmilling. Trades in livestock, vegetables, fruit. Site of cathedral (Nuestra Señora de los Ángeles) with noted stone figure (visited yearly by pilgrims). Founded 1563, it was a major center in colonial times and ⊙ Costa Rica until 1823. Destroyed frequently by Irazú volcano; last earthquake in 1910.

Cartago, Tunisia: see CARTHAGE.

Cartajima (kärtähē'mä), town (pop. 602), Málaga prov., S Spain, 6 mi. S of Ronda; chestnuts, cereals, wine, timber ,livestock.

Cártama (kär'tämä), town (pop. 2,090), Málaga prov., S Spain, near Guadalhorce R., 10 mi. W. of Málaga; cereals, oranges, lemons, almonds, olives.

Cartavio (kärtä'vyō), village (pop. 7,965), Libertad dept., NW Peru, on coastal plain, in irrigated Chicama R. valley, on railroad and 20 mi. NW of Trujillo; sugar-milling center; distilling.

Cartaxo (kärtä'shōō), town (pop. 5,706), Santarém dist., central Portugal, near railroad, 7 mi. SW of Santarém; winegrowing center; pottery mfg.

Cartaya (kärtī'ä), town (pop. 6,329), Huelva prov., SW Spain, fishing port near Atlantic inlet, 11 mi. W of Huelva. Processing, lumbering, and agr. center (cereals, figs, grapes, olives, corn). Liquor distilling, sawmilling, flour milling.

Carter. 1 County (□ 402; pop. 22,559), NE Ky.; ⊙ Grayson. Drained by Little Sandy R. and Tygarts Creek. Limestone caverns (Carter Cave State Park, Cascade Caves) and natural bridges attract tourists. Hilly agr. area (tobacco, corn, poultry, livestock, dairy products, lespedeza, clover, fruit, wheat); clay, sand, and gravel pits; stone quarries, coal mines, iron and asphalt deposits; timber tracts. Mfg. (especially stone, clay, and glass products). Formed 1838. **2** County (□ 506; pop. 4,777), S Mo.; ⊙ Van Buren. In the Ozarks; drained by Current R. Agr., livestock; lumber. Part of Clark Natl. Forest is here. Formed 1859. **3** County (□ 3,313; pop. 2,798), SE Mont.; ⊙ Ekalaka. Plains area bordering on S.Dak. and Wyo.; drained by Little Missouri R. Livestock. Two sections of Custer Natl. Forest here, one in N and the other in E. Formed 1917. **4** County (□ 829; pop. 36,455), S Okla.; ⊙ Ardmore. Drained by Washita R. and by small Walnut and Caddo creeks. Includes a section of the Arbuckle Mts. (recreation area) and part of L. Murray (state park; recreation). Stock raising. Oil and natural-gas wells; refineries, gasoline plants. Some agr. (cotton, grain, truck, corn, peanuts; dairy products). Mfg. at Ardmore. Formed 1907. **5** County (□ 355; pop. 42,432), NE Tenn.; ⊙ Elizabethton. Borders S and SE on N.C.; Unaka Mts. lie along boundary; Roan Mtn. in S; drained by Watauga and Doe rivers. Includes parts of Cherokee Natl. Forest and Watauga Reservoir. Timber, agr. (tobacco, grain, livestock, fruit); iron-ore deposits. Mfg. at Elizabethton. Formed 1796.

Carter. 1 Town (pop. 84), Carter co., NE Ky., 27 mi. W of Ashland; crushed stone. **2** Town (pop. 406), Beckham co., W Okla., 14 mi. SSW of Elk City, in agr. area; cotton ginning. **3** Town (pop. 16), Tripp co., S S.Dak., 17 mi. W of Winner.

Carter Caves State Park, Ky.: see OLIVE HILL.

Carter Dome, N.H.: see CARTER-MORIAH RANGE.

Carteret (kärtůrā'), village (pop. 910), Manche dept., NW France, fishing port on the Channel, on W coast of Cotentin Peninsula, 19 mi. SSW of Cherbourg; rail terminus and bathing resort. By its capture (June 17, 1944), Americans cut off Ger. garrison in Cherbourg area in Second World War.

Carteret (kärtůrĕt'), county (□ 532; pop. 23,059), E N.C., on the Atlantic; ⊙ Beaufort. Bounded S by Onslow Bay, E by Raleigh Bay, NE by Neuse R. and Pamlico Sound. Tidewater area bordered by Bogue and Portsmouth isls. and other barrier beaches; W part included in Croatan Natl. Forest. Shipbuilding (Beaufort, Morehead City), fishing, sawmilling, farming (tobacco, truck). Resorts along coast. Formed 1722.

Carteret, borough (pop. 13,030), Middlesex co., NE N.J., on Arthur Kill opposite Staten Isl., 5 mi. S of Elizabeth; mfg. (machinery, metal products, chemicals, fertilizer, textiles, clothing, paint, lumber, cigars); oil refinery. Inc. 1922.

Carteret, Cape of (kärtůrā'), rocky headland of Manche dept., NW France, on the Channel, on W coast of Cotentin Peninsula, 20 mi. SSW of Cherbourg; 49°23'N 1°48'W. Lighthouse.

Carter Fell, mountain (1,815 ft.) of Cheviot Hills, on border bet. Northumberland, England, and Roxburgh, Scotland, 11 mi. S of Jedburgh.

Carter Lake, town (pop. 1,183), Pottawattamie co., SW Iowa, on small oxbow lake of Missouri R., just NE of Omaha, Nebr.; ironworks.

Carter-Moriah Range (mŭrī'ŭ), Coos co., E N.H., range of White Mts. lying S of the Androscoggin, E of Presidential Range. Carter Dome (4,843 ft.), highest peak; others are Mt. Hight (4,690 ft.), South Carter Mtn. (4,458 ft.), Middle Carter Mtn. (4,621 ft.), North Carter Mtn. (4,539 ft.), Imp Mtn. (site of Imp Face, rock profile; 3,708 ft.), Mt. Moriah (4,041 ft.), Middle Moriah Mtn. (3,758 ft.), and Shelburne Moriah Mtn. (3,748 ft.).

Cartersville, city (pop. 7,270), ⊙ Bartow co., NW Ga., on Etowah R. and 37 mi. NW of Atlanta. Mining (barite, ochre, manganese, limestone, marble) and mfg. (bedspreads, underwear, yarn, cordage, mineral products) center. Allatoona Dam and Indian mounds near by. Founded 1832, inc. 1850.

Carterville. 1 City (pop. 2,716), Williamson co., S Ill., 5 mi. SW of Herrin, in bituminous-coal-mining and agr. area; corn, wheat, dairy products, fruit, timber. Crab Orchard L. is S. Inc. 1892. **2** City (pop. 1,552), Jasper co., SW Mo., near Spring R., just N of Joplin. Its mining activities have declined. Laid out 1875.

Carthage (kär'thĭj), ancient city-state on N shore of Africa, on the Gulf of Tunis, 9 mi. NE of modern Tunis. The Latin name, *Carthago* or *Cartago,* was derived from the Phoenician name, which meant "new city" (the old city being Utica). It was founded (traditionally by Dido) from Tyre in the 9th cent. B.C.; the date is usually conventionally set at either 850 B.C. or 814 B.C. Beginning in 6th cent. B.C., it sent its merchants and explorers across the seas (even as far as the W coast of Africa), and acquired control of Sardinia, Malta, the Balearic Isls., most of Sicily, and the African shore of the W Mediterranean. Despite Hamilcar's defeat at Himera (480 B.C.), Carthaginians continued to develop their seapower. The ensuing rivalry bet. Rome and Carthage resulted in the Punic Wars. The 1st of these (264–241 B.C.) cost Carthage all hold on Sicily, but Hamilcar Barca and later Hasdrubal conquered Spain to the Ebro. In 2d Punic War (218–201 B.C.), Carthaginians led by Hannibal were defeated by Roman generals Fabius and, especially, Scipio Africanus Major. During this war were fought the famous battles of Cannae (216 B.C.) and Zama (202 B.C.). The 3d Punic War (149–146 B.C.) ended in total destruction of Carthaginian power and in the razing of the city itself by the younger Scipio. A Roman project to build a new city (122 B.C.) failed, but Julius Caesar founded a colony which became a Roman administrative center under Augustus. Carthage was later (A.D. 439–533) capital of the Vandals, and was briefly recovered (533) for Byzantine Empire by Belisarius. Again destroyed by Arabs in 698. There are few remains of anc. Carthage. Those which are found are of the Roman city, and include vestiges of old harbor and a large aqueduct of Hadrian. Louis IX of France (St. Louis) died here in 1270 when on crusade. A chapel built (1841) in his honor stands on the hill which is traditionally identified as Byrsa Hill, site of anc. citadel. Here, too, stands the huge neo-byzantine cathedral (built 1886 by Cardinal Lavigerie), and the Lavigerie mus. of antiquities. Carthage today is a residential suburb (1946 pop. 4,873) of Tunis, noted for its archiepiscopal see and theological seminary.

Carthage. 1 Town (pop. 533), Dallas co., S central Ark., 29 mi. E of Arkadelphia. **2** City (pop. 3,214), ⊙ Hancock co., W Ill., near the Mississippi, 14 mi. E of Keokuk, Iowa; trade center in agr. area (corn, wheat, soybeans, livestock, poultry; dairy products); cigar mfg. Seat of Carthage Col. Laid out 1833, inc. 1837. In 1844, Joseph Smith, Mormon leader, and his brother were killed in the city jail by a mob; the old jail is now property of the Mormon Church. **3** Town (pop. 1,065), Rush co., E central Ind., on Big Blue R. and 32 mi. E of Indianapolis, in agr. area (livestock, grain, poultry); lumber, paperboard. **4** Town (pop. 339), Franklin co., W Maine, 11 mi. WNW of Wilton. Settled 1803, inc. 1826. **5** Town (pop. 1,925), ⊙ Leake co., central Miss., c.50 mi. NE of Jackson, near Pearl R., in agr. and timber area; lumber, brick; cotton ginning. Indian reservations near by. **6** City (pop. 11,188), ⊙ Jasper co., SW Mo., on Spring R. and 13 mi. NE of Joplin; industrial and shipping center, with resort activities. Agr.; mfg. (shoes, clothing, concrete, explosives); dairy, grain products; noted marble quarries, lead and zinc mines. Inc. 1873. **7** Paper-milling village (pop. 4,420), Jefferson co., N N.Y., on Black R. and 15 mi. E of Watertown, in agr. area; mfg. (paper, paperboard, wood and stone products, machinery, concrete, tile, cheese). Limestone, iron, talc deposits; timber. Small lakes (resorts) near by. Settled before 1801, inc. 1841. **8** Town (pop. 1,194), ⊙ Moore co., central N.C., 12 mi. N of Southern Pines; hosiery mfg., lumber milling. Settled 18th cent. **9** City (pop. 458), Miner co., E central S.Dak., 15 mi. NW of Howard and on branch of James R.; poultry, livestock, grain, dairy products. **10** Town (pop. 1,604), ⊙ Smith co., N central Tenn., on Cumberland R. (here crossed by Cordell Hull Bridge), near mouth of Caney Fork, and 45 mi. E of Nashville; tobacco market; cheese, wood products. Center Hill Dam near by. Founded 1804. **11** City (pop. 4,750), ⊙ Panola co., E Texas, near the Sabine, 27 mi. S of Marshall; trade center for oil, natural-gas, lumber, cotton area; woodworking, canning, basket mfg.; gasoline plant near. Founded 1848.

Carthage, Cape, rocky headland on the Gulf of Tunis, N Tunisia, near the site of anc. Carthage, 10 mi. ENE of Tunis; lighthouse; 36°52'N 10°22'E. Town of Sidi-bou-Saïd occupies headland.

Carthago, N Africa: see CARTHAGE.

Carthago Nova, Spain: see CARTAGENA.

Cartier Island, Australia: see ASHMORE AND CARTIER ISLANDS, TERRITORY OF.

Cartierville (kär'tyävĭl), NW suburb of Montreal, S Que., on Montreal Isl.; site of airport.

Cartina Lagoon, Honduras: see BRUS LAGOON.

Cartmel (kärt'mĕl), market town in Cartmel Fell parish (pop. 320), N Lancashire, England, near Morecambe Bay 6 mi. E of Ulverston. Site of Augustinian priory of medieval origin.

Cartuja, La (lä kärtōō'hä), W section of Seville, SW Spain, on right bank of the Guadalquivir. Has noted ceramics industry.

Cartura (kärtōō'rä), village (pop. 393), Padova prov., Veneto, N Italy, 9 mi. S of Padua; benzine.

Cartworth, England: see HOLMFIRTH.

Cartwright. 1 Village (pop. 183), SE Labrador, on S side of entrance of Sandwich Bay; 53°42'N 57°W. Lumbering. **2** Village (pop. estimate 400), S Man., on Badger Creek and 60 mi. SSE of Brandon, near N.Dak. border; grain, mixed farming.

Caruao (kärwä'ō), town (pop. 867), Federal Dist., N Venezuela, on the Caribbean, 40 mi. ENE of Caracas; cacao, goats.

Caruaru (kärōōŭrōō'), city (1950 pop. 44,595), E Pernambuco, NE Brazil, on railroad, 75 mi. WSW of Recife; commercial center; mfg. of rope and bags from caroa fibers, cotton and sugar milling, alcohol distilling.

Carumas (kärōō'mäs), town (pop. 901), Moquegua dept., S Peru, in Cordillera Occidental, 33 mi. NE of Moquegua; alt. 10,040 ft.; wheat, barley, livestock. Thermal springs.

Carúpano (kärōō'pänō), city (pop. 16,548), Sucre state, NE Venezuela, port on open roadstead of the Caribbean, 65 mi. ENE of Cumaná; 10°40'N 63°15'W. Shipping, trading, fishing, and mfg. (straw hats and other fiber products, soap, rum) center; exports cacao, coffee, sugar, tobacco, timber, hides; sawmills, potteries. Airport, customhouse. Salt and petroleum deposits in vicinity.

Carusa, Turkey: see GERZE.

Carutapera (kärōōtäpĕ'rŭ), city (pop. 1,133), northernmost Maranhão, Brazil, on an inlet of the Atlantic, near Pará border, and 150 mi. NW of São Luís; cotton, rice. Airfield. Gold mining in area bet. Gurupi and Turiaçu rivers.

Caruthersville (kůrŭ'dhŭrzvĭl), city (pop. 8,614), ⊙ Pemiscot co., extreme SE Mo., on Mississippi R. (levees) and 19 mi. NW of Dyersburg, Tenn.; agr. center; cotton processing, shoes; ships wood, sand products. Laid out 1857.

Carvajal, Venezuela: see SAN RAFAEL DE CARVAJAL.

Carvalhal Redondo (kärvälyäl' rĭdōn'dōō), village (pop. 1,338), Viseu dist., N central Portugal, 9 mi. S of Viseu; wine, olives, corn, rye.

Carver, county (□ 358; pop. 18,155), S central Minn.; ⊙ Chaska. Agr. area bounded SE by Minnesota R. and watered by small lakes. Dairy products, livestock, grain, potatoes, poultry. Formed 1855.

Carver. 1 Town (pop. 1,530), Plymouth co., SE Mass., 7 mi. SW of Plymouth; wooden boxes, cranberry-picking equipment. Includes North Carver village. Settled c.1660, inc. 1790. **2** Village (pop. 548), Carver co., S Minn., on Minnesota R. and 23 mi. SW of Minneapolis, in agr. area (corn, oats, barley, potatoes, livestock); dairy products.

Carville, village, Iberville parish, SE central La., on E bank (levee) of the Mississippi and 16 mi. SSE of Baton Rouge. Seat of Natl. Leprosarium, only leper colony in U.S., a Federal public health institution since 1921.

Carvin (kärvē'), town (pop. 14,063), Pas-de-Calais dept., N France, 10 mi. SSE of Lille; coal-mining center with textile industry (cottons, linens). Breweries, brickworks.

Carvoeiro, Cape (kärvwä'rōō), W tip of rocky Peniche peninsula, Leiria dist., W central Portugal, 2 mi. W of Peniche; 39°22'N 9°24'W.

Carway, village, SW Alta., on Mont. border, 55 mi. SSW of Lethbridge; coal mining.

Cary (kâ'rē). **1** Village (pop. 943), McHenry co., NE Ill., near Fox R., 12 mi. N of Elgin, in dairying and resort area; annual ski-jumping meet. **2** Plantation (pop. 278), Aroostook co., E Maine, 9 mi. S of Houlton, near N.B. line, in agr., lumbering area. **3** Town (pop. 390), Sharkey co., W Miss., 32 mi. N of Vicksburg. **4** Town (pop. 1,446), Wake co., central N.C., 8 mi. W of Raleigh. Walter Hines Page b. here. State fairgrounds near by. Founded 1852; inc. 1870.

Carystus, Greece: see KARYSTOS.

Caryville. 1 Town (pop. 525), Washington co., NW Fla., on Choctawhatchee R. and 7 mi. W of Bonifay; farming, lumbering. **2** Village (pop. 1,234), Campbell co., NE Tenn., 28 mi. NW of Knoxville; ships coal.

Casa (kā'sŭ), town (pop. 184), Perry co., central Ark., c.50 mi. NW of Little Rock.

Casabasciana (kä"zäbäshä'nä), village (pop. 525), Lucca prov., Tuscany, central Italy, 14 mi. NE of Lucca; paper mill, macaroni mfg.

Casabe (käsä'bā), village, Antioquia dept. NW central Colombia, on Magdalena R., opposite Barrancabermeja (Santander dept.): site of petroleum field. Sometimes Cazabe.

Casabermeja (kä"sävĕrmä'hä), town (pop. 2,681), Málaga prov., S Spain, on small Guadalmedina R. and 12 mi. N of Málaga; olives and olive oil, grapes, cereals, almonds, livestock.

Casablanca (kä"säbläng'kä), town (pop. 2,096), Valparaiso prov., central Chile, 22 mi. SE of Valparaiso; agr. (fruit, grain, vegetables, livestock).

Casa Blanca, town (pop. 3,433), Havana prov., W Cuba, on E shore of Havana Harbor, just opposite Havana (connected by ferry); coaling station. Site of Natl. Observatory of Meteorology, La Cabana Fort (N), and the Cuban Navy Yard.

Casablanca (käsŭblăng'kŭ, kăzŭ-, Sp. kä"säbläng'kä), Arabic *Dar el Beida*, largest city (pop. 551,322) of Fr. Morocco and of French North Africa, ⊙ Casablanca region (□ 11,947; pop. 2,043,278), on the Atlantic, 55 mi. SW of Rabat (⊙ Fr. Morocco) and 180 mi. SW of Tangier; 33°36'N 7°37'W. Morocco's leading commercial and industrial center, with a port handling over 3/4 of the Fr. protectorate's foreign trade and all its passenger traffic. One of the world's fastest-growing cities (1907 pop. 20,000; 1936 pop. 257,430), Casablanca owes much of its expansion to constant harbor development since 1913. Sheltered against prevailing NW winds by a jetty 1 1/2 mi. long, port is divided into 2 basins and an inner fishing port. Of 2 transversal docks, the outer one is used for phosphate, iron ore, and manganese shipment, and for coal storage, while the inner or commercial dock has warehouses and a modern silo. Phosphates (brought here by rail directly from Khouribga mines) have been (since 1923) chief export item. Casablanca's industries, concentrated mostly in E dists. (notably at Roches Noires, site of large electric-power plant) bet. port and railroad station and along highway to Rabat, include textile mills (cotton, wool, linen), Morocco's only glassworks and only blast furnace, a large cement mill, a tobacco factory, manganese-processing and superphosphate plants, brickworks. Fish canning, sawmilling, and furniture mfg. are also important. Beer, soft drinks, flour products, chocolate are made for local consumption. Carpet mfg. is the last remaining important handicraft industry. Casablanca has a pleasant Mediterranean subtropical climate (yearly average temp. 63°F.), with rainfall (17 inches) concentrated in winter months. On site of anc. *Anfa*, which Portuguese destroyed in 1468 and resettled in 1515, naming it Casa Branca [Port.,=white house]. Almost destroyed by earthquake in 1755; rebuilt (late 18th cent.) by Mohammed XVI. French occupation dates from 1907. Modern Casablanca was laid out in a semicircle around the old city. From the Place de France (center of business and amusement dist.) avenues radiate in all directions and lead to European residential dists. of Bourgogne, Racine, Maarif (W), fashionable Mers Sultan (S), and to the modern Moslem quarters in SE (Nouvelle Médina, Aïn Chock). The fine villa dist. of Anfa, near W city limits, was site of Roosevelt-Churchill conference (Jan., 1943), after Allied landing here in Nov., 1942. Casablanca international airport (Cazes), on air route to South America, is 4 mi. SW of city center.

Casabona (kä"zäbô'nä), village (pop. 2,718), Catanzaro prov., Calabria, S Italy, 5 mi. WSW of Strongoli; wine, dairying. Zinc mines near by.

Casa Branca (kä'zŭ brăng'kŭ), city (pop. 7,094), NE São Paulo, Brazil, 60 mi. SE of Ribeirão Prêto; rail junction; dairying center; mfg. of flour products, corn meal, textiles, furniture, tiles; coffee processing. Has old church.

Casa Branca. 1 Village (pop. 314), Évora dist., S central Portugal, 14 mi. WSW of Évora; rail junction (spur to Évora). **2** Village (pop. 1,690), Portalegre dist., central Portugal, 32 mi. SSW of Portalegre; grain, olives, cork.

Casacalenda (kä"zäkälĕn'dä), town (pop. 6,584), Campobasso prov., Abruzzi e Molise, S central Italy, 16 mi. NNE of Campobasso, in cereal-growing region.

Casa Grande (kä'sä grän'dā), village (pop. 9,251), Libertad dept., NW Peru, on coastal plain, in irrigated Chicama R. valley, on railroad and 30 mi. NNW of Trujillo; sugar- and cotton-production center; sugar mill, distillery, cottonseed-oil mill.

Casa Grande (kä'sŭ grän'dā), town (pop. 4,181), Pinal co., S central Ariz., near Santa Cruz R., 45 mi. SSE of Phoenix; health resort in irrigated agr. area (cotton, alfalfa, grain, livestock). Copper, gold, silver mines near by. CASA GRANDE NATIONAL MONUMENT and Casa Grande Farms (U.S. resettlement project) are 20 mi. E.

Casa Grande National Monument (472.5 acres; established 1918), S Ariz., near Florence, c.45 mi. SE of Phoenix. Adobe watchtower (the Casa Grande), built c.1350 by Salado Indians, is only prehistoric structure of its type still standing. Here are also ruins of villages and a mus. of Indian artifacts.

Casalanguida (kä"zäläng'gwēdä), village (pop. 1,528), Chieti prov., Abruzzi e Molise, S central Italy, 12 mi. WSW of Vasto.

Casalarreina (kä'sälärā'nä), town (pop. 1,419), Logroño prov., N Spain, 24 mi. WNW of Logroño; vegetables, fruit, wine, cereals, lumber. Has 16th-cent. Dominican convent and Renaissance palace.

Casalbordino (käzäl"bôrdē'nô), town (pop. 3,658), Chieti prov., Abruzzi e Molise, S central Italy, 7 mi. WNW of Vasto, in grape- and cereal-growing region.

Casalbuono (-bwô'nô), village (pop. 2,131), Salerno prov., Campania, S Italy, on Tanagro R. and 14 mi. SSE of Sala Consilina.

Casalbuttano (-bōōt-tä'nô), town (pop. 3,640), Cremona prov., Lombardy, N Italy, 8 mi. NNW of Cremona; silk and linen mills, sausage and shoe factories.

Casal di Principe (käzäl' dē prēn'chēpĕ), town (pop. 9,357), Caserta prov., Campania, S Italy, 13 mi. NW of Naples; agr. center.

Casalecchio di Reno (käzälĕk'kyô dē rā'nô), town (pop. 3,754), Bologna prov., Emilia-Romagna, N central Italy, on Reno R. and 3 mi. ESE of Bologna; mfg. (agr., textile, and marble-working machinery, zinc and iron plate, silverware, beer, perfume, stationery). Damaged in Second World War.

Casale Monferrato (käzä'lĕ mônfĕr-rä'tô), town (pop. 25,485), Alessandria prov., Piedmont, N Italy, on Po R. (head of navigation) and 18 mi. NNW of Alessandria. Rail junction; a major center of lime and Portland cement industry supplied from near-by limestone quarries; mfg. (agr. machinery, pianos, wine, sugar, macaroni, paper, cork, silk, rayon, shoes). Bishopric. Has 12th-cent. cathedral and seminary, 16th-cent. castle (now a barracks), 18th-cent. palaces, technical institute, mus. Became capital of marquisate of Montferrat in 1435; was strongly fortified.

Casale sul Sile (sōōl sē'lĕ), village (pop. 1,325), Treviso prov., Veneto, N Italy, on Sile R. and 6 mi. SSE of Treviso; alcohol distillery.

Casal Guidi (käzäl' gwē'dē) or **Casalguidi,** village (pop. 702), Pistoia prov., Tuscany, central Italy, 4 mi. S of Pistoia; ceramics industry.

Casalmaggiore (käzäl"mäd-jô'rĕ), town (pop. 5,281), Cremona prov., Lombardy, N Italy, on Po R. and 22 mi. ESE of Cremona; agr. trade center (wine, hemp, cereals, fodder); beet sugar; mfg. (majolica, glass, shoes); dairying.

Casalnuovo di Napoli (käzälnwô'vô dē nä'pôlē), town (pop. 9,085), Napoli prov., Campania, S Italy, 6 mi. NE of Naples.

Casalnuovo Monterotaro (môn"tĕrôtä'rô), town (pop. 5,156), Foggia prov., Apulia, S Italy, 15 mi. WSW of San Severo; copper working, wine making.

Casalpusterlengo (käzäl"pōōstĕrlĕn'gô), town (pop. 6,578), Milano prov., Lombardy, N Italy, 12 mi. SE of Lodi; rail junction; dairy products; macaroni, fertilizer, pottery, toys.

Casalvieri (käzäl"vyä'rē), village (pop. 421), Frosinone prov., Latium, S central Italy, 8 mi. SE of Sora; toymaking.

Casamance River (käzämăs'), S and SW Senegal, Fr. West Africa, rises in N outliers of Fouta Djallon massif, flows c.200 mi. W through basin (called the Casamance) bet. Br. Gambia (N) and Port. Guinea (S), past Kolda, Sedhiou, and Ziguinchor, to the Atlantic in wide marshy delta c.150 mi. SSE of Dakar. Principal port is Ziguinchor, c.40 mi. inland. Smaller vessels can proceed farther upstream to Sedhiou. Along its banks is luxuriant vegetation, and peanuts are grown. There are ilmenite deposits near its mouth.

Casamassima (kä"zämäs'sēmä), town (pop. 9,056), Bari prov., Apulia, S Italy, 12 mi. SSE of Bari; wine, olive oil.

Casamicciola (kä"zämēt'chôlä), town (pop. 4,086), on N coast of isl. of Ischia, Napoli prov., Campania, S Italy, 3 mi. WNW of Ischia; health resort with warm mineral springs and baths. Largely destroyed by earthquake of 1883. Has seismological observatory.

Casamozza (käsämōzä', It. käzämô'tsä), hamlet of NE Corsica, on the Golo and 12 mi. S of Bastia; rail junction.

Casanare (käsänä'rā), intendancy, NE Colombia; ⊙ Pore. Bounded N by Arauca (along Casanare R.), SE by Vichada and Meta (along Meta R.), and SW and W by Boyacá. Formed 1950 out of llanos section of Boyacá.

Casanare River (käsänä'rā), E Colombia, rises S of Sierra Nevada de Cocuy, flows c.200 mi. E along Arauca-Boyacá border to Meta R. at 6°2'N 69°51'W. Navigable for small craft.

Casanay (käsänī'), town (pop. 2,057), Sucre state, NE Venezuela, 15 mi. SSW of Carúpano; cacao, sugar cane, coconuts, corn. Sulphur deposits near by.

Casa Nova (kä'zŭ nô'vŭ), city (pop. 1,096), N Bahia, Brazil, on left bank of São Francisco R. (navigable) and 40 mi. W of Juàzeiro; stock, corn.

Casapalca (käsäpäl'kä), town (pop. 2,615), Lima dept., W central Peru, in Cordillera Occidental of the Andes, near source of Rímac R., on Lima–La Oroya RR and 35 mi. NE of Lima; alt. c.14,000 ft. Major copper-mining center, shipping ore to La Oroya.

Casa Pangue (kä'sä päng'gā), village, Llanquihue prov., S central Chile, in the Andes, at N foot of Monte Tronador (Argentina border), just W of L. Nahuel Huapí; tourist resort.

Casapulla (kä"zäpōōl'lä), town (pop. 3,314), Caserta prov., Campania, S Italy, 2 mi. W of Caserta; soap mfg.

Casarabonela (käsärävōnä'lä), town (pop. 3,370), Málaga prov., S Spain, 25 mi. W of Málaga; olives, cereals, truck produce. Has mineral springs.

Casarano (kä"zärä'nô), town (pop. 10,843), Lecce prov., Apulia, S Italy, 10 mi. SE of Gallipoli; agr. center; wine, olive oil, fruit.

Casar de Cáseres (käsär' dhā kä'thārĕs), village (pop. 4,736), Cáceres prov., W Spain, 6 mi. N of Cáceres; livestock market; cheese processing; cereals, olive oil.

Casar de Escalona, El (ĕl, ĕskälō'nä), town (pop. 1,635), Toledo prov., central Spain, 17 mi. ENE of Talavera de la Reina; grapes, olives, cereals, sheep. Lumbering, olive-oil pressing, dairying, meat-products mfg.

Casar de Palomero (pälōmā'rō), town (pop. 1,535), Cáceres prov., W Spain, 21 mi. NW of Plasencia; olive-oil processing, flour milling; fruit.

Casar de Talamanca, El (ĕl, tälämäng'kä), town (pop. 917), Guadalajara prov., central Spain, 24 mi. NE of Madrid; cereals, sheep, goats.

Casares (käsä'rĕs), village, Carazo dept., SW Nicaragua, on the Pacific, 15 mi. SW of Diriamba (linked by road); seaside resort.

Casares, town (pop. 3,606), Málaga prov., S Spain, at SW slopes of the Sierra Bermeja (spur of the Cordillera Penibética), 23 mi. N of Gibraltar; cereals, fruit, livestock. Mineral springs in vicinity.

Casariche (käsärē'chā), town (pop. 4,203), Seville prov., SW Spain, on railroad and 20 mi. E of Osuna; agr. center (olives, cereals); mfg. of soap, sweets, flour, plaster, charcoal.

Casarrubios del Monte (käsärōōv'yōs dhĕl mōn'tā), town (pop. 2,013), Toledo prov., central Spain, 25 mi. SW of Madrid; carobs, chick-peas, cereals, olives, grapes, livestock. Olive-oil pressing, wine making, tile mfg.

Casarza della Delizia (käzär'tsä dĕl-lä dĕlē'tsyä), village (pop. 1,535), Udine prov., Friuli-Venezia Giulia, 9 mi. E of Pordenone; rail junction; alcohol distilleries. Has church with frescoes by Pordenone.

Casas (kä'säs), town (pop. 211), Tamaulipas, NE Mexico, 25 mi. E of Ciudad Victoria, in agr. region (sugar cane, cereals, fruit).

Casas, Las, Mexico: see SAN CRISTÓBAL DE LAS CASAS.

Casas de Benítez (kä'säs dhā bānē'tĕth), town (pop. 1,458), Cuenca prov., E central Spain, 30 mi. NW of Albacete; exports cereals, olives, grapes; also raises sheep and goats.

Casas de Don Antonio (dhōn' äntō'nyō), town (pop. 1,120), Cáceres prov., W Spain, 18 mi. S of Cáceres; olive oil, wheat.

Casas de Don Pedro (pā'dhrō), town (pop. 3,235), Badajoz prov., W Spain, near the Guadiana, 55 mi. ENE of Mérida; olives, cereals, grapes, fruit.

Casas de Fernando Alonso (fĕrnän'dō älōn'sō), town (pop. 1,496), Cuenca prov., E central Spain, 36 mi. NW of Albacete; cereals, grapes, potatoes, sheep; lumbering, flour milling.

Casas de Juan Núñez (hwän' nōō'nyĕth), village (pop. 1,906), Albacete prov., SE central Spain, 18 mi. NE of Albacete; lumbering, stock raising; cereals, wine, saffron.

Casas del Castañar (kästänyär'), village (pop. 1,104), Cáceres prov., W Spain, 11 mi. NE of Plasencia; cattle and hog raising; olive oil, fruit, chestnuts.

Casas del Monte (mōn'tā), village (pop. 1,085), Cáceres prov., W Spain, 14 mi. NE of Plasencia; olive oil, fruit, pepper.

Casas de Millán (dhā mēlyän'), village (pop. 1,502), Cáceres prov., W Spain, 24 mi. NNE of Cáceres; olive oil, oranges, wine, cereals.

Casas de Reina (rā'nä), town (pop. 964), Badajoz prov., W Spain, 4 mi. SE of Llerena; cereals, chick-peas, olives, truck, stock.

Casas de Vés (vās), town (pop. 2,015), Albacete prov., SE central Spain, 35 mi. NE of Albacete; alcohol distilling; stock raising, lumbering; wine, cereals, saffron.

Casas Grandes (kä'säs grän'dĕs), town (pop. 1,126), Chihuahua, N Mexico, on interior plateau, on Casas Grandes R. and 130 mi. SW of Ciudad Juárez; cotton, cereals, livestock. Nueva Casas Grandes is 2½ mi. NE.

Casas Grandes River, Chihuahua, N Mexico, rises in Sierra Madre Occidental S of Buenaventura, flows N, past Casas Grandes and Nueva Casas Grandes, and, as it approaches Amer. border, curves E to L. Guzmán. Total length, c.250 mi. Used for irrigation.

Casas Ibáñez (kä'säs ēvä'nyĕth), town (pop. 3,808), Albacete prov., SE central Spain, 30 mi. NE of Albacete; alcohol distilling, flour- and saw-milling, chocolate mfg.; saffron, cereals, grapes.

Casasimarro (kä"säsēmä'rō), town (pop. 3,710), Cuenca prov., E central Spain, 29 mi. NNW of Albacete; agr. center (olives, saffron, cereals, grapes, fruit, livestock). Olive-oil pressing, liquor distilling, flour milling; mfg. of tiles and musical instruments.

Casasola de Arión (käsäsō'lä dhā äryōn'), town (pop. 1,346), Valladolid prov., N central Spain, 28 mi. WSW of Valladolid; cereals, wine, sheep.

Casatejada (käsätāhä'dhä), town (pop. 1,975), Cáceres prov., W Spain, 24 mi. SE of Plasencia; stock raising; olive oil, wine, vegetables.

Casavieja (käsävyā'hä), town (pop. 2,573), Ávila prov., central Spain, on SE slopes of the Sierra de Gredos, 22 mi. N of Talavera de la Reina; grapes, olives, fruit, livestock. Olive-oil pressing, flour milling, tile mfg.

Casbas (käz'bäs), town (pop. 2,005), W Buenos Aires prov., Argentina, 20 mi. N of Guaminí; grain, livestock; dairying.

Cascade, village (pop. estimate 200), S B.C., on Wash. border, on Kettle R. and 12 mi. E of Grand Forks; fruit, vegetables.

Cascade, town (pop. 2,000), Hanover parish, NW Jamaica, 6 mi. ESE of Lucea; rice, yams, fruit.

Cascade, village on E coast of Mahé Isl., Seychelles, 4½ mi. SE of Victoria; copra, essential oils; fisheries.

Cascade, county (□ 2,658; pop. 53,027), W central Mont.; ⊙ Great Falls. Agr. and mining region drained by Missouri, Sun, and Smith rivers. Livestock, grain, dairy products; coal, silver, zinc, lead, gold. Part of Lewis and Clark Natl. Forest and Little Belt Mts. in SE. Formed 1887.

Cascade. 1 Village (pop. 943), ⊙ Valley co., W central Idaho, 65 mi. N of Boise and on North Fork of Payette R.; alt. 4,800 ft. Trade center for lumber, agr., livestock area; dairying, lumber milling. Gold, silver, lead mines near by. Founded 1912–13 when Van Wyck, Crawford, and Thunder City joined; inc. 1917. Cascade Dam near by. **2** Town (pop. 1,299), on Dubuque-Jones co. line, E Iowa, on North Fork Maquoketa R. and 22 mi. SW of Dubuque; dairy products. Settled 1834, platted 1842, inc. 1881. **3** Town (pop. 447), Cascade co., W central Mont., on Missouri R. and 25 mi. SW of Great Falls; flour; dairy and poultry products, livestock, grain, potatoes. **4** Village (pop. 1,146, with adjacent Leaminburg), Yakima co., S Wash., near Yakima. Sometimes Cascade Mill. **5** Village (pop. 403), Sheboygan co., E Wis., on branch of Milwaukee R. and 15 mi. WSW of Sheboygan, in dairy and grain area.

Cascade Caverns, Texas: see BOERNE.

Cascade Caves, Ky.: see OLIVE HILL.

Cascade Dam, W Idaho, on North Fork of Payette R. just N of Cascade. Earth-fill dam (90 ft. high, 700 ft. long; completed 1949) forms reservoir (21 mi. long) used for power and for irrigation of c.110,000 acres in Boise project.

Cascade d'Argent, Vietnam: see TAMDAO.

Cascade Locks, city (pop. 733), Hood River co., N Oregon, on Columbia R. and 20 mi. W of Hood River. U.S. constructed (1896) a series of locks around rapids near here.

Cascade Mill, Wash.: see CASCADE.

Cascade Range, in Calif., Oregon, Wash., and B.C., extends more than 700 mi. N from LASSEN PEAK, where it meets the Sierra Nevada, through Oregon and Wash., to Fraser R. in B.C., whence it is continued by Coast Mts.; parallels the Pacific coast, c.100–150 mi. inland. Many of its peaks—Mt. RAINIER (14,408 ft.), the highest, Mt. SHASTA, Mt. ADAMS, Mt. HOOD, Mt. JEFFERSON, and Mt. St. Helens (9,671 ft.)—are snow-covered volcanic cones. Extensive glaciation has left many lakes, of which L. Chelan is largest; glaciers (notably those of Mt. Rainier) are found on higher peaks. CRATER LAKE NATIONAL PARK is in the S. The Klamath and Columbia rivers cut E-W through range. Chief resource is timber (fir, cedar, and pine); rivers of the Pacific slope (which receives most of the rainfall) are extensively used for hydroelectricity especially in Wash. The drier E slope in Wash. is cut by rivers into spurs (Chelan, Entiat, Wenatchee, and other ranges) separated by Methow, Chelan, Entiat, Wenatchee, and Yakima valleys, famous for their yields (esp. of apples), made possible by irrigation. Principal E-W crossings in Wash. are Cascade Tunnel (railroad) and Snoqualmie Pass (highway, railroad); Columbia R. gorge carries highways and rails along Wash.-Oregon line; in Oregon are Salt Creek Pass (5,128 ft.; 55 mi. SE of Eugene) and several other E-W routes.

Cascade River, rises in small lake in Cook co., NE Minn., flows 20 mi. S, through Superior Natl. Forest, to L. Superior at Cascade State Park, a recreational area extending along lake front.

Cascade Tunnel, central Wash., railroad tunnel c.8 mi. long, through the Cascades c.40 mi. NW of Wenatchee; completed 1929 to replace earlier tunnel (1897), it is one of longest in world.

Cascais (käsh-kīsh'), town (pop. 7,115), Lisboa dist., W central Portugal, on the Atlantic, 15 mi. W of Lisbon; electric railroad terminus; fashionable bathing resort along Port. Riviera; fishing and fish canning (sardines, lobster).

Cascajal (käskähäl') town (pop. 1,033), Las Villas prov., central Cuba, on Central Highway, on railroad and 38 mi. NW of Santa Clara; sugar cane, tobacco, stock.

Cascajal, village (pop. 1,230), Lambayeque dept., NW Peru, in W foothills of Cordillera Occidental, at E edge of Olmos Desert, on Pan American Highway and 7 mi. N of Olmos; corn, sugar cane, cattle.

Cascante (käskän'tā), city (pop. 3,651), Navarre prov., N Spain, 6 mi. SW of Tudela, in fertile agr. area (wine, cereals, fruit); mfg. of brandy, alcohol, soap; olive-oil processing, flour- and sawmilling.

Cascapedia, Que.: see GRAND CASCAPEDIA.

Cascapedia River (kă"skŭpē'dēŭ) or **Cascapédia River** (käskäpädēä'), E Que., on Gaspé Peninsula, rises in the Shickshock Mts., flows 75 mi. SSE, past Grand Cascapedia, to Chaleur Bay 24 mi. ENE of Dalhousie. Noted salmon stream.

Cascas (kä'skäs), village, N Senegal, Fr. West Africa, on Senegal R. (Mauritania border) and 60 mi. ESE of Podor; gum trading post.

Cascas (kä'skäs), city (pop. 2,162), Cajamarca dept., NW Peru, on W slopes of Cordillera Occidental, 7 mi. SSW of Contumasá; sugar cane, coffee.

Cascata, Brazil: see SÃO JOÃO DA BOA VISTA.

Cascatinha (käskŏotē'nyŭ), town (pop. 6,166), central Rio de Janeiro state, Brazil, in the Serra dos Orgãos, on railroad and 3 mi. NNE of Petrópolis; cotton-milling center; flower- and fruitgrowing.

Cascavel (käskävĕl'). **1** City (pop. 2,501), NE Ceará, Brazil, near the Atlantic, 32 mi. SE of Fortaleza; sugar, cotton, manioc, carnauba wax; kaolin deposits. Airfield. **2** Town, W Paraná, Brazil, on road, and 85 mi. ENE of Foz do Iguaçu; livestock. **3** City, Sãó Paulo, Brazil: see AGUAÍ.

Cascina (kä'shēnä), town (pop. 2,136), Pisa prov., Tuscany, central Italy, near the Arno, 8 mi. ESE of Pisa. Furniture mfg. and cotton-milling center; alcohol, lye, macaroni, pumps. Has 12th-cent. church, woodworking school. Florence defeated Pisa near by in 1364.

Casco (kă'skō). **1** Resort town (pop. 881), Cumberland co., SW Maine, on Sebago L. and 25 mi. NNW of Portland; agr. Includes part of Sebago L. State Park. Near South Casco village is Nathaniel Hawthorne's boyhood home, in Raymond town. **2** Village (pop. 389), Kewaunee co., E Wis., on Door Peninsula, 20 mi. E of Green Bay city, in dairying and farming area.

Casco Bay, SW Maine, bet. Cape Elizabeth (S) and Cape Small (N); 20 mi. wide, □ 200. Over 200 isls., many of them summer resorts. Principal harbor, Portland.

Cascorro (käskô'rō), town (pop. 2,075), Camagüey prov., E Cuba, on Central Highway and 32 mi. ESE of Camagüey; cattle raising, dairying.

Cascumpeque Bay (kă'skŭmpĕk), inlet (7 mi. long, 10 mi. wide at entrance) of the Gulf of St. Lawrence, NW P.E.I. At head of bay is Alberton.

Cáseda (kä'sā-dhä), town (pop. 1,640), Navarre prov., N Spain, near Aragon R., 25 mi. SE of Pamplona; wine, olive oil, livestock.

Casegas (käzā'gŭsh), village (pop. 1,525), Castelo Branco dist., central Portugal, in the Serra da Estrêla, 13 mi. SW of Covilhã; sheep and goat raising.

Caselle Torinese (käzĕl'lĕ tôrēnā'zĕ), village (pop. 2,908), Torino prov., Piedmont, NW Italy, 7 mi. N of Turin; silk industry.

Casellina (käzĕl-lē'nä), village (pop. 396), Firenze prov., Tuscany, central Italy, 4 mi. W of Florence; mfg. (macaroni, brooms).

Casentino (käzĕntē'nô), valley of upper Arno R., Tuscany, central Italy, E of the Pratomagno, S of Stia; c.20 mi. long.

Case-Pilote (käz-pēlôt'), town (pop. 620), W Martinique, 3 mi. NW of Fort-de-France; adjoining are large sugar estates, with mills and distilleries.

Caseros. 1 District, Buenos Aires prov., Argentina: see DAIREAUX. **2** Department, Santa Fe prov., Argentina: see CASILDA.

Caseros (käsā'rōs), city (pop. estimate 15,000) in greater Buenos Aires, Argentina, 11 mi. WNW of Buenos Aires; mfg. center (ceramics, insecticides, gloves, furniture). Site of defeat (1852) of the dictator Juan Manuel de Rosas.

Caserta (käzĕr'tä), province (□ 1,019; pop. 506,860), Campania, S Italy; ⊙ Caserta. On Gulf of Gaeta; coastal plain bordered by the Apennines, watered by Volturno R. Agr. (fruit, vegetables, grapes, olives, cereals, hemp, tobacco); livestock raising. Hydroelectric plants (Piedimonte d'Alife, Prata Sannita). Mfg. at Santa Maria Capua Vetere. A prov. until 1927, when it was abolished; reconstituted in 1945, mostly from Napoli prov. and also from Benevento and Campobasso provs.

Caserta, town (pop. 30,910), ⊙ Caserta prov., Campania, S Italy, 16 mi. N of Naples; 41°4'N 14°20'E. Rail junction; agr. trade center (cereals, citrus fruit, tobacco, hemp); macaroni, wine, olive oil; mfg. (scales, explosives, soap, tobacco products). Bishopric. Noted for its royal palace (1752–74) and park. Used as Allied headquarters in Second World War; palace and its period furnishings were considerably damaged. Here, on April 29, 1945, surrender of Ger. forces in Italy to the Allies was signed.

Casetas (käsā'täs), outer suburb (pop. 3,237) of Saragossa, Saragossa prov., NE Spain, 8 mi. NW of city center; sugar and flour mills; linen mfg. Railroad shops.

Caseville, village (pop. 482), Huron co., E Mich., at mouth of small Pigeon R., on Saginaw Bay, and 38 mi. NE of Bay City. Resort. State park near by.

Casey (kā'sē), county (□ 435; pop. 17,446), central Ky.; ⊙ Liberty. Bounded E by small Fishing Creek; drained by Green R. Hilly agr. area (livestock, corn, hay, burley tobacco); timber; stone quarries. Lumber mills at Liberty. Formed 1806.

Casey. **1** (kā'zē, kā'sē) City (pop. 2,734), Clark co., E Ill., 24 mi. ESE of Mattoon; oil, natural gas; mfg. (shoes, limestone products, hardware); agr. (grain, poultry; dairy products). Inc. 1896. Had oil boom in early-20th cent. **2** (kā'sē) Town (pop. 703), on Adair-Guthrie co. line, SW Iowa, c.45 mi. W of Des Moines, near Middle R., in agr. region (grain, hogs); feed milling.

Casey, Fort, Wash.: see PORT TOWNSEND.

Caseyville (kā'sēvĭl). **1** Village (pop. 1,209), St. Clair co., SW Ill., 7 mi. E of East St. Louis and within St. Louis metropolitan area. **2** Town (pop. 73), Union co., W Ky., on the Ohio just above Tradewater R. mouth, and 14 mi. SW of Morganfield.

Cash, town (pop. 188), Craighead co., NE Ark., 14 mi. WSW of Jonesboro, near Cache R.

Casheen Bay (kŭ-shēn'), inlet (2 mi. long) of Galway Bay, SW Co. Galway, Ireland, bet. Lettermullen and Gorumna isls.

Cashel (kă'shŭl), Gaelic *Caiseal Mumhan*, urban district (pop. 3,063), S central Co. Tipperary, Ireland, near Suir R., 12 mi. ENE of Tipperary; agr. market (dairying; potatoes, beets). Seat of R.C. archbishop and of Protestant bishop, and is famous shrine and anc. ⊙ of kings of Munster. In center of town rises the Rock of Cashel, limestone mount (300 ft.) crowned with ruins of 13th-cent. cathedral of St. Patrick, 14th-cent. bishop's castle, Cormac's Chapel (founded 1127 by Cormac MacCarthy, king of Desmond and bishop of Cashel), and of 10th-cent. round tower. Here also is anc. Cross of Cashel. Below The Rock are remains of Hore Abbey (1272). In town is Dominican priory (founded 1243) and modern R.C. church incorporating remains of Hacket's Friary (c.1250). St. Declan having founded 1st church here in 6th cent., Cashel early became fortified town; in 10th cent. it became stronghold of Brian Boru.

Cashen, Ireland: see FEALE RIVER.

Cashie River (kă'shē), NE N.C., rises in NW Bertie co., flows SE past Windsor (head of navigation), and ESE to Albemarle Sound 5 mi. N of Plymouth; c.50 mi. long. In lower course, connected with Roanoke R. by short passage.

Cashiers (kă'shŭrz), resort town (pop. 305), Jackson co., W N.C., 20 mi. SSE of Sylva, near Glenville Reservoir (Tuckasegee R.).

Cashion (kă'shŭn), town (pop. 182), Kingfisher co., central Okla., 24 mi. NNW of Oklahoma City, in agr. area.

Cashmere: see KASHMIR.

Cashmere, town (pop. 1,768), Chelan co., central Wash., on Wenatchee R. and 10 mi. above Wenatchee; fruit, apple confections; timber, wood products. Settled 1889, inc. 1904.

Cashton, village (pop. 836), Monroe co., S central Wis., 23 mi. ESE of La Crosse, in timber and dairy region (butter, cheese); mfg. of bowling pins.

Casiguran (käsēgōō'rän). **1** Town (1939 pop. 1,869; 1948 municipality pop. 5,643), Quezon prov., central Luzon, Philippines, at base of San Ildefonso Peninsula on E coast, 65 mi. ESE of Bayombong; sawmilling; fishing. **2** Town (1939 pop. 3,771; 1948 municipality pop. 12,940), Sorsogon prov., extreme SE Luzon, Philippines, on S shore of Sorsogon Bay, 27 mi. SE of Legaspi; fishing and hemp-growing center.

Casiguran Sound, inlet of Philippine Sea, in Philippines, bet. W coast of central Luzon and San Ildefonso Peninsula; 20 mi. long, 1–10 mi. wide. Cape San Ildefonso is at E side of entrance.

Casilda (käsēl'dä), town (1947 pop. 12,060), ⊙ Caseros dept. (□ 1,330; 1947 census 64,191), S Santa Fe prov., Argentina, 30 mi. WSW of Rosario; rail junction; agr. center (wheat, flax, corn, alfalfa, livestock); produces frozen meat, dairy products, sweets, toys, furniture, paper bags. Has agr. school.

Casilda, town (pop. 1,986), Las Villas prov., central Cuba, port for Trinidad (3 mi. N; linked by rail), on sheltered bay, 45 mi. S of Santa Clara. Fishing and seaside resort.

Casilinum, Italy: see CAPUA.

Casillas (käsē'yäs), town (1950 pop. 1,609), Santa Rosa dept., S Guatemala, in Pacific piedmont, on Esclavos R. and 10 mi. NNE of Cuilapa; sugar cane, grain, cattle.

Casillas (käsē'lyäs), town (pop. 1,417), Ávila prov., central Spain, in E Sierrra de Gredos, 24 mi. SSE of Ávila; fruit, grapes, chestnuts, resins, timber, livestock; flour milling.

Casillas de Coria (dhā kōr'yä), village (pop. 1,257), Cáceres prov., W Spain, 36 mi. NNW of Cáceres; olive oil, cereals, livestock.

Casillas de Flores (flō'rēs), town (pop. 1,296), Salamanca prov., W Spain, 19 mi. SW of Ciudad Rodrigo; cereals, lumber, livestock.

Casillas del Ángel (dhĕl än'hĕl), inland village (pop. 470), Fuerteventura, Canary Isls., 9 mi. WSW of Puerto de Cabras; cereals, alfalfa, vegetables, fruit; flour milling.

Casim, Bulgaria: see GENERAL TOSHEVO.

Casimiro de Abreu (kăzēmē'rōō dĭ ăbrē'ōō), city (pop. 458), E central Rio de Janeiro state, Brazil, on railroad and 25 mi. ESE of Nova Friburgo; coffee, manioc.

Casino (kŭsē'nō), municipality (pop. 6,698), NE New South Wales, Australia, on Richmond R. and 110 mi. S of Brisbane; rail junction; dairying center; bananas.

Casinos (käsē'nōs), village (pop. 1,962), Valencia prov., E Spain, 7 mi. NW of Liria; wine, olive oil, cereals. Mineral springs.

Casiquiare (käsēkyä'rā), river in Amazonas territory, S Venezuela, navigable waterway linking Orinoco and Amazon basins; branches off from the Orinoco 20 mi. W of Esmeralda at 3°10'N 65°50'W, flows 140 mi. SW and W to the Río Negro 7 mi. NNW of San Carlos.

Casitas (käsē'täs), village (pop. 421), Tumbes dept., NW Peru, in W foothills of the Andes, 17 mi. S of Zorritos; cattle and goat raising.

Caskets or **Casquets,** group of dangerous rocky isls. in English Channel, 7 mi. W of Alderney; lighthouse (49°43'N 2°23'W).

Caslav (chä'slăf), Czech *Čáslav*, Ger. *Czaslau* or *Tschaslau* (chä'slou), town (pop. 8,773), E Bohemia, Czechoslovakia, 18 mi. WSW of Pardubice; rail junction; center of agr. industries (sugar milling, distilling, food processing). Sapphires found in near-by hills. Has baroque town hall, memorial gate to Zizka. A Hussite parliament assembled here (1421) to repudiate Emperor Sigismund

Casma (käz'mä), city (pop. 2,929), ⊙ Huarmey prov. (organized in 1950), Ancash dept., W central Peru, on coastal plain, on Casma R. (short coastal stream; irrigation), on Pan American Highway and 50 mi. W of Huarás, in cotton- and rice-growing area; cotton ginning, rice milling. PUERTO CASMA is on Casma Bay (WNW) on the Pacific. Was ⊙ Santa prov. until 1950, when seat was moved to Chimbote.

Casnovia (kăznō'vēŭ), village (pop. 312), on Muskegon-Kent co. line, SW Mich., 20 mi. NNW of Grand Rapids, in fruitgrowing and dairying area.

Caso, Greece: see KASOS.

Casola in Lunigiana (kä'zôlä ēn lōōnējä'nä), village (pop. 336), Massa e Carrara prov., Tuscany, central Italy, 9 mi. NE of Carrara; mfg. (macaroni, cement).

Casola Valsenio (välsā'nyô), village (pop. 1,282), Ravenna prov., Emilia-Romagna, N central Italy, on Senio R. and 10 mi. SSW of Imola.

Casole d'Elsa (kä'zôlĕ dĕl'sä), village (pop. 863), Siena prov., Tuscany, central Italy, 14 mi. WNW of Siena; cement works. Marble quarries near by.

Casoli (kä'zôlē), town (pop. 2,690), Chieti prov., Abruzzi e Molise, S central Italy, 10 mi. SSW of Lanciano; cement.

Casorate Primo (käzôrä'tě prē'mô), village (pop. 3,472), Pavia prov., Lombardy, N Italy, 11 mi. NW of Pavia; mfg. (agr. machinery, artificial fruit).

Casorate Sempione (sěmpyô'ně), village (pop. 2,409), Varese prov., Lombardy, N Italy, 2 mi. WNW of Gallarate; rayon mfg.

Casoria (käzô'rēä), town (pop. 14,090), Napoli prov., Campania, S Italy, 4 mi. N of Naples; sausage, macaroni, vinegar.

Caspar, village (1940 pop. 565), Mendocino co., NW Calif., on the Pacific, 6 mi. S of Fort Bragg; lumber mill.

Caspar Roblesdiep, Netherlands: see KOLONELSDIEP.

Caspe (kä'spā), city (pop. 7,343), Saragossa prov., NE Spain, in Aragon, on the Ebro at mouth of Guadalope R., and 55 mi. SE of Saragossa; olive-oil production center; mfg. of soap, brandy, flour products; agr. trade (cereals, fruit, vegetables, livestock). Agreement of Caspe reached here (1412) by the Cortes brought Prince Ferdinand of Castile to throne of Aragon. Scene of heavy fighting in civil war, especially in 1938.

Casper, city (pop. 23,673), ⊙ Natrona co., central Wyo., on N.Platte R. just N of Laramie Mts., and 145 mi. NW of Cheyenne; alt. 5,123 ft. Second largest city in Wyo.; rail and distribution center for rich oil and livestock region; oil refineries; mfg. (tents, awnings, bricks, torpedoes, beverages). Site of pioneer crossing and military post on Oregon Trail. Founded 1888, inc. 1889. Growth as oil center dates from erection of oil well (1890) in near-by Salt Creek field. Other fields (including Big Muddy and celebrated TEAPOT DOME) were discovered and developed, and refineries and pipelines constructed. Production had spectacular increase in 1917 because of First World War, declined during late 1920s, rose again in late 1930s, and boomed in 1948 with development of Lost Soldier field in Sweetwater co. Has jr. col., state home for children. Air Force base near by. Important annual event is Wyoming-on-Parade, frontier pageant. Near-by points of interest: Fort Caspar (rebuilt 1938), recreation area on Casper Mtn. (c.8,000 ft.), Hell's Half Acre (picturesque, eroded area), Independence Rock (huge granite landmark on Oregon Trail), Devil's Gate (deep chasm in granite ridge). Kendrick project of Bureau of Reclamation irrigates 66,000 acres in vicinity; includes SEMINOE DAM and ALCOVA DAM. Kortes Dam, begun 1946 on N.Platte R., c.50 mi. SSW of Casper, is unit in Missouri R. basin project.

Caspian, village (pop. 1,608), Iron co., SW Upper Peninsula, Mich., on Iron R. and 15 mi. WSW of Crystal Falls. Resort, in area of small lakes. Inc. 1918.

Caspian Gates, Russian SFSR: see DERBENT.

Caspian Lake, NE Vt., resort lake in Greensboro town, 18 mi. NW of St. Johnsbury; c.2 mi. long.

Caspian Sea (kă'spēŭn), Rus. *Kaspiyskoye More*, Persian *Darya-i-Khazar*, anc. *Mare Caspium* or *Mare Hyrcanium*, largest salt-water lake and inland sea (□ 163,800) in the world, bet. Europe and Asia, in USSR (80% of shore line) and Iran, separated from the Black Sea (W) by the Caucasus; 750 mi. long, 130–300 mi. wide; surface is 92 ft. below sea level; maximum depth c.3,200 ft. (S). Chief tributaries (all delta-forming) are (N) the Ural and Volga rivers, (W) the Terek, Sulak, Samur, and Kura rivers, and (S, in Iran), the Sefid-Rud and the Atrek. The Caspian basin, which has no outlet, is divided morphologically into 3 sections: a N shallow portion (frozen 2–3 months), with low salinity and an abundance of marine life, and a middle section (mean depth 650 ft.) separated from the deep S section (mean depth 1,100 ft.) by a submarine ridge extending from Apsheron Peninsula to Krasnovodsk. The average salinity is 1.3%, with less sodium chloride, but more sulphates and carbonates than ocean water. The large E inlet KARA-BOGAZ-GOL acts as a natural evaporating basin, mainly for mirabilite (Glauber's salt). Fishing (in N shallow portion, at Volga delta) yields 35% of USSR catch, chiefly sturgeon (black caviar), herring, carp, salmon. Sealing is of lesser importance. The greater depths (below 1,500 ft.) are contaminated with hydrogen sulphide and therefore devoid of marine life. The Caspian Sea is of great importance in the Soviet economy as an inland water transportation route, accounting for ½ of USSR maritime freight turnover. The principal Soviet ports are Guryev, Astrakhan, Makhachkala, Baku, Lenkoran, Krasnovodsk, and Fort Shevchenko. On the Iranian coast, Pahlevi, Naushahr, Babulsar, and Bandar-Shah are the main harbors. Cargo consists of petroleum (chiefly bet. Baku and Astrakhan), grain, lumber, cotton, dried fruits. The present Caspian is the residual basin of a vast Miocene sea connected with the Black Sea (via the MANYCH DEPRESSION) and, more recently, with the Aral Sea (via the UZBOI). Tectonic processes and differential evaporation have long caused fluctuations in the lake level within a 4-ft. span. Since 1929, the lake level has steadily dropped from 85 ft. to 92 ft. below sea level. Corresponding variations in area resulted in considerable changes in the configuration of the low shore line. In view of the paramount economic importance of the Caspian Sea for the USSR, several large-scale projects were formulated after the Second World War to check the continuing lowering of the lake level. Among these is the diversion of the Amu Darya through the Uzboi to the Caspian Sea.

Casquets, Channel Isls.: see CASKETS.

Cass. **1** County (□ 370; pop. 15,097), W central Ill., bounded N by Sangamon R. and W by Illinois R.; ⊙ Virginia. Agr. (corn, wheat, soybeans, fruit, sweet potatoes, livestock, poultry; dairy products). Mfg. (flour, gloves, feed); commercial fisheries; river, rail shipping. Includes Treadway L. Formed 1837. **2** County (□ 415; pop. 38,793), N central Ind.; ⊙ Logansport. Intersected by the Wabash; drained by Eel R. and Deer Creek. Agr. area (livestock, grain, poultry, fruit, truck; dairy products); nurseries, timber. Mfg. and shipping at Logansport. Formed 1828. **3** County (□ 559; pop. 18,532), SW Iowa; ⊙ Atlantic. Prairie agr. area (cattle, hogs, poultry, corn) drained by East Nishnabotna and West Nodaway rivers; coal deposits. Formed 1851. **4** County (□ 488; pop. 28,185), SW Mich.; ⊙ Cassopolis. Bounded S by Ind. line; drained by St. Joseph R. and short Dowagiac Creek. A lake and farm region (grain, truck, peppermint, ginseng, fruit, livestock; dairy products). Mfg. at Dowagiac. Resorts. Formed 1829. **5** County (□ 2,053; pop. 19,468), N central Minn.; ⊙ Walker. Agr. area bounded S by Crow Wing R., N by Mississippi R. Dairy products, livestock, potatoes; peat deposits. Leech L. is in NW, part of Winnibigoshish L. in N and of Cass L. in NW. Area includes much of Greater Leech Lake Indian Reservation and Chippewa Natl. Forest. Formed 1851. **6** County (□ 698; pop. 19,325), W Mo.; ⊙ Harrisonville. Drained by South Grand R. Agr. (corn, wheat, oats), cattle, poultry; gas wells. Formed 1849. **7** County (□ 552; pop. 16,361), SE Nebr.; ⊙ Plattsmouth. Agr. region bounded E by Missouri R. and Iowa, N by Platte R. Grain, livestock, dairy products. Formed 1868. **8** County (□ 1,749; pop. 58,877), E N.Dak.; ⊙ Fargo. Rich agr. area bounded E by Red River of the North, drained by Maple and Sheyenne rivers. Formed 1873. **9** County (□ 965; pop. 26,732), NE Texas; ⊙ Linden. Bounded E by Ark. and La., N by Sulphur R. Rolling, partly forested area (lumbering); agr. (cotton, corn, peanuts, peas, sweet potatoes, fruit, truck); livestock (cattle, hogs, poultry); dairying. Oil, natural-gas wells; lignite, clay, iron deposits. Mfg., processing at Linden, Atlanta. Formed 1846.

Cass, town (pop. 417), Pocahontas co., E W.Va., on Greenbrier R. and 15 mi. NE of Marlinton., in agr. region.

Cassaba, Turkey: see TURGUTLU.
Cassadaga (kăsŭdā'gù), resort village (pop. 676), Chautauqua co., extreme W N.Y., on Cassadaga Lakes, 10 mi. S of Dunkirk; mfg. (feed, furniture, machinery, metal products).
Cassadaga Creek, N.Y.: see CASSADAGA LAKES.
Cassadaga Lakes, Chautauqua co., extreme W N.Y., 3 small lakes (Upper, Middle, and Lower Cassadaga lakes), 17 mi. N of Jamestown; resorts. Connected and drained by Cassadaga Creek, which flows c.30 mi. generally SE to Conewango Creek 5 mi. E of Jamestown.
Cassá de la Selva (käsä' dhā lä sĕl'vä), town (pop. 3,631), Gerona prov., NE Spain, 7 mi. SSE of Gerona; cork and wine processing; cereals.
Cassagnès-Begonhès (käsä'nyù-bāgōnĕs'), village (pop. 499), Aveyron dept., S France, on Ségala Plateau, 13 mi. S of Rodez; flour milling, dairying.
Cassaigne (käsā'nyù), village (pop. 2,050), Oran dept., NW Algeria, in the coastal Dahra range, 21 mi. NE of Mostaganem; winegrowing.
Cassaigne, village (pop. 69), Gers dept., SW France, 4 mi. SSW of Condom; Armagnac brandy distilling.
Cassai River, Angola and Belgian Congo: see KASAI RIVER.
Cassandra, in Gr. names, Greece: see KASSANDRA.
Cassandra (kùsăn'drù), borough (pop. 381), Cambria co., SW central Pa., 16 mi. ENE of Johnstown.
Cassandrea, Greece: see POTIDAEA.
Cassano al Ionio (käs-sä'nô äl yô'nyô), town (pop. 7,689), Cosenza prov., Calabria, S Italy, 6 mi. ESE of Castrovillari. Commercial center; wine, olive oil, citrus fruit, cereals; mfg. (agr. and wine-press machinery, cutlery). Bishopric. Has castle and warm mineral springs.
Cassano d'Adda (däd'dä), town (pop. 4,404), Milano prov., Lombardy, N Italy, on Adda R. and 17 mi. ENE of Milan, in grape- and silk-growing region. Stone and gravel quarries near by. Here in 1705 French under Vendôme defeated Imperialists led by Eugene of Savoy; in 1799 French under Moreau defeated Russians under Suvarov.
Cassano delle Murge (dĕl'lĕ mōōr'jĕ), town (pop. 6,136), Bari prov., Apulia, S Italy, 17 mi. S of Bari; wine, olive oil.
Cassano Magnago (mänyä'gô), town (pop. 6,067), Varese prov., Lombardy, N Italy, 4 mi. N of Busto Arsizio; woodworking, tanning, mfg. of chemicals, cotton textiles.
Cass City, village (pop. 1,762), Tuscola co., E Mich., on Cass R. and 35 mi. E of Bay City. Trade center for agr. area (livestock, poultry, grain; dairy products); mfg. of condensed milk. Settled 1866; inc. 1883.
Cassel (käsĕl'), village (pop. 1,794), Nord dept., N France, 11 mi. ENE of Saint-Omer, atop solitary hill (515 ft.) dominating Flanders plain; road junction; footwear mfg., dairying. Roman stronghold, medieval fortress, and old ⊙ of Maritime Flanders. Here French defeated Flemings in 1328. Here also they defeated William of Orange in the Dutch Wars (1677). Hq. of General Foch in 1914–15 and of Br. 2d Army in 1916–18. Its typically Flemish town hall destroyed in Second World War.
Cassel, Germany: see KASSEL.
Casselberry, town (pop. 407), Seminole co., central Fla., NE of Orlando.
Casselman, village (pop. 1,021), SE Ont., on South Nation R. and 30 mi. ESE of Ottawa; dairying, mixed farming.
Casselman (kă'sùlmùn), borough (pop. 130), Somerset co., SW Pa., 11 mi. SW of Somerset and on Casselman R.
Casselman River, NW Md. and SW Pa., formed by branches joining in N Garrett co., Md., flows c.60 mi. in a semicircle (NE past Salisbury and Meyersdale, Pa., NW to Rockwood, thence SW) to Youghiogheny R. at Confluence, Pa.
Casselton, city (pop. 1,373), Cass co., E N.Dak., 20 mi. W of Fargo; rail center; grain, dairy products. Inc. 1883.
Casseneuil (käsùnû'ē), village (pop. 906), Lot-et-Garonne dept., SW France, on the Lot and 5 mi. WNW of Villeneuve-sur-Lot; steel and copper rolling mill; fruit preserving.
Cássia (kä'syù), city (pop. 3,502), SW Minas Gerais, Brazil, near the Rio Grande and near São Paulo border, 20 mi. NW of Passos; agr. trade.
Cassia (kă'shù), county (□ 2,544; pop. 14,629), S Idaho; ⊙ Burley. Agr. area bordering on Utah and Nev., bounded N by Snake R. Irrigated regions are in N, along Snake R., and in W, along Goose Creek, around Oakley. Potatoes, sugar beets, dry beans, livestock. Parts of Minidoka Natl. Forest throughout. Co. formed 1879.
Cassiar Mountains (kăsēär'), small range, N B.C., near head of Stikine R., NE of Dease L. Gives its name to surrounding district.
Cassibile River (käs-sē'bēlĕ), SE Sicily, rises on SE slopes of Monti Iblei, flows 20 mi. ESE to Ionian Sea 4 mi. NE of Avola. Dammed in upper course for hydroelectric power.
Cassidy, village, SW B.C., on SE Vancouver Isl., 7 mi. SSE of Nanaimo; coal mining.
Cassillis, Scotland: see DALRYMPLE.
Cassine (käs-sē'nĕ), village (pop. 1,884), Alessandria prov., Piedmont, N Italy, near Bormida R., 12 mi. SSW of Alessandria; cork, organs, hardware. Has 13th-cent. church.
Cassino (käs-sē'nô), town (pop. 9,208), Frosinone prov., Latium, S central Italy, on Rapido R. and 75 mi. ESE of Rome; toy mfg. At end of 1943 both town and Benedictine abbey of MONTE CASSINO, on a near-by hill, were key defense points of Germans blocking Allied advance to Rome. Despite repeated, concentrated ground attacks started in Jan., 1944, the Allied attempt to divert Ger. troops from here by landings at ANZIO, and virtual destruction of town and abbey by air and artillery bombing, the Ger. positions held out until May 18, 1944. Reconstruction of part of the town was begun in 1945. Near by are British and Polish military cemeteries.
Cassis (käsēs'), town (pop. 2,063), Bouches-du-Rhône dept., SE France, port on the Mediterranean, 10 mi. SE of Marseilles; known for its white wines and picturesque shoreline. Resort slightly damaged in Second World War.
Cassiterides, England: see SCILLY ISLANDS.
Cass Lake, resort village (pop. 1,936), Cass co., N central Minn., on W shore of Cass L., in Chippewa Natl. Forest and Greater Leech Lake Indian Reservation, 15 mi. ESE of Bemidji; dairy products, lumber, potatoes. Consolidated Chippewa Agency here; forest experiment station and tree nursery near by. Inc. 1899.
Cass Lake. 1 Lake in Oakland co., SE Mich., 3 mi. SW of Pontiac; c.3 mi. long, 1 mi. wide; bathing, boating, fishing. A state park is here. **2** Lake (□ 25) in Cass and Beltrami counties, N central Minn., in Greater Leech Lake Indian Reservation and Chippewa Natl. Forest, 13 mi. E of Bemidji; 10 mi. long, 7 mi. wide. Has fishing, boating, and bathing resorts and is fed and drained by Mississippi R. Star Island (2.5 mi. long, 1 mi. wide; used as summer resort) is just off W shore.
Cassolnovo (käs-sôlnô'vô), town (pop. 4,626), Pavia prov., Lombardy, N Italy, near Ticino R., 11 mi. SE of Novara.
Cassopolis (kùsŏ'pùlĭs), village (pop. 1,527), ⊙ Cass co., SW Mich., on a small lake 22 mi. NE of South Bend, Ind., in agr. area (livestock, poultry, fruit, grain, truck, peppermint, ginseng); dairy products; timber. Summer resort. Settled 1831; inc. 1863.
Cass River, E central Mich., formed near Cass City by branches rising to E, flows c.80 mi. W and SW past Caro, Vassar, and Frankenmuth, to Saginaw R. just S of Saginaw city.
Casstown, village (pop. 368), Miami co., W Ohio, 4 mi. E of Troy, in agr. area.
Cassumit Lake, village, NW Ont., in Patricia dist., on Richardson L. (4 mi. long), 100 mi. NNW of Sioux Lookout; gold mining.
Cassville. 1 City (pop. 1,441), ⊙ Barry co., SW Mo., in the Ozarks, 45 mi. SE of Joplin; fishing resort; ships livestock, poultry, dairy products, fruit. State park and fish hatchery near by. Platted 1845. **2** Borough (pop. 158), Huntingdon co., S Pa., 14 mi. S of Huntingdon. **3** Village (1940 pop. 1,105), Monongalia co., N W.Va., 6 mi. WNW of Morgantown, in coal-mining region. **4** Village (pop. 984), Grant co., extreme SW Wis., on Mississippi R. and 22 mi. NW of Dubuque (Iowa), in agr. area; canned foods, beer, wood products. State park near by.
Castagnaro (kästänyä'rô), village (pop. 1,515), Verona prov., Veneto, N Italy, on Adige R. and 19 mi. WNW of Rovigo, in cereal, tobacco, and sugar-beet region; vegetable oils.
Castagneto Carducci (kästänyā'tô kärdōōt'chē), village (pop. 2,291), Livorno prov., Tuscany, central Italy, 11 mi. SSE of Cecina; chemicals, macaroni.
Castagnola (kästänyô'lä), town (pop. 2,358), Ticino canton, S Switzerland, on L. of Lugano; residential E suburb of Lugano; cement products, pastry.
Castalia (kăstā'lēù). **1** Town (pop. 221), Winneshiek co., NE Iowa, 15 mi. SSE of Decorah; milk receiving and shipping point. Limestone quarries near by. **2** Town (pop. 421), Nash co., N central N.C., 17 mi. WNW of Rocky Mount. **3** Village (pop. 736), Erie co., N Ohio, 7 mi. SW of Sandusky; Blue Hole Spring here attracts tourists.
Castalla (kästä'lyä), city (pop. 3,290), Alicante prov., E Spain, 13 mi. SW of Alcoy; mfg. of footwear, toys, tiles; olive-oil and wine processing. Wheat, almonds, vegetables. Gypsum quarries. In Peninsular War, Suchet was defeated (1813) here by the Spaniards.
Castana (kă"stă'nù), town (pop. 265), Monona co., W Iowa, on Maple R. and 39 mi. SE of Sioux City, in livestock and grain area.
Castañar de Ibor (kästänyär' dhā ēvōr'), town (pop. 1,678), Cáceres prov., W Spain, 29 mi. ENE of Trujillo; olive-oil processing, flour milling; stock raising; nuts, wine. Lead mining near by.
Castañares de Rioja (kästänyä'rĕs dhā ryō'hä), town (pop. 1,056), Logroño prov., N Spain, 24 mi. W of Logroño; flour mills; vegetables, fruit, potatoes, sheep.
Castanet-Tolosan (kästänā'-tôlôzä'), village (pop. 816), Haute-Garonne dept., S France, near the Canal du Midi, 6 mi. SSE of Toulouse; chemical laboratory, truck gardens.
Castanhal (kästùnyäl'), city (pop. 1,780), E Pará, Brazil, on Belém-Bragança RR and 40 mi. ENE of Belém; Brazil nuts, rubber, cacao, lumber.
Castanheira de Pêra (käshtänyā'rù dĭ pā'rù), town (pop. 894), Leiria dist., W central Portugal, 38 mi. NE of Leiria; mfg. of woolen goods.
Castanheira do Ribatejo (dōō rēbātā'zhōō), agr. village (pop. 1,079), Lisboa dist., central Portugal, near lower Tagus R., on railroad and 20 mi. NNE of Lisbon.
Castaño del Robledo (kästä'nyō dhĕl rōblā'dhō), town (pop. 488), Huelva prov., SW Spain, in Sierra de Aracena, 7 mi. W of Aracena; chestnuts, potatoes, pears. Iron-pyrite mining. Salting of pork.
Castano Primo (kä'stänô prē'mô), town (pop. 5,890), Milano prov., Lombardy, N Italy, 6 mi. SW of Busto Arsizio; foundry.
Castaño River (kästä'nyō), left headstream of San Juan R., W San Juan prov., Argentina, rises in the Andes, flows c.100 mi. SE to join the Río de los Patos 6 mi. N of Calingasta.
Castaños (kästä'nyōs), town (pop. 1,415), Coahuila, N Mexico, in NE foothills of Sierra Madre Oriental, on railroad and 8 mi. S of Monclova, in agr. region (cereals, fibers, cattle). Lead mining; also silver, zinc, iron deposits.
Castara (kăstä'rù), village (pop. 438), W central Tobago, B.W.I., on Castara Bay, 7 mi. NNE of Scarborough; cacao, coconuts.
Casteggio (kästĕd'jô), anc. *Clastidium*, village (pop. 3,192), Pavia prov., Lombardy, N Italy, 12 mi. S of Pavia; wine, shoes, agr. tools. Has castle and medieval ruins. Sulphur springs near by.
Castejón (kästāhōn'). **1** Town (pop. 1,003), Cuenca prov., E central Spain, 30 mi. NW of Cuenca; cereals, olives, grapes, livestock. **2** Village (pop. 2,168), Navarre prov., N Spain, rail junction near the Ebro, 9 mi. NNW of Tudela; wine, cereals.
Castejón de Monegros (dhā mōnā'grōs), town (pop. 1,412), Huesca prov., NE Spain, 36 mi. SSE of Huesca; lumbering, sheep raising; wine, honey.
Castelar (kästĕlär'), town (pop. estimate 2,500) in Greater Buenos Aires, Argentina, adjoining Morón, 15 mi. WSW of Buenos Aires; apicultural and agr. center; alfalfa, corn, oats, livestock.
Castel Baronia (kästĕl' bärōnē'ä), village (pop. 1,594), Avellino prov., Campania, S Italy, 9 mi. SSE of Ariano Irpino; textile machinery, combs.
Castelbellino (kästĕlbĕl-lē'nô), village (pop. 256), Ancona prov., The Marches, central Italy, 6 mi. WSW of Iesi; macaroni, canned tomatoes.
Castel Benito (kästĕl' bĕnē'tō), village, W Tripolitania, Libya, 15 mi. S of Tripoli; road junction; agr. center. Has airport.
Castel Bolognese (bôlônyā'zē), town (pop. 2,440), Ravenna prov., Emilia-Romagna, N central Italy, near Senio R., 5 mi. ESE of Imola; agr. machinery, meat and vegetable extracts. Badly damaged in Second World War.
Castelbuono (kästĕlbwô'nô), town (pop. 11,155), Palermo prov., N Sicily, in Madonie Mts., 8 mi. SSE of Cefalù, in cereal- and grape-growing region. Has 13th-cent. castle.
Casteldaccia (kästĕldät'chä), village (pop. 4,900), Palermo prov., N Sicily, 2 mi. SE of Bagheria; macaroni, wine.
Casteldelfino (kästĕl"dĕlfē'nô), village (pop. 202), Cuneo prov., Piedmont, NW Italy, on Varaita R., at S foot of Monte Viso, and 21 mi. WSW of Saluzzo; hydroelectric plant.
Castel del Piano (kästĕl' dĕl pyä'nô), town (pop. 3,098), Grosseto prov., Tuscany, central Italy, near Monte Amiata, 23 mi. ENE of Grosseto. Resort (alt. 2,073 ft.); macaroni, metal furniture.
Castel di Sangro (dē säng'grô), town (pop. 4,428), Aquila prov., Abruzzi e Molise, S central Italy, on Sangro R. and 15 mi. NW of Isernia; rail junction; mfg. (woolen textiles, fireworks). In Second World War largely destroyed (1943) by Ger. mines.
Castelfidardo (kästĕl"fēdä'rô), town (pop. 2,659), Ancona prov., The Marches, central Italy, 11 mi. S of Ancona; mfg. center of musical instruments (accordions, harmoniums, harmonicas). Here Piedmontese under Cialdini defeated (1860) papal forces led by Lamoricière.
Castelfiorentino (–fyôrĕntē'nô), town (pop. 5,278), Firenze prov., Tuscany, central Italy, on Elsa R. and 18 mi. SW of Florence; liquor, soap, cement, glass, harmonicas. Site of Amer. military cemetery, with c.5,000 dead of Second World War.
Castel Focognano (kästĕl' fôkônyä'nô), village (pop. 145), Arezzo prov., Tuscany, central Italy, 3 mi. SW of Bibbiena; cement mfg.
Castelforte (kästĕlfôr'tĕ), village (pop. 2,461), Latina prov., Latium, S central Italy, 14 mi. ENE of Gaeta.
Castelfranc (kästĕlfrã'), village (pop. 362), Lot dept., SW France, on the Lot and 11 mi. WNW of Cahors; lime and cement works, kaolin quarries.
Castelfranco dell'Emilia (kästĕlfräng'kô dĕlĕmē'lyä) town (pop. 4,980), Modena prov., Emilia-Romagna, N central Italy, near Panaro R., 6 mi. SE of Modena; wine, dairy products, paper.
Castelfranco di Sotto (dē sôt'tô), village (pop. 1,277), Pisa prov., Tuscany, central Italy, near the Arno, 17 mi. E of Pisa; mfg. (shoes, brooms).
Castelfranco in Miscano (ēn mēskä'nô), village (pop. 2,437), Benevento prov., Campania, S Italy, 20 mi. NE of Benevento.

Castelfranco Veneto (vě′nětô), town (pop. 4,670), Treviso prov., Veneto, N Italy, 15 mi. W of Treviso. Rail junction; mfg. (macaroni, shoes, cotton textiles, alcohol, pharmaceuticals, firearms, radio and telephone accessories). Market for raw silk and livestock. Has medieval walls, cathedral with frescoes by Paolo Veronese and a famous altarpiece by Giorgione, who was b. here.

Castel Frentano (kästĕ′′ frĕntä′nô), town (pop. 2,695), Chieti prov., Abruzzi e Molise, S central Italy, 3 mi. SW of Lanciano; machinery mfg.

Castel Gandolfo (gändôl′fô), village (pop. 1,862), Roma prov., Latium, central Italy, in Alban Hills, overlooking L. Albano, 15 mi. SE of Rome. Papal summer residence. Papal palace (17th cent.) and its beautiful gardens and the Villa Barberine have extraterritorial rights. A major astronomical observatory was established here 1936 by the Vatican. Town possibly occupies site of anc. Alba Longa. Damaged by air bombing (1944) in Second World War.

Castelgrande (kästĕlgrän′dĕ), village (pop. 2,598), Potenza prov., Basilicata, S Italy, 22 mi. NW of Potenza, in cereal- and grape-growing region.

Casteljaloux (kästĕlzhälōō′), town (pop. 3,633), Lot-et-Garonne dept., SW France, on edge of the LANDES, 13 mi. SSW of Marmande; woodworking center; mfg. of cabinetmaking equipment and hosiery, paper milling. Lumber trade. Has 13th-14th-cent. houses.

Castellammare, Gulf of (kästĕl″läm-mä′rĕ), inlet of Tyrrhenian Sea, W Sicily, bet. Cape San Vito and Punta Raisi; 20 mi. wide, 11 mi. long; tunny fisheries. Chief port, Castellammare del Golfo.

Castellammare Adriatico, Italy: see PESCARA, city.

Castellammare del Golfo (dĕl gôl′fô), town (pop. 16,430), Trapani prov., W Sicily, port on Gulf of Castellammare, 5 mi. NW of Alcamo, in agr. region (cereals, grapes, olives, vegetables); tunny fishing, wine making. Seaport for anc. Segesta (SE).

Castellammare di Stabia (dē stä′byä), city (pop. 36,469), Napoli prov., Campania, S Italy, port on Bay of Naples, 16 mi. SE of Naples. Industrial and commercial center; naval yards, arsenal; many macaroni factories; mfg. (machinery, marine motors, aeronautical equipment, cotton textiles, paper, packing boxes, cement, soap); sulphur refinery, tanneries. Exports macaroni, wine, fruit, cement. Bishopric. Its beautiful location and famous mineral baths, used since Roman times, make it a frequented resort. The royal villa Quisisana (built 1310; rebuilt 1820) is now a hotel. Near by was anc. *Stabiae*, a favorite Roman resort, buried in the eruption of Vesuvius in A.D. 79.

Castellamonte (kästĕl″lämôn′tĕ), town (pop. 2,315), Torino prov., Piedmont, NW Italy, near Orco R., 10 mi. SW of Ivrea; rail terminus; ceramics (crockery, kilns), tanneries, woolen mill, macaroni factory. Magnesite deposits near by.

Castellana (kästĕl-lä′nä), town (pop. 9,944), Bari prov., Apulia, S Italy, 9 mi. SW of Monopoli; wine, olive oil, macaroni, cotton textiles.

Castellane (kästĕlän′), village (pop. 804), Basses-Alpes dept., SE France, on the Verdon (10 mi. above its canyon) and 22 mi. SE of Digne, at foot of a rock 600 ft. high; tourist resort. Coal mining near by. Hydroelectric plant 3 mi. NNE.

Castellaneta (kästĕl″länā′tä), town (pop. 8,993), Ionio prov., Apulia, S Italy, 19 mi. NW of Taranto; olive oil, dairy products. Bishopric. Has 12th-cent. cathedral (rebuilt in 15th cent.).

Castellanos, department, Argentina: see RAFAELA.

Castellanza (kästĕl-län′tsä), town (pop. 4,601), Varese prov., Lombardy, N Italy, on Olona R. and 2 mi. E of Busto Arsizio; rail junction; foundries, cotton mill; mfg. (textile machinery, vegetable oils). Large thermoelectric station near by.

Castellar (kästälyär′), village (pop. 3,301), Barcelona prov., NE Spain, 8 mi. W of Manresa; lumbering; trades in wine, olive oil, fruit.

Castellarano (kästĕl″lärä′nô), village (pop. 1,070), Reggio nell'Emilia prov., Emilia-Romagna, N central Italy, near Secchia R., 13 mi. SW of Modena. Has old castle.

Castellar de la Frontera (kästälyär′ dhā lä frōntā′rä), town (pop. 521), Cádiz prov., SW Spain, 14 mi. NNW of Gibraltar; cereals, cork, timber, charcoal, livestock. Has sulphur springs. Situated on a hill topped by ruins of Moorish fortress.

Castellar de Santiago (säntyä′gō), town (pop. 3,827), Ciudad Real prov., S central Spain, 16 mi. SSE of Valdepeñas; agr. center (olives, cereals, grapes, livestock). Olive-oil extracting, cheese processing.

Castellar de Santisteban (säntēstä′vän), town (pop. 6,002), Jaén prov., S Spain, 9 mi. NNW of Villacarrillo; olive-oil processing center; soap mfg., sawmilling. Cereals, livestock. Gypsum quarries.

Castellare-di-Casinca (kästĕl-lä′rĕ-dē-käsēng′kä), village (pop. 358), NE Corsica, 16 mi. S of Bastia; winegrowing.

Castell'Arquato (kästĕl″ärkwä′tô), town (pop. 1,598), Piacenza prov., Emilia-Romagna, N central Italy, on Arda R. and 16 mi. SSE of Piacenza. Has Romanesque church (1122), 13th-cent. palace, and 14th-cent. castle.

Castell'Azzara (kästĕl″ätsä′rä), village (pop. 2,173), Grosseto prov., Tuscany, central Italy, near Monte Amiata, 8 mi. S of Abbadia San Salvatore. Mercury and antimony mines near by.

Castellazzo Bormida (kästĕl-lät′tsô bôr′mēdä), town (pop. 4,306), Alessandria prov., Piedmont, N Italy, near Bormida R., 5 mi. SSW of Alessandria, in cereal and silkworm-growing region; silk mills.

Castellbisbal (kästäl″vēzväl′), village (pop. 1,206), Barcelona prov., NE Spain, 12 mi. NW of Barcelona; knit-goods mfg.; wine, wheat, fruit.

Castelldáns (kästäldäns′), village (pop. 1,106), Lérida prov., NE Spain, 11 mi. SE of Lérida; olive-oil processing, almond shipping, sheep raising.

Castell de Ampurdá, Spain: see CASTELLÓ DE AMPURIAS.

Castell de Castells (kästäl′ dhā kästäls′), town (pop. 1,041), Alicante prov., E Spain, 15 mi. ENE of Alcoy; olive-oil processing. Gypsum quarries.

Castell de Ferro, Spain: see GUALCHOS.

Castelleone (kästĕl″lĕô′nĕ), town (pop. 4,619), Cremona prov., Lombardy, N Italy, 17 mi. NW of Cremona, in cereal- and mulberry-growing region; mfg. (cotton, linen, caramels, quince jam, agr. machinery); dairying. Market for cereals, grapes, cattle. Has church built 1551 (restored) and 13th-cent. tower.

Castelli (kästĕ′lē). **1** Town (pop. 3,328), ⊙ Castelli dist. (□ 797; pop. 6,741), E Buenos Aires prov., Argentina, 17 mi. NNW of Dolores; agr. center (sunflowers, corn, flax, cattle, sheep). **2** Town (pop. estimate 1,500), central Chaco natl. territory, Argentina, 55 mi. N of Presidencia Roque Sáenz Peña; rail terminus; cotton, corn; lumbering, cotton ginning. Formerly called Kilómetro 100; sometimes Colonia Castelli.

Castelli (kästĕl′lē), village (pop. 815), Teramo prov., Abruzzi e Molise, S central Italy, in Gran Sasso d'Italia, 12 mi. S of Teramo. Noted majolica center since 13th cent.

Castelli, Yugoslavia: see KASTELANSKA RIVIJERA.

Castellina in Chianti (kästĕl-lē′nä ēn kyän′tē), village (pop. 610), Siena prov., Tuscany, central Italy, 10 mi. NNW of Siena; wine, fertilizer, woolen textiles. Has 15th-cent. citadel (now town hall). Lignite mine near by.

Castellina Marittima (märēt′tēmä), village (pop. 1,201), Pisa prov., Tuscany, central Italy, 16 mi. SE of Leghorn. Alabaster quarries near by.

Castellnovo (kästälnō′vō), town (pop. 1,276), Castellón de la Plana prov., E Spain, 17 mi. NW of Sagunto; olive-oil processing, flour milling, basket-making; hemp, cereals, cattle.

Castello, Brazil: see CASTELO DO PIAUÍ.

Castello (kästĕl′lô), village (pop. 3,083), Firenze prov., Tuscany, central Italy, 3 mi. N of Florence; liquor.

Castelló de Ampurias (kästälyō′ dhā ämpōō′ryäs), Catalan *Castell de Ampurdá* (kästäl′ dhā ämpōōr-dhä′), town (pop. 1,844), Gerona prov., NE Spain, 11 mi. E of Gerona; lumber and cork trees; livestock, cereals, wine. Sometimes called San Martín de Llanares.

Castelló de Farfaña (färfä′nyä), town (pop. 1,106), Lérida prov., NE Spain, 5 mi. NW of Balaguer; sheep raising; wine, olive oil, hemp.

Castello di Fiemme (kästĕl′lô dē fyĕm′mĕ), village (pop. 698), Trento prov., Trentino–Alto Adige, N Italy, 1 mi. SW of Cavalese; box factories.

Castellón de la Plana (kästälyōn′ dhā lä plä′nä), province (□ 2,579; pop. 312,475), E Spain, in Valencia, on the Mediterranean; ⊙ Castellón de la Plana. Covered by mts. in N and W (E edge of central plateau), sloping to fertile, densely populated coastal plain. Has 2 good ports, El Grao de Castellón and Vinaroz. Drained by short, torrential rivers (Mijares, Palancia). Essentially agr.: forests and pastures (cattle and sheep raising) in the mts.; vineyards, olive groves, and grain fields in the hills; and fruit and vegetable orchards (extensive orange groves) and rice fields on the coastal plain, where several irrigation canals date from Moorish times. Few, mostly unexploited, mineral resources (lead, coal, barite); clay, limestone, and marble quarries. Besides agr. processing, there is mfg. of textiles, colored tiles and porcelain, cement, soap, and some paper; sericulture; hemp processing. Chief cities: Castellón de la Plana, Villarreal, Burriana, Vinaroz, Benicarló.

Castellón de la Plana, city (pop. 42,324), ⊙ Castellón de la Plana prov., E Spain, in Valencia, 3 mi. from the Mediterranean and 200 mi. ESE of Madrid, on fertile, irrigated plain yielding citrus and other fruit, wine, olive oil, cereals, and rice; 39°59′N 0°2′W. Connected by railroad with its harbor El Grao de Castellón (3 mi. E), exporting oranges, hemp, and colored tiles. Mfg. (cement, sandals, chemical fertilizers, perfumes, soap, textiles, knit goods, headgear, colored tiles). City is entirely modern (remains of anc. settlement near by). Has 17th-cent. town hall, church of Santa María with detached bell tower (1604), and botanical gardens. Conquered from Moors by James I of Aragon (1233). Suffered in the *communeros*' rising (16th cent.) and in Peninsular War (19th cent.). In Sp. civil war, fell to Franco in 1938.

Castellón de Rugat (dhā rōōgät′), village (pop. 1,496), Valencia prov., E Spain, 12 mi. SE of Játiva; olive-oil processing; wine, cereals, melons.

Castellorizo, Greece: see KASTELLORIZO.

Castellote (kästälyō′tā), town (pop. 1,080), Teruel prov., E Spain, near the Guadalope, 20 mi. SSW of Alcañiz; olive-oil processing; wine, apples, livestock. Lignite deposits near by.

Castellserá (kästälsärä′), village (pop. 1,369), Lérida prov., NE Spain, near Urgel Canal, 10 mi. ESE of Balaguer, in well-irrigated area (cereals, olive oil, wine, sugar beets); sheep raising.

Castelltersol (kästältĕrsôl′), town (pop. 1,605), Barcelona prov., NE Spain, 15 mi. ENE of Manresa; textile (cotton, woolen, linen) mfg., meat processing, flour milling, lumbering.

Castelluccio Acqua Borrana, Italy: see CASTELMAURO.

Castelluccio Inferiore (kästĕl-lōōt′chô ēnfĕrēô′rĕ), village (pop. 2,242), Potenza prov., Basilicata, S Italy, 6 mi. S of Latronico; woolen mill. Castelluccio Superiore (pop. 1,515) is just NW.

Castel Madama (kästĕl′ mädä′mä), village (pop. 4,215), Roma prov., Latium, central Italy, 4 mi. ENE of Tivoli. Near by, on Aniene R., is a major hydroelectric plant.

Castel Maggiore (mäd-jô′rĕ), town (pop. 1,450), Bologna prov., Emilia-Romagna, N central Italy, 5 mi. N of Bologna; mill machinery (rice, hemp), electric cranes, cement.

Castelmassa (kästĕlmäs′sä), village (pop. 1,396), Rovigo prov., Veneto, N Italy, on Po R. and 20 mi. NW of Ferrara; mfg. (potato starch, glucose). Formerly Massa Superiore.

Castelmauro (–mou′rô), town (pop. 4,979), Campobasso prov., Abruzzi e Molise, S central Italy, 19 mi. N of Campobasso. Formerly Castelluccio Acqua Borrana.

Castelmoron-sur-Lot (kästĕlmōrō′-sür-lôt′), village (pop. 686), Lot-et-Garonne dept., SW France, on the Lot and 10 mi. W of Villeneuve-sur-Lot; footwear mfg.; vegetable preserving.

Castelmuschio, Yugoslavia: see OMISALJ.

Castelnau or **Castelnau-de-Médoc** (kästĕlnō′-dü-mädôk′), village (pop. 1,085), Gironde dept., SW France, 17 mi. NW of Bordeaux; sawmilling.

Castelnaudary (kästĕlnōdärē′), town (pop. 6,306), Aude dept., S France, on the Canal du Midi and 21 mi. WNW of Carcassonne; road and commercial center (cereals, cattle, wool, wines); flour milling, pottery mfg.

Castelnau-d'Auzan (kästĕlnō′-dōzã′), village (pop. 388), Gers dept., SW France, 14 mi. W of Condom; Armagnac brandy mfg.

Castelnau-de-Médoc, France: see CASTELNAU.

Castelnau-de-Montmiral (–dü-mõmēräl′), village (pop. 369), Tarn dept., S France, 16 mi. W of Albi; winegrowing.

Castelnau-de-Montratier, France: see CASTELNAU-MONTRATIER.

Castelnau-Durban (–dürbã′), village (pop. 384), Ariège dept., S France, 10 mi. E of Saint-Girons; iron mining, marble and construction-material quarrying.

Castelnau-Magnoac (–mänyōäk′), village (pop. 664), Hautes-Pyrénées dept., SW France, on Lannemezan Plateau, 16 mi. SSE of Mirande; cereals, poultry; mule raising.

Castelnau-Montratier (–mõträtyā′), village (pop. 614), Lot dept., SW France, 13 mi. SSW of Cahors; grape growing, wool spinning, livestock raising. Also Castelnau-de-Montratier.

Castelnau-Rivière-Basse (–rēvyâr′-bäs′), village (pop. 302), Hautes-Pyrénées dept., SW France, near Adour R., 24 mi. NNW of Tarbes; winegrowing.

Castelnovo di Sotto (kästĕlnô′vô dē sôt′tô), town (pop. 1,466), Reggio nell'Emilia, N central Italy, 8 mi. NW of Reggio nell'Emilia; wine making.

Castelnovo ne' Monti (nĕmôn′tē), town (pop. 1,343), Reggio nell'Emilia, N central Italy, in Etruscan Apennines, 21 mi. SW of Reggio nell'Emilia; resort (alt. 2,297 ft.); sausage factories.

Castelnuovo, Yugoslavia: see HERCEG NOVI.

Castelnuovo Berardenga (kästĕlnwô′vô bĕrärdĕng′gä), town (pop. 1,132), Siena prov., Tuscany, central Italy, near upper Ombrone R., 9 mi. ENE of Siena; wine, liquor, cement, nails. Lignite mine near by.

Castelnuovo della Daunia (dĕl-lä dou′nyä), town (pop. 3,314), Foggia prov., Apulia, S Italy, 15 mi. SW of San Severo, in cereal-growing, stock-raising region.

Castelnuovo di Garfagnana (dē gärfänyä′nä), town (pop. 3,025), Lucca prov., Tuscany, central Italy, on Serchio R. and 16 mi. E of Carrara; chief center of the Garfagnana; foundry, paper mill; mfg. (briquettes, pumps). Has 16th-cent. cathedral (recently restored) and citadel.

Castelnuovo di Val di Cecina (väl dē chä′chēnä), village (pop. 1,428), Pisa prov., Tuscany, central Italy, 14 mi. S of Volterra. Has *soffioni* (113°F.) used for baths, extraction of boric acid, and producing of electricity. Near by are anc. mines of argentiferous lead, copper, and pyrite.

Castelnuovo di Verona (vĕrô′nä), village (pop. 1,322), Verona prov., Veneto, N Italy, 12 mi. W of Verona; alcohol distillery.

Castelnuovo Rangone (räng-gô′nĕ), village (pop. 107), Modena prov., Emilia-Romagna, N central Italy, 6 mi. S of Modena; sausage factories.

Castelnuovo Scrivia (skrē'vyä), town (pop. 4,232), Alessandria prov., Piedmont, N Italy, on Scrivia R. and 14 mi. ENE of Alessandria; shoes, musical instruments.

Castelo (kŏŏshtä'lŏŏ). **1** Town, Acre territory, Brazil: see MANUEL URBANO. **2** City (pop. 3,474), S central Espírito Santo, Brazil, terminus of rail spur, and 20 mi. N of Cachoeiro de Itapemirim; ships coffee, sugar cane, bananas. **3** City, Piauí, Brazil: see CASTELO DO PIAUÍ.

Castelo Branco (brāng'kŏŏ), district (□ 2,588; pop. 299,670), central Portugal, almost co-extensive with Beira Baixa prov.; ⊙ Castelo Branco. Bounded by Spain (E and SE), the Tagus (S), and Portugal's highest mtn. range (Serra da Estrêla; NW). Drained by right tributaries of the Tagus. Has extensive oak, chestnut, and pine forests. Agr. products are grain, corn, beans, livestock (especially sheep), olives, vinegar, wine. Woolen milling is main industry, concentrated at Covilhã, largest city in dist.

Castelo Branco, city (pop. 9,293), ⊙ Castelo Branco dist. and Beira Baixa prov., central Portugal, near Sp. border, on railroad and 120 mi. NE of Lisbon; agr. trading and processing center (cork, olive oil, cereals, cheese); mfg. of woolen goods (especially heavy blankets), candles, pottery, concrete, and furniture. Founded 1209 by Templars whose ruined castle is preserved. City also has episcopal palace and an archaeological mus.

Castelo de Paiva (dĭ pī'vŭ), town, Aveiro dist., N central Portugal, near the Douro, 20 mi. SE of Oporto; winegrowing.

Castelo de Vide (vē'dĭ), town (pop. 3,630), Portalegre dist., central Portugal, on N slope of Serra de São Mamede, on railroad and 9 mi. N of Portalegre; watering place; mfg. of rubber soles, cork, olive oil; pottery mfg., meat processing. Preserves medieval appearance (14th-cent. castle; old houses).

Castelo do Piauí (dŏŏ pyou-ē'), city (pop. 508), N central Piauí, Brazil, 90 mi. ESE of Teresina; carnauba wax, tiger and jaguar skins. Founded 1761. Until 1944, called Castelo (old spelling Castello), and, 1944–48, Marvão.

Castelo Novo (nō'vŏŏ), village (pop. 1,300), Castelo Branco dist., central Portugal, 18 mi. N of Castelo Branco; wheat, corn, olives. Has medieval watch tower and some 16th-cent. bldgs.

Castelo Point, easternmost point of the Azores, on Santa Maria Isl.; 36°55'N 25°1'W.

Castelo Rodrigo, Portugal: see FIGUEIRA DE CASTELO RODRIGO.

Castelpagano (kästĕl"pägä'nô), village (pop. 2,989), Benevento prov., Campania, S Italy, 14 mi. SE of Campobasso.

Castelraimondo (kästĕlrīmôn'dô), village (pop. 984), Macerata prov., The Marches, central Italy, on Potenza R. and 12 mi. SSE of Fabriano; rail junction; mfg. (cutlery, cement).

Castelrosso, Greece: see KASTELLORIZO.

Castel San Giorgio (kästĕl' sän jôr'jô), village (pop. 1,569), Salerno prov., Campania, S Italy, 8 mi. NNW of Salerno; food cannery.

Castel San Giovanni (jôvän'nē), town (pop. 5,441), Piacenza prov., Emilia-Romagna, N central Italy, near the Po, 12 mi. W of Piacenza, in sugar-beet region; wine, canned tomatoes, buttons; lime- and cementworks.

Castel San Pietro dell'Emilia (pyā'trô dĕlĕmē'lyä), town (pop. 4,135), Bologna prov., Emilia-Romagna, N central Italy, on Sillaro R. and 14 mi. SE of Bologna, at N foot of Etruscan Apennines; health resort (alt. 246 ft.) with mineral waters. Mfg. (agr. machinery, cement, packing boxes, umbrellas, canes).

Castel Sardo (sär'dô), village (pop. 2,692), Sassari prov., N Sardinia, port on Gulf of Asinara, 15 mi. NNE of Sassari. Fishing (tunny, lobster); domestic weaving, pottery making, tanning. Nuraghi found near by.

Castelsarrasin (kästĕlsäräzē'), town (pop. 4,751), Tarn-et-Garonne dept., SW France, on the Garonne Lateral Canal and 12 mi. W of Montauban; cattle market; metalworks, flour mills.

Castelserás (kästālsäräs'), town (pop. 1,414), Teruel prov., E Spain, 5 mi. S of Alcañiz; olive-oil processing; wine, fruit.

Casteltermini (kästĕltĕr'mēnē), town (pop. 11,559), Agrigento prov., SW central Sicily, near Platani R., 16 mi. N of Agrigento; cement, fertilizer. Many sulphur and rock salt mines near by.

Castelvetere, Reggio di Calabria prov., Italy: see CAULONIA.

Castelvetere in Val Fortore (kästĕlvā'tĕrĕ ēn väl fôrtô'rĕ), village (pop. 3,945), Benevento prov., Campania, S Italy, 17 mi. ESE of Campobasso.

Castelvetrano (kästĕl"vĕträ'nô), town (pop. 25,000), Trapani prov., W Sicily, 23 mi. SSW of Alcamo; rail junction; mfg. (Marsala wine; macaroni, furniture). Mus., 12th-cent. Norman church (restored) 2 mi. W.

Castelvetro di Modena (kästvĕlvā'trô dē mô'dĕnä), village (pop. 960), Modena prov., Emilia-Romagna, N central Italy, 10 mi. S of Modena; wine making, cement mfg.

Castelvetro Piacentino (pyächĕntē'nô), village (pop. 907), Piacenza prov., Emilia-Romagna, N central Italy, near the Po, 3 mi. SSW of Cremona; bicycle mfg.

Castel Viscardo (kästĕl' vēskär'dô), village (pop. 1,182), Terni prov., Umbria, central Italy, 7 mi. WNW of Orvieto; cementworks.

Castenaso (kästĕnä'zô), town (pop. 1,459), Bologna prov., Emilia-Romagna, N central Italy, on Idice R. and 5 mi. E of Bologna; pumps, wire, nets, fertilizer.

Castendo (kăshtān'dŏŏ), town (pop. 1,102), Viseu dist., N central Portugal, 12 mi. E of Viseu; rye, wheat, beans, wine, pine woods. Has 18th-cent. palace. Also called Penalva do Castelo.

Castenedolo (kästĕnā'dôlô), town (pop. 3,007), Brescia prov., Lombardy, N Italy, 6 mi. SE of Brescia, in grape-growing and sericulture region; agr. center.

Castéra-Verduzan (kästärä'-vĕrdüzä'), village (pop. 321), Gers dept., SW France, 14 mi. NNW of Auch; hot sulphur springs.

Casterton, town (pop. 2,083), SW Victoria, Australia, on Glenelg R. and 200 mi. W of Melbourne; rail terminus; cattle center; dairy plant.

Casterton, village and parish (pop. 278), S Westmorland, England, on the Lime and 11 mi. SE of Kendal; agr., cattle.

Castets (kästā'). **1** or **Castets-en-Dorthe** (–ā-dôrt'), village (pop. 495), Gironde dept., SW France, on the Garonne at W terminus of Garonne Lateral Canal, and 16 mi. WNW of Marmande; freight transshipments. Vineyards. **2** Village (pop. 773), Landes dept., SW France, 12 mi. NNW of Dax; lumbering, turpentine extracting, winegrowing.

Castex, Argentina: see EDUARDO CASTEX.

Castiglione (kästēlyō'nē), village (pop. 2,064), Alger dept., N central Algeria, small fishing port on the Mediterranean, 5 mi. W of Koléa; sardine canning, truck gardening. Bathing beach.

Castiglione d'Adda (kästēlyô'nĕdäd'dä), village (pop. 4,024), Milano prov., Lombardy, N Italy, near Adda R., 11 mi. SE of Lodi; mfg. (flour, carts, carriages, lace, embroidery).

Castiglione dei Pepoli (dā pä'pôlē), town (pop. 2,149), Bologna prov., Emilia-Romagna, N central Italy, in Etruscan Apennines, 26 mi. SSE of Bologna; resort (alt. 2,267 ft.) with mineral waters.

Castiglione del Lago (dĕl lä'gô), village (pop. 792), Perugia prov., Umbria, central Italy, port on W shore of lake Trasimeno, 17 mi. W of Perugia; resort. Has castle.

Castiglione della Pescaia (dĕl-lä pĕskä'yä), town (pop. 1,813), Grosseto prov., Tuscany, central Italy, port on Tyrrhenian Sea, 12 mi. W of Grosseto, in grape- and olive-growing region; bathing resort.

Castiglione delle Stiviere (dĕl-lĕ stēvyä'rĕ), town (pop. 4,127), Mantova prov., Lombardy, N Italy, 22 mi. NW of Mantua; silk, macaroni. Scene of Napoleon's brilliant victory over Austrians in 1796.

Castiglione di Sicilia (dē sēchē'lyä), village (pop. 5,805), Catania prov., NE Sicily, at NE foot of Mt. Etna, 19 mi. NNW of Acireale, in hazelnut and citrus-fruit region.

Castiglione Messer Marino (mĕs'sĕr märē 'nô), town (pop. 3,423), Chieti prov., Abruzzi e Molise, S central Italy, 27 mi. SSW of Vasto.

Castiglione Olona (ôlō'nä), village (pop. 1,219), Varese prov., Lombardy, N Italy, on Olona R. and 4 mi. SSE of Varese; mfg. (cotton goods, textile machinery, combs).

Castiglion Fibocchi (kästēlyôn' fēbôk'kē), village (pop. 434), Arezzo prov., Tuscany, central Italy, 7 mi. NW of Arezzo; alcohol.

Castiglion Fiorentino (fyôrĕntē'nô), town (pop. 3,076), Arezzo prov., Tuscany, central Italy, 9 mi. S of Arezzo; mfg. (alcohol, sulphur oils, fireworks, wire); lignite mining. Has palace with picture gall. Badly damaged in Second World War.

Castilblanco (kästēlbläng'kō), town (pop. 3,075), Badajoz prov., W Spain, near the upper Guadiana, 8 mi. N of Herrera del Duque; olives, cereals, livestock; flour milling.

Castilblanco de los Arroyos (dhā lōs äroi'ōs), town (pop. 3,661), Seville prov., SW Spain, 19 mi. N of Seville; agr. center (cereals, olives, chick-peas, cork, livestock).

Castile (kăstēl'), Sp. *Castilla* (kästē'lyä), region and former kingdom, N and central Spain, extending now from Bay of Biscay (Atlantic) southward to the Sierra Morena in Andalusia. Though of great physical variety, and far from having a geographic unity, it occupies mostly the great central plateau (Meseta) and has an average alt. of c.2,500 ft. The distinctive Castilian landscape is known for its bleak, monotonous plains, which possess an austere beauty. Its elevated plains are flanked by several ranges, among them the Cantabrian Mts. (N), Sierra de Culebra (NW), Sierra de Gata (W), Serranía de Cuenca (E). Across it NE-SW rise the rugged Sierra de Guadarrama and Sierra de Gredos, forming a natural boundary bet. Old Castile (N) and New Castile (S). The former is watered by the Ebro and Duero (Douro) rivers, the latter by the Tagus and Guadiana rivers. Though the political subdivisions are not clear-cut and have undergone several redefinitions (parts of Leon are in a certain sense typically Castilian), **Old Castile,** Sp. *Castilla la Vieja* (–lä vyā'hä) (□ 19,390; pop. 1,577,135), is generally considered, in modern times, to include the provs. of ÁVILA, BURGOS, LOGROÑO, SANTANDER, SEGOVIA, and SORIA, named after their principal cities; VALLADOLID and PALENCIA, in earlier times part of Castile and sometimes considered to be in Old Castile, are now usually placed in Leon. **New Castile,** Sp. *Castilla la Nueva* (–lä nwā'vä) (□ 27,933; pop. 3,129,170), comprises the provs. and cities of CIUDAD REAL, CUENCA, GUADALAJARA, MADRID, and TOLEDO. Castile has, apart from the N coastal strip, the features of an interior highland, characterized by a rigorous climate of cold, long winters and hot, dry summers. Droughts occur frequently. The entire region suffers from the ill effects of soil erosion and large landholdings. Irrigation, begun by the Moors, has decayed rather than progressed. Cereals, potatoes, olives (in S), and forage are grown widely. The irrigated sections and fertile valleys, particularly in S, produce grapes, saffron, hemp, fruit, and vegetables. Grazing (Merino sheep, goats), however, predominates. Scattered forests yield timber, acorns, and naval stores. Mineral resources include rich mercury mines of Almadén but are, except for some iron, coal, gypsum, and salt deposits, of little economic importance. Of the once famous industries (especially wool and silk textiles) centered in provincial cities, few have survived the expulsion of the Moriscos. Processing industries include flour milling, olive-oil pressing, alcohol and liquor distilling, wine making, meat packing, food canning, tanning. Since late 19th cent., Madrid has made great strides as a mfg. center 2d only to Barcelona. The history of Castile is to a large measure that of Spain. Its name is said to derive from the numerous castles built here by the Christian nobles as outposts against the Moors. Castile was originally a county of the kingdom of Leon, with Burgos as its ⊙. Under Fernán González (10th cent.) it began to expand, and secured virtual independence. Sancho III (el Mayor) of Navarre incorporated Old Castile into his kingdom, which reached to the Sierra de Guadarrama. Castile became an autonomous kingdom in 1035; a 1st union with Leon was effected in 1037, but because of dynastic rivalries the 2 realms were not permanently merged until much later (1230), under Ferdinand III. With conquest of Toledo (1085), former capital of a Moorish kingdom, New Castile evolved. Other territories, gradually wrested from the Moors, were sealed by the conquest of the Catholic Kings, Ferdinand and Isabella, under whose scepter the 2 kingdoms of Aragon and Castile were united. The royal govt. oscillated bet. Burgos, Valladolid, and Toledo, until Philip II moved (1561) the ⊙ permanently to the then obscure Madrid, where it has been ever since, apart from short residence (1601–06) at Valladolid. With a centralized regime at Madrid, Castile became the core of the Sp. monarchy. The Castilian dialect emerged as the literary language of all Spaniards, and has also been accepted—with some modifications—by most of the Latin American countries. The greatest example of Castilian literature is Cervantes' *Don Quixote de la Mancha.*

Castile (kăstīl'), village (pop. 1,072), Wyoming co., W N.Y., 11 mi. SSE of Warsaw; canned foods, textiles; ships dairy products, vegetables, apples. Summer resort. Letchworth State Park is near by.

Castile, Canal of (kăstēl'), in Palencia and Valladolid, N central Spain, starts from Pisuerga R. at Alar del Rey, and, enriched by waters from Carrión R., divides NW of Palencia into 2 branches, one flowing W across Tierra de Campos to Medina de Ríoseco, and one running S to rejoin the Pisuerga at Valladolid. Used mostly for irrigation, little for navigation.

Castilla, province, Peru: see APLAO.

Castilla (kästē'yä), town (pop. 8,892), Piura dept., NW Peru, on coastal plain, on Piura R. opposite Piura; cotton, corn, cattle.

Castilla, Sp. name for CASTILE.

Castilla, Punta, Honduras: see HONDURAS, CAPE.

Castilleja de Guzmán (kästēlyā'hä dhā gōōth-män'), town (pop. 232), Seville prov., SW Spain, 3½ mi. W of Seville; cereals, olives.

Castilleja de la Cuesta (dhā lä kwĕ'stä), town (pop. 3,248), Seville prov., SW Spain, 3 mi. W of Seville; agr. center (grapes, olives, horses, cattle); apiculture; mfg. of carpets, canned vegetables. Situated on elevated plain overlooking Seville. Occupies site of anc. Iberian town later settled by Romans; ruins remain. Cortes died here in 1547. The palace is now occupied by an Irish convent.

Castilleja del Campo (dhĕl käm'pō), town (pop. 681), Seville prov., SW Spain, near Huelva prov. border, 19 mi. W of Seville; olives, cereals, grapes.

Castilléjar (kästēlyā'här), town (pop. 2,111), Granada prov., S Spain, 18 mi. NE of Baza; flour mills; cereals, esparto, vegetables.

Castillejo de Robledo (kästēlyā'hō dhā rōblā'dhō), town (pop. 973), Soria prov., N central Spain, 14 mi. SE of Aranda de Duero; grain, wine.

Castillejos (kästēlyā'hōs), town (pop. 1,631), Yebala territory, NW Sp. Morocco, on the Mediterranean, on railroad and 4 mi. SSW of Ceuta; vegetable-fiber processing, pottery mfg.

Castilletes (kästīyā'tēs), village, Guajira commissary, N Colombia, on Gulf of Venezuela, at Venezuela border, 85 mi. N of Maracaibo; saltworks. Pearl banks near by.

Castillo (kästē'yō), town (1950 pop. 1,381), Duarte prov., E central Dominican Republic, in La Vega Real valley, 16 mi. ESE of San Francisco de Macorís; cacao, coffee, rice, corn.
Castillo, El, Nicaragua: see EL CASTILLO.
Castillo, Pampa de (päm'pä dā kästē'yō), arid Patagonian plateau in E Comodoro Rivadavia military zone, Argentina, S and E of L. Colhué Huapí; extends c.90 mi. SW (c.20 mi. wide) from Pico Salamanca to Colonia Las Heras. Oil-producing and sheep-raising region.
Castillo de Bayuela (kästē'lyō dhā bīwā'lä), town (pop. 1,694), Toledo prov., central Spain, 11 mi. NE of Talavera de la Reina; grapes, olives, garlic, bitter almonds. Liquor distilling, wine making, olive-oil pressing, flour milling.
Castillo de Garcimuñoz (gär-thēmōō'nyōth), town (pop. 1,206), Cuenca prov., E central Spain, 31 mi. SSW of Cuenca; olives, saffron, cereals, grapes. Has old castle. Near by is small lake Pozo Airón.
Castillo de las Guardas, El (läs gwär'dhäs), town (pop. 1,631), Seville prov., SW Spain, 27 mi. NW of Seville; cereals, olives, cork, acorns, timber, livestock.
Castillo de Locubín (lōkōōvēn'), city (pop. 5,447), Jaén prov., S Spain, 20 mi. SW of Jaén; olive-oil processing, flour milling, soap and plaster mfg.; cereals and fruit.
Castillo de San Marcos National Monument, Fla.: see SAINT AUGUSTINE.
Castillo de Teayo (kästē'yō dā tyī'ō), town (pop. 955), Veracruz, E Mexico, 20 mi. SW of Tuxpan, in agr. region (corn, sugar cane, tropical fruit, fiber plants).
Castillon (kästēyō'). **1** Agr. village (pop. 561), Ariège dept., S France, in central Pyrenees, on the Lez (small tributary of Salat R.) and 7 mi. SW of Saint-Girons; dairying. Winter sports. **2** Village (pop. 24), Basses-Alpes dept., SE France, on Verdon R. and 3 mi. NNE of Castellane. Hydroelectric dam (325 ft. high). **3** or **Castillon-et-Capitourlan** (-ā-käpētōōrlā'), town (pop. 2,731), Gironde dept., SW France, port on Dordogne R. and 11 mi. ESE of Libourne; wine and liqueur trade; fertilizer mfg. Scene of English defeat (1453) in final battle of Hundred Years War.
Castillonnès (kästēyônĕs'), village (pop. 935), Lot-et-Garonne dept., SW France, near Dropt R., 14 mi. SSE of Bergerac; poultry, plums, vegetables. A medieval stronghold (founded 1260).
Castillos or **San Vicente de Castillos** (sän vēsĕn'tā dā kästē'yōs), town (pop. 2,500), Rocha dept., SE Uruguay, on highway, and 35 mi. NE of Rocha; stock-raising center (cattle, sheep).
Castillos, Lake, fresh-water lagoon (□ c.30), Rocha dept., SE Uruguay, 7 mi. S of Castillos, near the Atlantic (linked by short channel).
Castine (kăstēn'). **1** Resort town (pop. 793), Hancock co., S Maine, on peninsula in Penobscot Bay opposite Belfast. Has state normal school, a mus., Fort Madison (1811; rebuilt in Civil War), Fort George (1779; British-built), Maine Maritime Acad. Plymouth Colony trading post near by, 1626; early French mission here; town changed hands several times among French, British, Dutch, and Americans. British held it in Revolution and in War of 1812. Named for Baron St. Castin or Castine, who settled here 1667; inc. 1796. **2** Village (pop. 146), Darke co., W Ohio, 12 mi. S of Greenville, in agr. area.
Castiñeiras (kästēnyā'räs), small port (pop. 1,210), La Coruña prov., NW Spain, on Arosa Bay of the Atlantic, 33 mi. SW of Santiago; fishing, lumbering, stock raising; vineyards.
Castle, town (pop. 144), Okfuskee co., central Okla., 25 mi. WSW of Okmulgee; cotton ginning.
Castle Air Force Base, Calif.: see MERCED, city.
Castlebar (kă"sŭlbär'), Gaelic *Caisleán an Bharraigh,* urban district (pop. 4,951), ⊙ Co. Mayo, Ireland, in central part of co., on Castlebar R. at E end of Castlebar or Lanagh Lough (3 mi. long), 140 mi. WNW of Dublin; agr. market in cattle-raising, potato-growing region. Sir Henry Bingham here surrendered (1641) to Irish Confederates under earl of Mayo; and French forces under General Humbert here defeated (1798) General Lake's troops in battle known as "Castlebar Races."
Castlebar River, Co. Mayo, Ireland, issues from E end of Castlebar Lough at Castlebar, flows 15 mi. NW to Lough Cullin.
Castlebay, Scotland: see BARRA.
Castlebellingham (kă"sŭlbĕ'lĭng-ŭm), Gaelic *Baile an Ghearlánaigh,* town (pop. 275), E Co. Louth, Ireland, on Dee R., near its mouth on Dundalk Bay, 8 mi. S of Dundalk; agr. market (wheat, barley, potatoes; cattle).
Castleberry. 1 Town (pop. 667), Conecuh co., S Ala., 32 mi. W of Andalusia; strawberry market. **2** City, Tarrant co., Texas: see RIVER OAKS.
Castleblakeney (kă"sŭlblāk'nē), Gaelic *Gallach Uí Cheallaigh,* agr. village, E Co. Galway, Ireland, 13 mi. NW of Ballinasloe; sheep; potatoes, beets.
Castleblayney (kă"sŭlblā'nē), Gaelic *Caisleán Mathghamhnach,* urban district (pop. 1,769), E Co. Monaghan, Ireland, on Fane R., on W shore of Lough Muckno, and 13 mi. SE of Monaghan; frontier station near border of Northern Ireland; linen milling; agr. market (flax, oats, potatoes).
Castle Bolton, agr. village and parish (pop. 121), North Riding, NW Yorkshire, England, 10 mi. SW of Richmond; site of 14th-cent. castle where Mary Queen of Scots was imprisoned, 1568–69.
Castle Bromwich (brŭ'mĭj), town and parish (pop. 678), N Warwick, England, 5 mi. ENE of Birmingham; machinery and soap industry. Site of annual British Industries Fair. Has church dating from 15th cent. In parish (NNW) is fruit-packing village of Tyburn.
Castle Bytham, agr. village and parish (pop. 490), Parts of Kesteven, SW Lincolnshire, England, 7 mi. W of Bourne; limestone quarries. Has church of Norman origin and remains of Norman castle, destroyed in Wars of the Roses.
Castle Carrock, village and parish (pop. 305), NE Cumberland, England, 9 mi. E of Carlisle; cattle, sheep, oats. Site of Carlisle reservoir and of excavations of early pit dwellings.
Castle Cary (kâ'rē), town and parish (pop. 1,664), E Somerset, England, 7 mi. S of Shepton Mallet; agr. market in dairying and flax-growing region; hemp and twine mfg.
Castlecary, agr. village, SE Stirling, Scotland, 7 mi. WSW of Falkirk. It is reputedly the anc. *Coria Damniorum,* important station on Wall of Antoninus. There is an old castle.
Castlecaulfield (kă"sŭlkô'fēld), agr. village (district pop. 1,218), SE Co. Tyrone, Northern Ireland, 3 mi. W of Dungannon; potatoes, flax, oats; cattle. Has ruins of Jacobean mansion, built on site of castle of the Donnellys, burned 1642.
Castlecomer (kă"sŭlkō'mŭr), Gaelic *Caisleán an Chumair,* town (pop. 718), N Co. Kilkenny, Ireland, 12 mi. WSW of Carlow; coal-mining center.
Castleconnell, Gaelic *Caisleán O gConaing,* town (pop. 245), NE Co. Limerick, Ireland, on the Shannon and 7 mi. NE of Limerick; salmon-fishing center. On isolated rock are remains of anc. castle of the O'Briens, kings of Thomond.
Castle Crags, Shasta co., N Calif., group of granite pinnacles (up to 6,000 ft.) in Klamath Mts., just S of Dunsmuir. State park here (□ c.50; campgrounds) is traversed by Sacramento R.
Castle Creek, S.Dak.: see RAPID CREEK.
Castle Dale, city (pop. 715), ⊙ Emery co., central Utah, on headstream of San Rafael R. and 30 mi. SSW of Price, in agr. area (fruit, grain); alt. 5,771 ft.; flour milling. Coal mines in vicinity. Deposits of radioactive ores near by.
Castledermot (kă"sŭldŭr'mŭt), Gaelic *Díseart Diarmada,* town (pop. 408), S Co. Kildare, Ireland, 6 mi. NE of Carlow; agr. market (cattle, horses; potatoes). Anc. residence of kings of Leinster, it has early-10th-cent. round tower, remains of Franciscan church (founded 1202), tower of Crutched Friary (dating from c.1200), and 2 sculptured crosses. St. Diarmuid founded monastery c.800; in 1182 Walter de Ridlesford founded a castle here. Town was scene of defeat (1316) of Edward Bruce by Sir Edmund Butler, and a Parliament was held here 1499. In vicinity are many monastic and castle ruins.
Castle Dome Mountains, Yuma co., SW Ariz., extend c.30 mi. S from Kofa Mts.; rise to 3,793 ft. in Castle Dome Peak, c.40 mi. NE of Yuma.
Castle Donington (dŏ'nĭngtŭn), town and parish (pop. 806), N Leicester, England, near Trent R., 7 mi. NW of Loughborough; hosiery industry. Has church begun c.1200 and some remains of Norman castle. Scene of automobile racing event.
Castle Dore, England: see FOWEY.
Castle Douglas, burgh (1931 pop. 3,008; 1951 census 3,322), S Kirkcudbright, Scotland, on Carlingwark Loch and 9 mi. NE of Kirkcudbright; agr. market, with agr. implement works. Just W, on isl. in Dee R., is 14th-cent. Threave Castle, stronghold of Douglas family.
Castlefin or **Castlefinn** (both: kă"sŭlfĭn'), Gaelic *Caisleán na Finne,* town (pop. 338), E Co. Donegal, Ireland, on Finn R. and 5 mi. WSW of Lifford; shirt mfg., flax scutching.
Castleford, urban district (1931 pop. 21,784; 1951 census 43,116), West Riding, S central Yorkshire, England, on Aire R. at mouth of Calder R., and 10 mi. ESE of Leeds; coal mining, metal casting; mfg. of bottles, pottery, machinery, chemicals for textile industry. Site of a Roman station.
Castle Gap, Texas: see CASTLE MOUNTAIN.
Castlegar, village (pop. estimate 350), S B.C., on Columbia R., near mouth of Kootenay R., and 16 mi. N of Trail, in mining (gold, silver, lead, zinc) and lumbering region.
Castle Gate, town (pop. 701), Carbon co., central Utah, 10 mi. NNW of Price and on Price R.; coal mines.
Castlegregory (kă"sŭlgrĕ'gŭrē), Gaelic *Caisleán Ghriaghaire,* town (pop. 294), W Co. Kerry, Ireland, on Tralee Bay, 14 mi. W of Tralee; fishing port, seaside resort.
Castle Gresley (grĕz'lē), town and parish (pop. 1,453), S Derby, England, 4 mi. SE of Burton-on-Trent; metalworking.
Castle Harbour, sheltered inlet (2½ mi. long, 2 mi. wide) of E Bermuda, bet. St. David's Isl. and Bermuda Isl., which are joined by causeway (N); entrance in S.
Castle Hayne (kă'sŭl hān'), village (1940 pop. 513), New Hanover co., SE N.C., 9 mi. NNE of Wilmington, near Northeast Cape Fear R.; truck, fruit, flowers.
Castle Heights, village (1940 pop. 319), McLennan co., E central Texas, S suburb of Waco.
Castle Hill. 1 Town (pop. 425), Black Hawk co., E central Iowa, just NW of Waterloo. **2** Town (pop. 581), Aroostook co., E Maine, 9 mi. W of Presque Isle, in agr., lumbering area.
Castleisland (kă'sŭl-ī'lŭnd), Gaelic *Oileán Ciarraighe,* town (pop. 1,427), E central Co. Kerry, Ireland, at foot of the Glanruddery Mts., 11 mi. ESE of Tralee; agr. market (grain, potatoes); dairying. Has ruins of anc. castle.
Castle Island, islet (1 mi. long) in Roaringwater Bay, SW Co. Cork, Ireland, 10 mi. WSW of Skibbereen.
Castle Island. 1 In Buteshire, Scotland: see LITTLE CUMBRAE. **2** In Kinross, Scotland: see LEVEN, LOCH.
Castle Island, E Mass., tip of a peninsula extending into Boston Bay in S.Boston. Recreational park; site of old Fort Independence, pre-Revolutionary fortification.
Castlelyons (kă"sŭl-lī'ŭnz), Gaelic *Caisleán Ua Liatháin,* town (pop. 111), E Co. Cork, Ireland, 4 mi. SSE of Fermoy; agr. market (dairying; oats, potatoes).
Castlemaine (kă"sŭlmān'), municipality (pop. 5,809), central Victoria, Australia, 65 mi. NW of Melbourne; rail junction; mfg. center; woolen and knitting mills, iron foundry. Art gall. Gold mines in vicinity; gold discovered here 1851.
Castlemaine, Gaelic *Caisleán na Mainge,* agr. village, central Co. Kerry, Ireland, on Maine R. and 7 mi. S of Tralee; dairying; potatoes, grain.
Castlemartyr (kă"sŭlmär'tŭr), Gaelic *Baile na Martra,* village (pop. 278), E Co. Cork, Ireland, 9 mi. WSW of Youghal; agr. market (dairying, cattle raising; oats, potatoes, beets). Henry Boyle, 1st earl of Shannon, and Roger Boyle, 1st earl of Orrery, b. here.
Castle Mountain, Alta.: see EISENHOWER, MOUNT.
Castle Mountain (7,326 ft.), on Alaska-B.C. border, in Coast Range, 30 mi. E of Petersburg; 56°52'N 132°7'W.
Castle Mountain (c.3,154 ft.), W Texas, near Pecos R., 6 mi. SSE of Crane. Gave its name to Castle Gap, adjacent pass used by westbound pioneers, which was scene of Indian and outlaw attacks.
Castle Peak (10,514 ft.), S Alaska, in Wrangell Mts., 100 mi. ENE of Valdez; 61°35'N 143°26'W.
Castle Peak. 1 Peak (9,038 ft.) in Nevada co., E Calif., a summit of the Sierra Nevada, 10 mi. WNW of Truckee, near Donner Pass. **2** Peak in Colo.: see CARBON, MOUNT. **3** Peak (11,820 ft.) in Sawtooth Mts., S central Idaho, c.40 mi. NNW of Hailey.
Castle Pinckney National Monument (3.5 acres), fortification on small isl. in harbor of Charleston, S.C. Built (1797) in anticipation of war with France. Seized by S.C. militia (1860); held by Confederates until 1865. Made a natl. monument in 1924.
Castlepoint, New Zealand: see TINUI.
Castle Point, N.Y.: see BEACON.
Castlepollard (kă"sŭlpŏ'lŭrd), Gaelic *Cionn Torc,* town (pop. 434), N Co. Westmeath, Ireland, 11 mi. N of Mullingar; agr. market (cattle; potatoes).
Castlerea or **Castlereagh** (both: kă"sŭlrā'), Gaelic *Caisleán Riabhach,* town (pop. 1,244), W Co. Roscommon, Ireland, on Suck R. and 15 mi. NW of Roscommon; agr. market (cattle, sheep; potatoes).
Castlereagh (kă"sŭlrā'), municipality (pop. 1,310), E New South Wales, Australia, 34 mi. WNW of Sydney, near Penrith; coal-mining center.
Castlereagh, Ireland: see CASTLEREA.
Castlereagh River, central New South Wales, Australia, rises in Liverpool Range, flows 341 mi. SW and NNW, past Coonabarabran, Gilgandra, and Coonamble, to Darling or Barwon R. 30 mi. W of Walgett. Drains sheep-raising area.
Castlerigg Saint John's and Wythburn (wĭdh'bŭrn, wī'-), parish (pop. 695), S central Cumberland, England, just S of Keswick.
Castle Rising, agr. village and parish (pop. 270), NW Norfolk, England, near The Wash, 4 mi. NE of King's Lynn. Formerly a seaport and market center, no longer on receding coast line. Has Norman church and ruins of Norman castle.
Castle Rock. 1 Town (pop. 741), ⊙ Douglas co., central Colo., on Plum Creek and 25 mi. SSE of Denver; alt. 6,000 ft. Dairy and poultry products, livestock, grain. Named for curiously eroded stone formation that served as pioneer landmark. **2** Town (pop. 1,255), Cowlitz co., SW Wash., 10 mi. N of Kelso and on Cowlitz R.; trade center for agr. region; livestock, dairy products, truck; alunite clay mining (for Longview aluminum plant); logging, wood products. Inc. 1890.
Castle Semple Loch, Scotland: see LOCHWINNOCH.
Castle Shannon, borough (pop. 5,459), Allegheny co., SW Pa., S suburb of Pittsburgh. Inc. 1919.
Castleton, village (pop. estimate 500), SE Ont., 28 mi. W of Belleville; dairying, fruitgrowing.
Castleton. 1 Village and parish (pop. 620), in The Peak, N Derby, England, 8 mi. NE of Buxton; lead and fluorspar mining. Near by is the Castle of

the Peak, or Peveril Castle, built by William Peveril, natural son of William the Conqueror; locale of Scott's *Peveril of the Peak*. Has Norman church with old library. Near by are Peak Cavern, Speedwell Mine, and Blue John Mine (in which fluospar is found), and other caverns. **2** Town, Lancashire, England: see ROCHDALE.

Castleton or **Castleton Gardens,** resort in St. Mary parish, E central Jamaica, 15 mi. N of Kingston; known for its tropical vegetation and lily pond.

Castleton, Scotland: see NEWCASTLETON.

Castleton. 1 Town (pop. 268), Marion co., central Ind., 10 mi. NE of Indianapolis. **2** Town (pop. 1,748), Rutland co., W Vt., 10 mi. W of Rutland, in L. Bomoseen summer resort area; lumber; fruit; slate quarries at Hydeville village. State normal school. Ethan Allen and Seth Warner met here (1775) to plan Ticonderoga attack. Chartered 1761, settled 1770.

Castleton Corners, SE N.Y., a section of Richmond borough of New York city, on N Staten Isl.

Castleton of Braemar, Scotland: see BRAEMAR.

Castleton-on-Hudson, village (pop. 1,751), Rensselaer co., E N.Y., on E bank of the Hudson and 9 mi. S of Albany; paper boxes. Settled by the Dutch c.1630; inc. 1827.

Castleton River, W Vt., rises W of Proctor, flows c.20 mi. S and W to Poultney R. near Fair Haven.

Castletown. 1 Town in Hylton parish (1931 pop. 3,041), NE Durham, England, on Wear R. and 2 mi. W of Sunderland; paper milling, ironworking. **2** Town district (1939 pop. 1,742), on S coast of Isle of Man, England, 9 mi. SW of Douglas; port and agr. market. Has 14th-cent. castle; King William's Col. was founded 1643. Town is of anc. origin and was formerly ⊙ Isle of Man.

Castletown, village, N Caithness, Scotland, on Dunnet Bay, 5 mi. E of Thurso; agr. market, with flagstone quarrying; seaside resort. Airfield.

Castletown Bere, Castletown Berehaven, or **Castletown Bearhaven** (kă'sůltůn bâr'; bâr'hāvůn), Gaelic *Baile Chaisleáin Bhéarra,* town (pop. 648), SW Co. Cork, Ireland, on N shore of Bantry Bay, at foot of Slieve Miskish mts., 20 mi. W of Bantry; fishing port. Barite mines near by. Port is protected by Bear Isl. Near-by Dunboy Castle was stronghold of the O'Sullivan Bere.

Castletown River, Ireland, rises near Newtown Hamilton, Co. Armagh, flows 25 mi. S and SE into Co. Louth, past Dundalk, to Dundalk Bay.

Castletownsend, Ireland: see CASTLETOWNSHEND.

Castletownshend or **Castletownsend** (both: kă″sůltoun'zůnd), Gaelic *Baile an Chaisleáin,* town (pop. 162), SW Co. Cork, Ireland, on the Atlantic, 4 mi. ESE of Skibbereen; fishing port.

Castlewellan (kă'sůlwě'lůn), town (pop. 1,660), S central Co. Down, Northern Ireland, 10 mi. SW of Downpatrick; agr. market (flax, oats). Just WNW is small Castlewellan Lough.

Castlewood, city (pop. 498), Hamlin co., E S.Dak., 13 mi. S of Watertown and on Big Sioux R.

Castor, town (pop. 647), SE Alta., 115 mi. SE of Edmonton; coal mining, oil drilling, flour milling, dairying, grain.

Castor, agr. village and parish (pop. 547) in the Soke of Peterborough, NE Northampton, England, 4 mi. W of Peterborough. On the Roman Ermine Street, it is thought to be the site of the Roman settlement *Durobrivae.* Has Norman church, with remains of 7th-cent. chapel.

Castor, village (pop. 171), Bienville parish, NW La., on Black Bayou and 37 mi. SE of Shreveport, in agr. area.

Castor, Bayou (bī'ō), N central La., rises in Jackson parish, flows SE and S c.65 mi., joining Dugdemona R. to form Little R. just above Rochelle.

Castorland (kă'stůrlănd″), village (pop. 308), Lewis co., N central N.Y., on Black R. and 21 mi. ESE of Watertown; paper products.

Castor River, SE Mo., rises in Ste. Genevieve co., flows c.100 mi. S and SE to the Mississippi floodplain drainage system in New Madrid co.

Castra Batava, Germany: see PASSAU.

Castra Caecilia, Spain: see CÁCERES, city.

Castra Regina, Germany: see REGENSBURG.

Castres (kä'strů), town (pop. 24,489), Tarn dept., S France, on Agout R. and 23 mi. SSE of Albi; textile mfg. center (woolen cloth, rayon, hosiery); furniture factories, foundries (textile machinery and tools), breweries. Mfg. of custom jewelry and leather belts, tanning. The cloth industry dates back to 14th cent. Protestant stronghold during 17th cent. Was ⊙ Tarn dept. 1790–1800 and long its largest town.

Castri, in Greek names: see KASTRI.

Castricum or **Kastrikum** (kä'strĭkům), village (pop. 5,532), North Holland prov., NW Netherlands, 16 mi. NW of Amsterdam, near North Sea. Has large lunatic asylum. Scene (1799) of Fr. victory over British.

Castries (kästrē'), village (pop. 1,010), Hérault dept., S France, 7 mi. NE of Montpellier; winegrowing. Has 17th-cent. castle.

Castries (kä'strēs, kästrē'), town (pop. 7,146; with environs 16,579), ⊙ SAINT LUCIA, Windward Isls., B.W.I., port on isl.'s NW coast, 40 mi. S of Fort-de-France, Martinique, and 440 mi. SE of San Juan, Puerto Rico; 14°1'N 60°59'W. Has excellent landlocked harbor; coaling station with modern docking facilities. Exports isl.'s products (sugar cane, rum, molasses, cacao, coconuts, copra, lime, lime juice, essential oils, bay rum, tropical fruits and vegetables). Processing of limes, sugar, rum, bay oil. Botanic station. Across narrow neck of land is popular Vigie Beach, a 3-mi. stretch of white sand. The town was largely destroyed by 1948 fire. Sometimes Port Castries.

Castrignano del Capo (kästrēnyä'nô děl kä'pô), village (pop. 2,890), Lecce prov., Apulia, S Italy, 25 mi. SE of Gallipoli.

Castril (kästrēl'), town (pop. 1,841), Granada prov., S Spain, 20 mi. N of Baza; flour milling; sheep raising; cereals.

Castro (kä'strōō), city (pop. 5,796), E central Paraná, Brazil, at SW foot of Serra Paranapiacaba, on railroad and 22 mi. NNE of Ponta Grossa; agr. trade center (maté, wine, cereals, jerked beef); sawmilling. Marble and clay quarries near by.

Castro (kä'strō), town (pop. 4,781), ⊙ Castro dept. (□ 2,123; pop. 51,867), Chiloé prov., S Chile, on E coast of Chiloé Isl., 45 mi. S of Ancud, at terminus of narrow-gauge railroad; 42°29'S 73°47'W. Port, trade and agr. center (potatoes, wheat, livestock). Ships potatoes and timber to mainland. Has sawmills and textile industry. Founded 1567, the town was sacked by Dutch pirates in 17th cent. and destroyed 1837 by earthquake.

Castro, Greece: see KASTRON.

Castro (käs'trô), village (pop. 1,286), Bergamo prov., Lombardy, N Italy, on NW shore of Lago d'Iseo, 1 mi. S of Lovere; ironworks, textiles.

Castro (kă'strō), county (□ 876; pop. 5,417), NW Texas; ⊙ Dimmitt. On Llano Estacado; alt. 3,500–4,000 ft.; cattle, wheat, grain sorghums; also irrigated agr. (cotton, potatoes, sugar beets, truck); some sheep, poultry. Organized 1891.

Castro Alves (kä'strōō äl'vĭs), city (pop. 7,208), E Bahia, Brazil, on railroad and 70 mi. WNW of Salvador; ships tobacco, corn, manioc. Graphite and rose-quartz deposits.

Castro Barros, Argentina: see AMINGA.

Castrocalbón (kästrōkälvōn'), town (pop. 1,269), Leon prov., NW Spain, 18 mi. SSE of Astorga; cereals, fruit, flax, lumber, livestock.

Castrocaro (käs″trōkä'rô), village, Forlì prov., Emilia-Romagna, N central Italy, on Montone R. and 6 mi. SSW of Forlì; health resort, noted for mineral waters and their salts, which are exported; macaroni mfg.

Castrocielo (käs″trôchā'lô), village (pop. 814), Frosinone prov., Latium, S central Italy, 19 mi. ESE of Frosinone; asphalt mining.

Castro Daire (käsh'trōō dī'rĭ), town (pop. 1,028), Viseu dist., N Portugal, 16 mi. N of Viseu; produces wax candles; wine, olives, rye.

Castro dei Volsci (kä'strô dā vôl'shē), village (pop. 789), Frosinone prov., Latium, S central Italy, 10 mi. SSE of Frosinone; asphalt mining.

Castro del Río (kä'strō dhěl rē'ō), town (pop. 15,916), Córdoba prov., S Spain, in Andalusia, agr. trade center on the Guadajoz and 20 mi. SE of Cordoba; olive-oil processing, flour- and sawmilling; mfg. of woolen cloth, soap, chocolate, plaster. Livestock market; cereals, vegetables, fruit, wine. Lumbering. Has remains of Moorish fortifications, and 15th-cent. parochial church.

Castrofilippo (kä″strôfēlēp'pô), village (pop. 4,377), Agrigento prov., S Sicily, 5 mi. W of Canicattì.

Castrogeriz or **Castrojeriz** (both: kästrōhārēth'), town (pop. 1,644), Burgos prov., N Spain, 23 mi. W of Burgos; cereals, vegetables, livestock. Sawmilling; mfg. of tiles, chocolate. Near by are ruins of anc. castle and fortress ascribed to Caesar. Fine parochial church. During 16th cent. town was residence of Castilian Council.

Castrogiovanni, Sicily: see ENNA, city.

Castrojeriz, Spain: see CASTROGERIZ.

Castro Marim (käsh'trōō mărēm'), town (pop. 1,373), Faro dist., S Portugal, near Spanish border, 2 mi. NNW of Vila Real de Santo António; fish canning. Its castle, built by Alfonso III, is a natl. monument.

Castronuño (kästrōnōō'nyō), town (pop. 2,332), Valladolid prov., N central Spain, on the Duero and 12 mi. SE of Toro; agr. trade (cereals, vegetables, fruit, wine); sheep raising.

Castronuovo or **Castronuovo di Sicilia** (kä″strônwô'vô dē sēchē'lyä), village (pop. 2,262), Palermo prov., central Sicily, near Platani R., 22 mi. S of Termini Imerese; marble quarries.

Castropignano (kä″strôpēnyä'nô), town (pop. 1,871), Campobasso prov., Abruzzi e Molise, S central Italy, near Biferno R., 7 mi. WNW of Campobasso.

Castropol (kästrōpōl'), town (pop. 611), Oviedo prov., NW Spain, on Eo R. estuary, opposite Ribadeo, 2 mi. from Bay of Biscay; cereals, cattle. Iron mines near by.

Castrop-Rauxel (käs'trôp-rouk'sůl), city (1950 pop. 69,547), in former Prussian prov. of Westphalia, W Germany, after 1945 in North Rhine-Westphalia, in the Ruhr, on Rhine-Herne (N) and Dortmund-Ems (E) canals, adjoining Bochum (SW) and Dortmund (S,E); coal-mining center; chemicals (gasoline, tar products, nitrates). Other mfg.: textiles, concrete, cigarettes, liqueur. Brickworks, sawmills. Distilling. Handicrafts industry. Has Renaissance castle. Formed 1926 through incorporation of Castrop or Kastrop (chartered 1484) and neighboring towns, including Rauxel.

Castroreale (kä″strôrěä'lě), village (pop. 1,695) and commune (pop. 9,044), Messina prov., NE Sicily, in Peloritani Mts., 20 mi. SW of Messina, in grape- and olive-growing region. Health resort (hot sulphur baths 3 mi. NW, at Castroreale Bagni). Kaolin-extraction plant in commune.

Castro Urdiales (kä'strō ōōr-dhyä'lěs), city (pop. 6,181, commune pop. 11,963), Santander prov., N Spain, in Old Castile, fishing and iron-shipping port on Bay of Biscay, 18 mi. NW of Bilbao; fish processing, *chacolí*-wine distilling, sawmilling. Cereals, apples, lumber, cattle in area. Bathing resort. Iron mines in vicinity. Has collegiate church and medieval mansions. Was Roman colony; had active trade in wheat and wool with Flanders in Middle Ages. Destroyed 1813 by French, was soon rebuilt.

Castro Valley (kă'strō), village (1940 pop. 4,145), Alameda co., W Calif., 2 mi. NE of Hayward; poultry, fruit.

Castro Verde (käsh'trōō věr'dĭ), town (pop. 2,792), Beja dist., S Portugal, 25 mi. SSW of Beja; cheese mfg. center.

Castroverde de Campos (kästrōvěr'dhā dhā käm'pōs), town (pop. 1,638), Zamora prov., NW Spain, on Valderaduey R. and 16 mi. WNW of Medina de Ríoseco; cereals, wine. Has 13th-cent. church.

Castrovillari (kä″strôvēl'lärē), town (pop. 10,508), Cosenza prov., Calabria, S Italy, at S foot of Pollino mts., near Coscile R., 36 mi. N of Cosenza. Commercial center; cereals, raw silk, wine, olive oil; mfg. (agr. tools, wagons, bricks). Has anc. Norman castle.

Castroville (kă'strůvĭl). **1** Village (pop. 1,865), Monterey co., W Calif., near Monterey Bay, 8 mi. NW of Salinas. **2** Village (pop. 985), Medina co., SW Texas, on Medina R. and 24 mi. W of San Antonio; market point in irrigated farm area. Settled 1844 by Alsatians and others, under Henry Castro; European influence is still evident in bldgs. and customs.

Castrovirreyna or **Castrovirreina** (kästrōvērā'nä), city (pop. 947), ⊙ Castrovirreyna prov. (□ 3,429; pop. 46,460), Huancavelica dept., S central Peru, in Cordillera Occidental, 38 mi. SSW of Huancavelica. Ore-concentrating mill; silver and lead mining; grain, alfalfa, tubers; cattle, sheep. Prov. ⊙ was moved here 1942 from Huaitará.

Castrum Peregrinorum, Palestine: see ATLIT.

Castua, Yugoslavia: see KASTAV.

Castuera (kästwä'rä), town (pop. 8,945), Badajoz prov., W Spain, in Estremadura, on La Serena plateau, 80 mi. E of Badajoz; processing and agr. center (wheat, barley, olives, oranges, acorns, livestock). Tanning, flour milling, olive-oil extracting; mfg. of pottery, ceramics, woolen goods, esparto products, soap, toys, bags. Copper, iron, and lead deposits near by.

Casuarinas, Las, Argentina: see LAS CASUARINAS.

Casupá (käsōōpä'), town (pop. 1,350), Florida dept., S central Uruguay, on railroad and 60 mi. NNE of Montevideo; trade center; wheat, corn, cattle, sheep.

Casupá, Arroyo (äroi'ō), river, S central Uruguay, rises in the Cuchilla Grande Principal 14 mi. WNW of Cerro Colorado, flows 55 mi. SW to Santa Lucía R. 6 mi. E of Fray Marcos.

Caswell (kăz'wůl), county (□ 435; pop. 20,870), N N.C.; ⊙ Yanceyville. In piedmont region; bounded N by Va.; drained by Dan R. and its tributary. Agr. (tobacco, corn, wheat, hay), timber (pine, oak); sawmilling. Formed 1777.

Caswell (kăz'wěl), plantation (pop. 687), Aroostook co., NE Maine, 9 mi. NE of Caribou, on N.B. line; produces lime.

Catacamas (kätäkä'mäs), city (pop. 2,039), Olancho dept., E central Honduras, in Olancho Valley, at S foot of Sierra de Agalta, on left affluent of Guayape R. and 26 mi. NE of Juticalpa; commercial center in livestock area; dairying (mainly cheese making); straw-hat mfg.; coffee, tobacco, rice. Airfield. Became city in 1898. Large model agr. settlement founded near by, c.1950.

Catacaos (kätäkä'ōs), city (pop. 8,526), Piura dept., NW Peru, on coastal plain, on Piura R. and 6 mi. SSW of Piura (connected by tramway), in irrigated cotton area; cotton gins; mfg. of Panama hats.

Catacocha (kätäkō'chä), town (1950 pop. 2,754), Loja prov., S Ecuador, in the Andes, 30 mi. W of Loja; cereals, potatoes, coffee, fruit, livestock.

Catacombs Mountain (10,800 ft.), W Alta., near B.C. border, in Rocky Mts., in Jasper Natl. Park, 35 mi. SSE of Jasper; 52°26'N 117°45'W.

Catadau (kätä-dhou'), town (pop. 1,783), Valencia prov., E Spain, 12 mi. NW of Alcira; shipping of oranges; olive oil, muscat grapes, truck produce.

Catadupa (kătůdū'pů,–dōō'pů), town (pop. 1,060), St. James parish, W Jamaica, on Kingston–Montego Bay RR and 15 mi. SSE of Montego Bay; banana growing.

Cataguases or **Cataguazes** (kätägwä'zĭs), city (pop. 8,972), SE Minas Gerais, Brazil, on Pomba R. and 50 mi. NE of Juiz de Fora; rail junction; prosperous agr.-processing center (coffee, sugar, cotton, cereals); textile milling. Kaolin and mica deposits.

Catahoula (kă'tủhōō'lů), parish (□ 732; pop. 11,834), E La.; ⊙ Harrisonburg. Bounded E by Black and Tensas rivers, S by Red R. and Big Saline Bayou; intersected by Ouachita and Little rivers; drained by Boeuf R. Includes L. Larto. Agr. area (cotton, corn, hay, sugar cane, livestock, poultry); lumbering; fisheries. Sand and gravel pits. Cotton and moss ginning. Formed 1808.

Catahoula Lake, La Salle parish, central La., 16 mi. NE of Alexandria; c.13 mi. long. Inlet: Little R. (SW end); outlets: Little R. (NE), Big Saline Bayou (SE). Recreation area; fishing.

Cataiñgan (kätäē'nyůgän), town (1939 pop. 1,180; 1948 municipality pop. 53,326), E Masbate isl., Philippines, 36 mi. SE of Masbate town, on Samar Sea; coal-mining and agr. center (rice, coconuts).

Catak (chätäk'), Turkish *Çatak*, village (pop. 340), Van prov., SE Turkey, on Buhtan R. and 34 mi. SSW of Van; grain. Also called Martanis. Formerly spelled Satak.

Catal (chätäl'), Turkish *Çatal*, rail junction, Smyrna prov., SW Turkey, 5 mi. N of Tire.

Catalan Bay (cätälän'), village (pop. c.300), E side of Gibraltar, on Catalan Bay, 2 mi. N of Europa Point, inhabitants, chiefly of Genoese origin, are engaged in fishing.

Catalão (kätälä'ō), city (pop. 4,280), SE Goiás, central Brazil, on railroad to Rio de Janeiro and 55 mi. NNE of Uberlândia (Minas Gerais); agr. trade center (cattle, hogs); tanning, meat processing (jerked beef, lard, sausages), dairying, distilling. Ships rice, coffee, alcohol, cotton. Iron and manganese deposits in area. Airfield.

Catalaunian Fields, France: see CHÂLONS-SUR-MARNE.

Catalca (chätäljä'), Turkish *Çatalca*, town (pop. 22,141), Istanbul prov., Turkey in Europe, 27 mi. WNW of Istanbul; military base. Also cement and glass mfg. Area is known for its watermelons. Here the Bulgarian advance on Istanbul was stopped by the Turks in the Balkan Wars. According to Treaty of Sèvres (1920), Catalca was to have marked limit of Turkey in Europe. Sometimes spelled Chatalja, Tchatalja.

Catalina (kätälē'nä), village (1930 pop. 399), Antofagasta prov., N Chile, in the Atacama Desert, 55 mi. ENE of Taltal; rail junction and nitrate-producing center.

Catalina or **Catalina de Güines** (dā gwē'něs), town (pop. 2,359), Havana prov., W Cuba, on Central Highway, on railroad and 28 mi. SE of Havana; potatoes, tomatoes, tobacco, sugar cane, cattle.

Catalina Channel, Calif.: see SAN PEDRO CHANNEL.

Catalina Island (kätälē'nä) (3 mi. long, 17 mi. wide; 1935 pop. 17), off SE coast of Dominican Republic, 4 mi. WSW of La Romana.

Catalina Island, Calif.: see SANTA CATALINA ISLAND.

Catalonia (kătůlō'nyů,–nēů), Sp. *Cataluña* (kätälōō'nyä), region (□ 12,332; pop. 2,890,974), NE Spain, stretching from the Pyrenees at Fr. border S along the Mediterranean. Comprises 4 provs.: BARCELONA, GERONA, LÉRIDA, TARRAGONA. Aragon is W, Valencia S. BARCELONA, the historic ⊙, is the chief city and port. Mostly hilly, with the S slopes of E Pyrenees and irregular coastal ranges, it also has some fertile plains (Ampurdán, Urgel, Tarragona). Drained by lower Ebro R. and its tributaries (Segre, Noguera Pallaresa), and by the Llobregat and the Ter. Partly low and sandy, partly high and rocky, coast is interrupted by Cape Creus (easternmost point of Spain), Gulf of Rosas, and Ebro delta; numerous bathing resorts. Forests and pastures (cattle raising) in Pyrenean valleys; irrigation canals (chiefly in Lérida prov.). The region produces ⅓ of the wines of Spain, and also olive oil, vegetables, rice (Ebro delta, Ampurdán), almonds, citrus and other fruit, sugar beets, cereals. Few mineral resources: coal (San Juan de las Abadesas, Llobregat valley), potash (Suria), salt (Cardona); lead, iron, maganese are little exploited; limestone is quarried. Mineral springs. Though lacking raw materials, Catalonia has hydroelectric power which has stimulated great industrial development (Barcelona is Spain's leading industrial center). Textile milling is chief industry (Barcelona, Manresa, Tarrasa, Sabadell); metallurgical industries (machinery, rolling stock, electrical equipment) in and near Barcelona. Other mfg.: chemicals (Barcelona, Badalona, Flix), cement (Igualada, Gerona), paper (El Prat de Llobregat), knitwear (Mataró), glass, leather, furniture. Agr. processing includes cork (throughout Gerona prov.), olive-oil (Tortosa), wine (Tarragona). Active trade in and exports of agr. products and manufactured goods. Trade has been active along the Catalan coast since Greek and Roman times. The history of medieval Catalonia (which took its name from its many castles) is that of counts of Barcelona, who emerged (9th cent.) as chief lords in the Spanish March founded by Charlemagne. United with ARAGON (1137), Catalonia nevertheless preserved its own laws and cortes, and its own language, akin to Provençal. Catalan art flourished in the Middle Ages. Catalan traders rivaled those of Genoa and Venice, and their maritime code became widely used in the Mediterranean in the 14th cent. After the union (1479) of Aragon and Castile, Catalonia declined. Agitation for autonomy, always strong, led to the establishment of an autonomous govt. (1932–39). A revolution (1934) for complete independence failed, but in 1936 autonomy was restored. In the civil war of 1936–39, Catalonia sided with the Loyalists and suffered heavily. Despite its valiant defense, Catalonia was in Franco's hands by Feb., 1939, and was fully inc. into his centralized state.

Cataluña, Spain: see CATALONIA.

Cataluña, Cape, N Majorca, Balearic Isls., 36 mi. NE of Palma; 39°57'N 3°11' E.

Catamaran (kă"tůmůrăn'), southernmost village of Tasmania, 50 mi. SSW of Hobart and on Recherche Bay (rů-shĕrsh') (3 mi. wide) of Tasman Sea; sawmills.

Catamarca (kätämär'kä), province (□ 45,829; pop. 147,213), NW Argentina; ⊙ Catamarca. Mountainous region in the Andes along the Chile border, including subandean ranges with arid plateaus (*puna*) and fertile valleys drained by the Cajón, Belén, Colorado rivers. Has dry, warm climate. Agr. activity in irrigated area of its main rivers: alfalfa, wheat, corn, grapes, fruit, wine, tobacco, spices; stock raising and dairying. Alcohol and wine distilleries. Produces also timber, textiles (hand-woven ponchos), charcoal, minerals. Mining plays dominant part in its economy, with tin (Fiambalá), tungsten, copper (Capillitas), kaolin, gypsum, mica, and iron deposits in the mts. Meat packing and tanning plants in Catamarca city. Mild winters attract tourists. Has no extensive railway net but good roads, the Agüita and San Francisco passes communicating with Chile. Antofagasta region in N was inc. into prov. in 1943, when Los Andes territory was dissolved.

Catamarca, city (pop. 30,177), ⊙ Catamarca prov. and Catamarca dept. (□ 404; pop. 31,316), NW Argentina, on railroad, on the Río del Valle and 1,000 mi. NW of Buenos Aires, 130 mi. SSW of Tucumán; 28°28'S 65°47'W; alt. 1,700 ft. Agr. (alfalfa, figs, cotton, wine) and dairying center in subandean valley, producing frozen meat, textiles, hand-woven ponchos, furniture, chocolate; leather tanning. Mica mines and thermal springs near by. An old colonial city, founded 1683, it has administrative bldgs., natl. col., archaeological mus., art gall., church of the Virgin of the Valley (shrine for pilgrims). Formerly sometimes called San Fernando de Catamarca.

Catamayo River, Ecuador: see GRANDE, Río.

Catana, Sicily: see CATANIA, city.

Catanauan (kätänä'wän), town (1939 pop. 3,850; 1948 municipality pop. 11,166), Quezon prov., S Luzon, Philippines, on Mompog Pass, 55 mi. ESE of Lucena; fishing, coconut growing.

Catanduanes (kätändwä'näs), island (□ 552; 1939 pop. 98,216, including offshore isls.), Philippines, in Philippine Sea, 5 mi. E of Rungus Point peninsula of SE Luzon across Maqueda Channel, on N shore of Lagonoy Gulf; 13°47'N 124°16'E; 40 mi. long, 22 mi. wide. Mountainous, rising to 2,506 ft. in W part of isl. Agr. (hemp, coconuts), copper mining. Catanduanes province (1948 pop. 112,121) includes Catanduanes isl. and several offshore isls., largest being PANAY; ⊙ VIRAC. Until 1946, Catanduanes was a sub-prov. of Albay prov.

Catanduva (kätändōō'vů), city (1950 pop. 22,186), central São Paulo, Brazil, on railroad and 75 mi. W of Ribeirão Prêto; coffee-processing center; livestock slaughtering, tanning, cotton ginning, rice milling, mfg. of furniture and pottery. Has 2 old churches.

Catania (kůtä'nyů, It. kätä'nyä), province (□ 1,377; pop. 713,131), E and SE central Sicily; ⊙ Catania. Mtn. terrain, rising to 10,705 ft. in Mt. Etna; divided by Plain of Catania in center; drained by Simeto R. and its tributaries. Agr. chiefly on lower slopes of Mt. Etna and in Plain of Catania. Sericulture; livestock (sheep, cattle); coral fisheries. Chief hydroelectric station of E Sicily on Alcantara R. Pozzuolana and sulphur mining. Industry concentrated at Catania, Acireale, Caltagirone. Antiquities at Catania and Adrano.

Catania, anc. *Catana* or *Catina*, second largest city (pop. 241,462) and port of Sicily, ⊙ Catania prov., at foot of Mt. Etna, on Gulf of Catania and 100 mi. SE of Palermo; 37°30'N 15°5'E. Transportation and industrial center; food processing (rice, macaroni); clothing mills (cotton, silk), sawmills; refineries (sugar, sulphur), shoe and tobacco factories, tanneries; coral fisheries, fish hatcheries; shipbuilding, paper and publishing industries; pozzuolana mining; power plant. Winter resort. Archbishopric, with Norman cathedral partly dating from 1091 (damaged in Second World War). The former Benedictine monastery of San Nicolò (rebuilt 1693–1735), housing mus. and observatory, was one of most extensive in Europe; its church (344 ft. long; transepts 157 ft.) is largest in Sicily. First univ. of isl. founded here by Alphonso of Aragon in 1434. Repeatedly destroyed by eruptions of Mt. Etna (especially in 1669) and by earthquakes (most disastrous one in 1693, when third of pop. perished), city has 18th-cent. appearance. Antiquities include ruins of Chalcidian necropolis, Greek and Roman theaters, Roman baths and aqueducts, early Christian cemetery. Founded by Chalcidians from Naxos in 8th cent. B.C.; conquered by Romans 263 B.C.; sacked by Normans 1169. In Second World War severely damaged (1943) by heavy bombing and fighting.

Catania, Gulf of, E Sicily, inlet of Ionian Sea, bet. Cape Campolato (S) and Cape Molini (N); 20 mi. long, 5 mi. wide; coral fisheries. Receives Simeto R. Chief port, Catania.

Catania, Plain of, Ital. *Piana di Catania*, largest lowland of Sicily, in Catania prov., S of Mt. Etna; extends 20 mi. W from Gulf of Catania; 10 mi. wide. Fertile soil, watered by Simeto R. and its tributaries; wheat, vineyards, citrus fruit. Malarial in summer. This is Laestrygonian Fields of the anc. world.

Catán-Lil, department, Argentina: see LAS COLORADAS.

Catán-Lil, Sierra de (syĕ'rä dā kätän'lēl), Andean range in S Neuquén natl. territory, Argentina, W of Las Coloradas; extends c.45 mi. N-S bet. Aluminé R. and Catán-Lil R.; rises to c.6,500 ft., The **Catán-Lil River** flows c.65 mi. S and SW, joining the Aluminé to form the Collón Curá.

Cataño (kätä'nyō), town (pop. 9,182), N Puerto Rico, on San Juan Bay, opposite San Juan (ferries); agr. center (sugar, pineapples, citrus fruit, corn); glass, paper, and cement plants; fishing.

Catanzaro (kätänzä'rô), province (□ 2,020; pop. 606,364), Calabria, S Italy; ⊙ Catanzaro. Bet. Ionian (Gulf of Squillace) and Tyrrhenian (Gulf of Sant'Eufemia) seas, in central part of toe of Italy. Traversed by the Apennines, including part of La SILA mts. (N); watered by Neto and Savuto rivers. Agr. (cereals, olives, grapes, citrus fruit, raw silk); stock raising (sheep, goats, pigs); forestry; fishing (Pizzo). Mining at Strongoli (sulphur) and Casabona (zinc); marble quarries at Gimigliano. Major hydroelectric plant near Cotronei. Mfg. at Crotone. Frequently damaged by earthquakes.

Catanzaro, town (pop. 27,907), ⊙ Catanzaro prov., Calabria, S Italy, in La Sila foothills, overlooking Gulf of Squillace, 32 mi. SE of Cosenza; 38°54'N 16°36'E. Rail junction; olive-oil trade. Until 17th cent. noted for its silk velvets and damasks. Its port is MARINA DI CATANZARO. Archbishopric. Has univ. and mus. of antiquities. Repeatedly struck by earthquakes (1783, 1905, 1907). In Second World War, damaged by bombs (1943) which devastated its early 19th-cent. cathedral.

Cataouatche, Lake (kătůhŏ'chē), SE La., 8 mi. SW of New Orleans, in marshy region; c.7 mi. long, 3 mi. wide. Joined by passages to the Mississippi (N) and to L. Salvador (S).

Catapilco (kätäpēl'kō), village (1930 pop. 403), Aconcagua prov., central Chile, on railroad and 8 mi. S of La Ligua; grain, potatoes, fruit, livestock. Copper deposits near by.

Cataractonium, England: see CATTERICK.

Catarama (kätärä'mä), town (1950 pop. 1,772), Los Ríos prov., W central Ecuador, in lowlands of the Guayas basin, 17 mi. N of Babahoyo; agr. center (cacao, rice, sugar cane, fruit); rice milling.

Cataraqui, Ont.: see KINGSTON.

Cataraqui River (kătůră'kwē, –rô'kwē,–rä'kwē), S Ont., issues from Rideau L., flows 70 mi. in a winding course SW to E end of L. Ontario at Kingston. Forms SW part of Rideau Canal.

Cataricahua (kätärēkä'wä), town (pop. c.3,200), Oruro dept., W Bolivia, in Cordillera de Azanaques, 3 mi. NE of Huanuni, in tin-mining dist.

Catarina (kätärē'nä), town (1950 pop. 621), San Marcos dept., SW Guatemala, in Pacific piedmont, 17 mi. WNW of Coatepeque; coffee, sugar cane, tropical fruit; cattle.

Catarina, town (1950 pop. 1,572), Masaya dept., SW Nicaragua, on L. Apayo, on railroad and 4 mi. SE of Masaya; residential summer resort; produces clay trinkets; sugar cane, rice, coffee.

Catarina (kătůrē'nů), city (pop. 380), Dimmit co., SW Texas, 25 mi. SSE of Crystal City; rail shipping point in irrigated truck-growing area.

Catarman (kätärmän'), town (1939 pop. 7,019; 1948 municipality pop. 33,153), N Samar isl., Philippines, on Philippine Sea, 55 mi. NNW of Catbalogan; agr. center (corn, rice).

Catarroja (kätärō'hä), outer S suburb (pop. 10,078), of Valencia, Valencia prov., E Spain; rice milling, vegetable canning; mfg. of bicycle rims, bonnets, knitwear, dyes. Cereals, rice, oranges in area.

Catasauqua (kătůsô'kwů), borough (pop. 4,923), Lehigh co., E Pa., 3 mi. NNE of Allentown and on Lehigh R.; silk, iron and steel products, beer. Inc. c.1853.

Catastrophe, Cape, on SE Eyre Peninsula, S South Australia, at W side of entrance to Spencer Gulf, opposite Thistle Isl.; 34°59'S 136°E.

Catatonk Creek (kă'tůtŏngk), S N.Y., drains Spencer L. N of Spencer, flows c.25 mi. S, E, and SE to Owego Creek just N of Owego.

Catatumbo River (kätätōōm'bō), in Colombia and Venezuela, rises in Cordillera Oriental of Colombia SE of Ocaña, flows N through foothills, then E into Maracaibo lowlands of Venezuela to L. Maracaibo 90 mi. S of Maracaibo; total length c.210 mi. Navigable in lower course, it is the chief outlet for upper Maracaibo basin and coffee country of NE Colombia. River port Encontrados is connected (S) by rail with Cúcuta. Oil wells in area, especially along Tarra R., a tributary. Receives Zulia R.

Cataumet, Mass.: see Bourne.
Catavi (kätä'vē), village (pop. c.6,600), Potosí dept., W central Bolivia, at E foot of Cordillera de Azanaques, 4 mi. N of Uncía (connected by railroad); alt. 13,280 ft. Newly developed tin-mining center, replacing Uncía and Llallagua as leading producer in Bolivia; satellite mining settlements include Cancañiri, Miraflores, Siglo Veinte.
Catawba (kùtô'bù), county (□ 406; pop. 61,794), W central N.C.; ⊙ Newton. In piedmont area; bounded E and N by Catawba R. (Hickory and Lookout Shoals lakes; hydroelectric plants). Agr. (tobacco, cotton, corn, wheat, hay; livestock, dairy products, poultry); timber (pine, oak). Textile and furniture mfg., lumber milling. Formed 1842.
Catawba. 1 Town (pop. 506), Catawba co., W central N.C., on Catawba R. and 16 mi. E of Hickory; hosiery mfg. **2** Village (pop. 313), Clark co., W central Ohio, 11 mi. ENE of Springfield, in agr. area. **3** Village, Roanoke co., SW Va., in Jefferson Natl. Forest, 11 mi. NW of Roanoke; state tuberculosis sanatorium. **4** Village (pop. 233), Price co., N Wis., 28 mi. SSW of Park Falls, in wooded area; dairying.
Catawba Island, resort village, Ottawa co., N Ohio, on N shore of Marblehead Peninsula on L. Erie, 12 mi. NW of Sandusky; vineyards, peach orchards.
Catawba River, in N.C. and S.C., rises in N.C. in the Blue Ridge S of Mt. Mitchell, flows E past Rhodhiss, and S past Mt. Holly, into S.C., past Great Falls (here becoming Wateree River), and joining Congaree R. 30 mi. SE of Columbia to form Santee R. Total length, c.295 mi.; length of Wateree R., c.75 mi. Dammed in N.C. course, forming a series of narrow reservoirs (hydroelectric plants): L. James (c.10 mi. long) is 8 mi. W of Morganton; Rhodhiss L. (c.15 mi. long) is W of Rhodhiss; Hickory L. (formerly Oxford L.; 11 mi. long) is near Hickory; Lookout Shoals L. (c.10 mi. long) is 10 mi. ENE of Hickory; Mountain Isl. L. (11 mi. long) is dammed above Mt. Holly; Catawba L., dammed in S.C. E of Fort Mill, extends c.20 mi. N, forming part of N.C.–S.C. boundary.
Catawissa (kătùwĭs'ù), borough (pop. 2,000), Columbia co., E central Pa., 3 mi. S of Bloomsburg and on Susquehanna R.; shoes, textiles. Laid out 1787, inc. 1892.
Catazajá (kätäsähä'), town (pop. 349), Chiapas, SE Mexico, in lowlands, on affluent of the Usumacinta and 17 mi. W of Emiliano Zapata (Tabasco); rubber, rice, tropical fruit, timber.
Catba Island or **Cacba Island** (kät'bä', käk'bä'), hilly island (15 mi. long, 13 mi. wide) in Gulf of Tonkin, off N Vietnam mainland (separated by Along Bay). **Phocatba** (fô'kät'bä') or **La Cacba,** town, at S extremity, is a fishing port.
Catbalogan (kätbälō'gän), town (1939 pop. 8,159; 1948 municipality pop. 26,839), ⊙ Samar prov., Philippines, on W Samar isl., port on Samar Sea, near Maqueda Bay, 38 mi. NNW of Tacloban, Leyte; 11°46'N 124°52'E. Trade center for agr. area (rice, hemp, coconuts). Exports copra, hemp.
Cat Cays (kăz, kēz), NW Bahama Isls., string of islets (60 mi. N-S) adjoining South Bimini isl., and administratively a part of the Biminis. Gun Cay has lighthouse at 25°34'N 79°18'W.
Cateau, Le (lù kätō'), town (pop. 7,682), Nord dept., N France, on the Selle and 15 mi. ESE of Cambrai; mfg. (tiles, furnaces, tulle, embroidered linen articles, hosiery). Has Renaissance town hall with 18th-cent. belfry. Here, in 1559, England, France, and Spain signed treaty of Cateau-Cambrésis (old name of Le Cateau). During First World War, British fought determined rearguard action near Le Cateau (1914). Recaptured 1918 with American assistance.
Catedral, Cerro (sĕ'rō kätādräl'), Andean peak (7,150 ft.), SW Río Negro natl. territory, Argentina, on S shore of L. Nahuel Huapí, 10 mi. W of San Carlos de Bariloche; popular skiing ground.
Cateechee (kùtē'chē), village (1940 pop. 588), Pickens co., NW S.C., 22 mi. WSW of Greenville; cotton mill.
Catel, Guernsey, Channel Isls.: see Saint Mary de Castro.
Catelet, Le (lù kätlā'), agr. village (pop. 194), Aisne dept., N France, on Escaut R. and 11 mi. NNW of Saint-Quentin. Captured (1918) by Americans and British in First World War.
Catemaco (kätämä'kō), town (pop. 5,374), Veracruz, SE Mexico, on L. Catemaco, at SE foot of Tuxtla Volcano, 8 mi. E of San Andrés Tuxtla; agr. center (fruit, high-grade tobacco). Airfield.
Catemaco, Lake (c.8 mi. long, 5 mi. wide), Veracruz, SE Mexico, at SE foot of Tuxtla Volcano, 8 mi. E of San Andrés Tuxtla.
Catemu (kätä'mōō), village (1930 pop. 381), Aconcagua prov., central Chile, 13 mi. WSW of San Felipe, in agr. area (fruit, wine, tobacco, hemp, livestock); copper deposits.
Catena (kätä'nä) [Ital.,=mtn. chain], in Italian names: for names beginning thus and not found here, see main part of name; e.g., for Catena del Marghine see Marghine, Catena del.
Catende (kätĕn'dĭ), city (pop. 5,238), E Pernambuco, NE Brazil, on railroad and 70 mi. SW of Recife; large sugar mill.
Caterham and Warlingham (kā'tùrùm, wôr'lĭng-ùm), residential urban district (1931 pop. 19,512; 1951 census 31,290), E Surrey, England, 7 mi. S of Croydon; site of insane asylum and military station. Warlingham has 13th-cent. church.
Catete (kätĕ'tä), town (pop. 716), Congo prov., NW Angola, on railroad and 40 mi. SE of Luanda; cotton-growing center.
Catfish River, Wis.: see Yahara River.
Catharina Sophia (kätärē'nä sōfē'ä), village (pop. 777), Saramacca dist., N Du. Guiana, on Saramacca R. and 27 mi. W of Paramaribo; cacao, coffee, rice.
Cathay (kăthā'), medieval name for China; derived from the Kitan (Khitan) or Kitai, the founders of the Liao dynasty (937–1125) of N China.
Cathay (kùthā'), village (pop. 209), Wells co., central N.Dak., 12 mi. ESE of Fessenden.
Cathays, Wales: see Cardiff.
Cathcart, S suburb (pop. 26,121) of Glasgow, Lanark, Scotland.
Cathcart, town (pop. 3,258), E Cape Prov., U. of So. Afr., 30 mi. SE of Queenstown; agr. center (stock, grain, fruit). Seat of local native-affairs council, established 1927, with jurisdiction over Cathcart dist. (□ 995; pop. 18,067; native pop. 14,847), included in Ciskeian General Council.
Cathedral City, village (pop. c.500), Riverside co., S Calif., in Coachella Valley, 6 mi. SE of Palm Springs.
Cathedral Peak, mountain (10,933 ft.) of the Sierra Nevada, in E Calif., 15 mi. WSW of Mono L., in Yosemite Natl. Park.
Cathedral Pines, Conn.: see Cornwall.
Cathedral Rocks, Calif.: see Yosemite National Park.
Catherine, Lake, W central Ark., 5 mi. SE of Hot Springs; created in Ouachita River by Remmel Dam; c.12 mi. long. State park (bathing, boating, fishing, camping) on S shore.
Catherine, Mount, Egypt: see Katherina, Gebel.
Catherine, Mount, peak (10,082 ft.) in Pavant Mts., central Utah, c.10 mi. ENE of Fillmore.
Catherine Canal, Russian SFSR: see Keltma.
Catherine Hall, sugar mill, St. James parish, NW Jamaica, just E of Montego Bay.
Catherine Harbor, Russian SFSR: see Kola Gulf.
Cathkin Peak or **Cathkin's Peak** (10,438 ft.), in the Drakensberg, W Natal, U. of So. Afr., on Basutoland border, 60 mi. SSE of Harrismith, 35 mi. SE of Mont-aux-Sources.
Cathlamet (kăthlă'mĭt), town (pop. 501), ⊙ Wahkiakum co., SW Wash., 22 mi. W of Longview and on Columbia R.; fishing, agr., lumbering, canning.
Catí (kätē'), town (pop. 1,186), Castellón de la Plana prov., E Spain, 22 mi. WSW of Vinaroz; hogs, cereals, potatoes. Mineral springs near by.
Ca' Tiepolo, Italy: see Porto Tolle.
Catillo or **Baños de Catillo** (bä'nyōs dā kätē'yō), village (1930 pop. 209), Linares prov., S central Chile, in Andean foothills, 27 mi. S of Linares; health resort; thermal springs.
Catina, Sicily: see Catania, city.
Catió (kùtyō'), village, SW Port. Guinea, 25 mi. SE of Bolama; rice.
Cat Island, long narrow island (50 mi. long, c.3 mi. wide) and district (□ 160; pop. 3,870), central Bahama Isls., bet. Eleuthera Isl. (NW) and San Salvador or Watling Isl. (E), 100 mi. ESE of Nassau. Rises at its N end to 400 ft., highest elevation in the Bahamas. Said to be the most fertile isl. of the archipelago, it produces coconuts and sisal; also sweet potatoes, pineapples, and bananas. The forests yield pine, cedar, mahogany. Main settlements: Arthur's Town (N), The Bight (center), Old Bight (S). Largely settled by loyalists from Florida (1783). Cat Isl. was long thought to be the isl. (called Guanahani by the Indians and San Salvador by Columbus) where Columbus made his 1st landfall; that honor has now generally been conceded to San Salvador or Watling Isl.
Cat Island (c.5 mi. long E–W), SE Miss., wooded anchor-shaped island in the Gulf of Mexico, one of isl. chain lying bet. Mississippi Sound (N) and Chandeleur Sound (S), 10 mi. S of Gulfport.
Cativá (kätēvä'), village (pop. 279), Colón prov., central Panama, near Canal Zone border, on Trans-Isthmian Highway and 4 mi. E of Colón; bananas, cacao, abacá; stock raising.
Catlabug or **Catlapug,** lagoon, Ukrainian SSR: see Katlabug Lagoon.
Catlettsburg (kăt'lĭtsbûrg), city (pop. 4,750), ⊙ Boyd co., NE Ky., bet. Huntington, W.Va. (E), and Ashland, Ky., on left bank (levee) of Ohio R. (toll bridge here) at mouth of Big Sandy R. (here Ky., Ohio, and W.Va. meet); mfg. of chemicals, concrete products, toys; oil refining. Near by is "Traipsin' Woman's Cabin," scene of annual American Folk Song Festival (June). Settled as trading post 1808.
Catlin, village (pop. 953), Vermilion co., E Ill., 6 mi. SW of Danville; bituminous-coal mines; agr. (corn, wheat, soybeans, livestock, poultry; dairy products).
Catmon (kätmōn'), town (1939 pop. 2,443; 1948 municipality pop. 11,761), N Cebu isl., Philippines, on Camotes Sea, 30 mi. NNE of Cebu city; agr. center (corn, coconuts).
Cato (kā'tō), village (pop. 431), Cayuga co., W central N.Y., 16 mi. N of Auburn; cheese, feed, timber, grain, cabbage.
Catoche, Cape (kätō'chā), headland on bar off NE extremity of Yucatan Peninsula, Quintana Roo, SE Mexico; 21°37'N 87°3'W. Said to be 1st site on Mex. soil discovered by the Spanish (1517).
Catoctin (kùtŏk'tĭn), village, Frederick co., N Md., at E base of Catoctin Mtn. and 11 mi. N of Frederick. Catoctin Furnace (opened 1774) produced armor for vessel *Monitor*.
Catoctin Creek, Frederick co., NW Md., rises in the Blue Ridge, flows c.35 mi. S, through Middletown Valley, to the Potomac 3 mi. E of Brunswick.
Catoctin Mountain, E prong of the Blue Ridge in Md.; extends c.37 mi. SSW from just S of the Pa. line in W Frederick co., Md., into Loudoun co., Va. Alt. declines from c.1,900 ft. in N to c.500 ft. in Va. Separated from W prong of Blue Ridge (South Mtn.) in Md. by Middletown Valley. Catoctin Recreational Demonstration Area (10,126 acres), just W of Thurmont, Md., is under jurisdiction of Natl. Capital Parks system; it includes "Shangri-La," President Roosevelt's retreat, which was scene of important World War II conferences.
Catolé do Rocha (kätôlĕ' dōō rô'shù), city (pop. 2,106), W Paraíba, NE Brazil, near Rio Grande do Norte border, 60 mi. NW of Patos; cotton, sugar.
Caton (kā'tùn), village and parish (pop. 1,209), N Lancashire, England, 4 mi. ENE of Lancaster; dairy farming, agr.
Catonsville (kā'tùnzvĭl), suburban village (1940 pop. 13,565), Baltimore co., central Md., just WSW of Baltimore; beverage plants, nurseries. Seat of Spring Grove state hosp. for the insane and St. Charles Col. (R.C.; men). Patapsco State Park is near by. Founded before 1729 as Johnnycake, renamed c.1800.
Catoosa (kùtōō'sù), county (□ 167; pop. 15,146), NW Ga.; ⊙ Ringgold. Bounded N by Tenn. line. Cotton, potatoes, corn, fruit, livestock; textile mfg. Includes parts of Chickamauga and Chattanooga Natl. Military Park and Chattahoochee Natl. Forest. Formed 1853.
Catoosa, town (pop. 438), Rogers co., NE Okla., near Verdigris R., 15 mi. E of Tulsa; agr. and coal mining.
Catorce (kätôr'sā), city (pop. 753), San Luis Potosí, N central Mexico, in spur of the Sierra Madre (Sierra de Catorce), 15 mi. W of Matehuala; alt. 9,045 ft. Situated in fabulously rich mining region, it produces silver and antimony; also gold, lead, and copper deposits. Depending on demand for silver, its pop. varies greatly. Its railroad station (pop. 1,064) is 6 mi. W. Sometimes called Real de Catorce.
Catota (kätō'tä), town, Bié prov., S central Angola, on central plateau, on road and 55 mi. ESE of Chitembo; wheat, potatoes.
Catral (käträl'), town (pop. 1,495), Alicante prov., E Spain, 10 mi. SW of Elche; olive-oil processing, fruit canning; hemp, wheat.
Catria, Monte (môn'tĕ kä'trēä), highest peak (5,584 ft.) in Umbrian Apennines, central Italy, near Scheggia Pass, 13 mi. NW of Fabriano.
Catriló (kätrēlō'), village (pop. estimate 1,800), ⊙ Catriló dept. (pop. 5,711), E La Pampa prov., Argentina, 50 mi. ENE of Santa Rosa; rail junction and agr. center (alfalfa, rye, corn, livestock); dairying, lumbering.
Catrimani (kätrēmä'nē), town, Rio Branco territory, N Brazil, on isl. in the Rio Branco at influx of Catrimani R., 170 mi. SSW of Boa Vista. Carmo airplane landing near by.
Catrine (kă'trĭn), town in Sorn parish (pop. 3,369), Central Ayrshire, Scotland, on Ayr R. and 4 mi. NW of Cumnock; coal mining, cotton milling. Near by is Ballochmyle.
Catron (kùtrōn'), county (□ 6,898; pop. 3,533), W N.Mex.; ⊙ Reserve. Stock-grazing, mining, and quarrying region; watered by San Francisco and Tularosa rivers; bounded W by Ariz. Includes parts of Gila and Apache natl. forests and Tularosa and Mogollon mts. Gila Cliff Dwellings Natl. Monument in SE. Co. formed 1921.
Catron (kă'trùn), city (pop. 278), New Madrid co., extreme SE Mo., near Mississippi R., 10 mi. W of New Madrid.
Cats, Mont des, France: see Godewaersvelde.
Catskill (kăt'skĭl), village (pop. 5,392), ⊙ Greene co., SE N.Y., on the Hudson at mouth of Catskill Creek, and 30 mi. S of Albany; gateway to resorts in Catskill Mts. (W); connected with Hudson city by Rip Van Winkle Bridge. Trade and shipping center for dairy, fruit, and truck region. Mfg.: liqueurs, cement products, machinery, clothing, flour. Settled by the Dutch in 17th cent.; inc. 1806.
Catskill Aqueduct, SE N.Y., a main unit of New York city water-supply system, extends 92 mi. from Ashokan Reservoir in the Catskills to Kensico Reservoir in Westchester and thence to Hillview Reservoir in Yonkers. Its waters are distributed to 4 New York city boroughs through tunnels cut in solid rock and to Staten Isl. via steel pipe line across the Narrows. Aqueduct passes under the Hudson at Storm King mtn. at a depth of 1,114 ft. Planned in 1905; 1st part was completed in 1917.
Catskill Creek, SE N.Y., rises in the Catskills in E

Schoharie co., flows c.40 mi. generally SE to the Hudson at Catskill.

Catskill Mountains, SE N.Y., range (general alt. c.3,000 ft.) of the Appalachian system, mainly in Greene and Ulster counties. A deeply dissected and glaciated portion of the Allegheny Plateau, here composed of Devonian sandstone, the Catskills descend abruptly to the Hudson on the E and extend N to the Mohawk valley, where the HELDERBERGS are N escarpment of the plateau. Generally rolling, wooded region, with some deep gorges (here called "cloves"), and many beautiful waterfalls. Highest peaks are Slide Mtn. (4,204 ft.), c.18 mi. W of Kingston, and Hunter Mtn. (4,025 ft.), 19 mi. W of Catskill. Drained by headstreams of Delaware R. and by Esopus, Schoharie, Rondout, and Catskill creeks. Water from Ashokan and Schoharie reservoirs is supplied to New York city by CATSKILL AQUEDUCT; DELAWARE AQUEDUCT carries supply from headstreams of Delaware R. Accessibility to New York city makes this one of most popular eastern summer- and winter-resort regions. Catskill Forest Preserve (232,423 acres) includes some of the range's finest scenery, including the region of the Rip Van Winkle legend.

Cattail Peak, N.C.: see BLACK MOUNTAINS.

Cattaraugus (kătûrô'gŭs), county (□ 1,335; pop. 77,901), W N.Y., bounded S by Pa. line; ⊙ Little Valley. Intersected by Allegheny R.; drained by Cattaraugus, Conewango, and Ischua creeks. Dairying, oil-producing (refineries), farming (fruit, hay, potatoes), stock- and poultry-raising area. Diversified mfg. especially at Olean, Salamanca. Natural-gas wells; sand and gravel pits. Includes Allegany State Park, Allegany Indian Reservation, and part of Cattaraugus Indian Reservation. Formed 1808.

Cattaraugus, village (pop. 1,190), Cattaraugus co., W N.Y., 29 mi. NW of Olean; mfg. of wood products, feed, machinery; lumber milling. Agr. (dairy products; poultry, hay, oats, potatoes). Cattaraugus Indian Reservation is NW. Settled 1851 during construction of Erie RR; inc. 1882.

Cattaraugus Creek, W N.Y., rises in Wyoming co., flows c.70 mi. SW and W, through Cattaraugus Indian Reservation, to L. Erie 12 mi. NE of Dunkirk. Receives South Branch near Gowanda.

Cattaro, Yugoslavia: see KOTOR, town, Montenegro.

Cattegat: see KATTEGAT.

Cattenom (kätnō'), Ger. *Kattenheim* (kä'tûnhīm), village (pop. 681), Moselle dept., NE France, near the Moselle, 5 mi. NE of Thionville.

Catterick, village and parish (pop. 849), North Riding, N Yorkshire, England, on Swale R. and 8 mi. WNW of Northallerton; military post is here. Site of Roman camp of *Cataractonium.* Has 14th-cent. church.

Cattewater, England: see PLYM RIVER.

Cattier, Belgian Congo: see KOLO.

Cattolica (kät-tô'lēkä), town (pop. 5,196), Forlì prov., Emilia-Romagna, N central Italy, on the Adriatic, 11 mi. SE of Rimini; bathing resort; fishing, boatbuilding, netmaking, cement mfg.

Cattolica Eraclea (ĕräklā'ä), town (pop. 9,856), Agrigento prov., S Sicily, near Platani R., 14 mi. NW of Agrigento. Sulphur mines, sandstone quarries near by.

Catton, England: see NORWICH.

Catuane (kätwä'nä), village, Sul do Save prov., S Mozambique, on Natal (U. of So. Afr.) border, 60 mi. SSW of Lourenço Marques.

Catuaro (kätwä'rō), town (pop. 551), Sucre state, NE Venezuela, in coastal range, 29 mi. SW of Carúpano; sugar cane, coffee, cacao.

Catubig (kätōō'bēg), town (1939 pop. 1,876; 1948 municipality pop. 23,456), N Samar isl., Philippines, 45 mi. NNE of Catbalogan; corn, rice, hemp.

Catuiçara (kätwēsä'rŭ), town (pop. 1,251), E Bahia, Brazil, rail-spur terminus 20 mi. NNE of Santo Amaro; kaolin quarries. Until 1944, called Bom Jardim.

Catumbela (kätōōmbĕl'lä), town, Benguela prov., W Angola, near the Atlantic, on Benguela RR and 6 mi. S of Lobito; sugar refining.

Catuna, Santa Rita de Catuna (sän'tä rē'tä dā kätōō'nä), or **Villa de Santa Rita** (vē'yä dā), village (pop. estimate 400), ⊙ General Ocampo dept. (□ 1,000; 1947 pop. 6,465), SE La Rioja prov., Argentina, 45 mi. S of Chamical, in irrigated area. Agr., stock raising (goats, cattle), fishing.

Catus (kätüs'), village (pop. 389), Lot dept., SW France, 9 mi. NW of Cahors; hosiery mfg.; tile works near by. Has 11th-14th-cent. church.

Cau, Song (shông' kou'), river of N Vietnam, rises near Backan, flows c.200 mi. SE, past Thainguyen, Dapcau (port of Bacninh) and Sept Pagodes, where it receives the name Thaibinh and empties into the Gulf of Tonkin via 4 main arms, on one of which is Haiphong. Linked by several channels with Red R.

Cauayan (käwä'yän). **1** Town (1939 pop. 1,232; 1948 municipality pop. 20,486), Isabela prov., N Luzon, Philippines, on small tributary of Cagayan R. and 11 mi. SSW of Ilagan; agr. center (rice, corn). **2** Town (1939 pop. 4,026; 1948 municipality pop. 34,946), Negros Occidental prov., W Negros isl., Philippines, on Panay Gulf, 22 mi. SW of Binalbagan; agr. center (rice, sugar cane).

Caub, Germany: see KAUB.

Cauca (kou'kä), department (□ 11,660; 1938 pop. 356,040; 1950 estimate 454,200), SW Colombia, on the Pacific; ⊙ Popayán. Drained by Cauca, Patía, and Caquetá rivers, which rise within its territory. Crossed N-S by Cordillera Occidental and Cordillera Central; includes Sotará and Puracé volcanoes. The high interior valleys and uplands have a healthy climate, the sparsely inhabited coastal lowlands are torrid and humid. Mineral resources include gold and platinum (Belalcázar, Timbiquí), copper (Santander), and silver, marble, sulphur, coal, and petroleum. Large-scale cattle raising; main agr. products are coffee, tobacco, sugar cane, cacao, bananas, corn, rice, fique, yucca, henequen, cotton; wheat, potatoes at higher alt.

Caucagua (koukä'gwä), town (pop. 2,229), Miranda state, N Venezuela, on affluent of Tuy R. and 40 mi. ESE of Caracas; sugar cane, cacao, rice, fruit.

Caucahué Island (koukäwā') (□ 16; pop. 1,055), off NE coast of Chiloé Isl., in Gulf of Ancud, Chiloé prov., S Chile, 25 mi. SE of Ancud; 6 mi. long. Potatoes, livestock; fishing.

Caucaia (koukī'ŭ), city (pop. 3,117), N Ceará, Brazil, on railroad and 9 mi. W of Fortaleza; cotton, sugar. Until 1944, called Soure.

Cauca River (kou'kä), Colombia, main tributary of MAGDALENA RIVER, rises in the Andes near source of the Magdalena at N foot of Páramo del Buey in Cordillera Central 32 mi. S of Popayán, flows c.600 mi. N through wide rift valley bet. Cordillera Occidental and Cordillera Central, receives Nechí R. in Caribbean lowlands, and enters left arm of the Magdalena (Brazo de Loba) 30 mi. SE of Magangué. Only partly navigable for small craft on its lower and mid-course. Its immensely fertile valley has a tropical climate with abundant rainfall, and is noted for rich gold placer mines and its variety of agr. crops (coffee on slopes of the Cordilleras, also tobacco, sugar cane, cotton, beans, chick-peas, bananas, yucca, hemp, fique, cacao) and cattle herds. Its main centers are Popayán, Cali, Palmira, Buga, Tuluá, Cartago, Antioquia. Along its lower course are rain forests and swamps.

Caucasian Gates, Georgian SSR: see DARYAL GORGE.

Caucasus (kô'kŭsŭs) or **Caucasia** (kôkā'zhŭ, -shŭ), Rus. *Kavkaz* (kŭfkäz'), major physiographic region in S European USSR, bet. the Black and Caspian seas, and bet. the Manych Depression (N) and Turkey and Iran (S). It consists of the Greater Caucasus (the main range and dominating feature), which separates the Northern Caucasus (with the Kuban Steppe and the Stavropol Plateau) from Transcaucasia (with the Colchis and Kura lowlands, the Lesser Caucasus, and the Armenian Highland). The **Greater Caucasus,** one of the great mtn. barriers of the world, is generally accepted as the natural boundary bet. Europe and Asia. It extends in a grandiose chain, c.750 mi. long (NW-SE), from the Taman Peninsula (bet. the Black Sea and Sea of Azov) to the Apsheron Peninsula (on the Caspian). Rising from a series of low hills at both extremities, the Greater Caucasus exceeds the elevation of Mont Blanc in its W central part (70–110 mi. wide), reaching its greatest height in Mt. Elbrus (18,481 ft.). Bet. Mt. Elbrus and Mt. Kazbek (16,545 ft.) are also the Dykh-Tau (17,054 ft.), Shkhara (17,037 ft.), Koshtan-Tau (16,880 ft.), Dzhanga (16,568 ft.), and Adai-Khokh (15,239 ft.). This high region consists of several parallel ranges N of the main divide. These are the front range (which contains the highest peaks), the rocky range (6,000–9,000 ft.), and the foothills known as Chernye Gory. On the Georgian (S) slope of the main divide, several spurs (Bzyb, Kodor, Svanetian, and Lechkhumi ranges) separate the upper Rion R. from the short Black Sea coastal streams. In the E, the Greater Caucasus widens to over 100 mi. in the complex mtn. system of Dagestan. Although railroads are forced to skirt the ends of the range, the Greater Caucasus is crossed by a few passes: the Klukhori Pass (9,239 ft.) on the Sukhumi Military Road, Mamison Pass (9,550 ft.) on the Ossetian Military Road, and the Pass of the Cross (7,815 ft.) on the Georgian Military Road (auto traffic). The gradual N slopes give rise to the Kuban, the Kuma, the Terek (one of whose tributaries, the Cherek, is fed by the Dykh-Su and Bezingi glaciers), and the Sulak and Samur rivers. On the steep S slopes are the sources of the Mzymta, Bzyb, Kodor and Ingur rivers (short Black Sea coastal streams), the Rion R., and the left affluents (Aragva, Iora, Alazan) of the Kura R. The climate becomes progressively drier toward the E, with the greatest rainfall (up to 100 inches yearly) on the Abkhaz (SW) slopes. There the most luxuriant vegetation is found, with mixed forests, beech, and conifers succeeding each other in altitudinal zones below the sub-alpine and alpine meadows. With the decreasing rainfall, the snow line rises from 9,000 ft. (W) to 11,000 ft. (E). Typical of the mountain fauna are the brown bear, wild goats (ibex, chamois), leopard, lynx, and jackals. The Caucasian bison is extinct. The leading mineral resource is petroleum, found at both extremities of the Greater Caucasus in Apsheron Peninsula (Baku) and Maikop field, and in N (Grozny, Makhachkala) and S (Mirzaani) foothills. Other deposits include coal (Tkibuli, Tkvarcheli), manganese (Chiatura), lead-zinc-silver (Sadon). Of great importance are mineral springs, notably those of Pyatigorsk, Kislovodsk, Yessentuki, and Zheleznovodsk, as well as Goryachi Klyuch and Matsesta (near Sochi). Formed essentially in the late Tertiary period as part of the Alpine orogenesis, the Greater Causasus consists of a crystalline core (granite, gneiss, schist) outcropping in the high W central section and flanked by cretaceous limestone (W) and Jurassic shale (E). Volcanism which accompanied the genesis of the Greater Caucasus—the Elbrus and Kazbek are extinct volcanoes—is still evident in the thermal springs and occasional earthquakes on S slopes. The Greater Caucasus is linked by the SURAMI RANGE with the **Lesser Caucasus,** a mtn. system formed by the N frontal ranges of the Armenian Highland and separated from the Greater Caucasus by the Colchis and Kura lowlands. The principal constituent ranges are the Adzhar-Imeretian and Trialet ranges (N), the Somkhet, Shakh-Dag (12,270 ft.) and Karabakh ranges. Unlike the Armenian Highland with its recent volcanic formations, the Lesser Caucasus consists of folded and block-faulted mountains of sedimentary and older igneous materials. The Caucasus was known to the anc. Greeks. According to their legends Prometheus was chained to a Caucasian rock and Jason and the Argonauts sought the Golden Fleece in Colchis. The early states of Iberia (present Georgia), Albania (present Azerbaijan), and Armenia had periods of independence and of subjection to Rome (later Byzantium), the Sassanids of Persia, the Arabs, the Mongols, and, after 16th cent., to Turkey and Persia. Russia had won partial control over the N lowlands by the 17th cent. and completed the conquest of the mountainous Caucasus and of Transcaucasia during the 19th cent. The numerous invasions and migrations that swept over the region have resulted in the ethnic and linguistic complexity that is reflected, since the Bolshevik Revolution, in its administrative structure. In addition to the later Slavic arrivals, there are several unrelated indigenous language families: the Japhetic (or Caucasian), which includes Adyge (Cherkess, Kabardian), Abkhaz, and the Dagestan mtn. groups of the North Caucasian family; Georgian, Mingrelian, and Svanetian of the South Caucasian family; the Indo-European, which includes Ossetic and Armenian; and the Turkic, represented by the Azerbaijani Turks. Politically the Caucasus can be divided into the Northern Caucasus (part of the Russian SFSR) and Transcaucasia. The **Northern Caucasus** or **Ciscaucasia** had been divided prior to 1917 into Dagestan and the divisions of Kuban, Stavropol, Terek, and Black Sea. Following the Bolshevik Revolution, there emerged (1924) the Northern Caucasus Territory, which included the entire region except autonomous Dagestan. This unit existed until the Azov-Black Sea territory was separated (1934) and the remainder renamed Ordzhonikidze Territory (1937) and Stavropol Territory (1943). The present administrative divisions of the Northern Caucasus are KRASNODAR Territory (including ADYGE AUTONOMOUS OBLAST), Stavropol Territory (including CHERKESS AUTONOMOUS OBLAST), KABARDIAN and NORTH OSSETIAN AUTONOMOUS SSRs, GROZNY oblast, and DAGESTAN AUTONOMOUS SSR. **Transcaucasia** (trănz"–, trăns"–) extends from the Greater Caucasus S to the Turkish and Iranian frontiers. Until the Bolshevik Revolution, it was divided into the Russian govts. of Baku, Erivan, Kars (after 1878), Kutais, Tiflis, and Yelizavetpol. It now comprises the Georgian SSR (including Abkhaz and Adzhar Autonomous SSRs and South Ossetian Autonomous Oblast), the Azerbaijan SSR (including Nakhichevan Autonomous SSR and Nagorno-Karabakh Autonomous Oblast), and the Armenian SSR. From 1922 until 1936, the 3 republics were associated in the Transcaucasian Soviet Federated Socialist Republic, one of the original constituent republics of the USSR.

Caucayá, Colombia: see LEGUÍZAMO.

Caucel (kousĕl'), town (pop. 1,075), Yucatan, SE Mexico, on railroad and 6 mi. NW of Mérida; henequen.

Caucete, Argentina: see VILLA COLÓN.

Caucomgomoc Lake (kôkŭmŭgŏ'mŭk), Piscataquis co., N central Maine, 50 mi. N of Greenville, in wilderness recreational area; 6 mi. long, 2 mi. wide.

Cauda (kou'dä'), village, Khanhhoa prov., S central Vietnam, minor South China Sea port, 4 mi. S of Nhatrang, on estuary sheltering roadstead from winter monsoon; it is winter harbor for Nhatrang.

Caudal River, Spain: see LENA RIVER.

Caudebec-en-Caux (kōdbĕk'-ā-kō'), village (pop. 1,575), Seine-Inférieure dept., N France, port on right bank of Seine R. and 18 mi. WNW of Rouen; aircraft plant. Heavily damaged (including 15th–16th-cent. church and picturesque old houses) in Second World War.

Caudebec-lès-Elbeuf (–lāz-ĕlbûf'), ESE suburb (pop. 8,881) of Elbeuf, Seine-Inférieure dept., N France; woolen milling, coffee drying, mustard mfg.

Caudéran (kōdārā'), W suburb (pop. 24,637) of Bordeaux, Gironde dept., SW France; hosiery, shoes, chemicals; brewing, canning, distilling.

Caudete (kou-dhā'tā), town (pop. 6,638), Albacete prov., SE central Spain, in Murcia, 8 mi. NW of Villena, in irrigated agr. dist. (cereals, wine, truck produce, potatoes). Mfg. of shoes, burlap, plaster; fruit and vegetable canning, meat processing, alcohol distilling. Livestock, lumber.

Caudete de las Fuentes (dhā läs fwĕn'tĕs), town (pop. 1,445), Valencia prov., E Spain, 11 mi. NW of Requena; olive-oil processing, sheep raising.

Caudiel (kou-dhyĕl'), town (pop. 1,217), Castellón de la Plana prov., E Spain, 30 mi. WSW of Castellón de la Plana; olive-oil processing; fruit, wine.

Caudine Forks (kô'dīn), narrow passes in the Apennines, S Italy, on road from Capua to Benevento. Here in 321 B.C. the Samnites routed the Romans.

Caudry (kōdrē'), town (pop. 12,091), Nord dept., N France, 9 mi. ESE of Cambrai; tulle and embroidery mfg. center. Sugar distilleries.

Caué, peak, Brazil: see ITABIRA.

Caughnawaga (kä'näwä"gŭ, käk"nŭwä'gŭ), village (pop. estimate 2,250), S Que., on L. St. Louis, opposite Lachine (bridge). Founded 1667 as refuge for Iroquois converted to Christianity, it is still an Indian village. In 1890 rule by tribal chief was changed to municipal govt.

Cauitan, Mount (käwē'tän) (8,427 ft.), Mountain Prov., N Luzon, Philippines, 45 mi. SE of Vigan.

Cauke (kou'kă'), town, Cantho prov., S Vietnam, in Mekong delta, 23 mi. SE of Cantho; rice.

Caulfield, municipality (pop. 79,913), S Victoria, Australia, 6 mi. SE of Melbourne, in metropolitan area; residential.

Caulfield's Hill, Malaya: see TAIPING.

Caulille, Belgium: see KAULILLE.

Caulker, Cay, Br. Honduras: see CAY CORKER.

Caulnes (kōn), village (pop. 645), Côtes-du-Nord dept., W France, on Rance R. and 13 mi. SSW of Dinan; tanning.

Caulonia (koulô'nyä), town (pop. 4,827), Reggio di Calabria prov., Calabria, S Italy, 10 mi. NNE of Siderno Marina, in agr. region (citrus fruit, olives, grapes). Ruins (walls, temple) of anc. Caulonia (an Achaean colony) are 9 mi. ENE, on Cape Stilo. Formerly called Castelvetere.

Caumont (kōmō'). **1** or **Caumont-l'Éventé** (–lāvātā'), village (pop. 558), Calvados dept., NW France, 13 mi. SSW of Bayeux; small-arms mfg., dairying. **2** or **Caumont-sur-Durance** (–sür-dürās'), village (pop. 948), Vaucluse dept., SE France, near right bank of the Durance, 8 mi. ESE of Avignon; winegrowing.

Caunao (kounou'), town (pop. 1,914), Las Villas prov., central Cuba, on railroad and 3½ mi. NE of Cienfuegos, in agr. region (sugar cane, coffee, tobacco, fruit).

Caunao River, Camagüey prov., E Cuba, rises NW of Camagüey city, flows c.70 mi. N to Jigüey Bay 15 mi. E of Cunagua.

Caunes-Minervois (kōn-mēnĕrvwä'), village (pop. 1,623), Aude dept., S France, on S slope of Montagne Noire, 12 mi. NE of Carcassonne; winegrowing. Noted marble quarries. Has 12th–15th-cent. church, part of former abbey.

Caunette, La (lä kōnĕt'), village (pop. 445), Hérault dept., S France, 16 mi. NW of Narbonne; lignite mining.

Caungan (kou'ngän'), village (1936 pop. 1,213), Travinh prov., S Vietnam, in Mekong delta, 12 mi. SE of Travinh. Badong beach resort is SE on South China Sea.

Caúngula (käōōng'gōōlŭ), town (pop. 3,903), Malange prov., N Angola, near Belgian Congo border, 170 mi. NE of Malange; rubber, almonds, beans, manioc; hog raising.

Caupolicán, Bolivia: see APOLO.

Caupolicán, Chile: see RENGO.

Cauquenes (koukä'nĕs). **1** Town (pop. 12,987), ⊙ Maule prov. and Cauquenes dept. (□ 805; pop. 33,116), S central Chile, in coastal range, 200 mi. SSW of Santiago; 35°58'S 72°19'W. Trading and agr. center (grain, potatoes, lentils, wine, sheep). Lumbering, flour milling, distilling. Its wines are considered to be the best in Chile. Town, heavily damaged in 1939 earthquake, has been rebuilt on modern lines. **2** or **Baños de Cauquenes** (bä'nyōs dā), village (1930 pop. 750), O'Higgins prov., central Chile, on Cachapoal R., in Andean foothills, 13 mi. ESE of Rancagua; spa (curative waters).

Caura, Spain: see CORIA, Seville prov.

Caura River (kou'rä), Bolívar state, SE Venezuela, rises as Merevari R. (märävä'rē) in range of Guiana Highlands near Brazil border, flows 465 mi. NNW, through dense tropical forests, to the Orinoco 100 mi. WSW of Ciudad Bolívar, at 7°38'N 64°53'W. Not navigable because of numerous rapids. Erebato R. is main affluent.

Caura Valley (kou'rŭ), N Trinidad, B.W.I., along small Caura R. and 8 mi. E of Port of Spain. Has luxuriant tropical vegetation. Once secluded picnic ground, now site of water reservoir.

Caurchari, Salar de (sälär' dā kourchä'rē), salt desert (□ 117; alt. 13,500 ft.) in the *puna*, SW Jujuy prov., Argentina, W of Jujuy; 50 mi. long, 6 mi. wide. Contains sodium and borax salts.

Cauri (kou'rē), town (pop. 413), Huánuco dept., central Peru, in Cordillera Occidental, on Marañón R. and 28 mi. SW of Huánuco; sugar cane, coffee. Sometimes San Miguel de Cauri.

Caurium, Spain: see CORIA, Cáceres prov.

Causani, Moldavian SSR: see KAUSHANY.

Causapscal (kōsäpskäl'), village (pop. 1,545), E Que., on Matapédia R. and 35 mi. NW of Campbellton; dairying, lumbering.

Causewayhead, village in Logie parish, NE Stirling, Scotland, on the Forth and 2 mi. NNE of Stirling; coal mining. Wallace monument commemorates assembly of Scottish troops here on eve of battle of Stirling Bridge (1297).

Caussade (kōsäd'), town (pop. 2,986), Tarn-et-Garonne dept., SW France, 13 mi. NE of Montauban; road center; produces straw hats, footwear, bricks and tiles, preserves. Known for its poultry.

Caussens (kōsā'), village (pop. 229), Gers dept., SW France, 3 mi. ESE of Condom; Armagnac brandy.

Causses (kōs), arid Jurassic limestone plateau of S and SW France, in S Massif Central, forming part of Lozère, Aveyron, Lot, and Tarn-et-Garonne depts. Of Karst-like topography, it features underground drainage, fissures, and pot-holes. It is divided by deeply intrenched streams into many smaller tablelands, which form 2 main groups, the E Causses, E of the Ségala Plateau, and the Causses du Quercy (W), chiefly in Lot dept. The E Causses (average alt. 3,000 ft.) include the Causse Méjan, bet. Tarn (N) and Jonte (S) rivers; the Causse de Sauveterre, SE of Millau, bet. the Lot (N) and the Tarn (S); the Causse du Comtal, N of Rodez; the Causse Noir, E of Millau, bet. Jonte (N) and Dourbie (S) rivers; and the Causse du Larzac, extending 25 mi. SE of Millau. The less arid Causses du Quercy (average alt. 1,500 ft.) contain the Causse de Martel, N of Dordogne R. and E of Souillac; the Causse de Gramat, bet. Lot (S) and Dordogne (N) rivers, NW of Figeac; and the Causse de Limogne, bet. Cahors and Villefranche-de-Rouergue. The region has severe climate, is sparsely populated, and has a sheep-raising economy. Known for Roquefort cheese and truffles (in Martel area). Chief towns, located in the valleys, are Mende, Rodez, Millau, Cahors. Tourists visit the numerous stalactite caverns, river gorges (especially of the Tarn) and the pilgrimage place of Rocamadour.

Cauterets (kōtŭrā'), village (pop. 1,012), Hautes-Pyrénées dept., SW France, near Sp. border, 8 mi. S of Argelès-Gazost; alt. 3,058 ft. Well-known spa and mtn. resort of central Pyrenees. Hot sulphur springs. Winter sports.

Cautín (koutēn'), province (□ 5,519; 1940 pop. 374,659, 1949 estimate 321,583), S central Chile; ⊙ TEMUCO. Situated bet. the Andes and the Pacific, it is drained by Cautín, Imperial, and Toltén rivers and includes N part of Chilean lake dist. (lakes Villarrica, Budi, Colico, and Caburgua). Mts. include Villarrica volcano. Has temperate, moist climate. Among its mineral resources, largely unexploited, are asbestos, talc, mica, and other silicates. It is a predominantly agr. area, a major Chilean center for wheat, oats, hogs, cattle, sheep. Grows also barley, rye, potatoes, peas, apples. Fishing in the lakes. Important forest areas. Flour milling, dairying, distilling, tanning, lumbering. Major resorts: Carahue, Toltén, Villarrica, and Pucón. Since conclusion of the Indian wars (treaty of Temuco, 1881), the prov. has become a noted resort area.

Cautín River, in Cautín and Malleco provs., S central Chile, rises in the Andes, flows c.100 mi. W and SW, past Lautaro, Cajón, and Temuco, to join the lesser Quepe R. 3 mi. SE of Nueva Imperial, forming IMPERIAL RIVER.

Cautivo (koutē'vō), oil town in Guayas prov., W Ecuador, on Santa Elena Peninsula; 2°12'S 80°53'W; petroleum refining.

Cauto River (kou'tō), Oriente prov., E Cuba, longest river in Cuba, rises in the Sierra Maestra near Caribbean coast 22 mi. W of Santiago de Cuba, flows c.150 mi. N and E, through alluvial swamps, to the Gulf of Guacanayabo 17 mi. NNW of Manzanillo. Navigable for small vessels c.40 mi. upstream.

Cauvery Falls (kô'vŭrē), 2 series of scenic rapids and cataracts, each on an arm of Cauvery R. surrounding SIVASAMUDRAM isl., on Mysore-Madras border, India, 35 mi. E of Mysore; each arm descends c.320 ft.; falls on left arm supply pivotal hydroelectric works.

Cauvery River or **Kaveri River** (both: kô'vŭrē), anc. *Chaberis*, S India, rises on Brahmagiri hill in Western Ghats WSW of Mercara, in Coorg; flows E and NE in Coorg, ESE through Mysore, past Krishnarajnagar, and generally SE through Madras, passing Kollegal, Mettur, Bhavani, Erode, and Trichinopoly, and at Srirangam Isl. divides to enter Bay of Bengal by several arms (northernmost and largest, the Coleroon), forming wide, fertile delta (□ c.4,000) S of Cuddalore. Delta's extensive irrigation-canal system, controlled by GRAND ANICUT, is powered by works just N of METTUR. In Mysore, river is dammed for irrigation at scenic resort of KRISHNARAJASAGARA; one of the noted CAUVERY FALLS, surrounding SIVASAMUDRAM isl., powers widespread hydroelectric network. Partly navigable by coracle in Madras and Mysore. Sacred stream to Hindus; often called Ganges of the South; main pilgrimage center is Srirangam Isl. Noted archaeological sites at Seringapatam. Chief tributaries: Lakshmantirtha, Amaravati, Bhavani, and Noyil (right) rivers.

Caux (kō), chalky tableland of Normandy, N France, in Seine-Inférieure dept., forming triangle bet. Rouen, Le Havre, and Dieppe, bounded by Seine R. (S) and English Channel (NW). Caudebec was old regional ⊙. Flax, cereals, pastures.

Caux, Fr. Guiana: see KAW.

Cava (kă'vŭ), island (pop. 14) of the Orkneys, Scotland, in Scapa Flow, bet. Hoy and Pomona isls.; 1 mi. long. Lighthouse (58°44'N 3°3'W).

Cava, La (lä kä'vä), village (pop. 3,498), Tarragona prov., NE Spain, in rice-growing Ebro R. delta, 14 mi. ESE of Tortosa.

Cava de' Tirreni (kä'vä dĕtēr-rā'nē), town (pop. 12,214), Salerno prov., Campania, S Italy, 3 mi. WNW of Salerno. Resort (alt. 640 ft.); textiles (cotton, linen), rope, soap, furniture, cement, macaroni, wine. Benedictine monastery of La Trinità della Cava (founded 1025) near by.

Cava d'Ispica, Sicily: see MODICA.

Cávado River (kä'vädōō), N Portugal, rises on Sp. border, flows 73 mi. WSW, past Amares and Barcelos, to the Atlantic at Esposende. Not navigable.

Cavaia, Albania: see KAVAJË.

Cavaillon (käväyō'), town (pop. 9,412), Vaucluse dept., SE France, near the Durance, 14 mi. SE of Avignon, at W foot of Montagne du Lubéron; fruit-shipping center (especially melons and grapes); mfg. of tin cans and aluminum kitchen utensils. Has 12th-cent. Romanesque church (former cathedral), and remains of Roman triumphal arch.

Cavaillon, agr. town (1950 census pop. 828), Sud dept., SW Haiti, on Tiburon Peninsula, near the coast, 6 mi. NE of Les Cayes; bananas, sugar cane grown here.

Cavalaire-sur-Mer (kävälâr'-sür-mâr'), village (pop. 546), Var dept., SE France, on Baie de Cavalaire (4 mi. wide, 2 mi. long) of the Mediterranean, 9 mi. SW of Saint-Tropez; Fr. Riviera resort damaged in Second World War.

Cavalcante (kävälkän'tĭ), city (pop. 278), E central Goiás, central Brazil, in the Chapada dos Veadeiros, 100 mi. N of Formosa; rock-crystal deposits.

Cavalese (kävälä'zĕ), town (pop. 2,124), Trento prov., Trentino–Alto Adige, N Italy, on Avisio R. and 15 mi. SSE of Bolzano; cement works. Resort (alt. 3,268 ft.). Chief center of Val di Fiemme. Has palace with 16th-cent. frescoes.

Cavalier (kă"vŭlēr'), county (□ 1,513; pop. 11,840), NE N.Dak., bordering on Manitoba; ⊙ Langdon; prairie area. Grain, dairy products, livestock. Agr. experiment station at Langdon. Formed 1873.

Cavalier, city (pop. 1,459), ⊙ Pembina co., NE N. Dak., 70 mi. NNW of Grand Forks and on Tongue R. Flour refining, dairy produce, livestock, potatoes. Founded 1875, inc. 1885.

Cavalla, Greece: see KAVALLA.

Cavalla River, Fr. West Africa: see CAVALLY RIVER.

Cavallermaggiore (käväl-lĕr"mäd-jô'rĕ), village (pop. 2,408), Cuneo prov., Piedmont, NW Italy, on Maira R. and 25 mi. S of Turin; rail junction; alcohol distillery.

Cavallino (käväl-lē'nô), village (pop. 2,821), Lecce prov., Apulia, S Italy, 3 mi. SSE of Lecce.

Cavallo, Cape (käväl'lô), headland, NE Algeria, on the Mediterranean, at E end of Gulf of Bougie, 10 mi. SW of Djidjelli; 36°46'N 5°36'E.

Cavally River (kŭvă'lē) or **Cavalla River** (kŭvă'lŭ), W Africa, flows S c.320 mi., mostly along Ivory Coast–Liberia border, to Gulf of Guinea 7 mi. E of Harper. Navigable for 80 mi. upstream.

Cava Manara (kä'vä mänä'rä), village (pop. 1,173), Pavia prov., Lombardy, N Italy, 4 mi. SW of Pavia; sausage, pharmaceuticals.

Cavan (kă'vŭn), Gaelic *an Chabhâin*, county (□ 729.9; pop. 70,355), Ulster, Ireland; ⊙ Cavan. Bounded by cos. Westmeath (S), Longford (SW), Leitrim (W), Fermanagh and Monaghan (N and NE), and Meath (SE). Drained by Annalee and Erne rivers. Among lakes are loughs Oughter, Ramor, and Sheelin. Surface is generally undulating, partly boggy, becoming mountainous in extreme NW; highest point, Cuilcagh (2,188 ft.). There are many mineral springs. Climate is notably damp. Cattle and hog raising, potato growing are main occupations. Industries include clay mining, mfg. of agr. implements, furniture, gypsum products, inks, waxes. Towns are Cavan, Cootehill, Belturbet, Kingscourt, and Bailieborough. On isl. in Lough Oughter are remains of anc. round tower.

Cavan, Gaelic *Cabhán* (kä'vän), urban district (pop. 3,477), ⊙ Co. Cavan, Ireland, 65 mi. NW of Dublin; agr. market (cattle, pigs; potatoes). Seat of R.C. bishop of Kilmore.

Cavanella Po (kävänĕl'lä pô'), village (pop. 560), Rovigo prov., Veneto, N Italy, on Po R. and 5 mi. ESE of Adria; beet-sugar refinery.

Cavareno (kävärā'nô), village (pop. 851), Trento prov., Trentino–Alto Adige, N Italy, 12 mi. SW of Bolzano; sawmill, box factory.

Cavarna, Bulgaria: see KAVARNA.

Cavarzere (kävärtsä'rĕ), town (pop. 4,973), Venezia prov., Veneto, N Italy, on Adige R. and 11 mi. SW of Chioggia; beet-sugar refinery, alcohol distillery, flax mill; agr. tools.

Cavaso del Tomba (kävä'zô dĕl tôm'bä), village (pop. 3,032), Treviso prov., Veneto, N Italy, 10 mi. NW of Montebelluna; canned fruit.

Cavazuccherina, Italy: see IESOLO.

Cave (kä'vĕ), village (pop. 4,333), Roma prov., Latium, central Italy, 2 mi. SE of Palestrina.

Cave City. 1 Town (pop. 372), Sharp co., N Ark., 13 mi. NNE of Batesville; resort. **2** Town (pop. 1,119), Barren co., S Ky., 10 mi. NNW of Glasgow; tourist center for limestone cave region of Ky. and an E gateway to MAMMOTH CAVE NATIONAL PARK. Near by are also Floyd Collins Crystal Cave (discovered 1917), with delicate formations of gypsum, crystal, and onyx; Great Onyx Cave, with formations of onyx, translucent alabaster, and white gypsum; Diamond Caverns; and other caves.

Cave Creek Dam, Ariz.: see SALT RIVER.

Cave del Predil (kä'vĕ dĕl prĕdĕl'), village (pop. 1,092), Udine prov., Friuli-Venezia Giulia, NE Italy, near Yugoslav border, in Julian Alps, 5 mi. S of Tarvisio. Zinc and lead mines.

Cave in Rock, village (pop. 550), Hardin co., extreme SE Ill., on Ohio R. (ferry here) and 26 mi. SE of Harrisburg, in agr. area. Cave in Rock State Park is near by.

Cave Junction, town (pop. 283), Josephine co., SW Oregon, 25 mi. SW of Grants Pass; lumber milling. Quartz mines in vicinity. Siskiyou Natl. Forest near by in Siskiyou Mts.

Cavendish (kă'vŭndĭsh), town (pop. 1,374), Windsor co., S central Vt., 25 mi. SE of Rutland and on Black R.; woolens, wood products; marble. Winter sports. Includes Proctorsville village (pop. 549) and Proctor-Piper state forest. Settled 1769.

Cavernes, France: see SAINT-LOUBÈS.

Cavers (kā'vŭrz), parish (pop. 1,179), central Roxburgh, Scotland. Includes KIRKTON.

Caversham, England: see READING.

Cave Spring or **Cave Springs**, city (pop. 959), Floyd co., NW Ga., 14 mi. SW of Rome, near Ala. line. Has state school for deaf. Limestone cave, here, has spring (source of city water supply).

Cave Springs, town (pop. 267), Benton co., extreme NW Ark., 14 mi. NNW of Fayetteville, in the Ozarks; fruit.

Cavetown, village (pop. c.250), Washington co., W Md., 7 mi. E of Hagerstown; cannery, grain and lumber mills.

Cave Valley, town, St. Ann parish, central Jamaica, 18 mi. SW of St. Ann's Bay, in rich agr. region (citrus fruit, corn, pimento, coffee, cattle).

Cavezzo (kävĕ'tsô), village (pop. 1,390), Modena prov., Emilia-Romagna, N central Italy, 14 mi. NNE of Modena; wine, hosiery.

Caviana Island (kävyä'nŏŏ) (□ c.1,900), in Amazon delta, NE Pará, Brazil, just N of Marajó isl., on the equator at long. 50°W.

Cavillargues (kävēyärg'), village (pop. 514), Gard dept., S France, 18 mi. NW of Avignon; lignite.

Cavinas (kävē'näs), mission, Beni dept., N Bolivia, near confluence of Madidi and Beni rivers, 115 mi. SSW of Riberalta. Rubber and quinine-bark collecting in region surrounding rivers.

Cavite (kävē'tä), province (□ 498; 1948 pop. 262,550), S Luzon, Philippines, bounded W by Manila Bay; ⊙ Cavite. Includes CORREGIDOR isl. Largely a fertile plain, producing rice, fruit, coconuts, sugar cane. U.S. naval station is at Sangley Point.

Cavite, city (1939 pop. 3,259; 1948 metropolitan area pop. 35,052), ⊙ Cavite prov., S Luzon, Philippines, on small peninsula on Cavite Harbor (inlet of Manila Bay), 10 mi. SW of Manila; 14°29'N 120°54'E. Naval base and trade center. A walled city, it has old Sp. forts. Principal suburbs of the city are Caridad (kärēdhädh') (1939 pop. 15,019) and San Roque (sän rō'kä) (1939 pop. 8,368), both W of city proper. After Spanish-American War in 1898, the U.S. established a major naval base at Sangley Point (14°29'N 120°54'E), just N of the city proper. In Second World War, the base was seized in Jan., 1942, by the Japanese; retaken in Feb., 1945, by U.S. forces. After the Philippines acquired independence, it was agreed (1947) that the U.S. would retain the base only as a limited operational area.

Caviúna, Brazil: see ROLÂNDIA.

Cavnic or **Capnic** (käv'nēk), Hung. *Kapnikbánya* (kŏp'nēk-bä"nyŏ), village (pop. 2,413), Baia-Mare prov., NW Rumania, 11 mi. E of Baia-Mare; mining (gold, silver); tourist center. Formerly major mining town, with pop. of 40,000. In Hungary, 1940–45.

Cavone River (kävô'nĕ), in Basilicata, S Italy, rises in the Apennines 9 mi. NW of Stigliano, flows 45 mi. NNE and ESE, bet. Basento and Agri rivers, to Gulf of Taranto 14 mi. ESE of Pisticci. In upper course called Salandrella R.

Cavour (kävōōr'), village (pop. 1,547), Torino prov., Piedmont, NW Italy, 7 mi. S of Pinerolo, in cereal-growing and sericulture region; silk industry. Giovanni Giolitti buried here. On near-by hill is ancestral castle of counts of Cavour.

Cavour, Peru: see SAN PEDRO, Libertad dept.

Cavour (kŭvōōr'), town (pop. 154), Beadle co., E central S.Dak., 10 mi. E of Huron.

Cavour Canal (kävōōr'), Italy, important irrigation canal in Piedmont; runs 55 mi. generally NE, from Po R. at Chivasso, across Dora Baltea, Sesia, and Agogna rivers, to Ticino R. near Galliate. Built 1863–66 to coordinate the spring high waters of the Po with the summer high waters of the Dora Baltea; canal system is over 900 mi. long and irrigates 1,250,000 acres. Made possible the rapid increase and predominance of rice growing in plains of Vercelli and Novara provs.

Cavriago (kävrēä'gô), town (pop. 3,312), Reggio nell'Emilia prov., Emilia-Romagna, N central Italy, 5 mi. W of Reggio nell'Emilia; cotton and hemp mills.

Cavriana (kävrēä'nä), village (pop. 1,425), Mantova prov., Lombardy, N Italy, 16 mi. NW of Mantua; peat digging.

Cavtat (tsäf'tät), Ital. *Ragusavecchia* (rägōō'zä-vĕk'kēä), Ger. *Altragusa* (ält'rägōō"zŭ), anc. *Epidaurus*, medieval *Civitas Vetus*, village, S Croatia, Yugoslavia, on Adriatic Sea, on railroad and 7 mi. SE of Dubrovnik, in Dalmatia; seaside resort. Has mausoleum built by Ivan Mestrovic, R.C. monastery, library. Legendary birthplace of Asclepius. A Gr. colony, it fell to the Romans, whose ruined baths and aqueduct remain. Following its destruction (7th cent.) by Avars, its inhabitants built city of DUBROVNIK.

Cavuscu, Lake (chävōōshchōō'), Turkish *Çavuşçu* (□ 20), W central Turkey, 45 mi. NW of Konya; 10 mi. long.

Cawdor, agr. village and parish (pop. 767), Nairnshire, Scotland, near Nairn R., 5 mi. SW of Nairn. Cawdor Castle, dating from 1454, is represented by Shakespeare, following tradition, as scene of murder of Duncan by Macbeth, which actually occurred in 1040. Near by is Kilravock Castle, built 1460.

Cawker City, city (pop. 691), Mitchell co., N Kansas, 17 mi. W of Beloit, in grain and livestock area; mfg. of farm appliances. Solomon R. formed just S by confluence of South Fork and North Fork.

Cawnpore (kôn'pŏŏr, kän'pŏŏr), since 1948 officially **Kanpur** (kän'pŏŏr), district (□ 2,372; pop. 1,556,247), S Uttar Pradesh, India; ⊙ Cawnpore. On Ganges Plain and Ganges-Jumna Doab; irrigated by Lower Ganges Canal and its distributaries. Agr. (gram, wheat, jowar, barley, mustard, corn, sesame, rice, pearl millet, sugar cane, cotton); dhak jungle, mango and mahua groves. Industrial center, Cawnpore. Other centers: Juhi, Bithur.

Cawnpore, since 1948 officially **Kanpur**, city (pop., including JUHI and cantonment, 487,324), ⊙ Cawnpore dist., S Uttar Pradesh, India, on the Ganges and 115 mi. NW of Allahabad. Rail and road junction; a major Indian industrial center for trade (grains, oilseeds, sugar cane, cotton, salt, saltpeter), woolen, cotton, and jute milling, tanneries (chief tanning material is babul bark), boot and shoe mfg. Also mfg. of chemicals, cement, hosiery, matches, shellac, textile machinery, plastics, electrical supplies, aluminum utensils, soap, cigarettes, glue, cardboard boxes, brushes, biscuits; oilseed milling, coach building, carpet weaving, sawmilling; iron and steel rolling mills, general engineering and ordnance factories, govt. harness and saddlery factory. Agr. col., law colleges, nurses training center, Central Textile Inst., govt. experimental farm. Technological institute at N suburb of Nawabganj. When ceded to British in 1801, Cawnpore was a village; grew rapidly to its present commercial importance. Entire Br. pop. of city, including women and children, slaughtered by Nana Sahib during Sepoy Rebellion of 1857.

Cawnpore Branch, India: see GANGES CANALS.

Cawood (kā'wŏŏd), agr. village and parish (pop. 923), West Riding, SE central Yorkshire, England, on Ouse R. and 4 mi. NW of Selby; site of remains of palace of archbishops of York, built before Norman conquest. It was Wolsey's summer residence.

Cawood (kā'wŏŏd), mining village (pop. 1,232), Harlan co., SE Ky., in the Cumberlands, 7 mi. SE of Harlan; bituminous coal.

Caxamarca, Peru: see CAJAMARCA, city.

Caxambu (käshămbōō'), city (pop. 5,866), S Minas Gerais, Brazil, on N slope of the Serra da Mantiqueira, on railroad and 40 mi. N of Cruzeiro (São Paulo); alt. 2,950 ft. One of Brazil's most frequented spas, noted for its curative mineral springs and dry, temperate climate. Effervescent waters are bottled. Direct air service to Rio de Janeiro (125 mi. SE) during Jan.–April season. Has fine church, meteorological observatory, broadcasting station.

Caxhuacán (käswäkän'), town (pop. 1,614), Puebla, central Mexico, in SE foothills of Sierra Madre Oriental, 29 mi. ESE of Huauchinango; sugar cane, coffee, tobacco, fruit.

Caxias (käshē'ŭsh). **1** City (pop. 7,042), E Maranhão, Brazil, head of regular navigation on right bank of Itapecuru R., on São Luís–Teresina RR, and 40 mi. WNW of Teresina; 4°53'S 43°22'W. Commercial and processing center of fertile agr. dist., with cotton mills, brickworks, and sugar refineries. Ships large quantities of babassu nuts; also tobacco, carnauba wax, and cereals. Airport. Road to Carolina. **2** City, Rio de Janeiro, Brazil: see DUQUE DE CAXIAS. **3** City, Rio Grande do Sul, Brazil: see CAXIAS DO SUL.

Caxias, town (pop. 1,507), Lisboa dist., W central Portugal, on right bank of Tagus estuary, on railroad and 7 mi. W of Lisbon; fishing. Has former royal summer palace.

Caxias do Sul (dōō sōōl'), city (1950 pop. 32,158), NE Rio Grande do Sul, Brazil, on S slope of Serra Geral, 60 mi. N of Pôrto Alegre; branch-railroad terminus; winegrowing center; cattle and hog slaughtering, lard mfg. Agates found near by. Founded c.1870 by Italian immigrant settlers. Called Caxias until 1944.

Caxine, Cape (käksēn'), headland of Alger dept., N central Algeria, on the Mediterranean, 6 mi. WNW of Algiers; 36°48'N 2°55'E.

Cayajabos (kīähä'bōs), town (pop. 775), Pinar del Río prov., W Cuba, 38 mi. SW of Havana; tobacco, sugar cane, fruit.

Cayaltí (kīältē'), village (pop. 3,877), Lambayeque dept., NW Peru, on coastal plain, on Saña R. (irrigation) and 2 mi. NE of Saña, on railroad from Puerto Eten; major sugar-producing center; sugar milling, distilling.

Cayamas, Las (läs kīä'mäs), keys off SW Cuba, in the Gulf of Batabanó, 35 mi. SSW of Havana; chain is c.10 mi. long, N-S.

Cayambe (kīäm'bā), town (1950 pop. 7,364), Pichincha prov., N central Ecuador, in Andes, at foot of Cayambe volcano, on Pan American Highway, on Quito-Ibarra RR, and 33 mi. NE of Quito; trading center in agr. region (wheat, corn, oats, potatoes, cattle); dairying, mfg. of straw hats.

Cayambe, extinct Andean volcano (19,014 ft.), N central Ecuador, just N of the equator, 40 mi. ENE of Quito. Town of Cayambe at NW foot. Now craterless, with square snow-capped top.

Cayapas River (kīä'päs), Esmeraldas prov., N Ecuador, rises in W outliers of the Andes near Imbabura prov. border, flows c.65 mi. W and N, through tropical lowland forests, to Santiago R. estuary 11 mi. WNW of Concepción. Navigable for shallow craft. Gold is washed along its course.

Cayari River, Colombia and Brazil: see UAUPÉS RIVER.

Cayasta (kīä'stä), town (pop. estimate 800), E central Santa Fe prov., Argentina, port on San Javier R. and 45 mi. NE of Santa Fe, in agr. area (peanuts, corn, flax, livestock).

Cayastacito (kīästäsē'tō), town (pop. estimate 700), central Santa Fe prov., Argentina, 35 mi. NNE of Santa Fe, in agr. area (corn, flax, wheat, livestock).

Caybasi (chībä-shŭ'), Turkish *Çaybaşı*, town (pop. 6,084), Rize prov., NE Turkey, on Black Sea, 13 mi. ENE of Rize; corn. Formerly Mapavri and Cayeli.

Cay Caulker, Br. Honduras: see CAY CORKER.

Cayce (kā'sē"). **1** Village, Fulton co., extreme SW Ky., 28 mi. WSW of Mayfield, in agr. area. Boyhood home of "Casey" Jones, railroad engineer famed in balladry; near by is monument to him. **2** Town (pop. 3,294), Lexington co., central S.C., on Congaree R. just SSW of Columbia, in cotton and corn area; lumber, fertilizer, foundry products.

Cay Corker, island (pop. 245) in Caribbean Sea, in Belize dist., N Br. Honduras, 15 mi. NNE of Belize; 8 mi. long, 1–2 mi. wide. Coconuts; lumbering. Cay Corker village is on E shore. Also spelled Cay Caulker.

Caycuma (chījōōmä'), Turkish *Çaycuma*, village (pop. 2,432), Zonguldak prov., N Turkey, on Yenice R., on railroad and 15 mi. E of Zonguldak; coal mines; grain, flax, hemp.

Cayeli, Turkey: see CAYBASI.

Cayemites Islands (kāmēt'), 2 islets (□ 17; 1950 pop. 1,951), W Haiti, in Gulf of Gonaïves, just off N Tiburon Peninsula, 90 mi. W of Port-au-Prince; 18°40'N 73°40'W. Just W of the larger, Grande Cayemite, is Petite Cayemite. Cotton growing.

Cayenne (kīĕn', kā–, Fr. käyĕn'), city (commune pop. 10,961), ⊙ Fr. Guiana, Atlantic port on NW coast of Cayenne Isl., at mouth of Cayenne R. (branch of Comté R.), 200 mi. ESE of Paramaribo; 4°56'N 52°20'W. Agr. region (coffee, cacao, rice, pepper, sugar cane, corn, tropical fruit); rum distilling, sawmilling. Exports principally gold; also some timber, rosewood essence, balata, rum, hides, cacao, bananas. Only ships of 15-ft. draught can dock; larger vessels anchor outside the harbor. Has international airport. Founded 1643 by the French, it was wiped out by the Indians soon after, and was permanently settled in 1664. It was long the center of Fr. penal settlements in Guiana; transportation of convicts ceased in 1935, and most of the penitentiaries were dissolved in 1946.

Cayenne Island (13 mi. long, c.5 mi. wide), on Atlantic coast of Fr. Guiana, formed by estuary of Comté R. and a branch, the small Cayenne R. An alluvial region with some low hills, it is the main settled region of Fr. Guiana, where sugar cane, coffee, cacao, corn, pepper, and tropical fruit are grown. Cayenne city is on NW coast.

Cayes, Les (lā kā'), or **Aux Cayes** (ō kā'), city (1950 census pop. 11,835), ⊙ Sud dept. (□ c.2,400; 1950 pop. 740,171), SW Haiti, Caribbean port on S coast of Tiburon Peninsula, 95 mi. WSW of Port-au-

Prince (linked by road); 18°12'N 73°45'W. The leading S port, shipping sugar, coffee, bananas, cotton, timber, dyewood, hides. Alcohol and liquor distilling. Laid out 1786. Sometimes simply Cayes.

Cayes-de-Jacmel (kā-dŭ-zhäkmĕl') or **Cayes-Jacmel,** town (1950 pop. 952), Ouest dept., S Haiti, on the coast, 10 mi. E of Jacmel, in banana region.

Cayetano Rubio (kīātä'nō rōō'byō), town (pop. 2,550), Querétaro, central Mexico, on interior plateau, 2 mi. E of Querétaro; cotton milling. Formerly called Hércules.

Cayeux-sur-Mer (käyû-sür-mâr'), town (pop. 2,255), Somme dept., N France, on English Channel just S of Somme R. estuary, 16 mi. WNW of Abbeville; bathing resort (boardwalk); fisheries.

Cayey (kīā'), town (pop. 18,429), E central Puerto Rico, in the Sierra de Cayey, 25 mi. S of San Juan; summer resort; sugar and tobacco center; also coffee; alcohol distilling. Just NE is U.S. Army Henry Barracks.

Cayey, Sierra de (syĕ'rä dā), mountain range, SE Puerto Rico, just N of Guayama, extending c.20 mi. W-E; rises to 2,963 ft. (Cerro La Santa). In the region are L. Carite reservoir and hydroelectric plants.

Caylar, Le (lŭ kĕlär'), village (pop. 397), Hérault dept., S France, in the Causse du Larzac, 9 mi. N of Lodève; sheep and horse raising.

Cayley, village (pop. 140), S Alta., 40 mi. S of Calgary; wheat, dairying.

Cay Lobos (kā' lō'bŭs, kē') or **Lobos Cay,** islet and district (including Cay Sal, □ 7; pop. 7), S Bahama Isls., on S fringe of the Great Bahama Bank, separated from Cuba by 20-mi.-wide Old Bahama Channel, 185 mi. S of Nassau; 22°24'N 77°37'W. Lighthouse.

Caylus (kĕlüs'), village (pop. 659), Tarn-et-Garonne dept., SW France, 16 mi. SW of Villefranche-de-Rouergue; cattle, vegetables. Has 14th-15th-cent. houses.

Cayma (kī'mä), town (pop. 1,781), Arequipa dept., S Peru, at SW foot of El Misti, on Chili R. and 2 mi. N of Arequipa; wheat, corn, potatoes, alfalfa. Sometimes Caima.

Cayman Brac (kā'mŭn brăk', kīmän'), island (□ 12.85; pop. 1,296) of Cayman Isls., dependency of Jamaica, B.W.I., easternmost of the group, separated by narrow channel from Little Cayman isl. (W) and 75 mi. ENE of Grand Cayman isl.; 19°45'N 79°50'W; c.11 mi. long, 1 mi. wide, rising to 130 ft. Exports turtle shells and coconuts.

Cayman Deep, Caribbean Sea: see BARTLETT TROUGH.

Cayman Islands (kā'mŭn, kīmän'), archipelago (□ 92.81; 1943 pop. 6,670; 1947 estimate 9,625), dependency of Jamaica, B.W.I.; ⊙ Georgetown. They lie c.150 mi. WNW of Jamaica and 100 mi. SW of Cape Cruz, Cuba; consist of 3 isls.—GRAND CAYMAN, LITTLE CAYMAN, CAYMAN BRAC—extending c.100 mi. WSW-ENE, bet. 19°15'–19°45'N and 79°45'–81°30'W. Average temp. about 80°F.; heaviest rains in Sept. and Oct. Principal industries are shark and turtle fishing, shipbuilding, ropemaking, lumbering (mahogany, cedar), coconut growing. The isls. were discovered on May 10, 1503, by Columbus. First called Las Tortugas because of the many turtles. Mainly settled from Jamaica in 1st half of 18th cent. Pop., though predominantly Negro, includes large number of white settlers.

Caymont, Palestine: see JOKNEAM.

Cayo [Sp.,=key]: for names beginning thus, see under main part of name; e.g., for Cayo Francés, see FRANCÉS, CAYO.

Cayo (kī'ō), district (□ 1,731; pop. 7,370) of central Br. Honduras; ⊙ Cayo. Bounded W by Guatemala, it is mostly mountainous (Maya Mts.) and jungle-covered. Drained by Belize R. Agr. (corn, rice, citrus fruit), chicle collecting, lumbering, stock raising (cattle, hogs). Principal centers are Cayo, Benque Viejo, and Soccoths.

Cayo or **El Cayo** (ĕl), town (pop. 1,548), ⊙ Cayo dist., central Br. Honduras, on Belize R. (river boat service) and 60 mi. SW of Belize, near Guatemala border. Trades in chicle, corn, beans, rice, livestock (cattle, hogs); lumbering. Entrepôt trade with Guatemala.

Cayolle, Col de la (kôl dŭ lä käyôl'), pass (alt. 7,634 ft.) in Provence Alps, SE France, on Basses-Alpes-Alpes-Maritimes dept. border, connecting Ubaye (N) and Var valleys, on Barcelonnette-Guillaumes road (*route des Alpes*).

Cayo Mambí (kī'ō mämbē'), town (pop. 1,362), Oriente prov., E Cuba, on landlocked inlet, 5 mi. NNW of Sagua de Tánamo; sugar cane, fruit.

Cayon (kāōn'), village (pop. 802), E St. Kitts, B.W.I., 4 mi. N of Basseterre, in agr. region (sugar cane, sea-island cotton, fruit).

Cayor (käyōr'), anc. native kingdom and region in W Senegal, Fr. West Africa, hinterland of Dakar. Now principal peanut-growing region.

Cayres (kâr), village (pop. 486), Haute-Loire dept., S central France, 9 mi. SSW of Le Puy; lacemaking.

Cayrol, Le (lŭ kĕrôl'), village (pop. 67), Aveyron dept., S France, 20 mi. NE of Rodez; slate quarries.

Cay Sal (kā" säl', kē") [Sp.,=salt key], uninhabited islet, Bahama Isls., on SW fringe of Cay Sal Bank, on 45-mi.-wide Nicholas Channel, separating the bank from Cuba, and 100 mi. SE of Key West, Fla. Belongs with Cay Lobos (200 mi. ESE) to Cay Lobos dist.

Cay Sal Bank, shoal (c.70 mi. long, up to 45 mi. wide) in the West Indies, bet. Florida (W) and Cuba (S), 100 mi. S of Miami; bounded by Straits of Florida (NW), Santaren Channel (E), and Nicholas Channel (S). Cay Sal reef is on its W fringe.

Cayster River, Turkey: see KUCUK MENDERES RIVER.

Cayuga (kāyōō'gŭ), village (pop. 709), ⊙ Haldimand co., S Ont., on Grand R. and 20 mi. S of Hamilton; natural-gas production, rug mfg., dairying, flour milling; limestone, gypsum, and sandstone quarries.

Cayuga (kīyōō'gŭ, kā-, kŭ-), county (□ 699; pop. 70,136), W central N.Y.; ⊙ Auburn. Bounded N by L. Ontario and extending S into Finger Lakes region; crossed by N.Y. State Barge Canal; drained by Seneca R. Dairying and farming (hay, grain, potatoes, truck) area, with diversified mfg. mainly at Auburn. Resorts on scenic Cayuga and Owasco lakes. Formed 1799.

Cayuga. 1 Town (pop. 1,022), Vermillion co., W Ind., near Wabash R., 34 mi. N of Terre Haute, in agr. and bituminous-coal area; canned goods, brick. **2** Resort village (pop. 534), Cayuga co., W central N.Y., on Cayuga L. near N end, 7 mi. W of Auburn. **3** Village (pop. 178), Sargent co., SE N.Dak., 16 mi. W of Lidgerwood.

Cayuga and Seneca Canal, N.Y.: see SENECA RIVER.

Cayuga Heights, residential village (pop. 1,131), Tompkins co., W central N.Y., on Cayuga L., just N of Ithaca, in Finger Lakes region.

Cayuga Lake, W central N.Y., longest (38 mi.) and 2d-largest (□ c.66) of the Finger Lakes, bet. Seneca and Owasco lakes, forming boundary of Seneca and Cayuga counties and extending into Tompkins co.; 1–3½ mi. wide, with cliff-like banks cut by entering streams. Joined via Seneca R. to Seneca L. (W), by Cayuga and Seneca Canal to the Barge Canal (N). Surrounding farm and fruit region has resorts. Cayuga Lake State Park is near Seneca Falls; Taughannock Falls and Buttermilk Falls state parks are near Ithaca. Cornell Univ. at Ithaca overlooks S end of lake, and Cayuga and Cayuga Heights villages are on its shores.

Cayuta Creek (kāyōō'tŭ), in N.Y. and Pa., rises in Cayuta L. (c.2 mi. long) SW of Ithaca, W central N.Y., flows c.35 mi. generally SE to Susquehanna R. at Sayre, Pa.

Cayutúe (kīōōtōō'ā), village, Llanquihue prov., S central Chile, resort on S arm of L. Todos los Santos, 40 mi. NE of Puerto Montt.

Cazabe, Colombia: see CASABE.

Cazaci or **Cazacii-Vechi,** Ukrainian SSR: see STARO-KAZACHYE.

Cazalegas (kä-thälā'gäs), village (pop. 1,104), Toledo prov., central Spain, on Alberche R. and 9 mi. ENE of Talavera de la Reina; olives, cereals, grapes, livestock.

Cazalilla (kä-thälē'lyä), town (pop. 1,650), Jaén prov., S Spain, 15 mi. SW of Linares; olive-oil processing; sheep and hog raising; cereals.

Cazalla de la Sierra (kä-thä'lyä dhä lä syĕ'rä), town (pop. 7,635), Seville prov., SW Spain, in the Sierra Morena, 39 mi. NNE of Seville; processing and agr. center (cereals, vegetables, olives, grapes, acorns, cork, timber, stock). Liquor distilling, mfg. of furniture and wooden boxes. Has mineral springs. Iron and copper deposits with foundries are near by. Sanctuary of the Virgin of the Mountain is 2 mi. SE.

Cazals (käzäl', -zäls'), village (pop. 316), Lot dept., SW France, 17 mi. NW of Cahors; sawmilling; iron deposits near by.

Cazane Defile (käzän'), narrow gorge (120–180 yards wide, c.8 mi. long) of the middle Danube, along border of Rumania and Yugoslavia, in outliers of W Transylvanian Alps, just SW of Orsova. One of the most impressive sights on the Danube, this passage is also of historic importance. Has remains of a road built by Trajan. Here Austrians won (1892) a victory over the Turks. Sometimes called Kazán.

Cazanesti (kŭzŭnĕsht'), Rum. *Căzănești,* village (pop. 2,278), Ialomita prov., SE Rumania, on railroad and 33 mi. NW of Calarasi; wheat, corn.

Cazaubon (käzōbō'), village (pop. 878), Gers dept., SW France, at edge of the Landes, 21 mi. E of Mont-de-Marsan; Armagnac brandy distilling, flour milling, horse breeding. Barbotan-les-Thermes (bärbôtä'-lā-târm'), a thermal station known for mud baths, is 2 mi. NE.

Cazaux (käzō), lake in Gironde and Landes depts., SW France, 35 mi. SW of Bordeaux; separated by dune belt (c.3 mi. wide) from Bay of Biscay; 7.5 mi. long, 6 mi. wide; fishing, duck hunting. Surrounded by pine forests.

Cazenovia (kăzŭnō'vēŭ). **1** Resort village (pop. 1,946), Madison co., central N.Y., at S end of Cazenovia L., 18 mi. SE of Syracuse, in farm and dairy area. Seat of Cazenovia Jr. Col. Settled 1793, inc. 1810. **2** Village (pop. 403), Richland co., S central Wis., 16 mi. NE of Richland Center, in dairy and livestock region.

Cazenovia Lake, Madison co., central N.Y., 15 mi. SE of Syracuse; 4 mi. long. Resort.

Cazères (käzâr'), town (pop. 2,314), Haute-Garonne dept., S France, on the Garonne and 19 mi. ENE of Saint-Gaudens; hosiery and furniture mfg., meat canning, tanning, hog raising.

Cazes, airport, Fr. Morocco: see CASABLANCA.

Cazes-Mondenard (käz'-mōdŭnär'), village (pop. 253), Tarn-et-Garonne dept., SW France, 15 mi. NNW of Montauban, in grape-growing region.

Cazilhac (käzēyäk'), village (pop. 84), Hérault dept., S France, in the Cévennes, 7 mi. SE of Le Vigan; silk-hose mfg.

Cazin or **Tsazin** (both: tsä'zĭn), town (pop. 2,780), NW Bosnia, Yugoslavia, 11 mi. NNE of Bihac; local trade center.

Cazma (chäz'mä), Serbo-Croatian *Čazma,* village (pop. 2,717), N Croatia, Yugoslavia, on Cazma R. and 15 mi. SW of Bjelovar, in Slavonia; trade center in winegrowing region. First mentioned in 12th cent. Formerly called Zacesan.

Cazma River or **Cesma River** (chĕz'mä), Serbo-Croatian *Čazma* or *Česma,* N Croatia, Yugoslavia, formed by junction of 2 headstreams 15 mi. WSW of Bjelovar, flows c.60 mi. SSW to Lonja R. 8 mi. NNE of Sisak.

Cazombo (käzŏm'bō), town (pop. 2,212), Bié prov., E Angola, on upper Zambezi R. and 200 mi. E of Vila Luso; 11°53'S 22°48'E.

Cazones (käsō'nĕs), town (pop. 1,202), Veracruz, Mexico, on small Cazones R., near Gulf of Mexico, 18 mi. SSE of Tuxpan; fruit, fiber plants, rubber.

Cazones, Gulf of, S Cuba, bet. Zapata Peninsula (N) and Jardines Bank (S), 45 mi. WSW of Cienfuegos; c.30 mi. long, up to 10 mi. wide. Fringed by keys. Its NW extension is called Ensenada de Cazones.

Cazorla (kä-thôr'lä), city (pop. 8,639), Jaén prov., S Spain, in Andalusia, on slope of the Sierra de Cazorla, 14 mi. SSE of Villacarrillo; agr. trade center. Olive-oil processing, flour- and sawmilling, plaster mfg. Cereals, fruit, livestock, lumber. Silver-lead ore mined near by. Dominated by ruins of Moorish castle.

Cazorla, Sierra de, Spain: see SEGURA, SIERRA DE.

Cazouls-lès-Béziers (käzōōl'-lā-bāzyā'), town (pop. 2,980), Hérault dept., S France, 7 mi. NW of Béziers; winegrowing.

Cazza, island, Yugoslavia: see SUSAC ISLAND.

Ccapacmarca or **Capacmarca** (both: käpäkmär'kä), town (pop. 741), Cuzco dept., S Peru, in the Andes, 25 mi. SSW of Cuzco; grain, stock.

Ccapi (kä'pē), town (pop. 638), Cuzco dept., S Peru, in the Andes, 23 mi. SSW of Cuzco; grain.

Cea, Greece: see KEA.

Ceadar-Lunga, Moldavian SSR: see CHADYR-LUNGA.

Ceahlau (chäkh'lŭōō), Rum. *Ceahlău,* picturesque mountain group in the Moldavian Carpathians, NE central Rumania, in Moldavia, 20 mi. NW of Piatra Neamt; rises to 6,245 ft. Noted in medieval times as refuge of numerous hermits and ascetics. Its bare ridges and fantastically shaped rocks gave rise to many Rumanian legends.

Ceanannus Mór (sē"ŭnă'nŭs mōr') or **Kells,** urban district (pop. 2,143), NW Co. Meath, Ireland, on the Blackwater and 10 mi. NW of An Uaimh; woolen milling; agr. market (cattle, horses; potatoes). Famous as early Celtic academic center; the *Book of Kells* (illuminated manuscript of the Latin Gospels, now in Trinity Col. library, Dublin) was produced here in 8th cent. Among noted bldgs. are St. Columba's House (c.800, relic of anc. monastery), a round tower, and remains of town walls. St. Columba founded monastery here c.550, which became important center of learning. In 9th cent monks of Iona, expelled by Danes, settled here; abbey was destroyed 1019 by Danes. In 1315 Edward Bruce burned the town; in 1551 the monastery was dissolved. Sometimes spelled Ceanannus Mór.

Ceará (sēärä'), state (□ 59,168; 1940 pop. 2,091,032; 1950 census 2,735,702), NE Brazil; ⊙ Fortaleza. Situated on N coast of Brazilian hump, it is bounded by states of Piauí (W), Rio Grande do Norte and Paraíba (E), and Pernambuco (S). Its narrow, sandy coastal plain is adjoined (S) by semiarid dissected interior plateau which rises to c.3,000 ft. in the Serra Grande and Serra do Araripe (along state's W and S border, respectively). Ceará is drained by Jaguaribe R., which enters the Atlantic below Aracati. Chief crops, grown by means of irrigation in interior and in more humid coastal areas, are cotton, sugar, and coffee. Important export products are carnauba wax, oiticica oil (chiefly from NE), vegetable fibers, castor beans, and maniçoba rubber. Livestock raised extensively in interior provides hides for shipment. Rutile and salt are the only minerals commercially exploited. Ceará has 2 railroad lines penetrating the interior from Fortaleza and Camocim, respectively. Has inadequate road net; no navigable rivers. Chief cities are Fortaleza, ports of Camocim and Aracati, and Sobral, Crateús, Crato, Juàzeiro do Norte, and Iguatu (inland). First settled by Portuguese early in 17th cent., and held by Dutch (1637–54), Ceará was part of Maranhão until it became (1680) a dependency of Pernambuco. An independent captaincy after 1799, it became a prov. in 1822, and a state of the federal republic in 1889. Ceará was one of 1st territories to abolish slavery in Brazil. Part of pop., forced to flee the interior (calamity area) during recurrent periods of drought, migrated to Amazonia (during rubber boom) and to S central states. Considerable irrigation work under federal supervision is now under way.

Ceará, city, Ceará state, Brazil: see Fortaleza.

Ceará Mirim (mĕrēm'), city (pop. 4,725), E Rio Grande do Norte, NE Brazil, on railroad and 22 mi. WNW of Natal; stock-raising and sugar-growing center; also ships cotton and tobacco. Diatomite deposits in area.

Ceará Mirim River, Rio Grande do Norte, NE Brazil, rises near Itaretama, flows c.90 mi. E, past Ceará Mirim, to the Atlantic 7 mi. N of Natal. Intermittent-flowing stream. Its sugar-growing valley is followed by railroad.

Cea River (thā'ä), N Spain, rises on S slopes of Cantabrian Mts. 4 mi. S of Riaño, flows 109 mi. SSW, through Leon, Valladolid, and Zamora provs., to the Esla 4 mi. W of Benavente.

Cébaco Island (sā'bäkō), in Pacific Ocean, off W central Panama, W of Azuero Peninsula, barring entrance to Montijo Gulf; 15 mi. long.

Cébala-du-Mornag, La (lä sābälä'-dü-môrnäg'), village, Tunis dist., N Tunisia, 10 mi. SE of Tunis, in fertile Mornag lowland along Miliane R.; wine-growing, stock raising; olives, wheat.

Cebelibereket, Turkey: see Osmaniye.

Ceboleira (thāvōlā'rä), SW suburb (pop. 1,313) of Vigo, Pontevedra prov., NW Spain. Dairy products, cattle, wine, vegetables in area.

Cebolla (thāvō'lyä), town (pop. 2,719), Toledo prov., central Spain, near the Tagus, 12 mi. E of Talavera de la Reina; olive- and winegrowing; flour milling. Hydroelectric station.

Cebollar (sĕbōyär'), village (1930 pop. 19), Antofagasta prov., N Chile, in the Andes, on railroad to Bolivia, at W edge of the salt desert Salar de Ascotán, 75 mi. NE of Calama; alt. 12,234 ft. Borax.

Cebollatí (sābōyätē'), town (pop. 1,000), Rocha dept., SE Uruguay, on Cebollatí R. and 32 mi. E of Treinta y Tres; stock raising (cattle, sheep, hogs), nutria hunting.

Cebollatí River, S and SE Uruguay, rises in the Cuchilla Grande Principal S of Illescas, flows c.130 mi. E and NE, through Lavalleja dept. and along Treinta y Tres-Rocha dept. border, to L. Mirim 40 mi. E of Treinta y Tres city. Navigable in lower course.

Cebollera, Sierra (syĕ'rä thāvrōlyā'rä), range on central plateau (Meseta) of Old Castile, N central Spain, on Soria-Logroño prov. border, 33 mi. SSW of Logroño; rises to 7,040 ft.

Cebolleta Mountains, N.Mex.: see San Mateo Mountains, Valencia co.

Ceboruco Volcano (sābōrōō'kō), twin peak (7,100 ft.), Nayarit, W Mexico, in Sierra Madre Occidental, 6 mi. NW of Ahuacatlán; 21°8'N 104°30'W. Active.

Cebreros (thāvrā'rōs), town (pop. 3,929), Ávila prov., central Spain, on SW slopes of the Sierra de Guadarrama, near Alberche R., 18 mi. SE of Ávila, in fertile region (principally grapes; also cereals, olives, vegetables, and all kinds of fruit). Olive-oil pressing, winemaking (*albillo*), alcohol and liquor distilling, flour milling, dairying. Hydroelectric plant. Has superb Renaissance church built by Herrera.

Cebu (sābōō'), island (□ 1,702; 1939 pop. 947,309) of Visayan Isls., Philippines, bet. Visayan Sea (N) and Mindanao Sea (S); separated from Negros isl. (W) by Tañon Strait, from Bohol isl. (SE) by Bohol Strait, and from Leyte isl. (E) by Camotes Sea; 10°39'–11°17'N 123°22'–124°3'E. Cebu is long (c.135 mi.) and narrow (22 mi. wide). The isl. is volcanic but largely overlaid with coral. Mountainous, rising to 3,324 ft. in Mt. Cabalasan. Agr. (corn, coconuts, sugar cane, hemp, tobacco), fishing. Coal is mined; there are oil deposits. Cebu province (□ 1,880; 1948 pop. 1,123,107) comprises Cebu isl. and near-by isls.—Mactan Island, Bantayan Island, Camotes Islands.

Cebu, city (1948 pop. 167,503), central Cebu isl., ⊙ Cebu prov., Philippines, port on Bohol Strait, opposite Mactan Isl., 350 mi. SE of Manila; 10°18'N 123°54'E; trade center for agr. area (coconuts, corn, hemp). Portland-cement mfg., coconut-oil extracting; exports copra and hemp. Has R.C. cathedral. Founded 1565 as San Miguel, Cebu was 1st permanent Sp. settlement in Philippines. It was ⊙ Sp. colony, 1565–71.

Ceccano (chĕk-kä'nô), town (pop. 5,487), Frosinone prov., Latium, S central Italy, on Sacco R. and 5 mi. S of Frosinone; mfg. (paper, soap, glycerin). Limestone quarries near by. Its late 12th-cent. church was destroyed by bombing (1944) in Second World War.

Cece (tsĕ'tsĕ), market town (pop. 4,062), Fejer co., W central Hungary, on Sarviz R. and 29 mi. N of Szekszard; potatoes, wheat, hemp, dairy farming. Formerly Czecze.

Ceceli, Turkey: see Karaisali.

Cechy, Czechoslovakia: see Bohemia.

Cecil (sē'sŭl), county (□ 352; pop. 33,356), extreme NE Md.; ⊙ Elkton. At head of Chesapeake Bay and at base of Eastern Shore, it is bounded S by Sassafras R., E by Del. line, N by Pa. line, W by the Susquehanna (forms lake N of Conowingo Dam). Drained by Elk R. (receives Chesapeake and Delaware Canal W of Chesapeake City), Northeast R., and Octoraro Creek. Stock raising, dairying, agr. (wheat, corn, hay, truck, fruit); granite quarries, kaolin and sand pits; some mfg. (especially at Elkton); commercial fisheries. Includes Elk Neck (state park and state forest here) and Susquehanna Flats (waterfowl hunting). Boundary dispute of 1702 (settled 1765 by Mason and Dixon line) bet. Lord Baltimore and William Penn was caused by lands in N part of co. Formed 1674.

Cecil. 1 (sē'sŭl) Town (pop. 254), Cook co., S Ga., 16 mi. NNW of Valdosta. **2** (sē'sŭl) Village (pop. 266), Paulding co., NW Ohio, near Maumee R., 12 mi. WSW of Defiance; lumber milling. **3** (sĕ'sŭl, sē'sŭl) Village (1940 pop. 716), Washington co., SW Pa., 13 mi. SW of Pittsburgh; bituminous-coal mines. **4** (sē'sŭl) Village (pop. 395), Shawano co., NE Wis., at E end of Shawano L., 30 mi. NW of Green Bay city; lumbering.

Cecilio Báez or **Doctor Cecilio Báez** (dōktōr' sāsē'lyō bīs'), town (pop. 3,529), Caaguazú dept., S central Paraguay, 32 mi. NNE of Coronel Oviedo; oranges, livestock; processing of oil of petitgrain. Formerly called Colonia Cecilio Báez.

Cecilton (sĭ'sŭltŭn), town (pop. 510), Cecil co., NE Md., 16 mi. SE of Havre de Grace. Near by are historic estates, including Bohemia Manor, granted 1676; Little Bohemia Manor (formerly Milligan Hall; built c.1740–45; restored). Near by are bathing beaches.

Cecina (chā'chēnä), town (pop. 5,570), Livorno prov., Tuscany, central Italy, on Cecina R., near its mouth in Ligurian Sea, and 19 mi. SSE of Leghorn; rail junction; canned foods, macaroni, soap, paint, lye, leather goods, cement.

Cecina River, Tuscany, central Italy, rises in Apennine hills 8 mi. NNE of Massa Marittima, flows 40 mi. N and W to Ligurian Sea 2 mi. SE of Cecina.

Cecir de Mer, Poulo (pōōlō' sāsēr' dŭ mâr'), Annamese *Culao Thu* (kōōlou' tōō'), Vietnam island (4 mi. long, 2 mi. wide), in South China Sea, 65 mi. ESE of Phanthiet, 10°32'N 108°49'E.

Cecir de Terre, Poulo (dŭ târ'), Annamese *Culao Cau* (kōōlou' kou'), small Vietnam island in South China Sea, 23 mi. SSW of Phanrang; 11°13'N 108°49'E.

Ceclavín (thāklävēn'), town (pop. 5,205), Cáceres prov., W Spain, near Alagón R., 33 mi. NW of Cáceres; agr. trade center (wine, cereals, fruit); olive-oil processing, flour milling. Mineral springs. Phosphate-rock quarries near by.

Cedar. 1 County (□ 585; pop. 16,910), E Iowa; ⊙ Tipton. Prairie agr. area (hogs, cattle, corn, oats, hay, wheat) drained by Cedar R.; limestone quarries. Formed 1837. **2** County (□ 496; pop. 10,663), W Mo., in Ozark region; ⊙ Stockton. Drained by Sac R. Agr. (corn, wheat, oats), livestock; hardwood timber; coal. Formed 1843. **3** County (□ 743; pop. 13,843), NE Nebr.; ⊙ Hartington. Agr. region bounded N by Missouri R. and S.Dak. Livestock, grain. Formed 1857.

Cedar. 1 City (pop. 86), Smith co., N Kansas, on North Fork Solomon R. and 10 mi. SW of Smith Center; grain, livestock. **2** Village (pop. c.250), Leelanau co., NW Mich., 10 mi. NW of Traverse City, in fruitgrowing, farming, and resort area.

Cedara (sĕdä'rä), village, central Natal, U. of So. Afr., 7 mi NW of Pietermaritzburg; site of agr. col. (1906) and govt. experimental farm (1903).

Cedar Bluff. 1 Town (pop. 563), Cherokee co., NE Ala., on Coosa R. and 27 mi. NE of Gadsden; farming, lumber. **2** Village (1940 pop. 126), Clay co., E Miss., 11 mi. W of West Point. **3** Town (pop. 1,083), Tazewell co., SW Va., in the Alleghenies, on Clinch R. and 32 mi. WSW of Bluefield; woolen mills (blankets).

Cedar Bluffs, village (pop. 505), Saunders co., E Nebr., 35 mi. WNW of Omaha, near Platte R.; livestock, grain.

Cedar Breaks National Monument (□ 9.6; established 1933), SW Utah, c.10 mi. E of Cedar City. Includes enormous amphitheater c.2,000 ft. deep, eroded in sandstone escarpment (Pink Cliffs) of Markagunt Plateau; strata of cliffs and eroded formations in amphitheater vary from white through many shades of orange, rose, and coral.

Cedarburg, city (pop. 2,810), Ozaukee co., E Wis., on tributary of Milwaukee R. and 17 mi. N of Milwaukee; trade center in dairying and farming area; mfg. (canned vegetables, electric motors, automobile parts; wire, paper, and wood products; shoes, textiles); limestone quarries. Settled 1842, inc. 1885.

Cedar City, town (pop. 6,106), Iron co., SW Utah, just W of Markagunt Plateau, just N of Kolob Terrace, 220 mi. SSW of Salt Lake City; alt. c. 5,800 ft. Seat of state agr. jr. col. and trade center for livestock and agr. area; dairy products; mfg. (plaster, wool products, lumber). Coal and iron mines are near by. Sections of Dixie Natl. Forest (hunting and fishing) are E and SW; Cedar Breaks Natl. Monument (E), Bryce Canyon Natl. Park (E), and Zion Natl. Park (S). Settled 1851, inc. 1868.

Cedar Creek. 1 In S Iowa, rises in Lucas co., flows E and generally N to Des Moines R., 9 mi. WSW of Oskaloosa; c.50 mi. long. **2** In SE Iowa, rises in Mahaska co., flows generally SE to Skunk R. in Henry co.; c.75 mi. long. **3** In N.Dak., rises in Slope co., SW N.Dak.; flows E c.200 mi. to Cannonball R. **4** In S Rockbridge co., Va., short left tributary of James R.; site of Natural Bridge. **5** In S Frederick co., Va., small N tributary of North Fork of Shenandoah R., near Middletown.

Cedaredge, town (pop. 574), Delta co., W Colo., on branch of Gunnison R. and 14 mi. NE of Delta; alt. 6,100 ft.

Cedar Falls, city (pop. 14,334), Black Hawk co., E central Iowa, on Cedar R. and 6 mi. WNW of Waterloo; mfg. center (farm equipment, pumps, auto seat covers, canned corn, feed, blankets). Seat of Iowa State Teachers Col. (1876). Settled 1845, laid out 1851, inc. 1857.

Cedar Gap, town (pop. 45), Wright co., S central Mo., in the Ozarks, 35 mi. E of Springfield; alt. 1,694 ft.

Cedar Grove. 1 Town (pop. 193), Franklin co., SE Ind., 33 mi. S of Richmond, in agr. area. **2** Township (pop. 8,022), Essex co., NE N.J., in Watchung Mts. 2 mi. N of Montclair; mfg. (gauges, brushes); stone quarry; truck, dairy products. Has hosp. for insane. **3** Town (pop. 1,738), Kanawha co., W W.Va., on Kanawha R. and 14 mi. SE of Charleston, in bituminous-coal, gas, and oil region. Site of Booker T. Washington's boyhood home is near by. Settled 1773. **4** Village (pop. 1,010), Sheboygan co., E Wis., 12 mi. SSW of Sheboygan, in dairy and grain area; furnace mfg.

Cedar Hammock, village (pop. 1,101), Manatee co., SW Fla.

Cedar Heights. 1 Village (1940 pop. 751), Prince Georges co., central Md., E suburb of Washington. **2** Village (pop. 1,553, with adjacent Spring Mill), Montgomery co., SE Pa., near Conshohocken.

Cedar Hill, town (pop. 732), Dallas co., N Texas, 18 mi. SW of Dallas, in agr. area.

Cedarhurst. 1 Village, Carroll co., N Md., 8 mi. SE of Westminster; mfg. of linoleum base, whisky. **2** Residential village (pop. 6,051), Nassau co., SE N.Y., on W Long Isl., near E shore of Jamaica Bay, 7 mi. SE of Jamaica; cement blocks. Inc. 1910.

Cedar Island. 1 Island in Maine: see Isles of Shoals. **2** Island in St. Lawrence co., N N.Y., one of the Thousand Isls., in the St. Lawrence, near Ont. line, just W of Chippewa Bay; c.½ mi. long. Site of Cedar Island State Park (recreational area). **3** Island in E Va., barrier island just off Atlantic shore of Accomack co., 5 mi. SE of Accomac; 6 mi. long. Metomkin Inlet along N, Wachapreague Inlet along S shores.

Cedar Key, city (pop. 900), Levy co., N Fla., 55 mi. SW of Gainesville, on small isl. connected by causeway with the Gulf coast; fishing; mfg. of palmetto brushes. Was a busy port and railroad station in mid-19th cent.

Cedar Lake (□ 537), W Man., 50 mi. SE of The Pas and 4 mi. N of L. Winnipegosis; 40 mi. long, 32 mi. wide. Drained E into L. Winnipeg by Saskatchewan R.

Cedar Lake. 1 Farm community, Morgan co., N Ala., 4 mi. S of Decatur. **2** Village (pop. 3,907), Lake co., NW Ind., on a small lake 18 mi. S of Gary.

Cedar Lake. 1 Lake in Minn.: see Koronis, Lake. **2** Lake in Wis.: see Slinger.

Cedar Mills, village (pop. 99), Meeker co., S central Minn., 11 mi. S of Litchfield.

Cedar Mountain, Va.: see Bull Run.

Cedar Park. 1 Suburb of Annapolis, Anne Arundel co., central Md. **2** Village, Williamson co., central Texas, 18 mi. NNW of Austin; ships cedar; limestone quarries.

Cedar Pines, resort village (pop. 1,369, with near-by Crestline), San Bernardino co., S Calif., in San Bernardino Mts. c.10 mi. N of San Bernardino.

Cedar Point. 1 Village (pop. 296), La Salle co., N Ill., 5 mi. S of La Salle, in agr. and bituminous-coal area. **2** City (pop. 107), Chase co., E central Kansas, on Cottonwood R. and 33 mi. WSW of Emporia; livestock, grain.

Cedar Point. 1 Low peninsula, St. Marys co., S Md., on S side of Patuxent R. entrance from Chesapeake Bay and 18 mi. N of Point Lookout. Site of Patuxent Naval Air Test Center. **2** Peninsula in Ohio: see Sandusky Bay.

Cedar Rapids. 1 City (pop. 72,296), ⊙ Linn co., E Iowa, on both banks of Cedar R. (dammed here for power) and c.65 mi. WNW of Davenport; a major industrial and commercial center of the state, noted for its cereal mills (particularly "Quaker Oats"). Has large factory making portable rock-crushing equipment. Also produces meat, corn, bakery, and dairy products; machinery (milling, dairy), furnaces, radio equipment and cabinets, steel office furniture, paper containers and photographic paper, sponge rubber, fur garments, feed, pharmaceuticals, concrete. Limestone quarries near by. Has railroad shops. Coe Col. (coeducational; 1881), a large Masonic library (1844), and an art gall. (with paintings by Grant Wood) are here. Landscaped Municipal Isl. is site of the courthouse and a neoclassic war memorial bldg. Settled in 1838; laid out as Rapids City in 1841; renamed and inc. as a town in 1849, as a city in 1856. Czechs came here early (1852), compose ⅓ of the pop. **2** Village (pop. 541), Boone co., E central Nebr., 11 mi. SW of Albion and on Cedar R.; dairy and poultry produce, livestock, grain, fruit.

Cedar River, resort village, Menominee co., SW Upper Peninsula, Mich., at mouth of Short Cedar R. on L. Michigan and 23 mi. NNE of Menominee; hunting, fishing. State park.

Cedar River. 1 In SW Upper Peninsula, Mich., rises in NW Menominee co., flows c.60 mi. SSE, past Powers, to Green Bay c.25 mi. NE of Menominee. **2** In S central Mich.: see RED CEDAR RIVER. **3** In Minn. and Iowa, rises in Dodge co., SE Minn., flows S, past Austin, Minn., then generally SE through E Iowa, past Charles City, Cedar Falls, Waterloo and Cedar Rapids, to Iowa R. at Columbus Junction, SE Iowa; 300 mi. long, not navigable. Sometimes known as Red Cedar R. Tributaries are Shell Rock and Little Cedar rivers. **4** In N central Nebr., rises in Garfield co., flows 120 mi. SE, past Belgrade, to Loup R. at Fullerton. **5** In W central Wash., rises in Cascade Range E of Tacoma, flows 45 mi. NW to L. Washington at Renton.

Cedars, village (pop. estimate 400), S Que., on St. Lawrence narrows bet. L. St. Francis and L. St. Louis, 5 mi. NE of Valleyfield; major hydroelectric station, supplying Montreal, on the Cedar Rapids.

Cedar Springs, village (pop. 1,378), Kent co., SW Mich., on small Cedar Creek and 18 mi. NNE of Grand Rapids, in resort and agr. area (livestock, truck, grain, potatoes, corn); dairy products; feed mill, poultry hatchery; timber. Settled 1859; inc. 1871.

Cedartown, city (pop. 9,470), ⊙ Polk co., NW Ga., 17 mi. SSW of Rome and on small Cedar Creek. Mfg. center; tire fabric, cotton and worsted goods, yarn, fertilizer, chemicals, furniture, agr. implements. Iron mines near by. Springs here furnish city water supply. Settled on site of Cherokee village.

Cedar Vale, city (pop. 1,010), Chautauqua co., SE Kansas, on Caney R. and 27 mi. E of Arkansas City, in grazing and grain region; mfg. of surgical instruments.

Cedarville. 1 Town (pop. 43), Crawford co., NW Ark., 13 mi. N of Fort Smith. **2** Village (pop. c.500), Modoc co., NE Calif., in Surprise Valley, 18 mi. E of Alturas; farming, stock raising. Gateway to Warner Mts. (W; hunting). **3** Village (pop. 466), Stephenson co., N Ill., 5 mi. N of Freeport, in agr. area. Birthplace of Jane Addams; her grave is here. **4** Village, Mackinac co., SE Upper Peninsula, Mich., on L. Huron and 20 mi. NE of St. Ignace. Tourist gateway to Les Cheneaux Isls. **5** Village (pop. 1,009), Cumberland co., S N.J., 7 mi. S of Bridgeton; market center for truck region; canned vegetables, fire-fighting equipment; sand pits, stone quarries. **6** Village (pop. 1,292), Greene co., S central Ohio, 11 mi. S of Springfield. Seat of Cedarville Col. Settled 1805.

Ceded Mile, name applied to a narrow, c.35-mi.-long strip of land in W Gambia, on right bank of Gambia R.; extends from Fr. Senegal border on Atlantic Ocean to area of Kerewan. Acquired 1826 by British as colony land, has been administered since 1897 as part of the protectorate.

Cedegolo (chĕdā'gôlô), village (pop. 733), Brescia prov., Lombardy, N Italy, in Val Camonica, on Oglio R. and 7 mi. S of Edolo; chemical industry; hydroelectric plant. Near by, at Sellero (pop. 659), is a copper mine.

Cedeira (thā-dhā'rä), town (pop. 1,479), La Coruña prov., NW Spain, fishing port on inlet of the Atlantic, and 15 mi. NE of El Ferrol; fish processing, sawmilling; cereals, potatoes, livestock.

Cedeño (sādā'nyō), village, Choluteca dept., S Honduras, on Gulf of Fonseca, 16 mi. SW of Choluteca; beach resort. Airfield.

Cedillo (thā-dhē'lyō), village (pop. 1,236), Cáceres prov., W Spain, near Tagus R. and Port. border, 13 mi. S of Castelo Branco (Portugal); olive-oil and cheese processing; cereals, honey, cork.

Cedillo del Condado (dhĕl kōndä'dhō), town (pop. 1,011), Toledo prov., central Spain, 24 mi. SW of Madrid; olives, cereals, grapes, livestock; olive oil.

Cedral (sĭdräl'), city (pop. 1,696), N São Paulo, Brazil, on railroad and 10 mi. SE of São José do Rio Prêto; mfg. of butter, soap, pottery; distilling; coffeegrowing.

Cedral (sādräl'), city (pop. 3,543), San Luis Potosí, N central Mexico, on railroad and 13 mi. NW of Matehuala; silver and lead mining.

Cedro (sā'drōō). **1** City (pop. 3,625), SE Ceará, Brazil, on Fortaleza-Crato RR at junction of spur to Patos (Paraíba), and 22 mi. SE of Iguatu; cotton. **2** City, Sergipe, Brazil: see DARCILENA.

Cedros (sā'drōs), city (pop. 1,095), Francisco Morazán dept., central Honduras, 33 mi. NNE of Tegucigalpa; alt. 3,199 ft. Trade center in agr. area; coffee, sugar cane, grain, livestock. A major Sp. colonial gold- and silver-mining center. First Honduras natl. assembly met here, 1824. Iron mining at Agalteca, 13 mi. SW.

Cedros (sā'drŏs), village, SW Trinidad, B.W.I., on N shore of SW peninsula (Cedros Bay), on the Serpent's Mouth, 45 mi. SW of Port of Spain, adjoined by Bonasse (E); coconut processing. A U.S. army base is just S.

Cedros Bay (sā'drŏs), inlet of Gulf of Paria, SW Trinidad, B.W.I., at SW peninsula, 45 mi. SW of Port of Spain. At its head is Bonasse. Bathing.

Cedros Island (sā'drōs) (□ 134), on Pacific coast of Lower California, NW Mexico, bordering on Sebastián Vizcaíno Bay (E), 15 mi. NW of Eugenia Point; extends 23 mi. N–S bet. 28°3'–28°22'N, up to 11 mi. wide; rises to 3,487 ft. Sparsely inhabited; has wild life (deer, reptiles, sea lions). Abalone shells are gathered.

Ceduna (sūdōō'nŭ, kē-), village (pop. 570), S South Australia, on Denial Bay of Great Australian Bight and 220 mi. NW of Port Lincoln, on spur of Port Lincoln–Penong RR; mfg. (plaster, shark-liver oil).

Cedynia (tsĕdĭ'nyä), Ger. *Zehden* (tsā'dŭn), town (1939 pop. 1,735; 1946 pop. 286) in Brandenburg, after 1945 in Szczecin prov., NW Poland, near the Oder, 30 mi. NNW of Küstrin (Kostrzyn); grain, potatoes, vegetables, livestock.

Cee (thā), town (pop. 1,373), La Coruña prov., NW Spain, on inlet of the Atlantic, and 32 mi. WNW of Santiago; fish processing, lumbering.

Ceepeecee, village (pop. estimate 100), W Vancouver Isl., SW B.C., on Hecate Channel, 20 mi. N of Nootka; fishing port; fish-reduction plant, fueling station.

Cefalo, Greece: see KEPHALOS.

Cefalù (chĕfälōō'), anc. *Cephaloedium*, town (pop. 9,654), Palermo prov., N Sicily, port on Tyrrhenian Sea, 18 mi. ENE of Termini Imerese, in grape- and olive-growing region; sardine fishing; macaroni. Bishopric. Has famous Norman cathedral built 1131–48 by Roger II, mus. of antiquities. Near by are ruins of temple dating from 9th or 8th cent. B.C. Cephaloedium, supposedly founded as an outpost of Himera, was taken by Romans in 254 B.C. during First Punic War and by Saracens in A.D. 858. Conquered in 1063 by Roger I, who rebuilt the town.

Cefn Bryn, Wales: see ARTHUR'S STONE.

Cefnllys, Wales: see LLANDRINDOD WELLS.

Cefn Mawr (kĕ'vŭn mour'), town in Cefn parish (pop. 6,526), SE Denbigh, Wales, 6 mi. SW of Wrexham; coal mining, mfg. of machinery, chemicals. Parish includes industrial town of Acrefair (äkrĕvīr'), just N of Cefn Mawr.

Ceggia (chĕd'jä), village (pop. 698), Venezia prov., Veneto, N Italy, 5 mi. NE of San Donà di Piave; beet-sugar refinery.

Cegled (tsĕg'lād), Hung. *Cegléd*, city (pop. 38,872), Pest-Pilis-Solt-Kiskun co., central Hungary, 40 mi. SE of Budapest; rail, agr., market center; distilleries, flour mills, brickworks. Grain, cattle, horses, truck farming (onions, cherries, mahalebs, grapes). Formerly spelled Czegled.

Ceglie del Campo (chā'lyĕ dĕl käm'pô), town (pop. 5,070), Bari prov., Apulia, S Italy, adjacent to Carbonara di Bari.

Ceglie Messapico (mĕs-sä'pēkô), town (pop. 16,327), Brindisi prov., Apulia, S Italy, 19 mi. NE of Taranto; agr. trade center; livestock, cereals, figs, wine, olive oil. Anc. remains (walls, necropolis).

Ceguaca (sāgwä'kä), town (pop. 1,024), Santa Barbara dept., W Honduras, near Ulúa R., 8 mi. S of Santa Bárbara; mfg. of harvest hats; sugar cane.

Cehegín (thāhēn'), city (pop. 7,724), Murcia prov., SE Spain, 25 mi. SW of Cieza; agr. trade center. Sandal mfg., essential-oil distilling, olive-oil processing, flour milling. Trades in livestock, lumber, wine, hemp, truck produce. Has Gothic church built by Herrera. Mineral springs.

Cehul-Silvaniei (chā'hōōl-sĕlvänyā'), Hung. *Szilágycseh* (sē'lädyŏochā), village (pop. 3,481), Baia-Mare prov., NW Rumania, 16 mi. NNE of Zalau; rail terminus; hide processing. Has ruins of royal fortress. In Hungary, 1940–45.

Ceiba (sā'bä), town (pop. 1,661), E Puerto Rico, near the coast, on railroad and 33 mi. ESE of San Juan; sugar growing. Adjoining E is U.S. naval reservation.

Ceiba, La, Dominican Republic: see HOSTOS.

Ceiba, La, Honduras, Venezuela: see LA CEIBA.

Ceiba del Agua (sā'bä dĕl ä'gwä), town (pop. 1,303), Havana prov., W Cuba, on Central Highway, on railroad and 25 mi. SW of Havana; tobacco, fruit, vegetables. Site of Cívico Militar Inst., with trade schools.

Ceiba Mocha (mō'chä), town (pop. 1,695), Matanzas prov., W Cuba, on railroad, on Central Highway and 10 mi. WSW of Matanzas; sugar cane, fruit, stock.

Ceica (chā'kä), Hung. *Magyarcséke* (mŏ'dyŏr-chā-kĕ), village (pop. 1,687), Bihor prov., W Rumania, on railroad and 17 mi. SE of Oradea; agr. center.

Ceja, La, Colombia: see LA CEJA.

Cejas, Las, Argentina: see LAS CEJAS.

Cejle-Kostelec, Czechoslovakia: see JIHLAVA.

Cekerek (chĕkĕrĕk'), Turkish *Çekerek*, village (pop. 1,329), Yozgat prov., central Turkey, 50 mi. ENE of Yozgat; mohair goats, grain.

Cekerek River, Turkish *Çekerek*, N central Turkey, rises 10 mi. SE of Tokat, flows 170 mi. WSW then NNE, past Artova, to the Yesil Irmak 8 mi. SW of Amasya.

Cekhira, La, Tunisia: see SKHIRA, LA.

Celadna (chĕ'lädnä), Czech *Čeladná*, village (pop. 2,449), NE Moravia, Czechoslovakia, on railroad and 20 mi. SSE of Ostrava; ironworks.

Celaenae, Turkey: see DINAR.

Celakovice (chĕ'läkôvĭtsĕ), Czech *Čelákovice*, town (pop. 6,041), N central Bohemia, Czechoslovakia, on Elbe R. and 16 mi. ENE of Prague; rail junction; mfg. of machinery; noted copper works.

Celanese Village (sĕ'lŭnēz), (pop. 1,945), Floyd co., NW Ga.

Celano (chĕlä'nô), town (pop. 9,784), Aquila prov., Abruzzi e Molise, S central Italy, near reclaimed Lago Fucino, 7 mi. ENE of Avezzano. Agr. trade center (cereals, potatoes, sugar beets, fruit); woolen mill. Largely destroyed (1915) by earthquake.

Celano, Lago di, Italy: see FUCINO, LAGO.

Celanova (thālänō'vä), town (pop. 3,679), Orense prov., NW Spain, 13 mi. SSW of Orense; agr. trade center (cereals, fruit, wine, flax); stock raising. Has Benedictine monastery, founded in 10th cent.

Celaque, Sierra de (syĕ'rä dā sālä'kä), section of main Andean divide in W Honduras, on Ocotepeque-Copán-Gracias dept. border; forms divide bet. Mocal R. (E) and Alash R. (upper Jicatuyo R.; W); rises to 10,000 ft.

Celaya (sālī'ä), city (pop. 22,766), Guanajuato, central Mexico, on interior plateau, near Laja R., 29 mi. W of Querétaro; alt. 5,764 ft. Rail junction, trading and processing center in fertile agr. region (grain, cotton, beans, sugar cane, fruit, livestock). Textile and flour milling, tanning, alcohol and liquor distilling; mfg. of sweets. Anc. colonial city (founded 1570), the city is noted as birthplace of Francisco Eduardo de Tresguerras (1765), architect and artist, who adorned it with remarkable bldgs., such as churches of El Carmen and San Francisco. Often involved in Mexican wars, Celaya was the first city to be captured (Sept. 28, 1810) by insurrectionary forces under Hidalgo y Costilla. In 1915 Villa, defeated at Celaya by Alvaro Obregón, began his long retreat northward.

Celbridge (sĕl'brĭj), Gaelic *Cill Droichid*, town (pop. 539), NE Co. Kildare, Ireland, on the Liffey and 12 mi. W of Dublin; woolen milling, clothing mfg. Celbridge Abbey was home of Esther Vanhomrigh, Swift's "Vanessa."

Celebes (sĕ'lŭbēz), Indonesian *Sulawesi* (sōōläwā'sē), island (□ 69,277; pop. 3,781,554) of Greater Sundas and province of Indonesia, bet. Celebes Sea (N), Flores Sea (S), Macassar Strait (W), and Molucca Sea (E), 90 mi. E of Borneo; 1°45'N–5°37'S 118°46'–125°14'E. Isl. is curiously shaped, consisting mainly of 4 large peninsulas extending E and S and separated by gulfs of Tomini, Tolo, and Bone. The principal peninsulas are the N projection (450 mi. long, 20–60 mi. wide) curving NE, and the SW peninsula (200 mi. long, 50–110 mi. wide). Mountainous terrain rises to 11,286 ft. at Mt. Rantemario in S central area. In central part of isl. are lakes Poso and Towuti, largest on isl. Interior is densely forested with oak, teak, cedar, ebony, sandalwood, bamboo, and upas (*Antiaris toxicaria*, a tree yielding poisonous juice). There are fertile valleys and rich grazing land in highlands. Climate is hot and humid, but relatively comfortable because of proximity of most areas to the sea. Temperature ranges from 70° to 90°F. Has heavy rainfall particularly during period of northeast monsoon. Annual rainfall ranges from 102 in. in N to 157 in. in S. Among wild animals are the ox-like anoa, marsupials known as cuscus, tailless baboons (peculiar to Celebes), and the swine-like babirusa. Inhabitants are Malayan, except for semi-civilized tribes (sometimes called Alfuros) in interior who have certain Negroid characteristics. Among the Malayan tribes are the Bugis and Macassars who are Moslem. In the N are the Christian Minahassa. Mineral resources include gold, silver, diamonds, coal, sulphur, nickel, iron. Major forest products are teak, resin, rattan. Agr.: copra, coffee, sago, vegetable oils, hemp. Cattle and ponies are raised in highlands. Valuable marine products are trepang and mother-of-pearl. Chief centers: MACASSAR, MANADO, GORONTALO, DONGGALA, PALOPO, KENDARI, PAREPARE. The first Europeans to visit the isl., the Portuguese, came 1512 and settled 1625 in Macassar area. The Dutch ousted them in 1660. In Second World War, isl. was occupied early 1942 by the Japanese who held it for duration of war. Celebes was briefly included in state of East Indonesia when it was created, 1946. In 1950, Celebes became part of the republic of Indonesia.

Celebes Sea, part of W Pacific Ocean, bounded N by Mindanao and Sulu Archipelago of the Philippines, W by Borneo, S by Celebes, E by Sangi Isls.; opens SW to Java Sea via Macassar Strait; c.400 mi. N–S, c.500 mi. E–W.

Celendín (sālĕndēn'), city (pop. 4,403), ⊙ Celendín prov. (□ 685; pop. 43,454), Cajamarca dept., NW Peru, at E slopes of Cordillera Occidental, on highway, and 32 mi. NE of Cajamarca; alt. 8,612 ft. Mfg. of straw hats; agr. trade (coca, sugar cane).

Celenza sul Trigno (chĕlĕn'tsä sōōl trē'nyō), village (pop. 1,633), Chieti prov., Abruzzi e Molise, S central Italy, 18 mi. SSW of Vasto.

Celenza Valfortore (välfôrtō'rĕ), village (pop. 3,006), Foggia prov., Apulia, S Italy, near Fortore R., 19 mi. W of Lucera; wine, olive oil, cheese.

Celerina (chĕlĕrē'nä), Romansh *Schlarigna*, village (pop. 633), Grisons canton, SE Switzerland, on Inn

R. and 1 mi. NE of St. Moritz; summer and winter resort (alt. 5,685 ft.) in Upper Engadine.

Célé River (sālā'), Cantal and Lot depts., SW France, rises 10 mi. S of Aurillac, flows 63 mi. WSW in deep valley, past Figeac, to the Lot 10 mi. E of Cahors. Strawberries, tobacco grown here.

Celeste (sůlěst'), town (pop. 729), Hunt co., NE Texas, 12 mi. NNW of Greenville; market point in agr. area.

Celestial Mountains, China and USSR: see TIEN SHAN.

Celestún (sālěstōōn'), town (pop. 872), Yucatan, SE Mexico, minor port on narrow bar off NW Yucatan Peninsula, 50 mi. W of Mérida; henequen growing, fishing.

Celethrum or **Celetrum,** Greece: see KASTORIA.

Celica (sālē'kä), town (1950 pop. 1,627), Loja, S Ecuador, in Andean spur, 50 mi. W of Loja; agr. center (cereals, sugar cane, cattle, sheep).

Celina. 1 (sůlī'nů) Village (pop. 5,703), ⊙ Mercer co., W Ohio, on Grand L., 27 mi. WSW of Lima; furniture, food products, optical goods, metal products, clothing, soap. Lake resort; fishing, hunting. Settled 1834. **2** (sůlē'nů) Town (pop. 1,136), ⊙ Clay co., N Tenn., on Cumberland R., at Obey R. mouth, and 95 mi. WNW of Knoxville, near Ky. line. Dale Hollow Reservoir is just E. **3** (sělī'nů) Town (pop. 1,051), Collin co., N Texas, 37 mi. N of Dallas; trade point in agr. area (cotton, dairy products, poultry).

Celje (tsě'lyě), Ger. and Ital. *Cilli* (chēl'lē), anc. *Claudia Celeia,* city (pop. 22,048), central Slovenia, Yugoslavia, on Savinja R. and 38 mi. ENE of Ljubljana. Junction of Maribor-Zagreb and Dravograd-Zagreb RRs; zinc smelter; light metal and ceramic industries; brewery. Brown-coal mining, winegrowing, and hop raising in vicinity. Has ruins of old castle and a new castle with fine paintings. Founded (1st cent. A.D.) by Roman emperor Claudius; seat (1333–1456) of powerful counts of Celje. Until 1918, in Styria.

Cella (thā'lyä), village (pop. 3,510), Teruel prov., E Spain, 12 mi. NW of Teruel; agr. trade center (sugar beets, hemp, saffron, cereals).

Cellan (kě'lůn), village and parish (pop. 350), S Cardigan, Wales, on Teifi R. and 3 mi. ENE of Lampeter; woolens.

Celldömölk (tsěl'dûmûlk), town (pop. 5,909), Vas co., W Hungary, 25 mi. E of Szombathely; rail center; artisan industry; honey, potatoes, dairy farming. Formerly Czelldömölk.

Celle (tsě'lů), city (1950 pop. 59,254), in former Prussian prov. of Hanover, NW Germany, after 1945 in Lower Saxony, on the Aller (head of navigation) and 22 mi. NE of Hanover; 52°37'N 10°5'E. Rail junction; refining and supply center for oil region; steel construction; mfg. of commercial and industrial chemicals, textiles, leather goods, flour products; textile bleaching, wax processing. Sericulture and horse breeding in vicinity. City's picturesque old section (E) has Gothic-baroque former ducal residence; 14th-cent. church with ducal burial vault; 16th-cent. town hall. Modern section (W) was damaged in Second World War. Founded and chartered 1292–94. Was residence (1371–1705) of dukes of Brunswick-Lüneburg.

Celle Ligure (chěl'lě lē'gōōrě), village (pop. 1,276), Savona prov., Liguria, NW Italy, port on Gulf of Genoa and 4 mi. NE of Savona; resort; mfg. (pianos, bicycles). Pope Sixtus IV b. here.

Celles-sur-Belle (sěl-sür-běl'), village (pop. 837), Deux-Sèvres dept., W France, 13 mi. ESE of Niort; woodworking, dairying.

Celles-sur-Durolle (-dürôl'), village (pop. 347), Puy-de-Dôme dept., central France, on Durolle R. and 6 mi. E of Thiers; cutlery mfg.

Cellino San Marco (chěl-lē'nô sän mär'kô), village (pop. 3,956), Brindisi prov., Apulia, S Italy, 12 mi. SSE of Brindisi; wine, olive oil.

Cellio (chěl'lyô), village (pop. 199), Vercelli prov., Piedmont, N Italy, 5 mi. SSE of Varallo; hemp mills.

Celo Dag (chělô' dä), Turkish *Çelo Dağ,* peak (10,660 ft.), SE Turkey, in Hakari Mts., 8 mi. SE of Satak.

Celorico da Beira (sălōrē'kōō dů bā'rů), town (pop. 1,959), Guarda dist., N central Portugal, near NE end of Serra da Estrêla, 9 mi. NW of Guarda; road junction; cheese making. Has 13th-cent. church.

Celorico de Basto (dĭ bäsh'tōō), town, Braga dist., N Portugal, near Tâmega R. 15 mi. NW of Vila Real; pottery, wax candles; resins.

Celoron (sě'lůrůn, -ŏn", -ŏn"), resort village (pop. 1,555), Chautauqua co., extreme W N.Y., on Chautauqua L., 3 mi. W of Jamestown; plywood. Inc. 1896.

Celrá (thälrä'), village (pop. 1,368), Gerona prov., NE Spain, 4 mi. NE of Gerona and on the Ter; cork and olive-oil processing, lumbering; cereals.

Cembra (chěm'brä), village (pop. 1,480), Trento prov., Trentino–Alto Adige, N Italy, near Avisio R., 9 mi. NE of Trent.

Cement or **Cement Siding,** township (pop. 405), Bulawayo prov., SW Southern Rhodesia, in Matabeleland, on railroad and 7 mi. ENE of Bulawayo; cement mill.

Cement (sĭměnt'). **1** Town (pop. 1,076), Caddo co., W central Okla., 12 mi. SW of Chickasha, in dairying and truck-farming area; oil and gas wells; oil refining, cotton ginning. **2** City (1940 pop. 249), Dallas co., N Texas, W suburb of Dallas.

Cement City, village (pop. c.500), Lenawee co., SE Mich., 13 mi. SSE of Jackson, in agr. area; cement mfg.

Cementon (sĭměn'tůn), village (1940 pop. 1,756), Lehigh co., E Pa., 5 mi. N of Allentown; cement, textiles.

Cemerna Planina or **Chemerna Planina** (both: chě'měrnä plä'nēnä), Serbo-Croatian *Čemerna Planina,* mountains in Dinaric Alps, W central Serbia, Yugoslavia, near left bank of Ibar R.; highest point (5,179 ft.) is 16 mi. SW of Rankovicevo town.

Cemernica Mountains or **Chemernitsa Mountains** (both: chě'měrnětsä), Serbo-Croatian *Čemernica Planina,* in Dinaric Alps, N Bosnia, Yugoslavia, along right bank of Vrbas R.; highest point, Veliki Vrh [Serbo-Croatian,=great peak] (4,389 ft.), is 17 mi. S of Banja Luka.

Cemetery Ridge, Pa.: see GETTYSBURG.

Cemiskezek (chěmĭsh'kězěk"), Turkish *Çemişkezek,* village (pop. 1,640), ⊙ Tunceli prov., E central Turkey, 31 mi. NNW of Elazig; wheat. Sometimes spelled Cemisgezek.

Cempoaltépetl, Mexico: see ZEMPOALTÉPETL.

Cenabum, France: see ORLÉANS.

Cendé, Páramo, Venezuela: see PÁRAMO CENDÉ.

Cendras (sădrä'), NNW suburb of Alès, Gard dept., S France, on the Gardon d'Alès; coal mines, iron foundries.

Cendre, Le (lů sä'drů), village (pop. 542), Puy-de-Dôme dept., central France, 7 mi. SE of Clermont-Ferrand; alcohol distilling.

Cene (chā'ně), village (pop. 2,399), Bergamo prov., Lombardy, N Italy, on Serio R. and 10 mi. NE of Bergamo; agr. tools. Marble quarries near by.

Ceneda, Italy: see VITTORIO VENETO.

Ceneri, Monte (môn'tě chā'něrē), mountain (2,063 ft.) in the Alps, S Switzerland, 6 mi. ESE of Locarno; pierced by several tunnels.

Cenia, La (lä thā'nyä), town (pop. 3,085), Tarragona prov., NE Spain, 18 mi. SW of Tortosa; soap and paper mfg., olive-oil and meat processing, sawmilling. Trades in ovines, cereals, fruit, wine, vegetables.

Cenicero (thānē-thā'rō), city (pop. 2,847), Logroño prov., N Spain, near Ebro R., 10 mi. W of Logroño; wine-production center; mfg. of alcohol, brandy. Fruit, vegetables, cereals, olive oil.

Cenicientos (thānē-thyěn'tōs), town (pop. 2,655), Madrid prov., central Spain, 7 mi. SSW of San Martín de Valdeiglesias; olive-, grain-, and wine-growing center; also stock raising, flour milling.

Cenis, Mont, France: see MONT CENIS.

Cenisio, Monte, France: see MONT CENIS.

Ceniza, Bocas de, Colombia: see BOCAS DE CENIZA.

Ceniza, Pico (pē'kō sänē'sä), peak (17,989 ft.), Aragua state, N Venezuela, in coastal range, 14 mi. NE of Maracay; highest elevation in state.

Cenizate (thānē-thä'tä), town (pop. 1,302), Albacete prov., SE central Spain, 24 mi. NE of Albacete; cereals, wine, saffron.

Cenon (sůnõ'), E suburb (pop. 10,051) of Bordeaux, Gironde dept., SW France, near right bank of Garonne R.; cement- and metalworks, distilleries. Oil storage tanks; rail freight yards. Vineyards.

Cenon-sur-Vienne (-sür-vyěn'), S suburb (pop. 243) of Châtellerault, Vienne dept., W central France, on Vienne R. at the mouth of the Clain; metalworks (cutlery, tractors, movie projectors).

Ceno River (chā'nô), N central Italy, rises in Ligurian Apennines 5 mi. S of Monte Maggiorasca, flows 35 mi. NE to Taro R. at Fornovo di Taro.

Cenotillo (sänōtē'yō), town (pop. 2,383), Yucatan, SE Mexico, 26 mi. E of Izamal; henequen.

Centallo (chěntäl'lô), village (pop. 1,712), Cuneo prov., Piedmont, NW Italy, 8 mi. N of Cuneo; mfg. of church organs.

Centa River, Italy: see ARROSCIA RIVER.

Centellas (thěntä'lyäs), town (pop. 2,367), Barcelona prov., NE Spain, 9 mi. SSW of Vich; cotton spinning and weaving, meat processing, sawmilling; truffles canning and shipping. Cereals, fruit in area. Mineral springs.

Centenario (sěntänär'yō), town (pop. estimate 1,000), E Neuquén natl. territory, Argentina, on Neuquén R. (irrigation area) and 12 mi. N of Neuquén; alfalfa, fruit, grapes.

Centenario, suburb (pop. 1,599) of Los Andes, Aconcagua prov., central Chile.

Centennial, village, Albany co., SE Wyo., in Snowy Range of Medicine Bow Mts., 28 mi. W of Laramie; alt. 8,076 ft. Trading point in gold-mining and ranching region.

Center. 1 Town (pop. 2,024), Saguache co., S Colo., near Rio Grande, W of Sangre de Cristo Mts., 23 mi. S of Saguache, in grain and livestock area of San Luis Valley; alt. 7,641 ft. Cheese, cattle feed, potatoes. Inc. 1907. **2** Town (pop. 112), Jackson co., NE central Ga., 7 mi. NNW of Athens. **3** City (pop. 415), Ralls co., NE Mo., near Salt R., 16 mi. SW of Hannibal; agr. **4** Village (pop. 148), ⊙ Knox co., NE Nebr., 45 mi. NNW of Norfolk and on Bazile Creek. **5** Village (pop. 492), ⊙ Oliver co., central N.Dak., 32 mi. NW of Bismarck and on Square Butte Creek; coal mines, livestock, poultry, wheat, corn, potatoes. **6** City (pop. 4,323), ⊙ Shelby co., E Texas, c.55 mi. S of Marshall; market, shipping center for pine timber, truck, cotton area; lumber milling, cotton ginning, mfg. of boxes, beverages, brooms. Founded 1866, inc. 1903.

Centerbrook, Conn.: see ESSEX.

Centerburg, village (pop. 887), Knox co., central Ohio, 13 mi. WSW of Mount Vernon and on North Fork of Licking R.; trade center for grain, livestock, dairy, and fruit area.

Center City, village (pop. 311), ⊙ Chisago co., E Minn., near St. Croix R., and 33 mi. NNE of St. Paul in region of resorts and lakes; grain, potatoes, livestock.

Center Conway, N.H.: see CONWAY.

Centerdale, R.I.: see NORTH PROVIDENCE.

Centerfield, town (pop. 601), Sanpete co., central Utah, near Sevier R., 15 mi. SW of Manti; alt. 5,125 ft.; beet sugar.

Center Harbor, town (pop. 451), Belknap co., central N.H., port and summer resort on N end of L. Winnipesaukee and 13 mi. N of Laconia.

Center Hill, city (pop. 522), Sumter co., central Fla., 13 mi. SW of Leesburg; agr. shipping point.

Center Hill Dam, De Kalb co., central Tenn., in Caney Fork, of Cumberland R., 14 mi. SE of Carthage; 246 ft. high, 2,172 ft. long; concrete, straight gravity, earthfill-wings construction. For flood control and power; controlled by U.S. Army Engineers. Center Hill Reservoir (□ 36; capacity 2,092,000 acre-feet) extends 64 mi. up Caney Fork and c.10 mi. up small Falling Water R., in De-Kalb, Putnam, White, and Warren counties. Great Falls Dam near S end.

Center Junction, town (pop. 153), Jones co., E Iowa, 10 mi. E of Anamosa; rail junction.

Center Line, residential city (pop. 7,659), Macomb co., SE Mich., 10 mi. N of Detroit; metal, tool, and die works. U.S. arsenal here. Inc. as village 1925, as city 1935.

Center Moriches (můrĭ'chēz), summer-resort village (pop. 1,761), Suffolk co., SE N.Y., on S Long Isl., on Moriches Bay, 11 mi. E of Patchogue; agr. (potatoes, cauliflower, beans).

Center Ossipee, N.H.: see OSSIPEE.

Center Point. 1 Town (pop. 162), Howard co., SW Ark., 8 mi. NW of Nashville. **2** Town (pop. 987), Linn co., E Iowa, near Cedar R., 16 mi. NNW of Cedar Rapids; canned corn, sorghum, feed. Limestone quarries near by. **3** Village (pop. c.650), Kerr co., SW Texas, 9 mi. SE of Kerrville and on Guadalupe R.; trade point in resort and ranching region.

Centerpoint, town (pop. 297), Clay co., W Ind., 18 mi. ESE of Terre Haute, in agr. and bituminous-coal area.

Centerport. 1 Resort village (1940 pop. 554), Nassau co., SE N.Y., on Centerport Harbor (SE arm of Huntington Bay) on N shore of W Long Isl., 3 mi. NE of Huntington. **2** Borough (pop. 226), Berks co., E central Pa., 11 mi. NNW of Reading.

Centerport Harbor, N.Y.: see CENTERPORT.

Center Rutland, Vt.: see RUTLAND, city.

Centerton, town (pop. 200), Benton co., extreme NW Ark., 22 mi. NNW of Fayetteville, in the Ozarks.

Centertown. 1 Town (pop. 370), Ohio co., W Ky., 26 mi. SSE of Owensboro, in coal and agr. area. **2** Town (pop. 248), Cole co., central Mo., near Missouri R., 13 mi. W of Jefferson City.

Center Valley, village (1940 pop. 622), Lehigh co., E Pa., 6 mi. S of Allentown; fruit, dairy products.

Centerview, town (pop. 179), Johnson co., W central Mo., near Blackwater R., 5 mi. W of Warrensburg.

Centerville. 1 Town, Bibb co., Ala.: see CENTREVILLE. **2** Village (pop. 1,401), Alameda co., W Calif., 22 mi. SE of Oakland; fruit packing, canning, shipping. **3** Village, New Castle co., N Del., near Pa. line, 5 mi. NNW of Wilmington; alt. 440 ft.; highest point in Del. **4** Town (pop. 1,386), Wayne co., E Ind., near a fork of Whitewater R., 6 mi. W of Richmond, in livestock, grain, poultry, and dairying area; furniture, dairy products, canned goods. **5** City (pop. 7,625), ⊙ Appanoose co., S Iowa, 32 mi. SW of Ottumwa, in agr. and coal-mining area; mfg. center (castings, bricks, plastic buttons, soybean products, dressed poultry, cheese, beverages); limestone quarrying. State park is SE. Has jr. col. Platted 1846, inc. 1855. **6** Town (pop. 63), Washington co., E Maine, 11 mi. W of Machias. **7** Town, Queen Annes co., Md.: see CENTREVILLE. **8** Village, Barnstable co., Mass.: see BARNSTABLE, town. **9** Village, St. Joseph co., Mich.: see CENTREVILLE. **10** Village (pop. 209), Anoka co., E Minn., 15 mi. N of St. Paul in lake region; grain, potatoes. **11** Village (pop. c.500), ⊙ Reynolds co., SE Mo., in the Ozarks, 34 mi. SE of Salem; resort. **12** Village (pop. 1,825, with adjoining Dublin Gulch), Silver Bow co., SW Mont., N suburb of Butte; copper mines. **13** Village, Gallia co., Ohio: see THURMAN. **14** Village (pop. 827), Montgomery co., W Ohio, 9 mi. S of Dayton, in agr. area. **15** Borough (pop. 245), Crawford co., NW Pa., on Oil Creek and 9 mi. NW of Titusville. **16** Agr. borough (pop. 5,845), Washington co., SW Pa., 28 mi. S of Pittsburgh and on Monongahela R.; bituminous coal. Settled 1766, laid out 1821, inc. 1895. **17** City (pop. 1,053), Turner co., SE S.Dak., 25 mi. NE of Yankton and on Vermillion R.; trade and livestock-shipping center for farming region; dairy products, poultry, corn. Founded 1883. **18** Town (pop. 1,532), ⊙ Hickman co., central Tenn., on Duck R. and 45 mi. SW of Nashville; trade center in fertile agr., lumbering, phosphate-mining area; makes shoes, clothing, agr. phosphate, cement blocks. **19** Town (pop. 961), ⊙ Leon co., E central Texas, c.70 mi. ESE of Waco; trade center in agr. and timber area; sawmills. **20** Town (pop. 1,262), Davis co., N Utah, near Great Salt L., 8 mi. N of Salt Lake City; alt. 4,246 ft.; cherries, truck, grain.

Cento (chĕn'tō), town (pop. 5,677), Ferrara prov., Emilia-Romagna, N central Italy, on Reno R. and 16 mi. NNW of Bologna; hemp and metal products. Has churches and art gall. with paintings by G. Francesco Barbieri, surnamed Guercino, who was b. here.

Central or **Central House,** village (pop. 45), E central Alaska, on Steese Highway and 25 mi. SW of Circle; junction for Circle Hot Springs.

Central (sĕnträl'), department (□ 1,024; pop. 163,131), S Paraguay; ⊙ Asunción, which forms a separate territorial div. Most populated section of Paraguay, bounded W by Paraguay R., NE by L. Ypacaraí, SE by L. Ypoá. Marshy lowlands with hilly outliers of central Brazilian plateau (NE). Has humid, subtropical climate. Fertile agr. area: cotton, sugar cane, tobacco, rice, oranges, bananas, cattle. Processing concentrated in its centers: Villeta, Capiatá, Luque, San Lorenzo, San Antonio. Areguá is a resort on L. Ypacaraí. The region has fine bldgs. dating from colonial times (Franciscan and Jesuit missions); heavily disputed during War of the Triple Alliance (1865–70).

Central, in Rus. names: see also Sredne-, Sredneye, Sredni, Sredniye, Srednyaya.

Central. 1 Village (pop. 1,511), Grant co., SW N.Mex., in foothills of Pinos Altos Mts., 7 mi. E of Silver City; alt. 6,068 ft. Copper, zinc, lead mining in vicinity. Part of Gila Natl. Forest is just N. **2** Town (pop. 1,263), Pickens co., NW S.C., 23 mi. WSW of Greenville; textiles, cottonseed oil; agr. Wesleyan Methodist jr. col. here. **3** Town (pop. 49), Washington co., SW Utah, 23 mi. N of St. George; alt. 5,345 ft.; livestock, agr.

Central, Cordillera (kôrdĭyä'rä sĕnträl'), name applied to several mtn. ranges in Spanish-speaking countries, notably in the Andes, bet. the Cordillera Occidental and Cordillera Oriental. In Peru, it refers to the middle Andean range bet. Nudo de Vilcanota and Nudo de Pasco and beyond to Ecuador border. In Colombia, it is the central of the 3 main cordilleras which fan out from near Ecuador border N to the Caribbean.

Central, Cordillera, 50-mi. section of continental divide in central Costa Rica, forming N side of central plateau. Includes volcanoes Poás, Barba, Irazú, and Turrialba.

Central, Cordillera, main interior range of the Dominican Republic, extends E c.220 mi. from Haiti border to Mona Passage. Densely wooded. Highest peaks: Monte Tina and Pico Trujillo, highest in the West Indies. Sometimes called Cibao Mts.

Central, Cordillera, Philippines, main range of Luzon, extending S from N coast to the central plain; rises to 9,606 ft. in Mt. Pulog. Formerly sometimes called Caraballo Mts., a name now more often limited to mts. in Nueva Vizcaya prov.

Central, Cordillera, mountain chain of Puerto Rico, extending c.80 mi. W–E through almost the entire length of the isl.; rises to 4,400 ft. in the Cerro de Punta. Subsidiary branches are the Sierra de Luquillo (NE) and Sierra de Cayey (SE). Known for its pleasant summer climate and scenery. There are several water reservoirs and hydroelectric plants. Tobacco, fruit, and sugar cane are grown.

Central Aimak (ī'mäk), Mongolian *Tub Aymag* or *Töb Aymag* (both: tûb ī'mäkh), aimak (□ 30,700; pop. 80,000), central Mongolian People's Republic; ⊙Dzun Modo. Situated in the steppe, except for wooded belt (N), the aimak lies on the plateau at SW foot of the Kentei Mts. It contains Ulan Bator, which constitutes an independent unit. Coal mining (Nalaikha); cement-rock, graphite, and oil-shale deposits.

Central America, narrow strip of land winding NW–SE bet. North America proper and the South American continent, bet. the Caribbean and the Pacific. The Gulf of Mexico is N. In a strictly geographic sense it is considered to include the transitional tract from the Isthmus of Tehuantepec to the Isthmus of Panama, thus comprising the Mexican states of Tabasco, Chiapas, Campeche, Yucatan, and the territory of Quintana Roo, as well as the 5 republics of Guatemala, Honduras, Salvador, Nicaragua, and Costa Rica, and the colony British Honduras. The term generally means, however, the 5 republics SE of Mexico and often includes the republic of Panama. Whatever its exact delineation, the tropical, mountainous region possesses an economic, ethnic, geological, and climatologic unity. It is crossed in its entire length by the main cordillera, which is—apart from the Sierra Madre in Guatemala—rather related to the volcanic ranges of the Antilles than to the continental divide of the Americas. Volcanoes are numerous, with the highest peak, Tajumulco, rising to 13,816 ft. Disastrous earthquakes have frequently occurred. There are several picturesque lakes, such as Atitlán, Amatitlán, and the largest, L. Nicaragua. Rivers, though small, are plentiful. Alt. largely determines the climate, which varies from hot, through temperate, to cool (*tierra caliente, tierra templada,* and *tierra fría*) zones. The jungle-covered lowlands (rich in hardwoods) have high rainfall, especially on the Caribbean side. Chief crops, introduced in 19th cent., are bananas, somewhat decreasing because of plant disease, and coffee, grown on the more temperate slopes. Racially, the mestizo element predominates, apart from Costa Rica, which is overwhelmingly white in its *meseta central;* the Negro element is strong on the Caribbean. Spanish is the principal language. The Central American NW was peopled by the highly advanced Mayas before the Sp. conquest. The Caribbean shore was visited (1502) by Columbus on his 4th voyage. Vasco Núñez de Balboa made (1513) his momentous voyage across the Isthmus of Panama to the Pacific. The Spanish organized (1st half of 16th cent.) the captaincy general of Guatemala (with Antigua as ⊙), which roughly included the area of the present-day 5 republics. Independence of Central America was declared (1821), the region was briefly annexed to Iturbide's Mexican Empire, and formed (1823) the Central American Federation (Costa Rica, Honduras, Nicaragua, Guatemala, Salvador), which fell apart in 1838. Since then the political history of the separate countries has been turbulent, with revolutions, coups d'état, and dictatorships. Attempts to re-establish a permanent federation have so far failed, though common interest would favor it. The 5 Central American nations have an area of c.191,000 sq. mi. and pop. of 8,300,000; with Panama, Br. Honduras, and the Panama Canal Zone they have an area of c.230,000 sq. mi. and pop. of c.9,000,000.

Central Asia or **Russian Central Asia** (ā'zhù, ā'shù), name formerly applied to an Asiatic division of the Russian Empire, constituting the governments-general of the Steppes and Russian Turkestan. After the Bolshevik revolution, the term **Central Asia** or **Soviet Central Asia** was applied to the newly created Soviet republics of Russian Turkestan: Kirghiz, Tadzhik, Turkmen, and Uzbek SSRs, and including sometimes Kazakh SSR.

Central Australia: see Northern Territory.

Central Black-Earth Oblast, Rus. *Tsentral'no-Chernozemnaya Oblast',* former administrative division of W central European Russian SFSR; ⊙ was Voronezh. Formed 1928 out of govts. of Voronezh, Kursk, Orel, and Tambov; dissolved 1934 into oblasts of Voronezh and Kursk.

Central Brahui Range, W Pakistan: see Brahui Range, Central.

Central Bridge, village, Schoharie co., E central N.Y., on Schoharie Creek at mouth of small Cobleskill Creek, and 30 mi. W of Albany. George Westinghouse b. here. Near by are the Howe and Secret caverns.

Central Butte, village (pop. 266), S Sask., 50 mi. NW of Moose Jaw; railroad junction; wheat.

Central City. 1 Town (pop. 371), ⊙ Gilpin co., N central Colo., on N fork of Clear Creek, in Front Range, and 26 mi. W of Denver; alt. 8,560 ft. Gold, silver, lead, copper, zinc, uranium mines. Near by, in Quartz Hill, is Glory Hole, huge mining pit c.1,000 ft. long, 300 ft. deep. City settled 1859, at time of Gregory gold strike; inc. 1886. Decline set in as gold production fell off, but there was increase of mining activity during Second World War. Play and music festival takes place annually (July) in old opera house (1878) now owned by Univ. of Denver. Next door is Teller House (1872), famous frontier hotel. **2** City (pop. 35), Grundy co., NE Ill., 24 mi. SSW of Joliet, in agr. and bituminous-coal area. **3** Village (pop. 1,231), Marion co., S Ill., on Crooked Creek and just N of Centralia, in agr., oil-producing, and bituminous-coal-mining area; large nurseries. Inc. 1857. **4** Town (pop. 965), Linn co., E Iowa, on Wapsipinicon R. and 17 mi. NNE of Cedar Rapids; ships poultry, eggs, butter. **5** Town (pop. 4,110), Muhlenberg co., W Ky., 33 mi. S of Owensboro; trade center in bituminous-coal-mining and agr. (truck, corn, tobacco, hay) area, with oil wells, hardwood timber. Rail junction (yards); makes tables, concrete blocks, soft drinks; lumber mill. Settled as Morehead's Horse Mill; renamed after 1870 with arrival of railroad. **6** City (pop. 2,394), ⊙ Merrick co., E central Nebr., 20 mi. NE of Grand Island and on Platte R.; flour; dairy produce, grain. Nebr. Central Col. here. Platted 1864. **7** Borough (pop. 1,935), Somerset co., SW Pa., 14 mi. SSE of Johnstown. Inc. 1918. **8** Town (pop. 218), Lawrence co., W S.Dak., 2 mi. W of Deadwood and on branch of Belle Fourche R., in Black Hills mining region.

Central Falls, industrial city (pop. 23,550), Providence co., NE R.I., on Blackstone R. (bridged here), adjoining Pawtucket, and 6 mi. N of Providence; textiles, thread, glass, glass fabrics, paper, leather and wood products, food products, beverages, plastics, toys, chemicals, machinery; printing, boatbuilding. Inc. 1895.

Centralhatchee, town (pop. 239), Heard co., W Ga., 22 mi. N of La Grange, near Chattahoochee R.

Central Heights, town (pop. 766), Cerro Gordo co., N Iowa, just W of Mason City.

Central House, Alaska: see Central.

Centralia (sĕntrā'lēù). **1** City (pop. 13,863), on Clinton-Marion co. line, S Ill., c.55 mi. E of East St. Louis; trade and shipping center; mfg. (metal products, shoes, flour, candy); oil refineries, railroad shops, meat-packing plants. Agr. (fruit, corn, wheat, livestock, poultry; dairy products. Bituminous-coal mines; oil fields (developed in boom of late 1930s). Has jr. col. Platted 1853, inc. 1859. Coal-mine explosion (1947), with loss of 111 lives, led to state and natl. investigations in which certain mines were declared unsafe. **2** Town (pop. 78), Dubuque co., E Iowa, 8 mi. W of Dubuque. **3** City (pop. 574), Nemaha co., NE Kansas, c.50 mi. NNW of Topeka, in livestock and grain region; dairying. **4** City (pop. 2,460), Boone co., central Mo., 20 mi. NNE of Columbia; grain; telephone-pole anchors, lumber products. Laid out 1857. **5** Town (pop. 124), Craig co., NE Okla., 15 mi. NW of Vinita. **6** Borough (pop. 1,986), Columbia co., E central Pa., just N of Ashland; anthracite. Inc. 1866. **7** City (pop. 8,657), Lewis co., SW Wash., 22 mi. S of Olympia, near Chehalis R.; timber, dairy products, oats, wheat. Site of jr. col. Settled 1866, inc. 1886.

Central India, former political agency (□ 51,946; pop. 7,486,303), India; hq. were at Indore. Comprised princely states of Indore, Rewa, and those in subordinate Bundelkhand Agency, Bhopal Agency, and Malwa Agency. Area was part of Asokan empire in 3d cent. B.C.; under Guptas, 4th–5th cent. A.D. In 7th–10th cent. several tribal dynasties arose; 1st Moslem invasion (Mahmud of Ghazni) in 1021. Kingdom of Malwa flourished in 15th cent., but later gave way to Mogul supremacy. Mahrattas overran country in 18th cent.; serious disorders resulted in Br. interference and subsequent establishment of Mahratta and Rajput states. States 1st grouped into separate agencies; in 1854 all were placed under agent to Governor-General in Central India. Scene of several skirmishes during Sepoy Rebellion (1857–59). Baghelkhand Agency, created 1871, was absorbed by Bundelkhand Agency in 1931; Gwalior separated 1921 from Central India. All states, except Bhopal and Makrai, joined Madhya Bharat and Vindhya Pradesh in 1948.

Central Industrial Oblast, Russian SFSR: see Moscow, oblast.

Central Islip (ī'slĭp), village (pop. 3,067), Suffolk co., SE N.Y., on central Long Isl., 5 mi. NNE of Bay Shore, in poultry-raising and dairying area. A state hosp. for the insane is here.

Central Karroo, U. of So. Afr.: see Great Karroo.

Central Lake, village (pop. 692), Antrim co., NW Mich., 27 mi. NE of Traverse City, and on W shore of Intermediate Lake (c.8 mi. long, 1 mi. wide), in agr. area (corn, potatoes, seed); flour mills, cannery.

Central Makran Range, W Pakistan: see Makran Range, Central.

Central Park. 1 Village (pop. 2,489), Vermilion co., E Ill. **2** Village, Nassau co., N.Y.: see Bethpage.

Central Patricia, village (pop. estimate 250), NW Ont., in Patricia dist., on Kawinogans R., 2 mi. NE of Pickle Lake and 120 mi. NE of Sioux Lookout; gold mining.

Central Point, town (pop. 1,667), Jackson co., SW Oregon, 5 mi. NW of Medford in truck and livestock area; cheese, lumber.

Central Province, administrative division (□2,290; pop., including estate pop., 1,132,127), central Ceylon; ⊙ Kandy. Largely in Ceylon Hill Country, with Hatton Plateau (SW), Horton Plains (SE), Piduru Ridges (E), Kandy Plateau (center), and Knuckles Group (N); drained by the Mahaweli Ganga. Largely agr.; tea, rubber, and cacao (principally in Dumbara and Matale valleys); rice, vegetables, cardamom, coconut and areca palms. Main centers: Kandy, Nuwara Eliya, Matale, Gampola, Nawalapitiya, Hatton (major tea-trade center of Ceylon). Land reclamation projects at Elahera and Minipe. Archaeological landmarks at Sigiriya, Dambulla, and Nalanda.

Central Provinces and Berar, India: see Madhya Pradesh.

Central Russian Upland, Rus. *Sredne-Russkaya Vozvyshennost,* hilly plateau in central European Russian SFSR, bet. Valdai Hills (N) and Donets Ridge (S); 500 mi. long, 270 mi. wide; rises to 1,900 ft. Of pre-glacial origin, it consists of Carboniferous, Jurassic, and Cretaceous formations, forming a divide bet. Black Sea and Caspian Sea basins. Gives rise to Oka and Don rivers and left affluents of the Dnieper. Main mineral deposits: coal, iron, limestone.

Central Saurashtra, India: see Madhya Saurashtra.

Central Siberian Plateau, vast uplands in E Siberia, Russian SFSR, E of the Yenisei and watered by Lena R.; average alt.: 1,000–1,500 ft. It corresponds to one of Asia's stable blocks of pre-Cambrian origin.

Central Square, village (pop. 665), Oswego co., N central N.Y., 15 mi. N of Syracuse, in dairying area.

Central Valley. 1 Village (pop. 2,202), Shasta co., N Calif., 8 mi. NE of Redding, just S of Shasta Dam and reservoir. 2 Village (1940 pop. 1,015), Orange co., SE N.Y., on Ramapo R. and 8 mi. WSW of Highland Falls; mfg. (dresses, machine parts, fishing tackle).

Central Valley or **Great Valley,** California's great longitudinal trough (c.450 mi. long, 50 mi. wide) bet. the Sierra Nevada (E) and the Coast Ranges; transverse Tehachapi Mts. (S) link E and W walls; on N, Cascade Range (extending N from the Sierra Nevada) meets Klamath Mts. (N of Calif. Coast Ranges) at head of valley. Section N of lat. of San Francisco known as Sacramento Valley, S part as San Joaquin Valley, after their principal streams; the SACRAMENTO RIVER and SAN JOAQUIN RIVER unite in a great delta just above their mouth on Suisun Bay, E arm of San Francisco Bay; the bay depression is the only major break in valley's mtn. walls. Level alluvial floor has ⅔ of state's farmland, most of it (except grain acreage) requiring irrigation, and producing virtually every type of crop (including some citrus fruit) grown in Calif. Sheltering mts. and tempering effect of ocean give N and S a relatively uniform climate; growing season is over 200 days in most of valley, but rainfall varies from less than 10 inches in S to over 20 inches in N. Falling water tables (especially in the San Joaquin), caused by excessive pumping for irrigation, forced abandonment of agr. on many acres and led to formulation by state and Federal authorities of Central Valley project for redistribution of water resources of region. The U.S. Bureau of Reclamation plan, authorized by Congress in 1935, hinges on use of abundant Sacramento R. waters (⅔ of Central Valley supply) on the farmlands (⅔ of valley total) of the San Joaquin Valley. In addition, the project's purposes are flood control, improvement of navigation on the Sacramento and the San Joaquin, development of hydroelectric power (to defray part of expense of supplying irrigation water), protection of farm lands in the Sacramento–San Joaquin delta from the invasion of sea water which has threatened their use for agr., and supply of water to cities. Chief developments in initial stage of long-term program are huge SHASTA DAM (completed 1945; first irrigation water released 1951) and smaller Keswick Dam (just downstream) on the upper Sacramento; the Delta Cross Channel, which combats soil salinity in the delta and conducts Sacramento R. water across delta to Tracy, where a pumping plant feeds DELTA-MENDOTA CANAL, leading S to the San Joaquin; the CONTRA COSTA CANAL (completed 1947), which conveys Sacramento R. water to Contra Costa co. farmlands and cities. On the upper San Joaquin is large FRIANT DAM (completed 1944), impounding Millerton L.; from dam, MADERA CANAL (in operation since 1945) leads NW, FRIANT-KERN CANAL leads S. FOLSOM DAM is on American R. At Antioch is a large steam-power plant of the project. The ultimate plan aims at developing c.3,000,000 more acres and providing power for increased pop. of Calif., and contemplates a total of 48 dams, 20 large canals, plus powerhouses and distribution works. Second stage (scheduled for 1945–60) includes following dams and reservoirs on E side of valley: Bidwell Bar, on North Fork Feather R.; New Bullards Bar, on North Yuba R.; Nashville, on Cosumnes R.; Buchanan, on Chowchilla R.; Tulloch, on the Stanislaus; Hidden, on Fresno R.; New Hogan, on the Calaveras; Pine Flat, on Kings R.; Terminus, on Kaweah R.; Success, on Tule R.; Isabella, on Kern R.; Rollins, on Bear R.; and enlargement of reservoir of Melones Dam, on the Stanislaus. On W side of valley are sites of Black Butte Reservoir, on Stony Creek; San Luis Reservoir, part of Delta-Mendota Canal system; and Monticello Dam, on Putah Creek.

Central Village. 1 Village, Windham co., Conn.: see PLAINFIELD. 2 Village, Bristol co., Mass.: see WESTPORT.

Centre, county (□ 1,115; pop. 65,922), central Pa.; ⊙ Bellefonte. Mtn. region, bounded NW by West Branch Susquehanna R.; drained by Bald Eagle Creek. Allegheny Mts. across NW part, paralleled by Bald Eagle Mtn. in central part and by Tussey Mtn. along part of S border. Limestone, bituminous coal, clay, sandstone; oats, swine; brass, matches, bakery products. Formed 1800.

Centre, town (pop. 1,672), ⊙ Cherokee co., NE Ala., near Coosa R., 22 mi. NE of Gadsden, in cotton and corn area; cotton products, lumber. Settled c.1840. Inc. 1937.

Centre, Canal du (känäl' dü sä'trů), canal in Saône-et-Loire dept., E central France, connecting Saône R. (at Chalon-sur-Saône) to Loire R. and LOIRE LATERAL CANAL (at Digoin) via valleys of the Dheune and the Bourbince. Total length 79 mi., with 68 locks. Passes through Chagny, Montchanin-les-Mines, Montceau-les-Mines, and Paray-le-Monial. Transports iron ore and coal to Le Creusot industrial dist., and construction materials to towns in Saône-Rhone valley.

Centre de Flacq, Mauritius: see FLACQ.

Centre Hall, borough (pop. 834), Centre co., central Pa., 6 mi. SE of Bellefonte, in fine hunting, fishing region. Penn's Cave is near by.

Centre Island, SE N.Y., peninsula on N shore of W Long Isl., enclosing part of Oyster Bay, N of Oyster Bay village; c.5 mi. long. Site of BAYVILLE and Centre Island (pop. 199) villages.

Centreville, village (pop. estimate c.250), W N.B., near Maine border, 20 mi. NNW of Woodstock; lumbering; potatoes.

Centreville. 1 or **Centerville,** town (pop. 1,160), ⊙ Bibb co., central Ala., on Cahaba R. and 30 mi. SE of Tuscaloosa; lumber, cotton. 2 or **Centerville,** town (pop. 1,804), ⊙ Queen Annes co., E Md., on the Eastern Shore 19 mi. N of Easton, and on Corsica R., in agr. area; makes sportswear, fertilizer; vegetable canneries. Historic houses near by include Poplar Grove (1700), with oldest boxwood garden in Md., and Walnut Grove (1681–85). Laid out 1792. 3 or **Centerville,** village (pop. 879), ⊙ St. Joseph co., SW Mich., on Prairie R. and 25 mi. S of Kalamazoo, in agr. area (grain, corn, mint); mfg. of clothing. Settled 1826. 4 Town (pop. 2,025), on Wilkinson-Amite co. line, SW Miss., near La. line, 37 mi. SSE of Natchez, in agr., timber, and cattle-raising area. Inc. 1880. 5 Industrial village in West Warwick town, Kent co., central R.I., on Pawtuxet R. and 11 mi. SSW of Providence; textile mfg. and finishing.

Centro, El, Colombia: see BARRANCABERMEJA.

Centum Cellae, Italy: see CIVITAVECCHIA.

Centuria (sĕntōōr'ēů), resort village (pop. 521), Polk co., NW Wis., near Balsam L., 35 mi. NNE of Hudson; dairying.

Centuripe (chĕntōōrē'pĕ), town (pop. 9,255), Enna prov., E central Sicily, 21 mi. NW of Catania. Sulphur mines are SE. Town is on site of anc. Centuripae, destroyed 1232 by Frederick II. Has a Hellenistic-Roman house with paintings of 2d–1st cent. B.C. Doric sarcophagus, Roman statues, terra cottas (3d cent. B.C.) in local mus.

Century. 1 Village (pop. 1,350), Escambia co., NW Fla., near Ala. line and Escambia R., 39 mi. N of Pensacola; lumber milling. Grew around sawmill established in 1900. 2 Village, Ottawa co., Okla.: see DOUTHAT.

Ceos, Greece: see KEA.

Ceotina River, Yugoslavia: see COTINA RIVER.

Cepeda (thāpā'dhä), town (pop. 1,305), Salamanca prov., W Spain, 16 mi. WNW of Béjar; olive presses, alcohol distilleries; wine, honey. Ruins of castle of Knights Templars near by.

Cephallenia, Greece: see CEPHALONIA.

Cephaloedium, Sicily: see CEFALÙ.

Cephalonia (sĕfůlō'nyů), Gr. *Kephallenia* or *Kefallinia* (both: kĕfälēnē'ä), Lat. *Cephallenia* (sĕfůlē'nyů), largest island (□ 289.4; pop. 57,384) of Ionian Isls., Greece, in Ionian Sea, off Gulf of Patras. Forms with near-by islets a nome (□ 306; pop. 58,437) of W central Greece; ⊙ Argostoli (38°10'N 20°30'E). Of irregular coastline (Argostoli Bay, W, is deepest inlet), isl. is 30 mi. long, 20 mi. wide, and rises to 5,315 ft. in Mt. Ainos (SE), a limestone formation. Agr. (chiefly near Argostoli): currants (leading export), wine, olive oil, cotton, citrus fruit, grain. Main towns are Argostoli, Lexourion, and Same. The traditional Same or Samos, Cephalonia was an ally of Athens in Peloponnesian War and later a member of Aetolian League. It was taken 189 B.C. by Rome, was held by Byzantium until captured (11th cent.) by Normans of Sicily. Subsequently ruled by various Ital. families (including the Tocchi of Naples), it passed 1479 to the Turks and 1499 to Venice, which held it until 1797. Its subsequent history is that of the Ionian Isls.

Cephisus River or **Cephissus River** (both: sĭfī'sůs), Gr. *Kephisos, Kifisos, Kephissos,* or *Kifissos* (kēfēsôs'), several streams in E central Greece. 1 In Attica, rises in the Pentelikon, flows 20 mi. SW, past Athens, to Bay of Phaleron of Saronic Gulf just E of Piraeus. Receives Eilissos R. (left). 2 In Attica, rises in the Patera massif, flows 17 mi. E and S to Bay of Eleusis of Saronic Gulf at Eleusis. Also called Sarandapotamos or Sarantapotamos. 3 Mainly in Boeotia, Greece, rises on N slopes of the Parnassus, flows 71 mi. ESE, through Phocis, Locris, and Boeotia, to N arm of Gulf of Euboea 10 mi. WNW of Chalcis. It forms lakes Hylike and Paralimne in lower course. Formerly the Cephisus ended in L. COPAIS (drained since 1880s). Formerly called Mavroneri.

Cepin (chĕ'pĭn) or **Cepinj** (chĕ'pĭnyů), Serbo-Croatian *Čepin* or *Čepinj,* village (pop. 5,041), NE Croatia, Yugoslavia, in Slavonia, on railroad and 7 mi. SW of Osijek, in the Podravina.

Cepo, Río del, Chile: see MAPOCHO RIVER.

Cépoy (sāpwä'), village (pop. 1,299), Loiret dept., N central France, on Loing R. and Loing Canal, and 4 mi. N of Montargis; glassworks. Lumbering.

Ceprano (chĕprä'nō), town (pop. 2,769), Frosinone prov., Latium, S central Italy, on Liri R. and 11 mi. SE of Frosinone; paper mills.

Ceptura or **Ceptura-de-Jos** (chĕptōō'rä-dā-zhôs'), village (pop. 2,019), Prahova prov., S central Rumania, 15 mi. NE of Ploesti; oil center.

Cer or **Tser** (both: tsĕr), mountain (2,253 ft.) in Dinaric Alps, W Serbia, Yugoslavia, 14 mi. SW of Sabac.

Ceram (sĕrăm', Du. sā'räm), island (□ 6,622), S Moluccas, Indonesia, bet. Ceram Sea (N) and Banda Sea (S), 100 mi. W of New Guinea; 2°46'–3°51'S 127°50'–130°52'E. Ceram census div. (□ 7,191; pop. 100,029) includes isls. of Boano, Kelang, Manipa, Ceram Laut, Watubela, and Goram. Ceram is 210 mi. long, 45 mi. wide, and traversed by central forested mtn. range rising to 10,205 ft. in Mt. Binaija. Indented by several wide bays; has generally narrow coastal plain. Principal products: copra, resin, fish, sago. Oil is exploited near BULA on NE coast. Chief port is WAHAI on N coast. Natives are Malay, many being partly of Papuan stock. Christianity and Mohammedanism are widespread. Portuguese missionaries were active here in 16th cent. Trading posts were established on isl. in early 17th cent. by the Dutch. Also spelled Seran and Serang.

Cerami (chĕrä'mē), village (pop. 3,869), Enna prov., N central Sicily, 21 mi. NNE of Enna. Cave dwellings near by.

Ceramicus Sinus or **Ceramic Gulf,** Turkey: see KOS, GULF OF.

Ceram Laut, island group (□ 100), S Moluccas, Indonesia, off SE coast of Ceram; 3°53'S 130°56'E; comprises c.15 isls., largest being Ceram Laut (□ 12; 4 mi. long, 3 mi. wide). Agr. (sago, sugar, coconuts), lumbering, trepang fishing. Sometimes spelled Serang Laut.

Ceram Sea, part of the Pacific, in Indonesia, bet. Halmahera (N) and Ceram (S) and bet. W coast of New Guinea (E) and Sula Isls.; merges with Molucca Sea (W) and Arafura Sea (SE). Formerly Pitt Passage.

Cerano (chĕrä'nô), town (pop. 5,562), Novara prov., Piedmont, N Italy, 8 mi. ESE of Novara, in irrigated region (fodder crops, wheat).

Cerano (särä'nō), town (pop. 2,153), Guanajuato, central Mexico, on interior plateau, 40 mi. S of Irapuato; cereals, vegetables, fruit.

Cerasus, Turkey: see GIRESUN, town.

Ceraunian Mountains (sĕrô'nēůn), coastal range of S Albania, in N Epirus, extends c.70 mi. from Gr. border to Strait of Otranto; rises to 6,726 ft. in Mt. Çikë (NW), where the range bifurcates into the ACROCERAUNIA and LUNGARA ranges. The name Acroceraunia is sometimes applied to the entire system.

Cerbat Mountains (sâr'bŏt), Mohave co., NW Ariz., just E of Black Mts.; extend c.25 mi. N from Kingman. Rise to 7,364 ft. in Mt. TIPTON, at N end.

Cerbère (sĕrbâr'), town (pop. 2,044), Pyrénées-Orientales dept., S France, on the Gulf of Lion, at E end of the Pyrenees, 22 mi. SE of Perpignan; rail and custom station on Sp. border. Smuggling center.

Cerbère, Cape, headland on Gulf of Lion, in Pyrénées-Orientales dept., S France, near Sp. border, formed by E spur of the Monts Albères just E of Cerbère; 42°24'N 3°10'E.

Cerboli (chĕr'bôlē), islet in Tuscan Archipelago, in Tyrrhenian Sea, off central Italy, 5 mi. S of Piombino.

Cercado (sĕrkä'dō). 1 Province, Beni dept., Bolivia: see TRINIDAD. 2 Province, Cochabamba dept., Bolivia; see COCHABAMBA, city. 3 Province, Oruro dept., Bolivia: see ORURO, city. 4 Province, Potosí dept., Bolivia: see POTOSÍ, city. 5 Province, Santa Cruz dept., Bolivia: see SANTA CRUZ, city. 6 Province, Tarija dept., Bolivia: see TARIJA, city.

Cercado, El, Dominican Republic: see EL CERCADO.

Cercal, Serra do (sĕ'rů dōō sĭrkäl'), coastal hill chain in S Portugal, extends along the Atlantic c.25 mi. bet. Santiago do Cacém (N) and Odemira (S). Rises to about 1,250 ft. Forested. Sparsely settled.

Cerca-la-Source (sĕrkä-lä-sōōrs'), agr. town (1950 census pop. 866), Nord dept., E Haiti, 14 mi. E of Hinche; coffee, timber.

Cercapuquio (sĕrkäpōō'kyō), village (pop. 237), Junín dept., central Peru, in Cordillera Occidental of the Andes, 29 mi. SW of Huancayo; cadmium-mining center.

Cercedilla (thĕrthā-dhē'lyä), town (pop. 2,125), Madrid prov., central Spain, in the Sierra de Guadarrama, 31 mi. NW of Madrid (linked by electric train); potatoes, cereals, rye, livestock. Lumbering. Sanatorium near by.

Cerchiara di Calabria (chĕrkyä'rä dē kälä'brēä), town (pop. 2,493), Cosenza prov., Calabria, S Italy, 10 mi. ENE of Castrovillari, in cereal-, fruit-, stock-raising region.

Cerchov (chĕr'khôf), Czech *Čerchov,* highest peak (3,408 ft.) of the *Český Les,* SW Bohemia, near Ger. border, and 7 mi. SW of Domazlice; numerous summer and winter resorts in E foothills.

Cercina, Tunisia: see KERKENNAH.

Cercy-la-Tour (sĕrsē'-lä-tōōr'), village (pop. 1,347), Nièvre dept., central France, on Aron R. and Nivernais Canal, and 9 mi. ENE of Decize; rail junction. Horse breeding.

Cerda (chĕr'dä), town (pop. 5,479), Palermo prov., N Sicily, near Torto R., 9 mi. SE of Termini Imerese; macaroni.

Cerdaña (thĕr-dhä'nyä), Fr. *Cerdagne* (sĕrdän'yů), high valley of the E Pyrenees and an historic region, now included in Pyrénées-Orientales dept. (S France) and in Gerona and Lérida provs. (NE Spain); chief city, Puigcerdá. Extends c.40 mi. ENE–WSW from Col de la Perche to Seo de Urgel. Average alt. 3,800 ft. Drained by upper Segre R. Stock raising (transhumance); dairying; fruit-, potato-, and winegrowing. On Perpignan-Lérida road. Frontier towns: Puigcerdá (Spain), Bourg-Madame (France). Old countship belonged to counts of Barcelona (11th cent.), then to kings of Aragon and Sp. crown. By Peace of the Pyrenees (1659), NE part of Cerdaña (except for Llivia enclave) passed to France.

Cerea (chĕrā'ä), village (pop. 1,942), Verona prov., Veneto, N Italy, 21 mi. E of Mantua; mfg. (phosphates, sulphuric acid, cotton textiles, awnings), canned vegetables, cement.

Cereal, village (pop. 111), SE Alta., 50 mi. ESE of Hanna; mixed farming.

Cerecinos de Campos (thārā-thē'nōs dhä käm'pōs), village (pop. 1,268), Zamora prov., NW Spain, 30 mi. NNE of Zamora; cereals, wine.

Ceredo (sĕr'ēdō), town (pop. 1,399), Wayne co., W W.Va., 6 mi. W of Huntington, near the Ohio, in agr. and bituminous-coal region. Founded 1857.

Ceremus River, Ukrainian SSR: see CHEREMOSH RIVER.

Cérences (särãs'), village (pop. 845), Manche dept., NW France, on Sienne R. and 9 mi. S of Coutances; dairying, mfg. of dairying equipment.

Cère River (sâr), Cantal and Lot depts., S central France, rises in the Massif du Cantal near Le Lioran, flows 70 mi. W, past Thiézac and Laroquebrou to the Dordogne 2 mi. below Bretenoux. Receives the Jordanne (right); important hydroelectric stations at Saint-Étienne-Cantalès, Lamativie, and Laval-de-Cère.

Ceres (sä'rĕs), town (pop. estimate 3,000), W central Santa Fe prov., Argentina, on railroad and 55 mi. NW of San Cristóbal; grain and livestock center; dairying, flour milling, lumbering. Clay deposits near by.

Ceres (sĭ'rĭs), town, central Goiás, central Brazil, 100 mi. NNW of Anápolis; natl. agr. colony, established here in 1941, has attracted numerous pioneer settlers.

Ceres (sē'rēz), agr. village and parish (pop. 1,425), E Fifeshire, Scotland, 3 mi. SE of Cupar.

Ceres (sĕr'ēs), town (pop. 4,063), SW Cape Prov., U. of So. Afr., on Dwars R. and 20 mi. NNW of Worcester, at foot of Hex River Mts.; resort; fruitgrowing center (apples, pears, nectarines); fruit processing, furniture and candy mfg. Hq. of Cape Town Ski Club. Matroosberg mtn. (7,386 ft.) is 20 mi. E.

Ceres (sēr'ēz). **1** City (pop. 2,351), Stanislaus co., central Calif., in San Joaquin Valley, 4 mi. SE of Modesto; grapes, peaches, figs, dates, poultry. Inc. 1918. **2** Village, Allegany co., N.Y., and McKean co., Pa., 9 mi. SE of Olean, N.Y.; post office is in N.Y.

Ceresco (sûrĕ'skō), village (pop. 374), Saunders co., E Nebr., 18 mi. N of Lincoln; livestock, grain.

Ceresio, Lago, Switzerland: see LUGANO, LAKE OF.

Ceresole Reale (chĕrĕzô'lĕ rĕä'lĕ), village (pop. 12), Torino prov., Piedmont, NW Italy, S of Gran Paradiso, 22 mi. SSW of Aosta. Alpine resort (alt. 5,291 ft.) on artificial lake formed on Orco R.; mineral springs.

Ceresville (sĕr'ēzvĭl), hamlet, Frederick co., N Md., on Monocacy R. and 3 mi. NE of Frederick. Grain mill here has operated since 1790.

Céret (sārĕ'), town (pop. 3,730), Pyrénées-Orientales dept., S France, bet. Massif du Canigou and Monts Albères (Sp. border), 16 mi. SSW of Perpignan; produces talc, corks, sandals, furniture. In truck- and cherry-growing valley. Tech R. is spanned by single-arch bridge, built 1321.

Cereté (sārātā'), town (pop. 4,503), Bolívar dept., N Colombia, on Sinú R., in Caribbean lowlands, and 9 mi. NNE of Montería; agr. center (cattle, corn, forest products).

Cerevic or **Cherevich** (both: chĕ'rĕvĭch), Serbo-Croatian *Čerević*, village, Vojvodina, N Serbia, Yugoslavia, on the Danube and 8 mi. W of Novi Sad, in the Srem, at N foot of Fruska Gora; coal.

Cerezo de Riotirón (thārā'thō dhä ryōtērōn'), town (pop. 1,593), Burgos prov., N Spain, on Tirón R. and 32 mi. ENE of Burgos; cereals, sheep, mules. Lumbering, mining of sodium sulphate, plaster mfg.

Cerf Island. **1** Outlying dependency of the Seychelles, near Farquhar Isls., in Indian Ocean, 225 mi. NNW of N tip of Madagascar; 9°30'S 51°E. Of coral origin. Copra; fisheries. **2** Island (290 acres), one of the Seychelles, in the Mahé group, off NE coast of Mahé Isl.; 4°38'S 55°30'E; granite.

Cerfontaine (sĕrfõtĕn'), village (pop. 1,786), Namur prov., S Belgium, 7 mi. WSW of Philippeville; marble quarrying.

Cerignola (chĕrēnyô'lä), town (pop. 37,163), Foggia prov., Apulia, S Italy, 23 mi. SE of Foggia; flour, macaroni, wine, olive oil; mfg. (shoes, cement, agr. machinery, fireworks). Bishopric. Near by, in 1503, Spanish defeated French under Louis XII.

Cerigo, Greece: see KYTHERA.

Cerigotto, Greece: see ANTIKYTHERA.

Cérilly (sārēyē'), village (pop. 1,051), Allier dept., central France, 17 mi. WSW of Saint-Amand-Montrond; woodworking.

Cerisiers (sûrēzyā'), village (pop. 457), Yonne dept., N central France, 10 mi. ESE of Sens; cider making.

Cerisy-la-Forêt (sûrēzē'-lä-fôrĕ'), village (pop. 679), Manche dept., NW France, 9 mi. NE of Saint-Lô. Has fine 11th-cent. Romanesque abbatial church and 13th-cent. conventual bldg. Just E is Forest of Cerisy (□ 8), scene of heavy fighting in Normandy campaign (June–July, 1944) of Second World War.

Cerisy-la-Salle (-lä-säl'), village (pop. 345), Manche dept., NW France, 11 mi. SW of Saint-Lô; apple orchards.

Cerizay (sûrēzā'), village (pop. 1,043), Deux-Sèvres dept., W France, 19 mi. SE of Cholet; shoe and cement pipe mfg. Heavily damaged in Second World War.

Cerkes (chĕrkĕsh'), Turkish *Çerkeş*, village (pop. 2,898), Cankiri prov., N central Turkey, on railroad and 60 mi. N of Ankara; grain, vetch, mohair goats; lignite near by.

Cerknica (tsĕrk'nĭtsä), Ital. *Circonico* (chērkônē'-kô), Ger. *Zirknitz* (tsĭrk'nĭts), village, SW Slovenia, Yugoslavia, 20 mi. SSW of Ljubljana; saltworks; lumbering. Cirknisko Jezero is 3 mi. S; numerous caverns near by. Until 1918, in Carniola.

Cerkno (tsĕrk'nô), Ital *Circhina* (chērkē'nä), village (1936 pop. 925), W Slovenia, Yugoslavia, 25 mi. W of Ljubljana. Until 1947, in Italy.

Cermeño (sĕrmā'nyō), village (pop. 331), Panama prov., central Panama, in Pacific lowland, 3 mi. SE of Capira; orange groves; stock raising.

Cermik (chĕrmĭk'), Turkish *Çermik*, village (pop. 3,320), Diyarbakir prov., E Turkey, 45 mi. WNW of Diyarbakir; cotton, potatoes, grain.

Cerna (chĕr'nä). **1** Czech *Černá*, village (pop. 230), S Bohemia, Czechoslovakia, in Bohemian Forest, near Austrian border, on railroad and 24 mi. SW of Budweis; graphite mining; glassmaking. **2** or **Cerna pri Cope** (prĭ'chôpĕ), Slovak *Černá pri Čope*, village (pop. 580), SE Slovakia, Czechoslovakia, 4 mi. W of Cop; frontier station.

Cerna Hora, Czechoslovakia: see JANSKE LAZNE.

Cernahora, Ukrainian SSR: see CHERNAGORA.

Cernatu (chĕrnä'tōō), Hung. *Csernátfalu* (chĕr'nätfŏ"lōō), village (pop. 2,532), Stalin prov., central Rumania, 6 mi. ESE of Stalin (Brasov); lumbering.

Cernauti, Ukrainian SSR: see CHERNOVTSY, city.

Cernavoda (chĕrnävô'dŭ), Rum. *Cernavodă*, town (1948 pop. 6,100), Constanta prov., SE Rumania, in Dobruja, on railroad, at junction of Danube R. and the Danube-Black Sea Canal, and 32 mi. WNW of Constanta; mfg. of cement, clay products, flour, screws and bolts; petroleum refining, stone quarrying. Former Turkish Bogazkoy. Remains of anc. Axiopolis lie 2 mi. SSW; ruins of anc. Capidava are c.10 mi. N. Noted as site of extensive finds of Neolithic period.

Cernay (sĕrnā'), Ger. *Sennheim* (zĕn'hīm), town (pop. 5,209), Haut-Rhin dept., E France, on the Thur and 9 mi. WNW of Mulhouse, at SE foot of the Vosges; road center; cotton milling, rayon processing, rubber mfg. Heavily damaged in First World War. Hartmannswillerkopf natl. cemetery 4 mi. N.

Cerne Abbas (sûrn' ă'bŭs), agr. village and parish (pop. 448), central Dorset, England, 7 mi. N of Dorchester. Has 15th-cent. church. Near by is Cerne Giant, 180-ft. figure (probably pre-Norman) cut into chalk hill.

Cernobbio (chĕrnôb'byô), village (pop. 2,447), Como prov., Lombardy, N Italy, port on SW shore of L. Como, 2 mi. N of Como. Resort with many villas, including 16th-cent. Villa d'Este (now a hotel). Paper and silk mills, paint factory, food and artificial-fruit industries.

Cernohorske Kupele, Czechoslovakia: see VONDRISEL.

Cernovice, Czechoslovakia: see BRNO.

Cernusco sul Naviglio (chĕrnōō'skō sōōl nävē'lyô), town (pop. 5,243), Milano prov., Lombardy, N Italy, 8 mi. ENE of Milan; mfg. (furniture, toys, paint, asbestos, textiles); dairy products.

Cérons (sārõ'), village (pop. 187), Gironde dept., SW France, on left bank of Garonne R. opposite Cadillac, 18 mi. SE of Bordeaux; sauterne wines.

Cerqueira César (sĕrkā'rŭ sĕ'zär), city (pop. 3,078), SW central São Paulo, Brazil, on railroad and 16 mi. W of Avaré; wine making, cotton ginning; coffee, rice, sugar cane. Also spelled Cerqueira Cezar.

Cerralbos, Los (lōs thĕräl'vōs), village (pop. 942), Toledo prov., central Spain, 14 mi. E of Talavera de la Reina; cereals, vegetables, olives, grapes. Olive-oil extracting, flour milling.

Cerralvo (sĕräl'vō), town (pop. 2,732), Nuevo León, NE Mexico, in NE foothills of Sierra Madre Oriental, 50 mi. NE of Monterrey; corn, cotton, sugar.

Cerralvo Island (□ 60), off SE Lower California, NW Mexico, in Gulf of California, 28 mi. E of La Paz; 19 mi. long NW-SE bet. 24°8'–24°23'N, up to 5 mi. wide. Uninhabited.

Cerredo, Torre de (tô'rā dhä thĕrā'dhō), highest peak (8,687 ft.) of Cantabrian Mts., N Spain, in the Picos de Europa (massif), on Leon-Santander prov. border, 12 mi. NE of Riaño. Sometimes called Peña de Cerredo.

Cerreto, Passo di (päs'sô dē chĕr-rā'tô), pass (alt. 4,137 ft.) in Etruscan Apennines, N central Italy, 17 mi. NNE of Carrara. Crossed by road bet. Sarzana and Castelnovo ne' Monti.

Cerreto d'Esi (dā'zē), village (pop. 1,766), Ancona prov., The Marches, central Italy, near Esino R., 4 mi. ESE of Fabriano; liquor.

Cerreto Guidi (gwē'dē), village (pop. 1,277), Firenze prov., Tuscany, central Italy, 4 mi. NW of Empoli; glass.

Cerreto Sannita (sän-nē'tä), town (pop. 3,110), Benevento prov., Campania, S Italy, 16 mi. NW of Benevento; mfg. (agr. tools, pharmaceuticals), wine, olive oil.

Cerrillos (sĕrē'yōs), village (pop. estimate 1,200), ⊙ Cerrillos dept. (□ 175; 1947 pop. 6,031), central Salta prov., Argentina, in Lerma Valley, 10 mi. SSW of Salta; rail junction and stock-raising center; flour milling; lime works.

Cerrillos. **1** Village (1930 pop. 635), Aconcagua prov., central Chile, 15 mi. WNW of San Felipe, in agr. area (fruit, wine, tobacco, hemp). Copper deposits near by. **2** Village (1930 pop. 292), Coquimbo prov., N central Chile, 12 mi. WNW of Ovalle; rail junction; grain, fruit, livestock.

Cerrillos, village (1940 pop. 660), Santa Fe co., N central N.Mex., on branch of Rio Grande and 21 mi. SSW of Santa Fe; alt. c.5,700 ft. Loading point in coal-mining region. Several Pueblo Indian villages in vicinity.

Cerrillos or **Los Cerrillos** (lōs), town (pop. 500), Canelones dept., S Uruguay, 22 mi. NNW of Montevideo, in rich agr. region (grain, wine, stock); dairying.

Cerrillos, Los, Chile: see SANTIAGO.

Cerrito (sĕrē'tōō), town (pop. 1,136), SE Rio Grande do Sul, Brazil, on railroad and 27 mi. W of Pelotas; gold washing.

Cerrito (sĕrē'tō), town (pop. 3,422), Valle del Cauca dept., W Colombia, in Cauca valley, 22 mi. NE of Cali; coffee, sugar cane, tobacco, cacao, fruit, cattle.

Cerrito, town (dist. pop. 2,249), Ñeembucú dept., S Paraguay, on Paraná R. (Argentina border) and 55 mi. SE of Pilar; fruit, livestock.

Cerritos (sĕrē'tōs), city (pop. 6,980), San Luis Potosí, N central Mexico, on interior plateau, on railroad and 50 mi. ENE of San Luis Potosí; alt. 3,783 ft. Agr. center (grain, cotton, fruit, stock).

Cerro [Span.,=hill], for names beginning thus and not found here: see under following part of the name.

Cerro or **Villa del Cerro** (vē'yä dĕl sĕ'rō), SW industrial section of Montevideo, S Uruguay, built on hill (486 ft.). Has meat-packing plants. Atop the hill are remains of anc. Portuguese fort, built 1717. Founded 1834.

Cerro, El, or **El Cerro de Andévalo** (ĕl thĕ'rō dhä ändā'välō), town (pop. 3,553), Huelva prov., SW Spain, in the Sierra Morena, 33 mi. N of Huelva; copper, antimony, manganese mining. Produces also wheat, barley, olives, timber; livestock, dairy products.

Cerro Agudo (sĕ'rō ägōō'dō), town (pop. 1,086), Sinaloa, NW Mexico, 17 mi. SSE of Sinaloa; corn, vegetables, sugar cane, fruit.

Cerro Alto, Texas: see HUECO MOUNTAINS.

Cerro Azul (sĕ'rō äsōōl'), town (pop. estimate 500), S Misiones natl. territory, Argentina, 37 mi. SE of Posadas; agr. (maté, rice, tobacco). Tobacco research station.

Cêrro Azul (sā'rōō äzōōl'), city (pop. 883), E Paraná, Brazil, near Ribeira R. and São Paulo border, 40 mi. N of Curitiba; brown-sugar mfg., distilling; corn, almonds, livestock. Marble quarries and iron mines near by. Old spelling, Serro Azul.

Cerro Azul (sĕ'rō äsōōl'), town (pop. 1,372), Lima dept., W central Peru, port on the Pacific, on highway, and 7 mi. WNW of Cañete; shipping point for sugar, cotton, and cotton products.

Cerro Castillo (sĕ'rō kästē'yō), village (1930 pop. 203), Magallanes prov., S Chile, on Argentina border, in Patagonian Andes, 33 mi. NNE of Puerto Natales; sheep raising; resort.

Cerro Chato (sĕ'rō chä'tō), town (pop. 2,000), central Uruguay, on border bet. Treinta y Tres, Florida, and Durazno depts., in the Cuchilla Grande Principal, on railroad and 135 mi. NNE of Montevideo, 75 mi. SW of Melo; road junction; grain, cattle, sheep.

Cerro Colorado (sĕ'rō kōlōrā'dō), village, Florida dept., S central Uruguay, in the Cuchilla Grande Principal, on railroad and 40 mi. SW of José Batlle y Ordóñez; grain, cattle, sheep.

Cerro de Andévalo, El, Spain: see CERRO, EL.

Cerro del Hierro, El (ĕl thĕ'rō dhĕl yĕ'rō), iron-mining village (pop. 101), Seville prov., SW Spain, in the Sierra Morena, 3 mi. SE of San Nicolás del Puerto (linked by rail).

Cerro de Pasco (sĕ'rō dŭ păs'kō, Sp. sĕ'rō dā pä'skō), city (pop. 19,187), ⊙ Pasco dept. and Pasco prov., central Peru, in Nudo de Pasco of the Andes, 110 mi. NE of Lima (connected by railroad and highway); 10°43'S 76°19'W; alt. 13,973 ft. One of the highest cities in the world, it is a major mining center, made famous by the great silver deposits discovered here in 1630. When silver mining declined late in 19th cent., the exploitation of other minerals—copper chiefly, and gold, lead, zinc, and bismuth—again made it Peru's leading mining center. Only Indians accustomed to the rarified air can be employed for any length of time in the mines. Smelter construction at LA OROYA (connected by railroad) stimulated its resurgence. Until 1931, ⊙ Junín dept. The vanadium-mining center of Mina Ragra is near by.

Cerro de San Antonio (sĕ'rō dā sän' äntō'nyō), town (pop. 2,508), Magdalena dept., N Colombia, on Magdalena R. and 45 mi. S of Barranquilla; corn, livestock.

Cerro de San Pedro (pā'drō) or **San Pedro,** town (pop. 1,757), San Luis Potosí, N central Mexico, on interior plateau, 12 mi. ENE of San Luis Potosí; alt. 6,719 ft. Silver, gold, lead mining.

Cerro Gordo (sĕ'rō gôr'dō), village and mountain pass, Veracruz, E Mexico, in foothills of the Sierra Madre Oriental, on highway to Mexico city, and 40 mi. WNW of Veracruz. Here was fought, April 17–18, 1847, a decisive battle of the Mexican War, in which Santa Anna unsuccessfully attempted to halt the advance of Gen. Winfield Scott. Taking part in the battle were the then Capt. R. E. Lee and Lt. U. S. Grant.

Cerro Gordo (sĕ"rŭ gôr'dŭ, –dō), county (□ 576; pop. 46,053), N Iowa; ⊙ Mason City. Rolling prairie agr. area (cattle, hogs, poultry, grain) drained by Shell Rock R. and Lime Creek. Limestone quarries, sand and gravel pits. Formed 1851.

Cerro Gordo. 1 Village (pop. 1,052), Piatt co., central Ill., 12 mi. ENE of Decatur, in rich agr. area; ships grain. Inc. 1873. **2** Town (pop. 265), Columbus co., SE N.C., 13 mi. W of Whiteville, near S.C. line.

Cerro Largo (sĕ'rō lär'gō), department (□ 5,764; pop. 97,256), NE Uruguay; ⊙ Melo. Bordered by the Río Negro (N and NW), by Brazil along Yaguarón R. (NE) and L. Mirim (SE). Tacuarí R. is in SE, the Cuchilla Grande Principal is S. Produces wheat, corn, oats; major cattle- and sheep-raising region. Main centers: Melo, Fraile Muerto, Río Branco. Dept. was formed 1837.

Cerro Maggiore (chĕr'rô mäd-jô'rĕ), town (pop. 5,409), Milano prov., Lombardy, N Italy, 2 mi. E of Legnano; shoe mfg. center; foundry, silk mill.

Cerro Negro (sĕ'rō nā'grō), village (1930 pop. 287), Ñuble prov., S central Chile, 35 mi. SW of Chillán; wheat, corn, fruit, wine, vegetables, livestock; lumbering.

Cerro Pelado, N.Mex.: see VALLE GRANDE MOUNTAINS.

Cerros Island, Mexico: see CEDROS ISLAND.

Cerro Vista (sĕ"rō vĭ'stŭ), peak (11,947 ft.), N N.Mex., in Sangre de Cristo Mts., 15 mi. SE of Taos.

Certaldo (chĕrtäl'dô), town (pop. 5,290), Firenze prov., Tuscany, central Italy, on Elsa R. and 19 mi. SW of Florence; wine, alcohol, macaroni, cement, glass, motors. Has palace and 13th-cent. church with works of Boccaccio, who was b. here.

Certosa di Pavia (chĕrtô'zä dē pävē'ä), village (pop. 140), Pavia prov., Lombardy, N Italy, 5 mi. N of Pavia; liquor, shoes. Near by is a splendid Carthusian monastery, the Certosa di Pavia, founded 1396 by Gian Galeazzo Visconti. One of Italy's most famous monuments, with 15th-cent. Lombard-Romanesque façade; ranks among finest creations of its kind.

Cerulean or **Cerulean Springs** (sûrōō'lēŭn), town (pop. 218), Trigg co., SW Ky., 15 mi. WNW of Hopkinsville, in agr. area; crushed limestone.

Cervantes (sĕrvän'tĕs), village (dist. pop. 2,015), Cartago prov., central Costa Rica, on branch of Inter-American Highway and 2 mi. S of Pacayas; potatoes, grain, livestock.

Cervaro (chĕrvä'rô), town (pop. 2,071), Frosinone prov., Latium, S central Italy, 30 mi. ESE of Frosinone.

Cervaro River, S Italy, rises in the Apennines 9 mi. ESE of Ariano Irpino, flows 55 mi. N, disappearing underground near coast of Gulf of Manfredonia, 9 mi. SSW of Manfredonia.

Cervasca (chĕrvä'skä), village (pop. 2,526), Cuneo prov., Piedmont, NW Italy, 4 mi. W of Cuneo.

Cervena Voda (chĕr'vĕnä vô'dä), Czech *Červená Voda,* village (pop. 1,423), N Moravia, Czechoslovakia, 13 mi. NNW of Zabreh; basketwork, brushes, brooms.

Cerveny Kostelec (chĕr'vĕnē kô'stĕlĕts), Czech *Červený Kostelec,* Ger. *Rothkosteletz* (rōt"kô'stŭlĕts), town (pop. 4,856), NE Bohemia, Czechoslovakia, in foothills of the Adlergebirge, 22 mi. NNE of Hradec Kralove; textiles (mainly linen).

Cervera (thĕrvä'rä), city (pop. 4,589), Lérida prov., NE Spain, in Catalonia, 19 mi. WNW of Igualada; cement, hat mfg.; olive-oil processing and exporting, almond shipping; agr. trade (cereals, wine, fruit). Philip V transferred here (1717) the universities of Barcelona, Lérida, and Solsona, later suppressed. Airport 9 mi. W.

Cervera del Llano (dhĕl lyä'nō), town (pop. 1,321), Cuenca prov., E central Spain, 35 mi. SW of Cuenca; cereals, fruit, livestock; flour milling, plaster mfg.

Cervera del Maestre (mäĕ'strā), town (pop. 1,860), Castellón de la Plana prov., E Spain, 9 mi. WSW of Vinaroz; olive oil; cereals, almonds, wine.

Cervera de los Montes (dhā lōs mōn'tĕs), town (pop. 783), Toledo prov., central Spain, 5 mi. N of Talavera de la Reina; cereals, forage, olives, livestock. Lime deposits.

Cervera del Río Alhama (dhĕl rē'ō älä'mä), town (pop. 4,770), Logroño prov., N Spain, 20 mi. S of Calahorra; agr. center with important hemp-sandal factories; other mfg.: cotton cloth, soap, chocolate, flour. Hemp, wine, vegetables, fruit, livestock in area. Has ruins of medieval castle. Mineral springs. Irrigation reservoir near by.

Cervera de Pisuerga (dhā pĕswĕr'gä), town (pop. 1,587), Palencia prov., N central Spain, on Pisuerga R. and 60 mi. N of Palencia; flour- and sawmills. Coal (anthracite and bituminous), iron, and lead mines near by.

Cerveteri (chĕrvā'tĕrē), anc. *Caere* (sē'rē), village (pop. 1,903), Roma prov., Latium, central Italy, 20 mi. WNW of Rome. Once a chief city of Etruria; has Etruscan necropolises with tombs of 7th to 3d cent. B.C. Formerly also Cervetri.

Cervi, island, Greece: see ELAPHONESOS.

Cervia (chĕr'vyä), town (pop. 2,920), Ravenna prov., Emilia-Romagna, N central Italy, 13 mi. SSE of Ravenna, bathing resort on the Adriatic. Its saltworks cover over 2,000 acres; among the most important in Italy. Bishopric.

Cerviá (thĕrvē'ä), village (pop. 1,536), Lérida prov., NE Spain, 6 mi. S of Borjas Blancas; olive-oil processing; cereals, almonds.

Cervignano del Friuli (chĕrvēnyä'nô dĕl frē'ōōlē), town (pop. 3,254), Udine prov., Friuli-Venezia Giulia, NE Italy, 17 mi. SSE of Udine; rail junction; mfg. (pottery, soap, macaroni, candy).

Cervin, Mont: see MATTERHORN.

Cervino, Monte: see MATTERHORN.

Cervione (sĕrvyôn'), village (pop. 1,157), E Corsica, near Tyrrhenian Sea, 25 mi. S of Bastia; orchards, vineyards. Has 15th-cent. church. Theodore, baron von Neuhof, installed himself as king of Corsica here.

Cesana Torinese (chĕzä'nä tôrēnā'zĕ), village (pop. 680), Torino prov., Piedmont, NW Italy, near Fr. border, on Montgenèvre Pass route, on Dora Riparia R. and 18 mi. SW of Susa.

Cesano Maderno (chĕsä'nô mädĕr'nô), town (pop. 5,771), Milano prov., Lombardy, N Italy, 12 mi. N of Milan. Furniture mfg. center; dyeworks, rayon factory.

Césares Island (sā'särĕs) (□ 7), in Anegada Bay, SW Buenos Aires prov., Argentina, 45 mi. NE of Carmen de Patagones; 7 mi. long.

Cesarò (chĕzärô'), village (pop. 4,596), Messina prov., NE central Sicily, 8 mi. NW of Bronte.

César River (sā'sär), Magdalena dept., N Colombia, rises on E slopes of Sierra Nevada de Santa Marta, flows c.200 mi. SW in irregular, meandering course, through Ciénaga de Zapatosa, to Magdalena R. at El Banco. Along its course are rich pasture lands.

Cesena (chĕzā'nä), town (pop. 20,043), Forlì prov., Emilia-Romagna, N central Italy, on Savio R. and 12 mi. SE of Forlì, on the Aemilian Way; mfg. (automobile chassis, electrical equipment, canned foods, macaroni, beet sugar, liquor, wine, hemp products). Sulphur mines near by. Bishopric. Has cathedral (14th–15th cent.), citadel, seminary, agr. and trade schools, and noted Malatesta library (1447–52; rich in MSS). Flourished under Malatesta family (1379–1465). Popes Pius VI and VII b. here.

Cesenatico (chĕzĕnä'tēkô), town (pop. 4,298), Forlì prov., Emilia-Romagna, N central Italy, on the Adriatic, 13 mi. NNW of Rimini; bathing resort; toy mfg.

Cesiomaggiore (chĕzyômäd-jô'rĕ), village (pop. 488), Belluno prov., Veneto, N Italy, 12 mi. SW of Belluno; alcohol.

Cesis or **Tsesis** (tsā'sēs), Lettish *Cēsis,* Ger. *Wenden,* city (pop. 8,748), N Latvia, in Vidzeme, 50 mi. NE of Riga, in the "Livonian Switzerland"; agr. center (foodstuffs, flax); mfg. (machinery, lime, woolens, leather goods), brewing, wine making. Has teachers col., castle ruins, medieval St. John church. Summer resort. Long the seat of Livonian Knights; passed in 1561 to Lithuania-Poland, 1629 to Sweden, and 1721 to Russia. Attacked (1577) by Ivan the Terrible, the fortress of Cesis was blown up by its own garrison. Here, in 1919, the Latvians defeated a German free corps.

Ceska Kamenice (chĕ'skä kä'mĕnyĭtsĕ), Czech *Česká Kamenice,* Ger. *Böhmisch-Kamnitz* (bû'mĭsh-käm'nĭts), town (pop. 4,885), N Bohemia, Czechoslovakia, in W foothills of Lusatian Mts., 19 mi. NE of Usti nad Labem. Rail junction; major paper mills; center of Bohemian cut-glass production; mfg. of textiles, knitwear. Picturesque summer resort. Has 14th-cent. church, 16th-cent. castle, mus.

Ceska Lipa (lē'pä), Czech *Česká Lípa,* Ger. *Böhmisch-Leipa* (bû"mĭsh-lī'pä), town (pop. 11,991), N Bohemia, Czechoslovakia, 22 mi. E of Usti nad Labem; rail junction (repair shops); textile center (cotton goods, knitwear); mfg. of leather goods, pianos, cardboard, wooden furniture. Extensive orchards in vicinity. Has old castle, 14th-cent. church, 15th-cent. Jewish cemetery, 17th-cent. Augustine monastery, remains of fortifications.

Ceska Skalice (skä'lĭtsĕ), Czech *Česká Skalice,* Ger. *Böhmisch-Skalitz* (bû'mĭsh-skä'lĭts), town (pop. 2,679), NE Bohemia, Czechoslovakia, in NW foothills of the Adlergebirge, on railroad, and 16 mi. NE of Hradec Kralove; summer resort; linen industry. Bozena Nemcova, 19th-cent. novelist, lived here.

Ceska Trebova (tûrzhĕ'bôvä), Czech *Česká Třebová,* Ger. *Böhmisch-Trübau* (bû"mĭsh-trü'bou), E Bohemia, Czechoslovakia, 35 mi. SE of Hradec Kralove; rail junction (repair shops); machinery mfg. Has rapidly developing textile industry (linen, cotton, silk).

Ceska Ves, Czechoslovakia: see JESENIK.

Ceske Budejovice, Czechoslovakia: see BUDWEIS.

Ceske Velenice (chĕ'skĕ vĕ'lĕnyĭtsĕ), Czech *České Velenice,* village (pop. 2,529), S Bohemia, Czechoslovakia, on Luznice R. and 26 mi. SE of Budweis, on Austrian border; rail junction (workshops); knitwear mfg., glass grinding, wood processing. Part of town of Gmünd under Austria-Hungary, and again, 1939–45.

Cesko-Moravska Vysocina (or **Vrchovina**), Czechoslovakia: see BOHEMIAN-MORAVIAN HEIGHTS.

Cesky Brod (chĕ'skē brôt"), Czech *Český Brod,* Ger. *Böhmisch-Brod* (bû"mĭsh-brōt'), town (pop. 5,754), E central Bohemia, Czechoslovakia, on railroad and 20 mi. E of Prague, in wheat and sugar-beet region; large sugar mills. Has 14th-cent. church, 16th-cent. belfry. Hussite chief, Procopius the Great, was killed in battle at Lipany (lĭ'pänĭ), 4 mi. SE.

Cesky Dub (dōōp"), Czech *Český Dub,* Ger. *Böhmisch-Aichel* (bû'mĭsh-ī'khŭl), village (pop. 1,835), N Bohemia, Czechoslovakia, 8 mi. SSW of Liberec; barley.

Cesky Krumlov (krōōm'lôf), Czech *Český Krumlov,* Ger. *Krummau* (krōō'mou), town (pop. 11,724), S Bohemia, Czechoslovakia, in foothills of Bohemian Forest, on Vltava (Moldau) R. and 13 mi. SSW of Budweis; mfg. (newsprint, chemicals), woodworking. Graphite and asbestos mining in vicinity. Its noted 12th-cent. castle, rebuilt in 16th cent., has large collection of paintings and tapestries, 18th-cent. theater, and a park. Also noteworthy are 14th-cent. church with cloister, 15th- and 18th-cent. churches, and Renaissance town hall.

Cesky Les, Czechoslovakia: see BOHEMIAN FOREST.

Cesky Raj, Czechoslovakia: see BOHEMIAN PARADISE.

Cesky Tesin (tyĕ'shēn), Czech *Český Těšín,* Ger. *Teschen* (tĕ'shŭn), town (pop. 9,986; urban commune 12,076), E Silesia, Czechoslovakia, on left bank of Olse R., opposite CIESZYN (Poland), and 16 mi. ESE of Ostrava. Important rail junction; mfg. (bentwood furniture, machinery, textiles), food processing, distilling; foundries. Awarded to Czechoslovakia by Conference of Ambassadors (Paris; 1920), together with part of TESCHEN territory. In Poland, 1938–39; inc. (1939–45) into Germany; returned to Czechoslovakia in 1945.

Cesma River, Yugoslavia: see CAZMA RIVER.

Cesme (chĕshmĕ'), Turkish *Çeşme,* village (pop. 4,029), Smyrna prov., W Turkey, port on Sakiz Strait (Aegean Sea), 45 mi. W of Smyrna, opposite Chios; tobacco, raisins, figs. Sometimes spelled Chesme.

Céspedes (sā'spādĕs), town (pop. 2,358), Camagüey prov., E Cuba, on Central Highway, on railroad and 4 mi. NW of Florida; sugar milling.

Cespedosa (thĕspā-dhō'sä), town (pop. 1,695), Salamanca prov., W Spain, 13 mi. NE of Béjar; flour mills; livestock, cereals.

Cessalto (chĕs-säl'tô), village (pop. 973), Treviso prov., Veneto, N Italy, 18 mi. E of Treviso; silk mill. Has palace designed by Palladio.

Cessenon (sĕsnō'), village (pop. 1,874), Hérault dept., S France, on Orb R. and 11 mi. NW of Béziers; brick and tile works. Lignite mining, marble quarrying.

Cessieu (sĕsyû'), village (pop. 658), Isère dept., SE France, on the Bourbre and 4 mi. W of La Tour-du-Pin; perfume mfg., iron founding, silk milling.

Cessnock (sĕs'nŏk), municipality (pop. 13,029), E New South Wales, Australia, 23 mi. W of Newcastle; rail terminus; coal mines; dairies.

Cess River, central Liberia, rises in Nimba Mts. on Fr. West Africa border, flows c.200 mi. S and SW to the Atlantic at River Cess town. Forms Liberia–Ivory Coast border in upper course. Formerly called Cestos R.

Cestona (thĕstō'nä), town (pop. 1,067), Guipúzcoa prov., N Spain, popular spa 15 mi. WSW of San Sebastián; iron-pipe and chocolate mfg., sawmilling. Lignite mines near by.

Cestos River, Liberia: see CESS RIVER.

Cetara (chĕtä'rä), village (pop. 2,298), Salerno prov., Campania, S Italy, on Gulf of Salerno, 4 mi. SW of Salerno.

Cetate (chĕtä'tā), village (pop. 5,819), Dolj prov., S Rumania, near Danube R. (Bulg. border), 10 mi. NNE of Calafat; agr. center, customs station.

Cetatea-Alba, Ukrainian SSR: see BELGOROD-DNESTROVSKI.

Cetatea Sucevii, Rumania: see SUCEAVA, town.

Cetin, Yugoslavia: see CETINGRAD.

Cetina (thātē'nä), town (pop. 2,261), Saragossa prov., NE Spain, on Jalón R. and 18 mi. WSW of Calatayud; sugar beets, wine, cereals, livestock.

Cetina River (tsĕ'tēnä), S Croatia, Yugoslavia, rises in Dinara mtn. range 12 mi. ESE of Knin, flows SSE, past Sestanovac, and W to Adriatic Sea at Omis; c.70 mi. long. Hydroelectric plant at Gubavica Falls, near SESTANOVAC.

Cetingrad (tsĕ'tēngrät), village, NW Croatia, Yugoslavia, 25 mi. SSE of Karlovac, near Bosnia border. Ruined castle. Scene of election (1527) by Croat nobility of Austrian archduke Ferdinand as king and 1st Hapsburg ruler of Croatia. Also called Cetin.

Cetinje or **Tsetinye** (both: tsĕ'tēnyĕ), town (pop. 9,109), SW Montenegro, Yugoslavia, 18 mi. W of Titograd, at E foot of the Lovcen, in a karst valley (alt. c.2,000 ft.). Has former royal palace (now a mus.), monastery of St. Gospodija (burial place of Montenegrin princes), and Orthodox Eastern church. Originally a monastery (built 1485). Former cultural center of Montenegro. Several times sacked by Turks; seat of Montenegrin princes and ⊙ Montenegro (and, 1929–41, Zeta banovina), until transfer of capital to Titograd after Second World War.

Cetona (chĕtô'nä), town (pop. 1,404), Siena prov., Tuscany, central Italy, at NE foot of Monte Cetona (3,766 ft.), 5 mi. SW of Chiusi. Has 13th-cent. church, 16th-cent. castle, palace with collection of Etruscan antiquities.

Cetraro (chĕträ'rô), town (pop. 2,729), Cosenza prov., Calabria, S Italy, on Tyrrhenian Sea, 24 mi. NW of Cosenza; fishing port.

Cette, France: see SÈTE.

Ceuta (syōō'tů, Sp. thā'ōōtä), Arabic *Sebta*, fortified city (□ 7.5; with suburbs: 1940 pop. 59,115; 1948 estimate 67,790), a Spanish possession on NW coast of Africa, an enclave in Sp. Morocco, strategically located at Mediterranean entrance to the Strait of Gibraltar, opposite (16 mi. S of) Gibraltar and 28 mi. ENE of Tangier; 35°54'N 5°18'W. An important military post, it is administratively part of Sp. province of Cádiz. Situated on a narrow peninsula extending 2 mi. E to Punta Almina (lighthouse), it has the best Sp.-owned harbor in N Africa, and is nearest port to European continent. It has active fisheries and is an important fueling station. A narrow-gauge railroad to Tetuán (22 mi. S) provides access to the mountainous hinterland (Rif) of Sp. Morocco. All of the city's economic activity is concentrated in the harbor, where fish are processed and canned and fishing vessels are built and repaired. On peninsula just E of harbor rises Mt. Acho (alt. 636 ft.), topped by a fort. It is probably the anc. *Abyla* or *Abila*, one of antiquity's Pillars of Hercules (Gibraltar was the other). On mainland, at base of peninsula, are Ceuta's military installations and defense works, which extend westward to the Jebel Musa (alt. 2,790 ft.), a prominent landmark from the sea. It, too, is often identified as one of the Pillars of Hercules. Ceuta preserves little of its Moorish appearance and tradition after 5 centuries of Christian rule. Founded by Phoenicians, it was held successively by Romans, Vandals, Byzantines, and Arabs (after 711). It prospered commercially during the Middle Ages. Taken by Portugal (1st permanent European conquest in Africa) in 1415, it passed (1580) to Spain and has remained Spanish despite several attacks, notably a long siege (1674–1701) by Sultan Ismail. Its commercial importance, however, has never reached its former heights.

Ceutí (thĕōōtē'), town (pop. 2,922), Murcia prov., SE Spain, near the Segura, 10 mi. NW of Murcia; fruit conserves; flour milling; olive oil, pepper.

Céüze, Pic de (pēk dů sāüz'), peak (6,624 ft.) of S Dauphiné Alps, Hautes-Alpes dept., SE France, bet. Petit Buëch (NW) and Durance (SE) river valleys, overlooking Gap (NE). Winter sports.

Ceva (chā'vä), village (pop. 2,982), Cuneo prov., Piedmont, NW Italy, on Tanaro R. and 11 mi. E of Mondovì; rail junction; silk mills; bricks, pottery.

Cevallos (sävä'yōs), village, Tungurahua prov., central Ecuador, in the Andes, on Guayaquil-Quito RR and 6 mi. SSW of Ambato, in fruitgrowing region (apples, grapes, oranges, etc.). Damaged in 1949 earthquake.

Cevedale, Monte (môn'tĕ chĕvĕdä'lĕ), glacier-topped peak (12,350 ft.) in center of ORTLES group, N Italy, 12 mi. ESE of Bormio.

Cévennes (sāvĕn'), mountain range of S France, limiting the Massif Central on the SE. The Cévennes proper occupy central section (extending c.40 mi. SW–NE across parts of Hérault, Gard, and Lozère depts., from the Causse du Larzac to the Ardèche) of a mtn. arc (average height, 3,000 ft.), swinging generally NE from the Montagne Noire (ESE of Toulouse) to the Monts du Vivarais (just S of Saint-Étienne) and overlooking the Rhone valley and Languedoc coastal lowland. Highest peaks are Mont Lozère (5,584 ft.) and Mont Aigoual (5,141 ft.). Mont Mézenc, in Vivarais, rises to 5,755 ft. The Loire, Allier, Lot, Tarn, Hérault, Gard, and Ardèche rivers all radiate from here. Olive, mulberry, and chestnut trees on SE slopes facing Mediterranean. Sheep pastures. Coal mined in La Grand' Combe-Bessèges area activates Alès industries. Pop., then largely Protestant, actively resisted revocation (1685) of Edict of Nantes until 1704.

Cevico de la Torre (thāvē'kō dhä lä tô'rā), town (pop. 1,630), Palencia prov., N central Spain, 13 mi. SE of Palencia; wine-production center. Also cereals and vegetables in area.

Cevicos (sāvē'kōs), village (1950 pop. 330), Duarte prov., E central Dominican Republic, on NE slopes of the Cordillera Central, 38 mi. ESE of La Vega; tobacco growing.

Cevizlik, Turkey: see MACKA.

Cevljanovici or **Chevlyanovichi** (both: chĕ'vlyänôvĭchē), Serbo-Croatian *Čevljanovići*, manganese-mining center, E central Bosnia, Yugoslavia, 12 mi. N of Sarajevo; connected by rail with SEMIZOVAC. Mines date from 1880.

Ceyhan (jāhän'), town (1950 pop. 17,860), Seyhan prov., S Turkey, on railroad on Ceyhan R., 26 mi. E of Adana; wheat, barley, oats, legumes, sesame, onions, tobacco, cotton. Formerly Hamidiye.

Ceyhan River, anc. *Pyramus* (pĭrā'můs), S Turkey rises in the Anti-Taurus Mts. 25 mi. NE of Elbistan, flows 295 mi. SW, past Elbistan and Ceyhan, to Gulf of Iskenderun 30 mi. SE of Adana. Receives Ergenez R. (left), Goksu R. (right). Formerly sometimes spelled Jihun, Jyhun, or Jaihan.

Ceylanpinar (jālän'pŭnär"), Turkish *Ceylânpınar*, village (pop. 1,397), Urfa prov., SE Turkey, 70 mi. ESE of Urfa and on railroad which follows the Syrian border, opposite town of Ras el 'Ain. Renamed c.1945 from Resulayn, Turkish *Resülayn*.

Ceylon (sēlŏn'), Sanskrit *Lanka*, anc. *Taprobane*, dominion of Br. Commonwealth of Nations, an island (□ 25,332; pop. 6,657,339) in Indian Ocean, just off extreme SE coast of India; ⊙ Colombo. Lying bet. 5°56'–9°50'N and 79°40'–81°53'E, Ceylon is separated from India by Palk Strait and Gulf of Mannar, but is also virtually connected with mainland by ADAM'S BRIDGE, a chain of rocky islets linking Mannar Isl. with Rameswaram Isl. of Madras. Ceylon is pear-shaped, measuring 270 mi. in length (N–S) and 140 mi. at its widest point. Consists of central mtn. mass of pre-Cambrian crystalline rocks surrounded by broad coastal plain covered with thick laterite soils. Along coast are many sand bars—chiefly Jaffna Peninsula, Mannar Isl., and Kalpitiya Peninsula—which enclose shallow lagoons and marshes. Mtn. section culminates in Pidurutalagala (8,291 ft.) and Kirigalpotta (7,857 ft.) peaks and ADAM'S PEAK (7,360 ft.), and gives rise to numerous streams, longest of which is the Mahaweli Ganga (206 mi.), flowing NNE to Koddiyar Bay S of Trincomalee. In the N, where there are extensive soft-limestone deposits, plain is fairly level, but elsewhere surface is broken by outcrops of central rock core. Ceylon's hot, tropical climate, tempered by sea breezes, is characterized by small diurnal and annual (75°–90°F.) ranges of temp. and generally heavy annual rainfall (40–200 in.). Seasons determined by SW monsoon (June–Oct.), from which SW coast and W mtn. slopes receive heaviest rainfall, and NE monsoon (Nov.–Dec.), during which E coast and E mtn. slopes have heaviest precipitation. NW and SE coastal areas receive less than 50 in. Vegetation varies from equatorial rain forest of hills and SW lowlands to xerophytic scrub of drier N and SE parts. Forests cover c.$^1/_5$ of area; rubber, ebony, halmalille, and satinwood are chief trees. Pop. is predominantly rural (85%) and agr. (60%). Of some 4,000,000 acres under cultivation, rice and coconuts comprise over 50%, followed by rubber, tea (Ceylon produces 12% of world's output), and lesser crops of millet, cinnamon, citronella, cacao, cardamon, areca nuts, tobacco, and fibers. Since rainfall is seasonal, numerous artificial irrigation tanks dot the countryside; multipurpose project on Gal Oya river is designed to bring large area in SE under irrigation. Ceylon's important cash crops depend on the heavy rainfall: coconuts are cultivated extensively along W and SW coasts, tea in the hills, especially bet. Kandy and Adam's Peak, rubber on the lower hill slopes of the SW, and cacao just N and E of Kandy. Over 1½ million head of cattle (oxen and buffaloes) are raised, primarily as draft animals; elephants (mostly tuskless), leopards, deer, and monkeys abound. The principal minerals are graphite (plumbago) and gems (sapphires, rubies, moonstones); RATNAPURA is major mining center. Other valuable deposits include iron ore, ilmenite, kaolin, limestone, salt (panned along coast), and mica. Ceylon's few mfg. industries comprise a steel-rolling mill, shark-oil extraction plant, and quinine factory (all in Colombo area), an acetic acid plant (at Madampe), and cementworks (at Kankesanturai), as well as small factories for agr. processing (tea, rubber, coconuts, tobacco); some mfg. of glass, ceramics, plywood, coir, leather, and textiles. Among the many handicraft industries are basket and mat making, cloth weaving, gem cutting, woodworking, and pottery mfg. Fishing is carried on in coastal waters, but dried fish is imported from Maldive Isls. and S India to meet local needs; there are noted pearl fisheries in Gulf of Mannar. Principal cities are COLOMBO, JAFFNA, KANDY, Moratuwa, GALLE, TRINCOMALEE, MATARA, ANURADHAPURA (famous Buddhist center), Badulla, NUWARA ELIYA (hill resort), and Batticaloa. Railroads link Colombo with all the larger cities, and there are air connections with Madras, Trichinopoly, Karachi, London, and Singapore; a ferry service operates bet. Ceylonese rail terminus of Talaimannar and Indian rail terminus of Dhanushkodi. Colombo, a major port of call on Europe–Far East shipping routes, handles bulk of Ceylon's exports (tea, rubber, coconut oil, copra, desiccated coconut, coir fibre, cacao, graphite) and imports (rice, cotton goods, sugar, fertilizers, coal, machinery). Ceylon's pop. is composed of Sinhalese (69%), Tamils (23%), Moors, and Burghers (Eurasians of partly Dutch lineage); also a few thousand Veddas, primitive aborigines living in the E parts. Majority of people are Buddhists (c.65%); some 20% are Hindus, 9% Christians, and 6% Moslems. Chief languages: Sinhalese and Tamil (N). Univ. of Ceylon, at Colombo, is leading educational institution. Literacy percentage (70%) is one of highest in Asia. Much of Ceylon's early history is recorded in the *Mahavansa*, a metrical chronicle written in Pali in 5th cent. A.D. and made known to Western world by a Ceylon civil servant in 1837. Lanka, as the isl. was called by anc. Brahman writers, figures prominently in the Hindu epic, *Ramayana*, and to Moslems isl. was abode of Adam and Eve after their expulsion from Paradise. In late 6th cent. B.C., Vijaya, an Aryan prince—probably from NE India—landed in N Ceylon, defeated aboriginal inhabitants, and established himself as 1st Sinhalese king. In 3d cent. B.C., Buddhism was introduced to the isl. and a branch of the sacred Bo tree from Buddh Gaya in Magadha was planted at Anuradhapura, the Sinhalese capital. Proximity to S India resulted in many invasions by various Tamil dynasties, including Cholan and Pandyan, and in Middle Ages capital was moved to POLONNARUWA. For short time in 12th cent. A.D. Sinhalese power was reaffirmed by Parakrama Bahu, an authoritarian ruler, in whose reign—often called "the golden age of Lanka"—numerous religious bldgs. and irrigation tanks were constructed. Soon, however, a Tamil kingdom arose in N Ceylon and the Sinhalese were driven to the SW parts. Ceylon was visited in 12th and 13th cent. by Arab traders, who called it *Serendib*, in 1505 by the Portuguese; later built (1517) trading post at Colombo, but religious proselytizing and bigotry led to almost constant warfare with Sinhalese kingdoms throughout 16th and early-17th cent. By 1658 all Port. coastal possessions had fallen to the Dutch, who, although primarily concerned with cinnamon trade, instituted some civil administration, the Roman-Dutch law code, and certain public works. Dutch settlements were in turn captured by the British, 1795–96, and were formally ceded to Britain by treaty of Amiens (1802). Coastal areas were at first administered by East India Co. from Madras, but in 1798 Ceylon became a crown colony. In 1815, Sinhalese kingdom of Kandy, which had maintained independence throughout Du. rule, surrendered to British and thus Britain annexed the whole isl. A growing nationalism among Ceylonese during 20th cent. led to several constitutional reforms, culminating in dominion status on Feb. 4, 1948. Divided into 9 provs.: Central, Eastern, North Central, Northern, North Western, Sabaragamuwa, Southern, Uva, Western. Maldive Isls., formerly subordinate to Ceylon, became Br. dependency in 1948.

Ceylon, village (pop. 286), S Sask., 40 mi. WSW of Weyburn; wheat.

Ceylon (sēlŏn', sĭ–), village (pop. 618), Martin co., S Minn., near Iowa line and East Des Moines R., 13 mi. SW of Fairmont, in grain, livestock, and poultry area; dairy products, cement blocks. Tuttle L. is just E.

Ceylon Hill Country, highest section of Ceylon, largely in Central Prov.; 90 mi. long N–S, up to 75 mi. wide; rises to highest point (8,291 ft.) in Pidurutakgala peak of Piduru Ridges, in S central area. Includes Hatton Plateau and Adam's Peak in SW, Horton Plains in S. Sabaragamuwa Hill Country is S extension; Una Basin and Lunugala Ridge are E extensions. NNW of Piduru Ridges lies Kandy Plateau, with Matale Valley to N. Knuckles group is NNE extension. Ceylon Hill Country is source of many rivers, including Amban Ganga, Deduru Oya, Gal Oya, Kalu Ganga, Kelani Ganga, Mahaweli Ganga, and Walawe Ganga.

Ceyras (sārās'), village (pop. 470), Hérault dept., S France, near the Hérault, 9 mi. SE of Lodève; woolen milling, barite quarrying.

Ceyzériat (sāzārēä'), village (pop. 655), Ain dept., E France, on S slope of the Revermont, 5 mi. ESE of Bourg; mfg. of biscuits, ladders, and toilet articles.

Cézallier, Monts du (mō dü sāzälyā'), basalt upland in Central Massif, S central France, on Puy-de-Dôme–Cantal dept. border bet. Monts Dore (N) and Massif du Cantal (S); extends S to Alagnon R. valley. Of volcanic origin, forms part of Auvergne Mts. Rises to 5,100 ft. Summer pastures.

Cèze River (sĕz), Gard dept., S France, rises on E slopes of Mont Lozère, in the Cévennes, flows 62 mi. SE, past Bessèges and Saint-Ambroix, through coal and asphalt mining dist., to the Rhone 6 mi. SE of Bagnols-sur-Cèze.

Chaadayevka (chädī'ůfků), town (1939 pop. over 2,000), E central Penza oblast, Russian SFSR, on Sura R. and 40 mi. E of Penza; sawmilling, distilling, meat packing. Developed in late 1930s.

Cha'ah (kä'ä), village (pop. 1,685), central Johore, Malaya, 26 mi. NNE of Bandar Penggaram; oil-palm center.

Chaa-Khol or **Chaa-Khol'** (chŭä"-khôl'), village, NW Tuva Autonomous Oblast, Russian SFSR, on Yenisei R. and 85 mi. W of Kyzyl; trading post.

Châalis, France: see ERMENONVILLE.

Chaba (chä'bä), village, central Himachal Pradesh, India, on Sutlej R. and 8 mi. N of Simla. Small hydroelectric plant near by, with transmission line to Simla.

Chabanais (shäbänä'), village (pop. 1,478), Charente dept., W France, on Vienne R. and 6 mi. WNW of Rouchchouart; mfg. of railroad ties, pit props, footwear. Damaged in Second World War.

Chaba Peak (10,540 ft.), on Alta.-B.C. border, in Rocky Mts., 50 mi. SSE of Jasper, in Columbia Icefield; 52°12'N 117°40'W.

Chabarovice (khä'bärzhô"vĭtsĕ), Czech *Chabařovice*, Ger. *Karbitz* (kär'bĭts), town (pop. 3,388), N Bohemia, Czechoslovakia, on railroad and 4 mi. W of Usti nad Labem.

Chabas (chä'bäs), town (pop. estimate 2,000), S Santa Fe prov., Argentina, 45 mi. WSW of Rosario; agr. center (corn, flax, wheat, sunflowers, vegetables, livestock); grain elevator.

Chaberis, river, India: see CAUVERY RIVER.

Chaberton (shäbĕrtō'), peak (10,285 ft.) of the Cottian Alps, on Fr.-Ital. border, 2 mi. NNE of Montgenèvre Pass. In Italy until 1947.

Chabeuil (shäbû'ē), village (pop. 1,290), Drôme dept., SE France, 7 mi. ESE of Valence; hosiery mfg., embroidering.

Chablais (shäblĕ'), limestone massif of the Savoy Alps, and region of Haute-Savoie dept., SE France, bounded by L. Geneva (N), Faucigny valley (S) and Switzerland (E). Average alt. 5,000 ft. Drained by Dranse R. Cattle raising, cheese mfg. Tourism and winter sports. Chief town: Thonon-les-Bains. Principal resort: Évian-les-Bains.

Châble, Le, Switzerland: see BAGNES.

Chablis (shäblē'), village (pop. 1,748), Yonne dept., N central France, on Serein R. and 10 mi. E of Auxerre. Famous for its white Burgundy wines. Has 12th-cent. early Gothic church, damaged in Second World War.

Chabot, Lake, Calif.: see SAN LEANDRO.

Chabris (shäbrē'), village (pop. 1,837), Indre dept., central France, near the Cher, 8 mi. SSW of Romorantin; woodworking, sheep raising; grain.

Chacabuco, department, Argentina: see CONCARÁN.

Chacabuco (chäkäbōō'kō), city (pop. 12,917), ⊙ Chacabuco dist. (□ 883; pop. 39,525), N Buenos Aires prov., Argentina, 28 mi. E of Junín, in agr. area (corn, wheat, cattle, sheep); meat packing, flour milling. Founded 1865 as settlement for natl. guardsmen.

Chacabuco, village (1930 pop. 684), Santiago prov., central Chile, at N end of the central valley, 28 mi. N of Santiago, in agr. area (wheat, alfalfa, fruit, livestock). Site of battle (1817) in War of Independence.

Chacachacare (chä"kächäkä'rā), islet (151 acres; pop. 501), off NW Trinidad, B.W.I., in the Dragon's Mouth, 13 mi. W of Port of Spain; 10°41'N 61°45'W; 2 mi. long, 2 mi. wide. Chacachacare village (center), once a whaling establishment, was turned into a leper settlement. The N and W part of the isl. is now a U.S. base.

Chacaltaya (chäkältī'ä), peak (15,224 ft.) in Cordillera de La Paz, W Bolivia, 15 mi. NNE of La Paz; ski resort.

Chacaltianguis (chäkältyäng'gēs), town (pop. 2,125), Veracruz, SE Mexico, on Papaloápam R. and 4 mi. SSW of Cosamaloapan; sugar, bananas, livestock.

Chacao (chäkou'), village (1930 pop. 86), Chiloé prov., S Chile, small port on NE Chiloé Isl., on Chacao Strait, 15 mi. ENE of Ancud; potatoes, livestock; fishing, lumbering.

Chacao, town (pop. 3,668), Miranda state, N Venezuela, 4 mi. E of Caracas, in agr. region (coffee, corn, sugar cane, fruit).

Chacao Strait, narrow channel bet. N Chiloé Isl. and mainland of Chile.

Chacas (chä'käs), town (pop. 1,095), Ancash dept., W central Peru, in Cordillera Blanca, 22 mi. NNE of Huarás; alt. 11,040 ft.; grain, alfalfa. Silver and lead mining near by.

Chacayal (chäkīäl'), village (1930 pop. 368), Osorno prov., S central Chile, on railroad and 7 mi. N of Osorno, in agr. area (wheat, livestock); dairying, lumbering.

Chacayán (chäkīän'), town (pop. 1,541), Pasco dept., central Peru, in Cordillera Central, 22 mi. NNW of Cerro de Pasco; grain, potatoes.

Chacha, volcano, Russian SFSR: see TYATINO.

Chachaclún, Guatemala: see SAN FRANCISCO.

Chachacomani (chächäkōmä'nē), peak (20,528 ft.) in Cordillera de La Paz, W Bolivia, 22 mi. SE of Sorata.

Chachak, Yugoslavia: see CACAK.

Chachani, Nevado de (nävä'dō dā chächä'nē), volcanic massif (19,960 ft.), Arequipa dept., S Peru, just NW of El Misti, 15 mi. N of Arequipa. Has meteorological station.

Chachapa (chächä'pä), town (pop. 1,408), Puebla, central Mexico, 7 mi. E of Puebla; grain, sugar, fruit, livestock.

Chachapoyas (chächäpoi'äs), city (pop. 5,494), ⊙ Amazonas dept. and Chachapoyas prov. (in 1940: □ 1,565; pop. 22,162), N Peru, in E Andean range, near Utcubamba R., on road, and 80 mi. NE of Cajamarca, 420 mi. N of Lima; 6°13'S 77°51'W; alt. 7,638 ft. With a cool mtn. climate, it is the leading city and trading center of an extensive agr. region (sugar cane, cacao, coca, cattle); *chancaca* and alcohol distilling, weaving of straw hats; apiculture. Airport. Bishopric. Dating back to pre-Incan settlement, Chachapoyas is considered the oldest Peruvian town E of the Andes, founded 1536–38. Gold-placer mines, coal deposits near by.

Chachas (chä'chäs), town (pop. 1,007), Arequipa dept., S Peru, 33 mi. NNE of Aplao; grain, potatoes; cattle, sheep, goats. Archaeological remains near by.

Chacha Village (chä'chü), S St. Thomas Isl., U.S. Virgin Isls., just W of Charlotte Amalie. Colony of Norman-French immigrants from St. Bartholomew, who live mostly by fishing; they still speak a Fr. dialect.

Chachoengsao (chä'chŭng'sou'), town (1947 pop. 12,083), ⊙ Chachoengsao prov. (□ 2,097; 1947 pop. 240,565), S Thailand, on right bank of Bang Pakong R. (low-water head of navigation) and on Bangkok-Pnompenh RR, 40 mi. E of Bangkok; head of road (S) to Trat; rice center. Site of pilgrimage (image of Buddha). Iron and salt deposits near by. Also spelled Chaxoengsao or Chajoengsao. Local name, Paet Riu, also spelled Petriu, Petriev, or Petriew.

Chachopo (chächō'pō), town (pop. 435), Mérida state, W Venezuela, in Andean spur, on Motatán R., on transandine highway and 37 mi. NE of Mérida; alt. 8,540 ft.; mica mining.

Chachora (chŭchō'rŭ), town (pop. 5,259), N Madhya Bharat, India, 40 mi. SSW of Guna; agr. (millet, wheat, gram). Sometimes spelled Chachaura.

Chachran (chŭchrän'), town (pop. 2,216), Bahawalpur state, W Pakistan, 80 mi. SW of Bahawalpur; rail spur terminus; wheat. Also spelled Chacharan; sometimes called Chachran Sharif.

Chachrauli, India: see CHHACHHRAULI.

Chaco or **Gran Chaco** (chä'kō, grän), extensive lowland plain of S central South America, divided among Paraguay, Bolivia, and Argentina. Bounded N by the tropical woodlands (c.18°S), S by the Río Salado (28°–30°S), E by the Paraguay R., and W by the Andean piedmont. Largely an area of scrub forest and grassland with tropical savanna climate, it has a very sparse pop. engaged in cattle raising and quebracho collecting. The Chaco is divided by the SE-flowing Pilcomayo and Bermejo rivers into the Chaco Boreal (Paraguay and Bolivia) and the Chaco Central and the Chaco Austral (Argentina). The **Chaco Boreal** (bōräl') (□ 100,000), N of the Pilcomayo, belongs almost entirely to Paraguay (PRESIDENTE HAYES, BOQUERÓN, and OLIMPO depts.), with only the W and N fringes in Bolivian territory. Although part of Bolivia after 1825, this section of the Chaco was gradually colonized by Paraguay. The dispute came to a head following the discovery of petroleum on the Chaco's W fringes and culminated in the Chaco War (1932–35). The award of Buenos Aires (1938) fixed the present boundaries. **Chaco Central** (sĕnträl') (□ 50,000), an elongated section bet. the Pilcomayo and Bermejo rivers, is traversed by the Embarcación-Formosa RR and corresponds to the Argentine natl. territory of FORMOSA and NE Salta prov. It passed 1889 from Bolivia to Argentina. The **Chaco Austral** (ousträl') (□ 100,000), bet. the Bermejo and the Río Salado, corresponds to Argentine natl. territory of Chaco and sections of Santa Fe, Santiago del Estero, and Salta provs.

Chaco, interior province (□ 38,041; pop. 430,555), N Argentina, in the Chaco Austral; ⊙ Resistencia. Bordered NE by Bermejo R. (or Teuco R.) and E by Paraguay and Paraná rivers; S boundary is 28°S latitude. Largely a humid, wooded plain, with a desert in NW, it has a warm subtropical climate. There are sand quarries at Barranqueras on Paraná R. and salt deposits in small lakes along Bermejo R. Agr.: cotton, corn, peanuts, sunflowers, tobacco (E, SE, and center), sugar (E). Stock raising (cattle, goats, horses, hogs) in S and center. Lumbering of subtropical hardwood (quebracho, laurel, carob, guaiacum, guava). Processing industries: tannin extracting (from quebracho), cotton ginning, lumbering, vegetable-oil pressing (peanuts, sunflowers, cotton, spurge), sugar refining (Las Palmas). Lead foundries at Puerto Vilelas. Tanneries (hides from domestic and wild animals), sawmills, tannin and food industries concentrated in Resistencia. Though cotton was introduced in the early colonial days, it has only in 20th cent. been cultivated on a large scale and has helped to make the province one of the fastest developing areas of Argentina. It was raised from the status of a natl. territory to that of a prov. in 1951.

Chaco Canyon National Monument (chä'kō) (□ 33.1; established 1907), NW N.Mex., on short Chaco R., in Chaco Canyon, and c.50 mi. NE of Gallup. Ruins of 13 pre-Columbian pueblos representing Pueblo Indian civilization at peak of development. Best known is Pueblo Bonito (11th cent. A.D.), D-shaped, masonry and timber structure laid out around court at base of sandstone cliff; contained 32 kivas and 800 rooms that accommodated c.1,200 persons. Fine turquoise ornaments and pottery have been found. Ruins of Chettro Kettle (large E-shaped pueblo) are just E.

Chacón, Lo, Chile: see LO CHACÓN.

Chacras de Coria (chä'kräs dā kōr'yä), town (pop. estimate 500), N Mendoza prov., Argentina, on railroad (Paso de los Andes station) and 8 mi. SSW of Mendoza; lumbering and agr. center (wine, alfalfa, fruit, livestock); wine making, dried-fruit processing; plant nurseries.

Chaczinkín (chäksēnkēn'), town (pop. 740), Yucatan, SE Mexico, 7 mi. E of Tekax; henequen, fruit.

Chad (chăd, chäd), Fr. *Tchad*, French overseas territory (□ 485,750; 1950 pop. 2,241,500), N Fr. Equatorial Africa; ⊙ Fort-Lamy. Bounded W by Fr. Cameroons, Nigeria (along L. Chad), and Fr. West Africa, N by Libya, E by Anglo-Egyptian Sudan; adjoins S on Ubangi-Shari territory. Much of it is semi-arid steppe. During the rainy season (July–Sept.) the main rivers of SW (Shari, Logone) overflow and the flat country is transformed into marshes and swamps. In E and NE is a belt of highlands with scattered clumps of shrub forests. Typical Saharan regions (□ c.140,000) lie in N and comprise beside sand desert the Bodélé depression and Tibesti Massif (11,204 ft.). Scarce rainfall; climate subject to cyclical changes and great diurnal ranges (122°F. to 10°F.) in desert zone. Characteristic fauna includes elephants, lions, rhinoceroses, giraffs, ostriches, etc. Principal products are livestock and (since 1931) cotton. Ivory, hides, ostrich feathers, dates, butter are also exported. Natives grow millet, sesame, vegetables (in irrigated localities), work iron, and weave and dye cotton. Shari and Logone rivers navigable by small steamers for part of the year. Principal caravan routes are the trans-Saharan tracks to Benghazi (Cyrenaica), and Tripoli, and pilgrimage route of W African Moslems to Mecca. In 1940–41 several roads were laid by Free French for strategic purposes. Chief centers are Fort-Lamy and Fort-Archambault; Abéché and Massénya are largest native towns. Pop. is Mohammedan and of Negroid-Arab stock and includes sedentary, seminomadic, and nomadic tribes. Native sultanates of WADAI, BAGUIRMI, KANEM, BORKOU were 1st visited by Gustav Nachtigal and Heinrich Barth in mid-19th cent. Senussism made numerous convents here after 1850. Long a bone of contention bet. Great Britain and France, Chad's E frontier was settled by Anglo-French agreement (1899); however, region bet. Darfur and Wadai was divided only in 1919 and its boundary demarcated in 1933. Area was part of Ubangi-Shari-Chad colony until 1920 and under military rule. Made separate colony 1920; acquired territorial status 1946, with representation in Fr. parliament. Chad was used (1940–41) by Free French troops as base of operations against S Libya. Some frontier adjustments with Ubangi-Shari in Fort-Archambault area were effected, 1946.

Chad (chät), village, SE Molotov oblast, Russian SFSR, on railroad and 20 mi. WSW of Krasnoufimsk; lumbering.

Chad, Lake (chăd, chäd), Fr. *Tchad*, large, shallow, freshwater lake (at low water □ c.4,000, at high water □ c.8,000), N central Africa, in the borderland of the Sahara and the Sudan and at meeting point of Fr. Equatorial Africa, Fr. West Africa, Fr. Cameroons, and Nigeria, bet. 12°40'–14°15'N and 13°–15°30'E; c.175 mi. long, 75 mi. wide, 13–22 ft. deep; alt. 800 ft. Fed by Shari-Logone system (S) and Komadugu Yobe (W); has no visible outlet but its waters seep underground to supply water points along Bahr el Ghazal (Soro) and in Bodélé depression. Occasionally, in high-water season, it communicates with Benue R. system through the Logone and Mayo-Kebbi. A remnant of a former inland sea, L. Chad expands and contracts according to seasons and water supply and seems also to be subject to a 10-year cycle. Its shoreline is undefined and marshy, aquatic vegetation and mudbanks encumber the middle, and a continuous chain of inhabited low isls. (□ c.1,500) runs along E coast. A navigable channel exists from mouth of the Shari to Bol. Fishing and natron extracting are carried on, and there is grazing on the isls. First reached by Europeans (Oudney, Chepperton, and Denham) in 1823. Reconnoitered by Gustav Nachtigal, 1870. Fr. explorer Jean Tilho made thorough survey of its hydrography, 1912–17.

Chadadé, Syria: see SHEDADI, TELL.

Chadan (chŭdän'), city (1945 pop. over 1,000), W Tuva Autonomous Oblast, Russian SFSR, 120 mi. WSW of Kyzyl, near Khemchik R., in agr. area Copper mining near by.

Chadbourn (chăd'bŭrn), town (pop. 2,103), Columbus co., SE N.C., 7 mi. W of Whiteville, near S.C. line; shipping center for strawberries. Inc. 1883.

Chadderton, urban district (1931 pop. 27,450; 1951 census 31,114), SE Lancashire, England, just WNW of Oldham; cotton milling, mfg. of pharmaceuticals.

Chadds Ford, village, Delaware co., SE Pa., 9 mi. NNW of Wilmington, Del., and on Brandywine Creek, where Howe defeated Washington, Sept. 11, 1777.

Chadileufú River, Argentina: see SALADO, Río.

Chadobets (chŭdŭbyĕts'), village (1939 pop. over 500), SE Krasnoyarsk Territory, Russian SFSR, on Angara R. and 285 mi. NE of Krasnoyarsk; lumbering.

Chadron (shă'drŭn), city (pop. 4,687), ⊙ Dawes co., NW Nebr., 50 mi. N of Alliance, near White R. and S.Dak. line, in Great Plains region; railroad div., trading point; oil refinery; flour; seed potatoes, dairy and poultry produce, livestock, grain. State teachers col. here. Near-by state park used for recreation. Founded 1885.

Chadwell Heath, England: see DAGENHAM.

Chadwick, village (pop. 607), Carroll co., NW Ill., 24 mi. SW of Freeport, in rich agr. area; feed mill.

Chadwicks. 1 Resort village, Ocean co., E N.J., on peninsula bet. Barnegat Bay and the Atlantic, N of Lavalette; fisheries. **2** Village (1940 pop. 654), Oneida co., central N.Y., 6 mi. S of Utica; textile milling.

Chadyr-Lunga (chŭdĭr"-lo͝on'gŭ), Rum. *Ceadâr-Lunga* (chädur"-lo͝on'gä), village (1941 pop. 7,667), S Moldavian SSR, on railroad and 20 mi. SE of Komrat, near Ukrainian border; flour milling. Pop. largely Gagauz (Turkish-speaking Christians).

Chaeronea (kĕrunē'ŭ), town of anc. Boeotia, Greece, in Cephisus valley, 4 mi. NNW of Levadia. Here Philip II of Macedon defeated (338 B.C.) the combined forces of Athens and Thebes, thus establishing Macedon's supremacy over Greece. In a 2d great battle, the Roman general Sulla defeated (86 B.C.) the forces of Mithridates of Pontus. Plutarch was a native of Chaeronea. A well-preserved theater and a colossal stone lion commemorating the battle of 338 B.C. have been excavated. On site is modern village of Chaironeia or Khaironia (pop. 668), formerly called Kapraina.

Chaeryong (chă'rĕung'), Jap. *Sainei*, town (1944 pop. 22,227), Hwanghae prov., central Korea, N of 38°N, 25 mi. NNW of Haeju; iron-mining center.

Chafarinas Islands (chäfärē'näs), group of 3 islets in the W Mediterranean, 2 mi. off coast of E Sp. Morocco, 30 mi. ESE of Melilla and 6 mi. NW of mouth of Muluya R. (Fr. Morocco border); 35°12'N 2°26'W; lighthouse. A possession of Spain, they are under direct Sp. administration. Only Isabel II Isl. (pop. 273) is inhabited. Other isls. are called Congreso and Rey. Occupied by Spain 1848. Also called Zafarin or Zaffarine Islands.

Chaffee, county (□ 1,039; pop. 7,168), central Colo.; ⊙ Buena Vista. Cattle area, drained by Arkansas R.; grain, truck. Includes parts of San Isabel and Cochetopa natl. forests. Part of Sawatch Mts. in W. Formed 1879.

Chaffee, city (pop. 3,134), Scott co., SE Mo., in Mississippi flood plain, 11 mi. SW of Cape Girardeau; agr. trade center; shoes, clothing. Laid out 1837, inc. 1906.

Chaffee, Camp, Ark.: see FORT SMITH.

Chaffers Island, Chile: see CHONOS ARCHIPELAGO.

Chafurray (chäfo͞orī'), airfield in Meta intendancy, central Colombia, on Ariari R., in llano lowlands, 80 mi. SSE of Villavicencio.

Chagai (chă'gī), dist. (□ 19,429; 1951 pop. 37,000), NW Baluchistan, W Pakistan; ⊙ Nushki. Bordered by Afghanistan (N), Iran (W), and Ras Koh hills (SE). Very dry, sandy area, with volcanic peaks (W) and barren hill ranges (N, SE). Scant rainfall; seasonal streams empty into depressions of the Hamun-i-Lora (NE) and Hamun-i-Mashkel (S). Mineral resources include sulphur ore, gypsum, alum, barite in Koh-i-Sultan area (N), copper, limestone in NW corner, and brine salt in the Hamun-i-Mashkel. Carpet weaving and dyeing; livestock raising. Chief villages: Nushki, Nok Kundi, Dalbandin. Pop. 95% Moslem, 4% Hindu.

Chagai, village, Chagai dist., N Baluchistan, W Pakistan, on W edge of the Hamun-i-Lora, 80 mi. WSW of Nushki; caravan center; trades in carpets, saddlebags, salt.

Chagai Hills, in N Chagai dist., NW Baluchistan, W Pakistan, on Afghan border; from the Hamun-i-Lora extend c.90 mi. W; 10–25 mi. wide. Average height 6,000 ft., rising to 8,060 ft. in W peak. Dry and barren; composed of igneous rock lying E of volcanic peak of Koh-i-Sultan.

Chagala (chŭgŭlä'), town (1941 pop. over 500), NW Ashkhabad oblast, Turkmen SSR, on N shore of Kara-Bogaz-Gol (gulf), 150 mi. NNE of Krasnovodsk; Glauber's salt extracted.

Chagan-Uzun (chŭgän"-o͞ozo͞on'), village, SE Gorno-Altai Autonomous Oblast, Altai Territory, Russian SFSR, on Chuya R. and 165 mi. SE of Gorno-Altaisk; mercury mining.

Chagda (chŭgdä'), town (1941 pop. over 500), SE Yakut Autonomous SSR, Russian SFSR, on Aldan R. and 185 mi. E of Aldan.

Chagford (chăg'fŭrd), town and parish (pop. 1,584), central Devon, England, on Teign R. and 3 mi. WNW of Moreton Hampstead; agr. market; tourist resort. Has medieval inn and 15th-cent. church.

Chagli, Greece: see ERETRIA.

Chagny (shänyē'), town (pop. 3,863), Saône-et-Loire dept., E central France, on Dheune R. and Canal du Centre, 10 mi. NW of Chalon-sur-Saône; railroad and wine-shipping center; produces cement pipes, fertilizer, bicycle parts, hosiery.

Chagoda (chä'gŭdŭ), town (1939 pop. over 2,000), SW Vologda oblast, Russian SFSR, on railroad, on Chagodoshcha R. and 27 mi. SW of Babayevo; center of glassworking dist.; glassworks, power plant. Until 1939, Bely Bychek.

Chagodoshcha River (chŭgŭdô'shchŭ), NW European Russian SFSR, rises in marshes SE of Tikhvin, flows 155 mi. ESE, past Chagoda, to Mologa R. NE of Ustyuzhna. Called Chagoda R. in upper course. Sominka R., a left affluent, is connected with Tikhvin R. by TIKHVIN CANAL. Part of historic water route bet. Baltic Sea and the Volga.

Chagos Archipelago (chä'gōs), dependency (□ 18; pop. 1,048) of Mauritius, c.1,200 mi. NE of Mauritius, in Indian Ocean, belonging to Great Britain; 4°40'–7°40'S 70°45'–72°50'E. Includes 5 main coral atolls: the inhabited Diego Garcia, Peros Banhos, and Salomon Isls., and the uninhabited Three Brothers and Six Isls. Coconut plantations; copra is exported. Sometimes called Oil Isls.

Chagres, Panama: see NUEVO CHAGRES.

Chagres River (chă'grĕs, Sp. chä'grĕs), Panama Canal Zone, now largely utilized by Panama Canal. Rises in Cordillera de San Blas of NE Panama c.45 mi. E of Colón, flows SE through artificial Madden L., reaching the Canal at Gamboa on Gatun L., which it leaves just W of Gatun at Gatun Dam, flowing c.10 mi. NW to the Caribbean at Fort San Lorenzo 7 mi. WSW of Colón. Receives numerous small streams, among them Gatun, Gatuncillo, and Pequení rivers. Not navigable in its uncanalized sections, where it is frequently interrupted by rapids.

Chagrin Falls (shŭgrĭn', shă'grĭn), village (pop. 3,085), Cuyahoga co., N Ohio, 16 mi. ESE of Cleveland and on Chagrin R.; paper, chemicals, pharmaceuticals, electrical goods, machinery.

Chagrin River, NE Ohio, rises S of Chardon, flows SW to Chagrin Falls, then N, through suburbs of Cleveland, to L. Erie just N of Willoughby; c.45 mi. long.

Chaguanas (chägwä'näs), village (pop. 1,840), W Trinidad, B.W.I., on railroad and 11 mi. SE of Port of Spain; sugar-cane growing and milling. A U.S. army base is just E.

Chaguaramal (chägwärämäl'), town (pop. 99), Monagas state, NE Venezuela, 14 mi. WNW of Maturín; zinc and cadmium deposits.

Chaguaramas Bay (chä"gwärä'mäs), inlet in NW Trinidad, B.W.I., on the Gulf of Paria, 8 mi. WNW of Port of Spain, in area leased 1940 to U.S. as naval base. Serves as transfer point for bauxite from the Guianas to Mobile, Ala. Here Sp. admiral Apadoca scuttled his fleet in 1797 on approach of the British.

Chagvan (chăg'văn), Indian fishing village (1939 pop. 12), SW Alaska, on SE shore of Kuskokwim Bay, S of Goodnews Bay; 58°48'N 161°38'W.

Chahar (chä'här'), Chinese *Ch'a-ha-erh*, province (□ 45,000; pop. 3,500,000) of N China; ⊙ Kalgan. Bounded N by Chahar section of Inner Mongolia, W by Suiyuan, SW by Shansi, SE by Hopeh, E by Jehol, Chahar lies mainly bet. 2 sections of the Great Wall in the drainage basins of Sangkan and Yang rivers, the headstreams of Yungting R. It has a continental climate, governed by the nearness of the Mongolian deserts. Next to Liaotung and Hupeh, Chahar ranks 3d as China's iron-ore producer, with mines extending from Süanhwa to Lungkwan. Coal is mined at Tatung, Yühsien, and at Chimingshan (near Süanhwa). Agr. yields primarily wheat, barley, kaoliang, beans, mushrooms, and rhubarb. Stock raising (cattle, sheep, horse, camels) is a leading branch of the economy, yielding the main export items, such as wool, hides, felt, and furs. The prov. lies on a traditional trade route bet. China proper and Mongolia, a route followed since 1920s by Peking-Suiyuan RR. Chief cities are Kalgan and Tatung, both served by the railroad. Tolun is an important caravan center (N). Pop. is entirely Chinese, speaking N Mandarin dialect. There are Mongol minorities along N margin, where Chinese agr. colonization has been encroaching upon the Mongolian plateau N of Kalgan. Chahar is named for the Mongolian Chahar league. It was originally formed in 1914 as a special Mongol administrative area and became a full prov. in 1928. As a result of considerable boundary changes (1949), Chahar consists of a NE section (in Chihli Hopeh, until 1928), and a SW section (in N Shansi until 1949). The original N Mongol section of Chahar, including the Chahar and Silingol leagues, was inc. 1949 into the Inner Mongolian Autonomous Region. During Sino-Japanese War, Chahar was occupied (1937–45) by the Japanese and was joined with Suiyuan into the Mongolian autonomous puppet govt. of Mengkiang.

Chahar, Mongolian league in SW Inner Mongolian Autonomous Region, Manchuria, on Chahar prov. border. Until 1949 in central Chahar.

Chahar Burjak or **Chahar Borjak** (chŭhär' bo͝or'jŭk), town (pop. over 2,000), Farah prov., SW Afghanistan, in small oasis on lower Helmand R., 140 mi. S of Farah, 35–40 mi. from Iran and Baluchistan lines, in Afghan Seistan. Sometimes spelled Charborjak.

Chahardeh (chŭhär'dā) or **Chardeh** (chär'dā), W suburban district of Kabul, Afghanistan; linked with city proper by Guzargah Pass and overlooked by Asmai (N) and Sherdarwaza (E) hills. A broad plain (8 mi. wide, 12 mi. long), it contains the univ. suburb of DAR-UL-FANUN, a tuberculosis sanatorium and dairy farm (at Aliabad), Baber's Garden with the Mogul's tomb (at foot of Sherdarwaza Hill), and the CHIHAL SATUN (Indaki) summer resort.

Chahba, Syria: see SHAHBA.

Chahbahar (chäbähär') or **Chahbar** (–bär'), town (1940 pop. 5,189), Eighth Prov., in Makran, SE Iran, minor port on Gulf of Oman, on SE point of small Chahbahar Bay, 60 mi. W of Pakistan line and 170 mi. NE of Muscat; 25°17'N 60°39'E. Fishing, some agr. (dates, oranges, mangoes, figs). Airfield. Planned port development.

Chah-i-Ab (chä'hī-äb'), town (pop. over 2,000), Afghan Badakhshan, NE Afghanistan, 50 mi. NW of Faizabad, near Panj R. (USSR line).

Chaho (chä'hô'), Jap. *Shako*, town (1944 pop. 20,328), S.Hamgyong prov., N Korea, on Sea of Japan, 60 mi. ENE of Hungnam; fishing and iron-mining center.

Chahuilco (chäwēl'kō), village (1930 pop. 1,370), Osorno prov., S central Chile, on railroad and 11 mi. S of Osorno; agr. center (grain, livestock); dairying, lumbering.

Chaianga River, Port. Guinea: see GEBA RIVER.

Chaibasa (chībä'sŭ), town (pop. 13,052), ⊙ Singhbhum dist., S Bihar, India, on tributary of Subarnarekha R. and 30 mi. WSW of Jamshedpur; road center; trades in rice, oilseeds, jowar, corn; silk growing (supply and research station); shellac mfg. Chromite mining in hill area (W). Cement mfg. 11 mi. S, at Jhinkpani.

Chai-Chai, Mozambique: see VILA DE JOÃO BELO.

Chaiguata, Lake (chīgwä'tä) (□ 15), on S Chiloé Isl., S Chile, 45 mi. SSW of Castro; 10 mi. long.

Chail (chīl), village, Allahabad dist., SE Uttar Pradesh, India, 12.5 mi. W of Allahabad city center; gram, rice, barley, wheat, pearl millet, sugar cane.

Chailey (chā'lē), agr. village and parish (pop. 1,760), central Sussex, England, 6 mi. NNW of Lewes. Site of hosp. and home for crippled children. Has 13th-cent. church.

Chaillac (shäyäk'), village (pop. 405), Indre dept., central France, 17 mi. SE of Le Blanc; iron and manganese deposits near by.

Chailland (shäyā'), village (pop. 380), Mayenne dept., W France, 11 mi. NNW of Laval; marble quarries.

Chaillé-les-Marais (shäyā'-lā-märĕ'), village (pop. 574), Vendée dept., W France, in the Marais Poitevin, 11 mi. WSW of Fontenay-le-Comte; dairying.

Chaillexon, Lake of, France and Switzerland: see BRENETS, LAKE OF.

Chaillol-le-Vieux, France: see CHAMPSAUR.

Chainat (chīnät'), town (1947 pop. 2,489), ⊙ Chainat prov. (□ 1,084; 1947 pop. 173, 413), central Thailand, on Chao Phraya R. and 105 mi. NNW of Bangkok, in rice-growing region, on road from railroad station of Ta Khli. Also spelled Chainad, Cheinat, or Jainad.

Chaîne [Fr.,=mountain range], for names beginning thus and not found here: see under following part of the name.

Chaîne des Puys, France: see DÔME, MONTS.

Chaîne Granitique (shĕn grānētēk'), low range, central Fr. Guiana, NE outlier of Guiana Highlands; extends c.50 mi. NE-SW; rises to over 1,300 ft.

Chainiche, Yugoslavia: see CAJNICE.

Chain Island, Tuamotu Isls.: see ANAA.

Chain Lakes, W Maine, 5-mi. series of narrow linked lakes in N Franklin co., near Que. line.

Chain-O'-Lakes, NE Ill., several lakes near Wis. line and NNW of Chicago, joined to each other by Fox R. Many popular resorts. Included are Fox (the largest), Grass, Nippersink, Pistakee lakes. Chain-O'-Lakes State Park is along shores of Fox and Grass lakes.

Chainpatia, India: see CHANPATIA.

Chairapata (chīräpä'tä), town (pop. c.3,900), Potosí dept., W central Bolivia, 7 mi. ESE of Colquechaca; corn, alpaca, sheep.

Chaise-Dieu, La (lä shāz-dyû'), village (pop. 768), Haute-Loire dept., S central France, on SW slopes of Monts du Forez, 21 mi. NNW of Le Puy; alt. 3,550 ft. Summer and winter-sports resort; woodworking. Has noteworthy Gothic church of St. Robert (14th cent.), which contains 15th-cent. frescoed stalls and 16th-cent. Flemish tapestries.

Chaivo or **Chayvo** (chī'vŭ), village (1948 pop. over 500), NE Sakhalin, Russian SFSR, minor port on Sea of Okhotsk, 80 mi. S of Okha; fish canneries. Petroleum deposits.

Chaiyaphum (chīyŭpoom'), town (1947 pop. 6,446), ⊙ Chaiyaphum prov. (□ 3,747; 1947 pop. 293,738), E Thailand, in Korat Plateau, 75 mi. SW of Khonkaen, and on road from rail station of Bua Yai; rice, cotton, cattle. Pop. is largely Lao. Sometimes spelled Chayabhum or Jayabhum.

Chajarí (chähärē'), town (1947 pop. 11,229), NE Entre Ríos prov., Argentina, on railroad and 45 mi. N of Concordia; agr. processing center (flax, corn, peanuts, tartago, olives, livestock). Produces vegetable oils (peanut, olive, sunflower); sawmilling, tobacco processing.

Chaj Doab (chŭj' dō'äb), alluvial tract in N Punjab, W Pakistan, bet. Jhelum R. (W) and Chenab R. (E). Irrigated by Upper and Lower Jhelum canal systems; agr. (wheat, millet, cotton). Comprises Gujrat and parts of Shahpur and Jhang dists. Sometimes called Jech Doab.

Chajoengsao, Thailand: see CHACHOENGSAO.

Chajul (chähōōl'), town (1950 pop. 3,391), Quiché dept., W central Guatemala, at E end of Cuchumatanes Mts., 11 mi. NNE of Sacapulas; alt. 7,875 ft.; corn, beans, livestock.

Chakachamna Lake (chăkŭchăm'nŭ) (17 mi. long, 2 mi. wide), S Alaska, 80 mi. W of Anchorage; 61°12'N 152°35'W; fed by surrounding glaciers; drained E by Chakachatna R.

Chakachatna River (chăkŭchăt'nŭ), S Alaska, issues from Chakachamna L. at 61°13'N 152°25'W; flows 40 mi. SE to Cook Inlet at Trading Bay.

Chakansur, Afghanistan: see CHAKHANSUR.

Chakari (chäkä'rē), village, Salisbury prov., central Southern Rhodesia, in Mashonaland, 20 mi. WNW of Hartley; tobacco, cotton, peanuts, dairy products. Gold mining near by.

Chakdaha (chäk'dŭhŭ), town (pop. 5,494), Nadia dist., E West Bengal, India, 36 mi. NNE of Calcutta; trades in rice, jute, linseed, sugar cane, wheat. Also spelled Chakdah.

Chake Chake (chä'kä chä'kä), town (pop. 3,014), on W coast of Pemba isl., Zanzibar protectorate; clove-growing center. Fisheries. Has hosp., govt. schools. Airfield.

Chakhansur (chŭkhŭnsōōr'), town (pop. over 2,000), Farah prov., SW Afghanistan, 85 mi. S of Farah, in Seistan lake depression, near Iran line; chief town of Afghan Seistan; irrigated agr. (cotton, sugar cane). Sometimes spelled Chakansur.

Chakhcharan, Afghanistan: see QALA AHANGARAN.

Chakhnaglyar (chŭkhnŭglyär'), town (1939 pop. over 500) in Kirov dist. of Greater Baku, Azerbaijan SSR, on W Apsheron Peninsula, 7 mi. NW of Baku; gas wells (linked to Baku by pipe line).

Chakia (chŭk'yŭ), town (pop. 3,066), Benares dist., SE Uttar Pradesh, India, 16 mi. SSE of Ramnagar; rice, barley, millet.

Chak Jhumra (chŭk jōōm'rŭ), town (pop. 4,764), Lyallpur dist., E central Punjab, W Pakistan, 11 mi. NNE of Lyallpur; wheat, cotton, gram; cotton ginning. Also called Jhumra.

Chaklala, W Pakistan: see RAWALPINDI, city.

Chaklasi (chŭklä'sē), village (pop. 10,578), Kaira dist., N Bombay, India, 17 mi. SE of Kaira; agr. market (millet, rice); dairy farming, butter mfg. Also spelled Chaklashi.

Chakradharpur (chŭkrŭdŭr'pōōr), town (pop., including rail settlement, 14,807), Singhbhum dist., S Bihar, India, 37 mi. WNW of Jamshedpur; trade center (sal timber, rice, oilseeds, corn).

Chakrata (chŭkrä'tŭ), town (pop. 957), Dehra Dun dist., N Uttar Pradesh, India, in W Kumaun Himalaya foothills (alt. c.6,890 ft.), 28 mi. NNW of Dehra; military hill station.

Chaksu, India: see CHATSU.

Chakva, Georgian SSR: see BATUM.

Chakwal (chŭkväl'), town (pop. 11,835), Jhelum dist., N Punjab, W Pakistan, on railroad and 50 mi. W of Jhelum; market center for wheat, millet, wool, cloth fabrics; hand-loom weaving; leather goods. Glass sand near by. Petroleum piped here from wells at Joya Mair and Balkassar transported by rail to refinery at Rawalpindi.

Chala (chä'lä), town (pop. 721), Arequipa dept., S Peru, on small Chala R., near the Pacific, on Pan-American Highway and 90 mi. NW of Ocoña; outlet for cotton and cattle region. Its landing on the rocky coast (4 mi. S) is a fishing base.

Chalabre (shälä'brŭ), village (pop. 1,562), Aude dept., S France, on the Hers and 12 mi. WSW of Limoux; mfg. of felt hats and footwear.

Chalainor or **Chalainoerh** (both: chälīnōr'), village, NW Inner Mongolian Autonomous Region, Manchuria, in the Barga, on Chinese Eastern RR and 18 mi. ESE of Manchouli, on channel linking lake Hulun Nor and Argun R.; coal-mining center.

Chalais (shälĕ'), village (pop. 1,519), Charente dept., W France, 17 mi. SE of Barbezieux; cattle raising.

Chalakazaki, Kirghiz SSR: see KIZYL-ASKER.

Chalakudi (chä'lŭkōōdē), town (pop. 7,429), S central Cochin, India, 20 mi. NNE of Ernakulam; trades in timber (teak, ebony), tea, coffee, cardamom from Anaimalai Hills (E); sawmilling, mfg. of plywood furniture, tiles, pottery. Also spelled Chalakkudi.

Chalamont (shälämō'), village (pop. 821), Ain dept., E France, in Dombes dist., 14 mi. S of Bourg; horse raising; pisciculture.

Chalan Bil (chŭlŭn' bēl'), marsh lake, Rajshahi dist., W East Bengal, E Pakistan, 15 mi. E of Nator; c.15 mi. long, 1–3 mi. wide; fed by Atrai R.; fish exported.

Chalandri or **Khalandri** (both: khŭlän'drē), NE suburb (pop. 11,793) of Athens, Greece, 5 mi. from city center, in metropolitan dist.; summer resort.

Chalanko (chä'längkō), Ital. *Ciallanco,* village (pop. 400), Harar prov., E central Ethiopia, in highlands 37 mi. W of Harar; coffee, cereals.

Chalantun, Manchuria: see YALU.

Chala Point (chä'lä), Pacific cape, Arequipa dept., S Peru, 13 mi. WSW of Chala; 15°48'S 72°27'W.

Chalastra or **Khalastra** (both: khŭlä'strŭ), town (pop. 3,987), Salonika nome, Macedonia, Greece, 10 mi. W of Salonika, in Vardar R. delta; wheat, silk, cotton. Formerly called Kouloukia.

Chalatenango (chälätänäng'gō), department (□ 1,292; pop. 129,473), N Salvador, on Honduras border; ⊙ Chalatenango. Bounded W and S by Lempa R., N by Sumpul R.; mainly mountainous (N and NE), sloping S to Lempa R. valley. Agr. (mainly grain; also sugar cane, manioc, sisal, indigo, coffee). Copper, lead, and limestone deposits. Main centers are Chalatenango and Tejutla, latter on road from San Salvador to Honduras border at Citalá. Formed 1855.

Chalatenango, city (pop. 4,263), ⊙ Chalatenango dept., N Salvador, near Honduras border, 30 mi. NE of San Salvador; alt. 1,660 ft.; 14°2'N 88°54'W. Commercial center; mfg. (pottery, rope), indigo processing; corn, beans, rice, manioc; livestock raising. Holds annual fair.

Chalcedon (kăl'sĭdŏn, kălsē'dŭn), anc. Greek city of Asia Minor, on the Bosporus, founded by Megara on the shore opposite Byzantium in 685 B.C.; KADIKOY, Turkey, is on the site. Taken by the Persians and recovered by the Greeks, it was later a possession of the kings of Bithynia, from whom it passed (74 B.C.) to Rome. The Council of Chalcedon was held here in A.D. 451.

Chalcedony Buttes (kălsĕ'dŭnē būts'), peak (10,400 ft.) in Rocky Mts., Park co., central Colo.

Chalchicomula, Mexico: see SERDÁN.

Chalchihuitán (chälchēwētän'), town (pop. 156), Chiapas, S Mexico, in N spur of Sierra Madre del Sur, 35 mi. NE of Tuxtla; corn. Formerly San Pablo.

Chalchihuites (chälchēwē'tĕs), town (pop. 3,816), Zacatecas, N central Mexico, on interior plateau, near Durango border, 95 mi. NW of Zacatecas; alt. 7,615 ft.; gold, silver, lead. Anc. ruins near by.

Chalchuapa (chälchwä'pä), city (pop. 10,300), Santa Ana dept., W Salvador, on railroad and highway, 8 mi. W of Santa Ana; alt. 2,100 ft.; coffee-growing center. Near-by remains of pre-Colombian city include pyramid of Tatzumal. President J. R. Barrios of Guatemala died here in battle (1885).

Chalcidice (kălsĭ'dĭsē), Gr. *Chalkidike, Chalkidiki,* or *Khalkidiki,* peninsula of NE Greece, projecting from Macedonia into Aegean Sea bet. Gulf of Salonika (W) and Strymonic Gulf (E); 60 mi. long, 30 mi. wide. Terminates SE in 3 characteristic 30-mi.-long prongs of Kassandra, Sithonia, and Akte (site of Mt. Athos), separated by Toronaic and Singitic gulfs of Aegean Sea. At its base are Salonika and lakes Volve and Koroneia. Administratively, N section of peninsula falls into Salonika nome and larger S portion forms nome of **Chalcidice** (□ 1,237, pop. 74,433; including MOUNT ATHOS, □ 1,368, pop. 79,179; ⊙ Polygyros). The nome produces wheat, tobacco, olive oil, and wine. Magnesite and chrome are mined at Gerakine, Vavdos, and Anthemous, iron pyrites at Stratoniki. Named for Chalcis, which established colonies here (7th–6th cent. B.C.). Olynthus (after late-5th cent. B.C., ⊙ Chalcidian league of cities) and Potidaea were leading centers. Passed (4th cent. B.C.) to Philip II of Macedon and (2d cent. B.C.) to Rome.

Chalcis (kăl'sĭs), Gr. *Chalkis* or *Khalkis* (both: khälkēs'), city (1951 pop. 26,097), ⊙ Euboea nome, Greece, port in W central Euboea, on Euripos strait, 35 mi. N of Athens. Rail terminus (station on mainland across strait) and trading center for alcoholic beverages, cereals, livestock, olives and olive oil, figs, wine, citrus; fisheries. Magnesite deposits (N). Medieval buildings of Venetian and Turkish construction. Originally a Phoenician settlement, Chalcis developed (after 7th cent. B.C.) into a flourishing commercial center, trading in dyes, pottery, and metal goods. It sent colonies to Chalcidice (which took its name from Chalcis), Sicily, and S Italy. A black wooden bridge, built 411 B.C. across the Euripos, was replaced in modern times by a steel structure. During the Middle Ages, the town was called Negropont, Ital. *Negroponte,* by Venetians, Egripo or Euripos by Greeks.

Chalco (chäl'kō), officially Chalco de Díaz Covarrubias, town (pop. 3,609), Mexico state, central Mexico, on railroad and 20 mi. SE of Mexico city, at edge of dry L. Chalco (a basin of Anáhuac region). Mfg. center (paper milling, coffee processing, iron and steel founding). Anc. Aztec town, with archaeological remains near by.

Chaldaea or **Chaldea** (both: kăldē'ŭ), properly the southernmost portion of the valley of the Tigris and the Euphrates. Sometimes it is extended to include BABYLONIA and thus comprises all S Mesopotamia, as in the Bible. The name is derived from the people who invaded the region in the 11th cent. B.C., and the restored kingdom of Babylonia is sometimes called the Chaldaean Empire.

Châlette-sur-Loing (shälĕt-sür-lwē'), N industrial suburb (pop. 2,861) of Montargis, Loiret dept., N central France, on Loing R., at junction of Briare and Orléans canals; tar and cider distilleries, fertilizer and refractory plants.

Chaleur Bay (shŭlûr', -lōōr'), inlet (90 mi. long, 15–25 mi. wide) of the Gulf of St. Lawrence, bet. the Gaspé Peninsula, E Que. (N), and N New Brunswick (S). It is a submerged valley of the Restigouche R., which it receives at its head. Has bold coastline, with several high capes. Noted fishing ground (cod, herring, mackerel, salmon). Chief towns on bay are Dalhousie, Campbellton, Bathurst, Caraquet (N), and Grand Cascapedia, New Richmond, and New Carlisle (S). Receives Cascapedia, Nisisiguit, and several smaller rivers. Near its mouth are Miscou and Shippigan isls. Discovered (1534) and named by Cartier.

Chalfant (chôl'fănt), borough (pop. 1,381), Allegheny co., SW Pa., E suburb of Pittsburgh.

Chalfont (chôl'fŏnt), agr. borough (pop. 828), Bucks co., SE Pa., on Neshaminy Creek and 5 mi. SW of Doylestown.

Chalfont Saint Giles (chăl'fŭnt sŭnt jīlz', chä'fŭnt–), residential town and parish (pop. 2,882), SE Buckingham, England, 7 mi. E of High Wycombe. Has cottage where Milton lived during the Great Plague and here finished *Paradise Lost.* Just SW is village of Jordans, with old Quaker meetinghouse and, in Quaker cemetery, grave of William Penn.

Chalfont Saint Peter, residential town and parish (pop. 6,217), SE Buckingham, England, 9 mi. E of High Wycombe. Has notable Georgian church.

Chalford, town and parish (pop. 2,736), central Gloucester, England, on Frome R. and 4 mi. ESE of Stroud; agr. market. Fishing resort.

Chalgrove, agr. village and parish (pop. 388), S Oxfordshire, England, 9 mi. SE of Oxford; flour milling. Scene of victory (1643) of Royalists under Prince Rupert over Parliamentarians under John Hampden, who was mortally wounded. Has church dating from 12th cent.

Chalhuanca (chälwäng'kä), town (pop. 2,756), ⊙ Aimaraes or Aymaraes prov. (□ 2,111; pop. 39,542), Apurímac dept., S central Peru, on affluent of Pachachaca R., in Cordillera Occidental, and 60 mi. SW of Abancay; alt. 9,020 ft. Gold and silver mining. Situated in agr. region (grain, potatoes, alfalfa, stock); mfg. of native textile goods.

Cha-liao, Tibet: see DRAYA.

Chalileo, Argentina: see SANTA ISABEL, La Pampa natl. territory.

Chalindrey (shälēdrā'), town (pop. 2,012), Haute-Marne dept., NE France, 7 mi. SE of Langres; rail and market center.

Chaling or **Ch'a-ling** (both: chä'lĭng'), town, ⊙ Chaling co. (pop. 196,549), E Hunan prov., China, 60 mi. E of Hengyang; rice, wheat, corn, beans. Copper, coal, tungsten deposits.

Cha-lin Hu, Tibet: see KYARING TSO.

Chalisgaon (chä'lĭsgoun), town (pop. 22,122), East Khandesh dist., E Bombay, India, 50 mi. SW of Jalgaon; rail junction; road center; trades in millet, wheat; cotton milling, match mfg.; ironworks.

Chalke or **Khalki** (both: khäl'kē), Ital. *Calchi* (käl'kē), Aegean island (□ 11.2; pop. 702) in the Dodecanese, Greece, off W coast of Rhodes; 36°14'N 27°35'E; 6 mi. long, 2 mi. wide; rises to 1,954 ft. (W). Produces figs, barley, wheat, olives and olive oil, grapes; sponge fishery; main village, Chalke (pop. 619), is on E shore.

Chalk Hills, SW outlier (□ c.10) of Shevaroy Hills, S central Madras, India, NW of Salem; rise to over 1,000 ft.; a major source of India's magnesite (calcined in kilns); chromite mines.

Chalkidike or **Chalkidiki,** Greece: see CHALCIDICE.

Chalkis, Greece: see CHALCIS.

Chalk River, village, SE Ont., on Chalk R., near its mouth on Ottawa R., and 95 mi. WNW of Ottawa. It is a govt. research establishment, operated by National Research Council of Canada for Atomic Energy Control Board; its chief feature, a large heavy water atomic pile, was brought into operation in 1947.

Chalky Inlet, bay of Tasman Sea, Fiordland Natl. Park, SW S.Isl., New Zealand; 10 mi. long, 6 mi. wide; branches into Edwardson and Cunaris sounds; contains several islets.

Chalkyitsik (chălkēĭt'sĭk), Indian village (1939 pop. 33), E Alaska, on Black R. and 40 mi. E of Fort Yukon, on Arctic Circle; 66°36'N 143°44'W; fishing, trapping. Formerly Fishhook.

Challacó (chäyäkō'), village (pop. estimate 400), E Neuquén natl. territory, Argentina, on railroad and 50 mi. W of Neuquén; stock raising; oil drilling and oil refining center.

Challacollo (chä'yäkō'yō), town (pop. c.3,500), Oruro dept., W Bolivia, in the Altiplano, on road and 10 mi. SW of Oruro; potatoes, sheep.

Challakere (chŭ'lŭkĕrĕ), town (pop. 4,257), Chitaldrug dist., N Mysore, India, 17 mi. ENE of Chitaldrug; cotton ginning, rice milling, cattle grazing. Formerly also spelled Chellakere.

Challana (chäyä'nä), village, La Paz dept., W Bolivia, on Challana R. (branch of the Mapiri) and 32 mi. ESE of Sorata; quina. Gold mine 10 mi. S.

Challans (shälā'), town (pop. 2,749), Vendée dept., W France, 24 mi. WNW of La Roche-sur-Yon; road center; livestock and poultry market.

Challao (chäyou'), village, N Mendoza prov., Argentina, 4 mi. NW of Mendoza; summer resort.

Challapata (chäyäpä'tä), town (pop. c.4,900), ⊙ Abaroa prov., Oruro dept., W Bolivia, in the Altiplano, 70 mi. SSE of Oruro, on Oruro-Uyuni RR; alt. 12,159 ft.; barley, corn, potatoes, quinoa.

Challes-les-Eaux (shäl'-lāzō'), village (pop. 945), Savoie dept., SE France, in Chambéry trough, 3 mi. SE of Chambéry; spa.

Challis (chă'lĭs), village (pop. 728), ⊙ Custer co., central Idaho, 50 mi. SSW of Salmon; alt. 5,400 ft. Hay, grain, livestock.

Challum Bay (chä'lŭm), Mandarin *Chelin* (jĕ'lĭn') inlet of S.China Sea, in Kwangtung prov., China near Fukien prov. border, NE of Swatow; 7 mi. wide, 7 mi. long. Ungkung is near N shore.

Chalma (chäl'mä), town (pop. 410), Veracruz, E Mexico, 5 mi. N of Huejutla; corn, fruit.

Chalmers, town (pop. 508), White co., NW central Ind., 17 mi. N of Lafayette, in agr. area.

Chalmette (shălmĕt'), village (pop. 1,695), St. Bernard parish, extreme SE La., on E bank (levee) of the Mississippi, just below New Orleans; large sugar refinery; mfg. of petroleum products, oil-field equipment. Chalmette National Historical Park (69.6 acres; established 1939) is here; it contains battlefield where Andrew Jackson defeated the British in 1815, just before ratification of Treaty of Ghent.

Chalmoux (shälmōō'), village (pop. 162), Saône-et-Loire dept., E central France, 11 mi. NW of Digoin; pyrites.

Chalna Anchorage, E Pakistan: see PORT JINNAH.

Chalon, Saône-et-Loire dept., France: see CHALON-SUR-SAÔNE.

Chalonnes-sur-Loire (shälôn'-sür-lwär'), town (pop. 2,210), Maine-et-Loire dept., W France, on branch of Loire R. and 13 mi. SW of Angers; noted for its white wines; mfg. (biscuits, shoes, barrels). Damaged in Second World War.

Châlons-sur-Marne (shälō'-sür-märn'), anc. *Catalaunum* or *Durocatalaunum,* town (pop. 28,257), ⊙ Marne dept., N France, on right bank of Marne R. and on its lateral canal, and 26 mi. SE of Rheims; commercial center (champagne wines, cereals); mfg. (beer, barrels, leather goods, barbed wire, wallpaper). Has 13th–17th-cent. cathedral (damaged in Second World War); 12th-cent. former collegiate church of Notre-Dame-en-Vaux; and a fine park known as Promenade du Jard. Except for fertile Marne valley, surrounding region (Champagne badlands) is barren and sparsely populated, and a battlefield of many wars. In 451, Huns under Attila were defeated by Aetius and Theodoric I in decisive battle of Catalaunian Fields (S of Châlons-sur-Marne; probably nearer present site of Troyes). In Middle Ages, town prospered under its bishops and was known for its woolen cloth. Was briefly occupied by Germans (1914).

Chalon-sur-Saône (shälō'-sür-sōn'), anc. *Cabillonum,* town (pop. 29,851), Saône-et-Loire dept., E central France, port on right bank of Saône R. at junction of the Canal du Centre, and 38 mi. SSW of Dijon; important transport and commercial center (wine, grains, livestock) for exchange of produce of N and S France. Has machine shops and foundries, glass and tile works, shipyards for river boats. Produces winegrowing equipment, hosiery, biscuits. Printing, brewing, tanning. Its 12th-15th-cent. church of St. Vincent was damaged during Second World War. Of pre-Roman origin, it was (6th cent.) ⊙ of kings of Burgundy, and (in 813) scene of church council convoked by Charlemagne. Bishopric was suppressed during Fr. Revolution. Sometimes called Chalon.

Chalosse (shälôs'), old region of Gascony prov., SW France, now forming S Landes dept., bet. Adour R. (N) and Gave de Pau (S); lies athwart foothills of the W Pyrenees. Dairying, hog and poultry raising, corn growing. Chief town is Saint-Sever.

Chalt (chŭlt), village, Hunza state, Gilgit Agency, NW Kashmir, in NW Karakoram mtn. system, on Hunza R. and 25 mi. N of Gilgit. Fort. Here in 1888 Hunza and Nagar states fought against Kashmir troops.

Chaltyr or **Chaltyr'** (chŭltĭr'), village (1926 pop. 9,328), SW Rostov oblast, Russian SFSR, 10 mi. WNW of Rostov; metalworks; truck produce.

Cha-lun, Tibet: see THOK JALUNG.

Châlus (shälüs'), village (pop. 1,405), Haute-Vienne dept., W central France, on the Tardoire and 18 mi. SW of Limoges; cattle raising. Has ruins of two 12th-cent. castles. Here Richard Cœur de Lion was mortally wounded in 1199. Also spelled Chalus.

Chalus (chälōōs'), town, First Prov., in W Mazanderan, N Iran, 34 mi. ESE of Shahsawar, near Caspian coast, at mouth of Chalus R. (torrential coastal stream), and on road from Karaj across Elburz range; major silk-milling center.

Chalybeate (shă'lŭbĕt), village (1940 pop. 199), Tippah co., N Miss., 20 mi. W of Corinth, near Tenn. line.

Chalybeate Springs (kŭlĭ'bēăt), town (pop. 255), Meriwether co., W Ga., 15 mi. W of Thomaston.

Chalysh (chŭlĭsh'), town (1948 pop. over 500), S Kara-Kalpak Autonomous SSR, Uzbek SSR, near Shabbaz; cotton.

Cham (khäm), town (pop. 8,916), Upper Palatinate, E Bavaria, Germany, in Bohemian Forest, on the Regen and 24 mi. NNE of Straubing; textile mfg., metal- and woodworking, printing, tanning, brewing. Summer resort. Has 14th-cent. gate and 15th-cent. town hall. Of Wendish origin; chartered in 10th cent.

Cham, town (pop. 4,645), Zug canton, N central Switzerland, at efflux of Lorze R. from L. of Zug, 3 mi. WNW of Zug; paper, metalworking. Has old church (rebuilt 1783–86).

Chama (chä'mü). **1** Village (1940 pop. 733), Costilla co., S Colo., in W foothills of Sangre de Cristo Mts., 5 mi. SE of San Luis, in truck-farming region. Sanchez Reservoir near by. **2** Village (1940 pop. 919), Rio Arriba co., N N.Mex., on Rio Chama, near Colo. line, and 55 mi. SW of Alamosa, Colo.; alt. c.7,850 ft. Shipping point for oil fields just over Colo. line; sawmill.

Chamá, Sierra de (syĕ'rä dā chämä'), range in Alta Verapaz dept., central Guatemala, N of Cobán; extends 70 mi. WSW-ENE, bet. Chixoy R. (W) and area of Cahabón (E); forms divide bet. Polochic R. (S) and Pasión R. (N). Rises to c.5,000 ft.

Chamácuaro (chämä'kwärō), town (pop. 1,156), Guanajuato, central Mexico, on railroad, on Lerma R. and 8 mi. NW of Acámbaro; alt. 6,053 ft.; corn, rice, sugar cane, fruit, vegetables, livestock. Sometimes Chamacuero.

Chamacuero de Comonfort, Mexico: see COMONFORT.

Cha Mai (chä' mī'), village (1937 pop. 3,249), Nakhon Sithammarat prov., S Thailand, in Malay Peninsula, on railroad (Tung Song or Thung Song station) and 27 mi. SW of Nakhon Sithammarat; rail junction (head of line to Kantang); tin-mining center.

Chamalières (shämälyâr'), W suburb (pop. 10,718) of Clermont-Ferrand, Puy-de-Dôme dept., central France; mfg. (rubberized clothing, electric motors, waxes). Ships strawberries, cherries, apricots.

Chaman (chŭmŭn'), town (pop., including cantonment area, 6,650), Quetta-Pishin dist., NE Baluchistan, W Pakistan, 60 mi. NW of Quetta, on Afghan border opposite Qala-i-Jadid; rail terminus; control post for traveling merchants.

Chamarajnagar or **Chamrajnagar** (chämŭräj'nŭgŭr), town (pop. 9,923), Mysore dist., S Mysore, India, 33 mi. SSE of Mysore, in silk-growing area; rail spur terminus; rice milling, cotton ginning, betel farming. Teak, sandalwood in near-by hills.

Chamarchi or **Chamurchi** (chŭmŭr'chē), village, SW Bhutan, 35 mi. NE of Jalpaiguri (India); rice, corn, millet. Fort ruins near by. Copper mines 4 mi. NW. Chamarchi area (also called Samchi), N of Western Duars, is roughly separated from Chirang area by the Sankosh; pop. mainly Nepalese. Sometimes spelled Chumurchi.

Chama River (chä'mä), Mérida state, W Venezuela, rises in Andean spur at S foot of Piedras Blancas massif, flows SW in fertile Andean valley, past Mucuchíes, Mérida, and Ejido, to Chiguará, then N, past El Vigía, to L. Maracaibo; 100 mi. long. The transandine highway follows its S course. Variety of crops produced in its valley.

Chamartín or **Chamartín de la Rosa** (chämärtēn' dhä lä rō'sä), town (pop. 64,480), Madrid prov., central Spain, just N of Madrid; industrial center; mfg. of engines, electric clocks, precision instruments, transformers, machinery. Has fine Jesuit col., formerly palace of duke of Osuna; Napoleon lived here in 1808. Among its leading sections are Tetuán de las Victorias and Ciudad Jardín.

Chamaya River, Peru: see HUANCABAMBA RIVER.

Chamba (chŭm'bŭ), district (□ 3,127; pop. 168,908), N Himachal Pradesh, India; ⊙ Chamba. Bordered N and W by Kashmir; separated from S dists. of state by Kangra dist. of Punjab (India). Until 1948 it was a princely state of Punjab States. A mountainous area, for centuries independent, it came under influence of Moguls, Sikhs, and (1846) British; since 1948, merged with Himachal Pradesh.

Chamba, town (pop. 6,597), ⊙ Chamba dist., N Himachal Pradesh, India, on Ravi R. and 115 mi. NW of Simla; trades in corn, rice, millet, wool, honey, timber; hand-loom weaving, fruitgrowing, mfg. of malaria pills, eye medicine. Mus. Was ⊙ former princely state of Chamba.

Chambak (chämbäk'), town, Takeo prov., SW Cambodia, 25 mi. SSW of Pnompenh; rice, lac, tobacco.

Chambal River (chŭm'bŭl), chief tributary of the Jumna, in W central India, rises in Vindhya Range 8 mi. SW of Mhow, in Madhya Bharat, flows N into SE Rajasthan, NE past Kotah, along Rajasthan–Madhya Bharat border, and ESE along Uttar Pradesh–Madhya Bharat border, to Jumna R. 16 mi. W of Auraiya; length, c.550 mi. Course winds through steep ravines and jungle-covered valleys. Subject to sudden floods after rains. Receives Sipra, Kali, Sindh, and Parbati (right), and Banas (left) rivers.

Chambas (chäm'bäs), town (pop. 2,182), Camagüey prov., E Cuba, on railroad and 17 mi. W of Morón; cattle raising.

Chamberlain (chām'bŭrlĭn), city (pop. 1,912), ⊙ Brule co., S S.Dak., 65 mi. W of Mitchell and on Missouri R.; resort; livestock-shipping center; dairy products. Large deposits of low-grade manganese near by. Hosp. and sanitarium. Inc. 1881.

Chamberlain Lake, Piscataquis co., N central Maine, 53 mi. NNE of Greenville, in wilderness recreational area; 13 mi. long, 1–2.5 mi. wide. Connected by streams to Allagash and Eagle lakes and Round Pond.

Chamberlin, Mount (9,131 ft.), NE Alaska, in Brooks Range; 69°17'N 144°52'W.

Chambers. 1 County (□ 598; pop. 39,528), E Ala.; ⊙ Lafayette. Drained (NW) by Tallapoosa R., bounded on E by Chattahoochee R. and Ga. Cotton; textile milling. Formed 1832. **2** County (□ 618; pop. 7,871), SE Texas; ⊙ Anahuac. On Gulf coastal plains, and bounded S by East Bay; indented by Galveston Bay, here receiving Trinity R. Crossed by Gulf Intracoastal Waterway. A leading Texas oil-producing co.; agr. (especially rice; also corn, wheat, citrus, truck, fruit); cattle, hogs; dairying. Natural gas, sulphur. Formed 1858.

Chambers. 1 Village, Bolivar co., Miss.: see WINSTONVILLE. **2** Village (pop. 395), Holt co., N central Nebr., 20 mi. SSW of O'Neill; meat and cold-storage products; grain.

Chambersburg. 1 Village (pop. 225), Gallia co., S Ohio, on the Ohio (locks and dam here) and 9 mi. S of Gallipolis. Also called Eureka. **2** Borough (pop. 17,212), ⊙ Franklin co., S Pa., in the Cumberland Valley c.50 mi. SW of Harrisburg; fruitgrowing; metal and paper products, machinery, clothing, food products, flour. Wilson Col., Letterkenny Ordnance Depot here. Has cabin (moved here 1925) in which James Buchanan was b. 1791, on site c.15 mi. W, now marked by state forest monument. John Brown's hq., 1859; burned in Confederate raid 1864. Settled 1730, laid out 1764, inc. 1803.

Chambers Island, Door co., NE Wis., in Green Bay, 12 mi. NE of Menominee, Mich.; 3 mi. long, 2 mi. wide.

Chambéry (shäbärē'), town (pop. 26,641), ⊙ Savoie dept., SE France, 28 mi. NNE of Grenoble, in Alpine trough (also occupied by Lac du Bourget) bet. Grande Chartreuse (SSW) and Bauges (NE) massifs, linking valleys of upper Rhone (N) and Isère (S) rivers. Communications center on Paris-Lyons-Italy RR. Aluminum and machinery (agr., cement, shoe, glove) plants; mfg. of clothing, flour and leather products, vermouth, pharmaceuticals, building material. Archiepiscopal see and historical ⊙ Savoy, with 15th-cent. ducal castle. Suffered some damage in Second World War. Les Charmettes (1 mi. S) noted for sojourn of Rousseau and Mme. de Warens.

Chambeshi River, Northern Rhodesia: see CHAMBEZI RIVER.

Chambeyron, Aiguille de, France; see AIGUILLE DE CHAMBEYRON.

Chambezi River (chămbē'zē, chämbĕ'zē) or **Chambeshi River** (–shē), N Northern Rhodesia, rises N of Isoka in hills on Tanganyika border, flows c.300 mi. SW, to L. Bangweulu swamps, where it merges with Luapula R. Chambezi Pontoon, a ferry road crossing 65 mi. NNW of Mpika, is site of old rubber factory (in operation 1915–16); marks southernmost advance (1918) of Ger. troops from Tanganyika.

Chambi, Djebel (jĕ'bĕl shämbē'), highest mountain (5,066 ft.) of Tunisia, in a spur of the Tebessa Mts., near Algerian border, 6 mi. WNW of Kasserine. Forms SW flank of Kasserine Pass.

Chamblee (chămblē'), city (pop. 3,445), De Kalb co., NW central Ga., 10 mi. NNE of Atlanta; mfg. (chemicals, furniture, mattresses, electrical equipment). Inc. as city 1922.

Chambley or **Chambley-Bussières** (shäblĕ'-büsyâr'), agr. village (pop. 446), Meurthe-et-Moselle dept., NE France, 14 mi. SW of Metz.

Chambly (shäblē'), county (□ 138; pop. 32,454), S Que., on St. Lawrence and Richelieu rivers; ⊙ Longueuil.

Chambly (shăm'blē, Fr. shäblē') or **Chambly Basin,** village (pop. 1,423), S Que., on Chambly Basin, small lake on Richelieu R., 14 mi. ESE of Montreal; agr. market (oats, apples, dairying). Fort Chambly, built 1665, was captured by American troops 1775, burned 1776; later became base for Carleton and Burgoyne; restored 1880. Near-by hydroelectric station supplies Montreal.

Chambly (shäblē'), town (pop. 3,465), Oise dept., N France, 10 mi. NE of Pontoise; dairying, woodworking, brick mfg. Has 13th-14th-cent. church.

Chambly Canton, village (pop. 1,185), S Que., on Richelieu R. and 16 mi. ESE of Montreal; agr. (oats, apples; dairying).

Chambois (shäbwä'), village (pop. 316), Orne dept., NW France, on the Dives and 7 mi. NE of Argentan. Here Allies sealed Argentan-Falaise pocket (Aug., 1944) in Second World War.

Chambolle-Musigny (shäbôl'-müzēnyē'), village (pop. 420), Côte-d'Or dept., E central France, on E slope of the Côte d'Or, 10 mi. SSW of Dijon; noted Burgundy wines.

Chambon Dam (shäbō'), Isère dept., SE France, on upper Romanche R. and 22 mi. SE of Grenoble, at foot of Massif du Pelvoux, in Dauphiné Alps. Completed 1935; 965 ft. long, 449 ft. high, and 230 ft. wide at base. Grenoble-Briançon road (Route des Alpes) crosses river along crest of dam. Installation is largest in France, after Génissiat. Activates several hydroelectric plants in Romanche R. valley.

Chambon-de-Tence, Le, France: see CHAMBON-SUR-LIGNON, LE.

Chambon-Feugerolles, Le (lŭ shäbō'-fûzhûrôl'), town (pop. 9,395), Loire dept., SE central France, on the Ondaine and 4 mi. SW of Saint-Étienne; metalworking center, with steel mills, ironworks; bronze smelting.

Chambon-le-Château (–lŭ-shätō'), village (pop. 462), Lozère dept., S France, on E slope of Montagnes de la Margeride, 17 mi. SW of Le Puy; pottery, tile.

Chambon-sur-Lignon, Le (–sür-lēnyō'), village (pop. 1,636), Haute-Loire dept., S central France, in Monts du Vivarais, on the Lignon and 10 mi. ESE of Yssingeaux; alt. 3,150 ft. Tourist resort. Formerly Le Chambon-de-Tence.

Chambon-sur-Voueize (–vwĕz'), village (pop. 906), Creuse dept., central France, on Tardes R. at mouth of the Voueize and 13 mi. SW of Montluçon; road center; mfg. of agr. implements. Gold mining at Châtelet, 2 mi. E. Has 11th-12th-cent. Romanesque church.

Chambord (shăbôr'), village (pop. 1,029), S central Que., on S shore of L. St. John, 10 mi. SE of Roberval; lumbering, dairying, pig raising.

Chambord, village (pop. 176), Loir-et-Cher dept., N central France, on Cosson R. and 9 mi. ENE of Blois. Known for its remarkable Renaissance château located in a fine walled-in park (□ 21). The castle, noted for its spiraling double stairway, was built under Francis I and became the residence of subsequent kings of France, until it was given to Marshal Saxe by Louis XV. It became state property in 1932.

Chambo River (chäm'bō), central Ecuador, rises in the Andes near Guamote, flows c.60 mi. NNE to join Patate R., forming the Pastaza 4 mi. W of Baños.

Chamboulive (shăbōōlēv'), village (pop. 725), Corrèze dept., S central France, 12 mi. NNW of Tulle; ships vegetables and fruit.

Chambre, La (lä shä'brù), village (pop. 714), Savoie dept., SE France, in Alpine Maurienne valley, on Arc R. and 6 mi. NNW of Saint-Jean-de-Maurienne; plaster and cheese mfg.

Chamchakly, Turkmen SSR: see UCH-ADZHI.

Chamdo or **Chhamdo** (chäm'dō), Chinese *Ch'a-mu-to* (chä'mōōdō), after 1913 *Changtu* or *Ch'ang-tu* (chäng'dōō'), town, E Tibet, 370 mi. ENE of Lhasa, 130 mi. NW of Paan, and on Mekong R.; alt. 10,600; 31°10'N 97°15'E. Chief town of Kham prov.; trade center at junction of routes to Lhasa and Jyekundo; exports musk and medicinal herbs. Farming, cattle raising; gold washing. Lamasery.

Chame (chä'mā), village (pop. 524), Panama prov., central Panama, in Pacific lowland, on Inter-American Highway and 35 mi. SW of Panama city; coffee, coconuts; stock raising.

Chamechaude, France: see GRANDE-CHARTREUSE.

Chamelco or **San Juan Chamelco** (sän hwän' chämĕl'kō), town (1950 pop. 1,055), Alta Verapaz dept., Guatemala, in N highlands, 3 mi. SE of Cobán; alt. 4,530 ft. Market center; net and rope weaving; coffee; livestock.

Chamelecón (chämālākōn'), village (pop. 1,688), Cortés dept., NW Honduras, on Chamelecón R., on railroad and 5 mi. S of San Pedro Sula, in banana zone; pineapple plantations.

Chamelecón River, NW Honduras, rises in Sierra del Gallinero SW of Florida, flows generally ENE, through Quimistán valley, past Chamelecón and La Lima, into Sula Valley, and N, parallel to Ulúa R., to Gulf of Honduras 11 mi. NE of Puerto Cortés; length, c.125 mi. Navigable for small craft in Sula Valley.

Chame Point (chä'mā), low headland at tip of Chame Peninsula, on SW coast of Bay of Panama of the Pacific, central Panama, 23 mi. SW of Panama city. It forms SE side of Chame Bay (marshy shores). Chame village is at base of the peninsula, W of Chame hill (1,770 ft.)

Chamical (chämēkäl'), town (1947 pop. 2,647), ⊙ Gobernador Gordillo dept. (□ 2,415; pop. 6,251), E La Rioja prov., Argentina, on railroad and 70 mi. SSE of La Rioja. Gypsum-mfg. center; stock raising (goats, sheep, cattle). Formerly called Gobernador Gordillo.

Chamita (chùmē'tù), village (pop. c.700), Rio Arriba co., N N.Mex., on W bank of Rio Grande, near mouth of Rio Chama, and 26 mi. NNW of Santa Fe; alt. c.5,700 ft. Fruit, livestock, chili, grain, beans. Settled 1595 as San Gabriel. Once capital of N.Mex. under Sp. rule. Valle Grande Mts. are W.

Chamiza or **La Chamiza** (lä chämē'sä), village (1930 pop. 109), Llanquihue prov., S central Chile, 9 mi. E of Puerto Montt, in Chilean lake dist.; military air base; lumbering, fishing.

Chamizo (chämē'sō), village (pop. 500), Florida dept., S central Uruguay, on railroad and 32 mi. NNE of Montevideo; road junction; wheat, corn, fruit, cattle.

Chamo, Lake (chä'mō), Ital. *Ciamo* (□ c.210), Gamu-Gofa prov., S Ethiopia, in Great Rift Valley, bet. lakes Abaya (3 mi. N) and Stefanie, 8 mi. NE of Gardula; alt. 4,045 ft.; 23 mi. long, 14 mi. wide. Receives (N) overflow of L. Abaya during periods of exceptional flood. At one time probably discharged into L. Stefanie through a headstream of the Galana Sagan, which now rises in a swamp E of lake and has an intermittent flow. Formerly also called Ruspoli, after its discoverer (1893), Prince Ruspoli. Sometimes Chama or Shamo.

Chamois (shùmoi'), city (pop. 621), Osage co., central Mo., on Missouri R. and 24 mi. ENE of Jefferson City; grain, potatoes, dairying.

Chamoli (chŭmō'lē), village, Garhwal dist., N Uttar Pradesh, India, on Alaknanda R. and 37 mi. NE of Pauri; wheat, rice, barley. Also called Lalsanga. Karnaprayag village, 12 mi. SSW, is on small Pindar R. (just above its mouth on the Alaknanda); one of 5 sacred confluences of the Alaknanda; has several Hindu temples. Two dams, one 200 and one 500 ft. high, are planned on the Pindar for hydroelectric power.

Chamonix or **Chamonix-Mont-Blanc** (shämônē'-mōblā'), town (pop. 2,654), Haute-Savoie dept., SE France, in scenic Chamonix valley of Arve R., bet. Mont Blanc massif (E, S) and Brévent–Aiguilles-Rouges range (N), 40 mi. SE of Geneva; alt. 3,402 ft. Leading winter and summer resort of Fr. Alps, and chief base for ascent of peaks in Mont Blanc group. Numerous hotels, Olympic skating rink. Principal excursions: Montenvers height (6,263 ft.; rack-and-pinion railway; hotel) at edge of MER DE GLACE; Mont Brévent (8,285 ft.; just NW of Chamonix; aerial tramway), and MONT BLANC (15,771 ft.)

Chamoson (shämōzō'), town (pop. 2,019), Valais canton, SW Switzerland, near the Rhone, 7 mi. WSW of Sion; farming.

Chamouilley (shämōōyā'), village (pop. 806), Haute-Marne dept., NE France, on Marne R. and Marne-Saône Canal, 5 mi. SE of Saint-Dizier; makes iron and wooden wheels.

Chamoux-sur-Gelon (shämōō'-sür-zhùlō'), village (pop. 491), Savoie dept., SE France, on N slope of Belledonne range, 14 mi. E of Chambéry, in Isère R. valley; flour products.

Champa (chŭm'pŭ), town (pop. 9,868), Bilaspur dist., E central Madhya Pradesh, India, 33 mi. E of Bilaspur; rice milling, mfg. of shellac, chemicals. Coal mining 20 mi. N, at village of Korba.

Champa, Indochina: see ANNAM.

Champadanga, India: see ARAMBAGH.

Champagnac-de-Bélair (shāpänyäk'-dù-bālâr'), village (pop. 237), Dordogne dept., SW France, on the Dronne and 14 mi. N of Périgueux; flour milling.

Champagnac-les-Mines (–lā-mēn'), village (pop. 455), Cantal dept., S central France, near Dordogne R., 10 mi. NNE of Mauriac; coal mining.

Champagne (shămpān'), Indian village, SW Yukon, 50 mi. W of Whitehorse, on Alaska Highway.

Champagne (shămpān', Fr. shāpä'nyù), region of NE France, bet. Lorraine plateau (E) and center of Paris Basin (W), extending from the Ardennes (N) to the Yonne (S). The region is not fully coextensive with old Champagne prov., which is now in Aube, Haute-Marne, and Marne depts., and in part of Ardennes, Aisne, Seine-et-Marne, and Yonne depts. Provincial ⊙ was Troyes. A generally arid, chalky plateau, sloping gently toward Paris, Champagne is divided into sub-regions by a series of parallel heights and crests. Just W of easternmost crest (Argonne, and heights bet. Bar-le-Duc and Bar-sur-Seine) is the Champagne Humide with fertile agr. areas around Brienne, Vitry-le-François, and Vouziers. Center is occupied by the bleak Champagne Pouilleuse (Champagne badlands), traditionally used for sheep raising. The famous champagne wines processed at Rheims and Épernay are grown in small area along westernmost crest (known as the Île-de-France crest). Cutting across these dissimilar sub-regions are the fertile alluvial valleys of the Aisne, Marne, Aube, and Seine rivers. Hosiery and champagne mfg. are principal industries. Chief towns are Rheims, Troyes, and Châlons-sur-Marne. Geographic position along approaches to Paris has given towns of Champagne great commercial importance despite agr. poverty of area. For same reason Champagne has been a major European battleground from invasion of the Huns, whom Aetius defeated near Châlons-sur-Marne in 451, to First World War, in which large areas were devastated. Medieval counts of Champagne ruled almost like independent sovereigns. They promoted the Fairs of Champagne which attracted merchants from afar. Cultural leadership was evidenced by works of Chrestien de Troyes and construction of cathedral of Rheims. Champagne was incorporated into Fr. royal domain in 1314 and declined in prosperity until revived by sudden popularity of its sparkling wines in 18th cent. Reclamation of its badlands through reforestation is well under way.

Champagne or **Champagne-en-Valromey** (–ã-välrōmā'), village (pop. 314), Ain dept., E France, in the S Jura, 10 mi. N of Belley; lumbering. Also spelled Champagne-en-Valromay.

Champagné (shāpänyā'), village (pop. 612), Sarthe dept., W France, on Huisne R. 6 mi. E of Le Mans; hemp and cotton spinning. Wilbur Wright, who made flights from near-by Camp d'Auvours, is commemorated by a monument.

Champagne Castle (shămpān'), mountain (11,075 ft.) in the Drakensberg, W Natal, U. of So. Afr., on Basutoland border, 60 mi. SSE of Harrismith, 35 mi. SE of Mont-aux-Sources, near Cathkin Peak. For a time thought to be highest in the range, but in 1951 Thabantshonyana, to SSW, was found to be higher.

Champagne-en-Valromey, Ain dept., France: see CHAMPAGNE, village.

Champagne-Mouton (shāpä'nyù-mōōtō'), village (pop. 646), Charente dept., W France, 12 mi. W of Confolens; woodworking; cattle raising.

Champagne-sur-Seine (–sür-sĕn'), town (pop. 2,803), Seine-et-Marne dept., N central France, on right bank of the Seine and 5 mi. E of Fontainebleau; mfg. of electrical equipment, winegrowing.

Champagney (shāpänyĕ'), village (pop. 1,412), Haute-Saône dept., E France, in Belfort Gap, 9 mi. NW of Belfort, at foot of the Vosges; aluminum works; hosiery mfg.

Champagnole (shāpänyôl'), town (pop. 4,750), Jura dept., E France, in the Jura, on Ain R. and 18 mi. ENE of Lons-le-Saunier; industrial center; steel milling, woodworking, clockmaking. Also produces shoes, cement, and barometers.

Champaign (shămpān'). **1** County (□ 1,000; pop. 106,100), E Ill.; ⊙ Urbana. Prairie agr. region (corn, wheat, soybeans, alfalfa, oats, livestock, poultry), with its mfg., commercial, and industrial center at the adjoining cities of Champaign and Urbana. Drained by Sangamon, Kaskaskia, and Embarrass rivers, and by South Fork of Vermilion R. Formed 1833. **2** County (□ 433; pop. 26,793), W central Ohio; ⊙ Urbana. Intersected by Mad R., Darby Creek, and small Buck and Little Darby creeks. Agr. area (livestock, corn, wheat, soybeans, poultry, honey; dairy products); mfg. at Urbana; sand and gravel pits. Includes Ohio Caverns and a state game farm. Formed 1805.

Champaign, city (pop. 39,563), Champaign co., E Ill., adjoining URBANA, with which it forms an economic and social unit; railroad, commercial, and industrial center in rich agr. area (corn, wheat, soybeans, alfalfa, oats, livestock, poultry). Mfg. of dairy and soybean products, tile, gloves, machinery, chemicals, trailers, bleaches, polishes, cleansers, concrete and metal products; railroad shops; oil refinery. Campus of Univ. of Illinois lies bet. Champaign and Urbana. Founded 1854, as West Urbana, with the coming of the railroad; inc. 1861.

Champaner (chämpä'nār), village, Panch Mahals dist., N Bombay, India, 20 mi. S of Godhra. Has ruins of 15th-cent. Rajput hill fortress, then noted for trade in silk products and sword blades; sacked 1535 by Humayun.

Champaquí, Cerro (sĕ'rō chämpäkē'), pampean peak (9,450 ft.) in W Córdoba prov., Argentina, 15 mi. E of Villa Dolores, in center of Cumbre de Achala, a range of the Sierra de Córdoba; highest point in Sierra de Córdoba.

Champaran (chŭmpä'rŭn), district (□ 3,553; pop. 2,397,569), NW Bihar, India, in Tirhut div.; ⊙ Motihari. On Ganges Plain; bounded N by Nepal (Himalayan foothills at NW corner), W by Gandak R.; drained by left tributaries of the Ganges. Mainly alluvial soil; rice, wheat, barley, corn, linseed, sugar cane, jute; tanning bark and timber in forest area (NW). Rice, sugar, and oilseed milling, cotton weaving. Main towns: Bettiah, Motihari; Raxaul is chief customs station for Nepal trade. Asokan stone column near Bettiah. English-Nepalese treaty of 1851 signed at Sagauli.

Champassak, province, Laos: see PAKSE.

Champawat (chŭmpä'vŭt), village, Almora dist., N Uttar Pradesh, India, 32 mi. SE of Almora; rice, wheat, barley. Noted Hindu temple (annual fair held) 15 mi. ENE, at village of Devi Dhura.

Champdani (chŭmpdä'nē), town (pop. 31,833), Hooghly dist., S central West Bengal, India, on Hooghly R. and 8 mi. SSW of Hooghly; jute-milling center.

Champ-de-Mars (shã-dù-märs'), former parade-ground, Paris, France, located in 7th *arrondissement*, bet. the École Militaire and left bank of the Seine. On its grounds several expositions were held, notably in 1889, when the Eiffel Tower was erected here.

Champdeniers (shădùnyā'), village (pop. 915), Deux-Sèvres dept., W France, 11 mi. NNE of Niort; leather working; cattle raising. Has 11th-cent. church with octagonal tower.

Champdepraz (shădùprä'), village (pop. 148), Val d'Aosta region, NW Italy, near Dora Baltea R., 17 mi. ESE of Aosta; copper mining.

Champeix (shăpĕ'), village (pop. 805), Puy-de-Dôme dept., central France, 6 mi. WNW of Issoire; mfg. of clothing.

Champerico (chämpärē'kō), town (1950 pop. 982), Retalhuleu dept., SW Guatemala, port on the Pacific, 23 mi. SW of Retalhuleu; 14°16'N 91°55' W; rail terminus; grain; livestock; fisheries, game hunting. Exports coffee, lumber, sugar. Beach.

Champéry (shăpārē'), village (pop. 810), Valais canton, SW Switzerland, 6 mi. SSW of Monthey, at foot of Dent du Midi; resort (alt. 3,450 ft.); winter sports.

Champex (shăpā'), resort (alt. 4,829 ft.), Valais canton, SW Switzerland, on small Champex L., 2 mi. W of Orsières.

Champigneulles (shăpēnyûl'), N suburb (pop. 4,886) of Nancy, Meurthe-et-Moselle dept., NE France, on Meurthe R. and Marne-Rhine Canal; breweries, tileworks. Iron mines near by.

Champigny-sur-Marne (shăpēnyē'-sür-märn'), town (pop. 29,207), Seine dept., N central France, an ESE suburb of Paris, 8 mi. from Notre Dame Cathedral, on left bank of the Marne; flour milling, mfg. (optical instruments, furniture, pharmaceuticals). Limestone quarries. Monuments commemorate siege (1870) of Paris.

Champigny-sur-Veude (–sür-vûd'), village (pop. 653), Indre-et-Loire dept., W central France, on small Veude R. and 8 mi. SSE of Chinon; dairying. Its 16th-cent. church is only remnant of an old castle demolished by Richelieu.
Champion, village (pop. 279), S Alta., 70 mi. SE of Calgary, in coal-mining region; cereal-foods mfg., wheat growing.
Champion, village (pop. c.750), Marquette co., NW Upper Peninsula, Mich., 27 mi. W of Marquette; ships potatoes. Copper mining; lumbering.
Champion Bay, Australia: see GEELVINK CHANNEL.
Champion Reef, India: see KOLAR GOLD FIELDS.
Champion's Hill, Miss.: see EDWARDS.
Champlain (shămplān', Fr. shăplē'), county (□ 8,586; pop. 68,057), central Que., extending N from the St. Lawrence; ⊙ Batiscan.
Champlain, village (pop. 692), S Que., on the St. Lawrence and 12 mi. NE of Trois Rivières; dairying, lumbering.
Champlain, village (pop. 1,505), Clinton co., extreme NE N.Y., on Great Chazy R., near L. Champlain and Que. line, and 20 mi. N of Plattsburg; port of entry. Lumber milling; mfg. of wood products, machinery. Settled 1789, inc. 1873.
Champlain, Lake (□ 435), in N.Y., Vt., and Que.; it lies in broad valley bet. the Adirondacks (W) and the Green Mts. (E), forms N.Y.-Vt. state line for c.100 mi., and extends into S Que.; 107 mi. long, ½–14 mi. wide. A link in Hudson–St. Lawrence waterway, the lake is entered from S at Whitehall by Champlain division of N.Y. State Barge Canal, which follows general route of the old Champlain Canal (1819) and connects with the Hudson at Fort Edward. Richelieu R., draining lake from N, connects it with the St. Lawrence. L. George drains into it via short channel. Plattsburg (N.Y.) and Burlington (Vt.) are on its shores; there are many resorts, and the region is a rich farm and orchard (applegrowing) area. Isls. in lake include GRAND ISLE and ISLE LA MOTTE (Vt.) and VALCOUR ISLAND (N.Y.). Named for Samuel de Champlain, who discovered it in 1609. Lake was scene of battles in French and Indian War and in the American Revolution, involving forts at CROWN POINT and TICONDEROGA; 1st American-British naval battle occurred here in 1776. In 1814, the victory at Cumberland Bay of an American fleet under Macdonough caused British to abandon invasion of New York.
Champlain Canal, N.Y.: see CHAMPLAIN, LAKE.
Champlin (chăm'plĭn), village (pop. 828), Hennepin co., E Minn., on Mississippi R., opposite Anoka (NE), and 16 mi. NNW of Minneapolis.
Champlitte-et-le-Prélot (shăplēt'-ā-lü-prālō'), village (pop. 1,336), Haute-Saône dept., E France, 12 mi. NNW of Gray; cattle, hogs. Marble quarried near by.
Champoeg Memorial State Park (chămpō'ĕg), NW Oregon, on the Willamette and 7 mi. SE of Newberg; commemorates 1st settlement of Willamette valley (in early 19th cent.) and establishment (1843) of 1st American provisional territorial govt. on Pacific coast. Historical mus. here.
Champotón (chämpōtōn'), town (pop. 2,071), Campeche, SE Mexico, on SW Yucatan Peninsula, minor port on Gulf of Campeche, 37 mi. SSW of Campeche; sugar, henequen, corn, tobacco, fruit, livestock; fishing. Pre-Columbian ruins are near by.
Champs (shã), village (pop. 1,286), Seine-et-Marne dept., N central France, near left bank of the Marne, 12 mi. E of Paris. Its 18th-cent. castle with fine garden (now state property) is summer residence of president of France.
Champsaur (shãzōr'), valley of the upper Drac R., in Hautes-Alpes dept., SE France, at S foot of Massif du Pelvoux, in Dauphiné Alps, extending c.25 mi. from Orcières (SE) to Corps (NW). Followed by Grenoble-Gap road. At N end is Sautet Dam and hydroelectric station. Mountain range just N is also called Champsaur and culminates in Chaillol-le-Vieux (10,378 ft.).
Champs-Élysées (shãzālēzā'), tree-lined avenue of Paris, France, leading from the Place de la Concorde to the Arc de Triomphe, and known for its elegant shops and cafés; just over 1 mi. long. Just off it is the Élysée palace, residence of president of France.
Champs-sur-Tarentaine (shã-sür-tärãtĕn'), village (pop. 353), Cantal dept., S central France, near the Rhue, 16 mi. NE of Mauriac; cattle, sheep.
Champtoceaux (shãtōsō'), village (pop. 373), Maine-et-Loire dept., W France, on Loire R. and 16 mi. NE of Nantes; barrelmaking; distilling, vegetable growing.
Champua (chămp'vŭ), village, Keonjhar dist., N Orissa, India, on Baitarani R. and 31 mi. N of Keonjhargarh; forest produce (lac, timber). Formerly called Champeswar.
Chamrajnagar, India: see CHAMARAJNAGAR.
Chamula, Mexico: see BOHOM.
Chamundi, hill, India: see MYSORE, city.
Chamurchi, Bhutan: see CHAMARCHI.
Chamusca (shămōōsh'kŭ), town (pop. 3,572), Santarém dist., central Portugal, on the Tagus and 14 mi. NE of Santarém, in fruit- and winegrowing area; fruit preserving, cork processing, cheese and pottery mfg.
Chamutang, China: see KUNGSHAN.
Ch'a-mu-to, Tibet: see CHAMDO.
Chamzinka (chăm'zĭn-kŭ), village (1948 pop. over 2,000), E central Mordvinian Autonomous SSR, Russian SFSR, on railroad and 28 mi. NE of Saransk; sawmilling; hemp, wheat.
Chanac (shänäk'), village (pop. 638), Lozère dept., S France, in the Causse de Sauveterre, near the Lot, 8 mi. WSW of Mende; cheese making.
Chanak, India: see BARRACKPORE.
Chanak Kalessi, Turkey: see CANAKKALE, town.
Chanal (chänäl'), town (pop. 3,880), Chiapas, S Mexico, in Sierra de Hueytepec, 32 mi. E of San Cristóbal de las Casas; alt. 6,500 ft. Agr. center (wheat, corn, sugar, tobacco, coffee, fruit, stock).
Chañar, town, Argentina: see PAMPA DEL CHAÑAR.
Chañar, El, Argentina: see EL CHAÑAR.
Chañar, El, Chile: see EL CHAÑAR.
Chañar, Lake (chänyär'), Mar Chiquita dist., on Buenos Aires–Santa Fe prov. border, Argentina, 14 mi. NNW of General Arenales; 5 mi. long, 1½ mi. wide. Source of the Río Salado.
Chañaral (chänyäräl'). **1** Town (1940 pop. 2,980), ⊙ Chañaral dept. (□ 9,930; pop. 23,904), NW Atacama prov., N Chile, port on the Pacific at mouth of the Quebrada del Salado, 70 mi. NNW of Copiapó; 26°21'S. Railhead; import and export center for inland mining region. Exports nitrate, copper, and gold ores. Sometimes called Chañaral de las Animas to distinguish it from the village of Chañaral in SW Atacama prov. Damaged in earthquake (1922). **2** Village (1930 pop. 9), SW Atacama prov., N Chile, minor port on Pacific coast, opposite Chañaral Isl.; 29°S.
Chañaral de las Animas, Chile: see CHAÑARAL.
Chañaral Island (c.2 mi. in diameter), off Pacific coast of N central Chile, 5 mi. off SW Atacama prov.; 29°S.
Chañarcillo (chänyärsē'yō), mining settlement (1930 pop. 11), Atacama prov., N Chile, on railroad and 35 mi. S of Copiapó; former noted silver-mining center (deposits discovered 1832), now almost wholly abandoned.
Chañar Ladeado (chänyär' lädää'dō), town (pop. estimate 1,500), S Santa Fe prov., Argentina, 85 mi. WSW of Rosario; agr. center (wheat, flax, corn, livestock); mfg. of sweets, biscuits.
Chanasma (chä'nŭsmŭ), town (pop. 9,922), Mehsana dist., N Bombay, India, 18 mi. WNW of Mehsana; rail junction; agr. market (millet, cotton, oilseeds); handicraft cloth weaving. Large Jain temple with elaborate carvings.
Chança River, Spain and Portugal: see CHANZA RIVER.
Chancay, province, Peru: see HUACHO.
Chancay (chängkī'). **1** Village, Cajamarca dept., Peru: see CHANCAYBAÑOS. **2** Town (pop. 2,761), Lima dept., W central Peru, on coastal plain, on Chancay R. (irrigation), on Pan-American Highway and 20 mi. NNW of Lima (connected by railroad); road junction in cotton-growing area; cotton ginning; fruit, vegetables; fisheries. Chancay port (pop. 171), on Chancay Point on the Pacific, is 1 mi. SW.
Chancaybaños (chängkībä'nyōs), village (pop. 427), Cajamarca dept., NW Peru, in Cordillera Occidental, near source of Chancay R., 13 mi. W of Chota; thermal springs. Until 1942, Chancay.
Chancay River (chängkī'). **1** In Cajamarca dept., NW Peru, rises in Cordillera Occidental near Chancaybaños, flows 40 mi. W, joining the Cumbil to form Lambayeque R. **2** In Lima dept., W central Peru, rises in Cordillera Occidental of the Andes 8 mi. WSW of Huarón, flows 70 mi. SW to the Pacific 4 mi. SSE of Chancay; used for irrigation in lower course.
Chance (chăns), village (1940 pop. 510), Somerset co., SE Md., on tidewater on the Eastern Shore, 23 mi. SW of Salisbury; bridge to Deal Isl. (just S), whose fishing, oystering fleet moors here.
Chancellor (chăn'sĭlŭr). **1** Town (pop. 193), Turner co., SE S.Dak., 18 mi. SW of Sioux Falls; corn, oats, potatoes. **2** Hamlet, Spotsylvania co., Va.: see CHANCELLORSVILLE.
Chancellorsville, crossroads hamlet (now known as Chancellor), in Spotsylvania co., NE Va., near Rappahannock R., 10 mi. W of Fredericksburg. Scene of Civil War battle of Chancellorsville (Apr. 27–May 6, 1863; sometimes called battle of Salem Church), in which Union army under Hooker was defeated in attempt to dislodge Lee's forces, S of the Rappahannock, and forced to retreat across river. Victory led to Confederate invasion of Pa. and to battle of Gettysburg. Part of battle area now included in Fredericksburg and Spotsylvania Co. Battlefield Memorial (hq. at FREDERICKSBURG). Stonewall Jackson Memorial Shrine, here, commemorates Confederate leader mortally wounded at Chancellorsville.
Chancha (chän'chä), Ital. *Cencia*, town, ⊙ Gamu-Gofa prov., S Ethiopia, bet. Mt. Gughe and L. Abaya, 110 mi. SE of Jimma; 6°6'N 37°39'E; alt. 8,963 ft. Formerly Dincha.
Chanchamayo River (chänchämī'ō), Junín dept., central Peru, formed by confluence of 3 headstreams at San Ramón, flows 20 mi. S, past La Merced, joining the Paucartambo to form PERENÉ RIVER. Coffee grown in valley.
Chan Chan (chän chän'), ruined city in Libertad dept., NW Peru, 4 mi. W of Trujillo, near the Pacific. Once a city of c.250,000 inhabitants, it was ⊙ Chimu empire, which was overcome by the Incas c.1400. Considered one of the most remarkable archaeological sites of Peru. Within the gigantic, now largely decayed walls are remains of palaces, fortresses, temples, storehouses, gardens, etc. Decorations of bldgs. and implements reveal great artistic merit. From some of the burial grounds the Spanish removed fabulous gold treasures. Sometimes spelled Chanchán.
Chanchán River (chän-chän'), central Ecuador, rises in the Andes E of Alausí, flows c.60 mi. W through narrow, steep Andean valley, past Huigra, to Chimbo R. 23 mi. ESE of Yaguachi. Its course is followed by the Guayaquil-Quito RR. On its upper course, near Sibambe, is the famed Nariz del Diablo (Devil's Nose) gorge.
Chan-chiang, China: see CHANKIANG.
Chanco (chäng'kō), town (pop. 1,931), ⊙ Chanco dept. (□ 375; pop. 10,978), Maule prov., S central Chile, 3 mi. from the coast, 25 mi. NW of Cauquenes. Resort with several beaches. Agr. center (grain, potatoes, wine, livestock). Noted for cheese mfg. Eucalyptus forests near by. Lumbering.
Chancos (chäng'kōs), village (pop. 47), Ancash dept., W central Peru, in the Callejón de Huaylas, near Santa R., 6 mi. ESE of Carhuás; mineral springs.
Chancy (shãsē'), village (pop. 286), Geneva canton, SW Switzerland, on the Rhone and 9 mi. WSW of Geneva, at Fr. border. Chancy-Pougny hydroelectric plant here.
Chanda (chän'dŭ), district (□ 9,205; pop. 873,284), S Madhya Pradesh, India, on Deccan Plateau; ⊙ Chanda. Bordered NW by Wardha R., SW by Pranhita R., S by Godavari R., and SE by Indravati R. NW plains area (cotton, millet, wheat) divided by Wainganga R. from thickly forested hills (teak, mahua, bamboo) of rest of dist. Rice and oilseeds (chiefly flax) along rivers. Dispersed sandstone, hematite, and fire-clay deposits. Rice and oilseed milling, cotton ginning, coal mining (largely in Wardha valley), sawmilling, handicraft silk weaving; limestone quarrying. Chanda is trade and mfg. center, Warora the main cotton-trade center. Has numerous architectural ruins of Gond dynasties (12th–18th cent.). Pop. 78% Hindu, 20% tribal (mainly Gond), 2% Moslem.
Chanda, town (pop. 35,730), ⊙ Chanda dist., S Madhya Pradesh, India, near Wardha R., 85 mi. S of Nagpur, in forest area; rail junction; trade center; coal mining, sawmilling, cotton ginning, rice and oilseed milling, mfg. of matches, electrical supplies, handicraft cloth and brassware. Annual cattle and tobacco market. Was seat of a Gond dynasty (12th–18th cent.); has 12th-cent. wall. S rail station called Chanda Fort. Ceramic works 16 mi. NW, at village of Bhandak; ruins of 10th-cent. Hindu temples.
Chandaburi, Thailand: see CHANTHABURI.
Chandalar River (shăn"dùlär'), N central Alaska, rises in 3 headstreams in Brooks Range. Longest headstream rises as East Chandalar R. near 69°N 144°10'W, flows SW to Venetie, where it is joined by combined Middle Fork and North Fork, and here becomes Chandalar R. proper, flowing SE to Yukon R. 20 mi. W of Fort Yukon; 280 mi. long to head of East Chandalar R.
Chandameta, India: see CHHINDWARA, town, Madhya Pradesh.
Chandan Chauki (chŭn'dŭn chou'kē), village, Kheri dist., N Uttar Pradesh, India, 14 mi. NE of Palia, on Nepal border; rail spur terminus; trades in rice, jute, oilseeds, vegetables, and sabai grass from Nepal. Also spelled Chandon Choki.
Chandauli (chŭndou'lē), village, Benares dist., SE Uttar Pradesh, India, 16 mi. E of Benares; rice, barley, gram, wheat, sugar cane.
Chandausi (chŭndou'sē), town (pop. 28,763), Moradabad dist., N central Uttar Pradesh, India, 27 mi. S of Moradabad; rail junction; trade center (wheat, rice, pearl millet, mustard, sugar cane, barley, salt); cotton ginning and pressing. Near by is hydroelectric station.
Chandbali (chänd'bälē), village, Balasore dist., NE Orissa, India, on Baitarani R. and 50 mi. SSW of Balasore; small port (trades in rice, fish, salt, cotton piece goods); rice milling.
Chandeleur Islands (shăndulōōr'), SE La., crescent-shaped archipelago (c.26 mi. long) in the Gulf of Mexico, c.40 mi. N of mouth of the Mississippi and 75 mi. E of New Orleans; frequented by fishermen, fur trappers. Lighthouse at N end of chain (30°3'N 80°52'W). W of isls. is **Chandeleur Sound** (c.20 mi. wide), an arm of the Gulf of Mexico, bet. La. coast (W) and Chandeleur Isls. (E). Adjoins Mississippi Sound (N), Breton Sound (SW).
Chanderi (chŭndā'rē), town (pop. 5,332), E Madhya Bharat, India, 50 mi. E of Guna; market center for cloth fabrics, oilseeds, millet; hand-loom weaving (notably muslins). Textile institute. Many ruins in vicinity attest to town's former importance; fort stands SW. Taken successively by Delhi sultanate in 1251, Malwa chieftain in 1438, Sesodia Rajputs in 1520, Babar c.1530, and Mahrattas in 1811 Ruins of old Chanderi fort lie 7 mi. NNW.

Chandernagore (chŭn″dŭrnŭgôr′, chŭn′dŭrnŭ″gŭr), Fr. *Chandernagor* (shänděrnägôr′), town and former Fr. settlement (pop., including GAURHATI, 44,786), Hooghly dist., S central West Bengal, India, on Hooghly R. and 21 mi. N of Calcutta city center; jute milling; ganja trade. Large ruined Hindu temple. Settled 1673 by French; expanded commercially under superintendentship of Dupleix. Captured 1757 and again, 1794, by English; restored to French in 1815. Following 1949 plebiscite, became part of India; inc. 1950 into Hooghly dist. Another Chandernagore (or Farashdanga), adjacent to the town, is S suburb of CHINSURA.

Chandigarh (chŭn′dēgŭr), village, Ambala dist., E Punjab, India, near Ghaggar R., 25 mi. NNE of Ambala; rail station on rail spur to Simla (31 mi. NE). Near by, in sparsely populated SW area, is site of projected ⊙ Punjab (plans drawn 1950), an entirely new city expected to have pop. of over 150,000 within 5 years of its completion.

Chandil, India: see BALARAMPUR.

Chandipur, India: see BALASORE, town.

Chandi Sewu or **Tjandi Sewoe** (both: chän′dē sĕwōō′), vast group of Buddhist temples in central Java, Indonesia, c.10 mi. NE of Jogjakarta. Consists of a large central temple surrounded by 4 rows of auxiliary temples, all richly decorated. Also called the Thousand Temples.

Chandla (chŭnd′lŭ), village, N Vindhya Pradesh, India, 24 mi. N of Panna; millet.

Chandler, village (pop. 1,858), E Que., on E Gaspé Peninsula, on the Gulf of St. Lawrence, at mouth of Grand Pabos R., 35 mi. SSW of Gaspé; pulp-milling center.

Chandler. 1 Resort town (pop. 3,799), Maricopa co., S central Ariz., 15 mi. SE of Phoenix, in irrigated agr. valley of Salt R.; cotton, alfalfa. Williams Air Force Base is E. Founded 1915, inc. 1920. **2** Village (1940 pop. 622), Warrick co., SW Ind., 13 mi. ENE of Evansville, in agr. and bituminous-coal area. **3** Village (pop. 331), Murray co., SW Minn., 11 mi. WSW of Slayton, in corn, oat, and barley area. **4** City (pop. 2,724), ⊙ Lincoln co., central Okla., 40 mi. ENE of Oklahoma City; trade, processing, shipping center for agr. area noted for pecans. Honey packing, cotton ginning, cottonseed-oil milling, meat packing, mfg. of metal products. Settled 1891. **5** Village (1940 pop. 663), Henderson co., E Texas, near Neches R., 11 mi. W of Tyler, in agr. area.

Chandler Bay, Maine: see WOHOA BAY.

Chandler's Ford, town and parish (pop. 3,148), S central Hampshire, England, 5 mi. N of Southampton; agr. market; brickworks. Sanitarium.

Chandlerville, village (pop. 788), Cass co., W central Ill., near Sangamon R., 30 mi. NW of Springfield, in agr. area.

Chandni (chänd′nē), village, Nimar dist., W Madhya Pradesh, India, 12 mi. NE of Burhanpur; industrial settlement in clearing in dense hardwood forest; established 1949 as site of India's 1st newsprint plant (construction begun early 1949).

Chandoline (shädôlēn′), hamlet, Valais canton, SW Switzerland, near Sion; hydroelectric plant.

Chandpur (chänd′pōōr). **1** Town (pop. 15,965), Bijnor dist., N Uttar Pradesh, India, 18 mi. SSE of Bijnor; trades in rice, wheat, gram, barley, sugar cane. Occupied by Pindaris in 1805. **2** Village, Jhansi dist., India: see DEOGARH.

Chandpur, town (pop. 40,434), Tippera dist., SE East Bengal, E Pakistan, on the Meghna and 37 mi. WSW of Comilla; rail spur terminus; major jute-pressing center; oilseed milling, mfg. of matches, chemicals, plywood; rice, jute, oil-seeds.

Chandraghona or **Chandragona** (chŭn″drŭgō′nŭ), village, Chittagong dist., SE East Bengal, E Pakistan, on Karnaphuli R. and 22 mi. ENE of Chittagong; large paper mill (construction begun 1951).

Chandragiri (chŭn′drŭgĭ″rē), village, Chittoor dist., central Madras, India, in a valley of Eastern Ghats, 30 mi. NNE of Chittoor. Site of anc. fort (A.D. c.1000) which was a refuge of Vijayanagar rulers after their defeat (1565) by Deccan sultans at battle of Talikota; became an important stronghold of rival Deccan powers in 17th and 18th cent.

Chandragiri, range, India: see BABA BUDAN RANGE.

Chandragiri Pass (alt. 7,400 ft.), in central Nepal Himalayas, central Nepal, 8 mi. WSW of Katmandu, on main India-Katmandu route; leads into Nepal Valley.

Chandrakona (chŭndrŭkō′nŭ), town (pop. 6,411), Midnapore dist., SW West Bengal, India, 25 mi. NNE of Midnapore; silk weaving, metalware mfg.; rice, wheat, pulse. Rice milling 14 mi. WSW, at Salbani.

Chandra River, India: see CHENAB RIVER.

Chandravalli, India: see CHITALDRUG, town.

Chandur (chän′dōōr), town (pop. 7,205), Amraoti dist., W Madhya Pradesh, India, on railway and 15 mi. SE of Amraoti; cotton, millet; oilseed milling. Sometimes called Chandur Railway.

Chandur Bazar (chän′dōōr bŭzär′), town (pop. 5,941), Amraoti dist., W Madhya Pradesh, India, 15 mi. E of Ellichpur; agr. market (cotton, millet, wheat). Also written Chandur-Bazar.

Chañe (chä′nyā), town (pop. 1,005), Segovia prov., central Spain, 31 mi. NW of Segovia; cereals, livestock; sawmilling, mfg. of resins.

Chanega, Alaska: see CHENEGA.

Chaneliak (chănĕlēăk′), village (pop. 99), W Alaska near Yukon R. delta.

Chanenga, Alaska: see CHENEGA.

Chang. 1 River, Kiangsi prov., China: see CHANG RIVER. **2** River, Kiangsi prov., China: see TSANG RIVER.

Chang, Ko (kô′ chäng′), island (1937 pop. 2,122), of Trat prov., S Thailand, in Gulf of Siam, 4 mi. off coast; 12°N 102°20′E; 20 mi. long, 5 mi. wide.

Changan or **Ch'ang-an** (chäng′än′). **1** Town, NW Chekiang prov., China, on railroad to Shanghai, on Grand Canal and 20 mi. NE of Hangchow; commercial center; silk, hemp, sugar cane, vegetable oil. **2** Town, ⊙ Changan co., (pop. 499,376), S central Shensi prov., China, at foot of the Tsinling, 12 mi. S of Sian; cotton and wool weaving, tanning; cattle raising; grain, ramie, tobacco, wax. Called Wangkü until 1942, when Changan co. seat was moved here from SIAN, which until then had also been called Changan.

Changanacheri (chŭng-gŭnä′chĕrē), city (pop. 28,381), W Travancore, India, 40 mi. N of Quilon; rice milling, cashew-nut processing, mfg. (coir rope and mats, pottery). Col. (affiliated with Univ. of Travancore). Jute growing near by. Also spelled Changanacherry.

Changbhakar (chäng′bŭkär′), former princely state (□ 899; pop. 21,266) of Chhattisgarh States, India; ⊙ was Bharatpur. Since 1948, inc. into Surguja dist. of Madhya Pradesh. Formerly Chang Bhakar.

Changchai, China: see CHANGSHUN.

Chang Chenmo Range (chäng′ chĕnmō′), SE extension of Kailas-Karakoram Range, E Kashmir and W Tibet; extends c.120 mi. W-E, bet. 78°20′E and 80°30′E; rises to 22,120 ft. in N; separated from Pangong Range (S) by Pangong Tso (lake).

Ch'ang-chi, China: see CHANGKI.

Ch'ang-chiang, town, China: see CHEONGKONG.

Ch'ang Chiang, river, China: see CHANG RIVER; YANGTZE RIVER.

Chang Chiang, river, China: see TSANG RIVER.

Changchih or **Ch'ang-chih** (chäng′jŭ′), town, ⊙ Changchih co. (pop. 189,678), SE Shansi prov., China, on railroad and 120 mi. SSE of Taiyüan; road center; silk weaving; winegrowing; medicinal herbs. Until 1912 called Luan.

Ch'ang-ch'ing, China: see CHANGTSING.

Chang-chiu, China: see CHANGKIU.

Changchow. 1 or **Chang-chou** (jäng′-jō′), town, Fukien prov., China: see LUNGKI. **2** or **Ch'ang-chou** (chäng′jō′), city (1938 pop. estimate 125,000), S Kiangsu prov., China, on railroad to Nanking, on Grand Canal, and 100 mi. WNW of Shanghai; industrial center; silk milling, machine and needle mfg., rice and flour milling. Traditionally known for its combs. An old walled town, on Marco Polo's route, Changchow became industrialized in late-19th cent. and developed into a mechanized textile-mfg. center. It was called Wutsin (wōō′jĭn′), 1912–49, while ⊙ Wutsin co. (1946 pop. 839,583). In 1949, it became an independent municipality, regaining its former name; and the co. seat was moved to Chishuyen, 8 mi. SE on railroad, thereafter called Wutsin.

Changchuen Island, China: see SAINT JOHN ISLAND.

Changchun or **Ch'ang-ch'un** (chäng′chōōn′), city (1947 pop. 630,049), ⊙ but independent of Changchun co. (1946 pop. 519,856), W Kirin prov., Manchuria, on South Manchuria RR and 145 mi. SW of Harbin, 175 mi. NE of Mukden; 43°53′N 125°20′E. Industrial and transportation center of central Manchuria; locomotive and rail shops; agr. processing (flour, soybeans, kaoliang, millet), matchmaking, sawmilling; mfg. of synthetic oil, magnesium alloys, electrical goods, ceramics, cotton goods. Has numerous higher educational institutions. City consists of the former Japanese railway zone adjoining the main station (N), the remains of the old Chinese city (E), and the new city (W and S). Dating from early 19th cent., Changchun was originally known as Kwancheng or Kwanchengtze. As the junction (after 1905) of the wide-gauge Chinese Eastern RR and of the standard-gauge South Manchuria RR, Changchun developed as a major rail transshipment point bet. N Manchuria and the S port cities. The lumber industry developed after 1912, when the city was linked with Kirin city and the E Manchurian highlands. Situated at the center of Manchuria, on the Itun R. (a left tributary of the Sungari) and at the hub of 4 rail lines, Changchun was selected in 1932 as the ⊙ Manchukuo and was renamed Hsinking [Chinese,=new capital]. Subsequently, the city was greatly enlarged and reconstructed in a grandiose building program which gave rise to broad avenues, large parks, sports grounds, and modern public bldgs.; and the city became the administrative and academic center of Manchuria, reaching a pop. of 862,600 in 1945. After Second World War, it declined slightly in importance, but remained an independent municipality.

Change Island (□ 9; pop. 946), E N.F., in Notre Dame Bay, 16 mi. E of Twillingate and 3 mi. W of Fogo Isl.; 49°37′N 54°27′W; 7 mi. long, 2 mi. wide. At N end is fishing village, site of lighthouse and radio station. With near-by islets, makes up group of Change Isles.

Changfengkai or **Chang-feng-chieh** (both: jäng′-fŭng′jyĕ′), town, westernmost Yunnan prov., China, on Burma line, 75 mi. SW of Tengchung. Officially known as Lungchwan or Lung-ch'uan (lōōng′chwän′) in summer and fall, when LUNGCHWAN dist. seat, moved from SHANMULUNG (30 mi. NE), is situated here.

Changhang (chäng′häng′), Jap. *Choko*, town (1949 pop. 17,965), S.Chungchong prov., S Korea, at mouth of Kum R., opposite Kunsan; rail terminus; agr. center known for fine grass linen.

Changhing or **Ch'ang-hsing** (both: chäng′shĭng′), town (pop. 12,368), ⊙ Changhing co. (pop. 237,030), northernmost Chekiang prov., China, near Anhwei-Kiangsi line, 55 mi. NNW of Hangchow, on Tai L.; coal mining; silk, rice, wheat, tea.

Changhowon (chäng′hō′wŭn′), Jap. *Chokoin*, town (1949 pop. 14,865), Kyonggi prov., central Korea, S of 38°N, 45 mi. SE of Seoul; grain, silk cocoons.

Changhsien (jäng′shyĕn′), town, ⊙ Changhsien co. (pop. 40,302), SE Kansu prov., China, 70 mi. WNW of Tienshui and on headstream of Wei R.; grain, medicinal herbs; cattle and sheep raising. Saltworks near by.

Ch'ang-hsing, China: see CHANGHING.

Ch'ang-hua, China: see CHANGHWA.

Changhung (chäng′hōōng′), Jap. *Choko*, town (1949 pop. 23,807), S.Cholla prov., S Korea, 30 mi. ESE of Mokpo; agr. center (soy beans, tobacco, ramie); paper and hemp-cloth making.

Changhwa or **Ch'ang-hua** (chäng′hwä′). **1** Town (pop. 5,646), ⊙ Changhwa co. (pop. 73,015), NW Chekiang prov., China, near Anhwei line, S of Tienmu Mts., 55 mi. W of Hangchow; rice, wheat, peaches, nuts. **2** Town, Hainan, Kwangtung prov., China: see CHEONGKONG. **3** Town, Sinkiang prov., China: see HUTUBI.

Changhwa or **Chang-hua** (jäng′hwä′), Jap. *Shoka* (shō′kä), town (1940 pop. 58,227), W central Formosa, on railroad and 10 mi. SW of Taichung; agr. processing center; rice and flour milling, weaving, hatmaking, sawmilling. Confucianist and Buddhist temples. Hot springs (SE). One of oldest towns of Formosa, dating from 17th cent. Its port is Lukang.

Changi or **Ch'ang-i** (chäng′yē′), town, ⊙ Changi co. (pop. 526,775), central Shantung prov., China, on road and 20 mi. NE of Weifang; silk weaving, straw plaiting, tanning; wheat, kaoliang, peanuts.

Changi (chäng′ē), village (pop. 1,337), at E tip of Singapore isl., 11 mi. NE of Singapore; has prison and Br. military cantonment. Site of one of civil airports of Singapore isl.

Changjin River (chäng′jēn′), Jap. *Cho-shin-ko*, Korean *Changjin-gang*, S.Hamgyong prov., N Korea, rises in mtn. range 25 mi. NW of Hamhung, flows c.160 mi. generally NE to Yalu R. c.30 mi. below Changpai (Manchuria); receives Puchon R. on right. Drains gold and silver mining area. In upper course are a reservoir (13 mi. long, 2 mi. wide) and hydroelectric plant feeding industrial Hungnam; fierce fighting here Nov.-Dec., 1950, in the Korean war.

Changki or **Ch'ang-chi** (both: chäng′jē′), town, ⊙ Changki co. (pop. 21,394), central Sinkiang prov., China, 30 mi. NW of Urumchi, and on highway N of the Tien Shan; silk-textile, paper mfg.; wheat, peas. Coal mining. Saltworks near by.

Changkiakow, China: see KALGAN.

Chang Kiang. 1 River, Kiangsi prov., China: see CHANG RIVER. **2** River, Kiangsi prov., China: see TSANG RIVER. **3** See also YANGTZE RIVER.

Changkiu or **Chang-chiu** (both: jäng′jyō′), town, ⊙ Changkiu co. (pop. 521,773), N Shantung prov., China, 30 mi. E of Tsinan and on railroad; coal-mining center (mines on rail spur; S). Rice, peanuts, wheat, millet. Called Mingshui until 1949, when co. seat was moved here from old Changkiu, 8 mi. NNW.

Changko or **Ch'ang-ko** (chäng′gwô′), town, ⊙ Changko co. (pop. 138,054), N Honan prov., China, 40 mi. S of Chengchow; wheat, kaoliang, millet.

Changku, China: see LUHO, Sikang prov.

Changkufeng or **Ch'ang-ku-feng,** Russian SFSR: see KHASAN, LAKE.

Changla, China: see SUNGPAN.

Changlaying, China: see SUNGPAN.

Changli or **Ch'ang-li** (chäng′lē′), town, ⊙ Changli co. (pop. 439,570), NE Hopeh prov., China, near Gulf of Chihli, 50 mi E of Tangshan, and on railroad; kaoliang, millet.

Changling or **Ch'ang-ling** (chäng′lĭng′), town, ⊙ Changling co. (pop. 160,000), W Kirin prov., Manchuria, 70 mi. WNW of Changchun; kaoliang, corn, beans.

Changlo or **Ch'ang-lo** (chäng′lŭ′). **1** Town, Fukien prov., China; see DIONGLOH. **2** Town, Hupeh prov., China: see WUFENG. **3** Town, ⊙ Changlo co. (pop. 225,362), N Shantung prov., China, 17 mi. W of Weifang and on Tsingtao-Tsinan RR; cotton and silk weaving; poultry.

Changlun (chänglōōn′), town (pop. 590) N Kedah, Malaya, 21 mi. N of Alor Star; road junction near Thailand line; rubber plantations.

Changming (jäng′mĭng′), town (pop. 7,443), ⊙ Changming co. (pop. 104,345), NW Szechwan prov., China, 45 mi. NNW of Santai and on Fow

R. (head of navigation); medicinal plants, rice, millet, wheat, indigo.

Changning or **Ch'ang-ning** (chăng'nĭng'). **1** Town, ⊙ Changning co. (pop. 329,773), S Hunan prov., China, 40 mi. SSW of Hengyang; rice, wheat, beans, cotton. SHUIKOWSHAN, major lead-zinc mining center, is 11 mi. NE. **2** Town (pop. 16,915), ⊙ Changning co. (pop. 232,280), SW Szechwan prov., China, 50 mi. SW of Luhsien; paper milling; rice, medicinal herbs, millet, sweet potatoes, wheat. Coal mines near by. **3** Town, ⊙ Changning co. (pop. 80,662), W Yunnan prov., China, 35 mi. SE of Paoshan; rice, millet, beans. Until 1935 called Yutien.

Changoreal, Sierra (syĕ'rä chăng'gōrääl"), subandean range in E central Catamarca prov., Argentina, S of Sierra del Hombre Muerto, 40 mi. NNE of Belén; extends 30 mi. SSW-NNE; rises to c.15,000 ft. Headstreams of Belén R. rise on W.

Changpai or **Ch'ang-pai** (chăng'bī'), town, ⊙ Changpai co. (pop. 42,066), E Liaotung prov., Manchuria, on right bank of Yalu R. (Korea border), opposite Hyesanjin, and 120 mi. E of Tunghwa, at S foot of Changpai mtn.; gold mining, lumbering.

Changpai Mountains, Chinese *Ch'ang-pai Shan* (shän) and *Pai-t'ou Shan* (bī'tō), Jap. *Hakuto-san* (hä'kōōtō"-sän'), Korean *Paektu-san* (păk'tōō-sän'), on Korea-Manchuria line, in upper reaches of Sungari, Yalu, and Tumen rivers. Rise to 9,003 ft. in Changpai mtn., 150 mi. SE of Kirin city; 42°1'N 128°5'E. The highest peak is an extinct volcano, containing the crater lake Tien Chih (T'ien Ch'ih).

Changpeh or **Changpei.** **1** (jäng'bā') Town, ⊙ Changpeh co. (pop. 111,898), N central Chahar prov., China, in Yin Mts., 20 mi. NNW of Kalgan; road junction and commercial center. Until 1918 called Sinho. **2** or **Ch'ang-pei** (all: chăng'bā'), town, ⊙ Changpeh co., N Liaosi prov., Manchuria, China, 30 mi. SW of Szeping.

Changping. **1** or **Chang-p'ing** (jäng'pĭng'), town (pop. 4,449), ⊙ Changping co. (pop. 76,394), S Fukien prov., China, on Kiulung R. and 70 mi. ESE of Changting; sweet potatoes, rice, sugar cane. Coal mines near by. **2** or **Ch'ang-p'ing** (chăng'pĭng'), town, ⊙ Changping co. (pop. 234,314), N Hopeh prov., China, 20 mi. NNW of Peking, and on railroad, near Great Wall (Chahar line); wheat, millet, kaoliang; manganese mining. Tombs of 13 Ming emperors are NE.

Changpu or **Chang-p'u** (jäng'pōō'), town (pop. 7,624), ⊙ Changpu co. (pop. 201,179), S Fukien prov., China, 40 mi. SW of Amoy; sweet potatoes, rice, peanuts. Bauxite mines near by.

Changra, Turkey: see CANKIRI, town.

Chang River (chăng), Chinese *Chang Kiang* or *Ch'ang Chiang* (both: jyäng), NE Kiangsi prov., China, rises on Anhwei prov. line, flows 100 mi. SW, past Fowliang, joining Loan R. to form short Po R. at Poyang, on Poyang L.

Changsan, Cape (chăng'sän'), Korean *Changsangot*, Jap. *Chozan-kan*, Hwanghae prov., central Korea, on small peninsula in Yellow Sea; 38°8'N 124°39'E.

Changsha or **Ch'ang-sha** (chăng'shä'), city (1946 pop. 421,616; 1947 pop. 396,465), ⊙ Hunan prov., China, port on right bank of Siang R., on railroad to Canton and 180 mi. SSW of Hankow; 28°12'N 112°59'E. Major trade and industrial center; smelting works (lead, zinc, antimony); mfg. of cotton goods, glass, flour; porcelain and embroidery handicrafts. Rice and tea trade. Has univ. and medical col. Known since 3d cent. B.C., Changsha was a noted literary and transit center on China's N-S Siang R. trade route. It was renamed (A.D. 700) Tanchow in the Tang dynasty, was ⊙ Chu kingdom in the Five Dynasties period (907–960), and since the Ming period has again been known as Changsha. It was unsuccessfully besieged (1852) during the Taiping rebellion and became an open port in 1904. During Second World War, it was briefly held (1941 and 1944–45) by the Japanese and was the site of several important battles. It passed to Communist control in 1949. The city became an independent municipality in 1933, when the seat of Changsha co. (1946 pop. 1,024,510) was moved to the town of Langli, 8 mi. ESE, thereafter also known as Changsha.

Changshan or **Ch'ang-shan** (chăng'shän'). **1** Town (pop. 12,173), ⊙ Changshan co. (pop. 128,905), SW Chekiang prov., China, on Kiangsi line, 22 mi. W of Chühsien, and on headstream of Tsientang R.; vegetable-tallow and tung-oil processing; rice, wheat, fruit. **2** Town, Shantung prov., China: see YAONAN.

Changshan Islands. **1** (jäng'shän') or **Miao Islands,** Chinese *Miao Tao* (myou' dou') or *Miao Lieh-tao* (lyĕ'–), island group in Yellow Sea, China, guarding entrance to Gulf of Chihli, bet. Liaotung peninsula (N) and Shantung prov., to which they belong. There are 15 isls., of which Changshan Isl. (7 mi. long, 2 mi. wide), 4 mi. N of Penglai, is the largest. **2** (chăng'shän') Chinese *Ch'ang-shan Lieh-tao*, island group in Korea Bay of Yellow Sea, off E coast of Liaotung peninsula; 39°25'N 122°30'E. Part of former Kwantung territory, they are situated, since 1945, within the limits of the Port Arthur naval base dist.

Changshow or **Ch'ang-shou** (both: chăng'shō'). **1** Town, Sungkiang prov., Manchuria, China: see YENSHOW. **2** Town (pop. 17,771), ⊙ Changshow co. (pop. 320,309), E Szechwan prov., China, on left bank of Yangtze R. and 35 mi. NE of Chungking; tobacco and tung-oil processing; rice, millet, sweet potatoes, wheat, sugar cane, oranges. Iron mines near by.

Changshu. **1** (jäng'shōō) Town, N central Kiangsi prov., China, 10 mi. ENE of Tsingkiang, and on Kan R. at crossing (rail bridge) of Chekiang-Kiangsi RR. **2** or **Ch'ang-shu** (chăng'shōō'), town (pop. 63,798), ⊙ Changshu co. (pop. 946,402), S Kiangsu prov., China, 25 mi. NNE of Soochow; rice-growing center; wheat, beans, rapeseed, cotton; silk spinning and weaving.

Chang Shui, China: see TSANG RIVER.

Changshun or **Ch'ang-shun** (chăng'shŏŏn'), town (pop. 5,145), ⊙ Changshun co. (pop. 74,745), S Kweichow prov., China, 45 mi. SSW of Kweiyang; pottery making; embroideries; wheat, beans, tea. Until 1942 called Changchai.

Changsong (chăng'sŭng'). **1** Jap. *Chojo*, town (1949 pop. 23,167), S. Cholla prov., S Korea, 45 mi. NNE of Mokpo; agr. center (rice, cotton, soybeans, tobacco); handicraft (lacquer ware, pottery, silk textiles, paper). **2** Jap. *Shojo*, township (1944 pop. 17,661), N.Pyongan prov., N Korea, on Yalu R. and 43 mi. NE of Sinuiju; gold mining, agr. (rice, soybeans, millet).

Changsungpo (chăng'sŏŏng'pō'), Jap. *Choshoho*, town (1949 pop. 15,213), on E coast of Koje Isl., S.Kyongsang prov., S Korea, fishing port on Korea Strait, 25 mi. SW of Pusan.

Changtai or **Ch'ang-t'ai** (chăng'tī'), town (pop. 3,901), ⊙ Changtai co. (pop. 57,167), S Fukien prov., China, 20 mi. WNW of Amoy, near Kiulung R.; rice, sweet potatoes, wheat.

Chang Tang or **Chang Thang** (both: chăng'tăng') [Tibetan, =northern plains], vast, arid plateau with numerous salt lakes, covering most of N Tibet; c.700 mi. long (E-W), c.300 mi. wide; average alt., 16,000 ft. Bounded N by Kunlun mts., S by Trans-Himalayas. Sparse herds (yaks, sheep, goats) and agr. (tubers).

Changteh. **1** or **Ch'ang-te** (chăng'dŭ'), town (1947 pop. estimate 50,000), ⊙ Changteh co. (1946 pop. 554,988), NW Hunan prov., China, on Yüan R., near Tungting L., and 105 mi. NW of Changsha; commercial center of Yüan R. valley and NW Hunan, on trade route from Yangtze port of Shasi (Hupeh) to Kweichow prov. Rice, wheat, beans, sugar cane, cotton. Gold mining near by. During Second World War the objective of several Jap. drives, it was briefly occupied in 1944. **2** City, Pingyuan prov., China: see ANYANG.

Changtien (jäng'dyĕn'), city, central Shantung prov., China, 60 mi. E of Tsinan and on railroad to Tsingtao; junction for Poshan coal-mining region; cotton and silk weaving; wheat, eggs.

Changting or **Ch'ang-t'ing** (chăng'tĭng'), town (pop. 26,749), ⊙ Changting co. (pop. 198,311), SW Fukien prov., China, near Kiangsi line, 190 mi. WSW of Foochow and on upper Ting R.; rice, wheat, sweet potatoes; exports tobacco, paper, bamboo. A center of the Hakka people. Until 1913 called Tingchow.

Changtsing or **Ch'ang-ch'ing** (both: chăng'chĭng'), town, ⊙ Changtsing co. (pop. 505,186), W Shantung prov., China, 17 mi. SW of Tsinan, near Yellow R.; commercial center; peanuts, fruit.

Changtu. **1** or **Ch'ang-t'u** (chăng'tōō'), town, ⊙ Changtu co. (pop. 617,068), N Liaosi prov., Manchuria, China, 35 mi. SSW of Szeping; soybeans, wheat. **2** or **Ch'ang-tu** (chăng'dōō'), town, Sikang prov., China: see CHAMDO.

Changtze or **Ch'ang-tzu** (chăng'dzŭ'). **1** Town, ⊙ Changtze co. (pop. 150,645), SE Shansi prov., China, 12 mi. WSW of Changchih; millet, kaoliang, corn. Coal mines near by. **2** Town, ⊙ Changtze co. (pop. 40,578), N Shensi prov., China, 40 mi. NNE of Yenan; wheat, millet, beans. Originally called Wayaopu, it was renamed Anting c.1940 and Changtze in 1949. The former co. seat (old Anting) is 5 mi. W.

Changuinola (chăng-gēnō'lä), village (pop. 182), Bocas del Toro prov., W Panama, on Changuinola R., on railroad and 19 mi. WNW of Bocas del Toro; bananas, cacao, abacá, coffee, coconuts, tobacco, rubber; stock raising, lumbering.

Changuinola River, W Panama, rises in continental divide N of the volcano Chiriquí, flows 45 mi. N, past Changuinola, to Caribbean Sea 13 mi. NW of Almirante.

Changwat, a civil division in Thailand: for Thai names beginning thus, see under following proper name.

Changwu. **1** (jäng'wōō') Town, ⊙ Changwu co. (pop. 188,204), W central Liaosi prov., Manchuria, China, 60 mi. NW of Mukden and on railroad; soybean oil, wheat flour, Chinese gin; buckwheat, corn, cotton. Chinese colonization of area (1902–03) caused the Mongolian Changwu rebellion. **2** or **Ch'ang-wu** (chăng'wōō'), town (pop. 8,205), ⊙ Changwu co. (pop. 60,317), W Shensi prov., China, on Kansu line, on King R. and 95 mi. NW of Sian, and on main road to Lanchow; wheat, millet, beans.

Changwucheng, Manchuria: see CHAOTUNG.

Changyang or **Ch'ang-yang** (chăng'yăng'), town (pop. 16,021), ⊙ Changyang co. (pop. 217,845), SW Hupeh prov., China, 15 mi. SSW of Ichang and on Ching R.; tea, beans, rice. Iron deposits near by.

Changyeh (jäng'yĕ'), town, ⊙ Changyeh co. (pop. 172,025), central Kansu prov., China, on Silk Road, 270 mi. NW of Lanchow, and on right bank of Hei R. (here known as Kanchow R.), near the Great Wall; 38°56'N 100°37'E. Rice- and licorice-producing center; cotton and wool weaving; hides, grain. Hot springs (S). Until 1913 called Kanchow.

Changyen (jäng'yĕn'), town, S Kiangsu prov., China, 33 mi. SSW of Shanghai, near Hangchow Bay; commercial center.

Changyon (chăng'yŭn'), Jap. *Choen*, town (1944 pop. 18,072), Hwanghae prov., central Korea, N of 38°N; rail terminus; gold-mining center. Monggumpo (mông'gōōm'pō'), is a popular beach resort 18 mi. WSW of Changyon.

Changyrtash (chŭn-gĭrtäsh'), town (1939 pop. over 500), S Dzhalal-Abad oblast, Kirghiz SSR, 15 mi. WSW of Dzhalal-Abad; oil field (producing since 1937); sulphur mine.

Changyüan or **Ch'ang-yüan** (chăng'yüăn'), town, ⊙ Changyüan co. (pop. 299,671), S Pingyuan prov., China, near Yellow R., 45 mi. ESE of Sinsiang; silk weaving; wheat, kaoliang, millet. Until 1949 in Hopeh prov.

Chanhassen, village (pop. 182), Carver co., S central Minn., near L. Minnetonka, 15 mi. W of Minneapolis; grain, livestock.

Chanhwa. **1** or **Ch'an-hua** (both: chăn'hwä'), town, ⊙ Chanhwa co. (pop. 162,000), NW Shantung prov., China, 20 mi. NE of Hweimin; peanuts, potatoes. Salines near by. **2** or **Chan-hua** (jän'-hwä'), town, ⊙ Chanhwa co. (pop. 14,229), Sikang prov., China, 65 mi. N of Lihwa and on Yalung R.; cattle raising; wheat. Gold washing near by. Until 1912 called Chantui; 1912–16, Hwaiju.

Chan-i, China: see CHANYI.

Chañí, Sierra de (syĕ'rä dā chänyē'), subandean mountain range on Salta-Jujuy prov. border, Argentina, W of Jujuy; rises to c.20,000 ft.

Chania, Crete: see CANEA.

Chanigot or **Chanigoth** (chŭnēgōt'), town (pop. 1,510), Bahawalpur state, W Pakistan, 45 mi. SW of Bahawalpur; wheat, millet. Sometimes called Goth Chani.

Chaniot, W Pakistan: see CHINIOT.

Chankiang or **Chan-chiang** (jän'jyäng'), Cantonese *Tsamkong* (jäm'gông'), municipality (□ 325; pop. 268,416), SW Kwangtung prov., China, port on Kwangchow Bay of S.China Sea, at base of Luichow Peninsula, 230 mi. WSW of Canton; 21°11'N 110°24'E. Trading and industrial center of SW Kwangtung; cotton milling and dyeing, match and leather mfg., rice milling. Main agr. products are rice, beans, sweet potatoes, sugar cane, sesame, and peanuts. Hog raising. Saltworks along coast. Chankiang is divided into 10 urban and rural dists., including SIYING (seat of govt.), CHIKHOM, and isls. of TUNGHAI and SIUNGCHOW. The territory, which now forms Chankiang municipality, was leased by China to France for 99 years in 1898–99 and was organized within the Fr. Union of Indochina as the territory of Kwangchowwan, Kwangchowan, or Kuang-chou-wan [Fr. *Kouang-Tchéou-Wan*]. The area was, however, restored to China in 1945 and constituted as a municipality.

Chan-Kom (chăng-kōm'), town (pop. 270), Yucatan, SE Mexico, 20 mi. WSW of Valladolid, in tropical forest.

Channagiri (chŭ'nŭgĭrē) or **Chennagiri** (chĕ'nŭgĭrē), town (pop. 5,057), Shimoga dist., N central Mysore, India, 25 mi. ENE of Shimoga; local trade in millet, rice, sugar cane. Has annual temple-festival market.

Channapatna (chĕ'nŭpŭtnŭ), town (pop. 16,485), Bangalore dist., SE Mysore, India, 35 mi. SW of Bangalore; silk-milling center; mfg. of silk and rayon yarn and cloth, lacquerware; rice and oilseed milling. Commercial col.; silk-growing research. Sometimes also spelled Chennapatna.

Channarayapatna (chŭnŭrä'yŭpŭtnŭ), town (pop. 4,134), Hassan dist., W central Mysore, India, 20 mi. ESE of Hassan; trades in grain, rice, oilseeds; mfg. of handicraft glass bangles, brass vessels, silk cloth. Sometimes spelled Chennarayapatna. Noted archaeological site of Sravana Belgola is 7 mi. SE.

Channel, town (pop. 1,309), at SW tip of N.F., 310 mi. W of St. John's and 8 mi. SE of Cape Ray, on Cabot Strait; cod and halibut fishing center. In 1945 Channel was inc. as a single municipality with near-by PORT AUX BASQUES.

Channel, village (pop. 1,218), Lake co., NE Ill., on Channel L.

Channel Islands or **Norman Isles,** Fr. *Îles Normandes* (ēl nôrmăd'), archipelago (□ 75.1; 1931 census pop. 93,205; 1945 census pop. 79,491; 1951 census 102,770) on S side of the English Channel, W of Cotentin Peninsula of Normandy, France, 80 mi. S of English coast, including isls. of JERSEY, GUERNSEY, ALDERNEY, SARK, JETHOU, HERM, and BRECHOU. With exception of the Chauseys the Channel Isls. belong to Great Britain. Christianization took place largely through the efforts of St. Helier and St. Sampson in 6th cent. In 10th cent. the isles were granted to the dukes of Normandy. They were the only part of Normandy remaining to England after 1204. Unsuccessful attempts were made by the French, in 14th cent. and later, to establish themselves on the isls. The mild and sunny climate (35–40 in. rainfall), the fertile soil, and the nearness to markets have made the growing of vegetables, flowers, and fruits an important industry. Dairying is also pursued; Guernsey, Jersey, and Alderney each has its famous breed of cattle. Fishing; granite quarrying. The climate and scenery have made them a popular resort area. Jersey, Guernsey, and smaller isls. have separate legislatures. Norman-French patois is generally spoken; French and English are official languages. In June, 1940, after collapse of France, military personnel and thousands of the inhabitants were evacuated to England prior to occupation by German forces, who remained in possession until May, 1945. With the defeat of Germany most of the inhabitants returned to the isls.

Channel Islands, Calif.: see SANTA BARBARA ISLANDS.

Channel Islands National Monument, Calif.: see SANTA BARBARA ISLANDS.

Channelkirk, parish (pop. 418), W Berwick, Scotland, at foot of Lammermuir Hills. Includes OXTON.

Channel Lake (c.2 mi. long), NE Ill., near Antioch, in resort area; connected by stream to Chain-O'-Lakes.

Channing. 1 Village (1940 pop. 683), Dickinson co., SW Upper Peninsula, Mich., 22 mi. N of Iron Mountain city, in forest and farm area. **2** Village (pop. c.500), ⊙ Hartley co., extreme N Texas, in high plains of the Panhandle, 45 mi. NW of Amarillo; market, shipping point for cattle, grain.

Chanonry Point, cape at narrow entrance to inner part of Moray Firth, E Ross and Cromarty, Scotland, 2 mi. E of Fortrose; 57°36'N 4°4'W.

Chanpatia (chänpät'yŭ), town (pop. 4,510), Champaran dist., NW Bihar, India, 8 mi. N of Bettiah; rice, wheat, barley, corn, oilseeds; sugar milling. Sometimes spelled Chainpatia; also called Chainpatia Bazar.

Chanpin (jŭn'bĕn'), Mandarin *Chenpien* (jŭn'byĕn'), town, ⊙ Chanpin co. (pop. 73,411), W Kwangsi prov., China, 55 mi. SW of Poseh, on Yunnan line; wheat, millet, beans.

Chanta, China: see LIENSHAN, Yunnan prov.

Chantabon, Chantaboon, Chantabun, or **Chantaburi,** Thailand: see CHANTHABURI.

Chantada (chäntä'dhä), town (pop. 1,552), Lugo prov., NW Spain, agr. center 20 mi. NNE of Orense; tanning, linen mfg., ham processing. Livestock, lumber, corn, potatoes in area. Mineral springs. E, 2.5 mi., is Roman bridge across Miño R.

Chantal (shätäl'), town (1950 pop. 643), Sud dept., SW Haiti, on Tiburon Peninsula, 10 mi. W of Les Cayes; bananas, sugar cane.

Chantavir, Yugoslavia: see CANTAVIR.

Chantburi, Thailand: see CHANTHABURI.

Chantelle (shätĕl'), agr. village (pop. 972), Allier dept., central France, in the fertile Limagne, on Bouble R. and 15 mi. NW of Vichy; winegrowing.

Chantenay-sur-Loire (shätünā'-sür-lwär'), W industrial section of Nantes, Loire-Inférieure dept., W France. Formerly a separate commune.

Chanthaburi (chän'tä'bōōrē'), town (1947 pop. 6,711), ⊙ Chanthaburi prov. (□ 2,325; 1947 pop. 110,808), SE Thailand, port on short Chanthaburi R. (near mouth on Gulf of Siam) and 135 mi. SE of Bangkok, S of Chanthaburi Range. Its deep-water harbor is Laem Sing. Agr. center; pepper, rubber, and coffee plantations; rice, kapok, fruit. Handicraft industry; fisheries. Semi-precious stones mined near by. Large Annamese and Cambodian pop. Originally part of Khmer Empire, passed 1576 to Thailand. Occupied (1893–1905) by French forces. Also spelled Chantburi, Chantaburi, and Chandaburi, and formerly Chantabon, Chantaboon, or Chantabun.

Chanthaburi Range, SE Thailand, extending c.80 mi. NW from Chanthaburi, bet. Gulf of Siam and Cambodian line; rises to 5,380 ft.

Chanthuk (chän'tŭk'), village (1937 pop. 3,713), Nakhon Ratchasima prov., central Thailand, on railroad and 27 mi. ESE of Nakhon Ratchasima; copper mining. Local name, Sikhiu.

Chantilly (shăntĭ'lē, Fr. shätēyē'), town (pop. 5,105), Oise dept., N France, at N edge of Forest of Chantilly, 24 mi. NNE of Paris, near Senlis; noted horse-racing center (the Newmarket of France) and favorite Parisian resort; porcelain mfg., sawmilling, mushroom shipping. Formerly known for its lace manufactures. Has large 18th-cent. stables. The château, rebuilt in 19th cent., contains the fine Condé art mus. Fr. general hq., 1914–17, in First World War.

Chantilly (shăntĭ'lē), battlefield, Fairfax co., N Va., 14 mi. W of Falls Church. In Civil War battle (Sept., 1862), Union troops retreating after 2d battle of Bull Run here checked pursuing Confederates under Stonewall Jackson.

Chantonnay (shätônē'), town (pop. 2,111), Vendée dept., W France, 17 mi. E of La Roche-sur-Yon; road center; poultry market; cereals, wine. Scene of a Republican defeat (1793) during the Vendean insurrection.

Chantrey Inlet, N Keewatin Dist., Northwest Territories, bay (100 mi. long, 50 mi. wide at mouth) of the Arctic Ocean, on E side of Adelaide Peninsula, sheltered by King William Isl.; 67°N 95°W. Receives Back R. at head; contains Montreal Isl.

Chantry Island, islet, SW Ont., in L. Huron, just W of Southampton; lighthouse (44°28'N 81°23'W).

Chantui, China: see CHANHWA, Sikang prov.

Chanu (shänü'), village (pop. 440), Orne dept., NW France, 6 mi. WSW of Flers; wrought-iron working, cider distilling.

Chanute (shŭnōōt'), city (pop. 10,109), Neosho co., SE Kansas, on Neosho R. and 41 mi. WNW of Pittsburg; trade and rail center (with railroad repair shops) in rich agr. and oil-producing region. Oil refining; mfg. of oil-drilling equipment, cement, clothing, gas and electric supplies, chemicals. Airport. Has jr. col. Settled c.1870, inc. 1872.

Chanute Air Force Base, Ill.: see RANTOUL.

Chany (chŭnē'), town (1939 pop. over 2,000), W Novosibirsk oblast, Russian SFSR, on Baraba Steppe, on Trans-Siberian RR and 30 mi. E of Tatarsk; dairy farming.

Chany, Lake, largest salt lake (□ 1,000) of Baraba Steppe, in Novosibirsk oblast, Russian SFSR, 28 mi. SW of Barabinsk; 65 mi. long, 35 mi. wide. Deeply indented, marshy shores enclose 3 sections: Kazanskoye L. (NE), Yudinskoye L. (W), and L. Malyye Chany, which receives Kargat and Chulym rivers. Salt content is lowest in SE, near mouths of inlets. The lake contains much plankton and abounds in fish. It is 33 ft. deep.

Chanyi or **Chan-i** (both: jän'yē'), town, ⊙ Chanyi co. (pop. 114,320), E Yunnan prov., China, on railroad and 8 mi. NNE of Kütsing; coal mines; chemical industry.

Chanyü (jän'yü'), town, ⊙ Chanyü co. (pop. 91,489), southwesternmost Heilungkiang prov., Manchuria, 55 mi. S of Taonan, near Kirin-Inner Mongolia line; kaoliang, millet, sheepskins, medicinal herbs. Until 1915 called Kaihwachen.

Chanza River (chän'thä), Port. *Chança* (chän'sŭ), flows c.40 mi. along S Portuguese-Spanish border after rising in the Sierra Morena of Huelva prov., S Spain, near Cortegana; joins the Guadiana c.30 mi. from the Atlantic at Pomarão; total length c.60 mi. Not navigable.

Chanzy (shänzē'), village (pop. 1,031), Oran dept., NW Algeria, on the Mékerra, on railroad and 17 mi. SSW of Sidi-bel-Abbès; winegrowing, lumber.

Chão, Madeira: see DESERTAS.

Chao (chou), village (pop. 123), Libertad dept., NW Peru, minor port on the Pacific, 13 mi. S of Virú; salt deposits.

Chaoan. 1 (jou'än') Town (pop. 23,085), ⊙ Chaoan co. (pop. 196,564), S Fukien prov., China, on Kwangtung line, 75 mi. SW of Amoy, near Chaoan Bay (or Tungshan Bay) of Formosa Strait; rice, sweet potatoes. **2** or **Ch'ao-an** (chou'än'), town (pop. 59,486), ⊙ Chaoan co. (pop. 620,785), E Kwangtung prov., China, at head of Han R. delta, 22 mi. N of Swatow (linked by railroad); commercial center; cotton milling, porcelain mfg., engraving. Produces indigo, bamboo. Embroidery work. Tin and tungsten mining, kaolin quarrying near by. A coast-wise port until 19th cent., when it was superseded by Swatow. Until 1914 called Chaochow.

Chaochen, China: see CHAOKIATU.

Chaocheng or **Chao-ch'eng** (jou'chŭng'). **1** Town, ⊙ Chaocheng co. (pop. 187,364), NE Pingyuan prov., China, 70 mi. ENE of Anyang; cotton and silk weaving; wheat, rice, millet, kaoliang, beans, timber. Until 1949 in Shantung prov. **2** Town, ⊙ Chaocheng co. (pop. 86,853), S Shansi prov., China, on Fen R. and 20 mi. NNE of Linfen, and on railroad; cotton weaving; wheat, kaoliang.

Chao-chiao, China: see CHAOKIOH.

Chao-chia-tu, China: see CHAOKIATU.

Chaochow. 1 or **Chao-chou** (jou'jō'), town, Hopeh prov., China: see CHAOHSIEN. **2** or **Chao-chou** (jou'jō'), town, ⊙ Chaochow co. (pop. 253,396), S Heilungkiang prov., Manchuria, 70 mi. W of Harbin, near Kirin-Sungkiang line; soybeans, wheat, hemp, corn, kaoliang. Called Laochengki until late 1930s. The name Chaochow was previously applied to a town, 20 mi. SW on Sungari R., originally called Erhtaichan and renamed Chaoyüan in late 1930s when Chaochow co. seat was moved to present site because of flood danger. **3** Town, Kwangtung prov., China: see CHAOAN. **4** Town, Yunnan prov., China: see FENGYI.

Chaochow or **Ch'ao-chou** (both: chou'jō'), Jap. *Choshu* (chō'shōō), town (1935 pop. 4,708), S Formosa, 9 mi. SE of Pingtung and on railroad; rice-milling center; sweet potatoes, sugar cane, bananas, livestock. Peopled by emigrants from Chaochow, Kwangtung prov., China.

Chaochwanpu, China: see LUNGKWAN.

Chaohsien. 1 or **Ch'ao-hsien** (chou'shyĕn'), town, ⊙ Chaohsien co. (pop. 374,424), N Anhwei prov., China, on E shore of Chao L., 40 mi. ESE of Hofei, and on railroad; rice-growing center; wheat, cotton, rapeseed. **2** (jou'shyĕn') Town, ⊙ Chaohsien co. (pop. 210,610), SW Hopeh prov., China, 25 mi. SE of Shihkiachwang; wheat, millet, beans, kaoliang. Until 1913 called Chaochow.

Ch'ao Hu, China: see CHAO LAKE.

Chaohwa or **Chao-hua** (both: jou'hwä'), town (pop. 8,726), ⊙ Chaohwa co. (pop. 96,285), N Szechwan prov., China, 30 mi. NNW of Langchung and on Kialing R.; tobacco and indigo center; rice, wheat, beans, potatoes, millet.

Chao-i, China: see CHAOYI.

Chao Island (chou), in Pacific Ocean, Libertad dept., NW Peru, WSW of Chao Point (8°46'S 48°47'W) and 18 mi. NW of Santa, 2 mi. offshore; 8°47'S 48°48'W; 2 mi. long, ½ mi. wide; guano.

Chaokiatu or **Chao-chia-tu** (both: jou'jyä'dōō'), town, W Szechwan prov., China, 30 mi. NE of Chengtu and on upper To R.; commercial center; medicinal plants, fruit. Sometimes Chaochen.

Chaoking, China: see KOYIU.

Chaokioh or **Chao-chiao** (both: jou'jyou'), town, ⊙ Chaokioh co. (pop. 59,010), SE Sikang prov., China, 45 mi. NE of Sichang and on tributary of Yangtze R.: rice, wheat, beans, kaoliang. Until 1938 in Szechwan.

Chaokow or **Chao-k'ou** (both: jou'kō'), village, N Honan prov., China, 20 mi. W of Kaifeng. Here the Yellow R. burst through its dikes (1938) on its SE course; was returned to old channel in 1947.

Chao Lake, Chinese *Ch'ao Hu* (chou'hōō'), N Anhwei prov., China, 65 mi. WSW of Nanking; 32 mi. long (E-W), 5–18 mi. wide; hilly isls. (SW). Its outlet, at Chaohsien (E), empties into Yangtze R. opposite Wuhu.

Chao Phraya River (chou' prŭyä'), commonly called **Mae Nam** or **Menam** (both: mă'näm') [Thai,=river], most important river of Thailand, used extensively for transportation and irrigation of one of Asia's leading rice-surplus areas; formed at Nakhon Sawan by confluence of the combined Ping-Wang and Nan-Yom rivers rising in mts. of N Thailand, flows 140 mi. S in tortuous course, past Chainat, Singburi, Angthong, Pathumthani, Nontburi, and Bangkok, to Gulf of Siam at Samutprakan. It is paralleled by several delta streams: the THA CHIN RIVER (Suphanburi), which branches off above Chainat, and flows to Gulf of Siam at Samutsakhon, and the Mae Nam Noi [=lesser river] (right) and the LOPBURI RIVER (left), which rejoin the main river in middle course. The Chao Phraya is linked with the Mae Klong R. (W) and the Bang Pakong R. (E) by extensive canal systems. Navigable in entire course for vessels of from 2–6 ft. draught (depending on season). Although lower course (below Bangkok) constitutes an excellent deep-water stream, lined with rice and saw mills and wharf and dock installations, a bar off mouth restricts ocean-going vessels exceeding 12.5-ft. draught to deep-water anchorage of Ko SICHANG. Also spelled Chao Phya.

Chaoping or **Chao-p'ing** (both: jou'pĭng'), town, ⊙ Chaoping co. (pop. 147,487), E Kwangsi prov., China, 55 mi. NW of Wuchow and on Kwei R.; cotton textiles; grain; coal. Iron deposits near by.

Chaosu, China: see KALMAK KURE.

Chaotung. 1 (jou'dōōng') Town, ⊙ Chaotung co. (pop. 229,638), S Heilungkiang prov., Manchuria, 50 mi. WNW of Harbin, near Sungkiang line; kaoliang, wheat, soybeans, corn, millet. Called Changwucheng until 1913. **2** or **Chao-t'ung** (jou'toong'), town, ⊙ Chaotung co. (pop. 198,951), NE Yunnan prov., China, 170 mi. NNE of Kunming, near the Yangtze; alt. 6,398 ft.; coal mines; chemical industry. Rice, buckwheat, millet, tobacco, fruit.

Chaouat (chäwät)'), village, Tunis dist., N Tunisia, on Tunis-Bizerte RR and 14 mi. WNW of Tunis; cereal- and winegrowing.

Chao Uda, Manchuria: see JOODA.

Chaource (shäōōrs'), village (pop. 635), Aube dept., NE central France, 17 mi. S of Troyes; cider distilling, sawmilling. Its Gothic and Renaissance church badly damaged in Second World War.

Chaoyang or **Ch'ao-yang** (chou'yäng'). **1** Town, ⊙ Chaoyang co. (pop. 283,303), E Jehol prov., Manchuria, 45 mi. NW of Chinchow and on railroad; trade center of E Jehol; wool, skins and hides, kaoliang, millet, beans. Brick and tile mfg. Lamasery; also remnants of Tang dynasty (618–906) pagodas, because of which the town was originally called Santsota [=three pagodas] until 1738. Formerly in Manchukuo's Chinchow prov. (1934–46). The Pehpiao coal field is 25 mi. NE. **2** Town (pop. 66,277), ⊙ Chaoyang co. (pop. 810,523), E Kwangtung prov., China, on coast, 8 mi. SW of Swatow; grass-cloth weaving; processing of local agr. products (rice, wheat, sugar cane, tobacco). Orange groves near by. Tin mining.

Chaoyangchwan, Manchuria: see SHULAN.

Chaoyi or **Chao-i** (both: jou'yē'), town (pop. 7,625), ⊙ Chaoyi co. (pop. 102,400), E Shensi prov., China, near Yellow R., 75 mi. ENE of Sian, and on Lo R. near its mouth on Wei R.; cotton, grain.

Chaoyüan (jou'yüän'). **1** Town, Heilungkiang prov., Manchuria: see CHAOCHOW. **2** Town, ⊙ Chaoyüan co. (pop. 372,631), E Shantung prov., China, 25 mi. S of Lungkow; gold-mining center; food processing (noodles, vegetable oil); kaoliang, peanuts, grain grown in area.

Chapa (shäpä'), village, Laokay prov., N Vietnam, hill station (12 mi. SSW) of Laokay, on slopes of the Fansipan; alt. c.5,000 ft.; hydroelectric station on small tributary of Red R.

Chapab (chäpäb'), town (pop. 1,568), Yucatan, SE Mexico, 10 mi. NE of Ticul; henequen, sugar, fruit.
Chapacura (chäpäkōō'rä), village, Pando dept., NW Bolivia, on Tahuamanu R. and 40 mi. SW of Cobija; rubber.
Chapada Diamantina (shäpä'dů dē"ůmäntē'nů), tableland, central Bahia, Brazil, extends c.75 mi. N from Lençóis; rises to c.3,000 ft. Leading black-diamond-mining region.
Chapa de Mota (chäpä dā mō'tä), town (pop. 1,472), Mexico state, central Mexico, 30 mi. NW of Mexico city; grain, maguey, stock.
Chapadinha (shäpädē'nyů), city (pop. 964), NE Maranhão, Brazil, 110 mi. SE of São Luís; cotton, rice, manioc flour.
Chapadmalal (chäpädh-mäläl'), town (pop. estimate 500), SE Buenos Aires prov., Argentina, 11 mi. W of Mar del Plata; stock-raising center; quartzite and sand quarries. Tourist resort.
Chapai Nawabganj, E Pakistan: see NAWABGANJ.
Chapala (chäpä'lä), town (pop. 4,217), Jalisco, central Mexico, on N shore of L. Chapala, 28 mi. SSE of Guadalajara; rail terminus; tourist resort; fishing. Hydroelectric plant.
Chapala, Lake (□ 417; 48 mi. long E-W, c.10 mi. wide), central Mexico, mostly in Jalisco but partly in Michoacán, on central plateau (alt. c.6,000 ft.), 30 mi. S and SE of Guadalajara. Largest lake in Mexico, it is fed by Lerma R., entering it at E shore and leaving as Santiago R. (or Río Grande de Santiago) at Ocotlán, at NE corner. Popular resort in beautiful scenery, with many isls. and good fishing grounds. The resort town Chapala is on NW shore.
Chapaleufú, Argentina: see INTENDENTE ALVEAR.
Chapanay (chäpänī'), town (pop. estimate 600), N Mendoza prov., Argentina, near Mendoza R. (irrigation area), on railroad and 25 mi. ESE of Mendoza; wine, fruit, alfalfa, livestock; apiculture; wine making, dried-fruit processing.
Chapantongo (chäpäntōng'gō), town (pop. 965), Hidalgo, central Mexico, 45 mi. WNW of Pachuca; alt. 7,037 ft.; corn, beans, maguey, livestock.
Chaparé, province, Bolivia: see SACABA.
Chaparé River (chäpärā'), Cochabamba dept., central Bolivia, rises in Cordillera de Cochabamba NE of Cochabamba, flows 180 mi. NE, mostly through tropical lowlands, past Todos Santos and San Antonio, joining Ichilo R. 80 mi. S of Trinidad to form MAMORÉ RIVER. Navigable for 90 mi. above mouth.
Chaparra (chäpä'rä), town (pop. 4,479), Oriente prov., E Cuba, near Chaparra Bay (N), 23 mi. NW of Holguín; has Cuba's largest sugar central.
Chaparral (chäpäräl'), town (pop. 5,506), Tolima dept., W central Colombia, on E slopes of Cordillera Central, 50 mi. SSW of Ibagué; coffeegrowing center; corn, rice, sugar cane, bananas, yucca, cacao; flour milling. Iron and copper mines, and petroleum deposits near by. Numerous curious grottoes are in vicinity.
Chaparro, El, Venezuela: see EL CHAPARRO.
Chaparrón or San Manuel Chaparrón (sän mänwěl' chäpärōn'), town (1950 pop. 741), Jalapa dept., E central Guatemala, in highlands, 17 mi. SE of Jalapa; corn, beans, livestock.
Chapayeva, Imeni (ē'mĭnyē chŏŏpī'ŭvä), town (1948 pop. over 500), S Mary oblast, Turkmen SSR, 60–70 mi. SE of Mary, on Kushka RR and Murgab R.; irrigated agr.
Chapayevo (chŏŏpī'ŭvŭ), village (1939 pop. over 500), central West Kazakhstan oblast, Kazakh SSR, on Ural R. and 70 mi. S of Uralsk, in agr. area (wheat, millet, mustard, cattle). Until 1940, Lbishchensk. Named for Soviet civil war leader who died here.
Chapayevsk (-ŭfsk). **1** City, Guryev oblast, Kazakh SSR: see GURYEV. **2** City (1926 pop. 13,530; 1939 pop. 57,995), central Kuibyshev oblast, Russian SFSR, on Chapayevka R. (left tributary of the Volga) and 25 mi. SW of Kuibyshev, on railroad; chemical mfg. (explosives, gunpowder, silicates). Originally called Ivashchenkovo; known 1919–27 as Trotsk.
Chapayevski or Chapayevskiy (-ŭfskē), town (1941 pop. over 500), N Chuvash Autonomous SSR, Russian SFSR, 4 mi. from (under jurisdiction of) Cheboksary; sawmilling.
Chapeau (shäpō'), village (pop. 471), SW Que., on Allumette Isl., in Ottawa R. and 7 mi. NNE of Pembroke; dairying; cattle, pigs.
Chapecó (shäpĭkô'), city (pop. 801), W Santa Catarina, Brazil, near Uruguay R., 70 mi. W of Joaçaba; maté, lumber, livestock. Also spelled Xapecó. Old name, Passo Bormann. In Iguaçu territory, 1943–46.
Chapecó River, W Santa Catarina, Brazil, flows c.170 mi. WSW to the Uruguay (right bank) 25 mi. W of Chapecó city. Also spelled Xapecó.
Chapei (jä'bā'), N residential suburb of Shanghai, China, N of former International Settlement.
Chapel-en-le-Frith (-ěn-lů-frĭth'), town and parish (pop. 5,662), NW Derby, England, 5 mi. N of Buxton; cotton milling, mfg. of automobile parts (clutches, brake linings). Has church dating from 14th cent. and remains of chapel founded 1226. Parish includes town of Dove Holes, 3 mi. NNE of Buxton, with chemical works, limestone and chalk quarries.
Chapel Hill. 1 University town (pop. 9,177), Orange co., N central N.C., 9 mi. SW of Durham. Seat of University of N.C. (chartered 1789; opened 1795). Founded 1792. **2** Town (pop. 603), Marshall co., central Tenn., 13 mi. NNE of Lewisburg, in farm region. Nathan Bedford Forrest b. here. **3** Village (pop. c.800), Washington co., S central Texas, 9 mi. E of Brenham, near the Brazos; trade point in agr. area.
Chapel Island (7 mi. long, 4 mi. wide), E N.F., in Notre Dame Bay, 14 mi. S of Twillingate; 49°27'N 54°45'W.
Chapelizod, Gaelic *Séipéal Isóilde*, W suburb of Dublin, Co. Dublin, Ireland, on the Liffey. Name reputedly derives from Isolde or Iseult, daughter of Irish king Aengus.
Chapelle, La (lä shäpěl'), agr. town (1950 census pop. 473), Artibonite dept., central Haiti, 20 mi. SE of Saint-Marc, on fertile plain (coffee, fruit).
Chapelle-d'Angillon, La (–däzhĭyō'), village (pop. 631), Cher dept., central France, on Petite Sauldre R. and 19 mi. N of Bourges; woodworking, poultry.
Chapelle-de-Guinchay, La (–dů-gēshě'), village (pop. 227), Saône-et-Loire dept., E central France, near Saône R., 7 mi. SSW of Mâcon; Burgundy wines.
Chapelle-en-Valgodemar, La, France: see VALGODEMAR.
Chapelle-en-Vercors, La (–ä-věrkôr'), village (pop. 247), Drôme dept., SE France, in Vercors massif (Dauphiné Pre-Alps), 15 mi. N of Die; alt. 3,120 ft. Winter sports. Grands Goulets gorge is 3 mi. N.
Chapelle-la-Reine, La (–lä-rěn'), agr. village (pop. 661), Seine-et-Marne dept., N central France, 16 mi. SSW of Melun. Has 15th-16th-cent. church.
Chapelle-lez-Herlaimont, (–lä-ěrlāmō'), town (pop. 7,858), Hainaut prov., S central Belgium, 9 mi. WNW of Charleroi; coal mining.
Chapelle-Saint-Mesmin, La (–sē-māmē'), W suburban commune (pop. 2,162) of Orléans, Loiret dept., N central France, on right bank of the Loire; glassworks.
Chapelle-sur-Erdre, La (–sür-âr'drů), village (pop. 495), Loire-Inférieure dept., W France, on Erdre R. and 6 mi. N of Nantes; truck gardens. Has 15th-cent. castle with belfry.
Chapel of Garioch, agr. village and parish (pop. 1,413), central Aberdeen, Scotland, on Urie R. and 3 mi. NW of Inverurie. Near by is battlefield of HARLAW.
Chapetona, Paso de la, Argentina-Chile: see AZUFRE NORTE, PASO DEL.
Chapimarca (chäpēmär'kä), town (pop. 824), Apurímac dept., S central Peru, in the Andes, 24 mi. SW of Abancay; potatoes, grain, alfalfa, stock.
Chapin (chā'pĭn). **1** Village (pop. 489), Morgan co., W central Ill., 10 mi. WNW of Jacksonville, in agr. area. **2** Village (pop. c.275), Franklin co., N central Iowa, 23 mi. S of Mason City; metal products. **3** Town (pop. 327), Lexington co., central S.C., 20 mi. WNW of Columbia; lumber.
Chapin, Mount, Colo.: see MUMMY RANGE.
Chapingo (chäpēng'gō), village (pop. 339), Mexico state, central Mexico, 2 mi. S of Texcoco. Seat of natl. agr. col.; murals by Diego Rivera adorn main bldg. and chapel.
Chapleau (shă'plō), village (pop. estimate 1,500), central Ont., 100 mi. NNE of Sault Ste. Marie; railroad division point; market for surrounding gold-mining region; lumber mills.
Chapleton (chă'pŭltŭn), town (pop. 1,130), Clarendon parish, central Jamaica, on affluent of Minho R., on railroad and 8 mi. NNW of May Pen; trades in bananas.
Chaplin, village (pop. 157), S Sask., on Chaplin L. (□ 66), 50 mi. W of Moose Jaw; sodium-sulphate production.
Chaplin, farming town (pop. 712), Windham co., E central Conn., on Natchaug R. and 7 mi. NNE of Willimantic. Has 19th-cent. buildings, state park, state forest.
Chaplin, Cape (chă'plyĭn), SE extremity of Chukchi Peninsula, NE Siberian Russian SFSR, in Bering Sea; 64°24'N 172°13'W. Site of village, Chaplino; govt. arctic station; airfield.
Chaplinka (chä'plyĭn-kŭ), village (1926 pop. 5,416), S Kherson oblast, Ukrainian SSR, 45 mi. SE of Kherson; metalworks.
Chaplino (chä'plyĭnŭ), town (1948 pop. over 10,000), E Dnepropetrovsk oblast, Ukrainian SSR, 60 mi. ESE of Dnepropetrovsk; rail center.
Chaplygin (chŏŏplĭ'gĭn), city (1939 pop. over 10,000), S Ryazan oblast, Russian SFSR, 70 mi. S of Ryazan; rail junction; metalworking center; textile milling. Founded 1702 as fortress against nomads; chartered 1745. Countryseat of A. D. Menshikov. Place of exile (after 1741) of Anna Leopoldovna and Ivan VI. Called Ranenburg until 1948; renamed for Soviet aeronautic scientist b. here.
Chaplyina, Yugoslavia: see CAPLJINA.
Chapman. 1 Town (pop. 943), Butler co., S Ala., 55 mi. SSW of Montgomery; lumber, lumber products. **2** City (pop. 990), Dickinson co., E central Kansas, on Smoky Hill R. and 11 mi. WSW of Junction City; trade center for livestock, grain, and dairy region; flour. **3** Town (pop. 381), Aroostook co., NE Maine, 8 mi. WSW of Presque Isle, in agr. area. **4** Village (pop. 274), Merrick co., SE central Nebr., 10 mi. NE of Grand Island and on Platte R. **5** Borough (pop. 285), Northampton co., E Pa., 10 mi. N of Bethlehem; slate quarries.
Chapman, Mount (10,150 ft.), SE B.C., in Selkirk Mts., near W side of Hamber Provincial Park, 65 mi. N of Revelstoke; 51°56'N 118°19'W.
Chapman, Mount, Tenn. and N.C.: see GREAT SMOKY MOUNTAINS NATIONAL PARK.
Chapman Camp, village (pop. 513), SE B.C., on St. Mary R. and 2 mi. SE of Kimberley; silver, lead, zinc mining.
Chapmanville, town (pop. 1,349), Logan co., SW W.Va., on Guyandot R. and 9 mi. N of Logan.
Chapo, Lake (chä'pō) (□ 40), Llanquihue prov., S central Chile, at S foot of Calbuco Volcano, 18 mi. E of Puerto Montt; c.12 mi. long.
Chapopotla (chäpōpōt'lä), town (pop. 1,884), Veracruz, SE Mexico, on Isthmus of Tehuantepec, 11 mi. ENE of Minatitlán; tropical fruit, livestock. Petroleum drilling. Ixhuatlán until 1938.
Chaporá (shäpōrä'), village, N Goa dist., Portuguese India, on Arabian Sea, at mouth of short Chaporá R., 10 mi. NNW of Pangim; local trade in fish, salt, timber, coconuts.
Chapovichi (chä'pŭvēchē), town (1926 pop. 9,369), E Zhitomir oblast, Ukrainian SSR, 16 mi. ESE of Korosten; furniture mfg. Also spelled Chepovichi.
Chappaqua (chă'pŭkwô), residential village (1940 pop. 2,286), Westchester co., SE N.Y., in New York city suburban area, 5 mi. E of Ossining; mfg. of paper products; nurseries.
Chappaquiddick Island (chăpŭkwĭ'dĭk) (c.5 mi. long), part of EDGARTOWN, Dukes co., SE Mass., off E Martha's Vineyard, from which a narrow channel separates it. Resort area. Cape Poge (pōg), at N tip, extends N into Nantucket Sound; has lighthouse (41°25'N 70°27'W).
Chappell (chă'pŭl), village (pop. 1,297), ⊙ Deuel co., W Nebr., 80 mi. SE of Scotts Bluff and on Lodgepole Creek, in Great Plains wheat-raising area; livestock, grain, dairy produce, sugar beets. Has memorial art gall. Platted 1884.
Chappells (chă'pŭlz), town (pop. 199), Newberry co., W central S.C., on Saluda R. and 18 mi. E of Greenwood. L. Greenwood is just W.
Chapra (chä'prŭ), city (pop. 55,142), ⊙ Saran dist., NW Bihar, India, on Gogra R. just above its mouth and 25 mi. WNW of Patna; rail and road junction; rice, wheat, barley, corn, sugar cane; saltpeter and linseed-oil processing. Sivaite temple.
Chaptico (chăp'tĭkō), village, St. Marys co., S Md., 10 mi. NW of Leonardtown. Christ Church, built c.1736 as one of original parish churches of Md., was designed by Christopher Wren.
Chapu or Cha-p'u (jä'pōō'), town, NE Chekiang prov., China, 55 mi. NE of Hangchow, on N shore of Hangchow Bay; considered a potential port for Hangchow.
Chapulco (chäpōōl'kō), town (pop. 1,172), Puebla, central Mexico, 11 mi. N of Tehuacán; corn, sugar, fruit, livestock.
Chapulhuacán (chäpōōlwäkän'), town (pop. 1,207), Hidalgo, central Mexico, in foothills of Sierra Madre Oriental, on Inter-American Highway, and 21 mi. NE of Jacala; corn, rice, sugar, tobacco, fruit. Picturesque Indian settlement.
Chapultenango (chäpōōltänäng'gō), town (pop. 941), Chiapas, S Mexico, in N spur of Sierra Madre, 40 mi. N of Tuxtla; orange growing.
Chapultepec (chäpōōl'täpěk'). **1** Officially San Miguel Chapultepec, town (pop. 1,142), Mexico state, central Mexico, 10 mi. SE of Toluca; cereals, livestock. **2** Town (pop. 658), Morelos, central Mexico, 2 mi. E of Cuernavaca; resort.
Chapultepec (chŭpōōl'tŭpěk, Sp. chäpōōl'täpěk'), rocky height just SW of Mexico city, central Mexico. One of world's largest and most beautiful parks, with splendid lakes and avenues, linked with the city by the Paseo de la Reforma. Developed as a playground for the last Aztec emperors, the hill became site (late 18th cent.) of a castle built as a summer house for Sp. viceroys and later used as a fortress and military acad. Chapultepec was a favorite resort of Maximilian, who beautified the grounds. As the last Mexican stronghold in the Mexican War, the castle fell to American forces after heavy fighting (Sept. 12–13, 1847), in which the defenders fought valiantly. At near-by MOLINO DEL REY (W) another battle of the Mexican War was fought (Sept. 8, 1847). After being occupied by Mexican presidents, the castle became (1937) a natl. mus., with historical, ethnographic, and other exhibits. Chapultepec Heights, a new residential colony, adjoins NW; it has a magnificent view over city and valley. Chapultepec was the 1st point in valley of Mexico to be occupied by Aztecs, who constructed several aqueducts to supply their capital, Tenochtitlán, with water. Here met the Inter-American conference (Feb. 21–March 8, 1945) of American republics, who signed the Act of Chapultepec, which declared "reciprocal assistance and American solidarity" and pledged to strengthen the Inter-American system. Argentina, who was not present, joined on April 4, 1945.
Chapurniki, Russian SFSR: see BOLSHIYE CHAPURNIKI.
Chaqui (chä'kē), town (pop. 7,800), Potosí dept., S central Bolivia, 15 mi. E of Potosí, and on Potosí-Sucre RR; barley.

Chara (chŭrä'), village, N Chita oblast, Russian SFSR, 225 mi. NNW of Mogocha and on Chara R. (left affluent of Olekma R.); lumbering.
Charadai (chärädī'), village (pop. estimate 600), S Chaco natl. territory, Argentina, 55 mi. WSW of Resistencia; rail junction; lumbering, livestock.
Charagua (chärä'gwä), town (pop. c.3,200), Santa Cruz dept., SE Bolivia, in Serranía de Charagua, on W edge of the Chaco, 33 mi. ESE of Lagunillas; corn, sugar cane, rice, fruit; cattle raising.
Charagua, Serranía de (sĕrănē'ä dä), range in SE Bolivia, on W edge of the Chaco, bet. Cordillera de Cochabamba (N) and Serranía de Aguaragüe (S); extends from Río Grande 50 mi. S to Parapetí R.; rises to 2,800 ft. One of major petroleum regions of Bolivia, with fields of Camiri and Saipurú and deposits at Guariri.
Charalá (chärälä'), town (pop. 2,479), Santander dept., N central Colombia, in W valley of Cordillera Oriental, 19 mi. S of San Gil; alt. 4,505 ft. Sugar cane, coffee, cotton, corn, vegetables, fruit, cattle.
Charallave (chäräyä'vä), town (pop. 1,733), Miranda state, N Venezuela, 19 mi. S of Caracas; cacao, coffee, sugar.
Charambirá Point (chärämbērä'), headland on Pacific coast of Chocó dept., W Colombia, on isl. in San Juan R. delta; 4°15'N 77°32'W; N point of Chocó Bay. Sometimes Chirambirá.
Charaña (chärä'nyä), village (pop. c.1,300), La Paz dept., W Bolivia, in the Altiplano, 85 mi. NE of Arica, on Arica–La Paz RR; alt. 13,251 ft. Customs station on Chilean border; alpaca wool trade.
Charanpur (chŭrŭn'po͝or), village, Burdwan dist., W West Bengal, India, 5 mi. NE of Asansol; coal mining; electrical-engineering factory.
Charapan (chärä'pän), town (pop. 1,715), Michoacán, central Mexico, 23 mi. S of Zamora; cereals, fruit, livestock.
Charapaya (chäräpī'ä), town (pop. c.4,700), Cochabamba dept., central Bolivia, on E slopes of Eastern Cordillera of the Andes, 20 mi. S of Independencia; corn, wheat, potatoes.
Charar Sharif, Kashmir: see TSRAR SHARIF.
Charasani, Bolivia: see VILLA PÉREZ.
Charata (chärä'tä), town (1947 pop. 3,419), SW Chaco natl. territory, Argentina, on railroad and 50 mi. SW of Presidencia Roque Sáenz Peña; cotton-ginning center; soap mfg.; farming (corn, cotton, sunflowers, spurge, peanuts), lumbering.
Charavines or **Charavines-les-Bains** (shärävēn'-lä-bē'), village (pop. 270), Isère dept., SE France, at S end of Paladru L., 10 mi. SSE of La Tour-du-Pin; summer resort in the Pre-Alps; paper milling, edge-tool mfg.
Charazani, Bolivia: see VILLA PÉREZ.
Charbagh, India: see LUCKNOW, city.
Charbonnières-les-Bains (shärbônyâr'-lä-bē'), outer NW suburb (pop. 671) of Lyons, Rhône dept., E central France; mineral springs.
Charbonnier-les-Mines (shärbônyā'-lā-mēn'), village (pop. 865), Puy-de-Dôme dept., central France, 9 mi. S of Issoire; coal mining.
Charborjak, Afghanistan: see CHAHAR BURJAK.
Charcas (chär'käs), Spanish colonial *audiencia* and presidency in South America, known also as Upper Peru and Chuquisaca. Roughly corresponded to modern Bolivia, but included parts of present Argentina, Chile, Peru, and Paraguay, a territorial jurisdiction leading to disputes and wars after independence had been won. Established 1559, it was attached to viceroyalty of Peru until joined (1776) to newly created viceroyalty of La Plata.
Charcas, province, Bolivia: see SAN PEDRO, Potosí dept.
Charcas, city, Bolivia: see SUCRE.
Charcas (chär'käs). **1** Village (pop. 1,321), Guanajuato, central Mexico, 20 mi. SE of San Luis de la Paz; grain, sugar, fruit, livestock. **2** City (pop. 6,081), San Luis Potosí, N central Mexico, on interior plateau, 70 mi. N of San Luis Potosí; alt. 6,748 ft.; mercury, lead, copper, silver, zinc mining.
Charchan, China: see CHERCHEN.
Charchemish, anc. city: see CARCHEMISH.
Charco, El, Argentina: see EL CHARCO.
Charco Azul Bay (chär'kō äso͞ol'), W inlet of Chiriquí Gulf of the Pacific, W Panama, E of Burica Peninsula; 30 mi. wide, 15 mi. long. Its port is Puerto Armuelles.
Charco Redondo, Mexico: see MELCHOR OCAMPO, Nuevo León.
Charcot Bay (shärkō'), inlet in Antarctica, on N coast of Palmer Peninsula bet. Danco Coast and Louis Philippe Peninsula; 63°50'S 59°30'W. Discovered 1903 by Otto Nordenskjöld.
Charcot Island (65 naut. mi. in diameter), Antarctica, in the South Pacific off W coast of Palmer Peninsula, NW of Alexander I Isl.; 70°S 75°W. Discovered 1910 by Dr. Jean B. Charcot, Fr. explorer, it was proved to be an isl. in 1929 by Sir Hubert Wilkins.
Chard, municipal borough (1931 pop. 4,054; 1951 census 5,218), S Somerset, England, 12 mi. SSE of Taunton; agr. market in dairying region; mfg. (agr. equipment, lace, brushes). Has 15th-cent. church and 17th-cent. grammar school.
Chardara (chŭrdŭrä'), village, S South Kazakhstan oblast, Kazakh SSR, at edge of Kyzyl-Kum (desert), on the Syr Darya and 70 mi. W of Tashkent; cotton, grain, livestock; metalworks.
Chardeh, Afghanistan: see CHAHARDEH.
Chardon (shär'dŭn), village (pop. 2,478), ⊙ Geauga co., NE Ohio, 25 mi. ENE of Cleveland; maple syrup and sugar; grain, dairy products, livestock, poultry, fruit. Mfg.: rubber products, lumber, metal products. Laid out c.1808.
Chardonnières (shärdônyâr'), village (1950 census pop. 1,431), Sud dept., SW Haiti, on SW coast of Tiburon Peninsula, 28 mi. W of Les Cayes; banana growing.
Charduar (chŭrdwär'), village, ⊙ Balipara frontier tract, N Assam, India, in Brahmaputra valley, 16 mi. N of Tezpur; rice, rape and mustard, tea.
Chardzhou (chŭrjô'o͞o), oblast (□ 35,900; 1946 pop. estimate 300,000), E Turkmen SSR; ⊙ Chardzhou. Drained by the Amu Darya flowing through Kara-Kum desert; intensive cotton and some wheat cultivation in its valley; sericulture. Cotton and silk processing at Chardzhou, Kerki, and Kerkichi. Sulphur mining and chemical industry (Gaurdak), coal (Kugitang). Goat and karakul-sheep raising on desert. Crossed by Trans-Caspian RR (N), Kagan-Stalinabad RR (S). Pop.: Turkmen, Uzbeks, Russians. Formed 1939.
Chardzhou, second largest city (1939 pop. 54,739) of Turkmen SSR, ⊙ Chardzhou oblast, major port on the Amu Darya, at crossing of Trans-Caspian RR, and 290 mi. ENE of Ashkhabad; 39°5'N 63°41'E. Transportation and industrial center; river-rail transshipment point; junction of railroad to Urgench and Kungrad. Cotton ginning and milling, silk spinning, karakul processing; mfg. (absorbent cotton, conveyor belts, plush, oxygen). Dist. produces noted cantaloupes. Shipyards and port installations at Farab-Pristan, across the river. Founded by Russians near present KAGANOVICHESK; called Chardzhui or Novy Chardzhui [new Chardzhui] until 1937, except for 1924–27, when it was known as Leninsk-Turkmenski.
Charemai, Mount, or **Mount Tjareme** (both: chärämä') (10,098 ft.), W Java, Indonesia, 16 mi. SW of Cheribon. Also called Peak of Cheribon.
Charente (shärãt'), department (□ 2,306; pop. 311,137), formed of Angoumois and part of Saintonge provinces, W France; ⊙ Angoulême. Level calcareous region with outliers of Massif Central in Confolens area (NE); drained by the Charente (center), Vienne (NE), and Dronne (S). Chief crops: wheat, oats, barley, and corn. Wine grown in limestone dist. surrounding Cognac is distilled into famous brandy. Cattle raising chiefly near Confolens and S of Barbezieux. Principal towns: Angoulême (paper mills), Cognac, and Jarnac (brandy distilling).
Charente-Maritime (–märētēm'), department (□ 2,792; pop. 416,187), W France, formed of Saintonge, Aunis, and part of old Poitou provinces; ⊙ La Rochelle. Bounded by Bay of Biscay (W) and the Girone (SW); includes several offshore isls. (Oléron, Ré, Aix, Madame). Level region drained by the Charente (center), the Seudre (SW), and the Sèvre Niortaise (N). Chiefly agr. (cereals, vegetables, forage crops, potatoes), dept. grows wine distilled into brandy. Cattle raising in coastal area; important dairy industry (especially casein mfg.). Saltworks (in islands) oyster and mussel-beds (Marennes area). Chief towns: La Rochelle, Rochefort, Saintes, Saint-Jean-d'Angély, and popular bathing resort of Royan. Until 1941, dept. named Charente-Inférieure.
Charente River, in Charente, Vienne, and Charente-Maritime depts., W France, rises 4 mi. SW of Rochechouart, flows 220 mi. generally W, past Civray, Angoulême, Cognac, Saintes, and Rochefort, into the Bay of Biscay opposite Île d' Oléron. Receives the Tardoire, Touvre, Seugne (left), and Boutonne (right). An important coastal stream, navigable below Angoulême, transports brandy from Cognac area to La Rochelle. Paper mills along its banks near Angoulême.
Charenton-du-Cher (shärãtō'-dü-shâr'), village pop. 817), Cher dept., central France, on Berry Canal and 7 mi. E of Saint-Amand-Montrond; cattle raising, sawmilling.
Charenton-le-Pont (–lü-pō'), town (pop. 20,891), Seine dept., N central France, just SE of Paris, 3 mi. from Notre Dame Cathedral, on right bank of Seine R. at influx of the Marne, and at SW edge of Bois de Vincennes; has freight yards, large storage depots and distilleries; fruit preserving and canning. The famous asylum of Charenton is at neighboring Saint-Maurice.
Chargoding La, Tibet: see DING LA.
Chargoggaggoggmanchaugagoggchaubunagungamaug, Lake, Mass.: see CHAUBUNAGUNGAMAUG, LAKE.
Chari, river, Fr. Equatorial Africa: see SHARI RIVER.
Chari-Baguirmi, Fr. Equatorial Africa: see BAGUIRMI, state.
Charikar (chä'rĭkär), town (pop. 20,000), Kabul prov., E Afghanistan, 35 mi. N of Kabul; alt. 5,260 ft.; administrative hq. of Samt-i-Shimali dist., in cotton- and winegrowing area; foundry (based on Ghorband iron ore); mfg. of metal products. Graphite found near by. Scene of massacre (1841) of British garrison in 1st Afghan war.
Charikot (chŭr'ĭkōt), town, E central Nepal, 45 mi. E of Katmandu; corn, barley, millet, buckwheat. Nepalese military post.
Charing (chă'rĭng, châ'rĭng), town and parish (pop. 1,442), central Kent, England, 5 mi. NW of Ashford; agr. market, with flour mills. There are few remains of 14th-cent. palace of archbishops of Canterbury, presented to Henry VIII by Cranmer. In Middle Ages it was important point on pilgrimage route to Canterbury. Town's records date from 757.
Charing Cross, district of Westminster metropolitan borough, in center of London, England, on N bank of the Thames, adjoining Trafalgar Square. Charing Cross station is an important London rail terminal; opposite station is Charing Cross Hosp. One of the Eleanor Crosses was erected here. Road distances from London are conventionally measured from Charing Cross.
Charité, La, or **La Charité-sur-Loire** (lä shärētā'-sür-lwär'), town (pop. 4,328), Nièvre dept., central France, on right bank of Loire R. and 15 mi. NNW of Nevers; mfg. (tools, furs, hosiery, canvas, cement). Lumber and coal trade. Has partly Romanesque abbatial church of Sainte-Croix. Built around 8th-cent. Benedictine abbey, it was vainly besieged by Joan of Arc, and suffered severely during Wars of Religion.
Chariton (shă'rĭtŭn, shâ–), county (□ 759; pop. 14,944), N central Mo.; ⊙ Keytesville. Bounded by Missouri R. (S) and Grand R. (W); drained by Chariton R. Corn, wheat, oats, livestock; bituminous coal. Formed 1820.
Chariton, city (pop. 5,320), ⊙ Lucas co., S Iowa, on Chariton R. and c.45 mi. SSE of Des Moines; agr. trade and coal-mining center; mfg. of work clothes, confectionery, chemicals, brooms; railroad shops. State park near by. Founded by Mormons in 1849; inc. in 1857.
Chariton River, N Mo. and S Iowa, rises in S central Iowa, flows c.280 mi. SE and S to Missouri R. above Glasgow; partly canalized in Missouri. Shortly above mouth, receives East Chariton R. (or East Fork), rising S of Kirksville, Mo., and flowing c.90 mi. S and SW.
Charity, village (pop. 838), Essequibo co., N Br. Guiana, on Pomeroon R., near the Atlantic, and 50 mi. NW of Georgetown, in tropical forest region; coconut plantations.
Charkhari (chŭrkä'rē), former princely state (□ 785; pop. 123,594) of Central India agency; ⊙ was Charkhari. In 1948, merged with Vindhya Pradesh; in 1950, large detached area inc. into Hamirpur dist. of Uttar Pradesh.
Charkhari, town (pop. 12,638), Hamirpur dist., S Uttar Pradesh, India, 45 mi. SSW of Hamirpur; trades in grain, cotton, oilseeds, ghee, cloth fabrics; hand-loom weaving. Was ⊙ former Central India state of Charkhari. Sometimes called Maharajnagar.
Charkhin (chŭr-khēn'), village (1939 pop. over 500), central Samarkand oblast, Russian SFSR, in Samarkand oasis, c.15 mi. W of Samarkand; cotton, fruit.
Charkhlik or **Charkhliq** (chärkhlĭk'), Chinese *Erh-ch'iang* (ŭr'chyäng') or *Ch'o-ch'iang* (chŭ'chyäng'), town, ⊙ Charkhlik co. (pop. 5,811), SE Sinkiang prov., China, at N foot of the Altyn Tagh, 210 mi. SSW of Kurla (linked by highway); road junction at E edge of Taklamakan Desert. Gold and coal mines near by.
Charlack, town (pop. 1,528), St. Louis co., E Mo., just NW of St. Louis.
Charlannes, France: see BOURBOULE, LA.
Charlbury, town and parish (pop. 1,271), W central Oxfordshire, England, on Evenlode R. and 13 mi. NW of Oxford; agr. market. Has Norman church. Near by is site of 15th-cent. house of Robert Dudley, earl of Leicester, rebuilt in 17th cent.
Charlemagne (shärlŭmān', Fr. shärlümä'nyü), village (pop. 1,150), S Que., on L'Assomption R., just N of its mouth on the St. Lawrence, 16 mi. NNE of Montreal; tobacco growing, dairying.
Charlemont (chärl'mŭnt), agr. village (district pop. 1,220), NW Co. Armagh, Northern Ireland, on Blackwater R. and 6 mi. N of Armagh; flax, potatoes, oats; cattle. Has fort built 1602.
Charlemont (chär'lŭmŏnt), agr. town (pop. 855), Franklin co., NW Mass., in hilly country, on Deerfield R. and 13 mi. ESE of North Adams; dairying; woodworking.
Charleroi (shärlŭrwä'), town (pop. 26,262), Hainaut prov., S central Belgium, on Sambre R., at S end of Charleroi-Brussels Canal, and 31 mi. S of Brussels. Rail junction; industrial center for coal-mining and steel-mfg. dist.; machine mfg., electrical equipment (motors, transformers, generators, cables), cement, window glass; brewing, flour milling. Has 17th-cent. Church of St-Christophe (built by order of Louis XIV), 17th-cent. chapel, archaeological mus., modern town hall (1936). A village called Charnoy during Middle Ages; renamed (1666) in honor of Charles II of Spain. Besieged many times in 17th cent.; was Napoleon's hq. for short time in 1818. First World War battle here (1914).
Charleroi (shärlŭroi', shär'lŭroi), borough (pop. 9,872), Washington co., SW Pa., 21 mi. S of Pittsburgh and on Monongahela R.; bituminous coal;

glass products, beverages, paper boxes, metal products; agr. Laid out 1890, inc. 1892.

Charleroi-Brussels Canal (shärlůrwä'), Belgium, runs 44 mi. N–S, bet. Sambre R. at Charleroi and S end of WILLEBROEK CANAL at Brussels; serves Seneffe, Tubize, Hal, and Anderlecht. Joined by Canal du Centre 1 mi. SW of Seneffe. Navigable for ships to 350 tons bet. Charleroi and Tubize, for ships to 600 tons bet. Tubize and Brussels.

Charles, county (□ 458; pop. 23,415), S Md.; ⊙ La Plata. On SW shore (Potomac R.; bridged here to Va.) of the Md. peninsula; co. is partly bounded SE by Wicomico R., E by Patuxent R., N by Mattawoman Creek. Tidewater agr. area (chiefly tobacco), with some lumbering, commercial fishing and oystering; tobacco markets at La Plata and Hughesville, naval ordnance installation at Indian Head. Swamps along streams (notably Wicomico R.) contain stands of timber and provide hunting. In region of earliest settlement in Md., co. contains many beautiful old buildings. Formed 1658.

Charles, city (pop. 20), Toombs co., E central Ga., just W of Vidalia.

Charles, Cape, E Va., S tip of Eastern Shore peninsula (Delmarva Peninsula), at N side of entrance to Chesapeake Bay, opposite Cape Henry; 37°7'N 75°57'W; Cape Charles lighthouse is on Smith Isl. (just SE). Terminus of Cape Charles ferries to Old Point Comfort and Norfolk at Cape Charles city, 10 mi. N.

Charles, Lake, La.: see CALCASIEU RIVER.

Charlesbourg (shärl'boorg), village (pop. 2,789), S Que., on short St. Charles R. and 5 mi. NNW of Quebec; fruitgrowing, dairying, poultry raising. One of the oldest parishes in Que., it was 1st settled 1659; originally called Bourg Royal.

Charles City, county (□ 184; pop. 4,676), E Va.; ⊙ Charles City. In tidewater region, on peninsula bet. James (S) and Chickahominy (N, E) rivers, which join at SE border. Agr., especially truck, poultry, dairy farming for Richmond market; also river fisheries, lumbering. Formed 1634 as one of 1st counties of Va.; has many beautiful old estates: "Westover," "Berkeley" (birthplace of Benjamin Harrison and William Henry Harrison), "Brandon," "Shirley."

Charles City. 1 City (pop. 10,309), ⊙ Floyd co., N Iowa, on Cedar R. and 28 mi. ESE of Mason City; rail junction; tractor-mfg. center; wood products, packed poultry, livestock remedies, pharmaceuticals, nurseries. Limestone quarries near by. Settled 1850, inc. 1869. **2** Hamlet, ⊙ Charles City co., E Va., 26 mi. SE of Richmond, near the James. Many fine old estates near by.

Charles Island (26 mi. long, 1–7 mi. wide), SE Franklin Dist., Northwest Territories, in Hudson Strait, off N Ungava Peninsula; 62°38'N 74°10'W.

Charles Island, Galápagos: see FLOREANA ISLAND.

Charles Mill Reservoir, Ohio: see MIFFLIN.

Charles Mix, county (□ 1,131; pop. 15,558), S S.Dak., on Nebr. line; ⊙ Lake Andes. Agr. area watered by L. Andes and bounded W by Missouri R. Grain, livestock, dairy products. Formed 1862.

Charles Mound, hill (1,241 ft.) in NW Ill., near Wis. line, 10 mi. NW of Galena; highest point in state.

Charles River. 1 In E Mass., rises in SW Norfolk co., follows winding course of c.60 mi. (N, E, NW, and E), past Cambridge and Boston, to W side of Boston Harbor. Navigable for c.10 mi. to Watertown; dam near its mouth has locks. Popular boating area; Harvard boat races held here. Lower ½ mi. has 35-ft. channel and wharves. **2** In R.I.: see PAWCATUCK RIVER.

Charleston, village, N Queensland, Australia, 185 mi. SW of Cairns; terminus of railroad from Cairns; cattle.

Charleston, county (□ 945; pop. 164,856), SE S.C.; ⊙ Charleston. Extends along Atlantic coast, bet. mouth of South Edisto R. (SW) and mouth of South Santee R. (NE). Intracoastal Waterway passes along coast among the SEA ISLANDS here (notably Edisto, Wadmalaw, Johns, James, Morris isls.). Has many popular coast resorts (notably Folly Beach and Isle of Palms); includes Castle Pinckney Natl. Monument and part of Francis Marion Natl. Forest. Was rich plantation region in ante-bellum days; now has chief mfg. and shipping center of the state (Charleston), some agr. (sweet potatoes, corn, vegetables), fisheries, hunting. Formed 1785.

Charleston. 1 Town (pop. 968), a ⊙ Franklin co., NW Ark., 21 mi. ESE of Fort Smith; ships livestock, poultry, eggs. Cotton ginning, coal mining; poultry hatchery. **2** City (pop. 9,164), ⊙ Coles co., E central Ill., near Embarrass R., 47 mi. ESE of Decatur; trade and rail center of rich agr., stock-raising, and dairying area; railroad shops; mfg. of shoes, brooms; lumber milling. Seat of Eastern Ill. State Col. Lincoln Log Cabin and Fox Ridge state parks are S. Inc. 1839. A Lincoln-Douglas debate was held here in 1858. **3** Agr. town (pop. 771), Penobscot co., central Maine, 22 mi. NW of Old Town. **4** City (pop. 2,629), a ⊙ Tallahatchie co., NW central Miss., 35 mi. N of Greenwood, in cotton, timber, and livestock area; clay, sand, fuller's-earth pits. Lumber milling, cotton ginning. **5** City (pop. 5,501), ⊙ Mississippi co., extreme SE Mo., near Mississippi R., 11 mi. SW of Cairo, Ill.; cotton center; shoes, staves, lumber products. State park near by. Laid out 1837. **6** A section of Richmond borough of New York city, SE N.Y., on SW Staten Isl.; makes tools, dies. **7** Seaport and 2d-largest city (pop. 70,174) of S.C., ⊙ Charleston co., 85 mi. NE of Savannah, Ga., on low narrow peninsula in Charleston Harbor, formed by confluence of Ashley R. and Cooper R. (bridged to mainland); 32°47'N 79°56'W. Chief mfg. and shipping center of S.C., one of chief ports of entry of the Southeast, and a year-round resort. Center of many transportation lines; through its excellent sheltered harbor is carried trade in timber, fruit, vegetables, seafood, fertilizers, cotton, sugar, and manufactured goods. Has foundries and machine shops, shipbuilding yards; mfg. (fertilizer, lumber products, pulp and paper, petroleum, chemicals, steel, ferroalloys, asbestos, paint, textiles, clothing, canned goods, cigars, food products), printing. At Charleston are: seaplane base and navy yard (just N, on Cooper R.); hq. of 6th naval dist. and southeast div. of U.S. Corps of Engineers; ordnance depot. Seat of Col. of Charleston (chartered 1785; oldest municipal col. in country), Medical Col. of S.C., The Citadel (state military col.). City dates from 1670, when English under William Sayle settled at Albemarle Point near by; in 1680 they moved to Oyster Point, where their capital, called Charles Town, had been laid out. It soon became center of wealth and culture in the South. In Revolutionary War it was defended successfully against Br. attacks in 1776 and 1779; taken and held (1780–82) by British. Inc. 1783 as city; was succeeded (1788) as ⊙ S.C. by Columbia, which had been so designated in 1786. Convention to proclaim state's secession from the Union met here 1860. First hostile act of Civil War, the firing on Fort Sumter, took place here April 12, 1861. Besieged by Union forces for more than 2 years (1863–65), city suffered partial destruction and fell in1865.Despite war damage, a violent earthquake on Aug. 31, 1886, and several destructive hurricanes and tornadoes, many of Charleston's fine old houses and places of historical interest survive. Among them are CASTLE PINCKNEY NATIONAL MONUMENT, old Fort SUMTER, the famous Battery (the water front), St. Michael's Episcopal church, Miles Brewton (or Pringle) house, and other old homes. In the vicinity are well-known Middleton, Magnolia, and Cypress gardens and remains of other rich ante-bellum plantations. Annual Azalea Festival is an important event. Resort beaches are near. Bordering or in Charleston Harbor are many isls., among them Sullivans Isl., site of old Fort MOULTRIE; James Isl., with U.S. quarantine station; Morris Isl., with lighthouse. **8** Village (1940 pop. 587), Bradley co., SE Tenn., on Hiwassee R. and 35 mi. NE of Chattanooga; hosiery finishing. **9** Town (pop. 201), Wasatch co., N central Utah, near Deer Creek Dam and Reservoir on Provo R. and 18 mi. NE of Provo; alt. 5,433 ft.; cattle, horses. **10** Town (pop. 764), Orleans co., N Vt., on Clyde R. and 8 mi. SE of Newport; lumber. **11** City (pop. 73,501), ⊙ W.Va. and Kanawha co., W W.Va., on Kanawha R. (bridges), at Elk R. mouth, and 45 mi. E of Huntington, in the Alleghenies; 38°22'N 81°38'W; alt. c.600 ft. State's 2d-largest city (after Huntington); industrial, shipping, and wholesale-distribution center for the Kanawha valley; huge chemical industries in city's outskirts and in many near-by "company towns" utilize region's resources of salt brine, bituminous coal, oil, natural gas; clay, sand, iron, and timber also in area. Oil refining; mfg. of ordnance, axes and other implements, glass, boilers, furniture, boats, paints, paper, rubber products; lumber milling. Seat of Morris Col. and Mason Col. of Music and Fine Arts. At Institute village, 8 mi. W, are W.Va. State Col., Booker T. Washington State Park, and large chemical plants. Among points of interest in Charleston is the new capitol (Ital. Renaissance; designed by Cass Gilbert; completed 1932). City grew around site of Fort Lee (1788); chartered 1794. Was (1870–75) ⊙ state; became permanent ⊙ in 1885. Daniel Boone lived here.

Charleston Harbor, land-locked inlet (□ 8) of the Atlantic at Charleston, S.C.; formed by junction of Ashley and Cooper rivers. Morris and Moultrie isls. shelter the entrance. U.S. navy yard is on Cooper R., 8 mi. above Charleston.

Charleston Peak, Nev.: see SPRING MOUNTAINS.

Charlestown, town (pop. 2,400), E New South Wales, Australia, 6 mi. SW of Newcastle; coal-mining center.

Charlestown, fishing port in St. Austell urban dist., S central Cornwall, England, on St. Austell Bay, 2 mi. E of St. Austell. Has 13th-cent. church.

Charlestown, Gaelic *Baile Chathail,* town (pop. 561), E Co. Mayo, Ireland, 22 mi. ENE of Castlebar; agr. market (cattle; potatoes).

Charlestown (chärlz'toun"), town (pop. 1,437), ⊙ Nevis isl., St. Kitts-Nevis presidency, Leeward Isls., B.W.I., port with open roadstead on isl.'s W coast, 13 mi. SE of Basseterre, St. Kitts; 17°9'N 62°37'W. Sugar milling. Known for hot springs. Alexander Hamilton b. at Charlestown; his ancestral estate is SE. Here Admiral Nelson was married.

Charlestown, town (pop. 2,642), NW Natal, near Transvaal border, U. of So. Afr., in Drakensberg range, on Buffalo R. and 4 mi. S of Volksrust; alt. 5,386 ft.; dairying, stock raising. Near by is Majuba Hill, scene of battle (1881) in Transvaal rebellion.

Charles Town, residential city (pop. 3,035), ⊙ Jefferson co., W.Va., in Eastern Panhandle, 13 mi. SSE of Martinsburg, in agr. and horse-breeding area; trade center for industrial RANSON (adjacent; N); flour and feed mills; dairy products; limestone and dolomite quarrying and processing; resort. Racing meets. John Brown was tried (1859) and hanged here. "Harewood," where Dolly Madison was married, is near by. Town laid out 1786.

Charlestown. 1 (chärlz'toun) Town (pop. 4,785), Clark co., SE Ind., near Ohio R., 15 mi. NE of New Albany; chemical mfg.; U.S. arsenal here. **2** (chärlz'toun) Town (pop. 551), Cecil co., NE Md., on Northeast R. and 26 mi. WSW of Wilmington, Del. Was 18th-cent. port and boat-building center. **3** (chärlz'toun) Part of BOSTON, Mass., just N of downtown Boston, and bet. Mystic and Charles rivers. Settled 1692, included in Boston 1874. Battle of Bunker (or Breed's) Hill was fought here, June 17, 1775; Bunker Hill Monument (221 ft. high) marks battlefield. Old frigate *Constitution* ("Old Ironsides") lies at anchor in U.S. navy yard here. **4** (chärlz'toun) Town (pop. 2,077), including Charlestown village (pop. 1,176), Sullivan co., SW N.H., on the Connecticut and 10 mi. S of Claremont. Settled 1740 as Township No. 4 and defended by Phineas Stevens against French and Indians, inc. 1753. **5** (chärlz'tůn) Town (pop. 1,598), Washington co., SW R.I., on Block Isl. Sound and 32 mi. SSW of Providence; resorts, agr., textile mfg.; dairy products, potatoes. Includes Kenyon and QUONOCHONTAUG villages and parts of CAROLINA and SHANNOCK villages. Charlestown Beach (summer colony) is on sandbar separated from mainland by Ninigret Pond (c.5 mi. long). Town has Indian burial ground, bird and game sanctuary. Inc. 1738. The 1938 hurricane took many lives here.

Charlestown of Aberlour, Scotland: see ABERLOUR.

Charlesville, village, Kasai prov., central Belgian Congo, on Kasai R. just below Wissmann-falls and 35 mi. W of Luebo; regional transshipment point (terminus of railroad from Makumbi), head of steam navigation on middle and lower Kasai. Has Protestant mission. Also known as Djoko Punda.

Charlesworth, town and parish (pop. 1,769), NW Derby, England, 2 mi. WSW of Glossop; coal.

Charleville (chärl'vĭl), town (pop. 3,460), S central Queensland, Australia, on Warrego R. and 425 mi. W of Brisbane; 26°24'S 146°15'E. Commercial center in livestock area.

Charleville (shärlvēl'), town (pop. 19,454), Ardennes dept., N France, on Meuse R. (canalized) and 50 mi. NE of Rheims, adjoining (N) MÉZIÈRES, its twin city; commercial and metalworking center; mfg. (hardware, stoves, motors, machine tools, brushes). Founded 1606 by Charles de Gonzague, duke of Rethel, and endowed with privileges which attracted economic activities to it from adjacent Mézières. Ger. army hq. during First World War. Rimbaud b. here.

Charleville, Ireland: see RÁTH LUIRC.

Charlevoix (shär'lůvoi), county (□ 414; pop. 13,475), NW Mich.; ⊙ Charlevoix. Bounded NW by L. Michigan; drained by short Boyne and Jordan rivers. Includes BEAVER ISLANDS group. Dairying, agr. (livestock, potatoes, cherries, apples, grain, corn, seed). Some mfg. at Charlevoix, Boyne City, and East Jordan. Flour, lumber mills; fisheries. Resorts. Charlevoix and Walloon lakes (fishing, boating, winter sports) near by. Organized 1869.

Charlevoix, city (pop. 2,695), ⊙ Charlevoix co., NW Mich., bet. L. Charlevoix and L. Michigan, 15 mi. SW of Petoskey, in agr. area (potatoes, grain, corn, seed). Resort. Flour, lumber mills; fisheries. Has Coast Guard station and U.S. fish hatchery. Ferry service to Beaver Isl. from here. Settled 1852; inc. as village 1879, as city 1905.

Charlevoix, Lake, NW Mich., extends c.14 mi. SE from Charlevoix city, which is on its short outlet to L. Michigan, to Boyne City; 2 mi. wide. Resort; fishing. Receives short Boyne R. in SE, short Jordan R. in narrow South Arm (c.8 mi. long).

Charlevoix East (shärlůvwä'), county (□ 719; pop. 13,077), E central Que., on the St. Lawrence; ⊙ Cap à l'Aigle.

Charlevoix West, county (□ 1,496; pop. 12,585), E central Que., on the St. Lawrence; ⊙ Baie St. Paul.

Charlieu (shärlyû'), town (pop. 4,313), Loire dept., SE central France, 9 mi. NNE of Roanne; silk-mfg. center and agr. market; processes and ships animal feed and seeds. Has remains of a Benedictine abbey (with 12th-cent. Romanesque portal) and 13th-16th-cent. wooden houses.

Charlois (shärlwä'), South Holland prov., W Netherlands, S suburb (pop. 21,657) of Rotterdam, on IJsselmonde isl., on left bank of New Maas R.

Charlotte, county (□ 1,243; pop. 22,728), SW N.B., on the Bay of Fundy and on Maine border (St. Croix R.); ⊙ St. Andrews. Includes Grand Manan, Deer, and Campobello isls.

Charlotte (shär'lŭt). **1** County (□ 705; pop. 4,286), S Fla., on Gulf of Mexico; ⊙ Punta Gorda. Lowland area with CHARLOTTE HARBOR in W. Cattle raising, vegetable growing, fishing. Formed 1921. **2** County (□ 468; pop. 14,057), S Va.; ⊙ Charlotte Court House. Rolling region, bounded W and S by Roanoke R. Agr. (especially tobacco; also corn, clover), beef cattle, dairying. Lumbering, lumber milling. Formed 1765.

Charlotte. 1 (shär'lŭt) Town (pop. 427), Clinton co., E Iowa, 16 mi. WNW of Clinton; dairy products, wagons. **2** (shär'lŭt) Town (pop. 252), Washington co., E Maine, 12 mi. SSE of Calais, in hunting, fishing area. **3** (shŭrlŏt') City (pop. 6,606), ⊙ Eaton co., S central Mich., 18 mi. SW of Lansing, in agr. area (grain, beans, corn). Maple-sugar distribution point. Mfg. of radios, machinery, electronic equipment, furniture, lumber, flour. The Kellogg Foundation's co. unit is here. Settled before 1840; inc. as village 1863, as city 1871. **4** (shär'lŭt) City (pop. 134,042), ⊙ Mecklenberg co., S N.C., in the piedmont, 90 mi. N of Columbia, S.C., near S.C. line and Catawba R. (supplies hydroelectric power); 35°14'N 80°50'W. Largest city in state; textile center; rail hub; a major distributing point for the Southeast; mfg. of cotton and woolen goods, hosiery, machinery, electrical equipment, dyestuffs, cottonseed oil, fertilizer, flour, paper boxes, furniture). Seat of Queens Col. (women; 1857) and Johnson C. Smith Univ. (Negro; coeducational; 1867). Settled c.1750; chartered 1768. **5** (shär'lŭt) Town (pop. 478), ⊙ Dickson co., N central Tenn., 33 mi. W of Nashville; lumbering. **6** (shär'lŭt) City (pop. 1,272), Atascosa co., SW Texas, c.40 mi. SSW of San Antonio; rail, trade point in cotton, truck, dairying area. Inc. after 1940. **7** (shŏrlŏt') Town (pop. 1,215), Chittenden co., NW Vt., 12 mi. S of Burlington and on L. Champlain; summer resort, fruitgrowing area; dairy products. Ferry to Essex, N.Y. Mt. Philo state park here. Chartered 1762, settled 1784.

Charlotte Amalie (shär'lŭt ŭmäl'yŭ), largest city (pop. 10,399) and ⊙ Virgin Isls. of the U.S., leading port on fine bay of S St. Thomas Isl., 70 mi. E of San Juan, Puerto Rico, and 1,075 mi. ESE of Miami, Fla.; 18°21'N 64°56'W. At head of St. Thomas Harbor, built on 3 low, volcanic spurs, and towered over by old Bluebeard's and Blackbeard's castles. For centuries a port of call of strategic importance, Charlotte Amalie is still a fueling station with good shipping facilities. Its healthful climate and picturesque, tropical scenery have made it more and more popular as a tourist resort. Main products: bay rum, rum, and handicraft products (embroideries, novelties). There are shipyards and machine shops; also an international cable station, and airport. Most of the bldgs. retain their quaint, Old World, mostly Danish, architecture. After unsuccessful attempts at settlement by the Dutch (1657) and the Danes (1666), the latter established (1672) a permanent colony called, for the consort of King Christian V, Charlotte Amalia or Amalienborg. Popularly it was referred to as St. Thomas, a name officially adopted in 1921 and officially abandoned in 1936, when the old name was restored. Charlotte Amalie was a free port, 1756–64; it prospered most before 1830. It was frequently visited by hurricanes. City has more than ¾ of isl.'s pop. Inhabitants are predominantly Negro.

Charlotte Court House or **Charlotte** (shär'lŭt), town (pop. 397), ⊙ Charlotte co., S Va., 37 mi. SE of Lynchburg; trade point in tobacco, timber area.

Charlotte Hall, village (pop. c.150), St. Marys co., S Md., 32 mi. SSE of Washington; seat of Charlotte Hall School, opened 1774.

Charlotte Harbor, SW Fla., shallow inlet (c.25 mi. long, 5 mi. wide) of the Gulf of Mexico, sheltered by the barrier isls. Gasparilla and Lacosta (W) and opening into Pine Island Sound (S) and Gasparilla Sound (N); 26°45'N 82°10'W. Channel dredged from S end of Gasparilla Isl. to PUNTA GORDA, the chief port. Receives Peace and Myakka rivers in N.

Charlottenberg (shärlô'tŭnbĕr"yŭ), village (pop. 1,024), Varmland co., W Sweden, 18 mi. NNW of Arvika; frontier station on Norwegian border, 5 mi. SE of Magnor, on Stockholm-Oslo main line. Sawmilling, woodworking, brick mfg.

Charlottenburg (shärlô'tŭnbûrkh"), village, Commewijne dist., N Du. Guiana, on Cottica R. and 27 mi. E of Paramaribo; sugar, coffee, rice.

Charlottenburg (shärlŏ'tŭnbûrg, Ger. shärlô'tŭnbŏŏrk), chief residential district (1939 pop. 299,955; 1946 pop. 208,453) of Berlin, Germany, on the Spree and 5 mi. W of city center. The 17th-cent. castle and mausoleum with graves of King Frederick William III and Queen Louise of Prussia, and of Emperor William I, was heavily damaged in Second World War. Originally called Lietzenburg, dist. was renamed for wife of Elector Frederick III. Chartered 1705; inc. 1920 into Berlin. Stadium here was scene of 1936 Olympic Games. Formerly noted for porcelain. After 1945 in British sector.

Charlotte River (shär'lŭt), E central N.Y., rises in W Schoharie co., flows c.30 mi. SW to the Susquehanna just E of Oneonta.

Charlottesville (shär'lŭtsvĭl), city (pop. 25,969), in but independent of Albemarle co., central Va., on Rivanna R. and 65 mi. NW of Richmond, in fruit-growing region of the piedmont. Co. courthouse here. Seat of Univ. of Virginia (founded by Thomas Jefferson; chartered 1819) and of Inst. of Textile Technology. Some mfg. (textiles, machinery, bakery and textile-mill equipment, wood products, clothing, food products, beverages, metal products); soapstone, slate quarrying. Near by are MONTICELLO (Jefferson's home), "Ash Lawn" (home of James Monroe), and state tuberculosis hosp. Birthplace of Meriwether Lewis is at Ivy, 7 mi. W, that of George Rogers Clark is 3 mi. NE. Founded 1762; chartered as town 1851, as city 1888. In the Revolution, Burgoyne's captured army was quartered near by, 1779–80; Tarleton raided here in 1781. Occupied by Union forces in Civil War.

Charlottetown, city (pop. 14,821), ⊙ Prince Edward Isl. and Queens co., on S central coast of the isl., at tip of a small peninsula bet. Hillsborough R. (E) and Yorke R. (W), 110 mi. NNE of Halifax; 46°15'N 63°8'W. The commercial and communications center of P.E.I., it is the chief port, shipping dairy products, seed potatoes, meat. Industries include shipbuilding, meat packing, woodworking. Seat of Prince of Wales Col. and, near by, St. Dunstan's Univ., affiliated with Laval Univ., Quebec. Noted bldgs. include Province Bldg., housing provincial legislature, and Govt. House (1833). Site of airport. There is rail communication with mainland via Port Borden–Cape Tormentine train ferry. Founded as French trading post in early 18th cent. near present site, the settlement, known as Port La Joie, grew rapidly after 1755 expulsion of Acadians from Nova Scotia and New Brunswick. Treaty of Paris (1763) assigned isl. to England. Present town was laid out 1768, named for Queen Charlotte, wife of George III. In 1864 city was scene of Charlottetown Conference of the Maritime Provinces, at which 1st steps toward confederation were taken.

Charlotte Town, Dominica, B.W.I.: see ROSEAU.

Charlotte Town, Grenada, B.W.I.: see GOUYAVE.

Charlotteville, village (pop. 1,360), NW Tobago, B.W.I., on Man of War Bay, 16 mi. NE of Scarborough; fishing.

Charlotte Waters, settlement, S Northern Territory, Australia, near South Australia line, 165 mi. SSE of Alice Springs; sheep.

Charlton, town (pop. 1,258), central Victoria, Australia, on Avoca R. and 140 mi. NW of Melbourne; flour mill.

Charlton, town (pop. 210), E Ont., 25 mi. S of Kirkland Lake, in silver-mining, farming region.

Charlton, county (□ 799; pop. 4,821), SE Ga.; ⊙ Folkston. Bounded S and SE by Fla. line (formed here by St. Marys R.) and NE by Satilla R.; W part included in Okefenokee Swamp. Flatwoods area drained by Suwanee R. (W); sawmilling, stock raising, farming (corn, tobacco). Formed 1854.

Charlton, agr. town (pop. 3,136), Worcester co., S central Mass., 12 mi. SW of Worcester; woolen goods. Settled c.1735, inc. 1755. Includes village of Dodge.

Charlton Heights, village (pop. 1,038, with adjacent Falls View), Fayette co., S central W.Va., on Kanawha R. and 26 mi. SE of Charleston.

Charlton Island (□ 113), SE Keewatin Dist., Northwest Territories, at head of James Bay; 51°58'N 79°25'W; 19 mi. long, 9 mi. wide. Terminal for ocean-going ships, transshipment point for rail-head at Moosonee, Ont. (70 mi. SW). Isl. is leased by Hudson's Bay Co. as beaver breeding-ground.

Charlton Kings, residential urban district (1931 pop. 4,763; 1951 census 5,836), N central Gloucester, England, on small Chelt R. just SE of Cheltenham. Has church with 15th-cent. tower.

Charlwood (chär'lĭwŏŏd), town and parish (pop. 2,284), S Surrey, England, 6 mi. S of Reigate; agr. market. Has Norman church with 13th-cent. wall paintings.

Charly (shärlē'), village (pop. 1,186), Aisne dept., N France, on right bank of the Marne and 7 mi. SW of Château-Thierry; plaster, lime, and cement mfg.

Charmes (shärm). **1** Town, Aisne dept., France: see FÈRE, LA. **2** Town (pop. 3,297), Vosges dept., E France, on Moselle R. and Canal de l'Est, and 15 mi. NNW of Épinal; brewing, cotton spinning, fruit preserving, flour milling. Its 15th–16th-cent. church and 18th-cent. bridge over the Moselle were badly damaged in 1944. Site of battle of Charmes in First World War. Maurice Barrès b. here.

Charminster, agr. village and parish (pop. 1,866), S central Dorset, England, 2 mi. NNW of Dorchester. Has 12th–15th-cent. church and 15th-cent. mansion.

Charmouth, agr. village and parish (pop. 719), W Dorset, England, on the Channel, at mouth of the short Char R., 2 mi. ENE of Lyme Regis.

Charneca (shärnā'kŭ), town (pop. 1,952), Setúbal dist., S central Portugal, 10 mi. SE of Lisbon; bee-keeping, saltworking.

Charneux (shärnû'), village (pop. 1,339), Liége prov., E Belgium, 5 mi. ESE of Verviers; agr. cattle raising, dairying. Has 13th-cent. Cistercian abbey.

Charnisay, Fort (chär'nĭsā), S N.B., on the Bay of Fundy, at mouth of St. John R., opposite St. John; built 1645 by Fr. governor Charnisay, abandoned in mid-18th cent. Rebuilt 1758 by General Monckton and named Fort Frederick, it was burned 1775 by the Americans; rebuilt 1778 and named Fort Howe; finally abandoned 1821.

Charnwood Forest, wooded region in NW Leicester, England, bet. Loughborough (NE), Coalville (W), and Groby (S). Coal mines and granite quarries.

Charny (shärnē'), village (pop. 2,831), S Que., on Chaudière R., near its mouth on the St. Lawrence, and 8 mi. SSW of Quebec; rail center.

Charny, village (pop. 1,033), Yonne dept., N central France, on Ouanne R. and 23 mi. WNW of Auxerre; cider mfg.; cattle raising.

Charny-sur-Meuse (–sür-mûz'), agr. village (pop. 269), Meuse dept., NE France, on the Meuse and Canal de l'Est, and 4 mi. NNW of Verdun. Also called Charny.

Charo (chä'rō), town (pop. 1,902), Michoacán, central Mexico, on railroad and 10 mi. NE of Morelia; alt. 6,105 ft.; cereals, fruit, livestock.

Charoda, Russian SFSR: see TSURIB.

Charolais or **Charollais** (both: shärôlĕ'), region and former county in E central France, now in Saône-et-Loire dept. Former ⊙ Charolles. Bounded by the Loire (W), the Monts du Mâconnais (E), and the Monts du Beaujolais (S), it is noted for its superior cattle. Acquired (1390) by Philip the Bold of Burgundy, it passed (1477) to the house of Hapsburg as part of Franche-Comté. In 17th cent. it was acquired from Spain by Louis XIV and incorporated into Burgundy prov.

Charollais, Monts du (mõ dü shärôlĕ'), hill range of the E Massif Central, E central France, extending c.30 mi. across Saône-et-Loire dept. in the area of Charolles, from the Loire (S) to Le Creusot industrial dist. (N). Average alt. 1,300 ft. Superior cattle raised here.

Charolles (shärôl'), town (pop. 2,622), Saône-et-Loire dept., E central France, 27 mi. WNW of Mâcon; livestock market. Pottery and hosiery mfg. Has ruined castle of counts of Charolais.

Charon (shärō'), village (pop. 753), Alger dept., N central Algeria, on railroad and 13 mi. SW of Orléansville; cereals, cotton. Irrigation dam on the Chéliff just N.

Charonda, Russian SFSR: see VOZHE, LAKE.

Charonne (shärôn'), an E quarter of Paris, France, comprised in 20th *arrondissement.*

Chârost (shärō'), village (pop. 1,052), Cher dept., central France, on Arnon R. and 7 mi. ENE of Issoudun; mfg. (brooms, candy, vegetable oil).

Charozero (chŭrō'zyĭrŭ), village, NW Vologda oblast, Russian SFSR, 45 mi. N of Kirillov; flax, wheat.

Charqueada, La, Uruguay: see GENERAL ENRIQUE MARTÍNEZ.

Charquemont (shärkŭmō'), village (pop. 1,542), Doubs dept., E France, near Swiss line, 8 mi. N of La Chaux-de-Fonds; watch mfg.

Charquito (chärkē'tō), village, Cundinamarca dept., central Colombia, on Bogotá R., E of Tequendama Falls, and 15 mi. WSW of Bogotá, on railroad; alt. 8,310 ft.; hydroelectric plant.

Charran, Asia Minor: see HARAN.

Charroux (shärōō'), village (pop. 1,086), Vienne dept., W central France, near Charente R., 15 mi. NW of Confolens; garment mfg., sawmilling. Has remains of abbey founded by Charlemagne, an 11th-cent. octagonal tower.

Charsadda (chär'sŭd-dŭ), town (pop. 16,845), Peshawar dist., central North-West Frontier Prov., W Pakistan, on Swat R., near its mouth, and 12 mi. NE of Peshawar; trade center for local agr. produce (wheat, corn, barley, sugar cane); handicrafts (felt mats, saddlecloths, leather goods); poultry farming. Near by is site of anc. city taken 326 B.C. by army of Alexander the Great; excavations here, 1903, were 1st in India carried out on modern scientific lines. Was hq. of Red Shirt movement, c.1930.

Charshanga (chŭrshŭn-gä'), village (1932 pop. estimate 980), SE Chardzhou oblast, Turkmen SSR, on the Amu Darya, on railroad and 50 mi. SE of Kerki; cotton.

Charski or **Charskiy** (chär'skē), town (1948 pop. over 2,000), N Semipalatinsk oblast, Kazakh SSR, on Turksib RR and 65 mi. SE of Semipalatinsk; metalworks; limestone quarrying.

Chartak (chär'täk), village (1939 pop. over 500), NE Namangan oblast, Uzbek SSR, on railroad and 10 mi. NE of Namangan; cotton.

Charter, village, Gwelo prov., E central Southern Rhodesia, in Mashonaland, NNE of Enkeldoorn; tobacco, wheat, dairy products, citrus fruit. Formerly called Fort Charter.

Charter Oak, town (pop. 710), Crawford co., W Iowa, 13 mi. WNW of Denison, in agr. area.

Charters Towers, city (pop. 7,561), E Queensland, Australia, 65 mi. SW of Townsville; mining center (copper, silver, gold). Formerly important gold-mining town. Gold discovered here 1871–72.

Chartham (chär'tŭm), town and parish (pop. 3,333), E Kent, England, on Great Stour R. and 3 mi. SW of Canterbury; paper mills. Site of mental hosp. Has 13th-14th-cent. church.

Charthawal (chŭr'tŭvŭl), town (pop. 8,257), Muzaffarnagar dist., N Uttar Pradesh, India, 8 mi. NW of Muzaffarnagar; wheat, gram, sugar cane, oilseeds.

Chartorisk or **Chartoriysk** (chŭrtŭrēsk'), Pol. *Czartorysk* (chärtôrĭsk'), village (1939 pop. over 500), E Volyn oblast, Ukrainian SSR, on Styr R. and 50 mi. E of Kovel; grain, potatoes; lumbering. Has ruins of castle. An old residence of Pol. gentry; passed to Russia (1795); scene of battles during First World War; reverted to Poland (1921); ceded to USSR in 1945.

Chartres (shärt, Fr. shär'trů), anc. *Autricum*, later *Carnutum*, city (pop. 23,509), ⊙ Eure-et-Loir dept., N central France, on the Eure and 50 mi. SW of Paris; chief commercial center (cereals, livestock) of the wheat-growing Beauce. Agr. machinery mfg., brewing, cider distilling, tanning. Noted for its turkey pies. Has famous 11th–13th-cent. cathedral of Notre Dame, remarkable for its 2 lofty spires (375 ft. and 350 ft.), its stained-glass windows, and its sculpture. In it St. Bernard of Clairvaux preached Second Crusade (1146) and Henry IV was crowned king of France (1594). The 12th–13th-cent. church of St. Pierre contains fine enamel paintings. Town has preserved many medieval and Renaissance houses. Its 17th-cent. town hall damaged in Second World War. Seat of the Carnutes (Gallic tribe) and probable center of Druid worship. Was ⊙ county, later duchy, of Chartres.

Chartre-sur-le-Loir, La (lä shär'trů-sür-lů-lwär'), village (pop. 1,210), Sarthe dept., W France, on Loir R. and 24 mi. N of Tours; mfg. (rubber, slaked lime). Trade in cattle, grains, wine.

Chartrettes (shärtrĕt'), village (pop. 791), Seine-et-Marne dept., N central France, on right bank of the Seine, 4 mi. SSE of Melun, resort at N edge of forest of Fontainebleau.

Chartreuse, La Grande-, France: see GRANDE-CHARTREUSE.

Chartridge, agr. village and parish (pop. 1,092), E central Buckingham, England, 2 mi. NW of Chesham.

Charybdis, Sicily: see GAROFALO.

Charysh River (chŭrĭsh'), S Altai Territory, Russian SFSR, rises in Altai Mts., flows WNW, past Charyshskoye, and NE, past Beloglazovo (head of navigation) and Ust-Kalmanka, to Ob R. at Ust-Charyshskaya Pristan; 268 mi. long. Copper and lead-zinc ores along its course.

Charyshskoye (chŭrĭsh'skŭyŭ), village (1939 pop. over 2,000), S Altai Territory, Russian SFSR, on Charysh R. and 100 mi. E of Rubtsovsk; dairy farming.

Charzykowy, Lake (khä-zhĭkô'vĭ), Pol. *Jezioro Charzykowskie* (yĕ-zhô'rô khä-zhĭkôf'skyĕ) (□5.5), Bydgoszcz prov., NW Poland, 3 mi. NW of Chojnice; 6 mi. long. Brda R. flows through N section.

Chasani, Greece: see ELLENIKON.

Chaschuil Valley (chäs-chwēl'), Andean river valley in W Catamarca prov., Argentina, starts 15 mi. E of Cerro Incahuasi (N) and extends S for c.40 mi. to a point 35 mi. W of Fiambalá.

Chascomús (chäskōmōōs'), town (pop. 9,064), ⊙ Chascomús dist. (□ 1,407; pop. 23,297), E Buenos Aires prov., Argentina, 45 mi. S of La Plata. Tourist and agr. center (sunflowers, flax, corn, wheat, livestock), dairying. Founded in 18th cent. Located on E shore of **Lake Chascomús** (□ 15) in popular resort area (bathing beaches, boating, fishing).

Chase, village (pop. estimate 350), S B.C., on South Thompson R. and 30 mi. ENE of Kamloops; lumbering, irrigated farming, fruitgrowing.

Chase. 1 County (□ 774; pop. 4,831), E central Kansas; ⊙ Cottonwood Falls. Hilly agr. area, drained by Cottonwood R. Livestock, grain. Scattered gas fields. Formed 1859. **2** County (□ 894; pop. 5,176), S Nebr.; ⊙ Imperial; agr. area bounded W by Colo. and drained by Frenchman Creek. Livestock, grain. Formed 1886.

Chase. 1 City (pop. 961), Rice co., central Kansas, 31 mi. NW of Hutchinson, in wheat and stock area. **2** Village (pop. c.300), Lake co., W central Mich., 6 mi. E of Reed City; livestock-trading and -shipping point.

Chaseburg, village (pop. 219), Vernon co., SW Wis., on small Coon Creek and 13 mi. SSE of La Crosse, in dairying and stock-raising region.

Chase City, town (pop. 2,519), Mecklenburg co., S Va., 55 mi. ENE of Danville; tobacco market; mfg. of wood products, footwear, clothing, food products. Inc. 1873.

Chashi (chŭshē'), village (1948 pop. over 2,000), N Kurgan oblast, Russian SFSR, 35 mi. NW of Kurgan; flour mill.

Chashniki (chäsh'nyĭkē), town (1926 pop. 2,974), W Vitebsk oblast, Belorussian SSR, on Ulla R. and 16 mi. E of Lepel; sawmilling center; peat; food products.

Chasia or **Khasia** (both: khäsēä'), mountain range on Macedonia-Thessaly line, Greece, forming divide bet. middle Aliakmon and upper Peneus rivers; rises to 5,131 ft. in the Kratsovon, 13 mi. NW of Kalambaka.

Chasicó, Arroyo (äroi'ō chäsēkō'), river in SW Buenos Aires prov., Argentina, rises in the Sierra de Curumalán near Saavedra at alt. of 1,400 ft., flows c.80 mi. SW, past Saavedra, to L. Chasicó (□ 16) 40 mi. W of Bahía Blanca.

Chaska (chă'skŭ), city (pop. 2,008), ⊙ Carver co., S central Minn., on Minnesota R. and 21 mi. SW of Minneapolis; trade and shipping point in agr. area; beet sugar, dairy products, canned vegetables, beverages, bricks. Settled 1853, inc. as village 1871, as city 1891. There are prehistoric Indian mounds in city park.

Chaskoi, Bulgaria: see KHASKOVO.

Chaskoi, Turkey: see HASKOY.

Chasov Yar (chŭsôf' yär''), city (1939 pop. over 10,000), N Stalino oblast, Ukrainian SSR, in the Donbas, 8 mi. W of Artemovsk; cement works; refractory clay.

Chassagne-Montrachet (shäsä'nyů-mōträshā'), village (pop. 451), Côte-d'Or dept., E central France, on SE slope of the Côte d'Or, 8 mi. SW of Beaune; Burgundy wines.

Chassal (shäsäl'), village (pop. 284), Jura dept., E France, on the Bienne and 4 mi. SW of Saint-Claude, in the central Jura; diamond cutting, brier pipe mfg., marble quarrying.

Chassart (shäsär'), village, Hainaut prov., S central Belgium, 8 mi. NNE of Charleroi; sugar-refining center. Commune center of Wagnelée (pop. 798) is 1 mi. NE.

Chassell (chă'sŭl), village (1940 pop. 636), Houghton co., NW Upper Peninsula, Mich., on Portage L. and 7 mi. SSE of Houghton; trade center for farm and resort area.

Chasseneuil (shäsnû'ē), village (pop. 1,081), Charente dept., W France, 18 mi. NE of Angoulême; tanning. Iron deposits.

Chasseneuil-du-Poitou (–dü-pwätōō'), village (pop. 649), Vienne dept., W central France, 5 mi. NE of Poitiers; mfg. (agr. machinery, electric batteries).

Chasseral (shäsůräl'), peak (5,284 ft.) in the Jura, W Switzerland, 8 mi. W of Biel.

Chasseron, Mont (mō shäsůrō'), peak (5,283 ft.) in the Jura, W Switzerland, 7 mi. NW of Yverdon.

Chasse-sur-Rhône (shäs-sür-rōn'), town (pop. 2,069), Isère dept., SE France, on left bank of the Rhone and 5 mi. NW of Vienne; rail junction; blast furnaces, forges. Winegrowing.

Chassezac River (shäsůzäk'), Lozère and Ardèche depts., S France, rises 5 mi. N of Le Bleymard, flows 47 mi. SE to the Ardèche 4 mi. WNW of Vallon.

Chassi River (shä'sē), small arm (c.12 mi. long) of Arabian Sea, separating Diu isl. from S shore of Kathiawar peninsula, W India.

Chastellet, Le, Palestine: see MISHMAR HAY YARDEN.

Chastiau Pelerin, Palestine: see ATLIT.

Chastoozerskoye (chŭ''stŭ-ŭzyôr'skŭyŭ), village (1948 pop. over 2,000), E Kurgan oblast, Russian SFSR, 35 mi. N of Petukhovo; metalworks.

Chastye or **Chastyye** (chä'stēŭ), village (1926 pop. 809), SW Molotov oblast, Russian SFSR, on left bank of Kama R. (landing) and 17 mi. WSW of Osa; food processing; rye, oats, flax, livestock.

Chasuta (chäsōō'tä), town (pop. 1,256), San Martín dept., N central Peru, landing on Huallaga R. and 17 mi. ESE of Tarapoto, on road; shipping point for Tarapoto region.

Chat, Cape (shä), on Gulf of St. Lawrence, E Que., on N Gaspé Peninsula, at S side of mouth of the St. Lawrence, 2 mi. W of Cap Chat village; 49°5'N 66°45'W; lighthouse.

Chat, Mont du (mō dü shä'), narrow limestone range in Savoie dept., SE France, extending c.10 mi. N-S along W shore of Lac du Bourget. Rises to 4,595 ft. at the Dent du Chat (opposite Aix-les-Bains). Continued by Montagne de l'Épine (S).

Châtaigneraie, La (lä shätĕnyůrĕ'), village (pop. 1,571), Vendée dept., W France, 13 mi. NNE of Fontenay-le-Comte; cattle raising, woodworking. Birthplace of Clemenceau near by.

Chatalja. 1 Town, Macedonia, Greece: see CHORISTE. **2** Town, Thessaly, Greece: see PHARSALA.

Chatalja, Turkey: see CATALCA.

Chatanika (chătŭnē'kŭ), village (1939 pop. 106), central Alaska, 20 mi. NNE of Fairbanks, on Steese Highway; large-scale placer gold mining.

Châtard (shätär'), village, Nord dept., N Haiti, 22 mi. SW of Cap-Haïtien, just S of Plaisance; coffee, cacao, fruit. Has agr. school.

Chatb, Egypt: see SHOTB.

Chatbazar, Kirghiz SSR: see BUDENNY.

Chatburn, village and parish (pop. 1,118), E Lancashire, England, on Ribble R. and 2 mi. NE of Clitheroe; cotton milling, lime burning.

Chatcolet (chăt''kŭlā'), town (pop. 92), Benewah co., N Idaho, 22 mi. S of Coeur d'Alene.

Château, Le, village, Charente-Maritime dept., France: see CHÂTEAU-D'OLÉRON, LE.

Château-Arnoux (shätō'-ärnōō'), commune (pop. 2,935), Basses-Alpes dept., SE France, on the Durance and 11 mi. W of Digne. Saint-Auban (2 mi. SSW), junction for rail branch to Digne, has large electrochemical works (magnesium) with workers' community (pop. 1,793).

Chateaubelair (shă''tōbŭlâr'), town (pop. 1,309), W St. Vincent, B.W.I., 8 mi. N of Kingstown; cotton, coconuts.

Châteaubourg (shätōbōōr'), village (pop. 855), Ille-et-Vilaine dept., W France, on Vilaine R. and 12 mi. E of Rennes; cattle raising. Slate quarries near by.

Châteaubriant (shätōbrēä'), town (pop. 7,965), Loire-Inférieure dept., W France, 36 mi. NNE of Nantes; railroad and agr. trade center; mfg. (hosiery, furniture, agr. implements), tanning, flour milling, printing. Iron deposits just N. Has remains of 11th-cent. castle and the Renaissance Château-Neuf, damaged in Second World War.

Château-Chalon, France: see VOITEUR.

Château-Chinon (shätō'-shēnō'), town (pop. 2,190), Nièvre dept., central France, in the Morvan, 19 mi. WNW of Autun, near the Yonne; alt. 1,752 ft. Cattle and lumber trade. Furniture mfg., rubber reclaiming (for heels and rubber mats). Hydroelectric plant. Tourists.

Château d'Eau (shätō' dō'), town (pop. 289), S Que., 9 mi. WNW of Quebec; dairying; vegetables, poultry.

Château d'If, France: see IF.

Château-d'Oex (shätō'-dā'), Ger. *Oesch* (ûsh), town (pop. 3,336), Vaud canton, W Switzerland, on Sarine R. and 24 mi. E of Lausanne; health resort (alt. 3,152 ft.) noted for fine views, rich flora.

Château-d'Oléron, Le (lů shätō'-dôlārō'), village (pop. 1,363), Charente-Maritime dept., W France, on SE coast of Île d'Oléron, 12 mi. WSW of Rochefort; island's chief port and bathing resort; oyster beds. Has 17th-cent. fortifications. Also called Le Château.

Château-du-Loir (shätō'-dü-lwär'), town (pop. 3,816), Sarthe dept., W France, near the Loir, 23 mi. SSE of Le Mans; hemp processing, sawmilling, winegrowing, mfg. of pharmaceuticals. Has cliff dwellings.

Châteaudun (shätōdŭ'), town (pop. 7,309), Eure-et-Loir dept., NW central France, on the Loir and 27 mi. SSW of Chartres; communications center; mfg. (telephone and optical equipment, machine tools, rubber). Livestock trade. Has 12th–16th-cent. castle of counts of Dunois (on rocky promontory overlooking river) and 12th-cent. Romanesque church of the Madeleine (burned in 1940). Sacked by Germans (Oct., 1870) after resisting a siege in Franco-Prussian War.

Châteaudun-du-Rhumel (–dü-rümĕl'), town (pop. 5,486), Constantine dept., NE Algeria, in the High Plateaus near headwaters of the Oued Rhumel, 30 mi. SW of Constantine; agr. market in cereal-growing region (wheat, barley). Also spelled Châteaudun-du-Rummel.

Chateaugay (shă'tŭgē'', –gā''), village (pop. 1,234), Franklin co., NE N.Y., on Chateaugay R., near Que. line, and 12 mi. NE of Malone; port of entry. Makes footwear. Summer resort. Agr. (dairy products; poultry, potatoes). Settled 1796, inc. 1869.

Chateaugay Lake, NE N.Y., 25 mi. W of Plattsburg, source of CHÂTEAUGUAY (or Chateaugay) RIVER; consists of Upper Chateaugay L. (4 mi. long) and, just N, Lower Chateaugay L. (3 mi. long).

Chateaugay River, N.Y.: see CHÂTEAUGUAY RIVER.

Châteaugiron (shätōzhērō'), village (pop. 1,112), Ille-et-Vilaine dept., W France, 9 mi. SE of Rennes; linen weaving. Has ruins of medieval fortifications.

Château-Gontier (shätō'-gōtyā'), town (pop. 6,282), Mayenne dept., W France, on Mayenne R. and 17 mi. SSE of Laval; road and commercial center; fruit preserving, textile milling, embroidering, oil refining. Has 11th–12th-cent. church (damaged in Second World War) with noteworthy crypt.

Châteauguay (shätōgā'), county (□ 265; pop. 14,443), S Que., on the St. Lawrence, near N.Y. border; ⊙ Ste. Martine.

Châteauguay, town (pop. 1,425), S Que., on Châteauguay R., near its mouth on L. St. Louis, 14 mi. SW of Montreal; market in dairying region.

Châteauguay River, in U.S. **Chateaugay River**, rises in Chateaugay L. in the Adirondacks, NE N.Y., W of Plattsburg, flows N into Que. and past Châteauguay to L. St. Louis (expansion of the St. Lawrence) 10 mi. SW of Montreal; c.50 mi. long. On the river in Quebec was fought (1813) the battle in which a large American invading force under Wade Hampton was defeated by a small Canadian-Indian force.

Château-Haut-Brion, France: see PESSAC.

Château-Lafite, France: see PAUILLAC.

Château-Landon (shätō'-lădō'), village (pop. 1,403), Seine-et-Marne dept., N central France, near Loing R., 18 mi. S of Fontainebleau; paper milling, sugar-beet distilling, mustard mfg. Has 11th–15th-cent. church, 13th-cent. houses, and ruins of medieval fortress and ramparts.

Château-Latour, France: see PAUILLAC.

Château-la-Vallière (shätō'-lä-välyâr'), village (pop. 1,035), Indre-et-Loire dept., W central France, 20 mi. NW of Tours; sawmilling. Iron mineral springs near by.

Châteaulin (shätōlĕ'), town (pop. 3,128), Finistère dept., W France, on Aulne R. and Brest-Nantes Canal, 13 mi. N of Quimper; mfg. (explosives, cider, food preserves). Slate quarries near by. Has a 15th–16th-cent. chapel with ossuary.

Château-Margaux, France: see MARGAUX.

Châteaumeillant (shätōmĕyä'), town (pop. 2,002), Cher dept., central France, 10 mi. E of La Châtre; cattle market; winegrowing. Small lead and copper deposits and stone quarry near by. Has 11th-cent. Romanesque church.

Châteauneuf (shätōnûf'). 1 or **Châteauneuf-du-Faou** (–dü-fou'), village (pop. 1,714), Finistère dept., W France, on Aulne R. and Brest-Nantes Canal, and 19 mi. NE. of Quimper; tourist center for Montagnes Noires dist. (SE). Woodworking. 2 or **Châteauneuf-les-Bains** (–lā-bē'), village (pop. 154), Puy-de-Dôme dept., central France, thermal station in Auvergne Mts., on Sioule R. and 14 mi. NW of Riom.

Châteauneuf-de-Randon (–dů-rãdō'), village (pop. 257), Lozère dept., S France, on S slopes of Montagnes de la Margeride, 12 mi. NE of Mende; cattle raising, cheese making. Du Guesclin died here during a siege (1380).

Châteauneuf-d'Ille-et-Vilaine (–dēl-ā-vēlěn'), village (pop. 523), Ille-et-Vilaine dept., W France, near Rance R. estuary, 7 mi. SSE of Saint-Malo; apple orchards and truck gardens.

Châteauneuf-du-Faou, France: see CHÂTEAUNEUF, Finistère dept.

Châteauneuf-du-Pape (–dü-päp'), village (pop. 1,583), Vaucluse dept., SE France, near left bank of the Rhone, 8 mi. N. of Avignon. Noted for its superior wines. Has ruins of 14th-cent. castle built by popes of Avignon.

Châteauneuf-en-Thymerais (–ã-tēmůrā'), village (pop. 1,438), Eure-et-Loir dept., NW central France, 12 mi. SSW of Dreux; dairying, poultry raising.

Châteauneuf-la-Forêt (–lä-fôrě'), village (pop. 1,190), Haute-Vienne dept., W central France, in Monts du Limousin, 18 mi. ESE of Limoges; mfg. (packing paper, cartons, bedsprings).

Châteauneuf-les-Bains, France: see CHÂTEAUNEUF, Pay-de-Dôme dept.

Châteauneuf-sur-Charente (–sür-shärãt'), town (pop. 2,095), Charente dept., W France, on Charente R. and 11 mi. WSW of Angoulême; brandy distilling; mfg. (footwear, felt, paper pulp). Has 12th–15th-cent. Romanesque and Gothic church.

Châteauneuf-sur-Cher (–sür-shâr'), village (pop. 1,737), Cher dept., central France, on Cher R. and 13 mi. NW of Saint-Amand-Montrond; mfg. (hardware, condensers, linen goods).

Châteauneuf-sur-Loire (–sür-lwär'), town (pop. 2,641), Loiret dept., N central France, on right bank of the Loire and 15 mi. ESE of Orléans; foundry. Metal stamping and cable-mfg. plants. Sawmilling. Damaged in Second World War.

Châteauneuf-sur-Sarthe (–sür-särt'), village (pop. 1,048), Maine-et-Loire dept., W France, on Sarthe R. and 14 mi. NNE of Angers; cattle raising; limekilns near by.

Châteauponsac (shätōpōsäk'), village (pop. 1,416), Haute-Vienne dept., W central France, on Gartempe R. and 11 mi. E of Bellac; electro-chemical works. Has 12th–15th-cent. church and early 17th-cent. bridge.

Château-Porcien (shätō'-pôrsyē'), village (pop. 579), Ardennes dept., N France, on the Aisne, on Ardennes Canal, and 6 mi. WNW of Rethel; brickworks.

Château-Regnault (–rünyō'), town (pop. 2,081), Ardennes dept., N France, on left bank of entrenched Meuse R. (canalized) and 6 mi. N of Mézières, in the Ardennes; ironworks, mfg. railroad equipment.

Châteaurenard (shätōrůnär'). 1 or **Châteaurenard-Provence** (–prôvãs'), town (pop. 4,848), Bouches-du-Rhône dept., SE France, near left bank of the Durance, 5 mi. SSE of Avignon; regional fruit and vegetable shipping center. 2 Village (pop. 1,129), Loiret dept., N central France, on Ouanne R. and 10 mi. ESE of Montargis; hog and poultry shipping, cider distilling.

Châteaurenault (shätōrůnō'), town (pop. 3,866), Indre-et-Loire dept., W central France, 17 mi. NE of Tours; tanning and leatherworking center; winegrowing. Also spelled Château-Renault.

Château Richer (shätō' rēshā'), village (pop. estimate 750), ⊙ Montmorency co., S central Que., on the St. Lawrence and 15 mi. NE of Quebec; stone quarrying; resort.

Châteauroux (shätōrōō'), town (pop. 31,195), ⊙ Indre dept., central France, on the Indre and 60 mi. SE of Tours; regional commercial and industrial center; makes woolen blankets and lingerie. Mfg. (agr. machinery, tobacco products); printing, tanning, food processing. Has 2 medieval churches (13th–15th cent.) and mus. containing an archaeological collection and Napoleonic souvenirs. Town owes its name and origin to a feudal castle (Château-Raoul), now occupied by the prefecture. Gen. Bertrand b. here. Suburban DÉOLS was early ⊙ of lower Berry and site of a 10th-cent. abbey.

Château-Salins (shätō'-sälē'), village (pop. 1,565), Moselle dept., NE France, 17 mi. NE of Nancy; rail and road junction; saltworks near by. Damaged in Second World War. Called Salzburgen under Ger. administration, 1940–44.

Château-Thierry (shätō'-tē'ůrē, Fr. shätō'-tyěrē'), town (pop. 7,283), Aisne dept., N France, on the Marne (canalized) and 24 mi. SSE of Soissons; mfg. (musical instruments, agr. tools, plaster). Has ruined castle of counts of Champagne and house of La Fontaine (b. here). Its history is one of captures and pillages. Shelled (1814) during Napoleonic Wars. Held briefly by Germans, Sept., 1914, during first battle of the Marne. Remembered for fierce struggle of May–July, 1918, in which French and Americans (who distinguished themselves in Hill 204–Belleau Wood sector) successfully barred road to Paris. Damaged in Second World War (including monument to U.S. 3d Division).

Châteauvillain (shätōvēlē'), village (pop. 1,032), Haute-Marne dept., NE France, 12 mi. SW of Chaumont; horse breeding.

Château-Yquem, France: see SAUTERNES.

Châtel (shätěl'). 1 Village (pop. 174), Haute-Savoie dept., SE France, in the Chablais, 18 mi. ESE of Thonon-les-Bains, near Swiss border; alt. 4,052 ft. Winter sports resort. Slate quarries. Just S is the Pas de Morgins, a pass (alt. 4,528 ft.) on road to Monthey. 2 or **Châtel-sur-Moselle** (–sür-mōzěl'), agr. village (pop. 831), Vosges dept., E France, on Moselle R. and Canal de l'Est, 10 mi. N of Épinal; damaged in Second World War.

Châtelaillon-Plage (shätěläyō'-plāzh'), town (pop. 3,818), Charente-Maritime dept., W France, on the Pertuis d'Antioche of Bay of Biscay, 7 mi. SSE of La Rochelle; bathing resort with oyster- and mussel-beds. Sometimes called Châtelaillon.

Châtelard, Le (lů shätůlär'), village (pop. 249), Savoie dept., SE France, in the Bauges, on Chéran R. and 13 mi. NE of Chambéry; alt. 2,484 ft.; resort.

Châtelard, Le, Switzerland: see MONTREUX.

Châtelaudren (shätělōdrã'), village (pop. 1,212), Côtes-du-Nord dept., W France, 9 mi. W of Saint-Brieuc; furniture mfg.; apple orchards.

Châteldon (shätěldō'), village (pop. 1,039), Puy-de-Dôme dept., central France, 9 mi. N of Thiers; cutlery mfg. Mineral waters.

Châtelet (shätůlā'), town (pop. 14,857), Hainaut prov., S central Belgium, on Sambre R. and 3 mi. E of Charleroi; chemical and metal industries.

Châtelet, Creuse dept., France: see CHAMBON-SUR-VOUEIZE.

Châtelet, Le (lů), agr. village (pop. 762), Cher dept., central France, 12 mi. WSW of Saint-Amand-Montrond; poultry shipping.

Châtelet-en-Brie (–ã-brē'), village (pop. 864), Seine-et-Marne dept., N central France, 7 mi. ESE of Melun; sawmilling.

Châtelguyon or **Châtel-Guyon** (shätělgēyō'), town (pop. 2,843), Puy-de-Dôme dept., central France, 3 mi. NW of Riom; noted thermal station with mineral springs.

Châtelineau (shätlēnō'), town (pop. 19,575), Hainaut prov., S central Belgium, on Sambre R. and 3 mi. E of Charleroi; coal mining; metal industry.

Châtellerault (shätělrō'), town (pop. 19,216), Vienne dept., W central France, on Vienne R. and 19 mi. NNE of Poitiers; industrial center with natl. firearms factory and cutlery plants; metal founding, goose and swan feather processing, textile milling. Was 16th-cent. ⊙ duchy given by Henry II to James Hamilton, regent of Scotland. Cutlery mfg. dates back to 14th cent.

Châtellier, Le (lů shätělyā'), commune (pop. 365), Orne dept., NW France, 6 mi. NNE of Domfront; iron mines.

Châtel-Montagne (shätěl'-mōtä'nyů), resort (pop. 226), Allier dept., central France, on the Besbre and 12 mi. E of Vichy; woodworking. Has 12th-cent. Romanesque church. Hydroelectric plant near by.

Châtel-Saint-Denis (shätěl'-sē-důnē'), town (pop. 2,885), Fribourg canton, W Switzerland, on short Veveyse R. and 13 mi. E of Lausanne; tobacco, woodworking.

Châtel-sur-Moselle, France: see CHÂTEL, Vosges dept.

Châtelus-le-Marcheix, France: see BOURGANEUF.

Châtelus-Malvaleix (shätůlü'-mälvälě'), agr. village (pop. 509), Creuse dept., central France, 12 mi. NE of Guéret; cider milling.

Châtenay-Malabry (shätůnā'-mäläbrē'), town (pop. 3,455), Seine dept., N central France, an outer SSW suburb of Paris, 7 mi. from Notre Dame Cathedral, just S of Sceaux; mfg. of insulators; strawberry growing.

Châtenois (shätůnwä'). 1 Ger. *Kestenholz* (kě'stůnhōlts), town (pop. 2,125), Bas-Rhin dept., E France, at E foot of the Vosges, 3 mi. WNW of Sélestat; mfg. (clothing, cartons, tiles, gingerbread). 2 Agr. village (pop. 682), Vosges dept., E France, 7 mi. SE of Neufchâteau; embroidering.

Châtenois-les-Forges (–lā-fôrzh'), village (pop. 1,866), Territory of Belfort, E France, in Belfort Gap, 6 mi. S of Belfort; metalworks, chemicals.

Chatfield. 1 City (pop. 1,605), Fillmore and Olmsted counties, SE Minn., on Root R. and 18 mi. SE of Rochester, in grain, livestock, and poultry area; dairy products. Founded before 1856. 2 Village (pop. 204), Crawford co., N central Ohio, 10 mi. N of Bucyrus.

Chatham (chă'tům), fishing village, SE Alaska near S end of Chichagof Isl., on Chatham Strait 35 mi. NNE of Sitka; 57°31'N 134°56'W.

Chatham (chă'tům). 1 Town (pop. 4,082), NE N.B., on Miramichi R. 12 mi. from its mouth, and 75 mi. NNW of Moncton; port, shipping lumber, fish, pulp. Lumber, pulp, paper mills; shipyards, foundries, sardine and lobster canneries, shoe factory. Has R.C. cathedral. Airfield. 2 City (pop. 17,369), ⊙ Kent co., S Ont., on Thames R. (head of navigation) and 40 mi. E of Detroit; sugar refining, dairying, tobacco processing, food canning, natural-gas production; mfg. of tractors, automobile parts, and other steel products; clothing, fertilizer. Commercial center for surrounding fruitgrowing and farming region. Has Ursuline academy and a business col. Thames R. gives it access to the Great Lakes.

Chatham, municipal borough (1931 pop. 42,999; 1951 census 46,940), N Kent, England, on Medway R. estuary and 30 mi. ESE of London; 51°23'N 0°32'E; major naval base, established by Queen Elizabeth in 1588, with important dockyards, drydocks, and shipbuilding works. Among notable bldgs. are St. Bartholomew's Hosp., with 11th-cent. chapel; 12th-cent. Gundulf's Hosp.; St. Mary's church, including some Norman parts. There are traces of Roman occupation. Chatham is closely associated with the adjoining towns of Rochester and Gillingham.

Chatham (chă'tům). 1 County (□ 441; pop. 151,481), E Ga.; ⊙ Savannah. Bounded N by S.C. line (formed here by Savannah R.), E by the Atlantic, and S by Ogeechee R.; includes Tybee and Skidaway isls. Mfg. and shipping at Savannah. Truck, dairy, and poultry farming. Fishing. Formed 1777. 2 County (□ 707; pop. 25,392), central N.C.; ⊙ Pittsboro. In piedmont area; drained by Deep and Haw rivers, joining at SE border to form Cape Fear R. Poultry raising, farming (tobacco, corn), textile mfg., sawmilling. Formed 1770.

Chatham (chă'tům). 1 Village (pop. 905), Sangamon co., central Ill., 9 mi. SSW of Springfield, in agr. and bituminous-coal area. 2 Town (pop. 833), Jackson parish, N central La., 24 mi. SW of Monroe, in natural-gas and agr. area; sawmills, cotton gins. 3 (also chăt'hăm") Town (pop. 2,457), including Chatham village (pop. 1,225), Barnstable co., SE Mass., on Atlantic shore of Cape Cod, 17 mi. E of Hyannis; summer resort; fishing; cranberries. Champlain landed here 1606. Has 18th-cent. bldgs. Settled 1665, inc. 1712. Includes villages of North Chatham, South Chatham, West Chatham. Monomoy Isl. (mŏ'nůmoi"), a sandspit extending 10 mi. S, has lighthouse (unused) and coast guard station at Monomoy Point; a lightship is just offshore. 4 Village, Alger co., N Upper Peninsula, Mich., 14 mi. SW of Munising, in agr. area. Mich. State Col. maintains an agr. experiment station here. 5 Town (pop. 177), Carroll co., E N.H., in White Mts., 15 mi. NE of Conway. 6 Residential borough (pop. 7,391), Morris co., NE N.J., on Passaic R. and 11 mi. W of Newark; hothouse flowers; mfg. (metal products, chemicals, cement blocks). Has pre-Revolutionary inn. Settled 1749, inc. 1897. 7 Village (pop. 2,304), Columbia co., SE N.Y., 22 mi. SE of Albany; railroad junction in diversified farm area; mfg. (boxboard, textiles, clothing, feed). Small lakes near by. Inc. 1869. 8 Town (pop. 1,456), ⊙ Pittsylvania co., S Va., 15 mi. N of Danville; trading center in rich agr. area; lumber milling. Preparatory schools for girls and boys here. Inc. 1852.

Chatham Island, off W coast of S Chile, NE of Hanover Isl., 95 mi. NW of Puerto Natales; 35 mi. long, c.12 mi. wide; 50°40'S 74°20'W. Uninhabited.

Chatham Island, Galápagos: see SAN CRISTÓBAL ISLAND.

Chatham Island, Western Samoa: see SAVAII.

Chatham Islands, Marshall Isls.: see ERIKUB.

Chatham Islands (chă'tům), volcanic group and county (□ 373; pop. 505) of New Zealand, in S Pacific, 422 mi. ESE of Wellington; 44°S 176°30'W. There are 2 inhabited isls., several uninhabited islets; forested hills, grassy plains. Largest, Chatham Isl. (□ 348), is site of chief town, Waitangi (wītăng'gē, wī'tŭng-ē); has large central lagoon. Pitt Isl. (□ 24) is 2d largest. Sheep raising. Discovered 1790.

Chatham Sound, W B.C., channel (40 mi. long, 8–15 mi. wide) of Dixon Entrance, extends N from Porcher Isl. to mouth of Portland Inlet, separating Dundas Isls. from Tsimpsean Peninsula.

Chatham Strait, SE Alaska, navigable channel extending 210 mi. N-S through NW portion of Alexander Archipelago, separating Admiralty Isl. from Chichagof and Baranof isls.; 134°50'W 56°10'–59°10'N; 7-8 mi. wide. Continued N by Lynn Canal and NW by Icy Strait. Named 1794 by Vancouver after Lord Chatham.

Chathastail, Scotland: see EIGG.

Châtillon or **Châtillon-sous-Bagneux** (shätēyō'-sōō-bänyû'), town (pop. 11,503), Seine dept., N central France, SSW suburb of Paris, 4.5 mi. from Notre Dame Cathedral; freight yards; mfg. of radios, electronic equipment, armaments; printing. Truck gardens. Has Renaissance church. Atomic energy pile established here in 1949.

Châtillon (shätēyō'), town (pop. 1,659), Val d'Aosta region, NW Italy, at mouth of the Valtournanche, near Dora Baltea R., 14 mi. E of Aosta; commercial center; mfg. (rayon, chemicals); hydroelectric plant. Resort with baths.

Châtillon-Coligny (–kôlēnyē'), village (pop. 1,540), Loiret dept., N central France, on Loing R. and

Briare Canal, and 13 mi. SSE of Montargis; agr. market. Gaspard de Coligny b. and buried here.

Châtillon-en-Bazois (-ā-bäzwä'), village (pop. 758), Nièvre dept., central France, on Nivernais Canal and 13 mi. W of Château-Chinon; cattle raising, lumbering.

Châtillon-en-Diois (-ā-dēwä'), village (pop. 607), Drôme dept., SE France, in Dauphiné Pre-Alps, 7 mi. SE of Die; wine, chestnuts.

Châtillon-le-Duc (-lü-dük'), village (pop. 132), Doubs dept., E France, 5 mi. NNW of Besançon; salt mines.

Châtillon-sous-Bagneux, Seine dept., France: see CHÂTILLON.

Châtillon-sur-Chalaronne (-sür-shälärôn'), village (pop. 1,566), Ain dept., E France, 14 mi. SW of Bourg; agr. market for Dombes dist.; mfg. of bicycle parts.

Châtillon-sur-Indre (-sür-ē'drü), town (pop. 2,206), Indre dept., central France, on Indre R. and 25 mi. NNE of Le Blanc; road center; wool carding and spinning, lingerie mfg., flour milling, tanning.

Châtillon-sur-Loire (-sür-lwär'), village (pop. 1,857), Loiret dept., N central France, on left bank of Loire R. and port on Loire Lateral Canal, 9 mi. SE of Gien; market. Cement-pipe mfg.

Châtillon-sur-Marne (-sür-märn'), village (pop. 602), Marne dept., N France, near the Marne, 14 mi. WNW of Épernay; winegrowing, woodworking. Pope Urban II b. here.

Châtillon-sur-Seine (-sür-sĕn'), town (pop. 3,860), Côte-d'Or dept., E central France, on Seine R. and 45 mi. NNW of Dijon; road center; foundries, with mfg. of agr. machinery and hardware. Has 10th-cent. church. Residence of early dukes of Burgundy. Scene (1814) of unsuccessful attempt at peace settlement bet. Napoleon I and Allies. Severly damaged in Second World War.

Châtillon-sur-Sèvre (-sür-sĕ'vrü), village (pop. 1,153), Deux-Sèvres dept., W France, near Sèvre Nantaise R., 11 mi. SSE of Cholet; road center; tanning, weaving, horse breeding. One of the hq. of Vendée insurrection (1793–94).

Chatkal Range (chŭtkäl'), branch of NW Tien Shan mountain system, in NW Kirghiz SSR and along Kazakh-Uzbek border; forms divide bet. Chatkal and Chirchik rivers (NW) and Naryn and Angren rivers (SE); extends 125 mi. SW from the Talas Ala-Tau to plain near Tashkent; rises to 13,385 ft.

Chatkal River, Talas oblast, Kirghiz SSR, and South Kazakhstan oblast, Kazakh SSR; rises in E Chatkal Range, flows c.125 mi. SW, past Yangi-Bazar, joining Pskem R. to form Chirchik R. E of Gazalkent. Irrigates the Chatkal valley, which abounds in wild-growing fruit and nut woods.

Chat Moss, peat bog (□ 12) in S Lancashire, England, 7 mi. W of Manchester, largely reclaimed 1793–1800. In 1829 George Stephenson constructed roadbed of Liverpool and Manchester railroad across the bog.

Chato Chico (chä'tō chē'kō), village (pop. 1,073), Piura dept., NW Peru, on coastal plain, near Piura R., 12 mi. S of Piura, in irrigated cotton area.

Chatom (chă'tŭm), town (pop. 609), ⊙ Washington co., SW Ala., 55 mi. NNW of Mobile; lumber, naval stores.

Chatou (shätōō'), town (pop. 12,754), Seine-et-Oise dept., N central France, a WNW suburb of Paris, 9 mi. from Notre Dame Cathedral, on right bank of the Seine (bridges), adjoining Le Vésinet (W); mfg. (radio receivers, printing and duplicating machines, headlights), dairying, mushroom shipping.

Chatra (chŭt'rŭ). **1** Town (pop. 9,638), Hazaribagh dist., central Bihar, India, 35 mi. NW of Hazaribagh; trade center (rice, rape and mustard, oilseeds, corn, sugar cane, barley); cattle. **2** Village, Hooghly dist., West Bengal, India: see SERAMPORE.

Chatra, village, SE Nepal, on KOSI RIVER and 26 mi. NNW of Biratnagar. Proposed 35-ft.-high barrage and headworks for 2 canals extending from both banks of the Kosi here; to irrigate 3–4 million acres of land in Nepal and Bihar. Eastern Kosi canal to include 3 power stations on falls, each with 40-ft. drop and installed capacity of 30,000 kw. Also spelled Chhatra.

Chatrapur (chŭt'rŭpōōr), town (pop. 6,227), ⊙ Ganjam dist., SE Orissa, India, 13 mi. ENE of Berhampur, near Bay of Bengal; local market for rice, coconuts; hand-loom weaving.

Châtre, La (lä shä'trü), town (pop. 3,611), Indre dept., central France, on the Indre and 18 mi. SE of Châteauroux; road center and livestock market; shirt mfg. Regional hiring place for seasonal agr. laborers.

Chats, Lac des (läk dā shä'), expansion (24 mi. long) of Ottawa R., SE Ont., 30 mi. E of Ottawa. Receives Madawaska and Mississippi rivers.

Chatsu (chät'sōō), town (pop. 4,416), E Rajasthan, India, 23 mi. SSE of Jaipur; agr. (millet, gram). Annual religious fair. Also called Chaksu.

Chatsworth, village (pop. 345), S Ont., 8 mi. SSE of Owen Sound; dairying, lumbering, mixed farming.

Chatsworth, seat of the dukes of Devonshire, near the Derwent, near Bakewell, N central Derby, England. The famous Chatsworth House, on site of house built in mid-16th cent., dates from 1688. Its gardens, libraries, picture galleries, and collections of sculpture are noted.

Chatsworth, village, Gwelo prov., E central Southern Rhodesia, in Mashonaland, on railroad and 32 mi. SE of Umvuma; alt. 4,518 ft. Tobacco, wheat, dairy products, citrus fruit.

Chatsworth. 1 Outlying section of LOS ANGELES city, Los Angeles co., S Calif., in San Fernando Valley, 9 mi. WSW of San Fernando; small fruit farms. **2** City (pop. 1,214), ⊙ Murray co., NW Ga., 11 mi. E of Dalton; talc-mining center; mfg. (bedspreads, lumber, metal products). State park and the site of a Moravian mission (1802–33) near by. **3** Town (pop. 1,119), Livingston co., E central Ill., 40 mi. NE of Bloomington, in agr., clay and bituminous-coal area; mfg. (brick, tile, tanks). Laid out 1858, inc. 1867. **4** Town (pop. 102), Sioux co., NW Iowa, near S.Dak. line, 29 mi. N of Sioux City.

Chattahoochee (chătŭhōō'chē), county (□ 253; pop. 12,149), W Ga.; ⊙ Cusseta. Bounded W by Ala. line (formed here by Chattahoochee R.); W part included in Fort Benning Military Reservation. Truck, dairy, and poultry farming. Formed 1854.

Chattahoochee or **River Junction**, town (pop. 8,473), Gadsden co., NW Fla., near Ga. line, on Apalachicola R. (formed just N by junction of Chattahoochee and Flint rivers) and 37 mi. WNW of Tallahassee; mfg. (furniture, lumber). Site of Florida State Hospital for the Insane. Dam (power, navigation) near by in Flint R.

Chattahoochee River, formed by confluence of several headstreams in Blue Ridge Mts., NE Ga., flows 235 mi. SW to West Point, then 201 mi. S, past Columbus at Ala. line, joining Flint R. at Chattahoochee, Fla., to form Apalachicola R.; 436 mi. long; navigable to Columbus. In lower course it is part of state boundary bet. Ga. and Ala. and bet. Ga. and Fla. Has several hydroelectric dams, including Bartlett's Ferry Dam (145 ft. high, 1,975 ft. long; completed 1926), 15 mi. N of Columbus, Ga.; just downstream is smaller Goat Rock Dam.

Chattanooga (chătŭnōō'gŭ). **1** Town (pop. 333), Comanche co., SW Okla., 19 mi. SW of Lawton, in agr. area; cotton ginning. **2** City (pop. 131,041), ⊙ Hamilton co., SE Tenn., on Moccasin Bend of Tennessee R. at Ga. line, and 100 mi. NNW of Atlanta, in Great Appalachian Valley just E of the Cumberlands. Chickamauga Reservoir, impounded by TVA's Chickamauga Dam in the Tennessee, is just NE. City is port of entry, railroad, industrial, commercial, and distributing center; hq. for TVA power system. Produces iron and steel products (boilers, sawmills, pumps, stoves, sheet-metal products), farm machinery, furniture, textiles, hosiery, ceramics, glass containers, wood products, cellulose. Iron, coal mines in region. Seat of Univ. of Chattanooga. Natl. and Confederate cemeteries for Civil War dead here. U.S. Fort Oglethorpe is just S, in Ga. Tennessee Cave (just SW) attracts tourists. Settled 1815 as trading post called Ross's Landing; laid out and renamed in 1837. First a river-shipping port, it expanded with coming of railroads in 1840s and 1850s. In Civil War, its strategic position in command of Confederate communications bet. the East and the Mississippi made it the objective of the Union armies' Chattanooga campaign, which culminated (1863) in series of decisive engagements in vicinity. Battle of Chickamauga (Sept., 1863) resulted in retreat of Union troops from CHICKAMAUGA, Ga., to Chattanooga, which was then besieged by Confederates. Battles of Lookout Mtn. ("Battle above the Clouds"), just S, and of Missionary Ridge, E, took place in Nov. and were won by Federals. Union-occupied through rest of war, city was base for Sherman's Atlanta campaign. Battlefields are now included in Chickamauga and Chattanooga Natl. Military Park (□ 2.9 in Tenn., □ 9.8 in Ga.). Point Park, at NE end of Lookout Mtn., Orchard Knob, just W of Missionary Ridge, and Signal Point, on Signal Mtn. (NW of city) are other battlefields in park area.

Chattaroy, mining village (pop. 1,484), Mingo co., SW W.Va., on Tug Fork just N of Williamson, in bituminous-coal region.

Chatteris (chă'tŭrĭs), urban district (1931 pop. 5,153; 1951 census 5,528), in Isle of Ely, N Cambridge, England, 10 mi. NW of Ely; agr. market; agr.-machinery and abrasives works.

Chattisgarh Plain, India: see CHHATTISGARH PLAIN.

Chattooga (chŭtōō'gŭ), county (□ 317; pop. 21,197), NW Ga., on Ala. line; ⊙ Summerville. Hilly area, including part of Chattahoochee Natl. Forest (E). Agr. (cotton, corn, hay, sweet potatoes, fruit, livestock), textile mfg., sawmilling. Formed 1838.

Chattooga River. 1. In Ga. and Ala. formed by confluence of several headstreams in Chattooga co., NW Ga., flows c.50 mi. SW, past Summerville, Ga., into Cherokee co., NE Ala., where it enters Coosa R. 3 mi. NNE of Centre. Little R. is tributary. **2** In Ga., N.C., and S.C., rises in the Blue Ridge in SW N.C., flows 40 mi. SW, mostly along Ga.-S.C. line, to a point just SE of Tallulah Falls, Ga., here joining Tallulah R. to form Tugaloo R.

Chatuge Dam (chătōō'gē), Clay co., SW N.C., in Hiwassee R., just SE of Hayesville. A major TVA dam (144 ft. high, 2,850 ft. long, completed 1942); concrete construction; for flood control. Impounds Chatuge Reservoir (□ c.11; 13 mi. long; capacity 247,800 acre-feet) extending into Towns co., Ga.

Chatwood, village (pop. 1,572), Chester co., SE Pa., near West Chester.

Chatyr-Dag (chŭtĭr"-däk'), central section of Crimean Mts., S Crimea, Russian SFSR; rises to 5,003 ft. in the Eklizi-Burun, 7 mi. NW of Alushta. Offers extensive panorama.

Chatyr-Kul or **Chatyr-Kul'** (-kōōl'), lake (□ 75) in SW Tyan-Shan oblast, Kirghiz SSR, near China border, 55 mi. SSW of Naryn; 14 mi. long, 7 mi. wide, alt. 11,435 ft. Meteorological post here.

Chaubattia, India: see RANIKHET.

Chaube Jagirs (chou'bā jä'gērz), group of former petty states of Central India agency, just W of Karwi; consisted of Bhaisaunda, Kamta Rajaula, Pahra, Paldeo, and Taraon. Established by British in 1812; in 1948 merged with Vindhya Pradesh; in 1950 largely inc. into Banda dist. of Uttar Pradesh.

Chaubunagungamaug, Lake (shùbŭn"ŭgŭn'gŭmŭg), Worcester co., S Mass., on Conn. line, just SE of Webster; c.3 mi. long; resort. Sometimes called L. Webster, sometimes L. Chargoggaggoggmanchaugagoggchaubunagungamaug (shŭgŏg'ŭgŏg-mănchŏg'ŭgŏg–).

Chauchina (chouchē'nä), village (pop. 2,912), Granada prov., S Spain, near Genil R., 9 mi. W of Granada; sugar beets, cereals, potatoes; lumber.

Chauddi, Portuguese India: see CANÁCONA.

Chaudeau, La, France: see AILLEVILLERS.

Chaudes-Aigues (shōdzĕg'), anc. *Calentes Aquae* village (pop. 752), Cantal dept., S central France, 13 mi. SSW of Saint-Flour; noted thermal station (185°F. mineral springs); hosiery mfg. Until 1935, spelled Chaudesaigues.

Chaudfontaine (shōfōtĕn'), town (pop. 1,936), Liége prov., E Belgium, on Vesdre R. and 4 mi. SE of Liége; steel-rolling mills; thermal springs.

Chaudière Falls (shōdyâr'), waterfalls, SE Ont., on Ottawa R. (bridges), at E end of L. Deschênes, bet. Ottawa and Hull. River here narrows to 200 ft. and has fall of c.50 ft. In the rapids is small Chaudière Isl.

Chaudière River, S Que., issues from L. Megantic at Megantic, flows 115 mi. N, past Bolduc, St. Joseph de Beauce, and Charny, to the St. Lawrence opposite Quebec. Four mi. above mouth are 130-ft. Chaudière Falls.

Chaudoc (chou'dōk'), town (1936 pop. 6,500), ⊙ Chaudoc prov. (□ 1,100; 1943 pop. 272,800), S Vietnam, in Cochin China, on Bassac R. (ferry) and 110 mi. W of Saigon, on Cambodia line, in fertile and irrigated area (canals); rice- and corn-growing center, linked with Hatien (on Gulf of Siam) by Vinhte Canal; castor beans, yams, sugar cane, kapok; distilling, sericulture and silk weaving; quarries; boat building. Has mixed Cambodian, Malay, and Chinese pop. Former Khmer dist., occupied 18th cent. by Annamese. Fell 1867 to French.

Chauen, Sp. Morocco: see XAUEN.

Chauffailles (shōfī'), town (pop. 2,411), Saône-et-Loire dept., E central France, in the Monts du Beaujolais, 17 mi. NE of Roanne; silk, woolen mills.

Chauk (chouk'), town (pop. 12,830), Magwe dist., Upper Burma, on left bank of Irrawaddy R. and 35 mi. SW of Pakokku, opposite mouth of Yaw R. Oil-production center in Singu oil fields; refinery (built after Second World War).

Chaukan Pass (chouk'-än) (alt. 7,980 ft.), on India-Burma border, 20 mi. SE of Putao; 27°10'N 97°10'E. Used by track linking Kachin State (Upper Burma) and Saikhoa Ghat near Sadiya (Assam).

Chauka River, India: see SARDA RIVER.

Chaulinec Island (choulēnĕk') (□ 12; pop. 1,650), bet. Chiloé Isl. and Chilean mainland, Chiloé prov., S Chile, 25 mi. SE of Castro; 42°38'S; 7 mi. long, c.2 mi. wide. Potatoes, livestock; fishing, lumber milling.

Chaullín Island (chouyēn') (□ 1.5; pop. 49), off SE coast of Chiloé Isl., Chiloé prov., S Chile, 45 mi. SSE of Castro; c.2 mi. long; potato growing, fishing.

Chaulnes (shōn), village (pop. 1,530), Somme dept., N France, 10 mi. SW of Péronne; rail junction, sharply contested by French and Germans, 1917.

Chaumergy (shōmĕr-zhē'), village (pop. 304), Jura dept., E France, in the Bresse dist., 12 mi. NNW of Lons-le-Saunier; cereals, cheese.

Chaumont (shōmō'). **1** or **Chaumont-en-Bassigny** (-ā-bäsēnyē'), town (pop. 15,068), ⊙ Haute-Marne dept., NE France, on height overlooking Marne R. and Marne-Saône Canal, 50 mi. ESE of Troyes; road center. Important tanneries and glove factory; paper milling, shoe mfg., printing. Has 13th–16th-cent. church. Just W is a remarkable 3-tier railroad viaduct (c.2,000 ft. long, 170 ft. high). Former seat of counts of Bassigny and of Champagne. Treaty of Chaumont, signed here 1814, laid foundation of Holy Alliance. In First World War Chaumont was American field hq. Damaged in Second World War. **2** or **Chaumont-en-Vexin** (-ā-vĕksē'), village (pop. 1,539), Oise dept., N France, 15 mi. SW of Beauvais; agr. market. Has 15th–16th-cent. church.

Chaumont, Switzerland: see NEUCHÂTEL, town.

Chaumont (shùmō'), resort village and fishing center (pop. 513), Jefferson co., N N.Y., on Chaumont Bay (inlet of L. Ontario) at mouth of small Chaumont R., 13 mi. NW of Watertown. State park near by.

Chaumont-Porcien (–pôrsyē′), agr. village (pop. 400), Ardennes dept., N France, 11 mi. NNW of Rethel.

Chaumont-sur-Loire (–sür-lwär′), village (pop. 198), Loir-et-Cher dept., N central France, on Loire R. and 10 mi. SW of Blois; winegrowing. Noted for its 15th-cent. château combining Gothic and Renaissance architecture. Residence (17th cent.) of Catherine de Medici and Diane de Poitiers and later the site of a well-known terra-cotta factory. Also called Chaumont.

Chaumu, India: see CHOMU.

Chaumuhani (chou′mōōhŭnē), village, Noakhali dist., SE East Bengal, E Pakistan, 9 mi. NNE of Noakhali; major cotton-weaving center; rice, jute, pulse, chili.

Chaun Bay (chŏŏn′), inlet of E.Siberian Sea, NE Siberian Russian SFSR; 69°25′N 170°E; 100 mi. long, 35 mi. wide. At entrance are Aion Isl. and several smaller isls. On shore are Pevek (E) and Chaunskaya Kultbaza (S), near mouth of **Chaun River**, which flows 100 mi. N from Northern Anyui Range, through reindeer-raising area.

Chauncey (chôn′sē). **1** Town (pop. 348), Dodge co., S central Ga., 10 mi. SE of Eastman, near Little Ocmulgee R. **2** Village (pop. 1,016), Athens co., SE Ohio, 5 mi. NNW of Athens, and on Hocking R., in coal-mining area.

Chaungu or **Chaung-u** (choung′ōō), village, Sagaing dist., Upper Burma, 50 mi. W of Mandalay, on railroad to Yeu, in rice-growing area.

Chaungzon (choung′zōn), village, Bilugyun Isl., Amherst dist., Lower Burma, 10 mi. SW of Moulmein.

Chaunskaya Kultbaza or **Chaunskaya Kul′tbaza** (chŏŏn′skĭŭ kōōltbä′zŭ), village, NW Chukchi Natl. Okrug, Kamchatka oblast, Khabarovsk Territory, Russian SFSR, on Chaun Bay of E. Siberian Sea, near mouth of Chaun R., 355 mi. NW of Anadyr. Trading post in reindeer-raising area.

Chauny (shōnē′), town (pop. 9,206), Aisne dept., N France, on the Oise and Oise-Sambre Canal, and 16 mi. SSW of Saint-Quentin; industrial center with chemical works (soda for Saint-Gobain glassworks, sulphuric and nitric acids, fertilizer) and glassworks (artificial pearls), foundries (agr. equipment, copper wire), and sugar refineries. Changed hands 4 times in First World War and was virtually leveled.

Chaupimarca (choupēmär′kä), town (pop. 915), Pasco dept., central Peru, in Cordillera Central, 24 mi. NW of Cerro de Pasco; potatoes, grain, stock.

Chauques Islands (chou′kĕs), archipelago (pop. 3,435) of 16 islands off E coast of Chiloé Isl., Chiloé prov., S Chile; 42°15′–42°21′S. Includes isls. of Mechuque (W), Cheniao (center), and Buta-Chauques (E). Agr. area (wheat, potatoes, livestock); fishing, lumbering.

Chaur Peak (chour) (11,966 ft.), in NW Kumaun Himalayas, in S Himachal Pradesh, India, 23 mi. SE of Simla.

Chausa, India: see BUXAR.

Chausey Islands (shōzā′), in English Channel, small archipelago of c.50 islets (300 at low tide), off NW France, forming part of Manche dept., and c.10 mi. WNW of Granville; 48°52′N 1°49′W. Only Grande-Île (2 hotels; lighthouse) is inhabited. Lobster fishing.

Chaussin (shōsē′), village (pop. 1,089), Jura dept., E France, near the Doubs, 9 mi. SSW of Dôle; cereals, beets. Poultry and horse raising.

Chausy (chŏŏ′sē), city (1926 pop. 5,409), central Mogilev oblast, Belorussian SSR, near Pronya R., 27 mi. ESE of Mogilev; linen milling, dairying.

Chautara (choutä′rŭ), town, N Nepal, 25 mi. ENE of Katmandu; corn, barley, buckwheat, rice, vegetables. Nepalese military post.

Chautauqua (shŭtô′kwŭ). **1** County (□ 647; pop. 7,376), SE Kansas; ⊙ Sedan. Hilly agr. area, bordered S by Okla.; drained by Caney R. Livestock, grain. Oil and natural-gas fields. Formed 1875. **2** County (□ 1,080; pop. 135,189), extreme W N.Y., bounded NW by L. Erie; ⊙ Mayville. Dairying and grape-growing area; mfg., especially at Jamestown and Dunkirk. Also general agr. (livestock, seed, truck); fisheries. Resorts on L. Erie and on Chautauqua L., site of Chautauqua Institution. Formed 1808.

Chautauqua. 1 City (pop. 215), Chautauqua co., SE Kansas, 30 mi. W of Coffeyville, near Okla. line, in livestock and grain area. **2** Resort village (pop. c.300), Chautauqua co., extreme W N.Y., 15 mi. NW of Jamestown; alt. c.1,300 ft. Has large summer colony. Here is Chautauqua Institution (1874), offering popular summer lectures and concerts, on W shore of **Chautauqua Lake** (18 mi. long; 1–3 mi. wide; alt. 1,308 ft.), 8 mi. from L. Erie; the lake extends bet. Mayville (NW) and Jamestown (SE), trade centers for surrounding resort and fruitgrowing region.

Chauvai or **Chauvay** (chŏŏvī′), town (1947 pop. over 500), N Osh oblast, Kirghiz SSR, 6 mi. S of Kizyl-Kiya; mercury, antimony mines.

Chauvigny (shōvēnyē′), town (pop. 3,877), Vienne dept., W central France, on Vienne R. and 14 mi. E of Poitiers; mfg. (furniture, parquetry, casein). Stone quarries. Has ruins of five castles which constituted a medieval stronghold. Former seat of bishops of Poitiers.

Chauvin (shō′vĭn, shô′–), village (pop. 383), E Alta., near Sask. border, 30 mi. ESE of Wainwright; grain elevators, dairying, oil drilling.

Chauvoncourt (shōvōkōōr′), village (pop. 105), Meuse dept., NE France, opposite Saint-Mihiel; German-held bridgehead on left bank of Meuse R. in First World War.

Chaux (shō), village (pop. 480), Territory of Belfort, E France, 5 mi. N of Belfort; hosiery mfg.

Chaux, Forest of, Jura dept., E France, bet. the Doubs (N) and the Loue (S), just E of Dôle; □ c.75. Traces of Celtic and Gallic habitations.

Chaux d'Abel (shō däbĕl′), mountainous region (3,379 ft.) in the Jura, Bern canton, W Switzerland, 5 to 9 mi. NE of La Chaux-de-Fonds.

Chaux-de-Fonds, La (lä-shō-dù-fō′), town (1950 pop. 33,154), Neuchâtel canton, W Switzerland, 9 mi. NNW of Neuchâtel, 2 mi. from Fr. border, in the Jura; alt. 3,271 ft. Large watch-mfg. center; radios, scales, flour, beer; printing. Art gall., historical mus., clock and watch mus.

Chavakachcheri (chä′vŭkŭ″chĕrē), town (pop. 5,440), Northern Prov., Ceylon, on S Jaffna Peninsula, on Jaffna Lagoon, 10 mi. E of Jaffna; extensive rice and coconut-palm plantations.

Chaval (shäväl′), town (pop. 1,609), N Ceará, Brazil, on the Atlantic, 33 mi. W of Camocim; rice, sugar.

Chavanay (shävänā′), village (pop. 829), Loire dept., SE central France, near right bank of Rhone R., 10 mi. SW of Vienne; noted wines.

Chavanges (shävãzh′), agr. village (pop. 609), Aube dept., NE central France, 15 mi. S of Vitry-le-François.

Chavanod (shävänōd′), village (pop. 49), Haute-Savoie dept., SE France, on the Fier and 4 mi. W of Annecy; cheese mfg. Hydroelectric plant near.

Chavanoz (shävänōz′), village (pop. 264), Isère dept., SE France, near the Rhone, 17 mi. E of Lyons; rayon plant.

Chavantes or **Xavantes** (both: shävăn′tĭs), city (pop. 1,908), SW central São Paulo, Brazil, on railroad and 10 mi. ESE of Ourinhos; coffee, alfalfa, rice.

Chavarría (chävärē′ä), town (pop. estimate 500), W central Corrientes prov., Argentina, on railroad and 35 mi. NW of Mercedes; agr. (corn, alfalfa, cotton, rice, livestock).

Chaves (shä′vĭsh), city (pop. 406), NE Pará, Brazil, on N coast of Marajó isl. in Amazon delta, 130 mi. NW of Belém, in cattle-raising area.

Chaves, anc. *Aquae Flaviae*, city (pop. 8,706), Vila Real dist., Trás-os-Montes e Alto Douro prov., N Portugal, on Tâmega R. and 35 mi. NNE of Vila Real; terminus of branch railroad; agr. trade and textile center (silks, linens); mfg. of chocolates and ceramics. Mineral springs. Airfield. Has medieval castle of dukes of Braganza and a Romanesque church. Convention of Chaves signed here 1837.

Chaves (chă′vĭs), county (□ 6,094; pop. 40,605), SE N.Mex.; ⊙ Roswell. Livestock and irrigated agr. area; watered by Pecos R. and Rio Hondo. Cotton, alfalfa, dairy products. Migratory waterfowl refuge and Bottomless Lakes State Park are near Roswell. Formed 1889.

Chaves Island (chä′vĕs), **Santa Cruz Island** (sän′tä krōōs′), or **Indefatigable Island** (□ 389; 1950 pop. 198), central Galápagos Isls., Ecuador, in the Pacific; 0°40′S 90°20′W. Circular in shape (25 mi. wide), of volcanic origin, it rises to c.2,300 ft. Agr. products: sugar cane, fruit; stock.

Chávez, Mexico: see FRANCISCO I. MADERO.

Chavies (chă′vēz), village (1940 pop. 886), Perry co., SE Ky., in Cumberland foothills, on North Fork Kentucky R. and 11 mi. NW of Hazard.

Chaville (shävēl′), town (pop. 13,111), Seine-et-Oise dept., N central France, a SW suburb of Paris, 8 mi. from Notre Dame Cathedral, and 2 mi. E of Versailles; electrical industry.

Chavín or **Chavín de Huantar** (chävēn′ dā wäntär′), town (pop. 916), Ancash dept., W central Peru, on E slopes of Cordillera Blanca, 23 mi. ESE of Huarás; alt. 10,531 ft.; cereals, potatoes.

Chaviña (chävē′nyä), town (pop. 1,529), Ayacucho dept., S Peru, in Cordillera Occidental, 32 mi. SE of Puquio (connected by road); grain, alfalfa; cattle raising.

Chavinda (chävēn′dä), town (pop. 5,131), Michoacán, central Mexico, on central plateau, on railroad, and 35 mi. SW of La Piedad; agr. center (grain, beans, sugar, fruit, livestock); flour milling.

Chavín de Huantar, Peru: see CHAVÍN.

Chawinda (chŭvĭn′dŭ), town (pop. 7,175), Sialkot dist., E Punjab, W Pakistan, 14 mi. SE of Sialkot; agr. (wheat, rice); limekilns.

Chaxoengsao, Thailand: see CHACHOENGSAO.

Chaya (chă′yä′), town (pop. 6,966), Okayama prefecture, SW Honshu, Japan, 8 mi. WSW of Okayama, in agr. area (rice, wheat, persimmons); spinning and textile mills; floor mats. Sometimes spelled Tyaya.

Chaya or **Ch'a-ya**, Tibet: see DRAYA.

Chayabhum, Thailand: see CHAIYAPHUM.

Chayala (chīä′lä), town (pop. c.4,100), Potosí dept., W central Bolivia, on Chayanta R. and 14 mi. NE of Colquechaca; corn, alpaca, sheep.

Chayan (chīän′), village (1939 pop. over 500), E South Kazakhstan oblast, Kazakh SSR, 50 mi. NNW of Chimkent; cotton, cattle.

Chayanta, province, Potosí dept., Bolivia: see COLQUECHACA.

Chayanta (chīän′tä), town (pop. c.8,600), Potosí dept., W central Bolivia, at E foot of Cordillera de Azanaques, 8 mi. E of Uncía; alt. 11,860 ft.

Chayanta River, Potosí dept., W central Bolivia, rises in E slopes of Cordillera de Azanaques E of Uncía, flows 80 mi. generally E, past Poroma, joining Caine R. at Pucara to form Río Grande. Receives San Pedro R. (left).

Chaya River, Bulgaria: see ASENOVITSA RIVER.

Chaya River (chī′ŭ), Tomsk oblast, Russian SFSR, formed by junction of Parbig and Bakchar rivers at Bakchar; flows 110 mi. NE, past Podgornoye, to Ob R. 10 mi. S of Kolpashevo. Navigable for entire length.

Chayek (chī′ŭk), village (1939 pop. over 500), NW Tyan-Shan oblast, Kirghiz SSR, on Dzhumgol R. and 85 mi. NW of Naryn; wheat.

Chayetina, Yugoslavia: see CAJETINA.

Chayniche, Yugoslavia: see CAJNICE.

Chayü or **Ch'a-yü**, Tibet: see RIMA.

Chayvo, Russian SFSR: see CHAIVO.

Chazelles-sur-Lyon (shäzĕl′-sür-lēō′), town (pop. 5,252), Loire dept., SE central France, 14 mi. N of Saint-Étienne; hat-making center.

Chazey-Bons (shäzā′-bō′), village (pop. 222), Ain dept., E France, in the S Jura, 3 mi. N of Belley.

Chazy (shā″zē′), village (pop. c.450), Clinton co., extreme NE N.Y., on Little Chazy R., near L. Champlain, and 14 mi. N of Plattsburg, in agr. area; metal products, lime, crushed stone.

Chazy Lake (□ c.2), Clinton co., extreme NE N.Y., in the Adirondacks, 18 mi. W of Plattsburg; 4 mi. long. Drained by Great Chazy R.

Cheadle (chē′dùl), town and parish (pop. 6,754), N Stafford, England, 8 mi. E of Stoke-on-Trent; cotton milling; coal mining; agr. market.

Cheadle and Gatley (chē′dùl, găt′lē), urban district (1931 pop. 18,473; 1951 census 31,508), NE Cheshire, England. Includes town of Cheadle, 2 mi. SSW of Stockport, with cotton milling, silk printing, mfg. of chemicals, pharmaceuticals, leather products; and town of Gatley, 3 mi. SSW of Stockport, with cotton mills.

Cheadle Heath, town in Cheadle and Gatley urban dist., NE Cheshire, England, just W of Stockport; textile bleaching, chemical making, mfg. of electric wire, concrete.

Cheaha Mountain (chē′hô), peak (2,407 ft.) in Talladega Mts., E Ala., 12 mi. S of Anniston. Highest point in Ala.; state park here.

Cheam, England: see SUTTON AND CHEAM.

Cheapside (chēp′sīd′), district and street in the City of London, England, running from St. Paul's churchyard to the Bank of England. Important market center of medieval London, it was scene of tournaments and of occasional executions. Here was one of the Eleanor Crosses. Cheapside was site of the Mermaid Tavern, frequented by Shakespeare. Milton was b. in one of its side streets. Some of its anc. guildhalls were destroyed or damaged in Second World War.

Cheatham (chē′tùm), county (□ 305; pop. 9,167), N central Tenn.; ⊙ Ashland City. Drained by Cumberland and Harpeth rivers. Agr. (grain, tobacco, livestock). Formed 1856.

Cheat Mountain, E W.Va., ridge (c.3,000 ft.) of the Allegheny; extends c.45 mi. NNE from point near head of Shavers Fork (which parallels ridge on E and cuts across it in N) to S Tucker co. line NE of Elkins. Rises to 4,830 ft. near S end, above 4,000 ft. in other summits. Civil War battle of Cheat Mtn. (a Union victory) was fought in Sept., 1861.

Cheat River, E W.Va. and SW Pa., formed by junction of Shavers Fork and Black Fork at Parsons, W.Va.; flows N past Rowlesburg, and NW to Monongahela R. at Point Marion, Pa.; c.75 mi. long. Used for hydroelectric power. Dammed in lower course NE of Morgantown, W.Va., to form Cheat L. or Lynn L. (resorts), extending c.10 mi. upstream; here river's gorge has 1,000-ft. walls. Civil War battle of Corrick's Ford fought at PARSONS.

Cheb (khĕp), Ger. *Eger* (ā′gùr), town (pop. 14,533), W Bohemia, Czechoslovakia, on Ohre R. and 90 mi. W of Prague, near Ger. border; rail junction; industrial center; mfg. of motorcycles, bicycles, agr. machinery, cotton and linen textiles, carpets, leather, beer; intensive trade. Peat cutting in near-by marshes. Has 11th-cent. castle, remains of fortifications, and mus. Wallenstein assassinated here, 1634. Exodus of its former large Ger. pop. began in 1933 and reached culminating point after Second World War.

Chebanse (shùbăns′), village (pop. 739), on Iroquois-Kankakee co. line, E Ill., 8 mi. SSW of Kankakee; ships grain.

Chebarkul or **Chebarkul′** (chĕbŭrkōōl′), town (1926 pop. 2,647), W central Chelyabinsk oblast, Russian SFSR, on small lake, 10 mi. E of Miass city, on railroad, in gold-placer region; iron and steel forgings. Several small health resorts near by.

Chebba, La (lä shĕb-bä′), village, Sfax dist., E Tunisia, on the Mediterranean, 39 mi. NE of Sfax; extensive olive groves; olive-oil pressing, mfg. of esparto products. Tuna fishing.

Chebeague Island, Maine: see GREAT CHEBEAGUE ISLAND.

Chebli (shĕblē'), village (pop. 940), Alger dept., N central Algeria, in the Mitidja plain, 14 mi. S of Algiers; citrus fruit, essential oils; olive oil.

Cheboksary (chĕbŭksä'rē), city (1939 pop. 31,040), ⊙ Chuvash Autonomous SSR, Russian SFSR, port on right bank of the Volga, opposite Sosnovka, and 360 mi. E of Moscow, on rail spur from Kanash; 56°9'N 47°14'E. Agr.-processing center (hides, sunflower oil, grain); mfg. (leather and electrical goods, liquor, bricks). Sawmilling, woodworking near by. Site of projected hydroelectric plant on Volga R. Teachers and agr. colleges. Has Chuvash mus., 16th-cent. monastery, and 17th-cent. cathedral. Founded 1556.

Cheboygan (shĭboi'gŭn), county (□ 725; pop. 13,731), N Mich.; ⊙ Cheboygan. Bounded N by Straits of Mackinac; drained by Cheboygan, Black, and Sturgeon rivers. Livestock, dairy products, potatoes, fruit. Mfg. at Cheboygan. Commercial fishing, limestone quarrying, sawmilling. Includes Burt, Mullett, Black, and Douglas lakes (resorts; fishing, boating); also state parks and state forests. Univ. of Mich. biological station is on Douglas L. Organized 1853.

Cheboygan, city (pop. 5,687), ⊙ Cheboygan co., N Mich., at mouth of Cheboygan R., on South Channel of the Straits of Mackinac, and c.65 mi. NW of Alpena. Port of entry and trade center for agr. (fruit, livestock; dairy products) and resort area. Mfg. of snow plows, paper, wood furniture, novelties, foundry products, clothing, feed; commercial fishing, limestone quarrying. Ships fish. On Douglas L. (SW) is Univ. of Mich. Biological Station. Important lumber center in late 19th cent. Settled 1857; inc. as village 1871, as city 1889.

Cheboygan River, N Mich., drains Mullett L., flows c.6 mi. N, past Cheboygan, into South Channel of the Straits of Mackinac.

Chebrolu (chĕbrō'lōō), town (pop. 12,305), Guntur dist., NE Madras, India, in Kistna R. delta, 8 mi. SE of Guntur; rice milling, cotton ginning; tobacco. Sometimes spelled Chebrole or Chibrolu.

Chebsara (chĕpsä'rŭ), town (1932 pop. estimate 2,030), SW Vologda oblast, Russian SFSR, on railroad and 36 mi. W of Vologda; flax processing.

Checa (chā'kä), town (pop. 830), Guadalajara prov., central Spain, on affluent of the Tagus and 18 mi. SSE of Molina; grain, livestock; flour milling. Has mineral springs and unexploited silver, iron-pyrite, graphite deposits.

Checacupe (chākäkōō'pā), town (pop. 1280), Cuzco dept., S Peru, on Vilcanota R., on railroad and 50 mi. SE of Cuzco; alt. 11,279 ft.; grain, potatoes. Silver deposits.

Checca (chā'kä), town (pop. 860), Cuzco dept., S Peru, in high Andean valley, 18 mi. SW of Sicuani, in agr. region (potatoes, grain); mfg. of woolen goods. Marble and ocher deposits.

Chech, Erg, Algeria: see ERG.

Chechaouene, Sp. Morocco: see XAUEN.

Chechelnik or **Chechel'nik** (chĭchĕl'nyĭk), town (1926 pop. 6,463), SE Vinnitsa oblast, Ukrainian SSR, 80 mi. SSE of Vinnitsa; sugar refining, distilling.

Checheng or **Che-ch'eng** (jŭ'chŭng'), town, ⊙ Checheng co. (pop. 256,699), NE Honan prov., China, near Anhwei line, on Kwo R. and 30 mi. SW of Shangkiu; cotton weaving; grain. Soda deposits near by.

Chechen-Ingush Autonomous Soviet Socialist Republic (chĭchĕn'-ĭng-gōōsh'), former administrative division (□ 6,100; 1939 pop. 697,408) of S European Russian SFSR; ⊙ Grozny. Pop. was largely Chechen (55%) and Ingush (10%). Originally part of Mountain Autonomous SSR, Chechen (created 1922) and Ingush (formed 1924) autonomous oblasts merged (1934) to form Chechen-Ingush Autonomous Oblast within North Caucasus Territory, and became an autonomous republic in 1936. Upon dissolution (1944) of the republic, following collaboration of local pop. with Germans, its major portion became part of GROZNY oblast, while border strips passed to neighboring North Ossetian (W) and Dagestan (E) Autonomous SSRs and to Georgian SSR (S).

Chechersk (chĭchĕrsk'), town (1926 pop. 3,682), E central Gomel oblast, Belorussian SSR, on Sozh R. and 34 mi. N of Gomel; fruit and vegetable canning. Beaver farm.

Che-chiang, China: see CHEKIANG.

Chechon (chā'chŭn'), Jap. *Teisen*, town (1949 pop. 28,391), N.Chungchong prov., S Korea, 19 mi. NE of Chungju; agr. (soy beans, cotton, tobacco), mining (silver, zinc), paper milling.

Checiny (khĕtsē'nĭ), Pol. *Chęciny*, Rus. *Khentsiny* (khĕntsē'nē), town (pop. 2,677), Kielce prov., SE central Poland, 9 mi. SW of Kielce; marble quarrying, copper mining; building materials. Castle ruins. Before Second World War, pop. 75% Jewish.

Checotah (shŭkō'tŭ), city (pop. 2,638), McIntosh co., E Okla., 21 mi. SSW of Muskogee; trade center for agr., and stock- and poultry-raising area; cotton ginning, feed milling, dairying; machine-shop products. Settled 1872.

Chedabucto Bay (shĕ"dŭbŭk'tō), inlet (15 mi. long, 10 mi. wide at entrance) of the Atlantic, E N.S., opposite S end of Cape Breton Isl., at S entrance to Strait of Canso. At head of bay is Guysborough.

Cheddar (chĕ'dŭr), town and parish (pop. 2,154), N Somerset, England, 10 mi. ESE of Weston-super-Mare, near Mendip Hills; agr. market in dairying region, famous for its cheese; tourist center. Has 15th-cent. church and market cross. Near by is CHEDDAR GORGE.

Cheddar Gorge, deep gorge in Mendip Hills, N Somerset, England, NE of Cheddar; limestone walls, rising over 400 ft., are pierced by large natural caves. Popular tourist attraction.

Chedde (shĕd), Alpine village of Haute-Savoie dept., SE France, at W end of upper Arve R. gorge, 7 mi. W of Chamonix; electrochemical (explosives) and electrometallurgical (aluminum) works.

Cheduba Island (chĕdōō'bŭ, chĕ'dōō-, Burmese chē'dōōbä), in Bay of Bengal, off Arakan coast, Lower Burma, in Kyaukpyu dist., 30 mi. W of Taungup and separated by Cheduba Strait from Ramree Isl. (N); 20 mi. long, 15 mi. wide. Agr., cattle raising on coast; mud volcanoes, oil deposits inland. Port and village of Cheduba, on NE coast, is linked by steamer with Kyaukpyu.

Cheeching, village (pop. 54), SW Alaska, near Bethel.

Cheektowaga (chēktŭwä'gŭ), village (1940 pop. 11,105), Erie co., W N.Y., 3 mi. E of Buffalo; mfg. (machinery, steel and wood products, lenses, canned foods); stone quarries; wheat growing.

Cheenik, Alaska: see GOLOVIN.

Cheesman Dam, central Colo., on South Platte R. and c.40 mi. SSW of Denver. Concrete dam (more than 200 ft. high, 710 ft. long) built 1904 by city of Denver for water supply. Forms L. Cheesman (4 mi. long, .5 mi. wide; sometimes spelled Cheeseman).

Cheetham (chē'tŭm), N suburb (pop. 23,374) of Manchester, SE Lancashire, England; cotton and wool milling, engineering; mfg. of chemicals, wax polishes, tobacco products.

Chef-Boutonne (shĕf-bōōtôn'), village (pop. 1,298), Deux-Sèvres dept., W France, 23 mi. SE of Niort; cider milling, dairying. Has Gallo-Roman ruins.

Chef Menteur Pass (shĕf' mŭntōōr', –tŭr'), navigable waterway in SE La., connecting L. Borgne and L. Pontchartrain; c.7 mi. long. Fort Macomb State Park is on its banks.

Chefoo, Chifu, Chih-fu, or **Chih-fou** (all: chē'fōō', chu'fō'), officially **Yentai** or **Yen-t'ai** (both: yĕn'tī'), city (1934 pop. 139,512; 1947 pop. estimate 227,000), E Shantung prov., China, port on Yellow Sea, on Shantung peninsula's N coast, 115 mi. NNE of Tsingtao; 37°32'N 121°24'E. Commercial center; exports wine, silk, straw plait, bean cake, vegetable oil, eggs. Fishing base with processing plants. City is situated on S shore of Chefoo Bay (2.5 mi. wide), sheltered by rocky promontory and Kungtung (K'ung-t'ung) Isl. with lighthouse. The name Chefoo is properly applied only to Chefoo village on promontory across the bay. This original site became inaccessible (19th cent.) as the result of silting, and a new harbor was built at Yentai, to which the name Chefoo continued to be applied. Chefoo was opened to foreign trade in 1858. By a convention signed here (1876), additional treaty ports were opened. City was held by the Japanese, 1937–45. Passed 1948 to Communist control. It became an independent municipality in 1946.

Chefornak (chĕfôr'näk), village (pop. 106), SW Alaska, near Bethel.

Chefuncte River, La.: see TCHEFUNCTA RIVER.

Chegem (chĭgyĕm'), village (1939 pop. over 2,000), N central Kabardian Autonomous SSR, Russian SFSR, on Chegem R. and 6 mi. NNW of Nalchik; truck produce, orchards.

Chegem River, Kabardian Autonomous SSR, Russian SFSR, rises in the central Greater Caucasus E of Mt. Elbrus, flows c.80 mi. NE, past Chegem, to Baksan R. NE of Nalchik. Floods during summer months; used for irrigation.

Chegoggin Point (shŭgŏ'gĭn), cape on the Atlantic, SW N.S., 3 mi. NW of Yarmouth; 43°51'N 66°9'W. Silica is mined.

Chehalis (chĭhā'lĭs), city (pop. 5,639), ⊙ Lewis co., SW Wash., on Chehalis R. and 4 mi. S of Centralia. State school for boys here. Lumber, brick, coal; food processing. Settled 1873, inc. 1890.

Chehalis River, SW Wash., rises in SW Chehalis co., flows N and NW c.115 mi., past Chehalis and Centralia, to Grays Harbor at Aberdeen.

Cheia, Rumania: see VALENI.

Cheichei (chā'chā), village, Sidamo-Borana prov., S Ethiopia, bet. lakes Awusa and Abaya, 17 mi. NW of Yirga-Alam. Caravan center (hides, coffee, wax).

Cheildag or **Cheyl'dag** (chāldäk'), town (1945 pop. over 500) in Molotov dist. of Greater Baku, E Azerbaijan SSR, c.20 mi. WSW of Baku; oil wells (developed in 1940s).

Cheimaditis, Lake, or **Lake Khimaditis** (both: khēmŭdhē'tĭs), lake (□ 4.6) in Greek Macedonia, 14 mi. SE of Phlorina; 4 mi. long, 1½ mi. wide. Formerly called Rudnik; also spelled Chimaditis.

Cheinat, Thailand: see CHAINAT.

Chejendé (chāhĕndā'), town (pop. 1,494), Trujillo state, W Venezuela, in Andean spur, 18 mi. N of Trujillo; coffee, corn, sugar cane, cacao.

Cheju (chā'jōō'), Jap. *Saishu*, town (1949 pop. 57,905), on N coast of Cheju Isl., Korea, on Cheju Strait; commercial center in agr. area (grains, soy beans, sweet potatoes); produces iodine and potash. Fishing, weaving.

Cheju Island, Korean *Cheju-do*, Jap. *Saishu-to* or *Saisyu-to*, island and province (□ 713, 1949 pop. 254,589, including offshore islets) of Korea, bet. Cheju Strait (N) and E.China Sea (S), 90 mi. S of Mokpo; 33°24'N 126°34'E; roughly oval, 45 mi. long, 18 mi. wide. An extinct volcano, the isl. is generally low, rising to 6,398 ft. at Mt. Halla in central forested area. Agr. (grains, soy beans, cotton), cattle raising, fishing, whaling. Chief town is Cheju on N coast. Isl. was separated (1946) from S.Cholla prov. and made a separate prov. Formerly called Quelpart Isl.

Chejung (jŭ'rōōng'), town (pop. 5,804), ⊙ Chejung co. (pop. 38,984), NE Fukien prov., China, on Chekiang line, 22 mi. NNW of Siapu; sweet potatoes, wheat, rice. Until 1945 town was called Cheyang.

Cheju Strait (chā'jōō'), Korean *Cheju-haehyop*, Jap. *Saishu-kaikyo*, channel connecting Korea Strait (E) with Yellow Sea (NW), bet. SW coast of Korean peninsula (N) and Cheju Isl. (S); c.50 mi. wide, contains many isls.

Chekalin (chĕkŭ'lyĕn'), city (1948 pop. over 2,000), W Tula oblast, Russian SFSR, on Oka R. (head of navigation) and 55 mi. WSW of Tula; limestone quarries. Chartered 1565; called Likhvin until 1944. Lignite mining at Cherepet, 6 mi. E.

Chekao (jŭ'gou'), town, N Anhwei prov., China, 15 mi. NW of Chaohsien; commercial center; rice, wheat, cotton, rapeseed.

Chekhov (chĕ'khŭf), city (1940 pop. 7,846), S Sakhalin, Russian SFSR, port on Sea of Japan, on W coast railroad and 27 mi. N of Kholmsk; pulp and paper milling. Coal mining near by; petroleum (N). Under Jap. rule (1905–45), called Noda.

Chekhov, Mount, Russian SFSR: see SUSUNAI RANGE.

Chekiang or **Che-chiang** (both: chĕ'kyăng', jŭ'-jyăng'), province (□ 40,000; pop. 20,000,000) of E China, on E.China Sea; ⊙ Hangchow. Bounded N by Kiangsu, W by Anhwei and Kiangsi, and S by Fukien, Chekiang lies in the zone of transition from the rocky, indented, isl.-strewn SE coast to the alluvial Yangtze plain of rivers and canals (N). The Fukien mtn. pattern continues in the S of Chekiang, where the NE outliers of the Bohea Hills terminate in the Kwatsang, Yentang, and Tientai mts., and extends into the sea as the Chusan Archipelago (major fishing grounds). This mtn. complex, drained by Wu, Ling, and Yung rivers, is separated by the Tsientang, Chekiang's main stream, from the broken S Yangtze hills (W), whose Tienmu Mts. and Mokan Shan fall within the Chekiang limits. The climate is subtropical and similar to that of Fukien in S, but becomes temperate, with colder winters, in N lowlands. Agr. is important, particularly on densely settled Yangtze delta plain, where rice, silk, cotton, tobacco, and hemp are raised. Tea grows mainly on the hill slopes, which also yield timber and bamboo. Coal (Changhing), soapstone (Tsingtien), and alum (Pingyang) are the only minerals produced. Leading port cities are Hangchow (noted for its silk and satin production), Ningpo (fishing port), and Wenchow (lumber exports). Pop. speaks the Wu (Shanghai) dialect. Main inland cities are Shaohing (rice wine), Kinhwa, and Kashing. The prov. is served by Chekiang-Kiangsi RR and by lines from Hangchow to Ningpo, Shanghai, and Soochow. Chekiang passed into the Chinese orbit in 3d cent. B.C., and flourished in 12th-13th cent. as the center of the Southern Sung dynasty. Originally called Yüeh for local tribes, it received its present name (the anc. name of Tsientang R.) in the Ming dynasty (1368–1644); it passed to Manchu control in 1645. During Sino-Japanese War, prov. was partly occupied by the Japanese. In 1949 it came under Communist regime.

Chekmagush (chĕkmŭgōōsh'), village (1926 pop. 3,141), NW Bashkir Autonomous SSR, Russian SFSR, 60 mi. NW of Ufa; wheat, rye, oats, livestock. Until 1945, Chekmagushi.

Chekunda (chĕkōōndä'), village (1939 pop. over 500), SW Khabarovsk Territory, Russian SFSR, on Bureya R. (head of navigation), on spur of Trans-Siberian RR and 210 mi. WSW of Komsomolsk, in Bureya coal basin.

Chela, Serra de (sĕ'rŭ dĭ shĕ'lŭ), W escarpment of Angola's central plateau, in Huíla prov. (SW Angola). Extends c.100 mi. from South-West Africa border to Sá da Bandeira area, parallel to and c.80 mi. inland from coast. Rises c.7,500 ft.

Chelamet, Eritrea: see KALAMAT.

Chelan (chĭlăn'), county (□ 2,931; pop. 39,301), central Wash.; ⊙ Wenatchee. Mtn. area in Cascade Range, including L. Chelan and parts of Chelan and Wenatchee natl. forests. Irrigated fruit-growing region; livestock; lumber; gold, copper. Formed 1899.

Chelan, town (pop. 2,157), Chelan co., central Wash., 15 mi. N of Waterville, near outlet of L. Chelan; trade center for recreational, agr. area. Copper mines; timber, fruit. Settled 1892, inc. 1902.

Chelan, Lake (c.50 mi. long, 0.5–1.5 mi. wide; alt. c.1,000 ft.), N central Wash., in deep glacial gorge of Cascade Range; resorts. Drains into Columbia R. SE of Chelan through Chelan R. (4 mi. long; used for hydroelectric power). Chelan Mts. (c.8,000 ft.), an E branch of Cascade Range, parallel lake on W.

Chelcic, Czechoslovakia: see VODNANY.

Cheleken (chĕlyĭkyĕn'), town (1926 pop. 2,728), W Ashkhabad oblast, Turkmen SSR, on E coast of Caspian Sea, on Cheleken peninsula (formerly an isl.; recently connected with mainland), 40 mi. S of Krasnovodsk, in oil fields; processing of iodine, bromine, and ozocerite.

Cheles (chā'lĕs), town (pop. 2,135), Badajoz prov., W Spain, near Port. border, 30 mi. SW of Badajoz; cereals, olives, olive oil, livestock. Mfg. of tiles.

Cheli or **Ch'e-li** (both: chŭ'lē'), town, ⊙ Cheli co. (pop. 30,170), southernmost Yunnan prov., China, on right bank of Mekong R., on route to Thailand, and 75 mi. S of Ningerh; cotton textiles; rice, millet, beans. Formerly called Kenghung.

Chélia, Djebel (jĕ'bĕl shālyä'), highest peak (7,641 ft.) of Algeria, in the Aurès massif, in Constantine dept., 30 mi. SE of Batna. Snow-covered part of the year. Cedar forests on slopes.

Chéliff River (shālĕf'), longest and most important stream of Algeria, and French North Africa's only river originating in the Saharan Atlas to reach the Mediterranean. Length, 450 mi. Rising as the Oued Sebgag in the Djebel Amour near Aflou, it flows N across the High Plateaus (where it loses most of its water) as the Oued Touïl. Replenished by the Oued Nahar Ouassel (which rises near Tiaret), it crosses the main axis of the Tell Atlas in a gorge bet. Boghari and Lavigerie. Thence, turning W, it parallels the coast, meandering through a widening floodplain, past Orléansville, and enters the sea 7 mi. N of Mostaganem. Ghrib Dam (213 ft. high; just above Dollfusville) stores water for irrigation and has hydroelectric plant since 1942. Cereals, cotton, and citrus fruit are intensively cultivated in lower valley, which is also irrigated from dams on the Chéliff's left tributaries (Oueds Fodda and Mina). Lower course followed by Oran-Algiers trunk railroad and highway. Also spelled Chélif and Sheliff.

Chelin Bay, China: see CHALLUM BAY.

Cheling Pass (jŭ'lĭng'), (alt. 1,000 ft.), S Hunan prov., China, in the Nan Ling, just N of Ichang, near Kwangtung line. A traditional route bet. Kwangtung and central and N China, it is used by Canton-Hankow RR.

Chelín Island (chālēn') (□ 4.4; pop. 738), just off E coast of Chiloé Isl., S Chile; 42°35'S 73°31'W.

Chelkar (chĭlkär'), city (1939 pop. over 10,000), S Aktyubinsk oblast, Kazakh SSR, on Trans-Caspian RR and 120 mi. NW of Aralsk; chemical industry based on salt production; metalworks; rubber goods, meat products, dairying.

Chelkar, Lake (□ 80), N West Kazakhstan oblast, Kazakh SSR, 40 mi. SSE of Uralsk; abounds in fish originating in Ural R. (connected by Solyanka R.) and Caspian Sea.

Chelkar-Tengiz (-tyĕngēs'), salt lake (□ c.700) in SE Aktyubinsk oblast, Kazakh SSR, 90 mi. NE of Aral Sea, in dry steppe and desert area. Receives Irgiz R. (W).

Chella (chä'lyä), town (pop. 2,950), Valencia prov., E Spain, 9 mi. WNW of Játiva; olive-oil processing, sawmilling, lumbering; cereals, vegetables, rice, oranges.

Chellakere, India: see CHALLAKERE.

Chellala, Algeria: see REIBELL.

Chelles (shĕl), anc. *Calae*, outermost E suburb (pop. 11,721) of Paris, France, 12 mi. E of Notre Dame cathedral, near right bank of the Marne; flour mills, forges; mfg. (millstones, mirrors, agr. equipment, soap). Prehistoric remains found near by gave name to Chellean epoch. Until French Revolution site of noted convent founded under Clovis.

Chelm (khĕ'ōōm), Pol. *Chełm*, Rus. *Kholm* (khôlm), city (pop. 23,329), Lublin prov., E Poland, 40 mi. ESE of Lublin. Rail junction; trade center; mfg. of agr. machinery, millstones, furniture; brewing, distilling, sawmilling, flour milling, brickworking. An early Slav settlement; founded (together with a castle and near-by fortifications) as a town and made an Orthodox Eastern bishopric (noted for its cathedral) in 13th cent. Passed (1795) to Austria and (1815) to Rus. Poland. In 1827, pop. was 2,200; development began at close of 19th cent. In 1909, Russia created Kholm govt. within Rus. Poland, and, claiming Orthodox Eastern pop. in that region, placed it (1912) in Russia proper. Chelm reverted to Poland in 1921. Before Second World War, pop. was 40% Jewish. First Pol. city to fall to Soviet army (1944); scene of proclamation (July 22, 1944) of new Pol. republic. After war, Poles evacuated some of Chelm's Ukrainian pop. to the USSR.

Chelmenti, Ukrainian SSR: see KELMENTSY.

Chelmer River, Essex, England, rises 3 mi. N of Thaxted, flows 35 mi. SE, past Great Dunmow and Chelmsford, to Blackwater R. at Maldon. Navigable below Chelmsford.

Chelmno (khĕ'ōōmnô), Pol. *Chełmno*, Ger. *Kulm* (kōōlm), town (pop. 11,634), Bydgoszcz prov., N central Poland, port on the Vistula and 24 mi. NE of Bydgoszcz, in area of small lakes. Rail terminus; mfg. of machinery, bricks, furniture; food processing, flour milling, sawmilling. Dates from 10th cent.; came (13th cent.) under Teutonic Knights, who established bishopric (present seat at Pelplin); passed 15th cent. to Poland, 1772 to Prussia; returned 1919 to Poland.

Chelmos, Greece: see AROANIA.

Chelmsford, town (pop. 905), S central Ont., 12 mi. NW of Sudbury; dairying center; nickel and copper mining.

Chelmsford (chĕlms'fùrd), residential municipal borough (1931 pop. 26,537; 1951 census 37,888), ⊙ Essex, England, in center of co., on Chelmer R. at mouth of Cann R., and 30 mi. ENE of London; agr. market; flour mills, mfg. of electrical equipment, hardware, tile. Has church built 1424 (a cathedral since 1914) and 16th-cent. grammar school.

Chelmsford (chĕmz'fùrd, chĕlmz'-), residential town (pop. 9,407), Middlesex co., NE Mass., 4 mi. SSW of Lowell; mfg. (beverages, wooden boxes), granite, wool processing; truck. Settled 1633, inc. 1655. Includes North Chelmsford village (1940 pop. 1,765).

Chelmsko Slaskie (khĕ'ōōmskô shlō'skyĕ), Pol. *Chełmsko Śląskie*, Ger. *Schömberg* (shûm'bĕrk), town (1939 pop. 2,099; 1946 pop. 2,299) in Lower Silesia, after 1945 in Wroclaw prov., SW Poland, near Czechoslovak border, at E foot of the Riesengebirge, 13 mi. SW of Waldenburg (Walbrzych); flax, hemp, and jute milling. After 1945, briefly called Szymrych.

Chelmza (khĕ'ōōm-zhä), Pol. *Chełmża*, Ger. *Kulmsee* (kōōlm'zā"), town (pop. 10,764), Bydgoszcz prov., N central Poland, 12 mi. N of Torun; rail junction; mfg. of machinery, bricks, roofing materials, combs, liquor, beet sugar, flour. L. Chelmza, Pol. *Jezioro Chełmżyńskie* (yĕzyô'rô khĕōōmzhĭ'nyùskyĕ), is just ESE; 4 mi. long.

Chelno-Vershiny (chĭlnô'-vyĭrshē'nē), village (1932 pop. estimate 2,500), NE Kuibyshev oblast, Russian SFSR, 32 mi. N of Sergiyevsk; wheat, sunflowers.

Chelny, Russian SFSR: see NABEREZHNYE CHELNY.

Chelsea (chĕl'sē), municipality (pop. 12,049), S Victoria, Australia, on E shore of Port Phillip Bay, 18 mi. SSE of Melbourne, in metropolitan area; commercial center for agr. region.

Chelsea, village (pop. estimate 300), SW Que., on Gatineau R. and 8 mi. NW of Ottawa; dairying, lumbering; cattle.

Chelsea, residential metropolitan borough (1931 pop. 59,031; 1951 census 50,912) of London, England, on N bank of the Thames (here crossed by Chelsea and Albert bridges), 3 mi. SW of Charing Cross. It is a literary and artistic quarter, with associations with Sir Thomas More, Carlyle, Rossetti, Whistler, Dickens, Kingsley, George Eliot, Mrs. Gaskell, and Oscar Wilde. It suffered considerable air-raid damage in 1940–41; 12th-cent. Chelsea Old Church was destroyed, and the Royal Hosp. for veteran soldiers (built 1682–92 by Wren) was damaged. Adjoining hosp. was RANELAGH, a center of entertainment in time of George III. District was also site of Henry VIII's Manor House.

Chelsea. 1 Town (pop. 482), Tama co., central Iowa, 28 mi. ESE of Marshalltown; feed milling. **2** Town (pop. 2,169), Kennebec co., S Maine, 5 mi. SE of Augusta, in agr., resort, lumbering area. Togus village is site of U.S. soldiers' home. Inc. 1850. **3** City (pop. 38,912), Suffolk co., E Mass., NE industrial and residential suburb of Boston, on estuary of Mystic R. (bridged to Charlestown). Produces elastic goods, shoes, rubber goods, chemicals, paints, wood products, food products; printing. Has naval hosp., soldiers' home. On April 12, 1908, fire destroyed much of city. Settled 1624, inc. as town 1739, as city 1857. **4** Village (pop. 2,580), Washtenaw co., SE Mich., 14 mi. WNW of Ann Arbor, in agr. area (livestock, poultry, grain); dairying. Mfg. of auto parts, flour, paper, metal products. Many small lakes near by. Settled c.1850; inc. before 1870, reincorporated 1889. **5** A section of Manhattan borough of New York city, SE N.Y., mainly bet. 14th and 28th streets, W of Avenue of the Americas; mainly residential. Site of General Theological Seminary and several pre-Civil War churches. **6** A section of Richmond borough of New York city, SE N.Y., on W Staten Isl. just NE of Carteret, N.J., across Arthur Kill. Richmond co. airport is just S. **7** City (pop. 1,437), Rogers co., NE Okla., 17 mi. WSW of Vinita, in petroleum-producing and agr. area (wheat, oats, barley, sweet potatoes); cotton ginning, feed milling. Coal mines. **8** Town (pop. 41), Faulk co., NE central S.Dak., 25 mi. SSW of Aberdeen. **9** Town (pop. 1,025), ⊙ Orange co., E central Vt., 20 mi. SSE of Montpelier and on First Branch of White R.; agr.; dairy and maple products; lumber. Settled 1784.

Chelsfield, residential town and parish (pop. 2,853), NW Kent, England, 2 mi. SE of Orpington. Church has 14th-cent. tower.

Chelsham (chĕl'sùm), residential town and parish (pop. 1,643), E Surrey, England, 5 mi. SE of Croydon. Has 14th–15th-cent. church.

Cheltenham (chĕlt'nùm), residential municipal borough (1931 pop. 49,418; 1951 census 62,823), N central Gloucester, England, near the Cotswolds, on Chelt R. (small tributary of the Severn) and 8 mi. ENE of Gloucester; resort (since 1716, when mineral springs were discovered here) and hunting center. Also mfg. of shoes, paper, printing, metal products, pharmaceuticals. Cheltenham Col. (1841) is a boys' public school; Cheltenham Ladies' Col. (1853) is a well-known public school for girls. Church of St. Mary is Norman to 14th cent.

Cheltenham (chĕl'tùnhăm"). **1** Village, Prince Georges co., central Md., 15 mi. SE of Washington. State reformatory for Negro boys. Near by is "Mt. Airy" (original wing built 1660; restored), whose garden was designed by Pierre L'Enfant. **2** Urban township (1950 pop. 22,854), Montgomery co., SE Pa., N residential suburb of Philadelphia. Includes communities of Cheltenham (1940 pop. 3,544), with mfg. of hosiery, tape, wood products; WYNCOTE; ELKINS PARK; Edge Hill (1940 pop. 2,681); Melrose Park (1940 pop. 2,509); La Mott (1940 pop. 1,618); Chelten Hills (1940 pop. 1,281).

Chelten Hills, Pa.: see CHELTENHAM.

Chelva (chĕl'vä), town (pop. 3,517), Valencia prov., E Spain, 24 mi. WNW of Liria; olive-oil processing; cereals, potatoes, grapes, livestock.

Chelyabinsk (chĭlyä'bĭnsk), oblast (□ 33,900; 1946 pop. estimate 2,100,000) in SW Siberian Russian SFSR; ⊙ Chelyabinsk. In E foothills of the S Urals; drained by the upper Ural, Ufa, Miass, and Ui rivers. Humid continental climate (short summers). Major industrial and mining region. Metallic ores, chiefly concentrated in the Urals (W, W panhandle), include magnetite (Magnitnaya mtn.), siderite and limonite (Bakal), copper (Karabash), nickel (Verkhni Ufalei), gold (Miass, Plast, Bredy), tungsten, titanium, corundum, chromium, and barite; lignite (Kopeisk, Korkino, Yemanzhelinka), anthracite (Kartaly), and other nonmetallic minerals (marble, marl, gypsum, talc, quartzite). Wheat, rye, oats (E), truck (around Chelyabinsk and Magnitogorsk), sheep (S); livestock, dairying. Forested in NW. Industry based on steel and pig-iron production. Local iron, alloys, limestone, and charcoal, combined with Karaganda and (to a lesser extent) Kuzbas coal, supply metallurgical plants of Magnitogorsk (leading in USSR), Chelyabinsk, Zlatoust, Verkhni Ufalei, Katav-Ivanovsk, Asha, and Kasli. Among noted industrial establishments are Chelyabinsk tractor works and Kyshtym copper refinery. Mfg. of machines and machine tools (Chelyabinsk, Magnitogorsk, Zlatoust, Kyshtym, Kopeisk, Sim), aircraft (Chelyabinsk), automobiles (Miass), railroad stock and streetcars (Ust-Katav), abrasives, chemicals, and building materials (including cement, concrete). Textile, leather, and food industries in major urban centers (Chelyabinsk, Magnitogorsk, Zlatoust). Agr.-processing centers: Verkhne-Uralsk, Troitsk. Numerous settlements developed around gold placers, small metalworks (in central part), and charcoal burners (in W panhandle). Served by S. Siberian RR and S branch of Trans-Siberian RR, with lateral line crossing at Chelyabinsk, Troitsk, and Kartaly. Formed 1934 out of Ural oblast. NE section separated (1943) to form Kurgan oblast.

Chelyabinsk, city (1926 pop. 59,307; 1939 pop. 273,127; 1946 pop. estimate 450,000), ⊙ Chelyabinsk oblast, Russian SFSR, in E foothills of the S Urals, on Miass R., on Trans-Siberian RR, and 900 mi. E of Moscow; 55°10'N 60°43'E. Rail junction; major metallurgical and industrial center of the Urals and of USSR; mfg. (tractors, aircraft, agr. and road-building machinery, abrasives, chemicals, lathes, watches); pipe rolling, cotton milling, sawmilling, agr. and food processing. Has machine building, medical, teachers, and agr. colleges, museums, and old churches. Plants producing pig iron and quality steels, and processing zinc and bauxite, form separate unit, on left Miass R. bank (N), called Metalurgicheski Gorodok [Rus., =metallurgical town]. City's S part, near small Smolino L., is main residential dist. (pop. c.300,000); light mfg. Tractor plant (leading in USSR; established 1930) and building-material works (cement, roofing, glass) based on local granite and refractory-clay deposits are in NE part of city. Founded 1658 as Rus. frontier stronghold; chartered 1745; developed as agr.-processing, grain- and coal-trading town. Major resettlement center for emigrants to Siberia in 19th cent. Building of Trans-Siberian RR (1892) and 1st metallurgical plant (1928) marked city's industrial beginnings. Level site, abundant fuel (KOPEISK lignite) and water supply, and transportation facilities stimulated further industrial construction, largely done in 1930s and after Second World War.

Chelyadz, Poland: see CZELADZ.

Chelyan (shĕl'yùn), village (pop., with adjacent Cabincreek, 1,616), Kanawha co., W W.Va., on the Kanawha and 14 mi. SE of Charleston, in coal-mining and industrial region.

Chelyuskin, Cape (chĭlyōō'skĭn), northernmost point (77°41'N 103°27'E) of Asiatic continent and continental USSR, in Krasnoyarsk Territory, Russian SFSR, on Boris Vilkitski Strait, at N end of Taimyr Peninsula. Govt. observation post; airfield. Originally called Northeast [Rus. *Severovostochny*] Cape; later named for 18th-cent. Rus. navigator.

Chemaïa (shāmäyä'), village, Marrakesh region, W Fr. Morocco, 37 mi. ESE of Safi; sheep and horse raising, barley growing. Saltworks at L. Zima (just W) for Safi fish-processing industry.

Chemainus (chùmā'nùs) town (pop. estimate 1,500), SW B.C., on Vancouver Isl., on Stuart Channel of Strait of Georgia, 40 mi. NNW of Victoria; lumbering center and lumber-shipping port; dairying, fruitgrowing.

Chemax (chāmäks'), town (pop. 1,573), Yucatan, SE Mexico, 18 mi. E of Valladolid; henequen, sugar, corn, fruit.

Chemayundung Chu, river, Tibet: see BRAHMAPUTRA RIVER.

Chemba (shĕm'bä), village, Manica and Sofala prov., W central Mozambique, on right bank of Zambezi R. and 190 mi. N of Beira; cotton.

Chembar, Russian SFSR: see BELINSKI.

Chembur (chăm'bŏŏr), town (pop. 6,198), Bombay Suburban dist., W Bombay, India, on S Salsette Isl., 9 mi. NNE of Bombay city center; chemical mfg., dyeing, yarn glazing, bone crushing.

Chemelil (chĕmĕlĭl'), village, Nyanza prov., W Kenya, on railroad and 25 mi. E of Kisumu; sugar cane, cotton, peanuts, sesame, corn. Also spelled Chemilil.

Chemerna Planina, Yugoslavia: see CEMERNA PLANINA.

Chemernitsa Mountains, Yugoslavia: see CEMERNICA MOUNTAINS.

Chemerovtsy (chĕmyĭrôf'tsē), town (1926 pop. 1,417), SW Kamenets-Podolski oblast, Ukrainian SSR, 24 mi. NNW of Kamenets-Podolski; metalworks.

Chemilil, Kenya: see CHEMELIL.

Chemillé (shùmēyā'), town (pop. 3,093), Maine-et-Loire dept., W France, 20 mi. SSW of Angers; road center and livestock market; mfg. (blankets, waterproof clothing). Here Vendeans defeated Republicans in 1793.

Chemin (shùmē'), village (pop. 140), Jura dept., E France, 11 mi. SW of Dôle; cheese mfg.

Chemin des Dames (shùmē-dā-däm'), ridge (c.600 ft.) in Aisne dept., N France, extending 12 mi. W from Craonne to Fort Malmaison bet. valleys of the Aisne (S) and the Ailette (N). Scene of desperate fighting in First World War. Captured by French in 1917, lost during battle of the Aisne (1918), and recaptured in Oct., 1918. Honeycombed with quarries. Through it passes the Oise-Aisne Canal in a tunnel.

Chemin Grenier (grùnyā'), village (pop. 2,717), S Mauritius, on road and 4 mi. WNW of Souillac; sugar milling, alcohol distilling.

Chemmis, Egypt: see AKHMIM.

Chemnitz (kĕm'nĭts), city (1939 pop. 337,657; 1946 pop. 250,188), Saxony, E central Germany, at N foot of the Erzgebirge, on Chemnitz R. and 40 mi. WSW of Dresden; 50°50'N 12°56'E. Rail junction; airfield (SW). Textile center, with important hosiery-, glove-, underwear-knitting and -finishing works; cotton, wool, silk, rayon, upholstery-fabric milling; carpets. Mfg. of textile machinery, machine tools, automobiles, bicycles, electrical equipment, glass, chemicals, musical instruments, food products. Distributing and finishing center for knitting industry of surrounding region. Near by are large lignite and coal fields. Heavily bombed (destruction about 45%) in Second World War; few of city's old bldgs.—which included 15th-cent. church of St. Jacob, 12th-cent. palace church, and palace (formerly Benedictine abbey; founded in early-12th cent. by Emperor Lothair)—remain. Of Wendish origin; chartered 1143 and granted linen-weaving monopoly. Passed in 1292 to Bohemia, in 1308 to margraves of Meissen. In Thirty Years War, scene (1639) of defeat of imperial forces by Swedes under Banér. Industrial growth dates from 17th cent., when knitting and cotton milling was introduced. Chief suburbs are Borna (NW), Hilbersdorf (NNE), and Gablenz (E).

Chemnitz River, E central Germany, rises in the Erzgebirge 3 mi. NE of Stollberg, flows 30 mi. N, past Chemnitz, to the Zwickauer Mulde 5 mi. S of Rochlitz. Sometimes called Chemnitzer Mulde (kĕm'nĭtsùr mōōl'dù).

Chemor (chĕmôr'), village (pop. 2,741), central Perak, Malaya, on railroad and 9 mi. NNE of Ipoh; tin mining; rubber plantations.

Chemquasabamticook Lake (chĕmkwä"sùbăm'tĭ-kōōk), Piscataquis co., NW Maine, in wilderness area 78 mi. WSW of Presque Isle; drains NE through **Chemquasabamticook Stream,** a tributary of the Allagash.

Chemtou, Tunisia: see OUED-MÉLIZ.

Chemulpo (chä'mōōl'pô') or **Inchon** (ĭn'chŏn', Korean ĕn'chŭn'), Jap. *Jinsen* or *Zinsen* (both: jēn'sän), city (1949 pop. 265,767), Kyonggi prov., central Korea, S of 38°N, on Yellow Sea (here characterized by high tide), 20 mi. WSW of Seoul; important port and industrial center (steel mills, textile and match factories, flour mills). Harbor is icefree and sheltered by several isls. Principal exports are rice, ginseng, dried fish, soy beans. Port was opened 1883 to foreign trade. Connected to the city proper by a causeway is Wolmi Isl. (Jap. *Getsubi-to*), c.1 mi. long, and once a popular summer resort; site of landing (1950) of U.N. forces in Korean war.

Chemung (shĭmŭng'), county (□ 412; pop. 86,827), S N.Y.; ⊙ Elmira. Rolling hilly area, bounded S by Pa. line, cut by Chemung R. valley; drained by Cayuta Creek and small Newtown and Wynkoop's creeks. Agr. (dairy products; poultry, apples); mfg., especially at Elmira; sand and gravel pits. Formed 1836.

Chemung River, in N.Y. and Pa., formed by junction of Cohocton and Tioga rivers at Painted Post, S N.Y., flows c.45 mi. SE, past Elmira, to the Susquehanna at Athens, Pa. Valley was scene of fighting in Sullivan's campaign in the American Revolution; battle of Newtown was fought near site of Elmira in 1779.

Chenab Canal, Lower (chā'năb), large irrigation channel in Punjab, W Pakistan; partly fed by Upper Jhelum Canal; from left bank of CHENAB RIVER (headworks at Khanki, Gujranwala dist.) runs 28 mi. SSW to just E of Hafizabad, where it divides into 2 main branches: E branch flows c.180 mi. S and SW, with numerous distributaries; W branch flows 12 mi. SW, then divides into 3 branches, largest extending c.130 mi. SW. System irrigates vast areas of Gujranwala, Sheikhupura, Lyallpur, and Jhang dists. in Rechna Doab. Opened 1892.

Chenab Canal, Upper, important irrigation channel in E Punjab, W Pakistan; from left bank of CHENAB RIVER (headworks near Marala, Sialkot dist.) runs 120 mi. SSW to Ravi R. (carried over by aqueduct), where it becomes Lower BARI DOAB CANAL. With several distributaries, it irrigates large areas of Sialkot, Gujranwala, and Sheikhupura dists. in Rechna Doab. Opened 1912.

Chenab River, anc. *Acesines*, in NW India, Kashmir, and W Pakistan, one of 5 rivers of the Punjab. Rises in 2 main headstreams (Chandra, S; Bhaga, N) near Bara Lacha La pass in Punjab Himalayas, NE Punjab, India. Flows NW, through N Himachal Pradesh, into S Kashmir, cutting through Pir Panjal Range near Kishtwar, thence W and S, past Riasi, into Pakistan Punjab, here flowing generally SW and receiving (from NW) Jhelum R. SW of Jhang-Maghiana and (from E) Ravi R. NNE of Multan, to Sutlej R. just E of Alipur; total length, c.675 mi. The combined stream (the Panjnad) flows 50 mi. SW to Indus R. The Chenab has noted irrigation system, begun in 1892 with Lower Chenab Canal (headworks at Khanki); later Upper Chenab Canal (headworks near Marala) and its extension, Lower Bari Doab Canal, were constructed, but, since amount of water left in river was insufficient to fill Lower Chenab Canal, Upper Jhelum Canal was built as a feeder to it.

Chenaga, Alaska: see CHENEGA.

Chenalhó (chānälō'), town (pop. 485), Chiapas, S Mexico, in Sierra de Hueytepec, 12 mi. NNE of San Cristóbal de las Casas; wheat, fruit.

Chenan (jŭn'än'). **1** Town, Kwangsi prov., China: see TIENPAO. **2** Town, Liaosi prov., Manchuria, China: see HEISHAN. **3** Town, ⊙ Chenan co. (pop. 96,819), S Shensi prov., China, 60 mi. SSE of Sian, in Tsinling mtn. region; wheat, millet, beans.

Chenango (shĭnăng'gō), county (□ 908; pop. 39,138), central N.Y.; ⊙ Norwich. Bounded E by Unadilla R.; drained by Susquehanna, Otselic, and Chenango rivers. A leading N.Y. dairying co.; also produces fruit, maple sugar, general farm crops, poultry. Some lumbering. Mfg. at Norwich, Bainbridge, Greene, Sherburne. Formed 1798.

Chenango Bridge, village (1940 pop. 735), Broome co., S N.Y., on Chenango R. and 5 mi. N of Binghamton, in dairying area.

Chenango Forks, village, Broome co., S N.Y., at junction of Tioughnioga and Chenango rivers, 11 mi. N of Binghamton.

Chenango River, central N.Y., rises SW of Utica, flows c.90 mi. S and SW, through a dairying and vegetable-growing valley, to the Susquehanna at Binghamton. Receives the Tioughnioga at Chenango Forks. Chenango Valley State Park (928 acres), S of Chenango Forks, is recreational area (camping, summer and winter sports). Chenango Canal, built in 1836–37 as a link in Erie Canal system and abandoned in 1878, joined Utica and Binghamton.

Chenango Valley State Park, N.Y.: see CHENANGO RIVER.

Chenani, Kashmir: see CHINENI.

Chenaran (chùnärän'), village, Ninth Prov., in Khurasan, NE Iran, 40 mi. NW of Meshed and on road to Quchan; grain, fruit.

Ch'en-ch'i, China: see CHENKI.

Chen-chiang, China: see CHINKIANG.

Chen-chieh, China: see CHENKIEH.

Chenchow. 1 Town, Honan prov., China: see HWAIYANG. **2** Town, Hunan prov., China: see CHENHSIEN.

Chenderiang (kùn'drùng), town (pop. 1,103), S central Perak, Malaya, 6 mi. SE of Kampar; tin mining.

Chenderoh (kùndrō'), village, N central Perak, Malaya, on Perak R. and 13 mi. NNE of Kuala Kangsar; site of hydroelectric dam backing up Chenderoh L. (10 mi. long) and supplying Kinta Valley tin centers with electricity.

Chendo (chĕn'dō'), Chinese *Chengto* or *Ch'eng-to* (both: chŭng'dô'), town, ⊙ Chendo co. (pop. 29,000), S Tsinghai prov., China, 30 mi. NNW of Jyekundo and on upper Yangtze R.

Chêne-Bougeries (shĕn-bōōzhùrē'), town (pop. 3,622), Geneva canton, SW Switzerland, just E of Geneva.

Chêne-Bourg (shĕn-bōōr'), town (pop. 2,136), Geneva canton, SW Switzerland, 3 mi. E of Geneva, at Fr. border; metal products, foodstuffs, chemicals.

Chenecey-Buillon (shĕnsā'-bwēyō'), village (pop. 157), Doubs dept., E France, 7 mi. SSW of Besançon; wire, cheese.

Chênée (shĕnā'), town (pop. 10,361), Liége prov., E Belgium, on Vesdre R. and 3 mi. SSE of Liége; rail junction; glassblowing industry.

Chenega (chùnē'gù), Indian fishing village (pop. 91), S Alaska, on S Chenega Isl., on Prince William Sound, 50 mi. ENE of Seward; 60°17'N 148°5'W. Indian School. Formerly also called Chanega, Chanenga, or Chenaga.

Chenega Island (7 mi. long, 4 mi. wide), S Alaska, in W Prince William Sound, bet. Kenai Peninsula (W) and Knight Isl. (E), 50 mi. ENE of Seward, 60°20'N 148°4'W; rises to 2,330 ft. Indian village in S.

Chenequa (chĕnē'kwù), village (pop. 270), Waukesha co., SE Wis., on Chenequa L., 23 mi. WNW of Milwaukee, in farm and lake-resort region.

Chénérailles (shānärī'), village (pop. 701), Creuse dept., central France, 11 mi. N of Aubusson; horse and cattle market.

Chénéville (shā'nāvĭl), village (pop. 589), SW Que., 28 mi. NE of Buckingham; lumbering, dairying, cattle, pigs.

Cheney (chē'nē). **1** City (pop. 777), Sedgwick co., S Kansas, 25 mi. W of Wichita, in grain, livestock, and dairy area. **2** City (pop. 2,797), Spokane co., E Wash., 11 mi. SSW of Spokane; mfg. (flour, farm implements). State teachers col. is here. Founded 1880, inc. 1883.

Cheneyville (chā'nēvĭl), town (pop. 918), Rapides parish, central La., on small Bayou Boeuf and 22 mi. SE of Alexandria; oil and natural-gas field; sugar mills, cotton gins; cotton and truck farms.

Chenfeng, China: see CHENGFENG.

Chengam (chăng'gŭm), village (pop. 4,276), North Arcot dist., E central Madras prov., India, on Cheyyar R. and 20 mi. WNW of Tiruvannamalai; trades in products (sandalwood, tanbark) of Javadi Hills (N).

Chengan. 1 or **Ch'eng-an** (both: chŭng'än'), town, ⊙ Chengan co. (pop. 92,335), SW Hopeh prov., China, on road and 45 mi. NNW of Anyang; wheat, millet, chestnuts, timber. **2** (jŭng'än') Town (pop. 14,072), ⊙ Chengan co. (pop. 216,288), N Kweichow prov., China, 65 mi. NE of Tsunyi; lacquer processing; silk textiles; rice, wheat, beans, millet.

Chengannur (chĕng'gùnōōr), town (pop. 12,543), W Travancore, India, 30 mi. N of Quilon; trades in coir rope and mats, rice, cassava; cashew-nut processing.

Chengcheng or **Ch'eng-ch'eng** (chŭng'chŭng'), town, ⊙ Chengcheng co. (pop. 95,642), E Shensi prov., China, 80 mi. NE of Sian, near Lo R.; rice, wheat, cotton, beans.

Ch'eng-chiang, China: see CHENGKIANG.

Chengchow or **Cheng-chou** (jŭng'jō'), city (1937 pop. 197,187), N Honan prov., China, near Yellow R., 40 mi. W of Kaifeng; rail center at junction of Lunghai and Peking-Hankow railroads; ships hides, sheepskins, grain, salt. Once an unimportant agr. town, Chengchow developed greatly as a processing and shipping center following construction of the rail lines. Called Chenghsien (jŭng'-shyĕn') from 1913 until created a separate municipality in 1949.

Chengfeng or **Chenfeng** (both: jŭng'fŭng'), town (pop. 6,097), ⊙ Chengfeng co. (pop. 101,546), SW Kweichow prov., China, 100 mi. SW of Kweiyang; tea center; cotton-textile, paper, and pottery making; sugar, tung oil. Coal deposits, kaolin quarry near by.

Ch'eng-hai, China: see TENGHAI.

Chengho (jŭng'hŭ'), town (pop. 3,846), ⊙ Chengho co. (pop. 68,176), N Fukien prov., China, near Chekiang line, 40 mi. ENE of Kienow, and on tributary of Min R.; rice, wheat. Zinc mines near.

Chenghsien. 1 or **Ch'eng-hsien** (chŭng'shyĕn'), town (pop. 14,567), ⊙ Chenghsien co. (pop. 379,528), NE central Chekiang prov., China, 50 mi. WSW of Ningpo; tanning, papermaking; rice, wheat, tea, bamboo shoots, medicinal herbs. **2** City, Honan prov., China: see CHENGCHOW. **3** or **Ch'eng-hsien** (chŭng'shyĕn'), town, ⊙ Chenghsien co. (pop. 120,045), SE Kansu prov., China, 50 mi. S of Tienshui, in region of upper reaches of Kialing R.; winegrowing center; paper mfg.; coal and iron mines. Saltworks near by.

Chenghwa, China: see SHARASUME.
Chengkiang or **Ch'eng-chiang** (both: chŭng'jyăng'), town, ⊙ Chengkiang co. (pop. 70,019), E central Yunnan prov., China, 28 mi. SE of Kunming, on N shore of L. Fusien (or L. Chengkiang); rice, wheat, millet, beans. Coal mines and bauxite deposits near by.
Chengkiang, Lake, China: see FUSIEN, LAKE.
Chengkiatun, Manchuria: see SHWANGLIAO.
Chengkow or **Ch'eng-k'ou** (both: chŭng'kō'), town (pop. 13,137), ⊙ Chengkow co. (pop. 91,164), NE Szechwan prov., China, at S foot of the Tapa Shan, 35 mi. ESE of Wanyüan; rice, potatoes, wheat, beans.
Chengku or **Ch'eng-ku** (chŭng'gōō'), town, ⊙ Chengku co. (pop. 196,791), SW Shensi prov., China, 15 mi. NE of Nancheng and on Han R.; cotton weaving; rice, wheat, beans.
Chengkung or **Ch'eng-kung** (both: chŭng'gōŏng'), town (pop. 1,898), ⊙ Chengkung co. (pop. 65,366), E central Yunnan prov., China, on railroad and 10 mi. SE of Kunming, on E shore of lake Tien Chih; alt. 6,155 ft.; cotton textiles; rice, wheat, beans. Coal mines near by.
Chenglingki or **Ch'eng-ling-chi** (both: chŭng'lĭng'jē'), town, NE Hunan prov., China, port on Yangtze R. at Yoyang canal (NE outlet of Tungting L.), and 5 mi. NE of Yoyang; exports rice, tea, tung oil.
Ch'eng-mai, China; see TSINGMAI.
Chengnai, Formosa: see TAIPEI.
Chengning (jŭng'nĭng'), town, ⊙ Chengning co. (pop. 46,158), SE Kansu prov., China, 85 mi. NNW of Sian, in mtn. region; wheat, beans.
Chengpu or **Ch'eng-pu** (both: chŭng'bōō'), town, ⊙ Chengpu co. (pop. 94,631), SW Hunan prov., China, near Kwangsi line, 75 mi. SE of Chihkiang; rice, wheat, beans, corn.
Cheng River (jŭng), N Kwangtung prov., China, rises in Tayü Mts. near Namyung, flows 75 mi. SW, past Namyung and Chihing, joining Wu R. at Kükong to form NORTH RIVER. Sometimes also called Yüan Shui.
Chengteh or **Ch'eng-te** (chŭng'dŭ'), city (1947 pop. estimate 60,000), ⊙ Jehol prov., Manchuria, and ⊙, but independent of, Chengteh co. (1946 pop. 162,195), on railroad and 90 mi. NE of Peking; 40°59'N 117°52'E. Second commercial center of Jehol (next to Chihfeng); wool trading and weaving, silk weaving, tanning, brick and tile mfg., woodworking. The former summer residence of the Manchu dynasty, Chengteh includes, N of the city proper, a large walled park containing the 18th-cent. palace, pavilions, and a lake. Formerly called Jehol, for the Je Ho [warm river], a small tributary of Lwan R., on which Chengteh is situated.
Chengting (jŭng'dĭng'), town, ⊙ Chengting co. (pop. 36,715), SW Hopeh prov., China, on Huto R. and 10 mi. NNE of Shihkiachwang, and on Peking-Hankow RR; wheat, beans, rice, kaoliang. An old city dating from 7th cent. A.D., it has been superseded by the rail center of Shihkiachwang.
Chengto, China: see CHENDO.
Chengtu or **Ch'eng-tu** (both: chŭng'dōō'), city (1948 pop. 647,877), ⊙ Szechwan prov., S China, port on arm of Min R. and 170 mi. NW of Chungking city (linked by railroad); 30°40'N 104°10'E. Center of the fertile Chengtu plain, irrigated by canalized arms of the Min R.; commercial hub for trade bet. mts. of NW Szechwan and Red Basin country. Mfg.: silk and cotton textiles, matches. Tea, tobacco, medicinal plants, mushrooms, rice, wheat, sweet potatoes, sugar cane are grown in surrounding agr. dist. A major educational center, Chengtu is seat of univ. of Szechwan, West China Union Univ., Chenghwa Univ., and col. of science. City became a municipality under prov. jurisdiction in 1930. Railroads to connect with Tienshui and Kangting are projected. Was U.S. air base in Second World War.
Chengwu or **Ch'eng-wu** (chŭng'wōō'), town, ⊙ Chengwu co. (pop. 222,810), SE Pingyuan prov., China, 30 mi. SE of Hotseh; cotton weaving; wheat, beans, millet, kaoliang. Until 1949 in Shantung prov.
Chengyang (jŭng'yăng'), town, ⊙ Chengyang co. (pop. 171,918), S Honan prov., China, 40 mi. NNE of Sinyang; wheat, beans, kaoliang.
Chengyangkwan or **Cheng-yang-kuan** (jŭng'yăng'-gwăn'), town, N Anhwei prov., China, 60 mi. SW of Pengpu, and on Hwai R. at mouths of Pi and Ying rivers; river transportation hub.
Chenhai, China: see CHINHAI.
Chen-hsi, China: see BARKOL.
Chenhsien or **Ch'en-hsien** (chŭn'shyĕn'), town, ⊙ Chenhsien co. (pop. 184,862), SE Hunan prov., China, on Hankow-Canton RR and 85 mi. SSE of Hengyang; rice, wheat, tobacco, hemp. Coal, sulphur, graphite, antimony, and tin are found near by. Until 1913 called Chenchow.
Chen-hsiung, China: see CHENSIUNG.
Chen-hua, China: see CHENHWA.
Chenhwa or **Chen-hua** (both: jŭn'hwä'), town, ⊙ Chenhwa co. (pop. 313,097), NW Shantung prov., China, 30 mi. NE of Tehchow; cotton, wheat, corn, beans. Until 1949, called Ningtsing, and in S Hopeh prov.
Cheniao Island, Chile: see CHAUQUES ISLANDS.
Chenies (chē'nēz, chā'–), agr. village and parish (pop. 366), E Buckingham, England, 4 mi. E of Amersham. The church was rebuilt in 15th cent. Here is seat of the Russell family.
Chenini-de-Gabès (shānēnē'-dů-găbĕs'), SW suburb of Gabès, E Tunisia,; date palms.
Chenit, Le (lů shůnē'), commune (pop. 4,176), Vaud canton, W Switzerland, near S end of Lac de Joux, on Orbe R and 20 mi. WNW of Lausanne; watches, metalworking. Includes villages of Le Sentier (lů sātyā') and Le Brassus (lů bräsü').
Chenju (jŭn'rōō'), town, S Kiangsu prov., China, 5 mi. WNW of Shanghai city and on Shanghai-Nanking RR; commercial center.
Chenkang or **Chen-k'ang** (jŭn'käng'), town, ⊙ Chenkang co. (pop. 62,467), W Yunnan prov., China, 70 mi. S of Paoshan; timber, rice, millet, beans. The name Chenkang was applied to a town 10 mi. NE, until 1914, when co. seat was moved to present location, previously known as Tehtang.
Chenki or **Ch'en-ch'i** (both: chŭn'chē'), town, ⊙ Chenki co. (pop. 164,333), W Hunan prov., China, on Yüan R. and 50 mi. NE of Chihkiang; rice, taro, buckwheat, oranges. Coal, gold, antimony, copper found near by.
Chenkiang, China: see CHINKIANG.
Chenkieh or **Chen-chieh** (both: jŭn'jyĕ'), town, ⊙ Chenkieh co. (pop. 88,404), SW Kwangsi prov., China, 65 mi. SE of Poseh; agr. products.
Chenlai (jŭn'lī'), town, ⊙ Chenlai co. (pop. 72,751), SW Heilungkiang prov., Manchuria, 110 mi. SSW of Tsitsihar and on railroad; kaoliang, beans. Called Chentung until 1949.
Chenliu or **Ch'en-liu** (chŭn'lyō'), town, ⊙ Chenliu co. (pop. 122,716), N Honan prov., China, 15 mi. SE of Kaifeng; silkgrowing; grain.
Chennagiri, India: see CHANNAGIRI.
Chennan (jŭn'nän'), town (pop. 5,336), ⊙ Chennan co. (pop. 83,995), central Yunnan prov., China, on Burma Road and 20 mi. NW of Tsuyung; alt. 6,299 ft.; rice, wheat, millet, beans. Iron mines near by.
Chennankwan or **Chen-nan-kuan** (jŭn'nän'gwän'), village, SW Kwangsi prov., China, on railroad and 100 mi. SW of Nanning, on N Vietnam border, at the pass Chennankwan, opposite Dongdang; major frontier-crossing point.
Chennapatna, India: see CHANNAPATNA.
Chennappattanam, India: see MADRAS, city.
Chennarayapatna, India: see CHANNARAYAPATNA.
Chennevières-sur-Marne (shĕnůvyâr'-sür-märn'), town (pop. 2,897), Seine-et-Oise dept., N central France, on left bank of Marne R. and 9 mi. ESE of Paris, with fine residential districts.
Chenning (jŭn'nĭng'), town (pop. 10,909), ⊙ Chenning co. (pop. 91,456), SW Kweichow prov., China, 10 mi. SW of Anshun and on road to Yunnan; alt. 4,255 ft.; paper mfg.; rice, wheat, millet, hides, medicinal herbs. Coal deposits near by.
Chenoa (shĭnō'ů), city (pop. 1,452), McLean co., central Ill., 23 mi. NE of Bloomington, in rich agr. and stock-raising area; canned corn; machine-shop products. Limestone quarry. Laid out 1856, inc. 1865.
Chenonceaux (shůnōsō'), village (pop. 220), Indre-et-Loire dept., W central France, on Cher R. and 18 mi. ESE of Tours. Famous for its château, the residence of Diane de Poitiers and Catherine de' Medici, to which Philibert Delorme in 1560 added a wing which bridges the Cher (c.200 ft. wide here). Slightly damaged in Second World War.
Chenoua-Plage, Algeria: see TIPASA.
Chenôve (shůnōv'), SW suburb (pop. 2,730) of Dijon, Côte-d'Or dept., E central France; Burgundy wines.
Chenpa (jŭn'bä'), town (pop. 2,509), ⊙ Chenpa co. (pop. 93,069), S Shensi prov., China, near Szechwan line, 55 mi. SE of Nancheng, in mtn. region; wheat, beans, millet. Iron deposits near by. Until 1913 called Tingyüan.
Chenpien. **1** Town, Kwangsi prov., China: see CHANPIN. **2** Town, Yunnan prov., China: see LANTSANG.
Chenping or **Chen-p'ing** (jŭn'pĭng'). **1** Town, ⊙ Chenping co. (pop. 307,394), SW Honan prov., China, 18 mi. WNW of Nanyang; wheat, kaoliang, beans. **2** Town, Kwangtung prov., China: see CHIULING. **3** Town, ⊙ Chenping co. (pop. 13,574), S Shensi prov., China, near Hupeh line, 65 mi. SE of Ankang, in mtn. region.
Chensi, China: see BARKOL.
Chensiung or **Chen-hsiung** (both: jŭn'shyŭng'), town, ⊙ Chensiung co. (pop. 215,915), northeasternmost Yunnan prov., China, 65 mi. ENE of Chaotung; alt. 5,807 ft.; timber, rice, wheat.
Chenstokhov, Poland: see CZESTOCHOWA.
Chentseh or **Chen-tse** (jŭn'dzŭ'), town, S Kiangsu prov., China, on Chekiang line, 28 mi. SSW of Soochow; silk-weaving center.
Chentung, Manchuria: see CHENLAI.
Chenyüan (jŭn'yüän'). **1** Town, ⊙ Chenyüan co. (pop. 152,321), SE Kansu prov., China, 30 mi. NE of Kingchwan; alt. 4,855 ft.; kaoliang, millet. **2** Town (pop. 10,752), ⊙ Chenyüan co. (pop. 77,429), E Kweichow prov., China, 110 mi. ENE of Kweiyang and on upper Yüan R. (head of navigation); major trade center; tung-oil and tobacco processing, paper and embroidery making; rice, wheat, millet. Iron and lead deposits, saltworks near by. **3** Town, ⊙ Chenyüan co. (pop. 21,694), SW central Yunnan prov., China, 50 mi. N of Ningerh; alt. 4,199 ft.; rice, wheat, millet, beans.
Chenyüeh (jŭn'yüĕ'), town, ⊙ Chenyüeh co. (pop. 19,010), southernmost Yunnan prov., China, 75 mi. SSE of Ningerh, near Laos border; timber, rice, millet, beans. Until 1929 called Yiwu.
Cheoah Dam (chēō'ů), Graham and Swain counties, W N.C., near Tenn. line, in Little Tennessee R., 8 mi. below Fontana Dam, E of Tapoco; 230 ft. high, 770 ft. long; completed 1919; concrete, arch, overflow type; for hydroelectric power. Impounds narrow L. Cheoah, extending E to Fontana Dam and receiving discharge of Fontana Reservoir.
Cheoah River, W N.C., rises in the mts. NE of Andrews, flows c.20 mi. NW past Robbinsville, through L. SANTEETLAH, to Little Tennessee R. just below Cheoah Dam.
Cheomksan (chômk'sän'), town (1941 pop. 2,189), Kompong Thom prov., N Cambodia, in Dangrek Mts. (Thailand frontier), 80 mi. NW of Stungtreng.
Cheongkong (chŭrng'gông'), Mandarin *Ch'ang-chiang* (chäng'jyäng'), town, ⊙ Cheongkong co. (pop. 45,659), W Hainan, Kwangtung prov., China, port on Gulf of Tonkin, at mouth of small Cheong R., 115 mi. SW of Kiungshan; rice, bananas, sweet potatoes; lumbering. Fisheries, saltworks. Iron mining at SHEKLUK, 23 mi. E. Called Changhwa until 1914.
Cheotina River, Yugoslavia: see COTINA RIVER.
Chepachet, village, R.I.: see GLOCESTER.
Chepachet River (chēpă'chĭt), NW R.I., rises in ponds in Glocester town, flows c.8 mi. generally NE, joining Pascoag R. near Oakland to form Branch R. Dammed S of Chepachet village to form Smith and Sayles Reservoir (c.1.5 mi. long).
Chepelare (chĕpĕlă'rĕ), village (pop. 3,489), Plovdiv dist., S Bulgaria, in E Rhodope Mts., on Asenovitsa R. and 10 mi. N of Smolyan; summer resort; tobacco, livestock; sawmilling. Health resort Narechenski-bani (pop. 273), just N, has radioactive thermal springs.
Chepelare River, Bulgaria: see ASENOVITSA RIVER.
Chepén (chāpĕn'), city (pop. 8,214), Libertad dept., NW Peru, in W foothills of Cordillera Occidental, in irrigated Jequetepeque R. valley, 13 mi. NNE of San Pedro, on railroad and Pan American Highway. Rice milling, cotton ginning, mfg. of chocolate, tanning; rice, fruit, vegetables. Sugar milling near by.
Chepes (chā'pĕs), town (1947 census pop. 2,089), ⊙ General Roca dept. (□ 2,170; 1947 census pop. 7,873), S La Rioja prov., Argentina, on railroad and 85 mi. SW of Serrezuela (Córdoba); stock raising (cattle, horses, sheep); sawmill. Meteorological station.
Chephren, Mount (10,715 ft.), SW Alta., near B.C. border, in Rocky Mts., in Banff Natl. Park, 70 mi. NW of Banff; 51°51'N 116°43'W.
Chépica (chā'pēkä), town (pop. 1,710), Colchagua prov., central Chile, 20 mi. SW of San Fernando; grain, fruit, wine, potatoes, livestock; dairying.
Chepigana (chāpēgä'nä), town (1950 pop. 2,490), Darién prov., E Panama, on Tuira R. and 12 mi. SE of La Palma; gold placers; sawmilling.
Chepino, Bulgaria: see VELINGRAD.
Chepino River (chĕ'pēnô), SW Bulgaria, formed S of Velingrad by confluence of streams rising in W Rhodope Mts.; flows 56 mi. generally NE, past Velingrad and Kamenitsa, to Maritsa R. 8 mi. WNW of Pazardzhik. Formerly called Yelidere R.; sometimes Ellidere. **Chepino Basin** (□ 15; average alt. 2,500 ft.), valley of upper Chepino R., is noted resort area with several thermal springs; pine forests; flax, vegetables, fruit.
Chepo (chā'pō), village (pop. 1,351), Panama prov., central Panama, 35 mi. ENE of Panama city, on Inter-American Highway (terminus of completed section); lumbering; stock raising.
Chepo River (chā'pō) or **Bayano River** (bäyä'nō), E Panama prov., central Panama, rises in the Cordillera de San Blas, flows 100 mi. WSW, past El Llano, to Bay of Panama. Navigable for 7-ft. draught 15 mi. upstream to vicinity of Chepo. On shores of upper reaches live Kuna Indians.
Chepovichi, Ukrainian SSR: see CHAPOVICHI.
Chepping Wycombe, England: see HIGH WYCOMBE.
Chepping Wycombe Rural, England: see LOUDWATER.
Chepstow (chĕp'stō), urban district (1931 pop. 4,302; 1951 census 5,285), SE Monmouth, England, on the Wye, near its influx into the Severn, and 14 mi. ENE of Newport; agr. market; asphalt works. On hill above river are ruins of 11th–14th-cent. Chepstow Castle. The 11th-cent. church was formerly part of Benedictine priory. TINTERN ABBEY is N. Built on a slope bet. steep cliffs, the town was long the site of forts. Wye R. here has unusually high tide or "bore." Chepstow is site of annual race meeting.
Cheptsa River (chĭptsä'), E central European Russian SFSR, rises W of Okhansk in W foothills of the central Urals, flows 310 mi. WNW, past Balezino and Glazov, to Vyatka R. at Kirovo-Chepetski; lumber floating.
Cheptura. **1** Station, Tadzhik SSR: see OKTYABRSKI, Stalinabad oblast. **2** Village, Tadzhik SSR: see SHAKHRINAU.

Chepu, Tjepu, or **Tjepoe** (all: chĕ′pōō), town (pop. 21,861), NE Java, Indonesia, on Solo R. and 80 mi. W of Surabaya, in major oil field; oil-refining center. Has railroad workshops. Extensive teak forests near by. Airfield.

Chequaga Falls, N.Y.: see MONTOUR FALLS.

Chequamegon Bay (shĭkwä′mŭgŭn), SW arm of L. Superior, N Wis., forming the harbor for Ashland (on SE shore); 12 mi. long, 1–5 mi. wide. Bay is sheltered by small narrow isl. (Long Isl.) just S of Apostle Isls. French explorers visited (17th cent.) the bay shores.

Chequers Court (chĕ′kûrz), locality and mansion, central Buckingham, England, 5 mi. SSE of Aylesbury, 30 mi. NW of London. Mansion, dating from 13th cent., is natl. property, used as country house for the prime minister.

Cher (shâr), department (□ 2,820; pop. 286,070), central France, formed of parts of old Berry and Bourbonnais provinces; ⊙ Bourges. A transitional region bet. Massif Central and Paris Basin, it is drained by the Cher and the middle Loire (Val de Loire). Contains a portion of the SOLOGNE and the SANCERROIS HILLS (E), renowned for their wines. Dept. grows small grains, vegetables, and forage crops; sheep, cattle. Has iron deposits. Important metallurgical industries at Vierzon (foundries, mfg. of railroad engines, agr. machinery) and Bourges (blast furnaces, arsenal, pyrotechnics). Cement, glass, porcelain, textiles are also produced.

Cher, river, France: see CHER RIVER.

Chera, India: see KERALA.

Chéragas (shārägäs′), village (pop. 3,418), Alger dept., N central Algeria, 6 mi. W of Algiers; grows table grapes, perfume plants.

Cherán (chārän′), town (pop. 3,388), Michoacán, central Mexico, on central plateau, 23 mi. N of Uruapan; corn, sugar, tobacco, fruit, livestock.

Cherangani Hills (chĕräng-gä′nē), section of W rim of Great Rift Valley, in W Kenya, E of Kitale; rise to over 11,000 ft.

Cherang Ruku (kûräng′ rōō′kōō), village (pop. 1,045), NE Kelantan, Malaya, port on South China Sea at mouth of small Semerak R., 25 mi. SE of Kota Bharu, near Trengganu line; coconuts, rice; fisheries. Sometimes called Semerak.

Cheranmahadevi, India: see SERMADEVI.

Chéran River (shārä′), Haute-Savoie and Savoie depts., SE France, rises in the Bauges, flows 25 mi. NW, past Le Châtelard and Alby, to the Fier below Rumilly.

Cheras (kûräs′), village, SE Selangor, Malaya, on road and 8 mi. SE of Kuala Lumpur, on Langat R.; rubber, rice.

Cherasco (kĕrä′skô), village (pop. 2,395), Cuneo prov., Piedmont, NW Italy, near confluence of Stura di Demonte and Tanaro rivers, 18 mi. E of Saluzzo, in sericulture region; silk, flour, and lumber mills, kilns, cheese factories. Has castle (begun 1348), hospitals dating from 1460 and 1739, church (1672), palaces, mus. (1868). Founded 1243 on site of anc. Clarascum.

Cherat (chä′rät), town (pop. 337), Peshawar dist., central North-West Frontier Prov., W Pakistan, 22 mi. SE of Peshawar; small military station; hill resort (alt. c.4,500 ft.); sanitarium.

Cheratte (shĕrät′), town (pop. 4,672), Liége prov., E Belgium, on Meuse R. and 6 mi. NNE of Liége; coal mining. Has 17th-cent. castle.

Cheraw (chĕr′ô, chĭrô′). **1** Town (pop. 174), Otero co., SE central Colo., near Arkansas R., 9 mi. N of La Junta; alt. 4,500 ft. **2** Town (pop. 4,836), Chesterfield co., NE S.C., on Pee Dee R. and 40 mi. N of Florence, in agr. area; lumber, wood products, cotton goods, cottonseed oil. Ships farm produce. Settled in mid-18th cent. by Welsh. Has fine old bldgs., notably St. David's Episcopal church (1770–73). Cheraw State Park (c.7,400 acres; recreational facilities) is S.

Cherbourg (shĕr′bōōrg, Fr. shĕrbōōr′), town (pop. 34,034), Manche dept., NW France, seaport on English Channel, 190 mi. WNW of Paris and 90 mi. S of Southampton, on N shore of Cotentin Peninsula; 49°38′N 1°37′W; major transatlantic port with well-sheltered harbor (□ 6) protected by breakwater 2¼ mi. long and capable of accommodating largest vessels (transatlantic pier with rail terminus heavily damaged in 1944). Commercial port imports coal and lumber, exports dairy produce and early vegetables, chiefly to England. Until Second World War, an important naval base and seaplane station. Its arsenal, with machine shops and armament works, was destroyed in 1944. Town dominated (S) by Montagne du Roule (alt. 465 ft.; old fort; panorama). Probably of Roman origin, Cherbourg became important under Louis XIV, who fortified it and began construction of breakwater (*digue*) completed during 1st half of 19th cent. Harbor was extended in 1889 and further strengthened (1940–44) by Ger. garrison. Capitulated to U.S. troops after brief siege (June, 1944), and became important Allied supply base after harbor was cleared of mines.

Cherchel or **Cherchell** (shĕrshĕl′), town (pop. 7,263), Alger dept., N central Algeria, fishing port on the Mediterranean, 50 mi. WSW of Algiers; rail-spur terminus; fish preserving; ships wine, truck produce. Has officer training school. The shallow, narrow harbor is exposed to N winds. Minor iron deposits in vicinity. Modern town is much smaller than anc. *Caesarea*, the flourishing chief city (pop. was c.100,000) of Mauretania under Juba II. Among Roman remains are an amphitheater, thermae, and statues (now housed in local mus. and in Algiers mus. of antiquities). City declined after sack by the Vandals. Occupied by French in 1840. Formerly also spelled Shershell.

Cherchen or **Cherchen Bazar** (chĕrchĕn′ bäzär′), Chinese *Chiehmo* or *Ch'ieh-mo* (both: chyĕ′mô′), town and oasis (pop. 10,959), S Sinkiang prov., China, on Cherchen R. and 145 mi. WSW of Charkhlik, and on route skirting S edge of Taklamakan Desert; 38°8′N 85°32′E. Sericulture; cattle raising; agr. products. Gold, mica mining. Also spelled Charchan.

Cherchen River or **Charchan River,** S Sinkiang prov., China, rises in central Kunlun mts. at 37°N 87°E, flows 300 mi. NE, past Cherchen, along SE edge of Taklamakan Desert, joining the Tarim just W of Lob Nor basin.

Chercher (chĕr′chĕr), forested highland region in E central Ethiopia, at edge of Great Rift Valley, W of Harar; includes Chercher Mts., rising to 9,775 ft. in Mt. Unde, near Asba Tafari. Agr. (coffee, durra, barley, fodder) and cattle raising. Native plants include tobacco, cotton, castor beans, agave, and sugar cane. Inhabited by the Galla. Chief centers: Deder and Asba Tafari.

Cherdakly (chĭrdäk′lē), village (1926 pop. 4,590), N Ulyanovsk oblast, Russian SFSR, 18 mi. E of Ulyanovsk; distilling, metalworking; grain, sunflowers, coriander, orchards.

Cherdoyak (chĕrdŭyäk′), town (1941 pop. over 500), central East Kazakhstan oblast, Kazakh SSR, near Kumashkino; tin mining.

Cherdyn or **Cherdyn'** (chĭrdĭn′yŭ, chĕr′dĭnyŭ), city (1926 pop. 3,884), N Molotov oblast, Russian SFSR, on Kolva R. (landing) just above its mouth and 50 mi. NNW of Solikamsk; trading center in lumber-floating, fishing, and hunting area. Minor shipyards near by, on Kolva R. Has regional mus. One of oldest Rus. settlements in the Urals, founded 1472. Developed in 16th cent. as center on N trade route to Siberia; declined in 18th cent., following southward shift of Siberian colonization.

Cherek River (chĕ′rĭk), Kabardian Autonomous SSR, Russian SFSR, rises in 2 headstreams in the central Greater Caucasus, on both sides of the Koshtan-Tau; flows 80 mi. NE, past Sovetskoye, to Baksan R. SE of Prokhladny.

Cheremisinovo (chĕrĭmē′sĭnŭvŭ), village (1926 pop. 227), N Kursk oblast, Russian SFSR, 45 mi. ENE of Kursk; sugar beets.

Cheremiss, in Rus. names: see MARI AUTONOMOUS SSR.

Cheremkhovo (chĕrĭmkhô′vŭ), city (1926 pop. 14,485; 1939 pop. 65,907), S Irkutsk oblast, Russian SFSR, on Trans-Siberian RR and 80 mi. NW of Irkutsk. Major coal-mining center; mfg. (machines, chemicals, flour, bricks, packed meats). Linked with near-by Angara R. by railroad spur. Center of **Cheremkhovo Coal Basin,** one of the largest USSR deposits (reserves of 75 billion tons) in exploitation; extends 300 mi. along Trans-Siberian RR from Nizhneudinsk to L. Baikal; up to 45 mi. wide.

Cheremosh River (chĭryĕ′mŭsh), Pol. *Czeremosz* (chĕrĕ′môsh), Rum. *Ceremuş* (chĕrĕ′mōōsh), SW Ukrainian SSR, formed 10 mi. E of Zhabye by confluence of White Cheremosh and Black Cheremosh rivers, rising in Chernagora mts.; flows c.45 mi. generally NE, past Kuty and Vashkovtsy, to Prut R. 6 mi. SE of Snyatyn. Logging. Formed (1921–39) Pol.-Rum. border.

Cheremshan (chĕrĭmshän′), village (1926 pop. 2,268), S Tatar Autonomous SSR, Russian SFSR, on Greater Cheremshan R. and 50 mi. W of Bugulma; wheat, livestock. A Rus. stronghold in 17th cent.

Cheremshanka (–kŭ), town (1946 pop. over 500), NW Chelyabinsk oblast, Russian SFSR, near (under jurisdiction of) Verkhni Ufalei, in nickel- and iron-mining region.

Cheremukhovo (chĭryô′mōōkhŭvŭ), town (1947 pop. over 500), N Sverdlovsk oblast, Russian SFSR, under jurisdiction of Severouralsk; bauxite-mining center, supplying Krasnoturinsk aluminum works.

Cheremushki (–mōōshkē), town (1939 pop. over 2,000), central Moscow oblast, Russian SFSR, adjoining (S of) Moscow; clay quarries, brickworks.

Cheren, Eritrea: see KEREN.

Cherente, Brazil: see MIRACEMA DO NORTE.

Cherepanovo (chĕrĭpä′nŭvŭ), city (1939 pop. over 10,000), SE Novosibirsk oblast, Russian SFSR, on Turksib RR and 55 mi. S of Novosibirsk; flour mill, brickworks; grain elevator, refrigerating plant. Chartered 1921.

Cherepet or **Cherepet'** (chĕ′rĭpĭtyŭ), town (1939 pop. over 2,000), W Tula oblast, Russian SFSR, 6 mi. E of Chekalin; metalworking center; lignite mining.

Cherepovets (chĕrĭpô′vyĭts, –pŭvyĕts′, chĭrĕ′pŭvyĭts), city (1926 pop. 21,783), SW Vologda oblast, Russian SFSR, port on Rybinsk Reservoir, at mouth of Sheksna R., on railroad and 70 mi. W of Vologda; river-rail transportation center in dairying region; machine works, shipyards; sawmilling, match mfg., distilling, food processing. Teachers col., regional mus. Dates from before 15th cent.; chartered 1777. Building (1941) of Rybinsk Reservoir speeded growth of city. Site of projected steel plant serving Leningrad region. Was ⊙ Cherepovets govt. (1918–1927).

Cherevich, Yugoslavia: see CEREVIC.

Cherevkovka (chĕrĭfkôf′kŭ), town, N Stalino oblast, Ukrainian SSR, in the Donbas, near Slavyansk.

Cherevkovo (–kô′vŭ), village (1939 pop. over 500), S Archangel oblast, Russian SFSR, on Northern Dvina R. and 55 mi. NW of Kotlas; coarse grain.

Chergui, island, Tunisia: see KERKENNAH.

Chergui, Chott ech (shôt′ ĕsh shĕrgē′) [Arabic,=eastern shott], marshy saline lake or salt flat, NW Algeria, in the High Plateaus along border of Oran dept. and Aïn-Sefra territory; c.100 mi. long. Area varies with amount of rainfall; no outlet. The shott is crossed at Le Kreider by narrow-gauge railroad to Colomb-Béchar.

Cherhill (chĕ′rĭl), agr. village and parish (pop. 251), N Wiltshire, England, 8 mi. ESE of Chippenham. On near-by chalk hill is cut the figure of a white horse, 129 ft. long, dating from 1780; visible from great distance.

Cherial or **Chiriyal** (both: chăr′yŭl), town (pop. 6,275), Nalgonda dist., central Hyderabad state, India, 19 mi. NW of Jangaon; rice, oilseeds. Sometimes spelled Chiryal.

Cheribon or **Tjirebon** (both: chĭrēbôn′), town (pop. 54,079), N Java, Indonesia, port on Java Sea, 125 mi. ESE of Jakarta, at foot of Mt. Charemai; 6°44′S 108°34′E; mfg. (chemicals, textiles, machine tools, cigars, cigarettes). Exports sugar, copra, rice. Formerly ⊙ sultanate of Cheribon, which was abolished 1815 by the British after series of uprisings against sultans' rule. Resort village of Linggajati or Linggadjati (lĭng-gŭjä′tē), 13 mi. SW of Cheribon, was scene of drafting (1946) of Du.-Indonesian agreement, sometimes called Cheribon Agreement. This pact recognized the original Republic of Indonesia (proclaimed Aug., 1945) and provided for eventual establishment of United States of Indonesia under Du. crown. Sometimes spelled Tjerebon.

Cheribon, Peak of, Indonesia: see CHAREMAI, MOUNT.

Cherikov (chĕrĭkôf′, chĕ′rēkŭf), city (1926 pop. 4,662), S central Mogilev oblast, Belorussian SSR, on Sozh R. and 45 mi. SE of Mogilev; dairying, wood distilling; chalk quarrying.

Cherim, Manchuria: see JERIM.

Cheriton, residential former urban district (1931 pop. 8,089), SE Kent, England, near the Channel, 2 mi. W of Folkestone.

Cheriton (chă′rētŭn), village, Northampton co., E Va., 5 mi. NE of Cape Charles town; canneries (seafood, vegetables).

Cherkasskoye (chĭrkä′skŭyŭ). **1** Village, Saratov oblast, Russian SFSR: see CHERKASY. **2** Town (1926 pop. 2,498), N Stalino oblast, Ukrainian SSR, in the Donbas, on railroad (Shidlovskaya station) and 9 mi. W of Slavyansk; chalk quarries. **3** Town (1926 pop. 4,316), S central Voroshilovgrad oblast, Ukrainian SSR, in the Donbas, on railroad (Zimogorye station) and 16 mi. W of Voroshilovgrad; coal mines.

Cherkassy (chĭrkä′sē), city (1926 pop. 39,511), SE Kiev oblast, Ukrainian SSR, port on high right bank of Dnieper R. and 95 mi. SE of Kiev. Sugar-refining and lumber center; tobacco products; shipbuilding, metalworking, sawmilling, clothing mfg. River and rail transportation junction. Teachers col., Shevchenko mus. Founded in mid-16th cent.; was ⊙ Ukraine until superseded by Chigirin in 17th cent. Passed 1793 to Russia. In Second World War, held (1941–43) by Germans.

Cherkasy (chĭrkä′sē), village (1926 pop. 4,945), N Saratov oblast, Russian SFSR, 28 mi. NNW of Volsk; metalworks; wheat, sunflowers. Also called Cherkasskoye.

Cherkesovski or **Cherkesovskiy** (chĭrkyĕ′sŭfskē), village, NW Stalingrad oblast, Russian SFSR, on railroad (Budarino station) and 12 mi. NNW of Novo-Annenski; metalworks; wheat, sunflowers. Until c.1940, Budarinskaya.

Cherkess Autonomous Oblast (chĭrkyĕs′), administrative division (□ 1,500; 1946 pop. estimate 150,000) of SW Stavropol Territory, European Russian SFSR, on N slopes of the W Greater Caucasus; ⊙ Cherkessk. Drained by Kuban R. and its left affluents, the Great and Little Zelenchuk; agr. (wheat, corn, sunflowers; N) and lumbering (S) on mtn. slopes. Industry largely based on agr. (flour, dairy, and other food products); also produces cement, sodium sulphate, shoes, furniture, clothing. Pop. largely Cherkess or Adyge (Circassian), Nogai Tatar, and Abaza (Circassian). One of the remaining Circassian ethnic areas (since 1825 under Russian rule), it was (after 1921) in Mountain Autonomous SSR, later became part of Karachai-Cherkess Autonomous Oblast (formed 1922); Cherkess unit became a natl. okrug upon separation (1926) of KARACHAI AUTONOMOUS OBLAST; raised to autonomous oblast in 1928. In 1944, it again absorbed parts of dissolved Karachai Autonomous Oblast.

Cherkessk (chĭrkyĕsk'), city (1939 pop. 28,646), ⊙ Cherkess Autonomous Oblast, Stavropol Territory, Russian SFSR, on right bank of Kuban R. and 55 mi. S of Stavropol, on railroad; industrial center; metalworking, mfg. of chemicals (based on near-by Glauber's salt deposits), flour milling, food processing, dairying. Teachers col. Founded 1825 and named Batalpashinsk; became city in 1926. Known briefly (1936–37) as Sulimov and (1938–39) as Yezhovo-Cherkessk. During Second World War, held (1942–43) by Germans.

Cherlak (chĭrläk'), town (1926 pop. 2,862), SE Omsk oblast, Russian SFSR, on Irtysh R. and 75 mi. SE of Omsk; metalworks, flour milling; river port.

Cherlakski or **Cherlakskiy** (chĭrläk'skē), town (1939 pop. over 2,000), SE Omsk oblast, Russian SFSR, 25 mi. SW of Cherlak, in agr. area.

Chermoz (chĭrmôs'), city (1939 pop. over 10,000), central Molotov oblast, Russian SFSR, port on right bank of Kama R. and 45 mi. NNW of Molotov; major charcoal-fed metallurgical center (steel, pig iron); fireproof-brick mfg.; peat digging. Developed prior to First World War as metallurgical works called Chermozski Zavod; became city in 1943.

Chern or **Chern'** (chĕr'nyů), village (1926 pop. 3,465), S Tula oblast, Russian SFSR, 60 mi. SSW of Tula; flour milling.

Cherna (chôr'nŭ), village (1926 pop. 3,931), W Odessa oblast, Ukrainian SSR, 26 mi. SW of Balta; wheat, fruit, vineyards. In Moldavian Autonomous SSR (1924–40).

Chernagora (chĕrnŭgô'rŭ), Czech *Černahora*, Pol. *Czarnohora* [all=black mountains], section of the Carpathians in SW Ukrainian SSR, extending NW-SE from Yablonitsa Pass to Stog peak, bet. Black Tissa and Black Cheremosh rivers; rises to 6,752 ft. in Goverla, to 6,647 ft. in Pop-Ivan peaks. Forms watershed bet. upper Tissa and Prut tributaries.

Chernatitsa Mountains (chĕrnätē'tsä), N spur of W Rhodope Mts., S Bulgaria; form divide bet. Vacha (W) and Asenovitsa (E) rivers. Rise to 6,804 ft. at Persenk peak, 9 mi. NE of Devin. Sometimes called Kara Balkan Mts.

Chernava (chĭrnä'vŭ). **1** Village (1939 pop. over 500), SE Orel oblast, Russian SFSR, on Sosna R. and 18 mi. ENE of Livny; starch plant. Also called Chernavsk. **2** Village (1926 pop. 5,614), W Ryazan oblast, Russian SFSR, 22 mi. SW of Skopin; distilling; wheat.

Chernaya Gansha River, Belorussia: see Czarna Hancza River.

Chernaya Kholunitsa (chôr'nīŭ khŭlōō'nyē'tsŭ), town (1948 pop. over 2,000), E Kirov oblast, Russian SFSR, 22 mi. NW of Omutninsk; iron milling (works in operation since 1766).

Chernaya River, S Crimea, Russian SFSR, rises in Ai-Petri section of Crimean Mts., flows c.25 mi. NW, past Chorgun, to Sevastopol Bay at Inkerman. Reservoir near its mouth supplies water to Sevastopol. Sometimes called Chorgun R. In its valley, near Chorgun, 8 mi. SE of Sevastopol, Russian troops suffered a defeat (Aug., 1855) in Crimean War.

Chernelitsa (chĕrnyĭlyē'tsŭ), Pol. *Czernelica* (chĕrnĕlyē'tsä), town (1931 pop. 3,320), E Stanislav oblast, Ukrainian SSR, 10 mi. NNW of Gorodenka; stone quarrying; cloth weaving, flour milling; fruit, truck. Has ruins of medieval castle.

Chernevo (chĕr'nyĭvŭ), town (1939 pop. over 500), NW Pskov oblast, Russian SFSR, on Plyussa R. and 15 mi. ESE of Gdov; match-mfg. center.

Chernevtsy (chĕr'nyĭftsē), village (1926 pop. 1,951), SW Vinnitsa oblast, Ukrainian SSR, 16 mi. ENE of Mogilev-Podolski; metalworks. Also spelled Chernovtsy.

Chernigov (chĭrnyē'gŭf), oblast (□ 12,200; 1946 pop. estimate 1,700,000), N Ukrainian SSR; ⊙ Chernigov. In Dnieper Lowland; bounded W by Dnieper R.; drained by Desna R. and its affluents; wooded steppe region. Chiefly agr., with grain (rye, oats, buckwheat) as basic crop; flax (N), hemp (NE), potatoes (center), sugar beets, tobacco, mint (SE); extensive livestock raising. Lumbering in wooded sections (N, W); peat digging along marshy river valleys. Sugar refining, flour milling, meat packing, hemp and flax processing; chief centers at Chernigov, Nezhin, and Priluki. Bakhmach is major rail junction. Formed 1932.

Chernigov, city (1939 pop. 67,356), ⊙ Chernigov oblast, Ukrainian SSR, port on high right bank of Desna R. and 80 mi. NNE of Kiev; 51°30'N 31°18'E. Agr. center in grain, flax, and potato region; mfg. (cotton textiles, knitwear, chemicals), distilling, fruit canning, flax processing, lumber milling; metal- and brickworks. Teachers col. River-port trade in lumber and grain. Inner city is site of Spasski Sobor (1024; Byzantine cathedral, one of oldest monuments in USSR) and several former govt. buildings, including 18th-cent. baroque Mazeppa House, state mus., and 17th-cent. cathedral. Numerous 10th-cent. tumuli in vicinity. One of oldest cities of USSR; became (1024) ⊙ independent principality; destroyed (1239) by Tatars; came under rule of Lithuania (14th cent.) and Muscovy (1503); held by Poland (1618–67). Scene (1905) of severe pogroms. Was ⊙ Chernigov govt. until 1925. In Second World War, occupied (1941–43) by Germans, who destroyed many of its anc. monuments.

Chernigovka (chĭrnyē'gŭfkŭ). **1** Village (1948 pop. over 10,000), SW Maritime Territory, Russian SFSR, on Trans-Siberian RR (Muchnaya station) and 50 mi. NNE of Voroshilov; metalworks, flour mill; grain, soybeans, sugar beets, rice, perilla. **2** Village (1939 pop. over 2,000), central Zaporozhe oblast, Ukrainian SSR, 22 mi. E of Bolshoi Tokmak; metalworks, dairy plant.

Chernigovskoye (–gŭfskŭyŭ), village (1926 pop. 2,733), SW Krasnodar Territory, Russian SFSR, on N slope of the W Greater Caucasus, 15 mi. S of Apsheronsk; lumber milling.

Chernikovsk (chĕrnyĭkôfsk'), city (1944 pop. over 10,000), central Bashkir Autonomous SSR, Russian SFSR, bet. Belaya and Ufa rivers, adjoining (NNE of) Ufa city. Industrial center; petroleum refining (light-oil products; pipe lines from Ishimbai and Oktyabrski), mfg. (combine and airplane motors, matches, chemicals, cellulose, plywood), sawmilling. Developed in 1930s, around woodpulp processing plant, as NE suburb of Ufa; became separate city in 1944.

Cherni Lom River, Bulgaria: see Rusenski Lom River.

Cherni Osam River, Bulgaria: see Osam River.

Cherni-vrakh (chĕr"nē-vräkh'), highest peak (alt. 7,506 ft.) in Vitosha Mts., W Bulgaria, 9 mi. S of Sofia. Struma R. rises at S foot.

Chernobai or **Chernobay** (chĕrnŭbī'), village (1926 pop. 7,002), W Poltava oblast, Ukrainian SSR, 13 mi. E of Zolotonosha; wheat, hemp, mint.

Chernobyl or **Chernobyl'** (chĭrnô'bĭl), city (1926 pop. 8,088), N Kiev oblast, Ukrainian SSR, port on Pripet R., at mouth of Uzh R., and 55 mi. NNW of Kiev; machine mfg., metalworking, shipbuilding; dairy products; clothing mills, sawmills.

Chernogorsk (chĕrnŭgôrsk'), city (1939 pop. over 10,000), E Khakass Autonomous Oblast, Krasnoyarsk Territory, Russian SFSR, 10 mi. NW of Abakan; coal-mining center on spur of Achinsk-Abakan RR.

Chernoistochinsk (chĕr"nŭēstŭchēnsk'), town (1926 pop. 7,479), W Sverdlovsk oblast, Russian SFSR, in the central Urals, on small lake, 13 mi. NE of Visim, on rail spur from Nizhni Tagil; copper and zinc mining, metalworking.

Chernomorskoye (chĕr"nŭmôr'skŭyŭ), village (1939 pop. over 2,000), W Crimea, Russian SFSR, minor Black Sea port, 40 mi. WNW of Yevpatoriya; wheat, livestock. Coquina deposits. Until 1944, Ak-Mechet.

Chernorechye or **Chernorech'ye** (chĭrnŭrĕ'chĭyĭ), town (1940 pop. over 500), S Grozny oblast, Russian SFSR, on Sunzha R. and 3 mi. SW of Grozny; center of Tashkala oil fields. Called Novye Aldy until 1940.

Chernovo, Ukrainian SSR: see Andreyevo-Ivanovka.

Chernovskiye Kopi (chĭrnôf'skēŭ kô'pē), W suburb (1939 pop. over 10,000) of Chita, W Chita oblast, Russian SFSR, on Trans-Siberian RR; lignite-mining center. Inc. c.1940 into Chita city.

Chernovskoye (chĭrnôf'skŭyŭ). **1** Village (1939 pop. over 500), W Kirov oblast, Russian SFSR, 45 mi. NW of Kotelnich; flax. **2** Village (1926 pop. 1,048), SW Molotov oblast, Russian SFSR, on right tributary of Kama R. and 36 mi. WNW of Osa; flax and food processing; grain, livestock.

Chernovtsy (chĭrnôf'tsē), oblast (□ 3,200; 1947 pop. estimate 900,000) of W Ukrainian SSR; ⊙ Chernovtsy. Bounded by Rumania (S), Cheremosh R. (W), and Dniester R. (N); extends from the Carpathians, across upper Sereth and Prut rivers, to the Dniester steppes. Agr. (corn, rye, wheat, sugar beets, hemp); cattle raising, beekeeping. Lumbering on Carpathian slopes (SW). Main centers (agr. processing, mfg.): Chernovtsy, Khotin, Storozhinets. Formed in 1940 (confirmed 1947) out of N Bukovina (including former Rum. Cernauti and Storojinet depts. and Putila and Gertsa dists.) and W section (□ c.1,000) of Bessarabian Hotin dept.

Chernovtsy. **1** Ger. *Czernowitz* (chĕr'nôvĭts), Rum. *Cernăuţi* (chĕrnŭ-ōōts'), city (1930 pop. 112,427; 1941 pop. 78,825), ⊙ Chernovtsy oblast, Ukrainian SSR, in N Bukovina, on right bank of Prut R., on main Lvov-Bucharest RR and 140 mi. SE of Lvov; 48°17'N 25°57'E. Commercial and industrial center; mfg. of cotton textiles, rubber products, varnishes, pharmaceuticals, furniture, nails, wire; lumber milling, food processing (sugar, meat, canned goods, sweets). Situated on hills overlooking the Prut; has 19th-cent. Gr. metropolitan's palace in Byzantine style, Orthodox cathedral (1864), univ. (1875), medical and teachers colleges. Industrial plants in N and NE suburbs. First mentioned in 15th cent.; became economic center of Moldavia. Rose to importance under Austrian rule (1775–1918), when it was ⊙ Bukovina. Until Second World War, pop. consisted largely of Germans and Jews. While in Rumania (1918–40, 1941–44), it was ⊙ Cernauti dept. (□ 684; 1941 pop. 267,486). Known by Russians as Chernovitsy from 1940 to 1944. **2** Village, Vinnitsa oblast, Ukrainian SSR: see Chernevtsy.

Chernoyerkovskaya, Russian SFSR: see Petrovskaya.

Chernukha (chĭrnōō'khŭ), village (1926 pop. 3,054), S Gorki oblast, Russian SFSR, on railroad (Serezha station) and 14 mi. N of Arzamas; sawmilling; potatoes, wheat.

Chernukhi (–khē), village (1926 pop. 3,391), N Poltava oblast, Ukrainian SSR, 18 mi. NNW of Lubny; grain.

Chernukhino (–khēnŭ), town (1926 pop. 4,108), SW Voroshilovgrad oblast, Ukrainian SSR, in the Donbas, 4 mi. E of Debaltsevo; coal mines.

Chernushka (–shkŭ), town (1939 pop. over 2,000), S Molotov oblast, Russian SFSR, on railroad and 60 mi. SSE of Osa; woodworking, sawmilling, flax and food processing.

Chernyakhov (chĕrnyŭkhôf'), town (1926 pop. 5,524), central Zhitomir oblast, Ukrainian SSR, on railroad (Gorbashi station) and 13 mi. N of Zhitomir; flour mill, food processing, metalworking.

Chernyakhovsk (chĕrnyŭkhôfsk'), city (1939 pop. 48,711), E central Kaliningrad oblast, Russian SFSR, 50 mi. E of Kaliningrad, on the Angerapp just above its union with the Inster, forming Pregel R. (head of navigation); rail junction; horse- and cattle-raising center; mfg. (chemicals, foundry goods, textiles), food processing (sugar, dairy products, meat, vinegar, mustard, beer). Stud farm in 14th-cent. fortress (N). Founded 1336 as fortress; chartered 1583. Until 1945, in East Prussia and called Insterburg (ĭn'stûrbōōrk); renamed for Soviet general Chernyakhovski, who captured it during Second World War.

Chernyanka (chĭrnyän'kŭ), village (1939 pop. over 2,000), E Kursk oblast, Russian SFSR, on Oskol R. and 22 mi. S of Stary Oskol; sunflower-oil press, flour mill, woodworking plant.

Chernye Bratya or **Chernyye Brat'ya** (chôr'nēŭ brä'tyŭ) [Rus.,=black brothers], Jap. *Chirihoi-to* (chērēhoi"tō'), group of 2 main isls. in central main Kurile Isls. chain, Russian SFSR; separated from Simushir Isl. (N) by Boussole Strait, from Urup Isl. (S) by Urup Strait; 46°30'N 150°52'E. Chirpoi Isl. (N; □ 4) is separated by 1.5-mi.-wide strait from Brat Chirpoyev Isl. (S; □ 9).

Chernye Gory or **Chernyye Gory** (gô'rĭ) [Rus.,= black mountains], N lateral outlier of W Greater Caucasus, in Krasnodar and Stavropol territories, Russian SFSR, extending from area of Maikop E to area of Pyatigorsk; rises to 5,000 ft.

Cherny Irtysh River, China and USSR: see Black Irtysh River.

Cherny Ostrov or **Chernyy Ostrov** (chôr'nē ô'strŭf), town (1926 pop. 2,061), central Kamenets-Podolski oblast, Ukrainian SSR, on the Southern Bug and 11 mi. WNW of Proskurov; clothing and leather industries; flour mill.

Cherny Otrog or **Chernyy Otrog** (ŭtrôk'), village (1948 pop. over 2,000), N central Chkalov oblast, Russian SFSR, on Sakmara R., on railroad and 35 mi. ENE of Chkalov; wheat, sunflowers, livestock.

Chernyshevskaya (chĕrnĭshĕf'skīŭ), village (1939 pop. over 500), NE Rostov oblast, Russian SFSR, on Chir R. and 37 mi. NNW of Oblivskaya; flour mill, metalworks; wheat, sunflowers, cattle.

Chernyshevskoye (–skŭyŭ), town (1939 pop. 4,922), E Kaliningrad oblast, Russian SFSR, on Lith. border opposite Kybartai, and 22 mi. E of Gusev. Was major Ger. railroad border station. Until 1945, in East Prussia where it was called Eydtkuhnen (īt'kōōnŭn) and, later (1938–45), Eydtkau (īt'kou).

Chernyshkovski or **Chernyshkovskiy** (–kôf'skē), village (1939 pop. over 500), SW Stalingrad oblast, Russian SFSR, on railroad (Chernyshkov station) and 40 mi. W of Nizhne-Chirskaya; dairying, metalworking; wheat, cotton, mustard.

Cherny Yar or **Chernyy Yar** (chôr'nē yär"), village (1926 pop. 3,387), N Astrakhan oblast, Russian SFSR, on right bank of Volga R. (landing) and 85 mi. SE of Stalingrad; fish-trading center; orchards; cattle. Until 1947, in Stalingrad oblast.

Cherokee (chĕ'rŭkē", chĕ"rŭkē'). **1** County (□ 600; pop. 17,634), NE Ala.; ⊙ Centre. Agr. area bordering on Ga., drained by Coosa, Chattooga, and Little rivers. Cotton, corn, livestock; lumber milling, iron mining. Deposits of coal and limestone. Formed 1836. **2** County (□ 428; pop. 20,750), NW Ga.; ⊙ Canton. Drained by Etowah R. (forms Allatoona Reservoir here). Piedmont agr. (cotton, corn, sweet potatoes, fruit, poultry, livestock) area; textile mfg.; marble quarries. Formed 1831. **3** County (□ 573; pop. 19,052), NW Iowa; ⊙ Cherokee. Prairie agr. area (hogs, cattle, poultry, corn, oats, soybeans) drained by Little Sioux and Maple rivers. Formed 1851. **4** County (□ 587; pop. 25,144), extreme SE Kansas; ⊙ Columbus. Gently rolling agr. area, bordered S by Okla. and E by Mo.; drained by headwaters of Spring R. Livestock, grain, poultry; dairying. Coal, lead, zinc deposits; timber. Formed 1866. **5** County (□ 467; pop. 18,294), extreme W N.C.; ⊙ Murphy. Partly in the Blue Ridge; bounded S by Ga., W and NW by Tenn.; Unicoi and Snowbird mts. in N; drained by Hiwassee R. (Apalachia and Hiwassee dams) and Nottely R. Includes Nantahala Natl. Forest. Largely forested (oak, pine); agr. (corn, hay, potatoes, apples, livestock, poultry); marble quarrying. Some mfg. at Murphy; sawmilling. Formed 1839. **6** County (□ 782; pop. 18,989), E Okla.; ⊙ Tahlequah. Bounded W by Neosho R.; intersected by Illinois R. Part of the Ozarks are in E. Stock raising, agr. (fruit, truck, corn, cotton, grain), dairying. Farm-products processing, mfg. at Tahlequah. Timber. Formed 1907. **7** County (□ 394; pop. 34,992), N S.C.; ⊙ Gaffney. Bounded N by N.C. line, S by Pacolet R.; drained by Broad R. Includes Cowpens Natl. Battlefield Site and part of Kings Mtn. Natl. Military Park. Agr. (especially cotton), grain, livestock, dairying; textile milling, some other mfg.; limestone, sand, feldspar. Formed 1798. **8** County (□ 1,054; pop. 38,694), E Texas; ⊙ Rusk. Bounded W by Neches R., partly E by Angelina R. Partly wooded (extensive lumbering). Agr. (especially tomatoes, other truck, fruit; also sweet potatoes, peanuts); rose growing, dairying, some livestock (cattle, poultry). Oil, natural-gas wells; minerals (iron, lignite, clay, silica, salt). Mfg., processing at Rusk, Jacksonville. Formed 1846.

Cherokee. 1 Town (pop. 748), Colbert co., NW Ala., 16 mi. W of Tuscumbia, near Tennessee R.; cotton goods. Sulphur wells, asphalt mines, marble quarries in vicinity. **2** City (pop. 7,705), ⊙ Cherokee co., NW Iowa, on Little Sioux R. and 45 mi. ENE of Sioux City; rail junction; trade center; processed poultry, metal products, beverages. Has state hosp. for the insane. Founded 1870, inc. 1873. **3** City (pop. 849), Crawford co., extreme SE Kansas, 8 mi. SW of Pittsburg, in agr. and coal-mining region. **4** Resort village (pop. c.300), Swain co., W N.C., 43 mi. WSW of Asheville; S gateway to Great Smoky Mts. Natl. Park; hq. of adjacent Cherokee Indian reservation here. **5** City (pop. 2,635), ⊙ Alfalfa co., N Okla., 37 mi. NW of Enid; trade, milling, shipping center for agr. area (wheat, corn, oats, alfalfa, sorghum, poultry; dairy products). Mfg. (farm machinery, lawn mowers, washing machines, underwear). The Great Salt Plains Dam, a wildlife refuge, and a fish hatchery are E.

Cherokee Dam, NE Tenn., in Holston R., 26 mi. NE of Knoxville, near Jefferson City. Major TVA dam (175 ft. high, 6,760 ft. long; completed 1942); used for flood control and hydroelectric power. Forms Cherokee Reservoir (□ 49; 59 mi. long, .5–2 mi. wide; capacity 1,565,400 acre-ft.).

Cherokee Falls, village (1940 pop. 632), Cherokee co., N S.C., on Broad R. and 6 mi. E of Gaffney; textiles.

Cherokees, Lake of the: see GRAND RIVER DAM.

Cherokee Sound, town (pop. 320), N Bahama Isls., on E shore of Great Abaco Isl., 18 mi. SSW of Hope Town; 26°16′N 77°3′W. Fishing.

Cherokee Strip or **Cherokee Outlet,** part of former Indian Territory of U.S., now part of N OKLAHOMA; bounded N by Kansas line, it was 50-mi.-wide strip extending more than 200 mi. E from base of Okla. Panhandle. Opened 1893 to white settlement, it became part of Okla. Territory and, later, part of state.

Chéroy (shārwä′), agr. village (pop. 458), Yonne dept., N central France, 13 mi. W of Sens.

Cherpista, Greece: see TERPNI.

Cherquenco (chĕrkĕng′kō), town (pop. 1,677), Cautín prov., S central Chile, 30 mi. E of Temuco; rail terminus and agr. center (cereals, vegetables, livestock); flour milling, lumbering.

Cherrapunji (chărŭpōōn′jē), village, Khasi and Jaintia Hills dist., W Assam, India, on S slope of Khasi Hills, 23 mi. SSW of Shillong; trades in rice, cotton, sesame. Coal deposits near by. Was ⊙ Khasi States until transferred 1864 to Shillong. Shares with WAIALEALE, Hawaii, the record of having the world's heaviest rainfall, yearly average, 450 in.

Cher River (shâr), central France, rises in Combrailles hills of Massif Central 14 mi. E of Aubusson, flows 200 mi. NNW, past Montluçon, Saint-Amand Montrond, Vierzon, and S suburbs of Tours, to the Loire 11 mi. below Tours. Receives the Tardes, Arnon (left), Yèvre, and Sauldre (right). The Cher is followed by the Berry Canal bet. Montluçon and Saint-Amand-Montrond, and again bet. Vierzon and Noyers, below which it is navigable to its mouth.

Cherry, county (□ 5,982; pop. 8,397), N Nebr.; ⊙ Valentine. Agr. region drained by N.Loup and Niobrara rivers; bounded N by S.Dak. Niobrara Div. of Nebr. Natl. Forest extends along Niobrara R. Livestock, grain. Formed 1877.

Cherry. 1 Village (pop. 520), Bureau co., N Ill., 7 mi. N of Spring Valley; bituminous-coal mines. Scene of mine disaster (1909) which killed 270 men. **2** Town (pop. 73), Washington co., E N.C., 18 mi. E of Plymouth, N of Phelps L.

Cherry Creek, village (pop. 631), Chautauqua co., extreme W N.Y., 15 mi. NNE of Jamestown; agr. (fruit, truck; dairy products), lumbering.

Cherry Creek, rises in high plateau in El Paso co., central Colo., flows 64 mi. N to South Platte R. in Denver. Cherry Creek Dam, 6 mi. SE of Denver, completed 1950, is 140 ft. high, 14,300 ft. long. Flood control, irrigation.

Cherry Creek Mountains (c.8,000 ft.), NE Nev., in Elko and White Pine counties. Copper, gold, lead, zinc have been mined here.

Cherryfield, town (pop. 904), Washington co., E Maine, bet. Machias and Ellsworth and on Narraguagus R.; blueberrying, lumbering. Settled c.1757, inc. 1816.

Cherry Fork, village (pop. 197), Adams co., S Ohio, 34 mi. WNW of Portsmouth.

Cherry Grove, N.Y.: see FIRE ISLAND.

Cherry Grove Beach, summer resort, Horry co., E S.C., on the coast, 23 mi. E of Conway.

Cherry Hills Village, town (pop. 750), Arapahoe co., N central Colo., a S suburb of Denver.

Cherry Hinton, residential town and parish (pop. 1,254), S Cambridge, England, 2 mi. SE of Cambridge. Has 13th-cent. church.

Cherry Mountain (3,600 ft.), in White Mts., N central N.H., NW of Presidential Range, near Carroll.

Cherrytree or **Cherry Tree,** borough (pop. 517), Indiana co., NW central Pa., 5 mi. NNW of Barnesboro. There is a village, Cherrytree, in Venango co., 8 mi. N of Oil City.

Cherryvale, city (pop. 2,952), Montgomery co., SE Kansas, 10 mi. ENE of Independence, in agr. area (livestock, grain, poultry; dairying); zinc refining, grain milling. Zinc mines, oil and gas wells in vicinity. Laid out by railroad in 1871, inc. 1880.

Cherry Valley, village, S Ont., on Spence L. (4 mi. long), near L. Ontario, 5 mi. SSW of Picton; fruit.

Cherry Valley. 1 Town (pop. 521), Cross co., E Ark., 12 mi. N of Wynne. **2** Village (pop. 741), Winnebago co., N Ill., on Kishwaukee R. (bridged here) and 7 mi. ESE of Rockford, in agr. area. **3** Village, Worcester co., Mass.: see LEICESTER. **4** Village (pop. 760), Otsego co., central N.Y., 11 mi. NE of Cooperstown; mfg. of chairs; summer resort. Settled c.1740. Tories and Indians led by Walter Butler and Joseph Brant burned village and massacred more than 40 people, on Nov. 11, 1778. **5** Borough (pop. 94), Butler co., W Pa., 21 mi. NNE of Butler.

Cherryville. 1 Town (pop. 25), Crawford co., E central Mo., in the Ozarks, 10 mi. SSE of Steelville. **2** Town (pop. 3,492), Gaston co., SW N.C., 11 mi. NE of Shelby; cotton mills. Inc. 1889.

Cherski Range or **Cherskiy Range** (chĕr′skē), NE Siberian Russian SFSR, arc-shaped mtn. system extending from Indigirka-Yana river divide SE to Kolyma R.; 625 mi. long, 90–125 mi. wide; cut by Indigirka R. N section, called Tas-Khayakhtakh Mts., rises to 6,500 ft.; S section culminates at Chen Peak (10,215 ft.). Rich in lead, zinc, molybdenum, coal. Named for Rus. geologist who 1st explored range, 1892.

Cherso, Yugoslavia: see CRES ISLAND.

Chersonese (kûrsùnēs′) or **Chersonesus** (kûrsùnē′sùs) [Gr.,=peninsula]. Name in anc. geography applied to several peninsulas: Chersonesus Aurea (MALAY PENINSULA), Chersonesus Cimbrica (JUTLAND), Chersonesus Heracleotica (SEVASTOPOL), Chersonesus Taurica (CRIMEA), Chersonesus Thracica (GALLIPOLI PENINSULA).

Chersonesus Aurea: see MALAY PENINSULA.

Chert (chĕrt), town (pop. 1,732), Castellón de la Plana prov., E Spain, 15 mi. WNW of Vinaroz; olive-oil processing, headgear and soap mfg.; cereals, wine, livestock. Jasper quarrying and anthracite mining. Prehistoric wall near by.

Cherta (chĕr′tä), town (pop. 2,030), Tarragona prov., NE Spain, on the Ebro and 6 mi. N of Tortosa; cementworks; nougat mfg., olive-oil processing, tanning; trades in cereals, fruit.

Chertkov, Ukrainian SSR: see CHORTKOV.

Chertkovo (chĭrtkô′vù), town (1926 pop. 2,254), NW Rostov oblast, Russian SFSR, on railroad and 35 mi. NNW of Millerovo, just NE of Melovoye (Ukrainian SSR); agr. center in wheat, sunflower, and cattle-raising area; flour milling, meat packing.

Chertsey (chûrt′sē), residential urban district (1931 pop. 17,133; 1951 census 31,029), N Surrey, England, on the Thames (bridged) and 18 mi. WSW of London; mfg. of electrical equipment; market gardening. There are remains of 7th-cent. Benedictine monastery, in which Henry VI was buried. Charles James Fox lived near by, and Abraham Cowley lived in Chertsey. In urban dist. (S) is residential town of Addlestone.

Cherusti (chĭrōō′styē), town (1939 pop. over 500), E Moscow oblast, Russian SFSR, 19 mi. E of Shatura; rail junction; sawmill.

Cherven, Bulgaria: see RUSE, city.

Cherven or **Cherven'** (chĕr′vĭnyù), city (1926 pop. 4,936), S Minsk oblast, Belorussian SSR, 38 mi. ESE of Minsk; sawmilling, food processing. Until 1920s, called Igumen.

Chervena-voda (chĕrvĕ′nä-vôdä′), village (pop. 2,836), Ruse dist., NE Bulgaria, 8 mi ESE of Ruse; sugar beets, sunflowers.

Cherven Bryag (chĕr′vĕn bryäk′), agr. city (pop. 5,268), Pleven dist., N Bulgaria, on Panega R. and 5 mi. NNW of Lukovit; rail junction; agr. and grain-trading center; flour milling, vegetable-oil extraction, tanning. Commercial school. Also called Cherven-bryag.

Chervonaya Kamenka (chĭrvô′nīŭ kä′myĭn-kŭ), village (1926 pop. 6,385), E Kirovograd oblast, Ukrainian SSR, 14 mi. E of Aleksandriya; flour. Formerly Krasnaya Kamenka; now also Chervona Kamenka.

Chervonoarmeisk or **Chervonoarmeysk** (chĭrvô″-nù-ŭrmyāsk′). **1** City (1931 pop. 5,409), SW Rovno oblast, Ukrainian SSR, 5 mi. NE of Brody; tanning, flour milling, sawmilling. Border station on Russo-Austro-Hungarian line prior to First World War. Until 1940, called Radzivilov, Pol. *Radziwiłłów* (rädzēvē′wōōf). **2** Town (1926 pop. 3,367), central Zhitomir oblast, Ukrainian SSR, 22 mi. NW of Zhitomir; flour mill. Until c.1935 Pulin. Pop. 25% German until Second World War.

Chervonoarmeiskoye or **Chervonoarmeyskoye** (–skŭyù). **1** E suburb (1939 pop. over 2,000) of Dnepropetrovsk, Dnepropetrovsk oblast, Ukrainian SSR, across the Dnieper, 6 mi. ENE of city center. **2** Town (1939 pop. over 2,000), N Zaporozhe oblast, Ukrainian SSR, on railroad (Sofiyevka station) and 15 mi. NE of Zaporozhe; agr. machinery works. Called Sofiyevka until c.1935, and after, until 1944, Krasnoarmeiskoye.

Chervono-Grigorovka (chĭrvô″nù-grēgô′rŭfkŭ), town (1926 pop. 5,679), S Dnepropetrovsk oblast, Ukrainian SSR, 7 mi. ENE of Nikopol, in manganese-mining dist. Until 1939, Krasnogrigoryevka.

Chervonoye (chĭrvô′nŭyù). **1** Village (1939 pop. over 500), NE Sumy oblast, Ukrainian SSR, 12 mi. NNE of Glukhov; hemp growing. **2** Town (1926 pop. 3,679), S Zhitomir oblast, Ukrainian SSR, 12 mi. ENE of Berdichev; sugar mill. Until c.1935, Krasnoye.

Cherwell River (chär′wŭl), Northampton and Oxfordshire, England, rises 12 mi. NE of Banbury, flows 30 mi. S, past Banbury, to the Thames (locally called the Isis) just S of Oxford.

Chesaning (chĕ′sùnĭng), village (pop. 2,264), Saginaw co., E central Mich., on Shiawassee R. and 19 mi. SW of Saginaw, in agr. area (sugar beets, corn, grain, livestock); coal mining; meat packing. Inc. 1869. Area formerly (1819–37) an Indian reservation.

Chesapeake (chĕ′sùpēk, chĕs′pēk). **1** Village (pop. 1,285), Lawrence co., S Ohio, on the Ohio (bridged), opposite Huntington, W.Va. Inc. 1908. **2** Town (pop. 2,566), Kanawha co., W W.Va., on the Kanawha and 10 mi. SSE of Charleston.

Chesapeake and Delaware Canal, N Del. and NE Md., a deep-water section of Intracoastal Waterway connecting Delaware R., 2 mi. S of Delaware City, Del., with Elk R. arm of Chesapeake Bay c.4 mi. W of Chesapeake City, Md.; 19 mi. long (including c.5 mi. in Back Creek, connecting canal and Elk R.). Opened 1829, bought 1919 by U.S. govt., enlarged 1935–39.

Chesapeake and Ohio Canal, former waterway bet. Washington, D.C., and Cumberland, W Md.; extended 185 mi. along E bank of Potomac R. Planned by George Washington; started 1828; finished 1850. Heaviest traffic (chiefly coal from mines near Cumberland) in 1860s; declined in volume after development of railroads. Abandoned (1924) because of flood damage. Purchased (1938) by U.S.; a part (restored) at Great Falls of the Potomac is a unit of system of Natl. Capital Parks. Lower 22 mi. of canal now used as recreational waterway.

Chesapeake Bay, great arm (c.195 mi. long N–S, 3–30 mi. wide) of the Atlantic penetrating N into E coast of U.S. (Md. and Va.). DELMARVA PENINSULA (called the Eastern Shore along the bay) separates the bay from the Atlantic, Delaware Bay, and Delaware R. on the E. Its entrance (13 mi. wide) from the Atlantic is bet. Cape Charles (N) and Cape Henry (S). The bay represents the drowned lower valley of the Susquehanna, which enters at its head. On W side, it is entered (N to S) by wide and deep estuaries of Patapsco R. (port of Baltimore), Severn R. (approach to U.S. Naval Acad. at Annapolis), Patuxent R., Potomac R. (approach to Washington), Rappahannock R., York R., and James R., whose estuary, together with those of Nansemond and Elizabeth rivers, enters great HAMPTON ROADS anchorage at S end of the bay. From the Eastern Shore, along which lie many isls. and sheltered Tangier and Pocomoke sounds, bay is entered by estuaries (N to S) of Northeast, Elk, Sassafras, Chester, Wye, Miles, Choptank, Nanticoke, and Pocomoke rivers and innumerable inlets, giving access to shipping centers (notably Crisfield, Salisbury, Cambridge) for bay's great sea-food industry (oysters, crabs, finfish). A part of sheltered route of Intracoastal Waterway, bay is connected near its head with Delaware R. by Chesapeake and Delaware Canal; from Norfolk on Hampton Roads, the Dismal Swamp Canal and the Chesapeake and Albemarle Canal connect it with Albemarle Sound (S). Naturally deep, bay requires dredging for deep-draft vessels only off harbor and canal entrances. Bay is famous as a sport fishing ground and recreational area; the Eastern Shore is known for its waterfowl hunting, and muskrats are trapped there. The bay region, one of earliest settled in the New World, is rich in historic sites. The English, who settled at Jamestown Isl., Va., on May 13, 1607, had anchored off Cape Henry on April 26; Capt. John Smith of the colony explored the bay in 1608. 1st permanent English settlement in Md. made 1631 at Kent Isl. Bay was route of British invasion in War of 1812. Many remote ways of life have persisted among fisherfolk and farmers on its isls. (especially Tangier, in Va., and Smith, in Md.) and on the Eastern Shore. The traditional isolation of the Eastern Shore has been lessened by construction (in early 1950s) of Chesapeake Bay Bridge (c.7 mi. long over all, more than 4 mi. long over water) bet. Sandy Point, Md. (W), and Kent Isl., Md. (E).

Chesapeake Beach. 1 Resort town (pop. 504), Calvert co., S Md., on Chesapeake Bay, 30 mi. ESE of Washington; sport fishing. 2 Resort, Northumberland co., E Va., on Chesapeake Bay at tip of Northern Neck peninsula, just E of Reedville.

Chesapeake City, town (pop. 1,154), Cecil co., NE Md., near terminus of Chesapeake and Delaware Canal and 21 mi. SW of Wilmington, Del.; boatyards. Near by are Port Herman (fishing village; bathing beach) and Hollywood Beach, summer resort.

Chesha Bay (chyô'shŭ), Rus. *Cheshskaya Guba*, inlet of Barents Sea, in NW Nenets Natl. Okrug, Archangel oblast, Russian SFSR, E of Kanin Peninsula; 70 mi. wide, 65 mi. long. Kolguyev Isl. is 85 mi. NNE of its entrance. Receives small Chesha R. (W).

Chesham (chĕ'sŭm, chĕ'shŭm), urban district (1931 pop. 8,812; 1951 census 11,428), E Buckingham, England, 26 mi. NW of London; shoes, machinery, furniture, cocoa products. Has 13th-cent. church.

Chesham Bois (chĕ'sŭm boiz'), residential town and parish (pop. 2,055), SE Buckingham, England, just S of Chesham. Has 14th-cent. church.

Cheshire (chĕ'shŭr) or **Chester,** county (□ 1,019.3; 1931 pop. 1,087,655; 1951 census 1,258,050), W England; ⊙ Chester. Bounded by Lancashire (N), Yorkshire (NE), Derby (E), Stafford (SE), Shropshire (S), Wales (W), and the Irish Sea (NW). Drained by Mersey, Dee, and Weaver rivers. Fertile grazing land; dairy farming and cheese mfg. (Cheshire cheese has long been famous). Main industries: textile mfg. (Macclesfield, Congleton, Hyde, Stockport), shipbuilding (Birkenhead), salt mining and mfg. of chemicals (Northwich, Winsford, Nantwich, Hyde, Sandbach), locomotive and railroad rolling-stock construction (Crewe), soap and oleomargerine mfg. (Port Sunlight), and petroleum refining (Stanlow and Ellesmere Port).

Cheshire, county (□ 717; pop. 38,811), SW N.H.; ⊙ Keene. Mfg. (textiles, wood products, shoes), mica and feldspar mining and processing, granite quarries; agr. Resorts on lakes. Drained by Connecticut and Ashuelot rivers (water power) and headwaters of the Contoocook. Formed 1769.

Cheshire. 1 Town (pop. 6,295), including Cheshire village (pop. 1,826), New Haven co., S central Conn., 13 mi. N of New Haven; agr., mfg. (metal and wire products). Cheshire Acad. for boys (1794), state reformatory here. Includes West Cheshire village (metal fasteners). Settled before 1700, inc. 1780. 2 Resort town (pop. 2,022), Berkshire co., NW Mass., on Hoosic R. and 9 mi. NNE of Pittsfield; dairying. Settled 1766, inc. 1793. Includes state park and village of Farnams (limestone).

Cheshskaya Guba, Russian SFSR: see CHESHA BAY.

Cheshunt (chĕ'sŭnt), residential urban district (1931 pop. 14,656; 1951 census 23,016), SE Hertford, England, 14 mi. N of London; truck gardens, iron foundries. Cheshunt Col. (theological), founded 1768 by Countess of Huntingdon, was here from 1792 to 1905, when it was transferred to Cambridge. Has 1420 church and remains of 13th-cent. Benedictine convent.

Chesières (shĕzyâr'), resort (alt. 4,000 ft.), Vaud canton, SW Switzerland, 16 mi. WNW of Sion.

Chesilhurst (chĕ'zŭl–), borough (pop. 314), Camden co., S N.J., 20 mi. SE of Camden; truck-farming center.

Chesley (chĕs'lē), town (pop. 1,701), S Ont., on North Saugeen R. and 20 mi. SSE of Owen Sound; knitting and flour mills; furniture mfg.

Chesma (chĭsmä'), village (1926 pop. 2,079), E Chelyabinsk oblast, Russian SFSR, 40 mi. SW of Troitsk; rye, oats, barley. Formerly Chesmenski.

Chesme, Turkey: see CESME.

Chesmenski, Russian SFSR: see CHESMA.

Chesnay, Le (lŭ shĕnā'), N suburb (pop. 8,315) of Versailles, Seine-et-Oise dept., N central France, 10 mi. WSW of Paris: mfg. (tractors, railroad equipment, brushes, rope).

Chesne, Le (lŭ shān'), agr. village (pop. 672), Ardennes dept., N France, on Ardennes Canal and 9 mi. NNE of Vouziers, at N edge of the Argonne.

Chesnee (chĕ'snē), town (pop. 1,051), Spartanburg co., NW S.C., 15 mi. N of Spartanburg; textiles, grain products. In 1781 British lost battle of Cowpens, just E.

Chesnokovka (chĕsnŭkôf'kŭ), city (1944 pop. over 10,000), NE Altai Territory, Russian SFSR, 5 mi. E of Barnaul (across Ob R.), at junction (Altaiskaya station) of Turksib RR and branch line to Bisk; agr.-processing center; flour milling. Developed during Second World War.

Chestatee River (chĕ'stŭtē), NE Ga., rises in the Blue Ridge, in N Lumpkin co., flows c.50 mi. S to Chattahoochee R. 7 mi. W of Gainesville.

Cheste (chĕ'stā), town (pop. 5,079), Valencia prov., E Spain, 16 mi. W of Valencia; agr. trade center (wine, olive oil, potatoes); shoe mfg., alcohol and brandy distilling, hog raising. Carlists defeated here (1832) by Queen Christina's troops.

Chester, town (pop. estimate 1,000), S N.S., at head of Mahone Bay, 30 mi. WSW of Halifax; seaside resort, tuna-fishing center: mfg. of marine engines, furniture. Settled c.1760.

Chester, county, England: see CHESHIRE.

Chester, county borough (1931 pop. 41,440; 1951 census 48,229) and city, ⊙ CHESHIRE, England, in W part of co., on a sandstone height above the Dee (here bridged), 16 mi. SSE of Liverpool; 53°12'N 2°53'W; railroad center; mfg. of leather goods, paint, synthetic fertilizer; nonferrous-metal refining, steel milling, machine making; important cheese market. An old town, occupied early by Britons and known as *Caerlon*, it was an important Roman fort (*Deva* or *Devana Castra*). Town sacked by Æthelfrith of Northumbria in 613 and by Danes in 894. Early in 10th cent. it was rebuilt by Æthelred and Æthelflæd of Mercia and was the last town in England to be taken by William the Conqueror in 1070. In the Civil War it was taken by Parliamentarians after long siege in 1646. Chester has a medieval aspect and is the only English town with city walls intact. Points of interest: Caesar's Tower, with remains of castle of Lupus; many 16th- and 17th-cent. timbered houses; cathedral dating from Norman times; St. John's church (formerly a cathedral); Grosvenor Mus.; Grosvenor Park; the "Rows," formed by the projection of the 2d stories of bldgs. along the main streets, in arcade fashion; and, across the Dee, Eaton Hall, seat of the duke of Westminster. The Chester plays, a cycle of miracle plays, originated here c.1400.

Chester. 1 County (□ 760; pop. 159,141), SE Pa.; ⊙ West Chester. Industrial and agricultural area, drained by Schuylkill R. (N) and BRANDYWINE CREEK. Chester Valley (35 mi. long, ½ to 2 mi. wide) extends WSW from Schuylkill R. below VALLEY FORGE. Iron and steel, canned goods, clothing; dairying, meat packing; granite, limestone. Formed 1682. 2 County (□ 585; pop. 32,597), N S.C.; ⊙ Chester. Bounded W by Broad R., E by Catawba R. Includes part of Sumter Natl. Forest. Mainly agr. area, with mfg. center at Chester; cotton, livestock, corn, oats, dairy products, hay (lespedeza). Great Falls is electric-power center. Formed 1785. 3 County (□ 285; pop. 11,149), SW Tenn.; ⊙ Henderson. Drained by South Fork of Forked Deer R. Timber, cotton, livestock. Contains part of Chickasaw State Park and State Forest. Formed 1879.

Chester. 1 Town (pop. 120), Crawford co., NW Ark., 24 mi. NNE of Fort Smith. 2 Village (pop. 1,197), Plumas co., NE Calif., in the Sierra Nevada, near L. Almanor, 30 mi. NW of Quincy; resort; lumbering. Lassen Volcanic Natl. Park in N. 3 Town (pop. 1,920), including Chester village (pop. 1,354), Middlesex co., S Conn., on the Connecticut and 15 mi. SE of Middletown; agr., mfg. (tools, hardware, brushes, needles, wire and wood products). State forest here. Settled 1692, inc. 1836. 4 Town (pop. 315), Dodge co., S central Ga., 17 mi. SW of Dublin. 5 City (pop. 5,389), ⊙ Randolph co., SW Ill., on the Mississippi near mouth of Kaskaskia R., and c.50 mi. SSE of St. Louis; trade and shipping center in agr., stock-raising, and dairying area; mfg. (clothing, leather goods, food products). Bituminous-coal mines, stone quarries. A branch of state penitentiary and a state hosp. are here. Near by are Fort Kaskaskia (near old site of KASKASKIA) and Fort Chartres state parks. Founded 1819, inc. 1835. 6 Town (pop. 226), Howard co., NE Iowa, near Minn. line, on Upper Iowa R. and 15 mi. NW of Cresco. Sand and gravel pits near by. 7 Town (pop. 256), Penobscot co., central Maine, on the Penobscot and 9 mi. SW of Mattawamkeag; agr., lumbering, camps. 8 Village, Queen Annes co., Md.: see KENT ISLAND. 9 Town (pop. 1,292), Hampden co., W Mass., in the Berkshires, on West Branch of Westfield R. and 18 mi. SE of Pittsfield; abrasives; mica, emery, granite; maple syrup. Settled 1760, inc. 1765. 10 Town (pop. 733), ⊙ Liberty co., N Mont., on branch of Marias R. and 70 mi. NNE of Great Falls; grain. 11 Village (pop. 539), Thayer co., SE Nebr., 10 mi. S of Hebron, at Kansas line; dairy, truck, and poultry produce, grain, livestock. 12 Town (pop. 807), Rockingham co., SE N.H., 11 mi. E of Manchester; agr. 13 Borough (pop. 754), Morris co., N central N.J., 11 mi. W of Morristown, in peach-growing region. 14 Village (pop. 1,215), Orange co., SE N.Y., 16 mi. SW of Newburgh, in farming, dairying, and horse-breeding area; summer resort. Hambletonian, famous trotter, was foaled and buried here. Inc. 1892. 15 Port city (pop. 66,039), Delaware co., SE Pa., 14 mi. SW of Philadelphia and on Delaware R.; port of entry; shipbuilding, oil refining, mfg. of locomotives, automobiles, electrical equipment, chemicals, machinery, steel products, glass, paper; aluminum plant; silk mills. Has Pennsylvania Military Col., Crozen Theological Seminary. William Penn landed here 1682; Penn's house, built 1683, still stands. Settled c.1644 as Uppland by Swedes, laid out 1686, inc. as borough 1795, as city 1866. 16 City (pop. 6,893), ⊙ Chester co., N S.C., 50 mi. NNW of Columbia; rail junction; textiles, fertilizer, cottonseed oil, foundry products, lumber and grain products. Settled in late 18th cent., inc. as town 1849, as city 1893. Hydroelectric power, developed on near-by rivers in early 20th cent., stimulated textile industry. 17 Resort town (pop. 1,981), including Chester village (pop. 796), Windsor co., SE Vt., on Williams R., just W of Springfield; wood products; talc; printing. Winter sports. 18 Village (pop. 1,168), Chesterfield co., E central Va., near the James, 14 mi. S of Richmond; rail junction; lumber milling. 19 Residential city (pop. 3,758), Hancock co., W.Va., in industrial Northern Panhandle, on the Ohio and 30 mi. WNW of Pittsburgh; makes pottery. Tomlinson Run State Park (c.1,350 acres) is 4 mi. S. City laid out 1896.

Chesterfield, municipal borough (1931 pop. 64,160; 1951 census 68,540), NE Derby, England, 10 mi. S of Sheffield; mfg. of steel, woolens, cotton, leather, machinery, paint, pottery. Near by are coal and lead mines. Has 14th-cent. church with twisted spire, a 16th-cent. grammar school, and Stephenson Memorial Hall, dedicated to George Stephenson, who died here (1848). In municipal borough (N) is town of Whittington (pop. 8,317) with steel mills and pottery works, and (NW) residential suburb of Newbold (pop. 6,555).

Chesterfield. 1 County (□ 793; pop. 36,236), N S.C., ⊙ Chesterfield. Bounded E by Pee Dee R., W by Lynches R., N by N.C.; in the Sand Hills. Cheraw is mfg. center. Mainly agr. (cotton, corn, tobacco); some timber. In S is Sand Hills Development Project for reforestation and game preservation. Formed 1798. 2 County (□ 475; pop. 40,400), E central Va.; ⊙ Chesterfield. Bounded SW, S, SE by Appomattox, N and NE by James rivers; adjoins Richmond (N), Petersburg and Hopewell (S) cities. Large tobacco-processing and rayon plants; stock and poultry raising, dairying, agr. (corn, tobacco, peanuts, some cotton). Fisheries. Bermuda Hundred and Drewry's Bluff were scenes of Civil War actions. Formed 1749.

Chesterfield. 1 Village (pop. 272), Macoupin co., SW Ill., 25 mi. NNE of Alton, in agr. and bituminous-coal area. 2 Town (pop. 1,086), Madison co., E central Ind., 39 mi. NE of Indianapolis. 3 Town (pop. 496), Hampshire co., W Mass., on Westfield R. and 12 mi. WNW of Northampton; agr., cattle raising; wood products. 4 Town (pop. 970), Cheshire co., SW N.H., on the Connecticut and 11 mi. WSW of Keene; agr.; resorts on Spofford L. Granted 1752 by Massachusetts Colony as Township No. 1 in the Connecticut valley, chartered and settled 1761. 5 Town (pop. 1,530), ⊙ Chesterfield co., N S.C., 42 mi. NNW of Florence, near N.C. line, in agr. area; lumber, cotton, tobacco. 6 Village (pop. c.150), ⊙ Chesterfield co., E central Va., 13 mi. S of Richmond. Sometimes called Chesterfield Court House.

Chesterfield Court House, Va.: see CHESTERFIELD, village.

Chesterfield Inlet, trading post (district native pop. 1,034), E Keewatin Dist., Northwest Territories, on Hudson Bay, at mouth of Chesterfield Inlet; 63°21'N 90°42'W. Govt. radio direction-finding and meteorological station, hosp., industrial home, Royal Canadian Mounted Police post. Site of R.C. mission.

Chesterfield Inlet, E Keewatin Dist., Northwest Territories, fjord (140 mi. long, 1–10 mi. wide) of Hudson Bay; extends WNW from Chesterfield Inlet trading post to Baker L.; with Baker L. it is over 200 mi. long.

Chesterfield Islands, uninhabited coral group (250 acres), SW Pacific, 340 mi. NW of New Caledonia, of which it is a dependency; 19°53'S 158°28'E; guano.

Chester Heights, borough (pop. 474), Delaware co., SE Pa., 6 mi. NW of Chester. Inc. 1946.

Chesterhill or **Chester Hill,** village (pop. 426), Morgan co., E central Ohio, 22 mi. WNW of Marietta.

Chester Hill, borough (pop. 954), Clearfield co., central Pa., just SW of Philipsburg.

Chester-le-Street (–lŭ–), urban district (1931 pop. 16,640; 1951 census 18,539), N Durham, England, 8 mi. S of Newcastle-upon-Tyne; coal and iron mining; mfg. of biscuits. Site of a Roman station and once seat of the Bishop of Bernicia. Just E is 14th-cent. Lumley Castle.

Chester River, W Del. and E Md., rises in NW Kent co., Del., flows c.55 mi. SW, past Millington (head of navigation), Crumpton, and Chestertown, to Chesapeake Bay; lower portion is wide estuary. Carries grain, produce schooners.

Chesterton. 1 Suburb, Cambridgeshire, England: see CAMBRIDGE, municipal borough. 2 Agr. village and parish (pop. 317), E Oxfordshire, England, 2 mi. SW of Bicester; bacon and ham curing. Church dates from 13th cent. Just S are remains of Roman town of Alchester.

Chesterton, town (pop. 3,175), Porter co., NW Ind., 15 mi. E of Gary, in agr. area (poultry, fruit; dairy products); makes printers' supplies.

Chestertown. 1 Town (pop. 3,143), ⊙ Kent co. (since 1696), E Md., on the Eastern Shore, on Chester R. and 30 mi. E of Baltimore. Trade center for resort and agr. area (tomatoes, wheat, corn); mfg. (fireworks, munitions, fertilizer, hosiery); vegetable and fish canneries. Seat of Washington Col. (chartered 1782), one of earliest colleges in U.S.; George Washington endowed it and received here an honorary degree in 1789. Protestant Episcopal Church of America adopted its name here in 1780. Laid out 1706; became port of entry 1708. Old customs house still stands. **2** Resort village, Warren co., E N.Y., in the Adirondacks, 25 mi. NNW of Glens Falls; wood products; lumbering.

Chesterville, village (pop. 1,067), SE Ont., on South Nation R. and 30 mi. SE of Ottawa; dairying, milk canning, leather mfg., lumbering.

Chesterville. 1 Town (pop. 588), Franklin co., W central Maine, 11 mi. SSE of Farmington in agr. area; wood products, canneries. **2** Village (pop. 208), Morrow co., central Ohio, 12 mi. WNW of Mount Vernon and on Kokosing R.

Chestnut Hill. 1 Village, Tolland co., Conn.: see COLUMBIA. **2** Beautiful residential suburb of Boston, E Mass.; partly in Newton and partly in Brookline. Main seat of Boston Col. **3** NW residential section of Philadelphia, Pa.

Chestnut Ridge (2,200–2,700 ft.), a ridge of the Alleghenies, SW Pa. and W.Va., runs 30 mi. NNE from Preston co., W.Va., to just E of Connellsville, Pa.; cut by Youghiogheny R. just S of Connellsville; natural gas.

Chestochina, Alaska: see CHISTOCHINA.

Chest Springs, borough (pop. 232), Cambria co., SW central Pa., 9 mi. NE of Ebensburg.

Chesuncook (chĭsŭn'ko͝ok), former plantation (pop. 16), Piscataquis co., N central Maine, on Chesuncook L. 43 mi. NE of Greenville, in hunting, fishing area.

Chesuncook Lake, Piscataquis co., N central Maine, 33 mi. NE of Greenville and on W branch of Penobscot R., in wilderness recreational area; 22 mi. long, 1–4 mi. wide. Joined at S end to Caribou and Ripogenus lakes.

Cheswick (chĕz'wĭk), residential borough (pop. 1,534), Allegheny co., SW central Pa., 12 mi. NE of Pittsburgh and on Allegheny R.; electrical supplies. Inc. 1902.

Cheswold (chĕz'wôld), town (pop. 292), Kent co., central Del., 5 mi. NNW of Dover, in fruitgrowing area.

Chetek (shĭtĕk', shĕ'tĕk), city (pop. 1,585), Barron co., NW Wis., on small Chetek L. and Chetek R. (tributary of the Red Cedar), and 36 mi. NNW of Eau Claire, in dairying and poultry-raising area; vegetable canning, mfg. of luggage. Summer resort. Settled 1863, inc. 1891.

Cheticamp (shĕ'tĭkămp), village (pop. estimate 600), NE N.S., on NW Cape Breton Isl., on the Gulf of St. Lawrence, 30 mi. NNE of Inverness; fishing port; gypsum quarrying, rug making. Acadian center. Just offshore is Cheticamp Isl.

Cheticamp Island (3 mi. long, 1 mi. wide), NE N.S., in the Gulf of St. Lawrence, off NW Cape Breton Isl., opposite Cheticamp; 46°38'N 61°2'W. Freestone quarrying.

Chetilla (chātē'yä), town (pop. 647), Cajamarca dept., NW Peru, in Cordillera Occidental, 9 mi. W of Cajamarca; thermal springs in agr. region (wheat, corn, potatoes).

Chetlat Island (chĕt'lŭt), coral island of Amin Divi group of Laccadive Isls., India, in Arabian Sea; 11°40'N 72°40'E. Administered by South Kanara dist., Madras; coir.

Chetma (shĕtmä'), village (pop. 1,289), Touggourt territory, NE Algeria, oasis in the Ziban region of the N Sahara, 4 mi. E of Biskra; date palms.

Chetopa (shĭtō'pů), city (pop. 1,671), Labette co., SE Kansas, near Okla. line, on Neosho R. and 26 mi. E of Coffeyville, in dairying and agr. area; woodworking. Coal, oak timber in vicinity. Settled 1857, laid out 1868, inc. 1870.

Chetpat, India: see CHETPUT.

Chetput or **Chetpat** (chĕtpŭt). **1** Section of MADRAS, city, India. **2** Town (pop. 8,815), North Arcot dist., E central Madras, India, 35 mi. SSE of Vellore; road center in agr. area (rice, cotton, peanuts). Formerly spelled Chetpet.

Chetumal (chāto͞omäl'), city (pop. 4,672), ⊙ Quintana Roo, SE Mexico, on E Yucatan Peninsula, port on Chetumal Bay at mouth of the Río Hondo, on Br. Honduras border, and 70 mi. N of Belize, 725 mi. E of Mexico city; 18°30'N 88°18'W. Agr. center (chicle, henequen, tropical fruit, hardwood; hogs, cattle). Airfield, radio station, customhouse. Founded 1898 as military post. Payo Obispo until 1935.

Chetumal Bay, inlet of Caribbean Sea, on E coast of Yucatan Peninsula, on border of Mexico and British Honduras; 35 mi. long N–S, 3–20 mi. wide. Ports of Corozal (Br. Honduras) and Chetumal (Mexico) are on W shore. Receives the Río Hondo.

Chetyrekhstolbovoi Island, Russian SFSR: see BEAR ISLANDS.

Cheurfas Dam, Oran dept., Algeria: see SAINT-DENIS-DU-SIG.

Chevagnes (shůvä'nyů), village (pop. 377), Allier dept., central France, in the Sologne Bourbonnaise, 11 mi. ENE of Moulins; mfg. of cement pipes.

Chevak (chĕväk'), village (pop. 228), W Alaska, near Yukon R. delta.

Cheverie (shĕvůrē'), village (pop. estimate 200), N central N.S., on Minas Basin, 6 mi. N of Hantsport; gypsum quarrying, lumbering.

Cheverly (shĕ'vůrlē), town (pop. 3,318), Prince Georges co., central Md., E suburb of Washington. Inc. 1931.

Cheverny (shůvĕrnē'), village (pop. 241), Loir-et-Cher dept., N central France, 8 mi. SE of Blois; winegrowing. Has remarkable château of regular dimensions suggesting the Louis-Quatorze style. It was built in 1634 and has fine tapestries and paintings.

Chevillon (shůvēyō'), village (pop. 664), Haute-Marne dept., NE France, near Marne R. and Marne-Saône Canal, 12 mi. SE of Saint-Dizier; steel- and iron-pipe mfg., cheese making. Stone quarried near by.

Chevilly-Larue (shůvēyē'-lärü'), town (pop. 2,630), Seine dept., N central France, an outer S suburb of Paris, 5.5 mi. from Notre Dame Cathedral; truck gardens, brickworks. Sanatorium. Scene of fighting 1870–71.

Cheviot (chĕv'yůt), township (pop. 294), ⊙ Cheviot co. (□ 327; pop. 1,248), E S.Isl., New Zealand, 60 mi. NNE of Christchurch; center of agr., sheep-raising area.

Cheviot (shĭ'vēůt, shĕ'–), city (pop. 9,944), Hamilton co., extreme SW Ohio, just W of Cincinnati; mfg. of packing boxes, clothes, rubber goods; meat-packing plant. Settled 1818.

Cheviot, The (chĕv'yůt), highest point (2,676 ft.) of Cheviot Hills, on border bet. Northumberland, England, and Roxburgh, Scotland, 6 mi. SW of Wooler.

Cheviot Hills, range extending 35 mi. NE–SW on Scotland-England border, in Northumberland and Roxburgh counties, scene of much strife in border warfare and site of forts and castles. Highest point is The Cheviot (2,676 ft.), 6 mi. SW of Wooler, in England. Grazing land, supporting a fine breed of sheep. Tyne, Tees, and Coquet rivers rise here.

Chevlyanovichi, Yugoslavia: see CEVLJANOVICI.

Chevreuil, Point, La.: see ATCHAFALAYA BAY.

Chevreuse (shĕvrûz'), village (pop. 1,820), Seine-et-Oise dept., N central France, resort on small Yvette R. and 8 mi. SSW of Versailles; truck gardens. Dominated by ruined castle with 12th-cent. keep.

Chevrolet (shĕv'rōlā), village (1940 pop. 962), Harlan co., SE Ky., in the Cumberlands, 3 mi. SE of Harlan, in bituminous-coal region.

Chevroz (shůvrō'), village (pop. 74), Doubs dept., E France, on the Ognon and 7 mi. N of Besançon; paper mill.

Chevy Chase, England: see OTTERBURN.

Chevy Chase (chĕ"vē chās'), residential village (pop. 1,971), Montgomery co., central Md., NW suburb of Washington; makes air-conditioning equipment. Inc. 1947.

Chevy Chase Heights, village (pop. 1,160), Indiana co., W central Pa.

Chewelah (chēwē'lů), town (pop. 1,683), Stevens co., NE Wash., 21 mi. SSE of Colville and on Colville R.; magnesite mills, quarries, timber, dairy products. Inc. 1903.

Chew Magna, agr. village and parish (pop. 1,596), NE Somerset, England, 6 mi. SSE of Bristol. Has 15th-cent. church.

Cheyang, China: see CHEJUNG.

Cheyenne (shīăn', –ĕn'). **1** County (□ 1,772; pop. 3,453), E Colo.; ⊙ Cheyenne Wells. Agr. area bordering on Kansas; drained by Big Sandy Creek. Wheat, livestock. Formed 1889. **2** County (□ 1,027; pop. 5,668), extreme NW Kansas; ⊙ St. Francis. Agr. region, bordered N by Nebr. and W by Colo.; drained by South Fork Republican R. Grain, livestock. Formed 1886. **3** County (□ 1,186; pop. 12,081), W Nebr.; ⊙ Sidney; agr. area bounded S by Colo.; drained by Lodgepole Creek. Grain, livestock, dairy produce. Formed 1870.

Cheyenne. 1 Town (pop. 1,133), Roger Mills co., W Okla., on Washita R., near Texas border, and 20 mi. NW of Elk City, in livestock, grain, and cotton area; mfg. of cement blocks, cotton ginning. Battle of the Washita (1868), bet. troops under Gen. Custer and the Cheyenne Indians, took place near by. Founded c.1892. **2** City (pop. 31,935), ⊙ Wyo. and Laramie co., SE Wyo., on Crow Creek, near Colo. and Nebr. lines, and 100 mi. N of Denver, Colo.; 41°8'N 104°49'W; alt. c.6,000 ft. Largest city in state, Cheyenne is transportation (rail, highway, air), trade, distribution center, and shipping point for sheep and cattle. Railroad shops, municipal airport, plane-servicing depot, oil refinery here. Mfg. includes dairy and bakery products, beverages, lumber. Selected (1867) as railroad div. point, city grew swiftly. It was inc. in same year; became territorial capital 1869, state capital 1890. Factors in its development were opening (c.1875) of gold fields in Black Hills, for which city was outfitting point, and growth of livestock industry. Frontier Days Celebration, 1st held 1897, takes place annually. Points of interest: St. Mary's Cathedral (R.C.), Supreme Court Building (also housing state historical mus. and state library), state capitol. Near by are veterans' hosp., Fort Francis E. Warren (large military post, Air Force Base, and reservation, formerly known as Fort D. A. Russell), U.S. horticultural field station, and Archer Field station (experimental farm run by state and U.S. Dept. of Agr.).

Cheyenne Agency, village (1940 pop. 630), Dewey co., N central S.Dak., 45 mi. N of Pierre and on Missouri R.; hq. for Cheyenne River Indian Reservation.

Cheyenne Mountain (c.9,500 ft.), peak of Front Range, just SW of Colorado Springs, central Colo. Halfway up mtn. is Shrine of the Sun Memorial, erected in memory of Will Rogers; consists of 100-ft. tower. Interior decorated with frescoes; has bust of Will Rogers sculptured by Jo Davidson.

Cheyenne River, in Wyo. and S.Dak., rises in E Wyo. as South Fork, flows 527 mi. E and NE into SW S.Dak., skirting S base of Black Hills, to Missouri R. N of Pierre; drains □ 25,500. Receives BELLE FOURCHE RIVER, its principal tributary, c.110 mi. upstream. Bridged at junction of Ziebach, Haakon, Pennington, and Meade counties by Four Corner Bridge, longest bridge (1 mi.) in S.Dak. Angostura Dam (begun 1946 as unit in Missouri R. basin irrigation project; to be 187 ft. high, 1,818 ft. long) is in Cheyenne R. near Hot Springs, SW S.Dak.

Cheyenne Wells, town (pop. 1,154), ⊙ Cheyenne co., E Colo., 160 mi. SE of Denver, near Kansas line; alt. 4,282 ft.; grain.

Cheylard, Le (lů shälär'), town (pop. 2,658), Ardèche dept., S France, in the Monts du Vivarais, on the Érieux and 15 mi. NW of Privas; tanning, leather working, silk weaving, jewelry mfg.

Cheylas, Le (lů shälä'), village (pop. 148), Isère dept., SE France, on Isère R. and 4 mi. SW of Allevard, in Grésivaudan valley; metallurgy.

Cheyl'dag, Azerbaijan SSR: see CHEILDAG.

Cheylus (shälü'), village, Tunis dist., N Tunisia, on Miliane R. and 18 mi. SSW of Tunis; silos. Cereals, wine, cattle.

Cheyney (chā'nē), village, Delaware co., SE Pa., 18 mi. W of Philadelphia. Seat of Cheyney Training School for Teachers.

Cheyram, Bhutan: see CHIRANG.

Cheyur (chā'yo͞or), town (pop. 6,166), Chingleput dist., E Madras, India, 14 mi. SE of Madurantakam. Large salt pans just E, near Buckingham Canal, on Coromandel Coast of Bay of Bengal. Also spelled Cheyyur or Cheyyar.

Cheyyar River (chā'yär), in North Arcot and Chingleput dists., E central Madras, India, rises on central plateau of Javadi Hills, flows 120 mi. NE, through agr. valley, past Chengam, Polur and Tiruvattiyur, to Palar R. 3 mi. SE of Walajabad.

Chèze, La (lä shĕz'), village (pop. 411), Côtes-du-Nord dept., W France, 15 mi. ENE of Pontivy; woodworking.

Chh-, for Indian names beginning thus and not found here: see under CH-.

Chhabra (chŭb'rů), town (pop. 6,107), SE Rajasthan, India, 75 mi. SE of Kotah; market center for wheat, millet, oranges; hand-loom weaving.

Chhachhrauli (chŭchrou'lē) or **Kalsia** (kŭls'yů) town (pop. 5,419), E Patiala and East Punjab States Union, India, 6 mi. NNE of Jagadhri; local market for wheat, gram, sugar, spices. Was ⊙ former Punjab state of Kalsia. Sometimes spelled Chachrauli.

Chhamdo, Tibet: see CHAMDO.

Chhapar (chä'pŭr), town (pop. 5,363), N central Rajasthan, India, 70 mi. ESE of Bikaner. Natural salt deposits near by.

Chharra (chŭr'rů), town (pop. 2,450), Aligarh dist. W Uttar Pradesh, India, 20 mi. E of Aligarh; wheat, barley, pearl millet, gram, corn. Formerly called Chharra Rafatpur.

Chhata (chä'tů), town (pop. 7,437), Muttra dist. W Uttar Pradesh, India, 19 mi. NNW of Muttra; gram, jowar, wheat, cotton, barley, oilseeds. Large fortlike serai.

Chhatak (chä'täk), village, Sylhet dist., E East Bengal, E Pakistan, in Surma Valley, on Surma R. and 16 mi. NW of Sylhet; trades in rice, tea, potatoes, oranges; cement mfg.

Chhatari (chŭtä'rē), town (pop. 5,045), Bulandshahr dist., W Uttar Pradesh, India, 26 mi. SW of Bulandshahr; wheat, oilseeds, cotton, barley, corn.

Chhatarpur (chŭ"tůpo͝or', chŭtŭr'po͝or), town (pop. 13,210), ⊙ Chhatarpur dist., N central Vindhya Pradesh, India, 110 mi. WNW of Rewa; road and trade center (wheat, millet, gram, cloth fabrics); hand-loom weaving. Was ⊙ former princely state of Chhatarpur (□ 1,170; pop. 184,720) of Central India agency; founded late-18th cent. since 1948, merged with Vindhya Pradesh.

Chhatra, Nepal: see CHATRA.

Chhattisgarh Plain (chŭt'tēsgŭr), E Madhya Pradesh and W Orissa, India, bet. Eastern Ghats (S), Chota Nagpur Plateau (N), and Satpura Range (NW); comprises upper Mahanadi R. basin; a broad, undulating tract of laterite soils. Partly irrigated, it produces rice, oilseeds, grain; sal forests. Bilaspur, Raipur, Raigarh, and Drug are chief towns. Long held by Hindu dynasty; invaded by Moguls (16th cent.) and Mahrattas (1740s). Sometimes spelled Chattisgarh.

Chhattisgarh States, subordinate agency (□ 37,688; pop. 4,050,000) of former Eastern States agency, India, surrounding Chhattisgarh Plain; hq. were at Raipur. Comprised princely states of Bastar, Changbhakar, Chhuikhadan, Jashpur, Kalahandi, Kanker, Kawardha, Khairagarh, Korea, Nandgaon, Patna, Raigarh, Sakti, Sarangarh, Surguja and Udaipur. Established 1936. In 1948, Kalahandi and Patna merged with Orissa, while rest merged with Central Provs. and Berar (now Madhya Pradesh).

Chhaya (chä'yŭ), suburb (pop. 2,651) of Porbandar, W Saurashtra, India. Was ⊙ Jethwa Rajputs from c.1574 to 1785, when they moved to Porbandar; has remains of old fort.

Chheharta (chā'hûrtŭ), industrial W suburb of Amritsar, Amritsar dist., W Punjab, India; mfg. of woolen textiles, carpets, silk and rayon fabrics, embroidered goods, metal products (chains, pails, drums, baling hoops); steel-rolling mill.

Chhibramau (chĭbrä'mou), town (pop. 7,202), Farrukhabad dist., central Uttar Pradesh, India, 17 mi. SSW of Farrukhabad; wheat, gram, jowar, corn, oilseeds. Serai.

Chhindwara (chĭndvä'rŭ), district (□ 7,933; pop. 1,034,040), central Madhya Pradesh, India, on Deccan Plateau; ⊙ Chhindwara. Mainly on central plateau of Satpura Range, which rises NW in rugged hills to over 3,800 ft. and slopes S to small alluvial plain broken by isolated outliers; drained mainly by Wainganga and Pench rivers. Agr. (wheat, millet, rice, oilseeds, cotton, sunnhemp); sal, bamboo, lac, myrobalan in dispersed forest areas. Important coal-mining area NW of Chhindwara (coal-shipping center); manganese mines and marble quarries near Sausar; bauxite deposits near Seoni. Cotton ginning, rice and oilseed milling, sawmilling, essential-oil (*rosha* or Andropogon) extraction and distilling, mfg. of sunn-hemp products (mats, cordage). Dist. enlarged in early 1930s by merger of former dist. of Seoni (E). Pop. 57% Hindu, 40% tribal (mainly Gond), 4% Moslem.

Chhindwara. **1** Town (pop. 21,916), ⊙ Chhindwara dist., central Madhya Pradesh, India, 65 mi. N of Nagpur, in central Satpura Range; road and rail junction; coal-shipping center; trades in cotton and sunn-hemp products (mats, cordage); cotton ginning, sawmilling. Rail spur to village of Barkuhi, 17 mi. NW, serves important coal mines in Pench valley (N); mining school just E of Barkuhi, at village of Chandameta. Experimental farm (chiefly sugar cane). Early Gond fort 18 mi. SW, at village of Deogarh. **2** or **Chhota Chhindwara** (chō'tŭ), town (pop., including railway settlement of Gotegaon, 4,461), Hoshangabad dist., NW Madhya Pradesh, India, 19 mi. ENE of Narsinghpur; cotton ginning; wheat, millet, oilseeds; cattle market.

Chhlong, Cambodia: see CHLONG.

Chhota Udaipur, India: see CHOTA UDAIPUR.

Chhoti Sadri (chō'tē sä'drē), S Rajasthan, India, 35 mi. S of Chitor; markets millet, corn, cotton, wheat; cotton ginning, hand-loom weaving.

Chhaprauli (chrŭprou'lē), town (pop. 7,484), Meerut dist., NW Uttar Pradesh, India, near the Jumna, 35 mi. WNW of Meerut; trade center (wheat, sugar, gram, oilseeds).

Chhuikhadan (chwē'kŭdän), town (pop. 3,190), Drug dist., E central Madhya Pradesh, India, 30 mi. NW of Drug; cotton, wheat, oilseeds; betel farming. Forested hills (W, N). Was ⊙ former princely state of Chhuikhadan (□ 153; pop. 32,731) of Chhattisgarh States, since 1948 inc. into Drug dist.

Chhushu, Tibet: see CHUSHUL.

Chi- or **Ch'i-,** for Chinese names beginning thus and not found here: see under KI-; TSI-.

Chi, province and city, China: see HOPEH.

Chia-, for Chinese names beginning thus and not found here: see under KIA-.

Chía (chē'ä), town (pop. 1,585), Cundinamarca dept., central Colombia, in Cordillera Oriental, 18 mi. N of Bogotá; alt. 9,544 ft.; wheat, potatoes, fruit, stock.

Chia-chi, China: see KACHEK.

Chia-chiang, China: see KIAKIANG.

Chia-hsiang, China: see KIASIANG.

Chia-hsing, China: see KASHING.

Chiaiano (kyä-yä'nô), village (pop. 3,442), Napoli prov., Campania, S Italy, 4 mi. NW of Naples.

Chiajna (kyäzh'nä), outer W rural suburb (1948 pop. 4,542) of Bucharest, S Rumania, on right bank of Dambovita R.; grain, dairying.

Chia Keng (chēä' kĕng'), village (pop. 7,405), Singapore isl., 5 mi. NE of Singapore and just NE of Paya Lebar; rubber. Pop. is Chinese.

Chia-li, Tibet: see LHARI.

Chia-ling Chiang, China: see KIALING RIVER.

Chiama Ngu Chu, Asia: see SALWEEN RIVER.

Chiamboni, Ras, Kenya and Ital. Somaliland: see DICKS HEAD.

Chiamis or **Tjiamis** (both: chēä'mĭs), town (pop. 13,864), W Java, Indonesia, in Preanger region, 60 mi. ESE of Bandung; trade center for agr. area (rubber, rice, corn, cassava).

Chiampo (kyäm'pô), village (pop. 1,850), Vicenza prov., Veneto, N Italy, on Chiampo R. and 13 mi. W of Vicenza, in Monti Lessini; woolen mill. Marble quarries near by.

Chiampo River, N Italy, rises in Monti Lessini 4 mi. SSE of Cima Carega, flows SSE, past Chiampo, and S, past San Bonifacio, to Adige R. near Albaredo d'Adige; 30 mi. long.

Chia-mu-ssu, Manchuria: see KIAMUSZE.

Chi-an. **1** City, Kiangsi prov., China: see KIAN. **2** Town, Liaotung prov., Manchuria, China: see TSIAN.

Chiana (kyä'nä), anc. *Clanis*, watercourse (mostly canalized) in Tuscany, central Italy, S of the Pratomagno. Flows bet. Arno R. 5 mi. NW of Arezzo, and the PAGLIA (affluent of the Tiber) at Orvieto; total length, c.50 mi. Connected with lakes of Montepulciano and Chiusi W of lake Trasimeno. Its valley, Val di Chiana, forms a natural projection of the uppermost Arno valley, the Casentino. In prehistoric times, the Arno flowed through it, until the deposition of its tributaries blocked the channel and turned the Arno NW. Part of its waters, however, continued to flow S. The valley became a fever-ridden swamp until it was reclaimed in 18th cent., becoming one of the most fertile in Italy. With the Tiber valley, it forms a major natural communications route bet. Rome and Florence.

Chianciano (kyänchä'nô), village (pop. 1,649), Siena prov., Tuscany, central Italy, 3 mi. SE of Montepulciano; cement, pottery. Health resort (alt. 1,499 ft.) with hot mineral baths 2 mi. SW. Marble quarries near by.

Chiang-, for Chinese names beginning thus and not found here: see under KIANG-; TSIANG-.

Chiang-ch'ia, Tibet: see MARKHAM.

Chiang-ching, China: see KIANGTSING.

Chiang-ch'uan, China: see KIANGCHWAN.

Chiang Dao (chēäng' dou'), village (1937 pop. 5,179), Chiangmai prov., N Thailand, on road and 40 mi. N of Chiangmai, at foot of Chiang Dao peak (7,160 ft.).

Chiang-hsi, China: see KIANGSI.

Chiang-hua, China: see KIANGHWA.

Chiang Khan (chēäng' kän'), village (1937 pop. 2,867), Loei prov., NE Thailand, 25 mi. N of Loei, on Mekong R. (Laos line); gold mining.

Chiang Khong (chēäng' kông'), village (1937 pop. 3,320), Chiangrai prov., N Thailand, on Mekong R. (Laos line) opposite Ban Houei Sai, 45 mi. NE of Chiangrai; gem deposits (rubies).

Chiang-lo, China: see TSIANGLO.

Chiangmai (chēäng' mī'), city (1947 pop. 26,062), ⊙ Chiangmai prov. (□ 8,861; 1947 pop. 534,628), N Thailand, on Ping R. and 360 mi. NNW of Bangkok (linked by railroad); 18°47'N 99°E. Rail terminus and largest city of N Thailand, in agr. dist. (rice, corn, soybean, tobacco, cotton); trade in teak and lac. Local handicraft industry; silk weaving, mfg. of pottery, silverware, and lacquerware. Pop. is largely Lao. Consists of 18th-cent. walled town on right bank, with ruins of 13th- and 14th-cent. temples, and modern left-bank town which developed after 1920s around railroad station. Founded 1296, it remained ⊙ separate Thai kingdom, flourishing in 16th cent., and was destroyed 1773 by Burmese. Rebuilt in 1790s, it then acknowledged suzerainty of Bangkok and became integral part of Thailand only in late 19th cent. Also spelled Chiengmai, Kiengmai, and Xiengmai.

Chiang-men, China: see SUNWUI.

Chiangrai (chēäng'rī'), town (1947 pop. 5,330), ⊙ Chiangrai prov. (□ 5,878; 1947 pop. 481,621), N Thailand, at foot of Khun Tan Range, on Kok R. and 95 mi. NE of Chiangmai, on Lampang-Kengtung (Burma) road; trading center; teak, lac, rice, coffee. Iron deposits near by. Also spelled Chiengrai.

Chiang Saen (chēäng' săn'), village, Chiangrai prov., N Thailand, near Burma border, on Mekong R. (Laos line), on road and 30 mi NE of Chiangrai; gold mining, teak. Sometimes spelled Chiengsen. In 1930s, called King Chiang Saen or Chiang Saen Luang, while name Chiang Saen was applied to Ban Kasa, a village adjoining MAE CHAN, 16 mi. SW.

Chiang-ta, Tibet: see GIAMDA.

Chiang-tzu, Tibet: see GYANGTSE.

Chianjur, Tjiandjur, or **Tjiandjoer** (all: chēän'jōōr), town (pop. 20,812), W Java, Indonesia, in Preanger region, 30 mi. W of Bandung, at foot of Mt. Pangrango; alt. 1,506 ft.; trade center for agr. area (rice, corn, tea, fruit).

Chianni (kyän'nē), village (pop. 1,245), Pisa prov., Tuscany, central Italy, 12 mi. NW of Volterra, in grape- and olive-growing region.

Chianti, Monti (môn'tē kyän'tē), small range of Apennines, Tuscany, central Italy, W of the Arno and the Pratomagno; c.15 mi. long; rises to 2,930 ft. in Monte San Michele (N). Gives its name to the famous wine produced on its slopes.

Chiantla (chyänt'lä), town (1950 pop. 1,552), Huehuetenango dept., W Guatemala, on S slope of Cuchumatanes Mts., 2 mi. NNE of Huehuetenango; alt. 6,250 ft. Market center (corn, beans, livestock); tanning, wool processing. Lead mining near by.

Chiao- or **Ch'iao-,** for Chinese names beginning thus and not found here: see under KIAO-; TSIAO-.

Chiao-ch'i, Formosa: see TSIAOKI.

Ch'iao-chia, China: see KIAOKIA.

Chiao-ling, China: see CHIULING.

Chiapa (chyä'pä). **1** or **Chiapa de Corzo** (dā kôr'sō), city (pop. 5,450), Chiapas, S Mexico, on the Grijalva an 1 8 mi. SE of Tuxtla; agr. center (mangoes, corn, cotton, sugar, coffee, fruit, livestock, timber). Picturesque city; has old cathedral, 16th-cent. fountain. Was an anc. Indian capital. Known as Nendiume. **2** Officially San José Chiapa, town (pop. 887), Puebla, central Mexico, on railroad and 32 mi. NE of Puebla; cereals, maguey.

Chiapa River, Mexico: see GRIJALVA RIVER.

Chiapas (chēä'pŭs, Sp. chyä'päs), state (□ 28,732; 1940 pop. 679,885; 1950 pop. 903,200), S Mexico; ⊙ Tuxtla. Located on Pacific bet. Isthmus of Tehuantepec and Guatemala. Bounded by Oaxaca and Veracruz (W), Tabasco (N). Main branch of Sierra Madre, which includes high volcano Tacaná on international border, towers over coastal lowland; area (N) adjoining Tabasco is a wild jungle plain. Well drained by Grijalva and Usumacinta rivers. Climate dry and tropical along coast, more temperate in interior, hot and humid in low country (N). Has rich mineral resources, but only salt deposits are of economic importance. Predominantly agr. region, producing coffee, cacao, henequen; also sugar, tobacco, vanilla, indigo, cotton, rice, corn, beans, bananas, fruit. Forests rich in dyewood and cabinet woods (ebony, mahogany, cedar, etc.); rubber in N. One of leading stock-raising (cattle, hogs, sheep) areas in Republic. Tuxtla, San Cristóbal de las Casas, Comitán, and Tapachula are processing centers. Famous PALENQUE Maya ruins in NE jungle. Chiapas became state of Mexican federation 1824. Boundaries with Guatemala fixed 1882.

Chiapas Valley, Chiapas, S Mexico, comprises N lowland of Sierra Madre along upper Grijalva R. (here sometimes Chiapa R.); bounded SE by Sierra de Hueytepec. The most densely populated area of the state, with Tuxtla as its center, it is extremely fertile, producing sugar, coffee, tobacco, cotton, cereals, vegetables, fruit, livestock.

Chiapilla (chyäpē'yä), town (pop. 1,211), Chiapas, S Mexico, on affluent of upper Grijalva R. and 29 mi. ESE of Tuxtla; corn, fruit, livestock.

Chiara (chyä'rä), town (pop. 750), Apurímac dept., S central Peru, on affluent of Pampas R. and 21 mi. SW of Andahuaylas; grain, stock.

Chiaramonte (kyärämôn'tē), village (pop. 1,189), Potenza prov., Basilicata, S Italy, 9 mi. SSW of Sant'Arcangelo; wine, olive oil.

Chiaramonte Gulfi (gōōl'fē), town (pop. 7,365), Ragusa prov., SE Sicily, 7 mi. N of Ragusa.

Chiaravalle (kyärävăl'lĕ), town (pop. 4,851), Ancona prov., The Marches, central Italy, near Esino R., 10 mi. W of Ancona; mfg. (chemicals, hardware, macaroni). Has anc. Cistercian abbey.

Chiaravalle Centrale (chĕnträ'lĕ), town (pop. 4,083), Catanzaro prov., Calabria, S Italy, 18 mi. SSW of Catanzaro, in agr. region (wheat, grapes, olives); power plant.

Chiaravalle Milanese (mēlänä'zĕ), SE suburb of Milan, Lombardy, N Italy. Noted for Cistercian monastery, founded 1135 by St. Bernard of Clairvaux.

Chiarenza, Greece: see KYLLENE.

Chiari (kyä'rē), town (pop. 7,097), Brescia prov., Lombardy, N Italy, near Oglio R., 14 mi. W of Brescia. Industrial center; silk and cotton mills, mfg. (carriages, textile machinery, fertilizer). Here Prince Eugene of Savoy defeated French under Villeroi in 1701.

Chia-shan, China: see KASHAN.

Chia-shih, China: see FAIZABAD.

Chiasso (kyäs'sô), town (pop. 5,625), Ticino canton, S Switzerland, on Ital. border, 3 mi. NW of Como, Italy; tobacco, pastry, flour, watches, chemicals; metalworking; wine trade.

Chiatura (chēŭtōō'rŭ), city (1932 pop. estimate 10,164), central Georgian SSR, on Kvirila R., on rail spur and 28 mi. ENE of Kutaisi, in Chiatura manganese basin (□ c.40). One of the largest manganese-mining centers of the world. Mines, located principally in Perevisi hills (SE) and Rgani hills (NW), are powered by Rion hydroelectric station. Manganese supplies Zestafoni ferromanganese works; exported via Poti and Batum on Black Sea. Production began in 1879. Formerly called Chiatury.

Chiautempan (chyoutĕm'pän), officially Santa Ana Chiautempan, town (pop. 4,762), Tlaxcala, central Mexico, on railroad and 3 mi. E of Tlaxcala; agr. center (corn, wheat, barley, alfalfa, beans, pulque, livestock).

Chiautla (chyout'lä). **1** Officially San Andrés Chiautla, town (pop. 629), Mexico state, central Mexico, 17 mi. NE of Mexico city; cereals, maguey, livestock. **2** Officially Chiautla de Tapia, town (pop. 3,306), Puebla, central Mexico, 24 mi. SSW of Matamoros; alt. 3,478 ft. Agr. center (rice, sugar, fruit, livestock); cheese mfg.

Chiautzingo (chyoutsĕng'gō), officially San Lorenzo Chiautzingo, town (pop. 1,806), Puebla, central Mexico, 20 mi. NW of Puebla; corn, wheat, maguey.

Chiavari (kyä'värē), town (pop. 14,042), Genova prov., Liguria, N Italy, port on Gulf of Rapallo and 16 mi. ESE of Genoa, on fertile plain (largest of Riviera di Levante) producing flowers, citrus fruit, vegetables. Industrial center: mills (silk, lace, linen), distilleries (liquor, olive oil), factories (cheese, wax, furniture), tanneries; shipbuilding; slate and coral working, metallurgical works; hydroelectric plant. Bishopric. Has cathedral (1613), seminary, mus., palaces, villas. Near by are late-

Romanesque church of San Salvatore (1244–52; founded by Pope Innocent IV) and wooden bridge built 1810 by Napoleon.

Chiavazza (kyävä'tsä), village (pop. 3,231), Vercelli prov., Piedmont, N Italy, 1 mi. NE of Biella; textile machinery; woolen and hemp mills.

Chiavenna (kyävĕn'nä), anc. *Clavenna*, town (pop. 3,803), Sondrio prov., Lombardy, N Italy, N of L. Como, on Mera R. and 25 mi. WNW of Sondrio. Rail terminus; tourist center (alt. 1,093 ft.) at junction of Splügen and Maloja roads to Switzerland. Produces beer, wine, barrels, skis, shoes, stoves, refrigerators, and woolen textiles. Feldspar quarries near by. Large Mese hydroelectric plant is 1 mi. SW, at mouth of Liro R.; regulated by reservoir on the LIRO.

Chiavenna River, N central Italy, rises in Ligurian Apennines 6 mi. SW of Castell'Arquato, flows 20 mi. N, past town of Caorso, to Po R. 8 mi. SW of Cremona.

Chiba (chē'bä), prefecture [Jap. *ken*] (□1,954; 1940 pop. 1,588,425; 1947 pop. 2,112,917), central Honshu, Japan; ⊙ Chiba. Bounded N by Tone R., W by Tokyo Bay and Sagami Sea; major part of prefecture is on Chiba Peninsula. Chief port, CHOSHI. Fertile coastal plains and river valleys produce rice, wheat, and market produce, largely for Tokyo area. Poultry raising, dairying, fishing. Numerous summer resorts on extensive coastline. Mfg. (textiles, soy sauce, flour). Principal centers: Chiba, Choshi, FUNABASHI, ICHIKAWA, TATEYAMA.

Chiba, city (1940 pop. 92,061; 1947 pop. 122,006), ⊙ Chiba prefecture, central Honshu, Japan, at NW base of Chiba Peninsula, 20 mi. E of Tokyo across Tokyo Bay; mfg. (cotton textiles, paper), woodworking, flour milling; fishing. Medical col., aviation school. Has 8th-cent. Buddhist temple. Includes (since 1937) former towns of Soga and Kemigawa. Sometimes spelled Tiba.

Chiba Peninsula, Jap. *Chiba-hanto,* Chiba prefecture, central Honshu, Japan, bet. Tokyo Bay and Sagami Sea (W) and the Pacific (E); 60 mi. long, 20–30 mi. wide. Primarily a resort area; fishing, agr. There are mounds of archaeological interest. Sometimes called Boso Peninsula.

Chibemba (shēbĕm'bä), town (pop. 354), Huíla prov., SW Angola, on road and 70 mi. SE of Sá da Bandeira. Also spelled Chivemba.

Chibi (chē'bē), village, Victoria prov., SE central Southern Rhodesia, in Mashonaland, 27 mi. SW of Fort Victoria; cattle, sheep, goats; corn.

Chibia (shē'byä), town (pop. 1,967), Huíla prov., SW Angola, on road and 22 mi. SE of Sá da Bandeira; cattle-raising center; corn milling; pottery mfg., dairying. R.C. mission.

Chibizhek (chĭbĕzhĕk'), town (1942 pop. over 500), S Krasnoyarsk Territory, Russian SFSR, near Artemovsk; gold mining.

Chibougamau (shĭbōō'gūmōō), settlement, central Que., on L. Doré, 140 mi. NW of Roberval, in lumbering and mining region. Airfield; radio station.

Chibougamau Lake (30 mi. long, 15 mi. wide), N Que., S of L. Mistassini, 160 mi. NW of Roberval. Drained W by Chibougamau R. (130 mi. long) into Waswanipi R.

Chibrolu, India: see CHEBROLU.

Chiburi-shima (chēbōōrē'shĭmä), island (□5; pop. 2,254) of Dozen group of the Oki-gunto, Shimane prefecture, Japan, in Sea of Japan, just S of Nishino-shima and Naka-no-shima; 4 mi. long, 2 mi. wide. Mountainous, forested. Rice, tea; sawmilling, fishing. Sometimes spelled Tiburi-sima.

Chibuto (shēbōō'tō), village, Sul do Save prov., S Mozambique, head of navigation on Limpopo R. and 110 mi. NNE of Lourenço Marques; sugar, corn, mafura, rice.

Chibwe (chē'bwä), township (pop. 17), Central Prov., Northern Rhodesia, on railroad and 20 mi. N of Broken Hill; tobacco, corn; cattle, sheep, goats.

Chib-Yu, Russian SFSR: see UKHTA, city.

Chica, Sierra (syĕ'rä chē'kä), pampean mountain range in Sierra de Córdoba system in W Córdoba prov., Argentina, extends c.55 mi. S from area SW of Deán Funes to area W of Córdoba; rises to c.6,000 ft.

Chicabasco, Mexico: see CHICAYASCO.

Chicacao (chēkäkä'ō), town (1950 pop. 1,642), Suchitepéquez dept., SW Guatemala, in Pacific piedmont, on left branch of Nahualate R. and 12 mi. E of Mazatenango; coffee, sugar cane, grain; livestock.

Chicacole (chĭkŭkōl'), city (pop. 22,249), Vizagapatam dist., NE Madras, India, port on Bay of Bengal, near mouth of Nagavali R., 35 mi. ENE of Vizianagaram; ships coir, grains, myrobalan; noted handicraft muslin. Casuarina plantations. Saltworks at Calingapatam (or Callingapatnam or Kalingapatam), port 15 mi. ENE, at mouth of Vamsadhara R.

Chicago (shĭkä'gō, –kô–), city (□ 211.3; 1950 pop. 3,620,962; 1940 pop. 3,396,808), ⊙ Cook co., NE Ill., on L. Michigan near its S tip, c.700 mi. W of New York city; 41°53'N 87°38'W; alt. c.600 ft. Nation's 2d city in size and importance and metropolis of the vast Midwest, Chicago is, in the words of Carl Sandburg,

Hog Butcher for the World
Tool Maker, Stacker of Wheat,
Player with Railroads and the
Nation's Freight Handler.

It is the world's greatest railroad center (23 trunk-line railroads, 17 belt and terminal lines), and a major highway focus (served by 500 truck and bus lines), air center (Midway, O'Hare, and Meigs airports), and Great Lakes port (connected with Mississippi R. by ILLINOIS WATERWAY system), with bulk of its shipping (coal, iron ore, limestone, grain) handled at Calumet (South Chicago) Harbor. Port of entry; seat of a Federal Reserve Bank, of world's largest grain and livestock markets, and of the Midwest stock exchange; a major U.S. wholesale and mail-order distribution point. Chicago, with its great Union Stockyards (opened 1865), is world's meat-packing center, and heart of one of nation's largest mfg. regions which extends SE into Ind. to encompass the CALUMET heavy-industry (iron and steel) dist. The "Windy City," whose climate is given to extremes (25°F. Jan. average, 73°F. July average) and to stiff breezes from the lake, is also a favorite U.S. convention city. After iron and steel making, largest of its industries produce industrial and agr. machinery and tools, electrical equipment and supplies, railroad cars and equipment, chemicals, textiles, clothing, musical instruments, furniture, food products, petroleum products, and printed matter, as well as an enormous quantity of consumer goods. Chicago proper extends for more than 20 mi. along L. Michigan from Evanston on the N to the Ind. line on SE; its industrial hinterland is estimated to cover more than □ 3,600. Residential suburbs to N include Evanston, Wilmette, Winnetka, Highland Park, Lake Forest; to NW, Arlington Heights, Des Plaines, Park Ridge; to W, Oak Park, Maywood, River Forest, Berwyn; to SW and S, Blue Island, Harvey, Chicago Heights. Downtown Chicago centers on the Loop dist., where the elevated rapid-transit lines make a huge rectangular circuit. In or near the city's center are the huge Public Library (more than 2,500,000 volumes), the John Crerar library of scientific books, the Auditorium (1889), Orchestra Hall (1904; home of the Chicago Symphony), St. Mary's Church (1865; one of few to survive the Great Fire), the Chicago Board of Trade Bldg. (world's largest grain exchange), the County and City Bldg., the Civic Opera Bldg. (1929), the U.S. courthouse, Union Station (1926), new Post Office bldg. (1934). La Salle St. is the financial center, State St. is known for its shops, and Randolph St. is the theatrical dist. Farther W are site of the Old Haymarket and St. Patrick's Church (1856; oldest in city). On the lake front is Grant Park (c.300 acres along Chicago Harbor, which is now used by pleasure craft); here are the Chicago Natural History Mus. (formerly Field Mus. of Natural History), Shedd Aquarium, Buckingham Memorial Fountain, the Chicago Art Inst. (with notable collections, libraries, and art school), and a seated figure of Lincoln by Saint-Gaudens (1907). Just S (in Burnham Park, c.600 acres) are Adler Planetarium and Astronomical Mus. (1930), and Soldier Field, a large stadium. Famed Michigan Blvd. (fine shops, hotels, apartments) runs along the lake front. Chicago's chain of lake-front parks also includes Calumet Park; Jackson Park (c.55 acres; created from swampland to be site of World's Columbian Exposition in 1893), which contains the Mus. of Science and Industry; and Lincoln Park (over 1,000 acres), containing the Chicago Historical Society Mus., Chicago Acad. of Sciences, Natural History Mus., Zoological Gardens, the Conservatory, a yacht basin, bathing beaches, and Saint-Gaudens' standing statue (1887) of Lincoln and the John P. Altgeld memorial monument (1915) by Gutzon Borglum. The sprawling residential quarters contain large communities of Polish, German, Scandinavian, Irish, Italian, Negro, and Jewish extraction. On the W side are Garfield and Humboldt parks and Hull House, 1st settlement house (1889) in U.S. The S side, containing the stockyards and the crowded dist. occupied by most of city's Negroes, and fringed with steel mills on the SE, also has Jackson Park and the campus of the Univ. of Chicago, largest of city's educational institutions. Also in Chicago are De Paul Univ., George Williams Col., Ill. Inst. of Technology, Loyola Univ., Mundelein Col., parts of Northwestern Univ., Roosevelt Col., St. Francis Xavier Col. for Women, parts of the Univ. of Ill., and theological seminaries, schools of music, art, and law, and several junior colleges and teachers colleges. Great Lakes Naval Training Station is near North Chicago. Chicago grew up at the mouth on L. Michigan of a shallow prairie stream (CHICAGO RIVER), that was, however, of great value because the narrow watershed between it and the Des Plaines R. (draining into the Mississippi through the Illinois R.) offered an easy portage for explorers, fur traders, and missionaries bound for the great central plains. Here came Father Marquette and Louis Jolliet in 1673, and the spot was well known for a century before Jean Baptiste Point Sable set up a trading post at the mouth of the river. John Kinzie, who succeeded him as a trader, is usually called the father of Chicago. The military post Fort Dearborn was established in 1803; in the War of 1812 its garrison perished in one of the most famous tragedies of Western history. Fort Dearborn was rebuilt in 1816, the building of the Erie Canal in the next decade speeded the settling of the Middle West, and Chicago began to grow; it was platted in 1830 and inc. as a village in 1833. Harbor improvements, lake traffic, and the peopling of the prairie farm lands boomed Chicago, which became a city in 1837. The Illinois and Michigan Canal was authorized by Congress in 1827 and was completed in 1848. By 1860 a number of railroad lines connected Chicago with the rest of the nation, and the city was launched on its career as the great mid-continent shipping center; it had long since started on a career as meat packer. A huge, shambling city built of wood, Chicago was wiped out by the great fire of 1871, which killed several hundred people and destroyed hundreds of millions of dollars in property. The city was rebuilt in stone and steel, industries sprang up, and the great inflow of immigrants started and climbed steadily. With industry came troubles over labor that were highlighted by the Haymarket Square riot of 1886 and the great strike at Pullman in 1894. Although proud of its reputation for brawling lustiness, Chicago was also the center of Middle Western culture. Theodore Thomas founded its symphony orchestra (1890) and writing flourished until, in the 20th cent., Chicago became a major leader in literature. Such men as Carl Sandburg, Edgar Lee Masters, and the much later realists including James T. Farrell have given a considerable literary lustre to Chicago's name. The World's Columbian Exposition of 1893 was notable in the development of American thought and taste in art. Louis H. Sullivan, with D. H. Burnham, John W. Root, and others, made Chicago, where the skyscraper came into being, a leader in architecture. The 1st decade of the 20th cent. saw the development of many agencies concerned with civic improvement, among them the City Club (1903), the Chicago Association of Commerce (1908), and the City Plan Commission (1909). Bet. the First World War and 1933, however, Chicago earned an unenviable renown as the home grounds of gangsters, Al Capone and his ilk, and the reputation for gangster warfare still clings, long after the event. Despite the world-wide depression Chicago's new world fair, the Century of Progress Exposition (1933–34), proved how greatly Chicago had prospered and progressed. In the Second World War all of the city's industrial and man-power resources were taxed to the utmost, and the metropolitan area grew considerably.

Chicago Drainage Canal, Ill.: see SANITARY AND SHIP CANAL.

Chicago-Gaika (gī'kä), S gold-mining suburb (pop. 1,180) of Que Que, Gwelo Prov., central Southern Rhodesia. Sometimes called Gaika.

Chicago Harbor, NE Ill., former commercial port of Chicago, now used mainly by pleasure boats, on L. Michigan at one-time mouth (now intake) of Chicago R.; some shipping enters river through locks here. Bulk of city's lake commerce is now handled by Calumet (South Chicago) Harbor, S.

Chicago Heights, industrial city (pop. 24,551), Cook co., NE Ill., S of Chicago and 22 mi. E of Joliet; steel and iron products, glass, chemicals, railroad equipment, textiles, soap, boxes, furniture, tile, asphalt, linseed products; truck farms. Settled in 1830s as Thorn Grove; renamed Bloom in 1849, and Chicago Heights in 1890; inc. 1901.

Chicago Ridge, village (pop. 888), Cook co., NE Ill., SW suburb of Chicago.

Chicago River, NE Ill., formed in downtown Chicago by North Branch (c.24 mi. long) and South Branch (c.10 mi. long); formerly flowed a short distance E to L. Michigan. Flow was reversed in 1900 into its South Branch and thence into SANITARY AND SHIP CANAL as a means of carrying Chicago's treated wastes to the Mississippi via navigable ILLINOIS WATERWAY system. Control locks (1938) at its former mouth on Chicago Harbor prevent pollution of L. Michigan and give lake vessels access to shipping terminals and industrial plants along the branches.

Chical-có, Argentina: see ALGARROBO DEL AGUILA.

Chicama (chēkä'mä), town (pop. 653), Libertad dept., NW Peru, on coastal plain, in irrigated Chicama R. valley, 20 mi. NW of Trujillo; rail junction; sugar cane; cattle raising.

Chicamacomico River (chĭ"kŭmŭkō'mĭkō), Dorchester co., E Md., on the Eastern Shore; rises just E of East New Market, flows c.25 mi. S and W to Transquaking R.

Chicama River (chēkä'mä), N Peru, formed by branches in Cordillera Occidental of the Andes 13 mi. S of Contumasá (Cajabamba dept.), flows 50 mi. SW, past Punta Moreno and Roma, to the Pacific 3 mi. WNW of Santiago de Cao. Its lower course feeds an irrigation system serving one of the major sugar-producing areas of Peru.

Chicamocha River (chēkämō'chä), in Boyacá and Santander depts., N central Colombia, rises W of Laguna de Tota, flows c.150 mi. N and NW to join Súarez R., forming Sogamoso R. SE of Zapatoca.

Chicapa River (chēkä'pä), Fr. *Tshikapa*, left tributary of Kasai R. in NE Angola and S Belgian Congo; rises just S of Alto Chicapa (Lunda dist.), flows c.400 mi. N, past Vila Henrique de Carvalho, forms section (30 mi. long) of Angola-Belgian Congo border, and enters the Kasai at Tshikapa village. Known for extensive diamond washings along its course, in exploitation since First World War. Sometimes spelled Chikapa.

Chicayasco (chēkïä'skō) or **Chicabasco** (chēkäbä'skō), town (pop. 1,601), Hidalgo, central Mexico, 15 mi. NW of Pachuca; corn, beans, maguey, livestock.

Chichagof (chĭ'chŭgôf), village (1939 pop. 63), SE Alaska, on W coast of Chichagof Isl., 50 mi. NW of Sitka; gold-mining camp.

Chichagof Harbor, settlement, SW Alaska, on NE Attu Isl., Aleutian Isls., on Bering Sea, at entrance of Holtz Bay; 52°56'N 173°15'E.

Chichagof Island (□ 2,104), SE Alaska, in Alexander Archipelago N of Baranof Isl., bounded by Chatham Strait (E), Icy Strait (NE), Cross Sound (NW), Gulf of Alaska (W), and Peril Strait (S); center near 57°51'N 135°34'W; 75 mi. long, 50 mi. wide; rises to 3,725 ft. (N). Hoonah village, NE. Fishing, fish processing, lumbering, gold mining. Tungsten and nickel deposits. Named for Admiral Vasili Chichagov.

Chichaoua (shĕshäwä'), village, Marrakesh region, SW Fr. Morocco, in the Haouz plain, 45 mi. W of Marrakesh; argan and olive groves; noted for its Moroccan carpets.

Chichas, Cordillera de (kôrdĭyä'rä dä chē'chäs), section of the Eastern Cordillera of the Andes, SW Bolivia, bet. Cordillera de los Frailes (N) and Cordillera de Lípez (S); extends c.100 mi. SSE from SE of Río Mulato to Portugalete. Rises to 18,422 ft. at Mt. Chorolque. Important mining region of Bolivia; contains towns of Quechisla (E), Huanchaca, Pulacayo (NW), Oploca, Chocaya, Tasna (W).

Chichawatni (chēchä'vŭtnē), town (pop. 7,986), Montgomery dist., SE Punjab, W Pakistan, 25 mi. WSW of Montgomery; local market for grain, cotton, sugar cane; cotton ginning. Forest plantation lies NE, W.

Chiché (chēchā'), town (1950 pop. 474), Quiché dept., W central Guatemala, in W highlands, on upper Motagua R. and 4 mi. E of Quiché; alt. 6,610 ft.; corn, beans; livestock market.

Chichén Itzá (chēchĕn' ētsä'), ruined Maya city in Yucatan, SE Mexico, 70 mi. ESE of Mérida. Hidden in dense tropical jungle, it is one of the continent's most famous archaeological sites, with pyramids and other ritual structures, including several temples and a sacred well used for human sacrifices. The bldgs. are decorated with bas-reliefs, cornices, and statues of great artistic merit. The sacred city is believed to have been founded in 6th cent. by the Itzá, from Guatemala; after having once been abandoned, the city was reoccupied in 10th cent. and flourished as the capital of Kukulcan. During war among the Maya nations the Itzá were defeated (c.1200) by the Mayapán and abandoned it for the last time. Near by are the ruins of Old Chichén, of even greater antiquity.

Chichester (chĭ'chĭstûr), municipal borough (1931 pop. 13,912; 1951 census 19,110) and city, ⊙ administrative county of West Sussex, England, on plain bet. the South Downs and the Channel, on Chichester Channel inlet, and 14 mi. ENE of Portsmouth. The Roman *Regnum*, it was conquered by Saxons in 477 and renamed *Cissaceaster* or *Cissanceaster* after Saxon king Cissa. The cathedral, begun c.1090, has detached bell tower. Anc. city walls, built on Roman foundations, are skirted by a promenade. There is market cross (1500). Roman amphitheater discovered outside the walls in 1935. William Collins b. in Chichester.

Chichester. 1 (chĭ'chĭstûr) Town (pop. 735), Merrimack co., S central N.H., on the Suncook and 8 mi. ENE of Concord. **2** (chĭ'chē"stûr) Resort village, Ulster co., SE N.Y., in the Catskills, near Esopus Creek, 20 mi. NW of Kingston; woodworking plant. Skiing near by.

Chichester Harbour, inlet (3 mi. wide, 5 mi. long) of the Channel, W Sussex, England, WSW of Chichester, bet. the Selsey peninsula and Hayling Isl. (Hampshire). The inlets of Bosham Channel and Chichester Channel extend inland. In Chichester Harbour is Thorney Isl., 1 mi. wide, 2 mi. long.

Chi-ch'i, China: see CHIKI.

Chi-chi, Formosa: see TSITSI.

Ch'i-chiang, China: see KIKIANG.

Ch'i-chiao-ching, China: see CHIKURTING.

Ch'i-chia-wan, China: see KIKIAWAN.

Chichibu (chē'chĭbōō), town (pop. 29,497), Saitama prefecture, central Honshu, Japan, 31 mi. WNW of Omiya; silk textiles.

Chichicastenango or **Santo Tomás Chichicastenango** (sän'tō tōmäs', chē"chēkästänäng'gō), town (1950 pop. 1,622), Quiché dept., W central Guatemala, in W highlands, 7 mi. SSE of Quiché; alt. 6,650 ft. Indian market center much visited by tourists; cotton and wool weaving; agr. (corn, beans). Became center of Quiché Indians following Sp. capture of Quiché.

Chichicaxtle (chēchēkä'slā), town (pop. 551), Veracruz, E Mexico, in Gulf lowland, 23 mi. NW of Veracruz; cereals, livestock.

Ch'i-ch'ien, Manchuria: see CHIKIEN.

Chichigalpa (chēchēgäl'pä), town (1950 pop. 4,352), Chinandega dept., W Nicaragua, on railroad and 7 mi. ESE of Chinandega; agr. center (sugar cane, corn, beans, rice). Near by (SW) are ruins of anc. colonial mission of Guadelupe. Sugar-milling and alcohol distilling at San Antonio, 3 mi. SSW.

Ch'i-ch'i-ha-erh, Manchuria: see TSITSIHAR.

Chichihualco (chēchēwäl'kō), town (pop. 2,815), Guerrero, SW Mexico, on N slopes of Sierra Madre del Sur, 14 mi. NW of Chilpancingo; alt. 3,950 ft.; cereals, sugar, tobacco, fruit, forest products (resin, rubber, vanilla).

Chichi-jima (chĭchē'jēmä), island (□ 9.5; pop. 4,302), one of Beechey Isls., W Pacific, 535 naut. mi. S of Tokyo; 27°5'N 142°13'E; largest of Bonin Isls. Omura on W coast is most important town in Bonin Isls. Produces sugar cane, coca, ornamental coral. Naval base and commercial harbor at Port Lloyd (Futami-minato) near Omura. Visited 1852 by Commodore Perry. In Second World War, site of Jap. air base. Formerly Peel Isl.

Chichi-jima-retto, Bonin Isls.: see BEECHEY ISLANDS.

Chichimilá (chēchēmēlä'), town (pop. 1,797), Yucatan, SE Mexico, 5 mi. SSW of Valladolid; henequen, sugar, fruit, timber.

Chichinales (chēchēnä'lĕs), village (pop. estimate 500), N Río Negro natl. territory, Argentina, on the Río Negro, on railroad and 35 mi. ESE of Fuerte General Roca; alfalfa, fruit, potatoes, sheep, cattle, goats.

Chichiquila (chēchēkē'lä), town (pop. 1,148), Puebla, central Mexico, 7 mi. NW of Huatusco; cereals, fruit.

Chichiriviche (chēchērēvē'chā), town (pop. 1,528), Falcón state, NW Venezuela, port on the Caribbean, 37 mi. NNW of Puerto Cabello; turtle fishing, oyster banks. Coal deposits near by.

Chichka, Tadzhik SSR: see OKTYABRSK.

Chichou, Formosa: see KICHOW.

Chichow, China: see ANKWO.

Chichoy Pass (chēchoi'), S central Guatemala, in central highlands, on branch of Inter-American Highway and 5 mi. NW of Tecpán; alt. c.10,000 ft. Offers panoramic view of volcanoes Agua and Fuego and L. Atitlán. Chichoy village at E end.

Chickahominy River (chĭkùhŏ'mĭnē), E Va., rises NW of Richmond, flows c.90 mi. generally SE to James R. 10 mi. W of Williamsburg. Navigable for shallow drafts; lumber, wood products are chief cargoes. On its banks were fought heavy engagements (in Peninsular campaign and Seven Days Battles) of Civil War.

Chickaloon (chĭkùlōōn'), village (1939 pop. 11), S Alaska, on Matanuska R., 25 mi. ENE of Palmer and on Glenn Highway; coal mining.

Chickamauga (chĭkùmô'gù), city (pop. 1,747), Walker co., NW Ga., 12 mi. S of Chattanooga, Tenn., in agr. area; textile milling, bleaching. Near by are Fort Oglethorpe (1903; U.S. Army post) and field of Civil War battle (1863) of Chickamauga, which preceded Union retreat to CHATTANOOGA. Battlefield is now part of Chickamauga and Chattanooga Natl. Military Park (□ 9.8 in Ga., □ 2.9 in Tenn.; established 1890). City inc. 1891.

Chickamauga Dam, SE Tenn., in Tennessee R., just NE of Chattanooga. Major TVA dam (129 ft. high, 5,800 ft. long; completed 1940); designed to aid navigation (has lock 360 ft. long, 60 ft. wide, providing max. lift of 53 ft.) and flood control and to supply hydroelectric power. Forms narrow Chickamauga Reservoir (□ 54; 59 mi. long; capacity 705,300 acre-ft.; sometimes known as L. Chickamauga).

Chickasaw (chĭ'kùsô). **1** County (□ 505; pop. 15,228), NE Iowa; ⊙ New Hampton. Rolling prairie dairying and agr. area (corn, hogs, cattle, grain, soybeans), with limestone quarries, sand and gravel pits. Drained by Cedar, Wapsipinicon, and Little Cedar rivers. Formed 1851. **2** County (□ 506; pop. 18,951), NE central Miss.; ⊙ Houston and Okolona. Drained by Yalobusha R. and tributaries of Tombigbee R. Agr. (cotton, corn), dairying, stock raising. Timber; clay, iron deposits. Formed 1836.

Chickasaw. 1 Town (pop. 4,920), Mobile co., SW Ala., 5 mi. N of Mobile; fishing, shipbuilding, steel exporting. **2** Village (pop. 166), Mercer co., W Ohio, 9 mi. SSE of Celina.

Chickasaw Bogue (bōg'), stream, SW Ala., rises in Marengo co., flows c.25 mi. W to Tombigbee R. 8 mi. W of Linden.

Chickasaw Creek, extreme SW Ala., rises in and flows c.40 mi. through Mobile co. S to Mobile Bay near Mobile. Navigable 9 mi. upstream. Terminal facilities near mouth.

Chickasawhay River (chĭ"kùsô'wā), SE Miss., formed by creeks N of Enterprise, flows c.210 mi. SE, S, and SW, joining Leaf R. to form Pascagoula R. in N George co. Formerly navigable.

Chickasha (chĭ'kùshā), city (pop. 15,842), ⊙ Grady co., central Okla., 36 mi. SW of Oklahoma City, and on Washita R.; processing and market center for rich petroleum-producing and agr. area (broomcorn, cotton, corn, wheat, oats, hay, alfalfa, livestock). Cotton ginning, cottonseed-oil milling, oil refining; mfg. of oil-field equipment, farm machinery, truck and trailer bodies, dairy products, flour, feed, bedding, wood products. Seat of Okla. Col. for Women. Shannoan Springs Park (boating, fishing) is near by. Inc. 1899.

Chicken, village (pop. 34), E Alaska, near Yukon border, 75 mi. W of Dawson; placer gold mining. Airfield. Important at time of Klondike gold rush; now nearly deserted.

Chickerell, agr. village and parish (pop. 1,192), S Dorset, England, 3 mi. NW of Weymouth.

Chick Springs, S.C.: see TAYLORS.

Chiclana or **Chiclana de la Frontera** (chēklä'nä dhā lä frōntä'rä), city (pop. 14,337), Cádiz prov., SW Spain, in Andalusia, near Atlantic coast, 10 mi. SE of Cádiz. Resort noted for its thermal springs (Fuente Amarga). Situated in fertile agr. region, surrounded by vineyards and pine forests. Chief products are grapes, wine, cereals, fruit, truck and dairy products, timber; salt from local saltworks. Founded 1303, probably on site of Roman town. Phoenician relics near by. The city is renowned for its bullfighters.

Chiclana de Segura (sāgōō'rä), town (pop. 1,948), Jaén prov., S Spain, 15 mi. NNE of Villacarrillo; olive-oil processing, soap mfg. Mineral springs. Lead mining near by.

Chiclayo (chēklī'ō), city (pop. 32,646), ⊙ Lambayeque dept. and Chiclayo prov. (□ 1,000; pop. 109,354), NW Peru, on coastal plain, in irrigated Lambayeque R. valley, on Pan American Highway and 400 mi. NNW of Lima; 6°46'S 79°51'W. Rail junction, connected with the ports of Pimentel and Puerto Eten. Leading commercial center of dept., in rice, cotton, and sugar-cane area; rice milling, cotton ginning, tanning, distilling, mfg. of soap, chocolate; condensed milk factory. Airport.

Chicligasta, Argentina: see CONCEPCIÓN, Tucumán prov.

Chiclín (chēklēn'), village (pop. 2,518), Libertad dept., NW Peru, on irrigated coastal plain, on Chicama R. and 23 mi. NW of Trujillo, on railroad; sugar milling; distilling. Archaeological mus.

Chico (chē'kō). **1** City (pop. 12,272), Butte co., N central Calif., in Sacramento Valley, c.80 mi. N of Sacramento; processing and packing center for agr. area (fruit, almonds, alfalfa, grain); lumber milling. mfg. of matches; railroad shops. Seat of Chico State Col. Bidwell Park has white oak tree reputed to be world's largest. Govt. plant introduction station near by. Gold mining in sierra foothills (E). Founded 1860, inc. 1872. **2** Village (pop. c.1,000), Wise co., N Texas, c.45 mi. NW of Fort Worth; ships crushed stone. L. Bridgeport (recreation area) is just SW. **3** Village (pop. 1,151), Kitsap co., W Wash., on an arm of Puget Sound and 5 mi. NW of Bremerton.

Chico, El, Mexico: see MINERAL DEL CHICO.

Chico, Río (rē'ō chē'kō). **1** River in Comodoro Rivadavia military zone and Chubut natl. territory, S Argentina, rises in L. Colhué Huapí, flows c.175 mi. NE through Patagonian highlands to Chubut R. 40 mi. ESE of Las Plumas. **2** Patagonian river in central Santa Cruz natl. territory, Argentina, rises in the Andes 25 mi. WSW of L. Strobel, flows 260 mi. SE, past Cañadón León, to Santa Cruz R. estuary N of Santa Cruz, 15 mi. from the Atlantic. **3** River, S Tucumán prov., Argentina, rises in several branches at E foot of the Nevado del Aconquija, flows c.60 mi. ESE, past Aguilares, to join Marapa R., forming the short Río Hondo 4 mi. WSW of Río Hondo town; the Río Hondo enters the Salí R. (upper course of the Río Dulce).

Chicoa (chēkō'ä), village, Manica and Sofala prov., NW Mozambique, 90 mi. WNW of Tete; downstream terminus of navigation on middle Zambezi R. just above Quebrabasa Rapids.

Chicoana (chēkwä'nä), town (pop. estimate 1,500), ⊙ Chicoana dept. (□ 375; 1947 pop. 9,465), central Salta prov., Argentina, in Lerma Valley, on railroad and 23 mi. SSW of Salta; tobacco, livestock center; lime factory. Tobacco research station.

Chicoloapan (chēkōlwä'pän), officially Chicoloapan de Juárez, town (pop. 2,135), Mexico state, central Mexico, on E shore of L. Texcoco, 14 mi. E of Mexico city; maguey, cereals, stock.

Chicoma Peak (chĭkō'mù) (11,950 ft.), N N.Mex., highest point in Valle Grande Mts., 34 mi. NW of Santa Fe.

Chicomo (chēkō'mō), village, Sul do Save prov., S Mozambique, railhead 50 mi. NE of Vila de João Belo; sugar, mafura, cotton, cashew nuts.

Chicomucelo (chēkōmōōsā'lō), town (pop. 558), Chiapas, S Mexico, on affluent of the Grijalva and 38 mi. S of Venustiano Carranza; cereals, fruit.

Chiconamel (chēkōnämĕl'), town (pop. 1,221), Veracruz, E Mexico, in E foothills of Sierra Madre Oriental, 17 mi. SW of Tantoyuca; cereals, tobacco, sugar, fruit.

Chiconcuac (chēkōngkwäk'), officially San Miguel Chiconcuac, town (pop. 1,872), Mexico state, central Mexico, 16 mi. NE of Mexico city; maguey, cereals, livestock. Weaving (serapes, blankets).

Chiconcuautla (chēkōngkwout'lä), town (pop. 1,665), Puebla, central Mexico, in Sierra Madre Oriental, 8 mi. SE of Huauchinango; sugar, coffee.

Chiconquiaco (chēkōngkyä'kō), town (pop. 1,109), Veracruz, E Mexico, in Sierra Madre Oriental, 21 mi. NE of Jalapa; corn, coffee, fruit.
Chicontepec (chēkōntāpĕk'), town (pop. 2,756), Veracruz, E Mexico, in Sierra Madre Oriental foothills, 50 mi. W of Tuxpan; corn, coffee, sugar, tobacco, fruit.
Chicopee (chĭ'kūpē). **1** Village (pop. 1,151), Hall co., N Ga., 3 mi. SW of Gainesville. **2** Industrial city (pop. 49,211), Hampden co., S Mass., at confluence of Connecticut and Chicopee rivers, just N of Springfield; tires, sporting goods, textiles, clothing, firearms, machinery, electrical apparatus. Includes villages of Chicopee (seat of Col. of Our Lady of the Elms), Chicopee Falls, Willimansett. Westover Field, U.S. air base, is here. Settled 1652, set off from Springfield 1848, inc. as city 1890.
Chicopee River, S Mass., formed at Three Rivers by junction of Quaboag and Ware rivers; flows c.18 mi. W to the Connecticut at Chicopee. Supplies water power to mfg. towns.
Chicora, Pa.: see MILLERSTOWN, Butler co.
Chico River (chē'kō), N Luzon, Philippines, rises in mts. in Mountain Prov. c.40 mi. NNE of Baguio, flows c.140 mi. generally NE to the Cagayan 26 mi. S of Aparri. Drains tobacco-growing area.
Chicot (shē'kō), county (□ 647; pop. 22,306), extreme SE Ark.; ⊙ Lake Village. Bounded S by La. line and E by Mississippi R. Includes L. Chicot (resort). Agr. (cotton, corn, truck, oats, hay); lumber milling, cotton ginning, pecan shelling. Formed 1823.
Chicot, Lake, extreme SE Ark., 8 mi. WSW of Greenville, Miss.; largest natural lake in Ark., formed by cut off of Mississippi R.; crescent-shaped, c.15 mi. long, 1 mi. wide. Resort (fishing, boating, bathing, hunting). Lake Village is on W shore.
Chicoutimi (shĭkōō'tĭmē), county (□ 17,800; pop. 78,881), S central Que., on Saguenay and Chicoutimi rivers; ⊙ Chicoutimi.
Chicoutimi, city (pop. 16,040), ⊙ Chicoutimi co., S central Que., on Saguenay R. (at head of navigation) at mouth of Chicoutimi R., and 120 mi. N of Quebec; pulp-milling center; lumbering, woolen milling; mfg. of shoes, furniture, cement, bricks, pottery; dairying; hydroelectric power center. Seat of R. C. bishop, with cathedral, seminary (affiliated with Laval Univ.), schools, and convents. Jesuit mission was established here 1670.
Chicoutimi River, S central Que., issues from Grand Lac Cartier, in Laurentian highlands, flows N to L. Kenogami, thence NE to Saguenay R. at Chicoutimi; 100 mi. long. Has 50-ft. falls just above Chicoutimi; hydroelectric power station. Its basin is heavily wooded and generally unsettled.
Chico Vecino (chē'kō vŭsē'nō), village (pop. 3,967), Butte co., N central Calif.
Chicxulub (chēksōōlōōb'), town (pop. 1,147), Yucatan, SE Mexico, 13 mi. NE of Mérida; henequen.
Chidambaram (chĭdŭm'bŭrŭm), city (pop. 26,212), South Arcot dist., SE Madras, India, in fertile delta bet. Coleroon and Vellar rivers, 23 mi. SSW of Cuddalore; rice milling, peanut-oil extraction. Large Dravidian temple complex (Sivaite and Vishnuite) contains 10th-cent. architectural landmarks, including noted shrine and statue of dancing Siva (Nataraja); major annual pilgrimage. Annamalai Univ. (1929) at Annamalainagar village, just SE, has engineering col., opened 1945. Was a strategic center in 18th cent. of French-English struggle for dominance in India.
Chiddingfold, town and parish (pop. 2,087), SW Surrey, England, 9 mi. SSW of Guildford; agr. market. Has 13th-cent. church and 14th-cent. inn. From 13th to 17th cent. it was center of glass industry, introduced by emigrants from Normandy and Lorraine. Also had important iron industry.
Chidester (chĭ'dĕ"stŭr), town (pop. 425), Ouachita co., S Ark., 13 mi. NW of Camden.
Chidguapi Island, Chile: see CHIDHUAPI ISLAND.
Chidhuapi Island (chēdh-wä'pē) (950 acres; pop. 446), Llanquihue prov., S central Chile, in Gulf of Ancud, 4 mi. S of Calbuco; 41° 50'S 73°6'W. Fishing. Sometimes spelled Chidguapi.
Chidley, Cape, NE extremity of Killinek Isl., SE Franklin Dist., Northwest Territories, on the Atlantic, near entrance to Hudson Strait; 60°23'N 64°26'W. Usually considered to be N extremity of Labrador. Just NE are 2 small Cape Chidley Isls.
Chiefland, town (pop. 843), Levy co., N Fla., 34 mi. WSW of Gainesville; mfg. (railroad crossties, telephone poles).
Chief's Head, Colo.: see FRONT RANGE.
Chieh, for Chinese names beginning thus and not found here: see under KIEH-.
Chiehchow, China: see CHIEHSIEN.
Chieh-hsien, China: see CHIEHSIEN.
Chieh-hsiu, China: see KIEHSIU.
Chiehmo, China: see CHERCHEN.
Chieh-shih Bay, China: see KITCHIOH BAY.
Chieh-shou, China: see KAISHOW.
Chiehsien or **Chieh-hsien** (jyĕ'shyĕn'), town, ⊙ Chiehsien co. (pop. 58,092), SW Shansi prov., China, 15 mi. SW of Anyi and on railroad: salt-extracting center, based on Lutsun salt pan; cotton weaving; wheat, corn, beans. Until 1912, Chiehchow.
Chieh-yang, China: see KITYANG.
Chiemsee (kēm'zā"), largest lake (□ 31) of Bavaria, Germany, 40 mi. ESE of Munich; 8.5 mi. long, 6 mi. wide, 241 ft. deep; alt. 1,699 ft. Inlet: small Ache R.; outlet: Alz R. Has 3 isls.; on largest, the Herreninsel, is magnificent castle built by Louis II of Bavaria in imitation of Versailles.
Chien- or **Ch'ien-,** for Chinese names beginning thus and not found here: see under KIEN-; TSIEN-.
Ch'ien, province, China: see KWEICHOW.
Chien Ch'i, China: see KIEN RIVER, Fukien prov.
Ch'ien-chiang. 1 Town, Hupeh prov., China: see TSIENKIANG. **2** Town, Kwangsi prov., China: see TSINKONG. **3** Town, Szechwan prov., China: see KIENKIANG.
Ch'ien Chiang, river, China: see KIEN RIVER, Kweichow prov.
Chien-ch'iao, China: see KIENKIAO.
Chien-ch'uan, China: see KIENCHWAN.
Chiengmai, Thailand: see CHIANGMAI.
Chiengrai, Thailand: see CHIANGRAI.
Chiengsen, Thailand: see CHIANG SAEN.
Ch'ien-hsi, China: see KIENSI.
Chiennamanur, India: see CHINNAMANUR.
Chien-ou, China: see KIENOW.
Chientang River, China: see TSIENTANG RIVER.
Chientao (jyĕn'dou'), region of E Manchuria, in E Kirin prov., on USSR and Korea borders, coextensive with left-bank drainage area of Tumen R. Its political center is Yenki, and its commercial hub, Lungching (Lungchingtsun). Coal and nonferrous metals are mined at Laotowkow and Towtaokow. Koreans, who emigrated here after 1910, constitute ⅔ of total pop. Separated from the old Kirin prov., Chientao became a separate prov. (□ 11,635; 1940 pop. 848,197) under Manchukuo regime. Passed 1946 to Sungkiang prov., and 1949 to the new Kirin prov.
Chien-te or **Ch'ien-te,** China: see KIENTEH.
Chienti River (kyĕn'tē), The Marches, central Italy, rises in the Apennines 7 mi. S of Monte Pennino, flows 60 mi. ENE, past Tolentino, to the Adriatic 1 mi. SE of Porto Civitanova.
Ch'ien-tsang, Tibet: see WEI.
Chieri (kyā'rē), town (pop. 9,601), Torino prov., Piedmont, NW Italy, 8 mi. SE of Turin, in agr. (grapes, cereals, hemp) and cattle-raising region; rail terminus. Cotton-milling and wine center; wagons, furniture, dyes, machinery (textile, agr.). Has Gothic cathedral (1405).
Chiers River (shyâr'), SW Luxembourg and N France, rises just S of Differdange (Luxembourg), crosses SE corner of Belgium S of Arthus, enters France above Mont-Saint-Martin, traverses Longwy metallurgical dist., forms Franco-Belg. border above Montmédy, and joins the Meuse 4 mi. SE of Sedan. Length, 70 mi.
Chiesa in Valmalenco (kyā'zä ēn välmälĕng'kō), village (pop. 306), Sondrio prov., Lombardy, N Italy, on Mallero R. (branch of upper Adda R.) and 6 mi. N of Sondrio; hydroelectric plant. Resort (alt. 3,156 ft.); base for Alpine excursions up nearby Disgrazia and Bernina peaks. Called Chiesa until c.1940.
Chiese River (kyā'zē), N Italy, rises in glaciers of Adamello mtn. group, 12 mi. ESE of Edolo, flows 100 mi. generally S, through Lago d'Idro, past Vobarno, Montichiari, and Asola, to Oglio R. 2 mi. E of Canneto sull'Oglio.
Chieti (kyā'tē), province (□ 997; pop. 374,729), Abruzzi e Molise, S central Italy; ⊙ Chieti. Mtn. and hill terrain with Maiella mts. in W; extends E to the Adriatic; watered by Sangro R. and its affluents. Agr. (cereals, olives, grapes, fruit); stock raising. Fishing (Ortona, Francavilla al Mare). Mfg. at Chieti, Lanciano, Ortona. Area reduced in 1927 to help form Pescara prov.
Chieti, anc. *Teate,* town (pop. 17,575), ⊙ Chieti prov., Abruzzi e Molise, S central Italy, 8 mi. SSW of Pescara; 42°21'N 14°10'E. Ironworks (agr. machinery), woolen mills, macaroni factory, brickworks, tobacco and cellulose industries. Archbishopric since 1526. Has ruins of Roman temples, Romanesque cathedral (11th cent.; restored 1936), and a noted music school. Order of Theatine Brothers named after anc. Teate. Damaged in Second World War by air and artillery bombing (1944).
Chietla (chyāt'lä), town (pop. 3,285), Puebla, central Mexico, on railroad and 9 mi. SW of Matamoros; agr. center (corn, rice, sugar, fruit, livestock).
Chieuti (kyā'ōōtē), village (pop. 1,912), Foggia prov., Apulia, S Italy, 16 mi. NW of San Severo.
Chièvres (shēĕ'vrŭ), town (pop. 2,862), Hainaut prov., SW Belgium, 11 mi. NW of Mons; agr. market. Has two 12th-cent. chapels, remains of 16th-cent. castle, 16th-cent. church, 18th-cent. town hall.
Chifeng, Manchuria: see CHIHFENG.
Chiffa, La (lä shēfä'), village (pop. 1,352), Alger dept., N central Algeria, in the Mitidja plain, 5 mi. WSW of Blida; vineyards, citrus groves, geranium gardens; paper milling. Just S is the scenic Chiffa gorge, traversed by road and railroad to Médéa.
Chifre, Serra do (sĕ'rŭ dōō shē'frĭ), range in NE Minas Gerais, Brazil, extending over 100 mi. NE from Teófilo Otoni toward Bahia border, and forming watershed bet. Jequitinhonha R. (N) and Mucuri R. (S); rises to 3,000 ft.
Chiftak (chĭf'täk), village (pop. 29), SW Alaska, near Bethel.
Chifu, China: see CHEFOO.
Chigasaki (chĭgä'sä'kē), town (pop. 43,315), Kanagawa prefecture, central Honshu, Japan, on N shore of Sagami Bay, bet. Hiratsuka (W) and Fujisawa (E); fashionable summer resort. Sometimes spelled Tigasaki.
Chigirin (chĭgĭrēn'), town (1926 pop. 7,961), N Kirovograd oblast, Ukrainian SSR, 23 mi. N of Znamenka; flour milling. Founded 1589 as fortress; rose to importance in 17th cent., when Bogdan Chmielnicki (Bogdan Khmelnitski) made it ⊙Ukraine.
Chigmecatitlán (chēgmäkätētlän'), town (pop. 2,116), Puebla, central Mexico, on Atoyac R. and 28 mi. SSE of Puebla; corn, sugar, livestock.
Chignahuapan (chēgnäwäpän'), town (pop. 4,156), Puebla, central Mexico, 55 mi. N of Puebla; alt. 7,415 ft.; corn, wheat, barley, beans, maguey.
Chignautla (chēgnout'lä), town (pop. 4,368), Puebla, central Mexico, 2 mi. W of Teziutlán; agr. center (corn, coffee, sugar, tobacco, fruit).
Chignecto, Cape (shĭgnĕk'tō), on the Bay of Fundy, NW N.S., bet. Chignecto Bay (N) and Minas Channel (S), 30 mi. NW of Kentville; 45°20'N 64°57'W.
Chignecto, Isthmus of, connects N.S. with Canadian mainland, bet. Northumberland Strait (N) and Chignecto Bay (S); c.15 mi. across at its narrowest point, near Amherst.
Chignecto Bay, inlet (50 mi. long, 10 mi. wide) of the Bay of Fundy, bet. SE N.B. and N.S. NE sections are Shepody Bay and Cumberland Basin. Noted for its high tides, sometimes rising 50 ft.
Chignik (chĭg'nĭk), village (pop. 243), SW Alaska, on Chignik Bay, on S Alaska Peninsula; 56°18'N 158°23'W; salmon fishing and canning. Has Russian Orthodox church.
Chignik Bay (20 mi. long, 18 mi. wide at mouth), SW Alaska, on E side of Alaska Peninsula, SW of Kodiak Isl., 56°23'N 158°10'W; salmon canneries. Chignik village, S.
Chignolo Po (kēnyô'lō pô'), village (pop. 2,216), Pavia prov., Lombardy, N Italy, near Po R., 12 mi. NW of Piacenza; silk mill.
Chigny-les-Roses (shēnyē'-lā-rōz'), village (pop. 565), Marne dept., N France, on N slope of the Montagne de Reims, 7 mi. S of Rheims; winegrowing (champagne).
Chiguana (chēgwä'nä), village, Potosí dept., SW Bolivia, in the Salar de Chiguana, 85 mi. SW of Uyuni, and on Antofagasta-Uyuni RR; alt. 12,090 ft.; alpaca, quinoa.
Chiguana, Salar de (sälär' dā), salt flat in Potosí dept., SW Bolivia, in the Altiplano, 60 mi. SW of Uyuni, on Chilean border; 40 mi. long, 6 mi. wide; alt. 12,090 ft. Crossed by Antofagasta-Uyuni RR. Chiguana village lies in center.
Chiguará (chēgwärä'), town (pop. 826), Mérida state, W Venezuela, in Chama R. valley, 28 mi. WSW of Mérida; sugar cane, coffee, fruit.
Chiguata, Peru: see CHIHUATA.
Chiguayante (chēgwīän'tā), town (pop. 3,697), Concepción prov., S central Chile, on Bío-Bío R., on railroad and 6 mi. SE of Concepción; paper mills, cotton yarn mills.
Chigwell, residential urban district (1951 census pop. 51,775), SW Essex, England, 12 mi. NE of London near Hainault Forest. King's Head Inn is the Maypole Inn of Dickens's *Barnaby Rudge.* William Penn attended the grammar school founded (1629) by Archbishop Harsnet of York. Formed 1933 out of Chigwell, Buckhurst Hill, and Loughton.
Chihal Satun (chĭhŭl' sŭtōōn'), SW suburb of Kabul, Afghanistan, on Chahardeh plain, 4 mi. SSW of city center and just E of Dar-ul-Fanun; summer resort; park. Formerly called Indaki.
Chihcheng or **Ch'ih-ch'eng** (chŭ'chŭng'), town, ⊙ Chihcheng co. (pop. 81,051), E Chahar prov. China, 50 mi. E of Kalgan, near Great Wall; cattle raising. Until 1928 in Chihli (Hopeh).
Ch'ih-ch'i, China: see CHIKKAI.
Chih-chiang, China: see CHIHKIANG.
Chih-chin, China: see CHIHKIN.
Chihchow, China: see KWEICHIH.
Chihfeng or **Ch'ih-feng** (chŭ'fŭng'), city, ⊙ but independent of Chihfeng co. (pop. 187,806), N central Jehol prov., Manchuria, 105 mi. NE of Chengteh; leading commercial center of Jehol and outlet for Mongolian goods; rail terminus on branch from Yehposhow junction. Trades in wool, furs, skins, cattle, grain, licorice. Gold and coal mining near by. Originally called Ulan Hada or Olan Khada, it was colonized by Chinese c.1778. Became independent municipality in 1949. Sometimes spelled Chifeng.
Chih-fou or **Chih-fu,** China: see CHEFOO.
Chihing (chē'hĭng'), Mandarin *Shih-hsing* (shŭ'-shĭng'), town (pop. 4,841), ⊙ Chihing co. (pop. 93,868), N Kwangtung prov., China, near Cheng R., 35 mi. ENE of Kükong; rice, beans. Tungsten and tin mining near by.
Ch'ih-k'an, China: see CHIKHOM.
Chihkiang or **Chih-chiang** (both: jŭ'jyäng'). **1** Town, ⊙ Chihkiang co. (pop. 160,406), W Hunan prov., China, near Kweichow line, on Yüan R. and 210 mi. WSW of Changsha; fruit, dried orange peel.

Coal and iron mining near by. Until 1913 called Yüanchow. **2** Town (pop. 19,478), ⊙ Chihkiang co. (pop. 191,115), SW Hupeh prov., China, 40 mi. W of Kiangling and on right bank of Yangtze R.; rice, wheat, cotton. Iron deposits near by.

Chihkin or **Chih-chin** (both: jû'jĭn'), town (pop. 10,657), ⊙ Chihkin co. (pop. 197,246), W Kweichow prov., China, 55 mi. WNW of Kweiyang; cotton-textile, paper, and pottery making; embroideries; inkstone. Rice, wheat, millet, beans. Coal and salt deposits. Until 1914, Pingyüan.

Chihli, province, China: see HOPEH.

Chihli, Gulf of (chē'lē', Chinese jû'lē'), Chinese *Po Hai* or *P'o Hai* (both: pô' hī'), arm of Yellow Sea, in NE China; bounded S by Shantung peninsula, W by Hopeh prov., NW by Liaosi prov., and NE by Liaotung peninsula; 300 mi. long, 180 mi. wide. Receives Yellow, Pai, Lwan (Lan), and Liao rivers. Its main ports are Yingkow, Hulutao, Chinwangtao, Tientsin (with outer ports of Taku and Tangku), Yangkiokow (in Yellow R. delta), and Lungkow on Shantung peninsula. Its N section is called Gulf of LIAOTUNG. The Gulf of Chihli is connected with the Yellow Sea by the **Strait of Chihli** or **Pohai Strait,** Chinese *P'o-hai Hai-hsia* (hī'shyä'), bet. Liaotung peninsula (N) and Shantung peninsula (S). It contains the Changshan (Miao) Isls.

Chihpen (jû'bŭn'), Jap. *Chippon* or *Chipon* (both: chēp'pōn), village, SE Formosa, on E coast, 7 mi. SW of Taitung, at foot of Mt. Chihpen (8,647 ft.); sugar refinery. Hot springs near by (SW).

Chihping or **Chih-p'ing** (jû'pĭng'), town, ⊙ Chihping co. (pop. 208,980), northeasternmost Pingyuan prov., China, 40 mi. WSW of Tsinan; cotton weaving; wheat, kaoliang, millet. Until 1949 in Shantung prov. Sometimes written Shihping.

Chihshui or **Ch'ih-shui** (chû'shwā'), town (pop. 11,642), ⊙ Chihshui co. (pop. 152,077), N Kweichow prov., China, on Szechwan line, 30 mi. SSE of Luhsien and on Ho R. (also called Chihshui R.; a tributary of Yangtze R.); trading center for lacquer, tung oil, hides, timber, pottery. Medicinal herbs, grain.

Ch'i-hsia, China: see TSISIA.

Chihsien. **1** (jû'shyĕn') Town, ⊙ Chihsien co. (pop. 165,918), SW Pingyuan prov., China, on Wei R. and 12 mi. NE of Sinsiang, and on railroad; cotton-growing center; cotton weaving; wheat, rice, beans. An anc. city, called Weihwei until 1913, it has been largely superseded by rail city of Sinsiang. Until 1949 in Honan prov. **2** or **Ch'i-hsien** (chē'shyĕn'), town, ⊙ Chihsien co. (pop. 71,821), W Pingyuan prov., China, 30 mi. NNE of Sinsiang and on Peking-Hankow RR; wheat, rice, millet. Until 1949 in Honan prov.

Chihtan (jû'dän'), town, ⊙ Chihtan co. (pop. 14,850), N Shensi prov., China, 38 mi. NW of Yenan; wheat, millet, beans. Oil and salt deposits near by. Until 1949 called Paoan. Was hq. briefly (1935–36) of Chinese Communists prior to transfer to Yenan.

Chihteh or **Chih-te** (jû'dŭ'), town, ⊙ Chihteh co. (pop. 81,469), S Anhwei prov., China, near Kiangsi line, 28 mi. S of Anking; tea, tung oil; vegetable-tallow processing (soap, candles). Until 1932 called Kiupu.

Chihuahua (chĭwä'wü, Sp. chēwä'wä), state (□ 94,831; 1940 pop. 623,944; 1950 pop. 841,077), N Mexico, on the Rio Grande; ⊙ Chihuahua. Bounded by N.Mex. and Texas (N), Coahuila (E), Durango (S), Sonora and Sinaloa (W). Includes Sierra Madre Occidental (W), with many broken subranges and plateaus in N and center, arid depression (Bolsón de Mapimí) in E. Watered by Conchos R., by the Río Verde, and Casas Grandes, Santa María, and Carmen rivers. Climate varies considerably: generally cool in mountainous W, mild in center, hot in desert (E); has long rainy season (June–Oct.). Largest and one of richest Mexican states; accounts for almost 40% of all mineral products. Abounds in silver; gold, silver, copper, zinc, lead mining centers in Aquiles Serdán, Hidalgo del Parral, Santa Bárbara, Guazapares, Cusihuiriáchic, Jiménez. Cattle raising (N, central) another important source of income. Irrigated river valleys are fertile; produce cotton, grain, beans, sugar, tobacco, fruit. Forested sierras (W) supply timber, resin, turpentine. Rural industries are mining, lumbering, flour milling, processing, dog breeding. Smelting, tanning, cementmaking, textile milling, cotton ginning, brewing concentrated in Ciudad Juárez, Chihuahua, Hidalgo del Parral, Camargo. Area belonged to Nueva Viscaya in early colonial days; became a state after war of independence. Largely occupied by American forces during Mexican War. Villa's civil war campaigns ruined cattle industry and retarded its development. Fierce Apache tribes still constitute large section of population.

Chihuahua, city (pop. 56,805), ⊙ Chihuahua, N Mexico, in valley, surrounded by E outliers of Sierra Madre Occidental, 220 mi. S of El Paso, Texas, and 780 mi. NW of Mexico city; 28°38'N 106°5'W; alt. 4,690 ft. Rail and commercial center for vast area in N Mexico, in rich mining (lead, zinc, silver, gold) and cattle-raising region; smelting, brewing, tanning, cement and textile milling, lumbering. Agr. products: cereals, fruit, vegetables. Airport. Famous for Chihuahua miniature dogs. Notable are: fine colonial bldgs., cathedral (begun 1717), Jesuit church, federal palace. Founded 1707 by Father Francisco Muñoz, the city played an important part in Mexican history. Hidalgo y Costilla, hero of struggle for independence, was executed here in 1811. During Fr. invasions, city was hq. of Benito Juárez, and later hq. of Villa. Has large American population today.

Chihuata (chēwä'tä), town (pop. 498), Arequipa dept., S Peru, on affluent of Vitor R., towered over by El Misti (N) and the Pichu Pichu (W), and 9 mi. E of Arequipa; grain, stock. Borax, gypsum deposits near by. Sometimes Chiguata.

Chiili (chĭ'ēlyē'), town (1948 pop. over 2,000), SE Kzyl-Orda oblast, Kazakh SSR, on Chiili arm of the Syr Darya, on Trans-Caspian RR and 75 mi. SE of Kzyl-Orda; rice; meat packing.

Chii-san, Korea: see CHIRI, MOUNT.

Chijiwa (chĭjē'wä), town (pop. 9,440), Nagasaki prefecture, W Kyushu, Japan, on W coast of Shimabara Peninsula, 18 mi. ENE of Nagasaki, across Tachibana Bay; fishing and agr. center. Sometimes spelled Tiziwa.

Chijiwa Bay, Japan: see TACHIBANA BAY.

Chik (chēk), town (1946 pop. over 500), E central Novosibirsk oblast, Russian SFSR, on Trans-Siberian RR and 15 mi. W of Novosibirsk; flour milling. Prokudskoye (1939 pop. over 2,000), a metalworking village, is just N.

Chikalda (chĭkŭl'dŭ), village, Amraoti dist., W Madhya Pradesh, India, 16 mi. NW of Ellichpur. Health resort (sanatorium) on plateau (alt. c.3,620 ft.) in central Satpura Range; acacia plantations (gum arabic). Fortress of Gawilgarh (just SE) was won (1803) by Wellesley from the Mahrattas.

Chikan, Manchuria: see CHIKIEN.

Chikapa River, Angola and Belgian Congo: see CHICAPA RIVER.

Chikaskia River (chĭkă'skēù), in Kansas and Okla., rises in Kingman co. in S Kansas, flows E and SE into Okla., past Blackwell, to Salt Fork of Arkansas R. 5 mi. SE of Tonkawa; 145 mi. long.

Chik Ballapur (chĭk' bŭläpŏŏr'), town (pop. 14,989), Kolar dist., E Mysore, India, 34 mi. NW of Kolar, in sugar-cane area; tobacco curing, oilseed milling, goldsmithing; handicraft glass bangles. Scenic health resort of Nandi or Nandi Hill (alt. c.4,800 ft.) is 5 mi. SW; has 18th-cent. fort; also called Nandidrug.

Chikchu, Hong Kong: see STANLEY.

Chike, Manchuria: see SÜNKO.

Chiker, Djebel, Fr. Morocco: see TAZA.

Chikhachevo (chēkhŭchô'vù), village (1939 pop. over 500), SE Pskov oblast, Russian SFSR, 37 mi. S of Dno; flax, wheat.

Chikhli (chĭk'lē). **1** Village, Surat dist., N Bombay, India, 32 mi. SSE of Surat; road center; trades in millet, wheat, sugar cane, fruit; handicraft cloth weaving. **2** Town (pop. 8,480), Buldana dist., W Madhya Pradesh, India, in Ajanta Hills, 14 mi. SSE of Buldana; millet, wheat; cotton ginning, oilseed milling. Also spelled Chikhali.

Chikhom (chĭk'hŭm'), Mandarin *Ch'ih-k'an* (chû'-kän'). **1** Fr. *Tchékam* (chākäm'), NW commercial district of CHANKIANG municipality, SW Kwangtung prov., China. **2** Town, S Kwangtung prov., China, port on Tam R. and 13 mi. NW of Toishan; commercial center.

Chiki or **Chi-ch'i** (both: jē'chē'), town, ⊙ Chiki co. (pop. 97,033), S Anhwei prov., China, near Chekiang line, 15 mi. NE of Sihsien, and on railroad; silkgrowing center; tea, corn, tung oil. Gold deposits near by. Also spelled Tsiki.

Chikien or **Ch'i-ch'ien** (both: chē'chyĕn'), town, ⊙ Chikien dist. (pop. 3,160), N Inner Mongolian Autonomous Region, Manchuria, in the Barga, on Argun R. (USSR line) and 220 mi. NNE of Hailar; gold placers. The name Chikien was applied until c.1920 to a village 70 mi. N, on Argun R. Present Chikien was formerly called Chikan.

Chikishlyar (chĭkēshlyär'), village, SW Ashkhabad oblast, Turkmen SSR, on Caspian Sea, 10 mi. NNW of Gasan-Kuli, near Iran border; former Rus. fortress. Natural-gas wells (N).

Chikjajur, India: see CHITALDRUG, town.

Chikkai (chĭk'kī'), Mandarin *Ch'ih-ch'i* (chû'chē'), town (pop. 3,783), ⊙ Chikkai co. (pop. 16,870), S Kwangtung prov., China, on coast, 22 mi. SE of Toishan; fisheries. Iron mining near by.

Chikmagalur (chĭk'mŭgŭlŏŏr), town (pop. 15,383), ⊙ Kadur dist., W Mysore, India, 90 mi. NW of Mysore; coffee-curing center; processing of fertilizer used by coffee, cardamom, and pepper estates in Baba Budan Range (NW); trades in rice, grain, sugar cane, coir products (rope, mats).

Chiknayakanhalli (chĭknä'yŭnhŭlē), town (pop. 3,313), Tumkur dist., central Mysore, India, 33 mi. WNW of Tumkur; hand-loom cotton and woolen weaving, handicrafts (pottery, goldsmithery, slate tiles, pencils); coconuts, areca palms. Manganese mining, gold prospecting in NE hills. Sometimes spelled Chiknaikanhalli.

Chiko, Manchuria: see SÜNKO.

Chikodi (chĭkō'dē), town (pop. 10,070), Belgaum dist., S Bombay, India, 40 mi. N of Belgaum; local market center (tobacco, millet, peanuts, betel leaf, sugar cane).

Chikoi or **Chikoy** (chēkoi'), town (1939 pop. over 500), SE Buryat-Mongol Autonomous SSR, Russian SFSR, on Chikoi R. and 23 mi. ESE of Kyakhta; tanning center.

Chikoi River or **Chikoy River,** SW Chita oblast and S Buryat-Mongol Autonomous SSR, Russian SFSR, rises in Borshchovochny Range, flows 350 mi. N and generally E, past Gutai and Chikoi, to Serenga R. 70 mi. SSW of Ulan-Ude.

Chikola (chēkô'lŭ), village (1939 pop. over 2,000), W North Ossetian Autonomous SSR, Russian SFSR, 20 mi. NW of Alagir; wheat, corn, orchards; sawmilling.

Ch'i-k'ou, China: see KIKOW.

Chikugo (chē'kŏŏgō), former province in N Kyushu, Japan; now part of Fukuoka prefecture.

Chikugo River, Jap. *Chikugo-gawa,* largest river of Kyushu, Japan; rises in mts. near Miyaji, central Kyushu; flows NW past Hida, W past Haki, Zendoji, and Kurume, and SW to the Ariakeno-umi 7 mi. SE of Saga; 88 mi. long. Drains major rice-growing area. Sometimes spelled Tikugo.

Chikuho (chēkōōhō'), largest coal field (□290) of Japan, in Fukuoka prefecture, N Kyushu, S of major industrial centers of Yawata, Wakamatsu, and Kokura, roughly bet. Fukuoka (W) and Kawara (E). Principal mining center, Tagawa. Chief outlets are Moji and Wakamatsu. Sometimes spelled Tikuho.

Chikumbi (chēkōōm'bē), township, Central Prov., Northern Rhodesia, on railroad and 14 mi. N of Lusaka; tobacco, wheat, corn; livestock.

Chikunan, Formosa: see CHUNAN.

Chikura (chēkōō'rä), town (pop. 9,746), Chiba prefecture, central Honshu, Japan, on SE Chiba Peninsula, fishing port on the Pacific, 6 mi. ESE of Tateyama; beach resort. Hot springs.

Chikurting (chēkōōrtĭng'), Chinese *Tsikiotsing* or *Ch'i-chiao-ching* (chē'jyou'jĭng'), town, ⊙ Chikurting co. (pop. 215), E Sinkiang prov., China, 100 mi. NW of Hami; junction on Silk Road; 43°28' N 91°36'E. Saltworks.

Chikuto, Formosa: see CHUTUNG.

Chikuzan, Formosa: see CHUSHAN.

Chikuzen (chē"kōō'zān), former province in N Kyushu, Japan; now part of Fukuoka prefecture.

Chikwawa (chēkwä'wä), administrative center, Southern Prov., Nyasaland, on left bank of Shire R. and 22 mi. SW of Blantyre, in cotton-growing area; tobacco, rice, corn. In 19th cent., head of navigation below Murchison Rapids of Shire R.

Chila (chē'lä). **1** Town (pop. 1,647), Puebla, central Mexico, 20 mi. SE of Acatlán; sugar, corn, fruit, livestock. **2** or **Chila de la Sal** (dā lä säl'), town (pop. 837), Puebla, central Mexico, on central plateau, 37 mi. S of Matamoros; corn, fruit, livestock. Pyramids and stone idols are near by.

Chilac (chēläk'), officially San Gabriel Chilac, town (pop. 6,091), Puebla, central Mexico, 10 mi. S of Tehuacán; alt. 3,904 ft.; agr. center (corn, rice, sugar, fruit, livestock).

Chilacachapa (chēläkächä'pä), town (pop. 2,701), Guerrero, SW Mexico, in Río de las Balsas valley, 17 mi. SW of Iguala; cereals, sugar, cotton, fruit, forest products (resin, vanilla).

Chilachap or **Tjilatjap** (both: chēlä'chäp), town (pop. 28,309), S Java, Indonesia, on inlet of Indian Ocean, 180 mi. SE of Batavia; 7°44'S 109°E; port for Preanger region, shipping copra, rubber, cassava, tea. Sheltered by NUSA KAMBANGAN isl., it has the only safe harbor on S coast. During final phase of battle of Java Sea (Feb., 1942) Chilachap was used as Allied fleet base.

Chila de la Sal, Mexico: see CHILA.

Chilai La (chēlī' lä'), pass (alt. c.12,000 ft.) in W Assam Himalayas, W Bhutan, 6 mi. SW of Paro, on main Ha-Paro road. Chilai La peak (13,475 ft.) is 1 mi. NW.

Chilakalurpet (chĭlŭkŭlŏŏr'pĕt), town (pop. 8,751), Guntur dist., NE Madras, India, 23 mi. SW of Guntur; road center; tobacco curing, cotton ginning. Steatite mines near by.

Chilamatal, El, Salvador: see CIUDAD ARCE.

Chilanga (chēläng'gä), town, Central Prov., Northern Rhodesia, on railroad and 10 mi. S of Lusaka; tobacco, wheat, corn; livestock. Cement plant near by.

Chilapa (chēlä'pä), officially Chilapa de Alvarez, city (pop. 6,094), Guerrero, SW Mexico, in Sierra Madre del Sur, 15 mi. E of Chilpancingo; alt. 4,658 ft. Agr. center (cereals, tobacco, coffee, fruit, livestock); tanneries; mfg. of shoes, cotton shawls.

Chilapa River, small stream in Tabasco, SE Mexico; flows, with small Chilapilla R., into the lower Grijalva E of Villahermosa; also linked with Usumacinta R.

Chilapilla River, Mexico: see CHILAPA RIVER.

Chilas (chĭläs'), feudatory state (□ 2,800; pop. 15,364) in Gilgit Agency, NW Kashmir; ⊙ Chilas. In W Punjab Himalayas; Nanga Parbat mtn. on SE border; traversed by the Indus. Agr. (wheat, corn, pulse, barley). After c.1850, under suzerainty of Kashmir; since 1948, held by Pakistan. Prevailing mother tongue, Shina.

Chilas, village, ⊙ Chilas state, Gilgit Agency, NW Kashmir, on the Indus and 36 mi. SSW of Gilgit; fort.

Chilaw (chĭlou'), town (pop. 9,041), ⊙ Chilaw dist. (□ 263; pop., including estate pop., 139,402), North Western Prov., Ceylon, on W coast, 45 mi. N of Colombo, at mouth of small lagoon; fishing center; trades in coconuts, rice, vegetables. Formerly an important cinnamon port, used (11th–12th cent.) by Moslem traders, who called it Salwat.

Chilca (chēl'kä), town (pop. 1,341), Lima dept., W central Peru, on coastal plain, just E of Chilca Point (2 mi. wide, 1 mi. long), on the Pacific, on Lima–Cañete highway and 45 mi. NNW of Cañete, in cotton-growing area. Thermal baths, salt deposits.

Chilca, Cordillera de (kôrdĭyā'rä dā), snow-capped Andean range, Arequipa dept., S Peru, 75 mi. N of Arequipa; forms a semicircle c.40 mi. long, reaching to Cuzco dept. border. Rises to c.20,000 ft.

Chilcaya (chēlkī'ä), borax-mining settlement (pop. 5), Tarapacá prov., N Chile, in Andes, near Bolivia border, 90 mi. ESE of Arica.

Chilches (chēl'chĕs), town (pop. 1,146), Castellón de la Plana prov., E Spain, 17 mi. SSW of Castellón de la Plana; soap mfg.; rice, olive oil, wine, oranges.

Chilchota (chēlkō'tä), town (pop. 2,479), Michoacán, central Mexico, 15 mi. SE of Zamora; cereals, sugar, fruit, stock.

Chilchotla, Mexico: see Rafael J. García.

Chilcotin River (chĭlkō'tĭn), SW B.C., rises in Coast Mts. W of Quesnel, flows 150 mi. SE to Fraser R. 30 mi. SSW of Williams Lake.

Chilcuautla (chēlkwout'lä), town (pop. 566), Hidalgo, central Mexico, on Tula R. and 35 mi. NW of Pachuca; alt. 6,181 ft.; corn, beans, fruit, livestock.

Childers (chĭl'dûrz), town (pop. 1,229), E Queensland, Australia, 160 mi. NNW of Brisbane; sugar-producing center.

Childersburg (chĭl'dûrzbûrg), town (1950 pop. 4,023; 1940 pop. 515), Talladega co., E central Ala., on Coosa R. and 30 mi. SE of Birmingham; paper, chemicals, fertilizer, rayon. It developed with bldg. of huge powder plant at near-by Coosa Pines. Plant was sold to private interests after Second World War. Large rayon and newsprint mills have been built.

Childress (chĭl'drĭs, chĭl'-), county (□ 701; pop. 12,123), extreme N Texas; ⊙ Childress. In rolling prairies of SE Panhandle; drained by Prairie Dog Town Fork of Red R. Agr. (cotton, wheat, grain sorghums, alfalfa; some fruit, truck); livestock raising (beef cattle, hogs, horses, poultry); some dairying. Formed 1876. Acquired part of Harmon co., Okla., in relocation of 100th meridian (1930).

Childress, city (pop. 7,619), ⊙ Childress co., extreme N Texas, in SE Panhandle c.100 mi. ESE of Amarillo, near Prairie Dog Town Fork of Red R.; trade and processing center for cattle, cotton, wheat, poultry, dairying region; railroad division point. Cotton gins and compresses; mfg. (cottonseed oil, flour, boots, dairy products, packed meat). Inc. 1888.

Childs, village, Cecil co., NE Md., 19 mi. WSW of Wilmington, Del.; paperboard factory.

Childs Hill, England: see Hendon.

Chile (chĭ'lē, Sp. chē'lā), republic (□ 286,396; 1940 pop. 5,023,539; 1950 pop. estimate 5,760,571) on SW coast of South America, administratively divided into 25 provs.; ⊙ Santiago. A long, narrow strip of land (never exceeding 250 mi. in width, and averaging 110 mi.) bet. the Pacific and the Andes, it stretches some 2,600 mi. southward from c.18°S to c.56°S at Cape Horn, which faces Antarctica, where Chile has claims. In the South Pacific it owns the Diego Ramírez Islands (60 mi. SW of Cape Horn), Juan Fernández Islands (c.400 mi. off the coast), San Félix Island and San Ambrosio Island (c.600 mi. W), Sala y Gómez Island (c.2,100 mi. W), and Easter Island (c.2,350 mi. W). Chile's long E boundary is with Argentina, while Peru is on N and Bolivia on NE. The climate and topography of Chile vary from arid tropical deserts to snow fields and rain-drenched subarctic tundras. The formidable Andes rise within a short distance of the coast to some of the hemisphere's highest peaks (e.g., Llullaillaco, Ojos de Salado, Tupungato, Maipo, Osorno; the great Aconcagua is just over the line in Argentina), most of them dormant or extinct snow-capped volcanoes on the Argentine boundary. The cordillera is crossed by the Transandine RR via Uspallata Pass to Valparaiso, and the Transandine RR of the North via Socompa Pass to Antofagasta. There are also rail connections to Peru and Bolivia. Towards Patagonia and Tierra del Fuego (largely in Chile and including the Strait of Magellan, which is entirely within Chilean territory) the Andes decrease in alt., splitting off into numerous isls. (e.g., Chiloé) and forming submerged valleys, glacier-fed lakes, and picturesque fjords. Parallel to the Andes runs the shorter and much lower coastal range. Numerous rivers cross the country horizontally, some navigable, among them Maipo River, Maule River, Ñuble River, Bío-Bío River, Palena River, Aysén River, and Baker River. Principal lakes of the celebrated lake dist. are the lakes Villarrica, Ranco, Puyehue, Llanquihue, and Todos los Santos (actually an inlet). Disastrous earthquakes, frequently followed by tidal waves, have occurred throughout Chilean history. Climatic conditions depend to a large degree on the cold Peruvian or Humboldt Current. Three major latitudinal, climatic, and topographic regions stand out. The excessively dry N region (sometimes without rainfall for a decade) extends from Peru to approximately 32°S near Coquimbo, a barren desert (Atacama Desert, Pampa del Tamarugal) containing the fabulously rich nitrate belt (exploited and refined at *oficinas* such as María Elena) and some of the world's most productive copper mines (Chuquicamata, Potrerillos). It also yields iodine as a by-product, besides substantial amounts of borax and salt and some gold, silver, mercury, sulphur, tungsten, manganese, lead, zinc, and guano. The high-grade ore of the El Tofo iron mines is shipped to the U.S. through Cruz Grande and to the recently-developed (1950) Huachipato steel mill near Concepción, c.550 mi. S. In small irrigated oases the fertile soil produces choice tropical fruit and sweet wines (Vallenar); and on the Andean slopes llamas, vicuñas, guanacos, and alpacas are grazed. In the Andes are the graceful *huemul* mtn. goat, which, together with the condor, adorns Chile's banner. There is excellent game fishing along the coast. Central Chile, by far the most important region, historically and demographically Chile proper, extends from c.32°S to 42°S near Puerto Montt. This is the nation's agr. heartland, a fertile, c.600-mi.-long plain of Mediterranean vegetation, known as the Central Valley for its location bet. the Andes and the coastal range. Here live almost 90% of the entire pop. (the total pop. of Chile is c.65% predominantly Sp. mestizo, 30% pure white, 5% pure Indian), centered on the country's 2 principal cities, the metropolis Santiago and the port Valparaiso, leading Pacific port on American coast S of San Francisco. With one of the globe's best climates (average temp. at Santiago is 57°F.) and a glorious landscape topped by the Aconcagua, the region compares favorably with California. Viña del Mar is a well-known fashionable resort. Irrigation is necessary in the N section of the Central Valley, where grapes are grown for Chile's fine wines. Other crops include vast amounts of subtropical fruit (citrus, olives, figs, apricots, peaches, plums, cherries, apples, melons), rice, corn, alfalfa, peas, beans. The more humid, forested S section is chiefly devoted to grain (wheat, barley, rye, oats) and potato growing and lumbering. In spite of the great agr. resources, Chilean peasantry is poverty stricken, since the Central Valley is still dominated by a quasi-feudal landholding system. About 90% of cultivated area is split into large estates, worked by the so-called *inquilinos*, whose lot is worse than that of ordinary tenant farmers. Land reforms have so far made little progress. Mass migration of the *inquilinos* to mines and cities have resulted in a large industrial proletariat. Though mining in the Central Valley is not as prominent as in the N deserts, it nevertheless plays an important part in central Chile's economy, particularly through the American-owned El Teniente copper mines in O'Higgins prov., and the coal deposits of Lota, Penco, and Coronel, which helped to develop the industrial cluster of Concepción-Talcahuano-San Vicente-Chiguayante. These deposits and the ones near Punta Arenas in the far S make Chile the leading coal producer of South America. Another steel mill is at Valdivia, progressive center of German immigrants. The principal mfg. dist., however, is grouped around Santiago-Valparaiso-Viña del Mar. Chile produces all kinds of consumer goods and has laid the foundations for a heavy industry. Only Brazil and Argentina surpass its output in South America. Few finished goods are shipped, however, and minerals (chiefly copper, nitrates, and iron) make up the bulk of exports. Chile imports machinery, vehicles, textiles, fibers, cloth, steel products and other metal goods, petroleum, coffee, tea, sugar. Most of the foreign trade—except for ore shipments— passes through Valparaiso. Santiago is also served by the port of San Antonio. Puerto Montt, entrepôt for the lake dist. of S Chile, ships lumber, paper, and fish. The densely forested S region of Chile supports only a scant pop.; here some timber is felled and wool is gathered from the large sheep herds grazed on the fine grasslands of humid Magallanes prov. Wool, frozen mutton, sheepskins, and sausage casings are processed and exported from Punta Arenas, an active trading center and coaling station, considered the southernmost city of the world—though the town of Ushuaia is farther S, on Beagle Channel. In S Chile survive the aboriginal Araucanian (or Mapuches) Indians, who had successively resisted Inca and Sp. incursions. Never properly conquered —but for alcohol and disease—they signed a treaty (1640) establishing the Bío-Bío R. as their N boundary, and remained hostile until near end of 19th cent. The region of present-day Chile was 1st entered (1536) by Diego de Almagro, a lieutenant of Pizarro, who crossed the N desert, but was forced to retreat by the warlike Indians. More successful was Pedro de Valdivia, who marched (1540) S, founding Santiago in 1541 and subsequently La Serena, Valparaiso, Concepción, Valdivia, and other towns—most of which were soon sacked by the Araucanians or destroyed by natural disasters. Chile became a part of the viceroyalty of Peru and later (1778) a separate captaincy general. Dutch and British (Drake) pirates attacked the coast frequently, and took advantage of the foreign restrictions decreed by mercantilist Spain. Finding little of the precious metals they sought, the Spaniards perforce developed a pastoral society based on large haciendas worked by Indian labor. As in most of Sp. South America, the movement toward independence began (1810) in the Napoleonic era—here notably under the leadership of Juan Martínez de Rosas and Bernardo O'Higgins. The patriots were 1st defeated (1814) at Rancagua. But through the assistance of Lord Cochrane, who commanded the newly established navy, and above all San Martín, who in 1817 crossed the Andes from Argentina to win the decisive battle of Maipú (1818), independence was attained. O'Higgins became supreme director of the nation until 1823, when a constitution (abolished 1833) was adopted. Since the downfall of O'Higgins the rich landowners have remained a determining factor, though more democratic practices have gradually evolved. Chile was victorious in the 1836–39 war with the Peru-Bolivian confederation, and took part (1866) in war against Spain. The more important War of the Pacific (1879–84) with Peru and Bolivia over the nitrate fields in the Atacama Desert gave Chile the vast N territory with Tacna and Arica; Tacna was returned to Peru in 1929 by Treaty of Lima. Long-standing boundary disputes with Argentina were finally settled in 1902, the peace symbolized by the Christ of the Andes, a statue in Uspallata Pass. European settlers, chiefly Germans, who had come to Chile since mid-19th cent., contributed greatly to the southern expansion. Chile's economy, however, came to be tenuously based on the copper and nitrate trade, from which practically all revenues were derived. Collapse of the market, chiefly as an outcome of the First World War and the then discovered ammonium synthesis, brought about a great depression. The liberal statesman Arturo Alessandri was 1st inaugurated in 1920, and Chile has since that time pushed social legislation energetically. A new constitution was drafted in 1925. After the disastrous 1939 earthquake an ambitious industrialization program (*fomento*) was introduced, and Chile has made great strides in industrialization, ranking 3d in South America. Chile broke (1943) diplomatic relations with the Axis countries and declared (1945) war on Japan, joining the U.N. in the same year. For further information see separate articles on cities, regions, physical features, and the following provs., listed here N–S: Tarapacá, Antofagasta, Atacama, Coquimbo, Aconcagua, Valparaíso, Santiago, O'Higgins, Colchagua, Curicó, Talca, Maule, Linares, Ñuble, Concepción, Arauco, Bío-Bío, Malleco, Cautín, Valdivia, Osorno, Llanquihue, Chiloé, Aysén, Magallanes.

Chile, Sierra del (syĕ'rä dĕl chē'lā), section of main Andean divide, central Honduras, bet. Jalán (NE) and Choluteca (SW) rivers; rises to c.3,500 ft.

Chile Chico (chē'lā chē'kō), village (1930 pop. 150), Aysén prov., S Chile, on S bank of L. Buenos Aires, at Argentina border, 95 mi. SE of Puerto Aysén; sheep raising, lumbering. Radio station.

Chilecito (chēlāsē'tō), town (1947 pop. 6,122), ⊙ Chilecito dept. (□ 1,860; 1947 pop. 13,983), central La Rioja prov., Argentina, at SE foot of Sierra de Famatina, in Famatina Valley, 45 mi. WNW of La Rioja. Rail terminus; tourist resort; agr., lumbering, and mining center; food canneries, sawmills. Copper and lead mines, quartzite deposits. Alfalfa, wine, fruit, vegetables, livestock. Funicular railway to Sierra de Famatina.

Chiledug, Tjiledug, or **Tjiledoeg** (all: chēlā'dŏŏg), town (pop. 20,002), NW Java, Indonesia, near Java Sea, 20 mi. SE of Cheribon; trade center for agr. area (sugar, rice, peanuts).

Chileka (chēlĕ'kä), village, Southern Prov., Nyasaland, on road and 7 mi. N of Blantyre. Site of chief Nyasaland airport.

Chiles, Los, Costa Rica: see Los Chiles.

Chiles, Nevado de (nävä'dō dā chē'lĕs), Andean peak (15,577 ft.) on Ecuador-Colombia border, 15 mi. W of Tulcán; 0°49'N 77°45'W. Extinct volcano.

Chilete (chēlā'tā), town (pop. 476), Cajamarca dept., NW Peru, on W slopes of Cordillera Occidental, on Jequetepeque R. and 23 mi. WSW of Cajamarca. Rail terminus; sugar cane, corn, wheat. Silver mining near by.

Chilga (chĭl'gä), town (pop. 3,000), Begemdir prov., NW Ethiopia, N of L. Tana, 27 mi. W of Gondar; trade center (coffee, honey, livestock). Lignite deposits near by.

Chilham (chĭ'lŭm), agr. village and parish (pop. 1,253), E central Kent, England, on Great Stour R. and 6 mi. WSW of Canterbury. Site of remains of Norman castle; has 15th-cent. church. Site of Roman fort.

Chilhowee (chĭl'houē), town (pop. 335), Johnson co., W central Mo., on railroad and 13 mi. SSW of Warrensburg.

Chilhowee Mountain (chĭl″hou′ē), E Tenn., ridge (1,500–3,000 ft.) in Great Appalachian Valley, bordering Great Smoky Mts.; from point c.5 mi. SW of Sevierville extends c.30 mi. SW to Little Tennessee R. Sometimes considered a range of Unaka Mts.

Chilhowie (chĭ′lŭwē), town (pop. 1,022), Smyth co., SW Va., on branch of Clinch R. and 10 mi. WSW of Marion; makes hosiery, fertilizer; ships fruit, cabbage.

Chilia-Noua: see KILIYA, Ukrainian SSR.

Chilianwala (chĭlyän′välŭ), village, Gujrat dist., NE Punjab, W Pakistan, 28 mi. WNW of Gujrat; wheat, millet, rice. Agr. seed farm. Indecisive battle fought (1849) just N, bet. Sikhs and British. Sometimes spelled Chillianwala.

Chilia-Veche: see KILIYA, Ukrainian SSR.

Chilibre (chēlē′brā), village (pop. 468), Panama prov., central Panama, on Trans-Isthmian Highway, near Canal Zone border, and 14 mi. NNW of Panama city; coffee; stock raising.

Chilik (chĭlyēk′). **1** Village (1939 pop. over 10,000), SE Alma-Ata oblast, Kazakh SSR, on Chilik R. and 70 mi. NE of Alma-Ata; irrigated agr. (wheat, tobacco); sheep. **2** Village (1948 pop. over 2,000), NE West Kazakhstan oblast, Kazakh SSR, on railroad and 110 mi. E of Uralsk; grain, cattle.

Chilik River, Alma-Ata oblast, Kazakh SSR, rises on Talgar peak of the Trans-Ili Ala-Tau, flows 140 mi. E and N, past Chilik, to Ili R.

Chililaya, Bolivia: see PUERTO PÉREZ.

Chilimanzi (chēlēmän′zē), village, Gwelo prov., central Southern Rhodesia, in Mashonaland, on road and 26 mi. SE of Umvuma; tobacco, wheat, dairy products, citrus fruit, livestock. Police post.

Chi-lin, Manchuria: see KIRIN.

Chiliodromia, Greece: see HALONNESOS.

Chili River, Peru: see VITOR RIVER.

Chilivani (kēlēvä′nē), village (pop. 297), Sassari prov., N Sardinia, on Mannu d'Ozieri R. and 21 mi. ESE of Sassari; rail junction.

Chilka Lake (chĭl′kŭ), lagoon in E Orissa, India, largely within Puri dist.; separated from Bay of Bengal by narrow spit, with 1 small outlet; 40 mi. long (NE-SW), 5-10 mi. wide, c.6 ft. deep. Receives seasonal drainage from near-by hills (W,S) and from S distributaries of Mahanadi R. (N); during dry months (Dec.-June) inflow of sea converts it to salt-water lake. Fisheries (mullet, pomfrets, prawns); salt pans along shores. Originally a bay of sea, since silted up by strong monsoon tides.

Chilkana (chĭlkä′nŭ), town (pop., including Sultanpur, 4,818), Saharanpur dist., N Uttar Pradesh, India, 9 mi. NW of Saharanpur; wheat, rice, rape, mustard, gram. Also spelled Chilkhana; sometimes called Chilkana-Sultanpur.

Chilkat Inlet (chĭl′kăt), SE Alaska, NW arm (15 mi. long) of Lynn Canal, NNW of Juneau; 59°7′N 135°23′W; extends from point 12 mi. SSE of Haines to mouth of Chilkat R. During 1890s it was the route to Chilkat Pass and Dalton Trail leading to the Klondike region.

Chilkat Pass (chĭl′kăt), in Coast Range, NW B.C., near Alaska and Yukon borders, 50 mi. WNW of Skagway. Discovered 1880; became important route from Haines, Alaska, to Yukon during Klondike gold rush in 1890s. Now crossed by Haines Cut-off, branch of Alaska Highway.

Chilkat River, SE Alaska, rises in Coast Range NW of Skagway, flows c.50 mi. generally SE, past Klukwan, to Chilkoot Inlet, arm of Lynn Canal, 4 mi. WNW of Haines. Navigable for boats to Klukwan.

Chilko Lake (□ 75; 40 mi. long, 1–4 mi. wide), SW B.C., in Coast Mts., 130 mi. NNW of Vancouver, at foot of mts. Goodhope and Queen Bess; drained N into Chilcotin R. by Chilko R.

Chilkoot or **Port Chilkoot** (chĭl′kōōt), village (pop. 92), SE Alaska, at head of Chilkoot Inlet, 13 mi. SW of Skagway; trading post.

Chilkoot Barracks, village (1939 pop. 337), SE Alaska, on W shore of Chilkoot Inlet, just S of Haines. Prior to Second World War it was the only U.S. army station in Alaska; afterwards became veterans' housing development. Formerly site of Fort William H. Seward.

Chilkoot Inlet, SE Alaska, NNW arm (20 mi. long) of Lynn Canal, NNW of Juneau; 59°15′N 135°20′W; extends from 12 mi. SSE of Haines to Chilkoot. N of Haines, Taiya Inlet extends 12 mi. NNE to Skagway. Route to Chilkoot Pass and Yukon during Klondike gold rush in 1890s.

Chilkoot Pass (3,500 ft.), in the Coast Mts. on border bet. SE Alaska and NW B.C., 20 mi. N of Skagway, bet. the coast and the Yukon valley; 59°42′N 135°16′W. On route to the Klondike from Skagway in the late 1890s.

Chillagoe (chĭ′lŭgō), town (pop. 204), NE Queensland, Australia, 80 mi. WSW of Cairns, in area producing tin, wolfram, bismuth, antimony, limestone. Coke smelting.

Chillán (chēyän′), city (1940 pop. 42,817, 1949 estimate 31,280), ⊙ Ñuble prov. and Chillán dept. (□ 1,191; 1940 pop. 86,158), S central Chile, in the central valley, on railroad and 55 mi. ENE of Concepción, c.240 mi. SSW of Santiago; 36°36′S 72°7′W. Rail, commercial, and agr. trade center (wine, fruit, grain, vegetables, livestock), with processing industries (shoe factories, tanneries, flour mills, alcohol distilleries, lumberyards). Founded c.1580, the town was moved (1835) to its present site from what is now CHILLÁN VIEJO, a SW suburb. It has been destroyed by earthquakes several times, most disastrously in 1939, when more than 10,000 people perished. There is a monument to Chilean liberator O'Higgins, who was born at Chillán Viejo. The sulphur baths, Baños de Chillán or Termas de Chillán, are 35 mi. SE in Andean foothills.

Chillán, Nevados de (nāvä′dōs dā), Andean range in Ñuble prov., S central Chile, 30 mi. SE of Chillán; extends c.20 mi. SE to Argentina border; rises to 10,370 ft. At its W foot are the famed sulphur baths Baños de Chillán or Termas de Chillán. Some of its slopes are popular skiing grounds. Among its peaks are active volcanoes. At foot of Chillán Volcano are sulphur deposits.

Chillán Viejo (vyā′hō), town (pop. 3,602), Ñuble prov., S central Chile, in the central valley, 2 mi. SW of Chillán, in agr. area (grain, wine, fruit, vegetables, livestock). The site of Chillán city until 1835; destroyed by 1830 earthquake. It is the birthplace of the Chilean hero Bernardo O'Higgins.

Chillar (chēyär′), town (pop. 2,301), S central Buenos Aires prov., Argentina, 38 mi. S of Azul; rail junction and agr. center; grain, livestock. Limestone deposits.

Chillicothe (chĭlĭkŏ′thē). **1** City (pop. 2,767), Peoria co., central Ill., on Illinois R., at N end of L. Peoria, and 15 mi. NNE of Peoria, in agr. and bituminous-coal area; sand, gravel pits; mfg. (brooms, clothing, concrete products); commercial fisheries. Inc. 1861. **2** Town (pop. 196), Wapello co., SE Iowa, on Des Moines R. and 8 mi. NW of Ottumwa; feed milling. **3** City (pop. 8,694), ⊙ Livingston co., N central Mo., near Grand R., 70 mi. NE of Kansas City; grain trading center; mfg. (wood, steel, and dairy products). Business col., state industrial school for girls. Founded 1837. **4** City (pop. 20,133), ⊙ Ross co., S Ohio, 45 mi. S of Columbus and on Scioto R. and Paint Creek; trade, industrial, and distribution center for stock-raising and farming area; pulp and paper products, shoes, food products, furniture, beer; railroad shops; poultry hatcheries. U.S. Industrial Reformatory, a U.S. veterans' hosp., and MOUND CITY GROUP NATIONAL MONUMENT are near by. Settled 1796, inc. 1802. Became ⊙ old Northwest Territory in 1800, and was twice ⊙ Ohio (1803–10, 1812–16). **5** Town (pop. 1,415), Hardeman co., N Texas, near Prairie Dog Town Fork of Red R., 13 mi. E of Quanah, in wheat, cotton area; grain elevators, cotton gins and compress, cottonseed-oil and flour mills. Has agr. experiment sta. Near by are L. Pauline (fishing, hunting) and Medicine Mound (Indian relics). Settled 1886, inc. 1907.

Chillingham (chĭ′lĭng-ŭm), agr. village and parish (pop. 782), N Northumberland, England, 11 mi. NW of Alnwick. Chillingham Castle (14th cent.), seat of Earl of Tankerville, was rebuilt by Inigo Jones. The large park has herd of wild cattle.

Chilliwack (chĭ′lĭwăk), city (pop. 3,675), SW B.C., on lower Fraser R. at mouth of Chilliwack R., and 50 mi. E of Vancouver; agr. center (dairying, stock, hops, fruit, tobacco); lumbering, fruit and milk canning, casein mfg.

Chillón (chēlyōn′), town (pop. 4,309), Ciudad Real prov. S central Spain, in the Sierra Morena, 2 mi. W of Almadén; agr. center (grain, olives, grapes, livestock); flour, olive oil.

Chillon (shĭlŏn′, Fr. shēyõ′), castle of W Switzerland, just S of Montreux, on E shore of L. Geneva. The 13th-cent. castle, now a mus., was once a stronghold of Savoy and a state prison; made famous by Byron's *Prisoner of Chillon.*

Chillos Valley (chē′yōs), in the high Andes of Pichincha prov., N central Ecuador, SE of Quito, with the bathing resort Tingo and processing center Sangolquí. Fertile grain-growing region with pleasant, cool climate.

Chillupar, India: see BARHALGANJ.

Chilmark, town (pop. 183), Dukes co., SE Mass., on SW Martha's Vineyard, 12 mi. WSW of Edgartown; fishing, agr.; summer resort. Includes village of Menemsha (mĭnĕm′shŭ).

Chiloango River (shēlwäng′gō), Fr. *Shiloango,* W central Africa, forming part of border bet. Belgian Congo and Cabinda (exclave of Angola); rises in Crystal Mts. 25 mi. ENE of Tshela (Belgian Congo), flows c.90 mi. SW and W to the Atlantic 25 mi. N of Cabinda.

Chilocco (shŭlŏ′kō), village, Kay co., N Okla., near Kansas line, 4 mi. S of Arkansas City, Kansas; seat of Chilocco School (vocational) for Indians.

Chiloé (chēlōā′), province (□ 9,053; 1940 pop. 101,706, 1949 estimate 96,242), S Chile; ⊙ ANCUD. Consists of a mainland part of the Patagonian Andes and numerous sparsely inhabited isls. in the Pacific just off the coast, notably Chiloé, the largest. Other isls. include: Chauques Isls., Guaitecas Isls., Guafo Isl., and the N part of the Chonos Archipelago. A mountainous area, with heavy rainfall, Chiloé has dense forests (which make it difficult to clear land for tillage) and a number of glaciers and snow-capped volcanic peaks, notably Minchinmávida and Corcovado. There are some coal deposits, but lumbering, agr. (especially potatoes, but also wheat, barley, and fruit), stock raising (sheep, cattle), and fishing are the main occupations. Potatoes, lumber, and fish are exported. Most of the inhabitants are on **Chiloé Island** (□ 3,241; 110 mi. long, 20-40 mi. wide), the largest isl. in Chile, c.30 mi. W of the mainland across the Gulf of Corcovado, and separated from a mainland peninsula (N) by a narrow channel 1 mi. wide; 41°45′–43°26′S 74°W. Guafo Gulf (S) separates it from the Guaitecas Isls. Principal centers are Ancud (N), on the Gulf of Ancud, and CASTRO (E coast), joined by narrow-gauge railroad. Wrested from the Indians by the Spaniards in 1567, Chiloé was the last foothold of the royalists in Chile after the War of Independence; they were not driven out until 1826.

Chiloeches (chēlōä′chĕs), town (pop. 872), Guadalajara prov., central Spain, 4 mi. S of Guadalajara; cereals, esparto; olive-oil pressing.

Chilón (chēlōn′), town (pop. c.700), Santa Cruz dept., central Bolivia, 50 mi. NW of Valle Grande; barley, corn, potatoes.

Chilón, town (pop. 596), Chiapas, S Mexico, in spur of Sierra Madre, 40 mi. NE of San Cristóbal de las Casas; corn, fruit; lumbering.

Chiloquin (chĭ′lōkwĭn), town (pop. 668), Klamath co., S Oregon, 25 mi. N of Klamath Falls and on Williamson R., in Klamath Indian Reservation; alt. 4,189 ft.; lumber.

Chilpancingo (chēlpänsĕng′gō), officially Chilpancingo de los Bravos, city (pop. 8,834), ⊙ Guerrero, SW Mexico, in valley of Sierra Madre del Sur, 55 mi. NNE of Acapulco, 135 mi. S of Mexico city; alt. 4,462 ft.; 17°33′N 99°30′W. Processing, lumbering, and agr. center (cereals, coffee, tobacco, sugar cane, vegetables, tropical fruit, livestock); tanning, vegetable-oil extracting, sawmilling, processing of forest products (rubber, vanilla, resin), printing. Airfield. Its official name honors the 3 Bravo brothers, heroes of war of independence. Ruins of high anc. pre-Aztec civilization near by. Has 16th-cent. bridge, old cemetery, govt. palace. First Mexican congress met here (1813) under Morelos y Pavón. Severely damaged by earthquake in 1902.

Chiltepe (chēltä′pā), SW Nicaragua, extinct volcano (2,297 ft.), on E end of Chiltepe Peninsula (8 mi. long, 7 mi. wide) in L. Managua, 5 mi. N of Managua. Small lakes of Apoyo and Jiloá occupy 2 craters near by.

Chiltern (chĭl′tŭrn), village (pop. 728), NE Victoria, Australia, 145 mi. NE of Melbourne; tin mines.

Chiltern Hills, range of chalk hills, S England, extending c.45 mi. NE from the Thames near Goring, through Oxford, Buckingham, Bedford, and N Hertford, to Suffolk border; 15-20 mi. wide. Highest elevation is Coombe Hill (852 ft.), 5 mi. SE of Aylesbury. Hills were at one time densely wooded, and a robbers' resort. To protect surrounding areas, office of Steward of the Chiltern Hundreds was created, now a nominal post. Chief towns in Chilterns are High Wycombe, Aylesbury, Berkhampstead, St. Albans, Luton, Stevenage, and Baldock. Beechwood in the area encouraged growth of furniture industry.

Chilton, county (□ 699; pop. 26,922), central Ala.; ⊙ Clanton. Agr. area bounded on E by Coosa R., drained (SW) by Mulberry R. Cotton, truck; lumber milling. Part of Talladega Natl. Forest in SW. Formed 1868.

Chilton. 1 Village (1940 pop. 681), Falls co., E central Texas, 19 mi. S of Waco, in agr. area. **2** City (pop. 2,367), ⊙ Calumet co., E Wis., on branch of Manitowoc R. and 23 mi. NE of Fond du Lac; trade center for dairying and farming area; mfg. (aluminum ware, wood products); dairy plants, canneries, breweries, poultry hatcheries. Settled 1847, inc. 1877.

Chilubula (chēlōōbōō′lä), mission station (European pop. 20), Northern Prov., NE Northern Rhodesia, 25 mi. W of Kasama; corn, wheat, potatoes. Site of White Fathers' mission (oldest in country); residence of bishop.

Chilung, Formosa: see KEELUNG.

Chi-lung, Tibet: see KYERONG.

Chilvers Coton, England: see NUNEATON.

Chilwa, Lake (chĭl′wä), or **Lake Shirwa** (shēr′wŭ), Port. *Chirua,* SE Nyasaland, on Mozambique border, 20 mi. E of Zomba; c.30 mi. long, c.16 mi. wide. Marshy shores; extent varies with rainfall and evaporation.

Chilwell, town and parish (pop. 2,584), S Nottingham, England, 5 mi. SW of Nottingham; lace industry.

Chimá (chēmä′), town (pop. 1,641), Bolívar dept., N Colombia, in Caribbean lowlands, 32 mi. NE of Montería; corn, cattle.

Chimaditis, Lake, Greece: see CHEIMADITIS, LAKE.

Chimahi or **Tjimahi** (both: chēmä′hē), town (pop. 21,994), W Java, Indonesia, in Preanger region, 5 mi. WNW of Bandung; trade center for agr. area (rubber, rice tea, cinchona); textile mills. Until 1949, it was a Du. military center.

Chimalhuacán (chēmälwäkän′), officially Santa María Chimalhuacán, town (pop. 1,462), Mexico state, central Mexico, on E shore of L. Texcoco, 13 mi. E of Mexico city; maguey, cereals. Formerly a Dominican mission. Chimal Falls are near by.

Chimalpa (chēmäl'pä), officially San Francisco Chimalpa, town (pop. 1,823), Mexico state, central Mexico, 15 mi. W of Mexico city; cereals, maguey, stock.

Chimaltenango (chēmältänäng'gō), department (□ 764; 1950 pop. 120,718), S central Guatemala; ⊙ Chimaltenango. In central highlands, sloping S to nearly 1,000 ft.; bounded N by Motagua R., W by Madre Vieja R., includes Acatenango volcano. Agr. (corn, wheat, black beans) in higher areas, coffee and sugar cane on S slopes; cattle, hogs, sheep. Flour milling and sawmilling near Tecpán and Patzicía; coffee processing. Main centers: Chimaltenango, Comalapa, Patzún.

Chimaltenango, city (1950 pop. 6,059), ⊙ Chimaltenango dept., S central Guatemala, on Inter-American Highway and 20 mi. W of Guatemala; 14°38'N 90°49'W; alt. 5,860 ft. Market center; brick making, tanning; grain, sugar cane. Agr. school in outskirts. Founded 1526 just S of old Indian fortress.

Chimaltitán (chēmältētän'), town (pop. 329), Jalisco, W Mexico, on N affluent of Santiago R. and 70 mi. NW of Guadalajara; grain, vegetables, stock. Airfield.

Chimán (chēmän'), village (pop. 417), Panama prov., central Panama, on Gulf of Panama of the Pacific, at mouth of Chimán R. (25 mi. long), 60 mi. ESE of Panama city.

Chimanas Islands (chēmä'näs), small archipelago in the Caribbean, off coast of Anzoátegui state, NE Venezuela, consisting of 4 islets 10 mi. NNE of Barcelona.

Chimanimani Mountains (chēmänēmä'nē), on Southern Rhodesia–Mozambique border, extend over 100 mi. N-S, forming left watershed of Sabi R.

Chimankend (chēmŭnkyĕnt'), village (1939 pop. over 500), S Armenian SSR, 24 mi. SE of Erivan, in irrigated zone; wheat, livestock.

Chimara, Albania: see HIMARË.

Chimay (shēmā'), town (pop. 3,222), Hainaut prov., S Belgium, 33 mi. SE of Mons; market center for dairying region; faïence, chemicals. Fortified town and ⊙ principality in Middle Ages. Has monument to Froissart, who died here. Trappist abbey established here in 1850.

Chimayo (chĭmī'ō), village (pop. c.2,000), Santa Fe and Rio Arriba counties, N N.Mex., near Rio Grande, in W foothills of Sangre de Cristo Mts., 21 mi. N of Santa Fe; alt. c.6,900 ft. Trading point in irrigated fruit region; also chili, grain, vegetables; weaving. Served as Sp. frontier post 1598–1695. Near by is El Santuário de Chimayó, adobe church built 1816.

Chimbai or **Chimbay** (chĭmbī'), city (1926 pop. 5,720), central Kara-Kalpak Autonomous SSR, Uzbek SSR, in the Amu Darya delta, 35 mi. N of Nukus; cotton ginning; lucerne seed. Teachers col.

Chimbarongo (chēmbärōng'gō), town (pop. 4,108), Colchagua prov., central Chile, on railroad and 10 mi. SSW of San Fernando; agr. center (grain, peas, potatoes, wine, fruit, tobacco, livestock). Flour milling, dairying, lumbering.

Chimbas (chēm'bäs), town, ⊙ Chimbas dept. (pop. 6,412; created c.1945), S San Juan prov., Argentina, just N of San Juan.

Chimbo, Ecuador: see SAN JOSÉ.

Chimborazo (chēmbōrä'sō), province (□ 2,685; 1950 pop. 213,495), central Ecuador, in Andes; ⊙ Riobamba. A high mtn. region, frequently shaken by earthquakes, it includes the Chimborazo, highest peak of the country. Climate is cool, temperate, with main rains Dec.-April. Among its mineral resources are large sulphur deposits (Alausí, Tixán). Predominantly agr., producing corn, wheat, barley, potatoes, fruit, fiber plants. Considerable cattle and sheep grazing. Rural industries: dairying, mfg. of woolen goods. Guano, Alausí, and Riobamba have textile mills.

Chimborazo, inactive Andean volcano (20,577 ft.) in Chimborazo prov., central Ecuador, highest peak of the Ecuadorian Andes, 18 mi. NW of Riobamba, frequently visible even from Quito and from the Pacific coast; 1°28'S 78°48'W. The majestic cone of the massif is partly covered by glaciers and well within the zone of permanent snow. Long a challenge to mountain climbers, it was ascended (1802) by Alexander von Humboldt, who was followed by many other mountaineers, but Whymper (1880) was 1st to reach its summit. Long believed to be the highest peak in the Andes, it is surpassed by several others (e.g., Aconcagua, Illampu, Tupungato).

Chimbo River (chēm'bō), central and S Ecuador, rises in the Andes near Chimborazo peak, flows S, past Guaranda, and turns W to coastal lowlands, joining the lower Guayas 5 mi. NW of Yaguachi; c.125 mi. long. Its lower (12 mi.) course is also called Yaguachi R.

Chimbote (chēmbō'tā), town (pop. 4,243), Ancash dept., W central Peru, port on sheltered Chimbote Bay or Ferrol Bay (7 mi. wide, 4 mi. long) of the Pacific, on Pan-American Highway and 34 mi. NW of Casma, 53 mi. WNW of Huarás. Rail head, shipping center for products of Santa dist. (sugar, cotton, rice) and for minerals of the Callejón de Huaylas, Cordillera Negra, and Cordillera Blanca regions; fisheries. Airport. Developing, in connection with Santa R. project, as an iron, steel, and coal center. Succeeded (1950) Casma as ⊙ Santa prov.

Chi-mei, China: see TSIMEI.

Chimeneas (chēmānā'äs), village (pop. 1,878), Granada prov., S Spain, 13 mi. WSW of Granada; olive-oil processing, flour milling; sheep raising.

Chimichagua (chēmēchä'gwä), town (pop. 2,478), Magdalena dept., N Colombia, on Ciénaga de Zapatosa, in Magdalena basin, 22 mi. NE of El Banco; sugar cane, stock; fisheries.

Chimingshan, China: see SÜANHWA.

Chimion (chĭmēôn'), oil town (1926 pop. 379), SE Fergana oblast, Uzbek SSR, 14 mi. SW of Fergana; health resort (baths). Near-by village of Chimion (1926 pop. 5,913) grows cotton and silk.

Chimishliya (chĭmēsh'lyēŭ), Rum. *Cimişlia* (chēmēsh'lyä), village (1941 pop. 5,221), S Moldavian SSR, on Kogalnik R. and 35 mi. S of Kishinev; vineyards, orchards.

Chimkent (chĭmkyĕnt'), city (1926 pop. 21,018; 1939 pop. 74,185), ⊙ South Kazakhstan oblast, Kazakh SSR, on Turksib RR and 380 mi. W of Alma-Ata, in cotton and fruit area; 42°20'N 69°35'E. Industrial center; large lead refinery (based on Achisai ore and Lenger coal), chemical plant (pharmaceutical products, santonin vermifuge), metalworks; cotton ginning, flour milling, fruit preserving. Has teachers col., building-trade school, mus., and remains of old citadel. The anc. Isfidzhab, ruled (8th-9th cent.) by Arabs; an important caravan center until captured (1864) by Russians.

Chimney Point, Vt.: see ADDISON, town.

Chimney Rock, village, Rutherford co., SW N.C., on Broad R. 20 mi. SE of Asheville; summer resort with handicraft industries (rugs, pottery, wood carving). Near by are Chimney Rock, a giant granite monolith ascended by trails, and Hickory Nut falls, c.400 ft. high.

Chimney Rock, height, Ky.: see CAMP NELSON.

Chimney Rock Peak, Wyo.: see WIND RIVER RANGE.

Chimoré River, Bolivia: see ICHILO RIVER.

Chimunai (jē'mōō'nī'), town, ⊙ Chimunai co. (pop. 10,675), northernmost Sinkiang prov., China, 120 mi. WSW of Sharasume, on USSR border, 40 mi. E of Zaisan (Kazakh SSR); livestock, grain. Formerly called Maikapchakai.

Chimur (chĭmōōr'), town (pop. 5,978), Chanda dist., S Madhya Pradesh, India, 40 mi. N of Chanda; rice, cotton, millet, oilseeds. Steatite deposits near.

Chin- or **Ch'in-**, for Chinese names beginning thus and not found here: see under KIN-; TSIN-.

Chin. 1 Province, China: see SHANSI. 2 or **Ch'in**, province, China: see SHENSI.

Chin. 1 River, Kiangsi prov., China: see KIN RIVER. 2 or **Ch'in**, river, Kwangtung prov., China: see YAM RIVER. 3 River, in Shansi and Pingyuan provs., China: see TSIN RIVER.

China (chī'nŭ), Chinese *Chung-kuo* [middle country] or *Hua-kuo* [flowery country], called after 1912 the Republic of China (Chinese *Chung-hua Min-kuo*) and, by the Communist regime, after 1949, the Chinese People's Republic (Chinese *Chung-hua Jen-min Kung-ho Kuo*), country (□ 3,800,000; pop. estimate 475,000,000) of E Asia, the most populous and 2d largest (after USSR) in the world; ⊙ PEKING (called Peiping, 1928–49). Massive in area, China extends from the Pacific Ocean W to the Pamir mtn. knot and from 20°N to 53°N (on Amur R.). It is bounded NE by Korea (along Yalu and Tumen rivers) and by the USSR (along Ussuri, Amur, and Argun rivers). Beyond the Mongolian People's Republic, China's border with the USSR continues along the mts. of the Altai, Tien Shan, and Pamir systems. In the SW, China borders, along the Karakoram and Himalaya systems, on Kashmir, India, Nepal, and the Indian-protected states of Sikkim and Bhutan; and in the S, on Burma and the Indochinese states of Laos and Vietnam. China's 4,000-mi. coast line fronts on the South China Sea (where it claims all isls. N of 4°N), the East China Sea, and the Yellow Sea (with its inlet, the Gulf of Chihli). Off the coast are the large Chinese isls. of HAINAN and FORMOSA. In broad physiographic terms, China consists of the following regions: the 12,000-ft.-high plateau of Tibet, bounded N by the Kunlun mtn. system and E by the great canyons and ranges of the Tahsüeh Mts.; the Tarim and Dzungarian basins of Sinkiang (Chinese Turkestan), separated by the Tien Shan; the vast Mongolian tableland; the E highlands and the central plain of Manchuria; and what has been traditionally called China proper. This last region, the country's most thickly populated, falls into 3 divisions, each oriented toward one of China's 3 great rivers. North China, which coincides with the Yellow R. basin and is bounded S by the Tsinling Mts. and their outliers, includes the NW loess plateau, the N China plain (consisting of the alluvial sediments of the Yellow R.), and the mts. of the Shantung peninsula. Central China, watered by the Yangtze, includes the mtn.-ringed Red Basin of Szechwan, the central Yangtze lowlands with the Tungting and Poyang lake basins, and the Yangtze delta region. South China, the hilliest of the 3 divisions, includes the plateau of Yunnan and Kweichow, the valleys of the West, North, and East rivers, and the small SE coastal plains. As a result of its location on Asia's E coast, China has a seasonal monsoon climate that is continental in winter and maritime in summer. Regional differences are found in the highlands of Tibet, the desert and steppes of Sinkiang and Mongolia, and in China proper. North China has very cold, rainless winters with strong winds causing dust storms, and hot, wet summers with a rainfall average of 25-30 in. S of the Tsinling Mts., Central China has a more moderate climate with 40-60 inches of precipitation (some in the winter). South China has a subtropical monsoon climate, distinguished by high rainfall (80 in.) and mild winters. In general terms, the Tsinling Mts. are the major dividing range not only bet. semiarid North China and more humid Central and South China, but also bet. the treeless loess (N) and the former forest soils (S). The original forest vegetation has been almost entirely removed, remaining only at higher elevations. Foremost among China's minerals is coal. Although Shansi (50%) and Shensi (30%) contain most of the country's reserves, production has developed mainly in the more accessible areas: in Manchuria (at Fushun and Pehpiao), in Hopeh (at the Kailan field and Tsingsing), in Shantung (at Poshan), and in Kiangsi (at Pingsiang). Petroleum is found in small fields at Yenchang (Shensi), Yümen (Kansu), and in Sinkiang; while oil shale is distilled at Fushun. Although potential hydroelectric power is available, the only development has been in Manchuria on the Sungari and Yalu rivers. The largest iron deposits are found in S Manchuria, where they are worked at Anshan and Penki. High-grade iron ore is also produced in the Süanhwa-Lungyen dist. of Chahar, at Tayeh (Hupeh), and in the Tientu and Shekluk (Shihlu) mines of Hainan. China's leading export minerals are tungsten (30–40% of world production), mined in Tayü area of S Kiangsi; antimony (60%), mined at Sikwangshan near Sinhwa (Hunan); tin, mined at Kokiu (Yunnan), and mercury, from Kweichow-Hunan border. Other important minerals are copper (Hweitseh), complex lead-zinc-silver ores (Shuikowshan), salt, soda, and gold. Agr. is by far the leading branch of China's economy, employing 80% of total pop., supplying the food needs of half a billion people, furnishing raw materials to industry, and comprising 75% of all exports. With only ¼ of her cultivable land under cultivation, China has the world's highest nutritional density (2 persons per cultivated acre), or, in the country's chief agr. areas, 3-4,000 per sq. mi. Of the 3 great food crops, rice, wheat, and millet, the latter two are grown in the N and rice in the S. The share of rice in the total crop area of the S varies from 40% in the diversified farming dist. of Szechwan's Red Basin to 90% in the extreme S, where rice is double-cropped. Secondary S crops are wheat, corn, silk, cotton, and opium in central China, silk, sugar cane, and sweet potatoes in double-cropping region, and tea in SE. Wheat, millet, and kaoliang share the N crop area, with emphasis on soybeans (export crop) in Manchuria; cotton and peanuts are secondary crops. Winter wheat is replaced by spring wheat in the drier inland areas. Until the late 19th cent., China was the world's leading tea exporter. Although it still produces half the world's tea, its world market has fallen largely to the newer producers of India and Ceylon. Except for the oasis agr. of Sinkiang, irrigated areas in Mongolia, and sheltered valleys in Tibet, agr. production is restricted to China proper. Livestock raising is mainly of the nomadic pastoral type (sheep, goats) in the outlying regions. Horses and mules are pack animals in N, while oxen and water buffaloes are used for ploughing, mainly in S. Hogs and poultry are widely raised in China proper, furnishing important export staples (hog bristles and egg products). Various types of vegetable oils, such as tung oil and tea oil, are also exported. Only 3% of pop. were employed in industry in 1950. Heavy industry and metallurgy have been developed in Manchuria (Anshan, Penki, Mukden) and in a few large cities of China proper (Tientsin, Shihkingshan near Peking). Cotton and silk spinning and weaving (Shanghai, Hankow, Canton, Tsingtao) are the leading light industries, while the processing of agr. products (soybeans, wheat, tobacco, tea, eggs) is also important. China's domestic handicraft industry occupies a special place in the economy, producing most of the consumer goods and such export products as porcelain and lacquer articles, straw hats, embroidery, matting, and fans. Most of China's large cities are also the country's main ports, situated at the mouths of the major rivers. Such are Canton in the West R. valley (S), Shanghai near the Yangtze R. mouth (center), and Tientsin at Pai R. mouth (N). Other leading ports are rail termini, such as Dairen, on South Manchuria RR; Tsingtao, on the line from Tsinan; and Lienyün, on Lunghai RR. Inland are the metropolises of Manchuria (Mukden, Harbin, Changchun), the capital cities of Peking, Nanking, and Chungking, and the great Wuhan tri-city area, comprising Hankow, Wuchang, and Hanyang. Though politically separate, Hong Kong has long been a major maritime outlet of S China. Foreign trade is overwhelmingly by sea. The main land-frontier crossings are in Manchuria on the Korean and USSR borders; others are on the Kalgan-Ulan-Bator trade route to the Mongolian People's Republic, on the USSR-Sinkiang line, the Lhasa-India route, Wanting on the Burma Road, and Hokow and Chennankwan on the Vietnam line. Transportation relies on coastwise shipping, river and canal navigation, particularly on the Yangtze, and on railroads in China proper and Manchuria (which has half the total lines). Caravan routes link China proper with the outlying territories. The greatest pop. density (3-4,000 per sq. mi.) is reached in the Yangtze delta, the Canton R. delta, the inland Red Basin of Szechwan, and the Tungting and Poyang lake basins, as well as the Yellow R. lowland. The Chinese proper (or Han, so called for the Han dynasty) constitute about 90% of the total pop. They are linguistically homogeneous in N where they speak the standard N Mandarin dialect. S of the Tsinling Mts., however, the Chinese speak a great variety of local dialects, including Southwest Mandarin (in Hupeh and Szechwan), East (or Lower Yangtze) Mandarin, the Wu dialect of Shanghai, the Kiangsi and North and South Fukien dialects, Hakka, and Cantonese. Written Chinese ideographs are common to all dialects. Among the main non-Chinese minorities are Thai tribes, Yao, Miao, and Lolo aborigenes in SW, Tibetans in the Tibet highlands, Uigurs, Kazakhs, Kalmyks, and Chinese Moslems (Dungans) in Sinkiang, Mongols in Inner Mongolia and in the Tsaidam section of Tsinghai, and Koreans and Tungusic tribes in Manchuria. Confucianism, Buddhism, and Taoism are the chief religions of China; they are generally practiced in an eclectic mixture making varying appeals. Mohammedanism, the largest monotheistic sect, is found chiefly in the NW. About 3,000,000 Chinese are Christians (mostly Catholics). While the earliest proto-human remains discovered in China are those of *Sinanthropus pekinensis* (Peking man), the ancestral home of the Chinese is generally placed in the area of the Wei, Lo, and middle Yellow rivers. The name China is thought to have been derived from the Ch'in (Ts'in) dynasty under which it became known to the West. The Romans called the country Serica and in the Middle Ages it was known as Cathay. Chinese history begins in the legendary period of the 3d millenium B.C. The 1st authenticated dynasty is the Hsia (2205–1766 B.C.), named for a town in S Shansi, though the following Shang dynasty (1766–1122 B.C.) is better documented. The Chow (Chou) dynasty (1122–249 B.C.) produced the philosophers Confucius, Laotze, and Mencius. A period of feudal strife in the 4th cent. B.C. ended in the rise of the Ch'in (Ts'in) state, whose dynasty (249–206 B.C.) 1st established a centralized imperial system. Its greatest emperor, Shih Hwangti (246–209 B.C.) completed the 1st Great Wall. The Han dynasty period (206 B.C.–221 A.D.), known as China's imperial age, was one of the most prosperous in the country's history, marked by peaceable rule and great artistic achievement. During this period, the country expanded greatly under Wu-ti (140–86), wars were waged against the Huns, 1st contacts made with the Roman Empire, and Buddhism was officially introduced. After a period of minor dynasties, the empire was reunited under the Sui (581–618) and the Tang (618–906), associated with the flowering of poetry. After another chaotic period, the Sung dynasty (960–1280), distinguished for its literature and philosophy, brought about another reunion. The Northern Sung dynasty (960–1127) was threatened along its N borders by the Kitan tribe, whose Liao dynasty was succeeded (1125) by the Chin dynasty of the Nuchen (or Juchen) tribe. The Chins conquered N China and restricted Southern Sung rule (1127–1280) to area S of the Yangtze. In early 13th cent. began the great Mongol conquest under Jenghiz Khan. His hordes defeated the Chins (1234), subdued the Southern Sungs (1280), and established the Mongol Yüan dynasty (1280–1368) under Kublai Khan over all China. The rich realm of this great Mongol ruler was described by Marco Polo. The Ming dynasty (1368–1644) reestablished native Chinese rule as far as the Great Wall. Initial territorial expansion was partly lost (15th cent.) to the resurgent Mongols and the 16th cent. saw increasing European trade and infiltration, as well as the arrival of the 1st missionaries (Jesuits). The Portuguese had reached Canton in 1516 and were allowed to settle (1557) in Macao. The union (1606) of Manchu tribes in E Manchuria laid the basis for the rising Manchu power that conquered all China in the course of the 17th cent., extending Chinese control over Tibet, Mongolia, and Formosa, and founded the last of China's imperial dynasties, the Ch'ing or Ts'ing (1644–1912). Its 2 great emperors, K'ang Hsi (1662–1723) and Ch'ien Lung (1736–96), sponsored reforms, but opposition to foreign trade (specifically opium imports) continued and culminated in the Opium War (1839–42) with Great Britain. By the Treaty of Nanking (1842), the 1st 5 ports (Canton, Amoy, Foochow, Ningpo, and Shanghai) were opened to foreign trade and Hong Kong ceded to Britain. The Taiping Rebellion (1850–64), aimed at the overthrow of the dynasty, ruined much of S China before it was subdued. In the meantime, a 2d war (1856–60) with Britain, joined by France, resulted in further Chinese concessions, including the opening of Tientsin to foreign trade. Thereafter it was the West that dictated the terms. Russia, having acquired (1858–60) her Far Eastern territories from China, obtained Manchurian railroad rights and the Port Arthur lease; Japan, successful in the Sino-Japanese War of 1895, obtained the cession of Formosa, the opening of additional ports and the independence of Korea; and in 1898, Germany secured the lease of Kiaochow, Britain Weihaiwei, and France Kwangchowan. The Boxer Rebellion (1900) was the last, unsuccessful effort to expel foreign influence. Manchu despotism was on the decline; the revolution, plotted by Sun Yat-sen and Yüan Shih-kai, broke out in 1911 and led to the Manchu abdication in 1912. The young republic, briefly led by Sun, and then by Yüan, entered upon a period of internal strife. Following Yüan's death (1916), the Peking regime passed into the hands of war lords, while in Canton, Sun strengthened his Kuomintang party after 1919. His successor, Chiang Kai-shek, engaged in a series of military operations (1926–28) that unified the country under Nationalist Kuomintang rule and made Nanking the capital. Shortly before, a split had developed bet. the Kuomintang and its Communist wing. The latter sought refuge in the mts. of S Kiangsi (hq. at Juikin) and in the middle 1930s made the long march W and N to N Shensi, where they set up hq. at Yenan. Japan, taking advantage of Chinese dissension, occupied (1931) Manchuria and there established (1932) the nominally independent state of Manchukuo. The Sino-Japanese War began (1937) when Japan fanned the minor Marco Polo Bridge incident into a major conflict that continued into the Second World War and led to Jap. occupation of China's most important economic areas. Free China, established in the W hinterland with ⊙ at Chungking, received U.S. and British aid, but Japan's power was not broken in China until the close of the Second World War. The rift bet. the Nationalists and Communists widened after 1945 and full-scale civil war developed. Though aided by the U.S., the Nationalists steadily lost ground through 1948 and 1949, were completely ejected from the mainland by early 1950, and sought refuge on Formosa. Since China was one of the 5 permanent members of the United Nations Security Council, the question of Chinese representation in the U.N. vexed the world. Though by 1950 Great Britain, the USSR, and India recognized the Communist regime as the govt. of China, the U.S. and most of the other nations of the world continued to recognize the Nationalists. Whatever the outcome, it seemed, in 1951, that the resolution of the conflict would leave deep scars among the nations of the world. China's modern provincial organization was 1st introduced under the Mongol Yüan dynasty. The number of provs. in China proper was 15 under the Mings and 18 under the Manchus. In addition to the 18 provs. of China proper, the country under the Manchus included the so-called outer dependencies of Manchuria, Mongolia, Sinkiang, and Tibet. After the Chinese Revolution, the new provs. of Jehol, Chahar, Suiyuan, and Ningsia were carved out of Inner Mongolia, and Tsinghai and Sikang out of E and NE Tibet. Tibet proper, though nominally under Chinese suzerainty, remained in fact independent until Chinese Communist invasion in 1950–51. Outer Mongolia, under Manchu control after 1691, seceded after the Chinese Revolution and became the Mongolian People's Republic. In 1949 the Chinese Communists undertook an administrative reorganization, grouping the existing provs. into large regional divisions. These divisions and their constituent provs. are as follows: MANCHURIA or the Northeast (Chinese *Tungpei;* ⊙ MUKDEN), including HEILUNGKIANG, JEHOL, KIRIN, LIAOSI, LIAOTUNG, SUNGKIANG, and the INNER MONGOLIAN AUTONOMOUS REGION; North China (Chinese *Hwapei;* ⊙ Peking), including CHAHAR, HOPEH, PINGYUAN (formed 1949), SHANSI, and SUIYUAN; Northwest China or the Northwest (Chinese *Sipei* or *Hsi-pei;* ⊙ Sian), including KANSU, NINGSIA, SHENSI, SINKIANG, and TSINGHAI; Southwest China or the Southwest (Chinese *Sinan* or *Hsi-nan;* ⊙ Chungking), including KWEICHOW, SIKANG (with its Tibetan autonomous dist.), SZECHWAN, and YUNNAN; Central and South China or the Center-South (Chinese *Chungnan;* ⊙ Hankow), including HONAN, HUNAN, HUPEH, KIANGSI, KWANGSI, and KWANGTUNG (with HAINAN); East China (Chinese *Hwatung;* ⊙ Shanghai), including N and S ANHWEI, CHEKIANG, FUKIEN, N and S KIANGSU, and SHANTUNG. See also TIBET.

China, peak, India: see NAINI TAL, town.

China (chē'nä), town (pop. 1,622), Nuevo León, N Mexico, in low country, 65 mi. E of Monterrey; cereals, cotton, sugar cane, cactus fibers.

China, resort town (pop. 1,375), Kennebec co., S Maine, at N end of China L., 8 mi. SE of Waterville. South China village at S end of lake. Settled 1774; known as Harlem, 1796–1818.

China, Gunong (gōōnōōng' chē'nä), or **Bukit China** (bōō'kĭt chē'nä), Thai *Buket China* or *Khao Chin* (kou"jĭn'), northernmost peak (2,370 ft.) of Malaya, on Perlis-Thailand border in Kalakhiri Range; 6°43'N 100°11' E. Tin is mined on slopes near Satun (Thailand) and Kaki Bukit (Perlis, Malaya).

Chinabad (chēnŭbät'), village (1926 pop. 1,704), N Andizhan oblast, Usbek SSR, near the Kara Darya, 20 mi. NW of Andizhan; cotton; sericulture.

China Bay, Ceylon: see TRINCOMALEE.

Chinácota (chēnä'kōtä), town (pop. 3,157), Norte de Santander dept., N Colombia, in valley of Cordillera Oriental, 20 mi. SSW of Cúcuta; alt. 4,363 ft. Coffee- and cacao-growing center; fique bags.

China Grove, town (pop. 1,491), Rowan co., central N.C., 10 mi. SW of Salisbury; mfg. of sheeting, cotton yarn.

China Lake. 1 In S central Calif., playa (c.11 mi. long) in Mojave Desert, c.10 mi. W of Trona. U.S. naval ordnance test station, airfield. **2** In Kennebec co., S Maine, lake in resort area near China, 8 mi. SE of Waterville; 8 mi. long.

Chinameca (chēnämä'kä), town (pop. 1,874), Veracruz, SE Mexico, on Isthmus of Tehuantepec, 9 mi. WNW of Minatitlán; fruit, livestock.

Chinameca, city (pop. 6,988), San Miguel dept., E Salvador, near Inter-American Highway, at N foot of volcano Chinameca (4,600 ft.), 12 mi. WNW of San Miguel; coffee-growing center. Earthquake, 1951.

Chinampa (chēnäm'pä), officially Chinampa de Gorostiza, town (pop. 1,662), Veracruz, E Mexico, in Gulf lowland, 34 mi. NW of Tuxpan; cereals, sugar cane, coffee, tobacco, fruit.

Chinandega (chēnändä'gä), department (□ 1,775; 1950 pop. 82,970), W Nicaragua, on the Pacific; ⊙ Chinandega. Bounded NW by Gulf of Fonseca, N by Honduras; includes Cosigüina Peninsula (W) and N section of Cordillera de los Marabios (SE); drained by Río Negro and the Estero Real (N) and by short coastal streams (S). One of chief agr. areas; produces corn, beans, sugar cane (principal mill at San Antonio), coffee, bananas, fruit, cotton, sesame; livestock raising; lumbering. Mfg. industries (agr. processing, metal- and woodworking, tanning) in Chinandega, Chichigalpa, and port of Corinto (all linked by rail). Puerto Morazán serves Gulf of Fonseca coastal trade.

Chinandega, city (1950 pop. 13,172), ⊙ Chinandega dept., W Nicaragua, 65 mi. NW of Managua; 12°37'N 87°8'W. Industrial and commercial center; rail junction (branch to Puerto Morazán) in grain and fruit (oranges) area. Mfg. of furniture, perfume, toilet water; sawmilling, metalworking, tanning, agr.-product processing (sugar, rice, coffee, cheese, alcohol). Has hosp., public market, several churches. Rail line to its port Corinto. Partly destroyed by fire in 1927 revolution.

Chinantla (chēnän'tlä), town (pop. 1,075), Puebla, central Mexico, 30 mi. SE of Matamoros; cereals, sugar cane, fruit, livestock.

China Sea, part of Pacific Ocean bordering on China, divided by Formosa into EAST CHINA SEA (N) and SOUTH CHINA SEA (S).

Chinati Mountains (chĭnä'tē), Presidio co., extreme W Texas, generally parallel to the Rio Grande, c.35 mi. SW of Marfa; Chinati Peak (7,730 ft.) is highest point. Silver mining.

Chinautla or **Santa Cruz Chinautla** (sän'tä krōōs' chēnout'lä), town (1950 pop. 1,639), Guatemala dept., S central Guatemala, 4 mi. N of Guatemala; alt. 3,800 ft. Pottery making, charcoal burning; corn, black beans; cattle.

Chinaz (chēnäs'), village (1926 pop. 3,191), N Tashkent oblast, Uzbek SSR, on Trans-Caspian RR, on the Syr Darya, at mouth of Chirchik R., and 40 mi. WSW of Tashkent; cotton, fiber plants.

Chincha Alta (chēn'chä äl'tä), city (pop. 12,768), ⊙ Chincha prov. (□ 1,188; pop. 42,579), Ica dept., SW Peru, on coastal plain, in San Juan (or Chincha) R. valley, on highway, and 50 mi. NW of Ica. Commercial center in important cotton- and wine-growing region; cotton ginning, distilling. Its port is TAMBO DE MORA.

Chincha Baja (bä'hä), town (pop. 590), Ica dept., SW Peru, on coastal plain, in San Juan (or Chincha) R. valley, 4 mi. SW of Chincha Alta (connected by highway); cotton ginning, soap mfg.

Chincha Islands, group of 3 small isls., in Pacific Ocean, 13 mi. off SW Peru, in Ica dept., 14 mi. WNW of Pisco; 13°39'S 76°25'W. Their large guano deposits have been heavily exploited.

Chinchani (chĭn'chŭnē), village (pop. 6,907), Thana dist., W Bombay, India, on Arabian Sea, 60 mi. N of Bombay; rice milling, fishing. Sometimes spelled Chinchni.

Chincha River, Peru: see SAN JUAN RIVER.

Chincheros (chēnchä'rōs), town (pop. 1,330), Apurímac dept., S central Peru, in Andean spur, 19 mi. NNW of Andahuaylas; grain, stock.

Chin-chi or **Chin-ch'i**, China: see KINKI.

Chin-chiang, town, China: see TSINKIANG.

Chin Chiang, river, Kiangsi prov., China: see KIN RIVER.

Ch'in Chiang, river, Kwangtung prov., China: see YAM RIVER.

Chinchilla (chĭnchĭ'lŭ), town (pop. 1,754), SE Queensland, Australia, 155 mi. WNW of Brisbane; rail junction in cattle-raising area.

Chinchilla de Monte Aragón (chēnchē'lyä dhä mōn'tä äragōn'), city (pop. 3,491), Albacete prov., SE central Spain, rail junction and agr. center 10 mi. SE of Albacete; alcohol distilling, sawmilling; cereals, wine, fruit. Built at foot of hill crowned by anc. castle, now a prison. Has cave dwellings and several 15th-cent. houses. Lignite mining.

Chinchiná (chēnchēnä'), town (pop. 4,146), Caldas dept., W central Colombia, on W slopes of Cordillera Central, on railroad and highway, and 8 mi. SW of Manizales; alt. 4,701 ft. Coffee center with coffee experiment station; sugar cane, silk, cereals, fruit. Coal deposits near by.

Chinchipe River (chēnchē'pā), rises in Ecuadorian Andes at SW foot of the Cordillera de Zamora, flows c.90 mi. SE into Peru, to the Marañón 12 mi. NE of Bellavista.

Chincholi (chĭnchō'lē), village (pop. 4,736), Gulbarga dist., W central Hyderabad state, India, 40 mi. ENE of Gulbarga. Cotton ginning, rice milling near by.

Chinchón (chēnchōn'), city (pop. 4,635), Madrid prov., central Spain, on railroad and 24 mi. SE of Madrid; viticultural center in prov.'s most fertile region. Known for its fine table wines and liquors. Region also grows cereals, garlic, potatoes, melons, olives, sugar beets. Sawmilling, alcohol distilling, flour milling; mfg. of soft drinks, plaster, soap.

Chinchorro Bank (chēnchô'rō), barrier reef in Caribbean Sea off E coast of Yucatan Peninsula, SE Mexico, 20 mi. off Quintana Roo coast, 100 mi. S of Cozumel Isl. Extends 28 mi. N-S, 4–10 mi. wide. Lighthouse is on an islet at 18°46'N 87°18'W.

Chinchoua (chēnchwä'), village, NW Gabon, Fr. Equatorial Africa, near Gabon R., 40 mi. SE of Libreville; lumbering (hardwood) and agr. center.

Chinchow or **Chin-chou** (both: jĭn'jō'). **1** City (1947 pop. 148,006), ⊙ Liaosi prov., Manchuria, and ⊙ but independent of Chinchow co. (1946 pop. 333,-224), 130 mi. SW of Mukden and on railroad to Peking; center of the Shanhaikwan corridor connecting Manchuria and N China, near Gulf of Liaotung; rail hub and industrial center. Flour and soybean milling, cotton weaving, tanning; mfg. of cement, glass, brick, tiles, paper and wood pulp. Coal mining at Tayaokow, 20 mi. W of Chinchow. An old city dating from 12th cent., it developed mainly after construction of Peking-Mukden RR. When in Manchukuo, it was (1934–46) ⊙ Chinchow prov. (□ 15,500; 1940 pop. 4,317,822); it became ⊙ Liaosi prov. in 1949. Sometimes spelled Kinchow, it was officially called Chinhsien from 1913 until it was created (1937; confirmed 1947) an independent municipality. **2** Town, in Port Arthur dist. at S tip of Liaotung peninsula, Manchuria: see Chinhsien.

Chin Chu, river, Bhutan: see Raidak River.

Chincolco (chēngkōl'kō), village (1930 pop. 846), Aconcagua prov., central Chile, 28 mi. NE of La Ligua, in agr. area (hemp, fruit, potatoes, livestock). Copper deposits near by.

Chincoteague (shĭng'kūtēg), town (pop. 2,724), Accomack co., E Va., 14 mi. SE of Pocomoke City, Md., on narrow Chincoteague Isl. (c.9 mi. long, in Chincoteague Bay), which is sheltered from the Atlantic by Assateague Isl. (E) and connected by causeway to Eastern Shore peninsula (W). Oyster fisheries; hunting, fishing. Here annually (July) is held a "pony-penning," a roundup and auction of wild ponies from Chincoteague and Assateague isls. Town inc. 1908.

Chincoteague Bay, E Md. and E Va., lagoon bordering Atlantic shore of Eastern Shore peninsula (Delmarva Peninsula), E of Snow Hill, Md.; 23 mi. long; sheltered E by Assateague Isl. Chincoteague Inlet (channel to ocean) and Chincoteague Isl. are at S end. Fishing, shellfishing.

Chinde (chēn'dā), town (1940 pop. 1,442), Zambézia prov., central Mozambique, seaport on navigable distributary (Chinde arm) of Zambezi R. delta, 60 mi. SSW of Quelimane and 130 mi. NE of Beira. Steamers go upstream to Tete. Ships sugar (grown on near-by plantations) and copra; fisheries. Formerly the principal outlet for Northern Rhodesia and Nyasaland, Chinde has now been superseded by Beira. Devastated 1922 by cyclone.

Chin-do, Korea: see Chin Island.

Chindwin, Lower, and **Chindwin, Upper**, districts, Burma: see Lower Chindwin and Upper Chindwin.

Chindwin River (chĭn'dwĭn'), main tributary of Irrawaddy R., Upper Burma; over 500 mi. long. Formed by network of headstreams rising in Patkai and Kumon ranges and draining the Hukawng Valley, flows generally S through Naga Hills gorges, past Singkaling, Homalin, Sittaung, Mawlaik, Kalewa, and Monywa, to the Irrawaddy NE of Pakokku. Receives Uyu and Myittha rivers. Navigable 380 mi. to Homalin; during dry season, 240 mi. to Kindat.

Chineni (chĭnä'nē), dependency (jagir) (□ 95; pop. 11,796) of Kashmir, an enclave within Udhampur dist., SW Kashmir, in S Punjab Himalayas; ⊙ Chineni. Agr. (corn, wheat, pulse, oilseeds, barley, rice). Main village, Chineni. Pop. 80% Hindu, 18% Moslem. Prevailing mother tongue, Dogri. Also spelled Chinani and Chenani.

Chineni, village, ⊙ Chineni jagir, SW Kashmir, in S Punjab Himalayas, near left tributary of the Chenab, 12 mi. NNE of Udhampur; corn, wheat, pulse, oilseeds. Also spelled Chinani and Chenani.

Chinese Changchun Railroad, Manchuria: see Chinese Eastern Railroad; South Manchuria Railroad.

Chinese Eastern Railroad, original name of the N Manchuria trunk line extending from Manchouli to Suifenho (built 1897–1903) via Harbin, from which city a branch (built 1903–7) extended S past Changchun to Dairen. Built by the Russians to provide a short route to Vladivostok and an exit to an ice-free port (Dairen). After the Russo-Japanese war (1904–5), the Dairen-Changchun section passed to Jap. control and became the South Manchuria Railroad. Manchukuo bought (1935) the rest of the Chinese Eastern line from the USSR. After the Second World War, the entire Manchurian rail system (renamed Chinese Changchun RR) passed to joint Soviet-Chinese control.

Chinese Turkestan: see Turkestan.

Ching- or **Ch'ing-**, for Chinese names beginning thus and not found here: see under King-; Tsing-.

Ching, river, China: see Ching River.

Ching-chiang or **Ch'ing-chiang**, town, China: see Tsingkiang.

Ch'ing Chiang, river, China: see Ching River.

Ch'ing-chien, China: see Tsingkien.

Ching-ch'uan, Kansu prov., China: see Kingchwan.

Ch'ing-ch'uan, Szechwan prov., China: see Tsingchwan.

Chingford, residential municipal borough (1931 pop. 22,053; 1951 census 48,330), SW Essex, England, on Lea R. and 10 mi. NE of London, on edge of Epping Forest. Site of half-timbered bldg. called Queen Elizabeth's Hunting Lodge and of large London water reservoir.

Ching-hsi, China: see Tsingsi.

Ching-hsing. **1** Town, Heilungkiang prov., Manchuria: see Kingsing. **2** Town, Hopeh prov., China: see Tsingsing.

Ching-hua, China: see Tsinghwa.

Chingis-Tau (chĭn-gēs-tou'), mountain range in Semipalatinsk oblast, Kazakh SSR; extends c.100 mi. W from Tarbagatai Range into Kazakh Hills; crystalline rocks rise to 4,100 ft. Forms divide bet. Irtysh R. and L. Balkhash basins.

Ching Kiang, China: see Ching River.

Chingleput (chĭng'gŭlpŏŏt), district (□ 3,074; pop. 1,823,955), E Madras, India; ⊙ Saidapet. On Coromandel Coast of Bay of Bengal; drained by Palar R. Madras dist. (coextensive with Madras city) is a coastal enclave. Agr.: rice, millet, oilseeds (sesame, peanuts). Salt pans in coastal backwaters and in Pulicat L.; numerous coastal fishing villages. Road-metal and building-stone quarrying in dispersed outcrops. Main centers: Saidapet, Sembiyam. Archaeological landmarks at Conjeeveram and Mahabalipuram.

Chingleput, city (pop. 17,829), Chingleput dist., E Madras, India, on Palar R. and 35 mi. SSW of Madras; rail junction; ships road metal and building stone (quarries near by); rice milling. Leprosy sanatorium; reformatory. Has ruined 16th-cent. fort; strategic center during English-Fr. struggle (18th cent.) for supremacy in India. Megalithic remains near by.

Chingo (chēng'gō), extinct volcano (5,840 ft.) on Guatemala-Salvador border, 16 mi. SE of Jutiapa.

Chingola (chĭng-gō'lä), township (pop. 798), Western Prov., N Northern Rhodesia, near Belgian Congo border, on rail spur and 60 mi. NW of Ndola; commercial center for adjoining copper-mining center of Nchanga. Govt. school.

Ching River, Chinese *Ching Kiang* or *Ch'ing Chiang* (both: chĭng' jyäng'), SW Hupeh prov., China, rises in 2 headstreams which join near Enshih, flows c.150 mi. E, past Changyang, to Yangtze R. at Itu.

Ching-te-chen, China: see Fowliang.

Chinguar (chĭng'gwär), town (pop. 1,675), Bié prov., central Angola, on railroad and 40 mi. WSW of Silva Pôrto; alt. 5,930 ft.; coffee, wheat, corn, beans, fruits.

Chinguetti (shĭng-gĕ'tē), village, central Mauritania, Fr. West Africa, in oasis of Adrar mtn. region, 45 mi. E of Atar; dates, subsistence crops, livestock. Airfield.

Ching-yen, China: see Tsingyüan.

Ch'ing-yüan, China: see Tsingyün.

Chinhae (chĕn'hä'), Jap. *Chinkai*, town (1949 pop. 38,357), S Kyongsang prov., S Korea, on Chinhae Bay, 20 mi. W of Pusan; site of naval base (established 1911); fishing.

Chinhae Bay, Korean *Chinhae-man*, Jap. *Chinkai-wan*, inlet of Korea Strait in S Kyongsang prov., S Korea, sheltered S by Koje Isl.; 20 mi. long, 15 mi. wide, broken into many coves. Masan and Chinhae are on N shore.

Chinhai or **Chenhai** (both: jŭn'hī'), town (pop. 13,987), ⊙ Chinhai co. (pop. 292,991), NE Chekiang prov., China, outer port (10 mi. NE) of Ningpo, on Hangchow Bay at mouth of Yung R.; saltworks, fisheries.

Chin Hills (chĭn), mountain ranges of Upper Burma, on Assam (India) border, bet. Manipur Hills (N) and the Arakan Yoma (S), bounded E by Myittha R. and separated from Indian Lushai Hills (W) by headstreams of Kaladan R.; rise to 10,018 ft. in Mt. Victoria. Consist of series of parallel ranges, broken by deep gorges (Manipur R.) with jungle on outer hills and villages and small-scale agr. on inner hills. Pop. is composed of Chins, a primitive Tibeto-Burman group speaking wide variety of dialects. Brought 1895 under Br. control, the Chin Hills were administered as a dist. (□ 10,675; 1941 pop. 186,405; ⊙ Falam) of Magwe div., Upper Burma. After Second World War, in accordance with Burma's 1947 constitution, the Chin Hills were set up as a separate administrative div. (□ 13,903; 1941 pop. 220,410; ⊙ Rangoon) of Upper Burma, including former Arakan Hill Tracts, and divided into dists. of Northern Chin Hills (⊙ Falam) and Southern Chin Hills (⊙ Kanpetlet).

Chin-hsi, Manchuria: see Chinsi.

Chin-hsiang, China: see Kinsiang.

Chinhsien (jĭn'shyĕn'). **1** Town in Port Arthur naval base dist., S Manchuria, China, at S tip of Liaotung peninsula, 15 mi. NE of Dairen, on inlet of Gulf of Chihli; rail junction and trade center; cotton spinning; saltworks. Called Kinchow, Chinchow, or Chinchou (all: jĭn'jō') (Jap. *Kinshu*) until 1945, while in Kwantung territory. **2** (jĭn'shyĕn') Town, Kiangsi prov., China: see Tsinsien. **3** or **Ch'in-hsien** (chĭn'shyĕn'), town, Kwangtung prov., China: see Yamhsien. **4** (jĭn'shyĕn') City, Liaosi prov., Manchuria, China: see Chinchow.

Chin-hua, China: see Kinhwa.

Ch'in-huang-tao, China: see Chinwangtao.

Chinhwai River, Chinese *Chinhwai Ho* or *Ch'in-huai Ho* (chĭn'hwī' hŭ'), S Kiangsu prov., China, rises in Shihkiu L. SW of Lishui, flows 50 mi. N, past Kiangning, to Yangtze R. at Nanking; flows through popular recreation area.

Chini (chē'nē), village, E Himachal Pradesh, India, near Sutlej R., 70 mi. ENE of Simla, on caravan route to Tibet; local trade in wool, rice, timber.

Chiniak, Cape (chĭ'nēăk), S Alaska, E extremity of Kodiak Isl., on Gulf of Alaska, 15 mi. SSW of Kodiak; 57°37'N 152°10'W.

Chiniak Bay, S Alaska, inlet (10 mi. long, 11 mi. wide at mouth) of Gulf of Alaska, NE Kodiak Isl.; 57°43'N 152°22'W. Kodiak village on N; Womens Bay (W arm) is site of naval base.

Chinicuila, Mexico: see Villa Victoria, Michoacán.

Chiniot (chĭnyōt'), town (pop. 34,437), Jhang dist., central Punjab, W Pakistan, near Chenab R., 50 mi. NE of Jhang-Maghiana; agr. market; trade center (wheat, cotton, millet); handicrafts (wood carving, ivory toys, brassware); cotton ginning; iron factory. Formerly noted for its masons. Sometimes spelled Chaniot.

Chínipas (chē'nēpäs), town (pop. 761), Chihuahua, N Mexico, in Sierra Madre Occidental, 175 mi. SW of Chihuahua; gold-placer mining, lumbering. Railroad to Palmarejo silver mine 6 mi. E.

Chinique (chēnē'kā), town (1950 pop. 517), Quiché dept., W central Guatemala, in Sierra de Chuacús, 5 mi. NE of Quiché; alt. 6,200 ft.; corn, beans, livestock.

Chin Island (chĕn), Korean *Chin-do*, Jap. *Chin-to*, island (□ 159; 1946 pop. 74,629), S.Cholla prov., Korea, in Yellow Sea, just off SW coast; 15 mi. long, 10 mi. wide; hilly, fertile. Cotton growing, building-stone quarrying.

Chinju (chĕn'jōō'), Jap. *Shinshu* or *Sinsyu* (both: shēn'shōō), city (1949 pop. 77,473), S.Kyongsang prov., S Korea, on small tributary of Naktong R. and 55 mi. W of Pusan; commercial center for agr. area (rice, cotton, tobacco, fruit).

Chinkai, Korea: see Chinhae.

Chinkiang (chĭn'kyăng', jĭn'jyäng'), **Chenkiang**, or **Chen-chiang** (both: jŭn'jyäng'), city (1948 pop. 179,059), S Kiangsu prov., China, port on right bank of Yangtze R. at junction of Grand Canal, on Shanghai-Nanking RR and 40 mi. E of Nanking; 32°12'N 119°28'E. Industrial and commercial center; rice and flour milling, vinegar distilling, silk-cloth weaving, tobacco and match mfg. Exports rice, wheat, beans. Seat of Kiangsu medical col. City consists of anc. walled section (E) and commercial quarter with river docks along the Yangtze (W). An old town, 1st mentioned under Sung dynasty (12th cent.) and reported by Marco Polo as Cinghian, it flourished under Ming and Manchu dynasties, was ravaged 1853 by the Taipings, and was opened 1859 to foreign trade. It declined in late-19th cent. when the Grand Canal ceased to be a major transportation artery, but flourished again as ⊙ Kiangsu (1928–49), succeeding Nanking. It is ⊙ Tantu (called Chinkiang co., 1928–49) co. (1948 pop. 511,219), from which it was separated in 1949 to become an independent municipality.

Chin Kiang, river, China: see Yam River.

Chinkuashih, Formosa: see Kinkwashih.

Chinle (chĭn"lē'), village, Apache co., NE Ariz., 90 mi. NNE of Holbrook; gateway to Canyon de Chelly Natl. Monument (E).

Chinley, town in parish of Chinley Bugsworth and Brownside (pop. 2,209), NW Derby, England, just WNW of Chapel-en-le-Frith; cotton milling.

Ch'in-ling Shan, China: see Tsinling Mountains.

Chin-men, China: see Quemoy.

Chinnai, Russian SFSR: see KRASNOGORSK, Sakhalin oblast.

Chinnamanur or **Chinnammanur** (chĭn″nŭmŭnōōr′), town (pop. 14,480), Madura dist., S Madras, India, 10 mi. NE of Cumbum, in Kambam Valley; sesame, tamarind, betel farms. Also spelled Chiennamanur.

Chinna-Merangi, India: see MERANGI.

Chinnampo (chĕn′näm′pô′), after 1945 often known as **Nampo,** city (1944 pop. 82,162), S.Pyongan prov., N Korea, at mouth of Taedong R. on Korea Bay of Yellow Sea, 27 mi. SW of Pyongyang; port for Pyongyang; industrial center (ironworks, fertilizer magnesium plants, gold refinery, vegetable-oil, rice and flour mills). Salt is produced near by; in surrounding country are large apple orchards. Exports rice, iron, coal, paper. Port was opened in 1897. Sometimes spelled Tinnanpo.

Chinna Salem (chĭn′nŭ sä′lŭm), town (pop. 8,232), South Arcot dist., S central Madras, India, 60 mi. WSW of Cuddalore; trades in timber and gum arabic from Kalrayan Hills (W; magnetite deposits). Also written Chinnasalem.

Chinnereth, town, Palestine: see GENOSSAR.

Chinnereth, Sea of, Palestine: see GALILEE, SEA OF.

Chinning (jĭn′nĭng′), town (pop. 5,615), ⊙ Chinning co. (pop. 51,511), E central Yunnan prov., China, 23 mi. S of Kunming, on SE shore of lake Tien Chih; rice, wheat, beans. Coal mines near by.

Chinnor (chĭ′nŭr), town and parish (pop. 1,124), S Oxfordshire, England, 4 mi. SE of Thame; cement-works. Has 13th-14th-cent. church with noted brasses.

Chinnur (chĭn-nōōr′), town, (pop. 8,369), Adilabad dist., NE Hyderabad state, India, on Godavari R. and 100 mi. SE of Adilabad; rice, mangoes. Bamboo (pulp used in paper mfg.) and timber (teak) forests near by.

Chino (chē′nō), city (pop. 5,784), San Bernardino co., S Calif., 30 mi. E of Los Angeles; walnuts, citrus fruit, truck, dairy products, sugar beets. State prison; state game-bird farms. Founded 1887, inc. 1910.

Chinobampo (chēnōbäm′pō), town (pop. 1,314), Sinaloa, NW Mexico, in Río del Fuerte basin (irrigation area), 18 mi. ESE of El Fuerte; sugar cane, corn, cotton, tomatoes, fruit.

Chinomiji, Russian SFSR: see TYATINO.

Chinon (shēnō′), town (pop. 4,312), Indre-et-Loire dept., W central France, on Vienne R. and 18 mi. ESE of Saumur; noted for its red wines. Its feudal castle, consisting of an oblong complex formed by 3 separate strongholds, towers above the river from a high rock. Castle was residence (12th cent.) of Henry II of England and resisted Philip II of France for a year (1204–5). It was the scene of Joan of Arc's interview (1429) with Charles VII. Later (1631–1789) it was a fief of the Richelieu family. Rabelais b. at near-by La Devinière.

Chinook (shĭnōōk′), village (pop. 130), SE Alta., 45 mi. ESE of Hanna; grain elevators, lumbering, farming.

Chinook, town (pop. 2,307), ⊙ Blaine co., N Mont., on Milk R. and 20 mi. E of Havre; gas wells; beet sugar; livestock, dairy and poultry products, grain, potatoes. Inc. 1901.

Chinook Pass (alt. 5,440 ft.), W central Wash., highway pass through Cascade Range, just E of Mt. Rainier.

Chin River, China: see TSIN RIVER.

Chinsali (chēnsä′lē), township (pop. 169), Northern Prov., NE Northern Rhodesia, in N Muchinga Mts., 65 mi. ESE Kasama; coffee, corn, wheat.

Chinshanchen, Manchuria: see HUMA.

Chinsi or **Chin-hsi** (both: jĭn′shē′), town, ⊙ Chinsi co. (pop. 234,887), SW Liaosi prov., Manchuria, 27 mi. SW of Chinchow and on railroad; junction for port of Hulutao; coal-mining center; cement plant. Lead and molybdenum mining near by. The name Chinsi was applied 1913–34 and 1946–49 to Hungkiatun, 15 mi. NW, at Jehol line. Present Chinsi was formerly called Lienshan.

Chinsura (chĭn′sōōrŭ), town (pop., including HOOGHLY, 49,081), ⊙ Hooghly dist., S central West Bengal, India, on Hooghly R. and 17 mi. N of Calcutta city center; rice milling. Hooghly Col. Former Dutch settlement, founded early 17th cent. Ceded in 1825, with other Du. settlements in India, to English in exchange for English settlements in Sumatra. Just S is Chandernagore (or Farashdanga), a major hand-loom cotton-weaving center adjacent to former Fr. settlement of CHANDERNAGORE.

Chintalapudi (chĭntŭlŭpōō′dē), village, West Godavari dist., NE Madras, India, 26 mi. NNW of Ellore; sheep raising, woolen-blanket weaving; chili, bamboo, myrobalan.

Chintamani (chĭntä′mŭnē), town (pop. 9,292), Kolar dist., E Mysore, India, 20 mi. NNW of Kolar; perfume mfg., goldsmithing, hand-loom silk weaving; silk growing.

Chinteche (chēntē′chē), town, Northern Prov., Nyasaland, port on W shore of L. Nyasa, 40 mi. E of Mzimba; fishing; cassava, corn; tung-oil development. Rubber plantation at near-by Vizara. Formerly spelled Chintechi.

Chinú (chēnōō′), town (pop. 3,953), Bolívar dept., N Colombia, 95 mi. S of Cartagena; stock-raising center. Old colonial city, founded 1534.

Chinwangtao or **Ch'in-huang-tao** (both: chĭn′hwäng′-dou′), city (1947 pop. estimate 100,000), NE Hopeh prov., China, near the Great Wall (Liaosi prov.), 10 mi. SE of Shanhaikwan, and on Tientsin-Mukden RR; major commercial port on Gulf of Chihli; 2d only to Tientsin, it is ice-free during the winter; ships coal from Kailan mining dist. Cement; peanuts. Opened 1907 to foreign trade.

Chiny (shēnē′), village (pop. 704), Luxembourg prov., SE Belgium, on Semois R. and 8 mi. SSW of Neufchâteau, in the Ardennes; lumbering.

Chinyadevo (chēnyŭdyô′vŭ), Czech *Čiňad'ovo* (chĭ′nyädyôvô), Hung. *Szentmiklós* (sĕntmĭ′klōsh), village (1941 pop. 2,850), W Transcarpathian Oblast, Ukrainian SSR, on Latoritsa R., on railroad, and 5 mi. NE of Mukachevo; lumbering; watch mfg. Has 16th-cent. castle. Sometimes called Chinadeyevo, Czech *Činadijevo.*

Chinyüan. 1 (jĭn′yüän′) Town, ⊙ Chinyüan co. (pop. 105,839), N central Shansi prov., China, 10 mi. SW of Taiyüan; wheat, kaoliang, beans, tobacco, rice; sericulture. Until 1947 called Taiyüan. **2** or **Ch'in-yuan** (chĭn′yüän′), town, ⊙ Chinyüan co. (pop. 80,319), S Shansi prov., China, on Tsin (Chin) R. and 55 mi. NE of Linfen; cotton weaving, flour milling; winegrowing; rice, wheat, kaoliang, corn, beans.

Chin-yün, China: see TSINYÜN.

Chiochis (kyô′kēsh), Rum. *Chiochiș,* Hung. *Kékes* (kā′kĕsh), village (pop. 980), Cluj prov., N Rumania, 15 mi. SE of Dej. In Hungary, 1940–45.

Chioggia (kyôd′jä), anc. *Fossa Claudia,* town (pop. 23,577), Venezia prov., Veneto, N Italy, port at S end of Lagoon of Venice, 15 mi. S of Venice, on isl. bridged to mainland. Rail terminus; a major fishing center of Italy; shipyards, soap and cement industries; agr. experimental station. Bishopric. Has Gothic church of San Martino (1392) and cathedral (rebuilt 1633–74). Harbor was scene of naval battles (1378–80), terminating rivalry of Venice and Genoa in favor of Venice.

Chios (kī′ŏs) or **Khios** (Gr. khē′ôs), Ital. *Scio* (shē′ō), Greek Aegean island (□ 321; pop. 72,777) off Karaburun Peninsula of Asiatic Turkey (separated by 5–15-mi. wide Chios Channel); 38°20′N 26°E. Forms, with near-by isls. of Psara and Oinousa, a nome (□ 348; pop. 75,853) of Aegean Isls. div. of Greece; ⊙ Chios. Mountainous in N (4,256 ft. in the Pelinaion), it forms a fertile plain in SE section; 32 mi. long, 8–17 mi. wide. Well cultivated, the isl. produces wine, olives and olive oil, mastic, silk cocoons, figs, citrus fruit, grain; sheep and goats are raised (tanning industry); fishing. Antimony (at Keramos), sulphur, and marble are the chief mineral resources. Chios, the chief port and trade center, is on E coast. Colonized by Ionians, it was a traditional ally of Miletus until it passed (546 B.C.) to Persian control under Cyrus. It participated in Ionian revolt, but was reannexed (494–479 B.C.) by the Persians. It became a member of the Delian League, and, after the Peloponnesian War, was again an ally of Athens in early 4th cent. Under Rome, it remained a free city until the time of Vespasian. From Byzantine Empire, it passed to Venetians and later to Genoese. The Turks conquered it in 1566 and held it until 1913. An anti-Turkish rebellion (1822) resulted in a ruthless massacre of Chian Christians. It suffered in an earthquake of 1881. Chios is one of the places which claims to be the birthplace of Homer, and, in antiquity, was known for its school of epic poets (the Homeridae) and its sculptors. Called Sakiz-Adasi [mastic isl.] under Turkish rule.

Chios or **Khios,** Ital. *Scio,* city (pop. 26,617), ⊙ Chios nome, Greece, port on E coast of Chios isl., on Chios Channel (separating it from Turkish Karaburun Peninsula); 38°22′N 26°8′E. Trade center, exporting mastic, wine, leather, fruit; winemaking and fruit-canning industries; boatbuilding. Seat of Gr. metropolitan. Remains of Genoese fortress. Formerly called Kastron. In antiquity Chios was (with the isl.) one of the 12 Ionian city-states.

Chipao (chēpä′ō), town (pop. 1,280), Ayacucho dept., S Peru, on E slopes of Cordillera Occidental, 38 mi. N of Puquio; corn, beans, barley, alfalfa, livestock (sheep, llamas, vicuñas).

Chipaque (chēpä′kä), village (pop. 973), Cundinamarca dept., central Colombia, in Cordillera Oriental, 11 mi. S of Bogotá; alt. 8,104 ft.; cereals, potatoes, stock.

Chip Chap River, Kashmir: see SHYOK RIVER.

Chiperceni, Moldavian SSR: see KIPERCHENY.

Chipewyan, Fort, Alta.: see FORT CHIPEWYAN.

Chipinga (chēpĭng′gä), village (pop. 447), Umtali prov., E Southern Rhodesia, in Mashonaland, 85 mi. S of Umtali (linked by road), in Chimanimani Mts.; farming center; tobacco, corn, wheat, citrus fruit, dairy products, livestock. Tanganda tea farm (NW).

Chipiona (chēpyō′nä), town (pop. 5,795), Cádiz prov., SW Spain, minor Atlantic port (Gulf of Cádiz) 15 mi. NNW of Cádiz. Ships and processes wine and cognac. Beach resort for Andalusian aristocracy. Has old monastery.

Chipley. 1 Town (pop. 2,959), ⊙ Washington co., NW Fla., c.45 mi. NNE of Panama City; shipping center for farm and timber area; lumber milling, brick mfg. Near by is egg-laying experiment station. Falling Water, 4 mi. S, is one of the state's rare waterfalls. **2** Town (pop. 817), Harris co., W Ga., 16 mi. SE of La Grange, in cotton and dairy area; clothing mfg. State park near by.

Chiplun (chĭp′lōōn), town (pop., including N suburban area, 15,528), Ratnagiri dist., W Bombay, India, 40 mi. NE of Ratnagiri, in the Konkan; trade center; agr. market (chiefly rice).

Chipman, village (pop. 194), central Alta., on Beaver Creek and 35 mi. ENE of Edmonton; mixed farming, dairying.

Chipoka (chēpō′kä), village, Central Prov., Nyasaland, port on L. Nyasa, on railroad and 50 mi. E of Lilongwe; 13°58′S 34°30′E; rail-steamer transfer point; tobacco, cotton, corn.

Chipola River (chĭpō′lŭ) (c.125 mi. long), in Ala. and Fla., rises in several branches near Dothan, SE Ala., flows S, across NW Fla., past Marianna, through DEAD LAKE, to Apalachicola R. 10 mi. SE of Wewahitchka. Lower course dredged and navigable for c.40 mi.

Chipon, Formosa: see CHIHPEN.

Chipongwe (chēpông′gwā), township (pop. 169), Central Prov., Northern Rhodesia, on railroad and 18 mi. S of Lusaka; tobacco, wheat, corn; cattle, sheep, goats.

Chiporov Mountains (chē′pôrôf), NW section of Balkan Mts., extend c.25 mi. NW-SE along Bulg.-Yugoslav border, SW of Chiporovtsi; rise to 7,111 ft. in Midzhur peak. Beech forests; lead-silver and iron deposits (worked in 14th-16th cent.). Also spelled Chiprov.

Chiporovtsi (chē′pôrôftsē), village (pop. 3,095), Vratsa dist., NW Bulgaria, in Chiporov Mts., 17 mi. W of Mikhailovgrad; carpet mfg.; sheep raising. Once a flourishing copper-mining center inhabited by Saxons; sacked by Turks following 17th-cent. revolt. Also spelled Chiprovtsi.

Chippawa or **Chippewa** (chĭ′pŭwô), village (pop. 1,385), S Ont., on Niagara R., SSE suburb of Niagara Falls, Ont., opposite Niagara Falls, N.Y. Airport. Scene of battle (1814) in which Americans defeated Anglo-Canadian force. Settled 1794.

Chippawa River, Ont.: see WELLAND RIVER.

Chippenham (chĭ′pŭnŭm), municipal borough (1931 pop. 8,493; 1951 census 11,850), NW Wiltshire, England, on the Avon and 12 mi. ENE of Bath; agr. market in dairying region. Mfg. of agr. machinery; cheese processing, bacon curing. Has 15th-cent. church (begun in 12th cent.) and old town hall.

Chippewa, Ont.: see CHIPPAWA.

Chippewa (chĭ′pŭwä″, –wŭ, –wô″). **1** County (□ 1,580; pop. 29,206), E Upper Peninsula, Mich.; ⊙ SAULT SAINTE MARIE. Bounded E by St. Marys R., N by Whitefish Bay, and S by L. Huron. Includes Sugar, Neebish, and Drummond isls. Contains part of Marquette Natl. Forest. Drained by Tahquamenon and Munuscong rivers. Port of entry, and mfg. and shipping at Sault Ste. Marie. Agr. (flax, potatoes), dairying, commercial fishing, lumbering. Resorts (hunting, fishing, boating). Co. is site of 2 state parks, Fort Brady, and a waterfowl refuge. Formed 1826. **2** County (□ 582; pop. 16,739), SW Minn.; ⊙ Montevideo. Agr. area bounded W by Minnesota R. and Lac qui Parle and drained by Chippewa R. Corn, oats, barley, livestock, poultry. Formed 1862. **3** County (□ 1,025; pop. 42,839), W central Wis.; ⊙ Chippewa Falls. Drained by Chippewa R. Dairying and stock-raising area; mfg. at Chippewa Falls (site of hydroelectric plant). There is a state park and several lakes, largest being L. Wissota. Formed 1845.

Chippewa, Lake, Sawyer co., NW Wis., 10 mi. SE of Hayward, in Lac Court Oreilles Indian Reservation; c.10 mi. long, with many sprawling arms; contains several islets.

Chippewa Bay, resort village, St. Lawrence co., N N.Y., 33 mi. N of Watertown, and on the St. Lawrence, in Thousand Isls. resort region. Cedar Island State Park is near by.

Chippewa Falls, city (pop. 11,088), ⊙ Chippewa co., W central Wis., on Chippewa R., near L. Wissota, and 9 mi. NE of Eau Claire; commercial center for dairying and farming area. Has important hydroelectric plant feeding transmission line system of W Wis. Mfg.: shoes, woolen goods, processed meat, wood products. State branch of Farmers Union is here. Formerly a lumbering center. Settled 1837; inc. as village in 1853, as city in 1869.

Chippewa Lake or **Chippewa-on-the-Lake,** village (pop. 107), Medina co., N Ohio, 5 mi. SSW of Medina, on small Chippewa L.; resort.

Chippewa River. 1 In central Mich., rises in NE Mecosta co., flows generally c.80 mi. ESE, past Barryton and Mt. Pleasant, to Tittabawassee R. at Midland. **2** In W and SW Minn., rises in lake region near Evansville, flows 120 mi. generally S, past Benson, to Minnesota R. at Montevideo. East Branch rises in small lake near Glenwood, W Minn., flows 60 mi. S and W to Chippewa R. at Benson. **3** In W central Wis., formed by streams rising in lake region in Lac Court Oreilles Indian Reservation, flows generally S and SW, past Chippewa Falls (hydroelectric plant), Eau Claire, and Durand, to the Mississippi at SE end of L. Pepin; c.200 mi. long. Largest of 3 dams forms L. Wissota near Chippewa Falls. Formerly important for log driving.

Chipping Barnet, England: see BARNET.

Chipping Campden (kăm′dŭn, kămp′–), town and parish (pop. 1,645), NE Gloucester, England, 8 mi. ESE of Evesham, in Cotswold Hills; agr. market, with flour mills. There are many beautiful old houses, and church dates from 13th cent.

Chipping Norton, municipal borough (1931 pop. 3,499; 1951 census 3,879), W Oxfordshire, England, 12 mi. SW of Banbury; woolen (tweed) milling, glove mfg.; agr. market. Has earthwork remains of 12th-cent. castle, 14th-15th-cent. church, and 17th-cent. almshouses. Near by are anc. stone monuments.

Chipping Ongar, England: see ONGAR.

Chipping Wycombe, England: see HIGH WYCOMBE.

Chippis (shēpē′), village (pop. 1,037), Valais canton, S Switzerland, on the Rhone opposite Sierre, at mouth of a small stream; hydroelectric plants; aluminum.

Chippon, Formosa: see CHIHPEN.

Chiprana (chēprä′nä), town (pop. 1,146), Saragossa prov., NE Spain, on the Ebro and 5 mi. WNW of Caspe; olive oil, cereals, fruit, livestock.

Chiprov Mountains, Bulgaria: see CHIPOROV MOUNTAINS.

Chipstead, residential town and parish (pop. 1,513), E central Surrey, England, 4 mi. NNE of Reigate. Has 12th-cent. church.

Chipurupalle (chē′po͝oro͝opŭlē), village, Vizagapatam dist., NE Madras, India, 17 mi. NE of Vizianagaram; oilseeds, millet, jute. Manganese mines just SW, near rail station of Garividi.

Chiputneticook Lakes (chĭpo͝otnē′tēko͝ok), E Maine and SW N.B., 28-mi. chain extending NW from Vanceboro (Maine) along international line; include North, Grand (17 mi. long), Spednik, and Palfrey lakes. Source of St. Croix R. Formerly called Schoodic Lakes (sko͞o′dĭk).

Chique-Chique, Brazil: see XIQUE-XIQUE.

Chiquián (chēkyän′), city (pop. 2,423), ⊙ Bolognesi prov. (□ 1,709; pop. 29,414), Ancash dept., W central Peru, in Cordillera Occidental, 50 mi. SE of Huarás; alt. 11,657 ft. Barley, potatoes, alfalfa. Silver mining near by.

Chiquilistlán (chēkēlēslän′), town (pop. 1,768), Jalisco, W Mexico, on central plateau, 32 mi. SSE of Ameca; grain, sugar cane, fruit, livestock.

Chiquimula (chēkēmo͞o′lä), department (□ 917; 1950 pop. 112,275), E Guatemala; ⊙ Chiquimula. On Honduras border, bounded S by Salvador; in E highlands; drained by Chiquimula R. Has volcanos Ipala and Quezaltepeque. Mainly agr. (corn, beans, fodder grasses, wheat); livestock. Coffee, sugar cane, bananas, tobacco, and rice grown in warmer valleys. Main centers: Chiquimula (on railroad to San Salvador), Esquipulas (pilgrimage town), Quezaltepeque.

Chiquimula, city (1950 pop. 8,848), ⊙ Chiquimula dept., E Guatemala, on Chiquimula R. and 65 mi. ENE of Guatemala, on railroad; 14°49′N 89°32′W; alt. 1,378 ft. Agr. center in fruit and cattle-raising region; tobacco, sugar cane, corn, wheat. Has ruins of colonial church, destroyed in 1765 earthquake. City suffered in 1773 earthquake.

Chiquimula River, E Guatemala, formed at Chiquimula by confluence of 2 branches rising in highlands; flows c.45 mi. N to the Motagua 5 mi. N of Zacapa. Sometimes called Río Grande de Zacapa.

Chiquimulilla (chēkēmo͞olē′yä), town (1950 pop. 3,486), Santa Rosa dept., S Guatemala, on coastal plain, near Esclavos R., 14 mi. SSW of Cuilapa; coffee, grain, livestock.

Chiquimulilla Canal, coastal lagoon in Santa Rosa dept., S Guatemala; separated by low, sandy isls. from Pacific Ocean; length c.70 mi., bet. San José (W) and Salvador border (Río de la Paz; E). Serves coastal trade (fish, salt).

Chiquinquirá (chēkēngkērä′), town (pop. 6,998), Boyacá dept., central Colombia, in W Cordillera Oriental, 75 mi. NNE of Bogotá, on highway and on Bogotá–Barbosa RR; alt. 8,432 ft. Commercial and agr. market (coffee, sugar cane, corn, wheat, potatoes, cotton, silk, stock). Airport. Pilgrimage center: many pilgrims visit the celebrated shrine of Our Lady of Chiquinquirá, in whose honor there is a beautiful church constructed of marble quarried near by. Founded 1586. Emerald mines in vicinity (SW).

Chiquinquirá, town (pop. 956), Zulia state, NW Venezuela, on NW shore of L. Maracaibo, 15 mi. S of Maracaibo; oil wells.

Chiquita, Mar, Argentina: see MAR CHIQUITA.

Chiquita, Mount, Colo.: see MUMMY RANGE.

Chiquitos, Bolivia: see SAN JOSÉ, Santa Cruz dept.

Chiquitoy (chēkētoi′), village (pop. 1,543), Libertad dept., NW Peru, on coastal plain, in irrigated Chicama R. valley, on railroad and 18 mi. NW of Trujillo; sugar-milling center; distilling.

Chira or **Chira Bazar** (chērä′ bäzär′), Chinese *Tsehleh* or *Ts'e-lo* (chĕ′lô′), town and oasis (pop. 60,185), SW Sinkiang prov., China, 50 mi. E of Khotan, and on highway skirting S edge of Taklamakan Desert; 37°2′N 80°53′E. Silk textiles.

Chiradzulu (chērädzo͞o′lo͞o), administrative center, Southern Prov., Nyasaland, 13 mi. NE of Blantyre, in agr. area; tobacco, tung, cotton, rice, corn.

Chiragidzor (chērä″gēdzôr′), town (1939 pop. over 500), W Azerbaijan SSR, on N slope of the Lesser Caucasus, 15 mi. S of Kirovabad; iron pyrite mine.

Chira Island (chē′rä), island (□ 20) in Gulf of Nicoya of the Pacific, NW Costa Rica, Puntarenas prov., 20 mi. NW of Puntarenas; 7 mi. long, 3 mi. wide. Agr. (corn, beans, manioc, fruit), stock raising, fishing; salines. Exported cedarwood in colonial times.

Chirak (chĭrŭk′), village, W Patiala and East Punjab States Union, India, 6 mi. S of Moga; wheat, millet.

Chirakchi (chērŭkchē′), village (1948 pop. over 2,000), NE Kashka-Darya oblast, Uzbek SSR, on the Kashka Darya and 13 mi. W of Shakhrisyabz; metalworks.

Chirala (chērä′lŭ), town (pop., including adjacent Perala, 27,086), Guntur dist., NE Madras, India, in Kistna R. delta, 33 mi. S of Guntur; tobacco curing; rice, palmyra, betel palms.

Chirambirá Point, Colombia: see CHARAMBIRÁ POINT.

Chiran (chē′rä), town (pop. 24,147), Kagoshima prefecture, S Kyushu, Japan, on S central Satsuma Peninsula, 15 mi. SSW of Kagoshima; rail terminus; mining center (gold, silver). Rice fields in vicinity. Sometimes spelled Tiran.

Chirang (chēräng′), village, S central Bhutan, near the Sankosh, 40 mi. SSE of Punakha; rice, corn; alt. c.5,000 ft. Chirang area, just N of Eastern Duars, is roughly separated from Chamarchi area by the Sankosh; inhabited by Nepalese settlers; main village, SARBHANG. Also called Cheyram.

Chira River (chē′rä), Piura dept., NW Peru, formed by confluence of the Río Grande or Catamayo R. and Macará R. at Peru-Ecuador border 20 mi. SW of Celica, flows c.100 mi. SW, through major cotton region, to the Pacific 5 mi. SW of Vichayal. It feeds numerous irrigation channels in middle and lower course. Forms part of Peru-Ecuador border in upper course, under 1942 boundary settlement.

Chirawa (chĭrä′vŭ), town (pop. 11,640), NE Rajasthan, India, 16 mi. NE of Jhunjhunu; trades in millet, wool, cotton, cattle; hand-loom weaving.

Chirchik (chĭrchēk′), city (1939 pop. over 10,000), N Tashkent oblast, Uzbek SSR, on Chirchik R. (hydroelectric plant) and 20 mi. NE of Tashkent (linked by railroad); modern industrial center; electro-chemical industry (nitrate fertilizer, ammonium compounds); mfg. of chemical and agr. machinery. Formerly a village called Kirgiz-Kulak, it was industrialized in 1930s.

Chirchik River, Kazakh and Uzbek SSRS, formed by junction of Pskem and Chatkal rivers E of Gazalkent; flows c.90 mi. SW, past Chirchik (hydroelectric plant), to the Syr Darya at Chinaz; irrigates Tashkent oasis.

Chireno (shĭrē′nō), village (pop.c.500), Nacogdoches co., E Texas, 19 mi. ESE of Nacogdoches, near Attoyac Bayou; farm trade point.

Chire River, Nyasaland and Mozambique: see SHIRE RIVER.

Chirgalandy (chĭrgŭlän′dē), village, SE Tuva Autonomous Oblast, Russian SFSR, 140 mi. SE of Kyzyl, in Tannu-Ola Range.

Chirgaon (chĕr′goun), town (pop. 4,674), Jhansi dist., S Uttar Pradesh, India, 12 mi. ENE of Jhansi; jowar, oilseeds, wheat, gram.

Chiri, Mount (chē′rē), Korean *Chiri-san*, Jap. *Chiisan*, peak (6,283 ft.), S.Kyongsang prov., S Korea, 20 mi. NW of Chinju; sacred to Buddhists. On its slopes are several anc. monasteries and pagodas.

Chiricahua Mountains (chĭrŭkä′wŭ), Cochise co., SE Ariz., N of Douglas. Separated from Dos Cabezas Mts. (NW) by APACHE PASS. Chief peaks: Cochise Head (8,100 ft.), Flys Peak (9,795 ft.), and Chiricahua Peak (9,795 ft.), 38 mi. NNE of Douglas. Range lies in part of Coronado Natl. Forest. Includes **Chiricahua National Monument** (□ 16.4; established 1924), area of remarkable rock shapes formed by volcanic action. Region long inhabited by Apache Indians, who, under leadership of Geronimo, Cochise, and Massai, attacked white settlements in vicinity during 2d half of 19th cent.

Chirie, Russian SFSR: see KOTIKOVO.

Chirignago (kērēnyä′gô), village (pop. 1,920), Venezia prov., Veneto, N Italy, 2 mi. W of Mestre; brush mfg.

Chiriguaná (chērēgwänä′), town (pop. 3,088), Magdalena dept., N Colombia, on small lake formed by César R., 38 mi. NE of El Banco; agr. center (cacao, coffee, pita fiber, stock).

Chirihoi-to, Russian SFSR: see CHERNYE BRATYA.

Chirikof Island (chĭ′rĭkôf) (11 mi. long, 3–7 mi. wide), S Alaska, in N Pacific, S of Alaska Peninsula, 180 mi. SW of Kodiak; 55°48′N 155°37′W.

Chirinda (chērĭndä′), village, N Evenki Natl. Okrug, Krasnoyarsk Territory, Russian SFSR, 240 mi. N of Tura, N of Arctic Circle, in reindeer-raising area.

Chirinkotan Island (chĭrēnkŭtän′), islet of N main Kurile Isls. group, Russian SFSR, 18 mi. W of Ekarma Isl.; 48°59′N 153°29′E; 1.5 mi. square. Has smoking volcano (2,434 ft.).

Chiriquí (chērēkē′), province (□ 3,693; 1950 pop. 137,422; 20% Indians), W Panama; ⊙ David. On Pacific slope, bounded W by Costa Rica and E by Tabasará R.; includes Chiriquí volcano. Drained by David, Chiriquí, and Chiriquí Viejo rivers, all flowing into Chiriquí Gulf of the Pacific. Agr.: bananas (Puerto Armuelles), coffee (Boquete), sugar cane, corn, rice, vegetables. Stock raising, lumbering. Mfg. principally at David. Prov. exports rice, corn, coffee, cattle. Railroad links main centers of Puerto Armuelles, David, Boquete, Potrerillos, and Pedregal. Motor launch from Puerto Armuelles and Pedregal to Panama city. Prov. traversed by Inter-American Highway. Formed 1850.

Chiriquí, village (pop. 922), Chiriquí prov., W Panama, on Inter-American Highway and 7 mi. ESE of David; coffee, bananas, cacao, livestock.

Chiriquí or **Barú** (bäro͞o′), inactive volcano and highest peak (11,410 ft.) of Panama, near Costa Rica border, just S of continental divide, 28 mi. NNW of David.

Chiriquí Grande (grän′dā), village (pop. 64), Bocas del Toro prov., W Panama, small Caribbean port in lowlands of Chiriquí Lagoon, 26 mi. SSE of Bocas del Toro. Bananas, cacao, abacá, coconuts, tobacco, rubber; stock raising, lumbering.

Chiriquí Gulf, inlet of Pacific Ocean in W Panama, E of Burica Peninsula; 80 mi. wide, 15 mi. long. Main ports are Puerto Armuelles (on Charco Azul Bay) and Pedregal.

Chiriquí Isthmus, W Panama, bet. Chiriquí Lagoon of the Caribbean (N) and Chiriquí Gulf (S); 45 mi. wide.

Chiriquí Lagoon, inlet of Caribbean Sea in W Panama, W of Valiente Peninsula and closed off by Bocas del Toro Archipelago; 32 mi. wide, 13 mi. long. Excellent natural harbor.

Chiriquí River, W Panama, rises in continental divide E of the Cerro Horqueta, flows 45 mi. S, past Gualaca, to the Pacific, forming a common delta with David R. Nonnavigable. Receives Caldera R. (right).

Chiriquí Viejo River (vyā′hō) [Sp.,=old Chiriquí], W Panama, near Costa Rica border, rises in continental divide bet. the Cerro Pando and the volcano Chiriquí, flows c.50 mi. S, past Progreso, to Charco Azul Bay of the Pacific. Navigable (in lower course) 6 mi. for 12-ft.-draught vessels.

Chiriu, Japan: see CHIRYU.

Chirivel (chērēvĕl′), town (pop. 1,265), Almería prov., S Spain, 12 mi. WSW of Vélez Rubio; sheep raising; cereals, esparto, potatoes.

Chirivella (chērēvä′lyä), W suburb (pop. 2,716) of Valencia, Valencia prov., E Spain, in truck-farming area; mfg. (silk textiles, insecticides, candles). Olive-oil, hemp, wheat.

Chi River (chē), E Thailand, rises in N Dong Phaya Yen Range, near Chaiyaphum, flows 250 mi. NE and SE through Korat Plateau, past Mahasarakham, to Mun R. 5 mi. W of Ubon; navigable up to 60 mi. from mouth.

Chiriyal, India: see CHERIAL.

Chirk, town and parish (pop. 2,955), SE Denbigh, Wales, 9 mi. SSW of Wrexham; coal mining. Near by is 14th-cent. Chirk Castle. Church dates from 15th cent.

Chirmiri (chĭr′mĭrē), town (pop. 10,044), Surguja dist., E Madhya Pradesh, India, 55 mi. W of Ambikapur; rail spur terminus; coal-mining center. Lac grown in surrounding dense sal forests (bamboo, khair).

Chirnside (chûrn′–), village and parish (pop. 1,414), E Berwick, Scotland, 6 mi. ENE of Duns; paper milling. Just E was ancestral home of David Hume.

Chiromo (chērō′mō), rail station, Southern Prov., Nyasaland, on Mozambique border, on the Shire (railroad bridge), at mouth of Ruo R., and 50 mi. SSE of Blantyre; cotton-growing center; cotton ginning; tobacco, tea, rice, corn. Important center at turn of 19th cent., it was river-trade port until 1907.

Chirpan (chĭrpän′), city (pop. 13,231), Stara Zagora dist., central Bulgaria, on S slope of Chirpan tableland (part of Sirnena Gora), 23 mi. SW of Stara Zagora; agr.- and livestock-trading center; wine making. Ruins of anc. Roman town of Pizus near by. A commercial center under Turkish rule; ceded to Bulgaria in 1877. Sometimes spelled Tchirpan.

Chirpoi Island, Russian SFSR: see CHERNYE BRATYA.

Chirripó Grande (chērēpō′ grän′dā), highest peak (12,533 ft.) of Costa Rica, in the Cordillera de Talamanca, 20 mi. NNW of Buenos Aires.

Chir River (chĕr), S European Russian SFSR, rises S of Migulinskaya, flows 215 mi. generally SE, in winding steppe course, past Chernyshevskaya, Oblivskaya, and Surovikino, to Don R. at Nizhne-Chirskaya. Floods in spring; nonnavigable.

Chirua, Lake, Nyasaland and Mozambique: see CHILWA, LAKE.

Chirundu (chēro͞on′do͞o), village, Salisbury prov., N Southern Rhodesia, in Mashonaland, on Zambezi R., at Northern Rhodesia border, and 125 mi. NW of Sinoia, on Salisbury-Kafue road. Site of Otto Beit Bridge, across Zambezi R.

Chiryal, India: see CHERIAL.

Chiryu (chērū′), town (pop. 15,988), Aichi prefecture, central Honshu, Japan, 12 mi. SE of Nagoya; commercial center in agr. area; raw silk, poultry. Sometimes spelled Chiriu.

Chisago (shĭsä'gō), county (□ 419; pop. 12,669), E Minn.; ⊙ Center City. Agr. area bounded E by St. Croix R. and Wis. and watered in S by small lakes. Dairy products, livestock, poultry, grain. Formed 1851.

Chisago City, village (pop. 703). Chisago co., E Minn., in lake region 31 mi. NNE of St. Paul; grain, livestock. Summer resorts near by.

Chisamba (chēsäm'bä), town, Central Prov., Northern Rhodesia, on railroad and 35 mi. S of Broken Hill; corn-growing center; tobacco, wheat, livestock.

Chisamula Island or **Chizmula Island** (chēzōōmōō'-lä) (pop. 1,157), in L. Nyasa, central Nyasaland, 35 mi. ESE of Chinteche; 3 mi. long, 1½ mi. wide. Fishing.

Chisana (chĭsă'nů, shōōshă'nů), village (1939 pop. 28), E Alaska, 100 mi. SSE of Tanacross, at foot of Wrangell Mts.; gold mining; supply point. Airfield.

Chisapani Ghari (chĭsä'pänē gŭr'ē), town, central Nepal, in Mahabharat Lekh range, 13 mi. SW of Katmandu, on main India-Katmandu route. Just N is pass (alt. c.6,000 ft.). Also called Sisagarhi.

Chisatau, Rumania: see CHIZATAU.

Chiscareni, Moldavian SSR: see KISHKARENY.

Chisekesi (chēsĕkĕ'sē), township (pop. 122), Southern Prov., Northern Rhodesia, c.45 mi. SSW of Mazabuka; corn-growing center; tobacco, potatoes, truck. Formerly called Mission.

Chishima-retto, Russian SFSR: see KURILE ISLANDS.

Chishmy (chĭshmē'), town (1932 pop. estimate 1,870), central Bashkir Autonomous SSR, Russian SFSR, 26 mi. SW of Ufa; rail junction; food processing (flour, meat).

Chisholm or **Chisholm Mills** (chĭ'zům), village (pop. estimate 200), central Alta., on Athabaska R. and 40 mi. WNW of Athabaska; wheat, stock.

Chisholm. 1 Village, Franklin co., Maine: see JAY. **2** City (pop. 6,861), St. Louis co., NE Minn., in Mesabi iron range, just NE of Hibbing, and c.60 mi. NW of Duluth; trading and mining point in grain and truck-product area; dairy products, beverages. Iron mines near by. Superior Natl. Forest is N. Settled 1898, inc. as town 1901, as city 1934.

Chisholm Trail, in U.S., old cattle trail over which herds of longhorns were driven from near San Antonio, Texas, to the railroad at Abilene, Kansas, for c.20 years after Civil War.

Chishuyen, China: see CHANGCHOW.

Chisimaio, Ital. Somaliland: see KISMAYU.

Chisinau, Moldavian SSR: see KISHINEV.

Chisineu-Cris (kē'shēnă"ōō-krēsh'), Rum. *Chişineu-Criş*, Hung. *Kisjenő* (kēsh'yĕ"nû), village (pop. 6,124), Arad prov., W Rumania, on White Körös R. and 25 mi. NNE of Arad; rail junction; mfg. of edible oils.

Chisledon (chĭ'zůldůn), agr. village and parish (pop. 2,075), NE Wiltshire, England, 4 mi. SE of Swindon. Has 13th-15th-cent. church.

Chislehurst (chĭ'zůl–), residential former urban district (1931 pop. 9,876) now in Chislehurst and Sidcup urban dist. (1951 census pop. 83,837), NW Kent, England, 3 mi. E of Bromley; various light industries. Napoleon III died here (1873) after short exile. Near-by noted chalk caves served as air-raid shelters in Second World War.

Chisos Mountains (chē'sůs), extreme W Texas, N-S range (□ c.40) in S Brewster co., lying within the Big Bend of the Rio Grande; 3d-highest range in state. Center of BIG BEND NATIONAL PARK; noted for unusual geological formations. Highest point is Emory Peak (7,835 ft.); just NE is Lost Mine Peak (7,750 ft.).

Chistian (chĭst'yŭn) or **Chishtian** (chĭsht'yŭn), town (pop. 6,245), Bahawalpur state, W Pakistan, 75 mi. ENE of Bahawalpur; wheat, cotton; handloom weaving. Also called Chishtian Mandi.

Chistochina (chĭstůchē'nů), village (1939 pop. 34), E Alaska, on upper Copper R. and at mouth of Chistochina R. (50 mi. long), 110 mi. NE of Valdez, on Tok Cut-off; supply point for prospectors and trappers. Formerly spelled Chestochina.

Chistoozernoye (chē"stůůzyôr'nůyů), town (1948 pop. over 2,000), SW Novosibirsk oblast, Russian SFSR, on Baraba Steppe, near L. Chany, on railroad and 40 mi. SE of Tatarsk; dairy farming.

Chistopol or **Chistopol'** (chēstô'půl), city (1939 pop. estimate 32,000), central Tatar Autonomous SSR, Russian SFSR, port on left bank of Kama R. and 65 mi. SE of Kazan; grain-trading center; shipyards; flour milling, sawmilling, metalworking, mfg. (furniture, knitwear). Floridin deposits near by. Has teachers col. and biological research station. Chartered 1781.

Chistoye (chē'stůyů), town (1939 pop. over 500), W Gorki oblast, Russian SFSR, 18 mi. SW of Chkalovsk; peat works.

Chistyakovo (chēstyä'kůvů), city (1926 pop. 2,121; 1939 pop. c.50,000), E Stalino oblast, Ukrainian SSR, in the Donbas, 38 mi. E of Stalino; coal-mining center; metal- and woodworking. Includes Krasnaya Zvezda and Pelageyevka suburbs (N).

Chiswick, England: see BRENTFORD AND CHISWICK.

Chita (chē'tä), town (pop. 1,013), Boyacá dept., central Colombia, in Cordillera Oriental, at SW foot of Sierra Nevada de Cocuy, 45 mi. NE of Sogamoso; alt. 9,859 ft. Wheat, potatoes, corn. Anc. Indian hamlet, settled 1621 by the Spanish.

Chita (chētä'), oblast (□ 168,200; pop. 1,050,000) in SE Siberian Russian SFSR; ⊙ Chita. Located in E Transbaikalia, on Mongolian and Manchurian frontiers; drained E by Shilka and Argun rivers (headstreams of the Amur), N by Vitim and Olekma rivers, SW by tributaries of Selenga R. Yablonovy Range (SW–NE) forms main drainage watershed. Includes AGA, Buryat-Mongol Natl. Okrug. Continental climate with little precipitation. Has largely coniferous forests, except for steppe vegetation in S. Extensive deposits of tin (Khapcheranga, Olovyannaya, Sherlovaya Gora), tungsten (Kolangui, Bukuka), molybdenum (Gutai), lead-zinc ores (Nerchinsk Range), gold, coal (Chernovskiye Kopi and Bukachacha), and iron. Industry and pop. (mainly Russians, with some Evenki in N) concentrated along Trans-Siberian RR, which crosses entire area W to E. Cattle and sheep raising important; some agr. along river valleys. Mining, lumbering, and tanning are chief industries. Formed 1937 out of E.Siberian Territory; NE gold-mining section (including Skovorodino) detached in 1948 to form Amur oblast.

Chita, city (1939 pop. 102,555; 1946 pop. estimate 150,000), ⊙ Chita oblast, Russian SFSR, on Trans-Siberian RR, on Ingoda R. and 3,000 mi. ESE of Moscow; 52°5'N 113°30'E. Industrial center; locomotive-repair and railroad shops, tanning (sheepskins, footwear), electromechanical works, meat plant, flour and sawmills. Trading and transportation center. Contains lignite mines of Chernovskiye Kopi (W; inc. c.1940). Site of regional mus., several technical schools. Picturesque location amid forested hills on E slopes of Yablonovy Range. Founded 1653 as Cossack stockade; developed after 1825 as place of exile of the Decembrists; was ⊙ Transbaikal govt. (1851–1926).

Chita Bay (chē'tä), Jap. *Chita-wan*, NE arm of Ise Bay, central Honshu, Japan; bounded W by Chita Peninsula; merges SE with Atsumi Bay; 10 mi. long, 5 mi. wide. Handa on W shore.

Chitai Lagoon, Ukrainian SSR: see KITAI LAGOON.

Chital (chĭt'ŭl), town (pop. 4,328), S central Saurashtra, India, 45 mi. SSE of Rajkot; millet, wheat, oilseeds.

Chitaldrug or **Chitaldroog** (chĭtŭl'drōōg), district (□ 4,179; pop. 725,104), N Mysore, India; ⊙ Chitaldrug. On Deccan Plateau; bordered NW by Tungabhadra R. An arid region, subject to famine; agr. (millet, gram, cotton) dependent on numerous reservoirs for storing small annual rainfall (c.22 in.). Cattle grazing, cotton ginning, handloom weaving. Manganese mined in S central chain of hills. Chief towns: Davangere, Chitaldrug, Harihar.

Chitaldrug or **Chitaldroog**, town (pop. 14,528), ⊙ Chitaldrug dist., N Mysore, India, 120 mi. NW of Bangalore; cotton-trade center, served by rail spur (junction at Chikjajur, 19 mi. WSW); cotton ginning and pressing, goldsmithing; handicraft leather footwear. Manganese and copper worked in near-by hills. Fortifications S of town used in 1770s by Hyder Ali. Buddhist coins discovered at site of anc. city of Chandravalli (just W) indicate its existence in 2d cent. A.D. Aimangala or Aymangala, village 14 mi. SE, is training center for revival of handspinning and weaving (khaddar).

Chitambo (chētäm'bä), mission station (pop. c.150), Central Prov., Northern Rhodesia, 20 mi. NNW of Serenje, off Great North Road. Old Chitambo village (pop. 60), 50 mi. NW, at S edge of L. Bangweulu swamps, is near site of Livingstone Memorial, which commemorates spot where David Livingstone died (1873).

Chita Peninsula (chē'tä), Jap. *Chita-hanto*, Aichi prefecture, central Honshu, Japan, bet. Ise Bay (W) and Chita Bay (E); 20 mi. N–S, 3–8 mi. E–W. Generally low and fertile; fish hatcheries. Handa on E shore. Sometimes spelled Tita.

Chitapur or **Chittapur** (both: chē'täpōōr), town (pop. 7,217), Gulbarga dist., W Hyderabad state, India, 22 mi. SE of Gulbarga; millet, cotton; limestone quarrying and dressing; noted hand-woven silk textiles.

Chitarum River or **Tjitarum River** (chētärōōm'), W Java, Indonesia, rises in mts. S of Bandung, in Preanger region, flows c.170 mi. generally NW to Java Sea, near Batavia Bay. Important for irrigation; major works are near Krawang.

Chitaura, India: see JANSATH.

Chit Baragaon (chēt bŭrä'goun), town (pop. 8,241), Ballia dist., E Uttar Pradesh, India, on Tons R. and 9 mi. WNW of Ballia; dal, rice, flour, and oilseed milling; rice, gram, barley, oilseeds. Also called Baragaon. Formerly Chit Firozpur.

Chitembo (chētĕm'bō), town (pop. 749), Bié prov., S central Angola, on road and 80 mi. S of Silva Pôrto; coffee, wheat, corn, beans.

Chit Firozpur, India: see CHIT BARAGAON.

Chitgopa, India: see MOINABAD.

Chitina (chĭt'nô), village (pop. 91), S Alaska, on Copper R. at mouth of Chitina R., and 65 mi. ENE of Valdez; SE terminus of Edgerton Highway, branch of Richardson Highway; supply and trading center for prospectors and trappers. On line of former Copper River and Northwestern RR (abandoned).

Chitina River, S Alaska, rises in St. Elias Mts. near 61°N 141°40'W, at foot of Logan Glacier, flows 120 mi. WNW to Copper R. at Chitina. Lower course is paralleled by Copper River and Northwestern RR (abandoned). Flows through copper-producing region.

Chitor (chĭtōr') or **Chitorgarh** (chĭtōr'gŭr), town (pop. 9,300), ⊙ Chitor dist., S Rajasthan, India, 65 mi. ENE of Udaipur; rail junction; market center (cotton, millet, corn, oilseeds); cotton ginning. Limestone deposits in vicinity. Just E, on long, rocky ridge (c.500 ft. above surrounding plain), is celebrated fort of Chitor, famous in Rajput history for its heroic resistance to Moslem assaults, when the women immolated themselves by fire and the men sallied forth to battle and death rather than surrender. Besieged and captured by Ala-ud-din Khilji in 1303, by Bahadur Shah of Gujarat in 1534, and by Mogul emperor Akbar in 1567–68. Old town was ⊙ Mewar from 8th cent. to 1568, when Udaipur succeeded it. Hill summit covered with ruins and monuments, notably 2 Jain pillars with remarkable sculpturing—Kirthi Stambh (Tower of Fame; c.12th cent.) and Jai Stambh(Tower of Victory; mid-15th cent.). Near village of Nagari, 7 mi. NNE, are anc. Buddhist ruins and Akbar's Lamp, a limestone pillar marking Akbar's hq. during siege of Chitor.

Chitose (chētō'sä), town (pop. 14,816), SW Hokkaido, Japan, 23 mi. SE of Sapporo, in forested area; lumbering.

Chitra (chē'trä), village (pop. 35), Veraguas prov., W central Panama, in Veraguas Mts., 20 mi. NNE of Calobre; coffee, livestock, lumber.

Chitrakut, India: see NARAINI.

Chitral (chĭträl'), princely state (□ 4,000; pop. 107,906) in N North-West Frontier Prov., W Pakistan, in Malakand agency, on S slope of the Hindu Kush; ⊙ Chitral. Bordered by Afghanistan (N,W), Kashmir (NE), Dir (SE); drained by upper Kunar R. A very mountainous area, with several N peaks and glaciers over 20,000 ft. high; Tirich Mir rises to 25,263 ft. Corn, rice, barley, wheat, fruit (apricots, melons, pears) grown in valleys; forests yield fine deodar timber. Mineral deposits (iron ore, lead, antimony, copper, alluvial gold); handicraft metalworking, embroidering, weaving. Exports daggers, metal utensils, cloth fabrics, timber, fruit.

Chitral, village, ⊙ Chitral state, N North-West Frontier Prov., W Pakistan, on Kunar R. and 125 mi. N of Peshawar; market center for grain, fruit, cloth fabrics; handicrafts (knives, sword hilts, embroideries). Small Br. force withstood siege here, 1895, by Afghan tribes.

Chitral River, Pakistan and Afghanistan: see KUNAR RIVER.

Chitré (chētrā'), town (1950 pop. 7,588), ⊙ Herrera prov., S Panama, on branch of Inter-American Highway, near Parita Gulf of the Pacific, 85 mi. SW of Panama city. Commercial center; agr. (onions, tomatoes, lettuce, corn, rice, beans, livestock). Mfg. of soap, ice, beverages; brandy distillery. Has electric power plant, radio station. Founded by Indians in 1821, it expanded very rapidly.

Chittagong (chĭt'ŭgông), dist. (□ 2,569; 1951 pop. 2,321,000), SE East Bengal, E Pakistan, on Burma border; ⊙ Chittagong. Bounded W by Bay of Bengal, N by Fenny R. and Tripura; drained by Karnaphuli and Sangu rivers. Mainly alluvial soil (rice, oilseeds, tobacco, jute, sugar cane, corn, betel leaves, hemp, vegetables); tea gardening; dispersed hill tracts (bamboo, gurjun-oil trees, betel palms). Small coal deposits. Chittagong (main port of E Pakistan) is mfg. center. Pilgrimage center at Sitakund (noted Hindu temples); Buddhist ruins near by. Originally part of anc. Hindu kingdom; conquered (9th cent.) by Buddhist king of Arakan; passed 13th cent. to Mogul empire; reabsorbed by Arakan in 16th cent. Reconquered by Moguls in 17th cent.; ceded to English in 1760. Figured in 1st Burmese War of 1784. Part of former Br. Bengal prov., India, until inc. 1947 into new Pakistan prov. of East Bengal, following creation of Pakistan.

Chittagong, city (1941 pop. 92,301; 1951 census pop., with suburbs, 269,000), ⊙ Chittagong dist., SE East Bengal, E Pakistan, on Karnaphuli R. and 120 mi. SE of Dacca, 8 mi. NNE of river's mouth in Bay of Bengal; 22°24'N 91°50'E. Main port of E Pakistan; rail terminus (spur junction at Sholashahar); trade (rice, oilseeds, jute, tobacco, sugar cane, tea, corn, vegetables) and industrial center; mfg. of chemicals, cotton cloth, soap, bricks, candles, ice); cotton ginning and baling, flour, oil, and rice milling, kerosene tinning and packing, jute pressing, sawmilling; general and electrical engineering factories; rail workshops. Main exports: jute, tea, hides. Similar mfg., tea processing, slate works in surrounding suburbs. Has col. Was 16th-cent. Arakanese pirate stronghold. Lighthouse 11 mi. S. Formerly called Islamabad by Moguls and Porto Grande (in 17th cent.) by the Portuguese, who traded here.

Chittagong Hills, name applied to series of parallel ridges in extreme SE East Pakistan, on Burma border; drained by Karnaphuli and Sangu rivers; rise to over 3,000 ft. Major part forms **Chittagong**

Hill Tracts, a district (□ 5,007; 1951 pop. 289,000) of East Bengal, E Pakistan; ⊙ Rangamati. Agr. (rice, cotton, oilseeds, tobacco, sugar cane, tea, corn); bamboo tracts (used in paper mfg.); gurjun, jarool, and toon trees; tea processing, plywood mfg. (in hill tracts); rice milling (at Rangamati). Main villages: Rangamati, Ramgarh. History consists mainly of tribal disturbances; most of dist. politically governed by tribal chiefs. Present dist. formed 1860. Part of former Br. Bengal prov., India, until inc. 1947 into new Pakistan prov. of East Bengal, following creation of Pakistan.

Chittapur, India: see CHITAPUR.

Chittaranjan (chĭ″tŭrŭn′jŭn), village, Santal Parganas dist., E Bihar, India, 14 mi. NW of Asansol; locomotive factory. Formerly called Mihijam.

Chittar River (chĭt-tär′), S Madras, India, rises on E slope of Western Ghats S of Shencottah, flows NE past Kuttalam (falls), and SE past Tenkasi, through fertile agr. valley, to Tambraparni R. 7 mi. NE of Palamcottah; 46 mi. long.

Chittavalsa, India: see BIMLIPATAM.

Chittenango (chĭtŭnăng′gō), village (pop. 1,307), Madison co., central N.Y., 15 mi. E of Syracuse, in farming and dairying area; summer resort. Chittenango Falls village, and a state park (122 acres) which includes scenic Chittenango Falls in small Chittenango Creek, are just S.

Chittenango Falls, N.Y.: see CHITTENANGO.

Chittenden, county (□ 532; pop. 62,570), NW Vt., bounded W by L. Champlain, with Green Mts. in E; ⊙ Burlington. Mfg. (textiles, wood and metal products, building materials, clothing), dairy and maple products, fruit; granite, talc. Lake and mtn. resorts. Drained by Winooski and Lamoille rivers. Organized 1782.

Chittenden, town (pop. 424), Rutland co., W central Vt., 6 mi. N of Rutland, partly in Green Mtn. Natl. Forest.

Chittim, Cyprus: see CITIUM.

Chittivalsa, India: see BIMLIPATAM.

Chittoor (chĭtōōr′), district (□ 5,951; pop. 1,632,395), W Madras, India; ⊙ Chittoor. On Deccan Plateau, crossed by S spurs of Eastern Ghats (rise to 3,863 ft. in peak NW of Chittoor). Agr.: rice, millet, oilseeds, sugar cane (intensive cultivation), cotton. Dyewood, sandalwood in forested hills. Main towns: Chittoor, Tirupati.

Chittoor, city (pop. 27,835), ⊙ Chittoor dist., W central Madras, India, 80 mi. WNW of Madras; road and trade center in agr. area; rice and oilseed milling. Rail junction of Pakala is 16 mi. N. Sandalwood, dyewood (red sanders) in near-by hills.

Chittur (chĭ′tōōr), city (pop. 12,732) in E exclave of Cochin, in SW Madras, India, 38 mi. ENE of Trichur; cotton ginning, rice and oilseed milling, tile mfg., hand-loom weaving.

Chitu or **Ch'i-tu** (chē′dōō′), Jap. *Shichito* (shē′chĭtō), village (1935 pop. 1,897), N Formosa, on Keelung R. and 3 mi. SW of Keelung, on railroad; coal, gold, and silver mining; rice, tea, livestock.

Chitung or **Ch'i-tung** (chē′dōōng′), town (pop. 54,857), ⊙ Chitung co. (pop. 98,349), N Kiangsu prov., China, 40 mi. NNE of Shanghai, across estuary of Yangtze R. (N), near Yellow Sea coast; cotton, corn, beans, wheat. Until 1929 called Hweilungchen.

Chiu- or **Ch'iu-,** for Chinese names beginning thus and not found here: see under KIU-.

Chiuchamayo River, Bolivia: see CINTI RIVER.

Chiu-chiang. 1 City, Kiangsi prov., China: see KIUKIANG. **2** Town, Kwangtung prov., China: see KOWKONG.

Chiu-chiang, Formosa: see KIUKANG.

Chiuchín (chyōōchēn′), town (pop. 115), Lima dept., W central Peru, in Cordillera Occidental, 80 mi. NNE of Lima; thermal springs.

Chiuchiu (chyōōchyōō′), village (1930 pop. 305), Antofagasta prov., N Chile, oasis on Loa R., 20 mi. NE of Calama, in Atacama Desert; Agr. center (grain, citrus fruit, wine, vegetables, sheep). Ruins of pre-Columbian city near by.

Chiuduno (kūdōō′nô), village (pop. 1,709), Bergamo prov., Lombardy, N Italy, 9 mi. ESE of Bergamo; button factories.

Chiuling (jyōō′lĭng′), Mandarin *Chiao-ling* (jyou′lĭng′), town (pop. 6,196), ⊙ Chiuling co. (pop. 103,384), NE Kwangtung prov., China, on branch of Mei R. and 24 mi. N of Meihsien; rice, wheat, sugar cane, oranges. Coal and manganese mining near by. Until 1914 called Chenping.

Ch'iung-, for Chinese names beginning thus and not found here: see under KIUNG-.

Chiuppano (kūp-pä′nô), village (pop. 1,503), Vicenza prov., Veneto, N Italy, on Astico R. and 15 mi. N of Vicenza; marmalade, mustard.

Chiuro (kū′rô), village (pop. 845), Sondrio prov., Lombardy, N Italy, in the Valtellina, 6 mi. E of Sondrio; sawmill, alcohol distillery.

Chiusa (kū′zä), Ger. *Klausen,* town (pop. 1,111), Bolzano prov., Trentino–Alto Adige, N Italy, on Isarco R. and 14 mi. NNE of Bolzano; woolen textiles, balsam sachets. Has 15th-16th-cent. houses, convent.

Chiusa di Pesio (dē pä′zyô), village (pop. 1,784), Cuneo prov., Piedmont, NW Italy, on branch of Tanaro R. and 8 mi. SE of Cuneo; pottery works, limekilns.

Chiusano di San Domenico (kūzä′nô dē sän dômä′nēkô), village (pop. 2,013), Avellino prov., Campania, S Italy, 7 mi. ENE of Avellino.

Chiusa Sclafani (kū′zä skläfä′nē), town (pop. 5,549), Palermo prov., W Sicily, 10 mi. S of Corleone.

Chiusi (kū′zē), anc. *Clusium,* town (pop. 2,534), Siena prov., Tuscany, central Italy, 23 mi. WSW of Perugia, near L. of Chiusi (□ 1; 2 mi. long; connected with the Chiana). Agr. center (wine, olive oil, macaroni); machinery mfg. Hydroelectric plant. Bishopric. Has catacombs, anc. cathedral, mus. of Etruscan antiquities. Once a powerful Etruscan town whose king, Lars Porsena, marched against Rome. Many tombs of the period (5th cent. B.C.) discovered here.

Chiuta, Lake (shēōō′tü), on Nyasaland-Mozambique border, SE Africa, 40 mi. SE of S tip of L. Nyasa; 40 mi. long, 2–8 mi. wide. Has indefinite, marshy S shore. Drained N by Lugenda R. L. Chilwa is 10 mi. S. Also called L. Amaramba.

Chiva (chē′vä), town (pop. 4,486), Valencia prov., E Spain, 19 mi. W of Valencia; mfg. of ceramics, soap, brandy; flour milling, olive-oil processing. Produces table wines. Has parochial church and palace of dukes of Medinasidonia.

Chivacoa (chēväkō′ä), town (pop. 2,425), Yaracuy state, N Venezuela, in coastal range, 16 mi. SW of San Felipe, in agr. region (coffee, sugar cane, cacao, corn, fruit). Lead deposits in vicinity.

Chivasso (kēväs′sô), town (pop, 6,002), Torino prov., Piedmont, NW Italy, at junction of Cavour Canal with Po R., 13 mi. NE of Turin, in cereal- and hemp-growing region; rail junction; steelworks, food cannery, textile mills; liquor, confectionery. Has cathedral begun 1415.

Chivay (chēvī′), town (pop. 2,088), ⊙ Cailloma prov. (□ 4,745; pop. 28,363), Arequipa dept., S Peru, in high Andean valley, at SE foot of Cordillera de Chilca, 60 mi. N of Arequipa; alt. 11,650 ft. Grain, potatoes, cattle, alpacas.

Chivé (chēvā′), village, Pando dept., NW Bolivia, on Madre de Dios R. and 10 mi. ENE of Puerto Heath; rubber.

Chivemba, Angola: see CHIBEMBA.

Chivilcoy (chēvēlkoi′), city (pop. 22,178), ⊙ Chivilcoy dist. (□ 771; pop. 46,594), N central Buenos Aires prov., Argentina, 95 mi. WSW of Buenos Aires; agr. center (sunflower seeds, grain, livestock); dairying, flour milling, meat packing, tanning; mfg. of ceramics, hosiery, furniture, sweets. Has natl. col.

Chiviyateru, Ceylon: see JAFFNA, town.

Chixoy River (chēchoi′), central Guatemala, rises SW of Huehuetenango as Río Negro, flows E, past Sacapulas, and N in winding course to Mex. border, here joining Pasión R. 25 mi. W of Sayaxché to form USUMACINTA RIVER Also called Salinas R. in lower course. Forms border bet. Quiché (W), Baja Verapaz and Alta Verapaz (E) depts., and bet. Mexico and Guatemala. Length, c.250 mi.; navigable c.140 mi. Receives Salamá R.

Chiyoda (chēyō′dä), town (pop. 11,196), Chiba prefecture, central Honshu, Japan, 7 mi. NE of Chiba; agr. center (rice, wheat); poultry.

Chizatau (kē′zütü″ōō), Rum. *Chizătău,* Hung. *Kiszető* (kĕsh′zĕtů), village (pop. 1,115), Timisoara prov., W Rumania, on railroad and 23 mi. E of Timisoara. Also spelled Chisatau.

Chizu (chē′zōō), town (pop. 12,739), Tottori prefecture, S Honshu, Japan, 16 mi. S of Tottori; agr. center (tea, rice); lumber (cryptomeria), arrowroot starch, raw silk. Sometimes spelled Tizu.

Chizumula Island, Nyasaland: see CHISAMULA ISLAND.

Chizzola (kētsô′lä), village (pop. 594), Trento prov., Trentino–Alto Adige, N Italy, on Adige R. and 6 mi. S of Rovereto; alcohol distillery.

Chkalov (chkä′lůf), oblast (□ 47,400; 1939 pop. 1,677,013) in SE European Russian SFSR; ⊙ Chkalov. In S foothills of the S Urals (E) and Obshchi Syrt hills (W); drained by Ural, Sakmara, Samara, Greater Kinel, and Ilek rivers. Humid continental (N; short summers) and steppe (S) climate. Minerals chiefly mined in Orsk-Khalilovo industrial dist.; include limonite, hematite, nickel, cobalt, copper, chromite, lignite, jasper, and limestone; salt (Sol-Iletsk), petroleum and asphalt (Buguruslan, Saraktash), gold (Aidyrlinski, Sini Shikhan), oil shale, phosphorite, gypsum, and fireproof clay (S, SE). Extensive agr. (wheat, millet, sunflowers) and cattle raising; sheep and goats (S); truck gardening (around Orsk and Chkalov). Lightly forested (NE, NW). Industries based on mining (metallurgy in Novo-Troitsk, nickel refining in Orsk, copper and sulphur works in Mednogorsk, saltworks in Sol-Iletsk) and agr. (flour milling, meat packing, distilling, food processing and preserving). Oil cracking (Orsk, Buguruslan), machine mfg. (Orsk, Buzuluk, Chkalov), light mfg. (Chkalov). Rural industries: wool weaving, sheepskin processing. Main urban centers: Chkalov, Orsk, Buzuluk, Buguruslan. Well-developed rail net; occasional spring navigation on Ural R. below Chkalov. Formed 1934 out of Middle Volga Territory, which had absorbed Orenburg govt. in 1928. Gained industrial importance following development of Orsk-Khalilovo dist. before Second World War.

Chkalov, city (1939 pop. 172,925), ⊙ Chkalov oblast, Russian SFSR, on right bank of Ural R. (occasional spring navigation), just E of Sakmara R. mouth, and 750 mi. ESE of Moscow; 51°46′N 55°7′E. Rail junction; N terminus of Trans-Caspian RR (locomotive and car repair shops); major flour-milling and agr.-processing (hides, meat, dairy products, grain, hops, animal feed) center; mfg. (aircraft and tractor parts, clothing, saddles, felt boots, rail ties). Medical, agr., and teachers colleges. Has museums, 18th-cent. cathedrals, old stone gate, churches, and mosque. Near by (W) is Menovoi Dvor, site of former caravan trading center. City founded (1735) on site of Orsk; moved (1743) to present location (formerly occupied by Rus. frontier stronghold of Berda); chartered in 1744. Assaulted by peasant rebels under Yemelyan Pugachev (1773). Noted caravan center on route from Central Asia to European Russia in 19th cent.; largely developed after building of Trans-Caspian RR (1905). Formerly called Orenburg; renamed 1938 for Rus. aviator Valeri Chkalov. Was ⊙ Orenburg govt. until 1928.

Chkalov Island, narrow, low-lying isl. at N end of Tatar Strait, in Khabarovsk Territory, Russian SFSR, 25 mi. NE of Nikodalyevsk; 10 mi. long. Fisheries; processing plant. Formerly called Udd Isl.; renamed for Soviet aviator who ended long-distance flight here, 1936. Near-by isls. named Baidukov (E) and Belyakov (NE).

Chkalovo (chkä′lůvů). **1** Village (1948 pop. over 2,000), N Kokchetav oblast, Kazakh SSR, 50 mi. ENE of Kokchetav; wheat; metalworks. Until 1939, Bogodukhovka. **2** Village (1947 pop. over 500), on W coast of S Sakhalin, Russian SFSR, on Sea of Japan, 20 mi. S of Nevelsk; fishing. Under Jap. rule (1905–45), called Kitose. **3** Village (1939 pop. over 2,000), S Dnepropetrovsk oblast, Ukrainian SSR, 8 mi. N of Nikopol, in manganese dist. Until 1939, Novo-Nikolayevka.

Chkalovsk (–lůfsk), town (1926 pop. 3,925), W Gorki oblast, Russian SFSR, on Volga R. and 40 mi. NW of Gorki; metalworking center. Until 1927, called Vasileva Sloboda and later, until 1937, Vasilevo.

Chkalovski or **Chkalovskiy** (chkä′lůfskē), town (1944 pop. over 500), central Leninabad oblast, Tadzhik SSR, 5 mi. E of Leninabad rail station, in cotton- and silkgrowing area. Until 1944 called Kostakoz.

Chkalovskoye (–skŭyů). **1** Village (1926 pop. 4,215), SE Chuvash Autonomous SSR, Russian SFSR, on left tributary of Sviyaga R. and 32 mi. S of Kanash; wheat. Phosphorite deposits near by (S). Until 1939, Shikhirdany. **2** Village (1939 pop. over 2,000), SW Maritime Territory, Russian SFSR, near Trans-Siberian RR (Sviyagino station) and 90 mi. NNE of Voroshilov, in agr. area (grain, soybeans, rice, sugar beets). Graphite deposits near by. Prior to 1939, Zenkovka.

Chkhari (chůkhä′rē), village (1926 pop. 1,362), W central Georgian SSR, 13 mi. E of Kutaisi; vineyards.

Chkhorotsku (chůkhŭrůtskōō′), village (1932 pop. estimate 1,800), W Georgian SSR, 35 mi. WNW of Kutaisi; tea. Sometimes spelled Chkhorotskhu.

Chlong or **Chhlong** (both: shlông), village, Kratie prov., SE Cambodia, on left bank of Mekong R. and 16 mi. S of Kratie; sawmilling center (hardwoods).

Chloride (klô′rīd), village (1940 pop. 719), Mohave co., W Ariz., 15 mi. NW of Kingman; alt. c.4,000 ft.; turquoise mines.

Chlumec (khlōō′mĕts), Ger. *Kulm* (kōōlm), village (pop. 539), NW Bohemia, Czechoslovakia, on railroad and 5 mi. NW of Usti nad Labem. Site of French defeat (1813) by allied Russian, Prussian, and Austrian armies.

Chlumec nad Cidlinou (nät′ tsĭ″dlĭnō), Ger. *Chlumetz an der Zidlina,* town (pop. 4,027), E Bohemia, Czechoslovakia, 16 mi. WSW of Hradec Kralove, in agr. area (oats, potatoes); rail junction; mfg. of agr. machinery. Fishing in near-by ponds.

Chmielnik (khůmyĕl′nēk) [Pol.,=hop field], Rus. *Khmelnik* or *Khmel'nik* (both: khmě′lyůněk), town (pop. 3,171), Kielce prov., SE Poland, 18 mi. SSE of Kielce; tanning, flour milling. Before the Second World War, 85% of the population was Jewish.

Choachí (chōächē′), village (pop. 722), Dundinamarca dept., central Colombia, in Cordillera Oriental, 13 mi. ESE of Bogotá; alt. 6,450 ft.; wheat, corn, potatoes, livestock. Thermal springs 3 mi. N.

Choápam (chōä′päm), officially Santiago Choápam, town (pop. 615), Oaxaca, S Mexico, in Sierra Madre del Sur, 55 mi. ENE of Oaxaca; cereals, sugar cane, coffee, fruit, livestock.

Choapa River (chwä′pä), Coquimbo prov., N central Chile, rises in the Andes near Argentina border, flows 65 mi. WNW, past Salamanca, to the Pacific 25 mi. SW of Illapel.

Choaspes, Iran: see KARKHEH RIVER.

Choban Bey (chōbän′ bā′) or **Juban Bey** (jōō′băn bā′), Fr. *Tchoban Bey,* village, Aleppo prov., NW Syria, near Turkish border, on railroad, and 32 mi. NNE of Aleppo; cotton, cereals.

Chobe (chō′bā), district (pop. 5,159), Bechuanaland Protectorate, adjoining Ngamiland.

Chobe River, S central Africa, rises in marshes near 18°30'S 23°30'E, flows c.120 mi. ENE along border of Bechuanaland Protectorate and South-West Africa's Caprivi Strip to the Zambezi (right bank) opposite Kasungula (Northern Rhodesia). It is usually considered the lower course of KWANDO RIVER.

Chobham (chŏ'bŭm), residential town and parish (pop. 4,724), NW Surrey, England, 3 mi. NW of Woking.

Chobien, Poland: see CHOBIENIA.

Chobienia (khôbyĕ'nyä), Ger. *Köben* or *Köben an der Oder* (kû'bŭn än dĕr ō'dûr), town (1939 pop. 1,649; 1946 pop. 338) in Lower Silesia, after 1945 in Wroclaw prov., SW Poland, on the Oder and 18 mi. SE of Glogau (Glogow); agr. market (grain, sugar beets, potatoes, livestock). Considerably damaged in Second World War. After 1945, briefly called Chobien, Pol. *Chobień*.

Chobo (chŭ'bô'), town, Hoabinh prov., N Vietnam, on Black R. and 45 mi. SW of Hanoi. Coal mining (SE); trade in lac, benzoin, cardamoms, horns.

Choc (shŏk), village, NW St. Lucia, B.W.I., 2 mi. NNE of Castries, on Choc Bay; sugar cane, limes, coconuts. The Union agr. experiment station is near by.

Chocamán (chōkämän'), town (pop. 2,538), Veracruz, E Mexico, at E foot of Pico de Orizaba, on railroad and 10 mi. NW of Córdoba; alt. 4,442 ft.; corn, coffee, sugar cane, fruit.

Chocaya (chōkī'ä), village, Potosí dept., SW Bolivia, on W slopes of Cordillera de Chichas 48 mi. SE of Uyuni, and on Villazon-Uyuni RR; alt. 12,251 ft. Major tin-mining center; shipping point for Oploca tin mines, 5 mi. SW.

Chocen (khô'tsĕnyŭ), Czech *Choceň*, Ger. *Chotzen* (khô'tsĭn), town (pop. 6,789), E Bohemia, Czechoslovakia, on Ticha Orlice R. and 20 mi. E of Pardubice; rail junction; aircraft mfg., cotton spinning; agr. center (notably barley for export).

Ch'o-ch'iang, China: see CHARKHLIK.

Chochiin, Korea: see CHOCHIWON.

Chochis, Cerro, Bolivia: see SANTIAGO, SERRANÍA DE.

Chochiwon (chô'chē'wŭn'), Jap. *Choshiin*, town (1949 pop. 18,276), S.Chungchong prov., S Korea, 10 mi. WSW of Chongju; rail junction; agr. center (rice, soybeans, tobacco, cotton); silk, cotton mills.

Chocholá (chōchōlä'), town (pop. 1,696), Yucatan, SE Mexico, 20 mi. SW of Mérida; henequen.

Chochow, China: see CHOHSIEN.

Chochu (chŭ'chōō'), town, Thainguyen prov., N Vietnam, 24 mi. NW of Thainguyen.

Chocianow (khôtsyä'nōōf), Pol. *Chocianów*, Ger. *Kotzenau* (kô'tsŭnou), town (1939 pop. 4,301; 1946 pop. 1,707) in Lower Silesia, after 1945 in Wroclaw prov., SW Poland, 19 mi. NW of Liegnitz (Legnica); agr. market (grain, potatoes, livestock).

Chociwel (khôtsē'vĕl), Ger. *Freienwalde* (frīŭnväl'dŭ), town (1939 pop. 3,406; 1946 pop. 402) in Pomerania, after 1945 in Szczecin prov., NW Poland, 15 mi. NE of Stargard; agr. market (grain, sugar beets, potatoes, livestock). Ruins of old town walls. After 1945, briefly called Chociwol.

Chocó (chōkō'), department (□ 17,981; 1938 pop. 111,216; 1950 estimate 112,420), W and NW Colombia, on the Pacific and the Caribbean; ⊙ Quibdó. Bordered NW by Panama; in E is Cordillera Occidental; N–S, through the length of Chocó, are Atrato and San Juan river valleys (both rivers are navigable), separated from coastal lowlands by Serranía de Baudó. A fertile, tropical region with year-round rains, it is little developed agriculturally. Main sources of income are its rich gold- and platinum-placer mines, making Colombia one of the world's leading platinum producers. Contains also silver, osmium, iridium, paladium, copper, iron, sulphur, lime, coal, petroleum deposits. Its luxuriant forests yield hardwood, tagua nuts (vegetable ivory), rubber, chicle, balsam, balata and other gums. Chocó is largely inhabited by primitive Indian tribes. Was administered as an intendancy until 1948.

Chocó, Farallones de, Colombia: see CITARÁ, FARALLONES DE.

Chocó Bay, indentation of the Pacific coast of W Colombia, extends 135 mi. S from Charambirá Point (4°15'N) in Chocó dept. to Guascama Point (2°38'N) in Nariño dept. Port of Buenaventura (Valle del Cauca dept.) is on its NE shore.

Chocolate Mountains. 1 In Yuma co., SW Ariz., W of Castle Dome Mts. and E of Colorado R.; rise to 2,820 ft. **2** In SE Calif., desert range extending c.70 mi. NW–SE along E side of Salton Sea and the Imperial Valley; mts. rise to c.2,000 ft. Gold mines. Barren Mts. are a spur at SE end, near Colorado R.

Chocontá (chōkōntä'), town (pop. 2,041), Cundinamarca dept., central Colombia, on Bogotá R., in Cordillera Oriental, on railroad, on Pan American Highway and 45 mi. NE of Bogotá; alt. 9,649 ft. Wheat, corn, potatoes, fruit, cattle; flour milling. Coal mines near by.

Chocope (chōkō'pā), town (pop. 1,302), Libertad dept., NW Peru, on coastal plain, in irrigated Chicama R. valley, 26 mi. NNW of Trujillo, on railroad and Pan American Highway. Sugar cane; cattle raising.

Chocorua (shŭkŏ'rōōŭ), resort village in Tamworth town, Carroll co., E N.H., 8 mi. SW of Conway and on small **Chocorua Lake.** To NW is **Mount Chocorua** (3,475 ft.) in Sandwich Range.

Chocques (shôk), outer W suburb (pop. 2,642) of Béthune, Pas-de-Calais dept., N France, in coal-mining area; chemical plant; sugar-beet distilling, brewing.

Choctaw (chŏk'tô). **1** County (□ 918; pop. 19,152), SW Ala.; ⊙ Butler. In Black Belt, bordering on Miss., bounded E by Tombigbee R. Cotton, corn, peanuts, livestock; lumber milling. Formed 1847. **2** County (□ 417; pop. 11,009), central Miss.; ⊙ Ackerman. Drained by Big Black, Noxubee, and Yockanookany rivers. Agr. (cotton, corn, lespedeza, sweet potatoes), stock raising, lumbering. Formed 1833. **3** County (□ 784; pop. 20,405), SE Okla.; ⊙ Hugo. Bounded S by Red R., here forming Texas line; drained by Muddy Boggy and Clear Boggy creeks and by Kiamichi R. Agr. (cotton, grain, livestock, peanuts, corn). Mfg., farm-products processing at Hugo. Timber. Formed 1907.

Choctaw, town (pop. 355), Oklahoma co., central Okla., 14 mi. E of Oklahoma City, in agr. area.

Choctawhatchee Bay (chŏktŭhă'chē, –tô–), NW Fla., arm (c.30 mi. long, 3–5 mi. wide) of the Gulf of Mexico, 35 mi. E of Pensacola, connected with Pensacola Bay via Santa Rosa Sound; E end of Santa Rosa Isl. extends almost across its mouth. Receives Choctawhatchee R. (E). Forms part of Gulf Intracoastal Waterway.

Choctawhatchee River, SE Ala. and NW Fla., rises in central Barbour co., flows SSW to Geneva, Ala. (here joined by Pea R.), thence S into Fla. and W to E end of Choctawhatchee Bay; 174 mi. long. Navigable in lower course; has formed large delta at mouth.

Chodau, Czechoslovakia: see CHODOV.

Chodavaram (chō'dŭvŭrŭm). **1** Village, East Godavari dist., NE Madras, India, 30 mi. N of Rajahmundry, in SE foothills of Eastern Ghats; supplies bamboo to paper mills at Rajahmundry. **2** Town (pop. 8,379), Vizagapatam dist., NE Madras, India, 26 mi. WNW of Vizagapatam; sugar, rice, and oilseed milling.

Chodecz (khô'dĕch), Rus. *Khodech* (khô'dĕch), town (pop. 1,551), Bydgoszcz prov., central Poland, 17 mi. S of Wloclawek; agr. market.

Chodien (chŭ'dyĕn'), village, Backan prov., N Vietnam, 20 mi. NW of Backan; zinc mines.

Chodorow, Ukrainian SSR: see KHODOROV.

Chodov (khô'dôf), Ger. *Chodau* (khō'dou), town (pop. 2,793), W Bohemia, Czechoslovakia, 6 mi. NE of Falknov; rail junction; porcelain mfg.

Chodziez (hô'jĕsh), Pol. *Chodzież*, Ger. *Kolmar* (kôl'mär), town (1946 pop. 7,694), Poznan prov., W Poland, 40 mi. N of Poznan; mfg. of bricks, machinery, furniture, porcelain, liqueur; flour milling, sawmilling.

Choele-Choel (chwā'lā-chwĕl'), village (pop. estimate 1,500), ⊙ Avellaneda dept., N Río Negro natl. territory, Argentina, inland port on the navigable Río Negro (whose arms here form a large isl., Choele-Choel), on railroad and 170 mi. NW of Viedma; agr. center (corn, alfalfa, fruit, wine, livestock; apiculture); trade in leather, wool, fruit; sawmills. Airport.

Choen, Korea: see CHANGYON.

Choerhcheng, Manchuria: see TALAI.

Chofu (chō'fōō). **1** Town (pop. 20,117), Greater Tokyo, central Honshu, Japan, just W of Tokyo; rice and mulberry fields; raw silk. **2** Town, Yamaguchi prefecture, Japan: see SHIMONOSEKI, city.

Chogao (chŭ'gou'), town, Mytho prov., S Vietnam, in Mekong delta, 7 mi. E of Mytho; rice.

Chohsien (jô'shyĕn'), town, ⊙ Chohsien co. (pop. 196,774), N Hopeh prov., China, 35 mi. SW of Peking and on Peking-Hankow RR; wheat, cotton, millet, rice. Until 1913 called Chochow.

Choibalsan (choi'bälsän), **Choibolsan** (–bōlsän), or **Choybalsan** (choi'bälsän), aimak (□ 47,500; pop. 50,000), E Mongolian People's Republic; ⊙ Choibalsan. Bounded N by Chita oblast of Russian SFSR and E by China's Inner Mongolian Autonomous Region, it is largely a steppe plateau drained by Kerulen R. Called Eastern Aimak until 1946.

Choibalsan, Choibolsan, Choybalsan, city (pop. c.10,000), ⊙ Choibalsan aimak, E Mongolian People's Republic, on Kerulen R. and 350 mi. E of Ulan Bator, and on railroad from Brozya (USSR); 2d-largest city of Mongolia; center of narrow-gauge rail lines to near-by coal mines. Formerly a monastery called San Beise or Kerulen; later (1931–46) known as Bayan Tumen or Bain Tumen; city was renamed (1946) for the Mongolian premier.

Choiceland, village (pop. 253), central Sask., 22 mi. WNW of Nipawin; dairying, wheat.

Choiren, Choirin (choi'rŭn), or **Choyron** (–rōn), village, Central Aimak, central Mongolian People's Republic, 150 mi. SE of Ulan Bator and on highway to Kalgan.

Choiseul (shwäzûl'), village (pop. 496), SW St. Lucia, B.W.I., 16 mi. SSW of Castries; coconuts, sugar cane, fruit; fishing.

Choiseul, volcanic island (□ 1,000; pop. c.4,000), Solomon Isls., SW Pacific, 30 mi. SE of Bougainville across Bougainville Strait; 90 mi. long, 20 mi. wide. Produces copra. In Second World War, isl. was occupied 1942 by Japan; taken 1943 by U.S.

Choiseul Sound, inlet (c.20 mi. long, 2 mi. wide), East Falkland Isl.

Choisy-le-Roi (shwäzē'-lŭ-rwä'), town (pop. 27,213), Seine dept., N central France, a SSE suburb of Paris, 7 mi. from Notre Dame Cathedral; port on the Seine; cycle and crystal works; mfg. of linoleum, varnish, hosiery, household appliances. Its ruined château, built by Mansard, was residence of Mlle de Montpensier.

Choix (choish), town (pop. 1,462), Sinaloa, NW Mexico, in W outliers of Sierra Madre Occidental, 28 mi. NE of El Fuerte; corn, chick-peas, sugar cane. Silver, gold, copper deposits near by (N).

Choja (chō'jä), town (pop. 4,514), Chiba prefecture, central Honshu, Japan, on E Chiba Peninsula, 3 mi. N of Chara; beach resort; agr., poultry raising.

Chojna (khoi'nä), Ger. *Königsberg* (kû'nĭkhsbĕrk), town (1939 pop. 6,767; 1946 pop. 1,484) in Brandenburg, after 1945 in Szczecin prov., NW Poland, 35 mi. S of Stettin; vegetable market; brewing. In Second World War, c.75% destroyed. After 1945, briefly called Chojnice Odrzanskie, Pol. *Chojnice Odrzańskie*.

Chojnice (khoinē'tsĕ), Ger. *Konitz* (kō'nĭts), town (pop. 12,444), Bydgoszcz prov., NW Poland, 45 mi. NNW of Bydgoszcz, in lake area; rail junction; mfg. (bricks, furniture, roofing materials, linen), food processing (beer, vinegar, candy), mineral-water bottling.

Chojnice Odrzanskie, Poland: see CHOJNA.

Chojnow (khoi'nōōf), Pol. *Chojnów*, Ger. *Haynau* (hī'nou), town (1939 pop. 11,114; 1946 pop. 5,467) in Lower Silesia, after 1945 in Wroclaw prov., SW Poland, 11 mi. WNW of Liegnitz (Legnica); metal- and woodworking, tanning, oil pressing. Has medieval castle, once residence of Pol. Piast princes.

Chojo, Korea: see CHANGSONG.

Choka, Yugoslavia: see COKA.

Choke Mountains (chō'kā), NW Ethiopia, in Gojjam prov., S of L. Tana, in a great bend of the Blue Nile. Chief peaks: Birhan (13,625 ft.), Tala (c.13,450 ft.).

Chokfactoly, Alaska: see CHUKFAKTOOLIK.

Chokhatauri (chŭkhä"tŏō'rē), town (1932 pop. estimate 6,210), SW Georgian SSR, in Guria region, 30 mi. SW of Kutsaisi; tea.

Chokio (chŭkī'ō), village (pop. 541), Stevens co., W Minn., 13 mi. W of Morris; dairy products.

Choko. 1 Town, S.Cholla prov., Korea: see CHANGHUNG. **2** Town, S.Chungchong prov., Korea: see CHANGHANG.

Chokoin, Korea: see CHANGHOWAN.

Chokurdakh (chŭkōōrdäkh'), settlement (1945 pop. under 500), N Yakut Autonomous SSR, Russian SFSR, on left bank of Indigirka R., just N of Allaikha, which it has supplanted as trading and arctic observation post. Fishing, reindeer raising; airfield. Developed in 1940s.

Cholach (chŭ'läk'), town, Vinhlong prov., S Vietnam, in Mekong delta, 10 mi. E of Vinhlong; rice. Sometimes spelled Cholac.

Cholan (jô'län'), Jap. *Takuran* (tä'kōōrän), village (1935 pop. 6,689), NW Formosa, 15 mi. NE of Taichung; tea processing, rice milling; bamboo and wooden articles; sericulture.

Cholar, El, Argentina: see EL CHOLAR.

Cholavandan, India: see SOLAVANDAN.

Cholburi, Thailand: see CHONBURI.

Cholchol (chōlchōl'), village (1930 pop. 1,043), Cautín prov., S central Chile, 17 mi. NW of Temuco; grain-growing center; also oats, peas, potatoes; livestock. Lumbering, flour milling, dairying.

Chole, India: see KALYAN.

Cholesey (chōl'zē), agr. village and parish (pop. 2,478), N Berkshire, England, 2 mi. SW of Wallingford. Has county mental hosp., Norman church.

Cholet (shôlā'), town (pop. 23,214), Maine-et-Loire dept., W France, 33 mi. SW of Angers; important textile center (cotton and linen goods) and cattle market. Other mfg.: cartons, footwear, toys, organic fertilizer. Cholet was completely destroyed in the wars of the Vendée (1793–95). Here in 1793 the Vendeans were defeated by Republicans. Town was rebuilt in 19th cent.

Cholguán (chōlgwän'), village (1930 pop. 343), Ñuble prov., S central Chile, on railroad, on Itata R. and 40 mi. S of Chillán; grain, wine, beans, livestock. The Salto de Laja, waterfalls on Laja R., are near by.

Cholila (chōlē'lä), village (pop. estimate 500), NW Chubut natl. territory, Argentina, in foothills of the Andes, 40 mi. N of Esquel; stock raising, lumbering. Coal deposits near by.

Cholla-namdo, Korea: see SOUTH CHOLLA.

Cholla-pukdo, Korea: see NORTH CHOLLA.

Cholm, Poland: see CHELM.

Cholmondeley (chŭm'lē), agr. village and parish (pop. 278), SW Cheshire, England, 8 mi. W of Nantwich. Castle is seat of marquess of Cholmondeley.

Cholo (chō'lō), administrative center, Southern Prov., Nyasaland, in Shire Highlands, 20 mi. SSE of Blantyre; alt. 3,100 ft. Former coffee-growing center, now tobacco; also tea, soybeans, tung, sisal, corn, rice.

Choloma (chōlō'mä), town (pop. 2,491), Cortés dept., NW Honduras, in Sula Valley, on railroad and 10 mi. NNE of San Pedro Sula; commercial center in banana zone. Called El Paraíso until early 1930s.

Cholomon or **Kholomon** (both: khôlômôn'), mountain in Greek Macedonia, on Chalcidice peninsula, rises to 3,819 ft. 7 mi. NE of Polygyros.

Cholon (chŭ'lŭn'), city (1936 pop. 145,254), S Vietnam, in Cochin China, on left bank of the Chinese Arroyo (affluent of Saigon R.), on railroad and 3 mi. SW of SAIGON, with which it is jointly administered (since 1932). Leading rice-processing and trading center and natural outlet for S Vietnam and Cambodia; rice milling, distilling, soap and tobacco processing. Pop. is ⅓ Chinese, who control most of rice industry and river vessels. Essentially a Chinese city, it was founded 1778 by Chinese emigrants from Bienhoa. Erected to a municipality in 1879, it rapidly merged with Saigon into a single urban complex.

Cholpon (chŭlpôn'), village, Tyan-San oblast, Kirghiz SSR, N of Naryn.

Cholpon-Ata (chŭlpôn'-ŭtä'), village (1939 pop. over 500), N Issyk-Kul oblast, Kirghiz SSR, on N shore of Issyk-Kul (lake), 45 mi. ENE of Rybachye; children's health resort; horse farm.

Cholsan (chŭl'sän'), Jap. *Tetsuzan*, township (1944 pop. 12,501), N.Pyongan prov., N Korea, 27 mi. SSE of Sinuiju; rice, soybeans, tobacco.

Cholu (chô'lōō'), town, ⊙ Cholu co. (pop. 107,101), central Chahar prov., China, 35 mi. SSE of Kalgan and on Sangkan R.; kaoliang, wheat, beans, corn. Called Paoan until 1914. Until 1928 in Chihli (Hopeh).

Cholula (chōlōō'lä), officially Cholula de Rivadavia, city (pop. 8,424), Puebla, central Mexico, on central plateau, on Inter-American Highway and 6 mi. W of Puebla; alt. 7,000 ft. Rail junction; processing and agr. center (cereals, maguey, fruit, vegetables, livestock); wine and liquor distilling, flour milling, mfg. of cotton fabrics. Site of a pre-Columbian pyramid of great antiquity. The town was an old Toltec city; at the time of Sp. conquest, it was the Aztec sacred city devoted to worship of Quetzalcoatl. Suspecting a native insurrection, Cortés destroyed the city. Atop the pyramid, the tallest (175 ft.) in Mexico, a church was built. Many churches dot the surrounding valley, and Cholula remains a place of pilgrimage.

Choluteca (chōlōōtä'kä), department (□ 1,966; 1950 pop. 117,998), S Honduras, on Gulf of Fonseca; ⊙ Choluteca. Bounded E by Nicaragua; drained by lower Choluteca R. and Río Negro. Mountainous (N and E), sloping SW into coastal lowland. Mainly agr. (corn, beans, rice, sugar cane, coffee, fruit); livestock (cattle, hogs, mules), dairying. Hardwood lumbering, saltworking in coastal area. Produces alcohol, cane syrup, and dividivi seed. Main centers (on Inter-American and Interoceanic highways): Choluteca, San Marcos, Pespire. Cedeño is popular beach resort. Dept. exports corn, cheese, cattle, mainly to Salvador. Formed 1825.

Choluteca, city (pop. 5,275) ⊙ Choluteca dept., S Honduras, on Inter-American Highway, on Choluteca R. (bridged) and 55 mi. S of Tegucigalpa; 13°18'N 87°12'W. Commercial center in agr. area; light mfg. (beverages, soap, bricks, tiles, furniture), dairying, tanning; sawmill. Apiculture. Has govt. buildings, public market, hosp., secondary col. Airfield. Founded 1537; became city in 1845.

Choluteca River, principal river of Pacific drainage basin of Honduras; rises in Sierra de Lepaterique as Río Grande, flows E and N, bet. Tegucigalpa and Comayagüela, thence E, past San Juan de Flores, SE and SW, past Morolica and Choluteca, to Gulf of Fonseca 15 mi. SW of Choluteca; length, c.175 mi. Navigable in lower course.

Choma (chō'mä), township (pop. 700), Southern Prov., Northern Rhodesia, on railroad and 105 mi. NE of Livingstone; tobacco center; tobacco processing; corn, wheat, potatoes, market gardening; dairy products. Mission school.

Chombal or **Tjombal** (chōmbäl'), island (□ c.35; 12 mi. long, 4 mi. wide), Riouw Archipelago, Indonesia, just E of Sugi, 25 mi. S of Singapore; lumbering, fishing.

Chomérac (shômäräk'), village (pop. 702), Ardèche dept., S France, 4 mi. SE of Privas; silk throwing and spinning. Fine stone, marble quarries nearby.

Chomes (chō'mĕs), village, Puntarenas prov., W Costa Rica, port on Gulf of Nicoya, 7 mi. NW of Puntarenas; salines.

Chomoi (chŭ'moi'), town, Longxuyen prov., S Vietnam, on right bank of Mekong R., 11 mi. N of Longxuyen; rice.

Chomo Lhari or **Jomolhari** (chō'mō lä'rē), mountain (23,997 ft.) in W Assam Himalayas, on undefined Bhutan-Tibet border, at 27°50'N 89°16'E. One of most sacred mts. of the Tibetans. First climbed in 1937. Formerly spelled Chumalhari.

Chomoling, Tibet: see LHASA.

Chomolungma, mountain, Tibet and Nepal: see EVEREST, MOUNT.

Chom Thong (chôm' tông'), village (1937 pop. 14,221), Chiangmai prov., N Thailand, on Ping R. and 30 mi. SW of Chiangmai, on highway to Mae Sariang. Local name, Luang.

Chomu (chō'mōō), town (pop. 9,671), E central Rajasthan, India, 17 mi. NNW of Jaipur; local trade in millet, gram, barley; handicraft cloth weaving. Also spelled Chaumu.

Chomutov (khô'mŏŏtôf), Ger. *Komotau* (kō'mōtou), city (pop. 26,697), NW Bohemia, Czechoslovakia, in E foothills of the Erzgebirge, 52 mi. NW of Prague. Rail junction; industrial center, with metallurgical works engaged primarily in finishing products of rolling mills of Kladno; mfg. of industrial pipes, wire cables, cutlery, turbines; textiles. Coal mining and hop growing in vicinity; extensive dahlia cultivation. Has 16th-cent. churches, old castle (now a mus.).

Chonan (chō'nä), town (pop. 4,407), Chiba prefecture, central Honshu, Japan, on central Chiba Peninsula, 4 mi. WSW of Mobara; rice, silk cocoons, poultry.

Chonan (chŭn'än'), Jap. *Tenan*, town (1949 pop. 26,589), S.Chungchong prov., S Korea, 50 mi. SSE of Seoul; rail center; mining center (gold, silver); agr. (rice, soybeans, fruit).

Chonburi (chôn'bŏŏrē'), town (1947 pop. 18,743), ⊙ Chonburi prov. (□ 1,730; 1947 pop. 210,244), S Thailand, on Gulf of Siam, S of Bang Pakong R., 40 mi. SE of Bangkok; road center; rice and sugarcane cultivation; rice milling, fisheries. Also spelled Cholburi or Jolburi. Local name, Bang Pla Soi.

Chonchi (chōn'chē), village (pop. 1,093), Chiloé prov., S Chile, on E coast of Chiloé Isl., 10 mi. S of Castro; fishing center; potatoes; timber.

Chonco (chōng'kō), W Nicaragua, volcano (3,537 ft.) in Cordillera de los Marabios, on SW slope of El Viejo, 7 mi. NE of Chinandega. Coffee plantations on slopes.

Chondwe (chōnd'wā), township (pop. 11), Western Prov., N Northern Rhodesia, near Belgian Congo border, on railroad and 18 mi. SSE of Ndola; tobacco, wheat, corn.

Chone (chō'nā), city (1950 pop. 8,030), Manabí prov., W Ecuador, in tropical lowlands, 38 mi. NE of Portoviejo, 23 mi. E of its Pacific port Bahía de Caráquez (linked by rail). Center of rich cacao-growing region, also producing sugar cane, coffee, rice, balsa wood, tagua nuts. Noted for mfg. of Panama hats. Sawmills.

Chone River, Manabí prov., W Ecuador, rises at NW foot of the Cordillera de Balzar, flows c.50 mi. W, past Chone, to the Pacific at Bahía de Caráquez.

Chongchon River (chŭng'chŭn'), Korean *Chongchon-gang*, Jap. *Seisen-ko*, N Korea, rises in mts. in N.Pyongan prov., c.45 mi. NW of Hamhung, flows 124 mi. generally SW, past Huichon, Anju, and Sinanju, to Korea Bay 15 mi. SW of Sinanju. In lower course, it forms boundary bet. North and South Pyongan provs.; drains agr. area.

Chongjin (chŭng'jĕn'), Jap. *Seishin* or *Seisin* (both: sā'shĕn'), city (1944 pop. 184,301), ⊙ N. Hamgyong prov., N Korea, 140 mi. SW of Vladivostok; 41°46'N 129°49'E; principal port of prov.; industrial center (pig iron, steel). There are match and staple-fiber factories, sardine canneries. Has marine experimental station. Exports iron, fish, cotton textiles, lumber. Port was opened in 1908. Since 1943, includes NANAM. Sometimes spelled Chungjin.

Chongju (chŭng'jōō'). **1** Jap. *Seishu* or *Seisyu*, city (1949 pop. 64,571), ⊙ N.Chungchong prov., S Korea, 70 mi. SSE of Seoul; 36°38'N 127°30'E; collection center for rice, soybeans, tobacco; sake brewing, meat packing, spinning. **2** Jap. *Teishu*, town (1944 pop. 18,633), N.Pyongan prov., N Korea, 50 mi. SE of Sinuiju; agr. center (rice, wheat, soybeans). Gold is mined near by.

Chonglok, China: see NGWA.

Chongmek (chông'māk'), village, Ubon prov., E Thailand, on Laos frontier, 40 mi. E of Ubon, on Ubon-Pakse highway.

Chongning, China: see SUNFUNG.

Chongos Alto (chōng'gōs äl'tō), town (pop. 774), Junín dept., central Peru, in Cordillera Occidental of the Andes, 17 mi. SSW of Huancayo; grain, alfalfa, cattle.

Chongos Bajo (bä'hō), town (pop. 2,796), Junín dept., central Peru, in Mantaro R. valley, 5 mi. SW of Huancayo; wheat, potatoes, cattle.

Chongoyape (chōng-goi-ä'pā), town (pop. 3,343), Lambayeque dept., NW Peru, on W slopes of Cordillera Occidental, near Lambayeque R., 33 mi. ENE of Chiclayo; rice milling.

Chongoyape River, Peru: see LAMBAYEQUE RIVER.

Chongsong (chông'sŭng'), Jap. *Shojo*, township (1944 pop. 6,834), N.Hamgyong prov., N Korea, on Tumen R. (Manchuria line) and 45 mi. NW of Unggi, in coal-mining and agr. area.

Chongup (chŭng'ŏŏp'), Jap. *Seiyu*, town (1949 pop. 31,579), N.Cholla prov., S Korea, 23 mi. SW of Chonju; rice, cotton, silk cocoons.

Chongyang (chŭng'yäng'), Jap. *Seiyo*, township (1946 pop. 9,172), S.Chungchong prov., S Korea, 36 mi. WNW of Taejon; tungsten mining.

Choni (jô'nē'), village, ⊙ Choni dist. (pop. 53,817), SE Kansu prov., China, 100 mi. S of Lanchow, and on Tao R., in mtn. region; grain.

Chonju (chŭn'jōō'), Jap. *Zenshu* or *Zensyu* (both: zän'shōō), city (1949 pop. 100,624), ⊙ N.Cholla prov., S Korea, 120 mi. S of Seoul; 35°48'N 127°8'E; handicraft center (silver and bamboo ware, fans, paper umbrellas, grass linen); silk reeling, sake brewing. Founder of Yi dynasty (last imperial line) is buried here. Sometimes spelled Chunju.

Chonoin Gol, Mongolia: see YUGODZYR.

Chonoplya, Yugoslavia: see CONOPLJA.

Chonos Archipelago (chō'nōs), island group in the Pacific, off W coast of Chiloé and Aysén provs., S Chile, bet. Guaitecas Isls. (N, sometimes considered part of the archipelago) and Taitao Peninsula (S), separated from the mainland by Moraleda Channel; extends c.130 mi. N-S bet. 44° and 46°S. Consists of over 1,000 isls. (uninhabited, except for a few transient Indians), the largest of which are, N-S: Forsyth, Chaffers, Concoto, Valverde, Jechica, Johnson, Level, Tahuenahuec, Cuptana, Tránsito (belonging to Chiloé prov.); and, S of King Channel: Ipun, Stokes, Benjamín, Jorge, James, Melchor, Victoria, Luz, Traiguén, Rivero, Humos, Fitzroy, Simpson (belonging to Aysén prov.). Guamblin Isl. is just W of the main group, across Adventure Bay. The small settlement Puerto Lagunas, on SE Melchor Isl., maintains a radio station.

Chontabamba (chōntäbäm'bä), village (pop. 27), Pasco dept., central Peru, in Cordillera Oriental, 6 mi. SSW of Oxapampa; coffee, cacao, fruit.

Chontales (chōntä'lĕs), department (□ until 1949, 4,170; 1950 pop. 50,411), S Nicaragua; ⊙ Juigalpa. Along E shore of L. Nicaragua; contains (N) Cordillera Ammerrique and Huapi Mts., parts of continental divide. Agr. largely in N (sugar cane, beans, corn, some coffee and bananas); livestock; cheese production. Lumbering (building timber, hardwood); rubber, chicle, balsam of Peru. Gold and silver mining at La Libertad and Santo Domingo (El Jabalí mine). Served by Juigalpa-Rama highway and L. Nicaragua shipping ports of Puerto Díaz, San Ubaldo). Chief urban centers: Juigalpa, La Libertad, Santo Domingo. In 1949 its S section (including San Carlos) became part of Río San Juan dept.

Chontla (chōn'tlä), town (pop. 797), Veracruz, E Mexico, in Sierra Madre Oriental foothills, 40 mi. NW of Tuxpan; cereals, sugar cane, fruit.

Choomphone, Thailand: see CHUMPHON.

Cho Oyu (chō' ōyōō'), peak (26,867 ft.) in NE Nepal Himalayas, on undefined Nepal-Tibet border, at 28°5'N 86°40'E. Up to 1950, unattempted by climbers.

Chop (chôp), Czech *Čop* (chôp), Hung. *Csap* (chŏp), village (1941 pop. 3,498), W Transcarpathian oblast, Ukrainian SSR, on Tissa R. and 14 mi. SSW of Uzhgorod; major rail junction at Hung.-Czech border; petroleum processing.

Chopawamsic Recreational Area, Va.: see DUMFRIES.

Chopda (chōp'dŭ), town (pop. 21,544), East Khandesh dist., NE Bombay, India, near S foothills of Satpura Range, 23 mi. NW of Jalgaon; market center for cotton, linseed, millet; cotton ginning, handicraft cloth weaving. Formerly called Chopra.

Choppington, England: see BEDLINGTONSHIRE.

Chopra, India: see CHOPDA.

Choptank River, in W Del. and E Md., rises SW of Dover, Del.; flows c.70 mi. generally SW, through Del. and Eastern Shore of Md., past Greensboro (head of navigation), Denton, and Cambridge (bridged here), to Chesapeake Bay S of Tilghman Isl. Tidal to Denton; estuary, more than 4 mi. wide at mouth, has many irregular inlets. Fishing, oystering.

Choqueyapu River, Bolivia: see LA PAZ RIVER.

Chora or **Khora** (both: khô'rŭ), town (pop. 3,963), Messenia nome, SW Peloponnesus, Greece, 23 mi. W of Kalamata; livestock raising (goats, hogs). Formerly Lygoudista or Lygudista.

Choranche or **Choranche-les-Bains** (shôräsh'-lā-bē'), village (pop. 74), Isère dept., SE France, on Bourne R. and 18 mi. SW of Grenoble, in the Pre-Alps; mineral springs.

Chorasmia, Uzbek SSR: see KHIVA.

Chora Sphakion, Crete: see SPHAKIA.

Chorazin (kōrā'zĭn), biblical locality, Lower Galilee, NW Palestine, 3 mi. NNW of Capernaum. Remains of anc. synagogue excavated here.

Chorba, Turkey: see KIZILCAHAMAM

Chordeleg (chôrdälĕg'), village, Azuay prov., S Ecuador, in the Andes, 9 mi. E of Cuenca; sugar cane, cereals, semitropical fruit. Site of pre-Inca ruins.

Chorges (shôrzh), agr. village (pop. 630), Hautes-Alpes dept., SE France, at S foot of Dauphiné Alps, 10 mi. E of Gap. Chief town of *Caturiges*, on Roman road from Arles to Briançon.

Chorgun River, Crimea, Russian SFSR: see CHERNAYA RIVER.

Choriste or **Khoristi** (both: khôrĭstē'), town (pop. 3,184), Drama nome, Macedonia, Greece, 3 mi. ESE of Drama; tobacco, barley; olive oil. Also spelled Choristi. Under Turkish rule, Chatalja.

Chorley (chôr'lē). **1** Village and parish (pop. 401), NE central Cheshire, England, just SW of Alderley Edge; dairy farming. **2** Municipal borough (1931 pop. 30,796; 1951 census 32,636), central Lancashire, England, on Lancaster Canal and 8 mi. NW of Bolton; cotton spinning and weaving, leather tanning, flour milling, mfg. of chemicals, paint, soap. Site of water reservoir for Liverpool. Has church with 15th-cent. tower and Norman font. Near by is mansion of Duxbury Hall (rebuilt in 16th cent.), birthplace of Miles Standish.

Chorleywood, residential urban district (1931 pop. 3,295; 1951 census 4,432), SW Hertford, England, 5 mi. W of Watford.

Chorlton-upon-Medlock, S suburb of Manchester, SE Lancashire, England; textile industry (cotton spinning, weaving, bleaching; mfg. of clothing); mfg. of chemicals, soap, paint. Just SW is industrial suburb of Chorlton cum Hardy.

Chorlu, Turkey: see CORLU.

Chorokh River: see CORUH RIVER, Turkey.

Chorolque, Mount (chōrōl'kä), in Cordillera de Chichas, SW Bolivia, just S of Quechisla; rises to 18,422 ft.; tin mines.

Choros Islands (chō'rōs), small archipelago off coast of Coquimbo prov., N central Chile, 45 mi. NW of La Serena; largest of 3 isls. is c.2 mi. long; 29°15'S.

Chorostkow, Ukrainian SSR: see KHOROSTKOV.

Choroszcz (khô'rôshch), Rus. *Khoroshch* (khô'rôshch), town (pop. 1,924), Bialystok prov., NE Poland, near Narew R., 7 mi. W of Bialystok. Castle ruins near by.

Chorrera, La, Panama: see LA CHORRERA.

Chorrie Island, Scotland: see ERIBOLL, LOCH.

Chorrillos (chōrē'yōs), village, Pando dept., NW Bolivia, on Madre de Dios R. and 65 mi. WSW of Riberalta; rubber. Formerly called Canadá.

Chorrillos, S suburb (pop. 6,996) of Lima, Lima dept., W central Peru, on Pacific coast, 8 mi. S of city center; fashionable bathing and boating resort, with La Herradura beach. Military school; monument to Unknown Soldier. Since 1940, inc. into Lima proper.

Chorro, El, Argentina: see EL CHORRO.

Chorro, El (ĕl chô'rō), gorge (c.10 mi. long, 200 ft. deep), Málaga prov., S Spain, along Guadalhorce R., in E outliers of the Sierra de Ronda, 3 mi. N of Álora. Tourist site. Has hydroelectric plants.

Chorsa, Turkey: see KARS, town.

Chortiates or **Khortiatis** (both: khôrtēä'tĭs), mountain in Greek Macedonia, at base of Chalcidice peninsula, S of L. Koroneia; rises to 3,937 ft. 10 mi. SE of Salonika. Also called Kissos. Village of Chortiates (pop 1,874) is at N foot.

Chortkov (chôrt'kûf), Pol. *Czortków* (chôrt'kōōf), city (1931 pop. 18,343), S Ternopol oblast, Ukrainian SSR, on Seret R. and 38 mi. SSE of Ternopol; grain-trading and -processing center; mfg. (cement, tiles, rubber goods), hatmaking, distilling. Has ruins of castle and monastery. Passed from Poland to Austria (1772); reverted to Poland (1919); called Chertkov (1939–44); ceded to USSR in 1945.

Chorukh-Dairon or **Chorukh-Dayron** (chŭrōōkh"-dīrôn'), town (1945 pop. over 500), N Leninabad oblast, Tadzhik SSR, on S slope of Kurama Range, 10 mi. NNE of Leninabad; tungsten mining. Also spelled Churukh-Dairon.

Chorum, Turkey: see CORUM.

Chorwad (chōr'väd), town (pop. 6,552), S Saurashtra, India, 37 mi. SSW of Junagarh; agr. (millet, betel vine, cotton). Sometimes spelled Chorvad.

Chorwon (chŭr'wŭn'), Jap. *Tetsugen,* town (1944 pop. 30,085), Kangwon prov., central Korea, N of 38°N, 50 mi. NNE of Seoul; rail junction; silk-reeling center.

Chorzele (khô-zhĕ'lĕ), Rus. *Khorzhele* (khôr-zhĕ'lĕ), town (pop. 2,187), Warszawa prov., NE central Poland, on Orzyc R. and 17 mi. N of Przasnysz; brewing, cement mfg., flour milling.

Chorzow (khô'zhōōf), Pol. *Chorzów,* city (1950 pop. c.142,000), Katowice prov., S Poland, 4 mi. NW of Katowice, in dense rail network. Industrial center; iron- and steelworks; mfg. of railroad cars, nitrate compounds, bricks, glass, liquer; coal mining, sawmilling, stone quarrying; coke, gas, and electrical works. First known as Krolewska Huta (krōōlĕf'skä hōō'tä), Pol. *Królewska Huta,* Ger. *Königshütte* (kû"nĭkhs-hü'tů); in Germany until 1921. Pop. rose from 1,000 in 1861 to 80,000 in 1931. In 1930s, Krolewska Huta and its 2 suburbs, Chorzow and Hajduki Wielkie (hīdōō'kē vyĕl'kyĕ), Ger. *Bismarckhütte* (bĭs"märk-hü'tů), joined to form city of Chorzow. Until 1939, Pol. frontier station opposite Beuthen and Hindenburg. In Second World War, relatively little damaged.

Chosa (chō'sä), town (pop. 13,071), Kagoshima prefecture, S Kyushu, Japan, on N shore of Kagoshima Bay, 12 mi. NNE of Kagoshima; commercial center in agr., livestock area; rice, raw silk, lumber.

Chosan (chō'sän'), Jap. *Sozan,* township (1944 pop. 18,239), N.Pyongan prov., N Korea, on Yalu R. and 90 mi. NE of Sinjuin; graphite mining.

Chosen: see KOREA.

Chosen, village (pop. 1,873), Palm Beach co., SE Fla., just NW of Belle Glade. Railroad name is Belle Glade-Chosen.

Chosen-kaikyo: see KOREA STRAIT.

Chosen-wan, Korea: see EAST KOREA BAY.

Choshi (chō'shē), city (1940 pop. 61,198; 1947 pop. 69,543), Chiba prefecture, central Honshu, Japan, at NE base of Chiba Peninsula, on the Pacific and at mouth of Tone R., 60 mi. E of Tokyo; major fishing port; large production of soy sauce. Sometimes spelled Tyosi.

Choshin-ko, Korea: see CHANGJIN RIVER.

Choshoho, Korea: see CHANGSUNGPO.

Choshu, Formosa: see CHAOCHOW.

Choshui River (jō'shwā'), Jap. *Dakusui* (däkōō'-sōōē), longest river of Formosa, rises in central mts. 20 mi. WNW of Hwalien, flows 102 mi. SW and W, past Silei, to Formosa Strait on W central coast.

Chosica (chōsē'kä), town (pop. 4,160), Lima dept., W central Peru, in Andean foothills, at confluence of Rímac and Santa Eulalia rivers, on Lima–La Oroya RR, on highway, and 27 mi. ENE of Lima; popular resort, situated above coastal mists; alt. c.2,800 ft. Has hydroelectric plant serving Lima; paper mill. Sugar cane, fruit. Pre-Columbian ruins near by.

Chos Malal (chōs mäläl'), town (pop. estimate 1,000), ⊙ Chos Malal dept. (1947 pop. 5,465), NW Neuquén natl. territory, Argentina, in outliers of the Andes, on Neuquén R. and 110 mi. NNW of Zapala; stock-raising and mining center. Gold, asphalt deposits. Hydroelectric station. Flour milling. The former capital of the territory, it has monuments to Sarmiento and San Martín.

Choson, Korea: see KOREA.

Choson-man, Korea: see EAST KOREA BAY.

Cho-so-t'u, Manchuria: see JOSOTO.

Choszczno (khôsh'chŭnō), Ger. *Arnswalde* (ärns'-väl"dů), town (1939 pop. 13,960; 1946 pop. 2,052) in Pomerania, after 1945 in Szczecin prov., NW Poland, on small lake, 20 mi. SE of Stargard; woolen milling; agr. market (grain, sugar beets, potatoes, livestock). Ruins of anc. town walls. In Second World War, c.80% destroyed.

Chota (chō'tä), city (pop. 2,944), ⊙ Chota prov. (□ 1,726; pop. 103,381), Cajamarca dept., NW Peru, in Cordillera Occidental, 40 mi. NNW of Cajamarca, on road from Hualgayoc; alt. 7,775 ft. Flour milling; agr. products (wheat, corn, alfalfa); cattle raising.

Chota Nagpur (chō'tŭ näg'pōōr), division (□ 27,112; pop. 7,516,349) of Bihar, India; ⊙ Ranchi. Comprises 5 dists.: HAZARIBAGH, RANCHI, PALAMAU, MANBHUM, SINGHBHUM.

Chota Nagpur Plateau, upland region (alt. 2,000–3,500 ft.), mainly in S Bihar and in NE Madhya Pradesh and N Orissa, India; extends E from Vindhya Range, bet. Ganges (N), Son (W, NW), and Mahanadi (S) river basins. Comprises extensive area of broken hill ranges, ravines, and valleys, drained by Rihand, North Koel, South Koel, Damodar, and Subarnarekha rivers. Annual rainfall 50–60 in. Forests (sal, bamboo) cover c.⅓ of area, forming India's major lac-producing section. Plateau is rich in mineral resources, especially iron ore, coal, mica, copper, limestone, cyanite, bauxite, and asbestos. Chief towns are Ranchi, Jamshedpur (iron and steel center), Hazaribagh, Daltonganj. Large tribal pop. is mainly Santal.

Chota Udaipur (chō'tŭ ōōdī'pōōr), village, Baroda dist., N Bombay, India, 50 mi. E of Baroda; rail terminus; market center (cotton, rice, timber); cotton ginning, oilseed pressing. Was ⊙ former princely state of Chota Udaipur (□ 894; pop. 162,177) in Gujarat States, Bombay; inc. 1949 into newly-created Baroda dist. Other spellings: Chhota Udaipur, Chhota Udepur, Chota-Udepur.

Choteau (shō'tō). **1** City (pop. 1,618), ⊙ Teton co., NW central Mont., on Teton R. and 50 mi. NW of Great Falls, in ranching region; dairy products, livestock, grain. Inc. 1913. **2** Town, Mayes co., Okla.: see CHOUTEAU.

Chotebor (khô'tyĕbôrsh), Czech *Chotěboř,* town (pop. 4,457), E Bohemia, Czechoslovakia, on railroad and 22 mi. SSW of Pardubice; barley, oats, potatoes; mfg. (starch, knit goods, hair nets). Cotton mills in vicinity.

Chotila (chō'tĭlŭ), village, N central Saurashtra, India, 26 mi. ENE of Rajkot; rail spur terminus; agr. (millet, cotton).

Chotina River, Yugoslavia: see COTINA RIVER.

Chott or **Shott** [Arabic,=lake or salt flat], for names in Fr. North Africa beginning thus, see following proper noun.

Chotusice (khô'tōōsĭtsĕ), Ger. *Chotusitz,* village (pop. 1,053), E Bohemia, Czechoslovakia, 2 mi. N of Caslav. Frederick the Great won victory here, 1742, over Austrians.

Chotzen, Czechoslovakia: see CHOCEN.

Chotzeshan, China: see LUNGSHENG, Suiyuan prov.

Chou-, for Chinese names beginning thus and not found here: see under CHOW-.

Chou-chia-ch'iao, China: see CHOWKIAKIAO.

Chou-chia-k'ou, China: see CHOWKIAKOW.

Choudrant (shōō'drŭnt), village (pop. 395), Lincoln parish, N La., 8 mi. E of Ruston, in cotton-growing area; cotton ginning, lumber milling.

Chouilly (shōōyē'), village (pop. 879), Marne dept., N France, near the Marne, 3 mi. ESE of Épernay; winegrowing (champagne).

Chouteau (shō'tō), county (□ 3,920; pop. 6,974), N central Mont.; ⊙ Fort Benton. Agr. area drained by Missouri, Teton, and Marias rivers. Grain, livestock. Formed 1865.

Chouteau, town (pop. 658), Mayes co., NE Okla., 37 mi. E of Tulsa; market center for farm area; cotton ginning. Formerly spelled Choteau.

Chouzé-sur-Loire (shōōzā'-sür-lwär'), village (pop. 944), Indre-et-Loire dept., W central France, on the Loire and 7 mi. NW of Chinon; winegrowing. Sometimes called Chouzé.

Chovet (chōvĕt'), town (pop. estimate 2,500), S Santa Fe prov., Argentina, 70 mi. SW of Rosario; agr. center (corn, wheat, flax, potatoes, vegetables, livestock).

Chovoreca, Cerro (sĕ'rō chōvōrā'kä), hill on Bolivia-Paraguay border, 85 mi. WSW of Puerto Suárez (Bolivia), in the Chaco; 19°11'S 59°8'W. Boundary marker established (1938) in Chaco Peace Conference.

Chowan (chō"wŏn'), county (□ 180; pop. 12,540), NE N.C.; ⊙ EDENTON. In coastal plain area; bounded W by Chowan R., S by Albemarle Sound. Agr. (peanuts, cotton, tobacco, corn), hog raising; timber (pine, gum). Sawmilling, fishing; some mfg. Formed 1672.

Chowan River, NE N.C., formed 11 mi. N of Winton, at Va. line, by confluence of Nottaway and Blackwater rivers; flows 52 mi. generally SSE past Winton, to W end of Albemarle Sound 4 mi. W of Edenton (here bridged). Navigable to Winton via. 10-ft. dredged channel.

Chowchih or **Chou-chih** (jō'jû'), town (pop. 6,364), ⊙ Chowchih co. (pop. 147,028), SW central Shensi prov., China, 45 mi. W of Sian and on Wei R.; rice, wheat, beans, kaoliang, millet.

Chowchilla (chouchĭ'lŭ), city (pop. 3,893), Madera co., central Calif., in San Joaquin Valley, 35 mi. NW of Fresno; cottonseed oil, evaporated milk; ships dairy products, potatoes, livestock. Inc. 1923.

Chowchilla River, central Calif., rises in S Mariposa co., flows SW and then NW to join San Joaquin R. 18 mi. SSW of Merced; c.65 mi. long. Site of projected Buchanan Dam of CENTRAL VALLEY project.

Chowhoctolik (chouhôk'tōlĭk), village (pop. 98), W Alaska, near Yukon R. delta.

Chowkiakiao or **Chou-chia-ch'iao** (both: jō'jyä'-chyou'), town, SE Kiangsu prov., China, 5 mi. W of Shanghai; commercial center.

Chowkiakow or **Chou-chia-k'ou** (both: jō'jyä'kō'), town (1922 pop. estimate 200,000), E Honan prov., China, 85 mi. SSE of Kaifeng, and on Ying R. (head of navigation) at mouth of Sha R. arm; leading commercial center on E agr. plain of Honan.

Chowkowtien or **Chou-k'ou-tien** (jō'kō'dyĕn'), town, N Hopeh prov., China, on railroad spur and 30 mi. SW of Peking; coal mining. Several bones of Peking Man (*Sinanthropus pekinensis*) were discovered here, 1928–29.

Chown, Mount (10,930 ft.), W Alta., near B.C. border, in Rocky Mts., in Jasper Natl. Park, 70 mi. WNW of Jasper; 53°24'N 119°25'W.

Chowning or **Chou-ning** (both: jō'nĭng'), town (pop. 3,855), ⊙ Chowning co. (pop. 45,395), NE Fukien prov., China, near Chekiang line, 50 mi. WNW of Siapu; rice, wheat, sweet potatoes. Until 1945 called Chowtun.

Chowra Island (chou'rů), small island of the Nicobars, in Bay of Bengal, 50 mi. SSE of Car Nicobar Isl.; pottery making; a center of interisland trade.

Chowtsun or **Chou-t'sun** (both: jō'tsōōn'), city (1934 pop. 56,620), N Shantung prov., China, 45 mi. E of Tsinan and on railroad to Tsingtao; major pongee-silk-weaving center; papermaking, cotton weaving, glass mfg. Opened to foreign trade in 1904. Became independent municipality in 1949.

Chowtun, China: see CHOWNING.

Choya, Argentina: see FRÍAS.

Choya (choi'ŭ), village, N Gorno-Altai Autonomous Oblast, Altai Territory, Russian SFSR, 25 mi. E of Gorno-Altaisk; dairy farming; tar and resin processing.

Choyron, Mongolia: see CHOIREN.

Chozan-kan, Korea: see CHANGSAN, CAPE.

Chozas de Canales (chō'thäs dhä känä'lĕs), town (pop. 1,307), Toledo prov., central Spain, 19 mi. SW of Madrid; cereals, grapes, olives, sheep, hogs; lumbering, cheese processing.

Chrapkowice, Poland: see KRAPKOWICE.

Chrastava (khră'stävä), Ger. *Kratzau* (krä'tsou), village (pop. 2,779), N Bohemia, Czechoslovakia, on Lusatian Neisse R., on railroad and 5 mi. NW of Liberec; oats, potatoes.

Chréa (shrăä'), village in the Mitidja Atlas, Alger dept., N central Algeria, 5 mi. SE of Blida, on NE slope of Abd-el-Kader peak; alt. c.5,100 ft. Health resort and winter-sports station. Center of animal and forest preserve.

Chrisman (krĭs'mŭn). **1** Village (pop. 4,211), Ventura co., S Calif. **2** City (pop. 1,071), Edgar co., E Ill., 22 mi. S of Danville; trade and shipping center in agr. area (corn, soybeans, wheat, poultry, livestock); feed mill. Platted 1872, inc. 1900.

Chrisney (krĭs'nē), town (pop. 439), Spencer co., SW Ind., 30 mi. E of Evansville, in agr. area.

Christburg, Poland: see DZIERZGON.

Christchurch (krĭs'chûrch, krīst'–). **1** Municipal borough (1931 pop. 9,190; 1951 census 20,506), SW Hampshire, England, at head of the Avon and Stour estuary (which here forms small harbor), bet. Poole Bay and Christchurch Bay of the Channel, 4 mi. ENE of Bournemouth; seaside resort with sandy beach. The 11th-cent. Augustinian priory church gave town its name. There are remains of castle (c.1100) and of Norman House (c.1150), probably residence of castle's governor. Promontory of Hengistbury Head is 2 mi. SE. **2** Residential town and parish (pop. 3,240), S Monmouth, England, near Usk R., 2 mi. ENE of Newport. Has 15th-cent. church.

Christchurch, city (pop. 112,681; metropolitan Christchurch 150,047), E S.Isl., New Zealand, at base of Banks Peninsula, just NW of Lyttelton, its port; 43°35'S 172°36'E. Seat of Canterbury Col. (1873), Christ's Col., School of Arts (1882), Robert McDougall Art Gall., Anglican and R.C. cathedrals, tuberculosis sanatorium. Tanneries, fertilizer plants, meat-freezing plants. Lincoln Agr. Col. near by. Founded 1850. Christchurch is ⊙ Heathcote co. (□ 20; pop. 5,206), but forms independent unit within co.

Christian, village (1939 pop. 34), in Chandalar dist., NE Alaska, 60 mi. N of Fort Yukon; 67°30'N 145°20'W; trapping and gold prospecting.

Christian. 1 County (□ 709; pop. 38,816), central Ill.; ⊙ Taylorville. Bounded N by Sangamon R.; drained by South Fork of Sangamon R. Agr.; (corn, wheat, oats, soybeans; dairy products; livestock, poultry). Bituminous-coal mining. Mfg. (clothing, mattresses, soybean products, tools, feed, paper, cigars, stationery); commercial rose growing. Formed 1839. **2** County (□ 726; pop. 42,359), SW Ky.; ⊙ HOPKINSVILLE. Bounded S by Tenn., NE by headstream of Pond R.; drained by Tradewater and Little rivers and branch of Red R. Gently rolling agr. area (dark tobacco, corn, wheat, livestock); coal mines, gas wells, hardwood timber; some mfg. at Hopkinsville. Includes U.S. Fort Campbell and part of Pennyrile State Forest. Formed 1796. **3** County (□ 567; pop. 12,412), SW Mo.; ⊙ Ozark. In the Ozarks; drained by James R. Resort area; agr. (corn, wheat, oats, strawberries), livestock, dairying; iron. Part of Mark Twain Natl. Forest is here. Formed 1860.

Christian, Cape, E Baffin Isl., SE Franklin Dist., Northwest Territories, on Davis Strait; 70°32'N 68°17'W. Site of govt. radio, meteorological, and ionospheric station. River Clyde trading post 9 mi. SW.

Christiana (krĭstyă'nŭ, krĭs-chēă'nŭ), town (pop. 2,825), Manchester parish, W central Jamaica, resort in uplands (alt. c.2,500 ft.), 9 mi. N of Mandeville. Ginger-growing center; also produces bananas, coffee, pimento, annatto, honey. Settled by Germans 1836–42.

Christiana, borough (pop. 1,043), Lancaster co., SE Pa., 9 mi. WSW of Coatesville; canned goods, textiles, metal products. Settled 1691, laid out 1833, inc. 1894.

Christiana River, Del.; see CHRISTINA RIVER.

Christianburg, village (pop., including adjoining Wismar, 1,458), Demerara co., N Br. Guiana, on left bank of Demerara R. and 55 mi. S of Georgetown. Large bauxite deposits worked here.

Christiania, Norway: see OSLO.

Christian Island (10 mi. long, 5 mi. wide), S central Ont., in Georgian Bay of L. Huron, on E side of entrance of Nottawasaga Bay, 40 mi. ENE of Owen Sound.

Christiansand, Norway: see KRISTIANSAND.

Christiansborg, Gold Coast: see ACCRA.

Christiansburg. 1 Village (pop. 666), Champaign co., W central Ohio, 9 mi. E of Troy, in agr. area. **2** Town (pop. 2,967), ⊙ Montgomery co., SW Va., near W base of the Blue Ridge, 27 mi. SW of Roanoke, in agr. and bituminous-coal area; canned goods, furniture, lumber, clothing; stockyards. Founded 1792; inc. 1916.

Christianshaab (krĭ'styäns-hôp"), Eskimo *Qasigiánguit,* settlement (pop. 181), ⊙ Christianshaab dist. (pop. 648), W Greenland, on Disko Bay, 40 mi. ENE of Egedesminde; 68°49'N 51°10'W. Fishing and hunting base; seal-oil refinery. Radio station. Settlement founded 1734.

Christianshavn, Denmark: see COPENHAGEN, city.

Christianstad, Sweden: see KRISTIANSTAD.

Christiansted (krĭs'chŭnstĕd"), city (pop. 4,126), ⊙ St. Croix Isl., U.S. Virgin Isls., port on N shore of the isl., 45 mi. SSE of Charlotte Amalie (St. Thomas Isl.), 11 mi. ENE of Frederiksted, in picturesque setting, built on amphitheater of sloping hills. Former ⊙ Danish West Indies and once the home of Alexander Hamilton. Sometimes called Bassin (băsĭn').

Christiansten, Norway: see TRONDHEIM.

Christiansund, Norway: see KRISTIANSUND.

Christina, Brazil: see CRISTINA.

Christina Lake (krĭstē'nŭ), Douglas and Grant counties, W Minn., just E of Pelican L., 23 mi. NW of Alexandria; 5 mi. long, 2 mi. wide.

Christina River, rises in Chester co., SE Pa., flows SE and NE, across NE tip of Md., through N Del., to Delaware R. at Wilmington, whose harbor it forms; c.35 mi. long. Receives Brandywine Creek near mouth. Formerly Christiana R.

Christine (krĭstēn'), city (pop. 289), Atascosa co., SW Texas, c.45 mi. S of San Antonio; farm trade point.

Christinehamn, Sweden: see KRISTINEHAMN.

Christinestad, Finland: see KRISTINESTAD.

Christmas Cove, Maine: see SOUTH BRISTOL.

Christmas Island, largest atoll (□ 222.6; pop. 52) in Pacific, one of Line Isls., central Pacific, 155 mi. SE of Fanning Isl.; 1°51'N 157°23'W. Bay of Wrecks on E shore. Coconuts, pandanus fruit. Discovered 1777 by Capt. Cook, claimed by U.S. under Guano Act (1856), included 1919 in Br. Gilbert and Ellice Isls. colony. U.S. questioned (1936) Br. ownership.

Christmas Island, isolated island (□ 60; pop. 866) of Singapore crown colony, in Indian Ocean, 260 mi. S of Java Head and 850 mi. SSE of Singapore; 10°30'S 105°40'E. Rising over 6,000 ft. from ocean bottom, it is steep-sided and densely wooded, in the shape of a rough parallelogram with deeply indented sides; 11 mi. long, 11 mi. wide; rises to 1,170 ft. Has extensive deposits of phosphate of lime which are worked and exported. Pop. (¾ Chinese) lives in settlement on NE shore. First mentioned 1666; annexed and settled (1888) by British and placed under Straits Settlements; inc. (1900) into Settlement of Singapore. Leased since 1897 to phosphate company. Occupied (1942–45) by Japanese. Originally called Moni; renamed by Capt. Cook on his visit, 1777.

Christmas Sound, S Tierra del Fuego, Chile, on W coast of Hoste Isl.; c.15 mi. long, 1–7 mi. wide.

Christopher. 1 City (pop. 3,545), Franklin co., S Ill., 11 mi. N of Herrin, in bituminous-coal-mining and agr. area. Inc. 1910. **2** Village (pop. 1,277, with near-by Fourseam), Perry co., SE Ky., in Cumberland foothills, on North Fork Kentucky R. just SE of Hazard, in bituminous-coal-mining area; oil and gas wells, timber.

Christoval (krĭstō'vŭl), village (pop. c.550), Tom Green co., W Texas, 26 mi. S of San Angelo and on South Concho R., in ranch, farm area. Tourist trade; mineral wells.

Chromepet, India: see PALLAVARAM.

Chrome Railway Block, township (pop. 1,025), Gwelo prov., central Southern Rhodesia, on railroad, near Selukwe; chrome mining.

Chropyne (khrô'pĭnyĕ), Czech *Chropyně,* village (pop. 2,286), W central Moravia, Czechoslovakia, on railroad and 17 mi. SSE of Olomouc; agr. center (barley, wheat, sugar beets).

Chrudim (khrŏŏ'dĭm), town (pop. 13,217), E Bohemia, Czechoslovakia, on Chrudimka R. and 6 mi. S of Pardubice, in sugar-beet area. Rail junction; large sugar mills and distilleries; cotton mills; mfg. (footwear, cables, rope), malt processing; embroidery. Has 16th-cent. baroque Capuchin abbey and baroque town hall.

Chrudimka River (-kä), E Bohemia, Czechoslovakia, rises in Bohemian-Moravian Heights at NW foot of Devet Skal mtn. flows c.65 mi. NW and NNE, past Chrudim, to Elbe R. at Pardubice. Dammed in upper course, S of Vapenny Podol.

Chruszczow (khrŏŏsh'chŏŏf), Pol. *Chruszczów,* Ger. *Schomberg* (shôm'bĕrk), commune (1939 pop. 7,437; 1946 pop. 5,701) in Upper Silesia, after 1945 in Katowice prov., S Poland, 2 mi. WSW of Beuthen (Bytom); coal, zinc, and lead mining.

Chryplin, Ukrainian SSR: see KHRYPLIN.

Chrysopolis, Turkey: see USKUDAR.

Chrysorrhoas, Syria: see BARADA.

Chrysos or **Khrisos** (both: khrĭsôs'), town (pop. 3,075), Serrai nome, Macedonia, Greece, 5 mi. ESE of Serrai; tobacco, cotton, corn, beans. Formerly called Topoliane (Topoliani); sometimes Chryssos.

Chrysoupolis or **Khrisoupolis** (both: khrĭsŏŏ'pôlĭs), town (pop. 3,017), Kavalla nome, Macedonia, Greece, on river and 15 mi. E of Kavalla; agr. center of lowland W of Mesta R. mouth; tobacco, cotton, wheat. Also spelled Chryssoupolis. Formerly called Sapai (Sapaioi) and, under Turkish rule, Sari Shaban.

Chryss-, in Greek names: see CHRYS-.

Chryzanow (khŭshä'nŏŏf), Pol. *Chrzanów,* town (pop. 12,121), Krakow prov., S Poland, 19 mi. ESE of Katowice. Center of coal-mining area; mfg. (locomotives, cardboard, leather, bricks). Abandoned mine (lead, calamine, galena) near by. Dolomite deposits (used for construction and as flux) in vicinity. In Second World War, under Ger. rule, called Krenau.

Chü- or **Ch'ü-,** for Chinese names beginning thus and not found here: see under KÜ-.

Ch'u-, for Chinese names beginning thus and not found here: see under TSU-.

Chu, river, Kwangtung prov., China: see CANTON RIVER.

Chü, river, Szechwan prov., China: see CHÜ RIVER.

Chu (chōō), town (1948 pop. over 10,000), E Dzhambul oblast, Kazakh SSR, on Chu R., on Turksib RR, near junction with Trans-Kazakhstan RR, and 130 mi. ENE of Dzhambul; cotton; metalworks; beet-sugar and meat processing.

Chuachan (chwŭ'chän'), town, Bienhoa prov., S Vietnam, at foot of Annamese Cordillera, on Saigon-Hanoi RR and 50 mi. ENE of Saigon.

Chuacús, Sierra de (syĕ'rä dā chwäkōōs'), range in Quiché and Baja Verapaz depts., central Guatemala; extends c.80 mi. E-W bet. Quiché and Salamá; forms divide bet. Chixoy R. (N) and Motagua R. (S); rises to c.8,000 ft. Continued E by Sierra de las Minas.

Chuadanga (chwädäng'gŭ), village, Kushtia dist., W East Bengal, E Pakistan, on upper Jamuna (Ichamati) R. and 25 mi. SW of Kushtia; trades in rice, jute, linseed, sugar cane. Until 1947, in Nadia dist. Large sugar-processing factory 9 mi. SSW, at Darsana.

Ch'uan-, for Chinese names beginning thus and not found here: see under CHWAN-.

Chüancheng or **Chüan-ch'eng** (jüăn'chŭng'), town, ⊙ Chüancheng co., central Pingyuan prov., China, near Yellow R., 20 mi. N of Hotseh; tobacco, peanuts, wheat. Until 1949 in Shantung prov.

Ch'üan-chiao, China: see CHÜANTSIAO.

Chüanchow, China: see TSINKIANG.

Chuang-, for Chinese names beginning thus and not found here: see under CHWANG-.

Chüanhsien or **Ch'üan-hsien** (both: chüăn'shyĕn'), town, ⊙ Chüanhsien co. (pop. 308,281), NE Kwangsi prov., China, near Hunan line, on railroad and 65 mi. NE of Kweilin, and on Siang R.; rice-growing center; cotton weaving; corn, wheat, potatoes, peanuts.

Chüanning, Manchuria: see WUTAN.

Chüantsiao or **Ch'üan-chiao** (both: chüăn'jyou'), town, ⊙ Chüantsiao co. (pop. 181,476), N Anhwei prov., China, near Kiangsu line, 28 mi. W of Nanking; rice, wheat, cotton.

Chuarrancho (chwärän'chō), town (1950 pop. 2,653), Guatemala dept., S central Guatemala, 13 mi. N of Guatemala; alt. 4,449 ft. Market center; corn, black beans, sugar cane, fruit.

Chubar-Kuduk, Kazakh SSR: see SHUBAR-KUDUK.

Chubarovka, Ukrainian SSR: see POLOGI.

Chubartau (chŏŏbŭrtou'), village, SW Semipalatinsk oblast, Kazakh SSR, 90 mi. W of Ayaguz; sheep.

Chubb Crater, Que.: see CRATER LAKE.

Chubbuck, town (pop. 120), Bannock co., SE Idaho, just N of Pocatello.

Chubek (chŏŏ'bĕk), village, SE Kulyab oblast, Tadzhik SSR, near Panj R. (Afghanistan line), 20 mi. SSW of Kulyab; center of agr. area (cotton, jute) placed under cultivation in 1940s.

Chubunshin, Korea: see CHUMUNJIN.

Chuburná (chōōbōōrnä'), officially Chuburná de Hidalgo, town (pop. 1,423), Yucatan, SE Mexico, 3 mi. N of Mérida; henequen.

Chubu-sangaku National Park (chōō'bōō-säng'gäkōō) (□656), central Honshu, Japan, in Nagano, Toyama, and Gifu prefectures; contains several high mts.; Mt. Hotaka (10,527 ft.), highest. Has alpine flora, hot springs. Winter sports. Sometimes spelled Tyubu-sangaku; also called Japanese Alps Natl. Park.

Chubut (chōōbōōt'), national territory (□ 65,669; pop. 58,856), S Argentina, on the Atlantic; ⊙ Rawson. Part of Patagonia, bet. the Andes and the Atlantic, bounded N by 42°S and S by 44°38'S. Crossed by Chubut R. In W is a noted lake region, including lakes of Puelo, Menéndez, General Paz, and Futalaufquén. In E, Valdés Peninsula juts into the Atlantic. Has a dry, cool climate. Mineral resources include coal (Cholila, Tecka, El Maitén, Epuyén), gold (Esquel, Tecka), lead (Gastre), salt (Valdés Peninsula). Some agr. activity along Chubut R. (irrigation area) and coast (alfalfa, grain, potatoes, fruit), but sheep raising predominates. Some cattle raising in lake dist. Meat packing and fish canning at Puerto Madryn. Lumbering in subandean forests (W). Mining, lumbering, dairying, flour milling. Los Alerces natl. park, in lake dist., was created 1937. Territory was set up in 1884 and largely colonized by Welsh immigrants. In 1946 the S part (□ 21,397) of Chubut was inc. into newly separated Comodoro Rivadavia military zone; prior to 1946 the Chubut S boundary was 46°S.

Chubut River, central Patagonia, Argentina, rises in the Andes SSE of San Carlos de Bariloche (Río Negro natl. territory) and crosses Chubut natl. territory, flowing SE to Paso de los Indios, then E, past Las Plumas, Dolavón, Gaimán, Trelew, and Rawson, to the Atlantic; c.500 mi. long; not navigable. Lower course is fertile agr. area, settled mostly by Welshmen. Affluents include the Tecka and the Chico.

Chucán, Cerro (sĕ'rō chōōkän'), Andean mountain (c.6,850 ft.) on Argentina-Chile border, S of Pino Hachado Pass; 38°41'S.

Chucándiro (chōōkän'dērō), town (pop. 1,861), Michoacán, central Mexico, on W bank of L. Cuitzeo, 18 mi. NW of Morelia; cereals, fruit, livestock.

Chucena (chōō-thā'nä), town (pop. 2,033), Huelva prov., SW Spain, near Seville prov. border, 22 mi. W of Seville; wine, olives, acorns, timber.

Chucheng or **Chu-ch'eng** (both: jōō'chŭng'), town (1922 pop. estimate 80,000), ⊙ Chucheng co. (pop. 816,577), SE Shantung prov., China, 50 mi. W of Tsingtao; silk weaving; trades in peanuts, millet, timber.

Chu-chi or **Chu-ch'i,** China: see CHUKI.

Ch'ü-ch'i, China: see KÜKI.

Chu-chia-chiao, China: see CHUKIAKIO.

Ch'ü-chiang, town, China: see KÜKONG.

Chu Chiang, river, Kwangtung prov., China: see CANTON RIVER.

Ch'ü Chiang, river, Szechwan prov., China: see CHÜ RIVER.

Ch'ü-ching, China: see KÜTSING.

Chuchkovo (cho͞och'kŭvŭ), village (1939 pop. over 2,000), E central Ryazan oblast, Russian SFSR, 19 mi. WSW of Sasovo; agr. implements.

Chuchow. 1 Town, Anhwei prov., China: see CHUHSIEN. 2 Town, Chekiang prov., China: see LISHUI. 3 or **Chu-chou** (jo͞o'jō'), town, E central Hunan prov., China, on Siang R. and 9 mi. ESE of Siangtan; railroad center on Hankow-Canton RR; junction for lines to Kiangsi and Kweichow.

Chüchow, China: see CHÜHSIEN.

Chüchüeh, China: see YUNGJEN.

Chuchuligovo, Bulgaria: see KULATA.

Chuckawalla Mountains (chŭkùwŏ'lù), SE Calif., small desert range just N of the Chocolate Mts., 30 mi. N of Calipatria; max. alt. 4,490 ft. The lower Little Chuckawalla Mts. are just SE.

Chuckchee Sea: see CHUKCHI SEA.

Chucuito, province, Peru: see JULI.

Chucuito (cho͞okwē'tō). 1 W section of Callao, W central Peru, on the Pacific, at base of La Punta peninsula. 2 Town (pop. 803), Puno dept., SE Peru, on NW shore of L. Titicaca, 9 mi. ESE of Puno; grain, potatoes, livestock.

Chucuito, Lake, Bolivia: see TITICACA, LAKE.

Chucunaque River (cho͞okoo͞nä'kä), Darién prov., E Panama, rises in the Cordillera de San Blas, flows c.90 mi. SE, past Yaviza, to Tuira R. near El Real. Navigable for 30 mi. above mouth. Its basin is inhabited by Kuna and Choco Indians.

Chuda (cho͝od'ŭ), town (pop. 8,129), NE Saurashtra, India, 15 mi. S of Wadhwan; local market for millet, cotton; hand-loom weaving. Was ⊙ former Eastern Kathiawar state of Chuda (□ 78; pop. 15,818) of Western India States agency, merged 1948 with Saurashtra.

Chudleigh (chŭd'lē), town and parish (pop. 1,944), S central Devon, England, on Teign R. and 9 mi. SW of Exeter; agr. market; flour mills. Has 14th-cent. church.

Chudnov (cho͞odnôf'), town (1926 pop. 7,867), SW Zhitomir oblast, Ukrainian SSR, on Teterev R. and 22 mi. WNW of Berdichev; distilling, food industries, light mfg.

Chudovo (cho͞o'dùvŭ), city (1939 pop. over 10,000), N Novgorod oblast, Russian SFSR, near Volkhov R., 45 mi. NNE of Novgorod; rail and road hub; match-mfg. center; glassworks, cement mill, metalworks, shoe factory. Became city in 1937. During Second World War, held (1941–44) by Germans.

Chudskoye Ozero, USSR: see PEIPUS, LAKE.

Chüeh-chiang, China: see CHÜEHKIANG.

Chüehkiang or **Chüeh-chiang** (both: jüĕ'jyäng'), town, S Kiangsu prov., China, 30 mi. NE of Nantung, near Yellow Sea; commercial center; saltworks, fisheries.

Ch'üeh-shan, China: see KIOSHAN.

Chuenpi (chwĕn'pē'), island at mouth of Canton R., S Kwangtung prov., China, S of Anunghoi isl., 35 mi. SE of Canton.

Ch'ü-fou, China: see KŪFOW.

Chufut-Kale, Russian SFSR: see BAKHCHISARAI.

Chugach Islands (cho͞o'găch), group of 3 small mountainous islands, S Alaska, off S Kenai Peninsula, in Gulf of Alaska; 59°8'N 151°40'W. Consists of Chugach Isl., Pearl Isl., and Elizabeth Isl.

Chugach Mountains, part of the Coast Ranges, S Alaska, extend 300 mi. E-W in crescent bet. Turnagain Arm and Cape Yakataga, N of Prince William Sound and S of Alaska Range; W continuation of St. Elias Mts. Highest peak is Mt. Marcus Baker (13,250 ft.). On S slope is Chugach Natl. Forest.

Chugach National Forest (□ 7,500), S Alaska, on S slope of Chugach Mts., on N shore of Prince William Sound, bet. Cape Suckling (E) and SE tip of Kenai Peninsula (W); includes offshore isls. Virgin forest, mainly western hemlock and Sitka spruce. Established 1907.

Chuginadak Island (cho͞ogĭ'nùdăk) (14 mi. long, 3–8 mi. wide), largest of Isls. of Four Mountains, Aleutian Isls., SW Alaska, 25 mi. W of Umnak Isl.; 52°50'N 169°44'W; rises to 5,680 ft. on Mt. Cleveland (W), active volcano which last erupted violently June 10, 1944.

Chugoku-katsuyama, Japan: see KATSUYAMA, Okayama prefecture.

Chuguchak (cho͞ogo͞ochäk') or **Tarbagatai** (tärbägätī'), Chinese *Tahcheng* or *T'a-ch'eng* (tä'chŭng'), town, ⊙ Chuguchak co. (pop. 48,327), N Sinkiang prov., China, in the Dzungaria, on USSR border, 300 mi. NW of Urumchi, 150 mi. SE of Ayaguz (on Turksib RR); major center for trade with USSR; exports fur, cotton, fruit. Mfg. (carpets, flour); camel raising. Gold mining near by. Situated at S foot of Tarbagatai Range, it is the administrative seat of Chuguchak dist., part of the former East Turkestan Republic (1944–50).

Chugunash (cho͞ogo͞onäsh'), town (1948 pop. over 2,000), S Kemerovo oblast, Russian SFSR, on branch of Trans-Siberian RR and 15 mi. NW of Tashtagol, in Gornaya Shoriya iron-mining dist.; quartz mine; sawmill.

Chuguyev (cho͞ogo͞o'yĭf), city (1926 pop. 14,412), N central Kharkov oblast, Ukrainian SSR, on the Northern Donets and 20 mi. ESE of Kharkov; food processing, metalworking. Soldier settlement in early 19th cent.

Chuguyevka (–kŭ), village (1948 pop. over 2,000), S Maritime Territory, Russian SFSR, on slope of Sikhote-Alin Range, on Ulukhe R. and 60 mi. ESE of Spassk-Dalni; grain, soybeans. Iron deposits near by.

Chugwater, town (pop. 283), Platte co., SE Wyo., on Chugwater Creek and 43 mi. N of Cheyenne, in ranching area; alt. c.5,290 ft.; grain, livestock.

Chugwater Creek, SE Wyo., rises in E Albany co., flows 81 mi. generally NE, past Chugwater, to Laramie R. near Wheatland.

Chuharkana or **Chuharkana Mandi** (cho͞ohŭrkä'nŭ mŭn'dē), town (pop., including SE suburb of Nokhar, 6,071), Sheikhupura dist., E Punjab, W Pakistan, 10 mi. WNW of Sheikhupura; agr. market (wheat, cotton, millet); cotton ginning. Also written Chuhar Kana.

Chuho, Formosa: see CHUNGPU.

Chuho, Manchuria: see SHANGCHIH.

Chuhsien or **Ch'u-hsien** (both: cho͞o'shyĕn'), town, ⊙ Chuhsien co. (pop. 145,641), N Anhwei prov., China, 30 mi. WNW of Nanking and on railroad; rice, wheat, kaoliang, beans, corn. Until 1912 called Chuchow.

Chühsien. 1 or **Ch'ü-hsien** (both: chü'shyĕn'), town (pop. 32,125), ⊙ Chühsien co. (pop. 322,056), SW Chekiang prov., China, on left headstream of Tsientang R. and 120 mi. SW of Hangchow, and on railroad; commercial center; mfg. (leather goods, tung oil). Tea, fruit, rice, wheat. Formerly called Chüchow or Küchow. 2 (jü'shyĕn') Town (pop. estimate 60,000), ⊙ Chühsien co. (pop. 896,185), S central Shantung prov., China, 45 mi. NE of Lini; cotton weaving; sericulture; wheat, millet. Until 1913 called Chüchow. 3 or **Ch'ü-hsien** (chü'-shyĕn'), town (pop. 10,634), ⊙ Chühsien co. (pop. 735,400), E central Szechwan prov., China, 70 mi. NE of Hochwan and on Chü R.; match mfg.; rice, wheat, sweet potatoes, millet. kaoliang. Gypsum quarrying, coal deposits near by.

Ch'u-hsiung, China: see TSUYUNG.

Chuí or **Xuí** (both: shwē), town (pop. 333), S Rio Grande do Sul, Brazil, on Uruguay border adjoining Chuy, bet. S tip of Mirim L. and the Atlantic, 11 mi. S of Santa Vitória do Palmar; southernmost settlement in Brazil; 33°41'S 53°27'W.

Ch'u-i, China: see CHUYI.

Chu-Ili Mountains (cho͞o"-ĭlyē'), branch of Tien Shan mountain system, in Dzhambul oblast, Kazakh SSR, W of the Trans-Ili Ala-Tau and NE of Chu R.; rise to 3,470 ft.

Chuit Island (□ 1.4; pop. 153), Chiloé prov., S Chile, bet. mainland and Chiloé Isl., 37 mi. SE of Castro; stock raising, fishing, lumbering.

Chüjung, China: see KÜYUNG.

Chukai (cho͞o"kī'), second largest town (pop. 6,635) of Trengganu, NE Malaya, on South China Sea at mouth of Kemaman R., just W of KUALA KEMAMAN (port) and 75 mi. SSE of Kuala Trengganu, near Pahang border; sawmilling, boat building; samshu distilling, cheroot mfg. Exports iron ore from Machang Satahun (10 mi. W) and tin from Bundi mine (17 mi. WSW). Sometimes called Kemaman.

Chukchi National Okrug (cho͞ok'chē), administrative division (□ 274,520; pop. c.20,000) of Kamchatka oblast, Khabarovsk Territory, Russian SFSR; ⊙ Anadyr. In NE extremity of Siberia, on Arctic Circle, in tundra zone, bet. E.Siberian, Chukchi, and Bering seas; drained by Anadyr and Anyui rivers; terminates NE in Chukchi Peninsula. Inhabited largely by Chukchi (Luoravetlany; a paleo-Asiatic tribe) and some Lamuts (SW); reindeer raising, fishing, hunting (furs). Coal mined on Anadyr Gulf. Occupied by Russians in 18th cent. Formed 1930 within former Far Eastern Territory. It passed in 1951 from Kamchatka oblast directly under Khabarovsk territorial administration.

Chukchi Peninsula, NE extremity of Asia and Siberia, in Chukchi Natl. Okrug, Khabarovsk Territory, Russian SFSR, at E end of Anadyr Range. Mountainous (to 5,000 ft.); severe climate; tundra vegetation: silver-lead ores, coal deposits. Its NE point is Cape DEZHNEV.

Chukchi Range, Russian SFSR: see ANADYR RANGE.

Chukchi Sea, Rus. *Chukotskoye More,* part of Arctic Ocean; bounded W by 180° long. at Wrangel Isl., S by NE Siberia and NW Alaska, E by Beaufort Sea, N by continental shelf; navigable Aug.–Sept. Joined by Bering Strait with Bering Sea. Also spelled Chuckchee Sea.

Chukfaktoolik or **Chokfactoly** (cho͞ofăk'tŏlĭk, –lē), village (pop. 59), SW Alaska, near Bethel.

Chukhloma (cho͞o'khlùmŭ), city (1926 pop. 2,259), NW Kostroma oblast, Russian SFSR, on L. Chukhloma (□ c.20), 30 mi. NNE of Galich; flour milling, flax retting. Dates from 1381.

Chuki. 1 or **Chu-chi** (both: jo͞o'jē'), town (pop. 30,377), ⊙ Chuki co. (pop. 493,720), N central Chekiang prov., China, 28 mi. SW of Shaohing and on railroad; rice, wheat, beans, silk, bamboo, timber. Zinc mines near by. 2 or **Chu-ch'i** (both: jo͞o'chē'), town (pop. 25,386), ⊙ Chuki co. (pop. 178,064), NW Hupeh prov., China, on Shensi line, 65 mi. WSW of Yünhsien; rice, wheat, cotton.

Chukiakio or **Chu-chia-chiao** (both: jo͞o'jyä'jyou'), town, SE Kiangsu prov., China, 28 mi. WSW of Shanghai, in lake area; commercial center.

Chu Kiang, Kwangtung prov., China: see CANTON RIVER.

Chü Kiang, Szechwan prov., China: see CHÜ RIVER.

Chuking, China: see KINSHAN.

Chukotskaya, Chukotski, Chukotskiy, or **Chukotskoye,** Rus. adjectival forms of CHUKCHI.

Ch'u-k'uang-k'eng, Formosa: see CHUKWANGKENG.

Chukwangkeng or **Ch'u-k'uang-k'eng** (both: cho͞o'-kwäng'kŭng'), Jap. *Shukkoko* (sho͞ok'kōkō), village (1935 pop. 1,486), NW Formosa, 7 mi. SE of Miaoli; oil-drilling center, with refinery.

Chula (cho͞o'lù), town (pop. 314), Livingston co., N central Mo., 10 mi. NNE of Chillicothe.

Chulakdoshchan, Kazakh SSR: see SMIRNOVSKI.

Chulak-Kurgan (cho͞oläk"-ko͞orgän'), village (1948 pop. over 2,000), N South Kazakhstan oblast, Kazakh SSR, in N foothills of the Kara-Tau, 55 mi. NE of Turkestan; cotton. Fell to Russians (1863).

Chulak-Tau (–tou'), town (1948 pop. c.6,000), W Dzhambul oblast, Kazakh SSR, in the Kara-Tau, 60 mi. NW of Dzhambul (connected by railroad); phosphorite-mining center, on reservoir of small Tamdy R.

Chula Vista (cho͞o"lù vĭ'stù), city (pop. 15,927), San Diego co., extreme S Calif., S of San Diego, on San Diego Bay; agr. (celery, citrus fruit; dairy products; poultry; flowers, bulbs); aircraft factory. Inc. 1911.

Chulilla (cho͞olē'lyä), town (pop. 1,278), Valencia prov., E Spain, 16 mi. WNW of Liria; brandy distilling; cereals, wine, olive oil, truck produce. Has mineral springs. The scenic Turia R. falls are near by.

Chulín Island (cho͞olēn') (□ 6.5; pop. 320), Chiloé prov., S Chile, bet. mainland and Chiloé Isl., 40 mi. ESE of Castro; 45°36'S; 4 mi. long. Potatoes, livestock; fishing, lumbering.

Chulitna River (cho͞olĭt'nù), S central Alaska, rises in McKinley glacier system, Alaska Range, near 62°54'N 150°W, flows 80 mi. S to Susitna R. at Talkeetna.

Chulman or **Chul'man** (cho͞olmän'), town (1941 pop. over 500), SE Yakut Autonomous SSR, Russian SFSR, on Yakutsk-Never highway and 125 mi. S of Aldan; graphite and lignite mines.

Chulmleigh (chŭm'lē), town and parish (pop. 1,165), N central Devon, England, on Taw R. and 13 mi. ESE of Torrington; agr. market. Has 15th-cent. church.

Chulucanas (cho͞olo͞okä'näs), city (pop. 12,622), ⊙ Morropón prov. (□ 1,315; pop. 62,980), Piura dept., NW Peru, on Piura R. and 33 mi. E of Piura, in rice region; cattle raising.

Chulumani (cho͞olo͞omä'nē), city (pop. c.6,500), ⊙ Sud Yungas or Sur Yungas prov., La Paz dept., W Bolivia, 40 mi. ENE of La Paz, on road; alt. 6,250 ft. Subtropical agr. center for coca, coffee, cacao, fruit, quina; tourist resort.

Chulym (cho͞olĭm'), city (1939 pop. over 10,000), central Novosibirsk oblast, Russian SFSR, on Chulym R., on Trans-Siberian RR and 75 mi. W of Novosibirsk; flour milling, dairying. Industrialized after 1935.

Chulym River. 1 In W Krasnoyarsk Territory and SE Tomsk oblast, Russian SFSR, rises in the Kuznetsk Ala-Tau at 6,500 ft., flows N in winding course, past Bogotol, Achinsk, and Birilyussy, and WNW, past Asino, to Ob R. near Mogochin; 1,177 mi. long. Receives Kiya R. (left). Navigable below Achinsk. 2 In Novosibirsk oblast, Russian SFSR, rises in E Baraba Steppe, flows 140 mi. SW, past Chulym, to SE L. Chany.

Chulyshman River, Russian SFSR: see TELETSKOYE LAKE.

Chuma (cho͞o'mä), town (pop. c.3,200), ⊙ Muñecas prov., La Paz dept., W Bolivia, 90 mi. NNW of La Paz; alt. c.11,500 ft.; *oca.*

Chumakovo (cho͞omŭkō'vù), village (1939 pop. over 500), central Novosibirsk oblast, Russian SFSR, on Om R. and 35 mi. NE of Barabinsk; dairying.

Chumalhari, mountain, Bhutan and Tibet: see CHOMO LHARI.

Chumatlán (cho͞omätlän'), village (pop. 1,242), Veracruz, E Mexico, in E foothills of Sierra Madre Oriental, 23 mi. SW of Papantla; corn, coffee, sugar.

Chumayel (cho͞omĭēl'), town (pop. 1,292), Yucatan, SE Mexico, 18 mi. E of Ticul; henequen, sugar cane, fruit.

Chumbi (cho͞om'bē), town, S Tibet, in Chumbi Valley, on upper Torsa (Amo Chu) R. and 37 mi. NE of Kalimpong (India), and on main India-Tibet trade route, bet. Sikkim and Bhutan.

Chumbicha (cho͞ombē'chä), town (pop. estimate 800), ⊙ Capayán dept. (□ 2,632; pop. 7,961), S Catamarca prov., Argentina, 31 mi. SW of Catamarca; rail junction and agr. center; livestock, wine, citrus fruit, tomatoes.

Chumbi Valley (cho͞om'bē) (□ 700), in W Assam Himalayas, in wedge-shaped section of S Tibet, bet. Bhutan (E) and Sikkim (W); extends c.30 mi. NNE to Tang La pass; alt. c.10,000 ft. Watered by headstream of Torsa R.; traversed by main India-Lhasa trade route. Agr.: barley, wheat, vegetables. Main towns: Chumbi, Phari, Yatung. Occupied 1904–8 by British.

Chumbivilcas, Peru: see SANTO TOMÁS, Cuzco dept.

Chumerna, rail station, Bulgaria: see BINKOS.

Chumerna (cho͞omĕr'nä), N central Bulgaria, highest peak (5,036 ft.) in Yelena Mts., 12 mi. SSE of Yelena. Coal mining.

Chumikan (cho͞omēkän'), village (1948 pop. over 500), SW Lower Amur oblast, Khabarovsk Territory, Russian SFSR, port on SW Sea of Okhotsk, at mouth of Uda R., and 245 mi. WNW of Nikolayevsk; gold mining.

Chumik Gyatsa, Nepal: see MUKTINATH.

Chumphon (cho͝om'pôn'), town (1947 pop. 5,219), ⊙ Chumphon prov. (□ 2,185; 1947 pop. 118,427), S Thailand, on E coast of Isthmus of Kra, on railroad and 95 mi. N of Suratthani; highway to Kraburi (on W coast). Fishing port on Gulf of Siam; also trade in rice, coconuts, fruit; charcoal burning. Tin mining (S). Also spelled Chumpon, Choomphone, or Jumbor.

Chumpi (cho͞om'pē), town (pop. 1,723), Ayacucho dept., S Peru, in Cordillera Occidental, 5 mi. S of Coracora; grain, alfalfa.

Chumunjin (cho͞o'mo͞on'jēn'), Jap. *Chubunshin*, town (1949 pop. 23,104), Kangwon prov., central Korea, S of 38°N, on Sea of Japan, 60 mi. E of Chunchon; fishing port.

Chumurchi, Bhutan: see CHAMARCHI.

Chumysh Dam, Kirghiz SSR: see CHU RIVER.

Chumysh River (cho͞omĭsh'), N Altai Territory, Russian SFSR, formed by union of 2 headstreams (Kara-Chumysh and Tom-Chumysh) on Salair Ridge; flows 380 mi. generally W, past Kytmanovo, Sorokino, and Talmenka, to Ob R. 25 mi. W of Barnaul.

Chün-, for Chinese names beginning thus and not found here: see under KÜN-.

Ch'u-na, Tibet: see TSONA.

Chunakam, Ceylon: see KANKESANTURAI.

Ch'un-an, China: see SHUNAN.

Chunan (jo͞o'nän'), Jap. *Chikunan* (chē'ko͞onän), village (1935 pop. 3,245), NW Formosa, on W coast, 10 mi. SW of Sinchu, and on railroad; sugar milling; bamboo products, hats, wooden articles; rice, sweet potatoes, peanuts.

Chunar (cho͞onär'), town (pop. 8,654), Mirzapur dist., SE Uttar Pradesh, India, on the Ganges and 20 mi. E of Mirzapur; mfg. of cement, glazed pottery, buttons; trades in rice, gram, barley, wheat, oilseeds. Mogul tomb. Fort (built on rock jutting into the Ganges) figured importantly in struggles bet. Mogul emperor Humayun and Afghan leader Sher Shah, who captured it in 1539; recovered (1575) by Moguls under Akbar. Under nawab of Oudh in 18th cent.; came under British rule in 1764. A favorite residence of Warren Hastings. Sandstone quarries near by.

Chuna River (cho͞onä'), W Irkutsk oblast and S Krasnoyarsk Territory, Russian SFSR, rises in Eastern Sayan Mts., flows N, past Nizhneudinsk, and NW, joining Biryusa R. to form Taseyeva R.; c.600 mi. long. Called Uda R. in upper course.

Chunchi (cho͞on'chē), town (1950 pop. 2,164), Chimborazo, S central Ecuador, in the Andes, on Pan American Highway and 9 mi. SW of Alausí; cereals, potatoes, stock.

Chunchon (cho͞on'chŭn'), Jap. *Shunsen* or *Syunsen* (both: sho͞on'sän), city (1949 pop. 54,539), ⊙ Kangwon prov., central Korea, S of 38°N, on Pukhan R. (tributary of Han R.) and 45 mi. NE of Seoul; 37°52'N 127°44'E; commercial center in agr. area (rice, millet, soybeans). Charcoal and honey are produced in vicinity. Has agr. school and agr. experiment station.

Chundzha (cho͞onjä'), village (1939 pop. over 500), SE Alma-Ata oblast, Kazakh SSR, 120 mi. E of Alma-Ata; sheep. Pop. largely Uigur.

Ch'ung-, for Chinese names beginning thus and not found here: see under TSUNG-.

Chung, river, China: see TO RIVER.

Chungan or **Ch'ung-an** (both: cho͝ong'än'), town (pop. 6,417), ⊙ Chungan co. (pop. 68,318), N Fukien prov., China, near Kiangsi line, 50 mi. NNW of Kienow, at foot of Bohea Hills; major tea center; rice, sweet potatoes, beans. Coal mining.

Chung-chiang, China: see CHUNGKIANG.

Chung-chien Island, China: see TRITON ISLAND.

Chung-ch'ing or **Ch'ung-ch'ing,** China: see CHUNGKING.

Chungchong-namdo, Korea: see SOUTH CHUNGCHONG.

Chungchong-pukdo, Korea: see NORTH CHUNGCHONG.

Chungchow, China: see CHUNGHSIEN.

Chung-hsiang, China: see CHUNGSIANG.

Chunghsien (jo͝ong'shyĕn'), town (pop. 17,335), ⊙ Chunghsien co. (pop. 467,280), E Szechwan prov., China, on left bank of Yangtze R. and 40 mi. SW of Wanhsien; tung-oil trading center; rice, millet, wheat, beans, kaoliang. Iron mines and saltworks near by. Until 1913 called Chungchow.

Ch'ung-hsin, China: see TSUNGSIN.

Ch'ung-i, China: see TSUNGYI.

Chungjin, Korea: see CHONGJIN.

Chungju (cho͝ong'jo͞o'), Jap. *Chushu*, town (1949 pop 41,227), N.Chungchong prov., S Korea, 65 mi. SE of Seoul; agr. center (tobacco, cotton, peaches, rice, soybeans). Has agr. school.

Chungkiang or **Chung-chiang** (both: jo͝ong'jyäng'), town (pop. 24,026), ⊙ Chungkiang co. (pop. 825,033), NW Szechwan prov., China, 45 mi. NE of Chengtu; spinning and weaving (ramie, cotton); rice, sweet potatoes, wheat, millet, beans. Saltworks near by.

Chung Kiang, river, China: see TO RIVER.

Chungkien Island, China: see TRITON ISLAND.

Chungking. 1 or **Chung-ch'ing** (cho͝ong'kĭng', jo͝ong'chĭng'), city (□ 115; 1947 pop. 1,000,101), ⊙ Southwest China, in but independent of Szechwan prov., China, on Yangtze R. at mouth of the Kialing, and 450 mi. WSW of Hankow; 29°34'N 106°35'E. Leading commercial center of SW China, it is the upstream head of regular navigation on the Yangtze and the natural outlet for the products of Szechwan. Its industries, dating largely from Second World War, include cotton and silk mills, and paper, match, iron, steel, and chemical plants. Among its leading exports are tung oil, hog bristles, tea, silk, hides, and medicinal plants. Situated on a rocky, 1-mi.-wide promontory at the Kialing-Yangtze confluence, it is seat of a univ. and a col. of education. Chungking was opened to foreign trade in 1891 and developed as a commercial center. It became a municipality under prov. jurisdiction in 1923 and under central govt. jurisdiction in 1939. The city became widely known during the Second World War, when it was (1937–46) the capital of war-time China and experienced a great economic boom. Officially known as Pahsien (bä'shyĕn') prior to 1936, when it was seat of Pahsien co. and included the N suburb of Kiangpei, across Kialing R. **2** or **Ch'ung-ch'ing** (cho͝ong'chĭng'), town (pop. 18,992), ⊙ Chungking co. (pop. 386,020), W Szechwan prov., China, 25 mi. W of Chengtu; match mfg.; rice, sugar cane, sweet potatoes, wheat, rapeseed. Coal mines near by. Also called Chungking West.

Chungli (jo͝ong'lē'), Jap. *Chureki* (cho͞orä'kē), town (1935 pop. 6,214), NW Formosa, 19 mi. NE of Sinchu; center of rice- and tea-growing dist.; sugar milling. Radio station.

Chungmow or **Chung-mou** (jo͝ong'mō'), town, ⊙ Chungmow co. (pop. 168,543), N Honan prov., China, on Lunghai RR and 20 mi. WSW of Kaifeng; millet, wheat, kaoliang, beans.

Chungning (jo͝ong'nĭng'), town (pop. 3,513), ⊙ Chungning co. (pop. 81,190), SE Ningsia prov., China, 80 mi. SW of Yinchwan and on right bank of Yellow R.; cattle raising; rice, wheat, kaoliang.

Chungpa (jo͝ong'bä'), town, N Szechwan prov., China, 7 mi. SSW of Kiangyu and on Fow R.; commercial center; exports medicinal plants, indigo, mushrooms.

Chungpu, China: see HWANGLING.

Chungpu (jo͝ong'bo͞o'), Jap. *Chuho* (cho͞o'hō), village (1935 pop. 664), W central Formosa, 7 mi. SE of Kiayi; tobacco center. Oil field near by.

Chungsan (cho͝ong'sän'), Jap. *Sosan*, township (1944 pop. 12,932), S.Pyongan prov., N Korea, 20 mi. WNW of Pyongyang; silk cocoons.

Chungsha, China: see MACCLESFIELD BANK.

Chungshan (jo͝ong'shän'). **1** Town, ⊙ Chungshan co. (pop. 178,396), E Kwangsi prov., China, 75 mi. N of Wuchow, near Hunan line; rice, wheat, beans, peanuts. Tin mines, coal deposits near by. **2** Town (pop. 84,219), ⊙ Chungshan co. (pop. 751,435), S Kwangtung prov., China, on Chungshan isl. of Canton R. delta, 40 mi. SSE of Canton. Produces rice, fruit, sea food. Sun Yat-sen b. here. The name Chungshan was applied (1930–34) to TANGKIAKWAN. Present co. seat was formerly called Shekki. Chungshan co., coextensive with isl., was known as Heungshan (Mandarin *Hsiang-shan*) until 1925. Isl. is sometimes called MACAO, for Portuguese colony at S tip.

Chungshankong, China: see TANGKIAKWAN.

Chungsiang or **Chung-hsiang** (both: jo͝ong'shyäng'), town (pop. 25,631), ⊙ Chungsiang co. (pop. 304,557), central Hupeh prov., China, 110 mi. WNW of Hankow and on left bank of Han R.; exports rice, cotton, ramie, charcoal. Until 1912 called Anlu.

Chungtang (cho͝ong'täng), village, E Sikkim, India, in E Nepal Himalayas, at confluence of rivers Lachen Chu and Lachung Chu, 20 mi. N of Gangtok; corn, rice, pulse. Noted lamasery of Tulung, with art collection, 12 mi. WNW. Also spelled Chunthang, Tsuntang; also called Tsetame.

Chungtien (jo͝ong'dyĕn'), town (pop. 2,827), ⊙ Chungtien co. (pop. 34,586), NW Yunnan prov., China, on Sikang line, 70 mi. NNE of Likiang, near Yangtze R.; alt. 11,057 ft.; lumbering center; rice, millet, beans.

Chungtu (jo͝ong'do͞o'), town, ⊙ Chungtu co. (pop. 37,809), NE central Kwangsi prov., China, 38 mi. NNE of Liuchow.

Chungwei (jo͝ong'wā'), town (pop. 10,575), SE Ningsia prov., China, on left bank of Yellow R. (head of navigation) and 90 mi. SW of Yinchwan, at the Great Wall; exports rice, wheat. millet, furs, wool, medicinal herbs. Coal and barite mining.

Chungyang (jo͝ong'yäng'), town, ⊙ Chungyang co. (pop. 70,671), W Shansi prov., China, 14 mi. S of Lishih; millet, wheat, beans, kaoliang. Coal mining near by. Until 1914 called Ningsiang.

Chünhsien, China: see SÜNHSIEN.

Chunhwa or **Ch'un-hua** (cho͞on'hwä'), town, ⊙ Chunhwa co. (pop. 38,195), central Shensi prov., China, 45 mi. NE of Sian; wheat, millet, beans.

Chunian (cho͞on'yän), town (pop. 10,093), Lahore dist., E Punjab, W Pakistan, 45 mi. SSW of Lahore; trades in wheat, cotton, gram, oilseeds; cotton ginning, hand-loom weaving.

Chunju, Korea: see CHONJU.

Chunky, village (pop. 258), Newton co., E central Miss., 13 mi. W of Meridian.

Chunnakam, Ceylon: see KANKESANTURAI.

Chunthang, India: see CHUNGTANG.

Chunya (cho͞o'nyä), town (pop. c.2,000), Southern Highlands prov., S Tanganyika, 25 mi. N of Mbeya; 8°31'S 33°25'E. Center of Lupa goldfield (discovered 1922). Agr. trade: tea, coffee, rice.

Chunya River (cho͞o'nyŏŏ), S Evenki Natl. Okrug, Krasnoyarsk Territory, Russian SFSR, rises on Central Siberian Plateau, flows 250 mi. generally W, past Strelka, to Stony Tunguska R. at Baikit.

Chupa (cho͞o'pŭ), town (1939 pop. over 500), N Karelo-Finnish SSR, port on inlet of White Sea, on Murmansk RR and 60 mi. SSE of Kandalaksha; extensive feldspar and mica quarries.

Chupaca (cho͞opä'kä), city (pop. 4,482), Junín dept., central Peru, in Mantaro R. valley, 5 mi. W of Huancayo; grain, alfalfa, sheep.

Chupadera Mesa (cho͞opŭdâ'rŭ mā'sŭ), high tableland (6–9,000 ft.) largely in E Socorro co., central N.Mex. Includes SIERRA OSCURA in SW, part of Cibola Natl. Forest in NE. Game is abundant.

Chupampa (cho͞opäm'pä), village (pop. 444), Herrera prov., S central Panama, in Pacific lowland, 20 mi. WNW of Chitré; corn, livestock.

Chupara Point (chŭpä'rŭ), cape, N Trinidad, B.W.I., 14 mi. NE of Port of Spain; 10°48'N 61°22'W.

Chupriya, Yugoslavia: see CUPRIJA.

Chuquiaguillo River, Bolivia: see LA PAZ RIVER.

Chuquiananta, Nevado (nävä'dō cho͞okyänän'tä), Andean peak (18,005 ft.), N Chile, near Bolivia border; 17°47'S.

Chuquibamba (cho͞okēbäm'bä), city (pop. 2,480), ⊙ Condesuyos prov. (□ 1,295; pop. 16,063), Arequipa dept., S Peru, at S foot of Nudo Coropuna, 90 mi. WNW of Arequipa (linked by highway); 15°51'S 72°39'W; alt. 9,586 ft. Agr. center (wheat, corn, potatoes, cattle). Archaeological remains near by.

Chuquibambilla (cho͞okēbämbē'yä), city (pop. 1,293), ⊙ Grau prov. (□ 1,367; pop. 69,683), Apurímac dept., S central Peru, in Andean valley, 33 mi. SSE of Abancay; alt. 10,825 ft. Grain, potatoes, stock.

Chuquicamata (cho͞okēkämä'tä), mining settlement (1930 pop. 13,346), Antofagasta prov., N Chile, on arid plateau on W slopes of the Andes (alt. 10,435 ft.), 135 mi. NE of Antofagasta, 10 mi. N of Calama. One of world's largest copper-mining and smelting centers. Receives power from Tocopilla and water through pipe lines from higher Andes. The settlement is company owned and has theater, hosp., and other facilities. Adjoining country is rich in pre-Columbian remains.

Chuquisaca (cho͞okēsä'kä), dept. (□ 19,140; 1949 pop. estimate 392,800), S central Bolivia; ⊙ Sucre. Includes part of the Chaco (E); drained by upper course of Pilcomayo and Pilaya rivers. W part, in outliers of Cordillera Real, contains fertile valleys which produce corn, potatoes, wheat, grapes. E part, bordering on Santa Cruz dept. and Paraguay, consists of tropical lowlands producing sugar cane and tobacco. Oil at Camatindi and Ñancorainza (SE). Until 1826 name Chuquisaca was also applied by Spaniards to SUCRE.

Chur (ko͞or), Fr. *Coire* (kwär), Ital. *Coira* (kōē'ra), Romansh *Cuera* (kwā'rä), town (1950 pop. 19,256), ⊙ Grisons, E Switzerland, on Plessur R., in the Rhine valley, among mts. A Roman settlement (*Curia Rhaetorum*); since early times an episcopal see; its bishops were princes of the Holy Roman Empire. Pop. largely German speaking and Protestant. Produces flour, beer, chocolate, metal goods, woolen textiles; woodworking, printing. Points of interest: government buildings (1752) with library and archives, town hall (1465), Rhaetian Mus., Grisons Mus., episcopal court (on site of a Roman castrum) with Gothic cathedral (1175–1282), St. Martin's church (8th cent.; remodeled 15th cent.).

Chur (cho͞or), town (1943 pop. over 500), central Udmurt Autonomous SSR, Russian SFSR, on railroad and 18 mi. NNW of Izhevsk; lumbering.

Churachiki (cho͞orä'chĭkē), village (1939 pop. over 500), central Chuvash Autonomous SSR, Russian SFSR, on Lesser Tsivil R. and 13 mi. N of Kanash; wheat. Formerly spelled Churatchiki.

Churapcha (cho͞orŭpchä'), village (1948 pop. over 500), E Yakut Autonomous SSR, Russian SFSR, 90 mi. E of Yakutsk, in agr. area; livestock raising.

Churatchiki, Russian SFSR: see CHURACHIKI.

Church, urban district (1931 pop. 6,187; 1951 census 5,199), E central Lancashire, England, just W of Accrington; cotton milling, mfg. of chemicals.

Churchbridge, village (pop. 202), SE Sask., near Man. border, 33 mi. SE of Yorkton; mixed farming.

Church Buttes (bŭts) (alt. 6,351 ft.), eroded sandstone cliffs in extreme SW Wyo., c.45 mi. WSW of Rock Springs. They rise, in form of cathedral, 75 ft. above surrounding hills.

Church Creek, town (pop. 187), Dorchester co., E Md., on Eastern Shore, 6 mi. SW of Cambridge, on inlet of Little Choptank R. Near by are Old

Trinity Church (built c.1680; restored 1850) and Blackwater Natl. Wildlife Refuge.

Churchdown, agr. village and parish (pop. 1,302), N central Gloucester, England, 4 mi. E of Gloucester. Has Norman church. On near-by hill are remains of Roman camp.

Church Gresley, England: see SWADLINCOTE DISTRICT.

Church Hill, town (pop. 271), Queen Annes co., E Md., 25 mi. W of Dover, Del., in agr. area. Church (built 1730–32; restored 1881) contains gifts from Queen Anne.

Church Hulme, England: see HOLMES CHAPEL.

Churchill, village, N Man., on Hudson Bay, at mouth of Churchill R., and c.600 mi. NNE of Winnipeg; 58°47'N 94°12'W; railroad terminal; major grain-shipping port, serving N Man. Shipping season mid-Aug. to mid-Oct. Mouth of CHURCHILL RIVER was discovered 1619 by Jens Munck; Hudson's Bay Co. established trading post here, 1688; burned and abandoned soon after. Wooden Fort Churchill was established 1718, replaced (1733) by near-by Fort Prince of Wales, heavily fortified stone structure. It was long Br. stronghold in N Canada, though captured for short period by the French under La Pérouse in 1782. Remains of fort are now historic memorial. Construction of Hudson Bay Railway was begun 1911: original terminal of Port Nelson was abandoned (1927) in favor of Churchill. Line was completed 1929, and grain shipments begun 1931.

Churchill, county (□ 4,907; pop. 6,161), W central Nev., in Great Basin; ⊙ Fallon. Irrigated agr. area watered in W by Carson R. and Lahontan Reservoir. Alfalfa, livestock; gold, silver. Carson Sink is in N. Clan Alpine Mts. are in E. Formed 1861.

Churchill, borough (pop. 1,733), Allegheny co., SW Pa., E suburb of Pittsburgh. Inc. 1933.

Churchill, Cape, N Man., on Hudson Bay, 33 mi. E of Churchill; 58°47'N 93°15'W.

Churchill Downs, Ky.: see LOUISVILLE.

Churchill Lake (□ 213), NW Sask., on Churchill R., 210 mi. N of North Battleford; 25 mi. long, 14 mi. wide.

Churchill Lake, Piscataquis co., N central Maine, 64 mi. SW of Presque Isle, in wilderness recreational area; triangular, with 3-mi. sides. Joined by Allagash R. to Eagle and Umsaskis lakes.

Churchill Peak (10,500 ft.), N B.C., in Rocky Mts.; 58°19'N 125°8'W.

Churchill River, Canada, in N Sask. and N Man., issues from Methy L., NW Sask., flows SE through Peter Pond L. and Churchill L. to L. Île-à-la-Crosse, thence E and NE, through Frobisher L., Granville L., and Southern Indian L., to Hudson Bay at CHURCHILL; 1,000 mi. long. There are hydroelectric power plants at Island Falls and Granville Falls. Its mouth was discovered 1619 by Jens Munck; upper course was 1st explored (1774–76) by Peter Pond, Alexander Henry, and the Frobisher brothers, who established fur-trade post at Frog L. for the North West Co. River became important fur-trading artery. It is called Missinipi R. by the natives.

Church Minshull (mĭnz'hŭl), village and parish (pop. 282), S central Cheshire, England, on Weaver R. and 4 mi. NNW of Crewe; dairying, cheese mfg.

Church Point, town (pop. 2,897), Acadia parish, S La., 16 mi. NNE of Crowley, in agr. area (rice, cotton, corn); rice and feed mills, cotton gins, machine and woodworking shops.

Churchs Ferry, village (pop. 223), Ramsey co., NE central N.Dak., 19 mi. NW of Devils Lake and on L. Irvine.

Church Stretton, urban district (1931 pop. 1,704; 1951 census 2,580), S central Shropshire, England, 12 mi. S of Shrewsbury; agr. market. Has 12th-cent. church. NE 2 mi. is Caer Caradoc Hill (1,506 ft.), site of anc. Br. camp.

Churchton, village (1940 pop. 566), Anne Arundel co., central Md., near Chesapeake Bay, 13 mi. S of Annapolis, in truck-farm area. Near by is Sudley, quaint old house built 1680, now restored.

Churchtown, Gaelic *Brugh Theineadh,* town (pop. 134), N Co. Cork, Ireland, 10 mi. NNW of Mallow; agr. market (dairying, cattle; oats, potatoes, beets).

Churchville, Village (pop. 755), Monroe co., W N.Y., 15 mi. WSW of Rochester, in agr. area. Frances E. Willard b. here.

Church Warsop, England: see WARSOP.

Church Wilne, England: see DRAYCOTT.

Churdan (shûrdăn'), town (pop. 593), Greene co., central Iowa, 10 mi. NNW of Jefferson.

Chureki, Formosa: see CHUNGLI.

Churfirsten (kŏŏr'fĭrstŭn), mountain in the Alps, E Switzerland, NW of Wallenstadt, overlooking L. of Wallenstadt. The Hinterrugg (7,578 ft.) is its highest peak.

Churia Range, Nepal: see SIWALIK RANGE.

Churín (chōōrēn'), town (pop. 217), Lima dept., W central Peru, in Cordillera Occidental, on road, and 28 mi. NE of Sayán; thermal baths.

Churintzio (chōōrēnts'yō), town (pop. 2,420), Michoacán, central Mexico, 12 mi. S of La Piedad; cereals, fruit, stock.

Chü River, Chinese *Chü Kiang* or *Ch'ü Chiang* (both: chü' jyäng'), Szechwan prov., China, rises on Shensi border, flows c.450 mi. SW, past Pingchang, Chühsien, and Kwangan, to Kialing R. near Hochwan. Navigable to Tahsien on a left headstream.

Chu River (chōō), Kirghiz and Kazakh SSR, rises in 2 branches in the W Terskei Ala-Tau, flows N, past Kochkorka (here called the Dzhuvan-Aryk), close to W end of lake Issyk-Kul (intermittent connection), through Boom Gorge (site of Orto-Tokoi reservoir), and WNW, along N foot of Kirghiz Range, past Tokmak and Georgiyevka, through irrigated Chu valley (sugar beets, fibers, essential oils), along Kirghiz-Kazakh border, into dry steppe of Kazakh SSR, turning N, past Chu, and W, bet. deserts Muyun-Kum (S) and Bet-Pak-Dala (N). After losing most of its water through evaporation in lower course, it enters a small salt lake 70 mi. E of the Syr Darya; c.700 mi. long. Important for irrigation of Chu valley, which it waters through 2 parallel (E-W) Chu canals (rising near Tokmak) and Atbashi and Georgiyevka canals, rising at Chumysh Dam just SE of Georgiyevka.

Churn River, England: see THAMES RIVER.

Churovichi (chōōrô'vēchē), village (1926 pop. 4,092), SW Bryansk oblast, Russian SFSR, 25 mi. S of Novozybkov; coarse grain, buckwheat.

Churriana de la Vega (chōōryä'nä dhā lä vā'gä), outer SW suburb (pop. 2,652) of Granada, S Spain; olive oil, sugar beets, hemp, tobacco, melons.

Churtan, Russian SFSR: see BEREZNIKI.

Churu (chōōr'ōō), town (pop. 28,269), ⊙ Churu dist., NE Rajasthan, India, 105 mi. ENE of Bikaner; trades in wool, millet, gram, cattle, salt; hand-loom weaving, pottery making; leather goods. Col.

Churubusco (chōōrōōbōō'skō), SE section of Mexico city, central Mexico; residential suburb of lovely gardens and fine colonial architecture. Has old Franciscan monastery (1678), colonial mus. A Mexican War battle took place here Aug. 20, 1847. Was anc. Aztec religious center dedicated to war-god Hutzilopochtli. Hydroelectric plant near by.

Churubusko (chōōrŭbŭ'skō, chĕrŭ-), residential town (pop. 1,232), Whitley co., NE Ind., 15 mi. NW of Fort Wayne, in agr. area; ships vegetables.

Churug, Yugoslavia: see CURUG.

Churuguara (chōōrōōgwä'rä), town (pop. 3,439), Falcón state, NW Venezuela, in N Andean outliers, 45 mi. SSE of Coro, in fertile agr. region (coffee, sugar cane, cacao, fruit).

Churukh-Dairon, Tadzhik SSR: see CHORUKH-DAIRON.

Churulia, India: see ASANSOL.

Churumuco (chōōrōōmōō'kō), town (pop. 1,106), Michoacán, central Mexico, near Río de las Balsas, 38 mi. SW of Tacámbaro; cereals, sugar cane, fruit.

Churwalden (kŏŏr'väldŭn), village (pop. 758), Grisons canton, E Switzerland, on Rabiusa R. (affluent of Plessur R.) and 5 mi. S of Chur; health resort (alt. 4,036 ft.). Remains of 12th-cent. convent, 15th-cent. church.

Chusan Archipelago (chōō'sän') or **Chushan Archipelago** (chōō'shän'), Chinese *Chou-shan* (jō'shän'), island group of Chekiang and Kiangsu provs., China, in E.China Sea, off Hangchow Bay bet. Yangtze estuary and Siangshan Bay. Includes Chusan, the main isl. (22 mi. long, 10 mi. wide), with the chief town TINGHAI; and numerous lesser isls., including Parker Isls., Saddle Isls., Jue Shan, Tai Shan, and Puto Shan. A considerable danger to navigation, the archipelago has strong tidal currents and frequent fogs. It is, however, one of the chief fishing grounds off the Chinese coast.

Chuschi (chōōs'chē), town (pop. 1,310), Ayacucho dept., S central Peru, on E slopes of Cordillera Occidental, 30 mi. SSW of Ayacucho; sugar cane, grain, livestock.

Chusei-hokudo, Korea: see NORTH CHUNGCHONG.

Chusei-nando, Korea: see SOUTH CHUNGCHONG.

Chushan (jōō'shän'), town (pop. 12,038), ⊙ Chushan co. (pop. 196,044), NW Hupeh prov., China, 45 mi. SW of Yünhsien; timber, wheat, millet. Copper deposits near by.

Ch'ü Shan, island, China: see JUE SHAN.

Chushan (jōō'shän'), Jap. *Takeyama* (täkā'yämä), sometimes *Chikuzan* (chē'kōōzän), town (1935 pop. 4,746), W central Formosa, 26 mi. S of Taichung; sugar milling; camphor, bamboo articles.

Chushan Archipelago, China: see CHUSAN ARCHIPELAGO.

Chushka Spit (chōōsh'kŭ), narrow land tongue of Krasnodar Territory, Russian SFSR; extends 9 mi. SW into Kerch Strait; fisheries.

Chushu, Korea: see CHUNGJU.

Chushul, Kashmir: see SHUSHAL.

Chushul (chōō'shōōl) or **Chhushu** (chōō'shōō), Chinese *Ch'ü-shui* (chü'shwā'), town [Tibetan *dzong*], S Tibet, near the Brahmaputra, on main India-Lhasa trade route and 31 mi. SW of Lhasa.

Chuska Mountains (chōō'skŭ), in Navajo Indian Reservation, NE Ariz. and NW N.Mex. Chief peaks are MATTHEWS PEAK (9,403 ft.) and ROOF BUTTE (9,576 ft.), both in Ariz.

Chusovaya River (chōōsŭvī'ŭ, -sô'vīŭ), Sverdlovsk and Molotov oblasts, Russian SFSR, formed 5 mi. SSE of Polevskoi by confluence of 2 streams rising in the central Urals; flows NW, through major industrial region of the central Urals, past Pervouralsk, Bilimbai, and Staroutkinsk, and W, past Chusovoi and Verkhne-Chusovskiye Gorodki, to Kama R. at Levshino (N section of Molotov city); c.480 mi. long. Lumber floating for c.380 mi.; seasonal navigation for c.250 mi. (northbound shipments include iron ore, pig iron, timber). Receives Utka, Serebryanka, Koiva, Usva (right) and Revda, Lysva, Sylva (left) rivers.

Chusovoi or **Chusovoy** (-voi'), city (1926 pop. 17,930; 1933 pop. estimate 41,620), E Molotov oblast, Russian SFSR, on right bank of Chusovaya R., at mouth of Usva R., on railroad (Chusovskaya station) and 55 mi. ENE of Molotov. Rail junction; metallurgical center (based on charcoal), producing quality steels, ferro-alloys, and pig iron; charcoal burning. Marl, refractory-clay, and peat deposits. Founded 1879 as ironworks called Chusovskoi Zavod; became city in 1933.

Chusovskiye Gorodki, Russian SFSR; see VERKHNE-CHUSOVSKIYE GORODKI.

Chust. 1 City, Ukrainian SSR: see KHUST. **2** (chōōst), city (1932 pop. estimate 18,400), central Namangan oblast, Uzbek SSR, in N Fergana Valley, 22 mi. W of Namangan, in grain, fruit, and cotton area; sericulture; quarrying. Home textile industry.

Chut or **Chutt** (chōōt'), village, Khanhhoa prov., S central Vietnam, minor South China Sea port, 3 mi. NE of Nhatrang, on promontory sheltering roadstead from summer monsoon; summer harbor of Nhatrang.

Chute à Caron (shüt ä kärō'), village, central Que., on Saguenay R. and 2 mi. NW of Arvida; hydroelectric plant.

Chute aux Outardes (shüt ōzōōtärd'), village (pop. estimate 250), E Que., on Outardes R., near its mouth on the St. Lawrence, and 12 mi. SW of Baie Comeau; hydroelectric station.

Chute Shipshaw (shüt shĭp'shô) or **Racine** (rŭsēn'), town (pop. 172), central Que., on Aulnets R. and 5 mi. NW of Arvida; hydroelectric-power center.

Chutovo (chōō'tŭvŭ), village (1926 pop. 3,967), E Poltava oblast, Ukrainian SSR, 27 mi. ENE of Poltava; sugar beets.

Chutt, Vietnam: see CHUT.

Chutung or **Tsutung** (both: jōō'dōōng'), Jap. *Chikuto* (chē'kōōtō), town (1935 pop. 5,747), NW Formosa, on railroad and 9 mi. SE of Sinchu; natural-gas-producing center (gasoline production); cement mfg., rice milling, tea processing.

Chutzeshan, Manchuria: see WEICHANG.

Chutzuchen, China: see WANHSIEN, Kansu prov.

Chuuronjang (chōō'ōō'rŏn'jäng'), Jap. *Shuotsuonjo, Shuotsu,* or *Syuotu,* township (1944 pop. 37,134), N.Hamgyong prov., Korea, 16 mi. SW of Chongjin; popular hot-springs resort.

Chuvash Autonomous Soviet Socialist Republic (chōōväsh'), administrative division (□ 7,100; 1939 pop. 1,077,614) of central European Russian SFSR; ⊙ Cheboksary. In middle Volga R. valley, S of Mari Autonomous SSR; bordered W by Sura R.; drained by Greater and Lesser Tsivil rivers. Humid continental climate (short summers). Mineral resources: phosphorite (center, W, SE), limestone (Kozlovka, Urmary, Yantikovo), oil shale (Irbesi), quartz sand (Sosnovka), tripoli (S). Extensive agr., with wheat (SW, SE, and around Tsivilsk), rye, oats, fodder crops, potatoes, flax, hemp, sunflowers, cattle (scattered), hogs (near Yadrin). Coniferous and deciduous (chiefly oak) forests (W, S, N). Industries based on agr. (flour milling, distilling, tanning, meat preserving, oil extracting, flax processing, starch mfg., sack- and matmaking), and lumber (woodworking, sawmilling, shipbuilding, tannin extracting); mfg. of phosphorite-based chemicals (Vurnary). Light mfg. and metalworking in main centers (Cheboksary, Alatyr, Kanash). Well developed rail- and roadnet. Pop. 80% Chuvash, 16% Russians; also Mordvinians and Tatars. The Chuvash are a Finnic group of Rus. culture and Greek Orthodox religion; dominated by Volga Bolgars (8th–10th cent.) and Golden Horde (13th–15th cent.). Area colonized by Russians in 16th cent.; became autonomous oblast in 1920; gained present status in 1925; part of Gorki Territory until 1936.

Chuviscar River (chōōvēskär'), Chihuahua, N Mexico, rises in E outliers of Sierra Madre Occidental NW of Chihuahua; flows c.100 mi. E, past Aldama, to Conchos R. 8 mi. N of Julimes. Irrigation.

Chuy (chwē), town, Rocha dept., SE Uruguay, adjoining Chí (Brazil), 13 mi S of Santa Vitória de Palmar, in stock-raising area (cattle, sheep). Customhouse. Beach.

Chuya Alps (chōō'yŭ), Rus. *Chuyskiye Belki,* one of highest ranges of Altai Mts., in SW Siberian Russian SFSR, S of Chuya R.; rises to 13,000 ft. at peaks Irbistu, Iiktu, and Dzhan-Iiktu.

Chuya River, SE Gorno-Altai Autonomous Oblast, Altai Territory, Russian SFSR, rises in Sailyugem Range of Altai Mts. at Mongolian border, flows c.150 mi. WNW, past Kosh-Agach, to Katun R. at Inya, 110 mi. SSE of Gorno-Altaisk. The Chuya highway, along its valley, links Bisk and Mongolia.

Chuyi or **Ch'u-i** (both: chōō'yē'), town, ⊙ Chuyi co. (pop. 269,800), N Anhwei prov., China, 65 mi. E of Pengpu and on lower Hwai R., near Hungtze L.; rice, wheat, beans, kaoliang, corn. Also written Suyi (or Hsü-i).

Chuzenji, Lake (chōōzän'jē), Jap. *Chuzenji-ko* (□5), Tochigi prefecture, central Honshu, Japan, in Nikko Natl. Park, 6 mi. W of Nikko; 4 mi. long, 1.5 mi. wide, alt. 4,000 ft.; surrounded by hills and cherry trees. Anc. Buddhist temple (Chuzen-ji) is on E shore. Near NE shore is scenic Kegon Waterfall (350 ft. high) on small Daiya R. Yachting, boating, fishing. Sometimes spelled Tyuzenzi.
Chuzik River, Russian SFSR: see PARABEL RIVER.
Chvaletice, Czechoslovakia: see PRELOUC.
Chvalsiny (khväl'shĭnĭ), Czech *Chvalšiny*, Ger. *Kalsching*, town (pop. 644), S Bohemia, Czechoslovakia, in Bohemian Forest, 15 mi. NE of Budweis.
Chvrstnitsa, Velika, mountain, Yugoslavia: see VELIKA CVRSTNICA.
Chwaka (chwä'kä), town (pop. 2,200), on E coast of Zanzibar, 17 mi. E of Zanzibar town; clove-growing center; citrus fruit, mangrove bark; matmaking, lime burning. Health resort. A slave-trade depot in mid-19th cent.
Chwaletitz, Czechoslovakia: see PRELOUC.
Chwangho or **Chuang-ho** (both: jwäng'hŭ'), town, ⊙ Chwangho co. (pop. 596,266), S Liaotung prov., Manchuria, on Liaotung peninsula, 95 mi. ENE of Dairen, on Yellow Sea; wild silk; chicken farming. Saltworks; asbestos deposits.
Chwanglang or **Chuang-lang** (both: jwäng'läng'), town, ⊙ Chwanglang co. (pop. 123,844), SE Kansu prov., China, 55 mi. N of Tienshui, in mtn. region; feltmaking; wheat, millet.
Chwankow, China: see MINHO.
Chwanpien, China: see SIKANG.
Chwanping, China: see LANKAO.
Chwansha or **Ch'uan-sha** (chwän'shä'), town (pop. 8,207), ⊙ Chwansha co. (pop. 136,779), S Kiangsu prov., China, 13 mi. E of Shanghai, near estuary of Yangtze R.; rice, wheat, beans, cotton, rapeseed.
Chyrow, Ukrainian SSR: see KHYROV.
Chyzne, Czechoslovakia: see JELSAVA.
Ciacova (chä'kôvä), Hung. *Csák* (chäk), village (pop. 3,787), Timisoara prov., W Rumania, on railroad and 17 mi. SSW of Timisoara; flour milling. Agr. institute near by.
Ciales (syä'lĕs), town (pop. 3,482), N central Puerto Rico, on the Manatí and 24 mi. WSW of San Juan; tobacco growing and shipping; mfg. of cigars. Damaged by 1867 earthquake. The coffee-growing village Cialitos is 6 mi. SSW.
Ciallanco, Ethiopia: see CHALANKO.
Ciamo, Lake, Ethiopia: see CHAMO, LAKE.
Ciampino (chämpē'nô), village (pop. 1,447), Roma prov., Latium, central Italy, 10 mi. SE of Rome; rail junction. An airport of Rome is located here.
Cianciana (chänchä'nä), town (pop. 7,376), Agrigento prov., S Sicily, 16 mi. NNW of Agrigento. Sulphur mine (NE).
Ciaño (thyä'nyō), village (pop. 2,016), Oviedo prov., NW Spain, on Nalón R. and 11 mi. SE of Oviedo, in Langreo coal-mining region.
Cibakhaza (tsĭ'bŏk-häzŏ), Hung. *Cibakháza*, town (pop. 5,618), Jasz-Nagykun-Szolnok co., E central Hungary, on Tisza R. and 15 mi. S of Szolnok; corn, hogs, fishing.
Cibao (sēbou'), lowland, N Dominican Republic, a broad valley bet. the Cordillera Setentrional (N) and Cordillera Central (S), along Yaque del Norte and Yuna rivers; extends 145 mi. ESE from Monte Cristi to Sánchez on Samaná Bay. The most fertile and densely populated region of the country, growing cacao, coffee, tobacco, corn, sugar cane, rice, tropical fruit. Its E section is sometimes called La Vega Real valley, a name given by Columbus.
Cibao Mountains, Dominican Republic: see CENTRAL, CORDILLERA.
Cibiana (chēbyä'nä), village (pop. 257), Belluno prov., Veneto, N Italy, 17 mi. N of Belluno; mfg. (spectacles, locks).
Cibinka, Poland: see CYBINKA.
Cibolo Creek (sĭ'bŭlō). **1** In S central Texas, rises on Edwards Plateau W of Boerne, flows c.125 mi. generally SE to San Antonio R., 5 mi. NNE of Karnes City. **2** In extreme W Texas, rises S of Marfa, flows c.40 mi. S to the Rio Grande at Presidio.
Ciboure (sēbōōr'), SW suburb (pop. 4,238) of Saint-Jean-de-Luz, Basses-Pyrénées dept., SW France; fishing port and bathing resort; fish canning, ceramics mfg.
Ciboux Island (sēbōō'), islet, NE N.S., off NE Cape Breton Isl., 4 mi. NE of Cape Dauphin; 46°23'N 60°22'W.
Cibyra (sĭ'bĭrŭ), anc. town of SW Asia Minor (now in Turkey), on Dalaman R. and 16 mi. WSW of Tefenni.
Cicagna (chēkä'nyä), village (pop. 550), Genova prov., Liguria, N Italy, 4 mi. N of Rapallo; slate-quarrying center; sawmills.
Cicarija (chēchä'rēä), Serbo-Croatian *Čičarija*, Ital. *Cicceria* (chēt-chĕr'-yä), region in NW Croatia, Yugoslavia, in N Istria, S of the Karst; extends c.30 mi. NW–SE; stony wasteland. Culminates (S) in UCKA peak.
Cicceria, Yugoslavia: see CICARIJA.
Cicciano (chēt-chä'nô), town (pop. 6,125), Napoli prov., Campania, S Italy, 3 mi. N of Nola, in agr. region (cereals, fruit).
Cicekdagi (chĭchĕk'däŭ), Turkish *Çiçekdağı*, village (pop. 784), Kirsehir prov., central Turkey, near railroad and Delice R., 35 mi. NNE of Kirsehir; forested dist.; mohair goats. Formerly Boyalik.
Cicero (sĭ'sŭrō). **1** Industrial town (pop. 67,544), Cook co., NE Ill., contiguous to Chicago (E); has large telephone, radio, and electrical-equipment plant; also mfg. of steel, iron, brass, and copper products; home appliances, building materials, tools, hardware, enamelware, printing machinery; clay, paper, rubber, asbestos, and wood products; paints and varnish, clothing, musical instruments. Seat of Morton Jr. Col. Founded 1857, inc. 1867. **2** Town (pop. 1,021), Hamilton co., central Ind., on Cicero Creek and 27 mi. NNE of Indianapolis, in agr. area. **3** Village (pop. c.500), Onondaga co., central N.Y., near Oneida L., 9 mi. N of Syracuse; makes cheese; agr. (potatoes, cabbage, corn, oats).
Cicero Creek, central Ind., rises in W Hamilton co., flows NE to Tipton, then S to West Fork of White R. near Noblesville; c.40 mi. long.
Cícero Dantas (sē'sĭrōō dän'tŭs), city (pop. 1,043), NE Bahia, Brazil, 90 mi. WNW of Aracaju (Sergipe); manioc, corn, livestock.
Cicia, Fiji: see THITHIA.
Cicié, Cape, France: see SICIÉ, CAPE.
Ciclova (chē'klôvä), village (pop. 3,718), Severin prov., SW Rumania, just SE of Oravita; beer.
Cicmany (chĭch'mänĭ), Slovak *Čičmany*, Hung. *Csicsmány* (chĭch'mänyŭ), village (pop. 999), W Slovakia, Czechoslovakia, in the Lesser Fatra, 11 mi. SSW of Rajec; picturesque community noted for unusual wooden buildings and old regional costumes.
Cidade de Minas, Brazil: see BELO HORIZONTE.
Cide (jĭdĕ'), village (pop. 1,796), Kastamonu prov., N Turkey, port on Black Sea, 55 mi. NW of Kastamonu; lignite; grain, hemp, beans.
Cidra (sē'drä), town (pop. 1,342), Matanzas prov., W Cuba, on railroad and 9 mi. SSE of Matanzas; sugar cane, fruit, cattle.
Cidra, town (pop. 3,146), E central Puerto Rico, on N slopes of the Sierra de Cayey, 9 mi. WSW of Caguas; summer resort in fine mtn. setting; tobacco- and fruitgrowing. Airfield NE.
Ciechanow (chĕ-khä'nōōf), Pol. *Ciechanów*, Rus. *Tsekhanov* (tsyĕ-khä'nŭf), town (pop. 11,831), Warszawa prov., NE central Poland, 50 mi. NNW of Warsaw. Rail junction; mfg. of agr. tools, ceramic goods, bricks; flour and sugar milling, brewing. Castle ruins near by. During Second World War, under administration of East Prussia, called Zichenau.
Ciechanowiec (chĕ-khänô'vyĕts), Rus. *Tsekhanovets* (tsyĕ-khänô'vyĕts), town (pop. 3,388), Bialystok prov., NE Poland, on Nurzec R. and 42 mi. SW of Bialystok; mfg. (cloth, liqueur, flour).
Ciechocinek (chĕ-khôtsē'nĕk), Rus. *Tsekhotsinek* (tsyĕ-khôtsē'nĕk), town (pop. 4,131), Bydgoszcz prov., N central Poland, on the Vistula and 12 mi. SE of Torun. Rail spur terminus; health resort with mineral springs, hot baths, and sanatoria; saltworks. During Second World War, under Ger. administration, called Hermannsbad.
Ciego de Ávila (syä'gō dā ä'vēlä), city (pop. 23,802), Camagüey prov., E Cuba, on Central Highway and 65 mi. WNW of Camagüey. Rail junction and commercial center for rich agr. region (sugar cane, molasses, bananas, oranges, pineapples, honey, beeswax, cattle). Sawmilling, distilling, bottling, making of jerked beef. Sugar centrals in outskirts. Has administrative bldgs., R.C. church, theater; airfield. Its port on the Caribbean is Júcaro (15 mi. SSW), linked by rail. Sometimes spelled Ciego de Avila.
Ciempozuelos (thyĕmpōth-wā'lōs), town (pop. 5,910), Madrid prov., central Spain, on railroad and 18 mi. S of Madrid; agr. center (grapes, olives, melons, artichokes, alfalfa, sugar beets, sheep, goats). Wine making, malt mfg. Insane asylum.
Ciénaga (syā'nägä) [Sp.,=swamp], city (pop. 22,783), Magdalena dept., N Colombia, port on Caribbean Sea, near mouth of Ciénaga Grande de Santa Marta, 17 mi. S of Santa Marta (connected by rail), 35 mi. E of Barranquilla; banana-shipping center in rich agr. region (bananas, cotton, tobacco, cacao); fishing. Marble deposits near by. Sometimes San Juan de Ciénaga.
Ciénaga, La, Argentina: see LA CIÉNAGA.
Ciénaga, La, Mexico: see RÍO, EL.
Ciénaga, La, Venezuela: see LA CIÉNAGA.
Ciénaga del Coro (dĕl kō'rō), agr. village (pop. estimate 500), ⊙ Minas dept. (□ c.1,500; pop. 7,836), NW Córdoba prov., Argentina, 70 mi. WNW of Córdoba.
Ciénaga de Oro (dā ō'rō), town (pop. 4,970), Bolívar dept., N Colombia, in Caribbean lowlands, 20 mi. ENE of Montería; sugar and cattle center; sugar refinery.
Ciénaga Grande de Santa Marta (grän'dā dā sän'tä mär'tä), lagoon inlet of Caribbean Sea, Magdalena dept., N Colombia, in alluvial lowlands of lower Magdalena R., 18 mi. E of Barranquilla; nearly closed off by long, narrow Salamanca Isl., which leaves a narrow channel 3 mi. SW of Ciénaga. Receives numerous arms of the Magdalena and small streams from W slopes of Sierra Nevada de Santa Marta.
Ciénega de Flores (dā flō'rĕs), town (pop. 1,590), Nuevo León, N Mexico, on Inter-American Highway, on Pesquería R. and 22 mi. NNE of Monterrey; grain, cotton, sugar cane.
Cieneguilla (syānāgē'yä), town (pop. 1,040), Hidalgo, central Mexico, 45 mi. NNE of Pachuca; corn, beans, maguey, stock.
Cienfuegos (syĕnfwā'gōs), city (pop. 52,910), Las Villas prov., central Cuba, major sugar port on fine, sheltered Cienfuegos or Jagua Bay (12 mi. long, c.3 mi. wide), and 30 mi. SW of Santa Clara, 140 mi. ESE of Havana; 22°8'N 80°28'W. Trades in sugar cane, molasses, coffee, tobacco, fruit, sisal, rice. Mfg. of cigars, liquor, soft drinks, canned fish, soap, bricks, tiles, candles, clothing, furniture. Sugar centrals in outskirts. Built upon a peninsula, the handsome city has boulevards, parks, cathedral, city hall, theater. Castillo de Jagua is near harbor entrance (SW). Its establishments include a naval dist., international airport, seaplane anchorage. Near by (E) at Central Soledad is a botanical garden. City was founded early in 16th cent., was frequently subjected to pirate attacks in 18th cent. Fr. settlers arriving in early 19th cent. contributed to its development. Copper and iron deposits are E, near Cumanayagua.
Cieplice Slaskie Zdroj (chĕplē'tsĕ shlō'skyĕ zdrōō'ē), Pol. *Cieplice Śląskie Zdrój*, Ger. *Bad Warmbrunn* (bät" värm'brōōn), town (1939 pop. 10,488; 1946 pop. 12,938) in Lower Silesia, after 1945 in Wroclaw prov., SW Poland, at N foot of the Riesengebirge, 4 mi. SSW of Hirschberg (Jelenia Gora); health resort with mineral springs, known since 13th cent.; mfg. of paper-milling machinery. Has 18th-cent. castle, bldgs. of former Cistercian monastery (founded 1403; secularized 1810).
Cierges (syârzh), village (pop. 111), Aisne dept., N France, 5 mi. ESE of Fère-en-Tardenois. Captured by Americans in 1918, after heavy fighting.
Cierny Vah River, Czechoslovakia: see VAH RIVER.
Cierp (syârp), village (pop. 789), Haute-Garonne dept., S France, 9 mi. N of Luchon; phosphate mining.
Cies Islands (thyās), just off Atlantic coast of Galicia, Pontevedra prov., NW Spain, at mouth of Vigo Bay; 3 islets, each c.1 mi. long, ½ mi. wide.
Cieszanow (chĕ-shä'nōōf), Pol. *Cieszanów*, town (pop. 958), Rzeszow prov., SE Poland, 6 mi. N of Lubaczow; flour mills; oil mill.
Cieszyn (chĕ'shĭn), Czech *Těšín* (tyĕ'shēn), Ger. *Teschen* (tĕ'shŭn), city (pop. 16,536), Katowice prov., S Poland, on right bank of Olza R. and 40 mi. SSW of Katowice, opposite CESKY TESIN (Czechoslovakia). Mfg. of metalware, machinery, electrotechnical equipment, watches, chemicals, furniture, wood products, paper; food processing, printing. Originally a part of TESCHEN territory, Cieszyn with adjoining agr. area along E bank of Olza R. was awarded to Poland by Conference of Ambassadors (Paris; 1920). After Munich Pact (1938) Poland also took the Czech portion, but in 1939 Germany annexed the whole region. After the war, Cieszyn was returned (1945) to Poland in accordance with pre-Munich status.
Cieux (syû'), village (pop. 347), Haute-Vienne dept., W central France, 9 mi. S of Bellac; tin, wolfram, and tungsten deposits.
Cieza (thyā'thä), city (pop. 18,561), Murcia prov., SE Spain, in fertile garden region on Segura R., and 24 mi. NW of Murcia; esparto-processing center (rope, baskets, fabrics). Mfg. of fruit conserves, knitwear, pottery, tiles, burlap, plaster; olive-oil processing, flour and sawmilling. Ships oranges and other fruit, hemp, olives. Remains of Roman fort on hill near by. Hydroelectric plants on Segura R. above and below city. Airport 3 mi. NW.
Ciftlik. 1 Village, Gumusane prov., Turkey: see KELKIT. **2** Village, Tokat prov., Turkey: see ARTOVA.
Cifuentes (sēfwĕn'tĕs), town (pop. 2,131), Las Villas prov., central Cuba, rail junction 15 mi. N of Santa Clara, in agr. region (sugar cane, cattle). Iron and manganese deposits and mineral springs near by.
Cifuentes (thēfwĕn'tĕs), town (pop. 1,315), Guadalajara prov., central Spain, in New Castile, 30 mi. ENE of Guadalajara; stock-raising and lumbering center, surrounded by forests. Known for its many springs. Also grows grapes, potatoes, grain; apiculture. Paper milling, woolen-goods mfg. Remains of old walls and castle.
Cigales (thēgä'lĕs), town (pop. 2,114), Valladolid prov., N central Spain, 7 mi. NNE of Valladolid; sawmills; cereals, wine. Has Romanesque church.
Cigand (tsĭ'gänd), Hung. *Cigánd*, town (pop. 5,114), Zemplen co., NE Hungary, on Tisza R. and 15 mi. SE of Satoraljaujhely; corn, barley, nuts, plums.
Cigliano (chēlyä'nô), village (pop. 3,691), Vercelli prov., Piedmont, N Italy, 20 mi. W of Vercelli, in irrigated region (cereals, fruit); sawmills, wooden-shoe and asbestos factories.
Cihanbeyli (jĭhän'bālē"), village (pop. 3,035), Konya prov., W central Turkey, 55 mi. NNE of Konya, near W shore of L. Tuz; wheat. Also called Inevi, formerly Esbikesan.
Cihuatlán (sēwätlän'), town (pop. 2,630), Jalisco, W Mexico, in Pacific lowland, on Colima border, 45 mi. SW of Autlán; corn, rice, sugar cane, tobacco, bananas.
Cijcloop Mountains, Netherlands New Guinea: see CYCLOPS MOUNTAINS.

Cijuela (thē-hwä′lä), village (pop. 1,306), Granada prov., S Spain, near Genil R., 12 mi. W of Granada; sugar beets, cereals, vegetables.

Çika, Mount, Albania: see ÇIKË, MOUNT.

Çikë, Mount (chē′kü), or **Mount Çika** (chē′kä), highest peak (6,726 ft.) of Ceraunian Mts., S Albania, 9 mi. NW of Hinarë. Here the range forks into Acroceraunia and Lungara prongs which enclose Bay of Valona.

Cikola River (chē′kôlä), Serbo-Croatian *Čikola*, W Croatia, Yugoslavia, in Dalmatia; rises 9 mi. SE of Drnis, flows NNW, past Drnis, and WSW to Krka R. opposite Skradin; c.25 mi. long.

Cilaos (seläōs′), village (pop. 4,975), central Réunion isl., on road and 11 mi. NNE of Saint-Louis, in Cilaos cirque of the central massif; alt. c.4,000 ft.; health resort (mineral springs); sanatorium.

Cilavegna (chēlävä′nyä), village (pop. 3,820), Pavia prov., Lombardy, N Italy, 4 mi. N of Mortara; liquor distillery.

Cilcennin (kĭlkĕ′nĭn), village and parish (pop. 353), W central Cardigan, Wales, 5 mi. ESE of Aberayron; woolen milling.

Cildir (chŭldŭr′), Turkish *Çıldır*, village (pop. 1,106), Kars prov., NE Turkey, bet. L. Cildir and Kura R., 36 mi. N of Kars; barley. Also Zurzuna.

Cildir, Lake, Turkish *Çıldır* (□ 46), NE Turkey, 26 mi. NNE of Kars; 12 mi. long; alt. 6,430 ft.

Ciledorugu (chĭlĕ′dôrōō″), Turkish *Çiledoruğu*, peak (6,411 ft.), NW Turkey, in Bolu Mts., 12 mi. NNE of Bolu.

Cilfrew (kĭlvrū′), town in Blaenhonddan parish (pop. 3,828), W Glamorgan, Wales, 2 mi. N of Neath; coal mining, tinplate mfg.

Cilicia (sĭlĭ′shù), region of SE Asia Minor now in S Asiatic Turkey, bet. the Mediterranean and Taurus Mts. It was successively under Assyrian, Persian, Greek, and Roman domination. Principal cities included Tarsus, Seleucia (modern Silifke), and Issus, which throve under Roman Empire. Later Cilicia was included in Byzantine Empire and was in 8th cent. invaded by Arabs. In 11th cent. an Armenian state was set up here which became a kingdom and is generally called Little Armenia; was conquered 1375 by the Mamelukes. In later cents., particularly in 20th cent., the Armenians suffered greatly at hands of the Turks, and most of them as well as the Greeks in Cilicia emigrated. In anc. times Pisidia and Pamphilia were to W, Lycaonia and Cappadocia to N.

Cilician Gates (sĭlĭ′shùn), anc. *Pylae Ciliciae*, Turkish *Gülek Boğaz* (gülĕk′ bôäz′), mountain pass over TAURUS MOUNTAINS, S Turkey, on an ancient highway N of Tarsus, bet. Cappadocia and Cilicia.

Cillero (thēlyä′rō), village (pop. 1,284), Lugo prov., NW Spain, on inlet of Bay of Biscay, 1 mi. N of Vivero; fish canning (anchovies, sardines).

Cilleros (thēlyä′rōs), town (pop. 3,703), Cáceres prov., W Spain, 40 mi. WNW of Plasencia; flour milling, chocolate and alcohol mfg.; olive oil, cereals, wine, honey.

Cilli, Yugoslavia: see CELJE.

Cillium, Tunisia: see KASSERINE.

Cilo Dag (jĭlô′dä), Turkish *Cilo Dağ*, peak (13,675 ft.), SE Turkey, in Hakari Mts., 16 mi. ESE of Hakari. Sometimes called Resko Dag.

Ciltaltepec (sēltältäpĕk′), town (pop. 1,811), Veracruz, E Mexico, in Sierra Madre Oriental foothills, 38 mi. NW of Tuxpan; cereals, sugar cane, tobacco, fruit, livestock.

Cilybebyll (kĭlubĕ′bĭl), town and parish (pop. 3,451), W Glamorgan, Wales, near Tawe R., 5 mi. N of Neath; coal.

Cilymaenllwyd (kĭlumän′thlōōĭd), village and parish (pop. 343), W Carmarthen, Wales, 3 mi. W of Llanboidy; woolen milling. Just E, on Taf R., is woolen-milling village of Login.

Cima [Ital.,=peak], for names beginning thus and not found here: see under following part of the name.

Cima di Cantone (chē′mä dē käntô′nĕ), peak (11,010 ft.) in the Alps, SE Switzerland, 9 mi. SSW of Sils im Engadin.

Cimarron (sĭ′mùrōn, sĭmùrōn′), county (□ 1,832; pop. 4,589), extreme NW Okla.; ⊙ Boise City. Bounded N by Colorado and Kansas, W by N.Mex., S by Texas. Comprised of high plains of the Panhandle (alt. c.4,000 ft.); includes the Black Mesa (alt. 4,978 ft.), highest point in Okla. Drained by Cimarron and North Canadian rivers. Stock raising, agr. (broomcorn, wheat, barley, corn). Formed 1907.

Cimarron. 1 City (pop. 1,189), ⊙ Gray co., SW Kansas, on Arkansas R. and 18 mi. W of Dodge City; grain, livestock. Inc. 1885. **2** Village (pop. 855), Colfax co., NE N.Mex., on smaller of 2 Cimarron rivers, in E foothills of Sangre de Cristo Mts., and 38 mi. SW of Raton; alt. c.6,400 ft.; livestock. Ruins of Maxwell House, famous frontier hotel, are here. Cimarron Canyon and Cimarron Palisades, rising 800 ft. above highway, are near-by scenic spots.

Cimarron, Territory of, U.S., now the Panhandle of OKLAHOMA. Area, then public land, was proposed (1887) as a separate territory by its settlers (many of them squatters), who attempted to create a territorial govt. at Beaver. Became part of Okla. Territory in 1890.

Cimarron River. 1 In NE N.Mex., rises in Eagle Nest L., in Colfax co., flows 55 mi. E, past Cimarron and Springer, to Canadian R. 6 mi. ESE of Springer. Eagle Nest Dam (140 ft. high; built 1918), 2 mi. SE of Eagle Nest village, is private project used for power and irrigation; forms Eagle Nest L. (capacity c.100,000 acre-ft.). **2** In N.Mex., Okla., Colo., Kansas, rises in high plateau in Union co., NE N.Mex.; flows generally E, through Okla. Panhandle (extreme NW Okla.) and SE Colo., across SW Kansas, re-entering Okla. near Buffalo, thence SE and E, through Okla., to Arkansas R. 17 mi. W of Tulsa, Okla.; 692 mi. long; not navigable. Tributaries: North Fork (Colo., Kansas; c.130 mi. long), Crooked Creek (Kansas, Okla.; 99 mi. long).

Cimbric Peninsula, Denmark: see JUTLAND.

Cimbrishamn, Sweden: see SIMRISHAMN.

Cime [Fr.,=peak], for names beginning thus and not found here: see under following part of the name.

Cime de l'Est (sēm dù lĕst′) [Fr.,=eastern peak] or **Dent Noire** (dã nwär′) [Fr.,=black tooth], 2d highest peak (10,433 ft.) of the Dent du Midi, in the Alps, SW Switzerland, 7 mi. NW of Martigny-Ville.

Cimena (chēmä′nä), village, Torino prov., Piedmont, NW Italy, on Po R. and 12 mi. NE of Turin; hydroelectric plant.

Cimiez, France: see NICE.

Ciminna (chēmēn′nä), village (pop. 5,585), Palermo prov., N Sicily, 9 mi. SW of Termini Imerese.

Cimislia, Moldavian SSR: see CHIMISHLIYA.

Cimitile (chēmētē′lĕ), town (pop. 4,258), Napoli prov., Campania, S Italy, 1 mi. N of Nola. Has basilica, built in 5th cent. from remains of Roman villa, and unearthed in 1890.

Cimmerian Bosporus, USSR: see KERCH STRAIT.

Cimolus, Greece: see KIMOLOS.

Cimone, Monte (môn′tĕ chēmô′nĕ), N central Italy, highest peak (7,096 ft.) in N Appennines, in Etruscan Apennines, 21 mi. NW of Pistoia.

Cinad'ovo, Ukrainian SSR: see CHINYADEVO.

Cinantécatl, Mexico: see TOLUCA, NEVADO DE.

Cinar (chŭnär′), Turkish *Çınar*, village (pop. 715), Diyarbakir prov., E Turkey, 23 mi. SE of Diyarbakir; grain, legumes. Formerly Hanakpinar.

Cincar or **Tsintsar** (tsēn′tär), mountain (6,580 ft.) in Dinaric Alps, SW Bosnia, Yugoslavia, 6 mi. NE of Livno. Also spelled Cincer and Tsintser.

Cinca River (thĭng′kä), Huesca prov., NE Spain, rises near Mont Perdu in the central Pyrenees near Fr. border, flows c.110 mi. S to Segre R. 6 mi. above Mequinenza (on the Ebro). Hydroelectric plants and irrigation reservoirs (Tella, Mediano). Receives Esera R. (left).

Cincinnati (sĭnsĭnă′tē, –tù). **1** Town (pop. 703), Appanoose co., S Iowa, near Mo. line, 7 mi. SSW of Centerville, in bituminous-coal-mining area. **2** City (□ 72; pop. 503,998), ⊙ Hamilton co., SW Ohio, on the Ohio (bridged), opposite Covington (Ky.), and c.220 mi. SW of Cleveland; 2d-largest (after Cleveland) city of Ohio, and river- and rail-shipping, industrial, distributing, and commercial metropolis of wide region in Ohio, Ky., and Ind. Port of entry. Diversified industries include production of alcoholic beverages, soap, packed meat (large stockyards here), machine tools, steel products, chemicals, plastics, watches, clothing, shoes, printing ink, paper, printed matter, vehicle bodies, machinery. Seat of Univ. of Cincinnati, Hebrew Union Col., Xavier Univ., Mt. St. Mary of the West (at NORWOOD), Cincinnati Conservatory of Music, Col. of Music of Cincinnati, Col. of Pharmacy, the Y.M.C.A. schools, Ohio Mechanics Inst., Our Lady of Cincinnati Col., a Catholic teachers col., and Col. of Mount St. Joseph-on-the-Ohio (at Mount St. Joseph). Built on terraces above a curve of the Ohio, city has expanded into encircling hills, where are most of its residential dists. In or near downtown Cincinnati, which centers on Fountain and Government squares, are the Music Hall and Exposition Bldg., where concerts of the Cincinnati Symphony Orchestra and a May Music Festival are held; Hamilton County Memorial Bldg., with historical collection; Ohio Mechanics Inst., with an industrial mus.; Taft House Mus.; Eden Park, with city art mus. and art acad.; the public library; Rookwood Potteries, known for fine ceramics. Other points of interest include the zoological garden, where summer opera is held; Union Station, known for its architecture; Lytle Park, with notable statue of Lincoln by George Grey Barnard; and many fine churches and parks. Laid out 1788 as Losantiville; settled 1789; renamed 1790. Early became a busy transshipment point for settlers, then a processing and shipping point for pork and grain after opening of Miami and Erie Canal. It was a center of Underground Railroad activities before Civil War. Many immigrants, especially Germans and Irish, came in mid-19th cent. The city has suffered from disastrous floods, notably in 1884 and 1937. A city-manager govt. (established 1924) ended a long period of boss control.

Cincinnatus (sĭn″sùnā′tùs), village (1940 pop. 668), Cortland co., central N.Y., on Otselic R. and 15 mi. ESE of Cortland; clothing, feed, dairy products.

Cinclare, La.: see BRUSLY.

Cinco Casas, Spain: see ARGAMASILLA DE ALBA.

Cinco Leguas, Cayos de las (kī′ōs dā läs sĭng′kō lā′gwās), keys (c.12 mi. long E–W), off NW Cuba, forming N bar of Santa Clara Bay, 20 mi. ENE of Cárdenas.

Cinco Pinos (sĭng′kō pē′nōs), town (1950 pop. 311), Chinandega dept., W Nicaragua, near Honduras border, 13 mi. N of Somotillo, on S slopes of main continental divide; corn, beans.

Cinco Saltos (säl′tōs), town (pop. estimate 2,500), N Río Negro natl. territory, Argentina, on Neuquén R. (irrigation area), on railroad and 30 mi. WNW of Fuerte General Roca; farming center: sand and gypsum quarrying, lumbering, wine making. Waterfalls near by.

Cinctorres (thēntô′rĕs), town (pop. 1,207), Castellón de la Plana prov., E Spain, 37 mi. WNW of Vinaroz; wool-cloth mfg.; cereals, almonds.

Cincul (chĕng′kōōl), Hung. *Nagysink* (nŏ′dyù-shĕngk), village (pop. 2,573), Sibiu prov., central Rumania, 9 mi. NW of Fagaras; vineyards.

Cine (chĭnĕ′), Turkish *Çine*, village (pop. 4,010), Aydin prov., W Turkey, 21 mi. SSE of Aydin; olives, figs, tobacco.

Ciñera, Spain: see POLA DE GORDÓN.

Ciney (sēnā′), town (pop. 6,106), Namur prov., S Belgium, 9 mi. ENE of Dinant; rail junction; horse and cattle market; metal industry. Has remains of 17th-cent. church with 13th-cent. tower. Market center since 16th cent.

Cinfalva, Austria: see SIEGENDORF IM BURGENLAND.

Cingoli (chēng′gôlē), anc. *Cingulum*, town (pop. 1,751), Macerata prov., The Marches, central Italy, near Musone R., 13 mi. WNW of Macerata; textile mills, macaroni factory. Bishopric. Has church rebuilt 1278.

Cinisello (chēnēzĕl′lô), town (pop. 6,438), Milano prov., Lombardy, N Italy, 7 mi. N of Milan; foundry; macaroni and soap factories.

Cinisi (chē′nēzē), town (pop. 7,115), Palermo prov., NW Sicily, 14 mi. WNW of Palermo, in cereal- and grape-growing region. Has anc. castle.

Cinkota (tsĭng′kôtŏ), town (pop. 6,783), Pest-Pilis-Solt-Kiskun co., N central Hungary, 7 mi. ENE of Budapest; wagon repairs; mfg. of chemicals.

Cinnamon Mountain (13,300 ft.), SW Colo., peak of San Juan Mts., 10 mi. NE of Silverton. Cinnamon Pass is near by.

Cinnamon Pass (12,300 ft.), in San Juan Mts., SW Colo., near Cinnamon Mtn., 11 mi. NE of Silverton. Crossed by road.

Cinq-Mars-la-Pile (sĕk-märs-lä-pēl′), village (pop. 803), Indre-et-Loire dept., W central France, on Loire R. and 11 mi. WSW of Tours; winegrowing. Has a square tower possibly of Roman origin. Numerous underground cliff dwellings near by.

Cinquefrondi (chĕng″kwĕfrôn′dē), town (pop. 5,480), Reggio di Calabria prov., Calabria, S Italy, 14 mi. ENE of Palmi, in olive-growing region; rail terminus; brick mfg. Limestone quarries near by. Severely damaged by earthquakes of 1783 and 1908. Formerly also Cinquefronde.

Cinque Ports (sĭngk) [Fr.,=five ports], group of maritime towns in Sussex and Kent, England. Originally they were: Hastings, Romney, Hythe, Dover, and Sandwich. They were chartered by Edward the Confessor and reorganized into an almost independent administrative division under a lord warden in time of William the Conqueror. Under Richard I, Winchelsea and Rye were added as "ancient towns." Other "limbs" or "members" were added later. In return for privileges they had to furnish ships for protection against invasion, before England had a permanent navy. From 1688 their importance declined, and their privileges were gradually taken away. Some of the Cinque Ports' court meetings were held at Dover Castle. Walmer Castle, near Deal, is official residence of the lord warden, now an honorary post, but once possessed of important civil, military, and naval powers. In recent times the court has continued to deal with salvaging cases.

Cintalapa (sēntälä′pä), city (pop. 5,043), Chiapas, S Mexico, on N slopes of Sierra Madre, 40 mi. W of Tuxtla; agr. center (corn, beans, sugar cane, fruit, livestock); forest products; alcohol and liquor distilling. Airfield.

Cintegabelle (sĕtùgäbĕl′), agr. village (pop. 595), Haute-Garonne dept., S France, on Ariège R. and 20 mi. SSE of Toulouse; flour milling.

Cinti River (sēn′tē), Chuquisaca dept., S Bolivia, rises in several branches on E slopes of Cordillera de Chichas, c.20 mi. ESE of Vitichi, flows 45 mi. S, past Camargo, to Cotagaita R. at Palca Grande. The name Cinti R. is sometimes applied to that part of Cotagaita R. below their confluence. Also called Chiuchamayo.

Cinto, Monte (môn′tĕ chēn′tô), highest peak (8,891 ft.) of Corsica, 12 mi. WNW of Corte. View of Maritime Alps 150 mi. NNW.

Cinto Euganeo (chēn′tô ĕōōgä′nĕō), village (pop. 199), Padova prov., Veneto, N Italy, in Euganean Hills, 14 mi. SW of Padua. Marble quarries.

Cintra (sēn′trù), Port. *Sintra*, town (pop. 6,307), Lisboa dist., central Portugal, resort on NE slope of the Serra de Sintra, 14 mi. WNW of Lisbon; rail terminus. Widely known for its remarkable site, picturesque bldgs., luxuriant vegetation, and mild climate, it has been rapturously described by Port. and foreign writers. It has noted marble quarries and is surrounded by orange groves and vineyards. Of special tourist interest is ruined Moorish castle high above town (1,490 ft.), and the 15th-16th-cent. palace of Cintra, the most interesting of Portugal's old royal palaces, built in Moorish-Gothic style. Near by there is an old convent surrounded by magnificent gardens. Once a flourishing Moorish city, Cintra was recaptured by Alfonso I in 1147, and became a favorite residence of Port. kings. Near here, during the Peninsular War, the Convention of Cintra was agreed upon (1808) by French, British, and Portuguese.

Cintruénigo (thēntrōōā'nēgō), town (pop. 3,846), Navarre prov., N Spain, 10 mi. W of Tudela; olive-oil- and wine-production center; alcohol mfg., flour milling; trades in sugar beets, cereals.

Cinvald (tsĭn'vält), Ger. *Zinnwald* (tsĭn'vält), village (pop. 615), NW Bohemia, Czechoslovakia, 7 mi. NNW of Teplice, on Ger. border; summer resort and popular winter-sports center (alt. 2,676 ft.) in the Erzgebirge. Tin, antimony, bismuth, and tungsten mining. Across the border is Ger. village of Zinnwald.

Cinzas (sēn'zŭs), city (pop. 851), NE Paraná, Brazil, 25 mi. SW of Jacarèzinho; grain milling, hog raising. Until 1944, called Jundiaí.

Cinzas, Rio das (rē'ōō däs), river in NE Paraná, Brazil, rises just N of Piraí do Sul, flows c.300 mi. NNW in a meandering course, past Tomazina, to the Paranapanema 15 mi. NW of Bandeirantes. Receives the Laranjinha (left). Coal deposits in valley.

Ciotat, La (lä syōtä'), town (pop. 10,819), Bouches-du-Rhône dept., SE France, 14 mi. SE of Marseilles; resort and shipbuilding center on sheltered bay of the Mediterranean; fishing. Wine, olives, and oranges grown in area. Damaged in Second World War.

Ciovo Island, Yugoslavia: see TROGIR.

Cipérez (thēpā'rĕth), town (pop. 1,032), Salamanca prov., W Spain, 32 mi. W of Salamanca; cereals, livestock.

Ciply (sēplē'), village (pop. 783), Hainaut prov., SW Belgium, 2 mi. S of Mons; quarrying of chalk phosphates.

Cipó (sēpô), city (pop. 1,183), NE Bahia, Brazil, on Itapicuru R. and 130 mi. N of Salvador; modern health resort with radioactive hot springs. Medical research station. Formerly spelled Sipó.

Cipolletti (sēpōyĕ'tē), town (1947 pop. 2,771), N Río Negro natl. territory, Argentina, on Neuquén R. (irrigation area) opposite Neuquén, and 25 mi. WNW of Fuerte General Roca. Rail junction, fruit- and winegrowing center; wine making, fruit packing, beekeeping.

Cirauqui (thērou'kē), town (pop. 1,234), Navarre prov., N Spain, 7 mi. E of Estella; olive-oil processing; wine, cereals.

Circars, Northern (sĭrkärz', sûr'kärz), historic region bet. Bay of Bengal and N Eastern Ghats, India, in NE Madras and SE Orissa. The Circars [Urdu *Sarkar*=govt.] were administrative areas (17th to early 18th cent.) under Mogul emperors. Here the English East India Co. 1st brought large territories under its control and called them Northern Circars as distinct from acquisitions in S Madras. Formally ceded to English in 1766 by nizam of Hyderabad.

Circasia (sērkä'syä), town (pop. 3,356), Caldas dept., W central Colombia, on W slopes of Cordillera Central, 6 mi. N of Armenia; alt. 5,308 ft.; coffeegrowing center; sericulture.

Circassia (sûrkă'shŭ), historical region of NW Caucasus, Russian SFSR, bet. Kuban R. (N) and Black Sea (SW). The Circassians, known as Kasogs until 15th cent. and as Adyge (Adighe) in their own tongue, are a Caucasian ethnic group of the Sunni Moslem religion. One of the last areas to resist Russian penetration into the Caucasus, the region was finally subjugated in 1864. This was followed by wholesale Circassian emigration to Turkey. Following the Bolshevik revolution, the remaining Circassian-majority areas were constituted as autonomous units, the Circassians proper (Cherkess or Adyge; 87,973 in 1939) forming the Adyge and Cherkess autonomous oblasts, and the related Kabardians (164,106 in 1939) comprising the Kabardian Autonomous SSR.

Circeo, Monte (môn'tē chĕrchä'ô), anc. *Circaeum Promontorium*, promontory at NW tip of Gulf of Gaeta, Latium, S central Italy, 12 mi. WSW of Terracina; rises to 1,775 ft. Site of natl. park. Resort area in anc. times; has remains of Roman town. Formerly also Circello.

Circhina, Yugoslavia: see CERKNO.

Circle, village (pop. 71), NE Alaska, on Yukon R. and 130 mi. ENE of Fairbanks, on the Yukon Flats; NE terminus of Steese Highway from Fairbanks; transshipment point for Yukon R. steamers; supply center for trapping, logging, placer gold-mining region. School; airfield. Established in 1890s following gold discovery near by.

Circle, town (pop. 856), ⊙ McCone co., E Mont., on Redwater Creek and 45 mi. NW of Glendive, in ranching region; shipping point for grain and livestock; dairy and poultry products.

Circle Hot Springs, village (1939 pop. 14), NE Alaska, near Yukon R., 100 mi. ENE of Fairbanks, on branch of Steese Highway; supply center for placer gold-mining region; truck farming. Resort; hot mineral springs near by. Airfield.

Circleville. 1 City (pop. 169), Jackson co., NE Kansas, 30 mi. NNW of Topeka; livestock, grain. **2** City (pop. 8,723), ⊙ Pickaway co., S central Ohio, 24 mi. S of Columbus and on Scioto R.; food products, glassware, paper containers, strawboard, brushes, brooms, feed; soybean processing. Laid out 1810 within remains of circular fort erected by mound builders; inc. as city in 1853. **3** Town (pop. 603), Piute co., S Utah, on Sevier R. and 5 mi. SSW of Junction; alt. 6,061 ft.; livestock. Circleville Mtn. (11,276 ft.) is 7 mi. WNW, in Tushar Mts.

Circonico, Yugoslavia: see CERKNICA.

Circular Head, headland, NW Tasmania, on E coast of peninsula in Bass Strait; c.480 ft. high. STANLEY town at base.

Cirenaica, Libya: see CYRENAICA.

Cirencester (sī'sĭtŭr, sī'rŭnsĕstŭr), urban district (1931 pop. 7,209; 1951 census 11,188), SE Gloucester, England, 13 mi. NW of Swindon; agr. market, with gravel quarries near by. Site of Roman settlement of *Corinium*, of which there are remains. Has 15th-cent. church and remains of 1117 abbey. Site of Royal Agr. Col.

Cirene, Cyrenaica: see CYRENE.

Cires, Point (thē'rĕs), headland of Sp. Morocco, on Strait of Gibraltar, at its narrowest point, opposite (8 mi. SE of) Point Marroquí (Spain); 35°54'N 5°29'W.

Cirey or **Cirey-sur-Vezouze** (sērĕ'-sür-vüzōōz'), town (pop. 2,178), Meurthe-et-Moselle dept., NE France, on the Vezouze and 21 mi. E of Lunéville; mirror-mfg. center; paper and carton milling, brewing. Residence (1734–49) of Voltaire and Mme du Châtelet.

Ciriè (chērēā'), town (pop. 6,131), Torino prov., Piedmont, NW Italy, 12 mi. N of Turin, in irrigated region (sericulture, stock raising). Silk, cotton, and paper mills, tanneries, foundry, alcohol distillery, dyeworks. There are several old churches, including 13th-cent. San Giovanni Battista.

Cirknisko Jezero (tsēr'knĭshkô yĕ'zĕrô), Slovenian *Cirkniško Jezero*, Ger. *Zirknitzer See* (tsĭrk'nitsŭr zā'), Ital. *Lago Periodico* (lä'gô pĕryō'dēkô), lake in SW Slovenia, Yugoslavia, 3 mi. S of Cerknica. Its surface varies bet. □ .2 and □ 11, depending on the season.

Cirò (chērō'), town (pop. 4,178), Catanzaro prov., Calabria, S Italy, 8 mi. N of Strongoli; mfg. of wine presses. **Cirò Marina** (pop. 3,938), its port, is 4 mi. E, on Gulf of Taranto; fishing.

Ciron River (sērō'), Gironde dept., SW France, rises in the Landes, flows 53 mi. NW, past Villandraut and Sauternes, to the Garonne 4 mi. below Langon. Navigable in lower course.

Cirque Mountain (sĕrk) (5,500 ft.), NE Labrador, highest peak of Torngat Mts.; 58°55'N 63°33'W.

Cirquenizza, Yugoslavia: see CRIKVENICA.

Cirrha (sĭ'rŭ), anc. town of Phocis, central Greece, port for Delphi, on Bay of Crisa (inlet of Gulf of Corinth), 1 mi. E of modern Itea. The taxes levied by Cirrha on pilgrims to Delphic oracle caused the first Sacred War, in which the Delphic Amphictyony destroyed Cirrha (c.590 B.C.). Its refugee pop. settled CRISA (with which it is often confused). On its site is modern Gr. village of Kyrra or Kirra (1928 pop. 520).

Cirrus, Mount, Colo.: see NEVER SUMMER MOUNTAINS.

Cirta, Algeria: see CONSTANTINE.

Ciruelas (sērwā'läs), village, Alajuela prov., central Costa Rica, on Turrúcares plain, 5 mi. SW of Alajuela; rail junction; grain, sugar cane, fruit, stock.

Cisa, La (lä chē'sä), pass (alt. 3,415 ft.) bet. Magra and Taro river valleys, in N Apennines, N Italy, 7 mi. NNE of Pontremoli. Separates Ligurian and Etruscan Apennines. Crossed by road bet. Pontremoli and Berceto.

Cisalpine Gaul, Italy: see GAUL; ITALY.

Cisalpine Republic (sĭsăl'pīn), Italian state created 1797 by Napoleon by uniting the Cispadane and Transpadane republics, which he had established (1796) N and S of the Po.

Ciscaucasia, Russian SFSR: see CAUCASUS.

Cisco (sĭ'skō). **1** Resort village, Placer co., E Calif., in the Sierra Nevada, 40 mi. NE of Auburn; winter sports. **2** Village (pop. 334), Piatt co., central Ill., 16 mi. NE of Decatur, in rich agr. area. **3** City (pop. 5,230), Eastland co., N central Texas, c.45 mi. E of Abilene; shipping, processing center for agr., livestock, petroleum area; mfg. (gloves, clay products, gasoline, brooms, flour); railroad shops; poultry packing and hatching, peanut processing; oil, natural-gas wells near. Seat of a jr. col. L. Cisco (bathing, fishing; state fish hatchery) is 5 mi. N. Settled 1851, inc. 1919; had oil boom, 1918.

Cisco, Lake, N central Texas, impounded by dam in a S tributary of Clear Fork of Brazos R., 5 mi. N of Cisco; c.2 mi. long; capacity 45,000 acre-ft.; recreational center; fishing.

Ciskei (sĭs'kā), SE division (□ 4,657; pop. 391,595; native pop. 322,410) of Cape Prov., U. of So. Afr., SW of Great Kei R. Division exists only in respect to administration of native affairs, carried out by Ciskeian General Council, federal body established 1934, with seat at Kingwilliamstown. Division includes dists. of East London, Kingwilliamstown, Peddie, Keiskamahoek, Middeldrift, Glen Gray, Herschel, Victoria East, most of which are not contiguous.

Cislago (chēslä'gô), village (pop. 3,610), Varese prov., Lombardy, N Italy, 13 mi. SSE of Varese; textile mfg.

Cisleithania (sĭs'lēthā'nēŭ), formerly part of Austria-Hungary W of Leitha R., an area now in Austria. The area E of Leitha R.—Transleithania—is now in Hungary.

Cismon River (chēzmôn'), N Italy, rises in the Dolomites 10 mi. ESE of Predazzo, flows 30 mi. S to Brenta R. 11 mi. N of Bassano.

Cisnadie (chēs'nûdyä), Rum. *Cisnădie*, Ger. *Heltau* (hĕl'tou), Hung. *Nagydisznód* (nŏ'dyŭdĕz"nôd), town (1948 pop. 7,284), Sibiu prov., central Rumania, in Transylvania, 5 mi. S of Sibiu; rail terminus; mfg. of broadcloth, rugs, blankets, shawls, ribbons; extensive orchards in vicinity. Has 13th-cent. fortified church.

Cisne (sĭs'nē), village (pop. 628), Wayne co., SE Ill., 28 mi. ENE of Mount Vernon, in agr. area; oil wells.

Cisne, Islas del, Honduras: see SWAN ISLANDS.

Cisneros (sēsnä'rōs), town (pop. 5,423), Antioquia dept., N central Colombia, on Nus R. (affluent of the Porce), in Cordillera Central, on railroad and 40 mi. NE of Medellín; alt. 3,543 ft. Agr. center (coffee, sugar, bananas, corn, beans). Starting point for 12,250-ft. railroad tunnel.

Cisneros (thēsnā'rōs), town (pop. 1,616), Palencia prov., N central Spain, 23 mi. NW of Palencia; flour mills; cereals, wine, lentils, sheep.

Cisnes River (sēs'nĕs), Aysén prov., S Chile, rises on Argentina border in mts. N of L. Fontana, flows 100 mi. WSW to Cay Channel, an inlet of Moraleda Channel. Because of rapids and cataracts, it is navigable only for 6 mi. upstream. Sheep raising in its valley.

Cissaceaster or **Cissanceaster**, England: see CHICHESTER.

Cissna Park (sĭs'nŭ), village (pop. 660), Iroquois co., E Ill., 37 mi. S of Kankakee, in agr. area; grain, livestock, dairy products. Center of a New Amish community.

Cista, Czechoslovakia: see KRASNO.

Cisterna (sēstĕr'nä), town (1930 pop. 1,960), Santiago prov., central Chile, on railroad and 6 mi. S of Santiago; residential suburb in agr. area (wheat, alfalfa, fruit, livestock); phosphate plant.

Cisterna di Latina (chēstĕr'nä dē lätē'nä), town (pop. 6,149), Latina prov., Latium, S central Italy, 15 mi. NE of Anzio. Rebuilt after being destroyed in Second World War. Formerly Cisterna di Littoria.

Cistérniga (thēstĕr'nēgä), town (pop. 1,063), Valladolid prov., N central Spain, near the Duero, 3 mi. SE of Valladolid; wheat, wine, sugar beets.

Cisternino (chēstĕrnē'nô), village (pop. 3,612), Brindisi prov., Apulia, S Italy, 16 mi. SSE of Monopoli, hosiery mfg.; wine, olive oil.

Cistierna (thēstyĕr'nä), town (pop. 2,671), Leon prov., NW Spain, on Esla R. and 28 mi. NE of Leon; coal briquettes, ceramics; cereals, lumber, livestock. Coal mines, limestone quarry near by.

Citalá (sētälä'), town (pop. 729), Chalatenango dept., NW Salvador, on Lempa R. and 45 mi. N of San Salvador (linked by road), near Honduras border; grain, indigo, livestock.

Citânia, Portugal: see BRAGA.

Citará, Farallones de (färäyō'nĕs' dä sĕtärä'), or **Farallones de Chocó** (chōkō'), Andean range on Chocó–Antioquia dept. border, W Colombia, in Cordillera Occidental, 45 mi. SW of Medellín; 28 mi. N–S; rises to 13,290 ft.

Cité, Île de la (ēl dü lä sētä'), island in Seine R., N central France, forming core of city of Paris; c.1,000 yds. long, 200 yds. wide. Site of Notre Dame Cathedral, Hôtel-Dieu, and Palais de Justice (containing Sainte-Chapelle and Conciergerie). Linked to city by 8 bridges, the westernmost of which is the famous Pont-Neuf. Just SE is the Île Saint-Louis.

Cîteaux, France: see NUITS-SAINT-GEORGES.

Cité de la Société du textile artificiel, France: see VAULX-EN-VELIN.

Cité du Bois-Dion, France: see OSTRICOURT.

Cité Jeanne-d'Arc, France: see SAINT-AVOLD.

Cité Saint-Éloi, France: see OSTRICOURT.

Cités Solvay, France: see TAVAUX.

Cithaeron (sĭthē'rŭn), Gr. *Kithairon* (kēthĕrôn'), mountain on Attica-Boeotia border, E central Greece; rises to 4,623 ft. 10 mi. SSW of Thebes. Mentioned in Gr. mythology, it was especially sacred to Dionysus. Formerly called Elatias.

Citium (sĭ'shēŭm), Gr. *Kition* (kē'tyôn), ruined city in SE Cyprus, now partly occupied by N section of Larnaca. Believed to have been founded during Mycenaean age before 1100 B.C., it became a Phoenecian center; its biblical name Chittim of Kittim also refers to the entire isl. Became administrative seat during Assyrian occupation (7th cent. B.C.). Besieged (449 B.C.) by an Athenian force, after it sided with Persia. Stoic philosopher Zeno b. here (335 B.C.). City was visited by earthquakes and declined with the silting up of its harbor.

Citlaltéptl, Mexico: see ORIZABA, PICO DE.
Citronelle (sĭt″rŭnĕl′), town (pop. 1,350), Mobile co., SW Ala., 30 mi. NNW of Mobile, in timber, livestock, and agr. area (cotton, truck, corn); resort with mineral springs; lumber, turpentine, tung oil (tung trees introduced 1906).
Citrus, county (□ 570; pop. 6,111), central Fla., on Gulf of Mexico and bounded N and E by Withlacoochee R.; ⊙ Inverness. Its swampy coast is dotted by Homosassa Isls.; contains Tsala Apopka L. in E. Agr. (corn, peanuts, citrus fruit, cattle, hogs), fishing, lumbering, quarrying (phosphate, limestone, clay). Formed 1887.
Cittadella (chēt-tädĕl′lä), town (pop. 4,588), Padova prov., Veneto, N Italy, near Brenta R., 14 mi. NE of Vicenza. Rail junction; mfg. (silk textiles, agr. and lumber machinery, chemicals). Founded 1220 by Paduans; encircled by medieval walls; has a cathedral.
Città della Pieve (chēt-tä′ dĕl-lä pyā′vĕ), town (pop. 2,457), Perugia prov., Umbria, central Italy, 17 mi. NNW of Orvieto; cement works. Bishopric. Has cathedral, church of Santa Maria dei Bianchi; both have works of Perugino, who was b. here.
Città di Castello (dē kästĕl′lō), town (pop. 8,816), Perugia prov., Umbria, central Italy, on the Tiber and 18 mi. E of Arezzo; mfg. (agr. machinery, metal furniture, cement, linen, macaroni). Bishopric. Has cathedral and several fine Vitelli palaces (15th–16th cent.).
Cittaducale (chēt-tä″dōōkä′lĕ), town (pop. 1,822), Rieti prov., Latium, central Italy, on Velino R. and 4 mi. E of Rieti; wine, olive oil. Has 15th-cent. cathedral. Hydroelectric plant near by.
Città Notabile, Malta: see MDINA.
Cittanova (chēt-tänô′vä), town (pop. 12,097), Reggio di Calabria prov., Calabria, S Italy, 13 mi. E of Palmi; agr. tools, bricks, olive oil, wine. Rebuilt after earthquake of 1783.
Cittanova, Slovenian *Novigrad* (nô′vĕgräd), anc. *Noventium*, town (pop. 1,502), S Free Territory of Trieste, fishing port on the Adriatic, at mouth of Quieto R., 25 mi. SW of Trieste, on Yugoslav border. Bauxite deposits (E). Placed 1947 under Yugoslav administration.
Città Sant'Angelo (chēt-tä′ säntän′jĕlō), town (pop. 2,469), Pescara prov., Abruzzi e Molise, S central Italy, near the Adriatic, 9 mi. WNW of Pescara; olive oil, flour, bricks. Has 14th-cent. church.
Città Vecchia, Malta: see MDINA.
Cittavecchia, Yugoslavia: see STARIGRAD, S Croatia.
City Bell, town (pop. 2,654), NE Buenos Aires prov., Argentina, 6 mi. NW of La Plata; agr. center (grain, livestock, poultry).
City Deep, SE suburb of Johannesburg, S Transvaal, U. of So. Afr.; gold mining.
City Island, SE N.Y., in Long Island Sound off E shore of the Bronx borough of New York city; connected with mainland by causeway. Boatbuilding, boating center; known for its seafood restaurants.
City Point, Va.: see HOPEWELL.
City View, village (pop. 8,471, with adjacent Riverside and Woodside), Greenville co., NW S.C., just W of Greenville.
Ciucas Peak (chōō′käsh), Rum. *Ciucaş*, highest peak (alt. 6,425 ft.) of the Moldavian Carpathians, in the Buzau Mts., SE central Rumania, 20 mi. SE of Brasov (Stalin).
Ciudad (Sp. thyōō-dhädh′; in Latin America usually syōōdädh′ or syōō-dhädh′) [Sp.,=city]: for names beginning thus and not found here, see under following part of the name.
Ciudad Altamirano, Mexico: see ALTAMIRANO, Guerrero.
Ciudad Antigua (äntē′gwä), town (1950 pop. 339), Nueva Segovia dept., NW Nicaragua, 10 mi. E of Ocotal: coffee, tobacco, sugar cane, grain.
Ciudad Arce (är′sä), town (pop. 3,310), La Libertad dept., W central Salvador, on railroad and Inter-American Highway, 14 mi. NW of Nueva San Salvador; commercial center; grain, sugar cane, livestock. Founded 1921. Until c.1948 called El Chilamatal.
Ciudad Barrios (bär′yōs), city (pop. 2,546), San Miguel dept., E Salvador, at W foot of volcano Cacaguatique (5,417 ft.), 21 mi. NNW of San Miguel; sugar milling; coffee, sugar cane, henequen. Until 1913, Cacaguatique.
Ciudad Bolívar (bōlē′vär), city (1941 pop. 19,789; 1950 census 31,009), ⊙ Bolívar state, E Venezuela, port on narrows of Orinoco R., on its right bank opposite Soledad, 262 mi. from the Orinoco's mouth, and 275 mi. SE of Caracas; 8°8′N 63°33′W. Accessible to ocean vessels. Has hot, tropical climate. Situated in cattle-grazing region. Commercial outlet for half the area of Venezuela—the Guiana Highlands and llanos of interior lowlands. Thriving port; focal point of Orinoco R. trade. Main exports are: cattle, hides, balata gum, tonka beans, medicinal plants, chicle, indigo, woods, gold, diamonds, egret plumes. Sawmilling, rice milling, tanning, furniture making, brewing. Airport. Colonial city; has cathedral and old Sp. palace. Founded 1764 and named Angostura for its location on narrowest point of the Orinoco. Became bishopric 1790. Played major part in struggle for independence. Simón Bolívar withdrew here after early defeat. It was site of Congress of Angostura (1819), which decreed formation of republic of Gran Colombia and elected Bolívar president. Name was changed to Ciudad Bolívar in 1864. Famous Angostura bitters invented here by local physician; distillery was later moved (1875) to Port of Spain.
Ciudad Bolivia (bōlē′vyä) or **Pedraza** (pādrä′sä), town (pop. 433), Barinas state, W Venezuela, 31 mi. SW of Barinas; cattle. Airfield.
Ciudad Camargo, Mexico: see CAMARGO, Tamaulipas.
Ciudad Darío (därē′ō), town (1950 pop. 1,766), Matagalpa dept., W central Nicaragua, 19 mi. SW of Matagalpa, on Inter-American Highway; agr. center (vegetables, potatoes, sugar cane, plantains); livestock. Ruben Darío b. here. Formerly called Metapa; sometimes Darío.
Ciudad de las Casas, Mexico: see SAN CRISTÓBAL DE LAS CASAS.
Ciudad del Maíz (dĕl mäēs′) or **General Magdaleno Cedillo** (hänäräl′ mägdälā′nō sādē′yō), city (pop. 2,804), San Luis Potosí, N central Mexico, in E outliers of Sierra Madre Oriental, 40 mi. NE of Río Verde; alt. 4,065 ft. Corn, wheat, beans, cotton, maguey. Sometimes Maíz.
Ciudad de Nutrias, Venezuela: see NUTRIAS.
Ciudad de Valles, Mexico: see VALLES.
Ciudadela (syōōdädhä′lä), city (pop. estimate 15,000) in W Greater Buenos Aires, Argentina, on W limits of federal dist.; industrial center: textiles (silk, cotton), bakelite, lime, toys, radios; distilling, meat packing.
Ciudadela (thyōōdhädhä′lä), anc. *Jamno*, city (pop. 9,289) on W coast of Minorca, Balearic Isls., 25 mi. WNW of Mahón (linked by road built by English in 18th cent.); fishing port with some industries. Mfg. of shoes, cheese, and butter; also flour, chocolate, ice, furniture, jewelry. Region produces cereals, tubers, grapes, timber, livestock. Historic city (once isl.'s ⊙) is a bishopric. Has fine Gothic cathedral (1287), remains of wall, and obelisk commemorating Turkish onslaught (1558). Vicinity is rich in Celtic and druid monuments, called *talaiots*.
Ciudad Encantada, Spain: see VALDECABRAS.
Ciudad Fernández (fĕrnän′dĕs), city (pop. 2,081), San Luis Potosí, N central Mexico, on the Río Verde and just NW of Río Verde; corn, wheat, cotton, beans, fruit, livestock.
Ciudad Flores, Guatemala: see FLORES.
Ciudad García, Mexico: see GARCÍA, Zacatecas.
Ciudad González, Mexico: see DOCTOR HERNÁNDEZ ALVAREZ.
Ciudad Guzmán, Mexico: see GUZMÁN.
Ciudad Hidalgo, Mexico: see HIDALGO, MICHOACÁN.
Ciudad Jardín, Spain: see CHAMARTÍN.
Ciudad Juárez or **Juárez** (wôrĕz′, Sp. hwä′rĕs), city (pop. 48,881), Chihuahua, N Mexico, on the Rio Grande (3 international bridges) opposite El Paso, Texas; alt. 3,717 ft. Rail terminus; customs station; commercial, shipping, and processing center. It is hemmed in by desert, except for the river valley, which, under intensive cultivation SE of city, produces cotton, cereals, corn, alfalfa, cattle. Has distilleries, vegetable-oil plants, flour mills, cotton gins, foundries. Developed (1659) as focal point for Sp. colonial expansion to N. Called originally El Paso del Norte, it included settlements on both sides of river, which were later separated by treaty of Guadalupe Hidalgo (1848) ending Mexican War. Name was changed (1888) to honor Benito Juárez; town was his capital during his exile from central Mexico. The capture of the city by Pascual Orozco and Francisco Villa was the final spark setting off the revolution in 1910.
Ciudad Lerdo, Mexico: see LERDO.
Ciudad Lineal (lĕnäăl′), E residential suburb (pop. 1,341) of Madrid, central Spain, linked by tramway. Sometimes considered to include sections of Vistalegre and Ventas.
Ciudad Madero (mädā′rō), city (pop. 28,075), Tamaulipas, NE Mexico, just N of Tampico; petroleum-producing and -refining center. Formerly Villa de Cecilia.
Ciudad Mante (män′tā), city (pop. 8,616), Tamaulipas, NE Mexico, on Inter-American Highway and 80 mi. NW of Tampico; agr. center (cereals, sugar cane, fruit, livestock); tanning, sugar refining, alcohol distilling. Formerly Villa Juárez.
Ciudad Manuel Doblado, Mexico: see MANUEL DOBLADO.
Ciudad Melchor Múzquiz, Mexico: see MÚZQUIZ.
Ciudad Mendoza, Mexico: see MENDOZA.
Ciudad Morelos, Mexico: see CUAUTLA, Morelos.
Ciudad Mutis, Colombia: see MUTIS.
Ciudad Obregón (ōbrāgōn′), city (pop. 12,497), Sonora, NW Mexico, in irrigated lowland of Gulf of California (Yaqui R. delta), on railroad and 65 mi. SE of Guaymas; agr. center (rice, fruit, winter vegetables, cotton, cattle); rice and flour milling, fruit canning. Copper mines near by. Sometimes called Cajeme (kähā′mā), name of the municipio.
Ciudad Ojeda, Venezuela: see LAGUNILLAS, Zulia state.
Ciudad Porfirio Díaz, Mexico: see PIEDRAS NEGRAS.
Ciudad Real (rääl′), province (□ 7,622; pop. 530,308), S central Spain, in New Castile; ⊙ Ciudad Real. Bounded S by Andalusia (Córdoba and Jaén provs.), it borders E on Albacete prov., NE on Cuenca prov., N on Toledo prov., and W on Estremadura (Badajoz prov.). Anchuras (NW) forms an enclave in Toledo prov. While mountainous in S and SW (Sierra Morena) and NW (Montes de Toledo), it is mostly occupied by the La Mancha (for which it is sometimes named), a monotonous, elevated plain reaching into Albacete and Cuenca provs. Watered by the Guadiana R. and its affluents (Javalón, Gigüela). Climate is dry, with hot summers and cool winters. A rich agr. region with many large processing towns. Besides grapes and olives, it raises cereals, chick-peas, saffron, esparto, hemp, pepper, potatoes, fruit. Sheep and goats are grazed. Prov. is among leading wine producers of Spain. Mineral resources also of great importance. The mercury mines of Almadén are considered the world's largest. Also mined are lead, iron, zinc, manganese, bituminous coal, lime, gypsum. Leading towns are Ciudad Real, Tomelloso, Manzanares, Daimiel, Alcázar de San Juan, Valdepeñas, Infantes, Piedrabuena, and Almodóvar del Campo. The prov. is crossed by Madrid-Seville RR via historic Despeñaperros pass. A center for reconquest of Spain from Moors; the Knights of Calatrava operated from here (see Campo de CALATRAVA). Much of its character has been captured by Cervantes in his *Don Quixote*. The prov. remained in Loyalist hands until the last phase of the Sp. civil war (1936–39).
Ciudad Real, city (pop. 30,015, with suburbs 32,931), ⊙ Ciudad Real prov., S central Spain, in New Castile, on central plateau (Meseta), near Guadiana R., rail and road junction 100 mi. S of Madrid; 38°59′N 3°55′W; alt. c.2,000 ft. A decayed provincial city, now a processing and trading center for agr. region (grapes, olives, forage, fruit, cereals, livstock). Lumbering. Flour milling, liquor distilling; mfg. of meat products, woolen and leather goods, cork articles, soap, ceramics; limekilns. Mineral springs near by. Still preserves some of its medieval walls, with imposing 14th-cent. Mudejar Toledo gate (declared a natl. monument). Has ruins of an alcazar. As a bishopric, it has a huge Gothic cathedral of simple outline and a bishop's palace. Apart from San Pedro, all other old churches have disappeared. Founded in 13th cent. as Villa Real by Alfonso X of Castile at site of Pozuelo de Don Gil, it was made hq. of the Santa Hermanidad [=holy brotherhood]. Under Ferdinand and Isabella, became seat of Inquisition tribunal, which was later transferred to Toledo. During Peninsular War the Spanish were defeated (1809) by the French in vicinity. The Alarcos shrine is 4 mi. WSW.
Ciudad Rodrigo (rōdhrē′gō), city (pop. 3,872; commune pop. 12,082), Salamanca prov., W Spain, in Leon, in strategic position near Port. border, 53 mi. SW of Salamanca; agr. trade center (cereals, vegetables, livestock, lumber). Mfg. of tiles, sandals; tanning, wood turning, flour- and sawmilling. Mineral springs, iron and lead deposits near by. Episcopal see. Has medieval walls and citadel, 12th-cent. cathedral (restored in 16th), several convents and anc. mansions. Bridge on Roman foundations spans Agueda R. Named after Count Rodrigo González, who resettled it in 12th cent. Taken (1706) by English; fell (1810) to French; its reconquest (1812) by Wellington earned him title of duke of Ciudad Rodrigo.
Ciudad Santos, Mexico: see GENERAL PEDRO ANTONIO SANTOS.
Ciudad Serdán, Mexico: see SERDÁN.
Ciudad Trujillo or **Trujillo** (trōōhē′yō), city (1945 pop. 116,217; 1950 pop. 181,533), ⊙ and largest city of Dominican Republic, Caribbean port on SE coast of Hispaniola isl., on right bank of small Ozama R., and 150 mi. E of Port-au-Prince (Haiti), 850 mi. ESE of Havana; 18°28′N 69°53′W. Political, social, cultural, and industrial center, in fertile, tropical sugar- and fruitgrowing region; served by natl. and international airlines and linked by highways with interior and coastal provs. of the republic. Its artificial harbor (completed 1937), with deep channel and modern docks, handles ⅔ of all imports; main exports are sugar, molasses, cacao, beeswax, hides, timber. Among the city's industries are alcohol (also anhydrous alcohol) and liquor distilling, brewing, meatpacking, tanning, cementmaking; mfg. of shoes, pharmaceuticals, soap, vegetable oil, chocolate, macaroni, coffee, clothing, hats, furniture. Fishing. A clean attractive city with a pleasant tropical climate (mean temp. 77°F.), it is also a popular resort, with fine beaches. Seat of papal nuncio and archbishop. Zoo and botanical garden (opened 1949). Fine example of a 16th-cent. Sp. town, retaining many anc. bldgs. and remains of historical interest, such as ruins of San Nicolás church (built 1502), San Francisco church (built 1504), the Alcázar of Columbus (seat of 1st viceroy), and Torre de Homenaje (Tower of Homage). The Renaissance cathedral, built 1514–40, has ornate tomb of Columbus. Outstanding modern structures are the new Palace of Justice, Palace for the Executive, University City (dating back to one of the 1st universities in the Americas, founded 1538), and the Perla Antilles race track

Across Ozama R. is the Cristóbal Colón airport; the large, new General Andrews airport is just W. Founded 1496 by Bartholomew Columbus, the city is the oldest continuously inhabited European settlement of the Western Hemisphere. It was long a center of Sp. activity in the New World, serving as the base for the expeditions of the conquistadors Velásquez, Cortés, Balboa, and others. It was captured by Drake in 1586. The 1930 hurricane devastated the city, which was then almost entirely rebuilt. Known for hundreds of years as Santo Domingo, name was changed 1936 to Ciudad Trujillo, named for Rafael Trujillo Molina.

Ciudad Victoria or **Victoria** (vēktōr'yä), city (pop. 19,513), ⊙ Tamaulipas, NE Mexico, at E foot of Sierra Madre Oriental, on railroad, on Inter-American Highway and 135 mi. NW of Tampico, 300 mi. N of Mexico city; 23°44'N 99°8'W; alt. 1,050 ft. Trading, mining (silver, gold, lead, copper), and agr. center (sugar cane, henequen, citrus fruit, cereals, livestock); tanning, henequen processing, textile milling. Radio station. Founded 1750.

Ciudad Vieja (vyā'hä), town (1950 pop. 4,267), Sacatepéquez dept., S central Guatemala, at N foot of volcano AGUA, on Guacalate R. (hydroelectric station) and 3 mi. SSW of Antigua; alt. 4,974 ft. Road center; coffee, grain, fodder grasses; cattle. Has oldest cathedral of Guatemala, built 1534. Founded 1527 on Indian site of Almolonga; ⊙ Guatemala until destroyed 1541 by flood during eruption of the Agua. A new capital was then founded at ANTIGUA.

Ciudmar (syōōdh-mär'), SE residential suburb of Santiago de Cuba, Oriente prov., E Cuba.

Civa, Cape (jüvä'), Turkish *Civa*, N Turkey, on Black Sea at mouth of Yesil Irmak, 17 mi. ENE of Samsun.

Civetta (chēvĕt'tä), mountain (alt. 10,558 ft.) in the Dolomites, N Italy, 19 mi. NNW of Belluno.

Civezzano (chĕvĕtsä'nô), village (pop. 761), Trento prov., Trentino-Alto Adige, N Italy, 3 mi. NE of Trent; sausage.

Cividale del Friuli (chēvēdä'lĕ dĕl frē'ōōlē), anc. *Forum Julii*, town (pop. 4,715), Udine prov., Friuli-Venezia Giulia, NE Italy, 9 mi. ENE of Udine; mfg. (alcohol, tanning extracts, soap, paper, cement). Has 8th-cent. octagonal baptistery, several old churches, cathedral (reconstructed 16th cent.), 14th-cent. palace, and a natl. archaeological mus. with Roman and barbarian antiquities. Anciently the capital of Friuli. Seat of Lombard duchy (569–774) and residence of patriarchs of Acquileia (beginning 730) and of Carolingian margraves. Paul the Deacon, Lombard historian, and Adelaide Ristori, actress, were b. here.

Cividate al Piano (chēvēdä'tĕ äl pyä'nô), village (pop. 2,744), Bergamo prov., Lombardy, N Italy, on Oglio R. and 13 mi. SE of Bergamo; agr. center.

Cividate Camuno (kämōō'nô), village (pop. 1,244), Brescia prov., Lombardy, N Italy, in Val Camonica, on Oglio R. and 1 mi. SW of Breno; a major Ital. hydroelectric plant here.

Civita (chē'vētä), village (pop. 2,279), Cosenza prov., Calabria, S Italy, 3 mi. N of Cassano al Ionio; olive oil, wine.

Civita Campomarano (käm"pômärä'nô), village (pop. 2,109), Campobasso prov., Abruzzi e Molise, S central Italy, 15 mi. N of Campobasso.

Civita Castellana (kästĕl-lä'nä), town (pop. 7,289), Viterbo prov., Latium, central Italy, 18 mi. ESE of Viterbo; mfg. (pottery, agr. tools, soap, macaroni); clay quarrying. Bishopric. Has 13th-cent. cathedral and citadel (1494–1512). Near by are sites of Etruscan Falerii Veteres, destroyed in 241 B.C. and rebuilt by Romans as Falerii Novi, with a theater and well-preserved walls and towers.

Civita Lavinia, Italy: see LANUVIO.

Civitanova del Sannio (chē"vētänō'vä dĕl sän'nyô), village (pop. 2,160), Campobasso prov., Abruzzi e Molise, S central Italy, near Trigno R., 11 mi. ENE of Isernia.

Civitanova Marche (mär'kĕ), town (pop. 2,184), Macerata prov., The Marches, central Italy, near the Adriatic, 12 mi. E of Macerata; foundry, celluloid factory.

Civitavecchia (chē"vētävĕk'kyä), anc. *Centum Cellae*, town (pop. 24,822), Roma prov., Latium, central Italy, on Tyrrhenian Sea, 38 mi. WNW of Rome. Rail junction; chief port for Rome and Terni, and for passenger service to Sardinia; foundries; mfg. (cement, soap, liquor); fishing. Bishopric. Has arsenal built by Bernini and citadel (houses Etruscan mus.) built by Bramante and Michelangelo. Its harbor was founded by Trajan. Badly damaged in Second World War by heavy air bombing (1943–44).

Civitella Casanova (chēvētĕl'lä kä"zänô'vä), village (pop. 923), Pescara prov., Abruzzi e Molise, S central Italy, 14 mi. W of Chieti; cementworks.

Civitella del Tronto (dĕl trôn'tô), town (pop. 729), Teramo prov., Abruzzi e Molise, S central Italy, 8 mi. N of Teramo, on castle-crowned hill in fruit-growing region.

Civitella di Romagna (dē rômä'nyä), village (pop. 1,156), Forlì prov., Emilia-Romagna, N central Italy, on Ronco R. and 16 mi. SSW of Forlì.

Civray (sēvrā'), town (pop. 2,491), Vienne dept., W central France, on Charente R. and 10 mi. NNE of Ruffec; cattle and mule market; metalworks; mfg. of linen fabrics. Has 12th-cent. church.

Civril (chĭvrĭl'), Turkish *Çivril*, village (pop. 4,241), Denizli prov., SW Turkey, rail terminus on Buyuk Menderes R. and 50 mi. NE of Denizli; wheat, barley, opium.

Ciz (chĭs), Slovak *Čiz*, Hung. *Csiz* (chĭz), village (pop. 706), S Slovakia, Czechoslovakia, on railroad and 26 mi. SSW of Roznava; health resort with iodine and bromine springs and baths.

Cize-Bolozon, France: see BOLOZON.

Cizre (chĭzrĕ'), village (pop. 4,419), Mardin prov., SE Turkey, on Tigris R. at Syrian border and 80 mi. E of Mardin; lignite; wheat, barley, millet, lentils, rice, chick-peas.

Clabecq (kläbĕk'), Flemish *Klabbeek* (klä'bāk), town (pop. 1,924), Brabant prov., central Belgium, 3 mi. S of Hal; steel foundries, rolling mills.

Clackamas (klă'kùmùs), county (□ 1,890; pop. 86,716), NW Oregon; ⊙ Oregon City. Cascade Range is in E; drained by Willamette and Clackamas rivers. Dairying, agr. (poultry, fruit, truck, grain, seeds, hay), paper mfg., quicksilver mining. Formed 1843.

Clackamas River, NW Oregon, formed SW of Mt. Hood, flows 81 mi. NW, past Estacada, to Willamette R. near Oregon City. Used for hydroelectric power.

Clackmannan or **Clackmannanshire** (klăkmă'nùn, -shĭr), county (□ 54.6; 1931 pop. 31,948; 1951 census 37,528), E central Scotland; ⊙ Clackmannan. Bounded by Stirling (SW and W), Perthshire (N and NE), Fifeshire (E). Drained by Forth and Devon rivers. Surface is mountainous in N (Ochil Hills, 2,363 ft.), leveling toward the Forth. Coal mining and woolen milling are principal industries; farming and cattle raising in Devon R. valley. Other towns are Alloa, Alva, Dollar, Tillicoultry. Smallest co. of Scotland.

Clackmannan, town and parish (pop. 2,858), ⊙ Clackmannanshire, Scotland, near the Forth, 2 mi. ESE of Alloa; coal mining; agr. market. Has 14th-cent. tower of the Bruce family and an anc. market cross.

Clackmannanshire, Scotland: see CLACKMANNAN, county.

Clacton or **Clacton-on-Sea,** town in residential urban dist. of Clacton (1931 pop. 15,848; 1951 census 24,065), E Essex, England, on North Sea and 13 mi. ESE of Colchester; seaside resort. Has Norman church. Paleolithic tools found near by. Near by is SAINT OSYTH, with remains of noted priory.

Cladonia, Mount (klùdō'nēù) (5,100 ft.), NE Labrador, on S shore of Nachvak Fiord; 58°58'N 63°34'W.

Clady (klă'dē), agr. village (district pop. 723), NW Co. Tyrone, Northern Ireland, on Finn R. and 4 mi. SW of Strabane; frontier point on Irish border; potatoes, flax, oats; cattle.

Claflin, city (pop. 921), Barton co., central Kansas, 15 mi. NE of Great Bend, in grain and poultry region; flour milling. Oil wells near by.

Claiborne (klā'bùrn). **1** Parish (□ 766; pop. 25,063), N La.; ⊙ Homer. On Ark. line (N); drained by Bayou D'Arbonne and its Middle Fork. Oil wells, natural-gas plants. Lumbering, cotton ginning. Agr. (cotton, corn, hay, peanuts). Formed 1828. **2** County (□ 486; pop. 11,944), SW Miss.; ⊙ Port Gibson. Bounded W by Mississippi R. (here the La. line), N by Big Black R.; also drained by Bayou Pierre. Agr. (cotton, corn), cattle raising, lumbering. Formed 1802. **3** County (□ 445; pop. 24,788), NE Tenn.; ⊙ Tazewell. Bounded N by Ky. and Va., S by Clinch R.; drained by Powell R. Includes part of Norris Reservoir. Traversed by Cumberland Mtn. in NW; rest of co. has ridges and valleys of the Appalachians. Coal mining, lumbering, woodworking, farming (corn, livestock, some tobacco). Formed 1801.

Claiborne, resort village (pop. c.150), Talbot co., E Md., 22 mi. NNW of Cambridge, on Eastern Bay; terminus of ferry to Kent Isl. Near by is tuberculosis preventorium for children.

Clain River (klē), Vienne dept., W central France, rises 5 mi. WNW of Confolens, flows 80 mi. generally N, past Poitiers, to the Vienne 3 mi. S of Châtellerault.

Clairac (klĕräk'), village (pop. 1,273), Lot-et-Garonne dept., SW France, on the Lot and 14 mi. SE of Marmande; tobacco- and winegrowing; fruit (chiefly plums) preserved and shipped.

Claire, Lake (□ 545), NE Alta., W of L. Athabaska, in Wood Buffalo Natl. Park; 58°30'N 112°W; 40 mi. long, 28 mi. wide. Drains E into L. Athabaska through Mamawi L. Formerly a deep lake, it is now much silted up.

Claire. Rivière, Vietnam: see CLEAR RIVER.

Claire City, town (pop. 109), Roberts co., NE S.Dak., 13 mi. N of Sisseton.

Clairemont, village (pop. c.200), ⊙ Kent co., NW Texas, 30 mi. NNE of Snyder and near Salt Fork of Brazos R.; trading point for cattle-ranching and agr. region (cotton, grain).

Clairoix (klĕrwä'), village (pop. 615), Oise dept., N France, on the Oise at mouth of Aisne R. and 2 mi. NE of Compiègne; tire plant.

Clairton, city (pop. 19,652), Allegheny co., SW Pa., 12 mi. SSE of Pittsburgh and on Monongahela R.; steel, coke by-products; bituminous coal; agr. Inc. as borough 1903, as city 1922.

Clairvaux, Aube dept., France: see VILLE-SOUS-LA-FERTÉ.

Clairvaux-les-Lacs (klĕrvō'-lā-läk'), village (pop. 985), Jura dept., E France, in the Jura, 12 mi. SE of Lons-le-Saunier; wood turning, diamond cutting, paper milling.

Claise River (klĕz), Indre and Indre-et-Loire depts., central France, rises 7 mi. SW of Châteauroux, flows 50 mi. W through the Brenne, past Mézières-en-Brenne, Preuilly-sur-Claise, and Le Grand Pressigny, to the Creuse 2 mi. above La Haye-Descartes.

Clallam (klă'lùm), county (□ 1,753; pop. 26,396), NW Wash.; ⊙ Port Angeles. Bounded W by Pacific Ocean and N by Juan de Fuca Strait; Olympic Mts. rise in S. Includes part of Olympic Natl. Park and Makah, Ozette, and Quillayute Indian reservations. Fish, lumber, manganese, paper, dairy products; resorts. Formed 1854.

Clamart (klämär'), residential town (pop. 32,638), Seine dept., N central France, a SSW suburb of Paris, 5 mi. from Notre Dame Cathedral.

Clamecy (klämsē'), town (pop. 5,314), Nièvre dept., central France, on Yonne R. and Nivernais Canal, and 23 mi. S of Auxerre; produces chemicals, parquetry, razors; meat processing, flour milling. Has steep, narrow streets and gabled houses. Until end of 19th cent. Morvan lumber was collected here and floated down the Yonne and Seine to Paris.

Clam River, NW and central Mich., drains L. Cadillac in Wexford co., flows c.40 mi. SE, through forest and farm region, to Muskegon R. in NW Clare co.

Clan Alpine Mountains, W central Nev., in Churchill co., E of Humboldt Sink. Highest peak is Mt. Grant (11,247 ft.), 53 mi. ENE of Fallon.

Clancey, village (pop. c.100), Jefferson co., SW central Mont., on Prickly Pear Creek and 10 mi. S of Helena; ore-shipping point in silver-mining dist.

Clandonald, village (pop. estimate 350), E Alta., 16 mi. NNE of Vermilion; grain, stock.

Clane, Gaelic *Claonadh*, town (pop. 112), NE Co. Kildare, Ireland, on the Liffey (bridged), on Grand Canal, and 14 mi. NE of Kildare; agr. market (cattle, horses, potatoes). Has remains of 13th-cent. monastery.

Clanfield, agr. village and parish (pop. 477), W Oxfordshire, England, near the Thames, 14 mi. W of Oxford; farm-implement works. Has Norman church with 14th-cent. tower.

Clanis, Italy: see CHIANA.

Clanton, town (pop. 4,640), ⊙ Chilton co., central Ala., 38 mi. NW of Montgomery, in cotton and fruit area; cotton milling, meat processing; wood products, feed. Ships fruit and vegetables. Small power dams are on near-by Coosa R. Inc. 1873.

Clanwilliam, town (pop. 1,452), SW Cape Prov., U. of So. Afr., on Olifants R. and 120 mi. NNE of Cape Town; grain, citrus fruit; viticulture. Near by are govt. cedar forests and Heerenlogement Cave, now natl. monument.

Clapham (klă'pùm), residential district of Wandsworth, London, England, S of the Thames, 4 mi. SSW of Charing Cross. Here are Clapham Common (c.200 acres) and Clapham Junction, S London rail center.

Clapier, Mont (mõ kläpyā'), peak (9,990 ft.) in Maritime Alps, on Fr.-Ital. border, 8 mi. WSW of Tenda Pass. Until 1947, border lay 5 mi. S of peak.

Clapperton Island (6 mi. long, 3 mi. wide), S central Ont., one of the Manitoulin Isls., in the North Channel of L. Huron, just N of Manitoulin Isl., 14 mi. W of Little Current.

Clapton, residential district of Hackney, London, England, N of the Thames, 4 mi. NE of Charing Cross.

Clara (klä'rä), town (pop. estimate 1,000), E central Entre Ríos prov., Argentina, on railroad and 13 mi. ENE of Villaguay; agr. (rice, corn, flax, livestock); tannery, soap factory.

Clara, Gaelic *Clárach*, town (pop. 1,635), N Co. Offaly, Ireland, on Brosna R. and 8 mi. NW of Tullamore; jute and flour milling, mfg. of rope and fish nets; agr. market (wheat, barley, potatoes; cattle).

Clara (klä'rä), town (pop. 1,000), Tacuarembó dept., N Uruguay, 35 mi. SSE of Tacuarembó; road junction; corn, wheat, cattle.

Clara, Cape, Canada: see GARRY, CAPE.

Clara City, village (pop. 1,106), Chippewa co., SW Minn., on small affluent of Minnesota R. and 19 mi. SW of Willmar, in grain, livestock, and poultry area; dairy products.

Clare (klâr), town (pop. 1,454), SE South Australia, 75 mi. N of Adelaide; wine center; orchards.

Clare, town and parish (pop. 1,252), SW Suffolk, England, on Stour R. and 7 mi. WNW of Sudbury; agr. market. Has 15th-cent. church, remains of Augustinian priory founded 1248, and earthwork remains of anc. castle.

Clare, Gaelic *an Chláir*, county (□ 1,230.9; pop. 85,064), Munster, W Ireland; ⊙ Ennis. On the Atlantic, bet. Galway Bay and the Shannon bounded by cos. Limerick and Kerry (S), Galway (N), and Tipperary (E). Drained by Fergus R. and other tributaries of the Shannon. Surface broken and hilly in NE and NW, with bogs and lakes, sloping toward fertile plain along the Shannon and Atlantic. Lough Derg, on the Shannon, is on NE border. Coastline is rocky and irregular. Dairying, grain and potato growing are carried on; salmon fisheries in the Shannon. Slate and marble quarried; some coal and lead mined in SW. Industries include woolen milling, mfg. of rope and fish net. Towns are Ennis, Kilrush, Kilkee (seaside resort), Killaloe, Newmarket-on-Fergus, and Ennistymon. Shannon Airport or Rineanna is one of world's most important international airports. At Ardnacrusha is major hydroelectric power station of the Shannon Power Scheme. Co. Clare, included in Connaught until 4th cent., later became part of kingdom of Thomond before being granted to the Clares. There are numerous remains of anc. castles, abbeys, and round towers; notable are monastic remains on Holy Isl. in Lough Derg. Among anc. stone forts is Cahercommaunfort (c.900), excavated by archaeologists in 1936.

Clare, town, Ireland: see CLARECASTLE.

Clare, county (□ 572; pop. 10,253), central Mich.; ⊙ Harrison. Drained by Muskegon R., Tobacco R., and small Cedar R. Livestock, dairy products, poultry, grain, potatoes, corn, beans, sugar beets. Some mfg. at Clare. Oil and gas wells. Many lakes (hunting, fishing); resorts. Has a state park. Organized 1871.

Clare. **1** Town (pop. 179), Webster co., central Iowa, 10 mi. NW of Fort Dodge; livestock, grain. **2** City (pop. 2,440), Clare co., central Mich., on Tobacco R. and 15 mi. N of Mt. Pleasant, in agr. area. (dairy products; fruit, livestock). Oil and gas wells. Mfg. of auto trailers, novelties. Many small lakes (resorts). Platted 1870; inc. as village 1879, as city 1891.

Clarecastle or **Clare** (klâr), Gaelic *Droichead an Chláir*, town (pop. 568), S Co. Clare, Ireland, on Fergus R. estuary (bridge), 2 mi. SSE of Ennis; agr. market (grain, potatoes; dairying). Ruins of anc. castle of the O'Briens on isl. in Fergus R.

Clare Island, Gaelic *Cliara*, island (4,024 acres; 4 mi. long, 2 mi. wide; rises to 1,520 ft.) at entrance to Clew Bay, W Co. Mayo, Ireland, 17 mi. W of Westport. At N extremity is lighthouse (53°49'N 10°W). There are ruins of 1224 Carmelite abbey, and of 16th-cent. castle.

Claremont, municipality (pop. 7,769), SW Western Australia, SW residential suburb of Perth.

Claremont, village (pop. estimate 500), S Ont., 24 mi. NE of Toronto; dairying, fruitgrowing.

Claremont, England: see ESHER.

Claremont, town (pop. 1,210), St. Ann parish, N Jamaica, 8 mi. S of St. Ann's Bay, in agr. region (citrus fruit, corn, pimento, coffee, cattle).

Claremont, town (pop. 931), SE Tasmania, 4 mi. NW of Hobart and on Derwent R.; chocolate factories.

Claremont. **1** City (pop. 6,327), Los Angeles co., S Calif., at base of San Gabriel Mts., 30 mi. E of Los Angeles and adjoining Pomona; ships citrus fruit. Seat of Claremont Col. (formerly Claremont Colleges; renamed 1944) and associated colleges: Claremont Men's Col. (1946), Pomona Col. (coeducational; chartered 1887), and Scripps Col. (for women; chartered 1926). City was inc. in 1907. **2** Village (pop. 249), Richland co., SE Ill., 6 mi. E of Olney, in agr. area (corn, wheat, livestock, apples). **3** Village (pop. 426), Dodge co., SE Minn., 27 mi. W of Rochester, in corn, oat, livestock region; dairy products. **4** City (pop. 12,811), Sullivan co., SW N.H., on Sugar R. (water power), near its junction with the Connecticut, and 20 mi. S of Lebanon. Mfg. (mining and milling machinery, textiles, shoes, paper); resort; winter sports. Includes West Claremont (paper mills). Has state's oldest Episcopal church bldg. (begun 1773) and oldest R.C. church (begun 1823). Settled 1762, inc. as town 1764, as city 1948. **5** Town (pop. 669), Catawba co., W central N.C., 11 mi. E of Hickory; hosiery mfg. **6** Town (pop. 236), Brown co., NE S.Dak., 27 mi. NE of Aberdeen. **7** Town (pop. 374), Surry co., SE Va., on the James and 25 mi. E of Petersburg. Claremont manor house, here, dates from mid-17th cent.

Claremore (klâr'mōr, klâ'rŭmōr), city (pop. 5,494), ⊙ Rogers co., NE Okla., 25 mi. ENE of Tulsa, in stock-raising and agr. area; cotton ginning, cottonseed-oil milling; mfg. of feed, chemicals, boilers. Health resort, with mineral springs. Oil, gas wells; sandstone quarries, strip coal mines. Will Rogers was b. near by and lived in Claremore; a memorial to him was dedicated in 1938. A U.S. Indian hosp. and Okla. Military Acad. are here. Settled in late 19th cent. on site of an Indian town; inc. as town 1896, as city 1908.

Claremorris (klârmô'rĭs), Gaelic *Clár Chloinne Mhuiris*, town (pop. 1,045), SE Co. Mayo, Ireland, 16 mi. SE of Castlebar; agr. market (cattle, potatoes); furniture mfg.

Clarence. **1** Town (pop. 791), Cedar co., E Iowa, 34 mi. NW of Davenport; dairy products, sausage. **2** City (pop. 1,123), Shelby co., NE Mo., near Salt R., 25 mi. NNE of Moberly. Ships grain, soy beans; livestock; coal. Founded 1857. **3** Village (pop. 1,018), Erie co., W N.Y., 15 mi. ENE of Buffalo; canned foods.

Clarence, Cape, NE extremity of Somerset Isl., E Franklin Dist., Northwest Territories, on Lancaster Sound, at N end of Prince Regent Inlet; 73°52'N 90°8'W.

Clarence, Port, bay (15 mi. long, 12 mi. wide) of Bering Strait, W Alaska, in W Seward Peninsula; 65°15'N 166°49'W. Teller village on E shore. SW side of bay protected by narrow spit of land. Ice-free June–Oct.

Clarence Center, village (pop. c.650), Erie co., W N.Y., 12 mi. NE of Buffalo; gypsum quarries.

Clarence Head, cape, SE Ellesmere Isl., NE Franklin Dist., Northwest Territories, on Baffin Bay; 76°50'N 77°45'W.

Clarence Island (17 naut. mi. long, 12 naut. mi. wide), easternmost of South Shetland Isls., off Palmer Peninsula, Antarctica; 61°10'S 54°5'W.

Clarence Island, in W Tierra del Fuego, Chile, on the Strait of Magellan; actually 2 isls. separated by narrow channel; 54°S 72°W. Rises to c.3,300 ft.

Clarence King, Mount, Calif.: see KING, MOUNT.

Clarence Peak, Sp. Guinea: see SANTA ISABEL PEAK.

Clarence River, NE New South Wales, Australia, rises in McPherson Range of Great Dividing Range, flows 245 mi. SE and NE, past Tabulam, Grafton, Ulmarra, and Maclean, to the Pacific 10 mi. E of Maclean. Navigable 45 mi. below Grafton by steamers carrying agr. and dairy products. Lighthouse at mouth, protected by breakwater.

Clarence River, E S.Isl., New Zealand, rises in Spenser Mts.; flows S and NE, bet. Kaikoura Ranges, to the Pacific 20 mi. N of Kaikoura; 125 mi. long.

Clarence Strait, SE Alaska, in Alexander Archipelago, E of Prince of Wales Isl., extends 125 mi. NW from Dixon Entrance to Sumner Strait.

Clarence Strait, channel connecting Timor Sea with Van Diemen Gulf, bet. Melville Isl. (N) and NW coast of Northern Territory, Australia (S); 90 mi. long, 16 mi. wide; contains Vernon Isls.

Clarence Strait, arm of Strait of Hormuz of Persian Gulf, SE Iran, bet. mainland and Quishm isl.; 70 mi. long, 5 mi. wide.

Clarence Town, town (pop. 344), S central Bahama Isls., on S Long Isl., 210 mi. SE of Nassau; 23°7'N 74°59'W. Livestock (goats, pigs, sheep), sisal.

Clarencetown, Sp. Guinea: see SANTA ISABEL.

Clarenceville, village (pop. 294), S Que., near Richelieu R., 14 mi. WSW of Bedford; dairying; pig raising.

Clarenceville, village (1940 pop. 1,535), Oakland co., SE Mich., just NW of Detroit and on the River Rouge.

Clarendon (klă'rŭndŭn), parish (□ 467.89; pop. 123,505), Middlesex co., central and S Jamaica; ⊙ May Pen. Includes Portland Ridge peninsula, southernmost section of the isl. The N region is mountainous; the S (Vere Plain), along lower Minho R., is irrigated lowland, where sugar cane is grown. Also produces bananas, citrus fruit, ginger, sisal, yams, breadfruit, cacao, coffee, honey; livestock. Copper mining in the uplands. May Pen, leading commercial center, has processing plants. Milk River spa is noted for its radioactive thermal springs. The parish is crossed by the Kingston–Montego Bay RR. Parts of its shore line (Portland Ridge) were leased as a base to the U.S. in 1940.

Clarendon, county (□ 694; pop. 32,215), E central S.C.; ⊙ Manning. Bounded S by L. Marion; drained by Black R. Agr. area (cotton, tobacco, truck), dairy products, timber. Formed 1856.

Clarendon. **1** City (pop. 2,547), ⊙ Monroe co., E central Ark., c.55 mi. E of Little Rock, at junction of Cache and White rivers, in rich agr. (cotton, corn, rice) area; timber. Commercial fishing; cotton ginning, lumber milling, mfg. of buttons. Has state game refuge. Settled c.1819. **2** Borough (pop. 748), Warren co., NW Pa., 5 mi. SE of Warren; oil refining. **3** City (pop. 2,577), ⊙ Donley co., extreme N Texas, in the Panhandle, 40 mi. S of Pampa. Commercial, processing, and shipping center for cattle, grain, and cotton region; cotton ginning. Clarendon jr. col. Founded 1878, moved to present site on railroad 1887, inc. 1901. **4** Town (pop. 1,102), Rutland co., W central Vt., on Otter Creek, just S of Rutland; fruit, lumber. **5** Village, Va.: see ARLINGTON, county.

Clarendon Hills, suburban village (pop. 2,437), Du Page co., NE Ill., W of Chicago and 17 mi. E of Aurora, in dairying area. Inc. 1924.

Clarendon Park, locality, SE Wiltshire, England, 3 mi. E of Salisbury. In hunting lodge, here, Great Council of Henry II met (1164), resulting in signature of Constitutions of Clarendon. Formerly site of royal forest. Excavations in ruins of royal palace have yielded objects of medieval art.

Clarendon River, W Vt., rises near Tinmouth, flows c.15 mi. N to Castleton R. W of Rutland.

Clarens (klärā'), resort village of MONTREUX, Vaud canton, W Switzerland, on E shore of L. Geneva; immortalized in Rousseau's *Nouvelle Héloïse*.

Clare River, Co. Galway, Ireland, rises 10 mi. E of Claremorris, flows S, then W, to Lough Corrib 4 mi. NNE of Galway; c.40 mi. long.

Claresholm (klârz'hōm), town (pop. 1,306), S Alta., 75 mi. SSE of Calgary; lumbering, dairying, cereal-foods mfg. Govt. mental hosp.

Claret (klärā'), village (pop. 359), Hérault dept., S France, 17 mi. N of Montpellier; olive oil.

Claridenstock (klä'rĭdŭnshtôk"), peak (10,728 ft.) in Glarus Alps, central Switzerland, 11 mi. E of Altdorf.

Claridge, village (pop. 1,039), Westmoreland co., SW Pa., 3 mi. N of Jeannette.

Clarie Coast (klă'rē), part of coast of Wilkes Land, Antarctica, just W of Adélie Coast, on Indian Ocean, bet. 131° and 136°20'E. Discovered 1840 by Dumont d'Urville, Fr. navigator.

Clarin (klä'rēn), town (1939 pop. 1,473; 1948 municipality pop. 15,005), N Bohol isl., Philippines, on Bohol Strait, 25 mi. NNE of Tagbilaran; agr. center (rice, corn, coconuts).

Clarin Bridge or **Clarinbridge**, Gaelic *Droichead an Chláirín*, agr. village, S Co. Galway, Ireland, on small inlet of Galway Bay, 8 mi. ESE of Galway; sheep; potatoes, beets.

Clarinda klŭrĭn'dŭ), city (pop. 5,086), ⊙ Page co., SW Iowa, on Nodaway R. (hydroelectric plant) and 17 mi. E of Shenandoah; rail junction; mfg. (dairy products, packed poultry, beverages, concrete, automotive tools). Bituminous-coal mines near by. Has a jr. col.; and a state hosp. for the insane. Inc. 1866.

Clarines (klärē'nās), town (pop. 1,142), Anzoátegui state, NE Venezuela, landing on Unare R. and 35 mi. WSW of Barcelona; cotton, sugar cane, cacao, corn, stock.

Clarington, village (pop. 478), Monroe co., E Ohio, on the Ohio and 18 mi. SSW of Woodsfield, in agr. area.

Clarion (klă'rēŭn), county (□ 599; pop. 38,344), W central Pa.; ⊙ Clarion. Coal-mining plateau area, drained by Clarion R.; bounded SW by Allegheny R., S by Redbank Creek. Settled after 1800 by Scotch-Irish; growth due to iron, lumber, and oil industries. Bituminous coal; glass products, rubber goods; clay, gas, oil; grain, dairy products. Formed 1839.

Clarion. **1** City (pop. 3,150), ⊙ Wright co., N central Iowa, 28 mi. NE of Fort Dodge; rail junction; livestock-shipping point; wood products. Inc. 1881. **2** Borough (pop. 4,409), ⊙ Clarion co., W Pa., 60 mi. NE of Pittsburgh and on Clarion R., in natural-gas, bituminous coal, clay area. Glass products, beverages, cement blocks, lumber; agr. State teachers col. Laid out 1840, inc. 1841.

Clarión Island, Mexico: see REVILLA GIGEDO ISLANDS.

Clarion River (klă'rēŭn), NW Pa., formed at Johnsonburg by confluence of East and West branches (each c.20 mi. long); flows c.110 mi. generally SW, past Ridgway and Clarion, to Allegheny R. 5 mi. S of Emlenton. Flood-control dam in East Branch.

Clarissa, village (pop. 650), Todd co., central Minn., on branch of Long Prairie R. and 12 mi. NNW of Long Prairie, in grain, livestock, poultry area; dairy products, potatoes.

Clark. **1** County (□ 878; pop. 22,998), S central Ark.; ⊙ Arkadelphia. Drained by Ouachita, Caddo, and Little Missouri rivers, and by Terre Noire Creek. Agr. (cotton, corn, truck, fruit, poultry, livestock); timber. Mfg. at Arkadelphia. Cinnabar mines. Formed 1823. **2** County (□ 1,751; pop. 918), E Idaho; ⊙ Dubois. Mtn. area bordering on Mont. Livestock (sheep, horses), lumber. Part of Targhee Natl. Forest in N. Formed 1919. **3** County (□ 505; pop. 17,362), E Ill.; ⊙ Marshall. Bounded SE by Wabash R.; drained by North Fork Embarrass R. Agr. (corn, wheat, oats, livestock, poultry); oil, natural-gas wells. Mfg. of shoes, limestone products, hardware, paint; oil refineries, storage and pumping stations. Formed 1819. **4** County (□ 384; pop. 48,330), SE Ind.; ⊙ Jeffersonville. Bounded SE by Ohio R. (here forming Ky. line); drained by Silver Creek and other small tributaries of the Ohio. Agr. (grain, tobacco, livestock). Mfg. at Charlestown and at Jeffersonville (river port). Formed 1801. **5** County (□ 984; pop. 3,946), SW Kansas; ⊙ Ashland. Level to gently rolling prairie region, bordered S by Okla.; drained (S) by Cimarron R. Livestock, grain. Oil and gas fields. Formed 1885. **6** County (□ 259; pop. 18,898), central Ky.; ⊙ Winchester. Bounded S by Kentucky R.; drained by several creeks. Gently rolling agr. area, in Bluegrass region; burley tobacco, bluegrass seed, livestock; limestone quarries. Mfg. at Winchester. Includes Daniel Boone Monument at Boonesboro. Formed 1792. **7** County (□ 509; pop. 9,003), extreme NE Mo.; ⊙ Kahoka. Bounded E by Mississippi and Des Moines rivers; drained by Fox and Wyaconda rivers; wheat, corn, oats, livestock. Formed 1818. **8** County (□ 7,927; pop. 48,289), SE Nev.; ⊙ Las Vegas. Mining and livestock-grazing area bordering on Ariz. and Calif., drained (E) by Colorado and Virgin rivers. Magnesium deposits. Dairy and truck products. L. Mead, created by Hoover Dam, is in E. Spring Mts. are in W, Sheep Range in N. Formed 1909. **9** County (□ 402; pop. 111,661), W central Ohio; ⊙ SPRINGFIELD. Intersected by Mad and Little Miami rivers and by small Buck, Beaver, and Honey creeks. Includes George Rogers Clark Memorial Park. Agr. (grain;

dairy products; livestock); mfg. at Springfield. Limestone quarrying; sand and gravel pits. Formed 1818. **10** County (□ 976; pop. 8,369), E central S.Dak.; ⊙ Clark. Agr. area watered by numerous intermittent creeks. Livestock, dairy products, poultry, corn, wheat, rye, oats, hay, potatoes. Formed 1873. **11** County (□ 633; pop. 85,307), SW Wash.; ⊙ Vancouver. Rolling hills sloping S to valley of Columbia R. Fruit, nuts, wood products, wool, cheese. Formed 1844. **12** County (□ 1,222; pop. 32,459), central Wis.; ⊙ Neillsville. Drained by Black and Eau Claire rivers. Principally a dairying area; cheese is chief product. Also lumbering, stock raising; vegetable canning. Formed 1853.

Clark. 1 City (pop. 276), Randolph co., N central Mo., 10 mi. SSE of Moberly. **2** Borough, Mercer co., Pa.: see CLARKSVILLE. **3** City (pop. 1,471), ⊙ Clark co., E central S.Dak., 30 mi. W of Watertown; trade center for grain and cattle area; dairy products, poultry, potatoes. Founded 1882. **4** Town (1940 pop. 715), McDowell co., S W.Va., c.8 mi. E of Welch, in coal-mining area. Post office at Northfork.

Clark, Fort, Texas: see BRACKETTVILLE.

Clark, Lake (50 mi. long, 1–4 mi. wide), S Alaska, 140 mi. WSW of Anchorage, on W slope of Aleutian Range; 60°18'N 154°10'W; Nondalton village (S) and Tanalian Point (E) are game-fishing resorts.

Clark, Mount (4,733 ft.), W Mackenzie Dist., Northwest Territories, near Mackenzie R., 50 mi. SE of Fort Norman; 64°25'N 124°11'W; highest peak of Franklin Mts.

Clarkdale. 1 Village (pop. 1,609), Yavapai co., central Ariz., 28 mi. NE of Prescott and on Verde R.; copper smelting (since 1915). Tuzigoot Natl. Monument is near. **2** Mill village (pop. c.700), Cobb co., NW central Ga., 15 mi. WNW of Atlanta; thread mfg.

Clarke, Argentina: see CARRIZALES.

Clarke. 1 County (□ 1,241; pop. 26,548), SW Ala.; ⊙ Grove Hill. Heavily forested area in Black Belt; bounded W by Tombigbee R., SE by Alabama R. Cotton, corn, livestock; lumber milling. Formed 1812. **2** County (□ 125; pop. 36,550), NE central Ga.; ⊙ Athens. Piedmont agr. (cotton, corn, truck, dairy products, poultry) area; textile mfg. Drained by Oconee R. Formed 1801. **3** County (□ 429; pop. 9,369), S Iowa; ⊙ Osceola. Rolling prairie agr. area (hogs, cattle, poultry, corn, wheat) with bituminous-coal deposits. Drained by Chariton and South rivers and Whitebreast Creek. Formed 1846. **4** County (□ 697; pop. 19,362), E Miss.; ⊙ Quitman. Borders E on Ala; drained by Chickasawhay R. Agr. (cotton, corn), lumbering. Includes a state park. Formed 1833. **5** County (□ 174; pop. 7,074), N Va.; ⊙ Berryville. In N Shenandoah Valley; bounded N by W.Va.; Blue Ridge in SE; traversed by Shenandoah R.; also drained by short Opequon Creek. Rich agr. area (apples, corn, wheat); dairying; horse breeding is important. Formed 1836.

Clarke City, village (pop. estimate 750), E Que., on Marguerite R., near its mouth on the St. Lawrence, and 110 mi. NNE of Matane, 300 mi. NE of Quebec; titanium mining, pulp milling, lumbering.

Clarke Island, southernmost island (□ 31), of Furneaux Isls., in Bass Strait, 13 mi. off NE coast of Tasmania across Banks Strait; 9 mi. long, 7 mi. wide; mountainous. Sheep raising.

Clarkes Harbour or **Clark's Harbour,** town (pop. 887), SW N.S., on W coast of Cape Sable Isl., 30 mi. SW of Shelburne; fishing port.

Clarkesville or **Clarksville,** resort city (pop. 1,106), ⊙ Habersham co., NE Ga., 11 mi. WNW of Toccoa; apple packing and shipping, sawmilling, toy mfg.

Clark Field, Philippines: see STOTSENBURG, FORT.

Clarkfield, village (pop. 1,012), Yellow Medicine co., SW Minn., 13 mi. W of Granite Falls, in grain, poultry, livestock area; dairy products.

Clark Fork or **Clarks Fork,** village (pop. 387), Bonner co., N Idaho, 35 mi. S of Bonners Ferry, near Pend Oreille L., and on Clark Fork of Columbia R.; center of agr., dairy, lumber area.

Clark Fork, river in Mont. and Idaho, part of Columbia R. system; rises in SW Mont., near Butte; flows c.360 mi. N and NW, past Deer Lodge and Missoula, Mont., and across panhandle region of N Idaho, to E side of Pend Oreille L. Principal tributaries are Flathead and Bitterroot rivers in Mont.; dammed at Frenchtown. Known as Silver Bow Creek near Butte and as Missoula R. near Missoula; part of its course is also called the Hell Gate. Sometimes defined to include Pend Oreille R., which leaves NW corner of Pend Oreille L., N Idaho, and flows W then N, through Pend Oreille co., NE Wash., to Columbia R. at British Columbia line. Total length of Pend Oreille R. and the Clark Fork is 479 mi.; their drainage basins total □ 25,820.

Clark Hill Dam, Ga. and S.C., built by U.S. Army Engineers in Savannah R. 22 mi. above Augusta, Ga.; 200 ft. high, 5,660 ft. long. For flood control and power; max. length of reservoir (capacity 2,900,000 acre-feet) is 36 mi.

Clark Island, (□ c.¼), Knox co., S Maine, just E of St. George town. Granite quarries; bridge to mainland.

Clark Mills, village (1940 pop. 929), Oneida co., central N.Y., on Oriskany Creek and 7 mi. W of Utica; textile milling.

Clarks. 1 Village (pop. 1,345), Caldwell parish, N La., 35 mi. S of Monroe. **2** Village (pop. 464), Merrick co., E central Nebr., 33 mi. NE of Grand Island and on Platte R.; dairy and poultry produce, livestock, grain.

Clarksburg, village (pop. estimate 500), S Ont., near Georgian Bay, 23 mi. E of Owen Sound; dairying, mixed farming.

Clarksburg. 1 Village, Yolo co., central Calif., on Sacramento R. and 10 mi. S of Sacramento; large beet-sugar refinery. **2** Town (pop. 1,630), Berkshire co., NW Mass., 22 mi. NNE of Pittsfield, near Vt. line; woolen mills. Briggsville village is pop. center. Settled 1769, inc. 1798. **3** City (pop. 366), Moniteau co., central Mo., 6 mi. W of California. **4** Village (pop. 391), Ross co., S Ohio, 15 mi. NW of Chillicothe, in agr. area. **5** Industrial city (pop. 32,014), ⊙ Harrison co., N W.Va., on the West Fork (headstream of the Monongahela) and 70 mi. E of Parkersburg, in bituminous-coal, oil, gas, clay, and limestone region. Mfg. of stone, clay, carbon, and glass products, oilfield equipment, mortuary equipment, tin plate, chemicals, precision instruments, clothing, and lumber, food, and paper products. Was important Union supply base in Civil War. Stonewall Jackson b. here. Chartered 1785.

Clarksdale. 1 City (pop. 16,539), ⊙ Coahoma co., NW Miss., on Sunflower R. and c.50 mi. NNW of Greenwood, in rich cotton region; shipping and processing center; mfg. of cottonseed products, farm implements; lumber mills, cotton gins and compress, grain elevators. Settled 1848 on site of Indian fortification; inc. 1882. Holds annual cotton festival. **2** Town (pop. 282), De Kalb co., NW Mo., 16 mi. ENE of St. Joseph.

Clarks Fork (of Yellowstone R.), river, Mont. and Wyo.; rises in NE spur of Absaroka Range, near Granite Peak, S Mont.; flows c.150 mi. SE into Wyo. thence NE into Mont., past Bridger and Fromberg, to Yellowstone R. near Laurel. Irrigates 132,000 acres; 11,360 acres in Wyo.

Clarks Green, borough (pop. 824), Lackawanna co., NE Pa., 6 mi. NNW of Scranton.

Clarks Grove, village (pop. 254), Freeborn co., S Minn., 9 mi. N of Albert Lea, in agr. area; dairy products.

Clark's Harbour, Nova Scotia: see CLARKES HARBOUR.

Clarks Hill, town (pop. 493), Tippecanoe co., W central Ind., 15 mi. SSE of Lafayette, in agr. area.

Clarkson. 1 Town (pop. 489), Grayson Co., W central Ky., 25 mi. WSW of Elizabethtown, in agr. area; makes tool handles. **2** Village (pop. 764), Colfax co., E Nebr., 20 mi. N of Schuyler and on branch of Elkhorn R.; feed, flour; grain.

Clarks Point, fishing village (pop. 117), SW Alaska, on Nushagak Bay, inlet of Bristol Bay, 16 mi. S of Dillingham.

Clarks River, SW Ky., formed in E McCracken co. by junction of East and West forks, flows 8 mi. N to Tennessee R. 4 mi. SE of Paducah. East Fork rises in Henry co., NW Tenn., flows c.60 mi. N and NW into Ky., past Murray and Benton, to West Fork; West Fork rises in Calloway co., SW Ky., flows 32 mi. N.

Clarks Summit, borough (pop. 2,940), Lackawanna co., NE Pa., 6 mi. NNW of Scranton; foundries; agr. Settled 1799, inc. 1911.

Clarkston. 1 Town (pop. 1,165), De Kalb co., NW central Ga., 9 mi. ENE of Atlanta. **2** Village (pop. 722), Oakland co., SE Mich., 9 mi. NW of Pontiac, in farm and lake-resort area. **3** Town (pop. 526), Cache co., N Utah, on Clarkston Creek, 17 mi. NW of Logan, near Idaho line; alt. 4,930 ft.; trading point for dairying and irrigated agr. area (wheat, alfalfa). **4** City (pop. 5,617), Asotin co., SE Wash., 22 mi. S of Pullman and on Snake R. opposite Lewiston, Idaho; ships and processes grain, fruit, livestock. Inc. 1902.

Clarkston Creek, rises in Cache co., N Utah, near Idaho line, flows 20 mi. SE, past Clarkston, to Bear R. near Newton. Newton Dam (101 ft. high, 3,360 ft. long, including dike; completed 1946), on creek 3 mi. N of Newton, is main unit in Newton irrigation project. Dam was built to replace structure constructed (1871) by Mormon pioneers.

Clark's Town, town (pop. 1,910), Trelawny parish, N Jamaica, 8 mi. SE of Falmouth; sugar cane, ginger, pimento, fruit.

Clarksville. 1 City (pop. 4,343), ⊙ Johnson co., NW Ark., c.55 mi. E of Fort Smith, near Arkansas R., in agr. area (cotton, fruit, livestock, poultry); cotton ginning, lumber milling. Gas wells, coal mines. Seat of Col. of the Ozarks. **2** City, Habersham co., Ga.: see CLARKESVILLE. **3** Town (pop. 5,905), Clark co., SE Ind., just E of New Albany and across the Ohio N of Louisville (Ky.), of whose metropolitan area it is a part. Laid out 1783. **4** Town (pop. 1,210), Butler co., N central Iowa, on Shell Rock R. and 26 mi. NW of Waterloo; rail junction; canned corn, feed; metal, concrete, and dairy products. Limestone quarries, sand and gravel pits near by. State park just S. Inc. 1874. **5** Village (pop. 339), Ionia co., S central Mich., 23 mi. SE of Grand Rapids, in farm area. **6** City (pop. 702), Pike co., E Mo., on Mississippi R. and 16 mi. E of Bowling Green; agr. **7** Town (pop. 171), Coos co., N N.H., on upper Connecticut R. and 38 mi. NNW of Berlin, in recreational area. **8** Village (pop. 510), Clinton Co., SW Ohio, 19 mi. S of Xenia. **9** Borough (pop. 428), Greene co., SW Pa., 9 mi. WSW of Brownsville. **10** or **Clark,** borough (pop. 345), Mercer co., W Pa., 5 mi. NE of Sharon and on Shenango R. **11** City (pop. 16,246), ⊙ Montgomery co., N Tenn., on the Cumberland, at Red R. mouth, and 40 mi. NW of Nashville. An important dark-tobacco market; mfg. of boots, work clothing, snuff, cigars, rubber goods, canned tomatoes, dairy products; flour milling; limestone quarries. Austin Peay State Col., state agr. experiment station here. U.S. Fort Campbell (formerly Camp Campbell) and Campbell Air Force Base are 10 mi. NW, in Ky.; Dunbar Cave is near by. Platted 1784. **12** City (pop. 4,353), ⊙ Red River co., NE Texas, 30 mi. E of Paris; processing center for cotton, truck, dairy, lumber area; cottonseed-oil and lumber milling, pecan shelling; cannery. Settled 1828, inc. 1837. **13** Town (pop. 1,035), Mecklenburg co., S Va., on Roanoke R. and 45 mi. E of Danville; tobacco market; textile finishing, pickle mfg. Buffalo Springs (resort) is 6 mi. W.

Clarkton. 1 City (pop. 1,004), Dunklin co., extreme SE Mo., on Mississippi R. and 16 mi. NNE of Kennett. **2** Town (pop. 589), Bladen co., S N.C., 23 mi. SE of Lumberton; tobacco market; lumber milling. Settled c.1760.

Clarkville, village (pop. 19), Kootenai co., N Idaho.

Claro, Río (rē'ō klä'rō), river, Talca prov., central Chile, rises in the Andes, flows c.100 mi. NW and SW, past Talca, to Maule R. 12 mi. WSW of Talca. Used for irrigation.

Claromecó (klärōmākō'), beach resort (pop. estimate 500), S Buenos Aires prov., Argentina, on Atlantic Ocean, 35 mi. SSE of Tres Arroyos.

Clary (klärē'), village (pop. 1,397), Nord dept., N France, 10 mi. SE of Cambrai; handkerchief, tulle, and lace mfg.

Claryville, town (pop. 16), Perry co., E Mo., on Mississippi R. opposite Chester, Ill.

Clase, Wales: see SWANSEA.

Clashmore (klăshmôr'), Gaelic *Clais Mhór,* town (pop. 75), SW Co. Waterford, Ireland, near the Blackwater, 4 mi. NNE of Youghal; agr. market in dairying, cattle-raising, potato-growing region.

Clason, Argentina: see CLASSON.

Clason Point (klā'sŭn, klô'–), SE N.Y., a residential section of S Bronx borough of New York city, at mouth of Bronx R. on East R. Sometimes called Clason's Point.

Classon, town (pop. estimate 500), S central Santa Fe prov., Argentina, 50 mi. NW of Rosario, in agr. area (corn, wheat, flax, livestock). Sometimes spelled Clason.

Clatonia, village (pop. 192), Gage co., SE Nebr., 25 mi. SSW of Lincoln, near Big Blue R.

Clatskanie (klătskā'nē), city (pop. 901), Columbia co., NW Oregon, 30 mi. E of Astoria and on Clatskanie R. (a small tributary of the Columbia); salmon fisheries; lumber, dairy products.

Clatsop, county (□ 820; pop. 30,776), NW Oregon; ⊙ Astoria. NW extremity of state, bounded N by Columbia R. and W by Pacific Ocean; drained by Nehalem R. Logging, dairying; salmon, tuna fisheries at Astoria. Formed 1844.

Clatsop Spit, NW Oregon, narrow arm of land at mouth of Columbia R., extending 2.5 mi. N from S shore of river.

Claude, city (pop. 820), ⊙ Armstrong co., extreme N Texas, in the Panhandle, 25 mi. ESE of Amarillo; trade, shipping center for livestock, grain area; poultry, dairy products. Has semi-annual stock shows.

Claudia Castra, England: see GLOUCESTER, city.

Cláudio (klou'dyŏŏ), city (pop. 2,034), S central Minas Gerais, Brazil, 22 mi. SSE of Divinópolis; rail-spur terminus; coffee, alcohol, lard.

Claudio Gay, Cordillera (kôrdīyā'rä klou'dyō gī'), W parallel spur of the Andes in Atacama prov., N Chile, extends 45 mi. N–S near Argentina border, forming E watershed of Salar de Pedernales and Salar de Maricunga; rises to over 18,000 ft.

Clausentum, England: see SOUTHAMPTON.

Claushavn (klous'houn"), Eskimo *Ilimanak,* fishing settlement (pop. 162), Christianshaab dist., W Greenland, on Disko Bay, 9 mi. S of Jakobshavn; 69°5'N 51°5'W. Radio station.

Clausthal-Zellerfeld (klous'täl"-tsĕ'lŭrfĕlt"), town (pop. 14,904), in former Prussian prov. of Hanover, W Germany, after 1945 in Lower Saxony, on a plateau in the upper Harz, 8 mi. SSW of Goslar; lead-, copper-, and silver-mining center; mfg. of metal goods, furniture, knitwear, paper; sawmilling, woodworking. Summer resort; winter sports. Zellerfeld (N) developed at the silver mines around Benedictine monastery Cella (founded in late-12th cent.); chartered 1532. Clausthal, chartered 1554, has mining acad. (founded 1775), large 17th-cent. wooden church. Towns were united 1924. Sometimes spelled Klaustal-Zellerfeld.

Clavaux, Les, France: see LIVET-ET-GAVET.

Clavenna, Italy: see CHIAVENNA.

Claverack (klä'vŭrĭk, –răk, klā'–), village (pop. c.400), Columbia co., SE N.Y., 3 mi. SE of Hudson.

Fine old bldgs. include Van Rensselaer manor house and former co. courthouse (built 1786).

Claveria (klävārē'ä), town (1939 pop. 3,741; 1948 municipality pop. 12,703), Cagayan prov., N Luzon, Philippines, on Babuyan Channel, 40 mi. WNW of Aparri; lumbering and agr. center (rice, tobacco). Sawmilling at near-by Pata (1939 pop. 1,371).

Clavering Island, Greenland: see DANEBORG.

Claverley, agr. village and parish (pop. 1,215), SE Shropshire, England, 5 mi. E of Bridgnorth; has Norman church.

Clavier (klävyā'), village (pop. 1,290), Liége prov., E central Belgium, 9 mi. SSE of Huy; dairying.

Claviere (klävyā'rē, Fr. klävyâr'), village (pop. 132), Torino prov., Piedmont, NW Italy, on Fr. border, 1 mi. E of Montgenèvre Pass; customs station. Summer resort (alt. 5,773 ft.); also winter sports. Until c.1936 written Clavières.

Clavo, El, Venezuela: see EL CLAVO.

Clavo, Rico, Honduras: see EL CORPUS.

Clawson, city (pop. 5,196), Oakland co., SE Mich., suburb 15 mi. NNW of downtown Detroit; machine shops. Inc. as village 1920, as city 1940.

Claxton, city (pop. 1,923), Evans co., E central Ga., 20 mi. SSW of Statesboro, near Canoochee R., in cotton and tobacco area.

Claxton Bay, village (pop. 594), W Trinidad, B.W.I., on the Gulf of Paria, on railroad and 23 mi. S of Port of Spain. Petroleum refining.

Clay. 1 County (□ 603; pop. 13,929), E Ala.; ⊙ Ashland. Mt. Cheaha (2,407 ft.) in Talladega Mts. (W) is highest point in state. Part of Talladega Natl. Forest is in W and N. Cotton, hogs, corn; lumber milling. Formed 1866. **2** County (□ 650; pop. 26,674), extreme NE Ark.; ⊙ Piggott and Corning. Bordered N and E by Mo. line; drained by St. Francis, Cache, Black, and Current rivers. Crowley's Ridge intersects the co. Agr. (fruit, cotton, grain, livestock; dairy products). Mfg. at Piggott, Corning. Hardwood timber. Formed 1873. **3** County (□ 598; pop. 14,323), NE Fla.; ⊙ Green Cove Springs. Bounded E by St. Johns R.; contains many small lakes in SW. Stock raising, dairying, farming (corn, vegetables, peanuts), lumbering; clay pits. Formed 1858. **4** County (□ 224; pop. 5,844), SW Ga.; ⊙ Fort Gaines. Bounded W by Ala. line, formed here by Chattahoochee R. Coastal plain agr. (cotton, corn, truck, peanuts, livestock) and timber area. Formed 1854. **5** County (□ 464; pop. 17,445), S central Ill.; ⊙ Louisville. Agr. (corn, wheat, fruit, redtop seed; dairy products; livestock). Oil, natural-gas wells. Mfg. (shoes, food products, underwear, furniture). Drained by Little Wabash R. Formed 1824. **6** County (□ 364; pop. 23,918), W Ind.; ⊙ Brazil. Agr. area (livestock, grain), with bituminous-coal mining, clay pits; mfg. (especially clay products). Drained by Eel R. and small Birch Creek. Formed 1825. **7** County (□ 571; pop. 18,103), NW Iowa; ⊙ Spencer. Rolling prairie agr. area (hogs, cattle, poultry, corn, oats, soybeans) drained by Little Sioux and Ocheyedan rivers. Formed 1851. **8** County (□ 658; pop. 11,697), N Kansas; ⊙ Clay Center. Rolling to hilly agr. region, drained by Republican R. Grain, livestock. Formed 1866. **9** County (□ 474; pop. 23,116), SE Ky.; ⊙ Manchester. In Cumberland foothills; drained by South Fork Kentucky R. and its headstreams. Mtn. agr. area (tobacco, corn, livestock, apples, hay). Bituminous-coal mines; hardwood timber. Formed 1806. **10** County (□ 1,050; pop. 30,363), W Minn.; ⊙ Moorhead. Agr. area bounded W by N.Dak. and Red River of the North and drained by Buffalo R. Wheat, livestock, dairy products, potatoes. Formed 1862. **11** County (□ 414; pop. 17,757), E Miss.; ⊙ West Point. Drained by Tombigbee R. and small affluents. Agr. (cotton, corn, hay), dairying, stock raising, lumbering. Formed 1871. **12** County (□ 413; pop. 45,221), W Mo., bounded S by Missouri R.; ⊙ Liberty. Agr. and mfg.; coal deposits. Formed 1822. **13** County (□ 570; pop. 8,700), S Nebr.; ⊙ Clay Center. Agr. area drained in SW by Little Blue R. Grain, livestock, dairy and poultry produce. Formed 1871. **14** County (□ 219; pop. 6,006), W N.C.; ⊙ Hayesville. Mtn. region; bounded S by Ga., NE by Nantahala R.; drained by Hiwassee R. (Chatuge dam and reservoir). Mostly included in Nantahala Natl. Forest. Farming (corn, hay, apples, livestock, dairy products, poultry), lumbering; resorts. Formed 1861. **15** County (□ 403; pop. 10,993), SE S.Dak., on Nebr. line; ⊙ Vermillion. Agr. area drained by Vermillion R. and bounded S by Missouri R. Grain, livestock, dairy products. Formed 1862. **16** County (□ 264; pop. 8,701), N Tenn.; ⊙ Celina. Bounded N by Ky.; drained by Obey and Cumberland rivers. Includes part of Dale Hollow Reservoir. Coal mining, lumbering, agr. (tobacco, grains), livestock raising. Formed 1870. **17** County (□ 1,101; pop. 9,896), N Texas; ⊙ Henrietta. Bounded N by Red R. (Okla. line); drained by Wichita and Little Wichita rivers. Livestock, agr., and oil-producing area: cattle, wheat, other grains, cotton, corn; dairying; horses, mules, sheep, hogs, poultry. Mfg. at Henrietta. Formed 1857. **18** County (□ 342; pop. 14,961), central W.Va.; ⊙ Clay. On Allegheny Plateau; drained by Elk R. Coal mines, natural-gas and oil wells; timber; some agr. (livestock, fruit, tobacco). Formed 1858.

Clay. 1 Town (pop. 1,291), Webster co., W Ky., 21 mi. WNW of Madisonville, in agr., coal, timber area; makes brooms, concrete blocks, ice cream. **2** Town (pop. 500), ⊙ Clay co., central W.Va., on Elk R. and 32 mi. ENE of Charleston; coal mines, gas and oil wells; timber; agr.

Clay, Mount, N. H.: see PRESIDENTIAL RANGE.

Clayburn, village (pop. estimate 200), SW B.C., in Fraser valley, 4 mi. SSE of Mission; brick and tile making, clay quarrying, fruitgrowing.

Clay Center. 1 City (pop. 4,528), ⊙ Clay co., N Kansas, on Republican R. and 30 mi. NW of Manhattan; shipping center for agr. and dairying area; flour milling, meat packing, bottling; mfg. of brooms. Laid out 1862, inc. 1875. **2** City (pop. 824), ⊙ Clay co., S Nebr., 18 mi. ESE of Hastings; small trade center; incubators, flour; dairy produce, grain. **3** Village (pop. 590), Ottawa co., N Ohio, 11 mi. ESE of Toledo.

Clay City. 1 Village (pop. 1,103), Clay co., S central Ill., near Little Wabash R., 14 mi. W of Olney; trade and shipping center; apples, pears, peaches, livestock, corn, wheat; oil, natural-gas wells. Settled in early 1830s; inc. 1869. Had oil boom in 1937. **2** Town (pop. 1,068), Clay co., W Ind., near Eel R., 22 mi. SE of Terre Haute, in agr. area; mfg. (concrete products, preserves, pottery); bituminous-coal mines, clay pits. Settled 1873, inc. 1888. **3** Town (pop. 636), Powell co., E central Ky., on Red R. and 35 mi. ESE of Lexington, in agr. area with oil wells, coal mines, oak timber. Ironworks formerly here. Near by is Indian Old Fields, site (c.1718–54) of Eskippakithiki, believed to have been last Indian village in Ky.

Claycomo, town (pop. 808), Clay co., NW Mo.

Clay Cross, urban district (1931 pop. 8,497; 1951 census 8,552), E central Derby, England, 5 mi. S of Chesterfield; steel milling. Coal mines near by.

Claye-Souilly (klĕ-sōōyē'), village (pop. 1,853), Seine-et-Marne dept., N central France, on Ourcq Canal and 17 mi. ENE of Paris; mfg. (electrical apparatus, plaster).

Clayette, La (lä klĕyĕt'), village (pop. 1,822), Saône-et-Loire dept., E central France, 10 mi. S of Charolles; rail junction. Mfg. of caps, rubber articles, hosiery, metal products.

Claymont, village (1940 pop. 3,736), New Castle co., NE Del., on Delaware R. and 6 mi. NE of Wilmington; mfg. (steel, chemicals), oil refining. State industrial school for girls here.

Clayoquot (klă'kwŭt), village, SW B.C., on Stubbs Isl. off W central Vancouver Isl., in Clayoquot Sound, just WNW of Tofino; fishing port.

Clayoquot Sound, SW B.C., inlet of the Pacific extending c.60 mi. along W central coast of Vancouver Isl., 50 mi. W of Port Alberni, near 49°15'N 126°W, in lumbering, gold-mining, and fishing area. Contains FLORES ISLAND, MEARES ISLAND, and VARGAS ISLAND. Several arms extend inland: Sydney Inlet, Shelter Inlet, and Herbert Inlet (N), Calmus Passage and Bedwell Sound (E), and Fortune Channel and Tofino Inlet (S).

Claypool, town (pop. 416), Kosciusko co., N Ind., c.45 mi. SSE of South Bend, in agr. area.

Claysburg. 1 Town (1940 pop. 597), Clark co., SE Ind., near Ohio R., just E of New Albany and 4 mi. N of Louisville (Ky.), of whose metropolitan area it is a part. **2** Village (pop. 1,355), Blair co., central Pa., 15 mi. S of Altoona; large firebrick plant.

Claysville, borough (pop. 963), Washington co., SW Pa., 9 mi. WSW of Washington.

Clayton. 1 E suburb of Manchester, SE Lancashire, England; chemical center (mfg. of aniline dyes, soap, pharmaceuticals); mfg. of leather, rubber products. Mansion of Clayton Hall dates from 16th cent. **2** Suburb, Yorkshire, England: see BRADFORD.

Clayton. 1 County (□ 149; pop. 22,872), NW central Ga.; ⊙ Jonesboro. Piedmont agr. (cotton, corn, potatoes, truck, fruit, livestock) and lumbering area drained by Flint R. Formed 1858. **2** County (□ 778; pop. 22,522), NE Iowa, bounded E by Mississippi R. (here forming Wis. line); ⊙ Elkader. Dairying and agr. area (hogs, cattle, corn, livestock, poultry, hay), with rugged, wooded "Little Switzerland" dist. in N; drained by Turkey and Volga rivers. Limestone quarries, sand and gravel pits, lead and zinc deposits. Includes state parks. Formed 1837.

Clayton. 1 Town (pop. 1,583), ⊙ Barbour co., SE Ala., 32 mi. ENE of Troy; lumber, peanuts and peanut butter. Founded 1833. **2** Town (pop. 825), Kent co., central Del., 11 mi. NNW of Dover, near Smyrna R., in agr. area. **3** City (pop. 1,302), ⊙ Rabun co., extreme NE Ga., 21 mi. N of Toccoa, in Blue Ridge Mts. and Chattahoochee Natl. Forest; mfg. (hosiery, barrel staves, lumber); ships apples. Resort. Inc. 1821. **4** Village (pop. 866), Adams co., W Ill., 25 mi. ENE of Quincy; corn, wheat, soybeans, livestock, poultry. **5** Town (pop. 598), Hendricks co., central Ind., 22 mi. WSW of Indianapolis; flour, timber, fruit, grain. **6** Town (pop. 136), Clayton co., NE Iowa, on the Mississippi and 37 mi. NW of Dubuque, in hog and dairy area. **7** City (pop. 157), on Decatur-Norton co. line, NW Kansas, on Prairie Dog Creek and 15 mi. WSW of Norton; agr., stock raising. **8** Village (pop. 657), Concordia parish, E central La., 11 mi. NNW of Vidalia. **9** Village (pop. 467), Lenawee co., SE Mich., 11 mi. WSW of Adrian, in agr. area. **10** City (pop. 16,035), ⊙ St. Louis co., E Mo., near Mississippi R., just W of St. Louis; agr. trade center; dairy, textile products. **11** Borough (pop. 3,023), Gloucester co., SW N.J., 4 mi. S of Glassboro; mfg. (brushes, brooms, clothing, blinds); truck farming. Settled c.1775, inc. 1924. **12** Town (pop. 3,515), ⊙ Union co., NE N.Mex., near Texas and Okla. lines, 75 mi. SE of Raton; rail, trade, and shipping center in grain and livestock region; dairy and poultry products, beans. Laid out 1887, inc. 1908. **13** Resort village (pop. 1,981), Jefferson co., N N.Y., on the St. Lawrence, in the Thousand Islands region, and 20 mi. NNW of Watertown; port of entry; mfg. (snowplows, fishing tackle, textiles, clothing, wood and paper products). Inc. 1872. **14** Town (pop. 2,229), Johnston co., central N.C., 13 mi. SE of Raleigh; cotton and lumber mills. State forest nursery near by. **15** Village (pop. 466), Montgomery co., W Ohio, 11 mi. NW of Dayton. **16** Town (pop. 612), Pushmataha co., SE Okla., 34 mi. SE of McAlester, and on Kiamichi R., in agr. and lumbering area of the Ouachita Mts.; cottonseed-oil and lumber milling. Near by is small L. Clayton (fishing). **17** Village (pop. 350), Polk co., NW Wis., 23 mi. SW of Rice Lake, in lake-resort and dairying area.

Clayton-le-Moors (–lŭ-mōōrz'), urban district (1931 pop. 7,909; 1951 census 6,823), E central Lancashire, England, 4 mi. ENE of Blackburn; cotton milling, coal mining, mfg. of chemicals, soap.

Clayton West, former urban district (1931 pop. 1,847), West Riding, S Yorkshire, England, 8 mi. ESE of Huddersfield; woolen milling. Inc. 1938 in Denby Dale.

Claytor Lake, Va.: see NEW RIVER.

Clayville, village (pop. 719), Oneida co., central N.Y., 9 mi. S of Utica; mfg. (paper and metal products, knit goods).

Clazomenae (klŭzŏ'mĭnē"), ancient city of W Asia Minor, some 20 mi. W of the present Smyrna, Turkey. It was one of cities of the Ionian Dodecapolis, but the later inhabitants were not Ionians. City was founded on mainland but was later moved to a small isl., and Alexander the Great built a causeway to it. Continued to flourish through the Hellenistic and Roman periods. Anaxagoras b. here. It was famous for its terra cotta sarcophagi.

Clear, Cape, Ireland: see CLEAR ISLAND.

Clear, Lake, N.Y.: see LAKE CLEAR JUNCTION.

Clear Boggy Creek, SE Okla., rises near Ada in Pontotoc co., flows c.125 mi. SE, receiving Muddy Boggy Creek in Choctaw co., to Red R. 8 mi. SW of Hugo. In combined stream (sometimes called Boggy Creek) is site of Boswell Reservoir, for flood control in Red R. basin.

Clearbrook, village (pop. 539), Clearwater co., NW Minn., 12 mi. N of Bagley, in agr. area; dairy products.

Clear Creek, county (□ 394; pop. 3,289), N central Colo.; ⊙ Georgetown. Mining and livestock-grazing area; drained by Clear Creek. Gold, silver, lead, copper, zinc mines. Includes parts of Pike Natl. Forest, Arapaho Natl. Forest, and Front Range. Formed 1861.

Clear Creek. 1 In N central Colo., rises in several branches near Grays Peak, in Front Range; flows E 68 mi., past Idaho Springs and Golden, to South Platte R. N of Denver. **2** In N Wyo., formed by its headstreams near Cloud Peak in Bighorn Mts., flows c.80 mi. NE, past Buffalo and Clearmont, to Powder R. near Mont. line.

Clearfield, county (□ 1,144; pop. 85,957), central Pa.; ⊙ Clearfield. Hilly upland, drained by West Branch of Susquehanna R. Bituminous coal; mfg. (metal products, leather, clay products); butter, buckwheat; natural gas, sandstone; recreation. Formed 1804.

Clearfield. 1 Town (pop. 547), on Taylor-Ringgold co. line, SW Iowa, 18 mi. SSW of Creston; wood products, feed. **2** Industrial borough (pop. 9,357), ⊙ Clearfield co., central Pa., 35 mi. N of Altoona and on West Branch of Susquehanna R.; railroad shops; bituminous coal; clay products, leather, electronic equipment, clothing. Laid out 1805, inc. 1840. **3** Town (pop. 4,723), Davis co., N Utah, 8 mi. S of Ogden; alt. 4,487 ft. Trading center for irrigated agr. area (alfalfa, forage crops); fruit and vegetable canning. U.S. arsenal near by. Inc. 1922.

Clear Fork of Brazos River, Texas: see BRAZOS RIVER.

Clear Island or **Cape Clear Island** (4,033 acres; 3 mi. long, 1 mi. wide; pop. c.700) in the Atlantic, off SW coast of Co. Cork, Ireland, 11 mi. SW of Skibbereen. At S tip is Cape Clear, with lighthouse on 438-ft. cliff (51°26'N 9°29'W). Near by are remains of 15th-cent. castle of the O'Driscolls.

Clear Lake. 1 Lake (7 mi. long, 3 mi. wide), SW Man., at SE edge of Riding Mtn. Natl. Park, 30 mi. S of Dauphin. Drains W into Minnedosa R. **2** Lake, Ont.: see STONY LAKE.

Clear Lake. 1 Resort town (pop. 151), Steuben co., extreme NE Ind., near Mich. line, on small Clear

L. **2** City (pop. 4,977), Cerro Gordo co., N Iowa, 9 mi. W of Mason City, on Clear L. (c.5 mi. long; state park, fish hatchery); popular summer resort; bakery and concrete products. Sand and gravel pits (E). Inc. 1871. **3** Village (pop. 297), Sherburne co., central Minn., near Mississippi R., 23 mi. NW of Elk River village, in agr. area; dairy products. Reformatory here. **4** City (pop. 1,105), ⊙ Deuel co., E S.Dak., 23 mi. ESE of Watertown and on Hidewood Creek; dairy products, livestock, grain. Annual co. fair. **5** Village (pop. 695), Polk co., NW Wis., 31 mi. NE of Hudson, in dairying and stock-raising area; produces cheese, feed, canned peas.

Clear Lake, NW Calif., c.80 mi. N of San Francisco; largest body of fresh water (c.21 mi. long, 1–10 mi. wide) entirely in state; alt. c.1,350 ft. Outlet (SE) is Cache Creek. Mt. Konochti on W shore. Fishing, bathing, boating resort.

Clear Lake Reservoir, NE Calif., formed in Modoc co. by dam on Lost R., 35 mi. SE of Klamath Falls, Oregon; c.10 mi. long.

Clearmont. 1 Town (pop. 283), Nodaway co., NW Mo., on Nodaway R. and 14 mi. NW of Maryville; grain, livestock. **2** Town (pop. 225), Sheridan co., N Wyo., on Clear Creek and 30 mi. ESE of Sheridan, in irrigated agr. region.

Clear River, Chinese *P'an-lung Chiang* (pän'lo͝ong' jyäng'), Fr. *Rivière Claire,* in Tonkin (N Vietnam), rises in China's Yunnan prov. N of Wenshan at alt. of c.4,000 ft., flows 250 mi. SE into Red R. at Viettri. Navigable for 5-ft.-draught boats up to Tuyenquang.

Clear Spring, town (pop. 558), Washington co., W Md., at E base of Bear Pond Mts., 12 mi. W of Hagerstown, in agr. area. Near by are Cushwa State Fish Hatchery and Fort Frederick State Park.

Clearwater. 1 County (□ 2,522; pop. 8,217), N Idaho; ⊙ Orofino. Mtn. area bounded on E by Bitterroot Range and Mont., crossed by North Fork of Clearwater R. Lumbering, stock raising, dairying. Clearwater Natl. Forest and Clearwater Mts. extend throughout much of co. Formed 1911. **2** County (□ 1,005; pop. 10,204), NW Minn.; ⊙ Bagley. Agr. area drained by Clearwater R. and, in SE, by headwaters of Mississippi R. Dairy products, livestock, potatoes; peat deposits. Includes part of Red Lake Indian Reservation in N, part of White Earth Indian Reservation in SW. Itasca State Park in SE encloses L. Itasca, on Mississippi R. and near its source. Formed 1902.

Clearwater. 1 Unincorporated town, Los Angeles co., S Calif., 11 mi. SSE of downtown Los Angeles, near Hynes; dairying; oil refining, mfg. of farm machinery. **2** City (pop. 15,581), ⊙ Pinellas co., W Fla., 20 mi. W of TAMPA, on Clearwater Bay, a lagoon of the Gulf of Mexico; resort, and citrus-fruit shipping center with packing houses and canneries; grows gladioli. A causeway crosses the lagoon to Clearwater Beach, a popular resort on a sandy key. City was settled after establishment here in 1841 of Fort Harrison; inc. 1891. **3** City (pop. 647), Sedgwick co., S Kansas, near Ninnescah R., 15 mi. SW of Wichita, in dairy and grain area. Oil wells in vicinity. **4** Village (pop. 224), Wright co., S central Minn., on Mississippi R. at mouth of Clearwater R., and 12 mi. SSE of St. Cloud, in grain, livestock, and poultry area; dairy products. **5** Village (pop. 472), Antelope co., NE Nebr., 10 mi. WNW of Neligh and on Elkhorn R.; livestock, poultry, grain. **6** Mill village (1940 pop. 804), Aiken co., W S.C., 9 mi. WSW of Aiken; textiles.

Clearwater Dam, Mo.: see BLACK RIVER.

Clearwater Lake. 1 Lake (16 mi. long, 1–2 mi. wide), E B.C., in Cariboo Mts., in Wells Gray Provincial Park, 100 mi. N of Kamloops. Drains S into North Thompson R. **2** Lake (□ 410), N Que.; 56°N 74°30'W; 45 mi. long, 20 mi. wide; alt. 790 ft. Contains several isls. Drains into Hudson Bay.

Clearwater Lake, Wright and Stearns counties, central Minn., c.45 mi. NW of Minneapolis; 5 mi. long, 2.5 mi. wide. Fishing resorts. Fed and drained by small Clearwater R.

Clearwater Mountains, largely in Idaho and Clearwater counties, N central Idaho, bounded S and W by Salmon R., E by Bitterroot Range. Includes parts of Nezperce, Clearwater, and Bitterroot natl. forests. Chief elevations (8–9,000 ft.) are in S near Salmon R. Gold, silver, lead, and copper are mined.

Clearwater River. 1 In NW Sask. and NE Alta., rises S of L. Athabaska in lat. 58°N, flows S, then W, crossing into Alta., to Athabaska R. at Fort McMurray; 230 mi. long. On its course are numerous rapids. Formerly an important link in the Churchill-Athabaska canoe route. **2** In W Alta., rises in Rocky Mts. S of Mt. Willingdon in Banff Natl. Park, flows 130 mi. in a winding course generally NE to North Saskatchewan R. at Rocky Mountain House.

Clearwater River. 1 In N central Idaho, formed by confluence of Middle Fork (100 mi. long; known in upper course as Lochsa R.) and South Fork (80 mi. long) at Kooskia, flows 90 mi. NNW, past Orofino, then W to Snake R. at Lewiston, on Oregon line. Important tributary is North Fork, rising near Mont. line in N half of Bitterroot Range and flowing 120 mi. generally W and SW to main stream near Orofino. Discovery of gold (1860) on small affluent caused gold rush and led to settlement of Orofino as mining camp. **2** In NW Minn., rises near Bagley, in Clearwater co., flows 205 mi. E, N, and W to Red Lake R. at city of Red Lake Falls. Drains several small lakes. **3** In S central Minn., rises in Meeker co., flows 20 mi. NNE, through Clearwater L., to Mississippi R. at Clearwater.

Cleaton, village (1940 pop. 767), Muhlenberg co., W Ky., 25 mi. ESE of Madisonville, in bituminous-coal and agr. area.

Cleator Moor (klē'tûr), former urban district (1931 pop. 6,581), W Cumberland, England, 4 mi. SE of Whitehaven; iron mining, smelting. Here is village of Cleator, with mfg. of shoes and linen thread.

Clebit (klē'bĭt), village (1940 pop. 630), McCurtain co., extreme SE Okla., 32 mi. N of Idabel, in Ouachita Mts.

Cleburne (klē'bûrn). **1** County (□ 574; pop. 11,904), E Ala.; ⊙ Heflin. Piedmont region crossed by Tallapoosa R., bordering on Ga. Part of Talladega Natl. Forest in W and N. Cotton, corn, livestock; lumber milling. Formed 1866. **2** County (□ 595; pop. 11,487), N central Ark.; ⊙ Heber Springs. Drained by Little Red R. and its tributaries; situated in Ozark region. Livestock, poultry, cotton; dairy products; cotton ginning, lumber milling and creosoting; stone quarries. Formed 1883.

Cleburne, city (pop. 12,905), ⊙ Johnson co., N central Texas, 28 mi. S of Fort Worth; shipping, processing center in blackland agr. area (cotton; also corn, grains); poultry, dairying. Cotton gins and compresses, cottonseed-oil mills, creameries, railroad shops; mfg. of clothing, mattresses, chairs, metal products, lime. Cleburne State Park (recreation) is c.12 mi. SW. Founded 1867.

Cléchère, La, Luxembourg: see LUXEMBOURG, city.

Cleckheaton, England: see SPENBOROUGH.

Clécy (kläsē'), village (pop. 264), Calvados dept., NW France, resort in Normandy Hills overlooking Orne R. and 19 mi. SSW of Caen.

Clee Hills, range of S Shropshire, England, extending 14 mi. N–S, 5 mi. E of Ludlow. Highest summits: Titterstone Clee Hill (1,749 ft.), 5 mi. ENE of Ludlow, and Brown Clee Hill (1,790 ft.), 9 mi. NE of Ludlow. Coal mines, stone quarries.

Cle Elum (klē" ĕ'lŭm), city (pop. 2,206), Kittitas co., central Wash., 22 mi. NW of Ellensburg and on Yakima R.; coal, lumber, dairy products, hothouse flowers. Founded 1885, inc. 1904.

Cle Elum River, central Wash., rises in Cascade Range; flows generally S to Cle Elum L. (8 mi. long; Cle Elum Dam, 160 ft. high, at S end), thence SE, past Cle Elum, to Yakima R.; c.28 mi. long.

Cleethorpes, municipal borough (1931 pop. 28,621; 1951 census 29,558), Parts of Lindsey, N Lincolnshire, England, on Humber R. and 2 mi. ESE of Grimsby; bathing resort. Has pier, pier gardens.

Clefmont (klĕmō'), agr. village (pop. 232), Haute-Marne dept., NE France, near Meuse R., 17 mi. E of Chaumont.

Cleggan (klĕ'gŭn), Gaelic *Cloigeann,* fishing village (district pop. 303), NW Co. Galway, Ireland, on Cleggan Bay of the Atlantic, 6 mi. NW of Clifden; herring, mackerel fishing.

Cleghorn, town (pop. 246), Cherokee co., NW Iowa, 9 mi. WNW of Cherokee.

Cléguérec (klāgārĕk'), village (pop. 698), Morbihan dept., W France, 6 mi. NW of Pontivy; horse raising.

Cleish (klēsh), agr. village and parish (pop. 483), Kinross, Scotland, 4 mi. SW of Kinross. Just S is 6-mi.-long range of Cleish Hills, rising to 1,241 ft.

Clejani (klāzhän'), village (pop. 2,964), Bucharest prov., S Rumania, 34 mi. NNW of Giurgiu; wheat.

Cleland, village in Shotts parish, NE Lanark, Scotland, 3 mi. E of Motherwell; coal mining, granite quarrying. Just N is coal-mining village of Omoa (ōmō'ŭ).

Clelles or **Clelles-en-Trièves** (klĕl-ā-trēĕv'), village (pop. 237), Isère dept., SE France, in the Dauphiné Alps, 13 mi. NE of Die; alt. 2,690 ft. Resort. Col de la Croix-Haute, a pass (alt. 3,826 ft.; road, railroad) separating Isère (N) and Durance (S) drainage basins, is 7 mi. SSE, and represents N limit of Mediterranean climate and vegetation.

Clemenceau (klĭmăn'sō), village (pop. 1,626, with adjacent Cottonwood), Yavapai co., central Ariz., on Verde R. and 29 mi. NE of Prescott.

Clémency (klāmäsē'), Ger. *Kuntzig* (ko͞on'tsĭkh), town (pop. 898), SW Luxembourg, near Belgian border, 12 mi. W of Luxembourg; agr. market (potatoes, wheat, oats, vegetables).

Clementon (klĕ'mŭntŭn), borough (pop. 3,191), Camden co., SW N.J., 11 mi. SE of Camden; makes charcoal (since 1879), hosiery, clothing. Inc. 1925.

Clements, village (pop. 239), Redwood co., SW Minn., 30 mi. WNW of New Ulm, in corn, oat, barley area.

Clementsport, village (pop. estimate 300), NW N.S., on Annapolis Basin, 7 mi. SW of Annapolis Royal; fishing port; apple growing. First settled 1784 by United Empire Loyalists.

Clementsvale, village (pop. estimate 550), NW N.S., 10 mi. SSW of Annapolis Royal; dairying, mixed farming; apples.

Clemons (klĕ'mŭnz), town (pop. 202), Marshall co., central Iowa, 13 mi. WNW of Marshalltown, in agr. area.

Clemson (klĕm'sŭn), town (pop. 1,204), Oconee and Pickens counties, NW S.C., 28 mi. WSW of Greenville, in agr. area; textile mill. Seat of Clemson Col. After 1940, absorbed adjacent town of Calhoun.

Clendenin (klĕndĕ'nĭn), town (pop. 1,475), Kanawha co., W central W.Va., on Elk R. and 19 mi. NE of Charleston; coal mines, oil and natural-gas wells. Inc. 1904.

Clendening Reservoir (klĕndĕn'nĭng), Harrison co., E Ohio, flood-control reservoir (capacity 54,000 acre-ft.) impounded in a tributary of Tuscarawas R. by dam c.14 mi. W of Cadiz.

Cleo, Okla.: see CLEO SPRINGS.

Cleobury Mortimer (klĭ'bürē, klĕ'–), town and parish (pop. 1,293), SE Shropshire, England, on Rea R. and 10 mi. E of Ludlow; agr. market. Church has 12th-cent. tower.

Cleona (klēō'nŭ), borough (pop. 1,483), Lebanon co., SE central Pa., 3 mi. W of Lebanon.

Cleo Springs or **Cleo** (klē'ō), town (pop. 310), Major co., NW Okla., 32 mi. W of Enid, near Cimarron R., in grain and livestock area.

Clerahan, Ireland: see CLERIHAN.

Clercken, Belgium: see KLERKEN.

Clères (klâr), village (pop. 820), Seine-Inférieure dept., N France, 11 mi. N of Rouen; dairying.

Clerf, village, Luxembourg: see CLERVAUX.

Clerf River (klĕrf), SE Belgium and N Luxembourg, rises 6 mi. NE of Bastogne (Belgium), flows 30 mi. ENE and S, past Clervaux and Wilwerwiltz, to Wiltz R. at Kautenbach. Not navigable.

Cléricy (klārēsē'), village (pop. estimate 500), W Que., 12 mi. NE of Rouyn; gold mining.

Clerihan or **Clerahan** (klĕ'rŭhăn), Gaelic *Baile Ui Chléireacháin,* agr. village, S Co. Tipperary, Ireland, 5 mi. NNW of Clonmel; dairying; cattle, potatoes, beets.

Clerkenwell (klär'kŭnwĕl), district in Finsbury, London, England, N of the Thames, 1.5 mi. NE of Charing Cross. Center for mfg. of watches, optical goods, jewelry. Was named for well at which parish clerks performed miracle plays. Here is Sadler's Wells theater.

Clerk Island, Gilbert Isls.: see ONOTOA.

Clermont (klûr'mŏnt), town (pop. 1,491), E Queensland, Australia, 185 mi. WNW of Rockhampton; mining center (coal, gold).

Clermont, village (pop. estimate 1,000), E Que., on Malbaie R. and 4 mi. NW of La Malbaie; copper mining.

Clermont (klĕrmō'), town (pop. 3,925), Oise dept., N France, 16 mi. ESE of Beauvais; agr. trade center. Mfg. (agr. machinery, plastics, furniture). Has 14th-16th-cent. church of St. Samson and large insane asylum. Its restored medieval town hall was built by Charles the Fair. Seat of powerful medieval countship. Damaged in Second World War.

Clermont (klâr'mŏnt), county (□ 458; pop. 42,182), SW Ohio; ⊙ Batavia. Bounded SW by Ohio R. (here forming Ky. line), NW by Little Miami R.; intersected by East Fork of Little Miami R. Agr. (livestock, corn, wheat, tobacco, fruit; dairy products); some mfg. at Batavia, Bethel, Milford, New Richmond; nurseries. Formed 1800.

Clermont. 1 City (pop. 2,168), Lake co., central Fla., 24 mi. W of Orlando; citrus-fruit shipping point with cannery. Diatomite found near by. **2** Town (pop. 323), Hall co., NE central Ga., 12 mi. NNE of Gainesville; sawmilling. **3** Town (pop. 824), Marion co., central Ind. **4** Town (pop. 625), Fayette co., NE Iowa, on Turkey R. and 9 mi. ENE of West Union; concrete and dairy products; sand and gravel pits. **5** (klĕr'–) Village (pop. c.200), Bullitt co., NW Ky., 23 mi. SSE of Louisville; makes whisky.

Clermont-en-Argonne (klĕrmō'-ānärgôn'), village (pop. 570), Meuse dept., NE France, near the Aire, 8 mi. ENE of Sainte-Menehould; horse raising. Strategically located at E end of defile across the Argonne, it was virtually leveled in First World War.

Clermont-Ferrand (–fĕrā'), city (pop. 93,695), ⊙ Puy-de-Dôme dept., central France, 210 mi. SSE of Paris; important industrial center (the "Akron" of France) with large rubber factories (tires, rubberized clothing), precision metalworks (hydraulic and mining machinery, bicycles, radio parts) and food-processing plants (preserves, candied fruits, fine chocolate); also makes furniture, work clothes, chemicals (sulphuric acid, superphosphates), photographic paper, jewelry, and flour products. Picturesquely situated at the foot of a range of extinct volcanoes (Monts Dôme), city is focus of Auvergne tourist trade. Founded by Romans near site of Gergovia (which Vercingetorix held against Julius Caesar and which was later dismantled), Clermont (anc. *Augustonemetum*) became episcopal see c.A.D. 250, and was site of several church councils, notably that of 1095, which gave rise to the Crusades. City became ⊙ duchy of Auvergne in 16th cent. and was merged in 1731 with neighboring Montferrand which dates back to 11th cent. Built largely of dark volcanic rock (quarried near by), city has distinctive character. Notable bldgs. are the Romanesque church of Notre Dame (12th cent.) and the Gothic cathedral (12th–15th cent.). Clermont has a univ., an archaeological mus., and a statue of Pascal (b. here). Montferrand (1.5 mi. E of Clermont, from which it is separated by industrial dist.) is remarkable for its well-preserved Gothic and Renaissance houses. In the hills 2 mi. W of Clermont is noted spa of Royat. City damaged in Second World War. Blaise Pascal b. here.

Clermont Harbor (klâr'mŏnt), resort village, Hancock co., SE Miss., 5 mi. SW of Bay St. Louis, on Mississippi Sound.

Clermont-lez-Aubel (klĕrmō'-lāzōbĕl'), village (pop. 1,620), Liége prov., E Belgium, 5 mi. NNE of Verviers; fruitgrowing; fruit-sirup mfg.

Clermont-l'Hérault (–lārō'), town (pop. 4,855), Hérault dept., S France, near Hérault R., 9 mi. SE of Lodève; woolen mills, tanneries, distilleries. Olive and grape shipping. Has 14th-cent. fortified church.

Clermont-Tonnerre, Tuamotu Isls.: see REAO.

Clerval (klĕrväl'), village (pop. 994), Doubs dept., E France, on Doubs R. and Rhone-Rhine Canal, and 16 mi. SW of Montbéliard; metalworking, sawmilling.

Clervaux (klĕrvō'), Ger. *Clerf* (klĕrf), village (pop. 996), N Luxembourg, on Clerf R. and 8 mi. NNE of Wiltz, in the Ardennes; gravel quarries, sawmills; market center for agr. area (rye, oats, buckwheat, potatoes, cattle). Has 12th-cent. castle, Benedictine abbey; both badly damaged (1944) in Second World War.

Cléry (klārē'), agr. village (pop. 1,336), Loiret dept., N central France, near left bank of Loire R., 9 mi. SW of Orléans; has 15th-cent. flamboyant basilica containing tombs of Louis XI and Dunois.

Cles (klĕs), town (pop. 2,613), Trento prov., Trentino–Alto Adige, N Italy, near Noce R., 18 mi. SW of Bolzano, in fruitgrowing region; resort (alt. 2,159 ft.). Tannery, wax and insecticide factories. Has 15th–16th-cent. palace and 16th-cent. church.

Cleve (klēv), village (pop. 276), S South Australia, on E Eyre Peninsula, 80 mi. NNE of Port Lincoln; wheat.

Cleve, Germany: see CLEVES.

Clevedale, textile village, Spartanburg co., NW S.C., 4 mi. W of Spartanburg.

Clevedon (klēv'dŭn), urban district (1931 pop. 7,029; 1951 census 9,467), N Somerset, England, on S shore of Bristol Channel and 12 mi. W of Bristol; seaside resort; agr. market in dairying region; shoe industry. "Clevedon Court" (14th cent.) is "Castlewood" of Thackeray's *Henry Esmond.* Arthur Hallam is buried in the Norman church. Coleridge lived here for some time.

Cleveland, hilly region (rising to c.1,900 ft.) in North Riding, NE Yorkshire, England, extending c.20 mi. W from North Sea coast near Whitby; important iron-mining and iron- and steel-milling area. Chief towns, Middlesbrough and Eston.

Cleveland. 1 County (□ 601; pop. 8,956), S central Ark.; ⊙ Rison. Bounded W by Moro Creek; intersected by Saline R. Agr. (cotton, corn, hay, livestock); cotton ginning, sawmilling; gravel, red clay. Formed 1873. **2** County (□ 466; pop. 64,357), SW N.C.; ⊙ Shelby. Bounded S by S.C.; drained by Broad R. and its affluents. In piedmont agr. (cotton, corn) region; timber. Textile mfg., sawmilling. Formed 1841. **3** County (□ 547; pop. 41,443), central Okla.; ⊙ Norman, seat of Univ. of Okla. Bounded SW by Canadian R.; drained by Little R. Diversified agr. (cotton, cattle, hogs, poultry, grain, sorghums, corn; dairy products). Some mfg., farm-products processing. Oil and natural-gas fields. Formed 1890.

Cleveland. 1 Town (pop. 59), Conway co., central Ark., 26 mi. ENE of Russellville. **2** Town (pop. 104), Charlotte co., S Fla., 2 mi. ENE of Punta Gorda, near Charlotte Harbor. **3** Resort town (pop. 589), ⊙ White co., NE Ga., 20 mi. N of Gainesville, in Blue Ridge foothills; lumber, pottery mfg. **4** Village (pop. 204), Henry co., NW Ill., on Rock R. and 12 mi. E of Rock Island. **5** Village (pop. 325), LeSueur co., S Minn., near Minnesota R., 14 mi. NE of Mankato; corn, oats, barley, potatoes, livestock, poultry. **6** City (pop. 6,747), a ⊙ Bolivar co., W Miss., 30 mi. NE of Greenville, in cotton-growing area; cotton gins and compress. Has a teachers col. Inc. as city since 1930. **7** Town (pop. 163), Cass co., W Mo., near South Grand R., 14 mi. W of Harrisonville. **8** Village (pop. 555), Oswego co., N central N.Y., on N shore of Oneida L., 22 mi. W of Rome, in dairy and fruit area. **9** Town (pop. 580), Rowan co., W central N.C., 11 mi. WNW of Salisbury, in agr. area; veneer mfg. **10** Village (pop. 181), Stutsman co., central N.Dak., 19 mi. W of Jamestown. **11** City (□ 73.1; pop. 914,808), ⊙ Cuyahoga co., N Ohio, on harbor on L. Erie at mouth of Cuyahoga R., 300 mi. E of Chicago; 41°30'N 81°42'W; alt. 865 ft. Largest city in Ohio, 7th-largest (in 1950) in U.S. A major Great Lakes port, it unloads iron ore for its large steel industry and for other Ohio and Pa. steel dists.; transships coal, grain, lumber. Port of entry. Airline and railroad hub (7 trunk rail lines; railroad shops); municipal airport is an air force base. In Cuyahoga valley (the Flats) to SW and S of city's center are huge steel mills (among world's largest), foundries, machine shops, oil refineries, lumberyards, slaughtering and meat-packing plants, warehouses, and plants producing cement, chemicals, freight-handling equipment, aircraft engines, automobiles and parts, electrical appliances and light bulbs, machine tools, paints and varnishes, textiles, clothing, and printed matter. Nela Park, research hq. of General Electric Company, is in adjacent East Cleveland. Seat of Western Reserve Univ., Case Inst. of Technology, Fenn Col. (Y.M.C.A.; coeducational; 1881), Ursuline Col. for women, John Carroll Univ. (at neighboring University Heights), Cleveland Inst. of Music, Cleveland Law School, Schauffler Col. of Religious and Social Work, and St. John Col. Near lake front, where breakwaters enclose the harbor, city's main arteries converge on the Public Square, which has statues of Moses Cleaveland and Tom L. Johnson; adjacent is Terminal Tower Bldg. (1930; 52 stories). To N, near lake front, is the Mall (Civic Center), whose bldgs. include a dist. Federal Reserve Bank, the noted Public Library, Federal Bldg. (1910), co. courthouse, City Hall, the Auditorium, and the Stadium. City has a mus. of natural history, the Western Reserve Historical Society Mus., Cleveland Mus. of Art (in Wade Park, also site of Fine Arts Garden); Rockefeller Park, enclosing the Cleveland Cultural Gardens, which commemorate city's many nationality groups; Severance Hall, home of Cleveland Symphony Orchestra; the Play House, a civic theater; zoological and horticultural gardens; Trinity Cathedral (Episcopal; 1910); and historical bldgs., including Weddell House (1847), where Lincoln spoke before his 1st inauguration and Dunham Tavern (1842; now a mus.). Tomb of President Garfield is in Lake View Cemetery. Principal communities adjacent and near by are Lakewood, Cleveland Heights, East Cleveland, Shaker Heights, Euclid, Parma, Rocky River, Bedford, South Euclid, University Heights. Cleveland was laid out in 1796 by Moses Cleaveland; chartered as city in 1836; annexed Ohio City (across Cuyahoga R.) in 1854. Coming of Ohio and Erie Canal (1832) and the railroad (1851) brought rapid development. Iron production began in 1850s, and large enterprises concerned with railroads, oil (Rockefeller began his dynasty here), and the electrical industry brought further growth. In 1936–37, Great Lakes Exposition was held in celebration of city's centenary. **12** City (pop. 2,464), Pawnee co., N Okla., 29 mi. WNW of Tulsa, near Arkansas R., in oil-producing and agr. area (cotton, fruit, grain). Oil refining; mfg. of plastic products, brick; cotton ginning. Settled 1893. **13** Hamlet, Greenville co., NW S.C., in the Blue Ridge, 17 mi. NNW of Greenville; rail terminus. **14** Industrial city (pop. 12,605), ⊙ Bradley co., SE Tenn., 25 mi. ENE of Chattanooga; trade center for timber and farm area; mfg. of stoves, caskets, wood products, textiles, processed foods; lumber milling, printing. Hq. of Cherokee Natl. Forest and of branch of Church of God (a fundamentalist group) here. Seat of Lee Col. Inc. 1838. **15** City (pop. 5,183), Liberty co., E Texas, near San Jacinto R., c.45 mi. NNE of Houston; lumbering; oil wells; oil refineries, lumber mills; mfg. of wood products. Inc. 1929. **16** Town (pop. 343), Emery co., central Utah, 6 mi. E of Huntington; alt. 6,000 ft. **17** Town (pop. 388), Russell co., SW Va., on Clinch R. and 35 mi. WNW of Marion.

Cleveland, Cape, E Queensland, Australia, in Coral Sea, forms E side of entrance to Cleveland Bay; 19°11'S 147°1'E.

Cleveland, Mount, Alaska: see CHUGINADAK ISLAND.

Cleveland, Mount, Mont.: see LEWIS RANGE.

Cleveland Bay, inlet of Coral Sea, E Queensland, Australia, bet. Magnetic Isl. (W) and Cape Cleveland (E); sheltered by Great Barrier Reef; connected with open sea by Flinders Passage; 10 mi. long, 8 mi. wide. Port of Townsville on SW shore.

Cleveland Heights, city (pop. 59,141), Cuyahoga co., N Ohio, E residential suburb of Cleveland. Inc. 1905 as village, 1921 as city.

Clevelândia (klĭvĭlăn'dyŭ), city (pop. 837), SW Paraná, Brazil, on Santa Catarina border, 80 mi. W of União da Vitória; livestock, maté, grain.

Cleveland Peninsula, SE Alaska, extends c.35 mi. SW into the Alexander Archipelago N of Ketchikan. On its Clarence Strait shore is fishing village Myers Chuck.

Cleveleys, England: see THORNTON CLEVELEYS.

Clever, town (pop. 273), Christian co., SW Mo., in the Ozarks, near James R., 16 mi. SW of Springfield.

Cleves (klēvz), Ger. *Kleve* or *Cleve* (klā'vŭ), town (pop. 23,154), in former Prussian Rhine Prov., W Germany, after 1945 in North Rhine-Westphalia, 12 mi. ESE of Nijmegen, Netherlands; connected with the Rhine by Spoy canal (built in 11th cent.); 51°47'N 6°8'E. Rail junction; food processing (margarine, biscuits, chocolate); mfg. of shoes, cigars, cigarettes. Second World War damage (about 80%) includes 14th–15th-cent. collegiate church, containing tombs of dukes of Cleves; and 11th-cent. Schwanenburg [swans' castle], associated with Lohengrin legend. Chartered 1242. Was residence of counts, since 1417 dukes, of Cleves until 1614, when duchy came to Brandenburg. Scene (Feb., 1945) of heavy fighting in Second World War.

Cleves, village (pop. 1,981), Hamilton co., extreme SW Ohio, on Great Miami R. and 13 mi. W of Cincinnati; petroleum refining. Platted 1818. William Henry Harrison Memorial Park near by.

Clew Bay, inlet (15 mi. long, 7 mi. wide) of the Atlantic on W coast of Co. Mayo, Ireland. At head of bay are ports of Westport and Newport; entrance is sheltered by Clare Isl. Near head of bay are c.300 cultivated islets.

Clewer, England: see WINDSOR.

Clewiston, city (pop. 2,499), Hendry co., S Fla., c.55 mi. W of West Palm Beach, on S shore of L. Okeechobee (diked here); resort and sugar-milling center in a large cane-growing region. Founded 1921.

Cley-next-the-Sea (klī, klā), town and parish (pop. 616), N Norfolk, England, on small Glave R. near North Sea, and 4 mi. NW of Holt; small resort. Important seaport (wool shipping) in 14th cent. Has 14th-cent. church and several old houses in Flemish style.

Clichy (klēshē'), anc. *Clippiacum,* industrial city (pop. 52,652), Seine dept., N central France, just NW of Paris, 4 mi. from Notre Dame Cathedral; port on right bank of the Seine opposite Asnières, bet. Saint-Owen (E) and Levallois-Perret (SW); metallurgical works (auto and aircraft parts and assembly, cables, sewing machines, electrical equipment). Railroad freight yards and workshops. Metropolitan gasworks. Has 17th-cent. church built by St. Vincent de Paul. One-time residence of Merovingian kings. Also called Clichy-la-Garenne and Clichy-sous-Bois.

Clichy-sous-Bois (–sōō-bwä'), town (pop. 3,573), Seine-et-Oise dept., N central France, outermost ENE suburb of Paris, 10 mi. from Notre Dame Cathedral; mfg. of chemicals.

Clifden (klĭf'dŭn), Gaelic *Clochán,* town (pop. 930), NW Co. Galway, Ireland, on Clifden Bay, inlet of the Atlantic, 45 mi. WNW of Galway; fishing port, seaside resort. Has radio station. Lobster fisheries. In 1919 Alcock and Brown landed here after 1st nonstop transatlantic flight, from St. John's, Newfoundland.

Cliff, village (pop. c.150), Grant co., SW N.Mex., near Gila R. and Ariz. line, 24 mi. NW of Silver City; livestock; agr. Gila Natl. Forest and Mogollon Mts. are N.

Cliff Haven, summer-resort village, Clinton co., extreme NE N.Y., on W shore of L. Champlain, 4 mi. S of Plattsburg.

Cliff Island, SW Maine, fishing and resort isl. in Casco Bay, NE of Portland; c.2 mi. long. Sometimes called Crotch Isl.

Clifford, village (pop. 464), S Ont., 16 mi. SE of Walkerton; dairying, lumber and flour milling.

Clifford, agr. village and parish (pop. 652), W Hereford, England, on Welsh border, on Wye R., and 17 mi. W of Hereford. Near by are ruins of Clifford Castle, a border stronghold in Norman times.

Clifford. 1 Town (pop. 232), Bartholomew co., S central Ind., 37 mi. SSE of Indianapolis, in agr. area. **2** Village (pop. 330), Lapeer co., E Mich., 19 mi. NNE of Lapeer, in agr. area. **3** Village (pop. 158), Traill co., E N.Dak., 17 mi. WSW of Hillsboro.

Cliffside, textile village (pop. 1,388), Rutherford co., SW N.C., near Broad R., 13 mi. WSW of Shelby; cotton mills.

Cliffside Park, suburban borough (pop. 17,116), Bergen co., NE N.J., near Hudson R., 7 mi. NNE of Jersey City; mfg. (monuments, embroideries, metal products). Inc. 1895.

Cliffs of Calvert (kăl'vûrt), S Md., highlands (c.100–150 ft. high) along W shore of Chesapeake Bay; extend c.30 mi. S from Chesapeake Beach to vicinity of Patuxent R. mouth.

Clifftop, W.Va.: see BABCOCK STATE PARK.

Cliffwood or **Cliffwood Beach,** resort village (pop. 1,448), Monmouth co., E N.J., on Raritan Bay near Keyport.

Clifton. 1 Agr. village and parish (pop. 1,309), E Bedford, England, 4 mi. SSW of Biggleswade. Has 14th-cent. church. **2** Spa resort and residential suburb (pop. 17,115) of Bristol, SW Gloucester, England, on high cliffs above Avon R. (bridged by Brunel's suspension bridge), NW of the city. Site of Clifton Col., a public school, and of zoological gardens. There are pharmaceutical works. **3** Town and parish (pop. 2,928), SE Lancashire, England, 5 mi. NW of Manchester; coal mining; mfg. of batteries, metal products. **4** Village and parish (pop. 2,199), West Riding, SW Yorkshire, England, just E of Brighouse; woolen and cotton milling.

Clifton, New Zealand: see WAITARA.

Clifton. 1 Town (pop. 3,466), ⊙ Greenlee co., SE Ariz., on San Francisco R., near N.Mex. line, 4 mi. SE of Morenci; copper mining, smelting. Hot springs here. Town settled 1872. **2** Village (pop. c.300), Mesa co., W Colo., on Colorado R. and 6 mi. E of Grand Junction; alt. c.4,750 ft.; fruit-shipping point. **3** Village (pop. 201), Franklin co., SE Idaho, 10 mi. NW of Preston; alt. 4,893 ft. **4** Village (pop. 734), Iroquois co., E Ill., 12 mi. SSW of Kankakee, in agr. area. **5** City (pop. 743), on Clay-Washington co. line, N Kansas, on Republican R. and 19 mi. E of Concordia; grain, livestock. **6** Former city, Campbell co., N Ky.; annexed 1935 by NEWPORT. **7** Town (pop. 193), Penobscot co., S Maine, 11 mi. E of Brewer; agr.; wood products. **8** Village, Essex co., Mass.: see MARBLEHEAD. **9** Industrial city (pop. 64,511), Passaic co., NE N.J., bet. Passaic and Paterson; airplane propellers, rubber goods, clothing, metal and paper products, radio parts, machine tools, textiles, pharmaceuticals, chemicals, cosmetics, food products; printing. Inc. 1917. **10** A section of Richmond borough of New York city, SE N.Y., in port dist. of NE Staten Isl. **11** Village (pop. 220), on Greene-Clark co. line, SW central Ohio, 9 mi. S of Springfield and on Little Miami R. **12** Mill village (pop. 1,707), Spartanburg co., NW S.C., on Pacolet R. and 7 mi. ENE of Spartanburg, in agr. area; textile mills. **13** City (pop. 818), Wayne co., S Tenn., on Tennessee R. and 14 mi. NW of Waynesboro; lumbering; makes railroad ties, buttons. **14** City (pop. 1,837), Bosque co., central Texas, on Bosque R. and 30 mi. NW of Waco; trade center in cotton, grain, cattle area; flour, feed milling, cotton ginning, rock quarrying. Seat of a jr. col. Settled 1880, inc. 1902. **15** Town (pop. 262), Fairfax co., N Va., near the Bull Run, 20 mi. WSW of Washington, D.C.

Cliftondale, Mass.: see SAUGUS.

Clifton Forge, city (pop. 5,795), in but independent of Alleghany co., W Va., in the Alleghenies, on Jackson R. and 37 mi. N of Roanoke, in coal-mining dist.; rail junction (shops); lumber and textile milling, clothing and uniform mfg. State park near by. Settled 1880; inc. 1884.

Clifton Heights, borough (pop. 7,549), Delaware co., SE Pa., just SW of Philadelphia. Largely residential; textiles, metal products. Settled c.1850, inc. 1885.

Clifton Hill, town (pop. 262), Randolph co., N central Mo., 12 mi. W of Moberly; grain, coal.

Clifton Springs, village (pop. 1,838), Ontario co., W central N.Y., 28 mi. SE of Rochester; mfg. of electrical and leather goods. Health and vacation resort, with mineral springs; Clifton Springs Sanitarium is here. Inc. 1859.

Cliftonville, England: see MARGATE.

Clifty, Ind.: see MILFORD, Decatur co.

Climax, village (pop. 308), SW Sask., 30 mi. S of Shaunavon, near Mont. border; alt. 3,064 ft.; wheat.

Climax. 1 Village (1940 pop. 860), Lake co., central Colo., in natl.-forest area of Rocky Mts., 10 mi. NNE of Leadville; alt. c.11,300 ft. Mine here is world's leading producer of molybdenum. High-altitude observatory here. Highway and railroad run through Fremont Pass (11,320 ft.) here. Quandary Peak and Mt. Lincoln near by. **2** Town (pop. 373), Decatur co., SW Ga., 8 mi. ESE of Bainbridge. **3** City (pop. 91), Greenwood co., SE Kansas, near Fall R., 7 mi. SSE of Eureka. **4** Village (pop. 524), Kalamazoo co., SW Mich., 13 mi. ESE of Kalamazoo, in agr. area (fruit, grain, livestock). **5** Village (pop. 271), Polk co., NW Minn., in Red R. valley, 14 mi. SW of Crookston, in grain area.

Climax Springs, town (pop. 151), Camden co., central Mo., 18 mi. WNW of Camdenton.

Clinch, county (□ 796; pop. 6,007), S Ga., on Fla. line; ⊙ Homerville. Flatwoods area drained by Suwannee R.; E part included in Okefenokee Swamp. Forestry (lumber, naval stores) and farming (livestock, corn, sweet potatoes). Formed 1850.

Clinchant (klĕshā′), village (pop. 821), Oran dept., NW Algeria, in irrigated Mina valley, 5 mi. W of Relizane; wine, olives, cereals.

Clinchco (klĭnch′kō), village (pop. 1,390, Dickenson co., SW Va., 15 mi. E of Jenkins, Ky., in bituminous-coal region.

Clinchfield. 1 Village, Houston co., central Ga., 7 mi. SE of Perry; limestone quarrying; cement mfg. **2** Village (pop. 1,033), McDowell co., W N.C., 2 mi. NE of Marion.

Clinch Mountain, in Va. and Tenn., ridge in Great Appalachian Valley, bet. Clinch and Holston rivers; from Burkes Garden, Va., extends c.145 mi. SW to Knoxville area; rises to 2,000 ft. in SW, to 3–4,700 ft. in NE.

Clinchport, town (pop. 359), Scott co., SW Va., on Clinch R. and 13 mi. S of Big Stone Gap. NATURAL TUNNEL is just N.

Clinch River, in Va. and Tenn., formed by forks joining in Tazewell co., SW Va.; flows c.300 mi. generally SW, through Great Appalachian Valley, into E. Tenn., here impounded by Norris Dam to form (with its tributary, Powell R.) Norris Reservoir, and thence into Watts Bar Reservoir, formed by Watts Bar Dam on Tennessee R. An important part of the TVA system.

Cline, village, Uvalde co., SW Texas, 19 mi. W of Uvalde; asphalt mining.

Cline, Mount (11,027 ft.), SW Alta., in Rocky Mts., near edge of Banff Natl. Park, 80 mi. SE of Jasper; 52°5′N 116°42′W.

Cline Town, Sierra Leone: see FREETOWN.

Clinge or **Klinge** (klĭng′ŭ), town (pop. 1,906), Zeeland prov., SW Netherlands, on Flanders mainland and 13 mi. ESE of Terneuzen, near Belg. border; knitting mills; building stone. Contiguous with Belg. town of Clinge.

Clingen (klĭng′ŭn), town (pop. 2,310), Thuringia, central Germany, 10 mi. SSE of Sondershausen; sugar beets; market gardening.

Clingmans Dome, highest point (6,642 ft.) in Tenn., in Great Smoky Mts., on N.C. line, 35 mi. SE of Knoxville; 35°34′N 83°30′W.

Clint, village (1940 pop. 745), El Paso co., extreme W Texas, near the Rio Grande, 20 mi. SE of El Paso; shipping point in irrigated agr. area.

Clinton. 1 Village (pop. estimate 300), S B.C., 32 mi. NNE of Lillooet, in lumbering, gold- and silver-mining region. **2** Town (pop. 1,896), S Ont., on Bayfield R. and 13 mi. SE of Goderich; mfg. of machinery, pianos, clothing, stockings. Salt wells near by.

Clinton. 1 County (□ 498; pop. 22,594), S Ill., bounded S by Kaskaskia R.; ⊙ Carlyle. Agr. area (corn, wheat, fruit, livestock, poultry; dairy products). Mfg. (flour, paper and glass containers, shoes, metal articles, food products). Bituminous-coal mines; oil wells and refineries. Formed 1824. **2** County (□ 407; pop. 29,734), central Ind.; ⊙ Frankfort. Agr. area (grain, livestock, soybeans, apples), with diversified mfg., including farm-products processing; oil refining at Frankfort. Bituminous-coal mines. Drained by Sugar Creek and forks of Wildcat Creek. Formed 1830. **3** County (□ 695; pop. 49,664), E Iowa; ⊙ Clinton. Bounded E by Mississippi R. (forms Ill. line here) and SW and S by Wapsipinicon R. Prairie agr. area (hogs, cattle, corn, oats); limestone quarries. Industry at Clinton. Formed 1840. **4** County (□ 206; pop. 10,605), S Ky.; ⊙ Albany. Bounded S by Tenn., NW by Cumberland R.; drained by several creeks. Includes part of Dale Hollow Reservoir. Hilly agr. region, in Cumberland foothills; livestock, grain, poultry, dairy products, burley tobacco; coal mines, timber. Formed 1836. **5** County (□ 571; pop. 31,195), S central Mich.; ⊙ St. Johns. Drained by Maple, Lookingglass, and Grand rivers, and by small Stony Creek. Agr. (grain, sugar beets, peppermint, beans, fruit, livestock); dairying. Mfg. at St. Johns and Ovid. Oil refining. Formed 1839. **6** County (□ 420; pop. 11,726), NW Mo.; ⊙ Plattsburg. Drained by Little Platte R.; agr. (corn, wheat, oats), mules. Formed 1833. **7** County (□ 1,059; pop. 53,622), extreme NE N.Y.; ⊙ Plattsburg. Bounded N by Que. line, E by L. Champlain (here forming Vt. line). Includes N Adirondacks; situated partly in Adirondack State Park and forest preserve. Has many mtn. and lake resorts and Ausable Chasm on Ausable R.; drained also by Saranac and Great Chazy rivers. Resort, dairying, farming, and lumbering area, with paper milling and other mfg., iron mining, some quarrying. Formed 1788. **8** County (□ 412; pop. 25,572), SW Ohio; ⊙ Wilmington. Drained by forks of Little Miami R. and small Caesar Creek. Stock raising (cattle, hogs), farming (grain), dairying; mfg. at Wilmington and Sabina. U.S. air force base at Wilmington. Includes Fort Ancient State Memorial Park. Formed 1810. **9** County (□ 902; pop. 36,532), N central Pa.; ⊙ Lock Haven. Forested mtn. area, drained by West Branch of Susquehanna R. and Bald Eagle Creek; Bald Eagle Mtn. crosses SE part. Clay, bituminous coal, limestone; lumber, paper, textiles, leather; agr., meat packing. Formed 1839.

Clinton. 1 City (pop. 853), ⊙ Van Buren co., N central Ark., c.60 mi. N of Little Rock, in diversified agr. area; lumber milling. Inc. as city 1938. **2** Resort town (pop. 2,466), Middlesex co., S Conn., on Clinton Harbor of Long Island Sound at mouth of Hammonasset R., and 20 mi. E of New Haven; agr. (potatoes, truck), mfg. (cosmetics), fishing. Settled 1663, set off from Killingworth 1838. **3** Village (pop. c.200), Jones co., central Ga., 13 mi. NNE of Macon. **4** City (pop. 5,945), ⊙ De Witt co., central Ill., 19 mi. N of Decatur; rail and trade center in agr. area; corn, wheat, soybeans, oats, livestock, dairy products; mfg. of clothing, patent medicines; railroad shops. Settled 1836, inc. 1855. Lincoln practiced law here. **5** City (pop. 6,462), Vermillion co., W Ind., on Wabash R. and 14 mi. N of Terre Haute; large-scale bituminous-coal mining; flour, clothing, packed meat. Site of Fort William Henry Harrison is near by. Settled 1818, laid out 1829. **6** City (pop. 30,379), ⊙ Clinton co., E Iowa, port on Mississippi R. (bridged here) and 28 mi. NE of Davenport; industrial and railroad center; structural steel, tubing, engines, pumps, machine tools, hardware, millwork, wooden toys, cellophane, wash dresses, wire cloth, corn (starch, syrup, oil) and soybean products, grain alcohol, packed poultry and eggs. Mt. St. Claire Jr. Col. is here. Laid out 1838, replatted 1855, inc. 1857. Grew as a sawmilling center in the 1880s. **7** Town (pop. 1,593), ⊙ Hickman co., SW Ky., 23 mi. WSW of Mayfield; trade center for agr. area; ships corn, cotton; mfg. of concrete products, poultry coops, soft drinks; lumber, flour, and feed mills. Columbus Belmont Battlefield State Park is near by. Platted 1826; inc. 1831. **8** Town (pop. 1,383), ⊙ East Feliciana parish, SE central La., 31 mi. NNE of Baton Rouge, in agr. and timber area; cotton ginning, feed- and sawmilling, cottonseed processing. Located 1825, inc. 1830, inc. as town 1852. **9** Town (pop. 1,623), Kennebec co., S Maine, 9 mi. NE of Waterville and on Sebasticook R.; wood products, textiles, canned foods. Settled c.1775, inc. 1795. **10** Town (pop. 12,287), Worcester co., central Mass., on S branch of Nashua R. and 12 mi. NNE of Worcester; metal products, chemicals, beverages, furniture. Settled 1654, inc. 1850. Formerly had one of largest cotton mills in U.S. Wachusett Reservoir is just S. **11** Village (pop. 1,344), Lenawee co., SE Mich., on Raisin R. and 18 mi. SW of Ann Arbor, in fertile farm area; woolen and flour mills. Wamplers L. (resort) is near by. Inc. 1838. **12** Village (pop. 718), Big Stone co., W Minn., 10 mi. N of Ortonville, in agr. area; dairy products. **13** Town (pop. 2,255), Hinds co., W Miss., 9 mi. WNW of Jackson. Seat of Mississippi Col. Settled c.1823 on site of an early Indian agency. **14** City (pop. 6,075), ⊙ Henry co., W central Mo., near South Grand R., 37 mi. SW of Sedalia; grain, dairy, poultry center; coal. **15** Village (pop. 36), Sheridan co., NW Nebr., 7 mi. ENE of Rushville. **16** Town (pop. 1,118), Hunterdon co., W N.J., on South Branch of Raritan R. and 16 mi. ESE of Phillipsburg. State corrective farm for women near by. Settled in mid-18th cent., inc. 1865. **17** Village (pop. 1,630), Oneida co., central N.Y., on Oriskany Creek and 8 mi. WSW of Utica. Seat of Hamilton Col. Mfg. (clothing, food products). Elihu Root was b. here. Inc. 1843. **18** Town (pop. 4,414), ⊙ Sampson co., SE central N.C., 32 mi. ESE of Fayetteville; sawmilling. Laid out 1818. **19** Village (pop. 397), Summit co., NE Ohio, 12 mi. SSW of Akron and on Tuscarawas R. **20** City (pop. 7,555), Custer co., W Okla., c.80 mi. W of Oklahoma City and on Washita R.; mfg. and shipping center for stock-raising, dairying, and agr. area (wheat, cotton, poultry). Mfg. of cottonseed and dairy products, feed, candy, brick, tile, beverages, packed poultry. U.S. soil-conservation camp, state hosp., state tuberculosis sanatorium, and an Indian hosp. are here. Founded 1903, inc. 1909. **21** Town (pop. 7,168), Laurens co., NW S.C., 33 mi. S of Spartanburg; center of agr. area (cotton, grain, peanuts, vegetables, dairy products, poultry); mfg. (textiles, clothing, flour, canned foods, fertilizer), printing. Seat of Presbyterian Col. and state school for feeble-minded. **22** Town (pop. 3,712), ⊙ Anderson co., E Tenn., near Clinch R., 15 mi. NW of Knoxville; trade and shipping point for timber, orchard, farm area; makes hosiery. OAK RIDGE and Norris Dam near by. **23** Town (pop. 670), Davis co., N Utah, 8 mi. SW of Ogden. **24** Village (pop. 1,138), Rock co., S Wis., 9 mi. NE of Beloit, near Ill. line, in dairying and farming area.

Clinton, Mount, N.H.: see PRESIDENTIAL RANGE.

Clinton-Colden Lake (20 mi. long, 5–20 mi. wide), E Mackenzie Dist., Northwest Territories, NE of Great Slave L.; 64°N 107°30′W. Drains S through Artillery L. into Great Slave L.

Clinton Corners, resort village, Dutchess co., SE N.Y., 13 mi. NE of Poughkeepsie. Small lakes near by.

Clintondale, village (1940 pop. 548), Ulster co., SE N.Y., 6 mi. W of Poughkeepsie, in fruitgrowing area.

Clinton River, SE Mich., rises in small lakes near Pontiac in Oakland co., flows c.30 mi. E, past Pontiac and Rochester, to Anchor Bay of L. St. Clair 5 mi. E of Mt. Clemens.

Clintonville. 1 Borough (pop. 307), Venango co., NW Pa., 13 mi. S of Franklin. **2** City (pop. 4,657), Waupaca co., E central Wis., on Pigeon R. (tributary of the Embarrass) and 30 mi. NNW of Appleton, in farm area; mfg. (trucks, trailers, conveyers, dairy products). Settled c.1855, inc. 1887.

Clintwood, town (pop. 1,366), ⊙ Dickenson co., SW Va., near Ky. line, 17 mi. NNE of Norton; bituminous coal, timber, agr. Inc. 1894.

Clio (klī′ō). **1** Town (pop. 840), Barbour co., SE Ala., 22 mi. ESE of Troy. **2** Town (pop. 162), Wayne co., S Iowa, near Mo. line, 11 mi. SW of Corydon, in agr. area. **3** City (pop. 1,963), Genesee co., SE central Mich., 11 mi. NNW of Flint, in agr. area. Inc. as village 1873, as city 1928. **4** Town (pop. 837), Marlboro co., NE S.C., 8 mi. ESE of Bennettsville; fertilizer.

Clippens, town in Paisley parish, central Renfrew, Scotland, just NNE of Johnstone; chemical mfg.

Clipperton Island, uninhabited atoll (□ c.2), Fr. Oceania, SE Pacific, 1,800 mi. W of Panama Canal; 10°18′N 109°13′W. Mexico and France claimed ownership of isl. when it became important with opening of Panama Canal. Italy arbitrated conflicting claims, decided (1930) in favor of France.

Clipstone, town and parish (pop. 3,443), central Nottingham, England, on Maun R. and 5 mi. NE of Mansfield; coal mining. Has remains of anc. palace, probably belonging to the kings of Northumbria. A parliament was held here 1290.

Clisham (klĭ′shŭm), mountain (2,622 ft.), on Lewis with Harris, Outer Hebrides, Scotland, 6 mi. NW of Tarbert.

Clissa, Yugoslavia: see KLIS.

Clisson (klēsō′), town (pop. 2,632), Loire-Inférieure dept., W France, on Sèvre Nantaise R. and 15 mi.

SE of Nantes; tanning, mfg. (soap, candles, slippers). Winegrowing. Has picturesque 14th-cent. bridges and ruins of medieval castle lived in by Olivier de Clisson in 14th cent.

Clitherall (klĭ'thrůl), village (pop. 175), Otter Tail co., W Minn., on L. Clitherall and 21 mi. E of Fergus Falls, in grain area.

Clitherall, Lake, Otter Tail co., W Minn., 18 mi. E of Fergus Falls; 3.5 mi. long, 1 mi. wide. Fishing, bathing resorts. Village of Clitherall at NE end of lake.

Clitheroe (klĭ'dhůrō), municipal borough (1931 pop. 12,008; 1951 census 12,057), E Lancashire, England, on Ribble R. just W of Pendle Hill (1,831 ft.), near Yorkshire boundary, 10 mi. NNE of Blackburn; 53°52'N 2°24'W; cotton and rayon milling; mfg. of cement. Has 16th-cent. grammar school and ruins of small Norman castle. Near by is Stonyhurst Col. (with observatory), founded in 17th cent.

Clive, village (pop. 227), S central Alta., 21 mi. NE of Red Deer; lumbering, dairying, farming.

Cliveden, England: see TAPLOW.

Cliviger (klĭ'vĭjůr), parish (pop. 1,569), E Lancashire, England, 3 mi. SSE of Burnley; coal mines; sheep raising.

Cliza (klē'sä), town (pop. c.14,600), ⊙ Germán Jordan (until c.1943 Cliza) prov., Cochabamba dept., central Bolivia, on S slopes of Cordillera de Cochabamba, 20 mi. SE of Cochabamba; alt. 8,934 ft. Junction point for railroads from Cochabamba to Arani and Villa Viscarra; local market center for general merchandise and agr. products (corn, wheat, potatoes). Alcohol distilling (W) in area bet. Tarata and Cliza.

Cloch Point, Scotland: see GOUROCK.

Clocolan (klŏkō'län), town (pop. 2,843), S Orange Free State, U. of So. Afr., near Basutoland border, 80 mi. E of Bloemfontein; alt. 5,304 ft.; wheat, rye, oats, malt, potatoes, fruit; grain elevator. Resort.

Clodomira (klōdōmē'rä), town (1947 pop. 3,549), central Santiago del Estero prov., Argentina, 12 mi. NE of Santiago del Estero; rail junction; agr. center (alfalfa, corn, cotton, wheat, livestock).

Cloete (klōā'tā), coal-mining settlement (pop. 2,464), Coahuila, N Mexico, on railroad and 6 mi. NW of Sabinas.

Clogh or **Clough** (klŏkh), agr. village (district pop. 1,305), central Co. Antrim, Northern Ireland, 7 mi. N of Ballymena; flax, potatoes, cattle.

Cloghan (klŏ'khůn), Gaelic *Clóchan*, town (pop. 172), W Co. Offaly, Ireland, 5 mi. NE of Banagher; agr. market (cattle; hops, barley, potatoes).

Clogheen (klŏ-khēn'), Gaelic *Cloich in an Mharghaid*, town (pop. 498), S Co. Tipperary, Ireland, 14 mi. WSW of Clonmel; agr. market (dairying; potatoes, beets).

Clogher (klŏ'khůr, klôr), Gaelic *Ceann Clochair*, town (pop. 586), SE Co. Louth, Ireland, on the Irish Sea, 7 mi. NE of Drogheda; fishing port. Just E is Clogher Head; 53°47'N 6°12'W.

Clogher, agr. village (district pop. 903), S Co. Tyrone, Northern Ireland, on Blackwater R. and 14 mi. NW of Monaghan; potatoes, oats, flax, cattle. A religious center since time of St. Patrick, it is seat of Protestant bishop, with cathedral rebuilt in 18th cent. R.C. bishop of Clogher has cathedral at Monaghan, Ireland.

Cloghjordan, Ireland: see CLOUGHJORDAN.

Clonakilty (klŏ"nůkĭl'tē), Gaelic *Clanna Chaoilte*, urban district (pop. 2,825), S Co. Cork, Ireland, on Clonakilty Bay, 25 mi. SW of Cork; small seaport and agr. market (dairying; potatoes, oats), with slate quarries. Founded 1614 by earl of Cork, town was almost destroyed in Anglo-Irish battle of 1641. Michael Collins b. here. Near by are Dunnycove and Dunowen castles.

Clonard (klŏ'nůrd), Gaelic *Cluain Ioraird*, agr. village, SW Co. Meath, Ireland, near the Boyne, 12 mi. SW of Trim. Fragmentary remains of abbey founded c.520.

Clonbrook, Br. Guiana: see ANN'S GROVE.

Cloncurry (klŏnkûr'ē), town (pop. 1,584), W central Queensland, Australia, 420 mi. WSW of Townsville; 20°42'S 140°28'E. Rail junction; gold-mining center; copper, silver, lead, zinc.

Clondalkin (klŏndô'kĭn, –dôl'kĭn), Gaelic *Cluain Dolcáin*, town (pop. 1,042), Co. Dublin, Ireland, on the Liffey and 5 mi. WSW of Dublin; paper mills. Has anc. round tower.

Clonderalaw Bay, inlet (4 mi. long) of the Shannon estuary, SW Co. Clare, Ireland, 5 mi. ESE of Kilrush.

Clones, Gaelic *Cluain Eois*, urban district (pop. 2,092), W Co. Monaghan, Ireland, on the Ulster Canal and 12 mi. WSW of Monaghan; rail center; agr. market (flax, oats, potatoes); mfg. of clothing and lace. Has anc. round tower and remains of 6th-cent. abbey.

Clonfert (klŏn'fůrt), Gaelic *Cluain Fhearta Bhréanainn*, agr. village (district pop. 462), SE Co. Galway, Ireland, on branch of the Grand Canal, near the Shannon, 5 mi. NW of Banagher; sheep; potatoes, beets. Has remains of medieval cathedral, on site of 6th-cent. monastery founded by St. Brendan. Name of see is still retained in title of bishop of Clonfert, Killaloe, Kilmacduagh, and Kilfenora.

Clonmacnoise (klŏn"mŭknoiz'), village (district pop. c.500), NW Co. Offaly, Ireland, on the Shannon and 21 mi. W of Tullamore. Important religious center, it is scene of annual feast of St. Kieran, attracting many pilgrims. It is site of ruins of the Seven Churches, oldest of which was built 904, of 2 anc. round towers, an abbey founded 541 by St. Kieran, the Episcopal Palace, a castle (destroyed by Cromwell), and a convent. Clonmacnoise suffered many Danish and English attacks. In 1568 the see was merged with that of Meath.

Clonmel (klŏnmĕl'), Gaelic *Cluain Meala*, urban district (pop. 9,857), ⊙ Co. Tipperary, Ireland, in S part of co., on Suir R. and 90 mi. SW of Dublin; agr. market in dairying region; woolen and flour milling, processing of dairy products, bacon and ham curing, mfg. of shoes and toys. It is tourist, salmon-fishing, and hunting center. Of anc. walls and gates only West Gate and part of rampart remain. Town was chartered and fortified by Edward I. In 1516 it was besieged by the British and in 1650 by Cromwell. Laurence Sterne b. here. In 1815 Charles Bianconi started public jaunting-car system bet. Clonmel and Cahir.

Clonmellon (klŏnmĕ'lůn), Gaelic *Cluain Mioláin*, town (pop. 271), E Co. Westmeath, Ireland, 7 mi. SW of Ceanannus Mór; agr. market.

Clontarf (klŏntärf'), NE suburb (pop. c.25,000) of Dublin, Co. Dublin, Ireland; scene of decisive defeat (1014) of the Danes by Irish under Brian Boru. Has castle (1835) on site of earlier structure.

Clontarf, village (pop. 206), Swift co., W Minn., on Chippewa R. and 6 mi. NW of Benson, in grain and potato area.

Cloppenburg (klô'pŭnbŏŏrk), town (pop. 12,529), in Oldenburg, NW Germany, after 1945 Lower Saxony, 21 mi. SSW of Oldenburg city; rail junction; mfg. of machinery, wool, wood products; meat processing.

Cloquet (klōkā'), city (pop. 7,685), Carlton co., NE Minn., on St. Louis R. and 18 mi. W of Duluth; trading and mfg. point in grain, potato, and poultry area; wood, paper, and dairy products, beverages. Near by are forest experiment station of state univ. and Indian hosp., on Fond du Lac Indian Reservation. Settled 1879, inc. as village 1880, as city 1904. Almost entirely destroyed (1918) by forest fire, rebuilt with state aid.

Cloquet River, rises in small lake in Lake co., NE Minn., flows 100 mi. SW, through Superior Natl. Forest, to St. Louis R. 10 mi. NNW of Cloquet city. Fish Lake Reservoir (4.5 mi. long, 2.5 mi. wide) is c.25 mi. upstream. Island Lake Reservoir (9 mi. long, max. width 4.5 mi.) is formed by dam 5 mi. further upstream. Boulder Lake Reservoir (4 mi. long, average width 1 mi.) is on small affluent of river and just NE of Island Lake Reservoir.

Clorinda (klōrēn'dä), town (1947 pop. 7,806), ⊙ Pilcomayo dept. (□ c.2,000; 1947 pop. 21,058), E Formosa natl. territory, Argentina, port on Pilcomayo R. near its influx into Paraguay R., and 5 mi. W of Asunción (Paraguay), in livestock and rice area; cotton processing, rice milling. PUERTO PILCOMAYO, its port, is at the junction of the rivers, 7 mi. SE.

Closeburn, agr. village and parish (pop. 1,074), W Dumfries, Scotland, 11 mi. NW of Dumfries. Site of anc. Closeburn Castle. Has ruins of Norman church.

Closepet (klō'sĕpĕt), town (pop. 8,882), Bangalore dist., SE Mysore, India, on tributary of Cauvery R. and 27 mi. SW of Bangalore, in silk-growing area; handicrafts (carpentry, weaving, paper, pottery, pith sun helmets). Poultry farm. Training center for rural health and welfare. Panther hunting in near-by scrub jungle. Also called Ramgiri.

Closplint (klō'splĭnt), mining village, Harlan co., SE Ky., on Clover Fork of Cumberland R. and 14 mi. ENE of Harlan; bituminous coal.

Closter (klō'stůr), residential borough (pop. 3,376), Bergen co., NE N.J., near Hudson R., 10 mi. NE of Paterson; mfg. (metal powders, curtains, cement). Inc. 1903.

Clotilde Island, Chile: see GUAITECAS ISLANDS.

Cloud, county (□ 711; pop. 16,104), N Kansas; ⊙ Concordia. Plains region, drained by Republican R. (N) and Solomon R. (SW). Wheat growing, stock raising. Formed 1867.

Cloud, Mount (6,110 ft.), SE Alaska, in Coast Range, 50 mi. ESE of Wrangell; 56°17'N 131°9'W.

Cloudcroft, village (pop. 251), Otero co., S N.Mex., in Sacramento Mts., 13 mi. ENE of Alamogordo, in Lincoln Natl. Forest; alt. 8,842 ft. Resort; timber-shipping point.

Cloud Lake, town (pop. 132), Palm Beach co., SE Fla.

Cloud Peak (13,165 ft.), N Wyo., 30 mi. SSW of Sheridan; highest point in Bighorn Mts.; has large glacier.

Clouds, Pass of the, Fr. *Col des Nuages* (kôl dā nüäzh'), Annamese *Deo Van* (dăō' vŭn'), pass (1,627 ft.) in spur of Annamese Cordillera, central Vietnam, on South China Sea coast, just N of Bay of Tourane; crossed by Tourane-Hue road. Just E is tunnel on Saigon-Hanoi RR.

Clouds Rest, Calif.: see YOSEMITE NATIONAL PARK.

Cloudveil Dome, Wyo.: see GRAND TETON NATIONAL PARK.

Cloudy Bay, inlet of Cook Strait, NE S.Isl., New Zealand, connected with Queen Charlotte Sound (N) by narrow channel; 15 mi. long, 5 mi. wide. Blenheim near SW shore.

Clough (klŏkh). **1** Village, Co. Antrim, Northern Ireland: see CLOGH. **2** Agr. village (district pop. 1,222), E central Co. Down, Northern Ireland, 6 mi. WSW of Downpatrick; flax, oats; sheep. There are ruins of anc. castle.

Cloughfold, England: see RAWTENSTALL.

Cloughjordan or **Cloghjordan** (klŏkh-jôr'důn), Gaelic *Cloch an tSiúrtánaigh*, town (pop. 442), N Co. Tipperary, Ireland, 9 mi. NE of Nenagh; agr. market (dairying, cattle raising; potatoes, beets).

Clovelly (klōvĕ'lē), village and parish (pop. 528), NW Devon, England, on Bideford Bay of Bristol Channel, and 9 mi. W of Bideford, on steep hillside; old fishing port and seaside resort. Has 14th-cent. Clovelly Court, old stone pier, and Norman church. Kingsley lived here as a youth.

Clovenfords, agr. village in Caddonfoot parish, NE Selkirk, Scotland, 3 mi. W of Galashiels; synthetic fertilizer mfg. and extensive grape growing (under glass). Just SW, on the Tweed, is Ashiestiel (ă"shēstēl'), residence of Sir Walter Scott while deputy sheriff of Selkirk. He here wrote a number of his works.

Clover. 1 Town (pop. 3,276), York co., N S.C., 8 mi. N of York, in agr. area; textiles. Mill villages and turkey farm near by. Kings Mtn. Natl. Military Park is W. **2** Town (pop. 274), Halifax co., S Va., 40 mi. NE of Danville, in agr. area.

Cloverdale, village (pop. estimate 700), SW B.C., 18 mi. SE of Vancouver; mixed farming; poultry, fruit, hops.

Cloverdale. 1 City (pop. 1,292), Sonoma co., W Calif., on Russian R. and 30 mi. NNW of Santa Rosa; fruit, sheep, wool, wine, hops. The Geysers and mineral springs (resorts) are near by (SE). **2** Village (pop. 1,432), Tazewell co., central Ill., 6 mi. SE of East Peoria. **3** Town (pop. 649), Putnam co., W central Ind., 33 mi. E of Terre Haute, in agr. area. **4** Village (pop. 200), Putnam co., NW Ohio, 18 mi. S of Defiance, near Auglaize R., in agr. region.

Clover Fork, SE Ky., rises in the Cumberlands in E Harlan co., flows c.35 mi. WSW past Highsplint, Evarts, and Harlan, joining Poor Fork just N of Harlan to form Cumberland R.

Cloverhills, town (pop. 408), Polk co., central Iowa, near Raccoon R., just W of Des Moines, in bituminous-coal-mining and agr. area.

Cloverport, city (pop. 1,357), Breckinridge co., NW Ky., on left bank (levee) of the Ohio and 27 mi. E of Owensboro, in agr. area (corn, burley tobacco, hay, livestock, cotton); rock quarrying; mfg. of tiles, furniture, roofing, pearl button blanks; flour and feed mills, cotton gins. Founded 1808.

Clovis (klō'vĭs). **1** City (pop. 2,766), Fresno co., central Calif., in San Joaquin Valley, 8 mi. NE of Fresno; orchards, truck farms, vineyards; packing plants, canneries, lumber mills. Inc. 1912. **2** City (pop. 17,318), ⊙ Curry co., E N.Mex., on Llano Estacado, near Texas line, 100 mi. NE of Roswell. Important trade and livestock-feeding center; railroad div. point, with repair shops; flour, dairy products, beverages. Artifacts of Folsom period found near by. Eastern N.Mex. State Park is 11 mi. S. Town settled 1907, inc. 1909. Grew with building of railroad shops and warehouses.

Clow Bridge, England: see DUNNOCKSHAW.

Clowne, town and parish (pop. 5,917), NE Derby, England, 12 mi. SE of Sheffield; coal-mining center. Has 12th-cent. church.

Cloyes-sur-le-Loir (klwä-sür-lů-lwär'), village (pop. 1,709), Eure-et-Loir dept., NW central France, on the Loir and 7 mi. SW of Châteaudun; market (cattle, poultry, cereals). Damaged in Second World War. Until 1938, called Cloyes.

Cloyne, Gaelic *Cluain Uamha*, village (pop. 620), SE Co. Cork, Ireland, 15 mi. E of Cork; agr. market (dairying; potatoes, oats). A bishopric founded by St. Colman, its 14th-cent. cathedral has memorial to Berkeley (bishop here 1734–53). Of interest are a round tower and, near by, limestone caves.

Clucellas (klōōsĕ'yäs), town (pop. estimate 1,500), central Santa Fe prov., Argentina, 60 mi. WNW of Sante Fe; agr. center (corn, flax, wheat, livestock).

Cluj (klōōzh), Ger. *Klausenburg* (klou'zůnbŏŏrk), Hung. *Kolozsvár* (kô'lôzh-vär), city (1948 pop. 117,915), ⊙ Cluj prov., W central Rumania, in NE foothills of Apuseni Mts., on Little Somes R., on railroad and 200 mi. NW of Bucharest; 46°47'N 23°37'E. Major cultural and commercial center, 2d largest town in Rumania and historical ⊙ Transylvania. Has large metallurgical industry producing munitions, automobile bodies, armor plate, hardware, silverware, wire cloth, pipes; also chemicals, textiles, footwear, furniture, electrical equipment, wooden toys, bricks, tiles, cardboard; processes foods, tobacco. Known for its educational establishments, which include several universities (one founded in 1872), music and art academy, 2 theological seminaries, agr. and deaf-mute institutes, teachers' col. Cluj is also the R.C., Greek-Catholic, Unitarian, and Reformed bishops' sees. Recently it has developed into a popular tourist center because of the picturesque countryside and the winter-sports facilities available near by. Most noted city landmarks are the central square (*Piața Unirii*) with 16th–18th-cent. houses and the large 15th–16th-cent. Gothic St. Michael church with 19th-cent. tower, remains of 13th-cent. and 15th–17th-cent. fortifications, National Opera bldg., Franciscan monastery, originally built in 13th-cent. and later restored in baroque, 18th-cent. Austrian fort (*Cetatuia*) on right bank of the Somes, and the house where Matthias Corvinus of Hungary was born. There are several noted museums and libraries, and fine botanical gardens. Possibly a Dacian and later a Roman colony. Cluj was one of the original 7 towns founded in 12th cent. by Ger. colonists in Transylvania and made a free city in 1408. Powerful craft guilds, notably the jewelers' guild, flourished in the city during Middle Ages. Introduction of Unitarian church (16th cent.) caused the departure of most of the Saxons and brought Magyars into prominence. Diet of Cluj proclaimed union of Transylvania with Hungary in 1848–49. Persecution of Rumanian nationals of Transylvania culminated in the historic trial of their leaders held here (1894). Cluj, transferred to Rumania in 1920, was again in Hungary 1940–45. Magyars still compose over 50% of pop.

Clun (klŭn), town and parish (pop. 1,723), SW Shropshire, England, on the small Clun R. and 14 mi. WNW of Ludlow; agr. market. Has ruins of Norman castle, and Norman church. Near by are remains of anc. Br. and Welsh camps.

Clunes (klōōnz), municipality (pop. 847), S central Victoria, Australia, 75 mi. WNW of Melbourne, in sheep-raising and gold-mining area; knitting mill. Formerly important mining town; gold discovered here 1851.

Cluny (klōō'nē), village (pop. 151), S Alta., near Bow R., 55 mi. ESE of Calgary; wheat, stock.

Cluny (klōō'nē, Fr. klünē'), town (pop. 3,420), Saône-et-Loire dept., E central France, on Grosne R. and 12 mi. NW of Mâcon, in the Monts du Mâconnais; cattle market. Furniture mfg., horse breeding, winegrowing. Former seat of the Benedictine Abbey of Cluny (founded 910), a leading religious and cultural center during Middle Ages. The remains of the impressive abbey church (10th cent. in part), the churches of Notre Dame (13th cent.) and of St. Marcellus (12th cent.), and the abbatial bldgs. (which now house a national school of arts and trades) were all damaged during Second World War.

Clusaz, La (lä klüzä'), village (pop. 375), Haute-Savoie dept., SE France, in the Bornes (Savoy Pre-Alps), 14 mi. E of Annecy; alt. 3,412 ft. Winter-sports resort. Col des Aravis (alt. 4,915 ft.) is 3 mi. SE on Annecy-Chamonix road.

Cluse-et-Mijoux, La (lä-klüz-ā-mēzhōō'), village (pop. 306), Doubs dept., E France, in a defile 2 mi. SSE of Pontarlier; sawmilling. The defile, traversed by Doubs R., road, and railroad, and providing access to Switzerland, is commanded by old fortress (Fort de Joux) in which Mirabeau and Toussaint l'Ouverture were imprisoned.

Cluses (klüz), town (pop. 2,646), Haute-Savoie dept., SE France, at N end of Arve R. gorge, 23 mi. ESE of Geneva, in Faucigny valley; clock-mfg. center. Natl. watchmaking school (founded 1848).

Clusium, Italy: see CHIUSI.

Clusone (klōōzô'nĕ), town (pop. 3,969), Bergamo prov., Lombardy, N Italy, in Serio R. valley, 19 mi. NE of Bergamo, in livestock-raising area; rail terminus; wool market. Marble quarries near by.

Clute, village (pop. c.1,000), Brazoria co., S Texas, near Brazos R., 5 mi. N of Freeport, in Brazosport industrial area (sulphur, chemicals).

Clutha, county, New Zealand: see BALCLUTHA.

Clutha River (klōō'thù), largest river of S.Isl., New Zealand; rises in L. Wanaka, flows 210 mi. SE, past Cromwell, Clyde, Alexandra, and Balclutha, to S Pacific near Kaitangata. Navigable by small steamers 45 mi. to Roxburgh; drains agr. area. Hydroelectric plant at Luggate, near its source. Sometimes called Molyneux R.

Clutier (klōōtēr', klōō'tēr), town (pop. 302), Tama co., central Iowa, 25 mi. E of Marshalltown; mfg. of farm equipment.

Clutterbuckganj, India: see BAREILLY, city.

Clutton, town and parish (pop. 1,220), NE Somerset, England, 5 mi. NW of Radstock; coal mining. Church is of Norman origin.

Clwydian Hills (klōōĭ'dēùn), range in Denbigh and Flint, Wales, extends 20 mi. NNW-SSE bet. upper Alyn R. valley and Prestatyn. Highest point is Moel Famman (moil vä'män), 4 mi. NE of Ruthin; there are traces of anc. British camps and of Roman quarries and lead mines.

Clwyd River (klōō'ĭd), Denbigh, Wales, rises 8 mi. SW of Ruthin, flows in a curve S and E, and finally N, past Ruthin, Rhuddlan, and St. Asaph, to Irish Sea at Rhyl; 30 mi. long. River is paralleled E by Clwydian Hills.

Clydach (klĭ'dākh), town in RHYNDWYCLYDACH parish, W Glamorgan, Wales, on Tawe R. and 5 mi. NE of Swansea; nickel and chemical works; coal mines. First Br. nickel refinery established here.

Clyde, village (pop. 150), central Alta., 40 mi. N of Edmonton; wheat, stock.

Clyde, township (pop. 328), ⊙ Vincent co. (□ 2,922; pop. 3,716), S central S.Isl., New Zealand, 70 mi. NW of Dunedin and on Clutha R.; fruitgrowing.

Clyde. **1** City (pop. 1,067), Cloud co., N Kansas, on Republican R. and 12 mi. E of Concordia, in wheat region; flour milling. Founded 1866, inc. 1869. **2** Town (pop. 115), Nodaway co., NW Mo., near Little Platte R., 13 mi. SE of Maryville. **3** Village (pop. 2,492), Wayne co., W central N.Y., on the Barge Canal and Clyde R., and 18 mi. NW of Auburn, in dairying and fruitgrowing area; mfg. (cheese, machinery, condiments, shoe counters and heels, canned foods). Summer resort. Inc. 1835. **4** Town (pop. 598), Haywood co., W N.C., on Pigeon R. and 20 mi. W of Asheville; ships cattle. **5** Village (pop. 4,083), Sandusky co., N Ohio, 17 mi. SW of Sandusky; trade center for agr. area (grain, fruit, truck); cutlery, canned foods, electric refrigerators, barrels, kegs. Settled c.1820. **6** Town (pop. 908), Callahan co., central Texas, 16 mi. E of Abilene; fruit, grain, peanuts; pecan nursery, chick hatchery.

Clyde, Firth of, Scotland: see CLYDE RIVER.

Clydebank, burgh (1931 pop. 46,952; 1951 census 44,625), SE Dumbarton, Scotland, on the Clyde and 6 mi. WNW of Glasgow; shipbuilding center, with largest British shipyards, and important sewing-machine and machinery works. The *Queen Mary* and *Queen Elizabeth* were built here. In Second World War, sustained severe air raids (1940–41).

Clyde Park or **Clydepark**, town (pop. 280), Park co., S Mont., on branch of Yellowstone R. and 15 mi. N of Livingston.

Clyde River, Northwest Territories: see RIVER CLYDE.

Clyde River, SW Scotland, rises as Daer Water (the main headstream) on Queensberry mtn. in S Lanark, 8 mi. ENE of Thornhill, flows 106 mi. generally N and NW, past Lanark, Hamilton, Glasgow, Renfrew, Clydebank, and Dumbarton, where it widens into the Firth of Clyde. Near Lanark are the Falls of Clyde, consisting of 4 series: Bonnington, Corra, Dundoff, and Stonebyres. Below Lanark the Clyde flows through fertile area, noted for its orchards, and then through most important Scottish industrial area, with coal mines and, below Glasgow, important shipyards and other heavy industries. This area was heavily bombed in 1940–41. The Clyde valley, or Clydesdale, is noted for Clydesdale horses, a leading draft breed. The river is navigable for ocean-going liners to Glasgow. A canal connects the river with the Forth. Below Dumbarton the Firth of Clyde extends 64 mi. (W and then S) to the North Channel at Ailsa Craig; it is generally 1–20 mi. wide, widening to c.35 mi. at its mouth. On its shores are the ports, industrial towns, and resorts of Greenock, Gourock, Largs, Saltcoats, Troon, and Ayr. The Cumbrae isls. are in the firth; Arran forms W shore of its lower course.

Clyde River. **1** In W central N.Y., continuation of outlet of CANANDAIGUA LAKE, flows c.37 mi. generally E from Lyons, past Clyde, to Seneca R. 7 mi. NE of Seneca Falls. Partly utilized by N.Y. State Barge Canal. **2** In NE Vt., rises in Island Pond in Essex co., flows c.25 mi. NW, past Charleston, to L. Memphremagog opposite Newport.

Clydesdale, Scotland: see CLYDE RIVER.

Clydey, village and parish (pop. 698), NE Pembroke, Wales, 5 mi. SW of Newcastle Emlyn; woolen milling.

Clyman (klī'măn), village (pop. 250), Dodge co., S central Wis., 12 mi. SSE of Beaver Dam, in dairying region.

Clymer (klī'mùr). **1** Village (pop. c.450), Chautauqua co., extreme W N.Y., 21 mi. WSW of Jamestown, near Pa. line; feed, lumber mills. **2** Borough (pop. 2,500), Indiana co., W central Pa., 8 mi. ENE of Indiana; bituminous coal, clay. Inc. 1905.

Clynder (klĭn'dùr), resort village, SW Dumbarton, Scotland, on Gare Loch, just NNW of Roseneath.

Clynekirkton, Scotland: see BRORA.

Clynnogfawr (klŭn"ŏgvour'), agr. village in Clynnog parish (pop. 1,281), W Caernarvon, Wales, on Lleyn Peninsula, on Caernarvon Bay of Irish Sea, 9 mi. SSW of Caernarvon. Has noted 16th-cent. church on site of church founded c.616.

Clytha, agr. parish (pop. 221), central Monmouth, England, 5 mi. N of Usk.

Clyth Ness (klĭth' nĕs'), headland on Moray Firth, SE Caithness, Scotland. Terminates in promontory of Halberry Head, 3 mi. E of Lybster, site of lighthouse (58°19'N 3°13'W).

Cnidus or **Cnidos** (both: nī'dùs), ancient Greek city of Caria, SW Asia Minor, on Cape Krio (tip of Resadiye Peninsula), in SW Asiatic Turkey; one of cities of the Dorian Hexapolis. Was built partly on an isl. made by cutting through the peninsula, partly on the peninsula itself. Had a large trade, particularly in wine, and was also noted for its medical school and other institutions of learning. It was famed for its statue of Aphrodite by Praxiteles. In the waters off Cnidus the Athenians under Conon defeated the Spartans under Pisander in 394 B.C. Sometimes spelled Gnidus.

Cnossus, **Cnossos**, or **Knossos** (all: nŏ'sùs), anc. city of Crete, 4 mi. SE of modern Candia. Occupied long before 3000 B.C., the site was center of an important Bronze Age culture. It was destroyed by earthquakes (c.1500 B.C.), but flourished until 4th cent. A.D. Excavations conducted after 1900 by A. J. Evans revealed the great palace (2000-1400 B.C.) of legendary King Minos, from which knowledge of the Minoan civilization has been drawn. The involved plan of the palace may be related to the Labyrinth of Gr. legend.

Coacalco (kwäkäl'kō), officially Coacalco de Berriozábal, town (pop. 1,152), Mexico state, central Mexico, 14 mi. N of Mexico city; cereals, maguey, livestock.

Coachella (kō-chĕ'lù), city (pop. 2,755), Riverside co., S Calif., in Coachella Valley, 70 mi. ESE of Riverside; ships dates, grapefruit, vegetables. Inc. 1946.

Coachella Valley, Riverside co., S Calif., desert trough (part of Colorado Desert) extending c.45 mi. NW from SALTON SEA, bet. Little San Bernardino Mts. (E), San Jacinto and Santa Rosa mts. (W); c.15 mi. wide; S part is c.120 ft. below sea level. Artesian irrigation (since 1890s) and a branch (Coachella Main Canal; completed 1948) of ALL-AMERICAN CANAL have made it a productive agr. region, known for its date gardens (Indio, Coachella dists.); also grows citrus fruit, truck, cotton, alfalfa. In N are desert resorts, notably PALM SPRINGS.

Coacoatzintla (kwäkwätsēn'tlä), town (pop. 667), Veracruz, E Mexico, in Sierra Madre Oriental, 9 mi. N of Jalapa; coffee.

Coacoyula (kwäkoiōō'lä), town (pop. 1,584), Guerrero, SW Mexico, in Río de las Balsas valley, 20 mi. SSW of Iguala; cereals, sugar cane, fruit.

Coacuilco (kwäkwēl'kō), town (pop. 2,316), Hidalgo, central Mexico, in foothills of Sierra Madre Oriental, 20 mi. WSW of Huejutla; corn, rice, sugar cane, tobacco, fruit.

Coahoma (kō"ùhō'mù), county (□ 570; pop. 49,361), NW Miss.; ⊙ Clarksdale. Bounded NW and W by Mississippi R., here forming Ark. line; drained by Sunflower R. Rich agr. area (cotton, corn, cattle, hogs); timber; cottonseed processing, lumber milling. Formed 1836.

Coahoma (kōhō'mù), town (pop. 802), Howard co., W Texas, 10 mi. ENE of Big Spring; shipping point in cattle-ranching, agr. and oil region.

Coahuayana (kwäwïä'nä), town (pop. 347), Michoacán, W Mexico, on Tuxpan (or Coahuayana) R. and 35 mi. S of Colima; rice, sugar cane, fruit are grown.

Coahuayana River, Mexico: see TUXPAN RIVER.

Coahuayutla (kwäwīōōt'lä), officially Coahuayutla de Guerrero, town (pop. 529), Guerrero, SW Mexico, in NW outliers of Sierra Madre del Sur, 65 mi. WSW of Huetamo; fruit; silver deposits.

Coahuila (kōùwē'lù, Sp. kwäwē'lä), state (□ 58,067; 1940 pop. 550,717; 1950 pop. 720,145), N Mexico, on the big bend of the Rio Grande, S of Texas; ⊙ Saltillo. Bounded by Chihuahua (W), Durango (SW), Zacatecas (S), and Nuevo León (E). Crossed by the Sierra Madre Oriental, which splits into many broken ranges. Mainly arid tableland with depressions or *bolsones* (NW), continuing Bolsón de Mapimí of Chihuahua. Mayrán depression (Laguna Dist.) in S is irrigated by Nazas and Aguanaval rivers. Climate hot and dry in N and center; mild and humid in S; cooler in sierras. Minerals include coal, of which state is Mexico's largest producer, mined at Sabinas, Nueva Rosita, Piedras Negras, Abasolo; silver, gold, copper, zinc, lead (Sierra Mojada, Monclova, Múzquiz, Ocampo, Saltillo). Predominantly a cattle-grazing region. The LAGUNA DISTRICT, a vast inland basin which absorbs rivers with no outlet to the sea, is S; it is Mexico's main cotton-growing center; also produces wheat, corn, sugar cane, tobacco, fruit; Torreón is its center. Wine is made at Nadadores and Parras. Fine timber in NE mts. Processing industries concentrated at Piedras Negras, Saltillo, Parras, Torreón; Monclova produces steel. Explored by the Spanish beginning in mid-16th cent., the area was claimed for Sp. crown. It was later in Nueva Vizcaya, until 1788; after Mex. independence it was combined with Texas. After Mexican War (battle of Buena Vista was fought S of Saltillo), Coahuila was combined (1857) with Nuevo León; it regained its autonomy in 1868.

Coajomulco, Mexico: see CUAXOMULCO.

Coakley Town, Bahama Isls.: see FRESH CREEK.

Coal, county (□ 526; pop. 8,056), S central Okla.; ⊙ Coalgate. Drained by Clear Boggy and Muddy Boggy creeks. Agr. (corn, cotton, sorghums, cattle, hogs, poultry). Some mfg. at Coalgate. Some coal mining. Oil, natural-gas wells. Formed 1907.

Coal Aston, agr. village (pop. 858), N Derby, England, 5 mi. S of Sheffield; abandoned coal pits.

Coalbrookdale, town and valley in Wellington urban dist., central Shropshire, England, near Severn R., 11 mi. SE of Shrewsbury; metallurgical industry; electrical-appliance works. Site of works founded 1709 by Abraham Darby where pig iron was smelted by the use of coke for the 1st time in England.

Coalburn, town in Lesmahagow parish, S central Lanark, Scotland, 3 mi. NW of Douglas; coal mining.

Coal Center, borough (pop. 584), Washington co., SW Pa., on Monongahela R. just WNW of California.

Coal City, city (pop. 2,220), Grundy co., NE Ill., 21 mi. SSW of Joliet, in agr., bituminous-coal-mining, and clay-producing area; mfg. (clay products, clothing, machinery, wire rope, wallpaper). Founded 1875, inc. 1881.

Coalcomán (kwälkōmän'), officially Coalcomán de Matamaros, town (pop. 2,994), Michoacán, W Mexico, in NW foothills of Sierra Madre del Sur, 50 mi. SE of Colima; alt. 3,530 ft.; cereals, fruit, coffee, sugar cane.

Coal Creek, village (pop. estimate 150), SE B.C., in Rocky Mts., 5 mi. E of Fernie; coal mining.

Coal Creek. 1 or **Coalcreek,** town (pop. 195), Fremont co., S central Colo., near Arkansas R., just NE of Wet Mts., 30 mi. WNW of Pueblo; alt. 5,600 ft. **2** Town, Anderson co., Tenn.: see LAKE CITY.

Coaldale, village (pop. 413), S Alta., 10 mi. E of Lethbridge; coal mining.

Coaldale. 1 Village, Fremont co., S central Colo., on Arkansas R., just E of Sangre de Cristo Mts., and 30 mi. WSW of Canon City; alt. 7,550 ft. Gypsum mines. **2** Borough (pop. 231), Bedford co., S Pa., 25 mi. SSE of Altoona. Post office is Six Mile Run. **3** Borough (pop. 5,318), Schuylkill co., E central Pa., 18 mi. NE of Pottsville; anthracite; clothing. Settled 1868, inc. 1871.

Coaley, agr. village and parish (pop. 605), central Gloucester, England, 5 mi. WSW of Stroud; flour milling. Has 14th-cent. church.

Coal Fork, village (pop. 1,185), Kanawha co., W W.Va., 6 mi. SE of Charleston.

Coalgate, city (pop. 1,984), ⊙ Coal co., S central Okla., 31 mi. ESE of Ada, near Muddy Boggy Creek; supply center for farm area (corn, cotton, livestock). Cotton ginning, pecan shelling and processing; mfg. of cottonseed oil, feed, lumber, concrete blocks. Oil wells. Formerly a coal-mining center; some coal still produced.

Coalgood, mining village, Harlan co., SE Ky., in the Cumberlands, 6 mi. ESE of Harlan; bituminous coal.

Coal Grove, village (pop. 2,492), Lawrence co., S Ohio, just N of Ashland (Ky.), across Ohio R.

Coal Hill, town (pop. 873), Johnson co., NW Ark., 40 mi. E of Fort Smith, near Arkansas R., in agr. area. Coal mining formerly important.

Coalhurst, village (pop. estimate 100), S Alta., 5 mi. NW of Lethbridge; coal mining.

Coalinga (kōlĭng'gŭ, kōŭ–), city (pop. 5,539), Fresno co., central Calif., in foothills of Coast Ranges, 50 mi. SW of Fresno; oil-field center; oil refining; mfg. of oil-well supplies, dairy products. Seat of Coalinga Col. Inc. 1906.

Coalisland (kōlī'lŭnd), town (pop. 2,234), E Co. Tyrone, Northern Ireland, 4 mi. NE of Dungannon; coal-mining center, with fire-clay quarrying, linen milling, brick mfg.

Coalmont, village (pop. estimate 250), SW B.C., in Cascade Mts., on Tulameen R. and 50 mi. W of Penticton; coal mining.

Coalmont. 1 Village (pop. c.200), Jackson co., N Colo., on headstream of N.Platte R. and 14 mi. SW of Walden; alt. 8,500 ft. Strip mining of coal. **2** Borough (pop. 207), Huntingdon co., S Pa., 21 mi. SSW of Huntingdon. **3** Village (1940 pop. 544), Grundy co., SE central Tenn., 31 mi. NW of Chattanooga.

Coalport, borough (pop. 1,052), Clearfield co., W central Pa., 17 mi. NNW of Altoona; bituminous coal. Inc. 1883.

Coal River, SW W.Va., rises in Raleigh co. W of Beckley, flows c.70 mi. NW, past Edwight and Whitesville, to Kanawha R. at St. Albans. Bituminous-coal mining in its valley.

Coalsnaughton (kōlznô'tŭn), village, Clackmannan, Scotland, on Devon R., just S of Tillicoultry; coal mining.

Coalspur, village, W Alta., in Rocky Mts., near Jasper Natl. Park, 35 mi. SW of Edson; railroad junction; coal mining.

Coalton. 1 Village (pop. 402), Montgomery co., S central Ill., 20 mi. ENE of Litchfield, in agr. and bituminous-coal area. **2** Village (pop. 628), Jackson co., S Ohio, 25 mi. SE of Chillicothe, in agr. and coal-mining area.

Coaltown of Wemyss (wēmz), town in Wemyss parish, central Fifeshire, Scotland, 5 mi. SW of Leven; coal mining.

Coal Valley, village, W Alta., in Rocky Mts., near Jasper Natl. Park, 40 mi. SW of Edson; coal.

Coal Valley, village (pop. 363), Rock Island co., NW Ill., 7 mi. SE of Rock Island, in agr. area.

Coalville, urban district (1931 pop. 21,880; 1951 census 25,739), NW Leicester, England, 12 mi. NW of Leicester; coal mines, metalworks, brickworks. Just NW is coal-mining town of Snibston, in Ravenstone with Snibston parish (pop. 1,777).

Coalville, town (pop. 2,930), S Transvaal, U. of So. Afr., 10 mi. SSW of Witbank; coal mining.

Coalville, town (pop. 850), ⊙ Summit co., N Utah, on Weber R., at S end of Echo Reservoir, and 37 mi. SE of Ogden, in livestock and poultry area; alt. 5,571 ft. Coal mine near by. Natl. forests in vicinity.

Coalwood, village (pop. 1,310), McDowell co., S W.Va., 6 mi. SW of Welch, in coal region.

Coamo (kwä'mō), town (pop. 11,592), S central Puerto Rico, in S foothills of the Cordillera Central, on Coamo R. and 17 mi. ENE of Ponce; trading center in sugar and tobacco region; mfg. of needlework. Known for its sulphur springs, Baños de Coamo, 3 mi. SSW. An old colonial town (founded 1580), once seat of a provincial govt.

Coamo River, S central Puerto Rico, rises in the Cordillera Central, flows c.20 mi. S, past Coamo, to the Caribbean W of Santa Isabel.

Coapilla (kwäpē'yä), town (pop. 746), Chiapas, S Mexico, in N spur of Sierra Madre, 25 mi. N of Tuxtla; corn, fruit.

Coari (kwärē'), city (pop. 1,443), central Amazonas, Brazil, steamer and hydroplane landing on right bank of the Amazon, and 220 mi. WSW of Manaus; rubber, sugar, manioc, rice. Formerly Coary.

Côa River (kō'ŭ), Guarda dist., N central Portugal, rises on Sp. border near Sabugal, flows 70 mi. N to the Douro near Vila Nova de Fozcôa.

Coarraze (kwäräz'), village (pop. 1,117), Basses-Pyrénées dept., SW France, on the Gave de Pau and 11 mi. SE of Pau; linen weaving, toy and furniture mfg.

Coary, Brazil: see COARI.

Coasa or **Coaza** (both: kōä'sä), town (pop. 1,472), Puno dept., SE Peru, on N slopes of Cordillera Oriental, 18 mi. E of Macusani; alt. 12,411 ft. Potatoes, corn; sheep and cattle raising. Gold mines near by.

Coast Fork, W Oregon, rises in Douglas co., on W slope of Cascade Range, flows 49 mi. N, past Cottage Grove, joining Middle Fork near Eugene to form Willamette R. Cottage Grove Dam, 6 mi. S of Cottage Grove, consists of rolled-earth embankment (1,750 ft. long, 95 ft. high) and concrete section (360 ft. long, 100 ft. high); total length 2,110 ft. Completed 1942 as unit in flood-control and navigation project in Willamette R. basin. Forms small reservoir (capacity 30,000 acre-ft.). On a tributary (Row R.) is Dorena Dam (145 ft. high, 3,388 ft. long), begun in 1947.

Coast Mountains, W B.C. and S Alaska, range extending c.1,000 mi. NW–SE bet. the Yukon border and the Fraser R. (where it meets N end of the structurally related Cascade Range), paralleling Pacific coast, to which it descends steeply, lining shores of the numerous fjords that extend inland; forms border bet. NW B.C. and S Alaska. Highest peak is Mt. Waddington (13,260 ft.); other high peaks are Mt. Tiedemann (12,000 ft.), Monarch Mtn. (11,714 ft.), Mt. Munday (11,000 ft.), Mt. Queen Bess (10,700 ft.), Mt. Goodhope (10,670 ft.), Razorback (10,667 ft.), Mt. Ratz (10,290 ft., highest point of N part of range), Mt. Grenville (10,200 ft.), and Mt. Gilbert (10,200 ft.) Range is continued NW by the Alaska and Aleutian ranges. The Coast Mts. are sometimes confused with the physiographically distinct COAST RANGES belt, which is represented in Alaska and B.C. by broken sections: Kodiak Isl., Kenai, Chugach, St. Elias ranges, and the isls. (Alexander Archipelago, Queen Charlotte and Vancouver isls.) sheltering the Inside Passage on W.

Coast Province (□ 26,651; pop. 498,744), SE Kenya; ⊙ Mombasa. A coastal strip on Indian Ocean drained by Tana and Athi rivers. Includes Lamu archipelago. Cultivable grasslands near seashore give way to an inland arid zone (alt. 500–3,000 ft.) known as the Nyika. Narrow palm belt and mangrove forest on coast. Chief products: copra, sisal, sugar cane, rice, corn. Fisheries. Main centers are Mombasa, Lamu, and Shimoni. A 10-mi.-wide coastal strip (including offshore isls.), under lease from sultan of Zanzibar, is called Kenya Protectorate.

Coast Ranges, W North America, mtn. belt extending along Pacific coast from Alaska southward through B.C., Wash., Oregon, and Calif., and into Lower California, Mexico. Beginning on NW with uplands (over 5,000 ft.) of Kodiak Isl., system is continued to E and SE by KENAI RANGE, CHUGACH RANGE, SAINT ELIAS MOUNTAINS (containing Mt. Logan, 19,850 ft., 2d highest peak of N.America); thence S along the coast of S Alaska and B.C. —where it is represented by isls. (Alexander Archipelago, Queen Charlotte and Vancouver isls.) and separated by the Inside Passage from the Coast Mts. (E)—until it reappears on the mainland as OLYMPIC MOUNTAINS (rising to 7,954 ft.) in Wash. The system continues S as generally low (2–4,000 ft.) mts. along Wash. and Oregon coasts to KLAMATH MOUNTAINS on Oregon-Calif. line. A NW–SE trend is assumed by the ridges in Calif., which lie in a belt c.50 mi. wide bet. the Central Valley and a narrow coastal strip for most of length of state. Calif. section includes Diablo Range (up to 3,400 ft.), Santa Lucia Range (to 5,844 ft.), San Rafael Mts. (up to 6,596 ft.), and Mt. Pinos (8,831 ft.), 40 mi. S of Bakersfield. S of San Rafael Mts. (at W end of transverse belt linking Coast Ranges with the Sierra Nevada to E), continuity in the ranges is lacking. It is sometimes considered that the Coast Ranges proper end here and sometimes that they continue through S Calif. so as to include the low Santa Ynez, Santa Monica, Santa Ana, and Laguna mts., and the high (over 10,000 ft.) San Gabriel, San Bernardino, and San Jacinto mts. N and E of Los Angeles. According to the latter view the uplands continuing S into W Lower California are also part of the Coast Ranges. Southernmost portions are sometimes called Los Angeles Ranges in vicinity of Los Angeles, and Peninsular Ranges farther S. From San Francisco N to S Alaska, abundant rainfall (up to c.150 in. in N) supports valuable forests, mainly conifers; the magnificent rain forest growth and wildlife of the Olympic Mts. is preserved in OLYMPIC NATIONAL PARK. Water power is extensively developed on streams bet. N Calif. and S B.C. S of San Francisco, dryness restricts forests to higher alts., but the valleys of the ranges, many of them opening out to the sea at their NW ends, contain valuable agr. land. Although the Coast Ranges are sometimes confused with the COAST MOUNTAINS of B.C., the 2 systems are distinct. Both belong to the geologically recent Pacific mtn. province, but the Coast Mts., along the mainland shore of B.C., are actually the N continuation of the Sierra Nevada and the Cascade Range, and are in turn continued in Alaska by the great Alaska and Aleutian ranges. The Coast Ranges, on the other hand, are represented in Canada by offshore isls. The Coast Mts. are separated for their entire length from the Coast Ranges to W by a series of lowlands (the Pacific troughs), represented by the Central Valley in Calif., by the Willamette valley in Oregon, by the Puget Sound lowland in Wash., by the waters of the Inside Passage in B.C. and Alaska, by deep valleys bet. the 2 mtn. belts in Alaska, and, ultimately, by the waters of Cook Inlet and Shelikof Strait. In the S, the Coast Ranges are composed mainly of geologically recent folded sedimentary rocks which still undergo considerable faulting (the cause of most Calif. earthquakes); there are portions (Klamath Mts.) formed by igneous intrusions, and areas of igneous and metamorphic formation (Olympic Mts.); farther N are ranges of both sedimentary and igneous origin, and the northwesternmost ranges contain active craters. Glaciation and sinking of the N Pacific coast has produced the isl. form assumed by the range in B.C. and S Alaska. The Coast Mts., however, are composed in their S part (B.C.) of a vast granitic batholith, and in the N (along B.C.-Alaska boundary) of sedimentary and volcanic formations; they have undergone extensive glaciation (producing the great fjords of the coast line), and their NW continuation (Alaska and Aleutian ranges, with highest peaks of N. America) abound in active volcanoes.

Coata River (kōä'tä), Puno dept., SE Peru, rises in Cordillera Occidental of the Andes, flows c.100 mi. E to L. Titicaca at Coata, NE of Puno. Its valley is used by Juliaca–Arequipa RR. Called Cabanilla R. in upper course.

Coatbridge, burgh (1931 pop. 43,056; 1951 census 47,538), N Lanark, Scotland, 9 mi. E of Glasgow; important coal-mining, steel-milling, chemical-mfg. center.

Coatepec (kwätāpĕk'). **1** Town (pop. 2,202), Guerrero, SW Mexico, 18 mi. WSW of Iguala; cereals, cotton, sugar cane, tobacco, fruit. **2** Officially Coatepec de las Bateas, town (pop. 1,921), Mexico state, central Mexico, 21 mi. SE of Toluca; cereals, livestock. **3** Officially Coatepec de Harinas, town (pop. 5,007), Mexico state, central Mexico, 28 mi. S of Toluca; agr. center (sugar cane, fruit, cereals, livestock). **4** Town (pop. 978), Puebla, central Mexico, in SE foothills of Sierra Madre Oriental, 22 mi. ESE of Huauchinango; sugar cane, fruit. **5** City (pop. 11,459), Veracruz, E Mexico, at E foot of Cofre de Perote, in Sierra Madre Oriental, 5 mi. SSW of Jalapa; alt. 4,019 ft. Rail junction; processing and agr. center (corn, sugar cane, coffee, oranges); sugar refining, coffee roasting, alcohol distilling, wine making, textile milling. Quaint Indian town in jungle area; famed for orchids.

Coatepeque (kwätāpā'kā), town (1950 pop. 6,714), Quezaltenango dept., SW Guatemala, in coastal plain, on Naranjo R. and 25 mi. WSW of Quezaltenango, on railroad; road center in agr. area (coffee, sugar cane, pineapples, plantains).

Coatepeque, city (pop. 2,426), Santa Ana dept., W Salvador, on railroad, 6 mi. SE of Santa Ana; coffee, sugar cane, grain. Fishing in near-by L. Coatepeque.

Coatepeque, Lake, W Salvador, on Santa Ana–Sonsonate dept. border, 25 mi. WNW of San Salvador; occupies circular crater at E foot of volcano Santa Ana; 3 mi. in diameter; alt. 2,205 ft. Popular summer resort; fisheries.

Coatesville (kōts'vĭl). **1** Town (pop. 444), Hendricks co., central Ind., 28 mi. WSW of Indianapolis, in dairy, grain, and livestock area; timber. **2** City (pop. 13,826), Chester co., SE Pa., 34 mi. W of Philadelphia and on W branch of Brandywine Creek. Has one of world's largest steel-plate rolling mills; textiles, paper, metal products. Veterans' hosp. here. Settled c.1717, inc. as borough 1867, as city 1915.

Coatetelco (kwätātĕl'kō), town (pop. 2,857), Morelos, central Mexico, 14 mi. SSW of Cuernavaca; sugar cane, rice, coffee, fruit, vegetables, livestock.

Coatham, England: see REDCAR.

Coaticook (kōă'tĭkōōk), town (pop. 4,414), ⊙ Stanstead co., S Que., on Coaticook R. and 19 mi. SSE of Sherbrooke, near Vt. border; textile milling, lumbering; mfg. of textile products, toys, furniture.

Coati Island (kōä'tē), in L. Titicaca, W Bolivia, off Copacabana Peninsula, 8 mi. N of Copacabana; 1½ mi. long, ½ mi. wide; archaeological site of Inca and pre-Inca civilizations. Also called Isla de la Luna [Sp.,=island of the moon].

Coatitla (kwätēt'lä), officially Santa Clara Coatitla, town (pop. 2,596), Mexico state, central Mexico, 11 mi. NNE of Mexico city; grain, maguey, livestock.

Coatlán del Río (kwätlän'dĕl rē'ō), town (pop. 983), Morelos, central Mexico, 18 mi. SW of Cuernavaca; rice, sugar cane, fruit.

Coats (kōts). **1** City (pop. 255), Pratt co., S Kansas, 10 mi. SSW of Pratt; wheat, grain, livestock. **2** Town (pop. 1,047), Harnett co., central N.C., 8 mi. NNW of Dunn; lumber, grain milling.

Coatsburg, village (pop. 194), Adams co., W Ill., 15 mi. ENE of Quincy, in agr. area; ships grain, livestock.

Coats Island (□ 1,544), E Keewatin Dist., Northwest Territories, in N part of Hudson Bay, S of Southampton Isl. across Fisher and Evans straits; 62°35'N 83°W; 80 mi. long, 13–30 mi. wide. Became reindeer reserve, 1920.

Coats Land, part of Antarctica, W of Queen Maud Land, bet. 16°30'E and 37°W. Forms E shore of Weddell Sea. Discovered 1904 by W. S. Bruce, Scottish explorer.

Coatzacoalcos (kwätsäkwäl'kōs), city (pop. 13,740), Veracruz, SE Mexico, at mouth of Coatzacoalcos R., on Gulf of Campeche, on Isthmus of Tehuantepec, 135 mi. SE of Veracruz; N terminus of transisthmian railroad to Pacific at Salina Cruz. Port of entry; exports hardwood, petroleum products, cereals, fruit, mainly to Yucatan. Mfg. (forest products, canned food, furniture, soap); fruitgrowing, stock raising. Petroleum wells near by. Formerly Puerto México.

Coatzacoalcos River, in Oaxaca and Veracruz, SE Mexico, the most important stream of the Isthmus of Tehuantepec; rises in headstreams in Sierra Madre del Sur N of Ixtepec, flows c.175 mi. NNE in meandering course, past Minatitlán, to Gulf of Campeche at Coatzacoalcos. Navigable 125 mi. Its course was early explored by Cortés.

Coatzingo (kwätsēng'gō), town (pop. 2,423), Puebla, central Mexico, near Atoyac R., 18 mi. E of Matamoros; agr. center (corn, sugar cane, rice, stock).

Coatzintla (kwätsēn'tlä), town (pop. 1,995), Veracruz, E Mexico, near Cazones R., 10 mi. WNW of Papantla; petroleum.

Coayuca (kwīōō'kä), officially San Pedro Cuayuca, town (pop. 1,362), Puebla, central Mexico, 20 mi. ESE of Matamoros; sugar cane, rice, fruit, stock.

Coaza, Peru: see COASA.

Cobalt (kō'bôlt), town (pop. 2,376), E Ont., 5 mi. SW of Haileybury, on hillside above Cobalt L.; mining center in one of world's richest silver regions, discovered 1903. Other ores mined include cobalt, arsenic, antimony, nickel, mercury, bismuth. Mines reached peak of output in 1911, when town's pop. was 5,638, including many Italian workers. Mining operations (silver, cobalt) were resumed 1946; a new smelter was later opened. Haileybury (connected by electric railroad) is region's residential center.

Cobán (kōbän'), city (1950 pop. 6,854), ⊙ Alta Verapaz dept., central Guatemala, in N highlands, 60 mi. N of Guatemala; 15°28'N 90°80'W; alt. 4,330 ft. Major commercial and agr. center in rich coffee-growing area; textiles, net and rope making, tanning, coffee processing; vanilla, tea, cacao, spices, grain, livestock. Has 17th-cent. church. Founded 1538; developed as chief urban center of N Guatemala, exporting its products via Polochic R. valley. Mayan remains near by.

Cobar (kō'bär), municipality (pop. 2,039), central New South Wales, Australia, 260 mi. ENE of Broken Hill; rail terminus; mining center (copper, gold).

Cobb, county (□ 348; pop. 61,830), NW central Ga.; ⊙ MARIETTA. Bounded SE by Chattahoochee R.; includes part of Allatoona Reservoir in NW. Piedmont agr. (cotton, corn, sweet potatoes, dairy products, poultry) and timber area; mfg. at Marietta. Contains Kennesaw Mtn. Natl. Battlefield Park and Marietta Natl. Military Cemetery. Formed 1832.

Cobb, village (pop. 284), Iowa co., SW Wis., near source of Pecatonica R., 10 mi. W of Dodgeville; makes cheese.

Cobberas, Mount (kŏ'bŭrŭs) (6,030 ft.), E Victoria, Australia, in Australian Alps, 190 mi. ENE of Melbourne, near New South Wales border. Sometimes called Mt. Cobboras.

Cobb Island, E Va., barrier island off Atlantic shore of Northampton co., S of Hog Isl., 13 mi. ENE of Cape Charles city; 5 mi. long. Coast Guard station, lighthouse. Great Machipongo Inlet at N, Sand Shoal Inlet at S end. Partially shelters Cobb Bay (W).

Cobble Hill, village (pop. estimate 300), SW B.C., on SE Vancouver Isl., 22 mi. NW of Victoria; lumbering, mixed farming, fruitgrowing.

Cobble Mountain Reservoir (c.5 mi. long), SW Mass.; impounded by Cobble Mtn. Dam (263 ft. high, 730 ft. long; completed 1932) in short Little R., 15 mi. W of Springfield, to which it supplies water and power.

Cobboras, Mount, Australia: see COBBERAS, MOUNT.

Cobbosseecontee, Lake (kŏb'ŭsēkŏn'tē), Kennebec co., S Maine, summer and winter resort center 8 mi. WSW of Augusta; 9 mi. long, 1 mi. average width, with many isls. Drains SE through **Cobbosseecontee Stream** into Pleasant Pond.

Cobb Town, Ala.: see WEST END ANNISTON.

Cobbtown, city (pop. 288), Tattnall co., E central Ga., 25 mi. WSW of Statesboro.

Cobden, village (pop. 656), SE Ont., at SE end of Muskrat L., 18 mi. SE of Pembroke; dairying, lumbering.

Cobden (kŏb'dŭn). **1** Village (pop. 1,104), Union co., S Ill., 36 mi. N of Cairo, in fruitgrowing area of Ill. Ozarks; ships fruit, truck, wheat, corn; mfg. of wood products, flour milling. Inc. 1875. **2** Village (pop. 118), Brown co., SW Minn., on small affluent of Cottonwood R. and 19 mi. W of New Ulm; corn, oats, barley, poultry.

Cobequid Bay (kŏ'bŭkwĭd), E arm (30 mi. long, 6 mi. wide) of the Minas Basin, central N.S., extending E to TRURO. Receives Shubenacadie R.

Cobequid Mountains, range in N N.S., extending 120 mi. E-W along Northumberland Strait, bet. Minas Basin and Antigonish; rises to 1,100 ft. 12 mi. W of Westville.

Cóbh (kōv), urban district (pop. 5,619), SE Co. Cork, Ireland, on S shore of Great Isl., in Cork Harbour, 9 mi. ESE of Cork; 51°51'N 8°20'W; seaport, with dock installations and excellent anchorage. Iron foundries. Situated on slopes above harbor and with a good climate, it is a popular seaside resort. St. Colman's Cathedral, begun 1868, completed 1919, contains grave of Charles Wolfe. Cóbh is seat of R.C. diocese of Cloyne, and is hq. of Royal Cork Yacht Club, founded 1720. Town became important during French and American wars as base for supply convoys. In 1838 the *Sirius* made one of the 1st steamship crossings of the Atlantic from here. Originally called Cove of Cork, the town was visited in 1849 by Queen Victoria, and its name was changed to Queenstown; it became Cóbh in 1922. Near by, in Cork Harbour, are Haulbowline Isl., with naval dockyard and repair installations, Spike Isl., and Rocky Isl. Until handed over to Ireland under 1938 agreement, isls. were garrisoned by the British.

Cobham (kŏ'bŭm). **1** Agr. village and parish (pop. 929), N Kent, England, 5 mi. W of Rochester. Church contains a notable collection of brasses, mainly of the Cobham family. **2** Residential town and parish (pop. 5,831), N central Surrey, England, on Mole R. and 6 mi. W of Epsom. Church (14th cent.) has Norman tower and memorial to Matthew Arnold.

Cobija (kōbē'hä), city (1949 pop. estimate 5,000), ⊙ PANDO dept., NW Bolivia, important port on Acre R. opposite Brasiléia (Brazil) and 380 mi. NNW of La Paz; 11°2'S 68°49'W. Airport; customhouse. Major rubber-trade center; local market for tropical products (rice, bananas).

Cobija, village (1930 pop. 30), Antofagasta prov., N Chile, minor port on the Pacific, and 34 mi. SSW of Tocopilla; 22°35'S; exports nitrates. In 19th cent., before the War of the Pacific, Cobija was an important Bolivian seaport.

Coblenz or **Koblenz** (kō'blĕnts"), city (1939 pop. 91,098; 1946 pop. 52,414; 1950 pop. 64,961), W Germany, was ⊙ former Rhine Prov. of Prussia and after 1945 temporary ⊙ French-occupied Rhineland-Palatinate (of which Mainz was formally named ⊙), on the Rhine (harbor), at mouth of Mosel R., and 34 mi. NW of Wiesbaden; 50°21'N 7°36'E. Rail junction; important trading point for Rhine wines; tourist center. Some mfg.: machinery, pianos, furniture, shoes, cigars; also food processing; potteries. Heavy Second World War destruction (about 80%) included 18th-cent. castle, Rhine mus., state archives. Has Romanesque basilica, 13th-cent. castle, 17th-cent. town hall. At the Rhine-Mosel confluence (*Deutsches Eck*) is a huge monument to William I. Coblenz, the Roman *Confluentes*, was founded (9 B.C.) by Drusus. Passed to archbishops of Trier in 1018; chartered 1214. Held by France in 1794. Became part of Prussia in 1815 and was ⊙ Prussian Rhine Prov. from 1824 to 1945. Occupied by U.S. (1919–23) and Fr. (1923–29) troops, and was seat of Inter-allied High Commission for the Rhineland. Captured by Americans in March, 1945, and later placed in French occupation zone. The fortress Ehrenbreitstein, across the Rhine, has been part of the city since 1937.

Cobleskill (kō'bulskĭl"), village (pop. 3,208), Schoharie co., E central N.Y., 36 mi. W of Albany, in dairying and truck-farming area; mfg. (refrigerators, silos, pancake flour, clothing). A state school of agr. is here. Howe Caverns are at Howes Cave (6 mi. E). Settled 1752, inc. 1868.

Coboconk (kō'bōkŏngk), village (pop. estimate 500), S Ont., near Balsam L., 20 mi. NNW of Lindsay; dairying, mixed farming.

Cobourg (kō'bûrg), town (pop. 5,973), ⊙ Northumberland co., S Ont., on L. Ontario, 65 mi. ENE of Toronto; port, with mfg. of leather, carpets, chemicals, rifles, knitted goods, patent medicines; popular resort and agr. market.

Cobourg Island or **Coburg Island** (both: kō'bûrg) (22 mi. long, 4–14 mi. wide), E Franklin Dist., Northwest Territories, in Baffin Bay, at entrance of Jones Sound, bet. Ellesmere and Devon isls.; 75°58'N 79°30'W. Mountainous. Large numbers of murres breed here.

Cobourg Peninsula (kō'bûrg), N Northern Territory, Australia, opposite Melville Isl. (W) across Dundas Strait; forms SW shore of Arafura Sea, N shore of Van Diemen Gulf; 50 mi. long, 25 mi. wide. Reserve for native flora and fauna. Port Essington inlet (19 mi. long, 7 mi. wide) on N coast. Sometimes spelled Coburg Peninsula.

Cobquecura (kōbkäkōō'rä), village (1930 pop. 692), Ñuble prov., S central Chile, on Pacific coast (Cobquecura Bay), 50 mi. NW of Chillán; minor port and seaside resort.

Cobram (kŏ'brŭm), village (pop. 995), N Victoria, Australia, 140 mi. NNE of Melbourne and on Murray R., near New South Wales border; tobacco.

Cobras Island (kô'brŭs), in Guanabara Bay, SE Brazil, connected by bridge with mainland at E end of Rio de Janeiro wharves. On it are naval establishments, arsenal, dry docks. Formerly fortified, it figured prominently in the naval revolt of 1893.

Cobre or **El Cobre** (ĕl kō'brā), town (pop. 1,990), Oriente prov., E Cuba, in the Sierra del Cobre (E Sierra Maestra), 8 mi. W of Santiago de Cuba; copper-mining center. Site of famous sanctuary of Our Lady of Charity, visited by pilgrims.

Cobre, El, Venezuela: see EL COBRE.

Cobre, Sierra del (syĕ'rä dĕl kō'brā), Oriente prov., E Cuba, the E section of the Sierra MAESTRA, just W of Santiago de Cuba, with town of Cobre (copper deposits) on its slopes.

Cobre River or **Rio Cobre** (rē'ō kō'brā), central and S Jamaica, rises 8 mi. S of Port Maria, flows c.35 mi. S and E, past Linstead, Bog Walk, Spanish Town, and Gregory Park, to Kingston Harbour 4 mi. W of Kingston. Used for irrigation.

Cobridge, N suburb of Stoke-on-Trent, N Stafford, England; pottery, glazed tiles; coal mining.

Cobscook Bay, Washington co., E Maine, inlet of Passamaquoddy Bay lying W of Eastport; c.7 mi. long. Average tidal range, 18 ft.; dams of Passamaquoddy Bay tidal power project were built here.

Cobscook River, Maine: see DENNYS BAY.

Coburg (kō'bûrg), municipality (pop. 49,597), S Victoria, Australia, 5 mi. N of Melbourne, in metropolitan area; mfg. center; woolen and knitting mills.

Coburg (kō'bŏŏrk), city (1950 pop. 44,789), Upper Franconia, N Bavaria, Germany, on the Itz and 55 mi. N of Nuremberg; 50°15'N 10°58'E. Rail junction; metal (auto bodies, machine tools, radios, precision and optical instruments) and glass (light bulbs, Christmas-tree decorations) industries. Other mfg.: ceramics, porcelain, textiles, furniture; lumber and paper milling, printing, brewing, tanning. Trades in basketware. Has 2 late-Gothic churches; mid-16th-cent. ducal castle, the Ehrenburg; late-16th-cent. city hall. The anc. fortress of Coburg, ducal residence until 1549, was Luther's home in 1530; renovated in 19th and 20th cent., it now houses a mus. First mentioned in 1056, Coburg was chartered before 1189; passed to house of Wettin in 1353. Part of Saxe-Coburg-Gotha (1826–1918), it alternated with Gotha as residence of rulers. Joined Bavaria in 1920. Captured by U.S. troops in April, 1945. Prince Albert, consort of Queen Victoria, was b. here. Sometimes spelled Koburg.

Coburg (kō'bûrg). **1** Town (pop. 83), Montgomery co., SW Iowa, near East Nishnabotna R., 7 mi. S of Red Oak, in agr. region. **2** City (pop. 693), Lane co., W Oregon, 5 mi. N of Eugene.

Coburg Island, Northwest Territories: see COBOURG ISLAND.

Coburg Peninsula, Australia: see COBOURG PENINSULA.

Coburn, gore (pop. 105), on Que. line, Franklin co., W Maine; includes lumbering village of Moosehorn.

Coburn Mountain (3,718 ft.), Somerset co., W Maine, 14 mi. SE of Jackman, in hunting, fishing area; lookout station.

Coca (kō'kä), village, Napo-Pastaza prov., E Ecuador, landing on Napo R. near mouth of Coca R., and 70 mi. NE of Tena; forest products (rubber, balata, chicle); cattle.

Coca, town (pop. 1,601), Segovia prov., central Spain, on Eresma R. and 28 mi. NW of Segovia; wheat, barley, grapes, chick-peas, pine kernels, sheep. Sawmilling. Turpentine and resin processing. Ruined Mudejar castle.

Coca, Pizzo di (pē'tsō dē kô'kä), highest peak (10,013 ft.) in Bergamasque Alps, Lombardy, N Italy, 9 mi. SE of Sondrio. Has several small glaciers.

Cocachacra (kōkächä'krä), town (pop. 2,470), Arequipa dept., S Peru, on lower Tambo R. (irrigation), on railroad and 50 mi. SSW of Arequipa;

agr. center (rice, cotton, sugar cane, corn, alfalfa). Copper, salt, gypsum, and magnesium deposits are near by.

Cocal, El, Panama: see EL COCAL.

Cocanada (kŏk″ünä′dŭ), since 1949 officially **Kakinada** (kŭkĭnä′dŭ), city (pop. 75,140), ⊙ East Godavari dist., NE Madras, India, port on Bay of Bengal, in E Godavari R. delta, 300 mi. NNE of Madras. Served by rail spur from Samalkot and by delta canal system; exports cotton, peanuts, castor seeds, sugar, tobacco; cotton, rice, and flour milling; iron foundry, saltworks. Col. and engineering institute (affiliated with Andhra Univ.). S suburb of Jagannathapuram was site of early Du. trading station; ceded to English in 1825. Former port of Coringa (important in 18th cent.; now destroyed by advance of Godavari R. silt) is 9 mi. S. Small-boat building 11 mi. S, at village of Tallarevu. Rail spur continues to Kotipalli village, 22 mi. S, on Gautami Godavari R.

Coca River (kō′kä), NE Ecuador, rises in the Andes at S foot of Antisana volcano, flows c.110 mi. E and SE to Napo R. at Coca.

Coccaglio (kôk-kä′lyô), village (pop. 2,327), Brescia prov., Lombardy, N Italy, 3 mi. NE of Chiari; alcohol distillery.

Cocentaina (kō-thĕntī′nä), town (pop. 5,209), Alicante prov., E Spain, 4 mi. N of Alcoy; mfg. of nougat candy, paper, footwear, colored tiles and ceramics; hemp growing and processing, brandy distilling, tanning, olive pressing. Livestock trade. Wine and cereals in area. Dominated by hill with anc. tower; has remains of Roman walls restored by Moors, and turreted palace of Medinaceli family, lords of anc. county of Cocentaina.

Cocha, La, Argentina: see LA COCHA.

Cocha, Laguna de la (lägōō′nä dā lä kō′chä), Andean lake (alt. c.6,500 ft.) in Putumayo commissary, SW Colombia, 10 mi. SE of Pasto; 10 mi. long, 1–4 mi. wide.

Cochabamba (kōchäbäm′bä), department (□ 23,030; 1949 pop. estimate 654,000), central Bolivia; ⊙ Cochabamba. Includes E branch of Cordillera Real, called Cordillera de Cochabamba, which crosses dept. in arc swinging W–SE, separating the mountainous part (W) from tropical valleys (*yungas*) and tropical lowlands (N and E). Drained by Santa Elena and Cotacajes rivers (W), Caine R. (S), Chaparé and Ichilo rivers (E). Its fertile valleys with mild climate make the dept. Bolivia's main agr. region, producing barley and potatoes in higher sections, coca, corn, wheat, and vegetables in lower region, sugar cane and cacao in tropical zones. Sheep, cattle, and horses are raised. In central and NE part, the dept. is covered by forests; some lumbering. Tin is mined at Berenguela (SW), tungsten deposits at Kami (W). Served by one of densest road nets of Bolivia, and by railroad from Oruro with branches to Villa Viscarra and Arani. Main centers: Cochabamba city and its satellite towns Quillacollo, Tarata, Cliza, and Punata; Mizque; Totora.

Cochabamba, city (1949 pop. estimate 80,300), ⊙ Cochabamba dept. and Cercado prov., central Bolivia, on S slopes of Cordillera de Cochabamba, on Rocha R. and 140 mi. SE of La Paz, 130 mi. NW of Sucre; 17°22′S 66°8′W; alt. 8,389 ft. Second largest city of Bolivia; terminus of railroad from Oruro and of lines to Tintín and Arani. Air center of domestic Bolivian and international lines; hub of highways to Santa Cruz, Sucre, Oruro, and Todos Santos, with river connection to Beni dept. Important distributing center for agr. products of near-by valleys, which represent Bolivia's main agr. region (potatoes, corn, wheat, fruit, vegetables). Ships lumber, mostly eucalyptus, used as pit props in Oruro mines. Commerce in general merchandise and imported goods; mfg. (cottons, woolens, carpets, cigarettes, soda water, leather, soap, chocolate); brewing, alcohol distilling. Famous for its beauty and mild climate, it is Bolivia's main tourist resort. Principal bldgs.: govt. palace, cathedral with colonial sculptures, univ., some major commercial bldgs., Patiño mansion. Cochabamba lies in fertile, cultivated region with subtropical fruit gardens (garden suburb of Calacala is N). Important near-by towns: Quillacollo and Vinto (W), Sipesipe (WSW), Sacaba (E). Founded 1574; 1st named Oropeza; changed 1786 to Cochabamba. Became bishopric, 1843.

Cochabamba, Cordillera de (kôrdĭyä′rä dā), E branch of the Eastern Cordillera of the Andes, in Cochabamba dept., central Bolivia; extends c.160 mi. in arc swinging W–SE from Cordillera de Tres Cruces to headwaters of Ichilo R. Rises to 17,060 ft. at Tunari peak. Tungsten deposits at Kami.

Cochamó (kōchämō′), village (1930 pop. 606), Llanquihue prov., S central Chile, on left bank of Reloncaví Sound and 32 mi. E of Puerto Montt; inland port and resort; dairying, lumbering.

Cocharca River, Bolivia: see MACHUPO RIVER.

Cocharcas (kōchär′käs), village (1930 pop. 91), Ñuble prov., S central Chile, on railroad and 6 mi. NNE of Chillán; grain, wine, fruit, livestock.

Cocheco River (kōchē′kō), E N.H., rises in N Strafford co., flows 30 mi. SE, past Dover (water power), to junction with Salmon Falls R., forming the Piscataqua.

Coche Island (kō′chā), Nueva Esparta state, NE Venezuela, in the Caribbean bet. Araya Peninsula and Margarita Isl., 11 mi. SSW of Porlamar; 7 mi. long, 2–3 mi. wide. Fisheries and saltworks at San Pedro (W).

Cochem (kō′khŭm), town (pop. 5,202), in former Prussian Rhine Prov., W Germany, after 1945 in Rhineland-Palatinate, on the Mosel and 23 mi. SW of Coblenz; wine. Has anc. castle, destroyed by French in 1689, rebuilt in 19th cent.

Cochetopa Pass (kō″chŭtō′pŭ, kō′chŭtōp″) (10,032 ft.), in Continental Divide, Saguache co., SW central Colo. Crossed by highway.

Cochin (kō′chĭn), administrative division (□ 1,493; pop. 1,422,875), N TRAVANCORE-COCHIN, India; ⊙ Ernakulam. Lies bet. MALABAR COAST of Arabian Sea (W) and Anaimalai Hills of Western Ghats (E); bordered N by Palghat Gap; Madras port of COCHIN is a coastal enclave. Alluvial coastal lowland (network of navigable lagoons, subject to floods during SW monsoon) is important coconut-producing area; mfg. of copra, coir mats and rope (factory and handicraft), jaggery (from coconut toddy). Central plains produce rice, betel nuts, mangoes, jack, cassava, peanuts, cashew nuts. Cotton in small exclave around Chittur in Palghat Gap. Extensive tea, coffee, cardamom, and rubber plantations in Anaimalai Hills (teak, ebony, blackwood forests; elephants, bison, cheetahs). Industries powered by Pallivasal hydroelectric works at Munnar; rice and oilseed milling, tile mfg., sawmilling, hand-loom weaving. Chief towns: Ernakulam, Mattancheri, Trichur (cotton-milling center). Princely state of Cochin, anc. *Kochchi*, founded c.6th cent. A.D., included N portion of Travancore. Trading agreements made early-16th cent. with Portuguese, who were succeeded by Dutch in late-17th cent.; English supremacy and present area established in 1790s, after wars with Tippoo Sahib of Mysore. In 1949, merged with Travancore to form Travancore-Cochin. Pop. 63% Hindu, 29% Christian, 7% Moslem. Chief languages: Malayalam (spoken by over 90% of pop.), Tamil, Telugu, Kanarese.

Cochin, city (pop. 26,320), Malabar dist., SW Madras, India, port on Malabar Coast of Arabian Sea, 670 mi. SSE of Bombay, 110 mi. NNW of Trivandrum, in coastal exclave (□ 2) within Cochin administrative div. of Travancore-Cochin. A major Indian seaport (rail terminus), serving coastal and mtn. hinterland; exports coir products (rope, mats), copra, tea, rubber, lemon-grass oil, spices (pepper, ginger), cashew nuts; mfg. of coir products, copra, plywood, military clothing supplies; shark-oil processing; large fishery (sardines, mackerel) with cold storage plant. Extensive development scheme (begun 1920) resulted in opening the natural harbor (served by system of coastal backwaters) to seagoing vessels in 1930. By 1940, modern wharfage and dry-dock facilities were completed and reclaimed land, called Willingdon Isl., added to original small isl. of Vendurutti, in inner harbor; enlarged isl. (c.900 acres) is now connected by rail bridges with Travancore-Cochin cities of ERNAKULAM (E) and Mattancheri (W); has airport and large naval training base. Portuguese trading station established here in 1502 by Vasco da Gama (fort built 1503 by Affonso de Albuquerque); St. Francis Xavier founded a missionary center in 1530. In 1635, English established a trading post beside Port. settlement; both expelled by Dutch in 1663; English recaptured city in 1795.

Cochin China (kō′chĭn chī′nŭ), Fr. *Cochinchine* (kôshĕshēn′), former Fr. colony (□ 24,750; 1943 pop. 5,579,000) in S Indochina, constituting (since 1949) S VIETNAM; ⊙ Saigon. Bounded NE by Annam, N and NW by Cambodia, SW by Gulf of Siam, and SE by South China Sea, it projects S as the flat Camau peninsula. Apart from the S spurs of the Moi Plateaux where European colonists cultivate rubber, tea, coffee, sugar cane, and oil palms, Cochin China is a flat, alluvial plain, one of the world's great rice-export areas, irrigated by the Mekong R., whose delta arms constitute also the chief means of communications. Coconuts, pepper, betel nuts, and cotton are other important crops. Only the Plaine des Joncs and the mangrove-covered Camau peninsula are not cultivated. Next to agr., fishing is an important occupation. The pop. is largely Annamese (85% of total); other groups are Cambodians and Chinese. Industry is concerned with rice milling (Cholon), fish curing, and silk and cotton spinning, Saigon-Cholon forming the only great conurbation. Originally part of the Khmer empire, modern Cochin China was annexed (1698, 1731) by the Hue dynasty of S Annam (theretofore itself known as Cochin China to Europeans). Following Fr. occupation of Saigon in 1859, the E portion of Cochin China, including Saigon, Mytho, and Bienhoa, was ceded by Annam to France in 1863, and the W portion, including Vinhlong, Chaudoc, and Hatien, in 1867. Cochin China became a Fr. colony and joined the Union of Indochina in 1887. Following the establishment (1945–46) of Vietnam after the Second World War, Cochin China was briefly a Fr. overseas territory (1946–49) before joining Vietnam.

Cochinoca, dept., Argentina: see ABRA PAMPA.

Cochinoca (kōchēnō′kä), village (pop. estimate 500), N Jujuy prov., Argentina, 45 mi. SSW of La Quiaca; stock-raising center; lime quarrying. Former ⊙ Cochinoca dept.; succeeded by ABRA PAMPA.

Cochinoca, Sierra de (syĕ′rä dā), subandean mountain range in NW Jujuy prov., Argentina; extends c.45 mi. NW-SE; rises to c.14,000 ft.

Cochinos, Cayos, or Islas Cochinos, Honduras: see HOG ISLANDS.

Cochinos Bay (kōchē′nōs), Caribbean inlet (15 mi. long N-S, up to 5 mi. wide), Las Villas prov., S Cuba, cutting off Zapata Peninsula (W) 45 mi. W of Cienfuegos.

Cochinos Point, southernmost point of Bataan Peninsula, central Luzon, Philippines, at W side of entrance to Mariveles Harbor (small inlet at entrance to Manila Bay); 14°24′N 120°30′E.

Cochise (kō′chēz″, kŏ″chēz′), county (□ 6,256; pop. 31,488), SE Ariz.; ⊙ Bisbee. Chief ranges are Chiricahua, Dos Cabezas, Dragoon, and Mule mts. Co. includes Chiricahua Natl. Monument (in E) and parts of Coronado Natl. Forest. Irrigated farming along San Pedro R. and San Simon Creek. Copper mined near Warren and Bisbee. Silver, gold, gypsum; livestock, alfalfa; dude ranching. Formed 1881.

Cochise Head, Ariz.: see CHIRICAHUA MOUNTAINS.

Cochiti (kōchĭtē′), pueblo (□ 35.6), Sandoval co., N central N.Mex. Cochiti village (1948 pop. 402) is on W bank of the Rio Grande and 23 mi. WSW of Santa Fe; alt. 5,600 ft. Pueblo Indians here make pottery and raise livestock and corn. Festival of San Buenaventura, patron saint, takes place in July in connection with rain dance. San Buenaventura de Cochití Mission dates from 17th cent. Village discovered 1598 by Juan de Oñate.

Cochituate, Mass.: see WAYLAND.

Cochituate, Lake (kŭ-chĭ′tōōwĭt), E Mass., 16 mi. W of Boston; c.3 mi. long. Part of water-supply system for Boston area.

Cochran (kŏ′krŭn), county (□ 782; pop. 5,928), NW Texas; ⊙ Morton. On Llano Estacado, and bounded W by N.Mex. line; alt. 3,500–3,800 ft. Cattle ranching, agr. (cotton, grain sorghums, wheat, some fruit, truck); hogs, poultry, some dairying. Oil wells. Formed 1876.

Cochran, city (pop. 3,357), ⊙ Bleckley co., central Ga., 34 mi. SSE of Macon, in farm area; mfg. (shirts, lumber, lime). Middle Ga. Col. here. Inc. 1870.

Cochrane (kŏ′krŭn), district (□ 52,237; pop. 14,075), NE Ont., on Que. border and on James Bay of the Hudson Bay; ⊙ Cochrane.

Cochrane. 1 Village (pop. 405), S Alta., on Bow R. and 20 mi. NW of Calgary; mixed farming, stock. **2** Town (pop. 2,844), ⊙ Cochrane dist., NE Ont., 45 mi. NNE of Timmins; commercial center of NE Ont. and W Que. mining region, with machinery mfg., pulp and paper milling, lumbering, woodworking, dairying. Starting point of prospecting and hunting parties. Founded 1908.

Cochrane, village (1930 pop. 43), Aysén prov., S Chile, in Andes, on W shore of L. Cochrane (W section of L. Pueyrredón), 130 mi. SSE of Puerto Aysén; sheep raising.

Cochrane, village (pop. 444), Buffalo co., W Wis., near the Mississippi, 41 mi. NW of La Crosse, in dairy and livestock area; timber.

Cochrane, Lake, Chile-Argentina: see PUEYRREDÓN, LAKE.

Cochranton (kŏ′krŭntŭn), agr. borough (pop. 1,092), Crawford co., NW Pa., 10 mi. SE of Meadville and on French Creek; metal and wood products; poultry, livestock.

Cochstedt (kôkh′shtĕt), town (pop. 2,605), in former Prussian Saxony prov., central Germany, after 1945 in Saxony-Anhalt, 9 mi. NNW of Aschersleben; lignite mining.

Cocibolca, Lake, Nicaragua: see NICARAGUA, LAKE.

Cockatoo Island (kŏ″kŭtōō′), in Port Jackson, E New South Wales, Australia, 1.5 mi. WNW of Sydney; ¾ mi. long, ½ mi. wide. Shipyards, aircraft plant, iron foundry here.

Cockburn, village (pop. 101), E South Australia, 190 mi. NE of Port Pirie, at New South Wales border, on Port Pirie–Broken Hill RR; wool.

Cockburn Channel, Tierra del Fuego, Chile, bet. Clarence Isl. and Brecknock Peninsula, leads from the Pacific to Strait of Magellan.

Cockburn Island (□ 53.5; pop. 210), S central Ont., one of the Manitoulin Isls., in L. Huron, 2 mi. W of Manitoulin Isl.; 11 mi. long, 10 mi. wide; rises to 1,020 ft. Dairying, mixed farming.

Cockburn Land, Northwest Territories: see BOOTHIA PENINSULA.

Cockburn Sound, inlet of Indian Ocean, bet. Garden Isl. (W) and SW coast of Western Australia, near Fremantle; 8 mi. N-S, 5 mi. E-W; Cape Peron at tip of SW shore.

Cocke (kŏk), county (□ 434; pop. 22,991), E Tenn.; ⊙ Newport. Borders SE on N.C.; Great Smoky and Bald mtn. ranges are along state line. Includes sections of Great Smoky Mts. Natl. Park, Cherokee Natl. Forest, and Douglas Reservoir. Drained by French Broad, Pigeon, and Nolichucky rivers. Forest and farm region, with iron-ore and granite deposits; corn, tobacco, fruit, dairy products, livestock. Formed 1797.

Cockenzie and Port Seton (kŏkĕn'zē, sē'tŭn), burgh (1931 pop. 2,526; 1951 census 3,180), W East Lothian, Scotland, on Firth of Forth. Includes fishing ports of Cockenzie, 7 mi. W of Haddington, and Port Seton, just E of Cockenzie. Just S of Port Seton is locality of Seton, with Seton Castle (1790), built on site of anc. Seton Palace. Church dates from 14th cent.

Cockermouth (kŏ'kŭrmouth, –mŭth), urban district (1931 pop. 4,789; 1951 census 5,234), W Cumberland, England, on Derwent R. at mouth of Cocker R., 23 mi. SW of Carlisle; textile industry (woolen weaving, linen-thread spinning); shoe mfg. Has ruins of 11th-cent. castle (prison of Mary Queen of Scots) and Pap Castle (with remains of Roman camp). Wordsworth b. here.

Cocker River, Cumberland, England, rises in the Cumbrians 7 mi. SW of Keswick, flows 15 mi. NW to the Derwent at Cockermouth. Flows through Buttermere and Crummock Water.

Cockeysville (kŏ'kēzvĭl), village, Baltimore co., N Md., near Loch Raven Reservoir, 13 mi. N of downtown Baltimore, in dairying area; makes wood products, cans vegetables; marble quarries near. Gunpowder Meeting House (Quaker; built 1773) is near.

Cockington, England: see TORQUAY.

Cockpen, parish (pop. 6,159), E Midlothian, Scotland. Includes ARNISTON ENGINE.

Cockpit Country, hilly region (c.200 sq. mi.), W central Jamaica, on S boundary of Trelawny parish. Composed of limestone rock with many sinks and caverns, it is known for its wild scenery. Rises to c.2,700 ft. Stronghold of maroons.

Cockrell Hill, city (pop. 2,207), Dallas co., N Texas, W suburb of Dallas.

Cockscomb Mountains, NE spur of Maya Mts. in central Br. Honduras; 10 mi. long (E–W); rise to 3,681 ft. in Victoria Peak, 30 mi. SW of Stann Creek. Lumbering. Summer resort region.

Cockspur Island, Chatham co., SE Ga., in mouth of Savannah R., bet. Tybee Isl. and Savannah. At E end is Fort Pulaski (built 1829–47), seized by Ga. troops (1861), captured (1862) by Union force; with surrender of fort, after 2-day bombardment in which rifled canon were used for 1st time, Federals gained control of Savannah. It is now Fort Pulaski Natl. Monument (□ 8.4; established 1924). During Second World War, fort was naval and coast-guard base.

Coclé (kōklā'), province (□ 1,354; 1950 pop. 72,-670), Panama, on Gulf of Panama of the Pacific; ⊙ Penonomé. Drained by the Río Grande and small streams descending from Coclé Mts. (N). Agr. (sugar cane, vegetables, corn, rice, coffee), stock raising. Hat making. Served by Inter-American Highway. Main centers are Penonomé, Aguadulce, Río Hato, and Antón. Formed 1855.

Coclé del Norte (dĕl nôr'tā), village (pop. 96), Colón prov., central Panama, minor port on Caribbean Sea, at mouth of Coclé del Norte R., and 17 mi. WSW of Donoso. Corn, rice, beans, coconuts; stock raising. Lead and mercury deposits.

Coclé del Norte River, Colón prov., central Panama, rises in continental divide 6 mi. WNW of La Pintada (Coclé prov.), flows c.50 mi. N to Caribbean Sea at Coclé del Norte. Navigable for 10-ft. draught 11 mi. upstream.

Coco, Cayo (kī'ō kō'kō), coral island (25 mi. long E-W, up to 8 mi. wide) off E Cuba, in Old Bahama Channel, 25 mi. N of Morón; separated by narrow strait from Cayo Romano (E). Low and swampy. Fishing. Belongs to Camagüey Archipelago.

Coco, El, Costa Rica: see EL COCO.

Cocoa, city (pop. 4,245), Brevard co., central Fla., c.40 mi. ESE of Orlando and on Indian R. lagoon; citrus-fruit shipping center, and resort. Inc. 1895. On Cape Canaveral, 15 mi. NE, is a military proving ground for guided missiles.

Cocoa Beach, resort town (pop. 246), Brevard co., central Fla., on barrier beach bet. Banana R. and the Atlantic, 8 mi. ESE of Cocoa.

Cocobeach, village, NW Gabon, Fr. Equatorial Africa, small port on Gulf of Guinea at mouth of Río Muni, opposite Kogo (Sp. Guinea); coconut plantations.

Coco Channel (kō'kō), seaway connecting Bay of Bengal (W) and Andaman Sea (E), bet. Coco Isls. (N) and N.Andaman Isl. (S).

Cocochillo, Peru: see CAMPORREDONDO.

Coco Islands, group of small isls. in E Bay of Bengal, N of Andaman Isls., lying (c.14°N) bet. Coco Channel (S) and Preparis South Channel (N).

Cocoli (kō'kūlē), village (pop. 1,240), Balboa dist., S Panama Canal Zone, on road to Miraflores, 3 mi. NW of Balboa; corn, rice, forage; livestock.

Cocoli River, Port. Guinea: see CORUBAL RIVER.

Coconino (kōkūnē'nō), county (□ 18,573; pop. 23,910), N Ariz.; ⊙ Flagstaff. Plateau and mesa area; highest elevation reached in SAN FRANCISCO PEAKS. Includes GRAND CANYON NATIONAL PARK and parts of GRAND CANYON NATIONAL MONUMENT, Hoover Dam Recreational Area, and Truxton Canyon Indian Reservation, which are on Colorado R. The PAINTED DESERT extends along right bank of Little Colorado R. Wupatki, Sunset Crater, and Walnut Canyon natl. monuments are in the co., as are parts of Navajo and Hopi Indian reservations. Lumber, stock, beans, potatoes; tourist trade. Formed 1891. 2d largest co. in U.S.

Coconino Plateau, high tableland (c.6,000 ft.) in N Ariz., S of Colorado R. and Grand Canyon. Extends throughout much of Coconino co. and includes natl. forest areas.

Coconucos, Los, Colombia: see LOS COCONUCOS.

Coconut Island, Hawaii: see HILO BAY.

Cocopás, Sierra de los (syĕ'rä dā lōs kōkōpäs'), precipitous range in N Lower California, NW Mexico, 10 mi. SW of Mexicali; extends c.40 mi. SE from U.S. border, E of Laguna Salada and Hardy R., S of Imperial Valley; rises to 3,475 ft. Sulphur deposits. Sometimes spelled Cucopas.

Cocorite (kō'kūrīt), W suburb of Port of Spain, NW Trinidad, B.W.I., seaplane base on the Gulf of Paria.

Coco River (kō'kō), N Nicaragua, rises near San Marcos de Colón (Honduras), flows over 300 mi. ENE, past Ocotal, Telpaneca, Bocay, Sansang, and Huaspán, to Caribbean Sea at Cabo Gracias a Dios, here forming a delta with several isls. and 3 main channels. Receives Jícaro and Poteca rivers (left), Estelí, Bocay, and Huaspuc rivers (right). A potential commercial route, it traverses remote undeveloped tropical forests and serves mainly for timber floating. Navigable for 140 mi. below Sansang (end of rapids in middle course). Has auriferous sands. Coco R. below Poteca R. confluence is claimed by Honduras as its international border with Nicaragua. Formerly called Segovia R. and Wanks R.

Cocorote (kōkōrō'tā), town (pop. 2,825), Yaracuy state, N Venezuela, in foothills of coastal range, 3 mi. SW of San Felipe, in agr. region (coffee, cacao, sugar cane, corn, tobacco, stock); has marble deposits.

Cocos Island (kō'kōs), Sp. *Isla del Coco* (ē'slä dĕl kō'kō), island (□ 10.4) in the Pacific, c.300 mi. SW of Osa Peninsula of Costa Rica, to whom it belongs; 5°30'N 87°W; 5 mi. long, 3 mi. wide; rises to 2,800 ft. Geologically a N outlier of the Galápagos Isls., Cocos Isl. has two natural harbors (Wafer and Chatham bays) on N coast. The reputed site of buried treasures, it has been the goal in the past of several fruitless expeditions.

Cocos Islands (kō'kōs) or **Keeling Islands,** isolated coral island group (□ 1.5; pop. 1,814) of Singapore crown colony, in Indian Ocean, 800 mi. WSW of Singapore; 11°50'–12°45'S 96°50'E. The largest of the 27 isls. are West Isl. (5 mi. long, ¼ mi. wide) with airstrip, Home Isl. (1¼ mi. long) with principal settlement, and Direction Isl. (1½ mi. long) with cable station. Pop. (almost all Malays) is employed in coconut plantations. Copra is the only export. Discovered 1609 by Br. Capt. Keeling; declared Br. possession, 1857. Attached 1878 to Ceylon, 1882 to Straits Settlements, inc. 1903 into Settlement of Singapore. In 1951 the isls. were transferred to Australia for development as a base for civil aviation. Were an important air base in Second World War. Isls. were granted in perpetuity (1886) to Scottish Ross family that had first settled there in 1827. Charles Darwin based his coral-reef formation theory on observations made during visit here, 1836. Sometimes called Cocos-Keeling Isls.

Coco Solo (kō"kū sō'lū), naval air station, Cristobal dist., N Panama Canal Zone, on Manzanillo Bay of the Caribbean, on railroad and 1½ mi. NE of Colón. Coco Solito town (pop. 1,303) is near by.

Cocotitlán (kōkōtētlän'), town (pop. 2,369), Mexico state, central Mexico, 23 mi. SE of Mexico city; cereals, vegetables, livestock.

Cocuina, Caño (kä'nyō kōkwē'nä), arm of Orinoco R. delta, Delta Amacuro territory, NE Venezuela; branches off from Caño Pedernales 13 mi. N of Tucupita, flows c.50 mi. N to the Atlantic at Serpent's Mouth.

Cocula (kōkōō'lä). **1** Town (pop. 1,956), Guerrero, SW Mexico, on affluent of the Río de las Balsas and 11 mi. SW of Iguala, on railroad; cereals, sugar cane, tobacco, tropical fruit. **2** City (pop. 7,706), Jalisco, W Mexico, on central plateau, on railroad and 35 mi. SW of Guadalajara; alt. 4,330 ft.; orange-growing center; wheat, sugar cane, beans, alfalfa, livestock.

Cocuy, El, town, Colombia: see EL COCUY.

Cocuy, Piedra del, or **Piedra del Cucuy** (pyā'drä dĕl kōkwē', kōō–), peak (1,516 ft.) at Brazil–Colombia–Venezuela border, on left bank of Río Negro and 50 mi. SSE of San Carlos (Venezuela); 1°14'N 66°49'W.

Cocuy, Sierra Nevada de (syĕ'rä nävä'dä dā), massif (18,021 ft.) in Boyacá dept., central Colombia, highest in Cordillera Oriental, 70 mi. SE of Bucaramanga, 175 mi. NE of Bogotá; snow-covered formation extending 15 mi. N–S.

Cod, Cape, Mass.: see CAPE COD.

Codaesti or **Codaesti-Targ** (kôdŭyĕsh'tĭ-tŭrg'), Rum. *Codăeşti-Târg,* village (pop. 2,207), Jassy prov., E Rumania, 15 mi. N of Vaslui; agr. center. The 15th-cent. Dobrovat Monastery is 7 mi. N.

Codajás (kōdäzhäs'), city (pop. 1,102), central Amazonas, Brazil, steamer and hydroplane landing on left bank of the Amazon, and 150 mi. WSW of Manaus; rubber, sugar, manioc, Brazil nuts. Also called Codajaz.

Codegua (kōdā'gwä), village (1930 pop. 729), O'Higgins prov., central Chile, 9 mi. NNE of Rancagua, in agr. area (grain, alfalfa, potatoes, cattle).

Codera Cape (kōdā'rä), headland on the Caribbean, N Venezuela, 60 mi. E of Caracas; 10°35'N 66°4'W.

Coderre, village (pop. 201), S Sask., 40 mi. WSW of Moose Jaw; wheat.

Codicote (kŭ'dĭkŭt), village and parish (pop. 1,441), W central Hertford, England, 8 mi. NW of Hertford; sand and gravel quarrying; asphalt mfg. Has 14th-cent. church.

Codigoro (kôdēgô'rô), town (pop. 5,692), Ferrara prov., Emilia-Romagna, N central Italy, on delta mouth of Po R. and 16 mi. S of Adria, in reclamation project area. Agr. center; beet-sugar refinery, flour and paper mills, cellulose factory; peat digging. Has large pumping works connected with canal system (over 100 mi. long) used to drain more than 125,000 acres of land.

Codihué, Chile: see ABTAO ISLAND.

Codington (kŏ'dĭngtŭn), county (□ 691; pop. 18,944), E S.Dak.; ⊙ Watertown. Agr. area drained by Big Sioux R.; has numerous lakes; includes S extremity of Sisseton Indian Reservation. Mfg. at Watertown; dairy products, poultry, corn, potatoes, soybeans, artichokes. Formed 1877.

Cod Island or **Ogualik Island** (ōgwä'lĭk) (11 mi. long, 10 mi. wide), NE Labrador; 57°45'N 61°45'W. Kaumajet Mts., rising to 4,000 ft., cover entire surface of isl.

Codlea (kôd'lēä), Ger. *Zeiden* (tsī'dŭn), Hung. *Feketehalom* (fĕ'kĕtĕhälôm), village (pop. 6,214), Stalin prov., central Rumania, in Transylvania, on railroad and 8 mi. NW of Stalin (Brasov); climatic resort in SW foothills of the Carpathians; mfg. of cloth, knitwear, soap, bricks, pottery; woodworking, food processing. Also floricultural center (greenhouses). Has noted 17th-cent. fortified church with 4 towers, partly destroyed. Large Ger. pop.

Codó (kōōdô'), city (pop. 3,405), E central Maranhão, Brazil, on São Luís–Teresina RR, on Itapecuru R. and 135 mi. SSE of São Luís; agr. trade center noted for its tobacco; cotton milling. Airfield. Bituminous schist deposits in area.

Codogno (kôdô'nyô), town (pop. 9,258), Milano prov., Lombardy, N Italy, 15 mi. SE of Lodi, bet. Adda and Po rivers. Rail junction; agr. and commercial center; dairy products, cattle feed; flour, silk, and cotton mills, cosmetic and candy factories.

Codosera, La (lä kō-dhōsä'rä), town (pop. 1,438), Badajoz prov., W Spain, just off Port. border, 25 mi. NNW of Badajoz; cereals, vegetables, fruit, olives, timber, livestock.

Codpa (kōd'pä), village (pop. 79), Tarapacá prov., N Chile, on Andean plateau, 45 mi. SE of Arica.

Codri, Moldavian SSR: see KODRY.

Codrington (kŏ'drĭngtŭn), village, central Barbuda, B.W.I., 37 mi. N of St. John's, Antigua; 17°38'N 61°50'W.

Codroipo (kôdrôē'pô), town (pop. 2,938), Udine prov., Friuli–Venezia Giulia, NE Italy, 14 mi. SW of Udine; agr. machinery, woolen textiles, organs, macaroni, liquor.

Cody (kō'dē). **1** Village (pop. 296), Cherry co., N Nebr., 35 mi. W of Valentine, near S.Dak. line; trading center for Rosebud Indian Reservation, S.Dak.; grain, cattle. Recreation area near by. **2** Town (pop. 3,872), ⊙ Park co., NW Wyo., on Shoshone R., just E of Absaroka Range, and 90 mi. SSW of Billings, Mont.; alt. c.5,000 ft. Tourist stop; oil-refining point in irrigated livestock and agr. area. Oil wells near by. Hq. of Shoshone Natl. Forest. Statue and former home of Col. William F. Cody (Buffalo Bill) are here; annual Frontier ball celebrates his birthday. Near by are Shoshone Cavern Natl. Monument, Shoshone Dam and Reservoir (of Shoshone irrigation project), Shoshone Canyon, and Shoshone Natl. Forest. Yellowstone Natl. Park is 55 mi. W. Platted c.1895, inc. 1901.

Coeburn, coal-mining town (pop. 760), Wise co., SW Va., 7 mi. SE of Wise; rail junction.

Coedffranc (koidfrängk'), parish (pop. 9,930), W Glamorgan, Wales, 3 mi. SW of Neath; coal and copper mining.

Coelemu (koilā'mōō), town (pop. 2,824), Concepción prov., S central Chile, on Itata R. and 30 mi. NE of Concepción; rail junction in agr. area (grain, wine, vegetables, livestock); flour milling, lumber.

Coele-Syria, Lebanon: see BEKAA.

Coelho da Rocha (kwā'lyōō dŭ rô'shŭ), NW suburb (1950 pop. 21,539) of Rio de Janeiro, Brazil, in Rio de Janeiro state, on federal dist. border.

Coelho Neto (kwā'lyōō nĕ'tōō), city (pop. 641), E Maranhão, Brazil, near left bank of Parnaíba R. (Piauí border), 50 mi. NNE of Caxias; ships babassu nuts, cotton, leather, lumber. Until 1939, called Curralinho.

Coen, village, N Queensland, Australia, on SE Cape York Peninsula, 265 mi. NW of Cairns; gold mine; cattle.

Coeneo (kwānā'ō), officially Coeneo de la Libertad, town (pop. 2,450), Michoacán, central Mexico, 30 mi. WNW of Morelia; cereals, fruit, livestock.

Coe River, Scotland: see GLENCOE.

Coeroeni River, Du. Guiana: see COURANTYNE RIVER.

Coesfeld (kōs'fĕlt″), town (pop. 12,053), in former Prussian prov. of Westphalia, NW Germany, after 1945 in North Rhine-Westphalia, on Berkel R. and 29 mi. W of Münster; rail junction; mfg. of linen, cotton, machinery; tanning, dairying. Has 17th-cent. church. Was member of Hanseatic League. Town almost completely destroyed in Second World War. Formerly also spelled Koesfeld.

Coëtivy Island (kwĕtēvē'), outlying dependency (pop. 167) of the Seychelles, in Indian Ocean, 650 mi. NE of N tip of Madagascar and 190 mi. SSE of Mahé Isl. (in Seychelles proper); 7°10'S 56°16'E; 7 mi. long, 2 mi. wide. Of coral origin. Copra; fisheries. Settlement on W coast. Formerly a dependency of Mauritius, it was transferred (1907) to the Seychelles.

Coëtquidan, France: see GUER.

Coëtzala (kwātsä'lä), town (pop. 638), Veracruz, E Mexico, 7 mi. S of Córdoba; coffee, fruit.

Coeur d'Alene (kûr dŭlān'), city (pop. 12,198), ⊙ Kootenai co., N Idaho, on N shore of Coeur d'Alene L. and 30 mi. E of Spokane, Wash. Woodworking center (lumber, shingles, railroad ties, boats) in mining (lead, silver, zinc) and irrigated agr. area; flour, dairy products, beverages. Hq. for Coeur d'Alene Natl. Forest (summer resort and winter-sports region in near-by Coeur d'Alene Mts.). Has steamboat connections. Founded in late 1870s as military outpost, inc. as city 1906. Growth followed discovery (1882) of lead and silver in vicinity and mining boom of 1884.

Coeur d'Alene Lake, Kootenai co., N Idaho, 25 mi. E of Spokane, Wash.; 24 mi. long, 1–3 mi. wide. Fed by Coeur d'Alene and St. Joe rivers, drained by Spokane R. Has small isl. in S half. City of Coeur d'Alene is at N end of lake.

Coeur d'Alene Mountains, N Idaho, extend S along Mont. line from Pend Oreille L. to St. Joe R., largely in Shoshone co. Coeur d'Alene Natl. Forest extends throughout most of range. Chief elevations (6–7,000 ft.) are in E. Coeur d'Alene mining district, including several mines in vicinity of Kellogg (smelting, refining center), is leading producer of lead, silver, and zinc.

Coeur d'Alene River, N Idaho, rises near Mont. line, flows SE, then WSW, to Coeur d'Alene L. at Harrison; c.110 mi. long.

Coevorden or **Koevorden** (both: kōō'vôrdûn), town (pop. 4,686), Drenthe prov., NE Netherlands, on Overijssel Canal and 24 mi. SSE of Assen, near Ger. border; center of petroleum industry (wells at OUD SCHOONEBEEK); mfg. (soap, potato flour, strawboard, cardboard, shirts); dairying, peat production; cattle and pig market. Played important part in 16th-cent. religious struggles.

Coevorden-Piccardie Canal (–pĭ'kärdē), in NW Germany and NE Netherlands, extends 15 mi. bet. Coevorden and Georgsdorf, linking Overijssel and Süd-Nord canals.

Coëvrons Hills (kôĕvrō'), Mayenne and Sarthe depts., W France, extend c.20 mi. WSW-ENE in a wooded ridge N of Sillé-le-Guillaume; rise to 900 ft.

Coeymans (kwē'mŭnz), village (1940 pop. 1,055), Albany co., E N.Y., on W bank of the Hudson and 12 mi. S of Albany; brickmaking.

Coffee. **1** County (□ 677; pop. 30,720), SE Ala.; ⊙ Elba and Enterprise. Coastal plain region drained by Pea R. Cotton, peanuts, hogs, timber; textiles. Formed 1841. **2** County (□ 613; pop. 23,961), S central Ga.; ⊙ Douglas. Bounded N by Ocmulgee R. Coastal plain farming (tobacco, cotton, corn, peanuts, livestock) and lumbering area drained by Satilla R. Formed 1854. **3** County (□ 435; pop. 23,049), central Tenn.; ⊙ Manchester. Partly in the Cumberlands; bounded SE by Elk R., drained by Duck R. Timber tracts, coal deposits. Agr. (corn, soybeans, tobacco, potatoes), livestock, dairying. Formed 1846.

Coffeen (kô'fēn), village (pop. 627), Montgomery co., S central Ill., 15 mi. ESE of Litchfield, in agr. and bituminous-coal area.

Coffee Springs, town (pop. 173), Geneva co., SE Ala., 33 mi. WSW of Dothan.

Coffeeville. **1** Town (pop. 211), Clarke co., SW Ala., near Tombigbee R., 75 mi. N of Mobile. **2** Town (pop. 739), a ⊙ Yalobusha co., N central Miss., 15 mi. NNE of Grenada.

Coffey, county (□ 656; pop. 10,408), E Kansas; ⊙ Burlington. Rolling plains area, drained by Neosho R. Livestock, grain; timber. Scattered oil fields in S. Formed 1859.

Coffeyville, city (pop. 17,113), Montgomery co., SE Kansas, on Verdigris R., near Okla. line, and 55 mi. W of Joplin, Mo.; trade, rail, and shipping center for agr. and oil-producing region. Flour milling, oil refining, meat processing; mfg. of gas and oil supplies, roofing, mattresses; smelting, wood planing. Has co. fairgrounds, and Coffeyville Col. Settled 1869, inc. 1872. Grew as cattle center after coming of railroad (1870), boomed with discovery (1902) of oil and natural gas in vicinity. In 1892 the Dalton gang was shot down here during attempted bank robbery.

Coffin Bay, inlet of Great Australian Bight; formed by W projection of SW Eyre Peninsula, South Australia; 8 mi. E–W, 6 mi. N–S. Opens into Port Douglas (S).

Coffin Island (4 mi. long, 1 mi. wide), in the Gulf of St. Lawrence, E Que., one of the Magdalen Isls., 80 mi. NNE of Prince Edward Isl.; 47°33'N 61°31'W.

Coff's Harbour, town and port (pop. 2,966), E New South Wales, Australia, on small inlet, 125 mi. NNE of Newcastle; dairying center; exports gold, dairy products.

Cofre de Perote, Mexico: see PEROTE, COFRE DE.

Cofrentes (kōfrĕn'tĕs), town (pop. 1,495), Valencia prov., E Spain, on Júcar R. and 19 mi. SSE of Requena; olive-oil processing; fruit, sheep, lumber. Mineral springs.

Cogalnic River, USSR: see KOGALNIK RIVER.

Cogealac (kôjä'läk), village (pop. 2,720), Constanta prov., SE Rumania, 26 mi. NNW of Constanta.

Cogeces del Monte (kōhā'thĕs dhĕl mōn'tā), town (pop. 1,476), Valladolid prov., N central Spain, 23 mi. ESE of Valladolid; cereals, wine, sugar beets.

Coggeshall (kŏ'gĭ-shûl, kŏk'sûl), town in Great Coggeshall parish (pop. 2,259), N central Essex, England, on Blackwater R. and 9 mi. W of Colchester; agr. market. Has 15th-cent. church and remains of Cistercian abbey (c.1140).

Coggiola (kôd'jôlä), village (pop. 1,950), Vercelli prov., Piedmont, N Italy, 10 mi. NE of Biella; woolen mills, foundry.

Coggon (kô'gŭn), town (pop. 604), Linn co., E Iowa, on Buffalo Creek and 22 mi. NNE of Cedar Rapids; dairy products.

Coghinas, Lake (kôgē'näs), artificial lake (□ 7.5) in Sassari prov., N Sardinia, 24 mi. E of Sassari; 10 mi. long, 3 mi. wide. Formed 1926 by 170-ft.-high masonry dam (site of hydroelectric plant) at N end. Inlets include MANNU D'OZIERI RIVER (S) and MANNU D'OSCHIRI RIVER (E). Outlet: COGHINAS RIVER (N).

Coghinas River, Sassari prov., N Sardinia, rises in L. Coghinas, flows c.25 mi. NNW to Gulf of Asinara 5 mi. E of Castel Sardo.

Coglians, Monte, on Austro-Ital. border: see KELLERWAND.

Cognac (kōn'yăk, kŏn'–, Fr. kônyäk'), town (pop. 16,106), Charente dept., W France, on Charente R. and 23 mi. W of Angoulême; leading distillery and export center of Fr. brandy, to which it has given its name; mfg. of winegrowing equipment, barrels, bottles. First brandy entrepôt established here in 1643. Birthplace of Francis I, who formed here (1526) alliance against Charles V. Huguenot stronghold in 16th cent. Near-by Jarnac and Segonzac also noted for their brandy.

Cogne (kô'nyĕ), village (pop. 617), Val d'Aosta region, NW Italy, 9 mi. S of Aosta, hydroelectric plant. Its rich iron mines supply iron and steel industry of Aosta. Resort (alt. 5,032 ft.) in scenic Val de Cogne (16 mi. long) of Gran Paradiso area, watered by small affluent of Dora Baltea R.

Cognin (kônyē'), W suburb (pop. 2,425) of Chambéry, Savoie dept., SE France; cutlery mfg., woodworking.

Cogoleto (kôgôlā'tô), village (pop. 2,147), Genova prov., Liguria, N Italy, port on Gulf of Genoa and 14 mi. W of Genoa; olive oil, dyes, fertilizer, paper. Quarries (serpentine, quartz) near by.

Cogolin (kôgôlē'), village (pop. 1,831), Var dept., SE France, on E slope of Monts des Maures, 6 mi. WSW of Saint-Tropez, near the Mediterranean; mfg. (rugs, olive oil, cork, pipes), winegrowing.

Cogollo del Cengio (kôgôl'lô dĕl chĕn'jô), village (pop. 1,185), Vicenza prov., Veneto, N Italy, on Astico R. and 6 mi. NNW of Thiene; shoe factory, woolen dyeworks.

Cogollos de Guadix (kōgō'lyōs dhā gwä-dhēks'), town (pop. 1,343), Granada prov., S Spain, 5 mi. SSW of Guadix; sheep; sugar beets, cereals. Iron mines.

Cogollos-Vega (–vā'gä), village (pop. 2,067), Granada prov., S Spain, 7 mi. NNE of Granada; olive-oil processing, flour milling, soap mfg. Summer resort.

Cogolludo (kōgōlyōō'dhō), town (pop. 785), Guadalajara prov., central Spain, 22 mi. N of Guadalajara, in fertile valley; cereals, olives, potatoes, sheep. Flour milling, mfg. of textile goods and pottery; alabaster quarrying. Anc. town, with 16th-cent. palace; also ruined castle.

Cogswell, village (pop. 393), Sargent co., SE N.Dak., 15 mi. E of Oakes; grain, livestock, dairy products.

Cogtong (kōgtōng'), town (1939 pop. 2,706) in Candijay municipality, E Bohol isl., Philippines, on small inlet of Canigao Channel, 50 mi. ENE of Tagbilaran; agr. center (rice, coconuts).

Cohansey Creek (kōhăn'zē), SW N.J., rises in SE Salem co., flows c.35 mi. S, past Bridgeton, and W to Delaware Bay. Navigable to Bridgeton. Chief freight: garden truck, seafood.

Cohasset. **1** (kōhă'sĭt) Town (pop. 3,731), including Cohasset village (pop. 2,009), in exclave of Norfolk co. in Plymouth co., E Mass., on Massachusetts Bay and 16 mi. SE of Boston; summer resort with summer theater; boatbuilding. Minots Ledge (mī'nŭts) lighthouse maintained offshore since 1850. Settled c.1647, inc. 1770. Includes village of North Cohasset. **2** (kōhă'sĭt) Village (pop. 484), Itasca co., N central Minn., on Mississippi R., 6 mi. WNW of Grand Rapids, and W of Mesabi iron range in lake and resort region; grain, potatoes.

Cohetzala (kōätsä'lä), officially Santa María Cohetzala, town (pop. 421), Puebla, central Mexico, on affluent of Atoyac R. and 37 mi. SW of Matamoros; corn, stock.

Cohocton (kûhŏk'tŭn, kō–), village (pop. 943), Steuben co., W central N.Y., on Cohocton R. and 15 mi. NNE of Hornell, in agr. area; flour, dairy products; sand and gravel. Summer resort.

Cohocton River, W central and S N.Y., rises in Livingston co., flows c.55 mi. generally SE, past Bath, joining the Tioga to form the Chemung at Painted Post.

Cohoes (kûhōz'), industrial city (pop. 21,272), Albany co., E N.Y., on W bank of the Hudson at mouth of the Mohawk (whose falls supply power), on the Barge Canal and 8 mi. N of Albany; knit goods, clothing, paper, wood products, machinery, brick, blankets, buttons, brushes. Boatbuilding (tugs, barges); railroad shops. Van Schaick mansion (1735) has historic relics. Settled by Dutch; inc. 1869.

Cohuna (kûhū'nû), town (pop. 1,278), N Victoria, Australia, 140 mi. NNW of Melbourne, near New South Wales border; rail terminus; livestock center.

Coi, Song, Vietnam: see RED RIVER.

Coiba Island (kwē'bä) (pop. 224), in Pacific Ocean, Veraguas prov., SW Panama, 15 mi. offshore, 35 mi. SW of Soná; 20 mi. long, 6 mi. wide; rises to 1,400 ft. Has observatory and federal penitentiary. Sometimes called Quibo Isl.

Coig River, Argentina: see COYLE RIVER.

Coigüe, Chile: see COIHÜE.

Coihüe or **Coigüe** (both: koiwā'), village (1930 pop. 138), Bío-Bío prov., S central Chile, on Bío-Bío R. and 15 mi. SW of Los Angeles; rail junction in agr. area (grain, peas, wine).

Coihueco (koiwā'kō), town (pop. 1,617), Ñuble prov., S central Chile, on railroad and 16 mi. E of Chillán; agr. (grain, vegetables, fruit, wine, livestock); lumbering, dairying.

Coilum, India: see QUILON.

Coimbatore (koĭm'bŭtōr), Tamil *Koyambattur*, district (□ 7,121; pop. 2,809,648), SW Madras, India; ⊙ Coimbatore. Crossed (N) by S Eastern Ghats; bordered E by Cauvery R.; Palghat Gap in SW. Fertile central plain is an important cotton area; also rice, millet, sugar cane, tobacco, peanuts. Tea, coffee, rubber, and cinchona plantations in Anaimalai Hills, on SW border. Industries mainly powered by Pykara hydroelectric system (linked at Erode with Mettur system). Construction of 160-ft. high dam (near confluence of Moyar and Bhavani rivers) and canal (to irrigate 200,000 acres) begun 1949. Main towns: Coimbatore, Erode, Tiruppur, Pollachi, Dharapuram, Kollegal.

Coimbatore, Tamil *Koyambattur*, city (pop. 130,348), ⊙ Coimbatore dist., SW Madras, India, on Noyil R. and 265 mi. SW of Madras; major cotton-textile and industrial center; silk weaving and dyeing, rice, flour, and peanut-oil milling, sugar processing; chemical (fertilizer), malt, coffee, match, and rubber factories, engineering workshops, tanneries; ceramics. Industries powered by PYKARA hydroelectric system (main receiving station here). Govt. col. and agr. col. (both affiliated with Madras Univ.). Madras Forest Col. (affiliated with Forest Research Inst. at Dehra Dun, Uttar Pradesh), polytechnic and serum institutes. Rail junction of Podanur is 4 mi. SE; cotton mills. Cement and soap factories at Madukarai (or Madukkarai) village, 7 mi. SSE. Sivaite temple (mainly built in 18th cent.) just SW, at village of Perur. Commanding approaches to Palghat Gap (SW) and mtn. pass to Mysore (N), city was strategic stronghold of successive Tamil kingdoms (9th–17th cent.) and was alternately besieged by Mysore sultans and English during 18th cent.; finally ceded to English in 1799.

Coimbra (kōēm'brû), old fort on Paraguay R. in SW Mato Grosso, Brazil, 65 mi. S of Corumbá, near Bolivia border. Repelled Spaniards in 1801; taken by Paraguayans in 1864.

Coimbra, district (□ 1,527; pop. 411,677), N central Portugal, mostly in Beira Litoral prov.; ⊙ Coimbra. Bounded by the Atlantic (W), and by the Serra da Lousã (E; outlier of Serra da Estrêla). Drained by Mondego R., which enters the Atlantic at Figueira da Foz. Agr. (grain, olives, wine) in Coimbra lowland. Fishing and salt panning along coast. Industry includes paper and wool milling, sardine canning, mfg. of earthenware.

Coimbra, city (pop. 35,437), ⊙ Coimbra dist. and Beira Litoral prov., N central Portugal, on right bank of Mondego R. and 110 mi. NNE of Lisbon; a leading cultural center and seat of Portugal's oldest univ. Episcopal see. Commercial center of a fertile lowland region producing wheat, corn, olives, wine. Mfg. (ceramics, brushes, flour products). City has many fine ecclesiastical buildings, including the church of Santa Cruz, the fortress-like Romanesque former cathedral, and the Sé Nova (cathedral since 1772) built after 1580 by Jesuits. The univ. (founded 1290 at Lisbon; established here permanently in 1537) occupies former royal palace atop hill overlooking the Mondego; for 5 centuries it was Portugal's only univ. A stone bridge links Coimbra with Santa Clara, the suburb where Inés de Castro was murdered in 1355. Known as *Aeminium* under Romans. Present name derived from near-by *Conimbriga*, former episcopal see transferred here in 9th cent. City was definitively freed from the Moors in 1064 by Ferdinand I of Castile aided by the Cid; ⊙ Portugal 1139–1385, though Lisbon became chief royal residence c.1260.

Coimbrões (kwẽmbrõ'ĭsh), S suburb (pop. 4,146) of Oporto, Pôrto dist., N Portugal, on left bank of Douro R.

Coín (kōēn'), city (pop. 9,631), Málaga prov., S Spain, in Andalusia, in S outliers of the Cordillera Penibética, 19 mi. W of Málaga (linked by rail). Picturesquely set in hilly country surrounded by vineyards and orchards (oranges, olives, figs, lemons). Trading and processing center; olive-oil pressing, flour milling, tanning; mfg. of food preserves, leatherwork, fiber articles, soap, shoes, cork products, tiles. Marble quarries in vicinity. Has old bishop's palace.

Coin, town (pop. 407), Page co., SW Iowa, near Tarkio R., 10 mi. SE of Shenandoah; rail junction.

Coinco (koing'kō), town (pop. 1,290), O'Higgins prov., central Chile, 15 mi. SW of Rancagua; agr. (wheat, oats, fruit, wine, livestock); flour milling, dairying, lumbering.

Coinjock, village, Currituck co., extreme NE N.C., 14 mi. E of Elizabeth City, on Albemarle and Chesapeake Canal; ships melons; sawmilling. Resort (hunting, fishing).

Cointrin (kwäntrē'), international airport in SW Switzerland, 3 mi. NW of Geneva.

Coipasa, Lake (koipä'sä), N part of Salar de Coipasa, Oruro dept., W Bolivia, in the Altiplano, 95 mi. SW of Oruro; 20 mi. long, 10 mi. wide; alt. 12,073 ft. Receives Lacahahuira (outlet of L. Poopó), Barras, and Lauca rivers.

Coipasa, Salar de (sälär' dā), second largest salt flat of Bolivia, in Oruro dept., W Bolivia, on Chilean border, in the Altiplano, and c.100 mi. SW of Oruro; 55 mi. long, 20–30 mi. wide; alt. c.12,000 ft. Receives Sabaya R. N section constitutes L. Coipasa; Coipasa peak (16,080 ft.) rises on isl. (W).

Coire, Switzerland: see CHUR.

Coiron, Monts du (mõ dü kwärõ'), volcanic spur of the Monts du Vivarais, in Ardèche dept., S France, extending 28 mi. SE from Mont GERBIER DE JONC to the Rhone at Rochemaure. Rises to 3,481 ft. 6 mi. W of Privas. Chestnut trees on slopes. Also called Chaîne des Coirons.

Coité, Brazil: see PARIPIRANGA.

Coity Higher, town and parish (pop. 2,501), S central Glamorgan, Wales, 2 mi. NE of Bridgend; agr. market. Has 13th-cent. castle, 14th-cent. church. Near by is megalithic tomb.

Coixtlahuaca (koisläwä'kä), town (pop. 2,596), Oaxaca, S Mexico, in Sierra Madre del Sur, 20 mi. NNW of Nochixtlán; alt. 6,988 ft.; cereals, beans, sugar cane, coffee, fruit.

Coja (kō'zhù), village (pop. 1,040), Coimbra dist., N central Portugal, 24 mi. ENE of Coimbra; resin extracting.

Cojedes (kōhā'dĕs), state (□ 5,710; 1941 pop. 49,-769; 1950 census pop. 52,022), N Venezuela; ⊙ San Carlos. Largely a llanos area; watered by secondary tributaries of Orinoco R. Has hot, humid climate; rainy season (May–Sept.). Principally a cattle-grazing region; produces sugar cane, cotton, corn, yuca, fruit; coffee plantations in N hills. Rich forests yield fine timber (cedar, carob, etc.) and vegetable fibers. Tinaquillo and San Carlos are its market centers.

Cojedes, town (pop. 198), Cojedes state, N Venezuela, landing on Cojedes R. and 23 mi. W of San Carlos; cattle raising.

Cojedes River, NW Venezuela, rises as Barquisimeto R. in Andean spur S of Barquisimeto, flows c.130 mi. SE, past Cojedes, Amparo, and El Baúl, to Portuguesa R. 13 mi. SSE of El Baúl. Navigable for small craft.

Cojímar (kōhē'mär), town (pop. 1,846), Havana prov., W Cuba, at mouth of small Cojímar R., 4 mi. ENE of Havana; summer resort; fishing. Cable station. Its fort (built 1646) was taken by English forces in 1762.

Cojocna (kôzhôk'nä), Ger. *Salzgrub* (zälts'grŏŏp), Hung. *Kolozs* (kô'lôsh), village (pop. 3,488), Cluj prov., W central Rumania, on railroad and 11 mi. ESE of Cluj; bathing resort on a salt lake; stud farm. In Hungary, 1940–45.

Cojumatlán (kōhōōmätlän'), town (pop. 3,666), Michoacán, central Mexico, on SE shore of L. Chapala and 17 mi. SSW of Ocotlán; cereals, fruit, livestock; lumbering.

Cojutepeque (kōhōōtāpā'kā), city (1950 pop. 10,-005), ⊙ Cuscatlán dept., Salvador, at N foot of volcano Cojutepeque or Las Pavas (recreation park), on railroad and Inter-American Highway, 17 mi. ENE of San Salvador; alt. 2,874 ft.; 13°44'N 88°56'W. Major market center; sugar milling, liquor distilling, cotton milling; agr. (sugar cane, coffee, grain). Cattle fair. Was ⊙ Salvador, 1834 and 1854; became ⊙ dept. in 1863.

Coka or **Choka** (chô'kä), Serbo-Croatian *Čoka*, Hung. *Csóka* (chō'kŏ), village, Vojvodina, N Serbia, Yugoslavia, on railroad, near Tisa R., opposite (3 mi. ENE) of Senta; meat packing. Tobacco growing in vicinity.

Cokato (kōkā'tō), village (pop. 1,403), Wright co., S central Minn., near small lake, c.45 mi. W of Minneapolis; trading and shipping point in agr. area; dairy products, flour, canned corn, beverages. Platted 1869, inc. 1878.

Coke, county (□ 915; pop. 4,045), W Texas; ⊙ Robert Lee. Colorado R. crosses NW–SE; alt. c.2,000 ft. Ranching area (sheep, goats, beef cattle); some hogs, poultry, dairying, agr. (grain sorghums, peanuts, fruit, truck, cotton). Some oil, natural gas, limestone, clay. Formed 1889.

Cokeburg, industrial borough (pop. 1,170), Washington co., SW Pa., 10 mi. ESE of Washington. Inc. 1906.

Cokedale, village (pop. 214), Las Animas co., S Colo., on Purgatoire R., near N.Mex. line, and 7 mi. WSW of Trinidad, in coal-mining region; alt. 6,350 ft.; coke.

Cokeville. **1** Village (1940 pop. 549), Westmoreland co., SW central Pa., on Conemaugh R. opposite Blairsville. **2** Town (pop. 440), Lincoln co., SW Wyo., on Bear R., near Idaho line, and 29 mi. NW of Kemmerer; alt. c.6,190 ft. Ranching, dairying; sheep, wool.

Coki (kō'kē), village, NW Senegal, Fr. West Africa, on railroad and 45 mi. SE of Saint-Louis; peanut growing. Sometimes spelled Coky or Koki.

Col [Fr.,=pass], for names beginning thus and not found here: see under following part of the name.

Col (tsôl), Ital. *Zolla* (tsôl'lä), village (1936 pop. 915), SW Slovenia, Yugoslavia, 26 mi. SW of Ljubljana. Until 1947, in Italy.

Colaba, India: see BOMBAY, city.

Colac (kōlăk'), municipality (pop. 6,381), S Victoria, Australia, 85 mi. WSW of Melbourne and on L. Colac (4 mi. long); rail junction in agr. (flax, potatoes) and dairying area; vegetable-dehydration and dairy plants.

Colachel or **Kolachel** (kō'lŭchĕl), city (pop. 11,377), S Travancore, India, port on Arabian Sea, 13 mi. W of Nagercoil; mfg. of coir rope and mats, copra, brushes, palmyra jaggery. Monazite and ilmenite workings near by.

Colair Lake (kōlâr'), Kistna dist., NE Madras, India, SE of Ellore, bet. Godavari and Kistna river deltas; during monsoon extends irregularly over □ c.100. Fishing (chiefly carp, prawns). Prawn processing at village of Akid or Akividu (SE, on railroad). Also spelled Kolleru.

Colán (kōlän'), village (pop. 398), Piura dept., NW Peru, minor port on the Pacific, and 7 mi. NNE of Paita (connected by railroad); salt mining, charcoal burning; vegetables.

Colangüil, Cordón de (kôrdōn' dā kōläng-gwēl'), Andean range in W San Juan prov., Argentina, NW of Rodeo; extends c.40 mi. NNE-SSW. Cerro Colangüil (29°52'S) rises to 17,160 ft.

Colares (kōlä'rĭsh), village (pop. 362), Lisboa dist., W central Portugal, near the Atlantic, 3 mi. W of Cintra; known for its table wines. Tourist center for excursions in Serra de Sintra.

Colatina (kôlätē'nù), city (pop. 3,913), central Espírito Santo, Brazil, on the Rio Doce (bridge), on railroad and 55 mi. NNW of Vitória; coffee and rice hulling, lumbering. Formerly Collatina.

Colavi (kōlä'vē), village (pop. c.3,100), Potosí dept., S central Bolivia, 21 mi. NE of Potosí, on branch of Potosí-Sucre road; alt. 11,975 ft.; tin placers. Also called San Felipe de Colavi.

Colayrac-Saint-Cirq (kōlärăk'-sē-sērk'), village (pop. 517), Lot-et-Garonne dept., SW France, on the Garonne and 3 mi. WNW of Agen; cauliflower, asparagus.

Colbeck, Cape (kōl'bĕk), headland, Antarctica, the NW tip of Edward VII Peninsula, on Ross Sea; 77°5'S 158°10'W. Discovered 1902 by R. F. Scott.

Colbert (kôlbâr'), agr. village (pop. 1,967), Constantine dept., NE Algeria, on N slope of Hodna Mts., 20 mi. SSW of Sétif; flour milling.

Colbert (kŏl'bûrt), county (□ 616; pop. 39,561), NW Ala.; ⊙ Tuscumbia. Bounded W by Miss.; in N are Pickwick Landing Reservoir and L. Wilson, both on Tennessee R. TVA developments have stimulated industry in region. Sheffield is mfg. center. There are deposits of asphalt, bauxite, and limestone. Fall line crosses co. N–S. Formed 1867.

Colbert. **1** Town (pop. 407), Madison co., NE Ga., 12 mi. ENE of Athens. **2** Town (pop. 748), Bryan co., S Okla., 12 mi. SW of Durant, near Red R. and L. Texoma. Denison Dam is 4 mi. W.

Colborne (kōl'bûrn), village (pop. 994), S Ont., on L. Ontario, 25 mi. WSW of Belleville; food canning, dairying, lumbering.

Colborne, Cape, SE Victoria Isl., SW Franklin Dist., Northwest Territories, on narrow passage bet. Dease Strait and Queen Maud Gulf, 12 mi. SSW of Cambridge Bay; 68°58'N 104°59'W.

Colbún (kōlbōōn'), village (1930 pop. 988), Linares prov., S central Chile, 16 mi. NE of Linares; rail terminus, agr. center (wheat, oats, chick-peas, wine, livestock).

Colby (kōl'bē). **1** City (pop. 3,859), ⊙ Thomas co., NW Kansas, 35 mi. E of Goodland; trading and shipping center for wheat and cattle region; mfg. (flour, butter, farm equipment). Agr. experiment station near by. Inc. 1886. **2** City (pop. 989), on Clark-Marathon co. line, central Wis., 34 mi. WSW of Wausau, in dairying region; cheese, butter, canned foods.

Colcapirhua (kōlkäpēr'wä), town (pop. c.5,000), Cochabamba dept., central Bolivia, on railroad and 6 mi. W of Cochabamba; grain, potatoes, livestock.

Colca River, Peru: see MAJES RIVER.

Colcha (kōl'chä), town (pop. 714), Cuzco dept., S Peru, 25 mi. SSE of Cuzco; wheat growing.

Colchagua (kōlchä'gwä), province (□ 3,255; 1940 pop. 131,248, 1949 estimate 136,822), central Chile, bet. the Andes and the Pacific; ⊙ San Fernando. Agr. area in the central valley, watered by Tinguiririca and Rupel rivers. Mild climate. Important corn-producing area; important also for wheat, barley, wine, cattle, sheep. Other products: potatoes, alfalfa, fruit, chick-peas. Dairying, flour milling, lumbering, wine making. On slopes of Tinguiririca Volcano are sulphur deposits. Prov. set up 1826.

Colcha "K" (kōl'chä kä'), town (pop. c.1,300), ⊙ Nor Lípez prov., Potosí dept., SW Bolivia, in the Altiplano, on S edge of Salar de Uyuni and 65 mi. WSW of Uyuni; alt. 12,697 ft.; alpaca, quinoa.

Colchester (kōl'chĭstûr), county (□ 1,451; pop. 30,124), N N.S., bet. Northumberland Strait and the Bay of Fundy; ⊙ Truro.

Colchester, municipal borough (1931 pop. 48,701; 1951 census 57,436), NE Sussex, England, on Colne R. and 50 mi. NE of London; agr. market; mfg. of agr. machinery, chemicals, boilers, shoes, cattle feed. Site of *Camulodunum*, 1st Roman colony in Britain, founded by Claudius at Colneceaster, fortified capital of Cunobelin (Shakespeare's *Cymbeline*). It was sacked by Boadicea in A.D. 62; in 931 a witenagemot met here. Town is traditionally associated with King Cole. Has Roman walls, the most complete in England; Norman castle, part of which is mus. of Roman antiquities; remains of 11th-cent. Augustinian St. Botolph's priory with Roman brickwork. In 1648 town was taken by Parliamentarians under Fairfax after long siege. It is an important military station. There are oyster fisheries in Colne R., and an annual oyster feast is held here.

Colchester. **1** (kōl'chē"stûr) Town (pop. 3,007), including Colchester borough (pop. 1,522), New London co., SE central Conn., on Salmon R. and 14 mi. WNW of Norwich; agr., mfg. (clothing, leather products, fiber board). Includes villages of North Westchester and Westchester. Settled and inc. 1699, borough inc. 1824. **2** (kōl'chē"stûr) City (pop. 1,551), McDonough co., W Ill., 6 mi. WSW of Macomb; bituminous-coal mines, clay pits; agr. (corn, wheat, hay, livestock, poultry; dairy products); mfg. (brick, tile). Inc. 1867. **3** (kōl'chĭstûr) Town (pop. 3,897), Chittenden co., NW Vt., on L. Champlain just above Burlington and Winooski; agr., dairy products. Ira Allen built mills and iron forge in area after 1783. Included Winooski until 1922.

Colchis (kŏl'kĭs), Rus. *Kolkhida* (kŭlkhē'dŭ), partly swampy lowland in W Georgian SSR, on Black Sea and along lower Rion R. Chief centers: Poti, Mikha-Tskhakaya, Samtredia. Swamp drainage and planting of moisture-absorbing eucalyptus render area malaria-free and open it to subtropical agr. (citrus fruit, tung oil). Anc. Colchis (sometimes identified with MINGRELIA) was mythical home of Medea and goal of the Argonauts.

Cold Ash, agr. village and parish (pop. 1,422), S Berkshire, England, 3 mi. NE of Newbury.

Cold Bay, inlet (20 mi. long, 4–8 mi. wide) of N Pacific in SW Alaska Peninsula, SW Alaska; 55°11'N 162°33'W. Air base, built here early in Second World War, played important part in repulse of initial Japanese attack on Aleutian Isls.

Cold Bokkeveld (bô"kŭfĕlt'), mountain range, SW Cape Prov., U. of So. Afr., at W edge of Great Karroo, extends 50 mi. NW from Hex River Mts., rises to 6,811 ft. on Great Winterhoek mtn., 20 mi. NW of Ceres. Continued N by Middelberg range.

Cold Branch Mountain (3,424 ft.), in the Blue Ridge, NW S.C., c.25 mi. NW of Greenville.

Cold Brook, village (pop. 342), Herkimer co., central N.Y., 14 mi. NE of Utica.

Colden, Mount (kōl'dùn) (4,713 ft.), Essex co., NE N.Y., in the Adirondacks just W of Mt. Marcy, 11 mi. S of Lake Placid village.

Cold Harbor, 2 localities (Old Cold Harbor, New Cold Harbor) c.10 mi. NE of Richmond, Va. Civil War battle of Gaines's Mill (1 of Seven Days Battles), a Confederate victory, was fought June, 1862, near Old Cold Harbor. New Cold Harbor was field of last battle (June 3, 1864) of Grant's WILDERNESS campaign, in which Union attack on Lee's strongly entrenched Confederates was repulsed with terrible losses to the attackers.

Coldingham (kôl'dĭng-ùm), town and parish (pop. 2,398), E Berwick, Scotland, near North Sea, 3 mi. WNW of Eyemouth; agr. market. Site of ruins of Benedictine priory, founded 1098 on site of 7th-cent. nunnery of St. Ebba.

Coldita Island (kōldē'tä) (□ 11.5; pop. 934), off SE coast of Chiloé Isl., Chiloé prov., S Chile, 50 mi. S of Castro; 43°13'S; lumbering, fishing.

Colditz (kôl'dĭts), town (pop. 6,971), Saxony, E central Germany, on the Zwickauer Mulde and 20 mi. NNW of Chemnitz, in lignite-mining region; woolen and cotton milling, ceramics mfg. Has 16th-cent. palace, now insane asylum.

Cold Lake (□ 136), on Alta.-Sask. line; 54°35'N 110°W; 16 mi. long, 11 mi. wide.

Cold Mountain, Mont.: see ABSAROKA RANGE.

Cold River, SW N.H., small stream, rises in S Sullivan co., flows SW c.20 mi. to the Connecticut above Walpole.

Cold Spring. 1 or **Cold Springs,** town (pop. 518), Campbell co., N Ky., 6 mi. SSE of Newport. **2** Resort village (pop. 1,488), Stearns co., central Minn., on Sauk R. and 15 mi. SW of St. Cloud, in grain, livestock area; dairy products, beverages. Granite quarries near by. **3** Village (pop. 1,788), Putnam co., SE N.Y., on E bank of the Hudson and 6 mi. S of Beacon, in dairying area; mfg. (metal products, textiles); crushed stone. Settled before the Revolution; inc. 1846.

Coldspring, village (pop. c.500), ⊙ San Jacinto co., E Texas, near San Jacinto R., c.60 mi. NNE of Houston, at edge of Sam Houston Natl. Forest, in agr., cattle, timber area.

Cold Spring Harbor, village (pop. c.1,000), Suffolk co., SE N.Y., on N shore of W Long Isl., on Cold Spring Harbor (SE arm of Oyster Bay), just W of Huntington village, in summer-resort area, part of Huntington town. Site of a marine biological station (part of the Long Isl. Biological Association), the dept. of genetics of Carnegie Inst., and a state fish hatchery. Was 19th-cent. whaling port.

Cold Spring Lake (□ 17), S N.F., 50 mi. SSE of Buchans; 7 mi. long, 4 mi. wide. Drains E into Round Pound.

Cold Springs, Ky.: see COLD SPRING.

Cold Springs Dam, Oregon: see UMATILLA RIVER.

Coldstream, burgh (1931 pop. 1,233; 1951 census 1,294), S Berwick, Scotland, on the Tweed (17th-cent. bridge and 1928 Royal Tweed Bridge) and 13 mi. SW of Berwick-on-Tweed; agr. market. An anc. border town, once noted for runaway marriages. In 1659–60 General Monk (or Monck), later duke of Albemarle, here raised troops for march into England which resulted in restoration to throne of Charles II; regiment became known as "Coldstream Guards," one of the guard regiments of the royal household.

Cold Stream Ponds, Penobscot co., central Maine, 20 mi. NNE of Old Town; include Cold Stream Pond (c.4 mi. long) and 2 small Upper Cold Stream Ponds.

Coldwater, village (pop. 549), S Ont., on Coldwater R. and 14 mi. NW of Orillia; dairying, lumbering, flour milling, limestone quarrying.

Coldwater. 1 City (pop. 1,208), ⊙ Comanche co., S Kansas, c.50 mi. SE of Dodge City; trade center for wheat and livestock area. Inc. 1884. **2** City (pop. 8,594), ⊙ Branch co., S Mich., on Coldwater R. and 28 mi. SSE of Battle Creek, in fruit- and grain-growing, and dairying area. Mfg. of cement, furnaces, marine engines, iron castings, furniture, plastics, shoes, clothing, flour. Coldwater State Home and Training School is here. Many lakes near by; Coldwater L., the largest, is at head of Coldwater R. Settled 1830; inc. as village in 1837, as city in 1861. **3** Town (pop. 949), Tate co., NW Miss., c.30 mi. S of Memphis (Tenn.), and on E shore of Arkabutla Reservoir. **4** Village (pop. 2,217), Mercer co., W Ohio, 5 mi. SW of Celina, in agr. area; mfg. (agr. machinery, overalls, food products).

Coldwater River. 1 In S Mich., rises in Coldwater L. (c.3 mi. long, 1 mi. wide; resort) in Branch co. near Ind. line, flows NW c.25 mi., past Coldwater, to St. Joseph R. at Union City. **2** In NW Miss., rises in Marshall co., flows SW and W to De Soto co., then generally S to Tallahatchie R. in Quitman co.; 220 mi. long. N of Arkabutla, the Arkabutla Dam (earth fill; 65 ft. high, 10,000 ft. long) impounds Arkabutla Reservoir (c.20 mi. long up main stream) in De Soto and Tate counties.

Cole, county (□ 385; pop. 35,464), central Mo.; ⊙ JEFFERSON CITY. In Ozark region; bounded by Missouri R. (N) and Osage R. (E). Agr. (wheat, corn), livestock; mfg. centered at Jefferson City; mining of zinc, lead, barite, copper, clay. Formed 1820.

Colebrook, village (pop. 459), SE Tasmania, 22 mi. NNE of Hobart; dairying center, livestock; zinc, lead.

Colebrook. 1 Resort town (pop. 592), Litchfield co., NW Conn., in Litchfield Hills, on Mass. line and 13 mi. N of Torrington. In Colebrook village 18th-cent. houses include home of younger Jonathan Edwards, pastor here 1795–99. Includes small villages of North Colebrook, Colebrook River, Mill Brook, and Robertsville. **2** Resort town (pop. 2,116), including Colebrook village (pop. 1,265), Coos co., NW N.H., on the Connecticut, at mouth of Mohawk R., and 22 mi. N of Northumberland; timber, dairy products, poultry. Granted 1770, inc. 1795.

Cole Camp, city (pop. 813), Benton co., central Mo., 17 mi. S of Sedalia.

Coleen River (kōlēn'), NE Alaska, rises in Davidson Mts. near 68°48'N 143°W, flows c.160 mi. S to Porcupine R. at 67°4'N 142°29'W.

Coleford, town and parish (pop. 2,777), W Gloucester, England, 5 mi. ESE of Monmouth; agr. market and chief town of Forest of DEAN. Has 17th-cent. town hall.

Colegio, El, Colombia: see EL COLEGIO.

Coleharbor, city (pop. 315), McLean co., central N.Dak., 20 mi. NNW of Washburn.

Colehill, agr. parish (pop. 1,675), E Dorset, England, just NE of Wimborne Minster.

Coleman, town (pop. 1,809), SW Alta., near B.C. border, in Rocky Mts., on Crowsnest R. and 100 mi. SSW of Calgary; alt. 4,312 ft.; coal mining, lumbering, ranching, dairying.

Coleman (kōl'mŭn), county (□ 1,282; pop. 15,503), central Texas; ⊙ Coleman. Bounded S by Colorado R. and drained by its tributaries; has flood-control reservoirs of Colorado R. project. Agr. (especially oats; also wheat, grain sorghums, cotton, vegetables, fruit, pecans); livestock (cattle, sheep, turkeys); some dairying. Oil, natural gas wells; silica (glass mfg.), clay mining; coal deposits. Formed 1858.

Coleman. 1 City (pop. 849), Sumter co., central Fla., 11 mi. W of Leesburg, near L. Panasoffkee; crate mfg. **2** Town (pop. 295), Randolph co., SW Ga., 9 mi. SW of Cuthbert. **3** City (pop. 1,024), Midland co., E central Mich., 19 mi. NW of Midland, in dairy and agr. area. Inc. 1905. **4** City (pop. 6,530), ⊙ Coleman co., central Texas, 26 mi. W of Brownwood; commercial, processing, shipping center for agr. (cotton, grains, truck), livestock (cattle, sheep, turkeys), oil-producing region; cotton ginning, cottonseed-oil and feed milling, mfg. of saddles, boots, clay products, iron products, clothing, dairy products. L. Scarborough (city reservoir) and Hords Creek Reservoir (begun 1947), units of Colorado R. flood-control project, are near. Founded 1876, inc. 1877. **5** Village (pop. 668), Marinette co., NE Wis., 20 mi. W of Marinette; dairying center.

Coleman, Mount (10,262 ft.), SW Alta., in Rocky Mts., near NE edge of Banff Natl. Park, 70 mi. SE of Jasper; 52°7'N 116°56'W.

Cole Mere, England: see ELLESMERE.

Colemerik, Turkey: see HAKARI, village.

Colenso (kōlĕn'sō), town (pop. 2,145), W Natal, U. of So. Afr., on Tugela R. and 13 mi. S of Ladysmith; agr. center in stock-raising region; important hydroelectric-power station. In South African War, British under Sir Redvers Buller were defeated (Dec., 1899) here by Boers under Botha while attempting to relieve Ladysmith; town was finally taken Feb. 20, 1900.

Colentina-Fundeni (kôlĕntē'nä-fōōndān'), outer NE urban suburb (1948 pop. 30,418) of Bucharest, S Rumania, on left bank of Colentina R.; dairy farming. Site of military airport. Has a 17th-cent. church; 16th-cent. monastery near by.

Colentina River, left tributary of Dambovita R., S Rumania, meandering c.50 mi. SE through N suburbs of Bucharest, past Baneasa, Herastrau, and Colentina-Fundeni. It widens to form a series of lakes bordered by parks.

Coleorton (kōlôr'tŭn), town and parish (pop. 764), N Leicester, England, 8 mi. W of Loughborough; coal mining; hosiery.

Colerain (kōl'rān), town (pop. 367), Bertie co., NE N.C., on Chowan R. and 29 mi. NNW of Williamston; fish canning.

Coleraine (kōl'rān), village (pop. 1,107), SW Victoria, Australia, 175 mi. W of Melbourne; rail terminus; cattle; dairy plant.

Coleraine, village (pop. estimate 300), S Que., 10 mi. SE of Thetford Mines; chromite mining.

Coleraine (kōlrān'), municipal borough (1937 pop. 9,180; 1951 census 10,748), NE Co. Londonderry, Northern Ireland, on Bann R. (4 mi. from its mouth) and 27 mi. ENE of Londonderry; seaport; linen milling, alcohol distilling, food canning, bog-iron mining, bacon and ham curing, mfg. of shirts, furniture; salmon fishing. In 1613 site was given to corporations of the City of London by James I; church was founded 1614. Near by is a rath, said to mark site of old castles.

Coleraine (kō"lŭrān'), village (pop. 1,321), Itasca co., N central Minn., on Trout L., at W end of Mesabi iron range, and 6 mi. NE of Grand Rapids; trading point and company town; iron mining, ore concentration. Junior col. is here. State forest is N.

Coleridge (kōl'rĭj), village (pop. 621), Cedar co., NE Nebr., 10 mi. SSE of Hartington; dairy and poultry produce, livestock, grain.

Coleridge, Lake (kōl'rĭj) (□ 18), central S.Isl., New Zealand, 55 mi. WNW of Christchurch; 11 mi. long; hydroelectric plant.

Coleroon River (kōlrōōn', kōl'rōōn, kō'lŭ–), Hindi *Kollidam,* northernmost and largest arm of CAUVERY RIVER, S India, separates from the Cauvery at W end of Srirangam Isl. (near whose E tip it is kept in its separate channel by the GRAND ANICUT) and flows c.100 mi. E and NE, entering Bay of Bengal in several mouths c.75 mi. S of Cuddalore.

Coles (kōlz), county (□ 507, pop. 40,328), E central Ill.; ⊙ Charleston. Drained by Kaskaskia, Embarrass, and Little Wabash rivers; includes Paradise L. (or L. Mattoon; fish hatchery here). Agr. (corn, wheat, broomcorn, soybeans, livestock, poultry; dairy products). Diversified mfg. Formed 1830.

Colesberg (kōlz'bûrg, –bĕrkh), town (pop. 3,155), E central Cape Prov., near Orange Free State border, U. of So. Afr., 130 mi. SW of Bloemfontein; agr. center (stock, wool, grain, fruit); ostrich farming formerly carried on here. Airfield. Founded 1829; scene (1899–1900) of operations in South African War.

Colesburg, town (pop. 326), Delaware co., E Iowa 28 mi. WNW of Dubuque; dairy products.

Coleshill (kōlz'hĭl). **1** Village, Buckingham, England: see AMERSHAM. **2** Town and parish (pop. 3,762), N Warwick, England, on Cole R. and 8 mi. E of Birmingham; metalworks.

Coleshill Fawr, Wales: see FLINT.

Coles Point (kō'lĕs), Pacific headland, Moquegua dept., S Peru, 6 mi. SSW of Ilo; 17°43'S 71°22'W.

Coleta (kōlē'tŭ), village (pop. 184), Whiteside co., NW Ill., 9 mi. NW of Sterling, in agr. area.

Colfax (kōl'făks). **1** County (□ 405; pop. 10,010), E Nebr.; ⊙ Schuyler. Agr. area bounded S by Platte R. Flour; grain, livestock. Formed 1869. **2** County (□ 3,765; pop. 16,761), NE N.Mex.; ⊙ Raton. Livestock, coal-mining area; borders on Colo.; drained by Canadian R. Includes part of Raton Mts. in N, Sangre de Cristo Mts. in W. Formed 1869.

Colfax. 1 City (pop. 820), Placer co., E central Calif., near Bear R., c.45 mi. NE of Sacramento; ships fruit. Health sanitariums here. **2** Village (pop. 819), McLean co., central Ill., on Mackinaw R. and 20 mi. ENE of Bloomington, in rich agr. area; makes cheese. **3** Town (pop. 725), Clinton co., central Ind., 19 mi. SSE of Lafayette, in agr. area; furniture mfg.; bituminous-coal mining. **4** City (pop. 2,279), Jasper co., central Iowa, on Skunk R. and 20 mi. ENE of Des Moines, in coal-mining area; packed poultry and eggs, feed, beverages. Developed with the exploitation of mineral wells. Inc. 1875. **5** Town (pop. 1,651), ⊙ Grant parish, central La., on Red R. and 22 mi. NW of Alexandria; mfg. of chemicals, creosoted and asphalt products; lumber milling, cotton ginning; sand, gravel. Agr.: livestock, truck, grain, cotton, pecans. Colfax riot (1873) was a bloody incident of the Reconstruction period. Founded c.1870, inc. 1878. **6** City (pop. 3,057), ⊙ Whitman co., SE Wash., 50 mi. S of Spokane and on Palouse R.; wheat, peas; flour mills. Settled 1870, inc. 1878. **7** Village (pop. 1,044), Dunn co., W Wis., on Red Cedar R. and 17 mi. NW of Eau Claire; dairying, grain growing.

Colgong (käl'gông), town (pop. 6,523), Bhagalpur dist., NE Bihar, India, on Ganges Plain, on Ganges R. and 17 mi. E of Bhagalpur; trades in rice, wheat, maize, barley, sugar cane, oilseeds.

Colhuapi, Lake, Argentina: see COLHUÉ HUAPÍ, LAKE.

Colhué Huapí, Lake (kōlwā' wäpē'), large fresh-water lake (□ 310; alt. 922 ft.) in Patagonian highlands, central Comodoro Rivadavia military zone, S Argentina, 7 mi. E of Sarmiento; extends c.35 mi. NW–SE (5–15 mi. wide) roughly parallel to L. Musters (6 mi. W), with which it is linked by short stream. Outlet: Río Chico, affluent of Chubut R. Sometimes called Colhuapi.

Colico (kōlē'kō), village (1930 pop. 229), Arauco prov., S central Chile, 25 mi. NE of Lebu; coal mining. Its railroad station is 3 mi. NW, adjoined W by San José de Colico (1930 pop. 199), also with coal mines.

Colico (kô'lēkō), village (pop. 1,016), Como prov., Lombardy, N Italy, port on N shore of L. Como, near influx of Adda and Mera rivers, on Splügen Road, 20 mi. N of Lecco; paper, silk textiles, electrical apparatus, liquor. Feldspar quarries near by.

Colico, Lake (kōlē'kō) (□ 30), Cautín prov., S central Chile, northernmost lake in Chilean lake dist., 35 mi. SE of Temuco; 12 mi. long, c.4 mi. wide. Resort.

Coligny (kôlēnyē'), village (pop. 714), Ain dept., E France, on W slope of Revermont, 14 mi. NNE of Bourg; cheese.

Coligny (kōlē'nē), town (pop. 2,202), SW Transvaal, U. of So. Afr., 16 mi. SE of Lichtenburg; rail junction; corn, stock; grain elevator.

Coligual (kōlēgwäl'), village (1930 pop. 1,324), Llanquihue prov., S central Chile, 15 mi. NW of Puerto Montt, in agr. area (cereals, flax, potatoes, livestock); dairying, lumbering.

Colihaut (kōlĭhôt'), village (pop. 757), NW Dominica, B.W.I., 14 mi. NNW of Roseau; limes, cacao.

Colijnsplaat, Netherlands: see NORTH BEVELAND.

Colima (kōlē'mä), state (□ 2,010; 1940 pop. 78,806; 1950 pop. 112,292), W Mexico, on the Pacific; ⊙ Colima. One of the smallest in area and the smallest in pop. of Mexican states. Situated bet. Jalisco, which nearly surrounds it, and Michoacán. Consists of foothills of the Sierra Madre Occidental and coastal lowlands; drained by Armería and Tuxpan (or Coahuayana) rivers. The Cuyutlán Lagoon, separated from the ocean by a narrow peninsula, extends along its coastline. Colima includes the REVILLA GIGEDO ISLANDS, 500 mi. off coast. Has a tropical to subtropical humid climate on plains, cooler in mts. Primarily agr. state: produces coffee, rice, corn, tobacco, sugar cane, cotton, beans, rubber, bananas, limes, cacao beans. Saltworks at coastal lagoons. Stock raising on mtn. slopes. Large-scale shark fishing based at Manzanillo, its major port. Also lumbering and mining (iron, copper, some gold). Colima became a territory in 1823, later a state.

Colima, city (pop. 22,601), ⊙ Colima, W Mexico, on Colima R. (affluent of the Armería), in W outliers of Sierra Madre Occidental, and 45 mi. NE of Manzanillo, 310 mi. W of Mexico city, on railroad; 19°14′N 103°48′W; alt. 1,575 ft. Processing and agr. center (corn, rice, sugar cane, coffee, cotton, fruit, livestock); tanning, rice milling, cotton ginning, alcohol distilling, saltmaking; mfg. of lemon extract, cigars, shoes, leatherware. Has cathedral, theater, parks, radio station, airfield. Old colonial city, founded 1523.

Colima, Nevado de (nävä′dō dā kōlē′mä), inactive volcano (14,240 ft.), Jalisco, W Mexico, near Colima border, 13 mi. SW of Guzmán. Just S is the **Volcán de Colima**, a smoking volcanic peak (12,631 ft.; another estimate, 12,750 ft.).

Colimes (kōlē′mĕs), village, Guayas prov., W Ecuador, landing on Daule R. at mouth of Colimes R., in tropical lowlands, 45 mi. N of Guayaquil, in agr. region (cacao, sugar cane, rice, tropical fruit, timber, cattle); rice milling.

Colín (kōlēn′), village (1930 pop. 633), Talca prov., central Chile, on railroad, on the Río Claro and 5 mi. SW of Talca, in agr. area (wheat, barley, wine, livestock); copper deposits.

Colina (kōōlē′nŭ), city (pop. 3,268), N São Paulo, Brazil, on railroad and 11 mi. S of Barretos; sugar milling, distilling, tile and pottery mfg.; coffee, cotton, corn. Formerly Collina.

Colina (kōlē′nä), village (1940 pop. 1,086), Santiago prov., central Chile, at N end of the central valley, 18 mi. N of Santiago, in agr. area (grain, fruit, livestock). Airport. The thermal springs Baños de Colina (1930 pop. 51) are 6 mi. ENE, and railroad station Colina (1930 pop. 81) is 8 mi. SW.

Colinas (kōōlē′nŭs), city (pop. 2,666), E central Maranhão, Brazil, head of navigation on upper Itapecuru R. and 90 mi. SW of Caxias; ships cotton, babassu nuts, cereals, and rubber. Roads to Caxias, Carolina, and Passagem Franca. Until 1944, called Picos.

Colinas (kōlē′näs), city (pop. 2,121), Santa Bárbara dept., W Honduras, on S slope of Sierra de Colinas, 10 mi. NNW of Santa Bárbara; commercial center in coffee zone; coffee processing; sugar cane. Also called San José Colinas.

Colinas, Sierra de (syĕ′rä dā), E branch of Sierra del Merendón, W Honduras; extends from Naranjito 55 mi. NE to Villanueva, forming watershed bet. Chamelecón R. (N) and Jicatuyo and Ulúa rivers (S); rises to over 5,000 ft.

Colindres (kōlēn′drĕs), town (pop. 1,470), Santander prov., N Spain, 18 mi. ESE of Santander; fish processing; corn, citrus fruit.

Colinton (kŏ′lĭntŭn), village (pop. estimate 200), central Alta., on Tawatinaw R. and 7 mi. S of Athabaska; mixed farming, wheat, stock.

Colinton, SW suburb (pop. 9,698) of Edinburgh, Scotland; paper mills.

Colipa (kōlē′pä), town (pop. 1,262), Veracruz, E Mexico, in Sierra Madre Oriental foothills, 31 mi. NNE of Jalapa; corn, beans, sugar cane, coffee.

Coliseo (kōlēsā′ō), town (pop. 1,433), Matanzas prov., W Cuba, 10 mi. SW of Cárdenas; rail junction in sugar-cane and cattle region.

Coll (kŏl), island (□ 28.6; pop. 322) and parish of Inner Hebrides, Argyll, Scotland, 7 mi. WNW of NW end of Mull; 12 mi. long, 4 mi. wide; rises to 339 ft. Crofting is chief occupation. There are remains of several early forts. Just off N shore is rocky islet of Suil Ghorm, with lighthouse.

Collado Mediano (kōlyä′dhō mādh-yä′nō), town (pop. 857), Madrid prov., central Spain, on E slopes of the Sierra de Guadarrama, 27 mi. NW of Madrid; cereals, livestock. Granite quarries.

Collado Villalba (vēlyäl′vä), town (pop. 841), Madrid prov., central Spain, summer resort near source of Guadarrama R., on Villalba hill, 23 mi. NW of Madrid; forage, cattle, sheep. Granite quarries; mfg. of cement products. Its railroad station (pop. 1,743), sometimes called Villalba, is 1 mi. S, point of bifurcation of Madrid railroad to Ávila and Segovia.

Collahuasi (kōyäwä′sē), former copper-mining area, Antofagasta prov., N Chile, in the Andes, near Bolivia border, on rail spur, and 100 mi. N of Calama; alt. c.15,000 ft.

Collarenebri (kŏlŭrĕ′nŭbrī), village (pop. 519), N New South Wales, Australia, on Darling or Barwon R. and 300 mi. NW of Newcastle; sheep-raising center.

Collaroy (kŏ″lŭroi′), town (pop. 3,014), New South Wales, Australia, on E coast 12 mi. N of Sydney; coal-mining center.

Collatina, Brazil: see COLATINA.

Collblanch-Torrasa (kōlblänch′-tôrä′sä), industrial suburb (pop. 10,218) of Barcelona, Barcelona prov., NE Spain, 3 mi. W of city center; mfg. of lamps, leather goods, paints, glass, candy; cotton spinning, tanning.

Collbran, town (pop. 237), Mesa co., W Colo., on branch of Colorado R. and 35 mi. ENE of Grand Junction; alt. 6,000 ft.; livestock. Pueblo Indian ruins near by.

Collecchio (kôl-lĕk′kyō), town (pop. 2,008), Parma prov., Emilia-Romagna, N central Italy, near Taro R., 6 mi. SW of Parma; canned foods, sausage, salami.

Collecorvino (kôl″lĕkôrvē′nō), village (pop. 647), Pescara prov., Abruzzi e Molise, S central Italy, 11 mi. W of Pescara; mfg. of agr. tools.

Cölleda, Germany: see KÖLLEDA.

Colle di Val d'Elsa (kôl′lĕ dē väl dĕl′sä), town (pop. 5,749), Siena prov., Tuscany, central Italy, near Elsa R., 12 mi. NW of Siena. Mfg. center; foundries, paper and woolen mills, cementworks, tannery; agr. and glass-furnace machinery, nails, pottery, glass, macaroni. Bishopric. Has cathedral and several old palaces.

Colleen Bawn, village, Bulawayo prov., S Southern Rhodesia, in Matabeleland, on railroad and 14 mi. ESE of Gwanda. Limestone-quarrying center; supplies cement mills at Cement, near Bulawayo.

College, village (pop. 405), central Alaska, near Tanana R., 3 mi. NW of Fairbanks, site of Univ. of Alaska (chartered 1917 and opened 1922 as Alaska Agr. College and School of Mines; became Univ. of Alaska 1935).

Collegeboro, Ga.: see STATESBORO.

College Corner, village (pop. 468), on Preble-Butler co. line, SW Ohio, at Ind. line, adjacent to West College Corner (Ind.) and 23 mi. W of Middletown.

Collegedale, village, Hamilton co., SE Tenn., 13 mi. E of Chattanooga. Has Southern Missionary Col.

College Gardens, village (pop. 5,046, with near-by North Modesto), Stanislaus co., central Calif., near Modesto.

College Heights. 1 Village (pop. 2,049, with adjacent Lincoln Gardens), Madison co., SW Ill. **2** Residential suburb (pop. 1,381), Darlington co., NE S.C., adjacent to Hartsville.

College Mound, town (pop. 89), Macon co., N central Mo., near branch of Chariton R., 10 mi. SSW of Macon.

College Park. 1 Village (pop. 1,214), St. Johns co., NE Fla., near St. Augustine. **2** City (pop. 14,535), Fulton and Clayton counties, NW central Ga., S suburb of Atlanta. Inc. 1891. **3** Village (pop. 1,058, with adjacent Highland Park), Saline co., S Ill. **4** Town (pop. 11,170), Prince Georges co., central Md., suburb NE of Washington; makes radio equipment; has airport. Seat of main campus of Univ. of Md. Inc. 1945.

College Place, town (pop. 3,174), Walla Walla co., SE Wash., just SW of Walla Walla. Seat of Walla Walla Col.; Whitman Natl. Monument is W.

College Point, SE N.Y., a residential section of N Queens borough of New York city, on Flushing Bay; some mfg. (clothing, printer's ink, paints, fur products, aircraft parts). Site of the Chisholm Mansion (1848).

College Springs, town (pop. 368), Page co., SW Iowa, near Mo. line, 9 mi. SSW of Clarinda.

College Station. 1 Village, Pulaski co., Ark.: see GENEVIA. **2** City (pop. 7,925), Brazos co., E central Texas, near Brazos R., 5 mi. S of Bryan. Seat of Agr. and Mechanical Col. of Texas. Inc. 1938.

Collegeville. 1 Village, Jasper co., NW Ind., on Iroquois R. and c.45 mi. S of Gary. Seat of St. Joseph's Col. **2** Hamlet, Stearns co., central Minn., on small affluent of Mississippi R. and 9 mi. W of St. Cloud, in agr. and dairying area. St. John's Univ. (R.C.) is here. **3** Borough (pop. 1,900), Montgomery co., SE Pa., 7 mi. NW of Norristown; metal products; agr. Ursinus Col.

Collegiate Range, Colo: see SAWATCH MOUNTAINS.

Collegno (kôl-lā′nyō) town (pop. 5,087), Torino prov., Piedmont, NW Italy, on Dora Riparia R. and 5 mi. WNW of Turin; foundries, mills (cotton, flour); liquor, marmalade. Has former Carthusian monastery (rebuilt 18th cent.); now an insane asylum.

Colle Salvetti (kôl′lĕ sälvĕt′tē), village (pop. 1,456), Livorno prov., Tuscany, central Italy, 9 mi. ENE of Leghorn; rail junction; foundry, food cannery, lye factory.

Colle Sannita (sän-nē′tä), village (pop. 3,016), Benevento prov., Campania, S Italy, 17 mi. N of Benevento.

Collesano (kôl-lĕzä′nō), town (pop. 5,970), Palermo prov., N Sicily, in Madonie Mts., 9 mi. SSW of Cefalù.

Collessie (kŏlĕ′sē), agr. village and parish (pop. 1,955, including Ladybank and Monkston burgh), N central Fifeshire, Scotland, 3 mi. NNW of Ladybank. Near by are remains of summer residence of archbishops of St. Andrews.

Collet-de-Dèze, Le, France: see SAINT-GERMAIN-DE-CALBERTE.

Colleton (kŏ′lŭtŭn), county (□ 1,048; pop. 28,242), S S.C.; ⊙ Walterboro. Bounded by Edisto R. (NE and E), Combahee R. (SW), and St. Helena Sound (S). Intracoastal Waterway passes along coast. Rural area, with timber, cotton, corn, livestock; hunting, fishing, tourist trade. Formed 1798.

Colletorto (kôl-lĕtôr′tō), town (pop. 3,959), Campobasso prov., Abruzzi e Molise, S central Italy, 10 mi. SSE of Larino.

Collevalenza (kôl″lĕvälĕn′tsä) or **Colvalenza**, village (pop. 121), Perugia prov., Umbria, central Italy, 5 mi. SE of Todi; cutlery mfg.

Colleville-Montgomery (kôlvēl′-mōgômārē′), village (pop. 367), Calvados dept., NW France, near English Channel, 7 mi. NNE of Caen. Captured (June 6, 1944) by British in Second World War. Until 1946, called Colleville-sur-Orne.

Colleville-sur-Mer (-sür-mâr′), village (pop. 173), Calvados dept., NW France, near Channel coast, 8 mi. NW of Bayeux. In Second World War American troops landed (June 6, 1944) at near-by Omaha Beach.

Colleville-sur-Orne, France: see COLLEVILLE-MONTGOMERY.

Colli a Volturno (kôl′lē ä vôltōōr′nō), village (pop. 1,226), Campobasso prov., Abruzzi e Molise, S central Italy, on Volturno R. and 7 mi. W of Isernia; paper mill.

Colli del Tronto (dĕl trôn′tō), village (pop. 588), Ascoli Piceno prov., The Marches, central Italy, 9 mi. ENE of Ascoli Piceno; dyeworks.

Collie, municipality (pop. 4,507), SW Western Australia, 100 mi. SSE of Perth; orchards, timber (karri eucalyptus); coal mines.

Collier, county (□ 2,032; pop. 6,488), S Fla., on Gulf of Mexico (W); ⊙ Everglades. Co. area mostly covered by Big Cypress Swamp and the Everglades; Ten Thousand Isls. along SW coast. Truck farming, fishing, lumbering. Oil wells at Sunniland. Formed 1923.

Collier Bay, inlet of Indian Ocean, NE Western Australia, NE of King Sound; 60 mi. E-W, 40 mi. N-S; broken into several small bays. Montgomery Isls. and Koolan Isl. at entrance.

Collier City, Fla.: see GOODLAND.

Collierville, town (pop. 1,153), Shelby co., SW Tenn., 20 mi. ESE of Memphis, in cotton, livestock, dairying region; chairs, cabinets; feed, cheese.

Colliguay (kōyĕgwī′), village (1930 pop. 356), Ñuble prov., S central Chile, on railroad and 17 mi. WSW of Chillán, in agr. area (grain, wine, vegetables, livestock). Also spelled Colliguai.

Collin (kŏ′lĭn), county (□ 886; pop. 41,692), N Texas; ⊙ McKinney. In rich blackland-prairie agr. region; drained by East Fork of the Trinity. A leading Texas corn-growing co.; also cotton, grains, alfalfa, pecans, fruit, truck (especially onions); extensive dairying; livestock (cattle, hogs, sheep, poultry). Formed 1846.

Collina, Brazil: see COLINA.

Collinée (kôlēnā′), village (pop. 393), Côtes-du-Nord dept., W France, 18 mi. SE of Saint-Brieuc; onions, cabbage.

Collingdale, borough (pop. 8,443), Delaware co., SE Pa., SW suburb of Philadelphia. Inc. 1891.

Collingswood, residential borough (pop. 15,800), Camden co., SW N.J., just SE of Camden; mfg. (leather products, thermometers). Settled 1682 by Quakers, inc. 1888.

Collingsworth, county (□ 899; pop. 9,139), extreme N Texas, in the Panhandle, on Okla. line; ⊙ Wellington. Drained by Salt Fork of Red R. Agr. (cotton, sorghum, peanuts, fruit, truck, beef cattle, poultry, hogs, dairy products). Formed 1876; acquired parts of Beckham and Harmon counties, Okla., in relocation of 100th meridian (1930).

Collingwood, municipality (pop. 29,758), S Victoria, Australia; NE suburb of Melbourne; mfg. center (woolens, hosiery).

Collingwood, town (pop. 6,270), S Ont., at S end of Georgian Bay of L. Huron, 36 mi. E of Owen Sound; important lake port, with large shipyards, grain elevators, and one of largest Canadian dry docks; food canning, dairying, lumbering. Resort. Site of govt. fish hatchery.

Collingwood, township (pop. 154), ⊙ Collingwood co. (□ 562; pop. 975), NW S.Isl., New Zealand, 12 mi. S of Cape Farewell, on Golden Bay; coal, silver mines.

Collingwood Channel (10 mi. long, 1-2 mi. wide), SW B.C., central entrance of Howe Sound from Strait of Georgia, separating Bowen Isl. (E) and Keats Isl. (W).

Collins. 1 Town (pop. 183), Drew co., SE Ark., 14 mi. SE of Monticello. **2** City (pop. 638), Tattnall co., E central Ga., 18 mi. E of Vidalia, in agr. area **3** Town (pop. 432), Story co., central Iowa, 27 mi. NE of Des Moines, in agr. area. **4** Town (pop. 1,293), ⊙ Covington co., S central Miss., on small Okatoma Creek and 28 mi. NNW of Hattiesburg; cotton, lumber, dairy products, truck. **5** Town (pop. 199), St. Clair co., W Mo., near Sac R., 12 mi. S of Osceola. **6** Village (1940 pop. 894), Erie co., W N.Y., on Cattaraugus Creek and 30 mi. S of Buffalo, near Cattaraugus Indian Reservation; canned foods, feed.

Collins, Mount, Tenn. and N.C.: see GREAT SMOKY MOUNTAINS NATIONAL PARK.

Collins Landing, village, Jefferson co., N N.Y., 22 mi. N of Watertown and on the St. Lawrence, here spanned by Thousand Islands International Bridge to a point 9 mi. E of Gananoque, Ont.

Collinston. 1 Village (pop. 546), Morehouse parish, NE La., 6 mi. SSE of Bastrop; agr. and lumbering. Natural-gas field near by. **2** Village (pop. c.300), Box Elder co., N Utah, near Bear R., 18 mi. N of Brigham City; alt. 4,460 ft.; shipping center for dry-farming and cattle-raising area.

Collinstown, N suburb of Dublin, Co. Dublin, Ireland; site of Dublin airport.

Collinsville, town (pop. 1,786), E Queensland, Australia, 110 mi. SSE of Townsville; state coal mines.

Collinsville. 1 Farming town (pop. 1,023), De Kalb co., NE Ala., 18 mi. NNE of Gadsden; hosiery, lumber mills; cotton. **2** Village, Hartford co.,

Conn.: see CANTON. **3** City (pop. 11,862), on Madison-St. Clair co. line, SW Ill., 10 mi. ENE of East St. Louis, within St. Louis metropolitan area; bituminous-coal-mining center; mfg. (chemicals, clothing, food products, brick, paint). Settled 1817; inc. as village in 1855, as city in 1872. **4** City (pop. 2,011), Tulsa co., NE Okla., 17 mi. NNE of Tulsa, in agr. area (grain, poultry, corn, livestock; dairy products); cottonseed oil, brick, tile; oil, natural-gas wells. **5** Town (pop. 561), Grayson co., N Texas, 19 mi. WSW of Sherman; oil wells; cotton ginning, grist milling.

Collinwood, town (pop. 589), Wayne co., S Tenn., 11 mi. S of Waynesboro, in hilly timber region; lumbering.

Collioure (kôlyo͞or'), anc. *Cauco Illiberis,* town (pop. 2,402), Pyrénées-Orientales dept., S France, fishing port on Gulf of Lion, at foot of Monts Albères, 15 mi. SE of Perpignan: sardine and anchovy processing center; olive preserving, winegrowing. The harbor, old quarter, and fortifications present an unusually picturesque site.

Collippo, Portugal: see LEIRIA.

Collipulli (kōyēpo͞o'yē), town (pop. 4,057), ⊙ Collipulli dept. (□ 739; pop. 21,983), Malleco prov., S central Chile, on Malleco R. (high bridge), on railroad and 19 mi. SE of Angol; agr. center (wheat, fruit, cattle); lumbering, flour milling. Gold and copper deposits near by.

Collo (kôl'lō), town (pop. 4,089), Constantine dept., NE Algeria, port on Gulf of Philippeville (Mediterranean Sea), in Little Kabylia, 21 mi. NW of Philippeville; ships cork stripped in surrounding cork-oak forests and processed here. Fish preserving, winegrowing. Town is overlooked by forested Djebel Goufi (alt. 3,900 ft.).

Collobrières (kôlōbrēâr'), village (pop. 892), Var dept., SE France, in Monts des Maures, 21 mi. ENE of Toulon; cork mfg., coal mining.

Collon (kŏ'lŭn), Gaelic *Collán,* town (pop. 241), S Co. Louth, Ireland, 7 mi. NW of Drogheda; agr. market (wheat, barley, potatoes; cattle).

Collón Curá, dept.: see PIEDRA DEL AGUILA.

Collón Curá River (kôyōn'-ko͞orä'), S Neuquén natl. territory, Argentina, formed by confluence of Aluminé and Catán-Lil rivers 13 mi. WNW of Junín de los Andes, flows c.50 mi. S to Limay R. 40 mi. SW of Piedra del Aguila.

Collondale, residential village (pop. 298), SE Cape Prov., U. of So. Afr., 4 mi. SW of East London; site of East London airport (33°3'S 27°59'E).

Collonges (kôlōzh'), village (pop. 410), Ain dept., E France, near the Rhone and Swiss border, 12 mi. WSW of Geneva; road and railroad junction; cheese mfg. Near by is the Écluse defile (commanded by old fort) in which the Rhone and the Lyons-Geneva RR cross chief range of the Jura.

Collooney (kŏlo͞o'nē), Gaelic *Cúil Mhaoile,* town (pop. 374), E Co. Sligo, Ireland, 6 mi. S of Sligo; agr. market (cattle; potatoes); woolen milling. In 1798 General Humbert's French force here fought engagement with Limerick militia.

Collpa (koi'pä), town (pop. c.3,020), Chuquisaca dept., S central Bolivia, near Pilcomayo R., 18 mi. WNW of Azurduy; vineyards; grain.

Collubi (kō'lo͞obē), village (pop. 600), Harar prov., E central Ethiopia, in highlands, 30 mi. W of Harar; barley, corn, durra.

Collyer, city (pop. 282), Trego co., W central Kansas, 11 mi. W of Wakeeney.

Colma (kōl'mŭ), town (pop. 297), San Mateo co., W Calif., 8 mi. S of San Francisco; cemeteries for the city are here. Large flower-growing industry. Formerly Lawndale, it took (1941) name of former town of Colma, which had been absorbed (1936) by Daly City.

Colman, city (pop. 509), Moody co., E S.Dak., 12 mi. WSW of Flandreau; grain market; livestock, dairy products, poultry.

Colmar (kôlmär'), city (pop. 43,514), ⊙ Haut-Rhin dept., E France, in Alsatian lowland near E foot of the Vosges, 24 mi. N of Mulhouse; textile center (factories in suburban Logelbach); other mfg.: starch, lubricating oils, dye extracts, sauerkraut. Kirsch distilling, brewing, flour milling, printing. Important commerce in Alsace wines (grown just W along slopes of the Vosges), and in Munster cheese (made in Fecht R. valley). Old section of Colmar has kept narrow winding streets and many anc. bldgs. (15th-cent. custom house, 16th-cent. Pfister mansion). St. Martin's church (13th cent.) contains the *Madonna of the Rose Arbor* by Schöngauer (who lived here). Outstanding mus., housed in 13th-14th-cent. former Dominican convent of Unterlinden, contains numerous masterpieces of Rhenish school of the 15th cent. and the Isenheim altarpiece by Grünewald. Became free imperial city in 13th cent. Annexed to France by Louis XIV in 1673. Seat of a prov. *parlement.* Inc. into Germany, 1871–1918, along with rest of Alsace. In Second World War, Colmar (at center of a Ger.-held pocket of resistance) was last Fr. city to be liberated (Feb., 1945) by Allies. Bartholdi b. here. Alternate Ger. spelling: Kolmar.

Colmar, village (pop. 322), central Luxembourg, on Alzette R. and 3 mi. S of Ettelbruck; chalk quarrying. Just W is village of Berg (pop. 230), with chalk quarries.

Colmar Manor (kōl'mŭr), town (pop. 1,732), Prince Georges co., central Md., NE suburb of Washington, on Anacostia R. Inc. 1927.

Colmars (kôlmär'), village (pop. 226), Basses-Alpes dept., SE France, on the Verdon and 14 mi. S of Barcelonnette, in Provence Alps; resort. Has 17th-cent. ramparts.

Colmena, La, Paraguay: see LA COLMENA.

Colmenar (kōlmānär'), town (pop. 3,275), Málaga prov., S Spain, 14 mi. NNE of Málaga; agr. center (grapes, wheat, almonds, tubers, oats, chick-peas, olives, livestock). Produces noted wines; also flour milling, olive-oil pressing, tanning.

Colmenar de Oreja (dhā ōrā'hä), city (pop. 5,569), Madrid prov., central Spain, 26 mi. SE of Madrid; rail terminus, processing and agr. (chiefly viticultural) center. Alcohol and liquor distilling, wine making, flour milling, olive-oil pressing; clay quarrying. Mfg. of tartaric acid, esparto goods, brooms, soap, plaster, pottery, meat products. Hydroelectric plant.

Colmenar Viejo (vyā'hō), town (pop. 7,469), Madrid prov., central Spain, near Manzanares, 17 mi. N of Madrid; agr. center (carobs, grapes, rye, wheat, chick-peas, honey, wax; sheep, cattle, bulls for the ring). Stone quarrying, sawmilling, tanning, brewing. Hydroelectric plant E, on the Manzanares.

Colmesneil (kōl'mŭnēl), village (pop. c.1,000), Tyler co., E Texas, 9 mi. N of Woodward, in lumbering, agr. area.

Colmonell (kŏlmŏnĕl'), agr. village and parish (pop. 1,713), S Ayrshire, Scotland, on Stinchar R. and 7 mi. SSW of Girvan. Near by are remains of 13th-cent. Craigneil Castle. Parish includes woolen-milling village of Barrhill, on Duisk R. and 10 mi. S of Girvan.

Coln, river, England: see COLN RIVER.

Cöln, Germany: see COLOGNE.

Colnbrook (kōln'–, kōn'–), residential town in parish of Horton (pop. 1,156), SE Buckingham, England, on Colne R. and 3 mi. SE of Slough; makes storage batteries. Just S is village of Horton, with Norman church. Milton lived here for some years, and here wrote *Comus* and *Lycidas.*

Colne (kōn, kōln), municipal borough (1931 pop. 23,791; 1951 census 20,674), NE Lancashire, England, near Yorkshire boundary 6 mi. NE of Burnley; textile industry (cotton, wool, silk, rayon); leather tanning. Slate and limestone quarries near by. Earthwork remains of Roman camp; Norman church with 13th- and 16th-cent. additions.

Colneceaster, England: see COLCHESTER.

Colne River (kōn, kōln). **1** In Essex, England, rises 4 mi. SSE of Haverhill, flows 35 mi. SE, past Halstead, Colchester, and Wivenhoe, to North Sea at Mersea Isl. Navigable below Colchester. **2** In Hertford and Middlesex, England, rises just W of Hatfield, flows 35 mi. SW, past Watford and Uxbridge, forming boundary bet. Middlesex and Buckingham, to the Thames at Staines. Receives Ver R. 4 mi. NE of Watford, and Gade R. at Rickmansworth. **3** In SW Yorkshire, England, rises 9 mi. WSW of Huddersfield, flows 14 mi. NE, past Huddersfield, to Calder R.

Colne Valley, urban district (1951 census pop. 22,184), West Riding, SW Yorkshire, England, on Colne R. and 5 mi. WSW of Huddersfield; woolen and cotton milling. Formed 1937 out of Golcar, Marsden, and Slaithwaite.

Colney Hatch, England: see FRIERN BARNET.

Coln River (kōln), England, a headstream of the Thames; rises 5 mi. ESE of Cheltenham, Gloucester, flows 20 mi. SE to the Thames near Lechlade.

Colo (kō'lō), town (pop. 538), Story co., central Iowa, 15 mi. E of Ames; grain milling.

Coloane Island (ko͞olō'ŭnē), island dependency (□ 2; pop. 2,764) of Macao colony, in S.China Sea, 8 mi. SSE of Macao peninsula. Fisheries. Small port of Coloane is on SW shore.

Cologna Veneta (kôlô'nyä vā'nĕtä), village (pop. 2,276), Verona prov., Veneto, N Italy, 21 mi. SE of Verona; beet-sugar refinery, tobacco factory, silk mill, cementworks.

Cologne (kôlô'nyŭ), village (pop. 383), Gers dept., SW France, 20 mi. ENE of Auch; fruitgrowing.

Cologne (kŭlōn'), Ger. *Köln* (kûln), anc. *Colonia Agrippinensis,* city (□ 97; 1939 pop. 772,221; 1946 pop. 491,380; 1950 pop. 590,825), in former Prussian Rhine Prov., W Germany, after 1945 in North Rhine-Westphalia, port on the Rhine and 295 mi. WSW of Berlin, 110 mi. E of Brussels; 50°56'N 6°57'E. For centuries the focal point of Lower Rhenish culture, it is a historical, religious, industrial, and commercial center at junction of E-W and N-S routes; airport (at NW suburb of Bickendorf). Industry is fueled by large, open-pit lignite deposits just W (mined at Brühl, Frechen, Hürth); iron, steel, and other metal foundries; mfg. of vehicles, railroad cars, Diesel motors, machine tools, cranes, cables; shipyards. Chemical industry includes mfg. of fertilizer, dyes, lacquer, pharmaceuticals, and perfume, especially the noted eau de Cologne (invented here c.1700). Textiles (artificial silk), clothing; devotional articles; candy, chocolate. City's 5 harbors accommodate small ocean-going craft (direct passenger and freight service to London, Bremen, Hamburg, Scandinavian ports); receive raw materials and half-finished products, export high-grade processed goods. Cologne, the metropolis of the Rhineland, was the 1st major target of Allied air raids in Second World War. Old town, comprising Roman and medieval city, was 90% destroyed. The famous cathedral, a masterpiece of Ger. Gothic containing the relics of the Wise Men of the East, sustained only slight damage. It was begun 1248 on site of 9th-cent. church; the choir, a replica of that of Amiens cathedral, was consecrated 1322; bldg. was completed according to original plans in 1880. The remarkable Romanesque basilicas of Holy Apostles, St. Maria in Kapitol (both 11th cent.), and Gross St. Martin were destroyed. Church of St. Ursula stands on burial place of the saint; St. Gereon's contains tomb of Albertus Magnus. Impressive 14th–17th-cent. city hall, 15th-cent. *Gürzenich* (banquet and reception hall of town council), and the Stapel House (one of Cologne's landmarks) were gutted. Univ., founded 1388, later discontinued, and reconstituted 1919, is situated in new outer town, which developed after construction of boulevards (after 1880). A Roman settlement, Cologne was created (A.D. 50) colony by Emperor Claudius. Became bishopric in 4th cent.; raised to archdiocese by Charlemagne. Its powerful archbishops were princes and electors of Holy Roman Empire. Constant feuds with the citizens resulted in transfer (1263) of their residence to Bonn. A flourishing member of the Hanseatic League, and created a free imperial city in 1474, town was birthplace of Cologne or Rhenish school of painting; masterpiece of its chief representative, Stephan Lochner, is in cathedral. Discriminations against Protestants lost town its trade with England; decline reached lowest point with capture of city by French in 1794. Secularized 1801; after annexation (1815) to Prussia, archdiocese was reorganized (1824). In 19th cent. Cologne developed into chief transit port and depot of W Germany, rivaled only by Frankfurt. First rail bridge over the Rhine was constructed here, 1855–59. Bet. 1888–1921, incorporation of surrounding towns (including Deutz, Kalk, and Mülheim on right bank) greatly increased city area. Occupied by Br. troops, 1918–26. Long known for its spectacular Mardi Gras celebrations, Cologne in 1924 held 1st of its noted commercial fairs. Captured by U.S. troops in March, 1945. Formerly also spelled Cöln in German.

Cologne, village (pop. 462), Carver co., S central Minn., 29 mi. SW of Minneapolis, in agr. area (corn, oats, barley, potatoes, livestock); dairy products.

Cologno al Serio (kôlô'nyô äl sä'rēô), village (pop. 3,222), Bergamo prov., Lombardy, N Italy, near Serio R., 8 mi. S of Bergamo; agr. center.

Cololo (kōlō'lō), peak (19,406 ft.) in Cordillera de La Paz, W Bolivia, 7 mi. SSW of Pelechuco.

Cololó, Arroyo (äroi'ō kōlōlō'), river, Soriano dept., SW Uruguay, rises in the Cuchilla Duraznito (a N outlier of the Cuchilla del Bizcocho) NNE of Egaña, flows 40 mi. NW to the Río Negro 11 mi. NNE of Mercedes.

Coloma or **La Coloma** (lä kōlō'mä), town (pop. 1,212), Pinar del Río prov., W Cuba, on S coast, 14 mi. SE of Pinar del Río; fishing; lobster canning.

Coloma (kŭlō'mŭ, kō–). **1** Village, El Dorado co., E Calif., on American R. and 45 mi. NE of Sacramento. At Sutter's Mill here, James W. Marshall discovered gold on Jan. 24, 1848. Marshall State Historic Monument commemorates the event. **2** City (pop. 1,041), Berrien co., extreme SW Mich., on Paw Paw R. and 9 mi. NE of Benton Harbor, in fruitgrowing region; fruit packing, canning; pickle factory. Near by is Paw Paw L. (resort; c.3 mi. long). City laid out 1855; inc. as village 1893, as city 1942. **3** Village (pop. 338), Waushara co., central Wis., 50 mi. W of Oshkosh, in dairy area.

Colomba (kōlōm'bä), town (1950 pop. 883), Quezaltenango dept., SW Guatemala, in Pacific piedmont, 17 mi. SW of Quezaltenango; road center; coffee, sugar cane, livestock.

Colomb-Béchar (kōlō'-bāshär'), town (pop. 14,604), ⊙ Aïn-Sefra territory, W Algeria, near Fr. Morocco border, 300 mi. SSW of Oran; 31°36'N 2°14'W. Algeria's only coal-mining center and temporary S terminus of trans-Saharan RR, projected to extend from Nemours (on the Mediterranean) to the great bend of the Niger in Fr. West Africa. Also linked by narrow-gauge line with Oran, via Aïn-Sefra. Mining operations (begun 1917 at near-by Kenadsa; accelerated during Second World War) are impeded by area's desert climate and remoteness from centers of pop. Town also ships dates, esparto grass, and handicraft jewelry. Military hosp. Trans-Saharan RR construction stopped 1943 in Kenadsa-Abadla stretch, just SSW.

Colombelles (kôlōbĕl'), village (pop. 1,165), Calvados dept., NW France, on the Orne and 3 mi. NE of Caen; large blast furnace processes locally mined iron. Portland cement mfg. Damaged in Second World War.

Colombes (kôlōb'), city (pop. 60,997), Seine dept., N central France, NW mfg. suburb of Paris, 7 mi. from Notre Dame Cathedral, within N bend of the Seine just WNW of Asnières; petroleum refining. Chief products: bicycles, aircraft, telephone equipment, chemicals, tires, hosiery, fountain pens, tennis rackets, perfumes.

Colombey-les-Belles (kôlōbā'-lā-bĕl'), agr. village (pop. 711), Meurthe-et-Moselle dept., NE France, 10 mi. S of Toul.

Colombey-les-deux-Églises (-lā-dûzāglēz'), agr. village (pop. 312), Haute-Marne dept., NE France, 8 mi. E of Bar-sur-Aube.

Colombia (kùlùm'bēù, Sp. kōlōm'byä), republic (□ 439,828; 1938 pop. 8,701,816; 1950 estimate 11,259,730), NW South America; ⊙ BOGOTÁ. The only South American country with a coast line both on the Atlantic and Pacific oceans, it is bounded NW by Panama (part of Colombia until 1903), NE and E by Venezuela. Its SE boundary with Brazil lies in the Amazon basin. In the S, where it borders on Ecuador and Peru, it is crossed by the equator. The tiny SAN ANDRÉS Y PROVIDENCIA archipelago, in the Caribbean c.115 mi. E of Nicaragua, belongs to Colombia. Truly a land of contrasts, Colombia consists roughly of 2 distinct regions, the humid, torrid plains and lofty Andean ranges, rising in the isolated Sierra Nevada de SANTA MARTA on the Caribbean to highest elevation (CRISTÓBAL COLÓN peak is 18,950 ft.) of the country. Disease-infected jungle lowlands make up ¾ of the entire area. E of the 3 great Andean chains which fan N from the Ecuadorian line at Galeras volcano, lies more than ½ of its territory, a vast, backward plain, dissected by navigable rivers tributary to the Orinoco and Amazon systems. This region's N section consists of savannas (*llanos*), which are increasingly used for cattle and sheep grazing, centered at VILLAVICENCIO. The densely forested transandean S (*selvas*), though interesting for its exotic fauna and flora, is of negligible importance, except for some balata and rubber gathered by primitive Indians. Physiographically somewhat similar are the coastal lowlands. Skirted by swamps, especially near the N coast, these alluvial sections are soaked by rain. Agr. is still little developed there, though cotton, rice, cacao, sugar cane, and bananas (notably near SANTA MARTA) thrive. The abundant forests yield all kinds of forest products–dye- and hardwoods, tonka beans, tagua nuts (vegetable ivory), vanilla, cinchona, sarsaparilla, kapok, palm fibers for Panama hats, balsam, resins, rubber, chicle, divi-divi, balata, and other gums. But of chief economic importance are the ample gold, and above all, platinum placers (Colombia is among the world's leading producers of that precious metal) in ATRATO RIVER and SAN JUAN RIVER valleys of the W coastal strip. These products are exported through BUENAVENTURA and, to a lesser extent, through TUMACO, the principal Pacific ports, which also ship coffee and cacao from the slopes of the cordilleras. A fine deep-sea port, Buenaventura is linked by rail with the interior upland towns, such as CALI, ARMENIA, and MANIZALES. But Colombia's chief transoceanic ports lie in the Caribbean north, where the Spanish made their 1st settlements—Santa Marta, CARTAGENA, and BARRANQUILLA. From these the main exports (coffee, petroleum, forest products, gold, hides) are shipped, predominantly to the U.S. Barranquilla is now the leading entrepôt and largest coastal city, with substantial processing industries. Situated on the all-important MAGDALENA RIVER, it has, since the dredging in the 1930s of the Boca de Ceniza, also been opened to deep-draft vessels, thus making its rail link with PUERTO COLOMBIA obsolete. Historic Cartagena, once the 1st port of colonial South America, is connected with the Magdalena by the Canal del DIQUE (long unnavigable but now again opened) and a railroad to Calamar. At adjacent Mamonal terminates the long pipe line from the rich BARRANCABERMEJA oil field. Colombia's petroleum industry is 2d only to Venezuela in South America. Santa Marta has grown as the outlet for near-by extensive banana plantations, but exports have declined in recent years because of plant disease. By far the most important region of Colombia is the healthful mountainous interior formed by the 3 great Andean chains, bet. which flow the Magdalena, still the republic's chief artery, and its formidable tributary, the CAUCA RIVER. This section, though occupying only about ¼ of the country's area, virtually dominates its social and economic life. Here lives the largest concentration of pop., mostly white or mestizo (whereas the coast is predominantly Negro), and Colombia's chief crop, coffee, is grown on large scale, accounting sometimes for 80% of its export volume. Colombia ranks next to Brazil as producer of coffee, but the high quality of its mild brand (used for blending in the U.S.) is little affected by Brazil's occasional overproduction and market slumps. Characteristic of the mts., as in all Latin America, is the altitudinal pattern of vegetation and climate. Above the tropical *tierra caliente* lies (3–7,000 ft.) the semitropical coffee belt; higher, up to 10,000 ft., is the grain- and potato-growing belt; still higher are the bleak, tundralike *páramos* (used for grazing), which yield to the perpetual snow fields. The Cordillera Occidental (Western Cordillera) is of the least economic consequence, especially N of Cali, an international air communications hub and chief distributing center of the sugar-growing south. The Cordillera Central, crowned by a chain of high volcanic peaks (e.g., TOLIMA, HUILA), separates the valleys of the Magdalena (E) and the Cauca (W); until late 19th cent. it was a backward region, but with better transport, the introduction of coffee culture, exploitation of rich gold and high-grade coal mines, and an enormous increase of the white pop., its cities, Manizales, and, principally, MEDELLÍN, have become the economic and industrial core of the republic. The Cordillera Oriental (Eastern Cordillera) is the longest chain, forking at Venezuela border N into the Sierra de Perijá and E into the Sierra de Mérida and coastal range of Venezuela. The W slopes yield coffee and the intramontane basins yield wheat, corn, barley, potatoes, cattle. The best-known of these basins, the Sabana de Bogotá, was the original home of the highly civilized Chibchas and foremost nucleus of Sp. culture in N South America. It also produces the world's largest quantity of emeralds from the famed MUZO mines. Rich saltworks are at ZIPAQUIRA. Important crops for local consumption are sugar cane, tobacco (chiefly around AMBALEMA, Tolima dept.), cacao, cotton, rice, indigo, oranges, pineapples, vegetables, fiber plants (HUILA), and silk (mostly around POPAYÁN). Among the leading cities of the interior are TUNJA, BUCARAMANGA, CÚCUTA (cradle of Gran Colombia), and, above all, Bogotá, the country's political and cultural focus, seat of an old univ. (founded 1572), and next to Medellín the principal mfg. center. Other univs. are at Medellín, Barranquilla, Cartagena, Popayán, and PASTO. Near Bogotá are famous TEQUENDAMA FALLS, a tourist site and power source. A steel mill is at PAZ DEL RÍO, Boyacá dept. Colombia's industrial activity has made great strides since the 1930s. While extracting and processing of the principal exports are most important, consumer industries (cotton textile milling, food processing, sugar refining, brewing, liquor distilling, mfg. of cement, clothing, chemicals, and pharmaceuticals) have developed, profiting from hydroelectric projects and improved communications. Communications have been a major problem throughout Colombia's history. Passenger and cargo still depend on the great Magdalena, a stream more than 1,000 mi. long, and navigable in long stretches only by flat-bottomed boats. Because of rapids, goods have to be transferred to railroads which circumvent falls at GIRARDOT, HONDA, and LA DORADO. Numerous small feeder lines and aerial cableways (e.g., Manizales-MARIQUITA) are a typical feature. Most transport follows a combined rail, river, and mule-track route. Railroads are few and expensive, but are developed energetically. Apart from a short mtn. stretch, traversed by highway, Bogotá is now linked by rail with Buenaventura on the Pacific and most of the interior centers. The Simón Bolívar Highway from Caracas (Venezuela) to Guayaquil (Ecuador) crosses the Andean region. One of the 1st commercial airlines was operated in Colombia. After the conquest of the Chibchas and the founding (1538) of Bogotá by Jiménez de Quesada, the region of Colombia became the nucleus of New Granada, which was to include present-day Panama, Venezuela, and Ecuador. New Granada was set up as viceroyalty in 1717 and 1739. Later the captaincy general of Venezuela was detached. First settlements were made on the coast at Santa Marta (1525) and Cartagena (1533). The struggle for independence began with the uprising at Bogotá (July 20, 1810), in which Antonio Nariño took a prominent part. During the long ensuing war Simón Bolívar assumed leadership. With the decisive victory at BOYACÁ in 1819 he secured the independence of Greater Colombia (*Gran Colombia*), of which Venezuela, Panama, and, after 1822, Ecuador formed a part. Santander administered the new nation, while Bolívar headed campaigns in Ecuador and Peru. Gran Colombia fell apart when in 1830 Venezuela and Ecuador became separate states. The remaining territory emerged as the Republic of New Granada, changing with constitutional shifts to confederation of Granadina in 1858, United States of New Granada (1861), United States of Colombia (1863), and finally the Republic of Colombia (1885). As have other South American countries, Colombia modeled its constitution after that of the U.S. Three statesmen stand out in 19th cent.—Mosquera, Rafael Núñez, and Reyes. While Núñez was president, a treaty was concluded (1846) granting the U.S. transit rights across the Isthmus of Panama. In 1903 the Republic of Panama was formed, after the U.S. had acquired rights to complete the canal. Colombia recognized the new nation's independence in 1914. It settled (1917) its boundary disputes with Ecuador. A border clash with Peru over the *Leticia Trapezium*, an outpost far S on the Amazon, was settled (1934) by the League of Nations. Colombia entered the Second World War on Allied side in 1943. A merchant fleet, jointly owned by Colombia, Ecuador, and Venezuela, was set up and the Quito Charter promised (1948) to establish close ties bet. former members of the Greater Colombia confederacy. During the Inter-American Conference at Bogotá (1948) violent street riots broke out following assassination of the liberal leader Jorge Gaitán. For further information see separate articles on cities, regions, physical features, and the following territorial units: depts. of ANTIOQUIA, ATLÁNTICO, BOLÍVAR, BOYACÁ, CALDAS, CAUCA, CUNDINAMARCA, CHOCÓ, HUILA, MAGDALENA, NARIÑO, NORTE DE SANTANDER, SANTANDER, TOLIMA, VALLE; intendancies of CASANARE, META, SAN ANDRÉS Y PROVIDENCIA; and the commissaries of ARAUCA, CAQUETÁ, GUAJIRA, PUTUMAYO, VAUPÉS, and VICHADA.

Colombia (kōlōm'byä), village (pop. 320), Nuevo León, N Mexico, on the Rio Grande opposite Darwin (Texas), on railroad and 20 mi. NW of Nuevo Laredo.

Colombier-Fontaine (kôlōbyā-fōtĕn'), village (pop. 887), Doubs dept., E France, on Doubs R. and Rhone-Rhine Canal, and 6 mi. SW of Montbéliard; cotton weaving; agr. machinery, furniture.

Colombo (kōōlōm'bōō), city (pop. 631), SE Paraná, Brazil, 10 mi. NNE of Curitiba; mfg. (ceramics, paints, soft drinks). Limestone quarries in area.

Colombo (kùlùm'bō), city (□ 13; pop. 355,374), ⊙ Ceylon, Western Prov., and Colombo dist. (□ 813; pop., including estate pop., 1,409,153), port on Indian Ocean, at mouth of the Kelani Ganga, 950 mi. SSE of Bombay, 1,200 mi. SSW of Calcutta; 6°55'N 79°52'E. Major rail and road junction; airport (at Ratmalana, 8 mi. SSE of city center); commercial center of Ceylon. Chief exports: tea, rubber, coconut products (copra, coconut oil, desiccated coconut, coir), cacao, graphite, cinnamon, citronella oil, areca nuts, cardamom, papain, kapok. Relatively poor industrially; steel-rolling mill and shark-liver oil extraction (MARADANA), leather mfg. (MATTAKULIYA), quinine and coir-rope mfg., gem cutting; fishing center at MUTWAL. Has artificial harbor (□ 1; completed 1912) with 4 breakwaters accommodating 36–40 ships; includes graving dock (built 1906; 723 ft. long, 85 ft. wide), coaling depot with coaling jetties, barge-repairing basin. Replaced Galle as principal port of Ceylon on completion of 1st breakwater (4,212 ft. long) in 1885. Principal business section (banks, govt. offices) is the Fort, in area of 17th-cent. Du. fort (demolished 1869), on coast just S of the harbor; has Queen's House (residence of governor-general) and clock tower (also a lighthouse). Just E of the Fort is the *pettah* (area with native bazaars). S of Fort and pettah is small Beira lake (St. Joseph's Col. on E bank), connected with harbor by canal bet. Fort and pettah; nearly bisected by promontory called Slave Isl. S of lake is residential area (Cinnamon Gardens), with Victoria Park (mus. built 1877; Ceylonese antiquities, products, and natural history; library), Univ. Col., Royal Col., Govt. Training Col., meteorological observatory. City also has Du. Wolfendahl church (built 1749 on site of former Port. church), Buddhist col., Hindu temples, large mosque, R.C. and Anglican cathedrals. Became in 1565 nominal ⊙ KOTTE kingdom, but actually was center of Port. power in Ceylon; captured 1656 by Dutch and surrendered 1796 to English. Selected as leading port of Ceylon because of its closeness to planting dists., especially the formerly-important cinnamon plantations. Main suburbs include DEHIWALA, MOUNT LAVINIA, Kotte, KELANIYA, and Kolonnawa. An extremely warm area, with an average temp. of c.80°F. Pop. mainly Singhalese.

Colombres (kōlōm'brĕs), town (pop. estimate 500), central Tucumán prov., Argentina, rail junction 7 mi. SE of Tucumán, in agr. area; cotton ginning, sugar refining.

Colome (kùlōm'), city (pop. 451), Tripp co., S S.Dak., 10 mi. SE of Winner; livestock, grain, poultry, dairy products.

Colomera (kōlōmā'rä), town (pop. 2,728), Granada prov., S Spain, 15 mi. NNW of Granada; olive-oil processing, flour milling; lumbering; stock raising. Gypsum quarries near by.

Colomi (kōlō'mē), town (pop. c.10,000), Cochabamba dept., central Bolivia, in Cordillera de Cochabamba, 18 mi. E of Sacaba, and on Cochabamba–Todos Santos road; alt. 10,892 ft.; barley, potatoes.

Colomoncagua (kōlōmōngkä'gwä), town (pop. 447), Intibucá dept., SW Honduras, 24 mi. SSE of La Esperanza, near Salvador border; commercial center; ropemaking; corn, beans, henequen.

Colón, department, Argentina: see JESÚS MARÍA.

Colón (kōlōn'). **1** Town (pop. 5,610), ⊙ Colón dist. (□ 384; pop. 16,549), N Buenos Aires prov., Argentina, near Santa Fe line, 30 mi. W of Pergamino, in agr. area (corn, cattle); meat-packing center. **2** Town (1947 census pop. 8,950), ⊙ Colón dept. (□ 1,225; 1947 census pop. 39,664), E Entre Ríos prov., Argentina, port on Uruguay R., opposite Paysandú (Uruguay), and 20 mi. NNE of Concepción del Uruguay; agr. center (grain, flax, grapes, olives, fruit, livestock, poultry; apiculture); rice milling, lumbering, meat canning. Airport. Has agr. and poultry school.

Colón, town (pop. 11,534), Matanzas prov., W Cuba, on the Llanura de Colón (interior plain), on Central Highway and 45 mi. ESE of Matanzas. Rail junction; trading and agr. center (sugar cane, fruit, tobacco, honey, poultry, cattle). Tobacco factories, fruit-dehydrating plant. Has polytechnic school.

Colón, department (□ 17,104; 1950 pop. 34,314), E Honduras; ⊙ Trujillo. On Caribbean Sea; bounded S by Nicaragua, (along COLÓN MOUNTAINS); includes MOSQUITO COAST region. Mountainous section (W) and coastal lowlands are drained by Aguán and Sico rivers (separated by Sierra de Esperanza) and by Bulaya, Plátano, and Patuca rivers. Main products: bananas (Aguán, Sico, Paulaya river valleys), coconuts (coastal zone), rice (mainly near Tocoa), corn, beans. Livestock raising and hardwood (mahogany, cedar) lumbering important in undeveloped Mosquito Coast region. Main centers: Trujillo, its new port of Puerto Castilla, Sabá and Sonaguera in banana zone. Formed 1881.

Colón, city (pop. 2,045), Querétaro, central Mexico, 27 mi. NE of Querétaro; agr. center (wheat, corn, sugar cane, cotton, beans, chicle, tobacco, fruit, stock).

Colón, province (□ 2,810; 1950 pop. 89,643; 25% Indians) of central Panama, on Caribbean coast; ⊙ Colón. Divided into W and E sections by Panama Canal Zone; drained by Coclé del Norte R. (W). E section includes SAN BLAS territory. Agr. (bananas, cacao, abacá, coconuts), stock raising. Mineral deposits (mercury, lead, iron, manganese, coal). Central section (greatest pop. density) is served by Trans-Isthmian Highway and Panama RR. Main centers are Colón, Lagarto, Portobelo, Nombre de Dios. Formed 1855.

Colón, second largest city (1950 pop. 52,035) of Panama, ⊙ Colón prov., and surrounded by the Canal Zone, at Caribbean end of Panama Canal, 38 mi. NW of Panama city (linked by Panama RR and Trans-Isthmian Highway). Major commercial center, exporting tropical fruit and hardwood. Situated on Manzanillo Isl. bet. Manzanillo Bay (E) and Limón Bay (W), it forms Panama republic enclave within Canal Zone, but in 1950 the highway to Panama itself was turned over to the republic. CRISTOBAL [Sp.,=Christopher], site of port installations, adjoins (S) in Canal Zone. Founded 1850 in connection with Panama RR construction, it was named (1852) Aspinwall and later adopted (after 1890) official name Colón.

Colon (kō'lŭn). **1** Village (pop. 1,000), St. Joseph co., SW Mich., on St. Joseph R. and 26 mi. SE of Kalamazoo, in mint-growing area; mfg. of clothing. Lake resort. **2** Village (pop. 127), Saunders co., E Nebr., 35 mi. N of Lincoln, S of Platte R. **3** Village, Lee co., central N.C., 3 mi. N of Sanford; brick- and tileworks.

Colón (kōlōn'). **1** Village, Lavalleja dept., SE Uruguay, 10 mi. SSE of Pirarajá; corn, wheat, cattle. **2** or **Villa Colón** (vē'yä), N residential suburb of Montevideo, Montevideo dept., S Uruguay, 7 mi. from city. Founded 1869.

Colón or **San Juan de Colón** (sän hwän' dā), town (pop. 4,118), Táchira state, W Venezuela, in Andean spur, 19 mi. N of San Cristóbal; coffeegrowing center.

Colón, Archipiélago de, Ecuador: see GALÁPAGOS ISLANDS.

Colona (kŭlō'nŭ), village (pop. 319), Henry co., NW Ill., 9 mi. E of Moline, in agr. area; livestock, corn.

Colonarie River (kŏlŭnâ'rē), rivulet, E St. Vincent, B.W.I., c.5 mi. NE of Kingstown; site of hydroelectric plant.

Colonelganj (kûr'nŭlgŭnj), town (pop. 7,760), Gonda dist., NE Uttar Pradesh, India, 15 mi. W of Gonda; rice milling; trades in rice, wheat, corn, oilseeds.

Colonel Hill, town (pop. 148), S Bahama Isls., on central Crooked Isl., 250 mi. SE of Nassau; 22°45'N 74°15'W. Produces cascarilla bark.

Colonel Light Gardens, town (pop. 4,724), SE South Australia, 4 mi. S of Adelaide, in metropolitan area; residential.

Colonia (kōlō'nyä), N suburb (pop. 1,465) of Coronel, Concepción prov., S central Chile, in coal-mining area.

Colonia, department (□ 2,194; pop. 130,325), SW Uruguay, on the Río de la Plata at mouth of Uruguay R., opposite Buenos Aires; ⊙ Colonia. One of the most populous depts. of the country, with fertile, well-watered, undulating lowlands. Predominantly stock raising (sheep, cattle) and agr. (wheat, corn, vegetables, grapes, fruit). Flour milling, dairying, wine making, sand and stone quarrying. Has many flourishing colonies settled by Eur. immigrants. Served by several fine ports, such as Nueva Palmira, Carmelo, Juan Lacaze, and Colonia. Puerto del Sauce has paper and textile industries. Dept. was set up 1816.

Colonia or **Colonia del Sacramento** (dĕl säkrämĕn'tō), city (pop. 8,000), ⊙ Colonia dept., SW Uruguay, port on peninsula jutting into the Río de la Plata, opposite Buenos Aires, and 100 mi. WNW of Montevideo (linked by railroad and highway); 34°38'S 57°51'W. Resort and center for rich stock-raising and agr. (cereals, vegetables) region. Dairy industry. Ships gravel and sand from near-by quarries. Airport. An old colonial town, founded 1680 by Portuguese, it has picturesque bldgs., Franciscan monastery, San Pedro fort. The summer resort Real de San Carlos, just N, has a bull ring and casino.

Colonia Alvear Oeste (älväär' wĕ'stä), town (pop. estimate 1,000), E central Mendoza prov., Argentina, on railroad (Colonia Alvear station) 50 mi. SE of San Rafael, in Atuel R. irrigation area, just S of General Alvear. Alfalfa, wine, fruit, grain, stock; wine making, dried-fruit processing.

Colonia Barón (bärōn'), town (pop. estimate 1,500), NE La Pampa natl. territory, Argentina, on railroad and 40 mi. NE of Santa Rosa; grain, livestock.

Colonia Benítez or **Benítez** (bānē'tĕs), town (pop. estimate 1,000), E Chaco natl. territory, Argentina, on railroad and 8 mi. N of Resistencia; cotton, corn, livestock; cotton ginning.

Colonia Berón de Astrada (bārōn' dā ästrä'dä), village (pop. estimate 600), SW Corrientes prov., Argentina, 75 mi. S of Goya; farming colony in cattle-raising area. Sometimes called Berón de Astrada, not to be confused with the BERÓN DE ASTRADA in N Corrientes.

Colonia Cabildo, Argentina: see CABILDO.

Colonia Caroya (käroi'ä) or **Caroya,** town (pop. estimate 1,500), N central Córdoba prov., Argentina, 22 mi. N of Córdoba; winegrowing center, with distilleries; cereals, potatoes, fruit, livestock.

Colonia Castelli, Argentina: see CASTELLI, Chaco natl. territory.

Colonia Cecilio Báez, Paraguay: see CECILIO BÁEZ.

Colonia del Sacramento, Uruguay: see COLONIA, city.

Colonia Dora (dō'rä), town (pop. estimate 1,200), S central Santiago del Estero prov., Argentina, in Río Salado irrigation area, on railroad, and 12 mi. SW of Añatuya; agr. center (cotton, alfalfa, livestock); cotton ginning.

Colonia Eldorado, Argentina: see ELDORADO.

Colonia Elía (ā'lyä), town (pop. estimate 1,000), E Entre Ríos prov., Argentina, 14 mi. SSW of Concepción del Uruguay; agr. center (grain, vegetables, fruit, livestock).

Colonia Elisa (ālē'sä), town (pop. estimate 1,000), E central Chaco natl. territory, Argentina, on railroad and 50 mi. NW of Resistencia; cotton growing, stock raising, lumbering; sawmills, cotton gins.

Colonia Ella, Argentina: see MALABRIGO.

Colonia General Delgado, Paraguay: see GENERAL DELGADO.

Colonia Hohenau, Paraguay: see HOHENAU.

Colonia Independencia, Paraguay: see INDEPENDENCIA.

Colonia Josefina (hōsāfē'nä), town (pop. estimate 1,000), W central Santa Fe prov., Argentina, on railroad (Josefina station) and 80 mi. WNW of Santa Fe; agr. center (wheat, flax, livestock).

Colonia La Colmena, Paraguay: see LA COLMENA.

Colonia Las Heras (läs ā'räs) or **Las Heras,** town, ⊙ Colonia Las Heras dept. (pop. 1,903), S Comodoro Rivadavia military zone, Argentina, at SW foot of Pampa de Castillo, 85 mi. SW of Comodoro Rivadavia; rail terminus; sheep raising. Airport.

Colonia Lavalleja, Uruguay: see LAVALLEJA, village.

Colonial Beach, resort town (pop. 1,464), Westmoreland co., E Va., on the Potomac and 28 mi. E of Fredericksburg; seafood packing, lumber milling. "Wakefield," restored birthplace of George Washington (a natl. monument), is 5 mi. SSE; "Stratford Hall," home (restored) of Lee family, is 9 mi. SE. Inc. 1892.

Colônia Leopoldina (kōlō'nyŭ lēōpōldē'nŭ), city (pop. 1,540), E Alagoas, NE Brazil, on Pernambuco border, 50 mi. N of Maceió; cotton and sugar growing. Until 1944, called Leopoldina.

Colonial Heights, residential city (pop. 6,077), independent of any co., E central Va., on the Appomattox (bridged) opposite Petersburg. Inc. 1926, made independent city 1948.

Colonial National Historical Park (□ 11.1; established 1936), SE Va., largely on peninsula bet. James and York rivers. Includes 4 areas (at JAMESTOWN ISLAND, WILLIAMSBURG, YORKTOWN, and Cape HENRY) important in development of colonial America, and the Colonial Parkway, extending E–W across peninsula and connecting Yorktown and Jamestown via Williamsburg.

Colonia Manuel González, Mexico: see MANUEL GONZÁLEZ.

Colonia Mennonita, Paraguay: see MENNONITE COLONIES.

Colônia Mineira, Brazil: see SIQUEIRA CAMPOS, Paraná.

Colonia Nueva Australia (–nyä nwä'vä ousträ'lyä), village, Caaguazú dept., Paraguay, 70 mi. ESE of Asunción; maté, cattle; lumbering. Sometimes Nueva Australia.

Colonia Nueva Colombia, Paraguay: see NUEVA COLOMBIA.

Colonia Patricia, Spain: see CÓRDOBA, city.

Colonia Piamontesa, Uruguay: see LA PAZ, Colonia dept.

Colonias, national territory, Bolivia: see PANDO; MADIDI RIVER.

Colonias, Las, department, Argentina: see ESPERANZA.

Colonia San Martín, Argentina: see JOSÉ DE SAN MARTÍN.

Colonia Sarmiento, Argentina: see SARMIENTO, town, Comodoro Rivadavia military zone.

Colonia Suiza (swē'sä), agr. settlement, Colonia dept., SW Uruguay, 40 mi. ENE of Colonia; a resort and model colony, noted for its fine surroundings and agr. products (meat, fruit, vegetables, wine, cheese, butter). Founded by German-Swiss settlers, it also includes a Russian colony. Has dairy school, theater, churches, and modern hotels. Its railroad station is N, adjoined by urban nucleus Nueva Helvecia.

Colonias Unidas (kōlō'nyäs ōōnē'däs), town (pop. estimate 500), E central Chaco natl. territory, Argentina, 70 mi. NW of Resistencia; cotton, corn, spurge; sawmills, cotton gins.

Colonia Tabay, Argentina: see TABAY.

Colonia Valdense (kōlō'nyä väldĕn'sā), agr. settlement, Colonia dept., SW Uruguay, 40 mi. ENE of Colonia and SW of Colonia Suiza; grain, fruit, stock. Settled 1858 by Piedmontese immigrants of the Waldensian sect, it is sometimes called Colonia Piamontesa. La Paz, its urban nucleus, is W.

Colonie (kŏlŭnē'), village (pop. 2,068), Albany co., E N.Y., 6 mi. NW of downtown Albany; makes chemicals. Inc. 1921.

Colón Island (kōlōn'), largest island of Bocas del Toro Archipelago, in Caribbean Sea, off NW Panama; 5 mi. long, 2.5 mi. wide; rises to 400 ft. Its main center, Bocas del Toro, is on SE coast.

Colón Mountains (kōlōn'), on Honduras-Nicaragua border, form section of watershed bet. Patuca (N) and Coco (S) rivers; rise to c.2,000 ft. An E extension of Sierra de Dipilto; Colón Mts. end (E) in Cabo Falso on Caribbean Sea.

Colonna, Cape, Greece: see SOUNION, CAPE.

Colonne, Cape (kôlôn'nĕ), Calabria, S Italy, at SE entrance to Gulf of Taranto, 5 mi. SE of Crotone; 39°2'N 17°13'E; lighthouse. Has single Doric column on anc. site of temple of Hera.

Colonsay (kŏ'lŭnzā), island (pop. 232) of the Inner Hebrides, Argyll, Scotland, forming parish of Colonsay and Oronsay (□ 17.3; pop. 238) with adjacent isl. of ORONSAY. Colonsay is 6 mi. N of Islay and 9 mi. W of Jura; it is 8 mi. long, 4 mi. wide, and rises to 470 ft. On E coast is fishing port of Scalasaig (skă'lŭsāg), site of lighthouse.

Colony, city (pop. 386), Anderson co., E Kansas, 25 mi. N of Chanute, in livestock, grain, and dairy region.

Colophon (kŏ'lŭfŏn), anc. town of Asia Minor, near Ephesus, on Bay of Kusada, 15 mi. SW of present-day Torbali, Turkey.

Colora (kŭlō'rŭ), village, Cecil co., NE Md., 8 mi. N of Havre de Grace, in truck-farm area; vegetable canneries.

Colorada, La, Mexico: see LA COLORADA.

Colorada, La, Panama: see LA COLORADA.

Colorada Grande, Laguna (lägōō'nä kōlōrä'dä grän'dā), lake (□ 50) in SE La Pampa natl. territory, Argentina, 20 mi. S of Bernasconi; c.20 mi. long, 2–4 mi. wide.

Coloradas, Las, Argentina: see LAS COLORADAS.

Colorado (kōlōrä'dō). **1** Village (dist. pop. 1,110), Guanacaste prov., NW Costa Rica, port on Gulf of Nicoya of the Pacific, and 11 mi. SW of Las Juntas. Exports gold from Abangares mines; salt pans. Lumbering, stock raising. **2** Village, Limón prov., Costa Rica: see BARRA DE COLORADO.

Colorado (kŏlŭrä'dŭ, –rä'dō, –ră'dō), state (land only □ 103,967; with inland waters □ 104,247; 1950 pop. 1,325,089; 1940 pop. 1,123,296), W U.S., bordered by Nebr. and Wyo. (N), N.Mex. and Okla. (S), Kansas and Nebr. (E), and Utah (W); 7th in area, 34th in pop.; admitted 1876 as 38th state; ⊙ Denver. The "Centennial State" or the "Silver State," a rectangle measuring 276 mi. N–S and 387 mi. E–W, is a Rocky Mtn. state crossed by the Continental Divide. Its average alt. (6,800 ft.) is highest in U.S., and Mt. ELBERT (14,431 ft.) here is 2d in alt. only to Mt. Whitney, Calif. E of the Rockies—which cross central and W central Colo. —lie the high Great Plains, while to W is the greatly dissected COLORADO PLATEAU. The 2 principal chains of the Colorado Rockies converge in the S. The E chain consists (N–S) largely of the FRONT RANGE, including Longs Peak (14,255 ft.) and PIKES PEAK (14,110 ft.), and partly of the Wet Mts. The W chain includes (N–S) Park Range, Sawatch Mts., and Sangre de Cristo Mts. The Rockies are a rugged, scenic region of coniferous forests (chiefly pine, fir, and spruce) and alpine meadows above which are expanses of barren rock culminating in snow-capped peaks. Most of the state's c.20,000,000 acres of forest land is here, largely in natl. forests. ROCKY MOUNTAIN NATIONAL PARK is NW of Denver. Bet. the E and W chains are large natural park lands—North Park, Middle Park, and South Park—separated by transverse ranges. Farther S is the arid SAN LUIS VALLEY, site of GREAT SAND DUNES NATIONAL MONUMENT. The valley extends into N.Mex. bet. the Sangre de Cristo and San Juan Mts. From the Rockies flow the South Platte and Arkansas rivers E across the Great Plains; the Rio Grande flows S through the San Luis Valley; and the Colorado, Yampa, Gunnison, San Miguel, and Dolores rivers flow generally W across the Colorado Plateau. Where these rivers cut through the Rockies they form deep, steep-walled gorges, such as the spectacular ROYAL GORGE (Arkansas R.), Gore Canyon (Colorado R.), and Black Canyon (Gunnison R.). Other notable water features of the Rockies are mineral springs (Pagosa Springs, Glenwood Springs, Steamboat Springs), reservoirs (e.g., Green Mtn.

Reservoir, Granby Reservoir, Grand Lake), and small glacial lakes. Highway passes include Independence Pass (12,095 ft.), Berthoud Pass (11,314 ft.), Cameron Pass, and Fremont Pass. The Mt. Evans highway ascends to 14,260 ft. Railroads go through the MOFFAT TUNNEL in the vicinity of Denver, the Royal Gorge, and Veta Pass (9,100 ft.) farther S. The Colorado Plateau is a rugged arid and semiarid region of lofty plateaus (UNCOMPAHGRE PLATEAU), steep-sided mesas (Grand Mesa, Mesa Verde), basins, and deep canyons. Evergreens clothe some of the higher plateaus, while the lower parts have scanty xerophytic vegetation. There are large areas of colorful rock. MESA VERDE NATIONAL PARK, COLORADO NATIONAL MONUMENT, and DINOSAUR NATIONAL MONUMENT are here. The high Great Plains of E Colo. are a rolling, semiarid grassland region which slopes gradually E from the Rocky Mtn. foothills. Colo. has a dry continental type climate (modified by the alt.) marked by hot summers, cold winters (severe only in the mts.), considerable sunshine, and relatively low humidity. The temp., characterized by a high diurnal range, averages 72°F. for July and 31°F. for Jan. The highly variable precipitation (heaviest in the spring) averages only 16.5 in. annually, ranging from 7 in. in the San Luis Valley to 27 in. in the San Juan Mts. Grand Junction (W) averages 189 frost-free days annually (the longest period in the state) and Arriba (E) has 141, while Steamboat Springs (in the Rockies) averages only 60 days. More than ⅔ of the pop. is concentrated in the E foothills of the Rockies in a belt some 30 mi. wide extending N–S across the state. With the exception of Grand Junction, all the larger cities are here, including (N–S) Fort Collins, Greeley, Boulder, Denver, Colorado Springs, Pueblo, and Trinidad. Here is most of the industrial activity—meat packing, mfg. of dairy products, beet-sugar refining, grain milling, vegetable canning, metal- and woodworking, oil refining, and ore processing (smelting, refining). Denver, the chief center in the state, is also the principal metropolis of the entire Rocky Mtn. region. Pueblo is one of the few centers in the West having an iron and steel industry. Colo. is primarily a stock-raising (especially beef cattle, sheep), farming, and mining state. The Federal govt. owns 38% of the area. Of the state's c.66,500,000 acres, some 26,000,000 acres (including c.7,500,000 acres federally owned) are grazing lands. Cattle raising predominates in the W Great Plains and is important in the Rocky Mtn. park lands and in the South Platte, Gunnison, Yampa, and San Luis valleys. Dairying is concentrated around the urban areas. Sheep are raised primarily in W Colo., although large numbers are also found in W plains. Grazing is also important in the natl. forests, where lumbering is also carried on. Increasing amounts of livestock are now fattened on alfalfa and sugar-beet pulp in the state's irrigated valleys. One of the largest cattle feeding areas is N of Greeley, while the N plains are used for sheep feeding. Poultry, hogs, and horses are also raised. Recently some fur farms have developed around Denver. The dry farming areas are in the E Great Plains, the irrigated areas in E Colo., in the valleys of the South Platte and Arkansas rivers. Wheat is the chief crop, grown on the c.7,000,000 acres of land dry farmed, but the yield is uncertain because of the vagaries of rainfall and the menace of insect pests, especially grasshoppers. Prolonged droughts made a large part of the region a dust bowl in the 1930s. More important than the dry farming, however, is the irrigation agr. Colo. ranks 2d (after Calif.) in irrigated lands, with more than 3,000,000 acres under irrigation. Numerous storage reservoirs and many miles of canals have been built. In addition, several tunnels carry water through the Rockies from the wetter W slopes to the drier E slopes; the largest is the 13-mi. Alva B. Adams Tunnel which conducts water through the Front Range from the headwaters of the Colorado R. to a tributary of the South Platte. The principal irrigated crop is alfalfa; others are hay, sugar beets (Colo. is chief U.S. producer), vegetables (onions, potatoes, beans, celery), fruit (cantaloupes, apples, peaches, cherries), and grain. Chief minerals are bituminous coal and petroleum, and Colo. is leading U.S. producer of uranium, radium, molybdenum, and vanadium; there are also gold, silver, lead, zinc, tungsten, lithium, fluorspar, and feldspar. The state has enormous deposits of oil shale in the W. A major source of the state's income is tourism. Numerous resorts include Aspen, Boulder, Colorado Springs, Steamboat Springs, Estes Park, Ouray, and Denver. The region is also becoming increasingly popular as a winter-sports region. The Basket Makers lived on Mesa Verde in SW Colo. around the beginning of the Christian era. When white men entered Colo., they found the Ute Indians in the mtn. areas, while the Comanche, Cheyenne, Arapaho, and Kiowa roamed the plains. The Ute Consolidated Agency in SW Colo. is the only Indian reservation in the state today. The bitter Indian resistance to white settlement was finally overcome in the early 1870s. Spaniards searched the San Juan Valley for gold in 1765, but the region was practically virgin territory when the U.S. bought the area N of the Arkansas and E of the Rockies in the Louisiana Purchase of 1803. Exploring parties were sent out by the Federal govt. under Zebulon M. Pike (1806), Stephen H. Long (1819–20), and John C. Fremont (1842–43, 1845). Settlement began when the U.S. acquired the remainder of present Colo. after the Mexican War in 1848 (with Texas yielding some territory in 1850); the area was separated from N.Mex. territory in 1861. People began entering Colo. in large numbers when the discovery of gold in 1858 on the present site of Denver led to a rush from the East accompanied by the slogan "Pike's Peak or Bust." Many towns, including Denver, were soon founded as mining camps. Some, such as CENTRAL CITY and LEADVILLE survived, others became ghost towns as the diggings became exhausted. The lean mining years were partially counterbalanced by the development of huge ranches, and farming was stimulated by increasing railroad construction in the 1870s. The discovery in 1875 of lead ore bearing silver in the Leadville dist. led to another boom. Pop. increased fivefold 1870–80 and Colo. established institutions of higher learning—Colo. Seminary, now the Univ. of Denver, the Colo. Agr. and Mechanical Col. at Fort Collins, the School of Mines at Golden, Colo. Col. at Colorado Springs, and Univ. of Colo. at Boulder. Prosperity was short-lived, for while the 1890s brought a rich silver strike at CREEDE and the discovery of the state's richest gold field at CRIPPLE CREEK, it also brought the collapse of the silver market, industrial strife, disputes over railroad franchises, and warfare bet. sheep and cattle interests. By 1910 Colo. had settled down to a predominantly agr. economy. In the First World War the price of silver and agr. products soared, stimulating mining and extending farming into the drier parts of the Great Plains. The stock-market crash of 1929 and the droughts of 1932–37 (which created extensive dust bowls in the plains) were a severe shock to the state's economy. The Second World War brought another period of prosperity to the mines and farms. After the war the state extended irrigation and power development. See also articles on cities, towns, and geographic features, and the 63 counties: ADAMS, ALAMOSA, ARAPAHOE, ARCHULETA, BACA, BENT, BOULDER, CHAFFEE, CHEYENNE, CLEAR CREEK, CONEJOS, COSTILLA, CROWLEY, CUSTER, DELTA, DENVER, DOLORES, DOUGLAS, EAGLE, ELBERT, EL PASO, FREMONT, GARFIELD, GILPIN, GRAND, GUNNISON, HINSDALE, HUERFANO, JACKSON, JEFFERSON, KIOWA, KIT CARSON, LAKE, LA PLATA, LARIMER, LAS ANIMAS, LINCOLN, LOGAN, MESA, MINERAL, MOFFAT, MONTEZUMA, MONTROSE, MORGAN, OTERO, OURAY, PARK, PHILLIPS, PITKIN, PROWERS, PUEBLO, RIO BLANCO, RIO GRANDE, ROUTT, SAGUACHE, SAN JUAN, SAN MIGUEL, SEDGWICK, SUMMIT, TELLER, WASHINGTON, WELD, YUMA.

Colorado (kŭ″lŭrā′dŭ, kŏ″lŭ–), county (□ 950; pop. 17,576), S Texas; ⊙ Columbus. Drained by Colorado and San Bernard rivers; includes Eagle L.; has waterfowl refuges. A leading Texas rice-producing co.; also potatoes, cotton, wheat, corn, grain sorghums, truck, fruit; livestock raising (cattle, hogs, poultry), dairying. Large gravel and sand-mining industry; natural-gas and oil production; lumbering. Formed 1836.

Colorado, city, Texas: see COLORADO CITY.

Colorado, Arroyo (kŏ″lŭrā′dŭ, –rä′dŭ), stream, extreme S Texas, flows c.50 mi. NE from vicinity of Mercedes, through Cameron co., to Laguna Madre 25 mi. NNW of Port Isabel. Canalized for c.20 mi. of lower course, it connects barge port of Harlingen to Gulf Intracoastal Waterway.

Colorado, Río (rē′ō kōlōrä′dō). **1** River, in Catamarca and La Rioja provs., NW Argentina, rises on E slopes of Sierra de Famatina as the Abaucán, flows S, past Fiambalá and Tinogasta, turning SE as the Río Colorado or Río Salado, and flowing intermittently S to lose itself in desert swamps W of the Salina la Antigua; c.200 mi. long. **2** River, S central Argentina, formed by union of Barrancas R. and Río Grande (which rise in the Andes on Chile border) on Mendoza-Neuquén prov. border 20 mi. N of Buta Ranquil, flows 530 mi. SE across N Patagonia, along borders of Mendoza-Neuquén and La Pampa–Río Negro, to the Atlantic (delta) 80 mi. S of Bahía Blanca. With the Río Grande it is 710 mi. long. **3** River, Tucumán prov., Argentina, rises at SE foot of Cumbre de Potrerillo, flows 35 mi. SE and S, past Río Colorado, to the Salí R. at Leales.

Colorado, Río, Curicó-Talca provs., Chile: see LONTUÉ RIVER.

Colorado, Río, navigable right (S) arm of lower San Juan R., NE Costa Rica, flows 25 mi. to the Caribbean at Barra de Colorado.

Colorado, Río, Honduras: see LEÁN RIVER.

Colorado City (kŭ″lŭrā′dŭ), city (pop. 6,774), ⊙ Mitchell co., W Texas, 22 mi. S of Snyder and on Colorado R.; cattle-shipping center and processing point for dairying, agr. (grain, peanuts, cotton), oil-producing region; oil refinery, cotton gins and compresses, cottonseed-oil mill. Inc. 1907. Also called Colorado.

Colorado Creek (kŏlŭră′dŭ, –ră′dō, –rä′dō), district (1939 pop. 16), W Alaska, N of Kuskokwim R., 45 mi. NNW of McGrath; 63°33′N 156°W; placer gold mining.

Colorado Desert, in SE Calif., and N Lower California, Mexico; depressed arid region (part of Great Basin) W of Colorado R., NW of Gulf of California, and meeting (N) the Mojave Desert; traversed by scattered mtn. ranges. Includes IMPERIAL VALLEY, COACHELLA VALLEY (irrigated agr.) and SALTON SEA. Its area is variously estimated at 2–3,000 sq. mi.

Colorado National Monument (□ 28.3; established 1911), W Colo., 5 mi. W of Grand Junction. Eroded sandstone formations, many of them vividly colored, include huge monoliths, stratified ramparts, and steep-walled canyons. Notable features are Independence Rock (500-ft. sandstone shaft), Window Rock, and Cold Shivers Point, 1,000-ft. elevation in SE. Dinosaur fossils have been discovered in monument area.

Colorado Plateau or **Colorado Plateaus,** SW U.S., vast arid upland (□ c.1,300; alt. 5–11,000 ft.) drained by the Colorado R. system, and including much of Ariz. and Utah and smaller parts of Colo. and N.Mex. It is bounded E by the S Rocky Mts. and the valley of the Rio Grande, W by the Great Basin, and is one of least populated and most inaccessible regions of U.S. The deep canyons and high plateaus which contribute to its scenic beauty have made railroad construction impossible over most of the plateau, and roads are few. Composed mainly of generally horizontal Paleozoic sediments (sandstones, shales, conglomerates, and limestones), plateau is underlain by very ancient (pre-Cambrian) metamorphic rocks (exposed in Grand Canyon) and is overlaid in places by later formations (Mesozoic, Tertiary) and volcanic materials. Faulting has raised portions above the general plateau surface, and the Colorado and its tributaries (Grand, Green, Gunnison, Little Colorado, San Juan rivers) have carved magnificent canyons, chief among them the stupendous GRAND CANYON of the Colorado in NW Ariz. Brilliantly colored strata carved by erosion into fantastic shapes are also exhibited in BRYCE CANYON NATIONAL PARK, ZION NATIONAL PARK, CEDAR BREAKS NATIONAL MONUMENT in Utah; in Ariz. are the PAINTED DESERT, Meteor Crater, and the Petrified Forest; Rainbow Bridge Natl. Monument (Utah) contains largest known natural bridge; Mesa Verde Natl. Park (Colo.), Canyon de Chelly Natl. Monument (Ariz.) preserve ancient cliff dwellings. In NE Ariz., S Utah, and NW N.Mex. are the vast, arid, colorful lands of the "Navajo country," containing the Navajo and Hopi Indian reservations, where sheep herds, a little agr., and handicrafts support an increasing Indian pop. Resources of region have been little developed for the most part, although some minerals are produced in Utah and Colo. portions. Good stands of pine grow at high alts. of Ariz. and N.Mex., and there is some lumbering.

Colorado River. 1 (kŏlŭră′dŭ, –rä′dō, –rä′dō) Great river of SW U.S., extending generally SW from Colo., through Utah and Ariz., and S to N tip of Gulf of California; c.1,400 mi. long; drains □ 242,000 in U.S., □ 2,000 in Mexico; total fall of more than 10,000 ft. from source to mouth. Rises in Continental Divide in NW corner of Rocky Mtn. Natl. Park, Grand co., N Colo., flows through W Colo. and SE Utah, enters N Ariz. through Marble Gorge, turns W through GRAND CANYON, then S at Hoover Dam, and forms boundaries bet. Nev. and Ariz., bet. Calif. and Ariz., and bet. Lower California (Mexico) and Sonora (Mexico), entering Gulf of California opposite Montague Isl. Forms small part of international line bet. Ariz. (S of Yuma) and Lower California. In Mexico its outlet is the HARDY RIVER. Traverses mtn. region, cutting numerous deep gorges, throughout most of its extent, and in lower course follows irregular, shifting channel through large delta which includes part of Imperial Valley. Receives Dolores R. and Gunnison R. in Colo., Green R. (from Wyo.; above influx of Green R., the Colorado was formerly known as Grand R.) and San Juan R. in Utah, Little Colorado R. and Gila R. in Ariz. River is used extensively for irrigation and power. Colorado–Big Thompson project (in N Colo.; authorized 1937; scheduled for completion in early 1950s) provides for diversion of water from headstream of Colorado R., on W slope of Continental Divide, through ALVA B. ADAMS TUNNEL to Big Thompson R. on E slope, where dams divert water for supplemental irrigation of 615,000 acres in basin of South Platte R., in NE Colo.; hydro-electric plants at Olympus Dam on Big Thompson R. and at Green Mountain Dam on Blue R. HOOVER DAM, bet. Nev. and Ariz., is key unit in program of flood control, power, and irrigation for basin of lower Colorado R.; other units are PARKER DAM (turning part of flow into Colorado River Aqueduct for distribution to Los Angeles and neighboring cities) and DAVIS DAM. Imperial Dam, N of Yuma, diverts water into ALL-AMERICAN CANAL for irrigation of IMPERIAL VALLEY. Before the building of dams, floods in lower course resulted in formation of SALTON SEA (S Calif.) and Laguna SALADA (Lower California). River was 1st explored (1540) by

Alarcón, who ascended it to a point not far below the Grand Canyon. **2** (kŭ"lurā'dŭ) River in Texas, rises on the Llano Estacado in NW Texas, flows 970 mi. generally SE, through Austin, to Matagorda Bay just below Matagorda; drains □ 41,500. Main tributaries: Concho, Pedernales, and San Saba rivers, Beals Creek, Pecan Bayou. Chief flood-control, power, irrigation, water supply projects (BUCHANAN DAM, ROY INKS DAM, MARSHALL FORD DAM impounding L. Travis, TOM MILLER DAM impounding L. Austin) are controlled by Lower Colorado River Authority, founded 1934 after repeated destruction of private power developments by floods. Other projects on river and tributaries are under jurisdiction of Central Colorado River Authority and Upper Colorado River Authority.

Colorado River Aqueduct (kŏlurā'dŭ, –rā'dō, –rä'dō), S Calif., great water-supply system, for Los Angeles basin; has its head at PARKER DAM on the lower Colorado. Main aqueduct (242 mi. long), with pumping stations raising water 1,600 ft., leads W, across Colorado Desert and through San Jacinto Mts., to L. Mathews S of Riverside; gravity then carries flow through 150 mi. of distribution lines to cities of Los Angeles area. Constructed by Metropolitan Water Dist. of S Calif. A major engineering achievement, it was begun in 1932, and the aqueduct completed in 1939; 1st water delivered to users in 1941.

Colorados, Cerro (sĕ'rō kōlōrä'dōs), Andean volcano (19,846 ft.) on Argentina-Chile border; 26°11'S. Sometimes Cerro Ceros Colorados.

Colorados, Los, or **Bajos de Los Colorados** (bä'hōs dā lōs), archipelago off NW Cuba, a chain of low coral reefs and keys stretching for c.140 mi from Cape San Antonio (W) along the coast, endangering navigation. On several islets are lighthouses. The group is also called Guaniguanico or Santa Isabel.

Colorado Springs (kŏlurā'dŭ, –rā'dō, –rä'dō), city (pop. 45,472), ⊙ El Paso co., central Colo., at junction of Fountain and Monument creeks, near base of Pikes Peak, c.60 mi. S of Denver; 38°50'N 104°49'W; alt. 5,900 ft. Famous health resort; hq. of Pike Natl. Forest. Mfg. of film, granite, concrete, wood, and dairy products, vaccines, chemicals, motor trucks, mechanical appliances; gold refining, meat packing are important industries. Gold, silver, and coal mines near by. City has Colorado Col., former home of Helen Hunt Jackson, Fine Arts Center, Union Printers Home, state school for deaf and blind, Fountain Valley School, 2 museums, several private sanitariums. Ent Air Force Base is hq. (since 1951) of Air Defense Command. Camp Carson is S. Near-by points of interest: Manitou Springs, PIKES PEAK, Ute Pass, GARDEN OF THE GODS (just NW), Will Rogers shrine (on CHEYENNE MOUNTAIN), North Cheyenne Canyon, South Cheyenne Canyon (with Seven Falls, dropping 266 ft.). City founded 1871 near Colorado City, a mfg. town founded 1859, annexed to Colorado Springs, 1917, and now known as industrial suburb of West Colorado Springs. Growth followed development of Cripple Creek gold fields and beginning of tourist trade. Inc. 1886.

Colorno (kôlôr'nô), town (pop. 3,839), Parma prov., Emilia-Romagna, N central Italy, on Parma R. and 9 mi. N of Parma; canned foods, cheese; agr. tools, lye. Has palace.

Coloso or **Caleta Coloso** (kälā'tä kōlō'sō), village (1930 pop. 422), Antofagasta prov., N Chile, minor port on the Pacific, adjoining cape of Coloso Point (23°46'S 70°28'W), 9 mi. S of Antofagasta; rail terminus; exports nitrate.

Coloso or **Central Coloso,** locality, NW Puerto Rico, 1½ mi. E of Aguada; sugar mill.

Colossae (kulŏ'sē), ancient city of SW Phrygia, Asia Minor, S of the Maeander (modern Buyuk Menderes), 4 mi. E of present-day Denizli, W Asiatic Turkey; flourished as trading town until eclipsed by neighboring Laodicea. It was to the congregation of the early Christian Church here that St. Paul addressed the Epistle to the Colossians.

Colotlán (kōlōtlän'), city (pop. 5,093), Jalisco, N central Mexico, on affluent of the Santiago, near Zacatecas border, and 60 mi. SW of Zacatecas; alt. 5,692 ft. Agr. center (cereals, alfalfa, vegetables, fruit, livestock). Airfield.

Colp (kŏlp), village (pop. 253), Williamson co., S Ill., 3 mi. W of Herrin, in bituminous-coal-mining and agr. area.

Colquechaca (kōlkāchä'kä), city (pop. c.1,500), ⊙ Chayanta prov., Potosí dept., W central Bolivia, 65 mi. WNW of Potosí, and on road from Challapata; alt. 13,533 ft. Once a prosperous silver-mining center.

Colquemarca (kōlkāmär'kä), town (pop. 580), Cuzco dept., S Peru, in Andean valley, 55 mi. SSW of Cuzco; gold washing; mfg. of woolen goods. Silver, iron, tin, lead, copper, salt deposits.

Colquiri (kōlkē'rē), village (pop. c.6,100), La Paz dept., W Bolivia, 38 mi. N of Oruro, in Cordillera de Tres Cruces; alt. 13,321 ft.; tin-mining center.

Colquitt (kŏl'kwĭt), county (□ 563; pop. 33,999), S Ga.; ⊙ Moultrie. Bounded E by Little R.; drained by Ochlockonee R. and its affluents. Coastal plain agr. (cotton, tobacco, corn, truck, melons, peanuts, livestock) and forestry (lumber, naval stores) area. Formed 1856.

Colquitt, city (pop. 1,664), ⊙ Miller co., SW Ga., 21 mi. NNW of Bainbridge and on Spring Creek; agr. trade center; peanut shelling, sawmilling. Founded 1856, inc. 1860.

Colrain (kōlrān'), town (pop. 1,546), Franklin co., NW Mass., in hills, 7 mi. NW of Greenfield. Includes villages of Griswoldville (cotton products) and Shattuckville. Settled 1735, inc. 1761.

Colsterworth, England: see WOOLSTHORPE.

Colston Basset (kŏl'stŭn), agr. village and parish (pop. 283), SE Nottingham, England, 4 mi. S of Bingham; cheese making.

Colstrip (kōl'strĭp), village, Rosebud co., SE Mont., on branch of Yellowstone R. and 25 mi. S of Forsyth; large quantities of lignite coal taken from open-pit mine.

Colt, town (pop. 267), St. Francis co., E Ark., 8 mi. N of Forrest City.

Coltauco (kōltou'kō), town (pop. 996), O'Higgins prov., central Chile, on Cachapoal R. and 25 mi. WSW of Rancagua; rail terminus, agr. center (wheat, alfalfa, beans, potatoes, fruit, livestock); flour milling, dairying.

Coltishall, agr. village and parish (pop. 951), NE Norfolk, England, on Bure R. and 7 mi. NNE of Norwich; site of important Royal Air Force station in Second World War. Has 13th–14th-cent. church.

Colt Island, islet of The Skerries, in the Irish Sea, just E of Skerries town, NE Co. Dublin, Ireland.

Colton (kōl'tŭn), village and parish (pop. 1,116), N Lancashire, England, 5 mi. NNE of Ulverston; cattle and sheep raising, agr. Has 17th-cent. church and 17th-cent. Baptist chapel.

Colton. 1 City (pop. 14,465), San Bernardino co., S Calif., just SW of San Bernardino; railroad junction; large cement plant; fruit canning, fruit and meat packing, flour milling; mfg. of furniture, mattresses. Inc. 1887. **2** City (pop. 521), Minnehaha co., E S.Dak., 20 mi. NNW of Sioux Falls; feed, livestock, dairy products, grain. **3** Town (pop. 207), Whitman co., SE Wash., 12 mi. S of Pullman, in agr. region.

Coltons Point (kōl'tŭnz), summer-resort village, St. Marys co., S Md., on the Potomac and 8 mi. SW of Leonardtown.

Columbia. 1 County (□ 768; pop. 28,770), SW Ark.; ⊙ Magnolia. Bounded S by La. line; drained by Bayou Dorcheat. Agr. (cotton, corn, hogs); timber; oil wells. Cotton ginning, oil refining; some mfg. Formed 1852. **2** County (□ 786; pop. 18,216), N Fla., on Ga. line, bet. Suwannee (NW) and Santa Fe (S) rivers; ⊙ Lake City. Flatwoods area partly containing Okefenokee Swamp (N) and Osceola Natl. Forest (E). Agr. (corn, peanuts, cotton, tobacco, livestock) and forestry (lumber, naval stores); phosphate deposits in S. Formed 1832. **3** County (□ 306; pop. 9,525), E Ga.; ⊙ Appling. Bounded E by Savannah R. (forms S.C. line here) and N by Little R. Farming (cotton, corn, potatoes, livestock) and sawmilling area intersected by the fall line. Clark Hill Dam (NE) under construction (1950) in Savannah R. Formed 1790. **4** County (□ 643; pop. 43,182), SE N.Y.; ⊙ Hudson. Bordered E by Mass., W by the Hudson; drained by Kinderhook Creek. Dairying, farming (apples, corn, grain, potatoes), poultry raising; limestone quarrying. Has summer and winter resorts; includes part of Taconic State Park and several small lakes Formed 1786. **5** County (□ 646; pop. 22,967), NW Oregon; ⊙ St. Helens. Columbia R. forms N and E boundary. Lumber milling, dairying; salmon fisheries at St. Helens. Iron-ore deposits. Formed 1854. **6** County (□ 484; pop. 53,460), E central Pa.; ⊙ Bloomsburg. Hilly region extending from Pocono plateau (N) to anthracite field (S); drained by Susquehanna R. Anthracite; metals, railroad parts, motor vehicles, textiles, carpets. Formed 1813. **7** County (□ 860; pop. 4,860), SE Wash., on Oregon line; ⊙ Dayton. Plateau area, with Blue Mts. in S; drained by Tucannon and Touchet rivers and bounded N by the Snake. Wheat, barley, fruit, livestock. Includes part of Umatilla Natl. Forest. Formed 1875. **8** County (□ 778; pop. 34,023), S central Wis.; ⊙ Portage. Drained by Wisconsin, Fox, Crawfish, and Baraboo rivers; contains resort lakes, notably Mud L. and L. Wisconsin, and part of Baraboo Range. Dairying, stock raising, farming (grain, potatoes, tobacco). Vegetable canning, processing of dairy products; other mfg. Formed 1846.

Columbia. 1 Town (pop. 849), Houston co., SE Ala., on Chattahoochee R. (here forming Ga. line) and 17 mi. ENE of Dothan. **2** Village (1940 pop. 531), Tuolumne co., central Calif., 4 mi. N of Sonora, in Mother Lode country; famous old gold-mining town which lost the race for state capital in 1854; its old bldgs. are well preserved. **3** Town (pop. 1,327), Tolland co., E central Conn., on Hop R., just W of Willimantic; agr. Includes small Columbia L. (resort), Hop River and Chestnut Hill villages. Eleazer Wheelock established here the school for Indians which became Dartmouth Col. Settled c.1695, organized 1804. **4** City (pop. 2,179), Monroe co., SW Ill., 12 mi. S of East St. Louis, in agr. area (corn, wheat, livestock); limestone quarries. Inc. as village in 1859, as city in 1933. **5** Town (pop. 2,167), ⊙ Adair co., S Ky., 36 mi. ENE of Glasgow, in agr. and timber area; lumber and flour milling, mfg. of quilted articles, soft drinks; airport. Seat of Lindsey Wilson Jr. Col. Settled c.1793. **6** Village (pop. 920), ⊙ Caldwell parish, NE central La., 28 mi. S of Monroe and on Ouachita R.; agr. (cotton, corn, truck); cotton ginning, lumber milling, furniture mfg. **7** Town (pop. 352), Washington co., E Maine, 16 mi. WSW of Machias, in blueberry-growing area. **8** City (pop. 6,124), ⊙ Marion co., S Miss., 32 mi. W of Hattiesburg, and on Pearl R., in agr. area; mfg. (clothing, hosiery, canned foods, veneer, naval stores); formerly a lumber center. A state industrial and training school is near by. Was ⊙ Miss. for part of 1821. **9** City (pop. 31,974), ⊙ Boone co., central Mo., near Missouri R., 20 mi. NW of Jefferson City. Trade center of farm and coal area; mfg. (shoes, clothing, dairy and grain products). Univ. of Missouri, Stephens Col., Christian Col., state cancer hosp. here. Laid out 1821, inc. 1826. **10** Town (pop. 495), Coos co., NW N.H., on the Connecticut and 28 mi. NW of Berlin. **11** Village (pop. c.300), Warren co., NW N.J., on Delaware R., at mouth of Paulins Kill (hydroelectric dam here), opposite Portland, Pa. Delaware Water Gap is 4 mi. NNW. **12** Town (pop. 1,161), ⊙ Tyrrell co., E N.C., 28 mi. E of Plymouth and on Scuppernong R., a navigable inlet of Albemarle Sound; sawmilling, fishing. A trading post before 1700; named Columbia in 1810. **13** City, Columbia co., Oregon: see COLUMBIA CITY. **14** Borough (pop. 11,993), Lancaster co., SE Pa., 10 mi. W of Lancaster and on Susquehanna R. (bridged); textiles, metal products, tobacco. Settled 1730, laid out 1788, inc. 1814. **15** Largest city (pop. 86,914) and ⊙ S.C. and Richland co., central S.C., on the fall line at head of navigation on the Congaree (formed here by junction of Broad and Saluda rivers), and 100 mi. NW of Charleston; 34°N 81°2'W; alt. 300 ft. It is a distributing, trade, and mfg. center, abundantly supplied with hydroelectric power; many large textile mills; other plants deal with lumber, clay, stone, and food products,fertilizer,cottonseed oil,printing;railroad shops, foundries, machine shops. U.S. Fort Jackson is E. Chosen as site of new capital in 1786, Columbia was founded here; legislature 1st met here in 1790. Most of city was burned by Sherman on night of Feb. 17, 1865, but out of the burning and the difficult years of Reconstruction its people built a more beautiful city. A cultural center from the first: Univ. of South Carolina, Allen Univ. (Negro), Benedict Col. (Negro), and Columbia Bible Col. here. City has state penitentiary, state hosp., U.S. veterans' hosp., fine airport. Notable buildings include: state house (begun 1851; an Ital. Renaissance structure); Woodrow Wilson Mus., boyhood home of the President; several antebellum houses. Near by are Fort Jackson (large U.S. army post), L. Murray, formed by dammed Saluda R., and Sesqui-Centennial State Park (1,500 acres; NE). Important annual events include state fairs and Columbia music festival. **16** City (pop. 270), Brown co., NE S.Dak., 14 mi. NE of Aberdeen and on James R.; trading point for agr. area. **17** City (pop. 10,911), ⊙ Maury co., central Tenn., on Duck R. and 40 mi. SSW of Nashville. A famous mule market; also trade and processing center for rich agr., dairying, livestock-raising, phosphate-mining area; mfg. of clothing, hosiery, chairs, aircraft parts, dairy products; flour milling. Home of James K. Polk here. Columbia Military Acad., and experiment station of Univ. of Tenn. near by. Settled 1807; inc. 1817. **18** Town (pop. 119), Fluvanna co., central Va., on the James, at Rivanna R. mouth, and 25 mi. SE of Charlottesville; canned foods, lumber.

Columbia, Cape, N Ellesmere Isl., NE Franklin Dist., Northwest Territories, on the Arctic Ocean; 83°7'N 70°28'W; northernmost point of Canada. Only N tip of Greenland is farther N.

Columbia, District of, U.S.: see DISTRICT OF COLUMBIA.

Columbia, Mount (12,294 ft.), on Alta.–B.C. line, in Rocky Mts., at S edge of Jasper Natl. Park, 60 mi. SSE of Jasper, in Columbia Icefield; 52°9'N 117°26'W. Athabaska R. rises here.

Columbia, Mount, peak (14,084 ft.), in Rocky Mts., Chaffee co., W central Colo.

Columbia Bay (5 mi. long, 3 mi. wide), S Alaska, on Prince William Sound, 30 mi. WSW of Valdez; 60°58'N 147°5'W. Receives scenic Columbia Glacier.

Columbia City. 1 City (pop. 4,745), ⊙ Whitley co., NE Ind., 20 mi. WNW of Fort Wayne, in agr. area (livestock, grain, poultry, soybeans; dairy products); mfg. (clothing, woolen goods, flour, condiments, automotive and aircraft products). **2** or **Columbia,** city (pop. 405), Columbia co., NW Oregon, on Columbia R. just N of St. Helens.

Columbia Falls. 1 Town (pop. 550), Washington co., E Maine, on Pleasant R. and 14 mi. WSW of Machias; agr.; blueberry canning. **2** Town (pop. 1,232), Flathead co., NW Mont., on Flathead R. and 15 mi. NNE of Kalispell; lumber mill; grain, fruit, vegetables.

Columbia Heights, city (pop. 8,175), Anoka co., E Minn., NE suburb of Minneapolis. Inc. 1921.

Columbia Mountains, B.C.: see ROCKY MOUNTAINS.

Columbiana (kúlŭm″bēă′nú), county (□ 535; pop. 98,920), E Ohio; ⊙ Lisbon. Bounded E by Pa. line, SE by Ohio R.; also drained by Little Beaver R. and by small Sandy and Yellow creeks. Agr. area (livestock; dairy products; fruit, grain, truck); mfg. at East Liverpool, Salem, East Palestine, Wellsville; coal mines, clay pits. Formed 1803.

Columbiana. 1 Town (pop. 1,761), ⊙ Shelby co., central Ala., 25 mi. SSE of Birmingham, in corn and cotton area; lumber milling. Founded c.1825. **2** Village (pop. 3,369), Columbiana co., E Ohio, 15 mi. S of Youngstown, in agr. and coal-mining area; machinery, furniture, pumps, boilers, tools. Settled 1802.

Columbia Plateau, Wash.: see COLUMBIA RIVER.

Columbia River, NW U.S. and SW Canada, rises in Rocky Mts. in British Columbia c.80 mi. N of U.S. line, flows c.1,200 mi. NW, S, W, SE, and W (forming Wash.-Oregon boundary) to the Pacific SW of Tacoma. Second to the Mississippi in volume among U.S. rivers, it drains a basin of □ 259,000, 85% of it in the U.S., and including nearly all of Idaho, most of Wash. and Oregon, and parts of Mont., Wyo., Nev., and Utah. It enters the U.S. near NE corner of Wash., and bet. the border and its junction with the Snake it is diverted into the "Big Bend" by an extensive lava basin (Columbia Plateau), which covers much of E Wash., E Oregon, and part (including Snake River Plain) of S Idaho. In Big Bend region is the Grand Coulee, dry prehistoric bed of part of river, now the site chosen for a large irrigation reservoir of the Columbia Basin project. The Columbia has many rapids and falls, and it has cut a great gorge, famed for its beauty, through the Cascade Range E of Portland, Oregon; the scenic Columbia R. Highway and railroads follow the gorge. Its mouth forms a deepwater harbor, with jetties (one is 7 mi. long) at entrance; ocean-going ships pass through a channel to the mouth of the Willamette R. and to the ports of Portland and Vancouver. Bonneville Dam is head of tidewater. Canals around obstructions (notably through the Cascade Range and at The Dalles) allow river boats to proceed farther upstream. Chief tributaries are the Kootenai, Clark Fork, Spokane, Okanogan, Yakima, Snake, Umatilla, John Day, Deschutes and Willamette rivers. Extensive fisheries (c.39,000,000 lbs. annually), mainly salmon, are protected by ladders and elevators for migrating fish at Bonneville and smaller dams, and by transplanting at Grand Coulee Dam. BONNEVILLE DAM (completed 1937), GRAND COULEE DAM (completed 1941), and MCNARY DAM (begun 1947) are part of vast Federal plan for developing the Columbia Basin; Rock Isl. Dam (privately owned) is on main stream, and many other dams and irrigation projects are on the Columbia's tributaries. Franklin D. Roosevelt L., the 151-mi. backwater of Grand Coulee Dam, is being developed as a recreational region. Federal plan for the basin's development contemplates 238 multiple-purpose projects, including 142 major dams; irrigation of 536,000,000 acres of land would be initiated or supplemented. Largest blocks of land which would be affected lie in central Wash. and N Oregon (including the Columbia Basin Project lands, 1,029,000 arid acres lying S of Grand Coulee Dam), areas in central Snake R. valley bet. Twin Falls and Boise, Idaho, and lands W of the Cascades, mainly in Oregon. Navigation on 600 mi. of waterways (principally the lower Columbia, Willamette, and Snake rivers), would be improved, flood control strengthened, and huge quantities of hydroelectric power added to the present output. An international joint commission considers problems and plans arising from Canadian and U.S. interests in development of the Columbia and its tributaries. Capt. Robert Gray discovered the mouth of the Columbia in 1792 and named it after his ship; Lt. William R. Broughton, an English naval officer, 1st entered it and mapped part of its course the same year. The Lewis and Clark expedition 1st reached it by land in 1805; its headwaters were discovered and its entire course explored 1807–11 by David Thompson. Before actual discovery, the river was known in traders' and explorers' legends as the River of the West or the Oregon.

Columbiaville, village (pop. 789), Lapeer co., E Mich., on Flint R. and 9 mi. NW of Lapeer, in agr. area.

Columbine, Cape, SW Cape Prov., U. of So. Afr., on the Atlantic, 90 mi. NNW of Cape Town; 32°48′S 17°51′E.

Columbretes (kōlōōmbrā′tĕs), archipelago of volcanic islets and rocks, in the W Mediterranean off E coast of Spain, 40 mi. E of Castellón de la Plana, at about 40°N 0°45′E. Known for vipers. Visited only by fishermen.

Columbus, county (□ 939; pop. 50,621), SE N.C.; ⊙ Whiteville. Bounded SW by S.C., NW by Lumber R.; forested and partly swampy tidewater area; drained by Waccamaw R. (forms small L. Waccamaw here). Farming (tobacco, corn, sweet potatoes); sawmilling. Formed 1808.

Columbus. 1 City (pop. 79,611), ⊙ Muscogee co., W Ga., c.90 mi. SSW of Atlanta and at head of navigation on Chattahoochee R., opposite Phenix City, Ala., at the fall line. Cotton market, and an industrial and shipping center, with textile mills, foundries, farm-products processing plants, and railroad shops. Mfg. of clothing, yarns, fabrics machinery, electrical equipment, agr. implements, fertilizer, food products, concrete products, bricks, lumber; meat packing, peanut processing. Hydroelectric power developments on CHATTAHOOCHEE RIVER have stimulated industrial growth. U.S. Fort Benning, with noted infantry training school, and Lawson Air Force Base are near by. Columbus was founded 1828 as a trading post on site of Creek Indian village. Its first textile mill was established 1838. A busy river traffic developed until the arrival of the railroads (1850s). During the Indian war of 1836, the Mexican War, and Civil War, Columbus was an important supply point. The city was taken by the Federals in April, 1865. **2** Village (pop. 83), Adams co., W Ill., 13 mi. E of Quincy. **3** City (pop. 18,370), ⊙ Bartholomew co., S central Ind., on East Fork of White R. and c.40 mi. SSE of Indianapolis, in agr. area; mfg. of Diesel engines, auto parts, wood and metal products, furniture, starch, clothing, cement products, canned goods; creosoting works, tanneries. Tipton Knoll, one of largest prehistoric Indian mounds in the state, is here. U.S. Camp Atterbury and Atterbury Air Force Base are 12 mi. NW. Settled c.1819. **4** City (pop. 3,490), ⊙ Cherokee co., extreme SE Kansas, 18 mi. SSW of Pittsburg; trade center for diversified agr. region; dairying; mfg. of work clothing, explosives. Coal mines and deposits of zinc and lead in vicinity. Laid out 1868, inc. 1871. **5** City (pop. 482), Hickman co., SW Ky., on the Mississippi and 28 mi. W of Mayfield, Ky., in agr. area. Columbus Belmont Battlefield State Park is near by, on old site of this community (now moved to higher ground); was a Confederate stronghold early in Civil War. **6** City (pop. 17,172), ⊙ Lowndes co., E Miss., on Tombigbee R. and c.80 mi. N of Meridian, near Ala. line; trade, transportation, and industrial center for cotton, livestock, and timber area; brick, clothing, creosoted and other wood products, cotton and dairy products; meat packing, marble cutting. Seat of Mississippi State Col. for Women and of Franklin Acad., which was 1st free school in state. Has a number of fine antebellum homes. Settled 1817, inc. 1821. **7** Town (pop. 1,097), ⊙ Stillwater co., S Mont., on Yellowstone R., at mouth of Stillwater R., and 40 mi. WSW of Billings; trade and shipping point; coal and copper mines; grain, sugar beets, livestock. **8** City (pop. 8,884), ⊙ Platte co., E Nebr., 70 mi. W of Omaha, in prairie region, at junction of Loup and Platte rivers; rail, mfg., trade center. Cement products, beverages, shoes, machine parts, feed; grain, livestock, dairy and poultry produce. Hq. for publicly owned power project on Loup R. City founded 1856. **9** Village (1940 pop. 595), Burlington co., W N.J., 7 mi. E of Burlington; farm trade center. **10** Village (pop. 251), Luna co., SW N.Mex., port of entry near Mex. line, 70 mi. W of El Paso, Texas. Gold, silver, copper, and onyx mined in Tres Hermanas Mts., just NW. **11** Town (pop. 486), ⊙ Polk co., W N.C., 15 mi. SE of Hendersonville, near S.C. line; large woolen mill; mfg. of drugs. **12** City (pop. 525), Burke co., NW N.Dak., 85 mi. NW of Minot; coal mines, truck and dairy farms, wheat, grain, oats, potatoes. **13** City (□ 39.5; pop. 375,901), ⊙ Ohio and Franklin co., central Ohio, on Scioto R. at mouth of Olentangy R., and 125 mi. SW of Cleveland; 39°56′N 83°W; alt. 800 ft. State's 3d-largest city (after Cleveland and Cincinnati); railroad hub, distribution center, with large jobbing and wholesale trade; port of entry. Seat of Ohio State Univ., Capital Univ. (at near-by Bexley), Col. of St. Mary of the Springs, Franklin Univ. Diversified industry: meat packing, printing and publishing, paper milling; mfg. of foundry products, aircraft, auto parts, electrical and heating equipment, glass, machinery, footwear, clothing. Trade center for rich farm area. City's center lies along a bend of the Scioto. Near river's E bank are the civic center and the capitol (Greek Revival; completed 1861), in 10-acre square; State Office Bldg., with state library; the Federal Bldg. Other points of interest: Columbus Gall. of Fine Arst (1931); Battelle Memorial Inst. (for industrial research); state institutions for the deaf and the blind; Ohio State Penitentiary; My Jewels Monument (to Ohio's noted soldiers and political figures); Memorial to William McKinley; Franklin County Memorial Hall; library and mus. of state archaeological and historical society; state fairgrounds; the zoo; Confederate cemetery, adjacent to site of Civil War Camp Chase. U.S. Fort Hayes is here; Lockbourne Air Force Base is at Lockbourne (S). City laid out in 1812, as site of state capital; govt. moved here in 1816 from Chillicothe. Inc. as borough in 1816, as city in 1834. Coming of feeder canal (1831) to Ohio and Erie Canal, the National Road (1833), and the 1st railroad (1850) stimulated its growth. City's suburbs include Bexley, Grandview Heights, Upper Arlington, Westerville, Worthington. **14** Town (pop. 2,878), ⊙ Colorado co., S Texas, c.70 mi. W of Houston and on Colorado R.; trade center for agr. area; cotton ginning, concrete mfg., lumber milling, gravel mining. Founded 1823, inc. 1928. **15** City (pop. 3,250), Columbia co., S central Wis., on Crawfish R. and 27 mi. NE of Madison, in diversified-farming area; machinery, dairy products, beer, canned vegetables. Louis H. Sullivan designed a local bank bldg. (1919). Settled c.1840, inc. 1874.

Columbus Bank, shoal (c.50 mi. NE-SW, up to 20 mi. wide), Bahama Isls., E and S of Great Ragged Isl.; continues Great Bahama Bank towards SE.

Columbus Belmont Battlefield State Park: see COLUMBUS, city, Ky.

Columbus City, town (pop. 350), Louisa co., SE Iowa, near Iowa R., 20 mi. WSW of Muscatine.

Columbus Grove. 1 Village (pop. 1,013), Monroe co., SE Mich. **2** Village (pop. 1,936), Putnam co., NW Ohio, 13 mi. N of Lima, in agr. area; dairy products, canned mushrooms, handles.

Columbus Junction, town (pop. 1,123), Louisa co., SE Iowa, on Iowa R. and 19 mi. WSW of Muscatine; tomato cannery.

Columna, La (lä kōlōōm′nä), or **Bolívar** (bōlē′vär), Andean peak (16,411 ft.) in Mérida state, W Venezuela, highest peak of Sierra Nevada de Mérida and of Venezuela, 8 mi. ESE of Mérida. Bolívar is name commonly given to highest of La Columna's twin peaks.

Colunga (kōlōōng′gä), town (pop. 867), Oviedo prov., N Spain, near Bay of Biscay, 20 mi. ESE of Gijón. Coal and iron mines near by. Corn, lumber, livestock.

Colusa (kúlōō′sú, kō–), county (□ 1,153; pop. 11,651), N central Calif.; ⊙ Colusa. Rises from lowlands along Sacramento R. (E boundary) to Coast Ranges in W. Includes parts of Mendocino Natl. Forest (W); and a wildlife refuge (N). Farming (rice, barley, sugar beets, alfalfa, almonds, prunes, vegetables); stock raising (sheep, cattle); dairying, beekeeping. Gold mining, sand and gravel quarrying. Hunting (waterfowl, pheasant, deer). Formed 1850.

Colusa, city (pop. 3,031), ⊙ Colusa co., N central Calif., on Sacramento R. and c.55 mi. NW of Sacramento; irrigated agr. (rice, fruit, grain, nuts). Inc. 1870.

Colvalenza, Italy: see COLLEVALENZA.

Colvend and Southwick (kŏlvĕnd′), parish (pop. 1,128), SE Kirkcudbright, Scotland. Includes DOUGLAS HALL and KIPPFORD.

Colver, village (pop. 1,708), Cambria co., W central Pa., 5 mi. N of Nanty Glo.

Colville (kŏl′vĭl), city (pop. 3,033), ⊙ Stevens co., NE Wash., 65 mi. NW of Spokane and on Colville R.; silver, lead, timber, wheat. Founded 1826 as a Hudson's Bay Company post, U.S. Fort Colville built 1859, inc. 1890.

Colville, Cape (kŏl′vĭl), N N.Isl., New Zealand, in Hauraki Gulf, at NW end of Coromandel peninsula; 36°29′S 175°21′E.

Colville, Lake (25 mi. long, 15 mi. wide), NW Mackenzie Dist., Northwest Territories, NW of Great Bear L.; 67°10′N 126°W. Outlet: Anderson R.

Colville Lake, Wash.: see SPRAGUE.

Colville Range, N N.Isl., New Zealand, central ridge of Coromandel peninsula; extends 40 mi. S from Coromandel to Waihi; rises to 2,680 ft.; forested slopes. Silver, gold.

Colville River (kŏl′vĭl, kōl′–), N Alaska, principal river draining Arctic slope; rises in several small streams in N Brooks Range, near 68°37′N, flows c.375 mi. ENE to Beaufort Sea of the Arctic Ocean at 70°30′N 150°10′W. Frozen most of year. Principal tributaries are Killik R. and Anaktuvuk R. River valley is part of Naval Oil Reserve.

Colville River, NE Wash., rises in S Stevens co., flows c.70 mi. NW, past Colville, to Columbia R. NW of the city.

Colvin, Mount (kŏl′vĭn) (4,074 ft.), Essex co., NE N.Y., in the Adirondacks c.4 mi. ESE of Mt. Marcy, c.15 mi. SE of Lake Placid village.

Colwall, town and parish (pop. 1,990), E Hereford, England, 4 mi. WSW of Great Malvern; agr. market. Church is partly Norman. Elizabeth Barrett Browning spent her childhood here.

Colwell (kŏl′wĕl), town (pop. 122), Floyd co., N Iowa, 8 mi. NE of Charles City; creamery.

Colwich (kŏl′wĭch), city (pop. 339), Sedgwick co., S Kansas, 13 mi. WNW of Wichita, in wheat region.

Colwick (kŏ′lĭk), residential town and parish (pop. 2,549), S Nottingham, England, on Trent R. and 3 mi. E of Nottingham; beet-sugar refining; soap, concrete.

Colwyn (kŏl′wĭn), borough (pop. 2,143), Delaware co., SE Pa., SW suburb of Philadelphia.

Colwyn Bay (kôl′wĭn), municipal borough (1931 pop. 20,886; 1951 census 22,276), NW Denbigh, Wales, on Colwyn Bay of Irish Sea, 5 mi. ESE of Llandudno; seaside resort, with beach, promenade, and piers. Urban dist. includes resort town of Llandrillo-yn-Rhos or Rhos (lăndrĭth′lō-ŭn-rōs′) (pop. 3,507), residential town of Eirias (ī′rēäs) (pop. 3,835), and quarrying town of Llysfaen (lĕsvīn′) (pop. 3,383).

Colyton (kŏ′lĭtŭn), town and parish (pop. 2,040), E Devon, England, 3 mi. N of Seaton; lace mfg., tanning; slate quarrying. Has 13th-cent. church.

Comacchio (kômäk'kyô), town (pop. 9,141), Ferrara prov., Emilia-Romagna, N central Italy, near the Adriatic, 29 mi. ESE of Ferrara, on islets in midst of Valli di Comacchio lagoon (19 mi. long, 5–10 mi. wide). Fishing center (eels); saltworks, woolen mill, macaroni factory. Bishopric. Has 16th-cent. cathedral. Its port is Porto Garibaldi.

Comal (kō'măl), county (□ 567; pop. 16,357), S central Texas; ⊙ New Braunfels. Crossed SW-NE by Balcones Escarpment, separating broken hilly region from agr. prairies of S and SE; alt. 700–1,400 ft.; drained by Guadalupe R., here receiving spring-fed Comal R. Ranching (sheep, goats; some cattle); agr. (corn, sorghum, oats, cotton, pecans); dairying; poultry, hogs. Timber (esp. cedar); limestone, clay. Mfg. at New Braunfels. Formed 1846.

Comala (kōmä'lä), town (pop. 2,829), Colima, W Mexico, in foothills, 7 mi. NW of Colima; alt. 2,050 ft.; corn, rice, beans, sugar cane, coffee, tobacco, fruit, livestock.

Comalapa or **San Juan Comalapa** (sän hwän' kōmälä'pä), town (1950 pop. 7,458), Chimaltenango dept., S central Guatemala, 9 mi. NNW of Chimaltenango; alt. 6,200 ft. Road and market center; brick making, cotton weaving; agr. (corn, beans, wheat).

Comalapa, Mexico: see FRONTERA COMALAPA.

Comalapa, town (1950 pop. 434), Chontales dept., S Nicaragua, 15 mi. NNW of Juigalpa; agr. center (coffee, vegetables); livestock. Beverage mfg., coffee processing.

Comalcalco (kōmälkäl'kō), city (pop. 3,364), Tabasco, SE Mexico, on the Río Seco (arm of Grijalva R.) and 28 mi. NW of Villahermosa; agr. center (rice, coffee, beans, fruit, stock).

Comallo (kōmä'yō), village (pop. estimate 500), SW Río Negro natl. territory, Argentina, on railroad and 55 mi. E of San Carlos de Bariloche; resort; stock-raising and lumbering center.

Comal River, Texas: see NEW BRAUNFELS.

Comana (kômä'nä), village (pop. 2,319), Bucharest prov., S Rumania, on railroad and 21 mi. NE of Giurgiu. Site of 18th-cent. monastery, several times restored.

Comanche (kůmăn'chē). **1** County (□ 800; pop. 3,888), S Kansas; ⊙ Coldwater. Level to rolling prairie region, bordered S by Okla.; drained by headstreams of Salt Fork of Arkansas R. Cattle raising, grain growing. Formed 1885. **2** County (□ 1,088; pop. 55,165), SW Okla.; ⊙ Lawton. Drained by Cache, West Cache, and Beaver creeks. Includes most of the Wichita Mts. U.S. Fort Sill, L. Lawtonka with Medicine Park resort, and a large wildlife refuge are in co. Some agr. (livestock, cotton, wheat, hay, oats, sorghums). Mfg. at Lawton. Granite and limestone quarries; oil wells; sand and gravel pits. Formed 1907. **3** County (□ 972; pop. 15,516), central Texas; ⊙ Comanche. Drained by Leon and South Leon rivers; mts. (c.1,800 ft.) in SW. A leading U.S. peanut-producing area; also fruit, pecans, grain, truck, livestock (cattle, sheep, goats, poultry, hogs); wool, mohair marketed. Oil, natural-gas wells; clay. Formed 1856.

Comanche. **1** City (pop. 2,083), Stephens co., S Okla., 9 mi. S of Duncan, in oil, farm, and ranch area; cotton ginning. Comanche L. is 4 mi. E. Founded 1892 on site of Indian village. **2** Town (pop. 3,840), ⊙ Comanche co., central Texas, 26 mi. ENE of Brownwood; shipping, processing center for diversified agr. co.: pecan and peanut shelling, grain milling, poultry and egg packing, cheese mfg. Founded 1858, inc. 1873.

Comanche Lake, Stephens co., S Okla., 4 mi. E of Comanche; c.2 mi. long.

Comandante Arbues, Brazil: see MIRANDÓPOLIS.

Comandante Fontana (kōmändän'tā fōntä'nä), town (pop. estimate 1,000), central Formosa natl. territory, Argentina, on railroad and 110 mi. NW of Formosa; cotton, corn, livestock; lumber.

Comandante Luis Piedrabuena (lōō-ēs' pyädräbwā'nä), village (pop. estimate 1,000), E Santa Cruz natl. territory, Argentina, port on Santa Cruz R. and 12 mi. NW of Santa Cruz; meat-packing and agr. center (alfalfa, potatoes, sheep, horses).

Comanesti (kômůněsht'), Rum. *Comăneşti*, village (pop. 1,451), Bacau prov., E central Rumania, in the Moldavian Carpathians, 4 mi. SW of Moinesti; rail junction and lignite-mining center; also lumbering.

Comapa (kōmä'pä), town (pop. 409), Veracruz, E Mexico, in Sierra Madre Oriental, 5 mi. E of Huatusco; fruit.

Coma Pedrosa, Puig de la (pōōch' dā lä kō'mä pādrō'sä), highest summit (alt. 9,665 ft.) of Andorra, in central Pyrenees, 7 mi. NW of Andorra la Vella, near Fr. and Sp. border.

Comarapa (kōmärä'pä), town (pop. c.3,100), Santa Cruz dept., central Bolivia, in E foothills of Cordillera de Cochabamba, 50 mi. NW of Valle Grande; grain, potatoes. Founded 1615.

Comares (kōmä'rěs), town (pop. 703), Málaga prov., S Spain, 13 mi. NE of Málaga; olives, raisins, figs, almonds.

Comarnic (kômär'nēk), village (pop. 4,022), Prahova prov., S central Rumania, on Prahova R., on railroad and 8 mi. SE of Sinaia; summer resort; mfg. of bricks and tiles, cement, plaster, lime.

Comasagua (kōmäsä'gwä), city (pop. 1,443), La Libertad dept., SW Salvador, in coastal range, 7 mi. SW of Nueva San Salvador; coffee, grain. Gypsum deposits near by.

Comayagua (kōmïä'gwä), department (□ 1,919; 1950 pop. 74,988), W central Honduras; ⊙ Comayagua. Bounded N by Sulaco R.; largely mountainous, with Sierra de Montecillos in W, Sierra de Comayagua in E; bisected N–S by Comayagua R. valley. Mainly agr. (wheat, corn, beans, rice, coffee, tobacco, sugar cane); dairy farming. Cacao, rubber, indigo, and vanilla grow wild on tropical hill slopes. Main centers (served by Tegucigalpa-Caribbean coast route) are Comayagua (mfg. center) and Siguatepeque. Its archaeological sites include Tenampúa. Formed 1825.

Comayagua, city (pop. 4,828), ⊙ Comayagua dept., W central Honduras, on Comayagua R. and 35 mi. NW of Tegucigalpa, on road; 14°24'N 87°38'W; alt. 2,067 ft. Commercial and industrial center in fertile Comayagua R. valley; mfg. of beverages, alcohol, soap, bricks, musical instruments, cigarettes; sawmilling, woodworking. Has 18th-cent. cathedral (formerly bishop's see), several 16th-cent. churches, col., and Sp. colonial buildings. Airfield. One of 1st inland cities founded by Spaniards in Honduras, it dates from early 16th cent. Was ⊙ Sp. prov. of Honduras and of republic (1543–1880), when it was called Valladolid.

Comayagua, Sierra de (syě'rä dā), N spur of main Andine divide, W central Honduras, E of Comayagua; rises to over 7,000 ft.; divide bet. Comayagua R. (W) and headstreams of Sulaco R. (E).

Comayagua River, central Honduras, rises W of Humuya in Sierra de Guajiquiro, flows over 100 mi. N, past Humuya (here called Humuya R.), through Comayagua valley, past Comayagua, to Ulúa R. 2 mi. SE of Pimienta. Also known as Humuya R. in entire course. Receives Sulaco R. (right).

Comayagüela (kōmïägwā'lä), city (pop., including Tegucigalpa, 55,755), Francisco Morazán dept., S central Honduras, on left bank of Choluteca R., opposite twin city of TEGUCIGALPA (administered jointly since 1938 as the Central District); commercial center; light mfg. Has old city hall, polyclinic, normal school, school of arts and crafts. An obelisk marks Honduras independence. Located in level terrain, it is laid out in checkerboard fashion. Developed in 19th cent.; called Villa de Concepción until 1897. Although declared (1898) integral part of Tegucigalpa, it kept own municipal govt. until 1938.

Combaconum, India: see KUMBAKONAM.

Combahee River (kům'bē), S S.C., formed 15 mi. SW of Walterboro by junction of Salkehatchie (sôl"kēhă'chē, popularly sôlt'kē"chůr) and Little Salkehatchie rivers; flows 40 mi. SE to Coosaw R. near its mouth on St. Helena Sound; navigable. Salkehatchie R. (60 mi. long) rises NNW of Barnwell; Little Salkehatchie R. (55 mi. long) rises NNE of Barnwell.

Combai, India: see KOMBAI.

Combapata (kōmbäpä'tä), town (pop. 1,224), Cuzco dept., S Peru, on Vilcanota R., on railroad and 55 mi. SE of Cuzco; grain, potatoes.

Combarbalá (kōmbärbälä'), town (pop. 2,112), ⊙ Combarbalá dept. (□ 886; pop. 19,527), Coquimbo prov., N central Chile, on railroad and 90 mi. S of La Serena. Health resort and agr. center (wheat, fruit, livestock). Silver mines near by.

Combeaufontaine (kōbōfōtěn'), village (pop. 429), Haute-Saône dept., E France, 14 mi. WNW of Vesoul; road junction. Cheese mfg.

Combe de Savoie (kōb dů sävwä'), glacial valley of middle Isère R., in Savoie dept., SE France, bet. the Bauges (N) and Belledonne (S) Alpine ranges, extending c.20 mi. from Albertville (NE) to junction with Chambéry trough near Montmélian (SW). Fruits, cereals, wine. Artery of communications (road to Mont Cenis and Little Saint Bernard passes).

Combe Martin (kōōm'), town and parish (pop. 1,920), N Devon, England, near Bristol Channel, 5 mi. E of Ilfracombe; agr. market in fruit- and vegetable-growing region. Has 13th-cent. church. Silver mining important in Middle Ages.

Comber (kŏm'bůr), village (pop. estimate 600), S Ont., 24 mi. E of Windsor; woodworking, dairying; corn, tobacco.

Comber (kům'bůr), town (pop. 2,690), NE Co. Down, Northern Ireland, near head of Strangford Lough, 8 mi. ESE of Belfast; linen milling, alcohol distilling, clothing mfg.

Combermere, Cape (kům'bůrmēr), SE Ellesmere Isl., NE Franklin Dist., Northwest Territories, on Baffin Bay; 76°59'N 78°15'W.

Combin, Grand (grã kōbē'), peak (14,164 ft.) in Pennine Alps, SW Switzerland, 1 mi. N of Ital. border, 10 mi. SE of Orsières; ascent from Bourg-St-Pierre (4 mi. W). **Petit Combin** (12,041 ft.) is 3 mi. NNW.

Combin de Corbassière (kōbē' dů kôrbäsyâr'), peak (12,200 ft.) in Pennine Alps, SW Switzerland, 7 mi. SE of Orsières.

Combined Locks, village (pop. 720), Outagamie co., E Wis., on Fox R. and 4 mi. E of Appleton; dairying, farming.

Comblain-au-Pont (kōblē'-ō-pō'), town (pop. 3,574), Liége prov., E central Belgium, on Ourthe R., near confluence with Amblève R., and 11 mi. S of Liége; tourist resort.

Comblanchien (kōblăshyē'), village (pop. 337), Côte-d'Or dept., E central France, on E slope of the Côte d'Or, 7 mi. NE of Beaune; vineyards. Has noted marble and stone quarries.

Combles (kō'blů), agr. village (pop. 762), Somme dept., N France, 6 mi. NW of Péronne. In First World War battle line.

Combourg (kōbōōr'), village (pop. 1,857), Ille-et-Vilaine dept., W France, 21 mi. N of Rennes; textile milling, dairying. In its 11th-15th-cent. castle Chateaubriand spent his boyhood.

Combrailles (kōbrī'), hilly district of the Massif Central, central France, bet. Monts du Limousin (SW) and Auvergne Mts. (E), extending c.35 mi. along Creuse–Puy-de-Dôme dept. border and into Allier dept. from Pontaumur (S) to Montmarault (N), bet. valleys of Cher (W) and Sioule (E) rivers. Coal deposits in Saint-Éloy-les-Mines area.

Combronde (kōbrōd'), village (pop. 1,019), Puy-de-Dôme dept., central France, 6 mi. N of Riom; mfg. of insecticides.

Combs (kōōm), agr. village and parish (pop. 1,899), central Suffolk, England, 2 mi. S of Stowmarket. Church contains noted 14th-cent. glass.

Combs, village, Perry co., SE Ky., in Cumberland foothills, on North Fork Kentucky R., just NW of Hazard; bituminous coal; oil and gas wells; sawmilling; concrete products.

Combs-la-Ville (kō-lä-vēl'), town (pop. 2,450), Seine-et-Marne dept., N central France, on the Yères and 10 mi. NNW of Melun; glass milling.

Come Caballos, Cerro (sě'rō kō'mā käbä'yōs), Andean peak (16,995 ft.) on Argentina-Chile border; 28°13'S.

Comechingones, Sierra de (syě'rä dā kōmāchēng-gō'nēs), pampean mountain range on San Luis–Córdoba prov. border, Argentina, in Sierra de Córdoba, S of the Cumbre de Achala; extends c.50 mi. N–S. Cerro Oveja is 7,237 ft. high.

Comeglians (kômālyäns'), village (pop. 256), Udine prov., Friuli-Venezia Giulia, NE Italy, on Degano R. and 10 mi. NW of Tolmezzo. Rail terminus; resort (alt. 1,814 ft.); sawmills, cutlery factory.

Comendador, Dominican Republic: see ELÍAS PIÑA.

Comer (kō'můr), town (pop. 882), Madison co., NE Ga., 16 mi. ENE of Athens; clothing, lumber.

Comeragh Mountains (kōōm'rů), range extending 15 mi. NW-SE in N Co. Waterford, Ireland, rises to 2,504 ft. in Knockanaffrin, 9 mi. SE of Clonmel.

Comerío (kōmārē'ō), town (pop. 5,031), E central Puerto Rico, in the Cordillera Central, on La Plata R. and 13 mi. W of Caguas; tobacco-growing and trading center. Kaolin deposits near by (SE).

Comet, village, E Queensland, Australia, 125 mi. WSW of Rockhampton and on Comet R., near its junction with Nogoa R.; cotton fields.

Comet Falls, W central Wash., waterfall more than 200 ft. high in small stream on S slope of Mt. Rainier, in Mt. Rainier Natl. Park.

Comet River, E central Queensland, Australia, rises in Carnarvon Range, flows 80 mi. N, past Comet, joining Nogoa R. near Comet to form Mackenzie R.

Comfort (kům'fůrt), village (1940 pop. 729), Kendall co., S central Texas, on Edwards Plateau, c.45 mi. NW of San Antonio and on Guadalupe R.; shipping point and tourist, health resort in sheep, goat ranching area. Fishing, hunting near by.

Comfort, Cape, NE Southampton Isl., E Keewatin Dist., Northwest Territories, on Foxe Channel; 65°8'N 83°20'W.

Comfort, Point, Monmouth co., E N.J., peninsula marking E limit of Raritan Bay, 8 mi. ESE of South Amboy; site of KEANSBURG borough.

Comfrey (kům'frē), village (pop. 642), Brown co., SW Minn., 26 mi. SW of New Ulm, in agr. area; dairy products, cattle feed.

Comilla (kōōmĭl'lů), town (pop. 48,462), ⊙ Tippera dist., SE East Bengal, E Pakistan, on Gumti R. (tributary of the Meghna) and 53 mi. ESE of Dacca; road and trade center (rice, jute, oilseeds, sugar cane, tobacco); mfg. of bell metal, electrical supplies, soap; general-engineering factory. Formerly spelled Kumilla.

Comillas (kōmē'lyäs), town (pop. 2,161), Santander prov., N Spain, on Bay of Biscay, and 12 mi. WNW of Torrelavega; fishing; corn, vegetables, cattle, lumber. Has fine palace and a Jesuit school. Zinc and lead mining in area.

Comines (kōmēn'), Flemish *Komen* (kō'můn), town in Flanders on Franco-Belg. border, 10 mi. NNW of Lille, and divided by Lys R.; the Fr. part (1946 pop. 5,409) is in Nord dept., the Belgian (1948 pop. 8,215), in West Flanders prov. Textile center (ribbons, straps, fringes; cotton yarn spinning, flax processing); beet-sugar distilling, copper smelting. Completely rebuilt in red brick after First World War. Philippe de Comines b. here.

Comino (kōmē'nō), Maltese *Kemmuna* (kēm'mōōnä), islet (□ 1; pop. 68) of the Maltese Isls., in the Mediterranean bet. Malta (SE) and Gozo (NW), separated by narrow channels, 11 mi. NW of Valletta. Produces beeswax, honey, grapes; goats, sheep. Fishing. Has 18th-cent. church and a fortified tower (1618).

Comino, Cape (kômē'nô), easternmost point of Sardinia, at N end of Gulf of Orosei; 40°32'N 9°49'E.
Cominotto (kōmēnôt'tō), tiny uninhabited islet of the Maltese Isls., in the Mediterranean just W of Comino Isl., 13 mi. NW of Valletta.
Comisa, Yugoslavia: see VIS ISLAND.
Comiso (kô'mēzô), town (pop. 21,914), Ragusa prov., SE Sicily, 7 mi. W of Ragusa; wine, olive oil; artisan industries (household utensils, textiles, soap). Limestone quarries near by. Anc. ruins, including Christian catacombs, are E.
Comitán (kōmētän'), officially Comitán de Domínguez, city (pop. 8,683), Chiapas, S Mexico, in Sierra Madre, near Guatemala border, 45 mi. SE of San Cristóbal de las Casas; alt. 5,538 ft. Trading, processing, and agr. center (lemons, corn, cotton, sugar cane, livestock); alcohol and liquor distilling, textile milling. Airfield. Has customhouse, colonial churches.
Comitini (kômētē'nē), village (pop. 1,480), Agrigento prov., S Sicily, 7 mi. NNE of Agrigento. Sulphur mines near by.
Commagene (kŏmŭjē'nē), district of ancient N Syria, on the Euphrates and S of Taurus Mts., now in SE Asiatic Turkey; chief city was Samosata. The fertile agr. dist. was made part of Assyrian Empire and later of Persian Empire. After Alexander the Great, it gradually assumed independence under the Seleucid kings of Syria and revolted, declaring absolute independence early in 2d cent. B.C. In A.D. 72 it was annexed to Roman prov. of Syria.
Commander Islands, Russian SFSR: see KOMANDORSKI ISLANDS.
Commentry (kômätrē'), town (pop. 6,934), Allier dept., central France, 7 mi. ESE of Montluçon; coal-mining center; forges (automotive steel plate, railroad equipment, chains, bolts); thermometer mfg. Furnishes coal to MONTLUÇON heavy industrial dist. Deposits, worked since 1827, are approaching exhaustion.
Commerce. **1** City (pop. 3,351), Jackson co., NE central Ga., 17 mi. NNW of Athens; mfg. (sheeting, overalls, lumber). Inc. 1883. **2** Village (pop. 1,075), Oakland co., SE Mich., 12 mi. W of Pontiac. **3** Town (pop. 360), Scott co., SE Mo., on Mississippi R. and 11 mi. SSE of Cape Girardeau. **4** City (pop. 2,442), Ottawa co., extreme NE Okla., 5 mi. N of Miami, in lead- and zinc-mining region; agr. (grain, poultry, livestock; dairy products). **5** City (pop. 5,889), Hunt co., NE Texas, 15 mi. NE of Greenville; trade, shipping point in cotton area; railroad shops, cotton gins, cottonseed-oil and grain mills. Seat of East Texas State Teachers Col. Settled 1874.
Commerce Bight, village (pop. 510), Stann Creek Dist., central Br. Honduras, on coast, 4 mi. S of Stann Creek; coconuts, bananas, citrus fruit; fisheries.
Commercial Point, village (pop. 238), Pickaway co., S central Ohio, 13 mi. S of Columbus.
Commercy (kômĕrsē'), town (pop. 5,857), Meuse dept., NE France, on left bank of Meuse R. and on Canal de l'Est, 19 mi. E of Bar-le-Duc; industrial center (forges, foundries, rolling mill) also known for its pastry (madeleine). Hand embroidering, woodworking. Its 18th-cent. castle (military barracks) was damaged in 1944.
Commewijne, district, Du. Guiana: see NIEUW AMSTERDAM.
Commewijne River (kômŭvī'nŭ), E Du. Guiana, rises 20 mi. N of Dam, flows c.100 mi. N and W, through tropical forests and alluvial lowland, to Surinam R. mouth at Nieuw Amsterdam. Its lower course, joined by Cottica R., is used by ocean vessels (carrying bauxite) of 15-ft. draught. Along its upper course are gold deposits.
Commissioners Lake (20 mi. long, 2 mi. wide), S central Que., 18 mi. S of Roberval; drains N into L. St. John by Ouiatchouanish R.
Committee Bay, Northwest Territories, inlet (130 mi. long, 80 mi. wide at mouth) of the Gulf of Boothia, in W side of Melville Peninsula; 67°10'-69°18'N 85°30'-88°20'W.
Como (kō'mō), village (pop. 481), SW Que., on L. of the Two Mountains, 7 mi. NW of Vaudreuil; dairying, potato growing.
Como (kō'mō, It. kô'mô), province (□ 798; pop. 501,752), Lombardy, N Italy; ⊙ Como. Borders Swiss canton of Ticino on NW. Mtn. and hill terrain, watered by Lambro R. and many streams. Contains several lakes, including Como and NE arm of Lugano. Agr. (cereals, raw silk, potatoes); cattle raising. Tourist resorts on L. Como. Industries include silk (Como), iron- and steelworks (Lecco), furniture (Cantù), hardware, cutlery. Area reduced 1927 to help form Varese prov.
Como, anc. *Comum,* city (pop. 42,569), ⊙ Como prov., Lombardy, N Italy, port on SW end of L. Como, 25 mi. N of Milan, near Swiss border; 45°48'N 9°5'E. Rail junction; tourist center; noted for its silk industry; mfg. (textile machinery, automobile chassis, furniture, glass, pottery, shoes, macaroni). Bishopric. Has cathedral (14th–18th cent.), town hall (1215), several Romanesque churches. Founded as a Roman colony. In 1335 conquered by Milan after frequent wars; later under Spanish and Austrian rule. Liberated by Garibaldi in 1859. Both Plinys, Volta, and several popes were b. here.
Como. **1** Town (pop. 39), Park co., central Colo., on headstream of Tarryall Creek, in Rocky Mts., and 55 mi. SW of Denver; alt. c.9,790 ft. Small-scale placer mining for gold. **2** Town (pop. 703), Panola co., NW Miss., c.45 mi. S of Memphis (Tenn.), in agr., timber, and dairying area. **3** Town (pop. 356), Hopkins co., NE Texas, 9 mi. SE of Sulphur Springs, in agr. area.
Como, Lake, Ital. *Lago di Como* or *Lario,* anc. *Larius Lacus,* third largest lake (□ 56) of Italy, in Como prov., Lombardy, 25 mi. N of Milan; c.30 mi. long, up to 2½ mi. wide, alt. 653 ft., max. depth 1,345 ft. Formed by Adda R., which enters near Colico and leaves at Lecco. Divided S by promontory of Bellagio into 2 arms, L. of Lecco (E) and L. Como (W). Surrounded by mts. which rise to 8,563 ft. in Monte Legnone (NE). Receives Mera R. (N). Fishing. Famous for its beauty and handsome villas. Has many noted resorts, including Como, Lecco, Bellagio, Cadenabbia, Tremezzo, Varenna.
Como, Lake. **1** Lake in Del.: see SMYRNA. **2** Resort lake in Walworth co., SE Wis., just N of L. Geneva; 3 mi. long, ½ mi. wide.
Comodoro Py (kōmōdō'rō pē'), town (pop. 2,488), N central Buenos Aires prov., Argentina, 14 mi. S of Bragado; wheat, corn, cattle.
Comodoro Rivadavia (rēvädä'vyä), military zone (□ 37,741; pop. 51,898), in Patagonia, S Argentina; ⊙ Comodoro Rivadavia. Located bet. the Andes and Gulf of San Jorge on the Atlantic; bounded N by 44°38'S, S by Deseado R. Contains several large lakes: L. Buenos Aires (SW), L. Musters and L. Colhué Huapí (center), L. Fontana (NW). Has dry, cool climate. It is the richest oil-producing area in Argentina, concentrated around town of Comodoro Rivadavia; other petroleum centers are: Pampa del Castillo, Astra, Yacimientos Petrolíferos, Caleta Olivia. Lime deposits at Puerto Deseado; lead on banks of L. Buenos Aires. The central region is a rich sheep-raising area, served by railroad, whose outlet is Puerto Deseado. Alfalfa and grain growing on coast and along lower Deseado R. (irrigation). Lumbering, flour milling, dairying. Established tentatively as a military zone in 1944, Comodoro Rivadavia's boundaries were determined in 1946, incorporating parts of Chubut and Santa Cruz.
Comodoro Rivadavia, town (pop. 25,210), ⊙ Comodoro Rivadavia zone and dept. (pop. 30,363), S Argentina, on Gulf of San Jorge on the Atlantic, and 900 mi. SSW of Buenos Aires, 350 mi. SSW of Viedma; 45°53'S 67°27'W. Important oil port and sheep-raising center at railhead. Site of main Argentinian petroleum wells; also lime deposits. Besides petroleum refineries, it has factories producing frozen meat, ceramics, soap, lime. Ships oil, wool, hides. Airport. Has seismographic station. Founded 1901; on Dec. 13, 1907, petroleum was accidentally struck.
Comoé River or **Komoé River** (kō'mwā), E Ivory Coast, Fr. West Africa, rises SW of Bobo-Dioulasso, Upper Volta, flows c.475 mi. S to Gulf of Guinea at Grand-Bassam. Navigable by small vessels 25 mi. upstream.
Comondú (kōmōndōō'), town (pop. 540), Southern Territory, Lower California, NW Mexico, 160 mi. NW of La Paz; copper mining, stock raising.
Comonfort (kōmōnfôr'), city (pop. 6,510), Guanajuato, central Mexico, on Laja R. and 37 mi. SE of Guanajuato, on railroad; alt. 5,889 ft. Agr. center (wheat, corn, alfalfa, beans, sugar cane, fruit, stock). Formerly Chamacuero de Comonfort.
Comores, Madagascar: see COMORO ISLANDS.
Comorin, Cape (kŏ'mŭrĭn), rocky headland, S Travancore-Cochin, India, southernmost point of Indian peninsula, in Indian Ocean, 8°5'N 77°33'E. Anc. temple on seashore is important Hindu pilgrimage site. Town of Cape Comorin or Kannijyakumari (pop. 4,283) is just inland.
Comoro Islands (kŏ'mŭrō), Fr. *Comores* (kômôr'), volcanic archipelago, a Fr. overseas territory (□ 830; pop. c.152,000); ⊙ Dzaoudzi. In Indian Ocean at N entrance of Mozambique Channel, c.300 mi. off N tip of Madagascar and 200 mi. off E coast of Africa; bet. 11° and 13°S and 43° and 45°30'E. Consist of 4 main isls., GRANDE COMORE, ANJOUAN ISLAND, MOHÉLI ISLAND, MAYOTTE ISLAND, and several small islets often fringed by coral reefs. Mountainous and very fertile; some parts are densely forested. Tropical climate, with dry (May–Oct.) and wet seasons pleasantly tempered by oceanic location. Exports are copra, coco fibers, vanilla, sisal, essential oils (ilang-ilang, citronella, bitter orange, basil), cacao, wild pepper, charcoal. Industries include sugar refining, rum distilling, sawmilling, fishing. Pop. is largely Moslem, of mixed Arab, Makwa, and Malagasy stock. Known to ancient navigators since 2d cent. Long under overwhelming Arab influence, the group was 1st visited by Europeans in 16th cent. Mayotte was occupied by France 1843, other islands came under Fr. protectorate 1886, were attached to Réunion 1896, to Madagascar 1908. In 1912 they were declared Fr. colonies (confirmed 1914); in Jan., 1947, they became a Fr. overseas territory (with a representative in the Fr. parliament), still, however, partly under the authority of the High Commissioner of Madagascar.
Comotay, India: see KAMATAPUR.
Comox (kō'mŏks), village (pop. estimate 700), SW B.C., on E central Vancouver Isl. with a harbor on Strait of Georgia at mouth of Courtenay R., 110 mi. NW of Victoria; coal-mining center; also lumbering, farming, dairying.
Compass Berg (bûrg, bĕrkh), mountain (8,209 ft.), SE central Cape Prov., U. of So. Afr., 35 mi. N of Graaff Reinet, in the Sneeuwberg mts., at E edge of Great Karroo; 31°46'S 24°33'E; highest peak of Cape Prov.
Compendium, France: see COMPIÈGNE.
Cómpeta (kōm'pātä), town (pop. 3,075), Málaga prov., S Spain, 26 mi. ENE of Málaga; raisins, grapes, wine, liquor, olives, olive oil.
Compiègne (kŏpyĕ'nyŭ), anc. *Compendium,* town (pop. 15,530), Oise dept., N France, on the Oise below mouth of Aisne R. and 45 mi. NE of Paris, at NW edge of Forest of Compiègne (□ 55); road center and fashionable resort for Parisians; sawmills, metalworks (sugar-refining machinery, automobile equipment, agr. tools), mfg. of rubber tires, biscuits, paper bags. Dating from Roman times, it has been a royal residence since Merovingian period. Has a château (rebuilt for Louis XV by Gabriel) which was used by Louis XVI, Napoleon I, and Napoleon III, and now houses a fine mus. of old carriages and early automobiles. The 16th-cent. early Renaissance town hall contains art mus. of Roman origin. Compiègne was site of a medieval Benedictine monastery. In 1430, Joan of Arc was captured here by Burgundians who sold her to the English. Armistice of Nov. 11, 1918, was signed on a rail siding (4.5 mi. E) in Forest of Compiègne; in 1940, Hitler forced the French to sign armistice of June 22 in same car, which had remained here as part of a natl. monument. The coach was removed by Germans, who also blew up the soldiers' monument, in their retreat from Paris in 1944; it has not been found. A slab, commemorating 1918 armistice, remains.
Compiobbi (kômpyôb'bē), village (pop. 656), Firenze prov., Tuscany, central Italy, 4 mi. W of Florence; cementworks.
Complutum, Spain: see ALCALÁ DE HENARES.
Compostela (kōmpōstā'lä), city (pop. 3,144), Nayarit, W Mexico, on low plateau near Pacific coast, on railroad and 20 mi. S of Tepic; mining (silver, gold, copper) and agr. center (corn, tobacco, beans, sugar cane, coffee, tobacco); tobacco factories. Founded 1535. Has San Jago church, built 1539 of red volcanic stone. Compostela was 1st ⊙ of Nueva Galicia, early Sp. colony.
Compostela, Santiago de, Spain: see SANTIAGO.
Comps-sur-Artuby (kŏps-sür-ärtübē'), village (pop. 165), Var dept., SE France, in Provence Alps, 12 mi. N of Draguignan.
Compstall, former urban district (1931 pop. 865), NE Cheshire, England, 5 mi. E of Stockport; dairy farming, cheese mfg. Inc. 1936 in Congleton.
Compton, county (□ 933; pop. 22,957), S Que., on N.H. border; ⊙ Cookshire.
Compton, village (pop. 425), S Que., on Coaticook R. and 12 mi. SSE of Sherbrooke; dairying; stock.
Compton, agr. village and parish (pop. 1,162), central Hampshire, England, near Itchen R., 3 mi. SSW of Winchester. Has small Norman church.
Compton. **1** City (pop. 47,991), Los Angeles co., S Calif., 12 mi. S of downtown Los Angeles, in industrial, and truck- and dairy-farm dist.; oil refining; mfg. of oil-well equipment, trucks, steel products, roofing, glass products. Has a jr. col. Settled 1867, inc. 1888. **2** Village (pop. 321), Lee co., N Ill., 24 mi. N of La Salle, in rich agr. area.
Comrat, Moldavian SSR: see KOMRAT.
Comrie (kŏm'rē). **1** Town in Carnock parish, SW Fifeshire, Scotland, 5 mi. W of Dunfermline; coal mining; site of one of most modern mines in Great Britain. **2** Town and parish (pop. 1,775), S central Perthshire, Scotland, on Earn R. and 5 mi. W of Crieff; agr. market and resort, at head of Glen Artney valley, one of scenes of Scott's *The Lady of the Lake.* Frequent earthquake shocks are registered here.
Comstock (kŏm'stŏk, kŭm'-). **1** Village (1940 pop. 1,774), Kalamazoo co., SW Mich., on Kalamazoo R. and 4 mi. E of Kalamazoo. Settled 1831. **2** Village (pop. 139), Clay co., W Minn., in Red R. valley, 15 mi. S of Fargo, N.Dak., in grain area. **3** Village (pop. 302), Custer co., central Nebr., 23 mi. NE of Broken Bow and on Middle Loup R.; poultry and dairy produce, livestock, grain, potatoes. **4** Village, Washington co., E N.Y., 12 mi. NE of Glens Falls. **5** Village (pop. c.400), Val Verde co., SW Texas, near the Rio Grande, 27 mi. NW of Del Rio; shipping point in goat- and sheep-raising area.
Comstock Lode, richest known silver deposit, W Nev., in Mt. Davidson of the Virginia Mts., just W of Virginia City. Discovered 1857 by miners who died before recording their claims, it was claimed (1859) and disposed of for a small sum by Henry Tompkins Paige Comstock. Miners and promoters flocked to the Lode, the enormous fortunes of the "silver kings" were founded, and Virginia City boomed and became a fabulous cente-

of wealth and luxury. The silver (and some gold) of the Comstock determined the development of Nev. until beginning (1873) of decline caused by wasteful mining and demonetization of silver; by 1898 it was virtually abandoned.

Comstock Park, village (1940 pop. 898), Kent co., SW Mich., just N of Grand Rapids, on Grand R.

Comtal, Causse du, France: see CAUSSES.

Comtat Venaissin, France: see VENAISSIN.

Comté River (kōtā'), N Fr. Guiana, rises at N foot of the Chaîne Granitique, flows c.75 mi. NNE to the Atlantic in 2 branches (including small Cayenne R.) which enclose Cayenne Isl.

Comum, Italy: see COMO, city.

Comunanza (kômōōnän'tsä), village (pop. 931), Ascoli Piceno prov., The Marches, central Italy, on Aso R. and 11 mi. NW of Ascoli Piceno; mfg. (woolen textiles, wine machinery). Called Comunanza del Littorio c.1937–45.

Conaica (kōnī'kä), town (pop. 1,644), Huancavelica dept., S central Peru, in Cordillera Occidental, on Huancayo–Huancavelica RR and 22 mi. N of Huancavelica; grain, corn, tubers, livestock.

Conakry (kŏ'nŭkrē, kônäkrē'), city (pop. c.38,050), ⊙ Fr. Guinea, Fr. West Africa, Atlantic port on offshore islet (Tombo, Toumbo, or Tumbou) linked by bridge to mainland, 440 mi. SE of Dakar (Fr. Senegal) and 80 mi. NNW of Freetown (Sierra Leone); 9°30'N 13°43'W. The Los Isls. are just W. Important entrepôt and shipping point for the colony; administrative and commercial center; terminus of railroad to Kankan 310 mi. ENE; head of intercolonial roads to Fr. Sudan, Senegal, and Ivory Coast. Principal exports are bananas and palm kernels, loaded at well-equipped wharves. Fertile region also produces millet, potatoes, corn, manioc; rubber, beeswax, honey; livestock, hides. Pleasant, well laid-out city shaded by tropical trees. Has fine botanical and experimental gardens. Airport; radio station. There are iron (exploited) and bauxite deposits in vicinity. Sometimes Konakri or Konakry.

Conanicut Island, R.I.: see JAMESTOWN.

Conasauga River (kŏnŭsô'gŭ), in Ga. and Tenn., rises in the Blue Ridge, Fannin co., N Ga., flows NW across Tenn. line, thence SSW into Ga., past Tilton to confluence with Coosawattee R. 3 mi. NE of Calhoun, forming Oostanaula R.; c.90 mi. long.

Concarán (kōngkärän'), town (pop. estimate 1,000), ⊙ Chacabuco dept. (□ 880; 1947 pop. 15,256), NE San Luis prov., Argentina, on railroad, on Conlara R. and 80 mi. NE of San Luis. Farming and tungsten-mining center. Corn, wheat, alfalfa, wine, livestock; dairying. Formerly Villa Dolores.

Concarneau (kōkärnō'), town (pop. 8,454), Finistère dept., W France, on Bay of Biscay, 12 mi. SE of Quimper; fishing port (sardines, tunny) and seaside resort; fish canning and smoking, handicraft lace mfg.; oyster beds. Old fortified town (14th-cent. ramparts) on offshore isl.; newer section on mainland. Much visited by artists.

Conceição (kōsäsä'ō). **1** City, Minas Gerais, Brazil: see CONCEIÇÃO DO MATO DENTRO. **2** City (pop. 1,146), W Paraíba, NE Brazil, 45 mi. S of Cajàzeiras; cotton, sugar, rice, beans.

Conceição da Aparecida (dä äpärĭsē'dŭ), city (pop. 2,107), SW Minas Gerais, Brazil, 40 mi. SE of Passos, in coffeegrowing dist.

Conceição da Barra (dä bä'rŭ), city (pop. 1,205), N Espírito Santo, Brazil, port on the Atlantic at mouth of São Mateus R., and 11 mi. NE of São Mateus; sawmilling. Lighthouse.

Conceição da Feira (fā'rŭ), city (pop. 2,080), E Bahia, Brazil, on rail spur and 10 mi. N of Cachoeira; cattle center; coffee, sugar, tobacco.

Conceição das Alagoas (däs älägō'ŭs), city (pop. 1,430), westernmost Minas Gerais, Brazil, in the Triângulo Mineiro, near the Rio Grande (São Paulo border), 35 mi. SW of Uberaba; cattle raising; diamond washings.

Conceição de Macabu (dĭ mäkäbōō'), town (pop. 2,298), E Rio de Janeiro state, Brazil, on railroad and 22 mi. N of Macaé; sugar, fruit. Until 1943, called Macabu. New dam and hydroelectric plant (opened 1944) on small Macabu R. (15 mi. WSW).

Conceição do Almeida (dōō älmā'dŭ), city (pop. 1,539), E Bahia, Brazil, 22 mi. NW of Nazaré; tobacco, coffee, manioc. Until 1944, called Afonso Pena (formerly spelled Affonso Penna).

Conceição do Araguaia (ärägwī'ŭ), city (pop. 1,074), SE Pará, Brazil, on Araguaia R. (Goiás border) and 450 mi. S of Belém; 8°15'S 49°15'W. Gold placers near by.

Conceição do Arroio, Brazil: see OSÓRIO.

Conceição do Coité (koitĕ'), city (pop. 1,095), NE Bahia, Brazil, near railroad, 70 mi. NW of Alagoinhas; corn, tobacco, livestock.

Conceição do Mato Dentro (mä'tōō dĕn'trōō), city (pop. 2,976), central Minas Gerais, Brazil, in the Serra do Espinhaço, 70 mi. NE of Belo Horizonte; important iron-ore deposits. Semiprecious stones, gold, bismuth in area. Until 1944, called Conceição.

Conceição do Paraíba, Brazil: see CAPELA, Alagoas.

Conceição do Rio Verde (rē'ōō vĕr'dĭ), city (pop. 2,574), S Minas Gerais, Brazil, on the Rio Verde, on railroad and 45 mi. NE of Itajubá; coffee, cereals. Asbestos deposits.

Concepción (kōnsĕpsyōn'). **1** Agr. village (pop. estimate 1,000), ⊙ Concepción dept. (□ c.2,000; pop. 14,892), N central Corrientes prov., Argentina, 55 mi. NNE of Mercedes; corn, sugar cane, cotton, livestock. **2** City, Entre Ríos prov., Argentina: see CONCEPCIÓN DEL URUGUAY. **3** or **Concepción de la Sierra** (dā lä syĕ'rä), town (pop. estimate 1,500), ⊙ Concepción dept. (1947 pop. 8,672), S Misiones natl. territory, Argentina, 45 mi. SSE of Posadas; farming center (corn, maté, sugar cane, rice, citrus fruit, livestock). **4** N suburb (pop. estimate 20,000) of San Juan, S San Juan prov., Argentina, on railroad; wine- and fruitgrowing center; wine making, flour milling. Hydroelectric station on branch of San Juan R. (irrigation area). Inc. c.1940 into San Juan city. **5** Town (1947 pop. 12,479), ⊙ Chicligasta dept. (□ c.1,000; 1947 census 48,032), S Tucumán prov., Argentina, 45 mi. SW of Tucumán; rail junction and agr. center (sugar cane, corn, rice, vegetables, tobacco, livestock); sugar refining, tanning, lumbering, flour milling.

Concepción. 1 Village (pop. c.200), Beni dept., N Bolivia, on Beni R. and 45 mi. SSW of Riberalta, opposite Exaltación; rubber; sugar-cane plantations and refineries. Alcohol distilleries near by. Sometimes called Barraca Concepción. **2** Town (pop. c.4,400), ⊙ Ñuflo de Chávez prov., Santa Cruz dept., E Bolivia, 130 mi. NE of Santa Cruz; rubber center; airport. Founded as Jesuit mission. **3** Town, Tarija dept., Bolivia: see URIONDO.

Concepción, province (□ 2,201; 1940 pop. 308,241; 1949 estimate 365,560), S central Chile, on the Pacific; ⊙ Concepción. Drained by Bío-Bío and Laja rivers, it is in part of the fertile central valley (wine, wheat, corn, oats, lentils, beans; some cattle and sheep raising). Coal mines near coast (Coronel, Lota, Penco), with some copper deposits. Lumbering inland, fishing on coast. Its important industries (textile, steel, and flour milling; fish canning, sugar refining, brewing, tanning) concentrated at Concepción and Talcahuano. Huachipato steel mill is near San Vicente. Tomé is known for textiles, Penco for ceramics. Resorts on coast. Has temperate climate. The area has suffered severely from earthquakes for centuries; most of its towns were destroyed in the 1939 catastrophe. Prov. was set up 1826.

Concepción, city (1940 pop. 85,813; 1949 estimate 87,620), ⊙ Concepción prov. and Concepción dept. (□ 510; 1940 pop. 121,597), S central Chile, on Bío-Bío R. 6 mi. above its mouth on the Pacific, and 220 mi. SW of Santiago; 36°49'S 73°3'W. Chile's third largest city, it is a major commercial, processing, and educational center; and, through its port TALCAHUANO (8 mi. NNW, at end of rail spur; site of modern Huachipato steel plant), it is an outlet for the hinterland agr. area (wine, grain). Mfg. includes: leather, shoes and other leather goods, textiles, flour and flour products, sugar, beer, wine, metal products, chemicals (fertilizer, pharmaceuticals). Productive coal mines near by. Has an old univ. and schools of agr. and textiles. It is an archiepiscopal see. Founded 1550 by Pedro de Valdivia at site of present-day Penco near by, Concepción was the target of raids by the Araucanian Indians. In 1570, 1730, and 1751, it was completely destroyed by earthquakes, that of 1730 causing removal to present site. After the 1939 earthquake, Concepción had to be almost completely rebuilt and is a city of fine modern bldgs. There are resorts near by.

Concepción, Costa Rica: see TEJAR.

Concepción, village, Esmeraldas prov., N Ecuador, on Santiago R. and 55 mi. E of Esmeraldas, in tropical lowland forests (balsa wood, tagua nuts, rubber); gold placer mines.

Concepción. 1 or **Concepción Las Minas** (läs mē'näs), town (1950 pop. 439), Chiquimula dept., E Guatemala, in highlands, 20 mi. SSE of Chiquimula; road center; corn, wheat, coffee, livestock. **2** Village (1940 pop. 3,000), Escuintla dept., S Guatemala, 2 mi N of Escuintla, on railroad; sugar-milling center. **3** Town (1950 pop. 1,854), Huehuetenango dept., W Guatemala, on W slopes of Cuchumatanes Mts., 25 mi. NNW of Huehuetenango; alt. 7,871 ft.; sheep raising; corn, wheat, beans. **4** or **Concepción Chiquirichapa** (chēkērēchä'pä), town (1950 pop. 1,186), Quezaltenango dept., SW Guatemala, 1 mi. SW of Ostuncalco; alt. 8,465 ft.; corn, wheat, fodder grasses; livestock. **5** Town (1950 pop. 513), Sololá dept., SW central Guatemala, 4 mi. E of Sololá; alt. 8,199 ft.; vegetables, grain, beans. Has 17th-cent. church.

Concepción, town (pop. 1,022), Sinaloa, NW Mexico, in coastal lowland, 21 mi. NE of Mazatlán; chickpeas, corn, tobacco, sugar cane, fruit, vegetables.

Concepción, SW Nicaragua, active volcano (5,577 ft.) on N Ometepe Isl. in L. Nicaragua, 3.5 mi. SSE of Alta Gracia Sometimes called Ometepe or Alta Gracia.

Concepción or **La Concepción** (lä), town (pop. 2,162), Chiriquí prov., W Panama, on Inter-American Highway, on railroad and 13 mi. NW of David; coffee, oranges, cacao, sugar cane, livestock.

Concepción, department (□ 6,970; pop. 46,479), central Paraguay; ⊙ Concepción. Bordered N by Apa R. (Brazil line), W by Paraguay R., S by Ypané R.; intersected by Aquidabán R. Mostly marshy lowland, with abundant rainfall. Stock raising, maté growing (also corn, alfalfa, tobacco), lumbering (hardwood, quebracho). Processing concentrated at Concepción city. Horqueta, Belén, and Loreto are cattle-raising centers.

Concepción, city (dist. pop. 18,922), ⊙ Concepción dept., central Paraguay, port on Paraguay R. near mouth of Ypané R. (5 mi. S), and 135 mi. NNE of Asunción; 23°24'S 57°28'W. Trading, processing, and cattle-raising center; sawmills, flour mills, cotton gins, sugar refineries, tanneries. A communication base for the Paraguayan Chaco, it trades in maté, lumber, quebracho, and livestock. Has customhouse, docks, airport. A short rail line runs E to Horqueta. Seat of bishop of Chaco; Salesian school and church. Founded 1773. Sometimes called Villa Concepción.

Concepción, city (pop. 3,317), Junín dept., central Peru, on Mantaro R. and 14 mi. SE of Jauja (connected by railroad); wheat, barley, corn. Trout hatcheries near by.

Concepcion (kŭnsĕp'shŭn, Sp. kōnsĕpsyōn'). **1** Town (1939 pop. 13,101) in Talisay municipality, Negros Occidental prov., W Negros isl., Philippines, 8 mi. ENE of Bacolod; agr. center (rice, sugar cane). **2** Town (1939 pop. 3,141; 1948 municipality pop. 30,785), Tarlac prov., central Luzon, Philippines, 12 mi. SSE of Tarlac; coconuts, rice, sugar cane.

Concepción (kōnthĕpthyōn'), town (pop. 509) on E coast of Fernando Po isl., Sp. Guinea, 25 mi. S of Santa Isabel; 3°22'N 8°45'E. Minor port. Cacao, coffee.

Concepción, Venezuela: see LA CONCEPCIÓN.

Concepción, Lake (kōnsĕpsyōn'), Santa Cruz dept., E Bolivia, c.45 mi. NW of San José; 13 mi. long, 8 mi. wide. Drains the Bañados de Izozog. Outlet: SAN MIGUEL RIVER.

Concepción Bay, inlet of the Pacific in Concepción prov., S central Chile, 6 mi. N of Concepción city; 9 mi. long, 7 mi. wide. At its entrance is Quiriquina Isl. On its shore are ports of Tomé (NE) and Talcahuano (SW).

Concepción Bay, inlet of Gulf of California, on E coast of Lower California, NW Mexico, 95 mi SE of Guaymas; 22 mi. long, 2–5 mi. wide.

Concepción Chiquirichapa, Guatemala: see CONCEPCIÓN, Quezaltenango dept.

Concepción de Ataco, Salvador: see ATACO.

Concepción de Buenos Aires (dā bwā'nōs ī'rĕs), town (pop. 3,310), Jalisco, central Mexico, in Sierra Madre Occidental, 20 mi. ENE of Sayula; grain, beans, fruit, stock.

Concepción de la Sierra, Argentina: see CONCEPCIÓN, Misiones natl. territory.

Concepción de la Vega, Dominican Republic: see LA VEGA, city.

Concepción del Oro (dĕl ō'rō), city (pop. 4,847), Zacatecas, N central Mexico, on interior plateau, near Coahuila border, 60 mi. SW of Saltillo; alt. 8,333 ft. Rail terminus and mining center (silver, copper, gold, lead, mercury, iron), with copper smelters.

Concepción del Uruguay (dĕl ōōrōōgwī'), city (pop. 30,939), ⊙ Uruguay dept. (□ 2,125; 1947 census pop. 72,623), E Entre Ríos prov., Argentina, port on Uruguay R. (Uruguay border) and 150 mi. N of Buenos Aires. Railhead; commercial, industrial, and agr. center in grain, flax, and livestock area. Frozen meat, dairy products, cider; maté and flour mills, sawmills; sand and stone quarries; lumbering. Trade in grain and beef. Import and export point for trade with Uruguay. Port accessible to ocean vessels. Has noted natl. col., cathedral, tomb of General Urquiza. It was ⊙ Argentine confederation, 1813–21 and 1860–83, during revolutionary and civil wars. Sometimes called simply Uruguay or Concepción.

Concepción de María (dā märē'ä), town (pop. 1,271), Choluteca dept., S Honduras, 15 mi. ESE of Choluteca, near Nicaragua border; pottery making; coffee, corn, beans; livestock.

Concepción Las Minas, Guatemala: see CONCEPCIÓN, Chiquimula dept.

Concepción River, Mexico: see MAGDALENA RIVER.

Concepción Strait or **Conception Strait,** inlet of the Pacific off coast of S Chile, bet. Madre de Dios Archipelago and Hanover Isl.; c.40 mi. long, 4–8 mi. wide.

Conception, Mo.: see CONCEPTION JUNCTION.

Conception, Point, SW Calif., promontory on Santa Barbara Channel and SW point of Santa Barbara co., 13 mi. S of Lompoc; lighthouse.

Conception Bay, inlet (50 mi. long, 20 mi. wide at entrance), SE N.F., in N part of Avalon Peninsula, 10 mi. W of St. John's; 47°45'N 53°W. Near SW shore is Bell Isl., with important iron mines. Chief towns on bay are Harbour Grace and Carbonear. There are numerous fishing settlements and salmon, cod, and lobster canneries.

Conception Island, islet, central Bahama Isls., 15 mi. NW of Rum Cay, 160 mi. SE of Nassau; 23°50'N 75°8'W. Lighthouse. Santa María de la Concepción was the name Columbus gave to RUM CAY.

Conception Island, one of the Seychelles, off NW coast of Mahé Isl., 6½ mi. WSW of Victoria; 4°39'S 55°22'E; 1 mi. long, ¾ mi. wide; rises to 482 ft.

Conception Junction, town (pop. 285), Nodaway co., NW Mo., on Little Platte R. and 10 mi. SE of Maryville. Benedictine abbey and seminary at near-by Conception.

Conception Strait, Chile: see CONCEPCIÓN STRAIT.

Concession, township (pop., including Amandas, 301), Salisbury prov., N Southern Rhodesia, in Mashonaland, on railroad and 31 mi. NNW of Salisbury; alt. 4,200 ft. Tobacco, corn, dairy products; livestock. Gold deposits. Police post. Amandas is just N of Concession rail station.

Concha, La (lä kōn'chä), Andean peak (16,148 ft.) in Mérida state, W Venezuela, in Sierra Nevada de Mérida, N of La Columna peak, 7 mi. ESE of Mérida.

Conchagua (kōnchä'gwä), active volcano (4,100 ft.) in La Unión dept., E Salvador, 4 mi. S of La Unión, on peninsula separating La Unión Bay (N) and Gulf of Fonseca (S). Erupted last in 1868.

Conchagüita Island (kōnchägwē'tä), in Gulf of Fonseca, E Salvador, 8 mi. SE of La Unión; 2.5 mi. long, 1.5 mi. wide; rises to 1,680 ft.

Conchalí (kōnchälē'), village (1930 pop. 420), Santiago prov., central Chile, 5 mi. N of Santiago, in agr. area (cereals, alfalfa, fruit, livestock). Copper mining (1930 mine pop. 41).

Conchas (kō'shŭs), city (pop. 2,129), S central São Paulo, Brazil, on railroad and 45 mi. NW of Sorocaba; cotton, rice, and coffee processing; pottery mfg.; corn milling.

Conchas, Las, Argentina: see TIGRE.

Conchas Dam (kŏn'chŭs), NE N.Mex., on Canadian R., 29 mi. WNW of Tucumcari. Unit in Tucumcari project of Army Engineers; concrete dam (235 ft. high, 1,250 ft. long, extended by earth dikes to length of c.4 mi.); completed 1940. Used for flood control and irrigation; forms Conchas Reservoir (□ c.25; capacity 600,000 acre-ft.), extending up valleys on Conchas and Canadian rivers.

Conchas River, NE central N.Mex., rises in high plateau in San Miguel co., flows 60 mi. S and E to Conchas Reservoir on Canadian R.

Conches or **Conches-en-Ouche** (kōsh-ānōōsh'), town (pop. 2,339), Eure dept., NW France, 10 mi. WSW of Évreux; road center; woodworking, mfg. of agr. equipment. Has 15th–16th-cent. Flamboyant church. Formerly called Douville. Just SW extends Forest of Conches (□ 25).

Conchillas (kōnchē'yäs), town, Colonia dept., SW Uruguay, 2 mi. inland from the Río de la Plata, 23 mi. NNW of Colonia; resort in agr., stock-raising region. Its port ships stone from near-by quarries to Buenos Aires, 33 mi. SW.

Concho (kōn'chō), town (pop. 1,497), Chihuahua, N Mexico, on Conchos R. and 45 mi. SE of Chihuahua; alt. 4,009 ft. Rail junction; corn, cotton, beans, cattle. Sometimes Conchos.

Concho (kŏn'chō), county (□ 1,004; pop. 5,078), W central Texas; ⊙ Paint Rock. On N Edwards Plateau; alt. c.1,600–2,100 ft. Bounded NE by Colorado R.; drained by Concho R. and Brady Creek. Stock raising (sheep, goats, cattle); wool, mohair marketed; some agr. (grain, grain sorghums, cotton), dairying, poultry raising. Formed 1858.

Concho, village (pop. c.200), Canadian co., central Okla., near North Canadian R., 30 mi. WNW of Oklahoma City; seat of a U.S. school for Indians.

Concho River, W Texas, formed at San Angelo by North Concho and Middle Concho rivers, flows c.55 mi. generally E to the Colorado 18 mi. SE of Ballinger. South Concho R., formerly joining the Middle Concho, now flows into an arm of L. Nasworthy (capacity 10,500 acre-ft.; municipal water supply), impounded by dam in the Middle Concho just SW of San Angelo.

Conchos River (kōn'chōs). **1** In Chihuahua, N Mexico, rises in Sierra Madre Occidental near Sonora border NE of Bocoyna, flows first E, through L. Toronto, then N and NE, past Camargo, to join Rio Grande at Ojinaga opposite Presidio (Texas); c.350 mi. long. Largely used for irrigation of arid but fertile plateaus. Along its middle course, near L. Toronto, are several dams and hydroelectric stations, including Boquilla. Receives Chuviscar and Florido rivers. **2** In Tamaulipas, Mexico: see SAN FERNANDO RIVER.

Conchucos (kōnchōō'kōs), town (pop. 1,939), Ancash dept., W central Peru, in Cordillera Occidental, 14 mi. NE of Cabana; barley, corn, alfalfa.

Concón (kōngkōn'), town (pop. 1,216), Valparaiso prov., central Chile, on the Pacific at mouth of Aconcagua R., and 12 mi. NNE of Valparaiso; seaside resort. Oil refinery.

Conconta, Cordón de (kōrdōn' dā kōngkōn'tä), Andean range in W San Juan prov., Argentina, W of Rodeo, N of Agua Negra Pass; rises to 17,437 ft.

Conconully (kŏn″kŭnōō'lē, kŏn-kō'nūlē), town (pop. 141), Okanogan co., N Wash., 18 mi. NW of Okanogan, near Conconully L.

Concord, municipality (pop. 29,401), E New South Wales, Australia, on S shore of Parramatta R. and 7 mi. W of Sydney, in metropolitan area; paint, varnish, lacquer.

Concord. 1 (kŏng'kŭrd) Town (pop. 6,953), Contra Costa co., W Calif., 17 mi. NE of Oakland, just S of Suisun Bay; shipping center for farming (grapes, berries, truck), dairying, and stock-raising area. Inc. 1905. **2** (kŏn'kôrd″) Town (pop. 360), Pike co., W central Ga., 15 mi. SW of Griffin; food canning, sawmilling. **3** (kŏng'kŭrd) Village (pop. 278), Morgan co., W central Ill., 10 mi. NW of Jacksonville, in agr. area. **4** (kŏn'kôrd″) Town (pop. 142), Lewis co., NE Ky., on left bank of Ohio R. and 25 mi. WSW of Portsmouth, Ohio. **5** (kŏng'kŭrd) Town (pop. 8,623), including Concord village (pop. 2,299), Middlesex co., E Mass., on Concord R., here formed by junction of Assabet and Sudbury rivers, 17 mi. WNW of Boston; mfg. of furniture, machinery, castings, chemicals; dairying, poultry, truck, fruit. Site of Revolutionary battle of Concord on April 19, 1775, is marked by bronze *Minuteman*. Hawthorne, Emerson, Thoreau, and the Alcotts lived here. Has many fine old houses. In Sleepy Hollow cemetery are graves of notable residents. WALDEN POND is just S. Town settled 1635. **6** (kŏng'kŭrd) Village (pop. 730), Jackson co., S Mich., on Kalamazoo R. and 13 mi. SW of Jackson, in stock-raising and grain-growing area; grain milling. **7** (kŏng'kŭrd) Village (pop. 194), Dixon co., NE Nebr., 30 mi. WSW of Sioux City, Iowa, and on Logan Creek. **8** (kŏng'kŭrd) City (pop. 27,988), ⊙ N.H. and Merrimack co., on right (W) bank of the Merrimack above Manchester; 43°12'N 71°32'W; alt. 67 ft. Rail, highway, trade center for agr. area. Seat of several state institutions, Rumford Press, granite quarries, factories (wood, metal, and leather products, machinery), handicraft establishments, state historical society and mus. (in Franklin Pierce's old home and office), state capitol (1819), St. Paul's preparatory school, Rolfe-Rumford home (built c.1764; Benjamin Thompson took his title from the town, 1791), bldgs. of Lewis Downing's old coach and wagon business (1813–1928), and, near by, childhood home of Mary Baker Eddy. Ski trails near. Settled 1725–27 as Penacook or Pennacook; inc. 1733 as Rumford, renamed Concord 1765; inc. 1853 as city. Capital since 1808. **9** (kŏn'kôrd″) City (pop. 16,486), ⊙ Cabarrus co., S central N.C., 18 mi. NE of Charlotte, in the piedmont. Textile center; mfg. of hosiery, cotton yarn, textiles, furniture, metal products. Barber-Scotia Jr. Col. (women). Settled 1796; inc. as town 1837, as city 1853. **10** (kŏng'kŭrd) Town (pop. 979), including Concord village (pop. 348), Essex co., NE Vt., 6 mi. E of St. Johnsbury and on Moose R. and (E) the Connecticut; agr.; wood products. Samuel R. Hall opened normal school here 1823. Chartered 1781, settled 1788.

Concordia (kōngkôr'dyä), city (pop. 51,573), ⊙ Concordia dept. (□ 2,645; 1947 census 86,999), E Entre Ríos prov., Argentina, port on Uruguay R., opposite Salto (Uruguay), and 155 mi. ENE of Paraná. Railhead, river port; trading, mfg., fishing, and agr. center. Produces vegetable oil (peanut, sunflower), candies, citrus extracts, dairy products, frozen meat, canned food, palm fibers, ceramics; has sawmills, tanneries, flour and rice mills, lime kilns. Ships cereals and citrus fruit. Trades with Brazil, Paraguay, Uruguay and transoceanic countries. The area produces cereals, maté, vegetables, grapes, and especially citrus fruit; stock raising and poultry farming. Airport. Has several institutions of higher learning, agr. research station, seismographic station, modern administrative bldgs., Gothic church, theater, parks (noted for their palms). Founded 1832, it is a leading city of the prov. It is visited by tourists, who value its salmon and dorado fishing in Uruguay R.

Concórdia (kōngkôr'dyŭ), city (pop. 914), W Santa Catarina, Brazil, near Uruguay R., 15 mi. W of Joaçaba.

Concordia (kōngkôr'dyä), town (pop. 4,827), Antioquia dept., NW central Colombia, on E slopes of Cordillera Occidental, near Cauca R., 28 mi. SW of Medellín; alt. 6,627 ft. Agr. center (coffee, corn, bananas, tobacco, yucca, cattle); starch mfg.

Concordia, town (pop. 328), Olancho dept., central Honduras, near Guayape R., 30 mi. W of Juticalpa; agr., livestock. Gold placers.

Concordia. 1 Village (pop. 1,136), Coahuila, N Mexico, in irrigated Laguna Dist., 25 mi. NE of Torreón; cotton, cereals, wine, vegetables. Cooperative settlement. **2** City (pop. 2,470), Sinaloa, NW Mexico, in coastal lowland, 23 mi. ENE of Mazatlán; agr. center (cotton, corn, tobacco, chickpeas, tomatoes, fruit); silver, gold, copper mining.

Concordia, village, Tacna dept., S Peru, in Pacific lowlands, on Pan-American Highway, on Chile border, and 10 mi. N of Arica.

Concordia (kŭnkôr'dēŭ), parish (□ 709; pop. 14,398), E central La.; ⊙ Vidalia. Bounded E by the Mississippi, W by Black and Tensas rivers, S by Red R. Oil and natural-gas fields; lumber; sand and gravel pits. Cotton ginning, lumber milling. Agr. (cotton, corn; dairy products; livestock). Oxbow lakes along the Mississippi (fishing). Formed 1805.

Concordia. 1 City (pop. 7,175), ⊙ Cloud co., N Kansas, on Republican R. and 45 mi. N of Salina; trade and produce-packing center for wheat, livestock, and poultry region; dairying; mfg. of concrete products, brooms. Founded 1870, inc. 1872. **2** City (pop. 1,218), Lafayette co., W central Mo., 25 mi. NW of Sedalia; dairy products; grain and livestock center. Has Lutheran acad. and jr. col. (St. Paul's Col.). Platted 1868.

Concordia, La, Mexico: see LA CONCORDIA.

Concordia, La, Nicaragua: see LA CONCORDIA.

Concordia, La, Salvador: see LA CONCORDIA.

Concordia Sagittaria (kôngkôr'dyä säjēt-tä'rēä), town (pop. 1,301), Venezia prov., Veneto, N Italy, 1 mi. S of Portogruaro; alcohol distillery, flax mill. Bishopric. Has Romanesque cathedral (much restored) and baptistery (restored 1880), Christian necropolis (discovered 1873), and Roman ruins. Once a Roman military station.

Concordia sulla Secchia (sōōl-lä sĕk'kyä), town (pop. 1,341), Modena prov., Emilia-Romagna, N central Italy, on Secchia R. and 4 mi. WNW of Mirandola; wine, furniture.

Concord River (kŏng'kŭrd), E Mass., formed at Concord by junction of Sudbury and Assabet rivers; flows c.15 mi. NE and N to Merrimack R. at Lowell.

Concorezzo (kôngkōrĕ'tsô), town (pop. 5,145), Milano prov., Lombardy, N Italy, 3 mi. E of Monza; ribbon, alcohol, soap.

Concoto Island, Chile: see CHONOS ARCHIPELAGO.

Concrete, town (pop. 760), Skagit co., NW Wash., 35 mi. SE of Bellingham, at confluence of Baker and Skagit rivers; cement, timber, dairy products. A gateway to Mt. Baker Natl. Forest.

Conda, village, Caribou co., SE Idaho, 8 mi. NE of Soda Springs; alt. 6,100 ft.; phosphate mines.

Condado (kōndä'dō), beach resort and S residential section of San Juan, NE Puerto Rico.

Condado de Treviño, enclave, Spain: see TREVIÑO.

Condamine, La (lä kōdämēn'), business district and bathing resort (pop. 9,421) of principality of Monaco, at head of Monaco harbor, bet. Monte Carlo (NE) and rock of Monaco (S).

Condamine River, Australia: see BALONNE RIVER.

Condat or **Condat-en-Féniers** (kōdä'-tā-fānyā'), village (pop. 1,077), Cantal dept., S central France, 22 mi. ENE of Mauriac; resort; linen-trading center; cheese mfg. Hydroelectric plant on the Rhue, 5 mi. W.

Conde (kōn'dĭ), city (pop. 2,732), NE Bahia, Brazil, on Itapicuru R. just above its mouth on the Atlantic, and 100 mi. NE of Salvador; ships alcohol, dried fish, coconuts, castor oil, livestock.

Conde (kŏn'dē″), city (pop. 409), Spink co., NE central S.Dak., 30 mi. NE of Redfield and on branch of James R.; dairy products, poultry, grain, cattle.

Condé-en-Brie (kōdā'-ā-brē'), agr. village (pop. 539), Aisne dept., N France, 8 mi. ESE of Château-Thierry.

Condega (kōndā'gä), town (1950 pop. 601), Estelí dept., W Nicaragua, 12 mi. N of Estelí, on Inter-American Highway; coffee, rice; mule raising.

Condeixa-a-Nova (kōndā'shä-nô'vŭ), town (pop. 1,580), Coimbra dist., N central Portugal, 8 mi. SSW of Coimbra; millstone mfg.; wheat, olives, wine, corn. Just S are ruins of Condeixa-a-Velha (anc. *Conimbriga*).

Condé-Mons Canal (kōdā-mōs'), SW Belgium, runs 16 mi. E–W bet. Scheldt (Escaut) R. (at Condé-sur-l'Escaut, France) and E end of Canal du Centre at Mons.

Condé-Smendou (kōdā'-smĕndōō'), village (pop. 1,531), Constantine dept., NE Algeria, on railroad and 13 mi. NNE of Constantine; flour mill.

Condé-sur-l'Escaut (-sür-lĕskō'), town (pop. 6,435), Nord dept., N France, on the Escaut at junction of Condé-Mons Canal, 7 mi. NNE of Valenciennes, near Belgian border; rayon, beer, and footwear mfg. Horse breeding in area. One mi. NW is industrial VIEUX-CONDÉ.

Condé-sur-Noireau (-nwärō'), town (pop. 2,650), Calvados dept., NW France, 16 mi. E of Vire; cotton-milling center; Calvados distilling, mfg. (optical equipment, chocolate). Almost leveled during Normandy campaign (summer, 1944) of Second World War.

Condesuyos, province, Peru: see CHUQUIBAMBA.

Condeúba (kōndĭōō'bŭ), city (pop. 1,169), S Bahia, Brazil, on Gavião R. and 65 mi. W of Vitória da Conquista; livestock center; sugar, coffee, manioc. Rock crystal deposits.

Condino (kôndē'nô), village (pop. 1,269), Trento prov., Trentino–Alto Adige, N Italy, on Chiese R. and 12 mi. W of Riva; cheese making.

Condivincum, France: see NANTES.

Condo (kōn'dō), town (pop. c.3,200), Oruro dept., W Bolivia, in the Altiplano, on road and 7 mi. SSE of Challapata; barley, corn, potatoes.

Condobolin (kŭndō'bŭlĭn), municipality (pop. 2,616), central New South Wales, Australia, on Lachlan R. and 240 mi. WNW of Sydney; mining center (silver-lead, gold).

Condom (kōdō'), town (pop. 4,250), Gers dept., SW France, on Baïse R. and 21 mi. SW of Agen; leading center for Armagnac brandy distilling and storing; foundry, furniture factories. Has 16th-cent. cathedral and cloister.

Condon, village, N Western Australia, 55 mi. NE of Port Hedland and on Indian Ocean; anchorage; sheep.

Condon, city (pop. 968), ⊙ Gilliam co., N Oregon, 35 mi. S of Columbia R. at Arlington; shipping point for grain, wool, livestock, timber.

Condong (kŏn'dŏng), village (pop. 538), NE New South Wales, Australia, near Queensland border, on Tweed R. and 70 mi. SSE of Brisbane; sugar.
Cóndor, Cordillera del (kôrdīyā'rä dĕl kōn'dôr), E Andean range on Peru-Ecuador border, 60 mi. SE of Cuenca, extends c.160 mi. bet. 3° and 5°S, rising in the Cerro Tres Cruces to 10,640 ft.
Condore, Poulo, Vietnam: see POULO CONDORE.
Cóndores, Los, Argentina: see LOS CÓNDORES.
Cóndores, Sierra de los (syĕ'rä dā lōs kōn'dōrĕs), pampean mountain range in W Córdoba prov., Argentina, an E range of the Sierra de Córdoba, S of the Sierra Chica; rises to c.2,700 ft.
Condoríaco (kōndōrē'äkō), village (1930 pop. 457), Coquimbo prov., N central Chile, 25 mi. NE of La Serena; gold, silver mining.
Condoriri (kōndōrē'rē), peak (21,998 ft.) in the Cordillera de la Paz of Bolivia, N of La Paz.
Cóndor Pass (kōn'dôr), one of highest railroad passes in the world; alt. 15,813 ft.; in Potosí dept., S central Bolivia, in Cordillera de los Frailes, on Río Mulato–Potosí RR and 31 mi. W of Potosí.
Condoto (kōndō'tō), town (pop. 1,558), Chocó dept., W Colombia, landing on affluent of San Juan R. and 40 mi. S of Quibdó; rich gold- and platinum-placer mines; banana growing.
Condove (kôndô'vĕ), village (pop. 2,143), Torino prov., Piedmont, NW Italy, in Val di Susa, 19 mi. WNW of Turin; ironworks, textile mills, chemical plant. Quartz mines near by.
Condrieu (kōdrēû'), town (pop. 2,038), Rhône dept., E central France, on right bank of Rhone R. and 7 mi. SW of Vienne; chemical and hat mfg. Wine trade.
Conecuh (kŭnē'kŭ), county (□ 850; pop. 21,776), S Ala.; ⊙ Evergreen. Coastal plain region drained by Sepulga R. Cotton, peanuts; lumber milling. Formed 1818.
Conecuh River, in SE Ala., and NW Fla., rises near Union Springs, Ala., flows SW into Fla. near Century, then S to Escambia Bay (ĕskăm'bēŭ), an arm of Pensacola Bay. In Fla. it is known as Escambia R. Total length, 231 mi. Dredged in lower course.
Conegliano (kônĕlyä'nô), town (pop. 7,544), Treviso prov., Veneto, N Italy, 15 mi. NNE of Treviso. Industrial and agr. center, noted for its wine; mfg. (agr. machinery, automobile chassis, stoves, paper, shoes, furniture, alcohol, cotton and silk textiles). Has cathedral (built 1352) with altarpiece by G. B. Cima, who was b. here, several 16th- and 18th-cent. palaces, castle with mus., and natl. viticulture school.
Conejos (kŭnā'ŭs, -hŭs, -hōs), county (□ 1,271; pop. 10,171), S. Colo.; ⊙ Conejos. Irrigated agr. area on N.Mex. line; bounded E by Rio Grande; drained by Conejos R. Livestock, hay, potatoes. San Luis Valley extends N-S. Includes part of San Juan Mts. (W) and parts of Rio Grande and San Juan natl. forests. Formed 1861.
Conejos, village (pop. c.150), S Colo., ⊙ Conejos co., in SE foothills of San Juan Mts., on Conejos R. and 27 mi. SSW of Alamosa, in San Luis Valley; alt. 7,880 ft. Church of Our Lady of Guadalupe (1856) here. Founded 1854, town is one of oldest in Colo.
Conejos Peak, (13,180 ft.), in San Juan Mts., Conejos co., S Colo.
Conejos River, S Colo., rises in several branches near Summit Peak, in S San Juan Mts.; flows c.75 mi. SE and NE, past Conejos and Manassa, to Rio Grande E of Sanford.
Conemaugh River (kŏ'nŭmô"), SW central Pa., rises in the Alleghenies near Cresson, flows c.70 mi. generally W, past Johnstown and Blairsville, joining Loyalhanna Creek at Saltsburg to form Kiskiminetas R. Johnstown flood occurred 1889, when dam at South Fork broke. River and tributaries now have flood-control works.
Conesa, Río Negro natl. territory, Argentina: see GENERAL CONESA.
Conestee (kŏ'nŭstē"), village (1940 pop. 660), Greenville co., NW S.C., on Reedy R. and 6 mi. S of Greenville; woolen mill.
Conestoga (kŏnŭstō'gŭ), village, Lancaster co., SE Pa., 7 mi. SSW of Lancaster. Once site of Indian village. Gave its name to Conestoga wagon, developed in this region before the Revolution.
Conestoga Creek, SE Pa., rises in E Lancaster co., flows c.50 mi. SW, past Lancaster, to Susquehanna R. near Safe Harbor.
Conesus Lake (kŭnē'sŭs), Livingston co., W central N.Y., the farthest W of the Finger Lakes, 30 mi. S of Rochester; 8 mi. long. Drains NW through outlet to Genesee R.
Conesville. 1 Town (pop. 252), Muscatine co., SE Iowa, near Cedar R., 15 mi. W of Muscatine. **2** Village (pop. 466), Coshocton co., central Ohio, on Muskingum R. and 7 mi. SSW of Coshocton.
Coneto (kōnā'tō), officially Coneto de Comonfort, town (pop. 433), Durango, N Mexico, 65 mi. N of Durango; silver mining.
Conetoe (kō'nētō), town (pop. 172), Edgecombe co., E central N.C., 7 mi. SE of Tarboro.
Conewango (kŏnĭwŏng'gō), village (pop. c.200), Cattaraugus co., W N.Y., on Conewango Creek and 15 mi. NE of Jamestown; feed milling.
Conewango Creek, in N.Y. and Pa., rises in W Cattaraugus co., W N.Y., flows NW, then generally S, past Kennedy and Frewsburg (N.Y.), to Allegheny R. at Warren, Pa.; c.65 mi. long.
Coney Island (½ mi. long), in Sligo Bay, N Co. Sligo, Ireland, 5 mi. WNW of Sligo. Sometimes called Inishmulclohy.
Coney Island (kō'nē), SE N.Y., a beach and amusement resort in S Brooklyn borough of New York city, on peninsula bet. Gravesend Bay (N) and Lower Bay (S). Has famed boardwalk (2 mi. long), innumerable amusement concessions, and 6-mi. bathing beach sometimes visited by c.1,000,000 persons daily. Became shore resort in 1840s; coming of subway extension (1920) made it a playground for New York city's throngs. Adjacent on W is Sea Gate, residential community; to E are Brighton Beach (residential and resort) and Manhattan Beach (resort).
Configni (kônfē'nyē), village (pop. 121), Rieti prov., Latium, central Italy, 12 mi. W of Rieti; hosiery.
Confital Bay (kōmfētäl'), small Atlantic inlet of N Grand Canary, Canary Isls., flanked E by Isleta peninsula, 3 mi. NW of Las Palmas.
Conflans (kōflä'). **1** Village (pop. 1,263), Meurthe-et-Moselle dept., NE France, on Orne R. and 7 mi. SSW of Briey; rail junction. **2** Town, Savoie dept., France: see ALBERTVILLE.
Conflans-Sainte-Honorine (-sĕtônôrēn'), town (pop. 10,547), Seine-et-Oise dept., N central France, on right bank of the Seine, above influx of Oise R. and 15 mi. NW of Paris; telephone-cable factory, foundries, cementworks. Damaged in Second World War.
Conflent (kōflä'), valley of upper Têt R., Pyrénées-Orientales dept., S France, extending c.30 mi. from Mont-Louis to Ille, N of Massif du Canigou. Sheep raising near its head (Mont-Louis area); corn, olives, fruit, wine in lower reaches. Extensive iron mining bet. Olette and Prades (chief town) on slopes of Mont Canigou. Hydroelectric works.
Confluence, borough (pop. 1,037), Somerset co., SW Pa., 20 mi. SW of Somerset and on Youghiogheny R., at mouth of Casselman R. Inc. 1873.
Confluencia, Argentina: see NEUQUÉN, town.
Confolens (kōfôlä'), town (pop. 2,274), Charente dept., W France, on Vienne R. and 30 mi. WNW of Limoges; road center and agr. market; paper milling. Has 2 medieval churches.
Confuso, Río (rē'ō kōmfōō'sō), river in Presidente Hayes dept., S central Paraguay, rises in the Chaco marshes of Estero Patiño on Argentina border, flows c.150 mi. SE, parallel to Pilcomayo R., to Paraguay R. 3 mi. SSW of Villa Hayes.
Cong (kŏng), Gaelic *Cunga Feichín*, town (pop. 164), S Co. Mayo, Ireland, at N end of Lough Corrib, 22 mi. NNW of Galway; lake port and market center in cattle-raising, potato-growing region. Has 14th-cent. market cross and remains of Cong Abbey, founded 1128.
Congaree River (kŏng"gŭrē'), central S.C., formed by confluence of Broad and Saluda rivers at Columbia; flows 52 mi. SE, joining Wateree R. 30 mi. SE of Columbia to form SANTEE RIVER. Navigable.
Congaz, Moldavian SSR: see KANGAZ.
Congella (kŏnjĕ'lŭ), S residential suburb of Durban, Natal, U. of So. Afr.
Conger (kŏn'jŭr), village (pop. 161), Freeborn co., S Minn., near Iowa line, 9 mi. WSW of Albert Lea; dairy products.
Congers (kŏng'gŭrz), village (pop. 1,949), Rockland co., SE N.Y., 3 mi. S of Haverstraw. Near by on W bank of the Hudson is a state park.
Congleton (kŏng'gŭl-), municipal borough (1931 pop. 12,885; 1951 census 15,492), E Cheshire, England, on Dane R. and 8 mi. SSW of Macclesfield; textile milling (silk, cotton, rayon, wool); mfg. of machine tools, tobacco, pharmaceuticals. Has 18th-cent. church.
Congl-y-Wal, Wales: see FFESTINIOG.
Congo (kŏng'gō), province (□ c.62,550; pop. 672,-535), NW Angola; ⊙ Uíge (since 1946). Bounded N and E by Belgian Congo, W by the Atlantic. Tropical coastal plain bordered E by a dissected tableland, drained by tributaries of Congo R. (especially the Kwango, which forms E boundary) and by coastal streams (M'Bridge, Cuanza). Congo estuary forms part of N border. Cotton, coffee, oilseeds, palm oil and kernels are exported. Chief ports are Luanda (⊙ Angola, and former prov.⊙), Santo António do Zaire, Ambriz, Ambrizete. Native kingdom of Congo (⊙ São Salvador) occupied region near N border. In 1946 Congo prov. (formerly called Luanda prov.) was administratively subdivided into 4 dists. (Zaire, Congo, Uíge, and Cuanza-Norte).
Congo, district, Angola: see MAQUELA DO ZOMBO.
Congo, El, Salvador: see EL CONGO.
Congo, French: see FRENCH EQUATORIAL AFRICA.
Congo Free State: see BELGIAN CONGO.
Congolón, Sierra de (syĕ'rä dā kōng-gōlōn'), W Honduras, S spur of main Andean divide; extends SSE from Sierra de Celaque, forming E watershed of Mocal R.; rises to 6,775 ft.
Congonhas (kōng-gō'nyŭs), city (pop. 2,831), S central Minas Gerais, Brazil, in the Serra do Espinhaço, on railroad and 12 mi. NNW of Conselheiro Lafaiete, in manganese- and iron-mining dist. Has 18th-cent. sanctuary of Senhor Bom Jesus de Matozinhos. noted for its wood sculptures by Aleijadinho. Until 1948, called Congonhas do Campo.
Congonhas, airport, Brazil: see SÃO PAULO, city.
Congonhinhas (kōng-gōōnyē'nyŭs), city (pop. 502), NE Paraná, Brazil, 45 mi. SE of Londrina; hogs; sawmilling. Coal mined at Cambuí (19 mi. S).
Congo River (kŏng'gō), Port. *Zaire* (zī'rā), great river of equatorial Africa, one of the world's longest (c.2,900 mi.) and second in Africa only to the Nile. Rises (alt. 4,650 ft.) as the Lualaba (lwälä'bä) on Katanga plateau, SE Belgian Congo, near Northern Rhodesia border, flows N parallel to the E central African lakes until it crosses the equator, and, thereafter known as the Congo, sweeps in a huge bow-like curve across the central African depression and turns SW, recrossing the equator and reaching the Atlantic Ocean through a narrow gorge in Crystal Mts. With its numerous tributaries, it drains a basin of c.1,450,000 sq. mi. (second in the world only to the Amazon), which extends from 12°S (source of Chambezi R.) to 8°N (source of Koto R.) and covers almost the whole of Belgian Congo, W part of Northern Rhodesia, N part of Angola, and a large section of French Equatorial Africa. Upper course of the Lualaba is marked by falls and rapids; the river becomes navigable at Bukama (for c.400 mi.). Henceforth it expands into a series of marshy lakes (Upemba, Kisale) periodically flooded and encumbered with papyrus and floating islands. It receives Lufira R. in L. Kisale and Luvua R. (draining Mweru L.) at Ankoro; L. Tanganyika waters are brought to it by Lukuga R. at Kabalo. Beyond Kongolo, the Lualaba enters a wild gorge (*Portes d'Enfer*) and is obstructed by rapids, although a navigable stretch exists bet. Kasongo and Kibombo. Here the river leaves the region of savannas and works its way through dense equatorial forest. At Kindu it becomes navigable again for 190 mi. to Ponthierville where STANLEY FALLS interrupt river's traffic. The falls are circumvented by a railroad and mark the end of the Lualaba and beginning of Congo proper. Below Stanleyville, the wide (c.10 mi. at Basoko) slow stream is unbroken by rapids for 1,090 mi. and is navigated year around by steamers up to 1,200 tons (mostly sternwheel); large islands (Bertha Isl.) and sandbars are frequent. In this section it receives the Lomami, Aruwimi, Itimbiri, and Mongala rivers. Below the mouth of the Mongala, its speed is further reduced by low gradient and accumulation of silt and it turns sluggishly SW, spreading in marshes and flooding bordering forest. Lulonga and Ruki rivers enter the Congo near Coquilhatville, and Ubangi R., its main N affluent, enters it at Irebu, where it also drains L. Tumba. Soon the river's 8-mi. width is constricted by cliffs to a width of 1 mi. at Liranga and Lukolela. From the mouth of the Ubangi it forms the Fr. Equatorial Africa border and receives the Sanga at Mossaka and the Kasai, its main S tributary, at Kwamouth. The river expands into STANLEY POOL c.350 mi. from its mouth; Leopoldville and Brazzaville, termini of inland navigation, are located here on SW and W shores. Beyond the pool begin the noted LIVINGSTONE FALLS, in which the river falls 852 ft. in 220 mi. to sea level. The Congo widens into an estuary of deltaic character c.100 mi. long and 6–10 mi. wide, with alluvial isls. and mangrove-bordered creeks, along Angola border. Ocean-going steamers ascend to Matadi, main port of the estuary, though navigation is hampered by a few violent whirlpools. Tide is felt as far as Boma, c.60 mi. upstream; at mouth the rise is 6 ft. Unlike most tropical rivers, Congo is noted for its constant flow, for its affluents bring it water from the rainy seasons of both N and S hemispheres. The Congo is the leading avenue of trade in Belgian Congo. Its nonnavigable stretches are circumvented by short railroads (Matadi-Leopoldville, Stanleyville-Ponthierville, Kindu-Kongolo). Together with its tributaries it represents c.8,000 mi. of navigable waterways. The Portuguese navigator Diogo Cão was 1st to discover (1482) the mouth of the Congo, naming it Zaire [corruption of native *Zadi*,=great water]. The British Capt. J. K. Tuckey reached Isangila (1816) from W seeking the sources of the Nile, David Livingstone explored lakes Mweru and Bangweulu (1866–71) and reached the Lualaba, but it remained for Henry M. Stanley to demonstrate the identity of Lualaba R. with the Congo through his epic journey down the river, begun at Nyangwe (1874) and ending at Boma (1877).
Congo-Ubangi, district, Belgian Congo: see LISALA.
Congresbury (kōōmz'bŭrē, kŏng'grĭs-), town and parish (pop. 1,274), N Somerset, England, on Yeo R. and 7 mi. ENE of Weston-super-Mare; agr. market in dairying region. Has 13th-cent. church and 15th-cent. vicarage.
Congress. 1 Village, Yavapai co., W central Ariz., 30 mi. SW of Prescott; gold mining. Near-by Congress Junction is sheep-shipping point. **2** Village (pop. 186), Wayne co., N central Ohio, 10 mi. NW of Wooster, in agr. area.
Conhelo, Argentina: see EDUARDO CASTEX.
Coni, Italy: see CUNEO, town.
Conil or **Conil de la Frontera** (kōnēl' dhā lä frōntā'-rä), town (pop. 5,562), Cádiz prov., SW Spain, land-

ing on the Atlantic, 20 mi. SE of Cádiz; seaside resort and agr. center (cereals, vegetables, grapes, livestock; agriculture). Fishing and fish canning (especially tuna). Has sawmills, limekilns. Unexploited sulphur and petroleum deposits in vicinity.

Conimbriga, Portugal: see COIMBRA.

Conimicut, R.I.: see WARWICK.

Conisborough or **Conisbrough** (both: kŏ'nĭsbrŭ), urban district (1931 pop. 18,174; 1951 census 16,412), West Riding, S Yorkshire, on Don R. and 5 mi. SW of Doncaster; coal mining; mfg. of bone by-products (glue, grease, fertilizer). Has ruins of 12th-cent. Norman castle.

Coniston (kŏ'nĭstŭn), town (pop. 2,245), SE central Ont., on Wanapitei R. and 7 mi. E of Sudbury; copper, nickel mining and smelting; hydroelectric station. Inc. 1934.

Coniston, resort village and parish (pop. 932), N Lancashire, England, on W shore of Coniston Water at foot of Old Man of Coniston (mountain, 2,633 ft.), in the Lake District, 19 mi. NNE of Barrow-in-Furness; sheep raising. Ruskin, who lived at Brantwood (on E shore of Coniston Water) is buried here. Near by is house in which Tennyson lived.

Coniston Water, lake, N Lancashire, England, in the Lake District 18 mi. NNE of Barrow-in-Furness; 6 mi. long, ½ mi. wide. Lake is a favorite trial ground for attempts on world motorboat speed record.

Conjeeveram (kŏnjē'vērŭm), anc. *Kanchi* (kŭn'chē), since 1949 officially **Kanchipuram** (-pōōrŭm), city (pop. 74,635), Chingleput dist., E Madras, India, on Palar R. and 40 mi. WSW of Madras. Famous archaeological site and pilgrimage center, one of the most sacred Hindu towns in India; proverbially known as the Benares of the South. Its many temples (mainly built by Pallava kings of 5th cent. A.D. and 16th-cent. rulers of Vijayanagar) provide a remarkably complete survey of Dravidian architecture; shrines are sacred to votaries of both Siva and Vishnu. An educational center since Buddhist times; Shankaracharya (8th-cent. A.D. Vedantic philosopher) founded one of his chief schools here. Still a center of Brahmanic culture; Sanskrit schools. Its hand-woven silk saris are known throughout India. Sometimes spelled Conjeevaram.

Conjo de Abajo (kōn'hō dhā ävä'hō), SW suburb (pop. 1,833) of Santiago, La Coruña prov., NW Spain. Near by is former monastery (12th cent.) and ruins of a fortified medieval castle.

Conkal (kōngkäl'), town (pop. 1,435), Yucatan, SE Mexico, 10 mi. NE of Mérida; rail junction; henequen.

Conklingville, village, Saratoga co., E N.Y., in foothills of the Adirondacks, 14 mi. W of Glens Falls. In Sacandaga R. here, Conklingville Dam (1,100 ft. long, 115 ft. high; completed 1930 for river control, power) impounds Sacandaga Reservoir.

Conlara River (kōnlä'rä), E San Luis prov., Argentina, rises at E foot of the Sierra de San Luis 15 mi. NW of La Toma, curves SE and NE, then flows N, past Renca, Concarán, and Santa Rosa, to lose itself near Córdoba prov. border 25 mi. E of Candelaria; c.100 mi. long. Used for irrigation and hydroelectric power.

Conlie (kōlē'), village (pop. 1,069), Sarthe dept., W France, 14 mi. NW of Le Mans; poultry, cattle, dairy products.

Conliège (kōlyĕzh'), village (pop. 773), Jura dept., E France, in a gorge of the W Jura, 3 mi. SE of Lons-le-Saunier; wood turning, button mfg. Sparkling wines.

Con Mine, Northwest Territories: see YELLOWKNIFE.

Conn, Lough (lŏkh), lake (9 mi. long, 4 mi. wide) in N central Co. Mayo, Ireland, 4 mi. W of Ballina and just N of Lough Cullin, with which it is connected by narrow channel.

Conna (kŏ'nŭ), Gaelic *Conaithe*, agr. village, E Co. Cork, Ireland, on Bride R. and 8 mi. ESE of Fermoy; dairying, cattle raising; oats, potatoes, beets.

Connacht or **Connaught** (both: kŏ'nôt), province (□ 6,610.7; pop. 492,797), W Ireland, including cos. Galway, Leitrim, Mayo, Roscommon, Sligo.

Connah's Quay, urban district (1931 pop. 5,980; 1951 census 7,365), Flint, Wales, on the Dee and 4 mi. SE of Flint; small port and agr. market, with fertilizer works. Urban dist. includes SHOTTON, agr. districts of Golftyn and Wepre and steel-milling town of Queensferry (SE), with tar and benzol refinery, dairying industry.

Connally Air Force Base, Texas: see WACO.

Connaught, Ireland: see CONNACHT.

Connaught Bridge, Malaya: see KLANG.

Connaught Tunnel (26,517 ft. long), SE B.C., in Selkirk Mts., under Mt. Macdonald, in Glacier Natl. Park, on Canadian Pacific RR, just NE of Glacier. Completed 1916.

Conneaut (kŏ'nēôt", –ôt"), city (pop. 10,230), Ashtabula co., extreme NE Ohio, c.55 mi. N of Youngstown, at mouth of Conneaut Creek on Conneaut Harbor of L. Erie, near Pa. line; important lake-rail transshipment center: receives L. Superior iron ore for Pittsburgh-Youngstown steel dist., ships coal and steel. Port of entry. Mfg. of tin cans, communications equipment, light bulbs, cutlery, clothing, agr. tools, leather, food products; railroad shops; fisheries; molding-sand pits. Settled 1799.

Conneaut Creek, in Pa. and Ohio, rises in Crawford co., NW Pa., flows N, then W into NE Ohio, then NE to Conneaut Harbor on L. Erie at Conneaut, c.50 mi. long.

Conneaut Lake, resort borough (pop. 676), Crawford co., NW Pa., 8 mi. WSW of Meadville and on Conneaut L., largest natural lake (929 acres) in Pa. Boat works; agr.

Conneautville, borough (pop. 1,177), Crawford co., NW Pa., 13 mi. NW of Meadville; agr. trading center; furniture, canned goods; corn, potatoes, buckwheat.

Connecticut (kŭnĕ'tĭkŭt), state (land □ 4,899; with inland waters □ 5,009; 1950 pop. 2,007,280; 1940 pop. 1,709,242), NE U.S., in New England; Bordered W by N.Y., N by Mass., E by R.I., S by Long Isl. Sound; 46th in area, 28th in pop.; one of 13 original states, it was the 5th to ratify (1788) the Constitution; ⊙ Hartford. The "Nutmeg State," roughly rectangular in shape, averages 90 mi. E–W and 55 mi. N–S. In the E and W are highlands, separated by a narrow lowland strip in the center. The upland areas, consisting of complex crystalline rocks (granite, schist), form the S part of the New England Upland physiographic prov., a peneplained surface, well dissected and sloping gently toward the S. The W section, rising to 2,355 ft. in Bear Mtn. in NW corner and including the Litchfield Hills (S extension of the Berkshires), is higher and more rugged than the hills of the E. The central lowland is drained by the CONNECTICUT RIVER as far as Middletown, where the river cuts SE through the uplands to the Sound. Conn.'s shore line is broken by river mouths and rocky inlets and contains some good harbors. The numerous lakes in the Conn. lowland are the result of the glaciation which covered the whole state. Besides the Connecticut R., the state is drained by the Thames R. system (E) and Housatonic R. and Naugatuck R. (W). Conn. has a humid continental climate, with an annual rainfall of 42–48 in. The growing season averages 155 days for most of the state, 175 days along the coast. Hartford (center) has mean temp. of 28°F. in Jan., 73°F. in July, and 43 in. of annual rainfall. Native vegetation was predominantly hardwood forest of chestnut, chestnut oak, and yellow poplar, with beech, birch, maple, and hemlock in the NE. Some 1,900,000 acres are now classified as forest land. Conn.'s generally hilly topography and stony soil have restricted its agr. to general farming (dairying, forage crops, potatoes) and the growing of specialized products. Almost ½ of the 22,000 farms are of the subsistence type. The best lands are in the Conn. lowland, where shade-grown tobacco (high-priced cigar leaf) is cultivated and market gardening carried on. Potatoes are also grown here, while corn, oats, and hay are raised throughout the state. Apples are important and peaches are found in some S hill sections. Poultry farming and dairying, however, are chief source of agr. income. Fishing in Long Isl. Sound yields a large annual catch of flounder, mackerel, shad, scup (porgy), bluefish, menhaden, and lobsters, oysters, and other shellfish. Conn.'s small mineral industry consists of the quarrying of sandstone (brownstone) and traprock (used for road metal) in central lowland, granite, limestone, feldspar, clay, sand, and gravel. Deposits of sheet mica and some iron ore occur but they are uneconomical to work. Conn. is primarily an industrial state, specializing in high-value products which require much skill. Although it imports coal (from Appalachian fields) and raw materials, it is favored by good road and rail facilities, large labor supply, and near-by urban markets. Principal manufactures are firearms and ammunition, brassware, clocks and watches, textiles, cutlery, silverware, hardware, machinery, jewelry, chemicals, precision tools, hats, boats, wire products, pins, and needles. The larger cities have a wide variety of light industries, many dating from 18th cent.: Bridgeport (firearms, sewing machines, electrical equipment), Hartford (firearms, typewriters), Waterbury (brass products, clocks), and New Haven (firearms, ammunition, hardware). Other important mfg. centers and large towns include Stamford, New Britain, Norwalk, Meriden, Bristol, West Hartford, East Hartford, New London, Manchester, Fairfield, Danbury, Derby, Ansonia, Naugatuck, Groton, Stratford, Greenwich, West Haven, Torrington, Middletown, and Hamden. Hydroelectric power is utilized in several areas; a power dam impounds L. Candlewood (W), largest in the state. Conn. is noted for its insurance companies, notably those at Hartford. The state's largely urban (77.6% in 1950) pop. is located in the central lowland and along the S shore; the residential communities in the SW corner are within commuting distance of metropolitan New York. The trim New England countryside and many fine lake and shore resorts attract numerous summer visitors to Conn., while in winter skiing is a popular sport. Leading educational institutions are Yale Univ. (New Haven), Univ. of Conn. (Storrs), Wesleyan Univ. (Middletown), and U.S. Coast Guard Acad. (New London). The Connecticut R. was discovered in 1614 by the Dutchman Adriaen Block and a Du. trading post was set up (1633) on the site of Hartford, but abandoned 1654. The 1st permanent settlements, however, were made by English colonists from Mass., who founded (1633–35) Windsor, Wethersfield, and Hartford in the Connecticut valley. A serious Indian threat was removed by the decisive defeat of the Pequots in 1637 (at present West Mystic). In 1638 New Haven colony was founded, and in the next year the Conn. valley towns adopted the Fundamental Orders, establishing a constitutional commonwealth. A member of the New England Confederation from 1643 to 1684, the Conn. colony received a royal charter in 1662, which included the New Haven colony and granted a strip of land extending W to the Pacific. Although under the rule of Gov. Andros from 1687 to 1689, Conn. successfully resisted crown efforts to control its affairs. Congregationalism was established as the official religion in 1708. Town meeting govt., dominated by the church, was characteristic. Economic self-sufficiency (subsistence farming and small handicrafts) and political isolation fostered provincialism and conservatism. With increasing trade relations, especially with the West Indies, Conn. became resentful of England's restrictive commercial and colonial policies and supported the Revolution; native sons Ethan Allen, Nathan Hale, and Benedict Arnold played active parts in the War of Independence. The state relinquished its claims to western lands in 1786, except for the WESTERN RESERVE, which it relinquished in 1800. Because of the prosperous carrying trade of the clipper ships, the embargo of 1807 was exceedingly unpopular in New England, as was the ensuing War of 1812, during which antiadministration feeling culminated in the Hartford Convention of 1814. The state adopted a new constitution in 1818, which is still in force today. Conn.'s legislature is unique in that the senate is elected from dists. based on pop., while the house of representatives is based on geographical distribution (i.e., the towns) and gives disproportionate representation to the older and smaller towns at the expense of the newer and larger cities. The decline of the shipping industry in the early 19th cent. forced many into mfg., and the ingenious Yankees began to turn out a variety of specialty goods (metalware, clocks) and "notions" (buttons, pins, needles)—the wares of the versatile Yankee peddler. Textiles were also important. Industry, which superseded agr. around 1840, received its greatest impetus with the coming of railroads and the influx of European workers. During the 19th cent. many Conn. farmers left the state for the richer lands of the west, but the overall pop. grew steadily as the trend toward industrialism and urban concentration increased rapidly. See also articles on the cities, towns, and geographic features, and on the 8 counties: FAIRFIELD, HARTFORD, LITCHFIELD, MIDDLESEX, NEW HAVEN, NEW LONDON, TOLLAND, WINDHAM.

Connecticut Lakes, N N.H., 3 lakes in hunting, fishing area of N Coos co.; sources of Connecticut R., which joins them. First Connecticut L. (4 mi. long) and Second Connecticut L. (3 mi. long) are power dam sites; Third Connecticut L. (1 mi. long) is near Que. line. Connecticut Lake State Park lies bet. Second and Third lakes.

Connecticut River, NE U.S., largest river of New England, rises in Connecticut Lakes in N N.H., flows S, forming Vt.-N.H. line, and across Mass. and Conn., to Long Island Sound at Old Saybrook, Conn.; 345 mi. long; navigable for 15-ft. drafts to Hartford, Conn. Springfield, Mass., and Brattleboro, Vt., are also on the river. Its right tributaries are Passumpsic, White, Deerfield, and Farmington rivers; left tributaries are the Ammonoosuc and the Chicopee. Extensive hydroelectric and flood-control developments in upper course include new dam at Wilder, Vt.; 385 ft. high, 2,100 ft. long, built 1948–50, the structure backs up reservoir 46 mi. long. Fifteen Mile Falls Dam at Barnet, Vt. is 178 ft. high, 2000 ft. long; it was completed 1930. Lower valley is rich agr. region; onions are important in Mass. part, and shade-grown tobacco is produced in Mass. and Conn. A disastrous flood in March, 1936, caused much destruction. A Federal flood-control project begun in 1936 is planned to include 20 dams and reservoirs on tributaries.

Connell (kŏnĕl'), town (pop. 465), Franklin co., SE Wash., 30 mi. NNE of Pasco, in Columbia basin agr. region.

Connellsville, industrial city (pop. 13,293), Fayette co., SW Pa., 36 mi. SE of Pittsburgh and on Youghiogheny R.; coke, metal products, glass, clothing, food products; railroad shops. Settled c.1770, inc. as borough 1806, as city 1911.

Connelsville, town (pop. 113), Adair co., N Mo., on Chariton R. and 8 mi. NW of Kirksville.

Connemara (kŏ"nĭmä'rŭ), wild mountainous region in W Co. Galway, Ireland, bet. the Atlantic and loughs Corrib and Mask, including mountain range of BENNA BEOLA. Coastline is rocky; interior has many picturesque glens. Population centers are along the coast; handloom weaving and kelp collecting (for iodine) are main occupations.

Connerré (kônĕrā'), village (pop. 1,745), Sarthe dept., W France, on Huisne R. and 15 mi. ENE of Le Mans; hog market; tanning. Megalithic monuments near by.

Conners Pass, Nev.: see SHELL CREEK RANGE.

Connersville, city (pop. 15,550), ⊙ Fayette co., E Ind., on Whitewater R. and c.55 mi. E of Indianapolis, in agr. area; railroad center, with mfg. (automobiles and equipment, metal and enamel products, machine-shop products, refrigerators, blowers, kitchen equipment, toys). Laid out 1817.

Connewitz (kô'nůvĭts), S suburb of Leipzig, Saxony, E central Germany.

Connoquenessing (kŏ"nůkůnĭ'sĭng), borough (pop. 441), Butler co., W Pa., 7 mi. WSW of Butler; oil. Also spelled Conoquenessing.

Connoquenessing Creek, W Pa., rises in E Butler co., flows SW, past Butler, and NW, past Ellwood City, to Beaver R. just W of Ellwood City; c.50 mi. long.

Connor, town (pop. 215), central Co. Antrim, Northern Ireland, 5 mi. SE of Ballymena; cattle; flax, potatoes.

Connor, township (pop. 630), Aroostook co., NE Maine, on Little Madawaska R. and 21 mi. N of Presque Isle, in agr. region.

Connors Pass, Nev.: see SHELL CREEK RANGE.

Conococheague Creek (kůnŏ'ků-chēg), rises in Franklin and Adams counties, S Pa., and winds c.80 mi. W and S, through Cumberland Valley, to the Potomac at Williamsport, Md. West Branch rises in N Franklin co., Pa., flows c.45 mi. generally S, entering the creek 3 mi. N of the Md. line.

Conodoguinet Creek (kŏnůdŏ'gwĭnůt), S Pa., rises in mts. in NW Franklin co., flows c.75 mi. generally ENE to Susquehanna R. near West Fairview.

Cononaco River (kōnōnä'kō), Napo-Pastaza prov., E Ecuador, left affluent (c.100 mi. long) of Curaray R., which it joins near Peru border.

Conon River (kŏ'nůn), Ross and Cromarty, Scotland, rises in Loch Fannich as Fannich Water, flows E, through Loch Luichard, to Cromarty Firth at Maryburgh; c.35 mi. long. Receives Orrin R. and Garve Water.

Conoplja or **Chonoplya'** (both: chô'nôplyä), Serbo-Croatian *Čonoplja*, Hung. *Csonoplya*, village (pop. 5,515), Vojvodina, N Serbia, Yugoslavia, 7 mi. ENE of Sombor, in the Backa.

Conoquenessing, Pa.: see CONNOQUENESSING.

Conos, Dos, Argentina: see DOS CONOS.

Conover (kŏ'nōvůr). **1** Town (pop. 1,164), Catawba co., W central N.C., 7 mi. ESE of Hickory; furniture and textile plants. **2** Village (pop. c.200), Vilas co., N Wis., 30 mi. NE of Rhinelander, in wooded lake region; trade center for resort area.

Conowingo (kŏnůwĭng'gō), village, Cecil co., NE Md., 9 mi. NNW of Havre de Grace. In the Susquehanna here is **Conowingo Dam** (4,675 ft. long, 99 ft. high; completed 1928), a hydroelectric dam which carries U.S. Route 1 across the river. Conowingo L. extends c.14 mi. upriver, into SE Pa.

Conques (kŏk'). **1** or **Conques-sur-Orbiel** (-sür-ôrbyĕl'), village (pop. 1,171), Aude dept., S France, 4 mi. NNE of Carcassonne; distilling, fruit- and winegrowing. **2** Village (pop. 248), Aveyron dept., S France, 19 mi. NNW of Rodez. Its noted 11th-cent. Romanesque church of Saint-Foy is place of pilgrimage. Seat of a powerful abbey during Middle Ages.

Conquest, village (pop. 240), S central Sask., 32 mi. E of Rosetown; railroad junction; wheat.

Conquet, Le (lů kōkā'), village (pop. 1,567), Finistère dept., W France, 13 mi. W of Brest; fishing port and resort; chemical works (fertilizer, salt, iodine).

Conquista (kōng-kē'stä), village (pop. c.1,500), Pando dept., NW Bolivia, on Madre de Dios R. and 40 mi. SE of Puerto Rico; rubber.

Conquista (kōng-kē'stů). **1** City, Bahia, Brazil: see VITÓRIA DA CONQUISTA. **2** City (pop. 2,489), W Minas Gerais, Brazil, near the Rio Grande (São Paulo border), in the Triângulo Mineiro, on railroad and 27 mi. SE of Uberaba; rice hulling, cattle raising.

Conquista (kōng-kē'stä), town (pop. 1,671), Córdoba prov., S Spain, 20 mi. E of Pozoblanco; cereals, livestock, lumber. Bismuth mining near by.

Conquista, La, Nicaragua: see LA CONQUISTA.

Conrad (kŏn'răd). **1** Town (pop. 649), Grundy co., central Iowa, on Wolf Creek and 33 mi. SW of Waterloo, in agr. area. Limestone quarry near by. **2** City (pop. 1,865), ⊙ Pondera co., N Mont., 55 mi. NNW of Great Falls; shipping point for grain and sugar beets; livestock, poultry; oil wells. Inc. 1910.

Conran, town (1940 pop. 129), New Madrid co., extreme SE Mo., near Mississippi R., 5 mi. NE of Portageville.

Conrath, village (pop. 114), Rusk co., N Wis., 35 mi. NE of Chippewa Falls; dairying.

Conroe (kŏn'rō), city (pop. 7,298), ⊙ Montgomery co., E Texas, 38 mi. NNW of Houston, near San Jacinto R.; trade, industrial center for oil and lumber-producing area; recycling plant; mfg. of gasoline, carbon black; also lumber mills, creosoting plant, foundries, furniture plant. Founded 1881, inc. 1906; oil discovery (1931) brought new growth.

Consata (kōnsä'tä), village, La Paz dept., W Bolivia, on Consata R. (branch of Mapiri R.) and 20 mi. NNE of Sorata; cacao, quina.

Conscripto Bernardi (kōnskrēp'tō bĕrnär'dē), town (pop. estimate 1,500), N central Entre Ríos prov., Argentina, on railroad and 100 mi. NE of Paraná; agr. center (wheat, flax, corn, livestock). Formerly Kilómetro 101.

Consecon (kŏnsē'kůn), village (pop. estimate 500), SE Ont., on Weller Bay of L. Ontario and on Consecon L. (5 mi. long), 14 mi. SW of Belleville; fishing, fruitgrowing.

Consegüina, in Nicaraguan names: see COSIGÜINA.

Consejo (kōnsä'hō), village (pop. 43), Northern Dist., Br. Honduras, on Chetumal Bay, 9 mi. NE of Corozal, near Hondo R. mouth; coconuts, sugar cane. Lighthouse.

Consejo, El, Venezuela: see EL CONSEJO.

Conselheiro Lafaiete (kōnsĭlyā'rōō lůfäyĕ'tĭ), city (pop. 14,352), S central Minas Gerais, Brazil, in the Serra do Espinhaço, on railroad and 45 mi. S of Belo Horizonte; leading manganese-mining center supplying Braz. steel industry and export shipments. Also has iron and ocher mines. Railroad workshops. Largest manganese mine at Morro da Mina (2 mi. NNE). Old name, Lafayette. Later called Queluz.

Conselheiro Pena (pā'nů), city (pop. 1,993), E Minas Gerais, Brazil, on the Rio Doce, on railroad and 36 mi. SE of Governador Valadares; exploitation of mica; semiprecious-stone deposits. Formerly called Lajão.

Conselice (kônsä'lēchĕ), town (pop. 2,183), Ravenna prov., Emilia-Romagna, N central Italy, 8 mi. NNW of Lugo; auto accessories.

Consell (kōnsäl'), town (pop. 1,519), Majorca, Balearic Isls., on railroad and 11 mi. NE of Palma; almonds, carobs, olives, cereals, vegetables, stock.

Conselve (kônsĕl'vĕ), town (pop. 2,622), Padova prov., Veneto, N Italy, 12 mi. S of Padua; mfg. (agr. machinery, wine presses, synthetic fuels), wine making.

Consentia, Italy: see COSENZA, town.

Consett, urban district (1931 pop. 12,354; 1951 census 39,456), N Durham, England, near Derwent R., 13 mi. SW of Newcastle-upon-Tyne; steel milling, coal mining, hosiery knitting. In urban dist. (since 1937) are Leadgate, with coal mines and ironworks, and Benfieldside, with coal mines.

Conshohocken (kŏn"shůhŏ'kůn), industrial borough (pop. 10,922), Montgomery co., SE Pa., 11 mi. NW of Philadelphia and on Schuylkill R.; steel mill; automobile tires, metal products, textiles, plastics, paper and cement products; agr. Settled 1831, inc. 1850.

Consigüina, in Nicaraguan names: see COSIGÜINA.

Consolacion (kōnsōläsyōn'), town (1939 pop. 2,293; 1948 municipality pop. 9,432), central Cebu isl., Philippines, 6 mi. NE of Cebu city, opposite Mactan Isl.; corn, coconuts.

Consolación del Norte, Cuba: see LA PALMA.

Consolación del Sur (dĕl sōōr'), town (pop. 5,392), Pinar del Río prov., W Cuba, on Central Highway and 12 mi. NE of Pinar del Río; commercial center in Vuelta Abajo tobacco-growing region; produces also bananas, pineapples, vegetables. Mfg. of cigars. Has airfield. Sulphurous springs and quarries near by.

Consort, village (pop. 325), SE Alta., near Sask. border, 60 mi. S of Wainwright; grain elevators, lumber and stockyards.

Constableville, village (pop. 378), Lewis co., N central N.Y., 30 mi. N of Rome, in timber and dairying area.

Constance, Ger. *Konstanz* (kôn'stänts), city (1950 pop. 42,209), S Baden, Germany, port on L. of Constance, at efflux of the Rhine (rail bridge), 25 mi. E of Schaffhausen, adjacent (S) to Kreuzlingen, Switzerland; 47°39'N 9°10'E. Rail junction; mfg. of textiles, clothing, machinery, chemicals, paper goods; metalworking, printing. Potteries. Active tourist trade. Old historic section of town is on left bank of Rhine with no land connection to Germany; modern section is on right bank (airport at N suburb of Petershausen). Cathedral, started in 11th cent., was completely rebuilt in 15th and 17th cent. Founded as Roman fort in 4th cent. A.D., Constance became episcopal see in 6th cent. Emperor Frederick I here recognized (1183) the Lombard League. Created free imperial city in 1192. Scene (1414–18) of Council of Constance, where John Huss was burned. Former Dominican convent, which housed Council, is now a hotel. City accepted Reformation; joined Schmalkaldic League in 1531. Deprived of its free imperial status and given to Austria by Charles V in 1548. Ceded to Baden in 1805. Bishopric was secularized 1802–03; diocese abolished 1827. The city, undamaged in Second World War, was captured by Fr. troops in spring, 1945. Count Zeppelin b. here.

Constance, Lake of, or **Lake Constance** (□ 208), Ger. *Bodensee* (bō'dùnzā"), anc. *Lacus Brigantinus*, bordering Switzerland, Germany, Austria; length (bet. Bregenz and Stein) 42 mi., widest c.8 mi.; average depth 295 ft., greatest depth 827 ft.; alt. 1,296 ft. Near Constance, in the W, it divides into 2 parts, the UNTERSEE (S) (ōōn'tůrzā") and the Überlinger See (N) (ü'bůrlĭng"ůr zā"). The large E and SE section, the main body of the lake, is called the Obersee (ō'bůrzā"). The whole lake is part of the course of the Rhine, which enters it in SE 4 mi. WSW of Bregenz and leaves in NW at Stein via the Untersee. Fruit and wine are raised on fertile shores; fishing; numerous resorts. Major cities: Constance, Lindau (on isl.), Friedrichshafen, Überlingen (Germany); Bregenz (Austria); Rorschach (Switzerland). Isl. of Mainau is N of Constance in the Überlinger See, isl. of Reichenau is W of Constance in the Untersee. Steamer service. There are remains of lake dwellings.

Constancia or **Central Constancia** (sĕnträl' kōnstän'syä), sugar-mill village (pop. 1,850), Las Villas prov., central Cuba, 9 mi. NW of Cienfuegos.

Constância (kōshtä'syů), town (pop. 771), Santarém dist., central Portugal, on the Tagus at influx of Zêzere R. and 9 mi. W of Abrantes; mfg. of soap and fishing nets, cork processing. The 12th-cent. castle of Almourol is 3 mi. WSW on an isl. in the Tagus.

Constancia (kōnstän'syä), village (pop. 150), Paysandú dept., NW Uruguay, on railroad and 9 mi. NNE of Paysandú; wheat, cattle.

Constanta (kônstän'tsä), Rum. *Constanța*, anc. *Tomis* and *Constantiniana*, former Turkish *Küstendje*, city (1948 pop. 78,586), ⊙ Constanta prov., SE Rumania, in Dobruja, on the Black Sea and c.125 mi. E of Bucharest, c.60 mi. SW of the Danube delta; 44°10'N 28°40'E. Chief Rum. Black Sea port, exporting oil, grain, lumber, and foodstuffs to the East; main Rumanian naval and air base; rail junction; and leading seaside resort of Rumania. An Orthodox bishopric since 4th cent. Its trading activities are more important than its industry, but it produces furniture, tiles and bricks, metal products, soap, mirrors, cordage, textiles; processes fruit, grain, meat, and hides. Its harbor has oil pipe line to Ploesti, huge grain elevators, and extensive docks. Airport at Hellenie. Numerous Byzantine and Roman remains are in and near Constanta. There are several mosques and synagogues, a fine beach and municipal casino, the regional mus. of Dobruja, and an open-air archæological mus. The anc. Milesian colony of Tomis was founded (7th cent. B.C.) here and came under Roman control in 72 B.C.; here Ovid lived in exile (A.D. 9–17). The city, rebuilt (4th cent.) by Constantine the Great as Constantiniana, was later destroyed again. Present Constanta began as a Turkish fishing village (1413–1878). Urban development dates from annexation of Dobruja by Rumania (1878). Popular bathing resort of Mamaia, with fine beach, is 5 mi. N. Sometimes spelled Constantsa and Constanza.

Constantí (kōnstäntē'), town (pop. 1,742), Tarragona prov., NE Spain, 4 mi. NNW of Tarragona; olive oil, wine, fruit, filberts.

Constantia (kônstän'tyä), village (pop. 332), Commewijne dist., N Du. Guiana, on Commewijne R. and 19 mi. ENE of Paramaribo; sugar cane, coffee.

Constantia, France: see COUTANCES.

Constantia (kůnstăn'shů, kônstän'tsēů), residential town (pop. 6,081), SW Cape Prov., U. of So. Afr., near False Bay, 8 mi. SSE of Cape Town; viticulture. Site of Groot Constantia House, built 1685 by Van der Stel.

Constantia (kůnstăn'shů), village (1940 pop. 647), Oswego co., N central N.Y., on N shore of Oneida L., 28 mi. W of Rome, in dairy and fruit area.

Constantiana, Rumania: see CONSTANTA, city.

Constantina (kōnstäntē'nä), city (pop. 11,425), Seville prov., SW Spain, in Andalusia, in spur of the Sierra Morena, 40 mi. NNE of Seville; trading and processing center in rich agr. region (olives, grapes, livestock); cork, timber. Flour- and sawmilling, tanning, liquor distilling (cognac, anisette); mfg. of soap and shoes. It is also a summer resort. Near by are iron, copper, lead, and coal deposits. Town was called *Constantina Julia* by the Romans.

Constantine (kŏn'stůntēn, -tīn), northeasternmost and largest department (□ 33,814; 1948 pop. 3,108,165) of Algeria, on the Mediterranean, bordering Tunisia (E); ⊙ Constantine. The Tell Atlas ranges, here broken into irregular chains and massifs, include Babor range of Little KABYLIA, Constantine Mts., Edough massif (NW of Bône), and Medjerda Mts. Here are Algeria's largest cork-oak forests. Valleys of short coastal streams (Soummam, Saf-Saf, Seybouse) grow wine, figs, truck produce. Olive groves on mtn. slopes. The TELL region of N Algeria widens here to 120 mi. The part of the High Plateaus (just S of the Tell Atlas) here is Algeria's chief wheat-growing region. The Rhumel is chief river. The Saharan Atlas, which here comes nearest to the coast, includes the AURÈS massif, with Algeria's highest summits. Further S lies the Sahara, which in the Hodna depression comes to within 80 mi. of the coast. Dept. has Algeria's leading phosphate deposits (worked at the Djebel Kouif and Djebel Dir near Tebessa) and iron mine (Djebel Ouenza). Minor deposits of lead, zinc, copper, antimony, and mercury. From the E–W trunk railroad linking Fr. Morocco with Tunisia, spurs reach port cities (Bougie, Philippeville, Bône) and inland centers (Tebessa, Khenchela, Biskra). There is flour milling in Constantine. Other towns are Guelma (livestock market); Souk-Ahras and Sétif in the High Plateaus; and Batna. Djidjelli, Collo, and La Calle are minor cork-exporting ports. Tourist attractions include Constantine, the Roman ruins of Lambèse and Timgad, and the rugged scenery of Kabylia and the Aurès. Moslems constitute (1948) 94% of total pop. Dept. was created 1848; localized Berber resistance (especially in the Aurès) to France continued until 1871.

Constantine, anc. *Cirta*, fortified city (pop. 80,233), ⊙ Constantine dept., NE Algeria, 200 mi. ESE of Algiers and 40 mi. SSW of Philippeville, its port on the Mediterranean; 36°22'N 6°37'E; average alt. 2,150 ft. Algeria's largest inland city, and chief market for products of the High Plateaus and the arid interior. Occupies a remarkable site atop a rocky ledge, set off from surrounding plateau by the precipitous gorge of the Rhumel (E and N) and of one of its tributaries (W). The ravine of the Rhumel (100–700 ft. below the city), with a scenic path cut into its sides, is city's leading tourist attraction. Besides natural bridges formed by its intermittently underground course, the Rhumel is crossed by El-Kantara bridge (built 19th cent., on site of original Roman bridge) and Sidi-M'Cid bridge (leading from the *casbah*, the old citadel). It leaves its gorge in a series of falls (260 ft. high) on which is a hydroelectric plant. Modern suburbs have grown up SW of the "isthmus" which leads to the adjacent plateau. Constantine is Algeria's 1st flour-milling center (mills in N, near falls) and grain market. Also chief seat of native handicraft industry (leather and textiles). Trades principally in grain, wool, leather and skins, esparto. Also metalworking (auto and railroad servicing, mfg. of agr. equipment), olive-oil pressing, mfg. of cement, tobacco products, burlap bags, flour paste. City is an episcopal see, has a Mohammedan seminary (Médersa), and an archaeological society. There are important remains of Roman fortifications. Airport is at Le Khroub (7 mi. SE). Anc. *Cirta* was prosperous chief city of Numidia, and later a Roman grain-shipping center. Destroyed (A.D. 311) in a civil war, it was rebuilt by Constantine I. During Middle Ages it was the seat of successive Moslem dynasties, and once again flourished under Turks in 18th cent. Taken 1837 by French after a costly siege. Of Algeria's chief cities, it has proportionately largest Moslem pop. (over 50%).

Constantine, town and parish (pop. 1,565), SW Cornwall, England, near the Channel, 5 mi. SW of Falmouth; agr. market in dairying region; granite quarrying. Has 15th-cent. church.

Constantine, village (pop. 1,514), St. Joseph co., SW Mich., on St. Joseph R. and 31 mi. SSW of Kalamazoo, in agr. area (grain, truck, livestock, poultry; dairy products). Mfg. of paper products, caskets. Settled 1828; inc. 1837.

Constantine, Mount (10,290 ft.), SW Yukon, near Alaska border, in St. Elias Mts., 200 mi. WNW of Whitehorse; 61°25'N 140°36'W.

Constantine Mountains, range of the Tell Atlas in Constantine dept., NE Algeria, extending c.60 mi. from Constantine area (WSW) to Guelma (ENE). The Djebel Chettaba (just SW of Constantine) rises to c.4,300 ft.

Constantinople (kŏn"stăntĭnō'pŭl), former ⊙ Byzantine Empire and Ottoman Empire, since 1930 officially named ISTANBUL, which see. The ⊙ Turkey was moved from Constantinople to ANKARA in 1922.

Constantinople, Straits of, Turkey: see BOSPORUS.

Constant Spring, town, St. Andrew parish, SE Jamaica, residential quarter in W foothill of Blue Mts., 5 mi. N of Kingston. Dairying.

Constanza (kōnstän'sä), village (pop. estimate 500), central Santa Fe prov., Argentina, on railroad and 26 mi. SSW of San Cristóbal, in flax-growing and stock-raising area.

Constanza, town (1950 pop. 961), La Vega prov., central Dominican Republic, in the Cordillera Central, on affluent of the Yaque del Sur, and 27 mi. SW of La Vega; mtn. resort in wheat-growing region.

Constitución, department, Argentina: see VILLA CONSTITUCIÓN.

Constitución (kōnstētōōsyōn'), town (pop. 7,053), ⊙ Constitución dept. (□ 993; pop. 26,403), Maule prov., S central Chile, port on the Pacific at mouth of Maule R., 43 mi. W of Talca; rail terminus, summer resort, and agr. center (wheat, wine, lentils, potatoes); shipyards. Exports grain and timber. Has a number of beaches noted for their picturesque rock formations. Town was founded 1794 as Nueva Bilbao. It was rebuilt after 1928 earthquake.

Constitución, town (pop. 1,600), Salto dept., NW Uruguay, on Uruguay R., on highway, and 23 mi. N of Salto; cereals; vineyards; cattle, sheep.

Constitution Island, SE N.Y., island (c.¾ mi. in diameter) in the Hudson, opposite West Point and separated from E bank of river by marshes; part of the U.S. military reservation. Ruins of old Fort Constitution (1775) here. In the Revolution, isl. was E anchorage of a chain stretched across river to prevent ascent of British ships. Susan and Anna B. Warner lived here.

Consuegra (kōnswā'grä), city (pop. 9,255), Toledo prov., central Spain, in New Castile, on small Amarguillo R. (irrigation) and 35 mi. SE of Toledo. Processing and agr. center (cereals, grapes, saffron, olives, sheep); olive-oil pressing, flour milling; limekilns; jasper and marble quarries. Hydroelectric plant. Has Roman ruins and near-by hermitage with shrine of Christ of the Cross. City was nearly destroyed (1891) by inundation from Amarguillo R.

Consuelo (kōnswā'lō), locality, San Pedro de Macorís prov., SE Dominican Republic, 8 mi. N of San Pedro de Macorís city; sugar mill.

Consulta, La, Argentina: see LA CONSULTA.

Contai (kän'tē), town (pop. 6,746), Midnapore dist., SW West Bengal, India, 50 mi. SE of Midnapore; rice, potatoes, mustard, chili. Has col. Was salt-mfg. center. Formerly called Kanthi. Lighthouse 13 mi. ENE, on Hooghly R.

Contamana (kōntämä'nä), city (pop. 3,076), ⊙ Ucayali prov. (in 1940: □ 53,392; enumerated pop. 54,033, plus estimated 30,000 Indians), Loreto dept., E central Peru, landing on Ucayali R. and 115 mi. ESE of Tarapoto (San Martín dept.); 7°15'S 74°52'W. Trading and rubber-gathering center, in agr. region (bananas, sugar cane, vegetables); liquor distilling. Airfield.

Contamines, Les (lā kōtämēn'), Alpine village (pop. 109), Haute-Savoie dept., SE France, resort on Bon-Nant R. (tributary of the Arve), at foot of Mont Blanc (6 mi. E) and of Mont Joly (just W), 10 mi. SW of Chamonix; alt. c.3,900 ft.; cheese mfg. Winter sports.

Contamine-sur-Arve (kōtämēn'-sür-ärv'), village (pop. 166), Haute-Savoie dept., SE France, on the Arve and 11 mi. SE of Geneva; winegrowing. Has 13th-cent. church. Near by are ruins of castle of Faucigny.

Contarina (kôntärē'nä), town (pop. 4,500), Rovigo prov., Veneto, N Italy, on Po R. and 8 mi. ESE of Adria; cereals, sugar beets, cattle. Was seat of Porto Viro commune formed 1938, abolished 1938.

Contas, Rio de (rē'ōō dĭ kōn'tŭs), river in S central and E Bahia, Brazil, rises on central plateau near 13°10'S 42°W, flows c.300 mi. generally ESE, past Jiquié, to the Atlantic at Itacaré. Receives the Gavião and Brumado (right). Cacao grown in lower valley. Gold placers in upper course.

Contepec (kōntāpĕk'), town (pop. 2,737), Michoacán, central Mexico, 13 mi. NNW of El Oro; cereals, livestock. Airfield.

Contern (kôn'tûrn), village (pop. 358), S Luxembourg, 4 mi. ESE of Luxembourg city; chalk quarrying; fruit (cherries).

Contes (kōt), village (pop. 1,298), Alpes-Maritimes dept., SE France, 8 mi. N of Nice; cement mfg., lumbering.

Contessa, Gulf of, Greece: see STRYMONIC GULF.

Contessa Entellina (kôntĕs'sä ĕntĕl-lē'nä), village (pop. 2,597), Palermo prov., SW central Sicily, 9 mi. SW of Corleone. Albanian colony founded 1450; still retains its language and customs. Surname taken in 1874 from near-by ruins of anc. Entella, destroyed 1224 by Frederick II.

Conthey (kōtā'), town (pop. 3,449), Valais canton, SW Switzerland, on short Morge R. and 3 mi. W of Sion; farming.

Contich, Belgium: see KONTICH.

Contin (kŏn'tĭn), agr. village and parish (pop. 1,105), SE Ross and Cromarty, Scotland, on Garve Water and 6 mi. WSW of Dingwall. Near by are picturesque Falls of Rogie, on Garve Water.

Continental, village (pop. 1,023), Putnam co., NW Ohio, 14 mi. SSE of Defiance, in diversified agr. area; food products, tile.

Continental Divide, in North America, the great ridge of the Rocky Mountain summits which separates W-flowing streams from E-flowing waters. In U.S., ridge has sometimes been called the Great Divide, a name also occasionally used for the whole Rocky Mtn. system, especially the S section where the high, rugged ranges presented a difficult barrier to west-bound explorers and settlers. Glacier, Yellowstone, and Rocky Mtn. natl. parks lie on the divide.

Contla (kōn'tlä), officially San Bernardino Contla, town (pop. 3,379), Tlaxcala, central Mexico, 5 mi. E of Tlaxcala; agr. center (corn, wheat, alfalfa, maguey, stock).

Conto, Colombia: see CACHIMBA.

Contoocook, village, N.H.: see HOPKINTON.

Contoocook River (kŭntōō'kŭk), S N.H., rises in SE Cheshire co., flows c.60 mi. generally NE to Merrimack R. at Penacook. Furnishes water power at Hillsboro, Peterboro, and other mfg. towns.

Contoy Island (kōntoi') (□ 1.6), in Yucatan Channel, off NE coast of Yucatan Peninsula, SE Mexico, 17 mi. ESE of Cape Catoche; 4 mi. long, c. ½ mi. wide; 21°32'N 86°49'W.

Contra Costa (kŏn'trŭ kŏ'stŭ), county (□ 734; pop. 298,984), W Calif.; ⊙ Martinez. Along 70-mi. waterfront on San Francisco, San Pablo, and Suisun bays and Carquinez Strait are important ports (notably RICHMOND) and industrial cities (PITTSBURG, with large steelworks; Antioch, Port Chicago, Martinez, Crockett, Hercules); and large oil refineries, shipyards, food-processing and explosives plants, smelters, and other diversified mfg. plants. Berkeley Hills are along W boundary; Mt. DIABLO (in state park) is in central section. In NE is part of fertile delta of San Joaquin R. Asparagus, truck, fruit, nuts, wine and table grapes, barley, alfalfa, sugar beets, dairy products, cattle, sheep, hogs. Quarrying of stone, clay, sand, gravel, pumice; natural-gas wells. Formed 1850.

Contra Costa Canal, W Calif., a unit (completed 1947) of CENTRAL VALLEY project, fed by pumped San Joaquin–Sacramento R. water from the delta near Oakley; flows 48 mi. W to reservoir at Martinez. Used for irrigation and for industrial and urban supply in Suisun Bay region.

Contra Estaca (kōn'trä ĕstä'kä), mining settlement (pop. 1,625), Sinaloa, NW Mexico, in W outliers of Sierra Madre Occidental, 55 mi. NNE of Mazatlán; silver and gold mining.

Contralmirante Villar, province, Peru: see ZORRITOS.

Contratación (kōnträtäsyōn'), town (pop. 5,238), Santander dept., N central Colombia, in W Cordillera Oriental, 19 mi. SW of Socorro; alt. 5,545 ft.; agr. center (rice, cotton, sugar cane, coffee, stock).

Contrecoeur (kōtrŭkûr'), village (pop. 1,043), S Que., on the St. Lawrence and 30 mi. NNE of Montreal; dairying, cattle raising; fruit, potatoes. Opposite, in the St. Lawrence, are the Contrecoeur Isls., group of 6 islets.

Contreras (kōntrā'räs), officially La Magdalena Contreras, town (pop. 7,831), Federal Dist., central Mexico, 10 mi. SSW of Mexico city. Textile mills use power from Magdalena R. Site of important battle of Mexican War (Aug. 19–20, 1847), enabling American advance under Winfield Scott.

Contreras Island, off S Chile, NW of Adelaide Isls.; 52°S 75°W; 35 mi. long, c.7 mi. wide; uninhabited.

Contres (kō'trŭ), village (pop. 1,935), Loir-et-Cher dept., N central France, 12 mi. SSE of Blois; meat salting and drying, fruit and vegetable preserving, asparagus growing.

Contrexéville (kōtrĕgzāvēl'), village (pop. 1,058), Vosges dept., E France, on N slope of Monts Faucilles, 3 mi. WSW of Vittel; noted watering place with cold mineral springs.

Controller Bay (18 mi. wide), S Alaska, in Gulf of Alaska, SE of Katalla.

Contulmo (kōntōōl'mō), village (1930 pop. 690), Arauco prov., S central Chile, near SE end of L. Lanalhue, at W foot of Cordillera de Nahuelbuta, 35 mi. SE of Lebu; tourist resort in agr. area (cereals, vegetables, livestock); lumbering.

Contumasá or **Contumazá** (both: kōntōōmäsä'), city (pop. 2,080), ⊙ Contumasá prov. (□ 875; pop. 30,332), Cajamarca dept., NW Peru, on W slopes of Cordillera Occidental, on road from Chilete, and 24 mi. SW of Cajamarca; alt. 5,586 ft. Agr. products (sugar cane, wheat, corn).

Contursi (kôntōōr'sē), town (pop. 2,348), Salerno prov., Campania, S Italy, on Sele R., near mouth of Tanagro R., and 25 mi. E of Salerno. Sulphur springs (baths) near by.

Contwoyto Lake (c.80 mi. long, 2-10 mi. wide), central Mackenzie Dist., Northwest Territories; near 66°N 110°W. Drained N into Bathurst Inlet by Burnside R. (c.150 mi. long).

Conty (kōtē'), village (pop. 1,191), Somme dept., N France, 12 mi. SSW of Amiens; agr. market; mfg. (felt hats, chemicals).

Convención (kōmvĕnsyōn'), town (pop. 3,210), Norte de Santander dept., N Colombia, in Cordillera Oriental, 16 mi. N of Ocaña; alt. 3,465 ft. Coffeegrowing center; cacao, corn, rubber; vegetable-oil pressing.

Convención, La, province, Peru: see QUILLABAMBA.

Convent, village (pop. c.900), ⊙ St. James parish, SE central La., on E bank (levee) of the Mississippi and 45 mi. W of New Orleans, in area growing perique tobacco. Oil, gas fields near by.

Convento or **El Convento** (ĕl kōmvĕn'tō), village (pop. 679), Santiago prov., central Chile, near the Pacific, 60 mi. WSW of Santiago, in agr. area (alfalfa, wheat, barley, fruit, livestock).

Convent Station, village, Morris co., N N.J., 2 mi. SE of Morristown. Col. of St. Elizabeth (Catholic, for women; 1899) here.

Conversano (kônvĕrsä'nô), town (pop. 13,234), Bari prov., Apulia, S Italy, 10 mi. W of Monopoli; agr. center (wine, olive oil, fruit, cereals); extensive trade in cherries. Bishopric. Has old cathedral, convent, medieval castle.

Converse (kŏn'vûrs), county (□ 4,167; pop. 5,933), E Wyo.; ⊙ Douglas. Grain, sugar-beet, livestock area, drained by N.Platte R. Coal, oil. Part of Laramie Mts. in S. Formed 1888.

Converse. 1 Town (pop. 979), Miami co., N central Ind., 10 mi. W of Marion, in livestock and grain area; canned goods, mops, milk-bottle caps. **2** Village (pop. 311), Sabine parish, W La., 50 mi. S of Shreveport; agr.; oil wells. **3** Textile-mill village (pop. 1,200), Spartanburg co., NW S.C., on Pacolet R. and 5 mi. ENE of Spartanburg. **4** Village (pop. c.200), Bexar co., S central Texas, 12 mi. NE of San Antonio; shipping point in agr. area. U.S. Randolph Field, one of world's largest military air fields, is just NE.

Convoy, Gaelic *Conmhagh,* town (pop. 508), E Co. Donegal, Ireland, 7 mi. WNW of Lifford; woolen milling; flax market.

Convoy, village (pop. 910), Van Wert co., W Ohio, 7 mi. WNW of Van Wert, near Ind. line; brick, tile, furniture.

Conway, county (□ 560; pop. 18,137), central Ark.; ⊙ Morrilton. Bounded S by Arkansas R.; drained by small Cadron Creek. Agr. (cotton, corn, hay, livestock); timber. Some mfg. at Morrilton. Part of Ozark Natl. Forest in NW. Formed 1825.

Conway. 1 City (pop. 8,610), ⊙ Faulkner co., central Ark., 27 mi. NNW of Little Rock; trade center for agr. area (cotton, livestock, poultry; dairy products); mfg. of shoes, bus bodies, lumber; cotton processing. Seat of Hendrix Col., Ark. State Teachers Col. Settled 1871, inc. 1875. **2** Town (pop. 168), Taylor co., SW Iowa, 7 mi. NE of Bedford, in agr. region. **3** Agr. town (pop. 873), Franklin co., W Mass., 14 mi. NNW of Northampton. **4** Resort village, Emmet co., NW Mich., on Crooked L. and 6 mi. NE of Petoskey. **5** Town (pop. 514), Laclede co., S central Mo., in the Ozarks, 15 mi. SW of Lebanon; wheat, corn, hay. **6** Town (pop. 4,109), including Conway village (pop. 1,238), Carroll co., E N.H., at confluence of Swift and Saco rivers, 19 mi. N of Ossipee, near Maine line in resort area; winter sports. Has summer theater. Includes villages of Redstone (granite quarries), Intervale, NORTH CONWAY, Center Conway, and KEARSARGE. Conway L., 4 mi. long, is SE. Settled 1764, inc. 1765. **7** Town (pop. 618), Northampton co., NE N.C., 25 mi. E of Roanoke Rapids. **8** Village (pop. 107), Walsh co., NE N.Dak., 37 mi. NW of Grand Forks. **9** Borough (pop. 1,570), Beaver co., W Pa., 20 mi. NW of Pittsburgh and on Ohio R.; railroad shops. **10** Town (pop. 6,073), ⊙ Horry co., E S.C., on Waccamaw R. (head of navigation) and 38 mi. NNE of Georgetown, in agr. area (tobacco, melons, truck); tourist center (hunting, fishing); lumber mills, woodworking plants, brickworks.

Conway or **Aberconway** (ă″bûrkŏn′wā), municipal borough (1931 pop. 8,772; 1951 census 10,237), NE Caernarvon, Wales, on Conway R. estuary (bridged), near Conway Bay of Irish Sea, 3 mi. S of Llandudno; agr. market and seaside resort, with granite quarrying. Has remains of 13th-cent. castle, 13th-cent. town walls, and 12th-cent. Cistercian abbey. Church dates from 13th cent. One of bridges was built by Telford, other by Stephenson. In Elizabethan manor of Plas Mawr is Royal Cambrian Academy of Art.

Conway, Cape, E Queensland, Australia, in Coral Sea; forms NE side of entrance to Repulse Bay; 20°32′S 148°57′E.

Conway River, Wales, rises 5 mi. E of Blaenau-Ffestiniog, flows 30 mi. N, past Llanwrst, to Irish Sea at Conway. Forms border bet. Denbigh and Caernarvon.

Conway Springs, city (pop. 816), Sumner co., S Kansas, 25 mi. SW of Wichita, in wheat region; dairying.

Conwil Caio (kŏn′wĭl kī′ō) or **Caio,** agr. village and parish (pop. 1,209), N Carmarthen, Wales, 7 mi. NW of Llandovery. Has mineral springs.

Conwil Elvet (ĕl′vĭt), town and parish (pop. 1,099), W central Carmarthen, Wales, 5 mi. NNW of Carmarthen; woolen milling. Woolen-milling village of Cwmduad (ko͝omdē′äd) is 3 mi. N.

Conyers (kŏn′yûrz), city (pop. 2003), ⊙ Rockdale co., N central Ga., 22 mi. ESE of Atlanta; textile and lumber milling. Inc. 1854.

Conyngham (kŏ′nĭng-hăm″), borough (pop. 935), Luzerne co., E central Pa., 4 mi. NW of Hazleton; agr.

Conz, Germany: see KONZ.

Coo, Greece: see KOS.

Coober Pedy, village (pop. 107), central South Australia, 335 mi. NW of Port Pirie, in Stuarts Range; opal mines.

Cooch Behar (ko͞och bĭhär′), district (□ 1,318; pop. 640,842), NE West Bengal, India; ⊙ Cooch Behar. Bounded E by Assam, S by East Bengal (E Pakistan); drained by Tista, Jaldhaka, and Torsa rivers. Alluvial plain; rice, jute, tobacco, oilseeds, sugar cane, pulse, corn. Sissoo, bamboo, areca palm, hidjal bark (*Barringtonia acutangula*) in dispersed forest area. Silk-cloth mfg. Main towns: Cooch Behar, Dinhata, Matabhanga. Early 15th-cent. fort and palace ruins at ruined city of Kamatapur. In 15th cent. under Afghans; in 16th cent. became Koch kingdom. English commissioner established 1788. Formerly a princely state in Bengal States of Eastern States agency; inc. 1949 into India as a chief commissioner's prov. and (Jan., 1950) as a dist. of West Bengal. Formerly spelled Kuch Bihar or Koch Bihar.

Cooch Behar, town (pop. 16,000), ⊙ Cooch Behar dist., NE West Bengal, India, on central plain, on Torsa R. and 88 mi. SE of Darjeeling; trade center (rice, jute, tobacco, oilseeds, sugar cane); mfg. of leather goods. Has col.

Cooch's Bridge, Del.: see NEWARK.

Coogee (ko͝o′jē), village, E New South Wales, Australia, on Coogee Bay, 5 mi. SSE of Sydney, in metropolitan area; summer resort; bathing beach.

Cook, county, New Zealand: see GISBORNE, borough.

Cook. 1 County (□ 226; pop. 12,201), S Ga.; ⊙ Adel. Drained by Little and Withlacoochee rivers. Coastal plain; agr. (tobacco, watermelons, truck, cotton, corn, peanuts, fruit), cattle, hogs, poultry; mfg. at Adel; sawmilling. Pine timber. Formed 1918. **2** County (□ 954; pop. 4,508,792), NE Ill.; ⊙ CHICAGO, 2d-largest city of U.S. and center of vast metropolitan area extending far beyond co. boundaries. Bounded E by L. Michigan and Ind. line; traversed by Chicago and Des Plaines rivers and other links in Illinois Waterway system. Industries of Chicago and suburbs earn county 1st rank among mfg. counties of U.S.; it also contains many residential communities, recreational areas, and truck-farming and dairying dists. Formed 1831. **3** County (□ 1,403; pop. 2,900), extreme NE Minn.; ⊙ Grand Marais. Agr. and resort area bounded S by L. Superior and on N by chain of lakes along Ont. line; watered by many lakes, including Brule and Saganaga. Forestry, fisheries; dairy products, poultry, potatoes. Lies largely within Superior Natl. Forest and is part of famous recreational area known as "Arrowhead Country." Grand Portage Indian Reservation is in E. Co. formed 1874.

Cook. 1 Village (pop. 482), Saint Louis co., NE Minn., on branch of Little Fork R. and 25 mi. NNW of Virginia, in grain and poultry area; dairy and wood products. Granite quarries near by. Superior Natl. Forest is S. **2** Village (pop. 332), Johnson co., SE Nebr., 35 mi. SE of Lincoln and on branch of Little Nemaha R.; livestock, grain, fruit, poultry products.

Cook, Cape, SW B.C., NW Vancouver Isl., at W extremity of Brooks Peninsula, 55 mi. SW of Alert Bay; 50°7′N 127°55′W.

Cook, Mount, highest peak (12,349 ft.) of New Zealand, in Southern Alps in Tasman Natl. Park, W central S.Isl. Sometimes called Aorangi.

Cook, Mount (13,760 ft.), on Yukon-Alaska border, in St. Elias Mts., 170 mi. WSW of Whitehorse, on SE edge of Seward Glacier; 60°11′N 139°58′W.

Cook Bay, Tierra del Fuego, Chile, inlet of the Pacific at W end of Beagle Channel, bet. Hoste Isl. and Londonderry Isl.

Cooke, county (□ 909; pop. 22,146), N Texas; ⊙ Gainesville. Bounded N by Red R. (here the Okla. line) and L. Texoma (recreation). Drained by Elm Fork of Trinity R. Agr. (especially small grains; also cotton, corn, peanuts, fruit, truck); dairying, livestock (cattle, hogs, poultry, sheep); oil, natural-gas wells; asphalt, clay, sand deposits; timber. Mfg., processing at Gainesville. Formed 1848.

Cooke, village (pop. c.100), Park co., S Mont., near Wyo. line and Yellowstone Natl. Park, in Absaroka Range, 55 mi. SE of Livingston; alt. 7,648 ft.

Cooke, Camp, Calif: see LOMPOC.

Cooke, Mount, Australia: see DARLING RANGE.

Cookeville, town (pop. 6,924), ⊙ Putnam co., central Tenn., 70 mi. E of Nashville; trade and industrial center in hilly farm, timber, coal, and granite region; mfg. of shirts, shoes, prefabricated houses, wood products, sporting goods, cheese, pottery; a poultry-shipping center. Seat of Tenn. Polytechnic Inst. Dale Hollow and Center Hill dams near by. Founded 1854.

Cookham, residential and resort town and parish (pop. 6,741), E Berkshire, England, on the Thames and 3 mi. N of Maidenhead. Church is Norman to 15th cent. A Saxon witenagemot met here.

Cookhouse, town (pop. 2,069), SE Cape Prov., U. of So. Afr., on Great Fish R. and 85 mi. N of Port Elizabeth; rail junction; stock raising, dairying; wool, fruit.

Cook Inlet (150 mi. long, 9–80 mi. wide), S Alaska, inlet of Gulf of Alaska, on W side of Kenai Peninsula; 59°10′–61°10′N 150°–154°W. From head at Anchorage, Turnagain Arm extends ESE, Knik Arm extends NE. Receives Susitna R. Sea lane to W Kenai Peninsula and Anchorage; salmon, herring fisheries. Explored (1778) by Capt. James Cook.

Cook Islands, group (□ 84; pop. 11,949; pop. with Manihiki group 14,088), S Pacific; 22°–19°S 157°–160°W. Composed of 2 volcanic isls., RAROTONGA and MANGAIA, and 6 coral isls., AITUTAKI, MANUAE, TAKUTEA, MITIARO, ATIU, and MAUKE. Some of isls. were discovered 1773 by Capt. Cook, others 1823 by John Williams, English missionary. Group was annexed 1901 to New Zealand. Rarotonga is seat of Cook Isls. administration, which also governs 7 isls. N of main group (see MANIHIKI). Polynesian inhabitants. Exports copra, fruits. Cook called group Hervey, a name now used as alternate for Manuae.

Cooksburg, village, Forest co., W central Pa., on Clarion R. and 14 mi. NNW of Brookville, at entrance to Cook Forest State Park; hq. for recreational area.

Cooks Falls, village (pop. c.200), Delaware co., S N.Y., in the Catskills, on Beaver Kill and c.50 mi. ESE of Binghamton; dyes, wood alcohol, charcoal, lime.

Cookshire, town (pop. 877), ⊙ Compton co., S Que., on Eaton R., a tributary of St. Francis R., and 14 mi. E of Sherbrooke; metalworking, lumbering. Agr. region (dairying; cattle, pigs).

Cooks Range, SW N.Mex., S extension of Mimbres Mts. Highest at Cooks Peak (8,400 ft.), 17 mi. N of Deming. Lead and zinc mined.

Cookstown, village (pop. estimate 600), S Ont., 15 mi. S of Barrie; dairying, mixed farming.

Cookstown, urban district (1937 pop. 3,369; 1951 census 4,221), NE Co. Tyrone, Northern Ireland, on Ballinderry R. and 10 mi. N of Dungannon; linen milling, hosiery mfg. Town was founded 1609. Near by is great rath of TULLAGHOGE.

Cook Strait, New Zealand, bet. N.Isl. and S.Isl.; 16 mi. wide at narrowest point.

Cooksville, village (pop. estimate 1,800), S Ont., 12 mi. WSW of Toronto; fruitgrowing, truck.

Cooksville, village (pop. 256), McLean co., central Ill., 14 mi. ENE of Bloomington, in rich agr. area.

Cooktown, village and port (pop. 397), NE Queensland, Australia, 105 mi. N of Cairns, on Coral Sea; rail terminus; exports tin, meat. Founded 1873 with discovery of gold near by.

Coolah (ko͞o′lů), village (pop. 851), E central New South Wales, Australia, 170 mi. NW of Sydney; rail terminus; dairying center. Zinc mines near by.

Coolamon (ko͞o′lůmŏn), town (pop. 1,064), S New South Wales, Australia, 125 mi. WNW of Canberra; sheep and agr. center.

Coolangatta (ko͞o″lŭn-gă′tů), town (pop. 4,053), SE Queensland, Australia, 60 mi. SSE of Brisbane, on coast, near Point Danger on New South Wales border, adjacent to Tweed Heads; rail terminus; seaside resort.

Cooleemee (ko͞o′lēmē″), village (pop. 1,925), Davie co., W central N.C., 12 mi. NNW of Salisbury, in agr. area; cotton textiles.

Cooley, village (pop. 113), Itasca co., N Minn., in Mesabi iron range, near Swan L., and 19 mi. ENE of Grand Rapids; iron-ore refining. Mines near by.

Cooley Point, cape on Irish Sea, at N end of Dundalk Bay, NE Co. Louth, Ireland, 11 mi. E of Dundalk; 53°58′N 6°8′W.

Coolgardie (ko͞olgär′dē), town (pop. 963), S central Western Australia, 22 mi. SW of Kalgoorlie; mining center in East Coolgardie Goldfield. Gold discovered here 1892.

Coolidge. 1 Town (pop. 4,306), Pinal co., S central Ariz., near Gila R., 9 mi. SW of Florence, in irrigated cotton and alfalfa area served by COOLIDGE DAM; cotton ginning. Casa Grande Natl. Monument and Casa Grande Farms (U.S. resettlement project) near by. Inc. since 1940. **2** Town (pop. 764), Thomas co., S Ga., 14 mi. NE of Thomasville. **3** City (pop. 168), Hamilton co., SW Kansas, R. and 15 mi. WNW of Syracuse, near Colo. line. **4** Town (pop. 1,062), Limestone co., E central Texas, 32 mi. NE of Waco; trade point in farm area (cotton, cattle, corn). Settled 1903, inc. 1905.

Coolidge Dam, E Ariz., on Gila R. and c.20 mi. SE of Globe; 1st multiple-dome-type dam, built (1928) as irrigation and power project; c.250 ft. high, c.900 ft. long; forms San Carlos Reservoir, used to irrigate 100,000 acres around towns of Coolidge, Casa Grande, and Florence and in San Carlos Indian Reservation.

Coolin Hills, Scotland: see CUILLIN HILLS.

Cool Ridge Heights, village (pop. 2,722, with adjacent Lincoln), Richland co., N central Ohio.

Coolscamp, Belgium: see KOOLSKAMP.

Coolville, village (pop. 469), Athens co., SE Ohio, on Hocking R. and 17 mi. ESE of Athens.

Cooma (ko͞o′mä, –mů), municipality (pop. 2,249), SE New South Wales, Australia, 65 mi. S of Canberra; livestock center. Gold mine near by.

Coomassie, Gold Coast: see KUMASI.

Coombe, England: see THE MALDENS AND COOMBE.

Coombe Hill (ko͞om) (852 ft.), central Buckingham, England, 5 mi. SE of Aylesbury; highest point of Chiltern Hills.

Coonabarabran (ko͞onůbă′růbrăn′), town (pop. 2,240), E central New South Wales, Australia, on Castlereagh R. and 210 mi. NW of Sydney; sheep-raising, agr. center. Sometimes spelled Coonabarrabran.

Coonamble (ko͞onăm′bůl), municipality (pop. 2,567), N central New South Wales, Australia, on Castlereagh R. and 260 mi. NW of Sydney; rail terminus; sheep-raising, agr. center.

Coondapoor (ko͞on′dŭpo͞or), town (pop. 9,537), South Kanara dist., W Madras, India, on Malabar Coast of Arabian Sea, 55 mi. NNW of Mangalore, at estuary mouth; fish curing (sardines, mackerel); coconuts, mangoes. Site of 17th- and 18th-cent. Port. and Du. trading posts. Commercial suburb of Gangoli (or Ganguli) is just N, across estuary. Clay pits (kaolin) near by. Also spelled Kundapur.

Coonoor (ko͞o′no͞or), city (pop 18,783), Nilgiri dist., SW Madras, India, 8 mi. SE of Ootacamund; hill resort (sanatorium) on scenic plateau (Nilgiri Hills); alt. c.6,000 ft. Tea and coffee plantations on slopes; eucalyptus-oil distilling. Has Pasteur Inst. (medical research center), Sims Park (noted botanical gardens; fruit research). Experimental farm (medicinal and rubber plants) is 4 mi. ESE, at suburb of Barliyar. Sericulture station and tea factory on Tiger Hill (or Hulikal Drug), 4 mi. SE.

Coon Rapids, town (pop. 1,676), Carroll co., W central Iowa, on Middle Raccoon R. and 17 mi. SSE of Carroll; hybrid seed corn, feed, concrete products. Inc. 1882.

Coon Valley, village (pop. 466), Vernon co., SW Wis., on small Coon Creek (tributary of the Mississippi) and 14 mi. SE of La Crosse, in tobacco-growing and dairying area; ships butter. Hq. of Coon Creek soil conservation project.

Cooper, county (□ 563; pop. 16,608), central Mo.; ⊙ Boonville. Bounded N by Missouri R.; drained by Lamine and Blackwater rivers. Agr. (wheat, corn, oats), cattle, poultry; barite; mfg. at Boonville. Formed 1818.

Cooper. 1 Town (pop. 128), Washington co., E Maine, 21 mi. N of Machias; molybdenum found here. **2** City (pop. 2,350), ⊙ Delta co., NE Texas, 21 mi. SSW of Paris; trade center for cotton area; cotton processing; cannery. Settled in 1870s.

Cooper, Lake, Ill. and Iowa: see Keokuk, city.

Cooper Creek, Camden co., SW N.J., rises near Lindenwold, flows c.20 mi. generally NW, through Camden, to Delaware R. Navigable 8 mi. above mouth.

Cooper Island, New Zealand: see Dusky Sound.

Cooper Island, islet, Br. Virgin Isls., 4 mi. SE of Tortola isl., bet. Salt Isl. (W) and Ginger Isl. (E); 18°23'N 64°30'W.

Cooper Landing, village (pop. 54), S Alaska, 30 mi. NNW of Seward, on Kenai Peninsula.

Cooper Mountain (10,100 ft.), SE B.C., in Selkirk Mts., 50 mi. N of Nelson; 50°11'N 117°11'W.

Cooper River, S.C.: see Santee River.

Coopersburg, borough (pop. 1,462), Lehigh co., E Pa., 8 mi. SE of Allentown; zinc, textiles. Settled 1780 as Fryburg, renamed 1832, inc. 1879.

Cooper's Creek, Australia: see Barcoo River.

Cooper's Hill, sand ridge (142 ft.), NW Surrey, England, on Berkshire border, near the Thames, just NW of Egham. Bldg. of former Royal Indian Engineering Col. is now residence. Celebrated in Sir John Denham's poem.

Cooperstown. 1 Village (pop. 2,727), ⊙ Otsego co., central N.Y., on the Susquehanna at its outlet from Otsego L., and c.60 mi. W of Albany; summer resort; lumber, gloves, food products. Seat of Knox School for girls. Natl. baseball mus. commemorates tradition that game was organized here. Here also are Farmers' Mus. and the quarters of the N.Y. State Historical Association. James Fenimore Cooper lived here and described the region in *Leatherstocking Tales.* Founded c.1790 by William Cooper; inc. 1807. **2** City (pop. 1,189), ⊙ Griggs co., E central N.Dak., 75 mi. NW of Fargo, near Sheyenne R. Machinery, livestock, dairy products, wheat, flax, barley. Settled 1882, inc. 1907. **3** Borough (pop. 271), Venango co., NW Pa., 10 mi. NW of Oil City.

Coopersville, village (pop. 1,371), Ottawa co., SW Mich., 15 mi. NW of Grand Rapids, in orchard and farm area (apples, peaches, grain, poultry; dairy products); cannery, flour mill, creamery. Settled 1845; inc. 1871.

Cooperton, town (pop. 129), Kiowa co., SW Okla., 16 mi. SE of Hobart, near the Wichita Mts., in agr. area; cotton ginning.

Coorg (kŏŏrg), Kanarese *Kodagu* (kō'dŭgōō), chief commissioner's state (□ 1,593; 1951 pop. 229,255), SW India; ⊙ Mercara. In Western Ghats; Mysore is on E, Madras (Malabar and South Kanara dists.) on W. Central plateau rises to 3,800 ft.; Tadiamol peak (5,724 ft.) in SW; drained by upper Cauvery R. and its tributaries, including Lakshmantirtha R.; average annual rainfall, c.120 in. Mainly agr.: rice (terrace farming), coffee, tea, cardamom, rubber, pepper; noted orange groves (mostly S); millet, tamarind along rivers. Deciduous forests (N, E; sandalwood and teak tracts); evergreen timber forests mainly W. Roads via Mercara and Virajpet lead to ports of Malabar Coast (W) and via Fraserpet (limestone quarries) to timber depot of Hunsur (in Mysore). Has numerous prehistoric cairns and inscriptions. From late-16th cent., except for brief 18th-cent. periods of occupation by Mysore sultans, the indigenous pop. (Coorgs or Kodagas) were ruled by independent Hindu dynasty, which the British overthrew in 1834, establishing area as a chief commissioner's prov. In 1950, constituted a chief commissioner's state. Pop. 90% Hindu (including Coorgs), 8% Moslem, 2% Christian. Sometimes spelled Kurg.

Coorong, the (kōō'rŏng), long, narrow lagoon (□ 80), SE South Australia, separated from Indian Ocean by sandspit; extends 80 mi. NW from N end of Lacepede Bay to L. Alexandrina, which it joins; 2.5 mi. wide, 3–10 ft. deep; outlet at Murray R. mouth.

Coos. 1 or **Coös** (kō'ŏs, kōōs') County (□ 1,825; pop. 35,932), N N.H., bordering on Vt., Que., and Maine; ⊙ Lancaster. Recreational region, including Presidential Range and part of White Mtn. Natl. Forest, with many resorts; hunting, fishing in Connecticut Lakes region in N. Mfg. (pulp and paper, wood products) mainly in Berlin, lumbering, agr. (dairy products, poultry, potatoes). Drained by Androscoggin (water power), Connecticut, and Upper Ammonoosuc rivers. Formed 1803. **2** (kōōs) County (□ 1,611; pop. 42,265), SW Oregon; ⊙ Coquille. Bounded W by the Pacific and E by Coast Range. Lumber, dairy, livestock. Formed 1853.

Coosa (kōō'sŭ), county (□ 648; pop. 11,766), E central Ala.; ⊙ Rockford. Bounded W by Coosa R. Cotton, corn, livestock; marble, granite. Tin mine (opened 1951) exploits cassiterite deposit. Formed 1832.

Coosa Pines, Ala.: see Childersburg.

Coosa River, meandering stream in NW Ga. and E Ala.; formed by confluence of Etowah and Oostanaula rivers at Rome, flows W into Cherokee co., Ala., then SW, past Gadsden, Childersburg, and Talladega Springs, turning SSE below Lay Dam and joining Tallapoosa R. 4 mi. SW of Wetumpka and 10 mi. N of Mountgomery to form Alabama R.; 286 mi. long. Drains fertile plateau area of Ala. and enters coastal plain at Wetumpka; receives Chattooga R. in Cherokee co. Its valley is southernmost portion of Great Appalachian Valley. System of locks and dams makes possible navigation for barges to Rome. Lay Dam, Mitchell Dam, and Jordan Dam are power dams in lower course, bet. Wetumpka and Talladega Springs. Allatoona Dam, in Etowah R., is initial unit in plan for development of Alabama-Coosa river system.

Coosawattee River (kōōsŭwä'tē), N Ga., formed at Ellijay by union of small Ellijay and Cartecay rivers, flows c.50 mi. WSW to confluence with Conasauga R. 3 mi. NE of Calhoun, forming Oostanaula R.

Coosawhatchie River (kōō"sŭhă'chē), S S.C., rises near Allendale, flows c.50 mi. SE to Broad R., tidal channel N of Port Royal Sound.

Coosaw River (kōō'sô"), S S.C., tidal channel bet. head of Broad R. channel (W) and St. Helena Sound (E), N of Port Royal Isl.; partly followed by Intracoastal Waterway.

Coos Bay (kōōs), city (pop. 6,223), Coos co., SW Oregon, on Coos Bay, near Pacific Ocean, c.75 mi. SW of Eugene; port of entry and trade center; lumber milling, salmon fisheries; wood novelties, cheese. Ships lumber, fish, fertilizer. Coal mining in vicinity. Siuslaw Natl. Forest is near by. Founded as Marshfield 1854, inc. 1874, renamed Coos Bay 1944. City of North Bend just N.

Coos Bay, SW Oregon, an indentation in Pacific coast; 13 mi. long, c.1 mi. wide. **Coos River** rises in Coast Range, flows 60 mi. W, entering the bay opposite Coos Bay city. North Bend and Coos Bay are trade and shipping points. Coal mining in vicinity.

Cootamundra (kōō"tŭmŭn'drŭ), municipality (pop. 5,250), SE New South Wales, Australia, 75 mi. NW of Canberra; rail center; sheep, agr.; dairy plant.

Cootehill, Gaelic *Muinchille,* urban district (pop. 1,565), NE Co. Cavan, Ireland, near Annalee R., 11 mi. NE of Cavan; agr. (cattle, pigs; potatoes); furniture mfg.

Cooter (kōō'tŭr), town (pop. 490), Pemiscot co., extreme SE Mo., near Mississippi R., 13 mi. SW of Caruthersville.

Coot-tha, Mount (kōō'thŭ) (740 ft.), SE Queensland, Australia, just SW of Brisbane. Zoo containing native fauna is near by.

Cooum River (kōō'ŭm) or **Kuvam River** (kōō'vŭm), E Madras, India, rises 10 mi. WNW of Conjeeveram, flows c.60 mi. generally E, through Chingleput dist. and center of Madras city, to Bay of Bengal just S of Fort St. George. Sometimes called Madras or Triplicane.

Cop, Ukrainian SSR: see Chop.

Copacabana (kōpŭkŭbă'nŭ, Sp. kōpäkäbä'nä), town (pop. c.14,320), La Paz dept., W Bolivia, port on L. Titicaca, on Copacabana Peninsula and 65 mi. WNW of La Paz; tourist resort; customs station near Peru border. Site of sanctuary of Virgen de la Candelaria (place of pilgrimage). Coal deposits near by.

Copacabana, town (pop. 1,763), Antioquia dept., NW central Colombia, in Cordillera Central, on railroad, on Porce R. and 8 mi. NNE of Medellín; alt. 4,770 ft. Agr. region (sugar cane, corn, coffee, beans, yucca, potatoes); dairying.

Copacabana Beach, Brazil: see Rio de Janeiro, city.

Copacabana Peninsula, on Bolivia-Peru border, extends E from 1.5-mi. neck at Yunguyo (Peru) into Bolivian part of L. Titicaca; separates lakes Chucuito and Uinamarca; 10 mi. long, 25 mi. wide. Copacabana is on W shore.

Copahué (kōpäwā'), village (pop. estimate 200), W Neuquén natl. territory, Argentina, near Copahué Pass (Chile border), at NE foot of Copahué Volcano, 55 mi. SW of Chos Malal; health resort with hot sulphur springs.

Copahué Pass (6,500–7,000 ft.), in the Andes, on Argentina-Chile border, at NE foot of **Copahué Volcano** (c.9,800 ft.); 37°49'S 71°7'W.

Copainalá (kōpĭnälä'), city (pop. 1,932), Chiapas, S Mexico, in Chiapas Valley, 23 mi. NNW of Tuxtla; corn, sugar cane, tobacco, fruit, livestock.

Copais, Lake (kōpā'ĭs), Gr. *Kopais* (kôpäēs'), drained lake of Boeotia, Greece, E of Levadia. Shallow in winter and nearly dry in summer, the lake was fed mainly by Boeotian Cephisus R. Anc. drainage works, generally ascribed to the Minyan pop. of Orchomenus, were destroyed by Thebes. The swampy lake was finally drained in 1830s. The area now produces cotton, vegetables, tobacco, and wheat.

Copake (kō'păk), village (1940 pop. 557), Columbia co., SE N.Y., 15 mi. SE of Hudson, in resort area. Copake Falls village (resort) is just NE. Taconic State Park is 1 mi. E. Copake L. (c.1½ mi. long) is c.2 mi. NW.

Copala (kōpä'lä), town (pop. 1,830), Guerrero, SW Mexico, in Pacific lowland, 55 mi. E of Acapulco; sugar cane, cotton, coffee, fruit, livestock.

Copalillo (kōpälē'yō), town (pop. 1,961), Guerrero, SW Mexico, on affluent of Mezcala R. (Río de las Balsas system), 40 mi. NE of Chilpancingo; cereals, sugar cane, fruit, forest products (vanilla, resins).

Copalnic-Manastur (kōpäl'nĕk-mŭnŭshtōōr'), Rum. *Copalnic-Mănăştur,* Hung. *Kápolnokmonostor* (kä'pôlnôkmônôstôr), village (pop. 1,141), Baia-Mare prov., NW Rumania, 43 mi. SE of Satu-Mare. In Hungary, 1940–45.

Copán (kōpän'), department (□ 1,430; 1950 pop. 105,468), W Honduras, on Guatemala border; ⊙ Santa Rosa. Largely mountainous; includes sierras del Gallinero (S) and del Espíritu Santo (N); drained by upper Chamelecón (N) and Jicatuyo (S) rivers. Chief tobacco region in Honduras; coffee, sugar cane, rice, cacao, fruit, grain; livestock raising. Cigar mfg. is main industry, coffee and rice processing at Corquín; antimony mine, limestone and gypsum quarries. Main centers: Santa Rosa, Corquín, Dulce Nombre, Trinidad. Includes ruins of Mayan city of Copán. Formed 1869.

Copán, city (pop. 1,045), Copán dept., W Honduras, near Guatemala border, on Copán R. (right tributary of the Chiquimula) and 22 mi. WNW of Santa Rosa, in tobacco area; tourist center. Has mus. of antiquities, airfield. Near by are noted ruins of Mayan city of Copán, including numerous sculptured steles, stone calendar, and Hieroglyphic Stairway, restored (1930s) by Carnegie Institution.

Copan (kō'păn"), town (pop. 459), Washington co., NE Okla., 10 mi. N of Bartlesville, in farm area.

Copanatoyac (kōpänätoiäk'), town (pop. 1,053), Guerrero, SW Mexico, in Sierra Madre del Sur, 38 mi. SE of Chilapa; cereals, fruit, livestock.

Copano Bay, Texas: see Aransas Bay.

Copco No. 1 Dam, Calif.: see Klamath River.

Cope, town (pop. 209), Orangeburg co., S central S.C., 11 mi. SW of Orangeburg.

Copé, El, Panama: see El Copé.

Copeland, city (pop. 242), Gray co., SW Kansas, 34 mi. SW of Dodge City, in grain area.

Copeland Islands, small group of islets in the Irish Sea at SE entrance to Belfast Lough, Co. Down, Northern Ireland. Largest is Great Copeland, 1 mi. long, just N of Donaghadee.

Copeland Park, suburb (pop. 7,115) of Newport News, Elizabeth City co., SE Va.

Copemish (kō'pŭmĭsh, kōp'mĭsh), village (pop. 255), Manistee co., NW Mich., on small Bear Creek and 26 mi. NE of Manistee, in agr. area.

Copenhagen (kō'pŭnhā"gŭn), Dan. *København,* formerly *Kjøbenhavn* (kûbŭnhoun'), amt (□ 482; 1950 pop. 509,764; pop. including Copenhagen city 1,275,344), NE Zealand, Denmark; includes Amager and Saltholm isls. Divided into Frederiksberg commune and dists. of Copenhagen and Roskilde. In, but independent of the amt, is its ⊙, Copenhagen, capital of Denmark. Roskilde is another important city. Fure L. is largest lake. Fertile flatlands in center; grain and dairy farming.

Copenhagen, Dan. *København,* formerly *Kjøbenhavn* [merchants' haven], largest city (pop. 765,580; with metropolitan area, 1,166,204) and ⊙ Denmark, in, but independent of, Copenhagen amt, on E Zealand and on N Amager isls., on the Oresund WNW of Malmo, Sweden; 55°41'N 12°35'E. Naval port; commercial, industrial, and communications center, with shipyards, iron foundries, machine shops, and mfg. (porcelain and pottery, chocolate, candy, paper, dairy and agr. products, chemicals, textiles, tobacco products, furniture, pianos, clocks, watches); auto assembly. First mentioned 1043 under name of *Hafnia,* Latinized from *Havn.* First fortifications built 1167 by Bishop Absalon; city chartered 1254 by Roskilde bishops; became ⊙ Denmark in 1443. From 13th to 16th cent. withstood numerous attacks by Hanseatic League; suffered from religious wars in 16th cent. Withstood Swedish siege 1658–59; Treaty of Copenhagen signed 1660. In 1700 attacked by joint English, Dutch, and Swedish fleet. Suffered severe fires in 1728 and 1795. Bombarded in 1801 by Br. fleet under Parker and Nelson in the battle of Copenhagen; bombarded again by Br. fleet in 1807. Older part of city radiates from a central square, Kongens Nytorv, touched by 12 streets and Nyhavn, an arm of the harbor. Near the square is 17th-cent. Charlottenborg Palace; now houses Art Acad. and royal theater. Bredegade (Broad Street), with a number of foreign legations, radiates NE from square to 17th-cent. citadel; midway is domed Marble Church (Dan. *Frederikskirke*), begun 1749, finished 1894. Near by is Palace of Amalienborg, the present royal residence. NW from Kongens Nytorv the Gotherspade leads to 17th-cent. Du. Renaissance Rosenborg palace, surrounded by Rosenborg Park and Botanical Gardens; Polytechnic Inst. and Communal Hosp. are near by. SW from Rosenborg, winding streets lead past

Trinity Church, with its famous 117-ft.-high Round Tower, to Copenhagen Univ. (founded 1479) and cathedral on 12th-cent. site (cathedral was almost completely rebuilt after 1807 bombardment). Further SW is Danish Renaissance Town Hall, built 1894–1903. On the harbor is Slottsholm (Castle Isl.), on which is Christiansborg Palace, originally built 1733–45, restored several times, last in 1903. Near by are Royal Library, Thorvaldsen Mus., 17th-cent. Exchange. The new NW suburbs are separated from the old city by 3 oblong lakes: Sankt Jorgens L., Peblinge L., and Sortedams L. Frederiksberg, a separate commune (pop. 113,584), is most important suburb; site of 17th-cent. Frederiksborg Palace. On Amager isl. is Christianshavn, a modern quarter which contains the fort. Since the opening of the free port in 1894, Copenhagen has become one of the most important Baltic ports. Center of Scandinavian culture; besides its univ. and museums, it has many technical schools and learned societies. In the Second World War Copenhagen was occupied (1940–45) by the Germans; the shipyards were bombed by the Allies, but otherwise the city—one of the handsomest in Europe—remained undamaged.

Copenhagen, village (pop. 690), Lewis co., N central N.Y., 12 mi. ESE of Watertown, in dairying and timber area.

Cöpenick, Germany: see KÖPENICK.

Copertino (kôpĕrtē'nô), town (pop. 11,889), Lecce prov., Apulia, S Italy, 9 mi. SW of Lecce; agr. center (cotton, tobacco, wine, olive oil, cheese); cotton milling. Has 16th-cent. castle.

Copey (kōpā'), village (pop. 958), San José prov., S central Costa Rica, in Cordillera de Talamanca, near Inter-American Highway, in Copey Pass (alt. 5,900 ft.), 5 mi. E of Santa María; stock raising, lumbering.

Cophus, Afghanistan and Pakistan: see KABUL RIVER.

Copiague or **Copiague Station** (kō'pĕg, -pāg), village (1940 pop. 1,584), Suffolk co., SE N.Y., near S shore of W Long Isl., just NE of Amityville.

Copiah (kùpī'ù, kō-), county (□ 781; pop. 30,493), SW Miss.; ⊙ Hazlehurst. Bounded E by Pearl R.; also drained by Homochitto R. and Bayou Pierre. Agr. (cotton, truck, fruit), lumbering, cattle raising. Formed 1823.

Copiapó (kōpyäpō'), town (pop. 15,693), ⊙ Atacama prov. and Copiapó dept. (□ 13,449; pop. 28,657), N central Chile, on Copiapó R., on railroad and 425 mi. N of Santiago, at S edge of the Atacama Desert; 27°22'S 70°21'W; alt. 1,215 ft. Trading and mining center (copper, gold). Airport. Hydroelectric power plant. Agr. in irrigated valley: corn, alfalfa, subtropical fruit. Has arid but mild climate. Its port is Caldera. Founded 1540 by Pedro de Valdivia, Copiapó has been frequently damaged in earthquakes (1819, 1922, 1939). With the discovery (1832) of the Chañarcillo silver mines, the town prospered in 19th cent. but later lost some of its importance. Formerly called San Francisco de Selva or Selva.

Copiapó, Cerro, Chile: see AZUFRE, CERRO.

Copiapó River, Atacama prov., N Chile, rises in Andean hills, flows c.110 mi. W, past Copiapó, to the Pacific 18 mi. SSW of Caldera. Usually considered the S boundary of the Atacama Desert. Its waters are used for irrigation and mining works (copper, silver). In its valley alfalfa, corn, and subtropical fruit are grown. Marble deposits along its course.

Copinsay (kŏ'pĭnzā), island (pop. 25) of the Orkneys, Scotland, 2 mi. SE of Pomona isl.; 1 mi. long. Lighthouse (58°54'N 2°39'W).

Copiulemu (kōpyōōlā'mōō), village (1930 pop. 91), Concepción prov., S central Chile, 20 mi. ESE of Concepción; grain, livestock.

Coplay (kŏp'lē), borough (pop. 2,994), Lehigh co., E Pa., 6 mi. NNW of Allentown and on Lehigh R.; cement mfg.

Copleston (kŏ'pùlztùn), village, S Ont., 3 mi. NNW of Petrolia; oil production.

Copley, England: see HALIFAX.

Coplin, plantation (pop. 64), Franklin co., W central Maine, on branch of Carrabassett R., in hunting area.

Copo, Argentina: see MONTE QUEMADO.

Coporaque (kōpōrä'kä), town (pop. 419), Cuzco dept., S Peru, in Cordillera Occidental, 7 mi. W of Yauri, in potato-growing region; some mining (silver, copper, iron, coal); alt. 12,893 ft.

Coporito (kōpōrē'tō), village (pop. 724), Delta Amacuro territory, NE Venezuela, landing on Caño Mánamo arm of Orinoco R. delta and 13 mi. SSE of Tucupita, in agr. region (corn, sugar cane, fruit).

Copou (kōpō'), suburb (pop. 1,212) of Jassy, Jassy prov., NE Rumania, 2 mi. NW of city center; food processing (notably meat); textile mills.

Copparo (kôp-pä'rô), town (pop. 4,618), Ferrara prov., Emilia-Romagna, N central Italy, 11 mi. ENE of Ferrara; rail terminus; hemp products, flour, auto supplies, pharmaceuticals.

Coppename River (kôpùnä'mù), Du. Guiana, rises in 2 headstreams in Wilhelmina Mts. at about 3°45'N, flows c.250 mi. N, through tropical forest region, to the Atlantic just SW of Saramacca R. mouth at 5°50'N 56°W. Many rapids in upper course; lower course navigable c.60 mi. for small boats. Linked by natural waterway with Nickerie R.

Coppenbrügge (kô'pùnbrü"gù), village (pop. 2,477), in former Prussian prov. of Hanover, W Germany, after 1945 in Lower Saxony, 8 mi. E of Hameln; sawmilling. Sometimes spelled Koppenbrügge.

Copperas Cove (kŏ'pùrùs), town (pop. 1,052), Coryell co., central Texas, c.50 mi. SW of Waco, in agr. area (oats, corn, cotton). U.S. Camp Hood is just E.

Copper Center, village (pop. 102), S Alaska, on Copper R. at mouth of Klutina R., and 70 mi. NNE of Valdez, on Richardson Highway; trading and supply center for prospectors; fur farming. Settled 1896, it became important when copper was discovered (1898) in region.

Copper City, village (pop. 336), Houghton co., NW Upper Peninsula, Mich., 14 mi. NE of Houghton, on Keweenaw Peninsula.

Copper Cliff, town (pop. 3,732), SE central Ont., 4 mi. WSW of Sudbury; nickel mining and smelting. Copper refinery, one of largest in British Commonwealth.

Coppercrown Mountain (10,218 ft.), SE B.C., in Selkirk Mts., 70 mi. NE of Nelson; 50°18'N 116°22'W.

Copper Falls State Park (1,080 acres), Ashland co., N Wis., near Mellen, in wooded area. Central feature is spectacular Copper Falls (65 ft. high) on Bad R.

Copper Harbor, resort village, Keweenaw co., Upper Peninsula, Mich., on L. Superior and 19 mi. ENE of Eagle River; boat connections with Isle Royale Natl. Park. Old Fort Wilkins (1844–63) is near by, in a state park.

Copperhill, town (pop. 924), Polk co., SE Tenn., near Ga.-N.C.-Tenn. border, on Ocoee R. (here dammed) and 50 mi. E of Chattanooga, in copper-mining region.

Copper Island, Turkey: see HEYBELI ISLAND.

Copper Island, Russian SFSR: see MEDNY ISLAND.

Coppermine, village, N Mackenzie Dist., Northwest Territories, on Coronation Gulf of the Beaufort Sea, at mouth of Coppermine R.; 67°40'N 115°5'W; trading post; govt. radio and meteorological station, Royal Canadian Mounted Police post; site of Anglican and R.C. missions. Extensive copper deposits in region.

Coppermine River, N central Mackenzie Dist., Northwest Territories, rises N of Great Slave L., flows 525 mi. in a winding course generally NW to Coronation Gulf of the Beaufort Sea at Coppermine. Discovered 1771 by Samuel Hearne.

Copper Mountain, village (pop. estimate 200), S B.C., in Cascade Mts., on Similkameen R. and 45 mi. WSW of Penticton; copper mining.

Copper Range, in Wis. and Mich., trap-rock ridge traceable for c.300 mi. from Minn.-Wis. line NE of Minneapolis, across NW Wis. and NW Upper Peninsula of Mich. near its Superior shore, and along the backbone of Keweenaw Peninsula (where it is most prominent) to its tip. On Keweenaw Peninsula (where it is sometimes called Keweenaw Range or Trap Range), its alt. is generally c.1,300 ft.; rises to 1,532 ft. S of Eagle Harbor. Here range is heart of the Mich. "copper country," where huge quantities of copper, a large part of U.S. supply, were produced in late 19th and early 20th cent.; peak production was in 1916–17.

Copper River, S Alaska, rises on N slope of Mt. Sanford in Wrangell Mts. near 62°20'N 144°W, circles the mts. and flows S past Chistochina, Gakona, Gulkana, Copper Center, and Chitina, through Chugach Mts. to Gulf of Alaska 30 mi. E of Cordova; c.300 mi. long. Receives Chistochina, Gakona, Gulkana, and Chitina rivers. Important copper deposits near upper course, 1st worked by Indians, later attracted attention of Russians and then of Americans. Copper River and Northwestern RR (built 1908–11, abandoned 1938, when mines were worked out) from Kennicott to Cordova, follows part of river valley.

Copper River, village, W B.C., on Skeena R. and 5 mi. ENE of Terrace; gold and silver mining.

Coppet (kôpā'), village (pop. 494), Vaud canton, SW Switzerland, on L. Geneva, 5 mi. SSW of Nyon. Known for its château, once residence of Madame de Staël.

Coppock (kŏ'pùk), town (pop. 81), on Henry-Jefferson-Washington co. line, SE Iowa, on Skunk R. and 9 mi. S of Washington; limestone quarry.

Coppull (kŏ'pùl), parish (pop. 5,101), central Lancashire, England. Includes village of Springfield, 3 mi. SE of Chorley; cattle raising, dairying, agr. Just SE is coal-mining village of Coppull Moor.

Copsa-Mica (kôp'shä-mē'kù), Rum. *Copşa-Mică*, Hung. *Kiskapus* (kēsh'kä"pōōsh), village (pop. 1,201), Sibiu prov., central Rumania, 27 mi. WSW of Sighisoara; rail junction; methane production, mfg. of munitions, dyes, varnishes, carbon black.

Coptos (kŏp'tùs, -tōs) or **Coptus** (kŏp'tùs), anc. city of Upper Egypt, on site of present-day village of QIFT, on the Nile 13 mi. SSE of Qena. It was a flourishing commercial town in Hellenistic times, when it was the starting point of the great caravan route through the Arabian Desert to Berenice, seaport on the Red Sea.

Copulhue Pass (kōpōōl'wā) (7,000 ft.), in the Andes, on Argentina-Chile border, 65 mi. ESE of Los Angeles, Chile; 37°35'S 71°7'W.

Copythorne, town and parish (pop. 2,130), SW Hampshire, England, 8 mi. WNW of Southampton; agr. market, with asphalt works.

Coquet, Palestine: see BELVOIR.

Coquet Island (kō'kùt, kŏ'-), small islet in North Sea, just off coast of Northumberland, England, near mouth of Coquet R., 2 mi. E of Amble; site of lighthouse (55°20'N 1°33'W). There are ruins of anc. Benedictine monastery.

Coquet River, Northumberland, England, rises on Carter Fell in the Cheviot Hills, flows 40 mi. NE, past Rothbury and Warkworth, to North Sea at Amble. Navigable below Warkworth.

Coquihalla (kōkùhă'lù), village, S B.C., in Cascade Mts., on Coquihalla R. and 55 mi. NE of Chilliwack; alt. 3,656 ft.; coal mining.

Coquilhatville, province, Belgian Congo: see EQUATOR PROVINCE.

Coquilhatville (kôkēlävēl'), native *Wangata* (wäng-gä'tä), town (1948 pop. 10,238), ⊙ Equator Prov., W Belgian Congo, on left bank of Congo R. at mouth of Ruki R., and 370 mi. NNE of Leopoldville; 0°4'N 18°20'E. Commercial center, particularly for trade in copal; river communications hub and center of native fisheries. Shipbuilding and repairing, mfg. of pharmaceuticals; printing. Airport with customs station. Seat of vicar apostolic of Equator Prov. Has R.C. and Protestant missions, hosp. and school for Europeans, medical and business schools for natives. Botanical gardens at EALA. Town was founded by Henry M. Stanley in 1883 and named Equateur or Equateurville.

Coquille (kō'kēl'), city (pop. 3,523), ⊙ Coos co., SW Oregon, on Coquille R. and 12 mi. S of Coos Bay, near Pacific Ocean; wood novelties, dairy products. Inc. 1901.

Coquille River, SW Oregon, formed by confluence of N.Fork (42 mi. long) and S.Fork (64 mi. long) near Myrtle Point, flows 35 mi. NW and W, through Klamath Mts., to Pacific Ocean at Bandon. Lumbering and dairying in river basin.

Coquimatlán (kōkēmätlän'), town (pop. 2,300), Colima, W Mexico, on affluent of Armería R. and 9 mi. SW of Colima, on railroad; rice, corn, beans, sugar cane, coffee, fruit, stock.

Coquimbito (kōkēmbē'tō), town (pop. estimate 500), N Mendoza prov., Argentina, in Mendoza R. valley (irrigation area), on railroad and 8 mi. SSE of Mendoza; wine, fruit; wine making, alcohol distilling.

Coquimbo (kōkēm'bō), province (□ 15,401; 1940 pop. 245,609, 1949 estimate 236,543), N central Chile, bet. the Pacific and the Andes; ⊙ LA SERENA. Watered by Elqui, Limarí, and Choapa rivers. Predominantly a mining area: copper (Andacollo, Tamaya), iron (El Tofo), lead (Las Cañas), gold (Guatulame), manganese (Cerro de Juan Soldado), lime. Mountainous area, with dry temperate climate, gives way W to irrigated river valleys, where grain, alfalfa, fruit (citrus, peaches, cherries, wine), livestock are raised. The prov. leads in raising of goats and mules, and sheep raising is important. Some industries (tanning, brewing, fruit processing, metal processing) at La Serena, Coquimbo, Ovalle.

Coquimbo, town (pop. 18,863), Coquimbo prov., N central Chile, on SW shore of Coquimbo Bay on the Pacific, and 8 mi. SW of La Serena, for which it is the port; 29°57'S. Railhead; commercial, industrial, and agr. center. Ships grain, fruit, copper, and manganese. Cement milling, tanning, food canning, soap making, wine making. Hydroelectric plant; airport. Its bay is winter hq. of Chilean navy. Coquimbo is adjoined S by Guayacán and La Herradura, minor ports and beach resorts. Town was severely damaged by tidal wave following 1922 earthquake.

Coquimbo River, Chile: see ELQUI RIVER.

Cora, village (pop. 4,201, with adjacent Mt. Gay), Logan co., SW W.Va., just W of Logan.

Corabia (kôrä'byä), town (1948 pop. 10,772), Dolj prov., S Rumania, in Walachia, on Danube R. (Bulg. border) and 25 mi. S of Caracal; rail terminus and river port, with trade in grain and lumber; mfg. of ceramics, tiles, rugs, alcohol, flour.

Coração de Jesus (kōōrùsä'ō dĭ zhä'zōōs), city (pop. 1,873), N Minas Gerais, Brazil, 40 mi. W of Montes Claros; cattle, lard. Formerly called Inconfidencia.

Coracora (kōräkō'rä), city (pop. 4,031), ⊙ Parinacochas prov. (□ 2,795; pop. 44,397), Ayacucho dept., S Peru, in Cordillera Occidental of the Andes, on road from Puquio, and 150 mi. SSE of Ayacucho; 15°1'S 73°47'W; alt. 10,500 ft. Weaving of native textiles; trade in sheep and vicuña wool; agr. products (grain, corn, alfalfa, livestock).

Cora Divh (kō'rù dĭv'), bank of the Laccadives, India, in Arabian Sea, bet. 13°–14°N and 72°–73°E.

Corail (kôrī'), town (1950 census pop. 1,209), Sud dept., SW Haiti, on NW coast of Tiburon Peninsula, 16 mi. ESE of Jérémie; manioc, coffee.

Coraki (kōră'kē), town (pop. 1,097), NE New South Wales, Australia, on Richmond R. and 110 mi. S of Brisbane; agr. center (bananas, sugar cane).

Coral Bay, large inlet of SE St. John Isl., U.S. Virgin Isls., 14 mi. E of Charlotte Amalie, which it matches as one of the finest harbors in the West Indies. Fishing ground, resort.

Coral Gables, city (pop. 19,837), Dade co., S Fla., resort and residential suburb on Biscayne Bay, just SW of Miami and part of Greater Miami; seat of Univ. of Miami. Some mfg. (concrete products, lumber, millwork products, shutters) and printing. City was planned and built during Fla. land boom of 1920s; inc. 1925. Tropical Park race track is near by.

Coral Harbour, trading post, S Southampton Isl., E Keewatin Dist., Northwest Territories, on Hudson Bay; 64°7'N 83°14'W. Radio station, Royal Canadian Mounted Police post. Site of Anglican and R.C. missions. Coral Harbour U.S.A.F. air base is 5 mi. NW, at Munn Bay; 64°9'N 83°17'W. Established during Second World War as base.

Coral Sea, SW arm of Pacific Ocean, E of Australia and New Guinea, W of New Hebrides and New Caledonia; connected with Arafura Sea by Torres Strait. In Second World War, scene of Jap. defeat by U.S. in naval battle (1942) fought near Louisiade Archipelago. Battle was fought entirely by aircraft; checked Jap. southward expansion.

Coralville, town (pop. 977), Johnson co., E Iowa, a suburb of Iowa City on Iowa R.

Coram, village (pop. c.200), Flathead co., NW Mont., on Flathead R. and 20 mi. NNE of Kalispell.

Corangamite, Lake (kŏrăng'gŭmĭt), salt lake (□ 90), S Victoria, Australia, 80 mi. WSW of Melbourne; 18 mi. long, 8 mi. wide; usually dry. Sometimes spelled Korangamite.

Corantijnpolder (kôrāntīn'pôl"dŭr), village (pop. 2,459), Nickerie dist., NW Du. Guiana, on Courantyne or Corantijn R. mouth on the Atlantic, and 4 mi. W of Nieuw Nickerie; rice center.

Corantijn River or **Corantyne River,** Br. and Du. Guiana: see COURANTYNE RIVER.

Coraopolis (kō"rēŏ'pŭlĭs), industrial borough (pop. 10,498), Allegheny co., W Pa., 10 mi. NW of Pittsburgh and on Ohio R.; metal products, glass, refined oil; bituminous coal, gas; Greater Pittsburgh Airport here is an Air Force base. Settled c.1760, inc. 1886.

Corato (kôrä'tô), city (pop. 43,907), Bari prov., Apulia, S Italy, 24 mi. W of Bari; agr. center (fruit, vegetables, almonds, cereals); wine, olive oil, machinery, cement, soap.

Corax, Greece: see VARDOUSIA.

Corazón, town, Ecuador: see EL CORAZÓN.

Corazón, Cerro (sĕ'rō kōräsōn'), Andean volcano (15,718 ft.), Pichincha prov., N central Ecuador, 25 mi. SSW of Quito; snow-capped twin peak, its crater lake containing sulphurous water.

Corbach, Germany: see KORBACH.

Corbehem (kôrbĕm'), SW suburb (pop. 1,592) of Douai, Pas-de-Calais dept., N France, at junction of Scarpe R. and Sensée Canal; sugar refining, paper milling, lubricant mfg.

Corbeil (kôrbā'), town (pop. 10,797), Seine-et-Oise dept., N central France, on left bank of the Seine at influx of Essonne R. and 18 mi. SSE of Paris; important flour-milling center. Its industrial SW suburb of Essonnes (pop. 9,900) has foundries, paper mills, furniture and chocolate factories. Slightly damaged in Second World War.

Corbelin, Cape (kôrbŭlē'), headland in Alger dept., N central Algeria, on the Mediterranean coast of Great Kabylia, just N of Port-Gueydon; 36°55'N 4°26'E; lighthouse.

Corbenay (kôrbŭnā'), village (pop. 621), Haute-Saône dept., E France, 16 mi. NNW of Lure; hardware, hand embroidery.

Corbera (kôrvā'rä), town (pop. 1,406), Tarragona prov., NE Spain, 2 mi. NE of Gandesa; rice milling, olive-oil processing; wine and almond shipping; lumbering.

Corbera de Alcira (dhā äl-thē'rä), town (pop. 2,691), Valencia prov., E Spain, 4 mi. E of Alcira, in rice-growing dist.; oranges, peanuts.

Corbetha, Germany: see GROSSKORBETHA.

Corbetta, Ethiopia: see KORBETTA.

Corbetta (kôrbĕt'tä), town (pop. 5,028), Milano prov., Lombardy, N Italy, 13 mi. W of Milan; mfg. (shoes, celluloid, liquor), metalworking.

Corbie (kôrbē'), town (pop. 3,909), Somme dept., N France, on canalized Somme R. near mouth of the Ancre, and 10 mi. E of Amiens; agr. trade and hosiery-mfg. center. Has relics of noted Benedictine abbey, founded 657. Heavily damaged in First World War.

Corbière Point (kôrbyâr'), promontory at SW extremity of Jersey, Channel Isls., 7 mi. W of St. Helier. Just SW is rocky islet of La Corbière, site of lighthouse (49°11'N 2°14'W).

Corbières (kôrbyâr'), outliers of E Pyrenees, Aude dept., S France, bounded by the Aude (W and N) and by the Gulf of Lion (E); rise to 4,038 ft. Of great aridity, one of France's most destitute and sparsely populated areas. Sheep raising; winegrowing in valleys and on N and E approaches. There are ruins of medieval abbeys and fortresses.

Corbigny (kôrbēnyē'), town (pop. 2,026), Nièvre dept., central France, near Nivernais Canal, 16 mi. SSE of Clamecy; cattle and lumber market. Sawmilling, cement mfg.

Corbii-Mare (kôr'bē-mä'rä), village (pop. 1,845), Bucharest prov., S Rumania, 30 mi. WNW of Bucharest.

Corbin, village, SE B.C., near Alta. border, in Rocky Mts., 18 mi. E of Fernie; coal mining.

Corbin, city (pop. 7,744), Knox and Whitley counties, SE Ky., in Cumberland foothills, near Laurel R., 33 mi. NW of Middlesboro. Rail junction (repair shops); trade center; shipping point for bituminous-coal-mining, agr. (corn, potatoes, hay, livestock), and timber area; mfg. of clothing, food products, soft drinks, concrete products; sawmilling. Near by are CUMBERLAND FALLS STATE PARK, Levi Jackson Wilderness Road State Park and Gatliff state fish hatchery. Situated on old Wilderness Road, Corbin developed with railroad's arrival (1883); inc. 1894.

Corbin City, city (pop. 238), Atlantic co., SE N.J., on Tuckahoe R. and 18 mi. WSW of Atlantic City, in cranberry region.

Corbola (kôr'bôlä), village (pop. 1,741), Rovigo prov., Veneto, N Italy, on Po R. and 3 mi. S of Adria.

Corbridge, town and parish (pop. 2,050), S Northumberland, England, on Tyne R. and 3 mi. E of Hexham; pottery works; agr. market. Has church with Saxon tower (A.D. 600–800) and tower arch, originally a Roman gateway.

Corby, urban district (1931 pop. 1,596; 1951 census 16,704), N central Northampton, England, 7 mi. N of Kettering; ironstone-quarrying center; shoe industry. Has 13th-cent. church. Expansion of the iron industry has led to town's rapid growth in 20th cent. Designated a model residential town after Second World War.

Corcagnano (kôrkänyä'nô), village (pop. 331), Parma prov., Emilia-Romagna, N central Italy, 5 mi. S of Parma; sawmill.

Corcaigh, Ireland: see CORK, city.

Corcelles-Cormondrèche (kôrsĕl'-kôrmõdrĕsh'), town (pop. 2,095), Neuchâtel canton, W Switzerland, near L. of Neuchâtel, 3 mi. W of Neuchâtel; watches.

Corcieux (kôrsyû'), village (pop. 408), Vosges dept., E France, 9 mi. SSW of Saint-Dié; linen mfg.

Corcoran (kôr'kŭrŭn), city (pop. 3,150), Kings co., S central Calif., in San Joaquin Valley, 15 mi. S of Hanford; cotton gins, cottonseed-oil mills. Tulare L. basin is just W. Inc. 1914.

Corcoran, Mount, Calif.: see LANGLEY, MOUNT.

Corcovado (kôrkōōvä'dōō) [Port.,=hunchback], granitic peak (2,310 ft.) overlooking Rio de Janeiro, Brazil. It is topped by a concrete statue of Christ (125 ft. high; inaugurated 1931; floodlit at night), one of Rio's distinguishing landmarks. Accessible by road and funicular railway up densely wooded back slope. Magnificent view from summit. Botafogo Bay and Botafogo residential dist. are at E foot; Rodrigo de Freitas Lagoon and Atlantic beaches are just S. Peak is part of Carioca range, which traverses the Federal Dist.

Corcovado, Gulf of (kôrkōvä'dō), bet. SE Chiloé Isl. and mainland of S Chile, opening on the Pacific through Guafo Gulf.

Corcovado Volcano, Andean peak (7,550 ft.), Chiloé, prov., S Chile, on E shore of Gulf of Corcovado, opposite Chiloé Isl.; 43°11'S.

Corcubión (kôrkōōvyōn'), town (pop. 1,073), La Coruña prov., NW Spain, fishing port and coaling station on inlet of the Atlantic, near Cape Finisterre, 32 mi. WNW of Santiago; fish processing and shipping; chemical works (calcium carbide); lace mfg. Mineral springs. Sea-bathing resort.

Corcyra, Greece: see CORFU.

Cordaville, Mass.: see SOUTHBORO.

Cordeiro (kôrdā'rōō). **1** City (pop. 2,259), N central Rio de Janeiro state, Brazil, in the Serra do Mar, 21 mi. NE of Nova Friburgo; rail junction; coffee, cattle; dairying. **2** City, São Paulo, Brazil: see CORDEIRÓPOLIS.

Cordeirópolis (kôrdārô'pōōlēs), city (pop. 1,330), E central São Paulo, Brazil, 5 mi. NNW of Limeira; rail junction; coffee, grain, cotton. Until 1944, Cordeiro.

Cordele (kôrdēl'), city (pop. 9,462), ⊙ Crisp co., S central Ga., 28 mi. ESE of Americus; market and processing center for farm and timber area; mfg. (clothing, farm machinery, foundry products, fertilizer, feed, lumber, naval stores); peanut milling. State park is 10 mi. W, on L. Blackshear, formed by power dam in Flint R. Founded 1888.

Cordell (kôrdĕl'), city (pop. 2,920), ⊙ Washita co., W Okla., 16 mi. S of Clinton, in agr. area (cotton, wheat, livestock, poultry; dairy products). Cotton ginning; mfg. of mattresses, flour, feed; meat and vegetable packing.

Cordenons (kôrdĕnôns'), town (pop. 4,736), Udine prov., Friuli–Venezia Giulia, NE Italy, 3 mi. NNE of Pordenone; agr. machinery, paper, lace, alcohol, macaroni.

Corder, city (pop. 541), Lafayette co., W central Mo., near Missouri R., 14 mi. SE of Lexington; agr.; coal.

Cordes (kôrd), village (pop. 1,042), Tarn dept., S France, on small Cérou R. and 14 mi. NW of Albi; embroidering, brick and tile mfg. Founded 1222 by counts of Toulouse; has many fine 14th-cent. bldgs.

Cordes Bay (kôr'dĕs), inlet of Strait of Magellan, S Chile, in SW Brunswick Peninsula, 30 mi. NW of Froward Cape.

Cordevole River (kôr"dĕvô'lĕ), N Italy, rises in the Dolomites 4 mi. NW of Marmolada peak, flows 40 mi. SE to Piave R. 8 mi. SW of Belluno. Used for hydroelectric power (Agordo).

Cordignano (kôrdēnyä'nô), village (pop. 871), Treviso prov., Veneto, N Italy, 6 mi. SE of Vittorio Veneto; chemicals.

Cordillera, for names of Spanish and Latin American mtn. ranges beginning thus, see under following part of name; e.g., for Cordillera Central, see CENTRAL, CORDILLERA.

Cordillera, province, Bolivia: see LAGUNILLAS.

Cordillera, La, dept., Paraguay: see LA CORDILLERA.

Cordillo Downs (kôrdĭ'lō), settlement, NE South Australia, near Queensland border, 470 mi. NNE of Port Pirie; cattle.

Cordisburgo (kôrdēzbōōr'gōō), city (pop. 1,314), central Minas Gerais, Brazil, on railroad and 60 mi. NNW of Belo Horizonte. The Maquiné cave, where prehistoric remains have been uncovered, is 10 mi. NNW.

Córdoba (kôr'dŭvŭ, kôrdō'vŭ, Sp. kôr'dhōvä), province (□ 64,894; pop. 1,497,987), central Argentina; ⊙ Córdoba. Its humid, fertile Pampa region, rising in W to ranges of the dry Sierra de Córdoba, gives way E and S to salt marshes. In NE is the salt lake Mar Chiquita, in NW is part of the salt desert Salinas Grandes. The rivers, some of which are used for irrigation and hydroelectric power, are the Río Primero (with one of the great dams of South America), Río Segundo, Río Tercero, Río Cuarto, and Río Quinto. Agr.: wheat, cereals, flax, alfalfa, tobacco, vegetables in the Pampa; peanuts, olives, fruit, wine near mts. Stock raising: cattle, horses, hogs mostly in S; goats and mules in hills. Rural industries: dairying, flour milling, fruit canning, wine making, distilling. Quarrying (marble, granite, limestone) in the sierras. Minerals include tungsten, beryllium, feldspar, mica, magnesium, salt. Mfg. centered mostly in Córdoba, Río Cuarto, and Villa María: textiles, cement, frozen meat, dairy products. Busy resort area in mts. W of Córdoba (e.g., Alta Gracia, Cosquín), with some mineral springs; hunting and fishing.

Córdoba, city (pop. 351,644), ⊙ Córdoba prov. and Córdoba dept. (□ c.220; pop. 362,688), central Argentina, on the Río Primero, on E slopes of Sierra de Córdoba, at W edge of the Pampa, 400 mi. NW of Buenos Aires; 31°25'S 64°12'W; alt. 1,450 ft. Third largest city of Argentina, it is a cultural, commercial, communication, and processing center, and popular health and tourist resort. Hydroelectric power from the great dam on the Río Primero (which also irrigates the surrounding orchard and grain area) has developed local industries: leather and leather goods, textiles, cement, ceramics, glass, frozen meat, dairy products, chocolate, candy, beer and liquor, flour, aircraft. Processes and exports grain, flax, wine, fruit, meat, hides, wood, lime, marble. Founded 1573 by Jerónimo Luis de Cabrera, Córdoba retains its picturesque colonial aspect because of its many old, beautiful bldgs., especially the cathedral. The univ. (founded 1613) early made the city an intellectual center of South America. There are also an agr. school, institute of mining, observatory, acad. of sciences.

Córdoba, town (pop. 1,548), Bolívar dept., N Colombia, on Magdalena R. and 23 mi. ESE of Carmen; cattle, corn, sugar cane.

Córdoba, city (pop. 17,865), Veracruz, E Mexico, in Sierra Madre Oriental, 55 mi. WSW of Veracruz; alt. 3,040 ft. Rail junction; processing and agr. center, known for coffee. Produces sugar cane, tobacco, bananas, mangoes, papayas, oranges, lemons; coffee roasting, rice milling, sugar refining, alcohol distilling, vegetable-oil extracting, textile milling, tanning, printing, lumbering, cigar making. Situated in picturesque tropical landscape of wild forests and clear streams. Has some fine colonial bldgs. Founded 1618. The treaty of Córdoba, establishing independence of Mexico, was signed here Aug. 24, 1821.

Córdoba or **Cordova** (kôr'dŭvŭ, kôrdō'vŭ, Sp. kôr'dhōvä), province (□ 5,297; pop. 761,150), S Spain, in Andalusia; ⊙ Córdoba. Divided by Guadalquivir R. into mountainous region (N) traversed by the Sierra Morena, and undulated fertile plain (S). Generally healthy climate, though summers are hot in S, winters cold in N. Predominantly agr., with forests and pastures prevailing in N, and olive, fruit, and vegetable orchards, vineyards, and grainfields covering S plain; some cork, tobacco, and cotton also grown. Livestock includes noted breed of horses. Mining is chief industry: anthracite, bituminous coal, silver-bearing lead (Peñarroya-Pueblonuevo, Bélmez, Espiel), copper (Córdoba), bismuth (Conquista), antimony, iron, and tungsten. Limestone, clay, and gypsum quarries. Except in industrial city of Córdoba, most industries of prov. are directly derived from agr.: flour, olive oil, wine (Montilla), brandy and liqueurs, fruit jellies and sweets (Puente-Genil), leather are chief products. Other mfg.: metal products, textiles and knitgoods, cement, soap, chemicals, pottery, furniture. Active trade favored by good communications. Tourist industry in Córdoba. Chief cities: Córdoba, Lucena, Puente-Genil, Peñarroya-Pueblonuevo, Montilla.

Córdoba or **Cordova,** anc. *Corduba* and *Colonia Patricia,* city (pop. 116,046), ⊙ Cordoba prov., S Spain, in Andalusia, on right bank of the Guadalquivir, at foot of the Sierra de Córdoba, and 200 mi. SSW of Madrid, 85 mi. NE of Seville; 37°53′N 4°46′W. An old city, famed for the brilliance of its Moorish period. Today it is an industrial, trade, and communications center on a fertile plain yielding cereals, grapes, olives, and truck products. Metalworking, and mfg. of machinery, chemicals, cement, pottery and tiles, toys, flour products, soap, leather goods (it was long known for its fine leather of goatskin—cordovan); has brewery, olive-oil and sugar refineries, distilleries (brandy, cognac, sirups), tanneries, flour mills, and sawmills. Copper and some lead and coal mines near by. Important exports are products of silver, gold, and leather work, traditional industries since Moorish times. It has an active tourist trade, attracted by its great monuments. Most of the city has old, narrow, winding streets, and Moorish-styled houses with fine patios; outlying dists. have broad promenades and modern bldgs. Suburb across river is reached by means of a fine Moorish stone bridge (16 arches; 730 ft. long; restored). The great edifice of Córdoba is its mosque—a cathedral since 1238—which was one of the greatest centers of Islam and the chief religious monument of Moorish architecture in Spain. Built in 8th cent. and added to in 9th and 10th cent., its main features are the hundreds of columns of its aisles, the *Patio de los Naranjos* (Court of Oranges), the Third *Mihrab* (prayer niche), and the Gate of Pardon. Notable, too, are ruins of Moorish citadel (alcazar), a Mudejar synagogue, episcopal palace (15th–18th cent.), and provincial art mus. Of Iberian origin, Córdoba prospered under Romans; passed to Visigoths (572) and Moors (711). Under Omayyad dynasty (756–1031), was seat of independent emirate (later called caliphate), including most of Moslem Spain. It reached its peak in 10th cent., flourishing as world-famous center of Moslem art and culture, with large, wealthy pop. Declined in 2d half of 11th cent., falling (1078) subject to Seville; conquered (1236) by Ferdinand III of Castile, it never recovered its former splendor. The two Senecas, and Lucan, Averroës, and Maimonides were b. here.

Córdoba, Sierra de (syĕ′rä dā), pampean mountain range of Argentina, largely in W Córdoba prov. and with outliers in San Luis, Tucumán, and Santiago del Estero provs. Extends c.300 mi. N–S, covering approximately □ 11,500. Comprises 3 parallel ridges running N–S: Sierra Chica (E); Sierra Grande, continuing S as the Sierra de Comechingones (center); Sierra de Guasapampa and Sierra de Pocho (W). Geologically older than the Andes, they are generally c.6,500 ft. high (highest peak, Cerro Champaquí, is 9,450 ft.), and are deeply eroded, including broad tablelands. Drained by the Río Primero, Río Segundo, Río Tercero, and Río Cuarto. There are mineral deposits, mostly marble and lime. Popular as resort area.

Córdoba Peninsula, Chile: see RIESCO ISLAND.

Cordobilla de Lacara (kôr-dhōvē′lyä dhä läkä′rä), town (pop. 1,693), Badajoz prov., W Spain, 23 mi. S of Cáceres; olives, cereals, fruit, honey, livestock; flour milling, meat salting.

Cordouan, Tour de (tōōr dù kôrdwä′), lighthouse off mouth of the Gironde, SW France, on rocky shoals 7 mi. WSW of Royan; 217 ft. high; 45°35′N 1°10′W. Weather station.

Cordova (kôrdō′vù), town (pop. 1,141), S Alaska, on Prince William Sound 150 mi. ESE of Anchorage; 60°33′N 145°46′W; fishing; fish cannery, cold-storage plant. Has hosp., Indian school. Founded 1908 as terminus of 197-mi. Copper River and Northwestern RR (ceased operations, 1938), serving copper-mining region, notably Kennicott area. Harbor was explored and named by Spaniards, 1792.

Cordova, Spain: see CÓRDOBA.

Cordova (kôrdō′vù, kùr-). **1** Town (pop. 3,156), Walker co., NW central Ala., on Mulberry Fork, 25 mi. NW of Birmingham, in coal area; cotton fabrics. Inc. 1902. **2** Village (pop. 475), Rock Island co., NW Ill., on the Mississippi and 17 mi. NE of Moline, in agr. area. **3** Village (pop. 147), Seward co., SE Nebr., 35 mi. WSW of Lincoln, near W. Fork of Big Blue R. **4** Village (1940 pop. 1,024), Richmond co., S N.C., 3 mi. SW of Rockingham, near Pee Dee R.; cotton milling. **5** Town (pop. 175), Orangeburg co., central S.C., 5 mi. SW of Orangeburg.

Cordovado (kôrdôvä′dô), village (pop. 1,347), Udine prov., Friuli–Venezia Giulia, NE Italy, 7 mi. NW of Latisana.

Cordova Mines (kôr′dōvù), village, SE Ont., 32 mi. NW of Belleville; diatomite mining.

Corduba, Spain: see CÓRDOBA, city.

Corduene, SW Asia: see KURDISTAN.

Coreaú (kōōrĭä-ōō′), city (pop. 1,022), NW Ceará, Brazil, 19 mi. WNW of Sobral; ships carnauba wax and lumber to Camocim. Until 1944, called Palma.

Core Banks, E N.C., section of the Outer Banks lying bet. Core Sound and the Atlantic, and terminating (SW) at Cape Lookout. Core Sound (c.25 mi. long) extends bet. Pamlico Sound (NE), Beaufort Harbor (SW), and is connected with the Atlantic by Drum Inlet through the banks.

Coreglia Antelminelli (kôrā′lyä äntĕlmēnĕl′lē), village (pop. 650), Lucca prov., Tuscany, central Italy, 15 mi. N of Lucca; marble working; furniture.

Corella (kōrā′lyä), city (pop. 5,663), Navarre prov., N Spain, 10 mi. WNW of Tudela; agr. trade center (wine, sugar beets, pepper, garlic); lumber. Olive-oil processing; mfg. of steel files, shoes, cement, tiles, brandy, alcohol, tartaric acid.

Corentyne River, Guiana: see COURANTYNE RIVER.

Coreses (kōrā′sĕs), village (pop. 1,490), Zamora prov., NW Spain, on Duero R. and 7 mi. ENE of Zamora; brandy distilling; cereals, lumber, cattle, sheep. Airport.

Coreytown, town (pop. 23), Pinellas co., W Fla.

Corfe Castle (kôrf), town and parish (pop. 1,409), SE Dorset, England, on Isle of Purbeck, 18 mi. ESE of Dorchester; agr. market. Has ruins of anc. castle, reputed scene of murder of Edward the Martyr (978). In 1643 the castle withstood long siege by Parliamentarians, who later took and partly destroyed it. There is 15th-cent. church.

Corfe Mullen, agr. village and parish (pop. 1,304), E Dorset, England, on Stour R. and 3 mi. WSW of Wimborne Minster. Has 15th-cent. church.

Corfinio (kôrfē′nyô), village (pop. 2,493), Aquila prov., Abruzzi e Molise, S central Italy, 7 mi. NW of Sulmona. Formerly Pentima.

Corfu (kôr′fōō, -fū), Gr. *Kerkyra* or *Kerkira* (both: kĕr′kērä), anc. *Corcyra* (kôrsī′rù), second largest island (□ 229; pop. 106,593) of Ionian group, Greece, forming with near-by isls. (Paxos, Antipaxos, Othonoi, Errikousai, Mathrake) a nome (□ 246; pop. 111,548) of Epirus-Corfu div.; ⊙ Corfu. The island's broad N section (17 mi. wide; rising to 2,974 ft. in the Pantokrator) reaches within 1.5 mi. of Albanian coast at Channel of Corfu. It continues S in a low 35-mi.-long, 3–4-mi.-wide extension. Mild climate with 50–60 in. annual rainfall. Agr.: olive oil, wine, fruit, grain. Stock raising; fisheries. Main economic center is Corfu city, on E central coast. Noted Achilleion villa of Elizabeth of Austria is at Gastourion. Corfu has been identified with Scheria, the isl. of the Phaeacians in Homer's *Odyssey*. Settled 734 B.C. by Corinth, the colony (Corcyra) shared with Corinth in the founding of Epidamnus (modern Durazzo), but became a competitor of Corinth in Adriatic Sea. The two rivals fought the first recorded (by Thucydides) naval battle (665 B.C.) and split (435 B.C.) over the control of Epidamnus. The subsequent alliance bet. Corcyra and Athens was one of the chief causes of the Peloponnesian War. Corfu passed (229 B.C.) to Rome, under whose rule it was eclipsed by the rising Nicopolis. It was seized from the Byzantines by the Normans of Sicily in 1080s and 1150s, by Venice (1206), and later by Epirus (1214–59) and the Angevins of Naples. The Venetians obtained (1386) a permanent hold that ended only in 1797 with the fall of the Venetian Republic. Under Venetian rule, Corfu had resisted 2 celebrated Turkish sieges (1537, 1716). Sharing the subsequent history of the Ionian Isls., Corfu passed to Greece in 1864. During First World War, French troops landed here (1916) in support of the Serbians, who were evacuated here and proclaimed their union with Croatia and Slovenia in 1917. Corfu was the object (1923) of an international incident bet. Greece and Italy, settled by council of ambassadors in Paris. In Second World War the isl. was bombed and occupied (1941–43) by the Italians.

Corfu, Gr. *Kerkyra* or *Kerkira,* anc. *Corcyra,* city (1951 pop. 30,739), ⊙ Corfu nome, chief town of Corfu isl., Greece, major port on Channel of Corfu, exporting chiefly olive oil; other trade in grain, wine, citrus fruit; mfg. (soap, paraffin); printing and engraving. Fisheries. Tourist trade. Airport. Seat of Greek and R.C. archbishops. Once surrounded by a wall, Corfu has largely kept a labyrinthine street lay-out. A broad esplanade (adjoined N by govt. palace) separates the town from the old Venetian isl. fortress (E). Site of anc. town (founded 734 B.C.) was on peninsula 2 mi. S. Corfu was ⊙ Ionian Isls., 1797-1864.

Corfu (kôr′fū), village (pop. 542), Genesee co., W N.Y., 12 mi. WSW of Batavia; flower growing.

Corfu, Channel of (kôr′fōō,–fū), arm of Ionian Sea, bet. Corfu and Albania and Gr. Epirus mainland; c.30 mi. long; 1.5 mi. wide at N entrance, 6 mi. wide at S entrance, and 17 mi. in center. Chief ports are Corfu city and Egoumenitsa. The damaging (1946) of 2 Br. destroyers by mines was a subject of an Albanian-British dispute, settled 1949 by International Court of Justice.

Corgnac-sur-l'Isle (kôrnyäk′-sür-lēl′), village (pop. 276), Dordogne dept., SW France, on Isle R. and 17 mi. NE of Périgueux; paper mills.

Corgo River (kôr′gōō), in Vila Real dist., N Portugal, rises near Vila Pouca de Aguiar, flows 25 mi. SSW, past Vila Real, to the Douro at Pêso da Régua; port-wine vineyards in valley.

Cori (kô′rē), anc. *Cora,* town (pop. 7,191), Latina prov., Latium, S central Italy, 20 mi. NE of Anzio, in grape- and olive-growing region; foundry. Has prehistoric and Roman ruins (walls, temples, bridge). Severely damaged in Second World War.

Coria (kō′ryä). **1** anc. *Caurium,* city (pop. 4,141), Cáceres prov., W Spain, in Estremadura, on Alagón R. and 35 mi. NNW of Cáceres; agr. trade center (chocolate, alcohol, cotton cloth); olive-oil processing. Episcopal see. Has remains of Roman walls; and Gothic cathedral (13th–15th cent.), episcopal palace and seminary. **2** or **Coria del Río** (dhĕl rē′ō), anc. *Caura,* town (pop. 10,053), Seville prov., SW Spain, on the Guadalquivir and 8 mi. SSW of Seville (linked by tramways); agr. center (cereals, olives, licorice, livestock). Lumbering, fishing, flour milling; mfg. of shoes. Has sericultural school. Known for its pottery.

Corigliano Calabro (kôrēlyä′nô kä′läbrô), town (pop. 12,698), Cosenza prov., Calabria, S Italy, near Gulf of Taranto, 26 mi. NE of Cosenza; agr. center; olive oil, canned tomatoes, licorice; shoe mfg. Has 15th-cent. castle (restored).

Corigliano d'Otranto (dô′träntô), town (pop. 4,493), Lecce prov., Apulia, S Italy, 14 mi. SSE of Lecce; wine, olive oil. Has ducal palace.

Coringa, India: see COCANADA.

Corinium, England: see CIRENCESTER.

Corinna (kùrĭ′nù), town (pop. 1,752), Penobscot co., S central Maine, 12 mi. NNE of Pittsfield woolen milling, wood products. Inc. 1816.

Corinne (kùrĭn′), city (pop. 427), Box Elder co., N Utah, 5 mi. NW of Brigham City and on Bear R.; alt. 4,299 ft.

Corinth (kŏ′rĭnth), Gr. *Korinthos* (kô′rĭnthôs), Lat. *Corinthus,* chief city (pop. 12,715) of N (Corinthia) sect. of Argolis and Corinthia nome, NE Peloponnesus, Greece, port on Gulf of Corinth near W end of Corinth Canal, on railroad, and 40 mi. W of Athens. Commercial center for trade in Zante currants (main exports), silk, citrus fruits, olive oil. Summer resort. Founded 1858 following destruction of Old Corinth by earthquake. The new city was also destroyed (1928) by earthquake and was later rebuilt. Formerly known as New Corinth. Old Corinth, Gr. *Palaia Korinthos,* is a village (pop. 1,473) at N foot of the ACROCORINTHUS, 3 mi. SW of the new city and on site of anc. Corinth. It was one of the oldest, most powerful, and wealthiest cities of ancient Greece, and a great intellectual center. A town of the Dorians, it existed as early as Homeric times. In the 8th and 7th cents. B.C., it became a strong and flourishing maritime power. It led in shipbuilding and had a great pottery industry. Syracuse, Corfu, Potidaea, and Apollonia were among its colonies. The natural rival of Athens, Corinth was traditionally allied with Sparta. Athenian assistance to the rebellious Corinthian colonies was direct cause of the Peloponnesian War, in which Corinth was aligned with Sparta. However, in the Corinthian war (395–387 B.C.) Corinth combined with Athens and Thebes against the tyrannical rule of Sparta. After the battle of Chaeronea (338 B.C.), Corinth became a leading Macedonian center. It became (in mid-3d cent. B.C.) a leading member of the Achaean League and was destroyed 146 B.C. by Rome. Julius Caesar refounded the city 44 B.C. as the Roman ⊙ of Achaea and reestablished the Isthmian games at near-by Isthmia. After 1204 Corinth was conquered by Geoffroi de Villehardouin as a sequel to the Fourth Crusade. It was held by various Latin princes, was taken by the Turks in 1458, and in 1687 was seized by Venice, which again lost it to the Turks in 1715. In 1822 it was taken by the Greek insurgents. In the days of its wealth and power, the city was a center of luxury and of intellectual and artistic life. Here St. Paul preached, and to the infant Corinthian church he wrote 2 epistles. The ruins (just S of Old Corinth) include market place, fountains, temple of Apollo, and Roman Amphitheater.

Corinth. 1 (kŏ′rĭnth) Town (pop. 135), Heard co., W Ga., 13 mi. NNE of La Grange. **2** (kŏ′rĭnth) Town (pop. 283), Grant co., N Ky., 16 mi. WNW of Cynthiana, in Bluegrass agr. region. **3** (kŏ′rĭnth) Town (pop. 1,167), Penobscot co., S central Maine, 15 mi. WNW of Old Town, in agr., recreational area. **4** (kŏ′rĭnth) City (pop. 9,785), ⊙ Alcorn co., NE Miss., near Tenn. line, c.85 mi. E of Memphis, Tenn.; shipping, mfg., and processing center for agr., livestock, dairying area; mfg. of clothing, hosiery, sawmill machinery, castings, brick, cottonseed products, lumber. Founded c.1855; was strategic railroad center in Civil War, abandoned by Confederate army after battle of Shiloh (May, 1862). **5** (kùrĭnth′, kŏ′rĭnth) Village (pop. 3,161), Saratoga co., E N.Y., in the Adirondack foothills, on the Hudson and 11 mi. SW of Glens Falls; summer resort; mfg. of clothing, lumber and paper milling. Inc. 1886. **6** (kùrĭnth′, kŏ′rĭnth) Town (pop. 786), Orange co., E central Vt., 16 mi. SE of Barre; wood products.

Corinth, Bay of (kŏ′rĭnth), on Gulf of Corinth, NE Peloponnesus, Greece, at W end of Corinth Canal; 5 mi. wide, 8 mi. long. Corinth on SE shore.

Corinth, Gulf of, inlet of Ionian Sea, Greece, bet. Peloponnesus (S) and central Greece (N), connects with Gulf of Patras (W) through Rion Strait and with Saronic Gulf (E) through Canal of Corinth; 3–20 mi. wide, 80 mi. long. Corinth and Aigion are on S shore, Naupaktos on N shore. Formerly called Gulf of Lepanto, (lĭpăn′tō, Ital. läpän′tô).

Corinth, Isthmus of, Greece, connects Peloponnesus (SW) with central Greece (NE), bet. Gulf of Corinth and Saronic Gulf; 20 mi. long, 4–8 mi. wide. Crossed by Corinth Canal. Main towns (on W coast) are Corinth and Loutrakion. Remains of anc. Isthmian wall (restored 3d–6th cent. A.D.) extend parallel to canal (N). Near E end of wall are ruins of Isthmian sanctuaries with temple of Poseidon, the site of the Isthmian games.

Corinth Canal, in NE Peloponnesus, Greece, crosses Isthmus of Corinth, joining Gulf of Corinth (NW) and Saronic Gulf (SE); 4 mi. long, 72 ft. wide, 26 ft. deep. Rail and road bridge. Ports of Poseidonia (NW end) and Isthmia (SE end) have developed since construction of canal (1881–93). Damaged in Second World War, it was out of commission 1944–48.

Corinthia, Greece: see ARGOLIS AND CORINTHIA; CORINTH.

Corintho, Brazil: see CORINTO.

Corinto (ko͝orēn′to͞o), city (pop. 5,047), central Minas Gerais, Brazil, near the Rio das Velhas, 110 mi. NNW of Belo Horizonte; important junction on railroad from Belo Horizonte (spurs to Pirapora, Montes Claros, and Diamantina); lumber trade. Airfield. Formerly spelled Corintho.

Corinto (kōrēn′tō), town (pop. 1,228), Cauca dept., SW Colombia, on W slopes of Cordillera Central, on highway to Popayán, 24 mi. SE of Cali; alt. 4,920 ft.; tobacco, cacao, sugar cane, coffee, cereals, fruit.

Corinto, town (1950 pop. 4,766), Chinandega dept., W Nicaragua, Pacific port on sheltered Corinto Bay, at SE end of low, offshore Aserradores Isl. (äsĕrädō′rĕs) (13 mi. long), 11 mi. SSW of Chinandega; 12°28′N 87°12′W. Principal Pacific port of Nicaragua; rail terminus, connected by bridge with mainland; exports mainly agr. products (coffee, sugar, hides). Has lighthouse, cement pier, customhouse. Site of U.S. naval base. Beach resorts of Miramar and Costa Azul are near by; resort of Paso Caballos is at rail bridge to mainland, 4 mi. NW. Founded 1840 and 1st called Punta Icacos (for point on which it is located); supplanted (1858) El Realejo as chief Pacific port of Nicaragua; later renamed Corinto.

Corio Bay (kō′rēō), S Victoria, Australia, W arm of Port Phillip Bay; 20 mi. long, 12 mi. wide; Geelong on W shore.

Coripata (kōrēpä′tä), town (pop. c.4,900), La Paz dept., W Bolivia, in the Yungas, 40 mi. ENE of La Paz, on road; alt. 5,295 ft. Trade and agr. center for coffee, cacao, quina, subtropical fruit.

Coripe (kōrē′pā), town (pop. 1,999), Seville prov., SW Spain, on affluent of the Guadalete, on railroad and 10 mi. WNW of Olvera (Cádiz prov.); wheat, olives, cereals, livestock, charcoal.

Coripós (ko͝orēpôs′), city (pop. 731), W Pernambuco, NE Brazil, down-river limit of navigation on upper section of São Francisco R. (Bahia border), c.180 mi. above Paulo Afonso Falls, and 60 mi. NE of Juàzeiro (Bahia). Until 1944, called Boa Vista.

Corisco (kōrē′skō), low island (□ 5.8; pop. 583) in Gulf of Guinea (Corisco Bay), 18 mi. off mouth of the Río Muni; belongs to continental Sp. Guinea; 0°55′N 9°22′E; 3 mi. long, 2 mi. wide. Coconuts, yucca. Fishing; silica-sand quarrying.

Corisco Bay, inlet of Gulf of Guinea, in Sp. Guinea and Gabon (Fr. Equatorial Africa), bounded by Cape San Juan (N) and Cape Esterias (S); 35 mi. wide, 20 mi. long. Corisco and Elobey isls. (Sp.) are in it, opposite Río Muni estuary.

Corityba, Brazil: see CURITIBA.

Corityabanos, Brazil: see CURITIBANOS.

Coriza, Albania: see KORITSA.

Cork, Gaelic *Chorcaigh*, largest county (□ 2,880.6; pop. 343,668) in Ireland, in Munster, on S coast, on the Atlantic; ⊙ Cork. Bounded by cos. Kerry (W), Limerick (N), Tipperary (NE), and Waterford (E). Drained by Blackwater, Bandon, Lee, and other rivers. Surface is mountainous in W and SW, rising to 2,239 ft. on Caherbarnagh, leveling toward E and coastal plain. Coastline is deeply indented; main inlets are Bantry Bay, Dunmanus Bay, Clonakilty Bay, Kinsale Harbour, Cork Harbour, and Youghal Harbour. Minerals include copper (Durrus, Killeen), barites (Bantry), coal, manganese, iron, lead. Red and gray marbles, slate, limestone are worked. Chief crops are potatoes, root vegetables, sugar beets, oats. Dairying and fishing are important. Industries include woolen milling, tanning, alcohol distilling, automobile construction, metalworking, mfg. of clothing, shoes, soap, chemicals, rope, food products. Youghal is noted for fine lace. Besides Cork, other towns are transatlantic port of Cóbh, Passage West, Youghal, Clonakilty, Bantry, Dripsey, Skibbereen, Macroom, Kinsale, Blarney, Mallow, Fermoy, and Mitchelstown. About 90% of pop. are R.C. Co. is co-extensive with anc. kingdom of the Desmonds; its strategic location resulted in early Anglo-Norman settlement and, later, attempts at invasion by Spain (1601) and France (1796). Cromwell (1649) and Marlborough (1690) fought here. Until 1938 isls. in Cork Harbour had Br. garrisons. Antiquities include 2 round towers and numerous remains of anc. castles, abbeys (Cloyne, Kilcrea), prehistoric monuments. Co. has associations with Edmund Spenser (Kilcolman Castle, Doneraile) and Sir Walter Raleigh (Youghal).

Cork, Gaelic *Corcaigh*, county borough (pop. 75,595) and city, ⊙ Co. Cork, Ireland, in SE central part of co., on Lee R. near its mouth on Lough Mahon, near Cork Harbour, and 130 mi. SW of Dublin; 51°54′N 8°28′W; seaport, with extensive dock installations and regular shipping services to Irish and British ports. Near-by ports of Passage West and Cóbh (for transatlantic ships) handle Cork's overseas trade. Chief exports are dairy produce, beef cattle, grain, cloth, fish. Industries include shipbuilding, woolen milling, tanning, alcohol distilling, automobile building; mfg. of agr. implements, metal products, chemicals, soap, shoes, clothing, shirts, hosiery, rope, oleomargerine, dairy products; marble polishing. Among city's noted features are Patrick Street, the main thoroughfare; St. Finbar's Cathedral (1879), seat of Protestant bishop, on site of earlier structure destroyed in 1690 bombardment; church of SS. Peter and Paul, by Pugin; 1835 courthouse; University Col. (1849, formerly Queen's Col.), constituent col. of the National Univ., with schools of science, art, agr.; church of St. Ann's Shandon (1726), containing grave of Francis Mahoney; St. Mary's Cathedral (1808). Near city is race course, and world's 1st yacht club was established at Cork 1720. In early 7th cent. St. Finbar reputedly founded monastery on isl. in Lee R., now forming oldest part of city and connected with mainland by numerous bridges. Monastery became target for Danish raids and in 9th cent. Danish trading colony was founded here. By 1172 Diarmuid MacCarthy, Lord of Desmond, had ousted Danes and sworn allegiance to Henry II, and Anglo-Norman settlement was established at Cork. In 1590 it became hq. of the Desmond rebellion. Cromwell occupied (1649) it without resistance; in 1690 it was taken by Marlborough after heavy bombardment. During 1920 disturbances many public bldgs. were destroyed and Lord Mayor of Cork murdered by constabulary. Spike Isl. and other Cork Harbour forts were occupied by the British until taken over by the Irish under 1938 agreement.

Corker, Cay, Br. Honduras: see CAY CORKER.

Cork Harbour, inlet (8 mi. long, up to 6 mi. wide) of the Atlantic on SE coast of Co. Cork, Ireland. It is one of best natural anchorages in the world. Contains several isls., including Great Isl. (on S shore of which is port of CÓBH), Haulbowline Isl., and Spike Isl. At NW end of Cork Harbour, at mouth of Lough Mahon, is port of Passage West. Until 1938 some isls. had British garrisons. Narrow entrance from the Atlantic is marked by Roche's Point light and is guarded by anc. Camden Fort (W) and Carlisle Fort (E).

Corlatesti (kôrlŭtĕsht′), Rum. *Corlătești*, SE suburb of Ploesti, Prahova prov., S central Rumania, in oil region.

Corlay (kôrlā′), village (pop. 768), Côtes-du-Nord dept., W France, 19 mi. SW of Saint-Brieuc; noted for its horses. Has yearly fairs and horse races. Slate quarries near by.

Corleone (kôrlĕō′nĕ), town (pop. 14,197), Palermo prov., W central Sicily, 21 mi. S of Palermo; agr. center; macaroni factories. Founded by Saracens c.840.

Corleto Perticara (kôrlā′tô pĕrtēkä′rä), town (pop. 4,657), Potenza prov., Basilicata, S Italy, 22 mi. SE of Potenza, in agr. (cereals, olives) and livestock region.

Corlu (chôrlo͞o′), Turkish *Çorlu*, anc. *Zurulum* or *Syrallum*, town (1950 pop. 10,956), Tekirdag, Turkey in Europe, on railroad and 20 mi. NE of Tekirdag; grain market. Formerly noted for its tiles. Sometimes spelled Chorlu, Tchorlu.

Cormack's Lake (6 mi. long, 2 mi. wide), SW N.F., 50 mi. S of Corner Brook.

Cormano (kôrmä′nô), village (pop. 1,532), Milano prov., Lombardy, N Italy, 6 mi. N of Milan; aluminum industry.

Cormantyn, Gold Coast: see SALTPOND.

Corme (kôr′mā), fishing port consisting of Corme village (pop. 688) and Corme port (pop. 2,420), La Coruña prov., NW Spain, on inlet of the Atlantic 28 mi. WSW of La Coruña; fishing, fish processing.

Cormeilles (kôrmā′), village (pop. 1,055), Eure dept., NW France, 10 mi. NE of Lisieux; alcohol, cheese.

Cormeilles-en-Parisis (–ā-pärēsē′), town (pop. 8,388), Seine-et-Oise dept., N central France, an outer NW suburb of Paris, 11 mi. from Notre Dame Cathedral, near right bank of the Seine; truck gardens (chiefly asparagus). Dominated by fort guarding approaches to Paris.

Cormery (kôrmůrē′), village (pop. 790), Indre-et-Loire dept., W central France, on the Indre and 11 mi. SE of Tours; basket and barrelmaking. Has a Romanesque belfry and ruins of a 13th-cent. cloister, originally part of a Benedictine abbey founded in 8th cent.

Cormicy (kôrmēsē′), village (pop. 647), Marne dept., N France, near Aisne-Marne Canal, 10 mi. NW of Rheims; winegrowing. Ger. stronghold dominating approaches to Rheims in First World War.

Cormons (kôrmôns′), town (pop. 4,635), Gorizia prov., Friuli–Venezia Giulia, NE Italy, near Yugoslav border, 7 mi. W of Gorizia; silk textiles, furniture, bricks, cement. Fruit trade.

Cormorant Island, B.C.: see ALERT BAY.

Cormorant Lake (□ 141), NW Man., 30 mi. NE of The Pas; 18 mi. long, 14 mi. wide.

Cormorant Lake, Becker co., W Minn., 9 mi. WSW of Detroit Lakes city; 4.5 mi. long, 2.5 mi. wide. Just W is Upper Cormorant L. (2.5 mi. long, 1 mi. wide).

Cornago (kôrnä′gō), town (pop. 1,509), Logroño prov., N Spain, 18 mi. SSW of Calahorra; olive oil, fruit, cereals, lumber. Mineral springs.

Corn Belt, important agr. region of the U.S., where the corn acreage (c.50,000,000) is more than that of any other single crop (e.g., oats or winter wheat). It lies in the N central plains of the Midwest, S of the hay and dairying belt, and extends through W Ohio, Ind., Ill., Iowa, N Mo., E Kansas, E Nebr., SE S.Dak., and S Minn. Favored by deep soil, adequate annual rainfall (c.30–35 in.), and long-summer type of continental climate, large-scale commercialized agr. prevails. Crops are raised primarily as feed for hogs and other livestock, which are the main source of cash income.

Corn Du, Wales: see BRECON BEACONS.

Cornedo Vicentino (kôrnā′dô vēchĕntē′nô), village (pop. 1,825), Vicenza prov., Veneto, N Italy, 11 mi. NW of Vicenza; silk and woolen mills. Marble quarries near by.

Corneilla-de-Conflent (kôrnāyä-dů-kōflā′), village (pop. 381), Pyrénées-Orientales dept., S France, in the CONFLENT valley, 4 mi. SW of Prades; marble and talc quarrying. Has fine Romanesque church.

Corneilla-la-Rivière (–lä-rēvyâr′), village (pop. 979), Pyrénées-Orientales dept., S France, on the Têt and 8 mi. W of Perpignan; Roussillon wines.

Corneille (kôrnā′), village (pop. 1,938), Constantine dept., NE Algeria, 15 mi. WNW of Batna; wheat.

Cornelia, city (pop. 2,424), Habersham co., NE Ga., 12 mi. WSW of Toccoa; trade center for apple-growing dist.; mfg. (plastics, furniture, brooms, lumber, veneer, shirts). State tuberculosis sanatorium near by. Inc. 1887.

Corneliano d'Alba (kôrnĕlyä′nô däl′bä), village (pop. 1,847), Cuneo prov., Piedmont, NW Italy, 5 mi. NW of Alba.

Cornelimünster, Germany: see KORNELIMÜNSTER.

Cornélio Procópio (kôrnĕ′lyo͞o pro͞okô′pyo͞o), city (pop. 3,818), N Paraná, Brazil, on railroad and 33 mi. ENE of Londrina, in pioneer coffee zone; coffee, corn, and rice processing, cotton milling, distilling.

Cornelio Saavedra, Bolivia: see BETANZOS.

Cornelius. 1 Town (pop. 1,548), Meckenburg co., S N.C., 17 mi. N of Charlotte; cotton milling. Settled 1880; inc. 1905. **2** City (pop. 998), Washington co., NW Oregon, 4 mi. W of Hillsboro; pickles, vinegar.

Cornell. 1 Village (pop. 458), Livingston co., central Ill., near Vermilion R., 9 mi. NNW of Pontiac, in agr. and bituminous-coal area. **2** Village (pop. 1,944), Chippewa co., W central Wis., on Chippewa R. and 19 mi. NE of Chippewa Falls, in dairying region; paper, wood products. Brunet Isl. and State Park is near by. Inc. 1913.

Cornellá or **Cornellá de Llobregat** (kôrnālyä′, dhā yōvrägät′), outer industrial suburb (pop. 4,719) of Barcelona, Barcelona prov., NE Spain, 6 mi. SW of city center, on Llobregat coastal plain. Mfg. of chemicals (dyes, pharmaceuticals), electrical equipment, auto accessories, knit goods, watches, ceramics; cotton milling, aluminum processing.

Corner Brook, town (pop. 8,635, including West Corner Brook), W N.F., on Humber R., near its mouth on the Bay of Islands in lumbering region, on railroad; 48°48′N 57°57′W. Second in size only to St. John's in N.F., it is important newsprint-milling center; also iron foundries, furniture works. Near by are limestone quarries and mink farms. Electric power from Deer L. Town has grown rapidly since 1925, when paper mills were erected. W suburb of West Corner Brook (pop. 5,439) became municipality in 1942; it is almost wholly inhabited by paper-mill employees.

Corner Inlet, inlet of Bass Strait, S Victoria, Australia, bet. Snake Isl. and Wilson's Promontory; 18 mi. long, 17 mi. wide; contains numerous mud flats.

Cornersville, town (pop. 358), Marshall co., central Tenn., 15 mi. NE of Pulaski, in farm area.

Cornesti, Moldavian SSR: see KORNESHTY.

Cornet Falls, Belgian Congo: see MWADINGUSHA.

Corneto or **Corneto Tarquinia,** Italy: see TARQUINIA.

Corney Bayou (bī′ō), in SW Ark. and N La., rises in headstreams SE of Magnolia, Ark., flows c.70 mi. SE, into La., to Bayou D'Arbonne just above Farmerville. Dam impounds Corney L. (c.5 mi. long) 7 mi. NW of Bernice, La.

Corney Lake, La.: see CORNEY BAYOU.

Cornfield Point, peninsula (2.5 mi. long) in Old Saybrook town, S Conn., at W side of Connecticut R. mouth, on Long Isl. Sound; summer resort, beaches.

Cornhill-on-Tweed, agr. village and parish (pop. 542), N Northumberland, England, on the Tweed, near Scottish border, just E of Coldstream.

Cornholme, England: see TODMORDEN.

Corniche, France: see RIVIERA.

Cornier, Grand, Switzerland: see GRAND CORNIER.

Cornigliano Ligure (kôrnēlyä'nô lē'goorē), town (pop. 23,898), Genova prov., Liguria, N Italy, port on Gulf of Genoa and 3 mi. W of Genoa, within Greater Genoa. Industrial center; metallurgical works, cotton mills, shipyards, rope factories. Has Genoese stadium (1928).

Cornil (kôrnē'), village (pop. 524), Corrèze dept., S central France, on Corrèze R. and 5 mi. SW of Tulle.

Cornillon (kôrnēō') or **Grand-Bois** (grã-bwä), village (1950 pop. 398), Ouest dept., S Haiti, 25 mi. ENE of Port-au-Prince; coffeegrowing, lumbering region.

Cornimont (kôrnēmō'), town (pop. 2,202), Vosges dept., E France, on Moselotte R. and 12 mi. ESE of Remiremont, in the central Vosges; cotton milling, granite- and metalworking.

Corning (kôr'nĭng). **1** City (pop. 2,045), a ⊙ Clay co., extreme NE Ark., 24 mi. NNW of Paragould, near Black R., at Mo. line, in diversified farming area; mfg. of buttons, pool tables; grain and lumber milling, cotton ginning. **2** City (pop. 2,537), Tehama co., N Calif., near Sacramento R., 17 mi. S of Red Bluff; processing center (oil extracting, canning) of extensive olive-growing area. Inc. 1907. **3** City (pop. 2,104), ⊙ Adams co., SW Iowa, on East Nodaway R. and 20 mi. WSW of Creston; grain-shipping center; mfg. (feed, concrete). Bituminous-coal mines, limestone quarries near by. An Icarian communist settlement, founded 1858 by Étienne Cabet, was situated near here until 1898. Platted 1855, inc. 1871. **4** City (pop. 254), Nemaha co., NE Kansas, 45 mi. NNW of Topeka; livestock, grain. **5** Town (pop. 184), Holt co., NW Mo., on Missouri R. and 45 mi. NW of St. Joseph. **6** Industrial city (pop. 17,684), Steuben co., S N.Y., on Chemung R. and 13 mi. WNW of Elmira; its large glass industry was begun in 1868. Produces also metal and wood products, chemicals, furnaces, machinery, fiber boxes; has railroad shops. Agr. (dairy products; hay, potatoes, tobacco); timber. The 200-inch telescope mirror for Mt. Palomar (Calif.) observatory was made at the Corning Glass Works here. Settled 1788; inc. as village in 1848, as city in 1890. **7** Village (pop. 1,215), Perry co., central Ohio, 23 mi. S of Zanesville and on small Sunday Creek; makes roofing tile; coal mining.

Cornish. 1 Agr. hamlet, Weld co., N Colo., 16 mi. ENE of Greeley; alt. 6,708 ft. Artifacts of Yuma man and Folsom man displayed annually (July) during Stone Age Fair. **2** Town (pop. 795), York co., SW Maine, on Ossipee R. and 26 mi. NW of Portland. Settled 1776, inc. 1794. **3** Town (pop. 989), Sullivan co., W N.H., near the Connecticut, 10 mi. N of Claremont; resort, art and literary colony. Seat of Augustus St. Gaudens' estate "Aspet," now a state memorial. Salmon P. Chase b. here. Inc. 1763. **4** Town (pop. 152), Jefferson co., S Okla., 26 mi. W of Ardmore, in farm area. **5** Town (pop. 181), Cache co., N Utah, near Idaho line, 20 mi. NNW of Logan and on Bear R.

Corn Islands, Sp. *Islas del Maíz*, group of 2 small isls. (1950 pop. 1,304) in Caribbean Sea off Nicaragua, in Zelaya dept., 50-55 mi. ENE of Bluefields. Consist of Great Corn Isl. and Little Corn Isl. (10 mi. NNE). Coconuts; coconut-oil mfg. Leased, after 1914, to U.S.

Cornlea, village (pop. 69), Platte co., E central Nebr., 20 mi. NNW of Columbus and on branch of Elkhorn R.

Corno, Monte (môn'tē kôr'nô), or **Corno Grande** (grän'dē), highest peak (9,560 ft.) in the Apennines, in Gran Sasso d'Italia, S central Italy, 12 mi. NE of Aquila. On its S slope is resort of Campo Imperatore (ascended by cable railway), where Mussolini was confined (Aug. 28, 1943) by the Badoglio government and later (Sept. 12, 1943) rescued by Ger. parachute troops. Resort lies at W edge of the Campo Imperatore, a large basin (17 mi. long, 5 mi. wide, average alt. 5,900 ft.) frequented for winter sports.

Cornouaille (kôrnwī'), historical region and medieval county of Brittany, W France, now forming part of Finistère, Côtes-du-Nord, and Morbihan depts.; ⊙ Quimper. So named by Britons who fled Cornwall c.500. Breton language still widely spoken here.

Cornú, Cerro (sĕ'rō kôrnoo'), Patagonian mountain (4,147 ft.) in S Tierra del Fuego natl. territory, Argentina, on S bank of L. Fagnano and 27 mi. ENE of Ushuaia; 54°45'S.

Cornucopia. 1 Town (1940 pop. 355), Baker co., NE Oregon, 35 mi. NE of Baker; alt. 4,800 ft.; gold mining. **2** Village, Bayfield co., extreme N Wis., on L. Superior and 45 mi. NE of Superior; fishing.

Cornuda (kôrnoo'dä), village (pop. 921), Treviso prov., Veneto, N Italy, 16 mi. NW of Treviso; shoe factory, tannery, silk mill; metal furniture.

Cornudella (kôrnoo-dhā'lyä), town (pop. 1,322), Tarragona prov., NE Spain, 13 mi. NW of Reus; olive-oil processing, alcohol distilling; agr. trade (wine, almonds, filberts, fruit, cereals). Has 17th-cent. parochial church.

Cornus (kôrnü'), village (pop. 244), Aveyron dept., S France, 14 mi. SSE of Millau; bituminous schist mining.

Cornville, town (pop. 563), Somerset co., central Maine, just N of Skowhegan; **agr.,** lumber mills.

Cornwall (–wôl, –wŭl), town (pop. 14,117), ⊙ Dundas, Glengarry, and Stormont cos., SE Ont., on the St. Lawrence, at SW end of L. St. Francis, opposite Cornwall Isl., and 55 mi. ESE of Ottawa; port, with dry dock; rayon, cotton, paper, and pulp milling, tanning; mfg. of clothing, bedding, chemicals, furniture, dairy products. Center of rich dairying, mixed-farming region. Founded 1783 by United Empire Loyalists. Noted Cornwall Grammar School was established here 1803. Town is at NE end of Cornwall Canal, 11 mi. long, with 6 locks, built 1834–43 to by-pass the long Sault rapids, and enlarged and deepened 1902. Opposite Cornwall is historic Indian village of St. Régis, in Que.

Cornwall (–wŭl, –wôl), county (□ 1,356.5; 1931 pop. 317,968; 1951 census 345,612), SW England; ⊙ Bodmin. Bounded by Atlantic (N and W), English Channel (S), and Devon (E). Includes Scilly Isls., 28 mi. SW of Land's End. A peninsula 75 mi. long and 45 mi. wide at the base, with moorlands and hills (N central), valleys (SW and central), plains (N and SW), and rocky coasts, the highest point (1,375 ft.) being in BODMIN MOOR. Drained by Tamar, Camel, Fowey, and Fal rivers. St. Ives Bay and Padstow Bay indent N shore, the Fowey estuary S shore. Has the mildest climate in England, producing subtropical gardens in the SCILLY ISLANDS, PENZANCE, and FALMOUTH. Tin, the chief mineral, is mined principally in CAMBORNE-REDRUTH area; smaller quantities of copper, lead, arsenic, and tungsten are found in NE and SW; large China-clay deposits in St. Austell area; stone and slate in Delabole and St. Dennis. Extensive fisheries (pilchard, mackerel, herring) located at Mevagissey, St. Ives, Padstow, and Newlyn. Dairy farming, flower growing. Other important towns are Truro, Launceston, Penryn. Especially rich in anc. Br. culture, having many druidical monuments, ruins of baronial castles, and legends of Arthurian romance, which make it a favorite tourist resort. Eldest son of the king of England bears title duke of Cornwall. Tin mining dates from Phoenician times. Cornish language (of Celtic origin) is no longer spoken, but a literature is preserved.

Cornwall, county (□ 1,565.07; pop. 353,052), W Jamaica, B.W.I., occupies W third of the isl., consists of St. Elizabeth, Trelawny, St. James, Hanover, and Westmoreland parishes. Set up 1758 for assize purposes, it is now a regional unit without administrative status.

Cornwall. 1 Town (pop. 896), Litchfield co., NW Conn., in Litchfield Hills, on Housatonic R. and 10 mi. W of Torrington; agr., resorts, fishing; winter sports center at Mohawk Mtn. State Park, on Appalachian Trail. Includes villages of Cornwall, Cornwall Center, Cornwall Bridge, Cornwall Hollow, North Cornwall, and West Cornwall. State forests in town include Cathedral Pines, one of finest U.S. stands of virgin white pine. **2** Village (pop. 2,211), Orange co., SE N.Y., near W bank of the Hudson, 5 mi. S of Newburgh; summer resort; mfg. of wood products. Seat of New York Military Acad., and 2 other boys' schools. Inc. 1884. Bet. Cornwall and the Hudson is village of Cornwall on the Hudson or Cornwall-on-Hudson. **3** Borough (pop. 1,760), Lebanon co., SE central Pa., 4 mi. SSE of Lebanon; rich deposits of magnetite. Inc. 1926. **4** Town (pop. 728), Addison co., W Vt., near Otter Creek, 5 mi. SW of Middlebury; agr.

Cornwall, village (pop. 250), E Tasmania, 55 mi. ESE of Launceston; coal mines.

Cornwall, Cape, headland, W Cornwall, England, on the Atlantic, 4 mi. N of Land's End; 50°7'N 5°41'W.

Cornwallis Island (□ 2,592), Parry Isls., central Franklin Dist., Northwest Territories, in the Arctic Ocean, bet. Bathurst Isl. (W), separated by McDougall Sound and Crozier Strait, Devon Isl. (E), separated by Wellington Channel, and Somerset Isl. (S), separated by Barrow Strait; 74°37'–75°38'N 93°40'–97°30'W. It is 70 mi. long, 30–60 mi. wide; on SE coast is U.S.-Canadian weather station of Resolute Bay; 74°42'N 94°34'W.

Cornwall Island. 1 Island (□ 720), N Franklin Dist., Northwest Territories, in the Arctic Ocean; 77°28'–77°49'N 93°50'–97°15'W; separated from Amund Ringnes Isl. (NW) by Hendriksen Strait and from Devon Isl. (S) by Belcher Channel. Isl. is 50 mi. long, 8–24 mi. wide; rises to over 1,000 ft. **2** Island (5 mi. long, 1 mi. wide), SE Ont., in the St. Lawrence, just S of Cornwall, at W end of L. St. Francis, opposite N.Y.-Que. border.

Cornwallis River, W central N.S., rises in North Mts., flows 30 mi. E, past Kentville, to Minas Basin at Wolfville.

Cornwall-on-Hudson, N.Y.: see CORNWALL.

Corny Point, S South Australia, in Spencer Gulf, forms NW end of SW projection of Yorke Peninsula; 34°54'S 137°1'E; lighthouse.

Coro (kō'rō), city (1941 pop. 18,962; 1950 census 28,307), ⊙ Falcón state, NW Venezuela, at base of Isthmus of Médanos S of Paraguaná Peninsula, bet. Gulf of Coro (W) and the Caribbean (E), 200 mi. WNW of Caracas; 11°25'N 69°42'W. Connected with its port La Vela (8 mi. ENE) by narrow-gauge railroad. Goat- and cattle-raising center; exports coffee, corn, hardwood, goatskins; mfg. of liquor (*aguardiente*). Salt and coal mines near by. Airport. Oldest city of W Venezuela, founded 1527. Became 1st bishopric. Remained colonial capital until 1578. Was base in early colonial times for Sp. exploration under Ger. mercenaries, notably Federmann.

Coro, Gulf of, E inlet of Gulf of Venezuela, Falcón state, NW Venezuela; bordered by Paraguaná Peninsula (N) and Isthmus of Médanos (E); 25 mi. long (W-E), up to 20 mi. wide.

Coroados (kooroōä'doos), city (pop. 1,267), NW São Paulo, Brazil, on railroad and 12 mi. SE of Araçatuba, in coffeegrowing region; cotton ginning, sawmilling, distilling, manioc-flour milling.

Coroatá (kooroōätä'), city (pop. 3,452), N central Maranhão, Brazil, on São Luís–Teresina RR, on left bank of Itapecuru R. and 110 mi. S of São Luís; cotton and sugar growing. Road to Barra do Corda.

Corocito (kōrōsē'tō), abandoned village, Colón dept., N Honduras, in Aguán R. valley, 15 mi. SE of Trujillo; rail junction; rice, sugar cane, bananas.

Corocoro (kōrōkō'rō), city (pop. c.6,900), ⊙ Pacajes prov., La Paz dept., W Bolivia, on high plateau 55 mi. SSW of La Paz, on spur of Arica–La Paz RR; alt. 13,190 ft.; major copper-mining center.

Coroico (kōroi'kō), city (pop. c.7,500), ⊙ Nor Yungas prov., La Paz dept., W Bolivia, 35 mi. NE of La Paz, on road; alt. 5,659 ft. Subtropical agr. center for coca, coffee, cacao, fruit; tourist resort. Has town hall, noted colonial church.

Coroico River, La Paz dept., W Bolivia, rises in several branches in outlier of Cordillera de La Paz, near Coroico; flows c.60 mi. N, past Caranavi, joining Mapiri R. at Puerto Ballivián to form Kaka R.

Coromandel (kooroomändĕl'), city (pop. 1,953), W Minas Gerais, Brazil, near Goiás border, 100 mi. NNE of Uberaba; center of well-known diamond-washing region; platinum and vanadium deposits. In 1938, the 727-carat Presidente Vargas diamond was found here.

Coromandel (kŏ"rōmăn'dŭl), township (pop. 721), ⊙ Coromandel co. (□ 439; pop. 2,271), N N.Isl., New Zealand, 42 mi. ENE of Auckland, on 50-mi.-long peninsula forming E shore of Firth of Thames; gold-mining center.

Coromandel Coast, E coast of Madras, India, bet. Point Calimere (S) and Kistna R. (N); c.450 mi. long; contains Cauvery R. delta and mouths of Ponnaiyar, Palar, and Penner rivers; subject to cyclones during NE monsoon (Oct.–April). Has no natural harbors; chief ports (S to N) are Negapatam, Cuddalore, Pondicherry, and Madras. Name believed to derive from *Cholamandalam* [Tamil, =Chola country] for the Cholas, a leading sea-going dynasty from early Christian era to mid-11th cent. Sometimes called CARNATIC coast.

Coron, Greece: see KORONE.

Coron, town, Philippines: see BUSUANGA ISLAND.

Corona (kŭrō'nŭ). **1** City (pop. 10,223), Riverside co., S Calif., 13 mi. SW of Riverside; ships citrus fruit, especially lemons; mfg. (pottery, glass, orchard equipment, chemicals). Sand, gravel, clay quarrying. Inc. 1896. **2** Village (pop. 530), Lincoln co., central N.Mex., 45 mi. NNE of Carrizozo; alt. c.6,660 ft. Trade and shipping point in bean and livestock area. Gallinas Peak 10 mi. W. Copper, lead, zinc mined near by. **3** A section of N Queens borough of New York city, SE N.Y.; residential; mfg. (clothing, scientific instruments, wood products, machinery). **4** Town (pop. 191), Roberts co., NE S.Dak., 26 mi. SE of Sisseton.

Corona, La (lä kōrō'nä), Andean peak in Mérida state, W Venezuela, in Sierra Nevada de Mérida N of La Columna peak, 10 mi. ESE of Mérida. Consists of 2 peaks: Humboldt (16,214 ft.), a name sometimes given to entire massif; and Bompland (16,040 ft.).

Corona, Villa, Mexico: see VILLA CORONA.

Coronaca (kŏ'rŭnē"kŭr, –kŭ), town (1940 pop. 192), Greenwood co., NW S.C., 6 mi. NE of Greenwood.

Coronada, La (lä kōrōnä'dhä), town (pop. 3,192), Badajoz prov., W Spain, 36 mi. E of Mérida; olives, grapes, livestock; mfg. of tiles.

Corona del Mar (kŭrō'nŭ dĕl mär'), resort village (pop. c.1,000), Orange co., S Calif., on Newport Bay, 10 mi. S of Santa Ana.

Coronado (kŏrŭnä'dō), residential and resort city (pop. 12,700), San Diego co., S Calif., on peninsula (Coronado Beach) across San Diego Bay from San Diego; fine beaches. North Isl. naval air station is adjacent. Inc. 1890.

Coronado, San Isidro de, Costa Rica: see SAN ISIDRO, San José prov.

Coronado Bay (kōrōnä'dō), bight of the Pacific in S Costa Rica, bet. Quepos and Osa Peninsula; 60 mi. wide, 20 mi. long. Receives Diquís R. Its ports are Dominical and La Uvita.

Coronado Beach (kŏrŭnä'dō), resort city (1940 pop. 328), Volusia co., NE Fla., on Atlantic coast, near New Smyrna Beach.

Coronado Islands or **Los Coronados** (lōs kōrōnä'dōs), small archipelago (□ 3) off Pacific coast of Lower California, NW Mexico, 20 mi. SSW of San Diego, Calif.; 4 barren rocks, rising to 672 ft. Guano deposits. Known for deep-sea fishing.

Coronados, Los, isls. of Mexico: see CORONADO ISLANDS.

Coronados Gulf (kōrōnä'dōs), inlet of the Pacific, S Chile, N of Chiloé Isl.; connected E with Gulf of Ancud by Chacao Strait. Receives Maullín R.

Coronanco (kōrōnäng'kō), officially Santa María Coronanco, town (pop. 2,072), Puebla, central Mexico, on railroad and 8 mi. NW of Puebla; cereals, maguey, stock.

Coronation, town (pop. 633), SE Alta., 100 mi. E of Red Deer; grain elevators, dairying. In coal- and oil-bearing region.

Coronation Gulf, SW Franklin Dist., Northwest Territories, arm (130 mi. long, 50–70 mi. wide) of the Arctic Ocean, separating Victoria Isl. (N) from Mackenzie Dist.; 67°42'–68°35'N 108°50'–113°30'W. Leads from Dolphin and Union Strait (W) to Queen Maud Gulf (E). Bathurst Inlet extends 120 mi. S. Gulf receives Coppermine R. at Coppermine village. It forms part of Northwest Passage through the Arctic Archipelago; passage was 1st completed by Roald Amundsen, 1903–06.

Coronation Island (30 naut. mi. long, 3–8 naut. mi. wide), largest of South Orkney Isls., in the South Atlantic; 60°37'S 45°30'W. Discovered 1821.

Coronda (kōrōn'dä), town (pop. estimate 4,000), ⊙ San Jerónimo dept. (□ 1,665; 1947 pop. 57,736), E Santa Fe prov., Argentina, on arm of the Paraná R. and 26 mi. SSW of Santa Fe; rail junction; agr. center (flax, corn, wheat, alfalfa, vegetables, livestock).

Coronda, Lake (□ 24), E Santa Fe prov., Argentina, formed by an arm of Paraná R. 25 mi. S of Santa Fe; 10 mi. long.

Corone, Greece: see KORONE.

Corone, Gulf of, Greece: see MESSENIA, GULF OF.

Coronea (kŏrùnē'ù), anc. town of Boeotia, Greece, 7 mi. SE of Levadia. Here the Thebans defeated (447 B.C.) the Athenians, and the Spartans under Agesilaus II won a victory (394 B.C.) over the Thebans and their allies. On site is modern village of Koroneia or Koronia (pop. 960), formerly called Koutoumoula.

Coronea, Lake, Greece: see KORONEIA, LAKE.

Coronel (kōrōnĕl'), town (pop. 14,799), ⊙ Coronel dept. (□ 467; pop. 71,613), Concepción prov., S central Chile, port on the Pacific (Arauco Gulf), 15 mi. SSW of Concepción; 37°2'S 73°8'W. Important coal-mining and shipping center, with a good harbor, it is chief coaling station on the Chilean coast. Principal mines at Schwager (N). Mfg.: flour mills, soap factory. Agr. products: cereals, cotton, wine; timber. In First World War, the Ger. Admiral von Spee defeated (Nov. 1, 1914) a Br. squadron off Coronel.

Coronel Aguirre, Argentina: see VILLA GOBERNADOR GÁLVEZ.

Coronel Bogado (bōgä'dō), town (pop. estimate 800), SE Santa Fe prov., Argentina, 25 mi. S of Rosario; agr. center (corn, flax, alfalfa, potatoes). Formerly Pueblo Navarro.

Coronel Bogado, town (dist. pop. 12,061), Itapúa dept., SE Paraguay, on railroad and 28 mi. WNW of Encarnación; lumbering, processing, and agr. center (tobacco, rice, cotton, fruit, stock).

Coronel Brandsen (brän'sĕn), **1** Town (pop. 3,692), ⊙ Brandsen dist. (□ 439; pop. 7,934), NE Buenos Aires prov., Argentina, on Samborombón R. and 24 mi. SW of La Plata; rail junction; agr. center (corn, oats, flax, livestock); dairying.

Coronel Dorrego (dôrā'gō). **1** Town (pop. 6,865), ⊙ Coronel Dorrego dist. (□ 2,315; pop. 21,420), S Buenos Aires prov., Argentina, 55 mi. E of Bahía Blanca; agr. center (grain, flax, sheep, cattle); flour milling. **2** Town (pop. 16,527), Mendoza prov., Argentina, just E of Mendoza. Also called Dorrego.

Coronel Eugenio Garay (ĕōōhä'nyō gärī'), town (dist. pop. 6,238), Guairá dept., S Paraguay, on railroad and 20 mi. SE of Villarrica, in agr. area (sugar cane, fruit, cattle).

Coronel Fabriciano (kōōrōōnĕl' fùbrēsyä'nōō), city (pop. 1,417), E central Minas Gerais, Brazil, on Piracicaba R. near its influx into the Rio Doce, on railroad and 90 mi. ENE of Belo Horizonte; site of new, special-steel plant; coke ovens. Manganese deposits.

Coronel Juan J. Gômez (kōrōnĕl' hwän' hō'tā gō'mĕs), village (pop. c.500), N Río Negro natl. territory, Argentina, in Río Negro valley (irrigation area), on railroad and 7 mi. W of Fuerte General Roca; wine making, dried-fruit processing; fruit, poultry, livestock. Has agr. school and research station.

Coronel L. Rosales, district, Argentina: see PUNTA ALTA.

Coronel Martínez (märtē'nĕs), town (dist. pop. 6,069), Guairá dept., S Paraguay, on railroad and 10 mi. W of Villarrica; sugar-growing and -refining center; stock raising.

Coronel Moldes (mōl'dĕs). **1** Town, Córdoba prov., Argentina: see MOLDES. **2** Town (pop. estimate 1,000), S central Salta prov., Argentina, on railroad and 35 mi. S of Salta; agr. center (tobacco, pepper, cotton, corn, wheat, alfalfa, livestock); flour mills. Has experimental farm. Formerly San Bernardo de Díaz.

Coronel Oviedo (ōvyä'dō), town (dist. pop. 34,681), ⊙ Caaguazú dept., S central Paraguay, 75 mi. E of Asunción; 25°25'S 56°28'W. Trading, lumbering, processing, and agr. center (oranges, tobacco, sugar cane, livestock). Sawmilling, sugar refining, oil of petitgrain extracting. Founded 1758.

Coronel Portillo, province, Peru: see PUCALLPA.

Coronel Pringles, department, Argentina: see CUATRO DE JUNIO.

Coronel Pringles (prĭng'glĕs). **1** City (pop. 12,727), ⊙ Coronel Pringles dist. (□ 2,032; pop. 23,601), S Buenos Aires prov., Argentina, 70 mi. NE of Bahía Blanca. Rail junction (railroad shops); stock raising; meat packing, dairying, winegrowing; grain elevator. Sometimes Pringles. **2** Village (pop. estimate 1,000), E Río Negro natl. territory, Argentina, on the Río Negro and 45 mi. NW of Viedma; alfalfa, fruit, wine, livestock. Sometimes Pringles.

Coronel Suárez (swä'rĕs), city (pop. 11,055), ⊙ Coronel Suárez dist. (□ 2,216; pop. 38,967), W central Buenos Aires prov., Argentina, 90 mi. NNE of Bahía Blanca; rail junction; agr. center (sheep, cattle); dairying, flour milling.

Coronel Vidal (vēdäl'), town (pop. 3,842), ⊙ Mar Chiquita dist. (□ 1,300; pop. 12,377), SE Buenos Aires prov., Argentina, 40 mi. NNE of Mar del Plata, near Mar Chiquita (lagoon of Atlantic Ocean); agr. center (flax, oats, wheat, livestock); dairying.

Coroneo (kōrōnā'ō), town (pop. 1,097), Guanajuato, central Mexico, 30 mi. SSE of Querétaro; alt. 6,519 ft.; grain, sugar cane, vegetables, livestock.

Corongo (kōrōng'gō), city (pop. 2,325), Ancash dept., W central Peru, in Cordillera Occidental, 12 mi. SE of Cabana; alt. 10,472 ft.; wheat, corn, alfalfa.

Coroni (kōrō'nē), town (pop. c.4,400), La Paz dept., W Bolivia, on W slopes of Eastern Cordillera of the Andes, near La Paz R., and 25 mi. SE of La Paz; fodder crops.

Coronie, district, Du. Guiana: see TOTNESS.

Coronil, El (ĕl kōrōnēl'), town (pop. 6,977), Seville prov., SW Spain, 29 mi. SE of Seville; grain, olive center. Has Moorish and Roman remains.

Coron Island, Philippines: see BUSUANGA ISLAND.

Coropuna, Nudo (nōō'dō kōrōpōō'nä), snow-capped Andean massif, Arequipa dept., S Peru, in Cordillera Occidental, 18 mi. N of Chuquibamba; has several peaks, highest rising to 21,696 ft.

Çorovodë (chôrôvô'dù) or **Çorovoda** (chôrôvô'dä), village, S central Albania, on Osum R. and 20 mi. SE of Berat; lignite mining. Sometimes called Skrapar or Skrapari, for surrounding dist.

Corowa (kŏ'rùwù), municipality (pop. 2,751), S New South Wales, Australia, on Murray R. and 165 mi. WSW of Canberra, on Victoria border; sheep and agr. center.

Corozal, district, Br. Honduras: see NORTHERN DISTRICT.

Corozal (kôrùzăl'), town (pop. 2,190), ⊙ Northern Dist., Br. Honduras, port on Chetumal Bay of Caribbean Sea, and 60 mi. NNW of Belize. Sugar milling, mfg. of mocassins and rum; fisheries. Exports coconuts, sugar, corn. Lighthouse. Has R.C. and Anglican churches. Until early 1940s, capital of former Corozal dist.

Corozal (kōrōsäl'), town (pop. 4,519), Bolívar dept., N Colombia, 80 mi. SSE of Cartagena; cattle-raising center. Old colonial town.

Corozal, village, Puntarenas prov., W Costa Rica, small Pacific port on Gulf of Nicoya, on Nicoya Peninsula, 21 mi. W of Puntarenas; lumbering.

Corozal, military reservation, Balboa dist., S Panama Canal Zone, on transisthmian railroad and 2 mi. NW of Panama city. Has military hosp. and a mental hosp.

Corozal, town (pop. 2,428), N central Puerto Rico, 15 mi. SW of San Juan, in tobacco- and fruit-growing region; fruit and vegetable canning. Gold, platinum, manganese, and copper deposits in vicinity.

Corpen Aike, department, Argentina: see SANTA CRUZ, town.

Corps (kôr), village (pop. 854), Isère dept., SE France, in upper Drac R. valley, 19 mi. NNW of Gap, on Grenoble-Gap road, in Dauphiné Alps; alt. 3,074 ft. On Drac R., 2 mi. W is SAUTET DAM. Basilica of Notre-Dame-de-la-Salette (built 19th cent.), a pilgrimage center, is 3.5 mi. NNE (alt. 5,807 ft.).

Corpus (kôr'pōōs), village (pop. estimate 1,500), S Misiones natl. territory, Argentina, near Alto Paraná R., 30 mi. NE of Posadas; farming center (corn, maté, sugar cane, tobacco, citrus fruit, cassava); sugar refining.

Corpus, El, Honduras: see EL CORPUS.

Corpus Christi (kôr'pùs krĭ'stē), city (1940 pop. 57,301; 1950 pop. 108,287), ⊙ Nueces co., S Texas, on Corpus Christi Bay at entrance to Nueces Bay, c.125 mi. SE of San Antonio; an important port, on Gulf Intracoastal Waterway and deepwater channel (completed 1926) to Gulf of Mexico at Aransas Pass. Port of entry; commercial, processing, distributing center for wide area. Ships cotton, fish, fruit, petroleum, zinc, sulphur, chemicals. Has oil refineries and carbon-black mfg. (supplied by local fields, pipelines from others), zinc refinery (ore from Mexico), foundries, alkali-chemicals and cement plants, sorghum-processing plant (starch, dextrose, feed), canneries, cotton gins, cottonseed-oil mills, creameries; mfg. of oil-field supplies, paint. Year-round resort, with fine beaches, fishing. Seat of Del Mar Col., Univ. of Corpus Christi. Huge naval air station (built 1941) caused boom in Second World War. Trading post founded here 1840 on Corpus Christi Bay (discovered 1519) on land claimed by Texas and Mexico; became port and wagon-train terminus, boomed in Mexican War; captured (1862) by Federal troops in Civil War. Shipping of livestock, wool marketing, fisheries, agr. increased in late 19th cent.; development of oil and natural gas in area (1923–30) and improvement of port stimulated industrial and commercial growth.

Corpus Christi, Lake, Texas: see NUECES RIVER.

Corpus Christi Bay, S Texas, an arm of Gulf of Mexico, forming harbor of Corpus Christi; c.25 mi. long E–W, 3–10 mi. wide. Mustang Isl. lies bet. bay and the Gulf. Traversed by deepwater Corpus Christi ship channel and by Gulf Intracoastal Waterway, which links it to Aransas Bay (N), Laguna Madre (S). Supplies oyster shell to chemical plants. Nueces Bay is W arm, crossed by bridge bet. Corpus Christi and Portland; receives Nueces R.

Corpusty, agr. village and parish (pop. 434), N Norfolk, England, on Bure R. and 12 mi. E of Fakenham.

Corque (kôr'kā), town (pop. c.5,800), ⊙ Carangas prov., Oruro dept., W Bolivia, in the Altiplano, 45 mi. SW of Oruro, on road; alt. 12,270 ft.; potatoes, alpaca.

Corquín (kôrkēn'), town (pop. 2,605), Copán dept., W Honduras, 12 mi. SSW of Santa Rosa; trade center in coffee area; tobacco, sugar cane, livestock.

Corral (kôräl'), town (pop. 3,317), Valdivia prov., S central Chile, port on Corral Bay (small Pacific inlet) at mouth of Valdivia R., and 12 mi. SW of Valdivia; 39°53'S 73°29'W. Beach resort, port, and mfg. center (iron- and steelworks). Site of old Sp. fort (1642) and victory of Admiral Cochrane's Chilean forces over Spaniards (1818). Sometimes called Puerto de Corral.

Corral de Almaguer (kôräl' dā älmägär'), town (pop. 7,837), Toledo prov., central Spain, in New Castille, on Riánsares R., on highway to Cartagena and 30 mi. SE of Aranjuez; agr. and processing center in fertile upper La Mancha; cereals, saffron, grapes, potatoes, sheep; beekeeping. Olive-oil pressing, flour milling, cheese processing, lumbering.

Corral de Bustos (bōō'stōs), town (pop. 4,087), SE Córdoba prov., Argentina, 45 mi. S of Marcos Juárez; wheat, flax, corn, potatoes, cattle, hogs.

Corral de Calatrava (käläträ'vä), town (pop. 2,388), Ciudad Real prov., S central Spain, 11 mi. SW of Ciudad Real; olives, cereals, grapes, livestock; apiculture. Alcohol distilling, flour milling, olive-oil pressing.

Corrales (kôrä'lĕs), town (pop. 1,262), Boyacá dept., central Colombia, in Cordillera Oriental, on Chicamocha R. and 10 mi. NE of Sogamoso; alt. 8,113 ft. Cereals, cotton, potatoes, silk, livestock; flour milling, tanning.

Corrales, Peru: see SAN PEDRO DE LOS INCAS.

Corrales. 1 Residential village (pop. 1,467), Huelva prov., SW Spain, on Odiel R. estuary, opposite and 2½ mi. W of Huelva; terminus of mining railroad from Tharsis and La Zarza. Sawmilling. **2** Village (pop. 1,723), Zamora prov., NW Spain, 10 mi. S of Zamora; brandy distilling; lumbering; cereals, wine, livestock.

Corrales. 1 Rail station, Lavalleja dept., Uruguay: see JOSÉ PEDRO VARELA. **2** or **Minas de Corrales** (mē'näs dā), village, Rivera dept., NE Uruguay, on the Arroyo Corrales, on road, and 50 mi. SSE of Rivera. Gold placers; agr. products (grapes, vegetables).

Corrales, Arroyo, river, Rivera dept., NE Uruguay, rises in the Cuchilla de Santa Ana NNW of Yaguarí, flows 60 mi. SW, past Corrales, to the Arroyo Cuñapirú 7 mi. below Cuñapirú.

Corrales, Los (lōs), town (pop. 3,620), Seville prov., SW Spain, on SW slopes of the Sierra de Yeguas, 11 mi. SSE of Osuna; olive, grain center. Gypsum quarries, mineral springs.

Corrales de Buelna, Los (dhä bwĕl'nä), village (pop. 2,527), Santander prov., N Spain, 7 mi. S of Torrelavega; steel mill and metalworks. Mineral springs at Caldas de Besaya (2 mi. N).

Corralillo (kôrälē'yō), town (pop. 1,073), Las Villas prov., central Cuba, near N coast, on railroad and 35 mi. WNW of Sagua la Grande, in agr. region (sugar cane, fruit, cattle).

Corral Nuevo (kôräl' nwā'vō), village (pop. 200), Matanzas prov., W Cuba, on railroad and 5 mi. W of Matanzas; sugar cane, cattle.

Corral Peak (11,333 ft.), in Rocky Mts., Grand co., N Colo.

Correa (kōrā'ä), town (pop. estimate 1,500), Santa Fe prov., Argentina, 36 mi. W of Rosario; agr. center (corn, wheat, flax).

Correctionville, town (pop. 992), Woodbury co., W Iowa, on Little Sioux R. and 32 mi. E of Sioux City, in livestock and grain area; mfg. (concrete products, feed). Sand and gravel pits near by.

Correggio (kôr-rĕd'jô), town (pop. 3,856), Reggio nell'Emilia prov., Emilia-Romagna, N central Italy, 9 mi. ENE of Reggio nell'Emilia; wine sausage, pharmaceuticals. Has 16th-cent. palace. Antonio Allegri, called Correggio, b. here 1494.

Corregidor (kŭrĕ'gĭdôr", Sp. kôrĕhĕdhôr'), fortress island (□ 2), Philippines, at entrance to Manila Bay, off Bataan Peninsula, in Cavite prov. Isl. consists of roughly circular main section (1.5 mi. in diameter) from which projects a narrow E peninsula. Fortified by the Spaniards, it was taken over 1898 by the U.S. In the Second World War, with the fall of Bataan (April 9, 1942), Gen. Wainwright and his remaining forces withdrew to Corregidor and fought on until May 6, when he surrendered to the Japanese with 11,500 troops. The isl. passed 1947 to the Philippine republic.

Corregidora (kôrāhĕdō'rä), town (pop. 4,298), Querétaro, central Mexico, on central plateau, 4 mi. SW of Querétaro; alt. 6,014 ft. Agr. center (wheat, corn, alfalfa, sugar cane, beans, fruit, stock). Anc. Indian ruins. Shrine of Our Lady of Pueblito here. Called El Pueblito until 1946.

Correll (kŭrĕl'), village (pop. 130), Big Stone co., SW Minn., on Marsh L., near S.Dak. line, 15 mi. ESE of Ortonville.

Corrente (kôrĕn'tĭ), city (pop. 1,080), southernmost Piauí, Brazil, on N slope of Serra da Gurgueia, 275 mi. SSE of Floriano, near Bahia border; cattle raising.

Corrente River, SW Bahia, Brazil, rises in the Serra Geral de Goiás, flows c.180 mi. NE to the São Francisco (left bank) below Bom Jesus da Lapa. Navigable below Santa Maria da Vitória.

Correntes (kôrĕn'tĭs), city (pop. 4,114), E Pernambuco, NE Brazil, near Alagoas border, 20 mi. SE of Garanhuns; coffee, cotton, corn, livestock.

Correnti (kôr-rĕn'tē), islet in Mediterranean Sea just off SE extremity of Sicily, 5 mi. S of Pachino. S point is Cape Correnti; 36°38'N 15°5'E; lighthouse.

Correntina (kôrĕntē'nŭ), city (pop. 1,641), SW Bahia, Brazil, on headstream of Corrente R. and 120 mi. SW of Paratinga; livestock, beans, rice, sugar. Gold panning.

Correntoso, Argentina: see VILLA LA ANGOSTURA.

Correntoso, Lake (kōrĕntō'sō) (□ 6; alt. 2,660 ft.), in the Andes, SW Neuquén natl. territory, Argentina, in the lake dist., separated from L. Nahuel Huapí by narrow sandbank; c.10 mi. long.

Corrèze (kôrĕz'), department (□ 2,273; pop. 254,601), in Limousin, S central France; ⊙ Tulle. Located in Massif Central and crossed by Monts du Limousin. Brive Basin, a fertile lowland, in SW. Drained by deeply incised Dordogne, Vézère, and Corrèze rivers which power large hydroelectric plants at Le Saillant, Marèges, L'Aigle, and Rochele-Peyroux. Rye, barley, and cattle raising in Tulle area. Wheat, corn, early vegetables, tobacco, fruits, and truffles near Brive-la-Gaillarde. Horse and hog raising. Potatoes. Slate quarries near Allassac. Chief industries: fruit and vegetable preserving, tanning, textile milling. Tulle has natl. arms factory. Brive-la-Gaillarde (largest town) is commercial and communications center.

Corrèze, village (pop. 788), Corrèze dept., S central France, in Monts de Monédières, on Corrèze R. and 9 mi. NE of Tulle; furniture mfg.; sheep raising. Granite quarries near by.

Corrèze River, Corrèze dept., S central France, rises in Plateau of Millevaches 6 mi. W of Meymac, flows 55 mi. SW, past Tulle, to the Vézère below Brive-la-Gaillarde. Hydroelectric plant at Bar.

Corrib, Lough (lŏkh kŏ'rĭb), irregular lake (□ 68; 27 mi. long, 1–10 mi. wide; 28 ft. deep) in W Co. Galway and S Co. Mayo, Ireland; drains into Galway Bay by short stream with navigable channel, and is connected with Lough Mask (N) by partly subterranean channel. Lough is navigable and is transportation route for produce of riparian region. Numerous isls. include Inchagoill, 4 mi. SSW of Cong, with remains of 2 anc. churches.

Corrick's Ford, W.Va.: see PARSONS.

Corridonia (kôr-rēdô'nyä), town (pop. 2,921), Macerata prov., The Marches, central Italy, 5 mi. SSE of Macerata; mfg. (shoes, furniture). Formerly Pausula.

Corrie (kŏ'rē), fishing village on E coast of Arran isl., Buteshire, Scotland, on the Firth of Clyde, 5 mi. N of Brodick.

Corrientes (kōryĕn'tĕs), province (□ 33,544; pop. 525,463), NE Argentina, in Mesopotamia; ⊙ Corrientes. Bounded E by Uruguay R. (Brazil border), N by Alto [upper] Paraná R. (Paraguay border), W by Paraná R. Includes the Esteros del Iberá (swamps) with the lakes Iberá and Luna. Marshy, fertile area with subtropical, humid climate; forests in N. Agr.: rice (N), cotton (NW), fruit, especially citrus (W, NE), tobacco (NW), corn (S), tung trees (E), maté (center and N); also sugar cane, olives, peanuts. Stock raising: sheep (S), cattle in whole prov. Rural industries: limestone and sandstone quarries (Mercedes, Monte Caseros), lumbering and sawmilling, tobacco processing, preparation of maté, pressing of tung oil, sugar refining. Some industries (tanning, meat packing) concentrated in Corrientes. Goya is known for cheese mfg.

Corrientes, city (pop. 56,425), ⊙ Corrientes prov. and Corrientes dept. (□ c.170; pop. 76,908), NE Argentina, port on Paraná R. 25 mi. below mouth of Paraguay R., opposite Barranqueras (port for Resistencia, Chaco prov.), on railroad and 480 mi. N of Buenos Aires, 170 mi. SSW of Asunción (Paraguay); 27°27'S 58°48'W. Commercial and agr. center. Exports tobacco, cotton, sugar cane, rice, maté, citrus fruit, hardwood, hides, livestock. Production of frozen meat, vegetable oil, ceramics, soap, footwear, textiles; tanning, sawmilling, flour milling, shipbuilding, fresh-water fishing. In farming, fruitgrowing, and stock-raising area. Has administrative bldgs., natl. col., mus., acad. of arts, seismographic station, basilica of Las Mercedes with Renaissance façade, pilgrimage church of La Cruz. City was founded 1588. Formerly sometimes called San Juan de Vera and San Juan de Corrientes.

Corrientes, Cape, headland on Atlantic Ocean, in SE Buenos Aires prov., Argentina, at Mar del Plata; 38°15'S.

Corrientes, Cape, on Pacific coast of Chocó dept., W Colombia, 65 mi. WSW of Quibdó; 5°28'N 77°33'W.

Corrientes, Cape, headland of S Guanahacabibes Peninsula, W Cuba, 30 mi. E of Cape San Antonio across Corrientes Bay; 21°46'N 84°30'W. Lighthouse.

Corrientes, Cape, Pacific headland, Jalisco, Mexico, at S entrance to Banderas Bay; 20°24'N 105°43'W.

Corrientes River, E Corrientes prov., Argentina, rises in the Esteros del Iberá (marshes), flows 150 mi. SW, through L. Itatí, to Paraná R. at Esquina.

Corrientes River, Loreto dept., NE Peru, rises in E Andean outliers near Ecuador border, meanders c.350 mi. SE and E through virgin tropical forests to Tigre R. at 3°42'S 74°45'W. Navigable for c.85 mi.

Corrievreckan or **Corrievrekin,** Scotland: see CORRYVRECKAN.

Corrigan, town (pop. 1,417), Polk co., E Texas, 24 mi. S of Lufkin; lumbering center; cattle. Inc. 1938.

Corriganville (kŏ'rĭgŭnvĭl), village (pop. c.500), Allegany co., W Md., on Wills Creek and 3 mi. NW of Cumberland; limestone quarries.

Corrigin (kŏ'rĭgĭn), town (pop. 409), SW Western Australia, 120 mi. ESE of Perth; rail junction; wheat, oats; orchards.

Corringham (kŏ'rŭnŭm), town and parish (pop. 1,897), S Essex, England, near the Thames, 7 mi. NE of Tilbury; agr. market.

Corropoli (kôr-rô'pôlē), village (pop. 913), Teramo prov., Abruzzi e Molise, S central Italy, 14 mi. NNE of Teramo; straw-hat mfg.

Corrora, Caroline Isls.: see KOROR.

Corrubedo, Cape (kôrōōvā'dhō), on Atlantic coast of Galicia, La Coruña prov., NW Spain, 25 mi. NW of Pontevedra; 42°35'N 9°5'W.

Corry (kŏ'rē), city (pop. 7,911), Erie co., NW Pa., 25 mi. SE of Erie; furniture, metal products, aircraft parts, leather, drugs. Settled 1795, inc. as borough 1863, as city 1866.

Corryong (kŏ"rēyŏng', –yông'), village (pop. 808), NE Victoria, Australia, 195 mi. NE of Melbourne, near Murray R.; dairy plant.

Corryvreckan, Corrievreckan, or **Corrievrekin** (kŏ"-rēvrĕ'kŭn), narrow strait and whirlpool bet. isls. of Jura (S) and Scarba (N), Inner Hebrides, Argyll, Scotland.

Corse, island, France: see CORSICA.

Corse, Cape (kôrs), anc. *Promontorium Sacrum,* northernmost tip of Corsica, 22 mi. N of Bastia and 100 mi. SSE of Genoa; 43°1'N 9°28'E. Finger-shaped Cape Corse peninsula (25 mi. long, 8 mi. wide), formed by N spur of central Corsican mtn. range, is island's most fertile area (vineyards, orchards, olive groves). At its base are Bastia (E) and Saint Florent (W). Just off Cape Corse is Giraglia islet (lighthouse).

Corsen, Pointe de (pwĕt dŭ kôrsĕn'), westernmost headland of France, in Finistère dept., 14 mi. WNW of Brest; 48°25'N 4°48'W.

Corsewall Point, Scotland: see GALLOWAY.

Corsham (kôr'sŭm), town and parish (pop. 3,754), W Wiltshire, England, 8 mi. ENE of Bath; agr. market in dairying region; stone quarrying. Has Norman church.

Corsica (kôr'sĭkŭ), Fr. *Corse* (kôrs), anc. *Cyrnus,* island (□ 3,367; pop. 267,873) of the Mediterranean, a department of metropolitan France, S of Gulf of Genoa and separated from Sardinia (S) by Strait of Bonifacio. Leaf-shaped, with stem-like Cape Corse peninsula (25 mi. long) pointing toward Genoa (100 mi. NNW), it extends 114 mi. S from Cape Corse (43°1'N) to Cape Pertusato (41°21'N); maximum width, 52 mi. Straight E coastline on Tyrrhenian Sea, with island's only important lowland (Aleria plain) near mouth of Tavignano R. Rocky W coast, into which descend several parallel mtn. ranges, is much indented (Gulfs of Porto, Sagone, Ajaccio, Valinco; Capes Senetosa, di Muro, de Feno, Rosso, and Pointe de la Revellata). Interior consists of a jumble of short mtn. chains, culminating in Monte Cinto (8,891 ft.) and Monte Rotondo (8,612 ft.). Principal streams are the Golo and Tavignano, both flowing E into Tyrrhenian Sea. Corsica has Mediterranean climate with Alpine influences in interior, where several peaks are snow-capped. Vegetation on lower slopes, consisting of almost impenetrable shrubbery [Fr. *maquis*], provided ideal hideout for bandits for which isl. has acquired notoriety. Olives, citrus fruit, and wine grown on Cape Corse peninsula, near W coast, and in some mtn. valleys. Primeval forests (though now greatly reduced) provide chestnuts and, for export, cork and lumber. Sheep and goats raised on upland pastures. Tuna, lobster, anchovy, and coral fisheries off N and W coasts. Mineral resources include antimony (Méria), arsenic (Matra), and asbestos mines (Canari), granite and marble quarries. Industry, aside from agr. processing, practically nonexistent. Chief towns, except Sartène and Corte, are seaports: Ajaccio (on W coast), Bastia (largest city, at base of Cape Corse peninsula), Calvi and L'Île-Rousse (on NW coast nearest France), Bonifacio (facing Sicily), and Porto-Vecchio. Poor communications in interior. Bastia, Ajaccio, Calvi, and Porto-Vecchio linked by railroad. Language spoken outside of chief towns is an Ital. dialect. Bloody feuds [Ital. *vendetta*], carried out by the *maquis,* were traditional until substantially suppressed by Fr. government. After having belonged to Romans (3d cent. B.C.–5th cent. A.D.), the Vandals (5th–9th cent.), and the Arabs (9th–11th cent.), it was ceded by the pope, who had claimed it, to Pisa in 1077. Pisans expelled (1312) by Genoese whose rule was marked by unrest. In 1755, Pasquale Paoli led a successful insurrection and from his capital at Corte controlled most of isl. until Fr. intervention led in 1768 to cession of Corsica to France. In 1769 Napoleon Bonaparte b. at Ajaccio. In 1794, Paoli having succeeded in expelling the French, Corsica voted to join Br. crown; recovered by France in 1796, and tacitly confirmed in latter's possession by Congress of Vienna. In Second World War, isl. occupied by Ital. and Ger. troops in 1942. In 1943 the people revolted and seized Ajaccio; a Free French task force came to their aid. Liberation of isl. completed by Allies in Oct., 1943, after which it became a base for Allied operations in Italy and S France.

Corsica. 1 Borough (pop. 421), Jefferson co., W central Pa., 7 mi. WNW of Brookville. **2** Town (pop. 551), Douglas co., SE S.Dak., 8 mi. NNW of Armour; dairy products, livestock, poultry, grain.

Corsicana (kôrsĭkă'nŭ), city (pop. 19,211), ⊙ Navarro co., E central Texas, c.50 mi. SSE of Dallas; commercial, shipping, processing center for agr. region (chiefly cotton; also cattle, poultry, grain, pecans); oil field near. Cotton, poultry, dairy-products processing, oil refining, textile, flour, cottonseed-oil milling, mfg. of oil-field machinery and supplies, steel products, refrigeration and farm equipment, brick, mattresses, clothing. Seat of Navarro Jr. Col., 2 childrens' homes. Inc. 1848. First commercial oil well (1895), 1st oil refinery (1898) in Texas were here.

Corsico (kôr'sēkô), town (pop. 6,987), Milano prov., Lombardy, N Italy, 4 mi. SW of Milan; paper mill, casein factory.

Corson, county (□ 2,525; pop. 6,168), N S.Dak., on N.Dak. line; ⊙ McIntosh. Agr. and cattle-raising area, with Standing Rock Indian Reservation in NE; drained by Grand R. and numerous creeks. Lignite mines; wheat, flax. Formed 1909.

Corsons Inlet, SE N.J., passage from the Atlantic to Ludlam Bay (SW) and Intracoastal Waterway channel, 4 mi. N of Sea Isle City; crossed by highway bridge.

Corstorphine (kôrstôr'fĭn), W suburb (pop. 7,381) of Edinburgh, Scotland.

Cort Adeler, Cape, or **Cape Cort Adelaer** (both: kôrt' ä'dŭlŭr), SE Greenland, on the Atlantic; 61°49'N 42°2'W. Rises to 2,313 ft. Meteorological and radio station.

Cortale (kôrtä'lĕ), town (pop. 4,091), Catanzaro prov., Calabria, S Italy, 11 mi. WSW of Catanzaro; olive oil, wine.

Cortazar (kôrtäsär'), city (pop. 9,044), Guanajuato, central Mexico, on central plateau, on Apaseo R. and 11 mi. WSW of Celaya; alt. 5,731; sugar-cane center.

Corte (kôrtā', It. kôr'tĕ), town (pop. 5,089), central Corsica, on Tavignano R. and 34 mi. NE of Ajaccio; alt. 1,300 ft. Largest inland town of isl., with trade in wine and cereals; produces brier pipestems. Large marble quarries near by. Castle rock (alt. 1,640 ft.) is crowned by 15th-cent. citadel. Seat of Paoli's insurgent govt. (1755–68).

Corteconcepción (kôrtākōn-thĕp-thyōn'), town (pop. 595), Huelva prov., SW Spain, in the Sierra de Aracena, 2½ mi. E of Aracena; chestnuts, walnuts, olives, grapes, timber, hogs. Charcoal burning. Hydroelectric plant near by.

Corte de Peleas (kôr'tā dhā pālā'äs), town (pop. 1,053), Badajoz prov., W Spain, in fertile Tierra de Barros, 14 mi. WNW of Almendralejo.

Corte do Pinto (kôr'tĭ dōō pēn'tōō), village (pop. 1,411), Beja dist., S Portugal, 30 mi. SE of Beja, near Chanza R. (Sp. border); grain, sheep.

Cortegana (kôrtāgä'nä), town (pop. 4,688), Huelva prov., SW Spain, in Andalusia, in the Sierra Morena, 45 mi. N of Huelva; sulphur, copper, graphite mining; sawmilling; mfg. of vegetable oil, bottle corks, salt pork, liquor. Potteries. The region produces cork, timber (chestnut, walnut), and livestock.

Cortelazor (kôrtälä-thōr'), town (pop. 640), Huelva prov., SW Spain, in the Sierra Morena, 5 mi. NW of Aracena; acorns, chestnuts, walnuts, olives, cereals, truck products, timber, livestock.

Corte Madera (kôr'tă mŭdâ'rŭ), residential town (pop. 1,933), Marin co., W Calif., N of San Francisco and 3 mi. S of San Rafael. Inc. 1916.

Cortemaggiore (kôr"tĕmäd-jô'rĕ), town (pop. 1,859), Piacenza prov., Emilia-Romagna, N central Italy, on Arda R. and 12 mi. ESE of Piacenza; agr. machinery. Has church with altarpieces by Pordenone. Oil and gas fields discovered near by, 1949.

Cortemarck, Belgium: see KORTEMARK.

Cortenuova (kôr"tĕnwô'vä), village (pop. 758), Bergamo prov., Lombardy, N Italy, 12 mi. SSE of Bergamo. Noted for victory of Frederick II over Lombard League in 1237.

Corteolona (kôr"tĕôlô'nä), village (pop. 1,493), Pavia prov., Lombardy, N Italy, on Olona R. and 11 mi. ESE of Pavia.

Cortês (kôrtās'), town (pop. 1,184), E Pernambuco, NE Brazil, 55 mi. SW of Recife; terminus (1948) of rail spur from Ribeirão (15 mi. E).

Cortés (kôrtās'), department (□ 2,350; 1950 pop. 146,291), NW Honduras, on Gulf of Honduras; ⊙ San Pedro Sula. Bounded NW by Guatemala, E by Comayagua and Ulúa rivers; mountainous (W and S; sierras de Omoa and Colinas); includes section of Sula Valley (E). Drained by Chamelecón and Ulúa rivers; includes part of L. Yojoa (S). One of chief banana areas of Honduras; also produces rice, sugar cane, fruit, vegetables, cotton (in Sula Valley), coconuts (on coastal plain), coffee, grain, beans (on hillsides). Livestock raising is important. Hardwood lumbering, chiefly mahogany. Served by main N-S railroad and highway joining at Potrerillos, and by network of plantation rail lines. Main commercial and mfg. centers are San Pedro Sula and Puerto Cortés, a major port. Formed 1893 out of Santa Bárbara dept.

Cortes (kôr'tĕs), town (pop. 2,110), Navarre prov., N Spain, on Imperial Canal and 13 mi. SE of Tudela; sugar and flour mills; cereals, fruit, sugar beets, wine.

Cortés, Ensenada de (ĕnsänä'dä dā kôrtās'), shallow inlet of SW Cuba, 20 mi. SW of Pinar del Río. The Laguna de Cortés is on its SW shore.

Cortés, Sea of, Mexico: see CALIFORNIA, GULF OF.

Cortés Bay, NW Honduras, inlet of Gulf of Honduras, in Cortés dept.; 3 mi. wide, 3 mi. long. Puerto Cortés is on N shore.

Cortes de la Frontera (kôr'tĕs dhā lä frōntä'rä), town (pop. 2,135), Málaga prov., S Spain, on S slopes of the Sierra de Ronda, 12 mi. SW of Ronda; olives, cereals, fruit, livestock. Its rail station is 2 mi. S on Guadiaro R.

Cortez (kôrtĕz'), town (pop. 2,680), ⊙ Montezuma co., SW Colo., 40 mi. W of Durango; alt. 6,198 ft. Trade center in fruit, grain, livestock region; dairy products, timber. Mesa Verde Natl. Park, Yucca House Natl. Monument, and Consolidated Ute Indian Reservation near by. Founded 1887, inc. 1902.

Cortez Mountains, N central Nev., in Eureka co., S of Humboldt R.; Mt. Tenabo (9,162 ft.), highest point, is 38 mi. SSE of Battle Mountain town.

Corticella (kôrtēchĕl'lä), town (pop. 2,228), Bologna prov., Emilia-Romagna, N central Italy, 3 mi. N of Bologna; liquor. Mineral springs.

Cortina d'Ampezzo (kôrtē'nä dämpĕ'tsô), town (pop. 1,552), Belluno prov., Veneto, N Italy, in center of the Dolomites, 45 mi. SE of Brenner Pass, 28 mi. N of Belluno. A leading summer and winter resort (alt. 3,970 ft.) of Ital. Alps; mfg. (shoes, furniture, wrought-iron products).

Cortland, county (□ 502; pop. 37,158), central N.Y.; ⊙ Cortland. Dairying and farming area (beans, potatoes, truck, clover); poultry raising; maple sugar. Diversified mfg. especially at Cortland. Drained by Tioughnioga R. Formed 1808.

Cortland. 1 Town (pop. 398), De Kalb co., N Ill., 22 mi. NW of Aurora, in rich agr. area. **2** Village (pop. 288), Gage co., SE Nebr., 20 mi. S of Lincoln; dairy and poultry produce, grain, livestock. **3** City (pop. 18,152), ⊙ Cortland co., central N.Y., on Tioughnioga R. and 30 mi. S of Syracuse; railroad center, in rich agr. area; dairy products, potatoes, cabbage. Mfg.: wire cloth; wood, metal, and paper products; sporting goods, clothing, trucks, burial vaults, chemicals, feed, flour, canned foods. Seat of a state teachers col. Settled 1791; inc. as a village in 1853, as a city in 1900. **4** Village (pop. 1,259), Trumbull co., NE Ohio, 15 mi. NNW of Youngstown, on Mosquito Creek Reservoir, in agr. area; flour, feed, handles, chemicals.

Cortona (kôrtô'nä), town (pop. 3,736), Arezzo prov., Tuscany, central Italy, on a hill N of L. Trasimeno, 14 mi. SSE of Arezzo; macaroni factory, hosiery mill. Has 13th-cent. palace (housing Etruscan mus.) and several churches with paintings by Fra Angelico and Luca Signorelli, who was b. here. One of 12 important Etruscan cities, with walls and a burial chamber of that period.

Corubal River (kōōrōōbäl'), longest river (c.300 mi.) of Port. Guinea, rises in the Fouta Djallon (Fr. Guinea), flows generally SW and joins Geba R. estuary 35 mi. E of Bissau. Interrupted by rapids. Also called Cocoli R.

Coruche (kōōrōō'shĭ), town (pop. 2,980), Santarém dist., central Portugal, on Sorraia R., on railroad and 21 mi. SSE of Santarém; agr. trade center; grain milling, cork processing.

Coruh (chôrōō'), Turk. *Çoruh*, prov. (□ 3,076; 1950 pop. 174,511), NE Turkey, on Black Sea; ⊙ Artvin. Bordered NE of USSR; drained by Coruh and Oltu rivers. Copper, lead, manganese; corn, tobacco. Formerly Artvin.

Coruh Mountains, Turkish *Çoruh*, NE Turkey, extend 110 mi. NE from Bayburt, with Coruh R. on NW; rise to 11,033 ft. in Deve Dag.

Coruh River, Turkish *Çoruh*, Rus. *Chorokh* (chôrôkh'), NE Turkey, rises in Coruh Mts. at Mt. Mescit 30 mi. W of Erzurum, flows 229 mi. NE, past Bayburt, Ispir, Artvin, and Borcka, into USSR, where it reaches Black Sea just S of Batum. Only 15 mi. of its course are in USSR. Sometimes spelled Zhorokh or Tchoruk.

Coruisk, Loch (lŏkh kŏrōōsk'), sea inlet on S coast of Skye, Inverness, Scotland, at foot of Cuillin Hills, 13 mi. S of Portree; extends 3 mi. inland.

Corullón (kōrōōlyōn'), town (pop. 1,251), Leon prov., NW Spain, 12 mi. WNW of Ponferrada; cereals, fruit, wine, livestock. Has 11th-cent. parochial church and ruins of 15th-cent. castle.

Corum or **Chorum** (both: chôrōōm'), Turkish *Çorum*, province (□ 4,245; 1950 pop. 342,290), N Turkey; ⊙ Corum. Drained by the Kizil Irmak. Mohair, wool, wheat, hemp.

Corum or **Chorum,** Turk. *Çorum*, town (1950 pop. 22,835), ⊙ Corum prov., N central Turkey, 115 mi. ENE of Ankara; earthenware, leather goods; wheat, barley, vetch, onions, mohair goats. An old town on the trade route from Kaysaria (Kayseri) to the Black Sea.

Corumbá (kôrōōmbä'). **1** City, Goiás, Brazil: see CORUMBÁ DE GOIÁS. **2** City (pop. 13,319), W Mato Grosso, Brazil, port on higher right bank of Paraguay R. and 250 mi. SSW of Cuiabá, in Paraguay flood plain, near Bolivia border; 19°0'S 57°38'W. Important distributing and shipping center at junction of railroad (almost completed in 1948) from São Paulo (E) with line from Santa Cruz (Bolivia; W). Transshipment point for regular Paraguay R. navigation upstream to Cuiabá, and downstream to Asunción (Paraguay) and Buenos Aires (Argentina). Ferry service to Puerto Suárez (10 mi. W in Bolivia) via Tamengo Canal. Exports all products of Brazilian interior and E Bolivian lowland, including dried meat, hides and skins, medicinal plants, rubber, lumber, gold, and diamonds. Enormous deposits of manganese and iron, mined since Second World War at Morro do Urucum (15 mi. SSE), shipped from Corumbá and Ladário (3 mi. E). City has new blast furnace, metalworks (chiefly for repair of rolling stock), lumber mills, and meat-packing plant. Customhouse, airport. Founded 1778; changed hands several times during war with Paraguay (1865–70).

Corumbá de Goiás (dĭ goi-äs'), city (pop. 986), S central Goiás, central Brazil, in the Serra dos Pireneus, 30 mi. N of Anápolis. Important rutile and diamond deposits along Corumbá R. near by. Gold 1st found here in 1774; placers no longer worked. Until 1944, called Corumbá.

Corumbaíba (kôrōōmbäē'bŭ), city (pop. 1,548), S Goiás, central Brazil, near Minas Gerais border, 38 mi. SW of Ipameri; cattle, hides, lard, rice. Diamond washings. Formerly spelled Corumbahyba.

Corumbalina, Brazil: see PIRES DO RIO.

Corumbá River (kôrōōmbä'), S Goiás, central Brazil, rises in the Serra dos Pireneus near Corumbá de Goiás, flows c.200 mi. S to the Paranaíba above Itumbiara. Diamond washings.

Coruña, La (lä kōrōō'nyä), or, often, in English, **Corunna** (kôrŭ'nŭ), province (□ 3,051; pop. 883,-090), NW Spain, in Galicia; ⊙ La Coruña. Bounded N and W by the Atlantic, S by Ulla R. Crossed by irregular, moderately elevated Galician Mts.; drained by many short rivers flowing N or W to the Atlantic; has rocky, deeply indented coast line formed by drowned valleys. Has greatest rainfall in Spain. Some tungsten, tin, and lignite are mined; but several mineral deposits, exploited in anc. times, are now abandoned. Fishing and fish processing are chief industries along coast, while stock raising (cattle, hogs, horses) and lumbering are carried on in mts. of interior. Agr. products include corn, rye, potatoes, vegetables, fruit, and some wine. Boatbuilding, tanning, meat processing; mfg. of dairy products, cotton and linen cloth, brandy, beer, candy. Chief cities: La Coruña, El Ferrol, Santiago, Betanzos.

Coruña, La, or, often, in English, **Corunna,** city (pop. 92,189), ⊙ La Coruña prov., in Galicia, NW Spain, Atlantic seaport on Coruña Bay (4 mi. long, 2–3 mi. wide), on N coast of Galicia, 320 mi. NW of Madrid; 43°22'N 8°24'W. Anc. fortifications are now dismantled. Consists of old town on promontory, and new sections on narrow isthmus (bet. Orzán Bay NW, and Coruña Bay SE) and on mainland; deep natural harbor on Coruña Bay, protected by breakwater and San Antón islet (former fort, now military prison), has shipyards and several piers. Exports fish, livestock, wine. Second largest fishing center of Spain, with large fish-processing plants. Tobacco (notably for cigars) and match factories, brewery, oil and sugar refineries, chemical works (acids, pharmaceuticals); boatbuilding, metalworking; also mfg. of rubber, glass, linen and cotton cloth, flour products, candy. Old town has two 12th–14th-cent. churches and tomb of Gen. Moore; new town has fine promenades and modern town hall. Houses have characteristic *miradores* or glazed window-balconies. On rock at NW end of peninsula is the Roman Tower of Hercules (157 ft.; lighthouse). The city, probably of Celtic origin, was occupied by the Romans; in Middle Ages was held by Moors and Normans; later flourished as cloth center and trading port with America. From La Coruña sailed the Sp. Armada in 1588, and in 1598 Drake sacked the city. In the Peninsular War, scene of battle (1809) when British under Moore (who was killed) escaped by sea after defeating the pursuing French. New economic prosperity dates from 18th cent. Formerly also called The Groyne.

Corunna (kôrŭ'nŭ). **1** Town (pop. 338), De Kalb co., NE Ind., 26 mi. N of Fort Wayne, in agr. area. **2** City (pop. 2,358), ⊙ Shiawassee co., S central Mich., on Shiawassee R. and 21 mi. W of Flint, in agr. area (beans, corn, wheat). Mfg.: refrigerator and radio cabinets, auto bodies, metal products, cigars, flour. Coal mining. Inc. as village 1858, as city 1869.

Corupá (kôrōōpä'), town (pop. 1,573), NE Santa Catarina, Brazil, on railroad and 25 mi. WSW of Joinvile. German agr. settlement. Until 1944, called Hansa.

Coruripe (kôrōōrē'pĭ), city (pop. 3,027), E Alagoas, NE Brazil, near the Atlantic, 30 mi. ENE of Penedo; grows sugar, cotton, and fruit (pineapples, mangoes).

Corvallis (kôrvă'lĭs), city (pop. 16,207), ⊙ Benton co., W Oregon, on Willamette R. and 28 mi. SSW of Salem, E of Coast Range; processing, trade center for agr., dairy, fruit, timber area. Seat of Oregon State Col.; hq. Siuslaw Natl. Forest. Settled 1846, platted 1851, inc. 1857.

Corveiro, Cape (kôrvā'rō), headland, Río de Oro, Sp. West Africa, 60 mi. N of Port-Étienne (Fr. West Africa); 21°48'N 16°58'W.

Corvey, Germany: see HÖXTER.

Corvo Island (kôr'vōō), smallest and northernmost isl. (□ 6.8; 1950 pop. 729) of Azores, in the Atlantic, forming, together with Flores Isl. (12 mi. S), the archipelago's W group; 39°42'N 31°7'W. Consists of a single extinct volcano (Monte Gordo, 2,549 ft.) whose crater floor (1 mi. wide) contains isl.-studded lake. Vila Nova de Corvo (on isl.'s SE shore) is only settlement; dairying, fishing, fish salting. Here Humboldt discovered (1749) what are believed to be Carthaginian coins of 3d or 4th cent. B.C. Corvo is part of Horta dist.

Corvol-l'Orgueilleux (kôrvôl'-lôrgûyû'), village (pop. 530), Nièvre dept., central France, 6 mi. SW of Clamecy; paper mill.

Corwen (kôr'wĕn), town and parish (pop. 2,534), NE Merioneth, Wales, on the Dee and 11 mi. NE of Bala; agr. market, angling resort. Has 13th-cent. church. Owen Glendower assembled his troops here before battle of Shrewsbury. Near by is prehistoric stone rampart of Caer Drewyn.

Corwin, village (pop. 326), Warren co., SW Ohio, 18 mi. SSE of Dayton and on Little Miami R.

Corwith, town (pop. 480), Hancock co., N Iowa, on Boone R. and 23 mi. N of Eagle Grove, in livestock and grain area; rail junction.

Corydon (kŏr'ĭdŭn). **1** Town (pop. 1,944), ⊙ Harrison co., S Ind., on Indian Creek and 17 mi. WSW of New Albany; center of grain, dairy, and poultry area; lumber milling; mfg. of furniture, wagons, glass, cheese, canned foods. Natural gas; limestone quarries; timber. WYANDOTTE CAVE is near by. Laid out 1808; was territorial ⊙ during 1813–16, and ⊙ Ind. until 1825. Scene of only Ind. battle of Civil War (July 8, 1863), when Confederate troops attacked. **2** Town (pop. 1,870), ⊙ Wayne co., S Iowa, 18 mi. S of Chariton; mfg. (batteries, gloves, metal products). Coal mines near by. Inc. 1862. **3** Town (pop. 742), Henderson co., W Ky., 9 mi. SW of Henderson, in agr. and bituminous-coal area.

Coryell (kôryĕl'), county (□ 1,043; pop. 16,284), central Texas; ⊙ Gatesville. Drained by Leon R. Agr. (oats, corn, sorghums, cotton, hay, peanuts); livestock (cattle, sheep, goats, horses), dairying, poultry raising. Includes Mother Neff State Park and part of U.S. Camp Hood. Hunting, fishing. Formed 1854.

Cory Peak, Nev.: see WASSUK RANGE.

Coryton, England: see STANFORD-LE-HOPE.

Corzo, Villa, Mexico: see VILLA CORZO.

Corzuela (kôrswä'lä), town (pop. estimate 500), S Chaco natl. territory, Argentina, on railroad and 35 mi. SW of Presidencia Roque Sáenz Peña; lumbering and agr. center (cotton, corn, spurge, sunflowers, livestock); sawmills.

Cos, Greece: see KOS.

Cos, Gulf of, Turkey: see KOS, GULF OF.

Cosalá (kōsälä'), town (pop. 1,911), Sinaloa, NW Mexico, in W outliers of Sierra Madre Occidental,

55 mi. ESE of Culiacán. Road center; agr. (corn, sugar cane, chick-peas). Copper mines near by; also lead, silver, gold deposits.

Cosamaloapan (kōsämälwä'pän), officially Cosamaloapam de Carpio, city (pop. 3,740), Veracruz, SE Mexico, on Papaloápam R., in Gulf lowland, and 40 mi. W of San Andrés Tuxtla; rail terminus; agr. center (sugar cane, bananas, livestock).

Cosautlán (kōsoutlän'), town (pop. 1,888), Veracruz, E Mexico, in Sierra Madre Oriental, 14 mi. S of Jalapa; alt. 4,294 ft.; coffee, fruit.

Cosby (kŏz'bē), town and parish (pop. 1,701), S Leicester, England, 7 mi. SSW of Leicester; shoe industry. Has church dating from 13th cent.

Cosby, town (pop. 142), Andrew co., NW Mo., on Little Platte R. and 11 mi. NE of St. Joseph.

Coscile River (kôshē'lĕ), anc. *Sybaris,* S Italy, rises in Pollino mts. 8 mi. NNW of Castrovillari, flows 30 mi. SE to Crati R. 4 mi. from Gulf of Taranto, near site of anc. Sybaris.

Cos Cob, Conn.: see GREENWICH.

Coscomatepec (kōskōmätäpĕk'), officially Coscomatepec de Bravo, city (pop. 5,266), Veracruz, E Mexico, in Sierra Madre Oriental, at E foot of Pico de Orizaba, 14 mi. NNW of Córdoba; alt. 5,019 ft. Rail terminus; agr. center (coffee, sugar cane, cereals, fruit).

Coseguina, Nicaragua: see COSIGÜINA.

Cosel, Poland: see KOZLE.

Coseley (kōz'lē), urban district (1931 pop. 25,137; 1951 census 34,414), S Stafford, England, 4 mi. SSE of Wolverhampton; steel casting, metalworking.

Cosenza (kôzĕn'tsä), province (□ 2,576; pop. 587,025), Calabria, S Italy; ⊙ Cosenza. Occupies N part of "toe" of Italy, bet. Tyrrhenian Sea and Gulf of Taranto. Mountainous and hill terrain, including most of La SILA and part of Pollino mts.; coastal plain in E. Watered by Crati, Lao, Neto, and Trionto rivers. Agr. (cereals, olives, fruit, silk), livestock (sheep, goats, pigs); forestry; fishing (Amantea, Cariati). Reservoirs in La Sila mts., on Arvo and Ampollino rivers; hydroelectric plant near San Giovanni in Fiore. Chief rock salt mines in Italy at Lungro.

Cosenza, anc. *Consentia,* town (pop. 30,038), ⊙ Cosenza prov., Calabria, S Italy, on W slope of La Sila mts., on Crati R., at mouth of Busento R., and 90 mi. NNE of Reggio di Calabria; 39°17'N 16°16'E. Agr. trade center (cereals, wine, olive oil, raw silk, fruit, livestock); mfg. (furniture, tannic acid, woolen textiles, soap). Archbishopric. Has castle of Frederick II, cathedral, and mus. of antiquities. Chief city of anc. Brutii; taken by Romans in 204 B.C. According to tradition, Alaric the Visigoth was buried here in the bed of Busento R. Town has suffered repeatedly from earthquakes. In Second World War badly damaged (1943) by bombs.

Cosham, England: see PORTSMOUTH.

Coshocton (kŭ-shŏk'tŭn), county (□ 562; pop. 31,141), central Ohio; ⊙ Coshocton. Drained by Muskingum, Tuscarawas, and Walhonding rivers. Agr. (livestock; dairy products; grain); mfg. at Coshocton; coal mines, sand and gravel pits. Formed 1811.

Coshocton, city (pop. 11,675), ⊙ Coshocton co., central Ohio, 24 mi. NNE of Zanesville, at confluence of Walhonding and Tuscarawas rivers; mfg. (iron and steel products, plastics, advertising novelties, lithographs, rubber goods, pottery, leather and paper products, electric lamps). Coal mines, gravel pits. U.S. soil erosion experiment station is near by. Laid out 1802, inc. 1902.

Cosigüina Peninsula (kōsēgwē'nä), W Nicaragua, bet. Pacific Ocean (S) and Gulf of Fonseca (N); 20 mi. long, 10–13 mi. wide. Terminates W in **Cosigüina Point** (12°55'N 87°42'W) and N in Rosario Point (13°5'N 87°35'W). Rises to 2,776 ft. in **Cosigüina Volcano,** known for its violent eruption of 1835. Sometimes spelled Consigüina; formerly also Coseguina and Conseguina.

Cosío (kōsē'ō), town (pop. 945), Aguascalientes, N central Mexico, 33 mi. N of Aguascalientes; corn, fruit, vegetables.

Cosmoledo Islands (kŏz"mōlā'dō, kŏŏzmŏŏlĕ'dŏŏ), outlying atoll dependency of the Seychelles, in the Aldabra group, in Indian Ocean, 200 mi. NW of N tip of Madagascar; copra; fisheries. Atoll is 11 mi. long, 8 mi. wide.

Cosmópolis (kôzmô'pŏŏlĕs), city (pop. 1,433), E central São Paulo, Brazil, on railroad and 20 mi. NNW of Campinas; cattle, coffee, oranges.

Cosmopolis (kŏzmŏ'pŭlĭs), town (pop. 1,164), Grays Harbor co., W Wash., on Chehalis R., near Aberdeen; sawmills.

Cosmos, village (pop. 382), Meeker co., S central Minn., on South Fork Crow R. and 15 mi. SW of Litchfield, in agr. area; dairy products.

Cosna (kŏz'nŭ), village (1939 pop. 38), central Alaska, on Tanana R. and 30 mi. SE of Tanana; placer gold mining.

Cosne (kōn), town (pop. 6,936), Nièvre dept., central France, on right bank of Loire R. and 30 mi. NNW of Nevers; industrial center mfg. tools, cables, bolts, furniture, agr. equipment. Printing, flour milling, distilling. Suffered some damage in Second World War.

Cosne-d'Allier (–dälyā'), town (pop. 2,004), Allier dept., central France, 14 mi. NE of Montluçon; road and market center. Formerly Cosne-sur-l'Oeil.

Cosnes-et-Romain (kōn-ā-rômē'), commune (pop. 1,194), Meurthe-et-Moselle dept., NE France, 2 mi. W of Longwy; blast furnaces, forges.

Cosolapa (kōsōlä'pä), town, Oaxaca, S Mexico, in N foothills of Sierra Madre del Sur, near Veracruz border, 55 mi. SW of Veracruz; agr. center (cereals, fruit, sugar cane, tobacco, livestock); tanning, alcohol distilling.

Cosoleacaque (kōsōläākä'kā), town (pop. 3,237), Veracruz, SE Mexico, on Gulf of Tehuantepec, 6 mi. W of Minatitlán; agr. center (rice, coffee, fruit, livestock).

Cospicua (kōspē'kwä), town (pop. 4,822), SE Malta, one of the "Three Cities," together with adjoining SENGLEA (NW) and VITTORIOSA (N), at head of Dockyard Creek, c.1½ mi. S of Valletta across Grand Harbour. Has naval arsenal and extensive ship repair yards. Town was heavily damaged in Second World War air raids. However, the parish church (1637), a near-by oratory (1731), and 17th-cent. monastery have survived, as have the unique Galley Houses, in which the Order of the Knights of Malta kept their ships. Other churches and most residential sections were destroyed. Town is sometimes called Bormla.

Cosquín (kōskēn'), town (pop. 9,321), ⊙ Punilla dept. (□ c.950; pop. 50,188), NW central Córdoba prov., Argentina, on small Cosquín R. and 22 mi. NW of Córdoba. Tourist resort and agr. center; granite quarrying; stock raising, dairying. Hydroelectric station near by on Cosquín R.

Cossa, Ethiopia: see KOSSA.

Cossack, town and port, NW Western Australia, 8 mi. N of Roebourne, on Indian Ocean; exports wool, pearl shell, horses.

Cossacks, Oblast of the Don, Russia: see DON COSSACKS, OBLAST OF THE.

Cossato (kôs-sä'tô), village (pop. 922), Vercelli prov., Piedmont, N Italy, 6 mi. E of Biella; woolen mills, dyeworks, foundry.

Cossayuna (kŏ"sŭyōō'nŭ), resort village, Washington co., E N.Y., on Cossayuna L. (c.3 mi. long), 14 mi. SE of Glens Falls.

Cossebaude (kô"sŭbou'dŭ), residential village (pop. 4,256), Saxony, E central Germany, on the Elbe and 6 mi. NW of Dresden; metalworking, furniture and leather mfg. Excursion resort.

Cossé-le-Vivien (kôsā'-lŭ-vēvyē'), village (pop. 1,408), Mayenne dept., W France, near the Oudon, 11 mi. SW of Laval; cider distilling, flour milling, horse raising.

Cossimbazar (kŏs'ĭmbŭzär') or **Kasimbazar** (kä'-sĭmbäzär'), village, Murshidabad dist., E West Bengal, India, near the Bhagirathi, 1 mi. NE of Berhampore. In 17th cent., major English trade center of Bengal; trade moved to Berhampore after sudden decline caused by change in river bed. Former town now marked by swamps and a few ruins. In late-17th cent., Fr. trading post established here; rights renounced 1947.

Cossipore (kä'sĭpôr), suburban ward (pop. 45,771) in Calcutta municipality, West Bengal, India, on the Hooghly and 4 mi. N of city center; gun and shell factories, shellac factory; extensive jute pressing, cotton milling, ginning, and baling, mfg. of leather goods, shoes, hosiery; large power-generating station. Also spelled Cossipur.

Cosson River (kôsō'), Loiret and Loir-et-Cher depts., N central France, rises SW of Sully-sur-Loire, flows 55 mi. WSW, past La Ferté-Saint-Aubin and Chambord, joining the Beuvron 1 mi. before emptying into the Loire 7 mi. below Blois.

Cossyra, Sicily: see PANTELLERIA.

Cost, Texas: see GONZALES.

Costa, Cayo, Fla.: see LACOSTA ISLAND.

Costa Azul, Uruguay: see LA FLORESTA.

Costacciaro (kôstät-chä'rô), village (pop. 1,059), Perugia prov., Umbria, central Italy, 7 mi. E of Gubbio; foundry. Iron mines near by.

Costa de Araujo (kō'stä dā ärou'hō), town (pop. estimate 500), N Mendoza prov., Argentina, on Mendoza R. (irrigation) and 27 mi. NE of Mendoza; alfalfa, wine, fruit, grain, livestock.

Costa di Rovigo (kô'stä dē rôvē'gô), village (pop. 2,015), Rovigo prov., Veneto, N Italy, 5 mi. WSW of Rovigo.

Costa Masnaga (kôs'tä mäznä'gä), village (pop. 887), Como prov., Lombardy, N Italy, 8 mi. SW of Lecco; cotton-milling center.

Costa Mesa (kŏ'stŭ mā'sŭ), village (pop. 11,844), Orange co., S Calif., near Newport Bay, 8 mi. S of Santa Ana; farming, dairying, citrus-fruit growing. Seat of Orange Coast Col.

Costa Rica (kŏ'stŭ rē'kŭ) [Sp., =rich coast], republic (□ c.19,650, including 43 sq. mi. of islets; 1950 pop. 800,875), Central America; ⊙ SAN JOSÉ. Occupies narrowing isthmus (minimal width c.75 mi.) bet. the Caribbean (E) and the Pacific (W and S), bordering N on Nicaragua (partly along SAN JUAN RIVER and just S of L. Nicaragua) and SE on Panama. Situated approximately bet. 8°N (Point BURICA) and 11°15'N and 82°30'W and 86°W. Cocos ISLAND is c.300 mi. SW in the Pacific. The marshy, alluvial Atlantic coast (c.130 mi. long) is comparatively straight, lined by lagoons; while the Pacific shoreline (c.630 mi.) is indented by the Gulf of NICOYA and GOLFO DULCE, flanked by Nicoya Peninsula and OSA PENINSULA. The main cordillera of Central America traverses the country NW-SE, in several ranges—Cordillera de GUANACASTE in N, with Miravalles volcano (6,627 ft.), and the Cordillera de TALAMANCA in S, which rises in the Chirripó Grande (12,533 ft.) to highest elevation in the country. In the center, E of the continental divide, is the short Cordillera Central, towered over by volcanic cones of little activity, such as IRAZÚ (11,260 ft.), TURRIALBA (10,974 ft.), BARBA (9,567 ft.), and POÁS (8,930 ft.). Disastrous earthquakes have frequently occurred. Against the volcanic chain nestles an intermontane basin (alt. c.3–5,000 ft.), the all important *meseta central,* covered by fertile volcanic ash. This is the heart of the country, where about 75% of the overwhelmingly white population—a rare instance in mestizo Central America—live. Costa Rica has numerous rivers. Tributary to the San Juan, the largest, is SAN CARLOS RIVER. The REVENTAZÓN RIVER empties into the Atlantic, and the Río Grande de TARZOLES into the Pacific. Though in the tropics, the country has a diverse climate, according to altitude. A humid climate with rainfall all year round (c.120 inches) prevails in the jungles of the Caribbean coast. Considerably drier, and somewhat milder, is the narrow Pacific lowland. The highlands W of the mtn. backbone have dry (Dec.–April) and rainy seasons. San José, at 3,838 ft. on the *meseta central,* has a delightful climate of perpetual spring; Jan. mean 65.3°F., July mean 67.3°F. About half of the entire area is wooded. Rich forest resources (balsa, cativo, cedar, guayacán, dyewood, rosewood, sandalwood, mahogany, oak, rubber) abound in the coastal plains and on lower slopes; only little—mostly in Pacific belt—is exploited. Valuable fisheries are based on the Pacific, centered at PUNTARENAS, which ships tuna. Costa Rica is, however, predominantly an agr. country, though approximately ¼ of the area is cultivated. Upon the 3 leading crops—bananas, coffee, cacao (in that order)—rests the economic life. Banana plantations, once prominent in the Caribbean area, where they were worked by Jamaican Negroes (c.5% of the pop.), have now, because of plant disease, been largely shifted to the Pacific (a mestizo region), from whence they are exported through the newly (1930s) constructed ports GOLFITO and QUEPOS. Cacao has somewhat superseded bananas on the E coast, but the Negroes—a socio-political problem because of the banana-leaf blight—have still to rely on subsistence crops. Coffee is raised in practically all provinces, foremost in upland sections of San José, Cartago, Alajuela, and Heredia provs. Sugar cane (principally from NW) and abacá (Manilla hemp) represent subsidiary exports; as do cattle (from Guanacaste prov.), hides, and skins. Among other crops are tobacco, corn, beans, rice, cinchona, potatoes. But while the govt. strives for self-sufficiency, corn, rice, and beans still have to be imported. Costa Rica contains a few rich gold fields, chiefly in the AGUACATE MOUNTAINS (W central). Occasionally also some silver and manganese are exported. Other minerals include copper, lead, nickel, zinc, iron, sulphur, granite, onyx, marble; coal in Cordillera de Talamanca. Petroleum deposits have been reported. Costa Rica, among the most progressive and potentially stable nations of Central America, retains an unfavorable trade balance. The U.S. takes c.75% of all exports and supplies the bulk (70–75%) of the imports (flour, cotton goods, metalware, vehicles, petroleum). Apart from the above-mentioned banana ports, foreign trade passes through LIMÓN (Puerto Limón) on the Caribbean and Puntarenas on the Pacific, which is also a favorite beach resort. Among industries, processing of primary products (sugar, coffee, cacao) leads. A few distilleries, cigarette factories, textile and clothing plants, mfg. of shoes and furniture, are centered at the principal cities: San José (seat of a univ.), CARTAGO (historical ⊙ until 1823, summer resort), ALAJUELA, HEREDIA, TURRIALBA (hq. of Inter-American Inst. of Agr. Sciences). Through the metropolis San José passes the Inter-American Highway and the intercoastal railroad to Limón and Puntarenas; it is also served by international airlines (at La Sabana airport). Costa Rica has the highest rate of literacy in Central America, c.75%. Natl. language is Spanish, the great majority R.C. The Caribbean coast was visited (1502) by Columbus, who landed at location of present-day Limón, and allegedly named the land Costa Rica. Not until 1563 was the region completely conquered by the Spanish and brought under the captaincy general of Guatemala. Since the few remaining Indians retreated into the mts., the colonists could not establish a hacienda system based on Indian labor and had to become relatively small landowners. With independence from Spain (1821) Costa Rica was nominally annexed to Iturbide's Mexican empire; became later a member (1823–38) of the Central American Federation. Helped to defeat (1857) the American filibuster William Walker. Coffee, introduced about 1800, and bananas, developed in 2d half of 19th cent. by

M. C. Keith, who founded Limón, contributed much to prosperity. Though there were short intervals of revolutions (last successful rebellion May, 1948) and strong-man rule, democracy is more firmly entrenched here than anywhere else in Central America, and Costa Rica is a leader in Pan Americanism. For further information see separate entries on towns, cities, physical features, and the 7 provinces: ALAJUELA, CARTAGO, GUANACASTE, HEREDIA, LIMÓN, PUNTARENAS, SAN JOSÉ.

Costa Rica (kō'stä rē'kä), village, Pando dept., NW Bolivia, on Tahuamanu R. and 36 mi. ESE of Cobija, on road; rubber.

Costerfield (kŏ'stûrfēld), village, central Victoria, Australia, 65 mi. N of Melbourne, near Heathcote; antimony mine.

Costermansville, province, Belgian Congo: see KIVU.

Costermansville (kôstĕrmänsvēl'), native *Bukavu* (bōōkä'vōō, –vōō'), town (1948 pop. 9,739), ⊙ Kivu prov. and Kivu dist. (□ 49,581; 1948 pop. c.1,177,000), E Belgian Congo, on SW shore of L. Kivu, near Ruanda-Urundi border, c.1,000 mi. ENE of Leopoldville; 28°55'E 2°30'S; alt. 4,768 ft. Commercial, distributing, and communications center (air, road, lake) in agr. and grazing region noted for its scenic beauty and as a major area of European settlement. Cinchona and food processing, brewing, mfg. of pharmaceuticals and insecticides, tin concentrating, printing. Tourist industry is important. Has 2 junior colleges, hospitals for Europeans and natives, meteorological station, branch of geological survey of Belgian Congo. Costermansville succeeded Rutshuru as administrative center of Kivu in 1925–30, and has rapidly grown with the opening of the region to white colonists. Its airport is at Kamembe, across Ruanda-Urundi border.

Costesti (kôstĕsht'), Rum. *Costeşti*, village (pop. 1,109), Arges prov., S central Rumania, 12 mi. S of Pitesti; rail junction.

Costigliole Saluzzo (kôstēlyô'lĕ sälōō'tsô), village (pop. 1,687), Cuneo prov., Piedmont, NW Italy, on Varaita R. and 6 mi. S of Saluzzo.

Costilla (kŏstē'ù), county (□ 1,215; pop. 6,067), S Colo.; ⊙ San Luis. Irrigated agr. area on N.Mex. line; bounded W by Rio Grande. Livestock, hay, potatoes. Part of San Luis Valley in W and of Sangre de Cristo Mts. in E. Formed 1861.

Costilla, village (1940 pop. 971), Taos co., N N.Mex., on Costilla Creek, in W foothills of Sangre de Cristo Mts., at S tip of San Luis Valley, and 40 mi. N of Taos, on Colo. line; alt. c.7,500 ft. Trade point in livestock and agr. region; beans, corn, chili. Ute Peak is 8 mi. WSW.

Costilla Creek, N N.Mex. and S Colo., rises in Sangre de Cristo Mts., N.Mex.; flows c.50 mi. NW, W, and S, crossing Colo. line above Costilla and recrossing it near Ute Peak, N.Mex., here joining Rio Grande. Also known as Rio Costilla.

Costilla Peak (12,634 ft.), N N.Mex., in Sangre de Cristo Mts., near Colo. line, 20 mi. SE of Costilla village.

Costitx (kōstēch'), town (pop. 882), Majorca, Balearic Isls., 17 mi. ENE of Palma; lumbering, stock raising, agr. (almonds, cereals, grapes); wood-pulp mfg.

Cosumnes River (kùsŭm'nĭs), central Calif., formed on W Sierra Nevada slope on El Dorado–Amador co. line by its North and South forks, flows c.50 mi. SW to Mokelumne R. 5 mi. W of Galt. The upper Cosumnes is site of projected Nashville Dam and reservoir of CENTRAL VALLEY project.

Coswig (kôs'vĭkh). **1** Town (pop. 14,591), in former Anhalt state, central Germany, after 1945 in Saxony-Anhalt, on the Elbe and 10 mi. ENE of Dessau; lignite mining; paper milling; mfg. of tires, chemicals, dyes, matches, pottery. **2** Town (pop. 11,705), Saxony, E central Germany, harbor on the Elbe, and 9 mi. NW of Dresden; rail junction; mfg. of paint, leather goods, wallpaper, electrical equipment; woolen milling.

Cot (kōt), village (dist. pop. 2,150), Cartago prov., central Costa Rica, on SW slopes of Irazú volcano, 2 mi. NE of San Rafael; corn, livestock. Pop. is largely Indian. Durán tuberculosis sanatorium N.

Cotabambas (kōtäbäm'bäs), town (pop. 1,187), Apurímac dept., S central Peru, in the Andes, 35 mi. ESE of Abancay; gold mining; sugar cane, fruit, livestock.

Cotabato (kōtäbä'tō), province (□ 8,868; 1948 pop. 439,669), S Mindanao, Philippines, bordering S on Celebes Sea, W on Moro Gulf and Illana Bay; ⊙ Cotabato. On its borders are 2 active volcanoes: Mt. Ragang (9,236 ft.) in N, Mt. Apo (9,690 ft.) in E. The Pulangi R. (Rio Grande de Mindanao) traverses it, draining its central area, a humid swamp. Rice, coconuts, rubber are grown. The prov., inhabited by Moros, is a rich but undeveloped agr. area, partly unexplored. Chief cities: Cotabato, Midsayap, Dulawan, Talayan, Buluan.

Cotabato, town (1939 pop. 8,144; 1948 municipality pop. 20,407), ⊙ Cotabato prov., Philippines, central Mindanao, 95 mi. W of Davao, on Moro Gulf, at mouth of N arm of Pulangi R.; river port and trade center; rice, corn, copra.

Cotacachi (kōtäkä'chē), town (1950 pop. 4,354), Imbabura prov., N Ecuador, in Andean valley, at SE foot of Cerro Cotacachi, 11 mi. WSW of Ibarra; alt. 8,038 ft. Textile and agr. center (cereals, fruit, coffee, cotton, incense); mfg. of cotton cloth, woolen ponchos, laces, cigarettes, leather suitcases. Has hot springs. Here was built (1840) the 1st cotton mill in Ecuador.

Cotacachi, Cerro, extinct Andean volcano (16,292 ft.) in Imbabura prov., N Ecuador, 15 mi. W of Ibarra. Has several craters and crater lakes. L. Cuicocha is at S foot.

Cotacajes River (kōtäkä'hĕs), on Cochabamba–La Paz dept. border, W central Bolivia; rises in several branches in Cordillera de Cochabamba W of Cochabamba; flows 120 mi. NNW to the Santa Elena 25 mi. SE of Huachi. Receives Ayopaya R. (left).

Cotagaita (kōtägī'tä), town (pop. c.7,000), ⊙ Nor Chichas prov., Potosí dept., S Bolivia, on E slopes of Cordillera de Chichas, on Cotagaita R. and c.40 mi. N of Tupiza; alt. 8,707 ft. Tin and antimony deposits.

Cotagaita River, S Bolivia, rises in several branches in Cordillera de Chichas, flows 75 mi. E, past Cotagaita, joining Tumusla R. c.15 mi. W of Palca Grande. The combined stream, which is sometimes considered (down to the influx of the Cinti) to be the Cotagaita and sometimes the Tumusla, flows E, past Palca Grande, and S, joining the San Juan just below Villa Abecia to form PILAYA RIVER.

Cotahuasi (kōtäwä'sē), city (pop. 1,395), ⊙ La Unión prov. (□ 1,136; pop. 21,077), S Peru, in high Andean valley, at N foot of Nudo Solimanca, 45 mi. NNW of Chuquibamba; 15°13'S 72°54'W; alt. 8,861 ft. Grain, potatoes, livestock; mfg. of native textile goods. Archaeological remains near by.

Cotahuasi River, Peru: see OCOÑA RIVER.

Cotarli, Portuguese India: see SANGUÉM.

Cotati (kōtä'tē), village (pop. c.1,000), Sonoma co., W Calif., 7 mi. S of Santa Rosa, in fruit and poultry dist.

Cotaxtla (kōtä'slä), town (pop. 337), Veracruz, E Mexico, in Gulf lowland, 30 mi. SW of Veracruz; fruit.

Cotchéry, Fr. India: see KOTTUCHCHERI.

Côte [Fr.,=coast], for names beginning thus and not found here: see under following part of the name.

Côte, La (lä kōt'), village (pop. 503), Haute-Saône dept., E France, 4 mi. E of Lure; weaving, plaster mfg.

Coteau (kùtō'), village (pop. 1,214), Terrebonne parish, SE La.

Coteau, Le (lù kōtō'), E suburb (pop. 6,071) of Roanne, Loire dept., SE central France, on right bank of Loire R.; mfg. of cotton textiles (chiefly hosiery), shoes, paints, varnishes, pottery, tar derivatives.

Coteau des Prairies (kō'tō dā prâr'ēz, kùtō'), plateau (alt. 2,000 ft.) in NE S.Dak. and W Minn.; begins as continuation of Drift Prairie, N.Dak.; extends S, past L. Traverse and Big Stone L., and bet. James and Minnesota rivers, to Blue Earth R., N Iowa. Occupies grain and livestock region in parts of Marshall, Roberts, Grant, Deuel counties, S.Dak., and Lincoln, Pipestone, Nobles, Jackson counties, Minn.

Coteau du Lac (kōtō' dü läk'), village (pop. 445), SW Que., on the St. Lawrence opposite Valleyfield; agr. (dairying; pigs, potatoes); resort.

Coteau du Missouri (kùtō' dù mĭzōō'rē), NW N.Dak., plateau (alt. 2,000 ft.), part of Missouri R. Plateau; lies W of Des Lacs R. and Missouri Escarpment, in grain and livestock region. Deposits of lignite, sodium sulphate, and bentonite here.

Coteau Landing (kōtō'), village (pop. 381), ⊙ Soulanges co., SW Que., on L. St. Francis, opposite Valleyfield; railroad workshops; agr. (dairying; pigs, potatoes). SW terminus of Soulanges Canal.

Coteau Station, village (pop. 796), SW Que., 5 mi. WNW of Valleyfield.

Côteaux (kōtō'), agr. town (1950 census pop. 1,877), Sud dept., SW Haiti, on SW coast of Tiburon Peninsula, 19 mi. W of Les Cayes; bananas. Sometimes Les Côteaux.

Cote Blanche Island (kōt" blänsh'), one of the Five Isls., in St. Mary parish, S La., a salt dome rising from sea marshes on N shore of West Cote Blanche Bay, 19 mi. SSE of New Iberia; alt. c.70 ft.

Côte d'Azur, France: see RIVIERA.

Côte des Neiges (kōt dā nĕzh'), W suburb of Montreal, S Que.

Côte-d'Or (kōt-dôr') [Fr.,=golden ridge], department (□ 3,392; pop. 335,602), in Burgundy, E central France; ⊙ DIJON. Abutting on the Monts du Morvan (SW), it extends to upper Saône R. valley (E and SE). Traversed by S part of Plateau of Langres (N of Dijon) and by the Côte d'Or (bet. Dijon and Chagny), latter of which forms divide bet. Saône, Seine, and Loire drainage basins. Celebrated vineyards of Beaune and Nuits-Saint-Georges lead agr. output. Vegetables grown in Dijon area, corn and oats throughout dept. Cattle and sheep raising. Dept. is crossed by Burgundy Canal, which connects the Saône with the Seine, and by a net of railroads converging on Dijon. Other towns are Beaune (wine center) and Montbard (metallurgy). Dijon, Semur-en-Auzois (medieval town), and Alise-Sainte-Reine (former site of Alesia) attract tourists.

Côte d'Or, hilly ridge in Côte-d'Or dept., E central France, extending 30 mi. from Dijon (NNE) to Chagny (SSW). Average alt. 1,500 ft. Its E slopes are lined with finest vineyards of Burgundy (Beaune, Nuits-Saint-Georges, Morey-Saint-Denis, Chambolle-Musigny, Pommard, Volnay, Puligny-Montrachet, Santenay).

Cotentin Peninsula (kôtätē'), NW France, forms N part of Manche dept., and juts into English Channel opposite Isle of Wight. Extreme N points: Cape La Hague (NW), Barfleur Point (NE). Rocky coastline (except in E) with silted embayments. CHERBOURG (on N shore), chief town, is only good port. Characterized by numerous hedgerows which divide hilly landscape into small fields and apple orchards. Stock raising and dairying in Douve R. valley, chiefly bet. Valognes and Carentan. An old Norman county, it is named after its former ⊙, Coutances. On E shore, bet. Saint-Marcouf and Carentan, American troops landed, June 6, 1944, in Normandy invasion.

Côte-Saint-André, La (lä kōt-sĕtädrä'), town (pop. 2,278), Isère dept., SE France, 15 mi. SW of La Tour-du-Pin; noted liqueur distilled in area; silk milling. Agr. school. Hector Berlioz b. here.

Côte Saint Luc (kōt sē lük'), residential village (pop. 776), S Que., W suburb of Montreal.

Côte Saint Michel (mĭshĕl') or **Saint Michel,** residential town (pop. 2,956), S Que., N suburb of Montreal.

Côtes-de-Fer (kōtùfĕr'), town (1950 census pop. 736), Ouest dept., SW Haiti, a minor port on Caribbean, 32 mi. W of Jacmel; cotton-growing region.

Côtes de Meuse (kōt dù mûz') [Fr.,=heights of the Meuse], Meuse dept., NE France, extend along right bank of the Meuse bet. Neufchâtel (S) and the Ardennes (N), forming one of several concentric ridge-lines at E edge of Paris Basin. Figured prominently in First World War during battles of Verdun (1916–17) and Saint-Mihiel (1918).

Côtes-du-Nord (–dü-nôr') [Fr.,=northern shores], department (□ 2,787; pop. 526,955), Brittany, W France; ⊙ Saint-Brieuc. Bounded N by English Channel; has indented coastline with numerous shoals and small offshore isls. Generally level, drained by short streams (Rance, Trieux) emptying into the Channel, and by longer ones flowing S into Bay of Biscay. Grows apples (for cider), flax and hemp, early root crops. Cattle and horse raising. Some lead and zinc mined at Trémuson. Fishing and textile industry (linen) on decline. Seaside resorts increasingly popular. Chief towns: Saint-Brieuc, Dinan, Guingamp.

Cotesfield, village (pop. 106), Howard co., E central Nebr., 15 mi. NW of St. Paul and on N.Loup R.

Cöthen, Germany: see KÖTHEN.

Cotia (kōōtē'ù), city (pop. 761), SE São Paulo, Brazil, 18 mi. W of São Paulo; mfg. of textiles and explosives; wine making.

Cotignac (kôtēnyäk'), village (pop. 1,018), Var dept., SE France, in Lower Provence Alps, 16 mi. W of Draguignan; olive and sericulture.

Cotignola (kôtēnyô'lä), town (pop. 1,647), Ravenna prov., Emilia-Romagna, N central Italy, on Senio R. and 3 mi. SE of Lugo.

Cotija or **Cotija de la Paz** (kōtē'hä dā lä päs'), city (pop. 4,567), Michoacán, central Mexico, on central plateau, 35 mi. SW of Zamora; agr. center (corn, sugar cane, fruit, tobacco, stock).

Cotilla Caves (kōtē'yä), caverns c.15 mi. SE of Havana, W Cuba.

Cotina River or **Chotina River** (both: chô'tēnä), Serbo-Croatian *Ćotina*, S Yugoslavia, rises in several headstreams in N Montenegro, joining SSE of Pljevlja; flows c.75 mi. WNW, past Pljevlja, to Drina R. at Foca. Formerly spelled Ceotina or Cheotina, Serbo-Croatian *Ćeotina*.

Cotinga River (kōōtĕng'gù), Rio Branco territory, northernmost Brazil, one of the headstreams of the Rio Branco, rises on S slopes of the Serra Pacaraima near Mt. Roraima (Venezuela–Br. Guiana border), flows c.180 mi. S to Tacutú R. 50 mi. above Boa Vista. Diamonds and gold found along its course.

Cotinguiba (kōōtĕng-gwē'bù), city (pop. 1,344), E Sergipe, NE Brazil, on railroad and 8 mi. NW of Aracaju; rock-salt mines supply Angra dos Reis (Rio de Janeiro) chemical works. Until 1944, called Socorro.

Cotinguiba River, Sergipe, NE Brazil, rises in the Serra Itabaiana, flows 30 mi. to the Atlantic just below Aracaju. Receives the Sergipe.

Cotiugenii-Mari, Moldavian SSR: see KOTYUZHANY.

Cotnari (kôt'närē), village (pop. 1,150), Jassy prov., NE Rumania, on railroad and 10 mi. NNW of Targu-Frumos; noted wine center. Has 15th-cent. church, rebuilt in 17th cent. Former summer residence of Stephen the Great.

Coto (kō'tō), village, Puntarenas prov., S Costa Rica, small Pacific port, 7 mi. SE of Golfito, on lower Coto R. (a tributary of the Golfo Dulce). Exports rice, bananas, coconuts.

Cotoca (kōtō'kä), town (pop. c.3,000), Santa Cruz dept., central Bolivia, on road and 15 mi. E of Santa Cruz; rice, corn, livestock. Religious sanctuary with Maryknoll mission.

Cotonou (kōtōnōō'), town (pop. c.22,900), S Dahomey, Fr. West Africa, port on Gulf of Guinea, built on narrow strip bet. the ocean and L. Nokoué, on railroad and 15 mi. WSW of Porto-Novo. Export center for rich agr. region (palm kernels, palm oil, copra, coffee, cotton). Mfg. of vegetable oil, soap, soda water, shoes; sawmilling. Has airport, customhouse, botanic garden, R.C. and Protestant missions. Sometimes Kotonu.

Cotopaxi (kōtōpăk'sē, kōtōpä'hē), province (□ 2,188; 1950 pop. 149,495), N central Ecuador, in Andes; ⊙ Latacunga. A mountainous prov. bounded NE by the active Cotopaxi volcano, and including a number of other snow-capped volcanoes. It is watered by Patate R. Frequently shaken by earthquakes, and damaged by volcanic eruptions, it has most recently been hit in 1949. Has a generally temperate climate, with rains Dec.–April. Among mineral resources are silver, gold, copper, and kaolin, but it is predominantly a stock-raising (cattle, sheep) and agr. region (corn, wheat, barley, potatoes, vegetables, fiber plants). Latacunga is the trading and processing center. The prov. was formerly called León.

Cotopaxi, active volcano (19,344 ft.), N central Ecuador, in the Andes, 30 mi. S of Quito; 0°40'S 78°26'W. Probably the world's highest live volcano, it is one of the most beautiful of Andean peaks, with a well-shaped, snow-capped cone broken by the Cabeza del Inca (Inca's Head). Frequently active and continuously emitting smoke, it has often caused severe damage. It was climbed by Reiss in 1872 and explored by Whymper in 1880.

Cotorro or **San Pedro del Cotorro** (sän pā'drō dĕl kōtôr'ō), town (pop. 3,714), Havana prov., W Cuba, 7½ mi. SE of Havana; dairying, sugar growing. Has mineral springs.

Cotrone, Italy: see CROTONE.

Cotronei (kôtrônā'), town (pop. 3,337), Catanzaro prov., Calabria, S Italy, in La Sila mts., 8 mi. SE of San Giovanni in Fiore. On Neto R., 1 mi. N, is important Timpa Grande hydroelectric plant; rail terminus.

Cotswold Hills (kŏts'wōld), a plateau of oölitic limestone hills, extending c.50 mi. NE from Bath, England, and rising to 1,083 ft. just NW of Cheltenham. Its crest (average alt. less than 600 ft.) is Thames-Severn watershed. Region is known for its picturesque countryside and houses and for its breed of sheep. There are many important long barrows and megalithic monuments. Among the anc. churches is Hayles Abbey, founded 1246. The Cotswold Games were held here from anc. times until 19th cent.

Cotta, Ceylon: see KOTTE.

Cottage, Cape, SW Maine, promontory on Casco Bay just S of South Portland; site of U.S. Fort Williams and Portland Head, with oldest lighthouse on Maine coast (1791).

Cottage City, town (pop. 1,249), Prince Georges co., central Md., suburb just NE of Washington, on Anacostia R.

Cottage Grove. **1** City (pop. 3,536), Lane co., W Oregon, 17 mi. S of Eugene and on COAST FORK of Willamette R.; lumbering, grazing, dairying, fruitgrowing. Inc. 1900. Cottage Grove Dam (100 ft. high, 2,110 ft. long; completed 1942), 6 mi. S, is unit in Willamette R. basin project for flood control and navigation. **2** Village (pop. 372), Dane co., S Wis., near small Koshkonong Creek, 9 mi. E of Madison, in dairy region.

Cottagegrove or **Cottage Grove,** town (pop. 126), Henry co., NW Tenn., 9 mi. NW of Paris.

Cottage Hills, village (pop. 3,357), Madison co., SW Ill., just E of Alton.

Cottageville, town (pop. 553), Colleton co., S S.C., 10 mi. ENE of Walterboro.

Cottam (kŏ'tům), village in Lea, Ashton, Ingol and Cottam parish (pop. 1,802), W Lancashire, England, 3 mi. NW of Preston; dairying.

Cottanello (kôt-tänĕl'lō), village (pop. 322), Rieti prov., Latium, central Italy, 9 mi. W of Rieti; marble quarrying.

Cottbus or **Kottbus** (both: kôt'bŏŏs), city (pop. 49,131), Brandenburg, E Germany, chief town of Lower Lusatia, at SE edge of Spree Forest, on the Spree and 70 mi. SE of Berlin; 51°45'N 14°20'E. Rail center; woolen milling, wood- and metalworking; mfg. of carpets, glass, food products. Vegetable and livestock market. Power station. Airport (NW). Has 14th- and 15th-cent. churches; remains of old town walls, including Spremberg Tower. First mentioned 1156; property (1199–1445) of margraves of Meissen, then passed to Brandenburg. Bombed in Second World War (destruction 25%). Captured April, 1945, by Soviet troops.

Cottel Island, N.F.: see COTTLE ISLAND.

Cottenham (kŏ'tůnům), town and parish (pop. 2,386), central Cambridge, England, 6 mi. N of Cambridge; agr. market in dairying and fruitgrowing region, famous for its cheese; there are also metal foundries. Has 15th-cent. church.

Cotter (kŏ'tůr). **1** Town (pop. 1,089), Baxter co., N Ark., 33 mi. E of Harrison, and on White R., in the Ozarks; railroad shops; mussel shells shipped for button mfg. **2** Town (pop. 49), Louisa co., SE Iowa, 12 mi. E of Washington. Limestone quarries near by.

Cottesloe (kŏts'lō), municipality (pop. 8,257), SW Western Australia, SW suburb of Perth, on N shore of Swan R.; summer resort; flour, rope.

Cottian Alps (kŏ'tēůn), Fr. *Alpes Cottiennes,* Ital. *Alpi Cozie,* division of Western Alps along Fr.-Ital. border; extend from Maritime Alps at Maddalena Pass (S) to Graian Alps at Mont Cenis (N). Highest peaks: Monte Viso (12,602 ft.), Aiguille de Chambeyron (11,155 ft.). Dauphiné Alps are W offshoots.

Cottica River (kôtē'kä), NE Du. Guiana, rises S of Moengo (head of navigation), flows c.100 mi. WNW and W, past Charlottenburg, to Commewijne R. 15 mi. E of Nieuw Amsterdam. Bauxite, from large deposits along its upper course, is shipped overseas from Moengo. Rice, coffee, and tropical fruit are grown along lower reaches.

Cottingham (kŏ'tĭng-ům), former urban district (1931 pop. 6,179), East Riding, SE Yorkshire, England, 4 mi. NW of Hull; woolen milling. Has church begun 1272, completed in 15th cent.; remains of Baynard Castle, built 1170. Inc. 1935 in Haltemprice.

Cottle (kŏ'tůl), county (□ 901; pop. 6,099), NW Texas; ⊙ Paducah. Rolling country, drained by Pease and Wichita rivers. Agr. (cotton, grain sorghums, wheat); beef cattle, horses, hogs, sheep, poultry; dairying. Formed 1876.

Cottle Island or **Cottel Island** (kŏ'tůl) (□ 7; pop. 656), E N.F., in Bonavista Bay, 30 mi. NW of Cape Bonavista; 48°50'N 53°44'W; 6 mi. long, 2 mi. wide. Fishing.

Cottle Knob, central W.Va., a summit (3,075 ft.) of the Alleghenies, 3 mi. SW of Camden on Gauley.

Cotton, county (□ 629; pop. 10,180), S Okla.; ⊙ Walters. Bounded S by Red R., here forming Texas line; drained by the Deep Red Run and by Beaver and Cache creeks. Agr. (livestock, cotton, wheat, poultry, oats). Mfg. at Walters. Oil wells. Formed 1912.

Cotton, town (pop. 146), Mitchell co., SW Ga., 6 mi. ENE of Pelham.

Cotton Belt, major agr. region of SE U.S., where cultivation of cotton is greater than that of any other single crop. It lies mainly in Atlantic and Gulf coastal plains and on the Piedmont upland, and extends through the Carolinas, Ga., Ala., Miss., W Tenn., E and S Ark., La., E half of Texas, and S Okla., with small areas in SE Va., N Fla., and SE Mo. Natural characteristics include humid subtropical climate, annual rainfall of 30–55 in., and growing season of at least 200 days. A modified plantation system prevails in most parts. Though cotton is dominant, there is considerable production of corn, wheat, tobacco, peanuts, and livestock. Up to 1793 (invention of cotton gin), Cotton Belt was confined to small coastal area in S.C. and Ga.; by time of Civil War it stretched from S Va. to E Texas; abolition of slavery, breakup of large estates, and advent of boll weevil in Gulf coast section have resulted in a steady W expansion of cotton. Cotton is also grown in irrigated S parts of N.Mex., Ariz., and Calif. Texas is leading producer, followed by Miss. and Ark.

Cottondale, town (pop. 747), Jackson co., NW Fla., 9 mi. W of Marianna; fertilizer mfg.

Cotton End, England: see EASTCOTTS.

Cotton Plant, town (pop. 1,838), Woodruff co., E central Ark., 26 mi. W of Forrest City, in agr. area (cotton, corn, hay); lumber milling, cotton ginning. Civil War battle took place here in 1862. Laid out 1840.

Cottonport, town (pop. 1,534), Avoyelles parish, E central La., 32 mi. SE of Alexandria, in cotton and sugar-cane area; cotton gins, sugar mill.

Cotton Valley, town (pop. 1,188), Webster parish, NW La., 29 mi. NE of Shreveport, near Bayou Dorcheat, in oil and natural-gas area; natural-gasoline and oil refineries; naval stores, lumber.

Cottonwood, county (□ 640; pop. 15,763), SW Minn.; ⊙ Windom. Agr. area watered by Des Moines R. Corn, oats, barley, livestock. Wildlife refuge in SW. Co. formed 1857.

Cottonwood. **1** Town (pop. 864), Houston co., SE Ala., 13 mi. SSE of Dothan, near Fla. line; naval stores. **2** Village (pop. 1,626, with adjacent Clemenceau), Yavapai co., central Ariz., on Verde R. and 29 mi. NE of Prescott; copper mining, agr., ranching. **3** Village (pop. 689), Idaho co., W Idaho, 12 mi. WNW of Grangeville, in grain, livestock, lumbering area. **4** Village (pop. 709), Lyon co., SW Minn., 13 mi. NNE of Marshall, in agr. area; dairy products. **5** Town (pop. 102), Jackson co., SW central S.Dak., 22 mi. WNW of Kadoka. Has substation of State Col. of Agr.

Cottonwood Creek, in S Calif., and N Lower Calif., Mexico; rises in Laguna Mts. of San Diego co., Calif., flows c.50 mi. generally SW to Tijuana R. E of Agua Caliente, Mexico. In U.S. section are 2 water-supply reservoirs for San Diego city: Barrett Reservoir is impounded by Barrett Dam (192 ft. high, 750 ft. long; completed 1922); Morena Reservoir (mûrē'nů) is formed by Morena Dam (279 ft. high, 550 ft. long; completed 1930).

Cottonwood Falls, city (pop. 957), ⊙ Chase co., E central Kansas, on Cottonwood R. and 20 mi. W of Emporia; trade and shipping center for livestock, poultry, and grain area. Knute Rockne Memorial is near by. Founded 1858 by Free State settlers, inc. 1872.

Cottonwood River. **1** In E central Kansas, rises in Marion co., flows SE, past Marion and Florence, then ENE and E, past Cottonwood Falls, to Neosho R. 7 mi. E of Emporia; c.140 mi. long. **2** In SW and S Minn., rises in Lyon co., flows 120 mi. E, past Sleepy Eye, to Minnesota R. near New Ulm.

Cotuí (kōtwē'), town (1950 pop. 2,268), Duarte prov., E central Dominican Republic, in fertile La Vega Real valley, 27 mi. ESE of La Vega, in rice- and cacao-growing region. Founded 1505. Silver, gold, and copper were mined near by in early colonial period. There are also iron pyrites, amber, and graphite deposits in vicinity.

Cotuit, Mass.: see BARNSTABLE, town.

Cotulla (kůtōō'lů), city (pop. 4,418), ⊙ La Salle co., SW Texas, on Nueces R. and c.65 mi. NNE of Laredo; shipping, trade center for winter-truck, cattle area; oil fields near. On Inter-American Highway, it has tourist trade. Inc. 1910.

Cotyora, Turkey: see ORDU, town.

Cotzal or **San Juan Cotzal** (sän hwän' kōtsäl'), town (1950 pop. 2,649), Quiché dept., W central Guatemala, at E end of Cuchumatanes Mts., 9 mi. NNE of Sacapulas; alt. 5,250 ft.; corn, beans, coffee, sugar cane; livestock.

Coubre, Pointe de la (pwĕt' dů lä kōō'brů), headland on Bay of Biscay, Charente-Maritime dept., W France, forming N lip of Gironde estuary. Main shipping lane into the Gironde c.1 mi. SW of lighthouse, 45°41'N, 1°15'W.

Couches-les-Mines (kōōsh-lā-mēn'), village (pop. 799), Saône-et-Loire dept., E central France, 8 mi. NE of Le Creusot; iron mines, no longer worked. Has 13th-cent. church, 15th-cent. castle.

Couchey (kōōshā'), village (pop. 532), Côte-d'Or dept., E central France, on E slope of the Côte d'Or, 5 mi. SW of Dijon; Burgundy wines.

Couchiching Lake (kōō'chĭching) (10 mi. long, 3 mi. wide), S Ont., in Muskoka lake region, 60 mi. N of Toronto and just N of L. Simcoe, with which it is joined. Drained N into Georgian Bay by Severn R. Resort; scene of annual conference for discussion of public questions.

Couckelaere, Belgium: see KOEKELARE.

Couço (kō'sōō), agr. village (pop. 1,284), Santarém dist., central Portugal, on the Sorraia and 27 mi. SE of Santarém.

Coucouron (kōōkōōrō'), village (pop. 364), Ardèche dept., S France, in the Monts du Velay, 17 mi. SSE of Le Puy; cattle, sheep; cheese making.

Coucy-le-Château (kōōsē'-lů-shätō'), village (pop. 757), Aisne dept., N France, on height near Ailette R., 10 mi. N of Soissons; flour milling, sugar distilling. Preserves medieval gateways and part of 13th-cent. walls. Its magnificent medieval castle (notorious for its robber barons in 12th cent.) was dynamited by Germans in 1917.

Coudekerque-Branche (kōōdkârk'-brãsh'), SE suburb (pop. 12,506) of Dunkirk, Nord dept., N France; tar and lubricant refining, cotton and jute weaving, vegetable canning, biscuit and borax mfg. Damaged (1940) in Second World War.

Couderay (kōō'důrā), village (pop. 133), Sawyer co., N Wis., 29 mi. E of Spooner, near small Lac Court Oreilles and Lac Court Oreilles Indian Reservation.

Coudersport (kou'důrzpôrt), resort borough (pop. 3,210), ⊙ Potter co., N Pa., 35 mi. ESE of Bradford and on Allegheny R.; agr.; tanning, toys, textiles, surgical appliances. Hunting, fishing near by. Laid out 1807, inc. 1848.

Coudray-Saint-Germer, Le (lů kōōdrĕ'-sē-zhĕrmā'), agr. village (pop. 269), Oise dept., N France, 12 mi. W of Beauvais; horse raising.

Coudres, Île aux (ēl ō kōō'drů), or **Coudres Island** (7 mi. long, 3 mi. wide), in the St. Lawrence, SE central Que., opposite Baie St. Paul and 55 mi. NE of Quebec; farming, fruitgrowing. At S end of isl. is village (pop. 200). Cartier landed here 1535.

Couëron (kōōĕrō'), town (pop. 4,820), Loire-Inférieure dept., W France, on Loire estuary, 8 mi. W of Nantes; ironworking center.

Couesnon River (kōōĕnō'), Ille-et-Vilaine and Manche depts., W France, rises 7 mi. E of Fougères, flows 55 mi. generally N, past Fougères and Antrain (head of navigation), to the English Channel just S of the Mont-Saint-Michel.

Couhé (kōōā'), village (pop. 1,622), Vienne dept., W central France, 21 mi. SSW of Poitiers; cattle and mule raising.

Couillet (kōōyā'), town (pop. 13,268), Hainaut prov., S central Belgium, on Sambre R., just SE of Charleroi; coal mining; blast furnaces, coke plants; soda mfg.

Couiza (kwēzä'), village (pop. 1,073), Aude dept., S France, on the Aude and 8 mi. S of Limoux; felt hats, wine.

Coulanges-la-Vineuse (kōōlãzh'-lä-vēnûz'), village (pop. 675), Yonne dept., N central France, 7 mi. S of Auxerre; noted Burgundy wines.

Coulanges-sur-Yonne (-sür-yôn'), village (pop. 499), Yonne dept., N central France, on Yonne R. and Nivernais Canal, and 5 mi. N of Clamecy; sheep, lumber.

Coulee City (kōō'lē), town (pop. 977), Grant co., E central Wash., 90 mi. W of Spokane, in the Grand Coulee 28 mi. SW of Grand Coulee Dam; wheat, apples, lumber. Dry Falls State Park, with huge prehistoric dry falls of the Columbia, is just W.

Coulee Dam, village (pop. c.3,500), Douglas co., central Wash., on Columbia R. adjacent to Grand Coulee Dam and opposite Mason City; hq. for Coulee Dam Natl. Recreational Area (□ 153.9; established 1946), and residential town for govt. employees.

Coulman Island (kōl′mŭn) (15 naut. mi. long, 19 naut. mi. wide), just off Victoria Land, Antarctica, near W shore of Ross Sea; 73°25′S 169°50′E. Discovered 1841 by Sir James C. Ross.

Coulogne (kōōlô′nyü), SE suburb (pop. 2,804) of Calais, Pas-de-Calais dept., N France, in intensive truck-farming area; chicory processing.

Coulommiers (kōōlômyā′), town (pop. 6,302), Seine-et-Marne dept., N central France, on the Grand-Morin and 14 mi. SE of Meaux; agr. trade center, in flower- and fruitgrowing area, noted for its Brie cheese; sugar milling.

Coulonge River (kōōlŏnj′, Fr. kōōlōzh′), SW Que., rises in a series of small lakes in the Laurentians, flows 120 mi. SSE, past Fort Coulonge, to Ottawa R. at Fort Coulonge.

Coulonges-sur-l'Autize (kōōlōzh′-sür-lōtēz′), village (pop. 1,336), Deux-Sèvres dept., W France, 10 mi. E of Fontenay-le-Comte; cattle raising.

Coulon River (kōōlō′) or **Calavon River** (kälävō′), Vaucluse dept., SE France, rises on E slopes of Monts de Vaucluse, flows c.35 mi. W, past Apt, to the Durance below Cavaillon.

Coulsdon and Purley (kōlz′dŭn, pûr′lē), residential urban district (1931 pop. 37,702; 1951 census 63,770), NE Surrey, England, 12 mi. S of London. Includes towns of Coulsdon, Purley, Kenley, Sanderstead, and Woodcote. Coulsdon has 13th-cent. church.

Coulter (kōl′tŭr), town (pop. 271), Franklin co., N central Iowa, 30 mi. SSW of Mason City; livestock.

Coulterville (kōl′tŭrvĭl). **1** Village (pop. c.375), Mariposa co., central Calif., old mining camp of gold rush days, 33 mi. NE of Merced. **2** Village (pop. 1,160), Randolph co., SW Ill., c.40 mi. SE of East St. Louis; corn, wheat, dairy products, livestock; bituminous-coal mines. Inc. 1874.

Council, village (pop. 36), W Alaska, on S Seward Peninsula, 60 mi. NE of Nome; placer gold mining. School; airstrip.

Council. 1 Village (pop. 748), ⊙ Adams co., W Idaho, 25 mi. NW of Cascade and on Weiser R.; lumber, apples, sugar beets. **2** Town (pop. 64), Bladen co., SE N.C., 34 mi. ESE of Lumberton.

Council Bluffs, city (pop. 45,429), ⊙ Pottawattamie co., SW Iowa, below steep bluffs along Missouri R. (bridged here), opposite Omaha, Nebr.; railroad, trade, and industrial center, with railroad repair shops, roundhouses, grain elevators, stockyards, food-processing plants. Mfg. also of agr. machinery, tools, car wheels and railway equipment, machinery, batteries, truck bodies, elevators, radio parts, canvas, wood and concrete construction materials, plastics, feed, livestock remedies, soft drinks, dairy products. Monuments commemorate council here (1804) bet. Lewis and Clark and the Indians, and Lincoln's visit (1859). State school for deaf (1868) is near by. Lake Manawa State Park is just S. Settled 1846 by Mormons on site of trading post (founded in late 1820s) and of an Indian mission established 1838–40 by Father de Smet. Mormons changed town's name from Hart's Bluff to Kanesville; it was named Council Bluffs (1852) after their departure for Utah, and inc. 1853. Important outfitting point during the gold rush (1849–50); grew rapidly after becoming E terminus of Union Pacific RR in 1863. Amelia Jenks Bloomer lived here, 1855–94.

Council Grove, city (pop. 2,722), ⊙ Morris co., E central Kansas, on Neosho R. and 24 mi. NW of Emporia; processing center for grain, poultry, and livestock area; egg packing, poultry dressing; flour, butter. Treaty with Osage Indians was concluded (1825) on site of city, which later became important camping station on Santa Fe Trail. Settled as trading post in 1847, inc. 1858. Methodist Indian mission (1849) is still standing.

Council Hill, town (pop. 166), Muskogee co., E Okla., 21 mi. SW of Muskogee, in agr. area.

Coundon (koun′–), town and parish (pop. 6,302), central Durham, England, 2 mi. E of Bishop Auckland; coal mining.

Countesthorpe, town and parish (pop. 1,921), S central Leicester, England, 6 mi. S of Leicester; textile printing.

Country Club Hills, town (pop. 1,731), St. Louis co., E Mo., just N of St. Louis.

Country Life Acres, town (pop. 57), St. Louis co., E Mo.

Countryside, city (1951 pop. c.350), Johnson co., E Kansas, a suburb of Kansas City.

Coupar-Angus (kōōpŭrăng′gŭs), burgh (1931 pop. 1,893; 1951 census 2,175), E Perthshire, Scotland, on Isla R. and 13 mi. NE of Perth; agr. market. Has remains of Cistercian abbey founded 1164. Near by are traces of Roman camp.

Coupeville (kōōp′vĭl), town (pop. 379), ⊙ Island co., NW Wash., on Whidbey Isl. and 25 mi. NW of Everett; shore resort; grain, poultry, dairy.

Couptrain (kōōtrē′), village (pop. 314), Mayenne dept., W France, on Mayenne R. and 19 mi. NE of Mayenne; candle mfg. Apple orchards.

Courantyne River or **Corantyne River** (kô′rŭntĭn), Du. *Corantijn* (kôräntīn′), river along Br. Guiana–Du. Guiana border, rises in the Serra Acaraí on Brazil border, flows c.450 mi. N, through dense tropical forests, to the Atlantic 5 mi. W of Nieuw Nickerie; in Du. Guiana, its uppermost section is called the Coeroeni (kōōrōō′nē). Navigable for large vessels to Orealla, 45 mi. upstream, for small boats for another 30 mi., and for canoes to Cow Falls, 126 mi. upstream. In its upper course are numerous falls. The region yields valuable timber (greenheart, mahogany, cedar, etc.) and is rich in bauxite deposits. Along the banks of its lower reaches sugar and rice are grown. Sometimes Corentyn and Corentyne.

Courbet (kōōrbā′), village (pop. 823), Alger dept., N central Algeria, near the Mediterranean coast, 7 mi. WNW of Bordj-Ménaïel; tobacco, wine.

Courbet, Port, inlet of Along Bay (Gulf of Tonkin), N Vietnam, in Quangyen anthracite basin. HONGAY is on E shore. Coal-loading facilities.

Courbevoie (kōōrbvwä′), city (pop. 54,025), Seine dept., N central France, a WNW suburb of Paris, 5 mi. from Notre Dame Cathedral, on left bank of Seine R. opposite Neuilly-sur-Seine; center of electrical industry; also mfg. of automobiles, bicycles, plumbing fixtures, canned food, soap, cosmetics. Monument commemorates defense (1870) of Paris.

Courcelles (kōōrsĕl′), town (pop. 16,675), Hainaut prov., S central Belgium, 5 mi. NNW of Charleroi; coal mining; glass mfg.

Courcelles-lès-Lens (kōōrsĕl′-lā-lā′), town (pop. 4,275), Pas-de-Calais dept., N France, 5 mi. NW of Douai; coal mines.

Courçon or **Courçon-d'Aunis** (kōōrsō′-dōnēs′), village (pop. 592), Charente-Maritime dept., W France, 17 mi. ENE of La Rochelle; mfg. (casein, fertilizer), dairying.

Courland or **Kurland** (kŏŏr′lănd), Lettish *Kurzeme* (kōōr′zāmā), region of W and S Latvia, bet. Baltic Sea and Western Dvina R., which separates it from Livonia. Agr. (grain, potatoes, sugar beets, flax) and wooded lowland, drained by Lielupe R. Chief centers are Liepaja, Ventspils, and Jelgava, its historic capital. Originally inhabited by Cours, an extinct Finno-Ugric group, the region was ruled (13th cent.) by Livonian Knights; became (1561–1795) a duchy under Pol. suzerainty; passed (1795) to Russia as a separate govt. In 1920 it became part of independent Latvia, except for small S coastal strip (including Palanga) which went to Lithuania; divided into KURZEME and ZEMGALE.

Courland Lagoon, Ger. *Kurisches Haff* (kōō′rĭshŏŏs häf′), Lith. *Kuršių Įlanka* or *Kuršių Marios*, Rus. *Kurskiy Zaliv*, large Baltic coastal lagoon (□ 625) on coasts of Lithuania and former East Prussia (Kaliningrad oblast, Russian SFSR), bet. Samland peninsula and Memel; 56 mi. long, 28 mi. wide (at S edge), up to 33 ft. deep. Low, marshy, wooded E coast constitutes Neman R. delta, site of elk reserves. Except for its outlet, 25-ft.-deep Memel channel (N), lagoon is separated from open Baltic by **Courland Spit,** Ger. *Kurische Nehrung* (kōō′rĭshŏŏ nā′rōōng), Lith. *Kuršių Neringa*, Rus. *Kurskaya Kosa*, a 60-mi.-long, narrow sandspit bet. Zelenogradsk (Cranz) and Memel; 1–2 mi. wide; shifting dunes rise to 217 ft. On it are fishing villages and summer resorts of Rybachi (Kaliningrad oblast), Nida, Preila, and Juodkrante (Lithuania).

Courmayeur (kōōrmäyûr′), village (pop. 509), Val d'Aosta region, NW Italy, at foot of Mont Blanc, on Dora Baltea R. and 17 mi. WNW of Aosta. Resort (alt. 4,028 ft.) noted for its scenery and mineral springs.

Courmont (kōōrmō′), village (pop. 132), Aisne dept., N France, 5 mi. SE of Fère-en-Tardenois.

Courneuve, La (lä kōōrnûv′), industrial town (pop. 16,609), Seine dept., N central France, a NNE suburb of Paris, 5 mi. from Notre Dame Cathedral, bet. Saint-Denis (NW) and Aubervilliers (S); mfg. (steel, railroad equipment, chemicals, cat gut); copper processing, distilling. Munitions dump exploded here in First World War.

Couronne, Cape (kōōrôn′), headland of Bouches-du-Rhône dept., SE France, on Gulf of Lion, 16 mi. W of Marseilles, at S foot of Chaîne de l'Estaque; 43°19′N 5°3′E. Lighthouse.

Couronne, La (lä–), town (pop. 2,046), Charente dept., W France, 4 mi. SW of Angoulême; paper mills, cement works, foundries. Has ruins of abbey (founded 12th cent.). Formerly called La Palud.

Courpière (kōōrpyâr′), town (pop. 2,144), Puy-de-Dôme dept., central France, on Dore R. and 7 mi. S of Thiers; mfg. (cutlery, pharmaceuticals). Mineral springs near by. Hydroelectric plant 3 mi. S.

Courrières (kōōrēâr′), town (pop. 4,248), Pas-de-Calais dept., N France, 5 mi. NE of Lens, in coal-mining dist.; sugar refining, mfg. of chemicals and building materials. Damaged in both world wars.

Cours (kōōr), town (pop. 4,041), Rhône dept., E central France, in the Monts du Beaujolais, 13 mi. ENE of Roanne; cotton-weaving center (blankets, quilts, shirts). Produces textile machinery and needles.

Coursan (kōōrsä′), town (pop. 3,101), Aude dept., S France, on Aude R. and 5 mi. NE of Narbonne; winegrowing center.

Coursegoules (kōōrsgōōl′), village (pop. 117), Alpes-Maritimes dept., SE France, in Provence Alps, 11 mi. NNE of Grasse.

Coursel, Belgium: see KOERSEL.

Courseulles or **Courseulles-sur-Mer** (kōōrsûl′-sür-mâr′), village (pop. 1,534), Calvados dept., NW France, resort on English Channel at mouth of Seulles R., 11 mi. NNW of Caen; sugar refining; oysters. In Second World War, Canadians landed here (June 6, 1944) in Normandy invasion.

Courson-les-Carrières (kōōrsō′-lā-kärēâr′), village (pop. 654), Yonne dept., N central France, 11 mi. N of Clamecy; dairying.

Courtdale, borough (pop. 982), Luzerne co., NE central Pa., 3 mi. N of Wilkes-Barre. Inc. 1897.

Courtenay (kôrt′nē), city (pop. 1,737), SW B.C., on E central Vancouver Isl., on Comox Harbour of Strait of Georgia at mouth of Courtenay R., 110 mi. NW of Victoria; rail terminus, center of coal-mining, lumbering, farming, and dairying area; sawmilling; lumber-shipping port. Sheet-metal works.

Courtenay (kōōrtŭnē′), village (pop. 1,833), Loiret dept., N central France, 15 mi. SW of Sens; cider distilling, flour milling; dairy equipment mfg.

Courtenay (kôrt′nē), village (pop. 229), Stutsman co., central N.Dak., 23 mi. NNE of Jamestown.

Courthézon (kōōrtāzō′), town (pop. 1,856), Vaucluse dept., SE France, 10 mi. NNE of Avignon; broom-mfg. center; winegrowing, fruit shipping. Has 16th-cent. walls.

Courtine, La (lä kōōrtēn′), village (pop. 446), Creuse dept., central France, on Plateau of Millevaches, 11 mi. NNW of Ussel; health resort. Artillery camp near by.

Courtland (kôrt′lŭnd). **1** Town (pop. 507), Lawrence co., NW Ala., near Tennessee R., 20 mi. WNW of Decatur. **2** Village (pop. c.600), Sacramento co., central Calif., on Sacramento R. and 15 mi. S of Sacramento; fruit, vegetable packing. **3** City (pop. 367), Republic co., N Kansas, 17 mi. NW of Concordia, near Republican R., in grain area. State park near by. **4** Village (pop. 251), Nicollet co., S Minn., on Minnesota R. and 19 mi. WNW of Mankato; dairy products. **5** Village (pop. 275), Panola co., NW Miss., 5 mi. S of Batesville, in agr. and timber area. **6** Town (pop. 443), ⊙ Southampton co., SE Va., on Nottoway R. and 27 mi. W of Suffolk; meat packing.

Courtmacsherry (kôrt″mŭk-shĕ′rē), Gaelic *Cúirt an tSéafraidh*, village (pop. 226), S Co. Cork, Ireland, on Courtmacsherry Bay, 21 mi. SW of Cork; fishing port and seaside resort.

Courtney, village (1940 pop. 500), Washington co., SW Pa., on Monongahela R. and 15 mi. S of Pittsburgh, in bituminous-coal area.

Courtomer (kōōrtômâr′), village (pop. 407), Orne dept., NW France, in the Perche hills, 12 mi. NW of Mortagne; horse breeding.

Courtown Cays, Colombia: see SAN ANDRÉS Y PROVIDENCIA.

Courtrai (kōōrtrā′), Flemish *Kortrijk* (kôrt′rīk), town (pop. 40,085), West Flanders prov., W Belgium, on Lys R. and 16 mi. NNW of Tournai; rail junction; furniture, textile center (linen and cotton spinning and weaving, artificial-silk mfg.); market center for flax-growing region. Has 13th-cent. church of Notre Dame, with famous Van Dyck painting (*Elevation of the Cross*); 15th-cent. church of St. Martin; two 15th-cent. towers; 16th-cent. Gothic town hall. Scene of 1st Battle of the Spurs (1302), when weavers of Ghent and Bruges defeated Fr. army under Count Robert of Artois. Town burned by French in 1382; captured again by French in 1793. In First World War, town taken by Germans in 1914; became an important base for Ypres front. Recaptured by British in October, 1918.

Courtright, village (pop. 325), S Ont., on St. Clair R. and 12 mi. SSW of Sarnia; sugar beets, corn; dairying.

Court-Saint-Étienne (kōōr-sĕtātyĕn′), town (pop. 4,841), Brabant prov., central Belgium, 5 mi. SSW of Wavre; steel foundries.

Courville or **Saint Louis de Courville** (sē lwē dü kōōrvēl′), residential town (pop. 2,011), S Que., on the St. Lawrence and 6 mi. NE of Quebec.

Courville-sur-Eure (kōōrvēl′-sür-ûr′), village (pop. 1,682), Eure-et-Loir dept., NW central France, on the Eure and 11 mi. W of Chartres; cereals, cattle raising.

Cousances-aux-Forges (kōōzãs-ō-fôrzh′), village (pop. 1,043), Meuse dept., NE France, 7 mi. ESE of Saint-Dizier; mfg. (agr. machinery, iron and wooden wheels).

Coushatta (kou″shă′tŭ), town (pop. 1,788), ⊙ Red River parish, NW La., 40 mi. SE of Shreveport and on Red R.; cotton-ginning and -shipping point; oil wells, sawmills. Settled c.1870.

Cousin River (kōōzē′), Yonne dept., N central France, rises in the Morvan SW of Saulieu, flows 30 mi. NW to the Cure 7 mi. below Avallon.

Cousins Island, SW Maine, resort isl. in Casco Bay off Yarmouth; 2 mi. long; bridge connects with Littlejohn Isl.

Cousolre (kōōsôr′), town (pop. 2,368), Nord dept., N France, frontier station on Belg. border, 8 mi. ESE of Maubeuge; marble quarrying.

Coussac-Bonneval (kōōsäk'-bônväl'), village (pop. 653), Haute-Vienne dept., W central France, 5 mi. W of St-Yrieix-la-Perche; gold mining, kaolin quarrying.

Coussey (kōōsĕ'), agr. village (pop. 591), Vosges dept., E France, on Meuse R. and 4 mi. N of Neufchâteau; sawmilling.

Coutances (kōōtäs'), anc. *Constantia*, town (pop. 4,689), Manche dept., NW France, on a hill near English Channel, 17 mi. WSW of Saint-Lô; road and commercial center (grain, dairy produce, livestock, apples, pears); furniture mfg., tanning. Episcopal see. Captured by Americans (July, 1944) after Saint-Lô break-through, it was ⅔ destroyed in Second World War. Its beautiful 13th-cent. Gothic cathedral (dominating town) and 2 other churches were heavily damaged. Coutances gives its name to Cotentin Peninsula.

Couthuin (kōōtwē'), village (pop. 2,435), Liége prov., E central Belgium, 5 mi. W of Huy; iron mining; agr.

Coutras (kōōträ'), town (pop. 3,790), Gironde dept., SW France, on Dronne R., near its influx into the Isle, and 10 mi. NNE of Libourne; commercial center; mfg. of vegetable oils, footwear, felt. Carton factory at Abzac (1.5 mi. S). Here Henry of Navarre defeated Henry III in 1587.

Coutts (kōōts), village (pop. estimate 350), S Alta., on Mont. border, near Milk R., 65 mi. SE of Lethbridge; oil refining; wheat.

Couture-Boussey, La (lä kōōtür'-bōōsā'), commune (pop. 554), Eure dept., NW France, 14 mi. SE of Évreux; mfg. of musical instruments.

Couva (kōō'vù), village, W Trinidad, B.W.I., on railroad and 17 mi. S of Port of Spain; sugar mill.

Couvet (kōōvā'), town (pop. 2,842), Neuchâtel canton, W Switzerland, on Areuse R., in Val de Travers, and 15 mi. WSW of Neuchâtel, in the Jura metal industry.

Couvin (kōōvē'), town (pop. 3,420), Namur prov., S Belgium on W slope of the Ardennes, 10 mi. S of Philippeville; iron mining; foundries.

Couze-et-Saint-Front (kōōz-ā-sē-frō'), village (pop. 579), Dordogne dept., SW France, near the Dordogne, 11 mi. E of Bergerac; paper mill (newsprint, filter paper, blotters).

Covadonga (kōvä-dhōng'gä), village (pop. 107), Oviedo prov., NW Spain, in Asturias, 18 mi. SW of Llanes. Pilgrimage place. In this area, at battle of Covadonga, King Pelayo inflicted, sometime bet. 718 and 725, the 1st decisive defeat upon the Moors, thus beginning the Christian reconquest of Spain.

Covaleda (kōvälā'dhä), town (pop. 1,453), Soria prov., N central Spain, near upper Duero R., 25 mi. WNW of Soria; stock raising, lumbering.

Cova-Lima, Portuguese Timor: see BALIBO.

Covarrubias (kōvärōō'vyäs), town (pop. 1,430), Burgos prov., N Spain, at foot of the Sierra de Covarrubias, on Arlanza R. and 21 mi. SE of Burgos; grapes, cereals, livestock. Liquor distilling, flour milling; fishing.

Covasna (kôväs'nä), Hung. *Kovászna* (kô'väznŏ), village (pop. 6,287), Stalin prov., central Rumania, in Transylvania, on railroad and 18 mi. E of Sfantu-Gheorghe; health resort (alt. 1,823 ft.) in W foothills of the Carpathians, with ferruginous and carbonic springs and baths; lumbering, sawmilling. In Hungary, 1940–45.

Covè (kō'vā), town (pop. c.16,600), S Dahomey, Fr. West Africa, on railroad and 55 mi. NNW of Porto-Novo; market center in agr. region; peanuts, palm kernels, palm oil, cotton, castor beans, coffee, corn. R.C. mission.

Cove, Kincardine, Scotland: see COVE BAY.

Cove. 1 Town (pop. 405), Polk co., W Ark., 14 mi. SW of Mena, near Okla. line. **2** Town (pop. 282), Union co., NE Oregon, 13 mi. E of La Grande; fruit.

Cove and Kilcreggan (kĭlkrĕ'gùn), burgh (1931 pop. 954; 1951 census 887), SW Dumbarton, Scotland. Includes fishing port of Cove, on Loch Long near its mouth on the Clyde, 5 mi. W of Helensburgh; and seaside resort of Kilcreggan, on the Clyde and 4 mi. WSW of Helensburgh.

Cove Bay or **Cove**, fishing village, NE Kincardine, Scotland, on the North Sea, 4 mi. S of Aberdeen.

Cove City, town (pop. 465), Craven co., SE N.C., 16 mi. WNW of New Bern, in agr. area; sawmilling.

Cove Island (4 mi. long, 2 mi. wide), S central Ont., in Lucas Channel, bet. L. Huron and Georgian Bay, 3 mi. N of extremity of Saugeen Peninsula, 60 mi. NW of Owen Sound.

Covelo (kō'vùlō), village (pop. c.600), Mendocino co., NW Calif., 38 mi. NE of Fort Bragg; cattle and sheep raising, farming, hunting, fishing. Round Valley Indian Reservation is near by.

Cove Mountain, S Pa. and NW Md., N–S ridge (c.1,500–2,000 ft.) of the Appalachians, extends c.15 mi. from S end of Tuscarora Mtn., Pa., to the Potomac in Md., along W side of Cumberland Valley.

Covena (kōvē'nù), agr. town (1940 pop. 105), Emanuel co., E central Ga., 9 mi. SW of Swainsboro.

Coveñas (kōvā'nyäs), town (pop. 746), Bolívar dept., N Colombia, minor port on Gulf of Morrosquillo, 11 mi. SW of Tolú; meat-packing plant. Terminus of oil pipe line from Petróla (Santander del Norte dept.).

Covendo (kōvĕn'dō), village, La Paz dept., W Bolivia, on Santa Elena R. and c.50 mi. NNE of Chulumani; quina. Site of mission.

Cove Neck, village (pop. 200), Nassau co., SE N.Y., on N shore of Long Isl., on Cove Neck peninsula (c.1½ mi. long) extending N into Oyster Bay. "Sagamore Hill," home of Theodore Roosevelt, is here.

Covent Garden (kŏ'vùnt), small district of Westminster, London, England, N of the Thames, just N of Charing Cross; site of London's chief vegetable, fruit, and flower market, and of the Royal Opera House (1st built 1732). On E side of Covent Garden is Bow Street, site of main London police court. In 17th and 18th cent. Covent Garden was site of several coffee houses frequented by artists and writers.

Coventry (kŏ'vùntrē), city and county borough (1931 pop. 167,083; 1951 census 258,211), central Warwick, England, 10 mi. NNE of Warwick; 52°25'N 1°30'W; industrial center, known for production (since 1914) of automobiles, aircraft, and aircraft engines. Has coal mining; produces machinery, nuts and bolts, chemicals, bricks, paint, concrete, bicycles, watches, electrical equipment, artificial silk. Its early industry was connected with textile mfg. ("Coventry true blue" woolens). On November 14, 1940, the city was subjected to a German air raid of intense destructiveness, in which many old bldgs. were seriously damaged, including the 14th-cent. cathedral (only the walls and tower remain), the 16th-cent. Ford's Hosp., and 14th-cent. Christ Church; homes, factories, hospitals, and public utilities were destroyed, and there were many casualties. In a later raid St. Mary's Hall, a guild meeting place in 14th cent., was destroyed. Scene of the Coventry Plays, dating from 15th cent. Site of a Benedictine abbey, founded c.1043 by Lady Godiva and her husband, Leofric, and locale of the legend of Lady Godiva's ride and Peeping Tom, celebrated by Tennyson. Later Coventry became seat of a bishopric; its monastic cathedral was demolished under Henry VIII. Here Bolingbroke and the duke of Norfolk met (related in Shakespeare's *Richard II*). Under Henry IV and Henry VI parliaments met here. The phrase *to send to Coventry*, meaning to ostracize socially, is of uncertain origin. County borough includes industrial suburbs of Longford (N), Foleshill (NNE), Stoke (E).

Coventry. 1 Town (pop. 4,043), Tolland co., E central Conn., on Willimantic R. and 16 mi. E of Hartford; agr., mfg. (yarn, fishline, silk goods). Monument to Nathan Hale, b. here. Near South Coventry village (pop. 1,617) is site of flood-control dam in the Willimantic. Settled c.1700, inc. 1711. **2** Town (pop. 9,869), Kent co., W central R.I., on Conn. line, on Flat and Pawtuxet rivers and 10 mi. SW of Providence; agr. in W; mfg. (woolens, cottons, elastic braid) in villages of Arkwright, Anthony (with Nathanael Greene's home), Greene, Summit, and WASHINGTON (administrative center). Flat R. Reservoir here. Set off from Warwick and inc. 1741. **3** Town (pop. 497), Orleans co., N Vt., on Black R., just SW of Newport; agr.

Cove of Cork, Ireland: see CÓBH.

Cove Point, promontory, Calvert co., S Md., on W shore of Chesapeake Bay at N side of Patuxent R. mouth, 15 mi. SE of Prince Frederick; lighthouse.

Covilhã (kōōvēlyă'), city (pop. 19,213), Castelo Branco dist., Beira Baixa prov., central Portugal, on SE slope of Serra da Estrêla, on railroad and 50 mi. E of Coimbra; Portugal's chief wool-milling center. Has dyeworks, textile school, sanatorium. Center for tourism and winter sports in near-by mts. and Zêzere R. valley. Had well-known fair.

Covina (kōvē'nù), city (pop. 3,956), Los Angeles co., S Calif., 20 mi. E of downtown Los Angeles, at base of San Gabriel Mts.; packing, shipping center for citrus fruit. Laid out 1885, inc. 1901.

Covington (kŭ'vĭngtùn). **1** County (□ 1,034; pop. 40,373), S Ala.; ⊙ Andalusia. Coastal plain area bordering on Fla., drained by Conecuh R. and Patsaliga Creek. Cotton, corn, hogs. Mfg. at Andalusia. Part of Conecuh Natl. Forest in S. Formed 1821. **2** County (□ 416; pop. 16,036), S central Miss.; ⊙ Collins. Drained by tributaries of Leaf R. Agr. (cotton, corn, truck), dairying, lumbering. Formed 1819.

Covington. 1 City (pop. 5,192), ⊙ Newton co., N central Ga., 32 mi. ESE of Atlanta; textile, lumber mills. Inc. as town 1822, as city 1854. **2** City (pop. 2,235), ⊙ Fountain co., W Ind., on the Wabash and c.50 mi. N of Terre Haute, in agr. and bituminous-coal area; ships canned goods, farm produce, fruit. Sand and gravel pits. Laid out 1826. **3** City (pop. 64,452), a ⊙ Kenton co., extreme N Ky., on left bank (levee) of the Ohio (bridged) opposite Cincinnati, at Licking R. mouth opposite Newport (E), to which it is also connected by bridges. Principal suburb within Cincinnati metropolitan dist.; 2d-largest city of Ky.; rail junction (shops); airport. An important industrial center, with tobacco and meat-packing plants, foundries, breweries, and distilleries; mfg. of X-ray equipment, prison equipment, machine tools, wire goods, food, metal, paper, and wood products, electrical equipment, tiles, bricks, asphalt, hardware, fertilizer. Oil refining at Latonia (S suburb). Seat of Northern Ky. State Vocational School, Villa Madonna Col., and several private acads. Points of interest include: suspension bridge to Cincinnati, designed by John A. Roebling and built 1866; Devou and George Rogers Clark memorial parks; tiny chapel at Monte Casino, reputedly world's smallest, seating 3; St. Mary's Cathedral (R.C.), modeled after Notre Dame de Paris, with one of world's largest stained-glass windows; Latonia Race Track (opened 1883); Carneal House (built 1815); Baker Hunt Foundation and Williams' Natural History Mus.; boyhood home of Dan Carter Beard; birthplace of Frank Duveneck, some of whose paintings are in city. A ferry and tavern built here c.1801; city settled 1812, laid out 1815, inc. 1834. **4** Town (pop. 5,113), ⊙ St. Tammany parish, SE La., 37 mi. N of New Orleans, and on the Bogue Falia, near L. Pontchartrain; strawberries, cotton, oranges; naval-stores and lumber milling; mfg. of charcoal wood preservatives, tung oil; resort. Settled 1769 inc. 1813. Has state park. **5** Village (pop. 2,172), Miami co., W Ohio, 6 mi. WSW of Piqua, at junction of Stillwater R. and Greenville Creek; grain, tobacco, dairy products, livestock, poultry; sawmill. Settled 1807, inc. 1835. **6** Town (pop. 769), Garfield co., N Okla., 17 mi. ESE of Enid; wheat, livestock, poultry; dairy products. Oil and natural-gas wells. **7** Town (pop. 4,379), ⊙ Tipton co., W Tenn., 35 mi. NE of Memphis, in cotton-growing, timber area; cotton yarn, cottonseed products, beverages. **8** Town (pop. 5,860), ⊙ Alleghany co., W Va., in Jackson R. valley, 35 mi. N of Roanoke, in the Alleghenies; mfg. center with large paper, pulp, and rayon-yarn plants; flour and textile milling, limestone quarrying. Iron and coal fields near by. Laid out 1819; inc. 1902.

Covington Mills, town (1940 pop. 317), Newton co., N central Ga., 2 mi. E of Covington.

Covunco Centro, Argentina: see MARIANO MORENO.

Cowal (kou'ùl), peninsula of SE Argyll, Scotland, bet. Loch Fyne (W) and Loch Long (E), bounded S by the Kyles of Bute and the Firth of Clyde; c.30 mi. long, up to 15 mi. wide. Dunoon is on SE shore.

Cowal, Lake (□ 23), SE central New South Wales, Australia, 140 mi. NW of Canberra; 16 mi. long, 5 mi. wide; shallow.

Cowan (kou'ùn), town (pop. 1,835), Franklin co., S Tenn., at edge of Cumberland Plateau, 40 mi. WNW of Chattanooga, in agr. area (potatoes, corn, clover); makes shoes, lime, cement. Settled 1826; inc. 1921.

Cowan Lake (kou'ùn) (32 mi. long, 1 mi. wide), central Sask., W of Prince Albert Natl. Park, 70 mi. NW of Prince Albert. Drains NW through Beaver R. into Churchill R.

Cowansville, town (pop. 3,486), S Que., on Yamaska R. and 25 mi. ESE of St. Jean; silk- and cotton-milling center; woodworking, furniture mfg.

Cowbridge, municipal borough (1931 pop. 1,018; 1951 census 1,055), S Glamorgan, Wales, 12 mi. W of Cardiff; agr. market. Has remains of 13th-14th-cent. town walls. Grammar school founded 1685.

Cow Creek, S central Kansas, rises in Barton co., flows 77 mi. SE, past Hutchinson, to Arkansas R. 7 mi. SE of Hutchinson.

Cowden (kou'dùn), village (pop. 619), Shelby co., central Ill., near Kaskaskia R., 40 mi. S of Decatur; agr., bituminous-coal mining.

Cowdenbeath (koudùnbēth'), burgh (1931 pop. 12,732; 1951 census 13,153), S Fifeshire, Scotland, 6 mi. NE of Dunfermline; coal-mining center.

Cowee Bald, N.C.: see COWEE MOUNTAINS.

Cowee Mountains (kō'ē), W N.C., transverse ridge of the Appalachians along Macon-Jackson co. border; from Tuckasegee R. near Bryson City extend SSE to a point near Highlands; included in Nantahala Natl. Forest. Rise to 5,145 ft. in Yellow Mtn., 5 mi. N of Highlands, to 5,085 ft. in Cowee Bald, 7 mi. WSW of Dillsboro.

Cowell (koul), town and port (pop. 501), S South Australia, on Franklin Harbour of E Eyre Peninsula, 72 mi. SW of Port Pirie across Spencer Gulf; asbestos. Exports sheep, silver. Small silver mine near by.

Cowen, town (pop. 632), Webster co., central W.Va., 9 mi. SW of Webster Springs, in coal-mining and agr. area.

Cowes, Australia: see PHILLIP ISLAND.

Cowes (kouz), urban district (1931 pop. 10,171; 1951 census 17,154), on N coast of Isle of Wight, Hampshire, England, on The Solent at mouth of Medina R., 10 mi. WSW of Portsmouth; port, seaside resort, and yacht-building center. Scene of annual regatta (Cowes Week), and hq. of Royal Yacht Squadron (established 1856), housed in castle built by Henry VIII. Founders of Maryland sailed from here in 1633. OSBORNE is in Cowes.

Cowesett, R.I.: see WARWICK.

Coweta (kouwē'tù), county (□ 443; pop. 27,786), W Ga.; ⊙ Newman. Bounded NW by Chattahoochee

R. Agr. (cotton, corn, melons, pecans, peaches, livestock) area. Textile mfg., sawmilling. Formed 1826.

Coweta (kōē′tŭ), town (pop. 1,601), Wagoner co., E Okla., 24 mi. SE of Tulsa, in agr. area (grain, cotton, corn); cotton ginning, flour and feed milling. Settled by Indians; inc. 1900.

Cowgill (kou′gĭl), town (pop. 241), Caldwell co., NW Mo., 25 mi. SW of Chillicothe.

Cowichan Lake (kou′ĭchŭn, kou-ĭ′chŭn) (□ 24), SW B.C., on S Vancouver Isl., 15 mi. WNW of Duncan, in lumbering area; 20 mi. long, 1–2 mi. wide. Drained E into Strait of Georgia by Cowichan R. (28 mi. long). Lake Cowichan village at E end, is trade center and fishing resort.

Cowick, England: see SNAITH AND COWICK.

Cowie Harbour (kou′ē), inlet (30 mi. long, 5–10 mi. wide) of Celebes Sea, NE Borneo; Tawau is on NE shore.

Cowlairs, NE suburb (pop. 22,512) of Glasgow, Lanark, Scotland.

Cowles, village (pop. 130), Webster co., S Nebr., 8 mi. NNE of Red Cloud.

Cowley, 1 Suburb, Middlesex, England: see UXBRIDGE. **2** Suburb, Oxfordshire, England: see OXFORD.

Cowley, county (□ 1,136; pop. 36,905), S Kansas; ⊙ Winfield. Gently rolling to hilly area, bordering S on Okla.; drained in W by Arkansas and Walnut rivers. Livestock, grain. Extensive oil and natural-gas fields. Formed 1870.

Cowley, town (pop. 463), Big Horn co., N Wyo., near Shoshone R. and Mont. line, 5 mi. NW of Lovell; food-processing point (flour and canned vegetables) in irrigated agr. region; sugar beets, beans, hay. Quarries near by.

Cowling (kō′lĭng), town and parish (pop. 1,745), West Riding, W Yorkshire, England, 6 mi. SSW of Skipton; cotton and rayon milling.

Cowlington (kou′lĭngtŭn), town (pop. 83), Le Flore co., SE Okla., 22 mi. WSW of Fort Smith (Ark.), in agr. area.

Cowlitz, county (□ 1,146; pop. 53,369), SW Wash.; ⊙ Kelso. Rolling hill area rising to foothills of Cascade Range in E; watered by Cowlitz, Lewis, and Columbia rivers. Timber, clay, fish, livestock, dairy products, fruit, hay, truck. Formed 1854.

Cowlitz River, SW Wash., rises in Cascade Range SE of Mt. Rainier, flows c.130 mi. W and S, past Kelso, to Columbia R. near Longview.

Cowpasture River, WVa., rises in the Alleghenies in NE Highland co., near W.Va. line; flows c.75 mi. SW, joining Jackson R. SE of Iron Gate to form James R.

Cowpen, England: see BLYTH.

Cowpens (kou′pĕnz, -pĭnz, kŭ′-), town (pop. 1,879), Spartanburg co., NW S.C., 9 mi. ENE of Spartanburg; textile mill. N, 8 mi., is Cowpens Natl. Battlefield Site (1 acre; established 1929) marking battle here (Jan. 17, 1781) in Carolina Campaign of Revolutionary War, in which British under Tarleton were defeated by Morgan.

Cowra (kou′rŭ), municipality (pop. 5,473), E central New South Wales, Australia, on Lachlan R. and 100 mi. NNW of Canberra; rail junction; copper-mining center; flour mill.

Cox (kôsh), village (pop. 2,592), Alicante prov., E Spain, 5 mi. NE of Orihuela; agr. trade (hemp, cereals, vegetables, potatoes).

Coxcatlán (kōskätlän′). **1** Town (pop. 1,741), Puebla, central Mexico, 21 mi. SE of Tehuacán; corn, sugar cane, fruit, livestock. **2** Town (pop. 1,102), San Luis Potosí, E Mexico, in fertile Gulf lowland, 32 mi. SSE of Valles: coffee, sugar cane, tobacco, fruit, livestock.

Coxilha, for Portuguese names beginning thus: see under following part of the name.

Coxim (kŏŏshēm′), city (pop. 684), S central Mato Grosso, Brazil, head of irregular navigation on Taquari R. and 180 mi. ENE of Corumbá; cattle. Diamonds, sapphires, rubies found in small Coxim R. Airfield. Called Herculânia or Herculânea, 1939–48.

Coxipó River (kŏŏshēpô′), central Mato Grosso, Brazil, small left tributary of Cuiabá R., which it enters c.20 mi. above Cuiabá; diamond washings.

Coxlodge, England: see GOSFORTH.

Coxquihui (kōskē′wē), town (pop. 3,136), Veracruz, E Mexico, in Sierra Madre Oriental foothills, on Puebla border, 26 mi. SW of Papantla; agr. center (corn, sugar cane, coffee, tobacco, fruit, livestock).

Coxsackie (kŏŏksŏ′kē), village (pop. 2,722), Greene co., SE N.Y., near W bank of the Hudson, 21 mi. S of Albany, in diversified-farming area; summer resort. Mfg.: valves, machinery, electrical appliances, clothing, food products, fertilizers. Granite quarrying; mushroom growing. Settled by the Dutch before 1700; inc. 1867.

Cox's Bazar, town (pop. 5,945), Chittagong dist., SE East Bengal, E Pakistan, on Bay of Bengal, 65 mi. S of Chittagong; trades in rice, oilseeds, sugar cane, tobacco. Track leads SE to Maungdaw on Burmese Arakan coast. Figured in 1st Burmese War of 1784. Lighthouse 30 mi. NNW, on isl.

Coxton, village (1940 pop. 1,196), Harlan co., SE Ky., in the Cumberlands, on Clover Fork of Cumberland R. and 30 mi. NE of Middlesboro, in bituminous-coal area.

Coxwold, agr. village and parish (pop. 240), North Riding, N central Yorkshire, England, 7 mi. ESE of Thirsk. Residence of Laurence Sterne. Has 15th-cent. church and Sterne's house, Shandy Hall.

Coxyde, Belgium: see KOKSIJDE.

Coyah (kō′yä), village, W Fr. Guinea, Fr. West Africa, 20 mi. ENE of Conakry; pineapple growing and canning; also bananas and palm kernels.

Coyame (koiä′mā), town (pop. 501), Chihuahua, N Mexico, on affluent of Conchos R. and 80 mi. NE of Chihuahua; corn, fruit, livestock.

Coychurch Higher, town and parish (pop. 1,301), S central Glamorgan, Wales, 5 mi. NE of Bridgend; coal mining. Has 13th-cent. church and remains of 2 anc. inscribed stones.

Coycoyan, Sierra de (syĕ′rä dā koikoi′än), range along Oaxaca-Guerrero border, S Mexico, in Sierra Madre del Sur, 30 mi. W of Tlaxiaco; c.45 mi. long; rises to 9,317 ft.

Coyhaique (koi-ī′kā), village (pop. 2,577), Aysén prov., S Chile, on Coyhaique R. (an affluent of Simpson R.), in the Andes, and 38 mi. ESE of Puerto Aysén, on road to Argentina. Tourist resort; sheep raising, lumbering. Radio station. Developed mainly in 1930s.

Coyle, town (pop. 360), Logan co., central Okla., 12 mi. NE of Guthrie, and on Cimarron R.; agr. and cotton ginning.

Coyle River or **Coig River,** Patagonian stream in S Santa Cruz natl. territory, Argentina, rises near Chile border, flows c.200 mi. generally E to the Atlantic at Puerto Coyle, 45 mi. N of Río Gallegos, forming 20-mi.-long estuary with good harbor facilities.

Coylton, agr. village and parish (pop. 2,366), central Ayrshire, Scotland, 6 mi. E of Ayr. Just N is agr. village of New Coylton.

Coyoacán (koiwäkän′), city (pop. 23,724), Federal Dist., central Mexico, 6 mi. S of Mexico city; residential suburb; paper-milling center. Anc. pre-Aztec town. First seat of Sp. govt. Cortés built a palace (now municipal palace) here. Other noteworthy colonial bldgs. are: San Juan Bautista church (1583), Dominican monastery (1530), and Casa de Alvarado, a colonial mansion, now a mus.

Coyolar, Costa Rica: see PUERTO COYOLAR.

Coyolate River (koī-ōlä′tā), S Guatemala, rises in highlands near Tecpán, flows c.70 mi. SSW, past Santa Ana Mixtán, to the Pacific 35 mi. W of San José.

Coyomeapan (koiōmää′pän), officially Santa María Coyomeapan, town (pop. 1,885), Puebla, central Mexico, in Sierra Madre, 30 mi. SE of Tehuacán; corn, sugar cane, fruit, livestock.

Coyote, Mexico: see EL COYOTE.

Coyote Creek (kīō′tē) or **Coyote River,** W Calif., rises in E Santa Clara co., flows S, through Coyote Reservoir (formed by a dam 6 mi. E of Morgan Hill), then NW, through Santa Clara Valley and past San Jose, to San Francisco Bay. Length, c.60 mi.

Coyote River, Calif.: see COYOTE CREEK.

Coyotepec (koiōtāpĕk′). **1** Town (pop. 4,159), Mexico state, central Mexico, 25 mi. N of Mexico city; agr. center (grain, maguey, fruit, livestock). **2** or **San Bartolo Coyotepec** (sän bärtō′lō), town, Oaxaca, S Mexico, in Sierra Madre del Sur, on railroad and 7 mi. S of Oaxaca; noted for black pottery. **3** Officially San Vicente Coyotepec, town (pop. 1,674), Puebla, central Mexico, 30 mi. W of Tehuacán; rice, corn, sugar cane, fruit, livestock.

Coytesville (koits′-), village (pop. c.2,000), Bergen co., NE N.J., near Hudson R., just N of Fort Lee, on S end of The Palisades.

Coyuca de Benítez (koiōō′kä dā bānē′tĕs), city (pop. 2,141), Guerrero, SW Mexico, in Pacific lowland, 26 mi. NW of Acapulco; rice, sugar cane, fruit, livestock.

Coyuca de Catalán (kätälän′), city (pop. 1,989), Guerrero, SW Mexico, on Río de las Balsas and 2 mi. SW of Altamirano; cereals, cotton, sugar cane, fruit. Ruins near by.

Coyuca Lagoon (20 mi. long), on Pacific coast of Guerrero, SW Mexico, just NW of Acapulco.

Coyutla (koiōōt′lä), town (pop. 4,363), Veracruz, E Mexico, in Sierra Madre Oriental foothills, 25 mi. SW of Papantla; agr. center (corn, beans, sugar cane, tobacco, coffee, stock).

Coyville, city (pop. 106), Wilson co., SE Kansas, on Verdigris R. and 24 mi. W of Chanute; livestock, grain.

Cozad (kōzăd′), city (pop. 2,910), Dawson co., S central Nebr., 13 mi. WNW of Lexington and on Platte R.; trading, hay-shipping point; dairy and poultry produce, livestock, alfalfa. Founded 1874.

Cózar (kō′thär), town (pop. 2,862), Ciudad Real prov., S central Spain, 18 mi. ESE of Valdepeñas; grapes, olives, cereals, sheep; liquor distilling, cheese processing.

Cozes (kōz), village (pop. 672), Charente-Maritime dept., W France, 15 mi. SW of Saintes; distilling.

Cozia, Rumania: see CALIMANESTI.

Cozie, Alpi, Italy and France: see COTTIAN ALPS.

Cozmeni, Ukrainian SSR: see KITSMAN.

Cozumel (kōsōōmĕl′), town (pop. 2,085), Quintana Roo, SE Mexico, on Cozumel Isl. (□ 189; 29 mi. long, 9 mi. wide), 11 mi. E of Yucatan Peninsula coast, in Caribbean Sea, 175 mi. ESE of Mérida. Trades in chicle, fine woods, stock. Airfield. Sometimes called San Miguel Cozumel. The isl., discovered 1517 by Fernández de Córdoba, has many Maya remains.

Cozzo, Cape (kô′tsô), Calabria, S Italy, at SW end of Gulf of Sant'Eufemia, 5 mi. NE of Tropea; 38°43′N 15°58′E.

Crabbs Cross, town in Feckenham parish (pop. 2,322), E Worcester, England, 2 mi. S of Redditch; light-metals industry.

Crab Island (544 acres), off Br. Guiana, at mouth of Berbice R.; 6°20′N 57°33′W.

Crab Orchard. 1 Town (pop. 757), Lincoln co., central Ky., 20 mi. SE of Danville, in Cumberland foothills; health resort, with mineral springs. On old Wilderness Road; near by is Whitley Home State Park, containing 18th-cent. Whitley House, once center of religious, political, and social life of Transylvania region. **2** Village (pop. 120), Johnson co., SE Nebr., 12 mi. W of Tecumseh and on branch of Nemaha R.; farm trade center. **3** Village (pop. 1,544), Raleigh co., S W.Va., 3 mi. S of Beckley, in coal region.

Crab Orchard Lake, Williamson co., S Ill., 8 mi. S of Herrin; 9 mi. long, 1–4 mi. wide. Impounded 1939 by dam in small Crab Orchard Creek.

Crab Orchard Mountains, E Tenn., ridge (2–3,000 ft.) of the Cumberlands, W of Harriman; lie bet. Pine Mtn. (NE), Walden Ridge (SW), Cumberland Plateau (N), and Great Appalachian Valley (S); highest point (3,100 ft.) is 11 mi. W of Rockwood. Source of Sequatchie R.

Crabtree, village (pop. 1,168), Westmoreland co., SW Pa., 6 mi. NE of Greensburg; bituminous coal.

Crabtree Bald, W N.C., peak (5,280 ft.) of Great Smoky Mts., 20 mi. WNW of Asheville.

Crac, Le, Jordan: see KERAK.

Cracow (krā′kō, -kou, krā′kō), village (pop. 417), E Queensland, Australia, 130 mi. S of Rockhampton, in mining area (gold, silver).

Cracow (krā′kō, krā′kou), Pol. *Kraków* (krä′kŏŏf), Ger. *Krakau* (krä′kou), Latin *Cracovia*, city (1950 pop. c.347,500), ⊙ KRAKOW prov., S Poland, on both banks of the Vistula and 155 mi. SSW of Warsaw; 50°5′N 19°55′E. An important rail junction, Cracow is chiefly a trade and commercial center; also has industries. Mfg. of railroad cars, boilers, agr. machinery, construction materials, paper, clothing, chemicals, wire, electrical goods; food, tobacco, and hemp processing, printing. Near by is a new metallurgical center, NOWA HUTA, built after 1949. The Univ. of Cracow (also known as Jagiellonian Univ.), founded 1364 by Pope Urban V, has long been a bulwark of Pol. culture and a leading European center of learning; Copernicus was one of its students. There are also academies of mining, fine art, and commerce. Standing on a hill, the Wawel, are the royal castle, rebuilt (16th cent.) in Ital. Renaissance style, and the Gothic cathedral (rebuilt 14th cent.), which contains the tombs of kings and other great Poles. On Rynek [market] square is 13th-cent. church of Our Lady with altar carvings by Veit Stoss; 14th-cent. Sukiennice [cloth hall]; and tower of 14th-cent. town hall. Cracow has also remains of former defensive walls. There are beautiful medieval bldgs., museums (including Natl. Mus.), galleries, and libraries (notably Jagiello Library). The tombs of Krakus and Wanda (legendary Pol. rulers), Kosciusko, and Pilsudski are near by. The city, allegedly founded c.700, was made (c.1000) a bishopric; in 14th cent. became residence of kings of Poland. Cracow fire in 1595 caused the transfer of the royal residence to Warsaw in 1609, but the kings continued to be crowned and buried in Cracow. The city passed (1795) to Austria; was included (1809) in grand duchy of Warsaw. In 1815, Congress of Vienna created the republic of Cracow, a protectorate of Russia, Prussia, and Austria, consisting of the city and vicinity; included (1846) in Austria as grand duchy of Cracow; in 1848, a center of revolution against Austria. City reverted to Poland in 1918 and became ⊙ Krakow prov. During Second World War, Cracow suffered relatively little damage.

Cracow Jura (jŏŏ′rŭ), Pol. *Jura Krakowska* (yōō′rä kräkôf′skä), mountain range, S Poland, extending c.60 mi. NNW-SSE, bet. Czestochowa and Cracow; highest point (1,653 ft.) is 6 mi. ESE of Zawierce. Also called Cracow-Czestochowa Highland, Pol. *Wyżyna Krakowsko-Częstochowska.*

Cracroft Island (□ 90), SW B.C., on N side of Johnstone Strait, at E end of Queen Charlotte Strait, opposite Vancouver Isl., 15 mi. E of Alert Bay; 20 mi. long, 1–5 mi. wide. On Port Harvey, bay on SE coast, is Cracroft fishing village.

Cradle Mountain (5,069 ft.), W central Tasmania, 45 mi. S of Burnie, on plateau (alt. 4,000 ft.) of natl. park. One of highest peaks in Tasmania; Legge Tor is highest.

Cradle Mountains, Wales and England: see BLACK MOUNTAINS.

Cradley, agr. village and parish (pop. 1,067), E Hereford, England, 4 mi. WNW of Great Malvern. Has 15th-cent. half-timbered parish hall. Church is of Norman origin.

Cradley Heath, town (pop. 9,749) in Rowley Regis municipal borough, S Stafford, England; machinery, pharmaceuticals.

Cradock, town (pop. 13,119), SE Cape Prov., U. of So. Afr., on Great Fish R. and 120 mi. N of Port Elizabeth; commercial center for large agr. region (stock, wool, mohair, grain, feed crops); scene of agr. fairs. Novelist Olive Schreiner lived here. Marlow Agr. Col. is 5 mi. NNW. Hot sulphur springs are 2 mi. N. Mountain Zebra Natl. Park is 15 mi. WNW.

Crafton, residential borough (pop. 8,066), Allegheny co., SW Pa., W suburb of Pittsburgh; paper boxes, bituminous coal, stoves. Inc. 1894.

Craftsbury, town (pop. 709), Orleans co., N Vt., on Black R. and 22 mi. SW of Newport; lumber, dairy products; winter sports. Craftsbury Acad. (1829) is here.

Craghead, town and parish (pop. 4,973), N Durham, England, 9 mi. S of Newcastle-upon-Tyne; coal mining.

Cragsmoor, resort village, Ulster co., SE N.Y., in the Shawangunk range, 3 mi. S of Ellenville.

Craig, town (pop. 370), SE Alaska, on W coast of Prince of Wales Isl., 60 mi. W of Ketchikan; 55°29′N 133°9′W; port of entry, with steamer services to Prince Rupert and U.S. and Alaskan ports; supply center for Alaskan fishing fleets. Sawmill, salmon canneries. Seaplane base.

Craig. 1 County (□ 764; pop. 18,263), NE Okla.; ⊙Vinita. Bounded N by Kansas line; drained by Neosho R. and small Cabin Creek. Stock raising, agr. (grain, poultry, corn; dairy products). Some mfg. at Vinita. Oil, natural-gas wells; coal mines; hardwood timber. Formed 1907. **2** County (□ 336; pop. 3,452), W Va.; ⊙ New Castle. In the Alleghenies, entirely within Jefferson Natl. Forest; bounded W by W.Va.; drained by Craig Creek. Grain, livestock, poultry (especially turkeys); timber; iron-ore deposits. Mtn. resorts, mineral springs; hunting, fishing. Formed 1851.

Craig. 1 Town (pop. 3,080), ⊙ Moffat co., NW Colo., on Yampa R. and 145 mi. WNW of Denver; alt. 6,200 ft. Livestock-shipping point; oil refineries, gas and oil wells. Inc. 1908. **2** Village, Fla.: see FLORIDA KEYS. **3** Town (pop. 142), Plymouth co., NW Iowa, 10 mi. NW of Le Mars; livestock, grain. **4** City (pop. 578), Holt co., NW Mo., on Tarkio R. and 40 mi. NW of St. Joseph; corn, wheat, dairy products, stock. **5** Village (pop. 384), Burt co., E Nebr., 40 mi. NNW of Omaha and on branch of Elkhorn R.; livestock, grain, poultry.

Craig, Mount (13,250 ft.), SW Yukon, near Alaska border, in St. Elias Mts., 200 mi. WNW of Whitehorse; 61°15′N 140°51′W.

Craig Air Force Base, Ala.: see SELMA.

Craig Beach, village (pop. 569), Mahoning co., E Ohio, 17 mi. W of Youngstown, near Milton Reservoir.

Craig Creek, W Va., rises in Montgomery co., flows c.75 mi. generally NW, past New Castle, to James R. opposite Eagle Rock.

Craigellachie (krāgĕlă′chē), agr. village, W Banffshire, Scotland, on the Spey and 2 mi. NE of Aberlour; whisky distilling. Near by is anc. fortalice, rebuilt in 19th cent.

Craigenputtock (krāgŭnpŭ′tŭk), agr. village in Dunscore parish (pop. 962), W Dumfries, Scotland, 6 mi. W of Dunscore. Site of farm where Carlyle lived, 1828–34, and wrote *Sartor Resartus*. His estate was left to Edinburgh Univ.

Craig Harbour, trading post, SE Ellesmere Isl., NE Franklin Dist., Northwest Territories, on Jones Sound of the Arctic Ocean; 76°12′N 81°2′W; former Royal Canadian Mounted Police post.

Craighead (krăg′hĕd), county (□ 717; pop. 50,613), NE Ark.; ⊙ JONESBORO and Lake City. Intersected by Crowley's Ridge; drained by St. Francis and Cache rivers. Agr. (cotton, corn, rice, fruit, poultry, livestock). Mfg. at Jonesboro. Gravel pits. Formed 1859.

Craighead Caverns, Tenn.: see SWEETWATER.

Craig Healing Springs, resort village, Craig co., W Va., in the Alleghenies, 22 mi. NW of Roanoke; mineral springs.

Craigmont, village (pop. 594), Lewis co., W Idaho, 28 mi. ESE of Lewiston; lumber, grain, potatoes.

Craigmore, village, Umtali prov., E Southern Rhodesia, in Mashonaland, 19 mi. SSW of Chipinga; tobacco, corn, wheat, citrus fruit, dairy products.

Craigmyle (krāg′mīl), village (pop. 140), S central Alta., 24 mi. NE of Drumheller; coal; paint mfg.

Craignair, Scotland: see DALBEATTIE.

Craignish Hills (krā′nĭsh), range (20 mi. long) in SW Cape Breton Isl., E N.S.; rises to 1,030 ft. on McIntyre Mtn., 12 mi. N of Port Hawkesbury.

Craig Phadrick, wooded hill (430 ft.), N Inverness, Scotland, 2 mi. W of Inverness. Site of anc. vitrified fortification.

Craigsville, village (1940 pop. 892), Augusta co., W Va., on Maury R. and 17 mi. WSW of Staunton; woolen milling.

Craigville, Mass.: see BARNSTABLE, town.

Craik, town (pop. 439), S Sask., near Arm R., 50 mi. NNW of Moose Jaw; grain elevators, lumbering.

Crail (krāl), burgh (1931 pop. 1,059; 1951 census 1,139), E Fifeshire, Scotland, on the Firth of Forth near its mouth on the North Sea, 9 mi. SE of St. Andrews; seaside resort and fishing center; agr. market. Near by is Fife Ness.

Crailsheim (krīls′hīm), town (pop. 8,653), N Württemberg, Germany, after 1945 in Württemberg-Baden, on the Jagst and 15 mi. E of Schwäbisch Hall; rail junction; steel construction. Mfg. of asbestos clothing, shoes, cement goods, door and window frames; lumber milling. Bombing and severe fighting here towards end of Second World War destroyed most of old city and historic bldgs. Of anc. origin; chartered 1338.

Crainville, village (pop. 433), Williamson co., S Ill., 5 mi. SSW of Herrin, in bituminous-coal-mining and agr. area. Crab Orchard L. is S.

Craiova (krăyô′vä), city (1948 pop., including suburbs, 84,574), ⊙ Dolj prov., S Rumania, in Walachia, on Jiu R. and 120 mi. WSW of Bucharest; economic and cultural center; major rail junction, grain market, and garrison town. Produces textiles, canned foods, agr. and industrial machinery, ceramics, furniture, cordage, brushes, leather goods, printed matter, stone work, soap, candles, confectionery, chocolate, vinegar. Has number of 16th- and 18th-cent. churches, noted 17th-cent. St. Demetrius church restored in 18th cent., 19th-cent. palace of justice, mus. with extensive medieval archaeological and natural science collections, rich library; 16th-cent. monastery near by. Seat of military and commercial schools, and of archaeological institute of Oltenia. Founded on the site of a Roman settlement, it was an important trading center by 14th cent. Became ⊙ Oltenia in 1492. S Dobruja was returned to Bulgaria by agreement signed here (1940).

Cramant (krämã′), village (pop. 942), Marne dept., N France, 5 mi. SSE of Épernay; winegrowing (champagne).

Cramerton (krā′mûrtŭn), textile village (pop. 3,211), Gaston co., S N.C., on arm of Catawba L., 13 mi. W of Charlotte.

Cramlington, former urban district (1931 pop. 8,238), SE Northumberland, England, 8 mi. N of Newcastle-upon-Tyne; coal-mining center. Here are coal-mining towns of East Cramlington (E), Hartford (N), and Shankhouse (NE). Cramlington inc. (1935) in Seaton Valley.

Cramond (krā′mŭnd, kră′–), W suburb (pop. 5,631) of Edinburgh, Scotland.

Crampel (krăpĕl′), village, NW Algeria, at border of Oran dept. and Southern Territories, S terminus of normal-gauge railroad from Oran, and 55 mi. S of Sidi-bel-Abbès; esparto depot; sheep raising. Also called Ras-el-Ma.

Cranae, Greece: see MARATHONISI.

Cranberry Glades, W.Va.: see RICHWOOD.

Cranberry Island, Knox co., S Maine, in Muscongus Bay, SSW of Friendship; c.1 mi. long.

Cranberry Isles, resort town (pop. 228), Hancock co., S Maine, on Great Cranberry, Little Cranberry, Baker (with lighthouse), and Sutton isls. and just S of Mt. Desert Isl. Islesford village, here, has Sawtelle Mus.

Cranberry Lake, N N.Y., resort lake (c.8 mi. long) with several arms, in the Adirondacks, 40 mi. W of Lake Placid village. Cranberry Lake and Wanakena villages and a state camp site are here. Entered and drained by Oswegatchie R.

Cranborne (–bôrn), agr. village and parish (pop. 596), NE Dorset, England, 9 mi. NNE of Wimborne Minster. Has 13th-15th-cent. church.

Cranbrook, city (pop. 2,568), SE B.C., at foot of Rocky Mts., 130 mi. SW of Calgary; alt. 3,019 ft.; railroad divisional point; lumbering, fruitgrowing; in mining (silver, gold, copper, lead) region. Distributing center for E Kootenay mining and agr.

Cranbrook, town and parish (pop. 3,878), S Kent, England, 12 mi. S of Maidstone; agr. market, with flour mills. Church dates from 13th cent., rebuilt in 15th cent. Bet. 14th and 17th cent. town was a center of cloth industry, introduced from Flanders. Near by is a pine arboretum.

Cranbury, residential village (1940 pop. 733), Middlesex co., central N.J., 15 mi. NE of Trenton, in agr. region (fruit, truck); pyrotechnic factory. Cranbury Inn (18th cent.) and First Presbyterian Church (1734) here. David Brainerd, Indian missionary, lived near by.

Crandall. 1 Town (pop. 202), Murray co., NW Ga., 14 mi. ENE of Dalton. **2** Town (pop. 149), Harrison co., S Ind., on Indian Creek and 14 mi. W of New Albany, in agr. area. **3** Village (pop. 727), Kaufman co., NE Texas, 22 mi. ESE of Dallas, near East Fork of Trinity R., in cotton, corn area.

Crandon, city (pop. 1,922), ⊙ Forest co., NE Wis., 25 mi. ESE of Rhinelander; resort in wooded-lake, lumbering, dairying, and potato-growing region; sawmilling, woodworking. Inc. 1898.

Crane or **The Crane**, village, SE Barbados, B.W.I., 11 mi. E of Bridgetown; popular bathing resort. Once a shipping place, hence its name. Historic Sam Lord's Castle, now a hotel, is just NE.

Crane, county (□ 796; pop. 3,965), W Texas; ⊙ Crane. On W part of Edwards Plateau, and bounded S by Pecos R.; alt. c.2,000 ft. Oil-producing and ranching (cattle, goats, sheep) region; salt production; some agr. (fruit, truck). Includes Castle Mtn., historic Castle Gap, and Horsehead Crossing of the Pecos. Formed 1887.

Crane. 1 City (pop. 939), Stone co., SW Mo., in the Ozarks, on branch of James R. and 27 mi. SW of Springfield. Tomatoes, strawberries; canning factories. **2** City (pop. 99), Harney co., E central Oregon, 25 mi. SE of Burns; alt. 4,132 ft.; sheep, cattle, horses, wool. **3** City (pop. 2,154), ⊙ Crane co., W Texas, on the Edwards Plateau, 45 mi. SSW of Midland; trade, shipping point of oil-producing region with ranches (sheep, cattle), agr. (grain, dairy products); creamery; gasoline plant near. Founded 1926, inc. 1933.

Craneco (krā′nēkō), village (pop. 1,115, with adjoining Lundale), Logan co., SW W.Va., 13 mi. ESE of Logan.

Crane Island, Que.: see GRUES, ÎLE AUX.

Crane Lake, St. Louis co., NE Minn., in state forest, near Ont. line, 40 mi. NW of Ely; 5 mi. long, 3 mi. wide. Has small isls. and fishing and hunting resorts. Receives Vermilion R. and has N outlet into chain of lakes on Can. line.

Cranenburg, Germany: see KRANENBURG.

Crane Neck, N.Y.: see SMITHTOWN BAY.

Cranesville, agr. borough (pop. 602), Erie co., NW Pa., 20 mi. SW of Erie.

Crane Valley Lake, Madera co., central Calif., reservoir (c.5 mi. long) impounded in a branch of San Joaquin R., 35 mi. NE of Madera, in the Sierra Nevada. Formerly called Bass L. Bass Lake (resort) is here.

Craney Island (krā′nē), SE Va., small island (partly artificial) in Elizabeth R., just W of Norfolk; quarantine station; oil wharves. Lighthouse offshore.

Cranfield, agr. village and parish (pop. 1,159), W Bedford, England, 7 mi. SW of Bedford; brickworks. Church dates from 12th cent.

Cranford, residential township (pop. 18,602), Union co., NE N.J., 5 mi. W of Elizabeth; printing, mfg. (metal products, heaters, razors, pin cushions). Jr. col. here. Inc. 1871.

Cranganur (krăng′gŭnōōr), town (pop. 10,876), SW Cochin, India, near Periyar R. mouth, 15 mi. N of Ernakulam; coir products (rope, mats), copra; fishing (in coastal lagoons). Trade with Persia in 15th cent. Also spelled Cranganore.

Crangasi (krŭng-gäsh′), Rum. *Crângaşi*, NW suburb (1948 pop. 5,181) of Bucharest, in Bucharest municipality, S Rumania, on left bank of Dambovita R.

Cran-Gevrier (krã–zhĕvrēā′), W suburb (pop. 3,153) of Annecy, Haute-Savoie dept., SE France, near the Fier; aluminum works; paper milling, cotton spinning.

Cranleigh (krăn′lē), town and parish (pop. 3,701), S Surrey, England, 8 mi. SE of Guildford; agr. market. Cranleigh School, here, is a public school.

Crannon (kră′nŭn), anc. town of central Thessaly, Greece, 10 mi. SW of modern Larissa. One of leading Thessalian cities, rivaling Larissa under the Scopadae family. Here Antipater won his final victory (322 B.C.) over the confederate Greeks in Lamian War. On site is modern Gr. village of Krannon or Kranon (1940 pop. 296).

Crans (krã), health resort (alt. 4,950 ft.), Valais canton, S Switzerland, 3 mi. WNW of Sierre; sports.

Cransac (krãsäk′), town (pop. 3,470), Aveyron dept., S France, 14 mi. ESE of Figeac; coal mines.

Cranston, industrial city (pop. 55,060), Providence co., E central R.I., on Pawtuxet R. and 4 mi. SW of Providence; textiles, mill machinery, beverages, chemicals, metal products, plumbing supplies, rubber goods, fire extinguishers, artificial leather, plastics, wood products, paper products; textile bleaching and finishing. Seat of state training schools, state mental hosp. Includes villages of Arlington, Auburn, Meshanticut Park (mĭshăn′tĭkŭt), and Pawtuxet (pŭtŭk′sĭt) (resort). Inc. as town 1754, as city 1910. Pre-Revolutionary bldgs. remain.

Cranwell, agr. village in Cranwell and Byard's Leap parish (pop. 1,907), Parts of Kesteven, S central Lincolnshire, England, 11 mi. NE of Grantham; site of Royal Air Force col.

Cranz, Russian SFSR: see ZELENOGRADSK.

Craon (krõ), town (pop. 2,991), Mayenne dept., W France, on the Oudon and 18 mi. SSW of Laval; road center; noted for its breed of pigs; dairying, cattle and horse raising. Has castle of the Louis XVI period. Birthplace of Volney.

Craonne (krän), agr. village (pop. 137), Aisne dept., N France, 12 mi. SE of Laon. Here Napoleon defeated Allies in 1814. In 1917 it was wrested from Germans by French in heavy fighting for the CHEMIN DES DAMES (W).

Crapaud (kră′pō), village, S P.E.I., 18 mi. W of Charlottetown; mixed farming, dairying; potatoes.

Craponne (kräpôn′), suburb (pop. 2,163) of Lyons, Rhône dept., E central France, 5 mi. W of city center; machine-tool mfg.

Craponne-sur-Arzon (–sür-ärzõ′), village (pop. 1,879), Haute-Loire dept., S central France, on S slopes of Monts du Forez, 16 mi. SSE of Ambert; lacemaking, lumber trade.

Crary, village (pop. 235), Ramsey co., NE central N.Dak., 10 mi. E of Devils Lake.

Crasna (kräs′nä), Hung. *Kraszna* (krŏz′nŏ), village (pop. 4,504), Cluj prov., NW Rumania, 8 mi. W of Zalau; agr. center. In Hungary, 1940–45.

Crasna River, Rumania: see KRASZNA RIVER.

Crater, main urban division (1946 pop. 36,231) of Aden town, on E shore of Aden peninsula, corresponding to the old historic Aden, the original settlement on the peninsula. Situated in the partly destroyed crater of an old volcano (2 mi. across), whose rock wall is pierced by a road to the MAALA and TAWAHI harbor areas of the peninsula. Pop. (nearly 60% of Aden town), which included nearly all Aden Jews prior to their partial emigration, engages in great variety of minor industries and trades. Crater has civil hosp., mosque, former residency bldg., Western Aden Protectorate office, and large native bazaar. On SW edge are the noted rock-carved water tanks, anc. reservoirs attributed to the Persians (A.D. c.600) and partly rebuilt after 1858. Small mus. near by contains anc. inscriptions and carvings. The crater rim has remains of 16th-cent. Turkish fortifications. It was at Crater that the British landed in 1839. With the subsequent development of the new harbor sections, Crater lost its former port activities, now only harbors fishing vessels.

Crater Lake, N Que., in Ungava, near Hudson Strait; 61°16'N 73°40'W; 850 ft. deep. Occupies bottom of Chubb Crater, of meteoric origin and 1,350 ft. in depth. Discovered 1949, the crater surpasses Meteor Crater, Ariz., in size.

Crater Lake National Park (□ 250.4), SW Oregon, in Cascade Range, c.50 mi. NNW of Klamath Falls. Circular Crater L. (6 mi. across; □ 20, depth 1,983 ft., alt. 6,164 ft.), famed for its deep-blue color, lies in enormous pit formed by destruction of summit of prehistoric volcano (now called Mt. Mazama). Varicolored cliffs 500–2,000 ft. high line lake's shore line. Without inlet or outlet, it was formed and is kept at near-constant level by rain and snowfall. Small Wizard Isl., near W shore, rises 776 ft. above surface of lake and has crater (90 ft. deep, 350 ft. in diameter) at top. Excellent views from rim drive, encircling lake, and from Cloudcap (8,070 ft.), prominent elevation on E rim. Mt. Scott (8,938 ft., near park's E boundary) is highest point among volcanic peaks here. Lake discovered (1855) by prospectors who named it Deep Blue L. Name changed to Crater L. 1869. Natl. park established 1902.

Craters of the Moon National Monument (□ 73.7; established 1924), SE central Idaho, c.20 mi. SSW of Arco (site of monument hq.). Area of cinder cones (largest 800 ft. high), vents, craters, lava flows, and lava tunnels caused by repeated eruptions of molten rock through a great rift in earth's crust.

Crateús (krŭtyōōs'), city (pop. 4,869), W Ceará, Brazil, on E slope of Serra Grande, 175 mi. SW of Fortaleza; transfer point on railroad from Camocim, projected to extend to Teresina, but completed only to Oiticica (Piauí), 30 mi. W. Cattle center; cotton. Formerly spelled Cratheús.

Cratheús, Brazil: see CRATEÚS.

Crathie and Braemar (kră'thē, brāmär'), parish (pop. 1,245), SW Aberdeen, Scotland, on the Dee. Includes agr. village of Crathie, on the Dee and 7 mi. W of Ballater. Also in parish are BRAEMAR and BALMORAL CASTLE.

Crati River (krä'tē), anc. *Crathis,* Calabria, S Italy, rises in La Sila mts. 8 mi. E of Cosenza, flows W, N, past Cosenza, and NE to Gulf of Taranto 13 mi. NW of Rossano; 50 mi. long. Receives Busento and Coscile (near site of anc. Sybaris) rivers.

Crato (krä'tōō), city (pop. 11,233), S Ceará, Brazil, on N slope of Serra do Araripe, 250 mi. SSW of Fortaleza; rail terminus and important commercial center for agr. produce of the interior (cattle, hides and skins, cotton, sugar, maniçoba rubber, tobacco); sugar milling, distilling. Has experimental livestock institute. Sulphur springs. Gypsum quarries near by. Bishopric.

Crato, town (pop. 2,286), Portalegre dist., central Portugal, on railroad and 11 mi. W of Portalegre; agr. trade (olives, cheese, flour); metalworking (olive-oil presses). Near-by monastery was hq. of Order of Crato, a branch of the Maltese Knights.

Crau (krō), boulder-strewn lowland (□ 80) of Bouches-du-Rhône dept., SE France, bounded by Rhone delta (W), Étang de Berre (E), and the Alpines (N). Mainly a desert, it has olive plantations along irrigation canals. Sheep raising.

Crau, La (lä krō'), village (pop. 1,958), Var dept., SE France, 8 mi. ENE of Toulon; rail junction (spur to Salins-d'Hyères); cork mfg., fruit shipping.

Crauthem (krōtĕm'), Ger. *Krauthem* (krou'tŭm), village (pop. 177), S Luxembourg, 5 mi. S of Luxembourg city; plant nurseries.

Craven (krā'vŭn), county (□ 725; pop. 48,823), E N.C., near Atlantic coast; ⊙ New Bern. Tidewater area drained by Neuse and Trent rivers; S part (several small lakes) included in Croatan Natl. Forest. Farming (tobacco, corn); timber (pine). Sawmilling, fishing. Formed 1712.

Cravinhos (krŭvē'nyōōs), city (pop. 4,068), NE São Paulo, Brazil, 13 mi. SSE of Ribeirão Prêto, in coffee zone; rail junction; mfg. of flour products, furniture; brandy distilling.

Cravo (krä'vō), village, Arauca commissary, E Colombia, on Casanare R. and 65 mi. SE of Arauca; cattle raising.

Crawfish River, central Wis., rises in Columbia co., flows c.50 mi. SE, past Columbus, to Rock R. at Jefferson.

Crawford, town and parish (pop. 1,572), S Lanark, Scotland, on the Clyde and 15 mi. SSE of Lanark; agr. market. Has remains of Tower Lindsay, anc. castle of earls of Crawford.

Crawford. 1 County (□ 598; pop. 22,727), NW Ark.; ⊙ Van Buren. Bounded W by Okla. line, S by Arkansas R.; Ozarks in N. Agr. (fruit, cotton, truck, livestock). Mfg. at Van Buren. Zinc smelters; natural-gas wells, hardwood timber. Mtn. resorts. Part of Ozark Natl. Forest is in N. Formed 1820. **2** County (□ 313; pop. 6,080), central Ga.; ⊙ Knoxville. Bounded SW by Flint R., NE by small Echeconnee Creek. Intersected by the fall line. Agr. (cotton, corn, vegetables, peaches, pecans, livestock) and timber area. Formed 1812. **3** County (□ 442; pop. 21,137), SE Ill.; ⊙ Robinson. Bounded E by Wabash R.; drained by Embarrass R. Agr. (livestock, corn, wheat, oats, hay, alfalfa, poultry; dairy products). Oil drilling, refining; mfg. of china, pottery, oil-well supplies, food products, glycerin, caskets; lumber milling. Wabash R. ports were important trade centers in 19th cent. Formed 1816. **4** County (□ 312; pop. 9,289), S Ind.; ⊙ English. Bounded S by Ohio R. (here forming Ky. line); drained by Blue R. and small Little Blue R. Agr. area (grain; dairy products; livestock, poultry, truck, tobacco). Mfg. (lime, concrete blocks, cement, wagon parts, baskets, canned foods). Timber; limestone quarries. Formed 1818. **5** County (□ 716; pop. 19,741), W Iowa; ⊙ Denison. Prairie agr. area (hogs, cattle; poultry, corn, oats, wheat) drained by Boyer R.; bituminous-coal deposits. Formed 1851. **6** County (□ 598; pop. 40,231), SE Kansas; ⊙ Girard. Agr. area bordering E on Mo. Stock, grain, and poultry raising; dairying. Extensive coal deposits, zinc and lead mines. Scattered gas and oil fields in W. Formed 1867. **7** County (□ 563; pop. 4,151), N central Mich.; ⊙ Grayling. Drained by North, Middle, and South branches of Au Sable R., and by Manistee R. Agr. (livestock, potatoes, grain, hay); dairy products; lumber mills. Includes part of Huron Natl. Forest, 2 state forests, and L. Margrethe. Organized 1879. **8** County (□ 760; pop. 11,615), E central Mo.; ⊙ Steelville. In the Ozarks; drained by Meramec R. Tourist, agr. region (wheat, corn, hay), livestock; oak timber; fire-clay, sulphur, iron mines. Part of Clark Natl. Forest is here. Formed 1829. **9** County (□ 404; pop. 38,738), N central Ohio; ⊙ Bucyrus. Drained by Sandusky and Olentangy rivers and small Sycamore Creek. Agr. area (livestock, dairy products, grain, poultry); mfg. at Bucyrus, Galion, and Crestline; hardwood timber. Formed 1815. **10** County (□ 1,016; pop. 78,948), NW Pa.; ⊙ Meadville. Mfg. and agr. area, drained by French Creek. Pymatuning Reservoir in Shenango R. is in SW part on Ohio border. Mfg. (metal products, textiles, food products, chemicals); dairy products; oil, gas, sand. Formed 1800. **11** County (□ 586; pop. 17,652), SW Wis.; ⊙ Prairie du Chien. Bounded W by Mississippi R. (here forming Iowa line), S by Wisconsin R., which enters the Mississippi at SE corner of co.; drained by Kickapoo R. Dairying and stock-raising area, with grain and tobacco growing, cheese making, processing of farm products, other mfg. Formed 1818.

Crawford. 1 Town (pop. 170), Delta co., W Colo., on branch of Gunnison R., in W foothills of West Elk Mts., and 25 mi. E of Delta; alt. 6,800 ft.; flour, potatoes, timber. **2** City (pop. 555), Oglethorpe co., NE Ga., 14 mi. SE of Athens; textile mfg. **3** Town (pop. 83), Washington co., E Maine, on Crawford L. (5 mi. long) and 23 mi. NNW of Machias. **4** Town (pop. 374), Lowndes co., E Miss., 17 mi. SW of Columbus. **5** City (pop. 1,824), Dawes co., NW Nebr., 22 mi. SW of Chadron and on White R., in irrigated grazing region; dairy and poultry produce, livestock, grain, potatoes. U.S. fish hatchery is here. Near by are Toadstool Park, Adelia Badlands, and Fort Robinson, historic military outpost. Relics of prehistoric man found in vicinity. Inc. 1885. **6** Town (pop. 423), McLennan co., E central Texas, 18 mi. W of Waco, in cotton, corn, grain area; limestone quarries.

Crawfordjohn, agr. village and parish (pop. 572), S Lanark, Scotland, on Duneaton Water (short tributary of the Clyde) and 12 mi. S of Lanark.

Crawford Notch, N central N.H., scenic pass in White Mts., W of Presidential Range and 17 mi. NW of Conway; c.5 mi. long. Saco R. rises here. Discovered 1771; 1st highway built during Revolution. Area made state forest in 1911. Winter sports.

Crawfordsburn, agr. village (district pop. 2,196), NE Co. Down, Northern Ireland, on Belfast Lough, 2 mi. W of Bangor.

Crawfordsville. 1 Town (pop. 680), Crittenden co., E Ark., 19 mi. WNW of Memphis, Tenn.; cotton. **2** City (pop. 12,851), ⊙ Montgomery co., W central Ind., on Sugar Creek and 27 mi. S of Lafayette; commercial center of agr. area (livestock, grain); mfg. of farm implements, foundry products, steel, wire, nails, fences, gates, elevating trucks, brick, caskets, conduits, clothing, food products; printing plants. Seat of Wabash Col. Has a memorial to Lew Wallace. Laid out c.1822. **3** Town (pop. 286), Washington co., SE Iowa, 10 mi. SE of Washington; concrete blocks.

Crawfordville. 1 Village, Wakulla co., NW Fla., 19 mi. SSW of Tallahassee, at edge of Apalachicola Natl. Forest; lumbering, farming. **2** City (pop. 966), ⊙ Taliaferro co., NE Ga., 38 mi. SE of Athens; sawmilling, clothes mfg. Alexander H. Stephens Memorial State Park (with "Liberty Hall," his home) is here. Inc. 1826.

Crawley, town (1951 pop. 10,701), N Sussex, England, 8 mi. NE of Horsham, in agr. area. Designated after Second World War as model residential community.

Crawshaw Booth, England: see RAWTENSTALL.

Crayford, urban district (1931 pop. 15,896; 1951 census 27,951), NW Kent, England, on Cray R. and 2 mi. W of Dartford; flour-milling center, with leather, wool-processing, and petroleum-refining industry. Has 15th-cent. church and moated manor dating from pre-Norman times.

Crazy Mountains, range of Rocky Mts. in S central Mont., rise just S of Musselshell R.; extend c.30 mi. S toward Yellowstone R. Lie within sec. of Absaroka Natl. Forest. Highest point, Crazy Peak (11,214 ft.).

Creagorry, Scotland: see BENBECULA.

Creal Springs, city (pop. 864), Williamson co., S Ill., 16 mi. SE of Herrin, in agr. area.

Crean Lake (krēn) (12 mi. long, 2–9 mi. wide), central Sask., in Prince Albert Natl. Park, 60 mi. NNW of Prince Albert. Drains NE through Montreal L. and Montreal R. into Churchill R.

Crécy, Crécy-en-Ponthieu (krĕ'sē, Fr. krāsē'-ā-pōtyû'), or **Cressy,** village (pop. 1,331), Somme dept., N France, on small Maye R. and 11 mi. N of Abbeville; flour milling, sugar-beet processing. Here, in 1346, Edward III of England defeated Philip VI of France in memorable battle.

Crécy-en-Brie (-brē'), village (pop. 923), Seine-et-Marne dept., N central France, on the Grand-Morin and 7 mi. S of Meaux; flour and sawmilling.

Crécy-en-Ponthieu, Somme dept., France: see CRÉCY.

Crécy-sur-Serre (-sür-sâr'), village (pop. 1,526), Aisne dept., N France, on the Serre and 9 mi. N of Laon; sugar beets.

Crediton (krĕ'dĭtŭn), village (pop. estimate 500) S Ont., on Ausable R. and 26 mi. NW of London; dairying, fruitgrowing.

Crediton, urban district (1931 pop. 3,490; 1951 census 3,992), central Devon, England, 7 mi. NW of Exeter; agr. market; tanneries and agr.-equipment works. Reputedly birthplace of St. Boniface. Seat of bishopric in 10th-11th cent. Has Norman church.

Credit River, S Ont., rises near Orangeville, flows 60 mi. SE, past Orangeville and Georgetown, to L. Ontario at Port Credit.

Creede, town (pop. 503), ⊙ Mineral co., SW Colo., on headstream of Rio Grande, in San Juan Mts., and 65 mi. NW of Alamosa; alt. 8,854 ft. Town founded 1890, when silver was discovered; had pop. of 8,000 in 1893. Mines closed down after 1893 with decline in price of silver; some have been worked since late 1920s. Near by is former (1908–50) Wheeler Natl. Monument, an area of fantastic rock formations and deep gorges created by volcanic action and erosion. Recreational area here is now administered by U.S. Forest Service.

Creedmoor. 1 (krēd'mōōr) A section of E Queens borough of New York city, SE N.Y. Site of a state hosp. for the insane. **2** (-môr) Town (pop. 852), Granville co., N N.C., 15 mi. NE of Durham.

Creek (krēk), county (□ 972; pop. 43,143), central Okla.; ⊙ Sapulpa. Drained by Cimarron and Arkansas rivers and by the Deep Fork. Diversified agr. (grain, cotton, corn, sorghums); stock raising, dairying. Extensive oil and natural-gas fields; refineries, pipe lines, gasoline plants. Mfg. at Sapulpa and Bristow. Formed 1907.

Creekside, borough (pop. 525), Indiana co., W central Pa., 5 mi. NNW of Indiana.

Cree Lake (□ 555), N Sask.; 57°30'N 107°W; 50 mi. long, up to 35 mi. wide. Drains N into Dubawnt R. through Cree R.

Creemore (krē'môr), village (pop. 629), S Ont., 40 mi. SE of Owen Sound; dairying, lumbering, fruit packing.

Cree River, in Ayrshire, Wigtown, and Kirkcudbright, Scotland, rises 11 mi. ESE of Girvan, flows 25 mi. SE, forming border bet. Wigtown and Kirkcudbright, past Newton Stewart and Creetown, to head of Wigtown Bay of Solway Firth.

Creetown, town in Kirkmabreck parish, SW Kirkcudbright, Scotland, on Wigtown Bay at mouth of Cree R., 4 mi. NE of Wigtown; granite quarrying. Dr. Thomas Brown b. near by.

Crefeld, Germany: see KREFELD.

Creglingen (krā'glĭng-ŭn), town (pop. 1,853), N Württemberg, Germany, after 1945 in Württemberg-Baden, on the Tauber and 11 mi. ESE of Mergentheim; spelt, oats. Has 14th-cent. church with carved late-Gothic altar.

Creidlitz (krīt'lĭts), village (pop. 1,499), Upper Franconia, N Bavaria, Germany, on Itz R. and 3 mi. SSE of Coburg; glassworks, paper mills; metal- and woodworking.

Creighton (krā'tŭn). **1** Town (pop. 269), Cass co., W Mo., near South Grand R., 18 mi. SE of Harrisonville. **2** City (pop. 1,401), Knox co., NE Nebr., 40 mi. NNW of Norfolk and on Bazile Creek; beverages; dairy and poultry produce, grain, livestock. Laid out 1885. **3** Village (1940 pop. 2,338), Allegheny co., W central Pa., opposite Arnold on Allegheny R. NE of Pittsburgh; glass.

Creighton Mine (krī'tŭn), village (pop. estimate 1,200), SE central Ont., 10 mi. ESE of Sudbury; nickel mining.

Creil (krā), town (pop. 9,476), Oise dept., N France, on the Oise and 29 mi. N of Paris; important rail junction with large railroad workshops. Also makes bridge-building equipment and precision instruments. Brewing, brick and carton mfg. Its 13th-16th-cent. Gothic church, along with dist. on right bank of Oise R., were heavily damaged in Second World War. Near-by Nogent-sur-Oise (1 mi. N) and Montataire (2 mi. W) are also metalworking centers.

Crema (krā'mä), town (pop. 13,541), Cremona prov., Lombardy, N Italy, on Serio R. and 23 mi. NW of Cremona. Agr. and industrial center; ironworks, hemp and linen mills; mfg. of agr. machinery, organs, soap, wax. Market for raw silk, rice, livestock. Cattle- and horse-breeding stations. Bishopric. Has cathedral (1284–1341) and palaces (15th-16th cent.). Destroyed by Frederick Barbarossa in 1160; rebuilt 1185.

Cremasto, Greece: see KREMASTE.

Crémieu (krāmyû'), village (pop. 1,251), Isère dept., SE France, 15 mi. NW of La Tour-du-Pin; market; belt mfg. Has picturesque 16th-cent. gateway, town hall, and church.

Cremona (krĭmō'nŭ, Ital. krĕmô'nä), province (□ 678; pop. 369,515), Lombardy, N Italy; ⊙ Cremona. Consists of fertile, irrigated Po plain lying bet. Oglio (E), Adda (W), and Po (S) rivers. Agr. (rice, wheat, corn, flax, raw silk) and stock raising (cattle, horses, swine) predominate. Mfg. at Cremona and Crema.

Cremona, city (pop. 54,564), ⊙ Cremona prov., Lombardy, N Italy, on Po R. and 46 mi. SE of Milan, in fertile agr. region; 45°8'N 10°2'E. Rail junction; agr. and industrial center noted for its *torrone* (candy) and French mustard. Mfg. (silk textiles, hats, bricks, pottery, musical instruments, stoves, firearms, fertilizer, sausage, macaroni); dairy products. Bishopric. In main square is cathedral (begun 12th cent.), octagonal baptistery (1167), city hall (1206–45), and the Torazzo (c.1250), highest campanile (almost 400 ft.) in Italy. Has scientific and technical institute, mus. Founded by Romans in 218 B.C.; became a center of learning in Middle Ages; in late Renaissance was site of Cremonese school of painting. The home of Amati, Guarneri, and Stradivari; long famous for violins made here. In Second World War, bombed (1944).

Crenshaw, county (□ 611; pop. 18,981), S central Ala.; ⊙ Luverne. Level farm region drained by Conecuh R. and Patsaliga Creek. Cotton, peanuts, corn, livestock; lumber milling. Formed 1866.

Crenshaw, town (pop. 740), Panola co., NW Miss., c.45 mi. S of Memphis (Tenn.), in agr. area; mfg. of clay and cottonseed products.

Créon (krāõ'), village (pop. 694), Gironde dept., SW France, in Entre-deux-Mers, 12 mi. ESE of Bordeaux; winegrowing, dairying; pottery.

Crépieux-la-Pape (krāpyû'-lä-päp'), outer NNE suburb (pop. 1,858) of Lyons, Ain dept., E France, on right bank of the Rhone; umbrellas; tanning.

Crépy or **Crépy-en-Laonnois** (krāpē'-ã-länwä'), village (pop. 1,250), Aisne dept., N France, 5 mi. WNW of Laon; sugar-beet growing. Here, in 1544, a treaty was signed bet. Charles V and Francis I. From a near-by height long-range Ger. railway guns shelled Paris in 1918. Old Fr. spelling, Crespy.

Crépy-en-Valois (–välwä'), town (pop. 5,395), Oise dept., N France, 13 mi. SSE of Compiègne; road junction and agr. market; furniture and footwear mfg. Has picturesque old houses and 2 churches. Medieval ⊙ Valois. Sacked by English in 1431. Resisted Prussians in 1814. Occupied by Germans in 1914. Damaged in Second World War.

Creran, Loch (lŏkh krĕr'ŭn), E inlet (9 mi. long, 1 mi. wide) of Loch Linnhe, Argyll, Scotland.

Cresaptown (krē'sŭptoun), village, Allegany co., W Md., on North Branch of the Potomac and 6 mi. SW of Cumberland, in apple-growing area.

Cresbard (krĕs'bärd), town (pop. 235), Faulk co., NE central S.Dak., 13 mi. NE of Faulkton; agr. trade center; wheat, barley, oats.

Crescent. 1 or **Crescent City**, village (pop. 324), Iroquois co., E Ill., 24 mi. S of Kankakee, in rich agr. area. **2** Village (pop. c.300), Pottawattamie co., SW Iowa, 7 mi. N of Council Bluffs, in agr. area. **3** Town (pop. 1,341), Logan co., central Okla., 11 mi. WNW of Guthrie, in oil-producing and agr. area (cotton, alfalfa, grain, livestock, fruit). Cotton ginning; mfg. of feed, petroleum products. Settled 1891, inc. 1893.

Crescent, Lake (□ 6), central Tasmania, 45 mi. N of Hobart, just S of L. Sorell; 3.5 mi. long, 2.5 mi. wide.

Crescent, Lake, NW Wash., in Olympic Natl. Park, 15 mi. W of Port Angeles; c.9 mi. long.

Crescent City. 1 City (pop. 1,706), ⊙ Del Norte co., NW Calif., on Pacific coast near Oregon line, c.65 mi. N of Eureka; fishing fleet (halibut, sole, salmon); lumber milling (redwood). Dairying, lumbering, hunting, game fishing in region. Crescent City Indian Reservation is near by. Laid out 1852, inc. 1854. **2** Town (pop. 1,393), Putnam co., N Fla., 34 mi. SSW of St. Augustine, on Crescent L.; orange-growing center, and resort. **3** Village, Iroquois co., Ill.: see CRESCENT.

Crescent Group, Chinese *Yunglo* (yŏŏng'lŭ'), western group of the Paracel Isls., China, in S.China Sea, 37 mi. SW of Woody Isl.; 16°30'N 111°40'E. Includes Drummond and Duncan isls. (SE), Robert Isl. (W), and Money Isl. (SW).

Crescent Heights, village (pop. 2,176, with adjacent Daisytown), Washington co., SW Pa., 5 mi. S of Charleroi.

Crescentino (krĕshĕntē'nô), village (pop. 2,117), Vercelli prov., Piedmont, NW Italy, near confluence of Dora Baltea and Po rivers, 18 mi. WSW of Vercelli, in irrigated region (rice, cereals); brickworks, bottling plant, rice-polishing mill.

Crescent Lake, N Fla., on Flagler-Putnam co. line, 6 mi. NE of L. George; c.14 mi. long, 1–3 mi. wide; drains into St. Johns R. through short outlet in N. Crescent City on W shore.

Crescent Springs, village (1940 pop. 953), Kenton co., N Ky., across the Ohio 5 mi. WSW of Cincinnati, within Cincinnati metropolitan dist.

Cresciúma, Brazil: see CRICIÚMA.

Cresco (krĕ'skō). **1** City (pop. 3,638), ⊙ Howard co., NE Iowa, near Turkey R., 17 mi. WNW of Decorah; agr. trade and mfg. center; farm equipment, dairy and wood products, feed, tankage, lime. Inc. 1868. **2** Village, Monroe co., NE Pa., 12 mi. NNW of Stroudsburg; mtn. resort (alt. 1,203 ft.).

Cres Island (tsrĕs), Ital. *Cherso* (kĕr'sô), island (□ c.150) in Adriatic Sea, NW Croatia, Yugoslavia; c.40 mi. long N-S; rises (N) to 2,060 ft.; northernmost point 11 mi. SSW of Rijeka (Fiume). Agr., fishing, stock raising (notably sheep). Part of Istria, it passed (1918) from Austria Hungary to Italy and (1947) to Yugoslavia. Chief village, Cres, is on W coast, 23 mi. S of Rijeka; has parts of Venetian walls, Renaissance cathedral, 16th-cent. palace. Osor, Ital. *Ossero*, village, on W coast, 18 mi. S of Cres, is linked by bridge with Losinj Isl.; has 15th-cent. cathedral (early Venetian Renaissance; damaged by bombing) and parts of Byzantine basilica.

Cresmont, village (pop. 1,022, with adjacent Altamont), Schuylkill co., E Pa.

Crespano del Grappa (krĕspä'nô dĕl gräp'pä), village (pop. 3,200), Treviso prov., Veneto, N Italy, 6 mi. NE of Bassano; silk mill, cementworks.

Crespin (krĕspē'), town (pop. 4,109), Nord dept., N France, on Belg. border, 8 mi. NE of Valenciennes; customhouse. Coal mines. Mfg. of railroad rolling stock and mining equipment. Railroad customs station at Blanc-Misseron (1 mi. S).

Crespino (krĕspē'nô), village (pop. 716), Rovigo prov., Veneto, N Italy, on Po R. and 8 mi. SE of Rovigo, in hemp-growing region.

Crespo (krĕ'spō). **1** or **Villa Crespo** (vē'yä), town (pop. estimate 2,000), W Entre Ríos prov., Argentina, 26 mi. SSE of Paraná; rail junction in grain and livestock area; flour milling. **2** Town, Santa Fe prov., Argentina: see GOBERNADOR CRESPO.

Crespo, Cerro (sĕ'rō), Andean peak (7,280 ft.) on Argentina-Chile border; 40°26'S.

Crespy, France: see CRÉPY.

Cresskill, suburban borough (pop. 3,534), Bergen co., NE N.J., near the Hudson, 5 mi. NE of Bergenfield. Inc. 1894.

Cresson. 1 Borough (pop. 2,569), Cambria co., SW central Pa., 10 mi. WSW of Altoona; railroad shops; bituminous coal; ice cream; resort. State tuberculosis sanatorium, Mount Aloysius Jr. Col. here. Birthplace of Robert E. Peary. Inc. 1906. **2** Village (pop. c.300), Hood co., N central Texas, 23 mi. SW of Fort Worth; rail point in agr. area.

Cressona (krŭsō'nŭ), borough (pop. 1,758), Schuylkill co., E central Pa., 3 mi. S of Pottsville and on Schuylkill R.; aluminum. Laid out 1847, inc. 1857.

Cressy, France: see CRÉCY.

Cressy (krĕ'sē), village (pop. 381), N central Tasmania, 18 mi. SSW of Launceston; cattle, flax. Agr. experiment station.

Crest (krĕst), town (pop. 3,821), Drôme dept., SE France, on the Drôme and 15 mi. SSE of Valence; market; textile milling, woodworking, distilling. Has picturesque old town and 12th-cent. dungeon. Damaged in Second World War.

Cresta (krĕ'stä), resort village (alt. 5,700 ft.), Grisons canton, E Switzerland, near St. Moritz, in Upper Engadine; noted for its long bobsled run.

Crested Butte (bŭt), town (pop. 730), Gunnison co., W central Colo., on Slate R., in Rocky Mts., and 22 mi. N of Gunnison; alt. 9,000 ft. Resort and coal-mining point; livestock. Rocky Mtn. Biological Laboratory near by. Growth stimulated by discovery of gold near by in 1880s.

Crested Butte, peak (12,172 ft.) in Rocky Mts., just NE of Crested Butte town, W central Colo.

Crestlawn, village (pop. 1,886, with adjoining Belvidere), Madison co., central Ind.

Crestline (krĕst'līn). **1** Resort village (pop. 1,369, with near-by Cedar Pines), San Bernardino co., S Calif., in San Bernardino Mts., 9 mi. N of San Bernardino. **2** Village (pop. 4,614), Crawford co., N central Ohio, 11 mi. W of Mansfield; railroad junction. Produces road machinery, furnaces, clothing, dairy foods. Laid out 1851.

Creston, village (pop. 1,153), SE B.C., near Wash. border, at foot of Selkirk Mts., near Kootenay R. and S end of Kootenay L., 45 mi. SE of Nelson; agr. center (strawberries, vegetables), with canneries, seed nurseries; woodworking.

Creston. 1 Village (pop. 362), Ogle co., N Ill., 24 mi. SSW of Rockford, in rich agr. area. **2** City (pop. 8,317), ⊙ Union co., S Iowa, c.55 mi. SW of Des Moines, near sources of Little Platte and Grand rivers, in a bluegrass region; commercial center and railroad divisional hq. (since 1869) with repair shops; dairy products, packed poultry and eggs, lubricators, concrete blocks. Has jr. col. Inc. 1871. **3** Village (pop. 228), Platte co., E Nebr., 20 mi. N of Columbus and on branch of Elkhorn R. **4** Village (pop. 1,300), Wayne co., N central Ohio, 13 mi. N of Wooster; makes baskets. **5** Town (pop. 268), Lincoln co., E Wash., 25 mi. WNW of Davenport, in Columbia basin agr. region.

Crestone, town (pop. 72), Saguache co., S central Colo., 25 mi. ESE of Saguache; alt. 7,500 ft. Just E in Sangre de Cristo Mts. are Crestone Peak (14,291 ft.), Crestone Needle (14,191 ft.).

Crestview, town (pop. 5,003), ⊙ Okaloosa co., NW Fla., c.45 mi. ENE of Pensacola; rail junction; clothing factory, fruit cannery. Choctawhatchee Natl. Forest is near by. Eglin Air Force Base is 20 mi. S.

Crestwood. 1 Village (pop. 739), Cook co., NE Ill., SW suburb of Chicago. **2** Town (pop. 1,645), St. Louis co., E Mo., just SW of St. Louis.

Creswell (krĕz'wŭl). **1** Town (pop. 425), Washington co., NE N.C., 20 mi. E of Plymouth; lumber mill. **2** Town (pop. 662), Lane co., W Oregon, 10 mi. SSE of Eugene.

Creswell Bay, SE Somerset Isl., E Franklin Dist., Northwest Territories, arm (45 mi. long, 50 mi. wide at mouth) of Prince Regent Inlet; 72°30'N 93°W.

Creswick (krĕz'wĭk), town (pop. 1,403), S central Victoria, Australia, 65 mi. WNW of Melbourne; rail junction; softwood plantations. Forestry school. Formerly gold-mining town.

Cretas (krā'täs), town (pop. 1,319), Teruel prov., E Spain, 20 mi. ESE of Alcañiz; olive oil, wine, almonds, fruit, honey.

Crêt de la Neige (krā dŭ lä nĕzh'), highest summit (5,652 ft.) of the Jura, in Ain dept., E France, 10 mi. WNW of Geneva. Splendid view of L. of Geneva and Mont Blanc (SE).

Crete (krēt), Gr. *Krete* or *Kriti* (both: krē'tē), Turkish *Kirid*, 4th largest island (□ 3,207; pop. 437,954) in Mediterranean Sea, at 35°15'N, bet. 23°30'E and 26°20'E. Including offshore isls., it forms an administrative division (□ 3,235; pop. 438,239) of Greece; ⊙ Canea. Largest of the isls. of Greece, it is at S limit of Aegean Sea, the southern part of which is known as Sea of Candia (a former name of Crete); it is 60 mi. from the Peloponnesus and 160 mi. from Cyrenaica coast of Africa; 160 mi. long, 7–35 mi. wide. Very mountainous and rugged, it rises to 8,058 ft. in Mt. Ida (center); other heights are Leuka (W) and Dikte (E). The few important agr. plains are those of Candia, Canea, and Mesara. The rocky coasts are deeply indented (N) in the gulfs of Kisamos, Canea, Suda, Almyros, Candia, and Mirabella. The Gulf Mesara is the only notable inlet on the less broken S coast. The climate is generally mild, with rainfall decreasing from W to E. The isl. is largely deforested. Gypsum, limestone, iron ore, and lignite are found. The relatively small agr. areas produce olive oil, wine, grapefruit, oranges, lemons, carobs, almonds, potatoes. Sheep and goats are raised (cheese). The leading urban centers (soap mfg.) are Candia (the largest city), Canea, and Rethymnon. They are linked by the N coastal road, the chief transportation artery. Crete had one of the world's earliest civilizations, the Minoan, named after the legendary King Minos, whose palace at CNOSSUS yielded invaluable finds. This early Cretan civilization flourished c.1500 B.C. and merged (c.1000 B.C.) with that of the Dorian Greeks. The leading city-states were Cnossus, Gortyna, and Cydonia (modern Canea). Though important as a station on Mediterranean trade routes, Crete remained outside of the main currents of Greek history. In 3d cent. B.C., the isl. accepted the unstable protection of Macedon and became a notorious pirates' haunt. Conquered 68–67 B.C. by the Romans, Crete fell A.D. 395 to Byzantium. It was invested 823–961 by the Saracens and, as a result of the Fourth Crusade, fell to Venice in 1204, under whose rule it became known as Candia, after the ruling duke's residence. The isl. was conquered by the Turks (1669) after a long war, but 2 tiny offshore island forts remained under Venetian control until 1715. A series of 19th-cent. revolts against the Turks climaxed in the insurrection of 1896–97 that led to war (1897) bet. Greece and Turkey, which ended in Gr. defeat. However, pressure exerted by the European powers forced Turkey to evacuate Crete 1898 and led to the formation of a Cretan autonomous state under Turkish sovereignty but governed by a high-commissioner of the occupying Great Powers (England, France, Russia, Italy). Following the Young Turk revolution of 1908, however, the Cretans proclaimed their union with Greece and foreign occupation troops were withdrawn (1909). The union was confirmed as a result of the Balkan Wars (1912–13). Cretan revolts against existing Greek regimes were suppressed (1935, 1938). During Second World War, British and Greek forces were evacuated here (1941) from Greece, but were soon overwhelmed by the Germans in an air-borne invasion, the 1st of its kind. Politically, Crete is divided into the nomes (from W to E) of CANEA, RETHYMNE, HERKLEION, and LASETHI.

Crete. **1** Village (pop. 2,298), Will co., NE Ill., near Ind. line, 30 mi. S of Chicago, in agr. area. Platted 1849, inc. 1880. Lincoln Field race track is near by. **2** City (pop. 3,692), Saline co., SE Nebr., 20 mi. SW of Lincoln and on Big Blue R.; camping equipment, flour, beer; dairy and poultry produce, livestock, grain. Doane Col. is here. City inc. 1871.

Crete, Sea of, Greece: see CANDIA, SEA OF.

Créteil (krātā'), town (pop. 9,995), Seine dept., N central France, a SE suburb of Paris, 7 mi. from Notre Dame Cathedral; port on left bank of the Marne; copper smelting, mfg. (silverware, pencils, oil paints, vinegar). Has 12th-cent. church.

Crétéville (krātāvēl') or **Haut-Mornag** (ō-mōrnäg'), village, Tunis dist., N Tunisia, 12 mi. SE of Tunis; winegrowing center in agr. region settled by Europeans; citrus groves. Grape processing, plaster mfg.

Creully (krûyē'), village (pop. 576), Calvados dept., NW France, on the Seulles and 11 mi. NW of Caen; dairying, Camembert cheese mfg.

Creus, Cape (krā'ōōs), easternmost point of Spain, on the Mediterranean, in Gerona prov., NE Spain, 18 mi. ENE of Figueras; 42°19'N 3°19'E. Lighthouse.

Creuse (krûz), department (□ 2,164; pop. 188,669), central France, formed of Marche and parts of Berry and Limousin; ⊙ Guéret. Crossed by W ranges of Massif Central (Monts du Limousin, Monts de la Marche), it contains the Plateau of Millevaches, France's central watershed. Drained by Creuse R. Agr.: potatoes, rye, chestnuts, forage crops. Cattle and sheep grazing in uplands; livestock fattening in valleys. Coal mining in Ahun basin. Chief towns are Guéret (commercial center) and Aubusson, with noted carpet factories.

Creuse River, central France, rises in Plateau of Millevaches 5 mi. NW of La Courtine (Creuse dept.), flows 160 mi. NNW, past Aubusson, Argenton, and Le Blanc, to the Vienne 7 mi. below La Haye-Descartes. Receives the Petite Creuse, Claise (right), and the Gartempe (left). Powers important hydroelectric station near Éguzon (Indre dept.). Picturesque gorge of upper Creuse R. bet. Ahun and Argenton was described by George Sand and attracts tourists.

Creusot, Le (lù krûzō'), town (pop. 17,133), Saône-et-Loire dept., E central France, 20 mi. W of Chalon-sur-Saône; a major metallurgical center of France, in coal-mining region, with large steel mills, railroad-engine and armament manufactures. Heavy industry was established here in 1836 by Schneider brothers. Le Creusot was severely damaged by Allied bombing during Second World War.

Creussen (kroi'sùn), town (pop. 1,969), Upper Franconia, N Bavaria, Germany, on the Red Main and 7 mi. SSE of Bayreuth; mfg. of precision instruments, metal and pottery working, brewing, tanning. Chartered 1358.

Creutzwald-la-Croix (krûzväld"-lä-krwä'), Ger. *Kreuzwald* (kroits'vält), town (pop. 7,080), Moselle dept., NE France, 9 mi. W of Forbach, on Saar border, in coal-mining region. Miners' residences. Also called Creutzwald.

Creux, Channel Isls.: see SARK.

Creux du Vent or **Creux du Van** (both: krû dü vã'), W Switzerland, craterlike rock amphitheater of the Jura, 4 mi. W of L. of Neuchâtel.

Creuzburg (kroits'bōōrk), town (pop. 2,267), Thuringia, central Germany, on the Werra and 7 mi. NW of Eisenach; cigar mfg.; tobacco growing. Has old palace.

Crevacuore (krĕväkwô'rĕ), village (pop. 1,355), Vercelli prov., Piedmont, N Italy, 13 mi. NE of Biella; woolen, cotton, and paper mills.

Crevalcore (krĕvälkô'rĕ), town (pop. 2,209), Bologna prov., Emilia-Romagna, N central Italy, 18 mi. NW of Bologna; rail junction.

Creve Coeur (krēv" kōōr'). **1** Village (pop. 5,499), Tazewell co., central Ill., on Illinois R. and 4 mi. S of Peoria, in agr. and bituminous-coal area. Inc. 1921. Near by is Fort Creve Coeur State Park, marking site of old Fort Crève Coeur built 1680 by La Salle. **2** Town (pop. 2,040), St. Louis co., E Mo., near the Missouri, 17 mi. NW of downtown St. Louis.

Crévecoeur-le-Grand (krĕvkûr'-lù-grã'), village (pop. 1,770), Oise dept., N France, 12 mi. N of Beauvais; wool milling.

Crévic (krāvēk'), village (pop. 489), Meurthe-et-Moselle dept., NE France, on Marne-Rhine Canal and 5 mi. NW of Lunéville; salt mines.

Crevillente (krāvēlyĕn'tā), town (pop. 10,145), Alicante prov., E Spain, in Valencia, in rich garden region, 7 mi. WSW of Elche; vegetable-fiber processing; mfg. of rugs and mats, hemp rope, footwear, olive pressing, flour milling; lumbering. Truck produce, wine, hemp, esparto, jute, coconuts in area. Probably of Roman origin; fell to Moors (8th cent.), liberated (1263) by Christians.

Crewe (krōō), municipal borough (1931 pop. 46,069; 1951 census 52,415), S central Cheshire, England, 28 mi. SSW of Manchester; railroad center, with major repair shops, machine shops, steel plants; also mfg. of chemicals, clothing, food products. Almost entirely dependent on railroads for industry and employment, town has grown from a small village within the past century. Has technical and art col. Near by is Crewe Hall, seat of the marquess of Crewe. Iron mines near-by.

Crewe (krōō), railroad town (pop. 2,030), Nottoway co., central Va., 40 mi. W of Petersburg; large railroad shops; mfg. (hosiery, clothing), lumber milling. Inc. 1888.

Crewkerne (krōō'kûrn), urban district (1931 pop. 3,509; 1951 census 3,838), S Somerset, England, 8 mi. WSW of Yeovil; agr. market in dairying region; mfg. (leather goods, agr. equipment, cheese), cotton milling. Has 15th-cent. church and 1499 grammar school.

Creysse (krĕs), village (pop. 316), Dordogne dept., SW France, on the Dordogne and 4 mi. E of Bergerac; paper mill.

Crézancy (krāzãsē'), village (pop. 305), Aisne dept., N France, near the Marne, 5 mi. E of Château-Thierry; foundry. Here Ger. bridgehead S of the Marne was contained (June, 1918) in First World War.

Criba Lagoon, Honduras: see SICO RIVER.

Criccieth (krĭk'yĕth), urban district (1931 pop. 1,449; 1951 census 1,651), on Lleyn Peninsula, S central Caernarvon, Wales, on Cardigan Bay of Irish Sea, 4 mi. W of Portmadoc; seaside resort. Has anc. castle, rebuilt 1285 by Edward I. Near by was home of Lloyd George.

Crichton (krī'tùn), agr. village and parish (pop. 797), E Midlothian, Scotland, 5 mi. SE of Dalkeith. Site of ruins of 14th-15th-cent. Crichton Castle, described in Scott's *Marmion.* Church dates from 15th cent.

Crichton, village (pop. c.1,000), Mobile co., extreme SW Ala., 4 mi. W of Mobile; wood-pulp and paper products.

Criciúma (krēsyōō'mù), city (pop. 4,340), SE Santa Catarina, Brazil, on railroad and 40 mi. WSW of Laguna; coal-mining center; hog and cattle raising; processing of hides, lard, and bacon. Settled c.1880 by Italians and Ukrainians. Formerly spelled Cresciúma.

Crickhowell (krĭk-hou'ùl), town and parish (pop. 1,076), SE Brecknock, Wales, on Usk R. and 13 mi. ESE of Brecknock; agr. market. Has 14th-cent. church and remains of 13th-cent. castle. Former flannel-milling center.

Cricklade, town and parish (pop. 1,399), N Wiltshire, England, on the Thames (here called the Isis) and 6 mi. NNW of Swindon; agr. market in dairying region. Has 12th-cent. church of St. Mary and 13th-15th-cent. church of St. Sampsons.

Cricklewood, England: see WILLESDEN.

Cridersville (krī'dùrzvĭl), village (pop. 684), Auglaize co., W Ohio, 7 mi. SSW of Lima.

Cridola, Monte (môn'tĕ krē'dôlä), peak (8,464 ft.) in SW Carnic Alps, N Italy, 15 mi. W of Ampezzo.

Crieff (krēf), burgh (1931 pop. 5,543; 1951 census 5,473), S central Perthshire, Scotland, on Earn R. and 16 mi. W of Perth; spa resort and agr. market; tanneries. Has 12th- and 17th-cent. market crosses, and Morrison's Acad. (1859). S are remains of Drummond Castle (1491), with famous gardens.

Criehaven, Maine: see MATINICUS ISLE.

Criel-sur-Mer (krēĕl'-sür-mâr'), village (pop. 846), Seine-Inférieure dept., N France, near English Channel, 13 mi. NE of Dieppe. Criel-Plage (1 mi. N; fine beach) damaged in Second World War.

Crigglestone, town and parish (pop. 4,630), West Riding, S central Yorkshire, England, near Calder R., 3 mi. SSW of Wakefield; coal mining; has benzol refinery.

Crikvenica (tsrēk'vĕnētsä), Ital. *Cirquenizza* (chērkwĕnēt'tsä), village (pop. 4,213), NW Croatia, Yugoslavia, on Adriatic Sea, 17 mi. SE of Rijeka (Fiume), opposite Krk Isl.; major resort, with 3-mi.-long bathing beach. Has 14th-cent. church and former monastery.

Crillon, Cape (krĭ'lùn, Fr. krēyõ'), Rus. *Krilon* or *Kril'on,* Jap. *Nishi-notoro-saki* (nē'shĭ-nōtō"rō'-sä'kē), southernmost point of Sakhalin, Russian SFSR, on La Pérouse Strait, W of Aniva Gulf; 45°53'N 142°05'E.

Crillon, Mount (krĭ'lùn) (12,725 ft.), SE Alaska, in Fairweather Range, 100 mi. WNW of Juneau, in Glacier Bay Natl. Monument; 58°39'N 137°10'W.

Crimea (krīmē'ù), Rus. *Krym* or *Krim* (krĭm), anc. *Chersonesus Taurica* [=Tauric Chersonese], peninsula and oblast (□ 10,000; 1946 pop. estimate 1,050,000) of S European Russian SFSR, on the Black Sea; ⊙ Simferopol. Connected with mainland (N) by narrow Perekop Isthmus; projects 120 mi. S into Black Sea and (with Kerch Peninsula; E) is 200 mi. long W-E. Bounded NE by Sea of Azov and its lagoonlike inlet, the Sivash; separated from Taman Peninsula (E) by Kerch Strait. The Crimea is divided into 4 distinct regions: dry, level steppe (N; 4/5 of total area) drained by intermittent streams, including Salgir R.; Crimean Mts., rising to over 5,000 ft., along S coast; subtropical Black Sea littoral at foot of steep S mtn. slopes; arid Kerch Peninsula, which contains minerals (iron at Kamysh-Burun, petroleum, gypsum, limestone). Fisheries (along its entire coast line) and salt deposits on Sivash lagoon are important resources. Grain (mainly quick-ripening, high quality wheat) and cotton in steppe portion; fruit orchards, vineyards, tobacco in foothill valleys and S coast. Sheep raising in Crimean Mts. Industry (except for heavy metallurgy at Kerch) largely based on agr. processing (fruit, vegetable, and fish canning, tobacco). Tourism is a major industry, mainly on S coast, the Rus. Riviera. Exports iron ore, salt, marble, canned goods, wine, tobacco. Since reduction of minorities (Tatars, Germans, Jews) during Second World War, pop. is largely Russian and Ukrainian. Chief cities: Sevastopol (Black Sea naval base), Simferopol, Kerch, Feodosiya, Yevpatoriya, Yalta (center of resort dist.). Known to anc. Greeks as the Tauric Chersonese; colonized successively by Scythians, Greeks (after 7th cent. B.C.; Chersonesus Heracleotica, Theodosia, Panticapaeum), kingdoms of Asia Minor (2d cent. B.C.), Rome, and Byzantium. Overrun by Goths, Huns, and Khazars during the great migrations. In 15th cent., Turks acquired existing Tatar khanate (dating from 13th cent.) and Genoese coastal colonies. Turkish rule continued until annexation (1783) by Russia, when Crimea was placed under Rus. govt. of Taurida. W Crimea, including Sevastopol, was scene (1854–56) of Crimean War bet. Russia and alliance of England, France, Turkey, and Sardinia. Rus. and Ukrainian settlement intensified after railroad construction (1880s). Crimea was last stronghold of Wrangel army in Rus. civil war. Following Soviet conquest (1921), the Crimean Autonomous SSR was created (within Russian SFSR) on basis of Tatar minority (25% of total pop.). Following Second World War, when it was occupied (1941–44) by Germans, Crimean Tatars (accused of collaboration) ceased to be recognized as an ethnic group and Crimea was reorganized (1945) as an oblast of Russian SFSR. The Crimea Conference (also known as Yalta Conference) bet. Roosevelt, Churchill, and Stalin took place (1945) at Livadiya, near Yalta.

Crimean Canal, Russian SFSR: see NORTH CRIMEAN CANAL.

Crimean Mountains, range of flat-topped limestone formations in S Crimea, Russian SFSR, extending c.80 mi. along S (Black Sea) coast; up to 30 mi. wide. Consist (W) of 3 parallel ridges, of which the highest (S) descends abruptly to subtropical resort coast, which it protects from N climatic influences. Principal elevations are Roman-Kosh (5,062 ft.), Chatyr-Dag (5,003 ft.), and Ai-Petri (4,045 ft.). Wooded slopes and sheep pastures (Tatar *yaila*) are to be found in the cooler higher altitudes. Sometimes called Yaila Mts.

Crimmitschau (krĭ'mĭchou), town (pop. 30,504), Saxony, E central Germany, on the Pleisse and 9 mi. NNW of Zwickau; textile center (cotton, woolen, rayon; carpets; silk milling, also knitting and dyeing); mfg. of machinery, musical instruments. Sometimes spelled Krimmitschau.

Crinan (krĭ'nùn), small port on **Loch Crinan** (2 mi. long, 2 mi. wide), inlet of the Sound of Jura, W Argyll, Scotland, 6 mi. NW of Lochgilphead; NW terminal of **Crinan Canal,** which extends 9 mi. SE across head of Kintyre peninsula, past Lochgilphead, to Loch Gilp (a small inlet of Loch Fyne) at Ardrishaig. Built 1793–1801, it is navigable for small ships only and is now rarely used.

Cripple, village (1939 pop. 13), S central Alaska, on upper Innoko R. and 60 mi. NNW of McGrath; placer gold-mining camp.

Cripple Creek, city (1940 pop. 2,358; 1950 pop. 853), ⊙ Teller co., central Colo., in Rocky Mts., 10 mi. SW of Pikes Peak, 20 mi. WSW of Colorado City; alt. 9,375 ft. It is in Cripple Creek dist., famous gold-producing region that was largely ignored by prospectors until 1891, when Bob Womack discovered El Paso lode. Womack sold his claim for $500, later dying in poverty; mine that was on it yielded more than $5,000,000 worth of gold. Other large producers were Gold Coin, Independence, and Cresson mines. Total production since 1891 has been estimated at more than $380,000,000. City reached pop. of 50,000 in 1901; later declined as deposits were exhausted. Ranching and farming (lettuce, potatoes, and grain) are now carried on; after 1934 new veins were found and worked. Near by is Carlton Tunnel (32,927 ft. long; finished 1941), built to drain mines in vicinity.

Criquetot-l'Esneval (krēktō'-lānùväl'), village (pop. 760), Seine-Inférieure dept., N France, 12 mi. NNE of Le Havre; cattle.

Crisa (krī'sŭ), anc. town of Phocis, central Greece, on road from port of Cirrha to Delphi, in plain sacred to Apollo. Settled (c.590 B.C.) by refugee pop. of CIRRHA (with which it is often confused), it was itself destroyed in the first Sacred War. The attempt (340 B.C.) by Amphissa to resettle Crisa led to the fourth Sacred (Amphissean) War (339–338 B.C.), in which Philip II of Macedon overwhelmed Greece. Near by is modern Gr. village of Chryson or Khrison (pop. 1,310).

Crisa, Gulf of, Gr. *Krissaios Kolpos*, inlet of Gulf of Corinth, central Greece, in Phocis nome; 8 mi. wide, 8 mi. long. Itea (port of Amphissa) is on N shore; Galaxeidion on W shore. Variously called Gulf of Amphissa, Galaxeidion, Itea, and Salona.

Crisana-Maramures (krēshä'nä-märmōō'rĕsh), Rum. *Crişana-Maramureş*, historical province (□ 9,241; 1948 pop. 1,391,672) of NW Rumania, bet. Transylvania and Hungary. Crisana is the easternmost part of the Alföld plain and is drained by Körös (Cris) and lower Mures rivers. The region is noted for its prosperous agr. and for its quality wines. Principal cities are Arad and Oradea. Maramures is extensively forested and drained by tributaries of the Tisa; its E section lies on W slopes of the Carpathians. Main centers are Sighet and Satu-Mare. Both Crisana and Maramures were part of Hungary until 1919 and included a strip of the present Salaj dept. (now entirely in Transylvania). Most of Crisana-Maramures was held for a short time (1940–45) by Hungary. Hung. minority is still important (365,745 persons in 1948).

Crisfield (krĭs'fēld), city (pop. 3,688), Somerset co., SE Md., on the Eastern Shore 31 mi. SSW of Salisbury, and on inlet of Tangier Sound; rail terminus; port of entry; ferries to Smith Isl. and Tangier Isl. (Va.). A center of seafood industry (fish, crabs, oysters) of Md. and Va.; has largest Chesapeake Bay fishing fleet, extensive processing, canning, shipping facilities. Diamondback terrapin are raised. Sport fishing, duck hunting. Mfg. of fishing equipment, boats, clothing, tents. Hinterland is rich truck-farming, dairying, poultry-raising area. Crisfield surveyed 1663.

Crisp, county (□ 296; pop. 17,663), S central Ga.; ⊙ Cordele. Bounded W by Flint R. (forms L. Blackshear here). Coastal plain agr. (cotton, corn, peanuts, pecans, truck, melons, fruit) and timber area. Formed 1905.

Crispi (krē'spē), village (1950 pop. 1,000), Tripolitania, Libya, near Gulf of Sidra, on coastal highway and 8 mi. S of Misurata, in fertile, irrigated region; agr. settlement (cereals, olives, fodder, vegetables) founded by Italians in 1938.

Crispiano (krēspyä'nô), town (pop. 5,699), Ionio prov., Apulia, S Italy, 9 mi. N of Taranto; wine, olive oil.

Cris River, Rumania and Hungary: see KÖRÖS RIVER.

Cristais, Serra dos (sĕ'rŭ dōōs krēstīs'), mountain range in SE Goiás, central Brazil, 90 mi. ESE of Anápolis; rises to 4,000 ft. Contains large quantities of rock crystals mined near Cristalina. Old spelling, Serra dos Crystaes.

Cristal, Sierra del (syĕ'rä dĕl krēstäl'), low range, Oriente prov., E Cuba, extending 20 mi. WSW from Sagua de Tánamo; rises to c.3,000 ft. Yields lumber. Nicaro nickel mines at N foot.

Cristalina (krēstŏŏlē'nŭ), city (pop. 1,339), SE Goiás, central Brazil, in the Serra dos Cristais, 90 mi. ESE of Anápolis; rock-crystal-mining center (large white-quartz reserves). Formerly spelled Crystalina.

Cristallo, Monte (môn'tĕ krēstäl'lô), glacier-topped mountain (alt. 10,551 ft.) in the Dolomites, Belluno prov., N Italy, 4 mi. NE of Cortina d'Ampezzo.

Cristianos, Los (lōs krēstyä'nōs), village (pop. 781), Tenerife, Canary Isls., 40 mi. SW of Santa Cruz de Tenerife; minor Atlantic port (Puerto de los Cristianos), serving Arona commune.

Cristina (krēstē'nŭ). **1** City (pop. 2,461), S Minas Gerais, Brazil, on N slope of Serra da Mantiqueira, on railroad and 20 mi. NE of Itajubá; dairy products, cereals. Formerly spelled Christina. **2** City, Sergipe, Brazil: see CRISTINÁPOLIS.

Cristina (krēstē'nä), town (pop. 639), Badajoz prov., W Spain, 15 mi. ESE of Mérida; cereals, olives.

Cristinápolis (krēstēnä'pōōlēs), city (pop. 721), S Sergipe, NE Brazil, near Bahia border, 22 mi. SW of Estância; sugar, tobacco, corn. Until 1944, called Cristina (formerly spelled Christina).

Cristo (krē'stō), town (pop. 3,382), Oriente prov., E Cuba, on railroad and 8 mi. NNE of Santiago de Cuba. Manganese mining, with large concentration plant.

Cristo, El, Panama: see EL CRISTO.

Cristobal (krĭstō'bŭl, Sp. krēstō'bäl), town (pop. 417), ⊙ Cristobal dist. (□ 140; pop. 15,029), Panama Canal Zone, at Atlantic end of Panama Canal, adjoining (S) Colón (Panama). Situated on isthmus connecting Manzanillo Isl. to mainland, it has rail yards and harbor installations (steel and concrete cargo piers and docks, bunker oil supplies) jutting W into Limon Bay. Other facilities (coaling plant, repair wharves) are on TELFERS ISLAND and at MOUNT HOPE on both sides of old Fr. canal mouth. Sometimes called Old Cristobal. NEW CRISTOBAL is a section of Colón.

Cristóbal Colón, Venezuela: see MACURO.

Cristóbal Colón, Pico (pē'kō krēstō'bäl kōlōn'), snow-capped Andean peak (18,950 ft.) in Magdalena dept., N Colombia, highest of the Sierra Nevada de Santa Marta and of Colombia, 70 mi. E of Barranquilla.

Crisul-Alb River, Rumania and Hungary: see KÖRÖS RIVER.

Crisul-Negru River, Rumania and Hungary: see KÖRÖS RIVER.

Crisul-Repede River, Rumania and Hungary: see KÖRÖS RIVER.

Crittenden (krĭ'tŭndŭn). **1** County (□ 623; pop. 47,184), E Ark.; ⊙ Marion. Situated in delta region bet. the Mississippi (E and S boundary) and the St. Francis; traversed by small Tyronza R. Agr. (cotton, corn, soybeans, hay). Mfg. at West Memphis. Hardwood timber. Formed 1825. **2** County (□ 365; pop. 10,818), W Ky.; ⊙ Marion. Bounded NW by Ohio R. (Ill. line), NE by Tradewater R., SW by Cumberland R. Rolling agr. area (livestock, poultry, grain, dairy products, burley tobacco); fluorspar mines, limestone quarries. Formed 1824.

Crittenden, town (pop. 287), Grant co., N Ky., 16 mi. E of Warsaw. Lloyd Reservation for preservation of native plant life is here.

Criuleni, Moldavian SSR: see KRYULYANY.

Crivesti (krēvĕsht'), Rum. *Criveşti*, village (pop. 529), Barlad prov., E Rumania, on Barlad R. and 10 mi. SW of Barlad.

Crivitz (krĭ'vĭts), town (pop. 5,879), Mecklenburg, N Germany, 10 mi. ESE of Schwerin; agr. market (stock, grain, potatoes).

Crivitz, village (1940 pop. 514), Marinette co., NE Wis., on Peshtigo R. and 21 mi. NW of Marinette; tourist center; fishing.

Crmnica or **Tsrmnitsa** (both: tsŭrm'nĭtsä), region in Dinaric Alps, SW Montenegro, Yugoslavia, extending c.10 mi. along NW coast of L. Scutari; vineyards. Largest village, VIR.

Crna or **Crna pri Prevaljah** (tsŭr'nä prē prĕ'välyäkh), Slovenian *Črna* or *Črna pri Prevaljah*, Ger. *Schwarzenbach* (shvär'tsŭnbäkh), village, N Slovenia, Yugoslavia, on Meza R. and 6 mi. SSW of Prevalje, in the Karawanken, near Austrian border. Forms, together with MEZICA, ore-mining and -smelting center. Formerly Crna pod Peco. Until 1918, in Carinthia.

Crna Gora, republic, Yugoslavia: see MONTENEGRO.

Crna Gora or **Tsrna Gora** (both: tsŭr'nä gô'rä) [Serbo-Croatian,=black mountain]. **1** Mountain in Dinaric Alps, W Bosnia, Yugoslavia; highest point (5,412 ft.) is 19 mi. ESE of Drvar. **2** Mountain, S Yugoslavia, on Macedonia-Serbia border; highest point (5,415 ft.) is 13 mi. N of Skoplje. Its S slope, called Skopska Crna Gora or Skopska Tsrna Gora, has chromium ore deposits; noted for embroideries done here.

Crna Reka or **Tsrna Reka** (rĕyĕ'kä) [Serbo-Croatian,=black river]. **1** River, Macedonia, Yugoslavia, rises WNW of Krusevo, flows SSE, through the Pelagonija, and NNE, across the Tikves, to Vardar R. near Gradsko; c.125 mi. long. Marsh-draining operations (1947–51) along its course. **2** or **Crni Timok** or **Tsrni Timok** (–nē, tē'môk) [Serbo-Croatian,=black Timok], river, E Serbia, Yugoslavia, rises 17 mi. E of Paracin, flows c.50 mi. E, joining Beli Timok R. just NNE of Zajecar to form TIMOK RIVER.

Crnica, Yugoslavia: see SIBENIK.

Crni Guber, Yugoslavia: see SREBRENICA.

Crni Timok, river, Yugoslavia: see CRNA REKA, Serbia.

Crni Vrh or **Tsrni Vrkh** (vŭrkh') [Serbo-Croatian,= black peak]. **1** Peak (1,791 ft.) in Dinaric Alps, N Bosnia, Yugoslavia, 8 mi. E of Banja Luka. **2** Peak, NW Bosnia, Yugoslavia: see GRMEC MOUNTAINS. **3** Peak (2,837 ft.) in N Croatia, Yugoslavia, 10 mi. E of Daruvar, in Slavonia. **4** Mountain (3,369 ft.) in E Serbia, Yugoslavia, 8 mi. WNW of Bor. **5** Peak, E Serbia, Yugoslavia: see DELI JOVAN.

Crnja, Tsrnya, or **Srpska Crnja,** or **Srpska Tsrnya** (all: tsŭr'nyä sŭrp'skä), Hung. *Csernye* (chĕrn'yĕ), village (pop. 7,998), Vojvodina, NE Serbia, Yugoslavia, on railroad and 13 mi. SE of Kikinda, near Rum. border, in the Banat.

Crnojevica Rijeka, Yugoslavia: see RIJEKA CRNOJEVICA.

Crno Jezero, Yugoslavia: see DURMITOR.

Crnomelj (chŭr'nômĕl, –mĕ'yŭ), Slovenian *Črnomelj*, Ger. *Tschernembl* (chĕr'nĕmbŭl), village (pop. 1,736), S Slovenia, Yugoslavia, near Croatia border, on railroad and 16 mi. S of Novo Mesto; lumbering. Old castle. Until 1918, in Carniola.

Croaghgorm (krō"ŭgôrm') or **Blue Stack Mountains,** range, S Co. Donegal, Ireland, extends 18 mi. WSW–ENE, rises to 2,219 ft. in Blue Stack, 7 mi. N of Donegal.

Croaghpatrick (krōpă'trĭk), mountain (2,510 ft.) in SW Co. Mayo, Ireland, near Clew Bay, 7 mi. WSW of Westport. In legend it is connected with St. Patrick; summit is a place of pilgrimage. On slope are ruins of 14th-cent. monastery.

Croatan Sound (krō"ŭtăn'), NE N.C., connects Albemarle (N) and Pamlico (S) sounds; bounded E by Roanoke Isl.; c.15 mi. long, 4 mi. wide; has dredged channel.

Croatia (krōā'shŭ), Serbo-Croatian *Hrvatska* (hŭr'vätskä), Ger. *Kroatien* (krōä'tsēŭn), Hung. *Horvátország* (hôr'vätôrshäg), constituent republic (□ 21,611; pop. 3,749,039), NW Yugoslavia; ⊙ Zagreb. Bounded by Free Territory of Trieste (NW), Slovenia and Hungary (N), Serbia (NE), Bosnia and Herzegovina (E), and Adriatic Sea (W, S). Includes Croatia proper, SLAVONIA, DALMATIA, and most of ISTRIA. Its coastline, which extends from mouth of Mirna R. to Gulf of Kotor (except for narrow corridor providing Herzegovina with an outlet to the Adriatic at Neum), is protected by many isls., the largest being Krk, Cres, and Brac. Its SW part, in Dinaric Alps, is mountainous and karstlike; its NE part, notably Slavonia, is mostly flat and fertile. Croatia is drained into the Danube by Sava and Drava rivers, into Adriatic Sea by Zrmanja, Krka, Cetina, and Neretva rivers. Predominantly agr., with grain (corn, wheat, oats, barley) as leading crop; vegetables (notably potatoes), industrial crops (sugar beets, flax, hemp, rape, chicory, etc.), fruit (both subtropical and temperate), nuts, and grapes (chiefly on coastland and isls. are also grown. Forestry, stock (notably dairy cattle) and poultry raising, beekeeping and fishing are well developed. Deposits of coal (at Siveric), lignite (bet. Sava and Drava rivers), petroleum (in Medjumurje, Bujavica, and Goilo), natural gas (in Bujavica and Goilo), iron ore (at Topusko), and sulphur (at Krapina). In addition, Dalmatia has deposits of bauxite, asphalt, limestone, gypsum, salt, and marble. Croatia has many health resorts, notably Topusko, Lipik, Daruvar, Varazdin, and Krapina. Chief hydroelectric stations are on CETINA and KRKA rivers. Home industry is an important branch of economy. Mfg. is better developed than in any other Yugoslav republic. There is a thick network of motor roads and railroads. Besides ZAGREB, chief cities are RIJEKA (Fiume), OSIJEK, SPLIT, KARLOVAC, and PULA; DUBROVNIK, SIBENIK, and ZADAR are also major seaports. Part of Roman Pannonia, Croatia was settled (7th cent.) by Croats, who in 9th cent. accepted Christianity. The fact that they accepted Roman Catholicism has ever since set the Croats apart from their neighbors, the Serbs, who also constitute a large minority within Croatia. A kingdom from 10th cent., Croatia conquered surrounding regions, notably Dalmatia (which was by 1420 under Venetian control). In 1091, Ladislaus I of Hungary conquered Croatia and in 1102 his successor was crowned king of Croatia. In the resulting personal union with Hungary, Croatia retained its own diet and was governed by a native *ban;* this system lasted, with interruptions and modifications, until 1918. From 1526 to 1699 most of Croatia (including Slavonia) was under Turkish rule; from 1809 to 1813 it was part of Napoleon's Illyrian Provs. Made an Austrian crownland in 1849, converted in 1868 into autonomous Hungarian crownland and titular kingdom of Croatia-Slavonia (□ 16,425). Included in Yugoslavia as prov. of Croatia-Slavonia in 1918. Croatia was nominally independent (under Italian protection) during Second World War. Became a people's republic in 1946, absorbing Dalmatia and (1947) most of Istria.

Croce, Monte (môn'tĕ krô'chĕ), peak (8,163 ft.) in the Dolomites, N Italy, 15 mi. NE of Trent.

Croce Carnico, Passo di Monte, Austro-Ital. border: see PLÖCKEN PASS.

Croce di Comelico, Passo di Monte (päs'sô dē môn'tĕ krô'chĕ dē kômä'lēkô), Ger. *Kreuzberg Pass*, pass (alt. 5,367 ft.) in Carnic Alps, Italy, near Austrian border, 7 mi. N of Auronzo. Crossed by road.

Crocetta del Montello (krôchĕt'tä dĕl môntĕl'lô), village (pop. 1,683), Treviso prov., Veneto, N Italy, 4 mi. N of Montebelluna; resort; silk mill, lime- and cementworks.

Croche River (krōsh), S central Que., rises W of L. St. John, flows 110 mi. S to St. Maurice R. 5 mi. N of La Tuque.

Crocheron (krōch'rŭn), fishing village, Dorchester co., E Md., on the Eastern Shore 23 mi. S of Cambridge; packs oysters, crabs.

Crocker, agr. city (pop. 712), Pulaski co., central Mo., in the Ozarks, near Gasconade R., 28 mi. ENE of Lebanon.

Crocker Mountain (4,168 ft.), Franklin co., W Maine, 26 mi. NW of Farmington.

Crocker Mountains, N Borneo, near W coast, extend c.40 mi. SSW from Marudu Bay; rise to Mt. Kinabalu (13,455 ft.), highest peak of isl.

Crockett (krŏ'kĭt). **1** County (□ 269; pop. 16,624), W Tenn.; ⊙ Alamo. Bounded NE by Middle Fork, SW by South Fork of Forked Deer R. Cotton, corn, livestock, truck; ships strawberries, tomatoes. Formed 1871. **2** County (□ 2,794; pop. 3,981), W Texas; ⊙ Ozona. Rough prairies and woodlands of Edwards Plateau, bounded W by Pecos R.; alt. c.1,500–2,500 ft. Oil, natural gas, livestock region (sheep, goats, cattle). Founded 1875.

Crockett. **1** Village (1940 pop. 4,105), Contra Costa co., W Calif., on Carquinez Strait (here bridged),

12 mi. NE of Richmond; "company town" for large sugar refinery; port facilities. **2** City (pop. 5,932), ⊙ Houston co., E Texas, 33 mi. SSE of Palestine; trade center of cotton, lumber, truck area; cottonseed oil and lumber mills, cotton gins, wood-working plants. Seat of Mary Allen Col. About 25 mi. NE (near Weches) is replica of 1st Sp. mission (1690) in E Texas. City founded in 1830s.

Crockett, Fort, Texas: see GALVESTON.

Crocodile River. 1 In U. of So. Afr., Bechuanaland, Southern Rhodesia, and Mozambique: see LIMPOPO RIVER. **2** In E Transvaal, U. of So. Afr., rises N of Belfast, flows c.175 mi. E, past Nelspruit, to Komati R. at Ressano Garcia, on Mozambique border. Lower course forms S boundary of Kruger Natl. Park.

Crocodilopolis, Egypt: see ARSINOË.

Crocq (krôk), village (pop. 571), Creuse dept., central France, on Plateau of Millevaches, 11 mi. ESE of Aubusson; hide and skin processing.

Crocus Hill, village, W Anguilla, B.W.I., 18°13'N 63°5'W; sea-island cotton.

Croda Rossa (krô'dä rôs'sä), peak (10,298 ft.) in the Dolomites, N Italy, 7 mi. N of Cortina d'Ampezzo.

Crofton. 1 Coal-mining town (pop. 500), Christian co., SW Ky., 13 mi. N of Hopkinsville. **2** Village (pop. 630), Knox co., NE Nebr., 60 mi. WNW of Sioux City, Iowa, near Missouri R.; dairy produce.

Croghan (krō'gŭn), village (pop. 772), Lewis co., N central N.Y., on Beaver R. and 8 mi. NE of Lowville; cheese, lumber, wood products, paper.

Croia, Albania: see KRUJË.

Croil Island, St. Lawrence co., N N.Y., in the St. Lawrence, at Ont. line, c.4 mi. NW of Massena; c.3½ mi. long, ¾–1¾ mi. wide.

Croisette, Cape (krwäzĕt'). **1** Headland on the Mediterranean, in Alpes-Maritimes dept., SE France, bet. Golfe de la Napoule (W) and Juan Gulf (E). Forms easternmost section of Cannes. Summer casino near its tip. 43°33'N 7°2'E. Just offshore are Îles de Lérins. **2** Rocky headland of Bouches-du-Rhône dept., SE France, on Gulf of Lion, 6 mi. SSW of Marseilles, at SW extremity of rugged, barren Massif de Marseilleveyre (alt. 1,434 ft.); 43°12'N 5°21'E. Several islets offshore.

Croisic, Le (lŭ krwäzēk'), town (pop. 3,335), Loire-Inférieure dept., W France, on Bay of Biscay and 14 mi. W of Saint-Nazaire; saltworks; oyster beds, sardine fisheries. Picturesque harbor and beaches attract tourists. Near by is a headland (47°18'N 2°33'W).

Croisilles (krwäzē'), village (pop. 716), Pas-de-Calais dept., N France, 8 mi. SSE of Arras; agr. tools.

Croissy-sur-Seine (krwäsē'-sür-sĕn'), town (pop. 3,960), Seine-et-Oise dept., N central France, a W suburb of Paris, 9 mi. from Notre Dame Cathedral, in bend of Seine R. just S of Chatou; metalworks; varnish mfg.

Croix (krwä), SE suburb (pop. 17,277) of Roubaix, Nord dept., N France, on canal and road to Lille (5 mi. SW); mfg. (agr. machines, furniture, biscuits), meat canning, cotton spinning. Cattle and poultry shipping.

Croix-des-Bouquets (krwä-dā-bōōkā'), town (1950 census pop. 1,455), Ouest dept., S Haiti, 8 mi. ENE of Port-au-Prince; cotton and sugar growing.

Croix-de-Vie (–dū-vē'), town (pop. 2,514), Vendée dept., W France, port and resort on Bay of Biscay at mouth of Vie R. and 17 mi. NNW of Les Sables-d'Olonne; sardine and tuna fishing; fish and vegetable preserving.

Croix-Haute, Col de la, France: see LUS-LA-CROIX-HAUTE.

Croker Island (krō'kŭr) (□ 126), in Arafura Sea, 1 mi. off NE shore of Cobourg Peninsula, N Northern Australia, across Bowen Strait; 27 mi. long, 10 mi. wide; forested. Aboriginal reservation.

Cro-Magnon, France: see EYZIES, LES.

Cromarty, county, Scotland: see ROSS AND CROMARTY.

Cromarty (krŏ'mŭrtē), burgh (1931 pop. 837; 1951 census 726), E Ross and Cromarty, Scotland, on Cromarty Firth, near its mouth on Moray Firth, on Black Isle, 16 mi. NNE of Inverness; 57°42'N 4°W; small port and naval station. Formerly a herring-fishing center.

Cromarty Firth, long, narrow inlet of Moray Firth, E Ross and Cromarty, Scotland, extends 18 mi. inland, 3–5 mi. wide. Narrow entrance is bet. Sutor Rocks headlands. Affords good anchorage, frequently used by Royal Navy. Naval base in First World War.

Cromdale, village, S Moray, Scotland, on the Spey and 2 mi. E of Grantown-on-Spey, at foot of Hills of Cromdale.

Cromdale, Hills of, range in S Moray, Scotland, extending 11 mi. SW-NE along Banffshire border. Highest point is 2,329 ft. Range includes peak of Cairn Tuairner (kârn' tûrn') (2,278 ft.), 5 mi. SE of Grantown-on-Spey. At foot of range is battlefield (1690) of the Haughs of Cromdale, 5 mi. E of Grantown-on-Spey.

Cromer (krō'mŭr), urban district (1931 pop. 4,176; 1951 census 4,658), N Norfolk, England, on North Sea, 21 mi. N of Norwich; seaside resort, fishing port, and lifeboat station. Site of lighthouse (52°56'N 1°18'E) with light visible over 23 mi. Has 15th-cent. church with 160-ft. tower. Town is on high cliffs and protected by a sea wall.

Cromford, England: see MATLOCK.

Crommyou, Cape, Cyprus: see KORMAKITI, CAPE.

Cromona (krŭmō'nŭ) or **Haymond,** village (pop. 1,321, with near-by Potters Fork), Letcher co., SE Ky., 3 mi. W of Jenkins.

Crompton (krŭmp'tŭn), urban district (1931 pop. 14,764; 1951 census 12,558), SE Lancashire, England, N suburb of Oldham. Includes cotton-milling towns of High Crompton and Shaw.

Crompton, industrial village in West Warwick town, Kent co., central R.I., 11 mi. SSW of Providence; mfg. (corduroys, velveteens, water repellents, soap, cleaning fluids).

Cromwell, borough (pop. 716), S central S.Isl., New Zealand, 85 mi. NW of Dunedin and on Clutha R.; terminus of railroad from Dunedin. Fruitgrowing center; small gold mine.

Cromwell. 1 Town (pop. 4,286), including Cromwell village (pop. 1,541), Middlesex co., central Conn., on Mattabesset and Connecticut rivers, just N of Middletown; hothouse flowers, toys, hardware. Settled c.1650, set off from Middletown 1851. **2** Town (pop. 449), Noble co., NE Ind., near Wawasee L., 33 mi. NW of Fort Wayne, in agr. area. **3** Town (pop. 147), Union co., S Iowa, 5 mi. W of Creston; livestock, grain. **4** Village (pop. 197), Carlton co., E Minn., on small lake and 37 mi. W of Duluth, in grain, livestock, and poultry area; dairy products. State forest near by. **5** Town (pop. 313), Seminole co., central Okla., 11 mi. NNE of Wewoka, in agr. area; cotton ginning.

Cronberg, Germany: see KRONBERG.

Cronberry, village in Auchinleck parish, E central Ayrshire, Scotland; barite mining.

Crone, Italy: see IDRO.

Cronenberg or **Kronenberg** (both: krō'nŭnbĕrk), SW section (1925 pop. 14,051) of WUPPERTAL, W Germany, 3.5 mi. SSW of Elberfeld; ironworking center (agr. and gardening implements. tools, screws, rivets); silk weaving. First mentioned 1225. Chartered 1827. Inc. (1929) with neighboring towns to form city of Wuppertal.

Cronin Mountain (krō'nĭn) (7,827 ft.), central B.C., 16 mi. NE of Smithers; 54°56'N 126°51'W; highest peak of Babine Mts.

Cronkhite, Fort, Calif., a sub-post of the Presidio of SAN FRANCISCO.

Cronstadt Island (krŏn'stăt"), islet off NW Trinidad, B.W.I., in the Gulf of Paria, just W of Carrera Isl., with which it forms the San Diego Isls., 7 mi. W of Port of Spain. Bathing resort.

Cronulla (krōnŭ'lŭ), town (pop. 7,330), E New South Wales, Australia, on W shore of Port Hacking and 12 mi. S of Sydney; summer resort.

Crook, England: see CROOK AND WILLINGTON.

Crook. 1 County (□ 2,980; pop. 8,991), central Oregon; ⊙ Prineville. Drained by Crooked R. Timber, livestock, dairy. Quicksilver mining. Includes parts of Ochoco Natl. Forest (E) in Blue Mts. Formed 1882. **2** County (□ 2,897; pop. 4,738), NE Wyo.; ⊙ Sundance. Grain, livestock region, bordering S.Dak. and Mont.; watered by Belle Fourche and Little Missouri rivers. Lumber, coal. Includes Devils Tower Natl. Monument. Sec. of Black Hills Natl. Forest and part of Black Hills in NE. Formed 1875.

Crook, town (pop. 259), Logan co., NE Colo., on S.Platte R. and 26 mi. NE of Sterling, near Nebr. line; sugar beets.

Crook, Lake, Texas: see PINE CREEK.

Crook and Willington, urban district (1951 census pop. 27,606), central Durham, England, 7 mi. SW of Durham; coal mines, chemical works. Formerly separate urban dists. of Crook (1931 pop. 11,690) and Willington (1931 pop. 8,964).

Crooked Creek, village (pop. 32), W Alaska, on Kuskokwim R. and 60 mi. ESE of Holy Cross; gold mining, fur farming.

Crooked Creek, village (pop. 1,134, with adjacent Smithfield), Huntingdon co., S central Pa.

Crooked Creek. 1 In S Ill., rises in Marion co., flows c.50 mi. S and SW, past Central City, to Kaskaskia R. 8 mi. SSW of Carlyle. **2** In Kansas and Okla.: see CIMARRON RIVER. **3** In W central Pa., rises in central Indiana co., flows c.50 mi. SW and NW to Allegheny R. just below Ford City. Flood-control dam (143 ft. high, 1,480 ft. long; completed 1940) is c.7 mi. above mouth.

Crooked Island, island (22 mi. long, up to 8 mi. wide) and district (□ 76; pop. 1,078), S Bahama Isls., in Crooked Island Passage, just W of Acklins Isl., and 250 mi. SE of Nassau. Exports cascarilla bark. Main settlements: Colonel Hill (center) and Landrail Point (NW). Visited by Columbus on Oct. 21, 1492. American loyalists settled here and grew cotton, but had to abandon their plantations because of insect pests. Sometimes Crooked Isl. group is considered to include also Acklins Isl. (E) and Long Cay (S), all grouped around a shoal.

Crooked Island Passage, deep channel (c.60 mi. long NE-SW), S central Bahama Isls., bounded by Samana Isl. (NE), Crooked Isl. (E), and Long Isl. (SW). Used by ships on way to Panama Canal.

Crooked Lake (□ 22), S central N.F., 40 mi. SE of Buchans; 48°22'N 56°15'W. S part of lake is called Great Burnt L. Connects N with Island Pond (4 mi. long, 2 mi. wide).

Crooked Lake. 1 In Polk co., central Fla., 5 mi. S of Lake Wales; c.7 mi. long, 2 mi. wide. Formerly also called Lake Caloosa. **2** In Emmet co., NW Mich., 6 mi. NE of Petoskey, in wooded resort area; c.4 mi. long, 1.5 mi. wide. Joined by streams to Pickerel L. (SE) and Burt L. (E). **3** In NE Minn. and W Ont., in chain of lakes on Can. line, 20 mi. N of Ely, Minn.; lies partly in St. Louis and Lake counties, Minn.; 25 mi. long, 4.5 mi. wide. Fishing resorts. Includes numerous isls. and inlets and has extremely irregular shore line. Bounded on S by Superior Natl. Forest.

Crooked Rhine River, Du. *Kromme Rijn* (krô'mŭ rīn'), central Netherlands, arm of the Rhine formed by forking of Lower Rhine R. into Crooked Rhine R. and Lek R. at Wijk bij Duurstede; flows 15 mi. NW to Utrecht, where it becomes OLD RHINE RIVER. Navigable by ships up to 30 tons.

Crooked River. 1 In SW Maine, rises in Songo Pond, W Oxford co.; flows c.40 mi. generally S to Sebago L. **2** In NW Mo., rises in Clinton co., flows c.60 mi. SE to the Missouri 4 mi. E of Lexington. **3** In central Oregon, rises in Blue Mts. in Crook co., flows W, N past Prineville, and W to Deschutes R. N of Redmond; 105 mi. long.

Crookham Church, town in Crookham parish (pop. 4,318), NE Hampshire, England, 3 mi. WNW of Aldershot. Part of Aldershot military camp here.

Crookhaven (krŏŏk'–), Gaelic *Cruachán*, town (pop. 72), SW Co. Cork, Ireland, on the Atlantic, 21 mi. WSW of Skibbereen; 51°28'N 9°43'W; fishing and yachting port.

Crook of Devon, Scotland: see DEVON RIVER.

Crookston. 1 City (pop. 7,352), ⊙ Polk co., NW Minn., on Red Lake R. and 24 mi. SE of Grand Forks, N.Dak.; trade center and shipping point in grain, sugar-beet, and potato area; food processing (flour, cattle feed, dairy products); beverages, wood products, monuments. Northwest School and Experiment Station of state univ. is here. Stock and produce show takes place annually. Settled 1872, inc. 1879. **2** Village (pop. 168), Cherry co., N Nebr., 10 mi. WNW of Valentine and on branch of Niobrara R., near S.Dak. line. Near by is Niobrara Div. of Nebr. Natl. Forest.

Crooksville, village (pop. 2,960), Perry co., central Ohio, 12 mi. SSW of Zanesville, in fruit, dairying, and truck area; makes pottery, chinaware; coal mining.

Crook Tower, W S.Dak., peak (7,140 ft.) in Black Hills, 35 mi. W of Rapid City.

Croom, Gaelic *Cromadh*, town (pop. 739), central Co. Limerick, Ireland, on Maigue R. and 10 mi. SSW of Limerick; agr. market (grain, potatoes; dairying). Has 12th-cent. castle of the Fitzgeralds, rebuilt in 19th cent.

Croppenstedt, Germany: see KROPPENSTEDT.

Cropredy (krŏp'rĕdē), agr. village and parish (pop. 425), N Oxfordshire, England, on Cherwell R. and 4 mi. N of Banbury; flour milling. Has 14th-cent. church. Site of Royalist victory at beginning of Civil War.

Cropunta (krōpōōn'tä), village, Colón dept., E Honduras, in Mosquitia, on Patuca R. and 60 mi. ESE of Iriona; livestock; lumbering.

Cropwell Bishop, agr. village and parish (pop. 573), SE Nottingham, England, 3 mi. SSW of Bingham; dairying, cheese making; gypsum quarrying, plaster mfg. Has church dating from 13th cent.

Crosby. 1 Village, Cumberland, England: see CROSSCANONBY. **2** Residential municipal borough (1951 census pop. 58,362), SW Lancashire, England, on Mersey R. estuary, just NNW of Bootle; flour milling, metalworking. Formed 1937 out of Great Crosby (1931 pop. 18,285) and Waterloo with Seaforth (1931 pop. 31,187). **3** Town, Lincolnshire, England: see SCUNTHORPE.

Crosby, county (□ 911; pop. 9,582), NW Texas; ⊙ Crosbyton. On edge of Llano Estacado, with E-facing Cap Rock escarpment curving from SW to N; alt. 2,100–3,400 ft. Drained by White R. and Double Mtn. Fork of Brazos R. Cattle ranching, agr. (cotton, grain sorghums, wheat, forage, some truck); some dairying; hogs, sheep, poultry. Includes a state park. Formed 1876.

Crosby. 1 Village (pop. 2,777), Crow Wing co., central Minn., in Cuyuna iron range, near Mississippi R., and 15 mi. NE of Brainerd in lake and forest region. Iron-mining and lumbering point; dairy products, beverages. Small lake here. Town's growth dates from 1st shipment (1911) of iron ore. **2** Town (pop. 1,152), on Amite-Wilkinson co. line, SW Miss., 26 mi. SE of Natchez, in Homochitto Natl. Forest; trade center for agr. and timber area; lumber milling. Until 1934 called Stephenson. **3** City (pop. 1,689), ⊙ Divide co., NW N. Dak., 55 mi. NNE of Williston, near Can. line; trade center and port of entry in farming area, flour refining, coal mines. Inc. 1911.

Crosby, Mount, Wyo.: see ABSAROKA RANGE.

Crosby Channel, England: see MERSEY RIVER.

Crosby Garrett, agr. village and parish (pop. 189), E Westmorland, England, on Eden R. and 7 mi. SSE of Appleby, at foot of Crosby Fell.

Crosby-on-Eden, parish (pop. 238), NE Cumberland, England. Includes dairying villages of High Crosby, on Eden R. and 4 mi. NE of Carlisle, and, just E, Low Crosby.

Crosby Ravensworth, village and parish (pop. 681), N central Westmorland, England, 4 mi. SW of Appleby; cattle, sheep. Has church dating from early 13th cent. Stone circles and other traces of early Britons have been found here.

Crosbyton (krôz'bĭtŭn, –bētŭn), town (pop. 1,879), ⊙ Crosby co., NW Texas, on the Llano Estacado, 35 mi. E of Lubbock; shipping center for cotton, grain, livestock region; cotton gins, mattress factory, grain elevator, rock-crushing plant. State park is 10 mi. N. Founded 1908.

Cros-de-Cagnes, France: see CAGNES-SUR-MER.

Crosland, town (pop. 127), Colquitt co., S Ga., 12 mi. NE of Moultrie.

Cross, county (□ 626; pop. 24,757), E Ark.; ⊙ Wynne. Intersected by Crowley's Ridge; drained by St. Francis and L'Anguille rivers. Agr. (fruit, cotton, corn, rice, hay); hardwood timber. Mfg. at Parkin and Wynne. Formed 1862.

Cross, Pass of the, Rus. *Krestovy Pereval* or *Krestovyy Pereval*, in main range of the central Greater Caucasus, N Georgian SSR, on Georgian Military Road and 55 mi. NNW of Tiflis; alt. 7,815 ft. Connects Terek (N) and Aragva (S) river valleys.

Crosscanonby, village and parish (pop. 862), W Cumberland, England, 3 mi. NE of Maryport; dairy farming. Parish includes coal-mining village of Crosby, near Ellen R., and dairying village of Birkby.

Cross City, town (pop. 1,522), ⊙ Dixie co., N Fla., c.50 mi. WNW of Gainesville; trade center for lumbering, farming, and fishing area. Inc. 1924.

Cross Creek, village (pop. 1,445), Brooke co., W. Va., in the Northern Panhandle, SE of Weirton.

Crossen, Poland: see KROSNO, Zielona Gora prov.

Crossett (krŏ'sĭt), town (pop. 4,619), Ashley co., SE Ark., 40 mi. ESE of El Dorado; a lumbering "company town," producing also chemicals, charcoal, paper pulp, cotton and paper bags. Scientific reforestation methods demonstrated here.

Crossfarnoge Point or **Forlorn Point,** cape on St. George's Channel, Ireland, 13 mi. SSW of Wexford; 52°10'N 6°36'W. Offshore are Saltee Isls.

Cross Fell, highest mountain (2,930 ft.) of the Pennines, E Cumberland, England, 11 mi. ENE of Penrith.

Crossfield, village (pop. 433), S central Alta., 25 mi. N of Calgary; grain elevators.

Cross-Florida Waterway, Fla.: see OKEECHOBEE WATERWAY.

Crossgar (krôsgär', krŏs–), agr. village (district pop. 1,451), E Co. Down, Northern Ireland, 6 mi. NNW of Downpatrick; oats, flax; sheep.

Crosshaven (krôs'–, krŏs'–), Gaelic *Bun tSabhairne*, fishing village (pop. 780), SE Co. Cork, Ireland, at entrance to Cork Harbour, 10 mi. SE of Cork; seaside resort.

Crosshill (krôs'hĭl', krŏs'–), S suburb (pop. 3,292) of Glasgow, Lanark, Scotland.

Cross Hill, town (pop. 543), Laurens co., NW central S.C., 14 mi. NNE of Greenwood.

Cross Island, Arctic islet (1939 pop. 10), NE Alaska, in Beaufort Sea, 30 mi. E of Beechey Point; 70°29'N 147°50'W; primitive Eskimo culture.

Cross Keys, Va.: see PORT REPUBLIC.

Cross Lake (68 mi. long, 6 mi. wide), central Man., 60 mi. N of L. Winnipeg. Drained N by Nelson R.

Cross Lake. 1 In Caddo parish, NW La., just W of Shreveport; c.8 mi. long; water-supply reservoir. Resort (fishing, boating). **2** In Maine: see FISH RIVER LAKES. **3** In Crow Wing co., central Minn., in state forest, 20 mi. N of Brainerd; 4.5 mi. long, 1 mi. wide. Fed and drained by Pine R. Has fishing and bathing resorts. Small village of Crosslake is on W shore. Lake is used as reservoir. Dam is on E outlet. **4** In central N.Y., 17 mi. WNW of Syracuse; 4½ mi. long, ½–1 mi. wide. Seneca R. (here part of Barge Canal) enters from W, discharges from E side of lake.

Crossmaglen (krôsmŭglĕn', krŏs–), town (pop. 626), SW Co. Armagh, Northern Ireland, 10 mi. WNW of Dundalk; cattle, potatoes.

Crossmichael (krôs'mī'kŭl, krŏs'–), agr. village and parish (pop. 1,160, including part of Castle Douglas burgh), central Kirkcudbright, Scotland, on Dee R. and 4 mi. NW of Castle Douglas.

Cross Mill, N.C.: see WEST MARION.

Crossmolina (–mōlē'nŭ), Gaelic *Cros Ui Mhaoilhíona*, town (pop. 742), N central Co. Mayo, Ireland, on Deel R. and 7 mi. W of Ballina; agr. market (cattle; potatoes); angling center.

Cross Mountain (3,350 ft.), in the Cumberlands, E central Tenn., 22 mi. NW of Knoxville.

Crossnore (krôs'nôr), town (pop. 240), Avery co., NW N.C., 23 mi. NW of Morganton.

Cross Plains. 1 Town (pop. 1,305), Callahan co., central Texas, 40 mi. SE of Abilene, in oil-producing and agr. area (cotton, fruit, truck, pecans); mfg. (machine-shop products, wood products, mattresses). Settled c.1876, inc. 1911. **2** Village (pop. 464), Dane co., S Wis., 15 mi. W of Madison, in dairy-farm area.

Cross Point, village (pop. estimate 150), E Que., SW Gaspé Peninsula, at head of Chaleur Bay, at mouth of Restigouche R., opposite Campbellton; fishing port.

Cross River, SE Nigeria, rises in S Bamenda highlands near Tinto, flows in winding course W, past Mamfe and Ikom (head of high-water navigation), and S, past Obubra, Ndibi Beach (port of Afikpo), and Itu (head of year-round navigation), to arm of Gulf of Guinea S of Calabar; length, c.300 mi. Forms network of tidal creeks at mouth with Calabar R. (left). Receives Ewayong R. (right; navigable to Bansara).

Cross Road, residential village (pop. 2,937, with near-by Bannertown), Surry co., NW N.C., suburb E of Mt. Airy.

Cross Roads, N suburb of Kingston, St. Andrew parish, SE Jamaica; mfg. of borax.

Cross Roads, borough (pop. 178), York co., S Pa., 13 mi. SE of York.

Cross Sound, SE Alaska, bet. Chichagof Isl. (S) and the mainland, extends 30 mi. NE from the Gulf of Alaska to Icy Strait.

Cross Timbers, town (pop. 179), Hickory co., W central Mo., 10 mi. NE of Hickory.

Crosstown, town (pop. 66), Perry co., E Mo., near Mississippi R., 8 mi. E of Perryville.

Cross Village, village (pop. c.250), Emmet co., NW Mich., on bluffs above L. Michigan, and 19 mi. NNW of Petoskey; fishing. Indian inhabitants hold annual festival and dances.

Crossville. 1 Town (pop. 609), De Kalb co., NE Ala., 18 mi. E of Guntersville. Ala. Polytechnic Inst. has an agr. experiment station here. **2** Village (pop. 866), White co., SE Ill., 24 mi. SW of Mount Carmel; agr. (corn, wheat, livestock). **3** Town (pop. 2,291), ⊙ Cumberland co., E central Tenn., 25 mi. E of Sparta, in the Cumberlands, in region of stone quarries, coal mines, timber, and small farms; makes wood and stone products, hosiery. Scenic state park, school for mtn. children, tuberculosis sanatorium near by. Founded c.1856; inc. 1901.

Crosswicks, village (pop. c.300), Burlington co., W N.J., on Crosswicks Creek and 7 mi. SE of Trenton; food products, bricks, feed. Has 18th-cent. Friends' meetinghouse. Settled before 1700. Hessians quartered here in Revolution.

Crosswicks Creek, W N.J., rises S of New Egypt, flows c.25 mi. N and WNW to Delaware R. near Bordentown.

Croston, former urban district (1931 pop. 1,934), W Lancashire, England, 8 mi. NE of Ormskirk; cotton milling. Has 15th-cent. church, 15th-cent. mansion (rebuilt in 19th cent.), and 17th-cent. almshouse.

Croswell (krŏz'–), city (pop. 1,775), Sanilac co., E Mich., on Black R. and 23 mi. NNW of Port Huron, in agr. area (sugar beets, grain, truck; dairy products); beet-sugar refining, flour milling, food canning. Inc. as village 1881, as city 1905.

Crotched Pond, S Maine, forked lake with two 3-mi. arms, bet. Lovejoy and Parker ponds, in 12-mi. chain stretching N from Androscoggin L., W Kennebec co.

Crotch Island, Maine: see CLIFF ISLAND.

Crothersville (krŭ'dhŭrzvĭl), town (pop. 1,276), Jackson co., S Ind., 28 mi. S of Columbus, in agr. area.

Croton (krō'tŭn). **1** Village, N.Y.: see CROTON-ON-HUDSON. **2** Village (pop. 356), Licking co., central Ohio, 19 mi. NW of Newark, in agr. area. Also called Hartford.

Crotona, Italy: see CROTONE.

Croton Aqueduct (krō'tŭn), SE N.Y., carries water of Croton R. reservoirs to New York city; 38 mi. long; built 1837–42. Begins at Croton L., parallels Croton R. to the Hudson, follows the Hudson to Yonkers and thence into New York city. Sometimes called Old Croton Aqueduct. Its flow is supplemented by New Croton Aqueduct (built 1885–91; c.30½ mi. long).

Croton Dam, N.Y.: see CROTON RIVER.

Crotone (krôtô'nĕ), anc. *Crotona* and *Croton*, town (pop. 19,163), Catanzaro prov., Calabria, S Italy, port on Gulf of Taranto, NW of Cape Colonne, 32 mi. ENE of Catanzaro. Industrial and commercial center; chemical plants (fertilizer, acids), zinc metallurgical works, agr. machinery factory; cereals, olive oil, dairy products, livestock. Hydroelectric power from reservoirs in La Sila mts. Sulphur mines near by. Bishopric. Has cathedral, castle, and mus. of antiquities. Founded 710 B.C. as colony of Achaea and noted for its devotion to athletic sports and as seat of school of Pythagoras. Conquered Sybaris in 510 B.C.; in 277 B.C. taken by Romans. Called Cotrone from Middle Ages until 1928.

Croton Falls (krō'tŭn), village (pop. c.500), Westchester co., SE N.Y., 12 mi. WSW of Danbury (Conn.), at S end of Croton Falls Reservoir (water supply for New York city), impounded in a branch of Croton R. by Croton Falls Dam (1,100 ft. long, 167 ft. high; completed 1911). Summer resort.

Croton Lake, N.Y.: see CROTON RIVER.

Croton-on-Hudson, residential village (pop. 4,837), Westchester co., SE N.Y., on E bank of the Hudson and 3 mi. N of Ossining; seat of Hessian Hills School. Mfg. of handbags and perfumes. Settled 1609, inc. 1898. Includes Harmon and New York Central railroad yards.

Croton Point, Westchester co., SE N.Y., peninsula (c.1½ mi. long) extending into the Hudson from its E bank, just above mouth of Croton R., S of Croton-on-Hudson; recreational park here.

Croton River, SE N.Y., rises in S Dutchess co. in West, Middle, and East branches, which flow S through Putnam co. to join near Westchester co. line; combined stream continues SW to the Hudson at Croton Point. New Croton Dam (2,168 ft. long, c.297 ft. high; completed 1905 to replace earlier structure), 3 mi. above mouth, impounds Croton L. (c.20 mi. long). Lake's waters, with those of West Branch, Middle Branch, East Branch, Croton Falls, Titicus, Cross River, Amawalk, and Bog Brook reservoirs and others in the river's watershed, are carried to New York city by CROTON AQUEDUCT.

Crotoy, Le (lŭ krôtwä'), town (pop. 2,107), Somme dept., N France, fishing port and resort on sandy mouth of the Somme, 12 mi. NW of Abbeville. Here Joan of Arc was imprisoned by British.

Crottendorf (krô'tŭndôrf), village (pop. 5,562) Saxony, E central Germany, in the Erzgebirge, [illegible] mi. SW of Annaberg, near Czechoslovak border, i[illegible] uranium-mining region; textile milling, knitting, and embroidering.

Crotty, village (pop. 1,435), La Salle co., N Ill., near Illinois R., 12 mi. ESE of Ottawa, in agr. and bituminous-coal area. Inc. 1865.

Crouch, village, Boise co., SW Idaho, 30 mi. NE of Emmett; agr., stock raising, lumbering. Inc. 1951.

Crouch End, England: see HORNSEY.

Crouch River, Essex, England, rises 3 mi. SE of Brentwood, flows 24 mi. E, past Burnham-on-Crouch, to North Sea at Foulness Point.

Crouse (krous), town (pop. 303), Lincoln co., SW N.C., 4 mi. SSW of Lincolnton.

Crouy (kro͞oē'), outer NE suburb (pop. 1,449) of Soissons, Aisne dept., N France, on the Aisne; metalworking.

Crow Agency, village, Big Horn co., SE Mont., on Little Bighorn R. and 12 mi. SSE of Hardin, in irrigated agr. region; grain, sugar beets. Hq. of Crow Indian Reservation. Custer Battlefield Natl. Monument near by.

Crowan, village and parish (pop. 1,838), W Cornwall, England, 3 mi. S of Camborne. Has 15th-cent. church.

Crowborough (krō'bŭrŭ), town and parish (pop. 6,095), NE Sussex, England, 9 mi. SE of East Grinstead; agr. market. Just S is Crowborough Beacon (792 ft.), highest point of Ashdown Forest.

Crow Creek, SE Wyo. and NE Colo., rises in Laramie Mts., flows E, past Cheyenne, and S to small lake in Weld co., Colo.; 140 mi. long.

Crowder (krou'dŭr). **1** Town (pop. 476), on Panola-Quitman co. line, NW Miss., 25 mi. E of Clarksdale and on Yocona R., in rich cotton area; lumber milling. **2** Town (pop. 133), Scott co., SE Mo., in Mississippi flood plain, 8 mi. NW of Sikeston. **3** Town (pop. 267), Pittsburg co., SE Okla., 14 mi. NNE of McAlester, in agr. area.

Crowdy Head (krou'dē), cape, E New South Wales, Australia, in Pacific Ocean; forms S end of Crowdy Bay (5 mi. wide); 31°51'S 152°46'E.

Crowell (krō'ŭl), city (pop. 1,912), ⊙ Foard co., N Texas, c.65 mi. W of Wichita Falls; rail, processing center in cattle-ranching and agr. area (grain, cotton, dairy products, poultry); oil, natural-gas wells. Settled 1887, inc. 1908; rebuilt after destructive tornado in 1942.

Crowland (krō'–) or **Croyland,** agr. village and rural district (pop. 2,809), Parts of Holland, S Lincolnshire, England, 7 mi. NNE of Peterborough. Has ruins of Benedictine abbey founded c.720 by King Æthelbald of Mercia; parts of it rebuilt into new church 1860 by Sir Gilbert Scott. Has 14th-cent. bridge.

Crowle (krōl), former urban district (1931 pop. 2,833), Parts of Lindsey, NW Lincolnshire, England, 7 mi. W of Scunthorpe; agr. market; brewing.

Crowley (krou'lē), county (□ 803; pop. 5,222), SE central Colo.; ⊙ Ordway. Irrigated agr. region, bounded S by Arkansas R. Livestock, sugar beets, feed grains. Formed 1911.

Crowley. 1 Town (pop. 379), Crowley co., SE central Colo., near Arkansas R., 5 mi. WSW of Ordway, in irrigated agr. region. **2** City (pop. 12,784), ⊙ Acadia parish, S La., c.70 mi. WSW of Baton Rouge, and on feeder canal to navigable Bayou Plaquemine Brule; processing, storage, and shipping center of a leading rice-growing area; also cotton, sugar cane, corn, sweet potatoes, peanuts. Sea-food packing; mfg. of machine-shop products, concrete blocks; cotton ginning. Oil and natural-gas wells. Rice experiment station. Founded 1886, inc. 1888.

Crowley, Lake, Calif.: see OWENS RIVER.

Crowley's Ridge (krō'lēz), SE Mo. and NE Ark., elevation (c.180 mi. long, 2–12 mi. wide) extending S from Scott co., Mo., to Phillips co., Ark., just W of Helena; highest point c.250 ft. above surrounding alluvial plain. Rich fruitgrowing region; contains many fossil beds. Crowley's Ridge State Park (established 1934) is on W slope near Walcott.

Crown City, village (pop. 301), Gallia co., S Ohio, 16 mi. SSW of Gallipolis and on the Ohio.

Crown Mountain, highest peak (1,550 ft.) of St. Thomas Isl., U.S. Virgin Isls., 3 mi. WNW of Charlotte Amalie.

Crown Point, headland at SW tip of Tobago, B.W.I., 8 mi. WSW of Scarborough; 11°8′N 60°50′W. Adjoining is the Crown Point civil airfield. Near bay with fine beach are the ruins of Milford Fort and the so-called "Robinson Crusoe's Cave." Cape is also called Brown's Point.

Crown Point. 1 Residential city (pop. 5,839), ⊙ Lake co., extreme NW Ind., 12 mi. S of Gary; some mfg. (monuments, signs, leather goods, grinders). Settled 1832, inc. 1868. **2** Resort town (1940 pop. 1,661), Essex co., NE N.Y., on L. Champlain, 7 mi. N of Ticonderoga. Crown Point village is chief center. Township includes Crown Point peninsula (now a state reservation), extending c.2 mi. into L. Champlain, which is bridged here to Chimney Point, Vt.; here are ruins of colonial forts, a mus., and recreational facilities. Champlain supported the Hurons in battle with the Iroquois here in 1609. Site was selected for French Fort St. Frederic (1731) because of location on N.Y.-Can. trail; after resisting British attacks (1755–56) in French and Indian War, fort was razed (1759) before advance of Sir Jeffrey Amherst. Fort Amherst (renamed Fort Crown Point) was begun by British in 1759; it was captured (May 12, 1775) in the Revolution by Seth Warner and the Green Mountain Boys, but was abandoned (1777) to Burgoyne in Saratoga campaign.

Crown Prince Christian Land, Dan. *Kronprins Christian Land*, peninsular region, NE Greenland, bounded by Danmark Fjord (NW) and Greenland Sea (E and SE); 80°–81°50′N 11°40′–26°W. It is c.180 mi. long (NE-SW), c.70 mi. wide. Greenland Sea coast line is indented by several deep fjords. Hilly, mostly glaciated. Entire NE part is covered by extensive Flade Glacier, Dan. *Flade Isblink*. At NE tip is Northeast Foreland.

Crown Prince Frederick Island (22 mi. long, 6 mi. wide), SE Franklin Dist., Northwest Territories, in the Gulf of Boothia, at W entrance of Fury and Hecla Strait, off NW Baffin Isl.; 70°8′N 86°40′W.

Crown-Prince Rudolf Land, Russian SFSR: see RUDOLF ISLAND.

Crownsville, village, Anne Arundel co., central Md., near Severn R., 7 mi. WNW of Annapolis. State mental hosp. for Negroes (established 1911).

Crow River, formed by confluence of North Fork and South Fork near Rockford, SE central Minn., flows 30 mi. NE to Mississippi R. 7 mi. NW of Anoka. South Fork rises in small lake in Kandiyohi co., SW central Minn., flows 100 mi. generally E, past Hutchinson, to North Fork, which rises in lake region of Pope co., SW central Minn., and flows 120 mi. ESE, through L. Koronis, to South Fork. Middle Fork, tributary of North Fork, rises in small lake near Belgrade, central Minn., flows 50 mi. S then E, through Green L., to North Fork in Meeker co.

Crows Nest, town (pop. 86), Marion co., central Ind., NW suburb of Indianapolis.

Crowsnest Mountain (9,138 ft.), SW Alta., near B.C. border, in Rocky Mts., 6 mi. NW of Coleman.

Crowsnest Pass (4,450 ft.), in Rocky Mts. bet. Alta. and B.C., 20 mi. NE of Fernie; 49°38′N 114°42′W. At E end of pass is village of Crows Nest or Crowsnest, B.C. (pop. estimate 250). Pass was discovered 1858 by the Palliser expedition; later used extensively by Northwest Mounted Police.

Crowsnest River, SE B.C. and SW Alta., rises in Rocky Mts. N of Crowsnest Pass, flows S to the pass, where it turns E and crosses into Alta., flowing past Coleman and Blairmore to Oldman R. near Macleod; 100 mi. long.

Crowthorne, residential town and parish (pop. 3,481), SE Berkshire, England, 10 mi. SE of Reading. Site of Wellington Col., a public school. Near by is Broadmoor insane asylum.

Crow Wing, county (□ 999; pop. 30,875), central Minn.; ⊙ Brainerd. Resort and agr. area drained by Mississippi R. and watered by numerous lakes. Dairy products, livestock, potatoes. Iron mining in E, near Crosby, in Cuyuna iron range. State forests extend throughout much of co. Formed 1857.

Crow Wing River, rises in chain of lakes in Hubbard co., NW central Minn., flows 100 mi. SE, past Motley and Pillager, to Mississippi R. 9 mi. SW of Brainerd. River is dammed above and below Pillager. Tributaries are Long Prairie and Leaf rivers.

Croy and Dalcross (dălkrôs′, –krŏs′), parish (pop. 911), partly in NW Nairnshire and NE Inverness, Scotland. Includes villages of Croy, 7 mi. SW of Nairn, and Dalcross, just S of Croy. Dalcross Castle was built 1621 by Lord Lovat.

Croydon (kroi′dŭn). **1** Village, N Queensland, Australia, 245 mi. WSW of Cairns; terminus of railroad from Normanton; tin. **2** Town (pop. 3,385), S Victoria, Australia, 17 mi. E of Melbourne; antimony mines.

Croydon, residential county borough (1931 pop. 233,032; 1951 census 249,592), NE Surrey, England, 9 mi. S of London; 51°22′N 0°5′W; mfg. of machinery, pharmaceuticals, leather, food products; metalworking. The airport here was formerly important, particularly during Second World War, when it was used for military purposes; sustained heavy air raids. After the war it was largely replaced by airports at Heath Row and Northolt. Croydon is site of palace of archbishops of Canterbury, founded in 11th cent., rebuilt in 14th cent., now used as girls' school. John Whitgift, buried in 15th-cent. church of St. John, founded the hosp. and grammar school. John Singleton Copley died here. Nearby is Bethlem Royal Hosp. (Bedlam). In county borough are residential dists. of Addington (pop. 2,791), former seat of archbishops of Canterbury, Addiscombe (pop. 14,048), Norbury (pop. 15,538), Upper Norwood (pop. 21,755), Thornton Heath (pop. 15,179), South Norwood (pop. 17,210), and Woodside (pop. 15,209).

Croydon. 1 Town (pop. 349), Sullivan co., W N.H., 7 mi. N of Newport. **2** Village (1940 pop. 2,412), Bucks co., SE Pa., 2 mi. W of Bristol; hosiery mfg.

Croyland, England: see CROWLAND.

Crozes-Hermitage (krōz-ĕrmētäzh′), village (pop. 93), Drôme dept., SE France, 2 mi. N of Tain-l'Hermitage; noted wines.

Crozet Islands (krōzā′), small archipelago, an outlying dependency of Madagascar, in subantarctic zone of S Indian Ocean, 1,500 mi. off SE coast of Africa, bet. Kerguelen Isls. and Prince Edward Isl., at approximately 46°S 51°E. Comprises several small islands of volcanic origin: Hog Isl., the Twelve Apostles, Penguin (Pingouin) Isl., Possession Isl., East Isl. Their steep cliffs, submarine reefs, and tempestuous waters have caused many wrecks. Still occasionally visited by whalers.

Crozier, Cape (krō′zhûr), headland, Antarctica, at E end of Ross Isl., in Ross Sea; 77°29′S 169°34′E. Discovered 1841 by Sir James C. Ross.

Crozier Channel, Northwest Territories: see FITZWILLIAM STRAIT.

Crozon (krôzō′), town (pop. 3,336), Finistère dept., W France, 9 mi. S of Brest; market center of Crozon Peninsula (fish, dairy products) and summer resort. Morgat just S.

Crozon Peninsula, Finistère dept., W France, a 3-pronged tongue of land projecting c.17 mi. into Atlantic Ocean, sheltering Brest Roads (N) and Bay of Douarnenez (S). On peninsula are the sardine-fishing ports of Crozon and Camaret-sur-Mer and the bathing resort of Morgat. Site of numerous megalithic monuments.

Cruas (krüä′), village (pop. 1,273), Ardèche dept., S France, near Rhone R. 10 mi. SE of Privas; cementworks; silk milling. Has 10th-cent. Romanesque abbey church.

Crucero Alto (krōōsā′rō äl′tō), hamlet, Arequipa dept., S Peru, highest point of Arequipa–Puno RR, 60 mi. W of Puno; alt. 14,665 ft.

Cruces (krōō′sĕs), town (pop. 9,043), Las Villas prov., central Cuba, on railroad and 13 mi. SW of Santa Clara; agr. trading center (sugar cane, tobacco, livestock). Sugar mills in outskirts. Mineral springs near by (SE).

Cruces, Las, Venezuela: see LAS CRUCES.

Cruces Point (krōō′sĕs) or **Peñita Point** (pānyē′tä), headland on Pacific coast of Chocó dept., W Colombia, N gate of Gulf of Cupica, 16 mi. SE of Cape Marzo; 6°39′N 77°32′W.

Cruces River, Valdivia prov., S central Chile, flows c.50 mi. SW, past San José de la Mariquina, joins CALLE-CALLE RIVER at Valdivia to form the Valdivia R.

Crucible, village (pop. 1,370), Greene co., SW Pa., on the Monongahela and 12 mi. ENE of Waynesburg.

Cruden (krōō′dŭn), parish (pop. 2,554), E Aberdeen, Scotland. Contains fishing port of Cruden Bay, on North Sea, 7 mi. SSW of Peterhead; seaside and golfing resort. There are remains of 17th-cent. Slains Castle, seat of earls of Erroll, hereditary High Constables of Scotland. Just SSE is fishing village of Port Erroll.

Cruger, town (pop. 494), Holmes co., central Miss., 14 mi. S of Greenwood, near Yazoo R.

Crugers, village, Westchester co., SE N.Y., near the Hudson, 4 mi. S of Peekskill. U.S. veterans' hosp.

Cruillas (krōōē′yäs), town (pop. 656), Tamaulipas, NE Mexico, 65 mi. ESE of Linares (Nuevo León); corn, sugar, livestock.

Crumlin, town (pop. 628), S Co. Antrim, Northern Ireland, 12 mi. W of Belfast; woolen milling.

Crum Lynne (krŭm″ lĭn′), residential village, Delaware co., SE Pa.; SW suburb of Philadelphia.

Crummies, mining village (1940 pop. 705), Harlan co., SE Ky., in the Cumberlands, 31 mi. ENE of Middlesboro; bituminous coal, lumber.

Crummock Water (krŭ′mŭk), lake on Cocker R. in the Lake District, SW Cumberland, England, 11 mi. E of Whitehaven; 2½ mi. long, 1 mi. wide; connected with and NNW of BUTTERMERE. On W side is the waterfall of Scale Force, one of highest (125 ft.) in the Lake District.

Crumpler, village (pop. 1,007), McDowell co., S W.Va., 14 mi. E of Welch, in coal region.

Crumpsall (krŭm′sŭl), N suburb (pop. 18,643) of Manchester, SE Lancashire, England; cotton milling, mfg. of chemicals, soap, biscuits, machinery.

Crumpton (krŭmp′tŭn), village (1940 pop. 243), Queen Annes co., E Md., on Chester R. and 22 mi. WNW of Dover, Del.

Cruseilles (krüzā′), village (pop. 724), Haute-Savoie dept., SE France, on S slopes of Mont Salève, 9 mi. N of Annecy; cheese mfg., industrial diamond cutting.

Crusinallo (krōōzēnäl′lô), village (pop. 2,859), Novara prov., Piedmont, N Italy, N of L. of Orta, near Omegna, 16 mi. SSE of Domodossola; cotton and paper mills, iron foundry, dyeworks.

Cruta (krōō′tä), village (pop. 59), Colón dept., E Honduras, in Mosquitia, on Cruta R. (Honduras-Nicaragua border) and 23 mi. NW of Cabo Gracias a Dios; livestock.

Cruta River, on Honduras-Nicaragua border, rises in E outliers of Colón Mts., flows c.50 mi. ENE, past Cruta (Honduras), to Caribbean Sea 13 mi. NW of Cape Gracias a Dios.

Cruybeke, Belgium: see KRUIBEKE.

Cruyshautem, Belgium: see KRUISHOUTEM.

Cruz, Cape (krōōs), S coast of Cuba, Oriente prov., at S entrance of the Gulf of Guacanayabo, 50 mi. SW of Manzanillo; 19°50′N 77°44′W. Lighthouse. Adjoining airfield.

Cruz, La, in Latin America: see LA CRUZ.

Cruz, La. 1 Town, Nariño dept., Colombia: see LA CRUZ. **2** Town, Norte de Santander dept., Colombia: see ABREGO.

Cruz, La, village, Spain: see GUALDÁCANO.

Cruz, Pico (pē′kō krōōth′), volcanic peak (7,710 ft.), Palma, Canary Isls., 5 mi. NW of Santa Cruz de la Palma.

Cruz Alta, department, Argentina: see ALDERETES.

Cruz Alta (krōōs′ äl′tä), town (pop. 4,242), E Córdoba prov., Argentina, on Carcarañá R. and 28 mi. SE of Marcos Juárez; wheat, corn, flax, alfalfa, vegetables, livestock; horticulture.

Cruz Alta (krōōs äl′tŭ), city (pop. 16,028), N central Rio Grande do Sul, Brazil, on SW slope of the Serra Geral, 75 mi. N of Santa Maria; rail junction; meat packing, mfg. of farm machinery, flour milling; processes hides, lard, rice. Airfield. Founded in 1830s.

Cruz Bay (krōōz), village (pop. 88), ⊙ St. John Isl., U.S. Virgin Isls., resort on fine bay at W extremity of the isl., on Pillsbury Sound, 18 mi. E of Charlotte Amalie; 18°20′N 64°47′W.

Cruz Chica, Argentina: see LA CUMBRE.

Cruz das Almas (krōōs′ däs äl′mŭs), city (pop. 4,299), E Bahia, Brazil, 12 mi. SW of Cachoeira; tobacco-growing center. Has agr. school founded 1860.

Cruz del Eje (krōōs′ dĕl ā′hā), city (pop. 16,429), ⊙ Cruz del Eje dept. (□ c.2,750; pop. 39,208), NW Córdoba prov., Argentina, on the short Cruz del Eje R. and 60 mi. NW of Córdoba. Rail junction and agr. center in irrigated area (grain, livestock; dairying). Marble and granite quarries. Dam (130 ft. high) on the river furnishes hydroelectric power.

Cruz del Padre, Cayo (kī′ō krōōs′ dĕl pä′drā), key off NW Cuba, just outside Cárdenas Bay, 23 mi. NE of Cárdenas; 23°15′N 80°55′W. Lighthouse.

Cruz del Río Grande, La, Nicaragua: see LA CRUZ.

Cruz de Piedra (krōōs′ dā pyā′drä), village (pop. estimate 500), N Mendoza prov., Argentina, on railroad, near Mendoza R. (irrigation), 10 mi. S of Mendoza; winegrowing center; olive groves.

Cruz de Taratara, La, Venezuela: see LA CRUZ DE TARATARA.

Cruz de Tejeda, peak, Canary Isls.: see TEJEDA.

Cruz do Espírito Santo (krōōs′ dōō ĭspē′rētōō săn′tōō), city (pop. 1,572), E Paraíba, NE Brazil, on Paraíba R. and 14 mi. W of João Pessoa; sugar, rice; pineapples, oranges, bananas. Until 1944, called Espírito Santo; and Maguari, 1944–48.

Cruzeiro (krōōzā′rōō). **1** City, Santa Catarina, Brazil: see JOAÇABA. **2** City (pop. 11,618), SE São Paulo, Brazil, on Paraíba R., at foot of the Serra da Mantiqueira, and 125 mi. ENE of São Paulo; junction on São Paulo–Rio de Janeiro RR (spur to Minas Gerais resort dist.). Railroad workshops. Livestock center (meat packing, lard mfg.); dairying, coffee roasting and grinding, alcohol distilling, mfg. of flour products.

Cruzeiro do Sul (dōō sōōl′). **1** City (pop. 2,765), NW Acre territory, westernmost Brazil, head of navigation and hydroplane landing on upper Juruá R. near Amazonas line; 7°40′S 72°35′W; rubber, gums, medicinal plants. Founded 1904. **2** City, Santa Catarina, Brazil: see JOAÇABA.

Cruz Grande (krōōs′ grän′dā), village (1930 pop. 432), Coquimbo prov., N central Chile, port on the Pacific, and 33 mi. NNW of La Serena; ships iron ore from mines at El Tofo, 5 mi. ENE.

Cruz Grande, town (pop. 1,064), Guerrero, SW Mexico, in Pacific lowland, 50 mi. E of Acapulco; sugar cane, fruit, livestock.

Cruzy-le-Châtel (krüzē′-lŭ-shätĕl′), village (pop. 409), Yonne dept., N central France, 11 mi. E of Tonnerre.

Crvanj Mountains, Tsrvan Mountains, or **Tsrvan′ Mountains** (all: tsŭr′vänyŭ), in Dinaric Alps, central Herzegovina, Yugoslavia; extend c.10 mi. along left bank of upper Neretva R. Highest peak, Zimomor (6,300 ft.), is 10 mi. NNE of Nevesinje.

Crvenka or **Tsrvenka** (both: tsŭr′vĕn-kä), Hung. *Cservenka* (chĕr′vĕnkō), village (pop. 7,279), Vojvodina, N Serbia, Yugoslavia, on Danube-Tisa Canal (railroad bridge) and 30 mi. S of Subotica, in the Backa; beet sugar, molasses, dried beet pulp.

Crynant, Wales: see DYLAIS HIGHER.

Crysler, village (pop. estimate 350), SE Ont., on South Nation R. and 30 mi. NW of Cornwall; dairying, mixed farming.

Crystaes, Serra dos, Brazil: see CRISTAIS, SERRA DOS.

Crystal. **1** Town (pop. 373), Aroostook co., E central Maine, 27 mi. WSW of Houlton. **2** Village (pop. 5,713), NW suburb of Minneapolis, Hennepin co., E Minn. **3** City (pop. 429), Pembina co., NE N.Dak., 14 mi. S of Cavalier and on branch of Park R.

Crystal I, air base, N Que., on Koksoak R., near its mouth on Ungava Bay, 6 mi. SW of Fort Chimo; 58°7'N 68°26'W.

Crystal II, air base, SE Baffin Isl., SE Franklin Dist., Northwest Territories, at head of Frobisher Bay, inlet of the Atlantic; 63°45'N 68°34'W; radio and meteorological station. Also called Frobisher Bay or Frobisher Airport.

Crystal III, air base, Padloping Isl., SE Franklin Dist., Northwest Territories, on Merchants Bay of Davis Strait, off Cumberland Peninsula, SE Baffin Isl.; 67°3'N 62°45'W; radio station.

Crystal Beach, village (pop. 618), S Ont., on L. Erie, 8 mi. WSW of Fort Erie; resort.

Crystal Brook, town (pop. 858), S South Australia, 15 mi. SE of Port Pirie; wheat, wool, wine, timber; pottery clay.

Crystal Caverns, Va.: see STRASBURG.

Crystal City, village (pop. estimate 650), S Man., in Pembina Mts., 65 mi. SSW of Portage la Prairie, near N.Dak. border; wheat, lumbering.

Crystal City. **1** City (pop. 3,499), Jefferson co., E Mo., on Mississippi R. and 30 mi. S of St. Louis; large plate-glass factory. Silica pits near. Company-owned; inc. 1911. **2** City (pop. 7,198), ⊙ Zavala co., SW Texas, 95 mi. SW of San Antonio; shipping center in irrigated Winter Garden area; claims to be "spinach capital of the world"; canneries. State experimental farm near by.

Crystal Falls, city (pop. 2,316), ⊙ Iron co., SW Upper Peninsula, Mich., 15 mi. E of Iron River city, near falls on Paint R., in the Menominee iron-mining region. Mfg. of woodenware; dairy and poultry farming. Its many lakes attract tourists. Inc. as village 1889, as city 1899.

Crystal Grottoes, Md.: see BOONSBORO.

Crystalina, Brazil: see CRISTALINA.

Crystal Lake. **1** Village, Tolland co., Conn.: see ELLINGTON. **2** Resort city (pop. 4,832), McHenry co., NE Ill., 13 mi. N of Elgin, on small Crystal L.; trade center in dairying area; some mfg. (radio and electrical appliances, auto parts, sporting goods). Inc. 1914. **3** Town (pop. 286), Hancock co., N Iowa, 30 mi. WNW of Mason City, on Crystal L. (1 mi. long; main source of Iowa R.); summer resort; has creamery.

Crystal Lake. **1** In Benzie co., NW Mich., 25 mi. SW of Traverse City, near L. Michigan; c.8 mi. long, 2 mi. wide; fishing. **2** In N Vt., resort lake (c.3 mi. long) near Barton, 23 mi. NNW of St. Johnsbury. Barton R. rises here; state forest is near by.

Crystal Lake Park, town (pop. 167), St. Louis co., E Mo., W of St. Louis.

Crystal Lakes, village (pop. 1,115), Clark co., NE Ohio.

Crystal Mountains, Fr. *Monts de Cristal,* belt of broken highlands in W central Africa, along the Atlantic coast; extend NNW-SSE (c.300 mi. wide) in Sp. Guinea (Río Muni), W Fr. Equatorial Africa, W Belgian Congo, and NW Angola. Rise to 4,500 ft. in Belgian Congo. Some copper, zinc, and lead deposits. Congo R. cuts a narrow gorge through the mts., forming the noted Livingstone Falls.

Crystal River, fishing town (pop. 1,026), Citrus co., central Fla., on Crystal R. (c.7 mi. long) near its mouth on the Gulf, and 34 mi. WSW of Ocala.

Crystal River, W central Colo., rises in Elk Mts. near Marble, flows c.40 mi. N to Roaring Fork R. at Carbondale.

Crystal Rock Caves, Ohio: see SANDUSKY, city.

Crystal Springs, town (pop. 3,676), Copiah co., SW Miss., 24 mi. SSW of Jackson; ships tomatoes; mfg. (boxes, shirts).

Crystal Terrace, village (pop. 2,086, with adjacent Fleetwing), Bucks co., SE Pa.

Csaba, Hungary: see BEKESCSABA.

Csabrendek (chŏ'brĕndĕk), town (pop. 3,315), Zala co., W Hungary, 29 mi. W of Veszprem; wine, nuts, apples, pears.

Csaca, Czechoslovakia: see CADCA.

Csak, Rumania: see CIACOVA.

Csakathurn, Yugoslavia: see CAKOVEC.

Csakigarbo, Rumania: see GARBOU.

Csaktornya, Yugoslavia: see CAKOVEC.

Csakvar (chäk'vär), Hung. *Csákvár,* town (pop. 5,084), Fejer co., N central Hungary, at SE foot of Vertes Mts., 13 mi. N of Szekesfehervar; flour mills; wheat, corn, hogs, sheep.

Csallóköz, Czechoslovakia: see SCHÜTT.

Csanad (chŏ'näd), Hung. *Csanád,* county (□ 724; pop. 168,064), SE Hungary; ⊙ Mako. Level region in S part of the Alföld; drained by Maros and Szaraz rivers. Agr. (grain, onions, hemp), livestock, poultry. Industry at Mezöhegyes.

Csanadapaca (chŏ'nädŏpätsŏ), Hung. *Csanádapáca,* town (pop. 4,629), Csanad co., SE Hungary, 13 mi. SW of Bekescsaba; red wine, onions.

Csanadpalota (chŏ'nätpŏ"lôtŏ), Hung. *Csanádpalota,* town (pop. 6,046), Csanad co., SE Hungary, 11 mi. E of Mako; ducks, geese, onions, grain.

Csantaver, Yugoslavia: see CANTAVIR.

Csanytelek (chŏ'nyûtĕlĕk), town (pop. 5,029), Csongrad co., S Hungary, 8 mi. S of Csongrad; basket weaving; tobacco, paprika.

Csap, Ukrainian SSR: see CHOP.

Csaszar (chä'sär), Hung. *Császár,* town (pop. 2,511), Komarom-Esztergom co., N Hungary, 26 mi. SE of Györ; wine, tobacco, eggs.

Csatad, Rumania: see LENAUHEIM.

Csatalja (chä'tŏlyŏ), Hung. *Csátalja,* town (pop. 2,758), Bacs-Bodrog co., S Hungary, 10 mi. S of Baja; wheat, onions, sheep, hogs.

Csenger (chĕng'gĕr), town (pop. 4,349), Szatmar-Bereg co., NE Hungary, on Szamos R. and 10 mi. WNW of Satu-Mare, Rumania; frontier station; grain, cattle, fruit.

Csepa (chä'pŏ), Hung. *Csépa,* town (pop. 3,284), Jasz-Nagykun-Szolnok co., E central Hungary, 22 mi. ESE of Kecskemet; wheat, cattle.

Csepel (chĕ'pĕl), industrial town (pop. 46,171), Pest-Pilis-Solt-Kiskun co., N central Hungary, on N tip of CSEPEL ISLAND and 5 mi. S of Budapest. Aluminum, iron, and steel mills; mfg. (munitions, cartridges, motors, airplanes, textiles, paper, canned goods); petroleum refineries. It has a 2,600-ft. coaling inlet. CSEPEL HARBOR is along the Danube.

Csepel Harbor, N central Hungary, on N tip of Csepel Isl., bet. town of Csepel and Budapest. Created international free port in 1928. Divided into 2 parts: 1 for inflammable materials (coal and petroleum storage, petroleum refineries); 1 for varied noninflammables (includes huge granary). Connected by 3 bridges to Pest.

Csepel Island (□ 99), N central Hungary, in the Danube, just S of Budapest; 30 mi. long, 4 mi. wide; agr. (grain, potatoes), cattle, hogs; fishing. Extreme N section is industrial, with town of CSEPEL and with CSEPEL HARBOR. Other towns: RACKEVE, SZIGETSZENTMIKLOS, TÖKÖL. Has large Serbian and Ger. pop. There are Roman remains.

Csepreg (chĕ'prĕg), town (pop. 4,010), Sopron co., W Hungary, on Repce R. and 20 mi. SSE of Sopron; tanneries; wheat, corn, dairy farming.

Cserehat Mountains (chĕ'rĕhät), Hung. *Cserehát,* NE Hungary, extend 25 mi. NE from Miskolc; average alt. 1,000 ft.

Cserhat Mountains (chĕr'hät), Hung. *Cserhát,* N Hungary, extend c.35 mi. NE from Vac, rising to 2,139 ft. in Mt. Nagyszal; forested slopes.

Csernatfalu, Rumania: see CERNATU.

Csernye, Yugoslavia: see CRNJA.

Cserszegtomaj (chĕr'sĕktômoi), town (pop. 2,036), Zala co., W Hungary, 18 mi. E of Zalaegerszeg; grain, wine.

Cservenka, Yugoslavia: see CRVENKA.

Csev (chāv), Hung. *Csév,* town (pop. 2,355), Komarom-Esztergom co., N Hungary, 9 mi. SE of Esztergom; vineyards, beans, potatoes, cattle.

Csikszentdomokos, Rumania: see SANDOMINIC.

Csikszentmarton, Rumania: see SANMARTIN.

Csikszereda, Rumania: see MERCUREA-CIUC.

Csillaghegy, Hungary: see BEKASMEGYER.

Csoka, Yugoslavia: see COKA.

Csökmö (chûk'mû), Hung. *Csökmő,* town (pop. 4,348), Bihar co., E Hungary, 31 mi. E of Mezötur; wheat, hemp, cattle.

Csokonyavisonta (chô'kònyŏvĭ"shôntŏ), agr. town (pop. 3,250), Somogy co., SW Hungary, 26 mi. SW of Kaposvar. Formed 1941 by union of Somogyvisonta and Erdöcsokonya.

Csolnok (chôl'nôk), town (pop. 3,845), Komarom-Esztergom co., N Hungary, 7 mi. S of Esztergom; lignite mine near by.

Csömör (chû'mûr), town (pop. 4,133), Pest-Pilis-Solt-Kiskun co., N central Hungary, 7 mi. NE of Budapest; wine, cherries, apples, pears.

Csongrad (chông'gräd), Hung. *Csongrád,* county (□ 728; pop. 152,438), S Hungary; ⊙ Szentes. Flat region in the Alföld; drained by Tisza R. Intensive agr. (grain, paprika, potatoes); cattle, horse, and sheep raising; garden products (wine, fruit, cloves); poultry. Extensive swamp-draining projects have added greatly to arable land. Carp and pike in artificial lakes. Industry, mainly flour mills, brickworks, distilleries, at SZEGED, Szentes, Csongrad, HODMEZÖVASARHELY.

Csongrad, Hung. *Csongrád,* city (pop. 25,594), Csongrad co., S Hungary, at confluence of Tisza (here bridged) and Körös rivers, 25 mi. SE of Kecskemet; rail, market center; flour, sawmills; brickworks. Wheat, tobacco, dairy farms near by.

Csonoplya, Yugoslavia: see CONOPLJA.

Csorbato, Czechoslovakia: see STRBA LAKE.

Csorna (chôr'nŏ), town (pop. 8,957), Sopron co., W Hungary, 31 mi. ESE of Sopron; rail center; distilleries, brickworks, flour mills; domestic lace. Has Premonstratensian monastery dating from 13th cent., R.C. monastic school.

Csorvas (chôr'väsh), Hung. *Csorvás,* town (pop. 7,269), Bekes co., SE Hungary, 13 mi. E of Bekescsaba; flour mill; grain, tobacco, cattle.

Csurgo (chŏŏr'gō), Hung. *Csurgó,* town (pop. 4,893), Somogy co., SW Hungary, 14 mi. SSE of Nagykanizsa; flax processing, flour mill.

Csurog, Yugoslavia: see CURUG.

Ctesiphon (tĕ'sĭfŏn), ruined anc. city, central Iraq, 20 mi. SE of Baghdad and on left bank of the Tigris opposite site of anc. SELEUCIA. After 129 B.C. it was winter residence of the Parthian kings and grew rapidly in renown and splendor. It rivaled Seleucia, but both cities were taken (A.D. 164) by the Romans. Ctesiphon became capital of the Sassanidae c.226. It grew in size and importance until it was taken (c.636) and plundered by the Arabs. The ruins of the Sassanid palace are impressive. Ctesiphon, scene of Turkish victory over the British in Nov., 1915, marks farthest advance of Great Britain against Turkey in First World War.

Cúa (kōō'ä), town (pop. 2,244), Miranda state, N Venezuela, on Tuy R. and 24 mi. S of Caracas; agr. center (coffee, cacao, sugar cane, corn).

Cuacnopalan (kwäknōpä'län), town (pop. 2,340), Puebla, central Mexico, 13 mi. SSW of Serdán; cereals, maguey, stock.

Cuacos (kwä'kōs), town (pop. 1,567), Cáceres prov., W Spain, 20 mi. ENE of Plasencia; olive-oil processing; pepper, wine, fruit. Yuste monastery just W.

Cuadro Nacional (kwä'drō näsyōnäl'), town (pop. estimate 500), central Mendoza prov., Argentina, on railroad and 3 mi. E of San Rafael, in Diamante R. irrigation area; wine, fruit, alfalfa.

Cuajimalpa (kwähēmäl'pä), town (pop. 2,156), Federal Dist., central Mexico, 13 mi. SW of Mexico city; cereals, fruit, stock.

Cuajinicuilapa (kwähēnēkwēlä'pä), town (pop. 1,148), Guerrero, SW Mexico, in Pacific lowland, 14 mi. S of Ometepec; fruit, sugar cane, livestock.

Cuajiniquilapa, Guatemala: see CUILAPA.

Cualac (kwäläk'), town (pop. 1,230), Guerrero, SW Mexico, in Sierra Madre del Sur, 40 mi. ENE of Chilapa; alt. 4,657 ft.; cereals, fruit.

Cuale (kwä'lā), village, Malange prov., N Angola, on road and 100 mi. N of Malange; manioc.

Cuando-Cubango, Angola: see SERPA PINTO.

Cuando River, Angola and Northern Rhodesia: see KWANDO RIVER.

Cuangar (kwŭng-gär'), town (pop. 136), Bié prov., S Angola, on Okovanggo R. (South-West Africa border) and 200 mi. SSE of Serpa Pinto.

Cuango (kwäng'gō), village, Congo prov., NW Angola, on Kwango R. (Belgian Congo border), and 150 mi. NE of Uíge; coffee, raffia, sesame.

Cuango (kwäng'gō), village (pop. 182), Colón prov., central Panama, on Caribbean Sea, at mouth of Cuango R. (small coastal stream), and 2 mi. E of Palenque; cacao, coconuts, abacá; stock raising.

Cuango River, Angola and Belgian Congo: see KWANGO RIVER.

Cuanza-Norte, Angola: see VILA SALAZAR.

Cuanza River (kwän'zä), central Angola, rises on Bié Plateau 50 mi. SE of Chitembo, flows N then W to the Atlantic 35 mi. S of Luanda; 600 mi. long. Navigable c.120 mi. below Dondo. Formerly also spelled Kuanza, Kwanza, and Coanza.

Cuanza-Sul, Angola: see NOVO REDONDO.

Cuapa (kwä'pä), village, Chontales dept., S Nicaragua, 13 mi. N of Juigalpa, at W foot of Cordillera Amerrique; sugar cane, livestock.

Cuapiaxtla (kwäpyä'slä), officially San Lorenzo Cuapiaxtla, town (pop. 1,972), Tlaxcala, central Mexico, on Puebla border, 33 mi. NE of Puebla; cereals, alfalfa, stock.

Cuarao (kōō'ú-rou'), town, Nghean prov., N central Vietnam, on the Song Ca (head of navigation), 85 mi. NW of Vinh, on road to Luang Prabang. Forestry (ebony, rattan); trade center for lac, benzoin, orchids, opium. Coal mines near by.

Cuareim (kwäräm'), village, Artigas dept., NW Uruguay, railroad station on Brazil border, just NE of BELLA UNIÓN, on Cuareim R. (railroad bridge) near its confluence with the Uruguay; river-rail transshipment point.

Cuareim River, Uruguay and Brazil: see QUARAÍ RIVER.

Cuaró (kwärō'), village, Artigas dept., NW Uruguay, on railroad and 29 mi. WSW of Artigas; cereals, cattle, sheep.

Cuaró Grande, Arroyo (äroi'ō kwärō' grän'dā), river, Artigas dept., NW Uruguay, rises in the Cuchilla de Belén 30 mi. SE of Cuaró, flows 75 mi. NW to Cuareim R. just SW below confluence of Arroyo Tres Cruces Grande.

Cuart de les Valls (kwärt' dhā lās väls'), village (pop. 1,107), Valencia prov., E Spain, 5 mi. N of Sagunto; rice, oranges, strawberries.

Cuart de Poblet (pōblĕt'), W suburb (pop. 3,674) of Valencia, Valencia prov., E Spain; mfg. of tiles and ceramics, brandy and liqueur; silk weaving. Olive and peanut oil, alfalfa, wheat, wine in area.

Cuartero (kwärtä'rō), town (1939 pop. 2,287; 1948 municipality pop. 9,985), Capiz prov., N central Panay isl., Philippines, on railroad and 18 mi. SSW of Capiz; rice-growing center.

Cuarto, Río (rē'ō kwär'tō), river in S Córdoba prov., Argentina, rises in Sierra de Comechingones

NW of Río Cuarto city, flows E, past Río Cuarto and La Carlota, through L. Olmos (where it becomes the Saladillo), then NE, joining the Río Tercero 30 mi. SE of Bell Ville to form CARCARAÑA RIVER; 150 mi. long.

Cuatreros, Argentina: see GENERAL CERRI.

Cuatretonda (kwätrātōn'dä), town (pop. 2,198), Valencia prov., E Spain, 7 mi. ESE of Játiva; olive-oil processing, sandal mfg.; ships grapes and melons. Marble quarries near by.

Cuatro Ciénegas or **Cuatro Ciénegas de Carranza** (kwä'trō syā'nägäs dā kärän'sä), town (pop. 2,783), Coahuila, N Mexico, on railroad and 130 mi. NE of Torreón; silver- and lead-mining center; cattle raising.

Cuatro de Junio, district, Argentina: see LANÚS.

Cuatro de Junio or **4 de Junio** (hōō'nyō), town (pop. estimate 1,500), ⊙ Pringles or Coronel Pringles dept. (□ 1,625; 1947 census 12,607), NE San Luis prov., Argentina, on railroad and 45 mi. ENE of San Luis. Farming and mining center. Agr. products: flax, wheat, corn, sunflowers, livestock. Travertine, granite, onyx, quartzite, feldspar, beryllium, strontium sulphate deposits near by. Until c.1945 called La Toma.

Cuatro Ojos (ō'hōs), town (pop. c.400), Santa Cruz dept., central Bolivia, port on Piray R. and 36 mi. NNW of Portachuelo; river-road transfer point.

Cuatro Vientos (vyěn'tōs), SW suburb (pop. 1,128) of Madrid, Madrid prov., central Spain, c.6 mi. SE of city center; mfg. of airplanes.

Cuauhtémoc (kwoutā'mōk). **1** Town (pop. 2,865), Chihuahua, N Mexico, in Sierra Madre Occidental, 50 mi. WSW of Chihuahua; alt. 6,752 ft. Rail junction, agr. center (corn, wheat, beans, fruit, livestock). Airfield. **2** Town (pop. 2,032), Colima, W Mexico, in W outliers of Sierra Madre Occidental, 10 mi. NE of Colima; alt. 3,180 ft.; agr. center (corn, beans, rice, sugar cane, fruit, livestock). **3** W residential section of Mexico city, Mexico, N of Paseo de la Reforma, on which stands the statue of Cuauhtémoc, last Aztec emperor.

Cuauhtémoc, Villa, Mexico: see VILLA CUAUHTÉMOC.

Cuautempan (kwoutěm'pän), officially San Esteban Cuautempan, town (pop. 1,832), Puebla, central Mexico, 10 mi. ESE of Zacatlán; corn, coffee, sugar cane, fruit.

Cuautepec (kwoutāpěk'). **1** Town (pop. 2,755), Federal Dist., central Mexico, 8 mi. N of Mexico city; cereals, maguey, livestock. Sometimes Cuauhtepec. **2** Town (pop. 1,457), Guerrero, SW Mexico, in Pacific lowland, 55 mi. E of Acapulco; sugar cane, fruit, livestock. **3** Town (pop. 2,698), Hidalgo, central Mexico, on railroad and 28 mi. ESE of Pachuca; cereals, maguey, livestock.

Cuautitlán (kwoutētlän'), officially Cuautitlán de Romero Rubio, town (pop. 3,816), Mexico state, central Mexico, 20 mi. N of Mexico city; rail terminus; agr. center (cereals, fruit, vegetables, livestock).

Cuautitlán River, Mexico state, central Mexico, canalized stream (c.35 mi.) draining L. Texcoco and L. Zumpango to Tula R. (Pánuco R. system) via Tequixquiac tunnel.

Cuautla (kwout'lä). **1** Town (pop. 1,027), Jalisco, W Mexico, 35 mi. SW of Ameca; alt. c.4,350 ft.; spa with sulphur springs. **2** or **Cuautla Morelos** (mōrā'lōs), city (pop. 6,431), Morelos, central Mexico, on S slope of central plateau, on railroad and 45 mi. SSE of Mexico city. Resort; agr. center (sugar cane, rice, wheat, wine, coffee, vegetables, stock); sugar refining, rice milling, wine making, alcohol distilling, cigar mfg., lumbering. Airfield. José María Morelos, hero of Mexican independence, made heroic defense against Spanish (1812) here. Thermal springs, mild climate, and picturesque scenery attract many tourists. Sometimes Ciudad Morelos.

Cuautlalpan (kwoutläl'pän). **1** Officially San Bartolo Cuautlalpan, town (pop. 1,730), Mexico state, central Mexico, 20 mi. NNW of Mexico city; cereals, stock. **2** Officially San Martín Cuautlalpan, town (pop. 1,556), Mexico state, central Mexico, 23 mi. SE of Mexico city; cereals, maguey, stock.

Cuautlancingo (kwoutlänsēng'gō), officially San Juan Cuautlancingo, town (pop. 2,726), Puebla, central Mexico, on railroad and 5 mi. NW of Puebla; grain, maguey, stock.

Cuautlixco (kwoutlē'skō), town (pop. 1,322), Morelos, central Mexico, 2 mi. NE of Cuautla; rail junction; sugar cane, fruit, livestock.

Cuaxomulco (kwähōmōōl'kō), officially San Antonio Cuaxomulco, town (pop. 1,033), Tlaxcala, central Mexico, 7 mi. NE of Tlaxcala; corn, wheat, maguey, stock. Sometimes Coajomulco.

Cuba (kū'bù, Sp. kōō'vä), island and republic (with Isle of Pines, □ 44,218; pop. 4,778,583) in the West Indies; ⊙ HAVANA. Westernmost of the West Indies and of the Greater Antilles, and larger than all other West Indian isls. combined. Strategically located on major sea routes, lying at entrance of the Gulf of Mexico, 120 mi. E of Yucatan (Mexico), and 90 mi. S of Key West (Fla.), separated by the Straits of Florida. The 50-mi.-wide Windward Passage separates isl.'s easternmost point (Cape Maisí) from Haiti (Cape St. Nicolas). Jamaica lies c.85 mi. S. Bounded N by Nicholas Channel and Old Bahama Channel of the Atlantic (Great Bahama Bank); S coast is washed by the Caribbean. Situated just below the Tropic of Cancer, Cuba extends c.700 mi. W-E (averaging 50 mi. in width) from Cape San Antonio (21°52'N 84°57'W) to Cape Maisí (20°15'N 74°8'W). Most of the isl. (c.60%) is level or gently rolling ground, well suited to large-scale farming. There are extensive marshes along the coast, and a few forested areas abounding in hardwood (mahogany, cedar, etc.), dyewood, and resins, but practically no large rivers, except for the Cauto in SE. Of the 3 major mtn. ranges, the Sierra Maestra, rising from S coast at the isl.'s E end to 6,560 ft. in the Pico Turquino (highest point of Cuba), represents, together with its outliers, the richest mining region of the country (chiefly iron, manganese, copper, nickel, chromium). In the W the Sierra de los Órganos is notable for its cliff-like calcareous formations and for the Vuelta Abajo tobacco-growing region along its piedmont. The Sierra de Trinidad with subranges forms the only mountainous area of the center. The low, frequently inundated coast is fringed by numerous coral isls. and keys, among which are the archipelagoes Los Colorados (NW), Sabana and Camagüey (N), Los Canarreos (SW), Jardines de la Reina (S). One of Cuba's outstanding features are the many bottlenecked bays, which provide excellent sheltered harbors on which are situated the leading ports, such as Havana, Matanzas, Cárdenas, Nuevitas, Guantánamo, Santiago de Cuba, and Cienfuegos. The climate is temperate and semitropical, and generally uniform, though somewhat warmer in E section. In Havana the mean annual temp. is 76°F. There are 2 distinct seasons, a rainy period May-Oct., and a cool and dry one Nov.-April. Rainfall averages c.50 inches, but increases inland. Hurricanes occur occasionally, especially in W and on Isle of Pines. By far the largest crop is sugar, accounting (with molasses and other derivatives) for ¾ of entire export volume, and placing Cuba in front rank of the world's sugar producers. More than 170 sugar mills, so-called centrals, served by a dense railroad net, dot the countryside; the foremost are in Havana, Matanzas, Las Villas, and Oriente provs. While sugar is still the base of the republic's entire economy, diversification is increasing. Tobacco (grown in pre-Columbian times) takes 2d place, with about 9% of the agr. output, chiefly centered in Pinar del Río prov. (W), which lies outside the sugar belt. Camagüey prov. has great stretches of fine pastures, with cattle raising and dairying (cheese, canned milk, and butter are exported). Sisal is grown in N Matanzas prov., coffee on mtn. slopes of Oriente prov. Fruit (bananas, pineapples, citrus fruit, etc.) is grown in all regions, and, together with winter vegetables (N Isle of Pines), is mainly shipped to the U.S. In most agr. products (cereals, cacao, potatoes, butter, cheese, eggs, honey, etc.) the country has now achieved self-sufficiency. Though natural power resources (coal, petroleum) rely on imports and the hydroelectric potential is negligible, mfg. has made great strides. Besides sugar milling and refining, the chief industries include rum distilling, processing of tobacco and sisal, sawmilling, mining, tanning, textile milling, food canning, metalworking; mfg. of famed cigars and cigarettes, sirup, alcohol, brandy, cement, cordage, leather and wooden products, chemicals. Apart from the rich mineral resources of the Sierra Maestra in Oriente prov., primary resources include gold, salt, asphalt, petroleum (Havana prov.), and building material. Thermal springs are found in all parts. The coastal waters yield lobsters, oysters, shrimps, etc. Deep-sea fisheries are based at several ports, and large-scale sponge fishing is carried on, chiefly off SW Caribbean coast and offshore reefs. Railway mileage is relatively one of the highest in the Americas. The great Central Highway (opened 1931) traverses the isl. E-W. Natl. and international air services are maintained. Because of its mild climate, picturesque cities, fine beaches, and proximity to the U.S., Cuba has developed a lucrative tourist trade. The isl., originally inhabited by Arawak Indians, was discovered (Oct., 1492) by Columbus, who landed near present-day Gibara. After having been given several Sp. names (Juana, Santiago, etc.), the anc. aboriginal name Cuba was restored. The Spanish had explored all the coast line by 1508 and gained a permanent foothold in 1511, under the leadership of Diego de Velázquez, who founded Baracoa near the E tip, and, soon after, Santiago de Cuba. Havana, settled at its present location in 1519, became an assembly point for the treasure fleets from the Viceroyalty of New Spain (of which Cuba formed a part), and thus offered a target for French and English buccaneers. The isl. flourished as a refuge for smugglers and pirates and was known as the "Pearl of the Antilles." Negro labor was introduced in early colonial days to replace the Indians, who had died off. Sugar, 1st planted in late 18th cent., chiefly by refugees from neighboring Haiti, turned Cuba into a one-crop country, bringing enormous riches to a few Cuban and foreign absentee owners; but the industry, depending on the world market, underwent severe crises, leading to social upheavals. With exception of a short British occupation (1762–63), Cuba remained a Sp. possession until 1898. The Ten Years War (1868–78), led by Carlos Manuel de Céspedes, who had proclaimed independence at Yara (Oct. 11, 1868), was unsuccessful. A new revolutionary bid was made in 1895 under the brilliant poet Martí, who fell the same year in battle. The hostilities resulted in the Spanish-American War, when the U.S. battleship *Maine* was blown up in Havana Harbor. The U.S. occupied the isl. from 1898 to 1902, whereupon the Republic of Cuba was formed, though the Platt Amendment, effective until 1934, infringed upon Cuba's sovereignty. A revolt brought about a 2d occupation (1906–08). Since 1903 a naval base has been leased to the U.S. at Guantánamo Bay. Cuba entered the First World War on the side of the Allies in 1917, at the time of its short-lived prosperity (based on sugar), the "Dance of Millions." Collapse of the sugar markets led to successive revolutions and dictatorships. Power was wielded by the dictator Gerardo Machado (1925–33) and by Fulgencio Batista (1940–44). With the democratically elected President Grau San Martín (1944–48), social reforms were introduced. Cuba declared war on the Axis powers in Dec., 1941. Economically Cuba is still a dependency of the U.S., which is responsible for about 75% of the isl.'s foreign trade, while tremendous American capital remains invested. The isl. is, for administrative purposes, divided into 6 provs., the Isle of Pines (since 1925 confirmed as Cuban) being a part of Havana prov. Its racial make-up is estimated at 75% white and mulatto, 24% Negro, and 1% Asiatic, chiefly Chinese. During the sugar harvest, foreign workers from other West Indian isls. are introduced to relieve labor shortage. Spanish is universally spoken, though English is a familiar tongue.

Cuba (kōō'bù), town (pop. 4,637), Beja dist., S Portugal, on railroad and 10 mi. N of Beja; wine-growing and agr. center; paper milling, cork processing, cheese and pottery mfg.

Cuba (kū'bù). **1** Town (pop. 525), Sumter co., W Ala., near Miss. line, 32 mi. WSW of Demopolis. **2** City (pop. 1,482), Fulton co., W central Ill., 34 mi. WSW of Peoria, in agr. and bituminous-coal-mining area; wood products. Inc. 1853. **3** City (pop. 345), Republic co., N Kansas, 17 mi. NE of Concordia, in corn and wheat region. **4** City (pop. 1,301), Crawford co., E central Mo., in the Ozarks, near Meramec R., 70 mi. SW of St. Louis; alt. 1,035 ft. Resort, agr. center. Inc. 1877. **5** Village (1940 pop. 733), Sandoval co., NW N.Mex., near the Rio Puerco, 70 mi. NNW of Albuquerque; alt. 6,898 ft.; livestock. Sections of Santa Fe Natl. Forest near by; Nacimiento Peak 7 mi. ENE. **6** Resort village (pop. 1,783), Allegany co., W N.Y., near Cuba L. (c.2 mi. long), 12 mi. NE of Olean; mfg. (cheese, boxes, feed, machinery, flour). Seneca Oil Spring is near by. Inc. 1850.

Cuba City, city (pop. 1,333), Grant co., extreme SW Wis., 19 mi. NE of Dubuque (Iowa), in agr. area (livestock, corn, alfalfa); processes dairy and farm products; zinc refinery. Inc. 1925.

Cubagua Island (kōōbä'gwä), federal dependency of Venezuela, in the Caribbean, bet. Margarita Isl. and Araya Peninsula, 22 mi. WSW of Porlamar; 5 mi. long W-E, c.2 mi. wide. Pearl fishing. A Sp. settlement made here 1520 was destroyed 1543 by earthquake and tidal wave.

Cubal (kōōbäl'), town (pop. 1,555), Benguela prov., W Angola, on Benguela RR and 70 mi. SE of Lobito; alt. 3,000 ft. Rice, sisal.

Cuba Lake, N.Y.: see CUBA.

Cubango River, Angola: see OKOVANGGO RIVER.

Cubatão (kōōbùtä'ō), city (pop. 1,887), SE São Paulo, Brazil, at foot of the Serra do Cubatão (section of great coastal escarpment), 7 mi. NW of Santos; junction of São Paulo–Santos and Sorocaba-Santos rail lines. Has Brazil's leading hydroelectric plant (one of finest in South America); water descends 2,378 ft. through penstocks from reservoir (formed by damming of tributaries of Tietê R.) just beyond crest of great escarpment. Plant supplies São Paulo and Santos with light and power. City also has paper mills, chemical works, and modern oil refinery.

Cub Cub, Eritrea: see KUBKUB.

Cube, Mount (2,911 ft.), Grafton co., W N.H., 6 mi. ESE of Orford. Formerly called Mt. Cuba.

Cubero (kōōbâ'rō), village (pop. c.500), Valencia co., W central N.Mex., near San Jose R., just S of San Mateo Mts., 50 mi. W of Albuquerque; alt. 5,929 ft. Laguna and Acoma Pueblo Indian villages near by. Part of Cibola Natl. Forest just N.

Cub Hill, village, Baltimore co., N Md., near Loch Raven Reservoir, 10 mi. NE of downtown Baltimore. Near by is Md. Training School for Boys (founded 1830).

Cubiro (kōōbē'rō), town (pop. 981), Lara state, NW Venezuela, 25 mi. SW of Barquisimeto; coffee, sugar, cereals, stock.

Cubitas, Sierra de (syě'rä dā kōōbē'täs), low range (750 ft.), Camagüey prov., E Cuba, 17 mi. N of Camagüey; c.20 mi. long WNW-ESE. Of calcareous formations with caverns. There are iron deposits here.

Cublize (küblēz'), village (pop. 590), Rhône dept., E central France, in the Monts du Beaujolais, 15 mi. E of Roanne; cotton milling.

Cub Mountain, peak (10,623 ft.) in Front Range, Jefferson co., N central Colo.

Cubo, El, Mexico: see El Cubo.

Cubo de Don Sancho, El (ĕl kōō'vō dhä dhōn' sän'chō), village (pop. 1,001), Salamanca prov., W Spain, 24 mi. NE of Ciudad Rodrigo; cereals, livestock, lumber.

Cubuk (chōōbŏŏk'), Turkish *Çubuk*, village (pop. 2,545), Ankara prov., central Turkey, on Cubuk R. and 23 mi. NNE of Ankara; dam and hydroelectric plant; grain, fruit, sugar beets, vetch; mohair goats.

Cubuk River, Turkish *Çubuk*, N central Turkey, rises in Koroglu Mts. 15 mi. N of Cubuk, flows 45 mi. S, past Cubuk, to Ankara R. at Ankara.

Cubulco (kōōbōōl'kō), town (1950 pop. 1,166), Baja Verapaz dept., central Guatemala, in N highlands, 21 mi. W of Salamá; grain, livestock raising.

Cuca (kōō'kä), village (pop. 577), Arges prov., S central Rumania, 18 mi. NW of Pitesti.

Cucalaya River (kōōkälī'ä), E Nicaragua, rises in E outlier of Cordillera Isabelia 8 mi. NE of Bonanza, flows c.100 mi. SE, through hardwood area, to Caribbean Sea at Huounta, here forming Cucalaya Lagoon. Also called Huounta R.

Cucamonga (kōōkùmŏng'gù), village (pop. 1,255), San Bernardino co., S Calif., in foothills of the San Gabriel Mts., just E of Upland; wineries; citrus-fruit packing.

Cucharas River (kùchâ'rùs, kùchä'rùs), S Colo., rises in Sangre de Cristo Mts. SSW of La Veta, flows c.70 mi. NE, past Walsenburg, to Huerfano R. 25 mi. S of Pueblo.

Cuchilla, for Spanish names beginning thus and not found here: see under following proper name.

Cuchilla, La, Uruguay: see Río Branco.

Cuchillo-Có (kōōchē'yō-kō'), village (pop. estimate 100), ⊙ Lihuel Calel dept. (pop. 1,061), SE La Pampa, prov., Argentina, 65 mi. S of General Acha, in stock-raising area.

Cuchu Ingenio or **Cucho Ingenio** (kōō'chōō ĭnhä'-nyō), village (pop. c.2,600), Potosí dept., S central Bolivia, 23 mi. S of Potosí; road junction in agr. area (potatoes, barley, vegetables).

Cuchumatanes Mountains (kōōchōōmätä'nĕs), in Huehuetenango and Quiché depts., W Guatemala; extend c.100 mi. NW-SE from area of Guatemala-Mexico border to Chixoy R.; rise to c.10,000 ft. N of Huehuetenango. Continued E by Sierra de Chamá.

Cucigliana (kōōchēlyä'nä), village (pop. 692), Pisa prov., Tuscany, central Italy, near the Arno, 7 mi. E of Pisa; ceramics.

Cuckfield (kŭk'–), urban district (1931 pop. 2,114; 1951 census 16,481), central Sussex, England, 13 mi. N of Brighton; agr. market. Has 15th-cent. church with 13th-cent. tower. Absorbed near-by areas in 1934, including Haywards Heath.

Cucuhy, Brazil: see Cucuí.

Cucuí (kōōkwē'), village, NW Amazonas, Brazil, on the Rio Negro, at Venezuela border, and 95 mi. N of Uaupés. Formerly spelled Cucuhy.

Cucumbi, Angola: see Trás os Montes.

Cucungará (kōōkōōng-gärä'), village (pop. 1,597), Piura dept., NW Peru, on coastal plain, near Piura R., 10 mi. S of Piura, in irrigated cotton area.

Cucurpe (kōōkōōr'pä), town (pop. 3,976), Sonora, NW Mexico, on San Miguel R. and 90 mi. N of Hermosillo; agr. center (wheat, corn, fruit, livestock); gold deposits.

Cúcuta (kōō'kōōtä), officially San José de Cúcuta, city (pop. 37,323), ⊙ Norte de Santander dept., N Colombia, on level plain on E slopes of Cordillera Oriental, on Pan American Highway from Bogotá to Caracas, on Pamplonita R. 3 mi. W of Venezuela border, and 250 mi. NNE of Bogotá; 7°53'N 72°30'W. Terminus of railroad to Puerto Villamizar and to L. Maracaibo (Venezuela). Leading communication, shipping, trading, processing, and agr. center (especially for coffee; other produce: cacao, tobacco, sugar cane, stock); coffee roasting, textile milling, soapmaking, brewing, printing. Active trade with Venezuela; coffee and hides are also shipped to Barranquilla via cableway to Gamarra on Magdalena R. Airport, customhouse. Founded 1733. Colonial town with parks and fine bldgs. (cathedral, govt. bldg., fine arts mus.). It was formerly a cinchona-growing center. Focal point of independence movement (Constituent Congress, 1821). Bolívar here addressed his troops before decisive battle on Feb. 28, 1813. Severely damaged by 1875 earthquake.

Cucuteni (kōōkōōtān'), village (pop. 678), Jassy prov., NE Rumania, 6 mi. NW of Targu-Frumos; site of extensive finds of the Neolithic period.

Cucuy, Piedra del, Venezuela: see Cocuy, Piedra del.

Cucuyagua (kōōkōōyä'gwä), town (pop. 1,421), Copán dept., W Honduras, on Higuito R. and 7 mi. SSW of Santa Rosa; cigar mfg.; tobacco, coffee, sugar cane. Gypsum quarries near by.

Cudahy (kŭ'dùhē), city (pop. 12,182), Milwaukee co., SE Wis., on L. Michigan, bet. Milwaukee and South Milwaukee; meat packing, forging; mfg. of leather products, knit goods, machinery, chemicals, beverages. Patrick Cudahy founded city and its meat-packing industry in 1892. Inc. 1906.

Cuddalore (kŭd'ùlôr), Tamil *Kudalur* (kōōdŭlōōr'), city (pop. 60,632), ⊙ South Arcot dist., SE Madras, India, port on Coromandel Coast of Bay of Bengal, at mouths of Ponnaiyar and Gadilam rivers, 100 mi. SSW of Madras. Chief exports: peanuts (kernels, oil cake), cashew nuts, textiles. Trade center for Casuarina plants; salt and experimental-weaving factories. Road-metal and building-stone quarries near by. Ruined 17th-cent. stronghold of Fort St. David (on coast; just SE) was held alternately by French, Mysore sultans, Nawabs of Arcot, and English, until finally ceded 1758 to English.

Cuddapah (kŭ'dùpä), district (□ 5,923; pop. 1,056,507), central Madras, India; ⊙ Cuddapah. On Deccan Plateau; Eastern Ghats in E; drained by Penner R. Agr.: millet, oilseeds (extensive peanut and castor-bean growing), rice, cotton. Barite and asbestos mining, limestone quarrying in dispersed outliers of Eastern Ghats; dyewood, satinwood. Main centers: Cuddapah, Proddatur.

Cuddapah, city (pop. 28,246), ⊙ Cuddapah dist., central Madras, India, near Penner R., 140 mi. NW of Madras; road center; rice and oilseed milling, betel farming; pottery; melon and orange orchards. Limestone quarrying, barite mining near by.

Cuddesdon (kŭdz'dùn), village and parish (pop. 284), SE Oxfordshire, England, 6 mi. ESE of Oxford. Has palace of bishops of Oxford and a theological col. The church is partly Norman.

Cuddington, residential town and parish (pop. 2,833), NE Surrey, England, just NE of Ewell.

Cudgewa, village (pop. 192), NE Victoria, Australia, 190 mi. NE of Melbourne; rail terminus; livestock.

Cudham (kŭ'dùm), town and parish (pop. 3,731), NW Kent, England, 5 mi. SSW of Orpington; agr. market. Church has 2 towers (c.10th cent.).

Cudillero (kōō-dhēlyā'rō), town (pop. 2,726), Oviedo prov., NW Spain, fishing port on Bay of Biscay, 20 mi. NW of Oviedo; fish processing, boatbuilding, mfg. of shark-liver oil; agr. trade.

Cudjoe Key, Fla.: see Florida Keys.

Cudjo's Cave, Ky., Tenn., and Va.: see Middlesboro, Ky.

Cudworth, village (pop. 532), S central Sask., 50 mi. NE of Saskatoon; mixed farming, dairying.

Cudworth, urban district (1931 pop. 9,377; 1951 census 8,757), West Riding, S Yorkshire, England, 3 mi. NE of Barnsley; coal mining.

Cue (kū), town (pop. 511), W central Western Australia, 220 mi. NE of Geraldton, on Geraldton-Wiluna RR; mining center in Murchison Goldfield.

Cuéllar (kwā'lyär), town (pop. 6,539), Segovia prov., central Spain, in Old Castile, on road to Valladolid, and 34 mi. NNW of Segovia. Processing and agr. center (wheat, barley, grapes, chicory, potatoes, sheep, goats); chicory processing, flour milling, tanning; mfg. of cement products. Forest industry (timber, naval stores). Has hydroelectric plant. Historic town of anc., perhaps Roman, origin. Among its distinguished bldgs. are Mudejar churches, castle, house in which Peter the Cruel married Juana de Castro, and remains of old walls. Was a center of resistance against Napoleon during Peninsular War. Hq. of Wellington when he was wounded. The shrine of Our Lady of Henor is 2½ mi. NNW.

Cuenca (kwĕng'kä), city (1950 pop. 46,428), ⊙ Azuay prov., S central Ecuador, in an Andean valley, on Pan American Highway and 75 mi. SE of Guayaquil, 190 mi. S of Quito; 2°53'S 78°58'W; alt. 8,468 ft. The 3d largest city of Ecuador, it has a pleasant subtropical climate and is an important cultural, commercial, and industrial center in a fertile agr. basin. Trades in sugar cane, cereals, coffee, fruit, cattle, hides, gold, and marble. Exports cinchona bark from the Amazon basin (E). Main industry is mfg. of Panama hats; also cotton and woolen textiles, lace, leather, gold and silver articles, cheese, flour, refined sugar, beer, alcohol, soft drinks. Airport. An old colonial town, founded 1557, it is a bishopric and has a fine cathedral, a univ. (schools of law, medicine, pharmacy, mining), and fine administrative edifices. A picturesque town with cobblestone streets, it preserves its anc. character, enhanced by weekly fairs. A rail line (under construction from Quito) supplements its highway connections.

Cuenca, province (□ 6,588; pop. 333,335), E central Spain, in New Castile; ⊙ Cuenca. Borders on Guadalajara prov. (N), Teruel prov. (NE), Valencia prov. (SE), Albacete prov. (S), Ciudad Real prov. (SW), Toledo prov. (W), and Madrid prov. (NW). Largely mountainous, it forms part of the great central plateau (Meseta); the N, less rugged section belongs to Alcarria; the S plain forms part of La Mancha. The Serranía de Cuenca crosses it in E and center. Watered by Tagus and Júcar rivers. Climate is of the rigorous continental type (hot summers, cold winters), but is much milder in the plains and valleys. Among the minerals mined, only rock salt (Minglanilla) and gypsum are of some economic importance. Grazing (chiefly sheep and goats) and forest industry (timber, paper, naval stores) are its mainstay. Agr. crops raised in lower sections include saffron, grapes, wheat, barley, potatoes, olives, beans, fruit. Honey, beeswax, goat cheese, and wool are major exports. Rail communications are poor. Prov. remained in Loyalist hands until last phase of the Sp. civil war (1936–39).

Cuenca, city (pop. 23,038), ⊙ Cuenca prov., E central Spain, in New Castile, on railroad to Madrid (85 mi. WNW), and 100 mi. WNW of Valencia; 40°5'N 2°8'W; alt. c.3,070 ft. The historic city is a bishopric. It has some minor industries, such as tanning, sawmilling, flour and paper milling; mfg. of furniture, soap, chocolate, woolen goods, hats, leather articles. Picturesquely built on steep slopes of a hill crowned by ruined castle and below which join Júcar and Huécar rivers. Beyond the gorges lies the Serranía de Cuenca. Retains its medieval character in its straight, narrow streets, clustered houses, and bridges. Most distinguished bldg. is the Gothic cathedral (begun 13th cent.). Also has bishop's palace, San Nicolás and Santa María de Gracia churches, Casa Ayuntamiento, and noted natl. institute. The modern, industrial section, called Carretaría, extends onto plain on left bank of the Huécar. Of unknown origin, the city was, in 9th cent., the Moorish fortress Conca. Taken 1177 by Alfonso VIII of Castile, it received, soon after, a liberal charter and became a bishopric. A cultural and textile center during Middle Ages, it decayed after 17th cent. Suffered frequently through warfare. Occupied (1706) by the British in War of Spanish Succession, and sacked by the French in Peninsular War (1808–14). The Carlists seized the city in 1874. During Sp. civil war of 1936–39, Cuenca remained in Loyalist hands almost to the very end; it fell after the capture of Valencia. In the vicinity (8 mi. NE), near Valdecabras, is the unique Ciudad Encantada ("enchanted city"), a fantastic agglomeration of eroded rocks, closely resembling a city with houses, palaces, squares, and streets.

Cuenca, Serranía de (sĕrānē'ä dhä), range in New Castile, E central Spain, part of the Cordillera Ibérica, on E edge of the great central plateau (Meseta) with Cuenca at its center; extends c.70 mi. N-S through Guadalajara and Cuenca provs., forming watershed bet. Tagus R. and Júcar R. Rises over 5,900 ft.

Cuenca de Campos (dhä käm'pōs), town (pop. 1,054), Valladolid prov., N central Spain, 13 mi. N of Medina de Ríoseco; sheep, cereals, wine.

Cuencamé (kwĕngkämā'), town (pop. 2,151), Durango, N Mexico, on interior plateau, 50 mi. SSW of Torreón; alt. 5,462 ft.; silver, gold, lead, copper, antimony mining; winegrowing.

Cuerámaro (kwārä'märō), town (pop. 4,576), Guanajuato, central Mexico, on central plateau, 35 mi. S of León; alt. 5,790 ft.; agr. center (wheat, corn, alfalfa, beans, sugar cane, fruit, stock).

Cuernavaca (kwĕrnävä'kä), city (pop. 14,336), ⊙ Morelos, central Mexico, on S slope of central plateau, on railroad and 37 mi. S of Mexico city; 18°55'N 99°13'W; alt. c.4,500 ft. Agr. center (sugar cane, rice, fruit, vegetables, stock) and major resort, noted for mild climate and beautiful scenery. Brewery, cement plant, sugar refineries, paper mill, cigar factory. There are fine anc. bldgs., a cathedral, and a palace (erected by Cortés) now adorned with murals by Diego Rivera; the formal Borda gardens were a favorite retreat of Maximilian and Carlotta. At Atlacomulco (2 mi. E), Cortés planted his 1st sugar cane and erected a refinery (1535).

Cuernos de Negros (kwĕr'nōs dā nā'grōs), extinct volcano (6,244 ft.), SE Negros isl., Philippines, c.10 mi. WSW of Dumaguete.

Cuero (kwâ'rō), city (pop. 7,498), ⊙ De Witt co., S Texas, on Guadalupe R. and 25 mi. NW of Victoria; processing center for poultry, dairy products; cotton gins; mfg. (dried eggs, textiles, cottonseed oil, saddles, concrete and metal products). Holds Turkey Trot (Nov.) to publicize poultry industry. Founded 1872, inc. 1873.

Cuers (kwâr'), town (pop. 2,744), Var dept., SE France, 11 mi. NE of Toulon; mfg. (cork, olive oil, footwear), winegrowing. Insane asylum 4 mi. E.

Cuerva (kwĕr'vä), town (pop. 1,870), Toledo prov., central Spain, 18 mi. SW of Toledo; cereals, grapes, potatoes, olives, sheep; tile mfg.

Cues, Germany: see Bernkastel-Kues.

Cuesmes (kwĕm'), town (pop. 10,659), Hainaut prov., SW Belgium, 2 mi. SW of Mons; coal mining.

Cuesta, La, Costa Rica: see La Cuesta.

Cueto (kwā'tō), town (pop. 3,798), Oriente prov., E Cuba, 25 mi. SE of Holguín; sugar milling.

Cuetzala (kwātsä'lä), officially Cuetzala del Progreso, town (pop. 2,186), Guerrero, SW Mexico, in Río de las Balsas valley, 28 mi. SW of Iguala; cereals, sugar cane, tobacco, fruit, forest products (resins, vanilla).

Cuetzalan (kwātsä'län), officially Cuetzalan del Progreso, town (pop. 7,087), Puebla, central Mexico, in SE foothills of Sierra Madre Oriental, 18 mi. NW of Teziutlán; agr. center (corn, coffee, tobacco, sugar cane, fruit).

Cuevas, Mexico: see San Pedro de la Cueva.

Cuevas, Las, Argentina: see Las Cuevas.

Cuevas, Las, Mexico: see Villa Matamoros.

Cuevas, Río de las (rē'ō dā läs kwā'väs), headstream of Mendoza R. in NW Mendoza prov., Argentina; rises from glaciers of the Aconcagua, flows c.30 mi. S and E to the Mendoza.

Cuevas Bajas (bä'häs), town (pop. 2,422), Málaga prov., S Spain, on Córdoba prov. border, in N Cordillera Penibética, 15 mi. NNE of Antequera; cereals, olives, vegetables; olive-oil pressing, flour milling, mfg. of plaster.

Cuevas del Almanzora (dhĕl älmänthō'rä), city (pop. 2,920), Almería prov., S Spain, on Almanzora R. and 7 mi. SE of Huércal-Overa; knitwear and soap mfg. Produces and ships fruit, vegetables, esparto. Lead, silver, iron mines in vicinity. Has Moorish castle. Formerly called Cuevas de Vera.

Cuevas del Becerro (bā-thĕ'rō), town (pop. 2,405), Málaga prov., S Spain, 10 mi. NE of Ronda; cereals, olives, livestock.

Cuevas del Valle (vä'lyā), town (pop. 925), Ávila prov., central Spain, in the Sierra de Gredos, 26 mi. NNW of Talavera de la Reina; grapes, olives, chestnuts, figs, walnuts, cereals, potatoes, livestock. Flour milling, olive-oil pressing.

Cuevas de San Marcos (dhā sän' mär'kōs), town (pop. 4,611), Málaga prov., S Spain, 20 mi. NNE of Antequera; olive and wine industry.

Cuevas de Vera, Spain: see CUEVAS DEL ALMANZORA.

Cuevas de Vinromá (vēnrōmä'), town (pop. 2,173), Castellón de la Plana prov., E Spain, 26 mi. NNE of Castellón de la Plana; olive-oil processing, flour milling; cereals, wine, fruit.

Cuevo (kwā'vō), village (pop. c.3,500), Santa Cruz dept., SE Bolivia, at N foot of Serranía de Aguaragüe, 55 mi. SSE of Lagunillas, on road; corn, fruit. Bishopric.

Cufra, Cyrenaica: see KUFRA.

Cufré (kōōfrā'), town, Colonia dept., SW Uruguay, on railroad and 16 mi. NE of Rosario, in agr. region (livestock, cereals). Granite deposits near by.

Cuggiono (kōōd-jô'nô), town (pop. 3,987), Milano prov., Lombardy, N Italy, 18 mi. W of Milan; mfg. (shoes, ribbon, macaroni).

Cugir (kōō'jēr), Hung. *Kudzsir* (kōō'jēr), village (pop. 7,712), Hunedoara prov., W central Rumania, 23 mi. ESE of Deva; rail terminus, metallurgical center; mfg. of munitions, pipes, bells.

Cuglieri (kōō'lyĕrē), village (pop. 4,895), Nuoro prov., W Sardinia, 12 mi. SW of Macomer; olive oil. Ruins of Roman town (Cornus) 13 mi. S.

Cuiabá (kōōyŭbä'). **1** City (1950 pop. 24,119), ⊙ Mato Grosso, W Brazil, head of navigation on Cuiabá R. and 950 mi. NW of Rio de Janeiro; 15°35'S 56°7'W. Linked by river boat with CORUMBÁ, and by road with Campo Grande. Airport. Ships cattle, skins, dried meat, sugar, alcohol, ipecac roots. Gold placers along Cuiabá R. in decline. City has tropical savanna climate, with heavy seasonal rainfall (63 inches). Chief bldgs. are Portuguese colonial-style govt. palace and cathedral. Founded c.1720, when large quantities of gold were found in near-by streams by prospectors from São Paulo. Capital was moved here from Mato Grosso city in 1820. Formerly spelled Cuyabá. **2** Town, Minas Gerais, Brazil: see MESTRE CAETANO.

Cuiabá River, central Mato Grosso, Brazil, rises near 14°20'S 55°10'W along the Amazon-Paraguay watershed, flows c.300 mi. generally SSW, past Cuiabá (head of regular navigation to Corumbá), to São Lourenço R., which crosses Paraguay flood plain in a braided course and enters the Paraguay 80 mi. N of Corumbá. The name Cuiabá is sometimes given to the combined courses of Cuiabá and São Lourenço rivers. Gold washings in headwaters. Formerly spelled Cuyabá.

Cuicas (kwē'käs), town (pop. 719), Trujillo state, W Venezuela, 26 mi. NNE of Trujillo; coffee, corn, fruit.

Cuicatlán (kwēkätlän'), town, Oaxaca, S Mexico, on railroad and 30 mi. NE of Nochixtlán; cereals, vegetables, sugar cane, fruit, livestock. Founded 1530. Church built 1600.

Cuichapa (kwēchä'pä), town (pop. 1,040), Veracruz, E Mexico, in Sierra Madre Oriental, on railroad and 9 mi. SSE of Córdoba; coffee, livestock.

Cuicocha, Lake (kwēkō'chä), small Andean lake in Imbabura prov., N Ecuador, 8 mi. NW of Otavalo, in a crater at S foot of Cerro Cotacachi; popular resort.

Cuicuilco, Mexico: see TLALPAN.

Cuicul, Algeria: see DJEMILA.

Cuijk, Netherlands: see CUYK.

Cuilapa (kwēlä'pä) or **Cuajiniguilapa** (kwähē"-nēgwēlä'pä), city (1950 pop. 2,709), ⊙ Santa Rosa dept., S Guatemala, in Pacific piedmont, on Inter-American Highway and 27 mi. SE of Guatemala, in bend formed by Esclavos R.; 14°17'N 90°18'W. Commercial and agr. center in coffee and sugar-cane area. On Esclavos R., 2 mi. SE, is massive 16th-cent. stone bridge. Dept. capital was moved here (1871) from Santa Rosa. Following destruction (1913) of Cuilapa by earthquake, Barbarena was temporary capital (until 1920).

Cuilápan or **Santiago Cuilápan** (säntyä'gō kwēlä'-pän), officially Cuilápan de Guerrero, town (pop. 3,521), Oaxaca, S Mexico, in Sierra Madre del Sur, 6 mi. SW of Oaxaca; fruit- and vegetable-growing dist. Has fine colonial church and ruins of Dominican monastery begun 1555. Destroyed 1604 by earthquake. Vicente Guerrero, revolutionary hero, was executed here Feb. 14, 1831. Sometimes Cuilápam.

Cuilcagh, mountain (2,188 ft.), NW Co. Cavan, Ireland, 12 mi. SW of Enniskillen. At its foot rises the Shannon.

Cuilco (kwēl'kō), town (1950 pop. 564), Huehuetenango dept., W Guatemala, on Cuilco R. (a headstream of Grijalva R.) and 33 mi. W of Huehuetenango; alt. 3,445 ft.; sugar refining, fishing, cattle raising.

Cuillin Hills or **Coolin Hills** (both: kōō'lĭn), mountain, S Isle of Skye, Inverness, Scotland, rising to 3,309 ft. in Sgur Alasdair (skûr' ălŭstâr').

Cuilo River, Angola and Belgian Congo: see KWILU RIVER.

Cuíma (kwē'mä), town, Benguela prov., W central Angola, on central plateau, 40 mi. S of Nova Lisboa; rice hulling. Agr. experiment station.

Cuiseaux (kwēzō'), village (pop. 794), Saône-et-Loire dept., E central France, in the Revermont, 12 mi. SE of Louhans.

Cuise-la-Motte (kwēz-lä-môt'), village (pop. 493), Oise dept., N France, 9 mi. ESE of Compiègne; mfg. of field glasses.

Cuisery (kwēzürē'), agr. village (pop. 685), Saône-et-Loire dept., E central France, on Seille R. and 11 mi. SW of Louhans; woodworking.

Cuisy (kwēzē'), village (pop. 78), Meuse dept., NE France, 12 mi. NW of Verdun.

Cuité (kwētĕ'), city (pop. 2,142), E Paraíba, NE Brazil, on Borborema Plateau, 55 mi. NNW of Campina Grande; cotton, agave fibers, beans, potatoes. Kaolin deposits.

Cuitláhuac (kwētlä'wäk), town (pop. 1,799), Veracruz, E Mexico, 15 mi. ESE of Córdoba; coffee, sugar cane, fruit. Formerly San Juan de la Punta.

Cuito Cuanavale (kwē'tōō kwŭnŭvä'lĭ), village, Bié prov., S central Angola, on Cuito R. and 100 mi. ESE of Serpa Pinto.

Cuito River, SE Angola, rises in central plateau, flows over 400 mi. generally SSE to the Okovanggo at Dirico (South-West Africa border). Not navigable.

Cuitzeo (kwētsä'ō), officially Cuitzeo del Porvenir, town (pop. 3,637), Michoacán, central Mexico, on W peninsula of L. Cuitzeo and 19 mi. N of Morelia; resort and agr. trade center; cereals, fruit, livestock; timber. Airfield.

Cuitzeo, Lake (□ 160; alt. 6,010 ft.), Michoacán, central Mexico, on central plateau, 15 mi. N of Morelia; of irregular shape, 30 mi. long (W-E), 2–7 mi. wide, but varies with rainy season. Resort and agr. region.

Cuitzeo de Abasolo, Mexico: see ABASOLO.

Cuivre River (kwĭ'vûr), E Mo.; formed in Lincoln co. by junction of West Fork and North Fork; flows c.55 mi. SE to Mississippi R. NW of St. Louis. Cuivre River Recreational Area (5,000 acres) is near Troy.

Cujillo (kōōhē'yō), town (pop. 127), Cajamarca dept., NW Peru, on E slopes of Cordillera Occidental, near Marañón R., 29 mi. NE of Cutervo; cacao, tobacco.

Cujmir or **Cujmiru** (kōōzhmēr'), agr. village (pop. 2,991), Dolj prov., SW Rumania, 30 mi. SSE of Turnu-Severin.

Cukmantl, Czechoslovakia: see ZLATE HORY.

Cularo, France: see GRENOBLE.

Culasi (kōōlä'sē, kōōläsē'), town (1939 pop. 2,278; 1948 municipality pop. 20,601), Antique prov., W Panay isl., Philippines, 50 mi. WSW of Capiz; agr. center (rice, sugar cane).

Culberson (kŭl'bûrsŭn), county (□ 3,848; pop. 1,825), extreme W Texas; ⊙ Van Horn. Fourth-largest co. in state; scenic mtn. and plateau region, bounded N by N. Mex. line. In N are Guadalupe Mts. (Guadalupe Peak, 8,751 ft., is highest point in Texas); Delaware and Apache mts. run NW–SE; part of Sierra Diablo is in W; Van Horn Mts. in SW. Cattle-ranching region, with tourist trade; also sheep, goat raising, mining (silver, copper, mica), saltworks (salt flats W of Guadalupe Mts. figured in Salt War, 1877); some timber. Formed 1911.

Culberson, town (pop. 150), Cherokee co., W N.C., 12 mi. SW of Murphy, at Ga. line.

Culbertson. 1 Town (pop. 779), Roosevelt co., NE Mont., on Missouri R. and 32 mi. E of Poplar; grain-shipping point; lumber mill; livestock. Near by is Missouri R. Bridge, 1,169 ft. long. **2** Village (pop. 770), Hitchcock co., S Nebr., 11 mi. W of McCook and on Republican R., at mouth of Frenchman Creek; dairy and truck produce, grain, livestock.

Culcairn (kŭlkârn'), town (pop. 1,054), S New South Wales, Australia, 125 mi. WSW of Canberra; rail junction; sheep, agr. center; wheat.

Culcheth (kĭl'shŭ), town and parish (pop. 2,730), S Lancashire, England, 5 mi. NE of Warrington; cotton milling.

Cul-de-Sac (kül-dŭ-säk'), plain in S Haiti, extending from Port-au-Prince to the depression of Étang Saumâtre and L. Enriquillo. Well irrigated, it is most fertile region of Haiti, with greatest pop. density. Grows mostly sugar cane, cotton, and subsistence crops; sisal in NW.

Culdesac (kŭl'dŭsăk"), village (pop. 175), Nez Perce co., NW Idaho, 18 mi. E of Lewiston; shipping point for agr. area.

Culebra (kōōlā'brä), village (pop. 241), Colón prov., central Panama, minor port on Caribbean Sea, 9 mi. ESE of Palenque; cacao, coconuts, abacá; stock raising.

Culebra, town, Puerto Rico: see DEWEY.

Culebra Cut, Panama Canal Zone: see GAILLARD CUT.

Culebra Gulf (kōōlā'brä) Pacific inlet, NW Costa Rica, S of Santa Elena Peninsula; 25 mi. wide, 15 mi. long. Forms Culebra Bay (E). Also called Papagayo Gulf.

Culebra Island (□ 11; pop. 877), belonging to Puerto Rico, 20 mi. E of the main isl., 50 mi. ESE of San Juan; c.7 mi. long, 2 mi. wide; rises to 650 ft. An almost barren volcanic isl., lacking in water; some coconut groves. Has good harbor. Main town is Dewey, formerly called Culebra. Isl. is a bird sanctuary. Just E is small Culebrita Isl.

Culebra Peak (kŭlĕ'brŭ, kūlē'brŭ) (14,069 ft.), S Colo., in Culebra Range of Sangre de Cristo Mts., 35 mi. W of Trinidad.

Culebra Range, Colo.: see SANGRE DE CRISTO MOUNTAINS.

Culebrinas River (kōōlābrē'näs), W Puerto Rico, rises SW of Lares, flows c.25 mi. WNW to Mona Passage SSW of Aguadilla.

Culebrita Island (kōōlābrē'tä), islet (1940 pop. 5) of E Puerto Rico, just off E shore of Culebra Isl.; lighthouse (18°18'N 65°14'W).

Culemborg (kü'lŭmbôrkh), town (pop. 10,430), Gelderland prov., central Netherlands, on Lek R. (rail bridge) and 12 mi. SSE of Utrecht; cigars, cigar boxes, furniture and other wood products, metalware, clothing. Has 16th-cent. town hall, 17th-cent. town gate. Van Diemen b. here. Sometimes spelled Culenborg, Kuilenburg, Kulemborg.

Culhuacán (kōōlwäkän'), town (pop. 1,990), Federal Dist., central Mexico, 7 mi. SSE of Mexico city; cereals, fruit, livestock.

Culiacán (kōōlyäkän'), city (pop. 22,025), ⊙ Sinaloa, NW Mexico, in semitropical lowland, 30 mi. from the coast, on Culiacán R. and 660 mi. NW of Mexico city; 24°48'N 107°28'W. Rail junction; commercial and agr. center (corn, cotton, tobacco, sugar cane, chick-peas, tomatoes, fruit); leather and textile industry; lumbering (dyewood, rubber). Mining near by (gold, silver, copper, lead, cobalt, iron). Altata, 35 mi. WSW, serves as its port. Culiacán was a stronghold of Colhua Indians in pre-conquest times. Founded 1531 by Guzmán, it played an important part in early Sp. colonial era, serving as base for the Coronado expedition (1540) up the Gulf of California. A well-built city with spacious plazas, cathedral, and luxuriant Rosales Park.

Culiacán, Cerro (sĕ'rō), peak (9,160 ft.), Guanajuato, central Mexico, in Sierra Madre, 15 mi. SW of Celaya.

Culiacán River, Sinaloa, NW Mexico; formed near Culiacán by 150-mi. headstreams, flows 50 mi. SW through coastal lowlands, past Navolato, to Gulf of California.

Culion Island (kōōlyōn') (□ 153; 24 mi. long; 1939 pop. 7,328), one of the Calamian Isls., Palawan prov., Philippines, bet. Palawan and Mindoro, just S of Busuanga Isl.; 11°50'N 120°E. On it is Culion Reservation (1948 pop. 3,279), a govt. leper colony for the Philippines, begun 1905, opened 1906. Climate is healthful. Rice, coconuts are grown. Isl. rises to 1,560 ft. Some manganese deposits.

Cúllar de Baza (kōō'lyär dhä bä'thä), town (pop. 4,782), Granada prov., S Spain, 13 mi. NE of Baza; olive-oil processing, flour milling, wool spinning. Lumbering, stock raising; agr. trade (cereals, sugar beets, hemp, vegetables, fruit).

Cullen, burgh (1931 pop. 1,688; 1951 census 1,555), N Banffshire, Scotland, on Cullen Bay of Moray Firth, 5 mi. W of Portsoy; fishing port, seaside resort. Cullen House has noted gardens. Church was founded by Robert the Bruce. Near by are ruins of anc. Findlater Castle. The Bin of Cullen, a hill (1,050 ft.), is 3 mi. SW of Cullen.

Cullen, village (1940 pop. 1,460), Webster parish, NW La., near Ark. line, 45 mi. NE of Shreveport.

Cullendale, village (pop. 3,225), Ouachita co., S Ark., 3 mi. S of Camden, near Ouachita R.; mfg. of paper and paper products.

Cullera (kōōlyä'rä), city (pop. 13,943), Valencia prov., E Spain, port on the Mediterranean at mouth of Júcar R., 23 mi. SSE of Valencia. Agr. trade center, shipping oranges and rice (river traffic on the Júcar). Rice milling, brandy distilling, furniture and leather-goods mfg. Has remains of anc. castle and fortifications.

Cullercoats, England: see TYNEMOUTH.

Cullin, Lough (lŏkh kŭ'lĭn), lake (2 mi. long, 2 mi. wide), central Co. Mayo, Ireland, 2 mi. W of Foxford, just S of Lough Conn, connected by narrow channel.

Cullinan (kŭ'lĭnŭn), town (pop. 1,134), S central Transvaal, U. of So. Afr., 22 mi. ENE of Pretoria; alt. c.4,800 ft.; site of Premier Mine, one of world's largest diamond mines. Operations began 1902; largest white diamond, the "Cullinan," found here 1905. Mine closed 1932, reopened 1948.

Cullison, city (pop. 174), Pratt co., S Kansas, 7 mi. W of Pratt; wheat, grain.

Cullman (kŭl'mŭn), county (□ 743; pop. 49,046), N Ala.; ⊙ Cullman. Hilly agr. area bounded on E by Mulberry Fork. Cotton, corn, strawberries; lumber milling. Coal deposits. Formed 1877.

Cullman, city (pop. 7,523), ⊙ Cullman co., N Ala., 45 mi. N of Birmingham; shipping center for strawberry, cotton, and timber region; wood, cottonseed, and dairy products, building materials, underwear, fertilizer. Jr. col. and Ave Maria Grotto near by. Coal and sandstone deposits in vicinity. Settled 1873.

Culloden (kŭ"lō'dŭn), agr. village (pop. 261), Monroe co., central Ga., 26 mi. W of Macon.

Culloden Moor or **Culloden Muir** (kŭlō'dŭn mūr'), moorland tract in Inverness, Scotland, at NE end of Drummossie Moor, 5 mi. E of Inverness. Scene (April 16, 1746) of decisive defeat of Highlanders under Prince Charles Edward (Young Pretender) by English troops under duke of Cumberland. Cumberland Stone commemorates battle. Near by are the Stones of Clava, 4 Bronze Age cairns.

Cullom, village (pop. 492), Livingston co., E central Ill., 18 mi. E of Pontiac, in agr. and bituminous-coal area.

Cullompton (kŭ'lŭmtŭn), town and parish (pop. 2,973), E Devon, England, on Culm R. (a tributary of Exe R.) and 12 mi. NE of Exeter; agr. market; woolen milling, tanning, bacon and ham curing, mfg. (leather goods, paper). Has 15th-cent. church.

Cullowhee (kŭ'lūwē), village (1940 pop. 542), Jackson co., W N.C., on Tuckasegee R. and 5 mi. SE of Sylva. Seat of Western Carolina Teachers Col.

Cullu, Turkey: see KARAYAZI.

Cully (külē'), resort town (pop. 1,102), Vaud canton, W Switzerland, on L. Geneva, 5 mi. ESE of Lausanne.

Culoz (kül), village (pop. 1,630), Ain dept., E France, near the Rhone, 8 mi. NE of Belley, at foot of the Grand Colombier; railroad junction; mfg. of cement pipes and heating equipment, distilling.

Culpeper (kŭl'pĕ"pŭr), county (□ 389; pop. 13,242), N Va.; ⊙ Culpeper. In the piedmont; bounded S by Rapidan R., N and NE by Rappahannock R.; drained by Thornton and short Hughes rivers. Rich livestock, dairying, agr. area (fruit, grain, tobacco, truck); poultry. Formed 1748; Madison co. set off 1792, Rappahannock co. set off 1833.

Culpeper, town (pop. 2,527), ⊙ Culpeper co., N Va., 30 mi. WNW of Fredericksburg. Rail and highway shipping center for rich livestock, dairying, fruit-growing area; mfg. of textiles, clothing, wood and wire products; flour milling. Natl. cemetery near by. Here in 1775 the Culpeper minutemen were organized. In Civil War, several engagements were fought near by, notably at BRANDY; Union forces occupied town. Founded 1759; inc. 1898.

Culpina (kōōlpē'nä), village (pop. c.3,700), Chuquisaca dept., S Bolivia, 20 mi. SE of Camargo; agr. center; sheep, cattle.

Culp's Hill, Pa.: see GETTYSBURG.

Culross (kōō'rŏs), burgh (1931 pop. 495; 1951 census 578), SW Fifeshire, Scotland, on the Firth of Forth, 6 mi. WSW of Dunfermline; resort town. It formerly had coal mines, saltworks, and shipyards, and was noted for "girdles" used in oat-cake baking. It is reputed birthplace of St. Kentigern, and has associations with St. Serf. Culross Abbey was founded 1217 by Malcolm, Earl of Fife; parts of abbey remains are incorporated in parish church. There are many 16th-17th-cent. houses. Near-by Dunimarle Castle contains noted collection of paintings.

Culter (kōō'tŭr), town in Peterculter parish, SE Aberdeen, Scotland, on the Dee and 6 mi. SW of Aberdeen; paper milling.

Cults (kŭlts), residential town in Peterculter parish, SE Aberdeen, Scotland, on the Dee and 3 mi. SW of Aberdeen. Site of 3 large cairns.

Cultus Lake (kŭl'tŭs) (3 mi. long, 1 mi. wide), SW B.C., 6 mi. SSE of Chilliwack. Drained into Fraser R. by Chilliwack R. Summer resort.

Culver. 1 Town (pop. 1,563), Marshall co., N Ind., on L. Maxinkuckee, 32 mi. SSW of South Bend; agr. (livestock; dairy products; apples); summer resort. Seat of Culver Military Acad. **2** City (pop. 153), Ottawa co., N central Kansas, on Saline R. and 12 mi. NW of Salina; livestock, grain. **3** City (pop. 301), Jefferson co., central Oregon, 32 mi. N of Bend, E of Cascade Range; alt. 2,633 ft.

Culver City, city (pop. 19,720), Los Angeles co., S Calif., 8 mi. SW of downtown Los Angeles, near the coast; motion-picture center, with several large studios; residential. Los Angeles International Airport. Laid out 1913, inc. 1917.

Culverden (kŭl'vŭrdŭn), township (pop. 286), ⊙ Amuri co. (□ 2,256; pop. 2,348), NE S.Isl., New Zealand, 55 mi. N of Christchurch; sheep.

Culvers Lake, NW N.J., resort lake just E of Kittatinny Mtn. ridge, 8 mi. N of Newton; 1½ mi. long.

Cuma (kōō'mä), town (pop. 2,772), Benguela prov., W central Angola, on Benguela RR and 50 mi. W of Nova Lisboa; alt. 4,700 ft. Pioneer agr. settlement.

Cumã Bay (kōōmã'), inlet of the Atlantic off Maranhão, NE Brazil, c.35 mi. NW of São Luís. On it are São João de Côrtes and Guimarães. Formerly spelled Cuman.

Cumae (kū'mē), anc. city of Campania, S Italy, near Gulf of Gaeta, 10 mi. W of Naples. Named by Strabo as earliest Greek settlement in Italy or Sicily. Graves have yielded 9th- and 8th-cent. B.C. pre-Hellenic (also Greek, Samnite, and Roman) burial treasures. From 7th to 5th cent. B.C. repulsed Etruscan and Umbrian attacks; in 474 B.C., with help of Hiero, defeated Etruscan and Carthaginian fleets. Conquered by Samnites in 417 B.C. Has some remains of Greek and Roman periods. A favorite resort in Roman times.

Cuman, Ukrainian SSR: see TSUMAN.

Cumaná (kōōmänä'), city (1941 pop. 25,893; 1950 census 46,416), ⊙ Sucre state, NE Venezuela, on both sides of Manzanares R. (near its mouth on the Gulf of Cariaco), 1 mi. from its port Puerto Sucre (connected by tramway), and 185 mi. E of Caracas; 10°27'N 64°10'W. Distributing, trading, and mfg. center in agr. region (coconuts, coffee, cacao, beans, sugar cane); exports fruit, coffee, tobacco, cacao, hides, rum, vegetable oil. Its industrial works include fish canneries, cotton mills, tobacco factories, coconut-oil factories. Airport. Bishopric. Founded 1521 as Nueva Toledo and rebuilt 1523 after having been destroyed by Indians, it is the oldest continuously inhabited European settlement in South America. Birthplace of revolutionist Antonio José de Sucre. Heavily damaged by earthquakes, most recently in 1929.

Cumanacoa (kōōmänäkō'ä), town (pop. 4,066), Sucre state, NE Venezuela, in coastal range, 23 mi. SE of Cumaná; sugar-growing center; coffee, cacao, vegetables. Founded 1717. Cuchivano grotto near by.

Cumanayagua (kōōmänïä'gwä), town (pop. 3,293), Las Villas prov., central Cuba, 15 mi. E of Cienfuegos; tobacco, sugar cane. Copper and iron deposits near by.

Cumaral (kōōmäräl'), village, Meta intendancy, central Colombia, at E foot of Cordillera Oriental, 13 mi. NE of Villavicencio; saltworks.

Cumarebo, Venezuela: see PUEBLO CUMAREBO.

Cumari (kōōmärē'), city (pop. 706), SE Goiás, central Brazil, on railroad to São Paulo and 15 mi. SW of Catalão.

Cumbal (kōōmbäl'), town (pop. 1,760), Nariño dept., SW Colombia, at SE foot of Nevado de Cumbal, in the Andes, near Ecuador border, 40 mi. SW of Pasto; alt. 9,947 ft. Wheat, potatoes, coffee, sugar cane, fruit, livestock.

Cumbal, Nevado de (nävä'dō dā), extinct Andean volcano (15,630 ft.) in Nariño dept., SW Colombia, near Ecuador border, 19 mi. WNW of Ipiales.

Cumbala Hill, India: see BOMBAY, city.

Cumbe, Brazil: see EUCLIDES DA CUNHA.

Cumberland, county (□ 1,683; pop. 39,476), N N.S., on N.B. border, bet. Northumberland Strait and the Bay of Fundy; ⊙ Amherst.

Cumberland, city (1941 pop. 885), SW B.C., on E Vancouver Isl., 4 mi. SSW of Courtenay; coal-mining center, with mines just N of city; lumbering, farming, dairying. Coal, discovered 1891 in the area, has declined in importance (1931 pop. 2,371).

Cumberland, county (□ 1,520.4; 1931 pop. 263,151; 1951 census 285,347), NW England, on Scottish border, on the Irish Sea and Solway Firth; ⊙ Carlisle. One of most picturesque counties of England, largely mountainous (except in NW), with part of LAKE DISTRICT and Cumbrian Mts. The coastal plain, flat fertile land with cattle raising and dairying, rises E towards the Pennines, where sheep and oats are raised. Co. is drained by Derwent, Eden, Ellen, and Esk rivers. Chief industries: coal and iron mining, granite quarrying, mfg. of iron, steel, metal products, wool textiles, leather. Chief towns: Maryport, Whitehaven, Cockermouth, Workington, Keswick (resort), Penrith, Silloth, Millom. For centuries Cumberland was scene of English-Scottish strife.

Cumberland. 1 County (□ 347; pop. 10,496), SE central Ill.; ⊙ Toledo. Agr. (livestock, fruit, poultry, redtop seed, broomcorn, hay, beans, corn, wheat). Mfg. (brooms, shoes, flour, cheese and other dairy products, gloves). Drained by Embarrass R. Formed 1843. **2** County (□ 313; pop. 9,309), S Ky.; ⊙ Burkesville. Bounded S by Tenn.; drained by Cumberland R. Includes part of Dale Hollow Reservoir. Hilly agr. area, in Cumberland foothills; livestock, grain, burley tobacco, poultry, fruit. Stone quarries, oil deposits. Formed 1798. **3** County (□ 881; pop. 169,201), SW Maine, most densely populated in state; ⊙PORTLAND. Mfg. (paper and wood products, shoes, furniture, hardware, clay products, textiles), food canning, fishing, printing and publishing at Portland, South Portland, and Westbrook; truck farming, dairying. CASCO BAY and Sebago L.–Long L. area are resort centers. Rivers: Fore (harbor of Portland), Presumpscot (water power), Nonesuch, Royal, Stroudwater. Formed 1760. **4** County (□ 503; pop. 88,597), S N.J., bounded SW by Delaware Bay; ⊙ Bridgeton. Mfg. (stone, concrete, glass, and iron products, textiles, clothing, canned foods); agr. (poultry, truck, fruit, dairy products); seafood. Drained by Maurice R. and Cohansey Creek. Includes part of pine barrens region (timber, cranberries, huckleberries). Formed 1748. **5** County (□ 661; pop. 96,006), S central N.C.; ⊙ Fayetteville. Sand-hill region; drained by Cape Fear and South rivers. Agr. (cotton, tobacco, corn); timber (pine, gum). Textile mfg., sawmilling. Fort Bragg military reservation in NW. Formed 1754. **6** County (□ 555; pop. 94,457), S Pa.; ⊙ CARLISLE. Agr. and mfg. area, bounded E by Susquehanna R.; drained by Conodoguinet Creek. Blue Mtn. lies along N border, South Mtn. in S part; bet. them lies Cumberland Valley (part of Great Appalachian Valley), famous 18th-cent. route to western territories. Agr. (grain, fruit); mfg. (metals and metal products, textiles, leather products, flour); clay, limestone. Formed 1750. **7** County (□ 679; pop. 18,877), E central Tenn.; ⊙ Crossville. On Cumberland Plateau; drained by Sequatchie R. and short Obed R. Stone quarries, coal deposits, timber tracts (lumbering); agr. (corn, hay, potatoes, livestock). Formed 1856. **8** County (□ 288; pop. 7,252), central Va.; ⊙ Cumberland. Bounded S and SE by Appomattox R., NE by James R.; drained by small Willis R. Agr. (mainly tobacco; also dairying, livestock); lumber milling Formed 1749.

Cumberland. 1 Town (pop. 493), Cass co., SW Iowa, 12 mi. SE of Atlantic, in agr. area. **2** City (pop. 4,249), Harlan co., SE Ky., in the Cumberlands near Pine Mtn., on Poor Fork of Cumberland R. and 50 mi. NE of Middlesboro, in region of bituminous-coal mining, some agr. (corn, tobacco, potatoes). Mfg. of concrete blocks, potato chips, peanut products, popcorn; sawmilling; airport. Near by are Pine Mtn. settlement school (1913; coeducational) and Kentenia State Forest. Settled as Poor Fork; renamed Cumberland 1926. **3** Town (pop. 2,030), Cumberland co., SW Maine, just N of Portland; mfg., meat packing. Inc. 1821. **4** City (pop. 37,679), ⊙ Allegany co., W Md., in the Appalachians, along a loop of North Branch of the Potomac (bridged to W.Va.), and c.45 mi. S of Johnstown, Pa. State's 2d-largest city, and metropolis of W Md., it is a rail and industrial center, shipping bituminous coal and limestone and mfg. rayon, clothing, tires, glassware, dairy products, beer; has railroad shops, lumber mills; airport. Grew up around trading post established 1750 by the Ohio Co. George Washington started (1754) to build Fort Cumberland, the base of operations for Braddock's ill-fated expedition (1755) in French and Indian War. Laid out 1785; inc. 1856. At natural gateway through the Appalachians to the Ohio valley, town became E terminus of old Cumberland (or National) Road (authorized 1806), a division point on the Baltimore and Ohio RR (arrived here 1842), and W terminus of Chesapeake and Ohio Canal (1850). Points of interest include Washington's restored hq. (in Riverside Park). Cumberland Narrows (route of old Cumberland Road) just NW, in Wills Mtn. Co. fairgrounds near by. Severe floods have necessitated repeated rebuilding of business section. **5** Village (1940 pop. 145), Webster co., central Miss., 25 mi. W of West Point. **6** Village (pop. 537), Guernsey co., E Ohio, 13 mi. SW of Cambridge; coal, limestone; timber. **7** Town (pop. 12,842), Providence co., NE R.I., bet. Blackstone R. and Mass. line, 10 mi. N of Providence; mfg. (silk, cotton, worsted, and rayon textiles, nuts, bolts, wire products, shovels). Includes mfg. villages of Ashton, Berkeley, VALLEY FALLS (administrative center), parts of LONSDALE and ALBION, and Arnold Mills (agr.). Ballou Meetinghouse dates from c.1740. Inc. 1747. **8** Village (pop. c.200), ⊙ Cumberland co., central Va., 40 mi. W of Richmond, in agr. area (tobacco). Also called Cumberland Court House. **9** City (pop. 1,872), Barron co., NW Wis., on Beaverdam L., 13 mi. W of Rice Lake, in dairying and farming area; cheese, wooden boxes, canned vegetables. Settled 1874, inc. 1885.

Cumberland Basin, SE arm (15 mi. long, 3 mi. wide) of Chignecto Bay, bet. SE N.B. and N.S. Near its head are Sackville and Amherst.

Cumberland Bay, Chile: see JUAN FERNÁNDEZ ISLANDS.

Cumberland Bay, NE N.Y., inlet in W shore of L. Champlain just NE of Plattsburg; c.2½ mi. wide at entrance, 3 mi. long. Here, on Sept. 11, 1814, was fought the naval engagement of battle of Plattsburg, in which Macdonough's American ships routed the British. Cumberland Beach is bathing resort.

Cumberland Court House, Va.: see CUMBERLAND, village.

Cumberland Falls State Park (c.700 acres; established 1930), Whitley and McCreary counties, SE Ky., in Cumberland Natl. Forest on both banks of Cumberland R., NE of Whitley City. Cumberland Falls (68 ft. high, c.125 ft. wide), in river here, are noted for moonbow (spectrum formed in mist at full moon).

Cumberland Gap, town (pop. 403), Claiborne co., NE Tenn., in the Cumberlands, at Va. line, 45 mi. NNE of Knoxville, near Cumberland Gap (NW).

Cumberland Gap, E U.S., natural passage (alt. c.1,700 ft.), now followed by railroad and highway, through Cumberland Mts. near point where Va.,

Ky., and Tenn. meet, bet. Middlesboro, Ky., and Cumberland Gap town, Tenn. Discovered 1750 by Dr. Thomas Walker; through it ran Boone's Wilderness Road. In Civil War, held alternately by Confederates (1861, 1861–63) and Federals (1861, 1863–65). Natl. historical park, here, authorized by Congress.

Cumberland Harbor, Cuba: see GUANTÁNAMO BAY.

Cumberland Island, largest (c.23 mi. long, 1–5 mi. wide) of the Sea Isls., in Camden co., SE Ga., just off the coast, bet. mouths of Satilla and St. Marys rivers; mostly privately owned.

Cumberland Islands, archipelago in Coral Sea, bet. Great Barrier Reef and Repulse Bay, off E coast of Queensland, Australia; comprise 60-mi. chain of 36 rocky isls. and scattered coral islets. Wooded, with high cliffs; coral gardens; tourist resorts.

Cumberland Mills, Maine: see WESTBROOK.

Cumberland Mountains, U.S.: see CUMBERLAND PLATEAU.

Cumberland Narrows, Md.: see WILLS MOUNTAIN.

Cumberland Peninsula, SE Baffin Isl., SE Franklin Dist., Northwest Territories, extends c.200 mi. E into Davis Strait, opposite Greenland, forming N shore of Cumberland Sound; 64°56'-67°57'N 61°56'-68°W; up to 150 mi. wide. Surface is mountainous, rising to over 8,500 ft. Pangnirtung trading post on S coast; off NE coast is Padloping Isl., with Crystal III air base.

Cumberland Plateau or **Cumberland Mountains,** SE U.S., southwesternmost division of the APPALACHIAN MOUNTAINS; a W-sloping upland c.450 mi. long NE–SW, c.50 mi. wide, the plateau extends from S W.Va. (where it is continuation of the Allegheny Plateau), through SE Ky. and SW Va., across Tenn. W of the Tennessee Valley, and into N Ala., where it merges with the Gulf Coast plain in the Birmingham region. Plateau, much of it rough and broken, slopes W to the interior basins of Ky. and Tenn. Highest portion, and region to which the name Cumberland Mts. is generally restricted, is narrow belt c.150 mi. long along the SE margin, along Ky.–Va. line and in NE Tenn.; here Cumberland Mtn., a linear ridge (alt. 2,500–3,450 ft.) forms E escarpment for c.100 mi., and is continued to NE by ridges called Sandy Ridge and Big Stone Mtn.; PINE MOUNTAIN (c.125 mi. long) extends along NW boundary of belt. Highest point in the Cumberlands and in Ky. is Big Black Mtn. (4,150 ft.), within this belt. SW of Cumberland Mts. portion and also along SE edge of plateau are WALDEN RIDGE and Crab Orchard Mts. (Tenn.), LOOKOUT MOUNTAIN (Tenn., Ga., and Ala.), and SAND MOUNTAIN (Ala.). Plateau is cut by Tennessee R., whose valley in N Ala. is occupied by large TVA reservoirs. Cumberland Gap (old westbound settlers' route) is at SW tip of Va. On the plateau rise the Cumberland and Kentucky rivers and tributaries of the Tennessee. Coal is chief mineral resource; timber (mainly hardwoods) is valuable. Inaccessibility of many parts of the Cumberlands, particularly in Ky. and Tenn., has preserved many old ways of life among the mountain people.

Cumberland River, in S Ky. and N Tenn., formed on Cumberland Plateau by confluence of Poor Fork (50 mi. long) and Clover Fork (30 mi. long) just N of Harlan; flows generally W past Barbourville, Burnside, and Burkesville, S into Tenn. past Celina (Dale Hollow Reservoir drains via Obey R. into Cumberland R. here) and Gainesboro, W past Carthage and Nashville, and NW past Clarksville, reentering Ky. in Trigg co., to Ohio R. at Smithland, 12 mi. ENE of Paducah; 693 mi. long; drains □ 18,080. Navigable to WOLF CREEK DAM (461 mi. upstream). Traverses diversified terrain (mts. in E, rolling highlands in W, alluvial valley at mouth); drops 68 ft. at Cumberland Falls, in CUMBERLAND FALLS STATE PARK, near Corbin, Ky. Tributaries: in Ky., Rockcastle, Laurel, and Little rivers; in Ky. and Tenn., South Fork Cumberland R. and Red R.; in Tenn., Caney Fork, Stones R., Harpeth R., and Obey R. System of locks, dams, levees, and canals completed in lower 335 mi. of river course has improved navigation and is used for flood control; further improvements, to include hydroelectric power, are planned. Important activities in river basin are agr. (grain, hay, tobacco, fruit, vegetables), livestock raising, and mining (coal, fluorite, phosphate rocks). Chief manufactures: cement, brick, chemicals; iron, steel, and wood products. Principal cities: Nashville, Clarksville. TVA is authorized to market power from generating plants at Wolf Creek Dam, Dale Hollow Dam in Obey R., and Center Hill Dam, in Caney Fork.

Cumberland Road, U.S.: see NATIONAL ROAD.

Cumberland Sound, SE Baffin Isl., SE Franklin Dist., Northwest Territories, inlet (170 mi. long, 100 mi. wide at mouth) of Davis Strait; 63°58'-66°30'N 64°37'-68°W. On N shore is Pangnirtung trading post.

Cumberland Valley (75 mi. long, 15–20 mi. wide), in NW Md. and S Pa., part of Great Appalachian Valley and N continuation of Shenandoah Valley of Va.; sweeps in great SW–NE arc bet. the Potomac in Md. and the Susquehanna in Pa. On NW are Bear Pond, Cove, Tuscarora, and Blue mts. and on SE is South Mtn. Drained by affluents of Potomac and Susquehanna rivers. Fertile agr. area. Hagerstown, Md., Chambersburg and Carlisle, Pa., are chief centers. Scene of much action in Civil War. In Md., called Hagerstown Valley.

Cumbernauld (kŭmbûrnôld'), agr. village and parish (pop. 4,829), in detached portion of Dumbarton, Scotland, 14 mi. NE of Glasgow.

Cumbil River, Peru: see CHANCAY RIVER.

Cumbraes, The (kŭmbrāz'), 2 islands of Buteshire, Scotland, in the Firth of Clyde. See GREAT CUMBRAE and LITTLE CUMBRAE.

Cumbre [Sp.,=peak], for names beginning thus and not found here: see under following part of the name.

Cumbre, La, town, Argentina: see LA CUMBRE.

Cumbre, La, pass, Chile–Argentina: see USPALLATA PASS.

Cumbre, La, Colombia: see LA CUMBRE.

Cumbre, La (lä kōōm'brā), town (pop. 2,718), Cáceres prov., W Spain, 6 mi. SW of Trujillo; livestock, cereals.

Cumbre Negra, Cerro (sĕ'rō kōōm'brā nā'grä), Andean peak (6,273 ft.) on Argentina-Chile border; 44°46'S.

Cumbres de en Medio (kōōm'brĕs dhā ĕn mā'dhyō), town (pop. 207), Huelva prov., SW Spain, in Sierra Morena, 15 mi. NW of Aracena; olives, livestock; cheese and meat products. Sometimes spelled Cumbres de Enmedio.

Cumbres de San Bartolomé (sän' bärtōlōmā'), town (pop. 1,331), Huelva prov., SW Spain, in Sierra Morena, 8 mi. SW of Fregenal de la Sierra (Badajoz prov.); wheat, olives, timber, wool, livestock.

Cumbres Mayores (mīō'rĕs), town (pop. 3,163), Huelva prov., SW Spain, in Sierra Morena, 7 mi. S of Fregenal de la Sierra (Badajoz prov.); meat industry (ham, sausages, salted meat). Region produces olives, cereals, livestock. Town has ruins of a convent and 13th-cent. castle (now a natl. monument), with a fine portal.

Cumbres Pass, Colo.: see SAN JUAN MOUNTAINS.

Cumbrian Mountains (kŭm'–), hills of the Lake District, Cumberland and Westmorland, England, extending from Solway Firth (N) into N Lancashire (S) and connected with the Pennines by a low ridge (SE). Central range runs along Cumberland-Westmorland border; the lakes radiate from this hub. SCAFELL (3,162 ft.) is highest elevation.

Cumbum (kŭm'bŭm). **1** Town (pop. 8,453), Kurnool dist., N Madras, India, in Gundlakamma R. valley, in Eastern Ghats, 70 mi. ESE of Kurnool; turmeric processing; tamarind, mangoes. Just W, on the Gundlakamma, is 16th-cent. reservoir with 57-ft.-high dam. Timber, bamboo, fibers in near-by forests. Barite and ocher deposits (E). **2** or **Kambam** (both: kŭm'bŭm), town (pop. 22,177), Madura dist., S Madras, India, 60 mi. WSW of Madura, in Kambam Valley; rice along Suruli R. (E); cardamom, teak, turmeric in Cardamom Hills (W).

Cumby (kŭm'bē), city (pop. 504), Hopkins co., NE Texas, 15 mi. E of Greenville, in agr. area.

Cumières (kümyâr'), village (pop. 978), Marne dept., N France, on Marne R. (canalized) and 3 mi. NW of Épernay; winegrowing (champagne).

Cumières-le-Mort-Homme (–lü-môrtôm'), village (pop. 4), Meuse dept., NE France, on left bank of the Meuse and 7 mi. NW of Verdun. Destroyed in First World War. Near-by Hill 304 and Le Mort-Homme (968 ft.) figured prominently in Fr. defense of Verdun in First World War.

Cuminá River, Brazil: see EREPECURU RIVER.

Cuminestown (kŭ'mĭnztoun), agr. village in Monquhitter parish (pop. 1,804), N Aberdeen, Scotland, 6 mi. E of Turriff.

Cuming (kŭ'mĭng), county (□ 571; pop. 12,994), NE Nebr.; ⊙ West Point. Agr. area drained by Elkhorn R. Grain, livestock, dairy produce. Formed 1855.

Cummerow Lake, Germany: see KUMMEROW LAKE.

Cumming. 1 Town (pop. 1,264), ⊙ Forsyth co., N Ga., 33 mi. NNE of Atlanta, in farm area. **2** Town (pop. 131), Warren co., S central Iowa, 11 mi. SW of Des Moines, in agr. area.

Cummington, agr. town (pop. 620), Hampshire co., W Mass., in hills, on Westfield R. and 18 mi. E of Pittsfield. William Cullen Bryant b. here; his home is a memorial.

Cummins (kŭ'mĭnz), village (pop. 489), S South Australia, on S Eyre Peninsula and 32 mi. NNW of Port Lincoln; rail junction; wheat.

Cumnock and Holmhead (kŭm'nŭk, hōm'–), burgh (1931 pop. 3,653; 1951 census 4,607), E central Ayrshire, Scotland, on Lugar Water and 15 mi. E of Ayr; coal-mining center, with iron foundries. Alexander ("the Prophet") Peden, 17th cent. Covenanter, is buried here. The parish is called Old Cumnock.

Cumnor (kŭm'nŭr), town and parish (pop. 2,027), N Berkshire, England, near the Thames, 4 mi. WSW of Oxford; brickworks. Has 13th-cent. church.

Cumpas (kōōm'päs), town (pop. 2,515), Sonora, NW Mexico, on affluent of Yaqui R. and 95 mi. NE of Hermosillo; agr. center (wheat, corn, livestock).

Cumpeo (kōōmpā'ō), village (1930 pop. 420), Talca prov., central Chile, 20 mi. NE of Talca, in agr. area (grain, wine, livestock).

Cumplida, Punta (pōōn'tä kōōmplē'dhä), NE point of Palma, Canary Isls., 10 mi. N of Santa Cruz de la Palma; 28°50'N 17°46'W. Lighthouse.

Cumra (chōōmrä'), Turkish *Çumra,* town (pop. 5,190), Konya prov., S central Turkey, near railroad, 22 mi. SSE of Konya; wheat, barley, legumes, vetch.

Cumstoun, Scotland: see TWYNHOLM.

Cumulus, Mount, Colo.: see NEVER SUMMER MOUNTAINS.

Cumuruxatiba, Brazil: see PRADO.

Cumuto (kümū'tō), village (pop. 2,520), N central Trinidad, B.W.I., on railroad and 21 mi. ESE of Port of Spain, in cacao-growing region. Adjoins U.S. army base Fort Read (N).

Cunagua or **Central Cunagua** (sĕnträl' kōōnä'gwä), sugar-mill village (pop. 1,283), Camagüey prov., E Cuba, in swampy coastlands, 19 mi. E of Morón. Rail terminus, airfield.

Cunani River (kōōnänē'), coastal stream in Amapá territory, N Brazil, empties into the Atlantic near 3°N 51°W. Length, c.75 mi. Gold found here.

Cuñapirú (kōōnyäpērōō'), village, Rivera dept., NE Uruguay, on the Arroyo Cuñapirú, on road, and 46 mi. S of Rivera. Gold placers; concentrating plant. Agr. (grain, vegetables; vineyards). Airport.

Cuñapirú, Arroyo, river, NE Uruguay, rises at Rivera city, flows 100 mi. S, across Rivera dept., past Cuñapirú, to the Tacuarembó.

Cunapo, Trinidad, B.W.I.: see SANGRE GRANDE.

Cunaxa (kūnăk'sŭ), town of Babylonia, near the Euphrates. It was scene of battle (401 B.C.) bet. Cyrus the Younger and Artaxerxes II, described by Xenophon in the *Anabasis.* The march northward of Clearchus and his Ten Thousand followed the battle.

Cunco (kōōng'kō), town (pop. 2,728), Cautín prov., S central Chile, 33 mi. ESE of Temuco; agr. center (wheat, barley, vegetables, livestock); flour milling, dairying, lumbering.

Cuncolim (kōōngkō'lĭm), town (pop. 10,730), S Goa dist., Portuguese India, 23 mi. SSE of Pangim; market center for rice, fish, timber, cashew and betel nuts.

Cuncunul (kōōngkōōnōōl'), town (pop. 502), Yucatan, SE Mexico, 7 mi. SW of Valladolid; sugar cane, henequen.

Cunday (kōōndī'), town (pop. 1,462), Tolima dept., W central Colombia, in Magdalena valley, at W foot of Cordillera Oriental, 18 mi. SSE of Girardot; coffee, livestock. Petroleum deposits near by.

Cundinamarca (kōōndēnämär'kä), department (□ 9,108; 1938 pop. 1,174,607; 1950 estimate 1,470,520), central Colombia; ⊙ Bogotá. Bounded by Magdalena R. (W), it is a mountainous region astride the Cordillera Oriental, which here forms the high plateau Sabana de Bogotá (alt. c.8,500 ft.), one of Colombia's healthiest and most densely populated areas. On Bogotá R. are the majestic Tequendama Falls; the Laguna de Fúquene, noted resort and fishing ground, lies N on Boyacá border. Climate varies with alt.: humid-tropical in Magdalena valley, cool-temperate on plateau, with heavy March-May and Sept.-Nov. rains. Notable among its rich mineral resources is salt (Zipaquirá, Nemocón, Sesquilé); also contains coal (Suesca, Chocontá, Soacha), iron (Pacho), sulphur (Gachalá), gold (Villeta), zinc (Ubaté). Fine timber and medicinal plants abound in its extensive forests. Mainly an agr. region, it grows wheat, corn, barley, potatoes, and fruit on the plateau, which also provides excellent pasture for large-scale cattle raising. In Magdalena lowlands the leading crops are bananas, sugar cane, tobacco, yucca, rubber, cotton, cacao. On slopes bet. river plains and high plateau (5-7,000 ft.) coffee is cultivated in large quantities. Girardot (an important landing and communication point on the Magdalena) and Facatativá are, next to Bogotá, the most important processing centers. Formerly a rather isolated region, Cundinamarca is now well served by river, highway, rail, and air communications. It was, in pre-Spanish period, the center of the Chibcha civilization.

Cunduacán (kōōndwäkän'), city (pop. 2,167), Tabasco, SE Mexico, on arm of Grijalva R. and 18 mi. WNW of Villahermosa; cacao-growing center.

Cunduc Lagoon, Ukrainian SSR: see SASYK LAGOON.

Cundys Harbor, Maine: see HARPSWELL.

Cunel (künĕl'), village (pop. 61), Meuse dept., NE France, 17 mi. NW of Verdun.

Cunén (kōōnĕn'), town (1950 pop. 1,691), Quiché dept., W central Guatemala, at E end of Cuchumatanes Mts., 5 mi. NNE of Sacapulas; alt. 5,600 ft.; corn, beans, livestock.

Cunene, district, Angola: see ROÇADAS.

Cunene River or **Kunene River** (kōōnĕ'nä), SW Africa, rises in W central Angola near Nova Lisboa, flows S, then turns W, forming Angola–South-West Africa border in its lower course to the Atlantic; length, 600-700 mi. Rua Cana cataract (c.400 ft. high), near 17°20'S 14°20'E, is largest of a series of falls, to be harnessed for hydroelectric power by both riparian countries.

Cuneo (kōō'nĕō), province (□ 2,669; pop. 604,638), Piedmont, NW Italy; ⊙ Cuneo. Mtn. terrain, including Maritime Alps (S and SW) and Cottian Alps (W), occupies over ½ of area; drained by many Alpine affluents of the Po, including Tanaro, Stura di Demonte, Varaita, and Maira rivers. A leading sericulture region of Italy; also produces forage crops, grain, hemp, fruit (grapes, pears, apples), chestnuts, truffles. Livestock raising (sheep, cattle). Quarries (marble, limestone, gneiss); mines (anthracite, graphite). Hydroelectric plants on Varaita and Maira rivers. Industry at Cuneo, Saluzzo, Mondovì, Fossano, Bra. Highways connect with France via Maddalena and Tenda (also rail) passes. Area (□ 202; pop. 4,274) in S and SW lost to France in treaty of 1947 included part of Tenda Pass and villages of Tenda, Briga, and San Dalmazzo di Tenda.

Cuneo, town (pop. 18,852), ⊙ Cuneo prov., Piedmont, NW Italy, on Stura di Demonte R. and 50 mi. S of Turin; 44°24'N 7°32'E. Road and rail junction; commercial and industrial center. A major raw-silk market of Italy; active trade in chestnuts, livestock; silk mills, metallurgical plants, candleworks, food-processing plants (cheese, macaroni, chocolate, potato flour, starch), breweries, distilleries; chemicals, fertilizer, furniture; printing; power station. Bishopric since 1817. Has Gothic cathedral and late-Romanesque Franciscan church of 1227, technical institute, mus. Founded 1189; had strong fortifications noted for repulsing 7 sieges, 16th–18th cent. Formerly called Coni.

Cunewalde (kōō"nŭvăl'dŭ), village (pop. 4,969), Saxony, E central Germany, in Upper Lusatia, 7 mi. SE of Bautzen; linen and cotton milling, carpet mfg.

Cunha (kōō'nyŭ), city (pop. 975), SE São Paulo, Brazil, 40 mi. E of Taubaté, in the Serra do Mar, near Rio de Janeiro border; mica, rose-quartz deposits; stock raising.

Cunlhat (kŭnlä'), village (pop. 784), Puy-de-Dôme dept., central France, in Massif du Livradois, 11 mi. NW of Ambert; dairying; cattle.

Cunnamulla (kŭ"nŭmŭ'lŭ), town (pop. 1,694), S Queensland, Australia, on Warrego R. and 120 mi. SSW of Charleville, near New South Wales border; rail terminus; sheep-raising center.

Cunningham, city (pop. 510), Kingman co., S Kansas, on South Fork Ninnescah R. and 15 mi. E of Pratt; wheat, oil, natural gas. State park near by.

Cunningham Mountain (3,314 ft.), highest peak in Dome Rock Mts., SW Ariz., near Colorado R. (Calif. line), 60 mi. NNE of Yuma.

Cuntis (kōōn'tēs), town (pop. 405), Pontevedra prov., NW Spain, 14 mi. NNE of Pontevedra, in rich agr. and stock-raising region. An old town, known for its thermal springs.

Cunuc-Yacu, Ecuador: see TUMBACO.

Cuñumbuqui (kōōnyōōmbōō'kē), town (pop. 717), San Martín dept., N central Peru, in E outliers of the Andes, 3 mi. SSE of Lamas; sugar cane, cotton, rice. Sometimes Cuñumbuque.

Cuorgnè (kwôrnyā'), town (pop. 3,278), Torino prov., Piedmont, NW Italy, on Orco R. and 12 mi. WSW of Ivrea; foundries, cotton and woolen mills, alcohol distillery.

Cupar (kōō'pŭr), village (pop. 369), S Sask., 40 mi. NNE of Regina; grain elevators, flour mills.

Cupar or **Cupar-Fife** (kōō'pär, -pŭr), burgh (1931 pop. 4,595; 1951 census 5,530), ⊙ Fifeshire, Scotland, in E part of co., on Eden R. and 27 mi. NNE of Edinburgh, 8 mi. WSW of St. Andrews; agr. market with tanneries, boilerworks, and synthetic fertilizer works. Bell Baxter Col., on School Hills, is on site of 12th-cent. castle of the MacDuffs. Near Cupar was estate of the poet Sir David Lindsay. Just NE of Cupar is Prestonhall, with beet-sugar refinery. At Dura Den, 2 mi. E, important fossils found in sandstone ravine.

Cupertino (kūpûrtē'nō, kōō–), village (pop. 2,438), Santa Clara co., W Calif., in Santa Clara Valley, 8 mi. W of San Jose; orchards, vineyards. Large cement plant at near-by Permanente.

Cupica, Gulf of (kōōpē'kä), inlet of the Pacific, Chocó dept., W Colombia, bounded E by Serranía de Baudó, 70 mi. NW of Quibdó; c.20 mi. long bet. 6°23' and 6°42'N. On its N shore, near little village of Cupica, salt is worked. Once considered as possible terminus of a transisthmian canal.

Cupra Marittima (kōō'prä märēt'tēmä), village (pop. 1,487), Ascoli Piceno prov., The Marches, central Italy, port on the Adriatic, 12 mi. SSE of Fermo; bathing resort; mfg. (liquor, lye, soap).

Cupramontana (kōōprämôntä'nä), town (pop. 2,180), Ancona prov., The Marches, central Italy, 8 mi. SW of Iesi; mfg. (silk textiles, shoes, macaroni).

Cuprija or **Chupriya** (both: chōō'prēä), Serbo-Croatian *Ćuprija*, town (pop. 9,819), E central Serbia, Yugoslavia, on Morava R., on railroad and 75 mi. SSE of Belgrade; mfg. of beet sugar, molasses, dried-beet pulp.

Cupsuptic Lake, Maine: see RANGELEY LAKES.

Cuptana Island, Chile: see CHONOS ARCHIPELAGO.

Cuq-Toulza (kük-tōōlzä'), agr. village (pop. 121), Tarn dept., S France, 18 mi. W of Castres.

Cuquenán, Venezuela–Br. Guiana: see KUKENAAM.

Cuquío (kōōkē'ō), town (pop. 2,230), Jalisco, central Mexico, 28 mi. NE of Guadalajara; bean-growing center; grain, fruit, livestock.

Cura, Venezuela: see VILLA DE CURA.

Curaçá (kōōrŭsä'), city (pop. 918), N Bahia, Brazil, landing on right bank of São Francisco R. (Pernambuco border) and 50 mi. NE of Juàzeiro; irrigated agr.; caroa fibers. Rock-crystal and copper deposits.

Curaçao (kūrŭsō', kōōräsou'), island (including Little Curaçao: □ 174.13; 1948 pop. estimate 95,000), largest and principal isl. of the isl. area of the Du. Antilles, until 1949 known as Curaçao territory (□ 366; 1948 pop. estimate 150,000); ⊙ Willemstad. It is 37 mi. long, up to 7 mi. wide, situated bet. Aruba (WNW) and Bonaire (E), 40 mi. N of Venezuela, bet. 12°3'–12°24'N and 68°45'–69°11'W. Tropical, semiarid climate, relieved by NE trade winds; mean annual temp. 81°F.; rainfall 22 inches. Generally flat, with low hills; its coastline provides good harbors, such as Sint Anna Bay. Main agr. products: sisal, divi-divi, limes, oranges, orange peel (for Curaçao liquor), livestock. Phosphate mining, ostrich farming, shipbuilding; mfg. of straw hats, tiles, cement. However, the petroleum industry (introduced 1916) has become the isl.'s leading industry—centered at Willemstad, a major trading point for the Caribbean. There are several oil refineries, counted among the world's largest, which receive crude oil in flat-bottomed lighters from Venezuelan sources, chiefly L. Maracaibo dist. The oil is transshipped from here (Willemstad, Bullen Bay, Caracas Bay). Sighted (1499) by both Ojeda and Amerigo Vespucci, it was settled (1527) by the Spanish, captured (1634) by the Dutch along with Aruba and Bonaire. In 1643 Peter Stuyvesant became its governor. Occupied by the British during Napoleonic Wars, restored to the Dutch in 1816. Its prosperity declined with abolition of slave trade (of which Curaçao was a hq.), but new impetus was received through the petroleum industry, on which depend most of its urbanized pop. Bet. 80% and 90% of the inhabitants are Negroes or mulattoes. While Dutch is the official language, Papiamento, a mixture of Dutch, English, Spanish, and French, serves as a lingua franca. The Curaçao territory (officially renamed Netherlands, or Dutch, Antilles in 1949), was a former colony, after 1922 being an integral part of the kingdom of the Netherlands, and comprising all Du. possessions in the Western Hemisphere except Du. Guiana. It consists of 2 widely separated units (c.550 mi. apart) in the Lesser Antilles: SABA, SAINT EUSTATIUS, and S half of SAINT MARTIN (Du. *Sint Maarten*) in the Leewards; and 3 isls. off N Venezuela coast, Curaçao, ARUBA, and BONAIRE. Only the latter group are of economic importance, having become a stepping stone to the South American continent, and flourishing through growth of Venezuelan oil fields. The N, more humid, group of small volcanic islets engages in subsistence agr. and stock raising; also fishing and salt panning. There English is generally spoken.

Curacautín (kōōräkoutēn'), town (pop. 5,740), ⊙ Curacautín dept. (□ 2,356; pop. 21,390), Malleco prov., S central Chile, at W foot of the Andes, 60 mi. SE of Angol; rail terminus on international road to Argentina (Zapala). Resort; agr. (wheat, fruit, cattle) and lumbering center; sawmills, flour mills. Thermal baths of Río Blanco and Tolhuaca are near by.

Curacaví (kōōräkävē'), town (pop. 1,586), Santiago prov., central Chile, 28 mi. W of Santiago; fruit- and winegrowing.

Cura-Có, Argentina: see PUELCHES.

Curaco or **Curaco de Vélez** (kōōrä'kō dā vā'lĕs), village (1930 pop. 222), Chiloé prov., S Chile, on NW QUINCHAO ISLAND, off E coast of Chiloé Isl., 9 mi. ENE of Castro; potatoes, livestock; fishing, lumbering.

Curacó River, Argentina: see SALADO, Río.

Curador, Brazil: see PRESIDENTE DUTRA.

Curahuara (kōōräwä'rä). **1** or **Curahuara de Pacajes** (dā päkä'hĕs), town (pop. c.5,700), La Paz dept., W Bolivia, in the Altiplano, 60 mi. WNW of Oruro; alt. 13,396 ft.; barley, sheep. **2** or **Curahuara de Carangas** (dā käräng'gäs), town (pop. c.1,800), Oruro dept., W Bolivia, on E slopes of Western Cordillera of the Andes and c.85 mi. W of Oruro; alt. 12,887 ft.; road center; potatoes, alpaca. Also Curaguara de Carangas.

Curanilahue (kōōränēlä'wä), town (pop. 3,995), Arauco prov., S central Chile, on railroad and 20 mi. NE of Lebu; coal-mining center in agr. area (grain, legumes, livestock); lumbering.

Curanipe (kōōränē'pä), village (1930 pop. 295), Maule prov., S central Chile, on the coast, 21 mi. NW of Cauquenes; resort. Gold-bearing sands.

Curaray River (kōōrärī'), in NE Ecuador and NE Peru, rises on E slopes of the Andes NE of Puyo (Napo-Pastaza prov.), flows c.500 mi. ESE, through virgin forests, to Napo R. at 2°30'S 74°8'W. Good navigability on its main lower course.

Curarigua (kōōrärē'gwä), town (pop. 742), Lara state, NW Venezuela, 45 mi. WSW of Barquisimeto; sugar, coffee, fruit, stock.

Curaumilla, Punta de (pōōn'tä dā kōōrämē'yä), headland on the Pacific, Valparaiso prov., central Chile, SW of Valparaiso; 33°5'S 71°44'W.

Cure, La, France: see ROUSSES, LES.

Cure, La, Switzerland: see SAINT-CERGUE.

Curé Island, T.H.: see KURE ISLAND.

Curema (kōōrā'mŭ), town (pop. 4,681), W Paraíba, NE Brazil, 40 mi. ESE of Cajàzeiras. Large irrigation dam and reservoir recently completed on Piancó R. (right tributary of Piranhas R.) here.

Curepe (kyōōrĕ'pē), village (pop. 5,579), NW Trinidad, B.W.I., 6 mi. E of Port of Spain, in sugar-growing region.

Curepipe, residential town (pop. 27,468), W central Mauritius, in central plateau, on railroad and 10 mi. S of Port Louis; tea plantations. Site of Royal Col. and R.C. St. Joseph's Col. Has botanical garden, Carnegie library, military barracks.

Curepto (kōōrĕp'tō), town (pop. 1,739), ⊙ Curepto dept. (□ 320; pop. 13,714), Talca prov., central Chile, 30 mi. NW of Talca; agr. center (wheat, barley, wine, livestock); dairying, flour milling.

Cure River (kür), Nièvre and Yonne depts., central France, rises in the Morvan, flows 70 mi. NNW to the Yonne 3 mi. below Vermenton. Dam 3 mi. SE of MONTSAUCHE forms Les Settons reservoir. Used for lumber floating. Receives the Cousin (right).

Curiapo (kōōryä'pō), town (pop. 216), Delta Amacuro territory, NE Venezuela, landing at mouth of Brazo Imataca on Boca Grande (arms of Orinoco R. delta), 80 mi. ESE of Tucupita; 8°35'N 61°W; in agr. region (corn, bananas, cacao).

Curibaya (kōōrēbī'ä), town (pop. 179), Tacna dept., S Peru, in Cordillera Occidental, on Locumba R. and 45 mi. E of Moquegua.

Curiche Liverpool, Bolivia: see LIVERPOOL, CURICHE.

Curicó (kōōrēkō'), province (□ 2,215; 1940 pop. 81,185, 1949 estimate 86,848), central Chile; ⊙ Curicó. Bet. the Andes and the Pacific, N of Lontué and Mataquito rivers, in the fertile central valley. Produces wine, wheat, barley, beans; livestock (cows, goats). Dairying, flour milling, wine making, lumbering. Salt lagoons near the coast, volcanoes in the Andes. Prov. set up 1865.

Curicó, city (1940 pop. 21,153, 1949 estimate 19,165), ⊙ Curicó prov. and Curicó dept. (□ 1,525; 1940 pop. 64,263), central Chile, in the central valley, on railroad and 115 mi. SSW of Santiago; 35°S 71°16'W. Agr., commercial, and processing center. Flour mills, distilleries, tanneries. Produces grain, peas, beans, wine; livestock. Trade in cattle. Founded 1743, Curicó was largely destroyed in 1928 earthquake and rebuilt.

Curiepe (kōōryā'pā), town (pop. 1,772), Miranda state, N Venezuela, in Caribbean lowlands, 50 mi. E of Caracas; cacao.

Curieuse Island (küryûz') (900 acres; pop. 90), one of the Seychelles, in Indian Ocean, 2 mi. N of Praslin Isl., 4°18'S 55°43'E. Copra, essential oils; fisheries. Has a leper settlement.

Curimeo (kōōrēmā'ō), town (pop. 1,852), Michoacán, central Mexico, 38 mi. E of Zamora; cereals, vegetables, fruit, stock.

Curimón (kōōrēmōn'), village (1930 pop. 834), Aconcagua prov., central Chile, on railroad, on Aconcagua R. and 4 mi. SE of San Felipe; agr. (grain, fruit, hemp, tobacco, livestock).

Curinga (kōōrēng'gä), village (pop. 3,717), Catanzaro prov., Calabria, S Italy, 16 mi. WSW of Catanzaro; wine, olive oil.

Curinhuás River (kōōrēnwäs'), E Nicaragua, rises in E outlier of Huapi Mts., flows c.80 mi. E to PEARL LAGOON off Caribbean Sea.

Curitiba (kōōrētē'bŭ), rapidly growing industrial city (1941 pop. 99,440; 1950 pop. 141,349), ⊙ Paraná, SE Brazil, on plateau (alt. 3,000 ft.) near headwaters of Iguassú R., 50 mi. W of Paranaguá, its port on the Atlantic, and 200 mi. SW of São Paulo; 25°26'S 49°16'W. Important commercial center processing maté, lumber, and livestock shipped from the hinterland. Mfg. of paper, furniture, textiles, Portland cement, matches, tobacco products, pharmaceuticals, ceramics; founding, metalworking, distilling, sugar refining, brewing. Dried maté is chief export. Gold deposits in area. City is linked by rail with its port (across Serra do Mar), with the neighboring states of São Paulo and Santa Catarina, and with the pioneer coffee zone of N Paraná. Air transport center. City has a truly temperate climate (mean temp. 59°F.). Founded 1654 as a gold-mining camp. Its most rapid growth has occurred since 1900 as a result of large-scale immigration (Germans, Slavs, Italians). City presents a modern appearance. Episcopal see and seat of state univ. (founded 1912). Became ⊙ Paraná in 1854. Formerly spelled Curityba, and sometimes Curytiba or Corityba.

Curitibanos (kōōrē"tēbä'nōōs), city (pop. 1,196), central Santa Catarina, Brazil, in the Serra Geral, 40 mi. NNW of Lajes; tobacco, cheese, jerked beef. Formerly spelled Curitybanos or Coritybanos.

Curityba, Brazil: see CURITIBA.

Curitybanos, Brazil: see CURITIBANOS.

Curium (kū'rēŭm), ruined city in Limassol dist., SW Cyprus, on Episkopi Bay, 9 mi. W of Limassol. Was a flourishing Mycenaean colony before 1100 B.C. Ruins include temple of Apollo Hylates. Some of the remains, excavated in mid-19th cent., are now exhibited in the N.Y. Metropolitan Mus. Three mi. E is the 15th-cent. Lusignan *Kolossi* tower, built by the Knights of St. John.

Curlew (kûrlōō'), town (pop. 151), Palo Alto co., NW Iowa, 23 mi. ESE of Spencer.

Curlew Mountains, range along border of cos. Sligo and Roscommon, Ireland, rising to 863 ft. 3 mi. WNW of Boyle.

Curling, town (pop. 1,265), W N.F., on Humber R. estuary and 3 mi. W of Corner Brook; fishing port, with fish-smoking plant; mfg. of beer, mineral water; lumbering.

Curllsville, borough (pop. 156), Clarion co., W central Pa., 8 mi. SSW of Clarion.

Curmi, Malta: see QORMI.

Curraes Novos, Brazil: see CURRAIS NOVOS.

Curragh, The (kûr'ů), undulating plain or common (4,885 acres; 6 mi. long, 2 mi. wide), central Co. Kildare, Ireland, 3 mi. E of Kildare. Military camp since 1646, and site of long-established race course.

Currais Novos (kōōrīs' nō'vōōs), city (pop. 2,643), central Rio Grande do Norte, NE Brazil, 95 mi. SW of Natal; mule-raising center; ships cotton, manioc, corn. Bismuth and beryl deposits in area. Sulphur mines, gypsum and kaolin quarries. Formerly spelled Curraes Novos.

Curral, Serra do (sĕ'rů dōō kōōräl'), offshoot range of the Serra do Espinhaço, S central Minas Gerais, Brazil, overlooking Belo Horizonte on SE. Rises to 4,560 ft. in Belo Horizonte peak. Gold mining on E slope. Also called Serra do Curral del Rei.

Curralinho (kōōrälē'nyōō). **1** City, Maranhão, Brazil: see COELHO NETO. **2** City (pop. 268), E Pará, Brazil, on S shore of Marajó isl in Amazon delta, 90 mi. WSW of Belém; cattle raising.

Current River, in SE Mo. and N Ark., rises in the Ozarks in Dent co., Mo.; flows c.225 mi. generally SE to Black R. just E of Pocahontas, Ark.; fishing traffic.

Curridabat (kōōrēdäbät'), town (1950 pop. 743), San José prov., Costa Rica, on central plateau, on Inter-American Highway and 3 mi. ESE of San José; coffee center.

Currie (kûr'ē), town and parish (pop. 3,261), NW Midlothian, Scotland, on Water of Leith and 6 mi. SW of Edinburgh; leather and paper mfg. Near-by Lennox Tower was frequent residence of Mary Queen of Scots.

Currie, largest town and port (pop. 513) of King Isl., Tasmania, on Bass Strait; sheep center.

Currie. 1 Village (pop. 551), Murray co., SW Minn., on Des Moines R. and 7 mi. NE of Slayton, in grain, livestock, and poultry area. L. Shetek near by. **2** Village, Pender co., SE N.C., 18 mi. NNW of Wilmington. Hq. for Moores Creek Natl. Military Park (30 acres; established 1926), commemorating battle (Feb., 1776) of Moores Creek Bridge, in which N.C. Tories were defeated by Whigs.

Currituck (kŭ'rētŭk"), county (□ 273; pop. 6,201), extreme NE N.C.; ⊙ Currituck. Bounded N by Va., E by the Atlantic, S by Albemarle Sound, SW by North R. (part of Intracoastal Waterway). Tidewater area, bordered by barrier beach enclosing Currituck Sound. Agr. (corn, soybeans, cotton, truck); timber (pine, gum). Sawmilling, fishing; resorts along coast (duck hunting). Formed 1672.

Currituck, village (pop. c.100), ⊙ Currituck co., extreme NE N.C., on Currituck Sound, 15 mi. NE of Elizabeth City; fishing and hunting resort.

Currituck Sound, NE N.C. and SE Va., salt-water arm (c.30 mi. long, 5 mi. wide) of the Atlantic, behind barrier beaches (E); joins Albemarle Sound (S); Intracoastal Waterway in NW; opens (NE) into Back Bay.

Curry, village (pop. 179), S Alaska, on Susitna R. and 100 mi. N of Anchorage; stop on Alaska RR bet. Anchorage and Fairbanks; hotel. Center of fishing and hunting region.

Curry. 1 County (□ 1,403; pop. 23,351), E N.Mex.; ⊙ Clovis. Agr. area, bordering on Texas; grain, livestock. Railroad repair shops at Clovis. Formed 1909. **2** County (□ 1,622; pop. 6,048), SW Oregon; ⊙ Gold Beach. SW extremity of state, bounded W by Pacific Ocean, S by Calif.; drained by Rogue R. Lumber milling, dairying. Siskiyou Natl. Forest throughout. Formed 1855.

Curry, resort village, Sullivan co., SE N.Y., near Neversink R., in the Catskills, 9 mi. NE of Liberty.

Curry Rivel (rī'vŭl), agr. village and parish (pop. 1,401), S Somerset, England, 11 mi. E of Taunton. Has 15th-cent. church.

Curryville, town (pop. 258), Pike co., E Mo., 8 mi. W of Bowling Green.

Curslack, Germany: see VIERLANDE.

Curt-Bunar, Bulgaria: see TERVEL.

Curtea-de-Argeş (kōōr'tyä-dä-är'jĕsh), Rum. *Curtea-de-Argeş*, town (1948 pop. 9,180), Arges prov., S central Rumania, in Walachia, on Arges R., on S slopes of the Transylvanian Alps, and 20 mi. NNW of Pitesti; rail terminus, climatic resort (alt. 1,476 ft.), and historic center. Woodworking, flour milling, pottery making. Its famed 16th-cent. Byzantine cathedral was repeatedly restored and finally reconstructed (1875–85) to become the burial place of Rumanian kings. Another 14th-cent. church, with 14th- and 15th-cent. frescoes, is preserved as historical monument. There are also noted remains of a Moorish-style palace. Founded in 14th cent., Curtea-de-Arges succeeded Campulung as ⊙ Walachia and was itself succeeded by Targoviste in 15th cent. Orthodox bishopric since 18th cent.; also R.C. bishopric.

Curtici (kōōr'tēch), Hung. *Kürtös* (kür'tûsh), village (pop. 8,050), Arad prov., W Rumania, on railroad and 10 mi. N of Arad, near Hung. border.

Curtina (kōōrtē'nä), village, Tacuarembó dept., N central Uruguay, on the Arroyo Malo, on highway, and 30 mi. SSW of Tacuarembó; road junction; grain, cattle.

Curtis, city (pop. 964), Frontier co., S Nebr., 30 mi. N of McCook and on Medicine Creek; flour, feed; truck and dairy produce, grain. Nebr. School of Agr. here.

Curtis, Port, Australia: see GLADSTONE.

Curtis Bay, Md.: see PATAPSCO RIVER.

Curtis Island (□ 18), in Pacific Ocean just off E coast of Queensland, Australia; forms SE shore of Keppel Bay; 30 mi. long, 10 mi. wide; rises to 425 ft.; sandy, wooded. Cape Capricorn (on Tropic of Capricorn) is NE point, forming SE side of entrance to Keppel Bay; lighthouse.

Curtis Islands, N.Z.: see KERMADEC ISLANDS.

Curtiss, village (pop. 139), Clark co., central Wis., 40 mi. W of Wausau, in dairying region.

Curtisville, village (pop. 1,477), Allegheny co., W Pa., 6 mi. NW of New Kensington.

Curtorim (kōōrtō'rĭm), town (pop. 7,772), central Goa dist., Portuguese India, 20 mi. SE of Pangim; rice, coconuts.

Curuçá (kōōrōōsä'), city (pop. 1,969), easternmost Pará, Brazil, on the Atlantic just E of the Amazon delta, 70 mi. NE of Belém; ships manioc flour, rice, salted fish, and cereals.

Curug or **Churug** (both: chōō'rōōk), Serbo-Croatian *Čurug*, Hung. *Csurog* (chōōr'ôg), village (pop. 7,602), Vojvodina, N Serbia, Yugoslavia, on the Tisa and 19 mi. NE of Novi Sad, in the Backa.

Curuguaty (kōōrōōgwätē'), town (dist. pop. 2,380), Caaguazú dept., S central Paraguay, 140 mi. NE of Asunción; tobacco-growing and -processing center; stock raising, lumbering, maté milling.

Curumalán, Sierra de, or **Sierra de Curumalal** (syĕ'rä dā kōōrōōmälän', –läl'), hill range in SW Buenos Aires prov., Argentina, NW of Sierra de la Ventana, extends c.25 mi. NW-SE, N of Tornquist; rises to 3,414 ft. Has caves with Indian designs.

Curundu (kūrŭn'dōō), village, Balboa dist., S Panama Canal Zone, 2 mi. N of Panama city; adjoins Albrook Field. Stock raising, dairying; corn, rice.

Cururupu (kōōrōōrōōpōō'), city (pop. 2,967), N Maranhão, Brazil, on inlet of the Atlantic, 65 mi. NW of São Luís; cotton and rice growing. Airfield. Gold mined near by.

Curutú, Cerro (sĕ'rō kōōrōōtōō'), peak (17,700 ft.) in the Andes, on Argentina-Chile border, 50 mi. NW of Susques; 23°11'S.

Curuzu (kōōrōōzōō'), town (pop. 538), NE Maranhão, Brazil, on Itapecuru Mirim–Brejo road, and 95 mi. SE of São Luís; cotton, babassu nuts. Until 1944, called São Benedito.

Curuzú Chali Island (kōōrōōsōō' chä'lē), in Paraná R., Entre Ríos prov., E Argentina, just N of La Paz; 23 mi. long, c.4 mi. wide; resort area.

Curuzú-Cuatiá (–kwätyä'), town (pop. 15,549), ⊙ Curuzu-Cuatiá dept. (□ c.3,500; pop. 39,538), S Corrientes prov., Argentina, 40 mi. S of Mercedes; rail junction; farming center (rice, cotton, jute, flax, stock); stone quarrying, corn milling. Airport.

Curvelo (kōōrvä'lōō), city (pop. 7,909), central Minas Gerais, Brazil, on railroad and 85 mi. NNW of Belo Horizonte; commercial center with cotton mills and tanneries. Ships dried meat, dairy products, sugar, tobacco, coffee. Rock-crystal deposits. Has dry, healthful climate. Formerly Curvello.

Curwensville (kûr'wĭnzvĭl"), borough (pop. 3,332), Clearfield co., W central Pa., 5 mi. SW of Clearfield and on West Branch of Susquehanna R.; brick and clay products, leather, clothing; sandstone. Settled c.1800, inc. c.1832.

Curytiba, Brazil: see CURITIBA.

Curzola, Yugoslavia: see KORCULA ISLAND.

Curzon Line (kûr'zŭn), demarcation line bet. POLAND and USSR anchored in center on Western Bug R. First proposed 1919 by Lord Curzon, Br. foreign secretary, during Soviet-Polish war, it was obviated by Polish victory (1920). During Second World War, it was used in part for Soviet-German partition (1939) of Poland, and was revived at Yalta Conference as basis for post-war Soviet-Polish boundary. The Potsdam Conference modified the line slightly in favor of Poland. In 1951, the line was further altered by a Polish-Soviet territorial exchange in USTRZYKI DOLNE and SOKAL areas.

Cusano Milanino (kōōzä'nô mēlänē'nô), town (pop. 5,554), Milano prov., Lombardy, N Italy, 6 mi. N of Milan; mfg. (celluloid, rubber articles, ribbon, macaroni).

Cusano Mutri (mōō'trē), village (pop. 1,070), Benevento prov., Campania, S Italy, 21 mi. NW of Benevento.

Cuscatlán (kōōskätlän'), department (□ 672; pop. 119,347), central Salvador; ⊙ Cojutepeque. Bounded N by Lempa R. (crossed by suspension bridge), SE by Jiboa R.; contains volcanoes Guazapa (NW) and Cojutepeque (SE), part of L. Ilopango (SW). Sugar cane is main crop; cotton, coffee, grain also grown. Main industries: sugar and cotton milling, mfg. (palm hats, mats, baskets). Main centers: Cojutepeque (on railroad and Inter-American Highway); Suchitoto. Formed 1853.

Cusco, Peru: see CUZCO.

Cush or **Kush** (kŭsh), in the Bible, refers mostly to the country of ETHIOPIA, then the region corresponding roughly to present-day Anglo-Egyptian Sudan. Cush is also the name of an Asiatic country, perhaps the one of similar name in E Mesopotamia which flourished c.1500 B.C.

Cushamén, department, Argentina: see LELEQUE.

Cushat Law (kŭ'shŭt), mountain (2,020 ft.) of Cheviot Hills, NW Northumberland, England, 10 mi. SSW of Wooler.

Cushendall (kōōshŭndôl'), fishing village, NE Co. Antrim, Northern Ireland, on Red Bay of the North Channel, 19 mi. NW of Larne, in iron-mining dist. Has anc. prison tower. Near by is sepulchral chamber called "Ossian's Grave."

Cushing (kōō'shĭng). **1** Town (pop. 248), Woodbury co., W Iowa, 38 mi. E of Sioux City; livestock, grain. **2** Resort town (pop. 376), Knox co., S Maine, on peninsula and 9 mi. SW of Rockland; includes Pleasant Point village. **3** Village, Essex co., Mass.: see SALISBURY. **4** Village (pop. 71), Howard co., E central Nebr., 7 mi. NNE of St. Paul, at junction of Middle Loup and N.Loup rivers, which here form Loup R. **5** City (pop. 8,414), Payne co., N central Okla., c.45 mi. WSW of Tulsa, near Cimarron R.; trade and industrial center for petroleum-producing, diversified agr., and stock-raising area. Oil and gas wells; refineries, pipe lines, storage tanks, reclaiming plants. Cotton ginning; mfg. of dairy products, metal products, beverages. Settled 1892; inc. as town 1894, as city 1913. **6** Town (pop. 479), Nacogdoches co., E Texas, near Angelina R., 18 mi. NW of Nacogdoches; cotton gins, sawmills.

Cushing Island. 1 Resort and residential island (c.1 mi. long), in Casco Bay, SW Maine, off South Portland; settled c.1682. Site of Fort Levett, built 1898. **2** Small uninhabited island, in Casco Bay, SW Maine, ½ mi. E of Great Chebeague Isl.

Cushman, town (pop. 314), Independence co., NE central Ark., 9 mi. NW of Batesville; manganese deposits near by.

Cushman Dam, Wash.: see SKOKOMISH RIVER.

Cusick (kū'zĭk, kū'sĭk), town (pop. 360), Pend Oreille co., NE Wash., 16 mi. NW of Newport and on Clark Fork R.; lumber, matches.

Cusihuiriáchic (kōōsēwēryä'chēk), town (pop. 1,131), Chihuahua, N Mexico, at E foot of Sierra Madre Occidental, 55 mi. SW of Chihuahua; rail terminus; gold, silver, lead, copper mining. Airfield.

Cusna, Monte (môn'tĕ kōōz'nä), peak (6,955 ft.) in Etruscan Apennines, N central Italy, 20 mi NNE of Carrara.

Cussabat or **Kussabat** (kōōsäbät'), Arabic *El Gusbat* or *Al-Gusbat*, town (pop. 2,365), central Tripolitania, Libya, near NE edge of the plateau Gebel Nefusa, on main road and 15 mi. WSW of Homs in agr. (olives, cereals) and livestock area; alt. c.1,130 ft.; olive-oil pressing, barracan weaving. Moslem religious center with Koranic col. and mosque. Fort built c.1530. Power station. Ruins of Roman olive-oil presses in region.

Cusset (küsā'), town (pop. 6,864), Allier dept. central France, 2 mi. ENE of Vichy; mfg. (machinery, furniture, rubber and plastic products, gingerbread); hemp spinning, distilling. Mineral springs. Building stone quarried near by.

Cusseta (kŭsē'tŭ), town (pop. 571), ⊙ Chattahoochee co., W Ga., 17 mi. SE of Columbus, near Ala. line; sawmilling.

Cussignacco (kōōs-sēnyäk'kô), village (pop. 2,063), Udine prov., Friuli–Venezia Giulia, NE Italy, 2 mi. S of Udine.

Custar (kŭ'stûr), village (pop. 263), Wood co., NW Ohio, 11 mi. SW of Bowling Green, in agr. area.

Custer. 1 County (□ 737; pop. 1,573), S central Colo.; ⊙ Silver Cliff. Livestock-grazing area drained by branches of Arkansas R. Part of Sangre de Cristo Mts. in W; part of Wet Mts. and of San Isabel Natl. Forest in E. Formed 1877. **2** County (□ 4,933; pop. 3,318), central Idaho; ⊙ Challis. Mtn. area crossed by Salmon R. Stock raising, mining (gold, silver, lead, copper). Lost River Range is in E; Salmon River Mts. are in N, in Challis Natl. Forest; Sawtooth and Pioneer mts. are in S, in Sawtooth Natl. Forest. Formed 1881. **3** County (□ 3,765; pop. 12,661), SE Mont.; ⊙ Miles City. Agr. region drained by Yellowstone, Tongue, and Powder rivers. Livestock. Formed 1877. **4** County (□ 2,562; pop. 19,170), central Nebr.; ⊙ Broken Bow. Agr. region drained by Middle Loup and S.Loup rivers and Mud Creek. Livestock, grain. Formed 1877. **5** County (□ 999; pop. 21,097), W Okla.; ⊙ Arapaho. Intersected by Washita and Canadian rivers. Agr. area (wheat, cotton, corn, rye, barley, oats, livestock, poultry). Mfg. at Clinton and Weatherford. Contains Red Moon Indian Reservation. Formed 1907. **6** County (□ 1,552; pop. 5,517), SW S.Dak., on Wyo. line; ⊙ Custer. Agr. and mining area includes S extremity of Black Hills and part of Harney Natl. Forest; watered by Cheyenne R. Mines at Custer; dairy products, livestock, poultry, grain, timber. Places of interest are Wind Cave Natl. Park and Jewel Cave Natl. Monument. Part of co. set aside as U.S. recreational demonstration area (Custer State Park). Formed 1875.

Custer. 1 Village (pop. 260), Mason co., W Mich., 12 mi. E of Ludington, near Pere Marquette R., in farm and resort area. 2 or **Custer City,** town (pop. 479), Custer co., W Okla., 11 mi. NNE of Clinton; wheat, cotton; flour milling. 3 City (pop. 2,017), ⊙ Custer co., SW S.Dak., 30 mi. SW of Rapid City, in Black Hills; alt. 5,301 ft. Resort; timber, feldspar, gold, rose quartz, mica, gypsum; dairy products, livestock, poultry, grain. Annual historical pageant celebrates discovery of gold (1874) in French Creek. State tuberculosis sanatorium 5 mi. S. Near by are Custer State Park, Harney Peak, Mt. Rushmore Natl. Memorial, Wind Cave Natl. Park, Jewel Cave and Fossil Cycad natl. monuments. Custer laid out 1875.

Custer, Fort, Mich.: see Battle Creek, city.

Custer Battlefield National Monument, Mont.: see Little Bighorn River.

Custer City, Okla.: see Custer.

Custer Peak (6,794 ft.), SW S.Dak., near Custer, in Black Hills.

Custódia (kōōstô'dyů), city (pop. 1,366), central Pernambuco, NE Brazil, 28 mi. W of Sertânia; cotton, tobacco, corn.

Custoza (kōōstô'tsä) or **Custozza,** village (pop. 320), Verona prov., Veneto, N Italy, 11 mi. SW of Verona. Scene of battles (1848, 1866) in which Austrians defeated Italians.

Cüstrin, Poland: see Küstrin.

Cútar (kōō'tär), town (pop. 601), Málaga prov., S Spain, 13 mi. ENE of Málaga; raisins, olives, cereals, fruit.

Cut Bank, town (pop. 3,721), ⊙ Glacier co., N Mont., on Marias R. and 95 mi. NNW of Great Falls. Near-by oil and gas fields supply gas for use in copper- and zinc-reduction plants in Great Falls, Helena, Anaconda, and Butte; oil products, wool, livestock, grain. Blackfeet Indian Reservation is just W. Inc. 1910.

Cutch or **Kutch** (kŭch), chief commissioner's state (less Rann of Cutch, □ 8,461; 1951 pop. 567,825), W India; ⊙ Bhuj. Bounded SW by Arabian Sea, N by Thar Desert and Sind (W Pakistan), S by Gulf of Cutch. Mostly treeless and barren, with rocky hills (S), its agr. yield (chiefly wheat, barley, cotton) is small. Salt panning (vast brine deposits in the Rann) is important occupation; also cattle raising, fishing (SW), embroidering, handicraft work (cloth weaving, silver products). Some gypsum mined. Mandvi and Kandla are main ports. Isolated from mainland by the Rann and rarely visited by trading ships, Cutch for centuries has been under local, independent dynasties and has played little part in the major events of Indian history. Since 13th cent., ruled by a Rajput clan. Made treaty 1815 with British; formerly one of Western India States; since 1948, administered by chief commissioner. Sometimes spelled Kachh.

Cutch, Gulf of, inlet of Arabian Sea on W coast of India, bet. Cutch (N) and Kathiawar peninsula (S); 110 mi. long, 10–40 mi. wide. Head and sides composed largely of mud flats. Ports at Mandvi, Kandla, Navlakhi, Bedi, and Okha. Has several isls. (S), including Beyt.

Cutch, Rann of (rŭn'ŭv kŭch'), large salt waste in S Sind (W Pakistan) and N and E Cutch (India); bounded W by Arabian Sea, N by Thar Desert. Larger N area, or Great Rann, is 220 mi. long, 25–50 mi. wide; smaller SE area, or Little Rann, is 65 mi. long, 35 mi. wide. Encloses small hill ranges (NE, S central). Originally a shallow arm of Arabian Sea; a navigable lake in Alexander the Great's time; since silted up to form an extensive mud flat. Inundated during monsoon season; has vast salt deposits when dry; saltworks. Also spelled Runn of Cutch.

Cutchi, W Pakistan: see Kachhi.

Cutchogue (kŭ-chäg', kŭ'chäg"), village (1940 pop. 1,050), Suffolk co., SE N.Y., on NE Long Isl., 11 mi. NE of Riverhead; farm, summer-resort area.

Cutervo (kōōtěr'vō), city (pop. 3,789), ⊙ Cutervo prov. (□ 1,352; pop. 57,459), Cajamarca dept., NW Peru, in Cordillera Occidental, 60 mi. NNW of Cajamarca; alt. 8,038 ft. Agr. products (wheat, corn, potatoes); cattle raising.

Cuth (kŭth) or **Cuthah** (kū'thů), anc. city of Mesopotamia, near Babylon. The inhabitants, when settled in Samaria, introduced the worship of Nergal. In later times the Jews called the Samaritans Cathites.

Cuthbert, city (pop. 4,025), ⊙ Randolph co., SW Ga., c.50 mi. SSE of Columbus; agr. trade center, with lumber and veneer mills, cotton gins. Jr. col. here. Inc. 1834.

Cut Knife, village (pop. 326), W Sask., 32 mi. W of North Battleford; alt. 2,096 ft.; grain elevators. Cutknife Hill, 6 mi. NE, was scene of engagement (1885) bet. Northwest Mounted Police and Cree Indians in the Riel Rebellion.

Cutler. 1 Village (pop. 1,768), Tulare co., S central Calif., in San Joaquin Valley, 14 mi. N of Visalia; ships fruit, truck. 2 Village (pop. 520), Perry co., SW Ill., 40 mi. SSW of Centralia, in agr. and bituminous-coal-mining area. 3 Agr. and fishing town (pop. 483), Washington co., E Maine, 14 mi. ESE of Machias.

Cutoff, village (pop. 66), W central Alaska, on Koyukuk R. and 110 mi. NE of Nulato; 66°N 155°45'W.

Cutral-Có (kōōträl-kō'), village (1947 pop. 3,733), E Neuquén natl. territory, Argentina, 2 mi. SW of Plaza Huincul; petroleum center, founded 1933.

Cutro (kōō'trô), town (pop. 5,999), Catanzaro prov., Calabria, S Italy, 8 mi. WSW of Crotone, in cereal-growing, stock-raising region.

Cutrofiano (kōō"trôfyä'nô), town (pop. 6,328), Lecce prov., Apulia, S Italy, 16 mi. S of Lecce; wine, olive oil.

Cuttack (kŭt'äk, kŭtäk'), district (□ 4,246; pop. 2,448,772), E Orissa, India; ⊙ Cuttack. Bounded E by Bay of Bengal, NE by Baitarani R.; largely deltaic tract of Mahanadi and Brahmani rivers; low hill ranges (W). Agr. (rice, jute); hand-loom weaving, fishing (mackerel, whitebait, seerfish, pomfret, mullet). Chief centers: Cuttack, Jajpur, Kendrapara. Territory of original dist. (□ 4,571; pop. 2,431,427) changed 1949 by inc. of former princely states (were in Orissa States) of Athgarh, Baramba, Narsinghpur, and Tigiria, and by transfer of detached Angul (N) subdivision to newly-created dist. of Dhenkanal.

Cuttack, city (pop. 74,291), ⊙ Cuttack dist., E Orissa, India, at apex of the Mahanadi delta mouth, 220 mi. SW of Calcutta; river port; trade center (rice, oilseeds, timber, lac, hides); rice, oilseed, and flour milling, tanning, mfg. of ice, biris, shoes, rubber stamps; engineering works. Handicrafts include silver and gold filigree work, cotton cloth, brassware. Has Utkal Univ. (founded 1943 as affiliating and examining body; to be moved to Bhubaneswar), Central Rice Research Inst., Orissa School of Engineering, medical and art cols. Near by, across Mahanadi R. and its distributaries, are weirs for flood control and canal irrigation. Ruined fort (NW; built c.10th cent.) became hq. of Mogul and Mahratta conquerors of Orissa; captured 1803 by British. City was former ⊙ Orissa (present ⊙ at Bhubaneswar).

Cutten, village, Humboldt co., NW Calif., just S of Eureka.

Cuttingsville, Vt.: see Shrewsbury.

Cuttyhunk Island, Mass.: see Elizabeth Islands.

Cutuco, Salvador: see La Unión, city.

Cutzamala (kōōtsämä'lä), officially Cutzamala de Pinzón, town (pop. 1,818), Guerrero, SW Mexico, on Cutzamala R., in Río de las Balsas basin, and 7 mi. NE of Altamirano; cereals, tobacco, coffee, sugar cane, fruit.

Cuvo River (kōō'vō), in W Angola, rises on Bié Plateau near Nova Lisboa, flows 210 mi. NW to the Atlantic S of Pôrto Amboim.

Cuxabexis Lake (kŭk"sůběk'sĭs), Piscataquis co., N central Maine, 47 mi. NNW of Greenville, in wilderness recreational area; 2 mi. long, 1 mi. wide. Stream connects with Chesuncook L. to SW.

Cuxhaven (kōōks-hä'fůn), city (1950 pop. 47,174), in former Prussian prov. of Hanover, NW Germany, after 1945 in Lower Saxony, North Sea tidal port at mouth of Elbe estuary, 22 mi. NNE of Bremerhaven; 53°53'N 8°42'E. Rail terminus; major fishing center; fish-processing industry; shipbuilding and -outfitting; mfg. of machinery, barrels, nets. Summer resort; tourist trade. Port installations include landing for small steamers and winter harbor for larger ocean vessels. Cuxhaven was harbor for Ritzebüttel, which was acquired by Hamburg in 1394. Inc. 1907 with neighboring Döse and chartered. Passed 1937 to Hanover prov. Frequently bombed by Allies in Second World War. Dike to Scharhörn isl. under construction. Sometimes spelled Kuxhaven.

Cuy, El, Argentina: see El Cuy.

Cuyabá, city, Brazil: see Cuiabá.

Cuyabá River, Brazil: see Cuiabá River.

Cuyaguateje River (kwēägwätā'hā) or **Guane River** (gwä'nā), Pinar del Río prov., W Cuba, rises in the Sierra de los Órganos, flows c.35 mi. S, past Guane, to the Ensenada de Cortés. Its upper course is partly subterranean.

Cuyahoga (kīhō'gů, –hô'gů, ků–, kīů–), county (□ 456; pop. 1,389,532), N Ohio; ⊙ Cleveland. Bounded N by L. Erie; drained by Cuyahoga and Rocky rivers. Agr. area (vegetables, poultry; dairying); mfg. (especially at Cleveland). Sand and gravel pits; salt wells. Formed 1810.

Cuyahoga Falls, city (pop. 29,195), Summit co., NE Ohio, just NE of Akron and on Cuyahoga R.; machinery, rubber products, tools, paper products, lumber, molds and dies, medical supplies. Inc. as village in 1868; became city in 1920.

Cuyahoga Heights, industrial village (pop. 713), Cuyahoga co., N Ohio, a S suburb of Cleveland; steel, aluminum, magnesium, and enamel products.

Cuyahoga River, NE Ohio, rises in Geauga co. near Chardon, flows SW to Cuyahoga Falls, thence N to L. Erie at Cleveland, where its mouth forms part of Cleveland's harbor; c.80 mi. long.

Cuyamaca Peak (kwēůmä'ků) (6,515 ft.), mountain in San Diego co., S Calif., 35 mi. ENE of San Diego, in state park (c.21,000 acres).

Cuyama River (kēä'mů, –ă'mů, kwē–, kōōyä'mů), SW Calif., rises in N Ventura co., flows c.85 mi. NW and SW, bet. the Coast Ranges, to Santa Maria R. just E of Santa Maria; flow is intermittent. Oil field in its valley was developed in 1948–49.

Cuyapo (kōōyäpō'), town (1939 pop. 5,122; 1948 municipality pop. 28,923), Nueva Ecija prov., central Luzon, Philippines, on railroad and 20 mi. NNE of Tarlac; rice, corn, tobacco.

Cuyavia, region, Poland: see Kujawy.

Cuyin Manzano, Sierra de (syĕ'rä dā kōō'yĭn mänsä'nō), spur of the Andes in S Neuquén natl. territory, Argentina, c.35 mi. long bet. L. Traful and L. Nahuel Huapí; rises to c.6,500 ft.

Cuyk (koik), town (pop. 3,450), North Brabant prov., E Netherlands, on Maas R. and 25 mi. E of 's Hertogenbosch; leather tanning; mfg. of industrial belting; stock-breeding center. Sometimes spelled Cuijk or Kuik.

Cuyoaco (kōōyōä'kō), town (pop. 737), Puebla, central Mexico, 24 mi. SW of Teziutlán; corn, maguey.

Cuyocuyo (kōōyōkōō'yō), town (pop. 809), Puno dept., SE Peru, on N slopes of Cordillera Oriental, 14 mi. SSW of Sandia; alt. 11,155 ft.; potatoes, quinoa, corn.

Cuyo East Pass (kōō'yō), channel bet. Cuyo Isls. and Panay, Philippines.

Cuyo Islands, archipelago (1948 pop. 22,445), in Palawan prov., Philippines, S of Mindoro, bet. Palawan (W) and Panay (E). Chiefly volcanic. Largest isl. is Cuyo (□ 22; c.9 mi. long), in S part of group, seat of chief town; 10°50'N 121°E. Other isls. include Agutaya, Quiniluban, Manamoc, and Putic. Trade and process rice and coconuts.

Cuyotenango (kōōyōtänäng'gō), town (1950 pop. 2,130), Suchitepéquez dept., SW Guatemala, in Pacific piedmont, on railroad and 4.5 mi. W of Mazatenango; coffee, sugar cane, grain, fodder grasses; livestock; lumbering.

Cuyo West Pass (kōō'yō), channel bet. Cuyo Isls. and Palawan, Philippines, bet. Sulu Sea (S) and Mindoro Strait (N).

Cuyuna (kůyōō'nů, kōōyōō'nů), village (pop. 112), Crow Wing co., central Minn., near Mississippi R., 18 mi. NE of Brainerd in region of woods and lakes. Iron mines near by in Cuyuna iron range.

Cuyuna Range, iron-mining area in Crow Wing co., central Minn., extends NE-SW along Mississippi R. bet. Aitkin and Brainerd. Manganiferous ore, mined here, used in production of spiegeleisen. First ore shipment took place in 1911. Chief mining point is Crosby.

Cuyuni River (kōōyōōnē'), Br. Guiana and Venezuela, rises in Venezuela in the Guiana Highlands near 6°N 61°30'W, flows a short distance N and then E, along the border and into Br. Guiana, through tropical forest region, past Aurora, to Mazaruni R. just before it joins the Essequibo 5 mi. W of Bartica; c.350 mi. long. Numerous rapids. Gold and diamonds along its course and its tributaries.

Cuyutlán (kōōyōōtlän'). 1 Town (pop. 2,168), Colima, W Mexico, 19 mi. ESE of Manzanillo, on a narrow strip of land bet. the Pacific and Cuyutlán Lagoon. Seaside resort. Major saltworks; fruitgrowing (bananas, limes, cacao). 2 Town (pop. 1,359), Jalisco, central Mexico, 19 mi. S of Guadalajara; wheat, corn, beans, chick-peas, livestock.

Cuzamá (kōōsämä'), town (pop. 960), Yucatan, SE Mexico, 25 mi. SE of Mérida; henequen.

Cuzco or **Cusco** (both: kōō'skō), department (□ 55,731; enumerated pop. 540,458, plus estimated 25,000 Indians), S and S central Peru; ⊙ Cuzco. Largely mountainous, and drained by Apurímac and Urubamba rivers, tributaries of the Amazon; here the Andes split into several high ranges (e.g., Cordillera de Carabaya, Cordillera de Vilcanota, Cordillera Vilcabamba). Climate ranges from tropical in N forests, to temperate in settled uplands, cool in high sierras. There is little mining of its minerals (gold, silver, copper, iron, mercury, tungsten, lead, kaolin, mica, asbestos, marble, salt, coal). Predominantly agr.; the high valleys grow wheat, barley, corn, potatoes, beans; the lower sections grow sugar cane, cotton, coffee, cacao, rice, coca, fruit; rubber in the montaña (N). Sheep, alpacas, vicuñas, and llamas are raised for their wool, which is exported, and from which also native textiles are made. Other industries include flour milling, sugar refining, liquor distilling, tanning—centered at Cuzco city. The region, formerly the heartland of the Inca empire, owes its fame to numerous archaeological treasures, among them the ruined city of Machupicchu, 50 mi. NW of Cuzco. Dept. set up 1822.

Cuzco or **Cusco,** city (pop. 45,158), ⊙ Cuzco dept. and Cuzco prov. (□118; pop. 60,679), S central Peru, in a deep Andean valley, on railroad from Puno, and 365 mi. ESE of Lima; 13°31'S 71°59'W; alt. 11,207 ft. The former ⊙ Inca empire, it is one of the most famed archaeological sites of the continent. Has a cool, pleasant climate (rains, Nov.–April). It is a communication and trading center (wool, hides, cacao, rubber, gold) of some importance; mfg. of woolen and cotton textiles, leather goods, soap, chocolate; breweries, soda-bottling plant, foundries, tanneries. Airport. Cuzco is immensely rich in historic and artistic treasures with a blending of anc. Inca and Hispanic colonial architecture. Among its noteworthy edifices are the lavishly decorated Temple of the Sun, now part of a Dominican monastery (severely damaged in 1950 earthquake); temples of the Moon, Stars, Thunder, Lightning, etc.; the cathedral (built 1564, reconstructed 1654); univ. (founded 1672) with archaeological mus.; many interesting churches and convents. The anc. Sacsahuamán fortress, in elevated N outskirts, commands the city. Cuzco was probably originally occupied by pre-Incan tribes, though it was founded, according to legend, by Manco Capac, first of the Incan dynasty. The city was taken by Pizarro in 1533, but declined shortly afterwards because of Incan rebellions and strife among the conquerors. Its population is still mainly Indian. With the discovery of other remarkable ruined cities in vicinity, Cuzco has become a mecca for tourists and students of history. Severely damaged by earthquakes, 1650, 1950. Just N of Cuzco are the Kencco or Kenco ruins of Inca origin; a former place of worship including temples, carved rocks (idols), and underground enclosures. Further N is Tambo Machay, an anc. Inca bathing resort with royal and public baths, galleries, terraces, and waterfalls.

Cuzcurrita-Río Tirón (kōōthkōōrē'tä-rē'ō tĕrōn'), town (pop. 1,032), Logroño prov., N Spain, 25 mi. WNW of Logroño; wine, vegetables, olive oil.

Cuzorn (küzôrn'), village (pop. 104), Lot-et-Garonne dept., SW France, 15 mi. NE of Villeneuve-sur-Lot; iron mining.

Cvikov (tsvĭ'kôf), Ger. *Zwickau* (tsvĭ'kou), town (pop. 2,995), N Bohemia, Czechoslovakia, on railroad and 27 mi. ENE of Usti nad Labem; glass mfg. (notably cut glass); textiles.

Cvrstnica, Velika; Cvrstnica, Mala, Yugoslavia: see VELIKA CVRSTNICA.

Cwmamman (kōōmă'mŭn), urban district (1931 pop. 5,217; 1951 census 4,593), SE Carmarthen, Wales. Includes coal-mining town of Glanamman, on Amman R. and 3 mi. ENE of Ammanford.

Cwmann, Wales: see LAMPETER.

Cwmavon (kōōmă'vŭn), town (pop. 5,583) in Port Talbot municipal borough, W central Glamorgan, Wales, on Afon R. and 2 mi. NE of Port Talbot; metallurgical and chemical industry. Just N is Foel (voil), hill (1,218 ft.) with large chimney, connected with metallurgical works by 1,100-yard flue.

Cwmbran (kōōmbrän'), urban district (1951 census pop. 13,162), S central Monmouth, England, 5 mi. N of Newport; coal mining, steel milling. Formed 1935 by combining Llanfrechfa Upper and Llantarnam, and designated as model residential community after Second World War.

Cwmdu, Wales: see MAESTEG.

Cwmduad, Wales: see CONWIL ELVET.

Cwm Nedd, Wales: see NEATH RIVER.

Cwmrheidol, Wales: see PONTERWYD.

Cwmsyfiog, England: see BEDWELLTY.

Cwmtillery, England: see ABERTILLERY.

Cybinka (tsĭbēn'kä), Ger. *Ziebingen* (tsē'bĭng-ŭn), town (1939 pop. 3,948; 1946 pop. 1,025) in Brandenburg, after 1945 in Zielona Gora prov., W Poland, near the Oder (E Germany border), 15 mi. SE of Frankfurt; agr. market (grain, potatoes, livestock). Chartered after 1945 and briefly spelled Cibinka.

Cyclades (sĭ'klŭdēz), Gr. *Kyklades* or *Kikladhes* (both: kĭklä'dhĭs) [=circular], Greek island group in Aegean Sea, regarded as circling around isl. of DELOS and extending SE from Attica and Euboea. The group forms a nome (□ 1,023; pop. 129,015; ⊙ Hermoupolis on SYROS isl.) of E central Greece. Largely mountainous, the isls. are composed of limestone, slate, and gneiss, except in S (MELOS, THERA), where they are of volcanic origin. Mild climate and light rainfall favor the production of wine, olive oil, figs, tobacco, citrus fruit. Mineral resources are of considerable importance: emery (NAXOS), Santorin earth, a volcanic tuff (Thera), marble (PAROS, TENOS), bauxite (AMORGOS), hematite (SERIPHOS), lead (SIPHNOS), and sulphur (Melos) are produced. Many of the N isls. quarry granite and furnish earths used as detergents since anc. times. According to tradition, the Cyclades were originally inhabited by Carians, later superseded by Minoans of Crete. Ionians occupied the N isls. c.1000 B.C., and Dorians from Laconia the southernmost volcanic isls. Variously ruled by Athens, Samos, and Naxos until Persian Wars. In 478–477, the isls. entered the Delian League under the leadership of Athens and were also enrolled (378–377) in the 2d Athenian Confederacy, ended by the rise of Macedon. In 3d cent. B.C. the isls. formed a separate League of Islanders, but suffered from the rivalries of Pergamum, Rhodes, and Syria. In 88 B.C. the isls. were reduced by Mithridates VI of Pontus. In the Middle Ages, most of the group constituted the Venetian Duchy of the Archipelago, with seat at Naxos; passed to Turks in 1566 and to Greece in 1832. The largest isls. are Naxos, ANDROS, Paros, Tenos, Melos, KEA, Amorgos, and Ios.

Cyclopean Islands, Sicily: see ACI CASTELLO.

Cyclops Mountains, N New Guinea, parallel the Pacific, extending c.20 mi. W from Hollandia to small Tanahmera Bay; rise to 7,086 ft. at Mt. Dafonsero. L. SENTANI is in S part of range. In Second World War, Jap. airfields in the area were taken (April, 1944) by U.S. forces. Sometimes spelled Cijcloop.

Cydnus, river, Turkey: see TARSUS RIVER.

Cydonia, Crete: see CANEA.

Cydweli, Wales: see KIDWELLY.

Cygnet (sĭg'nĭt), town and port (pop. 773), SE Tasmania, 23 mi. SSW of Hobart and on inlet of Huon R. estuary; fruit cannery. Small coal mines near by.

Cygnet, village (pop. 527), Wood co., NW Ohio, 9 mi. S of Bowling Green, in agr. area.

Cylinder, town (pop. 143), Palo Alto co., NW Iowa, 7 mi. E of Emmetsburg; livestock, grain.

Cyllene, Greece: see KYLLENE.

Cyme (sĭ'mē), anc. city of Aeolis, W Asia Minor, on Gulf of Candarli, 10 mi. ENE of Phocaea (modern Foca); according to Strabo, chief town of Aeolis.

Cymmer (kŭ'mŭr), town (pop. 4,738) in Glyncorwg urban dist., N central Glamorgan, Wales; coal mining.

Cymru: see WALES.

Cynfal River or **Cynfael River** (both: kŭn'văl), NW Merioneth, Wales, rises 4 mi. E of Ffestiniog, flows 6 mi. W to Dwyryd R. just W of Ffestiniog. Just S of Ffestiniog are Cynfal Falls, waterfalls noted for scenic beauty.

Cynon River (kŭ'nŏn), Glamorgan, Wales, rises 6 mi. NW of Aberdare, flows 18 mi. S and SE, past Aberdare, Aberaman, and Mountain Ash, to Taff R. 4 mi. SE Mountain Ash.

Cynoscephalae (sĭnŭsĕ'fŭlē, sĭnŭ–), Gr. *Kynos Kephalai* or *Kinos Kefalai* [=dog's heads], hills in SE Thessaly, Greece, rising to 2,382 ft. 14 mi. W of Volos. Here the Theban general Pelopidas was killed in battle in defeating (364 B.C.) Alexander, tyrant of Pherae, and the Roman consul Flamininus overwhelmed (197 B.C.) the army of Philip V of Macedon.

Cynthiana (sĭnthēă'nŭ). **1** Town (pop. 591), Posey co., SW Ind., 17 mi. NNW of Evansville, in agr. area. **2** City (pop. 4,847), ⊙ Harrison co., N Ky., on South Fork of Licking R. and 27 mi. NNE of Lexington, in Bluegrass agr. area (burley tobacco, livestock, dairy products, poultry). Distillery, tobacco warehouses; mfg. of soft drinks, dairy products, fertilizer, clothing, harness; flour, feed, and lumber milling. Stone quarries near by. Raided (1862, 1864) by Gen. John Hunt Morgan in Civil War. Points of interest: log house (1790) where Henry Clay appeared as a lawyer; covered bridge (c.1837); burying ground (established 1793). Founded 1793; inc. 1806.

Cynwyd, Pa.: see BALA-CYNWYD.

Cyparissiae, Greece: see KYPARISSIA.

Cypress. 1 Village (pop. 1,318), Orange co., S Calif., 10 mi. ENE of Long Beach; truck, dairy farms. **2** Town (pop. 262), Jackson co., NW Fla., 10 mi. ESE of Marianna, in agr. area. **3** Village (pop. 357), Johnson co., S Ill., 26 mi. NNE of Cairo, in rich agr. area.

Cypress, Point, Calif.: see MONTEREY PENINSULA.

Cypress Bayou (bī'ō) or **Cypress Creek,** in NE Texas and NW La., formed by headstreams rising N of Winnsboro, Texas; flows c.120 mi. generally SE, past Jefferson, to W end of Caddo L.; sometimes considered to continue from E end of Caddo L., through several bayous and channels, to Red R. at Shreveport, La. On it are sites of reservoirs of Red R. flood-control project: Ferrells Bridge Reservoir, 8 mi. W of Jefferson, Texas; and Mooringsport Reservoir, below Caddo L. and NW of Shreveport. Also called Big Cypress Bayou.

Cypress Hills, range, SW Sask. and SE Alta., extends 100 mi. E–W along Mont. border SE of Medicine Hat; rises to 4,810 ft. 30 mi. SE of Medicine Hat. In E part of range is the Shaunavon coal-mining area.

Cypress River, village (pop. estimate 300), SW Man., on Cypress R. and 45 mi. ESE of Brandon; grain, stock, poultry; lumbering.

Cyprus (sĭ'prŭs), Gr. *Kypros* (kē'prôs), British colony (□ 3,572; pop. 450,114), 3d largest Mediterranean isl. (after Sicily and Sardinia); ⊙ NICOSIA. It lies in E part of the Mediterranean, c.40 mi. S of Turkey, just outside the Gulf of Iskenderun, and c.65 mi. W of Syria, bet. 34°33'–35°41'N and 32°17'–34°35'E. Greatest length E–W, 140 mi.; greatest breadth, 60 mi. The port cities of Larnaca, Famagusta, and Akrotiri are on the principle bays which indent the coast. Long, narrow KARPAS PENINSULA (NE) projects c.50 mi. Among coastal promontories are Cape ANDREAS (NE), Cape GRECO (E), Cape GATA (S), Cape ARNAUTI (W), Cape KORMAKITI (N). Largely mountainous, the isl. is traversed by 2 ranges. The KYRENIA MOUNTAINS stretch for more than 100 mi. along the N coast. Loftier and older are the wooded OLYMPUS MOUNTAINS of the center, rising in Mt. TROODOS to 6,406 ft. The Olympus Mts., because of their cool summer climate, are a popular resort area (e.g., Pano PLATRES, PRODHROMOS, KAKOPETRIA, KALOPANAYIOTIS). They are also the principal mining region. Bet. these 2 ridges extends the fertile MESSAORIA depression, occupying about ⅓ of the isl. and representing the principal agr. area, centered on Nicosia. There are many rivers, mostly mountain streams, which are torrential in winter but run dry during the summer. Largest is PEDIAS RIVER, now feeding several reservoirs in lowland of Famagusta dist. (E). In the plains during the hot, dry summer, Messaoria takes on a sun-scorched appearance and irrigation becomes a main concern. Mean temp. is 66.7°F. Average rainfall—mostly Oct. to March—c.21 inches. Coniferous forests in elevated section largely depleted, still cover about ⅙ of entire area. Fairly rich in minerals, Cyprus has been known since anc. times for its copper [the word *copper* is derived from Cyprus]. Most important today are its iron-pyrite deposits (EVRYKHOU VALLEY, KALAVASOS). Cyprus also ships asbestos (AMIANDOS) chromite (Troodos), gypsum, terra umbra, ocher and zinc and copper concentrates. Salt is evaporated from saline ponds in LIMASSOL and LARNACA dists. Sponge fishing is carried on along the coast. Agr., however, dominates the isl.'s economy. About ½ of the land is cultivated. Principal crops are wheat, oats, barley, olives, cotton, tobacco; also potatoes, onions, beans, peas, raisins, flax, hemp, carobs, vetches, grapes, citrus fruit, pomegranates, almonds. Deciduous fruit are grown in the uplands. Cyprus wines enjoy a wide repute. Stock raising (sheep, goats, cattle, draught oxen, horses, mules, donkeys) is extensive, and mules find a ready market in countries of the Middle East. Spirits, cheese, olive oil, flax fibers, wool, and silk are among processed products. Though there is little industry, vegetable oils, buttons, artificial teeth, embroidery, and needlework are exported. Chief imports include cereals, dairy products, sugar, coffee, cigarettes, timber, pottery, glassware, iron, textiles, shoes, electrical appliances, machinery, vehicles, petroleum products, fertilizers, chemicals, paper. The trade balance is unfavorable. Trading and processing centers, besides Nicosia, are the ports FAMAGUSTA, LARNACA, LIMASSOL, KYRENIA, and PAPHOS, also capitals of their respective dists. The isl. has a net of fine highways converging on Nicosia. A railroad from Famagusta traverses the Messaoria plain via the capital. Cyprus is served by international air and shipping lines, linking it closely with countries of the Middle East. Schools are organized according to religious denominations, which roughly correspond to ethnic and linguistic divisions. The population included, according to 1946 census, 361,373 Greek Orthodox, 80,361 Moslems (Turks), and 3,686 Armenians. Illiteracy is over 40%, and there are no institutions of higher learning. Nicosia has a noted mus. testifying to Cyprus' colorful past. The isl. is a veritable treasure house of archaeological remains, ranging from Aphrodite temples to Gothic churches, Lusignan castles, Roman forums, mosques, and monasteries. Its ruined cities—AMATHUS, CITIUM, IDALIUM, CURIUM, SALAMIS, SOLI—were flourishing centers in antiquity. Excavations have proved the existence of a neolithic culture c.3000–4000 B.C., and several settlements are of Mycenaean origin. After 1500 B.C., contacts with Greece and Egypt are recorded. Phoenicians settled on the isl. c.800 B.C. Cyprus subsequently fell under Assyrian, Egyptian, and Persian rule. About 500 B.C. the Greek cities joined in revolt against Persians. Passed to Alexander the Great in 333 B.C. and to the Romans in 1st cent. B.C. Was later given by Antony to Cleopatra. Eventually became part of the Eastern Roman Empire. The apostles Paul and Barnabas introduced Christianity. Arab invasion began in 7th cent. In 1191 Richard I (Richard Lion-Heart) took Cyprus from the Byzantine Empire, and in 1192 it was bestowed as a kingdom on Guy of Lusignan, whose heirs ruled the isl. until 1489, when it was taken by Venice. The Turks conquered it in 1571. Placed (1878) under British administration, it was upon outbreak of First World War annexed (1914) by Britain. Formally made a colony in 1925. Legislative council was, because of disturbances, abolished (1931). Isl. became a stronghold for Br. navy during Second World War, when it suffered several air raids. A proposal (1947) for a more liberal govt. was rejected by a majority of the people, who instead demanded to be united with Greece. In 1945–49 Cyprus was used as a detention camp for "illegal" Jewish immigrants to Palestine. For further information see separate articles on the towns, regional and physical features, and the 6 districts.

Cypsela, Turkey: see IPSALA.

Cyr (sēr), plantation (pop. 256), Aroostook co., NE Maine, just S of Van Buren, 27 mi. N of Presque Isle.

Cyrenaica (sĭrŭnā'ĭkŭ, sĭrŭ–), Arabic *Barqa* or *Barqah*, Ital. *Cirenaica,* E division (□ c.300,000; 1947 pop. estimate 310,000) of LIBYA, on the Mediterranean; ⊙ BENGHAZI. Bounded E by Egypt and W by TRIPOLITANIA, it extends S deep into the Sahara (Libyan Desert), and includes the Kufra oases and part of the Tibesti Massif; it has desert boundaries with Anglo-Egyptian Sudan (SE) and Chad territory of Fr. Equatorial Africa (S). Pop. is concentrated in coastal area bet. Benghazi and Derna and in Gebel el AKHDAR plateau just S, where annual rainfall reaches 16 in. Here agr. settlements (Beda Littoria, Maddalena, Oberdan) were established by Italians in 1930s. Chief agr. products are barley, wheat, olives, grapes; dates from Gialo and Kufra oases. Nomadic stock raising (goats, sheep, camels) is principal occupation of Arab pop. Chief towns (Tobruk, Derna, Cyrene,

Barce, Benghazi) are linked by coastal highway which continues S and W along Gulf of Sidra to Tripoli. In the Benghazi plain, short rail lines (100 mi.) link Benghazi, Barce, and Soluch. Caravan tracks lead to the Saharan oases. Pop. is 98% Moslem; in 1947, there remained 4,580 Jews, less than 200 Italians. Coastal area was 1st settled by Greeks who founded Cyrene 631 B.C. After death of Alexander the Great, it passed to Ptolemies, who left it to Rome in 96 B.C. Became (67 B.C.) a Roman prov. (Cyrene or Cyrenaica) which included Crete. Conquered by Moslems in 7th cent. A.D. Nominally under Ottoman Empire bet. 16th cent. and 1911–12, when it became part of Ital. colony of Libya. Scene of seesaw battles bet. British and Axis forces during N African campaigns (1940–42) of Second World War. Under Br. military administration since 1942, Cyrenaica was designated one of the constituent units (Tripolitania and Fezzan are the others) of an independent federal kingdom of Libya established under U.N. auspices by 1952. The ruler of the Senusi (residing at Benghazi) was proclaimed (1950) king of Libya.

Cyrene (sīrē'nē), Arabic *Shahat*, Ital. *Cirene*, town (pop. 494), W Cyrenaica, Libya, on coastal road and 8 mi. SW of Apollonia; apiculture. Summer resort (alt. 2,037 ft.) with archaeological mus. and extensive Greek and Roman ruins, including temples (notably that of Apollo), baths, gymnasium, theater, necropolises, acropolis. Founded as a Greek colony, 631 B.C., by colonists from Thera and Crete, it was the original capital of Cyrenaica. Passed to the Ptolemies and later (96 B.C.) the Romans. Carried on important trade with Greece and Egypt; its port was Apollonia. Had noted medical school and was famous center of learning. Aristippus, Callimachus, Eratosthenes, and Synesius b. here. Bombed 1941 in Second World War.

Cyril (sī'rŭl), town (pop. 998), Caddo co., W central Okla., 18 mi. SW of Chickasha, in cotton-, wheat-, and oil-producing area; oil refining.

Cyrnus, France: see CORSICA.

Cyrus, river, Iran: see KUR RIVER.

Cyrus (sī'rŭs), village (pop. 363), Pope co., W Minn., on Chippewa R. and 17 mi. WSW of Glenwood, in grain and livestock area; dairy products, feed.

Cyrus River, Azerbaijan SSR: see KURA RIVER.

Cysoing (sēzwē'), town (pop. 2,420), Nord dept., N France, 8 mi. SE of Lille, near Belg. border; linen and cotton cloth weaving, tanning.

Cythera, Greece: see KYTHERA.

Cythnus, Greece: see KYTHNOS.

Cyzicus (sĭ'zĭkŭs), ancient city, at neck of Cyzicus Peninsula (modern Kapidagi), NW Turkey. Strategically situated, it rivaled Byzantium in commercial importance. Founded 756 B.C. by Greek colonist from Miletus, it was a member of the Delian League. Remained a free city under Roman rule until A.D. 25. In 410 B.C. Alcibiades defeated a Spartan fleet off Cyzicus, and in 74 B.C. the city withstood a siege by Mithridates VI of Pontus. Cyzicus was largely destroyed by the Arabs in A.D. 675. There are ruins of a large temple built by Emperor Hadrian and of other public buildings.

Cyzicus Peninsula, Turkey: see KAPIDAGI PENINSULA.

Czaplinek (chäplē'nĕk), Ger. *Tempelburg* (tĕm'pŭlbōork), town (1939 pop. 5,275; 1946 pop. 3,459) in Pomerania, after 1945 in Koszalin prov., NW Poland, on S shore of Drawsko L., 25 mi. WSW of Szczecinek; dairying; grain and cattle market. Founded late-13th cent. by Teutonic Knights. Until 1938, in former Prussian prov. of Grenzmark Posen–Westpreussen.

Czar (zär), village (pop. 121), E Alta., 26 mi. S of Wainwright; grain, mixed farming.

Czarna Hancza River (chär'nä hä'nyŭchä), Pol. *Czarna Hańcza*, Rus. *Chernaya Gansha* (chĭrnī'ŭ gän'shŭ), in NE Poland and W Belorussian SSR, rises 15 mi. NNW of Suwalki, Poland; flows SSE, past Suwalki, through L. Wigry, and E to Neman R. near Lith. border 15 mi. N of Grodno; 84 mi. long. Linked with Biebrza R. via Augustow Canal; part of Neman-Vistula waterway.

Czarna Prsemsza River (–pshĕm'shä), S Poland, rises just E of Zawierce, flows W and S, past Bedzin, Sosnowice, and Myslowice, joining the Biala Przemsza just SE of Myslowice to form Przemsza R.; 35 mi. long.

Czarna Woda, river, Poland: see WDA RIVER.

Czarne (chär'nĕ), Ger. *Hammerstein* (hä'mŭr-shtīn), town (1939 pop. 4,387; 1946 pop. 1,453) in Pomerania, after 1945 in Koszalin prov., NW Poland, 11 mi. E of Szczecinek; dairying; grain, livestock. Until 1938, in former Prussian prov. of Grenzmark Posen–Westpreussen.

Czarnkow (chärn'kōof), Pol. *Czarnków*, Ger. *Czarnikau* (chär'nĭkou), town (1946 pop. 4,394), Poznan prov., W Poland, on Notec R. and 38 mi. NNW of Poznan; cement mfg., flour milling, sawmilling, brewing; swine and grain trade.

Czarnohora, Ukrainian SSR: see CHERNAGORA.

Czarny Dunajec River, Poland: see DUNAJEC RIVER.

Czartorysk, Ukrainian SSR: see CHARTORISK.

Czaslau, Czechoslovakia: see CASLAV.

Czchow (chŭ-khōof'), Pol. *Czchów*, village, Krakow prov., S Poland, 15 mi. N of Nowy Sacz and on Dunajec R.; hydroelectric station.

Czechoslovakia (chĕk"ōslōvä'kēŭ, –vä'kēŭ), Czech *Československo* (chĕs'kōslō"vĕnskō), republic (□ 49,354; 1948 pop. 12,196,730), E central Europe; ⊙ PRAGUE. Since Dec., 1948, administratively divided into 2 sections: the Czech Lands (*České Země*), comprising the historic provs. of BOHEMIA, MORAVIA, and SILESIA; and the semi-autonomous SLOVAKIA (see the articles on these regions for detailed descriptions of history, geography, and economy). These are subdivided into 19 "regions." Its borders with surrounding countries are marked by natural boundaries: NW by the ERZGEBIRGE (Ore Mts.) on German Saxony, W by the Bohemian Forest on German Bavaria, N by the SUDETES and the CARPATHIANS on Poland (which returned the Czech section of TESCHEN after Second World War), S by the Danube on Austria and Hungary. Its former E prov. of RUTHENIA or Carpatho-Ukraine was inc. (1945) into the Ukrainian SSR. With a total frontier mileage of 3,553 mi. and greatest E-W extension of 418 mi., it is situated bet. 47°44'–51°3'N and 12°5'–22°34'E. Forests, which cover about ⅓ of the country, yield timber, wood pulp, paper, and naval stores. The heavily wooded Hercynian massifs enclose rolling peneplains—generally below 1,500 ft.—disrupted by fertile river valleys and traverse mtn. blocks, such as the BOHEMIAN-MORAVIAN HEIGHTS bet. Bohemia and Moravia and the Little Carpathians and White Carpathians, which merge with the BESKIDS bet. Moravia and Slovakia. The High Tatra, S of main Carpathian range, forms a separate knot of Alpine grandeur (favorite winter-sports area), reaching in Stalin Peak (8,737 ft.; formerly the Gerlachovka) the highest elevation of the republic. Through the navigable upper Elbe (NW), with its affluent, the Vltava (Moldau), and through the Oder (N) and the Danube (S), it has outlet to North Sea, Baltic Sea, and Black Sea respectively. Oder and Danube basins are linked bet. the Sudetes and Carpathians by the historic Moravian Gate, at whose entrance lies Moravska OSTRAVA. Though physiographically well defined, the country varies considerably culturally, socially, and climatologically from W to E. In climate the temperate W section shows an Atlantic influence; this becomes increasingly continental towards the E. Differences in temp. depend, however, largely on elevation. The shielded plains consitute the most equable sections, especially the Danube depression in the S, where grapes and corn thrive. Northernmost vineyards of Central Europe are near LITOMERICE (Bohemia). Winters are dry, with a comparatively low rainfall (c.20 in.), mostly in fall and spring. But there occur heavy snowfalls in the highlands. Annual mean temp. (1946 figures) is 48.9°F. at Prague and 51.6°F. at BRATISLAVA. Although it is heavily industrialized and has rich mineral resources, agr. plays an equal role, employing c.35% of the people, as do industry and mining. Bohemia, the country's most progressive part (it was the workshop, even, of the Austrian Empire), employs most intensive farming methods. About 50% of entire land is arable. The greater part of the agr. yield (c.60% of all crops) is grain (barley, wheat, rye, oats). Leading industrial crops are sugar beets, mostly in Moravia; followed by hops and malt (ZATEC, HANA region). Stock raising, dairying, and poultry farming are important. Apart from mineral and industrial output, Czechoslovakia exports barley, malt, hops, sugar; logs, timber, and pulp. It imports wheat, corn, lard, and pork. On its mineral resources depend the large-scale industries for which Czechoslovakia is world famous. Most important are the coal fields (bituminous and lignite) centered in Ostrava-KARVINA basin (Teschen), near ROSICE-OSLAVANY (S Silesia), and near PILSEN (Bohemia) and BRNO (Moravia). Iron ore is extracted from BEROUN basin SW of Prague, Silesia, and from the SLOVAK ORE MOUNTAINS. Other mineral resources, of secondary importance, include magnesite, copper, lead, antimony, silver, gold, mercury, vanadium, tin; limestone, semiprecious stones, natural gas. There are some oil wells near GBELY (Slovakia) and HODONIN (Moravia). JACHYMOV (Joachimsthal) in the Erzgebirge, long famous for its silver mines, has pitchblende ores containing radium and uranium. On near-by kaolin deposits is based the chinaware mfg. at CARLSBAD (Karlovy Vary). Prague, the leading city in culture, commerce, and industry, is outstanding for its baroque architecture and historic associations. Its varied industries include the mfg. of automobiles, gloves, chemicals, and motion pictures. Brno, the nation's 2d city, is the foremost textile center. Linen and cotton goods are made at LIBERICE and TRUTNOV. Leading steelworks are at Ostrava; also at CHOMUTOV. Pilsen, known for its beer, is site of the Skoda armament plants. Glass and crystal mfg. at JABLONEC, TEPLICE, and USTI NAD LABEM—the last, the chief port on the Elbe. GOTTWALDOV (formerly Zlin), capital of the shoe industry, also has mfg. of hosiery and rubber goods. BUDWEIS (Ceske Budejovice), with its graphite mines, turns out pencils; NOVY JICIN, hats; PROSTEJOV, clothing; KOSICE, wood pulp; MOST, synthetic gasoline. Bratislava, ⊙ Slovakia and republic's principal Danube port, has oil refining, shipbuilding, woodworking, printing, food processing, and metallurgical plants. The country is famed for its resorts and spas, among them Carlsbad, FRANTISKOVY LAZNE or Francensbad, MARIENBAD (Marianske Lazne), Jachymov, PODEBRADY, LUHACOVICE, PIESTANY, and TRENCIANSKE TEPLICE. There are univs. at Prague (famous Charles Univ., founded 1348), Brno, Bratislava, and OLOMOUC, some of which have faculties at HRADEC KRALOVE, Pilsen, and Ceske Budejovice; there are also several technical and theological institutions of higher learning. Mining acad. at Ostrava; agr. col. at Kosice. The countryside of Czechoslovakia, rich in scenic and historic sites, is dotted with medieval castles. Romanesque, Gothic, and baroque gems adorn the many old towns. An heir to the ethnic heterogeneity of the Austrian Empire, Czechoslovakia has included, since its emergence (1918) as separate state, large minorities of Germans, Hungarians, Poles, and Ruthenians. Even the closely related Slavic races of the Czechs and Slovaks show a great diversity. The Czechs represent the more enterprising section, with the lowest rate of illiteracy. There are now about 8,088,000 Czechs, 3,131,000 Slovaks, 115,000 Ukrainians, 85,000 Poles, 197,000 Germans, and 450,000 Hungarians. The majority belong to the R.C. church, but there are large Protestant (notably Hussite) groups in Bohemia and Moravia, and Orthodox Eastern and Uniate churches in Slovakia. During First World War Czech units fought on the Allied side. The liberation of Czechoslovakia from Austrian rulers was largely accomplished by its 1st and 2d presidents—T. G. Masaryk and Eduard Benes. Advent of Hitler to power in Germany sharpened the nationality problem and encouraged separatistic tendencies. By the Munich Pact (Sept., 1938) Czechoslovakia's allies gave the German-speaking Bohemian borderlands (SUDETENLAND) to Germany. Poland and Hungary shared in the spoils. In March, 1939, Germany dismantled the country by establishing Bohemia and Moravia as a protectorate, giving Slovakia short-lived independence, and transferring Ruthenia to Hungary. After outbreak of Second World War, Benes set up a provisional govt. in London. Czech contingents fought again on the Allied side. Though the country suffered under the harsh Ger. rule (the infamous LIDICE massacre is an instance), it was comparatively little damaged by the war. In April, 1944, Russian forces entered E Czechoslovakia, American forces entered (May, 1945) the W. The Potsdam Conference (1945) decreed the expulsion of c.3,-000,000 Germans and exchange of minorities with Hungary. In 1946 Communists emerged as the strongest single party, and, though still a minority, seized (Feb., 1948) control by means of a coup d'état. A new constitution on the Soviet model provided for a unicameral legislature. In 1950 about 97% of all industries were nationalized. For further information, see separate articles on the provs., cities, towns, and physical features.

Czecze, Hungary: see CECE.

Czegled, Hungary: see CEGLED.

Czeladz (chĕ'läj), Pol. *Czeladź*, Rus. *Chelyadz* (chĕl'yäj), town (pop. 16,624), Katowice prov., S Poland, 5 mi. NE of Katowice; coal mining; mfg. of bricks, ceramics; lime kiln.

Czelldömölk, Hungary: see CELLDÖMÖLK.

Czempin (chĕm'pēnyū), Pol. *Czempiń*, town (1946 pop. 2,380), Poznan prov., W Poland, 7 mi. NE of Koscian; rail junction; mfg. (agr. machinery, oxygen, brushes, candy, flour).

Czeremosz River, Ukrainian SSR: see CHEREMOSH RIVER.

Czernelica, Ukrainian SSR: see CHERNELITSA.

Czerniejewo (chĕrnyĕyĕ'vō), Ger. *Schwarzenau* (shvär'tsŭnou), town (1946 pop. 1,273), Poznan prov., W central Poland, 24 mi. E of Poznan. Castle ruins.

Czernina (chĕrnē'nä), Ger. *Lesten* (lĕ'stŭn), town (1939 pop. 840; 1946 pop. 1,860) in Lower Silesia, after 1945 in Wroclaw prov., W Poland, 9 mi. S of Leszno; agr. market (grain, sugar beets, potatoes, livestock). Until 1937, called Tschirnau.

Czernowitz, Ukrainian SSR: see CHERNOVTSY, city.

Czersk (chĕrsk), town (pop. 7,092), Bydgoszcz prov., NW Poland, 18 mi. ENE of Chojnice; rail junction; mfg. of furniture, bricks; distilling, brewing, flour milling.

Czestochowa (chĕstô-khô'vä), Pol. *Częstochowa*, Ger. *Tschenstochau* (chĕn"shtōkh'ou), Rus. *Chenstokhov* (chĕnstŭ-khôf'), city (pop. 101,255), Katowice prov., S Poland, on Warta R., on Warsaw-Vienna RR and 125 mi. SW of Warsaw. Rail junction; major industrial center at E end of iron-mining dist.; airport; ironworks; mfg. of bicycles, cotton textiles, hats, paper, chemicals, glass; food processing, sawmilling; cement mfg. near by. City is quadrangle-shaped; includes Nowa Czestochowa [New Czestochowa] (W, at foot of 938-ft. Jasna Gora [mountain of light]), its trade and tourist center, and Stara Czestochowa [Old Czestochowa] (E), which developed around its market place. Its 2 sections are connected by a mi.-long avenue along which the city has developed. Its monastery, on Jasna Gora, has in its chapel an image of the Virgin, supposedly painted by St. Luke, brought here in 14th cent.; attracts c.200,000 pilgrims yearly. In

1655, the monastery was successfully defended for 40 days against outnumbering Swedish soldiers; the image has since been venerated as the "Queen of Poland" and a symbol of natl. survival. Czestochowa was (1815–1919) in Rus. Poland. Although a battlefield in 1939, it suffered relatively little damage in Second World War. With enlargement of old ironworks (built 1895–99) after the Second World War, the city became one of Poland's chief iron and steel centers; construction of a new residential city was also begun near the steel mill.

Czlopa (chwô'pä), Pol. *Człopa*, Ger. *Schloppe* (shlô'pů), town (1939 pop. 2,986; 1946 pop. 715) in Pomerania, after 1945 in Koszalin prov., NW Poland, 25 mi. WSW of Schneidemühl (Pila); grain, sugar beets, potatoes, livestock; furniture mfg. Until 1938, in former Prussian prov. of Grenzmark Posen-Westpreussen.

Czluchow (chwōō'khōōf), Pol. *Człuchów*, Ger. *Schlochau* (shlôkh'ou), town (1939 pop. 6,029; 1946 pop. 3,711) in Pomerania, after 1945 in Koszalin prov., NW Poland, 30 mi. E of Szczecinek; rail junction; agr. market (grain, sugar beets, potatoes, livestock); sawmilling. Until 1938, in former Prussian prov. of Grenzmark Posen-Westpreussen; was (1919–39) Ger. frontier station on Pol. border. In the Second World War, c.60% of Czluchow was destroyed.

Czorsztyn (chôr'shtĕn), village, Krakow prov., S Poland, at foot of the Pieniny, 12 mi. ESE of Nowy Targ and on the Dunajec R.; site of a hydroelectric station.

Czortkow, Ukrainian SSR: see CHORTKOV.

D

Daanbantayan (dä-än'bäntäyän'), town (1939 pop. 1,418; 1948 municipality pop. 29,484), extreme N Cebu isl., Philippines, on Visayan Sea, 65 mi. NNE of Cebu city; corn, coconuts. Oil deposits in area.

Dab, Lake, Poland: see DAMM LAKE.

Daba, in Nigerian names: see DEBE.

Daba, Saudi Arabia: see DHABA.

Daba, El, Ed Daba, or **Al-Dab'ah** (all: ĕd dä'bů), town (1937 pop. 3,219), Western Desert prov., N Egypt, on coastal railroad and 85 mi. W of Alexandria. Airfield. An important objective (1941–42) in fighting during Second World War.

Dabajuro (däbähōō'rō), town (pop. 896), Falcón state, NW Venezuela, in Gulf of Venezuela lowland, 10 mi. SSW of Capatárida; goat grazing.

Dabakala (däbäkä'lä), village (pop. c.1,600), central Ivory Coast, Fr. West Africa, 45 mi. ENE of Katiola; produces essential oil from lemons.

Dabaro (däbä'rō), village, in the Mudugh, central Ital. Somaliland, on road and 70 mi. NNE of Obbia.

Dabasun Nor, China: see YENHAI TZE.

Dabat (dä'bät), village, Begemdir prov., NW Ethiopia, 31 mi. NE of Gondar.

Dabba, Saudi Arabia: see DHABA.

Dabeiba (däbä'bä), town (pop. 1,827), Antioquia dept., NW central Colombia, in valley of Cordillera Occidental, 45 mi. NW of Antioquia, in agr. region (coffee, cotton, hogs); alt. 4,429 ft. Cotton ginning, lumbering. Agr. research station.

Dabein (dä'băn), village, Insein dist., Lower Burma, on Pegu R. and 20 mi. NE of Rangoon, on railroad to Mandalay.

Daber, Poland: see DOBRA, Szczecin prov.

Dabhoi (dŭboi'), town (pop. 21,139), Baroda dist., N Bombay, India, 16 mi. SE of Baroda; rail junction; trades in cotton, rice, millet; cotton ginning, handicraft cloth weaving, wood carving, liquor distilling; copper and brass products. Noted carvings on gateways represent incarnations of Vishnu.

Dabie (dō'byĕ), Pol. *Dąbie*. **1** Rus. *Dombe* (dôm'byĕ), town (1946 pop. 2,628), Poznan prov., central Poland, on Ner R. and 35 mi. NW of Lodz; rail spur terminus; brewing, flour milling, liqueur mfg. **2** Ger. *Altdamm* (ält'däm), town (1939 pop. 11,982; 1946 pop. 1,366) in Pomerania, after 1945 in Szczecin prov., NW Poland, at S end of Damm L., 6 mi. ESE of Stettin. Rail junction; port; airport; potato-flour milling, food processing. Founded 1176; was fortress, 1249–1872. Inc. 1939 into Stettin; rechartered after 1945 and briefly called Dab Stary, Pol. *Dąb Stary*. After Second World War, evacuated by Ger. pop.

Dab'iya, El, Ed Dab'iya, or **Al-Dab'iyah** (all: ĕd däbē'yů), village (pop. 7,203), Qena prov., Upper Egypt, on W bank of the Nile and 5 mi. SW of Luxor; cereals, sugar cane, dates.

Dabo (däbō'), Ger. *Dagsburg* (däks'bŏŏrk), village (pop. 1,200), Moselle dept., NE France, in the N Vosges, 9 mi. SW of Saverne; resort in wooded area.

Dabo, Indonesia: see SINGKEP.

Dabo, W Pakistan: see HYDERABAD, city.

Dabola (däbō'lä), town (pop. c.3,800), central Fr. Guinea, Fr. West Africa, on Tinkisso R. (Niger affluent), on railroad, and 195 mi. ENE of Conakry. Exports honey, beeswax, hides, indigo, tobacco, rubber, peanuts.

Dabosingkep, Indonesia: see SINGKEP.

Dabou (dä'bōō), town (pop. c.4,600), S Ivory Coast, Fr. West Africa, landing on N shore of Ebrié Lagoon (Atlantic inlet), 25 mi. W of Abidjan; agr. center trading in palm oil and kernels; hardwood. Brickmaking. Customhouse.

Dabovo (dŭ'bôvô), village (pop. 2,120), Stara Zagora dist., central Bulgaria, in Kazanlik Basin, 12 mi. N of Stara Zagora; rail junction; grain, horticulture (roses, mint); chestnut groves. Oil-shale deposits E. Formerly Yaikanlii.

Daboya (däbō'yä), village, Northern Territories, N central Gold Coast, on White Volta R. and 40 mi. WNW of Tamale (linked by road); saltworking center.

Dabra, India: see PICHHOR.

Dabrowa Gornicza (dōbrô'vä gōōrnē'chä), Pol. *Dąbrowa Górnicza*, Rus. *Dombrova* (dŭmbrô'vŭ), city (1946 pop. 28,070), Katowice prov., S Poland, 9 mi. ENE of Katowice, just E of Bedzin. Rail junction; coal mines (dating from 1796), iron and zinc foundries; lumbering, food processing. Passed (1795) to Prussia and (1815) to Rus. Poland; returned 1919 to Poland. In 1937, pop. was 40,854.

Dabrowa Tarnowska (tärnôf'skä), Pol. *Dąbrowa Tarnowska*, town (pop. 4,520), Krakow prov., S Poland, 11 mi. N of Tarnow.

Dabrowica, Ukrainian SSR: see DUBROVITSA.

Dabrowno (dōbrôv'nô), Pol. *Dąbrowno*, Ger. *Gilgenburg* (gĭl'gůnbŏŏrk), town (1939 pop. 1,722; 1946 pop. 427) in East Prussia, after 1945 in Olsztyn prov., NE Poland, on small lake, 13 mi. SW of Allenstein (Olsztyn); grain and cattle market. Castle established here (1319) by Teutonic Knights. Was (1919–39) Ger. frontier station on Pol. border, 15 mi. NW of Dzialdowo.

Dab Stary, Poland: see DABIE, Szczecin prov.

Dabus River (dä'bōōs), Wallaga prov., W central Ethiopia, rises in highlands near Gadame, flows c.135 mi. NE to the Blue Nile 25 mi. E of Belfodio. Valley contains gold deposits mined E of Asosa.

Dabwali (dŭbvä'lē), town (pop. 6,655), Hissar dist., S Punjab, India, 80 mi. NW of Hissar; millet, cotton, gram, wheat; cotton ginning, mfg. of photographic materials. Sometimes called Nai Dab Wali.

Dacca (dăk'ů, dä'kŭ), district (□ 2,738; 1951 pop. 4,089,000), E central East Bengal, E Pakistan; ⊙ Dacca. Bounded W by Jamuna (main course of the Brahmaputra), E by Meghna, and S by Padma (Ganges) rivers; drained by Dhaleswari R. and its tributaries. Dist. subject to severe river inundations. Alluvial soil; rice, jute, oilseeds, sugar cane, wheat, tobacco, betel leaf. Madhupur Jungle in N; sal timber. Industrial centers at NARAYANGANJ (cotton-milling center) and Dacca (formerly known for hand-woven muslins); jute pressing, shipbuilding, mfg. of hosiery, chemicals, electrical supplies, buttons, glass, matches, filigreed silver, shell bracelets, ice; leather tanning; ironworks, general-engineering factories; rice milling (Madanganj), sugar milling (Kaliganj), cotton ginning and baling, oilseed milling; rail workshops. Besides city of Dacca, Rampal and Sonargaon were important old capitals and cultural centers. Dacca dist. was part of former Br. Bengal prov., India, until inc. 1947 into Pakistan prov. of East Bengal, following creation of Pakistan. Formerly spelled Dhaka.

Dacca, city (1941 pop., including administration area Ramna, 213,218), ⊙ East Bengal prov. and Dacca dist., E Pakistan, on Burhi Ganga R. (arm of the Dhaleswari) and 150 mi. NE of Calcutta; 23°43'N 90°25'E. Trade (rice, jute, oilseeds, hides, sugar cane) and industrial center; mfg. of shell bracelets, hand-woven muslin, silver filigree, chemicals, buttons, glass, matches, hosiery, electrical supplies, ice; jute pressing, leather tanning; oilseed; railroad shops. Airport. In late-19th cent., competition of British cloth virtually destroyed the mfg. of city's world-famed muslins. Has Dacca Univ., Jagannath Col., Madrasa School, engineering col., medical col. Noted 17th-cent. mosque and Mogul fort, large Hindu temple. Was Mogul ⊙ Bengal from 1608 until 1704, when ⊙ was moved to Murshidabad. In 1947, became ⊙ new Pakistan prov. of East Bengal, following formation of Pakistan. Fr. trading post established here in early 18th cent.; rights renounced in 1947. In late 1940s, Dacca and the surrounding area (including Narayanganj, SE) was formed into Greater Dacca (1951 pop. 401,000).

Dachau (dä'khou), town (pop. 18,158), Upper Bavaria, Germany, on the Amper and 10 mi. NNW of Munich; rail junction; mfg. of machinery, textiles, paper, ceramics; brewing, lumber milling, printing; mud baths. Has mid-16th-cent. castle, and early-17th-cent. town hall and church. Chartered 1391. Was site of notorious concentration camp under the Hitler regime.

Dachi (dä'chē), town (pop. 8,198), Gifu prefecture, central Honshu, Japan, 6 mi. E of Tajimi, in rice-growing area; pottery making.

Dachnoye (däch'nŭyů), agr. village (1947 pop. over 500), S Sakhalin, Russian SFSR, on E coast railroad and 9 mi. N of Korsakov; rail junction (branch to Aniva). Under Jap. rule (1905–45), called Shimba.

Dachsbach (däks'bäkh), village (pop. 773), Middle Franconia, W Bavaria, Germany, on the Aisch and 6 mi. NE of Neustadt; tanning, brewing, lumber and flour milling. Hops, sheep.

Dachsfelden, Switzerland: see TAVANNES.

Dachstein (däkh'shtīn), highest Alpine peak (9,829 ft.) in the Salzkammergut, in Austria, on borders of Styria, Upper Austria, and Salzburg; ascended from Hallstatt (N) or Schladming (S). Glacier.

Dacia (dā'shů), anc. name of the European region corresponding roughly to modern Rumania (including Transylvania) inhabited before the Christian era by people called Getae by the Greeks and Daci by the Romans. Trajan invaded the country, establishing colonies there in A.D. 105, and Dacia was a Roman prov. until abandoned to the Goths by Aurelian (270–275).

Dacice (dä'chĭtsĕ), Czech *Dačice*, Ger. *Datschitz* (dä'chĭts), town (pop. 2,796), SW Moravia, Czechoslovakia, on railroad, on headstream of Dyje R. and 23 mi. SSW of Jihlava; oats; lumbering.

Dacoma, town (pop. 256), Woods co., NW Okla., 11 mi. SE of Alva, in agr. area (wheat, sorghums, alfalfa).

Dacono (dăk'ůnō), town (pop. 258), Weld co., N central Colo., near South Platte R., 25 mi. N of Denver; alt. 4,500 ft.

Dacre (dā'kůr), village and parish (pop. 911), E Cumberland, England, 4 mi. WSW of Penrith; cattle, sheep, agr. The 14th-cent. castle was seat of the powerful lords called Dacre of the North, whose title derived from Acre in the Crusades.

Dacula (dăkū'lů), town (pop. 369), Gwinnett co., N central Ga., 32 mi. NE of Atlanta, near Apalachee R.; overalls mfg.

Dadahu (dŭdä'hōō), village, S Himachal Pradesh, India, on tributary of upper Jumna R. and 9 mi. ENE of Nahan; exports timber, rice, wheat; mahseer fishing.

Dadanawa, village, Essequibo co., S Br. Guiana, in the Guiana Highlands, on upper Rupununi R. and 280 mi. SSW of Georgetown; 2°49'N 59°29'W. Starting point for Rupununi cattle trail to Takama on the lower Berbice.

Daday (dädī'), village (pop. 1,402), Kastamonu prov., N Turkey, on the Gok Irmak and 17 mi. WNW of Kastamonu; wheat, barley, spelt; coal and chromium near by.

Daddato (däd'dätō), village, Assab div., SE Eritrea, near Fr. Somaliland border, 45 mi. S of Assab.

Dade (dād). **1** County (□ 2,504; pop. 495,084), S Fla., at tip of peninsula; ⊙ Miami. Lowland area bordered by Florida Keys enclosing Biscayne Bay (E) and part of Florida Bay (S). Coastal fringe is a tourist, truck, dairy, poultry, and citrus-fruit area, with limestone quarries and sand pits; interior lies in the Everglades and includes part of Everglades Natl. Park. Mfg. (food and wood products, building materials, clothing, chemicals) and fishing. Formed 1836. **2** County (□ 165; pop. 7,364), extreme NW Ga.; ⊙ Trenton. Bounded N by Tenn., W by Ala.; drained by Lookout Creek; crossed by Lookout Mtn. (coal mining) and Sand Mtn. Agr. (fruit, vegetables, corn, grain, cotton, livestock, poultry) and sawmilling area. Formed 1837. **3** County (□ 504; pop. 9,324), SW Mo.; ⊙ Greenfield. In Ozark region, drained by Sac R. Agr. (wheat, hay, corn), livestock; coal, limestone. Formed 1841.

Dade City, city (pop. 3,806), ⊙ Pasco co., W central Fla., 32 mi. NE of Tampa; shipping center (citrus fruit, truck); has packing houses and large citrus cannery. Dade Memorial Park is 20 mi. N, near Bushnell.

Dadeldhura, Nepal: see DANDELDHURA.

Dades, Cape, Cyprus: see KITI, CAPE.

Dadessa River (dädĕ'sä), Ital. *Didessa*, W central Ethiopia, rises in highlands 30 mi. WNW of Jimma, flows c.230 mi. NW to the Blue Nile 45 mi. NNE of Nejo.

Dadeville. **1** Town (pop. 2,354), ⊙ Tallapoosa co., E Ala., c.45 mi. NE of Montgomery, near Martin L., in timber and agr. area; lumber, building materials, fertilizer. Inc. 1837. State monument, 10 mi. N, at Horseshoe Bend (in Tallapoosa R.), marks site of battle in which Andrew Jackson defeated Creek Indians (March, 1814). **2** City (pop. 208), Dade co., SW Mo., near Sac R., 28 mi. NW of Springfield.

Dadhar (dä'dŭr), village, Kalat state, NE central Baluchistan, W Pakistan, 13 mi. WSW of Sibi, on N Kachhi plain; cattle raising; indigo.

Dadi, Greece: see AMPHIKLEIA.

Dadou River (dädōō'), Tarn dept., S France, rises on N slopes of Monts de Lacaune, flows 50 mi. W, past Graulhet, to the Agout below Lavaur.

Dadrá (dŭdrä'), town (pop. 984), Damão dist., Portuguese India, 10 mi. SE of Damão, in small enclave within Bombay state; rice, wheat.

Dadri (dä'drē). **1** or **Dalmia Dadri** (dŭlm'yŭ), town (pop. 8,712), S Patiala and East Punjab States Union, India, 13 mi. SSE of Bhiwani; market center for millet, gram, cattle; leather goods; cement works. **2** Town (pop. 4,419), Bulandshahr dist., W Uttar Pradesh, India, 21 mi. WNW of Bulandshahr; wheat, oilseeds, barley, cotton, jowar.

Dadu (dä'dōō), dist. (□ 7,370; 1951 pop. 419,000), W Sind, W Pakistan; ⊙ Dadu. Bounded W by Kirthar Range, E by Indus R., SW by Baran R.; crossed S (Kohistan) by E offshoots of Kirthar Range, including Lakhi Hills; irrigated by right-bank canals of Sukkur Barrage system. Lakes and marshes (notably Manchhar L.) in W section formed by seasonal drainage from near-by hills. Agr. (rice, millet, wheat, mangoes, dates); handicraft cloth and carpet weaving; fishing (chiefly shad) in the Indus; sheep and goats raised in hills. Kotri and Sehwan are small trade centers. Constituted a dist. in 1930s.

Dadu, town (pop. 10,896), ⊙ Dadu dist., W Sind, W Pakistan, on Dadu Canal and 140 mi. NNE of Karachi; market center (millet, wheat, rice, oilseeds, fish, mangoes); handicraft cloth weaving, cotton ginning, rice milling. Agr. farm.

Dadu Canal, irrigation canal of SUKKUR BARRAGE system, W Sind, W Pakistan; from right bank of Indus R. at Sukkur runs c.140 mi. SSW, through Sukkur, Larkana, and Dadu dists., to just N of Sehwan. Irrigates fields of millet, rice, wheat.

Daen Lao Range, Burma-Thailand: see TANEN TAUNGGYI RANGE.

Daer Water, Scotland: see CLYDE RIVER.

Daet (dä'āt), town (1939 pop. 5,621; 1948 municipality pop. 19,880), ⊙ Camarines Norte prov., SE Luzon, Philippines, 85 mi. NW of Legaspi; 14°6'N 122°57'E. Trade center for agr. area (coconuts, rice, abacá).

Dafla Hills (däflä'), extension of E Assam Himalayas in SE Balipara frontier tract, N Assam, India; separated from Miri Hills (N) by a right affluent of the Brahmaputra. Inhabited by Dafla and Aka tribes of Tibeto-Burman origin.

Dafna (däf'nä), settlement (pop. 600), Upper Galilee, NE Israel, near Syrian border, at SW foot of Mt. Hermon, 20 mi. NNE of Safad; brush mfg., trout breeding in near-by headwaters of the Jordan; mixed farming. Founded 1939; withstood Arab attacks (1948).

Dafni, Greece: see DAPHNE.

Dafonsero, Mount, Netherlands New Guinea: see CYCLOPS MOUNTAINS.

Dafundo (dŭfōōn'dōō), town (pop. 2,244), Lisboa dist., W central Portugal, on right bank of Tagus estuary, on railroad and 5 mi. W of Lisbon; fish canning, knitwear mfg. Aquarium.

Daga (dŭgä'), village, Bassein dist., Lower Burma, on Daga R. (arm of Irrawaddy delta), 20 mi. NE of Bassein and on railroad.

Daga (dä'gä), town (1939 pop. 5,062) in Cadiz municipality, Negros Occidental prov., N Negros isl., Philippines, on Visayan Sea, 30 mi. NE of Baccolod; agr. center (rice, sugar cane).

Dagahbur, Dagabur, or **Daggah Bur** (dä'gä bōōr'), town (pop. 2,000), Harar prov., SE Ethiopia, in the Ogaden, on Jerer R., on road, and 95 mi. SE of Jijiga; market center. Occupied by Italians (1936) in Italo-Ethiopian War and by British (1941) in Second World War.

Dagah Medo or **Daga Medo** (dä'gä mĕ'dō), Harar prov., SE Ethiopia, in the Ogaden, 40 mi. WSW of Dagabur, in pastoral region (camels, sheep); water hole. Also spelled Dagaha Modo.

Dagami (dägä'mē), town (1939 pop. 3,189; 1948 municipality pop. 20,361), E central Leyte, Philippines, 14 mi. SW of Tacloban; agr. center (rice, coconuts, corn).

Dagana (dägä'nä), town (pop. c.4,100), NW Senegal, Fr. West Africa, trading post and landing on left bank of Senegal R. (Mauritania border) and 70 mi. NE of Saint-Louis; fishing, hunting, stock raising.

Dagana-Kiik (dŭgŭnä"-kēk'), village, central Stalinabad oblast, Tadzhik SSR, 25 mi. S of Stalinabad (linked by narrow-gauge railroad); wheat, cattle, horses.

Dagania, Israel: see DEGANIYA.

Dagenham (dă'gŭnŭm), municipal borough (1931 pop. 89,362; 1951 census 114,588), SW Essex, England, on the Thames and 12 mi. ENE of London. With establishment here of huge Ford automobile plant in 1929, the city boomed (1921 pop. 9,127). There are also knitting mills and mfg. of chemicals and pharmaceuticals. On the Thames are dock installations. In the borough (N) is Chadwell Heath, with mfg. of electrical equipment, paint, tile.

Dagestan or **Daghestan** (dägŭstän', Rus. dŭgyĭstän') [Persian, =mountain land], autonomous soviet socialist republic (□ 14,750; 1946 pop. estimate 900,000), in S European Russian SFSR, bet. the E Greater Caucasus and Caspian Sea; ⊙ Makhachkala. A mountainous region (mean alt. 5,000 ft.), in triangle formed by main range of the Greater Caucasus (here up to 70 mi. wide), Andi Range, and Caspian Sea; except for narrow littoral belt (used by railroad) and low irrigated Sulak-Terek plain, it consists largely of denuded offshoots of the Greater Caucasus, difficult of access and separated by deep, narrow valleys. Drained by Sulak (N) and Samur (S) rivers, used extensively for irrigation in lower courses. Mtn. rivers offer great hydroelectric potentialities. Mineral resources include petroleum (Achi-Su, Izberbash), natural gas, sulphur, and nonferrous metals. Livestock grazing in mts.; orchards, vineyards, cotton, corn, and winter wheat in irrigated lowland; spring wheat and barley on mtn. slopes. Fisheries along coast. Industry: fruit and fish canning, cotton milling, glassworking (Dagestanskiye Ogni). Woolen and metalworking handicrafts in mts. Pop. comprises over 30 nationalities, including Avars (W center), Darghins (E center), Lezghians (S), Kumyk (N), Laks (S center), Andi (W), and Russians in cities and along littoral. Main centers: Makhachkala (with adjoining Kaspisk), Derbent, Buinaksk, Khasavyurt. Persian prov. of Dagestan was annexed (1813) by Russia, but Rus. rule over native khans was not entirely affirmed until suppression of revolts (1877). Scene of civil war (1918–20); came (1920) under Soviet rule; made autonomous republic in 1921. Dagestan included (1922–38) Kizlyar area, since 1944 part of Grozny oblast.

Dagestanskiye Ogni (-skēŭ ŭgnyē') [Rus.,=Dagestan fires], town (1926 pop. 1,048), SE Dagestan Autonomous SSR, Russian SFSR, on Caspian coastal railroad and 6 mi. NW of Derbent; glassworking center, served by local natural-gas wells and supplied with Glauber's salt from Kara-Bogaz-Gol (across Caspian Sea); fish canning.

Daggah Bur, Ethiopia: see DAGAHBUR.

Daggett, county (□ 764; pop. 364), NE Utah; ⊙ Manila. Mtn. area bordering on Wyo. and Colo., crossed by Green R. Uinta Mts. and Ashley Natl. Forest extend throughout most of co. Formed 1918.

Daggett. 1 Mining hamlet, San Bernardino co., S Calif., in Mojave Desert, 8 mi. E of Barstow. Silver mines near by. **2** Village (pop. 341), Menominee co., SW Upper Peninsula, Mich., on Little Cedar R. and 25 mi. N of Menominee.

Daghara, Iraq: see DAGHGHARA.

Daghestan, Russian SFSR: see DAGESTAN.

Daghghara or **Daghgharah** (däg-gä'rŭ), town, Diwaniya prov., SE central Iraq, 10 mi. N of Diwaniya; rice, dates. Also spelled Daghara.

Daghmar (dăgmär'), town, E Oman, on Gulf of Oman, 35 mi. SE of Muscat, at foot of Eastern Hajar hill country; dates, fruit, alfalfa, cotton.

Dago, Estonia: see HIIUMAA.

Dagomba, Gold Coast: see TAMALE.

Dagomys (dŭgŭmĭs'), village (1939 pop. over 500), S Krasnodar Territory, Russian SFSR, on Black Sea coastal railroad and 7 mi. NW of Sochi; steamer landing; tea processing, lumber milling.

Dagsboro, town (pop. 474), Sussex co., SE Del., 13 mi. SSE of Georgetown; distributing point in poultry region.

Dagsburg, France: see DABO.

Dagshai (dŭg'shī), town (pop. 1,047), E Patiala and East Punjab States Union, India, in Kumaun Himalayas, 17 mi. SSW of Simla. Acquired by British 1847 from Patiala state; used as cantonment.

Dagua (dä'gwä), town (pop. 2,173), Valle del Cauca dept., W Colombia, on railroad, on Dagua R. and 21 mi. NW of Cali; coffee, tobacco, sugar cane, corn, fruit, stock. Railroad workshops. Silver, gold, and platinum deposits near by.

Dagua River, Valle del Cauca dept., W Colombia, rises NW of Cali, flows c.60 mi. NW to the Pacific at Buenaventura. Cali-Buenaventura RR follows its course.

Dagupan (dägōō'pän), city (1939 pop. 6,323; 1948 municipality pop. 43,838) in but independent of Pangasinan prov., central Luzon, Philippines, near S shore of Lingayen Gulf, port on branch of Agno R., on railroad and 31 mi. SW of Baguio; 16°5'N 120°31'E. Trade center for agr. area (rice, copra, corn, sugar cane).

Dagus Mines (dā'gŭs), village (pop. 1,070, with adjacent Kersey), Elk co., N central Pa., 8 mi. SE of Ridgway, in bituminous-coal area.

Dahana, Dahanah, or **Dahna'** (dă'hŭnä), desert-type of Arabian Peninsula, consisting of a comparatively hard gravelly plain, covered at intervals with parallel red sand belts. It is most typical of E central Arabia, where it separates Nejd and Hasa in a belt 800 mi. long, 15–50 mi. wide. Its sands are stabilized in N, but consist largely of migratory dunes in S, where the Dahana broadens into the great S Arabian desert RUB' AL KHALI.

Dahanu (dähä'nōō), village (pop. 6,285), Thana dist., W Bombay, India, small port on Arabian Sea, 65 mi. N of Bombay; rice milling, machinery mfg., fishing.

Dahivadi (dŭhĭvŭ'dē), village, Satara North dist., central Bombay, India, 37 mi. E of Satara; market center for millet, wheat.

Dahlah (dä'lŭ), town, Kandahar prov., S Afghanistan, 25 mi. NE of Kandahar and on Arghandab R., in outliers of the Hindu Kush.

Dahlak Archipelago (dälăk'), Ital. *Dahalach*, group of 2 larger and 124 smaller flat, desert isls. (mostly uninhabited) in Red Sea, off coast of Eritrea at Massawa, bet. 15°30'N and 16°37'N. Noted for their fisheries (pearl, mother-of-pearl; marketed at Massawa). Contain traces of petroleum. On Nokra Isl. (near Dahlak Isl.) are stone quarries used to rebuild Massawa after earthquake of 1921. Chief isls. are Dahlak (□ c.290; 38 mi. long, 2–15 mi. wide) with fine natural harbor facing Massawa (35 mi. W), and near-by Norah (□ c.50; 15 mi. long, 2–10 mi. wide).

Dahlem (dä'lĕm), fine residential section of Zehlendorf dist., SW Berlin, Germany, 6 mi. SW of city center. Contains botanical gardens and several institutes of former Kaiser Wilhelm Inst. After 1945 in U.S. sector and site of U.S. army and administrative hq. for Berlin. Seat of Free Univ. of Berlin (founded after 1945).

Dahlen (dä'lŭn), town (pop. 4,571), Saxony, E central Germany, 13 mi. WNW of Riesa; mfg. of pharmaceuticals. Has 15th–16th-cent. church, 18th-cent. castle.

Dahlgren (dăl'grŭn, dăl'-). **1** Village (pop. 609), Hamilton co., SE Ill., 15 mi. ESE of Mou Vernon, in agr. area; mfg. (flour, building m terials). **2** Site of U.S. naval ordnance provi ground, King George co., E Va., along the Potom (bridged here to Charles co., Md.), 25 mi. S Washington, D.C.

Dahlhausen (däl"hou'zŭn), district (since 1929) of Bochum, W Germany, on the Ruhr and 4 mi. SSW of city center; coal mining; coking.

Dahlonega (dălŏ'nēgŭ), city (pop. 2,152), Lumpkin co., N Ga., 17 mi. NNW of Gainesville; trade center; gold mining, sawmilling. North Georgia Col. here. Settled with opening of mines in 1829; had U.S. mint 1836–61. Inc. 1833.

Dahme (dä'mŭ), town (pop. 6,391), Brandenburg, E Germany, on Dahme R. and 19 mi. SE of Luckenwalde; woolen milling, cigar mfg. Until late-19th cent., noted for handmade shoes. Has palace (rebuilt in 18th cent.); old town walls.

Dahme River, E Germany, rises in Lower Lusatia 3 mi. S of Dahme, flows c.60 mi. generally N, past Königs Wusterhausen, through several small lakes (including Seddin L., W terminus of Oder-Spree Canal), to the Spree at Köpenick dist. (SE) of Berlin. Connected with Scharmützel L. by Storkow Canal.

Dahn (dän), village (pop. 2,547), Rhenish Palatinate, W Germany, in Hardt Mts., on the Lauter and 9 mi. ESE of Pirmasens; tourist center; leather- and woodworking. Has ruined castle.

Dahna', Arabia: see DAHANA.

Dahomey (dŭhō'mē), French overseas territory (□ c.45,560; pop. c.1,458,000), SE Fr. West Africa, on Slave Coast of Gulf of Guinea; ⊙ PORTO-NOVO. A narrow strip of land bet. Fr. Togoland (W) and Nigeria (E) extending from coast (c.70 mi. long) 420 mi. N to the Niger, which separates it from Niger territory. Upper Volta is NW. Lat. 10°N divides it roughly into more elevated Upper Dahomey, with ATAKORA and other ranges, and Lower Dahomey, which stretches from flat marshy coastal belt (c.50 mi. wide) to gently rising forested interior. The coast is fringed by several large lagoons, linked by inland waterways. Principal river is the Ouémé. The climate, especially in populated coastal area, is equatorial, with a mean annual temp. above 80°F. There are 2 wet and 2 dry seasons, but humidity is always considerable. The N savannas in Niger basin are Saharan. Fertile Lower Dahomey yields most of the economically important products. Chief exports are palm kernels and palm oil; also coffee, cotton, shea nuts, shea-nut butter, peanuts, castor beans, copra, cacao, kapok. For local consumption natives grow millet, corn, yams, manioc, potatoes, beans, soya. Stock raising (cattle, sheep, goats, pigs) becomes more important in N highlands. Big game abounds. Vegetable-oil extracting, cotton ginning. Next to Porto-Novo ranks Cotonou, leading port and religious center. Other important settlements are Ouidah and Abomey. There is a railroad along the coast with an inland branch to Parakou. Until late 19th cent. the region was split into several powerful Negro kingdoms, on which Dahomey (with ⊙ Abomey) was supreme. Fr. claims were raised in early 1850s. After protectorates over native states were established, the coast was set up (1894) as Fr. colony. Boundaries were fixed soon after with German Togoland and the Br. possession of Lagos (now in Nigeria). The native rulers were removed. Dahomey was included 1904 in Fr. West Africa and is today represented in Fr. parliament. The Negro population speaks various Ewe languages and still adheres largely to an animistic religion.

Dahr, plateau, Yemen: see BEIDHA.

Dahr, Wadi, Yemen: see DHAHR, WADI.

Dahra (därä', dä'rä), rugged coastal region of N Algeria, mostly in Alger dept., extending ENE from mouth of the Chéliff to longitude of Ténès, bet. the Mediterranean and lower Chéliff valley. Average alt. 3,000 ft. Berber pop.

Dahra or **Dara,** village, W Senegal, Fr. West Africa, on railroad and 140 mi. ENE of Dakar; peanuts, gums.

Dahr el Qadib, Dahr eq Qadib (both: dä'hŭr ĕk-kädēb'), or **Zahr al-Qadib** (zä'hŭr), Fr. *Dahr el*

Kadib or *Dhor el Khodib*, mountain (c.10,000 ft.), Lebanon range, N Lebanon, 40 mi. NE of Beirut. At its foot are remains of the famous Cedars of Lebanon.

Dahshur or **Dashur** (dä'shŏŏr), town, Giza prov., Upper Egypt, on the Nile and 20 mi. S of Cairo; site of pyramid of Sesostris III (1887–49 B.C.).

Dai, Song, or **Song Day** (both: shông' dī'), major delta arm of Red R., N Vietnam, branches off below Sontay, flows over 100 mi. SSE, past Phuly and Ninhbinh to Gulf of Tonkin at 20°N.

Daibanretsu, Formosa: see TAPANLIEH.

Daido-ko, Korea: see TAEDONG RIVER.

Daigleville, village (pop. 4,809), Terrebonne parish, SE La.

Daigo (dī'gō), town (pop. 9,118), Ibaraki prefecture, central Honshu, Japan, 20 mi. NW of Hitachi; rice, wheat; charcoal, dried persimmons.

Daihanratsu, Formosa: see TAPANLIEH.

Daiji, Japan: see TAIJI.

Daik, Indonesia: see LINGGA.

Daikoji (dīkō'jē), town (pop. 5,896), Aomori prefecture, N Honshu, Japan, 5 mi. E of Hirosaki; rice, straw goods.

Daikon-shima (dīkō'shĭmä), island (□ 2; pop. 5,872, including near-by islet), Shimane prefecture, SW Honshu, Japan, in the lagoon Naka-no-umi, just E of Matsue; 1.5 mi. long, 1 mi. wide. Generally low, fertile. Agr. (rice, wheat, sweet potatoes, radishes); raw silk. Isl. has many varieties of tree peonies.

Daiku or **Daik-u** (dīkōō', dīk'ōō), town (pop. 5,025), Pegu dist., Lower Burma, on Rangoon-Mandalay RR and 33 mi. NNE of Rangoon. Sometimes spelled Deiku.

Dailekh or **Dailekha** (dīlā'kŭ), town, W Nepal, 55 mi. N of Nepalganj; corn, rice, millet, vegetables, fruit. Nepalese military post.

Dailly or **New Dailly** (dā'lē), agr. village and parish (pop. 1,726), S Ayrshire, Scotland, on Girvan Water and 6 mi. SSW of Maybole. Just N are ruins of 14th-cent. Dalquharran Castle. Parish includes agr. village of Old Dailly, 3 mi. ENE of Girvan, and coal-mining village of Barganny, just SW of Dailly.

Daimel (dīmyĕl'), city (pop. 19,277), Ciudad Real prov., S central Spain, in New Castile, on railroad and 17 mi. ENE of Ciudad Real; prosperous agr. center in La Mancha, surrounded by vineyards and olive groves. Region also raises cereals, vegetables, anise, saffron, livestock. Has important olive-oil and wine (vermouth, brandy, alcohol) industries. Other products include woolen and esparto goods, meat products, cheese, tartaric acid, soap, lime. Airfield.

Daimon (dīmō'), town (pop. 3,159), Toyama prefecture, central Honshu, Japan, just E of Takaoka; patent medicines.

Daingean, town (pop. 663), NE Co. Offaly, Ireland, on the Grand Canal, 9 mi. ENE of Tullamore; agr. market (barley, potatoes, hops; cattle). A former ⊙ Co. Offaly, it is also called Philipstown, named for Philip II. Has 16th-cent. castle.

Daingerfield, town (pop. 1,668), ⊙ Morris co., NE Texas, c.40 mi. NNW of Marshall; aircraft-engine plant; trade, shipping center in agr. (cotton, truck), lumbering area. About 10 mi. S are iron-ore deposits and large metallurgical plant built in Second World War. A state park is just SE.

Dainhat (dīn'hät), town (pop. 5,036), Burdwan dist., central West Bengal, India, on the Bhagirathi and 33 mi. NNE of Burdwan; rice, jute, gram, sugar cane; metalware mfg.

Daiquirí (dīkērē'), village (pop. 502), Oriente prov., E Cuba, on the Caribbean, 14 mi. ESE of Santiago de Cuba. Copper and iron deposits near by. In Spanish-American War, U.S. troops landed at near-by Siboney.

Daireaux (dârō'), town (pop. 4,714), ⊙ Caseros dist. (□ 1,502; pop. 14,578), W central Buenos Aires prov., Argentina, 45 mi. SW of Bolívar, in agr. region (wheat, sheep, cattle).

Dairen (dī'rĕn'), Chinese *Talien* (dä'lyĕn'), Rus. *Dalny* or *Dal'nyy* (däl'nyē), city (1947 pop. 543,690), S Manchuria, at S tip of Liaotung peninsula, in Port Arthur naval base dist., 23 mi. ENE of Port Arthur, 220 mi. SW of Mukden; 38°56'N 121°39'E. Premier port (open year round) and a leading industrial center of Manchuria, on Bay of Dairen, an inlet of Korea Bay of Yellow Sea; S terminus of South Manchuria RR. Its exports of soybean products (oil and cake), coal, and grain result in an overseas trade 2d only to that of Shanghai. Dairen is one of the world's leading soybean-processing centers, and also produces ceramic products, glass, cement, foundry goods, boilers, and other machinery. It has shipyards, railroad shops, an oil refinery, and chemical industries. The city, situated on sheltered S shore of the Bay of Dairen, consists of an administrative and business section adjoining the extensive harbor installations, and the Chinese residential city (W). Industrial sites are in the outskirts along the bay shore. Originally a small fishing village, Dairen was briefly occupied (1858) by the British fleet during the North China operations. Modern development was initiated by the Russians after the lease in 1898 of the Kwantung territory; and was continued after 1905 by the Japanese, who made Dairen a free port (1906) open to foreign trade. Under Jap. rule, the city boomed, particularly after the establishment of Manchukuo, with its pop. rising from 386,000 in 1931 to 872,600 in 1945, then including 188,000 Japanese. At the same time, however, Dairen lost its original industrial leadership to the rising Mukden industrial area. Following the Second World War, Dairen, while remaining a free port, was placed in the Port Arthur naval base dist.

Dairsie, Dairsiemuir (dâr'sēmūr'), or **Osnaburgh** (ŏz'nŭbûrg), agr. village in Dairsie parish (pop. 537), N Fifeshire, Scotland, on Eden R. (1522 bridge) and 3 mi. NE of Cupar. Has 1622 church and remains (mainly 16th cent.) of anc. Dairsie Castle. David II spent his youth here.

Dairut, Deirut, or **Dayrut** (all: dā'rōōt), twin towns, Dairut el Sherif (N; pop. 14,001) and Dairut el Mahatta or Dairut el Qibli (S; pop. 17,351), of Asyut prov., Upper Egypt, near the Nile, on railroad and 33 mi. NW of Asyut, on the Bahr Yusuf where it receives the Ibrahimiya Canal; cotton ginning, pottery making, wood and ivory carving; cereals, dates, sugar cane.

Dairyland, resort village, Ulster co., SE N.Y., in the Catskills, 13 mi. WNW of Ellenville.

Dai-sen (dī'sĕn), peak (5,653 ft.) in Tottori prefecture, SW Honshu, Japan, 13 mi. ESE of Yonago; winter sports on slopes. Site of 8th-cent. Buddhist temple. Peak is principal feature of Dai-sen Natl. Park (□ 47).

Daisetsu-zan (dīsā'tsōō-zä), collective name for several volcanic peaks in central Hokkaido, Japan; ASAHI-DAKE (7,513 ft.), highest. Peaks are central feature of Daisetsu-zan Natl. Park, largest (□ 895) in Japan, with hot springs, scenic gorges.

Daisetta (dĕsĕ'tŭ), town (pop. 1,764), Liberty co., E Texas, 32 mi. W of Beaumont, in farm, timber, oil area. Inc. since 1940.

Daishoji (dīshō'jē), town (pop. 13,864), Ishikawa prefecture, central Honshu, Japan, on Sea of Japan, 18 mi. NNE of Fukui; collection center for textiles and pottery. Sometimes spelled Daisyozi.

Dais Mountain (dās) (10,612 ft.), SW Alta., near B.C. border, in Rocky Mts., in Jasper Natl. Park, 45 mi. SSE of Jasper; 52°16'N 117°39'W.

Daisy. 1 Town (pop. 74), Pike co., SW Ark., c.43 mi. SW of Hot Springs. **2** Town (pop. 195), Evans co., E central Ga., 20 mi. S of Statesboro. **3** Town (pop. 52), Cape Girardeau co., SE Mo., bet. Mississippi and Whitewater rivers, 12 mi. NW of Jackson. **4** Village (pop. 1,336), Hamilton co., SE Tenn., 17 mi. NNE of Chattanooga; ships coal; makes tiles, bricks, textiles.

Daisyfield, village, Gwelo prov., central Southern Rhodesia, in Matabeleland, on railroad and 30 mi. SW of Gwelo; alt. 4,612 ft. Tobacco, corn, cotton, peanuts, citrus fruit, dairy products. Has Dutch Reformed Church orphanage.

Daisyozi, Japan: see DAISHOJI.

Daisytown. 1 Borough (pop. 442), Cambria co., SW central Pa., just E of Johnstown. **2** Village (pop. 2,176, with adjacent Crescent Heights), Washington co., SW Pa., 6 mi. S of Charleroi.

Daito (dītō'), town (pop. 4,917), Shimane prefecture, SW Honshu, Japan, 12 mi. SW of Matsue; agr. and livestock center; raw silk.

Daiton-zan, Formosa: see TATUN SHAN.

Daito-shima (dītō'shĭmä) or **Daito-jima** (–jĭmä), easternmost island group (□18; 1950 pop. 2,691) of Okinawa Isls., in the Ryukyus, Japan, in Philippine Sea, 195 mi. E of Okinawa; 34°56' N 127°50' E. Comprises Minami-daito-shima (sometimes called Minami-oagari-shima), Kita-daito-shima (Kita-oagari-shima), Okino-daito-shima (Okino-oagari-shima), and scattered islets. Minami-daito-shima (largest) is 4 mi. long, 3 mi. wide, has sugar refinery. Other isls. produce phosphate. Bombed in Second World War.

Daizenji (dī"zän'jē), town (pop. 5,528), Fukuoka prefecture, W Kyushu, Japan, just W of Kurume, on Chikugo R.; rice, wheat, barley, vegetable wax.

Dajabón (dähäbōn'), city (1950 pop. 1,691), ⊙ Libertador prov., NW Dominican Republic, on Haiti border, opposite Ouanaminthe, on Massacre R. and 20 mi. S of Monte Cristi; 19°32'N 71°42'W. Trades in timber, hides, bananas, honey, coffee. Center of resistance in struggle against Spain and Haiti. Since 1938, ⊙ prov.

Dajabón River, Dominican Republic and Haiti: see MASSACRE RIVER.

Dajal (dä'jŭl), town (pop. 6,378), Dera Ghazi Khan dist., SW Punjab, W Pakistan, 38 mi. SSW of Dera Ghazi Khan; wheat, millet; oilseed pressing, woolen-blanket weaving; sheep and camel breeding.

Dajarra (dŭjă'rŭ), village (pop. 182), W Queensland, Australia, 95 mi. SW of Cloncurry; rail terminus; livestock.

Dakar (däkär', dŭ–), city (pop. c.185,400, of which c.13,700 are Europeans), ⊙ Fr. West Africa, on coast of Senegal, a major Atlantic port at S extremity of Cape Verde peninsula (westernmost point of Africa), opposite Gorée isl., c.1,500 mi. SW of Casablanca, Fr. Morocco, and c.1,850 mi. ENE of Natal, Brazil; 14°40'N 17°25'W. An international air and maritime center on transoceanic lanes to Western Europe, Latin America, and South Africa. Also a naval base accommodating largest battleships, administrative hq. of governor general, and gate to France's African empire. Upon it converge railroads from Saint-Louis (110 mi. NE) and the upper Senegal and Niger basins of the Fr. Sudan. Through its modern harbor Dakar exports chiefly peanuts and also kapok, gum, sisal, hides, skins. Secondary industries include food processing, vegetable-oil extracting, brewing, meat packing, titanium refining, printing, mfg. of chocolate, ice, soap, cigarettes, oxygen, refrigerants, bricks. Railroad workshops, navy yard, drydock. The roadstead is flanked by jetties extending toward Gorée isl. Seat of Pasteur Institute, govt. school of medicine and pharmacy, missionary hospitals and schools. R.C. cathedral was consecrated 1936. Adjoining the European section with its partly suburban-French, partly colonial aspect, is Médina (NW), to which natives were removed (1914) after outbreak of pestilence. The new Yoff airport is 10 mi. NW, replacing Ouakam, 5½ mi. NW, now only a military base. Bel-Air arsenal adjoins N. Dakar has an exceedingly hot climate, with a rainy and dry season. The former is the hotter one, and lasts from mid-Nov. to end of June. Prevailing wind in dry season is the harmattan, sweeping S from the Sahara. Dakar was built by Faidherbe in 1857, though missionary and native settlements preceded it. First railroad to interior was begun 1882, and the naval base laid out 1899. Became ⊙ Fr. West Africa in 1902. From 1924 to 1946 it was part of the separate unit called "Dakar and Dependencies" which also included Rufisque and Gorée isl. In Second World War, after the fall of France, Dakar was held by Vichy forces. Following an ultimatum, the Fr. battleship *Richelieu* was damaged (July, 1940) here by the British. An attempt by Gen. Charles de Gaulle, aided by the British, to take the city (Sept. 1, 1940) failed. In Dec., 1942, Dakar joined the Allies. Since the war its population and trade have increased considerably.

Daka River (dä'kä), E Gold Coast, rises 40 mi. NNW of Yendi, flows c.200 mi. S, along W Br. Togoland border, to Volta R. 22 mi. ESE of Yeji. Until First World War, formed boundary bet. Gold Coast and Ger. Togoland.

Dakhineswar (dŭkĭnās'vŭr), village, 24-Parganas dist., SE West Bengal, India, on the Hooghly and 6 mi. N of Calcutta city center; mfg. of automobile parts. Has numerous temples; at the Kali temple, young Ramakrishna developed into a noted religious teacher.

Dakhin Shahbazpur Island (dŭkĭn' shäbäz'pŏŏr), E island of Ganges Delta, in Bakarganj dist., S East Bengal, E Pakistan, in Bay of Bengal, 14 mi. E of Barisal; 43 mi. long, 10–15 mi. wide; separated from Hatia Isl. (E) by Shahbazpur R. (an arm of Meghna R. delta mouth; 47 mi. long) and from mainland (W) by Tetulia R. (right arm of Meghna R. delta mouth; c.29 mi. long). Bhola town in NW. Steamer service to mainland. Subject to severe cyclones.

Dakhla (dă'khlŭ), **El Dakhla, Ed Dakhla,** or **Al-Dakhilah** (all: ĕd dă'–), oasis (pop. 21,136), S central Egypt, in Southern Desert prov., c.240 mi. W of Luxor; 25°30'N 29°E. Chief town is El Qasr. Most populous of Egyptian oases, it lies in a basin c.50 mi. long (E–W), 20 mi. wide (N–S). Caravan routes to Kharga and Farafra oases. Very fertile, with more than 40 sq. mi. in cultivation: dates, oranges, wheat, barley. Main urban centers: El Qasr, El Qalamun, Mut, Balat, El Gidida. SW of El Qasr is a large ruined temple of the Roman era.

Da Khure, Mongolia: see ULAN BATOR.

Dakka or **Loe Dakka** (lō'ä dŭk'kŭ), fortified town, Eastern Prov., Afghanistan, 37 mi. ESE of Jalalabad, and on Kabul R., near W entrance to Khyber Pass; military post. Also spelled Dekka.

Dakor (dä'kōr), town (pop. 10,135), Kaira dist., N Bombay, India, 30 mi. E of Kaira; cotton ginning. It is a pilgrimage center and has a large annual festival fair.

Dakota. 1 County (□ 571; pop. 49,019), SE Minn.; ⊙ Hastings. Agr. area bounded NE and N by Mississippi R. and NW by Minnesota R. Dairy products, livestock, grain. Food processing and mfg. at Hastings. Formed 1859. **2** County (□ 255; pop. 10,401), NE Nebr.; ⊙ Dakota City. Agr. region bounded E and NE by Missouri R., at Iowa-S.Dak. line. Food processing; grain, dairy products. Formed 1855.

Dakota. 1 Town (pop. 318), Stephenson co., N Ill., 8 mi. NE of Freeport, in agr. area. **2** Village (pop. c.300), Winona co., SE Minn., on Mississippi R. (Wis. line) and 17 mi. SE of Winona; dairy products. Wildlife refuge near by.

Dakota City. 1 Town (pop. 637), ⊙ Humboldt co., N central Iowa, on East Des Moines R., just E of Humboldt; livestock, grain. **2** Village (pop. 622), ⊙ Dakota co., NE Nebr., just S of Sioux City, Iowa, on Missouri R.; timber, grain. First Lutheran church in Nebr. (1860) is here.

Dakota River, N.Dak. and S.Dak.: see JAMES RIVER.

Dakovica, Yugoslavia: see DJAKOVICA.

Dakovo, Yugoslavia: see DJAKOVO.

Dakusui River, Formosa: see CHOSHUI RIVER.

Dal, river, Sweden: see DAL RIVER.

Dala', Aden: see DHALA.

Dala, Burma: see DALLA.

Dala (dä'lä), county [Icelandic *sýsla*] (pop. 1,207), W Iceland; ⊙ Budardalur. Extends E from Breidi Fjord. Mountainous. Sheep raising, sealing, fishing. Collection of eiderdown is important.
)alaas (däläs'), village (pop. 1,671), Vorarlberg, W Austria, 20 mi. ESE of Feldkirch; dairy farming.
)alaba (dälä'bä), town (pop. c.1,650), W central Fr. Guinea, Fr. West Africa, resort in Fouta Djallon mts., 130 mi. NE of Conakry; alt. c.3,850 ft. Botanical and zoological gardens. Protestant mission.
)ala-Fynnhyttan (dä'lä-fün'hü"tän), village (pop. 591), Kopparberg co., central Sweden, 10 mi. N of Avesta; iron mining. Includes mining villages of Gruvgarden (grüv'gôr"dün), Swed. *Gruvgården*, and Ryllshyttan (rüls'hü"tän).
)alaguete (dälägä'tä), town (1939 pop. 2,293; 1948 municipality pop. 29,333), S Cebu isl., Philippines, 24 mi. WNW of Tagbilaran across Bohol Strait; agr. center (corn, coconuts).
)alai Nor, Manchuria: see HULUN NOR.
)alaki (dä"läkē'), town (1945 pop. estimate 1,000), Seventh Prov., in Fars, S Iran, 45 mi. NE of Bushire and on Shiraz-Bushire road; dates, grain.
)alalven, Sweden: see DAL RIVER.
)alaman River (dälämän'), SW Turkey, rises 18 mi. S of Tefenni, flows 97 mi. N and SSW to Mediterranean Sea 10 mi. NW of Cape Kurtoglu, opposite Rhodes.
)alan Dzadagad (dä'län dzä'dägäd), town, ⊙ South Gobi aimak, S Mongolian People's Republic, in Gobi desert, 320 mi. SSW of Ulan Bator.
)alane (dä'länù) [Nor.,=the valleys], hilly region in Rogaland co., SW Norway, extending c.30 mi. NE from the coast at Egersund and Sogndal; traversed by many river valleys. Agr., cattle raising, lumbering, fishing. Formerly spelled Dalene.
)alark (dälärk'), town (pop. 142), Dallas co., S central Ark., 12 mi. SE of Arkadelphia.
)alarna (dä'lärnä") or **Dalecarlia** (dälùkär'lēù), province [Swedish *landskap*] (□ 12,017; pop. 255,356), central Sweden, on Norwegian border. Included in Kopparberg co. and NW part of Gavleborg co. Its noted scenic beauty and the many old customs and manner of dress preserved here, notably at RATTVIK, have made it a popular tourist resort area. Swedish revolt (1521) against Danes originated here, led by Gustavus Vasa.
)alaro (dä'lärü"), Swedish *Dalarö*, village (pop. 542), Stockholm co., E Sweden, on the Baltic, 18 mi. SE of Stockholm; seaside resort. Has 17th-cent. ramparts.
)alasagen, Sweden: see VANSBRO.
)alat (dälät'), town (pop. 2,570), central Sarawak, 10 mi. from S.China Sea and 135 mi. NE of Kuching; sago-producing center.
)alat (dä'lät'), city (1943 pop. 5,200), ⊙ Haut-Donnai prov. (□ 3,300; 1943 pop. 37,300), S central Vietnam, in Annam, in Moi Plateaus, 140 mi. NE of Saigon (connected by highway) and 45 mi. NW of Phanrang (linked by railroad and highway); alt. 4,940 ft. Summer capital of Vietnam and one of leading hill stations of SE Asia; chief town of Langbiang Plateau; govt. residences, villas, sanatorium; tea, coffee, and rubber plantations. Airport. Became (after 1946) ⊙ Hill Plateaus of South Indochina.
)ala Tando, Angola: see VILA SALAZAR.
)alauda (dŭlou'dŭ), village, W Madhya Bharat, India, 8 mi. SSE of Mandasor; sugar milling, cotton ginning.
)albandin (däl'bŭndēn), village, Chagai dist., N Baluchistan, W Pakistan, on railroad (workshop) and 110 mi. SW of Nushki; carpet weaving.
)albeattie (dùlbē'tē, dăl–), burgh (1931 pop. 3,011; 1951 census 3,288), SE Kirkcudbright, Scotland, on Urr Water and 13 mi. SW of Dumfries; agr. market; mfg. of fertilizer and spinning equipment. Just W are Craignair, granite-quarrying center, and Buittle (bĭ'tùl, bū'–), agr. village and parish (pop. 778), formerly site of castle, birthplace of John de Baliol and scene of signing of charter for Balliol Col., Oxford.
)albo, Lake, Sweden: see VANER, LAKE.
)albok Izvor (dùlbôk'-ēz'vôr), village (pop. 3,975), Plovdiv dist., S central Bulgaria, 8 mi. SW of Parvomai; tobacco, vineyards, fruit, truck. Formerly Koz-bunar.
)alby (dôl'bü), town (pop. 4,385), SE Queensland, Australia, 110 mi. WNW of Brisbane; rail center in wheat area.
)alby (däl'bü"), village (pop. 967), Malmohus co., S Sweden, 7 mi. ESE of Lund; rail junction; stone quarrying; grain, potatoes, stock. Has 11th-cent. church.
)alby (dăl'bē), town (pop. 13), Madison co., E Idaho, 7 mi. S of Rexburg.
)alcahue (dälkä'wä), village (1930 pop. 269), Chiloé prov., S Chile, on E coast of Chiloé Isl., 35 mi. SSE of Ancud; wheat, potatoes, livestock; lumbering.
)alcross, Scotland: see CROY AND DALCROSS.
)ale (dä'lù). **1** or **Dale i Bruvik** (ē brōō'vĭk), village (pop. 1,823) in Bruvik canton, Hordaland co., SW Norway, on railroad and 22 mi. NE of Bergen; woolen mills. At near-by waterfall is hydroelectric plant. **2** or **Dale i Sunnfjord** (sōōn'fyōr), village (pop. 666) in Fjaler canton (pop. 3,930), Sogn og Fjordane co., W Norway, on S shore of a fjord, 20 mi. SSE of Floro; shoe mfg. **3** Village in Luster canton, Sogn og Fjordane co., Norway: see SKJOLDEN.
Dale, county (□ 560; pop. 20,828), SE Ala.; ⊙ Ozark. Coastal plain drained by Choctawhatchee R. Cotton, peanuts, corn, hogs; lumber milling. Formed 1818.
Dale. 1 Town (pop. 850), Spencer co., SW Ind., 36 mi. ENE of Evansville; lumber, cheese, canned foods; poultry hatchery. **2** Borough (pop. 3,310), Cambria co., SW central Pa., on Stony Creek, surrounded by city of Johnstown; coal mines. Inc. 1891.
Dale, agr. village and parish (pop. 282), SW Pembroke, Wales, on Milford Haven, 6 mi. W of Milford Haven town. Earl of Richmond (Henry VII) landed near by in 1485 to claim English crown.
Dalecarlia, province, Sweden: see DALARNA.
Dale Hollow, town (pop. 5), Clay co., N Tenn.
Dale Hollow Dam, Clay co., N Tenn., near Ky. line, in Obey R., 7 mi. above its mouth, in foothills of Cumberland Mts.; 200 ft. high, 1,717 ft. long; concrete, straight gravity construction. Completed 1943 by U.S. Army Engineers; used for flood control and power. Impounds Dale Hollow Reservoir (□ 48; capacity 1,706,000 acre-feet) in Cumberland and Clinton counties, Ky., and Clay, Pickett, Overton, and Fentress counties, Tenn.; extends c.51 mi. up Obey R., 12 mi. up its East Fork, 6 mi. up its West Fork.
Dale i Bruvik, Norway: see DALE, Hordaland co.
Dale i Sunnfjord, Norway: see DALE, Sogn og Fjordane co.
Dale Lake, dry lake bed, San Bernardino co., S Calif., in Mojave Desert, 90 mi. E of San Bernardino; its saline deposits yield chemicals.
Dalen (dä'lùn), village (pop. 1,315), Drenthe prov., NE Netherlands, 3 mi. NNE of Coevorden; rye, oats, barley, buckwheat, potatoes.
Dalen, Norway: see LARDAL.
Dalence, Bolivia: see TENIENTE BULLAÍN.
Dalene, region, Norway: see DALANE.
Dalfsen (dälf'sùn), town (pop. 1,492), Overijssel prov., N central Netherlands, on Vecht R. and 7 mi. E of Zwolle; chicory drying, milk-powder mfg., dairy products. Has 14th-cent. Rechteren castle.
Dalga (dăl'gă, –gù), **Dilga** (dĭl'–), or **Dilja** (dĭl'jă), town (pop. 19,607), Asyut prov., central Upper Egypt, 9 mi. NW of Dairut; pottery making, wood and ivory carving; cereals, dates, sugar cane.
Dalgamun, El, Ed Dalgamun (both: ĕd dăl'gămōōn), or **Al-Daljamun** (ĕd dăl'jămōōn), village (pop. 12,059), Gharbiya prov., Lower Egypt, on El Baguriya Canal and 10 mi. W of Tanta; cotton, cereals, rice, fruit.
Dalgety (dùlgĕ'tē), parish (pop. 1,481), SW Fifeshire, Scotland. Includes SAINT DAVID'S.
Dalgopol (dùlgô'pôl), village (pop. 4,486), Stalin dist., E Bulgaria, on Golyama Kamchiya R. and 10 mi. SSW of Provadiya; grain, vineyards, livestock. Formerly Novo-selo.
Dalhart (dăl'härt), city (pop. 5,918), ⊙ Dallam co., and partly in Hartley co., extreme N Texas, on high plains of the Panhandle, 70 mi. NW of Amarillo, in irrigated farm area; alt. 3,985 ft. Railroad and trade center, with stockyards, grain elevators, hatchery. Founded 1901, inc. 1903. Near by, a dam in Rita Blanca Creek forms Rita Blanca L. (irrigation, recreation).
Dalheim (däl'hīm), rail junction, in former Prussian Rhine Prov., W Germany, after 1945 in North Rhine-Westphalia, 12 mi. W of Rheydt; customs station on Dutch border.
Dalhem (dälĕm'), village (pop. 951), Liége prov., E Belgium, 8 mi. NE of Liége; market for fruitgrowing area.
Dalhousie (dăLhou'zē, –sē, –hōō'zē), town (pop. 4,508), ⊙ Restigouche co., N N.B., at head of Chaleur Bay, at mouth of Restigouche R., 160 mi. NW of Moncton; 48°2'N 66°23'W; fishing port (lobster, cod, salmon, smelt); lumbering and newsprint milling. Seed potatoes are grown in region; lead and zinc mines near by. Resort. Inc. 1905.
Dalhousie, town (pop. 1,319), Gurdaspur dist., N Punjab, India, in small enclave near Chamba (Himachal Pradesh), 45 mi. NE of Gurdaspur; scenic resort (alt. c.7,500 ft.) in forested foothills of Punjab Himalayas; acquired by British in 1853. Cantonment of Balun (pop. 1,357) is just N.
Dalhousie (dùlhou'zē, dăl–, –hōō'zē), village in Lasswade parish, central Midlothian, Scotland, 8 mi. SE of Edinburgh; coal mining. Site of Dalhousie Castle, dating from 12th cent. (rebuilt), now a school.
Dali, Cyprus: see DHALI.
Dalia or **Daliah** (both: däl'yä), settlement (pop. 320), NW Israel, in Hills of Ephraim, 15 mi. SSE of Haifa; mfg. of water meters, precision instruments; grain, fruit; dairying. Founded 1939.
Daliao (dälē'ou, dälēä'ō, dälēou'), town (1939 pop. 5,603) in Davao city, Davao prov., S central Mindanao, Philippines, small port on Davao Gulf, 12 mi. WSW of Davao proper; abacá, coconuts.
Dalías (dälē'äs), city (pop. 3,863), Almería prov., S Spain, 5 mi. ESE of Berja; ships grapes, raisins, almonds. Flour mills. Cereals, fruit, vegetables. Lead mines, marble quarries in vicinity.
Dalijan or **Delijan** (both: dälējän'), village, Second Prov., in Mahallat, N central Iran, 45 mi. SSW of Qum and on road to Isfahan; road center; grain, fruit, tobacco. Airfield. Also spelled Dilijan.
Daling, India: see KUMAI.
Dalj (däl), Hung. *Dálya* (dä'yŏ), village (pop. 5,448), NE Croatia, Yugoslavia, on the Danube (Serbia border) and 14 mi. ESE of Osijek, in Slavonia; rail junction; trade center in winegrowing area; fishing.
Daljamun, Al-, Egypt: see DALGAMUN, EL.
Dalkeith (dùlkēth', dăl–), burgh (1931 pop. 7,502; 1951 census 8,786), NE Midlothian, Scotland, bet. South Esk R. and North Esk R., near their confluence, and 7 mi. SE of Edinburgh; important grain market, with metal foundries, in coal-mining region and near one of the few Br. oil fields. Just N is Dalkeith House, seat of dukes of Buccleuch, built c.1700 by Sir John Vanbrugh, replacing earlier 13th-cent. fortress.
Dalkey (dô'kē, dôl'–), Gaelic *Deilginis*, town, SE Co. Dublin, Ireland, on the Irish Sea, at S end of Dublin Bay, 9 mi. SE of Dublin; seaside resort. In Middle Ages it was important as port for passengers from England. Has ruins of anc. castle and of 2 churches. Just SE, in the Irish Sea, is Dalkey Isl. (22 acres), famous in 18th cent. for election of mock "King of Dalkey."
Dall (dôl), village (1939 pop. 13), central Alaska, 60 mi. SE of Bettles; 66°21'N 149°49'W; placer gold mining.
Dall, Mount (9,000 ft.), S central Alaska, in Alaska Range, 130 mi. NW of Anchorage; 62°37'N 152°19'W.
Dall, Point, cape, W Alaska, on Bering Sea, 150 mi. WNW of Bethel; 61°37'N 166°8'W.
Dalla or **Dallah** (dùlä'), S suburb of Rangoon, Lower Burma, on right bank of Rangoon R. opposite Rangoon; sawmilling and shipbuilding center of Irrawaddy R. flotilla; rice milling. Sometimes spelled Dala.
Dal Lake (dŭl) (□ 8), in Vale of Kashmir, just NE of Srinagar, W central Kashmir; 5 mi. long, 2 mi. wide. Comprises 2 sections, Lokut Dal (S) and Bod Dal (N; has Isle of Chenars, much visited by houseboats). Floating gardens in W, S of which are half-reclaimed marshes; in July and Aug. lake abounds with lotus. Near E bank are (S to N) famous Mogul gardens of Chasma-i-Shahi (built 1633 by Shah Jahan), Nishat Bagh (with 12 terraces, fountains, and garden house), and Shalimar Bagh (built by Jahangir; a favorite of Mogul emperors). Near W bank is Nasim Bagh, with large grove of chinar trees.
Dallam (dă'lùm), county (□ 1,494; pop. 7,640), extreme N Texas; ⊙ Dalhart. In high, treeless wheat and cattle plains of the Panhandle, on Okla. and N.Mex. lines; alt. 3,800–4,000 ft. Cattle, grain sorghums, wheat, corn, alfalfa, broomcorn, dairy products, hogs, poultry, sheep, horses, mules; some fruit, truck. Formed 1876.
Dallas, agr. village and parish (pop. 541), central Moray, Scotland, on Lossie R. and 7 mi. SE of Forres. In vicinity are extensive grouse moors.
Dallas (dă'lùs). **1** County (□ 976; pop. 56,270), S central Ala.; ⊙ Selma. Drained by Alabama and Cahaba rivers; in Black Belt. Cotton, dairy products, livestock, lumber. Formed 1818. **2** County (□ 672; pop. 12,416), S central Ark.; ⊙ Fordyce. Drained by Ouachita and Saline rivers, and by Moro Creek. Agr. (cotton, truck, fruit, livestock, poultry; dairy products); cotton ginning, sawmilling, mfg. of wood products. Hunting, fishing. Formed 1845. **3** County (□ 597; pop. 23,661), central Iowa; ⊙ Adel. Prairie agr. area (livestock, corn, oats, wheat) drained by Raccoon R. system and by Beaver Creek; coal mines. Formed 1846. **4** County (□ 537; pop. 10,392), SW central Mo.; ⊙ Buffalo. In the Ozarks; drained by Niangua and Little Niangua rivers. Agr. area; dairy cattle, poultry; oak timber. Formed 1842. **5** County (□ 893; pop. 614,799), N Texas; ⊙ DALLAS, 2d-largest Texas city, and a financial, commercial, industrial center. Rich blackland prairie, wooded in W; drained by Trinity R., here formed by Elm and West forks. Cotton, corn, grains, clover, much fruit, truck, pecans; extensive dairying, poultry raising; also beef cattle, hogs, sheep, horses. Clay, cement rock. Diversified industries in Dallas metropolitan area. Formed 1846.
Dallas. 1 Town (pop. 1,817), ⊙ Paulding co., NW Ga., 29 mi. WNW of Atlanta; textile and lumber mills. Inc. 1854. **2** Town (pop. 421), Marion co., S central Iowa, near Whitebreast Creek, 32 mi. SE of Des Moines, in bituminous-coal-mining and agr. area. **3** Plantation (pop. 81), Franklin co., W central Maine, near Rangeley L., 31 mi. NW of Farmington. **4** Town (pop. 2,454), Gaston co., S N.C., 3 mi. N of Gastonia; cotton milling. Inc. 1848. **5** City (pop. 4,793), ⊙ Polk co., NW Oregon, 13 mi. W of Salem, in fruit and grain area of Willamette valley; lumber products, leather. Founded 1852, inc. 1874. **6** Borough (pop. 1,674), Luzerne co., NE central Pa., 7 mi. NW of Wilkes-Barre; textiles; agr. Seat of College Misericordia. Inc. 1879. **7** City (pop. 244), Gregory co., S S.Dak., 4 mi. W of Gregory. **8** City (1940 pop. 294,734; 1950 pop. 434,462), ⊙ Dallas co., N Texas, 30 mi. E of

Fort Worth and 230 mi. NNW of Houston, at junction of Elm Fork and West Fork to form Trinity R.; 32°47′N 96°48′W; alt. 500 ft. Texas' 2d-largest city (after Houston), and a transportation, communications, commercial, insurance, financial, and industrial metropolis of the Southwest. Seat of a district Federal Reserve Bank. Airline and railroad focus; port of entry; a jobbing and wholesale center; one of world's largest inland cotton markets; has geophysical laboratories and hq. of several oil companies. Large cotton-gin mfg. industry; among other important industries are mfg. of cotton textiles and cottonseed products, packed meat, aircraft, automobiles (assembled here), auto and aircraft parts, leather goods, petroleum products, oil-field machinery, air-conditioning equipment, building materials, furniture, chemicals, and food products. As a regional U.S. fashion center, it is known for styling and manufacture of womens' clothing, particularly cotton dresses and hats. Seat of Southern Methodist Univ. (in suburban University Park), divisions of Baylor Univ., and Dallas Theological Seminary and Graduate School of Theology. Has a symphony orchestra and a Little Theater. State fairgrounds in State Park have bldgs. erected for Texas Centennial Exposition of 1936 and now occupied by museums. City's old reservoir, White Rock L., is now in large park; present water supply comes from reservoir (25 mi. N) in Trinity R. Has an Air Force base, Hensley Field (8 mi. SW, near Grand Prairie), and a naval air station. City's site settled 1841 by John Neely Bryan; early settlers were augmented by Fr. colonists who survived failure (1858) of Fourierist colony at near-by La Réunion. Grew as cotton-shipping center for rich blacklands region, especially after coming of railroads in 1870s. Oil interests came in 20th cent., and Second World War brought increased mfg. and expansion of pop. of city's metropolitan district (including Grand Prairie, Garland, other suburbs). A city improvement program was begun in 1920s. Inc. as town 1856, as city 1871. Annexed Preston Hollow in 1945. **9** Village (pop. 370), Barron co., NW Wis., 34 mi. NNW of Eau Claire, in dairying area.

Dallas, Lake, Texas: see TRINITY RIVER.

Dallas Center, town (pop. 944), Dallas co., central Iowa, 19 mi. WNW of Des Moines; feed mfg.

Dallas City, city (pop. 1,275), on Hancock-Henderson co. line, W Ill., on the Mississippi and 13 mi. S of Burlington (Iowa), in agr. and bituminous-coal-mining area; corn, wheat, soybeans, livestock, poultry, dairy products. Mfg. (buttons, handles); commercial fisheries; sand pits. Inc. 1859.

Dallas Mills, village (pop. 2,768, with near-by East Side), Madison co., N Ala., just NE of Huntsville.

Dallastown, borough (pop. 3,304), York co., S Pa., 6 mi. SE of York. Inc. 1867.

Dalle, Ethiopia: see YIRGA-ALAM.

Dalles, The, Oregon: see THE DALLES.

Dalles of the St. Croix, Wis. and Minn.: see INTERSTATE PARK.

Dalles of the Wisconsin, Wis.: see DELLS OF THE WISCONSIN.

Dall Island (43 mi. long, 2–8 mi. wide), SE Alaska, in Alexander Archipelago, W of Prince of Wales Isl.; 54°58′N 133°2′W; rises to 2,630 ft. View Cove village in E. Fishing, limestone quarrying.

Dallol (dä'lōl), village, Tigre prov., N Ethiopia, near Eritrean border, in Danakil desert, 45 mi. S of Merso Fatma (Eritrea); potash mining.

Dalma or **Dalmah** (dăl'mŭ), island in Persian Gulf, off Trucial Coast, belonging to Abu Dhabi sheikdom; 24°30′N 52°20′E. Pearl trade.

Dalmacio Vélez or **Dalmacio Vélez Sarsfield** (dälmä'syō vā'lĕs sär'fēl), village (pop. estimate 850), central Córdoba prov., Argentina, 23 mi. SW of Villa María; rail junction in grain and livestock area; cheese mfg.

Dalmally (dŭlmă'lē, dăl–), town in Glenorchy and Inishail parish (pop. 1,342), N central Argyll, Scotland, on Orchy R., near head of Loch Awe, 12 mi. NNE of Inveraray; market in sheep area. On near-by Loch Awe is 15th-cent. Kilchurn Castle.

Dalmarnock (dŭlmär'nŭk, dăl–), SE industrial suburb (pop. 35,824) of Glasgow, Lanark, Scotland, on N shore of the Clyde; chemical and paper works.

Dalmatia, village (pop. c.500), Northumberland co., E central Pa., on Susquehanna R. and 32 mi. N of Harrisburg.

Dalmatia (dălmā'shŭ), Serbo-Croatian *Dalmacija* (dälmä'tsēä), Ital. *Dalmazia* (dälmä'tsēä), Ger. *Dalmatien* (dälmä'tsyŭn), region of CROATIA, Yugoslavia, bet. Adriatic Sea and Bosnia and Herzegovina. The mainland, which extends from Velebit Channel (N) to Gulf of Kotor (S), consists of 2 unequal sections separated by a corridor which provides Herzegovina with an outlet to the sea near NEUM. Numerous isls. in Adriatic Sea, which constitute part of Dalmatia, include BRAC, HVAR, PAG, KORCULA, DUGI OTOK, RAB, VIS, and MLJET. Dalmatia lies entirely in DINARIC ALPS, culminating in the Troglav (6,275 ft.), which include several lowlands, notably the RAVNI KOTARI. The coast is famed for its scenic beauty and its resorts. Chief towns, all situated on the coast, are SPLIT, DUBROVNIK, SIBENIK, and ZADAR. The coast is linked with the interior by several navigable rivers (notably the NERETVA), railroads (termini at Sibenik, Split, KARDELJEVO, and Dubrovnik), and numerous roads. Dalmatia was made (34 B.C.) a Roman prov. under Augustus. It was overrun (5th cent. A.D.) by Ostrogoths, reconquered (6th cent.) by Byzantine Empire, and settled, except in coastal cities, in 7th cent. by Slavs. By 10th cent., it was divided bet. kingdoms of Croatia (N) and Serbia (S), while Venice held several ports and isls. After centuries of struggle, chiefly bet. Hungary-Croatia and Venice, the coastal isls. and most of the littoral were by 1420 under Venetian control, which was further extended (1699, 1718) by Turkish cession of interior dists. of Knin, Sinj, and Imotski. During Napoleonic era, Venetian Dalmatia passed in 1797 to Austria, in 1805 to Italy, became (1809) part of Illyrian Provs.; restored (1815) to Austria, where it was made a crownland and titular kingdom (□ 4,956; 1910 pop. 634,855; ⊙ Zara). In 1919, Yugoslavia received all Dalmatia save Zara, Lagosta, Cazza, and Pelagosa isls., which remained with Italy until 1947. Yugoslav Dalmatia constituted a separate prov. until 1921, and was divided (1929–41) into Sava, Primorje, and Zeta banovinas. During Second World War, it was part of Croatia, except for most isls. and main coastal towns (Sibenik, Split), which were temporarily annexed by Italy. In 1946, Dalmatia was inc. into Croatian people's republic; constituted (1949) as an oblast (⊙ Split).

Dalmatovo (dŭlmä'tŭvŭ), city (1926 pop. 5,458), NW Kurgan oblast, Russian SFSR, on Iset R., on Trans-Siberian RR and 28 mi. NW of Shadrinsk; agr. center; flour milling, dairying. Developed on site of Dolmatov monastery, founded 1644.

Dalmau (dŭl'mou), town (pop. 2,775), Rae Bareli dist., central Uttar Pradesh, India, on the Ganges and 17 mi. SW of Rae Bareli; trades in rice, wheat, barley, oilseeds. Ruins of anc. fort built on Buddhist stupa ruins, Moslem mosques and tombs. Annual fair.

Dalmellington (dŭlmĕ'lĭngtŭn, dăl–), town and parish (pop. 6,151), S central Ayrshire, Scotland, near Doon R., 13 mi. SE of Ayr; coal mines, ironworks.

Dalmeny (dăl'mŭnē), village (pop. 240), S central Sask., 16 mi. NNW of Saskatoon; wheat.

Dalmeny (dŭlmĕ'nē, dăl–), agr. village and parish (pop. 3,231, including part of Queensferry brugh), NE West Lothian, Scotland, near Firth of Forth, just SE of Queensferry. Has 12th-cent. Romanesque church. Near-by Dalmeny House (17th cent.) is seat of earl of Rosebery. Just NNW, on Firth of Forth, is New Halls, terminal of Firth of Forth car ferry to North Queensferry.

Dalmia Dadri, India: see DADRI.

Dalmianagar, India: see DEHRI.

Dalmiapuram, India: see LALGUDI.

Dalmine (däl'mĕnĕ), village (pop. 1,195), Bergamo prov., Lombardy, N Italy, 5 mi. SW of Bergamo; steel-tube mfg.

Dalmuir (dŭlmūr', dăl–), town in Old Kilpatrick parish, SE Dumbarton, Scotland, on the Clyde; NW suburb of Clydebank, with shipbuilding and machinery mfg.

Dalne-Konstantinovo or **Dal'ne-Konstantinovo** (däl'-nyĭ-kŭnstŭntyē'nŭvŭ), village (1926 pop. 1,099), S central Gorki oblast, Russian SFSR, 35 mi. S of Gorki; truck produce.

Dalny, Manchuria: see DAIREN.

Daloa (dä'lwä), town (pop. c.5,100), W central Ivory Coast, Fr. West Africa, on road and 135 mi. NNW of Sassandra, in fertile region (coffee, cacao, palm kernels, castor beans, rice, cotton, kola nuts, rubber). Gold deposits in vicinity.

Dalong Bay, Vietnam: see ALONG BAY.

Dalquharn, Scotland: see RENTON.

Dalquier (dälkyā'), village (pop. estimate 500), W Que., 8 mi. N of Amos; gold, copper mining.

Dal River, Swedish *Dalälven* (däl'ĕl"vŭn), central Sweden, rises in 2 headstreams (each 190 mi. long) on Norwegian border, E of Femund L.; the East Dal R., Swedish *Österdalälven* (û'stûrdälĕl"vŭn), flows SE past Sarna and Mora, through L. Silja, and past Leksand, to confluence with West Dal R. 10 mi. WNW of Borlange; the West Dal R., Swedish *Västerdalälven* (vĕ'stûrdälĕl"vŭn), flows SE to Vansbro, thence flows in winding course generally E to confluence with East Dal R. The combined stream, the Dal R. (140 mi. long), flows in winding course generally SE, past Borlange, Hedemora, and Avesta, to Krylbo, thence flows NE, through 1–4-mi.-wide estuary, to Gulf of Bothnia at Skutskar. It is important source of power for central Sweden's lumber-milling and iron industry; logging route. Major power station at Alvkarleby.

Dalroy, (dŭlroi', dăl–), village, Inverness, Scotland, on Nairn R. and 6 mi. E of Inverness; manganese mining.

Dalry (dŭlrī', dăl–). **1** Town and parish (pop. 6,827), N Ayrshire, Scotland, on Garnock R. and 7 mi. N of Irvine; ironworks, woolen mills; mfg. of agr. machinery and paint, textile dyeing. Coal mines near by. **2** Agr. village and parish (pop. 843), N central Kirkcudbright, Scotland, on Ken Water (branch of the Dee) and 3 mi. N of New Galloway.

Dalrymple (dŭlrĭm'pŭl, dăl–), agr. village anc parish (pop. 1,366), W Ayrshire, Scotland, on Door R. and 5 mi. SSE of Ayr. Cassillis House, 2 mi SW, is seat of Marquis of Ailsa.

Dalrymple, Mount, Australia: see LEICHHARD RANGE.

Dalrymple, Port, Tasmania: see TAMAR RIVER.

Dalsbruk (däls'brŭk), Finnish *Taalintehdas* (tä' lĭntĕ"däs, –tĕkh"däs), village in DRAGSFJARD com mune (pop. 4,645), Turku-Pori co., SW Finland on Gulf of Bothnia, 20 mi. NW of Hango; iron an steel milling, cable mfg.

Dalserf (dŭlsûrf'), village and parish (pop. 17,310) N central Lanark, Scotland, on the Clyde and mi. S of Wishaw; coal mining. Parish include LARKHALL.

Dalsfoss, Norway: see TOKE RIVER.

Dalsingpara, India: see RAJABHAT KHAWA.

Dalsjofors (däl"shû"fôrs',–fôsh'), Swedish *Dalsjöfors* village (pop. 1,564), Alvsborg co., SW Sweden, mi. E of Boras; linen milling.

Dalsland (däls'länd), province [Swedish *landskap* (□ 1,597; pop. 63,617), SW Sweden, on L. Vane and on Norwegian border. Included in N part c Alvsborg co.

Dals Rostock (däls" rōō'stôk"), village (pop. 710 Alvsborg co., SW Sweden, near SW shore of L Vaner, 20 mi. N of Vanersborg; health resort wit mineral springs and mud baths.

Dalston. **1** (dôl'–) Village and parish (pop. 1,631 N central Cumberland, England, 4 mi. SSW Carlisle; dairy farming. **2** (dôls' tŭn, dŏls'–) Indu trial and workers' residential district of Hackne London, England, N of the Thames, 3.5 mi. NE Charing Cross.

Dalton, Yorkshire, England: see HUDDERSFIELD.

Dalton (dôl'tŭn). **1** City (pop. 15,968), ⊙ Whitfiel co., NW Ga., 26 mi. SE of Chattanooga, Ten Major bedspread-mfg. center; also makes fabric yarn, hosiery, textile machinery, chairs, and lun ber. Dalton fell (1864) to Sherman in the Atlan campaign. Inc. 1847. **2** Town (pop. 4,772), i cluding Dalton village (pop. 4,285), Berkshire c W Mass., in the Berkshires, 5 mi. ENE of Pittsfiel resort; mfg. (paper, woolens). Settled 1755, in 1784. **3** Village (pop. 279), Otter Tail co., W Minn 11 mi. SE of Fergus Falls, in lake region; dai products. **4** Town (pop. 237), Chariton co., central Mo., near Missouri R., 8 mi. E of Brun wick. **5** Village (pop. 417), Cheyenne co., W Nebr 20 mi. N of Sidney, S of N.Platte R.; dairy an poultry produce, grain, livestock. **6** Town (po 557), Coos co., NW N.H., on the Connecticut an 22 mi. WSW of Berlin; agr. Includes Dalton Ran (2,169 ft.) and a state park. **7** Village (pop. 93 Wayne co., N central Ohio, 13 mi. E of Wooste in agr. area; pottery, grain products, electric goods. **8** Borough (pop. 1,109), Lackawanna c NE Pa., 9 mi. NNW of Scranton. Inc. c.1890.

Dalton City, village (pop. 384), Moultrie co., centr Ill., 10 mi. SE of Decatur, in agr. area.

Daltonganj (dôl'tŭngŭnj, dăl'tŭngŭnj), town (po 13,943), ⊙ Palamau dist., W Bihar, India, on Nor Koel R. and 80 mi. SW of Gaya; road and tra center (rice, corn, gram, oilseeds, barley, wheat lac growing, shellac mfg. Coal mining near b Portland-cement mfg. 34 mi. N, at Japla.

Dalton-in-Furness (dôl'–, fûr'nĭs), urban distri (1931 pop. 10,339; 1951 census 10,394), N Lanc shire, England, on Furness peninsula, 4 mi. NE Barrow-in-Furness; iron-mining and smelting ce ter; limestone quarrying.

Dalupiri Island (dälōōpē'rē). **1** Island (11 mi. lor 3.5 mi. wide; 1939 pop. 240) of Babuyan Isl Cagayan prov., Philippines, in Luzon Strait, 27 r N of Luzon; rises to 903 ft.; rice growing. **2** Isla (□ 11; 1939 pop. 6,421), Samar prov., Philippin in Samar Sea, just off NW coast of Samar isl., ne Capul Isl.; 12°24′N 124°15′E; 7 mi. long, 2 r wide. Generally low; coconuts.

Dalvik (däl'vēk"), Iceland *Dalvík*, town (pop. 61 Eyjafjardar co., N Iceland, on Eyja Fjord, 25 r NW of Akureyri; fishing port.

Dalwhinnie (dŭl-hwĭ'nē, dăl–), village, S Inverne Scotland, on Truim R., at NE end of Lo Ericht, 13 mi. SW of Kingussie; whisky distilli

Dalworthington Gardens, town (pop. 267), Tarra co., N Texas.

Dalworth Park (dăl'wûrth), former town, Dallas c N Texas, W suburb of Dallas, annexed 1943 GRAND PRAIRIE.

Daly, Mount, peak (13,193 ft.) in Rocky M Pitkin co., W central Colo.

Dalya, Yugoslavia: see DALJ.

Daly City, residential city (pop. 15,191), San Ma co., W Calif., S suburb of San Francisco; dairyi truck and flower growing. Absorbed former to of COLMA (whose name has been taken by anot town) in 1936.

Daly River (dā'lē), NW Northern Territory, A tralia, rises in hills 90 mi. W of Katherine, flows mi. NW to Anson Bay of Timor Sea.

Daly Waters, settlement (dist. pop. 51), N cent Northern Territory, Australia, 310 mi. SSE Darwin; peanuts.

Dalzell (dĕlzĕl', dŭzĕl'), village (pop. 543), Bur co., N Ill., 4 mi. WNW of La Salle, in agr. a bituminous-coal area.

Dalziel (dē-ĕl', dăl'zēl, dăl'yŭl), parish (pop. 45,116), N Lanark, Scotland; includes part of burgh of MOTHERWELL AND WISHAW.

Dam (dăm), village, Surinam dist., E central Du. Guiana, terminus of railroad from Paramaribo (80 mi. NNW, direct); serves near-by gold fields.

Dam (dăm), town, S Nejd, Saudi Arabia, in the Wadi Dawasir, 320 mi. SSW of Riyadh; 20°29'N 44°50'E. Chief town of the Wadi Dawasir; agr. (dates, vegetables, fruit), stock raising; handicrafts.

Damala, Greece: see TROIZEN.

Daman, Portuguese India: see DAMÃO.

Damanhur (dămănhŏŏr', dămăn'hŏŏr), town (pop. 84,983), ⊙ Beheira prov., Lower Egypt, 37 mi. ESE of Alexandria; 31°2'N 30°28'E. Center of rail and canal systems and important cotton and rice market; cotton ginning, wool weaving, carpentry, match mfg. Site of the anc. Hermopolis Parva.

Damão (dămã'ō) or **Daman** (dŭmăn'), district (□ 176; pop. 63,521), Port. India; ⊙ Damão. Consists of 3 separate enclaves lying bet. Arabian Sea and Western Ghats, at N end of the Konkan, in W Bombay state, India; Damão proper is on coast, Nagar Aveli at foot of the Ghats, and small area around town of Dadrá lies between. Rice, wheat, and tobacco are main crops. Fishing, hand-loom weaving, palm-mat and basket making. Teak forests in hills (E). Damão town seized by Portuguese in 1558; in 1559 surrounding area was annexed. Nagar Aveli ceded by Mahrattas in 1780.

Damão or **Daman,** town (pop. 4,757), ⊙ Damão dist., Portuguese India, small port at mouth of Gulf of Cambay, 100 mi. N of Bombay, India; trade center; exports teak, rice, wheat, tobacco, handicraft cloth fabrics; fishing (pomfrets, Bombay duck), palm-mat weaving; shipyard. Sacked by Portuguese in 1531 and finally taken in 1558; became prosperous port, trading mainly with E coast of Africa.

Damar (dămär'). **1** Island (9 mi. long, 6 mi. wide), N Moluccas, Indonesia, in Ceram Sea, 7 mi. S of S tip of Halmahera; 0°59'S 128°20'E. **2** Island, S Moluccas, Indonesia: see DAMAR ISLANDS.

Damar (dŭmär', dă'mär), city (pop. 305), Rooks co., N central Kansas, 14 mi. ESE of Hill City; wheat, livestock.

Damar, Yemen: see DHAMAR.

Damara (dămärä'), village, S Ubangi-Shari, Fr. Equatorial Africa, 45 mi. N of Bangui.

Damaraland (dŭmä'rŭlănd), region of central South-West Africa, N of Great Namaqualand, centered on Windhoek; named for the Berg Damaras, who were among earliest inhabitants of region.

Damariscotta (dă"mŭrĭskŏ'tŭ), town (pop. 1,113), Lincoln co., S Maine, 22 mi. SE of Augusta and on E bank of Damariscotta R.; clamming. Damariscotta Mills village is site of St. Patrick's church, said to be oldest R.C. church in New England (1803). Site of early trading posts; settled permanently c.1640.

Damariscotta Lake, S Maine, narrow lake (10 mi. long); center of resort area in central Lincoln co.

Damariscotta River, Lincoln co., S Maine, inlet extending c.20 mi. inland from point bet. Boothbay Harbor and South Bristol.

Damariscove Island (dă'mŭrĭskōv"), Lincoln co., S Maine, narrow isl. (2 mi. long), 5 mi. SSE of Boothbay Harbor.

Damar Islands (dămär'), group (□ 122; pop. 2,059), S Moluccas, Indonesia, in Banda Sea, 130 mi. NE of Timor; 7°9'S 128°37'E. Comprise the large volcanic isl. Damar (12 mi. long, 10 mi. wide, rising to 2,848 ft.) surrounded by several offshore islets. Group produces sago, corn. Also spelled Danmar and Dammer.

Damas (dămäs'), village (pop. 11,237), Daqahliya prov., Lower Egypt, 8 mi. NE of Mit Ghamr; cotton, cereals.

Damas, Syria: see DAMASCUS.

Damas, Paso de las (pä'sō dā läs dä'mäs), Andean pass (10,000 ft.), on Argentina-Chile border, on road bet. San Rafael (Argentina) and San Fernando (Chile); 34°53'S 70°20'W.

Damascus (dŭmă'skŭs), Arabic *Esh Sham, El Sham, Al-Sham* (all: ĕsh-shăm'), or *Dimashq*, Fr. *Damas*, province (□2,535; 1946 pop. 639,682), SW Syria, bordering W on Lebanon, E on Jordan; ⊙ Damascus. Bet. its E desert section and the Anti-Lebanon mts. on W is a fertile area watered by the Barada. The mts. have numerous summer resorts. In and around Damascus is some industry (tanning, canning, mfg. of textiles, cement, matches, and glass), but the region is principally agr. (sericulture, cotton, corn, wheat, millet, apricots, plums, figs, apples, oranges, mulberries, grapes, pears, olives, walnuts, melons).

Damascus, Arabic *Esh Sham, El Sham, Al-Sham,* or *Dimashq*, Fr. *Damas*, city (1946 pop. 303,952), ⊙ Syria and Damascus prov., in SW Syria, on Barada R., beautifully situated on a fruitful plain at E foot (alt. 2,260 ft.) of the Anti-Lebanon mts., on W edge of the desert, 50 mi. ESE of Beirut, 85 mi. NE of Haifa, and 185 mi. SSW of Aleppo; 33°30'N 36°18'E. The waters of the Barada and the A'waj (the Biblical "rivers of Damascus") irrigate wide orchards of apricots, figs, almonds, and pomegranates, and the white towers of the city rise above the green of the trees, a delight to the eyes of travelers. This favored spot has been inhabited since unknown antiquity. A city was here before the time of Abraham. It was probably held by the Egyptians before the Hittite period, and later it was under Israelite and Aramaean rule. Tiglath-pileser III made it (c.733 B.C.) a part of Assyrian territory. Later was a provincial capital of Persian Empire until it passed (332 B.C.) without a struggle to Alexander the Great. After his death Damascus was one of the prizes over which his successors fought bitterly. The Ptolemaic dynasty of Egypt tried to wrest it from the Seleucidae. When Seleucid power waned, Damascus was briefly an independent state but soon fell to new conquerors. Tigranes of Armenia took it, and after the surrender to the Romans, Damascus too went (64 B.C.) to the Romans under Pompey. It was usually under Roman influence until the break-up of the empire. A city of rich commerce, noted for its woolen cloth and its grain, it continued to thrive. It was early converted to Christianity, and it was on the road to Damascus—still a well-traveled highway—that Paul experienced his dramatic conversion. Emperor Theodosius I had a Christian church built (A.D. c.375) on the foundation of the Roman temple of Zeus, and Damascus was a Byzantine provincial capital. The Arabs took it in 635 and the city became Moslem; the great Christian church became the Great Mosque, now partly in ruins but still the principal "sight" of the city. Damascus was seat of the caliphate under the Omayyads from 661 to 750, when the triumphant Abbasids made Baghdad the center of the Moslem world. Damascus fell to the Egyptians, the Karmathians, and the Seljuk Turks. The Christian Crusaders failed to take the city but ravaged the rich plain several times, when the Saracen rulers, notably Nurredin and Saladin, were absent on campaigns. Damascus continued to prosper, with its bazaars selling the silks, wool, furniture inlaid with mother of pearl, and the famous swords and other ware of the Damascene metalworkers. In 1260 Damascus 1st fell to the Mongols under Hulagu Khan, and more than a century later it was sacked by Tamerlane, who took away the sword makers and armorers. In 1516 Damascus passed to the Ottoman Turks and for more than 300 years it remained in the Ottoman Empire fairly quietly, disturbed only by such events as the great massacres of the Christians and Jew in 1840 and 1860, and the disastrous fire of 1893, which damaged the Great Mosque. The city's great caravan trade from the East was greatly cut after the building of the Suez Canal in mid-18th cent. In the First World War, city was entered by the British in 1918. An independent Syrian government was set up but had to yield in 1920 to establishment of a French mandate. Damascus was the center of a state, which was joined in 1925 to the state centered on Aleppo. In 1925 the Damascenes joined the rebellion of the Druses. The French, shelling the city from the hills, did great damage then and again in May, 1926. In the Second World War, after the entrance of British and Free French forces in June, 1941, the independence of Syria was proclaimed in Sept., 1941, and Damascus became the capital of the new nation (confirmed 1943). Though it is reputedly the oldest continuously occupied city in the world, it has few marks of its long habitation, apart from the Great Mosque and the medieval citadel. The "street which is called Straight" still runs from the eastern to the western gate, flanked by bazaars. Damascus has a decidedly Oriental aspect, though as a center of commerce it is linked to the other cities of the Middle East by a good highway and by rail to Beirut and other cities. Damascene steel is known no more, but fine textiles, fruits, and Damascus ware are still the pride of the ancient city.

Damascus. 1 Town (pop. 402), Early co., SW Ga., 14 mi. ESE of Blakely; sawmilling. **2** Town (pop. 1,726), Washington co., SW Va., near Tenn. line, 22 mi. E of Bristol, Tenn., in dairying and agr. area; makes dyes, furniture, hosiery. Settled 1892; inc. 1904. White Top Mtn. and Mt. Rogers are E.

Damat (dămät'), village (pop. 6,093), Gharbiya prov., Lower Egypt, 11 mi. NNW of Tanta; cotton.

Damaturu (dămä'chŏŏrōō), town (pop. 2,379), Bornu prov., Northern Provinces, NE Nigeria, 50 mi. E of Potiskum; road center in peanut-growing dist.; cotton, millet, cassava, gum arabic; cattle raising. Peanut experimental station.

Damavand, Iran: see DEMAVEND.

Damazan (dămäzã'), village (pop. 733), Lot-et-Garonne dept., SW France, on Garonne Lateral Canal and 11 mi. NNW of Nérac; food canning, winegrowing, sawmilling.

Damba (däm'bä), town (pop. 1,367), Congo prov., NW Angola, 75 mi. N of Uíge; rubber, beans, rice.

Dambacha (däm'bächä), village, Gojjam prov., NW Ethiopia, in Choke Mts., 30 mi. NW of Debra Markos; trade center (coffee, hides, honey).

Dambach-la-Ville (dăbäk'-lä-vēl'), town (pop. 2,090), Bas-Rhin dept., E France, at E foot of the Vosges, 5 mi. NNW of Sélestat; noted vineyards; hosiery mfg. Retains old walls.

Dambadeniya (dŭmbŭdā'nĭyŭ), village (pop. 1,651), North Western Prov., Ceylon, 17 mi. WSW of Kurunegala; rice, coconuts. Was ⊙ Ceylon in mid-13th cent. under Singhalese, until ⊙ was moved to Yapahuwa.

Dambovicioara, Rumania: see RUCAR.

Dambovita River (dûm'bôvētsä), Rum. *Dâmbovița*, S central and S Rumania, in Muntenia, rises in Fagaras Mts. 13 mi. SW of Zarnesti, flows NE and S across the Transylvanian Alps, thence SE through Bucharest to Arges R. at Budesti; 155 mi. long. Sometimes spelled Dambovitsa.

Dambulla (dŭmbŏŏl'lŭ), village (pop., including near-by villages, 1,253), Central Prov., Ceylon, 38 mi. N of Kandy; rice, vegetables. Just W is Dambulla rock (1,148 ft.), a Buddhist pilgrimage center, with noted Buddhist cave temples dating from 1st cent. B.C.; sculptures include 47-ft.-long reclining Buddha.

Damdoi (däm'doi'), village, Baclieu prov., S Vietnam, on Camau Peninsula, 24 mi. SSE of Camau, in swamp forest area.

Damelevières (dămlŭvyâr'), town (pop. 2,513), Meurthe-et-Moselle dept., NE France, on the Meurthe and 6 mi. WSW of Lunéville; cotton-waste processing.

Dame-Marie (däm-märē'), town (1950 census pop. 1,918), Sud dept., SW Haiti, on W coast of Tiburon Peninsula, 20 mi. WSW of Jérémie; coffee, cacao.

Dame-Marie, Cape, on W tip of Tiburon Peninsula, SW Haiti, 20 mi. W of Jérémie; 18°38'N 74°26'W.

Damer, Ed, or **El Damer** (both: ĕd dă'mĕr), city (pop. 7,200), ⊙ Northern Prov., Anglo-Egyptian Sudan, on right bank of the Nile, on railroad and 165 mi. NNE of Khartoum; caravan route to Kassala (SE). Commercial and agr. center; native industry; cotton, wheat, barley, corn, fruits, durra; livestock. Large market town in 18th cent. Was ⊙ former Berber prov.

Damery (dămŭrē'), village (pop. 1,240), Marne dept., N France, on right bank of Marne R. and 4 mi. WNW of Épernay; wine-growing (champagne). Its 13th-cent. church damaged in Second World War. Adrienne Lecouvreur b. here.

Dames Quarter, village (pop. c.1,000), Somerset co., SE Md., on the Eastern Shore 21 mi. SW of Salisbury, on Monie Bay (NE arm of Tangier Sound); fishing, farming.

Damgarten (däm'gär"tŭn), town (pop. 5,723), in former Prussian Pomerania prov., N Germany, after 1945 in Mecklenburg, on the Saaler Bodden (inlet of the Baltic on S side of Darss peninsula), at mouth of small Recknitz R., 18 mi. NE of Rostock; seaside resort, fishing port.

Damghan (dămgän'), town (1941 pop. 12,235), Second Prov., in Samnan, N Iran, at S foot of Elburz mts., on road and railroad, and 165 mi. ENE of Teheran; alt. 3,767 ft. Trade center, noted for its pistachio nuts and almonds, in cotton and grain area. Identified with the anc. *Hecatompylus*, capital of Parthia, it was a flourishing city in Middle Ages, but was ruined (1723) in Afghan invasion.

Damiatte (dămyăt'), village (pop. 362), Tarn dept., S France, on Agout R. opposite Saint-Paul-Cap-de-Joux and 14 mi. WNW of Castres; brick and tile works. Wool spinning.

Damien (dămyẽ'), village, Ouest dept., S Haiti, 2 mi. NE of Port-au-Prince; has agr. school and experiment station.

Damienesti (dŭmyänĕsht'), Rum. *Dămienești*, village (pop. 1,022), Bacau prov., NE Rumania, 12 mi. SE of Roman; agr. market; lumbering.

Damietta (dămēĕ'tŭ, dămyĕ'tŭ), Arabic *Dumyat* (dŏŏm'yăt), city (pop. 53,620), coextensive with Damietta governorate, NE Egypt, on L. Manzala and on Damietta (anc. Phatnitic) mouth of the Nile, 8 mi. upstream from its mouth on the Mediterranean, and 100 mi. NNE of Cairo, 30 mi. WNW of Port Said; 31°25'N 31°48'E. Cotton ginning, silk weaving, rice milling, leather tanning, shoe making, dairying, fishing. Just N is the summer resort of Ras el Barr (or Ra's al-Barr), a peninsula jutting out bet. the Nile and the Mediterranean, with a large summer population; in winter it is partly submerged by the Mediterranean. Damietta is a few miles S of old Damietta (anc. Tamiathis), which was captured by the Crusaders 1219–21 and again in 1249; recovered and destroyed (1250) by the Egyptians, it was later reconstructed on its present site. It lost considerable importance after the construction (1819) of Mahmudiya Canal, which diverted most of Nile trade to Alexandria.

Damiya (dă'mĭyă), village (pop. c.600), N central Jordan, 12 mi. WNW of Salt; citrus fruits, vineyards. Damiya road bridge (Arabic *Jisr Damiya*), on the Jordan R. 1.5 mi. W, has frontier post.

Dammam (dăm-măm'), town in Hasa, Saudi Arabia, port on Persian Gulf, 8 mi. N of Dhahran; 26°25'N 50°7'E. Railhead (with 7-mi.-long, deepwater pier) for line to Dhahran, Abqaiq, Hofuf, and Riyadh; residential town for Arab oil-field workers; fisheries, stockyards, fruit and vegetable farms. Dammam oil field (S; discovered 1936) has its center at DHAHRAN. An anc. seaport, Dammam has remains of stone castle perched on coral reef. Its modern development began in late 1940s, when it supplanted Oqair.

Dammarie-les-Lys (dämärē'-lā-lēs'), town (pop. 5,666), Seine-et-Marne dept., N central France, near left bank of the Seine, 2 mi. SSW of Melun; industrial center mfg. radiators, pharmaceuticals, candy, rubber goods. Has 13th-cent. ruins of Cistercian Lys abbey.

Dammartin-en-Goële (dämärtē'-ā-gôĕl'), agr. village (pop. 1,215), Seine-et-Marne dept., N central France, on a hill 11 mi. NW of Meaux. Has 13th-15th-cent. church.

Dammastock (dä'mäshtôk"), peak (11,922 ft.) in Alps of the Four Forest Cantons, S central Switzerland, 12 mi. ESE of Meiringen.

Damme (dä'mů), village (commune pop. 9,282), in Oldenburg, NW Germany, after 1945 Lower Saxony, 14 mi. S of Vechta; distilling (brandy). Climatic resort.

Dammer Islands, Indonesia: see DAMAR ISLANDS.

Dammerkirch, France: see DANNEMARIE.

Damm Lake (däm), Ger. *Dammscher See* (däm'shůr zā'), or **Lake Dab**, Pol. *Jezioro Dąb* (yĕ-zhô'rô dōp') or *Jezioro Dąbskie* (dōp'skyĕ) (□ 21), in Pomerania, after 1945 in NW Poland, expansion of East Oder or Reglitz arm of Oder R. estuary, E of Stettin; from Dabie extends 10 mi. N. Efflux receives West Oder arm (N) and becomes canalized Oder R., entirely navigable.

Damm-Vorstadt, Poland: see SLUBICE.

Damnagar (däm'nŭgŭr), town (pop. 5,022), Amreli dist., NW Bombay, India, 21 mi. ENE of Amreli; millet, cotton, oilseeds; hand-loom weaving, calico printing.

Damodar River (dä'mōdär), Bihar and West Bengal, India, rises in Chota Nagpur Plateau c.15 mi. N of Lohardaga (Bihar), flows E to West Bengal border, then ESE past Raniganj and Burdwan, and S in several channels to Hooghly R. 25 mi. SW of Calcutta; c.340 mi. long. Receives combined stream of Konar R. (60 mi. long) and Bokaro R. (45 mi. long) 35 mi. W of Dhanbad and Barakar R. (155 mi. long) 11 mi. W of Asansol. Left-bank irrigation canal takes off from weir 25 mi. WNW of Burdwan, extends 50 mi. ESE and S, reentering the Damodar 16 mi. SSE of Burdwan. **Damodar Valley** (□ c.8,500; pop. c.5,000,000) includes one of India's most important mining areas (coal, mica) in central section and rich agr. tract (mainly rice) in lower reaches; traversed by Grand Trunk Road and Howrah-Benares railroad. In 1948 was begun the Damodar Valley development project of 8 multipurpose dams, a diversionary barrage, and an 80-mi.-long navigation canal linking coal fields with Hooghly R. near Calcutta. Scheme provides for flood control, hydroelectricity, a coal-fed power plant, irrigation (c.950,000 acres, mostly in West Bengal), afforestation, fish breeding, recreation, and general development of agr. and industry throughout valley. Project administered by independent corporation of central govt. All dam sites are in Bihar: 2 on Damodar R., 3 on Barakar R., 2 on Konar R., and 1 on Bokaro R. Irrigation barrage (c.2,500 ft. long, 25 ft. high) to span Damodar R. c.15 mi. SE of Raniganj near village of Durgapur in West Bengal.

Damodim (dŭmō'dĭm), volcanic cone, Chagai dist., NW Baluchistan, W Pakistan, just W of the Koh-i- Sultan; 4½ mi. wide at base; rises to c.6,000 ft. Sulphur-ore deposits on E slope. Several small, extinct volcanoes, including Koh-i-Dalil (4,870 ft.), are W; with Koh-i-Sultan and Damodim, form E extension of important volcanic region.

Damoh (dŭmō'), town (pop. 26,795), Saugor dist., Madhya Pradesh, India, 45 mi. E of Saugor; road and agr. trade center (wheat, oilseeds, cotton); oilseed milling; handicrafts (bell-metal vessels, pottery, weaving and dyeing); cattle market. Was ⊙ former Damoh dist. until merged in early 1930s with Saugor dist.

Damparis (dăpărē'), SW suburb (pop. 2,036) of Dôle, Jura dept., E France; makes plumbing fixtures.

Dampier, Mount (dăm'pyůr), peak (11,287 ft.) in Tasman Natl. Park, Southern Alps, W central S.Isl., New Zealand.

Dampier Archipelago, rocky group in Indian Ocean, just off NW coast of Western Australia, near Roebourne; 20°30'S 116°20'E. Comprises Enderby Isl. (largest; □ 21; 6 mi. long, 2 mi. wide), Legendre, Dolphin, Rosemary, Lewis, Delambre, and many smaller isls. Sheep runs on Lewis and Enderby isls.; wallabies.

Dampierre (dăpyâr'), village (pop. 264), Jura dept., E France, on the Doubs, on Rhone-Rhine Canal, and 12 mi. ENE of Dôle; lumbering.

Dampierre-sur-Salon (–sür-sälō'), village (pop. 729), Haute-Saône dept., E France, near Saône R., 9 mi. NNE of Gray; metalworking, alcohol distilling.

Dampier Strait, Bismarck Archipelago, SW Pacific, bet. New Britain and Umboi; 18 mi. wide.

Dampier Strait, channel connecting S end of Jailolo Passage with Pacific Ocean, bounded N by Waigeo isl. and S by Salawati isl. and NW Vogelkop peninsula of New Guinea; c.90 mi. long, 20–50 mi. wide.

Dampremy (dăprāmē'), town (pop. 11,559), Hainaut prov., S central Belgium, on Charleroi-Brussels Canal, just ENE of Charleroi; coal mining; glassworks, metallurgical industry.

Damprichard (dăprēshär'), village (pop. 925), Doubs dept., E France, near Swiss border, 10 mi. NNE of La Chaux-de-Fonds; watch and cheese mfg.

Damsay or **Damsay Holm** (dăm'zā hōm'), islet of the Orkneys, Scotland, in Bay of Firth, just off E coast of Pomona isl.

Damují River (dämōōhē'), central Cuba, rises W of Santa Clara, flows c.40 mi. SW and S, past Rodas and Abreus, to Cienfuegos Bay 6 mi. NW of Cienfuegos. Lower course is sometimes called Rodas.

Damville (dăvēl'), agr. village (pop. 1,061), Eure dept., NW France, on the Iton and 11 mi. SSW of Évreux.

Damvillers (dăvēlâr'), village (pop. 411), Meuse dept., NE France, on E slope of Côtes de Meuse, 13 mi. N of Verdun.

Dan (dăn, Hebrew dän), settlement (pop. 340), Upper Galilee, NE Israel, near Syrian border, at SW foot of Mt. Hermon, 20 mi. NE of Safad; shoe mfg.; agr.; trout breeding in near-by headwaters of the Jordan. Modern village founded 1939; withstood Arab attacks, May and Oct., 1948. Just N, on Syrian border, is Tell el Qadi or Tell el Kadi (both: tĕl' ĕl kä'dē), hill, reputed site of biblical locality of Dan (in earlier times called Laish or Leshem), then N extremity of Israelite territory (S extremity at Beersheba). Excavations have yielded finds dating from 17th cent. B.C.

Dan, Lough (lŏkh), lake (2 mi. long) in N Co. Wicklow, Ireland, 11 mi. NW of Wicklow; drained by Avonmore R., headstream of the Avoca.

Dana (dā'nů). **1** Village (pop. 246), La Salle co., central Ill., 13 mi. SSW of Streator, in agr. and bituminous-coal area. **2** Town (pop. 854), Vermillion co., W Ind., 24 mi. NNW of Terre Haute, near Ill. line. Atomic-energy installation under construction 1951. **3** Town (pop. 184), Greene co., central Iowa, 9 mi. NE of Jefferson, in agr. area. **4** Former town, Worcester co., central Mass.; site inundated 1937 by Quabbin Reservoir.

Dana, Mount (dā'nů), peak (13,055 ft.) of the Sierra Nevada, E Calif., 8 mi. SSW of Mono L., on E boundary of Yosemite Natl. Park.

Danakil (dă'nůkĭl, dä'näkĭl) or **Dankalia** (dängkä'-lyä), Ital. *Dancalia*, large desert region mostly in NE Ethiopia (Tigre, Wallo, Harar provs.) and partly in Eritrea and Fr. Somaliland bet. gulfs of Zula and Tadjoura. Bordered by Red Sea (N, E) and by escarpments of Great Rift Valley (S, W). Extends E of 40°E bet. 10°N and 15°N; c.350 mi. long, 50–250 mi. wide. Parallel to Red Sea coast, N of Fr. Somaliland, are a series of mtn. ranges (c.1,000–3,000 ft. high; c.150 mi. long, 10–50 mi. wide), sometimes called "Danakil Alps," containing some active and extinct volcanoes, and rising over 6,500 ft. in Afdera and Mussa Ali peaks. Bet. these ranges and the Ethiopian highlands is a large depression (section of Great Rift Valley), descending to c.500 ft. below sea level and containing salt lakes (Abbé, Assal, Gamarri, Arissa, Egogi Bad), marshes, hot springs, and several volcanoes; S part of depression is named AUSSA. Watered by Awash, Ererti, and Golima rivers. Inhabited by Nomadic Danakil or Afar tribe, who tend camels, sheep, goats, mules, and cattle. Salt extracting is widespread and potash is mined at Dallol. Crossed by Djibouti–Addis Ababa railroad and road in SE corner and by Dessye-Assab road in center.

Danané (dänä'nā), town (pop. c.3,600), W Ivory Coast, Fr. West Africa, 40 mi. W of Man; coffee, rice, kola nuts.

Danao (dänä'ō, dänou'), town (1939 pop. 2,631; 1948 municipality pop. 26,461), central Cebu isl., Philippines, on Camotes Sea, 17 mi. NE of Cebu city; agr. center (corn, coconuts).

Dana Point (dā'nů), high coastal promontory, S Calif., just SW of San Juan Capistrano. Dana Point village (pop. c.300) is near by.

Danapur, India: see DINAPORE.

Danbi (dŭnbē'), village, Henzada dist., Lower Burma, at crossing of Bassein R. by Henzada-Kyangin RR, 10 mi. W of Henzada.

Danburg, town (pop. 181), Wilkes co., NE Ga., 11 mi. NE of Washington.

Danbury, town and parish (pop. 1,807), central Essex, England, 5 mi. E of Chelmsford; agr. market. Has 14th–15th-cent. church. Just S are remains of Danish camp.

Danbury. 1 City (pop. 22,067), in Danbury town (pop. 30,337), a ⊙ Fairfield co., SW Conn., on Still R. and 20 mi. NW of Bridgeport; hat-making center since 18th cent., with diversified mfg. (machinery, metal products, silverware, clothing, chemicals, aircraft, rubber and paper products), agr. (poultry, truck, dairy products). L. Candlewood (resorts) is just N. Ski slopes near by. Settled 1684; inc. as town 1687, as city 1889. Military depot in Revolution; raided by Tryon in 1777. Noted annual fair, here, since early 19th cent. Has teachers col., U.S. prison (1940); state park near by. **2** Town (pop. 601), Woodbury co., W Iowa, c.40 mi. ESE of Sioux City; concrete products. **3** Village (pop. 218), Red Willow co., S Nebr., 15 mi. SE of McCook and on Beaver Creek, near Kansas line. **4** Town (pop. 496), Merrimack co., S central N.H., on Smith R. and 28 mi. NW of Concord; agr. **5** Village (pop. c.400), ⊙ Stokes co., N N.C., on Dan R. and 21 mi. N of Winston-Salem. Hanging Rock State Park near by. **6** Village, Burnett co., NW Wis., on St. Croix R. and 25 mi. NW of Spooner.

Danby, town (pop. 990), Rutland co., S central Vt., in valley bet. Green Mts. (E) and the Taconics, on Otter Creek and 18 mi. S of Rutland; wood products, dairying, marble quarrying, fern marketing. Chartered 1761, settled 1765.

Danby Lake, SE Calif., intermittently dry bed, in Mojave Desert, 50 mi. SW of Needles; c.15 mi. long.

Dancalia, region, Ethiopia, Eritrea, and Fr. Somaliland: see DANAKIL.

Dancalia Meridionale, Eritrea: see ASSAB.

Danco Coast (dăng'kō), NW coast of Palmer Peninsula, Antarctica, bet. Charcot Bay (63°50'S 59°30'W) and Cape Renard (65°5'S). Discovered 1898 by Adrien de Gerlache, Belgian explorer.

Dandagamuwa, Ceylon: see KULIYAPITIYA.

Dandara, Egypt: see DENDERA.

Dandei Sivaram, India: see WALAJABAD.

Dandeldhura (dŭndäl'dōōrŭ) or **Dadeldhura** (dŭd–), town, W Nepal, 24 mi. W of Doti; corn, rice, vegetables, fruit. Nepalese military post.

Dandeli (dŭndā'lē), village (pop. 40), Kanara dist., S Bombay, India, 31 mi. SW of Dharwar; rail spur terminus; timber depot (teak, sandalwood, bamboo, blackwood); sawmills.

Dandenong (dăn'dŭnŏng), town (pop. 6,512), S Victoria, Australia, 18 mi. SE of Melbourne; rail junction in dairying, agr. region; dairy plants, vegetable-dehydration plant, brickyards.

Danderyd (dän'dürüd"), residential town (pop. 6,302), Stockholm co., E Sweden, 5 mi. N of Stockholm city center; candy and chocolate mfg. Has medieval church. Near by are prehistoric stones with runic inscriptions.

Dandi (dŭn'dē), village, Surat dist., N Bombay, India, near Gulf of Cambay, 16 mi. NW of Surat; small port for coastal smacks. Here, in 1930, after march from Ahmadabad, Gandhi and followers made salt in symbolic defiance of govt. salt monopoly.

Dandot (dŭndōt'), village, Jhelum dist., N Punjab, W Pakistan, in Salt Range, 7 mi. NW of Pind Dadan Khan; cement works. Coal mines near by.

Dandridge, town (pop. 690), ⊙ Jefferson co., E Tenn., on Douglas Reservoir, 28 mi. E of Knoxville; canned vegetables, hosiery, flour.

Dane, county (□ 1,197; pop. 169,357), S Wis.; ⊙ Madison. Bounded NW by Wisconsin R; drained by Yahara and Sugar rivers and by Waterloo and Koshkonong creeks. Dairy-farming region; some mfg. in Madison and Stoughton. Includes several large lakes, notably the FOUR LAKES. Formed 1836.

Dane, village (pop. 305), Dane co., S Wis., 13 mi. NNW of Madison, in dairy region.

Daneborg (dä'nůbôr") or **Eskimonaes** (ĕ'skĭmônĕs"), meteorological and radio station, E Greenland, on S Clavering Isl. (35 mi. long, 25 mi. wide; rises to 5,261 ft.), on bay of Greenland Sea; 74°7'N 20°55'W. Near by are several whaling huts.

Danehill, agr. village and parish (pop. 1,153), central Sussex, England, 7 mi. S of East Grinstead.

Danelaw (dān'lô"), originally the body of law which prevailed in the part of England occupied by the Danes after the treaty of King Alfred with Guthrum in 886. It soon meant also the area in which Danish law prevailed; according to the treaty the boundary bet. England and Danelaw ran "up the Thames, and then up the Lea . . . to its source, then up the Ouse to Watling Street." The Danelaw contained 4 main regions: Northumbria; the shires dependent on the boroughs of Lincoln, Nottingham, Derby, Leicester, and Stamford; East Anglia; and the SE Midlands.

Dane River, Cheshire, England, rises 7 mi. SE of Macclesfield, flows 30 mi. W, past Congleton and Middlewich, to Weaver R. at Northwich.

Danforth, W suburb of Toronto, S Ont.

Danforth. 1 Village (pop. 385), Iroquois co., E Ill., 21 mi. SSW of Kankakee, in agr. area. **2** Town (pop. 1,174), Washington co., E Maine, 32 mi. S of Houlton, near Chiputneticook Lakes; lumber milling. Settled 1829, inc. 1860.

Dangara (dŭn-gŭrä'), village (1939 pop. over 500), W Kulyab oblast, Tadzhik SSR, 27 mi. NW of Kulyab; wheat, livestock; metalworks.

Dangé (dăzhā'), village (pop. 606), Vienne dept., W central France, on Vienne R. and 9 mi. NNE of Châtellerault; dairying.

Danger, Point. 1 Headland, NE New South Wales, Australia, on coast just S of Queensland border; forms E end of McPherson Range; 28°9'S 153°34'E. **2** Headland, SW Victoria, Australia, in Indian Ocean, forms W side of entrance to Portland Bay; 38°24'S 141°40'E.

Danger Island: see PUKAPUKA.

Danger Islands: see PUKAPUKA.

Dangerous Archipelago: see TUAMOTU ISLANDS.

Dang Ghorai, Nepal: see DHANGARHI.

Dangila (däng'gĭlä), town, Gojjam prov., NW Ethiopia, in Agaumdir dist., 100 mi. SW of Gondar; 11°18'N 36°55'E. Trade center (beeswax, honey, coffee, cereals).

Dangme Chu, river, Bhutan: see MANAS RIVER.

Dangra Yum, Tibet: see TANGRA TSO.

Dangrek Range (däng'rĕk), Thai *Dong Rak* (dông' räk'), forested hill range on Thailand-Cambodia line, forming S limit of Korat Plateau; extends c.200 mi. W from the Mekong and is continued W by San Kamphaeng Range; rises to over 2,000 ft. It slopes gradually N toward the Mun R., but forms abrupt scarp (S) on Cambodian plain.

Dangs (däṅgz, dŭngz), district (□ 667; pop. 40,498), N central Bombay, India; ⊙ Ahwa. Lies in N Western Ghats, bet. Surat dist. (N and W) and Nasik dist. (S and E). A forested, hilly tract, producing some millet, rice, and teak. Formerly was group of petty states of GUJARAT STATES agency; since 1949 merged in Bombay. Pop. 72% tribal, 27% Hindu.

Dania (dā'nēŭ), city (pop. 4,540), Broward co., S Fla., on Atlantic coast just S of Fort Lauderdale, 20 mi. N of Miami; canning, packing, and shipping center (vegetables, citrus fruit); mfg. of office machinery. Seminole Indian Reservation near by. Settled 1896 by Danes.

Daniel Carrión, Peru: see YANAHUANCA.

Daniels, county (□ 1,443; pop. 3,946), NE Mont.; ⊙ Scobey. Agr. area bordering on Sask.; drained by Poplar R. Grain, livestock. Formed 1920.

Daniels. 1 Village, Howard co., central Md., on Patapsco R. and 11 mi. W of downtown Baltimore; cotton-duck plant. Renamed 1940 from Alberton. **2** Village (pop. 1,159, with near-by Rhyne), Lincoln co., W central N.C., 5 mi. NW of Lincolnton.

Danielson, industrial borough (pop. 4,554) in Killingly town, Windham co., NE Conn., on Quinebaug R. and 18 mi. NE of Willimantic; textiles, machinery, cutlery, rubber products. Inc. 1854.

Danielstown, village (pop. 478), Essequibo co., N Br. Guiana, on Atlantic coast, 9 mi. N of Queenstown; coconut plantations.

Danielsville. 1 City (pop. 298), ⊙ Madison co., NE Ga., 14 mi. NE of Athens, in agr. area. **2** Village (1940 pop. 1,077), Northampton co., E Pa., 19 mi. N of Allentown; roofing slate.

Danilov (dŭnyē'lŭf), city (1939 pop. over 10,000), NE Yaroslavl oblast, Russian SFSR, 40 mi. NNE of Yaroslavl; rail junction; cattle-trading center; metalworking, clothing mfg., flax and food processing. Chartered 1777. Danilov Ridge, a moraine upland, extends from Volga R. at Tutayev c.75 mi. NE to Kostroma R.; rises to 525 ft.

Danilov Grad or **Danilovgrad** (dänē'lôfgrät), village (pop. 2,047), S central Montenegro, Yugoslavia, on Zeta R. and 11 mi. NW of Titograd, in the Bjelopavlici; local trade center.

Danilovka (dŭnyē'lŭfkŭ). **1** Town (1948 pop. over 2,000), N Akmolinsk oblast, Kazakh SSR, 30 mi. S of Stepnyak; gold mining. **2** Village (1926 pop. 3,221), S Penza oblast, Russian SFSR, 16 mi. N of Petrovsk; flour milling, distilling; wheat, sunflowers. **3** Village (1932 pop. estimate 5,400), N central Stalingrad oblast, Russian SFSR, on Medveditsa R. and 45 mi. NE of Mikhailovka; wheat, sunflowers.

Dänischenhagen (dā'nĭ-shŭnhä"gŭn), village (pop. 2,248), in Schleswig-Holstein, NW Germany, 7 mi. N of Kiel city center; sawmilling.

Danish West Indies, former possession of Denmark in Lesser Antilles just E of Puerto Rico, comprising SAINT CROIX, SAINT JOHN, and SAINT THOMAS isls., since 1917 the Virgin Isls. of the U.S.

Danjoutin (däzhōōtē'), S suburb (pop. 2,225) of Belfort, Territory of Belfort, E France; cotton milling, cable mfg., canning.

Dank, Oman: see DHANK.

Dankalia, region, Ethiopia, Eritrea, and Fr. Somaliland: see DANAKIL.

Dankama (däng-kä'mä), town (pop. 1,809), Katsina prov., Northern Provinces, N Nigeria, 25 mi. NNE of Katsina, on Fr. West Africa border; cotton, peanuts; cattle, skins.

Dankaur (dŭng'kour), town (pop. 5,289), Bulandshahr dist., W Uttar Pradesh, India, 19 mi. WSW of Bulandshahr; trades in wheat, oilseeds, sugar cane, barley, corn, ghee.

Dankhar (dŭng'kŭr), village, Kangra dist., NE Punjab, India, 110 mi. E of Dharmsala, on rocky spur of the Himalayas; hq. of Spiti subdivision. Buddhist monastery.

Dankov (dŭn-kôf'), town (1926 pop. 9,309), SW Ryazan oblast, Russian SFSR, on Don R. and 95 mi. SSW of Ryazan; flour milling; rubber-plant processing; limestone quarrying.

Danlí (dänlē'), city (pop. 3,759), El Paraíso dept., S Honduras, at S foot of Sierra del Chile, 45 mi. E of Tegucigalpa; 14°5'N 86°32'W. Commercial center in rich agr. area (tobacco, coffee, fruit); dairying. Has noted church and old aqueduct. Airfield. Dates from 17th cent.

Danmar Islands, Indonesia: see DAMAR ISLANDS.

Danmark: see DENMARK.

Danmark Fjord (dăn'märk fyōr'), inlet (130 mi. long, 1–20 mi. wide), NE Greenland; 80°25'–82°N 23°W; extends SW to edge of inland icecap, forms NW shore of Crown Prince Christian Land.

Danna, island (pop. 25), SW Argyll, Scotland, bet. Loch Sween (E) and the Sound of Jura (W), separated from mainland (N) by a narrow channel; 2 mi. long, 1 mi. wide.

Dannebrog (dă'nŭbrôg"), village (pop. 318), Howard co., E central Nebr., 7 mi. SW of St. Paul and on Middle Loup R., in grain and cattle region; dairy and poultry produce.

Dannemarie (dänmärē'), Ger. *Dammerkirch* (dä'mŭrkĭrkh), village (pop. 1,214), Haut-Rhin dept., E France, on Rhone-Rhine Canal and 6 mi. W of Altkirch; agr.-machinery mfg.

Dannemoine (dänŭmwăn'), village (pop. 351), Yonne dept., N central France, on Armançon R. and Burgundy Canal, and 3 mi. NNW of Tonnerre; large foundry.

Dannemora (dä'nŭmōō"rä), village (pop. 676), Uppsala co., E Sweden, on 4-mi.-long Dannemora L., 25 mi. NNE of Uppsala; important iron-mining center since 16th cent.

Dannemora (dă"nŭmô'rŭ), village (pop. 4,122), Clinton co., extreme NE N.Y., in the Adirondacks, 13 mi. W of Plattsburg. Seat of Clinton State Prison. Inc. 1881.

Dannenberg (dä'nŭnbĕrk), town (pop. 3,144), in former Prussian prov. of Hanover, NW Germany, after 1945 in Lower Saxony, near left bank of the Elbe, 30 mi. ESE of Lüneburg, 7 mi. WSW of Dömitz; rail junction; woodworking, food processing, dyeing. Has anc. ruined castle.

Dannevirke (dă'nŭvûrk), borough (pop. 4,334), ⊙ Dannevirke co. (□ 426; pop. 4,321), E N.Isl., New Zealand, 100 mi. NE of Wellington; dairies, sheep ranches, sawmills; airport.

Dannhauser (dän'houzŭr), town (pop. 1,558), NW Natal, U. of So. Afr., 15 mi. NW of Dundee; coal mining.

Dan River, in Va. and N.C., rises in the piedmont in Patrick co., S Va.; flows SE into N.C., NE into Va. past Danville, again briefly into N.C., then NE and E past South Boston, Va., to Roanoke R. above Clarksville; c.180 mi. long. At Pinnacles of Dan (in Patrick co.) on upper course is large hydroelectric project, completed 1938.

Dansalan (dänsä'län), town (1939 pop. 1,096; 1948 municipality pop. 19,657), ⊙ Lanao prov., W central Mindanao, Philippines, 40 mi. SW of Cagayan, near N shore of L. Lanao; rice, corn.

Danskoya (dänsk'ûyä), Nor. *Danskøya*, island (□ 15.5), Spitsbergen group, in Arctic Ocean, just off NW West Spitsbergen; 79°40'N 11°E. It is 6 mi. long, 4 mi. wide; rises to 1,132 ft. (N). Virgo Harbor (N) was starting point of S. A. Andrée's ill-fated attempt (July, 1897) to reach North Pole by balloon.

Dans Mountain, in NW Md. and S Pa., part of the E escarpment of the Alleghenies, rising to 2,898 ft. at Dans Rock c.5 mi. ENE of Lonaconing, Md.; runs NE c.30 mi. from North Branch of the Potomac just E of Westernport, Md., to Hyndman, Pa.

Dansville. 1 Village (pop. 433), Ingham co., S central Mich., 18 mi. SE of Lansing, in agr. area. **2** Village (pop. 5,230), Livingston co., W central N.Y., on Canaseraga Creek and 40 mi. S of Rochester; mfg. (shoes, paper, metal products); nurseries; agr. (beans, potatoes). Here Clara Barton founded (1881) 1st local chapter of the American Red Cross. Health resort. Near by is a state park. Settled 1795, inc. 1845.

Danta (dän'tŭ), town (pop. 2,312), Banas Kantha dist., N Bombay, India, 20 mi. E of Palanpur; local trade in grain, cloth fabrics, sugar cane; handloom weaving. Sometimes called Danta Bhavangadh. Was ⊙ former princely state of Danta (□347; pop. 31,110) in Rajputana States, inc. 1949 into Banas Kantha dist.

Dante, Ital. Somaliland: see HAFUN.

Dante. 1 (dän'tē) Town (pop. 140), Charles Mix co., SE S.Dak., 20 mi. SE of Lake Andes and on branch of Missouri R. **2** (dănt) Coal-mining village (pop. 2,405), Russell co., SW Va., in the Alleghenies, 19 mi. E of Norton.

Dantewara (dŭntāvä'rŭ), village, Bastar dist., SE Madhya Pradesh, India, 45 mi. WSW of Jagdalpur, in forested hills (sal, bamboo, myrobalan). Hematite deposits (S).

Danube (dă'nūb), village (pop. 437), Renville co., SW Minn., 6 mi. W of Olivia; dairy products.

Danube-Black Sea Canal (dă'nūb), Constanta prov., SE Rumania; seaway begun 1949 bet. Cernavoda and Cape Midia, to pass Medgidia and Poarta Alba. To be used for shipping and irrigation.

Danube Canal, Ger. *Donaukanal* (dō'noukänäl"), arm of the Danube at Vienna, Austria, forming an isl. on which Leopoldstadt and Brigittenau dists. of Vienna are located.

Danube-Oder Canal (-ō'dŭr), in S Poland and Czechoslovakia, is planned to run S from Kozle (Poland), via upper Oder R., Moravian Gate, and Morava R. valley, to the Danube at Morava mouth. N section, bet. Kozle and Ostrava, Czechoslovakia, was begun 1950.

Danube River (dă'nūb), Ger. *Donau* (dō'nou), Czech *Dunaj* (dōō'nī), Hungarian *Duna* (dōō'nŏ), Serbo-Croatian and Bulgarian *Dunav* (dōō'näv), Rumanian *Dunărea* (dōō'nŭryä), Russian *Dunai* (dōō'nī), anc. *Danubius* (dănū'bēŭs) and, in lower course, *Ister* (ĭ'stĕr), central and SE Europe, 2d longest (c.1,750 mi.) river (after the Volga) of the continent, with a drainage basin of c.320,000 sq. mi. The Danube waters some of Europe's principal granaries. It passes through or borders 8 countries (Germany, Austria, Czechoslovakia, Hungary, Yugoslavia, Rumania, Bulgaria, and the Ukraine of the USSR), and on it lie the capitals of 3 countries—VIENNA, BUDAPEST, and BELGRADE. It is formed by 2 headstreams (each c.25 mi. long), the BRIGACH RIVER and BREGE RIVER, which rise at alt. of c.2,200 ft. in the Black Forest of SW Germany and unite just below DONAUESCHINGEN only 20 mi. NNW of Schaffhausen on the Rhine. The Danube flows generally W-E, entering the Black Sea in a wide, marshy delta. In its upper course most of the water seeps away at IMMENDINGEN through subterranean channels to the small AACH RIVER and the near-by Rhine. It flows initially NE through Württemberg and Bavaria, past ULM (head of navigation) and REGENSBURG, where it turns SE to enter Austria below PASSAU while flanking the Bohemian Forest on S. It continues SE through Upper and Lower Austria, past LINZ, whence it follows a more easterly course to KREMS and Vienna. This section is particularly famous for its scenery, noted for its historical and literary (Niebelungenlied) associations. Near Vienna, outliers of the Alps—the Wienerwald—touch upon its right bank. It then forms short frontier bet. Austria and Czechoslovakia (whose major Danubian port is BRATISLAVA) and a longer frontier bet. Czechoslovakia and Hungary, passing KOMAROM and ESZTERGOM, to VAC, where it turns sharply S to separate with its meandering (partly canalized), widening course the Great Hungarian Plain or ALFÖLD (E) from the mts. and rolling hills of Transdanubia (Dunantul). Along this section are the Hungarian centers Budapest (with large CSEPEL ISLAND), BAJA, and MOHACS. It then enters Yugoslavia and cuts across the lowlands of E Croatia (Slavonia) and the Vojvodina (NE Serbia), past OSIJEK, VUKOVAR, PALANKA, NOVI SAD, and Belgrade. The Danube is joined in this region by some of its major navigable affluents, such as DRAVA RIVER, TISZA RIVER, SAVA RIVER, TIMIS RIVER, and MORAVA RIVER (or the Great Morava), interlaced by several canals. The Danube then reaches the Rumanian border, where it cuts a narrowing, swift course bet. the defiles of the W Transylvanian Alps and below ORSOVA pierces the famous c.2-mi.-long IRON GATE (since 1896 the rapids here have been removed and navigation facilitated by the lateral SIP CANAL). Beyond TURNU-SEVERIN the course becomes more gentle and broadens into the lower Danube that enters the great Walachian plain and forms most of the Rumanian-Bulgarian boundary, bounded on right bank by the fertile lowlands of N Bulgaria and the Deliorman piedmont. In this section are the Bulgarian towns of NIKOPOL, SVISHTOV, and RUSE, and the Rumanian towns of CORABIA and GIURGIU (principal port for Ploesti oilfields). Near SILISTRA it leaves the Bulgarian border and turns N, separating the Rumanian provs. of Dobruja (E) and Walachia (W); here the delta (□ 1,000 mi.) begins, the river splitting into several braided arms enclosing isls. and marshes which occasionally become a great flood plain (in this region the railroad from Bucharest to Constanta on Black Sea has to run across one of the globe's longest bridges). At BRAILA, Rumania's chief grain port, the web of streams unite, only to branch off again below GALATI after bending eastward and receiving the PRUT RIVER at the border of the Ukraine. Near TULCEA the 3 main arms—the Kiliya (the principal arm for shipping), the Sulina, and the St. George—are formed, carving out Letea Isl. (N) and St. George Isl. (S). On the northernmost Kiliya arms lie the Bessarabian towns IZMAIL, KILIYA, and VILKOVO, since 1940 belonging to USSR. The Sulina, the central arm of the delta, enters the Black Sea at town of Sulina (45°9'N 29°40'E). The deposition of alluvial matter is enormous. A region of floating isls. (*Baltas*), reeds, deciduous groves (beech, willow), it teems with bird life. Navigable for small craft from Ulm and for larger vessels from Regensburg, the Danube is a vital traffic artery and a link of many cultures. The volume of commerce, however, is far below that of the Rhine, owing to the relative backwardness of Eastern Europe, the complex political landscape, and the flow to a sea remote from the world's principal trade routes. Yet the economic importance to bordering countries is great, and physical conditions for navigation are excellent, since water supply as well as a good all-year passage are secured. Difficulties near its delta are planned to be overcome upon completion of the DANUBE-BLACK SEA CANAL from Cernavoda to Novodari at Cape Midia above Constanta; but ships drawing up to 22 ft. can now proceed via the Kiliya arm to Braila. The Danube is linked with other major European rivers, notably with the Main-Rhine rivers via the LUDWIG CANAL (partly Altmühl R.) and with the Oder through the DANUBE-ODER CANAL (begun 1950) via Moravian Gate. The Danube receives more than 300 affluents; among the major ones—apart from those already mentioned—are, on the right: ILLER RIVER, LECH RIVER, ISAR RIVER, INN RIVER, TRAUN RIVER, ENNS RIVER, LEITHA RIVER, RAAB RIVER, ISKER RIVER; on the left: ALTMÜHL RIVER, NAAB RIVER, REGEN RIVER, MORAVA RIVER (March R.), VAH RIVER, HRON RIVER, IPEL RIVER, JIU RIVER, OLT RIVER, IALOMITA RIVER, SIRET RIVER. Under the Roman Empire (when it was known as Danubius or Danuvius, and, in its section below the Iron Gate, by its Greek name *Ister*), the Danube formed the N defense line against the barbarian world. Along it were built fortified outposts, later to become the region's leading cities. As Rome declined, the Danubian plains for centuries attracted invading hordes—Goths, Huns, Avars, Magyars, Mongols, and others. The Turks gained control of its course from Hungary to the sea in 15th–16th cent. The European Commission of the Danube established (1856) an authority of 8 powers over the Mouths of the Danube. It was responsible for clearing obstructions and deepening the passage. After the Treaty of Versailles, the Danube was internationalized (1921) under the International Commission of the Danube with jurisdiction over the navigable course from Ulm to Braila. This commission had hq. at Vienna, while the European commission controlling the mouths remained at Galati. By the Sinaia agreement (1938) Rumania attained virtual control over the lower section. Germany, having repudiated the internationalization in 1936, also forced (1940) the International Commission to dissolve. Despite the provision made by 1947 peace treaty for the Danube's complete internationalization, a new Danube authority, set up 1948 upon instigation of the USSR, included only the riparian powers (except Germany and Austria). The Western Powers, who contested this decision, were not admitted.

Danube-Tisza Canal (–tĭ'sŏ) or **Danube-Tisa Canal** (–tē'sä). **1** In the Backa, Vojvodina, N Serbia, Yugoslavia; runs bet. Tisza R. at Becej (E), past Srbobran, Kula, and Sombor, and the Danube at Bezdan; 76 mi. long. Connects at Mali Stapar with branch canal SE to Novi Sad. Until 1945, called Franz Canal in Hungary, King Peter Canal in Yugoslavia. **2** In N central Hungary construction of another Danube-Tisza Canal, linking Dunaharaszti and Ujkecske, was begun 1950.

Danubian Principalities, name formerly applied to the principalities of WALACHIA and MOLDAVIA, now parts of RUMANIA.

Danubyu (dŏonyōō'bū), town (pop. 6,334), Maubin dist., Lower Burma, on right bank of Irrawaddy R. and 65 mi. NE of Bassein. Produces cheroots. Old Mon fort; captured 1825 by Br. forces in 1st Anglo-Burmese War.

Danum, England: see DONCASTER.

Danvers (dăn'vûrz). **1** Village (pop. 762), McLean co., central Ill., 9 mi. WNW of Bloomington, in rich agr. area; feed milling. **2** Residential town (pop. 15,720), Essex co., NE Mass., on tidewater inlet and 5 mi. NW of Salem; mfg. (shoes, leather, metal products). State insane asylum. Settled 1636, inc. 1757. Includes village of Danvers Port. **3** Village (pop. 162), Swift co., SW Minn., 8 mi. WSW of Benson, in grain and potato area.

Danville, village (pop. 1,332), S Que., 25 mi. N of Sherbrooke; asbestos mining, woodworking.

Danville. 1 Town (pop. 829), a ⊙ Yell co., W central Ark., 22 mi. SW of Russellville, and on Petit Jean R.; cotton ginning, lumber milling. Founded 1841. **2** Village (pop. c.1,200), Contra Costa co., W Calif., 15 mi. E of Oakland, in agr. region. **3** Town (pop. 461), Twiggs and Wilkinson counties, central Ga., 28 mi. ESE of Macon. **4** City (pop. 37,864), ⊙ Vermilion co., E Ill., on Vermilion R. (bridged here), at Ind. line, and c.75 mi. ENE of Decatur; commercial and industrial center in agr. and bituminous-coal-mining area; railroad shops; large brick and zinc plants. Mfg. also of food products, hoisting and mining machinery, hardware, paper boxes, shoes, foundry and machine-shop products, furnaces, textiles, clothing, auto supplies, transformers, chemicals, wood and metal products, fireworks, batteries. A natl. home for disabled soldiers is here. Near by are L. Vermilion (resort) and Kickapoo State Park. Platted on site of an Indian village and made co. seat in 1827; inc. 1839. Gurdon S. Hubbard had a trading post here (1828–33), and Joseph G. Cannon (whose home is preserved) lived here. Abraham Lincoln maintained a law office in Danville. **5** Town (pop. 2,802), ⊙ Hendricks co., central Ind., on a fork of Whitelick R. and 20 mi. W of Indianapolis; trading center in agr. area; mfg. (flour, oil dispensers, cement blocks). Seat of Canterbury Col. Settled 1824, inc. 1835. **6** Town (pop. 450), Des Moines co., SE Iowa, 10 mi. WNW of Burlington, in agr. area. Geode State Park near by. **7** City (pop. 122), Harper co., S Kansas, 40 mi. SW of Wichita, in wheat region. **8** City (pop. 8,686), ⊙ Boyle co., central Ky., 32 mi. SSW of Lexington. Railroad division point; industrial center in outer Bluegrass region (burley tobacco, wheat, livestock); mfg. of clothing, furniture, industrial gas-fired equipment, concrete blocks, beverages, prepared milk; flour, feed, and lumber milling; stockyards, tobacco warehouse; airport. Seat of Centre Col. of Ky. (chartered 1819; Presbyterian), state school for deaf, and Ky. state hosp. Other points of interest include Dr. Ephraim McDowell State Shrine (scene in 1809 of 1st successful ovariotomy) and Weisiger Memorial State Shrine (the old courthouse square), which preserves the setting of old seat of govt. W of the Alleghenies (1784–92), where Ky. constitutional conventions were held. Many fine ante-bellum houses. Near by is former site of Transylvania Col. (opened 1785), Herrington L., and a natl. cemetery. One of Ky.'s oldest communities; settled 1775, established 1787, inc. 1836. **9** Town (pop. 56), Montgomery co., E central Mo., 5 mi. S of Montgomery City. **10** Town (pop. 508), Rockingham co., SE N.H., 18 mi. ESE of Manchester; mfg. (yarn, shoes). **11** Village (pop. 853), Knox co., central Ohio, 13 mi. ENE of Mount Vernon, in agr. area; makes metal products. **12** Borough (pop. 6,994), ⊙ Montour co., E central Pa., 29 mi. SE of Williamsport and on Susquehanna R.; iron and steel works, machinery. State hosp. for insane. Laid out 1790, inc. 1849. **13** Town (pop. 1,312), Caledonia co., NE Vt., just W of St. Johnsbury; lumber, wood products. Thaddeus Stevens b. here. West Danville village is resort on Joe's Pond. Settled 1784. **14** City (pop. 35,066), in but independent of Pittsylvania co., S Va., near N.C. line, on Dan R. and 55 mi. S of Lynchburg. One of world's largest bright-leaf tobacco markets; important cotton-milling center; also produces hosiery, clothing, furniture, flour, fertilizers, tobacco products, elevators, foundry and lumber products, packed meat, beverages. City operates Pinnacles of Dan hydroelectric project (82 mi. W), completed 1938. Seat of 2 jr. colleges for girls, boys' preparatory school. Founded 1793; inc. as city 1870. For 7 days in April, 1865, was last capital of the Confederacy. **15** Village, Ferry co., NE Wash., port of entry near international line, 3 mi. SW of Grand Forks, British Columbia. **16** Town (pop. 544), Boone co., SW W.Va., just NNW of Madison; bituminous coal.

Danzig (dăn'sĭg, Ger. dän'tsĭkh) or **Gdansk** (gŭdä'-nyŭsk), Pol. *Gdańsk*, city (1941 pop. 267,251; 1946 pop. 117,894; 1950 pop. c.191,000), since 1945 ⊙ Gdansk prov., N Poland, Baltic port on Gulf of Danzig, at mouth of arm of Vistula estuary, 170 mi. NW of Warsaw; 54°20'N 18°40'E. Rail junction; one of the 2 largest ports (Gdynia is the other) of Poland; exports coal, lumber, grain, foodstuffs; imports iron and other raw materials. Transshipment point for Vistula steamers; ocean-going vessels dock at outer port of Nowy Port (Neufahrwasser). Airport (NW). Shipyards, grain elevator; food processing, distilling, construction industry. Seat of R.C. bishop. In Second World War, Danzig suffered, except in port dist., very heavy destruction; Church of St. Mary (1343) survived, heavily damaged. Prior to the war, city had retained its medieval architecture and aspect, with 14th-cent. city hall, old gates, numerous gabled houses, and narrow winding streets. First mentioned in 997, Danzig was ⊙ duchy of Pomerelia. After its settlement by Ger. merchants it joined (13th cent.) Hanseatic League and rapidly became important Baltic port. Passed (1308) to Teutonic Knights. Ceded (1466) to Poland, it became autonomous. Accepted Reformation in 16th cent. After Thirty Years War it declined. Resisted invasion (1655–60) of Poland by Charles X of Sweden. In War of the Polish Succession, King Stanislaus I took refuge here until Danzig fell (1734) to Russians after stubborn defense. Became free city (1772) in 1st partition of Poland; in 2d partition (1793) it passed to Prussia. Napoleon I again made it a free city, 1807–14. Reverted (1814) to Prussia and was fortified; until 1919, was ⊙ West Prussia prov. Under Treaty of Versailles (1919) it became ⊙ territory of the Free City of Danzig (□ 731; 1941 pop. 404,000), which also included ZOPPOT, OLIVA, NOWY DWOR (Neuhof), NOWY PORT (Neufahrwasser), NOWY STAW (Neuteich), and fortress of WESTERPLATTE, garrisoned by Poland. To give Poland a seaport, the free city was included in Pol. customs territory and railroads were placed under Pol. control; Danzig was placed under a high commissioner appointed by League of Nations, but had its own legislature. After 1933, it came under virtual Nazi control, as League of Nations authority declined. Hitler's demand for reunion of Danzig with Germany was principal immediate cause of Ger. invasion of Poland and outbreak of Second World War. Was ⊙ Ger. prov. of Danzig-Westpreussen from 1939 until its capture (1945) by Rus. army. After First World War, Danzig lost much trade through construction of rival Pol. port of GDYNIA. After 1945, when Danzig was given to Poland, Pol. plans envisaged the merging of Danzig, Gdynia, and Zoppot into a single city.

Danzig, Gulf of, Pol. *Zatoka Gdańska* (zätô'kä gŭdä'nyŭskä), Rus. *Gdanskaya Bukhta* (gŭdä'-nyŭskī"ŭ bōōkh'tŭ), Ger. *Danziger Bucht* (dän'-tsĭgŭr bŏŏkht'), inlet of Baltic Sea, bounded W, S, and SE by Poland, E by Kaliningrad oblast, Russian SFSR; c.40 mi. long N-S, 65 mi. wide; max. depth 370 ft. Includes Puck Bay (separated by Hel Peninsula) and Vistula Lagoon (separated by Vistula Spit and Samland peninsula). Receives Vistula R., and, through Vistula Lagoon, Nogat, Pasleka, and Pregel rivers. Gdynia, Zoppot, Danzig, Elbing, and Baltisk lie on or near its coast.

Danzig Corridor, Poland: see POLISH CORRIDOR.

Danziger Bucht, Poland: see DANZIG, GULF OF.

Dao (dä'ō, dou). **1** Town (1939 pop. 1,449; 1948 muncipality pop. 23,702), Antique prov., extreme SW Panay isl., Philippines, 45 mi. WSW of Iloilo; rice-growing center. **2** Town (1939 pop. 1,819; 1948 municipality pop. 13,706), Capiz prov., N Panay isl., Philippines, on railroad and 14 mi. SSW of Capiz; rice-growing center.

Dão River (dã'ō), in Viseu dist., N central Portugal, rises in Serra da Lapa, flows c.50 mi. SW to the Mondego. Winegrowing on valley slopes.

Daosa (dou'sŭ), town (pop. 8,844), E Rajasthan, India, 30 mi. E of Jaipur; trades in grain, marble, mica, cotton; marble sculpturing, hand-loom weaving. Also spelled Dausa. At village of Bhankri, 4 mi. NE, mica schist quarried.

Daoulas (doulās', dōō–), village (pop. 886), Finistère dept., W France, 10 mi. E of Brest; produces vegetables. Livestock fair. Kaolin and granite quarries near by. Has remains of 12th-cent. cloister. Damaged in Second World War.

Daoura, Oued ed, Fr. Morocco and Algeria: see ZIZ, OUED.

Daourat Dam, Fr. Morocco: see OUM ER RBIA.

Dapa (däpä', dä'pä), town (1939 pop. 3,165; 1948 municipality pop. 14,492), Surigao prov., Philippines, on Siargao Isl., just off NE tip of Mindanao.

Dapcau (däp'kou'), village, Bacninh prov., N Vietnam, port on the Song Cau and 3 mi. NE of Bacninh; mfg. (paper, fireworks).

Daphnae, Egypt: see TAHAPANES.

Daphne or **Dhafni** (both: dhäf'nē), town (pop. 2,360), Achaea nome, N Peloponnesus, Greece, 33 mi. SSE of Patras; summer resort; wine; sheep, goats. Also spelled Dafni; formerly Strezova.

Daphne (dăf'nē), farming town (pop. 1,041), Baldwin co., SW Ala., on E shore of Mobile Bay, 10 mi. SE of Mobile.

Dapitan (däpē'tän), town (1939 pop. 6,791; 1948 municipality pop. 37,984), Zamboanga prov., NW Mindanao, Philippines, small port on Mindanao Sea, 55 mi. N of Pagadian. Area has cattle, coconuts, rice, corn.

Dapoli (däpō'lē), village, Ratnagiri dist., W Bombay, India, near Arabian Sea, 55 mi. N of Ratnagiri; local market center for rice, fish. Former military station.

Daqadus (däkä'dōōs), village (pop. 6,022), Daqahliya prov., Lower Egypt, on Damietta branch of the Nile just NNE of Mit Ghamr; cotton, cereals.

Daqahliya or **Daqahliyah** (däkälē'yŭ), province (□ 1,014; pop. 1,416,226), NE Lower Egypt; ⊙ Mansura. Bounded W by Damietta branch of the Nile, N by L. MANZALA, E and S by Sharqiya prov. Cotton ginning, linen and sailcloth mfg.; fisheries; agr. (cotton, cereals). Main urban centers: Mansura, Mit Ghamr, Manzala. Served by Cairo-Damietta RR branch. Irrigated mainly by El Bahr el Saghir.

Dara, Fr. West Africa: see DAHRA.

Darab (däräb'), town (1940 pop. 7,403), Seventh Prov., in Fars, S Iran, 135 mi. ESE of Shiraz and 35 mi. SE of Niriz; grain, tobacco, dates, oranges, cotton, rice. Trade center, exporting figs, opium, wool, tobacco, and dried flowers. Near by is Sassanian bas-relief sculptured into rocks. Sometimes called Darabgird or Darabgerd.

Darabani (däräbän'), town (1948 pop. 11,379), Botosani prov., NE Rumania, near Prut R. (USSR border), 15 mi. NNE of Dorohoi; flour milling, metalworking, mfg. of carbonated drinks.

Daracya Peninsula (därächyä'), Turkish *Daraçya*, SW Turkey, extends S into Aegean Sea opposite Rhodes; 34 mi. long, 21 mi. wide; rises to 3,260 ft. Town of Marmaris on E shore.

Dara Dere, Bulgaria: see ZLATOGRAD.

Daraga, Philippines: see LEGASPI.

Daragaz (därägäz') or **Darajaz** (–jäz'), agr. district of Khurasan, Ninth Prov., NE Iran, on USSR line, 90 mi. NW of Meshed. Main towns are Muhammadabad (sometimes called Daragaz) and Lutfabad. Occasional earthquakes. Also spelled Dargaz.

Daragizy, Tadzhik SSR: see FAIZABAD.

Darahini, Turkey: see GENC.

Darajaz, Iran: see DARAGAZ.

Daralagez Range or **Daralagyaz Range** (där"-ŭlŭgyôs'), spur of the Lesser Caucasus, in Armenian and Nakhichevan Autonomous SSRs; extends from Karabakh Range c.40 mi. WSW to Aras R. valley; forms left watershed of the Eastern Arpa-Chai.

Dar al Amir (där' ăl ămēr'), village, Abdali sultanate, Western Aden Protectorate, just N of Sheikh Othman; Abdali customs station on Aden-Yemen trade route.

Daram Island (däräm') (1939 pop. 15,832), Samar prov., Philippines, in Samar Sea, just off W coast of Samar isl., 10 mi. SW of Catbalogan; 11°37'N 124°46'E; 15 mi. long, ½–6 mi. wide. Hilly, rises to 1,130 ft. Rice, coconuts.

Daran (därän'), town (1941 pop. 9,258), Tenth Prov., in Isfahan, W central Iran, 75 mi. WNW of Isfahan, in mountainous region and important grazing area; wild almond and oak forests. Pop. is Bakhtiari. Formerly called Faridan.

Daranagar (dä'rănŭgŭr). **1** Town (pop. 4,196), Allahabad dist., SE Uttar Pradesh, India, 35 mi. WNW of Allahabad; gram, rice, barley, wheat, oilseeds. **2** Town (pop., including adjacent village of Ganj, 1,359), Bijnor dist., N Uttar Pradesh, India, on the Ganges and 6 mi. SSW of Bijnor; rice, wheat, gram, barley, sugar cane. Also called Ganj Daranagar.

Darassa or **Darasa** (dä'räsä), village, Sidamo-Borana prov., S Ethiopia, in mts. E of L. Abaya, 9 mi. SW of Wando; coffee growing.

Darasun (dŭrŭsōōn'), town (1939 pop. over 10,000), S central Chita oblast, Russian SFSR, 95 mi. ENE of Chita; gold-mining center. Formerly Vershina Darasuna.

Darasun-Kurort (-kōōrôrt'), village (1948 pop. over 3,000), S Chita oblast, Russian SFSR, 60 mi. S of Chita; health resort (alt. 2,100 ft.); carbonated water.

Daraut-Kurgan (dŭrŭōōt"-kōōrgän'), village (1948 pop. over 2,000), S Osh oblast, Kirghiz SSR, on S slope of Alai Range, in Kyzyl-Su valley, 50 mi. S of Kizyl-Kiya; wheat.

Daraw (därou'), village (1937 pop. 2,902; 1947 commune pop. 17,289), Aswan prov., S Egypt, on W bank of the Nile, on railroad, and 22 mi. N of Aswan; cereals, dates. Sometimes spelled Darau.

Darawa or **Darawah** (dä'räwŭ), village (pop. 9,322), Minufiya prov., Lower Egypt, on tongue of land bet. Damietta and Rosetta branches of the Nile, on railroad, and 15 mi. NW of Cairo; cereals, cotton, flax.

Darazo (däräz'ō), town (pop. 4,766), Bauchi prov., Northern Provinces, NE central Nigeria, 60 mi. NE of Bauchi; road junction; cotton, peanuts, durra.

Darband (därbänd'), village, Second Prov., in Teheran, N Iran, 10 mi. N of Teheran, at foot of Elburz mts.; summer resort for Teheran; hotels. SAADABAD royal palace is just S.

Darbat 'Ali, Ras, Arabia: see DHARBAT 'ALI, RAS.

Dar bel Amri (där' bĕl ämrē'), village, Rabat region, NW Fr. Morocco, on the Oued Beth and 14 mi. W of Petitjean, in agr. area irrigated from El Kansera Dam (10 mi. S.). Oil struck here in 1947.

Darbhanga (dŭrbŭng'gŭ), district (□ 3,347; pop. 3,457,070), N Bihar, India, in Tirhut div.; ⊙ Darbhanga. On Ganges Plain; bounded N by Nepal, S by Ganges R.; drained by tributaries of the Ganges. Alluvial soil; rice, corn, sugar cane, wheat, barley, oilseeds, cotton, jute. Rice, sugar, jute, and oilseed milling. Main trade centers: Darbhanga, Madhubani.

Darbhanga, city (pop., including S suburb of Laheria-Sarai, 69,203), ⊙ Darbhanga dist., N Bihar, India, on Ganges tributary and 60 mi. NE of Patna; rail and road junction; trades in corn, wheat, barley, oilseeds; rice, jute, sugar milling. Medical col. Dist. hq. offices at Laheria-Sarai; rail station.

Darbisiyah, Syria: see DERBISIYE.

D'Arbonne, Bayou (bī'ō därbōn'), river in N La., rises in Claiborne parish, flows c.90 mi. SE to Ouachita R. just N of Monroe; navigable. Receives Middle Fork (c.50 mi. long) from NW in N Lincoln parish.

Darby. 1 Town (pop. 415), Ravalli co., W Mont., 15 mi. S of Hamilton, near Idaho line and Bitterroot Range, in rich agr. valley of Bitterroot R.; gold mining near by. **2** Borough (pop. 13,154), Delaware co., SE Pa., SW suburb of Philadelphia; boats, textiles, clothing. Settled 1682, inc. 1853.

Darby Creek, S central Ohio, rises in Logan co., flows c.70 mi. generally SE to Scioto R. just above Circleville. Sometimes called Big Darby Creek.

Darbyville, village (pop. 203), Pickaway co., S central Ohio, 11 mi. WNW of Circleville, and on Darby Creek, in agr. area.

Darcilena (därsēlā'nŭ), city (pop. 4,008), N Sergipe, NE Brazil, near railroad, 7 mi. SW of Propriá, in rice-growing dist. Until 1944, called Cedro.

Darda (där'dä), village, NE Croatia, Yugoslavia, near Drava R., on railroad and 5 mi. N of Osijek, in the Baranja; local trade center.

Dardanelle (därdŭnĕl'), city (pop. 1,772), a ⊙ Yell co., W central Ark., 4 mi. SSW of Russellville and on Arkansas R., in farm area; cotton ginning, sawmilling (pine and oak timber). Mt. Nebo State Park (recreation area) is near by. Platted 1843 on site of old Indian post.

Dardanelles (därdŭnĕlz'), anc. *Hellespont* (hĕ'lŭspŏnt), Turkish *Çanakkale Boğazı*, narrow strait in NW Turkey connecting Sea of Marmara and Aegean Sea, separating Gallipoli Peninsula (Turkey in Europe) from Asia Minor (Anatolia); 37 mi. long, 1.2–4 mi. wide. In Gr. mythology the Hellespont was scene of the legend of Hero and Leander. Modern name is derived from Dardanus, anc. Gr. city on its Asiatic shore. Controlling navigation bet. the Black Sea and the Mediterranean, the Dardanelles and the BOSPORUS straits have been of immense strategic and commercial importance since the dawn of history. Anc. Troy prospered near W entrance to the Hellespont. Xerxes I crossed (c.481 B.C.) it at Abydos on a bridge of boats, as did Alexander the Great in 334 B.C. Long important to the defense of Constantinople, the Dardanelles have been in the hands of the Turks since 15th cent. In 1841 the European powers agreed (confirmed 1856 at end of Crimean War) to close the straits to all but Turkish warships in peacetime. An Anglo-French attempt in 1915 to force the Dardanelles failed. Nominally a demilitarized zone of the Straits, 1920–36; the Montreux Convention (1936) formally allowed Turkey to remilitarize it. Important towns on it are Gallipoli, Canakkale, and Eceabat.

Dardanelles Cone, peak (9,502 ft.), Alpine co., E Calif., in the Sierra Nevada, c.40 mi. S of L. Tahoe.

Dardesheim (där'dŭs-hīm), town (pop. 1,832), in former Prussian Saxony prov., central Germany, after 1945 in Saxony-Anhalt, 11 mi. WNW of Halberstadt; flour milling; brickworks.

Dardistan (dŭr'dĭstän), name applied to area inhabited by tribes speaking mainly Dard languages. Comprises Gilgit Agency, Gilgit leased area, and Astor dist. in Kashmir, and Chitral and Dir states and upper reaches of Swat R. in North-West Frontier Prov., W Pakistan.

Dare, county (□ 388; pop. 5,405), NE N.C.; ⊙ Manteo. Bounded E by the Atlantic, N by Albemarle Sound, W by Alligator R. Includes Roanoke Isl., barrier beaches, and Cape HATTERAS. Forested (pine, cypress) and swampy tidewater area; dairying, farming (grapes, sweet potatoes, corn), fishing, sawmilling. Includes Cape Hatteras State Park, Fort Raleigh Natl. Historic Site, Kill Devil Hill Natl. Memorial. Formed 1870.

Dar el Beida, Fr. Morocco: see CASABLANCA.

Dar-el-Bey, Tunisia: see ENFIDAVILLE.

Darende (dărĕndĕ'). **1** Town, Konya prov., Turkey: see KARAMAN. **2** Town (pop. 6,182), Malatya prov., central Turkey, on Tohma R. and 45 mi. WNW of Malatya; grain.

Darenth (dă'rŭnth), town and parish (pop. 4,191), NW Kent, England, on Darent R. and 2 mi. SE of Dartford; paper-milling center. Church includes Roman and Saxon fragments. Just S, on Darent R., is paper-milling town of South Darenth.

Darent River (dă'rĕnt), Kent, England, rises just S of Westerham, flows 20 mi. NE and N, past Eynsford, South Darenth, and Darenth, to Thames R. just E of Erith. Many paper mills along course.

Dar es Salaam or **Dar-es-Salaam** (där'-ĕs-sŭläm') [Arabic,=haven of peace], largest town (pop. 69,227) and ⊙ of Tanganyika, major seaport on Indian Ocean, 45 mi. S of Zanzibar and 400 mi. SE of Nairobi (Kenya); 6°48'S 39°17'E. Ocean terminus of Central RR (773 mi. long) crossing Tanganyika to Kigoma on L. Tanganyika. Administrative and commercial center with modern European quarter. New deep-water berths have been added since late 1940s to congested, almost landlocked harbor. Handling over half of territory's exports, it ships sisal, cotton, copra, coffee, hides and skins, peanuts, papain, beeswax, and minerals (diamonds, gold, tin, mica). Agr. processing, mfg. of pharmaceuticals, beverages, furniture. Meat-packing plant at Msasani (N). Fishing. Fine botanical garden. Airport 3 mi. SW. Founded 1862 by Sultan of Zanzibar; occupied 1887 by German East Africa Co. Succeeded Bagamoyo as ⊙ German East Africa in 1891. Occupied (1916) by British during First World War. Non-native pop. (1948) 18,462, mostly Indian.

Darfield (där'-), urban district (1931 pop. 5,260; 1951 census 6,238), West Riding, S Yorkshire, England, 7 mi. N of Rotherham; coal mining. Church dates from 13th cent.

Darfield, township (pop. 324), E S.Isl., New Zealand, 27 mi. W of Christchurch; rail junction; agr.

Darfo (där'fô), town (pop. 3,193), Brescia prov., Lombardy, N Italy, in Val Camonica, on Oglio R. and 24 mi. N of Brescia; ironworks, chemical factory (calcium carbide, tannic acid), textile mill; large hydroelectric plant. Iron mines, red sandstone quarries near by.

Darfur (där'fōōr), province (□ 138,150; 1948 pop. estimate 910,565), W Anglo-Egyptian Sudan; ⊙ El Fasher. Bordered by Fr. Equatorial Africa (W). Consists of a vast rolling plain drained by intermittent streams. Marra Mts. in W. Vegetation ranges from bush forest (S) to scrub grass (N). Gum arabic and livestock are main resources. Some agr. (watermelons, dates, oilseeds, tobacco). Chief centers are El Fasher and Geneina. An independent kingdom until conquered by Egypt in 1874. Chiefly inhabited by Fur Moslems and Nuba Negro tribes.

Darfur (där'fŭr), village (pop. 150), Watonwan co., S Minn., near Watonwan R., 11 mi. WNW of St. James; dairy products.

Dargai (dŭrgī'), village, Swat state, N North-West Frontier Prov., W Pakistan, 4½ mi. SSW of Malakand, on Upper Swat Canal and 38 mi. NNE of Peshawar; rail terminus; hydroelectric plant.

Darganata (dŭrgŭnä'tŭ), village, NE Chardzhou oblast, Turkmen SSR, on railroad, on the Amu Darya and 120 mi. NW of Chardzhou; cotton; pistachio woods.

Dargaville (där'gŭvĭl), borough (pop. 2,370), ⊙ Hobson co. (□ 746; pop. 5,762), N N.Isl., New Zealand, 80 mi. NNW of Auckland and on Wairoa R.; timber, dairy products.

Dargaz, Iran: see DARAGAZ.

Dargilan, France: see MEYRUEIS.

Darg-Kokh (därk-kôkh'), village (1926 pop. 3,016), central North Ossetian Autonomous SSR, Russian SFSR, on Terek R. and 25 mi. NW of Dzaudzhikau, in hemp and soybean area; orchards, vineyards; starch processing. At Darg-Kokh rail junction (3 mi. W), Alagir spur leaves main line.

Dargun (där'gōōn), town (pop. 3,900), Mecklenburg, N Germany, 9 mi. W of Demmin; agr. market (grain, sugar beets, potatoes, stock); sawmilling. Health resort. Has 13th-cent. church and bldgs. of Cistercian monastery (founded 1172; secularized 1552; transformed into castle in 17th cent.). Connected with the Peene by short canal.

Darhan, Mongolia: see DARKHAN.

Dariapur, India: see AHMADABAD, city.

Daridere, Bulgaria: see ZLATOGRAD.

Dariel Gorge, Georgian SSR: see DARYAL GORGE.

Darien (dâ"rēĕn', dâ'rēĕn"), Sp. *Darién* (däryĕn'), E part of Panama; more properly only that part of the isthmus bet. Gulf of Darien on E coast and Gulf of San Miguel on W coast; 40 mi. wide at its narrowest point. The Gulf of Darien is a wide inlet of the Caribbean bet. Colombia and Panama; its S section is the Gulf of Urabá. Just back of the Caribbean coastal plain is the Serranía del Darién, a section of the continental divide extending c.140 mi. in semicircle W–SE through Panama and along Panama-Colombia border; rises to 7,480 ft. In E Panama, on Pacific slope of the Isthmus of Darien, is the Panamanian prov. of Darién (□ 5,994; 1950 pop. 14,108; 40% Indians); ⊙ La Palma. It is bordered N by the Cordillera de San Blas, E by the Cordillera de Tacarcuna (Colombia border), and W by the Pacific. Drained by Tuira, Chucunaque, and Sambú rivers. Agr. (plantains, corn, rice, beans), stock raising, lumbering, gold placer mining. Crossed by proposed route of Inter-American Highway, it is served largely by coastal shipping. Main centers (and ports) are La Palma, El Real, and Yaviza. Formed 1922 out of Panama prov.; temporarily recombined (1941–45).

Darien, railroad station, Balboa dist., central Panama Canal Zone, on transisthmian railroad, at E shore of the Canal, 19 mi. NW of Panama city. Radio station.

Darien. 1 (dâ"rēĕn') Residential town (pop. 11,767), Fairfield co., SW Conn., on Long Isl. Sound just E of Stamford; nurseries, metalworks. Includes Noroton (nŭrō'tŭn) village, site of soldiers' home and U.S. cemetery. Raided by British in Revolution; many 18th-cent. houses survive. Settled c.1641, inc. 1820. **2** (dā'rēyĭn") City (pop. 1,380), ⊙ McIntosh co., SE Ga., c.50 mi. SSW of Savannah, near mouth of Altamaha R. on the Atlantic; fishing port; seafood canning, sawmilling. State park and site of Fort King George (1721–27), the 1st English settlement in Ga., are near by. Founded 1736 by Scotch Highlanders recruited by James Oglethorpe to supersede Spanish influence in the area. **3** (dâ"rēĕn') Village (1940 pop. 534), Walworth co., SE Wis., 17 mi. ESE of Janesville, in dairying and hog-raising region.

Dariense, Cordillera (kôrdĭyā'rä däryĕn'sä), central Nicaragua, E spur of main continental divide; extends from Jinotega area c.100 mi. E, forming watershed bet. Tuma R. (N) and Río Grande (S); rises to 5,600 ft. in peak Musún. Other peaks are the Pancasán and Cangrejal. Sometimes called Sierra de Datanlí.

Darik (därēk') or **Dirik** (dē'rēk), Fr. *Dérik*, town, Jezire prov., NE Syria, near Turkish border, 90 mi. NE of El Haseke; sheep raising.

Darinski or **Dar'inskiy** (dŭrēn'skē), village (1939 pop. over 500), N West Kazakhstan oblast, Kazakh SSR, on Ural R. and 18 mi. NE of Uralsk; wheat, millet.

Dario, Nicaragua: see CIUDAD DARIO.

Dar'iyah, Saudi Arabia: see DERAYA.

Darjeeling (därjē'lĭng), district (□ 1,192; pop. 376,369), N West Bengal, India; ⊙ Darjeeling. Bounded N by Sikkim, W by Nepal, E by Bhutan, SW by Bihar (India); drained by Tista and Mahananda rivers. SE Nepal Himalayan foothills (W of Tista R.) and SW Assam Himalayan foothills (E of Tista R.) in N area; sal, teak, oak, cinchona (plantations near Kalimpong and Sonada), silver fir, orchids, and rhododendrons in extensive forest area; tea (a major tea-growing dist. of West Bengal), rice, corn, millet, cardamom, oranges, jute, wheat. Terai region (S); high malarial mortality. Coal and copper pyrite deposits near Kumai. Tea processing at Darjeeling, Kurseong, and Kalimpong (terminus of main trade route to Tibet; cotton-cloth weaving), sawmilling and rice milling at Siliguri; rail workshops at Tindharia. Dist. noted for wild game (elephants, tigers, leopards, rhinoceroses). Figured in Gurkha War of 1814–16. Present boundaries formed 1865. Pop. 55% Hindu, 45% tribal (Nepalese, Koch, Limbu, Lepcha, Bhotia).

Darjeeling, town (pop. 25,873), ⊙ Darjeeling dist., N West Bengal, India, 305 mi. N of Calcutta, in spur of SE Nepal Himalayan foothills; rail terminus; hill resort famous for its spectacular view of the great Himalayan range. Tea processing (extensive tea plantations on hill slopes), plywood mfg.; rice, corn, cardamom, oranges. Has col. Town was purchased 1835 from raja of Sikkim and built as a sanatorium for Br. troops; later expanded to include suburbs of JALAPAHAR and LEBONG. During intermittent clearing of mists, Kanchenjunga mtn., 46 mi. N, is visible. Mt. Everest, 106 mi. NW, may be seen from Jalapahar and from Tiger Hill (8,482 ft.; 13 mi. SE). Highest point in town (c.7,160 ft.) is Observatory Hill;

Buddhist monastery on its slope. Noted botanical gardens. Cutlery and tool mfg. 8 mi. S, at Ghum (or Ghoom) village.

Darke, county (□ 605; pop. 41,799), W Ohio; ⊙ Greenville. Drained by Greenville Creek, Stillwater and Mississinewa rivers. Rich agr. area (livestock, grain, tobacco, tomatoes, fruit); mfg. at Greenville; clay and gravel pits. Formed 1816.

Darkehmen, Russian SFSR: see OZERSK.

Darkhan or **Darhan** (där'khän), table mountain in E central Mongolian People's Republic, 150 mi. SE of Ulan Bator and 20 mi. NE of Choiren. Monument on top, honoring memory of Jenghiz Khan, attracts pilgrims.

Darkharbor, Maine: see ISLESBORO.

Darkoti (dŭrkō'tē), former princely state (□ 5; pop. 632) of Punjab Hill States, India, E of Simla. Since 1948, merged with Himachal Pradesh.

Darkot Pass (där'kŏt, dŭr'kōt), 15,380 ft. high, in range of E Hindu Kush, on Kashmir–North-West Frontier Prov. (Pakistan) border; lies on route bet. Gilgit (75 mi. SE) and Chitral.

Darkov (där'kôf), village (pop. 3,170), NE Silesia, Czechoslovakia, on railroad and 11 mi. E of Ostrava, near Pol. border; noted health resort, famous for iodine and salt treatments.

Darkush, Syria: see DERKUSH.

Darlac, province, Vietnam: see BANMETHUOT.

Darlac Plateau (därläk'), S central Vietnam, one of the Moi Plateaus, W of Annamese Cordillera; 13°N 108°20'E. Has average alt. of 2,500 ft. and forms watershed of left affluents of the Mekong. Inhabited by indigenous Moi tribes, the area is also a center of European colonization with tea, coffee, and rubber plantations. Chief town, Banmethuot.

Darlaston (där'lustun), urban district (1931 pop. 19,736; 1951 census 22,024), S Stafford, England, 4 mi. ESE of Wolverhampton; coal mines, steel-rolling mills, mfg. of nuts, bolts, automobile parts.

Darley, town (pop. c.5,000), central Derby, England, on Derwent R. and 3 mi. NW of Matlock, of which it has been part since 1934. Includes North Darley and South Darley. Lead mining and smelting, stone quarrying; resort with mineral springs. Stone quarries in use since Saxon and Roman times.

Darley Abbey, town and parish (pop. 699), S Derby, England, on Derwent R. just N of Derby; cotton milling. Has remains of 12th-cent. abbey.

Darling, village (pop. 1,201), SW Cape Prov., U. of So. Afr., 20 mi. WNW of Malmesbury; grain, tobacco, fruit.

Darling Downs, tableland (□ 27,610), SE Queensland, Australia, just W of Great Dividing Range, N of New South Wales border; alt. 2–3,000 ft. Wheat belt of Queensland; livestock. Toowoomba is commercial center.

Darlingford, village (pop. estimate 200), S Man., 50 mi. S of Portage la Prairie, in Pembina Mts.; grain, stock.

Darling Range, Western Australia, extends 200 mi. S from Gingin to Bridgetown, parallel with SW coast; rises to 1,910 ft. (Mt. Cooke). Site of Mundaring Weir, Canning Dam, and suburbs of Perth. Karri eucalyptus, sandalwood.

Darling River, SE Australia, longest tributary of MURRAY RIVER. Its headstreams, Dumaresq and Macintyre rivers, join at New South Wales-Queensland border 175 mi. SW of Brisbane; river thus formed flows W and SW along border and past Mungindi (here called both the Macintyre and the Barwon), thence SW through New South Wales, past Walgett, Brewarrina, and Bourke (known bet. Mungindi and Bourke as Barwon or Darling river), thence (known only as Darling R.) past Wilcannia and Menindee, to Murray R. at Wentworth. Length, 1,910 mi. Main tributaries: Gwydir, Namoi, Castlereagh, Macquarie, Bogan, and Warrego rivers. Important only for irrigation.

Darlington. **1** Municipality (pop. 3,032), E New South Wales, Australia, 2 mi. SSE of Sydney, in metropolitan area; sheet metal. **2** Residential town (pop. 747), SW Western Australia, 13 mi. E of Perth, in Darling Range; orchards.

Darlington, county borough (1931 pop. 72,086; 1951 census 84,861), S Durham, England, on Skerne R., near the junction with the Tees, and 17 mi. S of Durham; railroad center; locomotive works, steel mills and foundries, woolen mills, electrical-equipment plants. W terminal of the Stockton and Darlington railroad; *Locomotive No. 1*, which drew the 1st passenger train (1825), is exhibited at Bank Top Station. Has St. Cuthbert's Church (1180–1200), Elizabethan grammar school, technical and teachers colleges. In county borough (NE) is town of Haughton-le-Skerne (hô'tun-lu-skûrn'), with agr.-machinery works.

Darlington, county (□ 545; pop. 50,016), NE S.C.; ⊙ Darlington. Bounded E by Pee Dee R. Tobacco, cotton, corn, hogs, timber. Formed 1785.

Darlington. **1** Town (pop. 711), Montgomery co., W central Ind., on Sugar Creek and 9 mi. NE of Crawfordsville. **2** Village (pop. c.250), Harford co., NE Md., near the Susquehanna, 33 mi. NE of Baltimore; vegetable cannery, lumber mill. **3** Town (pop. 217), Gentry co., NW Mo., on Grand R. and 38 mi. NE of St. Joseph. **4** Village, Passaic co., NE N.J., on Ramapo R. just NW of Ramsey. Seat of Immaculate Conception Seminary. **5** Borough (pop. 354), Beaver co., W Pa., 6 mi. WNW of Beaver Falls. **6** Town (pop. 6,619), ⊙ Darlington co., NE S.C., 9 mi. NW of Florence; lumber, mfg. (chairs, textiles, paper cups, cottonseed oil, flour), printing; tobacco warehouses. Settled 1798, inc. 1835. **7** City (pop. 2,174), ⊙ Lafayette co., S Wis., on Pecatonica R. and c.45 mi. SW of Madison, in dairy-farming area; feed, cheese. Inc. 1877.

Darliston (där'lĭstun), town (pop. 1,170), Westmoreland parish, W Jamaica, 10 mi. ENE of Savanna-la-Mar; sugar cane, rice, breadfruit, stock.

Darlowo (därwô'vô), Pol. *Darlowo*, Ger. *Rügenwalde* (rü"gunväl'du), town (1939 pop. 8,363; 1946 pop. 5,262) in Pomerania, after 1945 in Koszalin prov., NW Poland, near the Baltic, 25 mi. W of Stolp (Slupsk); rail spur terminus; fishing port; metalworking. Has late-Gothic basilica with grave of King Eric of Pomerania (a king of the Scandinavian Union), former castle, old town gate. Chartered 1312; joined Hanseatic League in 1362; long-time residence of dukes of Pomerania. Formerly noted for its sausages.

Darmanesti (durmunĕsht'), Rum. *Dărmănești*. **1** Village (pop. 5,094), Bacau prov., E central Rumania, in the Moldavian Carpathians, on railroad and 10 mi. NW of Targu-Ocna; lignite mining, wood cracking, lumbering. **2** Village (pop. 2,835), Suceava prov., N Rumania, 8 mi. NW of Suceava; rail junction.

Dar Masalit, Anglo-Egyptian Sudan: see GENEINA.

Darmstadt (därm'shtät, -stăt, Ger. därm'shtät), city (1939 pop., including suburbs, 115,196; 1946 pop. 53,944, including suburbs 76,266; 1950 pop. 94,132), former ⊙ Hesse and of former Starkenburg prov., S Hesse, W Germany, at N tip of the Odenwald, 17 mi. S of Frankfurt; 49°52'N 8°39'E. Rail junction; steel construction; railroad repair shops; mfg. of Diesel motors, machinery, stoves, radios, pharmaceuticals, plastics. Oil slate quarried in vicinity. Has institute of technology. Second World War damage (about 75%) includes most noteworthy bldgs.: 16th–18th-cent. castle, 16th-cent. town hall, large Stadtkirche. Noted mus. with valuable collection of paintings was preserved. First mentioned in 8th cent. Passed to counts of Katzenellenbogen in 1257. Chartered 1330. Deeded to landgraves of Hesse in 1479. Residence of HESSE-DARMSTADT line (later grand dukes) from 1567 to 1918; then was ⊙ free state of Hesse until 1945. Captured by U.S. troops in March, 1945.

Darnall (där'nôl), town (pop. 23,695) in Sheffield county borough, West Riding, S Yorkshire, England, just E of Sheffield; coal mining, iron and steel industry; railroad rolling-stock construction.

Darnétal (därnätäl'), outer E suburb (pop. 7,469) of Rouen, Seine-Inférieure dept., N France; textile mills (cotton and linen cloth, shirts); tanning, metalworking, cider distilling, carton mfg.

Darney (därnē'), village (pop. 1,197), Vosges dept., E France, at foot of Monts Faucilles, 19 mi. WSW of Épinal, on Saône R.; metalworking, cheese mfg.

Darnitsa, Ukrainian SSR: see KIEV, city.

Darnley, Cape, headland on Indian Ocean, Antarctica, at NW entrance to Mackenzie Bay, on Mac-Robertson Coast; 67°42'S 69°30'E. Discovered 1931 by Sir Douglas Mawson.

Darnley Bay, NW Mackenzie Dist., Northwest Territories, inlet (28 mi. long, 20 mi. wide at mouth) of Amundsen Gulf, on E side of Parry Peninsula; 69°40'N 123°45'W.

Darnley Island (pop. 320), in Great Northeast Channel of Torres Strait, 110 mi. NE of Cape York Peninsula, N Queensland, Australia; 9°35'S 143°45'E. Circular, c.5 mi. in circumference; hilly, fertile. Produces trepangs, agr. products (sugar cane, yams, bananas).

Daroca (därō'kä), city (pop. 3,758), Saragossa prov., NE Spain, 20 mi. SE of Calatayud; agr. trade center (wine, sugar beets, fruit, grain, livestock); flour milling, lumbering. Has Moorish walls with towers and a fort, and Gothic church (13th cent.; restored in 16th). Founded by Iberians, prospered under Moors, freed by Christians (12th cent.).

Daror Valley or **Darror Valley** (därōr'), N Ital. Somaliland, extends from mts. at Br. Somaliland border across the Mijirtein to Indian Ocean S of Hafun peninsula. Has intermittent stream. Chief center is Skushuban.

Daros Island or **D'Arros Island** (därôs') (pop. 57), in central Amirantes, outlying dependency of the Seychelles, 150 mi. WSW of Mahé Isl.; 5°25'S 53°18'E; 1 mi. long, 1 mi. wide; coral. Copra.

Dar Ould Zidouh (där o͝old zēdo͞o'), village, Casablanca region, W central Fr. Morocco, on the Oued oum Rbia and 31 mi. W of Béni Mellal; cotton grown under irrigation.

Darovskoye (dŭrôf'skŭyu), village, W Kirov oblast, Russian SFSR, 35 mi. NNW of Kotelnich; flax.

Darr, village (pop. 39), Dawson co., S central Nebr., 7 mi. WNW of Lexington and on Platte R.

Darra-i-Suf or **Darrah-i-Suf** (dŭ'ru-ĭ-so͞of'), town (pop. over 2,000), Mazar-i-Sharif prov., N Afghanistan, in Afghan Turkestan, 60 mi. SSE of Mazar-i-Sharif, and on headstream of Balkh R.; irrigated agr. Coal and lead deposits near by. Sometimes called Qala Sarkari.

Darrang (dŭ'räng'), district (□ 2,806; pop. 736,791), NW Assam, India, in Brahmaputra valley; ⊙ Tezpur. Bounded N by Bhutan and Dafla Hills, S by Brahmaputra R. (main channel of trade). Alluvial soil; tea (extensive gardening), rice, rape and mustard, sugar cane, jute. Major tea-processing center; silk growing, rice and oilseed milling, brass-utensils mfg.; railroad workshops. Udalguri is S terminus of shortest trade route from India to Lhasa, Tibet. Tezpur was ⊙ div. of anc. Pal kingdom (A.D. c.1000); has 10th-cent. carvings, sculptures, and temple ruins. Pop. 47% Hindu, 16% Moslem, 35% Animist tribes.

Darregueira (därägā'rä), town (pop. 2,858), W Buenos Aires prov., Argentina, 23 mi. WSW of Puán; grain, livestock.

Darrell's Island (dă'rulz) (2½ mi. long, ⅛ mi. wide), W Bermuda, in Great Sound, 2.5 mi. WSW of Hamilton; seaplane base.

Darrington, town (pop. 921), Snohomish co., NW Wash., near Sauk R., 24 mi. E of Arlington.

Darro (dä'rō), town (pop. 1,557), Granada prov., S Spain, 20 mi. NE of Granada; cereals, esparto, olive oil.

Darro River, Granada prov., S Spain, small stream flowing across fertile plain of Granada and traversing city to join Genil R. Gold placer mining in anc. times.

Darror Valley, Ital. Somaliland: see DAROR VALLEY.

D'Arros Island, Seychelles: see DAROS ISLAND.

Darrouzett (dăro͞ozĕt'), town (pop. 328), Lipscomb co., N Texas, 28 mi. E of Perryton.

Darsana, E Pakistan: see CHUADANGA.

Darsi (dŭr'sē), village, Nellore dist., NE Madras, India, 31 mi. NW of Ongole; cattle, millet, cotton.

Darss (därs), peninsula (□ 30), N Germany, extending 20 mi. NE into the Baltic, 30 mi. W of Stralsund; 1–7 mi. wide; separated from mainland (S) by the Saaler Bodden (zä'lur bô'dun), 3–5-mi.-wide inlet of the Baltic. The cape Darsser Ort is its N tip. E portion also called Zingst peninsula.

Darsser Ort (där'sur ôrt'), N extremity of Darss peninsula, on the Baltic, N Germany, 25 mi. NW of Stralsund; 52°29'N 12°32'E. Lighthouse.

Dart, river, England: see DART RIVER.

Dartford, municipal borough (1931 pop. 28,871; 1951 census 40,544), NW Kent, England, ESE of London, on Darent R., near the Thames, and 7 mi. W of Gravesend; flour-milling center, with paper, leather, machinery, and pharmaceutical works. Town's history dates from Roman and Saxon times; in 1355 Edward III founded Augustinian convent; St. Edmund's Chantry was a place of pilgrimage. Wat Tyler's rebellion originated here in 14th cent. England's 1st paper mill was built here in time of Elizabeth.

Dartington, agr. village and parish (pop. 692), S Devon, England, on Dart R. and 3 mi. NW of Totnes; woolen milling. Dartington Hall, manor house dating from Saxon and Norman times, is now well-known coeducational school and hq. of ballet company. James Froude b. here.

Dartmoor, wild upland (□ 350), S Devon, England, bet. Plymouth and Exeter; consists of lofty granite masses (tors), with occasional heaths, woodlands, bogs. Dartmoor Forest is in the center. Highest points: High Willhays (2,039 ft.), 4 mi. S of Okehampton, and Yes Tor (2,029 ft.), 3 mi. S of Okehampton. There are tin, iron, copper mines, granite and China-clay quarries, and grazing lands. Site of prehistoric remains. At PRINCE TOWN is Dartmoor Prison.

Dartmouth (därt'muth), town (pop. 10,847), S N.S., just NE of Halifax, across Halifax Harbour; sugar refining, shipbuilding, iron founding; mfg. of carbon dioxide, rope, metalware. Site of airport and air-navigation radio station. Settled 1751, town became whaling port in late 18th cent.; inc. 1873. Montague gold mines are 4 mi. NE.

Dartmouth, port and municipal borough (1931 pop. 6,708; 1951 census 5,842), S Devon, England, on W shore of Dart R. estuary and 25 mi. E of Plymouth; 50°21'N 3°34'W. Shipbuilding; agr. market, tourist resort. Site of Royal Naval Col. Formerly one of England's greatest seaports. Dartmouth Castle (15th cent.) overlooks fine harbor. Has 14th-15th-cent. church. Dartmouth was starting point (1190) of Richard Coeur de Lion's crusades.

Dartmouth, town (pop. 11,115), Bristol co., SE Mass., on Buzzards Bay and 6 mi. SW of New Bedford; resort; dairying; sausage. Settled 1650, inc. 1664. Includes villages of Nonquitt, North Dartmouth (1940 pop. 1,936), South Dartmouth or Padanaram (pădunâ'rum) (1940 pop. 1,272), with boat yard, and Apponaganset (ŭpŏ"nugăn'sĭt) (1940 pop. 2,225).

Dartmouth, Mount (3,721 ft.), Coos co., N N.H., peak of White Mts. c.5 mi. NW of Mt. Washington.

Darton, urban district (1931 pop. 12,698; 1951 census 14,400), West Riding, S Yorkshire, England, on Dearne R. and 4 mi. NW of Barnsley; coal mining. Has early-16th-cent. church. In urban dist. and just S is chemical-mfg. town of Barugh (bärk).

Dart River, Devon, England, rises in Dartmoor, 4 mi. SSE of Okehampton, flows 37 mi. SE, past Totnes, to the Channel at Dartmouth. Navigable 11 mi. above mouth.

Dartuch, Cape (därtōōch'), SW point of Minorca, Balearic Isls., 23 mi. W of Mahón; 39°55'N 3°51'E.

Daru (dä'rōō), town, Territory of Papua, SE New Guinea, 270 mi. W of Port Moresby, on offshore inlet; 9°5'S 143°10'E; coconuts. Govt. station.

Daru (dä'rōō), town (pop. 1,401), South-Eastern Prov., E Sierra Leone, on Moa R. (here crossed by railroad) and 12 mi. SW of Pendembu; trade center; palm oil and kernels, cacao, coffee. Airfield.

Dar-ul-Fanun (där'-ōōl-fŭnōōn'), SW garden suburb of Kabul, Afghanistan, on Chahardeh plain, 5 mi. SW of city center. Seat of Kabul univ. and govt. offices; mus. Summer resort. Laid out in 1920s as the projected ⊙ Afghanistan, and originally called Dar-ul-Aman, it was temporarily linked with Kabul by Afghanistan's only railroad.

Daru'l Salam, Borneo: see BRUNEI, town.

Daruvar (dä'rōōvär), anc. *Aquae Balissae*, village (pop. 7,698), N Croatia, Yugoslavia, on railroad and 60 mi. E of Zagreb, at W foot of the Papuk, in Slavonia. Local trade center; health resort with mineral baths; glass mfg. Castle. Winegrowing in vicinity.

Darvaza (dŭrvä'zŭ), town (1941 pop. over 500), NE Ashkhabad oblast, Turkmen SSR, in the desert Kara-Kum, 140 mi. NNE of Ashkhabad; sulphur works.

Darvaza Range, branch of Pamir-Alai mountain system in S Garm oblast, Tadzhik SSR; extends from Stalin Peak c.110 mi. SW bet. Obi-Khingou and Panj rivers; rises to c.18,000 ft.; includes many glaciers. Stalinabad-Khorog highway, along Panj R., passes through Darvaza Gorge.

Darvel (där'vŭl), burgh (1931 pop. 3,232; 1951 census 3,237), E Ayrshire, Scotland, on Irvine R. and 9 mi. E of Kilmarnock; lace and carpet mfg. center. Loudoun Hill (1,034 ft.), 3 mi. E, is scene of defeat (1306) of Earl of Pembroke by Robert the Bruce.

Darvel Bay, inlet (40 mi. long, 30 mi. wide) of Celebes Sea, NE Borneo; Lahad Datu is on N shore. Has many isls.; largest, Timbun Mata.

Darwaz (dŭrwäz'), mountainous section of Afghan Badakhshan, NE Afghanistan, in bend of Panj R. (USSR line); 38°N 71°E. Across Panj R., which here flows in the Darwaz (Darvaza) Gorge, rises the DARVAZA RANGE of the Tadzhik SSR. The Darwaz area passed in 1895 from Bukhara to Afghanistan.

Darwen (där'wĭn), municipal borough (1931 pop. 36,012, 1951 census 30,827), central Lancashire, England, 4 mi. S of Blackburn; cotton milling; mfg. of paper, machinery, plastics, paint, soap.

Darwendale (där'wĕndāl), township (pop. 1,319), Salisbury prov., N Southern Rhodesia, in Mashonaland, in Umvukwe Range, on railroad and 35 mi. WNW of Salisbury; chrome mining.

Darwha (därv'hŭ), town (pop. 8,776), Yeotmal dist., SW Madhya Pradesh, India, 25 mi. WSW of Yeotmal; cotton ginning, oilseed milling. Industrial school. Rail station is Darwha Moti Bagh.

Darwin, city (pop. 2,538), ⊙ Northern Territory, Australia, at NE entrance to Port Darwin (inlet of Timor Sea), opposite Melville Isl. across Clarence Strait, 12°28'S 130°51'E. Chief port of Northern Territory; airport on Singapore-Sydney route. Produces pearl shell, bêche-de-mer, fish; exports peanuts, meat. Large Chinese pop. During Second World War, military airdrome, fuel oil installations, and a new wharf were built and Darwin became important Allied base. Founded 1872 as telegraph station; named for Charles Darwin. Formerly Palmerston.

Darwin, small outpost at head of Choiseul Sound, East Falkland Isl.; 51°50'S 58°57'W.

Darwin, district, Southern Rhodesia: see MOUNT DARWIN.

Darwin, village (pop. 273), Meeker co., S central Minn., near Washington L., c.55 mi. W of Minneapolis; dairy products.

Darwin, Mount, Patagonian peak (7,005 ft.) of the Andes, on SW peninsula of main isl. of Tierra del Fuego, S Chile, 40 mi. WNW of Ushuaia (Argentina).

Darwin, Mount, Calif.: see KINGS CANYON NATIONAL PARK.

Darwin Bay, inlet of the Pacific on coast of Aysén prov., S Chile, in Chonos Archipelago.

Darwin Peak, Wyo.: see GROS VENTRE RANGE.

Darwin Sound, strait (10 mi. long) in S Tierra del Fuego, Chile, continuing NW arm of Beagle Channel, 65 mi. W of Ushuaia.

Daryabad (dŭr'yäbäd), town (pop. 6,340), Bara Banki dist., central Uttar Pradesh, India, 22 mi. E of Nawabganj; rice, gram, wheat, oilseeds, corn. Founded 15th cent.

Daryal Gorge or **Dar'yal Gorge** (dŭryäl'), defile in the central Greater Caucasus, N Georgian SSR, on Terek R., on Georgian Military Road and 70 mi. N of Tiflis; 5,900 ft. deep; overlooked by Mt. Kazbek. It is probably the classical Caspian or Iberian Gates.

Daryapur (dŭryä'pōōr), town (pop., including adjacent railway settlement of Banosa or Vanosa, 11,625), Amraoti dist., W Madhya Pradesh, India, on railway and 25 mi. SSW of Ellichpur; cotton ginning.

Darzo (där'tsô), village (pop. 422), Trento prov., Trentino-Alto Adige, N Italy, 15 mi. WSW of Riva, near N end of Lago d'Idro; barite mining.

Dashava (dŭshä'vŭ), Pol. *Daszawa* (däshä'vä), town (1949 pop. over 500), E Drogobych oblast, Ukrainian SSR, 7 mi. E of Stry; natural-gas extracting center; head of 325-mi. gas pipe line to Kiev (past Ternopol, Staro-Konstantinov, Berdichev), constructed after Second World War. Minor pipe lines connect Dashava with Lvov, Borislav, Drogobych, and Khodorov.

Dashbrun (däshbrōōn'), town, Second Prov., in Gurgan, NE Iran, 33 mi. NW of Gunbad-i-Qawus, and on Atrek R. (USSR line), opposite Kizyl-Atrek; subtropical agr.

Dashev (dä'shĭf), village (1926 pop. 5,481), E Vinnitsa oblast, Ukrainian SSR, 45 mi. ESE of Vinnitsa; machine shops, flour and cotton mills. Until c.1930, Stary Dashev.

Dashkesan, Iran: see MARAGHEH.

Dashkesan (dŭshkyĭsän'), city (1948 pop. over 1,000), W Azerbaijan SSR, in the Lesser Caucasus, on N slope of the Shakh-Dag, on branch of Kura R. and 20 mi. SW of Kirovabad (linked by road); alt. 5,500 ft. Major magnetite-mining center, supplying Rustavi metallurgical industry. Formerly the small mtn. village of Verkhni Dashkesan, Azerbaijani *Yukhari-Dashkesan* [upper Dashkesan]; developed after 1945; renamed Dashkesan in 1948. The original (lower) town of Dashkesan (2 mi. N) is on road to KUSHCHI (4 mi. N), terminus of rail spur for Dashkesan mines.

Dashtidzhum (dŭshtyējōōm'), village (1939 pop. over 500), E Kulyab oblast, Tadzhik SSR, near Panj R. (Afghanistan border), 23 mi. ENE of Kulyab; wheat, truck produce.

Dasht-i-Kavir or **Dasht-e-Kavir** (both: däsht'ĕ-kävēr'), great salt desert of central Iranian plateau, in closed basin SE of Elburz range; 200 mi. across. The almost entire rainless climate and strong surface evaporation have created a salt crust covering salt marsh or mud. The marshes, because of their quicksand-like action, are dangerous to travelers, and the region is almost uninhabited and only partly explored. Settlement is confined to the surrounding mts. and hill ranges.

Dasht-i-Lut or **Dasht-e-Lut** (-lōōt'), great sandy and stony desert of E Iran, bet. Kerman, Seistan, and Khurasan; 200 mi. long, 100 mi. wide. Contains large salt depression.

Dasht-i-Margo (dŭsht'-ĭ-mär'gō), sandy desert in Farah prov., SW Afghanistan, bet. Khash and Helmand rivers; 170 mi. long, 90 mi. wide.

Dasht-i-Mishan or **Dasht-e-Mishan** (-mēshän'), Arab tribal district of Khuzistan, SW Iran, in bend of Karkheh R., NW of Ahwaz, near Iraq border. Inhabited by the Bani Turuf tribe. Main centers are Susangird, Hawizeh, and Bustan.

Dasht-i-Safed, Afghanistan: see KAMARD.

Dashtistan, Iran: see BORAZJAN.

Dasht River (dŭsht), in Makran, SW Baluchistan, W Pakistan, rises in S Central Makran Range, flows W, past Turbat, and SW to Gwatar Bay of Arabian Sea; c.265 mi. long; seasonal. In middle course, called Kech or Kej; waters valley of date palms. Receives Nihing R. (right).

Dashur, Egypt: see DAHSHUR.

Dashwood, village (pop. estimate 500), S Ont., 30 mi. NW of London; dairying, mixed farming.

Daska (dŭs'kŭ), town (pop. 13,719), Sialkot dist., E Punjab, W Pakistan, 15 mi. SW of Sialkot; agr. market center (wheat, rice, sugar cane); hand-loom weaving; brassware. Sometimes called Hardo Daska.

Dasna (dŭs'nŭ), town (pop. 4,990), Meerut dist., NW Uttar Pradesh, India, 13 mi. E of Delhi; wheat, gram, jowar, sugar cane, oilseeds.

Daso, Kashmir: see DASSU.

Dasol Bay (däsōl'), inlet of S.China Sea, Pangasinan prov., central Luzon, Philippines, at base of Cape Bolinao peninsula; 10 mi. long, 5 mi. wide.

Daspalla (dŭs'pŭl-lŭ), former princely state (□ 556; pop. 53,833) in Orissa States, India; ⊙ was Kunjabangarh. Inc. 1949 into Puri dist.

Daspalla, village, Puri dist., E central Orissa, India, 70 mi. WNW of Puri; mfg. of wooden bobbins.

Dassa-Zoumé (dä'sä-zōō'mā), village, S Dahomey, Fr. West Africa, on railroad and 90 mi. NNW of Porto-Novo; cotton, palm kernels, palm oil. Cotton ginning. R.C. and Protestant missions.

Dassel (dä'sŭl), town (pop. 3,610), in former Prussian prov. of Hanover, W Germany, after 1945 in Lower Saxony, 7 mi. W of Einbeck; iron mining; mfg. of machinery, furniture, pharmaceuticals, paper; weaving, food processing, sawmilling.

Dassel (dă'sŭl), village (pop. 962), Meeker co., S central Minn., near Washington L., c.50 mi. W of Minneapolis, in grain, livestock, poultry area; dairy products. Lake resort.

Dassen Island (c.200 acres), SW Cape Prov., U. of So. Afr., in the Atlantic, 40 mi. NW of Cape Town; 33°25'S 18°5'E; 2 mi. long, 1 mi. wide; guano.

Dasserat, Lake (däsürä') (7 mi. long, 3 mi. wide), W Que., 17 mi. W of Rouyn, near Ont. border. On shore are gold mines.

Dassow (dä'sō), town (pop. 4,364), Mecklenburg, N Germany, on Dassow L. (expansion of Trave R. estuary), 12 mi. ENE of Lübeck; fishing port; fish curing. Has 13th-cent. church.

Dassu or **Dusso** (both: dŭs'sō), village, Ladakh dist., N Kashmir, in main Karakoram mtn. system, on right tributary of the Indus and 30 mi. NNW of Skardu. Aquamarine mined near by. Small gold mines SW, near river's right bank. Also spelled Dasu and Daso. Another Dasu village is c.10 mi. SW, on the Indus.

Dastafyur, Azerbaijan SSR: see DOSTAFYUR.

Dastgird or **Dastgerd** (both: dästgĕrd'), village, Second Prov., in Qum, N Iran, 36 mi. WSW of Qum and on railroad; center of Khaljistan agr. area; grain, fruit; sheep raising. Sometimes spelled Dastjird or Dastjerd.

Dasu, Kashmir: see DASSU.

Dasuya (dŭsōō'yŭ), town (pop. 9,206), Hoshiarpur dist., N Punjab, India, 24 mi. NW of Hoshiarpur; agr. market (wheat, gram, corn); handicraft glass-work. Glass sands in hills (E).

Daszawa, Ukrainian SSR: see DASHAVA.

Dataganj (dä'tägŭnj), town (pop. 3,021), Budaun dist., central Uttar Pradesh, India, 17 mi. E of Budaun; wheat, pearl millet, mustard, barley, gram, jowar.

Datanlí, Sierra de, Nicaragua: see DARIENSE, CORDILLERA.

Datca (dätchä'), Turkish *Datça*, village (pop. 1,264), Mugla prov., SW Turkey, on Resadiye Peninsula, 50 mi. SW of Mugla; tobacco, millet. Formerly Resadiye and Dadya.

Datchet (dă'chĭt), residential town and parish (pop. 2,537), SE Buckingham, England, on the Thames, just E of Windsor. Has 14th-cent. church and several notable mansions. Locale of part of Shakespeare's *Merry Wives of Windsor.*

Date (dä'tā). **1** Town (pop. 3,902), Fukushima prefecture, N Honshu, Japan, 4 mi. N of Fukushima; mulberry fields. **2** Town (pop. 22,868), SW Hokkaido, Japan, on E shore of Uchiura Bay, 12 mi. NNW of Muroran; rice, soybeans; fishing.

Dathina or **Dathinah** (däthē'nŭ), tribal area (pop. 8,000) of Western Aden Protectorate, at S foot of the Kaur al Audhilla and SE of the Audhali country; 13°55'N 46°15'E. Local tribes, grouped in the Oleh confederation, include the Hasani (Hasanah) and Meisari (Meyasir) on the Mudia plain. The Dathina area came under Aden govt. control in 1944–45. Radio station at Quleita.

Datia (dŭt'yŭ), town (pop. 22,086), ⊙ Datu dist., NW Vindhya Pradesh, India, 16 mi. NNW of Jhansi; trades in grain, cloth fabrics, cotton; hand-loom weaving. Has fine Hindu palace. Was ⊙ former princely state of Datia (□ 846; pop. 174,072) of Central India agency, established c.1626 by Rajput chief, since 1948 merged with Vindhya Pradesh.

Datil (dă'tĭl), hamlet, Catron co., W N.Mex., near Gallina Mts., 55 mi. WNW of Socorro; alt. c.7,900 ft. Trade and supply point in ranching region. Part of Cibola Natl. Forest near by.

Datschitz, Czechoslovakia: see DACICE.

Datta (dä'tŭ), village (1939 pop. over 500), SE Khabarovsk Territory, Russian SFSR, port on Sea of Japan, 20 mi. N of Sovetskaya Gavan, near railroad; fish canning.

Dattapur (dŭt'täpōōr), town (pop., including adjacent railway settlement of Dhamangaon, 7,897), Amraoti dist., W Madhya Pradesh, India, on railway and 26 mi. ESE of Amraoti; cotton ginning, oilseed milling.

Datteln (dä'tŭln), town (pop. 21,106), in former Prussian prov. of Westphalia, W Germany, after 1945 in North Rhine-Westphalia, in the Ruhr, on Dortmund-Ems Canal and 7 mi. ENE of Recklinghausen; transshipment point at junction of Dortmund-Ems, Lippe Lateral, and Rhine-Herne canals; coal mining; coke works; extraction of coal-tar products. Mfg. of construction materials, chains, wire, insulating materials, trunks, leather goods. Coal trade. Second World War destruction c.50%. Chartered 1936.

Datto (dă'tō), town (pop. 176), Clay co., extreme NE Ark., 16 mi. NE of Pocahontas, bet. Black and Current rivers.

Datu, Cape (dä'tōō), promontory on S.China Sea, W Borneo, on border bet. Sarawak and Indonesian Borneo, 60 mi. WNW of Kuching; 4°13'N 108°15'E; lighthouse. Also called Tanjung Datu.

Daua Parma River, Ethiopia: see DAWA RIVER.

Dauba, Czechoslovakia: see DUBA.

Daubikhe River (doubēkhĕ'), Maritime Territory, Russian SFSR, rises in several branches in S Sikhote-Alin Range, flows 175 mi. N, past Anuchino, Semenovka, and Yakovlevka, joining Ulukhe R. SE of Kirovski to form Ussuri R.

Da'udi, Aden: see YAFA.

Daudnagar (doud'nŭgŭr), town (pop. 11,133), Gaya dist., W central Bihar, India, on Son R. (Patna Canal just SE) and 41 mi. WNW of Gaya; road center; trades in rice, gram, wheat, oilseeds, barley; mfg. of carpets, rugs, brass implements; silk-cloth weaving, sugar milling; silk growing.

Daufuskie Island (dŭfŭ'skē), S S.C., one of Sea Isls., at mouth of New R., 12 mi. E of Savannah, Ga.; c.5 mi. long. Daufuskie Island village on S shore.

Daugava River, USSR and Latvia: see DVINA RIVER (Western Dvina).

Daugavgriva (dou'gäfgrēvä), Lettish *Daugavgriva*, Ger. *Dünamünde* (dü'nämün'dŭ), Rus. (until 1917) *Ust-Dvinsk* or *Ust'-Dvinsk* (ōōst-dvĕnsk'), fortified outer port of Riga, Latvia, on left bank of the Western Dvina, at mouth of Lielupe R. (opposite Bolderaja), and 7 mi. NNW of Riga city center; timber shipping; shipyards. Winter harbor.

Daugavpils (dou'gäfpēls), Ger. *Dünaburg* (dü'näbōōrk"), Rus. *Dvinsk* (dvēnsk), city (pop. 45,160), SE Latvia, in Latgale, port on right bank of the Western Dvina opposite Griva, and 120 mi. SE of Riga; 55°52'N 26°32'E. Major transportation center; rail and highway junction; large railroad repair shops, foundries; mfg. (agr. machinery, hardware, woolen and silk goods, leather goods, furniture, cement ware); agr. processing (flour, sirups, beer, oilseeds, soap). Trades in flax, grain, timber. Laid out in rectangular pattern; has teachers col., castle, park, old fortress, and Jesuit church. Founded (1278) by Livonian Knights; became a strategic fortress, passing in 1561 to Lithuania-Poland and 1772 to Russia, where it was in Vitebsk govt. until 1920. Before 1914 city had c.115,000 inhabitants, but it was largely destroyed by the fighting in First World War and Russian Revolution. Became ⊙ Latgale in independent Latvia (1920–40). Pop. 25% Jewish until Second World War.

Dauin (dä'wēn), town (1939 pop. 1,473; 1948 municipality pop. 11,208), Negros Oriental prov., SE Negros isl., Philippines, on Mindanao Sea, 8 mi. SSW of Dumaguete; coconuts, corn, sugar cane.

Dauis, Philippines: see PANGLAO ISLAND.

Dauji, India: see BALDEO.

Daukli, Lake, Greece: see XYNIAS, LAKE.

Daulatabad or **Dawlatabad** (dou'lütäbäd"), town (pop. 10,000), Maimana prov., N Afghanistan, in Afghan Turkestan, on tributary of Qaisar R. and 35 mi. SSW of Andkhui; center of irrigated area; noted for its carpets.

Daulatabad (dou"lütäbäd'), village, Aurangabad dist., NW Hyderabad state, India, 8 mi. WNW of Aurangabad; site of hill fort which figured in 17th-cent. Mogul conquest of the Deccan; noted landmarks of Moslem architecture. Anc. city (was ⊙ 12th-cent. kingdom) called Deogiri or Devagiri until 1327.

Daulatabad, Iran: see MALAYER.

Daulatpur (dou'lütpōōr), village, Khulna dist., SW East Bengal, E Pakistan, on arm of Ganges Delta and 5 mi. NW of Khulna; rice, betel nuts, jute, oilseeds. Col.

Daule (dou'lā), town (1950 pop. 4,697), Guayas prov., W Ecuador, port on left bank of Daule R., and 25 mi. NNW of Guayaquil (linked by highway and ship); trading center for rich agr. region (rice, cacao, coffee, sugar cane, tobacco, rubber, cattle); sugar and rice milling. Mercury deposits near by.

Dauleia or **Dhavlia** (both: dhäv'lēü), village (pop. 2,602), Boeotia nome, E central Greece, 9 mi. NW of Levadia; tourist trade. Also spelled Davlia and Davleia.

Daule River (dou'lā), in Guayas and Manabí provs., W central Ecuador, rises on W slopes of the Andes W of Quito, flows c.175 mi. S through fertile tropical lowlands, past Balzar, Colimes, Daule, and Pascuales, to Guayas R. at Guayaquil. Navigable, especially during rainy season.

Daun-Gemünden (doun'-gümün'dün), town (pop. 2,069), in former Prussian Rhine Prov., W Germany, after 1945 in Rhineland-Palatinate, in the Eifel, 19 mi. WSW of Mayen; resort with mineral spring. In Middle Ages, Daun was residence of noted counts of Daun; Gemünden was joined to it in 1938.

Daunggyi (dounjē'), village, Henzada dist., Lower Burma, on right bank of Irrawaddy R. and 10 mi. SE of Henzada.

Dauntless Island (□ 1.8), off N Br. Guiana, in Essequibo R. estuary, near NE tip of Leguan Isl. Formed by gradual deposition of alluvial matter on the wreck of a schooner named *Dauntless*, it is now c.2 mi. long, 1 mi. wide.

Dauphin (dô'fĭn), town (pop. 4,637), SW Man., on Vermilion R. and 90 mi. N of Brandon; railroad center; lumber and flour milling, dairying; wheat, barley. Ridge Mountain Natl. Park is 10 mi. S.

Dauphin, county (□ 520; pop. 197,784), S central Pa.; ⊙ Harrisburg. Bounded W by Susquehanna R.; drained by Swatara Creek. Blue Mtn., running NE–SW across central part, divides mountainous anthracite region in N from agr. and industrial region in S. Long stone-arch bridge crosses Susquehanna R. at Rockville. Anthracite; mfg. (chocolate, metal products, shoes, clothing); dairying, slaughtering. Formed 1785.

Dauphin borough (pop. 667), Dauphin co., S central Pa., on Susquehanna R. and 8 mi. NNW of Harrisburg.

Dauphin, Cape (dô'fĭn), NE N.S., on NE coast of Cape Breton Isl., bet. St. Ann's Bay (W) and Great Bras d'Or (E), 12 mi. NW of Sydney Mines; 46° 21'N 60°25'W.

Dauphiné (dōfēnā'), region and former province of SE France, bordering on Italy (E) and on the Rhone (W and NW); ⊙ Grenoble. Now administratively divided into Isère, Drôme, and Hautes-Alpes depts. Lying chiefly in Dauphiné Alps, region contains, E-W, the Fr. slope of Cottian Alps, the Massif du Pelvoux (rising to 13,461 ft. at the Barre des Écrins), several pre-Alpine ranges, and E part of Rhone R. valley. Several deep river valleys (Grésivaudan, Oisans, Durance) penetrate high Alps, providing access to Italy over frontier passes (Montgenèvre). Agr. (fruit, olive, and mulberry trees) primarily in Rhone valley, also known for its fine vineyards (Tain-l'Hermitage). Cattle raising (transhumance) and dairying in uplands. Water power is exploited for electrometallurgy (Livet-et-Gavet, Grenoble, L'Argentière-la-Bessée) and chemical industry. Chief towns: Grenoble, Valence, Vienne. Comprised in kingdom of Provence (879), and after 933 in kingdom of Arles, it was nominally part of Holy Roman Empire. Its rulers assumed title of "dauphin" (from dolphins in their coat-of-arms). Sold (1349) by Dauphin Humbert II to Philip VI of France. Imperial suzerainty no longer recognized after 1378. Louis XI was last dauphin actually to rule Dauphiné (although eldest son of King of France bore title of Dauphin until 1830), which, after his reign, continued as a mere province under jurisdiction of *parlement* of Grenoble. Divided into present depts. in 1790. Sometimes spelled Dauphiny.

Dauphiné Alps, Fr. *Alpes du Dauphiné,* W offshoots of Cottian Alps, in SE France. Bounded N by Arc and Isère R. valleys, S by upper Durance R. valley. Contain the Massif du Pelvoux (highest peak, Barre des Écrins, 13,461 ft.), and the lower Belledonne and Grandes-Rousses ranges. Several piedmont ranges (Vercors, Dévoluy) overlooking Rhone valley are called Dauphiné Pre-Alps.

Dauphin Island (dô'fĭn), barrier beach (c.15 mi. long, average width .5 mi.) in Gulf of Mexico at entrance to Mobile Bay, SW Ala. Established as Fr. base (1699) for colonization of Louisiana; seized (1813) by Gen. Wilkinson for U.S. Now part of Mobile co. Fort Gaines, at E end of isl., was captured (1864) by Admiral Farragut during battle of Mobile Bay.

Dauphin Lake (□ 200), W Man., 11 mi. E of Dauphin; 26 mi. long, 12 mi. wide. Drains N into L. Winnipegosis.

Daura (dou'rä), town (pop. 4,851), Katsina prov., Northern Provinces, N Nigeria, near Fr. West Africa border, 50 mi. E of Katsina; road center; cotton, peanuts; cattle, skins. A large market center in 19th cent.

Dauria (däōō'rēü, Rus. dŭōō'rēü), name applied in 17th cent. to SE Siberia, E of L. Baikal. Treaty of Nerchinsk (1689) left W Dauria to Russia and E Dauria (on left bank of the Amur) to China. Named for Daurs of Manchu-Tungus stock, its original inhabitants.

Daurian Range (däōō'rēün), S Chita oblast, Russian SFSR, extends 150 mi. NE bet. Ingoda and Onon rivers; rises to 3,300 ft. Wooded slopes are rich in silver-lead ores and gold.

Daurskoye (dŭōōr'skŭyü), village (1948 pop. over 2,000), SW Krasnoyarsk Territory, Russian SFSR, on Yenisei R., and 85 mi. E of Uzhur; river port.

Dausa, India: see DAOSA.

Davaar Island, Scotland: see DAVARR ISLAND.

Davalu, Armenian SSR: see ARARAT, town.

Davangere (dä'vŭng-gĕrē), town (pop. 31,759), Chitaldrug dist., N Mysore, India, 150 mi. NW of Bangalore; agr. trade and cotton-milling center; mfg. of cotton textiles (since 1936), vegetable-oil processing, leather handicrafts. Sheep raising, hand-loom woolen and cotton weaving in surrounding villages.

Davao (dävou', dä'vou), province (□ 7,528; 1948 pop. 364,859), SE Mindanao, Philippines; ⊙ Davao. On the Pacific, and indented S by Davao Gulf. Mountainous, forested. Abacá, coconuts, lumber, rubber, pineapples. Iron, gold, sulphur deposits.

Davao, city (1939 pop. 24,521; 1948 municipality pop. 111,263), ⊙ Davao prov., SE central Mindanao, Philippines, 600 mi. SE of Manila, on Davao Gulf; 7°5'N 125°35'E. Chief commercial center of S Mindanao, and a busy port, shipping abacá, copra, lumber. Gold mine near by. Pineapple plantation in vicinity. "Davao City" is a municipality with an area equivalent to a county; in it are numerous towns. Scene of heavy fighting (1945) in Second World War, where Jap. forces continued to fight long after most of the Philippines had been liberated.

Davao Gulf, large inlet (90 mi. long, 30–50 mi. wide) in SE coast of Mindanao, Philippines. Davao city is on NW shore. Samal Isl. is in N.

Davark (dävärk'), village (pop. 700), Begemdir prov., NW Ethiopia, near source of Angareb R., on road and 45 mi. NE of Gondar; trade center.

Davarr Island or **Davaar Island** (dŭvär') (pop. 5), in Kilbrannan Sound, at entrance to Campbeltown Loch, S Argyll, Scotland, 3 mi. E of Campbeltown; 1 mi. long, ½ mi. wide; rises to 378 ft.

Davarzan (dä"värzän'), town, Ninth Prov., in Khurasan, NE Iran, 45 mi. W of Sabzawar and on Meshed-Teheran highway.

Daveluyville (dävülwē'vĭl), village (pop. 419), S Que., on Bécancour R. and 23 mi. E of Nicolet; dairying, cattle raising; wheat, potatoes.

Davenport (dă'vŭnpôrt). **1** Village (pop. c.650), Santa Cruz co., W Calif., on the Pacific, 10 mi. NW of Santa Cruz; large cement plant. **2** Town (pop. 760), Polk co., central Fla., 4 mi. NNE of Haines City; packs and cans citrus fruit, makes citrus candy. **3** City (pop. 74,549), ⊙ Scott co., E Iowa, c.160 mi. E of Des Moines and on Mississippi R. (here spanned by several bridges); largest of the Quad Cities (which also include ROCK ISLAND, MOLINE, and East Moline, all in Ill.). Industrial and commercial Davenport lies along the river (site of power plant), while the residential sections are on the limestone bluffs to the N. Produces locomotives, snowplows, washing machines, pumps, aluminum sheets and plate, wire, cameras, foundry products, millwork, cement, clothes, beer, cereals, flour, feed, packed meat, bakery and dairy products; other industry in the suburb BETTENDORF. Seat of St. Ambrose Col., Iowa Soldiers' Orphans' Home, Palmer School of Chiropractic, music organizations, art gall., and mus. Credit Isl., one of its parks, was site (1814) of battle in War of 1812. Near by are a large govt. roller-gate dam and locks and, on Rock Isl., a major U.S. arsenal. Founded 1836 by George Davenport on site of an early trading post, and inc. 1839. Prospered with arrival of 1st railroad to bridge the Mississippi (1856) and, after the Civil War, as a port and sawmilling center. The poet Arthur Davidson Ficke was b. here; the author Alice French lived here. **4** Village (pop. 459), Thayer co., S Nebr., 15 mi. NW of Hebron. **5** Village (pop. 150), Cass co., SE N.Dak., 15 mi. SW of Fargo. **6** Town (pop. 841), Lincoln co., central Okla., c.45 mi. ENE of Oklahoma City; has large gasoline plants. **7** Town (pop. 1,417), ⊙ Lincoln co., E Wash., 35 mi. W of Spokane, in agr., mining region; ships grain, flour.

Davenport Center, resort village, Delaware co., S N.Y., in the Catskills, on Charlotte R. and 7 mi. E of Oneonta.

Daventria, Netherlands: see DEVENTER.

Daventry (dă'vŭntrē, dān'trē), municipal borough (1931 pop. 3,609; 1951 census 4,078), W Northampton, England, 12 mi. W of Northampton; shoe mfg. There was an anc. Roman camp on Borough Hill (653 ft.), just E, now site of radio transmitter.

Daverkonda, India: see DEVARKONDA.

Davey, village (pop. 112), Lancaster co., E Nebr., 11 mi. N of Lincoln.

Davey, Port (dā'vē), bay of Indian Ocean, SW Tasmania, N of Southwest Cape, in mountainous, uninhabited area; 5 mi. long, 4 mi. wide; broken into many small bays. Connects with Bathurst Harbour (E) by narrow channel 8 mi. long.

David (dävēdh'), city (1950 pop. 16,193), ⊙ Chiriquí prov., W Panama, in lowland, on Inter-American Highway, on David R. (which forms common estuary with the Chiriquí), on railroad and 310 mi. WSW of Panama city. Commercial and industrial center, with seaport at Pedregal (4 mi. S). Mfg. of shoes, soap, clothing, furniture, ceramic products, beverages; sugar milling, tanning. Has modern hospital, electricity, water supply, radio station. Founded 1738 as gold-prospecting camp.

David City, city (pop. 2,321), ⊙ Butler co., E Nebr., 35 mi. NNW of Lincoln, in prairie region S of the Platte; farm trade center. Building materials, feed, flour; livestock, dairy produce, grain. Inc. 1878.

David-Gorodok (dŭvēt'-gŭrŭdôk'), Pol. *Dawidgródek* (dävēdgrōō'děk), city (1931 pop. 11,374), E Pinsk oblast, Belorussian SSR, in Pripet Marshes, on Goryn R. and 48 mi. E of Pinsk; grain- and lumber-trading center; tanning, flaxseed processing, flour milling, sawmilling, brick mfg. Passed (1793) from Poland to Russia; reverted (1921) to Poland; ceded to USSR in 1945.

David's Island, N.Y.: see NEW ROCHELLE.

Davidson, town (pop. 478), S central Sask., 65 mi. NNW of Moose Jaw; grain elevators.

Davidson. 1 County (□ 458; pop. 62,244), central N.C.; ⊙ Lexington. In piedmont region; bounded W by Yadkin R. Agr. (tobacco, corn, wheat, sweet potatoes, hay, dairy products), timber (pine, oak). Mfg. at Lexington and Thomasville; sawmilling. Formed 1822. **2** County (□ 532; pop. 321,758), N central Tenn.; ⊙ NASHVILLE, the state capital. Intersected by Cumberland R. Livestock, small grains, dairy products, tobacco; diversified mfg. at Nashville and Old Hickory. Formed 1783.

Davidson. 1 Town (pop. 2,423), Mecklenburg co., S N.C., 18 mi. N of Charlotte; mfg. of cotton yarn, asbestos; lumber. Seat of Davidson Col. (1837; men). **2** Town (pop. 490), Tillman co., SW Okla., 11 mi. SSW of Frederick, near Red R., in agr. area; cotton ginning.

Davidson, Mount (7,870 ft.), W Nev., in Virginia Range, just W of Virginia City; site of famed COMSTOCK LODE.

Davidson Glacier, SE Alaska, arm of Muir Glacier, at W side of mouth of Chilkat Inlet; 59°5'N 135°27'W.

Davidson Mountains, NE Alaska, NE part of Brooks Range, S of Arctic Ocean; 68°30'–69°N 141°30'–144°W; rises to over 8,000 ft.

Davidson's Mains, W suburb of Edinburgh, Scotland.

Davidstow, agr. village and parish (pop. 393), NE Cornwall, England, 4 mi. NE of Camelford. Prehistoric remains near by.

Davie (dā'vē), county (□ 264; pop. 15,420), central N.C.; ⊙ Mocksville. In piedmont region; bounded E by the Yadkin, SW by small South Yadkin R.

Agr. (tobacco, wheat, corn, cotton, hay); textile mfg. at Mocksville; sawmilling. Formed 1836.

Davie, village (1940 pop. 627), Broward co., S Fla., 8 mi. SW of Fort Lauderdale, in citrus-fruit area.

Daviess (dā'vĭs). **1** (also dā'vēŭs) County (□ 433; pop. 26,762), SW Ind., bounded S by East Fork of White R., W by West Fork of White R.; ⊙ Washington. Agr. and bituminous-coal area, with mfg. at Washington; natural-gas and oil wells; nurseries; grain, fruit, livestock. Formed 1816. **2** County (□ 466; pop. 57,241), NW Ky.; ⊙ OWENSBORO. Bounded N by Ohio R. (Ind. line), W by Green R.; drained by Panther Creek and its North and South forks. Rolling agr. area (tobacco, in which this co. ranks 2d in Ky.; corn, wheat, cattle, hogs). Oil and gas wells, coal mines; clay, sand, and gravel pits; timber. Industries at Owensboro. Formed 1815. **3** County (□ 563; pop. 11,180), NW Mo.; ⊙ Gallatin. Drained by Grand R.; agr. (corn, wheat, hay, oats, vegetables), livestock, dairy products. Formed 1836.

Davik (dä'vēk), village and canton (pop. 3,658), Sogn og Fjordane co., W Norway, on S shore of Nord Fjord, 27 mi. NNE of Floro.

Daviot (dāv'yŭt), agr. village and parish (pop. 557), central Aberdeen, Scotland, 4 mi. W of Old Meldrum.

Daviot and Dunlichity (dŭnlĭkh'ĭtē), parish (pop. 810), N Inverness, Scotland. Agr. village of Daviot, on Nairn R. and 5 mi. SE of Inverness, has remains of 15th-cent. Daviot Castle, stronghold of earls of Crawford.

Davis, main air base on NE ADAK ISLAND, Andreanof Isls., Aleutian Isls., SW Alaska; 51°52'N 176°39'W.

Davis. 1 County (□ 509; pop. 9,959), SE Iowa, on Mo. line (S); ⊙ Bloomfield. Stock-raising (sheep, hogs, cattle, poultry) and agr. (corn, soybeans, hay) area, drained by Des Moines, Fox, North Fabius, and Wyaconda rivers; bituminous-coal deposits mined in NE. Includes Lake Wapello State Park. Formed 1843. **2** County (□ 268; pop. 30,867), N Utah; ⊙ Farmington. Irrigated agr. area; includes SE corner of Great Salt L. (with Antelope Isl.) in W and part of Wasatch Range in E. Livestock, hay, sugar beets, fruit, truck; food processing. Formed 1850.

Davis. 1 City (pop. 3,554), Yolo co., central Calif., 13 mi. W of Sacramento; highway and railroad junction in agr. region (grain, sugar beets, tomatoes). Seat of Col. of Agr. of Univ. of Calif. Inc. 1917. **2** Village (pop. 348), Stephenson co., N Ill., 14 mi. NE of Freeport, in agr. area; cheese factories. **3** Town (pop. 1,928), Murray co., S Okla., at N base of the Arbuckle Mts., 23 mi. N of Ardmore, and on Washita R., in livestock area. Meat packing, cotton ginning; mfg. of brooms, sirup. Settled 1889. **4** Town (pop. 153), Turner co., SE S.Dak., 12 mi. SSE of Parker; grain-shipping point in farming area. **5** Town (pop. 1,271), Tucker co., N W.Va., 12 mi. ENE of Parsons, near Md. line. Highest community in state (alt. 3,101 ft.). Blackwater Falls State Park is just SW. Inc. 1889.

Davis, Mount (3,213 ft.), highest point in Pa., a peak of NEGRO MOUNTAIN, in Somerset co., S Pa., 15 mi. SSW of Somerset.

Davisboro, city (pop. 469), Washington co., E central Ga., 12 mi. E of Sandersville.

Davis Bridge Dam, Davis Bridge Reservoir, Vt.: see HARRIMAN DAM.

Davis City, town (pop. 432), Decatur co., S Iowa, near Mo. line, on Thompson R. and 8 mi. SSW of Leon, in livestock and grain area.

Davis Dam, in Colorado R. (here forming part of Ariz.-Nev. line), 67 mi. (by river) S of Hoover Dam, W of Kingman, Ariz. Rockfill and earthfill dam (200 ft. high, 1,600 ft. long) completed 1949. Built for hydroelectric power and for regulation of water from L. Mead for Parker and Imperial dams, downstream. Forms large reservoir.

Davis Inlet, bay (20 mi. long, 1 mi. wide) of the Atlantic, E Labrador; 55°55'N 60°50'W. In entrance of bay is UKASIKSALIK ISLAND, with fishing village (pop. 120) of Davis Inlet.

Davis-Monthan Air Force Base, Ariz.: see TUCSON.

Davis Mountains, extreme W Texas, mostly in Jeff Davis co., extend generally N c.45 mi. from region just N of Marfa; rise from plateau (alt. 4,000–5,000 ft.) to 8,382 ft. in Mt. LIVERMORE, 2d-highest peak in state, 19 mi. E of Valentine. Vacation region, with timbered peaks, scenic drives, including summit road to Mt. Locke (6,791 ft.), site of McDonald Observatory, 2 state parks, many springs, and noted Limpia, Madera, Cherry, and Musquiz canyons. Cattle grazing.

Davison, county (□ 432; pop. 16,522), SE central S.Dak.; ⊙ Mitchell. Agr. area watered by several creeks. Mfg. at Mitchell; livestock, dairy products, poultry, corn. Formed 1873.

Davison, city (pop. 1,745), Genesee co., SE central Mich., 9 mi. E of Flint, in agr. area. Has Rosemoor Park, with race track. Settled 1836; inc. as village 1889, as city 1939.

Davis Sea, in Indian Ocean, off coast of Antarctica, bet. Shackleton Shelf Ice and West Shelf Ice, off Queen Mary Coast and Wilhelm II Coast, in 66°S 92°E. Discovered 1912 by Sir Douglas Mawson.

Davis Strait, arm (400 mi. long, 180–400 mi. wide) of the Atlantic, bet. SE Baffin Isl., Northwest Territories, and SW Greenland; 64°–70°N 50°–65°W. Opens N on Baffin Bay, part of sea passage to the Arctic Ocean. Generally navigable from midsummer until late fall, quantities of ice are carried down from Baffin Bay by Labrador Current along Baffin Isl. shore; main shipping lane is along Greenland. Disko isl. is near Greenland shore. Discovered (1587) by John Davis.

Daviston (dā'vĭstŭn), town (pop. 110), Tallapoosa co., E Ala., near Tallapoosa R., c.35 mi. SE of Talladega; lumber.

Davisville, N suburb of Toronto, S Ont.

Davisville. 1 Village, Barnstable co., Mass.: see FALMOUTH. **2** Village, Washington co., R.I.: see NORTH KINGSTOWN.

Davle (däv'lĕ), village (pop. 1,490), S central Bohemia, Czechoslovakia, on Vltava (Moldau) R., at Sazava R. mouth, on railroad and 13 mi. S of Prague; popular summer resort; excursion center.

Davleia, Greece: see DAULEIA.

Davlekanovo (dŭvlyĭkä'nŭvŭ), city (1939 pop. over 10,000), W central Bashkir Autonomous SSR, Russian SFSR, on Dema R., on railroad and 50 mi. SW of Ufa; grain-export center; flour milling. Lignite deposits near by. Became city in 1942.

Davlia, Greece: see DAULEIA.

Davoli (dä'vôlē), village (pop. 2,471), Catanzaro prov., Calabria, S Italy, 19 mi. SSW of Catanzaro; wine, olive oil.

Davos (dävōs'), town and circle (1950 pop. 10,332), Grisons canton, E Switzerland, on Landwasser R. (tributary of Albula R.) and 14 mi. ESE of Chur; resort in Davos Valley among mts.; noted for curative climate, winter sports. Wood- and metal-working, printing. Town hall (16th cent.), parish church (15th cent.), 16th-cent church. Town consists of Davos Platz (alt. 5,115 ft.) and Davos Dorf (NE, alt. 5,164). German is generally spoken.

Davrath, Israel: see DOVRAT.

Davy, mining village (pop. 1,650), McDowell co., S W.Va., 5 mi. NW of Welch, semi-bituminous coal.

Davy Crockett Lake, Tenn.: see NOLICHUCKY RIVER.

Davydkovo, Russian SFSR: see TOLBUKHINO.

Davydovka (dŭvē'dŭfkŭ), village (1926 pop. 3,834), central Voronezh oblast, Russian SFSR, 35 mi. SSE of Voronezh, flour mill.

Davyhulme (dā'vēhŭm), town and parish (pop. 4,094), SE Lancashire, England, 6 mi. WSW of Manchester; cotton milling.

Davy Sound, Greenland. see KING OSCAR FJORD.

Dawaki Ta Kudu (däwäkē' tä ko͞oto͞o') [Hausa,= Dawaki South], town (pop. 4,890), Kano prov., Northern Provinces, N Nigeria, 10 mi. SSE of Kano; agr. trade center; cotton, peanuts, millet; cattle, skins.

Dawaki Ta Tofa (tōfä') [Hausa,=old Dawaki], town (pop. 3,320), Kano prov., Northern Provinces, N Nigeria, 12 mi. WNW of Kano; road center; cotton, peanuts, millet; cattle, skins.

Dawa River (dä'wä), Ital. *Daua Parma*, in Sidamo-Borana prov., S Ethiopia, rises in highlands 15 mi S of Hula, flows 360 mi. SE to Dolo where it unites with the Ganale Dorya to form Juba R. In lower course forms Kenya-Ethiopia boundary. Valley has gold deposits mined near Adola.

Dawasir, Wadi (wä'dē dăwă'sĭr), oasis district of S Nejd, Saudi Arabia, in valley of the Wadi Dawasir, at 20°30'N bet. 44°30' and 46°E; main towns, Sulaiyil and Dam.

Dawes, county (□ 1,389; pop. 9,708), NW Nebr.; ⊙ Chadron. Irrigated agr. area drained by White and Niobrara rivers; bounded N by S.Dak., badlands region in NW. Grain livestock, dairy and poultry produce, sugar beets, beans, potatoes. Formed 1885.

Dawhah, Qatar: see DOHA.

Dawidgrodek, Belorussian SSR: see DAVID-GORODOK.

Dawlatabad, Afghanistan: see DAULATABAD.

Dawley, urban district (1931 pop. 7,359; 1951 census 8,369), central Shropshire, England, 3 mi. SE of Wellington; agr. market; leather tanning.

Dawlish (dô'lĭsh), seaside resort and urban district (1931 pop. 4,580; 1951 census 7,512), S Devon, England, on the Channel, near mouth of Exe R., 4 mi. SW of Exmouth; agr. market in flower-, fruit-, and vegetable-growing region. Has 13th-cent. church. Near by is Luscombe Castle (18th cent.), built by Nash.

Dawna Range (dô'nä), in Tenasserim, Lower Burma, W of Thailand border; extension of Karenni Hills across Salween R., 120 mi. long (WNW-SSE); rises to 6,822 ft. Forms divide bet. Thaungyin and Gyaing rivers; crossed by Moulmein-Myawaddy road.

Dawson, city (pop. 1,043), ⊙ Yukon, in W part of the territory, on Yukon R. (here ½ mi. wide; ferry), at mouth of Klondike R., and 250 mi. ESE of Fairbanks, Alaska; 64°3'N 139°25'W; supply base, distributing and road center for the Klondike gold- and coal-mining region; truck gardening, farming (wheat, dairying). Has Anglican and R.C. churches, hosp., airfield, Royal Canadian Mounted Police post, radio and weather station. During navigation season (June–Oct.) there is steamer connection with Whitehorse, which in turn is reached from Skagway (Alaska) via the White Pass RR. Average summer temp. is 50–60°F., mean Jan. temp. –21°F. Average annual rainfall, 9–13 inches. In late June Dawson has 24 hours of daylight. Town was founded 1898 during Klondike gold rush; at height of the rush it was said to have population of c.20,000. Formerly called Dawson City, it was named after George M. Dawson. Opposite, on Yukon R., is West Dawson. Just SE of city Klondike R. receives Bonanza Creek, on which 1st gold strike in Yukon was made Aug. 17, 1896.

Dawson. 1 County (□ 213; pop. 3,712), N Ga.; ⊙ Dawsonville. Blue Ridge (N) and piedmont (S) area drained by Etowah and Chestatee rivers. Farming (cotton, corn, hay, sweet potatoes, poultry) and sawmilling. Chattahoochee Natl. Forest (N). Formed 1857. **2** County (□ 2,358; pop. 9,092), E Mont.; ⊙ Glendive. Agr. region drained by Yellowstone R. Grain, livestock. Oil field (in NW) discovered 1951. Formed 1869. **3** County (□ 983; pop. 19,393), S central Nebr.; ⊙ Lexington. Agr. area drained by Platte R. Grain, livestock, dairy and poultry produce. Formed 1871. **4** County (□ 899; pop. 19,113), NW Texas; ⊙ Lamesa. On high plains, with E-facing Cap Rock escarpment in E; co. alt. c.2,600–3,200 ft. Drained by intermittent Sulphur Springs Creek. Agr. (grain sorghums, cotton, soybeans, legumes, fruit, truck); livestock (cattle, hogs, poultry); dairying. Oil wells. Hunting. Formed 1876.

Dawson. 1 City (pop. 4,411), ⊙ Terrell co., SW Ga., 22 mi. NW of Albany; major peanut market and processing center, mfg. (peanut products, (cottonseed oil, lumber). Settled 1856, inc. 1872. **2** Village (pop. 374), Sangamon co., central Ill., 10 mi. ENE of Springfield, in agr. and bituminous-coal area. **3** Town (pop. 286), Dallas co., central Iowa, on Raccoon R., and 6 mi. W of Perry, in agr. area. **4** City (pop. 1,834), Lac qui Parle co., SW Minn., on Lac qui Parle R. and 9 mi. SE of Madison; trade center and shipping point for grain and livestock; dairy products. Inc. as village 1885, as city 1911. **5** Village (pop. 309), Richardson co., SE Nebr., 10 mi. WNW of Falls City and on N.Fork of Nemaha R.; grain, livestock. **6** Village (pop. 1,206), Colfax co., NE N.Mex., on Vermejo R., in E foothills of Sangre de Cristo Mts., 25 mi. SW of Raton; alt. c.6,390 ft.; coal mines. Vermejo Park, private club and game-preserve, is near by. **7** Village (pop. 280), Kidder co., central N.Dak., 8 mi. E of Steele. Airport is here. U.S. game reserve near by. **8** Town (1940 pop. 1,086), Tulsa co., NE Okla., just E of Tulsa. Inc. 1923. **9** Borough (pop. 723), Fayette co., SW Pa., 5 mi. WNW of Connellsville and on Youghiogheny R. **10** Town (pop. 1,107), Navarro co., E central Texas, 19 mi. SW of Corsicana; trade center in farm area (cotton, corn); cotton gins. Settled c.1882, inc. 1908.

Dawson, Mount (11,123 ft.), SE B.C., in Selkirk Mts., in Glacier Natl. Park, 35 mi. ENE of Revelstoke: 51°9'N 117°25'W.

Dawson Creek, village (pop. 518), E B.C., near Alta. border, on Dawson Creek and 170 mi. NE of Prince George, 300 mi. WNW of Edmonton; 55°46'N 120°14'W; S terminus of the newer part of Alaska Highway, connected by rail and highway with Edmonton; grain elevators, lumbering, meat packing, fur trading, mixed farming, stock raising.

Dawson Island (55 mi. long, 20 mi. wide), in central Tierra del Fuego archipelago, Chile, in middle of Strait of Magellan; 54°S 70°30'W; sheep raising.

Dawson-Lambton Glacier (lăm'tŭn) (40 naut. mi. wide), Antarctica, flows NW to Caird Coast of Coats Land, in 76°15'S 27°30'W. Discovered 1915 by Sir Ernest Shackleton.

Dawson River, E Queensland, Australia, rises in Carnavon Range, flows E, NE, and N, past Taroom, Theodore, and Boolburra, joining Mackenzie R. to form Fitzroy R.; 312 mi. long. Drains agr. land.

Dawson Springs, town (pop. 2,374), Hopkins co., W Ky., on Tradewater R. and 25 mi. NNW of Hopkinsville. Health resort, with mineral springs, in coal-mining and agr. (dairy products, fruit, burley tobacco, corn, hay) area; makes clothing, furniture; sawmilling. U.S. veterans' hosp., Dawson Springs State Park, and a state park in Pennyrile State Forest are near by.

Dawsonville, town (pop. 318), ⊙ Dawson co., N Ga., 19 mi. WNW of Gainesville; agr. trade center; sawmilling.

Dawu, China: see TAOFU.

Dax (däks), anc. *Aquæ Tarbellicæ* or *Aquæ Augustæ*, town (pop. 12,551), Landes dept., SW France, on the Adour and 27 mi. NE of Bayonne; noted spa and commercial (lumber and livestock) center Produces railroad ties, telegraph poles, pit props, turpentine; distilling, flour milling, meat processing and canning (pâté de foie gras). Its hot sulphur springs (147°F.) and mud baths were known to the Romans. In 10th–11th cent. Dax (then known as Civitas Aquensis, later contracted to d'Acqs and Dax) was capital of a viscountship. Held by the English until 1296. Saint-Paul-lès-Dax (1 mi. N on right bank of Adour R.) has the railroad station and a 15th-cent. church with a Romanesque apse.

Daxlanden (däks'län"dŭn), W suburb of Karlsruhe, Germany.

Day, county (□ 1,060; pop. 12,294), NE S.Dak.; ⊙ Webster. Agr. region watered by numerous lakes; located on E slope of Coteau des Prairies; part of Sisseton Indian Reservation in E. Resorts; dairy produce, grain. Formed 1875.

Day, Song, Vietnam: see DAI, SONG.

Dayal Bagh (dŭyäl' bäg'), village, Agra dist., W Uttar Pradesh, India, near the Jumna, 3 mi. N of Agra city center; mfg. of leather, dairy, and electrical goods, textiles, chemicals, soap, scientific balances and instruments, doors, bolts; tanneries. Hq. of Radhaswami Satsang Sabha sect. Also written Dayalbagh.

Daybrook, N suburb of Nottingham, S Nottingham, England; hosiery mfg.

Day Dawn, village, W central Western Australia, 220 mi. NE of Geraldton, on Geraldton-Wiluna RR; mining center in Murchison Goldfield.

Daykin, village (pop. 157), Jefferson co., SE Nebr., 13 mi. NNW of Fairbury; poultry produce, grain, livestock.

Daylesford, town (pop. 3,053), S central Victoria, Australia, 55 mi. NW of Melbourne; alt. 2,020 ft.; tourist resort (mineral springs); woolen mills. Gold mines in vicinity.

Daymán River (dīmän'), Salto dept., NW Uruguay, rises in a NW outlier of the Cuchilla de Haedo 35 mi. W of Tambores, flows 91 mi. W to Uruguay R. 9 mi. SW of Salto. Forms main part of Salto-Paysandú dept. border.

Dayr, Al-, Egypt: see DEIR, EL.

Dayr Abu Sa'id, Jordan: see DEIR ABU SA'ID.

Dayr al-Janadlah, Egypt: see DEIR EL GANADLA.

Dayr al-Qamar, Lebanon: see DEIR EL QAMER.

Dayr al-Zur, Syria: see DEIR EZ ZOR.

Dayr 'Awn Agha, Syria: see DEIR 'AWN AGHA.

Dayr Hafir, Syria: see DEIR HAFIR.

Dayr Mawas, Egypt: see DEIR MAWAS.

Dayrut, Egypt: see DAIRUT.

Day Shan, China: see TAI SHAN.

Daysland, town (pop. 464), central Alta., 27 mi. ESE of Camrose; grain elevators, cereal-food mfg.

Dayton. 1 Town (pop. 85), Marengo co., W Ala., 15 mi. SE of Demopolis. 2 Village (pop. 287), Franklin co., SE Idaho, 5 mi. WNW of Preston; alt. 4,745 ft.; peas, beans, sugar beets. 3 Town (pop. 793), Webster co., central Iowa, 17 mi. SSE of Fort Dodge; dairy products, feed. 4 City (pop. 8,977), Campbell co., N Ky., on left bank (levee) of the Ohio opposite Cincinnati, and within Cincinnati metropolitan dist.; mfg. of watch cases, compacts, cigarette cases, paint, varnish. Settled 1848; inc. 1867. 5 Town (pop. 502), York co., SW Maine, on Saco R. and 8 mi. NW of Biddeford. 6 Village (pop. 363), Hennepin and Wright counties, E Minn., on Mississippi R. at mouth of Crow R., and 23 mi. NNW of Minneapolis in grain, livestock, poultry area. 7 Village (pop. c.300), Lyon co., W Nev., on Carson R. and 10 mi. ENE of Carson City; alt. 4,400 ft.; trading point. Settled c.1850 as a mining town; ⊙ Lyon co. until 1911. 8 Village (pop. c.400), Middlesex co., central N.J., 9 mi. SSW of New Brunswick; ships potatoes. 9 City (pop. 243,872), ⊙ Montgomery co., W Ohio, on Great Miami R. at influx of Mad and Stillwater rivers, and c.45 mi. NNE of Cincinnati; industrial, railroad, and distributing center in fertile agr. area; port of entry. Chief U.S. aviation center; here or near by are U.S. military aeronautical laboratory (at Wright-Patterson Air Force Base), an air force service and supply center, several commercial airfields, and a municipal airport (1936). Chief industries produce cash registers, refrigerators and air-conditioning equipment, precision tools, lighting equipment, electric motors, aircraft and auto parts, printed matter, rubber goods, sports equipment, food products. Seat of Univ. of Dayton, Sinclair Col., and a large veterans' hosp. and home. Mound laboratory for atomic research is near by. Points of interest: Dayton Art Inst., Paul Laurence Dunbar Mus. (1938) in the poet's home; Newcom Tavern (1796), in Van Cleve Park; old courthouse (1850; Greek Revival); Woodlawn Cemetery, with graves of the Wright brothers and Dunbar. Settled 1796 and inc. 1805, Dayton grew with extension of canals in 1830s and 1840s, of the railroads (1850s), and with increased mfg. (farm machinery, railroad cars) for Civil War exigencies. Cash-register industry began c.1880, the making of electric motors in 1900s, and the Wright brothers' experimental airplane plant was established in 1911. Series of floods, culminating in one of especial destructiveness in 1913, gave rise to establishment of a flood-control dist. whose works now control the Miami valley. Dayton was 1st large city to adopt (1913) city-manager system of govt. Pop. of Dayton metropolitan dist. (including neighboring Oakwood, Miamisburg, West Carrollton, and other places) was 453,181 in 1950. 10 City (pop. 719), Yamhill co., NW Oregon, 6 mi. E of McMinnville and on Yamhill R. near its mouth in Willamette R.; fruit and vegetable processing, woodworking. 11 Borough (pop. 828), Armstrong co., W central Pa., 15 mi. ENE of Kittanning. 12 City (pop. 3,191), ⊙ Rhea co., E Tenn., near Tennessee R., 35 mi. NNE of Chattanooga, in fruit, coal, timber region; mfg. of hosiery, underwear, baskets. William Jennings Bryan Univ. here. In 1925, scene of the Scopes trial. Founded c.1884. 13 Town (pop. 1,820), Liberty co., E Texas, near Trinity R., 33 mi. ENE of Houston; trade, processing point in oil-producing and agr. area (cotton, rice, honey, poultry). Inc. 1925. 14 Town (pop. 788), Rockingham co., NW Va., in Shenandoah Valley, 19 mi. NNE of Staunton. 15 City (pop. 2,979), ⊙ Columbia co., SE Wash., 25 mi. NE of Walla Walla and on Touchet R.; timber, wheat, peas, apples, livestock. Inc. 1871. 16 Town (pop. 316), Sheridan co., N Wyo., on Tongue R. just E of Bighorn Mts., near Mont. line, and 15 mi. WNW of Sheridan; fruit, livestock. Near by are Tongue River Canyon, traversed by Tongue R. in gorge 2,000 ft. deep, and The Fallen City, picturesque jumble of rocks left on hillside by glacier.

Daytona Beach (dātō'nŭ), city (pop. 30,187), Volusia co., NE Fla., c.50 mi. SSE of St. Augustine, on the Atlantic and on both sides of Halifax R. (a lagoon; bridged here), in citrus-fruit and truck region; noted year-round resort; has boat yards. Seat of Bethune-Cookman Col. Town founded 1870 by Mathias Day; present city formed 1926 by consolidation of Seabreeze, Daytona Beach, and Daytona. Modern development came after arrival of railroad in 1890. Since 1903, automobile speed trials have been held on noted hard white beach here (c.25 mi. long and, at low tide, c.500 ft. wide).

Dayville, village (1939 pop. 54), S Alaska, on Port Valdez, 5 mi. SW of Valdez; fishing. Site of Fort Liscum, abandoned army base.

Dayville. 1 Village, Windham co., Conn.: see KILLINGLY. 2 Town (pop. 286), Grant co., NE central Oregon, 30 mi. W of Canyon City and on John Day R. at mouth of its South Fork.

Dayzangi, Afghanistan: see PANJAO.

Dazaifu (dä"zī'fōō), town (pop. 6,612), Fukuoka prefecture, N Kyushu, Japan, 9 mi. SE of Fukuoka; rail terminus; rice, raw silk.

Dazey, village (pop. 196), Barnes co., E central N.Dak., 20 mi. NNW of Valley City.

De Aar (dŭ är'), town (pop. 9,298), E central Cape Prov., U. of So. Afr., 140 mi. SSW of Kimberley; alt. 4,079 ft. One of Union's most important railroad centers, with extensive workshop; stock-raising center. Airfield. Of strategic importance in South African War.

Dea Augusta Vocontiorum, France: see DIE.

Dead Diamond River, N.H.: see SWIFT DIAMOND RIVER.

Dead Horse Mountains, Texas: see CARMEN, SIERRA DEL.

Dead Indian Peak, Wyo.: see ABSAROKA RANGE.

Dead Lake. 1 In NW Fla., widening (c.10 mi. long, 1 mi. wide) of Chipola R. (dredged here), in Calhoun and Gulf counties; S end, near Wewahitchka, is linked by cutoff with Apalachicola R. (1 mi. E). 2 In Otter Tail co., W Minn., lake (□ 12) near Otter Tail L., 16 mi. NE of Fergus Falls; 8.5 mi. long, 4 mi. wide.

Deadman's Cay (kā, kē), islet and town (pop. 474), S central Bahama Isls., off W Long Isl., 17 mi. NW of Clarence Town; 23°14'N 75°15'W. Stock raising, salt panning.

Dead River, former plantation (1940 pop. 76), Somerset co., W central Maine, 30 mi. NW of Skowhegan.

Dead River. 1 In Androscoggin co., SW Maine, small stream through which Androscoggin L. drains into Androscoggin R.; 6 mi. long. 2 In W Maine, rises in 2 branches in N Franklin co., flows c.45 mi. generally NE from their junction N of Stratton to Kennebec R. at The Forks. In middle course, Long Falls Dam (c.51 ft. high, ¼ mi. long; completed 1949; for power) backs up Flagstaff L. (c.25 mi. long), which covers □ 32 and inundates former site of Flagstaff. 3 In NW Upper Peninsula, Mich., rises in NW Marquette co., flows c.40 mi. SE to L. Superior 2 mi. N of Marquette. Power dams.

Dead Sea, Arabic *Bahret Lut* or *Birket Lut*, Hebrew *Yam ham Melah*, Lat. *Lacus Asphaltites*, salt lake (□ 405), S Palestine, on border of Jordan and Israel, 14 mi. E of Jerusalem; 49 mi. long (N–S), 3–10 mi. wide. Its surface is 1,292 ft. below sea level, and it is up to 1,300 ft. deep in N, though very shallow in S. High hills rise steeply from rocky E and W shores. Receives the Jordan (N) and several smaller intermittent streams, but has no outlet. The Dead Sea lies in part of the GREAT RIFT VALLEY, as does The Ghor, a great depression which extends N from the Dead Sea to the Sea of Galilee. The Dead Sea, with no outlet, is of 25% salinity, several times that of the ocean. It contains vast quantities of common salt, potassium chloride, magnesium salts, and bromide. Chemical plant at Sodom (S); similar plant at KALLIA (N) destroyed during Arab invasion, 1948. En-gedi (W) is health resort. Mentioned in the Bible as Salt Sea, Sea of the Plain, or East Sea.

Deadwood, city (pop. 3,288), ⊙ Lawrence co., W S.Dak., in Black Hills, just N of Lead, on branch of Belle Fourche R.; alt. 4,545 ft. Resort; trading point for mining and cattle region; jewelry; gold, quartz, cyanide. Near-by airport serves Deadwood, Lead, and Spearfish. Graves of such famous Western figures as Wild Bill Hickok, Calamity Jane, Preacher Smith, and Deadwood Dick are here; early history of town re-enacted annually in "Days of '76" celebration. Roosevelt Monument and Black Hills Natl. Forest are near by. Settled 1876 after discovery of gold in Deadwood Gulch.

Deadwood Dam, SW central Idaho, on Deadwood R. c.20 mi. upstream from mouth. Concrete arch dam (165 ft. high, 749 ft. long; completed 1930), unit in Payette div. of Boise irrigation project, forms Deadwood Reservoir (4 mi. long, 2 mi. wide; capacity c.164,000 acre-ft.). Deadwood River rises in Sawtooth Mts., flows 40 mi. S to South Fork of Payette R. in Boise co.

Deaf Smith, county (□ 1,507; pop. 9,111), extreme N Texas; ⊙ Hereford. In high plains of the Panhandle, on N.Mex. line; alt. 3,000–4,000 ft. Drained by Palo Duro and Tierra Blanca creeks. A leading Texas cattle and wheat co., producing also sheep, hogs, poultry, dairy products; irrigated lands produce potatoes, hay, fruit, truck. Includes Buffalo L. (recreation). Formed 1876.

Deal, municipal borough (1931 pop. 13,681; 1951 census 24,276), E Kent, England, on the coast 8 mi. NNE of Dover; seaside resort, with shipyards and naval station. It is reputed landing place (55 B.C.) of Caesar. It became one of the CINQUE PORTS; Walmer Castle, near by, is seat of lord warden of the Cinque Ports. Henry VIII built 3 castles here.

Deal, resort borough (pop. 1,064), Monmouth co., E N.J., on coast 2 mi. N of Asbury Park. Deal L. (c.2 mi. long) is just SW.

Deal Island, Somerset co., SE Md., low marshy isl. c.3 mi. long, 2 mi. wide, in Tangier Sound on N side of Manokin R. mouth; bridge to mainland at Chance. Large fishing fleet (crabs, oysters, clams, fish); seafood-packing houses; muskrat trapping; waterfowl hunting. Deal Isl. and Wenona (wēnō'nŭ) villages are here.

Deal Lake, N.J.: see DEAL.

Dean, village and parish (pop. 582), W Cumberland, England, 4 mi. SW of Cockermouth; dairy farming. Has church dating partly from 13th cent.

Dean, Forest of, wooded district and anc. royal forest in W Gloucester, England, bet. the Severn and the Wye; c.20 mi. long, 10 mi. wide. The area has been reforested; c.25,000 acres are crown land. There are coal and iron mines and stone quarries. Administratively the area is divided into parishes of East Dean (pop. 14,678) and West Dean (pop. 11,432).

Deandale, village (pop. 1,261, with adjacent Georges Run), Jefferson co., E Ohio, on the Ohio, 5 mi. S of Steubenville.

Deane cum Lostock (dēn' kŭm lŏ'stŭk), W suburb (pop. 5,873) of Bolton, S Lancashire, England; cotton milling, mfg. of chemicals, soap, aircraft accessories. Site of Bolton reservoir.

Deán Funes (dā-än' fōō'nĕs), city (pop. 13,064), ⊙ Ischilín dept. (□ c.2,200; pop. 27,256), N Córdoba prov., Argentina, 70 mi. N of Córdoba. Rail junction; mining and agr. center (corn, livestock); granite, marble, and lime quarrying.

Dean's Island, Tuamotu Isls.: see RANGIROA.

Deanston, Scotland: see DOUNE.

Dearborn (dĕr'bŭrn, dĕr'bôrn"), county (□ 306; pop. 25,141), SE Ind.; ⊙ Lawrenceburg. Bounded E by Ohio line and SE by Ky. line (here formed by Ohio R.); drained by Whitewater R. and small Laughery Creek. Agr. (livestock, tobacco, truck), with some mfg. (especially food products, wood products, whisky). Formed 1803.

Dearborn. 1 City (pop. 94,994), Wayne co., SE Mich., 10 mi. W of downtown Detroit, and on the River Rouge (freighter docks). Home of Ford Motor Company, whose immense River Rouge (or Rouge) plant is here. Also mfg. of aircraft parts, steel, metal products, brick. Edison Inst. of Technology, a jr. col., GREENFIELD VILLAGE, and a veterans' hosp. are here. Birthplace of Henry Ford has been restored. Settled 1795; inc. as village 1893, as city 1927. Grew in 1920s with expansion of Ford plant. Fordson city annexed 1929. 2 City (pop. 391), Platte co., W Mo., 17 mi. S of St. Joseph; grain.

Dearborn, Fort, Ill.: see CHICAGO.

Dearham (dĕr'ŭm), town and parish (pop. 1,923), W Cumberland, England, 2 mi. E of Maryport; coal mining. Has church begun in Norman times.

Dearing. 1 Town (pop. 325), McDuffie co., E Ga., 22 mi. W of Augusta; sawmilling. 2 City (pop. 261), Montgomery co., SE Kansas, 5 mi. WNW of Coffeyville, near Okla. line, in stock-raising and general agr. region. Oil and gas fields near by.

Dearne (dûrn), urban district (1951 census pop. 24,253), West Riding, S Yorkshire, England, 7 mi. N of Rotherham; coal mining. Formed 1937 out of the urban districts of Bolton-upon-Dearne and Thurnscoe.

Dearne River, SW Yorkshire, England, rises near Denby, flows 25 mi. SE, past Barnsley, to Don R. at Conisborough.

Deary, village (pop. 320), Latah co., N Idaho, 21 mi. ENE of Moscow; shipping point for lumber, agr., mining area.

Dease Lake (dēz) (25 mi. long, 1 mi. wide), NW B.C., 160 mi. E of Juneau, Alaska; drained N into Liard R. by Dease R. At S end of lake is trading post of Dease Lake; 58°27'N 130°2'W.

Dease Strait, S Franklin Dist., Northwest Territories, arm (130 mi. long, 12–30 mi. wide) of the Arctic Ocean, bet. Coronation Gulf (W) and Queen Maud Gulf (E); 69°N 104°30′–108°50′W. Separates Victoria Isl. (N) and Kent Peninsula of Mackenzie Dist. mainland (S). At E end of strait is Melbourne Isl. Dease Strait forms part of Northwest Passage through the Arctic Isls.

Death Valley or **Death Valley Junction,** unincorporated mining town, Inyo co., E Calif., in Amargosa Desert, near Nev. line, across Amargosa Range from Death Valley (W); borax works.

Death Valley National Monument (□ 2,906.4), E Calif. and S Nev., established 1933 in **Death Valley,** deep and arid desert basin (140 mi. long, 4–16 mi. wide, with □ 550 lying below sea level), extending generally NW from Mojave Desert and lying bet. Panamint Range (W) and Amargosa Range (E). A rift valley, formed by dropping of an earth block bet. parallel faults; part of Great Basin region. Badwater, 280 ft. below sea level, is lowest point in Western Hemisphere; c.15 mi. W rises Telescope Peak (11,045 ft.), highest point in monument. Has almost no rainfall (1.4 in. annual average), very high summer temperatures (134°F. recorded in 1913), but mild, healthful climate from Nov. to May. Amargosa R. and small Furnace Creek sink into valley floor; a few wells and springs are found. Includes numerous salt and alkali flats, great variety of colorful rock formations, unusual desert plants, considerable small animal life, and fossilized footprints of prehistoric animals. Other points of interest: in N, Ubehebe Crater (780 ft. deep), colorful Titus Canyon, and sand dunes; in E, Dantes View (5,700 ft.), on E rim of valley, Devils Golf Course (area of crystallized salt ridges and pinnacles) at base of E rim; and old Eagle and Harmony borax works. Resorts (Furnace Creek, Stovepipe Wells). Valley was named (1849) by party of gold seekers, some of whom died while trying to cross it. Later visited by prospectors who discovered gold, silver, and copper. In 1880s, large deposits of borax (no longer worked) were discovered. Panamint Indians (for centuries valley's only inhabitants) now occupy govt.-constructed village in E, just S of park hq. Scotty's Castle (lavish home built by ex-cowboy who did much to publicize region) is in N, near Nev. line. There are year-round tourist accommodations, highways, and an airport.

Deauville (dō′vĭl, Fr. dōvēl′), town (pop. 5,438), Calvados dept., NW France, on the Channel at mouth of Touques R., opposite TROUVILLE (NE), and 9 mi. S of Le Havre; leading bathing resort of Normandy, with fine gardens and beach (2 mi. long; boardwalk). A fashionable center with well-known race course.

Deaver (dē′vûr), (pop. 118), Big Horn co., N Wyo., near Mont. line, 11 mi. WNW of Lovell; alt. 4,105 ft. Supply point in oil and ranching area; sugar beets, beans, grain.

Deba, in Nigerian names: see DEBE.

De Baca (dĕbä′kŭ), county (□ 2,358; pop. 3,464), E N.Mex.; ⊙ Fort Sumner. Grazing, grain area, watered by Pecos R. Alamogordo Reservoir is in N, plateau (5,000 ft.) in W. Formed 1917.

Debai, Trucial Oman: see DIBAI.

Debaltsevo or **Debal'tsevo** (dyĕbŭltsyĕ′vŭ), city (1926 pop. 13,112), E Stalino oblast, Ukrainian SSR, in the Donbas, 37 mi. NE of Stalino; major rail center; metallurgical and metalworking industries.

Debar (dĕ′bûr), village (pop. 4,411), Plovdiv dist., S central Bulgaria, 2 mi. SSW of Parvomai; tobacco, vineyards, fruit, truck. Formerly Dervent.

Debar (dĕ′bär), Albanian and Turkish *Dibra,* anc. *Deborus,* town (pop. 4,628), W Macedonia, Yugoslavia, near confluence of Black Drin and Radika rivers, 55 mi. SW of Skoplje, near Albania border; commercial center for cattle and dairying region. First mentioned as Slav settlement in 1018; was medieval wood-carving center. Debarska Banja, health resort with sulphur springs, is near by.

Debarua (dĕbär′wä), Ital. *Debaroa,* village, Adi Ugri div., central Eritrea, on Gash R. (here called Mareb) and 18 mi. SSW of Asmara, on highway; alt. c.6,330 ft.; grain, vegetables, eucalyptus. Gold and copper mines near by.

Debba, Ed Debba, or **El Debba** (both: ĕd dĕb′bä), town, Northern Prov., Anglo-Egyptian Sudan, on left bank of the Nile at great bend, on road, and 75 mi. WSW of Merowe; starting point for direct caravan route to Omdurman; agr. and salt trade.

Debden (dĕb′dŭn), village (pop. 234), S central Sask., 50 mi. WNW of Prince Albert; mixed farming, dairying.

Debdou (dĕbdōō′), town (pop. 3,004), Oujda region, NE Fr. Morocco, in a NE outlier of the Middle Atlas, 30 mi. SSW of Taourirt; lumbering, alfa processing; essential oils. Lead deposits. Large Jewish pop. Occupied by French 1911.

Debe or **Débé** (dābā′), village (pop. 4,097), SW Trinidad, B.W.I., on railroad and 4 mi. S of San Fernando; marketing place in sugar-growing region. Petroleum deposits are near by (E).

Debe Fulani (dā′bä fōō′länē, fōōlä′nē), town (pop. 4,236), Bauchi prov., Northern Provinces, E central Nigeria, 25 m . ENE of Gombe, near Gongola R.; cassava, millet, durra. Sometimes spelled Daba Fulani.

Debe Habe (dā′bä hä′bē), town (pop. 11,257), Bauchi prov., Northern Provinces, E central Nigeria, 20 mi. ESE of Gombe; cassava, millet, durra. Sometimes spelled Daba Habe.

Debelets (dĕbĕlĕts′), village (pop. 2,378), Gorna Oryakhovitsa dist., N Bulgaria, on branch of Yantra R. and 3 mi. SW of Tirnovo; flour milling, fruit and vegetable canning; livestock.

Debeljaca or **Debelyacha** (both: dĕbĕ′lyächä), Serbo-Croatian *Debeljača,* Hung. *Torontálvásárhely* (tôr′ôntälvä″shärhĕē), village (pop. 5,942), Vojvodina, N Serbia, Yugoslavia, 13 mi. N of Pancevo, in the Banat.

Debenham (dĕb′nŭm), town and parish (pop. 1,016), central Suffolk, England, on Deben R. and 12 mi. N of Ipswich; agr. market. Has 14th–15th-cent. church.

Deben River (dē′bŭn), Suffolk, England, rises just N of Debenham, flows 30 mi. SE and S, past Wickham Market and Woodbridge, to North Sea 3 mi. NE of Felixstowe. Navigable below Woodbridge.

De Beque (dŭ bĕk′), town (pop. 253), Mesa co., W Colo., on Colorado R. and 26 mi. NE of Grand Junction; alt. 4,800 ft. Trade center in livestock region. Prehistoric fossils found near by. Oil-shale fields in vicinity. Grand Valley Dam, unit in Grand Valley irrigation project, is 14 mi. SSW.

Debert (dŭbûr′), agr. village (pop. estimate 300), N central N.S., on Debert R. and 10 mi. ENE of Truro; air base.

Debert River, N central N.S., rises in Cobequid Mts., flows 25 mi. S, past Debert, to Cobequid Bay 12 mi. W of Truro.

Debessy (dyĭbyĕ′sē), village (1926 pop. 2,033), E Udmurt Autonomous SSR, Russian SFSR, on Cheptsa R. and 60 mi. NNE of Izhevsk; wheat, flax, livestock.

Debhata (dābä′tŭ), town (pop. 6,286), Khulna dist., SW East Bengal, E Pakistan, on Jamuna R. and 40 mi. WSW of Khulna; sundari-wood trade center; rice, jute, oilseeds; lime kilns.

Debica (dĕbē′tsä), Pol. *Dębica,* town (pop. 9,924), Rzeszow prov., SE Poland, on Wisloka R. and 26 mi. W of Rzeszow; rail junction; airport; mfg. of rubber footwear; food processing; timber and synthetic rubber (planned before Second World War) industries. During Second World War, under Ger. rule, called Dembica.

De Bilt, Netherlands: see BILT.

Deblin (dĕ′blēn), Pol. *Dęblin,* village, Warszawa prov., E Poland, on the Vistula at Wieprz R. mouth, and 15 mi. SSE of Garwolin; rail and road junction. One of principal crossings of upper Vistula, it was formerly site of Rus. fortress (captured, 1915, by Germans) and called Ivangorod.

Deblois (dŭblois′), town (pop. 59), Washington co., E Maine, on Narraguagus R. and 29 mi. WNW of Machias.

Debno (dĕb′nô), Pol. *Dębno,* Ger. *Neudamm* (noi′däm), town (1939 pop. 7,493; 1946 pop. 3,341) in Brandenburg, after 1945 in Szczecin prov., NW Poland, 11 mi. N of Küstrin (Kostrzyn); fruit-growing and processing, hat mfg. Founded 16th cent.

Débo, Lake (dā′bō, dĕ′bō), central Fr. Sudan, Fr. West Africa, in lacustrine, frequently inundated depression (Macina) of upper Niger, 50 mi. N of Mopti.

Deborah, Mount (12,540 ft.), E Alaska, peak in Alaska Range, 90 mi. SSE of Fairbanks; 63°38′N 147°14′W.

Deborgia (dŭbôr′zhŭ), village (pop. c.100), Mineral co., W Mont., on branch of the Clark Fork and 75 mi. NW of Missoula near Idaho line. Near by is Savenac Forest Nursery, with annual capacity of 6,000,000 trees.

Deboyne Islands (dŭboin′), volcanic group, Louisiade Archipelago, Territory of Papua, SW Pacific, 110 mi. SE of New Guinea. Comprise c.6 isls.; largest is Panniet Isl. (5 mi. long, 3 mi. wide). In Second World War, lagoon in middle of group was site of Jap. seaplane base destroyed by U.S. forces after battle of Coral Sea (1942).

Debra Birhan (dĕ′brä bĭr′hän), town (pop. 3,000), Shoa prov., central Ethiopia, on road and 70 mi. NE of Addis Ababa; 9°40′N 39°31′E. Founded in mid-15th cent.

Debra Libanos (lĭbä′nōs), a major Coptic monastery and place of pilgrimage, Shoa prov., central Ethiopia. 45 mi. N of Addis Ababa. Has precious manuscripts.

Debra Markos (mär′kōs), town (pop. 10,000), ⊙ Gojjam prov., NW Ethiopia, on road, on S slope of Choke Mts., and 150 mi. NW of Addis Ababa; 10°15′N 37°49′E; alt. 8,251 ft. Trade center (coffee, cereals, hides, beeswax). Has old church surrounded by monastery. Airfield.

Debra Tabor (täbôr′), town (pop. 9,000), Begemdir prov., NW Ethiopia, E of L. Tana, on road and 65 mi. SE of Gondar, in cereal-growing and stock-raising (cattle, mules, sheep) region; 38°3′N 11°51′E; alt. 9,662 ft. Trade center. Has church and palace. Succeeded Gondar as capital of Ethiopia under Theodore II.

Debrecen (dĕb′rĕtsĕn), city (1941 pop. 125,936), ⊙ but independent of Hajdu co., E Hungary, 120 mi. E of Budapest; rail and market center for large agr. area. Tobacco warehouses and factory; mfg. of fertilizer, machinery, furniture; breweries, flour mills, soap and candleworks, brickworks, tanneries. Produces excellent salami. Experiment stations for tobacco and other agr. products; airport. Calvinist center; univ., founded 1588 as college, has schools of law, theology, philosophy, medicine; library contains 140,000 vols. Mus. houses city library. Seat of 1849 revolutionary govt.; scene of Kossuth's speech of independence. Pro-Allied provisional Hungarian govt. formed here Dec., 1944. Formerly spelled Debreczen. Was Hungary's 3d largest city until the administrative reorganization of 1950 separated its large rural suburban area and reduced its pop. to less than 100,000.

Debruce (dĭbrōōs′), resort village, Sullivan co., SE N.Y., on small Willowemoc Creek and 5 mi. E of Livingston Manor.

Debrzno (dĕbzh′nô), Ger. *Preussisch Friedland* (proi′sĭsh frēt′länt), town (1939 pop. 3,842; 1946 pop. 1,347) in Pomerania, after 1945 in Koszalin prov., NW Poland, 25 mi. ESE of Szczecinek; grain, sugar beets, potatoes, livestock. Until 1938, in former Prussian prov. of Grenzmark Posen–Westpreussen. After 1945, briefly called Frydlad, Pol. *Frydląd.*

Debsé, Syria: see DIBSE.

Debub (dĕbōōb′), village (pop. 600), Tigre prov., N Ethiopia, near source of Ererti R., 33 mi. SSE of Makale; cereals, coffee, cotton; livestock.

Debundscha (dĕbōōn′chä), village (pop. 230), S Br. Cameroons, administered as part of Eastern Provinces of Nigeria, on Gulf of Guinea, 16 mi. WNW of Victoria; lighthouse; 4°7′N 8°58′E. Average yearly rainfall, 400 in. Also spelled Debunscha, Debunja, and Debundja.

De Cade, Lake (dŭ kād′), Terrebonne parish, SE La., 14 mi. SW of Houma, in marshy coastal region; c.5 mi. long, 1–2 mi. wide. Connected by waterways with Gulf Intracoastal Waterway (N) and Gulf of Mexico (S).

Decamere (dĕkämĕ′rā), town (pop. 12,800), Asmara div., central Eritrea, 18 mi. SSE of Asmara, near Gura airport; alt. c.6,760 ft. Industrial and road center; foundry, automobile repair shops; vegetable-oil extracting, soap mfg. Market for grain, fruit, vegetables, flax. Developed rapidly as supply center in Italo-Ethiopian campaign (1935-36).

Decani or **Dechani** (both: dĕ′chänē), Serbo-Croatian *Dečani,* village, SW Serbia, Yugoslavia, 8 mi. S of Pec, in the Metohija. Chestnut growing in vicinity. Monastery of Visoki Decani is just NW.

Decapolis (dĕkă′pŭlĭs) [Gr.,=ten cities], confederacy of (originally) 10 anc. cities, all E of the Jordan, except Scythopolis. The others were (according to Pliny) Dion, Pella, Gadara, Hippos, Gerasa, Philadelphia, Damascus, Raphana, and Kanatha. The league was constituted after Pompey's campaign (65 B.C.–62 B.C.) as a protection against the Jews and the Arabian tribes and as a customs union. The Roman governor of Syria exercised general supervision of their affairs, and they were liable to Roman military service and taxation. The name was used for the general locality.

Decatur (dĕkā′tûr, dĭ–). **1** County (□ 467; pop. 23,620,) SW Ga.; ⊙ Bainbridge. Bounded S by Fla. line; intersected by Flint R. Coastal plain agr. (corn, sugar cane, peanuts, pecans, livestock) and forestry (lumber, naval stores) area with fuller's-earth mines. Formed 1823. **2** County (□ 370; pop. 18,218), SE central Ind.; ⊙ Greensburg. Drained by Flatrock and small Duck, Clifty, and Sand creeks. Agr. (grain, tobacco, livestock); some oil, natural gas; limestone quarries. Mfg. at Greensburg. Formed 1821. **3** County (□ 530; pop. 12,601), S Iowa, on Mo. line; ⊙ Leon. Rolling prairie agr. area (hogs, cattle, poultry, corn, alfalfa), with bituminous-coal deposits; drained by Thompson and Weldon rivers. Formed 1846. **4** County (□ 899; pop. 6,185), NW Kansas; ⊙ Oberlin. Flat to rolling area, bordered N by Nebr.; watered by Sappa and Beaver creeks. Grain, livestock. Formed 1879. **5** County (□ 346; pop. 9,442), W Tenn.; ⊙ Decaturville. Bounded E and S by Tennessee R.; drained by its tributaries. Includes part of Kentucky Reservoir. Livestock raising, dairying, agr. (cotton, corn, hay). Formed 1845.

Decatur. 1 City (pop. 19,974), ⊙ Morgan co., N Ala., on left bank of Tennessee R. and c.75 mi. N of Birmingham. Rail and processing center, with boat connections, in cotton and timber area. Manufactures tire-cord fabrics, copper tubing, hosiery, metal and wood products, fertilizer. Produces flour, corn meal, grits, peanut and cottonseed oil, evaporated milk. There are railroad shops, shipyard, and bottling works. Founded 1820 and named for Stephen Decatur by order of President Monroe; inc. 1826. Largely destroyed during Civil War. Industries stimulated by development of TVA. Keller Memorial Bridge across Tennessee R. was built 1928. **2** Town (pop. 350), Benton co., extreme NW Ark., 18 mi. W of Rogers, in the Ozarks. **3** City (pop. 21,635), ⊙ De Kalb co., NW central Ga., residential suburb of Atlanta, near Stone Mtn.; mfg. (furnaces, machinery, prefabricated houses). Agnes Scott Col. and Columbia

Theological Seminary here. Inc. as town 1823, as city 1922. **4** City (pop. 66,269), ⊙ Macon co., central Ill., 37 mi. E of Springfield and on Sangamon R., dammed here in 1923 to form L. Decatur (c.10 mi. long; recreation area); rail, industrial, trade, and distribution center in agr., oil, and coal area. Large railroad shops, corn- and soybean-processing plants; also mfg. of automobile accessories, chemicals, plastics; steel, iron, and brass products; plumbing fixtures, clothing, pumps, light fixtures, utilities equipment, farm machinery. James Millikin Univ. and a U.S. army supply depot are here. Spitler Woods State Park (c.200 acres) is SE. In Fairview Park is preserved the log-cabin courthouse where Lincoln practiced. Lincolniana collection in city library. The Grand Army of the Republic was organized here in 1866. Coal deposits 1st mined 1874. Founded 1829, inc. 1839. **5** City (pop. 7,271), ⊙ Adams co., E Ind., on St. Marys R. and 21 mi. SSE of Fort Wayne, in agr. area; mfg. (cement products, motors, electrical machinery, castings, wood products, cheese, soybean oil, beet sugar, tile, brick); timber. Settled 1837. City was a former home of Gene Stratton Porter. **6** or **Decatur City,** town (pop. 196), Decatur co., S Iowa, 35 mi. SE of Creston, in livestock area. Limestone quarries near by. **7** Village (pop. 1,664), Van Buren co., SW Mich., 24 mi. SW of Kalamazoo, in farm area (celery, onions, livestock); mfg. (celery crates, butter); celery cold-storage plants. Small lakes near by (resort). Inc. 1861. **8** Town (pop. 1,225), ⊙ Newton co., E central Miss., 24 mi. W of Meridian. A dist. jr. col. is here. **9** Village (pop. 808), Burt co., NE Nebr., 15 mi. N of Tekamah and on Missouri R.; livestock, grain. **10** Town (pop. 235), ⊙ Meigs co., SE Tenn., 45 mi. NE of Chattanooga, in farm area. **11** City (pop. 2,922), ⊙ Wise co., N Texas, 37 mi. NNW of Fort Worth; trade, shipping center for dairying, livestock, agr. area (truck, cotton); mfg. (dairy products, flour, mattresses, clothing, furniture, tile). Seat of Decatur Baptist Col. (1892).

Decaturville, town (pop. 514), ⊙ Decatur co., W Tenn., 38 mi. E of Jackson, near Kentucky Reservoir; sawmills, limestone quarries.

Decazeville (dûkäzvēl'), town (pop. 10,571), Aveyron dept., S France, 20 mi. NW of Rodez; coal-mining and ironworking center; chemical factories (ammonia, fertilizer, tar derivatives), cement-works.

Deccan Plateau (dĕ'kŭn, dĕ'kăn, -kăn), Sanskrit *Dakshin* [=south], triangular tableland covering most of peninsular India, enclosed at its apex (S) by junction of EASTERN GHATS and WESTERN GHATS, which spread out NE and NW respectively, forming its E and W escarpments. N limits (W-E), formed by SATPURA RANGE, overlooking Narbada valley (N), and by CHOTA NAGPUR PLATEAU, opens onto Chhattisgarh Plain N of Eastern Ghats. Area comprises Mysore, inland sections of central Madras and S Bombay, all of Hyderabad, all of Madhya Pradesh S of the Narbada, and those parts of S Bihar and N Orissa lying on Chota Nagpur Plateau. Mainly c.2,000 ft. high, the tableland slopes generally E from average alt. of 3,000 ft. in Western Ghats to average of 1,500 ft. in Eastern Ghats. Main rivers (N–S), the Godavari, Kistna, and Cauvery, rise in Western Ghats and flow to Bay of Bengal. A land surface since early-Paleozoic times; has late-Cretaceous and early-Tertiary lava beds (□ c.200,000), in NW characterized by water-retaining black cotton soil. Western Ghats precipitate most of rainfall of SW monsoon; less beneficial NE monsoon is admitted through Chhattisgarh Plain. As a historical term, Deccan refers to all peninsular India S of the Narbada. The Satpura and Vindhya ranges prevented early Aryans of Indo-Gangetic plain (HINDUSTAN) from invading the Dravidian South, but Aryan culture had permeated all of India by end of Asoka's empire (273–232 B.C.). The Delhi sultans extended their control over most of S India in 14th cent. and were succeeded in the area of the Deccan bet. Narbada and Kistna rivers by several rebel kings, the Deccan sultans, who combined to defeat the forces of Vijayanagar kingdom (S of the Kistna) at the battle of Talikota in 1565. In 17th cent., the Mogul empire united most of the Deccan under its administration. The CARNATIC became the scene of England's struggle with France, in 18th cent., for supremacy in India. The term Deccan is at times restricted to N domains of the Deccan sultans. Southern Deccan or Deccan proper is a term sometimes used for the area of the Mysore highlands. Formerly spelled Dekkan.

Deccan States, group of former princely states (total □ 10,870; pop. 2,785,428) situated within S and central Bombay, India. Comprised Akalkot, Aundh, Bhor, Jamkhandi, Janjira, Jath, Kolhapur, Kurandvad Senior, Kurandvad Junior, Miraj Senior, Miraj Junior, Mudhol, Phaltan, Ramdurg, Sangli, Savanur, Savantvadi, and Wadi Estate. Originally part of Mahratta confederacy; in 19th cent., entered into various individual and group relations with Br. administration; S group sometimes known as Southern Mahratta States. In 1933, all were formed into political agency (called Kolhapur and Deccan States Agency), with hq. at Kolhapur, under govt. of India. In 1947, 7 states formed United Deccan State; by Aug., 1949, all were inc. into various dists. of Bombay.

Decemvrie 30, 1947, outer E urban suburb (1948 pop. 12,613) of Bucharest, S Rumania, on right bank of Colentina R. Called Principele-Nicolae until 1948.

Deception Island, Sp. *Decepción* (dāsāpsyōn'), South Shetland Isls., 6 mi. S of Livingston Isl., off Palmer Peninsula, Antarctica; 62°56'S 60°34'W. Circular isl. (8–9 naut. mi. in diameter) enclosing a land-locked harbor. Claimed by Great Britain, Argentina, and Chile; all have maintained bases here.

Deception Pass, Wash.: see WHIDBEY ISLAND.

Decew Falls (dûkū'), village, S Ont., on Welland R. and 4 mi. SE of St. Catharines; hydroelectric-power center.

Dechani, Yugoslavia: see DECANI.

De Chartres, Fort, Ill.: see PRAIRIE DU ROCHER.

Dechen or **Dechhen Ling** (dĕ'chĕn lĭng'), Chinese *Te-ch'ing* (dŭ'chĭng'), town [Tibetan *dzong*], S Tibet, on the Kyi Chu and 13 mi. E of Lhasa; alt. 11,792 ft.

Decherd (dĕ'kûrd), town (pop. 1,435), Franklin co., S Tenn., 45 mi. WNW of Chattanooga; clothing mfg., cotton ginning.

De Chien, Bayou, or **Bayou du Chien** (dû shēn'), stream, SW Ky., rises in Graves co., flows c.35 mi. generally W to the Mississippi just NE of Hickman.

Dechy (dûshē'), outer ESE suburb (pop. 4,968) of Douai, Nord dept., N France, in coal-mining dist.; rail junction.

Decimomannu (dĕchēmōmän'nōō), village (pop. 2,144), Cagliari prov., S Sardinia, near Flumini Mannu R., 10 mi. NNW of Cagliari; rail junction.

Decin (dyĕ'chēn), Czech *Děčín*, Ger. *Tetschen* (tĕ'-chûn), city (pop. 10,639; urban area pop. 30,753), N Bohemia, Czechoslovakia, port on Elbe R. and 11 mi. NNE of Usti nad Labem; near Ger. border. Rail junction; noted chemical industry (soap, perfumes, drugs). Has 16th-cent. bridge, 11th-cent. church (rebuilt in 18th cent.), 18th-cent. castle with fine collections. River port is also known as Loubi (lō'bē), Czech *Loubí*.

Décines-Charpieu (dāsēn'-shärpyû'), town (pop. 6,156), Isère dept., SE France, 6 mi. E of Lyons; mfg. (rayon, chemicals, ink, biscuits).

Decize (dûsēz'), town (pop. 3,917), Nièvre dept., central France, 18 mi. SE of Nevers, on isl. in Loire R. at mouth of Arnon R.; port at junction of Nivernais Canal with Loire Lateral Canal; brick- and tile-mfg. center. Metalworking, parquetry and furniture mfg., flour milling. Trade in cattle, coal, iron, bldg. materials. Saint-Just b. here.

Decker, town (pop. 386), Knox co., SW Ind., on White R. and 11 mi. S of Vincennes, in agr. area.

Deckerville. **1** Town (pop. 46), Poinsett co., NE Ark., 9 mi. SE of Marked Tree. **2** Village (pop. 719), Sanilac co., E Mich., c.40 mi. NNW of Port Huron, in farm area (livestock, poultry, grain; dairy products).

Declo (dĕ'klō), village (pop. 219), Cassia co., S Idaho, 10 mi. E of Burley; wheat, sugar beets.

Decorah (dĭkō'rû), city (pop. 6,060), ⊙ Winneshiek co., NE Iowa, on Upper Iowa R. and c.60 mi. NNE of Waterloo; packed poultry, feed, beverages, mats, canvas products. Seat of Luther Col. (coeducational; 1861), with mus. devoted to early history of the city. Near by are limestone quarries, an "ice" cave, and state park with fish hatchery. Inc. 1857.

Decoto (dēkō'tō), village (pop. 2,830), Alameda co., W Calif., 20 mi. SE of Oakland; fruit canning and processing, tile mfg. Has Masonic home for aged.

Decs (dĕch), town (pop. 5,141), Tolna co., S Hungary, 5 mi. SE of Szekszard; wheat, corn, potatoes, poultry.

Dedaye (dā'dûyĕ'), town (pop. 6,778), Pyapon dist., Lower Burma, in Irrawaddy delta, 35 mi. SW of Rangoon.

Deddington, town and parish (pop. 1,234), N Oxfordshire, England, 6 mi. S of Banbury; agr. market. Has 14th-cent. church, several old houses, and remains of 12th-cent. castle.

Dedeagach, Greece: see ALEXANDROUPOLIS.

Dededo (dûdä'dō), town (pop. 988) and municipality (pop. 6,333), N Guam, on coast; coconut plantations.

Dedegol Dag (dĕdĕgûl' dä), Turkish *Dedegöl Dağ*, peak (9,780 ft.), S Turkey, in Taurus Mts., 28 mi. ESE of Egridir.

Dedemsvaart (dā'dûmsfärt'), town (pop. c.5,000), Overijssel prov., N Netherlands, on Dedemsvaart canal and 9 mi. ENE of Zwolle; strawboard, acetylene gas, cement tiles; knitting mills; peat processing; truck gardening.

Deder (dĕdĕr'), town (pop. 1,500), Harar prov., E central Ethiopia, 50 mi. W of Harar. A major center of Chercher highland; coffee market.

Dederkaly, Ukrainian SSR: see VELIKIYE DEDERKALY.

Dedham (dĕ'dûm), town and parish (pop. 1,556), NE Essex, England, on Stour R. and 6 mi. NE of Colchester; agr. market, with flour mills. Has 15th–16th-cent. church, one of Constable's favorite subjects.

Dedham. **1** Town (pop. 360), Carroll co., W central Iowa, 12 mi. S of Carroll. **2** Town (pop. 374), Hancock co., S Maine, 12 mi. SE of Bangor; includes Lucerne-in-Maine, resort village near Phillips L. **3** Residential town (pop. 18,487), ⊙ Norfolk co., E Mass., on Charles R. and 10 mi. SW of Boston; printing, mfg. (envelopes, paper goods, lightning rods); agr. Settled 1635, inc. 1636. Fairbanks house (built 1636) considered oldest frame house in U.S.

Dedilovo (dyĭdyē'lûvŭ), village (1939 pop. over 2,000), E Tula oblast, Russian SFSR, 20 mi. SE of Tula; truck produce, wheat. During Second World War, briefly held (1941) by Germans in Moscow campaign.

Dedinovo (dyĕ'dyĭnŭvŭ), village (pop. over 2,000), SE Moscow oblast, Russian SFSR, on Oka R. and 15 mi. ESE of Kolomna; hay and dairy farming. Dates from 15th cent.; early shipbuilding site.

Dedo de Deus, Brazil: see ORGÃOS, SERRA DOS.

Dedougou (dĕdōō'gōō), town (pop. c.2,700), W Upper Volta, Fr. West Africa, near Black Volta R., 100 mi. NNE of Bobo-Dioulasso. Peanut and shea-nut growing and processing; stock raising. R.C. and Protestant missions. Garrison.

Dedovichi (dyĕ'dûvēchē), town (1948 pop. over 2,000), SE Pskov oblast, Russian SFSR, 18 mi. S of Dno; flax processing, dairying.

Dedovita (dā'dôvētsä), Rum. *Dedovița*, village (pop. 255), Gorj prov., SW Rumania, 6 mi. NE of Turnu-Severin; lignite mines.

Dedovsk (dyĕ'dûfsk), city (1939 pop. over 10,000), central Moscow oblast, Russian SFSR, 20 mi. WNW of Moscow; cotton-milling center; tire-cord. Formerly named Guchkovo, and later called Dedovski, 1925–40.

Deduru Oya (dĕ'dōōrōō ō'yû), river, W Ceylon, rises in NW Ceylon Hill Country, NW of Kandy; flows 87 mi. NW and W to Indian Ocean 1 mi. N of Chilaw.

Dedyukhino, Russian SFSR: see BEREZNIKI.

Dedza (dĕ'dzä), town (pop. 682), Central Prov., Nyasaland, on Mozambique border, 50 mi. SE of Lilongwe; alt. 5,000 ft. Road center; tobacco, cotton, rice, corn; livestock. Bushman cave dwellings near by.

Dee, river: see DEE RIVER.

Deeg, India: see DIG.

Deel River. **1** Rises on Limerick-Cork border N of Newmarket, Ireland, flows 26 mi. N, past Rathkeale and Adare, to the Shannon 8 mi. W of Limerick. **2** In Co. Mayo, Ireland, rises NNE of Newport, flows 20 mi. N and ENE, past Crossmolina, to Moy R. at Ballina.

Deemston, borough (pop. 775), Washington co., SW Pa., just W of Centerville.

Deenish, islet (125 acres) of Hog Isls., SW Co. Kerry, Ireland, near mouth of Kenmare R., 3 mi. W of Lamb's Head.

Deep Bay, Chinese *Hauhoi Wan* (hou'hoi' wän'), inlet of S.China Sea, in northwesternmost Hong Kong colony; 9 mi. long, 5 mi. wide. Leased with New Territories to British in 1898.

Deep Bay, village, Northern Prov., Nyasaland, port on W shore of L. Nyasa, 40 mi. SSE of Karonga; fishing; rice, cassava, cotton.

Deep Creek, village (pop. c.500), Norfolk co., SE Va., 6 mi. S of Portsmouth and on short Deep Creek, a waterway connecting Dismal Swamp Canal (S) with South Branch of Elizabeth R. (N).

Deep Creek Lake (c.15 mi. long; c.4,000 acres; alt. c.2,450 ft.), Garrett co., NW Md., in the Alleghenies; formed by hydroelectric dam in small tributary of Youghiogheny R. McHenry (resort) is at N end.

Deep Creek Mountains, W Utah–E Nev., SW of Great Salt Lake Desert. HAYSTACK PEAK (12,101 ft.) is highest point.

Deep Fork, river in central and E Okla., rises in Oklahoma co., flows NE, E, and SE, past Okmulgee, to North Canadian R., of which it is principal tributary, c.6 mi. N of Eufaula; 236 mi. long.

Deep Gap (3,120 ft.), NW N.C., pass through the Blue Ridge, 20 mi. NW of Wilkesboro.

Deephaven, village (pop. 1,823), Hennepin co., E Minn., on E shore of L. Minnetonka and 13 mi. W of Minneapolis, in agr. area (corn, oats, barley, livestock, poultry).

Deep Red Run, stream in SW Okla., rises in W Comanche co., flows c.60 mi. generally SE, through Tillman and Cotton counties, to Cache Creek 10 mi. S of Walters. Receives West Cache Creek (c.55 mi. long) in Cotton co.

Deep River, town (pop. c.3,000), SE Ont., near Ottawa R., and 100 mi. WNW of Ottawa. Residential town for near-by Chalk River atomic research center.

Deep River. **1** Town (pop. 2,570), Middlesex co., S Conn., on the Connecticut and 16 mi. SE of Middletown. Includes Deep River village (pop. 2,034). Mfg. (piano and organ parts, gliders, electrical appliances, tools, lace, wire products), agr. (poultry, truck). State forest here. Settled 1635 as Saybrook colony on site of present OLD SAYBROOK; colony was sold to Conn. in 1644, and present town was inc. as Saybrook in 1899. Name changed 1947 to Deep River. **2** Town (pop. 368), Poweshiek co., central Iowa, 24 mi. NNE of Oskaloosa, in agr. area.

Deep River, N central N.C., rises near Kernersville, flows SE past Randleman and Franklinville, and E, joining Haw R. near Haywood to form Cape Fear R.; c.125 mi. long.

Deep Run, village (pop. 142), Lenoir co., E N.C., 12 mi. SW of Kinston, in agr. area.

Deepstep, town (pop. 159), Washington co., E central Ga., 10 mi. W of Sandersville, in farm area.

Deepwater, village (pop. 499), NE New South Wales, Australia, 160 mi. SW of Brisbane; tin mines; dairy products.

Deepwater. 1 City (pop. 885), Henry co., W central Mo., near South Grand R., 8 mi. S of Clinton. **2** Village (1940 pop. 798), Salem co., SW N.J., on Delaware R. and 3 mi. S of Penns Grove; large chemical plant (tetraethyl lead, dyes). Terminus of Del. Memorial Bridge and of N.J. Turnpike.

Deer, Scotland: see OLD DEER.

Deer Creek. 1 Village (pop. 501), on Tazewell-Woodford co. line, central Ill., 15 mi. ESE of Peoria, in agr. and bituminous-coal area. **2** Village (pop. 349), Otter Tail co., W Minn., 36 mi. ENE of Fergus Falls, in agr. area; dairy products. **3** Former town, St. Louis co., Mo.: see LADUE. **4** Town (pop. 209), Grant co., N Okla., 13 mi. W of Blackwell, in grain-producing area.

Deer Creek. 1 In N central Ind., rises in S Miami co., flows c.50 mi. W, past Delphi, to the Wabash just SW of Delphi. **2** In S central Ohio, rises in Madison co., flows c.70 mi. SE, past Mount Sterling and Williamsport, to Scioto R. in Ross co. **3** In S Pa. and NE Md., rises in S York co., Pa., flows c.50 mi. ESE, across Harford co., Md., to the Susquehanna just above Port Deposit.

Deer Creek Dam, Utah: see PROVO RIVER.

Deerfield. 1 Town, Broward co., Fla.: see DEERFIELD BEACH. **2** Village (pop. 3,288), Lake co., NE Ill., NNW of Chicago; mfg. of type molds, lumber milling; nurseries. Inc. 1903. **3** City (pop. 440), Kearny co., SW Kansas, on Arkansas R. and 14 mi. W of Garden City; grain, cattle. **4** Agr. town (pop. 3,086), Franklin co., NW Mass., on Deerfield R. and 16 mi. N of Northampton. In massacre of 1704, almost all inhabitants either killed or carried off. Has fine 18th-cent. houses. Deerfield Acad. for boys is here. Settled before 1670, inc. 1677. Includes South Deerfield village (pop. 1,418). **5** Village (pop. 725), Lenawee co., SE Mich., 13 mi. E of Adrian, near Raisin R., in farm area. **6** Town (pop. 706), Rockingham co., SE N.H., 16 mi. SE of Concord. **7** Village (pop. 614), Dane co., S Wis., 15 mi. E of Madison, in agr. area; farm tools, dairy products.

Deerfield Beach, town (pop. 2,088), Broward co., S Fla., on Atlantic coast, 14 mi. N of Fort Lauderdale; truck-farming center. Named Hillsborough until 1907; inc. 1925. Also called Deerfield.

Deerfield Dam, S.Dak.: see RAPID CREEK.

Deerfield River, in Vt. and Mass., rises in Windham co., S Vt., flows S into Mass., then S and E to Connecticut R. just SE of Greenfield, Mass.; c.70 mi. long. Extensive power developments on river include HARRIMAN DAM and SOMERSET DAM, both in Vt.

Deer Flat Reservoir, Canyon co., SW Idaho, 5 mi. W of Nampa; 9 mi. long, 2 mi. wide; capacity c.177,000 acre-ft. Formed by 3 earth-fill dams; fed by irrigation canal extending W from diversion dam on Boise R. 7 mi. SE of Boise. Supplies water for Arrowrock div. of Boise irrigation project. Also known as L. Lowell.

Deer Grove, village (pop. 72), Whiteside co., NW Ill., near Green R., 13 mi. S of Sterling, in agr. area.

Deering, village (pop. 173), NW Alaska, on S shore of Kotzebue Sound, N Seward Peninsula, 60 mi. S of Kotzebue; trapping; gold mining, some coal mining. School.

Deering. 1 Town (pop. 138), Pemiscot co., extreme SE Mo., in Mississippi flood plain, 13 mi. W of Caruthersville. **2** Town (pop. 392), Hillsboro co., S N.H., on the Contoocook and 20 mi. SW of Concord. **3** Village (pop. 136), McHenry co., N central N.Dak., 15 mi. NE of Minot and on Little Deep R.

Deer Island. 1 Island (pop. c.1,000; 8 mi. long, 3 mi. wide) in Passamaquoddy Bay of the Bay of Fundy, SW N.B., just off Maine coast, 6 mi. SSE of St. Andrews, N of Campobello Isl.; 44°52′N 66°57′W; surrounded by rocky islets. Pollock, sardine, herring, lobster fishing carried on. **2** Island (3 mi. long, 1 mi. wide), E N.F., in Bonavista Bay, 35 mi. E of Gander; 48°55′N 53°45′W; fishing, lobster canning.

Deer Island, Co. Clare, Ireland: see INISHMORE.

Deer Island. 1 In Hancock co., S Maine, island in Penobscot Bay, 20 mi. SE of Belfast; 10 mi. long, 3–5 mi. wide. On it are towns of STONINGTON and **Deer Isle** (pop. 1,234; settled 1762, inc. 1789); Deer Isle town includes Little Deer Isle village on Little Deer Isl., and smaller Beach, Bradbury, Butter, Eagle, and Great and Little Spruce Head isls. **2** In Piscataquis co., W central Maine, island (□ c.2.25) near S end of Moosehead L. Site of settlement of Capens. **3** In E Mass., former island (now connected to mainland to N by a fill) bet. Boston Bay (W) and Massachusetts Bay (E); c.1 mi. long. **4** In S Miss., island in the Gulf of Mexico just SE of Biloxi; c.5 mi. long.

Dee River, Ireland, rises in N Co. Meath, flows 25 mi. E, past Ardee and Castlebellingham, to Dundalk Bay of Irish Sea 2 mi. E of Castlebellingham.

Dee River. 1 In Aberdeen, Scotland, rises in Cairngorm Mts. on Ben Macdhui, flows 87 mi. E, past Braemar, Balmoral Castle, Ballater, and Banchory, to the North Sea through an artificial channel at Aberdeen. Forms border bet. Aberdeen and Kincardine. Noted for its scenic beauty and salmon fisheries. Its valley is called Deeside or Royal Deeside. **2** In Kirkcudbright, Scotland, rises 10 mi. WNW of Dalry, flows 50 mi. SE and S, past Kirkcudbright, to Kirkcudbright Bay of Solway Firth just S of Kirkcudbright.

Dee River, N Wales and Cheshire, England, rises in Bala L., Merioneth, Wales, flows 70 mi. E and N, past Corwen, Llangollen, Chester, and Flint, to Irish Sea at West Kirby; 13-mi.-long estuary.

Deer Lake, settlement (pop. 1,932), W N.F., at N end of Deer L., 27 mi. NE of Corner Brook, on Humber R. and at W end of Newfoundland Canal; lumbering, sawmilling center. Site of hydroelectric station, supplying power to Corner Brook paper mills, Buchans mines. Subsistence agr. in region.

Deer Lake. 1 Lake (□ 28; 15 mi. long, 3 mi. wide), W N.F., on Humber R. and 15 mi. ENE of Corner Brook; W terminal of Newfoundland Canal, which links it with Grand L. **2** Lake (35 mi. long, 5 mi. wide), NW Ont., in Patricia dist., near Man. border; 52°39′N 94°15′W; alt. 1,014 ft. Drained by Severn R.

Deer Lake, borough (pop. 174), Schuylkill co., E central Pa., 11 mi. ESE of Pottsville.

Deer Lake, Itasca co., N central Minn., in cluster of small lakes, 11 mi. NNW of Grand Rapids; 5 mi. long, 1.5 mi. wide. Fishing resorts.

Deerlijk (dār′līk), town (pop. 8,207), West Flanders prov., W Belgium, 5 mi. ENE of Courtrai; textiles; agr. market. Formerly spelled Deerlyck.

Deer Lodge, county (□ 738; pop. 16,553), SW Mont.; ⊙ Anaconda. Mining and agr. area drained by the Clark Fork. Livestock; copper and zinc smelting at Anaconda. Parts of Deerlodge Natl. Forest throughout. Flint Creek and Anaconda ranges in N and SW, respectively. Formed 1865.

Deer Lodge, city (pop. 3,779), ⊙ Powell co., W central Mont., 30 mi. NNW of Butte and on the Clark Fork, 10 mi. E of Flint Creek Range; lead and silver mines; lumber mill, railway workshops; livestock, dairy and poultry products, grain. State penitentiary here. Founded as La Barge 1862, named Deer Lodge 1864, inc. 1883.

Deer Park. 1 Town (pop. 320), Garrett co., W Md., in the Alleghenies near Deep Creek L., 35 mi. WSW of Cumberland; mtn. resort (alt. c.2,450 ft.). **2** Village (pop. 7,241), Hamilton co., extreme SW Ohio, a NE suburb of Cincinnati. **3** Town (pop. 736), Harris co., S Texas, industrial suburb E of Houston, near Houston Ship Channel; chemical mfg. (chlorine, caustic soda, glycerine, alcohols, acetone, acrolein). **4** Town (pop. 1,167), Spokane co., E Wash., 20 mi. N of Spokane; dairy products, lumber, grain, fruit. Inc. 1908. **5** Village (pop. 226), St. Croix co., W Wis., 23 mi. NE of Hudson; dairying.

Deer Pond (7 mi. long, up to 4 mi. wide), SE N.F., 30 mi. SSW of Gander; 48°31′N 54°45′W. Drains into L. St. John.

Deer River, village (pop. 1,033), Itasca co., N central Minn., near Mississippi R., 14 mi. WNW of Grand Rapids in region of lakes and forests; resort, supply point in grain, livestock, and poultry area; dairy and lumber products. Greater Leech Lake Indian Reservation is just W.

Deersville, village (pop. 149), Harrison co., E Ohio, 10 mi. WNW of Cadiz; livestock.

Deer Trail, town (pop. 421), Arapahoe co., E central Colo., 50 mi. E of Denver; alt. 5,183 ft. Grain, beans, livestock.

Deerwood, village (pop. 572), Crow Wing co., central Minn., on Serpent L., in state forest, and 17 mi. NE of Brainerd, in dairying and truck-farming area. Iron mines, resorts near by.

Dees, Rumania: see DEJ.

Deesa (dē′sŭ), town (pop. 5,638), Banas Kantha dist., N Bombay, India, near Banas R., 18 mi. WNW of Palanpur; rail spur terminus; rice, wheat; hand-loom weaving. Former Br. cantonment.

Deewhy (dē′wī), town (pop. 5,940), E New South Wales, Australia, 9 mi. N of Sydney, on coast; summer resort; bathing beach.

Deferiet (dĭfĕ′rēŭt, –rūt), village (pop. 616), Jefferson co., N N.Y., on Black R. (water power) and 12 mi. NE of Watertown; paper milling.

Defiance, county (□ 410; pop. 25,925), NW Ohio; ⊙ Defiance. Bounded W by Ind. line; intersected by Maumee, Auglaize, and Tiffin rivers. Agr. (livestock, grain, truck); diversified mfg., especially at Defiance. Formed 1845.

Defiance. 1 Town (pop. 368), Shelby co., W Iowa, 3 mi. N of Harlan, in agr. area. **2** City (pop. 11,265), ⊙ Defiance co., NW Ohio, c.50 mi. WSW of Toledo, at confluence of Auglaize and Tiffin rivers with the Maumee; machinery and machine tools, food and dairy products, beer, communications equipment, household appliances, metal products, hardware, auto parts. Seat of Defiance Col. Settled 1790; inc. 1836 as a city. Anthony Wayne built Fort Defiance here in 1794; it is now in Defiance City Park. William Henry Harrison built Fort Winchester (1812) near by.

De Forest, village (pop. 805), Dane co., S Wis., on Yahara R. and 12 mi. N of Madison, in tobacco-growing and dairying region; pea cannery, creamery.

De Funiak Springs (dē fū′nēăk), town (pop. 3,077), ⊙ Walton co., NW Fla., c.45 mi. NW of Panama City, in farm and timber area. Has large spring.

Deg (dăg), Hung. *Dég*, town (pop. 4,044), Veszprem co., W central Hungary, 22 mi. S of Szekesfehervar; distilleries; sugar beets, wheat, cattle, hogs in area.

Degache (dĕgăsh′), village, Tozeur dist., SW Tunisia, in El-Oudiane oasis, at N edge of the Chott Djerid, 6 mi. NE of Tozeur; date growing and shipping; olives, citrus fruit.

Degana (dāgä′nŭ), village, central Rajasthan, India, 90 mi. ENE of Jodhpur; rail junction (line to Ratangarh).

Deganiya "A," Deganya "A," or **Degania "A"** (all: dŭgänēyä′), settlement (pop. 400), NW Israel, Lower Galilee, on S shore of Sea of Galilee, at outflow of the Jordan, 6 mi. SSE of Tiberias; agr. (citrus fruit, grapes, bananas, vegetables, olives) and dairying center; poultry raising; carp ponds. Site of agr. school serving Jordan valley; natural mus. Founded 1909, it was 1st collective settlement (*kvutza*) in Palestine. Destroyed (1948) by Arab forces, subsequently recaptured and rebuilt by Israelis. Just SE is settlement of Deganiya "B" (pop. 500), founded 1920. Sometimes spelled Daganiya or Dagania. Immediate vicinity of settlements was site of Canaanite locality of *Beth Jerah* or *Beth-yerah*, the *Philoteria* of Roman times; scene of major archaeological finds. During Crusades, Bridge of Sennabra here crossed the Jordan.

Degano River (dĕgä′nô), NE Italy, rises in Carnic Alps on Monte Peralba, flows 20 mi. SSE, past Comeglians, to Tagliamento R. 5 mi. W of Tolmezzo.

Degeberga (dā″gŭbĕr′gä), village (pop. 483), Kristianstad co., S Sweden, 13 mi. S of Kristianstad; grain, potatoes, sugar beets, stock.

Dege Gonchen, China: see TEHKO.

Degema (dā′gyĕmä), town (pop. 432), Owerri prov., Eastern Provinces, S Nigeria, port on Sombrero R. and 18 mi. W of Port Harcourt; palm oil and kernels, hardwood, rubber. Has hosp. Former important port of entry.

Degerfors (dā″gŭrfôrs′, –fôsh′). **1** Town (pop. 7,216), Orebro co., S central Sweden, on Let R. and 7 mi. SSW of Karlskoga; iron and steel mills. **2** Village (pop. 433), Vasterbotten co., N Sweden, on Vindel R. and 30 mi. NW of Umea; grain, stock; dairying.

Degerhamn (dā″gŭrhä′mŭn), village (pop. 916), Kalmar co., SE Sweden, SW Oland isl., on Kalmar Sound, 20 mi. S of Kalmar; limestone quarrying, cement mfg. Includes Mockleby (mûk′lübü″), Swedish *Möckleby*, village.

Degerloch (dā′gŭrlôkh), S suburb of Stuttgart, Germany; summer resort.

Degersheim (dā′gŭrs-hīm), town (pop. 2,966), St. Gall canton, NE Switzerland, 9 mi. SW of St. Gall; embroideries, woolen textiles, knit goods, foodstuffs; metal- and woodworking.

Deggendorf (dĕ′gŭndôrf), city (1950 pop. 16,341), Lower Bavaria, Germany, at W foot of Bohemian Forest, on the Danube above mouth of the Isar, and 18 mi. E of Straubing; rail junction; textile mfg., metalworking, lumber milling, brewing. Granite quarries in area. Has Gothic and mid-17th-cent. churches, and mid-16th-cent. city hall. First mentioned 868; chartered c.1311.

Deglur (dā′gloor) or **Diglur** (dĭgloor′), town (pop. 8,573), Nander dist., N central Hyderabad state, India, on tributary of Manjra R. and 45 mi. SSE of Nander; millet, rice. Place of annual Moslem pilgrimage.

Dego (dā′gô), village (pop. 519), Savona prov., Liguria, NW Italy, on Bormida di Spigno R. and 13 mi. NNW of Savona; agr. tools. Napoleon defeated Austrians here, 1796.

Degollado (dāgōyä′dō), town (pop. 2,553), Jalisco, central Mexico, 10 mi. NW of La Piedad; alt. 5,594 ft.; orange-growing center.

De Graff, village (pop. 270), Swift co., SW Minn., 23 mi. NW of Willmar, in grain and potato area.

Degraff or **De Graff,** village (pop. 972), Logan co., W central Ohio, 9 mi. WSW of Bellefontaine, and on Great Miami R., in agr. area.

De Grey River, N Western Australia, rises in hills 50 mi. SE of Marble Bar, flows 190 mi. N and NW to Indian Ocean 28 mi. E of Port Hedland; intermittent.

Degtyanka (dyĭktyän′kŭ), village (1926 pop. 3,000), N central Tambov oblast, Russian SFSR, 21 mi. NW of Tambov; grain, sunflowers. Formerly Staraya Degtyanka.

Degtyarka (–tyär′kŭ), town (1944 pop. over 10,000), S Sverdlovsk oblast, Russian SFSR, 9 mi. SE of Revda; rail spur terminus; a major copper-mining and -processing center; woodworking. Pyrite deposits near by.

De Haven Point, SE extremity of Victoria Isl., S Franklin Dist., Northwest Territories, on Queen Maud Gulf, at S end of Victoria Strait; 69°39′N 101°34′W.

Deh Bid (dĕ' bēd'), village, Seventh Prov., in Fars, S Iran, 80 mi. NNE of Shiraz; grain, opium, fruit.

Dehdadi (dādä'dē), fortified town, Mazar-i-Sharif prov., N Afghanistan, 6 mi. WSW of Mazar-i-Sharif; cantonment. Founded 1912.

Dehesas de Guadix (dā'säs dhā gwä-dhĕks'), village (pop. 1,276), Granada prov., S Spain, 20 mi. N of Guadix; olive oil, cereals, esparto, grapes.

Dehesas Viejas (vyā'häs), village (pop. 1,486), Granada prov., S Spain, 20 mi. N of Granada; olive oil, cereals.

Deheza, Argentina: see GENERAL DEHEZA.

Dehgam (dā'gäm), town (pop. 6,771), Ahmadabad dist., N Bombay, India, 17 mi. NE of Ahmadabad; millet, pulse; oilseed milling, pottery mfg., cotton weaving.

Dehibat (dāhēbät'), Saharan outpost (pop. 1,360), in Southern Territories, S Tunisia, near Libyan border, 65 mi. SSE of Foum-Tatahouine; caravans; nomadic grazing; 32°1'N 10°42'E.

Dehiwala (dā'hĭvŭlŭ), town (pop. 13,268), Western Prov., Ceylon, on SW coast, 6 mi. S of Colombo city center; fishing; coconuts, rice, vegetables. Zoo. Urban council (pop. 56,503) includes town of Mt. Lavinia.

Dehkharegan, Iran: see AZARSHAHR.

Deh Kurd, Iran: see SHAHR-I-KURD.

Dehli, India: see DELHI.

Dehra or **Dehra Dun** (dā'rŭ dōōn'), city (pop., including cantonment area, 78,228), ⊙ Dehra Dun dist., N Uttar Pradesh, India, 37 mi. NE of Saharanpur; rail terminus, road center, hill resort; tea processing; wheat, rice, oilseeds, corn, gram, tea. The Indian Military Acad. (opened 1932) here was expanded in 1949 to include navy and air force officers' training; renamed Armed Forces Acad., it is India's West Point. Noted Forest Research Inst. includes Indian Forest Col. and Indian Forest Ranger Col.; controls Madras Forest Col. (at Coimbatore); grew out of forest school founded 1867. Has Archaeological Survey Laboratory, sericulture research station. City founded 17th cent. by dispossessed Sikh guru, Ram Rai (founder of Hindu Udasi sect). Noted sulphur spring with baths 6 mi. NE.

Dehra Dun, district (□ 1,202; pop. 266,244), N Uttar Pradesh, India; ⊙ Dehra. In W Kumaun Himalaya foothills, with valley bet. Himalayas and Siwalik Range (S); bounded E by the Ganges, W by the Jumna (Himachal Pradesh). Agr. (wheat, rice, oilseeds, tea, barley, corn, gram); valuable timber tracts (including sal, deodar, chir, khair, sissoo, and bahera). Main centers: Dehra, Mussoorie, Rikhikesh, Rajpur. Asokan stone edicts near Kalsi.

Dehri (dā'hŭrē), town (pop. 8,281), Shahabad dist., W Bihar, India, on Son R. (rail bridge) and 55 mi. SW of Arrah; rail junction (workshops; station called Dehri on Son); rice, wheat, barley, oilseeds, gram. Headworks and dam of Son Canals system just S. Dalmianagar, 1 mi. W, is industrial center; mfg. of cement, paper, chemicals, soap, plywood, playing cards, boxes; sugar milling, sawmilling, ghee processing.

Dehu, India: see TALEGAON DABHADE.

Dehzangi, Afghanistan: see PANJAO.

Deichow, Poland: see DYCHOW.

Deidesheim (dī'dŭs-hīm), town (pop. 2,809), Rhenish Palatinate, W Germany, at E foot of Hardt Mts., 4 mi. NNE of Neustadt; known for its wine. Has 15th-cent. church, 18th-cent. castle. Chartered in 14th cent. In 1908, extensive remains of prehistoric settlement were excavated near by.

Deifontes (dāfōn'tĕs), village (pop. 1,419), Granada prov., S Spain, 10 mi. N of Granada; lumbering, sheep raising; olive oil, sugar beets.

Deighton, England: see HUDDERSFIELD.

Deiku, Burma: see DAIKU.

Deilam, Bandar, Iran: see BANDAR DILAM.

Deima River or **Deime River,** Russian SFSR: see PREGEL RIVER.

Deinau or **Deynau** (dyānou'), town (1939 pop. over 500), E Chardzhou oblast, Turkmen SSR, on the Amu Darya and 24 mi. NW of Chardzhou; cotton.

Deinze (dīn'zŭ), town (pop. 5,552), East Flanders prov., W central Belgium, on Lys R. and 10 mi. WSW of Ghent; cotton weaving, artificial-silk mfg.; grain elevators. Formerly spelled Deynze.

Deir, El, Ed Deir, or **Al-Dayr** (all: ĕd dār'), village (pop. 10,445), Qena prov., Upper Egypt, on E bank of the Nile and 3 mi. NE of Isna; pottery making, sugar refining; cereals, sugar cane, dates.

Deira (dē'rŭ), Anglian kingdom bet. the Humber and the Tyne, united (late 6th cent.) with Bernicia to form NORTHUMBRIA.

Deir Abu Sa'id or **Dayr Abu Sa'id** (both: dār' ăbōō' sä-ēd'), town (pop. c.1,300), N Jordan, 10 mi. WSW of Irbid; wheat, olives.

Deir 'Awn Agha or **Dayr 'Awn Agha** (dār' oun' ä'gä), Fr. *Déroun Agha,* town, Jezire prov., NE Syria, on Turkish border, 70 mi. NE of El Haseke; sheep raising. Oil deposits.

Deir el Ganadla (dār' ĕl gănăd'lŭ) or **Dayr al-Janadlah** (jănăd'lŭ), village (pop. 7,993), Asyut prov., central Upper Egypt, 7 mi. SSW of Abu Tig; cereals, dates, sugar cane.

Deir el Kamar, Lebanon: see DEIR EL QAMER.

Deir el Qamer, Deir eq Qamer, or **Dayr al-Qamar** (all: dār' ĕk-kä'mŭr), Fr. *Deir el Kamar,* village (pop. 4,717), central Lebanon, 12 mi. S of Beirut; alt. 2,600 ft.; pine trees, vineyards. Has 17th-cent. castle, 17th-cent. mosque, old abbey.

Deir ez Zor, Deir el Zor (both: dār' ĕz-zōr'), or **Dayr al-Zur** (dār' ĕz-zōōr'), town (pop. c.7,500), ⊙ Euphrates prov., E Syria, on right bank of Euphrates R. and 175 mi. ESE of Aleppo. The rich oil deposits of the region are only beginning to be tapped. Has air base. Town was ⊙ Zor territory, a former region of Turkey now divided bet. Turkey and Syria.

Deir Hafir or **Dayr Hafir** (dār' hä'fĭr), village, Aleppo prov., NW Syria, 31 mi. E of Aleppo; cereals.

Deir Mawas or **Dayr Mawas** (both: dār' măwăs'), village (pop. 13,434), Asyut prov., central Upper Egypt, on railroad, on the Nile, and 6 mi. N of Dairut; pottery making, wood and ivory carving; cereals, dates, sugar cane. Across the Nile, 4 mi. E, are the famous ruins of TEL EL AMARNA.

Deirut, Egypt: see DAIRUT.

Deister (dī'stŭr), small low range of the Weser Mts., W Germany, c.10 mi. W of Hanover city; coal and salt mining at N foot (Barsinghausen, Egestorf).

Dej (dĕzh), Hung. *Des* (dĕsh) or *Deés* (dāsh), town (1948 pop. 14,681), ⊙ Cluj prov., N Rumania, in Transylvania, at confluence of the Great and Little Somes, 28 mi. NNE of Cluj, 200 mi. NW of Bucharest. Rail junction, market for hides, salt, grain, **fruit**, nuts; mfg. of thread, paper, flour, bricks, pottery; tanning, oil refining. Has 15th-cent. Gothic Calvinist church, 16th-cent. tower, mus. One of the oldest Hung. cities in Transylvania, it still has 50% Magyar pop. In Hungary, 1940–45. Ocna-Dejului (ôk'nä dä'zhōōlōōē), Hung. *Désakna* (dā'shăknŏ), saltworks and salt baths, exploited since 15th cent., are c.2 mi. S.

Deje (dā'ŭ), village (pop. 2,564), Varmland co., W Sweden, on Klar R. and 15 mi. N of Karlstad; rail junction; paper and pulp mills.

De-jima, Japan: see DE-SHIMA.

De Kalb (dē kălb'). **1** County (□ 778; pop. 45,048), NE Ala.; ⊙ Fort Payne. Hilly region bordering on Ga. Cotton, corn, livestock; deposits of coal, iron, limestone, fuller's earth. Sand Mtn. extends throughout most of co. Formed 1836. **2** County (□ 269; pop. 136,395), NW central Ga.; ⊙ Decatur. Includes part of Atlanta metropolitan area. Mfg., dairying, poultry, and truck region with granite quarries (Lithonia, Stone Mtn.). Formed 1822. **3** County (□ 636; pop. 40,781), N Ill.; ⊙ Sycamore. Agr. (livestock, grain, soybeans, poultry). Mfg. (dairy and other food products, farm machinery, metal products, clothing, pianos, wagons and trailers, heaters, electric motors, telephone equipment, brick, tile, cement products, feed). Drained by branches of Kishwaukee R. Formed 1837. **4** County (□ 365; pop. 26,023), NE Ind., bounded E by Ohio line; ⊙ Auburn. Agr. area (livestock, truck, poultry, soybeans, corn, wheat, oats; dairy products). Mfg., especially at Auburn, Butler, and Garrett. Drained by small Cedar and Fish creeks and by St. Joseph R. Formed 1835. **5** County (□ 423; pop. 8,047), NW Mo.; ⊙ Maysville. Drained by branches of Grand and Platte rivers; agr. (corn, wheat, oats). Formed 1845. **6** County (□ 317; pop. 11,680), central Tenn.; ⊙ Smithville. Drained by Caney Fork of Cumberland R. and includes part of Center Hill Reservoir. Lumbering, livestock raising, agr. (corn, small grains, tobacco); dairying. Formed 1837.

De Kalb. 1 City (pop. 11,708), De Kalb co., N Ill., on South Branch of Kishwaukee R. (bridged) and 24 mi. WSW of Elgin; trade, industrial, and shipping center in rich agr. area; mfg. (canned foods, electrical and farm machinery, wire products, gloves, bedding, musical instruments, wagons, women's handbags). Seat of Northern Ill. State Teachers Col.; has a memorial library. Inc. 1861. Twisted barbed wire, invented here in 1870s by Joseph Glidden, replaced older methods of fencing on the western plains and was of great importance in development of cattle industry. **2** Town (pop. 953), ⊙ Kemper co., E Miss., 28 mi. N of Meridian; sawmills, cotton gins. **3** Town (pop. 300), Buchanan co., NW Mo., near Missouri R., 12 mi. SSW of St. Joseph. **4** Town (pop. 1,928), Bowie co., NE Texas, near Red R., 34 mi. W of Texarkana; trade center in cotton, truck area; lumber milling.

De-Kastri (dyĕ-kŭstrē'), village (1948 pop. over 500), SE Lower Amur oblast, Khabarovsk Territory, Russian SFSR, port on Tatar Strait, 115 mi. SSE of Nikolayevsk; fish canneries.

Dekeleia or **Dhekelia** (both: dhĭkă'lēŭ), Lat. *Decelea* (dĕsŭlē'ŭ), village (1928 pop. 388), Attica nome, E central Greece, 15 mi. NNE of Athens. Summer resort of Greek monarchs; site of graves of kings George I and Alexander, it was made state property by Greek govt. Tatoi military airport is 4 mi. S. Also spelled Dekelia; formerly called Tatoi or Tatoion.

Dekese (dĕkĕ'sä), village, Kasai prov., central Belgian Congo, on right bank of Lukenie R. and 125 mi. N of Luebo; steamboat landing and trading center in copal-gathering area. R.C. mission.

Dekharegan, Iran: see AZARSHAHR.

Dekhkanabad (dyĕkhkŭnŭbät'), village (1948 pop. over 500), S Kashka-Darya oblast, Uzbek SSR, 50 mi. SE of Karshi; agr.; goats, horses. Until c.1935, called Tengi-Kharam.

Dekka, Afghanistan: see DAKKA.

Dekkan Plateau, India: see DECCAN PLATEAU.

Dekoa (dĕkwä'), village, central Ubangi-Shari, Fr. Equatorial Africa, 40 mi. N of Fort-Sibut; cotton center. Sometimes spelled Dekoua.

Dekoven or **DeKoven** (dŭ kō'vŭn), town (1940 pop. 296), Union co., W Ky., near left bank of the Ohio, 33 mi. SW of Henderson.

De La Beche, Mount (dĕ'lŭbĕsh') (10,058 ft.), W central S.Isl., New Zealand, in Southern Alps, near Malte Brun Range.

Delabole (dĕ'lŭbōl), village, N Cornwall, England, 2 mi. W of Camelford; slate-quarrying center.

Delafield, resort village (1940 pop. 508), Waukesha co., SE Wis., 24 mi. W of Milwaukee, on small lake in truck-farming region; wooden and aluminum toys. St. John's Military Acad., a state fish hatchery, and Cushing Memorial State Park are near by.

Delaford (dĕ'lŭfŭrd), village (pop. 1,135), NE Tobago, B.W.I., 13 mi. ENE of Scarborough; coconuts, cacao.

Delagoa Bay (dĭlŭgō'ŭ), sheltered inlet of Indian Ocean in S coast of Mozambique; 50 mi. wide, 20 mi. long. Inhaca Isl. at mouth. Receives Pongola, Umbeluzi, and Komati rivers. City of LOURENÇO MARQUES is near its head. Discovered 1502 by António do Campo (member of Vasco da Gama's expedition). Shoreline explored by Lourenço Marques, a Port. trader. Isls. in bay occupied by British in 1860s. Area disputed bet. England and Portugal until awarded to Port. by arbitration (1875). Also called Lourenço Marques Bay.

Delagua (dŭlä'gwŭ), town (pop. 239), Las Animas co., S Colo., just E of Culebra Range of Sangre de Cristo Mts., 14 mi. NW of Trinidad; alt. 6,700 ft.

Delake, city (pop. 644), Lincoln co., W Oregon, on the Pacific just S of Oceanlake, in resort area.

Delami (dĕlä'mē), town, Kordofan prov., central Anglo-Egyptian Sudan, in Nuba Mts., on road and 90 mi. SSE of El Obeid; gum arabic, peanuts, sesame.

De Lancey, village, Jefferson co., W central Pa., 2 mi. N of Punxsutawney, in bituminous-coal area.

Delanco (dŭlăn'kō), village (pop. 2,494), Burlington co., SW N.J., on Delaware R., N of mouth of Rancocas Creek, and 12 mi. NE of Camden.

De Land (dē lănd'). **1** City (pop. 8,652), ⊙ Volusia co., NE Fla., 21 mi. WSW of Daytona Beach; resort, and shipping center for citrus-fruit area; packing houses, lumber mill. John B. Stetson Univ. and the Royal French Mus. are here. Founded 1876. **2** Village (pop. 416), Piatt co., central Ill., 24 mi. NE of Decatur, in grain and livestock area.

Delano. 1 (dŭlä'nō, dĕ'lŭnō) City (pop. 8,717), Kern co., S central Calif., in San Joaquin Valley, 30 mi. NNW of Bakersfield; ships grain, truck, fruit; cotton gin, winery. Inc. 1915. **2** (dĕ'lŭnō) Village (pop. 1,386), Wright co., E Minn., on Crow R. and 27 mi. W of Minneapolis, in grain, livestock, poultry area; dairy products, cattle feed; granite monuments. Platted 1868, inc. 1885. **3** (dĕ'lŭnō) Village (1940 pop. 763), Schuylkill co., E central Pa., 4 mi. NE of Mahanoy City, in anthracite region.

Delano Peak (dĕ'lŭnō), highest point (12,173 ft.) in Tushar Mts., SW central Utah, 32 mi. SSW of Richfield.

Delanson (dĭlăn'sŭn), village (pop. 430), Schenectady co., E N.Y., 13 mi. WSW of Schenectady.

Delaplaine (dĕ'lŭplān), town (pop. 208), Greene co., NE Ark., 18 mi. NW of Paragould.

Delarof Islands (dĕ'lŭrŏf), SW Alaska, group of 7 small islands of the Aleutians, in N Pacific, bet. Andreanof Isls. (E) and Amchitka Pass (W), near 51°33'N 178°49'W. Main isls. are Gareloi, Ogliuga (emergency airfield), Ulak, and Amatignak.

Delaronde Lake (dĕ'lŭrŏnd″) (29 mi. long, 3 mi. wide), central Sask., 65 mi. NE of Prince Albert. Drains N into Beaver R.

Delatyn, Ukrainian SSR: see DELYATIN.

Delaval, England: see BLYTH.

Delavan (dĕ'lŭvŭn). **1** City (pop. 1,248), Tazewell co., central Ill., 23 mi. S of Peoria, in agr. and bituminous-coal area; mfg. of scales; poultry hatchery. Founded 1837, inc. 1888. **2** Village (pop. 302), Faribault co., S Minn., 10 mi. NE of Blue Earth; dairy products. **3** City (pop. 4,007), Walworth co., SE Wis., on Turtle Creek and 20 mi. E of Janesville, in dairying and stock-raising area; mfg. (knit goods, electrical equipment, clocks, cigars). A state school for the deaf is here. Settled 1836, inc. 1897. Just E of the city is Delavan L. (3½ mi. long), with the resort village Delavan Lake on its shores; winter and summer sports.

Delaware (dĕ'lŭwâr, –wŭr), state (land □ 1,978; with inland waters □ 2,057; 1950 pop. 318,085; 1940 pop. 266,505), E U.S., in Middle Atlantic region; bordered N by Pa., W by Md., S by Md., E by Atlantic Ocean, Delaware Bay, and Delaware R.; 47th in area, 46th in pop.; one of 13 original states, it was 1st to ratify (1787) the Constitution; ⊙ Dover. The "Diamond State" (or "Blue Hen State") extends 99 mi. N-S and 9–36 mi. E-W and comprises the NE third of the DELMARVA PENINSULA bet. Chesapeake Bay (W) and Delaware Bay and the Atlantic (E). The major portion of Del. lies in the Atlantic coastal plain, a low-lying area, while the extreme N is part of the Appalachian piedmont, a rolling upland which rises to 440 ft. near Centerville, the highest point in the state. Wilmington, by far the largest city, stands at the fall line bet. piedmont and coastal plain. The coast line is marked by much marshland, sandy beaches, and lagoons (e.g., Rehoboth Bay, Indian R. Bay), sheltered by narrow sand spits. Great Pocomoke Swamp stretches across S border into SE Md. A slight elevation along the W boundary, turning SE below center of state, forms Del.'s watershed; all streams, such as Brandywine Creek and Christina R. (N), are small. Climate is humid continental in N, humid subtropical in S, with annual rainfall (slight summer max.) of 40–45 in. Dover (center) has mean temp. of 36°F. in Jan. and 77°F. in July. The growing season varies bet. 180 and 195 days (N-S). General farming (corn, wheat, rye, barley, oats, hay, dairying) is characteristic of the N section, while to the S corn and some wheat are also grown; the sandy soils and moderate climate are better suited, however, to fruitgrowing and commercial market gardening. Peas, tomatoes, strawberries, potatoes, asparagus, beans, melons, and cucumbers are important truck crops; apples and peaches are the principal fruits. Poultry raising (especially broilers) is a major source of income. The large annual fish catch in Delaware Bay and Atlantic Ocean includes oysters and other shell fish, menhaden, shad, herring, and rockfish; Lewes is the chief fishing center. The state's small mineral resources are limited to clay, sand, gravel, and minor deposits of granite, feldspar, and kaolin. Del.'s industrial activity centers in and around Wilmington, a major port and transportation center, noted for its glazed kid and moroccan leather, braided rubber hose, cotton dyeing, shipyards, and chemical interests. Surrounding mfg. towns are Edge Moor and Newport (pigments, chemicals), Newark and Marshallton (vulcanized fiber), New Castle (rayon, steel, aircraft), and Claymont (steel, chemicals). Synthetic fibers are produced at Seaford, dental supplies at Milford. Other industries include mfg. of textiles, iron and steel products, boats, paper, machinery; railroad shops; oil refining. Most towns in the center (e.g., DOVER) and S (e.g., Laurel) are food-processing centers, and several have basketmaking and fertilizer factories. Because of the state's favorable incorporation and tax laws many large businesses, such as the Du Pont company, have their hq. in Wilmington. The CHESAPEAKE AND DELAWARE CANAL, part of the Intracoastal Waterway, cuts through N Del.; Del. Memorial Bridge, across the Delaware R. near New Castle, is an important highway link. Seaside resorts include Rehoboth, Bethany Beach, and Slaughter Beach. Univ. of Del. is at Newark. Delaware Bay was discovered 1609 by Henry Hudson. In 1631 the Dutch made a settlement near the present site of Lewes, but it was soon wiped out by the Indians. In 1638, a group of Swedes founded Port Christina (Wilmington), the 1st of the NEW SWEDEN settlements. The Dutch—led by Peter Stuyvesant—built Fort Casimir (New Castle) in 1651 and captured the Swedish colonies in 1655, but they in turn were driven out (1664) by the English. The region was part of the grant of the Duke of York until 1682, when it was transferred to the prov. of Pa. under William Penn. In 1703 the lower counties ("territories otherwise called Delaware") received the right to elect a separate assembly, a degree of autonomy maintained up to the Revolution. The colony became the sovereign state of Del. in 1776. Grain and lumber mills, especially on the Brandywine, were early industries, and by 1800 Wilmington was producing a variety of manufactures. Trade with the West Indies stimulated shipbuilding. A border state, Del. sided with the Union in the Civil War, although there was considerable proslavery sentiment. Improved transportation facilities helped develop mfg. industries in the N part of the state, but agr. declined somewhat. Del.'s pop. is characterized by a large immigrant element in the Wilmington area and predominantly homogeneous colonial stock, with a number of Negroes, throughout the rest of the state. See also articles on the cities, towns, geographic features, and the 3 counties: KENT, NEW CASTLE, SUSSEX.

Delaware. 1 County (□ 400; pop. 90,252), E Ind.; ⊙ MUNCIE. Drained by Mississinewa R., West Fork of White R., and small Kilbuck, Bell, and Buck creeks. Agr. (corn, grain, hogs, soybeans, tomatoes; dairy products). Diversified mfg. and shipping at Muncie. Formed 1827. **2** County (□ 573; pop. 17,734), E Iowa; ⊙ Manchester. Prairie agr. area (hogs, cattle, poultry, corn, oats, rye) drained by Maquoketa R.; limestone quarries. Has state parks. Formed 1837. **3** County (□ 1,470; pop. 44,420), S N.Y.; ⊙ Delhi. Situated in the W Catskills (resorts); bounded NW by Susquehanna R., SW by Delaware R. (here the Pa. line), which is formed in co. by junction of East and West branches; also drained by Beaver Kill and Charlotte R. A leading dairying co. of N.Y.; also produces hay, truck (especially cauliflower, potatoes), poultry. Blue-stone quarrying, some lumbering. Diversified mfg. at Sidney, Walton, Delhi, Hancock. Formed 1797. **4** County (□ 459; pop. 30,278), central Ohio; ⊙ Delaware. Intersected by Olentangy and Scioto rivers, and by small Big Walnut and Alum creeks. Agr. area (livestock, dairy products, grain, fruit); mfg. at Delaware; limestone quarries. Formed 1808. **5** County (□ 778; pop. 14,734), NE Okla.; ⊙ Jay. Partly (E) in the Ozarks; bounded E by Ark. and Mo. state lines. Includes part of Spavinaw L. (water supply for Tulsa) and also part of L. of the Cherokees, here receiving Elk R. Stock raising, dairying, some agr. (fruit, berries, corn, wheat, oats). Formed 1907. **6** County (□ 185; pop. 414,234), SE Pa.; ⊙ Media. Residential and industrial area; bounded E by Philadelphia, SE by Delaware R., S by state of Delaware. First white settlement in Pa. at ESSINGTON, 1643. Battle of Brandywine, 1777. Oil refining, shipbuilding; mfg. (textiles, metal and paper products). Formed 1789.

Delaware. 1 Town (pop. 192), Delaware co., E Iowa, 5 mi. E of Manchester, in livestock area. **2** City (pop. 11,804), ⊙ Delaware co., central Ohio, on Olentangy R. and 23 mi. N of Columbus; trade center for agr. area. Mfg.: motor vehicles, rubber goods, wood products, chairs, stoves, dairy products. Seat of Ohio Wesleyan Univ. Rutherford B. Hayes was b. here. Olentangy Caverns are near by. Laid out 1808, inc. 1903. **3** Town (pop. 582), Nowata co., NE Okla., 19 mi. E of Bartlesville; ships livestock, cotton, corn.

Delaware, Fort, Del.: see PEA PATCH ISLAND.

Delaware and Hudson Canal, in N.Y. and Pa., abandoned canal once extending c.107 mi. from the Delaware R. at Honesdale, Pa., to the Hudson at Kingston, N.Y. Built during 1825–29 to carry Pa. coal to N.Y. markets; enlarged in 1842 and 1850; rail competition caused abandonment in 1899.

Delaware and Raritan Canal, N.J., abandoned canal bet. Bordentown and New Brunswick, connecting Delaware and Raritan rivers; c.45 mi. long. Completed 1834; important inland waterway for a time in mid-19th cent.

Delaware Aqueduct, SE N.Y., part of water-supply system for New York city. Includes tunnels to carry waters impounded in Pepacton and Neversink reservoirs to Rondout Reservoir in Rondout Creek, from which main aqueduct then extends 85 mi. SE, passing under the Hudson N of Newburgh, and entering Kensico and Hillview reservoirs for distribution in city. Flows by gravity throughout. Construction was begun in 1937, suspended during Second World War; in 1944, partially complete system (from Rondout Creek to Hillview Reservoir) was put into emergency operation.

Delaware Bay, estuarine inlet of the Atlantic bet. N.J. and Del.; 52 mi. long; extends from mouth of Delaware R. (just below mouth of Alloway Creek) to entrance (c.12 mi. wide) bet. Cape May, N.J., and Cape Henlopen, Del.

Delaware Breakwater, Del.: see HENLOPEN, CAPE.

Delaware City, town (pop. 1,363), New Castle co., N Del., 10 mi. S of Wilmington and on Delaware R. Fort Du Pont, hq. of Delaware Bay and river defenses, is here; Fort Delaware is on near-by Pea Patch Isl. Laid out 1826, inc. 1851. E entrance to Chesapeake and Delaware Canal is 2 mi. S.

Delaware Memorial Bridge, across Delaware R. bet. New Castle, Del. and Pennsville, N.J., c.3 mi. below Wilmington, Del. Suspension structure 3½ mi. long over all, with center span 2,150 ft. long; completed 1951.

Delaware Mountains, extreme W Texas, barren range extending c.35 mi. SSE from Guadalupe Pass at S end of Guadalupe Mts.; rises to 5,870 ft. near S end. Part of E boundary of Diablo Bolson ; playas (salt flats) are just W.

Delaware River. 1 In E U.S., formed at Hancock, N.Y., by junction of East Branch (c.75 mi. long) and West Branch (c.90 mi. long), both rising in the Catskill Mts., SE N.Y.; flows SE from their junction, forming N.Y.–Pa. line, to Port Jervis, N.Y., then generally S bet. Pa. and N.J. to head of Delaware Bay; 315 mi. long; tidal to Trenton, N.J. (head of navigation); drains □ 12,300. Cities on its banks are Easton and Philadelphia, Pa., Camden, N.J., and Wilmington and New Castle, Del. Major bridges at Trenton, Philadelphia, Wilmington (DELAWARE MEMORIAL BRIDGE). Early important in commerce; Delaware and Raritan Canal (completed 1834; now abandoned) connected it with the Raritan, and Delaware and Hudson Canal (1828; abandoned) was its link with the Hudson. Chesapeake and Delaware Canal now links river with head of Chesapeake Bay. Reservoirs (Pepacton, in East Branch; Neversink, in Neversink R.) in headstreams are part of DELAWARE AQUEDUCT water-supply system for New York city. Interstate bodies have been formed to consider problems of water supply, conservation, and pollution control. DELAWARE WATER GAP, where river cuts through Kittatinny Mtn. ridge, is scenic resort area. Washington Crossing villages (N.J. and Pa.) are at point where Washington crossed river (Christmas night, 1776) to capture Trenton. **2** In NE Kansas, formed by confluence of several headstreams near Horton, flows 100 mi. S, past Valley Falls, to Kansas R. 15 mi. E of Topeka.

Delaware Water Gap, resort borough (pop. 734), Monroe co., E Pa., 3 mi. E of Stroudsburg and on Delaware R; lies 2 mi. NW of scenic Delaware Water Gap, where Delaware R. cuts through Kittatinny Mtn. Mt. Tammany (1,550 ft.) is on N.J. side, Mt. Minsi (1,480 ft.) on Pa. side.

Delbarton, mining village (pop. 1,353), Mingo co., SW W.Va., 5 mi. ENE of Williamson, in bituminous-coal region.

Del Bonita (dĕl bunē'tŭ), village, Glacier co., N Mont., port of entry at Alta. line, c.55 mi. NW of Shelby.

Delbrück (dĕl'brük), town (pop. 2,473), in former Prussian prov. of Westphalia, NW Germany, after 1945 in North Rhine-Westphalia, 9 mi. WNW of Paderborn.

Delburne, village (pop. 379), S central Alta., on small lake 25 mi. E of Red Deer; coal mining.

Delcambre (dĕl kăm'bŭr), village (pop. 1,463), on Vermilion-Iberia parish line, S La., 60 mi. SW of Baton Rouge, in the Acadian country; farming; sugar milling, cotton ginning, shrimp processing. Inc. 1907.

Del Carmen, Philippines: see LUBAO.

Delchev, Bulgaria: see NEVROKOP.

Del City or **Dell,** town (pop. 2,504), Oklahoma co. central Okla., near Oklahoma City.

Delco (dĕl'kō), town (pop. 257), Columbus co., SE N.C., 17 mi. WNW of Wilmington.

Delden (dĕl'dŭn), town (pop. 3,638), Overijssel prov., E Netherlands, 4 mi. W of Hengelo, near Twente Canal; textile center (cotton spinning, weaving, and processing; chemicals for textile industry); biscuits, butter; horse market. Twickel castle near by.

Dele, Belgian Congo: see MAKABA.

Deleau (dŭlō'), village (pop. estimate 200), SW Man., 35 mi. WSW of Brandon; grain, stock.

Delebio (dĕlā'byō), village (pop. 1,553), Sondrio prov., Lombardy, N Italy, in the Valtellina, 5 mi. W of Morbegno; cutlery.

Deleitosa (dālātō'sä), town (pop. 2,222), Cáceres prov., W Spain, 18 mi. NE of Trujillo; flour mills; cereals, olive oil, potatoes.

Delémont (dŭlāmō'), Ger. *Delsberg* (dĕls'bĕrk), town (pop. 6,625), Bern canton, NW Switzerland, on Sorne R. (tributary of Birs R.) and 14 mi. NNW of Solothurn; knives, watches. Town hall, church (both 18th cent.). Its old château once residence of prince-bishops of Basel (1528–1792).

Delenyes, Rumania: see DELINESTI.

De Leon (dē lēŏn'), city (pop. 2,241), Comanche co., central Texas, near Leon R., 35 mi. NE of Brownwood; shipping, processing center of peanut and truck region. Founded 1887, inc. as city 1919.

De Leon Springs or **Deleon Springs** (dŭlē'ŏn), village (1940 pop. 587), Volusia co., NE Fla., 22 mi. W of Daytona Beach; citrus-fruit packing. Site of large Ponce de Leon Springs.

De Léry (dŭ lārē'), town (pop. 816), S Que., on SW shore of L. St. Louis, 16 mi. SW of Montreal, in dairying region.

Delevan (dĕ'lŭvăn"), village (pop. 611), Cattaraugus co., W N.Y., 35 mi. SE of Buffalo; dairy products, printing type and supplies, lumber. Dairy and poultry farms.

Delfi, Greece: see DELPHI.

Delfín Gallo (dĕlfēn' gä'yō), town (pop. estimate 500), central Tucumán prov., Argentina, 7 mi. ESE of Tucumán; rail junction and sugar-refining center.

Delfinópolis (dĕlfēnô'pŏŏlēs), city (pop. 1,635), SW Minas Gerais, Brazil, near the Rio Grande, 22 mi. NNW of Passos.

Delfoi, Greece: see DELPHI.

Delfshaven (dĕlfs'hävŭn), South Holland prov., W Netherlands, SW suburb (pop. 8,396) of Rotterdam, on New Maas R. From here Pilgrims sailed for America. Sometimes spelled Delftshaven.

Delft (dĕlft), island (□ 18; pop. 6,372) in S Palk Strait, in Northern Prov., Ceylon, 21 mi. WSW of Jaffna; extensive coconut and palmyra-palm plantations. Main settlement, Maveiturai (NE).

Delft, town (pop. 62,018), South Holland prov., W Netherlands, 5 mi. SSE of The Hague; center of china and ceramics industry (delftware); ornamental tiles, glassware, paints, dyes, distilled liquors, yeast, amyl alcohol, machinery (railroad material, transformers), cables, leather goods, industrial belting; cattle and dairy market. Technical univ., 17th-cent. town hall and East Indian House, 15th-cent. Gothic church (*Nieuwe Kerk*) with tombs of William the Silent and Grotius, 13th-cent. Gothic church (*Oude Kerk*) with tombs of Admiral Tromp and Piet Hein, many other 16th- and 17th-cent. buildings. Grotius and painter Jan Vermeer b. here. Founded 1075, chartered 1246. Site (1584) of assassination of William the Silent. Trade center in 16th and 17th cent.; later superseded by Rotterdam. Ceramics industry introduced in mid-17th cent.

Delft Island, island (7 mi. long, 3 mi. wide) in Palk Strait, off NW shore of Ceylon, 22 mi. SW of Jaffna. Formerly called Neduntivu.

Delftshaven, Netherlands: see DELFSHAVEN.

Delfzijl (dĕlfzīl'), town (pop. 7,921) and port, Groningen prov., NE Netherlands, on Eems R. estuary, at E end of Eems Canal, and 17 mi. NE of Groningen; exports dairy and agr. products; lumber and trade center; shipbuilding, sugar refining, cement mfg. Sometimes spelled Delfzyl.

Delgada, Point (dĕlgä'dhä), N point of Alegranza Isl., northernmost of Canary Isls., 145 mi. NE of Las Palmas; 29°25'N 13°29'W.

Delgada, Point (dĕlgä'dŭ), NW Calif., promontory c.35 mi. SSE of Cape Mendocino.

Delgado, Cape (dĕlgä'dōō), low headland of northernmost Mozambique, on Mozambique Channel of Indian Ocean; 10°40'S 40°36'E. Mozambique-Tanganyika border reaches the sea 20 mi. NW, at mouth of Ruvuma R.

Delgany (dĕlgă'nē, -gā'ne), Gaelic *Deilgne*, town (pop. 180), NE Co. Wicklow, Ireland, near the Irish Sea, 5 mi. S of Bray; agr. market (cattle, sheep; dairying; potatoes) and golfing resort. Church dates from 1789.

Delger Mörön or **Delger Muren,** Mongolia: see MUREN, river.

Delgo (dĕl'gō), town, Northern Prov., Anglo-Egyptian Sudan, on right bank of the Nile, on road, and 65 mi. N of Dongola; cotton, grain; livestock. Important ruins near by.

Delhi (dĕl'hī), village (pop. 2,062), S Ont., on Big Creek and 34 mi. E of St. Thomas; tobacco processing, natural-gas production, glove mfg., lumbering.

Delhi (dĕ'lē), Hindi *Dilli* or *Dehli*, chief commissioner's state (□ 574; 1941 pop. 917,939; 1951 pop. 1,743,992), N India; ⊙ Delhi. Bordered N, W, and S by Indian Punjab, E by Uttar Pradesh. Crossed N-S near its E border by Jumna R. and SW-NE by Delhi Ridge (isolated outlier of Aravalli Range). Climate is tropical savanna, with yearly rainfall averaging 30 in. and mean temp. ranging from 60°F. in Dec. to 90°F. in May (summer max. often exceeds 110°F.). Mainly alluvial soil, drained by Jumna Canal system; gram, barley, wheat, millet, sugar cane. Building-stone and pottery-clay workings in Delhi Ridge. Handicraft cotton weaving, tanning, black-smithing, pottery, and glass-bangle making in towns (Mahrauli, Najafgarh, Narela, and Shahdara) and villages. In 1947–51, suburban industrial-training colonies, with prefabricated houses built in Delhi city, were established to rehabilitate refugees who had poured into state in the great migrations following partition of India and had taken shelter in historic buildings around Delhi and New Delhi cities; total of displaced persons in 1951, 509,767. Pop. (over 25% literate in 1941) is predominantly urban due to large administrative personnel required in NEW DELHI (⊙ India) and living mainly in DELHI city (important communications and commercial center); based on 1941 census figures, comprises Hindus (c.63%) and Moslems (c.33%); overall density in 1941, c.1,500 persons per sq. mi. Hindustani (lingua franca of India; composed of Hindi and Urdu) is spoken by over 90% of pop. and Punjabi by over 5%. Throughout India's history, Delhi has commanded roads to all parts of India; within 50 sq. mi., S of present Delhi city, are more important dynastic remains than exist in any other area in the country. Earliest site is the 12th-cent. Chauhan Rajput citadel (just N of present MAHRAULI) containing Lal Kot (red fort; erected 1052; sometimes confused with Shah Jehan's Red Fort in Delhi city) and the famous Kutb Minar and Iron Pillar. In 1193, Mohammed of Ghor captured the Rajput city and made it his ⊙ in 1206; thus began the long succession of Turko-Afghan rulers known as the Delhi sultans; the Slave kings (⊙ was Siri; 3 mi. NE of Mahrauli) were succeeded by the Tughlaks, who built Tughlakabad (5 mi. E of Mahrauli) in 1321 and (c.1350) Firozabad (8 mi. N of Tughlakabad). Invasion of Delhi by Tamerlane in 1398 put an end to Tughlak power; their successors, the Lodis, last of the Delhi sultans, gave way to the Moguls under Baber after battle of PANIPAT in 1526. Second Mogul emperor, Humayun, and his temporary supplanter, the Afghan Sher Shah, built Purana Kila (old fort; encloses Sher Shah's mosque) just E of New Delhi, on site believed to have been Indraprastha, the Pandava ⊙ described in the Mahabharata. Near by (4 mi. SSE of Delhi city center) is Humayun's tomb (built 1565–69; architectural prototype of the famous Taj Mahal of Agra). Early Moguls favored AGRA as their ⊙, and Delhi became their permanent ⊙ only after Shah Jehan built the walls of present Delhi city in 1638. Area around Delhi was carved out of Punjab in 1912, when building of New Delhi (completed 1929; city inaugurated 1931) was begun to replace Calcutta as seat of central Indian govt.; a small adjacent tract of land E of the Jumna was added in 1915. In 1950, in accordance with independent India's new constitution, Delhi was termed a chief commissioner's state.

Delhi, Hindi *Dilli* or *Dehli*, city (pop. 521,849; including cantonment and fort areas, 542,984), ⊙ Delhi state, India, on right (W) bank of Jumna R., on Grand Trunk Road, and 740 mi. NNE of Bombay, 800 mi. NW of Calcutta; 28°40'N 77°15'E; adjoins NEW DELHI (SSW: ⊙ India). Communications hub and commercial center; major rail and road junction; intercontinental airport at Palam (10 mi. WSW of New Delhi city center) and domestic airport at Safdar Jang (formerly Willingdon; just S of New Delhi). Cotton and woolen milling, mfg. of hosiery, military clothing, chemicals, pottery, brass and iron utensils; printing and publishing; noted handicrafts include gold and silver filigree, ivory carving, and embroidery. In 1950, a large plant was opened to produce prefabricated houses. Delhi's crowded city center (□ c.4) is enclosed by stone walls (built 1638 by Shah Jehan; towers made into bastions c.1810 by the British). In NE corner is the famous Red Fort (containing the imperial Mogul palace built mid-17th cent. by Shah Jehan and so called for its walls and gateways of red sandstone); most notable of the fort's edifices are the beautifully proportioned public audience hall (Diwan-i-Am) and the private audience hall (Diwan-i-Khas; entirely built of white marble); here stood the jewelled Peacock Throne, carried off 1739 by the Persian Nadir Shah. On the Jumna's bank, just S of the fort, is Rajghat, where Mahatma Gandhi's body was cremated on Jan. 31, 1948; now one of the most revered shrines in India. SW of the fort is the gracefully domed Jama Masjid, or great mosque (built 1644–58); of red sandstone inlaid with white marble and flanked by 2 minarets, it stands on a high base, approached by wide steps. Chandni Chauk, the bazaar where Delhi's noted gold- and silversmiths ply their wares, runs W from the fort. In NW, city fans out beyond the old walls into an open residential area; here are located hotels and clubs, Univ. of Delhi, and an amphitheater (built 1911) marking site of imperial durbars of 1877 (at which Victoria was proclaimed Empress of India), 1903, and 1911. Although other cities rose and fell from 12th to 17th cent. in S portion of DELHI state, actual present site did not become important until Shah Jehan (for whom it is sometimes called Shahjahanabad) made it ⊙ Mogul empire in 1638. City was sacked by Nadir Shah in 1739 and was held by Mahrattas from 1771 until taken by the British in 1803. Held by rebels for 5 months during Sepoy Rebellion of 1857. Was ⊙ India from 1912 (by proclamation of 1911) until New Delhi was officially inaugurated as ⊙ in 1931. Also called Old Delhi.

Delhi (dĕl'hī). **1** Town (pop. 383), Delaware co., E Iowa, near Maquoketa R., 8 mi. SE of Manchester. **2** Town (pop. 1,861), Richland parish, NE La., 36 mi. E of Monroe and on Bayou Macon; cotton, oats, corn; cotton gins, compresses, and warehouses; sawmills. Oil field. Fishing near by. Settled before the Civil War. **3** Village (pop. 152), Redwood co., SW Minn., near Minnesota R., 7 mi. NW of Redwood Falls; grain. **4** Village (pop. 2,223), ⊙ Delaware co., S N.Y., in the Catskills on West Branch of the Delaware and 14 mi. SE of Oneonta, in dairying and mtn.-resort area. Feed, barrels, dairy products. Site of a state agr. and technical institute. Settled c.1785, inc. 1821.

Delhi Ridge, narrow broken NE outlier of Aravalli Range, Delhi, India; extends c.15 mi. NE along W edge of Delhi and New Delhi cities; rises c.200 ft. above cities' level; building-stone and pottery-clay workings. Had strategic importance during many sieges of Delhi's history.

Deli (dä'lē), fertile region (□ c.660) in NE Sumatra, Indonesia; chief center, Medan. Known primarily as tobacco-growing area. Other products: rubber, palm oil, sugar, fibers.

Delia (dē'lyū), village (pop. 231), S central Alta., 18 mi. NE of Drumheller; coal mining; grain elevators, flour mills.

Delia (dĕ'lyä), village (pop. 6,428), Caltanissetta prov., S central Sicily, 12 mi. SSW of Caltanissetta. Has a Norman church. There are sulphur mines near by.

Delia (dē'lyū), city (pop. 164), Jackson co., NE Kansas, 20 mi. NW of Topeka; livestock, grain area.

Delianuova (dĕlyänwô'vä), commune (pop. 6,042), Reggio di Calabria prov., Calabria, S Italy, on N slope of the Aspromonte, 9 mi. SE of Palmi, in lumbering, livestock-raising region. Comprises adjacent villages of Paracorio and Pedavoli.

Delice River (dĕlĭjĕ'), N central Turkey, rises on Ak Dag 19 mi. S of Akdagmadeni, flows 190 mi. W and N, past Bogazliyan and Cicekdagi, to the Kizil Irmak 28 mi. ESE of Cankiri.

Deliceto (dĕlēchā'tô), town (pop. 6,152), Foggia prov., Apulia, S Italy, 3 mi. SE of Bovino; wine, olive oil.

Delicias (dālē'syäs), town (pop. 3,829), Oriente prov., E Cuba, near Atlantic inlet, 28 mi. NW of Holguín; sugar-milling center.

Delicias, city (pop. 6,020), Chihuahua, N Mexico, in irrigation area of Conchos R. valley, on railroad and 45 mi. SE of Chihuahua; alt. 3,842 ft. Cotton-growing center; corn, tobacco, sugar cane, beans, cattle; cotton ginning.

Delicias, Las, Argentina: see LAS DELICIAS.

Delight, town (pop. 574), Pike co., SW Ark., 25 mi. WSW of Arkadelphia.

Delijan, Iran: see DALIJAN.

Deli Jovan or **Deli Yovan** (both: dĕ'lē yô'vän), mountain, E Serbia, Yugoslavia; highest point Crni Vrh or Tsrni Vrkh (3,723 ft.), is 15 mi. W of Negotin.

Deli-Karpatok, Rumania: see TRANSYLVANIAN ALPS.

Deliktas Dag (dĕlĭktäsh' dä), Turkish *Deliktaş Dağ*, peak (7,392 ft.), S Turkey, in Taurus Mts., 16 mi. NNW of Anamur.

Delinesti (dălēnĕsht'), Rum. *Delineşti*, Hung. *Delényes* (dĕ'lānyĕsh), village (pop. 1,055), Severin prov., SW Rumania, 10 mi. NE of Resita; iron, copper, and manganese mining.

Delingat, El, Egypt: see DILINGAT, EL.

Deliorman (dĕlēôrmän'), hilly upland in NE Bulgaria, bet. Black Sea and the Danube, S of the Dobruja; rises to over 1,600 ft., 15 mi. E of Razgrad. Consisting largely of Cretaceous marls, the dry, sparsely populated region has oak forests (partly cleared) and some agr. (grain, tobacco).

Deli River (dä'lē), NE Sumatra, Indonesia, rises at Mt. Sibayak in N Barisan Mts., flows c.60 mi. N, past Medan and Labuan Deli, to Strait of Malacca at Belawan.

Délisle (dālēl') or **Saint Coeur de Marie** (sē kûr dů märē'), village (pop. 661), central Que., on Saguenay R. and 7 mi. NNW of St. Joseph d'Alma; dairying, pig raising.

Delisle (dŭlīl'), town (pop. 364), S central Sask., 24 mi. SW of Saskatoon; grain elevators.

Delitzsch (dā'lĭch), town (pop. 25,148), in former Prussian Saxony prov., central Germany, after 1945 in Saxony-Anhalt, 13 mi. N of Leipzig; sugar refining; market gardening; mfg. of shoes, chocolate, cigars. Spa.

Delium (dē'lēŭm), anc. town of Boeotia, Greece, on coast of S Gulf of Euboea, 9 mi. SSE of Chalcis. Here the Boeotians defeated the Athenians in 424 B.C. Modern village of Delesi (1928 pop. 52) here.

Deli Yovan, mountain, Yugoslavia: see DELI JOVAN.

Delizhan, Armenian SSR: see DILIZHAN.

Dell. 1 Town (pop. 384), Mississippi co., NE Ark., 9 mi. SW of Blytheville. **2** Village (pop. c.40), Beaverhead co., extreme SW Mont., on Red Rock R. in Jefferson R. system and 35 mi. S of Dillon; trading point in livestock range. Bitterroot Range just W. **3** Town, Oklahoma co., Okla.: see DEL CITY.

Dell Creek, Sauk co., S central Wis., rises c.20 mi. NW of Baraboo, flows SE, then NE, to Wisconsin R. near Lake Delton town; c.15 mi. long. Near its mouth, the stream widens to form L. Delton (2 mi. long, ½ mi. wide) and Mirror L. (2½ mi. long, c.¼ mi. wide), separated by a dam.

Delle (dĕl), town (pop. 3,165), Territory of Belfort, E France, on Swiss border, 11 mi. SE of Belfort, at foot of the N Jura; custom station; produces electrical equipment, safety pins, machine tools, hosiery.

Delligsen (dĕ'lĭgzŭn), village (pop. 3,523), in Brunswick, NW Germany, after 1945 in Lower Saxony, 4 mi. S of Alfeld; ironworks; wood products.

Dell Rapids, city (pop. 1,650), Minnehaha co., E S.Dak., 20 mi. N of Sioux Falls and on Big Sioux R.; rock quarries, diversified farming; animal feed, grain. Near by are the Dells, beautiful ravine cut by the river. Settled 1868, inc. 1879.

Dellroy, village (pop. 358), Carroll co., E Ohio, 17 mi. SSE of Canton, on Atwood Reservoir; coal mining.

Dells of the Wisconsin or **The Dells,** scenic gorge of Wisconsin R., in S central Wis., upstream from Wisconsin Dells city. Extending c.8 mi., it is c.150 ft. deep, walled by sandstone carved by the river into curious forms. Formerly sometimes called Dalles of the Wisconsin.

Dellview, town (pop. 7), Gaston co., S N.C., 10 mi. NE of Shelby.

Dellwood, village (pop. 245), Washington co., E Minn., on White Bear L. and 12 mi. NNE of St. Paul in agr. area.

Delly, Mount, India: see CANNANORE, city.

Dellys (dĕlēs'), town (pop. 5,269), Alger dept., N central Algeria, small port on the Mediterranean, 50 mi. ENE of Algiers; rail-spur terminus. Ships products of Great Kabylia: figs, olives, wines, truck. Basketmaking. The old Arab quarter is a labyrinth of narrow, steep alleys. Just W is Cape Bengut.

Del Mar (dĕl'mär"). **1** Village (pop. c.700), San Diego co., S Calif., on coast, 18 mi. N of downtown San Diego; race track. **2** Resort, Texas: see BRAZOS ISLAND.

Delmar. 1 Village (pop. 6,733, with adjacent Twin Lakes), Santa Cruz co., W Calif., on Monterey Bay, just E of Santa Cruz. **2** Town (pop. 415), Clinton co., E Iowa 23 mi. WNW of Clinton; mfg. (feed, boxes, gates). **3** Town (pop. 2,343; pop. in Wicomico co., Md., 1,328; in Sussex co., Del., 1,015), on Md.-Del. line, 7 mi. N of Salisbury, Md. Marketing and shipping center for truck-farming area (chiefly cantaloupes). Clothing mfg. Has 2 town govts. and 2 school systems. **4** Village (1940 pop. 2,992), Albany co., E N.Y., 5 mi. SW of downtown Albany; mfg. of bleaches, wood products.

Delmarva Peninsula (dĕlmär'vŭ), E U.S., extends c.180 mi. S from just S of Wilmington, Del., bet. Chesapeake Bay on the W and the Atlantic, Delaware Bay, and Delaware R. on the E; greatest width c.70 mi.; Cape Charles, Va., is S tip. Consists of most of Del. and parts (the Eastern Shore region along E side of Chesapeake Bay) of Md. and Va. Chesapeake and Delaware Canal cuts across peninsula's narrow neck (N). Tidewater agr. region (truck, fruit, potatoes) also noted for poultry raising (especially broilers); pine timber; large fishing and oystering industry; shore resorts. The Eastern Shore is famed for waterfowl hunting. Chesapeake Bay Bridge links peninsula to W shore of Chesapeake Bay.

Delme (dĕlm), village (pop. 553), Moselle dept., NE France, 7 mi. NW of Château-Salins; metalworking.

Delmenhorst (dĕl'mŭnhôrst), city (1950 pop. 60,864), in Oldenburg, NW Germany, after 1945 in Lower Saxony, 7 mi. W of Bremen; rail junction; industrial center. Processing of imported wool, jute spinning and weaving; mfg. of machinery, pharmaceuticals, cosmetics, soap, linoleum, cork, margarine. Founded in 13th cent. Industrial development started after 1850.

Delmiro (dĕlmē'rōō), town (pop. 3,448), W Alagoas, NE Brazil, on Petrolândia-Piranhas RR and 95 mi. W of Palmeira dos Índios. Road to Paulo Afonso Falls on São Francisco R. (14 mi. W). Until 1944, called Pedra.

Delmont. 1 Village (pop. c.300), Cumberland co., S N.J., in marshland near Delaware Bay, 13 mi. SSE of Millville; oysters; wood products. **2** Borough, Westmoreland co., Pa.: see NEW SALEM. **3** City (pop. 405), Douglas co., SE S.Dak., 10 mi. ESE of Armour and on branch of Missouri R.; ships cattle, grain.

Del Monte (dĕl mŏn'tē), resort, Monterey co., W Calif., on Monterey Peninsula, just E of Monterey.

Delnice (dĕl'nĭtsĕ), village (pop. 3,763), NW Croatia, Yugoslavia, on railroad and 19 mi. ENE of Rijeka (Fiume), in Gorski Kotar; climatic resort; local trade center; lumbering.

Del Norte (dĕl nôrt'), county (□ 1,003; pop. 8,078), NW Calif.; ⊙ Crescent City. Bounded N by Oregon line, W by Pacific Ocean; mountainous (Siskiyou and Klamath mts.), except for narrow coastal strip. Drained by Smith R. (NW), Klamath R. (SW). Includes parts of Siskiyou (N) and Klamath (S) natl. forests. Site of Smith River, Crescent City, and Lower Klamath Indian reservations. Redwood trees are preserved in 2 state parks. Lumbering and sawmilling (especially redwood); also fir, cedar, hemlock, spruce, and hardwoods. Dairying, cattle and sheep raising, mining (chromite, gold), quarrying (sand and gravel). Ocean fisheries (salmon, halibut, sole). Game fishing (salmon, steelhead, trout) and hunting attract vacationers. Processing industries (lumber, fish, dairy products). Formed 1857.

Del Norte, town (pop. 2,048), ⊙ Rio Grande co., S Colo., on Rio Grande, just E of San Juan Mts., and 30 mi. NW of Alamosa, in irrigated agr. area; alt. 7,778 ft. Dairy and truck products, livestock. Gold and silver mines in vicinity. Rio Grande Natl. Forest near by. Settled 1871–72, inc. 1885.

Del Norte Peak (12,378 ft.), SW Colo., in San Juan Mts., 13 mi. WSW of Del Norte.

Deloit (dŭloit'), town (pop. 235), Crawford co., W Iowa, on Boyer R. and 6 mi. N of Denison; honey.

De Long Fjord (dŭ lông' fyôr'), passage (30 mi. long, 2-5 mi. wide) of Arctic Ocean, bet. N Greenland and several small offshore isls.; 83°11'N 40°30'W.

De Long Islands, NE group of New Siberian Isls., in E.Siberian Sea, part of Yakut Autonomous SSR, Russian SFSR; 76°05'–77°N 149°–158°30'E. Include Bennett, Henrietta, and Jeannette isls. Named for U.S. navigator who discovered them in 1879.

De Long Mountains, NW Alaska, W part of Brooks Range, N of Kotzebue Sound; extend c.150 mi. E from Chukchi Sea, in 68°30'N; over 5,000 ft.

De Long Strait, Russian SFSR: see LONG STRAIT.

Deloraine (dĕ"lŭrān'), town (pop. 819), SW Man., 50 mi. SW of Brandon; wheat, barley, stock.

Deloraine, town (pop. 1,586), N central Tasmania, 25 mi. W of Launceston; center of livestock area; flax mill, sawmill, dairy plant.

Deloro (dŭlô'rō), village (pop. 333), SE Ont., 27 mi. NNW of Belleville; cobalt and arsenic smelting; dairying, stock raising.

Delos (dē'lŏs) or **Dhilos** (dhē'lôs), smallest island (□ 1.2) of the Cyclades, Greece, in Aegean Sea, 14 mi. E of Syros isl.; 37°22'N 25°16'E. Traditionally regarded as the center of the Cyclades. Delos was moored by Zeus as a birthplace for Apollo and Artemis. Sacred to Apollo from earliest times, Delos became the religious center of the Ionians and the site of annual festivals. It became (478–477) the treasury of the Delian League, a confederacy organized by Athens to continue naval war against Persia. The treasure was, however, removed to Athens in 454 B.C. and Delos became subject to Athens until late 4th cent. B.C. It flourished (3d-2d cent. B.C.) as an independent city-state and trade center and the political seat of the Cyclades. In 88 B.C. Delos was sacked by Mithridates VI of Pontus and never recovered. Excavations begun in 1870s have revealed remains of temples, commercial houses, theaters, and private buildings. Sometimes called Mikra [little] Delos as opposed to Megale Delos or RENEIA (W).

Delph, England: see SADDLEWORTH.

Delphi (dĕl'fī), anc. city in Phocis, central Greece, on S slope of the Parnassus, 7 mi. SE of Amphissa. Seat (after 8th cent. B.C.) of the Delphian or Delphic oracle, the most famous and powerful of anc. Greece, which played an important role in the social, religious, and political life of the country. Originally ascribed to the earth goddess Gaea, the oracle was regarded as the center ("navel") of the earth. It later passed to Apollo, according to some accounts after the god had slain the guardian dragon Python (for whom the oracle was originally called Pytho). Housed in 6th-cent. temple, the oracle was spoken by Pythia, a female medium, and transmitted in verse by priests. Delphi was the meeting place of the Delphic Amphictyony, the most important league of Greek states, originally a religious organization of 12 tribes, which (after 6th cent. B.C.) wielded great political influence. It waged a series of Sacred Wars against its members on the grounds of sacrilege against Apollo. The Amphictyony administered the temple of Apollo and conducted the Pythian Games, second only to the Olympic Games, which were held (after 582 B.C.) in memory of the victorious first Sacred War against Cirrha. Delphi accumulated rich gifts brought by those who consulted the oracle and housed the treasuries of the Greek states. These were despoiled in Roman times by Sulla (86 B.C.) and Nero. Following the advent of Christianity, the Delphic oracle was closed (A.D. 390) by Theodosius. Excavations begun in 1840 and continued through 19th cent. have unearthed the sacred precinct containing remains of the temple, a small theater, the treasuries, and commemorative monuments. Findings are housed in a near-by mus. Just S is the modern town of Delphoi or Dhelfoi (pop. 998), moved in 1892 from the ruin site to make way for the excavations; it was formerly called Kastri; sometimes spelled Delfi.

Delphi, mountain in Euboea, Greece: see DIRPHYS.

Delphi, town (pop. 2,530), ⊙ Carroll co., NW central Ind., on Deer Creek, near the Wabash, and 17 mi. NE of Lafayette, in agr. area; mfg. (decoys, food products, automobile bodies); poultry hatcheries.

Delphoi, Greece: see DELPHI.

Delphos (dĕl'fŭs). **1** Town (pop. 74), Ringgold co., S Iowa, near Grand R., 27 mi. S of Creston. **2** City (pop. 676), Ottawa co., N central Kansas, on Solomon R. and 29 mi. NNW of Salina, in livestock and grain region; grain milling. **3** City (pop. 6,220), on Allen–Van Wert co. line, W Ohio, 14 mi. WNW of Lima; motor trucks and equipment, food products, furniture, metal products, sporting goods, wood and fiber products. Limestone quarries; also grain, truck, dairy farming in region. Laid out 1845.

Delport's Hope, Afrikaans *Delportshoop* (dĕl"pôrts-hōp'), town (pop. 1,029), NE Cape Prov., U. of So. Afr., on Vaal R. at mouth of Hartz R., and 40 mi. NW of Kimberley, in Griqualand West, at edge of Kaap Plateau; diamond mining.

Delray Beach (dĕlrā'), resort city (pop. 6,312), Palm Beach co., SE Fla., 18 mi. S of West Palm Beach, in truck- and flower-growing area. A leading polo center. Holds annual gladioli festival.

Del Rey (dĕl rā'), village (pop. c.625), Fresno co., central Calif., in San Joaquin Valley, 12 mi. SE of Fresno; raisins.

Del Rio (dĕl rē'ō). **1** Village (pop. c.300), Cocke co., E Tenn., on French Broad R. and 10 mi. ESE of Newport, in Bald Mts. Grace Moore b. here. **2** City (pop. 14,211), ⊙ Val Verde co., SW Texas, on the Rio Grande (bridged) opposite Villa Acuña, Mexico, and c.140 mi. W of San Antonio. Port of entry; shipping center for wool, mohair, cattle from ranching area, with irrigated farms (fruit, alfalfa, truck, grapes), watered by San Felipe Springs in city's outskirts; wine making, mfg. of saddles, other leather goods; tourist trade. Founded 1868, inc. 1911.

Delsberg, Switzerland: see DELÉMONT.

Delsbo (dĕls'bōō"), village (pop. 737), Gavleborg co., E Sweden, on South Dell L., Swedish *Södra Dellen* (9 mi. long, 1-4 mi. wide), 18 mi. WNW of Hudiksvall; tourist resort; market gardens. Church has 18th-cent. tower.

Delson, village (pop. 570), S Que., near the St. Lawrence, 8 mi. SSE of Montreal; dairying; oats.

Delta, village (pop. estimate 500), SE Ont., bet. small Upper and Lower Beverley lakes, 20 mi. SSE of Smiths Falls; dairying, mixed farming.

Delta. 1 County (□ 1,157; pop. 17,365), W Colo.; ⊙ Delta. Coal-mining and agr. area, drained by Gunnison R. Fruit, beans, hay, livestock. Grand Mesa Natl. Forest in N. Formed 1883. **2** County (□ 1,180; pop. 32,913), S Upper Peninsula, Mich.; ⊙ Escanaba. Bounded S by L. Michigan and arms (Big Bay De Noc, Little Bay De Noc) of Green Bay; drained by Ford, Escanaba, and Whitefish rivers and small Days R. Includes part of Hiawatha Natl. Forest. Lumbering, dairying, agr. (fruit, potatoes, truck, livestock, poultry). Mfg. at Escanaba and Gladstone. Ships iron ore, grain. Fisheries. Resorts. Organized 1861. **3** County (□ 276; pop. 8,964), NE Texas; ⊙ Cooper. Rich prairie agr. region, bet. North and South forks of Sulphur R.; cotton; also corn, hay, feedstuffs, peanuts, fruit, truck; dairying; cattle, hogs, mules, poultry. Some lumbering. Formed 1870.

Delta. 1 City (pop. 4,097), ⊙ Delta co., W Colo., on Gunnison R., at mouth of Uncompahgre R., and 35 mi. SE of Grand Junction; alt. 4,980 ft. Trade and shipping center for diversified farming region; fruit, sugar beets, flour, dairy and wood products. City is hq. for Uncompahgre Natl. Forest. On small branch of Gunnison R., 8 mi. NE, is Fruit Growers Dam (55 ft. high, 1,520 ft. long; for irrigation; completed 1938). Inc. 1882. **2** Town (pop. 562), Keokuk co., SE Iowa, 17 mi. E of Oskaloosa; livestock, grain. **3** Village (pop. 150), Madison parish, NE La., on the Mississippi, opposite Vicksburg (Miss.); agr. (especially oats). **4** Town (pop. 453), Cape Girardeau co., SE Mo., in Mississippi flood plain, 13 mi. SW of Cape Girardeau. **5** Village (pop. 2,120), Fulton co., NW Ohio, 24 mi. WSW of Toledo; agr. (dairy products; wheat, corn); produces cutlery, gasoline-pumping equipment, motor-vehicle equipment, evaporated milk. **6** Borough (pop. 840), York co., S Pa., 28 mi. SE of York, on Md. border; agr.; slate and marble quarries; roofing, clothing. **7** Town (pop. 1,703), Millard co., W central Utah, on Sevier R. and c.80 mi. SW of Provo; alt. 4,649 ft. Trade and shipping center in livestock and irrigated agr. area; alfalfa-seed processing; dairy products. Settled 1906.

Delta, The, Miss.: see YAZOO RIVER.

Delta Amacuro (dĕl'tä ämäkōō'rō), territory (□ 15,520; 1941 pop. 28,165; 1950 census 30,957, excluding c.9,000 Indians), NE Venezuela; ⊙ Tucupita. Bordered by the Atlantic (E) and Br. Guiana (SE), opposite Trinidad (N). Consists largely of swampy Orinoco R. delta, forming vast triangle of 7,745 sq. mi. Among numerous arms of the delta are Caño Mánamo, Caño Macareo, Caño Araguao, Río Grande, Brazo Imataca. S section of territory comprises low Sierra Imataca and Atlantic lowlands, watered by Amacuro and Barima rivers. Climate generally hot and tropical, with rains all year round. Mineral resources include petroleum and asphalt (Pedernales), iron (Sierra Imataca and along Brazo Imataca), bauxite (SE). Its main crops are cacao, bananas, sugar cane, rice, corn, tobacco, coconuts. Tropical-rain forests yield gum, balata, divi-divi, mangrove bark. Egret plumes are collected. Native Indians ply by-streams of delta, living mainly on fish.

Delta Cross Channel, Calif.: see CENTRAL VALLEY.

Delta-Mendota Canal (dĕl'tŭ-mĕndō'tŭ), central Calif., an irrigation unit of CENTRAL VALLEY project; has its head near Tracy, where it receives water pumped from Delta Cross Channel; leads 120 mi. S, through W San Joaquin Valley, to San Joaquin R. near Mendota.

Delta River, E Alaska, rises in glaciers on N slope of Alaska Range, near 63°31'N 145°52'W, flows 50 mi. N to Tanana R. at Big Delta. Paralleled by Richardson Highway; before construction of highway, river when frozen was part of trail to interior gold fields.

Delton, Lake, Wis.: see DELL CREEK.

Deluz (dŭlüz'), village (pop. 502), Doubs dept., E France, on the Doubs and 9 mi. ENE of Besançon; paper mill.

Delvin (dĕl'vĭn), Gaelic *Dealbhna Mhór*, town (pop. 149), E Co. Westmeath, Ireland, 10 mi. ENE of Mullingar; agr. market (dairying; cattle, potatoes).

Delvinakion (dĕlvēnä'kēŏn), town (pop. 1,332), Ioannina nome, S Epirus, Greece, 33 mi. NNW of Ioannina, near Albanian border; timber; goat raising. Formerly called Pogonion.

Delvinë (dĕlvē'nŭ) or **Delvina** (dĕlvē'nä), Ital. *Delvino*, town (1945 pop. 2,501), S Albania, 9 mi. S of Argyrokastron; agr. center; olives, oranges, wine, tobacco. Ruins of Phoenice are 3 mi. SW.

Delwara, India: see ABU.

Delyatin (dyĭlyä'tyĭn), Pol. *Delatyn* (dĕlä'tĭn), town (1931 pop. 8,815), S central Stanislav oblast, Ukrainian SSR, on Prut R. and 19 mi. W of Kolomyya; rail junction; health resort; lumber-milling center; distilling, brick mfg. Salt deposits and mineral springs.

Dema, Russian SFSR: see UFA, city.

De-machi (dā'-mä'chē), town (pop. 6,562), Toyama prefecture, central Honshu, Japan, 17 mi. ENE of Kanazawa; textile mills.

Demak (dŭmäk'), town (pop. 8,783), central Java, Indonesia, near N coast, 15 mi. ENE of Semarang; trade center in agr. area (rice, sugar, corn). Here is noted mosque (completed 1468, rebuilt 1845) visited by pilgrims. Demak was ⊙ Moslem kingdom of Demak in late 15th cent.

De Malherbe (dŭ mälârb'), village (pop. 988), Oran dept., NW Algeria, 8 mi. SSE of Aïn-Témouchent; winegrowing.

Demanda, Sierra de la (syĕ'rä dhā lä dämän'dä), range of the Cordillera Ibérica, in Old Castile, N Spain, extends c.15 mi. along Logroño-Burgos prov. border, rising in the Cerro de San Lorenzo to 7,556 ft.

Demanova (dĕ'mänôvä), Slovak *Demänová*, Hung. *Deménfalu* (dĕ'mānfŏlōō), village (pop. 485), N central Slovakia, Czechoslovakia, at N foot of the Dumbier, 2 mi. SSW of Liptovsky Svaty Mikulas. Point of departure for excursions to near-by Demanova Caves (SE), a widely known labyrinth of stalactite and stalagmite caves and underground rivers and lakes.

Demar, Yemen: see DHAMAR.

Demarcation Point, small promontory, NE Alaska, just W of Yukon border, on Beaufort Sea of the Arctic Ocean; 69°42'N 141°18'W. Just SE is Gordon, Eskimo settlement and trading post (1939 pop. 25).

Demarest (dĕmūrĕst'), suburban borough (pop. 1,786), Bergen co., NE N.J., near Hudson R., 4 mi. N of Englewood; concrete products. Inc. 1903.

Dema River (dyĕ'mŭ), E European Russian SFSR, rises in W foothills of the S Urals, NW of Fedorovka (Bashkir Antonomous SSR); flows generally W, past Ponomarevka, and NNE, past Rayevski and Davlekanovo, to Belaya R. opposite Ufa; 233 mi. long.

Demavend or **Damavand** (both: dämävănd'), town (1941 pop. 9,998), Second Prov., in Teheran, N central Iran, 35 mi. E of Teheran, on S slopes of Mt. Demavend; fruit orchards; lumbering. Noted summer resort for Teheran; hot springs. In earthquake zone.

Demavend, Mount, or **Mount Demavand,** highest peak (18,600 ft.) of the Elburz range and of Iran, 45 mi. NE of Teheran. A dormant volcanic cone, it has a permanent snowcap. Demavend resort is at S foot.

Demba (dĕm'bä), village, Kasai prov., S Belgian Congo, on railroad and 60 mi. E of Luebo; cotton ginning, cottonseed-oil milling; coffee and fiber plantations. R.C. mission.

Dembea (dĕmbä'ä), fertile district in Begemdir prov., NW Ethiopia, bet. Gondar and L. Tana; cereals (millet, barley, wheat), livestock (cattle, sheep), butter, honey. Also name applied to L. Tana by Portuguese Jesuits in 16th-17th cent.

Dembica, Poland: see DEBICA.

Dembidollo, Ethiopia: see SAIO.

Demchok (dĕm'chōk) or **Demchhog** (–chōg), town, W Tibet, on the Indus, on main Leh-Lhasa trade route and 80 mi. NW of Gartok, near undefined Kashmir border; alt. 14,022 ft.

Demecser (dĕ'mĕchĕr), town (pop. 4,360), Szabolcs co., NE Hungary, 14 mi. NE of Nyiregyhaza; sugar refinery, starch mfg.; sugar beets, wheat, cattle, horses.

Demerara (dĕmūrâ'rū), county (□ 4,420; pop. 220,639), central and N Br. Guiana, on the Atlantic, along Demerara R.; ⊙ Georgetown. Smallest, but most populous and cultivated, section of Br. Guiana. Includes large sugar and rice plantations along the coast and bauxite deposits at Mackenzie and vicinity. First settled by the Dutch in 18th cent., it was (after 1773) a separate colony until united (1789) with Essequibo and (1831) with Berbice. Its name is sometimes applied to the whole colony of Br. Guiana. The co. (mainly of historical importance) comprises the administrative dists. of Georgetown and East Bank, East Demerara, and West Demerara.

Demerara River, central and N Br. Guiana, economically the most important stream of the colony, rises in densely forested interior at 4°42'N 58°21'W, flows c.200 mi. N, past Mackenzie and Vreed-en-Hoop, to the Atlantic at Georgetown, the country's main port. Adjoined by valuable forest country (greenheart, balata, etc.) in the upper region, where also alluvial gold is worked. Near Mackenzie are large bauxite and kaolin deposits. In its fertile lowlands along its mouth grow sugar cane, rice, tropical fruit. Navigable for ocean-going vessels to Mackenzie (65 mi.), where bauxite is loaded, and for smaller ships up to Malali (105 mi.). A railroad from Rockstone to Wismar carries goods from Essequibo R. to Demerara R.

Demer River (dā'mŭr), NE and central Belgium, rises near Bilzen, Limburg prov.; flows 60 mi. W, past Hasselt, Diest, and Aarschot, to Dyle R. at Werchter. Navigable below Diest.

Demetrias, Greece: see VOLOS.

Demetsana or **Dhimitsana** (both: dhēmētsä'nŭ), town (pop. 2,086), Arcadia nome, central Peloponnesus, Greece, 20 mi. WNW of Tripolis; tobacco, potatoes, wheat, wine; livestock (sheep, goats). Under Turks, site of important Gr. school and library. Also spelled Dimitsana.

Demidov (dyĭmē'dŭf), city (1948 pop. over 10,000), NW Smolensk oblast, Russian SFSR, on Kasplya R. (head of navigation) and 37 mi. NW of Smolensk; dairying center; flax processing; handicrafts (pottery, shoe-making). Chartered 1776; called Porechye until early 1920s.

Demidovka (–kŭ), Pol. *Demidówka* (dĕmēdōof'kä), village (1931 pop. 1,840), SW Rovno oblast, Ukrainian SSR, 17 mi. W of Dubno; flour milling.

Deming (dĕ'mĭng), village (pop. 5,672), ⊙ Luna co., SW N.Mex., in valley of Mimbres R., 85 mi. NW of El Paso, Texas; alt. c.4,330 ft. Health resort; rail junction; trade center in grain and livestock region; poultry, fruit, beans, cotton. Sanitarium is here. Mining (copper, zinc) in near-by mts.; fluorspar deposits. Settled 1880, inc. 1902. River, flowing underground here, is tapped for irrigation.

Demirci (dĕmĭrjē'), town (pop. 6,132), Manisa prov., W Turkey, 70 mi. ENE of Manisa; carpets; valonia, wheat, barley, potatoes; mica.

Demircikoy, Turkey: see CAL.

Demirci Mountains, W Turkey, extend 60 mi. ESE of Sindirgi, S of Simav R.; rise to 5,909 ft. in Simav Dag. Town of Simav on N slope. Emery, mica, chromium.

Demir Gate (dĕ'mĭr), Serbo-Croatian *Demir Kapija* (kä'pēyä), 12-mi.-long series of gorges along Vardar R., Macedonia, Yugoslavia, c.10 mi. SE of Negotin, below (SE of) the Tikves.

Demir Hissar, Greece: see SIDEROKASTRON.

Demirkoy (dĕmĭrkû'ē), Turkish *Demirköy*, village (pop. 1,401), Kirklareli prov., Turkey in Europe, 28 mi. ENE of Kirklareli, in forested dist. in Istranca Mts., near Black Sea and Bulgarian frontier. Formerly called Samakof, Samakov.

Demmin (dĕmēn'), town (pop. 18,006), in former Prussian Pomerania prov., N Germany, after 1945 in Mecklenburg, on the Peene (head of navigation), at mouth of Tollense R., and 20 mi. SW of Greifswald; sugar refining, brewing, distilling; mfg. of machinery, barrels, twine. Agr. center (grain, sugar beets, stock). Has 16th-cent. church and old town walls. Anc. Slav settlement, conquered by Saxons in 1164; chartered 1236. Was member of Hanseatic League.

Demnate (dĕmnät'), town (pop. 6,896), Marrakesh region, W central Fr. Morocco, at N foot of the High Atlas, 60 mi. E of Marrakesh; palm-fiber processing, olive-oil pressing. Trade in livestock, skins, wool, grapes, olives. Formerly spelled Demnat.

Democracia or **La Democracia** (lä dāmōkrä'syä), town (pop. 1,013), Escuintla dept., S Guatemala, in Pacific piedmont, 12 mi. SW of Escuintla, near railroad; sugar cane, grain. Citronella-oil press near by.

Democracia, La, Venezuela: see LA DEMOCRACIA.

Democrat, Mount, peak (14,142 ft.) in Park Range, central Colo., 10 mi. NW of Leadville.

Demonte (dĕmôn'tĕ), village (pop. 1,355), Cuneo prov., Piedmont, NW Italy, on Stura di Demonte R. and 14 mi. SW of Cuneo, in livestock region. Quarries (limestone, gypsum, slate), anthracite mines near by.

Demopolis (dēmŏ'pŭlĭs), city (pop. 5,004), Marengo co., W Ala., on Tombigbee R., at mouth of Black Warrior R., and 50 mi. SSW of Tuscaloosa; lumber and wood products, concrete building blocks, farm equipment; meat rendering. Navigation lock and dam begun 1950 on the Tombigbee here. Founded 1818 by Bonapartist exiles. Has fine Greek-revival homes built by cotton planters.

Demorest (dĕmūrĕst'), town (pop. 1,166), Habersham co., NE Ga., 13 mi. W of Toccoa, in apple-growing area. Piedmont Col. here.

Demotika, Greece: see DIDYMOTEIKHON.

Dempo, Mount (dĕm'pō), active volcanic peak (10,364 ft.), Barisan Mts., SW Sumatra, Indonesia, 65 mi. ESE of Benkulen; 4°1'S 103°7'E.

Demyanovka or **Dem'yanovka** (dyĭmyä'nŭfkŭ), village, NE Kustanai oblast, Kazakh SSR, 90 mi. NE of Kustanai; wheat, cattle.

Demyansk (dyĭmyänsk'), village (1926 pop. 2,472), S Novgorod oblast, Russian SFSR, 45 mi. ESE of Staraya Russa; clothing mfg., flax processing, dairying. During Second World War, held (1941–43) by Germans.

Denain (dūnē'), town (pop. 22,299), Nord dept., N France, on left bank of canalized Escaut R. and 6 mi. WSW of Valenciennes; major coal-mining and steel-milling center, and rail hub for surrounding industrial region. Produces railroad rolling stock, armaments. Sugar refining, brewing. Here French under Villars defeated the imperialists, 1712.

Denair (dĭnâr'), village (pop. c.500), Stanislaus co., central Calif., in San Joaquin Valley, 13 mi. SE of Modesto; dairying, irrigated farming.

Denali (dĭnä'lē, dĭ'nŭlē), village (1939 pop. 63), E Alaska, on upper Susitna R. and 120 mi. S of Fairbanks; supply point; airfield. The native name of Mt. MCKINLEY is Denali.

Denau (dyĭnou'), town (1939 pop. over 2,000), E Surkhan-Darya oblast, Uzbek SSR, on railroad and 80 mi. NNE of Termez; cotton-ginning center; sugar cane. Formerly spelled Dinau.

Den Berg, Netherlands: see GEERTRUIDENBERG.

Denbigh, village (1940 pop. 1,215), ⊙ Warwick co., SE Va., near the James, 12 mi. NNW of Newport News. U.S. Fort Eustis is 4 mi. NNW.

Denbigh or **Denbighshire** (dĕn'bē, –shĭr), county (□ 668.7; 1931 pop. 157,648; 1951 census pop. 170,699), NE Wales, on the Irish Sea; ⊙ Denbigh. Bounded by Caernarvon (W), Flint and Chester (NE), Shropshire (SE), Montgomery and Merioneth (S). Drained by Conway, Clwyd, and Dee rivers. Rugged terrain with fertile valleys. Coal mining is centered on Wrexham; other industries include steel milling, iron, copper, zinc, lead mining, slate quarrying, agr. Besides Denbigh, chief towns are Wrexham, Ruthin, Colwyn Bay (resort), Llangollen, Llanwrst, Abergele.

Denbigh, municipal borough (1931 pop. 7,249; 1951 census 8,127), ⊙ Denbighshire, Wales, in N part of co., 25 mi. SW of Liverpool, in Clwyd R. valley; agr. market. Has remains of town walls and of 13th-cent. castle built by Henry de Lacy, earl of Lincoln. Charles I stayed here after battle of Rowton Moor (1645). Henry Stanley b. here. Municipal borough includes Henllan (pop. 1,666).

Denbighshire, Wales: see DENBIGH, county.

Den Bosch, Netherlands: see 's HERTOGENBOSCH.

Den Briel, Netherlands: see BRIELLE.

Den Burg, Netherlands: see TEXEL.

Denby, town and parish (pop. 1,989), S central Derby, England, 3 mi. ESE of Belper; coal-mining center, with pottery works. Church dates partly from 14th cent.

Denby Dale, urban district (1931 pop. 3,396; 1951 census 9,651), West Riding, S Yorkshire, England, on Dearne R. and 7 mi. SE of Huddersfield; includes woolen-milling towns of Denby Dale, Denby, and Lower and Upper Cumberworth. Formerly called Denby and Cumberworth. Absorbed near-by areas in 1938.

Den Chai (dĕn' chī'), village (1937 pop. 5,033), Phrae prov., N Thailand, on Bangkok-Chiangmai RR and 40 mi. SE of Lampang; highway to Phrae and Nan.

Denchuka, Bhutan: see DORKHA.

Dendera (dĕn'dūrū), **Dandara,** or **Dandarah** (both: dĕn'därū), anc. *Tentyra*, village (pop. 16,320), Qena prov., Upper Egypt, on W bank of the Nile opposite Qena. Has large and well-preserved temple of Hathor, dating from time of Cleopatra and early Roman emperors, and a temple of Isis. In the temple of Hathor was the celebrated table of zodiacal signs now in Paris. Sometimes spelled Dendara.

Denderleeuw (dĕn'dūrlyōō), town (pop. 7,450), East Flanders prov., W central Belgium, on Dender R. and 13 mi. W of Brussels; agr. market (fruit, vegetables, poultry); textile milling.

Dendermonde (dĕn'dūrmōn"dū), Fr. *Termonde* (tĕrmōd'), town (pop. 9,330), East Flanders prov., N Belgium, on Scheldt R., at mouth of Dender R., and 17 mi. NW of Brussels; textile center (cotton spinning, carpet weaving). Has 14th-cent. town hall, 15th-cent. Gothic church. In 1667 town repulsed a siege by Louis XIV; was taken by Marlborough in 1706. Suffered looting and considerable destruction by Germans in 1914.

Dender River (dĕn'dūr), Fr. *Dendre* (dā'drū), W central Belgium, rises 6 mi. SW of Soignies, flows 55 mi. N past Ath, Lessines, Grammont, Ninove, and Alost, to Scheldt R. at Dendermonde. Lower course navigable.

Den Dolder, Netherlands: see DOLDER.

Dendre River, Belgium: see DENDER RIVER.

Dendron (dĕn'drūn), town (pop. 476), Surry co., SE Va., near Blackwater R., 30 mi. ESE of Petersburg.

Denekamp (dā'nūkämp), town (pop. 2,371), Overijssel prov., E Netherlands, 12 mi. NE of Hengelo, near Ger. border; cattle raising, truck gardening. Natura Docet rural mus. here.

Deneysville, town (pop. 406), NE Orange Free State, U. of So. Afr., on Transvaal border, 50 mi. SSE of Johannesburg, 20 mi. SE of Vereeniging, on NW side of Vaalbank Dam irrigation reservoir (□ 63); alt. 5,010 ft.; seaplane base for Johannesburg; resort. Town is of recent origin. Formerly Vaaldam.

Denezhkin Kamen or **Denezhkin Kamen'** (dĭnyĕ'-shkĭn kä'mĭnyū), peak (4,895 ft.) in central Urals, Russian SFSR; 60°30'N.

Dengkil (dĕng-kĭl'), village (pop. 677), S Selangor, Malaya, 18 mi. SSW of Kuala Lumpur; rubber.

Den Haag, Netherlands: see HAGUE, THE.

Denham (dĕ'nūm), village, W Western Australia, on W coast of Peron Peninsula, 210 mi. NNW of Geraldton; pearling center.

Denham, residential town and parish (pop. 2,609), SE Buckingham, England, on Colne R. and 3 mi. NNW of Uxbridge, 20 mi. WNW of London; center of Br. moving-picture industry. Also aircraft and electrical-equipment works. Has 15th-cent. church and 2 notable 17th-cent. mansions.

Denham, village (pop. 96), Pine co., E Minn., on affluent of Kettle R. and c.50 mi. SW of Duluth; dairy products.

Denham Sound, Australia: see SHARK BAY.

Denham Springs, town (pop. 2,053), Livingston parish, SE La., on Amite R. and 14 mi. E of Baton Rouge; agr. (fruit, truck); cotton gin; mfg. of wood products, boats, naval stores. Settled in early-19th cent. around mineral springs.

Den Helder, Netherlands: see HELDER.

Denholm (dĕ'nūm), village in Cavers parish (pop. 1,179), NE Roxburgh, Scotland, on Teviot R. and 5 mi. NE of Hawick.

Denholme (dĕ'nūm), urban district (1931 pop. 2,662; 1951 census 2,586), West Riding, W Yorkshire, England, 6 mi. W of Bradford; woolen and rayon milling.

Denia (dā'nyä), anc. *Dianium*, city (pop. 7,637), Alicante prov., E Spain, in Valencia, on side of hill near the Mediterranean, 18 mi. SE of Gandía; fruitgrowing and -shipping center (raisins, oranges, almonds). Toy mfg.; fishing and boatbuilding, fruit canning, sawmilling; also makes tiles and candy. Olive oil, peanuts, vegetables in area. Hill crowned by ruins of medieval castle; has baroque church with colored-tile dome. Probably of Iberian origin, became (6th cent. B.C.) flourishing Greek colony; Romans erected here temple to Diana (few inscriptions left); prospered also under Moors (8th-

13th cent.); was (14th cent.) seat of county of Denia. Declined in 18th cent., but has recently revived as important agr. trade center.

Denial Bay, inlet of Great Australian Bight, S South Australia, at NW base of Eyre Peninsula; sheltered by Nuyts Archipelago; 17mi. E–W. Splits into 3 small inlets. Thevenard and Ceduna on N shore.

Deniliquin (dŭnĭl'ĭkwĭn), municipality (pop. 3,668), S New South Wales, Australia, 160 mi. N of Melbourne; rail terminus; sheep, agr. center; dairy plant.

Denis Island or **Dennis Island** (340 acres; pop. 58), one of the Seychelles, in Indian Ocean, 50 mi. N of Victoria; 3°48'S 55°40'E; 1½ mi. long, 1½ mi. wide; granite formation. Copra. Lighthouse.

Denison, Australia: see DONGARA.

Denison. 1 City (pop. 4,554), ⊙ Crawford Co., W Iowa, on Boyer R. and c.60 mi. NNE of Council Bluffs; packed poultry, flour, feed, plastics, wood and metal products. Inc. 1876. **2** City (pop. 166), Jackson co., NE Kansas, 24 mi. N of Topeka, in livestock and grain region. **3** City (pop. 17,504), Grayson co., N Texas, 9 mi. N of Sherman; a trade, shipping, industrial center for fertile Red R. valley; railroad division point, with shops; milk and egg-processing plants (cheese making), pecan and peanut shelling, meat and poultry packing, grain milling, mfg. of machinery, metal products, textiles, creosoted products, furniture, mattresses, peanut butter, cottonseed oil, other foods. Dwight D. Eisenhower b. here (birthplace preserved). To NW is DENISON DAM. Grew around antebellum stagecoach station; inc. 1873.

Denison, Port, Australia: see BOWEN.

Denison Dam, in N Texas and S Okla., in the RED RIVER just N of Denison, Texas; completed 1943 for flood control and hydroelectric power, main dam is of earthfill construction 165 ft. high, 15,200 ft. long. Its reservoir, L. Texoma, covering □ 227 and with a capacity of 5,825,000 acre-ft., is one of largest in U.S.; has recreational facilities, wildlife refuges.

Denisovka (dyĭnyē'sŭfkŭ), village (1939 pop. over 500), NW Kustanai oblast, Kazakh SSR, on Tobol R. and 90 mi. SW of Kustanai; wheat, cattle.

Deniyaya (dā'nĭyŭyŭ), village (pop., including surrounding villages, 3,133), Southern Prov., Ceylon, in Sabaragamuwa Hill Country, 26 mi. N of Matara; extensive tea and rubber plantations; rice, vegetables; alexandrite deposits.

Denizli (dĕn"ĭzlē'), province (□ 4,244; 1950 pop. 340,010), SW Turkey; ⊙ Denizli. On SW are Mentese Mts.; drained by Menderes, Ak, and Dalaman rivers. Scattered deposits of chromium, sulphur, emery, copper, lignite; grain, cotton, raisins.

Denizli, town (1950 pop. 22,029), ⊙ Denizli prov., SW Turkey, on railroad, near Menderes R., 115 mi. ESE of Smyrna; cotton goods, lignite, tobacco, sesame, grain. Known for its luxuriant gardens. Near site of anc. Laodicea or Laodicea ad Lycum, which it succeeded as local center. An important center in Middle Ages, declined after 14th cent. Severe earthquake in 1715.

Denjong, India: see SIKKIM.

Denkendorf (dĕng'kŭndôrf), village (pop. 3,690), N Württemberg, Germany, after 1945 in Württemberg-Baden, 3 mi. S of Esslingen (linked by tramway); wine. Has former convent, with Romanesque church.

Denklingen (dĕngk'lĭng-ŭn), village (pop. 5,759), in former Prussian Rhine Prov., W Germany, after 1945 in North Rhine-Westphalia, 8 mi. SSE of Gummersbach; cattle.

Denman, town (pop. 705), E New South Wales, Australia, on Hunter R. and 70 mi. NW of Newcastle; dairying center.

Denman Glacier (40 naut. mi. long, 7 naut. mi. wide; alt. 3,000 ft.), Antarctica, flows into Shackleton Shelf Ice on Queen Mary Coast, in 66°45'S 99°10'E. Discovered 1912.

Denman Island (□ 19), SW B.C., in Strait of Georgia just off E coast of Vancouver Isl., 9 mi. SE of Courtenay; 12 mi. long; lumbering, fishing. Just E is Hornby Isl.

Denmark, Danish *Danmark* (dăn'märk), kingdom (□ 16,576; 1950 pop. 4,279,151), NW Europe, in S part of Scandinavia; ⊙ COPENHAGEN. It consists of JUTLAND peninsula, including N Schleswig, bounded S by Germany, bet. North Sea (W) and the Kattegat (E); and Baltic isls. of ZEALAND, FYN, FALSTER, LOLLAND, LANGELAND, and BORNHOLM. GREENLAND and FAEROE ISLANDS are Danish overseas possessions. The low and level surface of Denmark is continuation of North German plain; highest elevation is Mollehoj (561 ft.), in E Jutland. Chief straits of Denmark are Little Belt, bet. Jutland and Fyn isl., crossed by rail and road bridge; Great Belt, bet. Fyn and Zealand isls.; and Oresund, bet. Zealand and Sweden. Danish coast line is irregular and much indented; large Lim Fjord separates N tip from rest of Jutland. Moist maritime climate prevails; drift and pack ice in straits hinders navigation during severe winters. Danish soil is highly cultivated; stock raising (cattle, pigs), dairying, bacon production, poultry breeding are mainstay of Danish economy; butter, eggs, bacon, and condensed milk are country's chief exports. Other agr. products are fruit, barley, oats, rye, wheat, potatoes, feed crops, and sugar beets; large quantities of stock feed have to be imported. Fishing is important. Cooperative marketing and processing of agr. products are highly developed. Apart from some peat and lignite there is a virtual absence of domestically-produced fuel or other source of power. Denmark is a major producer of cement; and other bldg. materials (chalk, limestone, sandstone, granite, and clay) are quarried in quantities sufficient to cover domestic needs. Danish merchant fleet is considerable. Chief industries are brewing; meat, milk, and fish canning, shipbuilding, textile milling, tanning, sugar refining, tobacco processing; mfg. of machinery (marine engines, machine tools; dairying, agr., brewing, laundry, and refrigerating machinery), glass, soap, paint, fertilizer, margarine, bicycles, leather goods. Danish silver, porcelain, and cherry brandy are noted throughout the world. Dense rail network, supplemented by coastal-shipping lines, serves entire country; there are train ferries across the Great Belt (Korsor-Nyborg), across the Oresund to Sweden (Copenhagen-Malmo, Helsingor-Halsingborg), and across Mecklenburg Bay to Germany (Gedser-Warnemünde). Chief cities are Copenhagen (with over one quarter of country's total pop.), Aarhus, Odense, Aalborg, Esbjerg, Randers, Horsens, Kolding, Vejle, Roskilde, Fredericia, Svendborg, Silkeborg, Viborg, and Helsingor (Elsinore). Universities at Copenhagen and Aarhus; technical col. and veterinary and agr. col. at Copenhagen. Denmark is a constitutional monarchy; legislative power is vested in bicameral parliament (*Rigsdag*), consisting of upper chamber (*Landsting*) and lower chamber (*Folketing*). Established church is Lutheran; bishop of Roskilde is primate of Denmark. Administratively country is divided into 22 *amter* (counties) and the city of Copenhagen. Social legislation and education are on an exceptionally high level; social services include workmen's compensation insurance (introduced 1898), unemployment and sickness insurance, and old-age pensions. Danes played important part in Viking raids on W Europe and especially in invasion of England. Harold Bluetooth (d. c.985) was 1st Christian king of Denmark; his son, Sweyn, conquered England. Under King Canute (1018–35) Denmark, England, and Norway were united. S Sweden remained, with brief interruptions, in Danish hands until 1645 (SW Sweden) and until 1658 (SE Sweden). In late 12th and early 13th cent., kings Waldemar I and Waldemar II established Danish hegemony over large parts of N Europe. Under Waldemar IV (1340–75) Denmark again reached a peak of power, but had to yield (1370) to Hanseatic League in Treaty of Stralsund. Through Kalmar Union (1397) Queen Margaret effected personal union of Denmark, Norway, and Sweden and had Eric of Pomerania proclaimed king of the 3 countries; union was dissolved (1523) with accession of Gustavus I of Sweden, but Norway remained under Danish rule until 1814. Accession (1448) of Christian I established house of Oldenburg (from which present ruling family of Schleswig-Holstein-Sonderburg-Glücksburg is descended) on Danish throne; at same time duchies of Schleswig and Holstein came to Denmark. Under Christian III (1534–59) Reformation was introduced. Throughout 16th, 17th, and early 18th cent. Denmark was involved in periodic wars with Sweden and other neighbors; Danish participation in Thirty Years War and in concurrent wars with Sweden led to loss of her hegemony in Scandinavia to Sweden. A law (1665) defining royal powers transformed Denmark into absolute monarchy under Frederick III, aided by his minister, Count Griffenfeld. In 2d half of 18th cent. important social reforms were carried out by the elder and younger Bernstorff and by Struensee; serfdom was abolished 1788. In French Revolutionary and Napoleonic wars Denmark was attacked (1801 and 1807) by England; under Treaty of Kiel (1814) it had to cede Norway to Sweden. A constitution was adopted (1848) under Frederick VII. There followed a Prusso-Danish war (1848–49) over status of Schleswig-Holstein; Danish defeat led to London Protocol (1852), which granted the 2 duchies special status. New war (1864) bet. Denmark and Prussia and Austria resulted in Danish loss of Schleswig-Holstein. Early 19th cent. had seen Danish cultural renaissance, exemplified notably by the works of Kierkegaard, Andersen, and Thorvaldsen. There followed major agr. reorganization; specialized dairying economy was introduced, resulting in greatly increased prosperity, followed by rapid social progress. Educational basis for the drastic economic reorganization had been laid by the Folk Universities (founded by Grundtvig), which continued to exert great influence on modern Danish economic and cultural life. Later in 19th cent., growth of cooperative movement further strengthened Danish economy. Neutral in First World War, Denmark nevertheless recovered (1920) N Schleswig after a plebiscite. A new constitution had been introduced in 1915. Bet. the First and Second World wars the Social Democrats became major force in Danish politics. In Second World War neutral Denmark was invaded (April, 1940) by Germany. King Christian X and his govt. remained; at the same time the Danish minister in Washington, though disavowed by his govt., granted the United States military bases in Greenland, while c.40% of Danish merchant fleet served the Allies. In Aug., 1943, Germans established martial law in Denmark, arrested govt., and placed the king under house arrest; country was now treated as an enemy rather than as a "model protectorate." In May, 1945, Germans in Denmark surrendered to British. After Second World War Denmark entered (1945) the United Nations; later participated in European Recovery Program and became signatory of North Atlantic Treaty. Postwar economic recovery was comparatively rapid. In 1945, Iceland, until then in personal union with Denmark, became an independent republic. Virgin Isls. had been sold (1917) by Denmark to the United States. The 22 counties are: AABENRAA-SONDERBORG, AALBORG, AARHUS, BORNHOLM, COPENHAGEN, FAERO, FREDERIKSBORG, HADERSLEV, HJORRING, HOLBAEK, MARIBO, ODENSE, PRAESTO, RANDERS, RIBE, RINGKOBING, SORO, SVENDBORG, THISTED, TONDER, VEJLE, VIBORG.

Denmark, town (pop. 619), SW Western Australia, 220 mi. SSE of Perth and on inlet of Indian Ocean; butter factory, sawmills; dairy products, fruit, potatoes.

Denmark. 1 Village (pop. c.500), Lee co., SE Iowa, 13 mi. WSW of Burlington, in agr. area. **2** Town (pop. 447), Oxford co., W Maine, on the Saco and 31 mi. WSW of Auburn; farming, resort area. **3** Town (pop. 2,814), Bamberg co., S central S.C., 20 mi. SW of Orangeburg, in agr. area; rail junction; communications center; lumber products. Settled 1896, inc. 1903. **4** Town (pop. 69), Madison co., W Tenn., 12 mi. SW of Jackson, in farm area. **5** Village (pop. 1,012), Brown co., E Wis., at base of Door Peninsula, 15 mi. SE of Green Bay City, in dairy and farm area; dairy products, beer.

Denmark Strait, sea passage (180 mi. wide at narrowest point) bet. Greenland and Iceland, cut by Arctic Circle; c.300 mi. long. Icebergs are carried through strait by cold East Greenland Current. In Second World War German battleship *Bismarck* here sank (May, 1941) British battleship *Hood.*

Dennery, village (pop. 1,387), E St. Lucia, B.W.I., landing 9 mi. SE of Castries; limes, tropical fruit.

Dennewitz (dĕ'nŭvĭts), village (pop. 618), Brandenburg, E Germany, 4 mi. SW of Jüterbog. Scene (Sept., 1813) of victory of Prussians under Bülow over French forces under Marshal Ney.

Denning, town (pop. 268), Franklin co., NW Ark., 15 mi. W of Clarksville, near Arkansas R.

Dennis. 1 Resort town (pop. 2,499), Barnstable co., SE Mass., extending across central Cape Cod, 6 mi. ENE of Barnstable; cranberries. Has summer theater, Cape Playhouse (1927). Includes villages of Dennis Port (pop. 1,080), East Dennis, South Dennis, and West Dennis. Settled 1639, set off from Yarmouth 1793. **2** Village (pop. 158), Tishomingo co., NE Miss., 35 mi. NE of Tupelo; lumber milling.

Dennis Island, Seychelles: see DENIS ISLAND.

Dennison. 1 Village (pop. 163), Goodhue and Rice counties, SE Minn., c.40 mi. S of St. Paul; cheese. **2** Village (pop. 4,432), Tuscarawas co., E Ohio, on Stillwater Creek, opposite Uhrichsville; makes sewer pipe, chinaware, sheet-metal products. Founded 1864. About 5 mi. SE, a flood-control dam impounds Tappan Reservoir (capacity 61,600 acre-ft.) in Little Stillwater Creek.

Dennis Port, Mass.: see DENNIS.

Denniston, New Zealand: see WESTPORT.

Dennistown, plantation (pop. 24), Somerset co., W Maine, on Que. line just NW of Jackman; hunting, fishing.

Dennisville, village (pop. c.400), Cape May co., SE N.J., 19 mi. SE of Millville. Adjoins Great Cedar Swamp, which has giant prehistoric white cedars preserved in the mire.

Denny and Dunipace (dŭ'nĭpās), burgh (1931 pop. 5,512; 1951 census 6,692), E Stirling, Scotland. Includes Denny (pop. 4,277), on Carron R. and 5 mi. WNW of Falkirk, with coal mines, steel and paper mills. Just N is coal-mining town of Dunipace (pop. 1,235).

Denny Island (□ 51), SW B.C., in NE part of Queen Charlotte Sound; 52°7'N 128°W; 11 mi. long, 6 mi. wide. On NE coast is Bella Bella village.

Dennyloanhead, town in Denny parish, E Stirling, Scotland, 2 mi. S of Denny; coal mining.

Dennys Bay (dĕ'nĭs), Washington co., E Maine, inlet of Cobscook Bay; extends c.10 mi. N-S bet. Dennysville and Whiting. Formerly called Cobscook R.

Dennys River, Washington co., E Maine, rises in Meddybemps L., flows c.17 mi. S and E to Dennys Bay below Dennysville; noted for salmon fishing.

Dennysville, town (pop. 345), Washington co., E Maine, on Dennys R. and Dennys Bay; noted for salmon fishing.

Deno (dĕ'nô), peak (9,122 ft.) in E Rila Mts., W Bulgaria, 9 mi. SSE of Samokov.

Den Oever (dŭn ōō'vŭr), village (pop. 1,497), North Holland prov., NW Netherlands, on former Wieringen isl. and 12 mi. ESE of Helder, on the Ijsselmeer, at SW end of Ijsselmeer Dam; sluices and 46-ft.-wide navigation lock here. Fishing.

Denousa or **Dhenousa** (both: dhēnōō'sü), Aegean island (□ 5.5; pop. 213), in the Cyclades, Greece, E of Naxos isl.; 37°6'N 25°50'E; 4 mi. long, 4 mi. wide. Sometimes spelled Dinousa.

Denpasar (dĕnpä'sär), town (pop. 16,639), S Bali, Indonesia, 40 mi. SSE of Singaraja and 200 mi. ESE of Surabaya; 8°40'S 115°14'E; copra-trading center. Has numerous Hindu temples. Airport is near by. Conference held here 1946 established temporary state of East Indonesia.

Densu River (dĕn'sōō), S Gold Coast, rises NW of Koforidua, flows c.70 mi. S, past Nsawam, to Gulf of Guinea 7 mi. WSW of Accra. Water supply of Accra is furnished by Weija waterworks, 8 mi. WNW of Accra (linked by narrow-gauge railroad).

Dent, agr. village and parish (pop. 925), West Riding, NW Yorkshire, England, 4 mi. SE of Sedbergh.

Dent, county (□ 756; pop. 10,936), SE central Mo.; ⊙ Salem. In the Ozarks; drained by Meramec R. Agr. (corn, wheat, hay), livestock; oak, pine timber; iron mines. Part of Clark Natl. Forest is here. Formed 1851.

Dent, village (pop. 187), Otter Tail co., W Minn., 25 mi. NE of Fergus Falls, in lake region; dairy products.

Dent Blanche (dã blăsh'), peak (14,304 ft.) in Pennine Alps, S Switzerland, 7 mi. W of Zermatt.

Dent de Morcles (dã dů môr'klů), peak (9,777 ft.) in the Alps, SW Switzerland, 6 mi. N of Martigny-Ville; hamlet of Morcles is at WNW base.

Dent de Ruth (dã dů rüt'), peak (7,336 ft.) in the Alps, W Switzerland, 6 mi. W of Zweisimmen.

Dent d'Oche, La (lä dã dôsh'), peak (7,300 ft.) of the Chablais massif (Savoy Alps), near Swiss border, overlooking L. Geneva, 8 mi. ESE of Évian-les-Bains.

Dent du Midi (dã dü mēdē') [Fr.,=southern tooth] or **Dents du Midi**, mountain in the Western Alps, SW Switzerland near Fr. border. Its highest peak, the Haute Cime (10,695 ft.), is 8 mi. NW of Martigny-Ville. Other peaks include Cime de l'Est (or Dent Noire) (10,433 ft.), Forteresse (10,381 ft.), Cathédrale (10,387 ft.), Dent Jaune (10,456 ft.), and les Doigts (10,538 ft.).

Dent Noire, Switzerland: see CIME DE L'EST.

Denton. 1 Urban district (1931 pop. 17,384; 1951 census 25,612), SE Lancashire, England, near Cheshire boundary, just ESE of Manchester; cotton milling; coal mining; mfg. of leather, chemicals, machinery, dry batteries, hosiery; metallurgy. Has church dating partly from 16th cent. Site of Manchester reservoir. **2** Town, Northumberland, England: see NEWBURN. **3** Suburb, Sussex, England: see NEWHAVEN.

Denton, county (□ 942; pop. 41,365), N Texas; ⊙ Denton. Drained by Elm Fork of Trinity R., site of Garza–Little Elm project (under construction 1949), whose reservoir will engulf L. Dallas. Rich agr. area (cotton, wheat, oats, corn, hay, pecans, peanuts, fruit, truck); extensive dairying, poultry raising; also beef cattle, sheep, hogs. Some oil, natural gas; clay, limestone deposits. Formed 1846.

Denton. 1 City (pop. 273), Jeff Davis co., SE central Ga., 11 mi. SSW of Hazelhurst. **2** City (pop. 157), Doniphan co., extreme NE Kansas, 23 mi. W of St. Joseph, Mo.; apples. **3** Town (pop. 1,806), ⊙ Caroline co. (since 1791), E Md., on Delmarva Peninsula, 26 mi. NE of Cambridge and on Choptank R.; lumber mills, vegetable canneries, poultry-dressing plants. Settled c.1765. **4** Town (pop. 126), Pemiscot co., extreme SE Mo., in Mississippi flood plain, 16 mi. WSW of Caruthersville. **5** Town (pop. 435), Fergus co., central Mont., on branch of Judith R. and 30 mi. NW of Lewistown; shipping point for grain and livestock. **6** Village (pop. 101), Lancaster co., SE Nebr., 9 mi. WSW of Lincoln. **7** Town (pop. 766), Davidson co., central N.C., 15 mi. SSE of Lexington; hosiery and furniture mfg., lumber milling. **8** City (pop. 21,372), ⊙ Denton co., N Texas, 34 mi. NNE of Fort Worth. Seat of North Texas State Col. and Texas State Col. for Women. Processing center of agr. region (grain, cotton, corn, peanuts); peanut shelling, flour milling, mfg. of clay products, cheese, beverages, clothing, tanks. Agr. experiment station near by. Founded 1855, inc. 1866.

Denton Creek, N Texas, a W tributary of Elm Fork of Trinity River, rises in Montague co., flows c.75 mi. SE. Grapevine Reservoir, on the creek, is a unit of Trinity R. flood-control, conservation development.

D'Entrecasteaux Channel (dãtrůkästō'), inlet of Tasman Sea, bet. SE coast of Tasmania (W) and Bruny isl. (E); merges with Derwent R. estuary (N) and opens (NE) into Storm Bay; outlet for Huon R. estuary. Many small bays; Port Esperance is site of Dover.

D'Entrecasteaux Islands (dãtrůkästō'), volcanic group (□ c.1,200; pop. c.33,800), Territory of Papua, SW Pacific, 25 mi. SE of New Guinea; comprise FERGUSSON ISLAND (largest), GOODENOUGH ISLAND, NORMANBY ISLAND. Mountainous; highest peak (8,500 ft.) on Goodenough Isl. Extinct volcanoes, hot springs and geysers. Coconuts, pearl shell. Named for 18th-cent. Fr. navigator.

Dents de Veisivi (dã dů väsēvē'), 2 peaks in the Alps, S Switzerland, 9 mi. NW of the Matterhorn: Grande Dent de Veisivi (11,214 ft.) and Petite Dent de Veisivi (10,445 ft.).

Denu (dĕ'nōō), town, Eastern Prov., SE Gold Coast colony, on Gulf of Guinea, near Fr. Togoland border, 15 mi. NE of Keta; fishing; coconuts, cassava, corn.

Denver. 1 City (pop. 415,786), ⊙ Colo. and coextensive with Denver co. (□ 58), N central Colo., on South Platte R., at mouth of Cherry Creek, just E of Front Range of Rocky Mts., and c.550 mi. WNW of Kansas City, Mo.; 39°41'N 104°57'W; alt. 5,280 ft.; metropolis of the Rockies. Largest city in Colo., Denver was settled 1858, inc. 1861, and made state capital 1867; coextensive co. formed 1902. In 1870s and '80s it grew as mining center because of rich strikes in gold and silver in vicinity. Bet. 1880 and 1890 pop. increased from 35,629 to 106,713. Foundries, machine shops, and smelters were built, Tabor Grand Opera House was completed, and bonanza kings erected elaborate homes. After depression of 1890s city developed as distribution, financial, and industrial center for extensive livestock and agr. region. It is now served by several railroads, transcontinental airlines, and highways, and, by means of Moffat Tunnel and Dotsero cutoff, has direct rail route to Pacific coast. Mfg. of mining and farm machinery, tires and other rubber products, flour, feed, confectionery, furniture, electrical apparatus, explosives, clothing, and cotton, clay, and fiber products; large stockyards (especially for sheep); meat packing, canning (fruits and vegetables), oil refining; motor-car assembly. Fur market. Denver is financial center of the Rockies. Because of location and climate, it is a popular health resort and recreation center, with heavy tourist trade in summer. Administration hq. for numerous Federal agencies here; U.S. customhouse and mint. Has park system, with extensive mtn. areas. Educational institutions include Univ. of Denver, Loretto Heights Col., Regis Col., Iliff School of Theology (Methodist), Univ. of Colo. Medical School, women's jr. col., Rockmount Col., Westminster Law School, Emily Griffith Opportunity School (for education of those deprived of schooling). Points of interest: Palace Theater (1873), Windsor Hotel (1880), City and County Building (housing Denver Art Mus.), State Mus. Building (hq. of State Historical Society), civic center (with public library, theater, and Voorhies Memorial), capitol building, Cathedral of Immaculate Conception (R.C.), Cathedral of St. John's in the Wilderness (Protestant Episcopal), Temple Emanuel (Reformed Hebrew), Colo. Mus. of Natural History, zoological gardens, a naval air station, and Lowry Air Force Base. Near by are LOOKOUT MOUNTAIN, Fitzsimons General Hosp., Denver Home for indigents, Colo. School of Mines, and Fort Logan (summer training center for Reserve Officers Training Corps). City is also known for civic symphony orchestra and for its juvenile court. **2** Town (pop. 528), Miami co., N central Ind., on Eel R. and 8 mi. N of Peru; poultry, fruit, dairy products. **3** Town (pop. 635), Bremer co., NE Iowa, 12 mi. N of Waterloo; creamery, feed mill, machine shop. **4** Town (pop. 144), Worth co., NW Mo., on East Fork of Grand R. and 29 mi. ENE of Maryville. **5** Town (pop. 415), Lincoln co., S N.C., 13 mi. NE of Lincolnton. **6** Borough (pop. 1,658), Lancaster co., SE Pa., 14 mi. SW of Reading; clothing, shoes, flour, tobacco. Settled 1863, inc. 1900.

Denver City, town (pop. 1,855), Yoakum co., NW Texas, on the Llano Estacado, c.70 mi. SW of Lubbock; trade, supply point for oil region. Inc. after 1940.

Denville, resort village (1940 pop. 1,887), Morris co., N central N.J., on small Indian L. (c.½ mi. long), 6 mi. N of Morristown; fruit, truck, dairy products.

Denzil (dĕn'zĭl), village (pop. 226), W Sask., 70 mi. SW of North Battleford; wheat.

Denzlingen (dĕnts'lĭng-ůn), village (pop. 2,643), S Baden, Germany, on W slope of Black Forest, 4 mi. SSE of Emmendingen; rail junction; tobacco.

Deoband (dā'ōbŭnd), town (pop. 24,662), Saharanpur dist., N Uttar Pradesh, India, on railroad and 21 mi. SSE of Saharanpur; trades in wheat, rice, rape, mustard, gram; hand-loom cotton-weaving center. Noted Arabic Col., founded 1876. Annual religious festival near by.

Deodoro, Brazil: see PIRAQUARA.

Deodrug (dā'ōdrōōg), town (pop. 7,433), Raichur dist., SW Hyderabad state, India, 33 mi. WNW of Raichur; millet; cotton ginning, rice and oilseed milling. Sometimes spelled Deodurg.

Deogaon (dā'ōgoun), village, Azamgarh dist., E Uttar Pradesh, India, 26 mi. SSW of Azamgarh; rice, barley, wheat, sugar cane.

Deogarh (dā'ōgŭr). **1** Town, Bihar, India: see DEOGHAR. **2** Village, Madhya Pradesh, India: see CHHINDWARA, town. **3** Town (pop. 6,537), Sambalpur dist., N Orissa, India, 50 mi. E of Sambalpur; local market for rice, timber, lac. Was ⊙ former princely state of Bamra. **4** Town (pop. 5,742), S central Rajasthan, India, 65 mi. NNE of Udaipur, in Aravalli Range; local market (millet, corn, barley, cotton). **5** Village, Jhansi dist., S Uttar Pradesh, India, on the Betwa and 16 mi. SSW of Lalitpur. Here are ruins of Rajput fort held by Bundela Rajputs until captured (1811) by Mahrattas; also extensive Jain temple ruins, rock carvings, and inscriptions (date from A.D. 1097), some of which are important examples of Gupta period in Indian art. Chandel Rajput ruins and inscriptions (including one dated A.D. 868) at Chandpur village, 6 mi. ESE.

Deoghar or **Deogarh** (dā'ōgŭr), town (pop. 19,792), Santal Parganas dist., E Bihar, India, 55 mi. SSW of Bhagalpur; road junction; rice, corn, barley, oilseeds, rape and mustard. Coal mining near by. Pilgrimage center; Sivaite temples, Buddhist ruins. Rail station 4 mi. NW, at Baidyanathdham.

Deogiri, India: see DAULATABAD.

Deolali (dāōlä'lē, dāvlä'lē), town (pop. 16,292), Nasik dist., central Bombay, India, 6 mi. SSE of Nasik; military station; agr. market (chiefly millet, wheat, rice). Sometimes spelled Devlali.

Deolgaon-Raja, India: see DEULGAON RAJA.

Deoli (dā'ōlē). **1** Town (pop. 4,071), SE Ajmer state, India, 65 mi. SE of Ajmer; local agr. market (millet, corn, wheat, cotton). **2** Town (pop. 6,646), Wardha dist., central Madhya Pradesh, India, 10 mi. SW of Wardha; cotton ginning; hand-weaving cotton industry; large weekly cattle market; millet, wheat, oilseeds. Deoli was formerly also spelled Devli.

Deolia, India: see PARTABGARH, town, Rajasthan.

Déols (dāôl'), N suburb (pop. 3,206) of Châteauroux, Indre dept., central France, on right bank of Indre R. Has remarkable Romanesque tower with conical spire and 12th-cent. arches and columns which represent only remains of Cluniac abbey founded 917 and sacked by Huguenots in 1569. The 15th–16th-cent. church of Saint-Étienne contains the statue of Notre-Dame-de-Déols (goal of pilgrims) and Gallo-Roman crypts.

Deorha (dā'ōrhŭ), village, SE Himachel Pradesh, India, 30 mi. E of Simla, in W Kumaun Himalayas; exports timber (deodar) and rice. Was ⊙ former Punjab Hill state of Jubbal.

Deori (dā'ōrē). **1** Town (pop. 2,757), E Bhopal state, India, 80 mi. E of Bhopal; cotton, wheat. **2** Town (pop. 6,911), Saugor dist., N Madhya Pradesh, India, 35 mi. SSE of Saugor; wheat, oilseeds, millet.

Deoria (dā'ōryŭ), town (pop. 15,198), Gorakhpur dist., E Uttar Pradesh, India, 31 mi. SE of Gorakhpur; sugar milling; rice, wheat, barley, oilseeds.

Deorukh, India: see DEVRUKH.

Deosai Mountains (dā'ōsī), N lateral range of Punjab Himalayas, W central Kashmir; from Indus R. bend N of Bunji extend c.120 mi. SE to Suru R., which separates Deosai Mts. and Zaskar Range; several peaks rise to over 18,000 ft. Rondu, Skardu, and Kargil villages lie at foot; Burji La pass is SW of Skardu. Sometimes considered a trans-Indus extension of Ladakh Range or a trans-Suru extension of Zaskar Range.

Deo Van, Vietnam: see CLOUDS, PASS OF THE.

De Panne, Belgium: see PANNE, DE.

De Peel (dů pāl'), marshy area in North Brabant prov. and Limburg prov., SE Netherlands, bet. Deurne (NW), Meijel (SW), Kessel (SE), and Blerick (NE); c.7 mi. wide, 20 mi. long. Consists mostly of reclaimed fenland and heath, drained by a branch canal of the Zuid-Willemsvaart. Vegetable growing, strawboard mfg., peat digging. Chief village, Helenaveen (pop. 705), North Brabant prov., 14 mi. NNW of Roermond.

De Pere (dĭ pēr'), city (pop. 8,146), Brown co., E Wis., on Fox R. and 5 mi. SSW of Green Bay City; mfg. center (paper, boats, bricks, farm equipment, pharmaceuticals, flour). Has large hydroelectric plant. St. Norberts Col. is at near-by West De Pere. Father Allouez founded here in 1671 the St. Francis Xavier Mission. De Pere grew in 19th cent. as lumber town, port, and commercial center. Inc. 1883.

Depew (dĭpū'). **1** Industrial village (pop. 7,217), Erie co., W N.Y., just E of Buffalo; mfg. (textiles, castings, cereals, bags, cut and crushed stone, machinery, storage batteries, mattresses, feed); railroad shops. Inc. 1894. **2** Town (pop. 719), Creek co., central Okla., 37 mi. SW of Tulsa, in agr. area; cotton ginning; oil wells.

Depienne (dụpyĕn') or **Smindja** (smēnjä'), village, Zaghouan dist., N central Tunisia, 24 mi. SSW of Tunis; rail junction; cereals, wine. Agr. school.

De Pinte, Belgium: see PINTE, DE.

Deport (dē'pôrt), town (pop. 734), Lamar and Red River counties, NE Texas, 17 mi. SE of Paris; trade point in agr. area (cotton, cattle, corn, alfalfa); cotton gins.

Deposit, resort village (pop. 2,016), on Broome-Delaware co. line, S N.Y., on West Branch of the Delaware and 25 mi. ESE of Binghamton, near Pa. line; mfg. (feed, food products, lumber, machinery). Settled 1785, inc. 1811.

Depot Harbour (dē'pō), village (pop. estimate 450), S central Ont., on Parry Sound, inlet of Georgian Bay, 4 mi. WSW of Parry Sound town; grain and coal port.

Deptford (dĕt′fûrd), metropolitan borough (1931 pop. 106,891; 1951 census 75,694) of London, England, on S bank of the Thames, 4 mi. SE of Charing Cross. An industrial and residential section, noted in Elizabethan times for its cattle market and royal dockyard (built 1513, closed down 1869), where Peter the Great worked as shipwright. Christopher Marlowe was killed (in local inn) and is buried here.

Depue (dēpū′), village (pop. 2,163), Bureau co., N Ill., on Illinois R. and 11 mi. W of La Salle, in agr. and bituminous-coal area; zinc plant. L. Depue (c.3 mi. long), a bayou of Illinois R., is S. Inc. 1867.

De Queen (dē kwēn′), city (pop. 3,015), ⊙ Sevier co., SW Ark., c.45 mi. NNW of Texarkana, near Okla. line; rail center and shipping point for rich agr. area (fruit, vegetables, cotton, livestock, poultry; dairy products). Railroad shops, lumber and creosoting plants. Inc. 1897.

Dequen (dûkă′), village, central Que., 11 mi. SSE of Roberval; silica mining.

De Quincy (dĭ kwĭn′sē), town (pop. 3,837), Calcasieu parish, SW La., 20 mi. NW of Lake Charles city, in oil-producing and agr. area (truck, fruit, poultry, sheep, cattle); naval stores, wood products, tung oil. Settled 1898, inc. 1902.

Der'a (dĕr-ă′) or **Dir'a** (dĭr-ă′), Fr. *Déraa*, town (pop. c.5,000), ⊙ Hauran prov., SW Syria, near Jordan border, on railroad, and 60 mi. SSW of Damascus; cereals, wheat.

Dera Bassi, India: see BASI, E Patiala and East Punjab States Union.

Dera Ghazi Khan (dā′rŭ gä′zē khän′), district (□ 9,364, including W tribal area; 1951 pop. 628,000), SW Punjab, W Pakistan; ⊙ Dera Ghazi Khan. Bounded E by Indus R.; consists of alluvial tract (N section in Derajat plain) rising to Sulaiman Range (4–7,000 ft.) in W. Wheat, millet, rice, oilseeds grown in irrigated (E) area; date palms along the Indus. Hand-loom weaving; woolen products; cattle breeding. Chief towns: Dera Ghazi Khan, Jampur, Taunsa.

Dera Ghazi Khan, town (pop. 32,139), ⊙ Dera Ghazi Khan dist., SW Punjab, W Pakistan, 50 mi. WSW of Multan, in the Derajat; trade center (grain, cotton, dates, indigo, cloth fabrics); cotton ginning, rice husking, flour and oilseed milling, handicrafts (silk cloth, ivory bangles, woolen products). Has col. of arts. Cattle breeding near by. Formerly on Indus R. (7 mi. E); because of periodic floods, moved to present site in early 1900s.

Dera Ismail Khan (ĭsmīl′ khän′), district (□ 4,216; 1951 pop. 283,000), S North-West Frontier Prov., W Pakistan; ⊙ Dera Ismail Khan. Bordered by Sulaiman Range (W), Indus R. (E); mainly a level plain (the Derajat), partly irrigated, and producing wheat, millet, rapeseed. Hand-loom weaving, ghee mfg., camel breeding; petroleum in NE corner. Towns: Dera Ismail Khan, Tank, Kulachi. Held (early-19th cent.) by Sikhs under Ranjit Singh. Dist. exercises control over adjoining tribal area (pop. 48,000). Pop. 86% Moslem, 13% Hindu, 1% Sikh.

Dera Ismail Khan, city (pop. 49,238; including cantonment area, 51,306), ⊙ Dera Ismail Khan dist., S North-West Frontier Prov., W Pakistan, on the Indus and 150 mi. SSW of Peshawar; agr. market (wheat, millet, gram, oilseeds); trade center (grain, firewood, cloth fabrics, ghee); hand-loom weaving (turbans), fodder pressing, ice mfg., wood lacquering. Col.

Derajat (dā′rŭjät), alluvial plain in SW Punjab and SE North-West Frontier Prov., W Pakistan, in Dera Ghazi Khan and Dera Ismail Khan dists., bet. Indus R. (E) and Sulaiman Range (W); c.180 mi. long, c.40 mi. wide. Partly irrigated and drained by numerous seasonal streams; produces wheat, millet, rice, oilseeds.

Dera Nanak or **Dera Baba Nanak** (dā′rŭ bä′bŭ nä′nŭk), town (pop. 5,872), Gurdaspur dist., NW Punjab, India, near Ravi R., 22 mi. W of Gurdaspur; wheat, gram, corn; land-loom woolen weaving, embroidering. Built in memory of Guru Nanak, founder of Sikhism, who lived near by.

Dera Nawab or **Dera Nawab Sahib** (dā′rŭ nŭväb′ sŭhēb′), town (pop. 4,455), Bahawalpur state, W Pakistan, 3 mi. S of Ahmadpur East; cotton, wheat; leather goods; camel breeding. Dera Nawab rail station is ½ mi. NW of Ahmadpur East.

Derapur (dā′räpōōr), village, Cawnpore dist., S Uttar Pradesh, India, on tributary of the Jumna and 24 mi. W of Cawnpore; gram, wheat, jowar, mustard, barley.

Deravica, Albania-Yugoslavia: see DJERAVICA.

Deraya, Derayeh, or **Dar'iyah** (all: dĕr-ē′yŭ), village, central Nejd, Saudi Arabia, 10 mi. WNW of Riyadh, on site of flourishing old Wahabi capital, destroyed 1818 by Egyptian punitive expedition and succeeded by Riyadh.

Derazhno (dyĭräzh′nŭ), Pol. *Deraźne* (dĕräzh′nĕ), village (1939 pop. over 500), W Rovno oblast, Ukrainian SSR, on Goryn R. and 18 mi. NNW of Rovno; rye, wheat, oats, potatoes.

Derazhnya (–nyŭ), town (1926 pop. 5,659), E Kamenets-Podolski oblast, Ukrainian SSR, 22 mi. ESE of Proskurov; metalworks.

Derazne, Ukrainian SSR: see DERAZHNO.

Derbenevo, Russian SFSR: see KAMESHKOVO.

Derbent (dyĭrbyĕnt′), city (1926 pop. 23,097), SE Dagestan Autonomous SSR, Russian SFSR, on Caspian coastal railroad and 75 mi. SSE of Makhachkala; industrial center; fishing port; fruit and vegetable canning, woolen milling, mfg. of chemicals (nitrates), wine making, distilling. Cold-storage facilities. Agr. experimental station (grapes). Glassworks at Dagestanskiye Ogni, 6 mi. NW. Has remains of anc. Caucasian Wall or Alexander Wall, built 6th cent. by Persians as a bulwark against northern invaders. Derbent was founded (5th or 6th cent.) by Persians at the Caspian (or Iron) Gates, a defile at E end of the Greater Caucasus, on major commercial and migration route. Passed (728) to Arabs, who made it a center of arts and commerce, and in 1220 to Mongols. Briefly held (1722) by Peter the Great; besieged (1796) by Russians. Finally annexed by Russia in 1813.

Derbeshkinski or **Derbeshkinskiy** (dyĭrbyĕsh′-kĭnskē), town (1940 pop. over 500), NE Tatar Autonomous SSR, Russian SFSR, port on left bank of Kama R., near mouth of Belaya R., and 17 mi. NE of Menzelinsk; sawmilling, metalworking. Until 1940, Derbeshka.

Derbesiye (dĕrbĕ′sĭyĕ″), village (pop. 1,108), Mardin prov., SE Turkey, 8 mi. SSE of Kiziltepe; rail junction.

Derbinskoye, Russian SFSR: see TYMOVSKOYE.

Derbisiye or **Darbisiyah** (därbĭsē′yŭ), Fr. *Derbissié*, town, Jezire prov., NE Syria, on Turkish frontier, on railroad, and 40 mi. N of El Haseke; sheep raising; cereals. Oil deposits.

Derby (där′bē), port (pop. 326), N Western Australia, on W arm of King Sound, near mouth of Fitzroy R., and 600 mi. SW of Darwin; 17°20′S 123°40′E. Exports wool, cattle, gold. Airport.

Derby (dûr′bē), E N.B., on Southwest Miramichi R. and 9 mi. SW of Newcastle; freestone quarrying.

Derby or **Derbyshire** (där′bē,–shĭr,–shûr), county (□ 1,006; 1931 pop. 757,374; 1951 census 826,-336), central England; ⊙ Derby. Bounded by Yorkshire (N), Nottingham (E), Leicester (SE), Stafford (W), Cheshire (W and N). Drained by Derwent, Dove, Wye, and Trent rivers. Mountainous in N and NW (The PEAK), flat or undulating to S. Dairying and pasturing in hilly districts; arable farming. Has several mineral springs and resorts (Buxton, The Matlocks, Bakewell); important coal mines in N, E, and S; lead mining and limestone quarrying. Other industries are steel milling (Chesterfield, Whittington), cotton, silk, and artificial-silk milling, leather tanning, paper and pottery mfg., metal casting. Derby is a major engineering center. Other important towns: Ilkeston, Glossop, Swadlincote District, Long Eaton, Alfreton.

Derby, county borough (1931 pop. 142,403; 1951 census 141,264) and city, ⊙ Derby, England, in S part of co., on Derwent R. and 120 mi. NNW of London; 52°55′N 1°28′W; rail center with large repair shops; produces automobiles, automobile and aircraft engines, knitted goods, leather, pottery, cotton and silk yarns and threads, paint, soap, electrical appliances. Has Church of All Saints (1509–27), St. Mary's R.C. church (1838), built by Pugin, and an inn dating from 1530. The 1st silk mill in England was built here 1717. Henry Cavendish and Herbert Spencer were b. here, and Derby was the home of George Eliot. In county borough are towns of: Normanton (SW, pop. 7,649) with chemical industries; Little Chester (N; with optical glass-works), site of Roman station of *Derventio;* and Litchurch (SE; pop. 8,201).

Derby, town (pop. 593), NE Tasmania, 39 mi. NE of Launceston and on Ringarooma R.; tin mining, dairying.

Derby (dûr′bē). **1** Village (pop. 2,840), Adams co., N central Colo., a NE suburb of Denver. **2** Industrial city (pop. 10,259), coextensive with Derby town, New Haven co., SW Conn., on Housatonic R., at mouth of Naugatuck R., and 8 mi. W of New Haven. Mfg. (machinery, tools, rubber products, wire and metal products, chemicals, automobile and airplane parts, textiles, corsets). Yale Univ. spring regatta held on the Housatonic here. Founded 1642 as trading post; inc. as town 1675, as city 1893. **3** Town (pop. 194), Lucas co., S Iowa, near Chariton R., 10 mi. SW of Chariton. **4** City (pop. 432), Sedgwick co., S Kansas, on Arkansas R. and 11 mi. SSE of Wichita; wheat. Called El Paso until 1930. **5** Village, Piscataquis co., Maine: see MILO. **6** Village (1940 pop. 714), Erie co., W N.Y., near L. Erie, 15 mi. SSW of Buffalo, in grape-growing region. **7** Town (pop. 2,245), Orleans co., N Vt., at Que. line, just NE of Newport; granite, metal products. Includes villages of Derby Center (pop. 383) and Derby Line (pop. 767). Derby Line, on high (1,029 ft.) plateau, is port of entry; has Canadian-American World War memorial.

Derbyhaven or **Derby Haven** (där′bē–), fishing village on SE coast of Isle of Man, England, at neck of Langness peninsula. Site of Derby Fort (1645). Dreswick Point, 2 mi. S, has lighthouse (54°3′N 4°4′W). Near by is Isle of Man airport.

Derby Line, Vt.: see DERBY.

Derbyshire, England: see DERBY, county.

Derdap, Rumania: see IRON GATE.

Derdepoort (dĕr′dûpōōrt″), village, W Transvaal, U. of So. Afr., on Bechuanaland Protectorate border, 65 mi. NNE of Zeerust; scene (1849) of foundation of Vereenigde Bond [union] which became (1853) South African Republic.

Derdj, Fezzan: see DERG.

Derecske (dĕ′rĕch-kĕ), town (pop. 10,399), Bihar co., E Hungary, 13 mi. S of Debrecen; wheat, tobacco, cattle.

Dereham, England: see EAST DEREHAM.

Derekegyhaz (dĕ′rĕkĕdyûhäz), Hung. *Derekegyház*, town (pop. 1,937), Csongrad co., S Hungary, 11 mi. N of Hodmezövasarhely; wheat, corn, cattle.

Dereli, Greece: see GONNOS.

Derenburg (dā′rŭnbōōrk), town (pop. 4,057), in former Prussian Saxony prov., central Germany, after 1945 in Saxony-Anhalt, at N foot of the lower Harz, on the Holtemme and 7 mi. W of Halberstadt; agr. market (grain, potatoes, livestock).

Derendingen (dĕ′rĕndĭng″ŭn), town (pop. 3,741), Solothurn canton, NW Switzerland, on Emme R. and 2 mi. ESE of Solothurn; woolen textiles, pastry.

Derg or **Derdj** (both: dĕrj), village (pop. 937), N Fezzan, Libya, 55 mi. E of Ghadames, in an oasis; alt. c.1,640 ft. Caravan center; weaving (barracans, blankets, carpets), date growing.

Derg, Lough (lŏkh dûrg′). **1** Lake (23 mi. long, 1–5 mi. wide), Ireland, expansion of the Shannon bet. cos. Galway (NW), Clare (W), and Tipperary (E). W shore is mountainous, E shore is level. Numerous isls. in lough, including Holy Isl. or Iniscaltra, site of 10th-cent. round tower and of 7th-cent. monastic ruins. **2** Lake (3 mi. long, 3 mi. wide), S Co. Donegal, Ireland, 4 mi. WNW of Pettigo. Near S end of lake is Station Isl., place of pilgrimage.

Dergachi (dyĕrgŭchē′). **1** Village (1926 pop. 7,872), E Saratov oblast, Russian SFSR, 23 mi. ESE of Yershov; flour milling, metalworking; wheat, cattle, sheep. **2** Town (1926 pop. 11,958), N Kharkov oblast, Ukrainian SSR, 10 mi. NNW of Kharkov; metalworking center.

De Ridder, city (pop. 5,799), ⊙ Beauregard parish, W La., c.45 mi. N of Lake Charles city; wool market, and trade and processing center for sheep-raising, lumbering, and diversified-farming area (sweet potatoes, soybeans, grain, citrus fruit, livestock, truck). Also produces creosoted products, lumber, naval stores, cotton and cottonseed products, chemicals, mattresses, dairy products, pickles. Oil field near by. Inc. 1907.

Dérik, Syria: see DARIK.

Derik (dĕrĭk′), village (pop. 3,586), Mardin prov., SE Turkey, 25 mi. W of Mardin; wheat, barley, chick-peas, onions; mohair goats.

Dering Harbor (dĕr′ĭng), village (pop. 4), Suffolk co., SE N.Y., on N Shelter Isl., in summer-resort area.

Deritend (dĕrĭtĕnd′), E industrial suburb (pop. 39,309) of Birmingham, NW Warwick, England.

Derkush (dĕrkōōsh′) or **Darkush** (där–), Fr. *Derkouche*, village, Aleppo prov., NW Syria, on Turkish border, on Orontes R., and 45 mi. WSW of Aleppo; cereals.

Derma, town (pop. 494), Calhoun co., N central Miss., 30 mi. E of Grenada, near Yalobusha R.

Dermantsi (dĕrmän′tsē), village (pop. 5,0(0), Pleven dist., N Bulgaria, on Vit R. and 6 mi. SE of Lukovit; flour milling; livestock, truck.

Dermayo, Indonesia: see INDRAMAYU.

Dermott (dûr′mŭt), city (pop. 3,601), Chicot co., extreme SE Ark., 22 mi. WNW of Greenville, Miss., near the Bayou Bartholomew; trade center for agr. area (cotton, corn, oats, truck); sawmilling, woodworking, cotton ginning, pecan shelling. Settled 1832.

Derna (dĕr′nä), town (1950 pop. 20,782), E Cyrenaica, Libya, port on Mediterranean Sea, on coastal road and 60 mi. ENE of Benghazi, in an oasis (dates, figs, bananas, citrus, fruit); 32°45′N 22°34′E. Commercial center and winter resort; distilleries, limekilns, cementworks, flour mill, ice and soap factories; artisan metalworking. Has mosques (16th–17th cent.), modern European section, and airport. Occupied 1805 by U.S. after war against its pirates. Under Turkish rule until 1911, when it was taken by the Italians. Changed hands several times in fighting (1941–42) bet. Axis and British in Second World War; finally won by British in 1942.

Dernau (dĕr′nou), village (pop. 1,365), in former Prussian Rhine Prov., W Germany, after 1945 in Rhineland-Palatinate, on the Ahr and 2.5 mi. W of Ahrweiler; known for its red wine.

Dernis, Yugoslavia: see DRNIS.

Déroun Agha, Syria: see DEIR 'AWN AGHA.

Déroute, Passage de la (päsäzh′ dû lä dārōōt′), strait of English Channel, off NW France, bet. Channel Isls. (W) and coast of Cotentin Peninsula (E), extending approximately from Race of Alderney (N) to Chausey Isls. (S). Navigation hazards.

Derr, Egypt: see DIRR, EL.

Derravaragh, Lough (lŏkh dĕ″rŭvă′rä), lake (6 mi. long, up to 3 mi. wide), N central Co. Westmeath, Ireland, 6 mi. N of Mullingar.

Derry, Northern Ireland: see LONDONDERRY.

Derry. 1 Town (pop. 5,826), Rockingham co., SE N.H., 10 mi. SE of Manchester and on small Beaver Brook (water power), in agr. and resort area; shoe and textile mfg. has declined. Robert Frost taught at Pinkerton Acad. here. Horse races on ice held here. Set off 1827 from Londonderry. **2** Borough (pop. 3,752), Westmoreland co., SW central Pa., 13 mi. E of Greensburg; porcelain insulators; sandstone. Inc. 1881.

Derrynasaggart Mountains (dĕ″rēnŭsă′gûrt), range extending 15 mi. WSW–ENE along border of Co. Cork and Co. Kerry, Ireland, rising to 2,239 ft. in Caherbarnagh.

Derryveach Mountains (dĕ″rēvēch′), range extending 25 mi. NE–SW across NW Co. Donegal, Ireland; rise to 2,466 ft. in Mt. Errigail.

Dersim, province, Turkey: see TUNCELI.

Dersim, village, Turkey: see HOZAT.

Dersingham, town and parish (pop. 1,528), NW Norfolk, England, 7 mi. S of New Hunstanton; agr. market. Has 15th-cent. church.

Dertona, Italy: see TORTONA.

Dertosa, Spain: see TORTOSA.

Derudeb or **Derudeib** (both: dĕrŏŏdĕb′), village, Kassala prov., NE Anglo-Egyptian Sudan, on railroad and 145 mi. N of Kassala; livestock.

De Russy, Fort, S Oahu, T.H., at Waikiki; former hq. of Hawaiian Coast Artillery Command; established 1908.

Deruta (dĕrōō′tä), village (pop. 1,133), Perugia prov., Umbria, central Italy, near the Tiber, 9 mi. S of Perugia. Noted for its majolica industry since late Renaissance; also produces wrought-iron articles.

De Ruyter (dĭ rī′tûr), resort village (pop. 561), Madison co., central N.Y., 25 mi. SSE of Syracuse. Mfg. of cloth containers.

Derval (dĕrväl′), village (pop. 758), Loire-Inférieure dept., W France, 14 mi. WSW of Châteaubriant; road junction; dairying, hog raising.

Derventa (dĕr′vĕntä), town (pop. 9,085), N Bosnia, Yugoslavia, on Ukrina R., on railroad and 38 mi. ENE of Banja Luka; lumber milling; plum trade. First mentioned in 1473.

Derventio, England: see DERBY, city.

Dervio (dĕr′vyô), village (pop. 1,527), Como prov., Lombardy, N Italy, port on W shore of Lake Como, 16 mi. NNW of Lecco; mfg. of hydraulic turbines.

Dervock (dûr′vŭk), agr. village (district pop. 1,103), N Co. Antrim, Northern Ireland, 5 mi. NNE of Ballymoney.

Derwen (dĕr′wĕn), village and parish (pop. 441), S Denbigh, Wales, on Clwyd R. and 5 mi. N of Corwen; woolen milling. Has 15th-cent. church.

Derwent, village (pop. 207), E Alta., 22 mi. NNW of Vermilion; wheat, dairying, lumbering.

Derwenthaugh, England: see BLAYDON.

Derwent River (dûr′wŭnt). **1** In Cumberland, England, rises in the Cumbrians 9 mi. S of Keswick, flows 35 mi. N and W, through Derwentwater and Bassenthwaite L., past Keswick and Cockermouth, to Solway Firth at Workington. Receives Cocker R. at Cockermouth. **2** In Derby, England, rises on High Peak, flows 60 mi. S and SE, past The Matlocks, Belper, and Derby, to Trent R. just SW of Long Eaton. Receives the Wye at Great Rowsley. **3** In Durham, England, rises 6 mi. NE of Wolsingham, near Northumberland border, flows 30 mi. NE to Tyne R. at Derwenthaugh. **4** In E Yorkshire, England, rises in the Wolds 6 mi. S of Whitby, flows 60 mi. S, W, and S, past Malton, to Ouse R. 6 mi. NW of Goole.

Derwent River, S Tasmania, rises in L. St. Clair, flows 107 mi. SE, past New Norfolk, Claremont, Glenorchy, Bellerive, and Hobart, to Storm Bay of Tasman Sea; forms estuary 4 mi. wide, with sheltered inlet (E) 8 mi. wide; merges with NE opening of D'Entrecasteaux Channel. Floating bridge connects Hobart with E shore. Ouse, Clyde, and Jordan rivers, main tributaries.

Derwentwater or **Derwent Water,** picturesque lake in S Cumberland, England, on the Derwent just S of Keswick, surrounded by hills; 3 mi. long, 1 mi. wide. At N end are the Falls of Lodore. The lake contains Lord's Isle and Isle of St. Herbert, and Floating Isle, a mass of vegetation. Also called Keswick L.

Derygino, Russian SFSR: see PERVOAVGUSTOVSKI.

Derzhavino (dyĭrzhä′vĭnŭ), village (1939 pop. over 500), W Chkalov oblast, Russian SFSR, 30 mi. S of Buguruslan; wheat, livestock.

Des, Rumania: see DEJ.

Desaguadero (dāsägwädä′rō), village (pop. c.1,200), La Paz dept., W Bolivia, on L. Titicaca, at outlet of Desaguadero R., 60 mi. W of La Paz, on Peru border opposite Desaguadero (Peru); customs station; potatoes, barley, sheep.

Desaguadero, village (pop. 326), Puno dept., SE Peru, on L. Titicaca at outlet of Desaguadero R., opposite Desaguadero (Bolivia), c.75 mi. SE of Puno (connected by road); barley, potatoes, livestock.

Desaguadero River, Argentina: see SALADO, Río.

Desaguadero River, La Paz and Oruro depts., W Bolivia, rises in L. Titicaca (its only outlet) at Desaguadero, on Bolivia-Peru border; flows 200 mi. SE, across high plateau, past Calacoto and La Joya, to L. Poopó 32 mi. SSW of Oruro. Navigable for small vessels. Receives Mauri R. at Calacoto.

Desagüe River, Salvador: see GÜIJA, LAKE.

Desakna, Rumania: see DEJ.

Des Allemands, Bayou, La.: see DES ALLEMANDS, LAKE.

Des Allemands, Lake, or **Lac Des Allemands** (both: lăk′ dĕz ăl′mŭnz), SE La., 26 mi. W of New Orleans, near the Mississippi; c.7 mi. long, 6 mi. wide. Joined by Bayou Des Allemands (c.20 mi. long) to L. Salvador (SE).

Desamparados (dāsämpärä′dōs), W suburb (pop. estimate 12,000) of San Juan, S San Juan prov., Argentina, in San Juan R. irrigation area; fruit- and winegrowing center; wine making, alcohol distilling; flour mills, sawmills. Inc. c.1940 into San Juan city.

Desamparados, town (1950 pop. 1,320), San José prov., Costa Rica, on central plateau, 3 mi. SSE of San José; residential resort and industrial center in coffee zone; grain, cattle, hogs. Limekilns at Patarrá (S). Coal deposits and charcoal burning near by.

Des Arc. 1 (dāz ärk′) Town (pop. 1,612), ⊙ Prairie co., E central Ark., 33 mi. N of Stuttgart and on White R.; river port and rail center (ships lumber, farm products), in diversified farm area (cotton, corn, rice). Commercial fishing; stave- and sawmills. Settled in 1820s, inc. 1854. **2** (dĕ′zärk) Town (pop. 376), Iron co., SE central Mo., in the St. Francois Mts. 10 mi. N of Piedmont.

Des Arc, Bayou (bī′ō dāz ärk′), river in central Ark., rises W of Searcy, flows c.50 mi. SE to White R. just N of Des Arc.

Désarmes (dāzärm′), village, Artibonite dept., central Haiti, terminus of railroad from Saint-Marc (21 mi. WNW); coffee, bananas.

Desat or **Deshat** (dĕ′shät), Serbo-Croatian *Dešat*, mountain in the Pindus system, on Yugoslav-Albania border, N of Debar; rises to 7,820 ft.

Desbiens (dābyē′) or **Saint Emilien** (sĕtāmēlyē′), village (pop. 1,018), central Que., on S shore of L. St. John, at mouth of Metabetchouan R., 16 mi. SW of St. Joseph d'Alma; hydroelectric station; dairying, pig raising.

Desbordesville, Fr. Equatorial Africa: see IMPFONDO.

Desborough (dĕz′brŭ), urban district (1931 pop. 4,407; 1951 census 4,676), N central Northampton, England, 5 mi. NW of Kettering; shoe mfg., ironstone quarrying. Has 13th-cent. church. Site of Saxon settlement.

Descabezada Grande, Cerro (sĕ′rō dĕskäbäsä′dō grän′dä), Andean peak (12,565 ft.) in Talca prov., central Chile, near Argentina border, 50 mi. ESE of Talca. Cerro Descabezado Chico (10,660 ft.) is just NE.

Descalvado (dĭskälvä′dŏŏ), city (pop. 4,230), E São Paulo, Brazil, on railroad and 45 mi. NNW of Limeira; textile mfg.; cotton, coffee, grain, cattle.

Descartes (dākärt′), village (pop. 2,180), Oran dept., NW Algeria, in Tlemcen Mts., on railroad and 23 mi. ENE of Tlemcen; winegrowing.

Deschaillons (dāshäyō′), village (pop. 608), S Que., on the St. Lawrence and 26 mi. NE of Trois Rivières; dairying, pig raising. Adjoining is Deschaillons sur St. Laurent (sür sē lōrā′) (pop. 1,078).

Deschambault (dāshämbō′), village (pop. estimate 800), S central Que., on the St. Lawrence and 45 mi. WSW of Quebec; dairying; cattle, pigs, poultry.

Deschambault Lake (42 mi. long, 1–12 mi. wide), E Sask., near Man. border, 50 mi. W of Flin Flon. Drains N into Churchill R.

Deschênes, Lake (dāshān′), expansion (6 mi. long, up to 3 mi. wide) of Ottawa R., Que. and Ont., 6 mi. WSW of Ottawa.

Deschnaer Kuppe, mountain, Czechoslovakia: see VELKA DESTNA.

Deschutes (dā″shōōt′), county (□ 3,041; pop. 21,812), central Oregon; ⊙ Bend. Drained by Deschutes R. Lumber milling, agr. (potatoes, alfalfa), livestock grazing, diatomite quarrying; manganese, lead, zinc deposits. Includes part of Cascade Range (W) and much of Deschutes Natl. Forest. Formed 1916.

Deschutes River. 1 In N Oregon, rises in Cascade Range, flows 240 mi. NNE, past Bend and Redmond, to the Columbia 12 mi. E of The Dalles; used for power and irrigation. **2** In W Wash., rises in Snoqualmie Natl. Forest E of Chehalis, flows c.50 mi. NW to Puget Sound at Olympia.

Descubierta, La, Dominican Republic: see LA DESCUBIERTA.

Desdemona (dĕz′dŭmō′nŭ), town (1940 pop. 198), Eastland co., N central Texas, c.45 mi. NNE of Brownwood; rail point in cotton, cattle, petroleum area.

Deseado, Argentina: see PUERTO DESEADO.

Deseado, Cape (dāsā-ä′dō), NW headland of Desolation Isl., in Tierra del Fuego, Chile, on the Pacific, at W entrance to Strait of Magellan; 52°44′S 74°45′W.

Deseado River, in Patagonia, S Argentina, rises near Chile line in Andean hills S of L. Buenos Aires, flows NE, E, and SE, forming Santa Cruz-Comodoro Rivadavia boundary, to the Atlantic at Puerto Deseado; 380 mi. long. Its lower course (somewhat navigable) is used for irrigation.

Desecheo Island (dāsächā′ō), small islet (□ c.1) belonging to Puerto Rico, in Mona Passage, 17 mi. W of main isl.; 18°23′N 67°28′W. Bird sanctuary.

Desengaño (dāsĕngä′nyō), saddle depression (alt. 7,185 ft.) in the Central Cordillera, central Costa Rica, bet. Poás (W) and Barba (E) volcanoes, NW of San José. Through it passes San José–Sarapiquí road, an important traffic artery in middle 19th cent.

Desenzano del Garda (dĕsĕndzä′nô dĕl gär′dä), town (pop. 5,058), Brescia prov., Lombardy, N Italy, port on SW shore of Lago di Garda, 16 mi. ESE of Brescia; resort; mfg. (shoes, lubricating oils, marmalade, wine). Has medieval castle (now a barracks). Near by is 10th-cent. monastery. Until 1926 called Desenzano sul Lago.

Deseret (dĕ′zûrĕt, dĕzûrĕt′), a proposed state of the U.S., organized 1849 by a convention of Mormons; it would have included present-day Utah and much of the Southwest below the 42d parallel; proposed ⊙ was Salt Lake City. It was refused recognition by Congress, which instead set up Utah Territory (1850).

Deseret Peak (11,031 ft.), in Stansbury Mts., NW Utah, 19 mi. WSW of Tooele.

Deseronto (dĕzŭrŏn′tō), town (pop. 1,261), SE Ont., near Bay of Quinte of L. Ontario, 25 mi. W of Kingston; food canning, dairying, plastics mfg. Former lumbering center.

Deserta Grande, Madeira: see DESERTAS.

Desertas (dĭzĕr′tŭsh), group of 3 narrow uninhabited islands in the Atlantic, forming part of Madeira archipelago, c.20 mi. SE of Madeira isl., in 32°30′N 16°30′W. Named, N–S, Chão (1 mi. long, 340 ft. high), Deserta Grande (7 mi. long, 1,600 ft. high), and Bugio (5 mi. long, 1,350 ft. high).

Desert Hot Springs, resort village (pop. c.300), Riverside co., S Calif., in N Coachella Valley, 10 mi. N of Palm Springs. Railroad station is Garnet.

Désertines (dāzĕrtēn′), NE suburb (pop. 3,724) of Montluçon, Allier dept., central France; wax and hosiery mfg.

Desert of Maine, Maine: see FREEPORT.

Desert Peak, Utah: see NEWFOUNDLAND MOUNTAINS.

Desfina, Greece: see DESPHINA.

Desha (dŭshā′), county (□ 776; pop. 25,155), SE Ark.; ⊙ Arkansas City. Bounded E by Mississippi R.; drained by Arkansas and White rivers. Agr. (cotton, corn, hay, rice, livestock). Meat packing, rice and lumber milling, cotton ginning; railroad shops. Formed 1838.

Deshaies (dāzā′), town (commune pop. 1,593), NW Basse-Terre isl., Guadeloupe, 22 mi. NNW of Basse-Terre, in agr. region (coffee, cacao, vanilla); exports bananas. Sometimes spelled Deshayes.

Deshat, mountain, Yugoslavia and Albania: see DESAT.

Deshayes, Guadeloupe: see DESHAIES.

Deshikaga (dä′shĭkägä) or **Teshikaga** (tä′–), town (pop. 11,012), E Hokkaido, Japan, 35 mi. N of Kushiro; sulphur mining; lumbering. There are also hot springs.

De-shima (dā′shĭmä) or **De-jima** (dā′jĭmä), artificial islet in Nagasaki Harbor, Nagasaki prefecture, W Kyushu, Japan; c.⅛ mi. long, ⅕ mi. wide. Forms dist. of Nagasaki city; connected to rest of city by small bridge; docks on W shore. Early Du. traders restricted to islet (1641–1858). Sometimes spelled Desima.

Deshing (dā′shĭng), town (pop. 2,756), Satara South dist., S central Bombay, India, 17 mi. NE of Sangli; millet, sugar cane, cotton. Also spelled Desing.

Deshler. 1 Village (pop. 1,063), Thayer co., S Nebr., 7 mi. W of Hebron and on branch of Little Blue R., near Kansas line; brooms, flour; dairy and poultry produce, grain, livestock. **2** Village (pop. 1,623), Henry co., NW Ohio, 17 mi. SW of Bowling Green; metal products, grain and dairy products.

Deshnoke (dĕsh′nōk, dāsh′nōk), town (pop. 5,187), N central Rajasthan, India, 14 mi. S of Bikaner; pottery making. Also spelled Deshnok.

Desierto, Spain: see BARACALDO.

Desierto de los Leones (dāsyĕr′tō dā lōs lāō′nĕs), national park in Federal Dist., central Mexico, 18 mi. SW of Mexico city; pine-forested mtn. scenery; has ruins of old Carmelite monastery (built 1606).

Desima, Japan: see DE-SHIMA.

Desio (dā′zyō), town (pop. 11,788), Milano prov., Lombardy, N Italy, 11 mi. N of Milan; industrial center; textile mills, foundries, food cannery. Pope Pius XI b. here.

Désirade (dāzērād′), coral island (□ 10.5; pop. 1,581), dependency of Guadeloupe dept., Fr. West Indies, 5 mi. ENE of Grande-Terre; 7 mi. long, c.1 mi. wide. Rises to c.930 ft. Of little economic importance, it produces some sugar cane, cotton, sisal, and livestock. Coastal fishing. Its principal settlement, Grande-Anse, is in SW.

Des Joachims (dā zhôäshē′), locality, SW Que., on Ottawa R. (rapids) and 40 mi. NW of Pembroke; hydroelectric-power center.

Deskate or **Dheskati** (both: dhĭskä′tē), town (pop. 4,233), Larissa nome, N Thessaly, Greece, 25 mi. S of Kozane, in Kamvounia Mts.; timber, charcoal; wine; livestock products (milk, cheese, skins). Passed to Greece in 1913. Also spelled Deskati.

Deskford, agr. village and parish (pop. 541), N Banffshire, Scotland, 4 mi. S of Cullen.

Des Lacs (dŭ lăks′), village (pop. 180), Ward co., NW central N.Dak., 12 mi. W of Minot.

Des Lacs Lake, in SE Saskatchewan and N N.Dak., extends N and NW from Kenmare; largest of the Des Lacs lakes, sources of Des Lacs R.; 30 mi. long, ½ mi. wide. Migratory waterfowl project is here.
Des Lacs River, N N.Dak.; rises in Des Lacs lakes near Kenmare, flows 42 mi. SE to Souris R. 6 mi. WNW of Minot. Also known as Rivière des Lacs.
Desloge (dĕs″lōj′), lead-mining town (pop. 1,957), St. Francois co., E Mo., just SE of Bonne Terre. Inc. since 1940.
Desmeloizes (dāmĕlwäz′), village, W Que., 33 mi. NNW of Duparquet, near Ont. border; gold, copper, zinc mining.
De Smet (dĭ smĕt′), city (pop. 1,180), ⊙ Kingsbury co., E central S.Dak., 42 mi. SW of Watertown; center of dairying area; creameries; livestock, grain. Inc. 1880.
De Smet, Lake, N Wyo., just E of Bighorn Mts., 22 mi. SSE of Sheridan; 4 mi. long, 1 mi. wide.
Desmochados (dĕzmōchä′dōs), town (dist. pop. 2,464), Ñeembucú dept., S Paraguay, 27 mi. SE of Pilar; cattle-raising center.
Des Moines (dů moin′), county (□ 409; pop. 42,056), SE Iowa; ⊙ Burlington. Bounded E by the Mississippi (forms Ill. line here) and S by Skunk R. Prairie agr. area (hogs, cattle, corn, soybeans) with cutoff lakes in E; limestone quarries. Industry at Burlington. Formed 1834.
Des Moines. **1** City (□ c.55; pop. 177,965), ⊙ Iowa and Polk co., central Iowa, on Des Moines R. at mouth of Raccoon R., and c.300 mi. W of Chicago, in heart of Corn Belt and in bituminous-coal-mining area; 41°35′N 93°38′W; alt. c.800 ft. Largest city of state and an important center of transportation (rail, highway, air), commerce, industry, insurance, printing and publishing. Manufactures farm machinery and equipment, rubber tires and tubes, airplane parts, cement, brick, tile, millwork, dairy products, packed meats, feed, clothing, fur garments, cosmetics, leather goods. Places of interest include: the capitol (1871–84); the State Historical, Memorial, and Art Bldg.; and also the library, civic center, coliseum (1910), U.S. veterans' hosp., several war memorials, state fair grounds, and U.S. Fort Des Moines (established 1901; 1st WAC training center in Second World War). Seat of Drake Univ. (coeducational; founded 1881), Des Moines Still Col. of Osteopathy and Surgery, and Grant View jr. col. (coeducational). Near by are Camp Dodge (army camp) and Walnut Woods State Park. Established in 1843 as a military post (old Fort Des Moines); inc. as town in 1851; chartered as city in 1857; succeeded Iowa City as state ⊙ under terms of Iowa state constitution of 1857. In 1907, city adopted plan of municipal govt. known as Des Moines plan, a commission govt. **2** Village (pop. 282), Union co., NE N.Mex., 35 mi. ESE of Raton, near Colo. line, alt. c.6,620 ft. Trade and shipping point in agr., ranching region.
Des Moines River, in Iowa and Minn., rises NE of Pipestone, SW Minn., flows 535 mi. generally SSE through SW Minn. into Iowa, past Estherville, Fort Dodge, Des Moines, and Ottumwa to Mississippi R. at Keokuk, SE Iowa. Also known as West Fork or West Des Moines R. above Humboldt, Iowa. Important tributary is East Des Moines R. (or East Fork), which rises in Martin co., SW Minn., and flows 120 mi. SE and S through Tuttle L. into Iowa, past Algona, to Des Moines R. near Humboldt. No commercial navigation on either stream. Des Moines R. is used to generate hydroelectric power. Other tributaries are Boone and Raccoon rivers.
Desna River (dyĭsnä′), main left affluent of Dnieper R., W European USSR; rises near Yelnya in Smolensk-Moscow Upland, flows generally S, past Bryansk, Trubchevsk, and Novgorod-Severski, and SSW, past Chernigov, to Dnieper R. just above Kiev; 737 mi. long. Receives Seim and Bolva (left), Sudost and Snov (right) rivers. Navigable for 520 mi. below Bryansk; used chiefly for lumber.
Desneuf Island (dānûf′), southernmost of the Amirantes, outlying dependency of the Seychelles, 200 mi. SW of Mahé Isl.; 6°14′S 53°3′E; ½ mi. long, 1 mi. wide; coral formation. Uninhabited.
Desolation, Cape, on small isl., in SW Tierra del Fuego, Chile, 60 mi. SSW of Froward Cape; 54°46′S 71°38′W.
Desolation, Cape, Greenland: see NUNARSSUIT.
Desolation Island, long (80 mi.), narrow (10 mi.), bleak, uninhabited isl. in Tierra del Fuego, Chile, on the Pacific, at W end of Strait of Magellan. At its NW tip are Cape Deseado (52°44′S 74°45′W) and Cape Pillar (52°42′S 74°41′W).
Desolation Island, Indian Ocean: see KERGUELEN ISLANDS.
Desolation Valley (□ c.65), E. Calif., in the Sierra Nevada, just SW of L. Tahoe; alt. c.7,000 ft. Lake-dotted, forested glacial valley, accessible only by trails; preserved as a primitive area. Rubicon R. rises here.
De Soto (dē sō′tů, –tō, dĭ–). **1** County (□ 648; pop. 9,242), S central Fla.; ⊙ Arcadia. Rolling terrain, partly swampy, with many small lakes; drained by Peace R. Agr. (citrus fruit, vegetables, corn); cattle and poultry raising. Formed 1887. **2** Parish (□ 899; pop. 24,398), NW La.; ⊙ Mansfield. Bounded W by Texas line, SW by Sabine R., NE by Bayou Pierre and several lakes. Principal crops: cotton, corn, hay, peanuts. Oil, natural gas, lumber. Cotton ginning, lumber milling; other mfg. at Mansfield. Formed 1843. **3** County (□ 478; pop. 24,599), extreme NW Miss.; ⊙ Hernando. Bounded W by Mississippi R., here forming Ark. line; and N by Tenn. line. Drained by Coldwater R., here dammed into Arkabutla Reservoir. Agr. (cotton, corn), stock raising, dairying. Formed 1836.
De Soto. **1** Village (pop. 309), Sumter co., SW central Ga., 13 mi. SE of Americus. **2** Village (pop. 646), Jackson co., SW Ill., 11 mi. W of Herrin, in bituminous-coal-mining and agr. area. Devastated by tornado in 1925. **3** Town (pop. 280), Dallas co., central Iowa, 21 mi. W of Des Moines, in agr. area. **4** City (pop. 518), Johnson co., E Kansas, on Kansas R. and 20 mi. SW of Kansas City, Kansas; dairying, general agr. **5** City (pop. 5,357), Jefferson co., E Mo., bet. Mississippi and Big rivers, 35 mi. SSW of St. Louis; railroad shops; produces shoes, clothing, staves; stone quarries. State park near by. Founded 1857. **6** Town (pop. 298), Dallas co., N Texas, just S of Dallas. **7** Village (pop. 367), on Crawford-Vernon co. line, SW Wis., on the Mississippi and 28 mi. S of La Crosse. Black Hawk toll bridge to Lansing (Iowa) near by.
De Soto City, town (pop. 220), Highlands co., S central Fla., 4 mi. SSE of Sebring, in citrus-fruit area.
De Soto National Memorial, Fla.: see BRADENTON.
De Soto Park, village (pop. 1,065), Floyd co., NW Ga.
Despard (dĕ′spärd), village (pop. 1,976), Harrison co., N W.Va., a S suburb of Clarksburg.
Despatch, residential town (pop. 3,832), S Cape Prov., U. of So. Afr., on Brak R. and 4 mi. SE of Uitenhage.
Despeñaderos (dĕspĕnyädā′rōs), town (pop. estimate 1,200), central Córdoba prov., Argentina, 30 mi. S of Córdoba; rail junction and agr. center (corn, wheat, flax, peanuts, livestock).
Despeñaperros (dĕspĕnyäpĕ′rōs), mountain passage in S Spain, in the Sierra Morena, on Ciudad Real-Jaén prov. border, 22 mi. NNE of Linares, and linking New Castile (N) with Andalusia (S). Through the steep gorge passes railroad and highway from Madrid to Seville. Of strategic importance during Moorish wars and Peninsular War.
Des Peres (dů pâr′), town (pop. 1,172), St. Louis co., E Mo., W of St. Louis. Inc. 1934.
Desphina or **Dhesfina** (both: dhĭsfē′nä), town (pop. 3,590), Phocis nome, W central Greece, 6 mi. E of Itea; cattle, sheep, goats; wine; olive oil. Also spelled Desfina.
Des Plaines (dĕs plānz′), city (pop. 14,994), Cook co., NE Ill., NW suburb of Chicago, on Des Plaines R., in residential and industrial area; mfg. (radio and electrical equipment, cement blocks). Nurseries, greenhouses; truck, dairy products, mushrooms. Annual Methodist encampment held here since 1860. Forest preserve near by. Founded in 1830s as Rand; named Des Plaines in 1869; inc. as city in 1925.
Des Plaines River, in Wis. and Ill., rises in extreme SE Wis., flows S into Ill., through N and W suburbs of Chicago, to Forest View, thence SW, past Lockport and Joliet, joining Kankakee R. to form Illinois R.; c.110 mi. long. Below Lockport, where it is joined by Sanitary and Ship Canal from Chicago, the Des Plaines is part of ILLINOIS WATERWAY system.
d'Espoir, Bay (dĕspâr′, Fr. dĕspwär′), inlet (30 mi. long, 4 mi. wide at entrance), S N.F., N arm of Hermitage Bay. In it is Bois Isl. On shore are fishing settlements.
d'Espoir, Cape, at E end of Gaspé Peninsula, E Que., on N side of entrance of Chaleur Bay, 30 mi. SSE of Gaspé; 48°24′N 64°19′W.
Despotikon or **Dhespotikon** (both: dhĭspô′tĭkôn′), uninhabited Aegean island (□ 3.5) in the Cyclades, Greece, SW of Antiparos. Sometimes called Peresinthos.
Despoto Dagh, Bulgaria and Greece: see RHODOPE MOUNTAINS.
Despotovac or **Despotovats** (both: dĕspô′tôväts), village (pop. 3,537), E central Serbia, Yugoslavia, on Resava R. and 12 mi. NNE of Cuprija. Monastery near by (E).
Des Roches Island (dā rôsh′), outlying dependency (pop. 75) of the Seychelles, in Indian Ocean, E of the Amirantes, 575 mi. NNE of N tip of Madagascar and 150 mi. WSW of Mahé Isl. (in Seychelles proper); 5°41′S 53°40′E; 4 mi. long, ½ mi. wide. Of coral origin. Copra; fisheries. Isl. forms S side of atoll reef.
Dessalines (dāsälēn′), town (1950 census pop. 3,745), Artibonite dept., central Haiti, 18 mi. SE of Gonaïves; coffee, cotton, timber.
Dessau (dĕ′sou), city (pop. 88,139), ⊙ former Anhalt state, central Germany, after 1945 in Saxony-Anhalt, on the Mulde confluence with the Elbe, and 35 mi. N of Leipzig; 51°50′N 12°15′E. Rail center; airfield (W); harbor (at N suburb of Wallwitzhafen on the Elbe). Mfg.: railroad cars, machinery, chemicals, cooking ranges, heaters. Until 1945 site of large aircraft works, city was heavily bombed in Second World War. Home (1925–32) of the Bauhaus architectural school under Gropius. Originally a Sorb village; 1st mentioned 1213 as German settlement. Was ⊙ Anhalt-Dessau, after 1863 ANHALT, from 1603 to 1945. Moses Mendelssohn b. here. In Thirty Years War, Wallenstein forced (1626) Elbe crossing near by.
Desschel, Belgium: see DESSEL.
Dessel (dĕs′hĕl), town (pop. 5,088), Antwerp prov., NE Belgium, 10 mi. SE of Turnhout; agr. market (vegetables, potatoes). Formerly spelled Desschel.
Dessie, Ethiopia: see DESSYE.
Dessye (dĕs′yā), Ital. *Dessie*, town (pop. 40,000), ⊙ Wallo prov., NE Ethiopia, on W escarpment of Great Rift Valley, 155 mi. NE of Addis Ababa; 11°8′N 39°38′E; alt. c.8,000 ft. Commercial and communications center on Addis Ababa–Asmara road, joined here by road from Assab. Trade in salt, cereals, coffee, hides, and beeswax; has artisan industries (weaving, tanning, metalworking). Consists largely of scattered thatched huts with sprinkling of modern bldgs., several churches, and palaces.
De Steeg (dů stākh′), town (pop. 1,146), Gelderland prov., E central Netherlands, on Ijssel R. and 7 mi. ENE of Arnhem; mfg. of motors, ships, oil-drilling machinery.
Destelbergen (dĕ′stůlbĕrkhůn), town (pop. 5,412), East Flanders prov., NW Belgium, E suburb of Ghent.
Desterro, Brazil: see FLORIANÓPOLIS.
Destor (dĕstôr′), village, W Que., 13 mi. NNE of Rouyn; gold, copper mining.
Destrehan (dĕ′strēhăn″), village (1940 pop. 878), St. Charles parish, SE La., on E bank (levee) of the Mississippi and 16 mi. W of New Orleans; oil refining. Ferry to Luling.
Destriana (dĕstrēä′nä), town (pop. 1,338), Leon prov., NW Spain, 10 mi. SSW of Astorga; cereals, potatoes, sheep.
Desuq, Egypt: see DISUQ.
Desvres (dā′vrů), town (pop. 5,148), Pas-de-Calais dept., N France, 11 mi. ESE of Boulogne; faïence, tile, cement.
Deszk (dĕsk), town (pop. 2,823), Csanad co., S Hungary, 5 mi. E of Szeged, near Maros R.; grain, paprika, hogs.
Deta (dā′tä), Hung. *Detta* (dĕt′tŏ), village (pop. 4,328), Timisoara prov., W Rumania, on railroad and 25 mi. S of Timisoara; trading center; mfg. of soap, bricks, tiles; woodworking, clay quarrying.
Detchino (dyĕ′chĭnů), village (1926 pop. 405), NE Kaluga oblast, Russian SFSR, 20 mi. N of Kaluga; coarse grain.
Detmold (dĕt′môlt), town (pop. 26,807), ⊙ former LIPPE, NW Germany, after 1945 in North Rhine-Westphalia, on N slope of Teutoburg Forest, on the Werre and 16 mi. SE of Bielefeld; furniture-mfg. center; other products: machinery, pharmaceuticals, cosmetics, garments. Woodworking, food processing (fruit preserves, biscuits, flour, beer, spirits). Cement works. Summer resort. Has Renaissance former ducal residence; 18th-cent. new palace. Site of music acad. (founded 1946). House of Lippe acquired town c.1150. Chartered c.1350. Was residence of Lippe-Detmold line until 1918. On a hill, 2 mi. SW, is the Hermannsdenkmal, a monument commemorating the battle of the Teutoburg Forest (A.D. 9).
Detour (dētŏŏr′), village (pop. 611), Chippewa co., E Upper Peninsula, Mich., c.40 mi. SSE of Sault Ste. Marie, and on Detour Passage (S end of St. Marys R.) opposite Drummond Isl. (E). Lighthouse here. Fueling point for commercial shipping; resort.
Detour, Point, Mich.: see GARDEN PENINSULA.
Detour Passage, Mich.: see SAINT MARYS RIVER.
Detrick, Camp, Md.: see FREDERICK, city.
Détrie (dātrē′), village (pop. 1,693), Oran dept., NW Algeria, on the Mékerra and 5 mi. SW of Sidi-bel-Abbès; vineyards.
Detroit (dētroit′, dĭ–). **1** Village (pop. 126), Pike co., W Ill., 24 mi. WSW of Jacksonville, in agr. area. **2** Town (pop. 492), Somerset co., central Maine, 20 mi. E of Skowhegan. **3** City (□ 142; 1940 pop. 1,623,452; 1950 pop. 1,849,568), largest city of Mich. and 5th largest in U.S., ⊙ Wayne co., SE Mich., c.240 mi. ENE of Chicago, and on Detroit R., opposite Windsor, Ont.; 42°20′N 83°W; alt. c.600 ft. World's automobile-mfg. center; automotive industry developed here by Ford and others since early 1900s has expanded to many other cities beyond Detroit's metropolitan area, notably Flint and Lansing. Detroit is one of busiest ports of U.S., with harbor on Detroit R. (connecting lakes Erie and St. Clair; here up to 3 mi. wide), which is spanned by bridges and tunnels to Windsor. Port of entry. Has passenger steamer connections with chief Great Lakes ports, and is a rail (8 lines) and air transportation hub. It is center of a vast metropolitan area—including DEARBORN, RIVER ROUGE, WYANDOTTE, HAMTRAMCK, HIGHLAND PARK (latter 2 surrounded by Detroit), Ferndale, ECORSE, Royal Oak, and other places—which contains about ½ of pop. of Mich. Besides motor vehicles and parts (about 75% of its industrial output), Detroit makes aircraft and aircraft parts, railroad cars, rubber products, aluminum, steel, electrical and television equipment, adding machines, pharmaceuticals, home appliances, hardware, salt-based chemicals, varnish, furniture, clothing, packed

meat and other food products, tobacco products; it has oil refineries, shipyards, saltworks; and is an important seed-shipping center. Roughly triangular in shape, city lies along right bank of river (here flowing almost W), N of Windsor; residential suburbs are to E and NE along L. St. Clair (notably Grosse Pointe), and to N and NW; to W are Dearborn, Inkster, and Wayne, and to S are the predominantly industrial "downriver cities," including River Rouge, Ecorse, Wyandotte. Detroit is seat of Wayne Univ., Univ. of Detroit, Marygrove Col., Mercy Col., Detroit Inst. of Technology, Sacred Heart Seminary, Detroit Col. of Law, Merrill-Palmer School, and Detroit Inst. of Musical Art. Points of interest: Inst. of Arts, public library, Greater Penobscot Bldg. (47 stories; city's tallest), historical mus., St. Paul's Cathedral (Episcopal), Blessed Sacrament Cathedral (R.C.); several parks, notably Belle Isle (c.2 mi. long) in the river, on which are fine gardens, woodlands, a zoo, an aquarium, outdoor symphony shell, and extensive recreational facilities, including yacht basins; state fairgrounds; old Fort Wayne (completed 1851). Ambassador Bridge (2 mi. long; center suspension span 1,850 ft. long) was completed in 1929 to Windsor; highway tunnel (c.1 mi. long) under river was completed in 1930; railroad tunnel had been built in 1910. A fort (Pontchartrain) and settlement were founded 1701 by Antoine de la Mothe Cadillac and held by the French until 1760; became British in 1760, American in 1796 (by Jay's Treaty), British again in War of 1812, and finally American in 1813. It was territorial and then state capital, 1805–47. Despite destruction by fire in 1805, Detroit grew rapidly (especially in 1830s) with development of land and water transportation. In the latter half of 19th cent., Detroit assumed importance as a shipping, shipbuilding, and mfg. center. Its early carriage industry helped Henry Ford and others to make the city the world center of the automobile industry; other factors were its strategic location with respect to raw materials, transportation, and markets. Inc. as town in 1802, as city in 1806. **4** Town (pop. 679), Red River co., NE Texas, 16 mi. E of Paris, in cotton, corn, peanut, timber area; lumber mills.

Detroit Beach, village (pop. 1,966, with adjacent Woodland Beach), Monroe co., SE Mich., near Monroe.

Detroit Dam, Oregon: see SANTIAM RIVER.

Detroit Lake, Becker co., W Minn., at city of Detroit Lakes; 3 mi. long, 2.5 mi. wide. Fishing and bathing resorts. Pelican L. and L. Melissa are near by.

Detroit Lakes, city (pop. 5,787), ⊙ Becker co., W Minn., on Detroit L. and c.45 mi. E of Moorhead; trade center for farm and lake-resort area in which livestock, poultry, and vegetables are raised; dairy products, beverages; mfg. (agr. equipment, boats). There are 2 hospitals. Settled c.1858, inc. as village 1880, as city 1900.

Detroit River, bet. Mich. and Ont., drains L. St. Clair E of Detroit, flows SW and S, bet. Detroit and Windsor (Ont.), which are joined by rail, vehicular tunnels, and bridges, to W end of L. Erie; c.31 mi. long. Forms part of international boundary. Important artery for Great Lakes shipping.

Detskoye Selo, Russian SFSR: see PUSHKIN.

Dett, village, Bulawayo prov., W Southern Rhodesia, in Matabeleland, on railroad and 30 mi. SE of Wankie; cattle, sheep, goats; corn. Airfield.

Detta, Rumania: see DETA.

Dettelbach (dĕ'tůlbäkh), town (pop. 2,900), Lower Franconia, W Bavaria, Germany, on the Main (canalized) and 10 mi. E of Würzburg; leather mfg., brewing. Grain, potatoes, cattle, hogs. Chartered 1484. Has Gothic pilgrimage church and early-16th-cent. town hall.

Dettifoss (dĕ'tĭfŏs"), waterfall (over 200 ft.) on Jokulsa R., NE Iceland; 65°47'N 16°22'W. Noted for scenic beauty.

Dettingen (dĕ'tĭng-ůn). **1** or **Dettingen am Main** (äm mīn'), village (pop. 2,551), Lower Franconia, NW Bavaria, Germany, on the Main (canalized) and 7 mi. NW of Aschaffenburg; mfg. (textiles; metal, leather, and wood products). Lignite deposits near by. Here, in June, 1743, an English and German army under George II defeated the French under Marshal Noailles. **2** or **Dettingen an der Erms** (än dĕr ĕrms'), village (pop. 4,050), S Württemberg, Germany, after 1945 in Württemberg-Hohenzollern, in Swabian Jura, 6.5 mi. ENE of Reutlingen; textile and paper mfg.

Dettwiller (dĕtvēlâr'), Ger. *Dettweiler* (dĕt'vīlůr), town (pop. 2,169), Bas-Rhin dept., E France, on the Zorn, on Marne-Rhine Canal, and 5 mi. ENE of Saverne; shoe mfg.

Detva (dyĕt'vä), Hung. *Gyetva* (dyĕt'vŏ), town (pop. 7,605), S central Slovakia, Czechoslovakia, on railroad and 17 mi. SE of Banska Bystrica; noted for handicraft industries (embroidery, woodcarving, costume making) and well-preserved folkways; cheese making. Has picturesque church and cemetery with hand-carved and painted monuments. Colorful regional fairs held here.

De Twente, Netherlands: see TWENTE, DE.

De Twenthe, Netherlands: see TWENTE, DE.

Deuben (doi'bůn). **1** Town (pop. 3,762), in former Prussian Saxony prov., central Germany, after 1945 in Saxony-Anhalt, 5 mi. NW of Zeitz; lignite-mining center. Power station. **2** Village (pop. 1,195), Saxony, E central Germany, 2 mi. W of Wurzen; glass mfg.; synthetic-oil plant. **3** Town, Saxony, E central Germany: see FREITAL.

Deuel (dōō'ůl, dōō"ĕl', dū–). **1** County (□ 435; pop. 3,330), W Nebr.; ⊙ Chappell. Agr. area bounded S by Colo.; drained by Lodgepole Creek and S.Platte R. Grain, livestock, dairy produce, sugar beets. Formed 1888. **2** County (□ 636; pop. 7,689), E S.Dak., on Minn. line; ⊙ Clear Lake. Agr. area watered by numerous lakes and creeks; dairy produce, livestock, grain, potatoes. Formed 1862.

Deuil (dû'ē), town (pop. 9,338), Seine-et-Oise dept., N central France, bet. Enghien-les-Bains (SW) and Montmorency (N), 8 mi. N of Paris; fruit and vegetable shipping, woodworking, mfg. of railroad equipment.

Deûlémont (dûlāmõ'), village (pop. 700), Nord dept., N France, frontier station on Belg. border, 8 mi. NW of Lille, on the Lys at mouth of Deûle R. (canalized); boatbuilding, brick mfg.

Deûle River (dûl), Nord dept., N France, rises above Lens, flows 42 mi. NNE, past Lille, to the Lys at Deûlémont. Mostly canalized.

Deulgaon Raja (dā'ōōlgoun rä'jä), town (pop. 6,800), Buldana dist., W Madhya Pradesh, India, 32 mi. SSW of Buldana; millet, wheat; cotton ginning. Sometimes spelled Deolgaon-Raja.

Deurne (dûr'nů), town (pop. 57,362), Antwerp prov., N Belgium, industrial suburb 2 mi. E of Antwerp; airport.

Deurne, town (pop. 5,885), North Brabant prov., SE Netherlands, 6 mi. E of Helmond; weaving; mfg. (bricks, strawboard); dairying. Deep coal deposits near by.

Deutichem, Netherlands: see DOETINCHEM.

Deutsch Altenburg, Austria: see BAD DEUTSCH ALTENBURG.

Deutschbrod, Czechoslovakia: see HAVLICKUV BROD.

Deutsch Eylau, Poland: see ILAWA.

Deutschfeistritz (doich'fīs'trĭts), town (pop. 3,514), Styria, SE Austria, on Mur R. and 10 mi. NNW of Graz; iron- and steelworks, lead and zinc smelting (mines near by); summer resort; vineyards.

Deutsch Gabel, Czechoslovakia: see JABLONNE V PODJESTEDI.

Deutschkreutz (doich'kroits), Hung. *Németkeresztúr* (nā'mĕtkĕ"rĕstōōr), town (pop. 3,635), Burgenland, E Austria, near Hung. border, 6 mi. SSE of Sopron, Hungary; market center (wine, walnuts).

Deutsch Krone, Poland: see WALCZ.

Deutschland, Europe: see GERMANY.

Deutschlandsberg (doich'länts bĕrk), village (pop. 5,241), Styria, S Austria, 20 mi. SW of Graz; lumberyards, match factory, summer resort. Just S is 12th-cent. castle.

Deutsch-Oth, France: see AUDUN-LE-TICHE.

Deutsch Piekar, Poland: see PIEKARY.

Deutsch Przemysl, Poland: see PRZEMYSL.

Deutsch Wagram (doich' vä'gräm) or **Wagram,** town (pop. 3,917), E Lower Austria, 10 mi. NNE of Vienna, in the Marchfeld; airfield. On July 5–6, 1809, Napoleon here won decisive victory over the Austrians.

Deutz (doits), right-bank suburb of Cologne, W Germany, on the Rhine, just opposite city center; industrial harbor; junction for right-bank rail traffic; mfg. of motors. Has commercial fair grounds. Bridgehead of Cologne since Roman times.

Deutzen (doi'tsůn), village (pop. 4,005), Saxony, E central Germany, 4 mi. WSW of Borna; lignite mining; synthetic-oil plant.

Deux-Acren (dûzäkrã'), village (pop. 4,151), Hainaut prov., SW central Belgium, just NNE of Lessines; electric-power station.

Deux Frères, Les (lā dû' frâr'), two islets (Îlot Boisé and Îlot Aride) in South China Sea, 60 mi. S of Bassac R. mouth, S Vietnam.

Deux Montagnes (dû mōtä'nyů), county (□ 279; pop. 16,746), S Que., on the St. Lawrence; ⊙ Ste Scholastique.

Deux-Ponts, Germany: see ZWEIBRÜCKEN.

Deux Rivières (dōō" rĭvēâr', Fr. dû rēvyâr'). **1** Village, E central Ont., on Ottawa R. and 20 mi. E of Mattawa; lumbering. **2** Village, Que.: see SAINT STANISLAS DE CHAMPLAIN.

Deux-Sèvres (dû sĕ'vrů), department (□ 2,337; pop. 312,756), W France, formed of parts of Poitou, Angoumois, and Saintonge provinces; ⊙ Niort. Generally level region crossed (NW-SE) by low granitic Gâtine hills. Drained by the Thouet (NE) and the 2 Sèvre rivers (Sèvre Nantaise, Sèvre Niortaise) which give the dept. its name. An important dairying region raising high-grade cattle (Parthenay breed), horses, pigs, and mules. Chief towns (Niort, Thouars, and Parthenay) are livestock-shipping centers.

Deva, England: see CHESTER.

Deva (dā'vä), Ger. *Diemrich* (dēm'rĭkh), Hung. *Déva* (dā'vŏ), town (1948 pop. 12,959), ⊙ Hunedoara prov., W central Rumania, in Transylvania, on railroad, on Mures R. and 190 mi. NW of Bucharest; tourist and trading center (livestock, lumber, fruit, nuts); meat and vegetable processing, flour milling. Has 13th-cent. fortress, 17th-cent. Franciscan monastery and baroque castle, mus. with large archaeological and ethnographical collections. Former Roman settlement; chartered in 13th cent. Was a stronghold of Hunyadi family in 15th cent.

Deva (dā'vä), Basque town (pop. 1,549), Guipúzcoa prov., N Spain, on Bay of Biscay at mouth of small Deva R., 19 mi. W of San Sebastián; mfg. of celluloid and tortoise-shell articles, furniture; tanning, sawmilling. Bathing resort. Limestone and marble quarries near by.

Devagiri, India: see DAULATABAD.

Devakottai (dā"vŭkōt'tī), city (pop. 24,315), Ramnad dist., S Madras, India, 45 mi. E of Madura; residential and financial center of Chetty merchant community. Trade in foreign luxury goods.

De Valls Bluff (dē vălz'), town (pop. 830), Prairie co., E central Ark., c.45 mi. E of Little Rock and on White R.; ships fish, rice, cotton, hay.

Devana, Scotland: see ABERDEEN.

Devana Castra, England: see CHESTER.

Devanhalli (dā'vŭnhŭlē), town (pop. 6,931), Bangalore dist., E Mysore, India, 20 mi. NNE of Bangalore; rice milling; handicrafts (biris, lacquerware, pottery).

Devaprayag (dā"vŭprŭyäg'), village, Tehri dist., N Uttar Pradesh, India, in central Kumaun Himalaya foothills, at confluence of Alaknanda and Bhagirathi rivers to form the Ganges (one of 5 sacred confluences), 18 mi. SSE of Tehri; 30°9'N 78°37'E. Rice, wheat, barley, rape, mustard, potatoes. Pilgrimage center; anc. Hindu pyramid temple.

Devarayadurga, hill, India: see TUMKUR, town.

Deva River (dā'vä), in Santander and Oviedo provs., N Spain, rises on E slopes of the Picos de Europa, flows 40 mi. NNE to Bay of Biscay 6 mi. W of San Vicente de la Barquera.

Devarkonda (dāvŭrkōn'dŭ), village (pop. 4,313), Nalgonda dist., S Hyderabad state, India, 33 mi. SW of Nalgonda; rice, millet, castor beans. Sometimes spelled Daverkonda.

Devar Malai (dā'vär mŭlī'), peak (6,307 ft.) in S Western Ghats, on Travancore-Madras border, India, 18 mi. NNW of Tenkasi.

Devarshola, India: see GUDALUR, Madras.

Devavanya (dā'vŏvänyŏ), Hung. *Dévaványa*, town (pop. 15,202), Jasz-Nagykun-Szolnok co., E central Hungary, 16 mi. E of Mezötur; rail junction; wheat, corn, tobacco; cattle, horses.

Devdelija, Yugoslavia: see DJEVDJELIJA.

Deveci Dagi (dĕvĕjĕ' däŭ"), Turkish *Deveci Dağı*, mountain (6,207 ft.), N central Turkey, 15 mi. S of Zile.

Devecser (dĕ'vĕchĕr), town (pop. 4,427), Veszprem co., NW central Hungary, on Torna R. and 22 mi. W of Veszprem; wine, corn, sheep, hogs.

Deve Dag (dĕvĕ' dä), Turkish *Deve Dağ*, peak (11,033 ft.), NE Turkey, in Coruh Mts., 19 mi. ENE of Ispir.

Develi (dĕvĕlē'), town (pop. 11,362), Kayseri prov., central Turkey, 23 mi. S of Kayseri; iron, lignite; rye, wheat, legumes, vetch, onions. Formerly called Everek.

Devenish (dĕ'vŭnĭsh), island (123 acres; 1 mi. long) in Lower Lough Erne, central Co. Fermanagh, Northern Ireland, 2 mi. NW of Enniskillen. Site of ruins of 6th-cent. abbey of St. Molaise of Devenish, including 85-ft.-high round tower and tower of abbey church (1449).

Devens, Fort, Mass.: see AYER.

Deventer (dā'vŭntůr), Lat. *Daventria*, town (pop. 44,089), Overijssel prov., E central Netherlands, on Ijssel R. (bridge), at W end of Overijssel Canal, and 45 mi. ENE of Utrecht; rail junction; industrial center; machine shops and foundries, carpet and tapestry weaving, cotton spinning, meat packing, woodworking; bicycles, cigars, edible fats, honey cakes (a local specialty). Site of prov. butter-control station. Has church (*Groote Kerk*), originally built in 8th cent.; rebuilt in 11th, 15th, and 16th. cent. Also has 15th-cent. church (*Mariakerk*), 17th-cent. town hall, 16th-cent. weighthouse, other examples of Renaissance architecture. A Hanseatic commercial city in the Middle Ages, it was an educational center where Thomas à Kempis, Erasmus, and the later Pope Adrian VI studied.

Deveron River (dĕ'vůrůn), Banffshire and Aberdeen, Scotland, rises in S Banffshire 11 mi. SW of Huntly, flows 61 mi. NE, past Huntly, to North Sea bet. Banff and Macduff. Receives Isla R.

Devers (dĕ'vůrz), village (1940 pop. 687), Liberty co., E Texas, 30 mi. W of Beaumont, in oil-producing area.

Devesas (dĭvā'zůsh), S suburb (pop. 1,742) of Oporto, Pôrto dist., N Portugal, on left bank of Douro R. just S of Vila Nova de Gaia.

Devesel (dāvăsĕl'), agr. village (pop. 1,829), Gorj prov., SW Rumania, 11 mi. SSW of Turnu-Severin.

Devetaki (dĕvĕtä'kē), village (pop. 1,983), Pleven dist., N Bulgaria, on Osam R. and 11 mi. NE of Lovech; wheat, corn, livestock. Has grottoes with prehistoric remains.

Devetak Mountains (dĕvĕ'täk), in Dinaric Alps, SE Bosnia, Yugoslavia; extend c.10 mi. along left bank of the Drina. Highest peak, Devetak (4,648 ft.), is 13 mi. N of Rogatica.

Devet Skal (dĕ′vyĕt skäl″), Czech *Devĕt Skal,* highest mountain (2,745 ft.) in Bohemian-Moravian Heights, W Moravia, Czechoslovakia, 27 mi. NE of Jihlava. Svratka R. rises on S slope.
Devgad Bariya, India: see BARIYA, village.
Devgarh (dāv′gŭr), village, Ratnagiri dist., W Bombay, India, port on Arabian Sea, 40 mi. S of Ratnagiri; fish-supplying center; trades in hemp. Lighthouse (N). Also spelled Devgad.
Devi Dhura, India: see CHAMPAWAT.
Devihosur, India: see HAVERI.
Devikot (dā′vēkōt), anc. *Bannagar, Bangarh,* village, West Dinajpur dist., N West Bengal, India, on tributary of the Ganges and 38 mi. NE of English Bazar. Hindu temples and ruins, 13th-cent. mosque ruins. Early Afghan ruler of N Bengal died here, 1206. Moslem outpost at end of 15th cent.
Deville (dŭvēl′), village (pop. 1,439), Ardennes dept., N France, on left bank of entrenched Meuse R. (canalized) and 8 mi. N of Mézières, in the Ardennes; foundries.
Déville-lès-Rouen (dāvēl′-lā-rōōā′), NW suburb (pop. 7,491) of Rouen, Seine-Inférieure dept., N France; textile printing, cotton milling, barrel making.
Devil Postpile National Monument (c.800 acres; established 1911; alt. 7,600 ft.), E Calif., in Sierra Nevada, on Middle Fork of San Joaquin R. and 70 mi. NE of Fresno. Cluster of huge, prismatic columns (40–60 ft. high) on face of basaltic cliff. Rainbow Fall (140 ft. drop) is 2 mi. downstream. Yosemite Natl. Park is NW.
Devilsbit Mountains or **Devil's Bit Mountains,** short range, rising to 1,683 ft., N Co. Tipperary, Ireland, 11 mi. SSW of Roscrea; Suir R. rises here.
Devil's Bridge, Ger. *Teufelsbrücke* (toi′fŭls-brü′kŭ), over Reuss R., in the Alps, S central Switzerland, N of Andermatt; alt. 4,600 ft.; crossed by St. Gotthard Road. Named from an old bridle-path bridge below. Tall granite cross commemorates fighting here (1799) bet. Russians and French.
Devil's Bridge, village, Wales: see PONTERWYD.
Devil's Den State Park, NW Ark., recreational area (over 4,000 acres) in Boston Mts., 7 mi. W of Winslow; caves, unusual rock formations.
Devils Elbow, W Alaska, bend on lower Yukon R. and 50 mi. N of Bethel; 61°33′N 162°W. In 1939 pop. of dist. was 13.
Devils Head, mountain (9,174 ft.), SW Alta., near B.C. border, in Rocky Mts. near E edge of Banff Natl. Park, 18 mi. NE of Banff; 51°21′N 115°16′W.
Devils Island, Fr. *Île du Diable* (ēl dü dyä′blŭ), rocky islet off Atlantic coast of N Fr. Guiana, one of the Îles du Salut, 28 mi. NNW of Cayenne, 8 mi. off the mainland. Formerly a penal colony (where Dreyfus was imprisoned), abolished 1938–46.
Devils Lake. 1 Village (pop. 1,273), with adjacent Manitou Beach), Lenawee co., SE Mich., on Devils L. and 19 mi. SSE of Jackson. **2** City (pop. 6,427), ⊙ Ramsey co., NE central N.Dak., 85 mi. W of Grand Forks, near Devils L. Rail junction and resort. Sheet-metal products; grain, livestock, dairy products, poultry. State school for deaf; jr. col. Settled 1882, inc. 1887.
Devils Lake. 1 In Lenawee co., SE Mich., 15 mi. NW of Adrian; c.3 mi. long; summer resort. Devils Lake village is at N end. **2** In NE central N.Dak., largest (□ 30) of group of lakes which includes East Devils L. and Stump L. Occupies irregular basin 30 mi. long; max. depth, 7 ft. No longer used for commercial shipping, lake has been receding since turn of cent. Water is salty. Devils Lake Indian Reservation and game preserve are on S shore. **3** In Texas: see DEVILS RIVER.
Devils Lake State Park (1,440 acres), Sauk co., S central Wis., just S of Baraboo, in Baraboo Range. Central feature is spring-fed, oval-shaped Devils L. (c.1 mi. long); on its shores are Indian mounds and a resort village (Devils Lake). Summer and winter sports.
Devils Paw, mountain (8,584 ft.) on Alaska-B.C. border, in Coast Range, 35 mi. NE of Juneau; 58°44′N 133°50′W.
Devil's Punch Bowl, depression and lake on N side of Mangerton Mtn., Co. Kerry, Ireland, 5 mi. S of Killarney. Source of Killarney water supply, it is perhaps crater of a former volcano.
Devils River, SW Texas, rises in Sutton co., flows c.100 mi. generally S to the Rio Grande NW of Del Rio. Power dams form L. Walk (3,500 acre-ft.) and Devils L. or L. Hamilton (45,700 acre-ft.) in lower course. Dry Fork is an intermittent headstream.
Devils Thumb, mountain (9,077 ft.), on Alaska-B.C. border, in Coast Range, 30 mi. NE of Petersburg; 57°5′N 132°22′W.
Devil's Thumb, Dan. *Djaevelens Tommelfinger.* **1** Cape, NW Greenland, on Baffin Bay, 70 mi. N of Upernavik; 73°53′N 55°45′W. Rises to c.2,000 ft. **2** Island (4 mi. long, 1–2 mi. wide), NW Greenland, in Baffin Bay, 130 mi. N of Upernavik; 74°36′N 57°7′W.
Devils Tower National Monument (1,193.9 acres; established 1906), NE Wyo., on Belle Fourche R. and c.115 mi. ESE of Sheridan. Massive fluted tower of volcanic rock, 865 ft. high above base and 275 ft. in diameter at top, 1,000 ft. in diameter at bottom; alt. of summit, 5,117 ft. It was 1st natl. monument in U.S.
Devil's Woodyard, volcanic region, S central Trinidad, B.W.I., 10 mi. E of San Fernando; known for its tiny mud volcanoes, which erupt regularly.
Devin (dĕ′vēn), city (pop. 2,745), Plovdiv dist., SW Bulgaria, in W Rhodope Mts., on Vacha R. and 32 mi. SSW of Plovdiv; sawmill and lumber center in coniferous woodland; livestock. Cultural center of Bulg. Moslems. Until 1934, Dovlen.
Devin (dyĕ′vēn), Slovak *Devín,* Czech *Děvín,* Ger. *Theben* (tā′bŭn), Hung. *Dévény* (dā′vānyŭ), village (pop. 944), SW Slovakia, Czechoslovakia, near Austrian border, on the Danube, at Morava R. mouth, and 6 mi. WNW of Bratislava. Noted for ruins of 9th-cent. Devin castle (destroyed by French in 1809), reputedly seat of rulers of Great Moravian Empire. Site of 1st All-Slav Rally, in 1945. Roman and Bronze Age remains in vicinity.
Devin, Free Territory of Trieste: see DUINO.
Devine (dĭvīn′), city (pop. 1,672), Medina co., SW Texas, 32 mi. SW of San Antonio, in irrigated agr. area; dairy products, canned foods, beverages. Inc. 1904.
Devinière, La, France: see CHINON.
Devizes (dĭvī′zŭz), municipal borough (1931 pop. 6,058; 1951 census 7,892), central Wiltshire, England, on Kennet and Avon Canal and 16 mi. E of Bath; agr. market; bacon and ham curing, mfg. (dairy, tobacco, and wood products). Has 2 Norman churches, several 16th-cent. timbered houses, and remains of wooden Norman castle of bishops of Salisbury.
Devlali, India: see DEOLALI.
Devli, India: see DEOLI, Madhya Pradesh.
Devol or **Devoli,** river, Albania: see DEVOLL RIVER.
Devol (dĕvōl′), city (pop. 152), Cotton co., S Okla., near Red R., 19 mi. SW of Walters, in agr. area.
Devoll River (dĕ′vôl) or **Devolli River** (dĕ′vôlē), in S central Albania, rises S of Koritsa in the Grammos (Gr. border), flows over 100 mi. N and W through L. Maliq (reclamation project), and, cutting a torrentuous course through highlands, past Gramsh and Kuçovë (oilfield), joins the Osum 8 mi. NW of Berat to form Seman R. Also spelled Devol or Devoli.
Dévoluy (dāvôlwē′), limestone range of the Dauphiné Pre-Alps, in Isère and Hautes-Alpes depts., SE France, NW of Gap, bounded by Champsaur valley (E), by the Grand Buëch (SW) and the Petit Buëch (S). Highest summits are the Obiou (9,163 ft.), the Grand-Ferrand (9,058 ft.) and the Pic de Bure (8,898 ft.). An arid region suffering from depopulation. Saint-Étienne-en-Dévoluy is at its center.
Devon (dĕ′vŭn), residential town (pop. 2,337), S N.B., on St. John R. opposite Fredericton. Inc. 1917.
Devon or **Devonshire** (dĕ′vŭn, –shĭr,–shŭr), county (□ 2,611.5; 1931 pop. 732,968; 1951 census pop. 798,283), SW England; ⊙ Exeter. Bounded by Bristol Channel (N), Somerset (NE), Dorset (SE), English Channel (S), and Cornwall (W). Agr. and maritime co., with hills, fertile valleys, rocky coasts, reaching greatest height (2,039 ft.) in DARTMOOR; in NE is moorland area of Exmoor. Drained by Axe, Dart, Exe, Otter, Plym, Taw, Teign, Torridge, and Tavy rivers. Bideford Bay indents N shore; Plymouth Sound, Start Bay, Tor Bay, S shore. Dairy farming, cattle breeding (Devon cattle), fruitgrowing and cider making; mackerel and pilchard fishing (Brixham, Dartmouth, Plymouth), China-clay mining, granite and marble quarrying. Industries include mfg. of woolens, lace, paper, leather, shoes, and metalworking. Port of Plymouth is adjoined by naval base of Devonport. Seaside resorts: Ilfracombe, Barnstaple, Bideford, Torquay, Paignton, Dartmouth. Especially rich in anc. Br. culture (prehistoric, druidical remains) and English seafaring history (Raleigh, Drake, Hawkins, Grenville, Cook). The mild climate, pleasant scenery, and unspoiled villages make it a favorite tourist resort. Some of the fine landmarks of Plymouth and Exeter were destroyed by bombing during Second World War.
Devon, town (pop. 2,100), Manchester parish, W central Jamaica, in uplands, 9 mi. N of Mandeville; tropical fruit, spices.
Devon, Conn.: see MILFORD.
Devon Island (□ 21,606), E Franklin Dist., Northwest Territories, in the Arctic Ocean; 74°33′–77°4′N 79°40′–96°50′W; bounded E by Baffin Bay, separated from Baffin and Somerset isls. (S) by Lancaster Sound, from Cornwallis Isl. (SW) by Wellington Channel, from the Sverdrup Isls. (NW) by Belcher Channel, and from Ellesmere Isl. (N) by Jones Sound. Isl. is 320 mi. long, 80–100 mi. wide. Plateau, ice-covered in E, where it rises to c.3,000 ft.; in W it rises to 2,000 ft. Grinnell Peninsula, extending NW, was formerly considered to be separate isl. Dundas Harbour post (SE), on Lancaster Sound (74°31′N 82°25′W), is unoccupied. Formerly North Devon Isl.
Devonport, England: see PLYMOUTH.
Devonport (dĕ′vŭnpôrt), residential borough (pop. 11,662), N N.Isl., New Zealand, on NE shore of Waitemata Harbour; suburb of Auckland. Popularly called North Shore of Auckland.
Devonport, town and port (pop. 7,497), N Tasmania, 45 mi. NW of Launceston, at mouth of Mersey R.; vegetable-dehydration and dairy plants, sawmills, steam plant. Created 1890 by merging of Torquay and Formby, connected by bridge across Mersey R. Bathing beaches near by.
Devon River, Scotland, in Perthshire and Clackmannan, rises in Ochil Hills 3 mi. N of Alva, flows E, then turns sharply W at Kinross border, flows past Tillicoultry to the Forth at Cambus; 33 mi. long. There are noted waterfalls at Crook of Devon, 5 mi. WSW of Kinross.
Devonshire, parish (1939 pop. 3,059), central Bermuda.
Devonshire, England: see DEVON.
Devonside, Scotland: see TILLICOULTRY.
Devoto (dāvō′tō), town (pop. 2,505), E Córdoba prov., Argentina, 13 mi. W of San Francisco; agr. center (wheat, alfalfa, flax, livestock); mfg. of farm implements, liquor; flour milling, dairying.
Devrek (dĕvrĕk′), village (pop. 4,162), Zonguldak prov., N Turkey, on Devrek R. and 18 mi. SSE of Zonguldak; coal mines; grain, flax, hemp. Formerly Hamidiye.
Devrekani (dĕvrĕ′kănē), Turkish *Devrekâni,* village (pop. 1,203), Kastamonu prov., N Turkey, 15 mi. N of Kastamonu; wheat, barley.
Devrek River, N Turkey, rises in Bolu Mts. 10 mi. SW of Bolu, flows 80 mi. NE, past Bolu and Devrek, to Yenice R. 10 mi. NE of Devrek.
Devrez River (dĕvrĕz′), N central Turkey, rises on Yildirim Dag 13 mi. ENE of Kizilcahamam, flows 105 mi. ENE, past Ilgaz and Tosya, to the Kizil Irmak 5 mi. WSW of Kargi. Sometimes spelled Devres.
Devrukh (dāv′rōōk), village (pop. 5,303), Ratnagiri dist., S Bombay, India, 22 mi. ENE of Ratnagiri; agr. market (chiefly rice). Sometimes spelled Deorukh.
Devynock, agr. village in Maescar (mīskär′) parish (pop. 734), W Brecknock, Wales, on short tributary of Usk R. and 7 mi. W of Brecknock. Has 15th-cent. church. Just N is Senny Bridge, with remains of anc. stronghold of Senny Ddu.
Dewa (dā′vŭ), town (pop. 6,489), Bara Banki dist., central Uttar Pradesh, India, on branch of Sarda Canal and 8 mi. NNW of Nawabganj; rice, gram, wheat, oilseeds, corn.
Dewa (dā′wä), former province in N Honshu, Japan; now Akita prefecture and part of Aomori prefecture.
Dewangiri (dävăng′gĭrē), village, SE Bhutan, 50 mi. NNW of Gauhati (Assam), on trade route from Rangia. Dewangiri area was part of area annexed (1866) by the British after Bhutan War; it was part of Kamrup dist. (Assam) until 1949, when area was returned to Bhutan by India.
Dewar (dōō′ŭr, dū′ŭr), city (pop. 1,015), Okmulgee co., E central Okla., 3 mi. NE of Henryetta, in agr. area.
Dewas (dā′väs), former princely state (□ 866; pop. 173,021) of Central India agency, divided territorially and administratively into 2 separate branches, both sharing ⊙ at Dewas town. Acquired c.1730 by 2 brothers (Mahrattas) from Peshwa. In 1948, both branches, **Dewas Junior** (pop. 83,669) and **Dewas Senior** (pop. 89,352), were merged with Madhya Bharat.
Dewas, town (pop. 22,949), ⊙ Dewas dist., W central Madhya Bharat, India, on Malwa plateau, 20 mi. NNE of Indore; trade center for wheat, millet, cotton, cloth fabrics; cotton and flour milling, soap mfg., hand-loom weaving; engineering workshop. Was ⊙ former twin states of Dewas and was administered in 2 distinct parts, Dewas Senior (pop. 12,987) and Dewas Junior (pop. 9,962).
Dewdney, village, SW B.C., in lower Fraser R. valley, 5 mi. ENE of Mission; lumbering, dairying; vegetables, fruit.
Deweese (dŭwēz′), village (pop. 115), Clay co., S Nebr., 20 mi. SE of Hastings and on Little Blue R.
Dewees Island (dŭwēz′), Charleston co., SE S.C., swampy isl. (c.2 mi. long), 13 mi. ENE of Charleston, bet. Intracoastal Waterway channel and the Atlantic.
Dewetsdorp (dŭvĕts′dôrp), town (pop. 2,797), SW Orange Free State, U. of So. Afr., near Modder R., 40 mi. SE of Bloemfontein; alt. 4,990 ft.; stock, grain. Founded 1876.
Dewey, town (pop. 684), of Puerto Rico, on S Culebra Isl., 55 mi. E of San Juan; 18°17′N 65°18′W. U.S. naval base. Called Culebra until c.1940.
Dewey. 1 County (□ 990; pop. 8,789), W Okla.; ⊙ Taloga. Intersected by Canadian and North Canadian rivers. Agr. (wheat, broomcorn, cotton, oats), stock raising. Bentonite and fuller's-earth mining. Formed 1891. **2** County (□ 1,893; pop. 4,916), N central S.Dak.; ⊙ Timber Lake. Agr. and cattle-raising area drained by Moreau R. and numerous creeks and bounded E by Missouri R. Part of Cheyenne River. Indian Reservation in SW, and state game refuge along Little Moreau R. Lignite mines; dairy produce, flax, wheat. Formed 1883.
Dewey, city (pop. 2,513), Washington co., NE Okla., 4 mi. NE of Bartlesville, in farm and oil area; mfg. of gasoline, oil-field supplies, cement, metal products, dehydrated alfalfa. Has annual fair and rodeo. State fish hatchery near by. Founded 1899, inc. 1906.

Dewey Dam, Johnson co., E Ky., in Johns Creek (E tributary of Levisa Fork), 7 mi. SE of Paintsville. For flood control; 118 ft. high, 920 ft. long; begun 1946. Impounds Dewey Reservoir (capacity 88,000 acre-feet).

Dewey Park, village (pop. 1,589), Madison co., SW Ill.

Deweyville. **1** Village (1940 pop. 1,074), Newton co., E Texas, on Sabine and 26 mi. NE of Beaumont; lumber. **2** Town (pop. 233), Box Elder co., N Utah, near Bear R., 14 mi. N of Brigham City; alt. 4,323 ft.; agr., livestock.

De Witt. **1** County (□ 399; pop. 16,894), central Ill.; ⊙ Clinton. Grain-growing area, producing corn, wheat, soybeans, oats, livestock, poultry. Mfg. (dairy products, clothing, patent medicines). Drained by Salt Creek. Formed 1839. **2** County (□ 910; pop. 22,973), S Texas; ⊙ Cuero. Drained by Guadalupe R. Agr. (cotton, peanuts, corn, grain sorghums, fruit, truck); a leading poultry and egg-producing co. of state; also beef and dairy cattle, hogs, sheep. Oil, natural gas, sand, gravel. Formed 1846.

De Witt. **1** City (pop. 2,843), a ⊙ Arkansas co., E central Ark., 39 mi. E of Pine Bluff, in agr. area (rice, cotton, corn); cotton ginning, rice milling, sawmilling; ships timber, livestock. Federal bird refuge near by. Inc. as city in 1933. **2** Village (pop. 216), De Witt co., central Ill., 24 mi. NNE of Decatur, in agr. area. **3** City (pop. 2,644), Clinton co., E Iowa, 19 mi. N of Davenport; livestock shipping; calendar mfg. Settled 1837, platted 1841, inc. 1858. **4** Village (pop. 824), Clinton co., S central Mich., 7 mi. N of Lansing and on Lookingglass R., in agr. area. **5** City (pop. 254), Carroll co., NW central Mo., on Missouri R. and 15 mi. E of Carrollton. **6** Village (pop. 528), Saline co., SE Nebr., 30 mi. SSW of Lincoln and on Big Blue R.; mechanical appliances, flour; dairy and poultry produce, livestock, grain. **7** Village in De Witt town. (1940 pop. 10,836), Onondaga co., central N.Y., just E of Syracuse; paving materials; limestone quarries.

Dewsbury (dūz'bürē), county borough (1931 pop. 54,302; 1951 census 53,476), West Riding, S Yorkshire, England, on Calder R. and 8 mi. SSW of Leeds; woolen milling, coal mining; produces also shoddy, carpets, machinery, metal products, leather goods, chemicals, pharmaceuticals, soap, plastics. Has 13th-cent. Moot Hall; technical col.; church (rebuilt 1767) with stained glass dating from 13th-15th cent. In county borough are suburbs of Thornhill (S; pop. 11,040), Ravensthorpe (W; pop. 6,696), and Boothroyd (W), with metal-working and chemical industries.

Dexter. **1** Town (pop. 264), Laurens co., central Ga., 11 mi. SW of Dublin. **2** Town (pop. 643), Dallas co., central Iowa, 31 mi. W of Des Moines, in agr. area. **3** City (pop. 354), Cowley co., SE Kansas, 15 mi. ESE of Winfield; helium plant. **4** Town (pop. 277), Calloway co., SW Ky., near East Fork Clarks R., 30 mi. SE of Paducah. **5** Industrial town (pop. 4,126), including Dexter village (pop. 2,809), Penobscot co., central Maine, c.30 mi. NW of Bangor, near Wassookeag L.; woolen milling. Settled 1800, inc. 1816. **6** Village (pop. 1,307), Washtenaw co., SE Mich., 8 mi. NW of Ann Arbor and on Huron R., in agr. area (fruit, poultry, livestock; dairy products); sawmilling. Settled 1823; inc. 1855. **7** Village (pop. 316), Mower co., SE Minn., near Iowa line, 14 mi. ENE of Austin; dairy products. **8** City (pop. 4,624), Stoddard co., SE Mo., on Crowley's Ridge and 45 mi. WSW of Cairo; railroad junction; food and cotton processing, shirt factory. Founded 1873. **9** Town (pop. 784), Chaves co., SE N.Mex., near Pecos R., 16 mi. SSE of Roswell; trade point in cotton area; alfalfa mill, fish hatchery. **10** Village (pop. 1,038), Jefferson co., N N.Y., at mouth of Black R. on Black River Bay of L. Ontario, 7 mi. W of Watertown; paper milling. Inc. 1855.

Dexter City, village (pop. 170), Noble co., E Ohio, 17 mi. N of Marietta and on small Duck Creek.

Deyá (dĕyä'), town (pop. 418), Majorca, Balearic Isls., 12 mi. N of Palma; olives, carobs, lemons, oranges. Fishing; olive-oil pressing.

Deylam, Bandar, Iran: see BANDAR DILAM.

Deynau, Turkmen SSR: see DEINAU.

Deynze, Belgium: see DEINZE.

Deza (dā'thä), town (pop. 1,483), Soria prov., N central Spain, 30 mi. SE of Soria; grain growing, flour milling, stock raising, mfg. of tiles and pottery. Thermal springs near by.

Dezful, Iran: see DIZFUL.

Dezhnev, Cape (dyĕzh'nyĭf), northeasternmost point (on Chukchi Peninsula) of Asia and Siberia, Russian SFSR, on Bering Strait, 55 mi. WNW of Cape Prince of Wales (Alaska); 66°5'N 169°40'W. Called East Cape before 1898. Named for 17th-cent. Rus. navigator who 1st reached cape, 1648; commemorated by monument.

De Zusters, Du. Guiana: see DRIE GEZUSTERS.

Dhaba or **Daba** (both: dhăbä'), town, N Hejaz Saudi Arabia, in Madian, port on Red Sea, 90 mi. NNW of Wejh; hq. of a Bedouin tribe; dates, sorghum, wheat; fishing. Sometimes spelled Dabba, Dhuba, or Duba.

Dhafni, Greece: see DAPHNE.

Dhahira, Dhahirah, or **Zahirah** (dhähĭrä'), interior district of Oman, on landward side of the Western Hajar and extending to the desert Rub' al Khali; main towns, Ibri and Dhank.

Dhahr, Wadi, or **Wadi Dahr** (wä'dē dhä'hŭr), valley in Sana prov., central Yemen, on central plateau, 6 mi. NW of Sana; agr. dist. (citrus fruit, grapes). Summer residences.

Dhahran or **Zahran** (dhärän'), oil town (pop. 7,000) in Hasa, Saudi Arabia, 8 mi. S of Dammam and on railroad to Hofuf and Riyadh; 26°19'N 50°8'E. Hq. of Saudi Arabian oil operations, center of DAMMAM field (discovered 1938). International air hub; site of U.S. air base. Linked by pipe lines with Abqaiq, Ras Tanura, and Bahrein, and has stabilizing plant for removal of hydrogen sulphide. A modern desert settlement developed after 1938, Dhahran is the hq. community of the Arabian American Oil Company, well supplied with fresh water, meat, fruit, and vegetables.

Dhaid or **Dhayd** (dhīd), oasis of Sharja sheikdom, Trucial Oman, in central Oman Promontory, 30 mi. E of Sharja; date palms.

Dhak (dŭk), village, Shahpur dist., W central Punjab, W Pakistan, near Jhelum R., on railroad and 24 mi. NNW of Sargodha; shipping point for coal and rock salt mined in Salt Range (N; connected by tramway).

Dhaka, E Pakistan: see DACCA, district.

Dhala, Dhala', or **Dala'** (all: dhä'lä), town (pop. 2,500), ⊙ Amiri tribal area, Western Aden Protectorate, in hilly dist., 65 mi. NNW of Aden, near Yemen line; road terminus; airfield; radio station. Emir's residence on rocky hill overlooking town.

Dhaleswari River (dŭlā'svŭrē), arm of Jamuna R., central East Bengal, E Pakistan, leaves Jamuna R. (main course of the Brahmaputra) 8 mi. SSW of Tangail, flows 98 mi. SE, through extensive rice and jute area, past Munshiganj and Madanganj, to Meghna R. 5 mi. SE of Narayanganj. Receives an arm of old Brahmaputra R. just E of Narayanganj. Dacca is on Burhi Ganga R., a N arm of the Dhaleswari.

Dhali or **Dali** (dhä'lē), village (pop. 1,965), Nicosia dist., S central Cyprus, 13 mi. SSE of Nicosia, 15 mi. NW of Larnaca; wheat, barley, oats, olives; sheeps, goats. Near by is the site of anc. IDALIUM.

Dhalkisor River, India: see RUPNARAYAN RIVER.

Dhamangaon, India: see DATTAPUR.

Dhamar (dhămär'), town (pop. 5,000), Sana prov., S central Yemen, on central plateau, 60 mi. S of Sana and on motor road to Yarim; alt. 8,000 ft. Center of grain-growing dist.; tanning, rug weaving. Theological col. Noted for horse breeding. Sometimes spelled Damar and Demar.

Dhami (dä'mē), former princely state (□ 28; pop. 5,114) of Punjab Hill States, India, NW of Simla. Since 1948, merged with Himachal Pradesh.

Dhamnar, India: see SHAMGARH.

Dhampur (däm'pŏŏr), town (pop. 12,046), Bijnor dist., N Uttar Pradesh, India, 23 mi. E of Bijnor; hand-loom cotton-weaving center; sugar processing, brassware mfg.; trades in rice, wheat, gram, barley, sugar cane. Moguls defeated here c.1750 by Rohillas; sacked 1805 by Pindaris.

Dhamtari (dŭm'tŭrē), town (pop. 14,071), Raipur dist., E Madhya Pradesh, India, near Mahanadi R., 37 mi. S of Raipur; rail spur terminus; agr. trade center in canal-irrigated area; also trades in timber, lac, and myrobalan from near-by forests; rice and flour milling, shellac mfg. Industrial school. Lead deposits (SW).

Dhanaula (dŭnou'lŭ), town (pop. 9,560), central Patiala and East Punjab States Union, India, 50 mi. W of Patiala; local market for gram, wheat, millet; hand-loom weaving.

Dhanaura (dŭnou'rŭ), town (pop. 12,905), Moradabad dist., N central Uttar Pradesh, India, 13 mi. WNW of Sambhal; trades in wheat, rice, pearl millet, mustard, sugar cane.

Dhanbad (dän'bäd), town (pop., including rail settlement, 21,411), Manbhum dist., SE Bihar, India, in Damodar Valley, 31 mi. N of Purulia; rail and road junction; rice, corn, oilseeds, bajra, sugar cane; rice milling. Has Indian School of Mines and Applied Geology, Natl. Fuel Research Inst. Coal mining near by.

Dhandhuka (dŭn'dŏŏkŭ), town (pop. 11,150), Ahmadabad dist., N Bombay, India, 60 mi. SW of Ahmadabad; market center for millet and cotton; cotton ginning, handicrafts (cloth weaving, tanning, pottery), carpentry.

Dhangarhi (dŭng'gŭrhē), town, SW Nepal, in the Terai, on India border, 18 mi. NNE of Palia, 3 mi. W of Gauri Phanta (India) rail spur terminus; rice, jute, potatoes, sabai grass. Also called Dang Ghorai.

Dhangrot, W Pakistan: see TANGROT.

D'Hanis (dŭhä'nĭ, –hă'–, dă'nĭs), village (1940 pop. 655), Medina co., SW Texas, c.50 mi. W of San Antonio; shipping point in ranch and farm area; makes brick, tile.

Dhank or **Dank** (dhängk, dhänch), town (pop. 3,500), Dhahira dist., N Oman, 70 mi. SW of Sohar, across Western Hajar hill country; dates, limes, pomegranates; wheat, alfalfa.

Dhankuta (dŭng'kŏŏtŭ), town, SE Nepal, 35 mi. N of Biratnagar; handicraft paper mfg. Nepalese military station.

Dhanushkodi (dŭnŏŏshkō'dē), village (pop. 2,635), Ramnad dist., S Madras, India, port on SE point of Rameswaram Isl., 100 mi. SE of Madura, at W end of Adam's Bridge. Rail terminus; steamer service to Talaimannar (Ceylon) is main passenger route bet. India and Ceylon. Exports rice, dried fish, cotton goods.

Dhar (där), town (pop. 22,015), ⊙ Dhar dist., SW central Madhya Bharat, India, 36 mi. WSW of Indore; trade center for millet, corn, cotton, wheat, opium; cotton ginning, handicraft cloth weaving. Has several Hindu and Moslem monuments. Noted ⊙ Rajput clan (9th-14th cent.); later, under Moguls until c.1730, when it passed to Mahrattas. Birthplace (1775) of Baji Rao II, last of the Peshwas. Was ⊙ former princely state of Dhar (□ 1,798; pop. 253,210) of Central India agency, a Mahratta state, founded c.1730, since 1948 merged with Madhya Bharat.

Dharahra, India: see JAMALPUR.

Dharamjaygarh, India: see DHARMJAYGARH.

Dharampur (dŭrŭm'pŏŏr), village, Surat dist., N central Bombay, India, at NW foot of Western Ghats, 50 mi. SSE of Surat; local market center for rice, millet, pulse, timber; rice and oilseed milling, handicrafts (mats, baskets, fans, pottery); sawmills. Near-by forests have teak, blackwood, bamboo. Was ⊙ former princely state of Dharampur (□719; pop. 123,326) in Gujarat States, Bombay, inc. 1949 into Surat dist.

Dharampuri (dŭrŭm'pŏŏrē). **1** Town, Karimnagar dist., Hyderabad state, India: see DHARMAPURI. **2** Village, SW Madhya Bharat, India, on Narbada R. and 31 mi. S of Dhar; wheat, millet; cotton ginning.

Dharangaon (dŭrŭn'goun), town (pop. 19,840), East Khandesh dist., India, 18 mi. W of Jalgaon; trades in cotton and oilseeds with Jalgaon (linked by rail); cotton ginning, oilseed milling, handicraft cloth weaving. Wealthy market in late-17th cent.

Dharapuram (dä'räpŏŏrŭm), city (pop. 20,660), Coimbatore dist., S central Madras, India, on Amaravati R. and 45 mi. SE of Coimbatore; road and trade center in tobacco area; cotton, rice, millet; silk weaving; cattle market.

Dharavi, India: see BOMBAY, city.

Dharbat 'Ali, Ras, or **Ras Darbat 'Ali** (räs' dhärbăt' ălē'), cape on SE coast of Arabian Peninsula, on Arabian Sea; 16°38'N 53°4'E. Forms boundary bet. Aden Protectorate (W) and Oman sultanate (E).

Dhari (dä'rē), town (pop. 7,394), Amreli dist., NW Bombay, India, 22 mi. SSW of Amreli; millet, cotton; ironworking.

Dhariwal (dārē'vŭl), town (pop. 7,388), Gurdaspur dist., NW Punjab, India, on Upper Bari Doab Canal and 8 mi. SW of Gurdaspur; local market center; wheat, gram, sugar cane; large woolen mills turn out cloths, yarns, and clothing; hand-loom weaving, dyeing.

Dharla River, India and Pakistan: see JALDHAKA RIVER; TORSA RIVER.

Dharmaj (dŭr'mŭj), town (pop. 7,310), Kaira dist., N Bombay, India, 24 mi. SSE of Kaira; local market center for tobacco, millet, rice.

Dharmapuri (dŭr'mŭpŏŏrē). **1** or **Dharampuri** (dŭrŭm'pŏŏrē), town (pop. 5,577), Karimnagar dist., NE Hyderabad state, India, on Godavari R. and 35 mi. N of Karimnagar; rice, oilseeds. **2** Town (pop. 19,105), Salem dist., S central Madras, India, 34 mi. N of Salem; exports peanuts, sesame, castor beans, hides and skins; cattle breeding, woolen weaving. Corundum mined near by.

Dharmavaram (dŭr'mŭvŭrŭm), town (pop. 12,087), Anantapur dist., W Madras, India, 20 mi. SSE of Anantapur; rail junction; hand-loom silk-weaving center; oilseed milling.

Dharmjaygarh (dŭrmjī'gŭr), village, Raigarh dist., E Madhya Pradesh, India, 40 mi. NNW of Raigarh; rice, oilseeds. Was ⊙ former princely state of Udaipur, one of Chhattisgarh States. Limestone quarries near by. Sometimes spelled Dharamjaygarh or Dharamjaigarh. Formerly Rabkob.

Dharmkot (dŭrm'kōt), town (pop. 8,360), Ferozepore dist., W Punjab, India, 36 mi. E of Ferozepore; local trade in gram, wheat, cotton; hand-loom weaving.

Dharmsala (dŭrmsä'lŭ), town (pop., including N cantonment area, 9,653), ⊙ Kangra dist., N Punjab, India, on spur of E Punjab Himalayas, 75 mi. NNE of Jullundur; picturesque hill resort (highest point c.7,000 ft.); wheat, rice, tea; aerated-water mfg. Has col. of arts. Slate quarried near by. Average annual rainfall (c.120 inches) is heaviest in state. Severely damaged by earthquake in 1905. Sometimes spelled Dharamsala.

Dharsing, Nepal: see BHIMPHEDI.

Dharur (dä'rŏŏr). **1** Village (pop. 2,156), Atraf-i-Balda dist., central Hyderabad state, India, 45 mi. W of Hyderabad; rice, oilseeds. Vikarabad, rail junction, is 8 mi. E. **2** or **Fatehabad** (fŭtā'häbäd), town (pop. 6,894), Bir dist., NW Hyderabad state, India, 26 mi. SE of Bir; millet, cotton, wheat.

Dharwar (där'vär), district (□ 5,261; pop. 1,342,927), S Bombay, India, on W Deccan Plateau; ⊙ Dharwar. Bordered E by Hyderabad and Tungabhadra R., S by Mysore; drained mainly by right tributaries of Kistna R. Noted cotton area; also millet, wheat, chili, rice, oilseeds. Forests (W) produce teak and bamboo. Handicraft cloth weaving, cotton ginning. Hubli and Dharwar are cotton-milling centers and, with Gadag and Ranibennur, trade in local agr. products. Ruled (c.7th cent.) by early Chalukyan dynasty; later (14th-18th cent.) under Vijayanagar and Bijapur kingdoms, Mogul empire, and Mahrattas. Original dist. (□ 4,567; 1941 pop. 1,201,016) was enlarged by inc. (1949) of former Deccan states of Savanur and (parts of) Sangli, Miraj Senior, Miraj Junior, Jamkhandi, and Ramdurg. Pop. 84% Hindu, 14% Moslem, 1% Christian.

Dharwar, town (pop. 47,992), ⊙ Dharwar dist., S Bombay, India, 290 mi. SE of Bombay; road and trade center (cotton, timber, grain); cotton ginning and milling, rice and oilseed milling, mfg. of biris, perfume, glass bangles, handicraft cloth. Karnatak Col.; forest training col. Captured 1685 by Aurangzeb; taken 1778 from Mahrattas by Hyder Ali.

Dhasan River (dŭsän'), central India, rises in Vindhya Range in E Bhopal, flows c.235 mi. N, through NW Madhya Pradesh, W Vindhya Pradesh, and S Uttar Pradesh, to Betwa R. 13 mi. S of Orai.

Dhatu Pnom, Thailand: see THAT PHANOM.

Dhaulagiri (dou'lŭgĭ"rē), peak (26,810 ft.) in central Nepal Himalayas, N central Nepal, at 28°42'N 83°30'E.

Dhauli, India: see BHUBANESWAR.

Dhavlia, Greece: see DAULEIA.

Dhayd, Trucial Oman: see DHAID.

Dhebar Lake (dā'bŭr) or **Jai Samand** (jī' sŭmŭnd'), large artificial lake in SE Aravalli Range, S Rajasthan, India, 25 mi. SE of Udaipur; c.9 mi. long (NW-SE), 2–5 mi. wide when full. Formed by marble dam (SW; c.1,000 ft. long, 100 ft. high) built in late-17th cent.

Dhekelia, Greece: see DEKELEIA.

Dhekiajuli (dākyä'jŏŏlē), village, Darrang dist., NW Assam, India, 20 mi. WNW of Tezpur, in extensive tea-garden area; tea, rice, rape and mustard.

Dhelfoi, Greece: see DELPHI.

Dhenkanal (dāng'känäl), district (□ 4,161; pop. 741,900), central Orissa, India; ⊙ Dhenkanal. Bounded SW by Mahanadi R., E by Cuttack dist.; drained by Brahmani R.; cultivated valleys (rice, oilseeds) and several broken hill ranges (Malayagiri peak is N). Forests yield sal, bamboo, lac. Markets at Dhenkanal, Angul, Talcher (coal mines near by), and Bhuban. Created 1949 by merger of former princely states of Dhenkanal, Athmallik, Talcher, Pal Lahara, and Hindol, and former detached Angul subdivision of Cuttack dist.

Dhenkanal, town (pop. 8,422), ⊙ Dhenkanal dist., E central Orissa, India, 21 mi. NW of Cuttack; market center for rice, oilseeds, timber; hand-loom weaving. Was ⊙ former princely state of Dhenkanal (□ 1,428; pop. 324,212) in Orissa States, inc. 1949 into newly-created Dhenkanal dist.

Dhenousa, Greece: see DENOUSA.

Dherina (dhārē'nä), village (pop. 1,593), Famagusta dist., SE Cyprus, 35 mi. ESE of Nicosia; wheat, vetches, citrus; sheep, cattle.

Dhesfina, Greece: see DESPHINA.

Dheskati, Greece: see DESKATE.

Dhespotikon, Greece: see DESPOTIKON.

Dheune River (dûn), Saône-et-Loire dept., E central France, rises just E of Montchanin-les-Mines, flows c.35 mi. NE, past Saint-Léger-sur-Dheune and Chagny, to the Saône below Verdun-sur-le-Doubs. From its source to Chagny it is accompanied by the Canal du Centre.

Dhiakopton, Greece: see DIAKOPTON.

Dhiaporos, island, Greece: see DIAPOROS.

Dhiban (dhē'băn, zē'băn), anc. *Dibon,* village (pop. c.250), N central Jordan, 32 mi. SSW of Amman; wheat, barley, fruit. The Moabite Stone (with inscription from 850 B.C.) was discovered here, 1868. Sometimes spelled Diban.

Dhidhimotikhon, Greece: see DIDYMOTEIKHON.

Dhikti, Mount, Crete: see DIKTE, MOUNT.

Dhilos, Greece: see DELOS.

Dhimitsana, Greece: see DEMETSANA.

Dhinoj (dĭnōj'), town (pop. 5,544), Mehsana dist., N Bombay, India, 9 mi. NW of Mehsana; local market for millet, cotton, oilseeds. Sometimes spelled Dhinaj.

Dhirfis, Greece: see DIRPHYS.

Dhi Sifal or **Dhi Sufal,** Yemen: see DISUFAL.

Dhi Sura (dhē' sŏŏ'rü), town, ⊙ Dhubi sheikdom of Upper Yafa, Western Aden Protectorate, 3 mi. N of Mahjaba. Also spelled Disara.

Dhitiki Thraki, Greece: see THRACE.

Dhodhekanisos, Greece: see DODECANESE.

Dhofar, Dhufar, or **Zafar** (all: dhōfär'), southernmost district of Oman, on SE coast of Arabian Peninsula, extending 135 mi. bet. the capes Ras Nus (E) and Ras Dharbat 'Ali (W; marking limit of Aden Protectorate); consists of a coastal plain (20 mi. wide) backed by the hill country of the Jabal Samhan. In a more restricted sense, the name Dhofar applies to the coastal plain in the vicinity of Salala, the chief town, and Murbat, the chief port of the dist.

Dhoire, Northern Ireland: see LONDONDERRY, county borough.

Dhokos, Greece: see DOKOS.

Dhola (dō'lŭ), village, E Saurashtra, India, 27 mi. W of Bhaunagar; rail junction; sugar milling.

Dholera (dōlā'rŭ), town (pop. 3,884), Ahmadabad dist., N Bombay, India, 60 mi. SSW of Ahmadabad; cotton market; wheat, millet; trades inland via Dhandhuka and by sea (Gulf of Cambay, E).

Dholka (dōl'kŭ), town (pop. 17,222), Ahmadabad dist., N Bombay, India, 22 mi. SSW of Ahmadabad; trades in cotton, wheat, millet, rice; tanning, handicraft cloth weaving.

Dholpur (dōl'pŏŏr), city (pop. 21,311), E Rajasthan, India, 130 mi. ESE of Jaipur; rail junction (workshop); trade center (millet, gram, cotton, wheat, sandstone); hand-loom carpet weaving. Red sandstone quarried 3 mi. W. Ruins of anc. fort lie just S, near Chambal R. Was ⊙ former princely state of Dholpur (□ 1,173; pop. 286,901) in Rajputana States, India; Dholpur, a Jat state, made a treaty with British in 1803 and in 1949 joined union of Rajasthan.

Dhomokos, Greece: see DOMOKOS.

Dhond (dōnd), town (pop., including suburban area, 12,828), Poona dist., central Bombay, India, on Bhima R. and 45 mi. E of Poona; rail junction (workshops); trades in millet, gur, peanuts, wheat; brick mfg.

Dhone (dō'nā), town (pop. 4,828), Kurnool dist., N Madras, India, 32 mi. SSW of Kurnool. Rail junction (Dronachellam station); ships barite, ocher, and slate mined near by and 20 mi. ENE, near Betamcherla (rail station); ceramics, handicraft glass bangles. Bamboo, dyewood in near-by forests.

Dhopap, India: see SULTANPUR, town, Uttar Pradesh.

Dhoraji (dōrä'jē), town (pop. 37,647), W central Saurashtra, India, 45 mi. SSW of Rajkot; trade center (oilseeds, millet, cotton, cloth fabrics); hand-loom weaving, embroidering; copper- and brassware. Formerly in Gondal state.

Dhoran, Dhuran, or **Zuran** (all: dhōrän'), town, Sana prov., central Yemen, 40 mi. S of Sana; residence of a 17th-cent. Imam, whose tomb is on top of Jabal Dhoran (11,000 ft.; S).

Dhor el Khodib, Lebanon: see DAHR EL QADIB.

Dhoro Naro (dō'rō nä'rō), village, Thar Parkar dist., SE Sind, W Pakistan, on W edge of Thar Desert, 14 mi. NW of Umarkot; market center (cotton, millet, rice); cotton ginning, rice husking.

Dhour el Choueir, Lebanon: see DHUR EL SHUEIR.

Dhour Shouair, Lebanon: see DHUR EL SHUEIR.

Dhovista, Greece: see PAPPAS.

Dhoxaton, Greece: see DOXATON.

Dhrangadhra (drăng'gŭdrŭ), town (pop. 21,267), Zalawad dist., NE Saurashtra, India, on Kathiawar peninsula, 23 mi. NNW of Wadhwan. Rail junction; trades in cotton, salt, millet, building stone; chemical works (soda ash, caustic soda, sodium bicarbonate); cotton ginning, handicraft cloth weaving and embroidering. Built c.1730. Was ⊙ former princely state of Dhrangadhra (□ 1,167; pop. 94,417) of Western India States agency, founded late-11th cent. by Jhala Rajputs, merged 1948 with Saurashtra.

Dhrepanon, Cape, Greece: see DREPANON, CAPE.

Dhrol (drōl), town (pop. 9,741), NW Saurashtra, India, 23 mi. ENE of Jamnagar; market center for cotton, millet, sugar cane. Captured mid-16th cent. by Jadeja Rajputs. Was ⊙ former princely state of Dhrol (□ 283; pop. 33,617) of Western India States agency, merged 1948 with Saurashtra.

Dhuba, Saudi Arabia: see DHABA.

Dhubi (dhŏŏ'bē), sectional Upper Yafa sheikdom of Western Aden Protectorate; ⊙ Dhi Sura. Protectorate treaty concluded in 1903.

Dhubri (dŏŏb'rē), town (pop. 12,699), ⊙ Goalpara dist., W Assam, India, on the Brahmaputra and 110 mi. W of Gauhati; rail spur terminus; trade center (jute, fish, rice, mustard, tobacco, cotton, tea); large match factory.

Dhufar, Oman: see DHOFAR.

Dhuheartach, Scotland: see DUBH ARTACH.

Dhulia (dŏŏl'yŭ), city (pop., including suburban area, 54,406), ⊙ West Khandesh dist., NE Bombay, India, on Panjhra R. and 180 mi. NE of Bombay; rail terminus; road junction; cotton ginning and milling, oilseed milling, mfg. of biri, soap; handicraft cloth weaving and dyeing; markets millet, linseed, peanuts, wheat.

Dhulian (dŏŏlyän'), town (pop. 12,613), Murshidabad dist., W West Bengal, India, near the Ganges, 45 mi. NNW of Berhampore; cotton weaving; rice, gram, oilseeds, wheat, barley. Annual fair. Shellac mfg. 5 mi. SE, at Nimtita.

Dhulian, village, Attock dist., NW Punjab, W Pakistan, 5 mi. SE of Pindigheb; petroleum wells (in operation since 1937); oil pipe line to refinery at Rawalpindi, 50 mi. NE.

Dhulikhel (dŏŏlĭkāl'), town, E central Nepal, 15 mi. ESE of Katmandu; corn, rice, barley, vegetables. Nepalese military station.

Dhupgarh, peak, India: see PACHMARHI.

Dhuran, Yemen: see DHORAN.

Dhur el Shueir, Dhur esh Shueir or **Duhur al-Shuwayr** (all: dŏŏhŏŏr'ĕsh-shŏŏwär'), Fr. *Dhour el Choueir* or *Dhour Shouair,* village (pop. 2,142), central Lebanon, 16 mi. ENE of Beirut, alt. 4,100 ft.; popular summer resort. Also sericulture, cotton, cereals, tobacco, fruits.

Dhuri (dŏŏ'rē), town (pop. 7,649), central Patiala and East Punjab States Union, India, 33 mi. W of Patiala; rail junction; wheat, millet; cotton ginning, oilseed milling.

Dhursing, Nepal: see BHIMPHEDI.

Dhurwai (dŏŏr'vī), former petty state (□ 12; pop. 2,423) of Central India agency. In 1948, merged with Vindhya Pradesh; in 1950, inc. into Jhansi dist. of Uttar Pradesh.

Dia (dē'ü), uninhabited Aegean island (□ 6.6) off N coast of Crete, 10 mi. NNE of Candia; 35°28'N 25°14'E.

Diable, Île du, Fr. Guiana: see DEVILS ISLAND.

Diablerets (dyäblürā'), mountain in Bernese Alps, SW Switzerland; its highest peak (10,650 ft.) is Le Diableret (lü dyäblürā'), also known as Le Dôme (dōm), 9 mi. NW of Sion.

Diablerets, Les, health resort (alt. 3,790 ft.), Vaud canton, SW Switzerland, on Grande Eau R., NNW of the Diablerets, and 12 mi. NW of Sion.

Diablo, Mount (dēä'blō), peak (2,750 ft.), central Jamaica, 27 mi. NW of Kingston. At its N foot is the resort Moneague.

Diablo, Mount (dēä'blō, dĭă'–), W Calif., isolated peak (3,849 ft.) at N end of Diablo Range, c.20 mi. E of Oakland, in a state park (c.2,000 acres; recreational facilities). Road to summit.

Diablo Bolson (dēä'blō bōlsōn') or **Diablo Plateau,** extreme W Texas, basin with interior drainage into playas (salt flats) at W base of Guadalupe Mts.; alt. 3,500–5,000 ft.; bounded E by Guadalupe and Delaware Mts., E and S by Sierra Diablo, SW and W by Finlay Mts., W by Hueco Mts. Salt lakes here, worked for centuries, were disputed in Salt War, 1877.

Diablo Crater, Ariz.: see METEOR CRATER.

Diablo Dam (dĭă'blō), NW Wash., on Skagit R. and 65 mi. E of Bellingham. Part of hydroelectric project; the dam (386 ft. high, 1,180 ft. long) was built in 1930; owned by city of Seattle.

Diablo Heights (dēä'blō), town (pop. 1,647), Balboa dist., S Panama Canal Zone, 2 mi. NW of Panama city. Stock raising, dairying; corn, rice.

Diablo Plateau, Texas: see DIABLO BOLSON.

Diablo Range (dēä'blō, dĭă'–), W central Calif., one of the Coast Ranges, forms W wall of Central Valley for c.180 mi. from solitary Mt. Diablo E of Oakland to N end of Temblor Range in NW Kern co. General alt., 3–4,000 ft.; rises to 5,258 ft. in San Benito Mtn., c.20 mi. NNW of Coalinga. In N, range is double; its W arm (Mount Hamilton Range), which includes Mt. HAMILTON, bounds Santa Clara Valley on E.

Diablotin, Morne (môrn" dyäblôtē'), peak (4,747 ft.) of Dominica, B.W.I., 15 mi. N of Roseau; 15°30'N 61°25'W.

Diagonal, town (pop. 472), Ringgold co., S Iowa, 17 mi. S of Creston; livestock, grain.

Diakopton or **Dhiakopton** (both: dhēükôptôn'), village (pop. 1,874), Achaea nome, N Peloponnesus, Greece, at mouth of Vouraikos R., on railroad, and 25 mi. E of Patras; rail junction for Kalavryta. Zante currants, wine, livestock (sheep, goats). Formerly Diakophto or Dhiakofto.

Diakovar; Diakovo, Yugoslavia: see DJAKOVO.

Diala or **Dialah,** Iraq: see DIYALA.

Dial Pass (dēäl'), Andean pass (7,120 ft.) on Argentina-Chile border, 55 mi. SE of Linares; 36°25'S 70°56'W.

Diamant (dēämä'), town (pop. 614), S Martinique, on bay overlooking Rocher du Diamant (Diamond Rock), 9 mi. SSE of Fort-de-France; fishing; rum distilling. Sometimes called Le Diamant.

Diamant, Rocher du (rôshā' dü dēämä'), or **Diamond Rock,** SW promontory of Martinique, 10 mi. S of Fort-de-France. During war bet. Britain and France (1804), held successfully by Br. seamen.

Diamante (dyämän'tā), town (1947 pop. 13,503), ⊙ Diamante dept. (□ 960; 1947 census pop. 36,020), W Entre Ríos prov., Argentina, port on Paraná R. and 25 mi. S of Paraná. Rail junction; commercial and agr. center (flax, wheat, corn, fruit, olives, livestock, poultry); maté mills, sawmills, distillery. Clay quarries on Paraná R.

Diamante (dyämän'tě), village (pop. 2,203), Cosenza prov., Calabria, S Italy, fishing port on Tyrrhenian Sea, 10 mi. S of Scalea; wine, olive oil.

Diamante River (dyämän'tā), central Mendoza prov., W Argentina, rises in the Andes in small lake at foot of Maipo volcano, flows 200 mi. E, past San Rafael, to Río Salado 65 mi. E of Monte Coman. Used for irrigation and hydroelectric power.

Diamantina (dē"ümäntē'nü), city (pop. 9,663), central Minas Gerais, Brazil, in the Serra do Espinhaço, 120 mi. N of Belo Horizonte; alt. 4,144 ft. Terminus of rail spur from Corinto. Center of important diamond region. Known since early 18th cent., when diamonds were found in headstreams of near-by Jequitinhonha R. Also has rock-crystal and mica mines, and gold placers. Tanning, textile milling. Built in shape of an amphitheater. Known as Tejuco in colonial times.

Diamantina River (dī"ümŭntē'nü), E central Australia, rises in hills E of Selwyn, Queensland; flows 468 mi. generally SW, past Birdsville, to Goyder's Lagoon in NE South Australia.

Diamantino (dē"ümäntē'nŏŏ), city (pop. 644), N central Mato Grosso, Brazil, on a headstream of

Paraguay R. near the Amazon-Paraguay watershed, and 80 mi. NNW of Cuiabá. Its gold placers and diamond washings (important in 18th cent.) are now in decline.

Diamantpunt, Indonesia: see DIAMOND POINT.

Diamir, mountain, Kashmir: see NANGA PARBAT.

Diamond. 1 Village (pop. 107), Grundy co., NE Ill., 17 mi. SSW of Joliet, in agr. and bituminous-coal area. **2** Town (pop. 405), Newton co., SW Mo., 12 mi. SE of Joplin. **3** Industrial village, Kanawha co., W W.Va., on Kanawha R. and 12 mi. SE of Charleston; makes chemicals, plastics.

Diamond, Cape, on the St. Lawrence, S Que., at mouth of Charles R.; site of QUEBEC city.

Diamond Cave, Ark.: see HARRISON.

Diamond Caverns, Ky.: see PARK CITY.

Diamond Harbour, village, 24-Parganas dist., SE West Bengal, India, on Hooghly R. and 28 mi. SSW of Calcutta city center; rail spur terminus; rice milling; rice, pulse, chili. Customhouse and harbor master for ships proceeding to Calcutta. Main anchorage of East India Co. in Bengal. Falta village, 9 mi. NW, is rail spur terminus; rice milling; here English retreated, 1756, following capture of Calcutta by nawab of Bengal.

Diamond Head, promontory (alt. 761 ft.), on SE shore of Oahu, T.H.; extinct crater used by anc. Hawaiians as burial grounds. Site of lighthouse and U.S. Fort RUGER.

Diamond Island, reef in Andaman Sea, Lower Burma, off Bassein R. mouth of Irrawaddy delta; 15°22'N 94°17'E; pilot station and lighthouse. Turtle eggs.

Diamond Island (□ c.5), Henderson co., NW Ky., in Ohio R., 10 mi. W of Henderson; farming. Bandit refuge in early-19th cent.

Diamond Lake, Ill.: see MUNDELEIN.

Diamond Mountains, Korean *Kumgang-san,* Jap. *Kongo-san,* mountain range in Kangwon prov., central Korea, near Kosong, extending c.15 mi. parallel with E coast. Highest of numerous granite peaks is Mt. Piro (5,374 ft.). There are scenic ravines and canyons; on slopes are many anc. Buddhist temples.

Diamond Mountains, central Nev., NE of Eureka. Diamond Peak (10,626 ft.), highest point, is 9 mi. NE of Eureka.

Diamond Peak (8,792 ft.), W Oregon, in Cascade Range, 40 mi. N of Crater L.

Diamond Point, Du. *Diamantpunt,* promontory at NE tip of Sumatra, Indonesia, in Indian Ocean, at entrance to Strait of Malacca; 5°15'N 97°30'E; lighthouse. Important oil fields near by.

Diamond Rock, Martinique: see DIAMANT, ROCHER DU.

Diamond Shoal, N.C.: see HATTERAS, CAPE.

Diamond Springs, village (1940 pop. 594), El Dorado co., E central Calif., 3 mi. S of Placerville, in lumbering area.

Diamondville, town (pop. 415), S suburb of Kemmerer, Lincoln co., SW Wyo., on Hams Fork; alt. c.6,880 ft. Coal mines near by.

Diamouna, river, India: see JUMNA RIVER.

Dian, Vietnam: see THUDUC.

Diana Strait, Jap. *Shimushiru-kaikyo,* in central main Kurile chain, Russian SFSR, bet. Ketoi (N) and Simushir (S) isls.; 12 mi. wide.

Dianium, Spain: see DENIA.

Diano, Italy: see TEGGIANO.

Diano Marina (dyä'nô märē'nä), town (pop. 2,764), Imperia prov., Liguria, NW Italy, port on Gulf of Genoa and 3 mi. NE of Imperia, in olive-, grape-, flower-growing region; olive-oil market. Largely rebuilt since earthquake of 1887.

Diapaga (dyäpä'gä), town (pop. c.2,800), SE Upper Volta, Fr. West Africa, 90 mi. SSW of Niamey (Niger territory); peanuts, shea nuts, beeswax; cattle, sheep, goats.

Diaporos or **Dhiaporos** (both: dhēä'pôrôs), uninhabited Greek island (□ 1.6) in Singitic Gulf of Aegean Sea, off Sithonia arm of Chalcidice peninsula.

Diarbekr, Turkey: see DIYARBAKIR.

Díaz (dē'äs), town (pop. estimate 1,000), S central Santa Fe prov., Argentina, 45 mi. NNW of Rosario; agr. center (corn, flax, wheat, livestock).

Diba, Trucial Oman: see DIBBA.

Dibah, Trucial Oman: see DIBBA.

Dibai (dĭbī'), town (pop. 13,218), Bulandshahr dist., W Uttar Pradesh, India, 27 mi. ESE of Bulandshahr; trades in wheat, oilseeds, barley, jowar, cotton; cotton ginning and baling, oilseed milling. Headworks of Lower Ganges Canal 8 mi. E, at village of Naraura (or Narora).

Dibai or **Dubai** (both: dĭbī'), sheikdom (□ 1,000; pop. 20,000) of TRUCIAL OMAN, extending 50 mi. along Trucial Coast of Persian Gulf bet. the Khor al Ghanadha (Abu Dhabi border) and Abu Hail (Sharja border). Nearly all the settled pop. is concentrated in the town of Dibai, on coast, 8 mi. SW of Sharja; principal port and commercial center of Trucial Oman, port of call for Persian Gulf coastal trade; British post office; airfield, seaplane base. Petroleum exploration begun here in 1950. Sometimes spelled Debai.

Diban, Jordan: see DHIBAN.

Dibang River (dĭbäng'), NE Assam, India, rises in E Himalayan syntax on China border, flows 120 mi. S, through Mishmi Hills, joining Luhit R. W of Sadiya to form delta mouth at bend of Brahmaputra R. Also called Sikang.

Dibaya (dēbä'yä), village, Kasai prov., S Belgian Congo, near railroad, 105 mi. WSW of Kabinda; trading center. Cattle raised in vicinity, notably at Mazia Pata, 18 mi. SW.

Dibba or **Dibbah** (dĭb'bŭ), village, Trucial Oman, in Ras al Khaima sheikdom, on Gulf of Oman, 23 mi. SE of Ras al Khaima town across Oman Promontory; dates, livestock. Also spelled Diba or Dibah.

Dibble, town (pop. 148), McClain co., central Okla., 18 mi. E of Chickasha, in agr. area. Inc. 1937.

Dibden, town and parish (pop. 2,695), S Hampshire, England, near Southampton Water, 3 mi. SW of Southampton; agr. market. Has 13th-cent. church. In parish, on Southampton Water (E), is the commercial flying-boat base of Hythe.

Dibdiba or **Dibdibah** (dĭb'dĭbŭ), gravel plain in N Hasa, Saudi Arabia, on Kuwait and Iraq borders, adjoining (NE) Summan plateau; 150 mi. long (NW-SE), 100 mi. wide.

Dibe (dē'bē), village (pop. 3,215), NW Trinidad, B.W.I., just N of Port of Spain.

D'Iberville, village (pop. 1,429), Harrison co., SE Miss.

Diboll (dī'bŭl), village (pop. 2,391), Angelina co., E Texas, near the Neches and 11 mi. SSW of Lufkin; rail, trade point in lumbering area.

Dibon, Jordan: see DHIBAN.

Dibra, Yugoslavia: see DEBAR.

Dibrugarh (dĭb'rōōgŭr), town (pop. 23,191), ⊙ Lakhimpur dist., NE Assam, India, on Brahmaputra R. and 230 mi. NE of Shillong; rail and steamer terminus; airfield; road and trade center (tea, rice, jute, rape and mustard, sugar cane); tea processing, rice and oil milling. Medical school. Extensive tea gardens near by. Suffered greatly in 1950 earthquake.

Dibse or **Dibsah** (dĭb'sŭ), Fr. *Debsé,* village, Euphrates prov., E Syria, on right bank of Euphrates R. and 60 mi. ESE of Aleppo. Site of anc. *Thapsacus,* identified with the *Tiphsah* of the Bible. In anc. times, it was the principal crossing for hundreds of miles of the middle portion of the Euphrates.

Dicastillo (dēkästē'lyō), town (pop. 1,245), Navarre prov., N Spain, 5 mi. S of Estella; olive-oil, wine, cereals.

Dichato (dēchä'tō), village (1930 pop. 492), Concepción prov., S central Chile, minor port on the Pacific, on railroad and 20 mi. NNE of Concepción; seaside resort. Coal mines near by.

Diciosanmartin, Rumania: see TARNAVENI.

Dickelvenne, Belgium: see DIKKELVENNE.

Dickens, county (□ 930; pop. 7,177), NW Texas; ⊙ Dickens. Rolling plains, just Below Cap Rock escarpment of Llano Estacado; alt. 2,500–3,500 ft. Cattle-ranching and agr. area, including parts of huge Matador, Spur, and Pitchfork ranches. Cotton, grain sorghums, wheat, alfalfa, some fruit and truck; dairying, hogs, poultry. Gypsum, caliche, gravel deposits. Formed 1876.

Dickens. 1 Town (pop. 311), Clay co., NW Iowa, 6 mi. E of Spencer, in livestock and grain area. **2** Village (pop. 60), Lincoln co., SW central Nebr., 25 mi. SSW of North Platte. **3** Town (pop. 420), ⊙ Dickens co., NW Texas, on plain below Cap Rock escarpment, c.60 mi. E of Lubbock; a trading point for agr. and cattle-ranching area.

Dickenson, county (□ 335; pop. 23,393), SW Va.; ⊙ Clintwood. Bounded NW and N by Ky.; in the Cumberlands; drained by Russell Fork (a headstream of the Big Sandy; site of picturesque Breaks of Sandy) and its tributary Pound R. Bituminous-coal mining; agr. (grain, potatoes, livestock, fruit, tobacco); timber. Formed 1880.

Dickey, county (□ 1,144; pop. 9,121), SE N.Dak.; ⊙ Ellendale. Agr. area drained by James R. Grain and dairy products. State normal and industrial school at Ellendale. Formed 1881.

Dickey. 1 Town (pop. 135), Calhoun co., SW Ga., 27 mi. W of Albany, in farm area. **2** Village (pop. 165), La Moure co., SE central N.Dak., 15 mi. NNW of La Moure and on James R.

Dickey Peak, Idaho: see LOST RIVER RANGE.

Dickeyville, village (pop. 269), Grant co., extreme SW Wis., 9 mi. SW of Platteville, in agr. area. Here is an elaborately constructed shrine of Christ and His Mother.

Dickinson. 1 County (□ 382; pop. 12,756), NW Iowa, on Minn. line; ⊙ Spirit Lake. Glaciated, prairie agr. area (cattle, hogs, poultry, corn, oats, hay) drained by Little Sioux R. Chief lake region (Spirit, East and West Okoboji) of Iowa, with many state parks and resorts. Some lumbering; sand and gravel pits. Formed 1851. **2** County (□ 855; pop. 21,190), central Kansas; ⊙ Abilene. Gently rolling area, drained by Smoky Hill R. Grain, livestock. Formed 1857. **3** County (□ 757; pop. 24,844), SW Upper Peninsula, Mich.; ⊙ Iron Mountain. Bounded SW by Wis. line; drained by Menominee, Ford, and Escanaba rivers. Dairying and agr. area (livestock, poultry, potatoes, truck, hay, fruit). Mfg. at Iron Mountain. Some lumbering, iron mining. Resorts (hunting, fishing, winter sports). Organized 1891.

Dickinson. 1 City (pop. 7,469), ⊙ Stark co., W N.Dak., on Heart R. and 95 mi. W of Bismarck; wheat and livestock center. Lignite mines, brick and pottery plant, flour, dairy products, poultry. Seat of state teachers col. Agr. experiment station near by. Named Dickinson 1883, inc. 1919. **2** Village (pop. 2,704), Galveston co., S Texas, 18 mi. NW of Galveston; truck, fruit, dairy products; oil wells.

Dickoya, Ceylon: see HATTON, town.

Dicks Head or **Ras Chiamboni** (räs' kyämbō'nē), sandy headland on Indian Ocean at Kenya-Ital. Somaliland border; 1°39'S 41°36'E. Also spelled Dick's Head.

Dickson, county (□ 486; pop. 18,805), N central Tenn.; ⊙ Charlotte. Bounded NE by Cumberland R.; drained by Harpeth R. Livestock, dairy products, field crops; timber; iron-ore deposits, oil wells. Lumbering, mfg. of wood and textile products. Formed 1803.

Dickson, town (pop. 3,348), Dickson co., N central Tenn., 33 mi. W of Nashville, in timber, iron, oil, and farm area; mfg. of clothing, wood products, cigars; flour milling; railroad shops. Montgomery Bell recreation area near by. Inc. 1899.

Dickson City, borough (pop. 8,948), Lackawanna co., NE Pa., just N of Scranton on Lackawanna R.; anthracite; metal products. Founded 1859, inc. 1875.

Dickson Island or **Dikson Island,** in Kara Sea of Arctic Ocean, at mouth of Yenisei Gulf, in NW Taymyr Natl. Okrug, Krasnoyarsk Territory, Russian SFSR; 73°30'N 80°23'E; 4 mi. long, 3 mi. wide. On E side is Dickson Harbor, govt. polar station and coal depot on Arctic sea route. Named for Oskar Dickson, 19th-cent. Swedish merchant.

Dickson Mounds State Park, central Ill., 3 mi. SE of Lewistown. Here are extensive excavations of prehistoric burials, with skeletons and artifacts left in original positions.

Dicle River, Turkey: see TIGRIS RIVER.

Dicomano (dēkōmä'nō), town (pop. 1,377), Firenze prov., Tuscany, central Italy, on Sieve R. and 15 mi. NE of Florence; woolen mill. Badly damaged by bombing (1944) in Second World War.

Dicsoszentmarton, Rumania: see TARNAVENI.

Didam (dē'däm), village (pop. 2,331), Gelderland prov., E Netherlands, 10 mi. ESE of Arnhem; woodworking, strawboard mfg.; wheat, rye, oats, potatoes.

Didbiran (dyĭdbērän'), town (1939 pop. over 500), SE Lower Amur oblast, Khabarovsk Territory, Russian SFSR, 60 mi. SW of Bogorodskoye; gold mining.

Didcot (dĭd'kŭt), town and parish (pop. 1,655), N Berkshire, England, 10 mi. S of Oxford; agr. market. Govt. atomic research station at Harwell, 2 mi. W. Has 13th-cent. church.

Didessa, river, Ethiopia: see DADESSA RIVER.

Didia, Tanganyika: see LOHUMBO.

Didsbury, town (pop. 980), S central Alta., 40 mi. N of Calgary; stock and dairy-products shipping center; tanning, cereal-food mfg.

Didwana (dēdvä'nŭ), town (pop. 9,237), central Rajasthan, India, 120 mi. NE of Jodhpur; trades in salt, millet, oilseeds. On lake (just S) salt made by evaporation.

Didyme, Sicily: see SALINA.

Didymoteikhon or **Dhidhimotikhon** (both: dhĭdhĭmô'tĭkhôn), city (pop. 8,457), Hevros nome, W Thrace, Greece, on railroad and 23 mi. S of Adrianople (Edirne), on Maritsa R. (Turkish line); trading center for silk, wheat, barley, tobacco; mfg. of silk textiles. Bishopric. Flourished in Byzantine era. Following capture (1361) by Turks, it was briefly their European residence until fall of Adrianople. Called Demotika or Dimotika under Turkish and Bulg. rule; sometimes spelled Didymotichon.

Die (dē), anc. *Dea Augusta Vocontiorum,* town (pop. 2,502), Drôme dept., SE France, on right bank of the Drôme and 27 mi. SE of Valence, in Dauphiné Alps; noted claret and muscatel wines; furniture and hosiery mfg. Sericulture in area. Has restored Romanesque cathedral and Roman remains.

Diébougou (dyĕbōō'gōō), town (pop. c.1,800), SW Upper Volta, Fr. West Africa, 65 mi. E of Bobo-Dioulasso; peanuts, shea nuts, millet, corn, livestock. Market.

Dieburg (dē'bōōrk), town (pop. 7,884), S Hesse, W Germany, in former Starkenburg prov., on the Gersprenz and 8 mi. E of Darmstadt; mfg. of clothing; woodworking. Has old castle.

Dieciocho de Julio, Uruguay: see DIEZ Y OCHO DE JULIO.

Diedenhofen, France: see THIONVILLE.

Diedesfeld (dē'dŭsfĕlt), village (pop. 1,626), Rhenish Palatinate, W Germany, at E foot of Hardt Mts., 2 mi. S of Neustadt; wine; wheat, tobacco.

Diegem (dē'khŭm), town (pop. 4,296), Brabant prov., central Belgium, 5 mi. NE of Brussels; paper mfg. Formerly spelled Dieghem.

Diège River (dyĕzh), Corrèze dept., S central France, rises in Plateau of Millevaches 5 mi. W of La Courtine, flows c.30 mi. SSE to the Dordogne 8 mi. below Bort-les-Orgues. Powers hydroelectric plant at La Roche-le-Peyroux.

Dieghem, Belgium: see DIEGEM.

Diego Alvarez Island, S Atlantic: see GOUGH ISLAND.

Diego Álvaro (dyā'gō äl'värō), town (pop. 1,167), Ávila prov., central Spain, 27 mi. SE of Salamanca; vegetables, livestock; flour milling.

Diego Garcia (gärsē'ä), coral atoll (□ 11; pop. 501) in Chagos Archipelago of Indian Ocean, a dependency of Mauritius; 7°20'S 72°25'E. Encloses lagoon, 13 mi. long, 4–5 mi. wide. Exports copra, salt fish, tortoise shell. Served as Br. air base in Second World War.

Diego Martin (märtĕn'), village (pop. 5,774), NW Trinidad, B.W.I., 5 mi. NNW of Port of Spain, in cacao-growing region. Adjoined (W) by U.S. naval base (Chaguaramas Bay). Blue Basin waterfalls are 2 mi. ENE.

Diego Ramírez Islands (rämē'rĕs), small Chilean archipelago in the South Pacific, 60 mi. SW of Cape Horn; 56°30'S 68°43'W.

Diégo-Suarez (-swä'rĕs), town (1948 pop. 21,287), Majunga prov., N Madagascar, on S shore of Diégo-Suarez Bay (inlet of Indian Ocean), 20 mi. S of Cap d'Ambre, 310 mi. NE of Majunga; 12°10'S 49°20'E. Noted Fr. naval base (since 1901) with drydocks and coal and fuel depots; 2d port of Madagascar (after Tamatave). Mainly important as transshipment point bet. coastwise and overseas trade. Exports corn to Réunion, cattle to Egypt. Shipbuilding, printing; saltworks. Beef and sisal are processed in vicinity, and rice and cinchona are grown. Has military air base, large military camp, seaplane base. Seat of vicar apostolic. Town was laid out by Marshal Joffre. Diogo Soares, Portuguese explorer, gave his name (1543) to the bay, one of the world's best harbors; it is also sometimes known as British Sound. France occupied area in 1841 and Diégo-Suarez town became (1885) ⊙ of a Fr. colony called *Établissements français de Diégo-Suarez*. British troops occupied the port, 1942. Former native name of Antsirane (äntsērä'nä) or Antsirana (-nü) is still widely used.

Diehlstadt (dēl'stăt), town (pop. 165), Scott co., SE Mo., near Mississippi R., 5 mi. NW of Charleston.

Diekirch (dē'kĭrkh), town (pop. 3,793), ⊙ Diekirch dist., E central Luxembourg, on Sûre R. and 17 mi. N of Luxembourg city; metal foundries, mfg. (agr. machinery), meat canning, beer brewing; market center for wheat, pulse, potato, cattle region. Badly damaged in Second World War.

Diélette, France: see FLAMANVILLE.

Diemel River (dē'mŭl), W Germany, rises 8 mi. W of Korbach, flows c.65 mi. ENE to the Weser at Karlshafen. Dam at Helminghausen regulates (with Eder dam) water supply of Weser R.

Diemerbrug (dē'mŭrbrŭkh), town (pop. 3,572), North Holland prov., W Netherlands, 5 mi. SE of Amsterdam; coal-tar chemicals, asphalt, matches, cleaning materials, wood products.

Diemitz (dē'mĭts), village (pop. 5,604), in former Prussian Saxony prov., central Germany, after 1945 in Saxony-Anhalt, just E of Halle.

Diemrich, Rumania: see DEVA.

Dienbienphu (dyĕn'byĕn'fōō'), town, Laichau prov., N Vietnam, 50 mi. SSW of Laichau, near Laos line.

Dienville (dyēvēl'), village (pop. 854), Aube dept., NE central France, on Aube R. and 12 mi. NW of Bar-sur-Aube; grain; woodworking.

Diepenbeek (dē'pŭnbāk), town (pop. 7,808), Limburg prov., NE Belgium, on Demer R. and 4 mi. SE of Hasselt; agr. market. Has 12th-cent. castle, 16th-cent. Gothic church.

Diepenheim (dē'pŭnhīm), village (pop. 908), Overijssel prov., E Netherlands, 11 mi. WSW of Hengelo; agr., cattle raising. Near by is 17th-cent. castle (*Huis te Diepenheim*).

Diepholz (dēp'hôlts), town (pop. 8,052), in former Prussian prov. of Hanover, NW Germany, after 1945 in Lower Saxony, on the Hunte and 31 mi. NW of Minden, in peat region; rail junction.

Diepoldsau (dē'pôltsou'), town (pop. 2,715), St. Gall canton, NE Switzerland, on right bank of the Rhine, at Austrian border, and 13 mi. E of St. Gall; embroideries, toys.

Dieppe (dēēp', Fr. dyĕp), town (pop. 20,877), Seine-Inférieure dept., N France, on English Channel at mouth of Arques R., and 33 mi. N of Rouen; resort and fishing port, terminus of cross-Channel steamers to Newhaven, with bathing beach flanked by chalk cliffs; shipbuilding and repair yards; mfg. (fishing equipment, pharmaceuticals, faïence, vegetable oils, cider). France's leading port under Francis I, Dieppe became known for mfg. of carved ivory from imported tusks. Having adopted Protestantism, it suffered from revocation of Edict of Nantes. Bombarded (1694) by English fleet. Bombed repeatedly during Second World War; scene (Aug. 19, 1942) of an Allied commando raid which represented 1st important venture onto Continent since Dunkirk evacuation (1940). Town was heavily damaged, including 13th-16th-cent. church of St. Jacques, the 15th-cent. castle, and majority of hotels along beach.

Dieppe Bay (dēēp'), village (pop. 788), N St. Kitts, B.W.I., 10 mi. NW of Basseterre, in agr. region (sugar cane, sea-island cotton, fruit).

Dieppedalle-Croisset, France: see CANTELEU.

Dieren (dē'rŭn), town (pop. 6,352), Gelderland prov., E Netherlands, on Ijssel R. and 9 mi. NE of Arnhem; rail junction; bicycles, leather, fruit juices. Tourist resort.

Dierks (dûrks), city (pop. 1,253), Howard co., SW Ark., 16 mi. NW of Nashville, in timber and agr. area (fruit, cotton, corn, sorghum, livestock). Inc. 1907.

Diersbach (dērs'băkh), town (pop. 2,022), NW Upper Austria, 7 mi. ESE of Schärding; leather goods.

Diessen (dē'sŭn), village (pop. 5,599), Upper Bavaria, Germany, at SW tip of the Ammersee, near mouth of Ammer R., 13 mi. SE of Landsberg; lumber milling, printing, metal- and leatherworking; summer resort. Chartered 1317.

Diessenhofen (dē'sŭnhō"fŭn), village (pop. 1,860), Thurgau canton, N Switzerland, on the Rhine (Ger. border; bridge) and 5 mi. E of Schaffhausen; textile mfg., woodworking.

Diest (dēst), town (pop. 8,928), Brabant prov., N central Belgium, on Demer R. and 17 mi. NE of Louvain; wool carding, beer brewing. Has 15th-cent. church (with tomb of Prince Philip of Nassau), 14th-cent. Gothic market hall.

Dieterich (dē'drĭk, dē'trĭk), village (pop. 500), Effingham co., SE central Ill., 10 mi. ESE of Effingham; redtop-seed-cleaning plant; agr. (corn, wheat; dairy products; livestock); timber.

Dietfurt (dēt'fōort), town (pop. 2,027), Upper Palatinate, central Bavaria, Germany, on Altmühl R., at mouth of Ludwig Canal, and 23 mi. W of Regensburg; trout fishing. Chartered in early 15th cent. Limestone and dolomite quarried in area.

Dietharz, Germany: see TAMBACH-DIETHARZ.

Dietikon (dyē'tĕkôn), town (pop. 6,160), Zurich canton, N Switzerland, on Limmat R. and 6 mi. WNW of Zurich; metal and cement products, cotton textiles, clothing, canned goods, flour.

Dietlingen (dēt'lĭng-ŭn), village (pop. 2,798), N Baden, Germany, after 1945 in Württemberg-Baden, on N slope of Black Forest, 4 mi. W of Pforzheim; mfg. of costume jewelry.

Dietmannsried (dēt'mänsrēt'), village (pop. 1,634), Swabia, SW Bavaria, Germany, in the Allgäu, on the Iller and 5 mi. NNW of Kempten; dairying, printing, paper milling. Chartered 1586.

Dietrich (dē'trĭk), town (pop. 160), Lincoln co., S Idaho, 7 mi. E of Shoshone.

Dietrichsdorf, Germany: see NEUMÜHLEN-DIETRICHSDORF.

Dietz, Germany: see DIEZ.

Dietzenbach (dē'tsŭnbăkh), village (pop. 4,341), S Hesse, W Germany, in former Starkenburg prov., 6 mi. S of Offenbach; tanning.

Dieulefit (dyûlûfē'), village (pop. 1,801), Drôme dept., SE France, in the Baronnies, 12 mi. NNW of Nyons; pottery mfg., wool and silk milling.

Dieulouard (dyûlwär'), town (pop. 3,260), Meurthe-et-Moselle dept., NE France, on left bank of Moselle R. and 11 mi. NNW of Nancy; agr.-machine factory.

Dieuze (dyûz), town (pop. 2,444), Moselle dept., NE France, on the Seille and 16 mi. WNW of Sarrebourg; chemical mfg. based on near-by saltworks. Damaged in Second World War.

Dievenow, Poland: see DZIWNOW.

Dievenow River (dē'fŭnō) or **Dziwna River** (jēv'nä), right (E) arm of Oder R. estuary mouth, in Pomerania, after 1945 in NW Poland, bet. Wolin isl. (W) and mainland (E); connects Stettin Lagoon (S) with the Baltic; 22 mi. long N-S; rail and road bridges. Near Kamien Pomorski (Cammin), widens to form Kamien Lagoon; has strong current.

Diever (dē'vŭr), village (pop. 857), Drenthe prov., NE central Netherlands, near the Smildervaart, 12 mi. NNE of Meppel; cattle raising, dairying.

Diez (dēts), town (pop. 7,019), in former Prussian prov. of Hesse-Nassau, W Germany, after 1945 in Rhineland-Palatinate, on the Lahn and 2.5 mi. WSW of Limburg; main town of lower Lahn (Ger. *Unterlahn*) dist.; metalworking, marble polishing. Has 13th-cent. church, and former castle used since 1784 as house of correction. Sometimes spelled Dietz.

Dieze River, Netherlands: see DOMMEL RIVER.

Díez Gutiérrez, Mexico: see SOLEDAD DÍEZ GUTIÉRREZ.

Diezma (dyāth'mä), town (pop. 1,343), Granada prov., S Spain, 18 mi. NE of Granada; brandy distilling, lumbering; olive oil, cereals, wine.

Diez y Ocho de Julio, Dieciocho de Julio, or **18 de Julio** (all: dyāsēō'chō dā hōō'lyō), village, Rocha dept., SE Uruguay, near Brazil border, 12 mi. WNW of Chuy, in stock-raising region (cattle, sheep). Until 1909, called San Miguel. Just E are the ruins of old Portuguese fort San Miguel.

Dif (dĕf), Ital. *Diff*, village, S Ital. Somaliland, on Kenya border, 90 mi. NW of Afmadu; frontier station.

Differdange (dĭfürdäzh'), town (pop. 7,427), SW Luxembourg, 5 mi. WNW of Esch-sur-Alzette, near Fr. border; iron mining; steel center (blast furnaces, rolling mills); mfg. of synthetic fertilizer.

Diffie, Ga.: see WEST BAINBRIDGE.

Difícil, El, Colombia: see EL DIFÍCIL.

Difra or **Difrah** (dĭ'frŭ), village (pop. 4,988), Gharbiya prov., Lower Egypt, 4 mi. SSE of Tanta; cotton.

Difuntos, Laguna de los, Uruguay: see NEGRA, LAGUNA.

Dig (dēg), town (pop. 13,139), E Rajasthan, India, 20 mi. NNW of Bharatpur; agr. market (millet, gram, wheat, oilseeds); hand-loom cotton weaving; iron utensils. A walled town with several outstanding bldgs. Here, in 1804, British defeated Mahrattas. Sometimes spelled Deeg.

Digboi (dĭg'boi), village, Lakhimpur dist., NE Assam, India, 45 mi. E of Dibrugarh; petroleum-refining center (gasoline, kerosene, Diesel and lubricating oils; waxes, greases) in major Indian oil field; sulphuric acid mfg.

Digby, county (□ 970; pop. 19,472), W N.S., on the Bay of Fundy; ⊙ Digby.

Digby, town (pop. 1,657), ⊙ Digby co., W N.S., on Annapolis Basin of the Bay of Fundy, 60 mi. NNE of Yarmouth; fishing center (herring, scallops); seaside resort; terminal of car ferry from St. John, N.B. Lumbering, woodworking. Founded 1785 by United Empire Loyalists; inc. 1890. Extending SW from Digby is Digby Neck peninsula.

Digby Neck, peninsula (2 mi. wide) on the Bay of Fundy, W N.S., extends 30 mi. SW from Digby, forming St. Mary Bay. Opposite SW extremity is Long Isl.

Diges (dēzh), commune (pop. 1,059), Yonne dept., N central France, 9 mi. SW of Auxerre; ocher quarrying and processing.

Diggins, town (pop. 126), Webster co., S central Mo., in the Ozarks, 25 mi. E of Springfield.

Dighton (dī'tŭn). **1** City (pop. 1,246), ⊙ Lane co., W central Kansas, 40 mi. NNE of Garden City; grain, cattle. Inc. 1887. **2** Town (pop. 2,950), Bristol co., SE Mass., at mouth of Taunton R., 6 mi. S of Taunton; truck gardening; chemicals, dyeing and finishing textiles. Formerly shipbuilding. Origin of inscriptions, probably Indian, on Dighton Rock across the river has caused much speculation. Settled 1678, inc. 1712. Includes village of North Dighton (1940 pop. 1,181).

Diglur, India: see DEGLUR.

Dignano d'Istria, Yugoslavia: see VODNJAN.

Digne (dē'nyü), anc. *Dinia*, town (pop. 5,804), ⊙ Basses-Alpes dept., SE France, on left bank of Bléone R. and 70 mi. NE of Marseilles, in Provence Alps; rail terminus of branch line. Perfume and costume jewelry mfg., fruit drying and candying, beekeeping. Noted for sulphur springs (2 mi. E). Has church of Notre-Dame-du-Bourg (former cathedral built c.1200), and a 15th–19th cent. cathedral atop a central hill. Ruled by its bishops in Middle Ages. Damaged in Second World War.

Digoel River, Netherlands New Guinea: see DIGUL RIVER.

Digoin (dēgwē'), town (pop. 5,586), Saône-et-Loire dept., E central France, on Loire R. and 31 mi. N of Roanne; road center and port at junction of Loire Lateral Canal and Canal du Centre; pottery and chinaware mfg. center. Sandstone works.

Digor, Turkey: see POSOF.

Digora (dyēgŭrä'), village (1939 pop. over 2,000), W North Ossetian Autonomous SSR, Russian SFSR, 9 mi. NNW of Alagir; metalworks; wheat, corn, soybeans, orchards. Digora irrigation canal (NW) waters vegetable and fruit farms.

Digos (dē'gōs), town (1939 pop. 11,495), Davao prov., S central Mindanao, Philippines, 28 mi. SW of Davao, on Davao Gulf; abacá, coconuts.

Digras (dĭgrŭs'), town (pop. 10,705), Yeotmal dist., SW Madhya Pradesh, India 34 mi. SW of Yeotmal; cotton ginning; cattle market.

Digue Island, La, Seychelles: see LA DIGUE ISLAND.

Digul River or **Digoel River** (both: dēgōōl'), Netherlands New Guinea, rises in SE slopes of Orange Range, flows S and turns W to Arafura Sea, just N of Frederik Hendrik Isl.; c.400 mi. long; drains marshy area and extensive jungle region. The settlement of Digul or Digoel (7°16'S 139°25'E) is near its mouth.

Digwa (dĭg'wă) or **Dijwa** (dĭj'wă), village (pop. 6,321), Qalyubiya prov., Lower Egypt, 25 mi. NNW of Cairo; cotton, flax, cereals, fruit.

Digya or **Dygya** (dĭ'gyŭ), town (1939 pop. over 500) in Kirov dist. of Greater Baku, Azerbaijan SSR, on W Apsheron Peninsula, 8 mi. NNE of Baku; marlpits.

Dih, Turkey: see ERUH.

Dihang River, Tibet and India: see BRAHMAPUTRA RIVER.

Dijon (dēzhō'), city (pop. 92,686), ⊙ Côte-d'Or dept., E central France, on Ouche R. and Burgundy Canal, and 160 mi. SE of Paris; 47°21'N 5°2'E. Major transportation and commercial center, with important trade in Burgundy wines. Has various industries: metalworking (agr. and office machines, cycles, machine tools, electrical equipment), food (gingerbread, biscuits, mustard), chemicals (superphosphates, pharmaceuticals, fertilizer, ink); important railroad yards and workshops at Perrigny (just S); distilling, printing, tanning; mfg. of shoes, asbestos, and hosiery. Seat of univ. (founded 1722) and bishop (since 1731). Among its many fine public bldgs. are the 12th-cent. palace of dukes of Burgundy (largely rebuilt in 17th–18th cent.) now housing town hall and a noted mus. (founded 1783; celebrated sculptures by Sluter, Flemish paintings); the late-13th-cent. cathedral; the churches of Notre Dame (13th-cent. French Gothic) and St. Michael (Renaissance); and the 16th-cent. palace of justice, former seat of powerful *parlement* of Burgundy. Of Roman origin, Dijon flourished under dukes of Burgundy, who held a splendid court here (especially in 15th cent.). Reduced to prov. ⊙ after 1477, it remained a cultural center. Twice occupied by Germans in 1870. In Second World War it suffered from Allied air bombing. In Sept., 1944, 1st contact was established near by bet. Allied troops driving N and U.S. Third Army moving toward Ger. border. Dijon is birthplace of Bossuet, Rameau, Rude, and Crébillon.

Dijwa, Egypt: see DIGWA.

Dikanka or **Dikan'ka** (dyĭkä'nyŏŏkŭ), town (1926 pop. 4,951), E Poltava oblast, Ukrainian SSR, 15 mi. N of Poltava; flour mill, metalworks. Subject of Gogol stories.

Dike, town (pop. 517), Grundy co., central Iowa, 15 mi. W of Waterloo, in agr. area.

Dikhil (dēkēl'), village (pop. 500), S Fr. Somaliland, on road and 55 mi. SW of Djibouti; alt. 1,300 ft.; sheep, goats. Also spelled Dikkil.

Dikili (dĭkĭlē'), village (pop. 3,852), Smyrna prov., W Turkey, port on Mytilene Channel of Aegean Sea 50 mi. NNW of Smyrna; valonia, figs, tobacco.

Dikirnis (dĭkĭr'nĭs), town (pop. 10,681; with suburb, 11,264), Daqahliya prov., Lower Egypt, on El Bahr el Saghir and 13 mi. ENE of Mansura; cotton, cereals.

Dikkelvenne (dĭ'kŭlvĕ"nŭ), agr. village (pop. 1,632), East Flanders prov., NW Belgium, on Scheldt R. and 9 mi. S of Ghent. Formerly spelled Dickelvenne.

Dikoya, Ceylon: see HATTON, town.

Diksmuide, Belgium: see DIXMUDE.

Dikson Harbor, Russian SFSR: see DICKSON ISLAND.

Dikson Island, Russian SFSR: see DICKSON ISLAND.

Dikte, Mount, or **Mount Dhikti** (both: dhĭk'tē), highest peak (7,048 ft.) of E Crete, 25 mi. SE of Candia. Also called Lasithi.

Dikuluwe, Belgian Congo: see KOLWEZI.

Dikwa (dŭkwä'), town (pop. 5,242), N Br. Cameroons, administered as part of Bornu prov. of Nigeria, 55 mi. ENE of Maiduguri; cotton weaving, indigo dyeing, tanning; peanuts, cotton. An important center in old Bornu empire; ⊙ Bornu was moved here (1894–1902) from Kukawa. Since 1902, ⊙ Dikwa emirate. Dikwa division (□ 5,149; 1948 pop. estimate 228,100) is northernmost section of Br. Cameroons, administratively part of Nigeria's Bornu prov.

Dilam (dĭlăm'), town, S Nejd, Saudi Arabia, at S edge of Kharj oasis, 60 mi. SSE of Riyadh; trading center; grain (sorghum), dates, vegetables, and fruit; stock raising.

Dilam, Bandar, Iran: see BANDAR DILAM.

Dílar (dē'lär), village (pop. 1,337), Granada prov., S Spain, 7 mi. S of Granada; cereals, olive oil, sugar beets, fruit. Cinnabar, iron mining.

Dilaram (dĭlä'räm), town (pop. over 500), Farah prov., SW Afghanistan, in small oasis on the Khash Rud, 75 mi. E of Farah, and on road to Kandahar.

Dilbeek (dĭl'bāk), town (pop. 7,488), Brabant prov., central Belgium, 4 mi. W of Brussels; market for strawberry-growing area.

Dildo (dĭl'dō), village (pop. 536), SE N.F., at head of Trinity Bay, 40 mi. W of St. John's; cod-, salmon-fishing port. Sawmills near by.

Dilga, Egypt: see DALGA.

Dili or **Dilly** (dĭ'lē), city (pop. 1,795), ⊙ Portuguese Timor, and ⊙ Dili dist. (□ 475; pop. 32,661), on N coast of isl., on Ombai Strait; 8°34'S 125°35'E. Chief port and commercial center of colony. Mfg. of soap, perfume, pottery; coffee processing. Exports cotton, coffee, rice, wheat, sandalwood, wool, hides. In Second World War, city was occupied by Japan from Feb., 1942, until end of war. Sometimes spelled Dilli.

Diligent Strait, arm of Andaman Sea, bet. main group of Andaman Isls. (W) and Ritchie's Archipelago (E).

Dilijan, Iran: see DALIJAN.

Dilingat, El, Ed Dilingat (both: ĕd dĭlĭng-găt'), or **Al-Dilinjat** (dĭlĭnjăt'), village (pop. 10,636), Beheira prov., Lower Egypt, 15 mi. SSE of Damanhur; cotton ginning; cotton, rice, cereals. Sometimes El Delingat.

Dilizhan (dyĭlyĕzhän'), town (1926 pop. 6,464), NE Armenian SSR, in the Lesser Caucasus, near NW shore of L. Sevan, 45 mi. NNE of Erivan; highway junction; health resort (alt. 4,600 ft.), with mineral springs. Cattle-breeding station near by. Sometimes spelled Delizhan.

Dilj (dēl), mountain (1,506 ft.) in N Croatia, Yugoslavia; highest point is 10 mi. NNW of Slavonski Brod.

Dilja, Egypt: see DALGA.

Dill, Okla.: see DILL CITY.

Dilla (dĭ'lä), village (pop. 800), Sidamo-Borana prov., S Ethiopia, on road and 15 mi. WSW of Hula; flour mill. Sulphur springs near by.

Dillard (dĭ'lŭrd). **1** Resort town (pop. 186), Rabun co., extreme NE Ga., on Little Tennessee R. and 7 mi. N of Clayton, in the Blue Ridge and Chattahoochee Natl. Forest. **2** Town (pop. 51), Crawford co., E central Mo., in the Ozarks, 18 mi. SSE of Steelville; state park near by.

Dill City or **Dill,** city (pop. 453), Washita co., W Okla., 20 mi. SW of Clinton, in cotton and grain area; cotton ginning.

Dillenburg (dĭ'lŭnbŏŏrk), town (pop. 9,237), in former Prussian prov. of Hesse-Nassau, W Germany, after 1945 in Hesse, in the Westerwald, on the Dill and 16 mi. NW of Wetzlar; blast furnace; mfg. (ovens, stoves, wire; iron, steel, and other metal goods). Iron-ore mining. Has 15th-cent. church. William the Silent b. here.

Diller, village (pop. 314), Jefferson co., SE Nebr., 12 mi. E of Fairbury; dairy and poultry produce, livestock, grain.

Dilley (dĭ'lē), town (pop. 1,809), Frio co., SW Texas, c.65 mi. SW of San Antonio; rail, trade, shipping center for livestock and winter truck area (peas, melons, tomatoes). Settled 1880, inc. 1920.

Dilli, India: see DELHI.

Dilli, Portuguese Timor: see DILI.

Dilling (dĭl-lĭng'), town, Kordofan prov., central Anglo-Sudan, in Nuba Mts., 90 mi. SSW of El Obeid; trade center (gum arabic).

Dillingen or **Dillingen an der Donau** (dĭ'lĭng-ŭn än dĕr dō'nou), town (1950 pop. 9,673), Swabia, W Bavaria, Germany, on the Danube and 25 mi. ENE of Ulm; rail junction; woodworking, brewing, printing, tanning, lumber and flour milling. Has 13th–16th-cent. castle, former residence of archbishop of Augsburg; 2 early-17th-cent. churches; and univ. (1554–1804), now theological acad., controlled by Jesuits since 1564. First mentioned in 973, Dillingen was chartered c.1258. U.S. troops crossed the Danube here in April, 1945.

Dillingen, village (pop. 85), E Luxembourg, on Sûre R. and 7 mi. E of Diekirch, on Ger. border; building-stone quarrying.

Dillingen, town (pop. 12,917), W Saar, on Prims R. near its mouth on Saar R., and 15 mi. NW of Saarbrücken; rail junction; steel industry; mfg. of machinery, ceramics, chemicals; woodworking. Cannon-ball foundries here supplied French armies during Napoleonic era.

Dillingham, village (pop. 330), SW Alaska, on N shore of Nushagak Bay, inlet of Bristol Bay; 59°1'N 158°31'W; fishing; cannery; supply center for Nushagak R. trapping region. Airfield.

Dillingham Island, St. Lawrence co., N N.Y., in the St. Lawrence, at Ont. line, in group of islets just SW of Cardinal, Ont.; c.½ mi. long.

Dillon, county (□ 407; pop. 30,930), NE S.C.; ⊙ Dillon. Bounded NE by N.C.; drained by Little Pee Dee R. Agr. area (tobacco, cotton, corn, wheat, paprika); some timber. Formed 1910.

Dillon. 1 Town (pop. 191), Summit co., N central Colo., on Blue R., in Gore Range, and 9 mi. N of Breckenridge; alt. 8,600 ft.; resort. Gold, silver mines near by. **2** City (pop. 3,268), ⊙ Beaverhead co., SW Mont., on Beaverhead R. in Jefferson R. system and 55 mi. S of Butte; wool-shipping point; gold, silver, lead, copper mines; livestock. Western Mont. Col. of Education here. City founded 1880, inc. 1885. **3** Town (pop. 5,171), ⊙ Dillon co., NE S.C., 27 mi. NE of Florence; trade, processing, shipping center for agr. area producing cotton, tobacco, lumber, grain, paprika. Founded c.1886.

Dillon River, New Zealand: see WAIAU-UHA RIVER.

Dillonvale, village (pop. 1,407), Jefferson co., E Ohio, 12 mi. SSW of Steubenville, near Ohio R., in coal-mining area.

Dill River (dĭl), Hesse, W Germany, rises in the Westerwald 6 mi. N of Haiger, flows 30 mi. S and E to the Lahn at Wetzlar. Small iron-ore deposits in its valley.

Dillsboro. 1 Town (pop. 681), Dearborn co., SE Ind., 32 mi. SE of Greensburg, in agr. area. **2** Town (pop. 198), Jackson co., W N.C., on Tuckasegee R. and just W of Sylva, in mining (mica, talc) and resort area.

Dillsburg, borough (pop. 1,146), York co., S Pa., 14 mi. SW of Harrisburg; cigars, baskets; clay. Laid out 1880, inc. 1833.

Dillwyn (dĭl'wĭn), town (pop. 556), Buckingham co., central Va., 40 mi. ENE of Lynchburg; agr.; lumber milling.

Dilly, Portuguese Timor: see DILI.

Dilman, Iran: see SHAHPUR.

Dilolo-Gare (dĕlōlō'-gär'), town, Katanga prov., S Belgian Congo, on railroad, on Angola border opposite Teixera de Sousa, and 290 mi. WNW of Jadotville; customs station; trading center. Cotton ginning. Raising of native staples. Has R.C. and Protestant missions. Village of Dilolo, with cotton gins and R.C. mission, is 15 mi. NNE.

Dilos, Greece: see DELOS.

Dilton Marsh or **Dilton,** agr. parish (pop. 1,484), W Wiltshire, England, 2 mi. WSW of Westbury.

Dilworth, village (pop. 1,429), Clay co., W Minn., in Red R. valley, just E of Fargo, N.Dak.; railroad div. point in corn, oat, and barley area.

Dima (dē'mä), village, Leopoldville prov., W Belgian Congo, on left bank of the Kwa and 115 mi. SW of Inongo; trading and agr. center (mainly palm products), steamboat landing; shipbuilding, workshops. Has Jesuit mission.

Dimapur (dĭm'äpŏŏr), village, Naga Hills dist., E Assam, India, 28 mi. NW of Kohima, at junction of roads to Imphal and Burma; trades in rice, cotton, oranges, potatoes. Has 16th-cent. Kachari monuments and temple ruins. Was ⊙ Kachari kingdom until sacked 1536 by Ahoms (Shans). Rail station just NW, at Manipur Road.

Dimashq, Syria: see DAMASCUS.

Dimayrah, Egypt: see DIMEIRA.

Dimbelenge (dĕmbĕlĕng'gä), village, Kasai prov., central Belgian Congo, 50 mi. SSW of Lusambo; trading center; cotton.

Dimbokro (dĕmbō'krō), town (pop. c.1,200), S central Ivory Coast, Fr. West Africa, on railroad and 105 mi. NNW of Abidjan; cotton, palm kernels, palm oil, coffee, cacao, bananas, yams. Lumbering, cotton ginning. R.C. mission.

Dimboola (dĭmbōō'lŭ), town (pop. 1,710), W central Victoria, Australia, on Wimmera R. and 190 mi. WNW of Melbourne; rail junction in livestock area; salt, gypsum.

Dime Box, village (pop. c.400), Lee co., S central Texas, near Yegua Creek, c.55 mi. E of Austin; trade point in cotton, corn, truck area.

Dimeira or **Dimayrah** (dĭmā'rŭ), village (pop. 6,052), Gharbiya prov., Lower Egypt, 5 mi. NNW of Talkha; cotton.

Dimitrov Dam (dĭmē'trôv), dam in central Bulgaria, on Tundzha R. at Koprinka near Kazanlik. Projected reservoir (□ 5) to be linked by canal through the Sredna Gora with Stara Zagora plain (S).

Dimitrovgrad (dĭmē'trôvgrät), city (1946 pop. 3,672; 1950 estimate 40,000), Khaskovo dist., SE central Bulgaria, on the Maritsa and 9 mi. N of Khaskovo; rail junction and major industrial center; mfg. (cement, nitrate fertilizer, asbestos pipes); canning (fruit, vegetables). Coal mining; power plants. Originally called Kamenets, later Rakovski; named Dimitrovgrad in 1947 when large-scale industrial development began.

Dimitrovgrad (dĭmē'trôvgrät), village (pop. 4,430), SE Serbia, Yugoslavia, on Nisava R., on railroad and 14 mi. SE of Pirot, on Bulg. border. Black-coal mine is just WSW. In Bulgaria, 1913–19. Until 1950, called Caribrod or Tsaribrod.

Dimitrovo (dĭmē'trôvô). **1** City (pop. 28,504), Sofia dist., W Bulgaria, on Struma R. and 15 mi. WSW of Sofia; major industrial and coal-mining center in Dimitrovo Basin (□ 22; extensive lignite deposits); iron smelting, glassworks, mfg. of electrical equipment, briquettes. Has ruins of Byzantine fortress. Called Pernik until 1949. **2** Village (pop. 4,593), Sofia dist., W central Bulgaria, on E slope of Rila Mts., 10 mi. S of Ikhtiman; sawmilling, cutlery mfg. Health resort with thermal radioactive baths. Oil shale found near by. Its rail station (pop. 890), 3 mi. NW, on Maritsa R., has match, paper mills. Called Kostenets until 1950.

Dimitsana, Greece: see DEMETSANA.

Dimmit (dĭ'mĭt), county (□ 1,341; pop. 10,654), SW Texas, on plains of the Rio Grande; ⊙ Carrizo Springs. Drained by Nueces R. In Winter Garden truck area, irrigated by artesian wells; ships huge crops of onions, carrots, spinach, other vegetables, citrus; also cattle, dairy products, hogs, poultry. Formed 1858.

Dimmitt, town (pop. 1,461), ⊙ Castro co., NW Texas, on Llano Estacado, c.40 mi. NW of Plainview; trade and shipping point for wheat, cattle, and vegetable-growing area. Plains Memorial Hosp. is here.

Dimondale (dī'mŭndāl"), village (pop. 774), Eaton co., S central Mich., 7 mi. SW of Lansing and on Grand R., in farm area.

Dimotika, Greece: see DIDYMOTEIKHON.

Dimsdale, village, W Alta., 8 mi. W of Grande Prairie; coal mining.

Dinagat Island (dēnä'gät) (□ 309; 1939 pop. 14,606), Surigao prov., Philippines, just off NE Mindanao, opposite Surigao; 43 mi. long. A wooded range extends N-S, rising to 3,066 ft. in N. Coconut growing. Chromite and manganese deposits. Town of Dinagat (1939 pop. 3,521) is on W coast.

Dinahican Point (dē"nähēkän', –hē'kän), central Luzon, Philippines, on E coast, at tip of small peninsula at SW side of entrance to Polillo Strait; 14°41'N 121°43'E.

Dinajpur (dĭnäj'pŏŏr), district (□ c.2,600; 1951 pop. 1,380,000), NW East Bengal, E Pakistan; ⊙ Dinajpur. Bounded by West Bengal (W) and Bihar (NW), India; drained by Atrai and tributaries of Mahananda rivers. Alluvial agr. plain; rice, jute, sugar cane, rape and mustard, tobacco, corn, barley; low hill area S (sal, bamboo, and mango tracts). Rice, oilseed, and sugar milling, soap mfg. Main towns: Dinajpur, Parvatipur. Noted annual fairs at Nekmard and Alawakhawa. Hindu ruins at Ghoraghat; 18th-cent. Vishnuite temple at Kantanagar. Formed part of Buddhist Pal kingdom in 9th cent. A.D.; in 15th cent., under Raja Ganesh (Hindu convert to Islam). Original dist. (□ 3,953; 1941 pop. 1,926,833) was part of former Br. Bengal prov. until inc. (1947) into new Pakistan prov. of East Bengal; altered by transfer of W portion with Hindu majority to West Bengal, India, to form WEST DINAJPUR dist. and of S portion to Bogra dist., Pakistan, and by inc. of SW portion of Jalpaiguri dist. of West Bengal.

Dinajpur, town (1941 pop. 28,190), ⊙ Dinajpur dist., NW East Bengal, E Pakistan, on tributary of the Mahananda and 41 mi. WSW of Rangpur; road and agr. trade (rice, jute, sugar cane, rape and mustard, barley, corn) center; rice and oilseed milling, soap mfg. Col. Rice and sugar milling 11 mi. NW, at Setabganj.

Dinalupihan (dē″nälōōpē′hän), town (1939 pop. 3,041; 1948 municipality pop. 14,341), Bataan prov., S Luzon, Philippines, at base of Bataan Peninsula, 40 mi. WNW of Manila; agr. center (sugar cane, rice).

Dinamita (dēnämē′tä), mfg. settlement (pop. 1,716), Durango, N Mexico, 17 mi. NW of Torreón; explosives factory.

Dinan (dēnã′), town (pop. 11,111), Côtes-du-Nord dept., W France, port at head of Rance R. estuary, 29 mi. NW of Rennes; commercial and road center for tourists en route to seashore resorts; leather-working, mfg. of hosiery, agr. machinery; cider distilling, brewing. Granite quarries at near-by Le Hinglé. Fortified by dukes of Brittany; has preserved its medieval walls and towers, a 14th-cent. castle, and the Romanesque and Gothic church of Saint-Sauveur.

Dinanagar (dē′nänŭgŭr), town (pop. 6,968), Gurdaspur dist., NW Punjab, India, 7 mi. NNE of Gurdaspur; wheat, gram; hand-loom weaving; rice milling, embroidering. A summer resort of Ranjit Singh.

Dinant (dēnã′), town (pop. 6,925), Namur prov., S Belgium, on Meuse R. and 14 mi. S of Namur; rail junction; tourist center; mfg. (wool textiles, chocolate, beer); cattle market. Has 13th-cent. Gothic church, 17th-cent. town hall, and early-19th-cent. citadel. Fortified burgh in Merovingian and Carolingian times; fief of bishops of Liége from 1070 until Fr. Revolution. In Middle Ages, major market center noted for its copper-, brass-, and bronze ware, and for its wool trade. Sacked in 15th cent. by Charles the Bold, in 1914 by Germans.

Dinant (dī′nŭnt), village, central Alta., 8 mi. N of Camrose; coal mining.

Dinapore (dĭn′ŭpōōr, dunä′pōōr), town (pop., including cantonment, 40,057), Patna dist., N central Bihar, India, on Ganges R. and 6 mi. WNW of Patna; road center; rice, gram, barley, corn, wheat, millet; oilseed milling, furniture mfg.; metalworks. Also spelled Danapur.

Dinar (dīnär′), village (pop. 4,638), Afyonkarahisar prov., W central Turkey, near headwaters of the Maeander (Buyuk Menderes), on railroad and 50 mi. SSW of Afyonkarahisar; wheat, barley, opium, mohair goats. Sometimes spelled Dineir. It is on part of site of anc. Phrygian cities of Celaenae and Apamea, where Cyrus the Great had a palace. Alexander the Great conquered it in 333 B.C. Seleucus I moved inhabitants of Celaenae to Apamea, built near by.

Dinar, Kuh-i- (kōō′hĕdēnär′), mountain (c.14,000 ft.) in Zagros ranges, S Iran, 100 mi. NW of Shiraz.

Dinara (dē′närä), eponymous mountain range of Dinaric Alps, Yugoslavia; extends c.50 mi. along Bosnia-Dalmatia border. Highest peaks: Troglav (6,275 ft.; 20 mi. ESE of Knin); Kamesnica, Serbo-Croatian *Kamešnica* (6,065 ft.; 10 mi. E of Sinj); Dinara (6,006 ft.; 10 mi. NE of Knin).

Dinard (dēnär′), town (pop. 7,353), Ille-et-Vilaine dept., W France, on English Channel at mouth of Rance R. opposite Saint-Malo; Brittany's most fashionable bathing resort, catering to foreign tourists. Just W is smaller resort of Saint-Énogat.

Dinaric Alps (dĭnâ′rĭk), Serbo-Croatian *Dinara Planina*, Ital. *Alpi Dinariche*, SE division of Eastern Alps, almost entirely in Yugoslavia (small parts in Albania and Free Territory of Trieste), along E coast of Adriatic Sea. Linked in N to main Alpine system through the Julian Alps. Extend from Isonzo and Sava rivers (N) to Drin R. (S). Bounded (E) by Kolubara, Ibar, and Sitnica rivers. Occupy ⅓ of Yugoslavia, forming a great belt of limestone ranges and plateaus, including the KARST in NNW. The North Albanian Alps, southernmost and highest range, rise to 8,714 ft. at Djeravica peak. The Dinaric Alps constitute the most inhospitable barrier in Europe. Heavily indented coastline on the Adriatic produces numerous excellent natural harbors, but there is no natural access to productive agr. plains of the hinterland. Interior basins, though isolated, have fertile soil and dense population. Dinaric Alps are subdivided (from coast to interior) into maritime, central (highest), and ore-bearing ranges.

Dinas Mawddwy (dē′näs moudh′wē), village, S Merioneth, Wales, on Dovey R. and 11 mi. NE of Machynlleth, at foot of Maen Du (mīn dē′) mountain (2,213 ft.); slate quarrying; resort frequented by anglers and artists. Just NW is woolen-milling village of Dolobran.

Dinau, Uzbek SSR: see DENAU.

Dincha, Ethiopia: see CHANCHA.

Dinder River (dĭn′dĕr), central Anglo-Egyptian Sudan, rises on Ethiopian highlands W of L. Tana, flows W, past Dunkur, descends to Sudanese plain, and meanders NW to Blue Nile R. 12 mi. NE of Wad Abdalla; over 300 mi. long. Navigable c.120 mi. in lower course during flood season (late summer).

Dindigul (dĭn′dĭgŭl), city (pop. 56,275), Madura dist., S Madras, India, 32 mi. NNW of Madura; rail junction; trade and tobacco center; cigar mfg. Exports timber and agr. products (tea, coffee, cardamom) of Cardamom Hills and Palni Hills (SW) and Sirumalai Hills (S), hides and skins, brassware; cotton spinning, silk weaving, tanning. Fort (built early-17th cent.), on granite rock 280 ft. above plain, contested (1659–1792) by the Mahrattas, the Mysore sultans, and the English; passed to English in 1792.

Dindings (dĭn″dĭngz′), coastal district of W Perak, Malaya, on Strait of Malacca 80 mi. S of George Town. Includes 8-mi.-wide mainland strip astride Dindings R. (an inlet of the strait), PANGKOR ISLAND, 1 mi. off mainland across Dindings Channel, and SEMBILAN ISLANDS. Chief town, Lumut. Rubber, coconuts, rattan, fish. The original Dindings (□ 190; pop. 26,527) was ceded by Perak to Great Britain (the isls. in 1826, the mainland in 1874) and became part of Penang settlement. Following retrocession to Perak in 1935, the dist. was considerably enlarged.

Dindori (dĭndō′rē). **1** Village (pop. 2,661), Nasik dist., central Bombay, India, 14 mi. N of Nasik; millet, wheat, cotton. **2** Village, Mandla dist., NE Madhya Pradesh, India, on Narbada R. and 50 mi. NE of Mandla; rice, wheat, oilseeds. Lac cultivation near by, in dense sal forests.

Dineir, Turkey: see DINAR.

Dinga (dĭng′gŭ), town (pop. 8,545), Gujrat dist., NE Punjab, W Pakistan, 21 mi. WNW of Gujrat; market center (grain, cotton); hand-loom weaving.

Dingaans Kraal (dĭngänz′ kräl′), locality, Zululand, central Natal, U. of So. Afr., 35 mi. NNW of Eshowe; scene (Feb. 6, 1838) of massacre of advance party of Voortrekkers under Piet Retief by forces of Zulu chief Dingaan, who was later defeated at BLOOD RIVER.

Dingalan Bay (dĕng-gä′län), inlet of Philippine Sea, E Luzon, Philippines, merges with Polillo Strait (SE); 15 mi. long, 7 mi. wide.

Dingelstädt (dĭng′ŭl-shtĕt), town (pop. 5,602), in former Prussian Saxony prov., central Germany, after 1945 in Thuringia, on Unstrut R. and 10 mi. NW of Mühlhausen, at SW edge of the Eichsfeld; agr. market (tobacco, wheat, rye, potatoes, livestock); mfg. of machinery, cigars. Near by is 12th-cent. church of former Benedictine monastery.

Dingila (dĭng-gē′lä), village, Eastern Prov., N Belgian Congo, on left bank of Uele R. near influx of Bomokandi R. and 105 mi. NE of Buta; coffee and aleurite plantations, cotton processing.

Dingiwai (dĭn′gĭwī) or **Dinjiway** (dĭn′jĭwī), village (pop. 7,370), Gharbiya prov., Lower Egypt, on Damietta branch of the Nile just E of Shirbin; cotton.

Ding La (dĭng′ lä′) or **Chargoding La** (chär′gōdĭng), highest pass (alt. 19,308 ft.) of the Trans-Himalayas, SW Tibet, in N Kailas Range, 50 mi. NE of Tokchen, at 31°15′N 82°15′E.

Dingle (dĭng′gŭl), Gaelic *Daengean*, town (pop. 1,683), W Co. Kerry, Ireland, on Dingle Bay, at foot of Ballysitteragh mtn., 25 mi. WSW of Tralee; fishing center. Formerly a walled stronghold.

Dingle (dĭng′lē, dĭng′lā″), town (1939 pop. 1,438; 1948 municipality pop. 18,475), Iloilo prov., E Panay isl., Philippines, 22 mi. NNE of Iloilo; agr. center (rice, sugar cane); sugar milling.

Dingle Bay (dĭng′gŭl), inlet of the Atlantic, W Co. Kerry, Ireland; 18 mi. wide at entrance, extends 24 mi. inland to Castlemaine Harbour, a narrow extension (7 mi. long) of the bay. On N shore of bay is Dingle.

Dingli (dĭng′glē), village (pop. 1,869), W Malta, above coastal cliffs, 8 mi. WSW of Valletta. Has 17th-cent. churches. The isl.'s highest peak, Casal Dingli (817 ft.), is just S.

Dingmans Ferry, village, Pike co., NE Pa., on Delaware R. (bridged here) and 24 mi. NE of Stroudsburg. Near by are 2 noted waterfalls in short Dingmans Creek.

Dingolfing (dĭng′ôlfĭng″), town (pop. 7,477), Lower Bavaria, Germany, on the Isar and 19 mi. ENE of Landshut; metalworking, printing, tanning, brewing; candle- and brickworks. Has late-Gothic church, 15th-cent. castle. Chartered 1274.

Dingras (dĕng-gräs′), town (1939 pop. 4,308; 1948 municipality pop. 24,481), Ilocos Norte prov., NW Luzon, Philippines, 10 mi. SE of Laoag; rice-growing center.

Dingsperlo, Netherlands: see DINXPERLO.

Dinguiraye (dĭng-gērä′yä), town (pop. c.2,900), N Fr. Guinea, Fr. West Africa, 45 mi. NE of Dabola; cattle; peanuts, rubber, subsistence crops.

Dingwall (dĭng′wôl), village (pop. estimate 150), NE N.S., on Aspy Bay, N Cape Breton Isl., 9 mi. SSW of Cape North; gypsum-quarrying; fishing port.

Dingwall (dĭng′wŭl) [Scandinavian,=field of the assembly, or council], burgh (1931 pop. 2,553; 1951 census 3,367), ⊙ Ross and Cromarty, Scotland, in SE part of co., at head of Cromarty Firth, 11 mi. NW of Inverness; port and agr. market. It was created a royal burgh in 1226.

Dinhata (dēn′hätŭ), town (pop. 3,536), Cooch Behar dist., NE West Bengal, India, on tributary of the Jaldhaka and 13 mi. S of Cooch Behar; trades in rice, jute, tobacco, oilseeds, sugar cane.

Dinhlap (dĭng′läp′), town, Haininh prov., N Vietnam, 30 mi. SE of Langson, near China border.

Dinia, France: see DIGNE.

Dinjiway, Egypt: see DINGIWAI.

Dinkelsbühl (dĭng′kŭlsbül), town (pop. 6,928), Middle Franconia, W Bavaria, Germany, on the Wörnitz and 20 mi. SW of Ansbach; gingerbread mfg., weaving, tanning, brewing. Franconia's oldest city, it is still surrounded by early-10th-cent. walls with 12th-cent. towers, and completely retains its medieval character. The church of St. George (1444–99) is one of the most beautiful late-Gothic churches of S Germany. Has also 13th- and 14th-cent. churches. Town mill, formerly fortified, was built c.1390. The *Deutsche Haus* (mansion of late 14th or early 15th cent.) has a fine Renaissance lattice façade. Chartered before 928, Dinkelsbühl became a free imperial city c.1273; flourished in 14th and 15th cent. Town accepted the Reformation in 1532; was besieged 8 times during Thirty Years War.

Dinklage (dĭngk′lä″gŭ), village (commune pop. 7,313), in Oldenburg, NW Germany, after 1945 in Lower Saxony, 8 mi. SW of Vechta; mfg. of agr. machinery, cotton; meat processing. Has castle (c.1600).

Dinnet, agr. village, S Aberdeen, Scotland, on the Dee and 6 mi. ENE of Ballater. It is on edge of Dinnet Moor, with 2 small lakes noted for aquatic plants; remains of anc. lake dwellings and cairns have been found here.

Dinnington, town and parish (pop. 1,007), SE Northumberland, England, 7 mi. NNW of Newcastle-upon-Tyne; coal mining.

Dinorwic, Wales: see LLANBERIS.

Dinosaur National Monument (dī′nŭsôr) (□ 298.1; established 1915), NW Colo. and NE Utah, on Green R. at mouth of Yampa R., and c.140 mi. E of Salt Lake City. Set aside originally in Utah for preservation of rich deposits of dinosaur fossils, enlarged (1938) to include Canyon of Lodore (up to 2,000 ft. deep) of Green R. and Yampa Canyon (to 1,600 ft. deep), in Colo. Fossils are in Utah section (□ 71.7) of monument, near its W boundary; specimens are exhibited at fossil quarry.

Dinousa, Greece: see DENOUSA.

Dinozé (dēnôzā′), village (pop. 149), Vosges dept., E France, on Moselle R. and 3 mi. SSE of Épinal; metalworks.

Dinskaya (dyēn′skĭŭ), village (1926 pop. 12,527), central Krasnodar Territory, Russian SFSR, 18 mi. NE of Krasnodar; metalworks, flour mill; sugar beets, dairying. Village of Plastunovskaya (1926 pop. 12,385) is 6 mi. NE.

Dinslaken (dĭns′lä″kŭn), town (pop. 27,277), in former Prussian Rhine Prov., W Germany, after 1945 in North Rhine-Westphalia, in the Ruhr, 9 mi. N of Duisburg; coal mining; mfg. of steel-rolling equipment, pipes, nails, wire, shoes; sawmilling. Chartered 1273. Second World War destruction about 70%.

Dinsmore, village (pop. 231), S central Sask., 65 mi. SW of Saskatoon; wheat, stock.

Dinsmore, village (pop. 1,010), Duval co., NE Fla., 11 mi. N of Jacksonville.

Dinsor (dēnsōr′), village (pop. 500), in the Upper Juba, SW Ital. Somaliland, on road and 45 mi. E of Bardera, in stock-raising region.

Dintel Mark River, Netherlands: see MARK RIVER.

Dinteloord (dĭn′tŭlōrt), village (pop. 2,905), North Brabant prov., SW Netherlands, 8 mi. NNW of Roosendaal, near Dintel Mark R.; beet-sugar-refining center.

Dinting, England: see GLOSSOP.

Dinuba (dĭnōō′bŭ), city (pop. 4,971), Tulare co., S central Calif., in San Joaquin Valley, 25 mi. SE of Fresno; packing houses (raisins, figs, grapes, peaches), canneries, wineries. Inc. 1906.

Dinwiddie (dĭn′wĭ″dē, dĭn″wĭ′dē), county (□ 507; pop. 18,839), SE central Va.; ⊙ Dinwiddie. PETERSBURG is in but independent of co. Bounded N by Appomattox R., SW by Nottoway R. Agr. (tobacco, peanuts, cotton, hay, truck, livestock); lumber milling, granite quarrying. Mfg., processing industries at Petersburg. Battlefields at Five Forks (near Dinwiddie) and in Petersburg vicinity were scenes of last struggles (April, 1865) of Civil War. Formed 1752.

Dinwiddie, village (pop. c.250), ⊙ Dinwiddie co., SE central Va., 14 mi. SW of Petersburg. In Civil War, battle of Dinwiddie Court House (March 31, 1865) here was followed (April 1) by battle of Five Forks (at a near-by crossroads), in which Sheridan defeated Pickett.

Dinxperlo or **Dingsperlo** (both: dĭngks′pŭrlō), village (pop. 4,318), Gelderland prov., E Netherlands, 27 mi. ESE of Arnhem, on Ger. border; carpet weaving; wooden-shoe mfg. Adjoins Süderwick, Germany. Sometimes spelled Dingsperloo.

Dio (dē′ŭ″), Swedish *Diö*, village (pop. 508), Kronoberg co., S Sweden, on E side of L. Mockel, 17 mi. SE of Ljungby; sawmilling, woodworking, furniture mfg.

Diocaesarea, Palestine: see TSIPORI.

Dioïla (dyoi′lä), village (pop. c.300), S Fr. Sudan, Fr. West Africa, 80 mi. E of Bamako; peanuts, kapok, shea nuts.

Diomede, village, Alaska: see LITTLE DIOMEDE ISLAND.

Diomede Islands (dī′ŭmēd), island group in Bering Strait, midway bet. Asia (NE Siberia) and America (Alaska); consists of RATMANOV ISLAND (Russian SFSR) and LITTLE DIOMEDE ISLAND (Alaska), bet. which passes USSR-U.S. boundary and International Date Line. Fairway Rock lies 8 mi. SSE of

Little Diomede Isl. Inhabited chiefly by Chukchi. Discovered by Bering on St. Diomede's Day, 1728.

Dion (dī'ŏn), anc. city of Palestine, in upper reaches of Yarmuk R., 18 mi. E of Sea of Galilee; one of the Decapolis.

Diongloh (dyông'lō'), Mandarin *Ch'ang-lo* (chäng'-lŭ'), town (pop. 11,005), ⊙ Diongloh co. (pop. 209,609), E Fukien prov., China, 18 mi. SE of Foochow, near Min R. mouth on E.China Sea; wheat, rice, sweet potatoes. Coal mines near by.

Dionísio Cerqueira (dēōōnē'zyōō sĕrkā'rŭ), town (pop. 84), westernmost Santa Catarina, Brazil, on Argentina (W) and Paraná (N) border, adjoining Bernardo de Irigoyen (Argentina). Pepiri Guaçu R. (border stream) rises here.

Diosgyör (dĭ'ŏzh-dyûr), Hung. *Diósgyőr*, W suburb (pop. 26,538) of Miskolc, Borsod-Gömör co., NE Hungary, mfg. center; iron, steel, paper, and lumber mills. Lignite mines, thermal springs of Tapolca near by. Ruins of fortress built by Louis the Great in 14th cent.

Diosig (dyô'sēg), Hung. *Bihar-Diószeg* (bē'hŏr-dyō'sĕk), village (pop. 6,781), Bihor prov., W Rumania, near Hung. border, on railroad and 17 mi. NNE of Oradea, amidst extensive vineyards; center of wine production, with a school of viticulture. In Hungary, 1940–45.

Dioskurias, USSR: see SUKHUMI.

Diospolis, Egypt: see THEBES.

Diospolis, Palestine: see LYDDA.

Diosti (dyôsht'), Rum. *Dioşti*, village (pop. 1,803), Dolj prov., S Rumania, 8 mi. W of Caracal.

Diou (dyōō), village (pop. 904), Allier dept., central France, port on the Loire and 20 mi. E of Moulins; mfg. of cement pipes, quarrying and shipping of refractories. Oil storage depot.

Diouloulou (dyōōlōō'lōō), village, SW Senegal, Fr. West Africa, near Br. Gambia border, 37 mi. NW of Ziguinchor; peanut growing, lumbering.

Diourbel (dyōōrbĕl'), town (pop. c.15,700), W Senegal, Fr. West Africa, on Dakar-Niger RR and 80 mi. E of Dakar, in peanut-growing region. Ice plant, vegetable-oil factory. Airfield, mosque; medical center.

Dipal, Nepal: see DOTI.

Dipalpur (dē'pälpōōr), village, Montgomery dist., SE Punjab, W Pakistan, 33 mi. E of Montgomery; agr. market (cotton, wheat, millet); cotton ginning, hand-loom weaving. Has medieval fortress. Captured (1524) by Babar; held briefly (1758) by Mahrattas.

Dipalpur Canal, SE Punjab, W Pakistan, flows from right bank of Sutlej R. just NW of Ferozepore generally SW into Pakpattan Canal 4 mi. NW of Pakpattan; c.110 mi. long. Irrigates parts of Lahore and Montgomery dists.

Diphu (dĭpōō'), village, ⊙ Mikir Hills dist., central Assam, India, 20 mi. WSW of Dimapur.

Diphu Pass (dĭpōō'), northernmost crossing (14,280 ft.) on Burma-India border, at Tibet line, 55 mi. N of Putao; 28°10'N 97°20'E.

Dipilto (dēpēl'tō), town (1950 pop. 132), Nueva Segovia dept., NW Nicaragua, at S foot of Sierra de Dipilto, 5 mi. N of Ocotal; coffee, tobacco, sugar.

Dipilto, Sierra de (syĕ'rä dā), on Honduras-Nicaragua border, E spur of main continental divide; extends c.45 mi. from area of El Paraíso town (Honduras) NE to Teotecacinte peak; rises to over 7,000 ft. NE section is also called Sierra de Jalapa, with Jalapa town (Nicaragua) at its foot. Sierra de Dipilto is continued E by COLÓN MOUNTAINS.

Diplo (dĭp'lō), village, Thar Parkar dist., S Sind, W Pakistan, 60 mi. S of Umarkot, in SW Thar Desert; trades in millet, saddle cloths, dates. Extensive natural salt deposits (SW) form one of Sind's chief sources of supply.

Dipolog (dēpō'lōg), town (1939 pop. 6,534; 1948 municipality pop. 40,618), Zamboanga prov., NW Mindanao, Philippines, on Mindanao Sea, 50 mi. NNW of Pagadian; corn, rice, coconuts, cattle.

Dippoldiswalde (dĭpôl'dĭsväl"dŭ), town (pop. 5,937), Saxony, E central Germany, in the Erzgebirge, on Red Weisseritz R. (irrigation dam) and 11 mi. S of Dresden; woodworking, flour milling; mfg. of organs, agr. machinery, pharmaceuticals, straw hats. Has Romanesque and Gothic churches, Renaissance town hall and palace. Founded in 13th cent. as silver-mining settlement.

Dique, Canal del (känäl' dĕl dē'kā), natural water channel in Bolívar dept., N Colombia, connects Bay of Cartagena (Caribbean Sea) with Magdalena R.; c.60 mi. long, from point 10 mi. S of Cartagena to Calamar (E), running partly along Atlántico dept. border. In colonial times it contributed largely to the supreme position of Cartagena, but silted up during War of Independence. It has recently been dredged. Sometimes called El Dique.

Diquís River (dēkēs'), in SE Costa Rica, its stream on Pacific slope; formed SE of Buenos Aires by confluence of General (right) and Brus (left) rivers, flows over 30 mi. W, past El Palmar and Puerto Cortés (head of navigation), to Coronado Bay of the Pacific, forming swampy delta. Length, including headstreams, 100 mi. Also called Río Grande de Térraba.

Dir (dēr), princely state (□ 3,000; 1951 pop. 148,000), N North-West Frontier Prov., W Pakistan, in Malakand agency; ⊙ Dir. Bounded by Chitral (N, W), Afghanistan (SW), Swat (E); crossed by SE ranges of the Hindu Kush; drained by Panjkora R. Contains lofty mtn. ridges (N peaks over 13,000 ft.) and deep valleys. Fruit, wheat, barley, corn grown; forests yield good timber. Inhabited by Pathan tribes.

Dir, village, ⊙ Dir state, N North-West Frontier Prov., W Pakistan, 85 mi. NNE of Peshawar; local trade in fruit, rice, corn, timber.

Dir, Djebel (jĕ'bĕl dēr'), mountain in Constantine dept., NE Algeria, 6 mi. N of Tebessa. Phosphate mines. Also spelled Djebel Dyr.

Dir'a, Syria: see DER'A.

Dira, Djebel, Algeria: see TITERI.

Dirdal (dēr'däl), village in Forsand canton (pop. 1,845), Rogaland co., SW Norway, near head of Hogs Fjord (an arm of Bokn Fjord), 19 mi. SE of Stavanger; agr. (fruit, vegetables), animal husbandry (cattle, poultry).

Diré (dērā'), village, central Fr. Sudan, Fr. West Africa, landing on the Niger and 40 mi. SW of Timbuktu; millet, cotton, rice, peanuts; sheep fair. Cotton experiment station.

Direction, Cape, NE Queensland, Australia, on E coast of Cape York Peninsula, in Coral Sea; 12°52'S 143°33'E. Forms S tip of Lloyd Bay; rises to 490 ft.

Direction Island, Singapore colony: see COCOS ISLANDS.

Diredawa or **Dire Dawa** (dē'rā dä'wä), Ital. *Dire Daua*, town (pop. 25,000), Harar prov., E central Ethiopia, on Djibuti–Addis Ababa railroad and 26 mi. NW of Harar, on slope of Great Rift Valley; alt. c.3,950 ft.; 9°38'N 41°45'E. Road junction and commercial center, with large trade in coffee and hides; cotton gin, Sansevieria fiber factory, cement works, railroad shops, power plant, airfield. Has modern quarter, royal palace, Coptic church, and R.C. mission. Formerly a caravan center, it developed under French direction into a modern and sanitary town; in 1902 it was reached by railroad from Djibouti and became chief outlet for Harar's trade. Occupied by Italians (1936) in Italo-Ethiopian War and by British (1941) in Second World War; bombed 1940.

Diriá (dēryä'), town (1950 pop. 1,612), Granada dept., SW Nicaragua, 6 mi. SSE of Masaya; summer resort; grain; pottery and ropemaking.

Diriamba (dēryäm'bä), town (1950 pop. 7,566), Carazo dept., SW Nicaragua, on Inter-American Highway and 21 mi. SSE of Managua; rail terminus; major coffee center; processing plants; lumber trade. Limestone, saltworks near by.

Dirico (dērē'kō), village, Bié prov., SE Angola, on Okovanggo R. (South-West Africa border), at influx of the Cuito, 140 mi. ESE of Cuangar.

Dirik, Syria: see DARIK.

Dirikish, Syria: see DUREIKISH.

Dirillo River, Sicily: see ACATE RIVER.

Diriomo (dēryō'mō), town (1950 pop. 2,655), Granada dept., SW Nicaragua, 7 mi. SSE of Masaya; agr. center (grain, vegetables, tobacco); pottery and ropemaking. An important center at time of Sp. conquest.

Dirizhablstroi, Russian SFSR: see DOLGOPRUDNY.

Dirk Hartogs Island (dûrk här'tŏgz, –tōgz) (□ 239), in Indian Ocean, 1 mi. off W coast of Western Australia; forms SW shore of Shark Bay and S boundary of Naturaliste Channel; 48 mi. long, 6 mi. wide; rises to 608 ft. Sandstone cliffs. Lighthouse at Cape Inscription (N). Sheep run. Sometimes spelled Dirk Hartog's Isl.

Dirleton (dûrl'tŭn), agr. village and parish (pop. 2,824), N East Lothian, Scotland, near Firth of Forth, 3 mi. WSW of North Berwick. Has 17th-cent. church and ruins of 13th-cent. Dirleton Castle, dismantled 1650 by General Monk.

Dirmstein (dĭrm'shtīn), village (pop. 1,768), Rhenish Palatinate, W Germany, 5 mi. NW of Frankenthal; wine; sugar beets.

Dirphys or **Dhirfis** (both: dhĕr'fĭs), mountain in N central Euboea, Greece, rises to 5,718 ft. 16 mi. E of Chalcis. Formerly called Delphe, Dhelfi, or Delphi.

Dirr, El, Ed Dirr, or **Al-Dirr** (all: ĕd dĭr'), village (pop. 1,126), Aswan prov., S Egypt, on W bank of the Nile and 19 mi. ENE of 'Ineiba. Site of rock temple built (c.1250 B.C.) by Ramses II. Also spelled Derr.

Dirranbandi (dûr"ŭnbăn'dī), village (pop. 514), S Queensland, Australia, on Balonne R. and 190 mi. SE of Charleville; rail terminus; livestock.

Dirschau, Poland: see TCZEW.

Dirty Devil River, SE central Utah, formed by confluence of Muddy Creek and Fremont R., flows 80 mi. SE and S to Colorado R. 17 mi. E of Mt. Hillers. Sometimes called part of Fremont R.

Dis (dēs), town, Quaiti state, Eastern Aden Protectorate, near Sharma Bay of Gulf of Aden, 22 mi. ENE of Shihr. Its port is Al Qarn.

Disappointment, Cape, SW Wash., point (46°18'N 124°4'W) at N side of Columbia R. mouth; lighthouse. Discovered and named in 1788 by English voyagers searching for "River of the West," later located and named Columbia R.

Disappointment, Lake (□ 100), N central Western Australia, 325 mi. SE of Port Hedland; 45 mi. long; usually dry.

Disappointment Islands, isolated coral group (pop 250), N Tuamotu Isls., Fr. Oceania, S Pacific; 14°8'S 141°20'W; comprise Napuka and Tepoto. Discovered 1765 by Byron.

Disara, Aden: see DHI SURA.

Disaster Bay, inlet of Tasman Sea, SE New South Wales, Australia; Green Cape at NE side of entrance; 16 mi. long, 4 mi. wide.

Disco, Greenland: see DISKO.

Discovery, village, NW B.C., 6 mi. E of Atlin; gold mining.

Discovery Bay, wide inlet of Indian Ocean, SE Australia, bet. Cape Northumberland, South Australia, and Cape Bridgewater, Victoria; 45 mi. long E-W, 8 mi. wide; receives Glenelg R. Port MacDonnell on W shore.

Discovery Harbour, small bay on N side of Lady Franklin Bay, near its entrance on Robeson Channel, NE Ellesmere Isl., Franklin Dist., Northwest Territories; 81°44'N 64°45'W. First entered by Nares, whose expedition vessel *Discovery* wintered here, 1875–76. Greely established his expedition hq. and meteorological station, FORT CONGER, at head of inlet, 1881; it was also one of principal bases of Peary's expedition, 1898–1902. Visited 1934–35 by Oxford Univ. Ellesmere Land Expedition. Entrance is protected by small Bellot Isl.

Discovery Island, islet, SW B.C., in S part of Harc Strait, just off SE Vancouver Isl., 4 mi. E of Victoria; lighthouse (48°25'N 123°13'W).

Discovery Passage, SW B.C., channel on E coast o Vancouver Isl., joining Johnstone Strait with mair body of Strait of Georgia at Campbell River vil lage; 26 mi. long. Narrowest part of the channel Seymour Narrows (700 yards wide), is just NE o Bloedel. Here are strong tidal currents.

Disenchantment Bay (20 mi. long), SE Alaska, a head of Yakutat Bay, 20 mi. NE of Yakutat; 60°N 139°32'W. Russell Fiord extends 35 mi. SSE fron head of bay. Named 1791 by Malaspina, Spanisl explorer, when it proved not to be the Northwes Passage he was seeking.

Disentis (dē'sĕntĭs), Romansh *Mustèr* (mōōsh-tĕr') town (pop. 2,173), Grisons canton, E centra Switzerland, on the Vorderrhein and 35 mi. WSV of Chur; health resort, winter sports center; alt 3,772 ft. Benedictine abbey (founded 720; rebuil 17th cent.) with church (17th-18th cent.).

Disgrazia, Monte (môn'tĕ dēsgrä'tsyä), peak (12,06 ft.) in Rhaetian Alps, N Italy, near Swiss borde near Bernina Alps, 9 mi. NW of Sondrio. Has sev eral glaciers.

Dishergarh, India: see KULTI.

Dishna (dĭsh'nă), town (pop. 16,336), Qena prov Upper Egypt, on E bank of the Nile, on railroa and 16 mi. W of Qena; sugar refining, pottery mak ing; cereals, sugar cane, dates.

Disko (dĭ'skō), island (□ 3,312; pop. 1,450), just o W Greenland across Disko Bay (SE) and th Vaigat (NE), in Davis Strait; 69°14'–70°20' 51°50'–55°W. It is 80 mi. long, 20–75 mi. wid rises to 6,296 ft. Generally mountainous an partly glaciated. Godhavn (S) is chief town; li nite mining at Kutdligssat (NE). Telluric irc deposits. First reached (bet. 982 and 985) by Er the Red. Sometimes spelled Disco.

Disko Bay, inlet (120 mi. long, 50 mi. wide at mout of Davis Strait, W Greenland, separating Disko is from mainland; continued NW by the Vaigat.

Diskofjorden (dĭ'skôfyō"rŭn) or **Diskofjord,** fishi settlement (pop. 63), Godhavn dist., off W Gree land, on SW Disko isl., on Disko Fjord (35 m long), near its mouth on Davis Strait, 20 mi. N of Godhavn; 69°30'N 53°55'W.

Disley (dĭs'lē), residential town and parish (po c.3,000), NE Cheshire, England, 6 mi. ESE Stockport; paper mfg. Church has tower dati from 16th cent.; 16th-cent. mansion contains Gre and Egyptian marbles, a 14th-cent. Bible, a relics from Stuart times.

Dismal River, central Nebr., rises in Hooker c flows 75 mi. E to Middle Loup R. near Dunning.

Dismal Swamp, in SE Va. and NE N.C., coast swamp (c.20 mi. long) lying bet. Norfolk, Va. (N and Elizabeth City, N.C. (S). Near its center L. Drummond (c.3 mi. in diameter), connected a branch channel with Dismal Swamp Canal, N waterway connecting Chesapeake Bay with A bemarle Sound. Swamp, now partially reclaime was once much larger (□ c.2,000), heavily woode and almost impenetrable. Visited (1728) by W liam Byrd and surveyed (1763) by George Was ington, who was a member of a company organiz to drain it. Canal (completed 1828) and, later, railroad and highway facilitated lumbering (press, black gum, pine) and partial clearing truck farms. Hunting (deer, bear, raccoons), fis ing. Sometimes called Great Dismal Swamp.

Dismal Swamp Canal, in SE Va. and NE N.C., alternate section (c.22 mi. long) of Intracoas Waterway; connects Hampton Roads and Che peake Bay (via short Deep Creek and Southe Branch of Elizabeth R.) with Albemarle Sou (via Pasquotank R.); completed 1828 through th densely-wooded Dismal Swamp.

Disna (dyĭsnä', dyē'snŭ), Pol. *Dzisna* (jēs'nä), c (1931 pop. 4,788), central Polotsk oblast, Be russian SSR, on Western Dvina R., at mouth

Disna R., and 17 mi. WNW of Polotsk; flax- and grain-trading center; tanning, flour milling, woolen weaving. Phosphorite deposits near by. Passed (1793) from Poland to Russia; reverted (1921) to Poland; ceded to USSR in 1945.

Disna River, Lith. *Dysna* (dĭ'snä), Pol. *Dzisna*, in Lithuania and Belorussian SSR, rises in L. Disna (□9) just S of Dukstos, Lithuania; flows 95 mi. generally W, past Sharkovshehina, Belorussian SSR, to Western Dvina R. at Disna.

Disney (dĭz'nē), village (1940 pop. 1,510), Mayes co., NE Okla., 13 mi. SSE of Vinita, near Grand River Dam.

Dison (dēzō'), town (pop. 10,102), Liége prov., E Belgium, just N of Verviers; wool spinning and weaving; shoe mfg.

Disraeli (dĭzrā'lē), village (pop. 1,338), S Que., on St. Francis R., at N end of L. Aylmer, 30 mi. NW of Megantic; woodworking; market in dairying, cattle-raising, potato-growing region; resort.

Disraeli, Mount, New Guinea: see FINISTERRE RANGE.

Diss (dĭs), urban district (1931 pop. 3,421; 1951 census 3,505), S Norfolk, England, on Waveney R. and 19 mi. SSW of Norwich; agr. market, with agr.-machinery and pottery works. Has church dating from c.1290; John Skelton was rector here.

Diss, Djebel (jĕ'bĕl dēs'), mountain (alt. 2,036 ft.) in the Medjerda Mts., Tabarka dist., NW Tunisia, 17 mi. SSW of Tabarka. Zinc mining.

Distaghil (dēstägēl'), peak (25,868 ft.) in main range of Karakoram mtn. system, N Kashmir, 28 mi. E of Baltit.

Distington, town and parish (pop. 1,821), W Cumberland, England, 4 mi. NNE of Whitehaven; coal mining, iron smelting.

District Heights, town (pop. 1,735), Prince Georges co., central Md., SE suburb of Washington. Inc. 1936.

District of Columbia, E U.S., federal dist. (□ 61; with inland waters □ 69; 1950 pop. 802,178; 1940 pop. 663,091), on the Potomac and bounded by Va. and Md.; coextensive with city of WASHINGTON, capital of U.S. Established by Congressional acts of 1790 and 1791; territorial govt. was set up 1871, and present system of govt. by Congress, through an executive board of Presidential appointees, was established 1878.

Disufal, Dhi Sifal, or Dhi Sufal (all: dhĭsōōfăl'), town (pop. 2,500), Ibb prov., S Yemen, 15 mi. SW of Ibb, on seaward slope of maritime range.

Disuq (dĭsōōk'), town (pop. 23,992; with suburbs, 31,654), Gharbiya prov., Lower Egypt, on Rosetta branch of the Nile and 12 mi. NE of Damanhur; cotton ginning, cigarette mfg. Also spelled Desuq.

Disznoshorvat (dĭz'nōsh-hôrvät), Hung. *Disznóshorvát*, mining town (pop. 4,388), Borsod-Gömör co., NE Hungary, 15 mi. NNW of Miskolc; lignite mines.

Ditchling, agr. village and parish (pop. 1,683), central Sussex, England, 7 mi. N of Brighton. Has 13th-cent. church and 16th-cent. mansion, residence of Anne of Cleves. Just S is the hill of Ditchling Beacon (813 ft.), site of anc. Br. camp.

Dithmarschen (dĭt'mär"shŭn), region (□ 607; pop. 186,674) of W Schleswig-Holstein, NW Germany, bounded by the Eider (N), Kiel Canal (E), Elbe estuary (S), and the North Sea (W). Predominantly agr. (winter wheat, oats), with intensive vegetable growing (cabbage, beans, peas); cattle raising; horticulture (tulips, carnations, begonias). Major towns are Heide (in oil region), Meldorf (harbor), Marne, and Brunsbüttelkoog (at mouth of Kiel Canal into Elbe estuary). Resort of Büsum has important fisheries. Region was known as Nordalbingia when it was conquered by Charlemagne and Christianized. Was independent peasant state (⊙ Heide) until 1559. Sometimes called Ditmarsh in English.

Ditmarsh, Germany: see DITHMARSCHEN.

Ditrau (dē'trŭōō), Rum. *Ditrău*, Hung. *Ditró* (dē'trō), village (pop. 7,537), Mures prov., E central Rumania, in Transylvania, on railroad and 7 mi. NW of Gheorgheni; lumbering, stone quarrying. Renaissance church. In Hungary, 1940–45.

Dittaino River (dēt-täē'nô), central Sicily, rises in several branches near Leonforte, flows 50 mi. ESE to Simeto R. in Plain of Catania 8 mi. from its mouth.

Ditton. 1 Town and parish (pop. 848), central Kent, England, 4 mi. NW of Maidstone; tar works, paper mills. Has 13th-cent. church. **2** Town, Lancashire, England: see WIDNES.

Dittons, The, England: see ESHER.

Dittweiler (dĭt'vī"lŭr), village (pop. 713), Rhenish Palatinate, W Germany, 11 mi. WNW of Landstuhl; diamond grinding.

Ditzenbach, Bad, Germany: see BAD DITZENBACH.

Ditzingen (dĭ'tsĭng-ŭn), village (pop. 4,461), N Württemberg, Germany, after 1945 in Württemberg-Baden, 6 mi. NW of Stuttgart; grain, cattle. Has two 15th-cent. churches.

Diu (dē'ōō), small isl. of Portuguese India off S tip of Kathiawar peninsula, W India, and separated from it by arm of Arabian Sea (Chassi R.); c.8 mi. long (E-W), 2 mi. wide. Millet, coconuts, rice; fishing (pomfrets, Bombay duck), salt drying. **Diu** district (□ 14; pop. 19,731), ⊙ Diu, comprises Diu isl. and small detached sections of GOGOLA and SIMBOR on S Kathiawar peninsula.

Diu, town (pop. 4,856), ⊙ Diu dist., Portuguese India, at mouth of Gulf of Cambay, 170 mi. NW of Bombay, India; coastal trade in coconuts, salt, millet; fishing. Has cathedral built 1601; fort stands just E. Acquired by Portuguese in 1535 from Bahadur Shah of Gujarat. Importance as trade center has steadily declined.

Divaca (dēvä'chä), Slovenian *Divača*, Ital. *Divaccia* (dēvät'chä), village (1936 pop. 496), SW Slovenia, Yugoslavia, 9 mi. E of Trieste; rail junction. Until 1947, in Italy. Caves and cataracts at Skocjan, Slovenian *Skocjan*, Ital. *San Canziano*, a village (1936 pop. 83) 2 mi. SE, form one of finest natural structures of the Karst; here Reka river disappears underground.

Divalá (dēvälä'), village (pop. 387), Chiriquí prov., W Panama, 10 mi. WNW of Alanje; road terminus; bananas, coffee, livestock.

Divandarreh (dēvän"därĕ'), village, Fifth Prov., in Kurdistan, W Iran, on road and 40 mi. N of Sanandaj; grain, tobacco, gums; sheep raising; handmade rugs.

Divenié (dēvĕnyā'), village, W Middle Congo territory, Fr. Equatorial Africa, 110 mi. NW of Dolisie. In Gabon colony until 1946.

Dive River (dēv), Vienne and Maine-et-Loire depts., W central France, rises 3 mi. E of Thénezay, flows c.40 mi. N, past Moncontour, to the Thouet 6 mi. below Montreuil-Bellay. Partially canalized. Also called Dive-du-Nord.

Divernon (dīvûr'nŭn), village (pop. 1,013), Sangamon co., central Ill., 15 mi. S of Springfield, in agr. and bituminous-coal area. Inc. 1900.

Diversion Reservoir, Texas: see WICHITA RIVER.

Dives River (dēv), Orne and Calvados depts., NW France, rises near Exmes, flows c.60 mi. generally N, past Trun, Mézidon, and Troarn, through marshy Auge Valley, to the Channel just below Dives-sur-Mer. Receives the Vie (right).

Dives-sur-Mer (-sür-mâr'), town (pop. 4,870), Calvados dept., NW France, on right bank of the Dives near its mouth on the Channel, and 14 mi. NE of Caen; electrometallurgical works (copper and brass smelting); cider distilling, printing. Here, in 1066, William the Conqueror embarked for conquest of England.

Diveyevo (dyĭvyā'ŭvŭ), village (1926 pop. 694), SW Gorki oblast, Russian SFSR, 33 mi. SW of Arzamas; wheat, potatoes.

Diviaky (dĭ'vyäkĭ), Hung. *Turócdivék* (tōō'rōts-dĭvāk), village (pop. 742), N Slovakia, Czechoslovakia, 25 mi. SSE of Zilina; sawmills.

Divichi (dyĭvē'chē), town (1926 pop. 830), NE Azerbaijan SSR, on railroad and 70 mi. NNW of Baku, on Samur-Divichi Canal, near Caspian Sea; fisheries, fish canning; cotton; metalworks.

Divide, county (□ 1,303; pop. 5,967), extreme NW N.Dak.; ⊙ Crosby. Hilly area watered by small creeks and lakes. Lignite mines; farming, dairying, stock raising, grain. Formed 1910.

Divide. 1 Village (pop. c.75), Teller co., central Colo., in Front Range, 10 mi. NW of Pikes Peak, 20 mi. WNW of Colorado Springs; alt. 9,183 ft. Shipping point for lettuce, potatoes, and hay. **2** Village, Silver Bow co., SW Mont., 20 mi. SSW of Butte and on Big Hole R., just NE of Pioneer Mts.; livestock-shipping point for valley of Big Hole R.

Dividing Creek, village (1940 pop. 580), Cumberland co., S N.J., on small stream and 9 mi. SSW of Millville, in farm area.

Dividing Range, Australia: see GREAT DIVIDING RANGE.

Dividive, El, Venezuela: see EL DIVIDIVE.

Divin (dyē'vĭn), Pol. *Dywin* (dĭ'vēn), village (1939 pop. over 500), SE Brest oblast, Belorussian SSR, in Pripet Marshes, 15 mi. SSE of Kobrin; flour milling; rye, oats, potatoes, flax.

Divina Pastora (dēvē'nŭ pästô'rŭ), city (pop. 1,183), central Sergipe, NE Brazil, 21 mi. NW of Aracaju; sugar, cotton.

Divinópolis (dēvēnō'pōōlēs), city (1950 pop. 20,550), central Minas Gerais, Brazil, 65 mi. WSW of Belo Horizonte; rail junction; agr. trade center.

Divion (dēvyō'), town (pop. 10,111), Pas-de-Calais dept., N France, 7 mi. SW of Béthune; coal-mining center.

Divisa (dēvē'sä), village, Herrera prov., S central Panama, in Santa María R. valley, 20 mi. E of Santiago. Junction of Inter-American Highway and branch serving Herrera and Los Santos provs.

Divisadero, El, Salvador: see EL DIVISADERO.

Divisaderos (dēvēsädā'rōs), town (pop. 702), Sonora, NW Mexico, 115 mi. NE of Hermosillo; cattle, corn, wheat.

Diviso, El, Colombia: see EL DIVISO.

Divisoria (dēvēsōr'yä), town (pop. estimate 500), S San Juan prov., Argentina, in San Juan R. valley (irrigation area), on railroad and 17 mi. SE of San Juan; wine, wheat, oats, melons, livestock; apiculture.

Divnoye (dyēv'nŭyŭ), village (1926 pop. 7,127), N Stavropol Territory, Russian SFSR, in Manych Depression, 90 mi. NE of Stavropol (connected by rail); rail terminus; agr. center in wheat and cotton region; dairying. Village of Apanasenkovskoye (1939 pop. over 2,000) is 15 mi. SE.

Divo (dē'vō), village (pop. c.2,200), S Ivory Coast, Fr. West Africa, 50 mi. NNW of Grand-Lahou; cacao, coffee, palm kernels, palm oil, hardwoods.

Divocha Orlice River (dyĭ'vôkhä ôr'lĭtsĕ), Ger. *Wilde Adler* (vĭl'dĕ äd'lĕr), SW Poland and E Bohemia, Czechoslovakia, rises near SE foot of the Adlergebirge, just across Pol. border, 3 mi. NNE of Velka Destna mtn., flows SSE, along Pol.-Czechoslovak border, into Bohemia, and W, past Zamberk, joining Ticha Orlice R. 1 mi. above Tyniste nad Orlici to form Orlice R.; c.65 mi. long. In upper course, separates the Adlergebirge and Habelschwerdt Mts.

Divodurum, France: see METZ.

Divona, France: see CAHORS.

Divonne-les-Bains (dēvôn-lā-bē'), village (pop. 910), Ain dept., E France, near Swiss border and L. Geneva, 11 mi. N of Geneva, on E slope of the Jura; spa with cold mineral springs; hotels, hydrotherapy.

Divrigi (dĭvrē'), Turkish *Divriği*, town (pop. 6,804), Sivas prov., central Turkey, on railroad, on Calti R., and 65 mi. ESE of Sivas; wheat, barley. Iron-mining center supplying Karabuk mills. Divrigi Mts. (S), W and N of the Euphrates, rise to 8,930 ft.

Diwaniya or Diwaniyah (dĭwänē'yŭ), province (□ 5,765; pop. 383,787), central Iraq; ⊙ Diwaniya. Rich agr. area, watered in NE by the Euphrates. Dates, rice, corn, millet, sesame. Served by Baghdad-Basra RR. In it are sites of anc. Babylonian cities of ISIN and NIPPUR.

Diwaniya, Ad Diwaniya, Al Diwaniya, or Al-Diwaniyah (all: äd-), city (pop. 20,015), ⊙ Diwaniya prov., central Iraq, on the Hilla (branch of the Euphrates), on railroad, and 100 mi. SSE of Baghdad; rice, dates.

Diwaynah, Egypt: see DIWEINA.

Diwayr, Al-, Egypt: see DIWEIR, EL.

Diweina or Diwaynah (both: dĭwā'nŭ), village (pop. 9,617), Asyut prov., central Upper Egypt, 3 mi. NW of Abu Tig; cereals, dates, sugar cane.

Diweir, El, Ed Diweir, or Al-Diwayr (all: ĕd dĭwār'), village (pop. 9,616), Girga prov., central Upper Egypt, 6 mi. SSE of Abu Tig; cereals, dates, sugar.

Dix, village (pop. 270), Kimball co., W Nebr., 8 mi. E of Kimball and on Lodgepole Creek.

Dix, Fort, N.J.: see WRIGHTSTOWN.

Dixcove (dĭks'kōv), village, Western Prov., SW Gold Coast colony, on Gulf of Guinea, 15 mi. SW of Takoradi; wharf. Br. trading station in 18th–19th cent.

Dix Dam, Ky.: see DIX RIVER.

Dixfield, town (pop. 2,022), including Dixfield village (pop. 1,377), Oxford co., W Maine, on the Androscoggin just below Rumford, in farming, recreational area; wood products. Settled 1787–89, inc. 1803.

Dixiana, village (pop. 1,325, with adjacent Bradford), Jefferson co., N central Ala., 16 mi. NNE of Birmingham.

Dixie, county (□ 688; pop. 3,928), N Fla., on Gulf of Mexico (S, W) and bounded E by Suwannee R.; ⊙ Cross City. Flatwoods area, with swamps in central part and small lakes in NE. Cattle raising, lumbering, farming (corn, peanuts), and fishing. Formed 1921.

Dixie, town (pop. 261), Brooks co., S Ga., 20 mi. ESE of Thomasville, near Fla. line; sawmilling.

Dixie Caverns, Va.: see SALEM.

Dix Island, Knox co., S Maine, in Penobscot Bay, 3 mi. SE of South Thomaston; ½ mi. long.

Dixmont (dēmō'), village (pop. 274), Yonne dept., N central France, 10 mi. SE of Sens; lignite deposits.

Dixmont (dĭks'mŏnt"), town (pop. 631), Penobscot co., S Maine, 18 mi. WSW of Bangor, in agr. region.

Dixmont Hills, S Maine, low range near Penobscot-Waldo co. line; Mt. Harris (1,233 ft.) and Pickard Mtn. (1,221 ft.) are principal summits.

Dixmoor, village (pop. 1,327), Cook co., NE Ill., S suburb of Chicago. Inc. 1922.

Dix Mountain (4,842 ft.), Essex co., NE N.Y., in the Adirondacks, 8 mi. ESE of Mt. Marcy and 18 mi. SE of Lake Placid village.

Dixmude (dēksmüd'), Flemish *Diksmuide* (dĭks'-moidŭ), town (pop. 3,573), West Flanders prov., W Belgium, on Yser R. and 20 mi. SW of Bruges; butter market. In First World War, almost totally destroyed (1914) by heavy fighting; since rebuilt. Mentioned as town in 1120; medieval textile center and member of Hanseatic League; destroyed by fire in 1333. Has Episcopal col.

Dixon, county (□ 480; pop. 9,129), NE Nebr.; ⊙ Ponca. Agr. region bounded N by Missouri R. and S.Dak.; watered by Logan Creek. Livestock, grain. Formed 1888.

Dixon. 1 Town (pop. 1,714), Solano co., central Calif., in Sacramento Valley, 20 mi. WSW of Sacramento; livestock, grain, dairy products, eggs. Inc. 1878. **2** City (pop. 11,523), ⊙ Lee co., N Ill., on Rock R. (bridged here) and 35 mi. SW of Rockford, in rich agr. area (grain, livestock, poultry); mfg. (wire, cement, shoes, dairy products, farm machinery, metal products, caskets). Sand, gravel pits. A state hosp. is near by. Founded 1830, inc. 1857. On site of Dixon Blockhouse is a statue of Abraham Lincoln as a captain in the Black Hawk War. **3** Town (pop. 208), Scott co., E Iowa, 17 mi. NW of Davenport. Limestone quarries near by. **4** Town (pop. 624), ⊙ Webster co., W Ky., 24 mi. SSW of Henderson, in agr., timber, and coal-mining area. **5** City (pop. 988), Pulaski co., central Mo., in the Ozarks, near Gasconade R., 18 mi. W of Rolla; ships livestock; flour, stave mills. **6** Village (pop. c.150), Sanders co., W Mont., on Flathead R. and 35 mi. NNW of Missoula; shipping point for grain and livestock; hq. of Flathead Indian Reservation. Natl. Bison Range, with hq. at Moiese (mōēz'), is near by. **7** Village (pop. 159), Dixon co., NE Nebr., 30 mi. W of Sioux City, Iowa, and on Logan Creek. **8** Town (pop. 124), Carbon co., S Wyo., on Little Snake R., near Colo. line and 55 mi. S of Rawlins; alt. 6,324 ft.; hay, potatoes.

Dixon Entrance, strait (c.50 mi. long, c.50 mi. wide) in N Pacific at Alaska-Canada line, bet. Alexander Archipelago (N) and Queen Charlotte Isls. (S); leads from the ocean to Hecate Strait and the Inside Passage; 54°30'N. Forms main approach to Prince Rupert.

Dixon Island, St. Lawrence co., N N.Y., one of a group of islets in the St. Lawrence, at Ont. line, just SW of Cardinal, Ont.; c.½ mi. long.

Dix River, central Ky., rises in Rockcastle co., flows 77 mi. generally NW to Kentucky R. at High Bridge. On river 7 mi. E of Harrodsburg is Dix River (or Harrodsburg) Dam, 275 ft. high, 1,020 ft. long, completed 1925 for hydroelectric power. Impounds Herrington L. (c.35 mi. long) upstream in Boyle, Garrard, and Mercer counties; resorts (fishing, boating) on lake.

Dixville, village (pop. 385), S Que., on Coaticook R. and 5 mi. SSE of Coaticook, near Vt. border; dairying.

Dixville Notch, Coos co., N N.H., scenic pass in outlying range of White Mts., 10 mi. ESE of Colebrook; c.2 mi. long. State forest area; resorts at Dixville Notch village.

Diyadin (dēädĭn'), village (pop. 1,235), Agri prov., E Turkey, on Murat R. and 36 mi. ESE of Karakose; mineral springs.

Diyala (dĭyä'lä), province (□ 6,154; pop. 273,336), E Iraq, bordering Iran; ⊙ Ba'quba. A rich oil area, with a refinery at Khanaqin. There is also agr. along Diyala R. valley; dates, oranges, apples, plums; stock. Sometimes spelled Diala, Dialah.

Diyala, village, Baghdad prov., central Iraq, on the Tigris at mouth of Diyala R. and 10 mi. SE of Baghdad; dates, fruit, livestock. Sometimes spelled Diala or Dialah.

Diyala River, rises in Kurdistan in W Iran as the Sirwan, flows SW into Iraq to the Tigris at village of Diyala, 10 mi. SE of Baghdad; total length, c.275 mi. Sometimes spelled Diala.

Diyaluma Falls (dĭyä'lōōmŭ), noted waterfall (570 ft.), Ceylon, in SE Ceylon Hill Country, on upper right tributary of the Kirindi Oya and 1.5 mi. SE of Koslanda.

Diyarbakir (dĭyär'bäkĭr"), Turkish *Diyarbakır*, prov. (□ 5,629; 1950 pop. 294,618), E Turkey; ⊙ Diyarbakir. Bordered N by Bitlis Mts., W by Euphrates R.; also drained by Tigris and Batman rivers. Rich copper deposits at Ergani; also some silver and chromium. Wheat, barley, millet, rice, lentils, chick-peas, watermelons, walnuts. Pop. predominantly Kurds. Sometimes spelled Diyarbekir and Diarbekr.

Diyarbakir, Turk. *Diyarbakır*, anc. *Amida* (ă'mĭdŭ, ŭmī'dŭ), city (1950 pop. 45,495), ⊙ Diyarbakir prov., E Turkey, in Kurdistan, on Tigris R. and 110 mi. ESE of Malatya; 37°50'N 40°10'E. Rail and agr. center (wheat, barley, millet, rice, chick-peas, lentils; wool, mohair). Noted since anc. times for goldsmithing and silversmithing. Later known for cotton industry and leather products. Has Pasteur institute. Made a Roman colony A.D. 230; later besieged and captured (A.D. 363) by Shapur II of Persia. Sometimes spelled Diyarbekir and Diarbekr. Formerly also called Kara-Amid.

Diyarb Nigm (dĭyärb' nĭ'gŭm) or **Diyarb Nijm** (nĭ'jŭm), village (pop. 8,482), Daqahliya prov., Lower Egypt, 9 mi. SSW of El Simbillawein; cotton, cereals.

Diyatalawa (dĭyŭtŭlä'vŭ), village, Uva Prov., S central Ceylon, in Uva Basin, 15 mi. SSW of Badulla; hill station (alt. 4,367 ft.); extensive tea gardens; rice, vegetables; rubber plantations. Meteorological observatory. Prisoner-of-war camp for Boers during Boer War.

Diz, Ab-i-, Iran: see AB-I-DIZ.

Dizangué, Fr. Cameroons: see EDÉA.

Dizful or **Dezful** (dĭzfōōl', dĕz-) [Persian,=fort bridge], town (1940 pop. 31,800), Sixth Prov., in Khuzistan, SW Iran, 75 mi. N of Ahwaz and on the Ab-i-Diz, near Trans-Iranian RR (Andimishk station); trade center; flour milling; oranges, rice, onions. A Sassanian stone bridge dating from 3d cent. A.D. crosses the Ab-i-Diz here. Dizful flourished in 19th cent. as an administrative center and an exporter of indigo, having eclipsed the formerly important Shushtar.

Dizy-Magenta (dēzē'-mäzhătä'), N suburb (pop. 2,188) of Épernay, Marne dept., N France, on S slope of Montagne de Reims; winegrowing (champagne), petroleum refining.

Dj-, for names beginning thus: see also under J–.

Djado (jä'dō), village, E Niger territory, Fr. West Africa, oasis in the Sahara, on desert road and 175 mi. N of Bilma; dates.

Djailolo, Indonesia: see HALMAHERA.

Djailolo Passage, Indonesia: see JAILOLO PASSAGE.

Djakarta, Indonesia: see JAKARTA.

Djakovica or **Dyakovitsa** (both: dyäkô'vĭtsä), Serbo-Croatian *Đakovica*, town (pop. 14,497), SW Serbia, Yugoslavia, 40 mi. WSW of Pristina, near Albania border, in the Metohija. Chromium and pyrite mined in vicinity. Under Turkish rule (until 1913), called Djakova, Turkish *Yakova*. In Montenegro (1913–29), in Albania (1941–44).

Djakovo (dyä'kôvô), Serbo-Croatian *Đakovo*, Hung. *Diakovár* (dē'ŏkôvär), town (pop. 8,942), N Croatia, Yugoslavia, on railroad and 21 mi. SSW of Osijek, in Slavonia; local trade center. R.C. bishopric since 1252. Has 13th-cent. church; 19th-cent. cathedral built by Bishop Strossmayer. Sometimes spelled Diakovo.

Djalma Dutra. **1** City, E central Bahia, Brazil: see MIGUEL CALMON. **2** City, SE Bahia, Brazil: see POÇÕES.

Djalta (jältä'), village, Bizerte dist., N Tunisia, 23 mi. SW of Bizerte; cereals, livestock. Lead mining.

Djambala (jămbälä'), town, ⊙ Alima region (□ 15,830; 1950 pop. 73,100), SE Middle Congo territory, Fr. Equatorial Africa, 125 mi. NNW of Brazzaville; native tobacco market; potatoes.

Djambi, Indonesia: see JAMBI.

Djambi River, Indonesia: see HARI RIVER.

Djamour el Kebir, Tunisia: see ZEMBRA.

Djampea, Indonesia: see TANA JAMPEA.

Djanet (jănĕt') or **Fort Charlet** (shärlā'), oasis (pop. 74), Saharan Oases territory, southeasternmost Algeria, near Fezzan border, 50 mi. SW of Ghat; 24°41'N 9°25'E. Date palms. Caravan and automobile refueling station. French military post since 1911.

Djapara, Indonesia: see JAPARA.

Djaravica or **Dyaravitsa** (dyä'rävĭtsä), Serbo-Croatian *Đaravica*, highest peak (8,714 ft.) of North Albanian Alps, in Montenegro, Yugoslavia, near Albania line, 11 mi. SW of Pec.

Dja River, Fr. Cameroons and Fr. Equatorial Africa: see N'GOKO RIVER.

Djatiwangi, Indonesia: see JATIWANGI.

Djaul, Bismarck Archipelago: see DYAUL.

Djawa, Indonesia: see JAVA.

Djébail, Lebanon: see BYBLOS.

Djebba (jĕb-bä'), village, Teboursouk dist., N central Tunisia, 6 mi. WNW of Teboursouk; calamine and galena mining.

Djebel [Arabic,=mountain], for all names beginning thus and not listed below: see under following part of the name.

Djebel-Abiod (jĕ'bĕl-äbyôd'), village, Béja dist., N Tunisia, in the Medjerda Mts., 18 mi. NNW of Béja. Iron, lead, and zinc mining.

Djebel-Djelloud (–jĕl-lōōd'), SE industrial suburb of Tunis, N Tunisia, on S shore of L. of Tunis; sulphur refinery, cement- and metalworks, flour mills. Railroad yards.

Djebel-Hallouf (–häl-lōōf'), village, Souk-el-Arba dist., NW Tunisia, 12 mi. W of Béja; lead mining and smelting.

Djebel-M'Dilla, Tunisia: see M'DILLA.

Djebeniana (jĕbĕnyänä'), village, Sfax dist., E Tunisia, in the coastal strip (*sahel*), 22 mi. NNE of Sfax; olive-oil pressing.

Djéblé, Syria: see JEBLE.

Djedeïda (jĕdädä'), village, Tunis dist., N Tunisia, on the Medjerda and 13 mi. W of Tunis; road and rail junction. Truck-farming center. Ruins of Roman aqueduct near by. Dam and bridge over Medjerda R. destroyed during Second World War.

Djedeide, Lebanon: see JUDEIDE.

Djedi, Oued (wĕd' jĕdē'), Saharan wadi in Southern Territories, central Algeria, rises in the Djebel Amour (Saharan Atlas) near Aflou, flows intermittently ENE, past Ouled-Djellal and the southernmost Ziban oases, to NW edge of the Chott Melrhir.

Djedita, Lebanon: see JEDITA.

Djelfa (jĕlfä'), town (pop. 6,212), Ghardaïa territory, N central Algeria, in Saharan Atlas (Ouled-Naïl Mts.), 140 mi. S of Algiers; 34°40'N 3°15'E; alt. 3,800 ft. S terminus of railroad from Blida; roads to Bou-Saâda (NE) and Laghouat (SSW); market center (wool, horses, esparto, pine lumber, handicraft products; dates from Saharan oases). Salt deposits at the Rocher de Sel, 15 mi. NW. Established 1852 as a military post.

Djem, El- (ĕl-jĕm'), anc. *Thysdrus* or *Tysdrus*, town (pop. 5,122), Mahdia dist., E Tunisia, in the coastal region (*sahel*), on railroad and 36 mi. S of Sousse; olive-oil pressing; sheep and cattle raising; agr. trade. Has remains of large amphitheater (one of the finest Roman ruins in N Africa). Thysdrus prospered (3d cent. A.D.) from its olive trade.

Djemadja, Indonesia: see ANAMBAS ISLANDS.

Djember, Indonesia: see JEMBER.

Djemila (jĕmēlä'), anc. *Cuicul*, village, Constantine dept., NE Algeria, in the Tell Atlas, 20 mi. NE of Sétif. Its Roman ruins include a triumphal arch, a temple (3d cent. A.D.), and a forum.

Djemmal (jĕm-mäl'), town (pop. 9,234), Sousse dist., E Tunisia, in the coastal region (*sahel*), 15 mi. SSE of Sousse; commercial center in olive-growing region; oil presses; brick, tile, and plaster works. Trade in wool, skins, cereals.

Djenné or **Jenné** (both: jĕnā'), town (pop. c.5,000), S Fr. Sudan, Fr. West Africa, on Bani R. and 220 mi. SSW of Timbuktu, 250 mi. ENE of Bamako. Founded 765, it flourished in later centuries as a great market for gold and slaves, and it rivaled Timbuktu in Moslem learning. Known for its monumental mosque and other examples of Moorish architecture. Today it is market for rice, millet, livestock, hides; some native leatherwork. The Guinea coast may have been named for the town.

Djepara, Indonesia: see JAPARA.

Djérablous, Syria: see JERABLUS.

Djérada or **Jérada** (järädä'), town (pop. 12,606), Oujda region, NE Fr. Morocco, 26 mi. SSW of Oujda; the protectorate's major coal-mining center, yielding high-grade anthracite. Mining operations, begun 1931, were greatly expanded during Second World War. Coal is taken by cable car to Aïn Guenfouda (10 mi. NNE, on railroad to Oujda), where a washing and briquette-mfg. plant was built 1936. Town formerly called El Aouïnet.

Djeravica or **Dyeravitsa** (both: dyĕrăvē'tsä), Serbo-Croatian *Đeravica*, Albanian *Kozi Rtarij*, highest peak (8,714 ft.) of North Albanian Alps and Dinaric Alps, on Albanian-Yugoslav border, 11 mi. SW of Pec.

Djerba (jûr'bŭ, Fr. jĕrbä'), anc. *Meninx*, island (□ 197; pop. 59,331) in the central Mediterranean, just off S coast of Tunisia (of which it forms an administrative dist.), at S entrance to the Gulf of Gabès, 40 mi. E of Gabès; ⊙ Houmt-Souk (or Djerba). It is 17 mi. long, 16 mi. wide. Its fertile soil and abundant artesian water make it a Mediterranean paradise, covered with vineyards, fig and pomegranate trees, date palms, orchards, and olive groves. Sponge and oyster fishing. Berber pop. is noted for handmade pottery, wool and silk cloth, jewelry, and esparto products. Access to mainland is across narrow channels at Adjim (1 mi. wide) and El-Kantara (4.5 mi. wide) on S shore. A sizable Jewish community (1946 pop. 4,294) is concentrated in Hara-Sghira and Hara-Kebira villages. One legend makes Djerba the land of the lotus-eaters in the *Odyssey*. Djerba preserves remains of Roman civilization. Sometimes spelled Jerba or Gerba.

Djerba, town, Tunisia: see HOUMT-SOUK.

Djerid, region, Tunisia: see BLED-EL-DJERID.

Djerid, Chott (shôt' jĕrēd'), anc. *Tritonis Palus*, large saline lake (□ c.1900) in Southern Territories, SW Tunisia, forming together with the Chott el Fedjedj (E) and the Chott el Rharsa (NW), a continuous depression (former arm of the sea) bet. the Gulf of Gabès and Algeria. Covered with water only in lowest areas, and after period of rainfall, it is an extensive salt flat, crossed by several tracks (especially bet. Tozeur, NW, and Kébili, SE). Preliminary exploration for potash deposits was begun 1949. Chief oases along its shores are BLED-EL-DJERID and NEFZAOUA. Also called Chott el Djerid.

Djérissa (järēsä'), village, Le Kef dist., W Tunisia, 23 mi. S of Le Kef; important iron-mining center. Also called Djebel-Djérissa.

Djerma, Fezzan: see GERMA.

Djerman or **Dyerman** (both: dyĕr'män), Serbo-Croatian *Đerman*, mountain, Macedonia, Yugoslavia, bet. Pcinja R. and the Kriva Reka; highest peak (5,074 ft.) is 7 mi. NW of Kriva Palanka.

Djevdjelija or **Dyevdyeliya** (both: dyĕvdyĕ'lĭyä), Serbo-Croatian *Đevđelija*, Macedonian *Gevgelija* (gĕvgĕ'lēä) or *Gevgeli* (–lē), village (pop. 5,149), Macedonia, Yugoslavia, on Vardar R. and 40 mi. NNW of Salonika, on Greek border, in fertile valley (figs, cotton, silkworms). Trade center of Djevdjelija Plain; silk spinning. Yugoslav frontier station on Belgrade-Salonika RR, N of Eidomene (Greece). Sometimes spelled Gjevgjelija.

Djéziret, province, Syria: see JEZIRE.

Djezzine, Lebanon: see JEZZIN.

Djibo (jē'bō), village, N Upper Volta, Fr. West Africa, near Fr. Sudan border, 115 mi. N of Ouagadougou. Raises cotton, shea nuts; livestock.

Djibouti or **Jibuti** (jĭbōō'tē, Fr. jēbōōtē'), town (1948 pop. estimate 22,000), ⊙ Fr. Somaliland, on S shore of Gulf of Tadjoura (inlet of Gulf of Aden), and S of Bab el Mandeb strait (outlet of Red Sea), 150 mi. SW of Aden and 350 mi. NE of Addis Ababa (linked by rail); 11°36'N 43°8'E. Major port on shipping lanes to Suez Canal and principal outlet for Ethiopian exports (coffee, skins, beeswax, musk); coffee processing, salt-working. It is a free port. Town is situated on coral peninsula jutting 2.5 mi. N into sea. Artificial harbor (on peninsula's E side) is guarded by battery on Heron Isl. Near Djibouti are Ambouli (SW; water-pumping station, truck gardens) and Gabode (SE; airfield). Founded c.1888, city succeeded (1892) Obock as ⊙ Fr. Somaliland and became (1897) official port of Ethiopia. Rail link with Addis Ababa completed 1917.

Djidjelli (jĭjĕlē'), town (pop. 15,215), Constantine dept., NE Algeria, port on the Mediterranean, 38 mi. ENE of Bougie, in Little Kabylia; 36°49'N 5°45'E. Important cork-processing and exporting center. Also ships tanbark, charcoal. Flour milling. Granite quarries and lead mine in vicinity. Port facilities built after 1928. Founded by Carthaginians, it became Roman colony of *Igilgili* under Augustus. In 16th cent., it was 1st capital of Barbarossa. Repulsed French punitive expedition in 1664. Occupied by French in 1839, but isolated by native tribes until 1851. Sometimes spelled Jijelli.

Djin, Tell, Syria: see JIN, TELL.

Djiring (jĭr′ĭng), town, Haut-Donnai prov., S central Vietnam, in Moi Plateaus, 40 mi. N of Phanthiet and 110 mi. NE of Saigon; alt. 3,314 ft. Chief town of Djiring Plateau; coffee, tea, rubber plantations. Formerly spelled Jiring.

Djiring Plateau, S central Vietnam, one of the Moi Plateaus, SW of Annamese Cordillera, rises to 4,659 ft.; red residual soils support tea, coffee, and rubber plantations.

Djisr el Choghour, Syria: see JISR ESH SHUGHUR.

Djoje or **Dsodse** (jō′jā), town, Eastern Prov., SE Gold Coast Colony, near Fr. Togoland border, 20 mi. N of Keta; palm oil and kernels, cotton, cassava. Also spelled Dsoje.

Djokjakarta, Indonesia: see JOGJAKARTA.

Djoko Punda, Belgian Congo: see CHARLESVILLE.

Djoliba River, West Africa: see NIGER RIVER.

Djolu (jō′lōō), village, Equator Prov., NW Belgian Congo, on tributary of Lopori R. and 290 mi. ENE of Coquilhatville; trading post; rubber plantations near by. Also known as Lifake.

Djombang, Indonesia: see JOMBANG.

Djoubeil, Lebanon: see BYBLOS.

Djougou (jōō′gōō), town (pop. c.5,400), W central Dahomey, Fr. West Africa, road junction 70 mi. WNW of Parakou, in agr. region; cotton, peanuts, shea nuts, kapok, livestock. Cotton ginning; mfg. of mats. Sleeping-sickness clinic.

Djoum (jōōm), village, N'Tem region, S Fr. Cameroons, 100 mi. ESE of Ebolowa; trade center.

Djoungo, Fr. Cameroons: see N'KONGSAMBA.

Djouni, Lebanon: see JUNIYE.

Djugu (jōō′gōō), village, Eastern Prov., NE Belgian Congo, on a headstream of the Ituri and 60 mi. NE of Irumu, in gold-mining area; trading center; coffee plantations near by.

Djulfa, Iran: see JULFA, Azerbaijan.

Djuma (jōō′mä), village, Leopoldville prov., SW Belgian Congo, on right bank of Kwilu R., and 75 mi. NNW of Kikwit, in fiber-growing region. Mission center, with mission schools.

Djumaysah, Iraq: see SUWAIRA.

Djupene (jōō′pĭnĭ), Faeroese *Djúpini,* strait (c.15 mi. long) of the Faeroe Isls., separating Ostero and Kalso isls.; c.2 mi. wide.

Djup Lake (dyōōp), Nor. *Djupvatn* or *Djupevatn* [=deep lake], frozen lake in More og Romsdal co., W Norway, 5 mi. SE of Geiranger; 1 mi. long, ½ mi. wide; alt. c.3,400 ft. Tourist center at Djupvasshytta village on N shore.

Djurdjevac (dyōōr′dyĕväts), Serbo-Croatian *Đurđevac,* Hung. *Gjurgjevac* (dyōōr′dyĕvŏts), Ger. *Sankt Georgen* (zängkt gäôr′gūn), village (pop. 7,100), N Croatia, Yugoslavia, in the Podravina, at N foot of Bilo Gora, on railroad and 14 mi. SE of Koprivnica, in Slavonia, in lignite area. Trade center in winegrowing region; cattle market; flour milling.

Djurdjevik or **Dyurdyevik** (dyōōr′dyĕvĭk), Serbo-Croatian *Đurđevik,* village, (pop. 5,041), NE Bosnia, Yugoslavia, 9 mi. S of Tuzla.

Djurdjura or **Djurjura** (jürjürä′), anc. *Mons Ferratus,* highest range (average alt. 6,500 ft.) of Great Kabylia, in Alger dept., N central Algeria, c.60 mi. ESE of Algiers, overlooking the Oued Sahel valley (S); c.30 mi. long. Rises to 7,572 ft. in the Lella Khedidja, highest peak of Algeria's coastal ranges. Scenic limestone formations. Also spelled Jurjura.

Djursholm (yürs′hôlm″), residential city (pop. 6,679), Stockholm co., E Sweden, on Askrike Fjord (äskrē′kü), Swedish *Askrikefjärden,* 15-mi.-long inlet of the Baltic, 5 mi. N of Stockholm city center. In winter, iceboat races held offshore. Private estate, with 16th-cent. castle, until 19th cent.; inc. 1914.

Djursland (jōōrs′lăn), peninsula, E Jutland, Denmark, jutting into the Kattegat, bet. Aarhus Bay and Randers Fjord. Fertile soil; forest near center. Grenaa, chief city. Sometimes called Dyrsland or Grenaa Peninsula.

Djuwaymisah, Iraq: see SUWAIRA.

D'lo or **Dlo** (both: dē′lō), town (pop. 516), Simpson co., S central Miss., 27 mi. SE of Jackson, near Strong R.

Dmanisi (dŭmŭnyē′sē), village (1932 pop. estimate 670), S Georgian SSR, 40 mi. SW of Tiflis; livestock, wheat. Until 1947, Bashkicheti or Bashkichety. Another, smaller Dmanisi or Dumanisi village is 8 mi. ENE.

Dmitri Laptev Strait or **Dmitriy Laptev Strait** (dŭmē′trē läp′tyĭf), joins Laptev (W) and E. Siberian (E) seas of Arctic Ocean at 73°N lat.; separates Bolshoi Lyakhov Isl. and mainland of Yakut Autonomous SSR, Russian SFSR; 80 mi. long, 30 mi. wide. Also called Laptev Strait.

Dmitriyevka (dŭmē′trēŭfkŭ), village (1926 pop. 3,826), SE Chernigov oblast, Ukrainian SSR, 20 mi. SSE of Bakhmach; flour milling.

Dmitriyev-Lgovski or **Dmitriyev-L'govskiy** (dŭmē′-trēŭf-ŭlgôf′skē), city (1926 pop. 4,738), NW Kursk oblast, Russian SFSR, on Svana R. (right affluent of the Seim) and 50 mi. NW of Kursk; distilleries, machine shops, clothing and hemp mills, phosphate fertilizer works. Chartered 1779; formerly called Dmitriyev.

Dmitriyevsk, Ukrainian SSR: see MAKEYEVKA, city.

Dmitriyevskoye. 1 City, Talas oblast, Kirghiz SSR: see TALAS, city. **2** Village, Stavropol Territory, Russian SFSR: see TAKHTA, Stavropol Territory.

Dmitrov (dŭmē′trŭf), city (1939 pop. over 10,000), N Moscow oblast, Russian SFSR, port on E bank of Moscow Canal, 40 mi. N of Moscow; mfg. of lathes, excavators, nails, wire, clothing; food processing. Has old castle and wall, 15th-cent. cathedral, regional mus. Chartered 1154. During Second World War, W bank briefly held (1941) by Germans in Moscow campaign.

Dmitrovski Pogost or **Dmitrovskiy Pogost** (–skē pŭgôst′), village (1939 pop. over 500), E Moscow oblast, Russian SFSR, 20 mi. SE of Shatura; potatoes, flax; lumbering.

Dmitrovsk-Orlovski or **Dmitrovsk-Orlovskiy** (–sk-ŭrlôf′skē), city (1926 pop. 4,995), SW Orel oblast, Russian SFSR, 50 mi. SW of Orel; distilling center; sugar refining, lumber milling, metalworking. Chartered 1782. Formerly called Dmitrovsk.

Dmitryashevka (dŭmē′tryŭshĭfkŭ), village (1926 pop. 4,000), NW Voronezh oblast, Russian SFSR, on Don R. and 33 mi. NNW of Voronezh; wheat.

Dnepr, USSR: see DNIEPER RIVER.

Dneprodzerzhinsk (dŭnyĕ″prŭdzĭrzhēnsk′), city (1926 pop. 34,150; 1939 pop. 147,829), central Dnepropetrovsk oblast, Ukrainian SSR, on right bank of Dnieper R. and 15 mi. W of Dnepropetrovsk. Major metallurgical center (full iron and steel production cycle); freight-car building; coke ovens, chemical industry (nitrate fertilizers, plastics), metal construction, cement mfg. Metallurgical trade school. Granite quarries near by. Founded in 1880s. Until c.1935, Kamenskoye. In Second World War, held (1941–43) by Germans.

Dneproges (dŭnyĕprŭgĕs′) [Rus. abbr.,=Dnieper hydroelectric station], right-bank suburb (formerly Kichkas village) of Zaporozhe, Zaporozhe oblast, Ukrainian SSR, on Dnieper R., site of largest dam and power station of Europe. Dneproges dam is over ½ mi. long, 200 ft. high; power-station capacity, over 500,000 kilowatts. Construction of dam (1927–32; then called Dneprostroi) raised upstream level of Dnieper R. 123 ft. over rapids which formerly impeded through navigation. River traffic now passes through left-bank locks and river port (Port Imeni Lenina) of Zaporozhe. In Second World War, installations were destroyed (1941) in Rus. retreat; recaptured 1943. By 1947 dam was rebuilt and 1st turbine put into operation.

Dnepropetrovsk (dŭnyĕ″prŭpētrôfsk′), oblast (□ 12,590; 1946 pop. estimate 2,200,000), E central Ukrainian SSR; ⊙ Dnepropetrovsk. In Dnieper Lowland; extends E to Donets Basin. Dnieper R. divides oblast into 2 parts. Agr. includes wheat, sunflowers, corn, cotton (SW), hemp (NE), truck produce near metropolitan centers. Major Ukrainian industrial region outside of coal-supplying Donets Basin; metallurgy and machine production at Dnepropetrovsk and Dneprodzerzhinsk, iron mining in Krivoi Rog dist., manganese mining in Nikopol dist. Agr. industries (flour milling, meat packing, dairying) in rural areas. Dense rail network. Formed 1932.

Dnepropetrovsk, city (1926 pop. 232,925; 1939 pop. 500,662), ⊙ Dnepropetrovsk oblast, Ukrainian SSR, on right bank of Dnieper R. bend, at mouth of the Samara, and 110 mi. SSW of Kharkov, 230 mi. SE of Kiev; 48°28′N 35°E. Major industrial and river-rail center; metallurgical works (full iron and steel production cycle); pipe rolling; mfg. (automobiles, machinery, chemicals, clothing, flour). Has state univ., mining, metallurgical, medical, chemical, construction, and rail transportation schools, agr. and teachers colleges. City includes left-bank section, called Amur-Nizhne-Dneprovsk; main metallurgical plants are on right bank, W of city. Founded 1787 by Catherine II as center of lands newly won from Turkey, and named Yekaterinoslav; became govt. ⊙ (until 1925). Rapid growth began with industrialization (end of 19th cent.) due to location bet. Donbas coal, Nikopol manganese, and Krivoi Rog iron-mining areas; industrial development increased after completion (1932) of Dneproges dam and power station. City renamed (1926) for Ukrainian Bolshevik Petrovski. In Second World War, held (1941–43) by Germans.

Dneprostroi, Ukrainian SSR: see DNEPROGES.

Dnestr, river, Ukrainian SSR: see DNIESTER RIVER.

Dnieper, river, USSR: see DNIEPER RIVER.

Dnieper-Bug Canal (nē′pŭr-bōōg′, Rus. dŭnyĕ′pŭr–), Pol. *Kanał Królewski,* W Belorussian SSR, in Pripet Marshes, bet. Pina (E) and Mukhavets (W) rivers; 50 mi. long; built 1784.

Dnieper Liman (Rus. dŭnyĕ′pŭr lyĭmän′), inlet of Black Sea in S Ukrainian SSR; 40 mi. long, 8 mi. wide; receives swampy delta mouth of Dnieper R. (E) and BUG LIMAN (N); opens W into Black Sea through 2.5-mi. passage bet. the Kinburn Kosa and city of Ochakov.

Dnieper Lowland (nē′pŭr, Rus. dŭnyĕ′pŭr), W European USSR, extends c.500 mi. along middle course of Dnieper R. (chiefly on left bank), bet. Central Russian Upland (NW) and Volyn-Podolian Upland (SE). Drained by lower courses of Dnieper R. affluents (Berezina, Desna, Sula, Psel, and Vorskla rivers).

Dnieper River (nē′pŭr), Rus. *Dnepr* (dŭnyĕ′pŭr), anc. *Borysthenes,* third longest (1,420 mi.) of Europe, in W European USSR; rises W of Sychevka (Smolensk oblast), in Valdai Hills; flows S and W, past Dorogobuzh (head of navigation) and Smolensk, through Belorussian SSR, turning S at Orsha, past Mogilev, Zhlobin, and Rechitsa, through Ukrainian SSR (of which it is the main stream) in a vast bend SE, past Kiev, Cherkassy, Kremenchug, and Dnepropetrovsk, S, past Zaporozhe (site of Dneproges dam), and SW, past Nikopol, entering DNIEPER LIMAN through swampy delta mouth below Kherson. Chief affluents are Berezina, Pripet, Teterev, and Ingulets (right) and Sozh, Desna, Sula, Psel, Vorskla, Orel, and Samara (left) rivers. Right bank is generally low, left bank high. Width varies from 300 yds. to 1 mi. bet. Kiev and Dnepropetrovsk. Forms isls. below Kiev and numerous branches in lower course. Navigable for entire course since construction (1932) of DNEPROGES dam and flooding of rapids bet. Dnepropetrovsk and Zaporozhe. Carries lumber, grain, metals, and machinery for 240 days a year in upper reaches, for 265 days in lower course. Dnieper R. basin is linked with Bug (Western Bug) R. by Dnieper-Bug Canal, with Neman R. by Oginski Canal, and with Western Dvina R. by BEREZINA CANAL.

Dniepro-, in Rus. names: see DNEPRO-.

Dniester Liman (nē′stŭr, Rus. dŭnyĕ′stŭr lyĭmän′), shallow lagoon-shaped estuary of Dniester R., in SW Ukrainian SSR, on Black Sea, 20 mi. SW of Odessa; 25 mi. long, 6 mi. wide; opens into Black Sea through 2 narrow passages separated by sandbank. Ovidiopol on E bank, Belgorod-Dnestrovski on W bank. Fisheries.

Dniester River, Rus. *Dnestr* (dŭnyĕ′stŭr), Pol. *Dniestr,* Rum. *Nistru,* anc. *Tyras,* in W European USSR, rises NW of Turka (Drogobych oblast) in Carpathian Mts., flows 876 mi. generally SE, through W Ukrainian SSR, past Sambor, Galich, Khotin, and Mogilev-Podolski, through E Moldavian SSR, past Bendery and Tiraspol, to DNIESTER LIMAN of Black Sea. Tortuous, shallow course. Receives Stry, Reut, and Botna (right) and Seret, Zbruch, and Smotrich (left) rivers. Navigable for c.500 mi. below Mogilev-Podolski (chiefly lumber and grain). Freezes Dec.–March. Formed Rumania-USSR border, 1918-40.

Dno (ŭdnô′), city (1939 pop. over 10,000), E Pskov oblast, Russian SFSR, 60 mi. E of Pskov; rail junction; railroad shops; flax processing, flour milling. During Second World War, held (1941–44) by Germans.

Doab, India: see GANGES-JUMNA DOAB.

Doab Mekh-i-Zarin (dōäb′-mākh′-ĭ-zŭrēn′), village, Kabul prov., E Afghanistan, on highway and 85 mi. NW of Kabul, at N foot of Shikari Pass of the Hindu Kush; 35°15′N 68°E. Road center at junction of Surkhab, Saighan, and Kamard valleys.

Doagh Isle (dō′ŭ), peninsula (4 mi. long, 3 mi. wide) on the Atlantic, N Co. Donegal, Ireland, on W side of Trawbreaga Bay, 4 mi. S of Malin Head.

Doan, Wadi, Aden: see DUAN, WADI.

Doana River, Greece: see ERYMANTHOS RIVER.

Doba (dōbä′), village, SW Chad territory, Fr. Equatorial Africa, on Pendé R. and 50 mi. E of Moundou; cotton ginning. R.C. and Protestant missions, center for treatment of trypanosomiasis. Until 1946, in Ubangi-Shari colony.

Dobbiaco (dôb-byä′kô), Ger. *Toblach,* town (pop. 1,009), Bolzano prov., Trentino–Alto Adige, N Italy, near Rienza R., 15 mi. ESE of Brunico. Resort (alt. c.4,000 ft.), on plateau forming watershed bet. Drave and Rienza rivers. Paper mill.

Dobbs Ferry, residential village (pop. 6,268), Westchester co., SE N.Y., on E bank of the Hudson and c.6 mi. N of downtown Yonkers; mfg. (chemicals, electrical and electronic equipment). Masters School for girls and Children's Village, a rehabilitation school for problem boys, are here. Inc. 1873.

Dobbyn, village, NW Queensland, Australia, 70 mi. NNW of Cloncurry; rail terminus; livestock.

Dobcross, England: see SADDLEWORTH.

Dobczyce (dôpchĭ′tsĕ), town (pop. 2,791), Krakow prov., S Poland, on Raba R. and 14 mi. SSE of Cracow; tanning, flour milling.

Dobele (dō′bālā), Ger. *Doblen,* city (pop. 2,470), W central Latvia, in Zemgale, on branch of the Lielupe and 17 mi. W of Jelgava; dairying, brickworking. Has castle ruins, 15th-cent. church.

Döbeln (dû′bŭln), town (pop. 28,841), Saxony, E central Germany, on the Freiberger Mulde and 30 mi. W of Dresden; rail junction; industrial center; mfg. of steel products, agr. machinery, machine tools, glass, soap, shoes, musical instruments, cigars; sugar refining. Has late-Gothic church. Chartered 1294. Sacked by Hussites in 1429 during the Hussite Wars.

Doberan, Bad, Germany: see BAD DOBERAN.

Doberdò del Lago (dôbĕrdô' dĕl lä'gô), village (pop. 771), Gorizia prov., Friuli–Venezia Giulia, NE Italy, near Yugoslav border, 8 mi. SSW of Gorizia.
Döberitz (dû'bûrĭts), village (pop. 1,107), Brandenburg, E Germany, on the Havel and 6 mi. S of Rathenow; chemical mfg. Formerly site of military training ground. During 1936 Olympic Games in Berlin, residential village for participants was established here.
Doberlug (dō'bûrlōōk), town (pop. 2,909), Brandenburg, E Germany, in Lower Lusatia, 7 mi. WSW of Finsterwalde; rail junction; lignite mining; glass mfg. Exploitation of coal deposits, discovered after Second World War, begun 1949. Has 13th-cent. church of former Cistercian monastery (founded 1165; dissolved 1540; destroyed 1852 by fire); 17th-cent. former palace of dukes of Saxe-Merseburg. Called Dobrilugk until 1937.
Döbern (dû'bûrn), town (pop. 3,738), Brandenburg, E Germany, in Lower Lusatia, on Malxe R. and 9 mi. SSW of Forst; lignite mining; glass mfg.
Dobiegniew (dôbyĕg'nyĕf), Ger. *Woldenberg* (vôl'dûnbĕrk), town (1939 pop. 5,334; 1946 pop. 1,222) in Pomerania, after 1945 in Zielona Gora prov., W Poland, 30 mi. NE of Landsberg (Gorzow Wielkopolski), in lake region; agr. market (grain, potatoes, sugar beets, livestock). Founded c.1300. Has 14th-cent. church. In Second World War, c.80% destroyed. After 1945, briefly called Dobiegniewo.
Doblen, Latvia: see DOBELE.
Döbling (dû'blĭng), outer W district (□ 9; pop. 59,023) of Vienna, Austria, on S slope of the Wiener Wald; observatory. Vineyards.
Dobo (dō'bō), chief town of ARU ISLANDS, S Moluccas, Indonesia, on NE coast of Wamar isl., port on Arafura Sea; 5°46'S 134°13'E. Trading center (sago, copra, rattan, trepang), with exports of pearls, mother-of-pearl, and tortoise shell. Occupied by the Japanese early in Second World War; virtually destroyed (1943) by Allied bombing.
Dobogokö (dô'bôgökû), Hung. *Dobogókő*, village, N central Hungary, 9 mi. WNW of Szentendre; health resort (alt. 2,300 ft.) in Pilis Mts.
Doboj, Doboi, or **Doboy** (all: dô'boi), town (pop. 7,289), N Bosnia, Yugoslavia, on Bosna R., near Usora and Spreca river mouths, and 43 mi. E of Banja Luka; trade and rail center. First mentioned in 15th cent. Usora, its S suburb, produces sugar, molasses, dried beet pulp.
Doborjan (dô'bôryän"), Hung. *Doborján*, village, Sopron co., W Hungary, near Sopron; Liszt b. here.
Dobosnica or **Doboshnitsa** (both: dôbôsh'nĭtsä), Serbo-Croatian *Dobošnica*, village (pop. 5,052), NE Bosnia, Yugoslavia, 8 mi. WNW of Tuzla.
Doboy, Yugoslavia: see DOBOJ.
Doboz (dô'bôz), town (pop. 6,802), Bekes co., SE Hungary, on White Körös R. and 8 mi. ENE of Bekescsaba; flour mills. One of Hungary's oldest communities.
Dobra (dôb'rä). **1** Town (1946 pop. 1,850), Poznan prov., central Poland, 37 mi. WNW of Lodz; flour milling. **2** Ger. *Daber* (dä'bûr), town (1939 pop. 2,528; 1946 pop. 1,553) in Pomerania, after 1945 in Szczecin prov., NW Poland, 20 mi. NNE of Stargard; agr. market (grain, sugar beets, potatoes, livestock).
Dobra (dô'brä), village (pop. 1,710), Hunedoara prov., W central Rumania, on Mures R., on railroad and 16 mi. W of Deva; limestone quarrying.
Dobra (dô'brä), hamlet, E Serbia, Yugoslavia, on the Danube (Rum. border) and 70 mi. E of Belgrade; lignite mine.
Döbraberg (dû'bräbĕrk), highest peak (2,608 ft.) of Franconian Forest, Germany, 5 mi. SW of Selbitz.
Dobrany (dô'bûrzhänĭ), Czech *Dobřany*, Ger. *Wiesengrund* (vē'sûngrōōnt), town (pop. 3,983), W Bohemia, Czechoslovakia, on Radbuza R., on railroad and 7 mi. SSW of Pilsen; coal and kaolin mining. Has insane asylum.
Dobra River (dô'brä), NW Croatia, Yugoslavia, rises in the Velika Kapela near Brod Moravice, flows SSE, past Ogulin, and NNE to Kupa R. 5 mi. N of Karlovac; c.60 mi. long. Below Ogulin, flows c.20 mi. underground.
Dobratsch (dō'brăch), peak (7,106 ft.) in Carinthia, S Austria, W of Villach; highest of VILLACH ALP.
Dobra Voda (dô'brä vô'dä), mountain, Macedonia, Yugoslavia, bet. Gostivar-Kicevo RR and Treska R., highest point (6,763 ft.) is 12 mi. SSE of Gostivar.
Dobre Miasto (dôb'rĕ myä'stô), Ger. *Guttstadt* (gōōt'shtät), town (1939 pop. 5,932; 1946 pop. 966) in East Prussia, after 1945 in Olsztyn prov., NE Poland, on Lyna R. and 15 mi. N of Allenstein (Olsztyn); machinery mfg., sawmilling. Until 1811, seat of chapter of Ermland bishopric. Evacuated by Ger. pop. after Second World War.
Dobresti (dôbrĕsht'), Rum. *Dobreşti*, Hung. *Bihardobrosd* (bē'hŏrdô'brâsht), village (pop. 1,350), Bihor prov., W Rumania, 21 mi. SE of Oradea; rail terminus; bauxite, titanium, and zinc mining. Bauxite is also mined at near-by Rosia (rô'shä), Rum. *Roşia*, 6 mi. SE.
Dobrich, Bulgaria: see TOLBUKHIN.
Dobrilugk, Germany: see DOBERLUG.
Dobrina (dôbrēnä'), village (pop. 1,264), Stalin dist., E Bulgaria, on Provadiya R. and 2 mi. S of Provadiya; vineyards; saltworks. Has ruins of old churches. Once a commercial town; declined following emigration of Albanian pop. after Russo-Turkish War (1828). Formerly Dzhizelar-koi.
Dobrinishte (dôbrē'nĭshtĕ), village (pop. 2,218), Gorna Dzhumaya dist., SW Bulgaria, in Pirin Mts., 4 mi. ESE of Bansko; livestock raising, lumbering. Has thermal springs and baths. Sometimes spelled Dobrinishta.
Dobrinka (dŭbrēn'kŭ). **1** Village (1926 pop. 4,212), NE Stalingrad oblast, Russian SFSR, on right bank of Volga R. and 21 mi. NE of Kamyshin; grain shipping point; flour milling. One of oldest German Volga settlements; founded 1764. Until c.1940, called Nizhnyaya Dobrinka. **2** Village (1926 pop. 1,458), NW Stalingrad oblast, Russian SFSR, on Khoper R. and 7 mi. WNW of Uryupinsk; wheat, sunflowers. **3** Village (1926 pop. 1,458), N Voronezh oblast, Russian SFSR, 30 mi. SE of Gryazi; flour mill.
Dobris (dô'bûrzhĕsh), Czech *Dobříš*, town (pop. 4,130), central Bohemia, Czechoslovakia, 10 mi. NE of Pribram; rail terminus; mfg. (rope, knitted gloves), especially for export; coal mining. Lake fishing in vicinity. Summer excursion center for the Brdy. Has 14th- and 18th-cent. castles. Small amounts of gold are extracted from river sands at Novy Knin, 5 mi. E.
Dobrljin or **Dobrlyin** (both: dô'bûrlyĭn), village, NW Bosnia, Yugoslavia, on Una R., on railroad and 9 mi. NNE of Novi, on Croatia border; lumbering; brown-coal mining.
Dobrna (dô'bûrnä), Ger. *Neuhaus* (noi'hous), village, N Slovenia, Yugoslavia, 8 mi. N of Celje. Until 1918, in Styria. Health resort of Toplice Dobrna, Ger. *Bad Neuhaus*, just N of village, has hot springs.
Dobrodzien (dôbrô'jĕnyû), Polish *Dobrodzień*, Ger. *Guttentag* (gōō'tûntäk), town (1939 pop. 4,307; 1946 pop. 3,277) in Upper Silesia, after 1945 in Katowice prov., S Poland, 11 mi. WNW of Lubliniec; agr. market (grain, potatoes, livestock); sawmilling.
Dobroesti (dôbrôĕsht'), Rum. *Dobroeşti*, outer E rural suburb (1948 pop. 2,224) of Bucharest, Bucharest prov., S Rumania, on left bank of Colentina R.
Dobrogea, Rumania and Bulgaria: see DOBRUJA.
Döbrököz (dû'brûkûz), town (pop. 4,374), Tolna co., SW central Hungary, on Kapos R. and 22 mi. WNW of Szekszard; potatoes, wine.
Dobromierz, Poland: see HOHENFRIEDEBERG.
Dobromil or **Dobromil'** (dŭbrŭmēl'), city (1931 pop. 5,531), W Drogobych oblast, Ukrainian SSR, on N slope of E Beskids, 20 mi. WNW of Sambor, in woodland near Pol. border; summer resort; sawmilling, woodworking, agr. processing (cereals, hops), saltworks, cement. Has ruins of old castle. Passed from Austria to Poland in 1919; ceded to USSR in 1945.
Dobromirka (dôbrômĕr'kä), village (pop. 3,065), Gorna Oryakhovitsa dist., N Bulgaria, 9 mi. ENE of Sevliyevo; flour milling; fruit, truck, livestock.
Dobropolye or **Dobropol'ye** (dŭbrŭpô'lyĭ). **1** Village (1939 pop. over 500), W Stalino oblast, Ukrainian SSR, in the Donbas, 11 mi. NW of Krasnoarmeiskoye; dairy farming. **2** Village (1939 pop. over 500), central Zaporozhe oblast, Ukrainian SSR, 17 mi. SE of Bolshoi Tokmak; wheat, cotton, dairying. A Ger. agr. settlement originally called Valdgeim (Waldheim), and later (c.1935–41), Rot-Front.
Dobrosesti, Rumania: see SNAGOV.
Dobrovat, Rumania: see CODAESTI.
Dobrovelichkovka (dŭbrŭvyĭlyēch'kŭfkŭ), village (1926 pop. 4,669), W Kirovograd oblast, Ukrainian SSR, on road and 50 mi. WSW of Kirovograd; metalworks.
Dobrovice (dô'brôvĭtsĕ), village (pop. 2,137), N Bohemia, Czechoslovakia, 28 mi. SSW of Liberec; rail junction; sugar beets, potatoes.
Dobrovolsk or **Dobrovol'sk** (dŭbrŭvôlsk'), town (1939 pop. 5,833), E Kaliningrad oblast, Russian SFSR, on railroad and 10 mi. NNW of Nesterov; agr. market; brickworks. First mentioned in 16th cent.; chartered 1724. Until 1945, in East Prussia where it was called Pillkallen (pĭl'kälûn) and, later (1938–45), Schlossberg (shlôs'bĕrk).
Dobroye (dô'brŭyŭ). **1** Fishing village, Sakhalin oblast, Russian SFSR, on Iturup Isl., S main Kurile Isls., on SW coast, 50 mi. SW of Kurilsk. Under Jap. rule (until 1945), called Naibo. **2** Village (1926 pop. 6,323), SW Ryazan oblast, Russian SFSR, on Voronezh R. and 27 mi. SSW of Chaplygin; wheat, sugar beets.
Dobruja or **Dobrudja** (dō'brōōjä, dô–), Bulg. *Dobrudzha* (dôbrōō'jä), Rum. *Dobrogea* (dôbrô'jä), region (□ c.9,000; pop. c.850,000) of SE Rumania and NE Bulgaria, bet. the lower Danube and the Black Sea, bounded S by the Deliorman upland. Chief city, Constanta. Adjoining the swampy Danube delta, the low N lagoon coast is backed by the Tulcea hills (1,496 ft.), an old eroded crystalline massif. In its low central portion bet. Cernavoda and Constanta, the Dobruja is crossed by the Danube-Black Sea Canal. In S, the terrain rises again in karst-like Sarmatian formations toward the Deliorman uplands. Largely agr. (wheat, rye, barley, corn, beans, flaxseed), the Dobruja is a grain-surplus region. Copper is mined in Tulcea hills; limestone and building stone are quarried. Fisheries along coast. Pop. includes Rumanians, Bulgars, Turks, and Tatars. The Rumanian (N) Dobruja forms a historic province (□ 5,998; 1948 pop. 503,217; ⊙ Constanta). The Bulgarian (S) Dobruja (□ 2,971; 1940 pop. 318,772; chief city, Tolbukhin) forms part of Ruse and Stalin dists. of Bulgaria. Originally part of the Roman prov. of Moesia Inferior, the Dobruja later belonged to the Byzantine Empire, to medieval Bulgaria, and (after 15th cent.) to Ottoman Empire, and was a frequent battleground in Russo-Turkish wars of 18th and 19th cents. N Dobruja was awarded to Rumania by Congress of Berlin (1878). S Dobruja, which had become part (1878) of the newly created principality of Bulgaria, was also ceded (1913; confirmed 1919 by Treaty of Neuilly) to Rumania as a result of Second Balkan War, but was returned to Bulgaria in 1940 by the Treaty of Craiova.
Dobrush (dô'brōōsh), city (1939 pop. over 10,000), SE Gomel oblast, Belorussian SSR, on Iput R. (head of navigation) and 13 mi. E of Gomel; paper-milling center.
Dobruska (dô'brōōshkä), Czech *Dobruška*, town (pop. 3,317), E Bohemia, Czechoslovakia, 16 mi. ENE of Hradec Kralove; rail terminus; textile industry. Has 15th-cent. town hall.
Dobryanka (dŭbryän'kŭ). **1** City (1926 pop. 6,812), central Molotov oblast, Russian SFSR, port on left bank of Kama R. and 27 mi. N of Molotov; metallurgical center, based on charcoal. Founded 1752 as copper-smelting plant; shifted to pig-iron (later, steel) production after exhaustion of copper deposits. Became city in 1943. Ceramic industry 10 mi. WNW, on right Kama R. bank, at Ust-Garevaya (1939 pop. under 500). **2** Town (1926 pop. 4,996), NW Chernigov oblast, Ukrainian SSR, 40 mi. N of Chernigov; grain.
Dobrzany (dôb-zhä'nĭ), Ger. *Jacobshagen* (yä'kôps-hä"gûn), town (1939 pop. 1,984; 1946 pop. 342) in Pomerania, after 1945 in Szczecin prov., NW Poland, 16 mi. E of Stargard; agr. market (grain, sugar beets, potatoes, livestock). After 1945, briefly called Dobrzanek.
Dobrzyn (dôb'zhĭn), Rus. *Dobrzhin* or *Dobrzhin'* (dôbûr-zhē'nyû). **1** or **Dobrzyn nad Drweca** (näd dûrvĕ'tsä), Pol. *Dobrzyń nad Drwęca*, town, Bydgoszcz prov., N central Poland: see GOLUB. **2** or **Dobrzyn nad Wisla** (näd vĭs'wō), Pol. *Dobrzyń nad Wisłą*, town (pop. 2,339), Bydgoszcz prov., central Poland, port on the Vistula and 11 mi. E of Wloclawek; cattle and horse trade; mfg. of caps.
Dobsina (dôp'shĭnä), Slovak *Dobšiná*, Ger. *Dobschau* (dôp'shou), village (pop. 3,957), E central Slovakia, Czechoslovakia, in Slovak Ore Mts., on Slana (Sajo) R. and 40 mi. WNW of Kosice; rail terminus; iron foundries; long-established mining center (iron, copper, asbestos). Ice-cavern of Dobsina (4 mi. NW), with stalactite and stalagmite formations, was discovered in late-19th cent.; became a popular tourist attraction.
Dobson, town (pop. 609), ⊙ Surry co., N N.C., 34 mi. NW of Winston-Salem, near Va. line.
Dobtra (dōb'trä'), Chinese *To-p'a-t'e-la* (dô'pä'tŭ-lä'), town, S Tibet, near the lake Tsomo Tretung, 70 mi. SW of Shigatse; junction of a Nepal-Sikkim trade route; alt. 14,700 ft.
Doce, Rio (rē'ōō dō'sĭ), river of E Brazil, rises on E slope of the Serra do Espinhaço above Ponte Nova (Minas Gerais), flows NE to Governador Valadares (head of navigation), then SE along S edge of the Serra dos Aimorés, and across central Espírito Santo to the Atlantic 60 mi. NE of Vitória. Length, c.360 mi. Interrupted by rapids. Chief tributary: Piracicaba R. (left). River is paralleled along most of its course by Belo Horizonte–Vitória RR (recently modernized), used for iron-ore shipments from Itabira to the coast. Semiprecious-stone deposits in valley.
Doce Leguas, Cayos de las (kī'ōs dā läs dō'sā lä'gwäs), coral reefs off Caribbean coast of E Cuba, 70 mi. SW of Camagüey. The keys form 2 groups: Cayos de las Doce Leguas (NW) and Laberinto de las Doce Leguas (SE), divided by the Canal de Caballones, and forming in their entirety the Jardines de la Reina (c.85 mi. long NW–SE), which are sometimes considered to include the Gran Banco de Buena Esperanza.
Docelles (dôsĕl'), village (pop. 940), Vosges dept., E France, 8 mi. ESE of Épinal; paper milling, hosiery mfg.
Docena, village (pop. 1,551), Jefferson co., N central Ala., a NW suburb of Birmingham.
Dochart River (dŏkh'ûrt), Perthshire, Scotland, rises on Ben Lui, flows 25 mi. E, through Loch Dochart (3 mi. long), to Loch Tay at Killin. Headstream of the Tay. Upper course of the Dochart is called Fillan.
Dochet Island, Maine: see SAINT CROIX ISLAND.
Dock Junction, village (pop. 4,160), Glynn co., SE Ga., near Brunswick.
Dock Sud (dôk'sōōdh'), port section (pop. estimate, 20,000) of AVELLANEDA, in Greater Buenos Aires, Argentina, on Río de la Plata at mouth of Riachuelo R.

Doctor Arroyo (dōktôr' äroi'ō), city (pop. 2,912), Nuevo León, N Mexico, in Sierra Madre Oriental, 30 mi. E of Matehuala (Zacatecas); alt. 5,794 ft.; tanning, lumbering, garment making, printing; cigars, sweets, machinery.

Doctor Belisario Domínguez (dōktôr' bālēsär'yō dōmēng'gĕs), town (pop. 532), Chihuahua, N Mexico, 40 mi. SW of Chihuahua; corn, beans, fruit, livestock. Copper deposits. Formerly San Lorenzo.

Doctor Cecilio Báez, Paraguay: see CECILIO BÁEZ.

Doctor Coss (kōs), town (pop. 636), Nuevo León, N Mexico, on San Juan R. and 70 mi. ENE of Monterrey; cotton, sugar cane, corn, cactus fibers. Its railroad station is 10 mi. NE.

Doctor Facundo Zuviría, Argentina: see FACUNDO ZUVIRÍA.

Doctor Francisco Soca, Uruguay: see SOCA.

Doctor González (gōnsä'lĕs), town (pop. 1,205), Nuevo León, N Mexico, 26 mi. NE of Monterrey; cereals, cactus fibers, stock.

Doctor Hernández Álvarez (ĕrnän'dĕs äl'värĕs), officially Ciudad Doctor Hernández Álvarez, city (pop. 5,737), Guanajuato, central Mexico, in Sierra Madre Occidental, 32 mi. N of Guanajuato; alt. 6,890 ft. Agr. center (corn, wheat, barley, potatoes, maguey); tequila and mescal distilling. Formerly San Felipe; later, until 1938, Ciudad González. Its railroad station, San Felipe, is 4 mi. E.

Doctor Moisés S. Bertoni (moisās' ĕ'sĕ bĕrtō'nē) or **Moisés Bertoni,** town (dist. pop. 3,551), Caazapá dept., S Paraguay, 110 mi. SE of Asunción, S of Caazapá; lumber, fruit, livestock.

Doctor's Cave, Jamaica: see MONTEGO BAY.

Doda (dō'dŭ), district (□ 4,162; pop. 181,204), Jammu prov., SW Kashmir; ⊙ Doda. In S Punjab Himalayas; drained by Chenab R. Agr. (corn, wheat, barley, rice, oilseeds, gram); fruit orchards. Valuable deodar forest near Kishtwar. Sapphire mines near Sumjam; slate deposits SE of BANIHAL. Main towns: Kishtwar, Bhadarwah. Created in late 1940s out of Udhampur dist. Prevailing mother tongues, Kashmiri and Bhadrawahi.

Doda, village, ⊙ Doda dist., SW Kashmir, in Pir Panjal foothills, on Chenab R. and 50 mi. NE of Jammu; corn, wheat, barley, rice, fruit.

Dodabetta (dō'dŭbĕt-tŭ), highest peak (8,640 ft.) in Nilgiri Hills, SW Madras, India, just E of Ootacamund.

Doda Falls, Sweden: see RAGUNDA.

Dodanduwa (dōdän'dōōvŭ), village (pop., including near-by villages, 2,100), Southern Prov., Ceylon, on SW coast, 7 mi. NW of Galle; coir-rope mfg.; vegetables, rice, coconuts, citronella grass. Graphite mining near by.

Dodangaslanda (dōdŭng-gŭslŭn'dŭ), village, North Western Prov., Ceylon, 12 mi. NE of Kurunegala; graphite-mining center.

Dodballapur or **Dod Ballapur** (dōd' bŭ'lŭpōōr), town (pop. 11,866), Bangalore dist., E central Mysore, India, 20 mi. N of Bangalore; silk, rice, and oilseed milling, tobacco curing; sheep breeding. Handicraft training center (weaving, lacquerware, leather goods).

Dodd City, town (pop. 329), Fannin co., NE Texas, 6 mi. E of Bonham, in agr. area.

Dodderhill, England: see DROITWICH.

Doddington, town and parish (pop. 1,459), in Isle of Ely, N Cambridge, England, 4 mi. SSW of March; agr. market. Has church dating mainly from 15th cent.

Doddridge, county (□ 319; pop. 9,026), W W.Va.; ⊙ West Union. On Allegheny Plateau; drained by Middle Island Creek and South Fork of Hughes R. Agr. (livestock, fruit, potatoes, corn, tobacco); natural-gas and oil wells, some bituminous coal; timber. Formed 1845.

Dodds, village, central Alta., 19 mi. NE of Camrose; coal mining.

Doddsville, town (pop. 201), Sunflower co., W Miss., 22 mi. WNW of Greenwood, in cotton area.

Dodecanese (dōdĕ"kŭnēs', –nēz, dō"dĕ–), Gr. *Dodekanesos, Dodekanisos,* or *Dhodhekanisos* (Gr. dhôdhĕkä'nēsôs) [=12 islands], isl. group (□ 1,044; 1951 pop. 120,100) of Greece, in SE Aegean Sea, bet. Turkey and Crete; ⊙ Rhodes. Despite its name, it consists of 14 main isls. and c.40 islets and reefs. The major isls. are ASTYPALAIA, CHALKE, KALYMNOS, KARPATHOS, KASOS, KOS (2d largest), LEROS, LEIPSOS, NISYROS, PATMOS, RHODES (the largest), SYME, and TELOS. The tiny KASTELLORIZO is the easternmost isl., separate from the rest of the group. The group's extreme points are 37°28'N on Gaidaro isl., 35°20'N at S cape of Kasos isl., 26°8'E on Ophidousa isl., and 29°35'E on Kastellorizo. Largely mountainous, the isls. are very picturesque, crowned in part by medieval monasteries and knights' castles. Except for Rhodes, they are deforested and poorly watered. Earthquakes are common at Kos; near-by Nisyros is volcanic. Pop. is largely Greek; agr. (olives, wine, fruit), stock raising, and sponge fishing are the main sources of livelihood. The Dodecanese, consisting of the major (S) portion of the Southern Sporades, passed (1522–23) from the control of the Knights Hospitalers to the Turks. The group was occupied (1912; except for Kastellorizo) by the Italians in the Italo-Turkish war of 1911–12 and was formally awarded to the Italians by the Treaty of Sèvres (1920; confirmed by Treaty of Lausanne, 1923). In the Second World War, after the surrender of Italy, the group was garrisoned by German troops, which surrendered only in May, 1945. On the basis of their Greek pop., the isls. were awarded to Greece in the Allied peace treaty with Italy in 1947 and formally transferred in 1948 from provisional British military govt. Known under Ital. rule as Possedimenti Italiani dell'Egeo [=Ital. possessions in the Aegean].

Dodewaard (dō'dŭvärt), town (pop. 2,213), Gelderland prov., E central Netherlands, on Waal R. and 10 mi. WNW of Nijmegen; cigars, jam, canned food; truck gardening. Sometimes spelled Doodewaard.

Dodge. 1 County (□ 499; pop. 17,865), S central Ga.; ⊙ Eastman. Bounded SW by Ocmulgee R.; drained by Little Ocmulgee R. Coastal plain agr. (cotton, corn, peanuts, pecans, livestock) and lumber area; textile mfg. at Eastman. Formed 1870. **2** County (□ 435; pop. 12,624), SE Minn.; ⊙ Mantorville. Agr. area drained by branches of Zumbro R. Dairy products, livestock, grain. Formed 1855. **3** County (□ 529; pop. 26,265), E Nebr.; ⊙ Fremont. Agr. region bounded S by Platte R.; drained by Elkhorn R. Flour; grain, livestock, dairy and poultry produce. Formed 1854. **4** County (□ 892; pop. 57,611), S central Wis.; ⊙ Juneau. Drained by Rock R. and its tributaries, including Crawfish R.; contains Beaverdam, Fox, and Sinissippi lakes, and Horicon Natl. Wildlife Refuge. Dairying, stock-raising, grain-growing area. Processing of farm products, mfg., iron mining. Formed 1836.

Dodge. 1 Village, Worcester co., Mass.: see CHARLTON. **2** Village (pop. 633), Dodge co., E Nebr., 27 mi. NW of Fremont and on branch of Elkhorn R.; dairy and poultry produce, grain, livestock. **3** Village (pop. 251), Dunn co., W central N.Dak., 40 mi. NE of Dickinson and on Spring Creek. **4** Village (1940 pop. 507), San Jacinto co., E Texas, 10 mi. E of Huntsville, in Sam Houston Natl. Forest, in cotton-growing, lumbering area.

Dodge, Camp, Iowa: see JOHNSTON.

Dodge Center, village (pop. 1,151), Dodge co., SE Minn., 20 mi. W of Rochester; shipping point for livestock and truck and dairy products; canned corn and peas. Settled 1853, inc. 1872.

Dodge City, city (pop. 11,262), ⊙ Ford co., SW Kansas, on Arkansas R. and c.150 mi. W of Wichita; distribution center for extensive wheat-growing and stock-raising area; flour milling, dairying; mfg. of agr. equipment, tents, awnings; railroad maintenance. Has jr. col. Laid out 1872 near Fort Dodge (established 1864 on Santa Fe Trail), it flourished as cattle town and railhead of Atchison, Topeka, and Santa Fe RR. Inc. 1875.

Dodgeville. 1 Village (1940 pop. 536), Houghton co., NW Upper Peninsula, Mich., 2 mi. SSW of Houghton, in copper-mining area. **2** City (pop. 2,532), ⊙ Iowa co., S Wis., 38 mi. WSW of Madison; trade center for farm area (livestock, poultry; butter, cheese). Settled 1827; inc. as village in 1858, as city in 1889. Was center of early lead-mining industry.

Dodici, Cima (chē'mä dô'dēchē), mountains in N Italy. **1** Peak (10,151 ft.) in the E Alps, on Bolzano-Belluno prov. border, 12 mi. NE of Cortina d'Ampezzo. **2** Highest peak (7,680 ft.) of Asiago plateau (Sette Comuni), on Trento-Vicenza prov. border, 4 mi. S of Borgo. Formerly on Austro-Ital. frontier; scene of fighting in First World War.

Dodola (dōdō'lä), village (pop. 150), Harar prov., S Ethiopia, near upper Webi Shebeli (here called Wabi), 60 mi. W of Goba, in cereal-growing region.

Dodoma (dōdō'mä), town (pop. 9,414), ⊙ Central Prov. (□ 36,410; pop. 820,551), central Tanganyika, on railroad and 100 mi. WNW of Kilosa; alt. 3,713 ft.; 6°10'S 35°45'E. Communications center on railroad from Dar es Salaam and on N-S road; livestock market; peanuts, millet, gum arabic. Seat of Anglican bishopric. Mental hosp. Airfield. Gold and corundum deposits near by. New peanut-growing scheme at Kongwa and Hogora (50–60 mi. E).

Dodona (dōdō'nŭ), anc. city of S Epirus, Greece, 10 mi. SSW of modern Ioannina, at N foot of the Tomaros. Center of Pelasgian worship; site of oldest Greek oracle, dedicated to Zeus and dating from c.1500 B.C. Temple was destroyed 219 B.C. by Aetolians, but oracle continued until 6th cent. A.D. Excavations date from 1878. Near by is modern Gr. village of Dodone or Dhodhoni (pop. 512).

Dodowa (dōdō'wä), town, Eastern Prov., S Gold Coast colony, in Akwapim Hills, on road and 25 mi. NNE of Accra; cacao, palm oil and kernels, cassava.

Dodsland, village (pop. 214), SW Sask., 27 mi. NE of Kindersley; railroad junction; wheat, stock.

Dodson. 1 Village (pop. 375), Winn parish, N central La., 32 mi. S of Ruston, in agr. area. **2** Town (pop. 330), Phillips co., N Mont., on Milk R. and 17 mi. W of Malta. Fort Belknap Indian Reservation is near. **3** or **Dodsonville,** village (pop. 336), Collingsworth co., extreme N Texas, near Okla. line, 25 mi. NNE of Childress and on Salt Fork of Red R., in grain and cattle area.

Dodworth, urban district (1931 pop. 4,245; 1951 census 4,262), West Riding, S Yorkshire, England, 2 mi. W of Barnsley; coal mining.

Doe River, NE Tenn., rises on Roan Mtn. in Carter co., flows NNW around S end of Iron Mts., to Watauga R. at Elizabethton; c.30 mi. long.

Doerun (dō'rŭn"), city (pop. 902), Colquitt co., S Ga., 12 mi. NW of Moultrie, in agr. area; mfg. (naval stores, fertilizer).

Doesburg (dōōs'bûrkh), town (pop. 5,721), Gelderland prov., E Netherlands, on Ijssel R., at mouth of Old Ijssel R., and 10 mi. ENE of Arnhem; shipbuilding; mfg. (varnishes, ironware, mustard).

Doetinchem (dōō'tĭ-khŭm), town (pop. 13,089), Gelderland prov., E Netherlands, on Old Ijssel R. and 16 mi. E of Arnhem; meat canning, metal stamping and enameling, mfg. of bricks, asphalt, leather goods, wood products, motors, bicycle tires; printing. Sometimes spelled Deutichem.

Dogansehir (dōän'shĕhĭr"), Turkish *Doğanşehir,* village (pop. 943), Malatya prov., E central Turkey, on railroad and 30 mi. SW of Malatya; grain. Formerly Viransehir.

Dogdyke, agr. village and parish (pop. 162), Parts of Kesteven, central Lincolnshire, England, on Witham R. and 10 mi. NW of Boston; synthetic-fertilizer works.

Dogern (dō'gûrn), village (pop. 856), S Baden, Germany, at S foot of Black Forest, on the Rhine (Swiss border) and 2.5 mi. WSW of Waldshut. Bet. here and Albbruck is hydroelectric plant Albbruck-Dogern.

Dogger Bank, extensive sand bank, central North Sea, bet. England and Denmark, covered by shallow water. Notable for its fisheries.

Dog Island, islet of Leeward group, B.W.I., on Anegada Passage, 12 mi. W of Anguilla; 18°17'N 63°16'W.

Dog Island (c.7 mi. long), Franklin co., NW Fla., in the Gulf of Mexico; partly shelters St. George Sound.

Dog Lake (16 mi. long, 5 mi. wide), W Ont., 22 mi. NW of Port Arthur; drained S by Kaministikwia R. into L. Superior.

Dogliana (dôlyä'nē), village (pop. 2,253), Cuneo prov., Piedmont, NW Italy, near Tanaro R., 13 mi. SSW of Alba; agr. center for wine, livestock, fruit (pears, apples), truffles.

Dognecea (dôgnä'chä), Hung. *Dognácska* (dôg'-näch-kŏ), village (pop. 2,720), Severin prov., SW Rumania, 8 mi. SW of Resita; popular tourist center. Also molybdenum and bismuth mining, marble quarrying.

Dogo, town, Japan: see DOGOYUNO-MACHI.

Dogo (dō'gō), largest island (□94; pop. 22,584) of isl. group Oki-gunto, Shimane prefecture, Japan, just NE of Dozen group, 47 mi. NNE of Matsue, off SW Honshu; roughly circular, 11 mi. in diameter. Mountainous, forested; raw silk, lumber, charcoal; fishing. Formerly sometimes called Oki Shima. Saigo, on SE coast, is chief town and port of Oki-gunto.

Dogondoutchi (dōgōndōō'chē), town (pop. c.4,000), SW Niger territory, Fr. West Africa, 125 mi. E of Niamey; peanuts, kapok; goats.

Dogoyuno-machi (dō'gōyōō"nō-mächē), town (1940 pop. 8,410), Ehime prefecture, NW Shikoku, Japan, just NE of Matsuyama; health resort (alkaline hot springs). Site of 14th-cent. castle. Called Dogo until 1923. Since c.1947 it is part of Matsuyama.

Dog River. 1 In Ala. and Miss.: see ESCATAWPA RIVER. **2** In central Vt., rises in SW Washington co., flows c.25 mi. NNE to the Winooski at Montpelier.

Dogs, Isle of, district in Poplar, London, England, formed by bend of the Thames, 4 mi. ESE of Charing Cross, opposite Greenwich (joined by tunnel for pedestrians); contains shipyards and West India and Millwall docks. Formerly site of royal kennels.

Dogubayazit (dôōō'bäyäzŭt"), Turkish *Doğubayazıt,* village (pop. 5,723), Agri prov., E Turkey, in Armenia, 150 mi. E of Erzurum, 15 mi. SSW of Mt. Ararat; transit station for Iranian frontier, 8 mi. S; mineral springs. Once an important trading town, it was taken several times by Russia, last in 1914. Formerly Bayazit or Bayazid.

Doha, Dohah, or **Dawhah** (all: dō'hŭ), town (pop. 10,000), ⊙ Qatar, Persian Gulf port on E coast of Qatar peninsula; 25°18'N 51°31'E. Chief commercial center of Qatar; pearling, fishing; metal-working; coastal trade. Has old Turkish fort (built 1850). Formerly called Bida, for its oldest constituent quarter.

Dohad (dō'hŭd), town (pop. 12,666), Panch Mahals dist., N Bombay, India, 40 mi. E of Godhra; road center; grain market (corn, rice, wheat, millet); flour and oilseed milling; ordnance factory. Timber forests near by.

Dohah, Qatar: see DOHA.

Dohan (dōä'), village (pop. 236), Luxembourg prov., SE Belgium, in the Ardennes, on Semois R. and 14 mi. WSW of Neufchâteau, in tobacco-growing region.

Dohazari, E Pakistan: see SHOLASHAHAR.

Dohinob (dōhĭ'nŏb, dōhēnōb'), town (1939 pop. 6,794) in Katipunan municipality, Zamboanga prov., NW Mindanao, Philippines, 50 mi. NNW of Pagadian; coconuts, rice, corn.

Döhlen, Germany: see FREITAL.

Dohna (dō'nä), town (pop. 5,534), Saxony, E central Germany, in Saxonian Switzerland, 4 mi. W of Pirna; fluorspar processing, metalworking; mfg. of chemicals, glass, cellulose. Has remains of anc. castle.

Dohrighat (dō'rēgät), town (pop. 3,025), Azamgarh dist., E Uttar Pradesh, India, on the Gogra and 23 mi. NE of Azamgarh; rail spur terminus; trades in rice, wheat, barley, sugar cane, salt, oilseeds.

Doi, Japan: see TOI, town.

Doicesti (doichĕst'), Rum. *Doiceşti,* village (pop. 2,041), Prahova prov., S central Rumania, on Ialomita R., on railroad and 5 mi. N of Targoviste; oil-production center; oil refining, mfg. of cotton textiles.

Doiran, Yugoslavia: see DOJRAN.

Doiranes or **Doiranis,** lake, Greece-Yugoslavia: see DOJRAN, LAKE.

Doisanagar, India: see RANCHI, city.

Dois Côrregos (dois kô'rĭgo͝os), city (pop. 5,591), central São Paulo, Brazil, on railroad and 55 mi. WNW of Piracicaba; leatherworking center (chiefly shoes); also makes flour paste, furniture.

Dois Irmãos, Serra dos (sĕ'rŭ do͝os dois ērmā'ōs), hill range of NE Brazil, on Piauí-Pernambuco border, separating the São Francisco and Parnaíba drainage basins. Rises to c.3,000 ft. Diatomite deposits. Crossed by Petrolina-Paulistana RR. Sometimes called Serra dos Irmãos.

Dojran, Doiran, or **Doyran** (all: doi'rän), anc. *Assorus,* village, Macedonia, Yugoslavia, on L. Dojran and 17 mi. S of Strumica, near Greek border; fishing. Fig raising in vicinity. Traces of prehistoric and anc. lake dwellings.

Dojran, Lake, Serbo-Croatian *Dojransko Jezero,* Gr. *Doiranes, Doiranis* (both: doirä'nĭs), or *Prasias* (präsēäs'), Macedonian Lake (□ 17) on Yugoslav-Gr. border, bet. Vardar R. and the Belasica; 5 mi. long, 4 mi. wide, 33 ft. deep; alt. 485 ft. Fishing. Dojran village is on SW shore.

Doka (dō'kä), village, Kassala prov., NE Anglo-Egyptian Sudan, on road and 45 mi. SE of Gedaref.

Dokkum (dô'kŭm), town (pop. 5,587), Friesland prov., N Netherlands, 12 mi. NE of Leeuwarden; dairying; mfg. (cement, cigars, chocolate, sugar). Site of slaying (775) of Bonifacius by the Frisians.

Dokos or **Dhokos** (both: dhôkôs'), anc. *Aperopia,* island (□ 5.4; pop. 41) in Aegean Sea at mouth of Gulf of Argolis, E Peloponnesus, Greece, in Attica nome, 1 mi. off mainland bet. Hydra isl. and Argolis Peninsula; 4 mi. long, 1–1.5 mi. wide; goats.

Dokri (dō'krē), village, Larkana dist., NW Sind, W Pakistan, 12 mi. SSW of Larkana; rice, millet, wheat, gram. Agr. research station.

Dokshitsy (dŭkshē'tsē), Pol. *Dokszyce* (dôkshĭ'tsĕ), city (1931 pop. 3,235), S Polotsk oblast, Belorussian SSR, 17 mi. SSE of Glubokoye; agr. processing (hides, flax, grain, hops), sawmilling, woodworking. Has old churches and synagogue. Passed (1793) from Poland to Russia; reverted (1921) to Poland; ceded to USSR in 1945.

Dokshukino (dŭkshōo'kēnŭ), town (1939 pop. over 2,000), central Kabardian Autonomous SSR, Russian SFSR, on railroad and 15 mi. NE of Nalchik; industrial center; corn-alcohol distilling, fruit and vegetable canning, bast-fiber processing; wood- and metalworking. Power station. Developed in late 1930s.

Doksy (dôk'sĭ), village (pop. 3,061), N Bohemia, Czechoslovakia, at NW foot of Bezdez Mtn., on railroad and 26 mi. ESE of Usti nad Labem; popular summer resort; pond-fishing industry. Has 16th-cent. Wallenstein castle (with library), biological institute. Health resort of Stare Splavy (stä'rā splä'vĭ), Czech *Staré Splavy,* Ger. *Hammer am See* (hä'mŭr äm zā'), is 2 mi. NNW.

Dokszyce, Belorussian SSR: see DOKSHITSY.

Dol, France: see DOL-DE-BRETAGNE.

Dol, Yugoslavia: see HRASTNIK.

Dol, Marais de (märĕ' dŭ dôl'), former tidal marsh in Ille-et-Vilaine dept., W France, on English Channel, extending 20 mi. from Rance R. estuary to mouth of Couesnon R. and c.5 mi. inland. Protected by a dike, it is now a fertile agr. region. In its center rises granitic Mont-Dol, formerly an island.

Doland, city (pop. 535), Spink co., NE central S.Dak., 20 mi. E of Redfield; trade and wool-shipping point in productive agr. region; dairy produce, livestock, poultry, grain.

Dólar (dō'lär), town (pop. 1,173), Granada prov., S Spain, 12 mi. SE of Guadix; sugar beets, cereals, esparto; sheep raising. Iron mines near by.

Dölau (dû'lou), village (pop. 4,378), in former Prussian Saxony prov., central Germany, after 1945 in Saxony-Anhalt, 4 mi. WNW of Halle, in lignite-mining region.

Dolavón (dōlävōn'), town (pop. estimate 1,000), E Chubut natl. territory, Argentina, on railroad, on Chubut R. (irrigation area) and 30 mi. W of Rawson; wheat, alfalfa, fruit, sheep, cattle; flour milling, dairying. Founded by Welsh settlers.

Dolban, Russian SFSR: see LIMAN, Astrakhan.

Dolbeau (dŏlbō'), town (pop. 2,847), S central Que., on Mistassini R., near its mouth on L. St. John, at mouth of Mistassibi R., 60 mi. NW of Arvida; pulp and paper milling; market in dairying region. Inc. 1927.

Dolbenmaen (dôlbŭnmīn'), town and parish (pop. 1,460), S central Caernarvon, Wales, 3 mi. N of Criccieth; slate quarrying.

Dolceacqua (dôl″chĕä'kwä), village (pop. 1,970), Imperia prov., Liguria, NW Italy, 8 mi. NW of San Remo.

Dol-de-Bretagne (dôl dŭ brŭtä'nyŭ), town (pop. 3,627), Ille-et-Vilaine dept., W France, near English Channel, at edge of the Marais de Dol, 14 mi. ESE of Saint-Malo; tanning, printing and bookbinding; saltworks. Its 13th-16th-cent. cathedral of St. Samson has fine stained-glass windows. Also called Dol.

Doldenhorn (dôl'dŭnhôrn″), peak (11,966 ft.) in Bernese Alps, S central Switzerland, 3 mi. SE of Kandersteg.

Dolder or **Den Dolder** (dŭn dōl'dŭr), village (pop. 794), Utrecht prov., central Netherlands, 6 mi. NE of Utrecht; rail junction; soap mfg.

Dôle or **Dole** (dōl), town (pop. 16,340), Jura dept., E France, on the Doubs, on Rhone-Rhine Canal, and 26 mi. WSW of Besançon; industrial, transportation, and agr.-processing center. Has foundries and metalworks; also flour milling, tanning, meat processing, biscuit mfg. Important chemical factory at Tavaux (6 mi. SW). Stone quarries near by. The early seat of the counts of Burgundy, Dôle became ⊙ and fortified stronghold of Franche-Comté in 14th cent. Captured and razed (1479) by Louis XI. Its walls, rebuilt by Charles V in 16th cent., were dismantled by Louis XIV, who conquered Franche-Comté from Spain in 1674, and shifted its *parlement* and univ. of Dôle (founded 1422 or 1423) to Besançon. Louis Pasteur b. here. Sometimes called Dôle-du-Jura.

Dôle or **La Dôle** (lä dōl'), peak (5,513 ft.), 2d highest in the Swiss Jura, 7 mi. WNW of Nyon, near Fr. border.

Dôle-du-Jura, France: see DÔLE.

Dolefjell, Norway: see SOGNEFJELL.

Dolega (dōlā'gä), village (pop. 723), Chiriquí prov., W Panama, on railroad, on David R. and 9 mi. N of David; coffee, bananas, cacao, livestock.

Dolenji Logatec (dô'lĕnyĭ lô'gätĕts), Ital. *Longatico Inferiore* (lônggä'tēkō ēnfĕrēō'rĕ), Ger. *Unterloitsch* (o͝on'tŭrloich″), anc. *Longaticum,* village, W Slovenia, Yugoslavia, on railroad and 15 mi. SW of Ljubljana; local trade center. Until 1918, in Carniola. Village of Gorenji Logatec is just SW.

Dolenjske Toplice, Yugoslavia: see TOPLICE.

Dolent, Mont (mō dôlā'), Alpine peak (12,342 ft.) of Mont Blanc massif, 8 mi. E of Chamonix. Here France, Italy, and Switzerland meet. From it descends Argentière glacier.

Dolen Tsibar, Bulgaria: see DOLNI TSIBAR.

Dolfusville, Algeria: see DOLLFUSVILLE.

Dolgan-Nenets National Okrug, Russian SFSR: see TAIMYR NATIONAL OKRUG.

Dolgarrog (dŏlgă'rŏg), town and parish (pop. 572), NE Caernarvon, Wales, on Conway R. and 6 mi. S of Conway; aluminum milling.

Dolgaya (dôl'gīŭ), town (1926 pop. 2,873), S Orel oblast, Russian SFSR, 24 mi. S of Livny, in potato area; starch plant.

Dolgaya Kosa (kŭsä') [Rus.,=long spit], low-lying, pointed peninsula in Sea of Azov, in Krasnodar Territory, Russian SFSR, 25 mi. W of Yeisk. Site of village of Dolzhanskaya (1926 pop. 10,319); wheat, sunflowers, cotton. Fisheries. Offshore is long sandy Dolgi Isl.

Dolgelley (dŏlgĕth'lē,-gĕ'lē), urban district (1931 pop. 2,260; 1951 census 2,246), ⊙ Merionethshire, Wales, in W part of co., on Wnion R. and 60 mi. SW of Liverpool, at N foot of Cader Idris; agr. market and tourist center; leather works. Has anc. church (rebuilt in 18th cent.) and 17th-cent. almshouses. Scene of conference (1404) bet. Owen Glendower and the French. Sometimes spelled Dolgelly.

Dolgeville (dŏlj'vĭl, dŏlz'–), village (pop. 3,204), on Fulton-Herkimer co. line, central N.Y., on East Canada Creek and 23 mi. E of Utica; mfg. (felt goods, footwear, wood products, piano parts, dairy products). Summer resort. Inc. 1891.

Dolgi Most or **Dolgiy Most** (dôl″gē môst'), village (1939 pop. over 500), SE Krasnoyarsk Territory, Russian SFSR, 55 mi. NE of Kansk.

Dolginovo (dŭlgē'nŭvŭ), Pol. *Dołhinów* (dôwhē'no͝of), town (1931 pop. 3,000), E Molodechno oblast, Belorussian SSR, 25 mi. ENE of Vileika; flour milling, fruitgrowing.

Dolgintsevo (dŭlgēn'tsyĭvŭ), E suburb (1926 pop. 5,154) of Krivoi Rog, Dnepropetrovsk oblast, Ukrainian SSR, 5 mi. E of city center; major rail junction; workshops. Called Bukharino (1920s–c.1935).

Dolgiy Most, Russian SFSR: see DOLGI MOST.

Dolgoderevenskoye (dôl″gŭdyĕrĭvyĕn'skŭyŭ), village (1939 pop. over 500), E central Chelyabinsk oblast, Russian SFSR, on Miass R. and 13 mi. NNW of Chelyabinsk; truck, livestock. Gold placers near by (N).

Dolgoprudny or **Dolgoprudnyy** (–pro͞od'nē), residential town (1939 pop. over 500), central Moscow oblast, Russian SFSR, 14 mi. NNW of Moscow; mfg. of dirigibles; airport. Developed in 1930s; called Dirizhablstroi until 1938.

Dolgorukovo (–ro͞o'kŭvŭ), village (1939 pop. over 500), SE Orel oblast, Russian SFSR, 22 mi. SSW of Yelets; wheat, tobacco, potatoes.

Dolgoshchelye or **Dolgoshchel'ye** (–shchĕ'lyĭ), village (1939 pop. over 500), N Archangel oblast, Russian SFSR, on Mezen Bay, at mouth of Kuloi R., 25 mi. NW of Mezen; fisheries.

Dolhain (dōlē'), town, Liége prov., E Belgium, on Vesdre R. and 4 mi. ENE of Verviers; wool spinning and weaving.

Dolhasca (dôl-khä'skä), village (pop. 2,385), Suceava prov., NE Rumania, on Siret R., and 13 mi. E of Falticeni; rail junction. Noted 16th-cent. fortified monastery of Probota is 8 mi. SE.

Dolhinow, Belorussian SSR: see DOLGINOVO.

Dolianova (dôlyänô'vä), village (pop. 4,459), Cagliari prov., S Sardinia, 11 mi. NNE of Cagliari. Has 13th-cent. church of San Pantaleo.

Dolina, Free Territory of Trieste: see SAN DORLIGO DELLA VALLE.

Dolina (dŭlyē'nŭ), city (1931 pop. 9,616), W Stanislav oblast, Ukrainian SSR, at N foot of E Beskids, 21 mi. SSE of Stry; rail junction; mining center (salt and potash deposits); petroleum refining, natural-gas extracting, potash-fertilizer mfg., flour milling, sawmilling; saltworks. Iron foundry just SW.

Dolinsk (dŭlyēnsk'), city (1940 pop. 22,295), S Sakhalin, Russian SFSR, on E coast railroad and 25 mi. N of Yuzhno-Sakhalinsk, in agr. area (grain, potatoes, hemp, sugar beets); paper and pulp milling. Under Jap. rule (1905–45), called Ochiai (ōchyī').

Dolinskaya (–īŭ), town (1926 pop. 4,237), SE Kirovograd oblast, Ukrainian SSR, 36 mi. SE of Kirovograd; rail junction; food processing. Kaolin quarries. Called Shevchenkovo in middle 1920s and again c.1940–44.

Dolinskoye (–ŭyŭ), village (1926 pop. 15,266), W Odessa oblast, Ukrainian SSR, 32 mi. SSE of Balta; flour mill. In Moldavian Autonomous SSR (1924–40); called Valegotsulovo until 1945.

Dolisie (dôlēzē'), town (1949 pop. c.7,000), ⊙ Niari region (□ 19,690; 1950 pop. 142,100), SW Middle Congo territory, Fr. Equatorial Africa, on railroad and 180 mi. W of Brazzaville, 70 mi. NE of Pointe-Noire. Founded 1934, it is a growing center of a mining (gold, lead) and agr. region; tanning, fiber processing, stock raising; sisal plantations. School for natives.

Dolj, Rumania: see CRAIOVA.

Dollar, burgh (1931 pop. 1,485; 1951 census 1,385), Clackmannan, Scotland, near Devon R., 6 mi. NE of Alloa, at foot of Ochil Hills; agr. market. Dollar Academy has noted Greek bldgs. Near by are remains of Castle Campbell or Castle Gloom, with 12th-cent. keep.

Dollar Bay, village (1940 pop. 713), Houghton co., NW Upper Peninsula, Mich., 3 mi. E of Houghton, across Keweenaw Waterway.

Dollard (dŏ'lŭrd), village (pop. 140), SW Sask., in the Cypress Hills, 8 mi. W of Shaunavon; alt. 3,029 ft.; coal mining.

Dollard, Netherlands-Germany: see DOLLART.

Dollar Law, Scotland: see MOFFAT HILLS.

Dollart (dô'lärt), baylike enlargement of Ems estuary, on German-Netherlands border; c.13 mi. long, 5 mi. wide. Formed by North Sea inundations (especially 1362, 1377) bet. 1277 and 1509. Land reclamation begun in 16th cent. and continued until late-19th cent. has greatly reduced size of bay. Also spelled Dollard.

Dollbergen (dôl'bĕr″gŭn), village (pop. 1,525), in former Prussian prov. of Hanover, NW Germany, after 1945 in Lower Saxony, 6 mi. NNW of Peine, in oil-producing region; petroleum refining.

Dolleman Island (dŏl'mŭn) (13 naut. mi. long), Antarctica, in Weddell Sea, just off E coast of Palmer Peninsula; 70°35'S 60°45'W. Discovered 1940 by U.S. expedition.

Dollfusville (dôlfüsvēl'), village, Alger dept., N central Algeria, on the Chéliff and 13 mi. SW of Médéa. Ghrib Dam is just S. Also spelled Dolfusville.

Dollis Brook, England: see BRENT RIVER.

Dolliver, town (pop. 130), Emmet co., NW Iowa, near Minn. line, 12 mi. ENE of Estherville. State park on near-by Tuttle L.

Döllnitz (dûl'nĭts), village (pop. 2,729), in former Prussian Saxony prov., central Germany, after 1945 in Saxony-Anhalt, on the White Elster and 6 mi. SSE of Halle; lignite mining. Site of a power station.

Dolmatovski or **Dolmatovskiy** (dŭlmä'tŭfskē), town (1941 pop. over 500), NE Ivanovo oblast, Russian SFSR, 6 mi. NE of Kineshma; cotton milling.

Dolna-banya (dôl'nä-bä'nyä), village (pop. 4,044), Sofia dist., W central Bulgaria, at N foot of Rila Mts., on Maritsa R. and 9 mi. SSW of Ikhtiman; health resort with thermal radioactive springs; livestock, truck. Has woodworking school. Sometimes called Banya.

Dolna Lipnitsa (lēp'nĭtsä), village (pop. 3,292), Gorna Oryakhovitsa dist., N Bulgaria, 20 mi. NW of Tirnovo; wheat, corn.

Dolna-makhala (–mäkhlä'), village (pop. 803), Plovdiv dist., central Bulgaria, on Strema R. and 15 mi. S of Karlovo; rail junction; rye, livestock, fruit, truck.

Dolna Mitropoliya (mētrôpôlē'ä), village (pop. 2,472), Pleven dist., N Bulgaria, on Vit R. and 6 mi. WNW of Pleven; sugar refining, flour milling; truck, poultry.

Dolna Oryakhovitsa (ôryä'khôvētsä), village (pop. 5,035), Gorna Oryakhovitsa dist., N Bulgaria, on Yantra R. and 4 mi. NNE of Gorna Oryakhovitsa; truck, sugar beets; poultry, livestock.

Dolni Becva River, Czechoslovakia: see Becva River.

Dolni-chiflik (dôl'nē-chĭflēk'), village (pop. 3,253), Stalin dist., E Bulgaria, in S part of Longosa alluvial flood plain, 16 mi. SSW of Varna; sawmilling, lumbering. Rail terminus Staro Oryakhovo (pop. 1,443) is 4 mi. E.

Dolni Dabnik (dŭbnĕk'), village (pop. 6,105), Pleven dist., N Bulgaria, on branch of Vit R. and 10 mi. W of Pleven; flour milling; truck, livestock.

Dolni Hricov, Czechoslovakia: see Bytca.

Dolni Kounice (dôl'nyē kō'nyĭtsĕ), Czech *Dolní Kounice,* village (pop. 2,635), S Moravia, Czechoslovakia, on Jihlava R., on railroad and 11 mi. SW of Brno; milling industry. Has castle.

Dolni Kralovice (krä'lôvĭtsĕ), Czech *Dolní Kralovice,* town (pop. 1,437), SE Bohemia, Czechoslovakia, on railroad and 19 mi. WNW of Havlickuv Brod; rail terminus; barley, oats.

Dolni Kubin (dôl'nē kōō'bēn), Slovak *Dolný Kubín,* Hung. *Alsókubin* (ŏl'shōkōōbĭn), town (pop. 2,018), N Slovakia, Czechoslovakia, on Orava R., on railroad and 25 mi. E of Zilina; lumbering.

Dolni Lipova (dôl'nyē lĭ'pôvä), Czech *Dolní Lipová,* Ger. *Nieder Lindewiese* (nē"dŭr-lĭn'dŭvēsŭ), town (pop. 2,046), W Silesia, Czechoslovakia, 3 mi. W of Jesenik; rail junction; health resort (alt. 1,640 ft.) in the Jeseniky.

Dolni Listna, Czechoslovakia: see Trinec.

Dolni Litvinov, Czechoslovakia: see Litvinov.

Dolni Lukovit (dôl'nē lōō'kôvēt), village (pop. 4,450), Vratsa dist., N Bulgaria, on the Iskar and 20 mi. SE of Oryakhovo; vineyards, grain, livestock.

Dolni Poustevna (dôl'nyē pō'stĕvnä), Czech *Dolní Poustevna,* village (pop. 1,357), N Bohemia, Czechoslovakia, on railroad and 25 mi. NNE of Usti nad Labem, near Ger. border, opposite Sebnitz; mfg. of artificial flowers and feather ornaments. Village of Horni Poustevna, Czech *Horní Poustevna,* is NNE.

Dolni Smokovec, Slovak *Dolní Smokovec,* Ger. *Unterschmecks* (ōōn'tŭr-shmĕks), Hung. *Alsótátrafüred* (ŏl'shōtätrōfü"rĕd), village, N Slovakia, Czechoslovakia, on SE slope of the High Tatra, on rack-and-pinion railroad and 6 mi. NNW of Poprad; part of commune of Vysoke Tatry. Has sanatorium for tubercular children (alt. 2,985 ft.).

Dolni Tsibar (dôl'nē tsē'bŭr), village (pop. 1,885), Vidin dist., NW Bulgaria, on the Danube (landing), at mouth of Tsibritsa R., and 13 mi. E of Lom; vineyards; fisheries. Also called Dolen Tsibar.

Dolni Vestonice, Czechoslovakia: see Hustopece.

Dolnja Lendava, Yugoslavia: see Lendava, village.

Dolno Yezerovo (dôl'nô yĕ'zĕrôvô), village (pop. 1,683), Burgas dist., E Bulgaria, 5 mi. W of Burgas; grain, sugar beets, flax. Formerly called Vayakoi or Bajakeui. Lies on N shore of Burgas L. (□ 11), a W lagoon of Gulf of Burgas.

Dolo, Belgian Congo: see Leopoldville, city.

Dolo (dō'lō), village (pop. 350), Harar prov., S Ethiopia, on Ital. Somaliland border, at confluence of Ganale Dorya and Dawa rivers (here forming the Juba), 20 mi. NE of Mandera (Kenya), in corn-growing region. Occupied (1941) by British in Second World War.

Dolo (dô'lô), town (pop. 2,670), Venezia prov., Veneto, N Italy, on Naviglio di Brenta and 12 mi. W of Venice; alcohol distillery.

Dolobran, Wales: see Dinas Mawddwy.

Dolomieu (dôlômyû'), village (pop. 486), Isère dept., SE France, 4 mi. NNE of La Tour-du-Pin; silk spinning; fiber products.

Dolomite (dŏ'lŭmĭt), village (1940 pop. 2,229), Jefferson co., N central Ala., just SW of Birmingham.

Dolomites or **Dolomite Alps** (dō'lŭmĭts, –mĭt), N Italy, division of Eastern Alps, SW of Carnic Alps, bet. Isarco and Adige (W), Rienza (N), Piave (E), and Brenta (S) rivers; a dolomitic limestone formation. Noted for its striking scenery and for its beautiful colors at sunrise and sunset. Chief peaks: glacier-topped Marmolada (10,964 ft.), Antelao (10,705 ft.), and Le Tofane (10,640 ft.). A popular tourist and mountain-climbing region. Cortina d'Ampezzo is chief resort.

Dolon or **Dolonnor,** China: see Tolun.

Dolores (dōlō'rĕs). **1** City (pop. 14,369), ⊙ Dolores dist. (□ 762; pop. 21,740), E Buenos Aires prov., Argentina, 130 mi. SSE of Buenos Aires; agr. center (cattle, sheep, sunflowers, oats, flax). Dairying (butter, cheese, casein, milk powder), meat packing, flour milling; mfg. of chocolate, soap, cigarettes, sweets. Has natl. col. Founded 1818, town was destroyed by Indians (1821), played active part in 1839 revolution. **2** Village, Catamarca prov., Argentina: see San Isidro.

Dolores, town (1950 pop. 512), Petén dept., N Guatemala, 40 mi. SE of Flores; agr., lumbering, chicle collecting.

Dolores, town (pop. 522), Copán dept., W Honduras, 9 mi. NNW of Santa Rosa; tobacco growing.

Dolores, town (1950 pop. 755), Carazo dept., SW Nicaragua, just off Inter-American Highway, 1 mi. E of Diriamba, in coffee zone.

Dolores, town (1939 pop. 2,275; 1948 municipality pop. 13,124), E Samar isl., Philippines, on Philippine Sea, 8 mi. SSE of Oras; agr. center (rice, coconuts, corn).

Dolores, town (pop. 2,126), Alicante prov., E Spain, 10 mi. SW of Elche, in irrigated truck-farming area; flour milling, fruit canning. Also hemp, olives, cereals in area.

Dolores (dŭlō'rŭs), county (□ 1,028; pop. 1,966), SW Colo.; ⊙ Rico. Zinc-mining and agr. area, drained by Dolores R. San Miguel Range in NE. Includes parts of Montezuma Natl. Forest. Formed 1881.

Dolores, town (pop. 729), Montezuma co., SW Colo., on Dolores R. and 37 mi. WNW of Durango, in livestock region; alt. 6,957 ft.; flour, lumber.

Dolores (dōlō'rĕs), city (pop. 11,500), Soriano dept., SW Uruguay, port on San Salvador R. and 21 mi. SSW of Mercedes (connected by highway); major shipping center for grain; flour mill; sheep and cattle raising.

Dolores, town (pop. 540), Barinas state, W Venezuela, in llanos, 50 mi. ESE of Barinas; cattle.

Dolores, Los (lōs), NW suburb (pop. 4,737) of Cartagena, Murcia prov., SE Spain; brandy distilleries, sawmills; ships fruit and pepper.

Dolores, Mission, Calif.: see San Francisco.

Dolores Hidalgo (ēdäl'gō), city (pop. 5,915), Guanajuato, central Mexico, on central plateau, on railroad and 23 mi. NE of Guanajuato; alt. 6,233 ft. Agr. center (wheat, corn, sugar cane, vegetables, fruit, livestock); flour milling, tanning, mfg. of chinaware. Miguel Hidalgo y Costilla here initiated struggle for independence on Sept. 16, 1810.

Dolores Peak, Colo.: see San Miguel Mountains.

Dolores River (dŭlō'rŭs), in Colo. and Utah, rises near Dolores Peak in San Miguel Mts. of SW Colo., flows c.250 mi. SW and NNW, past Dolores and Gateway, Colo., to Colorado R. NE of Moab, Utah. San Miguel R. is tributary.

Dolo River (dô'lô), N central Italy, rises in Etruscan Apennines near Monte Cusna, flows 20 mi. N to Secchia River 4 mi. N of Montefiorino. Receives Dragone R. (right). Used for hydroelectric power (plant at Farneta).

Dolovo (dô'lôvô), Hung. *Dolova* (dô'lôvŏ), village (pop. 5,718), Vojvodina, N Serbia, Yugoslavia, 11 mi. ENE of Pancevo, in the Banat.

Dolphin and Union Strait (dŏl'fĭn), SW Franklin Dist., Northwest Territories, arm (100 mi. long, 20–40 mi. wide) of the Arctic Ocean, bet. Amundsen Gulf (W) and Coronation Gulf (E), separating Victoria Isl. (N) from Mackenzie Dist. mainland; 69°N 113°30'–116°30'W. Strait forms part of Northwest Passage through the Arctic Isls.

Dolphin's Nose, India: see Vizagapatam, city.

Dolsk (dôlsk), Ger. *Dolzig* (dôl'tsĭkh), town (1946 pop. 1,656), Poznan prov., W Poland, on small lake, 30 mi. SSE of Poznan; flour milling, sawmilling, candy mfg.

Dolton (dôl'tŭn). **1** Residential village (pop. 5,558), Cook co., NE Ill., S suburb of Chicago; truck farming. Inc. 1892. **2** Town (pop. 93), Turner co., SE S.Dak., 14 mi. WNW of Parker.

Doluong (dō'lōō'ŭng), village, Nghean prov., N central Vietnam, on the Song Ca (navigation head for large river craft), 27 mi. NW of Vinh; cotton growing, trading (rice, corn, tea).

Dolwyddelan (dôlwĭdh-ĕ'lăn), village and parish (pop. 836), E Caernarvon, Wales, 4 mi. SW of Bettws-y-Coed; slate quarrying. Reputed birthplace of Llewelyn the Great. Has 16th-cent. church and remains of Dolwyddelan Castle, built c.1170.

Dolzhanskaya, Russian SFSR: see Dolgaya Kosa.

Dolzhok (dŭlzhôk'), village (1926 pop. 2,425), SW Kamenets-Podolski oblast, Ukrainian SSR, 3 mi. W of Kamenets-Podolski; distilling.

Dolzig, Poland: see Dolsk.

Dom (dōm), peak (14,923 ft.), S Switzerland, 7 mi. NNE of Zermatt; highest in the Mischabelhörner, 3d highest in the Alps, and highest situated entirely in Switzerland. First scaled in 1858. Domjoch, a pass (14,056 ft.), is S, and WNW is Dom Hütte (9,617 ft.).

Domachevo (dŭmŭchĕ'vŭ), Pol. *Domaczewo* (dômächĕ'vô), town (1939 pop. over 500), SW Brest oblast, Belorussian SSR, on Bug R. (Pol. border) and 25 mi. S of Brest; rye, oats, potatoes.

Doman (dō'män), village (pop. 1,239), Severin prov., SW Rumania, 2 mi. S of Resita; lignite and coal mining.

Domanevka (dŭmä'nyĭfkŭ), village (1926 pop. 2,853), E Odessa oblast, Ukrainian SSR, 30 mi. S of Pervomaisk; metalworks.

Domar (dō'mär), town (pop. 1,693), Rangpur dist., N East Bengal, E Pakistan, 36 mi. NW of Rangpur; rice milling, jute pressing; jute trade center; trades in rice, tobacco, oilseeds.

Domariaganj (dōmŭryä'gŭnj), village, Basti dist., NE Uttar Pradesh, India, on Rapti R. and 30 mi. N of Basti; rice, wheat, barley, sugar cane.

Domart or **Domart-en-Ponthieu** (dômär'-ã-pōtyû'), village (pop. 1,022), Somme dept., N France, 15 mi. NW of Amiens; hemp spinning, furniture mfg.

Domashni Island or **Domashniy Island** (dŭmäsh'-nyē), in Kara Sea of Arctic Ocean, 15 mi. off W Severnaya Zemlya archipelago, in Krasnoyarsk Territory, Russian SFSR; 79°30'N 90°45'E. Govt. observation post.

Domasnia Pass, Rumania: see Porta Orientalis.

Domazlice (dô'mäzhlĭtsĕ), Czech *Domažlice,* Ger. *Taus* (tous), town (pop. 7,228), SW Bohemia, Czechoslovakia, 29 mi. SSW of Pisen, near Ger. border; rail junction; mfg. (machinery, furniture, kitchen ware, wooden articles), glass- and lace-making. Has 13th-cent. Gothic church, 12th-cent. castle, 166-ft. tower mus. Hussites defeated Crusaders near by, 1431. In Middle Ages, regional pop., called Chods, played important part in safeguarding Bohemian border; still retain colorful dress and customs.

Dombaas, Norway: see Dombas.

Dombarovski or **Dombarovskiy** (dŭmbä'rŭfskē), town (1939 pop. over 500), SE Chkalov oblast, Russian SFSR, 40 mi. SE of Orsk, in Orsk-Khalilovo industrial dist., on rail spur to Profintern (10 mi. SE; coal mines); bituminous-coal-mining center. Until 1939, Dombarovka.

Dombas (dôm'bôs, dôm'môs), Nor. *Dombås,* village (pop. 419) in Dovre canton, Opland co., S central Norway, at head of the Gudbrandsdal, at S foot of the Dovrefjell, on Lagen R. and 80 mi. SE of Kristiansund; rail junction; ski resort, in thickly wooded region. Site of sanitarium. Sometimes spelled Dombaas.

Dombasle (dõbäl'), village (pop. 1,355), Oran dept.; NW Algeria, in the Tell Atlas, 20 mi. E of Mascara; cereals.

Dombasle or **Dombasle-sur-Meurthe** (dõbäl'-sür-mûrt'), town (pop. 7,622), Meurthe-et-Moselle dept., NE France, on Meurthe R., at junction of Marne-Rhine Canal, and 9 mi. SE of Nancy; chemical works (soda); mfg. (metal bldg. materials).

Dombe, Poland: see Dabie, Poznan prov.

Dombegyhaz (dôm'bĕdyûhäz), Hung. *Dombegyház,* town (pop. 5,313), Csanad co., SE Hungary, 24 mi. S of Bekescsaba; market center for agr. (grain, onions), livestock region.

Dombes (dõb), lake-studded plateau in Ain dept., E France, bet. Saône (W), Rhone (S), and Ain (E) rivers, characterized by glacial deposits. Chief activity is fish breeding. Lakes are alternately drained and refilled. When dry, land is in crops and pasture. Pop. centers chiefly located along periphery.

Dombovar (dôm'bōvär), Hung. *Dombóvár,* town (pop. 8,859), Tolna co., SW central Hungary, on Kapos R. and 16 mi. E of Kaposvar; rail center; vegetable fats, bricks. Farms, vineyards near by.

Dombrad (dôm'bräd), Hung. *Dombrád,* town (pop. 6,688), Szabolcs co., NE Hungary, near the Tisza, 21 mi. NNE of Nyiregyhaza; flour mill; wheat, tobacco, hogs.

Dombrowa, Poland: see Dabrowa Gornicza.

Domburg (dôm'bûrkh), village (pop. 1,019), Surinam dist., N Du. Guiana, on left bank of Surinam R. and 10 mi. SE of Paramaribo; coffee, rice, fruit.

Domburg, town (pop. 1,429), Zeeland prov., SW Netherlands, on N coast of Walcheren isl. and 7 mi. NW of Middelburg; seaside resort, surrounded by woods.

Dôme, Le, Switzerland: see Diablerets.

Dôme, Monts (mõdōm'), or **Chaîne des Puys** (shĕn dā pwē'), division of Auvergne Mts., central France, in Puy-de-Dôme dept.; consists of c.50 extinct volcanoes extending 20 mi. N-S, W of Clermont-Ferrand. Highest peak, Puy de Dôme (4,806 ft.). Tourist area.

Dôme, Puy de, France: see Puy de Dôme.

Domegge (dômĕd'jĕ), village (pop. 1,461), Belluno prov., Veneto, N Italy, on Piave R. and 24 mi. NNE of Belluno; mfg. (celluloid, spectacles, paper lace).

Domegliara (dômĕlyä'rä), village (pop. 886), Verona prov., Veneto, N Italy, 10 mi. NW of Verona; marble quarries.

Domel Island (dō'mŭl), in central Mergui Archipelago, Lower Burma, in Andaman Sea, 50 mi. SSW of Mergui town; 25 mi. long, 2–6 mi. wide; mountainous (highest point 2,020 ft.), forested.

Dome Mines, Ont.: see Porcupine.

Domène (dômĕn'), town (pop. 2,759), Isère dept., SE France, in the Grésivaudan valley on slopes of Belledonne range, 6 mi. E of Grenoble; paper mills, metalworks.

Dome Peak (9,000 ft.), SW Mackenzie Dist., Northwest Territories, in Mackenzie Mts.; 61°32'N 126°56'W.

Dome Rock Range, N extension of Trigo Mts. in Yuma co., SW Ariz., near Colorado R. (Calif. line), just E of Colorado River Indian Reservation. Rises to 3,314 ft. in Cunningham Mountain.

Domesnas, cape, Latvia: see Kolka, Cape.

Domèvre-en-Haye (dômĕ'vrä-ĕ'), agr. village (pop. 170), Meurthe-et-Moselle dept., NE France, 10 mi. N of Toul.

Domeyko (dōmā'kō), town (pop. 1,517), Atacama prov., N central Chile, on railroad and 26 mi.

SSW of Vallenar; copper and gold mining; agr. (alfalfa, clover, corn, goats).

Domeyko, Cordillera de (kōrdĭyā'rä dā), W spur of the Andes in Antofagasta and Atacama provs., N Chile, extends c.230 mi. NNE-SSW from 20 mi. W of San Pedro de Atacama to Salar de Pedernales (Atacama prov.), forming W divide of Salar de Atacama; rises to over 16,000 ft. It separates the Atacama Desert (W) and the Puna de Atacama (E).

Domfront (dōfrō'), town (pop. 2,600), Orne dept., NW France, 20 mi. N of Mayenne, on rocky spur overlooking small Varenne R.; road center and livestock market; cider distilling. Quartzite quarries and iron mines in area. Has ruins of 11th-cent. fortress (captured by William the Conqueror) and medieval town walls. Heavily damaged in Second World War. Near-by 11th-cent. Romanesque church was also damaged.

Domica Caverns, Czechoslovakia: see SLOVAKIAN KARST.

Domingo Pérez (dōmēng'gō pā'rĕth), town (pop. 1,173), Toledo prov., central Spain, 26 mi. WNW of Toledo; olives, cereals, grapes, sheep, hogs; lumbering.

Domingos Martins (dŏŏmēng'gŏŏs märtēns'), city (pop. 512), central Espírito Santo, Brazil, on railroad and 14 mi. W of Vitória; coffee, oranges, bananas. Bauxite deposits. Formerly Vila Campinho.

Domínguez (dōmēng'gĕs), town (pop. estimate 1,000), central Entre Ríos prov., Argentina, on railroad and 9 mi. SSE of Villaguay; agr. (grain, livestock, poultry); dairying.

Dominica (dōmĭ'nĭkŭ, dŭ–, dŏmĭnē'kŭ), island (29 mi. long, 16 mi. wide) and Br. colony (□ 304.7; pop. 47,624), largest of the Windward Isls., B.W.I.; ⊙ Roseau. In central Lesser Antilles, bet. Guadeloupe (N) and Martinique (SSE), 400 mi. SE of San Juan, Puerto Rico; bet. 15°10'–15°40'N and 61°14'–61°30'W. The climate is healthful; temp. on the coast varies bet. 70° and 90°F.; cooler in the hills. Rainfall ranges bet. 80 and 250 inches in different sections. Of volcanic formation, with a mountainous backbone running N-S, the rugged isl. rises in the Morne Diablotin to 4,747 ft. The isl., noted for its beautiful, little-explored scenery, abounds in forested plateaus, and ravines, waterfalls, craters, thermal springs, *solfataras*, and torrential rivers. It has fertile soil, but only its coastline has been settled and thoroughly cultivated. While coffee was staple of early Fr. settlers, limes now account for about 80% of the agr. output; also grown are bananas, cacao, coconuts, oranges, mangoes, avocados, vanilla, and spices. Main industries: mfg. of lime juice, citrates, lime oil, rum, copra, bay oil, exported through Roseau. The isl.'s name stems from its discovery by Columbus on Sunday, Nov. 3, 1493. It was included in the grant made (1627) to the earl of Carlisle, but initial attempts to subdue the aboriginal Caribs proved unsuccessful, and the Treaty of Aix-la-Chapelle (1748) agreed to its remaining neutral. However, Fr. settlers soon gained a foothold, only to have the isl. wrested from them by the English (1759), an action legalized by the Treaty of Paris 4 years later. There followed several abortive attempts by the French to recapture it. In 1833 Dominica was made a part of the Leeward Isls. colony, of which it formed a presidency until it became (1940) a colony of the Windward Isls., with a legislative council of its own. The pop. is predominantly Negro; a few Carib Indians, concentrated on a reserve on NE coast near Marigot, remain. English is the official language, though a Fr. patois is spoken widely.

Dominical (dōmēnēkäl'), village, Puntarenas prov., W Costa Rica, small Pacific port 25 mi. NW of Puerto Cortés, linked by road with El General. Exports tobacco. Stock raising.

Dominican Republic (dŭmĭ'nĭkŭn), Sp. *República Dominicana*, republic (□ 19,129; 1935 pop. 1,479,417; 1950 pop. 2,121,083), West Indies, comprising the eastern ⅔ of HISPANIOLA; ⊙ Ciudad Trujillo (formerly Santo Domingo). Borders E on Mona Passage (75 mi. wide to Puerto Rico), W on Haiti, bet. 17°36'–19°58'N and 68°19'–72°W. Though within the tropical zone, it has a generally healthy climate, relieved by NE trade winds. Average annual temp. 77°F. in lowlands, cooler in mts.; intermittent rains May-Sept. More arid is the W and SW, where irrigation becomes necessary. Otherwise it is a mountainous isl., well watered by many rivers, among them the Yaque del Norte, Camú, Yuna, Ozama, and Yaque del Sur. Extending E-W through its length is the wooded Cordillera Central, rising to highest elevation in the West Indies (see Monte TINA and Pico TRUJILLO). There are fertile interior valleys, such as the Cibao and La Vega Real (N) and San Juan valleys (W). The Seibo lowland (main sugar-growing region) stretches SE along the Caribbean. The country is predominantly agr., with sugar still accounting for about 60% of all its exports. Other important crops, principally grown in the densely populated Cibao region, are: coffee, cacao, tobacco, rice, corn, chick-peas, cotton, bananas, and other tropical fruit. There is some stock raising (cattle, hogs, goats) in E and in uplands. Exported also are molasses, liquor, beeswax, honey, hides, and fine timber (mahogany, lignum vitae, satinwood, cedar, dyewood). Aside from the sugar centrals and refineries, industries are few, but foodstuffs (yucca starch, meat, flour, dairy products, essential oils, chocolate) and cigars, cigarettes, and leather are increasingly processed. Fishing along the coast. Gold has been washed since early colonial days, and there are several saltworks, but the other mineral deposits (iron, copper, manganese, chromium, nickel, tin, zinc, cobalt, coal) remain so far little exploited. Petroleum has been discovered in the S. Principal city and port, and the social, political, industrial, and commercial center of the republic, is Ciudad Trujillo, which is also becoming an international resort. San Pedro de Macorís is the leading sugar port, and, together with La Romana, hq. of the sugar industry. Santiago or Santiago de los Caballeros, the country's 2d city, the center of the N, dominating the Cibao region, is linked by rail with its port on the Atlantic, Puerto Plata, and with other towns of the Cibao such as La Vega, San Francisco de Macorís, and Sánchez. Since Columbus discovered (Dec. 5, 1492) Hispaniola isl., which he called La Espaniola, the country has had a varied history. The native Indians were soon, after initial revolts, exterminated or absorbed; Negro labor was introduced in 1505. The Spanish made here some of the 1st settlements in the Americas, such as the now-ruined town Isabela (1493), and Ciudad Trujillo, then Santo Domingo, in 1496 by Bartholomew Columbus. Early incursions were made by privateers, who gained a foothold in present-day Haiti and later on attained Fr. protection, legalized by Treaty of Ryswick (1697). In 1777 the frontiers of the Fr. and Sp. possessions were defined, and by the Treaty of Basel (1795) Spain also ceded the colony of Santo Domingo to France. The Haitian insurgents under Toussaint L'Ouverture embarked upon conquest of the entire isl. in 1801. An expeditionary force was sent over by Napoleon and was assisted by the Spanish. By 1808 the Sp. rule was reestablished. One year later, with help of a Br. squadron, the Dominicans set up their 1st short-lived republic. Spain regained her title in 1814, but had to yield again in 1821. The 2d Dominican Republic lasted only 1 year. Haitians ruled from 1822 to 1844. Since then, apart from another Sp. regime, 1861–63, and an occupation by U.S. marines, 1916–34 (though the U.S. maintained a customs receivership, 1905–41), the Dominican Republic kept its independence, although frequently torn by interior strife and disorder. In 1930 Rafael Trujillo Molina took absolute control of the govt. Border clashes culminated in the violence of 1937, when Dominican troops crossed into Haiti and massacred over 10,000 Haitians. Due to overpopulation of the adjoining country, pressure from the W is great. Dominicans have therefore encouraged settlements along its border, and have invited European refugees. The Spanish-speaking Dominican pop. is, in contrast to the predominantly Negro Haitians, mulatto with strong European and Indian elements. The Republic is sometimes called Santo Domingo (its name as a Sp. colony), which also occasionally designates the entire isl. of Hispaniola.

Dominica Passage, channel (c.20 mi. wide) in Lesser Antilles, West Indies, bounded by Guadeloupe and Marie-Galante (N) and Dominica (S).

Dominion, town (pop. 3,279), NE N.S., on NE coast of Cape Breton Isl., near E side of Glace Bay, 15 mi. E of Sydney; coal-mining center. Inc. 1906.

Dominion, Md.: see KENT ISLAND.

Dominion City, village (pop. estimate 500), S Man., on Roseau R. and 50 mi. S of Winnipeg; grain elevators, lumbering.

Domino Harbour, settlement on Isl. of Ponds (10 mi. long, 9 mi. wide), off SE Labrador; 53°27'N 55°45'W; fishing port and seaplane anchorage. Lighthouse.

Domira Bay (dōmē'rä), village Central Prov., Nyasaland, port on L. Nyasa, 55 mi. NE of Lilongwe; fishing; cotton, tobacco, corn. Projected rail terminus.

Dömitz (dû'mĭts), town (pop. 4,585), Mecklenburg, N Germany, on the Elbe, at mouth of canalized Neue ELDE RIVER, and 25 mi. WNW of Wittenberge, 7 mi. ENE of Dannenberg; mfg. of chemicals, bricks, furniture; sawmilling, basket weaving. Has remains of former fortress, in which novelist Reuter was imprisoned (1839–40).

Domjoch, Switzerland: see DOM.

Domkonda (dōm'kōndŭ), town (pop. 5,118), Nizamabad dist., central Hyderabad state, India, 36 mi. SE of Nizamabad; rice, millet, oilseeds.

Dom-le-Mesnil (dō-lŭ-mānēl'), village (pop. 916), Ardennes dept., N France, 6 mi. SE of Mézières, on left bank of Meuse R. (canalized) at junction of Ardennes Canal.

Domleschg (dōm'lĕshk), valley, Grisons canton, E Switzerland, extends along Hinterrhein R. from mouth of Albula R. to its confluence with Vorderrhein R. Mountainous W side is called Heinzenberg. Administratively Heinzenberg is a dist. (pop. 7,526) and Domleschg is one of its circles (pop. 3,044).

Domman-Asfaltovy Zavod, Russian SFSR: see LENINSKI, Tula oblast.

Dommartin-le-Franc (dômärtē-lŭ-frā'), village (pop. 304), Haute-Marne dept., NE France, on Blaise R. and 15 mi. S of Saint-Dizier; mfg. (stoves, kitchen ranges).

Dommartin-sur-Yèvre (–sür-yĕ'vrŭ), village (pop. 156), Marne dept., N France, 9 mi. SW of Sainte-Menehould.

Dommary-Baroncourt (dômärē'-bärōkŏŏr'), commune (pop. 1,027), Meuse dept., NE France, in Briey iron basin, 11 mi. WNW of Briey; iron mines.

Domme (dôm), village (pop. 511), Dordogne dept., SW France, on the Dordogne and 6 mi. S of Sarlat in tobacco area; cement mill. Has 13th-cent. fortifications.

Dommeldange (dômŭldäzh'), town, S Luxembourg, on Alzette R. and 2 mi. N of Luxembourg city; steel center (blast furnaces, rolling mills), metal forging and stamping, processing of nonferrous metals, brick mfg.

Dommel River (dô'mŭl), S Netherlands, rises 3 mi. NW of Weert, flows 51 mi. NNW, past Eindhoven and Boxtel, joining Aa R. and the Zuid-Willemsvaart at 's Hertogenbosch to form Dieze R. (dē'zŭ), which flows 4.5 mi. NNW to Maas R. Near its source it is known as the Kleine Dommel.

Dommitzsch (dô'mĭch), town (pop. 3,606), in former Prussian Saxony prov., central Germany, after 1945 in Saxony-Anhalt, near the Elbe, 8 mi. NW of Torgau; agr. market (grain, sugar beets, potatoes, livestock); brick mfg.

Domnarvet, Sweden: see BORLANGE.

Domnau, Russian SFSR: see DOMNOVO.

Domnesti (dōmnĕsht'), Rum. *Domneşti.* **1** Village (pop. 2,951), Arges prov., S Rumania, 12 mi. SE of Campulung; orchards (notably apple trees). **2** or **Domnesti-de-Sus** (–dā-sōōs'), village (pop. 462), Bucharest prov., S Rumania, 10 mi. W of Bucharest; agr. center; dairying. Also spelled Domnestii-de-Sus.

Domnita-Maria (dōm"nētsä-märē'ä), Rum. *Domniţa-Maria,* agr. village (pop. 4,213), Bacau prov., E central Rumania, on Bistrita R. and 2 mi. SE of Bacau.

Domnovo (dôm'nŭvŭ), town (1939 pop. 2,990), SW Kaliningrad oblast, Russian SFSR, 23 mi. SE of Kaliningrad; cattle market. Largely destroyed during First World War. Until 1945, in East Prussia and called Domnau (dôm'nou).

Domodedovo (dŭmŭdyĕ'dŭvŭ), city (1947 pop. over 2,000), central Moscow oblast, Russian SFSR, 22 mi. SSE of Moscow; brickworks; fireproof tiles. Became city in 1947.

Domodossola (dô"môdôs'sôlä), anc. *Oscela,* town (pop. 9,193), Novara prov., Piedmont, N Italy, NW of Lago Maggiore, near Toce R., on Simplon rail route to Brig (Switzerland) and 50 mi. NNW of Novara. Rail junction; mfg. (iron furniture, fertilizers, shoes, clothing, cement). Marble, granite quarries near by. Has trade schools, mus., geophysical observatory, and hydroelectric plant.

Domohani, India: see JALPAIGURI, town.

Domokos or **Dhomokos** (both: dhômôkôs'), anc. *Thaumaci,* town (pop. 1,820), Phthiotis nome, central Greece, on railroad and 17 mi. NNW of Lamia; summer resort. Besieged unsuccessfully 198 B.C. by Philip V of Macedon. Passed 1881 to Greece. Greek-Turkish War of 1897 ended here.

Domont (dômō'), town (pop. 3,184), Seine-et-Oise dept., N central France, outermost N suburb of Paris, 12 mi. from Notre Dame Cathedral; mfg. (bricks, paints, cattle feed), poultry raising.

Dompaire (dōpâr'), village (pop. 955), Vosges dept., E France, 11 mi. WNW of Épinal; brush mfg.

Dom Pedrito (dō pĭdrē'tŏŏ), city (pop. 10,030), S Rio Grande do Sul, Brazil, near Uruguay border, 40 mi. NW of Bagé; rail-spur terminus; stock-raising center; slaughtering, woolshearing. Mineral deposits (agates, gold, silver, lead) in vicinity. Airfield.

Dompierre-sur-Besbre (dōpyâr'-sür-bĕ'brŭ), town (pop. 2,249), Allier dept., central France, on the Besbre near Loire Lateral Canal, and 17 mi. E of Moulins; mfg. of agr. machinery, sawmilling. Near-by model farm organized by Trappists has pioneered in reclamation of Sologne Bourbonnaise.

Domremy, village (pop. 232), central Sask., near small Pelican L., 28 mi. S of Prince Albert; mixed farming, dairying.

Domrémy-la-Pucelle (dōrāmē'-lä-püsĕl'), village (pop. 185), Vosges dept., E France, on the Meuse and 6 mi. N of Neufchâteau. Preserves house in which Joan of Arc was born in 1412. Near by is the basilica of St. Joan of Arc, begun in 1881.

Dom Silvério (dō sēlvĕ'ryŏŏ), city (pop. 2,210), SE central Minas Gerais, Brazil, 18 mi. N of Ponte Nova; rail-spur terminus; coffee shipping. Manganese mine. Formerly called Saúde.

Domsjo (dŏŏm'shû"), Swedish *Domsjö,* village (pop. 2,335), Vasternorrland co., NE Sweden, on small inlet of Gulf of Bothnia, 2 mi. S of Ornskoldsvik; lumber and pulp mills, sulphite works.

Dömsöd (dûm'shûd), town (pop. 5,913), Pest-Pilis-Solt-Kiskun co., central Hungary, on arm of the Danube and 28 mi. S of Budapest; wheat, corn, horses, cattle; fishing.

Domusnovas (dô″mōōsnō′väs), village (pop. 3,483), Cagliari prov., SW Sardinia, 6 mi. E of Iglesias; paper mills. Lead-zinc-silver mine 3 mi. NW; iron deposits near by.

Domuyo, Cerro (sĕ′rō dōmōō′yō), Andean volcano (c.15,500 ft.), NW Neuquén natl. territory, Argentina, 45 mi. NW of Buta Ranquil; 36°38′S. Several geysers on its slopes.

Domzale (dôm′zhälĕ), Slovenian *Domžale*, village, central Slovenia, Yugoslavia, on railroad and 7 mi. NE of Ljubljana; mfg. of straw hats. Until 1918, in Carniola.

Don, river: see DON RIVER.

Don, oblast, Russia: see DON COSSACKS, OBLAST OF THE.

Dona Ana (dō′nyŭ ă′nŭ), county (□ 3,804; pop. 39,557), SW N.Mex.; ⊙ Las Cruces. Irrigated agr. and livestock area; watered by Rio Grande; bounded S by Texas and Mexico. Cotton, alfalfa, dairy products. Organ Mts. in E, part of White Sands Natl. Monument in NE. Formed 1852.

Doña Ana, Cerro (sĕ′rō dō′nyä ä′nä), Andean peak (18,670 ft.) on Coquimbo-Atacama prov. border, N central Chile, near Argentine line; 29°47′S.

Donada (dônä′dä), village (pop. 2,300), Rovigo prov., Veneto, N Italy, 8 mi. ESE of Adria; brick mfg.

Donadeu (dōnädĕ′ōō), town (pop. estimate 500), N Santiago del Estero prov., Argentina, 25 mi. N of Tintina; rail junction in stock-raising and lumbering area; sawmills.

Doña Francisca, Brazil: see JOINVILE.

Donaghadee (dŏ″nŭkhŭdē′), urban district (1937 pop. 2,533; 1951 census 3,398), NE Co. Down, Northern Ireland, on the Irish Sea, 16 mi. ENE of Belfast; 54°38′N 5°32′W; seaport and seaside resort. It is nearest Irish port to Great Britain; until 1849 it was terminal of mail steamers from Portpatrick, Scotland, with which it is linked by submarine cable. Has parish church founded 1626, 70-ft.-high rath, and Holy Well. There is trade in cattle and farm produce.

Donaghmore (dŏ″nŭkhmôr′, dŭ″nŭmôr′), village (district pop. 806), Co. Meath, Ireland, on the Boyne 2 mi. NE of An Uaimh; site of 10th-cent. round tower and 13th-cent. church, replacing earlier church.

Donaghmore (dŏ″nŭkhmôr′), town (pop. 1,316), E Co. Tyrone, Northern Ireland, 3 mi. NW of Dungannon; agr. market (flax, potatoes, oats; cattle), soap mfg. St. Patrick founded abbey here, of which a cross is preserved.

Donahue (dŏ′nŭ-hū), town (pop. 105), Scott co., E Iowa, 12 mi. NNW of Davenport, in agr. area.

Doña Juana (dō′nyä hwä′nä), cascades, rivulet, reservoir, mountain (over 3,500 ft.), and recreational area, central Puerto Rico, 32 mi. SW of San Juan. Near by (W) is one of the Toro Negro hydroelectric plants.

Donald, town (pop. 1,308), W central Victoria, Australia, 150 mi. NW of Melbourne; trading center for livestock area; meat-packing plant.

Donald, town (pop. 187), Marion co., NW Oregon, 25 mi. SSW of Portland.

Donalda (dŭnăl′dŭ), village (pop. 220), S central Alta., near Buffalo L., 30 mi. SSE of Camrose; coal mining.

Donalds, agr. town (pop. 332), Abbeville co., NW S.C., 33 mi. S of Greenville.

Donaldson. **1** Village (pop. 128), Kittson co., NW Minn., 14 mi. S of Hallock, in Red R. valley; grain. **2** Village (1940 pop. 901), Schuylkill co., E central Pa., 12 mi. WSW of Pottsville; clothing mfg.

Donaldsonville, city (pop. 4,150), ⊙ Ascension parish, SE La., on W bank (levee) of the Mississippi (ferry here) and 27 mi. SSE of Baton Rouge, in agr. area (sugar cane, rice, cotton, vegetables, corn); sugar milling; mfg. of foundry and machine-shop products, agr. machinery, candy, feed. Oil and natural-gas wells near by. Annual state fair held here. Founded 1806 as trading post; inc. 1822; was temporary ⊙ La. in 1830. H. H. Richardson b. near by.

Donalsonville, city (pop. 2,569), ⊙ Seminole co., extreme SW Ga., 21 mi. WNW of Bainbridge; trade center for agr. and timber area; peanut shelling, sawmilling. Inc. 1897.

Don Álvaro (dōn äl′värō), town (pop. 922), Badajoz prov., W Spain, on the Guadiana, on railroad and 6 mi. SSE of Mérida; cereals, olives, grapes, vegetables, sheep.

Doña María-Ocaña (dō′nyä märē′ä-ōkä′nyä), village (pop. 1,093), Almería prov., S Spain, 25 mi. NW of Almería; olive oil, fruit, cereals, lumber. Lead and iron mines 10 mi. SW (aerial tramway).

Doña Mencía (mĕnthē′ä), town (pop. 5,611), Córdoba prov., S Spain, 4 mi. SSW of Baena; olive-oil processing, brandy distilling. Agr. trade (wine, cereals, almonds, honey); stock raising.

Don Army, Oblast of the, Russia: see DON COSSACKS, OBLAST OF THE.

Doña Rosa, Cordillera de (kôrdĭyä′rä dā dō′nyä rō′sä), Andean range in Coquimbo prov., N central Chile, extends c.20 mi. WSW from Argentina border; rises to over 15,000 ft. in 30°40′S.

Donau, Ger. name of DANUBE RIVER.

Donaueschingen (dō″nou-ĕ′shĭng-ŭn), town (pop. 6,911), S Baden, Germany, in Black Forest, on the Brigach just above its confluence with the Breg (where the Danube is formed), and 7 mi. SSE of Villingen; rail junction; metal- and woodworking, brewing. Resort (alt. 2,277 ft.) with salt springs and baths. Staircase behind choir of 18th-cent. church leads to a powerful spring, whose waters are led underground to the Danube. Castle (18th cent.) of princes Fürstenberg was renovated 1893–96. Fürstenberg library contains 160,000 volumes, 500 incunabula, 1,600 manuscripts.

Donaukanal, Austria: see DANUBE CANAL.

Donaustauf (dō″nou-shtouf′), village (pop. 2,051), Upper Palatinate, E Bavaria, Germany, on the Danube and 5 mi. E of Regensburg; winegrowing. Has ruins of Romanesque castle. Just N is large tuberculosis sanatorium. To W (1 mi.), and overlooking the Danube, is the Walhalla, resembling the Parthenon, built (1830–42) by Louis I of Bavaria.

Donauwörth (dō″nouvûrt′), town (pop. 7,298), Swabia, W Bavaria, Germany, port on the Danube, at mouth of the Wörnitz, and 24 mi. NNW of Augsburg; rail junction; mfg. of dolls, lace trimmings, chemicals; metalworking, printing, brewing; cattle trade. Has early-14th-cent. town hall, several 15th-cent. churches, and Fugger House (1537–39). Developed around 9th-cent. fort, the Mangoldstein. Became seat of dukes of Upper Bavaria in mid-13th cent.; created free imperial city in 1348. Adopted Reformation in 1555; political riots ensuing from attempts (1607) at re-Catholicizing the pop. became one of the causes of the Thirty Years War. Passed to Bavaria in early 18th cent.

Donawitz, Austria: see LEOBEN.

Donbas or **Donbass,** USSR: see DONETS BASIN.

Don Benito (dōn′ bānē′tō), city (pop. 20,613), Badajoz prov., W Spain, in Estremadura, on Madrid-Badajoz RR and 60 mi. E of Badajoz; agr. center picturesquely situated on La Serena plain, and trading in cereals, vegetables, corn, cotton, grapes, olives, livestock. Industries include olive-oil processing, alcohol distilling, tanning; mfg. of shoes, chocolate, soap, furniture, musical instruments, hats.

Doncaster (dŏng′kŭstŭr), town (pop. 917), S Victoria, Australia, 9 mi. ENE of Melbourne, in metropolitan area; fruitgrowing center.

Doncaster, county borough (1931 pop. 63,316; 1951 census 81,896), West Riding, S Yorkshire, England, on Don R. and 17 mi. NE of Sheffield; coal mining, metalworking. Has important railroad shops, rayon mills, steel mills, machinery, plastics, and paint industries. Site of race course where the St. Leger stakes, a race founded 1776, are run. Has 19th-cent. parish church with 170-ft. tower, technical col., art gall., and library. Site of Roman station of *Danum.* On Don R. and 2 mi. SW is industrial suburb of Balby, and on Don R., 2 mi. NE, industrial suburb of Wheatley.

Donchery (dōshŭrē′), village (pop. 1,295), Ardennes dept., N France, on the Meuse and 3 mi. W of Sedan; enamelware mfg. Here capitulation of Sedan was signed, 1870, in Franco-Prussian War.

Donck, Belgium: see DONK.

Don Cossacks, Oblast of the, or **Oblast of the Don Army,** Rus. *Donskogo Voiska Oblast′* or *Donskogo Voyska Oblast′*, former government (□ 63,532; 1897 pop. 1,870,764) of S European Russia; ⊙ Novocherkassk. Formed 1802; its area (largely included in present ROSTOV oblast) was inc. (1924) into North Caucasus Territory. Called Don oblast in early 1920s.

Dondaicha (dōndī′chŭ), town (pop. 6,801), West Khandesh dist., NE Bombay, India, 32 mi. NNW of Dhulia; market center for millet, cotton, wheat; cotton ginning, oilseed milling.

Don Diego (dōn dyā′gō), village, Potosí dept., S central Bolivia, 11 mi. NE of Potosí, on road and on Potosí-Sucre RR; sulphur springs.

Dondo (dōn′dō), town (pop. 645), Congo prov., NW Angola, head of navigation of Cuanza R. and 100 mi. SE of Luanda; rail-spur terminus; cotton, sisal, sugar, palm oil.

Dondo, village, Manica and Sofala prov., central Mozambique, 17 mi. NW of Beira; junction of Beira and Trans-Zambezia railroads.

Dondon (dōdō′), agr. town (1950 census pop. 1,689), Nord dept., N Haiti, in the Massif du Nord, 18 mi. S of Cap-Haïtien; banana- and coffeegrowing.

Dondra (dōn′drŭ), village (pop., including near-by villages, 7,690), Southern Prov., Ceylon, on S coast, 3 mi. ESE of Matara; fishing; vegetables, rice, coconuts. Hindu pilgrimage center; Vishnuite temple, here, destroyed 1587 by Portuguese. Village is on **Dondra Head,** promontory (5°55′N 80°35′E), southernmost point of Ceylon; lighthouse (built 1889).

Done, Se, river, Laos: see KHONG SEDONE.

Donegal (dŏnĭgôl′, dŏ′-), Gaelic *Dhún na nGall*, county (□ 1,864.9; pop. 136,317), Ulster, Ireland; ⊙ Lifford. On the Atlantic bounded by Donegal Bay (S), Lough Foyle and Co. Londonderry (NE), cos. Tyrone (E) and Fermanagh (SE). Drained by Foyle, Finn, and Erne rivers and numerous small streams. Lough Derg is largest of many lakes. Surface is barren and mountainous, with some fertile valleys. Chief elevations are Derryveach and Blue Stack mts.; highest peak is Mt. Errigal (2,466 ft.). Coastline is rocky and deeply indented; Donegal Bay, Sheep Haven, and loughs Swilly and Foyle are chief inlets. Malin Head is northernmost point of Ireland. Of numerous isls. offshore, Tory and Aran are most important. Sea fisheries and kelp collecting (for iodine) are important; granite and sandstone are quarried. Cattle and sheep raising; growing of flax, oats, potatoes. Industries include textile milling (woolen, linen, muslin), potato-alcohol distilling, flax scutching, tobacco processing, peat digging, mfg. of clothing, shirts, furniture. Towns are Lifford, Donegal, Ballyshanon, Letterkenny, Dungloe, Moville, Dunfanaghy, Buncrana, Ballybofey, Stranolar, Ardara, and Bundoran. There are numerous anc. castles, round towers, and monastic remains.

Donegal, Gaelic *Dún na nGall*, town (pop. 1,182), S Co. Donegal, Ireland, at head of Donegal Bay, 120 mi. NW of Dublin; 54°39′N 8°7′W; seaport, with woolen milling, mfg. of shirts, carpets. Has castle, rebuilt 1610 from earlier stronghold of the O'Donnells, whose hq. were here. There are ruins of Franciscan monastery founded 1474 by Hugh O'-Donnell; here originated (c.1636) the *Annals of Donegal* or *Annals of the Four Masters*, history of the world up to 1616.

Donegal (dŏ′nĭgŭl), borough (pop. 198), Westmoreland co., SW Pa., 13 mi. ESE of Mount Pleasant.

Donegal Bay, inlet (25 mi. long, 21 mi. wide at mouth) of the Atlantic, in Ireland, bet. cos. Donegal (N and E), Leitrim (SE), and Sligo (S); receives Erne R. just W of Ballyshannon. At head of bay is Donegal town.

Donelly (dŏ′nŭlē), village (pop. estimate 500), W Alta., 35 mi. S of Peace River; lumbering, mixed farming, wheat.

Donelson (dŏ′nŭlsŭn), village (pop. 1,765), Davidson co., N central Tenn., just E of Nashville.

Donelson, Fort, Tenn.: see FORT DONELSON NATIONAL PARK.

Doneraile (dŭ′nŭrāl), Gaelic *Dúnaraill*, village (pop. 801), N Co. Cork, Ireland, 6 mi. NNE of Mallow; agr. market (dairying; potatoes, oats).

Doneraile (dŏ′nŭrāl), residential suburb (pop. 1,-086), Darlington co., NE S.C., adjacent to Darlington.

Don Esteban, Arroyo (äroi′ō dōn′ ĕstā′bän), river, Río Negro dept., W Uruguay, rises in the Cuchilla de Haedo SE of Algorta, flows 30 mi. SSW, past Paso de la Cruz, to the Río Negro.

Donets, river, USSR: see DONETS RIVER.

Donets Basin (dŏnĕts′, dō–; Rus. dŭnyĕts′), Rus. *Donetskiy Basseyn*, abbreviated as **Donbas** or **Donbass** (dŏn′băs, Rus. dŭnbäs′), basin (□ 10,-000), one of principal coal-producing and industrial areas of USSR, SW of lower Donets or Northern Donets R., extending through STALINO and VOROSHILOVGRAD oblasts of Ukrainian SSR and ROSTOV oblast of Russian SFSR. Coal deposits extend NW-SE; 235 mi. long, 100 mi. wide; reserves estimated at 90 billion tons; coking coal in N and W, anthracite E and S. Principal coal centers: Stalino, Makeyevka, Yenakiyevo, Gorlovka, Kadiyevka, Chistyakovo, Krasny Luch, Krasnodon, Novoshakhtinsk, Shakhty. Industries include steel mills (Stalino, Makeyevka, Voroshilovsk, Krasny Sulin), heavy machinery works (Kramatorsk, Voroshilovgrad), chemical plants (Artemovsk, Lisichansk), power plants (Zugres, Shtergres). Also mined are dolomite, fireproof clays, kaolin, salt, gypsum, mercury (Nikitovka), and lead-zinc ores. Region has one of densest rail networks of USSR. Developed after 1870s with construction of 1st blast furnaces and rail lines. In Second World War, held (1941–43) by Germans. The Donets Basin was formerly administered as a govt. (1919–25), later as an oblast (1932–38) of the Ukrainian SSR. The oblast was divided (1938) into Stalino and Voroshilovgrad oblasts.

Donetsko-Amvrosiyevka, Ukrainian SSR: see AMVROSIYEVKA.

Donets Ridge, Rus. *Donetskiy Kryazh*, hilly eroded plateau in SE Ukrainian SSR; extends 230 mi. parallel to lower course of Northern Donets R., which breaks through extreme E section; rises to 1,210 ft. Sandstone, clay schists, and limestone formations. Site of DONETS BASIN coal and industrial area.

Donets River or **Northern Donets River,** Rus. *Severnyy Donets*, chief affluent of Don R., in SW European USSR, rises NW of Korocha in Central Russian Upland, flows S, past Belgorod and Chuguyev, and SE, past Izyum, Lisichansk, and Kamensk-Shakhtinski, through E Donets Ridge, to Don R. W of Konstantinovski (Rostov oblast); 631 mi. long. Navigable for 140 mi. above mouth (locks in operation since 1914); fisheries. Receives Oskol and Aidar (left) and Lugan (right) rivers.

Don Fernando de Taos, N. Mex.: see TAOS, village.

Donga (dŏgä′), town (pop. 2,894), Benue prov., Northern Provinces, E central Nigeria, on Donga R. (left affluent of Benue R.) and 22 mi. SE of Wukari; shea nuts, sesame, cassava, durra, yams.

Donga La (dôngä′lä′) or **Drongkhya La** (drông′chä′), pass (alt. 12,500 ft.) in central Assam Himalayas, E Bhutan, 37 mi. E of Byakar.

Dongala, Indonesia: see DONGGALA.

Dongan Hills (dŭng'gŭn), SE N.Y., a section of Richmond borough of New York city, on E Staten Isl., 4 mi. SSW of St. George. Todt Hill (c.409 ft.), highest point of isl., is here.

Dongara or **Dongarra** (dŏn-gä'rŭ), port (pop. 269), W Western Australia, 38 mi. SSE of Geraldton, on Indian Ocean; grain center. Denison is adjacent to Dongara.

Dongargarh (dōng'gŭrgŭr), town (pop. 9,891), Drug dist., E central Madhya Pradesh, India, 34 mi. W of Drug; agr. market; railway settlement. Bamboo forests near by. Sometimes spelled Dongergarh.

Dongarra, Australia: see DONGARA.

Dongdang (dông' däng'), town, Langson prov., N Vietnam, on Hanoi-Nacham RR and 8 mi. NW of Langson, on China frontier at the Chennankwan pass; junction connecting with the Chinese rail system.

Dongen (dōng'ŭn), town (pop. 9,697), North Brabant prov., SW Netherlands, on Donge R. and Wilhelmina Canal, and 7 mi. ENE of Breda; leather tanning, shoe mfg.

Donge River (dōng'ŭ), North Brabant prov., S Netherlands, rises near Baarle-Nassau, flows 36 mi. N, past Dongen, 's Gravenmoer, and Geertruidenberg, to Bergsche Maas R. just N of Geertruidenberg. Navigable below 's Gravenmoer. Crossed by Wilhelmina Canal near Dongen.

Donges (dōzh), village (pop. 434), Loire-Inférieure dept., W France, on Loire R. estuary, 7 mi. ENE of Saint-Nazaire; petroleum refinery; produces tar and derivatives. Site of American landings during First World War.

Donggala (dông-gä'lŭ), town (pop. 3,821), W Celebes, Indonesia, port on Palu Bay (narrow inlet of Macassar Strait), 310 mi. N of Macassar at base of N peninsula; 0°39'S 119°41'E; trade center, shipping copra. Sometimes spelled Dongala.

Dongha (dông'hä'), village, Quangtri prov., central Vietnam, 8 mi. NW of Quangtri; major road center; terminus of highway to Savannakhet (Laos).

Donghoi (dông-hû'ē), town, ⊙ Quangbinh prov. (□ 3,200; 1943 pop. 255,200), N central Vietnam, in Annam, port on Gulf of Tonkin, on railroad and 95 mi. NW of Hue. Fishing and coastal port; fish curing, woodcarving; trading center (rice, corn). Zinc mines, phosphate deposits, granite quarries near by. Pop. mostly Chinese. Has Annamese citadel (1825). Formerly called Quangbinh.

Dongkhe (dông'khā'), town, Caobang prov., N Vietnam, 20 mi. SE of Caobang.

Dongkya Range (dôngchä'), S spur of W Assam Himalayas, along Sikkim (India)-Tibet border; c.40 mi. long N-S. Highest point (23,385 ft.), Pauhunri (pouhōōn'rē) or Pawohumri (päwō-hōōm'rē) peak, is 18 mi. NNE of Lachung.

Dongnai River or **Donnai River** (both: dông'nī'), S Vietnam, rises as the Dadung in Annamese Cordillera, NW of Dalat, flows W and S c.300 mi., past Bienhoa (head of navigation), forming a joint delta with Saigon R. on South China Sea; rapids in upper course.

Dongo (dông'gō), village, Equator Prov., NW Belgian Congo, on left bank of Ubangi R., at mouth of Lua R. and 215 mi. WNW of Lisala; steamboat landing and trading post in copal-gathering area.

Dongo (dông'gô), village (pop. 1,062), Como prov., Lombardy, N Italy, port on W shore of L. Como, 24 mi. NNE of Como; ironworks, paper and silk mills. Near here, on April 27, 1945, Mussolini and several other leading fascists were captured by Italian partisans as they fled N in a German convoy, and were executed the next day near TREMEZZO.

Dongola (dông'gōlä), town, Northern Prov., Anglo-Egyptian Sudan, on left bank of the Nile 45 mi. above 3d Cataract, and 105 mi. NW of Merowe; trade and caravan center. Airfield. Town, also called New Dongola, was ⊙ former Dongola prov. (inc. 1930s into Northern Prov.); its pop. is Nubian. Old Dongola (c.70 mi. S), now in ruins, was ⊙ Christian Kingdom of Dongola or Makurra (6th–14th cent.). Kingdom was later conquered by Egyptians and ruled by Moslems. Region was held by Mahdists 1885–96.

Dongola (dŏng-gō'lŭ), village (pop. 704), Union co., S Ill., 25 mi. N of Cairo, in Ill. Ozarks; fruit, sweet potatoes, truck; flour mill.

Dongou (dông-gōō'), village, N Middle Congo territory, Fr. Equatorial Africa, on Ubangi R. and 30 mi. N of Impfondo; native market for palm products.

Dong Phaya Yen Range (dông' pŭyä'yĕn'), E central Thailand. Forming 150-mi. section of SW boundary of Korat Plateau, it consists of series of flat-topped, densely forested peaks rising to 4,062 ft., 25 mi. NE of Nakhon Nayok. The Mun and Chi rivers of Korat Plateau rise here. Also Dong Phraya Yen.

Dong Rak Range, Thailand-Cambodia: see DANGREK RANGE.

Dongtrieu (dông'tryō'), town, Haiduong prov., N Vietnam, in Tonkin, 45 mi. E of Hanoi, at W end of Quangyen anthracite basin; tea and coffee plantations, cattle raising, sericulture. Coal mining at Maokhe and Uongbi (ESE).

Dongtrieu Hills, low, denuded coastal range, N Vietnam, on Gulf of Tonkin, extending 60 mi. E from Dongtrieu; rises to 3,500 ft. Quangyen coal basin is on S slopes.

Donguzskaya, rail station, Russian SFSR: see PERVOMAISKI, Chkalov oblast.

Dongvan (dông'vän'), town, Hagiang prov., N Vietnam, on China frontier, 40 mi. NW of Hagiang.

Doniambo, New Caledonia: see KONÉ.

Donibristle, Scotland: see SAINT DAVID'S.

Doñihue (dōnyē'wā), town (pop. 3,890), O'Higgins prov., central Chile, on Cachapoal R., in the central valley, on railroad, and 13 mi. SW of Rancagua; agr. center (wheat, alfalfa, potatoes, beans, fruit, livestock). Flour milling, dairying. Mfg. of ponchos and native textile goods.

Donington, Cape (dŏ'nĭngtŭn), on SE Eyre Peninsula, S South Australia, in Spencer Gulf, on peninsula forming E shore of Boston Bay; 34°42'S 136°1'E.

Doniphan (dŏ'nĭfŭn), county (□ 391; pop. 10,499), extreme NE Kansas; ⊙ Troy. Fertile agr. area (hilly in E), bounded E and N by Missouri R. and Mo. Livestock, grain, apples; dairying. Formed 1855.

Doniphan. 1 City (pop. 1,611), ⊙ Ripley co., S Mo., in Ozark region, on Current R. and 27 mi. SW of Poplar Bluff; resort, agr. center; lumber products; gravel quarries. Settled c.1847. **2** Village (pop. 412), Hall co., S central Nebr., 10 mi. S of Grand Island and on Platte R. Near by is Stolley State Park, used for recreation.

Donja Gusterica or **Donya Gushteritsa** (both: dô'nyä gōō'shtĕrĭtsä), Serbo-Croatian *Donja Gušterica*, village (pop. 5,630), SW Serbia, Yugoslavia, 8 mi. S of Pristina, in the Kosovo.

Donja Lendava, Yugoslavia: see LENDAVA, village.

Donja Stubica (stōō'bētsä), village (pop. 2,821), N Croatia, Yugoslavia, on railroad and 11 mi. N of Zagreb; local trade center; health resort. Gornja Stubica is 2 mi. E.

Donjek River (dŏn'jĕk), SW Yukon, rises in St. Elias Mts. near 61°15'N 139°35'W, flows 150 mi. generally N to White R. 20 mi. NE of Snag.

Donji Lapac (dô'nyĭ lä'päts), village (pop. 1,436), W Croatia, Yugoslavia, at SE foot of the Pljesevica, 27 mi. E of Gospic, near Bosnia border; local trade center. Gornji Lapac is 3 mi. SSE.

Donji Miholjac (mē'hôlyäts), village (pop. 4,370), N Croatia, Yugoslavia, in the Podravina, near Drava R., on railroad and 28 mi. WNW of Osijek, near Hung. border, in Slavonia; local trade center. Castle.

Donji Milanovac, Yugoslavia: see MILANOVAC, E Serbia.

Donji Vakuf or **Donyi Vakuf** (vä'kōōf), village, W central Bosnia, Yugoslavia, on Vrbas R., on railroad and 55 mi. NW of Sarajevo. Copper mines near by.

Donjon, Le (lŭ dōzhō'), village (pop. 791), Allier dept., central France, 10 mi. NE of Lapalisse; hogs, oats, potatoes.

Donk (dōngk), village (pop. 1,034), Limburg prov., NE Belgium, 9 mi. W of Hasselt; bottle mfg.; fruit-growing. Formerly spelled Donck.

Donkin (dŏng'kĭn), village (pop. estimate 800), NE N.S., on Glace Bay, 2 mi. SE of Glace Bay town; coal mining.

Donkyr, China: see HWANGYÜAN.

Donley (dŏn'lē), county (□ 909; pop. 6,216), N Texas, in the Panhandle; ⊙ Clarendon. Lies just below the high plains; alt. 2,500–3,200 ft. Traversed by Salt Fork of Red R. Grain, cotton, cattle, and hog-raising region, with some dairying, poultry raising. Formed 1876.

Don Martín Dam, Mexico: see SABINAS RIVER.

Don Martín Island (dōn märtēn'), Lima dept., W central Peru, 2 mi. W of Végueta; 11°2'S 77°40'W; 1 mi. wide, 1½ mi. long. Large guano deposits.

Don Matías (dōn' mätē'äs), town (pop. 1,581), Antioquia dept., NW central Colombia, in Cordillera Central, 21 mi. NE of Medellín; alt. 7,237 ft. Corn, beans, coffee, sugar cane, yucca, potatoes, cattle; ships milk to Medellín. Gold placer mines near by.

Don Muang (dôn' mŭäng'), village, Phra Nakhon prov., S Thailand, on railroad and 15 mi. NNE of Bangkok; civil and military airport of Bangkok.

Donna (dûn'nä), Nor. *Dønna*, island (□ 52; pop. 2,156) in the North Sea, Nordland co., N central Norway, at mouth of Ran Fjord, 25 mi. NW of Mosjoen; 15 mi. long, 5 mi. wide; 66°7'N. Peat bogs cover large part of isl. Fishing (cod, herring), cattle raising, dairying, guano collecting. Formerly called Donnesoy, Nor. *Dønnesøy*.

Donna (dŏ'nŭ), city (pop. 7,171), Hidalgo co., extreme S Texas, 12 mi. E of McAllen in lower Rio Grande valley; a shipping, processing center in rich irrigated citrus, truck, cotton area; canneries, dehydrating plants. Founded c.1902.

Donnacona (dŏ"nŭkō'nŭ), town (pop. 3,064), S Que., on the St. Lawrence, at mouth of Jacques Cartier R., and 26 mi. WSW of Quebec; pulp milling, dairying center.

Donnai River, Vietnam: see DONGNAI RIVER.

Donnan, town (pop. 36), Fayette co., NE Iowa, 5 mi. SW of West Union; rail junction.

Donnaz (dônä'), village (pop. 388), Val d'Aosta region, NW Italy, on Dora Baltea R. and 11 mi. N of Ivrea; copper smelting; wine.

Donnellson (dŏ'nŭlsŭn). **1** Village (pop. 336), on Bond-Montgomery co. line, S central Ill., 20 mi. WNW of Vandalia, in agr. area (corn, wheat; dairy products; poultry, livestock). **2** Town (pop. 589), Lee co., SE Iowa, 12 mi. W of Fort Madison, in livestock and grain area.

Donnelly, village (pop. 396), Stevens co., W Minn., 8 mi. NW of Morris, in grain area; dairy products.

Donnelly's Crossing, village (pop. 148), N N.Isl., New Zealand, 100 mi. NW of Auckland; rail terminus; kauri pine.

Donnelsville, village (pop. 285), Clark co., W central Ohio, 6 mi. W of Springfield; limestone quarrying.

Donnemarie-en-Montois (dônmärē'-ā-mōtwä'), village (pop. 844), Seine-et-Marne dept., N central France, 9 mi. SW of Provins.

Donner Lake, glacial lake (c.3 mi. long; alt. 5,939 ft.), Nevada co., E Calif., summer and winter resort in the Sierra Nevada, 13 mi. NW of L. Tahoe. Site of state monument in honor of ill-fated Donner party, which perished here (1846).

Donner Pass (alt. 7,135 ft.), Nevada co., E Calif., highway pass in the Sierra Nevada, c.35 mi. WSW of Reno, Nev.; U.S. Weather Bureau observatory here. Norden Tunnel carries railroad under summit of pass. Donner L. is just E.

Donner und Blitzen River, SE Oregon, rises near Steens Mtn., flows c.60 mi. N to Malheur L.

Donnesoy, Norway: see DONNA.

Donnybrook (dŏ'nēbrōōk), town (pop. 1,065), SW Western Australia, 110 mi. S of Perth; orchards; gold.

Donnybrook, Gaelic *Domhnach Broc*, SE suburb of Dublin, part of Pembroke district, Co. Dublin, Ireland; famous for fair, founded 1204 by King John, and suppressed 1855 because of its notorious disorderliness.

Donnybrook, village (pop. 207), Ward co., NW central N.Dak., 33 mi. NW of Minot and on Des Lacs R.

Donnybrook Place, village (pop. 1,392), Harris co., S Texas.

Donon, Le (lŭ dônō'), flat summit (3,307 ft.) of the central Vosges, Bas-Rhin dept., E France, overlooking Bruche R. valley, 3 mi. NW of Schirmeck. **Col du Donon** or **Schirmeck Pass** (alt. 2,425 ft.) on Schirmeck–Raon-l'Étape road is 1 mi. W. Winter sports.

Donora (dŭnô'rŭ), borough (pop. 12,186), Washington co., SW Pa., 19 mi. SSE of Pittsburgh and on Monongahela R.; wire, steel and zinc products; milk, corn, wheat. Inc. 1901.

Donore (dŏnôr'), Gaelic *Dún Uabhair*, agr. village in E Co. Meath, Ireland, 4 mi. WSW of Drogheda. James II stayed here night before battle of the Boyne (1690), fought just N at OLDBRIDGE.

Donori (dônô'rē), village (pop. 1,218), Cagliari prov., S Sardinia, 14 mi. N of Cagliari.

Donoso (dōnō'sō), village (pop. 139), Colón prov., central Panama, on Caribbean Sea, 28 mi. SW of Colón; road terminus; corn, coconuts, livestock. Also called Miguel de la Borda.

Donovan, village (pop. 327), Iroquois co., E Ill., 20 mi. SE of Kankakee, near Ind. line; agr. (corn, oats, soybeans).

Don Pedro Dam; Don Pedro Reservoir, Calif.: see TUOLUMNE RIVER.

Don River (dŏn), S Yorkshire, England, rises on moor near Penistone, flows SE to Sheffield, turns NE, and flows past Rotherham and Doncaster to the Ouse at Goole. Receives Dearne R. at Conisborough. Length, 70 mi.

Don River (dõ), Loire-Inférieure dept., W France, rises 6 mi. NW of Candé, flows 55 mi. W, past Moisdon-la-Rivière and Guéméné-Penfao, to Vilaine R. 7 mi. ENE of Redon, forming a marshy lake at confluence.

Don River (dŏn), Aberdeen, Scotland, on Banffshire border W of Strathdon, flows 82 mi. E, past Strathdon, Alford, Kemnay, and Kintore, to the North Sea at Old Aberdeen. Receives Urie R. just S of Inverurie. Noted angling stream.

Don River (dŏn, Rus. dôn), anc. *Tanaïs*, one of the great streams (length, 1,222 mi.) of Europe, in S central European Russian SFSR; rises in Central Russian Upland near Stalinogorsk (Moscow oblast), flows generally S, past Dankov, Zadonsk (head of navigation), and Liski, here making wide eastward bend, past Boguchar and Serafimovich, and SW, past Kalach (Stalingrad oblast; here linked by canal with Volga R. at Stalingrad), Tsimlyanskaya, Konstantinovski (Rostov oblast), and Rostov, to Sea of Azov, forming delta mouth. Chief affluents are Sosna, Northern Donets and Chir (right), and Voronezh, Bityug, Khoper, Medveditsa, Sal, and Western Manych (left) rivers. A typical quiet steppe river, navigable for boats carrying grain, coal, bldg. materials, and lumber, except during low summer stage and while frozen (Dec.–March). Don R. delta mouth (□ c.100) admits sea-going vessels, via S arm, as far as Rostov.

Donskogo Voiska Oblast, Russia: see DON COSSACKS, OBLAST OF THE.

Donskoi or **Donskoy** (dŭnskoi'), city (1939 pop. over 10,000), S Moscow oblast, Russian SFSR, on railroad (Bobrik-Donskoi station) and 7 mi. SE of Stalinogorsk; lignite-mining center.

Donskoye (–skoi′ŭ). **1** Village, N Aktyubinsk oblast, Kazakh SSR, on rail spur from Nikel-Tau and 60 mi. E of Aktyubinsk; chromium mining. **2** Village (1939 pop. 642), W Kaliningrad oblast, Russian SFSR, on Baltic Sea, 27 mi. NW of Kaliningrad, near headland (190-ft. lighthouse). Until 1945, in East Prussia and called Gross Dirschkeim (grōs dĭrsh′kīm).

Donso (dōōns′û″), Swedish *Donsö*, fishing village (pop. 908), Goteborg och Bohus co., SW Sweden, on isl. (469 acres) of Donso in the Kattegat, 9 mi. SW of Goteborg.

Donsol (dōnsōl′), town (1939 pop. 4,338; 1948 municipality pop. 20,681), Sorsogon prov., extreme SE Luzon, Philippines, on Burias Pass, 18 mi. SW of Legaspi; agr. center (abacá, coconuts, rice).

Donville-les-Bains (dõvēl′-lā-bē′), town (pop. 2,341), Manche dept., NW France, resort on the Channel 2 mi. NE of Granville.

Don-Volga Canal, Russian SFSR: see VOLGA-DON CANAL.

Donya, in Yugoslav names: see DONJA.

Donyi, in Yugoslav names: see DONJI.

Donzdorf (dônts′dôrf), village (pop. 6,070), N Württemberg, Germany, after 1945 in Württemberg-Baden, 7 mi. E of Göppingen; grain, cattle.

Donzenac (dõznäk′), village (pop. 1,122), Corrèze dept., S central France, in Brive Basin, 5 mi. N of Brive-la-Gaillarde; fruit and vegetable shipping. Slate quarrying at Travassac (1 mi. E). Has 12th-13th-cent. church.

Donzère (dõzâr′), village (pop. 807), Drôme dept., SE France, on left bank of the Rhone and 8 mi. S of Montélimar; nougat and carton mfg. Cistercian abbey of Aiguebelle (founded 1137; restored 19th cent.) is 6 mi. ENE. Dam and hydroelectric plant under construction (1950) bet. here and Mondragon (15 mi. S) on Rhone R.

Donzy (dõzē′), village (pop. 1,268), Nièvre dept., central France, 10 mi. ESE of Cosne; cheese mfg., woodworking. Cattle and lumber trade.

Dooars, India: see DUARS.

Doodewaard, Netherlands: see DODEWAARD.

Dookie, village (pop. 199), N Victoria, Australia, 115 mi. NNE of Melbourne, in agr. area. Agr. col.

Doolittle, town (pop. 237), Phelps co., central Mo., 7 mi. SW of Rolla.

Dooly, county (□ 394; pop. 14,159), central Ga.; ⊙ Vienna. Bounded W by Flint R. Coastal plain agr. (cotton, corn, peanuts, pecans, truck) and forestry (lumber, naval stores) area. Formed 1821.

Doom Dooma, India: see DUM DUMA.

Doon, village (pop. estimate 400), S Ont., 6 mi. SE of Kitchener; dairying, mixed farming.

Doon, town (pop. 517), Lyon co., NW Iowa, 11 mi. SSW of Rock Rapids, near confluence of Little Rock and Rock rivers, in livestock and grain area.

Doon, Loch (lŏkh), lake, S Ayrshire, Scotland, 3 mi. S of Dalmellington, enclosed by Carrick and Glenkens mts.; 5 mi. long, ½ mi. wide. On islet at S end are ruins of anc. Doon Castle. Outlet: Doon R.

Doone Valley, England, NW of Exmoor, forming part of Devon-Somerset boundary.

Doon Hill, Scotland: see DUNBAR.

Doon River, Ayrshire, Scotland, rises in Loch Doon, flows 27 mi. NW, past Dalmellington, Patna, and Dalrymple, to Firth of Clyde at Alloway just S of Ayr. Its beauties were sung by Burns.

Door (dôr), county (□ 491; pop. 20,870), NE Wis., on Door Peninsula, bounded E by L. Michigan, W by Green Bay; ⊙ Sturgeon Bay. Includes Washington and Chambers isls. Cherry growing, fishing, dairying; shipbuilding and quarrying at Sturgeon Bay city. A resort area, the co. contains Peninsula and Potawatomi state parks. Formed 1851.

Doorn (dōrn), village (pop. 4,535), Utrecht prov., central Netherlands, 11 mi. SE of Utrecht. Retreat of William II of Germany from 1919 till his death in 1941.

Doornijk, Belgium: see TOURNAI.

Doornkop (dōōrn′kôp), hill (5,366 ft.), S Transvaal, U. of So. Afr., 9 mi. WSW of Johannesburg. Jameson Raid in support of Johannesburg *Uitlanders* ended here (Jan. 2, 1896) with capture of Dr. Jameson and his men. Scene (1900) of engagement during Lord Roberts' advance on Johannesburg in South African War.

Doornspijk (dōrn′spīk), village (pop. 775), Gelderland prov., central Netherlands, near the Ijsselmeer, 9 mi. NE of Harderwijk; cattle raising, dairying, agr. Sometimes spelled Doornspyk.

Door Peninsula (dôr), NE Wis., bet. Green Bay (W) and L. Michigan (E); 80 mi. long, c.30 mi. wide at base, tapering to a point. It is crossed E–W by waterway at Sturgeon Bay. Partly wooded, with rolling terrain, the peninsula is known as a major cherry-growing region. Door co. comprises N area; Kewaunee co. and part of Brown and Manitowoc counties are at the base. Peninsula was visited in 17th cent. by French explorers and missionaries.

Dor, Palestine: see NASHOLIM.

d'Or, Cape (dôr), on Bay of Fundy, NW N.S., on N side of entrance of Minas Channel, 20 mi. NW of Kentville; 45°18′N 64°46′W.

Dora, Formosa: see TUNGLO.

Dora, town (pop. 984), Walker co., NW central Ala., 20 mi. NW of Birmingham, in industrial area.

Dora, Lake (c.6 mi. long, 1 mi. wide), Lake co., central Fla., near Tavares; connected by waterways with lakes Eustis (N) and Apopka (S), it is part of central Fla. lake system drained by Oklawaha R.

Dora Baltea River (dô′rä bäl′tĕä), anc. *Duria Major*, NW Italy, formed by junction of 2 Alpine streams 1 mi. N of Courmayeur, near Mont Blanc; flows E, through Val d'Aosta, past Aosta, and S, past Ivrea, to Po R. 1 mi. SW of Crescentino; length, 100 mi. Used for irrigation in conjunction with CAVOUR CANAL and for hydroelectric power.

Dorada, La, Colombia: see LA DORADA.

Dorado (dōrä′dō), town (pop. 2,537), N Puerto Rico, at mouth of the La Plata, on railroad and 10 mi. W of San Juan; sugar and tobacco growing. Airport 1½ mi. W.

Dorado, El, Venezuela: see EL DORADO.

Doraha, India: see DURAHA.

Dorah Pass (dō′rŭ), mountain pass (alt. c.14,900 ft.) in the Hindu Kush, on Afghanistan-Pakistan frontier, 35 mi. NW of Chitral, on trade route (closed winter and spring) bet. Badakhshan and Chitral state.

Doran, village (pop. 126), Wilkin co., W Minn., bet. Otter Tail and Bois de Sioux rivers, 7 mi. SE of Breckenridge, in corn, oat, and barley area.

Doranda, India: see RANCHI, city.

Dora Riparia River (dô′rä rēpä′rēä), anc. *Duria Minor*, NW Italy, rises in Cottian Alps 2 mi. N of Montgenèvre Pass, flows 75 mi. generally E, past Susa and Bussoleno, to Po R. at Turin. Furnishes power to many hydroelectric plants, including those at Turin, Susa, and Bussoleno. Also used for irrigation. In upper reaches, forms Val di Susa.

Dorasamudra, India: see BELUR, Mysore.

Dorat, Le (lû dôrä′), village (pop. 1,533), Haute-Vienne dept., W central France, 6 mi. N of Bellac; road junction and agr. market. Has 11th-12th-cent. Romanesque church and part of 15th-cent. walls.

Doraville, town (pop. 472), De Kalb co., NW central Ga., 11 mi. NNE of Atlanta; auto assembly plant.

D'Orbigny (dôr′bēnē), village (pop. c.370), Tarija dept., SE Bolivia, in the Chaco, on Pilcomayo R. and 65 mi. SE of Villa Montes, on Argentina border; cattle. Sometimes called Fortín D'Orbigny.

Dorcheat, Bayou (bī′ō dôr′chĕt), river in Ark. and La., rises in SW Ark., flows c.115 mi. generally S into La., through Webster parish, to N end of L. Bistineau.

Dorchester (dôr′chĭstŭr), county (□ 842; pop. 29,869), S Que., on Maine border; ⊙ Ste. Hénédine.

Dorchester, village (pop. estimate c.1,100), ⊙ Westmorland co., N.B., on Memramcook R., just above its mouth on Shepody Bay, 18 mi. SE of Moncton, in wheat-growing region. Dominion penitentiary. Near by are sandstone quarries, salt and copper mines.

Dorchester. 1 Municipal borough (1931 pop. 10,030; 1951 census 11,623), ⊙ Dorset, England, in S part of co., on Frome R. and 50 mi. WSW of Southampton; agr. market. Has 15th-cent. church containing tomb of Rev. John White, founder of Dorchester, Mass. There are associations with William Barnes, the poet, and it is the "Casterbridge" of Hardy's Wessex novels. Site of remains of Roman station of *Durnovaria;* near by, at Maumbury Rings, was amphitheater. Just SW is anc. earthwork of MAIDEN CASTLE. Hardy lived in Dorchester. **2** Agr. village and parish (pop. 774), S Oxfordshire, England, on the Thames at mouth of the Thame, and 9 mi. SE of Oxford. Has Augustinian abbey church dating from Norman times, built on site of Saxon cathedral founded in late 7th cent. Site of Roman station of *Dorocina* or *Durocina*. Remains of Iron Age settlement found near by.

Dorchester (dôr′chĕ″stŭr, dôr′chĭstŭr). **1** County (□ 580; pop. 27,815), E Md.; ⊙ Cambridge, Marsh-fringed peninsula on the Eastern Shore, bounded E by Del. line. In Chesapeake Bay are Taylors, Hoopers, Bloodsworth, and other isls. Shores are indented by many inlets. Fruit (especially cantaloupes), vegetables (especially tomatoes), other truck, corn, wheat, dairy products, poultry; timber; has large seafood industry (fish, crabs, oysters, diamondback terrapin). Vegetable and seafood canneries and packing houses, lumber and flour mills, boatyards. Marshes (W half of co.) are center of state's muskrat-trapping industry. Sport fishing, duck hunting, yachting attract visitors. Includes Blackwater Natl. Wildlife Refuge. Formed 1668. **2** County (□ 569; pop. 22,601), SE central S.C.; ⊙ St. George. Bounded W by Edisto R.; drained by Ashley R. Agr. area, formerly (18th and 19th cent.) seat of rich rice and indigo plantations; now small farming (cotton, tobacco, corn), livestock raising, lumbering. Summerville is center of winter-resort area. Formed 1897.

Dorchester. 1 Village (pop. 162), Macoupin co., SW Ill., 20 mi. NE of Alton, in agr. and bituminous-coal area. **2** District of BOSTON, Mass. **3** Village (pop. 478), Saline co., SE Nebr., 25 mi. WSW of Lincoln; flour, grain. **4** Town (pop. 133), Grafton co., W central N.H., 25 mi. NW of Grafton, in agr., recreational region. **5** Village (pop. c.200), Cumberland co., S N.J., on Maurice R. and 9 mi. SSE of Millville; shipbuilding; sand pits. **6** Village, Dorchester co., SE central S.C., 15 mi. NW of Summerville; brick mfg. Forestry demonstration area. **7** Village (pop. 1,129), Wise co., SW Va., 10 mi. ENE of Big Stone Gap. **8** Village (pop. 457), Clark co., central Wis., 35 mi. W of Wausau, in dairying region; makes cheese, butter, dairy equipment, canned vegetables. Poultry hatchery; stone quarries.

Dorchester, Cape (dôr′chĭstŭr), SW Baffin Isl., Northwest Territories, NW extremity of Foxe Peninsula, on Foxe Channel; 65°29′N 77°50′W.

Dorchester Bay, Mass.: see BOSTON BAY.

Dorchester Station, village (pop. estimate 400), S Ont., on Middle Thames R. and 10 mi. E of London; dairying, mixed farming, fruitgrowing.

Dordogne (dôrdô′nyû), department (□ 3,561; pop. 387,643), SW France; ⊙ Périgueux. A dry, stony hill land, sloping SW from Massif Central to Aquitaine basin, and dissected by fertile valleys of Dordogne, Vézère, Isle, Auvézère, and Dronne rivers, where wine, vegetables, tobacco, wheat, and corn are grown; hog raising, cattle fattening. Dept. ships wines, walnuts, and truffles. Industries: paper milling, food processing and canning, woodworking. Chief towns are Périgueux (truffles) and Bergerac (wines). Prehistoric sites at Les Eyzies and scenic river valleys attract tourists. Dept. was formed 1790 mainly from old dist. of Périgord.

Dordogne River, central and SW France, rises in Auvergne Mts. S of Le Mont-Dore (Puy-de-Dôme dept.), flows c.300 mi. SW and W, past La Bourboule, Bort-les-Orgues, Bergerac (head of navigation), and Libourne, to unite with the Garonne at the Bec d'Ambès (14 mi. N of Bordeaux) to form the Gironde. Receives the Rhue, Maronne, and Cère (left), the Diège, Vézère, and Isle (right). Bet. Saint-Sauves and Beaulieu-sur-Dordogne, the Dordogne follows a narrow, uninhabited gorge for c.100 mi. Vineyards along lower course. River harnessed for water power.

Dordrecht (dôr′drĕkht), town (pop. 68,217), South Holland prov., SW Netherlands, at point where Lower Merwede R. divides to form Noord R. and Old Maas R., 12 mi. SE of Rotterdam; rail junction; inland port. Heavy machine mfg. center (machinery, boilers, bridging material, electric motors); chemicals (plastics, nitrogen compounds, asphalt and tar products); shipbuilding; food industries; electric-power station. Has 14th-cent. Gothic church (*Groote Kerk*), art mus. Town founded 1008, chartered 1220. Declared for Reformed Church in 1572; captured in same year by Beggars of the Sea. Scene (1572) of 1st assembly of United Provinces. Site (1618–19) of Synod of Dort (Arminius). Johan de Witt b. here. Sometimes called Dort or Dordt (shortened forms).

Dordrecht, town (pop. 3,172), E Cape Prov., U. of So. Afr., 40 mi. NNE of Queenstown, near SW end of Drakensberg range; alt. 5,289 ft.; sheep-raising, wool-producing center; health resort. Several near-by caves contain old Bushman paintings.

Dordsche Kil River, Netherlands: see DORTSCHE KIL RIVER.

Dordt, Netherlands: see DORDRECHT.

Dore, Monts (mõ dôr′), or **Massif du Mont-Dore** (mäsēf″ dü–), highest range of Auvergne Mts., Puy-de-Dôme dept., central France, bet. the Monts Dôme (N) and the Monts du Cézallier (S); formed by eroded remnants of large Tertiary volcanic cone (base diameter c.20 mi.); has several craters, crater lakes, and basalt flows. Forms drainage divide bet. Loire and Garonne basins. Highest peak, Puy de Sancy (6,187 ft.). Mineral springs at La Bourboule and Mont-Dore. Sometimes spelled Monts Dores.

Doré Lake (dôrā′) (□ 248), central Sask., 120 mi. NNW of Prince Albert; 24 mi. long, 18 mi. wide.

Dorena Dam, Oregon: see COAST FORK.

Dorepotagala Peak, Ceylon: see LUNUGALA.

Dore River (dôr), Puy-de-Dôme dept., central France, rises in Massif du Livradois 3 mi. NE of St-Germain-l'Herm, flows 85 mi. N, past Ambert and Olliergues, to the Allier 8 mi. S of Vichy.

Dores, agr. village and parish (pop. 572), N Inverness, Scotland, on NE shore of Loch Ness, 8 mi. SW of Inverness.

Dores da Boa Esperança, Brazil: see BOA ESPERANÇA, Minas Gerais.

Dores do Indaiá (dô′rĭs dōō ēndīä′), city (pop. 5,377), W central Minas Gerais, Brazil, on rail spur, and 110 mi. WNW of Belo Horizonte; coffee, cotton, livestock. Has normal school.

Dorfen (dôr′fûn), village (pop. 4,039), Upper Bavaria, Germany, on the Isen and 11 mi. ESE of Erding; rail junction; pottery mfg., brewing, lumber milling. Has pilgrimage church. Chartered c.1331.

Dorfmark (dôrf′märk), village (pop. 3,491), in former Prussian prov. of Hanover, NW Germany, after 1945 in Lower Saxony, 8 mi. ENE of Walsrode; woodworking. Rye, potatoes, sheep.

Dorgali (dôrgä′lē), town (pop. 6,057), Nuoro prov., E Sardinia, 14 mi. E of Nuoro; domestic leather-working, ceramics; hot mineral springs. Three grottos (including Grotta del Bue Marino), numerous nuraghi in vicinity.

Dori (dō'rē), town (pop. c.3,600), N Upper Volta, Fr. West Africa, near Niger territory border, 150 mi. NE of Ouagadougou. Exports beef and mutton. Livestock fair. Airstrip; climatological station.

Dorion (dŏ'rēō), town (pop. 1,292), S Que., on Ottawa R., opposite Isle Perrot, 25 mi. WSW of Montreal; truck gardening.

Dorion Peak, Idaho: see LOST RIVER RANGE.

Dorion Station, village (pop. estimate 200), W central Ont., on Black Bay of L. Superior, 40 mi. NE of Port Arthur; wheat growing, dairying.

Doris, a small mtn. district of W central Greece, bet. Oeta and Parnassus massifs, at headwaters of Cephissus R. Regarded as the traditional home of the Dorians, one of the Great Hellenic races, who may have stopped here in their invasion of Greece. It was championed by Sparta.

Doris, anc. district on coast of SW Asia Minor, consisting of Dorian settlements on mainland and nearby isls. Six of these towns formed a league, the Dorian hexapolis, including Cnidus, Halicarnassus on mainland, Cos, and Lindus, Ialysus, and Camirus on Rhodes.

Doristhal, Russian SFSR: see RAZINO.

Dorkha (dōr'kŭ), village, SW Bhutan, on the Torsa and 45 mi. NE of Jalpaiguri (India); rice, corn, millet. Chief stronghold of Nepalese settlement in W Bhutan; pop. mainly Rais. Just across river (E) is Denchuka, a Nepalese settlement of Limbus.

Dorking, residential urban district (1931 pop. 10,411; 1951 census 20,252), central Surrey, England, on Mole R. and 18 mi. SSW of London, near foot of Box Hill (590 ft., just NNE), at edge of the North Downs; agr. market, with electric-cable works. It was home of Malthus and of George Meredith, who is buried here. Near by is "Deepdene" mansion. There is 15th-cent. inn.

Dormagen (dôr'mä"gŭn), village (pop. 7,233), in former Prussian Rhine Prov., W Germany, after 1945 in North Rhine-Westphalia, near the Rhine, 9 mi. S of Düsseldorf; mfg. of synthetic fiber.

Dormans (dôrmã'), village (pop. 1,391), Marne dept., N France, on left bank of the Marne and 11 mi. E of Château-Thierry; woodworking. Has chapel commemorating battles of the Marne (1914 and 1918) during which it was briefly held by Germans. Damaged in Second World War.

Dormanstown, England: see REDCAR.

Dormida, La, Argentina: see LA DORMIDA.

Dormidontovka (dŭrmēdôn'tŭfkŭ), town (1939 pop. over 500), S Khabarovsk Territory, Russian SFSR, on Trans-Siberian RR and 50 mi. S of Khabarovsk; sawmilling; truck, wheat, perilla.

Dormont, residential borough (pop. 13,405), Allegheny co., SW Pa., SW suburb of Pittsburgh. Settled c.1790, inc. 1909.

Dornach (dôr'näkh), town (pop. 3,056), Solothurn canton, N Switzerland, on Birs R. and 5 mi. S of Basel; copper products. Acad. of anthroposophy. Consists of Dornach proper and Dornachbrugg.

Dornakal (dōr'nŭkŭl), village, Warangal dist., SE Hyderabad state, India, 15 mi. SW of Yellandlapad; rail junction (workshops) in Singareni coal field; spur lines serve mining centers of Yellandlapad and Kottagudem.

Dorna-Vatra, Rumania: see VATRA-DORNEI.

Dornbirn (dôrn'bĭrn), city (pop. 22,516) and market center, Vorarlberg, W Austria, 6 mi. S of Bregenz; textile (silk, cotton, velvet), machine mfg.; breweries. Hydroelectric plant. Customs station. Spectacular Rappenloch Gorge near by.

Dornburg (dôrn'bŏŏrk), town (pop. 1,271), Thuringia, central Germany, on the Thuringian Saale and 6 mi. NE of Jena; grain, sugar beets, livestock. Noted for 3 palaces, the oldest of which dates from 11th cent., was formerly property of dukes of Saxe-Weimar, and was often visited by Goethe.

Dornes (dôrn), agr. village (pop. 438), Nièvre dept., central France, 10 mi. SSW of Decize.

Dornhan (dôrn'hän), town (pop. 1,737), S Württemberg, Germany, after 1945 in Württemberg-Hohenzollern, in Black Forest, 9 mi. SE of Freudenstadt; cattle.

Dornie, fishing village, SW Ross and Cromarty, Scotland, at head of Loch Alsh, 7 mi. E of Kyle.

Dorno (dôr'nô), town (pop. 3,387), Pavia prov., Lombardy, N Italy, 10 mi. WSW of Pavia.

Dornoch (dôr'nŏkh, –nŏk), burgh (1931 pop. 725; 1951 census 793), ⊙ Sutherland, Scotland, in SE part of co., on Dornoch Firth, 29 mi. NNE of Inverness; seaside resort, with famous golf course. Once seat of bishops of Caithness; of their palace, destroyed 1570, tower remains. The cathedral, begun c.1224, was burned 1570, rebuilt 1837 as parish church. Dornoch was scene of last witch-burning in Scotland, 1722.

Dornoch Firth, Scotland, inlet of Moray Firth, bet. Embo, Sutherland (W), and Tarbat Ness, Ross and Cromarty (E); 22 mi. long, 9 mi. wide at mouth. Chief riparian towns: Dornoch, Tain, Edderton, Bonar Bridge.

Dornock (dôr'nŏk), agr. village and parish (pop. 1,688), S Dumfries, Scotland, 3 mi. E of Annan.

Dornot Gobi, Mongolia: see EAST GOBI.

Dornstetten (dôrn'shtĕ"tŭn), town (pop. 1,583), S Württemberg, Germany, after 1945 in Württemberg-Hohenzollern, in Black Forest, 4 mi. E of Freudenstadt; woodworking. Climatic health resort and skiing center (alt. 2,067 ft.). Has 15th-cent. church.

Doro, Cape, Greece: see KAPHEREUS, CAPE.

Dorobantu (dôrôbänts'), Rum. *Dorobanţu,* village (pop. 1,271), Constanta prov., SE Rumania, 22 mi. W of Babadag; cotton growing.

Doro Channel, Greece: see KAPHEREUS CHANNEL.

Dorog (dô'rôg), town (pop. 8,182), Komarom-Esztergom co., N Hungary, 5 mi. S of Esztergom; mining center, rail junction; limestone quarries, quicklime kilns, lumberyards. Lignite mines near by in use since 1850.

Dorogobuzh (dŭrôgŭbōōsh'), city (1926 pop. 7,850), central Smolensk oblast, Russian SFSR, on Dnieper R. (head of navigation) and 50 mi. ENE of Smolensk, on rail spur from Dorogobuzh station (13 mi. N; on Smolensk-Moscow RR); dairying center. Lignite deposits near by. Has old Rus. stone church. Dates from mid-11th cent.; changed hands frequently (15th–17th cent.) bet. Poland and Russia, to which it finally passed in 1667.

Doro Gorge, Japan: see KUMANO RIVER.

Dorohoi (dôrôhoi'), town (1948 pop. 15,036), Botosani prov., NE Rumania, in Moldavia, c.75 mi. NW of Jassy; rail terminus, with trade in grain, lumber, livestock; mfg. of candles, soap, hats, stoves, ceramics; flour milling, tanning. Has 15th- and 18th-cent. churches. Founded in 14th cent. About 25% pop. are Jews.

Dorokawa, Russian SFSR: see ULYANOVSKOYE.

Dorokhovo (dŏ'rŭkhŭvŭ), town (1939 pop. over 500), SW Moscow oblast, Russian SFSR, 50 mi. WSW of Moscow; ceramic industry.

Doron de Beaufort River (dôrō' dŭ bōfôr'), Savoie dept., SE France, rises in Beaufortin massif of Savoy Alps, flows 15 mi. SW, past Beaufort, to the Arly above Albertville.

Doron de Bozel River (bôzĕl'), Savoie dept., SE France, rises in Massif de la Vanoise (Savoy Alps), flows 20 mi. NW, past Bozel, to the Isère at Moutiers. Hydroelectric plants.

Doronod Gobi, Mongolia: see EAST GOBI.

Dorot or **Doroth** (both: dōrōt'), settlement (pop. 300), SW Israel, in Judaean Plain, at NW edge of the Negev, 10 mi. E of Gaza; metalworking; grain, fruit, vegetables; on Negev water pipe line. Founded 1941.

Dorotea (dōō"rōōtā'ä", dō"rō–), village (pop. 847), Vasterbotten co., N Sweden, 70 mi. WSW of Lycksele; cattle; dairying.

Doroth, Israel: see DOROT.

Dorothy, village (1940 pop. 1,042), Raleigh co., S W.Va., 20 mi. SSE of Charleston, in coal-mining region.

Dorowati, Mount, Indonesia: see WILLIS MOUNTAINS.

Dorpat, Estonia: see TARTU.

Dorrance, city (pop. 365), Russell co., central Kansas, 15 mi. E of Russell, near Smoky Hill R., in livestock and grain region.

Dorrego, Argentina: see CORONEL DORREGO.

Dorre Island (dôr) (□ 22), in Indian Ocean, 32 mi. off W coast of Western Australia, just S of Bernier Isl.; forms W shore of Shark Bay and N boundary of Naturaliste Channel.

Dorris, town (pop. 892), Siskiyou co., N Calif., 20 mi. SSW of Klamath Falls, Oregon; agr.; lumber milling.

Dorrisville, Ill.: see HARRISBURG.

Dorset or **Dorsetshire** (–shĭr), county (□ 973.2; 1931 pop. 239,352; 1951 census 291,157), SW England; ⊙ Dorchester. Bounded by Devon (W), Somerset (NW), Wiltshire (NE), Hampshire (E), and English Channel (S). Drained by Stour R. and Frome R. Crossed E-W by chalk hills in N and center, with fertile valleys; important dairying region, supplying butter for London market. Sheep are also raised. Portland stone and marble are quarried. Industries include mfg. of leather, paper, silk, pottery, tiles. Besides Dorchester, important towns are: ports of Poole, Portland, and Weymouth; resorts of Lyme Regis and Swanage; market towns of Blandford, Shaftesbury, Sherborne, Wareham, and Wimborne Minster. There are many early Br. and Roman remains. Co. is closely associated with works of Thomas Hardy.

Dorset, town (pop. 1,150), Bennington co., SW Vt., just N of Manchester, in a valley of Taconic Mts.; resort, especially for artists and writers; wood and dairy products, fruit, maple sugar. Dorset Mtn. (3,804 ft.) is NE of Dorset village. First commercial marble quarry in U.S. opened here, 1785. Conventions which led to independent Vt. held in Dorset, 1775 and 1776.

Dorset Mountain, Vt.: see DORSET, town.

Dorsetshire, England: see DORSET.

Dorsten (dôr'stŭn), town (pop. 24,707), in former Prussian prov. of Westphalia, W Germany, after 1945 in North Rhine-Westphalia, in the Ruhr, on Lippe Lateral Canal and 6 mi. N of Gladbeck; rail junction; dairying; vegetables.

Dort, Netherlands: see DORDRECHT.

Dortan (dôrtã'), village (pop. 254), Ain dept., E France, on the Bienne and 12 mi. NNE of Nantua; its wood-turning artisans produce chessmen, precision tools.

Dortmund (dôrt'mŏŏnt), city (□ 105; 1939 pop. 542,261; 1946 pop. 436,491; 1950 pop. 500,150), in former Prussian prov. of Westphalia, W Germany, after 1945 in North Rhine-Westphalia, port at head of Dortmund-Ems Canal, c.20 mi. E of Essen; 51°31'N 7°27'E. Rail hub; a focal point of Ruhr coal and iron-ore mining; steel plants, coke works. Brewing center; refining of natural petroleum, mfg. of synthetic oil. Extensive port installations at NW suburb Huckarde. Severe Second World War destruction includes noted 12th-, 13th-, and 14th-cent. churches. First mentioned 879. Became free imperial city in 1220 and soon after joined Hanseatic League. Passed to Prussia in 1815.

Dortmund-Ems Canal (–ĕms'), major transportation artery of NW Germany, extends from Dortmund (Ruhr region) to Emden (North Sea port); 165 mi. long, 82 ft. deep; navigable until Bergeshövede for vessels up to 1,000 tons, thence for 750-ton vessels. From Dortmund, canal flows to Datteln, where it is connected with the Rhine via Lippe Lateral and Rhine-Herne canals, then continues past Münster and Bergeshövede (junction with Ems-Weser Canal 1 mi. NW) to Meppen, whence it utilizes regulated bed of Ems R. until head of river's estuary, reaching Emden in short lateral canal. Transports coal N, ores S. Built 1892–99 to give the Rhine a mouth in Germany.

Dortsche Kil River or **Dordsche Kil River** (both: dôrt'sŭ kĭl'), SW Netherlands, navigable branch of Old Maas R.; leaves main stream 1 mi. SW of Dordrecht; flows 6 mi. S to the Hollandschdiep at Willemsdorp. Forms E boundary of Beijerland isl.

Dortyol (dûrtyôl'), Turkish *Dörtyol,* village (pop. 4,410), Hatay prov., S Turkey, on railroad, near head of Gulf of Iskenderun, 50 mi. ESE of Adana; wheat, barley.

Doru (dō'rōō), town (pop. 2,280), Anantnag dist., SW central Kashmir, in Vale of Kashmir, on tributary of upper Jhelum R. and 12 mi. SSE of Anantnag; rice, corn, oilseeds, wheat. Sometimes Duru.

Dorud, Iran: see DURUD.

Dorum (dō'rōōm), village (pop. 3,400), in former Prussian prov. of Hanover, NW Germany, after 1945 in Lower Saxony, 10 mi. N of Bremerhaven; sawmilling, food processing. Has Romanesque church.

Doruma (dōrōō'mä), village, Eastern Prov., N Belgian Congo, near Anglo-Egyptian Sudan border, 235 mi. NE of Buta; cotton center. Has Dominican mission. Former seat of African chief Doruma, ally of the Arab slave traders, who fought a protracted war (until 1896) against Congo Free State.

Dorunda, India: see RANCHI, city.

Dorval (dôrväl'), town (pop. 2,048), S Que., on S shore of Montreal Isl., on L. St. Louis, 10 mi. SW of Montreal; 45°27'N 73°46'W; site of Montreal internatl. airport; resort. Just offshore is islet of Dorval, a resort.

Dörverden (dûr'fĕr"dŭn), village (pop. 2,077), in former Prussian prov. of Hanover, NW Germany, after 1945 in Lower Saxony, on right bank of the Weser and 5 mi. S of Verden; woodworking, flour milling.

Dorylaeum, Turkey: see ESKISEHIR, city.

Dos Amigos or **Central Dos Amigos** (sĕnträl' dōs' ämē'gōs), sugar-mill village (pop. 1,340), Oriente prov., E Cuba, just NE of Campechuela, 13 mi. SW of Manzanillo.

Dos Bahías, Cabo (kä'bō dōs bäē'äs), Atlantic cape in N Comodoro Rivadavia military zone, Argentina, at N edge of Gulf of San Jorge; 44°56'S 65°31'W.

Dosbarrios (dōzvä'ryōs), town (pop. 2,608), Toledo prov., central Spain, 14 mi. SE of Aranjuez; olives, oats, barley, wheat, grapes, goats, sheep. Olive-oil pressing; mfg. of arrope (sweets).

Dos Bocas (dōs bō'käs), hydroelectric project, NW central Puerto Rico, at confluence of Arecibo R. and Caonillas R., 10 mi. S of Arecibo. Consists of artificial lake, dam, and hydroelectric plant. Completed 1943. Caonillas dam, reservoir, and hydroelectric plant, just SE, was dedicated 1949.

Dos Cabezas (dōs' kŭbā'sŭs), village, Cochise co., SE Ariz., 80 mi. E of Tucson. Chiricahua (chĭrŭkä'wŭ) Natl. Monument is SE.

Dos Cabezas Mountains, SE Ariz., c.15 mi. E of Wilcox. Separated from Chiricahua Mts. by APACHE PASS. Highest point is Dos Cabezas, peak with 2 summits, 8,369 ft. and 8,363 ft.

Dos Caminos (dōs' kämē'nōs), town (pop. 1,468), Oriente prov., E Cuba, on railroad and 12 mi. N of Santiago de Cuba; sugar cane, coffee, fruit.

Dos Caminos del Cobre (dĕl kō'brā), town (pop. 2,872), Oriente prov., E Cuba, 2 mi. NW of Santiago de Cuba; sugar cane, fruit.

Doschatoye (dŭshchä'tŭyŭ), town (1926 pop. 2,166), SW Gorki oblast, Russian SFSR, on Oka R. and 5 mi. NW of Vyksa; ironworks, shipyards.

Dos Conos (dōs kō'nōs), volcano (19,350 ft.), Catamarca prov., NW Argentina, in the Puna de Atacama, 70 mi. SW of Antofagasta de la Sierra.

Dos de Mayo, Peru: see LA UNIÓN, city, Huánuco dept.

Döse, Germany: see CUXHAVEN.

Dosewallips River (dōzĭwŏ'lŭps, dōsĭ–), NW Wash., rises in Olympic Natl. Park E of Mt. Olympus, flows c.35 mi. SE to Hood Canal.

Doshan Tepe, Iran: see TEHERAN.

Dos Hermanas (dōs' ĕrmä'näs), town (pop. 16,456), Seville prov., SW Spain, 8 mi. SSE of Seville; processing and agr. center in fertile region of lower Guadalquivir basin. Chiefly a center for olive industry. Also sawmilling, liquor distilling, vegetable canning, textile milling; mfg. of meat products, shoes. Lime quarrying.

Dos Hermanas, Cerro (sĕ'rō), Andean volcano (18,175 ft.) on Argentina-Chile border, 55 mi. SW of Cerro Incahuasi; 27°31'S.

Dos Hermanos (-nōs), town (1939 pop. 12,811) in Talisay municipality, Negros Occidental, Negros isl., Philippines, 7 mi. NE of Bacolod; agr. center (rice, sugar cane).

Doshi or **Dushi** (dō'shē), town (pop. over 2,000), Kataghan prov., NE Afghanistan, on N slopes of the Hindu Kush, 80 mi. NNW of Kabul, and on main highway to Mazar-i-Sharif; road center at junction of Surkhab and Andarab valleys. Coal mined near by at Ishpushta.

Dosing (dō'shĭng'), Mandarin *Tu-ch'eng* (dōō'-chŭng'), town, W Kwangtung prov., China, on West R. and 18 mi. SSE of Fungchün; commercial center; exports grain, fruit, tobacco, silk.

Dos Lagunas (dōs' lägōō'näs), village, Petén dept., NE Guatemala, c.60 mi. NNE of Flores; airfield for chicle shipments.

Doson (dô'shŭn'), town, Kienan prov., N Vietnam, on Gulf of Tonkin, 65 mi. ESE of Hanoi. Seaside resort; summer residence.

Dos Palos (dôs pă'lŭs), city (pop. 1,394), Merced co., central Calif., in San Joaquin Valley, 23 mi. SSW of Merced; dairying, alfalfa and truck growing. Rail station is South Dos Palos (2 mi. SW). Inc. 1935.

Dospat Dagh, Bulgaria and Greece: see RHODOPE MOUNTAINS.

Dospat Pass (dôspät'), S Bulgaria, in W Rhodope Mts., 12 mi. SW of Devin, on road to Nevrokop.

Dosquet (dŏskā'), village (pop. estimate 500), S Que., 28 mi. SW of Quebec; lumbering, dairying.

Dos Ríos (dōs' rē'ōs), village, Oriente prov., E Cuba, 40 mi. NW of Santiago de Cuba. Site of 1895 battle in which Martí, hero of Cuban independence, was killed. Has monument to him.

Dossenheim (dô'sŭnhīm), village (pop. 5,601), N Baden, Germany, after 1945 in Württemberg-Baden, at W foot of the Odenwald, 3 mi. N of Heidelberg; mfg. of fountain pens, pencils, vegetable preserves; paper milling; red-porphyry quarrying.

Dosse River (dô'sŭ), E Germany, rises NW of Wittstock, flows 75 mi. generally S, past Wittstock and Neustadt, to the Havel 7 mi. ESE of Havelberg. Navigable for 10 mi. above mouth.

Dosso (dō'sō), town (pop. c.1,900), SW Niger territory, Fr. West Africa, 80 mi. ESE of Niamey; peanuts, kapok, millet, melons; goats. Airfield.

Dossor (dŭsôr'), oil town (1932 pop. estimate 12,000), N Guryev oblast, Kazakh SSR, on railroad and 55 mi. NE of Guryev, in Emba oil field; pipe lines to Orsk and Guryev.

Dostafyur (dŭstŭfyōōr'), village (1939 pop. over 500), W Azerbaijan SSR, on N slope of the Lesser Caucasus, 18 mi. SW of Kirovabad; livestock, wheat, potatoes; lumbering. Formerly spelled Dastafyur.

Dos-Torres (dōs-tô'rĕs), town (pop. 3,519), Córdoba prov., S Spain, 6 mi. NW of Pozoblanco; olive-oil processing, flour milling; stock raising; wheat, vegetables, potatoes.

Dota, Santa María de, Costa Rica: see SANTA MARÍA.

Dothan (dō'thŭn), city (pop. 21,584), ⊙ Houston co., SE Ala., 95 mi. SE of Montgomery; trade center for livestock and agr. area (cotton, peanuts); mfg. of fertilizer, cottonseed oil and cottonseed products, lumber; food processing (dairy and meat products, flour, beverages). Inc. 1885. Grew after arrival of railroad (1889).

Doti or **Silgarhi Doti** (sĭl'gŭrhē dō'tē), town, W Nepal, near Seti R. (tributary of Karnali or Gogra R.), 90 mi. E of Naini Tal, India; rice, corn, millet, buckwheat, vegetables. Nepalese military station. Sometimes called Dipal for adjoining village.

Dotis, Hungary: see TATA.

Dotnuva (dôt'nōōvä), village (pop. c.500), central Lithuania, on railroad and 33 mi. N of Kaunas. Lithuanian agr. acad. (1924) here, prior to its removal (1940s) to Kaunas.

Dotsero (dŏtsĕ'rō), village (pop. c.75), Eagle co., NW Colo., on Colorado R., at mouth of Eagle R., and 12 mi. W of Eagle; alt. 6,160 ft. Dotsero cutoff (completed 1934) is 38-mi. stretch of track extending NE from Dotsero along Colorado R. It links 2 railroads and, with Moffat Tunnel, shortens route from Denver to Salt Lake City, Utah, by 173 mi.

Dottenijs, Belgium: see DOTTIGNIES.

Dottignies (dôtēnyē'), Flemish *Dottenijs* (dô'tŭnīs), town (pop. 5,926), West Flanders prov., W Belgium, 8 mi. S of Courtrai; wool industry; agr. market. Has 12th-cent. Romanesque church. Waloon community in Flemish-speaking area.

Dotzheim (dôts'hīm), residential suburb (pop. 8,281) of Wiesbaden, W Germany, 2 mi. W of city center.

Douai (dōōā'), anc. *Duacum*, town (pop. 35,509), Nord dept., N France, on Scarpe R. (canalized) and 18 mi. S of Lille, in coal-mining basin; large metalworks (mining and agr. machinery, automotive springs), breweries, glassworks. Mfg. (varnishes, industrial oils, flour products, sugar, embroidery). Coal mined in suburban Dorignies (coke ovens). Its 15th-cent. town hall (partly rebuilt in 19th cent.) has 15th-cent. belfry. Town was substantially rebuilt in 18th cent. Its univ. (founded 1562 by Philip II of Spain) and Roman Catholic col. (where Douai Bible was prepared) were suppressed in French Revolution; univ. was relocated at Lille in 1887. Douai still has natl. agr. school, conservatory of music, teachers colleges, and fine arts academy. Successful resistance to siege (1479) by Louis XI is celebrated yearly in the Gayant feast. Seized (1667) by Louis XIV; capitulated (1710) to Marlborough; retaken (1712) by Villars, and restored to France by Peace of Utrecht. Held by Germans 1914–18 and 1940–44, it was heavily damaged in both wars. Old spelling, Douay.

Douala or **Duala** (dōōä'lä), town (pop. estimate c.45,000), ⊙ Wouri region, SW Fr. Cameroons, on left shore of Wouri R. estuary (Cameroon River) and 130 mi. W of Yaoundé; 4°5'N 9°40'E. Chief seaport of Fr. Cameroons, with deepwater harbor; commercial center. Ships hardwoods, cacao, coffee, palm oil and kernels, ivory. Here converge the 2 railroads of the trust territory, one from Yaoundé, another from N'Kongsamba (terminating at suburb of BONABERI). Sawmilling, palm-oil milling; mfg. of beer, cotton textiles, carbonated drinks, bricks; food processing, fishing. Rubber plantations in vicinity, large palm groves N. Airport, seaplane base. Has R.C. and Protestant missions, technical and agr. school, jr. col. for girls, meteorological station, health institute. Seat of vicar apostolic. By 19th cent. it was already known for its British and German factories. Nachtigal planted Ger. flag here, 1884. Former ⊙ Ger. Cameroons (1901–16) and ⊙ Fr. Cameroons (1940–46) under Free French.

Douarnenez (dwärnŭnĕz'), town (pop. 17,687), Finistère dept., W France, 12 mi. NW of Quimper, port on Douarnenez Bay (7–10 mi. wide, 13 mi. long) of the Atlantic with important sardine, tunny, and lobster fisheries; fish canning, smoking, and salting; construction of fishing boats; mfg. (tin cans, flour products, pharmaceuticals). Picturesque harbor dist.

Douaumont (dōō-ōmō'), fort on Verdun battlefield (First World War), Meuse dept., NE France, 5 mi. NE of Verdun. Lost and recaptured by French in 1916. Near by are a cemetery (with remains of 10,000 unidentified soldiers), and the renowned Trench of Bayonets (in which a Fr. unit was buried alive).

Douay, France: see DOUAI.

Double (dōō'blŭ), poorly drained region of Dordogne dept., SW France, bet. Isle and Dronne rivers, SW of Ribérac; cattle grazing, cheese making. Drainage of its 100 ponds begun by Trappists during reign of Napoleon III, but discontinued in 1902.

Double Island Point, SE Queensland, Australia, in Pacific Ocean, 13 mi. SE of Fraser Isl.; 25°56'S 153°13'E.

Double Mer (dōō'blŭ mâr'), lake (35 mi. long, 4 mi. wide), SE Labrador, N of L. Melville and W of Hamilton Inlet, into which it drains, at Rigolet, through 20-mi.-long channel; 54°5'N 59°W.

Double Mountain Fork of Brazos River, Texas: see BRAZOS RIVER.

Double Springs, town (pop. 524), ⊙ Winston co., NW Ala., 32 mi. W of Cullman; lumber, cotton.

Double Top Mountain (3,905 ft.), Ulster co., SE N.Y., in the Catskills, 27 mi. WNW of Kingston.

Doubletop Peak (11,715 ft.), W Wyo., 26 mi. ESE of Jackson; highest point in Gros Ventre Range.

Doubrava (dō'brävä), town (pop. 4,397), NE Silesia, Czechoslovakia, on railroad and 8 mi. ENE of Ostrava; intensive coal mining; large power plant, established 1896.

Doubs (dōō), department (□ 2,031; pop. 298,255), in old Franche-Comté prov., E France; ⊙ Besançon. Borders on Switzerland (E). Occupied by the central and N Jura. Drained NE-SW by Doubs, Loue, and Ognon rivers. Livestock raising, Gruyère cheese mfg., and lumbering carried on in mts. Lowland agr. (cereals, potatoes, wine) N of Doubs R. Dept. has important metallurgical dist. (centered on Montbéliard and extending along Doubs valley from Pont-de-Roide to L'Isle-sur-le-Doubs), which produces automobiles (Sochaux, Audincourt), bicycles (Beaulieu), hardware, auto parts and accessories (Seloncourt, Valentigney, Hérimoncourt). Besançon, center of France's watch and clock industry, also has artificial-silk mills. Montbeliard (strategically located in Belfort Gap) has metal, cotton, and clock factories. Pontarlier is known for its liqueur distilleries, and Morteau for its precision instruments. Smaller towns have cotton mills and clock workshops.

Doubs River, 270 mi. long, in Doubs, Jura, and Saône-et-Loire depts., E France, rises in the E Jura above Mouthe (just 55 mi., as the crow flies, from its mouth), flows NE, through L. of Saint-Point, past Pontarlier and Morteau. Below Lacou-Villers it forms L. of BRENETS (2.5 mi. long, ending in falls 88 ft. high) and Franco-Swiss border for c.25 mi. Throwing a loop into Switzerland S of Porrentruy, it then flows W, crossing the Lomont range, and enters Montbéliard industrial dist. at Pont-de-Roide. As far as L'Isle-sur-le-Doubs its valley is lined with metallurgical factories. Below Audincourt it turns SW, flowing parallel to its early course, past Besançon and Dôle, to the Saône at Verdun-sur-le-Doubs. Bet. Voujeaucourt and Dôle it is accompanied by (or lends its channel to) the Rhone-Rhine Canal. Receives the Loue (left).

Doubt, River of, Brazil: see ROOSEVELT RIVER.

Doubtful Sound, inlet of Tasman Sea, Fiordland Natl. Park, SW S.Isl., New Zealand; separated from Thompson Sound by Secretary Isl.; 20 mi. long, 2 mi. wide.

Douce Mountain (2,384 ft.), NE Co. Wicklow, Ireland, 8 mi. SW of Bray.

Doucette (dōōsĕt'), village (1940 pop. 566), Tyler co., E Texas, c.55 mi. NNW of Beaumont, in agr., lumbering area.

Douchy-les-Mines (dōōshē'-lā-mēn'), town (pop. 3,846), Nord dept., N France, on Selle R. near its mouth on the Escaut, and 2 mi. S of Denain; coal-mining center. Until 1938, called Douchy.

Doudeville (dōōdvēl'), village (pop. 1,271), Seine-Inférieure dept., N France, 19 mi. SW of Dieppe; dairying.

Doué-la-Fontaine (dōōā'-lä-fōtĕn'), town (pop. 3,297), Maine-et-Loire dept., W France, 10 mi. WSW of Saumur; dairying, alcohol distilling, cement mfg. Lignite and coal deposits near by. Built atop abandoned stone quarry in which theatrical performances were held in 15th–17th cent. Until 1933, called Doué.

Douentza (dwĕntsä'), village (pop. c.2,250), S Fr. Sudan, Fr. West Africa, 120 mi. S of Timbuktu; market, mfg. of leatherwork.

Douéra (dwārä'), village (pop. 2,658), Alger dept., N central Algeria, 10 mi. SW of Algiers; wine-growing.

Dougga (dōōg-gä'), anc. *Thugga*, ruined city in N central Tunisia, 4 mi. SSW of Teboursouk. Preserved are a Punic mausoleum (2d cent. B.C.); temples, arches, a theater (with Corinthian columns), an aqueduct of Roman times, and a Byzantine fortress.

Doughbraneen, Ireland: see BLACK HEAD.

Dougherty (dŏ'rŭrtē), county (□ 326; pop. 43,617), SW Ga.; ⊙ Albany. Coastal plain agr. (pecans, peanuts, corn, cattle) and timber area intersected by Flint R.; mfg. at Albany. Formed 1853.

Dougherty. **1** (dô'rŭtē) Town (pop. 212), Cerro Gordo co., N Iowa, 18 mi. SSE of Mason City; dairy products, feed; sand and gravel pits. **2** (dô'ŭrtē, -hŭr-) Town (pop. 341), Murray co., S Okla., 16 mi. NNE of Ardmore, and on Washita R.

Douglas, town (pop. 690), SE Alaska, on E Douglas Isl., in Alexander Archipelago, on Gastineau Channel (bridge), opposite Juneau; residential section for Juneau gold miners and mill employees. Salmon cannery, foundry. Grew up after 1881 during operation of TREADWELL mines.

Douglas, village (pop. 204), Northern Dist., Br. Honduras, on Hondo R. and 9 mi. WSW of Corozal; corn, sugar cane.

Douglas, village (pop. estimate 500), SE Ont., on Bonnechère R. and 23 mi. SE of Pembroke; dairying, mixed farming.

Douglas, town district (1939 pop. 20,012), ⊙ Isle of Man, England, on SE coast, 50 mi. W of Barrow-in-Furness; 54°10'N 4°29'W; port and seaside resort, with metalworking, rope making, and pharmaceutical mfg. Has piers, long esplanade, Tower of Refuge (built by founder of Royal Natl. Lifeboat Inst.), and Manx Mus. Scene of annual automobile race. Just SE is promontory of Douglas Head, site of lighthouse.

Douglas, Gaelic *Dubhghlas*, town (pop. 816), SE central Co. Cork, Ireland, 2 mi. SE of Cork; woolen milling, clothing mfg.

Douglas, town and parish (pop. 2,948), S central Lanark, Scotland, on Douglas Water and 9 mi. SSW of Lanark; agr. market; coal mining. Douglas Castle, Scott's "Castle Dangerous," has been replaced by modern mansion of earls of Home. Church of St. Bride (12th cent.) contains many graves of Douglas family. Cameronian Regiment was raised here in 1689 (monument).

Douglas, town (pop. 2,537), NE Cape Prov., U. of So. Afr., on Vaal R. (bridge) and 7 mi. E of its mouth on Orange R., 65 mi. WSW of Kimberley, in Griqualand West; agr. center (stock, grain, fruit, cotton); dairying, lime mfg. Town changed hands several times during South African War.

Douglas. **1** County (□ 843; pop. 3,507), central Colo.; ⊙ Castle Rock. Wheat and livestock area, bounded W by South Platte R. Part of Pike Natl. Forest in W. Formed 1861. **2** County (□ 201; pop. 12,173), NW central Ga.; ⊙ Douglasville. Bounded SE by Chattahoochee R. Piedmont agr. (cotton, corn, melons, vegetables, apples, peaches), livestock, poultry, and timber area. Formed 1870. **3** County (□ 420; pop. 16,706), E central Ill.; ⊙ Tuscola. Agr. (corn, wheat, soybeans, broomcorn, livestock, poultry; dairy products). Mfg. (brooms, road machinery, oil tanks, burial vaults, caskets, office equipment, food products, wood products). Drained by Embarrass and Kaskaskia rivers. Formed 1859. **4** County (□ 468; pop. 34,086), E Kansas; ⊙ Lawrence. Gently sloping agr. area, bounded on N by Kansas R. Grain, livestock, truck. Scattered oil and gas fields (E). Formed 1855. **5** County (□ 637; pop. 21,304), W Minn.; ⊙ Alexandria. Resort and agr. area watered by Long Prairie R. and numerous lakes. Dairy products, livestock, grain, poultry. Formed 1858. **6** County (□ 809; pop. 12,638), S Mo.; ⊙ Ava. In the Ozarks; drained by North Fork of White R. Resort, agr. region (especially dairy cattle, poultry, corn); pine, oak timber. Parts of Mark Twain Natl. Forest are here. Formed 1857. **7** County (□ 335; pop. 281,020), E Nebr.; ⊙ Omaha. Industrial region bounded W by Platte R., E by Missouri R. and Iowa; drained by Elkhorn R. Mfg. and food processing at Omaha; livestock, grain. Formed 1854. **8** County (□ 724; pop. 2,029), W Nev.; ⊙ Minden. Irrigated region bordering on Calif. and watered by Carson R. Livestock, dairy products. Foothills of Sierra Nevada throughout, part of L. Tahoe in NW. Formed 1851. **9** County (□ 5,062; pop. 54,549), SW Oregon; ⊙ Roseburg. Mtn. area bounded W by the Pacific; crossed by Umpqua R. Fruit, poultry; lumber milling. Part of Siuslaw Natl. Forest is in W, in Coast Range; part of Umpqua Natl. Forest is in E, in Cascade Range. Formed 1852. **10** County (□ 435; pop. 5,636), SE S.Dak.; ⊙ Armour; agr. and cattle-raising area. Livestock, cattle feed, dairy produce, poultry, grain. Formed 1883. **11** County (□ 1,841; pop. 10,817), central Wash.; ⊙ Waterville. Plateau area bounded N and W by Columbia R. Fruit, wheat, hay, oats, cattle; clay, limestone. Formed 1883. **12** County (□ 1,310; pop. 46,715), extreme NW Wis.; ⊙ Superior. Bounded W by Minn., N by St. Louis R. (on Minn. border) and L. Superior. Generally wooded lake area, drained by St. Croix, Eau Claire, and Black rivers. Dairying, cattle raising, limited farming on cutover forest land. Heavy industry at Superior, a major port. Pattison State Park containing Big Manitou Falls is here. Formed 1854.

Douglas. 1 City (pop. 9,442), Cochise co., SE Ariz., on Mex. line and c.105 mi. SE of Tucson; alt. 4,026 ft. Copper-smelting center, resort, and port of entry (with immigration and agr. quarantine stations) in livestock area; mfg. (gypsum products, furniture, clothing, bricks). Copper and gypsum mines, lime quarries in vicinity. Founded c.1900, inc. 1905. Has international airport. **2** Town (pop. 1), Lincoln co., SE Ark., on Arkansas R. and 29 mi. ESE of Pine Bluff. **3** City (pop. 7,428), ⊙ Coffee co., S central Ga., 34 mi. NW of Waycross; tobacco market and processing center; mfg. of clothing, naval stores, lumber. Railroad, machine shops. Has state jr. col. Inc. as town 1895, as city 1897. **4** Town (pop. 2,624), Worcester co., S Mass., 14 mi. SSE of Worcester, near R.I. line; woolens. Settled c.1721, inc. 1746. Includes village of East Douglas (pop. 1,846). **5** Village (pop. 447), Allegan co., SW Mich., 19 mi. WNW of Allegan, and on Kalamazoo R. near its mouth on L. Michigan; peach packing. Resort, with art colony. **6** Village (pop. 213), Otoe co., SE Nebr., 20 mi. SE of Lincoln and on branch of Little Nemaha R. **7** Village (pop. 236), Ward co., central N.Dak., 30 mi. SSW of Minot. **8** Town (pop. 114), Garfield co., N Okla., 15 mi. SE of Enid, in agr. area. **9** Town (pop. 2,544), ⊙ Converse co., E central Wyo., on N.Platte R. and 50 mi. E of Casper; alt. 4,815 ft. Trade center in livestock and oil region; dairy and poultry products, grain, clover seed, timber, beverages. State fairgrounds are here. Near by are Ayer's Park Natural Bridge and site of Fort Fetterman, important supply depot (1867–82) during Indian Wars. Town laid out 1886 with coming of railroad.

Douglas, Cape, S Alaska, at base of Alaska Peninsula, at N end of Shelikof Strait 80 mi. NNW of Kodiak; 58°51′N 153°16′W.

Douglas, Fort, Utah: see SALT LAKE CITY.

Douglas Dam, Sevier co., E Tenn., in French Broad R., 22 mi. E of Knoxville. A major TVA dam (202 ft. high, 1,705 ft. long) for flood control and power; completed 1943. Impounds Douglas Reservoir (□ 49; capacity 1,514,100 acre-ft.; 43.1 mi. long) in Sevier, Jefferson, and Cocke counties.

Douglas Hall, village in Colvend and Southwick parish, SE Kirkcudbright, Scotland, on Solway Firth, 6 mi. SE of Dalbeattie; seaside resort.

Douglas Island (18 mi. long, 3–7 mi. wide), SE Alaska, bet. Admiralty Isl. (NE) and mainland (SW), W of Juneau across Gastineau Channel (bridge); 58°16′N 134°30′W; rises to 3,515 ft. Douglas town in E. Fishing, fish processing. Site of famous TREADWELL mine.

Douglas Lake, Cheboygan co., N Mich., 10 mi. SW of Cheboygan, in wooded resort area; c.4 mi. long, 2 mi. wide; fishing, boating. Univ. of Mich. Biological Station is here.

Douglas Reef, Pacific Ocean: see PARECE VELA.

Douglass, city (pop. 729), Butler co., SE Kansas, on Walnut R. and 21 mi. SE of Wichita; livestock, grain. Oil wells near by.

Douglas Station, village (pop. estimate 150), SW Man., 12 mi. ENE of Brandon; grain, stock.

Douglaston (dŭ′glŭstŭn), SE N.Y., a residential section of NE Queens borough of New York city, on Little Neck Bay.

Douglastown, village (pop. estimate c.500), NE N.B., on Miramichi R. and 3 mi. W of Chatham; timber-shipping port.

Douglasville, town (pop. 3,400), ⊙ Douglas co., NW central Ga., 21 mi. W of Atlanta; clothing mfg. Inc. 1875.

Douglas Water, village in Douglas parish, S Lanark, Scotland, on Douglas Water and 5 mi. S of Lanark; coal mining.

Douglas Water, river, Lanark, Scotland, rises 6 mi. SW of Douglas near Ayrshire border, flows 20 mi. NE, past Douglas, to the Clyde 3 mi. S of Lanark.

Douglas West, village in Douglas parish, S Lanark, Scotland, near Douglas Water, just W of Douglas; coal mining.

Doukato, Cape, or **Cape Doukaton** (do͞okä′tôn), S tip of Leukas, one of Ionian Isls., Greece; 38°34′N 20°32′E. Ruins of temple of Apollo. The anc. Cape Leucadia, a promontory from which, in legend, Sappho threw herself. Sometimes spelled Ducato.

Doukkala, Fr. Morocco: see MAZAGAN.

Doulaincourt (do͞olĕko͞or′), village (pop. 872), Haute-Marne dept., NE France, 15 mi. NNE of Chaumont; small metalworks; lingerie mfg.

Doulevant-le-Château (do͞olůvä′-lů-shätō′), village (pop. 462), Haute-Marne dept., NE France, on Blaise R. and 14 mi. NE of Bar-sur-Aube; agr. tools.

Doullens (do͞olã′), town (pop. 3,955), Somme dept., N France, on the Authie and 18 mi. N of Amiens; cotton spinning, fertilizer mfg. (from local phosphate). Has 16th–17th-cent. citadel and town hall. Here, in 1918, Foch was appointed commander-in-chief of Allied armies. Heavily damaged in Second World War.

Doullut Canal, La.: see EMPIRE.

Douma, Syria: see DUMA.

Doumé (do͞o′mā), village, Haut-Nyong region, SE central Fr. Cameroons, 30 mi. NE of Abong-M'Bang; trade center in coffee-growing area. Sawmills near by (NE).

Doumeira, Cape (do͞omā′rä), on Red Sea at Fr. Somaliland–Eritrea line, at N end of Bab el Mandeb strait; 12°42′N 43°9′E. Police post. Offshore is small Doumeira Isl., belonging to Fr. Somaliland.

Doummar, Syria: see DUMMAR.

Doune (do͞on), burgh (1931 pop. 822; 1951 census 834), S Perthshire, Scotland, on Teith R. (16th-cent. bridge) and 4 mi. W of Dunblane; agr. market, formerly noted for mfg. of Highland pistols and as Highland cattle market. Has remains of 15th-cent. Doune Castle, built by duke of Albany and figuring in Scott's *Waverley*. Just W is cotton-milling village of Deanston.

Doupov (dō′pôf), Ger. *Duppau* (do͞o′pou), town (pop. 525), W Bohemia, Czechoslovakia, 10 mi. SW of Kadan; rail terminus.

Dour (do͞or), town (pop. 11,876), Hainaut prov., SW Belgium, 9 mi. WSW of Mons; coal mining; cable mfg.

Doura, Syria: see DURA.

Dourado (dōrä′do͞o), city (pop. 2,500), E central São Paulo, Brazil, on railroad spur, and 27 mi. WSW of São Carlos; oranges, livestock.

Dourados (dōrä′do͞os), city (pop. 1,821), S Mato Grosso, Brazil, 55 mi. NE of Ponta Porã; maté-shipping center. In Ponta-Porã territory, 1943–46.

Dourados River, Brazil: see IVINHEMA RIVER.

Dourbie River (do͞orbē′), Gard and Aveyron depts., S France, rises in Cévennes near Valleraugue, flows 50 mi. W in canyon bet. Causse Noir (N) and Causse du Larzac (S), to the Tarn at Millau.

Dourdan (do͞ordã′), town (pop. 3,166), Seine-et-Oise dept., N central France, 12 mi. SW of Rambouillet, at SE edge of Forest of Rambouillet; cattle market. Has 13th-cent. castle (slightly damaged 1939–45) and 12th–16th-cent. church.

Dourges (do͞orzh), town (pop. 4,602), Pas-de-Calais dept., N France, on Haute-Deûle Canal and 7 mi. E of Lens; coal mines, metalworks.

Dourgne (do͞or′nyů), village (pop. 635), Tarn dept., S France, on W slope of Montagne Noire, 10 mi. SSW of Castres; hosiery mfg. Slate and stone quarries. Near by are 2 modern Benedictine abbeys.

Douro Litoral (dō′ro͞o lĕto͞oräl′), province (□ 1,269; 1940 pop. 1,104,925), N Portugal, formed 1936 from S part of old Entre Douro e Minho prov. and from NW part of old Beira prov.; ⊙ Oporto. It contains Pôrto dist. and small sections of Aveiro and Viseu dists. Cities: Oporto, Penafiel.

Douro River (Port. dō′ro͞o), Sp. *Duero* (dwā′rō), anc. *Durius*, in Spain and Portugal, one of the longest (c.475 mi.) rivers of the Iberian Peninsula. Flows generally W to the Atlantic. From its source high in the Sierra de Urbión in Old Castile, N central Spain, it turns southward in a wide curve of c.75 mi., flowing past anc. ruins of Numantia and the city of Soria to Almazán, then W, past Aranda de Duero and Zamora, draining the entire N section of the central plateau (Meseta) in Old Castile and Leon, to the Port. border, which it follows in a SW course for c.70 mi. before again turning W through N Portugal, emptying into the Atlantic at Foz de Douro 3 mi. W of Oporto, the major port on its estuary. While its mid-course is relatively even, its upper course and, especially, lower course in Portugal, cut through steep gorges, interrupted by cataracts of difficult, intermittent navigability. Its drainage basin occupies roughly 30,500 sq. mi. Among the chief tributaries are: right—Pisuerga, Arlanzón, Esla; left—Eresma-Adaja, Tormes. The Douro system is used extensively for irrigation and hydroelectric power.

Douskon (do͞o′skôn), Albanian *Nemërçkë* (nä′mûrchkû) or *Nemërçka* (nä′mûrchkä), mountain ridge in S Albania and Epirus, Greece, SW of Aoos (Vijosë) R.; rises to 7,247 ft. in Mt. Merope (Meropi), 13 mi. W of Konitsa.

Dousman (douz′mŭn), village (pop. 328), Waukesha co., SE Wis., on Bark R. and 28 mi. W of Milwaukee, in farm area.

Doussard (do͞osär′), village (pop. 304), Haute-Savoie dept., SE France, near S tip of L. of Annecy, 10 mi. SSE of Annecy; summer resort; cheese mfg.

Douthat (dou′thĭt) or **Century,** mining village (pop. c.700), Ottawa co., extreme NE Okla., 7 mi. NNE of Miami; lead, zinc.

Douvaine (do͞ovĕn′), village (pop. 619), Haute-Savoie dept., SE France, near S shore of L. Geneva and Swiss border, 10 mi. NE of Geneva; cheese mfg.

Douve River (do͞ov), Manche dept., NW France, rises in Cotentin Peninsula 4 mi. S of Cherbourg, flows 40 mi. SE, past Saint-Sauveur-le-Vicomte, to the Vire (near its marshy mouth) NE of Carentan. Also called Ouve R.

Douvres (do͞o′vrů), village (pop. 841), Calvados dept., NW France, near English Channel, 8 mi. N of Caen. Stubbornly defended by Germans in Normandy invasion (June, 1944) of Second World War. La Délivrande (1 mi. NE) is a pilgrimage place with 19th-cent. basilica (damaged).

Douvrin (do͞ovrē′), town (pop. 3,704), Pas-de-Calais dept., N France, 9 mi. E of Béthune; refractories.

Doux River (do͞o), Ardèche dept., S France, rises in the Monts du Vivarais, flows c.35 mi. generally E, past Lamastre, to the Rhone just above Tournon.

Douz (do͞oz), village, SW Tunisia, in the Nefzaoua oasis, near SE edge of the Chott Djerid, 60 mi. SE of Tozeur; dates, olives.

Douzy (do͞ozē′), village (pop. 757), Ardennes dept., N France, on the Chiers and 5 mi. ESE of Sedan; makes agr. machinery and tools.

Dovadola (dôvä′dôlä), town (pop. 1,872), Forlì prov., Emilia-Romagna, N central Italy, on Montone R. and 11 mi. S of Faenza.

Dovbysh (dôv′bĭsh), town (1926 pop. 2,075), W Zhitomir oblast, Ukrainian SSR, 32 mi. WNW of Zhitomir; ceramic industry. Until 1944, Markhlevsk. Pop. largely Polish.

Dove, river: see DOVE RIVER.

Dove Bay (dŭv) (50 mi. wide at mouth, extends c.50 mi. inland), NE Greenland; 76°30′N 20°30′W. Mouth protected by Great Koldewey isl.; Germania Land peninsula forms N shore. Inland ice-cap descends to E shore of bay.

Dove Creek, town (pop. 702), Dolores co., SW Colo., bet. Dolores R. and Utah line, 65 mi. NW of Durango; alt. c.6,850 ft. Diversified farming; beans, wheat, potatoes; timber.

Dovedale, England: see DOVE RIVER.

Dove Holes, England: see CHAPEL-EN-LE-FRITH.

Dover, anc. *Dubris* or *Portus Dubris*, municipal borough (1931 pop. 41,097; 1951 census 35,217), E Kent, England, 65 mi. ESE of London, on the Strait of Dover, at foot of fortified chalk cliffs; 51°7′N 1°19′E. Chief of the CINQUE PORTS and most important English Channel port, closest to France (Calais is 22 mi.). Terminal of cross-Channel services to Calais and Ostend, and of train ferry to Dunkirk. Extensive harbor, improved in late 19th and early 20th cent., is protected by breakwaters (Admiralty and Prince of Wales piers). Industries: mfg. of paper, chemicals, concrete, and flour. Just W is well-known Shakespeare Cliff where the 1st coal in Kent was discovered (1822). Small Dover R., which flows through town, gave it its name. Dover was site of Roman and Saxon forts; in 1216 Hubert de Burgh defended it against Fr. attack. In Civil War it was captured 1642 by Parliamentarians. Charles II landed here 1660. In First World War it was an important naval base ("Dover Patrol"). In Second World War it was chief port for Dunkirk evacuation, and was under constant fire, 1940–44, from Ger. long-range guns in France. A series of subterranean caves and tunnels in the cliffs served as shelters. Among town's features are Dover Castle, of Roman or Saxon origin; 13th-cent. Maison Dieu Hall of Hubert de Burgh; the partly Roman lighthouse, reputedly built c.43 A.D.; and anc. church of St. Mary-in-Castro, rebuilt 1051.

Dover, town and port (pop. 586), SE Tasmania, 35 mi. SSW of Hobart and on Port Esperance (inlet of D'Entrecasteaux Channel); fruit cannery, sawmills. Crayfish.

Dover. 1 Town (pop. 510), Pope co., N central Ark., 8 mi. N of Russellville. **2** City (pop. 6,223), ⊙ Delaware and Kent co., central Del., 40 mi. S of Wilmington and on St. Jones R., at head of navigation, near Silver L.; 39°10′N 75°31′W; alt. 34 ft.; second-largest city in state. Market and shipping center in rich agr. and fruitgrowing region; canning, cheese-making, mfg. (hosiery, paint, rubber products). Air Force base. Old statehouse (partly dating from 1722) has been capitol since 1777. Has children's home. State col. for Negroes is near by. Settled 1683, laid out 1717, inc. as town 1829, as city 1929. **3** Village (pop. 191), Bureau co., N Ill., 6 mi. NE of Princeton, in agr. and bituminous-coal area. **4** Town (pop. 334), Mason co., NE Ky., on the Ohio and 10 mi. NW of Maysville. **5** Former village, Piscataquis co., Maine: see DOVER-FOXCROFT. **6** Residential town (pop. 1,722), Norfolk co., E Mass., on Charles R. and 14 mi. SW of Boston. Settled c.1635, set off from Dedham 1784. **7** Village (pop. 263), Olmsted co., SE Minn., 17 mi. ESE of Rochester; dairy products. **8** Town (pop. 173), Lafayette co., W central Mo., near Missouri R., 10 mi. E of Lexington. **9** City (pop. 15,874), ⊙ Strafford co., SE N.H., 10 mi. NW of Portsmouth, at falls (33-ft. drop) of Cocheco R., near its confluence with Piscataqua R. Mfg. (textiles, wood products, leather goods, machinery, monuments). Has 17th-cent. garrison house, 18th-cent. Friends' meetinghouse. Settled 1623, one of 1st towns in N.H.; inc. as city 1855. Many near-by towns were formerly in Dover. **10** Industrial town (pop. 11,174), Morris co., N central N.J., on Rockaway R. and 7 mi. NW of Morristown; metal products, machinery, rock wool, wood products, clothing; truck, dairy products. Formerly an iron center; near-by explosives plants brought expansion in early 1940s. Picatinny Arsenal and U.S. naval rocket experiment station (at Lake Denmark) are near. Settled 1722, inc. 1869. Grew as port on old Morris Canal. **11** Town (pop. 638), Craven co., E N.C., 9 mi. SE of Kinston, sawmilling. **12** Village, Cuyahoga co., Ohio: see WESTLAKE. **13** City (pop. 9,852), Tuscarawas co., E Ohio, just NW of New Philadelphia, and on Tuscarawas R., in mining (coal, fire clay) area; mfg. of steel, electric-light bulbs, clay products, chemicals, cheese, wood products, vacuum cleaners; oil refining. Laid out 1807. Dover Reservoir (capacity 203,000 acre-ft.) is impounded by near-by flood-control dam on the Tuscarawas. **14** Borough (pop. 809), York co., S Pa., 6 mi. WNW of York. **15** Village (1940 pop. 709), ⊙ Stewart co., NW Tenn., on Cumberland R. and 27 mi. W of Clarksville, in agr. area. FORT DONELSON NATIONAL MILITARY PARK is near by. **16** Town (pop. 252), Windham co., SE Vt., 13 mi. NW of Brattleboro; lumber. Partly in Green Mtn. Natl. Forest.

Dover, Strait of, Fr. *Pas de Calais* (pä dü kälā'), anc. *Fretum Gallicum*, strait separating England from France and connecting English Channel with North Sea. Narrowest points, bet. Dover and Cape Gris-Nez and bet. South Foreland and Cape Gris-Nez, both 21 mi. wide. Chief riparian ports: Dover, Folkestone, Calais, and Boulogne. Ridge Shoals, a central shallow, are marked by Varne Lightship (50°55'N 1°10'E), 11 mi. SSE of Folkestone. Strait has been scene of several naval actions: in 1216 Hubert de Burgh defeated invading French; in 1588 the Armada received 1st major check here. In May–June, 1940, the Allied evacuation from Dunkirk was made across the Strait of Dover. Regular shipping services: Folkestone–Boulogne, Dover–Calais, Ostend–Dunkirk (train ferry).

Dover Center, Ohio: see WESTLAKE.

Dovercourt, England: see HARWICH.

Dover-Foxcroft, town (pop. 4,218), including Dover-Foxcroft village (pop. 2,566), ⊙ Piscataquis co., central Maine, c.35 mi. NW of Bangor, astride Piscataquis R., which furnishes power for woolen and wood-products mills; potatoes shipped. Formed 1922 by union of Foxcroft (settled 1806, inc. 1812) and Dover (settled 1803, inc. 1822).

Dove River (dŭv, dōv), Derby and Stafford, England, rises 4 mi. SW of Buxton, flows 40 mi. S and SE, forming much of Derby-Stafford boundary, to Trent R. 3 mi. NE of Burton-upon-Trent. It is associated with Izaak Walton; the valley of Dovedale, below Hartington, has been a favorite theme for painters and poets.

Dover Plains, village (1940 pop. 730), Dutchess co., SE N.Y., near Conn. line, 19 mi. ENE of Poughkeepsie; mfg. of paper; cider, dairy products, poultry, truck.

Dovey River, Welsh *Dyfi River* (dŭ'vē), Merioneth and Montgomery, Wales, rises 9 mi. ENE of Dolgelley, flows 30 mi. S and SW, past Mallwyd and Machynlleth, to Cardigan Bay of Irish Sea at Aberdovey.

Dovista, Greece: see PAPPAS.

Dovje, Yugoslavia: see MOJSTRANA.

Dovlen, Bulgaria: see DEVIN.

Dovolenskoye, Russian SFSR: see DOVOLNOYE.

Dovolnoye or **Dovol'noye** (dŭvôl'nŭyŭ), village (1939 pop. over 2,000), S Novosibirsk oblast, Russian SFSR, 55 mi. SSW of Kargat; dairy farming. Also called Dovolenskoye.

Dovrat (dōvrät') or **Davrath** (dävrät'), agr. settlement (pop. 120), Lower Galilee, N Israel, near S foot of Mt. Tabor, 5 mi. SE of Nazareth. Founded 1946.

Dovray (dŭv'rē), village (pop. 127), Murray co., SW Minn., 12 mi. ENE of Slayton; dairy products.

Dovre (dôv'rŭ), village (pop. 216; canton pop. 3,019), Opland co., S central Norway, in the Gudbrandsdal, on Lagen R., on railroad and 75 mi. NW of Lillehammer, at S foot of the Dovrefjell; dairying. Has church built in 1740.

Dovrefjell (dôv'rŭfyĕl), mountain plateau (c.100 mi. long, 40 mi. wide) in Opland, Hedmark, and More og Romsdal counties, S central Norway, extends bet. Romsdal Fjord (W), the Romsdal and Gudbrandsdal (SW), the Osterdal (E), and the Trollheimen (N). Rises to 7,498 ft. in the Snohetta (snû'hĕt-tä), Nor. *Snøhetta*, 70 mi. SE of Kristiansund; 62°19'N 9°15'E. Skrimkolla (skrĭm'-kôl-lä) mtn., 8 mi. WNW of the Snohetta, rises to 6,509 ft. Plateau is crossed N–S by Dovre RR (opened 1921) bet. Oslo and Trondheim, which follows anc. royal coronation route to Trondheim.

Dowa (dō'wä), town, Central Prov., Nyasaland, 25 mi. NNE of Lilongwe; tobacco, cotton, corn. African hosp.

Dowager Island (□ 53), SW B.C., in SE arm of Hecate Strait, 20 mi. NNW of Bella Bella; 52°25'N 128°22'W; 10 mi. long, 5 mi. wide; rises to 2,360 ft.

Dowagiac (dōwô'jăk), city (pop. 6,542), Cass co., SW Mich., 34 mi. SW of Kalamazoo, on short Dowagiac Creek, in farm area (wheat, corn, celery). Mfg. (stoves, furnaces, hot-water heaters, air-conditioning equipment, rifle barrels, sporting goods, flour); timber. Resort. Settled 1848; inc. as village 1863, as city 1877.

Dowally, Scotland: see DUNKELD AND DOWALLY.

Dow City, town (pop. 524), Crawford co., W Iowa, on Boyer R. and 9 mi. SW of Denison, in agr. area.

Dowell (dou'ŭl), mining village (pop. 616), Jackson co., SW Ill., 15 mi. NW of Herrin, in bituminous-coal and agr. area.

Dowelltown (doul'tŭn), town (pop. 262), De Kalb co., central Tenn., 8 mi. NW of Smithville.

Dowlais (dou'lŭs), town (pop. 10,220) in Merthyr Tydfil county borough, NE Glamorgan, Wales; steel milling, coal mining.

Dowlaiswaram or **Dowlaishwaram** (doulĭsh'vŭrŭm), town (pop. 11,383), East Godavari dist., NE Madras, India, on left bank of Godavari R., at head of delta, and 4 mi. S of Rajahmundry; rice milling; engineering works. Headworks (including dam completed 1850) of delta's navigable irrigation-canal system are just S. Building-stone quarries near by. Fruit-canning plant 3 mi. SE, at Kadiam (rail station). Formerly spelled Dowlaishweram.

Dowling Lake (6 mi. long, 5 mi. wide), SE central Alta., 35 mi. NE of Drumheller and 8 mi. S of Sullivan L. Drains S into Red Deer R.

Down, county (□ 951.6; 1937 pop. 210,687; 1951 census 241,105), Ulster, SE Northern Ireland; ⊙ Downpatrick. Bounded by the Irish Sea (E and SE), Carlingford Lough (S), and cos. Armagh (W) and Antrim (N). Drained by Bann, Newry, and Lagan rivers. Coastline is deeply indented by Belfast Lough, Strangford Lough, Dundrum Bay, and Carlingford Lough. Surface is irregular and hilly, with fertile valleys along the rivers. In SE are Mourne Mts., rising to 2,796 ft. on Slieve Donard. Flax, oats, potatoes are chief crops; sheep are raised. Granite is quarried in Mourne Mts.; there is some iron mining. Sea fisheries are important. Leading industries are linen, cotton, woolen milling; mfg. of leather, hosiery, lace, shirts, rope, fish nets, agr. implements. Towns are Downpatrick, Newry, Newtownards, Bangor, Warrenpoint, Banbridge, and Dromore. There are many ruins of anc. castles, abbeys, raths, and stone monuments. Downpatrick and Dromore are religious centers with associations with St. Patrick. Population is largely Protestant.

Downend, England: see MANGOTSFIELD.

Downers Grove, residential village (pop. 11,886), Du Page co., NE Ill., W of Chicago and 15 mi. E of Aurora, in dairying, poultry- and truck-farming area; mfg. (tools, portable buildings, electric hoists and machinery, foot remedies); nurseries. Settled 1832, inc. 1873.

Downey. **1** Unincorporated town (1940 pop. 9,364), Los Angeles co., S Calif., suburb 10 mi. SE of downtown Los Angeles, in industrial and agr. (truck, citrus fruit) dist.; mfg. (aircraft, cement and asbestos products, machinery, soap). **2** Village (pop. 748), Bannock co., SE Idaho, 15 mi. NE of Malad City in agr. and grazing area; alt. 4,860 ft.; cheese.

Downfield, Scotland: see DUNDEE.

Downham (dou'nŭm), town and parish (pop. 2,044), in Isle of Ely, N Cambridge, England, 3 mi. NNW of Ely; agr. market. Has remains of 15th-cent. palace of bishops of Ely, and 13th–14th-cent. church. Also called Little Downham.

Downham Market, urban district (1931 pop. 2,465; 1951 census 2,759), W Norfolk, England, on Ouse R. and 11 mi. S of King's Lynn; agr. market, with farm-implement works and flour mills. Has 15th-cent. church.

Downhill, fishing village, N Co. Londonderry, Northern Ireland, on the coast 7 mi. WNW of Coleraine; resort.

Downieville (dou'nēvĭl), village (pop.c. 350), ⊙ Sierra co., NE Calif., in the Sierra Nevada, on North Yuba R. and 25 mi. SW of Portola. Gold mining (since gold rush days) in region. Winter-sports area near by.

Downing. **1** City (pop. 453), Schuyler co., N Mo., near North Fabius R., 9 mi. ESE of Lancaster. **2** Village (pop. 295), Dunn co., W Wis., 14 mi. NW of Menomonie; dairying.

Downings, Gaelic *Na Dúine*, locality in N Co. Donegal, Ireland, on E shore of Sheep Haven, 5 mi. E of Dunfanaghy; fishing port; fish curing.

Downingtown, borough (pop. 4,948), Chester co., SE Pa., 28 mi. W of Philadelphia and on E branch of Brandywine Creek; paper, textiles, metal products. Inc. 1859.

Downpatrick (dounpă'trĭk), urban district (1937 pop. 3,372; 1951 census 3,878), ⊙ Co. Down, Northern Ireland, in E part of co., near Quoile R. just above its mouth on Strangford Lough, 21 mi. SE of Belfast; agr. market (oats, flax; sheep), with linen mills; hunting center. Seat of diocese of Down, it has long been a religious center; St. Patrick is said to have founded a church here c.440. Present cathedral dates from 1790. Downpatrick is one of chief centers of pilgrimage in Ireland; St. Patrick, St. Columba, and Bridget of Kildare are buried here; tall granite monolith is said to mark St. Patrick's grave. Near by are remains of Inch Abbey, founded 1180 by Sir John de Courcy, and of Monastery of Saul, reputedly founded by St. Patrick. There are also noted earthworks and Holy Wells of Struell. Town was of early importance and was residence of anc. kings of Ulster. Quoile Quay, 2 mi. NNE of Downpatrick, on Quoile R., is its port.

Downpatrick Head, promontory on the Atlantic, NW Co. Mayo, Ireland, 9 mi. NNW of Killala; 54°20'N 9°20'W.

Downs, 2 parallel low chalk hill ranges (average alt., 500 ft.) in S England, extending E from mid-Hampshire to the Channel coast, across Surrey, Sussex, and Kent. The North Downs, in Surrey and Kent, terminate at Dover, the South Downs, largely in Sussex, at Beachy Head. The 2 ranges enclose The Weald, and are cut by several small rivers, including Darent, Medway, and Great and Little Stour (North Downs), and Arun, Adur, and Ouse (South Downs). They provide excellent sheep pasturage ("Southdown sheep").

Downs. **1** Village (pop. 209), McLean co., central Ill., 8 mi. SE of Bloomington, in rich agr. area. **2** City (pop. 1,221), Osborne co., N Kansas, on North Fork Solomon R. and 22 mi. W of Beloit; produce-packing center in grain and livestock area; railroad repair shops, monument works. Inc. 1879.

Downs, The, roadstead bet. North Foreland and South Foreland in English Channel off Deal, E Kent, England; 8 mi. long, c.6 mi. wide, protected (except from strong south wind) by the Goodwin Sands. Scene of naval battles bet. Netherlands and Spain (1639), and bet. England and Netherlands (1666).

Downs Mountain, Wyo.: see WIND RIVER RANGE.

Downsview, N suburb (pop. estimate 500) of Toronto, S Ont.

Downsville. **1** Village (pop. 720), Delaware co., S N.Y., c.45 mi. E of Binghamton, in a resort area of the Catskills. Downsville Dam impounds PEPACTON RESERVOIR near here. **2** Village (pop. c.200), Dunn co., W Wis., on Red Cedar R. and 7 mi. S of Menomonie; granite quarrying.

Downton, town and parish (pop. 1,352), SE Wiltshire, England, on the Avon and 6 mi. SSE of Salisbury; agr. market in dairying and sheep-raising region; tanneries, agr.-implement works. Has medieval church; site of Saxon earthworks. Near by is prehistoric earthwork of Cleobury Ring.

Dows (douz), town (pop. 948), on Franklin-Wright co. line, N central Iowa, on Iowa R. and 37 mi. SSW of Mason City; dairy products, feed.

Doxaton or **Dhoxaton** (both: dhôksä'tôn), town (pop. 4,760), Drama nome, Macedonia, Greece, 6 mi. SE of Drama; tobacco, olive oil, beans, grain. Site of battle bet. Bulgarians and Greeks during the Second Balkan War, 1913.

Doyhof (doi'hŏf), fishing village (1939 pop. 57), SE Alaska, on W shore of Mitkof Isl., on Wrangell Narrows, just SW of Petersburg.

Doyle Colony, village (pop. 2,100, with adjacent Plane), Tulare co., central Calif.

Doylestown. **1** Village (pop. 1,358), Wayne co., N central Ohio, 12 mi. SE of Akron, in stock-raising and farming area. **2** Borough (pop. 5,262), ⊙ Bucks co., SE Pa., 23 mi. N of Philadelphia; agr., dairying; large seed farm; textiles, tapestries, paint. Settled 1735, laid out 1778, inc. 1838. **3** Village (pop. 261), Columbia co., S central Wis., near Crawfish R., 17 mi. SE of Portage, in farm area.

Doyline (doi'līn), village (pop. 1,170), Webster parish, NW La., 20 mi. E of Shreveport. Inc. after 1940.

Doyran, Yugoslavia: see DOJRAN.

Dozen (dō'zăn), island group (□51; pop. 16,068) of isl. group Oki-gunto, Shimane prefecture, Japan, in Sea of Japan, just SW of Dogo, 35 mi. N of Matsue, off SW Honshu. Includes NISHI-NO-SHIMA (largest isl.), NAKA-NO-SHIMA, CHIBURI-SHIMA, and several scattered islets. Generally mountainous, forested. Cattle raising, lumbering, fishing; rice, tea, raw silk, charcoal.

Dozier (dō'zhŭr), town (pop. 362), Crenshaw co., S Ala., on Conecuh R. and 14 mi. NE of Andalusia.

Dozmary Pool, lake, Cornwall, England: see BODMIN MOOR.

Dozulé (dôzülā'), village (pop. 559), Calvados dept., NW France, 15 mi. ENE of Caen; brick mfg., cider distilling.

Dozza (dô'tsä), village (pop. 493), Bologna prov., Emilia-Romagna, N central Italy, 4 mi. W of Imola; explosives.

Dra, wadi, Fr. Morocco: see DRA, OUED.

Dra, Cape (drä), sandy headland of southwesternmost Fr. Morocco, just NE of mouth of the Oued Dra, which marks border of Spanish Southern Protectorate of Morocco; 28°14'N 11°5'W. Also spelled Draa.

Dra, Oued, or **Oued Draa** (wĕd' drä'), Sp. *Uad Dráa,* intermittent stream (wadi) of NW Africa, forming Fr. Morocco's S border with Algeria and with SPANISH WEST AFRICA. Formed E of Ouarzazate by junction of 2 headstreams (Dadès and Imini) which rise on S slope of the High Atlas, it flows 1st SE in S Fr. Morocco across Saharan border ranges and past Zagora oasis, then turns abruptly SW near 30°N 5°30'W, and, henceforth a frontier stream, continues to the Atlantic SW of Cape Dra at 28°40'N 11°7'W; length, c.700 mi. Except in upper course, the Dra usually carries no water. Sometimes confused with the Uad Nun.

Drabble, Uruguay: see RODÓ.

Drabenderhöhe (drä'bĕn'dûrhû"ù), village (pop. 8,545), in former Prussian Rhine Prov., W Germany, after 1945 in North Rhine-Westphalia, 8 mi. SW of Gummersbach; forestry.

Drabescus, Greece: see DRAMA.

Drable, Uruguay: see RODÓ.

Drabov (drä'bûf), village (1926 pop. 5,921), W Poltava Oblast, Ukrainian SSR, 18 mi. N of Zolotonosha; metalworks.

Drachenfels (drä'khûnfĕls") [Ger.,=dragon's rock], mountain (1,053 ft.) in the Siebengebirge, W Germany, on right bank of the Rhine, just N of Honnef; crowned by 12th-cent. ruined fortress Drachenburg; well-known excursion point. Scene (according to legend) of Siegfried's triumph over the dragon.

Drachten (dräkh'tûn), town, Friesland prov., N Netherlands, 14 mi. ESE of Leeuwarden; limekilns, linseed-oil mills; mfg. of tobacco, leather products; food canning.

Drac River (dräk), Hautes-Alpes and Isère depts., SE France, rises on S slopes of Massif du Pelvoux in Dauphiné Alps, flows c.95 mi. generally NNW, through alternating valleys (Champsaur) and gorges to the Isère just below Grenoble. Subject to severe floods until construction of Sautet Dam. Hydroelectric plants 2 mi. S of La Mure, at Avignonet and Pont-de-Claix (electrochemical works). Receives the Bonne and the Romanche.

Dracut (drā'kŭt), town (pop. 8,666), Middlesex co., NE Mass., on the Merrimack, just N of Lowell; textile dyeing and printing; agr. trade. Settled 1664, inc. 1702.

Dra-el-Mizan (drä'-ĕl-mēzän'), village (pop. 1,373), Alger dept., N central Algeria, in Great Kabylia, 17 mi. SW of Tizi-Ouzou; rail-spur terminus. Olive-oil processing.

Drafa (drä'fû), village, W central Saurashtra, India, 35 mi. S of Jamnagar. Was ⊙ former petty state of Drafa, since 1948 merged with Saurashtra.

Dragalevtsi (drägälĕf'tsĕ), village (pop. 3,306), Sofia dist., W Bulgaria, S suburb of Sofia, at N foot of Vitosha Mts.; grain, livestock, truck. Has 14th-cent. monastery.

Draganesti (drûgûnĕsht'), Rum. *Drăgănești.* **1** Village (pop. 3,965), Bucharest prov., S Rumania, on railroad and 15 mi. NW of Giurgiu, in grain and tobacco region. **2** Village (pop. 5,003), Teleorman prov., S Rumania, 20 mi. SSE of Slatina; agr.

Draganesti-de-Targ (-dä-tûrg'), Rum. *Drăgănești-de-Târg,* village (pop. 1,364), Prahova prov., S central Rumania, on railroad and 14 mi. SE of Ploesti.

Draganovo (drägä'nôvô), village (pop. 5,465), Gorna Oryakhovitsa dist., N Bulgaria, on Yantra R. and 7 mi. NNE of Gorna Oryakhovitsa; fruit, truck, grain; oil-bearing plants.

Dragas or **Dragash** (both: drä'gäsh), Serbo-Croatian *Dragaš,* village (pop. 3,472), SW Serbia, Yugoslavia, at W foot of Shar Mts., 11 mi. SSW of Prizren, in the Metohija, near Albanian border.

Dragasani (drûgûshän'), Rum. *Drăgășani,* town (1948 pop. 9,737), Valcea prov., S central Rumania, in Walachia, on railroad and 30 mi. S of Ramnicu-Valcea; noted for its wine production (notably champagne) and extensive vineyards; flour milling. Tobacco growing in vicinity.

Drage River, Poland: see DRAWA RIVER.

Dragerton, village (pop. 3,453), Carbon co., central Utah, 22 mi. E of Price; coal-mining area.

Dragocaj, Dragochai, or **Dragochay** (all: drä'gôchī), Serbo-Croatian *Dragočaj,* village (pop. 5,808), NW Bosnia, Yugoslavia, 7 mi. NW of Banja Luka.

Dragogna River (drägô'nyä), Slovenian *Dragonja* (drä'gônyä), main river in Free Territory of Trieste, flows 20 mi. W to Gulf of Trieste of the Adriatic, forming Pirano Bay (salines).

Dragoman (drä'gômän), village (pop. 1,513), Sofia dist., W Bulgaria, 25 mi. NW of Sofia, in poorly drained area at Yugoslav border; customs rail station; rye, potatoes. Site of battles (1885) bet. Bulg. and Serbian armies.

Dragomerfalva, Rumania: see DRAGOMIRESTI.

Dragomesto, Greece: see ASTAKOS.

Dragomiresti (drägômērĕsht'), Rum. *Dragomirești.* **1** Village (pop. 884), Prahova prov., S central Rumania, near Dambovita R., 7 mi. W of Targoviste; oil and natural-gas wells. **2** Hung. *Dragomérfalva* (drŏ'gômârfŏl"vŏ), village (pop. 3,335), Rodna prov., NW Rumania, 25 mi. SE of Sighet; health resort with ferruginous springs on the W slopes of the Carpathians; also petroleum production. Has 18th-cent. wooden church. In Hungary, 1940–45.

Dragomirna, Rumania: see SUCEAVA, town.

Dragomirovo (drä'gômē"rôvô), village (pop. 3,084), Pleven dist., N Bulgaria, 8 mi. SSW of Svishtov; grain, hemp, livestock.

Dragomirovo, Tadzhik SSR: see PROLETARSK, Leninabad oblast.

Dragón, Bocas del, Venezuela-Trinidad: see DRAGON'S MOUTH.

Dragonera Island (drägōnā'rä), barren islet (c.2 mi. long, ⅓ mi. wide; pop. 4) off W Majorca, Balearic Isls., 17 mi. W of Palma.

Dragonja River, Free Territory of Trieste: see DRAGOGNA RIVER.

Dragon Run, Va.: see PIANKATANK RIVER.

Dragon's Mouth, Sp. *Bocas del Dragón* (bō'käs dĕl drägōn'), channel (c.12 mi. wide) of the Caribbean, bet. E tip of Paria Peninsula, NE Venezuela, and NW tip of Trinidad; links Gulf of Paria with the ocean.

Dragoon Mountains (drŭgōōn'), small range in Cochise co., NNE of Tombstone, SE Ariz. Mt. GLEN (7,520 ft.) is highest point. Copper is mined in Little Dragoon Mts., which form N extension of range.

Dragopsa (drägôp'sù), village (pop. 337), Ioannina nome, S Epirus, Greece, 10 mi. SW of Ioannina; petroleum deposits.

Dragor (drä'wûr), Dan. *Dragør,* town (pop. 2,149), Copenhagen amt, Denmark, on SE coast of Amager isl. and 7 mi. SE of Copenhagen, on the Oresund; fisheries.

Dragos-Voda (drä'gôsh-vô'dù), Rum. *Dragoș-Vodă,* village (pop. 2,210), Ialomita prov., SE Rumania, 18 mi. NNW of Calarasi; corn, barley, wheat.

Dragotsenka, Manchuria: see NALEMUTU.

Dragsfjard (dräks'fyërd"), Swedish *Dragsfjärd,* Finnish *Dragsfjärdi* (träks'fyërdē), commune (pop. 4,645), Turku-Pori co., SW Finland, on Gulf of Bothnia, 25 mi. NW of Hango. Includes BJORKBODA and DALSBRUK villages.

Draguignan (drägēnyä'), town (pop. 8,879), ⊙ Var dept., SE France, in Provence Alps, 40 mi. NE of Toulon; terminus of rail spur. Mfg. (olive oil, flour products, straw hats, soap), tanning; sericulture. Located at foot of Malmont (1,995 ft.), with picturesque old town preserving two 13th-cent. gates and part of a synagogue. Verdon R. gorge is 15 mi. N. U.S. military cemetery (Second World War) near by.

Dragutinovo, Yugoslavia: see MILOSEVO.

Drain, town (pop. 1,150), Douglas co., SW Oregon, 30 mi. SSW of Eugene; shipping point for turkeys, lumber; lumber milling.

Drake, village (pop. 112), NE New South Wales, Australia, 110 mi. SSW of Brisbane; mining center (gold, copper).

Drake, city (pop. 831), McHenry co., central N.Dak., 48 mi. ESE of Minot. Railway division point; cooperative creamery, diversified farming, livestock, poultry, wheat.

Drake Creek, S Ky., formed in S Warren co. by junction of West Fork and Trammel Fork headstreams; flows c.26 mi. generally N to Barren R. 5 mi. E of Bowling Green. Trammel Fork rises in NW Macon co., N Tenn., flows c.45 mi. NNW. West Fork rises in Sumner co., N Tenn., flows c.50 mi. generally N.

Drakensberg (drä'kûnsbĕrkh"), main mountain range of U. of So. Afr., in Transvaal, Natal, and Cape Prov., extends c.700 mi. NE–SW from Tropic of Capricorn in E Transvaal to S Cape Prov.; forms W border of Swaziland and SE border of Basutoland. One of Union's main watersheds, it is source of Orange R., flowing into the Atlantic, and its tributaries, Vaal and Caledon rivers; Tugela R. flows to the Indian Ocean. In 1951 Thabantshonyana (11,425 ft.), in Basutoland, was found to be the highest peak; for some time Mont-aux-Sources (10,822 ft.), 50 mi. SE of Bethlehem, and Cathkin Peak, to SE, were considered highest; other near-by peaks over 10,000 ft. high are Champagne Castle and Giant's Castle. Near Mont-aux-Sources is Natal Natl. Park, with splendid mtn. scenery, including gorge and falls of Tugela R.

Drake Passage, Antarctic strait (c.500 mi. long, 400 mi. wide) off South America bet. Cape Horn and South Shetland Isls., joining the South Pacific and the South Atlantic.

Drakes Bay, indentation in coast of Marin co., W Calif., c.30 mi. WNW of San Francisco. Point Reyes forms a natural breakwater in NW. Visited 1579 by Sir Francis Drake; in 1933, an engraved brass tablet, believed to be that left by Drake in claiming region for England was found near by.

Drakesboro, mining town (pop. 1,102), Muhlenberg co., W Ky., 27 mi. ESE of Madisonville; bituminous coal.

Drakes Branch, town (pop. 410), Charlotte co., S Va., on railroad and 40 mi. SE of Lynchburg; market center in tobacco, timber area.

Drakesville, town (pop. 222), Davis co., SE Iowa, near Fox R., 15 mi. SSW of Ottumwa, in sheep-raising area. Lake Wapello State Park near by.

Drama (drä'mù), nome (□ 1,350; pop. 145,653), Macedonia, Greece; ⊙ Drama. Bordered N by Bulgaria, W by Menikion Mts., it is drained by Mesta R. and contains the Phalakron massif. Known for its tobacco grown mainly in agr. lowland W and S of Drama; cotton, olive oil, and wine are lesser products. Main centers are Drama (on Salonika-Adrianople RR) and Prosotsane.

Drama, anc. *Drabescus,* city (1951 pop. 32,895), ⊙ Drama nome, Macedonia, on railroad and 70 mi. ENE of Salonika at S foot of the Phalakron; major tobacco center; cotton milling, tobacco processing, cigarette mfg.; trade in cotton, olive oil, wine, potatoes. Manganese mining near by. Airfield. Bishopric. Under Turkish rule, 15th cent. to Balkan Wars (1912–13).

Dramburg, Poland: see DRAWSKO.

Drammen (dräm'mùn), city (pop. 26,994), ⊙ Buskerud co., SE Norway, at head of Drammen Fjord, at mouth of Drammen R., 20 mi. SW of Oslo; 59°45'N 10°14'E. Port and railroad terminus; paper-milling center; mfg. of wood pulp, cellulose, plastics, abrasives; textile and lumber mills, machine shops, foundries, tanneries, breweries. Granite quarried near by. Known in 13th cent.; inc. 1811, when dists. of Bragernes (N), Stromso (Nor. *Strømsø*) (S), and Tangen (SE) were merged.

Drammen Fjord or **Drams Fjord,** SE Norway, NW arm (20 mi. long, 1–3 mi. wide) of Oslo Fjord, extends NNW to Drammen, receiving Drammen R.

Drammen River or **Drams River,** Buskerud co., SE Norway, rises as Hallingdal R. on S slope of Hallingskarv mts., flows ENE to Gol, then SSE, past Nesbyen, and through the lake Kroderen (here stream becomes Drammen R.), to Drammen Fjord at Drammen; 190 mi. long. One of Norway's best-regulated streams, its several falls are used by hydroelectric plants and lumber and paper mills.

Drams Fjord, Norway: see DRAMMEN FJORD.

Drams River, Norway: see DRAMMEN RIVER.

Dran (drän), village, Haut-Donnai prov., S central Vietnam, in Moi Plateaus, 10 mi. SE of Dalat and on railroad; road junction.

Drance River or **Dranse River** (both: drãs), SW Switzerland, rises near Great St. Bernard Pass, flows 27 mi. N to the Rhone N of Martigny-Ville. Drance de Ferret and Drance de Bagnes rivers join it. Orsières and Martigny hydroelectric plants are on river.

Drancy (drãsē'), city (pop. 42,096), Seine dept., N central France, NE suburb of Paris, 6 mi. from Notre Dame Cathedral; aircraft construction; distilling, printing, mfg. (toys, brushes, paints, hardware).

Drangajokull (droung'gäyû"kütùl), Icelandic *Drangajökull,* glacier, NW Iceland, in N part of Vestfjarde Peninsula; rises to 3,035 ft. at 66°10'N 22°17'W.

Drangeid, Norway: see LOGA.

Drangey (droung'gā"), islet, N Iceland, in Skaga Fjord; 65°57'N 19°42'W. Bird nesting-ground. In Icelandic history noted as hideout of outlaws.

Drangiana, Iran and Afghanistan: see SEISTAN.

Drango, China: see LUHO, Sikang prov.

Dranitsi, Greece: see PALAIOKHORION.

Drann River, Yugoslavia: see DRAVINJA RIVER.

Dranse River (drãs), Haute-Savoie dept., SE France, rises in the Chablais above Morzine, flows 25 mi. NNW to L. Geneva just NE of Thonon-les-Bains.

Dranse River, Switzerland: see DRANCE RIVER.

Dransfeld (dräns'fĕlt), town (pop. 2,249), in former Prussian prov. of Hanover, W Germany, after 1945 in Lower Saxony, 8 mi. WSW of Göttingen; woodworking; quarrying.

Draper. 1 City (pop. 3,629), Rockingham co., N N.C., near Dan R. and Va. line, 11 mi. N of Reidsville; textile mfg. Inc. 1949. **2** Town (pop. 252), Jones co., S central S.Dak., 32 mi. SSW of Pierre; small trading point; grain, dairy produce, livestock, poultry. **3** Village (1940 pop. 1,444), Salt Lake co., N central Utah, 18 mi. S of Salt Lake City; alt. 4,525 ft. Dairy, poultry, sugar beets, truck. Alpine Peak (11,253 ft.) is 5 mi. E in Wasatch Range. **4** Town (pop. 258), Pulaski co., SW Va., near New R., 3 mi. S of Pulaski, in agr., timber area.

Draperstown, town (pop. 1,307), S Co. Londonderry, Northern Ireland, 26 mi. SE of Londonderry; market in agr. area (flax, potatoes, oats). Town was founded by Draper's Company of London in 17th cent.

Draperville, town (pop. 201), Linn co., W Oregon.

Drashovicë (dräshôvē'tsù) or **Drashovica** (–vē'tsä), Ital. *Drasciovizza,* village (1930 pop. 357), S Albania, 5 mi. SE of Valona; petroleum and bitumen deposits.

Dratzig, Lake, Poland: see DRAWSKO, LAKE.

Drau River, S central Europe: see DRAVA RIVER.

Drausen, Lake, Poland: see DRUZNO, LAKE.

Drava River or **Drave River** (both: drä'vù), Ger. *Drau* (drou), Hung. *Dráva* (drä'vŏ), S central Europe, rises in Carnic Alps near Dobiacco (Italy); flows E, into Austria, through Tyrol and Carinthia, past Lienz, Spittal, and Villach, into Yugoslavia (above Dravograd), thence ESE, through Slovenia and Croatia, past Maribor, Ptuj, Varazdin, and Osijek, through the Podravina, to the Danube 11 mi. E of Osijek; length, c.450 mi. Receives Mur R. Forms Yugoslav-Hungarian frontier intermittently from mouth of Mur R. to vicinity of Siklos. Navigable for freight below Barcs, for passengers below Osijek.

Draveil (drävā'), town (pop. 9,708), Seine-et-Oise dept., N central France, on right bank of Seine R., opposite Juvisy-sur-Orge, and 12 mi. SSE of Paris; mfg. (electric cables, agr. instruments, paper, furniture, paints, and varnishes).

Drave River, S central Europe: see DRAVA RIVER.

Dravinja River (drä'vēnyä), Ger. *Drann* (drän), NE Slovenia, Yugoslavia, rises 8 mi. NW of Konjice, flows c.50 mi. E, past Konjice, to Drava R. 4.5 mi. SE of Ptuj.

Dravograd (drä'vôgrät), Ger. *Unterdrauburg* (ŏŏn'tûrdrou"bŏŏrk), village (pop. 2,508), N Slovenia, Yugoslavia, on the Drava, at Meza R. mouth and 30 mi. W of Maribor, near Austrian frontier. Junction of Vienna-Zagreb and Klagenfurt-Maribor RRs; hydroelectric plant; health resort. Sometimes called Spodnji Dravograd. Until 1918, in Carinthia. Hamlet of Meza, Slovenian *Meža*, Ger. *Miss*, adjoins village.

Dravosburg (drūvōs'bûrg), borough (pop. 3,786), Allegheny co., SW Pa., 8 mi. S of Pittsburgh and on Monongahela R.; iron, steel. Inc. 1903.

Drawa River (drä'vä), Ger. *Drage* (drä'gù), in Pomerania, after 1945 in NW Poland, rises 10 mi. N of Czaplinek, flows S, W, through numerous lakes, past Zlocieniec and Drawsko, and S past Drawno, to Notec R. SW of Krzyz; 100 mi. long.

Drawno (dräv'nô), Ger. *Neuwedell* (noi'vā'dùl), town (1939 pop. 2,711; 1946 pop. 1,241) in Pomerania, after 1945 in Szczecin prov., NW Poland, on Drawa R. and 30 mi. ESE of Stargard; agr. market (grain, sugar beets, potatoes, livestock); woolen milling. After 1945, briefly called Nowe nad Drawa, Pol. *Nowe nad Drawą*.

Drawsko (dräf'skô), Ger. *Dramburg* (dräm'bŏŏrk), town (1939 pop. 8,088; 1946 pop. 3,504) in Pomerania, after 1945 in Koszalin prov., NW Poland, in lake region, on Drawa R. and 35 mi. ENE of Stargard; woolen milling. In Second World War, c.35% destroyed.

Drawsko, Lake (dräf'skô), Ger. *Dratzig* (drä'tsĭkh) (□ 7), in Pomerania, after 1945 in NW Poland, NW of Czaplinek; 7 mi. long, up to 3 mi. wide. Drawa R. flows through.

Draya or **Draya Yamdun** (drä'yä yäm'dŏŏn), Chinese *Cha-liao* (jä'lyou'), after 1913 *Chaya* or *Ch'a-ya* (chä'yä'), town, E Tibet, in Kham prov., 60 mi. SE of Chamdo; stock raising; agr. products.

Draycott, town in parish of Draycott and Church Wilne (pop. 2,339), SE Derby, England, on Derwent R. and 6 mi. ESE of Derby; hosiery and lace knitting. Parish includes cotton-milling town of Borrowash, on Derwent R. and 2 mi. WNW of Draycott, and agr. village of Church Wilne, just SE of Draycott.

Drayton (drā'tùn), village (pop. 504), S Ont., 23 mi. NNW of Kitchener; knitting mills; dairying, lumbering.

Drayton. 1 City (pop. 875), Pembina co., NE N.Dak., 45 mi. N of Grand Forks and on Red River of the North; livestock, dairy produce, wheat, sugar beets, potatoes. **2** Mill village (pop. 1,228), Spartanburg co., NW S.C., just NE of Spartanburg; textiles.

Drayton Plains, residential village (1940 pop. 1,603), Oakland co., SE Mich., 5 mi. NW of Pontiac and on Clinton R., in area of many lakes. Has state fish hatchery. Settled 1823.

Drebkau (drāp'kou), town (pop. 2,518), Brandenburg, E Germany, in Lower Lusatia, 9 mi. SW of Cottbus; lignite mining; glass mfg.

Dre Chu, China: see YANGTZE RIVER.

Drefach, Wales: see LLANGELER.

Dreghorn, town and parish (pop. 4,338), NW Ayrshire, Scotland, 2 mi. E of Irvine; coal mining. Parish includes agr. village of Dykehead, 4 mi. NE of Irvine.

Dreher Shoals Dam, S.C.: see SALUDA RIVER.

Dreibrunnen, France: see TROIS-FONTAINES.

Dreiherrnspitze (drī'hěrn'shpĭtsù), Ital. *Pizzo dei Tre Signori*, peak (11,499 ft.) on Austro-Ital. border, at W end of the Hohe Tauern, and at head of Valle Aurina (Italy).

Dreikich, Syria: see DUREIKISH.

Dreiländerspitze (drī'lěnd'ùrshpĭtsù) [Ger.,=peak of 3 countries], peak (c.10,500 ft.) in Silvretta Group of Rhaetian Alps, on Swiss-Austrian border, E of Piz Buin. On Austrian side it forms Tyrol-Vorarlberg boundary.

Dreisam River (drī'zäm), S Baden, Germany, formed c.5 mi. E of Freiburg by several mtn. streams, flows 20 mi. generally N (canalized below Freiburg) to Riegel, where it receives the canalized ELZ RIVER and becomes the Leopold Canal, flowing 7 mi. NNW to the Rhine.

Dreketi River, Fiji: see NDREKETI RIVER.

Drem, agr. village in Athelstaneford parish, East Lothian, Scotland, 4 mi. N of Haddington; rail junction.

Dren (drĕn), village (pop. 3,174), Sofia dist., W Bulgaria, in Radomir Basin, 14 mi. SSE of Radomir; livestock, hemp, truck.

Drenova, Bulgaria: see DRYANOVO.

Drensteinfurt (drän'shtīnfŏŏrt"), town (pop. 2,455), in former Prussian prov. of Westphalia, NW Germany, after 1945 in North Rhine-Westphalia, 7 mi. NW of Ahlen; grain, cattle, hogs. Has 18th-cent. castle.

Drenthe or **Drente** (both: drĕn'tù), province (□ 1,010.9; pop. 271,909), NE Netherlands; ⊙ Assen. Bounded by Groningen prov. (N, NE), Germany (E), Overijssel prov. (S), Friesland prov. (W). Heath country with large fenland areas; drained by the Smildervaart, Noord-Willems Canal, Oranje Canal. Agr. (potatoes, vegetables); cattle raising, dairying; food canning; mfg. of potato flour, strawboard; peat production; petroleum industry (centered at Coevorden). Main towns: Assen, Coevorden, Emmen. Came into possession of bishops of Utrecht in 1046; under governorship of provincial nobles until 1395, when it was again directly administered by bishops; passed (1536) to Emperor Charles V. After 1581, joined in struggle against Spain, nominating its own stadholder; gained provincial status in 1796. Its economic importance began with drainage of fen areas in mid-18th cent. Oil industry developed after Second World War.

Drentsche Hoofdvaart, Netherlands: see SMILDERVAART.

Drepanon, Cape, or **Cape Dhrepanon** (both: dhrĕ'pùnôn). **1** SE extremity of Sithonia prong of Chalcidice peninsula, Greek Macedonia, on Aegean Sea; 39°56'N 23°56'E. **2** Northernmost point of Peloponnesus, Greece, on Gulf of Corinth; 38°21'N 21°51'E.

Drepanum, Sicily: see TRAPANI, city.

Drepung (drĕ'pŏŏng) [Tibetan,=rice heap], Chinese *Pieh-pang Ssu* (byĕ'bäng'sŭ'), lamasery (pop. c.10,-000), S Tibet, near the Kyi Chu, 5 mi. WNW of Lhasa; alt. c.12,000 ft. One of the 3 great lamaseries of Tibet (the others are Sera and Ganden). Founded in 15th cent. by the 2d Dalai Lama, Ganden Truppa.

Dresden (drĕz'dùn), town (pop. 1,662), S Ont., on Sydenham R. and 12 mi. N of Chatham; food canning, flour milling, dairying, lumbering, natural-gas production. Hydroelectric station.

Dresden (drĕz'dùn, Ger. drās'dùn), city (1939 pop. 630,216; 1946 pop. 467,966), ⊙ Saxony, E central Germany, on the Elbe, at mouth of Weisseritz R., and 100 mi. S of Berlin, 65 mi. ESE of Leipzig; 51°3'N 13°44'E. Large inland port and rail junction. Cultural center, formerly noted for its extensive art collections and baroque and rococo architecture. City gives its name to china products, especially figurines, called "Dresden china" though made at Meissen (14 mi. NW). Industries include mfg. of optical and precision instruments, glass, chemicals, pharmaceuticals, pianos, organs, machine tools, electrical equipment, typewriters, textiles, leather, abrasives, cigarettes, food products. Site of state musical col., art col., and technical col. City sustained heavy air-raid and later artillery damage (destruction about 60%) in Second World War; the 18th-cent. basilica of Our Lady (*Frauenkirche*), 16th-cent. Saxonian state library, opera house (Wagner conductor here, 1843–49), and city- and technical-col. libraries were among bldgs. destroyed. Of Dresden's many well-known museums, almost all were heavily damaged, including the Zwinger (which housed Raphael's *Sistine Madonna*) and State Mus. Other features of Dresden, many of which received bomb or shell damage, are the Brühl Terrace, built 1738 along the Elbe; Kreuzkirche (c.1200; rebuilt 1900 after fire); 16th-cent. former royal palace. Most of Dresden's fabulous art treasures were safely kept through the war outside of Dresden, but many art objects were afterward removed to Russia. Some remaining art objects were assembled (1947) in the mus. of former royal hunting lodge at Moritzburg (8 mi. NNW). Schiller resided (1785–87) in Dresden and here wrote *Ode to Joy* and *Don Carlos;* Schumann taught (1844–50) at conservatory. Originally Slav swamp settlement of *Drezdzane*, the town is 1st mentioned 1206 as German fortified place established by margraves of Meissen. Chartered 1403; was residence (1485–1918) of electors, later kings, of Saxony. Accepted Reformation in 1539. In late 17th and 18th cent., particularly under the electors Frederick Augustus I and Frederick Augustus II, Dresden became a center of the arts and an outstanding example of baroque and rococo architecture. Dresden was occupied by Prussians in Second Silesian War (ended 1745 by Treaty of Dresden), and again in 1756. Shelled (1760) during Seven Years War. Napoleon defeated (Aug., 1813) Allied army near the city before his defeat at Leipzig. Occupied by Prussia in War of 1866. In late 19th cent., Dresden became a center of sculpture under leadership of Johannes Schilling. At close of Second World War, it was captured by Soviet forces after heavy shelling. Among chief suburbs are Loschwitz, Blasewitz, and Weisser Hirsch (E), climatic health resorts; Plauen (S), with coal mines; and Löbtau (W).

Dresden (drĕz'dùn). **1** City (pop. 162), Decatur co., NW Kansas, 15 mi. SSE of Oberlin, in agr. and livestock area. **2** Town (pop. 729), Lincoln co., S Maine, on the Kennebec and 10 mi. above Bath; boatbuilding, summer camps. **3** Village (pop. 373), Yates co., W central N.Y., on W shore of Seneca L., 12 mi. S of Geneva. **4** Village (pop. 1,310), Muskingum co., central Ohio, 12 mi. N of Zanesville, at head of navigation on Muskingum R.; woolen and paper mills; poultry hatcheries. Coal mines, sand and gravel pits. **5** Town (pop. 1,509), ⊙ Weakley co., NW Tenn., 21 mi. SE of Union City; trade center in timber, clay, agr. (cotton, corn, sweet potatoes) area; makes barrel staves, cigars. Laid out 1825.

Dresser, village (pop. 365), Polk co., NW Wis., 26 mi. N of Hudson, in dairying area. Until 1940, called Dresser Junction.

Dreswick Point, Isle of Man: see DERBYHAVEN.

Dreumel (drû'mùl), village (pop. 1,323), Gelderland prov., central Netherlands, near Waal R., 2.5 mi. S of Tiel; mfg. of bricks, wooden shoes; agr. First mentioned in 893.

Dreux (drû), town (pop. 11,528), Eure-et-Loir dept., NW central France, on braided Blaise R. (tributary of the Eure) and 21 mi. NNW of Chartres; industrial and communications center; foundries (railroad and agr. equipment), biscuit and shoe factories; brewing, cider distilling. Important trade in grain and poultry. Has 16th-cent. belfry and a richly ornamented 19th-cent. chapel containing Orléans family vault. François de Guise defeated (1562) Protestants under Louis I de Condé, who was captured. Damaged in Second World War.

Drew, county (□ 836; pop. 17,959), SE Ark.; ⊙ Monticello. Drained by the Bayou Bartholomew and Saline R. Agr. (cotton, hay, corn, truck, fruit, livestock); timber. Formed 1846.

Drew. 1 Plantation (pop. 72), Penobscot co., central Maine, 3 mi. ESE of Millinocket; agr., lumbering. **2** Town (pop. 1,681), Sunflower co., W Miss., 28 mi. NW of Greenwood, in rich cotton-growing area; mfg. of cottonseed products, clothing; grain elevator, cotton compress and gins. State penal farm near by.

Drewenz River, Poland: see DRWECA RIVER.

Drewrys Bluff, village, Chesterfield co., E central Va., on the James and 9 mi. S of Richmond. Large rayon plant near by. A height above river, here, was scene of 2 Civil War engagements, a repulse of Union gunboats (May 15, 1862) in Peninsular Campaign and Beauregard's defeat (May 16, 1864) of Butler's Union Army of the James, which was forced to retreat to Bermuda Hundred. The bluff is also called Drewry Bluff; also spelled Drury's Bluff.

Drewsey (drŏŏ'zē), town (pop. 64), Harney co., E Oregon, 37 mi. NE of Burns; alt. 3,516 ft.

Drewsteignton (drŏŏz'tān'tùn), agr. village and parish (pop. 674), central Devon, England, 12 mi. W of Exeter. Spinster's Rock (2 mi. W) is only erect cromlech in Devon.

Drexel (drĕk'sùl). **1** City (pop. 456), Cass co., W Mo., 19 mi. SW of Harrisonville; grain, livestock; gas wells. **2** Town (pop. 988), Burke co., W central N.C., 5 mi. E of Morganton; hosiery and furniture mfg.

Drexel Hill, Pa.: see HAVERFORD.

Drezdenko (drĕzdĕn'kô), Ger. *Driesen* (drē'zùn), town (1939 pop. 5,674; 1946 pop. 1,908) in Pomerania, after 1945 in Zielona Gora prov., W Poland, on Notec R. and 25 mi. ENE of Landsberg (Gorzow Wielkopolski), in marshy region; agr. market (grain, potatoes, sugar beets, livestock); metal- and woodworking. First mentioned 1092. Has 14th-cent. castle, held 1620–50 by Swedes.

Drezna (dryĕz'nù), city (1939 pop. over 10,000), E Moscow oblast, Russian SFSR, 7 mi. SW of Orekhovo-Zuyevo; cotton-milling center; peat works. Became city in 1940.

Driana (drēä'nä), anc. *Adrianopoli*, village (pop. 1,400), W Cyrenaica, Libya, near Mediterranean Sea, on coastal road and 22 mi. NE of Benghazi. Has 2 ruined forts. Was an agr. colony in Hadrian's time.

Dribin (drē'bĭn), village (1926 pop. 1,418), NE Mogilev oblast, Belorussian SSR, on Pronya R., and 35 mi. NE of Mogilev; dairying.

Driburg, Bad, Germany: see BAD DRIBURG.

Driebergen (drē'bĕrkh-ùn), residential village, Utrecht prov., central Netherlands, 8 mi. ESE of Utrecht.

Driebes (drēā'vĕs), town (pop. 889), Guadalajara prov., central Spain, 35 mi. ESE of Madrid; cereals, hemp, grapes, olives, sugar beets, livestock. Olive-oil pressing, dairying.

Drie Gezusters (drē gùzû'stûrs), landing in Nickerie dist., NW Du. Guiana, on Courantyne R. and 20 mi. SSW of Nieuw Nickerie, opposite 3 small isls. (The Three Sisters) in Br. Guiana; timber, balata. Sometimes called De Zusters.

Driel, Netherlands: see KERK-DRIEL.

Driesen, Poland: see DREZDENKO.

Drietabbetje (drētä'bĕtyù), village, Marowijne dist., E Du. Guiana, on Tapanahoni R. and 45 mi. SSE of Dam; hq. of Bush Negroes.

Driffield or **Great Driffield** (drĭ′fĭl), urban district (1931 pop. 5,915; 1951 census 6,888), East Riding, E Yorkshire, England, 20 mi. NNW of Hull; agr. market; has flour, linseed-oil, feed-cake mills, agr.-machinery works.

Driftless Area (□ c.13,000), largely in SW Wis., but extending into SE Minn., NE Iowa, and NW Ill.; has residual, well-drained soil, and numerous caves and sinkholes. So called because area was untouched by continental glaciers that covered surrounding region in Pleistocene times.

Drifton, village (pop. c.1,000), Luzerne co., E central Pa., 5 mi. NE of Hazleton, in anthracite region.

Drift Prairie, in N N.Dak. and S Manitoba, sandy, rolling plain. Varies in width from 70 to 200 mi.; extends S to headwaters of James and Sheyenne rivers; in N are Devils L. and Stump L., basis of an interior drainage system.

Driftsands, airport, S Cape Prov., U. of So. Afr., just S of Port Elizabeth; 33°59′S 25°37′E.

Driftwood. 1 Town (pop. 69), Alfalfa co., N Okla., 18 mi. ENE of Alva, in grain and livestock area. **2** Borough (pop. 289), Cameron co., N central Pa., 12 mi. SSE of Emporium and on Sinnemahoning Creek.

Driftwood River, Ind.: see WHITE RIVER.

Drigg and Carleton, parish (pop. 420), SW Cumberland, England. Includes dairying village of Drigg, 2 mi. NW of Ravenglass, with church of Norman origin, enlarged in 13th cent. Near by is a large bird sanctuary.

Driggs, village (pop. 941), ⊙ Teton co., E Idaho, near Wyo. line, c.50 mi. ENE of Idaho Falls, in valley of Teton R.; trade center for farm, dairy area; cheese, flour. Large coal bed near by.

Drighlington (drĭg′lĭngtŭn, drĭ′–), former urban district (1931 pop. 4,091), West Riding, S central Yorkshire, England, 5 mi. SE of Bradford; woolen milling, metal casting. Inc. 1937 in Morley. On near-by Adwalton Moor a Civil War battle was fought (1643).

Drim, river, Albania: see DRIN RIVER.

Drimkol (drēm′kôl), region of Macedonia, Yugoslavia, extending c.20 mi. NNW from L. Ochrida, bet. E foot of the Jablanica (Albanian border) and left bank of the Black Drin.

Drimoleague (drĭmùlēg′), Gaelic *Druim Dhá Liag*, village, SW Co. Cork, Ireland, 8 mi. E of Bantry; slate quarrying.

Drim River, Albania: see DRIN RIVER.

Drin, river, Albania: see DRIN RIVER.

Drina River (drē′nä), E Bosnia, Yugoslavia; formed by junction of Tara and Piva rivers on Montenegro border, 8 mi. NE of peak Maglic; flows 285 mi. generally N, past Foca, Visegrad, and Zvornik, through the PODRINJE, to Sava R. 12 mi. NNE of Bijeljina. Navigable for 206 mi. Receives Cotina and Lim rivers (right). Lower course forms Bosnia-Serbia border. Hydroelectric plant planned (1947) at Zvornik.

Drin Gulf (drēn), Albanian *Gji i Drinit* or *Pellg i Drinit*, inlet of the Adriatic in NW Albania, bet. Ulcinj (Yugoslavia) and Cape Rodoni (S); 20 mi. wide, 10 mi. long. Low E shore is formed by deltas of Drin, Mat, and Ishm rivers. Receives Bojana R. (Yugoslav-Albanian border; N). Shëngjin is the chief port.

Drinjaca River or **Drinyacha River** (both: drē′nyächä), Serbo-Croatian *Drinjača*, E Bosnia, Yugoslavia, rises on E slope of the Konjuh, flows c.50 mi. generally E, past Kladanj, to Drina R. 7 mi. SSE of Zvornik. Receives Jadar R. (right).

Drinnan (drĭ′nŭn), village, W Alta., in Rocky Mts., near E side of Jasper Natl. Park, on Athabaska R. and 45 mi. NE of Jasper; coal mining.

Drin River (drēn). **1** Albanian *Drin* or *Drini*, Serbo-Croatian *Drim*, anc. *Drilon*, longest river of Albania, formed at Kukës by WHITE DRIN RIVER and BLACK DRIN RIVER, flows 65 mi. generally W through deep gorges to plain of Scutari. Here the old Drin continues 30 mi. S, past Lesh, to Drin Gulf of the Adriatic (delta). Since 1858–59, the major outlet of the Drin is the Drinassa [Albanian *Drin i madh;* Serbo-Croatian *Drimac*], a braided arm (7 mi. long) which joins the Bojana just below its efflux from L. Scutari. Total length, 95 mi.; including either headstream, 175 mi. **2** Gr. *Dhrino*, left affluent of the Vijosë, in S Albania, rises just across border in Greece, flows c.50 mi. NW, past Argyrokastron, to the Vijosë near Tepelenë.

Drinyacha River, Yugoslavia: see DRINJACA RIVER.

Dripping Springs, village (pop. c.250), Hays co., S central Texas, 22 mi. WSW of Austin; trade point in livestock, agr. area.

Dripsey (drĭp′sē), Gaelic *Druipseach*, village (district pop. 730), S central Co. Cork, Ireland, near Lee R., 12 mi. W of Cork; woolen milling.

Driscoll (drĭ′skŭl), village (1940 pop. 505), Nueces co., S Texas, 23 mi. WSW of Corpus Christi; rail point in oil, cotton area.

Drisht (drēsht) or **Drishti** (drēsh′tē), Ital. *Drivasto*, village (1930 pop. 1,204), N Albania, on Kiri R. and 6 mi. NE of Scutari. Flourished under Venetian rule (1396–1477) as fortified bishopric. Declined under Turkish domination.

Driskill Mountain (drĭ′skŭl), Bienville parish, NW La., 6 mi. NE of Bienville; highest point (535 ft.) in state.

Drissa (drē′sŭ), city (1926 pop. 2,548), N Polotsk oblast, Belorussian SSR, on Western Dvina R. (former Pol. border) and 39 mi. NW of Polotsk; dairying, flax processing.

Drisvyaty, Lake (drēsvyä′tē), Lith. *Drukšiai* (drōōk′shyā), Pol. *Dryświaty*, lake (□ 13) on Lithuania–Belorussian SSR border, 17 mi. W of Braslav (Belorussian SSR); c.6 mi. long, up to 5 mi. wide; fisheries.

Driva River (drē′vä), More og Romsdal co., W Norway, rises on slope of Snohetta in the Dovrefjell, flows c.100 mi. N and WNW to head of Sunndals Fjord (inlet of North Sea), 40 mi. SE of Kristiansund. Sometimes called Sunndal R.

Drivasto, Albania: see DRISHT.

Drivyaty, Lake (drĭvyä′tē), Pol. *Drywiaty* (drĭvyä′tē), lake (□ 13) in W Belorussian SSR, 70 mi. WNW of Polotsk; c.5 mi. long, up to 4 mi. wide; fisheries. Braslav is on S shore.

Drjenovo, Bulgaria: see DRYANOVO.

Drnava, Czechoslovakia: see ROZNAVA.

Drnis (dŭr′nĭsh), Serbo-Croatian *Drniš*, Ital. *Dernis* (dĕrnēs′), village (pop. 3,053), W Croatia, Yugoslavia, on Cikola R., on railroad and 16 mi. ENE of Sibenik, in Dalmatia; trade center in winegrowing region. Center of bauxite-mining area (Kalun and Umci mines); gypsum deposits. Brown-coal mine at near-by Siveric. Has old castle, partly destroyed by Venetians. Sometimes spelled Drnish.

Dro (drô), village (pop. 1,290), Trento prov., Trentino–Alto Adige, N Italy, on Sarca R. and 8 mi. NW of Rovereto, in olive-growing region.

Drobak (drû′bäk), Nor. *Drøbak*, city (pop. 2,032), Akershus co., SE Norway, on E shore of Oslo Fjord narrows, 18 mi. S of Oslo; port and seaside resort. Mfg. of printer's ink and ski wax; ships lumber, cement. Site of marine biological station of Oslo Univ. Just offshore, on islet, is Oscarsborg fortress. Sometimes spelled Drobakk, Nor. *Drøbakk*.

Drobyshevo (drŭbĭ′shĭvŭ). **1** Village (1939 pop. over 500), SE Omsk oblast, Russian SFSR, 15 mi. SW of Cherlak, in agr. area. **2** Town (1926 pop. 5,072), N Stalino oblast, Ukrainian SSR, 5 mi. NW of Krasny Liman.

Drochia, Moldavian SSR: see NADUSHITA.

Drochtersen (drôkh′tûrzŭn), village (pop. 6,545), in former Prussian prov. of Hanover, NW Germany, after 1945 in Lower Saxony, on arm of Elbe estuary, 8 mi. NNW of Stade; building materials; brewing.

Drogden (drôg′dŭn), strait, Denmark, branch of the Oresund bet. Amager and Saltholm isls.; 3 mi. wide.

Drogenbosch (drō′gŭnbōs), town (pop. 3,571), Brabant prov., central Belgium, 4 mi. S of Brussels; chemical industry; electric-power station. Formerly spelled Droogenbosch.

Drogheda (drô′ùdù, droi′–), Gaelic *Droichead Átha*, urban district (pop. 15,715), SE Co. Louth, Ireland, on the Boyne 4 mi. above its mouth on the Irish Sea, and 25 mi. N of Dublin; 53°43′N 6°21′W; seaport, with dock installations; tanning, iron founding, shipbuilding, brewing; linen, cotton, flour milling; oil pressing; mfg. of machinery, chemicals, fertilizer, soap, shoes, clothing, rope, cement, cattle feed; cattle and beef are exported. Noted features of town are: St. Lawrence's Gate and other ruins of anc. town walls; ruins of Abbey of St. Mary d'Urso; Magdalen Steeple, relic of Dominican abbey founded 1224; and 17th-cent. St. Peter's Church. In 911 Drogheda became Danish stronghold; later Anglo-Normans established bridgehead here. In 1395 chief Irish princes here submitted to Richard II; in 1494 a Parliament held here passed Poynings's Law, making future Irish legislation subject to approval of English Privy Council. Drogheda was besieged 1641 by Sir Phelim O'Neill; in 1649 Cromwell stormed town and massacred or deported inhabitants. Held for James II, town surrendered after the battle of Boyne (1690), fought at near-by OLDBRIDGE.

Drogichin, Poland: see DROHICZYN.

Drogichin (drŭgĭ′chēn′), Pol. *Drohiczyn* or *Drohiczyn Poleski* (drôhē′chĭn pôlĕs′kē), town (1937 pop. 3,100), SW Pinsk oblast, Belorussian SSR, 42 mi. WNW of Pinsk; flour milling, brick mfg.

Drogobych (drŭgŭbĭch′), oblast (□ 3,800; 1946 pop. estimate 1,200,000), W Ukrainian SSR; ⊙ Drogobych. On N slopes of E Beskids (S); bounded W by Poland, SW by San R.; drained by upper Dniester R and its tributaries (Stryyazh and Stry rivers). Humid continental climate (short summers). Mining region: petroleum, natural gas, ozocerite, salt, potassium (Stebnik, Morshin), kainite and sylvanite (Drogobych); iron-ore deposits (near Sambor). Gas pipe lines connect major extracting centers (Borislav, Dashava) with Kiev and Lvov. Oats, rye, potatoes, flax, livestock (N), sheep (in mts.). Industries based on mining (petroleum refining, saltworks), agr. (tanning, distilling, flour milling), and coniferous forests (sawmilling, furniture, mfg.). Metalworking and light industries in main urban centers (Drogobych, Borislav, Stry, Sambor). Health resorts with mineral springs (Truskavets, Morshin). Formed (1939) out of parts of Pol. Lwow and Stanislawow provs., following Soviet occupation of E Poland; held by Germany (1941–44); ceded to USSR in 1945. In 1951 the oblast ceded Ustrzyki Dolne area (□ 185) to Rzeszow prov., Poland.

Drogobych, Pol. *Drohobycz* (drôhô′bĭch), city (1931 pop. 32,622), ⊙ Drogobych oblast, Ukrainian SSR, on right tributary of Dniester R. and 42 mi. SSW of Lvov; 49°20′N 23°30′E. Rail junction; major petroleum and natural-gas extracting center, linked by gas pipe lines with Borislav, Stebnik, and Dashava. Kainite and sylvanite mining; petroleum refining (gasoline, artificial asphalt, lubricating oil, paraffin), coppersmithing, iron casting, mfg. (metalware, chemicals, rubber goods, cardboard, soap, candles); agr. trading (sheep, grain) and processing (cereals, vegetable and animal fats, hides); saltmaking, sawmilling, stone quarrying, tile and brickworking. Teachers col., technical schools. Has 14th-cent. Gothic church, old castle. A livestock-trading and salt-mining settlement, it passed from Poland to Austria in 1772. Developed in 19th cent. as center of petroleum-producing dist. Reverted to Poland in 1919; ceded to USSR in 1945.

Drohiczyn or **Drohiczyn nad Bugiem** (drôhē′chĭn näd bōō′gyĕm), Rus. *Drogichin* (drŭgē′chĭn), town (pop. 1,634), Bialystok prov., E Poland, on Bug R. and 55 mi. SSW of Bialystok.

Drohiczyn, Belorussian SSR: see DROGICHIN.

Drohobycz, Ukrainian SSR: see DROGOBYCH, city.

Droichead Nua, Ireland: see NEWBRIDGE.

Droit, Montagne du (mōtä′nyù dü drwä′), range in the Jura, NW Switzerland, extending generally NE from La Chaux-de-Fonds to NW of Biel, along upper Suze R. Mont Soleil (Ger. *Sonnenberg*) (4,238 ft.), plateau, is highest point.

Droitwich (droit′wĭch), municipal borough (1931 pop. 4,515; 1951 census 6,453), central Worcester, England, on Salwarpe R. 7 mi. NNE of Worcester; has brine baths, salt and soap works. Town is connected with Severn R. by Droitwich Canal, built 18th cent. by James Brindley. Has several medieval churches. The important Droitwich radio transmitter is at Wychbold, 2 mi. NE, in Dodderhill parish (pop. 1,604).

Drokiya, Moldavian SSR: see NADUSHITA.

Drolshagen (drôls′hä″gŭn), town (pop. 2,116), in former Prussian prov. of Westphalia, W Germany, after 1945 in North Rhine-Westphalia, 3 mi. W of Olpe; forestry.

Dromahair or **Drumahaire** (drŭ″mùhâr′), Gaelic *Druim Dhá Eithiar*, town (pop. 275), W Co. Leitrim, Ireland, near Lough Gill, 7 mi. ESE of Sligo; agr. market (dairying, cattle raising, potato growing). Old Hall (1626) is on site of 12th-cent. Breffni Castle of the O'Rourkes. Creevelea Abbey was built 1508.

Drôme (drōm), department (□ 2,533; pop. 268,233), in Dauphiné, SE France; ⊙ Valence. Traversed in E half by westernmost spurs (Vercors, Baronnies) of Dauphiné Alps, surface slopes gradually toward Rhone R. which bounds dept. on the W. Drained by Isère, Drôme, Roubion, Lez, and Aygues rivers, all left tributaries of the Rhone. Vineyards (Tain-l'Hermitage), olive and mulberry groves, and orchards in Rhone valley. Extensive upland pastures. Dept. grows truffles and colza. Numerous cementworks. Mfg.: shoes at Romans-sur-Isère, felt hats at Bourg-de-Péage, well-known nougats at Montélimar. Wide-spread silk milling. Chief towns: Valence, Romans-sur-Isère, Montélimar.

Drôme River, Drôme dept., SE France, rises in Dauphiné Pre-Alps just E of Col de Cabre, flows 63 mi. generally WNW, past Die and Saillans, to the Rhone 4 mi. below Livron.

Dromod (drŭ′mŭd), Gaelic *Dromad*, agr. village, S Co. Leitrim, Ireland, on the Shannon and 9 mi. SE of Carrick-on-Shannon; dairying, cattle raising, potato growing. Formerly site of noted ironworks; now popular angling resort.

Dromore (drōmôr′, drō′môr). **1** Urban district (1937 pop. 2,176; 1951 census 2,390), NW Co. Down, Northern Ireland, on Lagan R. and 16 mi. SW of Belfast; agr. market (flax, oats; sheep), with linen mills. It is anc. religious center of Co. Down and was site of abbey reputedly founded c.600 by St. Colman, destroyed in 1641 civil wars. Present church was built 1641 by Jeremy Taylor, who is buried here, together with Bishop Thomas Percy. **2** Agr. village (district pop. 928), SW Co. Tyrone, Northern Ireland, 9 mi. SW of Omagh; oats, flax, potatoes; cattle.

Dromore West or **Dromore,** Gaelic *Druim Mór*, fishing village (district pop. 531), NW Co. Sligo, Ireland, on the coast, 17 mi. W of Sligo.

Dron (drōn), agr. village in Dunbarney parish, SE Perthshire, Scotland, 5 mi. SSE of Perth.

Dronachellam, India: see DHONE.

Dronero (drônā′rô), village (pop. 2,889), Cuneo prov., Piedmont, NW Italy, on Maira R. and 11 mi. NW of Cuneo; rail terminus; agr. tools, cutlery, macaroni, wine, silk. Quarries (marble, talc) near.

Dronfield, urban district (1931 pop. 4,530; 1951 census 7,628), N Derby, England, 6 mi. S of Sheffield; steel milling, coal mining. Has 14th-cent. church.

Dronfield Woodhouse, town and parish (pop. 976), N Derby, England, 6 mi. SSW of Sheffield; coal mining.

Drongan (drŏng'gŭn), village in Ochiltree parish, central Ayrshire, Scotland, 7 mi. ESE of Ayr; coal mining.

Drongen (drōng'ŭn), Fr. *Tronchiennes* (trōshyĕn'), town (pop. 6,977), East Flanders prov., NW Belgium, on Lys R. and 2 mi. W of Ghent; textile industry; agr., cattle market. Has 12th- and 13th-cent. buildings of an old abbey.

Drongkhya La, pass, Bhutan: see DONGA LA.

Dronne River (drōn), Dordogne and Gironde depts., SW France, rises near Chalus, flows 115 mi. SW, past Brantôme and Saint-Aulaye, to the Isle just below Coutras.

Dronninggaard, Denmark: see HOLTE.

Dronninglund (drô'nĭng-lo͝on), town (pop. 1,339), Hjorring amt, N Jutland, Denmark, 23 mi. SSE of Hjorring.

Dronrijp (drōn'rīp), town (pop. 1,630), Friesland prov., N Netherlands, on the Harlinger Trekvaart and 6 mi. W of Leeuwarden; dairying; potato-flour mfg. Birthplace of painter Alma-Tadema. Sometimes spelled Dronryp.

Drontheim, Norway: see TRONDHEIM.

Droogenbosch, Belgium: see DROGENBOSCH.

Droop Mountain Battlefield State Park (265 acres), Pocahontas co., E W.Va., just SW of Hillsboro. Here on slope of Droop Mtn. (c.3,100 ft.) is preserved the battlefield where Union troops defeated (Nov. 6, 1863) a Confederate army.

Dropt River or **Drot River** (both: drō), Lot-et-Garonne and Gironde depts., SW France, rises near Monpazier (Dordogne dept.), flows 78 mi. W, past Villeréal and Monségur, to the Garonne 3 mi. W of La Réole.

Drosh (drōsh), village, Chitral state, N North-West Frontier Prov., W Pakistan, on Kunar R. and 110 mi. N of Peshawar; trade in fruit, timber, grain.

Drösing (drû'zĭng), village (pop. 1,359), NE Lower Austria, near Czechoslovak border, 32 mi. NE of Vienna; rail junction; oil refinery.

Droskovo (drô'skŭvŭ), village (1926 pop. 2,105), S central Orel oblast, Russian SFSR, 22 mi. W of Livny; hemp milling.

Drossen, Poland: see OSNO.

Drot River, France: see DROPT RIVER.

Drottningholm (drôt'nĭng-hôlm"), residential village (pop. 322), Stockholm co., E Sweden, on Lovo (lo͞ov'û"), Swedish *Lovö*, isl. (□ 10; pop. 1,085) in E part of L. Malar, 7 mi. W of Stockholm city center. Site of royal palace of Drottningholm (1662–81), with large park, theater, and Chinese pavilion.

Drottningskar (drôt'nĭng-shâr"), Swedish *Drottningskär*, fishing village (pop. 638), Blekinge co., S Sweden, on Aspo (äsp'û"), Swedish *Aspö*, isl. (□ 3; pop. 859) in the Baltic, 3 mi. SSW of Karlskrona.

Droué (dro͞oā'), village (pop. 655), Loir-et-Cher dept., N central France, 12 mi. W of Châteaudun; cattle market. Has castle built under Henry IV.

Drouin (dro͞o'ĭn), town (pop. 1,638), S Victoria, Australia, 52 mi. SE of Melbourne; livestock, fruit; flax, cheese.

Drovyanaya (drŭvyŭnī'ŭ), town (1948 pop. over 2,000), SW Chita oblast, Russian SFSR, 37 mi. SSW of Chita; sawmills.

Droylsden, urban district (1931 pop. 13,274; 1951 census 26,365), SE Lancashire, England, on Rochdale Canal just E of Manchester; cotton textile industry; steel milling, mfg. of chemicals.

Drozhzhanoye (drŭzhä'nŭyŭ), village (1939 pop. over 2,000), SW Tatar Autonomous SSR, Russian SFSR, 34 mi. SW of Buinsk; grain, livestock. Phosphorite deposits near by. Until c.1940, Drozhzhanovo.

Drug (dro͞og), district (□ 7,580; pop. 1,415,552), E central Madhya Pradesh, India, on Deccan Plateau; ⊙ Drug. Bordered W and N by forested E foothills of Satpura Range; drained by Seonath R. and its numerous tributaries. Rice and oilseeds (chiefly flax) along rivers (canal irrigation); wheat, cotton, bamboo, sal, myrobalan in W hills. Hematite, steatite, limestone, and ceramic clay deposits (S, E); hematite, bauxite, copper, and red ocher deposits in W hills. Raj-Nandgaon is a cotton-textile center; Drug (experimental farm) is main agr. market. Original dist. (□ 4,830; 1941 pop. 928,851) enlarged 1948 by inc. of former Chhattisgarh States of Chhuikhadan, Kawardha, Khairagarh, and Nandgaon. Pop. 80% Hindu, 18% tribal (mainly Gond), 2% Moslem.

Drug, town (pop. 16,766), ⊙ Drug dist., E central Madhya Pradesh, India, near Seonath R., 140 mi. E of Nagpur, in Chhattisgarh Plain; rice market; rice and dal milling. Experimental farm (rice, betel; silk growing). Construction of large steel-milling plant begun 1950 at village of Bhilai (on railroad, 9 mi. E).

Druid Hills, N.C.: see BALFOUR, Henderson co.

Druif (droif), village, NW Aruba, Du. West Indies, 2 mi. NW of Oranjestad; petroleum refinery.

Druim Fiaclach, mountain (2,852 ft.), highest elevation of Moidart region, W Inverness, Scotland, 10 mi. SE of Arisaig.

Druja, Belorussian SSR: see DRUYA.

Drukgye, Bhutan: see DUKYE.

Drulingen (drülĕzhĕn', Ger. dro͞o'lĭng-ŭn), village (pop. 664), Bas-Rhin dept., E France, 12 mi. NW of Saverne; makes stoves.

Drum, agr. village in Drumoak parish (pop. 798), SE Aberdeen, Scotland, near the Dee, 2 mi. WSW of Peterculter. Drum Castle dates from 1619, has 14th-cent. tower.

Drum, Camp, N.Y.: see GREAT BEND.

Drum, Mount (12,002 ft.), E Alaska, in Wrangell Mts., 85 mi. NE of Valdez; 62°8'N 144°38'W.

Drumahaire, Ireland: see DROMAHAIR.

Drumblade (drŭmblād'), agr. village and parish (pop. 828), N Aberdeen, Scotland, 4 mi. E of Huntly.

Drumbo (drŭm'bō), village (pop. estimate 500), S Ont., 16 mi. S of Kitchener; dairying, farming.

Drumcliff or **Drumcliffe** (drŭmklĭf'), Gaelic *Druim Cliabh*, fishing village (district pop. c.1,300), NE Co. Sligo, Ireland, on Drumcliff Bay (inlet of Sligo Bay), 4 mi. N of Sligo. There are slight remains of round tower, monastery (founded 575 by St. Columba), and scrolled cross.

Drumclog (drŭmklŏg'), moorland tract in W Lanark, Scotland, 5 mi. SW of Strathaven. An obelisk commemorates defeat (1679) here of Claverhouse by the Covenanters.

Drumcondra (drŭmkŏn'drŭ), Gaelic *Druim Chonnrach*, N suburb (pop. c.30,000) of Dublin, Co. Dublin, Ireland.

Drum Ddu, Wales: see MYNYDD EPPYNT.

Drumelzier (drŭmĕl'yŭr), agr. village and parish (pop. 200), W Peebles, Scotland, on the Tweed and 7 mi. ESE of Biggar. Has remains of 16th-cent. Drumelzier Castle, seat of Tweedie family. Just E are remains of Tinnis Castle, destroyed 1592 by order of James VI.

Drumheller (drŭm"hĕ'lŭr), city (pop. 2,659), S central Alta., on Red Deer R. and 65 mi. NE of Calgary; center of coal- and clay-mining and farming area; grain elevators.

Drumin (drŭ'mĭn), agr. village, W Banffshire, Scotland, on the Avon at head of GLENLIVET.

Drum Inlet, E N.C., channel through the Outer Banks, connects Core Sound with the Atlantic just E of Atlantic town.

Drumkeeran or **Drumkeerin** (both: drŭmkēr'ŭn), Gaelic *Druim Caorthainn*, village, central Co. Leitrim, Ireland, on NW shore of Lough Allen, 15 mi. ESE of Sligo; dairying; cattle, potatoes.

Drumlemble, village, S Argyll, Scotland, on Kintyre peninsula, 2 mi. WSW of Campbeltown; coal mining.

Drumley, village in Tarbolton parish, central Ayrshire, Scotland, 4 mi. NE of Ayr; coal mining.

Drumlish (-lĭsh'), Gaelic *Druim Lis*, town (pop. 212), NW Co. Longford, Ireland, 7 mi. NNE of Longford; agr. market (dairying; potatoes).

Drumlithie, Scotland: see GLENBERVIE.

Drummond, county (□ 532; pop. 36,683), S Que., on St. Francis R.; ⊙ Drummondville.

Drummond. **1** Village (pop. 59), Fremont co., E Idaho, 15 mi. E of St. Anthony; alt. 5,603 ft.; dry farming (wheat). **2** Village, Chippewa co., Mich.: see DRUMMOND ISLAND. **3** Town (pop. 531), Granite co., W Mont., on the Clark Fork and 55 mi. W of Helena; phosphate mines; silver, sapphires, and phosphates in near-by Sapphire Mts. **4** Town (pop. 314), Garfield co., N Okla., 11 mi. SW of Enid, and on Turkey Creek, in agr. area. **5** Village, Bayfield co., N Wis., 25 mi. SW of Ashland, in Chequamegon Natl. Forest; lumbering. Govt.-owned farms are near by.

Drummond, Lake, Va.: see DISMAL SWAMP.

Drummond Island, China: see CRESCENT GROUP.

Drummond Island, Chippewa co., SE Upper Peninsula, Mich., bet. North Channel and main body of L. Huron, just E of St. Marys R.; only U.S. isl. of the MANITOULIN ISLANDS; c.20 mi. long, 11 mi. wide. Drummond, the only village (pop. c.350), is on Potagannissing Bay, which indents isl.'s NW shore. Resort (hunting, fishing, boating); lumbering, stone quarrying. Occupied by Br. troops in 1815, became American in 1828.

Drummondville, city (pop. 10,555), ⊙ Drummond co., S Que., on St. Francis R. and 60 mi. ENE of Montreal; rayon-milling center; textile printing, lumbering, dairying, mfg. of hosiery, tire cord, fish nets. Hydroelectric station.

Drummore (drŭm-môr'), village in Kirkmaiden parish, SW Wigtown, Scotland, on the Rhinns of Galloway and on Luce Bay of Solway Firth, just E of Kirkmaiden; fishing port.

Drummossie Moor or **Drummossie Muir** (drŭm-mô'sē mūr'), moorland tract in N Inverness, Scotland. Its NE part is called CULLODEN MOOR.

Drummoyne (drŭmoin'), municipality (pop. 32,985), E New South Wales, Australia, on S shore of Parramatta R. and 3 mi. W of Sydney, in metropolitan area; shipyards, woolen mills. Connected by bridge with Hunter's Hill (N).

Drumoak, Scotland: see DRUM.

Drum Point, low headland, Calvert co., S Md., on N shore of Patuxent R. estuary and 18 mi. SSE of Prince Frederick; lighthouse.

Drumright, city (pop. 5,028), Creek co., central Okla., c.40 mi. WSW of Tulsa, in oil region; oil refining. Founded c.1913.

Drumshambo or **Drumshanbo** (drŭm-shăm'bō), Gaelic *Druim Sean-bhó*, town (pop. 495), central Co. Leitrim, Ireland, on the Shannon at S end of Lough Allen, and 7 mi. NNE of Carrick-on-Shannon; coal, iron mining, limestone quarrying, iron founding.

Drunen (drü'nŭn), town (pop. 3,227), North Brabant prov., S Netherlands, 7 mi. W of 's Hertogenbosch; leather tanning, shoe mfg.

Druse, Jebel, Syria: see JEBEL ED DRUZ.

Drusenheim (drüzünĕm', Ger. dro͞o'zŭnhīm), town (pop. 2,060), Bas-Rhin dept., E France, on the Moder near its influx into the Rhine (Ger. border), and 9 mi. SE of Haguenau; wool spinning, cement pipe mfg.

Druskininkai or **Druskininkay** (dro͞oskēnēn'kī), Pol. *Druskieniki*, city (1931 pop. 2,053), S Lithuania, near Belorussian border, on right bank of Neman R. and 24 mi. N of Grodno, on rail spur from Porechye (on main Grodno-Vilna RR); noted health resort. In Rus. Grodno govt. until it passed to Poland in 1921, to Belorussian SSR in 1939, and to Lithuania in 1940.

Druten (drü'tŭn), town (pop. 3,337), Gelderland prov., E central Netherlands, on Waal R. and 12 mi. WNW of Nijmegen; leather tanning, shipbuilding, cement mfg.

Drut River or **Drut' River** (dro͞ot'yŭ), E Belorussian SSR, rises N of Tolochin in Smolensk-Moscow Upland, flows 180 mi. S, past Belynichi, to Dnieper R. at Rogachev. Navigable in lower course.

Druya (dro͞o'yŭ), Pol. *Druja* (dro͞o'yä), town (1931 pop. 2,500), W Polotsk oblast, Belorussian SSR, on Western Dvina R. (landing) and 35 mi. ESE of Daugavpils; tanning, flour milling, brick mfg. Has ruins of castle and several old churches. Pol. frontier town on Latvian border prior to Second World War.

Druz, Jebel ed, Syria: see JEBEL ED DRUZ.

Druze, Jebel, Syria: see JEBEL ED DRUZ.

Druzhba (dro͞ozh'bŭ), town (1939 pop. 2,694), S central Kaliningrad oblast, Russian SFSR, on the Lyna (head of navigation), at mouth of Masurian Canal, and 31 mi. ESE of Kaliningrad; sawmilling, dairying; trade in agr. products, wool, horses, and cattle. Founded 1407. Until 1945, in East Prussia and called Allenburg (ä'lŭnbo͝ork).

Druzhina (dro͞ozhē'nŭ), town (1947 pop. over 500), NE Yakut Autonomous SSR, Russian SFSR, N of Arctic Circle, on Indigirka R. and 220 mi. WNW of Sredne-Kolymsk; reindeer farms.

Druzhinino (dro͞ozhē'nyĭnŭ), town (1938 pop. over 500), SW Sverdlovsk oblast, Russian SFSR, in the central Urals, 11 mi. NE of Nizhniye Sergi; rail junction; lumbering. Gold placers near by.

Druzhkovka (dro͞oshkôf'kŭ), city (1939 pop. over 10,000), N central Stalino oblast, Ukrainian SSR, in the Donbas, 45 mi. NNW of Stalino; steel foundry; ironworks. Until 1930s, Gavrilovski Zavod.

Druzhnaya Gorka (dro͞ozh'nīŭ gôr'kŭ), town (1948 pop. over 2,000), W central Leningrad oblast, Russian SFSR, 18 mi. S of Gatchina; glassworking.

Druzno, Lake (dro͞ozh'nô), Pol. *Drużno*, Ger. *Drausen* (drou'zŭn) (□ 7), in East Prussia, after 1945 in N Poland, 2 mi. S of Elbing; 8 mi. long.

Drvar (dŭr'vär), town (pop. 2,136), W Bosnia, Yugoslavia, on Unac R., on railroad and 50 mi. SW of Banja Luka; woodworking and trade center. Hq. of Marshal Tito in Second World War.

Drvenik Island, Yugoslavia: see VELIKI DRVENIK ISLAND.

Drweca River (dŭrvĕ'tsä), Pol. *Drwęca*, Ger. *Drewenz* (drā'vĕnts), N Poland, rises 14 mi. SSE of Ostroda, flows NNW past Ostroda, and SW through several lakes, past Brodnica and Golub, to Vistula R. 4 mi. E of Torun; 152 mi. long.

Dryanovo (dryä'nôvô), city (pop. 3,741), Gorna Oryakhovitsa dist., N central Bulgaria, on N slope of central Balkan Mts., 10 mi. NE of Gabrovo; health resort; winegrowing, horticulture. Has old houses with wood carvings. Handicraft center under Turkish rule. Dryanovski monastery (2 mi. SW) is site of monument to Bulg. revolution. Sometimes spelled Drenova or Drjenovo.

Dryazgi, Russian SFSR: see MOLOTOVO, Voronezh oblast.

Dry Bay, SE Alaska, inlet (10 mi. long, 14 mi. wide at mouth) of Gulf of Alaska, 50 mi. SE of Yakutat; 59°10'N 138°25'W; moraine delta at mouth of Alsek R.

Dryberry Lake (22 mi. long, 6 mi. wide), W Ont., 20 mi. E of L. of the Woods, 30 mi. ESE of Kenora.

Dry Branch, village, Bibb co., central Ga., 7 mi. E of Macon; kaolin-mining center.

Dryburgh Abbey (drī'bŭrŭ), ruins of Premonstratensian abbey in S Berwick, Scotland, on the Tweed and 4 mi. SE of Melrose. Founded 1150, several times destroyed and rebuilt. In early 18th cent. it became property of Scott family, who later retained only burial rights here. Abbey contains tombs of Sir Walter Scott and his family, and of Earl Haig.

Dryden, town (pop. 1,641), NW Ont., on Wabigoon L., 75 mi. E of Kenora; paper, pulp, and lumber milling, dairying. Site of govt. experimental farm. In gold-mining region.

Dryden. **1** Town (pop. 43), Craighead co., NE Ark., 11 mi. W of Jonesboro. **2** Village (pop. 476), Lapeer co., E Mich., 12 mi. SE of Lapeer; trade center for agr. and horse-breeding area. **3** Village (pop. 976), Tompkins co., W central N.Y., in Finger Lakes region, 10 mi. ENE of Ithaca; mfg. of tools, clothing, feed, dairy products; lumber milling. Agr. (fruit, poultry).

Dry Falls State Park, Wash.: see COULEE CITY.

Dryfesdale, Scotland: see LOCKERBIE.

Dry Fork, river, SW W.Va., rises near Va. line 15 mi. W of Bluefield, flows c.35 mi. NW, past War and Bradshaw, to Tug Fork opposite Iaeger. Extensive semibituminous-coal mining in its valley. A headstream of Black Fork of Cheat R. is also called Dry Fork.

Drygalski Crest (drügäl'skē, drĭgăl'skē), mountain (4,669 ft.), NW West Spitsbergen, Spitsbergen group, near Kross Fjord (15-mi.-long inlet of Arctic Ocean), 85 mi. NW of Longyear City; 79°17'N 12°35'E.

Drygalski Island (drĭgăl'skē) (9 naut. mi. long), off Antarctica, 45 naut. mi. off Queen Mary Coast, in Indian Ocean; 65°43'S 92°30'E. Rises to c.1,200 ft. Discovered 1914 by Sir Douglas Mawson.

Dry Harbour, village, St. Ann parish, N Jamaica, 13 mi. W of St. Ann's Bay, on fine bay, where Columbus on his 2d voyage made (May 4, 1494) his 1st landing in Jamaica and took possession of the isl. for Spain. There are caves with aboriginal remains near by. The adjoining interior uplands are called Dry Harbour Mts.

Drymen (drĭ'mŭn), agr. village and parish (pop. 1,128), W Stirling, Scotland, near Loch Lomond, 10 mi. NE of Dumbarton.

Dry Mills, Maine: see GRAY.

Dry Prong, village (pop. 377), Grant parish, central La., 20 mi. NNW of Alexandria.

Dry Ridge, town (pop. 640), Grant co., N Ky., 19 mi. ESE of Warsaw, in Bluegrass agr. region.

Dryswiaty, Lake, Lithuania and Belorussian SSR: see DRISVYATY, LAKE.

Dry Tortugas (tôrtōō'gŭz), small island group in the Gulf of Mexico, off S Fla., c.65 mi. W of Key West; included in FORT JEFFERSON NATIONAL MONUMENT. Loggerhead Key, the largest isl. (c.1 mi. long), has a lighthouse (24°38'N 82°55'W). On Garden Key is old Fort Jefferson. Large sea-bird rookeries on Bush Key. Sometimes group is called Tortugas.

Drywiaty, Lake, Belorussian SSR: see DRIVYATY, LAKE.

Dschang (jäng), town, ⊙ Bamileké region, W Fr. Cameroons, 155 mi. NW of Yaoundé, near Br. Cameroons border; alt. 4,525 ft. Health resort, tourist center, and center of native trade, notably in coffee and kola nuts; also communications point. Brick mfg., coffee growing, experimental cinchona plantations. R.C. mission, hosp. for natives, hydroelectric power plant. International Conference on Nutrition held here, 1949.

Dsodse, Gold Coast: see DJOJE.

Dsoje, Gold Coast: see DJOJE.

Duaca (dwä'kä), town (pop. 3,205), Lara state, NW Venezuela, at SW foot of Sierra de Aroa, on Barquisimeto-Tucacas RR and 19 mi. NE of Barquisimeto; agr. center (coffee, sugar cane, corn, fruit, stock).

Duacum, France: see DOUAI.

Duagh (dōō'ŭ), Gaelic *Dubháth,* town (pop. 127), NE Co. Kerry, Ireland, on Feale R. and 5 mi. ESE of Listowel; grain, potatoes; dairying.

Duala, Fr. Cameroons: see DOUALA.

Duan, Wadi, or **Wadi Du'an** (wă'dē dōō'ăn), river valley in the Quaiti state, Eastern Aden Protectorate, extending a distance of 55 mi. from plateau 60 mi. NW of Mukalla N to the main Wadi Hadhramaut. Major honey-producing dist.; date groves. With its right tributary valley, the Wadi Leisar, the upper Wadi Duan constitutes Duan prov. (⊙ Masna'a 'Aura) of Quaiti state. Sometimes spelled Doan.

Duars (dwärz), region (□ 3,432) at foot of W Assam Himalayas, India. Divided into EASTERN DUARS and WESTERN DUARS. Also spelled Dwars and Dooars.

Duarte (dwär'tā), province (□ 1,090; 1935 pop. 111,957; 1950 pop. 165,433), central Dominican Republic; ⊙ San Francisco de Macorís. Camú R. here forms fertile E section of La Vega Real valley, bounded by Cordillera Setentrional (N) and Cordillera Central (S). Main crops of the densely populated agr. region: cacao, coffee, rice, tropical fruit. Iron deposits near Cotuí. It is traversed by Sánchez-Santiago RR. The prov., formerly Pacificador dist., was set up 1936.

Duarte (dwär'tē), unincorporated town (pop. c.1,-970), Los Angeles co., S Calif., 16 mi. ENE of downtown Los Angeles, bet. Monrovia (NE) and Azusa (E); citrus-fruit and avocado packing; poultry.

Duartina (dwärtē'nŭ), city (pop. 2,957), W central São Paulo, Brazil, on railroad and 22 mi. WSW of Bauru; coffee, cotton, and rice processing.

Duas Barras (dōō'ŭs bä'rŭs), city (pop. 485), N Rio de Janeiro state, Brazil, 20 mi. N of Nova Friburgo; coffee, rice, tobacco, sugar. Has fine church.

Duba (dōō'bä), Czech *Dubá,* Ger. *Dauba* (dou'bä), town (pop. 1,237), N Bohemia, Czechoslovakia, 23 mi. ESE of Usti nad Labem; hops. Has fine Italian-style church.

Duba, Saudi Arabia: see DHABA.

Dubach (dōō'bŏk), town (pop. 703), Lincoln parish, N La., 11 mi. N of Ruston; farming; timber; cotton ginning, lumber milling.

Dubai, Trucial Oman: see DIBAI.

Dubaini, Aden: see DUBEINI.

Dubawnt Lake (dōōbônt') (□ 1,600), W Keewatin Dist., Northwest Territories, on Mackenzie Dist. boundary; 62°46'–63°34'N 100°40'–102°12'W; 60 mi. long, 3–38 mi. wide. Drains NE into Thelon R. by Dubawnt R.

Dubawnt River, SE Mackenzie Dist. and W Keewatin Dist., Northwest Territories, rises NE of L. Athabaska, near Sask. border, flows 580 mi. NE, through Dubawnt L., to Thelon R. just W of Aberdeen L.

Dubayni, Aden: see DUBEINI.

Dubbeln, Latvia: see RIGAS JURMALA.

Dubbo (dŭ'bō), municipality (pop. 9,545), E central New South Wales, Australia, on Macquarie R. and 190 mi. NW of Sydney; rail junction, flour and woolen mills, dairy plants.

Dubeini, Dubaini, or **Dubayni** (dōōbā'nē), petty sheikdom of SUBEIHI tribal area, Western Aden Protectorate; ⊙ Tafih. Protectorate treaty concluded in 1912.

Dubele, Belgian Congo: see WATSA.

Düben, Bad, Germany: see BAD DÜBEN.

Dübendorf (dü'bŭndôrf"), town (pop. 5,143), Zurich canton, N Switzerland, on Glatt R. and 4 mi. E of Zurich; metal- and woodworking; chemicals, tobacco. Airport for Zurich here.

Dubenka, Poland: see DUBIENKA.

Dubenki (dōō'byĭnkē), village (1926 pop. 2,678), E Mordvinian Autonomous SSR, Russian SFSR, 31 mi. SSW of Alatyr, hemp processing; hemp, wheat, potatoes.

Dubenski or **Dubenskiy** (dōōbyĕn'skē), town (1944 pop. over 500), N Chkalov oblast, Russian SFSR, near Sakmara R., on railroad (Dubinovka station) and 20 mi. WNW of Mednogorsk; gypsum and limestone quarrying.

Dubh Artach or **Dhuheartach,** rocky islet (pop. 3) of the Inner Hebrides, Argyll, Scotland, 15 mi. SW of Iona.

Dubi (dōō'bē), Czech *Dubí.* **1** Ger. *Eichwald* (īkh'vält), village (pop. 2,483), NW Bohemia, Czechoslovakia, on railroad and 4 mi. NW of Teplice, near Ger. border; health resort (alt. 1,387 ft.) in the Erzgebirge. **2** Town (pop. 6,978), central Bohemia, Czechoslovakia, on railroad and 15 mi. WNW of Prague, in urban area of Kladno.

Dubica or **Dubitsa** (dōō'bētsä). **1** or **Bosanska Dubica** or **Bosanska Dubitsa** (bô'sänskä), town (pop. 4,620), N Bosnia, Yugoslavia, on Una R. opposite Dubica (Croatia) and 33 mi. NNW of Banja Luka; local trade center. **2** Village, N Croatia, Yugoslavia, on Una R. opposite Dubica (Bosnia), on railroad; local trade center.

Dubienka (dōōbyĕn'kä), Rus. *Dubenka* (dōōbyĕn'-kŭ), town (pop. 4,096), Lublin prov., E Poland, on Bug R. (Ukrainian SSR border) and 19 mi. ESE of Chelm; hat mfg., flour milling, brickworks. Once an important river crossing. In 1792, Poles under Kosciusko defeated here by Russians. Before Second World War, pop. 50% Jewish.

Dubinovka, Russian SFSR: see DUBENSKI.

Dubisa River, Lithuania: see DUBYSA RIVER.

Dublán (dōōblän'), village (pop. 1,206), Chihuahua, N Mexico, on Casas Grandes R. (irrigation) and 125 mi. SW of Ciudad Juárez, on railroad; cotton-growing center; cereals, cattle.

Dublany, Ukrainian SSR: see DUBLYANY.

Dublin [=black pool], Gaelic *Baile Átha Cliath* (bä'lĕ ä klē'), county (□ 355.8; pop. 636,193, including Dublin city), Leinster, E Ireland; ⊙ Dublin. Bounded by cos. Wicklow (S), Kildare and Meath (W and N), and the Irish Sea (E). Drained by the Liffey. Surface is generally level, with large bog areas; rises toward Wicklow Hills (S). Coastline is irregular; largest inlet, Dublin Bay. Limestone and granite are quarried. Sea fisheries are important; cattle raising, farming are main agr. occupations. Outside of industrial center of Dublin city, hosiery industry of Balbriggan is notable. Besides Dublin, other towns are Dún Laoghaire (port), Balbriggan, Swords, Skerries, Lucan, Clondalkin, Clontarf, Rush, and Malahide. History of co. is closely associated with that of Dublin city.

Dublin, Gaelic *Baile Átha Cliath* [=town of the hurdle ford] (bä'lĕ ä klē'), county borough (pop. 506,051) and city, ⊙ Ireland and Co. Dublin, on E coast of co., on Dublin Bay of the Irish Sea, at mouth of the Liffey; 53°20'N 6°15'W. The cultural, administrative, and communications center of the country, Dublin is also a seaport, with extensive dock installations (begun 1714) and shipyards; connected with interior by Royal and Grand canals, as well as by railroad It is important center of brewing (huge Guinness breweries are well known) and poplin-milling (introduced by Huguenot refugees in 17th cent.). Other industries include whisky distilling; woolen, rayon, jute, and paper milling; food canning, tobacco processing; mfg. of chemicals, soap, shoes, clothing, thread, lace, carpets, machinery, agr. implements. Chief exports are cattle, beef, beer, whisky, leather, wood products. City is Irish literary, art, and academic center; its bldgs. mostly date from 18th cent. and later. Univ. of Dublin, or Trinity Col. (founded 1591 by Queen Elizabeth on site of 12th-cent. monastery), has in its noted library (1712) the *Book of Kells.* University Col. (R.C.) was inc. 1909 as part of National Univ. of Ireland (1849). Notable are Natl. Mus., Municipal Art Gall., and Natl. Gall. of Art. Abbey Theatre, founded 1904, is center of Irish dramatic art. Dublin Castle, built c.1200, was residence of lords lieutenant of Ireland until 1922; it now houses government offices. Christ Church, founded 1038 by Sigtryg, is cathedral of Protestant diocese of Dublin and Glendalough; oldest extant parts were built 1172 by Strongbow, who is buried here. St. Patrick's Cathedral, founded 1190 by Archbishop Comyn, is national cathedral of Protestant Church of Ireland; Swift was dean here, 1713–45, and it contains his grave and that of "Stella." Metropolitan Pro-Cathedral, seat of R.C. archdiocese of Dublin, dates from 1816. Leinster House (1745) is seat of Dáil Éireann, the Irish Parliament. Noted Phoenix Park, with former viceregal residence, is surrounded by military establishments. The main thoroughfare is O'Connell St. (formerly Sackville St.), and the Circular Road, 9 mi. long, skirts the city. Among famous Dublin citizens were Thomas Moore, Oscar Wilde, W. B. Yeats, G. B. Shaw, R. B. Sheridan, Edmund Burke, Lady Gregory, Jonathan Swift, Synge, Steele, Wolfe Tone, Robert Emmet, duke of Wellington, James Joyce. Reputed to be the anc. *Eblana,* Dublin became important with 9th-cent. Danish invasion. Danes settled here, surviving 1014 defeat at Clontarf, until expelled (1170) by Anglo-Normans under Strongbow. In 1172 Henry II gave city to the men of Bristol and made it ⊙ English-held part of Ireland and center of the Pale. Dublin suffered numerous attacks. In 1209 English inhabitants were attacked in Black Monday massacre. In Civil War city surrendered (1647) to Parliamentarians and Cromwell landed here (1649). In 1689 James II held his last Parliament here; later city was taken by William III. The 19th-cent. history of Dublin was violent; it was hq. of Repeal movement and scene of execution of Robert Emmet after 1803 rebellion, and of imprisonment of O'Connell and Parnell. In 1867 the Fenian uprising began here. In 1873 1st Home Rule conference was held in the Rotunda, where (1905) Sinn Fein movement was founded. In 1882 Lord Frederick Cavendish and Thomas Burke were murdered in Phoenix Park. In 1916 Dublin was scene of Easter Monday disturbances; in 1919 1st Sinn Fein parliament met here under de Valera. Violence continued until founding of Irish Free State (1922); last major riot was in 1927. In Second World War German air raids (1941) caused damage and casualties. Among city's chief suburbs are Clontarf, scene of 1014 defeat of Danes by Brian Boru; Donnybrook, once site of famous fair; Blanchardstown, site of Dunsink Observatory (53°23'N 6°20'W) of Trinity Col.; Sandymount, Rathmines, Rathgar, Rathfarnham, Lucan, Clondalkin, Palmerstown, Glasnevin, Finglas, Sutton, Chapelizod, and Ranelagh. Dublin airport is at Collinstown. Extending E into the Irish Sea is the peninsula Hill of HOWTH. Suburb of Howth became part of Dublin in 1940.

Dublin. **1** City (pop. 10,232), ⊙ Laurens co., central Ga., on Oconee R. and c.45 mi. ESE of Macon; market and processing center for farm and timber area; cotton ginning, mfg. of woolen textiles, lumber, cottonseed oil, fertilizer. Inc. 1812. **2** Town (pop. 993), Wayne co., E Ind., 17 mi. W of Richmond, in agr. area. **3** Resort town (pop. 675), Cheshire co., SW N.H., 12 mi. ESE of Keene and on small Dublin Pond; one of state's highest towns (alt. 1,485 ft.). Mt. Monadnock is SW. **4** Village (pop. 289), Franklin co., central Ohio, 11 mi. NW of Columbus and on Scioto R. **5** Town (pop. 243), Bladen co., SE N.C., 16 mi. E of Lumberton, in agr. area. **6** Borough (pop. 400), Bucks co., SE Pa., 6 mi. NW of Doylestown. **7** City (pop. 2,761), Erath co., N central Texas, c.45 mi. NE of Brownwood; rail junction; trade, processing center in agr., dairying, cattle-ranching region; peanut and grain milling, cotton ginning, mfg. of cheese, potato chips. Founded 1856, inc. 1889. **8** Town (pop. 1,313), Pulaski co., SW Va., 7 mi. WSW of Radford; textile finishing.

Dublin Bay, inlet (6 mi. wide, 5 mi. long) of the Irish Sea, on E coast of Co. Dublin, Ireland, bet. Hill of Howth (N) and Dalkey (S); receives the Liffey at Dublin. On S shore is port of Dún Laoghaire.

Dublineau (dŭblĕnō'), village (pop. 1,185), Oran dept., NW Algeria, on railroad and 11 mi. NW of Mascara; citrus groves; brick mfg.

Dublin Gulch, Mont.: see CENTERVILLE.

Dublon, Caroline Isls.: see TRUK.

Dublyany (dōōblyä'nē), Pol. *Dublany* (dōōblä'nē), village (1939 pop. over 500), central Drogobych oblast, Ukrainian SSR, 12 mi. NNW of Drogobych; processing (grain, potatoes). Agr. school.

Dubna (dōōb'nŭ), town (1926 pop. 2,074), W Tula oblast, Russian SFSR, 25 mi. W of Tula; metal-working center; iron foundry. During Second World War, briefly held (1941) by Germans in Moscow campaign.

Dubnany (do͞ob'nyänĭ), Czech *Dubňany*, village (pop. 3,804), SE Moravia, Czechoslovakia, on railroad and 5 mi. N of Hodonin; lignite mining.
Dubnik, Bulgaria: see Gorni Dabnik.
Dubnik, Czechoslovakia: see Presov.
Dubno (do͞ob'nŭ), city (1931 pop. 12,696), SW Rovno oblast, Ukrainian SSR, on Ikva R. and 25 mi. WSW of Rovno; agr. center; tobacco and food (cereals, meat, hops, vegetable-oil, fruit) processing; tanning, sawmilling, tile and brick mfg. Ruins of old castle. Founded in 11th cent.; became a commercial center in 18th cent. Passed from Poland to Russia in 1795; site of several battles during Russo-Polish War (1919–20); reverted to Poland in 1921; ceded to USSR in 1945. Pop. largely Jewish prior to Second World War.
Dubois (do͞obois'), county (□ 433; pop. 23,785), SW Ind.; ⊙ Jasper. Bounded partly N by East Fork of White R.; drained by Patoka R. and small Huntley, Little Pigeon, and Pokeberry creeks. Agr. area with bituminous-coal mines, clay pits, timber, and stone quarries; diversified mfg. Formed 1817.
Du Bois. 1 or **Dubois** (do͞o'boiz), village (pop. 282), Washington co., SW Ill., 20 mi. S of Centralia, in agr. and bituminous-coal area. **2** or **Dubois** (dŭbois'), village (pop. 236), Pawnee co., SE Nebr., 7 mi. SE of Pawnee City and on branch of Nemaha R., near Kansas line. **3** (do͞o'bois, dŭbois') City (pop. 11,497), Clearfield co., W central Pa., in the Allegheny Plateau region, 75 mi. NE of Pittsburgh. Railroad shops; metal products, bituminous coal, textiles, china, fertilizer, luggage, rubber goods; recreation. Seat of Du Bois Undergraduate Center of Pa. State Col. Settled 1812, laid out 1872, inc. 1881.
Dubois. 1 (dŭbois') Village (pop. 430), ⊙ Clark co., E Idaho, 35 mi. NW of Rexburg; alt. 5,147 ft.; livestock, grain. **2** Village, Ill.: see Du Bois. **3** (do͞obois') Village (1940 pop. 504), Dubois co., SW Ind., on Patoka R. and 8 mi. NE of Jasper, in agr. and bituminous-coal area. **4** Village, Nebr.: see Du Bois. **5** (dŭbois') Town (pop. 279), Fremont co., W Wyo., on Wind R., in Wind River Range, and 65 mi. NW of Lander; alt. 6,917 ft.; sheep, cattle. Archaeological field laboratory here. Large state fish hatchery near by.
Duboistown (do͞o'boistoun, do͞obois'–), borough (pop. 1,140), Lycoming co., N central Pa., on West Branch of Susquehanna R. opposite Williamsport. Settled 1773, inc. 1878.
Dubossary (do͞obŭsä'rē), town (1926 pop. 4,530), E Moldavian SSR, on left bank of Dniester R., opposite Reut R. mouth, and 22 mi. NE of Kishinev; wine center; fruit canning, flour milling, dairying, metalworking, furniture mfg.
Dubovka (do͞obôf'kŭ). **1** Town (1944 pop. over 500), S Moscow oblast, Russian SFSR, 4 mi. WSW of Uzlovaya; lignite mines. **2** (do͞o'bŭfkŭ) City (1926 pop. 11,364), central Stalingrad oblast, Russian SFSR, on right bank of Volga R. (landing) and 25 mi. NNE of central Stalingrad, in melon dist.; lumber milling, wool washing, flour and oilseed milling. Founded in 1st half of 18th cent.; an early center of the Volga Cossacks; chartered 1803. Became an important center for Volga-Don trade, until rise of Stalingrad in late-19th cent.
Dubovski or **Dubovskiy** (do͞obôf'skē), town (1948 pop. over 500), SW Mari Autonomous SSR, Russian SFSR, on Volga R. and 8 mi. E of Kozmodemyansk, on lumber railroad; sawmilling center.
Dubovskoye (–skŭyŭ), village (1948 pop. over 2,000), SE Rostov oblast, Russian SFSR, on Sal R., on railroad (Remontnaya station) and 25 mi. SW of Kotelnikovski; flour milling; wheat, cotton; cattle and sheep raising.
Dubovyazovka (do͞o″bŭvyä'zŭfkŭ), village (1939 pop. over 2,000), W Sumy oblast, Ukrainian SSR, 11 mi. SE of Konotop; sugar refining, distilling.
Dubovy Umet or **Dubovyy Umet** (do͞obô'vē o͞omyôt'), village (1926 pop. 3,789), central Kuibyshev oblast, Russian SFSR, 15 mi. SSE of Kuibyshev; wheat, sunflowers.
Dubrajpur (do͞obräj'po͝or), town (pop. 10,812), Birbhum dist., W West Bengal, India, 12 mi. SW of Suri; rice and oilseed milling, cotton weaving, pottery and metalware mfg.; trades in rice, wheat, gram, sugar cane. Hindu temple just S, on large isolated rock.
Dubrave (do͞o'brävĕ), village (pop. 5,304), NE Bosnia, Yugoslavia, 4 mi. SSE of Tuzla.
Dubréka (do͞obrā'kä), village (pop. c.800), W Fr. Guinea, Fr. West Africa, on an Atlantic bay, on railroad, and 22 mi. NE of Conakry; bananas.
Dubris, England: see Dover.
Dubrovitsa (do͞obrô'vētsŭ), city (1931 pop. 2,914), N Rovno oblast, Ukrainian SSR, on Goryn R. and 15 mi. N of Sarny; rail junction; tanning, vegetable-oil processing, flour milling, sawmilling. Until 1944, Dombrovitsa, Pol. *Dąbrowica*.
Dubrovka (do͞obrôf'kŭ). **1** Town (1948 pop. over 2,000), N Bryansk oblast, Russian SFSR, 45 mi. NW of Bryansk; hemp milling, woodworking, distilling. **2** Town (1926 pop. 2,070), N Leningrad oblast, Russian SFSR, on Neva R. and 22 mi. ESE of Leningrad; rail terminus; lumber and paper mills. Has peat-fed power station.
Dubrovnik (do͞o'brôvnĭk), Ital. *Ragusa* (rägo͞o'sä), anc. *Ragusium*, town (pop. 16,060), S Croatia, Yugoslavia, in Dalmatia, on Adriatic Sea, 100 mi. NE of Split, near Herzegovina border. Major seaport; terminus of narrow-gauge railroad to Sarajevo; tourist and seaside resort, with bathing beaches and small harbor. Its commercial port, and only modern harbor on S coast of Yugoslavia, is at suburb of Gruz, Serbo-Croatian *Gruž*, Ital. *Gravosa;* naval acad. here. Dubrovnik has 14th-cent. custom house and mint, rectors' palace (1464), cloisters of 14th-cent. Franciscan and Dominican monasteries, old churches, ports, walls, towers, and gates. Just off city lies small Lokrum Isl., Ital. *Lacroma*, where Richard I was allegedly shipwrecked (1190); has former Austrian imperial chateau. Dubrovnik was built (c.614) on site called Ragusium by Greek refugees from Epidaurus (present Cavtat), which had been destroyed by Avars. Passed (867) to Byzantine Empire and in 874 repulsed attack by Saracens. After rise of Venice, it warred against Dalmatian pirates, Venice, and Byzantine Empire; became an international trade center, with a great merchant fleet, situated at end of trade route leading to Constantinople. Its wealthy and educated nobility represented (13th–18th cent.) the intellectual elite of southern Slavs. A semi-independent republic, it passed under nominal rule of various powers: Venice (1205), Hungary (1326), Turkey (1526), and, in 1570, both Christian and Moslem sovereigns. City suffered severely in earthquake of 1667. Fell to French in 1806; inc. into Illyrian Provs. (1808), Austria (1815) as part of Dalmatia, and Yugoslavia (1919). In Middle Ages called Arragosa or Arragourse (hence *argosy*).
Dubrovno (do͞obrôv'nŭ), city (1926 pop. 7,921), SE Vitebsk oblast, Belorussian SSR, on Dnieper R. and 13 mi. ENE of Orsha; linen-milling center.
Dubrovnoye (–nŭyŭ), village (1939 pop. over 500), SE Tyumen oblast, Russian SFSR, on Irtysh R. and 45 mi. ESE of Tobolsk, in agr. area (flax, grain, livestock).
Dubuisson (dŭbwēsõ'), village, W Que., on L. Dubuisson (6 mi. long, 5 mi. wide), 6 mi. WSW of Val d'Or; gold mining.
Dubulti, Latvia: see Rigas Jurmala.
Dubuque (dŭbūk'), county (□ 608; pop. 71,337), E Iowa, bounded E by Mississippi R. (forms Wis. and Ill. lines here); ⊙ Dubuque. Prairie agr. area (hogs, cattle, corn, oats) drained by North Fork Maquoketa R.; lead and zinc deposits around Dubuque; many limestone quarries. Industry at Dubuque. Formed 1834.
Dubuque, city (pop. 49,671), ⊙ Dubuque co., E Iowa, opposite junction of Ill. and Wis. lines, port on Mississippi R. (bridged here) and c.70 mi. N of Davenport; industrial, trade, and rail center, with wood- and metalworking factories, railroad shops, shipyards, meat- and poultry-packing plants, creameries. Mfg. also of tractors, machinery, radio parts, clothing, mirrors, soap, fertilizer. Lead and zinc deposits, limestone quarries in vicinity. Loras Col. (Catholic; men; 1839), Clarke Col. (Catholic; women; 1843), Univ. of Dubuque (Presbyterian; coeducational; 1852), and Wartburg Theological Seminary (Lutheran; 1854) are here. City has library with collection of paintings, St. Raphaels Cathedral (1857), and Eagle Point Park, containing one of oldest houses in Iowa. A hotel fire in 1946 took many lives. Near by are Crystal Lake Cave, U.S. locks and dam, grave of Julien Dubuque, and the Trappist monastery New Melleray Abbey (founded 1849). Organized 1837 and chartered 1841, it is one of the oldest towns in Iowa and is named for Julien Dubuque, who settled near by in 1788. The 1st newspaper in the state, the *Dubuque Visitor* was founded here in 1836. Town developed as a mining and sawmilling center.
Dubyazy or **Dub'yazy** (do͞obyä'zē), village (1926 pop. 1,299), NW Tatar Autonomous SSR, Russian SFSR, 22 mi. N of Kazan; grain, cattle. Distilling and tanning near by.
Dubysa River or **Dubisa River** (do͞obē'sä), central Lithuania, rises in swamps S of Siauliai, flows 89 mi. S to Neman R. 24 mi. NW of Kaunas. Joined with Venta R. in upper course by 25-mi. canal.
Ducato, Cape, Greece: see Doukato, Cape.
Ducey (düsā'), village (pop. 1,178), Manche dept., NW France, on the Sélune and 6 mi. SE of Avranches; cider distilling. Dam and 2 hydroelectric stations near Vezins (2 mi. SE).
Duchcov, Czechoslovakia: see Duchkov.
Ducherow (do͞o'khŭrō), village (pop. 3,510), in former Prussian Pomerania prov., N Germany, after 1945 in Mecklenburg, 8 mi. SE of Anklam; rail junction; grain, potatoes, sugar beets, stock.
Duchesnay (düshānā'), village, S central Que., on L. St. Joseph (4 mi. long), 20 mi. WNW of Quebec; gold mining.
Duchesne (do͞oshĕn', dŭshĕn'), county (□ 3,260; pop. 8,134), NE Utah; ⊙ Duchesne. Agr. area bordering on Colo. and served by irrigation projects on Strawberry and Duchesne rivers and Lake Fork. Livestock, wheat, hay, alfalfa, sugar beets, dairy products. Uinta Mts. and Uintah and Ouray Indian Reservation are in N, part of West Tavaputs Plateau in S. Co. formed 1914.
Duchesne, town (pop. 804), ⊙ Duchesne co., NE Utah, 45 mi. NNE of Price, near junction of Strawberry and Duchesne rivers; alt. 5,517 ft.; ranch-outfitting center in irrigated agr. area (grain, alfalfa seed); flour, dairy products.
Duchesne River, NE Utah, rises in foothills of Uinta Mts., flows c.100 mi. generally E, past Duchesne and Myton, to Green R. 22 mi. SE of Roosevelt. Strawberry R. joins Duchesne R. near Duchesne. Small irrigation dam and dike are 10 mi. E of Duchesne.
Duchess, village, W Queensland, Australia, 60 mi. SW of Cloncurry; rail junction; copper mine. Formerly important mining town.
Duchess, village (pop. 207), S Alta., 70 mi. NW of Medicine Hat; ranching.
Duchess Hill, village, Salisbury prov., central Southern Rhodesia, in Mashonaland, 10 mi. SSE of Hartley; tobacco, cotton, peanuts, dairy products, citrus fruit. Gold mining.
Du Chien, Bayou, Ky.: see De Chien, Bayou.
Duchin Wai (do͞o'shĭn wā), town (pop. 1,338), Zaria prov., Northern Provinces, N central Nigeria, on railroad and 40 mi. SE of Zaria; agr. trade center (cotton, ginger, peanuts). Sometimes spelled Duchi-N-Wai and Dutsan Wei.
Duchkov or **Duchcov** (do͝okh'kôf, –tsôf), Ger. *Dux* (do͝oks), town (pop. 8,229), NW Bohemia, Czechoslovakia, 4 mi. SW of Teplice; rail junction; intensive coal mining; sugar refining, china and glass mfg. Has picturesque castle, formerly of counts Waldstein or Wallenstein.
Duchoa (do͝ok'hwä), town, Cholon prov., S Vietnam, 15 mi. WNW of Saigon; rice.
Duchray Water, Scotland: see Forth River.
Ducie Island: see Pitcairn Island.
Duckabush River, NW Wash., rises in Olympic Natl. Park N of L. Cushman, flows generally E through recreational area to Hood Canal; c.30 mi. long.
Duck Bay, Tasmania: see Perkins Bay.
Duck Hill, town (pop. 537), Montgomery co., central Miss., 10 mi. N of Winona.
Duck Island. 1 Islet, just off SW N.F., 3 mi. SW of Burgeo; 47°35'N 57°42'W; lighthouse. **2** Island (3 mi. long, 2 mi. wide), E N.F., in Notre Dame Bay, 35 mi. SE of Cape St. John; 49°31'N 55°7'W. Chief fishing settlement is Exploits (pop. 289), on NE coast.
Duck Island, Maine: see Isles of Shoals.
Duck Islands, Ont.: see Great Duck Island; Western Duck Island.
Duck Lake, town (pop. 561), central Sask., near Duck L. (6 mi. long), 33 mi. SW of Prince Albert; lumbering, woodworking, grain. Scene of 1st engagement in the Riel Rebellion (1885).
Duck Lake. 1 In Grand Traverse co., NW Mich., just SE of Interlochen, in resort area; c.3 mi. long, 1.5 mi. wide. State park and forest here; camping, fishing. Joined by stream to Green L. (W). **2** In Utah: see Navajo Lake.
Duckmanton: see Sutton cum Duckmanton.
Duck Mountain, range, W Man., extends 50 mi. N-S along Sask. border. Highest point is Baldy Mtn. (2,727 ft.), 36 mi. NW of Dauphin.
Duck River, central Tenn., rises c.15 mi. NNW of Manchester, flows S and generally WNW, past Shelbyville, Columbia, and Centerville, to Kentucky Reservoir (Tennessee R.) 7 mi. SW of Waverly; c.250 mi. long. Receives Buffalo R.
Ducktown. 1 Town (pop. 58), Forsyth co., N Ga., 12 mi. E of Canton. **2** Village (pop. 1,064), Polk co., SE Tenn., near Ga.-N.C.-Tenn. border, 50 mi. E of Chattanooga; smelting center in copper-mining region; large sulphuric-acid plant. Smelter fumes, by destroying plant growth, have caused deep erosion of region.
Duckwater, Nev.: see White Pine Mountains.
Duclair (dŭklâr'), village (pop. 1,452), Seine-Inférieure dept., N France, port on Seine R. and 11 mi. WNW of Rouen; hardware and leatherette mfg. Damaged in Second World War.
Ducos (dükō'), town (pop. 490), S Martinique, 6 mi. ESE of Fort-de-France; bananas, sugar cane; rum distilling.
Duddingston, town in Musselburgh burgh, NE Midlothian, Scotland, on Firth of Forth, near Edinburgh; seaside resort.
Duddon, village and parish (pop. 194), W Cheshire, England, 7 mi. E of Chester; dairy farming, cheese.
Duddon River, Cumberland and Lancashire, England, rises in the Cumbrian Mts. 7 mi. W of Ambleside, flows 20 mi. SW, past Broughton-in-Furness and Millom, to the Irish Sea 4 mi. SW of Millom. Its estuary, 8 mi. long, is 4 mi. wide at mouth. River has been celebrated by Wordsworth.
Dudelange (düdŭläzh'), town (pop. 12,878), S Luxembourg, 5 mi. ESE of Esch-sur-Alzette, near Fr. border; iron mining; steel center (blast furnaces, rolling mills); mfg. of synthetic fertilizer, tobacco products, beer.
Dudenhofen (do͞o″dŭnhō'fŭn), village (pop. 2,700), Rhenish Palatinate, W Germany, on Speyer R. and 2 mi. W of Speyer; wine; also corn, tobacco.
Dudergof, Russian SFSR: see Nagornoye.
Duderstadt (do͞o'dŭr-shtät), town (pop. 10,003), in former Prussian prov. of Hanover, W Germany, after 1945 in Lower Saxony, in the Eichsfeld, 13 mi. E of Göttingen; mfg. of textiles, chemicals, tobacco; food processing (flour products, beer, spirits), metal- and woodworking, paper milling. Has 2 Gothic churches, 13th–16th-cent. town hall.

Dudesti-Cioplea (dōōdĕsh'tĭ-chô'plēä), Rum. *Dudeşti Cioplea*, outer SE urban suburb (pop. 14,103) of Bucharest, S Rumania, on left bank of Dambovita R.; cotton milling, dairying.

Dudhani (dōōd'ŭnē), town (pop. 4,682), Sholapur dist., E Bombay, India, 36 mi. SE of Sholapur; agr. market (millet, wheat, cotton, peanuts). Also spelled Dudhni.

Dudhi (dōō'dē), village, Mirzapur dist., SE Uttar Pradesh, India, 75 mi. SE of Mirzapur; rice, gram, barley, wheat, sugar cane.

Dudh Kosi River, Nepal: see Sun Kosi River.

Dudhkumar River, E Pakistan: see Torsa River.

Düdingen (dü'dĭng-ŭn), Fr. *Guin* (gē), town (pop. 3,634), Fribourg canton, W Switzerland, 3 mi. NNE of Fribourg; matches, tiles, cement.

Dudinka (dōōdyĕn'kŭ), village (1948 pop. over 2,000), ⊙ Taimyr Natl. Okrug, Krasnoyarsk Territory, Russian SFSR, N of Arctic Circle, on Yenisei R., 100 mi. from its mouth, in reindeer-raising area. Ore port for Norilsk nickel mines (linked by railroad).

Dudley. 1 Town, Northumberland, England: see Weetslade. **2** Town, Stafford, England: see Tipton. **3** County borough (1931 pop. 59,583; 1951 census 62,536), in an enclave of Worcestershire located in S Staffordshire, England, in the Black Country 8 mi. WNW of Birmingham; coal mines, steel, iron, and brass foundries, machinery and brickworks. Has old Dudley Castle and remains of 12th-cent. Cluniac priory. In county borough (S) is town of Netherton (pop. 15,935), with foundries and chemical works.

Dudley. 1 Town (pop. 272), Laurens co., central Ga., 10 mi. W of Dublin. **2** Town (pop. 5,261), Worcester co., S Mass., 17 mi. SSW of Worcester, near Conn. line; woolens, paper, towels. Has a jr. col. Quinebaug R. skirts township. Settled 1714, inc. 1732. Includes Merino Village (pop. 3,118) and Perryville. **3** Town (pop. 319), Stoddard co., SE Mo., in Mississippi flood plain, 7 mi. W of Dexter. **4** Town (pop. 133), Wayne co., E central N.C., 8 mi. SSW of Goldsboro. **5** Borough (pop. 350), Huntingdon co., S central Pa., 22 mi. S of Huntingdon.

Dudley Port, England: see Tipton.

Dudorovski or **Dudorovskiy** (dōō'dŭrŭfskē), town (1926 pop. 1,275), SE Kaluga oblast, Russian SFSR, 28 mi. S of Sukhinichi; glassworks.

Dudweiler (dōōt'vī"lŭr), town (pop. 26,017), S Saar, on Sulz R. and 5 mi. NE of Saarbrücken; coal-mining center; metal- and woodworking; mfg. of electrical equipment, precision instruments, garments. Town was the *Duodonisvillare* of the Romans. Near by is the "burning mtn.," a coal vein on fire continuously since 1680.

Dudzele (dŭd'zūlŭ), agr. village (pop. 2,051), West Flanders prov., NW Belgium, 5 mi. N of Bruges. Ruins of 12th-cent. Romanesque church. Formerly spelled Dudzeele.

Due (dōōĕ'), town (1939 pop. over 2,000, N Sakhalin, Russian SFSR, on Tatar Strait, 5 mi. S of Aleksandrovsk; coal mines.

Dueim or **Ed Dueim** (ĕd dōōwām'), town (pop. 15,700), Blue Nile prov., E central Anglo-Egyptian Sudan, on left bank of the White Nile, on road and 85 mi. WSW of Wad Medani; cotton, barley, corn, durra, gum arabic; livestock. Was ⊙ White Nile prov. (now part of Blue Nile prov.).

Duékoué (dwĕ'kwā), village (pop. c.300), W Ivory Coast, Fr. West Africa, 45 mi. SSE of Man; rice, coffee, kola nuts.

Dueñas or **San Miguel Dueñas** (sän mēgĕl', dwā'nyäs), town (1950 pop. 2,164), Sacatepéquez dept., central Guatemala, at foot of volcano Acatenango, 5 mi. SW of Antigua; alt. 4,724 ft.; coffee, sugar cane, grain; beekeeping.

Dueñas, town (1939 pop. 1,534; 1948 municipality pop. 17,842), Iloilo prov., E central Panay isl., Philippines, on railroad and 25 mi. NNE of Iloilo; rice-growing center.

Dueñas, city (pop. 3,357), Palencia prov., N central Spain, near confluence of Carrión and Pisuerga rivers, 10 mi. SSW of Palencia, in fertile agr. area (cereals, wine, vegetables, fruit). Has Romanesque-Gothic church (13th–15th cent.), the Medinaceli and other mansions. Castle and convent of San Isidro near by.

Duero River, Spain and Portugal: see Douro River.

Dueville (dōōĕvēl'lĕ), village (pop. 1,595), Vicenza prov., Veneto, N Italy, 6 mi. N of Vicenza; paper mill, agr. machinery factory.

Due West, agr. town (pop. 1,033), Abbeville co., NW S.C., 37 mi. S of Greenville. Seat of Erskine Col.

Duffel (dŭ'fŭl), town (pop. 12,199), Antwerp prov., N Belgium, on Nèthe R. and 9 mi. SSE of Antwerp; nickel-refining center; paper mfg.

Dufferin (dŭ'fŭrĭn), county (□ 557; pop. 14,075), S Ont., on Grand R.; ⊙ Orangeville.

Duffield, town and parish (pop. 2,485), S central Derby, England, on Derwent R. and 5 mi. N of Derby; mfg. of dyes and colors. Has two 17th-cent. almshouses, 14th–15th-cent. church, and remains of a major Norman fortress.

Duffield, town (pop. 176), Scott co., SW Va., 11 mi. S of Big Stone Gap.

Duff Islands, small volcanic group, Solomon Isls., SW Pacific, 60 mi. NE of Santa Cruz Isls.; largest isl. c.1 mi. long.

Duffryn (dŭ'frĭn), town (pop. 4,374) in Mountain Ash urban dist., NE Glamorgan, Wales, on Taff R.; coal mining.

Dufftown (dŭf'toun), burgh (1931 pop. 1,454; 1951 census 1,460), central Banffshire, Scotland, 9 mi. SW of Keith; woolen milling, whisky distilling, lime mfg.; summer resort. Town was founded 1817 by James Duff, 4th Earl of Fife. Near by are ruins of 15th-cent. Balvenie Castle.

Duffus (dŭ'fŭs), agr. village, N Moray, Scotland, near Moray Firth, 4 mi. E of Burghead. Near by are ruins of 14th-cent. Duffus Castle.

Dufile (dōōfē'lā), village, Northern Prov., NW Uganda, at Anglo-Egyptian Sudan border, on the Albert Nile and 6 mi. WSW of (opposite) Nimule; cotton, peanuts, sesame.

Dufourspitze (dōōfōōr'shpĭ"tsŭ), Ital. *Punta Dufour*, highest peak (15,203 ft.) of Monte Rosa group and of Pennine Alps, on Italo-Swiss border, 28 mi. SSW of Brig. Also 2d highest Alpine peak (after Mont Blanc).

Dufresnoy (düfrĕnwä'), village, W Que., 10 mi. NE of Rouyn; copper, zinc, pyrite mining.

Dufrost (dōō'frôst), village, SE Man., 35 mi. S of Winnipeg; dairying; grain.

Dufur (dōō'fûr), town (pop. 422), Wasco co., N Oregon, 10 mi. S of The Dalles; wheat.

Dugald (dōō'gŭld), village (pop. estimate 500), SE Man., 14 mi. E of Winnipeg; dairying; grain.

Duga Resa or **Dugaresa** (dōō'gärĕ'sä), village (pop. 5,461), NW Croatia, Yugoslavia, on Mreznica R., on railroad and 4 mi. SW of Karlovac; mfg. of cotton textiles.

Dugdemona River (dŭgdŭmō'nŭ), N central La., rises SW of Ruston, flows c.85 mi. SE, joining Bayou Castor to form Little R. just above Rochelle.

Dugger (dŭ'gŭr), town (pop. 1,204), Sullivan co., SW Ind., 8 mi. E of Sullivan, in agr. area; crushed stone.

Duggirala (dōō'gĭrä"lŭ), village, Guntur dist., NE Madras, India, on railroad and 6 mi. N of Tenali; headworks of Kistna canal system.

Duggye, Bhutan: see Dukye.

Dugi Otok (dōō'gē ô'tôk) [Serbo-Croatian, =long island], Ital. *Isola Lunga* (ē'zôlä lōōng'gä) or *Isola Grossa* (grôs'sä), Dalmatian island (□ 71) in Adriatic Sea, W Croatia, Yugoslavia; 27 mi. long. Fishing villages, seaside resorts; Sali, largest, is on SE coast, 14 mi. SSW of Zadar.

Dugirat, Yugoslavia: see Omis.

Dugna (dōōg'nŭ), town (1926 pop. 1,401), E Kaluga oblast, Russian SFSR, near Oka R., 23 mi. ESE of Kaluga; metalworks.

Dugort, Ireland: see Achill Island.

Dugo Selo or **Dugoselo** (dōō'gô sĕ'lô), village (pop. 2,510), N Croatia, Yugoslavia, 12 mi. E of Zagreb; rail junction; local trade center.

Duhur al-Shuwayr, Lebanon: see Dhur el Shueir.

Duich, Loch, lake (6 mi. long, 1 mi. wide) in SW Ross and Cromarty, Scotland, extending SE from junction with Loch Alsh at Dornie. At its head is Kintail Forest.

Duida, Cerro (sĕ'rō dwē'dä), mountain (7,861 ft.), Amazonas territory, S Venezuela, N of Esmeralda, c.200 mi. SE of Puerto Ayacucho; 3°20'N 65°40'W. At its SW foot occurs the bifurcation of Orinoco R., where the Casiquiare R. branches off and flows SW to join Río Negro, thus linking the Orinoco and Amazon systems.

Duinbergen, Belgium: see Heist.

Duingt (dwē), village (pop. 155), Haute-Savoie dept., SE France, resort on W shore of L. of Annecy, 6 mi. SE of Annecy.

Duino (dwē'nō), Slovenian *Devin* (dĕ'vēn), Ger. *Tibein* (tē'bīn), village (pop. 371), on Gulf of Trieste, N Free Territory of Trieste, on railroad and 12 mi. NW of Trieste, near Yugoslav and Ital. borders; seaside resort. Has 15th-cent. castle (residence, after 1945, of Anglo-American zone commander).

Duisburg (dōōz'bûrg, Ger. düs'bōōrk), city (□ 56; 1939 pop. 434,646; 1946 pop. 356,408; 1950 pop. 408,877), in former Prussian Rhine Prov., W Germany, after 1945 in North Rhine-Westphalia, port on right bank of the Rhine (head of deep-sea navigation), at mouth of Ruhr R. and Rhine-Herne Canal, and 10 mi. W of Essen, adjoining Oberhausen (NE) and Mülheim (E); 51°26'N 6°45'E. Transshipment point of the Ruhr; has one of world's largest inland harbors. Coal-mining and integrated steel-mfg. center, producing pig iron, steel, steel products (notably heavy industrial machinery and lifting appliances); copper, zinc, and tin refining; shipbuilding. Other products: chemicals, textiles, tobacco. Flour milling, brewing, distilling. Imports ore, petroleum, gasoline, grain, timber; exports coal, steel, and iron products. Coal shafts, blast furnaces, and steel mills dominate scenery of city. Duisburg, with dists. of Hochfeld (S), Düssern (W), Neudorf (SW), and S outer dists. (all inc. 1929), is located S of Ruhr R. Ruhrort and Meiderich (both inc. 1905) are N of Ruhr R., adjoined (N) by outer suburb of Hamborn (inc. 1929). Of anc. origin, Duisburg passed to duchy of Cleves in 1290 and with it to Brandenburg in 1614. Residence (1559–94) of Mercator. Seat of univ. (1655–1818). Founding of Thyssen concern here in 19th cent. aided rapid industrial development. Occupied by Belgian troops 1921–25. Called Duisburg-Hamborn 1929–35. Subjected to severe Allied aerial attacks throughout Second World War (destruction about 75%).

Duitama (dwētä'mä), town (pop. 3,773), Boyacá dept., central Colombia, on Pan-American Highway, on railroad from Bogotá, in Cordillera Oriental, and 30 mi. NE of Tunja; alt. 8,500 ft. Resort; fruitgrowing center; wheat, corn, tobacco, potatoes, cattle; flour milling, cigar making. Silver and copper deposits near by. Fine colonial bldgs. Paipa thermal springs are 6 mi. WSW.

Duiveland (doi'vŭlänt), island (□ 23), Zeeland prov., SW Netherlands, NW of Bergen op Zoom; bounded by Schouwen isl. (W), the Eastern Scheldt (S), the Mastgat (E), the Grevelingen (NE); forms, with Schouwen isl., isl. of Schouwen-Duiveland. Agr. (vegetables, grains, sugar beets, potatoes, flax); dairying. Chief village, Zijpe. Flooded in Second World War.

Duiven (doi'vŭn), village (pop. 900), Gelderland prov., E central Netherlands, 5 mi. ESE of Arnhem; bricks, tiles; cattle raising, agr.

Duizend Eilanden, Indonesia: see Thousand Islands.

Dujail or **Dujayl** (dōōjīl') village, Baghdad prov., central Iraq, on railroad and 35 mi. NNW of Baghdad; dates, livestock. Also called Sumaika or Sumaykah.

Dujana (dōōjä'nŭ), town (pop. 4,278), Rohtak dist., SE Punjab, India, 15 mi. S of Rohtak; millet, cotton, oilseeds. Was ⊙ former princely state of Dujana (□ 91; pop. 30,666) of Punjab States; the state comprised 3 detached areas and in 1948 was inc. into Rohtak dist.

Duke, village (pop. c.350), Jackson co., SW Okla., 13 mi. WNW of Altus, near East Duke.

Duke Center, village (pop. c.1,200), McKean co., N Pa., 8 mi. E of Bradford, in oil-producing area.

Duke Island (12 mi. long, 8 mi. wide), SE Alaska, Gravina Isls., Alexander Archipelago, 30 mi. SSE of Ketchikan; 54°56'N 131°20'W; rises to 1,778 ft.

Dukelsky, Prusmyk, pass, Poland and Czechoslovakia: see Dukla.

Duke of Clarence Island: see Nukunono.

Duke of Gloucester Islands (glôs'tŭr) or **Anou Islands** (änōō'), small coral group, Tuamotu Isls., Fr. Oceania, S Pacific, 470 mi. SE of Tahiti; 20°40'S 143°20'W; consist of 3 islets: Anuanuraro, Anuanurunga, Nukutipipi.

Duke of York Island, Sp. *Isla Duque de York*, off coast of S Chile, at entrance to Concepción Strait, 140 mi. NW of Puerto Natales; 50°40'S 75°20'W; 23 mi. long. Uninhabited. Sometimes considered part of Madre de Dios Archipelago.

Duke of York Island, Tokelau group: see Atafu.

Duke of York Islands, coral group (□ 23; pop. c.1,100), New Britain dist., Bismarck Archipelago, Territory of New Guinea, SW Pacific, 15 mi. NE of New Britain, in St. George Channel. Comprise Duke of York Isl. (largest, 5 mi. long), Makada, Ulu, Kabakon, Kerawara. Coconut plantations. Formerly Neu Lauenburg.

Dukeries, The (dū'kŭrēz), park district of Sherwood Forest, NW Nottingham, England, bet. Warsop and Worksop, containing a number of ducal seats, including Clumber, Thoresby, Welbeck, Worksop.

Dukes, county (□ 106; pop. 5,633), SE Mass.; ⊙ Edgartown. Comprises isl. of Martha's Vineyard and Elizabeth Islands; former lying c.5 mi. S of SW angle of Cape Cod. Summer resorts; agr. fishing. Formed 1695.

Duke Town, Nigeria: see Calabar, town.

Dukhan or **Jabal Dukhan** (jă'băl dōōkhän'), oil field on W coast of Qatar peninsula, on Gulf of Bahrein; 25°25'N 50°45'E. Oil was struck here (1939) at Hawar well, but commercial development began only after Second World War. Field is linked by pipe line with loading terminal at Umm Said.

Dukhan, Jabal, highest point (445 ft.) of Bahrein, in central basin. Oil field adjoins.

Dukhovnitskoye (dōō"khŭvnyēt'skŭyŭ), village (1939 pop. over 2,000), N Saratov oblast, Russian SFSR, on arm of Volga R., opposite Khvalynsk; wheat, sunflowers, cattle.

Dukhovshchina (dōōkhŭfshchē'nŭ), village (1926 pop. 2,906), central Smolensk oblast, Russian SFSR, 13 mi. NW of Yartsevo; dairying, flax processing. Peat works near by. Chartered 1777.

Duki (dōōk'ē), village, Loralai dist., NE Baluchistan, W Pakistan, 13 mi. S of Loralai; wheat; making of mats, felt.

Dukielska, Przelecz, pass, Poland and Czechoslovakia: see Dukla.

Dukinfield (dŭ'kĭn–), municipal borough (1931 pop. 19,311; 1951 census 18,445), NE Cheshire, England, on Tame R. and 7 mi. E of Manchester; cotton milling, machine making, ironworking, mfg. of aluminum products, soap, storage batteries, bricks and tiles.

Dukku, Nigeria: see Duku.

Dukla (dōō'klä), town (pop. 699), Rzeszow prov., SE Poland, 36 mi. SSW of Rzeszow; brewing, distilling. Monastery. **Dukla Pass,** Pol. *Przełęcz*

Dukielska, Slovak *Průsmyk Dukelský* (alt. 1,647 ft.), in E Beskids, is 10 mi. S, on Czechoslovak border.

Dukstos or **Dukshtos** (do͝ok'shtōs), Lith. *Dukštos*, Pol. *Duksztý*, village, E Lithuania, on railroad and 25 mi. SSW of Daugavpils; junction of rail line to Druya.

Duku (do͞o'ko͞o'), town (pop. 7,504), Bauchi prov., Northern Provinces, E central Nigeria, 40 mi. NW of Gombe, on road; cassava, millet, durra. Sometimes spelled Dukku.

Dukwan, India: see JHANSI, city.

Dukye (do͝okyā'), fortified village [Bhutanese *dzong*], W Bhutan, on right tributary of the Raidak and 8 mi. NW of Paro, on main Phari-Punakha route. Reputedly oldest of feudal castles of Bhutan. Site of important victory of Bhutanese over Tibetans. Sometimes called Duggye and Drukgye.

Dulag (do͞o'läg), town (1939 pop. 4,861; 1948 municipality pop. 31,185), E Leyte, Philippines, on Leyte Gulf, 20 mi. S of Tacloban; agr. center (coconuts, rice, corn).

Dulaim or **Dulaym** (do͞olīm'), province (□ 27,488; pop. 193,294), central Iraq, extending from the edge of the Tigris valley W into the Syrian Desert (the desert, which extends to the Syrian, Jordan, and Saudi Arabian boundaries, is not included in the prov. area); ⊙ Ramadi. The Euphrates crosses its E section, NW–SE, and here are grown dates, corn, millet, wheat, barley; stock raising. The oil pipe line from Kirkuk to the Mediterranean crosses the prov. A legend holds that the Garden of Eden was in the Mesopotamia region W of Baghdad.

Dulais, Wales: see PONTARDULAIS.

Du Large, Bayou (bī'ō dü lärzh'), stream in Terrebonne parish, SE La., rises S of Houma, flows c.35 mi. SW to an outlet to the Gulf of Mexico, SW of Caillou L.; partly navigable for shallow-draught vessels. In lower course, joined by channels to Mechant and Caillou lakes.

Dulawan or **Dulauan** (both: do͞olä'wän), town (1939 pop. 17,927; 1948 municipality pop. 42,858), Cotabato prov., S central Mindanao, Philippines, 75 mi. W of Davao, in a swampy area on Pulangi R.; rice growing.

Dulaym, Iraq: see DULAIM.

Dulce (dŭl'sē), village (pop. c.150), Rio Arriba co., NW N.Mex., on branch of San Juan R., near Colo. line, 29 mi. NW of Tierra Amarilla; alt. c.6,800 ft.; hq. of Jicarilla Indian Reservation. San Juan Mts. near by.

Dulce, Golfo (gōl'fō do͞ol'sä), or **Osa Gulf** (ō'sä), inlet of the Pacific in S Costa Rica, bet. Osa Peninsula and mainland; 30 mi. long, c.10 mi. wide. Its ports are Golfito (on small El Golfito gulf) and Puerto Jiménez. Receives Coto R.

Dulce, Río (rē'ō), river, N Argentina, rises as the Salí in mts. of Tucumán prov. NW of Tucumán, flows SE past Tucumán, through Santiago del Estero prov., past Santiago del Estero city, into Córdoba prov. and through the salty Porongos lake region to the Mar Chiquita; 400 mi. long. In Santiago del Estero prov. it is sometimes called the Río Hondo (for a right affluent) and an arm, the Saladillo, intersects the Salinas Grandes before rejoining the main stream. The Dulce is much used for irrigation. The name Río Saladillo is also used for the whole stream.

Dulce, Río, outlet of L. IZABAL, in Izabal dept., E Guatemala; leaves NE end of lake at San Felipe, flows 22 mi. NE in winding course to Bay of Amatique (inlet of Caribbean Sea) at Lívingston. Widens in middle course to form the Golfete [Sp.,= little gulf], a lake 10 mi. long, 2–4 mi. wide. The name Río Dulce sometimes restricted to lower course, below the Golfete.

Dulce Nombre (do͞ol'sä nōm'brā). **1** Town (pop. 2,978), Copán dept., W Honduras, 7 mi. N of Santa Rosa; trade and cigar-mfg. center in tobacco area; footwear, furniture, string instruments. Limestone quarries. **2** Town (pop. 77), Olancho dept., E central Honduras, 55 mi. NE of Juticalpa; livestock; lumbering. Sometimes called Dulce Nombre de Culmí.

Dulce Nombre de María (dā märē'ä), town (pop. 1,576), Chalatenango dept., NW Salvador, 10 mi. W of Chalatenango; grain, sugar cane, coffee.

Dulcigno, Yugoslavia: see ULCINJ.

Duldurga or **Dul'durga** (do͝oldo͝orgä'), village, SW Aga Buryat-Mongol Natl. Okrug, Chita oblast, Russian SFSR, 95 mi. S of Chita, in livestock-raising area.

Duleek (dūlēk'), Gaelic *Daimhliag Chianáin*, town (pop. 295), E Co. Meath, Ireland, 5 mi. SW of Drogheda; agr. market in cattle, horse, potato region. Remains of 1182 priory.

Dülken (dül'kŭn), town (pop. 16,729), in former Prussian Rhine Prov., W Germany, after 1945 in North Rhine-Westphalia, 6 mi. NW of München Gladbach; textile mfg.

Dull, agr. village, central Perthshire, Scotland, 3 mi. W of Aberfeldy. It was site of an abbey founded c.700 (no remains).

Dullabchara or **Dullabcherra** (do͞ol–lŭb'chŭrŭ), village, Cachar dist., S Assam, India, on tributary of the Kusiyara and 32 mi. SW of Silchar; rail spur terminus; rice, tea. Until 1947, in Sylhet dist.

Dülmen (dül'mŭn), town (pop. 9,248), in former Prussian prov. of Westphalia, NW Germany, after 1945 in North Rhine-Westphalia, 17 mi. SW of Münster; rail junction; mfg. of machinery; dairying. Was almost pulverized in Second World War.

Dulnan River (dŭl'nŭn), Inverness, Scotland, rises in Monadhliath Mts. 6 mi. NW of Kingussie, flows 28 mi. E, past Carrbridge and Duthill, to the Spey 3 mi. SW of Grantown-on-Spey.

Duluth (dŭlo͞oth'). **1** Town (pop. 842), Gwinnett co., N central Ga., 21 mi. NE of Atlanta; mfg. (buffing wheels, clothing). **2** City (pop. 104,511), ⊙ St. Louis co., NE Minn., at mouth of St. Louis R., at W end of L. Superior, c.140 mi. NNE of St. Paul; 46°48'N 92°6'W; alt. 609 ft. Third largest city in Minn., it is built on rocky bluffs along lake at head of lake navigation. Has large harbor (Superior and St. Louis bays), shared with Superior, Wis., protected by sandspits called Minnesota Point and Wisconsin Point. Site of city visited in 17th cent. by early explorers, including the sieur Duluth, or DuLhut, for whom city was named; permanently settled after 1850. Grew as trade and shipping center for lumber area. Inc. as city 1870, returned to village status 1877, inc. again as city 1887. Adopted commission form of govt. 1912. Became one of world's leading ore-shipping points in 1890s after discovery of iron in Mesabi and Vermilion iron ranges. Numerous foundries, factories, and mills were established and in 1915 large plant and town (Morgan Park) were built in vicinity by U.S. Steel Corp. City is now commercial and industrial center of N Minn., port of entry, and entrance to resort area. Harbor, icebound for an average of 4 months yearly, has extensive dock facilities for handling enormous shipments of ore, grain, flour, and dairy products. Manufactures farm and telephone equipment, metal and wood products, clothing, beverages, and cement, and has flour and lumber mills, cold-storage plants, canneries, creameries, and shipyards. Oil refinery (begun 1951) near by. Prominent feature of harbor is Aerial Lift Bridge (over-all length 510 ft., vertical clearance 138 ft.), elevator bridge that spans ship canal and connects Minnesota Point with mainland of Minn. Skyline Parkway is scenic boulevard extending above city and affording good views of Duluth and lake. Other points of interest are zoological gardens and civic center (with courthouse containing mus. and library), city hall, and Federal Building (1930), which includes post office. City has Little Theater, children's mus., and civic symphony orchestra and choral society. Airport, seaplane base, U.S. fish hatchery, and U.S. coast guard, naval and weather stations are here. Institutions of education are junior col., state teachers col., and Col. of St. Scholastica. Demonstration farm and experiment station of Univ. of Minn. are near by. Jay Cooke State Park is just SW.

Dulverton, town and parish (pop. 1,502), W Somerset, England, on Barle R. and 10 mi. NNW of Tiverton; agr. market in cattle-raising region; shooting and fishing center on fringe of Exmoor. Has 13th-cent. church.

Dulwich (dŭ'lĭj), residential district of Camberwell, London, England, S of the Thames, 5 mi. SSE of Charing Cross. Has large park and is site of Dulwich Col., public school founded 1619 by Edward Alleyn. Its art gall. contains noted Dutch and Flemish paintings.

Dulyapino (do͞o'lyŭpēnŭ), town (1939 pop. over 500), NW Ivanovo oblast, Russian SFSR, 11 mi. W of Furmanov; cotton milling.

Duma (do͞o'mä), Fr. *Douma*, town (pop. c.15,000), Damascus prov., SW Syria, on Damascus-Homs road and 7 mi. NE of Damascus, in the fertile Ghuta valley; grapes.

Dumaguete (do͞omägā'tā), city (1939 pop. 6,135; 1948 metropolitan pop. 24,838), ⊙ NEGROS ORIENTAL prov., SE Negros isl., Philippines, port on Mindanao Sea, near entrance to Tañon Strait, 95 mi. SSE of Bacolod; 9°18'N 123°18'E. Trade center for agr. area. Exports hemp, copra, sugar. Here is Silliman Univ. (1901).

Dumalag (do͞omä'läg), town (1939 pop. 1,463; 1948 municipality pop. 13,103), Capiz prov., central Panay isl., Philippines, 21 mi. SSW of Capiz; sugar milling.

Dumangas (do͞omäng'gäs), town (1939 pop. 1,444; 1948 municipality pop. 29,336), Iloilo prov., E Panay isl., Philippines, 13 mi. NE of Iloilo; rice-growing center.

Dumanjug (do͞omänghōōg'), town (1939 pop. 1,791; 1948 municipality pop. 19,630), central Cebu isl., Philippines, on Tañon Strait, 36 mi. SW of Cebu city; agr. center (corn, coconuts).

Dumanquilas Bay (do͞omängkē'läs), wide inlet of Moro Gulf in SW Mindanao, Philippines.

Dumaran Island (do͞omärän') (□ 126; 1948 pop. 3,497), Palawan prov., Philippines, just off NE coast of Palawan; 10°30'N 119°45'E. On E coast is village of Dumaran or Araceli (pop. c.1,000); on W coast is another Dumaran village. Isl. is 18 mi. long, 15 mi. wide, generally low, wooded, and fertile (rice, coconuts). Pearl fishing.

Dumarao (do͞omärä'ō, –rou'), town (1939 pop. 1,415; 1948 municipality pop. 16,308), Capiz prov., central Panay isl., Philippines, 23 mi. SSW of Capiz, near railroad; rice-growing center.

Dumaresq River (do͞omĕ'rĭk) or **Severn River**, E Australia, rises in McPherson Range in Queensland, flows c.110 mi. SW and NW, past Texas (forming part of New South Wales–Queensland border), to Macintyre or Barwon R. (see DARLING RIVER).

Dumas (do͞o'mŭs). **1** Town (pop. 2,512), Desha co., SE Ark., 39 mi. SE of Pine Bluff, in agr. area (cotton, corn, hay); cotton ginning, feed and sawmilling. Founded c.1876. **2** City (pop. 6,127), ⊙ Moore co., extreme N Texas, in high plains of the Panhandle, 45 mi. N of Amarillo; oil, natural gas, and wheat center; zinc smelter, refinery; carbon-black, nitrate, helium, and gasoline plants. U.S. ordnance works at near-by Etter. Settled 1892, inc. 1930.

Dumbara Valley (do͞om'bŭrŭ), agr. area (□ 20), S central Ceylon, E of Kandy; alt. 700–1,500 ft.; extensive tea, cacao, rubber, rice, and tobacco plantations. Chief settlement, Teldeniya.

Dumbarton or **Dumbartonshire** (dŭmbär'tŭn, –shĭr), county (□ 244; 1931 pop. 147,744; 1951 census 164,263), W Scotland; ⊙ Dumbarton. Bounded by the Clyde (S), Argyll (W), Perthshire (N), Stirling (E), and Lanark (SE), and including a detached section bet. Lanark and Stirling. Drained by Clyde and Leven rivers. Mountainous in N, with several peaks over 3,000 ft. high, including Ben Vorlich; lochs Lomond, Long, and Gare are in Dumbarton. Industries include large shipyards (Clydebank and Dumbarton); coal mining (in detached section of co.), dyeing (especially red), bleaching, and printing of cotton textiles (in Leven R. valley), fishing, quarrying. There are numerous resorts along the lochs. Other towns are Clydebank, Alexandria, Helensburgh, Milngavie, Kirkintilloch, Jamestown, and Bonhill. On Roseneath peninsula is castle of duke of Argyll. Co. is associated with Tobias Smollett, b. at Dalquharn. There are traces of the Wall of Antoninus. Name of co. is sometimes spelled Dunbarton; its former name is Lennox, the name also of a district which comprises parts of Stirling, Perthshire, and Renfrew.

Dumbarton, burgh (1931 pop. 21,546; 1951 census 23,703), ⊙ Dumbartonshire, Scotland, in S part of co., on the Clyde at mouth of Leven R., 14 mi. WNW of Glasgow; shipbuilding center, with mfg. of aircraft, hosiery, soap, pharmaceuticals, and whisky. On isolated rock above Leven R. are remains of very old Dumbarton Castle; Wallace was imprisoned here in 1305, and Mary Queen of Scots was secretly taken to France from here in 1548. Under Treaty of Union (1707) castle was to be maintained as chief Scottish fortress. St. Patrick's Church dates from 1450 (rebuilt). Town is anc. British *Alcluith*, was ⊙ kingdom of Strathclyde.

Dumbarton Bridge, Calif.: see PALO ALTO.

Dumbartonshire, Scotland: see DUMBARTON, county.

Dumbéa, La (lä do͞om'bā-ä'), village (dist. pop. 390), SW New Caledonia, 7 mi. N of Nouméa; terminus of railroad from Nouméa; agr. products, livestock.

Dumbier (dyo͞om'byĕr), Slovak *Ďumbier*, Hung. *Gyömber* (dyûm'bĕr), highest peak (6,707 ft.) of the Low Tatra, in central Slovakia, Czechoslovakia, 18 mi. SE of Ruzomberok. Demanova Caves at N foot.

Dumbraveni (do͞ombrŭvän'), Rum. *Dumbrăveni*, Ger. *Elisabethstadt* (ālē'zäbĕt-shtät"), Hung. *Erzsébetváros* (ĕr'zhābĕt-vä"rōsh), town (1948 pop. 4,562), Sibiu prov., central Rumania, in Transylvania, on railroad and 31 mi. ENE of Blaj; trading center (grain, livestock, wine, wool, hides); mfg. of vinegar, bricks, tiles, flour, smoked meats; tanning; methane production. Former Armenian colony, it still has 18th-cent. Catholic Armenian church and monastery. About 25% of pop. are Magyars.

Dumdum or **Dum-Dum** (dŭm'dŭm), town (pop. 39,434), 24-Parganas dist., SE West Bengal, India, 6 mi. NE of Calcutta city center; airport for Calcutta; jute milling, mfg. of glass, matches, soap; iron- and steel-rolling works, tannery. In 19th cent., arsenal here made 1st dumdum bullets, lead-nosed cartridges which spread on impact, causing tearing wounds, 1st used by British in North-West Frontier Prov. against the tribes; prohibition of their use was adopted (1899) by 1st Hague Conference. Silk-growing research station 3 mi. ENE, at Narayanpur.

Dum Duma or **Doom Dooma** (do͞om' do͞om'ŭ), town (pop. 2,177), Lakhimpur dist., NE Assam, India, in Brahmaputra valley, on tributary of the Brahmaputra and 41 mi. E of Dibrugarh; trades in tea, rice, rape and mustard, jute, sugar cane; tea processing. Extensive tea gardens near by.

Dume, Point (do͞om, dūm), S Calif., promontory on N shore of Santa Monica Bay, 18 mi. W of Santa Monica.

Dumesnil (do͞omĕznēl'), town (pop. estimate 500), central Córdoba prov., Argentina, on Río Primero and 10 mi. NW of Córdoba; granite and limestone quarrying; cement factory; stock raising.

Dumfries or **Dumfriesshire** (dŭmfrēs', –shĭr), county (□ 1,073.4; 1931 pop. 81,047; 1951 census 85,656), S Scotland; ⊙ Dumfries. Bordering SE on England (Cumberland) and S on Solway Firth, it is bounded by Kirkcudbright (SW), Ayrshire (NW), Lanark, Peebles, and Selkirk (N), and Roxburgh (E). Drained by Annan, Esk, and Nith rivers. Surface is generally bare and hilly, rising to Lowther Hills and Moffat Hills in N; coastline is low and sandy. Has several small lochs. Farming and grazing are leading industries. There are salmon fishing, mining of coal (Sanquhar) and lead (Leadhills); sandstone and limestone quarrying. Other industries are woolen (tweed) and hosiery milling (Dumfries). Other towns are Annan, Moffat, Thornhill, Gretna Green, Lochmaben, Lockerbie, Langholm. There are many anc. castles and relics of early occupation, including Roman station at Birrens. Co. played part in border warfare and in struggle of the Covenanters. In literature it has many associations with Carlyle, who was b. at Ecclefechan and lived at Craigenputtock; Burns died at Dumfries; James Macpherson lived at Moffat.

Dumfries, burgh (1931 pop. 22,795; 1951 census 26,320), ⊙ Dumfriesshire, Scotland, on Nith R. and 30 mi. NW of Carlisle; agr. market with woolen (tweed) and hosiery mills and agr. machinery works. St. Michael's churchyard has mausoleum of Robert Burns, who lived in Dumfries from 1791 until his death. Other features are: Burns's House; Mid Steeple, old town hall built 1707; Dumfries Acad.; Greyfriars Church, built on site of anc. castle. Bridges over Nith R. include one dating from 13th cent. On W bank of Nith R., in Kirkcudbright, but inc. in Dumfries since 1929, is suburb of Maxwelltown, site of mus. and observatory (55°2'N 3°38'W).

Dumfries (-frēz'), town (pop. 1,585, with near-by Triangle), Prince William co., N Va., near the Potomac, 27 mi. SW of Washington, D.C. U.S. fish hatchery. Prince William Forest Park (formerly Chopawamsic Recreational Area) is just W.

Dumfriesshire, Scotland: see DUMFRIES, county.

Duminichi (dōōmē'nyĭchē), town (1926 pop. 1,483), S Kaluga oblast, Russian SFSR, 16 mi. SW of Sukhinichi; metalworking.

Dumitresti (dōōmētrĕsht'), Rum. *Dumitreşti* or *Dumitreşti-de-Jos*, village (pop. 646), Ramnicu-Buzau prov., E central Rumania, 14 mi. NNW of Ramnicu-Sarat; agr. center. Also spelled Dumitrestii-de-Jos.

Dumka (dōōm'kŭ), town (pop. 10,811), ⊙ Santal Parganas dist., E Bihar, India, in S Rajmahal Hills, on Mor R. and 70 mi. SSE of Bhagalpur; road junction; rice, corn, barley, oilseeds, rape and mustard. Also called Naya Dumka. Reservoir for MOR RIVER irrigation project is just S.

Dummar (dōōm'mär), Fr. *Dommar*, village (pop. c.500), Damascus prov., SW Syria, 3 mi. NW of Damascus; alt. 2,460 ft. Cement plant.

Dummer, town (pop. 229), Coos co., N N.H., on the Androscoggin and 10 mi. N of Berlin, in hunting, fishing region.

Dummerston, town (pop. 790), Windham co., SE Vt., on the Connecticut, just N of Brattleboro; wood products.

Dumont (dōō'mŏnt). **1** Town (pop. 718), Butler co., N central Iowa, 31 mi. SSE of Mason City; creamery. **2** Village (pop. 223), Traverse co., W Minn., on branch of Mustinka R. and 7 mi. SE of Wheaton; dairy products. **3** Suburban borough (pop. 13,013), Bergen co., NE N.J., 5 mi. NNE of Hackensack; makes dresses, cement blocks. Has old church (1801). Settled 1730, inc. 1894.

Dumraon (dōōm'roun), town (pop. 16,316), Shahabad dist., W Bihar, India, on Son Canals branch and 32 mi. W of Arrah; rice, wheat, gram, oilseeds, barley, sugar cane. Experimental agr. farm near by. Large annual cattle fair at Barahpur (or Barhampur), 10 mi. ENE.

Dumyat, Egypt: see DAMIETTA.

Dun, agr. village and parish (pop. 419), E Angus, Scotland, near Montrose Basin, 3 mi. WNW of Montrose. John Erskine (Erskine of Dun) b. here.

Duna, Hungarian name of DANUBE RIVER.

Duna (dōō'nä), fortified village [Bhutanese *dzong*], SW Bhutan, on tributary of the Torsa and 50 mi. SW of Punakha; lamasery.

Düna, Tibet: see TUNA.

Dünaburg, Latvia: see DAUGAVPILS.

Dunaff Head (dŭnăf'), promontory on the Atlantic, NE Co. Donegal, Ireland, on E side of entrance to Lough Swilly, 11 mi. NNW of Buncrana; 55°17'N 7°32'W.

Dunaföldvar (dōō'nŏfûld"vär), Hung. *Dunaföldvár*, town (pop. 11,480), Tolna co., central Hungary, on the Danube and 35 mi. SE of Szekesfehervar; market center; hemp and flax mfg.; fisheries. Extensive wheat growing, cattle raising near by. Railroad bridge (S) across the Danube.

Dunaharaszti (dōō'nŏhŏrŏstĭ), town (pop. 10,018), Pest-Pilis-Solt-Kiskun co., N central Hungary, on arm of the Danube and 10 mi. S of Budapest; mfg. (furniture, baskets); grain, cattle. Terminus of Danube-Tisza Canal.

Dunai, town, Russian SFSR: see SMOLYANINOVO.

Dunai, Russian name of DANUBE RIVER.

Dunaj, Czech name of DANUBE RIVER.

Dunajec River (dōōnä'yĕts), Krakow prov., S Poland, formed at Nowy Targ by junction of Czarny Dunajec [Pol.,=black Dunajec] and Bialy Dunajec [Pol.,=white Dunajec] rivers rising in the High Tatra; flows generally E along S foot of the Pieniny, and NNE past Nowy Sacz, to Vistula R. 10 mi. NNW of Zabno; 128 mi. long. Dammed at ROZNOW, CZCHOW, and CZORSZTYN for hydroelectric power. Beautiful scenery along upper course. Main tributaries, Poprad and Biala (right) rivers.

Dunajska Streda (dōō'nīskä strĕ'dä), Slovak *Dunajská Streda*, Hung. *Dunaszerdahely* (dōō'nŏsĕr"-dŏhä), town (pop. 5,691), SW Slovakia, Czechoslovakia, on railroad and 25 mi. ESE of Bratislava; agr. trade center for Great Schütt isl.

Dunakeszi (dōō'nŏkĕsĭ), town (pop. 8,365), Pest-Pilis-Solt-Kiskun co., N central Hungary, near the Danube, 9 mi. N of Budapest; rail center; vegetable, fruit canning.

Dunalastair (dŭnălŭstâr'), agr. village in Fortingall parish, N Perthshire, Scotland, on Tummel R. and 3 mi. E of Kinloch Rannoch, at foot of Schiehallion.

Dunalley (dŭnă'lē), town (pop. 285), SE Tasmania, 25 mi. E of Hobart and on SW shore of Blackman Bay, near N base of Forestier Peninsula; fish cannery.

Dunamase, Rock of, rocky hill (200 ft. high), central Co. Laoighis, Ireland, 3 mi. E of Port Laoighise, with ruins of anc. castle of Diarmuid MacMurrough, king of Leinster; later property of Strongbow. Destroyed 1650, after changing hands several times in Civil War.

Dünamünde, Latvia: see DAUGAVGRIVA.

Dunantul (dōō'näntōōl) or **Transdanubia,** Hung. *Dunántúl*, fertile hilly region in Hungary bet. Danube and Austrian border. Agr., livestock, wine; peat bogs around L. Balaton.

Dunany Point (dŭnă'nē, -ā'nē), cape on the Irish Sea, at S end of Dundalk Bay, E Co. Louth, Ireland, 12 mi. SE of Dundalk; 53°51'N 6°13'W.

Dunapataj (dōō'nŏpŏtoi), town (pop. 6,152), Pest-Pilis-Solt-Kiskun co., S central Hungary, on the Danube and 31 mi. N of Baja; rail terminus; flour mills; wheat, corn, cattle, hogs.

Dunapentele (dōō'nŏpĕn"tĕlĕ), town (pop. 3,981), Fejer co., central Hungary, on the Danube and 28 mi. SE of Szekesfehervar; river port; industry (developed after Second World War) includes iron, steel, chemical works; fishing, agr., poultry raising.

Dunarea, Rumanian name of DANUBE RIVER.

Düna River, USSR and Latvia: see DVINA RIVER (Western Dvina).

Dunaszekcsö (dōō'nŏsĕk-chû), Hung. *Dunaszekcső*, town (pop. 5,552), Baranya co., S Hungary, on the Danube and 7 mi. NNE of Mohacs; river port; fisheries.

Dunaszerdahely, Czechoslovakia: see DUNAJSKA STREDA.

Dunav, Serbo-Croatian and Bulgarian name of DANUBE RIVER.

Dunavecse (dōō'nŏvĕ-chĕ), town (pop. 4,377), Pest-Pilis-Solt-Kiskun co., central Hungary, on the Danube and 34 mi. W of Kecskemet; river port; flour mills. Roman camp ruins.

Dunayevtsy (dōōnī'ŭftsē), town (1926 pop. 8,574), S Kamenets-Podolski oblast, Ukrainian SSR, 18 mi. NNE of Kamenets-Podolski; road hub; woolen mill, machine shop.

Dunbar (dŭnbär'), burgh (1931 pop. 3,751; 1951 census 4,115), E East Lothian, Scotland, on North Sea at mouth of Firth of Forth, 25 mi. E of Edinburgh; fishing port and seaside resort. On rock above harbor are remains of anc. castle, defended 1339 for 6 weeks by "Black Agnes," countess of Dunbar, against English siege. In 1314, after battle of Bannockburn, Edward II here embarked for England. Mary Queen of Scots fled here 1566 with Darnley after murder of Rizzio, and was brought to Dunbar by Bothwell in 1567. In 1568 Moray destroyed castle. At Doon Hill, 2 mi. S of Dunbar, Cromwell defeated (1650) Leslie's Covenanters in battle of Dunbar. Dunbar House, former seat of earls of Lauderdale, is now barracks.

Dunbar (dŭn'bär). **1** Village (pop. 228), Otoe co., SE Nebr., 8 mi. W of Nebraska City and on branch of Little Nemaha R. Near by is state fruit-farm experimental station. **2** Borough (pop. 1,363), Fayette co., SW Pa., bet. Connellsville and Uniontown. **3** Industrial city (pop. 8,032), Kanawha co., W W.Va., on Kanawha R. and 6 mi. WNW of Charleston, in coal-mining region; oil wells; mfg. of farm implements, glass products, enamelware. Inc. 1921.

Dunbarney, parish (pop. 1,085), SE Perthshire, Scotland. Includes DRON and BRIDGE OF EARN.

Dunbarton, Scotland: see DUMBARTON, county.

Dunbarton (dŭn'bär"tŭn). **1** Town (pop. 533), Merrimack co., S central N.H., 9 mi. SW of Concord. **2** Former town (1950 pop. 262), Barnwell co., W S.C., 25 mi. SSE of Aiken, in area taken over (1951–52) by U.S. Atomic Energy Commission for its Savannah R. Plant (hydrogen-bomb materials).

Dunbeath (dŭnbēth'), fishing village, S Caithness, Scotland, on Moray Firth, 18 mi. SW of Wick. Dunbeath Castle dates from 15th cent. (rebuilt).

Dunblane (dŭnblăn'), burgh (1931 pop. 2,692; 1951 census 2,985), S Perthshire, Scotland, on Allan Water and 5 mi. N of Stirling; agr. market and spa resort. Has cathedral founded c.1150 by David I; Celtic cross (c.900); and remains of anc. bishops' palace. Field of Sheriffmuir (shĕ'rĭfmūr), 2 mi. E, was scene of indecisive battle (1715) bet. the Jacobites under the earl of Mar and king of England's forces under the duke of Argyll.

Dunboyne (dŭnboin'), Gaelic *Dún Bóinne*, town (pop. 336), S Co. Meath, Ireland, 10 mi. NW of Dublin; agr. market in cattle, horse, potato region.

Duncan, city (pop. 2,189), SW B.C., on SE Vancouver Isl., on Cowichan R., near its mouth on Saanich Inlet, and 30 mi. NW of Victoria; railroad junction, trade center for dairying, ranching, and poultry-raising area; lumbering, woodworking.

Duncan (dŭng'kŭn). **1** Town (pop. 941), Greenlee co., SE Ariz., on Gila R., near N.Mex. line, and 32 mi. SSE of Morenci; trade center and cattle-shipping point in irrigated agr. area. **2** Town (pop. 436), Bolivar co., NW Miss., 15 mi. SW of Clarksdale, in agr. area. **3** Village (pop. 228), Platte co., E central Nebr., 6 mi. WSW of Columbus and on Platte R. **4** City (pop. 15,325), ⊙ Stephens co., S Okla., 38 mi. S of Chickasha; trade center and supply point for oil and agr. area (cotton, grain, livestock; dairy products). Oil refining, cotton ginning; mfg. of oil-field equipment, cottonseed oil. Duncan L. is 5 mi. E. Founded 1892. **5** or **Duncan Mills,** village (pop. 3,950), Greenville co., NW S.C., near Greenville. **6** Town (pop. 599), Spartanburg co., NW S.C., 12 mi. W of Spartanburg. Power plant here.

Duncan Canal, SE Alaska, inlet (30 mi. long, 2 mi. wide) in S coast of Kupreanof Isl., Alexander Archipelago.

Duncan Falls, village (1940 pop. 689), Muskingum co., central Ohio, on Muskingum R. and 7 mi. SE of Zanesville; coal mines, oil wells.

Duncan Island, China: see CRESCENT GROUP.

Duncan Lake, Stephens co., S Okla., 5 mi. E of Duncan; c.3.5 mi. long.

Duncan Mills, S.C.: see DUNCAN, Greenville co.

Duncannon (dŭnkă'nŭn), Gaelic *Dun Conáin*, town (pop. 228), SW Co. Wexford, Ireland, on Waterford Harbour, 8 mi. ESE of Waterford; fishing port, with anc. fort.

Duncannon (dŭn"kă'nŭn), borough (pop. 1,852), Perry co., S central Pa., on Susquehanna R., just below mouth of Juniata R., and 13 mi. NW of Harrisburg; metal products, flour. Inc. 1844.

Duncan Passage, channel connecting Bay of Bengal and Andaman Sea, bet. main group of Andaman Isls. (N) and Little Andaman Isl. (S).

Duncans, town (pop. 1,650), Trelawny parish, N Jamaica, near the coast, 8 mi. E of Falmouth; sugar cane, ginger, pimento, fruit. Adjoining NE is the now-abandoned Braco airfield.

Duncansbay Head or **Duncansby Head,** NE extremity of Scotland, NE Caithness, on Pentland Firth, 14 mi. N of Wick; 210 ft. high. Site of lighthouse (58°39'N 3°2'W).

Duncansville, residential borough (pop. 1,391), Blair co., S central Pa., 5 mi. SSW of Altoona; mfg. of radiators. Laid out 1831.

Duncan Town, settlement on Great Ragged Isl. or Ragged Isl., S Bahama Isls., c.225 mi. SE of Nassau; 22°12'N 75°44'W. Salt panning.

Duncanville, town (pop. 841), Dallas co., N Texas, just SW of Dallas.

Duncombe (dŭn'kŭm), town (pop. 378), Webster co., central Iowa, 10 mi. ESE of Fort Dodge.

Duncormick (dŭnkŏr'mĭk), Gaelic *Dún Cormaic*, agr. village (district pop. 416), S Co. Wexford, Ireland, near the coast, 11 mi. SW of Wexford; dairying, wheat, barley, potatoes.

Duncow (dŭnkō'), agr. village in Kirkmahoe parish (pop. 1,075), central Dumfries, Scotland, 5 mi. N of Dumfries.

Duncrue (dŭnkrōō'), village, E Co. Antrim, Northern Ireland, 2 mi. NW of Carrickfergus; rock-salt mining.

Dunda Gobi, Mongolia: see MIDDLE GOBI.

Dundalk (dŭndôk', -dôlk'), village (pop. 688), S Ont., 35 mi. SE of Owen Sound; dairying; lumber.

Dundalk, Gaelic *Dún Dealgan*, urban district (pop. 18,562), ⊙ Co. Louth, Ireland, on Castletown R., near its mouth on Dundalk Bay of the Irish Sea, 50 mi. N of Dublin; 54°N 5°24'W; seaport with dock installations, exporting cattle, beef, grain, butter, eggs; fishing port and rail center, with railroad shops. Also linen milling, brewing, tobacco, processing, bacon curing, mfg. of hosiery, clothing, shoes, chemicals, soap, lace, furniture, cattle feed. Features are Pro-Cathedral of St. Patrick; Church of St. Nicholas; "Seatown Castle," tower of 1240 Franciscan abbey; and fortified Castletown House. Reputed birthplace of the legendary hero Cuchulain (killed here). Dundalk became hq. (1315) of Edward Bruce, who was killed in its defense (1318). It was walled by Henry IV, and suffered numerous sieges until walls were razed in 1747. In 1922–23 civil war Dundalk suffered destruction from fire.

Dundalk (dŭn'dôk), industrial suburb, Baltimore co., central Md., near Patapsco R., 6 mi. SE of downtown Baltimore; boat building, mfg. of sheet metal products, welding wire, engines, whisky. Harbor Field airport is just SW.

Dundalk Bay (dŭndôk', -dôlk'), inlet (7 mi. long) of the Irish Sea, NE Co. Louth, Ireland, bet. Dunany Point (S) and Cooley Point (N), receiving Castletown, Dee, and Fane rivers. On Castletown R., near its mouth on the bay, is Dundalk town. There are oyster fisheries.

Dundarrach (dŭn"dâ'rŭk), village (pop. 134), Hoke co., S N.C., 18 mi. SW of Fayetteville.

Dundas (dŭndăs′, dŭn′dăs), municipality (pop. 7,635), E New South Wales, Australia, 11 mi. WNW of Sydney, in metropolitan area; coal-mining center; brickyards, confectioneries.
Dundas (dŭn′dŭs), county (□ 384; pop. 16,210), SE Ont., on the St. Lawrence and on N.Y. border; ⊙ Cornwall.
Dundas, town (pop. 5,276), S Ont., 10 mi. W of Hamilton; textile knitting; mfg. of machinery, clothing, gloves, furniture. Laid out 1801, it is at head of Desjardins Canal, a position which made it an important lake port before building of railroad.
Dundas, village (pop. 469), Rice co., S Minn., on Cannon R. and 10 mi. NNE of Faribault, in agr. area (corn, oats, barley, livestock, poultry).
Dundas, Cape, N Prince of Wales Isl., central Franklin Dist., Northwest Territories, on Barrow Strait; 73°58′N 99°57′W.
Dundas Harbour (dŭn′dŭs), trading post, SE Devon Isl., E Franklin Dist., Northwest Territories, on Lancaster Sound; 74°31′N 82°25′W; Royal Canadian Mounted Police post, now unused.
Dundas Islands, W B.C., group of 4 isls. and numerous islets and rocks, in Dixon Entrance of the Pacific, NW of Prince Rupert. Largest, Dundas Isl. (□ 58; 14 mi. long, 8 mi. wide; rises to 1,523 ft.), is 25 mi. NW of Prince Rupert and 12 mi. S of Cape Fox, S extremity of Alaska mainland, separated from Canadian mainland by Chatham Sound (15 mi. wide). Just SE are the small Baron, Dunira, and Melville isls.
Dundas Strait, channel connecting Timor Sea with Van Diemen Gulf, bet. Melville Isl. (W) and Cobourg Peninsula, N Northern Territory, Australia; 40 mi. long, 18 mi. wide.
Dundee (dŭndē′), burgh (1931 pop. 175,585; 1951 census 177,333) and co. of itself, S Angus, Scotland, on N shore of the Firth of Tay, 40 mi. NNE of Edinburgh; 56°27′N 2°58′W. Third largest city of Scotland, Dundee is a commercial and jute-milling center, with port and dock installations; other industries include shipbuilding, petroleum refining, tar distilling, metal casting, textile bleaching, and mfg. of textile machinery, electrical appliances, biscuits. Dundee marmalade is famous. Near by are fish canneries. Notable are: University Col. (part of St. Andrews Univ.), founded 1883; Town Hall (1734), built by John Adam; St. Mary's Church, with famous 15th-cent. "Old Steeple"; Albert Inst. (1867), by Sir Gilbert Scott; and modern Caird Hall. Dundee was 1st town in Scotland to adopt Reformation doctrines, largely through influence of George Wishart. In 1547 it was taken and sacked by forces of Henry VIII; in 1651 it was occupied by General Monk. Claverhouse (Bonnie Dundee) became its hereditary constable in 1683. It was created a city in 1889. Hector Boece b. here. Suburbs include Downfield (N), site of mental hosp., and Lochee (WNW) with fish canneries and textile-machinery works. Burgh includes residential and resort town of Broughty Ferry (brô′tē), on the Firth of Tay, 4 mi. E of Dundee; terminal of ferry to Tayport, Fifeshire, and site of 15th-cent. Broughty Castle, taken (1547) by the English after battle of Pinkie. From Dundee the land slopes W to Dundee Law (571 ft. high). Dundee is at N end of the Tay Bridge, a railroad bridge over the Firth of Tay to Wormit, Fifeshire. Built 1882–88, it is over 2 mi. long and replaces earlier structure (1871–78), blown down 1879 in a gale, along with an entire passenger train.
Dundee, town (pop. 6,797), NW Natal, U. of So. Afr., 40 mi. NE of Ladysmith; coal- and iron-mining center; mfg. of glass, bricks, tiles, soap, candy, dairy products; agr. market. Airfield. Scene (1899) of South African War battle; in vicinity are numerous battle sites of Zulu (1879) and South African (1899–1902) wars.
Dundee. 1 Town (pop. 1,152), Polk co., central Fla., 7 mi. E of Winter Haven; packs citrus fruit. **2** Village, Kane co., NE Ill., just N of Elgin, in agr. area; composed of EAST DUNDEE and WEST DUNDEE, separately inc. villages on either side of Fox R. **3** Town (pop. 176), Delaware co., E Iowa, on Maquoketa R. and 7 mi. NW of Manchester. Backbone State Park with fish hatchery (N). **4** Village (pop. 1,975), Monroe co., extreme SE Mich., 14 mi. WNW of Monroe and on Raisin R., in agr. area (grain, truck, hay, livestock; dairy products). Alfalfa and feed mills; poultry hatcheries; cannery; mfg. of auto parts; salt beds. Settled 1827; inc. 1855. **5** Village (pop. 179), Nobles co., SW Minn., near Des Moines R., 17 mi. NNE of Worthington in grain and potato area. Small lakes near by. **6** Village (pop. 1,165), Yates co., W central N.Y., 24 mi. S of Geneva, in Finger Lakes grape-growing region; summer resort. Mfg. (metal products, clothing, flour, boats). Inc. 1847. **7** City (pop. 308), Yamhill co., NW Oregon, 10 mi. NE of McMinnville; walnuts, filberts, prunes. **8** Village (pop. c.300), Archer co., N Texas, 25 mi. WSW of Wichita Falls. State fish hatchery on Wichita R. (N) is near.
Dundee Island (15 naut. mi. long, 10 naut. mi. wide), Antarctica, off E of tip of Palmer Peninsula, SW of Joinville Isl.; 63°25′S 56°10′W. Discovered 1893 by Thomas Robertson, Scottish explorer.
Dunderlandsdal (dōōn′nürlänsdäl″), valley of lower Rana R., in Nordland co., N central Norway, extends c.30 mi. NE from Ran Fjord at Mo; traversed by railroad. Iron deposits. Stalactite caverns have been formed by river, which flows partly underground.
Dund Gobi, Mongolia: see MIDDLE GOBI.
Dundit (dōōn′dēt), village (pop. 9,684), Daqahliya prov., Lower Egypt, on railroad and 3 mi. SE of Mit Ghamr; cotton, cereals.
Dundo (dōōn′dō), town (pop. 2,821), Malange prov., northeasternmost Angola, near Belgian Congo border, just S of Portugália, in diamond-washing region.
Dundonald (dŭndŏ′nŭld), town (pop. 1,535), NE Co. Down, Northern Ireland, 5 mi. E of Belfast; agr. market (flax, oats), with chalybeate springs. An annual automobile race is held here. Near by is Kempe Stone, anc. dolmen.
Dundonald, agr. village, W Ayrshire, Scotland, 4 mi. SW of Kilmarnock. Has ruins of 14th-cent. castle, where Robert II, 1st Stuart king of Scotland, lived and died.
Dundrennan (dŭndrĕ′nŭn), agr. village in Rerrick parish, S Kirkcudbright, Scotland, 5 mi. SE of Kirkcudbright. Site of ruins of Dundrennan Abbey, founded 1142 for Cistercian monks.
Dundrum (dŭndrŭm′), Gaelic *Dún Droma,* SE residential suburb (pop. 733) of Dublin, Co. Dublin, Ireland.
Dundrum, fishing village (district pop. 1,291), SE Co. Down, Northern Ireland, on Inner Bay, narrow inlet of Dundrum Bay of the Irish Sea, 7 mi. SW of Downpatrick.
Dundrum Bay, inlet (12 mi. wide, 5 mi. long) of the Irish Sea, on SE coast of Co. Down, Northern Ireland. Chief ports: Dundrum and Newcastle. At NE end of bay is St. John's Point, 7 mi. SSE of Downpatrick; lighthouse (54°14′N 5°39′W).
Dundurn (dŭndûrn′), village (pop. 343), S Sask., 23 mi. SSE of Saskatoon; wheat.
Dundwaraganj (dōōndvä′rägŭnj), town (pop. 8,519), Etah dist., W Uttar Pradesh, India, 19 mi. ESE of Kasganj; trades in wheat, pearl millet, barley, corn, jowar, cotton. Also called Ganj Dundwara (also written Ganjdundwara).
Dundy, county (□ 921; pop. 4,354), S Nebr.; ⊙ Benkelman. Agr. area bordering on Kansas and Colo.; drained by Republican R. Grain, livestock, dairy and poultry produce. Formed 1873.
Dune Acres, town (pop. 86), Porter co., NW Ind., on L. Michigan, 13 mi. ENE of Gary.
Duneaton Water, Scotland: see CRAWFORDJOHN.
Dunecht, Scotland: see ECHT.
Dunedin (dŭnē′dĭn), city (pop. 65,771; metropolitan Dunedin 83,351), on SE coast of S.Isl., New Zealand, at base of Otago Peninsula, which forms long, sheltered Otago Harbour; 45°52′S 170°31′E. Near-by Port Chalmers is its port. Mfg. center; iron and brass foundries, woolen mills, clothing and shoe factories. Univ. of Otago (1869), School of Medicine (affiliated with Univ. of New Zealand), School of Mines, Knox Col. (theological seminary), Anglican and R.C. cathedrals. Founded 1848 by Scottish settlers.
Dunedin, Scotland: see EDINBURGH.
Dunedin, city (pop. 3,202), Pinellas co., W Fla., on Gulf coast, adjacent to Clearwater; resort; processes citrus fruit, makes canning and packing machinery. Settled c.1865, inc. 1899.
Dunedoo, village (pop. 752), E central New South Wales, Australia, 165 mi. NW of Sydney; mining center (silver, lead, zinc).
Dunellen (dŭnĕ′lŭn), borough (pop. 6,291), Middlesex co., NE N.J., 18 mi. SW of Newark, adjoining Plainfield; mfg. (concrete mixers, adhesives, pumps, printing presses, lace curtains); commercial printing; agr. (nursery products, poultry, fruit, truck). Laid out 1868, inc. 1887.
Dunes Park, village (pop. 1,762), Lake co., NE Ill., on L. Michigan and 5 mi. N of Waukegan.
Dunfanaghy (dŭn-fă′nŭhē), Gaelic *Dún Fheannachaidh,* town (pop. 362), N Co. Donegal, Ireland, on Sheep Haven (bay of the Atlantic), 18 mi. NW of Letterkenny; fishing port, seaside resort, and agr. market (cattle, sheep; oats, potatoes).
Dunfermline (dŭnfûrm′lĭn, dŭm–), burgh (1931 pop. 35,058; 1951 census 44,710), SW Fifeshire, Scotland, near the Firth of Forth, 13 mi. NW of Edinburgh; textile center (linen, silk, rayon; textile machinery), with metal foundries and food-processing works (ham and bacon); agr. market. Dunfermline Abbey was founded 1072 by Malcolm Canmore and his queen, St. Margaret, and was rebuilt by Davis I in 1150; Robert the Bruce and other Scottish kings are buried here. There are remains of 11th-cent. palace; David I and James I b. here. In 11th cent. Dunfermline became royal residence of Scottish kings. Andrew Carnegie, b. here, made many gifts to the town, which is hq. of the Carnegie Trusts.
Dunfermline (dŭnfûrm′lĭn –fûr′lĭn, –fûrlĭn′), village (pop. 292), Fulton co., W central Ill., 28 mi. SW of Peoria.
Dunga (dōōng′gä), town, central Zanzibar, on road and 10 mi. ENE of Zanzibar town; clove-growing center; copra. Ruins of 19th-cent. palace near by.
Dungannon (dŭn-gă′nŭn), village (pop. estimate 450), S Ont., 10 mi. NE of Goderich; dairying, mixed farming.
Dungannon, urban district (1937 pop. 3,930; 1951 census 5,674), SE Co. Tyrone, Northern Ireland, 12 mi. NNW of Armagh, in coal-mining region; linen and woolen milling, pottery mfg. Has Royal School, founded by Charles I. Until 17th cent. town was chief stronghold of the O'Neills, who had castle here.
Dungannon, town (pop. 431), Scott co., SW Va., on Clinch R. and 23 mi. WSW of Lebanon.
Dungarpur (dōōng′gŭrpōōr), former princely state (□ 1,460; pop. 274,282) in Rajputana States, India; ⊙ was Dungarpur. Before c.1530, territories included Banswara state; under Mahratta control in late-18th cent. In 1948, merged with union of Rajasthan.
Dungarpur, town (pop. 8,670), ⊙ Dungarpur dist., S Rajasthan, India, 50 mi. S of Udaipur, at SE end of Aravalli Range; markets corn, rice, barley, gram; handicrafts (woodwork, metalware, stone images). Was ⊙ former Rajputana state of Dungarpur.
Dungarvan (dŭn-gär′vŭn), Gaelic *Dún Garbháin,* urban district (pop. 5,276), S Co. Waterford, Ireland, on Dungarvan Bay, 25 mi. WSW of Waterford; 52°5′N 7°37′W; fishing port and market center; tanning and tobacco processing. Has remains of castle built by King John. Just E is suburb of Abbeyside, with ruins of 13th-cent. castle of the MacGraths, and a priory.
Dungeness, Australia: see LUCINDA POINT.
Dungeness (dŭnj′nĕs′), flat shingle headland, forming S tip of Kent, England, on the Channel 11 mi. E of Rye; lighthouse (55°55′N 0°58′E). Off Dungeness the Dutch, under Admiral Tromp, defeated the English in 1652.
Dungeness (dŭn″jŭnĕs′), fishing village, Clallam co., NW Wash., on Juan de Fuca Strait, at mouth of Dungeness R. (c.35 mi. long), and 15 mi. ENE of Port Angeles; ships crabs. Dungeness Spit has lighthouse.
Dungeness, Point (dŭnj′nĕs′), cape on Argentina-Chile border, SE point of South American mainland at E entrance to Strait of Magellan, 4 mi. SW of Cabo Vírgenes; 52°23′27″S 68°24′42″W.
Dungiven (dŭn-gĭ′vŭn), town (pop. 775), central Co. Londonderry, Northern Ireland, on Roe R. and 8 mi. S of Limavady; agr. market (flax, potatoes, oats). Has remains of fortified house of the Skinner's Company of London (1618) and of priory founded c.1100, restored 1397.
Dungloe or **Dunglow** (dŭn-glō′), Gaelic *Clochán Liath,* town (pop. 586), W Co. Donegal, Ireland, on inlet of the Atlantic, 25 mi. W of Letterkenny; fishing port.
Dungog (dŭn-gŏg′, dŭn′gŏg), municipality (pop. 2,041), E New South Wales, Australia, 35 mi. N of Newcastle; agr. center; fruit, hardwood timber.
Dungu (dōōng′gōō), village, Eastern Prov., NE Belgian Congo, at confluence of Dungu R. and Kibali R., on Congo-Nile highway and 260 mi. ENE of Buta; cotton ginning, fishing; corn, manioc. Has Dominican and Protestant missions with schools and small seminary for natives. Former Congo Free State fort during the campaign against Arab slave-traders (1890–94).
Dungun, Malaya: see KUALA DUNGUN.
Dungunab (dōōng-gōōnăb′), village, Kassala prov., NE Anglo-Egyptian Sudan, minor port on Red Sea, on road and 140 mi. N of Port Sudan; fishing.
Dungu River (dōōng′gōō), NE Belgian Congo, rises near Anglo-Egyptian Sudan border 15 mi. SE of Aba, flows c.150 mi. W, past Faradje and Gangala na Bodio, to Kibali R. at Dungu.
Dunham (dŭ′nŭm), village (pop. 377), S Que., 9 mi. ENE of Bedford; dairying, pig raising.
Dunhinda Falls, Ceylon: see BADULLA.
Dunholme, England: see DURHAM, city.
Dunières (dünyâr′), village (pop. 1,873), Haute-Loire dept., S central France, 15 mi. S of Saint-Étienne; silk spinning and weaving, woodworking.
Dunilovichi (dōōnyĕ′lŭvĕchē), Pol. *Dunilowicze* (dōōnyēwôvē′chĕ), town (1931 pop. 2,250), SW Polotsk oblast, Belorussian SSR, 19 mi. WSW of Glubokoye; tanning, flour milling, sawmilling.
Dunipace, Scotland: see DENNY AND DUNIPACE.
Dunkeld (dŭnkĕld′), village in Dunkeld and Dowally parish (pop. 946), E central Perthshire, Scotland, on the Tay (bridge by Telford) and 13 mi. NNW of Perth, near Birnam. Has cathedral, partly dating from 12th cent. and formerly seat of a bishop. Dunkeld House is seat of duke of Atholl. Agr. village of Dowally is 4 mi. NNW of Dunkeld, on the Tay.
Dunkerque, France: see DUNKIRK.
Dunkerton, town (pop. 409), Black Hawk co., E central Iowa, 10 mi. ENE of Waterloo, in agr. area.
Dunkery Beacon, mountain (1,708 ft.), W Somerset, England, on Exmoor, 6 mi. SW of Minehead. Highest point in Somerset; surmounted by anc. cairn.
Dunkineely (dŭn-kĭnē′lē), Gaelic *Dún Geannfhaolaidh,* town (pop. 226), SW Co. Donegal, Ireland, on small inlet of Donegal Bay, 11 mi. W of Donegal; fishing port. Near by is anc. castle.
Dunkirk (dŭn′kûrk), Fr. *Dunkerque,* formerly also spelled *Dunquerque* (both: dŭkârk′), coastal town

(1946 pop. 9,869; 1936 pop. 28,450), Nord dept., N France, on the North Sea 24 mi. ENE of Calais, near Belg. border; northernmost and, until 1940, one of France's principal seaports. It is in flat, low region (drained by canals and dikes) which can be flooded for defense purposes. Economic activities, now chiefly carried on in suburbs of Rosendaël (E), Coudekerque-Branche (S), and Saint-Pol-sur-Mer (W), include boat building, mfg. of fishing equipment, jute and cotton milling, canning and drying (vegetables, fish), petroleum refining, chicory and cod-liver oil processing, metal- and woodworking. Suburban Malo-les-Bains is a beach resort (heavily damaged). Founded c.10th cent., often fortified, it was key stronghold in long struggle among France, Holy Roman Empire, Spain, England, and the Netherlands. Frequently changed hands, generally sharing history of FLANDERS. Permanently acquired for France by Louis XIV in 1662. Withstood Anglo-Dutch bombardment in 1694, and numerous Ger. shellings and air raids in First World War. Scene of memorable evacuation to England (May 26-June 4, 1940) of more than 300,000 Allied troops, cut off from retreat on land by Ger. break-through to Fr. Channel ports. In 1944-45, isolated Ger. garrison held out in Dunkirk to deny Allies use of port facilities until after Ger. surrender in May, 1945. As a result of Second World War, not a single building remained undamaged and harbor was completely gutted. Jean Bart b. here.

Dunkirk. 1 City (pop. 3,048), on Jay-Blackford co. line, E Ind., 16 mi. NNE of Muncie, in agr. area (livestock, dairy, poultry farms; soybeans, grain); mfg. (brick, tile, glass). **2** Industrial city (pop. 18,007), Chautauqua co., extreme W N.Y., on L. Erie, 38 mi. SW of Buffalo; mfg. (radiators, boilers, machinery, silk, tool steel, glass); fisheries; agr. (dairy products; tomatoes, grapes). Seat of Holy Cross Preparatory Seminary. Bathing beaches. A state park is near by. Inc. as village in 1837, as city in 1880. **3** Village (pop. 972), Hardin co., W central Ohio, 24 mi. E of Lima, in agr. area; mfg. of transportation equipment. Limestone quarry.

Dunk Island, uninhabited island (4 mi. long, c.1 mi. wide) in Coral Sea, bet. Great Barrier Reef and E coast of Queensland, Australia, at N side of entrance to Rockingham Bay; rises to 900 ft. Wooded; bird sanctuary.

Dunklin, county (□ 543; pop. 45,329), extreme SE Mo.; ⊙ Kennett. Bounded W by St. Francis R.; in Mississippi flood plain, with drainage canals. Grows and processes cotton; corn, wheat, melons, strawberries, livestock. Formed 1845.

Dunkur (dōōng'kōōr), village (pop. 300), Gojjam prov., NW Ethiopia, on Dinder R. and 65 mi. NE of Qubba, in cotton-growing region.

Dunkwa (dōōng'kwä), town (pop. 6,714), Western Prov., S central Gold Coast colony, on Ofin R. (rail bridge) and 75 mi. N of Takoradi; rail junction (branch to Awaso bauxite mines); gold mining; sawmill; rubber and cacao trade.

Dún Laoghaire (dōōnlâ'rē, dŭnlâ'rŭ), formerly Kingstown or Dunleary (dŭnlē'rē), borough (pop. 44,674), SE Co. Dublin, Ireland, on the Irish Sea, 7 mi. SE of Dublin; 53°17'N 6°8'W; principal passenger port for Dublin, with 2 piers and extensive dock installations; seaside resort, fishing and yachting center. Has chemical works. Port is terminal of mail steamers from Holyhead, Wales. Originally called Dunleary, town was named Kingstown when George IV landed here in 1821. Harborworks, built by Rennie, were begun 1817, completed 1859.

Dunlap. 1 Village (pop. 1,154), Elkhart co., N Ind., 4 mi. SE of Elkhart. **2** Town (pop. 1,409), Harrison co., W Iowa, c.45 mi. NNE of Council Bluffs; foundry, feed mill. Inc. 1871. **3** City (pop. 134), Morris co., E central Kansas, near Neosho R., 16 mi. NW of Emporia, in grazing and farming region. **4** City (pop. 873), ⊙ Sequatchie co., E Tenn., on Sequatchie R. and 23 mi. N of Chattanooga, in fertile agr., livestock, timber region; wood products.

Dunlavin (dŭnlă'vŭn), Gaelic *Dún Luadháin*, town (pop. 404), W Co. Wicklow, Ireland, 11 mi. SE of Kildare; cattle, sheep; dairying; potatoes.

Dun Law, Scotland: see MOFFAT HILLS.

Dunleary, Ireland: see DÚN LAOGHAIRE.

Dunleer (dŭnlēr'), Gaelic *Dún Léire*, town (pop. 411), S central Co. Louth, Ireland, 8 mi. NNW of Drogheda; wheat, barley, potatoes; cattle.

Dun-le-Palleteau (dū-lŭ-pältō'), village (pop. 965), Creuse dept., central France, 13 mi. NW of Guéret; horse breeding.

Dunlevy (dŭn"lĕ'vē), borough (pop. 379), Washington co., SW Pa., 3 mi. SE of Charleroi.

Dunlo, village (pop. c.1,400), Cambria co., SW central Pa., 10 mi. E of Johnstown.

Dunlop, agr. village and parish (pop. 1,224), N Ayrshire, Scotland, 7 mi. N of Kilmarnock, in dairying area noted for its cheese.

Dunloy (dŭnloi'), village (district pop. 1,022), NW Co. Antrim, Northern Ireland, 6 mi. SE of Ballymoney; lignite mining.

Dunmanus Bay (dŭnmă'nŭs), inlet (15 mi. long, 3 mi. wide) of the Atlantic, on SW coast of Co. Cork, Ireland. Entrance lies bet. Sheep Head (N) and Mizen Head (S). At head of bay is Durrus.

Dunmanway (dŭnmăn'wē), Gaelic *Dún Maonmhuighe*, town (pop. 1,475), SW Co. Cork, Ireland, on Bandon R. and 14 mi. NNE of Skibbereen; agr. market (potatoes, oats; dairying).

Dunmore (dŭnmôr'), Gaelic *Dún Mór*. **1** Town (pop. 465), N Co. Galway, Ireland, 8 mi. NE of Tuam; agr. market (sheep; beets, potatoes). Has remains of abbey founded 1428 on site of anc. monastery. **2** Town, Co. Waterford, Ireland: see DUNMORE EAST.

Dunmore, agr. village in Airth Parish, E Stirling, Scotland, on the Forth and 7 mi. ESE of Stirling. Has small port.

Dunmore, borough (pop. 20,305), Lackawanna co., NE Pa., just E of Scranton; anthracite mines; silk and rayon mfg. Settled 1783 as Buckstown, renamed 1840.

Dunmore, Lake, Addison co., W Vt., lake (3.5 mi. long) and resort village, 8 mi. SSE of Middlebury, partly in Green Mtn. Natl. Forest.

Dunmore East or **Dunmore,** Gaelic *Dún Mór*, town (pop. 288), SE Co. Waterford, Ireland, on the coast at entrance to Waterford Harbour, 9 mi. SE of Waterford; 52°9'N 7°W; fishing center and resort. Formerly important as terminal of mail-ship service from Milford Haven, England.

Dunmore Head, promontory on the Atlantic, W Co. Kerry, Ireland, 35 mi. WSW of Tralee, just NW of Slea Head; 52°6'N 10°29'W; W extremity of Irish mainland.

Dunmore Town, chief settlement of Harbour Isl., central Bahama Isls., 33 mi. NE of Nassau; 25°30'N 76°38'W. Winter resort with fine harbor; grows tomatoes, fruit.

Dunmow or **Great Dunmow** (–mō), town and parish (pop. 2,882), W Essex, England, on Chelmer R. and 8 mi. W of Braintree; agr. market. Has 14th-15th-cent. church. Agr. village and parish of Little Dunmow (pop. 408), 2 mi. ESE, has remains of Augustinian priory (founded 1104) and Norman church. The annual Dunmow Flitch trials are held here; a flitch of bacon is awarded the couple who testify that they had not quarreled or regretted their marriage for a year and a day after their wedding. Custom is described in *Piers Plowman*.

Dunmurry (dŭnmûr'ē), town (pop. 2,645), S Co. Antrim, Northern Ireland, near Lagan R., 4 mi. SSW of Belfast; linen milling.

Dunn. 1 County (□ 2,068; pop. 7,212), W central N.Dak.; ⊙ Manning. Agr. area drained by Little Missouri and Knife rivers. Coal mines; livestock, dairy products, poultry, wheat, flax, oats. Fort Berthold Indian Reservation in N. Formed 1883. **2** County (□ 858; pop. 27,341), W Wis.; ⊙ Menomonie. Drained by Red Cedar and Chippewa rivers. Predominantly a dairying region, with some stock raising and lumbering; mfg. at Menomonie. Formed 1854.

Dunn, town (pop. 6,316), Harnett co., central N.C., 23 mi. NE of Fayetteville; trade center for agr. area (cotton, corn, tobacco); mfg. of hosiery, farm implements; flour and sawmilling.

Dunn Center, village (pop. 246), Dunn co., W central N.Dak., 33 mi. N of Dickinson.

Dunnell (dŭnĕl'), village (pop. 242), Martin co., S Minn., near Iowa line, 18 mi. WSW of Fairmont; dairy products.

Dunnellon (dŭnĕ'lŭn), town (pop. 1,110), Marion co., N central Fla., on Withlacoochee R. and 22 mi. WSW of Ocala; sawmilling, quarrying (phosphate, limestone), fertilizer mfg. Rainbow Springs near by. Inc. 1909.

Dunnet, town and parish (pop. 928), N Caithness, Scotland, on Dunnet Bay of the Atlantic, 7 mi. ENE of Thurso; agr. market. Near by is DUNNET HEAD.

Dunnet Head, promontory at N extremity of the island of Britain, N Caithness, Scotland, at W end of Pentland Firth, 8 mi. NE of Thurso; site of naval signal station and of lighthouse (58°41'N 3°22'W).

Dunnichen (dŭnĭkh'ŭn), agr. village and parish (pop. 978), central Angus, Scotland, 3 mi. SE of Forfar.

Dunning, agr. village and parish (pop. 1,056), SE Perthshire, Scotland, near Earn R., 8 mi. SW of Perth.

Dunning, village (pop. 254), Blaine co., central Nebr., 15 mi. SW of Brewster and on Middle Loup R., at mouth of Dismal R.; dairy and poultry produce, fruit, livestock. Near by is Halsey Div. of Nebr. Natl. Forest.

Dunnings Mountain, S central Pa., N–S ridge (1,-900–2,200 ft.), runs c.15 mi. S from Roaring Spring, Blair co.; joins Evitts Mtn. NE of Bedford; quartzite.

Dunnockshaw, town and parish (pop. 429), E Lancashire, England, 3 mi. SSW of Burnley; cotton spinning; coal mining. In parish (NE) is cotton-weaving village of Clow Bridge, site of Burnley reservoir.

Dunnose, high headland on SE coast of Isle of Wight, England, just E of Ventnor.

Dunnottar (dŭnŏ'tŭr), town and parish (pop 1,987, including part of Stonehaven burgh), E Kincardine, Scotland, on North Sea, just SW of Stonehaven; fishing port and agr. market. On rock above the sea are ruins of Dunnottar Castle; present structure dates partly from late 14th cent. An earlier bldg. was taken by Wallace in 1297. During civil war the Scottish regalia were hidden here; they were smuggled out when castle surrendered to Parliamentarians in 1652. In Whigs' Vault dungeon over 100 Covenanters were imprisoned in 1685; 9 of them are buried in churchyard here.

Dunn Point, promontory, SE N.F., at S end of Merasheen Isl., in Placentia Bay; 47°25'N 54°22'W.

Dunnville, town (pop. 4,028), S Ont., on Grand R., near its mouth on L. Erie, and 27 mi. SSE of Hamilton; port; woolen milling and knitting, food canning, dairying; mfg. of clothing, stockings, cement, iron castings.

Dunnville, village (pop. c.200), Casey co., central Ky., on Green R. and 20 mi. WNW of Somerset; wood products, furniture.

Dunolly (dŭnŏ'lē), village (pop. 832), central Victoria, Australia, 95 mi. NW of Melbourne; rail junction in gold-mining region. Large nuggets found in 1906 at near-by Poseidon.

Dunoon (dŭnōōn'), burgh (1931 pop. 8,780; 1951 census 9,940), E Argyll, Scotland, on the Firth of Clyde, 27 mi. WNW of Glasgow; bathing resort and yachting center. Scene of annual Cowal games. On Castle Hill are remains of 12th-cent. castle; at foot of hill is statue of Burns's "Highland Mary," b. here. Burgh includes resorts of Kirn, just N of Dunoon, and Hunter's Quay, 2 mi. NNE of Dunoon, both on the Firth of Clyde. Hunter's Quay is hq. of Royal Clyde Yacht Club.

Dunquerque, France: see DUNKIRK.

Dunragit (dŭnră'gĭt), village in Old Luce parish, W Wigtown, Scotland, 6 mi. ESE of Stranraer; dairying and oleomargarine mfg. Near by is 17th-cent. Castle Kennedy.

Dunraven, Mount, Colo.: see MUMMY RANGE.

Dunraven Pass, Wyo.: see WASHBURN RANGE.

Dunrea (dŭnrā'), village (pop. estimate 250), SW Man., 30 mi. SSE of Brandon; grain, stock.

Dunreith (dŭn'rēth), town (pop. 196), Henry co., E Ind., 9 mi. SSW of New Castle, in agr. area.

Dunrobin Castle, Scotland: see GOLSPIE.

Dunrossness (dŭnrŏs"nĕs'), parish (pop. 2,704, including Fair Isle) and district, at S end of Mainland isl., Shetlands, Scotland, terminating S in Sumburgh Head.

Duns (dŭns, dŭnz), burgh (1931 pop. 1,788; 1951 census 2,028), ⊙ Berwick, Scotland, 13 mi. W of Berwick-on-Tweed; agr. market. It is at foot of Duns Law (713-ft. hill), on which town was originally located until destroyed 1545 by the English; it was founded 1588 on present site. Duns Law was camping place of Alexander Leslie and the Covenanters in 1639; site is marked by Covenanters' Stone.

Dunsany (dŭnsā'nē, –sā'nē), Gaelic *Dún Samhna*, agr. village, S central Co. Meath, Ireland, 9 mi. SSE of An Uaimh; cattle, horses, potatoes. Dunsany Castle, here, was founded by Hugh de Lacy.

Dunscore, agr. village and parish (pop. 962), W Dumfries, Scotland, 9 mi. NW of Dumfries. Parish includes CRAIGENPUTTOCK.

Dunsden Green, England: see SONNING EYE.

Dunseith (dŭnsēth'), city (pop. 713), Rolette co., N N.Dak., port of entry 20 mi. WSW of Rolla and bordering on Turtle Mts.; 12 mi. N, on Can. border, is International Peace Garden.

Dunshaughlin (dŭn-shôkh'lĭn), Gaelic *Domhnach Seachlainn*, town (pop. 184), SE Co. Meath, Ireland, 11 mi. SE of An Uaimh; agr. market (cattle, horses; potatoes). Near by is Killeen Castle, founded by Hugh de Lacy.

Dunsinane (dŭnsĭ'nŭn, dŭnsĭnān'), elevation (1,012 ft.) in the Sidlaw Hills, SE Perthshire, Scotland, 7 mi. NE of Perth. On summit are ruins of anc. castle, called Macbeth's Castle, reputed scene of Macbeth's defeat by the earl of Northumbria, as related by Shakespeare.

Dunsink (dŭnsĭngk'), elevation in Blanchardstown, NW suburb of Dublin, Co. Dublin, Ireland; site of observatory (founded 1782) belonging to Trinity Col.; 53°23'N 6°20'W.

Duns Law, Scotland: see DUNS.

Dunsmuir (dŭnz'mūr), city (pop. 2,256), Siskiyou co., N Calif., in canyon of Sacramento R., near W base of Cascade Range, 15 mi. S of Mt. Shasta; railroad division hq.; lumber milling; hunting, fishing resort. Castle Crags State Park is S, Lava Beds Natl. Monument is NE. Inc. as town in 1909, as city in 1935.

Dunstable (dŭn'stŭbŭl), municipal borough (1931 pop. 8,976; 1951 census 17,108), S Bedford, England, at foot of Chiltern Hills, 5 mi. W of Luton; printing center, also producing straw hats, automobiles, chemicals, paint. Near by are limestone quarries. Priory church includes part of Augustinian priory founded 1131. Town is at intersection of the anc. Icknield Way and Watling Street. Stone and Bronze Age relics have been found near by. One of the Eleanor Crosses erected at Dunstable. Whipsnade, with large zoo, 3 mi. S.

Dunstable, farming town (pop. 522), Middlesex co., NE Mass., 8 mi. WNW of Lowell.

Dunstaffnage Castle (dŭnstăf'nĭj), ruins of anc. stronghold in W Argyll, Scotland, on rocky promontory on inlet of the Firth of Lorne, near mouth of Loch Etive 3 mi. NE of Oban. Castle is ascribed to 13th cent.; ruins date mainly from 15th cent.

Dunstan, Maine: see SCARBORO.

Dunster, town and parish (pop. 839), NW Somerset, England, near Bridgwater Bay of Bristol Channel, 2 mi. SE of Minehead; agr. market in cattle-raising region. Has 14th-cent. castle, incorporating remains of Norman structure mentioned in Hardy's *Laodicean*. Church (mainly 15th cent.) was formerly part of Benedictine priory. Old Yarn Market dates from c.1600.

Dunston, England: see GATESHEAD.

Dun-sur-Auron (dŭ-sür-ōrō'), town (pop. 2,791), Cher dept., central France, near Auron R. and Berry Canal, 12 mi. NNE of Saint-Amand-Montrond; road center; woodworking, truck gardening. Has 11th-cent. Romanesque church and 16th-cent. clock tower. Scene of defenestration (1427) of Pierre de Giac. Formerly Dun-le-Roi.

Dun-sur-Meuse (–mûz'), village (pop. 621), Meuse dept., NE France, on Meuse R. (canalized) and 18 mi. NNW of Verdun; dairying, sawmilling.

Duntocher (dŭntŏkh'ŭr), town in Old Kilpatrick parish, SE Dumbarton, Scotland, N suburb of Clydebank.

Dunton Green, agr. village and parish (pop. 1,496), W Kent, England, on Darent R. and 2 mi. NW of Sevenoaks.

Dunvegan, Scotland: see SKYE, ISLE OF.

Dunwich (dŭ'nĭch), agr. village and parish (pop. 174), E Suffolk, England, on North Sea, 4 mi. SSW of Southwold. Has remains of 12th-cent. St. James's Hosp. and of 13th-cent. Franciscan priory. Was seat of 1st East Anglican bishopric, established c.630. Most of former town submerged by sea in 12th cent.

Duong (zûng', yûng'), village, Phanthiet prov., S central Vietnam, on South China Sea coast, 5 mi. E of Phanri; fishing port; salt extraction, fish curing.

Duongdong, Vietnam: see PHUQUOC.

Du Page (dōō pāj'), county (□ 331; pop. 154,599), NE Ill., partly in Chicago suburban area; ⊙ Wheaton. Agr. and dairying area (truck, grain, fruit, livestock, poultry), with many residential communities. Diversified mfg.; railroad shops; limestone quarries; nurseries. Drained by Du Page R. Formed 1839.

Du Page River, NE Ill., rises in 2 branches W of Chicago, flows c.30 mi. SW from their junction N of Joliet to Des Plaines R. just above its confluence with Kankakee R. West Branch (c.30 mi. long) flows generally S, past Naperville. East Branch (c.20 mi. long) flows S and SW to West Branch.

Duparquet (dü"pärkā'), town (pop. 1,384), W Que., on L. Duparquet (6 mi. long, 6 mi. wide), 20 mi. NNW of Rouyn; gold-mining center.

Duperré (düpĕrā'), village (pop. 2,170), Alger dept., N central Algeria, in Chéliff valley, on railroad and 15 mi. WSW of Miliana; cereal and winegrowing. Iron mining.

Duplin (dŭ'plĭn), county (□ 822; pop. 41,074), E N.C.; ⊙ Kenansville. Forested (pine, gum), partly swampy coastal plain; drained by Northeast Cape Fear R. Agr. (especially tobacco; also corn, cotton); sawmilling. Formed 1749.

Dupnitsa, Bulgaria: see MAREK.

Dupo (dōō'pō), village (pop. 2,239), St. Clair co., SW Ill., on the Mississippi and 6 mi. S of East St. Louis, within St. Louis metropolitan area; large railroad classification yard; limestone quarries. Inc. 1907.

Du Pont (dū'pŏnt", dū"pŏnt'), town (pop. 285), Clinch co., S Ga., 27 mi. ENE of Valdosta and on small Suwanoochee Creek.

Dupont. **1** Village (pop. 225), Putnam co., NW Ohio, 15 mi. S of Defiance and on Auglaize R.; mfg. of drain tile. **2** Borough (pop. 4,107), Luzerne co., NE Pa., 8 mi. SSW of Scranton; munitions; anthracite. Inc. 1917.

Du Pont, Fort, Del.: see DELAWARE CITY.

Duppau, Czechoslovakia: see DOUPOV.

Düppel (dü'pŭl) Dan. *Dybbøl*, village (pop. 116), SE Denmark, in Schleswig 4 mi. W of Sonderborg. Here in 1849 the Danes were defeated by Saxon and Bavarian troops and again, in 1864, by the Prussians. It passed to Denmark in 1920.

Dupplin Moor (dŭ'plĭn), locality in SE Perthshire, Scotland, 5 mi. WSW of Perth. In 1332 Edward Baliol and the "disinherited barons" here defeated the earl of Mar. Dupplin Castle dates from 1832.

Duprat (düprä'), village, W Que., 5 mi. NW of Rouyn; gold, copper, zinc, pyrite mining.

Dupree (dōōprē'), town (pop. 438), ⊙ Ziebach co., N central S.Dak., 80 mi. NW of Pierre and on Elm Creek; trading center; livestock, poultry, flax, wheat, dairy produce.

Dupuy (düpwē'), village (pop. estimate 850), W Que., 45 mi. NNW of Rouyn, near Ont. border; gold, copper, zinc mining.

Dupuyer (dŭpōō'yŭr), village (pop. c.200), Pondera co., N Mont., on branch of Marias R. and 26 mi. W of Conrad; supply point in rich livestock region.

Duque de Bragança (dōō'kĭ dĭ brŭgän'sŭ), town (pop. 2,037), Malange prov., N Angola, 45 mi. NNW of Malange; corn, beans, soya beans, tobacco.

Duque de Caxias (käsh'yŭs), city (1950 pop. 74,-557), S Rio de Janeiro state, Brazil, near Guanabara Bay, 10 mi. NNW of center of Rio, on Federal Dist. line; mfg. of motors; flax and jute milling; orange groves. Formerly called Caxias.

Duque de York, Isla, Chile: see DUKE OF YORK ISLAND.

Duquesne (dükĕn'), village (pop. 637), Constantine dept., NE Algeria, 4 mi. SE of Djidjelli; wine, olives.

Duquesne (dŭkān', dōō–, dū–), city (pop. 17,620), Allegheny co., SW Pa., on Monongahela R. opposite McKeesport; steel, iron, drugs, chemicals. Settled 1789, inc. as borough 1891, as city 1910.

Duquesne, Fort, Pa.: see PITTSBURGH.

Du Quoin (dōō koin', kwoin'), city (pop. 7,147), Perry co., SW Ill., 35 mi. S of Centralia; trade and mfg. center in bituminous-coal-mining and agr. area; machinery, explosives, cigars, dairy and other food products; corn, wheat, livestock. Inc. 1861.

Dura (dōō'rä, dōō'rŭ), **Europus** or **Europos** (yōōrō'-pŭs), or **Dura-Europus,** ruined city of E Syria, on right bank of the Euphrates and 135 mi. E of Palmyra, 50 mi. SE of Deir ez Zor, near Iraq line; modern village of Salihiye or Qal'at es Salihiye is on site. Founded c.300 B.C. by a general of Seleucus I, it prospered. In the 2d cent. A.D. the Parthians took it. Later taken by Rome; a Roman city until seized (A.D. c.257) by Shapur I. It was then abandoned to the desert. Excavations begun 1922 yielded rich finds supplying much information on life, history, and art in upper Mesopotamia from Hellenistic through Roman times. The name is also spelled Doura.

Dura Den, Scotland: see CUPAR.

Duraha (dōōrä'hŭ), town (pop. 2,155), N Bhopal state, India, 18 mi. NW of Bhopal; wheat, gram. Sometimes spelled Doraha.

Durán (dōōrän') or **Alfaro** (älfä'rō), village, Guayas prov., W Ecuador, river port on Guayas R. (ferry) opposite Guayaquil, in fertile agr. region (cacao and rice plantations); rice milling. Terminus of the Andean railroad to Quito. Sometimes called Eloy Alfaro.

Duran (dŭrăn'), village (pop. c.400), Torrance co., central N.Mex., 50 mi. SW of Santa Rosa; alt. 6,000 ft.; wool-shipping point.

Durance River (dürãs'), SE France, rises at foot of Montgenèvre Pass near Ital. border, flows SSW through the Provence Alps, past Briançon and Sisteron, veers W at the Montagne du Lubéron, entering the Rhone 3 mi. SW of Avignon; c.180 mi. long. Receives Guisane, Buëch (right), Ubaye, Bléone, Asse, and Verdon rivers (left). Hydroelectric plants in upper course. Used for irrigation and Marseilles water supply.

Durand (dyōōrănd', dŭ–). **1** Town (pop. 186), Meriwether co., W Ga., 16 mi. ESE of La Grange. **2** Village (pop. 679), Winnebago co., N Ill., 17 mi. NW of Rockford, in dairying and grain area. **3** City (pop. 3,194), Shiawassee co., S central Mich., 15 mi. SW of Flint, in farm area (beans, corn, wheat); mfg. of machinery; railroad shops, grain elevators. Inc. as village 1887, as city 1933. **4** City (pop. 1,961), ⊙ Pepin co., W Wis., on Chippewa R. and 27 mi. SW of Eau Claire, in dairy and livestock area; dairy products, canned vegetables, feed, beverages. Settled c.1850, inc. 1887.

Durango (dŭrăng'gō, dŭ–, Sp. dōōräng'gō), state (□ 47,691; 1940 pop. 483,829; 1950 pop. 629,502), N Mexico; ⊙ Durango. Bounded by Chihuahua (N), Coahuila (E), Zacatecas (SE), Nayarit (SW), Sinaloa (W). W part is dominated by the Sierra Madre Occidental, a rich mining region. Vast semiarid plains of E part are excellent ranching country. The extremely fertile Laguna Dist. is farther E, on border of Coahuila; there tremendous desert basin lands are irrigated by Nazas R. Other streams are: Mezquital R. (S) and Aguanaval R. (SE). Climate generally temperate: arid in outliers of Bolsón de Mapimí (N), cool in mts., subtropical in fertile Laguna Dist. and in S. Rich mtn. mines (silver, gold, lead, copper, mercury, antimony) are centered near Durango, Cuencamé, Santiago Papasquiaro, El Oro, Guanaceví. The famed Cerro de Mercado, in the outskirts of Durango, consists of almost pure iron ore. Vast plains provide excellent pastures for livestock (cattle, sheep, horses, mules). Agr. highly developed in Nazas R. valley and near Durango; grows cotton principally, also wheat, corn, barley, chick-peas, sugar cane, tobacco, alfalfa, wine, fruit. Maguey, candelilla wax, and guayule rubber are produced in more arid sections. Metallurgical and processing industries are concentrated at Gómez Palacio, Lerdo, Durango. The Spanish explored the region in 1562; it formed, during colonial epoch, together with Chihuahua, the province of Nueva Viscaya. With independence, Durango was set up (1823) as a separate state.

Durango, city (pop. 33,412), ⊙ Durango state, N Mexico, on fertile interior plateau of Sierra Madre Occidental, 180 mi. ESE of Culiacán, 500 mi. NW of Mexico city; 24°3'N 104°40'W; alt. 6,197 ft. Rail junction; resort; commercial, industrial, lumbering, and agr. center (grain, cotton, sugar cane, tobacco, fruit, vegetables, stock). Iron and steel mills process ore from the famed iron deposits at Cerro de Mercado, 2 mi. N, a hill (640 ft.) of almost solid iron ore. Copper, silver, and lead foundries, textile and flour mills, lumber works, vegetable-oil plants, glassworks, tanneries, sugar refineries, tobacco factories. Notable are the 18th-cent. cathedral, govt. palace, mint (founded 1811). Alonzo Pacheco, serving under Ibarra, founded the city (1563); it was for some time ⊙ Nueva Viscaya. The city is sometimes called Victoria de Durango or Ciudad de Victoria.

Durango, town (pop. 5,965), Vizcaya prov., N Spain, 18 mi. SE of Bilbao; mfg. of hardware, furniture, candy; tanning. Cereals, fruit, sugar beets, cattle in area. Iron and lignite mines. Church of San Pedro de Tavira, near by, is one of oldest in Basque Provs. Hq. of Carlists and scene of bitter fighting during Carlist Wars (19th cent.). Severely damaged in civil war of 1936-39.

Durango (dōōrăng'gō). **1** City (pop. 7,459), ⊙ La Plata co., SW Colo., on Animas R., in W foothills of San Juan Mts., and c.130 mi. SSE of Grand Junction; alt. 6,505 ft. Shipping center and resort in livestock, fruit, and grain region; flour, metal products, beverages, timber. U.S. uranium and vanadium processing plant and hq. of San Juan Natl. Forest here. Carnotite deposits and gold, silver, lead, and coal mines in vicinity; Fort Lewis agr. school is near by; Mesa Verde Natl. Park 25 mi. W. City founded by railroad 1880, inc. 1881. **2** Town (pop. 71), Dubuque co., E Iowa, 6 mi. NW of Dubuque.

Durania (dōōrä'nyä), town (pop. 1,724), Norte de Santander dept., N Colombia, 15 mi. SW of Cúcuta; corn, coffee, tobacco.

Durant. **1** (dŭ'rănt) Town (pop. 1,075), Cedar co., E Iowa, 17 mi. WNW of Davenport; dairy products, feed, iron castings. **2** (dyōōrănt', dŭ–) Town (pop. 2,311), Holmes co., central Miss., 36 mi. SSE of Greenwood, and on Big Black R., in agr. and timber area: mfg. of wagons, trailers, hosiery, chenille articles; railroad shops. State park near by. Founded 1858. **3** (dŭrănt') City (pop. 10,541), ⊙ Bryan co., S Okla., 27 mi. NNE of Sherman, Texas; market and processing center for agr. area (cotton, peanuts, livestock, grain, hay, potatoes). Cotton ginning; cottonseed-oil, flour, feed, and lumber milling; peanut and pecan shelling, meat packing; mfg. of wood products, furniture, mattresses, dairy products, soap. Seat of Southeastern State Col. and of Okla. Presbyterian Col. for women. Denison Dam (impounding L. Texoma) is 15 mi. SW. Settled c.1870.

Duras (dürä'), village (pop. 556), Lot-et-Garonne dept., SW France, near Dropt R., 12 mi. N of Marmande; winegrowing.

Durasovka (dōōrä'sŭfkŭ), village (1939 pop. over 500), W central Saratov oblast, Russian SFSR, on Medveditsa R. and 13 mi. SSW of Atkarsk; wheat, sunflowers, cattle.

Durazno (dōōrä'snō), department (□ 5,527; pop. 95,148), central Uruguay; ⊙ Durazno. Bordered by the Río Negro reservoir (N and NW) and Yí R. (S and SW). The Cuchilla Grande del Durazno crosses dept. E-W. Produces wheat, corn, grain; cattle and sheep are raised on large scale Main centers: Durazno, Carmen, Sarandí del Yí.

Durazno or **San Pedro de Durazno** (sän pā'drō dā), city (pop. 27,000), ⊙ Durazno dept., central Uruguay, on Yí R. (bridge) and 105 mi. NNW of Montevideo; 33°21'S 56°31'W. Processing and trade center; rail and road junction of lines from Florida and Trinidad. Dairying, grain milling, meat packing; mfg. of shoes, mosaics; limekilns; trade in lumber, firewood, hides, grain. Military air base (SE). Has col., a subsidiary of Montevideo Univ. Founded 1821.

Durazzo (dŭră'zō, dōōrät'tsō), Albanian *Durrës* (dōōr'ŭs) or *Durrësi* (dōōr'ŭsē), Serbo-Croatian *Drač*, Turkish *Dradj*, *Draj*, or *Draç*, anc. *Epidamnus*, later *Dyrrachium* or *Dyrrhachium*, city (1945 pop. 14,031) and chief port of Albania, on the Adriatic, 19 mi. W of Tirana, on N shore of Gulf of Durazzo; leading Albanian commercial and communications center, serving Tirana and central Albania. Linked by railroads with Tirana and Elbasan. Mfg. of flour, soap, alcohol, cigarettes; power plant. Exports olive oil, grain, skins, tobacco. Seat of R.C. bishop (since 449) and Greek metropolitan. Pop. is largely Moslem. Built on rocky promontory on S slopes of Mt. Durazzo [Albanian *Mal i Durrësit*; 607 ft.], Durazzo is of Oriental character; has great mosque (1939), and on hill spur above town, a former royal villa and remains of Byzantine-Venetian fortifications. Seaside resort on gulf, 5 mi. SE. Founded (c.627 B.C.) as Epidamnus as a joint colony of Corinth and Corcyra (Corfu), it developed as the chief port of Illyria. The quarrel bet. the two colonizers helped to precipitate (431 B.C.) the Peloponnesian War. Under Romans (after 229 B.C.), it was known as Dyrrachium, a military base (remains of anc. port channel) and terminus of the Via Egnatia (leading to Salonika and Byzantium). Pompey made a stand here (48 B.C.) against Caesar. During Byzantine period, Durazzo was held intermittently by Goths, Serbs, Bulgars, Normans (1082), by the crusaders in the Fourth Crusade, by Venice, and by the Angevins of Naples, who made it a duchy in 1267. Venice again held it from 1392 until 1501, when it passed to the Turks. The majority of the citizens accepted Islam, which still prevails. Under Turkish rule Durazzo declined rapidly and almost disappeared. It was occupied (1912) by the Serbs in the First

Balkan War, was assigned to Albania in 1913, and was (1914) the residence of William, prince of Wied. It subsequently revived as the main Albanian port (modernized 1928–34). Occupied, with the rest of Albania, by Italy (1939-43) and by German troops (1943–44), Durazzo was severely bombarded by the British navy in 1943.

Durbach (do͞or'bäkh), village (pop. 2,074), S Baden, Germany, on W slope of Black Forest, 4 mi. NE of Offenburg; noted for its wine.

Durban (dûr'bŭn, -băn, dûrbăn'), city (pop. 339,247; including suburbs 372,269), E Natal, U. of So. Afr., on Natal Bay (5 mi. long, 2 mi. wide) of Indian Ocean, 300 mi. SE of Johannesburg; 29°53'S 31°2'E; largest city and commercial center of Natal; chief eastern seaport of U. of So. Afr., serving Witwatersrand industrial region. Extensive dock facilities on sheltered bay (protected by breakwaters) include floating dock, wharves, oil docks, whaling station, ship-repair yards, terminal grain elevators, coal docks. Salisbury Isl. in bay has naval installations. Coal, manganese, chrome are among exports. Industries include large railroad workshops, sugar refineries, auto-assembly plants, breweries; mfg. of machinery, metalware, furniture, rubber products, plastics, chemicals, soap, paint, wattle extract, glass, paper, textiles, clothing, food products. City is also important resort with racecourses, tourist and sports facilities, and marine esplanade. Site of Natal Univ. Col. (1909; affiliated with Univ. of South Africa) and M.S. Sultan Technical Col. Features include Municipal Art Gallery, Botanical Gardens (50 acres), Snake Park, aquarium, several parks, and Old Fort (1842). In SE part rises the Berea, hill c.500 ft. high, main residential section. Suburbs include Stamford Hill (N), site of Durban airport, Morningside, and Congella. Mean temp. ranges from 64°F. (July) to 77°F. (Feb.); average annual rainfall 43.13 in. Settlement of Port Natal established here 1824; town site laid out 1835 and named for Sir Benjamin D'Urban, then governor of Cape Colony. Municipality created 1854; port construction begun 1855. In recent years city has been scene of much civic unrest, the result of repressive measures imposed on the large Indian community; scene (1949) of native riots.

Durban-Corbières (dürbã'-kôrbyâr'), village (pop. 723), Aude dept., S France, in the Corbières, 16 mi. SW of Narbonne; winegrowing.

Durbanville, residential town (pop. 1,667), SW Cape Prov., U. of So. Afr., 12 mi. NE of Cape Town, in wheat-growing region.

Durbari (do͞orbä'rē), village, N Rajasthan, India, near Jamsar; kunkur and lime factory.

Durbe (do͞or'bā), Ger. *Durben*, city (pop. 525), W Latvia, in Kurzeme, 14 mi. ENE of Liepaja, at S end of small Durbe L.; wool processing, flour milling. Seaplane base. Has castle ruins.

Durbin, lumber town (pop. 540), Pocahontas co., E W.Va., 27 mi. NNE of Marlinton.

Durbuldjin or **Durbuljin** (do͞orbo͝oljĭn'), Chinese *Omin* (ŭ'mĭn') or *Omileiho* (ŭ'mē'lā'hŭ'), town, ⊙ Durbuldjin co. (pop. 50,554), N Sinkiang prov., China, 35 mi. ESE of Tarbagatai and on highway; cattle raising; timber; carpets. Sometimes Hoshang.

Durbuy (dürbwē'), town (pop. 323), Luxembourg prov., SE Belgium, on Ourthe R. and 10 mi. NNE of Marche; agr. market; tourist center. Smallest township in Belgium. Ruins of anc. castle, two 17th-cent. monasteries. Fortified outpost in Roman times; became ⊙ small co. in 11th cent.; retained considerable independence until 14th cent., when it came under rule of dukes of Luxemburg.

Dúrcal (do͞or'käl), village (pop. 4,692), Granada prov., S Spain, 13 mi. S of Granada; terminus of aerial tramway to seaport of Motril. Olive-oil processing, flour milling; mfg. of soap, flour products, liqueurs. Cereals, truck products; livestock.

Durdevac, Yugoslavia: see DJURDJEVAC.

Durdevik, Yugoslavia: see DJURDJEVIK.

Dureikish (do͞orā'kēsh) or **Dirikish** (dĭrē'kēsh), Fr. *Dreikich*, town, Latakia prov., W Syria, 50 mi. SSE of Latakia; sericulture, cereals.

Düren (dü'rŭn), city (1939 pop. 45,321; 1946 pop. 27,653), in former Prussian Rhine Prov., W Germany, after 1945 in North Rhine-Westphalia, on the Rur and 17 mi. E of Aachen; 50°48'N 6°29'E. Rail junction; iron foundries, iron- and steelworks; mfg. of cloth and paper. An important center under the Frankish kings, it came to duke of Jülich in 1242. Was subjected to heavy air bombing and artillery shelling in Nov., 1944. Most of city was obliterated, and no bldg. remained unharmed.

Durfee Hill (804 ft.), NW R.I., in Glocester town, 17 mi. WNW of Providence.

Durga Nor, Durge Nur, or **Dürge Nuur** (all: dûr'gŭ nōr', no͞or'), salt lake (□ 115) in W Mongolian People's Republic, 80 mi. ESE of Kobdo; connected with KHARA NOR (N); 14 mi. long.

Durgapur (do͞or'gäpo͞or), village, Burdwan dist., W West Bengal, India, on the Damodar and 15 mi. SE of Raniganj; brick and tile mfg.; rice, sugar cane, wheat, potatoes. Barrage site for DAMODAR VALLEY project near by.

Durge Nur or **Dürge Nuur,** Mongolia: see DURGA NOR.

Durham (dŭ'rŭm), county (□ 629; pop. 25,215), S Ont., on L. Ontario; ⊙ Port Hope.

Durham, town (pop. 1,700), S Ont., 28 mi. SSE of Owen Sound; dairying, lumbering, metalworking; candy, furniture mfg.

Durham, county (□ 1,014.9; 1931 pop. 1,486,175; 1951 census 1,463,416), NE England; ⊙ Durham. Bounded by Cumberland (W), Northumberland (N), the North Sea (E), Yorkshire (S), and Westmorland (SW). Drained by Tees, Tyne, and Derwent rivers. Hill ranges in W, level land to E; fertile land in river valleys (cattle raising). Major English coal-mining area; lead, iron, and marble are also found. Other important industries are shipbuilding (Sunderland, Hartlepool, Gateshead), steel milling (Stockton-on-Tees, Consett), chemicals (Billingham), paper, machinery, pottery, glass. Ports include South Shields, Sunderland, Hartlepool, West Hartlepool. The co., part of the earldom of Northumbria (547–827), was a county palatine until the 1830s.

Durham, municipal borough (1931 pop. 16,224; 1951 census 19,283), ⊙ Durham, England, in center of co., on hillside almost surrounded by Wear R., 13 mi. S of Newcastle-upon-Tyne; 54°46'N 1°34'W; coal mining, carpet weaving; leather, machinery, pharmaceutical industries. The cathedral (begun 1093), built on site of shrine of St. Cuthbert, whose relics were brought to Durham (then Dunholme) in 995, is one of finest examples of Norman architecture. Castle, dating from 1072, is now occupied by Durham Univ., with mining col. and observatory. St. Giles's and St. Margaret's are 2 Norman churches. Wear R. is crossed by 2 anc. bridges, dating from 1230 and c.1390.

Durham (dŭ'rŭm), county (□ 299; pop. 101,639), N central N.C.; ⊙ Durham. In fertile piedmont region; drained by headstreams of Neuse R. Agr. (tobacco, corn); pine forests; mfg. at Durham. Formed 1881.

Durham. **1** (dŭ'rŭm) Village (1940 pop. 953), Butte co., N central Calif., in Sacramento Valley, 6 mi. S of Chico; plums, almonds. **2** (do͞o'rŭm) Town (pop. 1,804), Middlesex co., S central Conn., 5 mi. S of Middletown; metal products; farming. State park here. Public library dates from 1733. Settled 1698, inc. 1708. **3** (dŭ'rŭm) City (pop. 229), Marion co., central Kansas, on Cottonwood R. and 28 mi. S of Abilene; grain, livestock. **4** (do͞o'rŭm) Town (pop. 1,050), Androscoggin co., SW Maine, on the Androscoggin and 10 mi. SE of Auburn; agr. **5** (do͞o'rŭm, dŭ'rŭm) Town (pop. 4,770), Strafford co., SE N.H., just S of Dover and on Oyster R. Agr. (truck, poultry), cannery. Seat of Univ. of N.H.; has 18th-cent. home of Gen. John Sullivan. Settled 1635 as Oyster River parish of Dover, inc. as town of Durham 1732. Settlement suffered greatly in Indian wars. **6** (dŭ'rŭm) City (pop. 71,311), ⊙ Durham co., N central N.C., 50 mi. E of Greensboro, in piedmont region; 36°N 78°35'W. Port of entry; a major cigarette-mfg. and tobacco-marketing and -processing center, producing c.25% of U.S. cigarettes; hosiery and textile mills; also mfg. of paper boxes, pharmaceuticals, machinery; lumber and grain milling. Seat of Duke Univ. and N.C. Col. for Negroes. Negroes have extensive business and industrial enterprises; hq. of largest Negro life insurance company in the country is here. Settled c.1852 in area which was settled c.1750, Durham was only a hamlet until after the Civil War, when the tobacco industry began its great development, with the Duke family a leading manufacturer. Inc. 1867.

Durham South, village (pop. 341), S Que., 16 mi. SSE of Drummondville; dairying.

Durhamville (dŭ'rŭmvĭl), village (1940 pop. 533), Oneida co., central N.Y., on Oneida Creek, just NW of Oneida; canned foods.

Duria Major, Italy: see DORA BALTEA RIVER.

Duria Minor, Italy: see DORA RIPARIA RIVER.

Durika (do͞orē'kä), peak (12,726 ft.) in the Cordillera de Talamanca, SE Costa Rica, 13 mi NNE of Buenos Aires.

Durius, river, Spain: see DOURO RIVER.

Dürkheim, Bad, Germany: see BAD DÜRKHEIM.

Durlach (do͞or'läkh), E district (since 1938) of KARLSRUHE, Germany, on the Pfinz; railroad repair shops; mfg. of sewing machines, dental equipment, margarine; leatherworking. Has ruins of 16th-cent. castle (destroyed by French in 1689). Residence of margraves of Baden-Durlach 1565–1715.

Durlstone Head, England: see SWANAGE.

Durmersheim (do͞or'mürs-hīm), village (pop. 4,262), S Baden, Germany, 8 mi. SW of Karlsruhe; woodworking.

Durmitor (do͞or'mētôr), highest mountain in Montenegro, Yugoslavia, in Dinaric Alps, bet. Tara and Piva rivers, in the Brda; highest point, Bobotov Kuk (8,272 ft.), is 5 mi. WSW of Zabljak. Small lake Crno Jezero or Tsrno Yezero [Serbo-Croatian, = black lake] is 3 mi. ENE of peak.

Dürnberg (dürn'bĕrk), S suburb of Hallein, Salzburg, W Austria, near Ger. border; customs station. Large salt mines near by.

Durness (dûrnĕs'), agr. village and parish (pop. 529), NW Sutherland, Scotland, on the Atlantic, 45 mi. W of Thurso. Has ruins of 17th-cent. church.

Durnford Point, promontory, Río de Oro, Sp. West Africa, at S tip of peninsula 5 mi. SSW of Villa Cisneros; 23°38'N 15°W.

Dürnkrut (dürn'kro͞ot), village (pop. 1,988), NE Lower Austria, near Czechoslovak border and March R., 28 mi. NE of Vienna; sugar refinery.

Durnovaria, England: see DORCHESTER.

Dürnstein (dürn'shtīn), village (pop. 638), central Lower Austria, on the Danube and 4 mi. WSW of Krems; wine. According to legend, Richard Coeur de Lion was imprisoned in Dürnstein fortress, now in ruins.

Dürnten (dürn'tŭn), town (pop. 3,006), Zurich canton, N Switzerland, 15 mi. ESE of Zurich; textiles, woodworking.

Duro, Serra do, Brazil: see GERAL DE GOIÁS, SERRA.

Durobrivae, England: see ROCHESTER.

Durocatalaunum, France: see CHÂLONS-SUR-MARNE.

Durocortorum, France: see RHEIMS.

Durolipons, England: see GODMANCHESTER.

Duror (do͞o'rŭr), fishing village, N Argyll, Scotland, in Appin dist., on Loch Linnhe, 17 mi. NNE of Oban.

Durostor, department, Rumania: see SILISTRA.

Durostorum, Bulgaria: see SILISTRA.

Durovernum Cantiaciorum, England: see CANTERBURY.

Dürrenberg, Bad, Germany: see BAD DÜRRENBERG.

Dürrenstein (dü'rŭnshtīn), Alpine peak (6,160 ft.), SW Lower Austria, S of Lunz, near Styrian line.

Durrës or **Durrësi,** Albania: see DURAZZO.

Dürrheim, Bad, Germany: see BAD DÜRRHEIM.

Durrington. **1** Suburb, Sussex, England: see WORTHING. **2** Agr. village and parish (pop. 3,846), E Wiltshire, England, on the Avon and 9 mi. N of Salisbury. Has 13th–15th-cent. church. Near by is prehistoric earthwork of Woodhenge.

Durris, Scotland: see KIRKTON OF DURRIS.

Durrow (dûr'ō), Gaelic *Darmhagh Ua nDuach.* **1** Town (pop. 413), S Co. Laoighis, Ireland, 14 mi. SSW of Port Laoighise; agr. market (wheat, barley, potatoes, beets). **2** Agr. village (district pop. 468), N Co. Offaly, Ireland, near Brosna R., 4 mi. NNW of Tullamore; cattle, barley, potatoes. Durrow Abbey was founded by St. Columba; in 7th cent. the *Book of Durrow* (now in Trinity Col. Library, Dublin) was written here.

Durrus (dûr'ŭs), Gaelic *Dubhros*, village (pop. 114), SW Co. Cork, Ireland, at head of Dunmanus Bay, 5 mi. SW of Bantry; copper-mining center.

Dursey (dûr'sē), island (1,402 acres; 4 mi. long, 1 mi. wide) just off SW coast of Co. Cork, Ireland, 11 mi. WSW of Castletown Bere. At SW tip is Dursey Head, 51°35'N 10°13'W.

Dur Sharrukin, Iraq: see KHORSABAD.

Dursley, town and parish (pop. 3,288), SW Gloucester, England, 19 mi. NE of Bristol; carpet weaving; agr.-machinery and electrical-equipment works. Has 15th-cent. chapel.

Dursunbey (do͞orso͞onbā'), village (pop. 4,541), Balikesir prov., NW Turkey, on railroad and 40 mi. E of Balikesir; cereals. Formerly Balat.

Durtal (dürtäl'), village (pop. 1,760), Maine-et-Loire dept., W France, on Loir R. and 20 mi. NE of Angers; brick- and tileworks. Has 14th-cent. bridge spanning the Loir.

Duru, Kashmir: see DORU.

Durud or **Dorud** (both: dōro͞od'), village, Sixth Prov., in Luristan, SW Iran, on the Ab-i-Diz and 38 mi. SE of Burujird, for which it serves as station on Trans-Iranian RR; grain- and fruitgrowing area.

Durunka or **Durunkah** (do͞oro͞ong'kŭ), village (pop. 10,603), Asyut prov., central Upper Egypt, 11 mi. NW of Abu Tig; cereals, dates, sugar cane.

Duruz, Jabal al-, Syria: see JEBEL ED DRUZ.

d'Urville, Cape (dûr'vĭl), E Ellesmere Isl., NE Franklin Dist., Northwest Territories, on Kane Basin, at entrance of small Allman Bay; 79°28'N 74°10'W. Peary's expedition vessel the *Windward* wintered offshore, 1898–99.

D'Urville, Cape, NW New Guinea, in the Pacific, near NE side of entrance to Geelvink Bay; 1°27'S 137°53'E.

D'Urville Island, Antarctica, off NE tip of Palmer Peninsula, N of Joinville Isl., in the South Atlantic; 63°2'S 56°15'W; 13 naut. mi. long, 5 naut. mi. wide. Discovered 1902 by Otto Nordenskjöld, Swedish explorer.

D'Urville Island (pop. 132), in Tasman Sea, c.1 mi. off N coast of S.Isl., New Zealand, at E entrance to Tasman Bay; 18 mi. long, 5 mi. wide; lumber milling.

Duryea (do͞or'yā, dûryā'), borough (pop. 6,655), Luzerne co., NE Pa., 8 mi. WSW of Scranton and on Lackawanna R., near its mouth on the Susquehanna; anthracite mines; silk mills. Inc. 1891.

Dushak (do͞oshäk'), town (1939 pop. over 500), SE Ashkhabad oblast, Turkmen SSR, on Trans-Caspian RR and 105 mi. SE of Ashkhabad.

Dushamba or **Dushamba Bazar** (do͞oshämbä'bäzär'), Chinese *Sinho* or *Hsin-ho* (both: shĭn'hŭ'), town and oasis (pop. 48,137), W central Sinkiang prov., China, 17 mi. SW of Kucha and on Muzart R.; cattle raising; fruit, grain.

Dusheti (do͞oshā'tyē), city (1926 pop. 2,100), E central Georgian SSR, on Georgian Military Road and 25 mi. N of Tiflis, in wooded area. Excursion base. Site of old fortress. Until 1936, Dushet.

Dushi, Afghanistan: see Doshi.

Dushore (do͞o'shôr), borough (pop. 759), Sullivan co., NE Pa., 17 mi. S of Towanda; silk mills; dairying.

Duside (do͞o'sīd), residential village, Montserrado co., W Liberia, 25 mi. E of Monrovia, in rubber plantations.

Dusky Sound, inlet of Tasman Sea, Fiordland Natl. Park, SW S.Isl., New Zealand; 25 mi. long, 12 mi. wide. Resolution Isl. at entrance. In it are Long Isl. (largest; c.8 mi. long), Anchor Isl., Cooper Isl., and several smaller isls. Formerly visited by sealers.

Duson (do͞o'sŏn), village (pop. 707), Lafayette parish, S La., 10 mi. W of Lafayette, in agr. area; cotton ginning. Natural-gas field near by.

Dusse-Alin, Russian SFSR: see Bureya Range.

Düsseldorf (do͞o'sŭldôrf, Ger. dü'sŭldôrf), city (□ 61; 1939 pop. 541,410; 1946 pop. 420,909; 1950 pop. 498,347), in former Prussian Rhine Prov., W Germany, after 1945 ⊙ North Rhine-Westphalia, port on the Rhine and 21 mi. NNW of Cologne; 51°13'N 6°47'E. Business center for the Ruhr; rail hub with airport (N outskirts); integrated steel-mfg. center (pig iron, steel, steel products). Other mfg.: chemicals (especially sulphuric acid), plate and industrial glass, ceramics, textiles; food processing. Large harbor (accommodating ocean-going vessels) trades in iron, steel, machinery, pipes, chemicals, grain, and wood of the Wupper region. Noted for its numerous parks, Düsseldorf is situated mainly on right bank of the Rhine, except suburbs of Heerdt, Niederkassel, and Oberkassel. Built around core comprising the 4 historical dists.: Altstadt (with bldg. of art acad.; house where poet Heine was born; 16th-cent. town hall), Neustadt, Friedrichstadt, and Karlstadt. Industry concentrated in E suburbs. Until 1945 a center of Ger. war industry (ordnance, U-boat sections), city was subjected (1943–45) to severe aerial bombing in Second World War (destruction about 65%). First mentioned in 12th cent.; chartered 1288. Was ⊙ duchy of Berg from 1511 to 1609, when it passed to Palatinate-Neuburg line. Came to Prussia in 1814. Noted art acad., founded 1819, gave its name in 19th cent. to Düsseldorf school of painting. Under Fr. occupation (1921–25) city was a center of Rhenish Separatist movement. Captured by U.S. troops March-April, 1945.

Dusso, Kashmir: see Dassu.

Dust Bowl, in U.S., name given to semi-arid regions of the plains states where wind storms may carry off enormous quantities of topsoil. The droughts of 1934, 1936, and 1937 in W Kansas and in the Texas and Okla. panhandles led to much suffering and migration of many farm families to other areas. Measures such as planting of windbreaks and soil-holding plants and the return to grassland of large areas unsuited to agr. have aided in combating soil destruction.

Dustin, town (pop. 524), Hughes co., central Okla., 12 mi. S of Henryetta, in agr. area; cotton ginning.

Duston, residential town and parish (pop. 2,095), central Northampton, England, 2 mi. W of Northampton; roller-bearing works. Has church dating from 13th cent.

Dusun Tua (do͞osōon' to͞oä'), village, E Selangor, Malaya, 9 mi. E of Kuala Lumpur, on Langat R.; health resort; hot springs.

Duszniki Zdroj (do͞oshnē'kē zdro͞o'ē), Pol. *Duszniki Zdrój*, Ger. *Bad Reinerz* (bät" rīn'ärts"), town (1939 pop. 4,690; 1946 pop. 5,926) in Lower Silesia, after 1945 in Wroclaw prov., SW Poland, near Czechoslovak border, at NW foot of Habelschwerdt Mts., 12 mi. WSW of Glatz (Klodzko); health resort; mfg. of electrical equipment, chemicals. Has 18th-cent. church. Iron formerly mined here.

Dutch Antilles, West Indies: see Curaçao.

Dutch Bay, Ceylon, S inlet of Gulf of Mannar, bet. Kalpitiya Peninsula (W) and Ceylon mainland (E); 7 mi. long, up to 5 mi. wide; extends S into Puttalam Lagoon. Receives the Kala Oya.

Dutch Borneo: see Borneo.

Dutch East Indies: see Indonesia.

Dutchess (dŭ'chĭs), county (□ 816; pop. 136,781), SE N.Y.; ⊙ Poughkeepsie. Bounded W by the Hudson, E by Conn. line; includes part of the Taconic Mts. (state park here) and part of highlands of the Hudson. Drained by Wappinger and Fishkill creeks. Dairying, poultry raising, diversified farming (fruit, grain, potatoes, truck, clover); hothouse flowers. Limestone; timber. Mfg. at Poughkeepsie, Beacon. Includes small lakes, resorts. At Hyde Park, the home and grave of Franklin D. Roosevelt and the Vanderbilt Mansion are natl. historic sites. Formed 1683.

Dutch Gap Canal, Va.: see James River.

Dutch Guiana: see Guiana, Dutch.

Dutch Harbor, village (1939 pop. 52), on small Amaknak Isl., in Unalaska Bay, NE Unalaska Isl., Aleutian Isls., SW Alaska; 53°53'N 166°32'W. Known to early fur traders and whalers, it became transshipment port for Nome after 1899. In 1940 U.S. here established a base which became an important air and naval base for operations in the Second World War. Also has Fort Mears army base. Attacked (June 3, 1942) by Japanese carrier-based planes, 1st attack on the Aleutian Isls.

Dutch Island, S R.I., small island (c.1 mi. long) in Narragansett Bay, c.1 mi. W of Conanicut Isl.; site of old Fort Greble (1863).

Dutchman Peak, Oregon: see Siskiyou Mountains.

Dutch New Guinea: see New Guinea, Netherlands.

Dutch West Indies: see Curaçao; West Indies.

Duthie (do͞o'thē), mining camp, Shoshone co., N Idaho, 16 mi. NE of Wallace, near Mont. line, in mtn. region; alt. 4,200 ft.; silver, lead, zinc.

Duthil and Rothiemurchus (dŭ'thĭl, rŏ-thēmûr'kŭs), parish (pop. 2,136), E Inverness, Scotland. Includes agr. village of Duthil, on Dulnan R. and 7 mi. WSW of Grantown-on-Spey, and resort of Boat-of-Garten, 8 mi. SW of Grantown-on-Spey.

Dutoitspan or **Du Toits Pan** (dŭtwēs"păn', Afrikaans –pän'), SE suburb of Kimberley, NE Cape Prov., U. of So. Afr.; important diamond mine.

Dutsan Wei, Nigeria: see Duchin Wai.

Dutton, village (pop. 787), S Ont., near L. Erie, 18 mi. WSW of St. Thomas; milk canning, dairying, lumbering.

Dutton, parish (pop. 231), W Lancashire, England. Includes village of Lower Dutton, 5 mi. NW of Blackburn; dairy farming.

Dutton, town (pop. 431), Teton co., N central Mont., near Teton R., 30 mi. NW of Great Falls; wheat-shipping point. Inc. 1935.

Dutton, Mount, Utah: see Sevier Plateau.

Duval. 1 (do͞ovăl') County (□ 777; pop. 304,029), NE Fla., on the Atlantic (E); ⊙ Jacksonville. Lowland area bordered by Talbot Isl. (E) and drained by St. Johns R.; coast partly swampy. Agr. (dairy and poultry products, corn, vegetables), forestry (naval stores, lumber; furniture), and fishing. Industry at Jacksonville. Resorts along coast. Formed 1822. **2** (dŭvăl') County (□ 1,818; pop. 15,643), S Texas; ⊙ San Diego. Livestock area (beef, dairy cattle), and a leading petroleum-producing co. of Texas; also horses, sheep, agr. (cotton, peanuts, corn, grain sorghums, some fruit and truck). Sulphur, salt mining. Hunting. Formed 1858.

Duvall (do͞o"vŏl'), town (pop. 236), King co., W, central Wash., 18 mi. NE of Seattle, near Snoqualmie R.; timber.

Duvan (do͞ovän'), village (1948 pop. over 2,000), NE Bashkir Autonomous SSR, Russian SFSR, 100 mi. NE of Ufa; agr. processing (grain, livestock).

Duvauchelle (do͞o"vūshĕl'), village (pop. 165), ⊙ Akaroa co. (□ 169; pop. 1,446), E S.Isl., New Zealand, 26 mi. SE of Christchurch, on N shore of Akaroa harbor on Banks Peninsula; dairy products, sheep. Also spelled Duvauchelle's.

Duvbo (düv'bo͞o"), residential village (pop. 2,121), Stockholm co., E Sweden, 5 mi. NW of Stockholm.

Duved (dü'väd"), village (pop. 360), Jamtland co., NW Sweden, in mts. near Norwegian border, on Indal R. and 55 mi. WNW of Ostersund; tourist resort. Tannforsen falls near by.

Duvergé (do͞ovĕrhā'), town (1950 pop. 4,876), Bahoruco prov., SW Dominican Republic, near E shore of L. Enriquillo, 8 mi. S of Neiba, in fertile, irrigated agr. region (corn, coffee, rice, fruit); lumbering. Salt mine near by.

Dúvida, Rio da, Brazil: see Roosevelt River.

Duvivier (düvēvyā'), village (pop. 815), Constantine dept., NE Algeria, on the Oued Seybouse, 30 mi. S of Bône; rail junction; olive-oil milling.

Duvnas (düv'nĕs"), Swedish *Duvnäs*, residential village (pop. 2,031), Stockholm co., E Sweden, 5 mi. ESE of Stockholm city center.

Duvno (do͞ov'nô), town (pop. 1,260), SW Bosnia, Yugoslavia, 50 mi. E of Split; local trade center. Called Tomislavgrad or Tomislav Grad from 1930s to c.1945.

Duwadami (do͞owădămē'), village, central Nejd, Saudi Arabia, 150 mi. W of Riyadh and on main highway to Mecca; agr. oasis.

Duwamish River (dŭwä'mĭsh), W Wash., formed by White and Green rivers, flows c.25 mi. N to Elliott Bay at Seattle. Lower section (dredged channel) is part of Seattle harbor.

Dux, Czechoslovakia: see Duchkov.

Duxbury (dŭks'brē, dŭks'bĕ"rē). **1** Town (pop. 3,167), Plymouth co., E Mass., on Duxbury Bay and 30 mi. SE of Boston; summer resort; poultry, cranberries. Formerly shipbuilding. Plymouth colonists here included Miles Standish, William Brewster, John Alden. Alden's house is still standing. Settled c.1624, inc. 1637. Includes villages of Millbrook and South Duxbury. **2** Town (pop. 489), Washington co., N central Vt., 11 mi. NW of Montpelier, in Green Mts. Camels Hump (4,083 ft.) is here.

Duxbury Bay, Mass.: see Plymouth Bay.

Duxford, town and parish (pop. 740), S Cambridge, England, on Cam R. and 8 mi. S of Cambridge; agr. market, with flour mills. Site of a Royal Air Force station. Has two 14th–15th-cent. churches with Norman towers.

Duzce (düzjĕ'), Turkish *Düzce*, town (1950 pop. 10,153), Bolu prov., NW Turkey, 25 mi. WNW of Bolu; agr. center (tobacco, corn, flax, garlic).

Duzdab, Iran: see Zahidan.

Duzerville (düzârvēl'), village (pop. 1,173), Constantine dept., NE Algeria, 7 mi. S of Bône; truck-gardening, winegrowing.

Duzkend, Armenian SSR: see Akhuryan.

Dve-mogili (dvĕ'-môgē'lē), village (pop. 3,903), Ruse dist., NE Bulgaria, 16 mi. SSW of Ruse; wheat, rye, sunflowers.

Dvigatelstroi, Russian SFSR: see Kaspisk.

Dvin (dvēn), village, S Armenian SSR, 9 mi. SE of Erivan, in orchard and cotton zone. Near by are ruins of anc. Dvin, ⊙ Armenia in 7th cent., under the Arabs.

Dvina Bay (dvēnä'), SE inlet of White Sea, in N European Russian SFSR, E of Onega Peninsula; 80 mi. wide, 65 mi. long; straight forested shores. Receives Northern Dvina R. Formerly also called Archangel Bay.

Dvina River. 1 or **Northern Dvina River,** Rus. *Severnaya Dvina*, in N European Russian SFSR, formed at Veliki Ustyug by union of Sukhona and Yug rivers; flows 455 mi. NW, past Krasavino, Kotlas, Semenovskoye, Yemetsk, and Kholmogory, to Dvina Bay 25 mi. below Archangel, forming vast delta mouth (□ 4,250; 5 main channels, including deep-draught Korabl and Maimaksa branches). Navigable (May–Nov.) in entire course; connected with Mariinsk canal system via Sukhona River (with which the Northern Dvina is 803 mi. long) and Northern Dvina Canal. Receives Vychegda and Pinega (right), Vaga and Yemtsa (left) rivers. Called Lesser [Rus. *Malaya*] Northern Dvina R. above mouth of Vychegda R. **2** or **Western Dvina River,** Rus. *Zapadnaya Dvina*, Lettish *Daugava* (dou'gävä), Ger. *Düna* (dü'nä), in W European USSR and Latvia, rises in Valdai Hills N of Andreapol (Velikiye Luki oblast), flows SSW, past Zapadnaya Dvina and Velizh (head of navigation), and WNW, through N Belorussia, past Vitebsk and Polotsk, through Latvia, past Daugavpils, Kegums (hydroelectric station), and Riga, to Gulf of Riga; length, 633 mi. (in Latvia, 228 mi.). Receives Drissa, Aiviekste, and Ogre (right), Ulla and Disna (left) rivers; forms common mouth with Lielupe R. Except for Berezina Canal, 19th-cent. waterways linking the Western Dvina with Volga and Neman rivers and L. Ilmen have become obsolete. Used mainly for logging; frozen Dec.–April. In lower course, formed (after 1561) border bet. Livonia and Courland.

Dvinsk, Latvia: see Daugavpils.

Dvor or **Dvor na Uni** (dvôr nä o͞o'nē), village (pop. 1,963), N Croatia, Yugoslavia, on Una R. and 2 mi. N of Novi (Bosnia).

Dvorce (dvôr'tsĕ), Ger. *Hof* (hōf), village (pop. 1,058), N Moravia, Czechoslovakia, 21 mi. NNE of Olomouc; oats.

Dvory nad Zitavou (dvô'rĭ näd' zhĭtävō), Slovak *Dvory nad Žitavou*, Hung. *Udvard* (o͞od'vŏrd), village (pop. 5,769), S Slovakia, Czechoslovakia, on railroad and 11 mi. NNE of Komarno; wheat. Has Gothic church.

Dvurechnaya (dvo͝oryĕch'nīŭ), village (1926 pop. 3,506), E Kharkov oblast, Ukrainian SSR, on Oskol R. and 11 mi. NNE of Kupyansk; flour milling, metalworking.

Dvur Kralove or **Dvur Kralove nad Labem** (dvo͝or' krä'lôvā näd' läbĕm), Czech *Dvůr Králové nad Labem*, Ger. *Königinhof* or *Königinhof an der Elbe* (kû"nĕgĭnhōf' än dĕr ĕl'bŭ), town (pop. 13,675), NE Bohemia, Czechoslovakia, on Elbe R., on railroad and 15 mi. N of Hradec Kralove; important linen trade; mfg. of linen, cotton, silk, and jute textiles (notably printed materials). Originally founded by Wenceslaus II. Site of Prussian victory (1866) over Austrians.

Dwangwa River (dwäng'gwä), central Nyasaland, rises NW of Kasungu on Northern Rhodesia border, flows 100 mi. ENE to L. Nyasa 25 mi. NNW of Kota Kota.

Dwarahat, India: see Ranikhet.

Dwarasamudra, India: see Belur, Mysore.

Dwarka (dwär'kŭ, dvär'–), town (pop. 10,876), Amreli dist., NW Bombay, India, port on Arabian Sea, at W end of Kathiawar peninsula, 70 mi. WSW of Jamnagar; exports millet, ghee, oilseeds, salt; large cement works. One of 7 sacred Hindu centers of India; an important Hindu pilgrimage center; noted Vishnuite temples, including one dedicated to Krishna. Shankaracharya (8th-cent. A.D. Vedantic philosopher) founded one of his main schools here. Lighthouse 1 mi. W. Sometimes called Jigat.

Dwarka River, in Bihar and West Bengal, India, rises in NE Chota Nagpur Plateau foothills in headstreams joining 27 mi. W of Berhampore, flows c.100 mi. E and S to Bhagirathi R. 5 mi. NNE of Katwa. Receives Brahmani R. 16 mi. WNW of Berhampore and Mor R. 7 mi. E of Kandi.

Dwarkeswar River, India: see Rupnarayan River.

Dwars, India: see Duars.

Dwars-in-den-Weg, Indonesia: see Sangiang.

Dwight. 1 Village (pop. 2,843), Livingston co., NE central Ill., 30 mi. W of Kankakee, in agr. and bituminous-coal area; granite products. Seat of Keeley Inst. and a veterans hosp. Near by is the state reformatory for women. Inc. 1869. **2** City (pop. 281), Morris co., E central Kansas, 18 mi. SE of Junction City, in grazing and agr. region. **3** Village (pop. 218), Butler co., E Nebr., 25 mi. NW of

Lincoln. **4** Village (pop. 129), Richland co., SE N.Dak., 6 mi. WNW of Wahpeton.

Dwingelo (dwĭng'ŭlō), town (pop. 893), Drenthe prov., NE central Netherlands, on the Smildervaart and 12 mi. NNE of Meppel; center of dairy industry. Sometimes spelled Dwingeloo.

Dworp (dwôrp), Fr. *Tourneppe* (tōōrnĕp'), town (pop. 3,583), Brabant prov., central Belgium, 7 mi. S of Brussels; metal industry; agr. market. Has 17th-cent. castle.

Dwory (dvô'rē), village, Krakow prov., S Poland, 3 mi. E of Oswiecim; gasoline plant.

Dwyryd River (dōō'ĭrĭd), NW Merioneth, Wales, rises just S of Blaenau-Ffestiniog, flows 14 mi. SW and WSW, past Maentwrog, to Cardigan Bay of Irish Sea 3 mi. SW of Portmadoc. Receives Cynfal R. just W of Ffestiniog; below this junction its valley is known as Vale of Ffestiniog (3 mi. long), noted for scenic beauty. Estuarial section is called Traeth Bach (trīth băkh').

Dyakonovo or **D'yakonovo** (dyä'kŭnŭvŭ), village (1926 pop. 5,929), central Kursk oblast, Russian SFSR, on Seim R. and 15 mi. WSW of Kursk; fruit canning.

Dyakovitsa, Yugoslavia: see DJAKOVICA.

Dyakovskaya or **D'yakovskaya** (dyä'kŭfskīŭ) or **Syamzha** (syäm'zhŭ), village (1939 pop. over 500), central Vologda oblast, Russian SFSR, 70 mi. NNE of Vologda, on Archangel highway; flax; dairying.

Dyaravitsa, Yugoslavia: see DJARAVICA.

Dyardanes, river, S Asia: see BRAHMAPUTRA RIVER.

Dyatkovo or **Dyat'kovo** (dyät'yŭkŭvŭ), city (1939 pop. over 10,000), NE Bryansk oblast, Russian SFSR, 25 mi. N of Bryansk; center of glass-producing region; glassworks, sawmills. Glassworks (NW, W) at Bytosh, Ivot, and Star.

Dyatlovo (dyä'tlŭvŭ), Pol. *Zdzięciół* (zdzyĕ'tsyōōōō), town (1931 pop. 3,746), W Baranovichi oblast, Belorussian SSR, 20 mi. SW of Novogrudok; tanning, food processing (flour, butter), mfg. (parchment, tiles). Has old castle.

Dyaul (joul), volcanic island (□ 42; pop. c.600), New Ireland dist., Bismarck Archipelago, Territory of New Guinea, SW Pacific, 8 mi. SW of New Ireland; 15 mi. long; coconut plantation. Sometimes spelled Djaul.

Dybbol, Denmark: see DÜPPEL.

Dybso Fjord (düb'sû), inlet of Smaalandsfarvand strait, SE Zealand, Denmark; 6 mi. long. N arm, deepened by canal to mouth of Sus R., navigable to Naestved.

Dybvaag, Norway: see DYPVAG.

Dybvad (düp'vädh), town (pop. 1,021), Hjorring amt, N Jutland, Denmark, 20 mi. SE of Hjorring; lumber mills.

Dyce (dīs), town and parish (pop. 1,256), SE Aberdeen, Scotland, near Don R., 6 mi. NW of Aberdeen; agr. market; bacon and ham curing. Site of Aberdeen city airport.

Dychow (dē'khōōf), Pol. *Dychów*, Ger. *Deichow* (dī'khō), village (1939 pop. 646), in Brandenburg, after 1945 in Zielona Gora prov., 5 mi. S of Krosno and on Bobrawa R. (hydroelectric station).

Dycusburg, town (pop. 147), Crittenden co., W Ky., on Cumberland R. and 24 mi. ENE of Paducah.

Dyer (dī'ŭr), county (□ 527; pop. 33,473), NW Tenn.; ⊙ Dyersburg. Bounded W by the Mississippi, SW by Forked Deer R.; drained by Obion R. Fertile cotton-growing area; livestock raising. Some mfg. at Dyersburg. Formed 1823.

Dyer. 1 Town (pop. 398), Crawford co., NW Ark., 17 mi. NE of Fort Smith, near Arkansas R. **2** Town (pop. 1,556), Lake co., extreme NW Ind., near Ill. line, 10 mi. S of Hammond. **3** Town (pop. 1,864), Gibson co., NW Tenn., 6 mi. N of Trenton, in farm area; makes shoes, shipping containers.

Dyer, Cape, E extremity of Baffin Isl., SE Franklin Dist., Northwest Territories, at tip of Cumberland Peninsula, on Davis Strait; 66°37'N 61°19'W.

Dyer, Cape, on NW Campana Isl., Aysén prov., S Chile; 48°6'S 75°30'W.

Dyeravitsa, Albania-Yugoslavia: see DJERAVICA.

Dyer Brook, town (pop. 219), Aroostook co., E Maine, 18 mi. WSW of Houlton; ships potatoes; agr.

Dyer Island, Knox co., S Maine, just W of and bridged to Vinalhaven Isl.; ½ mi. long.

Dyerman, mountain, Yugoslavia: see DJERMAN.

Dyersburg, city (pop. 10,885), ⊙ Dyer co., NW Tenn., on North Fork of Forked Deer R. and 70 mi. NNE of Memphis; trade and processing center for fertile timber and agr. (cotton, grain, corn, dairy products) area; produces staves, textiles, cottonseed oil, canned foods. Holds annual cotton festival. Laid out 1825; inc. 1836.

Dyersville, city (pop. 2,416), on Delaware-Dubuque co. line, E Iowa, on North Fork Maquoketa R. and 22 mi. W of Dubuque; livestock shipping; mfg. (shirts, concrete blocks, butter tubs). Limestone quarries near by. Settled 1837–38 by English; laid out 1851; inc. 1892.

Dyerville, hamlet, Humboldt co., NW Calif., at junction of Eel R. and its South Fork, 33 mi. SSE of Eureka; hq. of HUMBOLDT STATE REDWOOD PARK. Near by is Founders' Tree (364 ft.), tallest tree in world.

Dyevdyeliya, Yugoslavia: see DJEVDJELIJA.

Dyffryn Clydach (dŭ'frĭn klĭ'dăkh), town and parish (pop. 1,964), W Glamorgan, Wales, 2 mi. NNW of Neath; coal mining.

Dyfi River, Wales: see DOVEY RIVER.

Dygya, Azerbaijan SSR: see DIGYA.

Dyhernfurth, Poland: see BRZEG DOLNY.

Dyje River (dĭ'yĕ), Ger. *Thaya* (tī'ä) principal tributary of Moravia R., in N Austria and W and S Moravia, Czechoslovakia; formed by junction of Austrian and Moravian branches in Lower Austria, 10 mi. NE of Waidhofen an der Thaya; flows NE, into Czechoslovakia, and generally E, past Znojmo and Breclav, forming parts of Czechoslovak-Austrian border, to Morava R. 18 mi. SSW of Hodonin; c.175 mi. long. Receives Svratka R. (left). Large dam, hydroelectric works, and reservoir are just W of Vranov.

Dyke, agr. village in Dyke and Moy parish (pop. 987), NW Moray, Scotland, 3 mi. W of Forres.

Dykehead. 1 Town, Ayrshire, Scotland: see DREGHORN. **2** Town in Shotts parish, NE Lanark, Scotland, 7 mi. ENE of Motherwell; coal mining, steel milling.

Dykh-Tau (dĭkh-tou'), peak (17,054 ft.) in front range of the central Greater Caucasus, on Russian SFSR–Georgian SSR border, 40 mi. SW of Nalchik, just NW of Shkhara (peak); 43°2'N 43°6'E.

Dylais Higher (dŭ'lĭs), parish (pop. 6,629), NW Glamorgan, Wales, 7 mi. NE of Neath; coal mining. Includes coal-mining town of Crynant (krŭn'ŭnt), 5 mi. NE of Neath.

Dyle River (Fr. dēl, Fl. dī'lŭ), central Belgium, rises just SW of Genappe, flows 60 mi. NE, past Genappe, Ottignies, Wavre, Louvain, and Mechlin, joining Nèthe R. at Rumst to form RUPEL RIVER.

Dylym (dĭlĭm'), village (1932 pop. estimate 1,160), W Dagestan Autonomous SSR, Russian SFSR, 12 mi. S of Khasavyurt; wheat, livestock.

Dymer (dĭ'myĭr), agr. town (1926 pop. 3,613), N Kiev oblast, Ukrainian SSR, on road and 25 mi. NNW of Kiev.

Dymock (dĭ'mŭk), agr. village and parish (pop. 1,149), NW Gloucester, England, 12 mi. NW of Gloucester. Church dates from Norman times.

Dyna, Norway: see AL.

Dynas, Sweden: see VAJA.

Dynevor Park, Wales: see LLANDILO.

Dyngjufoll, Iceland: see ASKJA.

Dynow (dĭ'nōōf), Pol. *Dynów*, town (pop. 4,960), Rzeszow prov., SE Poland, on San R. and 23 mi. SSE of Rzeszow; rail spur terminus; sawmilling, woodworking, brick mfg., flour milling.

Dypvag (düp'vôg), Nor. *Dypvåg*, village and canton (pop. 2,067), Aust-Agder co., S Norway, on an inlet of the Skagerrak, 18 mi. NE of Arendal; shipping, fishing. Formerly spelled Dyvag (Nor. *Dyvåg*) and Dybvaag. At Gjeving (yă'vĕng), formerly Giving, village (pop. 235), 3 mi. NE: mfg. of wood pulp. LYNGOR, in the canton, is just offshore.

Dyr, Djebel, Algeria: see DIR, DJEBEL.

Dyrholaey (dĭr'hō"lăä"), Icelandic *Dyrhólœy*, or **Portland**, cape at S extremity of Iceland, near S foot of Myrdalsjokull; 63°24'N 19°7'W

Dyrnesvagen, Norway: see SMOLA.

Dyrrachium or **Dyrrhachium**, Albania: see DURAZZO.

Dyrsland, Denmark: see DJURSLAND.

Dysart, village (pop. 273), S Sask., 40 mi. NE of Regina; wheat, mixed farming.

Dysart (dī'zŭrt), town, S Fifeshire, Scotland, on the Firth of Forth, just NE of Kirkcaldy; coal-shipping port, with coal mining and linen milling. Has remains of 15th-cent. St. Serf's church. Dysart House was residence of earl of Rosslyn. Town is former burgh, incorporated with Kirkcaldy in 1930. Just N is coal-mining town of Gallatown.

Dysart, town (pop. 1,089), Tama co., central Iowa, 22 mi. S of Waterloo; feed milling.

Dyserth (dĭ'sĕrth), town and parish (pop. 1,413), Flint, Wales, 2 mi. SSW of Prestatyn; agr. market. Church contains 15th-cent. Jesse window. Near by are remains of castle built 1241 by Henry III, destroyed 1263.

Dysna River, Lithuania and Belorussian SSR: see DISNA RIVER.

Dytike Thrake, Greece: see THRACE.

Dyulty-Dag or **Dyul'ty-Dag** (dyōōltē"-däk'), N outlier of the E Greater Caucasus, in Dagestan Autonomous SSR, Russian SFSR; rises to c.13,500 ft. at Taklik peak, 20 mi. WSW of Kuli. Avar Koisu and Samur rivers rise on its slopes.

Dyurbeldzhin or **Dyurbel'dzhin** (dyōōrbĕljēn'), village, W Tyan-Shan oblast, Kirghiz SSR, in N foothills of the Dzhaman-Tau (section of Tien Shan mtn. system), 55 mi. WSW of Naryn; wheat.

Dyurdyevik, Yugoslavia: see DJURDJEVIK.

Dyurtyuli (dyōōrtyōō'lyē), village (1948 pop. over 2,000), NW Bashkir Autonomous SSR, Russian SFSR, on Belaya R. (landing) and 65 mi. NW of Ufa; rye, oats.

Dyushambe, Tadzhik SSR: see STALINABAD, city.

Dyushambinka River, Tadzhik SSR: see KAFIRNIGAN RIVER.

Dyvag, Norway: see DYPVAG.

Dywin, Belorussian SSR: see DIVIN.

Dzabkhan or **Dzabhan** (dzäb'khän), aimak (□ 37,-200; pop. 80,000), W Mongolian People's Republic; ⊙ Uliassutai. Bounded N by Tuva Autonomous Oblast of Russian SFSR, it contains W part of Khangai Mts. and is drained (S) by Dzabkhan R. Vegetation varies from alpine meadows in high mts. (E) to desert along the lakes Khara Nor and Durga Nor (W). Pop.: Khalkha Mongols.

Dzabkhan River or **Dzabhan River**, W Mongolian People's Republic, rises on S slopes of the Khangai Mts. E of Uliassutai, flows 500 mi. S and NW to the Airik Nor.

Dza Chu, Tibet: see MEKONG RIVER.

Dzagidzor (dzŭgĕdzôr'), town (1947 pop. over 500), N Armenian SSR, on railroad and 8 mi. S of Alaverdi. Near by is Dzora hydroelectric station.

Dzam, Mexico: see DZAN.

Dzamandzar (dzämändzär'), village, Majunga prov., N Madagascar, on SE shore of Nossi-Bé Isl., 8 mi. NW of Hellville; sugar milling.

Dzamyn Ude or **Dzamiin Üüde** (dzä'mĭn ŭ'dā), village, East Gobi aimak, SE Mongolian People's Republic, 60 mi. SE of Sain Shanda, and on Ulan Bator–Kalgan highway, at China border Formerly called Ude or Udde, Chinese *Wuteh*.

Dzan (tsän), town (pop. 1,186), Yucatan, SE Mexico, 4 mi. E of Ticul; henequen, sugar cane, corn. Sometimes Dzam.

Dzaoudzi (dzoud'zē), town (pop. c.3,000), ⊙ Comoro Isls. and main town of Mayotte Isl., on small Pamanzi islet, 2 mi. offshore; 12°45'S 45°15'E. Trading center and small port. R.C. mission.

Dzasaktu Khan, Mongolia: see YUSUN BULAK.

Dzaudzhikau (dzoujĭkou'), city (1939 pop. 127,172), ⊙ North Ossetian Autonomous SSR, Russian SFSR, on Terek R., at its issue from the Greater Caucasus, and 375 mi. SE of Rostov, 900 mi. SSE of Moscow; 43°1'N 44°41'E. Rail terminus; N end of Georgian Military Road; industrial center; electric zinc smelter, lead and silver refineries for Sadon mines, car repair shops; food processing (fruit, starch), woodworking, glassware mfg. Industry powered by Gizeldon hydroelectric station (S) and by gas pipe line from Malgobek. Has agr., medical, and teachers col., nonferrous metals institute, regional mus. Offers fine views of Mt. Kazbek (SSW). Pop. largely Russian, Ossetian, Armenian, and Georgian. Founded 1784 as fortress in Caucasus wars and named Vladikavkaz [Rus.,= rule the Caucasus]; long the military and political center of Rus. Caucasus. After introduction (1920) of Soviet rule, it was (1921–24) ⊙ Mountain Autonomous SSR and later, ⊙ North Caucasus Territory. In Second World War, Germans came within c.10 mi. of city in their farthest advance in the Caucasus. Called Ordzhonikidze 1930–44.

Dzemul (tsāmōōl'), town (pop. 1,732), Yucatan, SE Mexico, 27 mi. NE of Mérida; henequen growing.

Dzerzhinsk (dzĭrzhĕnsk'). **1** City (1926 pop. 5,483), W Minsk oblast, Belorussian SSR, 23 mi. SW of Minsk; metalworks; food processing, clothing and light mfg. Until c.1935, called Kaidanovo or Koidanovo. **2** City (1926 pop. 8,910; 1939 pop. 103,415), W Gorki oblast, Russian SFSR, on Oka R. and 20 mi. WSW of Gorki; chemical industry (phosphate fertilizers); rope mfg., sawmilling, flour milling. Alabaster production, based on local gypsum quarries. Formed 1930 by union of town of Rastyapino (formerly Chernoye) and its industrial suburbs of Imeni Sverdlova and Chernorechenski Zavod. Boomed during 1930s. **3** City (1926 pop. 12,806), central Stalino oblast, Ukrainian SSR, in the Donbas, 28 mi. N of Stalino; coal-mining center; chemical works. Formerly called Shcherbinovka and later, until 1938, Imeni Dzerzhinskogo. **4** Town (1926 pop. 7,559), SW Zhitomir oblast, Ukrainian SSR, 34 mi. WSW of Zhitomir; ceramic industry. Until c.1935, Romanov.

Dzerzhinski or **Dzherzhinskiy** (dzĭrzhĕn'skē), district of Greater Baku, Azerbaijan SSR, on SW Apsheron Peninsula, just NW of Baku; oil fields. Main center, Baladzhary.

Dzerzhinski or **Dzerzhinskiy**, town (1939 pop. over 500), central Moscow oblast, Russian SFSR, 9 mi. S of Lyubertsy, near Moskva R. Until 1938, Trudovaya Kommuna Imeni Dzerzhinskogo.

Dzerzhinski Rudnik or **Dzerzhinskiy Rudnik** (rōōd-nyĭk'), town (1939 pop. over 500), S Voroshilovgrad oblast, Ukrainian SSR, in the Donbas, 4 mi. SSE of Rovenki; coal mines.

Dzerzhinskoye (dzĭrzhĕn'skŭyŭ). **1** Village (1948 pop. over 2,000), NE Taldy-Kurgan oblast, Kazakh SSR, in the Dzungarian Ala-Tau, W of the Ala-Kul (lake), 145 mi. NE of Taldy-Kurgan; irrigated agr. (wheat). Formerly Kolpakovskoye. **2** Village (1926 pop. 577), SE Krasnoyarsk Territory, Russian SFSR, 45 mi. NNW of Kansk, in agr. area. Formerly Rozhdestvenskoye.

Dzhaferitsa, Bulgaria: see SLAV.

Dzhalagash (jŭlŭgăsh'), village, central Kzyl-Orda oblast, Kazakh SSR, on the Syr Darya, on Trans-Caspian RR and 40 mi. WNW of Kzyl-Orda; rice.

Dzhalal-Abad (jŭlăl"-ŭbăt'), oblast (□ 9,200; 1946 pop. estimate 200,000), NW Kirghiz SSR; ⊙ Dzhalal-Abad. Mostly mountainous; Chatkal Range (NW), the Talas Ala-Tau (N), Fergana Range (E); includes NE section of Fergana Valley; drained by Naryn R. Wheat, barley, and cotton grown in mtn. valleys and lower irrigated areas; cattle and goat raising; nut and almond woods; some sericulture. Coal mines at Tashkumyr and

Kok-Yangak, oil fields and sulphur mines at Changyrtash and Mailisai; vanadium mined at Mailisai. Mfg. at Dzhalal-Abad. Pop.: Kirghiz, Uzbeks. Formed 1939.

Dzhalal-Abad, city (1939 pop. 14,961), ⊙ Dzhalal-Abad oblast, Kirghiz SSR, in E Fergana Valley, on railroad and 34 mi. ENE of Andizhan, 155 mi. SSW of Frunze; 40°57'N 73°E. Industrial center; cotton ginning, food processing (canned goods, meat, dairy products, vitamins), mfg. (tobacco products, clothing, paper, shoes). Health resort (hot springs) near by. Until 1937 spelled Dzhalyal-Abad. Prior to industrialization in 1930s, known chiefly for its resort.

Dzhalinda (jŭlyēn'dŭ), village (1939 pop. over 500), NW Amur oblast, Russian SFSR, on Amur R. and 35 mi. S of Skovorodino, to which it is joined by railroad; river port. Founded 1858 as Cossack village of Reinovo.

Dzhama, peak, Bulgaria and Yugoslavia: see ILOVRAKH.

Dzhambai, Uzbek SSR: see KHASHDALA.

Dzhambeity or **Dzhambeyty** (jŭmbyā'tē), village (1926 pop. 2,388), West Kazakhstan oblast, Kazakh SSR, 80 mi. SE of Uralsk; cattle. Also called Dzhambeita or Dzhambeyta.

Dzhambul (jŭmbōōl'), oblast (□ 52,000; pop. c.300,000), S Kazakh SSR; ⊙ Dzhambul. Drained by lower Chu, Talas, and Assa rivers; bounded S by Kirghiz SSR; bet. the Kara-Tau (W) and Chu-Ili Mts. (E). Includes, in N, clay steppe (Bet-Pak-Dala) and sandy desert (Muyun-Kum), in S, irrigated agr. areas (sugar beets, cotton, wheat, rice, tobacco, fiber plants). Raising of sheep, cattle, horses, and camels is important. Phosphorite mining (Chulak-Tau). Industry (sugar refining, tanning, cement mfg.) along Turksib RR, which crosses S section. Pop.: Kazakhs, Russians, Ukrainians, Uzbeks. Formed 1939.

Dzhambul, city (1926 pop. 24,761; 1939 pop. 62,723), ⊙ Dzhambul oblast, Kazakh SSR, on Turksib RR, on Talas R. and 280 mi. W of Alma-Ata; 42°53'N 71°24'E. Center of sugar-beet and orchard area; mfg. of phosphate fertilizer; sugar refining, fruit canning, wool washing, metalworking, distilling. Linked by rail with phosphorite mines of Chulak-Tau. City site, dating from 5th cent., first occupied by Taraz (ruled by Arabs, 8th–9th cent.), later called Yany (Yangi); followed by modern Kazakh city of Aulie-Ata or Auliye-Ata; renamed Mirzoyan (1933) and Dzhambul (1937). Fell to Russians (1864).

Dzhandar, Uzbek SSR: see SVERDLOVSK, village.

Dzhanga (jŭn-gä'), town (1939 pop. over 500), W Ashkhabad oblast, Turkmen SSR, on Trans-Caspian RR, on N Krasnovodsk Gulf, 7 mi. E of Krasnovodsk; fisheries, salt extraction.

Dzhanga, peak (16,568 ft.) in main range of central Greater Caucasus, on Russian SFSR–Georgian SSR line, bet. Tetnuld and Shkhara peaks.

Dzhangi-Dzhol (jŭn-gē-jôl'), village (1948 pop. over 500), W Dzhalal-Abad oblast, Kirghiz SSR, near Naryn R., 15 mi. NNE of Tashkumyr; pastures. Until 1942, Chon-Ak-Dzhol.

Dzhankoi or **Dzhankoy** (jŭn-koi'), city (1939 pop. over 10,000), N Crimea, Russian SFSR, 55 mi. NNE of Simferopol; rail center in wheat and cotton area; railroad and agr.-machine workshops; cotton ginning, flour milling. Developed with construction of railroad. Until Second World War, center of Jewish colonization of N Crimea.

Dzhanybek (jŭnĭbyĕk'), village (1948 pop. over 2,000), W West Kazakhstan oblast, Kazakh SSR, on railroad and 110 mi. NE of Stalingrad; cattle, horses.

Dzharat (jŭrät'), town (1939 pop. over 500) in Sumgait dist. of Greater Baku, Azerbaijan SSR, on N shore of Apsheron Peninsula, 15 mi. NNW of Baku; vineyards. Formerly spelled Dzhorat.

Dzhargalan (jŭrgŭlän'), village, E Issyk-Kul oblast, Kirghiz SSR, on Tyup R. and 35 mi. E of Przhevalsk (linked by narrow-gauge railroad); coal mining. Also spelled Dzhergalan.

Dzharkent, Kazakh SSR: see PANFILOV.

Dzhar-Kurgan (jŭr-kōōrgän'), village (1939 pop. over 2,000), S Surkhan-Darya oblast, Uzbek SSR, on railroad, on the Surkhan Darya and 22 mi. NNE of Termez; agr., food processing.

Dzharma, Kazakh SSR: see ZHARMA.

Dzhava (jŭvä'), village (1948 pop. over 2,000), central South Ossetian Autonomous Oblast, Georgian SSR, 11 mi. N of Stalinir; health resort (mineral springs).

Dzhebel (jĕ'bĕl), village (pop. 487), Khaskovo dist., S Bulgaria, in E Rhodope Mts., 6 mi. SW of Momchilgrad; noted for high-grade tobacco (experiment station). Formerly Shekh-Dzhumaya.

Dzhebel (jĭbyĕl'), town (1932 pop. estimate 3,900), W Ashkhabad oblast, Turkmen SSR, in the desert Kara-Kum, on Trans-Caspian RR and 10 mi. NW of Nebit-Dag; railroad shops; salt extraction. Just SW is health resort Molla-Kara.

Dzhebrail (jĕbrĭēl'), village (1932 pop. estimate 580), S Azerbaijan SSR, at S end of Karabakh Range, 40 mi. S of Agdam, near Aras R (Iranian border); wheat, stock; rug mfg. Marble quarries.

Dzhekonda (jĕkŭndä'), town (1948 pop. over 2,000), SE Yakut Autonomous SSR, Russian SFSR, 25 mi. ESE of Aldan; gold mining.

Dzhema, Bulgaria, Yugoslavia: see ILOVVRAKH.

Dzhergalan, Kirghiz SSR: see DZHARGALAN.

Dzherman River (jĕrmän'), W Bulgaria, rises in small alpine lake in NW Rila Mts., N of Mt. Malovitsa; flows W in an arc, past Marek, and SSW to Struma R. 2 mi. SE of Boboshevo; 30 mi. long.

Dzhermuk (jĕrmōōk'), village, E Armenian SSR, in Daralagez Range, 20 mi. ENE of Mikoyan; health resort (alt. c.7,000 ft.).

Dzhetygara (jĕtĭgŭrä'), city (1939 pop. over 10,000), NW Kustanai oblast, Kazakh SSR, near Tobol R., 115 mi. SW of Kustanai; cattle; gold-mining center.

Dzhety-Oguz (jĕtē"-ŭgōōs'), village, central Issyk-Kul oblast, Kirghiz SSR, on N slope of the Terskei Ala-Tau, 10 mi. SW of Przhevalsk. Health resort of Dzhety-Oguz is 7 mi. S of village.

Dzhety-Su (-sōō') [Kazakh,=seven rivers], Rus. *Semirech'ye*, sandy desert plain in Alma-Ata and Taldy-Kurgan oblasts, Kazakh SSR, bet. the N Tien Shan and L. Balkhash; 350 mi. long, 70–150 mi. wide; includes Sary-Ishik-Otrau (desert). Fishing in L. Balkhash and sheep breeding are chief activities of pop. Semirechye was an oblast which became a govt. in 1917; in 1922 it was renamed Dzhetysu and in 1928 was abolished; it extended from L. Balkhash S to Issyk-Kul (lake). Named for 7 rivers which flow through area into L. Balkhash.

Dzhezdinski or **Dzhezdinskiy** (jĭzdyēn'skē), town (1945 pop. over 500), W Karaganda oblast, Kazakh SSR, on rail spur and 20 mi. NE of Karsakpai; manganese-mining center. Developed during Second World War. Also called Dzhesdy.

Dzhezkazgan (jĕskŭzgän'), town (1948 pop. over 2,000), W Karaganda oblast, Kazakh SSR, on railroad and 20 mi. E of Karsakpay; copper-mining center (in exploitation since 1847). Near by (15 mi. SE) is copper-smelter town of Bolshoi Dzhezkazgan or Bol'shoy Dzhezkazgan [Rus.,=greater Dzhezkazgan] (1948 pop. over 2,000); developed during Second World War.

Dzhibkhalantu, Mongolia: see ULIASSUTAI.

Dzhida River (jē'dŭ), S Buryat-Mongol Autonomous SSR, Russian SFSR, rises in Eastern Sayan Mts., flows 300 mi. E, past Tsakir and Torei, to Selenga River 20 mi. S of Selenduma. Rich tungsten deposits (mined at Gorodok) along upper course.

Dzhilikul or **Dzhilikul'** (jĭlyĕkōōl'), village (1932 pop. estimate 1,980), S Stalinabad oblast, Tadzhik SSR, on Vakhsh R. and 18 mi. SSW of Kurgan-Tyube (linked by narrow-gauge railroad); long-staple-cotton center; truck produce.

Dzhirgalantu, Mongolia: see KOBDO, city.

Dzhirgatal or **Dzhirgatal'** (jĭrgŭtäl'), village (1932 pop. estimate 890), N Garm oblast, Tadzhik SSR, near Surkhab R., 45 mi. ENE of Garm; wheat, sheep, goats.

Dzhizak (jēzäk'), city (1932 pop. estimate 17,500), NE Samarkand oblast, Uzbek SSR, on Trans-Caspian RR and 55 mi. NE of Samarkand; metalworks, tobacco products; cotton. Hot climate. Until late 19th cent., a major trade center at junction of caravan routes; declined following construction of railroad. Fell to Russians (1866).

Dzhugdzhur Range (jōōgjōōr'), E continuation of Stanovoi Range, in E Siberian Russian SFSR; extends from Maya R. (left affluent of Uda R.) 500 mi. NNE in an arc along Sea of Okhotsk coast; forms watershed of Maya R. (right affluent of Aldan R.); rises to 7,200 ft. Formed mainly by mesozoic effusives (diabase, andesite).

Dzhugeli, Georgian SSR: see ZESTAFONI.

Dzhulfa or **Dzhul'fa** (jōōl'fŭ), city (1932 pop. estimate 1,450), SE Nakhichevan Autonomous SSR, Azerbaijan SSR, on Aras R. and 20 mi. SE of Nakhichevan, on Iranian border; commercial and communication center; railroads to Tiflis, Alyaty-Baku, and Tabriz. Arsenic mining (N).

Dzhulinka (jōō'lyĭnkŭ), village (1926 pop. 4,413), SE Vinnitsa oblast, Ukrainian SSR, 8 mi. NW of Gaivoron; metalworks.

Dzhulyunitsa (jōōlyōōnē'tsä), village (pop. 4,555), Gorna Oryakhovitsa dist., N Bulgaria, on headstream of Bregovitsa R. and 10 mi. E of Gorna Oryakhovitsa; horticultural center (tomatoes, onions, peppers, vervain mallow); tomato paste.

Dzhuma (jōōmä'), town (1926 pop. 2,310), S Samarkand oblast, Uzbek SSR, on Trans-Caspian RR and 16 mi. WNW of Samarkand; cotton; metalworks, flour mill. Called Ikramovo in 1930s.

Dzhumaya, Greece: see HERACLEIA.

Dzhumgol River (jōōmgôl'), N Tyan-Shan oblast, Kirghiz SSR, rises N of Son-Kul (lake), flows c.50 mi. W, past Chayek, to Kokomeren R. (left tributary of Naryn R.); in fertile agr. and grazing valley. **Dzhumgol-Tau** range (N) rises to c.13,000 ft.

Dzhungarski Ala-Tau, Kazakh SSR: see DZUNGARIAN ALA-TAU.

Dzhurin (jōō'rĭn), village (1926 pop. 5,761), SW Vinnitsa oblast, Ukrainian SSR, 28 mi. NE of Mogilev-Podolski; sugar refining.

Dzhurun (jōōrōōn'), village (1948 pop. over 2,000), central Aktyubinsk oblast, Kazakh SSR, on Trans-Caspian RR and 70 mi. S of Aktyubinsk; phosphorite deposits; grain, livestock.

Dzhusaly (jōōsŭlē'), town (1948 pop. over 2,000), central Kzyl-Orda oblast, Kazakh SSR, on the Syr Darya, on Trans-Caspian RR and 85 mi. NW of Kzyl-Orda; rice, sheep; saltpeter extraction.

Dzialdowka River, Poland: see WKRA RIVER.

Dzialdowo (joudô'vô), Pol. *Działdowo*, Ger. *Soldau* (zôl'dou), town (pop. 5,139), Olsztyn prov., N Poland, on Wkra R. and 40 mi. SSW of Allenstein (Olsztyn); rail junction; mfg. of railroad cars, sawmilling, flour milling.

Dzialoszyce (jäwô-shĭ'tsĕ), Pol. *Działoszyce*, Rus. *Dzyaloshitse* (dzyŭlŭshĭ'tsĕ), town (pop. 2,306), Kielce prov., S central Poland, 37 mi. SSW of Kielce; tanning, flour milling. Before Second World War, pop. 80% Jewish.

Dzibalchén (tsēbälchĕn'), town (pop. 1,296), Campeche, SE Mexico, on Yucatan Peninsula, 55 mi. SE of Campeche; timber, henequen, chicle, fruit.

Dzidzantún (tsētsäntōōn'), town (pop. 2,757), Yucatan, SE Mexico, 40 mi. ENE of Mérida; henequen, sugar cane, corn.

Dzierzgon (jĕzh'gônyŭ), Pol. *Dzierzgoń*, Ger. *Christburg* (krĭst'bōōrk), town (1939 pop. 3,604; 1946 pop. 810) in East Prussia, after 1945 in Gdansk prov., N Poland, 16 mi. ESE of Marienburg (Malbork); gravel quarrying. Teutonic Knights founded castle here in 1248 (destroyed 1410); town founded 1267. Until 1919, in West Prussia.

Dzierzoniow, Poland: see REICHENBACH.

Dzilam or **Dzilam González** (tsēläm' gōnsä'lĕs), town (pop. 1,520), Yucatan, SE Mexico, 50 mi. ENE of Mérida; henequen.

Dzilam de Bravo (dā brä'vō), town (pop. 374), Yucatan, SE Mexico, on a bar off the coast, 30 mi. N of Izamal; picturesque fishing village with fine beaches.

Dzisna, Belorussian SSR: see DISNA.

Dzitás (tsētäs'), town (pop. 1,648), Yucatan, SE Mexico, 23 mi. NW of Valladolid; rail junction; henequen, corn, sugar.

Dzitbalché (tsētbälchā'), town (pop. 3,514), Campeche, SE Mexico, on NW Yucatan Peninsula, 55 mi. SW of Mérida; corn, sugar cane, henequen, tobacco, fruit, livestock.

Dziwna River, Poland: see DIEVENOW RIVER.

Dziwnow (jēv'nōōf), Pol. *Dziwnów*, Ger. *Dievenow* (dē'fŭnō), town (1939 pop. 1,587; 1946 pop. 136) in Pomerania, after 1945 in Szczecin prov., NW Poland, on Baltic Sea, at Dievenow mouth of Oder R., 3 mi. NNW of Kamien Pomorski; fishing port. Inc. after 1946.

Dzoncauich (tsōnkouēch'), town (pop. 1,038), Yucatan, SE Mexico, 16 mi. NNE of Izamal; henequen.

Dzongka, Tibet: see JONGKA.

Dzora, Armenian SSR: see DZAGIDZOR.

Dzungaria (zōōng-gâ'rēŭ, dzōōng–, zŭng–), Rus. *Dzhungariya* (jōōn-gä'rēyŭ), semi-desert plateau region of N Sinkiang prov., China, bet. the Tien Shan (S) and the Altai Mts. (N), bounded W by USSR and E by Mongolia. Its few rivers drain largely into inland salt lakes; only the Black Irtysh (through the Irtysh) reaches the sea. Pop. is Kazakh and Mongol (Torgut and Dzungar tribes) and is largely engaged in nomadic pastoralism. The chief centers are Urumchi (at N foot of the Tien Shan), Chuguchak, and Sharasume. Passed under Chinese rule in 1750s. Considered part of Mongolia until it passed to Sinkiang in 1878. Also spelled Jungaria, Sungaria, and Zungaria.

Dzungarian Ala-Tau (–rēŭn ä'lä-tou'), Rus. *Dzhungarski Ala-Tau*, northernmost branch of Tien Shan mtn. system, on USSR-China line separated from main Tien Shan range by Ili R.; extends from Dzungarian Gates 250 mi. SW to Ili R. bend; forms 130-mi. section of USSR-China border in E. Rises to 16,550 ft. Silver-lead ores and hot springs.

Dzungarian Gates, defile on USSR-China border, at E end of the Dzungarian Ala-Tau; links lakes Ebi Nor (Sinkiang) and Ala-Kul (Kazakh SSR).

Dzun Modo or **Dzuun Modo** (dzōōn' mō'dō), town, ⊙ Central Aimak, central Mongolian People's Republic, 15 mi. SSW of Ulan Bator.

Dzyaloshitse, Poland: see DZIALOSZYCE.

E

E¹, peak (27,890 ft.) on undefined Tibet-Nepal border, in S Mt. Everest massif, 27°58′N 86°56′E. Tibetan name Lhotse sometimes attributed to E¹.

Eads (ēdz), town (pop. 1,015), ⊙ Kiowa co., E Colo., 55 mi. NE of La Junta; alt. 4,262 ft. Grain, livestock, dairy and poultry products.

Eagar (ē′gûr), town (pop. 637), Apache co., E Ariz., on headstream of Little Colorado R. and 27 mi. S of St. Johns; livestock.

Eagerville (ē′gûrvĭl), village (pop. 187), Macoupin co., SW Ill., 27 mi. NE of Alton, in agr. and bituminous-coal area.

Eagle, city (pop. 54), E Alaska, near Yukon border, on Yukon R. and 70 mi. NW of Dawson; fur-trading post and supply center for placer gold-mining operations on upper Yukon; port of entry. Has Episcopal mission, U.S. customs office, school, airfield. Eagle Native Village is 3 mi. E.

Eagle, county (□ 1,685; pop. 4,488), W central Colo.; ⊙ Eagle. Livestock-grazing and mining area, drained by Colorado and Eagle rivers. Silver, gold, lead, copper, zinc. Includes parts of Holy Cross, Arapaho, and White River natl. forests. Ranges of Rocky Mts. are in E and S, Holy Cross Natl. Monument in SE, near Redcliff. Formed 1883.

Eagle. 1 Town (pop. 445), ⊙ Eagle co., W central Colo., on Eagle R., near Colorado R., and 40 mi. NW of Leadville; alt. 6,602 ft. Trading point in grain and potato region; silver, gold mines. **2** Village (pop. 145), Clinton co., S central Mich., 13 mi. WNW of Lansing, near Grand R. **3** Village (pop. 255), Cass co., SE Nebr., 13 mi. E of Lincoln. **4** Village (pop. 460), Waukesha co., SE Wis., 30 mi. WSW of Milwaukee, in agr. and lake-resort region. Eagle L. is SE.

Eagle, Mount, highest peak (1,165 ft.) of St. Croix Isl., U.S. Virgin Isls., 7 mi. W of Christiansted; 17°45′N 64°49′W.

Eagle Bay, resort village, Herkimer co., N central N.Y., in the Adirondacks, on Fourth L. (part of Fulton Chain of Lakes), c.50 mi. NNE of Utica.

Eagle Bend, village (pop. 691), Todd co., W central Minn., on branch of long Prairie R. and 16 mi. NW of Long Prairie, in grain, livestock, poultry area; dairy products.

Eagle Butte (būt), town (pop. 375), Dewey co., N central S.Dak., 30 mi. SSW of Timber Lake; grain, livestock.

Eagle Cap, Oregon: see WALLOWA MOUNTAINS.

Eagle Creek, N Ky., rises in Scott co., flows NNW and SW, past Sparta and Worthville, to Kentucky R. just SW of Worthville; 87 mi. long.

Eagle Ford, city, Dallas co., N Texas, a W suburb of Dallas.

Eagle Grove, city (pop. 4,176), Wright co., N central Iowa, near Boone R., 18 mi. NE of Fort Dodge; railroad junction; livestock shipping. Poultry packing; mfg. of feed, fertilizer, wood and metal products. Sand and gravel pits near by. Inc. 1882.

Eagle Harbor. 1 Town (pop. 7), Prince Georges co., central Md., on the Patuxent and 15 mi. E of La Plata. **2** Resort village, Keweenaw co., NW Upper Peninsula, Mich., on L. Superior and 17 mi. NE of Houghton. Former copper-shipping point.

Eaglehawk, Australia: see BENDIGO.

Eaglehawk Neck, Tasmania: see FORESTIER PENINSULA.

Eagle Island, islet in Atlantic, NW Co. Mayo, Ireland, 6 mi. NW of Belmullet; lighthouse (54°16′N 10°5′W).

Eagle Island. 1 In Cumberland co., SW Maine, small island in Casco Bay, SW of Harpswell. Site of Admiral Peary's summer home, containing many trophies. **2** In Hancock co., Maine: see DEER ISLAND.

Eagle Lake (□ 130), W Ont., 10 mi. WSW of Dryden, in gold-mining region; 30 mi. long, 10 mi. wide. At N end is Vermilion Bay village.

Eagle Lake. 1 Town (pop. 1,060), Polk co., central Fla., 8 mi. NE of Bartow, near several small lakes. **2** Town (pop. 1,516), including Eagle Lake village (pop. 1,014), Aroostook co., N Maine, on Eagle L. and 15 mi. S of Fort Kent, in hunting, fishing area. Seat of Northern Maine General Hosp. Settled 1840, inc. 1911. **3** Village (pop. 310), Blue Earth co., S Minn., on small lake and 6 mi. E of Mankato in agr. area. **4** City (pop. 2,787), Colorado co., S Texas, 60 mi. W of Houston and on Eagle L. (c.2.5 mi. long). Railroad junction; rice-milling center; also ships potatoes; meat packing, cotton ginning. Founded c.1840.

Eagle Lake. 1 In central Lassen co., NE Calif., c.35 mi. E of Lassen Peak; c.13 mi. long, 2-6 mi. wide. **2** In Aroostook co., Maine: see FISH RIVER LAKES. **3** In Piscataquis co., N central Maine, 60 mi. NNE of Greenville, in wilderness recreational area; 9 mi. long, 2 mi. wide. Joined to Churchill and Chamberlain lakes.

Eagle Mountain Lake (□ 15, capacity 716,000 acre-ft.), N Texas, in West Fork of Trinity R. just above L. Worth and 10 mi. NW of Fort Worth. Impounded by Eagle Mtn. Dam (earth fill; 127 ft. high, 4,350 ft. long), completed 1933; for flood control, water supply to Fort Worth, irrigation. State fish hatchery.

Eagle Mountains, Texas: see EAGLE PEAK.

Eagle Nest, village (pop. c.200), Colfax co., N N.Mex., in Sangre de Cristo Mts., 50 mi. SW of Raton; alt. c.8,500 ft.; livestock, coal. U.S. fish hatchery here. Eagle Nest L. and Dam just S; Wheeler Peak and part of Carson Natl. Forest W. Called Therma until 1935.

Eagle Nest Dam, N.Mex.: see CIMARRON RIVER, Colfax co.

Eagle Pass, city (pop. 7,276), ⊙ Maverick co., SW Texas, c.130 mi. WSW of San Antonio and on the Rio Grande (bridged) opposite Piedras Negras, Mexico. Port of entry; connected by rail and highway with Saltillo and Mexico city. Tourist center; trade, shipping, hub of rich irrigated agr. part of Winter Garden area; known for huge spinach shipments. Cold-storage and freezing plants, cotton gins, creameries; mfg. of brick, wood products, mattresses. Has annual internatl. fair, horse show, races. Founded as Camp California near old Fort Duncan (est. 1849; now in a park) on old gold-rush trail; laid out 1850 as El Paso del Aguila (Eagle Pass).

Eagle Peak. 1 Mountain in Mariposa co., Calif.: see YOSEMITE NATIONAL PARK. **2** Mountain in Modoc co., Calif.: see WARNER MOUNTAINS. **3** Mountain (11,825 ft.) in Mono co., E Calif., in the Sierra Nevada, 18 mi. NW of Mono L. **4** Mountain (9,802 ft.) in W N.Mex., in Tularosa Mts., 11 mi. E of Reserve. **5** Mountain (7,510 ft.) in S Hudspeth co., extreme W Texas, near the Rio Grande, 16 mi. SW of Van Horn; highest peak of Eagle Mts., small range (c.15 mi. long NW-SE) lying bet. Quitman Mts. (NW) and Van Horn Mts. (SE).

Eagle Point, town (pop. 607), Jackson co., SW Oregon, 10 mi. N of Medford.

Eagle River. 1 Village (pop. c.200), ⊙ Keweenaw co., NW Upper Peninsula, Mich., 24 mi. NE of Houghton, on L. Superior on NW shore of Keweenaw Peninsula. Shipping and distribution point. Summer resort. **2** City (pop. 1,469), ⊙ Vilas co., N Wis., on small Eagle R. and 20 mi. NE of Rhinelander, in dairying and lumbering area; year-round resort and sports center. Near by is a chain of 27 lakes. Inc. as village in 1923, as city in 1937.

Eagle River, W central Colo., rises S of Mt. of the Holy Cross in Sawatch Mts., flows c.70 mi. NW and W, past Minturn and Eagle, to Colorado R. at Dotsero.

Eagle River Peak, Colo.: see JACQUE PEAK.

Eagle Rock. 1 N residential section of LOS ANGELES city, Los Angeles co., S Calif., near Glendale; seat of Occidental Col. Annexed 1923 by Los Angeles. **2** Village (pop. c.600), Botetourt co., W Va., on the James and 25 mi. N of Roanoke; limestone quarrying, lime burning.

Eaglesham (ē′gŭl-shŭm), village (pop. estimate 250), W Alta., near Peace R., 40 mi. SW of Peace River town; lumbering, mixed farming, wheat.

Eaglesham, agr. village and parish (pop. 1,671), SE Renfrew, Scotland, 8 mi. S of Glasgow; bacon and ham curing.

Eagles Mere, resort borough (pop. 157), Sullivan co., NE Pa., 28 mi. ENE of Williamsport and on Eagles Mere L.; alt. 2,000 ft.

Eagle's Nest, wooded cliff (1,200 ft. high), central Co. Kerry, Ireland, overlooking Upper Lake, one of the Lakes of Killarney, 6 mi. SW of Killarney. Here is noted echo.

Eagleton Village, village (pop. 3,503, with Blount Hills), Blount co., E Tenn.

Eagleville. 1 Village, Tolland co., Conn.: see MANSFIELD. **2** Town (pop. 360), Harrison co., NW Mo., 14 mi. N of Bethany. **3** City (pop. 378), Rutherford co., central Tenn., 16 mi. SW of Murfreesboro.

Eakly (ē′klē), town (pop. 191), Caddo co., W central Okla., 23 mi. NW of Anadarko, in agr. area; cotton ginning. Inc. 1930.

Eala (ää′lä), village, Equator Prov., W Belgian Congo, on Ruki R., on E outskirts of Coquilhatville; center of agr. research with botanical gardens, experimental plantations, entomology and mycology laboratories.

Ealing, residential municipal borough (1931 pop. 117,707; 1951 census 187,306), Middlesex, England, 8 mi. W of London. Has several parks. Thomas Huxley b. here. In municipal borough are towns of Greenford (NW), on Brent R., with glass industry; NORTHOLT (WNW); and Hanwell (S).

Earby (ēr′bē), urban district (1931 pop. 5,522; 1951 census 5,348), West Riding, W Yorkshire, England, on Earby Beck, a tributary of the Aire, 6 mi. SW of Skipton; cotton milling.

Eardley (ûrd′lē), village, SW Que., on L. Deschênes, 18 mi. WNW of Ottawa; molybdenum mining.

Earith, England: see BLUNTISHAM.

Earle, town (pop. 2,375), Crittenden co., E Ark., 27 mi. WNW of Memphis, Tenn., in cotton- and corn-growing area; cotton ginning, storage, and marketing center. Inc. 1905.

Earlestown, England: see NEWTON-LE-WILLOWS.

Earleton, Kansas: see EARLTON.

Earl Grey, village (pop. 233), S Sask., 33 mi. N of Regina; wheat, stock.

Earlham (ûr′lŭm). **1** Community, Wayne co., Ind.: see RICHMOND. **2** Town (pop. 771), Madison co., S central Iowa, 27 mi. WSW of Des Moines, in agr. area. Limestone quarries near by.

Earlimart (ûr′lēmärt″), village (pop. 2,162), Tulare co., S central Calif., in San Joaquin Valley, 22 mi. S of Tulare; cotton ginning; ships truck, fruit.

Earling, town (pop. 341), Shelby co., W Iowa, 10 mi. NW of Harlan; hybrid seed corn.

Earlington (ûr′lĭngtŭn), city (pop. 2,753), Hopkins co., W Ky., 30 mi. N of Hopkinsville, in coal-mining and agr. (dairy products, livestock) area; rail junction. Fishing in near-by small lake.

Earl Park, town (pop. 488), Benton co., W Ind., on small Sugar Creek and 34 mi. NW of Lafayette, in agr. area.

Earlsboro, town (pop. 278), Pottawatomie co., central Okla., 8 mi. SE of Shawnee, in grain-growing, dairying, and truck-farming area; oil wells and refineries.

Earls Colne (ûrlz′ kōn′), town and parish (pop. 1,655), N Essex, England, on Colne R. and 9 mi. WNW of Colchester; agr. market, with iron foundries.

Earlsferry, Scotland: see ELIE AND EARLSFERRY.

Earl Shilton, town and parish (pop. 4,838), SW Leicester, England, 8 mi. SW of Leicester; hosiery and shoe center. Just S is shoe-mfg. village and parish of Elmesthorpe (pop. 134).

Earl's Seat, Scotland: see LENNOX HILLS.

Earlston, town and parish (pop. 1,689), SW Berwick, Scotland, in Lauderdale, on Leader Water and 6 mi. ENE of Galashiels; woolen milling. Rhymer's Tower (remains) was traditional home of Thomas of Erceldoune or Thomas the Rhymer. Formerly Erceldoune or Ercildoune (ûr′sŭldōōn).

Earlton, city (pop. 141), Neosho co., SE Kansas, 7 mi. S of Chanute; stock raising, agr. Sometimes Earleton.

Earlville. 1 City (pop. 1,217), La Salle co., N Ill., 16 mi. NNW of Ottawa, in agr. and bituminous-coal area; railroad junction; processes cheese, butter; corn, oats, soybeans, livestock, poultry. Founded c.1854, inc. 1869. **2** Town (pop. 661), Delaware co., E Iowa, 30 mi. W of Dubuque; creamery, poultry hatchery. **3** Village (pop. 945) on Madison-Chenango co. line, central N.Y., on the Susquehanna and 28 mi. SSW of Utica, in dairying area; makes paper boxes.

Early, county (□ 526; pop. 17,413), SW Ga.; ⊙ Blakely. Bounded W by Ala. line, formed here by Chattahoochee R. Coastal plain agr. (cotton, corn, peanuts, pecans) and sawmilling area drained by Spring Creek. Formed 1818.

Early, town (pop. 742), Sac co., W Iowa, near Boyer R., 8 mi. WNW of Sac City; grain elevator.

Earn, Loch (lŏkh ûrn′), lake (7 mi. long, 1 mi. wide, 287 ft. deep), in central Perthshire, Scotland, 13 mi. W of Crieff; drained by Earn R.; surrounded by hills. At E end is village of St. Fillans, named for Irish missionary. On S shore is hamlet of Ardvorlich (ärdvôr′lĭkh), site of Ardvorlich House.

Earn River (ûrn), Perthshire, Scotland, rises in Loch Earn, flows 46 mi. E, past Comrie, Crieff, and Bridge of Earn, to the Tay 3 mi. W of Newburgh. Its valley is called Strathearn.

Earnslaw, Mount (ûrnz′lô) (9,250 ft.), W central S Isl., New Zealand, near Glenorchy, at head of L. Wakatipu; glaciers.

Earsdon (ûrz′dŭn, ērz′–), former urban district (1931 pop. 13,086), SE Northumberland, England, 7 mi. NE of Newcastle-upon-Tyne; coal mining. Here are coal-mining towns of Holywell (N) and Backworth (W). Earsdon inc. (1935) in Seaton Valley.

Earswick (ērz′wĭk), agr. village and parish (pop. 261), North Riding, central Yorkshire, England, on Fosse R. and 4 mi. N of York; leather tanning.

Earth, town (pop. 539), Lamb co., NW Texas, 2[illegible] mi. NNW of Littlefield.

Easdale, islet (pop. 78) of the Inner Hebrides, Argyll, Scotland, in the Firth of Lorne just off Seil. Its slate quarries, worked since 17th cent., extend below sea level.

Easebourne (ĕz′bôrn), agr. village and parish (pop. 1,537), W Sussex, England, near Rother R., just NE of Midhurst. Site of ruins of 16th-cent. Cowdray Castle, with large park.

Easington, town and parish (pop. 11,986), E Durham, England, 9 mi. E of Durham; coal mining. Has 13th-cent. church.

Easington (ē′zĭngtŭn), town, St. Thomas parish, SE Jamaica, 14 mi. E of Kingston, in fruitgrowing region (bananas, coconuts, sugar cane, coffee).

Easington Lane, England: see HETTON.

Easingwold, town and parish (pop. 2,043), North Riding, central Yorkshire, England, 13 mi. NNW of York; agr. market. Has 14th-cent. church and many picturesque old houses.

Easky (ē′skē), Gaelic *Iasgach*, town (pop. 140), NW Co. Sligo, Ireland, on the Atlantic, 20 mi W of Sligo; fishing port. Near by are several castle ruins.

Easley (ēz′lē), city (pop. 6,316), Pickens co., NW S.C., 12 mi. W of Greenville. Cotton-milling cente[illegible] in agr. area; mfg. (clothing, textile supplies, cottonseed oil, bldg. supplies, flour and feed). Founded 1874.

East, for names beginning thus and not found here: see under EASTERN.

East, Eastern, in Rus. names: see also VOSTOCHN-.

East, Cape, headland, NE Madagascar; part of Masoala Peninsula; 15°18′S 50°25′E. Lighthouse.

East Africa Protectorate, former name of KENYA.

East Albany, village (pop. 1,177), Dougherty co., SW Ga., near Albany.

East Alliance, village (pop. 1,474), Mahoning co., E Ohio.

East Alligator River, Australia: see SOUTH ALLIGATOR RIVER.

East Alton (ôl′tŭn), village (pop. 7,290), Madison co., SW Ill., on the Mississippi and 4 mi. E of Alton; ammunition, brass products. Inc. 1894.

East Andover, N.H.: see ANDOVER.

East and West Molesey (mōl′zē), residential former urban district (1931 pop. 8,464), NE Surrey, England, 3 mi. WSW of Kingston-on-Thames. East Molesey, on the Thames at mouth of Mole R., has electric-cable and pharmaceutical works. Here is race course of Hurst Park. Inc. 1933 in Esher.

East Anglia (ăng′glēŭ), old Anglo-Saxon kingdom, one of the Heptarchy, in SE England, comprising the modern Norfolk and Suffolk. Settled by Angles in late 5th cent.; by virtue of its large size and protection by fens it probably became one of the most powerful kingdoms by late 6th cent. Its brief power was eclipsed by the rise of Mercia, of which it became an underkingdom for long periods after 650 and c.794. It rebelled (825) from Mercia to submit to Egbert of Wessex. Great Danish invading army was quartered (865–66) in East Anglia and returned (869) to conquer state completely. After Danes were 1st decisively defeated (878) by King Alfred, they retired under Guthrum to a region which included East Anglia; treaty of 886 confirmed it as part of the Danelaw. Its Danes aided (893) Viking invaders and continued to harass Wessex until Edward the Elder finally defeated them in 917. East Anglia was subsequently an earldom of England. In modern times the term is applied to cos. of Suffolk and Norfolk, which form peninsula on the North Sea bet. Thames estuary (S) and the Wash (N). Noted for its fertile soil (producing sugar beets, potatoes, grain; stock raising) and its important herring fisheries, based on Yarmouth and Lowestoft.

East Angus (ăng′gŭs), town (pop. 3,501), S Que., on St. Francis R. and 13 mi. ENE of Sherbrooke; pulp and paper milling, brick making; dairying, pig-raising region.

East Ann Arbor, city (pop. 1,826), Washtenaw co., SE Mich., suburb of Ann Arbor. Inc. 1946.

East Ashtabula (ăsh″tŭbū′lŭ), village (pop. 2,390), Ashtabula co., NE Ohio.

East Aspetuck River (ă′spĭtŭk″), W Conn., rises in W Litchfield co. N of Warren, flows c.18 mi. generally S, joining West Aspetuck R. just above junction with the Housatonic near New Milford. ASPETUCK RIVER is S, in Fairfield co.

Eastatoe (ēstă′tō), summer resort, Pickens co., NW S.C., in the Blue Ridge, 32 mi. NW of Greenville.

East Aurora (ŭrō′rŭ), village (pop. 5,962), Erie co., W N.Y., 15 mi. SE of Buffalo; mfg. (metal and leather goods, wood products, toys, feed); agr. (potatoes, truck); summer resort. Site (1895–1939) of the Roycroft Shops, founded by Elbert Hubbard. Inc. 1874.

East Australian Current, in Tasman Sea of Pacific Ocean, forming part of counterclockwise circulation of Tasman Sea; flows S along SE coast of Australia.

East Avon River, England: see AVON RIVER.

East Bakersfield, village (pop. 38,177), Kern co., S central Calif., near Bakersfield.

East Bangor (băng′gŭr), borough (pop. 988), Northampton co., E Pa., 13 mi. N of Easton.

East Bank, town (pop. 735), Kanawha co., W W.Va., on the Kanawha and 14 mi. SE of Charleston, in coal-mining region.

East Barnet Valley (bär′nĭt), residential urban district (1931 pop. 18,549; 1951 census 40,414), S Hertford, England, 10 mi. N of London; includes residential dists. of East Barnet, Hadley, and New Barnet.

East Barre (bă′rē), village of BARRE town, Washington co., central Vt.; granite. Flood-control dam of Winooski R. system here.

East Baton Rouge (bă′tŭn rōōzh″), parish (□ 462; pop. 158,236), SE central La.; ⊙ BATON ROUGE, shipping, industrial, and commercial center for large region. Bounded E by Amite R., S by Bayou Manchac, W by Mississippi R. Diversified industry; oil and gas fields; lumber. Agr.: corn, cotton, sugar cane, poultry, cattle, hay, sweet potatoes; dairy products. Formed 1810.

East Battle Lake, Minn.: see BATTLE LAKE.

East Bay, Texas: see GALVESTON BAY.

East Bend, town (pop. 475), Yadkin co., NW N.C., 16 mi. NW of Winston-Salem.

East Bengal, E Pakistan: see BENGAL.

East Benhar (bĕnhär′), village in Whitburn parish, SW West Lothian, Scotland, 2 mi. NE of Fauldhouse; coal mining.

East Bergholt, agr. village and parish (pop. 1,474), S Suffolk, England, on Stour R. and 8 mi. SW of Ipswich. Has 15th-cent. church. John Constable b. here.

East Berlin (bûr′lĭn). **1** Village, Hartford co., Conn.: see BERLIN. **2** Borough (pop. 913), Adams co., S Pa., 13 mi. W of York; shoes, feed.

East Bernard (bŭrnärd′), village (1940 pop. 634), Wharton co., S Texas, 15 mi. N of Wharton; trade point in agr., cattle-ranching area.

East Bernstadt (bûrn′stăt), village (pop. c.800), Laurel co., SE Ky., in Cumberland foothills, 16 mi. N of Corbin, in agr., coal, timber region.

East Berwick, village (pop. 1,077), Luzerne co., E central Pa.

East Blatchington, England: see SEAFORD.

East Bloomfield, village (pop. 425), Ontario co., W central N.Y., 20 mi. SSE of Rochester, in fruit-growing region.

East Boldon, England: see BOLDON COLLIERY.

Eastborough, city (pop. 708), Sedgwick co., S Kansas, E suburb of Wichita. Oil discovered here in 1930.

East Boston, Mass.: see BOSTON.

Eastbourne, county borough (pop. 57,435; 1951 census 57,801), SE Sussex, England, on the Channel, backed by the South Downs, 19 mi. E of Brighton, and 66 mi. by rail S of London. Seaside resort, sheltered by Beachy Head, with 3-mi. promenade along terraced sea front. City developed during late 19th cent. because of efforts of 7th duke of Devonshire. Devonshire Park contains winter gardens and is scene of tennis tournaments. The parish church is partly Norman. Traces of Roman occupation exist.

Eastbourne, borough (pop. 2,561), S N.Isl., New Zealand, on E shore of Wellington harbor; summer resort.

East Brady, borough (pop. 1,400), Clarion co., W central Pa., 13 mi. NE of Butler and on Allegheny R.; rubber products; bituminous coal, limestone, oil, gas; timber, bricks. Capt. Samuel Brady, Indian fighter, lived near here. Laid out 1866.

East Braintree, Mass.: see BRAINTREE.

East Brewster, Mass.: see BREWSTER.

East Brewton, town (pop. 2,173), Escambia co., S Ala., c.65 mi. NE of Mobile, near Conecuh R.; suburb of Brewton.

East Bridgewater, town (pop. 4,412), including East Bridgewater village (pop. 1,570), Plymouth co., E Mass., 23 mi. S of Boston, just SE of Brockton; machinery mfg.; dairying, fruit farming. Settled 1649, set off from Bridgewater 1823.

East Brimfield Dam, Mass.: see QUINEBAUG RIVER.

East Brisbane, suburb (pop. 12,438) of Brisbane, SE Queensland, Australia.

Eastbrook, town (pop. 199), Hancock co., S Maine, 27 mi. SE of Bangor, in recreational area.

East Brookfield, town (pop. 1,243), Worcester co., S central Mass., 12 mi. WSW of Worcester. Settled 1664, set off from Brookfield 1920.

East Brooklyn. 1 Village, Windham co., Conn.: see BROOKLYN. **2** Village (pop. 65), Grundy co., NE Ill., 25 mi. SSW of Joliet, in agr. and bituminous-coal area.

East Broughton (brô′tŭn), village (pop. estimate 3,000), S Que., 15 mi. NE of Thetford Mines; asbestos mining, lumbering, maple-sugar making. Adjacent is East Broughton Station.

East Burke, Vt.: see BURKE.

East Burra, Scotland: see WEST BURRA.

East Butler, borough (pop. 758), Butler co., W Pa., 3 mi. ENE of Butler.

East Caicos (kī′kōs, kī′kŭs), uninhabited island, Turks and Caicos Isls., dependency of Jamaica, E of Middle Caicos, on Turk Island Passage; 21°40′N 71°30′W.

East Caister, England: see CAISTER-ON-SEA.

East Canaan, Conn.: see NORTH CANAAN.

East Canada Creek, E central N.Y., rises in the Adirondacks in S Hamilton co., flows c.35 mi. generally SW, past Dolgeville, to Mohawk R. 4 mi. W of St. Johnsville. Dams impound small lakes in lower course.

East Canon (kăn′yŭn), E suburb (pop. 761) of Canon City, Fremont co., S central Colo., on Arkansas R., just N of Wet Mts.

East Canton, village (pop. 1,001), Stark co., E central Ohio, 5 mi. E of Canton; clay products, tools, cheese. Founded 1805.

East Cape, easternmost point of New Guinea, at N side of entrance to Milne Bay, opposite Normanby Isl. across narrow Goschen Strait; 10°13′S 150°53′E.

East Cape, NE N.Isl., New Zealand, easternmost point of New Zealand proper; 40°S 178°25′E; lighthouse.

East Cape, Russian SFSR: see DEZHNEV, CAPE.

East Caroga Lake, N.Y.: see CAROGA LAKE.

East Carondelet (kărŏndŭlĕt′), village (pop. 401), St. Clair co., SW Ill., on the Mississippi and 5 mi. S of East St. Louis.

East Carroll, parish (□ 432; pop. 16,302), extreme NE La.; ⊙ Lake Providence. Bounded E by the Mississippi, W by Bayou Macon, N by Ark. line; drained by Tensas R. Farming (cotton, corn, oats, soybeans), stock raising, lumbering; cotton ginning; commercial fishing. Natural-gas wells. Formed 1877.

Eastchester (ēst′chĕ″stŭr), village (pop. 3,096), S Alaska, just SE of Anchorage.

Eastchester, residential town (1940 pop. 23,492), Westchester co., SE N.Y., just E of Yonkers; includes BRONXVILLE and TUCKAHOE villages. Once a township (formed 1788) extending from the present Bronx N to Scarsdale; Mt. Vernon city was separated from it in 1892; the section S of Mt. Vernon was annexed by New York city in 1895.

Eastchester Bay, SE N.Y., an inlet of Long Island Sound in E shore of the Bronx borough of New York city; sheltered on E by Rodman's Neck and City Isl. Receives Hutchinson R. Pelham Bay Park is on its shores.

East Chevington, England: see BROOMHILL.

East Chicago, industrial city (pop. 54,263), Lake co., extreme NW Ind., on L. Michigan, SSE of Chicago (of whose metropolitan area it is a part) and just W of Gary, in CALUMET industrial region. Has state's largest port (Indiana Harbor), connected by 3-mi. ship canal with Grand Calumet R. (S) and thence to South Chicago Harbor (NW) and Illinois Waterway system. Receives iron ore, coal, limestone, gypsum, wood pulp; ships steel, petroleum products. Has steel mills, oil refineries, railroad-car repair shops, smelters and refineries for lead and other metals, meat-packing plant, shipyard; also plants producing coke, chemicals, insulation, firebrick, cement, automobiles, hardware, cleansers, metal products. Settled 1888, inc. 1889.

East Chicago Heights, village (pop. 1,548), Cook co., NE Ill., near Chicago. Inc. since 1940.

East Chillicothe (chĭ″lĭkŏ′thē), village (pop. 2,13 Ross co., S central Ohio.

East China Sea, Chinese *Tung Hai* (dŏŏng′ h [eastern sea], arm of Pacific Ocean, bet. E Chin coast (W) and Kyushu and Ryukyu Isls. (E); 300–500 mi. wide, 600 mi. long; □ 480,000; deepest 8,920 ft.; mean depth 615 ft. Connected SW with South China Sea by Formosa Strait, it merges N with the Yellow Sea and is linked NE with Sea of Japan by Korea Strait. It receives Yangtze, Tsientang, Wu, and Min rivers. Its main ports are Shanghai, Hangchow, Ningpo, Wenchow, and Foochow on China mainland, and Keelung on Formosa.

East Chop, headland, N Martha's Vineyard, SE Mass., on E side of entrance to harbor of Vineyard Haven; lighthouse.

Eastchurch, town and parish (pop. 1,572), N Kent, England, on Isle of Sheppey, 5 mi. SE of Sheerness; agr. market. Has 15th-cent. church.

East Cleveland. 1 City (pop. 40,047), Cuyahoga co., N Ohio, adjacent to CLEVELAND; mainly residential; mfg. of foundry products. Nela Park (nē′lŭ), seat of General Electric experimental laboratories, and Forrest Hill Park (recreation) are here. Inc. as village in 1895, as city in 1911. **2** Village (pop. 1,667), Bradley co., SE Tenn.

East Coast, residency (□ 16,150; 1931 pop. 74,711), Br. North Borneo; ⊙ SANDAKAN.

East Columbia, Texas: see WEST COLUMBIA.

East Conemaugh (kŏ′nŭmô), borough (pop. 4,101), Cambria co., SW central Pa., on Conemaugh R. just NE of Johnstown; coal mining. Inc. 1891.

East Coolgardie Goldfield (kōōlgär′dē), S central Western Australia, richest gold field (□ 632) in Australia. Chief mining center is municipality of KALGOORLIE AND BOULDER. Gold discovered here 1892; large area, called Coolgardie Goldfield, placed (1894) under govt. control and leased to mining interests. E.Coolgardie Goldfield separated (1896) from Coolgardie Goldfield.

Eastcote, England: see RUISLIP NORTHWOOD.

East Cote Blanche Bay (kōt″ blänsh′), arm of the Gulf of Mexico, in St. Mary parish, S La., c.30 mi. SSE of New Iberia; 12 mi. wide at entrance. Peninsula (NW) separates it from West Cote Blanche Bay.

Eastcotts, agr. parish (pop. 1,660), central Bedford, England. Includes agr. village of Cotton End, 4 mi. SE of Bedford.

East Coulée (kōōlā′), town (pop. estimate 1,400), S Alta., on Red Deer R. and 14 mi. SE of Drumheller; coal mining.

East Cowes (kouz′), former urban district (1931 pop. 4,604), on Isle of Wight, Hampshire, England, on The Solent at mouth of Medina R., opposite Cowes; seaside resort, with shipyards for small craft, especially lifeboats. There are two 18th-cent. castles. Inc. 1932 in Cowes.

East Cramlington, England: see CRAMLINGTON

East Dal River, Sweden: see DAL RIVER.

East Dean, England: see DEAN, FOREST OF.

East Demerara (dĕmūră′rŭ), district (□ 1,333; pop., including Georgetown, 163,919), Demerara co., N Br. Guiana; ⊙ Enmore. Drained by Mahaica and Mahaicony rivers.

East Dennis, Mass.: see DENNIS.

East Dereham or **Dereham** (dĕr′ŭm), urban district (1931 pop. 5,643; 1951 census 6,441), central Norfolk, England, 15 mi. W of Norwich; agr. market, with farm-implement works and flour mills. Site of 7th-cent. convent, destroyed by the Danes. Has church dating from 12th cent. and 17th-cent. Corn Hall. Church contains tomb of William Cowper.

East Des Moines River, Minn. and Iowa: see DES MOINES RIVER.

East Detroit (dētroit′, dĭ–), city (pop. 21,461), Macomb co., SE Mich., 10 mi. NNE of Detroit; residential suburb. Truck and poultry farming. Settled 1827; inc. as Halfway village 1924, as East Detroit city 1928.

East Donyland, parish (pop. 1,511), NE Essex, England. Includes market town and small river port of Rowhedge, on Colne R. estuary, 3 mi. SE of Colchester.

East Douglas, Mass.: see DOUGLAS.

East Dubuque (dŭbūk′), residential city (pop. 1,697), Jo Daviess co., extreme NW Ill., near Wis. line, on the Mississippi, opposite Dubuque (Iowa; connected by bridge), in agr. area (livestock, grain; dairy products). A natl. wildlife refuge (resort area) is near by. Inc. 1865.

East Duke, town (pop. 325), Jackson co., SW Okla., 8 mi. WNW of Altus, near Duke.

East Dundee (dŭndē′), village (pop. 1,466), Kane co., NE Ill., on Fox R. and c.35 mi. WNW of Chicago, in agr. area (dairy products; livestock); makes pottery. Inc. 1887. With WEST DUNDEE, across river, it composes community known as Dundee.

East Durham (dŭ′rŭm, dōō′rŭm), resort village, Greene co., SE N.Y., in the Catskills, 16 mi. NW of Catskill.

East Ellijay, town (pop. 549), Gilmer co., N Ga., just SE of Ellijay.

East Ely (ē′lē), village (1940 pop. 873), White Pine co., E Nev., just NE of Ely; alt. 6,415 ft.; railroad shops.

Eastend, town (pop. 589), SW Sask., in the Cypress Hills, on Frenchman R. and 20 mi. WSW of Shaunavon; coal and clay mining; grain elevators.

East End, Cayman Isls., B.W.I.: see GRAND CAYMAN.

Eastend, village, E St. John Isl., U.S. Virgin Isls., 17 mi. E of Charlotte Amalie; 18°21′N 64°40′W. A Moravian settlement, with school.

Easter Island, Sp. *Isla de Pascua* (ē′slä dā pä′skōōä) (□ 45.5; pop. 563), in the South Pacific, c.2,350 mi. W of Chile, to which it belongs; 27°3′–27°12′S 109°14′–109°28′W. Administered as part of Valparaiso prov. Roughly triangular in shape (c.15 mi. long, 11 mi. wide), of volcanic origin (rises to 1,765 ft.), it is a fertile isl. swept by trade winds that occasionally bring days of rain. The inhabitants, mostly Polynesians, raise tobacco, sugar cane, potatoes, yams, taro roots, and tropical fruit. Good fishing off the coasts. Isl. was visited 1686 or 1687 by the English buccaneer Edward Davis and named by the Du. navigator Roggeveen on Easter day, 1722. Spain claimed it 1770, Cook (1774) and La Pérouse (1786) visited it, and Chile finally (1888) took possession of it. It has long been known for the indecipherable petroglyphs and remarkable monolithic stone heads, 30–40 ft. tall, which have evoked all kinds of legends and theories as to their origin. Carved from tufa, they weigh bet. 5 and 8 tons. The SW part of the isl. is called by the natives Rapa Nui [Great Rapa; Sp. *Gran Rapa*] (a name often applied to the whole isl.), and other names include Teapi and Waihu.

Easter Islands, in Indian Ocean, one of coral groups of HOUTMAN ABROLHOS, 45 mi. off W coast of Western Australia. Consist of Rat Isl. (largest; c.½ mi. long), Coral Isl., Wooded Isl., several smaller islets and reefs. Tourist resort.

Eastern, for names beginning thus and not found here: see under EAST.

Eastern, in Rus. names: see also VOSTOCHN.

Eastern Aden Protectorate: see ADEN PROTECTORATE.

Eastern Aimak, Mongolia: see CHOIBALSAN, aimak.

Eastern Arpa-Chai, river, USSR: see ARPA-CHAI.

Eastern Bay, E Md., irregular Chesapeake Bay inlet (c.5 mi. long, 7 mi. wide), indenting the Eastern Shore to S and E of Kent Isl.; connected with Chester R. (N) by narrow channel. Miles R., other estuaries enter it. Oystering, fishing.

Eastern Bengal and Assam, former prov., Br. India: see BENGAL; ASSAM.

Eastern Bosphorus (bŏs′fŭrŭs), Rus. *Bosfor Vostochny,* strait of Peter the Great Bay of Sea of Japan, Russian SFSR; connects S Amur and Ussuri bays; separates Russian Isl. (S) from mainland (Muravyev-Amurski Peninsula; N); 7 mi. long, 2–3 mi. wide. Golden Horn Bay (N inlet) is harbor of Vladivostok.

Eastern Duars (dwärz), region (□ 1,570) at foot of W Assam Himalayas, W Assam, India, N of Dhubri; separated from Western or Bengal Duars by Sankosh R. Bounded N by Bhutan, E by Manas R., S by Brahmaputra valley; Terai soil (sal and cotton trees). Inhabited mainly by Mech tribes. Formally ceded to British by Bhutan in 1866, after Bhutan War. Also spelled Dwars and Dooars.

Eastern Ghats, India: see GHATS.

Eastern Hajar, Oman: see HAJAR.

Eastern Island (□ 6; pop. 30), one of the St. Barbe or Horse Isls., NE N.F., at entrance of White Bay, 20 mi. NW of Cape St. John; 50°13′N 55°47′W; 4 mi. long, 2 mi. wide, rises to 550 ft.

Eastern Kathiawar Agency (kä′tyäwär), subdivision (□ 2,845; pop. 323,019) of former Western India States agency, on Kathiawar peninsula, India; hq. were at Wadhwan Camp. Comprised princely states of Bajana, Chuda, Lakhtar, Lathi, Muli, Patdi, Sayla, Vala, and numerous petty states. Merged 1948 with Saurashtra.

Eastern Manych River, Russian SFSR: see MANYCH RIVER.

Eastern Nara Canal (nä′rŭ), irrigation canal of SUKKUR BARRAGE system, E Sind, W Pakistan; extends from left bank of Indus R. at Sukkur c.230 mi. S, through Khairpur state, to c.12 mi. SSW of Umarkot. Feeds Jamrao Canal and other branches which irrigate large tracts (millet, cotton, rice) in Nawabashah and Thar Parkar dists.

Eastern Neck Island, sparsely wooded isl. (c.3 mi. long, c.2 mi. wide), Kent co., E Md., in Chesapeake Bay c.15 mi. ENE of Annapolis; separated from mainland by narrow channel (bridged). Hunting.

Eastern Panhandle, W.Va., state's E extension (□ c.3,500), with its W base at Tucker and Randolph counties; Md. (Potomac R.) is on N and E, Va. on E and S. Includes Pendleton, Grant, Mineral, Hardy, Hampshire, Morgan, Berkeley, and Jefferson counties; Martinsburg is largest city. Near its W base are highest summits of the Alleghenies in W.Va. (including Spruce Knob); to E, beyond Allegheny Front and Allegheny Mtn., are ridges of the Appalachians; in extreme E is part of Great Appalachian Valley. Drained by Shenandoah, Cacapon, and Moorefield rivers and South Branch of the Potomac. In W is part of Monongahela Natl. Forest, including scenic Smoke Hole, Seneca Caverns, Seneca Rocks, and Blackwater Falls State Park.

Eastern Point, Mass.: see GLOUCESTER.

Eastern Province, Pashto *Samt-i-Mashriqi* (sŭmt′-ĭ-mŭshrĭkē′), province (□ 10,000; pop. 1,100,000), Afghanistan; ⊙ Jalalabad. Bounded N by the Hindu Kush, E and S (along Safed Koh range) by Pakistan, it falls into 2 distinct regions: the wooded, mountainous Nuristan (Kafiristan; N), and the alluvial, partly irrigated Kabul R. valley (S). This mountain-ringed plain is Afghanistan's only subtropical area, and produces citrus fruit, figs, bananas, and sugar cane in vicinity of Jalalabad. The valley lies astride the major Kabul–Khyber Pass route to Pakistan.

Eastern Province, Fr. *Orientale,* province (□ 204,164; 1948 pop. 2,310,007), NE and N Belgian Congo; ⊙ Stanleyville. Borders NE on Anglo-Egyptian Sudan, E on Uganda along Semliki R. and L. Albert, N on Fr. Equatorial Africa along Bomu R. Drained by Uele-Kibali, Aruwimi-Ituri, and Congo-Lualaba rivers. Covered by equatorial rain forest in center and S, by savannas in N. Cotton cultivation and gold mining industry (Kilo-Moto goldfields) are important. Also palm kernels, rice, fibers, peanuts, sesame, coffee, rubber, cacao. In NE region of high plateaus (to 8,070 ft.), an area of European agr. settlement, vegetables, potatoes, essential-oil plants are grown and cattle raised. Experimental plantations of cinchona, tea, and tobacco. Main navigable waterways are the Congo-Lualaba (except in the sector of Stanley Falls), Lomami, L. Albert, and lower Itimbiri. Railroads include the Ponthierville-Stanleyville section and a secondary system in N. Chief towns are Stanleyville, Buta, Irumu, and Bunia. Yangambi and Nioka are centers of tropical agr. research. Prov. was called Stanleyville, 1935–47.

Eastern Province, administrative division (□ 3,840; pop., including estate pop., 271,732), E Ceylon; ⊙ TRINCOMALEE. Long, narrow strip along E and SE coast, bounded E by Indian Ocean; many coastal lagoons; drained by Mahaweli Ganga and Gal Oya rivers. Largely agr. (rice, coconuts, vegetables, tobacco); extensive timber and scrub jungles. Served by extensive irrigation lakes, including Kantalai and Unnichchai (land development project) tanks. Main settlements (on coast): Trincomalee, Batticaloa, Kalmunai. Large govt. saltern at Nilaveli; ilmenite deposits at Pulmoddai. Pop. includes Tamils, Moors, and Veddas (SW area). Created 1833.

Eastern Provinces, major administrative division (□ 45,752; 1931 pop. 4,721,414) of Nigeria, on Gulf of Guinea; ⊙ Enugu. Prov. includes part (□ 16,581; 1931 pop. 382,501; 1948 pop. estimate 481,000) of Br. Cameroons. Bounded W by lower Niger R., E by Fr. Cameroons. Includes Nigerian provs. of CALABAR, OGOJA, ONITSHA, OWERRI, and CAMEROONS of Br. Cameroons. Situated in equatorial forest belt, with mangrove forest (S) graduating northward into rain forest, deciduous forest, and savanna; drained by Niger delta and Cross R. Produces palm oil and kernels, kola nuts, hardwood, rubber, cacao. Chief food crops are corn, yams, plantains. Coal mining at Enugu; lead, zinc, and silver mining at Abakaliki; lignite, limestone, salt, and monazite deposits. Main centers: Port Harcourt (major port and rail terminus), Enugu, Onitsha, Calabar, Afikpo, Buea. Pop. largely Ibo (NW), Ijo (SW), and Ibibio (S). Formed 1939 out of E section of Southern Provinces of Nigeria.

Eastern Pyrenees, department, France: see PYRÉNÉES-ORIENTALES.

Eastern Rajputana States, India: see RAJPUTANA STATES.

Eastern River, S Maine, rises in NW Lincoln co., flows 18 mi. SW to Kennebec R. near Dresden.

Eastern Rumelia (rōōmē′lyŭ), former autonomous Turkish province on Balkan Peninsula; ⊙ Plovdiv. Bounded E by Black Sea, N by Balkan Mts., it included upper Maritsa R. valley (Thracian Plain). Separated in 1878 from Thracian section of Rumelia by Treaty of Berlin, following defeat of Turkey by Russia; ceded to Bulgaria in 1885.

Eastern Sayan Mountains, Russian SFSR: see SAYAN MOUNTAINS.

Eastern Scheldt (–skĕlt), Du. *Ooster Schelde* (ōst′ŭr skhĕl′dŭ), SW Netherlands, inlet of North Sea; separates Schouwen, Duiveland, and Tholen isls. from North Beveland and South Beveland isls.; former branch of Scheldt R. estuary. Bergen op Zoom at its E end. Linked to Western Scheldt by South Beveland Canal.

Eastern Shore, Md. and Va., the tidewater region along E shore of CHESAPEAKE BAY; includes all of Md. and Va. E of the bay, and, with Del., comprises DELMARVA PENINSULA.

Eastern States, former political agency (□ 65,243; pop. 9,218,560), India; hq. were at Calcutta. Comprised 42 princely states, grouped into subordinate agencies of BENGAL STATES, CHHATTISGARH STATES, and ORISSA STATES. Created 1933.

Eastern Townships, S Que., collective name of townships S of the St. Lawrence, centered on Sherbrooke, 1st surveyed after 1791, when English land laws briefly replaced French system of seigneural tenure. Name was used to distinguish region from the Western Townships, N of the St. Lawrence and on the Bay of Quinte, Ont., surveyed 1783–84; latter designation is no longer used.

Eastern Turkestan, China: see TURKESTAN.

East Falkland Island: see FALKLAND ISLANDS.

East Falmouth, Mass.: see FALMOUTH.

East Farnham (fär′nŭm), village (pop. 221), S Que., near Yamaska R., 12 mi. SSW of Granby; dairying.

East Fayu (fä′yōō), small, uninhabited coral island, Truk dist., E Caroline Isls., W Pacific, 19 mi. W of Nomwin.

East Feliciana (fĭlĭ′shēănŭ), parish (□ 454; pop. 19,133), SE central La.; ⊙ Clinton. Bounded E by Amite R., N by Miss. line. Agr. (cotton, corn, hay, sweet potatoes). Timber; sand, gravel. Cotton ginning; sawmills. Formed 1824.

East Flanders, Flemish *Oost-Vlaanderen* (ōst-vlän′dŭrŭn), Fr. *Flandre Orientale* (flã′drŭ ôrēätäl′), province (□ 1,147; pop. 1,223,073), NW Belgium; ⊙ Ghent. Bounded by the Netherlands (N), Antwerp and Brabant provs. (E), Hainaut prov. (S), West Flanders prov. (W). Highly fertile soil, drained by Scheldt, Dender, and Lys rivers. Produces wheat, oats, flax, potatoes, pigs, cattle, dairy products. Mfg. of woolen, linen, and cotton textiles; carpets, chemicals; engineering industry. Important towns: Ghent, Dendermonde, St-Nicolas, Eekloo, Lokeren, Oudenaarde, Renaix, Alost, Ninove (textile centers). Prov. mainly Flemish-speaking.

East Flatbush, N.Y.: see FLATBUSH.

East Flat Rock, town (1940 pop. 1,103), Henderson co., SW N.C., 3 mi. SSE of Hendersonville, in resort area; hosiery mfg.

Eastford, town (pop. 598), Windham co., NE Conn., on Natchaug R. and 14 mi. NNE of Willimantic; agr., wood products. State park, state forest here.

East Fork, Minn. and Iowa: see DES MOINES RIVER.

East Fork of Trinity River, Texas: see TRINITY RIVER.

East Fork of White River, Ind.: see WHITE RIVER.

East Fork Owyhee River (ōwī′ē, ōwī′hē), in Nev. and Idaho, rises in N part of Elko co., NE Nev., flows c.110 mi. NW, past Mountain City and Owyhee, into Owyhee co., SW Idaho, and joins South Fork Owyhee R. near Oregon line. Artificial reservoir in upper course, 12 mi. SE of Mountain City.

East Fork Sevier River (sŭvēr′), S Utah, rises in Paunsaugunt Plateau near Bryce Canyon Natl. Park, flows N, past Antimony, then W, through Sevier Plateau, to Sevier R. near Junction; 90 mi. long. Dam on lower course forms Otter Creek Reservoir.

East Fork Virgin River, SW Utah, rises in Kane co., W of Alton, flows SW and W, joining North Fork just S of Zion Natl. Park to form Virgin R.; 50 mi. long.

East Freetown, Mass.: see FREETOWN.

East Friesland (frēz′lŭnd), Ger. *Ostfriesland* (ōst′-frēs′länt), historic region (□ c.1,100; pop. 415,000) of NW Germany, on North Sea, bet. Ems estuary (Dutch border) and Jade Bay; includes East Frisian Isls. Historic ⊙ was Aurich. Low, level region; agr. (grain) and cattle raising in fertile reclaimed marshland near coastline; extensive moors (peat cutting) inland. Traversed (E-W) by Ems-Jade Canal. Industry (connected with shipping and fishing) is centered at Emden (W) and Wilhelmshaven (E), the chief ports. Once part of historic Friesland, which extended W to the Ijsselmeer, East Friesland became (15th cent.) a county of Holy Roman Empire. Raised to duchy in 16th cent.; passed to Prussia in 1744, to Hanover in 1815. Predominantly Frisian pop.

East Frisian Islands, Germany: see FRISIAN ISLANDS.

East Fultonham, Ohio: see UNIONTOWN.

East Gaffney or **Limestone,** village (pop. 4,289), Cherokee co., N S.C., just E of Gaffney.

East Galesburg, village (pop. 651), Knox co., NW central Ill., just E of Galesburg. Formerly Randall.

East Gary (gâ'rē), town (pop. 5,635), Lake co., extreme NW Ind., just SE of Gary, in the Calumet industrial area; surgical instruments, food products, cement blocks.

East Gastonia (găstō'nēŭ), village (pop. 3,733), Gaston co., S N.C., near Gastonia.

East Germantown, town (pop. 389), Wayne co., E Ind., 12 mi. W of Richmond, in agr. area.

East Gillespie (gĭlĭ'spē), village (pop. 224), Macoupin co., SW central Ill., just N of Gillespie, in agr. and bituminous-coal area.

East Glacier Park, village (pop. c.400), Glacier co., NW Mont., 40 mi. WSW of Cut Bank; resort; E entrance to Glacier Natl. Park. Formerly Glacier Park.

East Gobi (gō'bē), Mongolian *Dornot Gobi* or *Doronod Gobi* (dōr'nōt), aimak (□ 42,700; pop. 35,000), SE Mongolian People's Republic; ⊙ Sain Shanda. Bounded SE by China's Suiyuan prov. and Inner Mongolian Autonomous Region, it lies entirely in the Gobi desert and is traversed by the Kalgan–Ulan Bator highway.

East Godavari (gōdä'vŭrē), district (□ 6,322; pop. 2,161,863), NE Madras, India; ⊙ Cocanada. Largely in Godavari R. delta (extensive canal irrigation), bet. Eastern Ghats (NW) and Bay of Bengal (SE). Agr. (rice, millet, oilseeds, sugar cane, tobacco, coconuts); forest produce (teak, sal, bamboo, myrobalan). Main towns: Cocanada, Rajahmundry, Samalkot, Peddapuram. French settlement of Yanam is near mouth of Gautami Godavari R. Called Godavari dist. until 1925, when original Kistna dist. was divided into West Godavari and present Kistna dists.

East Granby, town (pop. 1,327), Hartford co., N Conn., 13 mi. N of Hartford. Newgate Prison, copper mine used as prison 1773–1827, is here. Set off from Granby 1858.

East Grand Forks, city (pop. 5,049), Polk co., NW Minn., on Red R. at mouth of Red Lake R., opposite Grand Forks, N.Dak.; shipping point in wheat, potato, and sugar-beet area; beet sugar, dairy products. Settled 1870.

East Grand Rapids, city (pop. 6,403), Kent co., SW Mich., residential suburb just ESE of Grand Rapids. Settled 1835; inc. as village 1891, as city 1926.

East Greenbush, village (1940 pop. 837), Rensselaer co., E N.Y., 10 mi. S of Troy, in fruitgrowing area.

East Greenland Current, cold ocean current of North Atlantic Ocean, rises in Arctic Ocean, flows S and SW along E coast of Greenland through Greenland Sea and Denmark Strait. A branch of current turns Cape Farewell and becomes the WEST GREENLAND CURRENT. Carries many icebergs originating in Greenland.

East Greenville, borough (pop. 1,945), Montgomery co., SE Pa., 14 mi. S of Allentown. Settled 1850, inc. 1875.

East Greenwich (grĕ'nĭch, grĭ–), town (pop. 4,923), ⊙ Kent co., central R.I., on Greenwich Bay and 11 mi. S of Providence; industrial center in agr. area; textile machinery, worsteds, woolens, wire staplers, lawn mowers, tools, wire, chemicals; textile dyeing, bleaching; dairy products, poultry, corn, potatoes, fruit, truck; clam and oyster fisheries. East Greenwich Acad. (1802) here; Northeastern Naval Air Station at near-by QUONSET POINT. Includes village of East Greenwich. Inc. 1677. Textile industry dates from 1790.

East Griffin, village (pop. 1,539), Spalding co., W central Ga., near Griffin.

East Grinstead, residential urban district (1931 pop. 7,902; 1951 census 10,845), N Sussex, England, 25 mi. S of London; brick and tile mfg., brewing. Site of Sackville Col., a 17th-cent. almshouse and orphanage. In Middle Ages town was a center of iron industry. Near by is Royal Ashdown Forest Golf Club.

East Gull Lake, village (pop. 238), Cass co., central Minn., on Gull L. and 8 mi. WNW of Brainerd.

East Haddam (hă'dŭm), town (pop. 2,554), Middlesex co., S Conn., on the Connecticut (here bridged), at mouth of Salmon R., and 12 mi. SE of Middletown; textiles, farming. Includes MOODUS, Leesville, and Millington villages, Devil's Hopyard State Park. Settled c.1670, set off from Haddam 1734.

East Hagbourne, agr. village and parish (pop. 2,579), England, 5 mi. W of Wallingford. Has 13th-cent. church.

Eastham (ēst'hŭm), town and parish (pop. 2,990), NW Cheshire, England, on Mersey R. at W end of Manchester Ship Canal, 6 mi. SSE of Birkenhead. Site of 3 canal locks.

East Ham (ēst' hăm'), county borough (1931 pop. 142,394; 1951 census 120,873), SW Essex, England, on the Thames at mouth of Roding R. and 9 mi. ENE of London; extensive shipyards, docks, chemical factories, ironworks. In county borough (N) is residential dist. of Manor Park (pop. 13,922).

Eastham (ēs'tăm", ēs'tŭm), town (pop. 860), Barnstable co., SE Mass., on N arm of Cape Cod, 19 mi. ENE of Barnstable; summer resort; agr. Formerly shipping and fishing port. Has lighthouse and coast guard station. Settled 1644, inc. 1651. Includes North Eastham village.

East Hamburg, N.Y.: see ORCHARD PARK.

Easthampstead, agr. village and parish (pop. 1,978), E Berkshire, England, 4 mi. ESE of Wokingham. Modern church has windows by Burne-Jones. Near by is prehistoric encampment.

East Hampton (ēst" hămp'tŭn). **1** Town (pop. 4,000), including East Hampton village (pop. 1,481), Middlesex co., S central Conn., on the Connecticut opposite Middletown; mfg. (bells, thread, toys, machine parts, boxes, witch hazel), agr. (fruit, dairy products, poultry). Includes Middle Haddam village, once a shipbuilding center. Pocotopaug L. (resort), state park here. Settled c.1710, inc. 1767 as Chatham, renamed 1915. **2** Resort and residential village (pop. 1,737), Suffolk co., SE N.Y., near S shore of Long Isl., 6 mi. SE of Sag Harbor, in diversified-farming area; mfg. of aircraft parts, machinery; sea-food cannery. Birthplace of John Howard Payne, whose home is now a mus. Contains other historic bldgs. Settled 1648, inc. 1920. **3** Village (pop. 3,437, with near-by North Phoebus), Elizabeth City co., SE Va., near Hampton.

Easthampton, town (pop. 10,694), Hampshire co., W central Mass., just S of Northampton; mfg. (textiles, metal products). Williston Acad. for boys here. Settled 1664, inc. 1809. Includes part of Mt. Tom State Park and Mount Tom village.

East Harbor, Indonesia: see PANJANG.

East Hartford, town (pop. 29,933), Hartford co., central Conn., on the Connecticut opposite Hartford, at mouth of Hockanum R.; mfg. (airplanes and airplane motors, paper, machinery, furniture, awnings, food products), agr. (tobacco, truck, poultry, dairy products, livestock); railroad shops. Includes villages of Hockanum (residential) and Burnside (paper products). Settled c.1640, inc. 1783.

East Hartland, Conn.: see HARTLAND.

East Harwich, Mass.: see HARWICH.

East Haven. 1 Town (pop. 12,212), New Haven co., S Conn., on Long Isl. Sound, just E of New Haven; truck farming; oil refining, mfg. (metal products, cigars). Includes Momauguin (mŭmô'gwĭn), shore resort. L. Saltonstall here. Inc. 1785. **2** Town (pop. 85), Essex co., NE Vt., on Passumpsic R. and 17 mi. N of St. Johnsbury.

East Hazelcrest, village (pop. 1,066), Cook co., NE Ill., S suburb of Chicago, just E of Hazel Crest.

East Helena (hĕ'lŭnŭ), town (pop. 1,216), Lewis and Clark co., SW central Mont., on Prickly Pear Creek, near Missouri R., and 5 mi. E of Helena; industrial suburb of Helena; here silver, zinc, lead, and gold ores are reduced. Inc. 1927.

East Hills, village (pop. 2,547), Nassau co., SE N.Y., on W Long Isl., 4 mi. NNE of Mineola. Inc. 1931.

East Hope, village (pop. 149), Bonner co., N Idaho, 9 mi. NW of Clark Fork and on E shore of Pend Oreille L.

East Horseley, residential town and parish (pop. 1,196), central Surrey, England, 7 mi. ENE of Guildford. Has old church.

East Hsingan (shĭng'än'), former province (□ 42,125; 1940 pop. 199,530) of NW Manchukuo, in Inner Mongolia; ⊙ was Yalu (Chalantun). See HSINGAN prov. The area of East Hsingan was coextensive with Mongolian BUTEHA league.

East Humboldt Range, NE Nev., in Elko co., E of Elko. Rises to 11,276 ft. Lies in part of Humboldt Natl. Forest. Ruby Range is just S.

East Ilsley, village and parish (pop. 403), W Berkshire, England, 9 mi. N of Newbury; sheep market. Has 13th-cent. church.

East Indian Island (□ 4; pop. 190), E N.F. at mouth of Notre Dame Bay, 3 mi. S of Fogo Isl.; 49°32'N 54°14'W; 2 mi. long, 2 mi. wide. On N coast is fishing settlement of Indian Island Harbour. Just W is West Indian Isl.

East Indies, a name which has had various meanings over the years. It first meant India, then, by extension, SE Asia, and, finally, the MALAY ARCHIPELAGO. It is often used, in a political sense, to refer to the Netherlands East Indies—the isls. of the Malay Archipelago which became the republic of INDONESIA after Second World War.

East Island (5 mi. long, 2 mi. wide), in Gulf of St. Lawrence, E Que., one of Magdalen Isls., bet. Grosse Isl. and Coffin Isl., 85 mi. NNE of Prince Edward Isl.; 47°37'N 61°27'W.

East Islip (ī'slĭp), village (pop. 2,834), Suffolk co., SE N.Y., near S shore of Long Isl., just E of Islip, in summer-resort area; mfg. (wood boxes, toys). Heckscher State Park is near by.

East Jaffrey, village (pop. 1,866), of JAFFREY town, Cheshire co., SW N.H., on the Contoocook (water power); textiles, wood and metal products, agr.; resort.

East Jewett, resort village, Greene co., SE N.Y., in the Catskills, 9 mi. W of Catskill. Lakes near by.

East Jordan, city (pop. 1,779), Charlevoix co., NW Mich., 18 mi. SSW of Petoskey, at mouth of Jordan R. on South Arm of L. Charlevoix, in fruitgrowing and dairying area. Mfg. (castings, canned goods, pickles, butter). Resort; fishing. Inc. as village 1889, as city 1911.

East Juliette, town (pop. 303), Jones co., central Ga., 20 mi. NNW of Macon, on Ocmulgee R.

East Kansas City, town (pop. 206), Clay co., W Mo., on left bank of Missouri R., opposite Kansas City, Mo.

East Kazakhstan (käzäkstän'), Rus. *Vostochno-Kazakhstan,* oblast (□ 37,300; 1946 pop. estimate 500,000), E Kazakh SSR; ⊙ Ust-Kamenogorsk. Mainly mountainous (Altai Mts.), except for L. Zaisan depression (S); drained by Irtysh R. One of most important mining areas of Kazakh SSR: extensive lead-zinc (Leninogorsk, Zyryanovsk, Belousovka), tin and tungsten (Kalba Range), copper, and gold mines, coal deposits (Kenderlyk R.). Some irrigated agr. on N slopes of Tarbagatai Range; cattle and sheep raising. Lead-zinc refining at Leninogorsk and Ust-Kamenogorsk. Pop.: Kazakhs, Russians, Ukrainians. Formed 1932.

East Keansburg, village (pop. 2,596), Monmouth co., E N.J., just E of Keansburg.

East Kennebago Mountain (kĕnŭbā'gō) (3,825 ft.), Franklin co., W Maine, 10 mi. NE of Rangely L.

East Khandesh (khän'dāsh), district (□ 4,598; pop. 1,327,722), NE Bombay, India, on Deccan Plateau; ⊙ Jalgaon. Bordered N by Satpura Range, S by Ajanta Hills; drained by Tapti and Girna rivers (Jamda irrigation system begins 8 mi. NNW of Chalisgaon). Agr. (cotton, peanuts, millet, wheat, mangoes); timber in forests at foot of Satpura Range (markets at Yaval, Faizpur). Cotton ginning, handicraft cloth weaving, oilseed milling, dyeing, tanning. Amalner, Chalisgaon, Jalgaon, and Bhusawal are trade centers and cotton markets. Annexed 1601 to Mogul empire by Akbar; under Mahrattas in late-17th cent. Formerly joined with West Khandesh in one dist. called Khandesh; divided 1906. Boundaries altered 1950 by exchange of enclaves with Hyderabad. Pop. 83% Hindu, 11% Moslem, 6% tribal.

East Kilbride, town and parish (pop. 5,300), N Lanark, Scotland, 7 mi. SSE of Glasgow; coal mining; large agr.-machinery and automotive works.

East Killingly, Conn.: see KILLINGLY.

East Kilpatrick, Scotland: see NEW KILPATRICK.

East Kingsford, village (pop. 1,279, with adjacent Skidmore), Dickinson co., SW Upper Peninsula, Mich.

East Kingston, town (pop. 449), Rockingham co., SE N.H., 15 mi. SW of Portsmouth.

East Kirkby, England: see KIRKBY-IN-ASHFIELD.

East Korea Bay, Jap. *Higashi-Chosen-wan,* Korean *Tongjoson-man* and *Choson-man,* wide inlet of Sea of Japan, S.Hamgyong prov., N Korea; 100 mi. long, 50 mi. wide. Hungnam is on W shore; Wonsan is on its SW inlet (Yonghung Bay). Formerly sometimes called Broughton Bay.

East Lake, village, Dare co., NE N.C., 16 mi. E of Columbia and on Alligator R. (ferry); fishing, lumbering.

Eastlake. 1 or **East Lake,** village (pop. 376), Manistee co., NW Mich., E of Manistee, across Manistee L. **2** City (pop. 7,486), Lake co., NE Ohio, 18 mi. NE of Cleveland, on L. Erie. Inc. 1948. Post office is Willoughby.

Eastland, county (□ 955; pop. 23,942), N central Texas; ⊙ Eastland. Drained by Leon R. Agr. (especially peanuts; also cotton, corn, oats, grain sorghums, vetch seed); dairying; poultry, hogs; ranching (cattle, sheep, goats); wool, mohair marketed. Includes L. Cisco (recreation). Oil, natural-gas wells, refineries; mfg., processing at Ranger, Cisco, Eastland. Formed 1858.

Eastland, city (pop. 3,626), Eastland co., N central Texas, on South Leon R. and c.50 mi. E of Abilene; trade, processing center in petroleum-producing and agr. area (peanuts, truck, vetch seed, cotton, dairy products); gasoline plant; mfg. of clothing, pottery. Laid out 1875, inc. 1897.

East Lansdowne, borough (pop. 3,527), Delaware co., SE Pa., SW suburb of Philadelphia.

East Lansing, residential city (pop. 20,325), Ingham co., S central Mich., 4 mi. E of LANSING, and on Red Cedar R. Seat of Mich. State Col. of Agr. and Applied Science, the oldest state agr. col. in U.S. (opened 1857). Mich. state police hq. here. Settled c.1850, inc. as city 1907.

East Laurinburg (lŏ'rĭnbûrg), town (pop. 745), Scotland co., S N.C., just SE of Laurinburg.

Eastlawn, village (pop. 4,127), Washtenaw co., SE Mich.

East Layton, town (pop. 217), Davis co., N Utah, near Layton.

East Leake, town and parish (pop. 1,162), S Nottingham, England, 4 mi. NNE of Loughborough; hosiery milling, basket weaving. Has 13th-cent. church.

East Lee, Mass.: see LEE.

Eastleigh (ēst'lē), municipal borough (1951 census 30,557), formerly urban dist. of Eastleigh and Bishopstoke (1931 pop. 18,335), S central Hampshire, England, 5 mi. NNE of Southampton; site of important railroad workshops; also processes bacon and ham.

Eastleigh, airport, Kenya: see NAIROBI.

Eastleigh, U. of So. Afr.: see ORKNEY.

East Linton, burgh (1931 pop. 882; 1951 census 990), NE East Lothian, Scotland, on Tyne R. and

5 mi. ENE of Haddington; agr. market. Near by are remains of Hailes Castle, one-time residence of Mary Queen of Scots.

East Livermore, Maine: see LIVERMORE FALLS.

East Liverpool, city (pop. 24,217), Columbiana co., E Ohio, on the Ohio and 18 mi. N of Steubenville; clay-products mfg. center; also makes machinery, steel, paper cartons, barrels, chemicals; coal mining. A mus. houses a historical pottery collection. Settled 1798; inc. as village in 1834, as city in 1882.

East Loch Tarbert. 1 Inlet, Argyll, Scotland: see TARBERT, Argyll. **2** Inlet on E coast of Harris, Lewis with Harris isl., Outer Hebrides, Scotland, extending 6 mi. inland to narrow isthmus at Tarbert which separates it from West Loch Tarbert.

East Lomond, Scotland: see LOMOND HILLS.

East London, Afrikaans *Oos-Londen* (ōs-lôn'dů), city (pop. 76,105; including suburbs 79,205), SE Cape Prov., U. of So. Afr., on Indian Ocean, at mouth of Buffalo R. (bridge), 150 mi. ENE of Port Elizabeth, 300 mi. SW of Durban; 33°2'S 27°55'E. Major seaport with extensive dock facilities, including Princess Elizabeth graving dock (1947), cold-storage installations; fishing port. Commercial center for rich agr. region (including Transkei), its chief exports are wool, hides, citrus fruits, chilled meat, dairy products. Industries include railroad workshops, foundries; mfg. of soap, candles, furniture, leather goods, clothing, electric batteries, toys, food products. Seat of local native-affairs council, established 1932, with jurisdiction over East London dist. (pop. 118,280; native pop. 67,011), included in Ciskeian General Council. Site of technical col. Among notable features are East London Mus. (1921), aquarium, city hall, permanent wool exhibition, Queen's Park (80 acres), and Fort Glamorgan (1847). Founded 1846 as Port Rex, it became base of operations (1847) for Kaffir War; renamed East London when established as town, 1848. Originally on W bank of Buffalo R., center of pop. shifted to E bank (then called Panmure) when railroad station was built there. Chief suburbs are Collondale (airport), Cambridge, Amalinda, Woodbrook.

East Longmeadow, town (pop. 4,881), Hampden co., SW Mass., 4 mi. SE of Springfield. Settled c.1740, inc. 1894.

East Looe, England: see LOOE.

East Los Angeles (lŏs ăng'gůlůs, ăn'jůlůs, –lēz), unincorporated E suburb (1940 pop. 41,507), of Los Angeles city, S Calif.

East Lothian (lō'dhēůn), formerly **Haddington** or **Haddingtonshire,** county (□ 267.1; 1931 pop. 47,338; 1951 census 52,240), SE Scotland; ⊙ Haddington. On S shore of the Firth of Forth, bounded by Berwick (S) and Midlothian (W). Drained by Tyne R. Surface is flat in N, rising to the Lammermuir Hills in S. Agr. is important, and there are also sheep raising, coal mining, and fishing; other industries are quarrying, lumbering, whisky distilling, brewing, brick and pottery mfg. Other towns are Dunbar, North Berwick, Tranent, and Prestonpans. There are anc. castles (Dirleton, Tantallon) and traces of Roman and Celtic occupation. Co. is associated with John Knox and the poet William Dunbar. It was site of battles of Dunbar (1650) and Prestonpans (1745).

East Luangwa, former province, Northern Rhodesia: see FORT JAMESON.

East Lumberton, town (pop. 1,106), Robeson co., S N.C., just SE of Lumberton, near Lumber R.

East Lyme (līm), town (pop. 3,870), New London co., SE Conn., on Niantic R. (nīăn'tĭk), W of Niantic Bay, and 5 mi. W of New London; mfg. (surgical dressings, steam gauges). Includes Niantic (pop. 1,746), resort village. Has state farm for women, state park and forest, state guard military reservation. Many old houses, 18th-cent. schoolhouse here. Settled c.1660, inc. 1839.

East Lynne (lĭn), town (pop. 204), Cass co., W Mo., 6 mi. E of Harrisonville.

East Machias (můchī'ůs), town (pop. 1,101), Washington co., E Maine, on E. Machias R. and 34 mi. SSW of Calais, 10 mi. from the ocean; lumbering, canning. Inc. 1826.

East Machias River, E Maine, rises in lakes of central Washington co., flows c.35 mi. generally SE to Machias Bay at East Machias.

East McKeesport, residential borough (pop. 3,171), Allegheny co., SW Pa., 5 mi. NE of McKeesport. Inc. 1895.

Eastmain River, in central and W Que., rises in Otish Mts., on St. Lawrence-Hudson Bay watershed, flows 375 mi. W to James Bay. Near mouth is Eastmain (52°14'N 78°31'W), one of oldest of Hudson's Bay Co. posts, founded 1685.

East Maitland, Australia: see MAITLAND.

East Malling (môl'lĭng), town and parish (pop. 2,305), central Kent, England, 4 mi. WNW of Maidstone; agr. market, with flour mills and pharmaceutical works. Site of fruit cold-storage experimental station.

Eastman, village (pop. 517), S Que., on Missiquoi R. and 20 mi. ESE of Granby; dairying.

Eastman. 1 City (pop. 3,597), ⊙ Dodge co., S central Ga., c.50 mi. SSE of Macon, in agr. and timber area; cotton ginning, naval stores, lumber, canned goods. Founded 1871, inc. 1873. **2** Village (pop. 359), Crawford co., SW Wis., 10 mi. NE of Prairie du Chien, in livestock and dairy area.

East Marion, village (pop. 2,901), McDowell co., W N.C., just E of Marion.

East Mattapoisett, Mass.: see MATTAPOISETT.

East Mauch Chunk (môk' chŭngk', mô" chŭngk'), borough (pop. 3,132), Carbon co., E Pa., on Lehigh R. opposite Mauch Chunk. Inc. 1853.

East Meadows, residential village (1940 pop. 3,145), Nassau co., SE N.Y., on W Long Isl., c.2 mi. E of Hempstead.

East Middletown, village (pop. 1,485), Orange co., SE N.Y.

East Millinocket (mĭ"lĭnŏ'kĭt), town (pop. 1,358), Penobscot co., central Maine, on the Penobscot and 55 mi. N of Bangor. Inc. 1907, when dam and paper mill were built.

East Millstone, town (1940 pop. 387), Somerset co., central N.J., on Millstone R. and 7 mi. W of New Brunswick; rubber works.

East Milton, Mass.: see MILTON.

East Mobridge, town (pop. 51), Walworth co., N S.Dak., 80 mi. N of Pierre, near Missouri R.; suburb of Mobridge.

East Moline (mōlēn'), city (pop. 13,913), Rock Island co., NW Ill., on the Mississippi, adjacent to MOLINE, of which it is an industrial suburb (farm equipment, trucks, pumps, engines). A state hosp. and Campbell's Isl. State Park are here. Inc. 1907.

East Montpelier (mŏntpĕl'yůr), town (pop. 1,128), Washington co., central Vt., on Winooski R., just E of Montpelier. First settled c.1788, set off from Montpelier 1848.

East Moriches (můrĭ'chēz), village (1940 pop. 943), Suffolk co., SE N.Y., on SE Long Isl., on Moriches Bay, just E of Center Moriches, in shore-resort and duck-farming area.

East Morton, England: see BINGLEY.

East Mountain (1,840 ft.), SW Mass., in East Mtn. State Forest (1,553 acres), just SE of Great Barrington, in the Berkshires; winter sports center.

East Murton, town and parish (pop. 9,344), NE Durham, England, 8 mi. ENE of Durham; coal mining.

East Newark (nōō'ůrk), borough (pop. 2,173), Hudson co., NE N.J., across Passaic R. from Newark; mfg. (clothing, textiles, yarn, metal products, light bulbs), rug dyeing. Inc. 1895.

East New Market, town (pop. 264), Dorchester co., E Md., 9 mi. ENE of Cambridge; ships truck; vegetable canneries.

East Newnan, village (pop. 1,525), Coweta co., W Ga., near Newnan.

East New York, SE N.Y., a residential section of N Brooklyn borough of New York city.

East Nishnabotna River, Iowa: see NISHNABOTNA RIVER.

East Northfield, Mass.: see NORTHFIELD.

East Northport, residential village (pop. 3,842), Suffolk co., SE N.Y., on N shore of W Long Isl., 2 mi. SE of Northport.

East Oder River (ō'důr) or **Reglitz River** (rā'glĭts), Pol. *Regalica* (rĕgälē'tsä), in Pomerania, after 1945 in NW Poland, right arm of lower Oder R., which divides near Hohensaaten (E Germany); flows 20 mi. N, past Podjucky and Gryfino, to Damm L.

East Okoboji Lake, Iowa: see OKOBOJI.

East Omaha (ō'můhä), NE suburb (pop. 2,262) of Omaha, Douglas co., E Nebr., on Missouri R.

Easton. 1 Town (pop. 2,165), Fairfield co., SW Conn., on Aspetuck R. and 8 mi. NW of Bridgeport. Settled c.1757. **2** Village (pop. 371), Mason co., central Ill., 31 mi. NNW of Springfield, in agr. area. **3** City (pop. 255), Leavenworth co., NE Kansas, on small affluent of Kansas R. and 11 mi. WNW of Leavenworth; grain, livestock. **4** Agr. town (pop. 1,664), Aroostook co., NE Maine, just E of Presque Isle. Inc. 1864. **5** Town (pop. 4,836), ⊙ Talbot co., E Md., on the Eastern Shore near head of Tred Avon R., 15 mi. N of Cambridge; trade center for agr. (wheat, corn, tomatoes) and summer-home area; canneries; hosiery, clothing, and lumber plants; airport near by. Quaker meetinghouse here was built c.1683. Settled 1710, inc. 1906. **6** Town (pop. 6,244), Bristol co., SE Mass., 6 mi. SW of Brockton; castings, molds, tools; dairying. Settled 1694, inc. 1725. Includes village of North Easton (1940 pop. 1,895). **7** Village (pop. 379), Faribault co., S Minn., 13 mi. NE of Blue Earth; dairy products. **8** Town (pop. 173), Buchanan co., NW Mo., near Little Platte R., 11 mi. E of St. Joseph. **9** Town (pop. 94), Grafton co., NW N.H., on Wild Ammonoosuc R., in recreational area just W of Franconia Notch. **10** City (pop. 35,632), ⊙ Northampton co., E Pa., on Delaware R. (bridged here) and 50 mi. N of Philadelphia, at mouth of Lehigh R.; machinery, metal products, slate, cement, electrical devices, textiles, leather, paper, clothing, food products, chemicals; railroad shops. Lafayette Col. here. Scene of frontier conferences with Indians. Laid out 1752, inc. as borough 1789, as city 1886. **11** Town (pop. 203), on Gregg-Rusk co. line, E Texas, 17 mi. E of Kilgore.

Easton-in-Gordano, residential town and parish (pop. 2,471), N Somerset, England, 5 mi. WNW of Bristol. Has 15th-cent. church.

Easton-on-the-Hill, village and parish (pop. 814), N Northumberland, England, 2 mi. SW of Stamford; ironstone quarrying. Has church dating from 14th cent.

East Orange, city (pop. 79,340), Essex co., NE N.J., adjoining Newark on NW; residential, industrial (metal products, machinery, electric motors, clothing, concrete products, paint, insecticides). Upsala Col. and Panzer Col. of Physical Education and Hygiene here. Municipal Center (1929) includes city hall and post office. Settled 1678, separated from Orange 1863, inc. 1899.

East Orleans, Mass.: see ORLEANS.

East Otto, village (pop. c.300), Cattaraugus co., W N.Y., 36 mi. S of Buffalo; canned foods.

Eastover, town (pop. 564), Richland co., central S.C., 20 mi. ESE of Columbia.

East Palatka (půlăt'ků), village (pop. c.1,200), Putnam co., N Fla., on St. Johns R., opposite Palatka; shipping (citrus fruit, vegetables); lumber milling.

East Palestine (pă'lůstīn), city (pop. 5,195), Columbiana co., E Ohio, at Pa. line, 20 mi. SSE of Youngstown, in dairy and orchard area; clay products, fireproofing materials, metal products, tires, models and patterns, furniture. Coal mining; clay pits. Founded 1828; inc. as city in 1875.

East Park Dam, Calif.: see STONY CREEK.

East Parsonfield, Maine: see PARSONSFIELD.

East Patchogue (pă'chäg", –chôg"), residential village (pop. 4,124), Suffolk co., SE N.Y., on S Long Isl., on Great South Bay just E of Patchogue, in shore-resort area; concrete blocks.

East Paterson (pă'tůrsůn), borough (pop. 15,386), Bergen co., NE N.J., industrial suburb of Paterson, across Passaic R.; mfg. (paper products, leather goods, metal products, cosmetics, cement pipe); dairying. Inc. 1916.

East Pearl River, La.: see PEARL RIVER.

East Peckham, town and parish (pop. 1,924), W central Kent, England, near Medway R., 5 mi. ENE of Tonbridge; agr.

East Pensacola (pĕnsůkō'lů), village (pop. 1,695), Escambia co., extreme NW Fla., near Pensacola.

East Peoria (pēō'rēů), city (pop. 8,698), Tazewell co., central Ill., on Illinois R. (bridged here), opposite Peoria, in agr. and bituminous-coal area; mfg. of tractors. Inc. 1919. Fort Creve Coeur State Park is near by.

East Pepperell, Mass.: see PEPPERELL.

East Peru, town (pop. 204), Madison co., S central Iowa, 30 mi. SSW of Des Moines, in agr. area.

East Petersburg, borough (pop. 1,268), Lancaster co., SE Pa., 4 mi. N of Lancaster. Inc. 1946.

East Pittsburgh (pĭts'bûrg), industrial borough (pop. 5,259), Allegheny co., SW Pa., SE suburb of Pittsburgh; electrical equipment. Braddock defeated near here (1755) by French and Indians. Inc. 1895.

East Point. 1 Cape at E extremity of P.E.I., on the Gulf of St. Lawrence, 15 mi. NE of Souris; 46°27'N 61°58'W; lighthouse. **2** Cape at E extremity of Anticosti Isl., E Que., on the Gulf of St. Lawrence; 49°8'N 61°41'W.

East Point, city (pop. 21,080), Fulton co., NW central Ga., 6 mi. SSW of Atlanta; creosoting; mfg. (yarn, cottonseed oil, fertilizer, metal products, furniture, batteries). Inc. 1887.

Eastport. 1 Village, Boundary co., N Idaho, port of entry at British Columbia line, 22 mi. NNE of Bonners Ferry. **2** City (pop. 3,123), Washington co., E Maine, on Moose Isl. in SE PASSAMAQUODDY BAY, 24 mi. SSE of Calais; fishing, sardine canning, resort activities. Ships lumber, fish; port of entry. Has artists' colony. First sardine cannery in U.S. built here c.1875. Site of old Fort Sullivan (1808). Tidal variation averages 18 ft. Settled c.1780, town inc. 1798, city 1893. **3** Village (pop. 4,594), Anne Arundel co., central Md., on Severn R. just SE of Annapolis; boatyards. **4** Village (pop. 1,042, with adjacent Speonk), Suffolk co., SE N.Y., on SE Long Isl., on Moriches Bay, 15 mi. E of Patchogue, in summer-resort and duck-farming area; mfg. of feed, fertilizer, barrels; poultry packing.

East Port Chester, Conn.: see GREENWICH.

East Prairie, city (pop. 3,033), Mississippi co., extreme SE Mo., in Mississippi flood plain, 10 mi. S of Charleston; cotton gins, flour mills, lumber mills.

East Prospect, borough (pop. 500), York co., S Pa., 12 mi. E of York.

East Providence, town (pop. 35,871), Providence co., E R.I., along Seekonk and Providence rivers, opposite Providence; mfg. (building materials, chemicals, petroleum products, wire and steel products, insulating board, paper, feed, flour, roofing, lumber, machinery, paint); textile dyeing and printing; shipbuilding; dairy products. Includes residential, industrial villages of Phillipsdale, Rumford, and Riverside. Settled as a Mass. town; inc. 1862.

East Prussia (prŭ'shů), Ger. *Ostpreussen* (ôst'-proi"sůn), former province (□ 14,283; 1939 pop. 2,333,301, excluding Memel dist.) of Prussia, NE Germany; ⊙ was Königsberg. Bordered N on the Baltic, NE on Lithuania, and S and W on Poland; separated from rest of Germany by Polish Corridor and Free City of Danzig. After 1945 divided bet. Pol. Olsztyn prov. (□ 8,106; pop. 441,651), with ⊙ Allenstein (Olsztyn), and Kaliningrad oblast

(□ c.6,100; 1947 pop. estimate 600,000), Russian SFSR, with ⊙ Kaliningrad (Königsberg). Small E section was added to Pol. Bialystok prov. Surface has low rolling hills, partly forested, dotted with many small lakes. In E part is extensive MASURIAN LAKES region. Drained by Nogat, Pasleka (Passarge), Lyna (Alle), Pregel, and Neman rivers. Coast line is deeply indented by Vistula Lagoon, protected by Vistula Spit, and by Kurland Lagoon, protected by Kurland Spit. Principal cities: Marienburg (Malbork), Elbing (Elblag), Allenstein (Olsztyn), after 1945 in Poland; and Königsberg (Kaliningrad), Tilsit (Sovetsk), Insterburg (Chernyakhovsk), Gumbinnen (Gusev), Pillau (Baltiysk), and seaside resort of Rauschen (Svetlogorsk), after 1945 in Russian SFSR. Chief industries: shipbuilding, sawmilling, woodworking, fishing, stock raising. Peat, amber, and lignite are worked. Crops include rye, potatoes, oats, and barley. Region was conquered in 13th cent. from the Old Prussians (a people related to the Liths) by the Teutonic Knights, who displaced original pop. and made territory a fief of their order. In 1466 they ceded Pomerelia (later West Prussia) and WARMIA to Poland and accepted Pol. suzerainty over rest of their domain. Albert of Brandenburg, after secularizing Teutonic order, took (1525) title of duke of Prussia; in 1618 elector of Brandenburg inherited duchy. At Peace of Oliva (1660), Frederick William, the Great Elector, won full sovereignty over the duchy, and his son was crowned (1701) as King Frederick I of Prussia at Königsberg. Region was henceforth known as East Prussia. It became a stronghold of Prussian *Junkers*, a land-owning and military aristocracy, who had vast estates here. In First World War, scene (1914–15) of heavy battles (Tannenberg, Masurian Lakes). After the war E part of West Prussia prov. was added to East Prussia. In 1920, Memel (Klaipeda) dist. passed to Lithuania; Soldau (Suwalki) dist. passed to Poland. Under heavy Ger. pressure Lithuania returned Memel dist. to East Prussia in 1939, before outbreak of Second World War. During the war a section of NE Poland was annexed to East Prussia (whose area in 1943 was □ 20,361), while formerly West Prussian section was added to Danzig–West Prussia prov. created 1939. With the partition in 1945 most of the Germans left the region.

East Quogue (kwäg), resort village, Suffolk co., SE N.Y., on SE Long Isl., on Shinnecock Bay, 6 mi. SE of Riverhead; yachting, duck hunting.

East Radford, Va.: see RADFORD.

East Rainelle (rānĕl′), town (pop. 1,695), Greenbrier co., SE W.Va., 20 mi. NW of Lewisburg, just E of Rainelle, in coal, timber, agr. region; casket mfg. State park near by. Inc. 1921.

East Randolph, village (pop. 628), Cattaraugus co., W N.Y., 15 mi. ENE of Jamestown; feed and lumber milling.

East Retford (rĕt′fûrd), municipal borough (1931 pop. 14,229; 1951 census 16,312), N Nottingham, England, on Idle R. and 8 mi. E of Worksop; agr. market; leather tanning. Has church founded 1258 but dating mainly from 15th cent.; 17th-cent. Holy Trinity Hosp.; notable 18th-cent. town hall; and grammar school founded c.1550.

East Ridge, town (pop. 9,645), Hamilton co., SE Tenn., a S suburb of Chattanooga. Inc. 1921.

East Riding, administrative division of Yorkshire, England, covering SE part of county. See YORK, county.

East River, Chinese *Tung Kiang* or *Tung Chiang* (both: dŏŏng′jyäng′), S China, rises in 2 branches on N slopes of Kiulien Mts. in S Kiangsi prov. (W branch near Tingnan, E branch near Sünwu), flows 250 mi. SW and W, past Laolung, Hoyün, and Waiyeung, and below Sheklung empties through delta into Canton R. Receives Tseng R. (right). Navigable for 200 mi. below Laolung.

East River, village, Conn.: see MADISON.

East River, in New York city, SE N.Y., navigable tidal strait (c.16 mi. long, 600–4,000 ft. wide) connecting Upper New York Bay and Long Island Sound and separating the boroughs of Manhattan and the Bronx from Brooklyn and Queens boroughs on Long Isl. Connected with Hudson R. by Harlem R. and Spuyten Duyvil Creek at N end of Manhattan isl. Welfare, Wards, Randalls, and Rikers isls. are in the river, which is crossed by Brooklyn, Manhattan, Williamsburg, Queensboro, Triborough, and Bronx-Whitestone highway bridges and by Hell Gate railroad bridge. Subway, railroad, and vehicular tunnels pass under it. Extensive port facilities along its S portions include U.S. navy yard on Brooklyn shore. Indenting Queens shore is FLUSHING BAY, site of La Guardia Field, the municipal airport. East River Drive (7½ mi. long; opened 1942) extends along right bank in Manhattan. There are several parks on both banks and on Randalls and Wards isls.

East Riverdale, village (1940 pop. 1,424), Prince Georges co., central Md., NE of Washington.

East River Mountain, in SW Va. and SE W.Va., ridge (c.3–4,000 ft.) of the Alleghenies; from point SW of Bluefield extends c.35 mi. NE along state line to gorge of New R. Its NE continuation is Peters Mtn.

East Rochester (rŏ′chĕ″stûr, rŏ′chĭstûr). **1** Village (pop. 7,022), Monroe co., W N.Y., 7 mi. SE of Rochester, in agr. area; mfg. (pianos, farm machinery, chemicals, metal and paper products, flour, filter plates). Inc. 1906. **2** Borough (pop 985), Beaver co., W Pa., on Ohio R. just above Rochester.

East Rockaway, resort and residential village (pop. 7,970), Nassau co., SE N.Y., near S shore of W Long Isl., 8 mi. SE of Jamaica. Mfg. of sashes, screens. Inc. 1900.

East Rockingham (rŏ′kĭng-hăm″), village (pop. 5,180, with adjacent Mills), Richmond co., S N.C., near Rockingham.

East Rupert, Vt.: see RUPERT.

East Rutherford (rŭ′thûrfûrd), industrial borough (pop. 7,438), Bergen co., NE N.J., 8 mi. NNE of Newark; clothing, chemicals, metal products, ink, asbestos products. Includes Carlton Hill, mfg. village (hosiery; bleaching and dyeing works). Inc. 1894.

Eastry, town and parish (pop. 1,567), E Kent, England, 3 mi. SW of Sandwich; agr. market. Has Norman church.

East Ryegate, Vt.: see RYEGATE.

East Saint Louis (lōō′ĭs), city (pop. 82,295), St. Clair co., SW Ill., on left bank of the Mississippi (levees), opposite SAINT LOUIS (several bridges); important processing, mfg., trade, and shipping (air, river, rail, highway) point, surrounded by other industrial suburbs of St. Louis. Large alumina refinery; railroad yards, meat-packing plants, foundries, machine shops, steelworks and rolling mills, oil refineries, grain mills. Mfg. of chemicals, fertilizer, paint, glass, roofing material; power-plant, refinery, and railroad equipment; prefabricated houses, rubber products, boxes. Livestock market (especially horses, mules). Rock quarries, coal mines near by. Seat of Parks Col. of Aeronautical Technology (of St. Louis Univ.). Cahokia Mounds State Park is in vicinity. Platted as Illinoistown in 1816; inc. as a town in 1859; reincorporated as East St. Louis in 1865, after absorption of East St. Louistown (platted 1859). Commission govt. adopted 1917. Many Negroes were killed in violent race riot here in 1917.

East Salinas (sùlē′nùs), unincorporated village (pop. c.5,000), Monterey co., W Calif., adjoining Salinas. Settled after 1933 by migratory agr. workers from the Midwest.

East Saltney, Wales: see SALTNEY.

East Sandwich, Mass.: see SANDWICH.

East Sarasota (să″rùsō′tù), village (pop. 1,073), Sarasota co., SW Fla., near Sarasota.

East Saugus, Mass.: see SAUGUS.

East Sayan Mountains, Russian SFSR: see SAYAN MOUNTAINS.

East Sea, Palestine: see DEAD SEA.

East Setauket (sētô′kĭt, sĭ–), village (1940 pop. 704), Suffolk co., SE N.Y., on N Long Isl., on Port Jefferson Harbor, bet. Port Jefferson (E) and Setauket, in summer-resort area.

East Siberian Sea, Rus. *Vostochno-Sibirskoye More*, section of Arctic Ocean, bounded W by New Siberian Isls., S by N coast of NE Siberia, E by Wrangel Isl., N by edge of continental shelf; receives Indigirka, Kolyma, and Chaun rivers. W section is very shallow, deepening toward E. Navigable during ice-free Aug.–Sept. Main port, Ambarchik.

East Siberian Territory, Rus. *Vostochno-Sibirskiy Kray*, former administrative division of E Asiatic Russian SFSR; ⊙ was Irkutsk. Formed 1930 out of E part of Siberian Territory which contained Vitim-Olekma, Taimyr, and Evenki natl. okrugs and Buryat-Mongol Autonomous SSR; reduced 1934 by separation from it of Krasnoyarsk Territory. Upon separation in 1936 of Buryat-Mongol Autonomous SSR, it was converted into East Siberian Oblast (Rus. *Vostochno-Sibirskaya Oblast′*) and finally dissolved in 1937 into Irkutsk and Chita oblasts.

East Side. 1 Village (pop. 2,768, with adjacent Dallas Mills), Madison co., N Ala., just NE of Huntsville. **2** Village (pop. 1,215), Jackson co., SE Miss., near the coast just NE of Pascagoula. **3** Borough (pop. 286), Carbon co., E Pa., 14 mi. SSE of Wilkes-Barre and on Lehigh R.

Eastside. 1 City (pop. 890), Coos co., SW Oregon, just E of Coos Bay. **2** Village (pop. 1,926), Thurston co., W Wash.

East Spanish Peak, Colo.: see SPANISH PEAKS.

East Sparta, village (pop. 811), Stark co., E central Ohio, 9 mi. S of Canton and on small Nimishellen Creek; clay products.

East Spencer, town (pop. 2,444), Rowan co., central N.C., just E of Spencer, near High Rock L., in cotton and tobacco area; brick mfg.

East Springfield. 1 Resort village, Otsego co., central N.Y., 11 mi. NNE of Cooperstown. Ostego L. is 4 mi. SW. **2** Borough (pop. 499), Erie co., NW Pa., 20 mi. WSW of Erie, near L. Erie; potatoes.

East Stanwood, town (pop. 378), Snohomish co., NW Wash., 18 mi. NNW of Everett, in pea-growing region; canneries.

East Stonehouse, England: see PLYMOUTH.

East Stroudsburg, borough (pop. 7,274), Monroe co., E Pa., 21 mi. N of Easton, just N of Stroudsburg; railroad shops; printing, textiles, metal-working shops. State teachers col. here. Settled 1737, inc. 1870.

East Sumner, Maine: see SUMNER.

East Syracuse (sĭ′rùkūs, sē′–), village (pop. 4,766), Onondaga co., central N.Y., just E of Syracuse; mfg. (steel products, screws, machinery). Inc. 1881.

East Tallassee (tălùsē′), village (1940 pop. 2,301), Tallapoosa co., E Ala., across Tallapoosa R. from Tallassee.

East Taunton, Mass.: see RAYNHAM.

East Tavaputs Plateau (tă′vùpōōts), high tableland (7–9,000 ft.) in Grand and Uintah counties, E Utah; bounded S by Book Cliffs, W by Green R. and West Tavaputs Plateau. Forms W continuation of Roan Plateau in W Colo.

East Tawas (tô′wùs, tä′–), city (pop. 2,040), Iosco co., NE Mich., c.50 mi. NE of Bay City, on Tawas Bay, in agr. area (hay, grain, potatoes); railroad shops; fisheries. Resort. Contains U.S. forest nursery and state park. Settled 1864; inc. as village 1887, as city 1895.

East Templeton, village (pop. estimate 500), SW Que., on Ottawa R. and 7 mi. ENE of Hull; quartz mining.

East Templeton, Mass.: see TEMPLETON.

East Thermopolis (thûrmŏ′pùlĭs), town (pop. 246), Hot Springs co., N central Wyo., a suburb of Thermopolis.

East Thomaston, village (pop. 3,082), Upson co., W central Ga., just NE of Thomaston.

East Timbalier Island, La.: see TIMBALIER ISLAND.

East Tohopekaliga Lake, Fla.: see TOHOPEKALIGA LAKE.

East Toronto (tùrŏn′tō), E suburb of Toronto, S Ont.; merged with Toronto 1908.

East Troy, village (pop. 1,052), Walworth co., SE Wis., on Honey Creek (tributary of Fox R.) and 30 mi. SW of Milwaukee, in dairy and livestock area; makes stainless-steel products, condensed milk, feed. Resort lakes near by.

East Tupelo (tū′pùlō, tōō′–), town (1940 pop. 1,108), Lee co., NE Miss., just E of Tupelo.

East Turkestan Republic, China: see SINKIANG, province.

East Tyrol, Austria: see TYROL.

East Uniontown, village (pop. 2,138), Fayette co., SW Pa., near Uniontown.

Eastvale, borough (pop. 533), Beaver co., W Pa., on Beaver R. opposite Beaver Falls.

East Vandergrift, borough (pop. 1,665), Westmoreland co., W central Pa., on Kiskiminetas R. adjoining Vandergrift. Inc. 1901.

East Vaughn, village (pop. c.500), Guadalupe co., central N.Mex., 38 mi. SW of Santa Rosa; alt. c.6,000 ft. Rail junction in sheep-raising area.

East Verde River (vĕr′dē, vûr′dē), central Ariz., rises in Mogollon Plateau, flows c.50 mi. SW and W to Verde R. 37 mi. S of Cottonwood.

Eastview, town (pop. 7,966), SE Ont., on Ottawa R., at N end of Rideau Canal, NE suburb of Ottawa; woodworking, lumbering, flour milling.

East View, village (pop. 1,642), Harrison co., N W.Va., just E of Clarksburg.

East Village, Mass.: see WEBSTER.

Eastville. 1 Town (pop. 96), Oconee co., NE central Ga., 9 mi. SW of Athens. **2** Town (pop. 311), ⊙ Northampton co., E Va., 7 mi. NE of Cape Charles town, in truck-farming region. Co. records beginning 1632 are preserved here.

East Walker River, in E Calif. and W Nev., rises in Sierra Nevada near Mono L., Calif., flows c.70 mi. generally N into Nev., joining West Walker R. in Lyon co. 7 mi. S of Yerington to form Walker R. Dam in upper course (Calif.) forms Bridgeport Reservoir (c.3 mi. long).

East Wallingford, Vt.: see WALLINGFORD.

East Walpole, Mass.: see WALPOLE.

East Wareham, Mass.: see WAREHAM.

East Washington, borough (pop. 2,304), Washington co., SW Pa., just NE of Washington. Inc. 1892.

East Weissport, village (pop. 1,814), Carbon co., E Pa., near Mahoning.

East Wellington, village (pop. estimate 200), SW B.C., on SE Vancouver Isl., 4 mi. WNW of Nanaimo; coal mining.

East Wemyss (wēmz), town in Wemyss parish, central Fifeshire, Scotland, on the Firth of Forth, 4 mi. SW of Leven; fishing port, with coal mines. Modern Wemyss Castle replaces earlier structure.

East Wenatchee (wĭnă′chē), town (pop. 389), Douglas co., central Wash., across Columbia R. (here bridged) from WENATCHEE.

East Weymouth, Mass.: see WEYMOUTH.

East Williston, village (pop. 1,734), Nassau co., SE N.Y., on W Long Isl., just N of Mineola; residential. Inc. 1926.

East Wilmington, village (pop. 1,623), New Hanover co., SE N.C., near Wilmington.

East Windham (wĭn′dùm), resort village, Greene co., SE N.Y., in the Catskills, 17 mi. NW of Catskill.

East Windsor (wĭn′zûr), E suburb of Windsor, S Ont., on Detroit R., opposite Detroit; automobile-mfg. center. Formerly one of the Border Cities, it was named Ford in 1913, later became Ford City. Name was changed to East Windsor 1929; merged with Windsor 1935.

East Windsor, farming town (pop. 4,859), Hartford co., N Conn., on Connecticut (here bridged) and Scantic rivers and 10 mi. NNE of Hartford; tobacco. Mfg., tobacco packing at villages of Scantic, Warehouse Point (pop. 1,283; hardware, thread), and Broad Brook (woolens). Set off from Windsor 1768.

Eastwood, municipality (pop. 4,108), E New South Wales, Australia, 10 mi. NE of Sydney, in metropolitan area; chemicals.

Eastwood. 1 Town and parish (pop. 3,887), S Essex, England, 3 mi. NW of Southend, agr. market. Has Norman church. **2** Urban district (1931 pop. 5,360; 1951 census 9,896), W Nottingham, England, 9 mi. NW of Nottingham; coal mining; pharmaceutical industry. D. H. Lawrence b. here.

Eastwood, parish (pop. 26,496, including part of Glasgow burgh), E Renfrew, Scotland. Includes THORNLIEBANK.

East Youngstown, Ohio: see CAMPBELL.

Eaton, county (□ 567; pop. 40,023), S central Mich.; ⊙ Charlotte. Drained by Grand and Thornapple rivers, and by the Battle Creek. Agr. area (maple sugar, grain, corn, beans, sugar beets, fruit, poultry); dairy products; stock breeding. Mfg. at Charlotte, Eaton Rapids, and Grand Ledge. Sandstone, clay, coal deposits; mineral springs. Organized 1837.

Eaton. 1 Town (pop. 1,276), Weld co., N Colo., near Cache la Poudre R., 7 mi. N of Greeley, in grain and livestock region; alt. 4,750 ft. Beet sugar, flour, dairy and poultry products, potatoes, beans. Artifacts of Yuma man and Folsom man discovered near by. Founded 1881, inc. 1892. **2** Town (pop. 1,598), Delaware co., E Ind., on Mississinewa R. and 11 mi. N of Muncie; livestock, grain; mfg. (paper products, canned goods, glass jars). **3** Town (pop. 221), Carroll co., E N.H., on Conway L., in recreational area just SE of Conway. **4** Village (pop. 4,242), ⊙ Preble co., W Ohio, 23 mi. W of Dayton and on small Seven Mile Creek; trading center for agr. area (tobacco, grain); mfg. (fertilizer, gloves, tobacco boxes, food products). Fort St. Clair State Park is near by. Founded 1806.

Eaton, Lake, NE central Hamilton co., N central N.Y., in the Adirondacks, c.2 mi. W of Long Lake village; c.1 mi. in diameter. State camp site here.

Eaton Bray, agr. village and parish (pop. 1,042), S Bedford, England, 3 mi. W of Dunstable. Has 13th-cent. church.

Eaton Hall, England: see CHESTER.

Eatonia (ētō'nēŭ), village (pop. 329), SW Sask., 20 mi. SW of Kindersley; wheat, stock.

Eaton Rapids, city (pop. 3,509), Eaton co., S central Mich., 17 mi. SSW of Lansing and on Grand R., in sheep-raising area. Mfg. (woolen goods, metal parts, food products); dairy, poultry, fruit farming. Mineral springs. Natl. home for children of Veterans of Foreign Wars is near by. Settled 1837; inc. as village 1871, as city 1881.

Eatons Neck, SE N.Y., irregular sandspit (¼–1½ mi. wide). extending c.3½ mi. NW from N shore of W Long Isl., and sheltering Huntington and Northport bays (W). At its tip is Eatons Neck Point (lighthouse). Site of Asharoken (resort).

Eaton Socon, town and parish (pop. 2,240), NE Bedford, England, on Ouse R., just SW of St. Neots; agr. market. Has remains of 12th-cent. Bushmead Priory.

Eatonton, city (pop. 2,749), ⊙ Putnam co., central Ga., 37 mi. NNE of Macon; cotton and lumber milling. Has monument to Joel Chandler Harris, who was b. here. Inc. 1809.

Eatontown, borough (pop. 3,044), Monmouth co., E N.J., 3 mi. S of Red Bank; truck farming. U.S. Fort Monmouth is near by. Settled 1670, inc. 1926.

Eatonville, town (pop. 1,048), Pierce co., W central Wash., 28 mi. SSE of Tacoma, in foothills of Cascade Range; agr., timber, dairy products.

Eaubonne (ōbôn'), town (pop. 9,348), Seine-et-Oise dept., N central France, outer NNW residential suburb of Paris, 10 mi. from Notre Dame Cathedral; perfume factories. Race track.

Eau Claire (ō"klâr'), county (□ 649; pop. 54,187), W central Wis.; ⊙ Eau Claire. Drained by Chippewa and Eau Claire rivers. Dairying (most important industry), stock raising, farming (clover, corn, oats). Eau Claire city has diversified mfg. Formed 1856.

Eau Claire. 1 Village (pop. 480), Berrien co., extreme SW Mich., 12 mi. SE of Benton Harbor. **2** Borough (pop. 403), Butler co., W Pa., 19 mi. NNE of Butler. **3** Town (pop. 9,238), Richland co., central S.C.; N residential suburb of Columbia. Seat of Columbia Col. and a Lutheran seminary. Inc. 1897. **4** City (pop. 36,058), ⊙ Eau Claire co., W central Wis., at confluence of Chippewa and Eau Claire rivers, 70 mi. NNW of La Crosse; commercial center for dairying and stock-raising area. Mfg. (automobile parts, rubber and leather goods, machinery, aluminum ware, paper). A state teachers col. and state fish hatchery are here. Trading post in late-18th cent., city developed as lumbering center. Inc. 1872.

Eau Claire River. 1 In central Wis., rises in lake region in Langlade co., flows c.55 mi. generally SW to Wisconsin R. at Schofield. **2** In W Wis., formed by 2 forks joining near Eau Claire-Clark co. line, flows c.40 mi. W to Chippewa R. at Eau Claire.

Eau Galle River (ō găl'), W Wis., rises in St. Croix co., flows c.35 mi. SE, past Elmwood (hydroelectric plant), to Chippewa R. near Durand.

Eau Gallie (ō gă'lē), city (pop. 1,554), Brevard co., central Fla., 4 mi. N of Melbourne and on Indian R. lagoon.

Eau Pleine River (ō plān'), central Wis., rises in Marathon co., flows c.35 mi. SE to Wisconsin R. 17 mi. SSW of Wausau. Near its mouth, the river widens to form Big Eau Pleine Reservoir (9 mi. long, ½–2 mi. wide).

Eauripik (ĕou'rēpĕk), atoll (pop. 125), Yap dist., W Caroline Isls., W Pacific, 600 mi. W of Truk; 6°42'N 143°4'E; 5.5 mi. long, 1.5 mi. wide; 6 islets on reef. Sometimes spelled Iuripick.

Eaux-Bonnes, Les (lāzō'-bôn'), village (pop. 172), Basses-Pyrénées dept., SW France, in central Pyrenees at the foot of Pic de Ger, 18 mi. SE of Oloron-Sainte-Marie; winter-sports resort and spa with sulphurous hot springs.

Eaux-Chaudes, Les (–shōd'), village (pop. 753), Basses-Pyrénées dept., SW France, in Ossau valley of central Pyrenees, on road to Spain via Pourtalet pass, and 18 mi. SSE of Oloron-Sainte-Marie; alt. 2,152 ft.; spa with hot sulphur springs. Hydroelectric station.

Eauze (ōz), anc. *Elusa,* village (pop. 1,708), Gers dept., SW France, near the Gélise, 15 mi. WSW of Condom; Armagnac brandy trading center; canning (pâté de foie gras), hosiery mfg. Was capital of Roman prov. of Novempopulana.

Eawy, Forest of, France: see SAINT-SAËNS.

Eba, Mount, Australia: see MOUNT EBA.

Ebal, Mount (ē'bŭl) (3,084 ft.), in Palestine, after 1948 in W Jordan, in Samarian Hills, just NE of Nablus.

Ebange, France: see FLORANGE.

Ebano (ābä'nō), village (pop. 2,696), San Luis Potosí, E Mexico, in fertile Gulf plain, on railroad and 35 mi. W of Tampico; sugar cane, tobacco, coffee, vegetables, fruit, cattle. Formerly petroleum production.

Ebara (ābä'rä) or **Ehara** (āhä'rä), town (pop. 8,720) Tokushima prefecture, E Shikoku, Japan, 22 mi. WNW of Tokushima; agr. center (rice, wheat, tobacco); raw silk; kaolin.

Ebba-Ksour (ĕb-bä'ksōōr'), town (pop. 2,700), Le Kef dist., W Tunisia, on railroad and 17 mi. SSE of Le Kef; agr. trade center (livestock, wool, cereals); flour mill. Experimental stock-raising station. Ruins of Roman *Althiburos* near by.

Ebbe, Sweden: see STENSHOLM.

Ebbegunbaeg, Lake (12 mi. long, 1 mi. wide), S central N.F., 50 mi. SSE of Buchans; 48°12'N 56°28'W. Drains NW into Meelpaeg L.

Ebbetts Pass or **Ebbett Pass,** E Calif., highway pass (alt. 8,800 ft.) across the Sierra Nevada, in Alpine co., c.40 mi. S of Carson City, Nev.

Ebbsfleet, village, NE Kent, England, on Pegwell Bay of the Channel, 2½ mi. WSW of Ramsgate; reputed landing place (A.D. 449) of the Saxons under Hengist and Horsa. St. Augustine landed here 597.

Ebbw River (ĕ'bōō), Monmouth, England, rises in 2 headstreams on Brecon border N of Ebbw Vale, flows 24 mi. SE, past Ebbw Vale and Risca, to the Usk 2 mi. S of Newport. Receives Sirhowy R. just W of Risca.

Ebbw Vale, urban district (1931 pop. 31,686; 1951 census 29,205), W Monmouth, England, on Ebbw R. and 20 mi. N of Cardiff; steel-rolling and tinplate-mfg. center; coal mining.

Ebebiyín (ābābēyēn'), town (pop. 150), continental Sp. Guinea, on Fr. Cameroons and Gabon border, 110 mi. ENE of Bata; 2°11'N 11°20'E. Cacao, coffee. Also spelled Ebibeyín.

Ebeleben (ā'bŭlā"bŭn), town (pop. 2,535), Thuringia, central Germany, 9 mi. SW of Sondershausen, in sugar-beet growing region; sugar refining. Has 16th–18th-cent. palace.

Ebeltoft, Denmark: see AEBELTOFT.

Ebenezer (ĕbŭnē'zŭr). **1** Village (pop. 95), Holmes co., central Miss., 20 mi. ENE of Yazoo City. **2** Village (1940 pop. 1,818), Erie co., W N.Y., 6 mi. SE of Buffalo; glassware, wood containers. **3** Town (pop. 680), York co., N S.C.; NW residential suburb of Rock Hill.

Ebenfurth (ā'bŭnfōōrt), town (pop. 2,360), E Lower Austria, on Leitha R. and 7 mi. NE of Wiener Neustadt; rail junction; flour mill.

Ebenhausen (ā"bŭnhou'zŭn), village (pop. 1,229), Upper Bavaria, Germany, on Paar R. and 6 mi. S of Ingolstadt; glass and porcelain mfg.

Ebenrode, Russian SFSR: see NESTEROV.

Ebensburg (ĕ'bŭnzbûrg), residential borough (pop. 4,086), ⊙ Cambria co., SW central Pa., 15 mi. NE of Johnstown; agr.; bituminous coal, timber; summer resort. Settled 1796, laid out 1806, inc. 1825.

Ebensee (ā'bŭnzā), city (pop. 10,545), S Upper Austria, on S shore of L. Traun, at influx of Traun R., and 8 mi. S of Gmunden; saltworks, mfg. (soda, ammonia, clocks), wood carving. Salt baths. Suspension railway to Feuerkogel, mtn.

Eber, Lake (ĕbĕr') (□ 40), W central Turkey, 30 mi. ESE of Afyonkarahisar; 11 mi. long, 8 mi. wide; alt. 3,270 ft. Connected with L. Akhisar.

Eberbach (ā'bŭrbäkh), town (pop. 10,440), N Baden, Germany, after 1945 in Württemberg-Baden, in the Odenwald, at W foot of the Katzenbuckel, on the canalized Neckar, at mouth of small Itter R., and 14 mi. ENE of Heidelberg; rail junction; mfg. of chemicals, textiles, pottery; metal- and woodworking. Basalt quarries. Timber trade. Has ruined castle; towers of medieval fortifications. Was free imperial city.

Ebergassing (ā"bŭrgä'sĭng), town (pop. 1,598), after 1938 in Schwechat dist. of Vienna, Austria, on Fischa R. and 13 mi. SE of city center; rug mfg. Château with large park.

Ebermannstadt (ā'bŭrmän"shtät'), town (pop. 2,302), Upper Franconia, N Bavaria, Germany, on the Wiesent and 7 mi. NE of Forchheim; textile mfg., brewing. Chartered 1323.

Ebern (ā'bŭrn), village (pop. 2,022), Lower Franconia, N Bavaria, Germany, 15 mi. NNW of Bamberg; wood-fiber mfg.; lumber, paper, and flour milling; brewing, tanning. Cattle. Has late-Gothic church and Renaissance town hall.

Ebernburg (ā'bŭrnbŏŏrk), village (pop. 1,025), Rhenish Palatinate, W Germany, on the Nahe and 3 mi. SW of Bad Kreuznach; wine. Has medieval castle. Franz von Sickingen b. here.

Eberndorf (ā'bŭrndôrf), town (pop. 4,154), Carinthia, S Austria, 16 mi. ESE of Klagenfurt; summer resort. Old monastery near by.

Ebersbach (ā'bŭrsbäkh). **1** Town (pop. 11,315), Saxony, E central Germany, in Upper Lusatia, in Lusatian Mts., on the upper Spree and 12 mi. NW of Zittau; frontier station on Czechoslovak border, opposite Jirikov; cotton- and linen-milling center; mfg. of artificial flowers, pianos, glass. **2** or **Ebersbach an der Fils** (än dĕr fĭls'), village (pop. 6,148), N Württemberg, Germany, after 1945 in Württemberg-Baden, on the Fils and 5.5 mi. W of Göppingen; grain, cattle.

Ebersberg (ā'bŭrsbĕrk), village (pop. 3,827), Upper Bavaria, Germany, 20 mi. ESE of Munich; printing, woodworking, brewing. Former Benedictine monastery (founded c.934) has late-Romanesque church.

Eberschwang (ā'bŭrshväng), town (pop. 3,820), central Upper Austria, 5 mi. SE of Ried, in Hausruck Mts.; potatoes, hogs.

Eberstadt (ā'bŭr-shtät), S suburb (pop. 12,067) of Darmstadt, W Germany, 3.5 mi. S of city center. Inc. 1937 into Darmstadt.

Eberstein (ā'bŭrshtīn), village (pop. 2,078), Carinthia, S Austria, 17 mi. NE of Klagenfurt; summer resort.

Eberswalde (ā"bŭrsväl'dŭ), city (1939 pop. 40,615; 1946 pop. 30,186), Brandenburg, E Germany, on Finow Canal, near Hohenzollern Canal, 30 mi. NE of Berlin; 52°50'N 13°48'E. Rail junction; railroad workshops; mfg. of steel products, machinery, chemicals, plastics, roofing materials, paper and cardboard products, bricks; lumber milling, brewing. Site of Berlin Univ. forestry school. Has 14th-cent. church and 18th-cent. town hall. In 1913 an important find of gold utensils, assigned to 6th cent. B.C. (in some cases to 11th–9th cent. B.C.), was made here. Town chartered in mid-13th cent. Formerly called Neustadt-Eberswalde.

Ebetsu (ābā'tsōō), town (pop. 28,815), W Hokkaido, Japan, on Ishikari R. and 11 mi. ENE of Sapporo; paper-milling center; dairying.

Ebha, Saudi Arabia: see ABHA.

Ebi (ā'bē), town (pop. 3,618), Aichi prefecture, central Honshu, Japan, 20 mi. NNE of Toyohashi; raw silk, rice, wheat.

Ebibeyín, Sp. Guinea: see EBEBIYÍN.

Ebikon (ā'bēkôn), residential town (pop. 2,655), Lucerne canton, central Switzerland, 3 mi. NE of Lucerne.

Ebina (ābē'nä), town (pop. 9,552), Kanagawa prefecture, central Honshu, Japan, 13 mi. W of Yokohama; rice, mulberry trees.

Ebinayon, Sp. Guinea: see EVINAYONG.

Ebing (ā'bĭng), village (pop. 834), Upper Franconia, N Bavaria, Germany, on the Main and 8 mi. N of Bamberg; grain, hogs.

Ebingen (ā'bĭng-ŭn), town (pop. 14,028), S Württemberg, Germany, after 1945 in Württemberg-Hohenzollern, in Swabian Jura, 20 mi. S of Tübingen; rail junction; a center of Ger. knitwear industry. Other mfg.: velvet, precision instruments, needles. Has 16th-cent. town hall. Damaged in Second World War.

Ebi Nor (ĕbē' nôr') or **Ebi Nur** (nōōr'), Chinese *Ai-pi Hu* (ī'bē' hōō'), salt lake in NW Sinkiang, China, near USSR border, N of Tsingho; 40 mi. long, 15 mi. wide. Connected by Dzungarian Gates with lake Ala-Kul (Kazakh SSR).

Ebisu, Japan: see RYOTSU.

Ebnat (ĕbnä'), town (pop. 2,582), St. Gall canton, NE Switzerland, on Thur R. and 3 mi. SSE of Wattwil; cotton textiles, clothes, beer, flour, pastry; woodworking.

Ebnefluh (āb'nŭflōō), cliff (13,003 ft.) in Bernese Alps, S central Switzerland, 13 mi. S of Interlaken.

Eboli (ā'bôlē), town (pop. 12,057), Salerno prov., Campania, S Italy, 17 mi. ESE of Salerno; macaroni mfg. Has old castle. Badly damaged in Second World War, during fighting in the Salerno landings (1943).

Ebolowa (ĕbōlō'wä), town, ⊙ N'Tem region, SW central Fr. Cameroons, 70 mi. SSW of Yaoundé; 2°57'N 11°14'E. Center of cacao trade; communications point; sawmills. Its agr. school has large experimental plantations for elaeis palms, cacao, and African food staples (manioc, plantains, yams). R.C. and Protestant (founded 1885) missions.

Ebon (ĕ'bŏn), southernmost atoll (□ 2; pop. 784) of Ralik Chain, Majuro dist., Marshall Isls., W central Pacific; 4°39'N 168°42'E; c.25 mi. in circumference; formerly chief port of Marshall Isls. Produces copra; some phosphate deposits. Ebon isl. (5 mi. long) is largest of atoll's 22 islets; site of 1st mission station (1857) in group. Formerly Boston Isl.

Ebora, Portugal: see Évora, city.

Eboracum, England: see York.

Éboulements, Les (läzāboolmä'), village (pop. estimate 500), E Que., on the St. Lawrence and 7 mi. ENE of Baie St. Paul; dairying, lumbering; hydroelectric station.

Ebreichsdorf (ĕ'brīkhsdôrf), village (pop. 1,977), E Lower Austria, on Piesting R. and 8 mi. ESE of Baden; vineyards.

Ébreuil (äbrû'ē), village (pop. 911), Allier dept., central France, on the Sioule and 15 mi. N of Riom; fruit- and winegrowing. Has abbatial church with 15th-cent. frescoes.

Ebrié Lagoon (ĕbrēä'), along Ivory Coast, Fr. West Africa, flanked by narrow spit and linked with ocean through channel at Grand-Bassam (Comoé R. mouth); 70 mi. long. On its inland shore is Abidjan, served by its new port Port-Bouet. Navigable.

Ebro, Monte (môn'tĕ ā'brô), peak (5,581 ft.) in Ligurian Apennines, N central Italy, 9 mi. S of Varzi.

Ebro River (ē'brō, ā'brō), anc. *Iberus*, longest river entirely in Spain; generally considered 2d largest on Iberian Peninsula, though some estimates of its length (500–575 mi.) slightly exceed some estimates of the Tagus. Rising in the Cantabrian Mts. (Peña Labra) in N Spain, it flows SE in a broad valley bet. the Pyrenees and the Iberian Mts. to the Mediterranean. In its upper course it flows bet. provs. of Álava and Navarre (left) and Logroño (right), then enters the arid plains of Aragon (extensively irrigated by canals, especially in the *vega* around Saragossa) and meanders into Catalonia at Mequinenza, where it widens and turns SSE, branching off, below Tortosa, into a wide delta (about 150 sq. mi.) c.80 mi. SW of Barcelona. Besides Saragossa and Tortosa, cities on it include Miranda de Ebro, Logroño, Calahorra, Tudela, and Caspe. The largely canalized delta projects into the sea (Cape Tortosa). Chief port at its mouth is San Carlos de la Rápita. Though the Ebro is said to have once been navigable upstream to Logroño, ocean-going vessels can now only proceed to Tortosa c.20 mi. inland. Its drainage area of about 33,100 sq. mi. occupies roughly 1/6 of Spain. Among the chief tributaries are: left—Aragon, Gállego, and Segre rivers; right —Jalón, Huerva, Guadalope rivers. The Ebro system supplies about half of the nation's hydroelectric power and is an invaluable source of irrigation. In Roman times the river constituted the boundary bet. Hispania Citerior and Hispania Ulterior. It has always played a major part as strategic defense line. During the Sp. civil war, a decisive battle was fought here Aug.–Nov., 1938.

Ebstorf (ĕps'tôrf), village (pop. 4,404), in former Prussian prov. of Hanover, NW Germany, after 1945 in Lower Saxony, 15 mi. S of Lüneburg; woodworking, mfg. of chemicals.

Ebudae, Scotland: see Hebrides.

Eburru (ĕbōō'rōō), town, Rift Valley prov., W Kenya, on railroad and 18 mi. NW of Naivasha; wheat, coffee, corn. Thermal springs.

Ebusus, Balearic Isls.: see Iviza, island.

Ebute Metta (ăbōōtä mĕ'tä), residential town (pop. 18,398) in Lagos township, Nigeria colony, on Lagos Lagoon NW of Lagos; brickworks. Has R.C. mission; hq. of Nigerian railway. Iganmu rail siding (1.5 mi. SW) has a brewery.

Ecatepec Morelos (ākätāpĕk' mōrā'lōs), town (pop. 1,422), Mexico state, central Mexico, 12 mi. NNE of Mexico city; grain, maguey, livestock. Morelos, the revolutionary hero, was imprisoned and executed here. Sometimes San Cristóbal Ecatepec.

Ecatzingo (ākätsēng'gō), officially Ecatzingo de Hidalgo, town (pop. 1,518), Mexico state, central Mexico, 40 mi. SE of Mexico city; sugar cane, cereals, stock.

Écaussines-d'Enghien (ākōsēn'-dägyē'), town (pop. 6,896), Hainaut prov., S central Belgium, 4 mi. E of Soignies; granite quarrying. Contiguous with village of Écaussines-Lalaing (-lālē') (pop. 1,048).

Ecbatana, Iran: see Hamadan.

Ecclefechan (ĕ"kŭlfĕkh'ŭn, -kŭn), town in Hoddom parish (pop. 1,242), S Dumfries, Scotland, 5 mi. N of Annan; agr. market. Has grave of Thomas Carlyle, b. here. Hoddam Castle (15th cent.), now youth hostel, is 2 mi. SW.

Eccles (ĕ'kŭlz), municipal borough (1931 pop. 44,416; 1951 census 43,927), SE Lancashire, England, on Irwell R., on Manchester Ship Canal, and 5 mi. W of Manchester; cotton milling, textile printing; mfg. of chemicals for textile, leather, and plastics industries; pharmaceuticals, machinery. Site of Manchester airport. Has 14th-cent. church with 15th-cent. tower. Eccles cakes originated here.

Eccles, agr. village and parish (pop. 1,182), S Berwick, Scotland, 5 mi. WNW of Coldstream.

Eccles, mining village (pop. 1,885), Raleigh co., S W.Va., 4 mi. W of Beckley; coal area.

Ecclesall, SW suburb (pop. 19,293) of Sheffield, West Riding, S Yorkshire, England; steel milling.

Ecclesfield, town and parish (pop. 16,019), West Riding, S Yorkshire, England, 4 mi. N of Sheffield; coal-mining center. Has 14th–15th-cent. church, called Minster of the Moors. Parish includes Thorncliffe.

Eccleshall (ĕ'kŭl-shŭl, -shôl), town and parish (pop. 3,508), W central Stafford, England, on Sow R. and 7 mi. NW of Stafford; agr. market. Has castle (begun 1315), until 1867 residence of bishops of Lichfield; in 1459 it was the refuge of Margaret of Anjou.

Eccleshill (ĕ'kŭlz-hĭl). **1** Parish (pop. 305), central Lancashire, England. Includes paper-mfg. village of Lower Darwen, 2 mi. SSE of Blackburn. **2** Suburb, Yorkshire, England: see Bradford.

Ecclesmachan (ĕkŭlzmäkh'ŭn), agr. village and parish (pop. 1,793), N West Lothian, Scotland, 5 mi. ESE of Linlithgow.

Eccleston. **1** Residential town and parish (pop. 5,004), SW Lancashire, England, just W of St. Helens; site of sanitarium. **2** Village and parish (pop. 1,411), W central Lancashire, England, 4 mi. W of Chorley; dairying, agr. Just SSE is agr. village of Eccleston Moor.

Eceabat (ĕjĕ'äbät"), village (pop. 5,090), Canakkale prov., Turkey in Europe, on the Dardanelles opposite Canakkale; agr. center (wheat, oats, barley, beans). Site of anc. Sestos just NE. Sometimes spelled Edje-Abad. Formerly Maydos or Maidos.

Echagüe or **Gobernador Echagüe** (gōbĕrnädōr' ächä'gwā), town (pop. estimate 500), S central Entre Ríos prov., Argentina, on railroad and 50 mi. N of Gualeguay; wheat, flax, sunflowers, stock.

Echague (ächä'gwā), town (1939 pop. 2,827; 1948 municipality pop. 16,311), Isabela prov., N Luzon, Philippines, on Cagayan R. and 65 mi. S of Tuguegarao; agr. center (rice, corn).

Echallens (ā-shälä'), Ger. *Tscherlitz* (chĕr'lĭts), town (pop. 1,217), Vaud canton, W Switzerland, 8 mi. N of Lausanne.

Echaporã (ĭshäpōō'rã'), city (pop. 567), W São Paulo, Brazil, 22 mi. SW of Marília, in pioneer zone; cotton, coffee, and rice processing; sawmilling, distilling. Until 1944, Bela Vista.

Echarate (āchärä'tā), town (pop. 133), Cuzco dept., S central Peru, on Urubamba R. and 5 mi. NNE of Quillabamba, in agr. region (sugar cane, cacao, coca, coffee); sugar milling, alcohol distilling. Iron deposits. Sometimes Echarati.

Echarri-Aranaz (ächärē-äränäth'), town (pop. 1,327), Navarre prov., N Spain, 16 mi. S of Tolosa; cheese processing, flour- and sawmilling; cereals, potatoes, livestock. Iron, lead, silver deposits and marble quarries near by.

Echedoros River or **Ekhedhoros River** (both: ĕkhĕ'dhôrôs), anc. *Achedorus*, in Macedonia, Greece, rises in S outlier of the Belasica, flows 45 mi. S to the Gulf of Salonika 4 mi. W of Salonika. Also called Gallikos.

Échelles, Les (lāzāshĕl'), village (pop 825), Savoie dept., SE France, on the Guiers and 12 mi. SSW of Chambéry, on NW slope of the Grande Chartreuse; razor-strap mfg. Grottoes 2 mi. NE.

Echigawa (āchē'gäwŭ), town (pop. 7,320), Shiga prefecture, S Honshu, Japan, 8 mi. SSW of Hikone; rice.

Echigo (ā'chĭgō), former province in N Honshu, Japan; now Niigata prefecture.

Echizen (āchē'zän), former province in S Honshu, Japan; now part of Fukui prefecture.

Echizen Point, Jap. *Echizen-zaki*, in Fukui prefecture, S Honshu, Japan, in Sea of Japan; forms E side of entrance to Wakasa Bay; 35°59'N 135°57'E; lighthouse.

Echka, Yugoslavia: see Ecka.

Echmiadzin (ĕch"mēŭdzēn'), city (1926 pop. 8,436), central Armenian SSR, 12 mi. W of Erivan; highway center; distilling (wines, brandies); metalworks. Near-by walled Echmiadzin monastery (founded 6th cent. A.D.) is traditional seat of primate of Armenian church; site of cruciform 4th-cent. cathedral, mus., and library (former archives of Armenian MSS; now transferred to Erivan). City dates from 6th cent. B.C.; fortified (2d cent. A.D.) and renamed Vagarshapat; was ⊙ Armenia (2d–4th cent.). Modern city renamed Echmiadzin in 1945.

Echo. **1** Village (pop. 490), Yellow Medicine co., SW Minn., 15 mi. SSE of Granite Falls; dairy products, flour. **2** City (pop. 457), Umatilla co., N Oregon, 20 mi. WNW of Pendleton and on Umatilla R.; ships wool, wheat. **3** or **Echo City**, village (pop. c.225), Summit co., N Utah, NNW of Coalville and on Weber R., at Echo Dam; alt. 5,460 ft.

Echo, Lake (□ 12), central Tasmania, 55 mi. NW of Hobart, in mountainous region; 6.5 mi. long, 3 mi. wide.

Echo Dam, Utah: see Weber River.

Echo Lake. **1** In E Calif., small lake in the Sierra Nevada, 7 mi. S of L. Tahoe. Echo Lake village (resort) is near S shore. **2** In N.H.: see Franconia Notch.

Echols (ĕ'kŭlz), county (□ 425; pop. 2,494), S Ga., on Fla. line; ⊙ Statenville. Coastal plain agr. (corn, truck, tobacco, livestock) and forestry (lumber, naval stores) area drained by Alapaha and Suwannee rivers. Formed 1858.

Echt (ĕkht), village (pop. 5,024), Limburg prov., SE Netherlands, 8 mi. SW of Roermond; bricks, strawboard; vegetable growing.

Echt (ĕkt), village and parish (pop. 1,111), SE Aberdeen, Scotland, 12 mi. W of Aberdeen; granite quarrying. Just N is granite-quarrying village of Dunecht, with 19th-cent. mansion and observatory (57°9'N 2°25'W).

Echterdingen (ĕkh'tŭrdĭng"ŭn), village (pop. 3,895), N Württemberg, Germany, after 1945 in Württemberg-Baden, 6 mi. S of Stuttgart; site (after 1945) of Stuttgart airport.

Echternach (-näkh), town (pop. 3,002), E Luxembourg, on Sûre R. and 19 mi. NE of Luxembourg city, on Ger. border; farinaceous food products, plastics; market center for agr. (barley, pulse, beets) region; mineral springs. Noted for annual pilgrimage and dancing procession (dates from medieval times; held on Whit-Tuesday) commemorating cure of a disease in dist. Has 11th-cent. church of St. Willibrord, 16th-cent. town hall. In Roman times, popular vacation resort for Treves. Badly damaged in Second World War.

Echuca (ŭchōō'kŭ), municipality (pop. 4,490), N Victoria, Australia, on New South Wales border, opposite Moama, and 105 mi. N of Melbourne, at confluence of Campaspe and Murray rivers. Rail center for agr., livestock area; flour mill, vegetable cannery.

Echunga (ĕchŏŏng'gŭ), suburb (pop. 474) of Adelaide, SE South Australia, 17 mi. SE of Adelaide; dairy products, livestock.

Écija (ā'thēhä), anc. *Astigis*, city (pop. 25,165), Seville prov., SW Spain, in Andalusia, on navigable Genil R., on railroad and 50 mi. E of Seville; agr. and industrial center in one of the hottest regions of Spain. Known for its horse breeding. The fertile region produces cereals, fruit, beet sugar, olives, cotton, tobacco, vegetables, timber, livestock. There are sawmills, lime quarries, iron foundries. Mfg. of ceramics, textile goods, soap, vegetable oil, sweets, chocolate, meat products, cheese. Picturesque city, with notable bldgs. such as Santa Cruz church in Mudejar style, Chapel of Our Lady of the Valley, and 15th-cent. Gothic church. It was successively settled by Greeks, Celts, and Romans. Taken (1240) by Ferdinand III.

Ecilda Paullier (āsēl'dä pouyĕr'), town (pop. 1,000), San José dept., S Uruguay, 19 mi. W of San José, in agr. region (grain, sheep, cattle). Founded 1881. Sometimes Santa Ecilda.

Eck, Loch (lŏkh), lake (7 mi. long) in S Argyll, Scotland, on Cowal peninsula, bet. lochs Long (E) and Fyne (W).

Ecka or **Echka** (both: ĕch'kä), Serbo-Croatian *Ečka*, Hung. *Écska* (āch'kŏ), village, Vojvodina, N Serbia, Yugoslavia, on canalized Begej R. and 5 mi. SSE of Zrenjanin, in the Banat.

Eckartsberga (ĕ'kärtsbĕr"gä), town (pop. 2,838), in former Prussian Saxony prov., central Germany, after 1945 in Saxony-Anhalt, 7 mi. NNE of Apolda; flour milling; sugar beets, grain, potatoes, livestock. Has remains of castle founded 998 by margraves of Meissen.

Eckenhagen (ĕ"kŭnhä'gŭn), village (pop. 7,516), in former Prussian Rhine Prov., W Germany, after 1945 in North Rhine-Westphalia, 6 mi. SE of Gummersbach; forestry.

Eckernförde (ĕ"kŭrnfûr'dŭ), town (pop. 24,394), in Schleswig-Holstein, NW Germany, harbor on isthmus at end of Eckernförde Bay (Baltic inlet), 15 mi. NW of Kiel; popular seaside resort (with N suburb Borby); fishing fleet; boatbuilding; mfg. of machinery and motors. Food processing (smoked and canned fish, flour, spirits); woodworking. Glass and ceramics works. Has Gothic church. Founded in 12th cent. Here, in 1849, two Schleswig-Holstein coastal batteries defeated a Danish fleet.

Eckero (ĕ'kŭrû"), Swedish *Eckerö*, fishing village (commune pop. 1,060), Aland co., SW Finland, on S shore of Eckero, isl. (□ 42) of Aland group, just off Aland isl., 15 mi. NW of Mariehamn.

Eckert, Colo.: see Orchard City.

Eckertal (ĕ'kŭrtäl), rail station, in Brunswick, NW Germany, after 1945 Lower Saxony, at N foot of the upper Harz, 4 mi. ENE of Bad Harzburg, just W of Stapelburg; woodworking. Formerly also spelled Eckerthal.

Eckhart Mines, bituminous coal-mining village (pop. c.1,500), Allegany co., W Md., in the Alleghenies 8 mi. W of Cumberland.

Eckington, town and parish (pop. 12,016), NE Derby, England, 7 mi. SE of Sheffield; coal-mining center. Has 13th-cent. church with Norman parts. In parish (SE) is steel-milling town of Renishaw, site of abandoned colliery.

Eckley. **1** Town (pop. 295), Yuma co., NE Colo., 14 mi. W of Wray. **2** Village (1940 pop. 893), Luzerne co., E central Pa., 6 mi. ENE of Hazleton, in anthracite region.

Eckman. **1** Village (pop. 55), Bottineau co., N N.Dak., 30 mi. WSW of Bottineau. **2** Mining village (pop. 1,574), McDowell co., S W.Va., 7 mi. ESE of Welch; semibituminous coal.

Eckmühl, Germany: see EGGMÜHL.

Eckville, agr. village (pop. 195), S central Alta., on Medicine R. and 24 mi. W of Red Deer.

Eclectic, town (pop. 715), Elmore co., E central Ala., near Martin L., 22 mi. NE of Montgomery.

Eclipse Sound, N Baffin Isl., SE Franklin Dist., Northwest Territories, arm (60 mi. long, 40 mi. wide) of Baffin Bay, S of Bylot Isl.; 72°30'N 80°W.

Écluse, France: see COLLONGES.

Écluse, L', Netherlands: see SLUIS.

Ecnomus, Sicily: see LICATA.

Écommoy (ākômwä'), village (pop. 1,924), Sarthe dept., W France, 12 mi. SSE of Le Mans; grain and livestock market; apple orchards.

Economy, village (pop. estimate 200), N central N.S., on Cobequid Bay, at mouth of Economy R., 30 mi. W of Truro; dairying, mixed farming.

Economy. **1** Town (pop. 285), Wayne co., E Ind., on a fork of Whitewater R. and 15 mi. NW of Richmond, in agr. area. **2** Former settlement, Beaver co., Pa.: see AMBRIDGE.

Ecorse (ēkôrs'), city (pop. 17,948), Wayne co., SE Mich., 7 mi. SW of downtown Detroit and on Detroit R.; industrial products include steel, chemicals, auto parts, tools, luggage. Settled c.1815; inc. as village 1903, as city 1941.

Écos (ākō'), village (pop. 385), Eure dept., NW France, 11 mi. SE of Les Andelys; dairying.

Écouché (ākōōshā'), village (pop. 1,077), Orne dept., NW France, on the Orne and 5 mi. WSW of Argentan; limekilns.

Écouen (ākwä'), town (pop. 2,077), Seine-et-Oise dept., N central France, outermost N suburb of Paris, 11 mi. from Notre Dame Cathedral; its 16th-cent. Renaissance château now houses school for children of members of Legion of Honor. Old fort.

Écouis (ākwē'), village (pop. 454), Eure dept., NW France, 5 mi. N of Les Andelys; lumbering. Its 14th-cent. church contains fine sculptures and woodwork.

Écouves, Forest of, France: see ALENÇON.

Ecrehou Islands (ākrĕhōō'), uninhabited islets, Channel Isls., NE of Jersey in the Passage de la Déroute. France and Britain have joint fishery rights here under 1839 treaty.

Écrins, Barre des, France: see BARRE DES ÉCRINS.

Ecru (ĕ'krōō), town (pop. 494), Pontotoc co., N Miss., 8 mi. N of Pontotoc, in agr. area.

Ecsed Marsh (ā'chĕd), Hung. *Ecsedi láp* (ĕ'chĕdē läp), Rum. *Ecsedul* (ā'chĕdōōl), NE Hungary and W Rumania, large swampy region (31 mi. long, 19 mi. wide) bet. Szamos and Kraszna rivers. Peat cutting.

Ecseg (ĕ'chĕg), town (pop. 1,842), Nograd-Hont co., N Hungary, on tributary of Zagyva R. and 19 mi. SE of Balassagyarmat; potatoes, honey, hogs.

Ecska, Yugoslavia: see ECKA.

Ector, county (□ 907; pop. 42,102), W Texas; ⊙ Odessa. Here S Llano Estacado meets Edwards Plateau; alt. c.2,500-3,000 ft.; sand dunes in SW. A leading petroleum-producing co. of Texas, with great fields in Odessa region. Oil refining, mfg. of carbon black, oil-field supplies. Cattle ranching, little agr. (grain sorghums, some truck). Large potash deposits. S of Odessa is huge meteor crater. Co. formed 1887.

Ector, town (pop. 430), Fannin co., NE Texas, 5 mi. W of Bonham, in agr. area.

Ecuador (ĕ'kwŭdôr) [Sp.,=equator], republic (□ 108,478; 1950 census pop. 3,076,933), NW South America, on the Pacific; ⊙ QUITO. Borders N on Colombia, E and S on Peru. Includes the GALÁPAGOS ISLANDS, c.650 mi. off the coast. The country is c.350 mi. N–S, crossed in N by the equator. Like all Andean countries, climate and vegetation depend chiefly on altitude, and Ecuador includes steaming jungles and perpetual snowfields. The 2 large lowland regions, along the coast and in the upper Amazon basin, are separated by the Andes, whose majestic summits are grouped in a double file, rising in the inactive volcano CHIMBORAZO to 20,577 ft. There are more than 20 active volcanoes, among them SANGAY (17,454 ft.) and the famous COTOPAXI (19,344 ft.), considered the highest active volcano of the globe. Other well-known peaks are ANTISANA, CAYAMBE, TUNGURAHUA, and PICHINCHA, on whose slopes the decisive battle of Ecuador's independence was fought (May 24, 1822). The 2 parallel N–S cordilleras (Oriental and Occidental) enclose a narrow, longitudinal tableland (20–30 mi. wide), which is broken by transverse ridges into 10 well-drained intermontane basins, having an alt. of 7,500–9,000 ft. In this healthful region live more than 60% of the country's pop. Yearly temp. range is less than 1°. Quito has a mean of 54.6°F. and enjoys a pleasant spring all year round. But frequent earthquakes, the most recent in 1949 (which levelled Ambato), cause great havoc. All kinds of minerals occur, but only silver (from Cerro PILSHUM), some gold, and copper have achieved economic importance. Sulphur abounds in Chimborazo area and in the Galápagos. The plateaus produce subsistence crops—wheat, barley, forage, potatoes, grapes, vegetables, and fruit. Cotton, sugar cane, and coffee in lower sections. Beyond 10,500 ft., in the *páramos*, grazing of cattle and sheep (also llamas) predominates. The AMBATO region is noted for its choice fruit (apples, pears, peaches, strawberries, citrus). CUENCA, the country's 3d largest city, is hq. for the mfg. of Panama or Jipijapa hats (made from toquilla straw), a leading export article also made at JIPIJAPA, MONTECRISTI, and TABACUNDO. In the upland cities, such as IBARRA, LATACUNGA, RIOBAMBA, and LOJA, is concentrated the principal industry, textile milling. All these cities are linked by Pan American Highway with Quito, Ecuador's political and religious center, 2d most populous city of the republic, seat of a univ. (founded 1787). BAÑOS, a favorite spa within a stock-raising and fruitgrowing zone, serves as gateway to the vast transandean lowland, the so-called ORIENTE. This much-disputed region, uninhabited apart from scattered Indian tribes (the Jivaro), is potentially the richest of the republic. Its jungles and savannas are traversed by long navigable rivers, notably the NAPO RIVER and PASTAZA RIVER, tributary to the Amazon. Petroleum is drilled near MERA, which also has a refinery. But Ecuador's main oil resources are in the Pacific lowlands on SANTA ELENA PENINSULA. Petroleum, refined at SALINAS (also a beach resort) and LA LIBERTAD, is shipped to other Latin American countries. Petroleum, gold, and cyanide precipitates are the leading mineral exports. Santa Elena also has extensive saltworks, besides gold, platinum, and sulphur deposits. The humid maritime lowland (c.100 mi. wide) is, however, primarily agr., its fertile soil yielding the chief commercial crops for foreign trade, cacao and rice. Coffee is grown in the lower Andean slopes. Next to these rank the rich forest products, especially tagua nuts (vegetable ivory), the light balsa wood (on which Ecuador has a virtual monopoly), hardwood, rubber, kapok, annatto seed, toquilla straw, and mangrove bark (for tannin). The most productive areas are along the GUAYAS RIVER, one of the largest systems of the South American W coast, in reality a network of navigable rivers such as DAULE RIVER, VINCES RIVER, and BABAHOYO RIVER, along whose banks also thrive bananas, sugar cane, cotton, mangoes, pineapples. Climate is here entirely tropical with a mean temp. of 78.3°F. at Guayaquil. Rainy period Dec.–April. The lowland near S border marks the transition to the arid coastal strip of Peru and Chile, influenced by the cold Peru or Humboldt Current. All trade converges on Guayaquil, largest city of the republic and its chief transoceanic port (45 mi. inland from the Gulf of Guayaquil), a major processing and communications center, handling the bulk of all exports and imports (foodstuffs, chemicals, pharmaceuticals, textiles, vehicles, machinery, paper, beverages). Secondary ports are MANTA, ESMERALDAS, Salinas, PUERTO BOLÍVAR. From DURÁN (Eloy Alfaro) opposite Guayaquil across the Guayas (linked by ferries) begins the Andean railroad, climbing dizzily through deep gorges and tunnels above 10,000 ft. to Quito and the other upland centers. Estimates about the country's racial composition vary. Negroes living exclusively in the coastal belt are listed as comprising from 1% to 12 or 15% (including mulattoes). The majority, c.60%, are pure Indian, the rest being white and mestizo. Present-day Ecuador had been a center of the Quito Indian civilization before being conquered by the Incas in about mid-15th cent. At the time of the Sp. invasion (1533) under Francisco Pizarro's subordinate Benalcázar, it was ruled by Atahualpa. The region was established (1563) as the presidency of Quito, at various times subject to the viceroyalty of Peru or New Granada. Following an abortive independence movement in 1809, it remained under Sp. control until liberated by Sucre at Pichincha (1822) and joined by Bolívar to Greater Colombia (*Gran Colombia*), of which Colombia, Venezuela, and Panama formed a part. That union was dissolved, and Ecuador became (1830) an independent republic under a constitution promulgated by its 1st president, Juan José Flores. Ecuador fought (1832) an unsuccessful war with Colombia, but in the same year acquired the Galápagos Isls. Its most notable 19th-cent. presidents were Gabriel García Moreno and, particularly, Eloy Alfaro, who during his 2d term completed the Guayaquil-Quito RR. But a small white land-owning class remained in control of the govt., split into personal cliques and party factions struggling for dominance; and the rivalry bet. coast and highlands, i.e., Guayaquil and Quito, is still virulent. There have been long boundary disputes with Colombia and Peru. With the latter an agreement over Oriente was reached (1942) and signed (1944). The U.S. acquired (1942) naval and air bases in the Galápagos Isls. and on the mainland. The establishment of a Gran Colombia merchant fleet (jointly owned by Colombia, Ecuador, and Venezuela) and the signing (1948) of the Quito Charter recommending closer economic ties, were moves toward material and political stabilization. For further information see separate articles on cities, towns, physical features, and the following provs.: AZUAY, BOLÍVAR, CAÑAR, CARCHI, CHIMBORAZO, COTOPAXI, EL ORO, ESMERALDAS, GUAYAS, IMBABURA, LOJA, LOS RÍOS, MANABÍ, NAPO-PASTAZA, PICHINCHA, SANTIAGO-ZAMORA, TUNGURAHUA.

Ecuandureo (ākwändōōrā'ō), town (pop. 3,372), Michoacán, central Mexico, on central plateau, 14 mi. SW of La Piedad; grain, fruit, livestock.

Écueillé (ākûyā'), village (pop. 1,210), Indre dept., France, 25 mi. NW of Châteauroux; brewing.

Écuisses (ākwēs'), village (pop. 1,485), Saône-et-Loire dept., E central France, near the Canal du Centre, 6 mi. SE of Le Creusot; brick and tile works.

Écury-sur-Coole (ākürē'-sür-kōl'), agr. village (pop. 269), Marne dept., N France, 5 mi. SSW of Châlons-sur-Marne; sheep.

Ed [Arabic,=the], for Arabic names beginning thus: see under following part of the name.

Ed (ād), village (pop. 585), Alvsborg co., SW Sweden, at S end of L. Stora Le, 30 mi. WSW of Amal; tourist resort.

Eda, Japan: see ETA.

Eda (ā'dä''), village (pop. 356), Varmland co., W Sweden, on Norwegian border, 2 mi. NNW of Charlottenberg, 20 mi. NW of Arvika; glassworks. Norwegian-Swedish peace monument, erected 1914.

Edale, village and parish (pop. 422), NW Derby, England, 9 mi. NNE of Buxton; cotton milling.

Edam (ē'dăm), village (pop. 192), W Sask., on Turtlelake R. and 35 mi. NW of North Battleford; wheat, mixed farming.

Edam (ē'dŭm, -dăm, Du. ādäm'), town (pop. 3,741; commune pop. 10,895), North Holland prov., NW Netherlands, on the Ijsselmeer and 12 mi. NNE of Amsterdam; noted for its cheese. Has fine 14th-cent. church. Fishing port until construction of Ijsselmeer Dam.

Edappadi, India: see IDAPPADI.

Eday (ē'dā), island (□ 12.2, including FARA isl.; pop. 430) of the Orkneys, Scotland, bet. Sanday and Westray; 7 mi. long, up to 3 mi. wide; rises to 334 ft. Noted for peat beds, supplying surrounding isls. with fuel. Just off NE coast is isl. of Calf of Eday, 2 mi. long, 1 mi. wide.

Edberg, village (pop. 163), S central Alta., 17 mi. S of Camrose; coal mining.

Edcouch (ĕd'kouch'), town (pop. 2,925), Hidalgo co., extreme S Texas, in the lower Rio Grande valley, 12 mi. E of Edinburg; a trade, shipping center in irrigated citrus, truck, cotton area. Inc. 1928.

Edd (ĕd), village, Assab div., SE Eritrea, fishing port on Red Sea, 75 mi. NW of Assab. Has mosque. Hot springs near by.

Ed Damer, Anglo-Egyptian Sudan: see DAMER, ED.

Edderton, agr. village and parish (pop. 485), NE Ross and Cromarty, Scotland, on Dornoch Firth, 6 mi. WSW of Dornoch.

Eddesse (ĕ'dĕ''sŭ), village (pop. 1,045), in former Prussian prov. of Hanover, NW Germany, after 1945 in Lower Saxony, 6 mi. N of Peine; oil wells.

Eddington, agr. town (pop. 664), Penobscot co., S Maine, on the Penobscot just above Brewer.

Eddiville, village (pop. 10), Kootenai co., N Idaho.

Eddleston, agr. village and parish (pop. 452), N Peebles, Scotland, 4 mi. N of Peebles. Site of 17th-cent. Darnhall mansion, now a hotel.

Eddrachillis (ĕdrŭkĭ'lĭs), parish (pop. 967), W Sutherland, Scotland, on Eddrachillis Bay.

Ed Dueim, Anglo-Egyptian Sudan: see DUEIM.

Eddy. **1** County (□ 4,163; pop. 40,640), SE N.Mex.; ⊙ Carlsbad. Irrigated agr. and livestock region; watered by Pecos R.; borders on Texas. Cotton, alfalfa, dairy products. Potash mines near Carlsbad. Carlsbad Caverns Natl. Park, Guadalupe Mts., and part of Lincoln Natl. Forest in SW. Formed 1889. **2** County (□ 643; pop. 5,372), central N.Dak.; ⊙ New Rockford. Agr. area drained by Sheyenne and James rivers. Dairy products, wheat, poultry, livestock. Formed 1885.

Eddy, Mount, Calif.: see KLAMATH MOUNTAINS.

Eddystone, borough (pop. 3,014), Delaware co., SE Pa., on Delaware R. just above Chester; railroad shops; steel products. Inc. 1889.

Eddystone Point (ĕ'dĭstŭn), NE Tasmania, in Banks Strait, SE of Cape Portland; 40°59'S 148°18'E; lighthouse.

Eddystone Rocks (ĕ'dĭstŭn), SE Cornwall, England, in the Channel, 14 mi. SSW of Plymouth; dangerous reef. Lighthouse (alt. 133 ft.; 50°11'N 4°16'W) is visible for 17 mi.

Eddyville. **1** Village (pop. 106), Pope co., extreme S Ill., 17 mi. S of Harrisburg, in Ill. Ozarks. **2** Town (pop. 941), on Mahaska-Wapello co. line, S central Iowa, on Des Moines R. and 15 mi. NW of Ottumwa; feed milling. Bituminous-coal mines, limestone quarries near by. **3** City (pop. 1,840), ⊙ Lyon co., W Ky., on Cumberland R. and 29 mi. E of Paducah, in agr. area (burley tobacco, corn) with limestone quarries, hardwood timber; mfg. harness, shirts, brooms; sawmilling. State penitentiary here. Near by are Kentucky Dam, Kentucky Woodlands Wildlife Refuge (largest game preserve in Ky.), and ruins of iron furnace where William Kelly discovered his method (later known as Bessemer process) of making steel. **4** Village (pop. 188), Dawson co., S central Nebr., 15 mi. NNE of Lexington and on Wood R.

Ede (ā'dü), town (pop. 15,608), Gelderland prov., central Netherlands, 11 mi. WNW of Arnhem; rail junction; egg market; metal industry, artificial-silk mfg.; dairying.

Ede (ā'dā), town (pop. 52,392), Oyo prov., Western Provinces, SW Nigeria, on railroad and 45 mi. NE of Ibadan; road center; cotton weaving, cacao, palm-oil and palm-kernel processing; cotton. Yoruba pop.

Edéa (ĕdā'ä), town, ⊙ Sanaga-Maritime region, SW Fr. Cameroons, on left bank of Sanaga R., on railroad, and 100 mi. W of Yaoundé, 35 mi. SE of Douala; 3°49'N 10°13'E. Commercial center, head of steamboat navigation on lower Sanaga, and road communications point; palm-oil milling, hardwood lumbering, stone quarrying. Cacao plantations in vicinity. Large rubber plantations and rubber processing plant at near-by Dizanqué. Has hosp., R.C. and Protestant missions, meteorological station, hydroelectric power plant.

Edeghem or **Edegem** (both: ā'dü-khŭm), residential town (pop. 7,969), Antwerp prov., N Belgium, 5 mi. SSE of Antwerp. Has 15th-16th-cent. church and Terlinden Castle, built 1768.

Edeleny (ĕ'dĕlänyü), Hung. *Edelény*, town (pop. 3,280), Borsod-Gömör co., NE Hungary, on Bodva R. and 13 mi. N of Miskolc; lignite mines near by. Has 13th-cent. church.

Edemissen (ā'dümĭ"sŭn), village (pop., including Ölheim, 2,097), in former Prussian prov. of Hanover, NW Germany, after 1945 in Lower Saxony, 4.5 mi. NNE of Peine. Oil wells at near-by Ölheim (ûl'hīm).

Eden, town and port (pop. 993), SE New South Wales, Australia, on Twofold Bay, 230 mi. SSW of Sydney; exports dairy products. Summer resort.

Eden, New Zealand: see AUCKLAND, city.

Eden. 1 Town (pop. 621), St. Clair co., NE central Ala., 28 mi. ENE of Birmingham. **2** Village (pop. 456), Jerome co., S Idaho, 18 mi. SE of Jerome; potatoes, onions, beets; dairy. **3** Village (pop. 306), Yazoo co., W central Miss., 11 mi. NNE of Yazoo City, near Yazoo R. **4** Village (pop. 1,394), Erie co., W N.Y., 18 mi. S of Buffalo; aircraft parts, canned foods. **5** Town (pop. 149), Marshall co., NE S.Dak., 20 mi. SE of Britton. **6** Village (pop. 1,993), Concho co., W central Texas, on Edwards Plateau c.40 mi. ESE of San Angelo; trade, shipping center in ranch, farm area (sheep, goats, poultry, cotton, grain). **7** Town (pop. 496), Lamoille co., N Vt., in Green Mts., 24 mi. SW of Newport; asbestos. L. Eden (2 mi. long) here. **8** Village (pop. 234), Fond du Lac co., E Wis., 6 mi. SE of Fond du Lac, in farm area; canned vegetables; lime. **9** Village (pop. c.200), Sweetwater co., SW central Wyo., near Sandy Creek, 33 mi. NNW of Rock Springs; alt. 6,590 ft. On fertile, irrigated plateau extensively cultivated by state agr. experiment station; clover, alfalfa.

Edenborn, village (pop. 1,315), Fayette co., SW Pa., 9 mi. WSW of Uniontown.

Edenbridge (ēd'–), town and parish (pop. 3,222), W Kent, England, on Eden R., a small tributary of Medway R., and 10 mi. WNW of Tunbridge Wells; agr. market. Site of 15th-cent. Hever Castle. Church dates mostly from 13th cent.

Edenburg, town (pop. 2,392), SW Orange Free State, U. of So. Afr., 45 mi. SSW of Bloemfontein; alt. 4,514 ft.; grain, stock.

Edenburg, Pa.: see KNOX.

Edendale, residential town (pop. 14,043), central Natal, U. of So. Afr., 5 mi. SW of Pietermaritzburg; site of mission station.

Edenderry (ē"dündĕ'rē), Gaelic *Éadan Doire*, town (pop. 2,996), E Co. Offaly, Ireland, on the Grand Canal and 14 mi. NNW of Kildare; agr. market (barley, potatoes; cattle). Has old castle; Boyne R. rises in castle grounds.

Edenfield, England: see BURY.

Edenhall, village and parish (pop. 216), E Cumberland, England, on Eden R. and 3 mi. ENE of Penrith; castle, sheep, agr. Has church begun in Norman times. Site of former mansion of Eden Hall which contained glass cup named The Luck of Eden Hall, property of the Musgrave family whose luck, according to legend, depended on the cup remaining unbroken. The cup, now in South Kensington Mus. in London, is the subject of Uhland's poem *Das Glück von Edenhall*, translated by Longfellow.

Edenkoben (ā'dün-kō"bün), village (pop. 5,433), Rhenish Palatinate, W Germany, on E slope of Hardt Mts., 6 mi. N of Landau; mfg. of machinery, chemicals, furniture; damask weaving, woodworking. Wine growing. Resort (sulphur spring; grape cure). Near by (W) is 19th-cent. château Ludwigshöhe.

Eden Park, borough (pop. 1,531), Allegheny co., SW Pa., on Youghiogheny R., just SE of McKeesport. Inc. 1944.

Eden River. 1 In Surrey and Kent, England: see MEDWAY RIVER. **2** In Westmorland and Cumberland, England, rises on E border of Westmorland 10 mi. SE of Appleby, flows 65 mi. NW, bet. the Pennines and the Cumbrians, past Appleby, Lazonby, and Carlisle, to Solway Firth 7 mi. NW of Carlisle.

Eden River, Fifeshire, Scotland, rises in Lomond Hills, flows 30 mi. NE, past Cupar, Dairsie, and Guard Bridge, to North Sea 2 mi. NW of St. Andrews.

Edenton (ē'düntŭn), town (pop. 4,468), ⊙ Chowan co., NE N.C., on inlet of Albemarle Sound, 27 mi. SW of Elizabeth City, near Chowan R. mouth (bridged). Largest peanut market in state; trade center for agr. (peanuts, cotton) area; cotton-yarn mfg., lumber milling, shad and herring fishing. Has St. Paul's Church (1736), old court house (1767), other historic bldgs. U.S. fish hatchery near by. Settled c.1658, inc. 1722.

Edenvale, residential town (pop. 5,567), S Transvaal, U. of So. Afr., on Witwatersrand, 5 mi. NNW of Germiston.

Eden Valley, village (pop. 792), Meeker and Stearns counties, S central Minn., 14 mi. N of Litchfield, in lake region; resort; dairy products.

Edenville, Iowa: see RHODES.

Edenwald (ē'dünwôld), SE N.Y., a residential section of N Bronx borough of New York city.

Eder, river, Mongolia: see IDER RIVER.

Ederkopf (ā'dürkôpf), mountain (2,218 ft.), W Germany, in the Rothaargebirge, 10 mi. NE of Siegen. Eder, Lahn, and Sieg rivers rise here.

Eder River (ā'dür), W Germany, rises on the Ederkopf, flows 110 mi. generally E to the Fulda near Grifte. Dam at Hemfurth (hydroelectric plant), forming one of Germany's largest reservoirs, regulates (with Diemel dam) water supply of Weser R. and feeds Ems-Weser Canal. Eder dam was damaged by aerial attacks in May, 1943.

Edesheim (ā'dūs-hīm), village (pop. 2,422), Rhenish Palatinate, W Germany, on E slope of Hardt Mts., 4 mi. N of Landau; wine; also wheat, tobacco.

Edessa or **Edhessa** (both: ĕdĕ'sü, Gr. ĕ'dhĕsü), Macedonian *Vodena*, city (pop. 12,994), ⊙ Pella nome, Macedonia, Greece, 50 mi. WNW of Salonika, on railroad to Phlorina; trade center at W edge of Giannitsa lowland, at foot of Voros-Vermion mtn. region; mfg. of cotton textiles, carpets, tobacco products. Trade in wheat, wine, cherries. Bishopric. The anc. Aegae, it was the earliest seat of the Macedonian kings (ruins of royal tombs).

Edessa, Turkey: see URFA, city.

Edewecht (ā'düvĕkht), village (commune pop. 8,609), in Oldenburg, NW Germany, after 1945 in Lower Saxony, 9 mi. W of Oldenburg city; meat processing (ham, sausage).

Edfa, Egypt: see IDFA.

Edfina, Egypt: see IDFINA.

Edfu, Egypt: see IDFU.

Edgar, county (□ 628; pop. 23,407), E Ill., on Ind. line (E); ⊙ Paris. Agr. (corn, wheat, broomcorn, soybeans, livestock, poultry). Meat packing; mfg. of shoes, brooms, farm machinery, metal products, streetcars, buses. Bituminous-coal mining. Drained by small tributaries of the Wabash. Formed 1823.

Edgar. 1 City (pop. 724), Clay co., S Nebr., 25 mi. SE of Hastings; grain. Rail junction. **2** Village (pop. 705), Marathon co., central Wis., 16 mi. W of Wausau; cheese, processed meat, wood products.

Edgard (ĕd'gärd), village (pop. c.300), ⊙ St. John the Baptist parish, SE La., on the Mississippi and 28 mi. WNW of New Orleans, in sugar-cane area; sugar refining.

Edgartown, town (pop. 1,508), ⊙ Dukes co., SE Mass., on SE Martha's Vineyard and 27 mi. SE of New Bedford; main center (village pop. 1,264) of the isl.; summer resort, fishing community; good harbor. Steamer connections with Woods Hole. Boatbuilding, canning; state forest. Includes CHAPPAQUIDDICK ISLAND. Old homes, built when town was whaling port, survive. Settled 1642, inc. 1671.

Edgbaston (ĕj'bŭstŭn), SW industrial suburb (pop. 35,539) of Birmingham, NW Warwick, England.

Edgecomb (ĕj'kŭm), town (pop. 447), Lincoln co., S Maine, 10 mi. NE of Bath; includes North Edgecomb village. Fort Edgecomb, wooden blockhouse built 1808–09, is near.

Edgecombe (ĕj'kŭm), county (□ 511; pop. 51,634), E central N.C.; ⊙ Tarboro. On coastal plain; bounded N by Fishing Creek; crossed by Tar R. Half forested (pine, gum), partly swampy; agr. (tobacco, peanuts, cotton, corn, soybeans); sawmilling. Tobacco markets, industries at Rocky Mount and Tarboro. Formed 1735.

Edgecumbe, Cape, SE Alaska, SW tip of Kruzof Isl., on Gulf of Alaska, at mouth of Sitka Sound, 20 mi. W across Sitka Sound from Sitka; 57°N 135°51'W.

Edgecumbe, Mount, extinct volcano (3,271 ft.), SE Alaska, on S Kruzof Isl., 16 mi. W of Sitka; 57°3'N 135°45'W.

Edgecumbe, Mount (ĕj'kŭm), promontory, SE Cornwall, England, on Plymouth Sound, 2 mi. WSW of Plymouth.

Edgecumbe Bay, inlet of Coral Sea, E Queensland, Australia, bet. Cape Gloucester (SE) and Cape Edgecumbe (NW); 11 mi. E-W, 10 mi. N-S. NW inlet (Port Denison) is site of Bowen.

Edgefield, county (□ 481; pop. 16,591), W S.C.; ⊙ Edgefield. Bounded SW by Savannah R.; includes part of Sumter Natl. Forest. Sparsely settled agr. region (cotton, asparagus, peaches), timber). Some mfg. (textiles, lumber). Formed 1785.

Edgefield, town (pop. 2,518), ⊙ Edgefield co., W S.C., 20 mi. NNW of Aiken, in agr. area; textiles, lumber products; cotton gins. Settled in 18th cent.

Edgehill, hilly ridge in S Warwick, England, 8 mi. NW of Banbury. Site of 1st battle (1642) bet. Charles I and Parliamentary forces. The large figure of a horse cut into side of the hill gives adjoining valley name of Vale of Red Horse.

Edge Hill, Pa.: see CHELTENHAM.

Edge Island, Nor. *Edgeøya* (ĕd'yü-ûyä), island (□ 1,942) in the Spitsbergen group, in Barents Sea of Arctic Ocean, off SE West Spitsbergen, S of Barents Isl.; 77°15'–78°14'N 20°50'–24°50'E. It is 70 mi. long (N-S), 25–65 mi. wide; rises to 2,349 ft. near S tip. Large ice field extends along SE coast; interior of isl. uncharted.

Edgeley, city (pop. 943), La Moure co., SE central N.Dak., 20 mi. W of La Moure; grain, dairy products.

Edgely, village (pop. 1,368), Bucks co., SE Pa., on Delaware R., just above Bristol.

Edgemere (ĕj'mēr). **1** Suburban industrial village (1940 pop. 5,698), Baltimore co., central Md., on Back R. and 10 mi. ESE of downtown Baltimore; makes wooden boxes, welding rods. **2** A section of S Queens borough of New York city, SE N.Y., near base of Rockaway Peninsula.

Edgemont. 1 Town (pop. 89), Cleburne co., N central Ark., 33 mi. WSW of Batesville. **2** Summer resort, Washington co., W Md., on South Mtn., 10 mi. ENE of Hagerstown. **3** City (pop. 1,158), Fall River co., SW S.Dak., 20 mi. SW of Hot Springs, just S of Black Hills, and on Cheyenne R., near Wyo. line. Trading point for agr. area; sandstone quarries; dairy produce, livestock, poultry, grain. Sulphur hot-springs sanitarium is here. Black Hills Ordnance Depot is 8 mi. S. at Igloo.

Edge Moor, village, New Castle co., N Del., just NE of Wilmington; mfg. (pigments, chemicals); railroad yards.

Edgemoor, town (pop. 258), Chester co., N S.C., 10 mi. S of Rock Hill. Post Office name formerly Edgmoor.

Edgerton, village (pop. 273), E Alta., near Sask. border, 18 mi. ESE of Wainwright; mixed farming, grain.

Edgerton (ĕ'jürtŭn). **1** City (pop. 266), Johnson co., E Kansas, 29 mi. SW of Kansas City, Kansas; dairying, farming. **2** Village (pop. 961), Pipestone co., SW Minn., on Rock R. and 13 mi. SE of Pipestone; dairy products. **3** City (pop. 408), Platte co., W Mo., on Little Platte R. and 28 mi. N of Kansas City. **4** Village (pop. 1,246), Williams co., extreme NW Ohio, on St. Joseph R. and 10 mi. W of Bryan, near Ind. line; baskets, lumber, canned foods. **5** City (pop. 3,507), Rock co., S Wis., 23 mi. SE of Madison, near L. Koshkonong (resort), in tobacco-growing area; mfg. (trailer trucks, shoes, pharmaceuticals); tobacco warehouses. Settled 1836, laid out 1854, inc. 1883. **6** Town (pop. 203), Natrona co., central Wyo., on Salt Creek and 40 mi. N of Casper, in oil field.

Edgerton Highway, S Alaska, extends 39 mi. NW from Chitina to Richardson Highway 60 mi. NE of Valdez. Serves gold- and copper-mining region.

Edgewater. 1 Village (pop. 1,984), Jefferson co., N central Ala., near Birmingham. **2** W suburb (pop. 2,580) of Denver, Jefferson co., N central Colo.; alt. 5,353 ft.; within Denver metropolitan area. Inc. 1904 as town. **3** Resort town (pop. 837), Volusia co., NE Fla., near the Atlantic, on Hillsborough R. (lagoon) and 17 mi. SSE of Daytona Beach. **4** Borough (pop. 3,952), Bergen co., NE N.J., on Hudson R. just S of Fort Lee; mfg. (chemicals, food products, boats, automobile parts, metal products, linseed oil); petroleum, sugar refining; shad fishing. Inc. 1899.

Edgewater Park, resort, Harrison co., SE Miss., on Mississippi Sound, c.5 mi. W of Biloxi.

Edgewood, village (pop. estimate 200), S B.C., on Lower Arrow L. (Columbia R.), 40 mi. NW of Nelson; silver, lead, zinc mining.

Edgewood. 1 Town (pop. 217), Orange co., central Fla., suburb of Orlando. **2** Village (pop. 515), Effingham co., SE central Ill., 15 mi. SSW of Effingham, in agr. area. **3** Residential town (pop. 796), Madison co., E central Ind., just W of Anderson. **4** Town (pop. 696), on Clayton-Delaware co. line, NE Iowa, 27 mi. E of Oelwein; mfg. (dairy products, packed poultry, feed). Limestone quarry near by. Bixby State Park is N. **5** Village, Harford co., NE Md., near Bush R., 19 mi. ENE of Baltimore. Near-by Army Chemical Center (adjacent to Aberdeen Proving Ground) on Chesapeake Bay is a chemical warfare station which grew up around Edgewood Arsenal, established 1917. **6** Borough (pop. 5,292), Allegheny co., SW Pa., just E of Pittsburgh. Inc. 1888. **7** Village, Northumberland co., E central Pa. **8** Town (pop. 834), Van Zandt co., NE Texas, 24 mi. E of Terrell, in grain, truck-farming area; makes and ships pickles.

Edgeworth, residential borough (pop. 1,466), Allegheny co., W Pa., 13 mi. NW of Pittsburgh and on Ohio R. First municipality in Pa. to adopt borough-manager govt. Inc. 1904.

Edgeworthstown, Gaelic *Meathus Truim,* town (pop. 490), E Co. Longford, Ireland, 8 mi. ESE of Longford; agr. market (dairying; potatoes).
Edgmoor, S.C.: see EDGEMOOR.
Edgware, England: see HENDON.
Edh [Arabic,=the], for Arabic names beginning thus: see under following part of the name.
Edhessa, Greece: see EDESSA.
Edie Creek, small stream of NE New Guinea, 40 mi. SW of Salamaua, where gold was discovered 1926.
Edina (ēdī'nů), village, Grand Bassa co., S Liberia, on Atlantic Ocean, 4 mi. NNW of Buchanan; palm oil and kernels, cassava, rice.
Edina (ēdī'nů, ĭ–). **1** Village (pop. 9,744), SW suburb of Minneapolis, Hennepin co., E Minn. **2** City (pop. 1,607), ⊙ Knox co., NE Mo., on South Fabius R. and 20 mi. E of Kirksville; agr., lumber. Inc. 1857.
Edinboro (ĕ'dĭn–), resort borough (pop. 1,567), Erie co., NW Pa., 17 mi. S of Erie; lumber. State teachers col. here.
Edinburg, Latvia: see RIGAS JURMALA.
Edinburg (ĕ'dĭnbûrg). **1** Village (pop. 921), Christian co., central Ill., 15 mi. SE of Springfield; grain, soybeans, livestock. **2** Town (pop. 3,283), on Johnson-Bartholomew co. line, S central Ind., 31 mi. SSE of Indianapolis and on East Fork of White R., in grain, livestock, and dairying area. Mfg. of wood products, canned foods. U.S. Camp Atterbury is just W. Settled 1821. **3** Agr. town (pop. 36), Penobscot co., S central Maine, on the Penobscot and 14 mi. above Old Town; lumbering. **4** Village (pop. 343), Walsh co., NE N.Dak., 22 mi. WNW of Grafton. **5** City (pop. 12,383), ⊙ Hidalgo co., extreme S Texas, in lower Rio Grande valley, c.50 mi. WNW of Brownsville; trade, packing, processing center in rich irrigated citrus, truck, cotton area; cotton gins; cottonseed-oil mills; canneries. Oil, natural-gas wells in area. Seat of a jr. col. Inc. 1908 as Chapin; renamed 1911. **6** Town (pop. 533), Shenandoah co., NW Va., near North Fork of Shenandoah R., 5 mi. SW of Woodstock, in agr. area.
Edinburgh (ĕ'dĭnbůrů), city and burgh (1931 pop. 439,010; 1951 census 466,770), ⊙ Scotland and co. of Midlothian, on the Firth of Forth, 42 mi. E of Glasgow; 55°57'N 3°12'W; a co. of itself. In literature it is often called "Dunedin," Gaelic form of the name; its popular nickname is "Auld Reekie." City is built on a series of ridges, with Castle Rock (445 ft.) at W edge of the old town and Calton Hill on the E. It is primarily a cultural, academic, and administrative center, of great historical, architectural, and artistic importance. Among its famous art collections are the Royal Scottish Academy, Natl. Gall. of Scotland, and Royal Scottish Mus.; the Natl. Library contains many valuable manuscripts. There are numerous parks and public gardens, including noted Princes Street Gardens, paralleling Princes Street, city's renowned main thoroughfare. On Calton Hill are City Observatory, the Natl. Monument, and 102-ft.-high Nelson Monument. In S of city are bldgs. of Univ. of Edinburgh, founded 1583 under James VI and including famous col. of medicine, as well as those of law, divinity, art, science, agr., and music. Edinburgh Castle is on Castle Rock, in anc. times site of the *Castrum Puellarum,* retreat of the daughters of Pictish kings. Edwin of Northumbria established a military post here c.617, around which a settlement grew. In 1174 castle was surrendered to Henry II by William the Lion under Treaty of Falaise. Edinburgh became a burgh in 1329 under Robert the Bruce and in 1437 superseded Perth as ⊙ of Scotland. Town walls were begun 1450. In 1544 the city was sacked by the English. In 1573 the castle was held for Mary Queen of Scots and was surrendered after being much damaged. In 1650 Cromwell captured the castle; in Napoleonic wars it held Fr. prisoners of war. The town declined in importance with departure of James VI (who was b. here) to England in 1603. Parliament House was completed in 1640; Scottish Parliament met here until the Act of Union (1707); it now houses supreme courts of Scotland. Holyrood Palace, chief royal residence in Scotland, was begun c.1500 by James IV; was residence of Mary Queen of Scots 1561–67, and was scene of her interview with Knox, her marriage to Bothwell, and of murder of Rizzio. Prince Charles Edward held court here in 1745 and for some years after Fr. Revolution. Near by are ruins of Holyrood Abbey, founded 1128 by David I; extant are remains of the structure begun 1501 by James IV. Royal vault contains tombs of David II, James II, James V, Darnley, and Rizzio. James II and Charles I were crowned here. Other notable features of Edinburgh are: Norman chapel of St. Margaret, on Castle Rock; 12th-cent. St. Giles's church; and 19th-cent. Cathedral of St. Mary. In 18th and 19th cent. Edinburgh's literary and academic fame grew; among its notable men were David Hume, Adam Smith, Francis Jeffrey, John Wilson, Sir Walter Scott, Allan Ramsay, Tobias Smollett, and James Hogg. The *Edinburgh Review,* founded 1802, added to city's literary reputation. Since Second World War it has been scene of annual music festival. Industries include tanning, whisky distilling, mfg. of machinery, machine tools, paper, food products, chemicals. Tourist trade is important. Burgh includes the port of LEITH and the industrial suburbs of Colinton, Liberton, and Portobello (also a popular resort).
Edinburghshire, Scotland: see MIDLOTHIAN.
Edineti, Moldavian SSR: see YEDINTSY.
Edingen, Belgium: see ENGHIEN.
Edingen (ā'dĭng-ůn), village (pop. 4,441), N Baden, Germany, after 1945 in Württemberg-Baden, on the canalized Neckar and 6 mi. ESE of Mannheim; tobacco.
Edington (ĕ'dĭngtůn), agr. village and parish (pop. 714), W central Wiltshire, England, 4 mi. ENE of Westbury. Has 12th-cent. church. Scene of final defeat (9th cent.) of Danes by Alfred.
Edirne, Turkey: see ADRIANOPLE.
Edison. 1 City (pop. 1,247), Calhoun co., SW Ga., 32 mi. W of Albany; mfg. (fertilizer, lumber); peanut shelling. **2** Village (pop. 302), Furnas co., S Nebr., 45 mi. E of McCook and on Republican R.; dairying; livestock, grain. **3** Village (pop. 471), Morrow co., central Ohio, 13 mi. E of Marion, in agr. area.
Edisto Beach, S.C.: see EDISTO ISLAND.
Edisto Island (ĕ'dĭstō), Charleston co., S S.C., one of Sea Isls., bet. mouths of North and South Edisto rivers, N of St. Helena Sound, 22 mi. SW of Charleston; c.10 mi. long, 10 mi. wide. Highway connects with Little Edisto Isl. (just N) and mainland. Here are Edisto Island village, Edisto Beach (resort), and Edisto Beach State Park (c.1,250 acres). Ante-bellum plantation area; truck farming, fishing.
Edisto River, S S.C., formed 15 mi. S of Orangeburg by junction of its North and South forks; flows 90 mi. SE and S to the Atlantic, dividing near coast into 2 channels (called North Edisto R. and South Edisto R.) which embrace Edisto Isl. South Fork (c.65 mi. long) rises SE of Johnston; North Fork rises near Batesburg. Navigable. Drains □ 6,150.
Edithburgh, village and port (pop. 497), S South Australia, on SE coast of Yorke Peninsula, 50 mi. WSW of Adelaide across Gulf St. Vincent; salt; wheat, wool.
Edith Cavell, Mount (kă'vůl) (11,033 ft.), W Alta., near B.C. border, in Rocky Mts., in Jasper Natl. Park, 15 mi. S of Jasper; 52°40'N 118°3'W.
Edith Ronne Land (rō'nů), Antarctica, extends from base of Palmer Peninsula SE to Coats Land, bet. 40° and 60°W. Discovered 1948 by expedition (U.S.) under Finn Ronne.
Ediz Hook, Wash.: see PORT ANGELES.
Edje-Abad, Turkey: see ECEABAT.
Edku, Egypt: see IDKU.
Edlabad, India: see ADILABAD, town.
Edlington, town and parish (pop. 7,422), West Riding, S Yorkshire, England, near Don R. 4 mi. SW of Doncaster; coal-mining center; brickworks.
Edmeston (ĕd'můstůn), village (1940 pop. 573), Otsego co., central N.Y., 28 mi. S of Utica, in farming and dairying area; makes cheese.
Edmond. 1 City (pop. 110), Norton co., NW Kansas, on North Fork Solomon R. and 14 mi. SSE of Norton; corn, hogs. **2** City (pop. 6,086), Oklahoma co., central Okla., 12 mi. N of Oklahoma City; trade center for agr. area, with large oil fields near by. Produces petroleum products, flour, feed, wood products, concrete blocks. Seat of Central State Col. A memorial to Wiley Post is near by. Settled 1889.
Edmonds, city (pop. 2,057), Snohomish co., NW Wash., 15 mi. N of Seattle and on Puget Sound; lumber, dairy products, poultry. Settled 1866.
Edmondsley (–lē), town and parish (pop. 2,389), N central Durham, England, 5 mi. NNW of Durham; coal mining.
Edmondson or **Edmonson** (both: ĕd'můnsůn), town (pop. 283), Crittenden co., E Ark., 15 mi. W of Memphis (Tenn.).
Edmonson, county (□ 304; pop. 9,376), central Ky.; ⊙ Brownsville. Drained by Green and Nolin rivers and Bear Creek. Agr. (livestock, dairy products, grain, poultry, burley tobacco); leading Ky. co. in asphalt mining. Resorts; includes most of MAMMOTH CAVE NATIONAL PARK. Formed 1825.
Edmonson, town, Ark.: see EDMONDSON.
Edmonston (ĕd'můnztůn), town (pop. 1,190), Prince Georges co., central Md., NE of Washington.
Edmonton (ĕd'můntůn), city (pop. 113,116), ⊙ Alberta, in central part of prov., on both banks of North Saskatchewan R.; 53°33'N 113°30'W; alt. 2,182 ft. Industrial and trading center for agr. region (wheat, stock, mixed farming, dairying), with large grain elevators, lumber and flour mills. Near by are coal mines, oil and gas wells. Important fur-trade center; city's industries include oil refining, brewing, woodworking, meat packing, tanning, brewing; mfg. of butter, cereal foods, furniture, machinery, sheet-metal products, chemicals, soap, paint, clothing, knitted goods. Edmonton is S terminus of the Alaska Highway, distributing and transportation center for Peace and Athabaska rivers region (N) and for the N Mackenzie dist., and outfitting point for northern expeditions. Major airport. Site of Univ. of Alberta (1906) and of R.C. seminary. Notable features include Legislative Bldg. (1912), on bluff overlooking the river and on site of Edmonton House, built by the Hudson's Bay Co.; McDougall Memorial Church (1871), 1st bldg. erected outside Fort Edmonton palisades; and many modern commercial bldgs. There are several museums. Fort Edmonton was built 1794 by the Hudson's Bay Co. on North Saskatchewan R., 25 mi. below site of present city; destroyed 1807 by Blood Indians, it was rebuilt 1819 on present site and became important trading post. Reached 1891 by Canadian Pacific RR, and chosen ⊙ Alberta in 1905. It was united with city of Strathcona, on S bank of river, in 1912. Development was rapid: 1901 pop. 2,626; 1911 pop. 24,900; 1931 pop. 79,197.
Edmonton, residential municipal borough (1931 pop. 77,658; 1951 census 104,244), Middlesex, England, 8 mi. N of London. It was residence of Keats, of Cowper (who made Bell Inn famous by his "Diverting History of John Gilpin"), and of Charles Lamb, who died here. The public library was built as memorial to Keats and Lamb.
Edmonton, town (pop. 519), ⊙ Metcalfe co., S Ky., 17 mi. E of Glasgow, in agr. and timber area; corn, burley tobacco, wheat; lumber, staves.
Edmore. 1 Village (pop. 971), Montcalm co., central Mich., 18 mi. SW of Mt. Pleasant, in dairy, poultry, and grain area; oil and gas wells and refineries; grain mills. **2** City (pop. 458), Ramsey co., NE N.Dak., 27 mi. NE of Devils Lake; livestock, dairy products, poultry, grain.
Edmunds, county (□ 1,153; pop. 7,275), N central S.Dak.; ⊙ Ipswich. Agr. area drained in E by intermittent creeks. Dairy produce, livestock, poultry, grain. Formed 1873.
Edmunds, village, Washington co., E Maine, on Dennys Bay and 10 mi. WSW of Eastport; township (pop. 288) includes part of Moosehorn Natl. Wild Life Refuge.
Edmundson, town (pop. 621), St. Louis co., E Mo.
Edmundston (ĕd'můnztůn), town (pop. 7,096), ⊙ Madawaska co., NW N.B., on St. John R. (Maine border) at mouth of Madawaska R., opposite Madawaska, Maine, and 65 mi. ESE of Rivière du Loup; pulp-milling center. Pulp is transported to Madawaska by pipeline. Fishing and hunting base. Has R.C. cathedral. Pop. is largely French-speaking. Settled by Acadians c.1785, town, originally called Petit Sault or Little Falls, was renamed Edmundston 1848; inc. 1905.
Edna. 1 City (pop. 422), Labette co., SE Kansas, 15 mi. E of Coffeyville; dairying, general agr. **2** Town (pop. 3,855), ⊙ Jackson co., S Texas, 35 mi. NE of Victoria; trade, shipping point in oil, cattle, cotton area; cotton gins. Inc. 1926.
Edna Bay, village (pop. 41), SE Alaska, on SE shore of Kosciusko Isl., 38 mi. NNW of Craig.
Ednam, Scotland: see KELSO.
Edo, Japan: see TOKYO.
Edö, Norway: see EDOY.
Edolo (ā'dôlô), town (pop. 1,873), Brescia prov., Lombardy, N Italy, in Val Camonica, on Oglio R. and 22 mi. E of Sondrio. Rail terminus; resort (alt. 2,264 ft.) and winter-sports center at W foot of Monte Adamello. Ironworks (agr. machinery; iron supplied from near-by mines), furniture and macaroni factories; livestock market.
Edom (ē'dŏm), **Idumaea,** or **Idumea** (both: īdūmē'-ů), mountainous country of Palestine, called also Mt. Seir, given to Esau and his descendants. It extended along E border of the Araba valley from the Dead Sea to Elath on Gulf of Aqaba.
Edon (ē'důn), village (pop. 645), Williams co., extreme NW Ohio, 13 mi. WNW of Bryan; machine tools, poultry equipment, food products.
Edosaki (ādō'sä'kē), town (pop. 4,448), Ibaraki prefecture, central Honshu, Japan, on SW arm of lagoon Katsumi-ga-ura, 8 mi. NE of Ryugasaki; rice. Has agr. school.
Edough (ĕdōōg'), coastal range of the Tell Atlas, in Constantine dept., NE Algeria, extending 30 mi. along the Mediterranean from Bône (E) to the Cap de Fer (W). Rises to 3,307 ft. Receives heavy rainfall (up to 70 in. annually); covered by cork-oak forests. Resort of Bugeaud near E end.
Edoy (äd'ûü), Nor. *Edøy,* village, More og Romsdal co., W Norway, on Edoy isl. (□ 3; pop. 152) just S of Smola isl., 20 mi. NE of Kristiansund; fishing, fish canning; sheep raising. Formerly spelled Edö. Edoy canton (pop. 1,170) includes near-by isls. and part of Smola.
Edremit (ĕdrĕmĭt'), anc. *Adramyttium* (ădrůmĭ'-tēům) or *Adramyti* (ădrůmĭ'tē, –mē'tē), town (pop. 12,847), Balikesir prov., NW Turkey, on railroad near Gulf of Edremit, 45 mi. W of Balikesir; cereals, olives; soap factories; iron deposits. Sometimes spelled Edremid. At Adramyttium Paul's ship was built.
Edremit, Gulf of, NW Turkey, inlet of Aegean Sea, 50 mi. W of Balikesir; 20 mi. wide, 27 mi. long. Opens on the straits of Muselim Remma and Mytilene Channel, which enclose the Greek island of Lesbos.
Edrenos River, Turkey: see KIRMASTI RIVER.
Edri (ĕ'drē), town (pop. 486), central Fezzan, Libya, 80 mi. WNW of Sebha, in an oasis at edge of the Hammada el Hamra region of the Sahara; caravan center; dates, cereals, vegetables; sheep, camels, poultry. Has ruined fort.

Edrom (ĕd'drŭm), agr. village and parish (pop. 1,015), E central Berwick, Scotland, 2 mi. ENE of Duns.
Edsbyn (āts'bün"), village (pop. 2,419), Gavleborg co., E Sweden, on Voxna R. 18 mi. W of Bollnas; wood- and metalworking, sawmilling.
Edsel Ford Ranges (ĕd'sŭl), Antarctica, in NW Marie Byrd Land, E of Sulzberger Bay; centers in 77°S 145°W. Discovered 1929 by R. E. Byrd, U.S. explorer.
Edsin Gol, China: see ETSIN GOL.
Edson (ĕd'sŭn), town (pop. 1,571), W Alta., near McLeod R., 120 mi. W of Edmonton, in coal-mining region; also lumbering, cereal-food mfg., farms.
Edsvalla (āts'vä"lä), village (pop. 909), Varmland co., W Sweden, on Nor R. and 9 mi. WNW of Karlstad; pulp mills, sulphite works.
Eduardo Castex (ĕdwär'dō kästĕks') or **Castex**, town (1947 pop. 3,717), ⊙ Conhelo dept. (pop. 15,667), NE La Pampa prov., Argentina, on railroad and 50 mi. N of Santa Rosa; agr. center (grain, alfalfa, wine, livestock); wine making, sawmilling.
Edwa, El, El 'Idwa, or **Al-'Idwah** (all: ĕl ĭd'wŭ), village (pop. 5,677), Faiyum prov., Upper Egypt, 6 mi. NE of Faiyum; cotton ginning; cotton, cereals, sugar cane, fruits.
Edward, town (pop. 155), Beaufort co., E N.C., 18 mi. SE of Washington.
Edward, Lake, or **Edward Nyanza** (nīăn'zŭ, nē–, nyän'zä), lake (□ 830), E central Africa, on Belgian Congo–Uganda border W of L. Victoria and N of L. Kivu in W Great Rift Valley; c.50 mi. long, 30 mi. wide; alt. c.3,000 ft., depth c.365 ft. Receives Ruindi and Rutshuru rivers (S), drains L. George through Kazinga channel (NE), empties NNW through Semliki R. into L. Albert. Abundant in fish, it is noted as bird-gathering grounds and for its large flocks of hippopotami. Entire Belgian Congo shore is within Albert Natl. Park and has been evacuated because of the spread of sleeping sickness. No navigation on lake. Discovered 1889 by Henry Stanley. Formerly called L. Albert Edward or Albert Edward Nyanza.
Edward VII Peninsula, Antarctica, extends NW from Marie Byrd Land into Ross Sea, W of Sulzberger Bay; 77°45'S 156°W. Discovered 1902 by Robert F. Scott, Br. explorer, who named it King Edward VII Land.
Edward VIII Bay, inlet (15 naut. mi. long, 12 naut. mi. wide) of Antarctica, on Indian Ocean, bet. Kemp Coast and Enderby Land; 66°50'S 57°20'E. Discovered 1936 by Br. expedition, which called it King Edward VIII Gulf.
Edwardesabad, W Pakistan: see BANNU, town.
Edwards. 1 County (□ 225; pop. 9,056), SE Ill.; ⊙ Albion. Agr. (livestock, corn, wheat, fruit, poultry; dairy products). Mfg. (clothing, textiles, flour, brick, buttons, wood products). Fisheries. Drained by Little Wabash R. and Bonpas Creek (co.'s E boundary). Formed 1814. **2** County (□ 614; pop. 5,936), S central Kansas; ⊙ Kinsley. Prairie area, drained by Arkansas R. Wheat, livestock. Formed 1874. **3** County (□ 2,075; pop. 2,908), SW Texas; ⊙ Rocksprings. On Edwards Plateau; alt. c.2,000–2,500 ft.; drained by South Llano and Nueces rivers. A leading Texas co. in angora-goat raising; also sheep, beef cattle, horses. Some oil; deposits of silver, iron, sulphur, coal, kaolin. Hunting, fishing, fur trapping. Formed 1858.
Edwards. 1 Town (pop. 1,002), Hinds co., W Miss., 16 mi. E of Vicksburg, in agr., timber, and cattle-raising area. Southern Christian Inst. is here. The Civil War battle of Champion's Hill (May, 1863) in Grant's Vicksburg campaign was fought near by. **2** Village (pop. 584), St. Lawrence co., N N.Y., on Oswegatchie R. and 28 mi. SSE of Ogdensburg, in dairying area.
Edwards, Camp, Mass.: see FALMOUTH.
Edwards Air Force Base, Calif.: see MUROC.
Edwardsburg, village (pop. 616), Cass co., SW Mich., 10 mi. ESE of Niles, near Ind. line, in farm and lake area.
Edwards Plateau, SW Texas, SE extension of the Great Plains, lying to S and SE of the South Plains (S Llano Estacado), and bounded on S by the Rio Grande valley, SE by the Balcones Escarpment, overlooking the coastal plain; drained by Colorado, Concho, San Saba, Llano, Nueces, Guadalupe rivers. Max. alt. c.2,500 ft. (in Edwards co.). W extension, across canyon of Pecos R., is the Stockton Plateau country (alt. c.2,000–4,000 ft.) of W Texas, bounded S by the Rio Grande and W by Davis Mts. Much of it semi-arid, plateau is largely devoted to stock raising (cattle, sheep, goats) and is chief mohair-producing area of state. In region just above escarpment on SE, streams have carved the scenic terrain of the hill country, known for its many springs and its wild-game hunting.
Edwardsport, village (1940 pop. 697), Knox co., SW Ind., on West Fork of White R. and 17 mi. ENE of Vincennes, in agr., oil, natural-gas, and bituminous-coal area; power plant here.
Edwards River, NW Ill., rises in SE Henry co., flows c.75 mi. WNW and generally W, through Mercer co., to the Mississippi just S of New Boston.
Edwardstone, England: see GROTON.
Edwardsville. 1 Town (pop. 179), Cleburne co., E Ala., 18 mi. E of Anniston, in cotton and corn area. Talladega Natl. Forest near by. **2** City (pop. 8,776), ⊙ Madison co., SW Ill., on Cahokia Creek and 17 mi. NE of East St. Louis, within St. Louis metropolitan area; bituminous-coal-mining center; mfg. (metal products, brick, creosoted products, clothing, candy). Co. historical mus. is here. Settled 1800, platted 1813, inc. 1837. **3** City (pop. 274), Wyandotte co., NE Kansas, on Kansas R. and 10 mi. WSW of Kansas City, Kansas; general agr. **4** Borough (pop. 6,686), Luzerne co., NE central Pa., on Susquehanna R. opposite Wilkes-Barre; anthracite. Inc. 1884.
Edwight, coal-mining village (1940 pop. 1,294), Raleigh co., S W.Va., 20 mi. WNW of Beckley.
Edwinstone, town and parish (pop. 2,818), central Nottingham, England, on Maun R. and 7 mi. NE of Mansfield; coal mining. Town is in Sherwood Forest and is associated with a number of legends. Has church dating from 14th cent.
Edzell (ĕd'zŭl), town and parish (pop. 891), NE Angus, Scotland, on North Esk R. and 6 mi. N of Brechin; agr. market. Just W are remains of Edzell Castle.
Eeckeren, Belgium: see EKEREN.
Eek, Eskimo village (pop. 141), W Alaska, at head of Kuskokwim Bay, 45 mi. SSW of Bethel; trapping and fishing. Eek school for natives 6 mi. E.
Eeklo (āk'lō), town (pop. 16,953), East Flanders prov., NW Belgium, 12 mi. NW of Ghent; textile center (wool combing and carding; linen and carpet weaving). Formerly spelled Eecloo or Eekloo.
Eelde (āl'dŭ), village (pop. 1,632), Drenthe prov., N Netherlands, 6 mi. S of Groningen; agr., cattle raising. Site of Groningen airport.
Eel River. 1 In NW Calif., rises in N Mendocino co., flows SE and W to L. Pillsbury, then W and NW, past Scotia, to the Pacific 13 mi. SSW of Eureka; c.200 mi. long. Upper course formerly called South Eel R. Near Dyerville, receives South Fork (c.90 mi. long), which flows N, generally parallel to main stream, through redwood groves. **2** In W central and SW Ind., rises in Boone co., flows generally SW, passing near Greencastle, to SW central Clay co., then SE to West Fork of White R. at Worthington; 110 mi. long. **3** In N central Ind., rises in S Noble co., flows c.100 mi. SW to the Wabash at Logansport.
Eems Canal (āms) or **Groot-Scheepvaart Canal** (grōt'-skhāp'värt), N Netherlands; extends 17 mi. WSW-ENE bet. Groningen and Ems (Eems) R. estuary at Delfzijl; joined by Van Starkenborgh Canal 1.5 mi. ENE of Groningen; 14.8 ft. deep; built 1866–76.
Eems River, Netherlands: see EMS RIVER.
Eemst, Netherlands: see EMST.
Eerken, Belgium: see ARCHENNES.
Eersterust (âr'stûrŭst"), residential town (pop. 5,049), S central Transvaal, U. of So. Afr., 8 mi. ENE of Pretoria.
Eesti: see ESTONIA.
Efate (ĕfä'tē), Fr. *Vaté* (vätā'), volcanic island (pop. 1,940), most important isl. of NEW HEBRIDES, SW Pacific, 155 mi. SE of Espiritu Santo; 17°40'S 168°23'E; 50 mi. long, 20 mi. wide. Seat of Vila, ⊙ Anglo-Fr. condominium. Contains group's finest harbors: Havannah (developed during Second World War) in NW and Vila in Mele Bay in SW. Produces copra, coffee, cacao, sandalwood. Formerly Sandwich Isl.
Eferding (ĕ'fûrdĭng), town (pop. 3,685), N central Upper Austria, near the Danube, 12 mi. W of Linz; rail junction; leather goods. Gothic church. Ruins of medieval Schaumburg castle near by.
Effie, resort village (pop. 202), Itasca co., N Minn., c.40 mi. N of Grand Rapids, near Big Fork R.
Effigy Mounds National Monument (1,000 acres; established 1949), NE Iowa, atop bluffs overlooking Mississippi R. just N of McGregor. Prehistoric Indian mounds 2–4 ft. high, up to 200 ft. in diameter; many of them are in shapes of birds and animals, and are believed to be burial mounds. Artifacts (including bone, copper, and stone tools) have been found.
Effingham (ĕ'fĭng-ŭm), residential town and parish (pop. 1,144), central Surrey, England, 4 mi. NW of Dorking. Church is partly 13th cent.
Effingham (ĕ'fĭnghăm"). **1** County (□ 480; pop. 9,133), E Ga.; ⊙ Springfield. Bounded E by Savannah R. (forms S.C. line here) and W by Ogeechee R. Coastal plain agr. (truck, fruit, livestock, poultry) and timber area. Formed 1777. **2** County (□ 483; pop. 21,675), SE central Ill.; ⊙ Effingham. Agr. area (corn, wheat, oats, poultry, livestock). Mfg. (dairy and other food products, lumber and wood products, road machinery, clothing). Oil field; petroleum production and refining. Drained by Little Wabash R. Formed 1831.
Effingham. 1 City (pop. 6,892), ⊙ Effingham co., SE central Ill., 26 mi. SSW of Mattoon; trade, railroad, and mfg. center (food products, lumber, road machinery, shoe lasts and heels, golf clubs, gloves, church fixtures). Situated in agr. area (dairy products; corn, wheat, poultry, livestock). Small L. Kanaga (resort) is just W. Inc. 1861. **2** City (pop. 525), Atchison co., extreme NE Kansas, 15 mi. W of Atchison, in corn belt; corn, livestock. **3** Town (pop. 341), Carroll co., E N.H., 30 mi. NE of Laconia, in resort area. Effingham Falls village, in the town, is on Ossipee L., at outlet of Ossipee R.
Efimovskaya, Russian SFSR: see YEFIMOVSKAYA.
Efon Alaiye (ĕ'fō älī'yĕ), town, Ondo prov., Western Provinces, S Nigeria, 25 mi. ESE of Oshogbo; cacao-producing center; palm oil and kernels, timber, rubber, cotton.
Eforia (ĕfô'rēä), town (1948 pop. 428), Constanta prov., SE Rumania, on Black Sea, and on Techirgiol lake, on railroad and 6 mi. S of Constanta; bathing and health resort with mineral springs and mud baths. Former summer residence of Carol II.
Efrem-, in Rus. names: see YEFREM-.
Efsus, Turkey: see AFSIN.
Egadi Islands (ā'gädē), **Aegadian Islands**, or **Aegadean Islands** (both: ēgā'dēŭn), anc. *Aegates* (□ 15; pop. 6,196), in Mediterranean Sea, 6–23 mi. off W Sicily, in Trapani prov. Principal isls.: FAVIGNANA, MARETTIMO, LEVANZO. Major tunny fisheries of Sicily. Site of Roman naval victory (241 B.C.) over Carthaginians which ended First Punic War.
Egan, city (pop. 347), Moody co., E S.Dak., 5 mi. SSW of Flandreau and on Big Sioux R. Large school is here.
Egaña (āgä'nyä), village (pop. 350), Soriano dept., SW Uruguay, in the Cuchilla del Bizcocho, on railroad and 33 mi. SE of Mercedes; wheat, corn, barley, linseed; sheep and cattle raising.
Egan Range (6–10,000 ft.), E Nev., in White Pine co., just W of Ely; extends c.100 mi. S from Cherry Creek Mts. Copper mines near Ely.
Eganville (ē'gŭnvĭl), village (pop. 1,088), SE Ont., on Bonnechère R. and 20 mi. S of Pembroke; pulp and lumber milling, dairying, lime production.
Ega River (ā'gä), in Álava and Navarre provs., N Spain, rises in E spurs of the Cantabrian Mts. SE of Vitoria, flows E to Estella, then S to the Ebro near San Adrián; 75 mi. long.
Egavik (ēgä'vĭk), Eskimo village (1939 pop. 23), W Alaska, on E shore of Norton Sound, 13 mi. N of Unalakleet; supply point; trapping.
Egba, Nigeria: see ABEOKUTA, province.
Egbe (ĕgbĕ'), town (pop. 6,444), Kabba prov., Northern Provinces, SW central Nigeria, 45 mi. NW of Kabba; tin-mining center; columbite and tantalite also mined; shea-nut processing; cotton, durra, cassava, yams.
Egbunda (ĕgbōōn'dä), village, Eastern Prov., NE Belgian Congo, on railroad and 155 mi. E of Buta; coffee plantations. Cotton gins and R.C. mission at Viadana, 7 mi. NW.
Egea de los Caballeros, Spain: see EJEA DE LOS CABALLEROS.
Egede and Rothe Fjord (ā'gŭdhŭ, rō'tŭ), Dan. *Egede og Rothes Fjord*, inlet (65 mi. long, 5–10 mi. wide) of Denmark Strait, SE Greenland; 66°N 37°40'W. Extends NNE to edge of inland icecap. Also called Sermilik (sĕr'mēlēk). Angmagssalik Isl. is on E side of mouth.
Ege Denizi, Greece: see AEGEAN SEA.
Egedesminde (ā'gŭdhŭsmĭ"nŭ), Eskimo *Ausiait*, town (pop. 670) and district (pop. 2,413), W Greenland, on small isl. on SW side of mouth of Disko Bay, near Davis Strait; 68°37'N 52°50'W; fishing port, hunting base; seal-oil refinery. Meteorological and radio station. Founded 1763, named for Hans Egede, missionary.
Egegik (ĭ'gĕgĭk, ēgĭg'ĭk), village (pop. 116), SW Alaska on W shore of Alaska Peninsula, at mouth of King Salmon R., 40 mi. SSW of Naknek; salmon fishing and canning.
Ege-Khaya (ĕgyĕ'-khī'ŭ), town (1942 pop. over 500), N Yakut Autonomous SSR, Russian SFSR, N of Arctic Circle, 40 mi. E of Verkhoyansk; tin and tungsten mining.
Egeland (ĕg'lŭnd), village (pop. 248), Towner co., N N.Dak., 10 mi. NNE of Cando.
Egeln (ā'gŭln), town (pop. 7,650), in former Prussian Saxony prov., central Germany, after 1945 in Saxony-Anhalt, near the Bode, 15 mi. SW of Magdeburg; lignite and potash mining; sugar refining.
Egelsbach (ā'gŭlsbäkh), village (pop. 4,376), S Hesse, W Germany, in former Starkenburg prov., 7 mi. N of Darmstadt; tanning.
Egendy-Bulak, Kazakh SSR: see YEGENDY-BULAK.
Eger, town, Czechoslovakia: see CHEB.
Eger (ĕ'gĕr), Ger. *Erlau* (ĕr'lou), city (pop. 32,482), ⊙ Heves co., N Hungary, on Eger R. and 24 mi. SW of Miskolc; market center, horse-breeding station; tobacco, flour, soap, candles. Known for its red Erlauer wine. Archbishopric. Its many churches have earned it the name "Rome of Hungary." Cathedral dates from early 1830s. Old fort, now in ruins, withstood heavy siege from Turks, 1552–53. Turkish minaret is memento of sultan's rule, 1596–1687.
Egerdir, Turkey: see EGRIDIR.
Egeres, Rumania: see AGHIRESU.
Egerisee, Switzerland: see AEGERISEE.
Egernsund (ā'gŭrnsōōn), town (pop. 1,280), Aabenraa-Sonderborg amt, S Jutland, Denmark, 7 mi. W of Sonderborg; clay products.
Eger River (ā'gŭr), Czech *Ohře* (ôr'zhĕ), in Bavaria, Germany, and W Bohemia, Czechoslovakia; rises

in the Fichtelgebirge in Bavaria; flows generally E c.25 mi., into Czechoslovakia, past Cheb, generally NE, past Sokolov, Carlsbad, and Klasterec nad Ohri, E, past Zatec and Louny, and N, past Terezin, to Elbe R. opposite Litomerice; total length, 159 mi.

Eger River (ĕ'gĕr), NE Hungary, rises in Bükk Mts., flows 50 mi. S, past Eger, to the Tisza 9 mi. SW of Tiszafüred.

Egersund (ā'gůrsōōn), town (pop. 3,419), Rogaland co., SW Norway, port on North Sea, protected by isl. of Eigeroy, on railroad and 37 mi. SSE of Stavanger; fishing and lobstering center; mfg. of furniture, china, pottery. The center of the Dalane region, it has Dalane folk mus. Mentioned in 13th-cent. *Edda*. Formerly spelled Ekersund and Eigersund.

Egestorf (ā'gůstôrf), village (pop. 3,897), in former Prussian prov. of Hanover, W Germany, after 1945 in Lower Saxony, at N foot of the Deister, 11 mi. WSW of Hanover; salt mining.

Egg (ĕk), town (pop. 2,333), Vorarlberg, W Austria, on river Bregenzer Ache and 9 mi. ESE of Bregenz; brewery; embroidery, straw hats. Gothic church.

Egg, village (pop. 903), Lower Bavaria, Germany, on SW slope of the Bohemian Forest, 4 mi. NNW of Deggendorf; granite quarrying. Near by is 12th-cent. castle.

Egg, Scotland: see EIGG.

Egg (ĕk), town (pop. 2,194), Zurich canton, N Switzerland, 8 mi. SE of Zurich; silk textiles.

Eggan (ĕgä'), town, Kabba prov., Northern Provinces, W central Nigeria, port on Niger R., opposite Katcha, and 70 mi. NNW of Lokoja; shea-nut processing, wine, sackmaking.

Eggebogen (ĕg'gůbōgůn), village (pop. 766) in Egge canton (pop. 2,475), Nord-Trondelag co., central Norway, at head of Beitstad Fjord (an extension of Trondheim Fjord), 1 mi. WNW of Steinkjer; lumber milling. Has medieval church.

Eggemoggin Reach, Hancock co., S Maine, passage bet. Deer Isl. and Brooklin and Sargentville towns; connects Penobscot and Jericho bays; c.12 mi. long.

Eggenberg, Austria: see GRAZ.

Eggenburg (ĕ'gůnbōōrk), town (pop. 3,829), N Lower Austria, 19 mi. NNE of Krems; ceramics. Mus. of folk art, late-Gothic church.

Eggenfelden (ĕ'gůnfĕl"důn), town (pop. 5,326), Lower Bavaria, Germany, on Rott R. and 15 mi. NE of Mühldorf; mfg. of textiles, paint, pottery, bricks; leather-, metal-, and woodworking; brewing, printing. Has 15th-cent. church.

Eggenstein (ĕ'gůn-shtīn), village (pop. 3,359), N Baden, Germany, after 1945 in Württemberg-Baden, 5 mi. N of Karlsruhe; asparagus, strawberries.

Eggertsville, village (1940 pop. 5,708), Erie co., W N.Y., just N of Buffalo.

Eggesin (ĕ"gůzēn'), village (pop. 4,671), in former Prussian Pomerania prov., N Germany, after 1945 in Mecklenburg, near Uecker R., 4 mi. SSE of Ueckermünde; grain, potatoes, sugar beets, stock; peat digging, brick mfg.

Egg Harbor, resort village (pop. c.200), Door co., NE Wis., on Door Peninsula, on Green Bay, 16 mi. NNE of Sturgeon Bay city.

Egg Harbor City, inland city (pop. 3,838), Atlantic co., SE N.J., 15 mi. NW of Atlantic City; wine-making center; fruit, poultry, truck. Annual agr. fair. Great Egg Harbor Bay lies S, near Ocean City, and Little Egg Harbor NE, near Tuckerton. Settled 1854 by Germans, inc. 1856.

Eggishorn (ĕ'gĭs-hôrn"), peak (9,613 ft.) in Bernese Alps, S Switzerland, 9 mi. NE of Brig.

Egg Island, islet in central Bahama Isls., off N tip of Eleuthera Isl., just W of Royal Isl., 40 mi. NE of Nassau; 25°30'N 76°53'W. Belongs to Spanish Wells dist.

Egg Island Point, S N.J., low headland with lighthouse, on N shore of Delaware Bay 7 mi. SW of Port Norris.

Eggiwil (ĕ'gĭvēl'), town (pop. 2,579), Bern canton, central Switzerland, 18 mi. ESE of Bern; farming.

Eggmühl (ĕk'mül"), village (pop. 595), Lower Bavaria, Germany, on Great Laaber R. and 13 mi. SSE of Regensburg; rail junction; barley, wheat, cattle. After his victory over the Austrians here in April, 1809, Davout was created prince of Eckmühl. Sometimes spelled Eckmühl.

Egham (ĕ'gům), residential urban district (1931 pop. 15,916; 1951 census 24,515), NW Surrey, England, on the Thames and 19 mi. WSW of London. Near by are Cooper's Hill (subject of poem by John Denham) and Royal Holloway Col. for Women (1886). Church contains shields of Magna Carta barons. Along river is level stretch of meadow called Runnymede or Runnimede; either here, or on Magna Charta Isl. (just N, in the Thames), King John accepted (1215) Magna Carta. In urban dist. are residential towns of Hythe (E) and Virginia Water (SSW), with artificial lake.

Egholm (ĕg'hôlm), island (□ 2.4; pop. 124) in E Lim Fjord, Denmark, just WNW of Aalborg; in center is Egholm town, with mill, dairy transportation center, and school.

Egido, Venezuela: see EJIDO.

Egiin Gol, Mongolia: see EGIN GOL.

Egil (ĕyĭl'), Turkish *Eğil*, village (pop. 2,110), Diyarbakir prov., E Turkey, on Tigris R. and 25 mi. NNW of Diyarbakir; grain, legumes. Also called Egilselman. Formerly called Piran.

Egilsay (ĕ'gĭlsā), island (pop. 85) of the Orkneys, Scotland, just E of ROUSAY; 2½ mi. long, 1½ mi. wide. Has old church.

Egin, Turkey: see KEMALIYE.

Egin Gol or **Egiin Gol** (ĕ'gĕn gōl'), left tributary of Selenga R., in NW Mongolian People's Republic; rises at S end of L. Khubsugul at Khadkhal, flows 295 mi. generally E to Selenga R. 180 mi. NW of Ulan Bator. Freezes Nov.–April.

Egirdir, Turkey: see EGRIDIR.

Egisheim, France: see EGUISHEIM.

Égletons (āglůtõ'), town (pop. 2,406), Corrèze dept., S central France, in Monts de Monédières, 17 mi. NE of Tulle; agr. trade center (fruits, vegetables); mfg. of electrical equipment. Ruins of feudal Ventadour fortress near by.

Eglin Air Force Base, Fla.: see VALPARAISO.

Eglinton (ĕ'glĭntůn), fishing village (district pop. 1,357), NW Co. Londonderry, Northern Ireland, on S shore of Lough Foyle, 7 mi. NE of Londonderry.

Eglinton Island (□ 504), Parry Isls., W Franklin Dist., Northwest Territories, in the Arctic Ocean; 75°28'–76°10'N 117°35'–119°30'W; separated from Melville Isl. (E) by Kellett Strait and from Prince Patrick Isl. (W) by Crozier Channel; 50 mi. long, 10–20 mi. wide.

Eglisau (ā'glēzou"), village (pop. 1,444), Zurich canton, N Switzerland, on N bank of the Rhine (dam; bridge) and 14 mi. N of Zurich, near Ger. border; hydroelectric plant; clothes, flour.

Églisottes-et-Chalaures, Les (lāzāglēzôt'-ē-shälōr'), village (pop. 310), Gironde dept., SW France, on the Dronne and 17 mi. NE of Libourne; paper and tire mfg.

Egmond aan Zee (ĕg'mōnt än zā'), resort village (pop. 3,052), North Holland prov., NW Netherlands, on North Sea, 5 mi. W of Alkmaar, in sandy region; fishing, agr., cattle raising. Lighthouse (built 1833).

Egmondville (ĕg'můnd–), village, SW Ont., S suburb of Seaforth.

Egmont, Cape (ĕg'mŏnt), W extremity of P.E.I., on Northumberland Strait, on S side of Egmont Bay, 17 mi. W of Summerside; 46°24'N 64°8'W; Lighthouse.

Egmont, Cape, W N.Isl., New Zealand, separates N. and S. Taranaki bights of Tasman Sea; 39°16'S 173°42'E.

Egmont, Mount, extinct volcanic cone (8,260 ft.), in Egmont Natl. Park, W N.Isl., New Zealand, near New Plymouth. Surrounded by forest belt. Named 1770 by Capt. Cook.

Egmont Bay, inlet (12 mi. long, 19 mi. wide at entrance) of Northumberland Strait, W P.E.I., 17 mi. W of Summerside, bet. West Point and Cape Egmont.

Egmont Islands, in Indian Ocean: see SIX ISLANDS.

Egmont Key (c.2 mi. long), W Fla., 3 mi. N of Anna Maria Key, at entrance to Tampa Bay; lighthouse at 27°36'N 82°45'E.

Egmont National Park (□ 12), W N.Isl., New Zealand, near New Plymouth, on wide peninsula bet. N. and S. Taranaki bights of Tasman Sea; contains Mt. EGMONT.

Egna (ĕ'nyä), Ger. *Neumarkt*, village (pop. 1,547), Bolzano prov., Trentino–Alto Adige, N Italy, on Adige R. and 13 mi. SSW of Bolzano.

Egnach (ĕg'näkh), town (pop. 3,136), Thurgau canton, NE Switzerland, near L. Constance, 8 mi. N of St. Gall; foodstuffs, embroideries, clothes; woodworking.

Egogi Bad (ĕ'gōgē bäd'), Ital. *Afreda, Afrera*, and *Giulietti*, salt lake in Danakil desert, NE Ethiopia, near Eritrean border, in Tigre prov., 60 mi. SW of Edd (Eritrea); 13°18'N 41°3'E; c.460 ft. below sea level; 10 mi. long, 5 mi. wide. Largely fed by hot springs. Enclosed by mts., including Mt. Afrera (c.3,935 ft.) in S.

Egor-, in Rus. names: see YEGOR-.

Egorevsk, Russian SFSR: see YEGORYEVSK.

Egoumenitsa or **Igoumenitsa** (both: ēgōōmĕnē'tsů), town (pop. 1,353), ⊙ Thesprotia nome, S Epirus, Greece, port on inlet of Strait of Corfu and 33 mi. WSW of Ioannina; timber, barley, corn; olive oil; fisheries.

Egremont (ĕ'grůmŏnt). **1** Town, Cheshire, England: see WALLASEY. **2** Former urban district (1931 pop. 6,017), W Cumberland, England, on Ehen R. and 5 mi. SSE of Whitehaven; iron-mining and smelting center; agr. market. Has ruins of 12th-cent. castle.

Egremont, resort town (pop. 731), Berkshire co., SW Mass., in the Berkshires, 21 mi. SSW of Pittsfield, near N.Y. line. Its villages are North Egremont and South Egremont.

Egridere, Yugoslavia: see KRIVA PALANKA.

Egridir (ārĭdĭr') or **Egirdir** (āĭrdĭr'), Turkish *Eğridir* or *Eğirdir*, town (pop. 5,739), Isparta prov., W central Turkey, rail terminus at S end of L. Egridir, 18 mi. NE of Isparta; wheat, barley, potatoes, chick-peas.

Egridir, Lake, or **Lake Egirdir**, Turkish *Eğridir* or *Eğirdir* (□ 200), W central Turkey, 20 mi. NE of Isparta; 22 mi. long, 10 mi. wide; alt. 3,031 ft. Its N part is called Hoyran (hoirän'). Outlet, Aksu R. Sometimes spelled Egerdir.

Egrigoz, village, Turkey: see EMET.

Egrigoz Dag (ārĭgûz'dä), Turkish *Eğrigöz Dağ*, peak (7,155 ft.), NW Turkey, 8 mi. WNW of Emet.

Egripo, Greece: see EUBOEA; CHALCIS.

Eguisheim (āgēsĕm'), Ger. *Egisheim* (ā'gĭs-hīm), village (pop. 1,313), Haut-Rhin dept., E France, 3 mi. SW of Colmar, at E foot of Vosges; tile mfg. Alsace wines grown in area.

Éguzon (āgüzõ'), village (pop. 669), Indre dept., central France, 22 mi. WSW of La Châtre. Important dam (200 ft. high, 985 ft. long) and hydroelectric station on Creuse R., 1.5 mi. NE.

Egwanga, Nigeria: see OPOBO.

Egyek (ĕ'dyĕk), town (pop. 7,473), Hajdu co., E Hungary, 35 mi. WNW of Debrecen; grain, potatoes, cattle.

Egypt (ē'jĭpt), Arabic *Misr* (mĭs'rů) or *Masr* (măs'rů), anc. *Aegyptus* (ējĭp'tůs), biblical *Mizraim* (mĭzrā'ĭm), kingdom (□ 386,198; pop. 19,087,304, including an estimated 49,320 nomads), occupying NE corner of Africa and the SINAI peninsula in SW Asia, separated by the Suez Canal; ⊙ CAIRO. It borders W on Libya and S on the ANGLO-EGYPTIAN SUDAN, a condominium Egypt shares with Great Britain. Its c.1,300-mi.-long coast line is washed on E, opposite Saudi Arabia, by the Red Sea and the Gulf of Suez, and on N by the Mediterranean. The Sinai peninsula has the Gulf of Aqaba on SE, Israel on NE. Of the former mandate of PALESTINE Egypt holds a small strip (□ c.135) along the Mediterranean around the town of GAZA. Crossed by the Tropic of Cancer, the country is roughly a square—c.675 mi. N–S, c.700 mi. E–W—bet. 21°35'–31°35'N and 25°–36°E. Only about 13,600 sq. mi. (c.3.5%) of Egypt's vast territory are inhabited cultivated land, the rest being desert, where a few nomads eke out a precarious living. Egypt proper is really an elongated, immensely fertile oasis (from less than 1 mi. to 10–15 mi. wide) along the NILE RIVER (c.930 mi. long in Egypt) from just below the 2d Cataract near Wadi Halfa N to Cairo, whence it widens into the great Nile delta (□ c.8,500). The ecological pattern is still very much the same as in antiquity, when Herodotus aptly called Egypt a "gift of the Nile." The delta area is called Lower Egypt, the rest of the Nile valley Upper Egypt. Some 95% of the pop. lives along the Nile, and while the density in Egypt as a whole (c.50 persons per sq. mi.) is not large, the density within the Nile zone (average c.700 per sq. mi.) is among the greatest in the world, and in Lower Egypt is over 1,000 persons per sq. mi. The WESTERN DESERT, W of the Nile, forms part of the LIBYAN DESERT—all part of the Sahara—and is in its minute settled areas administratively divided into the few "frontier dists." which comprise fertile oases—SIWA, BAHARIYA, FARAFRA, DAKHLA, and KHARGA—where cereals and fruit thrive. FAIYUM, SW of Cairo, though surrounded by desert, may be considered part of the Nile valley, with which it is linked by the c.150-mi.-long BAHR YUSUF irrigation arm. The Libyan Desert is occasionally pierced by rock, reaching 6,256 ft. in the Gebel Uweinat on SW border. Large depressions, particularly the Qattara (440 ft. below sea level), characterize the N section. Here, along the Mediterranean coast—heavily disputed during Second World War—are a few minor towns and ports, such as SALUM, SIDI BARRANI, MATRUH, and ALAMEIN, all linked by railroad with the leading port of ALEXANDRIA. E of the Nile is the Eastern Desert or Arabian Desert, bisected by many wadis leading to the Red Sea. The highest peaks, a range of granitic and porphyritic mts., border the E shore, where they attain 7,165 ft. (Shayib) just W of the oil-producing center Hurghada. Other petroleum wells, also on the Gulf of Suez, are Gemsa and Ras Gharib. The Eastern Desert has considerable mineral wealth, of which the phosphates mined at SAFAGA and KOSSEIR (both on the Red Sea) are the most valuable for foreign trade. Also extracted are nitrates (near QENA), building stone from the crystalline ridge (which forms the famous cataracts) near Aswan. Iron deposits have been found E of Aswan. There are limestone quarries bet. Cairo and HELWAN (sulphur springs). Elsewhere in the desert occur natron (Wadi el NATRUN, NW of Cairo) and other minerals, little exploited except for manganese: tungsten, titanium, gold, lead, zinc, chromite, asbestos, kaolin, talc, barium sulphate, alabaster, emeralds (anc. Sikait mines), alum. Marine salt is extracted near Alexandria and PORT SAID. In the rugged and virtually uninhabited Sinai peninsula petroleum is drilled at Abu Durba, Asl, and Sudr along the Gulf of Suez. Sinai also yields some iron and manganese, mined near ABU ZENIMA, and gypsum and anhydrites. In Sinai rise some of the highest peaks in Egypt, e.g., Gebel KATHERINA (8,651 ft.) and Gebel MUSA (c.7,400 ft.). The SUEZ CANAL is entirely on Egyptian territory, though largely British controlled. Port Said, Port Fuad, and SUEZ are the chief ports on the canal, and at ISMAILIA the ISMAILIA CANAL runs to the Nile at Cairo. Bordering the Nile delta are marshy salt lakes (L. MANZALA, L. BURULLUS, L. IDKU, L. MARYUT). There are now 2 main navigable channels in the Nile delta, the Rosetta (W) and the Damietta (E), both c.150 mi. long. Alexandria, at delta's edge, is connected by MAHMUDIYA CANAL (completed 1820) with the Rosetta branch. Since all the farming of arid Egypt depends on the Nile, the regime of the river rather than climatic or seasonal features condition its vegetation. The river itself has no tributary in Egypt. Rainfall is scarce, particularly in Upper Egypt; Cairo has 1.2 inches annually, Alexandria 8 inches. Cairo has an annual mean temp. of 69°F., Alexandria 73°F. There are diurnal changes of as much as 30°F. In the desert, temperatures of over 120°F. are brought about by the scorching *khamsin* wind. Egypt's dry atmosphere is renowned for its beneficial effects on pulmonary diseases. Malaria is almost unknown. The floods of the Nile take place generally from late Aug. to early Sept. From anc. times the overflow was controlled by diversion into basins which watered the farmlands, also adding fertile silt carried by the river. This system has now largely been replaced by "perennial" irrigation, serving about 80% of cultivated area and making 2 or 3 crops a year possible. Nile waters are today stored by the great reservoirs at Jebel Aulia, Sennar (Sudan), and at Aswan (Upper Egypt), while a series of barrages (Isna, Nag Hammadi, Asyut, Zifta, and at head of delta below Cairo) divert waters regularly throughout the year into a net of irrigation canals. Projects to construct even larger reservoirs by damming outlets of some of the great central African lakes are under consideration, chiefly to meet the growing needs of Egypt. Building of a major dam and hydroelectric station at Owen Falls on the Victoria Nile (Uganda), financed jointly by Egypt and Uganda, was inaugurated 1949. Agr. development has not kept up with country's rapidly increasing population, whose large *fellahin* class still lives on a miserable, semifeudal level. The nation's economy also suffers from the unstable world market in cotton, its chief cash crop, which occupies c.30% of all arable land. The quality of Egyptian cotton is one of the world's finest. The bulk is raised in Lower Egypt. Besides accounting for c.80% of all exports, cotton supplies the country's leading industry (textiles) and furnishes valuable cottonseed oil and oil cake. Other agr. products, partly exported, include rice (N delta), sugar cane (Upper Egypt), onions, potatoes, flax, sesame, peanuts, and dates (Faiyum). Principal subsistence crop is corn, followed by rice, wheat, millet, sorghum, barley, beans, lentils, peas, and forage. The oases, in particular, yield choice fruit, among them oranges, tangerines, grapes, figs, melons, pomegranates. Jute, Indian hemp, and sugar beets have been successfully introduced. There is considerable stock raising (sheep, cows, buffaloes, goats, donkeys, camels, pigs, horses). Fishing has gained some importance, chiefly in L. Manzala and in the Nile. The Nile waters also teem with electric eels; the crocodile and the hippopotamus are now rarely met N of Aswan. The indigenous fauna of Egypt is preeminently of the African type, but lions and leopards have retreated to the Sudan. More common are jackals, hyenas, antelopes, gazelles, and ibexes in the desert area. There is a rich bird life. Egypt's industry, employing c.500,000 people and principally based at Cairo and Alexandria, is devoted almost entirely to textile milling (cotton, wool, silk, rayon) and food processing. Consumer industries developing since 1940s include cigarette mfg., petroleum refining (Suez), distilling of aromatic oil (mint, thyme), cement milling, tanning, non-ferrous metal refining (Alexandria), mfg. of chemicals, fertilizers, pharmaceuticals, light bulbs, matches, candles, glass, paper, pottery. Egypt also has a substantial publishing and film industry of its own. Alexandria is the largest port, handling c.60% of all freight and most of its foreign trade. Imports are mainly machinery, vehicles, timber, leather, chemicals, luxury goods, petroleum products, coal. Alexandria—founded 332 B.C. by Alexander—once the metropolis of Hellenistic civilization, is a popular resort, where most of the Egyptian govt. agencies move to in summer. Here is Farouk univ. Cairo, the largest city of Africa, is the commercial, political, and cultural capital, one of the globe's great air hubs (Farouk and Almaza airports), and seat of El Azhar Moslem univ. (founded 972). The city houses also secular Fuad Univ., an American univ., a People's univ., and outstanding archaeological museums. Among other leading commercial and industrial towns are: in Lower Egypt—Mahalla, Tanta, Mansura, Zifta, Damanhur, Zagazig, Benha, Shibin el Kom, Kafr el Zayat, Rosetta, and Damietta; in less urbanized Upper Egypt—Giza, Faiyum, Beni Suef, Minya, Asyut, Sohag, Qena, Aswan. The country has a good highway and railroad system, with more than 5,000 mi. of railroads, mostly state owned. It now reaches to El SHALLAL beyond Aswan, but a 310-mi. extension to WadiHalfa in the Anglo-Egyptian Sudan is planned. Transverse railroads link the Nile valley with Safaga on the Red Sea, Kharga oasis in the Western Desert, and Ismailia and Suez on the Suez Canal. Rails on both sides of the canal are joined to Eastern Mediterranean railroads (Haifa, Beirut). Some 91% of the Egyptian people are Moslems (of the Sunnite sect); Christians, chiefly of the Coptic Church, form about 8%. The Jews are a small minority, and quite a few Egyptian citizens are of Armenian, Greek, Moslem, Sudanese, Syrian, Palestinian, and Turkish stock. Egypt's dry climate accounts for the preservation of so many remarkable monuments studding the Nile valley. Testifying to one of the globe's most anc. and continuous civilizations, they are an inexhaustible attraction to tourists and archaeologists. Different epochs are associated with such sites as THEBES, MEMPHIS, KARNAK, TEL EL AMARNA, the Pyramids of GIZA, the Valley of the Tombs near LUXOR, and the PHAROS of Alexandria. There is an Egypt of the Pharaos, of Hellenism, and of Islam. While the site of the beginning of Western Civilization can only be surmised, Egypt's place as the seat of one of the oldest civilizations is rivaled only by Mesopotamia. Egypt enters history as an advanced culture at the earliest historic date known to man, set at 4241 B.C., when it adopted the calendar. Conventionally, Egyptian history up to Alexander the Great is chronologically divided into 30 dynasties. There are, however, many gaps and not all rulers are known. By c.3400 B.C. Menes united Upper and Lower Egypt, making Memphis his capital. Egyptian culture reached a peak during the IV dynasty (2900 B.C.), which is the age of the great Pyramids. Eventually a rising nobility weakened the monarchy towards mid-3d millennium B.C. Around 2445 B.C. Heracleopolis evolved as capital and was replaced c.2160 B.C. (XI dynasty) by Thebes, when a strengthened state rose once more, particularly during the Middle Kingdom (or Middle Empire), from 2000 onward (XII dynasty kings Amenemhet I-IV and Sesostris I–III). This was a period of considerable cultural and commercial activity, interrupted (1675–1575) by the foreign rule of the probably Semitic Hyksos. Under the XVIII dynasty (after 1580) Egypt expanded its domain into Syria and Mesopotamia, and built the gigantic temples of Luxor and Karnak. Among those kings who inaugurated the New Kingdom were the Amenhoteps and Thutmoses. A remarkable interlude was brought about by the reign of Amenhotep IV (c.1375–58), who called himself Ikhnaton and tried to install a monotheistic sun cult; he moved his capital to Akhetaton (Tel el Amarna). His reforms—which had also given a fresh stimulus to the arts—were, however, short lived. With his successors, notably Tut-Ankh-Amen (known through his sumptuous tomb, excavated in 20th cent.), Egypt reverted to the traditional beliefs guarded by a rigid priesthood. The XIX dynasty (1350 B.C.) brought Ramses I and Ramses II to the throne. Around 1200 (XX dynasty) the New Kingdom began to decline steadily, falling prey in turn to Libyan, Nubian, Assyrian, and Persian invaders (Cambyses, Darius, Xerxes). Most of the time SAÏS was the capital. It was during this period that Herodotus visited Egypt. The last dynasty (XXX) was swept away by the conquest (332 B.C.) of Alexander the Great. In the wars of his successors (Diadochi) his general Ptolemy became king. The Ptolemies maintained a formidable empire for more than 2 centuries. Alexandria developed into a progressive center of a somewhat diluted but progressive Hellenistic culture, distinguished by its scientific and philological researches. It had a large Jewish community. The rising power of Rome early exercised its influence over Egypt. Through Pompey's aid (58 B.C.) to Ptolemy XI Rome gained an actual foothold. Cleopatra, the daughter of Ptolemy XI, tried to win back power for Egypt, especially through Julius Caesar and Marc Antony. Octavian (later Emperor Augustus) annexed the country to Rome. Egypt became a granary for the empire, the irrigation system was raised to great efficiency, and Trajan reopened the Nile–Red Sea canal. Christianity was welcomed in Egypt, which contributed several of the most celebrated Doctors of the Church, and which also gave rise to the Arian and Nestorian heresies. Gnosticism flourished for a time. Out of Monophysitism developed the still surviving Coptic Church. Only some 20 years after the rise of Islam Egypt was conquered (639–42) by the Arabs, becoming an integral part of the Moslem World. Though many of the people continued under the Omayyad their adherence to the Coptic Church, the Greek and Coptic languages went out of use, and Arabic alone was spoken. The Abbasid caliphate (founded 750) held Egypt until replaced in 10th cent. by Fatimites, who invaded from the W and founded Cairo in 969. They established there in 972 the Mosque of El Azhar, a great (and still active) Moslem center of Higher Learning, which might be termed the world's oldest univ. The Crusaders raided Egypt several times, and for brief periods occupied (13th cent.) Damietta, then the leading port. During the reign of the Ayyubites control was eventually seized (1250) by the Mamelukes, former slaves from Asia who had become influential soldiers and advisers. The Mamelukes maintained their turbulent rule until 1517, when Egypt was conquered by the Ottoman Turks; but even afterwards they continued to wield power as beys (princes) administering the provinces. With ascent of Ali Bey (1768–73) the Ottoman hold remained only nominal. It was under the pretext of reestablishing Turkish rule that Napoleon Bonaparte undertook the Fr. occupation of Egypt (1798–1801), though his real object was to cut off the Br. trade and ultimately Br. India. In the end the Turks joined the British to throw out the French after Napoleon's fleet was decisively defeated (1798) by Nelson outside Abukir. After Fr. withdrawal occurred the meteoric rise of Mohamed Ali (founder of the present Egyptian royal line), a former common soldier of Albanian descent, who was appointed (1805) Egyptian pasha by the Ottoman emperor. He massacred the Mamelukes and even threatened Turkey proper. He introduced cotton from India, redistributed land, improved irrigation, and had a large share in the country's modernization. In 1866 Ismail Pasha was granted the title khedive (viceroy), symbolizing greater independence from Turkey. Ismail's extravagance forced him (1875) to sell his shares in the Suez Canal to Great Britain, who had at 1st opposed its construction. Tewfik Pasha submitted (1880) to joint British-French control over Egypt's finances. Ensuing riots in Alexandria precipitated a Br. intervention. The British consolidated their control during the period (1883–1907) when able Lord Cromer was, as consul general, de facto ruler. Lord Kitchener at this time accomplished the conquest of the Sudan, which was constituted as the Anglo-Egyptian Sudan. He later (1911–14) became consul general in Egypt. In the First World War, when Turkey joined the Central Powers, Great Britain declared Egypt a Br. protectorate. But after the war Egyptian nationalists of the Wafd party pushed demands for freedom. A treaty providing for independence was concluded (1922) and went into effect the next year. Egypt became a constitutional kingdom under Fuad I. Great Britain could still station troops in the country; it refused, however, to consider exclusive Egyptian claims to the Anglo-Egyptian Sudan. The Br. protectorate was retained until the treaty of 1936, which promised eventual withdrawal of Br. troops. In the Second World War Great Britain undertook the defense of Egypt, which declared war only in 1945, despite almost continuous danger of Axis engulfment until the Br. victory at Alamein (Oct., 1942) hurled the enemy back. Friction bet. Great Britain and Egypt continued after the war, mainly over the Suez Canal and the Anglo-Egyptian Sudan. An Egyptian appeal (1947) to the Security Council of the United Nations was rejected. Egypt bitterly opposed the United Nations' partition (1948) of Palestine, and, joining its forces with the other members of the Arab League, sent troops into S Negev, where it was on the whole unsuccessful against the newly-formed state of Israel. By virtue of 1949 truce Egypt occupied the tiny Gaza strip on the Mediterranean which the partition plan had designated as Arab territory. For further information see separate entries on cities, towns, ruined sites, and physical features. Egypt is administratively divided into the 6 provs. of Lower Egypt (Beheira, Daqaliya, Gharbiya, Minufiya, Qalyubiya, Sharqiya), the 8 provs. of Upper Egypt (Aswan, Asyut, Beni Suef, Faiyum, Girga, Giza, Minya, Qena), 5 governorates (Alexandria, Cairo, Canal, Damietta, Suez), and 5 frontier dists. (Bahariya Oases, Red Sea or Coast, Sinai, Southern Desert, Western Desert).

Egypt. 1 Village, Plymouth co., Mass.: see SCITUATE. 2 Village (1940 pop. 1,189), Lehigh co., E Pa., near Lehigh R., 6 mi. N of Allentown; clothing mfg.

Ehara, Japan: see EBARA.

Ehdène, Lebanon: see IHDEN.

Ehen River (ē'ŭn), SW Cumberland, England, flows 12 mi. S from Ennerdale Water, past Egremont, to Irish Sea near Beckermet Saint John.

Ehime (āhē'mā), prefecture [Jap. *ken*] (□ 2,188; 1940 pop. 1,178,705; 1947 pop. 1,453,887), NW Shikoku, Japan; chief port and ⊙ MATSUYAMA. Bounded N by Hiuchi and Iyo seas of Inland Sea, W by Hoyo Strait; includes offshore isls. of O-SHIMA, NAKA-SHIMA, GOGO-SHIMA, OMI-SHIMA. Mountainous terrain, rising to 6,497 ft. at Mt. Ishizuchi (highest peak of isl.); drained by Yoshino, Shimando, and Niyodo rivers. Extensive forests of white fir, pine, Jap. cedar; fruit trees (plum, pear, cherry, orange). Besshi (N) is one of the few copper fields in Japan; centers on NIIHAMA. Limited mining of gold, silver, pyrite. Widespread cultivation of rice, wheat, tea, soybeans; sweet potatoes, tobacco grown on some offshore isls. and on W coast. Extensive paper milling and livestock-breeding. Principal products: textiles, paper, woodwork, sake, soy sauce, pottery, dried bonito. Most of its towns are ports, the smaller being fishing ports. Hot springs at DOGAYUNO-MACHI (NW).

Mfg. centers: Matsuyama (NW), IMABARI (N), UWAJIMA (W), SAIJO (N), YAWATAHAMA (W).

Ehingen or **Ehingen an der Donau** (ā'ĭng-ŭn än dĕr dō'nou), town (pop. 6,729), S Württemberg, Germany, after 1945 in Württemberg-Hohenzollern, at S foot of Swabian Jura, on the Danube and 15 mi. SW of Ulm; mfg. of wood fiber, cellulose. Has 18th-cent. church. Austrian until 1805.

Ehlershausen, Germany: see RAMLINGEN MIT EHLERSHAUSEN.

Ehrang (ā'räng), village (pop. 4,523), in former Prussian Rhine Prov., W Germany, after 1945 in Rhineland-Palatinate, 4 mi. NNE of Trier; wine.

Ehrenberg, Germany: see BÖHLITZ-EHRENBERG.

Ehrenbreitstein (ā"rŭnbrīt'shtīn), fortress, W Germany, on right bank of the Rhine, opposite Coblenz. First built in 12th cent.; rebuilt 1816–26. Occupied after First World War by Allies. Inc. 1937 into Coblenz.

Ehrenfeld (ā'rŭnfĕlt), NW industrial suburb of Cologne, W Germany; glassworks.

Ehrenfeld (â'rŭnfĕld), village (pop. 1,159), Cambria co., central Pa., 7 mi. ENE of Johnstown.

Ehrenforst, Poland: see SLAWIECICE.

Ehrenfriedersdorf (ā"rŭnfrē'dŭrsdôrf"), town (pop. 5,730), Saxony, E central Germany, in the Erzgebirge, 13 mi. S of Chemnitz; textile-mfg. center (cotton, wool, silk, stockings, lace, embroidery). Tin and tungsten mining. Just W are noted granite rock formations. Has late-Gothic church.

Ehrhardt (ĕr'härt), town (pop. 510), Bamberg co., S central S.C., 29 mi. SSW of Orangeburg; cooperage.

Ehringsdorf (ā'rĭngsdôrf), suburb of Weimar, Thuringia, central Germany, 2 mi. SE of city center; site of excavation of early Stone Age skeletons and relics. Here is BELVEDERE hunting lodge.

Ehrwald (âr'vält), village (pop. 1,869), Tyrol, W Austria, at W foot of the Zugspitze (aerial tramway), 24 mi. WNW of Innsbruck, near Ger. border.

Ei (ā'ē), town (pop. 4,381), on W Awaji-shima, Hyogo prefecture, Japan, on Harima Sea, 9 mi. NNW of Sumoto; rice, wheat.

Eiao (ā'ou'), uninhabited island, Marquesas Isls., Fr. Oceania, S Pacific, 56 mi. NW of Nuku Hiva; 6 mi. long, 2 mi. wide; central ridge rises to 2,000 ft. Wild sheep, cattle, hogs. Formerly Fr. prison isl., called Masse Isl.

Eibar (āvär'), Basque town (pop. 10,607), Guipúzcoa prov., N Spain, 20 mi. WNW of Tolosa, in fertile agr. area; metallurgical center (armaments, sewing machines, auto and bicycle parts, hardware and surgical instruments). Other mfg.: electrical equipment and steel furniture. Noted for its decorative metal-engraving industry. Suffered heavily in civil war of 1936–39.

Eibau (ī'bou), village (pop. 5,394), Saxony, E central Germany, in Upper Lusatia, in Lusatian Mts., 9 mi. NW of Zittau, near Czechoslovak border; linen and cotton milling and dyeing. Just SE is Neueibau village (pop. 1,129).

Eibenschitz, Czechoslovakia: see IVANCICE.

Eibenstock (ī'bŭn-shtôk), town (pop. 8,250), Saxony, E central Germany, in the Erzgebirge, 8 mi. SW of Aue, near Czechoslovak border, in uranium- and wolframite-mining region; embroidery center; metalworking.

Eibergen (ī'bĕrkh-ŭn), town (pop. 3,075), Gelderland prov., E Netherlands, on the Berkel, 8 mi. NNW of Winterswijk; leather, textiles.

Eibiswald (ī'bĭsvält), village (pop. 1,124), Styria, S Austria, 15 mi. WSW of Leibnitz; ironworks, brewery; vineyards.

Eich (īsh), N suburb of Luxembourg city, S Luxembourg; steel mills, processing of nonferrous metals, beer brewing; rose growing.

Eichenberg (ī'khŭnbĕrk), village (pop. 908), in former Prussian prov. of Hesse-Nassau, W Germany, after 1945 in Hesse, 2.5 mi. NE of Witzenhausen, 10 mi. W of Heiligenstadt; rail junction.

Eichendorf (ī'khŭndôrf), village (pop. 2,032), Lower Bavaria, Germany, on the Great Vils and 22 mi. SE of Straubing; barley, wheat, cattle, horses. Has Gothic church.

Eichsfeld (īkhs'fĕlt), hilly region in central Germany, drained by Leine, Unstrut, and Wipper rivers. Tobacco growing, home weaving are chief rural occupations. Centers at Heiligenstadt and Duderstadt. It is predominantly R.C. enclave in generally Protestant part of Germany. Became (1294) principality, property of electors of Mainz; after 1540, Heiligenstadt was its ⊙. Passed to Prussia in 1802.

Eichstädt, Germany: see EICHSTÄTT.

Eichstätt (īkh'shtĕt), town (1950 pop. 10,684), Middle Franconia, central Bavaria, Germany, on the Altmühl and 38 mi. S of Nuremberg; rail junction; textile mfg., paper milling, printing, metalworking. The Romanesque and early-Gothic cathedral was consecrated in 1060, renovated 1881–1903. Church of Benedictine abbey (founded 870) contains tomb of St. Walburga. Has mid-15th-cent. town hall. Site of theological acad. Episcopal see was founded 740 by St. Boniface. Town was chartered 908. Sometimes spelled Eichstädt. On hill (NW) are ruins of mid-14th-cent. castle Willibaldsburg. Dolomite and slate quarries in area.

Eichstetten (īkh'shtĕ"tŭn), village (pop. 1,892), S Baden, Germany, at E foot of the Kaiserstuhl, 8 mi. NW of Freiburg; wine.

Eichwald, Czechoslovakia: see DUBI.

Eichwalde (īkh'väl"dŭ), village (pop. 5,847), Brandenburg, E Germany, near Seddin L., 13 mi. SE of Berlin; ceramics mfg.; market gardening.

Eickel, Germany: see WANNE-EICKEL.

Eid. 1 Canton, More og Romsdal co., Norway: see TORVIK. **2** Canton, Sogn og Fjordane co., Norway: see NORDFJORDEID.

Eidanger (ā'däng"ŭr), village and canton (pop. 7,196), Telemark co., S Norway, 7 mi. SSE of Skien, near Porsgrunn; truck produce; mfg. of cement, lime, fertilizer; tanning.

Eider River (ī'dŭr), NW Germany, rises near Baltic coast 8 mi. S of Kiel, flows N to Kiel Canal, which uses its course to Rendsburg, whence it meanders (generally E) to the North Sea, 3 mi. below Tönning. Length 117 mi., for most of which it is navigable; regulated in lower course. Eiderkanal (built 1777–84), bet. Rendsburg and the Baltic below Kiel, was 22 mi. long; has been supplanted by Kiel Canal. Eider R. is historic boundary bet. Schleswig (N) and Holstein (S).

Eiderstedt (ī'dŭr-shtĕt), peninsular district (□ 130; pop. 29,720) of W Schleswig-Holstein, NW Germany, just SW of Husum; bounded by North Sea (N,W) and by Eider R. and its estuary (S). Stock raising (meat cattle, horses, sheep). Main town: Tönning. Consisted originally of 3 isls.; connected since 1489 to mainland.

Eidfjord (ād'fyōr), village and canton (pop. 1,164), Hordaland co., SW Norway, at head of Hardanger Fjord, 60 mi. E of Bergen; tourist center at foot of the Hardangervidda. Formerly spelled Ejdfjord. FOSSLI village is in canton.

Eido, Korea: see YONGDONG.

Eidomene or **Idhomeni** (both: ēdhômĕ'nē), village (pop. 1,016), Kilkis nome, Macedonia, Greece, on railroad and 21 mi. WNW of Kilkis, on Yugoslav border, just S of Djevdjelija. Also spelled Idomeni; formerly Sechovon (Sekhovon).

Eidsfjord (āts'fyōr), village in Hadsel canton, Nordland co., N Norway, on S Langoy (Vesteralen group), on Vesteral Fjord, 30 mi. NNE of Svolvaer; fishing port (herring, eels); fish-oil processing.

Eidsfoss (āts'fôs), village (pop. 175) in Hof canton (pop. 2,357), Vestfold co., SE Norway, 12 mi. SSW of Drammen, at falls which drop 49 ft. from a small lake into the lake Eikeren. Falls power iron foundry, machine shop, railroad-car works; also supply current to Oslo-Kongsberg RR. Ironworks date from 1697.

Eidskog, Norway: see MAGNOR.

Eidsvag, Norway: see SALHUS.

Eidsvold, village (pop. 487), SE Queensland, Australia, on Burnett R. and 190 mi. NW of Brisbane; gold.

Eidsvoll or **Eidsvold** (both: āts'vôl), village (pop. 237; canton pop. 11,175), Akershus co., SE Norway, on Vorma R. S of L. Mjosa, on railroad and 30 mi. NE of Oslo. Scene (April, 1814) of natl. assembly at which a constitution was drafted and proclaimed (May 17, 1814) at manor house, now a natl. monument. From about 1st cent. A.D. one of oldest Norse confederacies, *Eidsivalag,* met at Eidsvoll, then also a pagan worship ground. In Middle Ages it was seat of Opland *storting.* Terminus of 1st Norwegian railroad (1854). Has agr.-implement and woodworking plants. In 17th cent. ironworks were established here, and later abandoned. Poet Wergeland b. here.

Eielson Air Force Base (ī'ŭlsŭn), central Alaska, 25 mi. SE of Fairbanks; 64°39'N 147°6'W. Construction begun after Second World War. Connected with Alaska R.R.

Eierland, Netherlands: see TEXEL.

Eierlandschegat (ī'ŭrlänt"sŭ-khät'), strait (1.5 mi. wide) of North Sea, NW Netherlands, bet. Texel isl. (SW) and Vlieland isl. (NE); leads from North Sea to the Waddenzee. Formerly spelled Eijerlandschegat.

Eifel (ī'fŭl), plateau, W Germany, bet. the Rhine (E), the Mosel (S), and the Ardennes (W); rises to 2,447 ft. in the Hohe Acht. Desolate region characterized by deep valleys, extinct volcanoes, and crater lakes. Sometimes divided into Hohe Eifel (NE), Schnee Eifel (NW), and Voreifel (S). Geologically it is considered part of Rhenish Slate Mts.

Eifel, peak, Wales: see NEVIN.

Eiffel Flats (ī'fŭl), township (pop. 3,169), Salisbury prov., central Southern Rhodesia, in Mashonaland, on rail spur and 5 mi. ENE of Gatooma. Goldmining center; site of noted Cam and Motor Mine.

Eigelshoven, Netherlands: see EYGELSHOVEN.

Eigenbrakel, Belgium: see BRAINE-L'ALLEUD.

Eiger (ī'gŭr), peak (13,036 ft.) in Bernese Alps, S central Switzerland, 10 mi. SE of Interlaken; N wall is one of most formidable in the Alps. Klein Eiger (peak), Eigerjoch (pass), and Eiger Glacier are near by.

Eigersund, Norway: see EGERSUND.

Eigg or **Egg** (both: ĕg), island (pop. 138), Inner Hebrides, Inverness, Scotland, separated from mainland by 7-mi.-wide channel, 10 mi. W of Arisaig; 6 mi. long, 3½ mi. wide; rises to 1,289 ft. (S). SE promontory of Chathastail is site of lighthouse (56°56'N 6°6'W).

Eight Degree Channel, channel in Arabian Sea at 8°N, bet. Minicoy Isl. of the Laccadives (N) and Maldive Isls. (S).

Eight-Mile Rock, town (pop. 189), Grand Bahama Isl., NW Bahama Isls., on SW shore of the isl., at picturesque Hawksbill Creek, 27 mi. SE of West End; fishing, lumbering.

Eights Coast, Antarctica, along S shore of Bellingshausen Sea, bet. 88° and 97°W.

Eijerland, Netherlands: see TEXEL.

Eijerlandschegat, Netherlands: see EIERLANDSCHEGAT.

Eijgelshoven, Netherlands: see EYGELSHOVEN.

Eijsden or **Eisden** (both: īz'dŭn), town (pop. 1,389), Limburg prov., SE Netherlands, on Maas R. and 5 mi. S of Maastricht; frontier station on Belg. border; mfg. of refined zinc, lithopone, syrups; fruitgrowing. Also spelled Eysden.

Eikelandsosen (ā'kŭlänsō"sŭn), village in Fusa canton (pop. 1,449), Hordaland co., SW Norway, on an arm of Bjorna Fjord, 18 mi. SE of Bergen; fish and meat canneries, barrel factory; exports dairy products.

Eikeren (ā'krŭn), lake (□ 11) in Buskerud and Vestfold counties, SE Norway, 10 mi. WSW of Drammen; 12 mi. long, 1–2 mi. wide, up to 518 ft. deep. Drained N into Drammen R. by short stream. At S end is Eidsfoss village (waterfalls), with major hydroelectric plant, powering Oslo-Kongsberg RR. Steamers ply lake.

Eikesdal Lake (ā'kŭsdäl), Nor. *Eikesdalsvatn* (□ 9), More og Romsdal co., W Norway, on Aura R.; extends c.12 mi. N from Eikesdal village, 37 mi. SE of Molde; tourist center. Mts. (5,900 ft.) tower over lake. Formerly spelled Eikisdal or Ejkisdal.

Eikisdal Lake, Norway: see EIKESDAL LAKE.

Eiko, Korea: see YONGHUNG.

Eiko-wan, Korea: see YONGHUNG BAY.

Eil (āl), town (pop. 350), in the Mijirtein, N Ital. Somaliland, on Negro Bay of Indian Ocean, 95 mi. ESE of Garoe. Has ruined forts.

Eil, Loch, Scotland: see LINNHE, LOCH.

Eilam, Iran: see ILAM.

Eilat, Israel: see ELATH.

Eilbeck (īl'bĕk), residential district (since 1894) of Hamburg, NW Germany, adjoining Barmbeck (N) and Wandsbek (E) dists.

Eildon Hills (ēl'dŭn), short range in N Roxburgh, Scotland, just S of Melrose, consisting of 3 conical summits: N peak is 1,327 ft. high, central peak 1,385 ft., and S peak 1,216 ft. On N summit are traces of prehistoric settlement. Near by was site of Roman camp of Trimontium. Hills are associated with legends of Thomas the Rhymer (Thomas of Erceldoune).

Eildon Reservoir, Australia: see EILDON WEIR.

Eildon Weir (wēr'), village (pop. 148), central Victoria, Australia, on Goulburn R. and 65 mi. NE of Melbourne; irrigation center. Site of dam (2,000 ft. long, 135 ft. high) on W side of Eildon Reservoir (sometimes called Sugarloaf Reservoir), which is c.35 mi. long, 2 mi. wide. Hydroelectric plant.

Eileen (īlēn'), village (pop. 332), Grundy co., NE Ill., 16 mi. SSW of Joliet, in agr. and bituminous-coal area.

Eilenburg (ī'lŭnbo͝ork), town (pop. 19,980), in former Prussian Saxony prov., central Germany, after 1945 in Saxony-Anhalt, on the Mulde and 13 mi. NE of Leipzig; rail junction; mfg. of plastics, machinery, furniture, candy; cotton printing, metalworking. Heavily bombed in Second World War (destruction c.55%). Has remains of anc. castle. Composer Abt b. here. First mentioned as fortress against the Sorbs in reign of Henry I. Passed 1396 to margraves of Meissen, and became part of Prussia in 1815.

Eilendorf (ī'lŭndôrf), village (pop. 9,468), in former Prussian Rhine Prov., W Germany, after 1945 in North Rhine-Westphalia, 3 mi. E of Aachen. Ironworks near by.

Eiler Rasmussen, Cape (ā'lŭr räs'mo͞osŭn), E extremity of Peary Land, N Greenland, on Greenland Sea; 82°34'N 20°5'W.

Eilerts de Haan Mountains (ī'lŭrts dŭ hän'), S Du. Guiana, spurs of the Guiana Highlands; extend c.60 mi. N from Tumuc-Humac Mts. (Brazil line) to Wilhelmina Mts.; rise to over 3,200 ft.

Eilissos River or **Ilissos River** (both: ĭlĭsôs'), Lat. *Ilissus,* in Attica, E central Greece, rises in Hymettus, flows 10 mi. WSW to Cephisus R. just SW of Athens.

Eilon (ālōn'), settlement (pop. 350), Upper Galilee, NW Israel, near Lebanese border, 21 mi. NE of Haifa; mfg. of precision instruments, agr. implements; fruit, vegetables. Founded 1938.

Eilsen, Bad, Germany: see BAD EILSEN.

Eilsleben (īls'lā"bŭn), village (pop. 4,335), in former Prussian Saxony prov., central Germany, after 1945 in Saxony-Anhalt, 9 mi. N of Oschersleben; rail junction; potash mining.

Eimeo, Society Isls.: see MOOREA.

Eimsbüttel (īms'bü"tŭl), NW district (since 1894) of Hamburg, NW Germany, adjoining Altona (S), Rotherbaum and Harvestehude (E) dists.

'Einat, 'Ainat, or **'Aynat** (all: ī'nät), town (pop. 5,000) Quaiti state, Eastern Aden Protectorate, in the Wadi Hadhramaut, 10 mi. E of the Kathiri town of Tarim; agr. center.

Einbeck (īn'bĕk), town (pop. 16,166), in former Prussian prov. of Hanover, W Germany, after 1945 in Lower Saxony, 20 mi. N of Göttingen; textile mills; mfg. of machinery, tools, wood products, chemicals, leather goods, paper; brewing. Has 2 Gothic churches; numerous half-timbered houses; remnants of old fortifications. Chartered c.1250. Joined Hanseatic League in 14th cent. Was known for its beer.

Eindhoven (īnt'hōvůn), city (pop. 134,527), North Brabant prov., S Netherlands, on Dommel R. and 18 mi. ESE of Tilburg; rail junction; airport at Welschap, 2 mi. W. Industrial center; mfg. (radio and electric appliances, plastics, textiles, cigars, cigarettes, heating apparatus, bicycles, leather, glass, matches, soap), woodworking, machine shops. Provincial butter-control station. Town chartered 1232. Rapid growth followed industrialization: 1910, pop. 5,700; 1920, pop. 47,964; 1930, pop. 95,565. In Second World War city was one of chief targets in the landing (Sept., 1944) of the First Allied Airborne Army.

Ein Dor, Israel: see EN-DOR.

Eine (ī'nů), town (pop. 3,981), East Flanders prov., W central Belgium, 2 mi. NNE of Oudenaarde, near Scheldt R.; textiles. Formerly spelled Eyne.

Einfeld (īn'fĕlt), village (pop. 5,148), in Schleswig-Holstein, NW Germany, on the small Einfelder See, 4 mi. N of Neumünster; chemicals, leather goods.

Ein Gedi, Israel: see EN-GEDI.

Ein Gev (ān' gĕv'), settlement (pop. 450), NE Israel, near Syrian border, on E shore of Sea of Galilee, 6 mi. E of Tiberias; fishing center; banana growing; winter resort. Scene of annual music festival. Founded 1937; suffered heavy attacks during Arab riots, 1936–39, and during Arab invasion, 1948. Near by (SE) is anc. locality of *Hippos*, town of the Decapolis, mentioned in Talmud as Sussita.

Ein Haemek, Israel: see RIHANIYA.

Ein Hahoresh or **'Ein ha Horesh** (both: ān' hä hō-rĕsh'), settlement (pop. 450), W Israel, in Plain of Sharon, 3 mi. SSE of Hadera; mfg. of agr. and poultry-breeding equipment; mixed farming. Founded 1931.

Ein Hamifratz or **'Ein ha Mifrats** (both: ān' hämē-fräts'), settlement (pop. 400), NW Israel, in Zebulun Valley, near Mediterranean, 9 mi. NE of Haifa; brick mfg.; mixed farming, fish breeding. Founded 1938. Sometimes spelled Ein Hamifrats.

Ein Hanatziv or **'Ein han Natsiv** (both: ān'hänätsēv'), settlement (pop. 175), NE Israel, in Jordan valley, 2 mi. SSW of Beisan; grain growing. Founded 1946.

Ein Haoved, Israel: see AVIHAYIL.

Ein Harod or **'Ein Harod** (both: ān' härōd'), settlement (pop. 1,120), N Israel, in SE part of Plain of Jezreel, near N foot of Mts. of Gilboa, on railroad and 7 mi. ESE of Afula; dairying and agr. center (viticulture; citrus fruit, grain, olives, vegetables, stock, poultry); woodworking, printing. Has natural history and art mus. During 1936–39 Arab riots it was hq. of Wingate's special police; during Arab invasion (1948) important Israeli defense base. Founded 1921 on reclaimed swamp land. Biblical *Well of Harod* was located in vicinity of near-by settlement of GILBOA.

Ein Hashofet or **'Ein ha Shofet** (both: ān' häshōfĕt'), settlement (pop. 450), NW Israel, in Hills of Ephraim, 16 mi. SSE of Haifa; dairying, poultry; grain, fruit, sheep. Afforestation; light industries. Founded 1937; heavily attacked by Arabs, 1948. Also spelled 'Ein Hashofet.

Ein Iron or **'Ein 'Iron** (ān' ērōn'), settlement (pop. 250), W Israel, in Plain of Sharon, 6 mi. NE of Hadera; mixed farming. Founded 1934.

Einme (ānmĕ'), village, Myaungmya dist., Lower Burma, in Irrawaddy delta, 30 mi. ENE of Bassein.

Einöd (īn'ût"), town (pop. 1,794), SE Saar, on Blies R., frontier station on Ger. border, opposite and 2.5 mi. NW of Zweibrücken; rail junction; mfg. (ceramics, tobacco products). Near by are remains of 13th-cent. Cistercian monastery (burned 1614).

Einödriegel (īn'ût"rē'gůl), mountain (3,704 ft.), Bavaria, Germany, highest peak of Bavarian Forest range of Bohemian Forest, 5 mi. SW of Regen.

Ein Sara or **'Ein Sara** (ān' särä'), agr. settlement, W Galilee, NW Israel, near Mediterranean, 12 mi. NNW of Haifa, just S of Nahariya.

Ein Shemer 'Ein Shemer (ān' shĕ'mĕr), settlement (pop. 430), W Israel, in Plain of Sharon, 5 mi. ENE of Hadera; mixed farming; glucose and starch mfg. Airfield near by. Founded 1927.

Einsiedel (īn'zē"důl), village (pop. 4,999), Saxony, E central Germany, at N foot of the Erzgebirge, on Chemnitz R. (dam) and 5 mi. SSE of Chemnitz; hosiery knitting, machinery mfg.

Einsiedeln (īn'zē"důln), town (pop. 8,392), Schwyz canton, NE central Switzerland, near the Sihlsee, 8 mi. NNE of Schwyz; largest pilgrim resort in Switzerland; printing, candles. Benedictine abbey, above village, was founded in 9th cent. and has an 18th-cent. church (baroque interior) noted for its black-marble chapel with sacred image of the "Black Virgin." Abbey has a fine library.

'Ein Vared (ān' värĕd') or **'Ein Vered** (vĕ'rĕd), settlement (pop. 450), W Israel, in Plain of Sharon, 6 mi. SE of Natanya; mixed farming, citriculture. Founded 1930. Also spelled Ein Vared or Ein Vered.

Einville-au-Jard (ĕvēl'-ō-zhär'), village (pop. 987), Meurthe-et-Moselle dept., NE France, on Marne-Rhine Canal and 5 mi. N of Lunéville; salt mines.

Ein Zeitim or **'Ein Zeitim** (ān' zātēm'), agr. settlement (pop. 100), Upper Galilee, N Israel, just N of Safad; founded 1891, abandoned during First World War, resettled 1946. Heavily attacked during Arab invasion, 1948.

Eipel, Czechoslovakia: see UPICE.

Eipel River, Czechoslovakia and Hungary: see IPEL RIVER.

Eire: see IRELAND.

Eirias, Wales: see COLWYN BAY.

Eiriksjokull (ā'rēksyû"kütůl), Icelandic *Eiríksjökull*, glacier, W Iceland, 60 mi. NE of Reykjavik; rises to 5,495 ft. at 64°46'N 20°25'W. Adjoins extensive lava field of Hallmundarhraun (hä'tůlmüntärhů-rû"ün) or Halmundarhraun (häl'müntär–). Noted cave (1 mi. long) of Surtshellir (sürs'hĕt"lĭr), 8 mi. W of peak, has interesting ice formations.

Eiris Fjord, Norway: see NAUSTE.

Eirunepé (ärōōnĭpĕ'), city (pop. 1,095), SW Amazonas, Brazil, on Juruá R. (navigable) and 200 mi. NE of Cruzeiro do Sul; rubber, sugar, vegetable ivory. Called São Felippe (other spellings, São Felipe and São Philippe) until 1939, and João Pessoa from 1939 to 1943.

Eisack, Italy: see ISARCO RIVER.

Eisden (īz'důn), town (pop. 8,197), Limburg prov., NE Belgium, near the Zuid-Willemsvaart, 8 mi. SSW of Maaseik; coal mining; machine mfg. Formerly spelled Eysden.

Eisden, Netherlands: see EIJSDEN.

Eisei, Formosa: see YUNGTSING.

Eisen, Korea: see YONGCHON.

Eisenach (ī'zůnäkh), city (pop. 51,834), Thuringia, central Germany, at NW end of Thuringian Forest, on small Hörsel R. near its mouth on the Werra, and 30 mi. W of Erfurt, at foot of the WARTBURG; 50°58'N 10°19'E. Rail junction; rock-salt mining; metal- and woodworking, distilling, food canning; mfg. of automobiles, machine tools, light bulbs, glass. Spa. Has 12th-cent. churches of St. Nicholas and St. George; house where J. S. Bach was born (now mus. with large collection of early musical instruments); Luther's residence (1498–1501); 18th-cent. former grand-ducal castle; villa of novelist Reuter (who lived here, 1863–74). Chartered in late-12th cent., Eisenach passed in 1440 from local counts to house of Wettin. Went to Ernestine branch of Saxony in 1485; passed to Saxe-Weimar (later Saxe-Weimar-Eisenach) in 1741. Scene (1869) of Congress of Eisenach, at which August Bebel and Wilhelm Liebknecht founded Ger. Social Democratic party.

Eisenberg (ī'zůnbĕrk). **1** Village (pop. 4,046), Rhenish Palatinate, W Germany, 13 mi. W of Frankenthal; ironworks; pottery, paper mills. Remains of a Jupiter temple excavated here (1764). **2** Town (pop. 15,299), Thuringia, central Germany, 10 mi. NW of Gera; woolen milling, woodworking; mfg. of china, pianos, furniture, photographic equipment, sausages, toys. Has 15th-cent. church; 16th-cent. former town hall; 17th-cent. Christiansburg palace, now town hall. Chartered 1182. Was ⊙ duchy of Saxe-Eisenberg, 1680–1707; passed to Saxe-Altenburg in 1826.

Eisenbrod, Czechoslovakia: see ZELEZNY BROD.

Eisenburg, Hungary: see VASVAR.

Eisenerz (ī'zůnĕrts), mining town (pop. 12,917), Styria, central Austria, at N foot of the ERZBERG, 15 mi. NW of Leoben. Large ironworks here use deposits mined for over 1,000 years.

Eisenerz Alps, range of Eastern Alps, in Styria, central Austria, S of Eisenerz. Rise to 7,106 ft. at the Reichenstein. Contains the Erzberg [Ger.,=ore mtn.], Austria's largest iron mine.

Eisenhower, Mount (ī'zůnhou"ůr) (9,390 ft.), SW Alta., near B.C. border, in Rocky Mts., in Banff Natl. Park, 18 mi. WNW of Banff; 51°18'N 115°56'W. Renamed 1946 from Castle Mtn.

Eisenhut (ī'zůnhōōt), highest peak (8,008 ft.) of Gurktal Alps (and of Noric Alps), SE Austria, at Styria-Carinthia border, 25 mi. N of Villach.

Eisenkappel (ī'zůnkäpĕl'), village (pop. 1,376), Carinthia, S Austria, 17 mi. SE of Klagenfurt; summer resort with mineral springs. Lead mined near by.

Eisenmarkt, Rumania: see HUNEDOARA, town.

Eisenstadt (ī'zůnshtät), Hung. *Kismarton* (kĭsh'-märtôn), city (pop. 7,626), ⊙ Burgenland, E Austria, at S foot of Leitha Mts., 25 mi. S of Vienna. Has fine Esterhazy castle in large park. Haydn lived here many years.

Eisenstein, Czechoslovakia: see ZELEZNA RUDA.

Eisenstein or **Bayrisch Eisenstein** (bī'rĭsh ī'zůn-shtīn), village (pop. 2,294), Lower Bavaria, Germany, in Bohemian Forest, at NE foot of the Great Arber, 8 mi. NNW of Zwiesel, on the Czechoslovak border, opposite Zelezna Ruda; well-known summer and winter resort (alt. 2,375 ft.).

Eiserfeld (ī'zůrfĕlt), village (pop. 7,866), in former Prussian prov. of Westphalia, W Germany, after 1945 in North Rhine-Westphalia, 4 mi. SW of Siegen; blast furnaces. Iron mining.

Eisernes Tor, Rumania: see IRON GATE.

Eisfeld (īs'fĕlt), town (pop. 5,586), Thuringia, central Germany, at foot of Thuringian Forest, on the Werra and 12 mi. N of Coburg (Bavaria); mfg. of china, optical and precision instruments, lace, toys; woodworking. Has 15th-cent. church and remains of 16th-cent. church. Otto Ludwig b. here.

Eishishkes, Lithuania: see EISISKES.

Eishu, Korea: see YONGJU.

Eisiskes, Eishishkes, or **Eyshishkes** (ā'shēshkĕs), Lith. *Eišiškes*, Pol. *Ejszyszki*, city (1930 pop. 2,382), S Lithuania, 37 mi. SSW of Vilna, on Belorussian border; road junction; cement mfg., tanning, flour milling. In Rus. Vilna govt. until it passed in 1921 to Poland, in 1939 to Lithuania.

Eisk-, in Rus. names: see YEISK-.

Eisleben (īs'lā"bůn), city (pop. 29,652), in former Prussian Saxony prov., central Germany, after 1945 in Saxony-Anhalt, at E foot of the lower Harz, 19 mi. W of Halle; 51°31'N 11°34'E. Copper-slate mining and smelting center (since 1200); food canning; mfg. of clothing, vinegar, mustard. Seed nurseries. Has houses where Luther was born and where he died, and the 15th-cent. church where he was baptized; also several other Gothic churches. Of anc. Slav origin. First mentioned as town in 1180. Was ⊙ county of Mansfeld (12th cent. to 1780), then passed to Saxony. Went to Prussia in 1815.

Eislingen (īs'lĭng-ůn), town (pop. 12,335), N Württemberg, Germany, after 1945 in Württemberg-Baden, on the Fils and 2.5 mi. E of Göppingen; mineral-oil refineries, iron foundry; produces machinery, vehicles, piston pins, electrical household goods, radios, batteries, chemicals (coal cracking, rubber and asbestos processing). Also enameling; mfg. of textiles (artificial fiber), clothing, candy, chairs; printing, leather- and woodworking, lumber and paper milling. Chartered after unification of Grosseislingen and Kleineislingen (1933).

Eitorf (ī'tôrf), village (pop. 11,101), in former Prussian Rhine Prov., W Germany, after 1945 in North Rhine-Westphalia, on the Sieg and 15 mi. E of Bonn; grain.

Eitrheim (ā'tůrhäm), village in Odda canton, Hordaland co., SW Norway, on Sor Fjord, 2 mi. NNW of Odda village; zinc-mining and -smelting center, producing zinc, cadmium, copper matte, lead sulphate, sulphuric acid.

Eitzen, village (pop. 151), Houston co., extreme SE Minn., near Iowa line, 9 mi. SSE of Caledonia.

Eivindvik (ā'vĭnvēk), village in Gulen canton (pop. 2,975), Sogn og Fjordane co., W Norway, on an inlet of North Sea, c.6 mi. S of entrance to Sogne Fjord, 40 mi. N of Bergen; medieval seat of regional parliament. Formerly spelled Evenvik.

Eixo (ā'shōō), village (pop. 1,575), Aveiro dist., N central Portugal, on branch railroad and 4 mi. ESE of Aveiro; produces chicory.

Eizanho, Korea: see YONSANPO.

Ejby (ī'bü), town (pop. 1,196), Odense amt, Denmark, on Fyn isl. and 18 mi. WNW of Odense; leather tanning, furniture mfg.

Ejdfjord, Norway: see EIDFJORD.

Ejea de los Caballeros or **Egea de los Caballeros** (both: āhā'ä dhā lōs kävälyā'rōs), town (pop. 7,398), Saragossa prov., N Spain, 35 mi. NNW of Saragossa; agr. trade center (cereals, livestock, potatoes, sugar beets); farm-implement mfg.; flour mills. Irrigation reservoir near by.

Ejemplo or **Central Ejemplo** (āhĕm'plō), locality, E Puerto Rico, just S of Humacao; sugar mill.

Ejido or **Egido** (both: āhē'dō), town (pop. 2,719), Mérida state, W Venezuela, on Chama R., on transandine highway, at SW foot of Sierra Nevada de Mérida, and 6 mi. SW of Mérida; sugar cane.

Ejinrin (ā'jūrēn), town (pop. 2,330), Nigeria colony, port on coastal lagoon and 15 mi. S of Ijebu-Ode; market center; cacao, palm oil and kernels, rice. Bitumen deposits.

Ejisu, town, Ashanti, S central Gold Coast, on railroad and 10 mi. E of Kumasi; cacao, cassava, corn. Gold deposits.

Ejkisdal Lake, Norway: see EIKESDAL LAKE.

Ejszyszki, Lithuania: see EISISKES.

Ejuanema, Mount, Gold Coast: see MPRAESO.

Ejura (ĕjōō'rä), village, Ashanti, central Gold Coast, 50 mi. NNE of Kumasi; hill station.

Ejutla (āhōōt'lä). **1** Town (pop. 1,048), Jalisco, W Mexico, on central plateau, 18 mi. NE of Autlán; grain, sugar cane, fruit, vegetables. **2** or **Ejutla de Crespo** (dā krĕ'spō), city (pop. 3,942), Oaxaca, S Mexico, in Atoyac valley, 33 mi. S of Oaxaca; alt. 4,724 ft. Rail terminus; agr. center (cereals, coffee, sugar cane, vegetables, fruit, livestock). Silver and gold deposits.

Ekalaka (ē'kůlă"ků), town (pop. 904), ⊙ Carter co., SE Mont., 70 mi. SE of Miles City; timber, livestock, grain. Local mus. contains animal fossils.

Ekarma Island (ĕkŭrmä'), Jap. *Ekaruma-to* (ākä-rōōmä-tō') (□ 6), one of N main Kurile Isls. group, Russian SFSR; separated from Shiashkotan Isl. (E) by 4.5-mi.-wide Ekarma Strait; 48°57'N 153°57'E; 5 mi. long, 3 mi. wide; volcanic cone rises 3,839 ft.

Ekaterin-, in Rus. names: see YEKATERIN-.

Ekaterinburg, Russian SFSR: see SVERDLOVSK, city, Sverdlovsk oblast.

Ekaterinodar, Russian SFSR: see KRASNODAR, city.

Ekdil (āk'dĭl), town (pop. 3,737), Etawah dist., W Uttar Pradesh, India, 5 mi. ESE of Etawah; pearl millet, wheat, barley, corn, gram. Also called Sarai Ekdil.

Ekeby (ā'kübü"), village (pop. 567), Uppsala co., E Sweden, 18 mi. N of Uppsala; grain, potatoes, stock. Includes Eriksberg (ā'rĭksbĕr"yù) village.

Ekecek Dag (ĕkĕjĕk' dä), Turkish *Ekecek Dağ*, peak (6,998 ft.), central Turkey, 33 mi. SE of Kochisar.

Ekeli, India: see ZAHIRABAD.

Ekenas (ā"künĕs'), Swedish *Ekenäs*, Finnish *Tammisaari* (täm'mĭsä"rē), city (pop. 4,442), Uusimaa co., S Finland, on Pojo Bay of Gulf of Finland, at base of Hango peninsula, 50 mi. SE of Turku; woolen mills; seaside resort. Site of Swedish teachers seminary. Has church (c.1650). Majority of pop. is Swedish-speaking.

Ekenassjon (ā'künĕs"shûn"), Swedish *Ekenässjön*, village (pop. 508), Jonkoping co., S Sweden, on small Ekenas L., 6 mi. NNW of Vetlanda; grain, stock.

Ekeren (ā'kürün), residential town (pop. 16,174), Antwerp prov., N Belgium, 4 mi. N of Antwerp; truck gardening. Has 16th-cent. church. Site of defeats (1703, 1747) of Dutch by French. Formerly spelled Eeckeren.

Ekersund, Norway: see EGERSUND.

Eket (ĕ'kĕt), town (pop. 301), Calabar prov., Eastern Provinces, SE Nigeria, minor port on mouth of Kwa Ibo R. and 35 mi. SW of Calabar; palm oil and kernels, hardwood, rubber. Fisheries.

Eketahuna (ĕ"kùtùhōō'nù), borough (pop. 682), ⊙ Eketahuna co. (□ 311; pop. 1,827), S N.Isl., New Zealand, 65 mi. NE of Wellington; timber, sheep, dairy products.

Eketanga (ā'kùtông"ù), Swedish *Eketånga*, village (pop. 691), Halland co., SW Sweden, on Laholm Bay of Kattegat, 3 mi. WSW of Halmstad; stone quarrying.

Ekhabi (ĕkhä'bē), oil town (1944 pop. over 500), N Sakhalin, Russian SFSR, on Sea of Okhotsk, 10 mi. S of Okha.

Ekhedhoros River, Greece: see ECHEDOROS RIVER.

Ekhmim, Egypt: see AKHMIM.

Ekibastuz (ĕkēbäs'tōōs), town (1948 pop. c.10,000), W Pavlodar oblast, Russian SFSR, on S. Siberian RR and 75 mi. SW of Pavlodar; coal-mining center. Large-scale exploitation developed after construction (late 1940s) of railroad.

Ekimchan (ĕkĕmchän'), village (1948 pop. over 500), E Amur oblast, Russian SFSR, on upper Selemdzha R. (head of navigation) and 240 mi. NE of Svobodny; center of gold-mining region.

Ekimovichi, Russian SFSR: see YEKIMOVICHI.

Eklingji (āk'lĭngjē), village, S Rajasthan, India, 11 mi. N of Udaipur; contains noted group of white marble temples, carved in fine detail.

Eklutna (ēklōōt'nù), village (pop. 27), S Alaska on Knik Arm, 25 mi. NE of Anchorage, on Glenn Highway. Eklutna Industrial School for natives was closed, 1946.

Eko, Nigeria: see LAGOS.

Ekornnes, Norway: see IKORNNES.

Ekpoma (ĕk-pō'mä), town, Benin prov., Western Provinces, S Nigeria, 16 mi. WNW of Ubiaja; road center; palm oil and kernels, hardwood, rubber, cacao, kola nuts, cotton.

Ekron, Israel: see EQRON.

Ekron (ĕ'krŏn), town (pop. 188), Meade co., NW Ky., 24 mi. NW of Elizabethtown; makes whisky.

Eksaarde (ĕksär'dù), village (pop. 4,839), East Flanders prov., NW Belgium, 8 mi. NW of Dendermonde; agr., cattle raising. Has 14th-cent. church. Formerly spelled Exaerde.

Eksere, Turkey: see GUNDOGMUS.

Eksjo (āk'shû"), Swedish *Eksjö*, city (pop. 7,898), Jonkoping co., S Sweden, 30 mi. ESE of Jonkoping; machinery mfg., woodworking. Has church (1521) and mus. Chartered in 14th cent., city was burned (1570) by Danes.

Ektorp, Sweden: see SKURU.

Ekwangatana (ĕkwäng-gätä'nä), village, Eastern Prov., N Belgian Congo, on Rubi R., on railroad, on Congo-Nile highway, and 45 mi. W of Buta; coffee and rubber plantations; coffee processing.

Ekwan River (ĕ'kwän), N Ont., rises in Patricia dist., flows 300 mi. NE and E to James Bay opposite Akimiski Isl.

Ekwendeni (ĕkwĕndĕ'nē), village, Northern Prov., N central Nyasaland, 25 mi. NNE of Mzimba; cassava, corn. Church of Scotland mission station, with school, hosp.

Ekwok (ĕk'wŏk), village (pop. 55), SW Alaska on Nushagak R. and 40 mi. NE of Dillingham; supply point for trappers.

El [Arabic,=the], for Arabic names beginning thus: see under following part of the name.

Ela (ā'lä), village, Yamethin dist., Upper Burma, 9 mi. S of Pyinmana and on railroad.

Ela Bared (ĕ'lä bärĕd') or **Ela Behred** (bĕrĕd'), village, Keren div., N Eritrea, near Anseba R., on railroad and 20 mi. ESE of Keren, in agr. region (citrus fruit, vegetables, agave); fiber working.

Elabuga, Russian SFSR: see YELABUGA.

El Aceituno (ĕl äsātōō'nō), village (pop. 390), Valle dept., S Honduras, minor Pacific port on Gulf of Fonseca, 14 mi. WSW of Nacaome; saltworks; fisheries.

El Adelanto, Guatemala: see ADELANTO.

Elafonisos, Greece: see ELAPHONESOS.

Elahera (ālŭhä'rŭ), village (pop. 813), Central Prov., Ceylon, on the Amban Ganga and 20 mi. NNE of Matale; rice, vegetables. Headworks of a canal (in anc. times much larger) just S; land reclamation (□ 15) project. Anc. Buddhist ruins of monastery, temple, large reclining Buddha near by.

Elaine, town (pop. 744), Phillips co., E Ark., 21 mi. SW of Helena, near the Mississippi; cotton ginning.

Elaiya, Br. Somaliland: see ELAYU.

El Alamein, Egypt: see ALAMEIN.

El Alto (ĕl äl'tō), village (pop. estimate 500), ⊙ El Alto dept. (□ 680; pop. 4,670), SE Catamarca prov., Argentina, 26 mi. NE of Catamarca; stock-raising center. Granite quarries near by.

El Alto, Bolivia: see LA PAZ, city.

El Alto, town (pop. 4,897), Piura dept., NW Peru, in W foothills of Cordillera Occidental, E of Cabo Blanco–Restín oil fields, 22 mi. N of Talara; oil wells. Petroleum is shipped through LOBITOS (connected by railroad).

El Alto, town (pop. 558), Trujillo state, W Venezuela, in Andean spur, 5 mi. W of Valera; coffee, fruit.

Elam (ē'lăm), anc. country of SW Asia, N of the head of the Persian Gulf and E of the Tigris, and now in SW Iran, where it coincides roughly with modern Khuzistan. The language of the Elamites, which survives in cuneiform inscriptions, remains undeciphered. Their capital was SUSA, and from this the country became known as Susiana in classical times. In the historical period, Elam was a rival of Babylonia, which it helped to overthrow in 18th cent. B.C. Elam reached its golden age after 1200 B.C. Threatened by the rising power of Assyria, it fell (645 B.C.) to Assur-bani-pal, but revived under the Achaemenian Persian empire, which made Susa one of its residences.

Elam, town, Iran: see ILAM.

Elamanchili, India: see YELLAMANCHILI.

El Amparo (ĕl ämpä'rō). **1** Officially El Amparo de Apure, town (pop. 631), Apure state, W central Venezuela, landing on Arauca R., opposite town of Arauca (Colombia), and 9 mi. S of Guadualito; cattle raising. **2** or **Amparo,** village (pop. 108), Cojedes state, N Venezuela, landing on Cojedes R. and 29 mi. SSW of San Carlos; cattle raising.

Elan-, in Rus. names: see YELAN-.

Eland (ē'lùnd), village (pop. 232), Shawano co., E central Wis., 22 mi. ESE of Wausau, in lumbering and agr. area.

Elandslaagte (ē'läntslākh"tù), agr. village, W Natal, U. of So. Afr., 15 mi. NE of Ladysmith; scene (Oct. 21, 1899) of South African War battle in which British under General French defeated Boer force.

Elandsputte, U. of So. Afr.: see BAKERSVILLE AND ELANDSPUTTE.

El Angel (ĕl än'hĕl), town (1950 pop. 3,769), Carchi prov., N Ecuador, in the Andes, on branch of Pan American Highway, and 20 mi. SW of Tulcán; agr. center (cereals, potatoes, sugar cane, coffee, livestock); mfg. of native woolen goods (rugs, ponchos).

Elaphonesos or Elafonisos (both: ĕlä'fô'nĭsôs), Ital. *Cervi* (chĕr'vē), island (□ 8.5; pop. 457), in Laconia nome, in E Gulf of Laconia, 1 mi. off SE Peloponnesus, Greece; 4 mi. long, 3 mi. wide. Elaphonesos village on N shore. Formerly Elaphonisi.

El Arañado (ĕl äränyä'dō), town (pop. estimate 2,000), E central Córdoba prov., Argentina, 80 mi. ESE of Córdoba; agr. center (dairy products; wheat, flax, alfalfa, livestock). Formerly San Alberto.

El Arenal or **Arenal** (ĕl, äränäl'). **1** Town (pop. 1,050), Hidalgo, central Mexico, 13 mi. NW of Pachuca; corn, beans, maguey, stock. **2** Village (pop. 2,045), Jalisco, W Mexico, on railroad and 24 mi. WNW of Guadalajara; alt. 4,600 ft.; grain, beans, livestock.

El Asintal, Guatemala: see ASINTAL.

Elasson (ĕläsôn'), anc. *Oloosson*, town (pop. 3,939), Larissa nome, N Thessaly, Greece, on highway and 22 mi. NNW of Larissa, on W slope of the Lower Olympus; olives, vegetables, fruit, grain, livestock.

Elasy, Russian SFSR: see YELASY.

Elatea (ĕlùtē'ù), anc. ⊙ city of Phocis, Greece, next in importance to Delphi. Strategically located, it guarded pass bet. Sperchios and Cephisus valleys. Its capture (339 B.C.) by Philip II of Macedon blocked all routes from Boeotia northward. Onomarchus, Phocian statesman, b. here (4th cent. B.C.). On its site is modern village of Elateia or Elatia (pop. 1,759), formerly Drachmani, of Phthiotis nome.

Elath (ē'lăth) or **Eilat** (ālät'), seaport at S extremity of Israel, at head of Gulf of Aqaba of the Red Sea, 150 mi. S of Jerusalem; 19°33'N 34°57'E; near borders of Egypt, Jordan, and Saudi Arabia. Fisheries. Modern settlement founded 1948 near AQABA, Jordan, which is probably on site of anc. port of Elath. Near by is site of biblical port of EZION-GEBER.

Elatias, mountains, Greece: see CITHAERON.

Elatma, Russian SFSR: see YELATMA.

Elato (ĕlä'tō), double atoll (pop. 36), Yap dist., W Caroline Isls., W Pacific, 5 mi. W of Lamotrek; consists of Elato and Toas atolls; 7°29'N 146°10'E; lagoon is 4.5 mi. long, 1 mi. wide.

Elayu (ĕlä'yōō), village, NE Br. Somaliland, minor port on Makhir Coast of Gulf of Aden, on Ital. Somaliland border (just W of Bender Ziada), 45 mi. E of Las Khoreh; gums (frankincense, myrrh); fisheries. Customs and police posts. Formerly spelled Elaiya.

Elazig (ĕläzū'), Turkish *Elazığ* or *Elâzığ*, province (□ 3,554; 1950 pop. 212,400), E Turkey, in Kurdistan; ⊙ Elazig. Bordered N by Euphrates, Murat, and Peri rivers, SE by Taurus Mts., SW by Euphrates R.; also drained by Tigris R. Mountainous; lignite, chromium. Cereals, legumes; apricots, apples, pears, plums; cotton. Formerly spelled Elaziz and Mamuret-el-Aziz.

Elazig, Turkish *Elazığ* or *Elâzığ*, city (1950 pop. 29,044), ⊙ Elazig prov., E Turkey, 55 mi. ENE of Malatya; rail terminus and agr. center (grain, legumes, fruit). Formerly called Mezre, Mezere, or Yeni Harput.

Elba (ĕl'bä), anc. *Ilva* and *Aethalia*, largest island (□ 86; pop. 29,462) of Tuscan Archipelago, in Tyrrhenian Sea, Italy, in Livorno prov., 7 mi. SW of Piombino; 42°47'N 10°17'E; 18 mi. long, 11.5 mi. wide. Mountainous, rising to 3,343 ft. in Monte Capanne (W). Produces 90% of Italy's iron ore, mined here since Etruscan times; principal mines in E, around Rio Marina. Also noted for its wine. Fisheries (tunny, sardine) along deeply indented coast. Chief town and port, PORTOFERRAIO, on N coast. Steamer service to other isls. of the archipelago, to Leghorn, and to Piombino. Under many foreign rulers throughout its history; briefly (1814–15) a sovereign principality under the exiled Napoleon I.

Elba. 1 City (pop. 2,936), ⊙ Coffee co., SE Ala., on Pea R. and 42 mi. WNW of Dothan; trading point in cotton, peanut, and livestock area; agr. equipment, lumber; peanut butter, meat products. Became co. seat 1852. **2** Village (pop. 147), Winona co., SE Minn., on small affluent of Mississippi R. and 22 mi. ENE of Rochester; dairy products. **3** Village (pop. 216), Howard co., E central Nebr., 7 mi. NW of St. Paul and on N.Loup R.; pheasant hunting near by. **4** Village (pop. 569), Genesee co., W N.Y., on Oak Orchard Creek and 5 mi. N of Batavia, in agr. area.

Elba, Ras, Anglo-Egyptian Sudan: see HADARBA, RAS.

El Balde, Argentina: see BALDE.

El Banco (ĕl bäng'kō), town (pop. 5,626), Magdalena dept., N Colombia, river port on Magdalena R., at mouth of César R., on Barrancabermeja–Cartagena pipe line, and 36 mi. ESE of Mompós; trading, fishing, and stock-raising center; dried fish, mats, mangrove bark.

El Barco (ĕl bär'kō), town (pop. estimate 800), NE Tucumán prov., Argentina, on railroad and 25 mi. NE of Tucumán; agr. center (sugar cane, corn, livestock); lime deposits.

Elbasan (ĕlbäsän') or **Elbasani** (ĕlbäsä'nē), city (1945 pop. 14,968), central Albania, on Shkumbi R. and 20 mi. SE of Tirana (linked by highway), on railroad from Durazzo; transportation and agr. center in fertile valley (vegetables, olives, tobacco, wine); leather, silk, wool, handicrafts; flour milling, olive-oil pressing, cigarette mfg.; power plant. Hot sulphur springs at Llixhë (SE). Chrome and iron mining at Labinot (NE). Has 15th-cent. Turkish fortress (partly dismantled 1832) and active bazaar. The anc. Scampa, it is sometimes identified with Albanopolis, the anc. ⊙ (c.130 A.D.) of the Albanians. Became bishopric (5th cent.); destroyed (10th cent.) by Bulgars, it passed (15th cent.) to Turks who gave it its modern name.

El Batatal (ĕl bätätäl'), town (pop. 540), Trujillo state, W Venezuela, 20 mi. ESE of Trujillo; grain, potatoes.

El Baúl (ĕl bäōōl'), village (pop. 1,100), Escuintla dept., S Guatemala, 3 mi. N of Santa Lucía; sugar milling.

El Baúl, town (pop. 780), Cojedes state, N Venezuela, river port at confluence of Tirgua R. with Cojedes R., 55 mi. SSE of San Carlos; cattle raising.

Elbe-Lübeck Kanal, Germany: see ELBE-TRAVE CANAL.

Elberfeld (ĕl'bùrfĕlt), central section (1925 pop. 167,577) of WUPPERTAL, W Germany, on the Wupper; textile- and chemical-mfg. center; metalworking. Chartered 1610. Industrial development began after 1750. Elberfeld system of poor relief was developed here in 1852. Inc. (1929) with Barmen (just E) and other neighboring towns to form city of Wuppertal.

Elberfeld (ĕl'bùrfēld), town (pop. 499), Warrick co., SW Ind., 14 mi. NNE of Evansville, in agr. and bituminous-coal area.

Elbe River (ĕl'bù), Czech *Labe* (lä'bĕ), a major river of central Europe, rises at c.4,600 ft. in the Riesengebirge on Bohemian-Silesian line 5 mi. NW of Spindleruv Mlyn, flows in general NW course through NW Czechoslovakia and central Germany to the North Sea at Cuxhaven, 55 mi. NW of Hamburg. Length, until junction with Kiel Canal (at Brunsbüttelkoog), is 691 mi.; until Cuxhaven, 706 mi. River forms wide arc (c.225 mi. long) in Czechoslovakia, flowing past Dvur Kralove, Hradec Kralove, Kolin, and Melnik, turns N above Usti nad Labem, and continues past Decin to Czechoslovak–German border, which it forms for c.2 mi. Entering Germany (in which it is c.475 mi. long) bet. Hrensko and Schöna, the Elbe cuts through limestone mts. of Saxonian Switzerland into N German lowlands, flows in large meanders generally NW, past Dresden, Torgau, Dessau, and

Magdeburg, to Hamburg, which it traverses in 2 arms, the Norderelbe and the Süderelbe; it continues in c.60-mi.-long estuary to North Sea at Cuxhaven, where it is 10 mi. wide. Chief tributaries are: Eger, Ilmenau, Mulde, Saxonian Saale, and Vltava (Moldau) rivers (left); Black Elster, Elde, Havel, and Jizera rivers (right). A major European waterway, the Elbe is navigable over 500 mi. for barges below Kolin, for river boats below Melnik; dammed below Hostinne and at Strekov. It is linked with the Weser and the Rhine via the Mittelland Canal system, with the Oder via Havel-Hohenzollern and Plaue-Havel-Spree waterways; the Elbe-Trave and Kiel canals connect it with Baltic ports of Lübeck and Kiel, respectively. The *Albis* of the Romans, the Elbe marked limit of Roman advance into Germany, and, later, of Charlemagne's conquests. By Treaty of Versailles (1919), river was internationalized from mouth of Vltava (at Melnik) to North Sea; Germany repudiated internationalization after Munich Pact (1938).

Elberon (ĕl'bûrŏn). **1** Town (pop. 225), Tama co., central Iowa, 8 mi. N of Belle Plaine, in agr. area. **2** Community, Monmouth co., N.J.: see LONG BRANCH.

Elbert. 1 County (□ 1,864; pop. 4,477), E central Colo.; ⊙ Kiowa. Wheat and livestock area. Formed 1874. **2** County (□ 362; pop. 18,585), NE Ga.; ⊙ Elberton. Bounded E by S.C. line (formed here by Savannah R.) and W by Broad R. Farming (cotton, corn, oats, fruit) and granite-quarrying (ELBERTON) area. Formed 1790.

Elbert, village (pop. 1,565), McDowell co., S W.Va., 6 mi. S of Welch.

Elbert, Mount (14,431 ft.), central Colo., in SAWATCH MOUNTAINS, 5 mi. SSE of Mt. Massive, 12 mi. SW of Leadville. Highest peak in Colo. and in Rocky Mts. of U.S.

Elberta, village (pop. 597), Benzie co., NW Mich., opposite Frankfort on Betsie R. at its mouth on L. Michigan.

Elberton. 1 City (pop. 6,772), ⊙ Elbert co., NE Ga., 31 mi. ENE of Athens, near S.C. line. A major granite-quarrying and processing center of the U.S.; mfg. (monuments, clothing, yarns, tapestry). Nancy Hart Forest Park near by. Settled 1780s. **2** Town (pop. 145), Whitman co., SE Wash., 8 mi. NE of Colfax and on Palouse R.

Elbe-Trave Canal (ĕl'bù-trä'vù), NW Germany, connecting the Elbe (at Lauenburg) with the Baltic (through Trave estuary) at Lübeck; 40 mi. long; 7 locks. Built 1895–1900 to replace old Stecknitz Canal (built 1391–98). In Ger. sometimes also called *Elbe-Lübeck Kanal* (–lü'bĕk känäl').

Elbeuf (ĕlbûf'), town (pop. 15,341), Seine-Inférieure dept., N France, on left bank of a Seine R. bend and 11 mi. SSW of Rouen; a leading woolen-milling center, especially known for its fine woolen fabrics. Also produces machinery and dyes for textile industry. Damaged in Second World War by bombings and by short but desperate stand of retreating Germans in Aug., 1944. Has important suburbs of Caudebec-lès-Elbeuf (ESE), Saint-Aubin-lès-Elbeuf (N; paper and pencil mfg.), and Saint-Pierre-lès-Elbeuf (3 mi. SE).

Elbing (ĕl'bĭng) or **Elblag** (ĕl'blŏk), Pol. *Elbląg*, town (1939 pop. 85,952; 1946 pop. 20,924) in East Prussia, after 1945 in Gdansk prov., N Poland, on Elbing R. just below its mouth on Vistula Lagoon, at E edge of Vistula estuary, and 35 mi. ESE of Danzig; 54°9'N 19°24'E. Rail junction; seaport; shipbuilding, metalworking, sawmilling, brewing, mfg. of railroad cars, ship machinery; power station. Castle, founded 1237 by Teutonic Knights, destroyed c.1440. Town chartered 1246; joined Hanseatic League in late-13th cent. Passed 1466 to Poland; Reformation introduced c.1520. In 1580 became chief East Prussian port for trade with England. In Thirty Years War, captured (1626) by Gustavus Adolphus; fortified and held by Swedes until 1636. Passed 1772 to Prussia. After Second World War, during which it was c.70% destroyed, its Ger. pop. was evacuated.

Elbing, city (pop. 98), Butler co., SE central Kansas, 26 mi. NNE of Wichita; grain, livestock.

Elbingerode (ĕl"bĭngûrō'dù), town (pop. 4,291), in former Prussian Saxony prov., central Germany, after 1945 in Saxony-Anhalt, in the lower Harz, 5 mi. S of Wernigerode; iron- and sulphuric-ore mining; lime and cement works.

Elbing River or **Elblag River**, in East Prussia, after 1945 in N Poland, leaves L. Druzno 2 mi. S of Elbing, flows 7 mi. N, past Elbing (head of ocean-going navigation), to SW arm of Vistula Lagoon.

Elbistan (ĕlbĭstän') [Turkish,=the garden], town (pop. 6,655), Maras prov., S central Turkey, 45 mi. NNE of Maras, in Taurus Mts.; alt. 3,775 ft.; wheat, barley, rye, vetch, potatoes, sugar beets. Formerly sometimes spelled El-Bostan, Al-Bostan, or Al-Bistan.

Elblag, Poland: see ELBING.

El Bluff (ĕl bloof'), town, Zelaya dept., E Nicaragua, outer port (5 mi. E) of BLUEFIELDS, on Caribbean Sea, on promontory forming breakwater for Bluefields Bay. Has lighthouse, customhouse.

Elbogen, Czechoslovakia: see LOKET.

El Bolsón (ĕl bōlsōn'), town (pop. estimate 500), SW Río Negro natl. territory, Argentina, in Argentinian lake district, 60 mi. SSW of San Carlos de Bariloche. Hydroelectric station; sawmills, flour mills. Agr.: wheat, oats, alfalfa, fruit, livestock. Coal deposits. Waterfall near by.

El Boom (ĕl boom'), village, Cabo Gracias a Dios territory, Zelaya dept., NE Nicaragua, on Coco R. and 32 mi. W of Cabo Gracias a Dios; lumbering. Airfield.

El Borbollón (ĕl bôrdōyōn'), village (pop. estimate 600), N Mendoza prov., Argentina, 8 mi. NE of Mendoza; health resort (mineral waters); agr.

El Borracho or **Paso del Borracho** (pä'sō dĕl bôrä'chō), village, Tacuarembó dept., NE Uruguay, on Tacuarembó R. and 35 mi. ESE of Tacuarembó; grain, cattle, sheep.

El Bosque (ĕl bō'skā), town (pop. 873), Chiapas, S Mexico, in spur of Sierra Madre, 33 mi. NE of Tuxtla; cereals, fruit.

El-Bostan, Turkey: see ELBISTAN.

Elbow, village (pop. 260), S Sask., on South Saskatchewan R. and 70 mi. NW of Moose Jaw; grain.

Elbow Lake, village (pop. 1,398), ⊙ Grant co., W Minn., on small lake and 21 mi. S of Fergus Falls; farm trading point; dairy products.

Elbow Lake, Becker co., W Minn., 25 mi. NE of Detroit Lakes city, in White Earth Indian Reservation; 5 mi. long, ½ mi. wide. Fed and drained by Otter Trail R.

Elbowoods, village (pop. c.150), McLean co., W N.Dak., on Missouri R. and c.45 mi. W of Garrison. Hq. of Fort Berthold Indian Reservation. Nonprofit flour mill and experimental farm are maintained for education of Indians in agr. methods.

Elbridge, village (pop. 586), Onondaga co., central N.Y., 16 mi. W of Syracuse, in agr. area.

Elbrus, Mount, or **Mount El'brus** (ĕl'broos, ăl'broos), highest peak of Caucasus mts. and of Europe, in NW Georgian SSR, 12 mi. N of main range of the central Greater Caucasus, 40 mi. SSW of Kislovodsk; 43°21'N 42°27'E. Formed by 2 conical peaks rising to 18,481 ft. (W) and 18,356 ft. (E); extinct volcanoes covered by laval flows, with crystalline rock base. Its glaciers give rise to Kuban, Malka, and Baksan rivers. Snow-line at 10,500 ft. on S slope, at 11,500 ft. on N slope.

Elbsandsteingebirge, Germany: see SAXONIAN SWITZERLAND.

El Bur, Ital. Somaliland: see BUR, EL.

Elburg (ĕl'bûrkh), town (pop. 2,758), Gelderland prov., central Netherlands, on the Ijsselmeer and 18 mi. NNW of Apeldoorn; fishing, fish curing, cattle raising. Town charter dates from 1233.

Elburgon (ĕlboor'gŏn), village, Rift Valley prov., W Kenya, on railroad and 18 mi. WSW of Nakuru; hardwood industry; coffee, tea, wheat, corn.

Elburn, village (pop. 792), Kane co., NE Ill., 12 mi. NW of Aurora, in agr. area; meat-packing plant.

El Burrero (ĕl boorā'rō), town (pop. 613), Trujillo state, W Venezuela, in Andean spur, 11 mi. SW of Trujillo; alt. 3,678 ft.; coffee, wheat, potatoes.

Elburz (ĕlboorz') or **Alborz** (älbōrz'), major mountain range in N Iran, separating Caspian Sea from central Iranian plateau; rises to 18,600 ft. in Mt. Demavend. Consists of narrow series of steep parallel ranges disposed in form of shallow crescent along S border of Caspian coastal provs. of Gilan and Mazanderan. Rainy and forested slopes of N section are deeply dissected by erosion and short torrential Caspian coastal streams; S slopes receive scanty rainfall. The Elburz is continued NW by the Talysh Mts., and extends E to c.56°E.

El Cacao (ĕl käkou'), village, Alajuela prov., central Costa Rica, on central plateau, on Inter-American Highway and 2 mi. W of Alajuela; sugar-milling center; sugar and tapioca mill; pineapples.

El Cadillal (ĕl kädĭyäl'), village (pop. estimate 300), central Tucumán prov., Argentina, on the Salí and 15 mi. N of Tucumán; site of irrigation dam.

El Cafetal, Bolivia: see PUERTO VILLAZÓN.

El Caín (ĕl käēn'), village (pop. estimate 500), S Río Negro natl. territory, Argentina, 35 mi. SE of Maquinchao; sheep, goats.

El Cairo, Costa Rica: see CAIRO.

El Cajon (ĕl kùhōn'), city (pop. 5,600), San Diego co., S Calif., 12 mi. E of San Diego; packs and ships avocados, citrus fruit, grapes, vegetables; sawmills. Inc. 1912.

El Calafate (ĕl käläfä'tā) or **Lago Argentino** (lä'gō ärhĕntē'nō), village (pop. estimate 300), ⊙ Lago Argentino dept. (1947 pop. 2,181), W Santa Cruz natl. territory, Argentina, on S shore of L. Argentino, 175 mi. WSW of Santa Cruz. Resort in natl. park; sheep-raising and fruitgrowing center. Sawmills. Airport. Coal mines near by.

El Callao (ĕl käyä'ō), town (pop. 5,121), Bolívar state, SE Venezuela, landing on Yuruari R. and 135 mi. ESE of Ciudad Bolívar; 7°18'N 61°46'W; gold-mining center. Once (1885) greatest gold producer in the world; although mines were later considered exhausted, they are again operating profitably.

El Calvario (ĕl kälvär'yō), village (pop. 186), Meta intendancy, central Colombia, on E slopes of Cordillera Oriental, 15 mi. N of Villavicencio; cattle raising.

El Campo (ĕl kăm'pō), city (pop. 6,237), Wharton co., S Texas, c.65 mi. SW of Houston; trade, processing, market center; oil-producing, cattle-ranching, dairying, agr. area (rice, cotton, pecans); rice, cottonseed-oil, and feed milling, cotton ginning, meat packing, dairying, mfg. of metal products, beverages. Founded 1884, inc. 1905.

El Caney, Cuba: see CANEY.

El Cano, Cuba: see CANO.

El Caño (ĕl kä'nyō), village (pop. 520), Coclé prov., central Panama, in Pacific lowland, 13 mi. SW of Penonomé, on Inter-American Highway; sugar cane, corn, rice, beans, livestock.

El Capitan. 1 (ĕl kăpĭtăn') Peak in Calif.: see YOSEMITE NATIONAL PARK. **2** (ĕl kăpĭtăn') Peak in Mont.: see BITTERROOT RANGE. **3** (ĕl kăpĭtăn') Peak (8,078) in W Texas, in Guadalupe Mts.

El Capitan Dam, Calif.: see SAN DIEGO RIVER.

El Carate (ĕl kärä'tā), village (pop. 419), Los Santos prov., S central Panama, in Pacific lowland, 4.5 mi. SSW of Las Tablas; sugar cane, coffee; stock.

El Carmen or **Perico del Carmen** (ĕl, pārē'kō dĕl kär'mĕn), village (pop. estimate 500), ⊙ El Carmen dept. (□ 370; 1947 pop. 12,548), SE Jujuy prov., Argentina, 14 mi. SSE of Jujuy; agr. center (grain, sugar cane, livestock); sawmills, flour mills.

El Carmen (ĕl kär'mĕn), town (pop. 1,172), Ñuble prov., S central Chile, 20 mi. SSW of Chillán; agr. (grain, wine, potatoes, beans, livestock).

El Carmen. 1 Town, Bolívar dept., Colombia: see CARMEN. **2** Village, Chocó intendancy, Colombia: see CARMEN. **3** Town (pop. 2,432), Norte de Santander dept., N Colombia, 6 mi. SW of Cúcuta; coffee.

El Carmen, village (pop. 147), San Marcos dept., SW Guatemala, in lower Pacific piedmont, on Inter-American Highway and 6 mi. WNW of Malacatán near Mex. border. Customs station; coffee, sugar cane, grain; cattle raising.

El Carmen, town (pop. 2,667), Tlaxcala, central Mexico, 40 mi. NE of Puebla; cereals, alfalfa, beans, livestock.

El Carmen, town (1950 pop. 392), Managua dept., SW Nicaragua, 18 mi. SW of Managua; sugar cane, cacao, livestock; lumbering. Sugar mill of Apante is just SE.

El Carro, Mexico: see VILLA GONZÁLEZ ORTEGA.

El Castillo (ĕl kästē'yō), town (pop. 224), Río San Juan dept., S Nicaragua, 28 mi. ESE of San Carlos and on San Juan R. (rapids); lumbering; livestock.

El Cayo, Br. Honduras: see CAYO, town.

El Centro, Colombia: see BARRANCABERMEJA.

El Centro (ĕl sĕn'trō), city (pop. 12,590), ⊙ Imperial co., S Calif., near Mexico line, c.25 mi. S of Salton Sea; a shipping center for IMPERIAL VALLEY truck and livestock. Central Jr. Col. and an experiment station of Univ. of California Col. of Agr. are here. Mfg. of flax-fiber cigarette paper; dairying; poultry hatchery.

El Cercado (ĕl sĕrkä'dō), officially San Pedro del Cercado, town (1950 pop. 1,697), Benefactor prov., W Dominican Republic, on N slopes of the Sierra de Neiba, 19 mi. WSW of San Juan, in agr. region (coffee, bananas, potatoes, vegetables); sawmilling.

El Cerrito (ĕl sûrē'tō), city (pop. 18,011), Contra Costa co., W Calif., residential suburb of Richmond, on San Francisco Bay; clay products, lumber; nurseries. Inc. 1917.

El Chaco, Argentina-Paraguay-Bolivia: see CHACO.

El Chañar (ĕl chänyär'), town (pop. estimate 500), central Tucumán prov., Argentina, on railroad and 10 mi. WNW of Tucumán; agr. center (sugar cane, cotton, corn, livestock).

El Chañar, abandoned village, Coquimbo prov., N central Chile, on railroad and 55 mi. NNE of La Serena; iron deposits.

El Chaparro (ĕl chäpä'rō), town (pop. 919), Anzoátegui state, NE Venezuela, on affluent of Unare R. and 25 mi. SSW of Aragua de Barcelona; cotton, sugar cane, cacao, cattle.

El Charco (ĕl chär'kō), village (pop. estimate 600), W Santiago del Estero prov., Argentina, on railroad and 45 mi. NW of Santiago del Estero; stock raising (sheep, goats, cattle), lumbering.

Elche (ĕl'chā), anc. *Ilici*, city (pop. 31,275), Alicante prov., E Spain, in Valencia, in fertile oasis, 13 mi. SW of Alicante; circled by extensive date-palm plantation, only one of its kind in Europe; dates and palm leaves (sold for Easter throughout Spain) are shipped; pomegranates, figs, and other fruit also grown here. Footwear mfg. is chief industry; also makes chemical fertilizers, cotton cloth, cement, toys, furniture, ceramics, artificial flowers; has olive-oil presses, fruit cannery, flour- and sawmills. Has Moorish aspect because of white, flat-roofed houses; 17th-cent. church and former palace of dukes of Altamira are notable. Of Iberian origin, was Greek colony; besieged (229 B.C.) by Carthaginian general Hamilcar Barca, who died here; later Roman colony. Many Iberian, Greek, Roman, and Arabic findings in vicinity—most important is the sculpture *Dama de Elche*, found in 1897.

Elche de la Sierra (dhā lä syĕ'rä), town (pop. 4,066), Albacete prov., SE central Spain, 20 mi. WSW of Hellín; esparto processing, flour milling, tanning, olive pressing; sericulture. Hemp, cereals, saffron; and peat in area.

Elcherot, Belgium: see NOBRESSART.

El Chico, Mexico: see MINERAL DEL CHICO.

El Chilamatal, Salvador: see CIUDAD ARCE.

Elcho (ĕl'kō), resort village (1940 pop. 556), Langlade co., NE Wis., 20 mi. N of Antigo, in wooded lake region. Near by are the privately owned Kraftwood Gardens.

Elcho Island (ĕl'kō), in Arafura Sea; separated from Napier Peninsula of Arnhem Land, N Northern Territory, Australia, by Cadell Strait (2 mi. wide); 30 mi. long, 7 mi. wide; aboriginal reservation.

El Cholar (ĕl chōlär'), village (pop. estimate 200), NW Neuquén natl. territory, Argentina, in Andes foothills, 20 mi. WSW of Chos Malal; stock raising.

El Chorro (ĕl chô'rō), village (pop. estimate 200), ⊙ Ramón Lista dept. (□ c.1900; 1947 pop. 697), extreme NW Formosa natl. territory, Argentina, on Salta prov. line, 330 mi. NW of Formosa, in agr. area (corn, cotton, livestock); lumbering.

Elciego (ĕl-thyā'gō), town (pop. 1,455), Álava prov., N Spain, near the Ebro, 10 mi. WNW of Logroño; winegrowing center; chocolate mfg.

El Clavo (ĕl klä'vō), town (pop. 724), Miranda state, N Venezuela, 55 mi. ESE of Caracas; cacao, sugar.

Elco, borough (pop. 596), Washington co., SW Pa., 4 mi. S of Charleroi and on Monongahela R.

El Cobre, Cuba: see COBRE.

El Cobre (ĕl kō'brā), town (pop. 792), Táchira state, W Venezuela, in Andean spur, 23 mi. NE of San Cristóbal; alt. 6,309 ft.; in agr. region (wheat, cotton, tobacco, apples, apricots, peaches). Founded 1576. Copper mines near by were worked in colonial times. Frequent earthquakes.

El Cocal (ĕl kōkäl'), village (pop. 501), Los Santos prov., S central Panama, in Pacific lowland, 3 mi. SSW of Las Tablas; sugar cane, coffee, livestock.

El Coco (ĕl kō'kō), village, Guanacaste prov., NW Costa Rica, port on Papagayo Gulf of the Pacific, 12 mi. NW of Filadelfia; livestock.

El Cocuy (ĕl kōkwē'), town (pop. 2,358), Boyacá dept., central Colombia, at W foot of Sierra Nevada de Cocuy, in Cordillera Oriental, 55 mi. NE of Sogamoso; alt. 9,019 ft. Wheat, potatoes, corn, barley, peas, silk, cattle, sheep; mfg. of woolen goods. Coal, lime, gypsum, sulphur, gold, and silver deposits near by.

El Colegio (ĕl kōlā'hēō), town (pop. 1,046), Cundinamarca dept., central Colombia, on W slopes of Cordillera Oriental, 27 mi. W of Bogotá; sugar cane, coffee, fruit, stock.

El Congo (ĕl kōng'gō), town (pop. 2,780), Santa Ana dept., W Salvador, on railroad and 7 mi. SSE of Santa Ana; agr. (coffee, sugar cane, grain), livestock raising. Transfer point for tourist traffic to L. Coatepeque, just SW.

El Consejo (ĕl kōnsā'hō), town (pop. 1,699), Aragua state, N Venezuela, on railroad and highway, on Tuy R. and 30 mi. SW of Caracas; coffee, corn, sugar cane, cacao.

El Convento, Chile: see CONVENTO.

El Copé (ĕl kōpā'), village (pop. 70), Coclé prov., central Panama, on lower slopes of Coclé Mts., 8 mi. ENE of Penonomé; rice, corn, beans, livestock.

El Corazón or **Corazón** (kōräsōn'), town (1950 pop. 1,051), Cotopaxi prov., N central Ecuador, on W slopes of the Andes, 40 mi. WSW of Latacunga, in grain-growing and dairying area.

El Corpus (ĕl kôr'pōōs), town (pop. 1,289), Choluteca dept., S Honduras, 10 mi. E of Choluteca; coffee, livestock. Near by is Clavo Rico, a Sp. colonial gold-mining center.

El Coyote (ĕl koiō'tā) or **Coyote,** village (pop. 1,653), Coahuila, N Mexico, in irrigated Laguna Dist., on railroad and 13 mi. NE of Torreón; cotton, cereals, vegetables, fruit.

El Cristo (ĕl krē'stō), village (pop. 633), Coclé prov., central Panama, in Pacific lowland, 5 mi. WNW of Aguadulce; sugar cane, corn, rice, beans, livestock.

El Cubo (ĕl kōō'bō), mining settlement (pop. 1,836), Guanajuato, central Mexico, in Sierra Madre Occidental, 5 mi. SE of Guanajuato; gold, silver, lead mines.

El Cuy (ĕl kwē'), village (pop. estimate 150), W central Río Negro natl. territory, Argentina, 75 mi. SW of Fuerte General Roca; stock raising (sheep, goats).

Elda (ĕl'dä), city (pop. 18,443), Alicante prov., E Spain, in Valencia, on fertile plain, 20 mi. NW of Alicante; shoe-mfg. center. Tanning, paper and furniture mfg., esparto processing, flour milling. Olive oil, wine, fruit, cereals in area. Has greendomed church, ruins of Moorish castle, and 17th-cent. Franciscan convent. Of Iberian origin; fell to Moors (8th cent.), was liberated (1265) by Christians, who called it *Ella.*

Eldagsen (ĕl'däg"zŭn), town (pop. 3,921), in former Prussian prov. of Hanover, W Germany, after 1945 in Lower Saxony, 14 mi. S of Hanover; cattle.

Eldama Ravine (ĕldä'mä), town, Rift Valley prov., W Kenya, near railroad, 35 mi. NW of Nakuru, at S end of the Eldama Ravine (section of Great Rift Valley); agr. trade center; corn, coffee, wheat.

El Dara (ĕl dâ'rŭ), village (pop. 137), Pike co., W Ill., 29 mi. SE of Quincy, in agr. area.

Eldena (ĕl'dünä), district (since 1945) of Greifswald, N Germany, 3 mi. E of city center. Has remains of Cistercian abbey of Hilda (founded 1199 by Danish monks), a cultural center of Pomerania until destroyed (1638) in Thirty Years War.

Elden Mountain, peak (9,280 ft.), in Coconino Natl. Forest, N central Ariz., just NE of Flagstaff; pueblo ruins at base of mountain.

Elde River (ĕl'dù), N Germany, formed by several headstreams c.10 mi. S of Malchow, flows in an arc through several lakes (including Müritz, Kölpin, and Plau lakes), continues generally SE in regulated meandering course, past Plau, Parchim, and Neustadt-Glewe. Divides below Grabow into the canalized Neue Elde (noi'ù), built 1568–72, which flows to the Elbe at Dömitz; and into the Alte Elde (äl'tù), which continues in original bed to an arm of the Elbe 2 mi. WNW of Lenzen. Length, c.150 mi. Connected by short canals with Havel R. and Schwerin L.

Elderon (ĕl'dùrŏn), village (pop. 212), Marathon co., central Wis., 23 mi. SE of Wausau, in dairying region.

Elderslie, town in Paisley parish, N Renfrew, Scotland, 2 mi. W of Paisley; carpet weaving. It was family seat of Wallace family and reputed birthplace of William Wallace.

Elderton, borough (pop. 336), Armstrong co., W central Pa., 12 mi. SE of Kittanning; bituminous coal.

Eldey (ĕlt'ā"), islet, SW Iceland, 8 mi. SW of Reykjanesta cape; 63°44'N 22°57'W. Submarine volcanic activity near by.

El Diente (ĕl dēĕn'tē), peak (14,200 ft.) in Rocky Mts., Dolores co., SW Colo.

El Difícil (ĕl dēfē'sēl), village (pop. 1,584), Magdalena dept., N Colombia, at SW foot of Sierra Nevada de Santa Marta, 85 mi. SE of Barranquilla; oil wells.

Eldikan or **El'dikan** (ĕldyēkän'), town (1948 pop. over 500), SE Yakut Autonomous SSR, Russian SFSR, on Eldikan R. (right subtributary of Aldan R.) and c.50 mi. WSW of Allakh-Yun; gold-mining center. Developed in 1940s.

El Dividive (ĕl dēvēdē'vā), town (pop. 1,696), Trujillo state, W Venezuela, on railroad and 22 mi. WNW of Trujillo; sugar cane, corn, livestock.

El Divisadero (ĕl dēvēsädā'rō), village, Morazán dept., E Salvador, on spur of Inter-American Highway and 2 mi. WSW of Jocoro; gold and silver mining.

El Diviso (ĕl dēvē'sō), village (pop. 858), Nariño dept., SW Colombia, in W foothills of Cordillera Occidental, 22 mi. S of Barbacoas. Terminus of railroad from Tumaco (Pacific port); linked by highway to Pasto; another road leads N to Barbacoas.

Eldon. 1 City (pop. 1,457), Wapello co., SE Iowa, on Des Moines R. and 12 mi. SE of Ottumwa; metal products. Bituminous-coal mines near by. Inc. 1877. **2** City (pop. 2,766), Miller co., central Mo., near Osage R., 28 mi. SW of Jefferson City; railroad division point; cheese, clothing; barite mines. Founded c.1880.

Eldora (ĕldô'rù). **1** Town (1940 pop. 31), Boulder co., N central Colo., in Front Range, 35 mi. NW of Denver; alt. 8,700 ft.; gold mining. **2** City (pop. 3,107), ⊙ Hardin co., central Iowa, on Iowa R. and 24 mi. NNW of Marshalltown; dairy, concrete, and wood products. Has state training school for boys. Pine Lake State Park (with fish hatchery) is near by. Limestone quarries, sand pits in area. Settled 1851, inc. 1896.

Eldorado (ĕldôrä'dō), agr. town (pop. estimate 2,500), central Misiones natl. territory, Argentina, on Alto Paraná R. (Paraguay border) and 95 mi. NE of Posadas; farming center (maté, tobacco, corn, tung trees, citrus fruit, honey); lumbering.

Eldorado (ĕl"dôrä'dō), village (pop. 337), N Victoria, Australia, 135 mi. NE of Melbourne, near Beechworth; gold and tin mines.

Eldorado (ĕldōōrä'dōō), city (pop. 1,306), S São Paulo, Brazil, head of navigation on the Ribeira de Iguape and 65 mi. S of Itapetininga; dairy processing, sugar milling. Until 1948, called Xiririca.

Eldorado, Northwest Territories: see PORT RADIUM.

Eldorado (ĕl"dōrä'dō), village, Salisbury prov., N Southern Rhodesia, in Mashonaland, on railroad and 4 mi. ENE of Sinoia; gold mining.

El Dorado (ĕl dôrä'dō), village (pop. 3,678), NW Trinidad, B.W.I., on railroad and 8 mi. E of Port of Spain, in sugar-growing region.

El Dorado (ĕl" dùrā'dō, –rä'dō), county (□ 1,725; pop. 16,207), E and E central Calif.; ⊙ Placerville. Rises from the Sierra Nevada foothills (W) to crest of range; includes Pyramid Peak (10,020 ft.), Freel Peak (10,900 ft.). Many lakes, among them L. TAHOE, and small Fallen Leaf and Echo lakes. Drained by American, Rubicon, and Cosumnes rivers. Parts of El Dorado Natl. Forest and Desolation Valley primitive area are here. Winter sports, hunting, fishing, camping, hiking. Lumbering; limestone quarrying (a leading Calif. co.), gold and copper mining, slate quarrying. Livestock, fruit (especially Bartlett pears). Coloma, site of gold discovery (1848) which began the gold rush, and other old mining towns of the Mother Lode survive. Formed 1850.

El Dorado (ĕl" dùrā'dù). **1** City (pop. 23,076), ⊙ Union co., S Ark., c.80 mi. NE of Shreveport, La. Hq. of oil industry in state (drilling, refining; mfg. of oil-well equipment and petroleum products). Also trade center for lumber and farm area (cotton, sweet potatoes, corn, peanuts, livestock); cotton processing, lumber milling, making of fertilizers. Has jr. col. Founded c.1843, inc. 1851. **2** City (pop. 11,037), ⊙ Butler co., SE Kansas, on Walnut R. and 26 mi. ENE of Wichita; trade and oil-refining center; gasoline, oil products, oil-field equipment. Oil wells and quarries near by. Laid out 1868, inc. 1870. Grew as refining and shipping point for petroleum after discovery (1915) of oil in vicinity.

Eldorado. 1 (ĕl"dùrā'dō) City (pop. 4,500), Saline co., SE Ill., 7 mi. NE of Harrisburg; trade center of bituminous-coal-mining and agr. area; corn, wheat, oats, poultry. Inc. 1873. **2** (ĕl"dùrā'dù) Town (pop. 79), Dorchester co., E Md., 16 mi. E of Cambridge and on Marshyhope Creek; vegetable cannery. **3** (ĕl"dùrā'dù) Village (pop. 364), Preble co., W Ohio, 14 mi. SSW of Greenville. **4** (ĕl"dùrā'dō) City (pop. 732), Jackson co., SW Okla., 21 mi. WSW of Altus, near Texas line, in agr. area (grain, cotton, poultry); dairying, cotton ginning. **5** (ĕl"-dùrā'dù) Town (pop. 1,663), ⊙ Schleicher co., W Texas, on the Edwards Plateau, 40 mi. S of San Angelo; shipping point for cattle, sheep, and goat ranching region; woolen mill. Founded near by as Verand; moved here and changed name, 1895.

El Dorado (ĕl dôrä'dō), town (pop. 227), SE Venezuela, on Cuyuni R. and 40 mi. SSE of El Callao, in tropical forests. Gold deposit near by.

Eldorado Mountains (ĕl"dùrä'dō) (3–4,000 ft.), SE Nev., W of Colorado R., S of Boulder City. Gold, silver, copper, and lead have been mined. Sometimes written El Dorado.

Eldorado Springs (ĕl"dùrā'dù), city (pop. 2,618), Cedar co., W Mo., in Ozark region, 19 mi. E of Nevada. Health resort; grain; coal. Founded 1881.

Eldoret (ĕldōrĕt'), town (pop. 8,193), Rift Valley prov., W Kenya, on Uasin Gishu Plateau, on railroad and 80 mi. NW of Nakuru; alt. 6,875 ft.; 0°32'N 35°16'E. Road and trade center; dairying, flour milling; coffee, wheat, corn, tea, wattle growing. Airport. Area settled by European farmers. Healthful climate. Kakamega gold field (W).

Eldred (ĕl'drĭd). **1** Village (pop. 298), Greene co., W Ill., near Illinois R., 32 mi. NW of Alton, in agr. area. **2** Borough (pop. 1,199), McKean co., N Pa., 8 mi. SSE of Olean, N.Y., and on Allegheny R.; oil wells and refining, natural gas; dairying. Inc. 1880.

Eldred Passage, S Alaska, arm (10 mi. long) of Kachemak Bay, S Kenai Peninsula, 10 mi. ENE of Seldovia; salmon fishing.

Eldridge, town (pop. 376), Scott co., E Iowa, 8 mi. N of Davenport, in agr. area.

Elea (ē'lēä), anc. town in Lucania, Italy, where Xenophanes founded his Eleatic school of pre-Socratic philosophy; Parmenides, Zeno, and Melissus were its later leading thinkers.

Eleanor, Lake, E Calif., in W Yosemite Natl. Park; a reservoir (c.3 mi. long) impounded in a tributary of Tuolumne R., it supplies water to San Francisco.

Electoral Hesse, Germany: see HESSE-KASSEL.

Electra, city (pop. 4,970), Wichita co., N Texas, 26 mi. WNW of Wichita Falls, in oil, agr. region; mfg. (oil-field supplies and machinery, gasoline, petroleum products); ships poultry, wheat. Founded 1890, inc. 1910; had oil boom, 1911.

Electric City, village (pop. 1,484), Grant co., E central Wash., near the Columbia, 5 mi. SW of Grand Coulee Dam.

Electric Mills, town (1940 pop. 1,205), Kemper co., E Miss., 32 mi. NNE of Meridian, near Ala. line, in agr. and timber area.

Electric Peak (11,155 ft.), highest point in Gallatin Range, SW Mont., in NW part of Yellowstone Natl. Park, c.45 mi. S of Bozeman, Mont.

Electrona (ĭlĕktrō'nù), village (pop. 118), SE Tasmania, 13 mi. SSW of Hobart and on D'Entrecasteaux Channel; carbide works.

Eleele (ā'lā-ā'lā), village (pop. 992), S Kauai, T.H.; agr.

Elefantos, Rio dos, Mozambique: see OLIFANTS RIVER.

Elefsis, Greece: see ELEUSIS.

Eleftheroupolis, Greece: see ELEUTHEROUPOLIS.

Eleia, Greece: see ELIS, nome.

Elek (ĕ'lĕk), town (pop. 9,327), Bekes co., SE Hungary, 8 mi. S of Gyula; flour mills, brickworks; grain, cattle.

Elekmonar (ĕlyĕkmŭnär'), village (1939 pop. over 500), NW Gorno-Altai Autonomous Oblast, Altai Territory, Russian SFSR, on Katun R. and 35 mi. S of Gorno-Altaisk; livestock raising.

Elektrogorsk (ĕlyĕktrŭgôrsk'), city (1939 pop. over 10,000), E Moscow oblast, Russian SFSR, 13 mi. E of Noginsk; large peat-fed power plant. Until 1946, Elektroperedacha.

Elektroperedacha, Russian SFSR: see ELEKTROGORSK.

Elektrostal or **Elektrostal'** (ĕlyĕktrŭstäl'), city (1939 pop. over 10,000), E central Moscow oblast, Russian SFSR, 5 mi. S of Noginsk; steel-milling center (stainless steel products, instruments, tractor parts). Developed in 1920s; became city 1938.

Elektrougli (–ōō′glyē), town (1939 pop. over 500), E central Moscow oblast, Russian SFSR, on railroad (Kudinovo station) and 23 mi. E of Moscow; ceramics, chemicals. Until 1935, called Kudinovo.

Elektrovoz, Russian SFSR: see STUPINO.

Elen-, in Rus. names: see YELEN-.

Elena (ālā′nä), town (pop. estimate 1,500), W Córdoba prov., Argentina, 40 mi. N of Río Cuarto; cereals, flax, sunflowers, livestock.

Elena, Bulgaria: see YELENA.

Elena, village (1930 pop. 66), Magallanes prov., S Chile, on Riesco Isl., on Skyring Sound and 55 mi. NW of Punta Arenas; coal mining.

Elend (ā′lĕnt), village (pop. 551), in former Prussian Saxony prov., central Germany, after 1945 in Saxony-Anhalt, in the upper Harz, at SE foot of the Brocken, 8 mi. SW of Wernigerode; popular summer resort and winter-sports center.

Elephanta (ĕlūfăn′tŭ), island, Kolaba dist., W Bombay, India, in Bombay Harbour, 5 mi. E of Bombay city center; 1½ mi. long, 1 mi. wide. Famous Brahmanic caves carved in side of hill 250 ft. above sea level. Main hall dates from 8th cent.; supported by 6 rows of columns; has several large statues of Siva. Isl. also called Gharapuri (gä′räpōōrē).

Elephant Butte Dam (būt), SW N.Mex., main unit of RIO GRANDE reclamation project, just E of Truth or Consequences. Concrete dam 306 ft. high, 1,674 ft. long; completed 1916; used for irrigation, power, flood control. Impounds Elephant Butte Reservoir (capacity 2,198,000 acre-ft.), sometimes called Hall L.; recreational area (boating, fishing).

Elephantine (ĕ″lūfăntī′nē), island, S Egypt, in the Nile opposite ASWAN, below Aswan dam and 1st Cataract. There are important Egyptian and Roman ruins, including a temple built by Trajan. On the isl. the Nubians used to trade with the anc. Egyptians. Here was the Nilometer (dating from the Ptolemies and which gauged the depth of the Nile), restored 1870 by Ismail Pasha.

Elephant Island (28 naut. mi. long, 15 naut. mi. wide), E South Shetland Isls., off Palmer Peninsula, Antarctica; 61°5′S 55°10′W.

Elephant Pass, causeway across E Jaffna Lagoon, Ceylon, 28 mi. ESE of Jaffna; connects Jaffna Peninsula via rail and road with Ceylon proper. Large govt. saltern just S.

Elephant Point, village (pop. 99), W Alaska, on S shore of Eschscholtz Bay, 55 mi. SE of Kotzebue.

Elephant Range, isolated southern offshoot of Cardamom Mts., SW Cambodia, extends c.70 mi. N from Kampot on Gulf of Siam; highest point, Bokor Peak (3,511 ft.), N of Bokor hill station.

Elephant Rock or **Etagala** (ĕtŭgä′lŭ), isolated rock (1,101 ft.) overlooking Kurunegala, W central Ceylon; in early-14th cent., when Kurunegala was ⊙ Ceylon, used as fortress. Also called Kurunegala Rock.

El Escobal, Panama: see ESCOBAL.

Elesd, Rumania: see ALESD.

Eleshnitsa, Bulgaria: see YELESHNITSA.

Eleskirt (ĕlĕshkĭrt′), Turkish *Eleşkirt*, village (pop. 1,865), Agri prov., E Turkey, 15 mi. NW of Karakose; lead deposits. Formerly Aleskirt.

El Espino (ĕl ĕspē′nō), village, Madríz dept., NW Nicaragua, on Inter-American Highway, 9 mi. WSW of Somoto; customs station on Honduras border.

El Estor (ĕl ĕstōr′), town (1950 pop. 384), Izabal dept., E Guatemala, on NW shore of L. Izabal and 50 mi. WSW of Puerto Barrios; fisheries, lumbering; grain, bananas. Transferred from Alta Verapaz dept. 1945.

Elesvaram (ĕlĕs′vŭrŭm) or **Yeleshwaram** (yĕlĕsh′vŭrŭm), town (pop. 6,838), East Godavari dist., NE Madras, India, 15 mi. NNW of Peddapuram, in Eluru R. valley; rice milling; sugar cane, castor beans. Also spelled Yelleswaram.

Elets, Russian SFSR: see YELETS.

Éleu-dit-Leauwette (ālû′-dē-lōvĕt′), S suburb (pop. 2,283) of Lens, Pas-de-Calais dept., N France; coal mines.

Eleusis or **Elevsis** (ēlū′sĭs, Gr. ĕlĕf′sĭs), town (pop. 9,154), Attica nome, E central Greece, port on Bay of Eleusis, at mouth of Cephisus R., 11 mi. WNW of Athens. Industrial center; mfg. of cement, soap, olive oil, liquor; rice milling. Ruins of anc. city include temple of Demeter, scene of Eleusinian Mysteries. One of oldest cities of Attica, it is mentioned in Gr. mythology and was separated (1000 B.C.) from Athens under friendly alliance. Home of Aeschylus (b. here 525 B.C.), it became (c.400 B.C.) place of worship of Demeter. Partly destroyed c.395 B.C. by Visigoths. Formerly called Levsina; sometimes spelled Elefsis.

Eleusis, Bay of, inlet of Saronic Gulf, Attica nome, E central Greece, 7 mi. W of Athens, nearly closed off by Salamis isl.; 6 mi. wide, 4 mi. long. Eleusis is on N shore.

Eleuthera Island (ēlū′thŭrŭ), island and district (□ 164; pop. 6,430), central Bahama Isls., bet. Great Abaco Isl. (NW) and Cat Isl. (SE), its N tip 50 mi. NE of Nassau; a narrow, curved bar, c.80 mi. long, up to 6 mi. wide. Produces tomatoes, pineapples, dairy products. Main settlements: Governor's Harbour and Palmetto Point (center), Tarpum Bay and Rock Sound (S center), Gregory Town and Hatchet Bay (N). Eleuthera was one of the 1st isls. to be settled by Englishmen (1647; from Bermuda) in the Bahamas. Most of the settlers, driven out by the Spaniards (1680), emigrated to Boston. Harbour Isl. is off its NE tip.

Eleutheropolis, Palestine: see BEIT JIBRIN.

Eleutheroupolis or **Elevtheroupolis** (both: ĕlĕfthĕrōō′pôlĭs), town (pop. 4,999), Kavalla nome, Macedonia, Greece, 8 mi. WSW of Kavalla; tobacco, corn, citrus fruits; livestock. Also spelled Eleftheroupolis. Formerly called Pravi or Pravion, and, under Turkish rule, Pravishta or Pravista.

Eleva (ĕlē′vŭ), village (pop. 479), Trempealeau co., W Wis., on Buffalo R. and 16 mi. S of Eau Claire, in dairy, poultry, and grain area.

Eleven Mile Reservoir, central Colo., in Colo., in canyon of South Platte R., 60 mi. SSW of Denver; 6 mi. long, 1 mi. wide; alt. 8,564 ft. Formed by concrete dam (112 ft. high). Unit in water-supply system of Denver.

Eleven Point River, S Mo. and N Ark., rises in Howell co., Mo., flows c.115 mi. E and S to Spring R. above Black Rock, Ark. Flood-control dam in its lower course.

Elevi, Turkey: see GORELE.

Elevsis, Greece: see ELEUSIS.

Elevtheroupolis, Greece: see ELEUTHEROUPOLIS.

Elfeld, Germany: see ELTVILLE.

Elfin Cove, village (pop. 64), SE Alaska, on NW tip of Chichagof Isl., on Cross Sound, 70 mi. W of Juneau; fishing, fish processing; supply point for fur trappers.

Elfkarleby, Sweden: see ALVKARLEBY.

Elfros (ĕl′frŏs), village (pop. 268), SE central Sask., near the Quill Lakes, 15 mi. E of Wynyard; mixed farming, dairying.

Elfsborg, country, Sweden: see ALVSBORG.

El Fuerte (ĕl fwĕr′tā), city (pop. 2,936), Sinaloa, NW Mexico, on the Río del Fuerte (irrigation area) and 140 mi. NW of Culiacán; sugar-cane center; corn, chick-peas, tomatoes, fruit.

Elfus, Turkey: see AFSIN.

El Gabriel, Cuba: see GABRIEL.

El Galpón (ĕl gälpōn′) or **Galpón**, town (pop. estimate 1,000), S central Salta prov., Argentina, on the Pasaje or Juramento R., on railroad and 65 mi. SE of Salta; agr. center (corn, alfalfa, rice, cotton, sugar, livestock). Curative waters.

El Gato, Chile: see RÍO GATO.

El General (ĕl hānārāl′), village (dist. pop. 1,324), San José prov., S central Costa Rica, on Inter-American Highway and 50 mi. SE of San José. Junction for road to Pacific port of Dominical. Rice, corn, beans, tobacco, livestock.

Elgeyo Escarpment (ĕlgā′yō), section of W rim of Great Rift Valley, in W Kenya, E of Eldoret. The N continuation of Mau Escarpment, it rises to over 8,000 ft., overlooking Eldama Ravine (E).

Elghena (ĕlgĕ′nä) or **Alghena** (äl–), village, Keren div., N Eritrea, 25 mi. SSE of Karora; cattle.

Elgin (ĕl′gĭn), county (□ 720; pop. 46,150), S Ont., on L. Erie and on Thames R.; ⊙ St. Thomas.

Elgin. 1 Village (pop. estimate 400), SW Man., on Elgin Creek and 30 mi. SSW of Brandon; grain, stock. **2** Village (pop. estimate 300), SE Ont., 30 mi. NE of Kingston; dairying, mixed farming.

Elgin, county, Scotland: see MORAY.

Elgin (ĕl′gĭn), burgh (1931 pop. 8,810; 1951 census 10,535), ⊙ Morayshire, Scotland, in N part of co., on Lossie R. and 36 mi. ENE of Inverness; agr. market, with woolen mills, sawmills, whisky distilleries, breweries, iron foundries. The Cathedral of Moray was founded here 1224, partly burned 1270, and again 1390 by the Wolf of Badenoch, Alexander Stuart. In 16th cent. the bldg. fell into decay, and in 1711 the central tower collapsed. There are also ruins of bishops' palace and of 12th-cent. Greyfriars' Monastery. A column marks site of castle where Edward I stayed in 1296. Other notable features are: Anderson's Institution (endowed by Andrew Anderson), mus. of the Elgin Literary Society, hosp., asylum.

Elgin. 1 (ĕl′jĭn) Industrial city (pop. 44,223), on Cook-Kane co. line, NE Ill., on Fox R. and 36 mi. WNW of Chicago, in agr. area (dairy products; livestock); printing; mfg. of watches, electrical appliances, shoes, clothing, hardware, metal castings, pianos, machinery, tools, radios, auto accessories, chemicals, thread, wood products, toiletries, paper products; dairy-products processing center. Seat of one of state's oldest preparatory schools for boys (opened 1856). A state hosp. for the insane is here. Founded 1835; inc. as village in 1847, as city in 1854. **2** (ĕl′jĭn) Town (pop. 642), Fayette co., NE Iowa, on Turkey R. and 9 mi. E of West Union; corn cannery, feed mill. **3** (ĕl′jĭn) City (pop. 212), Chautauqua co., SE Kansas, on Caney R., at Okla. line, and c.40 mi. E of Arkansas City; livestock, grain. **4** (ĕl′jĭn) Village (pop. 438), Wabasha co., SE Minn., 13 mi. NE of Rochester; dairy products. **5** (ĕl′jĭn) Village (pop. 820), Antelope co., NE central Nebr., 10 mi. S of Neligh and on branch of Elkhorn R.; dairy and poultry produce, livestock, grain. **6** (ĕl′jĭn) City (pop. 882), Grant co., S N.Dak., 57 mi. WSW of Bismarck; stock raising, dairy farms, grain, poultry, wheat, flax. **7** (ĕl′jĭn) Village (pop. 126), Van Wert co., W Ohio, 10 mi. SSE of Van Wert. **8** (ĕl′jĭn) Town (pop. 428), Comanche co., SW Okla., 14 mi. NNE of Lawton, in agr. area; cotton ginning. **9** (ĕl′jĭn) City (pop. 1,223), Union co., NE Oregon, 20 mi. NNE of La Grande and on Grande Ronde R.; alt. 2,670 ft.; shipping point for apples; lumber milling. Wallowa Mts. SE. **10** (ĕl′jĭn) Borough (pop. 202), Erie co., NW Pa., 5 mi. WSW of Corry. **11** (ĕl′gĭn) City (pop. 3,168), Bastrop co., S central Texas, 23 mi. ENE of Austin; trade, shipping, processing center for agr. area (truck, dairy products, cotton); clay products, cottonseed oil; lignite mines. Settled 1867, inc. 1890.

Elgin Falls, Ceylon: see AMBAWELA.

Elginshire, Scotland: see MORAY.

Elgoibar (ĕlgoivär′), town (pop. 2,617), Guipúzcoa prov., N Spain, 18 mi. WNW of Tolosa; mfg. (armaments, bicycle parts, hardware). Mineral springs near by.

El Golfito, Costa Rica: see GOLFITO.

Elgon, Mount (ĕl′gŏn), huge extinct volcanic cone (14,178 ft.) on Uganda-Kenya frontier, rising above E African plateau NE of L. Victoria; c.50 mi. in diameter. Crater is 5 mi. across and nearly 2,000 ft. deep. Coffee is grown on its slopes. First scaled by Kmunke and Stigler (Austrians) in 1911. Ascended from Kitale at SE foot.

El Granada (ĕl grŭnä′dŭ), resort village (pop. c.150), San Mateo co., W Calif., on the Pacific, c.20 mi. SSW of downtown San Francisco.

El Grullo (ĕl grōō′yō), town (pop. 5,433), Jalisco, W Mexico, in W outliers of Sierra Madre Occidental, 9 mi. SE of Autlán; agr. center (grain, sugar cane, cotton, fruit, stock).

El Guaje, Mexico: see VILLAGRÁN, Guanajuato.

El Guamo, Colombia: see GUAMO, Bolívar dept.

El Guapo (ĕl gwä′pō) or **Guapo**, town (pop. 365), Miranda state, N Venezuela, 70 mi. ESE of Caracas; terminus of railroad from Higuerote (25 mi. NW); in cacao-growing region.

El Guarco, canton, Costa Rica: see TEJAR.

El Hatillo (ĕl ätē′yō). **1** Town (pop. 656), Anzoátegui state, NE Venezuela, on narrow bar bet. Unare Lagoon and the Caribbean, 37 mi. W of Barcelona; fishing. **2** Town (pop. 815), Miranda state, N Venezuela, 8 mi. SE of Caracas; coffee, grain.

Elhovo, Bulgaria: see YELKHOVO.

El Huecú (ĕl wākōō′), village (pop. estimate 500), ⊙ Ñorquín dept., NW Neuquén natl. territory, Argentina, 90 mi. NNW of Zapala; stock raising.

Elías Piña (ālē′äs pē′nyä), town (1935 pop. 397; 1950 pop. 1,469), ⊙ San Rafael prov., W Dominican Republic, near Haiti border, on Ciudad Trujillo–Port-au-Prince highway, and 120 mi. WNW of Ciudad Trujillo; 18°57′N 71°43′W. In agr. region of San Juan valley (cotton, sugar cane, coffee, fruit). Until 1930, Comendador. Since 1942, ⊙ prov.

Elida. 1 (ĭlī′dŭ) Village (pop. 430), Roosevelt co., E N.Mex., 25 mi. SW of Portales; trade point in ranching region. **2** (ē′līdŭ) Village (pop. 607), Allen co., W Ohio, 6 mi. WNW of Lima and on Ottawa R.

Elie and Earlsferry (ē′lē), burgh (1931 pop. 1,098; 1951 census 1,190), E Fifeshire, Scotland, on the Firth of Forth, 7 mi. E of Leven; seaside resorts, noted for garnets found on beaches. Just S of Elie, on the Firth of Forth, is promontory of Sauchar Point, with lighthouse (56°11′N 2°49′W).

Elie de Beaumont (ē′lē dŭ bō′mŭn), mountain (10,200 ft.), W central S.Isl., New Zealand, in Southern Alps, near Malte Brun Range.

Elikon, Greece: see HELICON.

Elila (ēlē′lä), village, Kivu prov., E Belgian Congo, on right bank of Lualaba R. just N of mouth of Elila R., and 130 mi. NNW of Kasongo, in tin-mining area; steamboat landing and agr. center (rice, palm products); palm-oil mills.

Elila River, E tributary of Lualaba R., in E Belgian Congo, rises on the high plateaus NW of L. Tanganyika, c.15 mi. SW of Uvira, flows in wide curves generally W past Itula and Kama to Lualaba R. at Elila village; c.285 mi. long. Together with Ulindi R., drains important tin- and gold-mining area.

Elim (ē′lĭm), village (pop. 154), W Alaska, on SE Seward Peninsula, at mouth of Norton Bay, 95 mi. E of Nome; supply point for trappers and prospectors.

Elim (ē′lĭm), town (pop. 1,024), SW Cape Prov., U. of So. Afr., 16 mi. WSW of Bredasdorp; agr. market (grain, sheep).

Eling, town and parish (pop. 5,586), SW Hampshire, England, on Test R. estuary and 4 mi. W of Southampton; agr. market, with chemical works. In parish (N) is market and residential town of Totton.

Eliock, Scotland: see SANQUHAR.

Eliot. 1 Town (pop. 2,509), York co., extreme SW Maine, on Piscataqua R. just above Portsmouth, N.H. Includes South Eliot village (pop. 1,331). Set off from Kittery 1810. **2** Village, Middlesex co., Mass.: see NEWTON.

Eliot, Mount (4,554 ft.), E Labrador, 10 mi. N of Nachvak Fiord; 59°10′N 63°49′W.

Elis (ē′lĭs), Gr. *Eleia* or *Ilia* (both: ĭlē′ŭ), nome (□ 1,178; pop. 185,085), W Peloponnesus, Greece; ⊙ Pyrgos. Bordered E by Alpheus R. and its affluent, the Erymanthos, and W by Ionian Sea. The lowland (W along coast), drained by Alpheus and Peneus rivers, is fertile agr. region producing Zante currants (chief crop), figs, citrus fruits, olives, wine. Grains (wheat, corn) and livestock (cattle, sheep, goats) raised on mtn. slopes. Mineral springs, lignite mines. Pyrgos is industrial and commercial center. Modern Elis is administratively part of W Central Greece. Anc. country of Elis (⊙ Elis) was bordered N by Achaea, E by Arcadia, S by Messenia, and included Olympia and Pisa. It was divided into Hollow Elis or Elis proper (N), Pisatis (center), and Triphylia (S). It was noted for horse breeding and flax growing. Eleans established supremacy in area at end of 8th cent. B.C. and wrested control over Olympic Games from Pisa in 572 B.C. Originally in Spartan League, Elis excluded Sparta from Olympic Games at 420 B.C., fought Sparta in Peloponnesian War, and lost control (399 B.C.) over Triphylia to Arcadia. Accepted Macedonian supremacy and later joined Aetolian League. Conquered (A.D. 145) by Romans, it declined after suppression (394) of Olympic Games. During early Middle Ages, it was under French control and, 1460–1828, under Turkish rule. Modern nome formed part of nome of Achaea and Elis until c.1930.

Elis, anc. city of Peloponnesus, Greece, on Peneus R. and 14 mi. NNW of Pyrgos. Has ruins of acropolis and temple of Athena. Founded 471 B.C., it became ⊙ anc. Elis, supplanting Olympia. Modern village of Ilis or Eleis (pop. 219), formerly called Palaeopolis or Palaiopolis, is on the site.

Elisa (ālē'sä), town (pop. estimate 1,000), central Santa Fe prov., Argentina, on railroad and 30 mi. SSE of San Cristóbal, in agr. area (alfalfa, flax, sunflowers, wheat, livestock).

Elisabetha (ālēzäbĕtä'), village, Eastern Prov., N Belgian Congo, on left bank of Congo R. opposite Basoko and 120 mi. WNW of Stanleyville; center of palm-oil industry; extensive harbor installations for export of palm products; rubber plantations. R.C. mission, hosp. for Europeans.

Elisabethstadt, Rumania: see Dumbraveni.

Elisabethville, prov., Belg. Congo: see Katanga.

Elisabethville, city (1948 pop. 67,989), ⊙ Katanga prov. and Upper Katanga dist. (□ 28,918; 1948 pop. c.220,000), Belgian Congo, c.950 mi. SE of Leopoldville, near Northern Rhodesia border; 11°40'S 27°28'E; alt. 5,008 ft. Commercial and industrial center, second largest town in Belgian Congo, on railroad; air hub. Woodworking, cabinet making, brewing, food processing, printing, stone quarrying, mfg. of building materials and soap; large flour mills for manioc, corn, and grain; various construction and repair workshops. Just outside urban limits (SW) are the copper smelters of Lubumbashi, which name is sometimes extended to city itself. Elisabethville has several R.C. and Protestant missions, hospitals and schools for Europeans and Africans (notably junior college and air navigation school), synagogue, mus. of native art, observatory. Founded 1910; has prospered with development of Katanga copper-mining industry.

Eliseina, Bulgaria: see Yeliseina.

Elisenvaara (ĕ'lyĕsyĭnvüä"rŭ), village (1948 pop. over 500), SW Karelo-Finnish SSR, 35 mi. SW of Sortavala; rail junction. In Finland until 1940.

Elista, Russian SFSR: see Stepnoi.

Elizabeth. 1 Town (pop. 253), Elbert co., central Colo., 35 mi. SE of Denver; alt. 6,400 ft. **2** Village (pop. 1,067), Cobb co., NW central Ga., just N of Marietta. **3** Village (pop. 723), Jo Daviess co., NW Ill., on Apple R. (bridged here) and 25 mi. ESE of Dubuque, Iowa; dairy products; lead mines; timber. **4** Town (pop. 211), Harrison co., S Ind., 14 mi. SW of New Albany, in agr. area. **5** Village (pop. 1,113), Allen parish, SW central La., 35 mi. SW of Alexandria; paper milling. **6** Village (pop. 168), Otter Tail co., W Minn., on Pelican R. and 7 mi. N of Fergus Falls; dairy products. **7** City (pop. 112,817), ⊙ Union co., NE N.J., on Newark Bay and Arthur Kill (bridged 1928 to Staten Isl.), adjacent to Newark. Residential, industrial; machinery, sewing machines, printing presses and type, paper containers, chemicals, furniture, clothing; radio, auto, and aircraft parts; oil refining; bookbinding; railroad shops. Vocational school here. Settled on site purchased from Indians, 1664; known as Elizabethtown until 1740; inc. as borough 1789, as city 1855. First provincial capital of N.J.; assembly met here 1668–82. School that became Princeton Univ. opened here 1747. Raided repeatedly and partly burned in Revolution. Tanning and brewing began in late 17th cent.; industrialization came in late 19th cent. A Singer sewing-machine plant opened 1873. Points of interest: Elias Boudinot's home (c.1750); Belcher Mansion (before 1750); Nathaniel Bonnell House (before 1682); *Minute Man* statue; pre-Revolutionary First Presbyterian church (restored after fire in 1946). Nicholas Murray Butler and M. W. Baldwin b. here. **8** Residential borough (pop. 2,615), Allegheny co., SW Pa., 13 mi. SSE of Pittsburgh and on Monongahela R.; limestone, bituminous coal; agr. Pioneer boatbuilding center after 1778. Settled 1769, inc. 1834. **9** Town (pop. 755), ⊙ Wirt co., W W.Va., on Little Kanawha R. and 17 mi. SE of Parkersburg, in agr. area; lumber milling.

Elizabeth, Cape, R SFSR: see Yelizaveta, Cape.

Elizabeth City, county (□ 56; pop. 55,028), SE Va.; co. courthouse is at Hampton, in but independent of co. On SE shore of peninsula bounded NE by York R., NW by James R., S by Hampton Roads, E by Chesapeake Bay; co. adjoins Newport News city (SW). Ferries to Norfolk, Cape Charles town. Residential; resorts (notably Old Point Comfort); extensive fisheries. Phoebus, Hampton are ports. Includes U.S. Fort Monroe. Truck, fruit, tobacco; dairying, poultry raising. Formed 1634.

Elizabeth City, town (pop. 12,685), ⊙ Pasquotank co., NE N.C., near Dismal Swamp, on navigable Pasquotank R. and 40 mi. S of Norfolk, Va. Port of entry; commercial and fishing center; lumber, hosiery, and cotton mills; tourist resort; yacht basin. U.S. Coast Guard hq., with shipyard and supply base. State Teachers col. Founded 1793.

Elizabeth Islands, SE Mass., island chain (□ 14) extending c.15 mi. SW from SW tip of Cape Cod, bet. Buzzards Bay and Vineyard Sound. Best known isls., frequented as summer resorts, are: Naushon (nô'shŭn), largest; Cuttyhunk (kŭ'tēhŭngk), westernmost, reached by Gosnold 1602, and site of Cuttyhunk, only village on isls.; Penikese (pĕ"nŭkēs'), former seat of summer school of marine biology established 1873 by Louis Agassiz; Nashawena (nă"shuwē'nŭ); Pasque (păsk); Nonamesset (nŏ"nümĕ'sĭt). First permanent settlers in 1641. Isls. constitute Gosnold town.

Elizabeth River, Va., short branching river entering Hampton Roads bet. cities of Norfolk and Portsmouth, whose port dists. are along river and its Western, Southern, and Eastern branches (dredged channels). Southern Branch is connecting link bet. Hampton Roads and 2 inland waterways (Dismal Swamp Canal, Albemarle and Chesapeake Canal) leading S to Albemarle Sound, N.C.

Elizabethton, city (pop. 10,754), ⊙ Carter co., NE Tenn., at junction of Watauga and Doe rivers, and 8 mi. E of Johnson City; industrial center in timber and farm area; mfg. of rayon and synthetic yarn, wood products; lumber milling. Watauga Reservoir is E. In one of earliest-settled regions in Tenn.; one of 1st independent civil govts., Watauga Assn., formed here in 1772. Inc. 1905.

Elizabethtown. 1 Village (pop. 583), ⊙ Hardin co., extreme SE Ill., on Ohio R. and 23 mi. SSE of Harrisburg; mining (lead, fluorspar, zinc), farming (wheat, corn; dairy products; poultry). Cave in Rock State Park is E. **2** Town (pop. 323), Bartholomew co., S central Ind., 8 mi. SE of Columbus, in agr. area. **3** City (pop. 5,807), ⊙ Hardin co., central Ky., 40 mi. S of Louisville; trade center for agr. area (livestock, burley tobacco, corn, wheat); limestone quarries; mfg. of clothing, quilted articles, dairy products, phonograph records, concrete blocks; bottling works. Fort Knox is near by. Town's Union garrison was captured by Gen. John H. Morgan's Confederate cavalry in Dec. 1862. Settled 1780, platted 1793. **4** Resort village (pop. 665), ⊙ Essex co., NE N.Y., in the Adirondacks, on Bouquet R. and 34 mi. SSW of Plattsburg; lumber. **5** Town (pop. 1,611), ⊙ Bladen co., SE N.C., on Cape Fear R. (head of navigation) and 33 mi. SSE of Fayetteville, in agr., timber, and lake area; lumber milling, peanut processing. Settled c.1738. **6** Borough (pop. 5,083), Lancaster co., SE central Pa., 16 mi. SE of Harrisburg; dairy products, tobacco, shoes, confectionery, clothing. Elizabethtown Col., Masonic homes, hosp. for crippled children here. Laid out 1751, inc. 1827.

Elizabethville, agr. borough (pop. 1,506), Dauphin co., S central Pa., 20 mi. NNE of Harrisburg; shirts, wagons. Settled 1817.

Elizalde (ĕlē-thäl'dā), village (pop. 1,748), Guipúzcoa prov., N Spain, 7 mi. ESE of San Sebastián; corn, potatoes, apples, lumber, livestock. Iron mines in area.

Elizavet-, in Rus. names: see Yelizavet-.

Elizondo (ĕlē-thōn'dō), village (pop. 1,645), Navarre prov., N Spain, in the W Pyrenees, on Bidassoa R. and 24 mi. NNE of Pamplona; meat packing, chocolate mfg.; corn, chestnut, lumber trade.

Elizovo, USSR: see Yelizovo.

El Jabalí, Nicaragua: see Santo Domingo.

El Jaguito (ĕl hägē'tō), village (pop. 299), Coclé prov., central Panama, in Santa María R. valley, 1.5 mi. NW of El Roble; sugar cane, corn, rice, beans; stock raising.

El Jaral (ĕl häräl'), village (pop. 383), Cortés dept., W central Honduras, port on N shore of L. Yojoa, on road and 38 mi. S of San Pedro Sula. Ferry service to Pito Solo on S shore.

Eljas (ĕl'häs), town (pop. 1,830), Cáceres prov., W Spain, 30 mi. SW of Ciudad Rodrigo; olive-oil processing, flour milling; stock raising; wool trade; cereals, wine. Has anc. castle. Local dialect is mixture of Castilian and anc. Portuguese.

El Jicaral (ĕl hēkäräl'), town (1950 pop. 206), León dept., W Nicaragua, 35 mi. NE of León; road junction; corn, beans.

El Jícaro or **Jícaro** (ĕl hē'kärō), town (1950 pop. 1,464), El Progreso dept., E central Guatemala, on Motagua R. and 15 mi. ENE of El Progreso, on railroad; corn, beans, livestock.

El Jícaro, town (1950 pop. 638), Nueva Segovia dept., NW Nicaragua, on Jícaro R. and 26 mi. ENE of Ocotal; important gold- and silver-mining center; coffee, sugar cane, livestock. San Albino, 3 mi. SE, has mines.

El Jovero, Dominican Republic: see Miches.

Elk (ĕ'ŏŏk), Pol. *Ełk*, Ger. *Lyck* (lĭk), town (1939 pop. 16,482; 1946 pop. 6,104) in East Prussia, after 1945 in Bialystok prov., NE Poland, in Masurian Lakes region, on small Elk L., 60 mi. NW of Bialystok, 60 mi. SSE of Chernyakhovsk; rail junction; grain and cattle market; sawmilling. On isl. in lake, Teutonic Knights established castle in 14th cent. In First World War, town was a center of action (Feb., 1915) during battle of Masurian Lakes. After Second World War, when it was c.50% destroyed, its Ger. pop. was evacuated.

Elk. 1 County (□ 647; pop. 6,679), SE Kansas; ⊙ Howard. Gently rolling agr. area, watered by Elk R. Cattle, grain. Oil and natural-gas fields. Formed 1875. **2** County (□ 809; pop. 34,503), N central Pa.; ⊙ Ridgway. Forested upland, drained by Clarion R. Mfg. (paper, leather, metal and rubber products); bituminous coal, clay, sandstone, limestone, oil, natural gas. Formed 1843.

Elkader (ĕlkā'dŭr, –kā'–), town (pop. 1,584), ⊙ Clayton co., NE Iowa, on Turkey R. (bridged here) and 29 mi. ENE of Oelwein; livestock shipping; mfg. (concrete blocks, millwork); limestone quarries. Inc. 1868. Near by are ruins of Communia, a cooperative town settled c.1850.

Elk Basin, village (pop. c.100), Park co., NW Wyo., on Mont. line, in E foothills of Absaroka Range, 33 mi. NNE of Cody. Gasoline plant here. Elk Basin oil field near by.

Elk City. 1 City (pop. 524), Montgomery co., SE Kansas, on Elk R. and 12 mi. WNW of Independence; livestock, grain. Oil and gas fields in vicinity. Near by is site of flood-control reservoir in Elk R. **2** City (pop. 7,962), Beckham co., W Okla., 27 mi. WSW of Clinton, and on Elk Creek; processing and distribution center for agr. and dairying area. Mfg. of cottonseed and dairy products, brooms, concrete blocks, mattresses, cotton-gin equipment; cotton ginning and compressing. Has a cooperative medical center. A Cheyenne Indian reservation is near by. Inc. 1907.

Elk Creek, village (pop. 176), Johnson co., SE Nebr., 5 mi. SSE of Tecumseh and on N. Fork of Nemaha R.

Elk Creek, river in SW Okla., rises in E Beckham co., flows c.65 mi. SE and S, past Elk City, to North Fork of Red R. 15 mi. S of Hobart.

Elk Falls, city (pop. 276), Elk co., SE Kansas, on Elk R. and 25 mi. WNW of Independence; livestock, grain.

Elk Garden, town (pop. 318), Mineral co., NE W. Va., 9 mi. WSW of Keyser.

Elk Grove, village (1940 pop. 575), Sacramento co., central Calif., 12 mi. SE of Sacramento; wineries.

Elkhart (ĕl'kärt", ĕlk'härt"), county (□ 468; pop. 84,512), N Ind., bounded N by Mich. line; ⊙ Goshen. Agr. area (dairy products; livestock, soybeans, corn, wheat, oats, potatoes, hay, mint, onions); diversified mfg. (especially at Elkhart and Goshen); timber. Drained by Elkhart and St. Joseph rivers. Formed 1830.

Elkhart. 1 Village, Logan co., Ill.: see Elkhart City. **2** City (pop. 35,646), Elkhart co., N Ind., at confluence of Elkhart and St. Joseph rivers, 15 mi. E of South Bend; shipping and trading center in agr. area (livestock; dairy products; soybeans, grain). Mfg.: electrical appliances, musical instruments, industrial machinery; rubber, clay, paper, brass, and sheet-metal products; castings, plastics, pharmaceuticals, railroad and automobile equipment, fishing tackle. Division point (with shops) for New York Central RR. Settled and platted 1832, inc. 1877. **3** Town (pop. 222), Polk co., central Iowa, 15 mi. NNE of Des Moines, in agr. area. **4** City (pop. 1,132), Morton co., extreme SW Kansas, at Okla. line, 50 mi. W of Liberal, in grain region; flour milling. Inc. 1913. **5** Town (pop. 776), Anderson co., E Texas, near the Trinity, 10 mi. S of Palestine; shipping point for truck; lumber milling.

Elkhart City or **Elkhart,** village (pop. 420), Logan co., central Ill., 17 mi. NNE of Springfield, in agr. and bituminous-coal area. Richard J. Oglesby b. and buried here.

Elkhart Lake, village (pop. 587), Sheboygan co., E Wis., on Elkhart L. (resort), 16 mi. NW of Sheboygan, in dairy and grain area; cannery.

Elkhart River, N Ind., rises in E Noble co., flows c.100 mi. generally W and NW, past Goshen, to St. Joseph R. at Elkhart.

Elkhorn, village (pop. 592), SW Man., 60 mi. W of Brandon; grain elevators; dairying, stock raising.

Elk Horn, town (pop. 566), Shelby co., W Iowa, 13 mi. N of Atlantic, in agr. area.

Elkhorn. 1 Village (pop. 476), Douglas co., E Nebr., 15 mi. W of Omaha and on Elkhorn R., near Platte R. **2** Coal-mining village (pop. 1,035), McDowell co., S W.Va., 10 mi. SE of Welch. **3** City (pop. 2,935), ⊙ Walworth co., SE Wis., near L. Geneva, 40 mi. SW of Milwaukee, in dairy, grain, and poultry area; mfg. of band instruments and equipment; canneries; fish hatchery. Resort lakes near by.

Settled 1837; inc. as village in 1852, as city in 1897.
Elkhorn, Mount (7,200 ft.), SW B.C., on central Vancouver Isl., in Strathcona Provincial Park, 40 mi. WNW of Courtenay; 49°47'N 125°51'W.
Elkhorn City, Ky.: see PRAISE.
Elkhorn Creek. 1 In NW Ill., rises in W Ogle co., flows c.55 mi. generally SW and S to Rock R. c.5 mi. SW of Sterling. 2 In N Ky., rises in Fayette co. W of Lexington, flows 85 mi. NNW to Kentucky R. 9 mi. N of Frankfort.
Elkhorn Peak, Idaho: see TETON RANGE.
Elkhorn Ridge, NE Oregon, range of Blue Mts. in Baker co., W of Baker. Chief peaks: Angell Peak (8,675 ft.), Twin Mtn. (8,920 ft.), and ROCK CREEK BUTTE (9,097 ft.). Lies in Whitman Natl. Forest.
Elkhorn River, NE Nebr., rises in Rock co., flows 333 mi. ESE and S, past O'Neill, Norfolk and West Point, to Platte R. near Omaha. Logan Creek is tributary.
Elkhorn Tavern, Ark.: see PEA RIDGE.
Elkhotovo or **El'khotovo** (ĕlkhô'tüvŭ), village (1926 pop. 4,891), W Ossetian Autonomous SSR, Russian SFSR, on railroad, on Terek R. and 32 mi. NW of Dzaudzhikau; fruit and vegetable processing; metalworks.
Elkhovka, Russian SFSR: see YELKHOVKA.
Elki, Turkey: see BEYTUSSEBAP.
Elkin (ĕl'kĭn), town (pop. 2,842), Surry co., N N.C., on Yadkin R. and 35 mi. WNW of Winston-Salem; cotton and woolen mills, furniture mfg.; noted for its woolen blankets.
Elkins, city (pop. 9,121), ⊙ Randolph co., E W.Va., on Tygart R. and 36 mi. SE of Clarksburg; rail junction (shops); trade and distributing center for coal-mining and timber area; foundry and lumber products; tannery, Has Davis and Elkins Col., state home for children. A gateway to Monongahela Natl. Forest. Inc. 1890.
Elkins Park or **Ogontz** (ō'gŏnts), village (1940 pop. 3,286) in CHELTENHAM township, Montgomery co., SE Pa.; N suburb of Philadelphia. Has Quaker meetinghouse built 1682.
Elk Island National Park (□ 75), central Alta., 20 mi. E of Edmonton. Largest fenced animal preserve in Canada; 10 mi. long, 6 mi. wide. Contains several lakes. Sandy Beach, on Astotin L., is park's chief resort. Sanctuary for buffalo, elk, moose, mule deer, weasels, muskrats, porcupines, and other fauna. Reserved 1906 and established 1913, park became home of a herd of buffalo purchased 1907 by Dominion govt. Park was enlarged 1922 and again 1947. During Second World War the Dominion govt. buffalo herd from Buffalo Natl. Park was transferred here.
Elk Lake, NW Mich., 12 mi. NE of Traverse City, in resort area; c.9 mi. long, 2 mi. wide. Drains W into East Arm of Grand Traverse Bay through Elk R. (c.2 mi. long). Joined by passage to Round L. (SE; 3½ mi. in diameter), thence to Torch L. (E).
Elkland, borough (pop. 2,326), Tioga co., N Pa., 27 mi. WSW of Elmira, N.Y., on N.Y. border. Large sole-leather tannery; gloves. Inc. 1850.
Elk Mills, village (pop. c.500), Cecil co., NE Md., on Elk R. near Del. line and 17 mi. WSW of Wilmington, Del.; cotton velours mill. Near by is Elk Forge (c.1761), where guns for the Continental Army were made.
Elkmont. 1 Town (pop. 179), Limestone co., N Ala., 9 mi. N of Athens, near Elk R. and Tenn. line. 2 Mountain resort (alt. c.2,150 ft.), Sevier co., E Tenn., in Great Smoky Mts. Natl. Park, on Little R. and 14 mi. S of Sevierville. Mt. Le Conte and Newfound Gap near by.
Elk Mound, village (pop. 390), Dunn co., W Wis., 10 mi. WNW of Eau Claire, on sandy plain; vegetable canning. A small co. park is near by.
Elk Mountain, town (pop. 196), Carbon co., S Wyo., on Medicine Bow R. and 45 mi. ESE of Rawlins; alt. c.7,000 ft. Elk Mtn. is 7 mi. WSW.
Elk Mountain. 1 Peak (6,423 ft.) in W S.Dak., near Wyo. line, in Black Hills. 2 Outlying peak (11,162 ft.) in NNW tip of Medicine Bow Mts., S Wyo., 7 mi. WSW of Elk Mountain town. Peak has long served as landmark.
Elk Mountains, range of Rocky Mts. in Pitkin and Gunnison counties, W central Colo., just W of Sawatch Mts. Chief peaks: Sopris Peak (12,823 ft.); PYRAMID PEAK (14,000 ft.); SNOWMASS PEAK (14,077 ft.); Capitol Peak (14,100 ft.); MAROON PEAK (14,126 ft.); Mt. CARBON (14,259 ft.; also called Castle Peak), highest point in range. SW extension, called West Elk Mts., rises to 12,714 ft. in Mt. GUNNISON.
Elk Neck, Cecil co., NE Md., peninsula c.12 mi. long, at head of Chesapeake Bay bet. Northeast R. and Elk R., just SW of Elkton; terminates at Turkey Point (lighthouse). State forest and park.
Elko, village (pop. estimate 200), SE B.C., on Elk R. and 14 mi. SSW of Fernie; iron, coal, copper deposits.
Elko, county (□ 17,140; pop. 11,654), NE Nev.; ⊙ Elko. Mtn. and plateau area crossed by Humboldt R., bordering on Idaho and Utah. Part of Duck Valley Indian Reservation is in N, on Idaho line; part of Goshute Indian Reservation is in E, on Utah line. South Fork Indian Reservation is S of Elko. Sections of Humboldt Natl. Forest are in S (in Ruby Mts.) and N. Livestock grazing. Formed 1869.
Elko. 1 Town (pop. 188), Houston co., central Ga., 8 mi. S of Perry. 2 Village (pop. 111), Scott co., SE Minn., 20 mi. SE of Shakopee. 3 City (pop. 5,393), ⊙ Elko co., NE Nev., on Humboldt R. and c.200 mi. W of Salt Lake City; alt. 5,063 ft.; trade center and shipping point for cattle, sheep, and wool. Has railroad repair shops. Copper, gold, silver mines in vicinity. Industrial school for boys is near by. Founded 1868, when railroad arrived; inc. 1917. Univ. of Nevada (now at Reno) was here 1873–85. 4 Town (pop. 142), Barnwell co., W S.C., 30 mi. WSW of Orangeburg.
Elk Park, town (pop. 545), Avery co., NW N.C., 17 mi. WSW of Boone, near Tenn. line; mtn. resort.
Elk Point, village (pop. 338), E Alta., near North Saskatchewan R., 40 mi. N of Vermilion; wheat, dairying, lumbering.
Elk Point, city (pop. 1,367), ⊙ Union co., SE S. Dak., 20 mi. NW of Sioux City, Iowa, near Missouri R.; livestock, poultry, grain. Founded 1861.
Elkport, town (pop. 99), Clayton co., NE Iowa, near confluence of Turkey and Volga rivers, 9 mi. WSW of Guttenberg. Limestone quarries near by.
Elk Rapids, village (pop. 889), Antrim co., NW Mich., 13 mi. NE of Traverse City, bet. Elk L. and East Arm of Grand Traverse Bay; agr. (potatoes, beans, cherries); resort.
Elkridge. 1 Village (1940 pop. 1,541), Howard co., central Md., on Patapsco R. and 8 mi. SW of downtown Baltimore. Residential; some light mfg. 2 Village, McDowell co., W.Va.: see ALGOMA.
Elk Ridge (c.1,500 ft.), NW Md., N continuation of the Blue Ridge of Va.; extends 10 mi. NNE from the Potomac opposite Harpers Ferry, W.Va., to just S of Keedysville, Md.
Elk River. 1 Village (pop. 312), Clearwater co., N Idaho, 21 mi. N of Orofino; railroad terminus. Grazing, lumber. 2 Village (pop. 1,399), ⊙ Sherburne co., E Minn., on Mississippi R., at mouth of Elk R., and 28 mi. NW of Minneapolis; farm trading point; dairy products. Platted 1865, inc. 1881.
Elk River. 1 In SE Kansas, formed by confluence of several headstreams in Elk co. near Howard, flows c.80 mi. ESE, past Elk City, to Verdigris R. just N of Independence. 2 In central Minn., rises in marshy area of Benton co., flows 70 mi. S and SE to Mississippi R. at Elk River village. 3 In SW Mo. and NE Okla., rises in McDonald co., Mo., flows 80 mi. W to L. of the Cherokees in Delaware co., Okla. 4 In SE Pa. and NE Md., rises in S Chester co., Pa., flows c.35 mi. S and SW, past Elkton, Md. (head of navigation), to Chesapeake Bay near its head. Lower section (9 mi.) serves as connecting channel (27 ft. deep) bet. the bay and Chesapeake and Delaware Canal. 5 In S Tenn. and N Ala., rises on W slope of Cumberland Mts. in Grundy co., Tenn.; meanders c.200 mi. generally WSW past Fayetteville, into Ala., to Wheeler Reservoir (Tennessee R.) 6 mi. E of Wheeler Dam; lower course forms part of reservoir. 6 In central W.Va., rises in the Alleghenies N of Marlinton, flows N, W past Webster Springs, generally NW past Sutton, and SW past Clendenin, to Kanawha R. at Charleston; 172 mi. long.
Elkton (ĕlk'tŭn). 1 City (pop. 1,312), ⊙ Todd co., S Ky., 17 mi. ESE of Hopkinsville, in agr. area (dark tobacco, grain, fruit, Jersey cattle); stone quarries, timber; mfg. of clothing, agr. lime, road stone; flour, feed, and lumber mills. Blue and Gray State Park is near by; Jefferson Davis State Monument is W, at Fairview. 2 Town (pop. 5,245), ⊙ Cecil co. (since 1786), NE Md., at head of navigation on Elk R. and 19 mi. WSW of Wilmington, Del., in wheat-growing area, with large sand and gravel pits. Mfg. (rubber toys, paper, clothing, fireworks, spark plugs, radios). Until 1938, when Md. passed a revised marriage law, Elkton was the Gretna Green of the East. Near by are Md. terminus of Chesapeake and Delaware Canal and Elk Neck, site of a state forest, state park, and Turkey Point Lighthouse (erected 1834). Founded 1681. 3 Village (pop. 854), Huron co., E Mich., 39 mi. NE of Bay City, near Saginaw Bay, in agr. area; grain elevators; dairy products; tile mfg. 4 Village (pop. 141), Mower co., SE Minn., near Iowa line, 13 mi. E of Austin, in corn, oat, barley area. 5 City (pop. 201), Douglas co., W Oregon, on Umpqua R. and 32 mi. NNW of Roseburg; trading point in agr. area. 6 City (pop. 657), Brookings co., E S.Dak., 16 mi. ESE of Brookings, near Minn. line; dairy produce, poultry, livestock, grain. 7 Town (pop. 168), Giles co., S Tenn., near Ala. line, 13 mi. SE of Pulaski. 8 Town (pop. 1,361), Rockingham co., NW Va., in Shenandoah Valley, on South Fork of Shenandoah R. and 14 mi. E of Harrisonburg; mfg. of pharmaceuticals, clothing. Inc. 1908.
Elkville, village (pop. 934), Jackson co., SW Ill., 13 mi. NW of Herrin; bituminous-coal mining; agr. (grain, poultry, fruit, truck).
Ellamaa or **Ellama** (ĕ'lämä), village (pop. 83), NW Estonia, on railroad and 32 mi. SW of Tallinn; peat-fed power plant.
Ellamar (ĕ'lümär), village (pop. 34), S Alaska, on Prince William Sound, 20 mi. SW of Valdez; fishing, canning.
Elland (ĕ'lünd), urban district (1931 pop. 10,326; 1951 census 19,273), West Riding, SW Yorkshire, England, on Calder R. and 3 mi. SE of Halifax; woolen and cotton milling, metal casting; mfg. of clothing. Near by are stone and clay quarries.
Ellange (ĕlãzh'), village (pop. 247), SE Luxembourg, 10 mi. SE of Luxembourg city; vineyards.
Ellasar, Iraq: see LARSA.
Ellaville, city (pop. 886), ⊙ Schley co., W central Ga., 12 mi. NNW of Americus, in farm and timber area.
Ellefeld (ĕ'lüfĕlt), village (pop. 5,023), Saxony, E central Germany, in the Erzgebirge, 2 mi. SSW of Auerbach; cotton and woolen milling, embroidering, machinery mfg.
Ellef Ringnes Island (□ 4,266), Sverdrup Isls., N Franklin Dist., Northwest Territories, in the Arctic Ocean; 77°44'–79°25'N 99°–106°30'W; separated from Axel Heiberg Isl. (NE) by Peary Channel, from Amund Ringnes Isl. (SE) by Hassel Sound, from Bathurst Isl. (S) by Maclean Strait, and from Borden Isl. (W) by the Gustav Adolph Sea. Isl. is 150 mi. long, 20–70 mi. wide; surface rises to c.2,000 ft. on central plateau. Isachsen Peninsula (□ 1,008; 55 mi. long, 40 mi. wide), extending NW, was formerly believed to be separate isl. Near Cape Isachsen, NW extremity (79°25'N 105°30'W), is U.S.–Canadian weather station.
Ellel, England: see GALGATE.
Ellen, Mount. 1 Summit in Vt.: see LINCOLN MOUNTAIN. 2 Highest peak (11,485 ft.) in Henry Mts., S Utah, c.50 mi. NE of Escalante.
Ellenboro. 1 Town (pop. 537), Rutherford co., SW N.C., 12 mi. W of Shelby. 2 Town (pop. 307), Ritchie co., NW W.Va., 27 mi. E of Parkersburg.
Ellendale. 1 Town (pop. 321), Sussex co., S central Del., 7 mi. S of Milford. Ellendale Swamp, here, is noted for southern flora and fauna. 2 Village (pop. 476), Steele co., SE Minn., 15 mi. SSW of Owatonna, in agr. area; dairy products. 3 City (pop. 1,759), ⊙ Dickey co., SE N.Dak., 37 mi. N of Aberdeen, near S.Dak. line; dairy products, livestock. State Normal and Industrial Col. Inc. 1889.
Ellenikon or **Ellinikon** (both: ĕlĕnēkôn'), village (pop. 3,441), Attica nome, E central Greece, 6 mi. S of Athens. Site of Athens international airport. Ellenikon includes the village of Chasani, Hasani, or Khasani, for which the airport was formerly named.
Ellen River, Cumberland, England, rises in the Cumbrians 7 mi. N of Keswick, flows 20 mi. NW and W to Solway Firth at Maryport.
Ellensburg, city (pop. 8,430), ⊙ Kittitas co., central Wash., 28 mi. N of Yakima, near Yakima R.; timber, agr., dairying; center of Yakima reclamation project. Mines (coal, gold) near by. Has state teachers col. Ginkgo Petrified Forest State Park c.25 mi. E. Platted 1875.
Ellen's Isle, islet at E end of Loch KATRINE, SW Perthshire, Scotland, principal scene of Scott's *The Lady of the Lake.* Its size was decreased when level of loch was raised, 1859.
Ellenton. 1 Town (pop. 429), Colquitt co., S Ga., 11 mi. E of Moultrie; lumber, naval stores. 2 Former town (1950 pop. 746), Aiken co., SW S.C., near Savannah R., 23 mi. S of Aiken, in area taken over (1951–52) by U.S. Atomic Energy Commission for huge Savannah R. Plant (hydrogen-bomb materials).
Ellenville, resort village (pop. 4,225), Ulster co., SE N.Y., in the Shawangunk range, 25 mi. SW of Kingston; mfg. of cutlery, wood products, clothing, umbrellas, beverages. Inc. 1856.
Ellerbee (ĕ'lürbē), town (pop. 773), Richmond co., S N.C., 9 mi. N of Rockingham; hosiery and lumber mills.
Ellerbek, GERMANY: see KIEL.
Ellerslie (ĕ'lürzlē), village (pop. estimate 150), W P.E.I., near Malpeque Bay, 16 mi. NW of Summerside; lobster fishing and canning.
Ellerslie, borough (pop. 3,119), N N.Isl., New Zealand; SE suburb of Auckland; horse racing.
Ellerslie, village (1940 pop. 718), Allegany co., W Md., on Wills Creek at Pa. line, 5 mi. NNW of Cumberland; limestone quarries near.
Ellesmere (ĕlz'mēr), urban district (1931 pop. 1,872; 1951 census 2,159), NW Shropshire, England, 15 mi. NNW of Shrewsbury and on Ellesmere Canal, which connects Severn R. and Mersey R., crossing Vale of Llangollen by Telford's aqueduct; agr. market in dairying region. Was site of Norman castle. Its 13th-cent. church was built on foundations of a Norman church. Near by is group of lakes, the largest of which are The Mere, White Mere, Blake Mere, and Cole Mere.
Ellesmere, county, New Zealand: see LEESTON.
Ellesmere, Lake, lagoon (□ 107.5), E S.Isl., New Zealand, 16 mi. SSW of Christchurch; 16 mi. long, 10 mi. wide, 45 ft. deep; nearly closed off from Canterbury Bight by sandspit.
Ellesmere Island (□ 77,392), NE Franklin Dist., Northwest Territories, in the Arctic Ocean, just W of NW Greenland; northernmost isl. of America; 76°15'–83°7'N 60°30'–90°20'W. Separated from Devon Isl. (S) by James Sound, from Axel Hei-

berg Isl. (W) by Eureka and Nansen sounds, and from Greenland (E) by Robeson and Kennedy channels, Kane Basin, Smith Sound, and Baffin Bay. Isl. is 500 mi. long, 25–300 mi. wide; coastline is indented by numerous fjords. Surface is mountainous and largely ice-covered; S part of isl. is generally over 2,000 ft. high, while United States Range (N) rises to over 11,000 ft. Chief subdivisions of isl. are King Oscar Land (SW), Ellesmere Land (SE), Grinnell Land (center), and Grant Land (N). In ice-free regions there is considerable vegetation, supporting large musk-ox herds. Settlements at Craig Harbour (SE) and Buchanan Bay (E); on Eureka Sound is U.S.–Canadian weather station. Fort Conger (NE; 81°43′N 64°43′W) was site (1881–83) of meteorological station established by A. W. Greely. Cape Columbia (83°7′N 70°28′W) is northernmost point of Canada. E coast of Ellesmere Isl. was 1st explored by Sir E. A. Inglefield (1852), the Grinnell expedition (1853–56), Sir G. S. Nares (1875–76), C. F. Hall (1871–73), and A. W. Greely and R. E. Peary. Otto Sverdrup explored W coast (1898–1902).

Ellesmere Port, formerly Ellesmere Port and Whitby, urban district (1931 pop. 18,911; 1951 census 32,594), NW Cheshire, England, on Manchester Ship Canal and 9 mi. SSE of Liverpool; flour-milling center; has important petroleum docks and refinery; mfg. of asphalt and petroleum products, paper. In it (S) is residential town of Whitby. Just E, on Manchester Ship Canal and included in urban dist., is the major petroleum refinery and oil-storage dock of Stanlow.

Ellettsville, town (pop. 855), Monroe co., S central Ind., 6 mi. NW of Bloomington, in agr. area; limestone, timber.

Ellezelles (ĕlzĕl′), Flemish *Elzele* (ĕl′zēlü), town (pop. 4,444), Hainaut prov., SW central Belgium, 4 mi. E of Renaix; textiles; agr. market.

Ellice Island (ĕ′lĭs) (24 mi. long, 4–11 mi. wide), NW Mackenzie Dist., Northwest Territories, in Beaufort Sea of the Arctic Ocean, off mouth of Mackenzie R.; 65°5′N 135°40′W.

Ellice Islands (ĕ′lĭs), group of atolls (□ 9.5; pop. 4,487) in Br. colony of GILBERT AND ELLICE ISLANDS, SW Pacific, 9°39′–10°45′S 176°8′–179°30′E. Include 9 isls.: FUNAFUTI (port of entry and ⊙), NANUMANGA, NANUMEA, NUI, NIUTAO, VAITUPU, NUKUFETAU, NUKULAELAE, NIULAKITA. Isls. generally low; some rise to 90 ft. Pandanus, coconut groves; chief export, copra. Polynesian natives. Discovered 1764 by Capt. Byron, became 1892 Br. protectorate, included 1915 in Gilbert and Ellice Isls. colony. In Second World War, group escaped Japanese invasion. Nanumea and Funafuti were occupied 1943 by U.S. forces who established naval and air bases. Formerly Lagoon Isls.

Ellichpur (ĭl′lĭchpŏŏr), town (pop. 31,475), Amraoti dist., W Madhya Pradesh, India, 28 mi. NW of Amraoti; cotton-trade center in major Indian cotton-growing tract; cotton and oilseed milling; sawmills (timber in Satpura Range, N). Seat (13th–15th cent.) of several Deccan dynasties. Was ⊙ former dist. of Ellichpur (mid-19th cent. to 1905).

Ellichpur Camp, India: see PARATWADA.

Ellicott City (ĕ′lĭkŭt), village (1940 pop. 2,682), ⊙ Howard co., in Baltimore and Howard counties, central Md., on Patapsco R. and 11 mi. WSW of downtown Baltimore; trade center in agr. area (wheat, corn, hay); mfg. (doughnut machines, prepared flour mixes, feed, shirts). Near by are Doughoregan Manor (built c.1720), home of Charles Carroll of Carrollton; a Franciscan monastery (1930); and Patapsco State Park. Flour mill built here (1774) was nucleus of settlement of Ellicott Mills; inc. and renamed 1867; reverted (1935) to unincorporated status.

Ellicottville, village (pop. 1,073), Cattaraugus co., W N.Y., 9 mi. NNE of Salamanca, in dairying and poultry area; summer resort; some mfg. (cheese, feed, wood products, baskets, cutlery, heaters). Inc. 1881.

Ellidere River, Bulgaria: see CHEPINO RIVER.

Ellijay, city (pop. 1,527), ⊙ Gilmer co., N Ga., on Coosawattee R. and c.50 mi. NE of Rome; mfg. (bedspreads, lumber). Inc. 1834.

El Limón (ĕl lēmōn′), town (pop. 2,362), Jalisco, W Mexico, in W outliers of Sierra Madre Occidental, 12 mi. NE of Autlán; grain, sugar cane, fruit, tobacco.

El Limón, village, León dept., W Nicaragua, near railroad, 25 mi. NNE of León; gold- and silver-mining center.

Ellingen (ĕ′lĭng-ŭn), town (pop. 1,879), Middle Franconia, W central Bavaria, Germany, on the Swabian Rezat and 2 mi. N of Weissenburg; brewing, flour milling. Has mid-18th-cent. town hall and church. Chartered 1378.

Ellinger (ĕ′lĭnjŭr), town (pop. 219), Fayette co., S central Texas, 28 mi. SW of Brenham, in agr. area.

Ellington. 1 Town (pop. 3,099), Tolland co., N Conn., 15 mi. NNE of Hartford; agr. (tobacco, potatoes). Includes Crystal Lake, resort village on Crystal L. (c.1 mi. long), parts of Shenipsit L. and state forest. Settled c.1720, inc. 1786. **2** Town (pop. 777), Reynolds co., SE Mo., in the Ozarks, 16 mi. WNW of Piedmont; ships farm products. **3** Village in Ellington town (1940 pop. 1,073), Chautauqua co., extreme W N.Y., 11 mi. NE of Jamestown, in dairying and fruitgrowing area.

Ellington Air Force Base, Texas: see HOUSTON.

Ellinikon, Greece: see ELLENIKON.

Ellinwood, city (pop. 2,569), Barton co., central Kansas, on Arkansas R. and 10 mi. E of Great Bend; mfg. oil-well equipment, flour. Founded 1871, inc. 1878. Boomed in 1930s with development of oil fields.

Elliot, Scotland: see ARBROATH.

Elliot, town (pop. 2,361), E Cape Prov., U. of So. Afr., in Drakensberg range, 80 mi. SE of Aliwal North, near Transkeian Territories; stock-raising, dairying center; alt. 4,761 ft.

Elliott, county (□ 240; pop. 7,085), NE Ky.; ⊙ Sandy Hook. Drained by Little Sandy R. and several creeks. Hilly agr. area (tobacco, corn, hay, livestock, fruit); timber, coal mines. Includes part of Cumberland Natl. Forest. Formed 1869.

Elliott. 1 Village (pop. 337), Ford co., E central Ill., 23 mi. N of Champaign, in rich agr. area. **2** Town (pop. 482), Montgomery co., SW Iowa, on East Nishnabotna R. and 10 mi. NNE of Red Oak, in agr. region. **3** Village (pop. 87), Ransom co., SE N.Dak., 8 mi. WSW of Lisbon. **4** Town (1940 pop. 270), Lee co., central S.C., 15 mi. NE of Sumter.

Elliott Bay, Wash., inlet of Puget Sound forming harbor of Seattle; 6 mi. wide at entrance, 4 mi. long. Receives Duwamish R.

Elliott Highway (72 mi. long), central Alaska, NNW extension of Alaska Highway network from Fairbanks to Livengood. Serves gold-mining region.

Elliott Key (c.8 mi. long), in the Florida Keys, S Fla., c.20 mi. S of Miami. Sometimes called Elliotts Key.

Elliottsville, plantation (pop. 39), Piscataquis co., central Maine, 17 mi. NW of Dover-Foxcroft, in hunting, fishing area. Includes Onawa village on Onawa L. (3 mi. long).

Ellis. 1 County (□ 900; pop. 19,043), W central Kansas; ⊙ Hays. Prairie region, drained in N by Saline R., in S by Smoky Hill R. Wheat, livestock. Oil fields in NE. Formed 1867. **2** County (□ 1,222; pop. 7,326), NW Okla.; ⊙ Arnett. Bounded W by Texas line, S by Canadian R.; drained by Wolf Creek. Agr. area (livestock, wheat, barley, broomcorn, poultry). Some mfg. at Shattuck. Formed 1907. **3** County (□ 953; pop. 45,645), N Texas; ⊙ Waxahachie. In rich blackland agr. region; bounded E by Trinity R. Cotton, corn, grains, clover seed, pecans, fruit, truck (especially onions); dairying, livestock (cattle, sheep, hogs, poultry); beekeeping. Limestone quarrying, clay mining; large brick industry. Mfg., processing at Waxahachie, Ennis, Ferris. Formed 1849.

Ellis, city (pop. 2,649), Ellis co., W central Kansas, on the Big Creek, and 14 mi. WNW of Hays, in wheat and livestock region; railroad repair shops. Oil wells near by. Founded 1867, inc. 1888.

Ellisburg, village (pop. 285), Jefferson co., N N.Y., 20 mi. SSW of Watertown, near L. Ontario; wood products.

Ellis Grove or Ellisgrove, village (pop. 258), Randolph co., SW Ill., near the Mississippi, c.45 mi. SSE of East St. Louis, in agr. area.

Ellis Island (c.27 acres), SE N.Y., in Upper New York Bay, c.1 mi. SW of the Battery of Manhattan; ferry connections. Govt. property since 1808, it was 1st site of an arsenal and fort, later (1892–1943) the chief immigration station of U.S.; now used as detention station for deportees and immigrants without proper entry permission.

Ellisland, farm, Dumfries co., Scotland, 6 mi. NW of Dumfries. Robert Burns lived here 1788–91. Became natl. property 1928.

Ellison Bay, fishing village, Door co., NE Wis., on Door Peninsula, on Green Bay, 33 mi. NE of Sturgeon Bay city.

Ellis River, Carroll co., E N.H., rises in S Pinkham Notch in White Mts., flows 12 mi. S to Saco R. E of Bartlett. Glen Ellis Falls (70 ft.), scenic feature.

Elliston, village (pop. 127), S South Australia, on W Eyre Peninsula, 90 mi. NW of Port Lincoln, on small inlet of Great Australian Bight; some livestock.

Elliston, village (pop. c.150), Powell co., W central Mont., on branch of the Clark Fork and 20 mi. W of Helena; lime quarry. Gold-quartz and placer mining in vicinity.

Ellisville. 1 Village (pop. 157), Fulton co., W central Ill., on Spoon R. (bridged here) and 16 mi. WNW of Canton, in agr. and bituminous-coal area. **2** City (pop. 3,579), a ⊙ Jones co., SE Miss., 7 mi. SSW of Laurel, near Tallahala Creek; hosiery mills. Seat of a jr. col.; has state school for feeble-minded. **3** Town (pop. 628), St. Louis co., E Mo., near Missouri R., 18 mi. W of St. Louis.

El Llano (ĕl yä′nō), town (pop. 1,378), Hidalgo, central Mexico, 38 mi. W of Pachuca; corn, sugar, cotton, fruit, stock.

El Llano, village (pop. 200), Panama prov., central Panama, on Bayano R. and 10 mi. ENE of Chepo, on proposed route of Inter-American Highway; lumbering; stock raising.

Ellmauer Haltspitze, Austria: see KAISERGEBIRGE.

Ellon, burgh (1931 pop. 1,300; 1951 census 1,491), E Aberdeen, Scotland, on Ythan R. and 16 mi. N of Aberdeen; agr. market, with shoe mfg.

Ellora (ĕlō′rŭ), village, Aurangabad dist., NW Hyderabad state, India, 10 mi. NW of Aurangabad. Famous rock-cut shrines on sloping hills, just SE, consist of 3 distinct groups: Buddhist (c.3d–6th cent.), Hindu (c.6th–8th cent.), and Jain (c.8th–13th cent.). Kailasa temple, in Hindu group, is carved from monolithic mass left standing in center of large excavation dug vertically from top of hill; contains fine frescoes. Also spelled Elura.

Ellore (ĕlōr′), since 1949 officially **Eluru** (ĕlōō′rōō), city (pop. 64,911), ⊙ West Godavari dist., NE Madras, India, at junction of navigable irrigation-canal system of Godavari and Kistna rivers; agr. trade center (rice, oilseeds, tobacco, sugar); noted pile carpets; rice, sunn-hemp (jute substitute), and cotton milling, mfg. of electrical supplies; tanneries. Has col. affiliated with Andhra Univ. Buddhist archaeological remains 5 mi. N, at village of Pedda Vegi.

Elloree (ĕ′lūrē), town (pop. 1,127), Orangeburg co., central S.C., 17 mi. E of Orangeburg, near Santee R.; lumber, veneer.

Ellos (ĕl′ŭs″), Swedish *Ellös*, fishing village (pop. 402), Goteborg och Bohus co., SW Sweden, on NW coast of Orust isl., on the Skagerrak, 6 mi. SSE of Lysekil; fish canning.

Elloughton with Brough (ĕ′lŭtŭn, brŭf), parish (pop. 1,375), East Riding, SE Yorkshire, England. Includes agr. village of Elloughton, 9 mi. W of Hull, and town of Brough, just S on Humber R., with aircraft-parts industry.

Ellport, borough (pop. 1,122), Lawrence co., W Pa., on Connoquenessing Creek just E of Ellwood City.

Ellrich (ĕl′rĭkh), town (pop. 5,963), in former Prussian Saxony prov., central Germany, after 1945 in Thuringia, at S foot of the lower Harz, 8 mi. NW of Nordhausen, opposite Walkenried; cotton milling, woodworking; gypsum quarrying.

Ellsinore (ĕl′sĭnôr″), town (pop. 299), Carter co., S Mo., in Ozark region, near Black R., 23 mi. NW of Poplar Bluff; lumber.

Ellston, town (pop. 158), Ringgold co., S Iowa, 20 mi. SE of Creston; livestock, grain.

Ellsworth, county (□ 723; pop. 8,465), central Kansas; ⊙ Ellsworth. Rolling-plain area, drained by Smoky Hill R. Livestock, wheat. Oil and gas fields, limestone quarries. Formed 1867.

Ellsworth. 1 Village (pop. 199), McLean co., central Ill., 14 mi. E of Bloomington, in rich agr. area. **2** Town (pop. 439), Hamilton co., central Iowa, on Skunk R. and 17 mi. SE of Webster City. **3** City (pop. 2,193), ⊙ Ellsworth co., central Kansas, on Smoky Hill R. and 35 mi. WSW of Salina; marketing center for livestock and winter-wheat region. Oil and gas fields, and limestone in vicinity. Laid out 1867, inc. 1868. **4** City (pop. 3,936), ⊙ Hancock co., S Maine, bet. Bangor and Mt. Desert Isl., on Union R. (falls here); resort center, dairy and wood products, machinery. Black Mansion (1802) is colonial mus. Settled 1763, town inc. 1800, city 1869. **5** Village (pop. 369), Antrim co., NW Mich., 33 mi. NNE of Traverse City, in resort and farm area. **6** Village (pop. 630), Nobles co., SW Minn., just N of Iowa line, 23 mi. WSW of Worthington, in grain area. **7** Town (pop. 24), Grafton co., central N.H., 18 mi. NW of Meredith. **8** Borough (pop. 1,670), Washington co., SW Pa., 12 mi. ESE of Washington. Inc. 1900. **9** Village (pop. 1,475), ⊙ Pierce co., W Wis., 35 mi. ESE of St. Paul, Minn.; dairying, stock raising. Inc. 1887.

Ellsworth Highland, Antarctica, extends SSW from base of Palmer Peninsula to Rockefeller Plateau. Discovered 1935 by Lincoln Ellsworth.

Ellwangen (ĕl′väng″ŭn), town (pop. 9,415), N Württemberg, Germany, after 1945 in Württemberg-Baden, on the Jagst and 9 mi. N of Aalen; mfg. of furniture, stockings; lumber milling. Has 12th–13th-cent. collegiate church; 17th-cent. pilgrimage church; anc. fortress, rebuilt into Renaissance castle. Developed around 8th-cent. abbey, which was transformed into col. of secular canons in 1460, secularized in 1802.

Ellwood City, borough (pop. 12,945), Lawrence and Beaver counties, W Pa., 10 mi. SSE of New Castle and on Connoquenessing Creek; metal products, pipe, wire; limestone, sandstone; dairying. Settled 1890, inc. 1892.

Elm, town and parish (pop. 2,570), in Isle of Ely, N Cambridge, England, 2 mi. SSE of Wisbech; agr. market in fruitgrowing region. Has 13th-cent. church.

Elm (ĕlm), village (pop. 1,424), in former Prussian prov. of Hanover, NW Germany, after 1945 in Lower Saxony, 3 mi. NE of Bremervörde; knitwear mfg.

Elma. 1 Town (pop. 731), Howard co., NE Iowa, 18 mi. NE of Charles City; concrete blocks. Limestone quarry, sand and gravel pits near by. **2** Town (pop. 1,543), Grays Harbor co., W Wash., 25 mi. W of Olympia, near Chehalis R.; lumber, dairy products, poultry, truck, bulbs. Settled c.1886.

Elmadagi (ĕlmä′däŭ″), Turkish *Elmadağı*, town (pop. 4,058), Ankara prov., central Turkey, 20 mi. E of Ankara; mfg. town in agr. area. Formerly Kucukyozgat.

Elma Dagi, Turkish *Elma Dağı*, peak (6,086 ft.), central Turkey, 11 mi. SE of Ankara.

El Maitén (ĕl mītĕn′) or **Maitén,** village (pop. estimate 500), NW Chubut natl. territory, Argentina, on railroad, on Chubut R. and 60 mi. N of Esquel; farming and coal-mining center. Alfalfa, sheep, cattle; fishing, flour milling.

Elmali (ĕlmälŭ′), Turkish *Elmalı*, town (pop. 5,217), Antalya prov., SW Turkey, 45 mi. W of Antalya; wheat, barley, chick-peas, vetch. Sometime spelled Elmalu or Almali.

Elmali Mountains, Turkish *Elmalı*, SW Turkey, extend 55 mi. SSW from L. Sogut; rise to 10,021 ft. in Ak Dag. Chromium in S.

El Mamey, Mexico: see MINATITLÁN, Colima.

El Manteco (ĕl mäntä′kō) or **Manteco,** town (pop. 516), Bolívar state, SE Venezuela, on Caroní R. and 55 mi. SE of Ciudad Bolívar; rubber, balata gum, fruit.

El Marqués (ĕl märkās′) or **Marqués,** officially Villa del Marqués, town (pop. 1,688), Querétaro, central Mexico, on Querétaro R. (affluent of Apaseo R.) and 3 mi. E of Querétaro (connected by tramway). Produces flowers, fruit. Resort noted for thermal springs. Formerly La Cañada.

Elm City, town (pop. 839), Wilson co., E central N.C., 6 mi. NNE of Wilson.

Elm Creek, village (pop. estimate 400), S Man., 40 mi. WSW of Winnipeg; grain, stock.

Elm Creek, village (pop. 799), Buffalo co., S central Nebr., 15 mi. W of Kearney and on Platte R.; alfalfa meal; dairy and poultry produce, grain, livestock.

Elm Creek, rises NE of Jackson, SW Minn., flows 60 mi. E to Blue Earth R. at Winnebago.

Elmdale. 1 City (pop. 180), Chase co., E central Kansas, on Cottonwood R. and 25 mi. W of Emporia; livestock, grain. **2** Village (pop. 119), Morrison co., central Minn., 11 mi. SW of Little Falls.

Elmdale Village, town (pop. 641), St. Louis co., E Mo.

El Médano (ĕl mā′dänō), island (2 mi. long) in the Mar Chiquita, NE Córdoba prov., Argentina, at mouth of the Río Primero, 10 mi. NW of Miramar.

El Melón (ĕl mālōn′) or **Melón,** village (1930 pop. 279), Valparaíso prov., central Chile, on railroad and 35 mi. NE of Valparaíso; lime-quarrying center; cement plant. Copper deposits near by.

Elmendorf, village (pop. c.300), Bexar co., S central Texas, 15 mi. SE of San Antonio, in agr. area; makes brick, tile.

Elmendorf Field, air base and commercial airport for Anchorage, S Alaska, near Knik Inlet, 4 mi. NE of Anchorage; 61°15′N 149°51′W.

El Mene (ĕl mā′nā), town (pop. 2,734), Falcón state, NW Venezuela, in Maracaibo lowlands, 40 mi. E of Maracaibo; linked by railroad and pipe line with Altagracia on L. Maracaibo. Petroleum wells. Media, Hombre Pintado, and Las Palmas oil fields, now also connected with Altagracia pipe line, are NE.

Elmenteita (ĕlmĕntā′tä), village, Rift Valley prov., W central Kenya, on railroad, W of L. Elmenteita and 15 mi. SSE of Nakuru; wheat, coffee, corn. Thermal springs. Diatomite deposits.

Elmer. 1 Town (pop. 295), Macon co., N central Mo., on Chariton R. and 18 mi. NW of Macon. **2** Borough (pop. 1,460), Salem co., SW N.J., 15 mi. E of Salem; agr. shipping center (truck, grain, dairy products). Inc. 1893. **3** Town (pop. 145), Jackson co., SW Okla., 10 mi. S of Altus, near junction of Salt and Prairie Dog Town forks to form Red R., in cotton and grain area.

Elmer City, town (pop. 513), Okanogan co., N Wash., on the Columbia just below Grand Coulee Dam.

El Mesón (ĕl māsōn′), town (pop. 1,430), Veracruz, SE Mexico, in Sotavento lowlands, 18 mi. NW of San Andrés Tuxtla; fruit, cattle.

Elmesthorpe, England: see EARL SHILTON.

Elm Fork of Red River, Texas and Okla.: see NORTH FORK OF RED RIVER.

Elm Grove, residential village (1940 pop. 1,004), Waukesha co., SE Wis., 8 mi. W of Milwaukee.

Elmham, England: see NORTH ELMHAM.

Elmhurst. 1 Residential city (pop. 21,273), Du Page co., NE Ill., suburb W of Chicago and 8 mi. E of Wheaton, in truck-farming area; mfg. (sprinklers, fertilizer); greenhouses; limestone quarry. Seat of Elmhurst Col. Settled 1843, inc. 1910. **2** A section of N Queens borough of New York City, SE N.Y.; mainly residential; some mfg. (clothing, radio equipment; wood, fiber, and rubber products; machinery). **3** Former borough, Lackawanna co., NE Pa., 6 mi. ESE of Scranton; reverted to township status, 1941.

El Milagro, Argentina: see MILAGRO.

Elmina (ĕlmē′nŭ), town (1931 pop. 4,797), Western Prov., S Gold Coast colony, on Gulf of Guinea, 7 mi. W of Cape Coast; fishing center; cassava, corn. St. George's Castle (built 1482) still serves as govt. office. Founded 1471 by Portuguese; 1st major European post on Gold Coast. Developed as major gold-trading center; passed 1637 to Dutch (becoming hq. of their possessions), 1872 to British.

Elmira (ĕlmī′rŭ), town (pop. 2,012), S Ont., 11 mi. N of Kitchener; felt-shoe mfg. center; mfg. of chemicals, aluminum products, furniture; dairying, woodworking.

Elmira (ĕlmī′rŭ). **1** Town (pop. 128), Ray co., NW Mo., on Crooked R. and 18 mi. NNW of Richmond. **2** City (pop. 49,716), ⊙ Chemung co., S N.Y., near Pa. line, on Chemung R. and 45 mi. W of Binghamton; distributing and mfg. center (milk bottles, fire-fighting equipment and chemicals, office equipment, business machines, metal products, trucks, munitions, gliders, textiles); railroad shops. Sand and gravel, limestone quarries. Annual glider contest held near by. Site of Elmira State Reformatory. Here are also Arnot Art Gall., Elmira Col. for women (1855). Near by is Newtown Battlefield Reservation, commemorating battle (1779) bet. Sullivan-Clinton expedition and Indians. Mark Twain is buried in Elmira. Settled 1788, inc. 1864.

Elmira Heights, village (pop. 5,009), Chemung co., S N.Y., just N of Elmira; machinery, metal products. Settled 1779, inc. 1896.

Elmo. 1 Town (pop. 258), Nodaway co., NW Mo., near Nodaway R., 18 mi. NW of Maryville; grain. **2** Town (pop. 170), Emery co., central Utah, 16 mi. NE of Castle Dale. **3** Town (pop. 213), Carbon co., S Wyo., in N outlier of Medicine Bow Mts., 38 mi. ENE of Rawlins; alt. c.7,000 ft.

El Mochito (ĕl mōchē′tō), mining settlement, Santa Bárbara dept., W Honduras, 10 mi. SE of Santa Bárbara, W of L. Yojoa; silver-mining center, linked by road with San Pedro Sula. Gold and lead are by-products. Developed in 1940s.

El Modena (ĕl mōdē′nŭ), village (pop. c.650), Orange co., S Calif., just NE of Santa Ana; citrus-fruit groves.

El Moján, Venezuela: see SAN RAFAEL, Zulia state.

El Molino, Mexico: see VISTA HERMOSA DE NEGRETE.

Elmont, residential village (1940 pop. 8,957), Nassau co., SE N.Y., on W Long Isl., just E of Jamaica; mfg. of clothing. Belmont Park Race Track is near by.

El Monte (ĕl mōn′tā), town (pop. 2,543), Santiago prov., central Chile, on railroad and 25 mi. SW of Santiago; resort and fruitgrowing center.

El Monte (ĕl mŏn′tē). **1** Village (pop. 2,502), Contra Costa co., W Calif. **2** City (pop. 8,101), Los Angeles co., S Calif., 12 mi. E of downtown Los Angeles; dairy and truck farms; also walnuts, poultry. Large lion farm near by. Founded 1842, inc. 1912.

Elmore, town (pop. 702), N Victoria, Australia, on Campaspe R. and 95 mi. NNW of Melbourne; rail junction in livestock, agr. area; flour mill.

Elmore. 1 County (□ 628; pop. 31,649), E central Ala.; ⊙ Wetumpka. Coastal plain bounded on E and S by Tallapoosa R., drained by Coosa R. Part of Martin L. is in NE; fall line crosses co. E-W. Cotton, corn, livestock; textiles. Formed 1866. **2** County (□ 2,968; pop. 6,687), SW Idaho; ⊙ Mountain Home. Livestock-grazing region bounded N by Boise R., S by Snake R., which drains SE corner. Mtn. area in N, occupying part of Boise Natl. Forest, contains deposits of gold, silver, copper, lead, zinc. Irrigated regions are in NW, around ARROWROCK DAM, and in SE (King Hill project). Co. formed 1889.

Elmore. 1 Village (pop. 1,074), Faribault co., S Minn., on branch of Blue Earth R., on Iowa line, and 9 mi. S of Blue Earth, in grain, potato, livestock area; dairy products. **2** Village (pop. 1,215), Ottawa co., N Ohio, 18 mi. SE of Toledo, and on Portage R., in agr. area; machinery, baskets, cement blocks, meat products. **3** Town (pop. 312), Lamoille co., N central Vt., 19 mi. N of Montpelier. Includes Lake Elmore, resort on small L. Elmore; state forest near by.

Elmore City or **Elmore,** town (pop. 743), Garvin co., S central Okla., 13 mi. SW of Pauls Valley, in agr. area; cotton ginning.

El Morrito, Nicaragua: see MORRITO.

El Morro (ĕl mô′rō), village (pop. estimate 500), N San Luis prov., Argentina, on railroad and 45 mi. E of San Luis; stock raising, tungsten mining.

El Morro (ĕl mô′rō), town (pop. 934), Trujillo state, W Venezuela, in Andean spur, on Pan-American Highway and 27 mi. E of Trujillo; alt. 3,556 ft.; coffee, grain, potatoes, fruit.

El Morro National Monument (ĕl mŏ′rō) (240 acres; established 1906), W N.Mex., c.40 mi. SE of Gallup. Includes Inscription Rock, soft sandstone monolith covering 12 acres, with inscriptions (earliest c.1605) carved by Sp. explorers and early Amer. settlers. Prehistoric petroglyphs and ruins of 2 pueblos are also here.

Elmsford, residential village (pop. 3,147), Westchester co., SE N.Y., 3 mi. NW of White Plains; mfg. (hearing aids, piano parts). Inc. 1910.

Elmshorn (ĕlms′hôrn), town (pop. 33,759), in Schleswig-Holstein, NW Germany, harbor on short navigable tributary of Elbe estuary, 20 mi. NW of Hamburg; rail junction; industrial center; shipbuilding and -outfitting; food processing (flour, margarine, meat, canned goods, dairy products). Also mfg. of textiles, machinery, leather goods, paper, wood products. Horse breeding. First mentioned 1141. Chartered 1878. Second World War damage about 25%.

Elm Springs, town (pop. 217), Washington co., NW Ark., 10 mi. NNW of Fayetteville.

Elmstein (ĕlm′shtīn), village (pop. 2,773), Rhenish Palatinate, W Germany, in Hardt Mts., on the Speyer and 9 mi. W of Neustadt; rail terminus; wine; apricots, peaches.

Elmton, town and parish (pop. 5,399), NE Derby, England, 8 mi. N of Mansfield; coal mining.

Elmvale, village (pop. estimate 800), S Ont., 23 mi. W of Orillia; lumber and flour milling, dairying.

Elmwood, village (pop. estimate 400), S Ont., 23 mi. S of Owen Sound; dairying, mixed farming.

Elmwood. 1 City (pop. 1,613), Peoria co., central Ill., 19 mi. WNW of Peoria, in agr., bituminous-coal-mining, and timber area; makes granite memorials. Inc. 1867. Lorado Taft b. here; his statue *Pioneers of the Prairies* (1928) is in city park. **2** Village (pop. 445), Cass co., SE Nebr., 20 mi. E of Lincoln and on Weeping Water Creek; livestock, grain. **3** Village (pop. 772), Pierce co., W Wis., on Eau Galle R. and 33 mi. W of Eau Claire, in lumbering, dairying, and poultry-raising area; hydroelectric plant.

Elmwood Park, residential village (pop. 18,801), Cook co., NE Ill., suburb just W of Chicago. Inc. 1914.

Elmwood Place, village (pop. 4,113), Hamilton co., extreme SW Ohio, within but administratively independent of Cincinnati; machinery, foundry products. Settled 1875, inc. 1890.

Eln-, in Rus. names: see YELN-.

El Nancito, Panama: see NANCITO.

Elne (ĕln), anc. *Illiberis*, later *Helena*, town (pop. 3,724), Pyrénées-Orientales dept., S France, near the Tech, 8 mi. SSE of Perpignan; commercial center; distilling, metalworking, fruit and vegetable shipping. In winegrowing area. Has former cathedral of Sainte-Eulalie (11th–12th cent.) and remarkable 12th-cent. Romanesque cloister. Episcopal see, 571–1602. Here Hannibal 1st encamped after crossing the Pyrenees. Constantine rebuilt the town (4th cent.) and named it after his mother, Helena.

El Negrito (ĕl nägrē′tō), town (pop. 1,089), Yoro dept., NW Honduras, 14 mi. SE of Progreso; coffee, tobacco, grain, livestock.

El Níspero (ĕl nē′spärō), town (pop. 1,108), Santa Bárbara dept., W Honduras, 12 mi. SW of Santa Bárbara; corn, beans, tobacco, coffee.

Elnora (ĕlnô′rŭ), village (pop. 201), S central Alta., 32 mi. SE of Red Deer; wheat, mixed farming.

Elnora, town (pop. 849), Daviess co., SW Ind., near West Fork of White R., 28 mi. ENE of Vincennes, in farming and dairying area; concrete products, flour, packed poultry.

El Norte or **San Antonio del Norte** (sän äntō′nyō dĕl nôr′tä), town (pop. 966), La Paz dept., SW Honduras, near Goascorán R., 20 mi. NNE of Goascorán; palm-hat mfg., ropemaking; coffee, livestock.

Elobey Islands (älōbā′), 2 low islets in Corisco Bay of Gulf of Guinea, just off mouth of the Río Muni; belong to continental Sp. Guinea; 0°59′N 9°33′E. Called Elobey Grande (□ .9; pop. 202) and Elobey Chico (uninhabited; until 1928, seat of sub-governor of continental Sp. Guinea).

El Ocotal, Mexico: see OCOTAL.

Elogui River, Russian SFSR: see YELOGUI RIVER.

Elói Mendes (ĭloi′ măn′dĭs), city (pop. 2,718), S Minas Gerais, Brazil, 10 mi. WSW of Varginha; coffee, corn, hogs. Formerly spelled Eloy Mendes.

Eloise, village (1940 pop. 1,233), Wayne co., SE Mich., 2 mi. E of Wayne and on a branch of the River Rouge. Mental hosp is here.

Elon College (ē′lŏn), town (pop. 1,109), Alamance co., N central N.C., 4 mi. W of Burlington. Seat of Elon Col.

Elöpatak, Rumania: see VALCELE.

Elora (ēlô′rŭ), village (pop. 1,247), S Ont., on Grand R. and 14 mi. NW of Guelph; cattle center; mfg. of farm implements, furniture; resort.

El Oratorio, Guatemala: see ORATORIO.

Elorn River (ālôrn′), Finistère dept., W France, rises in Montagnes d'Arrée, flows 40 mi. W, past Landerneau, to the Brest Roads (inlet of the Atlantic).

El Oro (ĕl ō′rō), prov. (□ 3,134; 1950 pop. 88,565), S Ecuador, on a Pacific inlet; ⊙ Machala. Consists of coastal plains (W) and Andean uplands (E). Climate ranges from arid-tropical to more temperate in highlands. It is the chief mining section of Ecuador, with gold mines in the Zaruma dist., where there are also silver, copper, and lead deposits. Main agr. products are: cacao, coffee, sugar cane, rice, fibers, tropical fruit, tagua nuts, and rubber; livestock. Main centers are Machala, Santa Rosa, and Pasaje; Puerto Bolívar is the port. Boundary with Peru was adjusted 1942.

El Oro. 1 Officially Santa María del Oro, town (pop. 1,800), Durango, N Mexico, 60 mi. N of Santiago Papasquiaro; alt. 5,790 ft.; silver, gold, lead, copper mining. **2** Officially El Oro de Hidalgo, city (pop. 8,638), Mexico state, central Mexico, on central plateau near Michoacán border, on railroad and 70 mi. NW of Mexico city; silver, gold, copper mining center; shoe mfg., tanning. Airfield. Sometimes Real del Oro.

El Oro de Hidalgo, Mexico: see EL ORO.

Elorrio (ĕlôr′yō), town (pop. 1,490), Vizcaya prov., N Spain, 22 mi. SE of Bilbao; metalworking (hardware, electric fans). Cereals, fruit, cattle in area. Mineral springs.

Elortondo (ālôrtōn'dō), town (pop. estimate 2,500), S Santa Fe prov., Argentina, 75 mi. SW of Rosario. Agr. center: corn, wheat, flax, alfalfa, oats; fruit (cherries, plums, pears, apples, figs); livestock, poultry.

Elorza (ālôr'sä), town (pop. 485), Apure state, W central Venezuela, on S bank of Arauca R. and 85 mi. E of Arauca (Colombia); cattle raising.

Előszallas (ĕ'lûsälăsh), Hung. *Előszállás*, town (pop. 3,880), Fejer co., W central Hungary, 31 mi. SE of Szekesfehervar; corn, hemp, potatoes, cattle.

Elota (ālō'tä), town (pop. 656), Sinaloa, NW Mexico, in coastal lowland, on Elota R. and 75 mi. SE of Culiacán; lumbering (dyewood) and agr. (corn, chick-peas, fruit).

Elota River, W Mexico, rises in Sierra Madre Occidental in Durango near Sinaloa border, flows c.100 mi. SW through fertile coastal lowlands of Sinaloa, past Elota, El Roble, and La Cruz, to the Pacific 4 mi. SW of La Cruz.

Élouges (ālōōzh'), town (pop. 5,278), Hainaut prov., SW Belgium, 9 mi. WSW of Mons; mfg. of mine and cable rolling stock, explosives.

Elovo, Russian SFSR: see YELOVO.

Eloxochitlán (ālōhōchētlän'). **1** Town (pop. 1,533), Hidalgo, central Mexico, in Sierra Madre Oriental, 20 mi. NNW of Metztitlán; cereals, beans, fruit, livestock. **2** Town (pop. 227), Puebla, central Mexico, on E slope of Sierra Madre, on Veracruz border, 30 mi. E of Tehuacán; corn, sugar cane, livestock.

Eloy (ē'loi), town (pop. 3,580), Pinal co., S Ariz., on Santa Cruz R. and 48 mi. NW of Tucson in agr. area (wheat, alfalfa, cotton, truck products); vegetable packing, cotton processing. Inc. since 1940.

Eloy Alfaro, Ecuador: see DURÁN.

Éloyes (ālwä'), town (pop. 2,476), Vosges dept., E France, on the Moselle and 6 mi. N of Remiremont in the W Vosges; cotton weaving, woodworking.

Eloy Mendes, Brazil: see ELÓI MENDES.

El Palmar (ĕl pälmär'), village (pop. c.1,100), Tarija dept., SE Bolivia, 12 mi. NNE of Yacuiba; tropical agr. products (rice, sugar cane, fruit).

El Palmar, town, Puntarenas prov., S Costa Rica, on lower Diquís R., opposite Puerto Cortés, and 40 mi. NW of Golfito (linked by rail); banana-growing center, developed after 1938.

El Palmar, town (1950 pop. 1,276), Quezaltenango dept., SW Guatemala, in Pacific piedmont, 13 mi. SSW of Quezaltenango; livestock, coffee, sugar cane. Sulphur springs near by.

El Palmar, town (pop. 815), Bolívar state, SE Venezuela, 36 mi. E of Upata; cattle raising. Mica deposits near by.

El Palmito (ĕl pälmē'tō), town (pop. 4,021), Durango, N Mexico, on Nazas R. (here dammed) and 45 mi. NE of Santiago Papasquiaro; agr. center (grain, sugar cane, fruit, cotton, beans, tobacco).

El Palomar (ĕl' pälōmär'), town (pop. estimate 2,500) in Greater Buenos Aires, Argentina, adjoining Caseros, 13 mi. WNW of Buenos Aires; air base with military acad. The former hq. of Gen. Juan Manuel de Rosas is now a natl. shrine.

El Pao (ĕl pä'ō). **1** Town (pop. 445), Anzoátegui state, NE Venezuela, 25 mi. WSW of El Tigre, in agr. area. **2** Iron-mining town, Bolívar state, SE Venezuela, in W Sierra Imataca, 12 mi. WNW of Upata, 20 mi. SSE of San Félix. Rail line for ore shipment completed 1949 to Palua, on Orinoco R. **3** or **Pao**, town (pop. 312), Cojedes state, N Venezuela, on Pao R. and 40 mi. S of Valencia; cattle raising.

El Paraíso (ĕl päräē'sō), department (□ 3,310; 1950 pop. 90,829), S Honduras, on Nicaragua border; ⊙ Yuscarán. Bordered S by Sierra de Diplito; largely mountainous; contains Sierra del Chile; drained by Jalán (N) and Choluteca (W) rivers and by Guayambre R. (right headstream of the Patuca; E). Agr. (coffee, tobacco, beans, corn, oranges, quince). Gold mining at Agua Fría, silver at Yuscarán. Main centers, Yuscarán and Danlí (in agr. zone), linked by road with Tegucigalpa. Formed 1869.

El Paraíso. **1** Town, Cortés dept., Honduras: see CHOLOMA. **2** Town (pop. 1,617), El Paraíso dept., S Honduras, on N slopes of Sierra de Dipilto (Nicaragua border), 13 mi. S of Danlí (linked by road); tobacco, corn, beans. Airfield.

El Paso (ĕl pä'sō), town (pop. c.3,600), Cochabamba dept., central Bolivia, on S slopes of Cordillera de Cochabamba, 11 mi. WNW of Cochabamba; grain, potatoes, cattle.

El Paso, Canary Isls.: see PASO, EL.

El Paso (ĕl pă'sō). **1** County (□ 2,158; pop. 74,523), E central Colo.; ⊙ Colorado Springs. Wheat and livestock area, drained by Fountain Creek. Coal mining; mfg. and tourist trade at Colorado Springs. Includes part of Pike Natl. Forest in W. Pikes Peak is a prominent landmark. Formed 1861. **2** County (□ 1,054; pop. 194,968), westernmost co. of Texas; ⊙ EL PASO, commercial, transportation, industrial, tourist center of border region. Bounded N by N.Mex. line, W and S by the Rio Grande (Mex. border). High plateau (alt. 3,500–7,100 ft.), with Hueco Mts. in NE, Franklin Mts. in NW. Irrigated agr. (water from Elephant Butte Reservoir, N.Mex.) in Rio Grande valley. A leading cotton-producing Texas co.; also alfalfa, seeds, fruit, truck, poultry, dairy products; cattle ranching. Some minerals (copper, tin, lead, zinc, borax, limestone, clay, glass sand). Includes Ysleta, Socorro, and San Elizario, oldest communities in Texas. Formed 1850.

El Paso. **1** City (pop. 1,818), Woodford co., central Ill., 30 mi. E of Peoria, in agr. and bituminous-coal area; ships grain, hybrid seed corn. Poultry hatchery; mfg. (tile, concrete blocks, canned foods). Inc. 1861. **2** City, Sedgwick co., Kansas: see DERBY. **3** City (1940 pop. 96,810; 1950 pop. 130,485), ⊙ El Paso co., near extreme W tip of Texas, at foot of Franklin Mts. on the Rio Grande opposite Juárez, Mexico (bridges), and c.225 mi. S of Albuquerque, N.Mex.; alt. 3,762 ft. Largest of the U.S.-Mex. border cities, with a large pop. of Mex. descent; gateway to N Mexico, and internatl. trade and transportation (rail, highway, air) center and port of entry; imports Mex. timber, ore; exports manufactured goods, foods. In cattle-raising and irrigated agr. area (water from Elephant Butte Reservoir, N.Mex.). Large copper refineries, smelters, oil refineries; railroad shops; mfg. of cement, glass products, textiles, clothing, footwear, flour, canned foods, packed meat, beverages, dairy products, cottonseed products; Mex. handicrafts (pottery, textiles, leather). Tourist and health resort (mean annual temp. c.65°F.). Here or near by are Texas Western Col. (a branch of Univ. of Texas), U.S. Fort Bliss (with guided-missile experiment station and a natl. cemetery), an army hosp. (Beaumont Gen. Hosp.), a military airfield (Biggs Air Force Base). At near-by Ysleta, Socorro, and San Elizario, oldest settlements in state, are old Sp. missions. Has annual livestock show (March), Sun Carnival (Dec.). In 17th cent., missionaries, soldiers, and traders came to Juárez–El Paso region, then known as El Paso del Norte, because of pass through mts. to N; 1st mission settlement on present U.S. side of the river was established 1681 or 1682 at Ysleta, 10 mi. SE. The area of El Paso, however, was settled 1st on the S side of the river, on the site of Juárez; 1st bldg. on what is now the U.S. side at El Paso was not built until 1827. Region remained under Mex. jurisdiction until surrender (1846) to U.S. forces in Mexican War. U.S. infantry post (later Fort Bliss) est. 1849; town (then known as Franklin) was important stagecoach station during Gold Rush. Alternately occupied by Federal and Confederate forces in Civil War. Coming of 1st railroad (1881) stimulated growth of the modern commercial city.

El Paso del Norte, Mexico: see CIUDAD JUÁREZ.

El Pedegral, Chile: see PEDEGRAL.

El Petén, Guatemala: see PETÉN.

Elphin (ĕlfĭn'), Gaelic *Ailfionn*, town (pop. 577), N central Co. Roscommon, Ireland, 10 mi. SSE of Boyle; agr. market (cattle, sheep; potatoes). Town has been see of R.C. bishopric (cathedral at Sligo) since time of St. Patrick.

Elphinstone, Scotland: see ORMISTON.

Elphinstone Island, in central Mergui Archipelago, Lower Burma, in Andaman Sea, 35 mi. W of Mergui town; 13 mi. long, 2–5 mi. wide.

El Pilar (ĕl pēlär'). **1** Town (pop. 621), Anzoátegui state, NE Venezuela, 16 mi. SSW of Barcelona; cotton, cattle. **2** Town (pop. 1,418), on Margarita Isl., Nueva Esparta state, NE Venezuela, 2½ mi. inland from Pampatar; sugar cane, coconuts, cotton, corn, fruit. Formerly Robles. **3** Town (pop. 1,481), Sucre state, NE Venezuela, 10 mi. SSE of Carúpano; cacao growing. Sulphur deposits of the Azufrales (äsōōfrä'läs) volcano, which emits sulphuric gases and hot springs, are 3 mi. SW.

El Pintado (ĕl pēntä'dō), village (pop. estimate 100), ⊙ Río Teuco dept. (pop. 20,425), N Chaco prov., Argentina, on Bermejo R., opposite San Camilo, and 160 mi. NNW of Presidencia Roque Sáenz Peña; livestock center.

Elpitiya (ĕlpĭt'ĭyŭ), village (pop., including near-by villages, 2,944), Southern Prov., Ceylon, 7 mi. ENE of Ambalangoda; extensive rubber and tea plantations; coconuts, vegetables, rice.

El Plateado (ĕl plätää'dō), town (pop. 461), Zacatecas, N central Mexico, 65 mi. SW of Zacatecas; grain, stock.

El Playón, Salvador: see NEJAPA.

El Plumerillo (ĕl plōōmĕrē'yō) or **Plumerillo**, town (pop. estimate 500), N Mendoza prov., Argentina, on railroad and 8 mi. NE of Mendoza, in fruit- and winegrowing region; wine making, dried-fruit processing. Military air base. San Martín camped here before crossing the Andes.

El Portal (ĕl pôrtăl'), town (pop. 1,371), Dade co., S Fla., a N suburb of Miami.

El Porvenir (ĕl pôrvänēr'), town (pop. 346), Atlántida dept., N Honduras, minor port on Caribbean coast, 5 mi. WSW of La Ceiba (linked by rail); coconuts, plantains, corn, beans.

El Porvenir, town (pop. 274), Chiapas, S Mexico, in Sierra Madre, 8 mi. N of Motozintla; fruit.

El Porvenir, village (pop. 51), ⊙ San Blas territory, E Panama, situated on small isl. in Caribbean Sea, 55 mi. NE of Panama city; fishing. Pop. largely Indian.

El Potrero (ĕl pōtrā'rō), village (pop. c.500), Veracruz, E Mexico, in foothills of Sierra Madre Oriental, 20 mi. N of Tantoyuca; has sugar plantations and huge refinery.

El Potrero, village (pop. 277), Panama prov., central Panama, at E foot of Trinidad peak, off Inter-American Highway, 2 mi. W of Capira; orange groves; stock raising.

El Progreso (ĕl prōgrā'sō), department (□ 742; 1950 pop. 46,555), E central Guatemala; ⊙ El Progreso. In upper Motagua R. valley, bet. Sierra de Chuacús and Sierra de las Minas (N) and highlands (S). Has a warm, dry climate. Mainly agr. (corn, beans, sugar cane, fodder grasses); livestock raising. Chief centers: El Progreso and Sanarate, on Guatemala–Puerto Barrios RR. Formed 1934–35.

El Progreso or **Progreso**. **1** Town (1950 pop. 2,233), Jutiapa dept., SE Guatemala, in highlands, 6 mi. NE of Jutiapa; alt. 3,652 ft. Road center; corn, beans, livestock. **2** City (1950 pop. 2,461), ⊙ El Progreso dept., E central Guatemala, on Guastatoya R. (a right affluent of the Motagua) and 35 mi. ENE of Guatemala, on railroad; 14°50'N 90°3'W; alt. 1,696 ft. Commercial center; corn, beans, livestock, dairying. Until c.1920, Guastatoya.

El Progreso, Honduras: see PROGRESO.

El Progreso Industrial (ĕndōōstrēäl') or **Progreso**, town (pop. 1,462), Mexico state, central Mexico, 1½ mi. NW of Nicolás Romero; paper-milling and pulp-mfg. center.

El Pueblito, Mexico: see CORREGIDORA.

El Puente (ĕl pwĕn'tā), town (pop. c.1,100), Santa Cruz dept., E central Bolivia, 60 mi. W of Concepción; rubber.

El Puente, Nicaragua: see PUENTE REAL.

El Quebrachal (ĕl kābrächäl') or **Quebrachal**, town (pop. estimate 700), SE Salta prov., Argentina, on Pasaje or Juramento R., on railroad, and 95 mi. ESE of Salta; lumbering and agr. center (rice, cotton, alfalfa, corn, livestock); sawmills.

El Quelite, Mexico: see QUELITE.

El Quemado (ĕl kämä'dō), village (pop. estimate 200), SE Jujuy prov., Argentina, on railroad and 30 mi. ENE of Jujuy, in agr. area (sugar cane, alfalfa, livestock). Oil wells near by.

El Quetzal (ĕl kātsäl'), town (1950 pop. 340), San Marcos dept., SW Guatemala, in Pacific piedmont, 9 mi. NE of Coatepeque; coffee, sugar cane, grain; livestock.

Elqui, department, Chile: see VICUÑA.

El Quiché, Guatemala: see QUICHÉ, dept.

Elqui River (ĕl'kē), Coquimbo prov., N central Chile, formed at Rivadavia by the Río Turbio and the Río Claro, which rise in the Andes near Argentina border; flows c.50 mi. W, past Vicuña, to the Pacific at Coquimbo Bay, 1½ mi. W. of La Serena; length with longest tributary, 130 mi. Not navigable. Fruit, grain, livestock raised in its valley. Sometimes called Coquimbo R.

El Rama, Nicaragua: see RAMA.

El Rancho, Guatemala: see RANCHO.

El Real or **El Real de Santa María** (ĕl rääl', dā sän'tä märē'ä), town (pop. 622), Darién prov., E Panama, on proposed route of Inter-American Highway, on Tuira R. and 32 mi. SE of La Palma. Plantains, corn, rice, beans; stock raising; lumber.

El Real, town (pop. 89), Barinas state, W Venezuela, on Santo Domingo R. and 20 mi. SE of Barinas. Annual pilgrimages to shrine of the Virgin.

El Real de Santa María, Panama: see EL REAL.

El Realejo (ĕl räälā'hō), town (1950 pop. 271), Chinandega dept., W Nicaragua, on Pacific coast, 4 mi. N of Corinto, across Corinto Bay, amid mangrove swamps. Founded 1534; developed as main Pacific port of Nicaragua; frequently attacked and fired by pirates. Flourished (pop. c.15,000; shipbuilding) during colonial period; later declined; replaced (1858) by Corinto.

El Recreo (ĕl rĕkrā'ō), village, Zelaya dept., E Nicaragua, on Mico R. and 10 mi. W of Rama, on road; sugar cane, livestock; lumbering. Agr. experimental station.

El Recreo or **Sabana Grande** (säbä'nä grän'dā), city (pop. 26,414), Federal Dist., N Venezuela, E residential suburb of Caracas (2½ mi. W), on Guaire R., in intermontane basin of coastal range.

El Reno (ĕl rē'nō), city (pop. 10,991), ⊙ Canadian co., central Okla., 25 mi. W of Oklahoma City, near North Canadian R.; processing, shipping, and marketing center for agr. area (dairy products, wheat, oats, barley, alfalfa, corn, sorghums, livestock, cotton). Flour and feed milling, dairying, meat packing; mfg. of chemicals, metal products; poultry hatcheries; railroad shops. Seat of El Reno Jr. Col. Near by are: a U.S. reformatory; U.S. Fort Reno (just NW); and a state game farm. Settled 1889, inc. 1893.

El Rey Island, Panama: see SAN MIGUEL ISLAND.

El Rincón (ĕl rēngkōn'), town (pop. 671), Sucre state, NE Venezuela, 6 mi. S of Carúpano; cacao growing.

El Rio (ĕl rē'ō). **1** Suburb (pop. 5,466, with near-by Pasqua Village) of Tucson, Pima co., SE Ariz. **2** Village (pop. 1,376), Ventura co., S Calif., N suburb of Oxnard.

El Rito (ĕl" rē'tō), village (1940 pop. 707), Rio Arriba co., N N.Mex., in S foothills of San Juan Mts., 31 mi. SE of Tierra Amarilla; alt. c.7,000 ft. Trading point in livestock and agr. region; grain, beans. Part of Carson Natl. Forest near by.

El Roble (ĕl rō'blā), town (pop. 2,197), Sinaloa, NW Mexico, on Presidio R., in coastal lowland, and 13 mi. ENE of Mazatlán; agr. center (corn, chick-peas, cotton, tobacco, vegetables); lumber.

El Roble, village (pop. 348), Coclé prov., central Panama, on Inter-American Highway, in Santa María R. valley, and 10 mi. SW of Aguadulce; sugar cane, corn, rice, beans, livestock.

El Roble, oil field in Anzoátegui state, NE Venezuela, 20 mi. E of Aragua de Barcelona.

El Rodeo (ĕl rōdā'ō), village (pop. estimate 500), SE Catamarca prov., Argentina, 22 mi. NNW of Catamarca; cattle raising, fruitgrowing.

El Rodeo, Guatemala: see RODEO.

Elro-i or **Elroi** (ĕlrō'ē), residential settlement (pop. 440), NW Israel, bet. Zebulun Valley and Plain of Jezreel, at SE foot of Mt. Carmel, on Kishon R., on railroad and 9 mi. SE of Haifa. Founded 1935.

El Romeral, Chile: see ROMERAL, Coquimbo prov.

Elrosa, village (pop. 173), Stearns co., central Minn., 37 mi. W of St. Cloud; dairy products.

El Rosario, Chile: see ROSARIO.

El Rosario (ĕl rōsär'yō), town (pop. 947), Comayagua dept., W central Honduras, 11 mi. NW of Comayagua, near Comayagua R.; commercial center; sugar milling; wheat, tobacco, sugar cane.

El Rosario, town (1950 pop. 691), Carazo dept., SW Nicaragua, 5 mi. E of Jinotepe; sugar cane.

Elrose, village (pop. 304), SW Sask., 50 mi. ESE of Kindersley; wheat, mixed farming.

Elroy, city (pop. 1,654), Juneau co., S central Wis., on Baraboo R. and c.50 mi. ESE of La Crosse, in timber and farm area (dairy products; poultry, livestock); railroad shops. Settled 1854, inc. 1885.

Els-, in Rus. names: see YELS-.

Elsa (ĕl'sù), town (pop. 3,179), Hidalgo co., extreme S Texas, in lower Rio Grande valley, 10 mi. E of Edinburg; trade, shipping center in irrigated citrus, truck, cotton area. Settled 1927, inc. 1933.

El Sabino (ĕl säbē'nō) or **Sabino**, village (pop. 2,696), Guanajuato, central Mexico, on Lerma R. and 20 mi. SSW of Celaya; rice, corn, alfalfa, sugar cane, vegetables, fruit. Cooperative settlement.

Elsah (ĕl'zù), village (pop. 520), Jersey co., W Ill., on the Mississippi and 10 mi. WNW of Alton, in agr. area. Seat of Principia Col.

El Salado (ĕl sälä'dō), village (pop. 929), San Luis Potosí, N Mexico, on interior plateau, on railroad and 80 mi. S of Saltillo; alt. 6,033 ft.; silver, copper, lead mining.

El Salto. 1 Village, Llanquihue prov., Chile: see PUERTO TOLEDO. **2** Village, Santiago prov., Chile: see SALTO.

El Salto, Guatemala: see SALTO.

El Salto (ĕl säl'tō), town (pop. 6,070), Durango, N Mexico, in Sierra Madre Occidental, 55 mi. SW of Durango; alt. 8,327 ft. Agr. center (corn, cotton, sugar cane, tobacco, vegetables, fruit, livestock).

El Salvador, Central American republic: see SALVADOR.

El Salvador (ĕl sälvädhôr'), town (pop. 1,953), Zacatecas, N central Mexico, on railroad and 65 mi. S of Saltillo; maguey, corn, stock. Sometimes San Salvador.

El Salvador (ĕl săl'vùdôr, Sp. ĕl sälvädhôr'), town (1939 pop. 5,053) in Cagayan municipality, Misamis Oriental prov., N Mindanao, Philippines, on Macajalar Bay, 10 mi. NW of Cagayan; agr. center (corn, coconuts).

El Samán (ĕl sämän'), officially El Samán de Apure, town (pop. 549), Apure state, W central Venezuela, near S bank of Apure R., and 85 mi. W of San Fernando; cattle raising.

El Santo, Cuba: see SANTO.

Elsa River (ĕl'sä), Tuscany, central Italy, rises in the Apennines 9 mi. WSW of Siena, flows N, past Poggibonsi, and NNW, past Certaldo and Castelfiorentino, to Arno R. 3 mi. W of Empoli; 39 mi. long. Used in mfg. and for irrigation.

Elsass, France: see ALSACE.

Elsasser Belchen, France: see ALSACE, BALLON D'.

Elsass-Lothringen, France: see ALSACE-LORRAINE.

El Sauce (ĕl sou'sä), town (1950 pop. 1,781), León dept., W Nicaragua, on railroad and 40 mi. NE of León; road junction; agr. center in irrigated area (coffee, corn, rice, sesame, beans); dairying, cheese making. Has church with colonial records. Annual commercial fair.

El Sauzal (ĕl sousäl') or **Sauzal**, village, O'Higgins prov., central Chile, on Cachapoal R., in Andean foothills, on railroad and 10 mi. SE of Rancagua. Hydroelectric plant supplying Santiago.

Elsberry, city (pop. 1,565), Lincoln co., E Mo., near Mississippi R., 17 mi. NW of Troy; grain, apples; shoes, gloves, limestone products. Has a U.S. nursery. Laid out 1871.

Elsburg (ĕlz'bûrg, Afrikaans ĕls'bûrkh), residential town (pop. 2,205), S Transvaal, U. of So. Afr., on Witwatersrand, 3 mi. SSE of Germiston.

El Seco (ĕl sā'kō), officially San Salvador El Seco, town (pop. 4,365), Puebla, central Mexico, 38 mi. ENE of Puebla; agr. center (cereals, beans, maguey).

El Segundo (ĕl sigŭn'dō, -gōōn'dō), city (pop. 8,011), Los Angeles co., S Calif., on the coast, 13 mi. SW of downtown Los Angeles; large oil refineries, with offshore pipelines for loading tankers; aircraft plant; mfg. of chemicals, truck parts. Founded 1911 by Standard Oil Company; inc. 1917.

El Seibo, Dominican Republic: see SEIBO.

Elsene, Belgium: see IXELLES.

Elsenz River (ĕl'zĕnts), N Baden, Germany, rises 4 mi. W of Eppingen, flows 35 mi. generally N to the Neckar at Neckargemünd.

El Sesteadero (ĕl sästäädä'rō), village (pop. 609), Los Santos prov., S central Panama, in Pacific lowland, just S of Las Tablas; sugar cane, livestock.

Elsfleth (ĕls'flāt), town (pop. 5,636), in Oldenburg, NW Germany, after 1945 in Lower Saxony, port on left bank of the Weser, at mouth of Hunte R., and 18 mi. NW of Bremen; shipbuilding; fruit and vegetable canning. Dispatches herring fleet.

Elsie. 1 Village (pop. 911), Clinton co., S central Mich., 26 mi. NNE of Lansing and on Maple R., in farm area (dairy products; grain, sugar beets); oil refining. **2** Village (pop. 219), Perkins co., SW central Nebr., 18 mi. E of Grant.

Elsinore, Denmark: see HELSINGØR.

Elsinore (ĕl'sĭnôr). **1** City (pop. 2,068), Riverside co., S Calif., 22 mi. S of Riverside; resort on L. Elsinore (c.6 mi. long), near hot mineral springs. Clay quarrying. Inc. 1888. **2** Town (pop. 657), Sevier co., central Utah, near Sevier R., 8 mi. SSW of Richfield; alt. 5,335 ft.; sugar beets, grain mill. Pavant Mts. just W.

Elsinore, Lake, Calif.: see ELSINORE.

Elsmere (ĕlz'mēr). **1** Residential town (pop. 5,314), New Castle co., N Del., just W of Wilmington. Co. workhouse near by. Inc. 1909. **2** Town (pop. 3,483), Kenton co., N Ky., a SW suburb of Covington. **3** Village (1940 pop. 1,941), Albany co., E N.Y., 4 mi. SW of downtown Albany.

Elsmore, city (pop. 152), Allen co., SE Kansas, 18 mi. NE of Chanute, in livestock, grain, and dairy region.

El Soco or **Baños de Soco** (bä'nyōs dā sō'kō), village, Coquimbo prov., N central Chile, 18 mi. WSW of Ovalle; thermal springs.

El Socorro (ĕl sōkô'rō, sù-), village (pop. 5,550), NW Trinidad, B.W.I., 3 mi. E of Port of Spain, in agr. region (coconuts, sugar cane).

El Socorro (ĕl sōkô'rō), town (pop. 1,335), Guárico state, central Venezuela, in llanos, 38 mi. SW of Zaraza; cattle, sugar cane, fruit; mfg. of straw hats; trade in hides.

El Sombrero (ĕl sōmbrā'rō), town (pop. 1,713), Guárico state, N central Venezuela, landing on Guárico R. and 45 mi. SSE of San Juan de los Morros; cattle raising.

El Sosneado (ĕl sōsnā-ä'dō), village (pop. estimate 300), W Mendoza prov., Argentina, on Atuel R. and 80 mi. WSW of San Rafael. Health resort with sulphur springs; sulphur and petroleum deposits. Hydroelectric station on Atuel R.

Elspe (ĕl'spù), village (pop. 8,758), in former Prussian prov. of Westphalia, W Germany, after 1945 in North Rhine-Westphalia, 16 mi. S of Arnsberg; forestry.

Elstead, agr. village and parish (pop. 1,291), W Surrey, England, on Wey R. and 4 mi. W of Godalming. Church dates partly from 15th cent.

Elster, Bad, Germany: see BAD ELSTER.

Elsterberg (ĕl'stûrbĕrk), town (pop. 6,081), Saxony, E central Germany, on the White Elster and 8 mi. N of Plauen; textile milling (cotton, wool, rayon, silk); mfg. of stoves, leather goods, synthetic fiber. Has remains of anc. castle.

Elster River (ĕl'stûr). **1** or **White Elster River**, Ger. *Weisse Elster* (vī'sù), E central Germany, rises on Czechoslovak-German border 4 mi. SE of As, flows generally N, past Oelsnitz, Plauen, Greiz, Gera, and Zeitz, turns WNW at Leipzig, and continues to the Saxonian Saale 4 mi. S of Halle. Sometimes called just Elster below Leipzig. Total length, 153 mi.; above Leipzig, 121 mi. Receives the Pleisse and the Parthe (right). After battle of Leipzig (1813), Poniatowski was killed while crossing river. **2** or **Black Elster River**, Ger. *Schwarze Elster* (shvär'tsù), central Germany, rises in Upper Lusatia SSW of Elstra, flows 116 mi. N, W, and NW, past Kamenz, Senftenberg, and Elsterwerda, to the Elbe 6 mi. WNW of Jessen.

Elsterwerda (ĕl"stûrvĕr'dä), town (pop. 9,749), in former Prussian Saxony prov., central Germany, after 1945 in Saxony-Anhalt, on the Black Elster and 15 mi. NE of Riesa; rail junction; mfg. of textile machinery, screws; sawmilling. Sand and gravel quarrying. Has 18th-cent. castle.

Elstow (ĕl'stù), residential village and parish (pop. 513), central Bedford, England, just S of Bedford. Church, of Norman origin, includes parts of former Benedictine abbey. John Bunyan b. here.

Elstra (ĕl'strä), town (pop. 1,889), Saxony, E central Germany, in Upper Lusatia, on the Black Elster and 4 mi. SSE of Kamenz; linen milling; mfg. of china, shoes.

Elstree (ĕlz'trē), residential town and parish (pop. 3,457), S Hertford, England. In the parish is Borehamwood, site of important moving-picture studios. Elstree makes hosiery, pharmaceuticals, electrical equipment.

Elswick, England: see NEWCASTLE-UPON-TYNE.

El Tabacal (ĕl täbäkäl') or **Tabacal**, town (pop. estimate 500), N Salta prov., Argentina, on railroad and 10 mi. SSE of Orán; sugar-refining center; stock raising, lumbering.

El Tambo (ĕl täm'bō). **1** Town (pop. 1,323), Cauca dept., SW Colombia, bet. Cordillera Occidental and Cordillera Central, 15 mi. W of Popayán; alt. 5,577 ft. Cacao, coffee, tobacco, sugar cane, livestock. **2** Town, Nariño dept., Colombia: see TAMBO.

El Tambo, Ecuador: see TAMBO.

El Tejar, Costa Rica: see TEJAR.

El Tejar (ĕl tāhär'), agr. town (1950 pop. 898), Chimaltenango dept., S central Guatemala, on Inter-American Highway and 2.5 mi. ESE of Chimaltenango; alt. 5,600 ft.; corn, wheat, black beans.

El Teniente (ĕl tānyĕn'tā), mining settlement (1930 pop. 2,121), O'Higgins prov., central Chile, in the Andes, at Santiago prov. border, 25 mi. ENE of Rancagua. Copper-mining and smelting center, with hydroelectric plant. Also molybdenite.

Elterlein (ĕl'tûrlīn), town (pop. 2,625), Saxony, E central Germany, in the Erzgebirge, 6 mi. W of Annaberg, in uranium-mining region; lace, ribbon mfg.

Eltham (ĕl'thùm), borough (pop. 1,855), ⊙ Eltham co. (□ 207; pop. 3,342), W N.Isl., New Zealand, 28 mi. SSE of New Plymouth; dairying center.

El Tigre (ĕl tē'grā), town (pop. 10,140), Anzoátegui state, NE Venezuela, 90 mi. SSE of Barcelona; petroleum center in Oficina (ōfēsē'nä) oil field, connected by pipe line with Puerto La Cruz on the Caribbean.

Eltingville, SE N.Y., a section of Richmond borough of New York city, on SE Staten Isl., 8 mi. SW of St. George; makes machinery. Marine Park is just E.

Eltmann (ĕlt'män), town (pop. 2,941), Lower Franconia, N Bavaria, Germany, on the Main and 11 mi. NE of Bamberg; metalworking, pottery mfg., stone cutting, brewing, flour milling. Chartered 1335. Sand- and grindstone quarries near by. On hill (S) is watchtower of 13th-cent. castle which was razed in 1777.

El Tocuyo, Venezuela: see TOCUYO.

El Tofo (ĕl tō'fō), mining settlement (1930 pop. 1,081), Coquimbo prov., N central Chile, 35 mi. N of La Serena; major iron-mining center (hematite and magnetite deposits). Ore is shipped by rail to its port Cruz Grande, and from there to smelters at Corral in Valdivia prov.

Elton. 1 Agr. village and parish (pop. 462), central Derby, England, 5 mi. W of Matlock; dairying. **2** Town, Lancashire, England: see BURY.

Elton or **El'ton** (ĕl'tŭn), village (1939 pop. over 2,000), E Stalingrad oblast, Russian SFSR, on railroad and 110 mi. ENE of Stalingrad, on salt steppe; sheep raising. Health resort (linked by rail spur) is 3 mi. NW, on L. Elton; mineral and mud baths. Salt and gypsum deposits. In Second World War, a major Rus. supply base in siege of Stalingrad (1942–43).

Elton, town (pop. 1,434), Jefferson Davis parish, SW La., 35 mi. NE of Lake Charles city; cotton ginning; lumber, rice, and feed milling. Natural-gas field near by.

Elton, Lake, or **Lake El'ton**, salt lake (□ c.58) in E Stalingrad oblast, Russian SFSR, near Kazakh SSR border, 95 mi. ENE of Stalingrad; c.10 mi. in diameter; 60 ft. below sea level. Salt content, 23–27%; a source of salt supply in 17th cent.; later supplanted by L. Baskunchak (opened 1881).

El Toro, Chile: see TORO.

El Toro (ĕl tô'rō), village, Orange co., S Calif., 14 mi. SE of Santa Ana; U.S. marine corps airfield here.

El Toro (ĕl tō'rō), town (pop. 1,196), Zulia state, NW Venezuela, on small Toas Isl. in Tablazo Bay (part of narrows bet. L. Maracaibo and Gulf of Venezuela), 22 mi. N of Maracaibo; cement plant.

El Tránsito, Chile: see TRÁNSITO.

El Tránsito, Honduras: see NACAOME.

El Tránsito (ĕl trän'sētō), town (pop. 3,023), San Miguel dept., SE Salvador, on railroad and 7 mi. E of Usulután; grain, livestock and poultry raising. Founded 1914.

El Trébol (ĕl trā'bōl), town (pop. estimate 3,000), S central Santa Fe prov., Argentina, 80 mi. NW of Rosario. Agr. center (alfalfa, wheat, corn, rye, sunflowers, livestock); produces casein, butter, cheese.

El Triunfo (ĕl trēōōm'fō), town (pop. 893), Choluteca dept., S Honduras, 19 mi. SE of Choluteca, near Nicaragua border; coffee, corn, beans.

El Triunfo or **Triunfo**, town (pop. 599), Southern Territory, Lower California, NW Mexico, 28 mi. SSE of La Paz; silver, lead, gold mining; stock grazing; corn, beans.

El Triunfo, Salvador: see PUERTO EL TRIUNFO.

Eltsovka, Russian SFSR: see YALTSOVKA.

El Tule (ĕl tōō'lā), town (pop. 1,054), Chihuahua, N Mexico, in wide valley on E slopes of Sierra Madre Occidental, 34 mi. W of Hidalgo del Parral; corn, cotton, sugar cane, beans, cattle. Formerly San Antonio del Tule.

El Tumbador, Guatemala: see TUMBADOR.

El Turbio (ĕl tōōr'byō), village (pop. estimate 50), SW Santa Cruz natl. territory, Argentina, near Puerto Natales (Chile) and 120 mi. W of Río

Gallegos; sheep-raising center. Airport. Coal mines near by on Turbio R., a headstream of the Gallegos; manganese, iron, salt deposits. Río Turbio coal field developed greatly after completion (1951) of rail link to port of Río Gallegos.

Eltville (ĕlt'vĭl), town (pop. 6,304), in former Prussian prov. of Hesse-Nassau, W Germany, after 1945 in Hesse, on right bank of the Rhine (landing) and 6 mi. WSW of Wiesbaden; main town of the Rheingau. Noted for its sparkling wine. Has 14th-cent. church; 14th-cent. castle (destroyed 1635). In 15th cent., frequently residence of archbishops of Mainz. One of earliest printing presses established here c.1460. Also called Elfeld (ĕl'fĕlt).

Elura, India: see ELLORA.

Eluru, India: see ELLORE.

Eluru River (ĕ'lōōrōō), NE Madras, India, rises in Eastern Ghats NNW of Addatigala, flows c.80 mi. SE to Bay of Bengal 5 mi. ESE of Pithapuram. Formerly spelled Yeleru.

Elva or **El'va** (ĕl'vä), Ger. *Elwa*, city (pop. 1,746), SE Estonia, on railroad and 15 mi. SW of Tartu; agr. market, oats, orchards, dairying.

El Vado Dam, N.Mex.: see RIO CHAMA.

El Valle, Mexico: see VALLE DE JUÁREZ.

El Valle (ĕl vä'yä). **1** Town (pop. 11,682), Federal Dist., N Venezuela, S residential suburb of Caracas, in picturesque mtn. valley, 2½ mi. S of Caracas. Agr. research station. **2** or **Espíritu Santo** (ĕspē'rētōō sän'tō), town (pop. 1,227), on Margarita Isl., Nueva Esparta state, NE Venezuela, 4 mi. NW of Porlamar; sugar cane, corn, fruit. Famous shrine with fine neo-Gothic church.

Elvanfoot, agr. village, S Lanark, Scotland, on the Clyde and 2 mi. S of Crawford, at foot of Lowther Hills.

Elvanlar, Turkey: see ESME.

Elvas (ĕl'vŭsh), city (pop. 11,272), Portalegre dist., Alto Alentejo prov., E central Portugal, on railroad (customs station near Sp. border) and 21 mi. W of Badajoz (Spain). Formerly known as Portugal's strongest fortress, it preserves a Moorish castle (built on Roman foundations), a 15th–17th-cent. aqueduct (partially in 4 tiers), and the late-Gothic cathedral. Two 18th-cent. forts overlook the city from adjoining hills. Elvas is now an agr. processing center, specializing in fruit preserving, drying, and candying. Also makes biscuits, brooms. Livestock market. Recaptured from the Moors c.1230. Unsuccessfully besieged by Spaniards in 1581, and again 1658–59. Captured by French in 1808.

Elvaston (ĕl'vŭstŭn), village (pop. 238), Hancock co., W Ill., 7 mi. E of Keokuk (Iowa), in agr. and bituminous-coal area.

Elvebakken (ĕl'vŭbäk-kŭn), fishing village (pop. 930) in Alta canton, Finnmark co., N Norway, on Alta Fjord, 4 mi. ENE of Alta, 50 mi. S of Hammerfest.

Elven (ĕlvĕ'), agr. village (pop. 1,108), Morbihan dept., W France, 9 mi. NE of Vannes. Ruins of medieval Largoët castle and of Kerlo manor house (home of Descartes) near by.

Elvend, Iran: see ALWAND.

El Verano (ĕl vŭrä'nō), village (1940 pop. 796), Sonoma co., W Calif., 17 mi. SE of Santa Rosa.

El Verde (ĕl vĕr'dā). **1** Officially San Salvador el Verde, town (pop. 528), Puebla, central Mexico, 24 mi. NW of Puebla; wheat, corn, maguey. **2** Town (pop. 1,413), Sinaloa, NW Mexico, in coastal lowland, 22 mi. NE of Mazatlán; cotton, corn, chickpeas, sugar cane, fruit, vegetables; lumbering.

Elversberg (ĕl'vŭrsbĕrk), town (pop. 8,287), E Saar, 3.5 mi. SW of Neunkirchen; coal mining.

Elverson, borough (pop. 370), Chester co., SE Pa., 13 mi. SSE of Reading.

Elverum (ĕl'vŭrōōm), village (pop. 3,538; canton pop. 12,048), Hedmark co., SE Norway, on Glomma R. and 17 mi. ENE of Hamar; rail junction; sawmilling; agr. market. Has Glomdal folk mus. and 18th-cent. church. Formerly site of Christiansfeld fortress (built 1685). After Ger. capture of Oslo (April, 1940), it was briefly seat of Norwegian king, govt., and parliament, and was heavily bombed by Germans.

El Viejo (ĕl vyā'hō), town (1950 pop. 4,358), Chinandega dept., W Nicaragua, on branch railroad to Puerto Morazán and 3 mi. NW of Chinandega; agr. center (coffee, sugar cane, fruit, grain). Has anc. colonial church.

El Viejo, highest volcano (5,839 ft.) of Nicaragua, in Cordillera de los Marabios, 10 mi. NE of Chinandega. Coffee plantations on slopes. Also called San Cristóbal.

El Vigía (ĕl vēhē'ä), village (pop. 668), Mérida state, W Venezuela, in Maracaibo lowlands, 34 mi. W of Mérida; terminus of railroad from San Carlos (Zulia state); rice, cotton, stock.

Elvins, city (pop. 1,977), St. Francois co., E Mo., in the St. Francois Mts. just S of Flat River; agr., timber. Inc. 1903.

Elvira, Cape (ĕlvī'rŭ), NE extremity of Victoria Isl., central Franklin Dist., Northwest Territories, on Viscount Melville Sound; 73°16'N 107°5'W.

El Volcán (ĕl vōlkän'), village (1930 pop. 399), Santiago prov., central Chile, in the Andes, 38 mi. SE of Santiago. Summer and winter resort. Copper mining (1930 mine pop. 350). Gypsum deposits.

El Volcán, village (pop. 71), Chiriquí prov., W Panama, on Inter-American Highway, at W foot of Chiriquí volcano, and 18 mi. N of Concepción; resort (hotels); sawmilling.

Elwa, Estonia: see ELVA.

Elwell, Mount (7,846 ft.), peak of the Sierra Nevada, NE Calif., 13 mi. SW of Portola, in recreational region; trail to summit.

Elwha River (ĕl'wä), NW Wash., rises N of Mt. Olympus, flows c.15 mi. N to Juan de Fuca Strait W of Port Angeles; near source, Glines Canyon Dam (completed 1927; 210 ft. high, 508 ft. long) forms reservoir, furnishes power.

Elwood. **1** Village (pop. 420), Will co., NE Ill., 9 mi. S of Joliet, in agr. and bituminous-coal-mining area. **2** City (pop. 11,362), Madison co., E central Ind., c.40 mi. NNE of Indianapolis; canning center in tomato-growing area; ships livestock, grain, tomatoes. Mfg. (trailers, tractors, tin plate, kitchen equipment, wire goods, boxes, glass, buffing wheels, cigars). Wendell L. Willkie was b. here. **3** City (pop. 1,020), Doniphan co., extreme NE Kansas, on right bank of Missouri R. and 18 mi. NE of Atchison; residential suburb of St. Joseph, Mo. (across river). Founded 1856, inc. 1873. **4** Village (pop. 562), ⊙ Gosper co., S Nebr., 40 mi. WSW of Kearney; grain, livestock, poultry products. Near by are Plum Creek Reservoir and Johnson Canyon Power Plant, part of tri-co. irrigation and power project. **5** Village (1940 pop. 573), Atlantic co., SE N.J., 27 mi. NW of Atlantic City; sawmilling, hosiery mfg. **6** Town (pop. 393), Box Elder co., N Utah, 16 mi. W of Logan and on Bear R.; alt. 4,290 ft.; farming.

Ely (ē'lē), urban district (1931 pop. 8,381; 1951 census 9,989), in Isle of Ely (administrative county), N Cambridge, England, on Ouse R. and 15 mi. NNE of Cambridge. A monastery founded here 673 was destroyed by Danes (870). In 970 a Benedictine monastery was established; in 1109 its church became cathedral of bishop of Ely. The present building embodies styles from Norman to Perpendicular; within the grounds are Tudor bishops' palace, theological col., and King's Grammar School (founded 1541). Ely is a beet-sugar refining center and agr. market, with leather and shoe industries. The **Isle of Ely** (□ 375; 1931 pop. 77,698; 1951 census 89,038) is an administrative co. of Cambridgeshire, on elevated ground surrounded by fenland. Here the Saxons, under Hereward the Wake, made their last stand against William the Conqueror.

Ely. **1** Town (pop. 155), Linn co., E Iowa, 8 mi. SSE of Cedar Rapids; feed milling. **2** City (pop. 5,474), St. Louis co., NE Minn., on Shagawa L., at E end of Vermilion iron range, in Superior Natl. Forest, and c.40 mi. NE of Virginia; iron-mining center, with mines within city limits. Also resort activities. Has junior col. and hq. of Superior Natl. Forest. Settled 1885, inc. as village 1888, as city 1891. **3** City (pop. 3,558), ⊙ White Pine co., E Nev., 120 mi. SSE of Elko, in E foothills of Egan Range; alt. 6,433 ft.; trade center for mining, dairying, livestock area. Extremely productive copper mines and gold, silver, lead mines near by. Wheeler Peak and Lehman Caves Natl. Monument are SE, in Snake Range. Settled 1868, inc. 1907.

Ely, Isle of, England: see ELY.

El Yagual (ĕl yägwäl'), town (pop. 357), Apure state, W central Venezuela, on N bank of Arauca R. and 70 mi. WSW of San Fernando; cattle raising.

Elyashiv (ĕlyäshēv'), settlement (pop. 350), W Israel, in Plain of Sharon, 5 mi. NE of Natanya; mixed farming. Founded 1933.

Elyria (ĭlĭr'ēŭ). **1** Village (pop. 87), Valley co., central Nebr., 7 mi. NNW of Ord and on N.Loup R. **2** City (pop. 30,307), ⊙ Lorain co., N Ohio, on Black R. and 23 mi. WSW of Cleveland; railroad and industrial center, in agr. area. Mfg.: aircraft, electrical products, motor vehicles, metal and plastic products, bicycle equipment, pumps, tools, chemicals, air-conditioning units. Gates Memorial Hosp. for crippled children and Cascade Park are here. Settled 1817; inc. as city in 1892.

Ely's Harbour (ē'lēz), inlet, W Bermuda, bet. Somerset Isl. and NW end of Bermuda Isl.

Elysian (ĭlĭ'zhŭn), resort village (pop. 402), Le-Sueur co., S Minn., at N end of L. Elysian and 16 mi. E of Mankato, in grain, livestock, poultry area; dairy products.

El Yunque, peak, Puerto Rico: see YUNQUE, EL.

Elz (ĕlts), village (pop. 4,808), in former Prussian prov. of Hesse-Nassau, W Germany, after 1945 in Hesse, 2 mi. NNW of Limburg; chemicals.

El Zapallar (ĕl säpäyär') or **Zapallar**, town (pop. estimate 2,000), ⊙ Tobas dept. (pop. 20,045), E central Chaco prov., Argentina, 70 mi. NNW of Resistencia. Rail terminus; agr. center (cotton, corn, citrus fruit, livestock).

El Zapallo (ĕl säpä'yō), village (1930 pop. 6), Coquimbo prov., N central Chile, 40 mi. NNE of La Serena; high-grade iron-ore deposits.

El Zapotal (ĕl säpōtäl'), town (pop. 1,044), Chiapas, S Mexico, at S foot of Sierra de Hueytepec, 8 mi. SW of San Cristóbal de las Casas; cereals, fruit, stock. Formerly San Lucas.

Elze (ĕl'tsŭ), town (pop. 5,397), in former Prussian prov. of Hanover, NW Germany, after 1945 in Lower Saxony, 9 mi. WSW of Hildesheim; rail junction; foundry; food processing (canned goods, sugar, beer), spinning.

Elzele, Belgium: see ELLEZELLES.

Elz River (ĕlts), S Baden, Germany, rises in Black Forest 3 mi. WNW of Triberg, flows 60 mi. SW and NW to the Rhine, 6 mi. W of Lahr. Middle course canalized. Partly discharges into the canalized DREISAM RIVER at Riegel to form Leopold Canal.

Emajogi River, Estonia: see EMA RIVER.

Emali (ĕmä'lē), village, Central Prov., S central Kenya, on railroad and 70 mi. SE of Nairobi; sisal, rubber, wheat, corn.

Eman, river, Sweden: see EM RIVER.

Eman-, in Rus. names: see YEMAN-.

Emaneswaram (āmŭnās'vŭrŭm), town (pop. 6,739), Ramnad dist., S Madras, India, on Vaigai R. opposite Paramagudi; betel farms.

Emangak (ĕmän-gäk'), village (pop. 68), W Alaska, near Yukon R. delta.

Emania, Northern Ireland: see NAVAN FORT.

Emanuel (ēmă'nūŭl), county (□ 686; pop. 19,789), E central Ga.; ⊙ Swainsboro. Bounded NE by Ogeechee R.; drained by Ohoopee and Canoochee rivers. Coastal plain; agr. (cotton, corn, tobacco, sweet potatoes, peanuts, hogs, cattle), and lumbering area. Formed 1812.

Ema River (ĕ'mŭ), Est. *Emajõgi* (ĕ'mäyŭgē), Ger. *Embach* (ĕm'bäkh), S Estonia, rises in Otepaa hills, flows 49 mi. SSW and N to lake Vortsjarv, leaving it at NE shore, and 60 mi. E, past Tartu, to L. Peipus. Was a medieval trade route. Navigable for flat-bottomed craft.

Ematheia, Greece: see HEMATHEIA.

Emaus, Pa.: see EMMAUS.

Emba (ĕm'bŭ), town (1948 pop. over 2,000), central Aktyubinsk oblast, Kazakh SSR, on Trans-Caspian RR, near Emba R., and 110 mi. SSE of Aktyubinsk; metalworks.

Embach, river, Estonia: see EMA RIVER.

Embarcación (ĕmbärkäsyōn'), town (1947 pop. 3,805), N Salta prov., Argentina, on Bermejo R. and 15 mi. SE of Orán; rail junction; stock-raising center; sawmills, oil refinery.

Embarcadero de Banes (ĕmbärkädä'rō dā bä'nĕs), port for Banes, Oriente prov., E Cuba, on sheltered Banes Bay, 38 mi. E of Holguín. Ships sugar and tropical fruit.

Emba River (ĕm'bŭ), Aktyubinsk and Guryev oblasts, Kazakh SSR, rises in S Mugodzhar Hills, flows 384 mi. SW, through rich oil area, past Zharkamys, to Caspian Sea near Zhilaya Kosa. Receives Temir R. (right). In lower course (irrigation) is Emba oil field, with main centers at Dossor, Makat, and Koschagyl.

Embarrass (ĕmbă'rŭs), village (pop. 303), Waupaca co., central Wis., on Embarrass R. and 8 mi. SSW of Shawano; lumbering.

Embarrass River. **1** or **Embarras River** (ăm'brô), in E Ill., rises near Urbana, flows 185 mi. generally S and SE, past Newton and Lawrenceville, to the Wabash 6 mi. SW of Vincennes, Ind. Receives North Fork (55 mi. long) SE of Newton. **2** (ĕmbă'-rŭs), in E central Wis., formed by several branches rising in Shawano co., flows E and S to Wolf R. at New London; c.45 mi. long.

Embden, town (pop. 303), Somerset co., central Maine on the Kennebec and 12 mi. NNW of Skowhegan; resort area.

Embleton, village and parish (pop. 383), W Cumberland, England, 2 mi. E of Cockermouth; granite quarrying, cattle and sheep raising.

Embo, fishing village, SE Sutherland, Scotland, on Dornoch Firth, 2 mi. NE of Dornoch. Stone commemorates early-13th-cent. battle against Danes.

Emboscada (ĕmbōskä'dä), town (dist. pop. 5,419), La Cordillera dept., S central Paraguay, 20 mi. NE of Asunción; agr. center (oranges, tobacco, livestock); liquor distilling.

Embreeville, village (pop. 1,273), Washington co., NE Tenn., on Nolichucky R. and 11 mi. SSW of Johnson City; iron, lead, zinc, manganese deposits.

Embro, village (pop. 464), S Ont., on Middle Thames R. and 8 mi. WNW of Woodstock; dairying; grain.

Embrun (ĕm'brŭn), village (pop. estimate 500), SE Ont., 23 mi. ESE of Ottawa; dairying.

Embrun (ābrŭ'), anc. *Ebrodunum*, town (pop. 2,166), Hautes-Alpes dept., SE France, on a terrace overlooking Alpine Durance R. valley, 21 mi. E of Gap; alt. 2,855 ft. Flour and sawmilling, cutlery mfg. Winter sports. Has 12th-cent. Romanesque church (former cathedral and pilgrimage place). Important town of the *Caturiges*, and military stronghold since Roman times. Archiepiscopal see until 1790.

Embu (ĕm'bōō), town (1948 pop. c.1,000), Central Prov., S central Kenya, 70 mi. NNE of Nairobi, at S foot of Mt. Kenya; agr. center; coffee, sisal, wheat, corn; dairying.

Emden (ĕm'dŭn), city (1950 pop. 36,762), in former Prussian prov. of Hanover, NW Germany, after 1945 in Lower Saxony, in East Friesland, artificial port on Ems R. estuary, terminus of Dortmund-Ems and Ems-Jade canals, near Dutch border, 40 mi. WSW of Wilhelmshaven; 53°23'N 7°13'E. Germany's 3d-largest North Sea port after Hamburg and Bremen, importing ores, grain, and timber, and exporting coal and coke; shipbuilding; herring fisheries; mfg. of agr. machinery, barrels, containers, fruit and vegetable preserves; brickworks. Steamer to Borkum isl. Second World War destruction (about 80%) included 12th-cent. church, 16th-cent. town hall, and other historic bldgs., but harbor installations emerged undamaged. First mentioned in 10th cent. Went to East Friesland in 15th cent. Received (1494) storage and customs rights. Was hq., in 16th cent., of Europe's largest merchant fleet. Passed to Prussia in 1744, to Hanover in 1815. Captured by Canadian troops in April, 1945.

Emden, village (pop. 406), Logan co., central Ill., 20 mi. SSE of Pekin, in agr. and bituminous-coal area.

Emden Deep, Pacific Ocean: see MINDANAO TRENCH.

Eme-, in Rus. names: see YEME-.

Emelgem (ĕ'mŭl-khŭm), town (pop. 4,158), West Flanders prov., NW Belgium, 5 mi. ESE of Roulers; agr. market (grain, stock).

Emerald, town (pop. 1,336), E Queensland, Australia, 150 mi. W of Rockhampton and on Nogoa R.; rail center in sheep-raising area. Some cotton grown in vicinity.

Emerald Bay, resort village, El Dorado co., E Calif., in the Sierra Nevada, on Emerald Bay (an arm of L. Tahoe). State park at Rubicon Point (N).

Emerald Island (c.20 mi. long, 5–10 mi. wide), W Franklin Dist., Northwest Territories, in Ballantyne Strait of the Arctic Ocean, at mouth of Fitzwilliam Strait, bet. Prince Patrick Isl. and Melville Isl.; 76°46'N 114°30'W.

Emerald Lake, resort village, SE B.C., near Alta. border, in Rocky Mts., in Yoho Natl. Park, on small Emerald L., 4 mi. NW of Field.

Emerita Augusta, Spain: see MÉRIDA.

Emerson, town (pop. 847), SE Man., on Red R. and 65 mi. S of Winnipeg, at Minn.–N.Dak. line; dairying center; mixed farming, stock raising.

Emerson. 1 Town (pop. 523), Columbia co., SW Ark., 32 mi. WSW of El Dorado, in cotton area; sawmilling. **2** City (pop. 508), Bartow co., NW Ga., 4 mi. SE of Cartersville. **3** Town (pop. 556), Mills co., SW Iowa, 30 mi. SE of Council Bluffs, in corn and livestock region. **4** Village (pop. 784), Dakota, Dixon, Thurston counties, NE Nebr., 23 mi. SW of Sioux City, Iowa, near Logan Creek; livestock, grain. **5** Borough (pop. 1,744), Bergen co., NE N.J., 6 mi. N of Hackensack; building blocks. Settled 1875, inc. 1909.

Emery, county (□ 4,442; pop. 6,304), central Utah; ⊙ Castle Dale. Drained by Price and San Rafael rivers and Muddy Creek. Agr. (livestock, grain), coal mining. Part of Wasatch Plateau and Manti Natl. Forest in NW. Co. formed 1880.

Emery. 1 City (pop. 480), Hanson co., SE central S.Dak., 22 mi. ESE of Mitchell; dairy products, livestock, poultry, grain. **2** Town (pop. 488), Emery co., central Utah, 25 mi. SSW of Castle Dale; alt. 6,247 ft.; coal.

Emeryville (ĕm'rēvĭl), industrial town (pop. 2,889), Alameda co., W Calif., on San Francisco Bay, just N of Oakland; paper, electrical equipment, linoleum, food products, industrial gases, steel products, calculating machinery. Petroleum research laboratory. Inc. 1896.

Emesa, Syria: see HOMS, city.

Emet (ĕmĕt'), village (pop. 2,834), Kutahya prov., W Turkey, 38 mi. W of Kutahya; lignite; wheat, barley. Formerly Egrigoz.

Emhouse, town (pop. 198), Navarro co., E central Texas, 8 mi. NW of Corsicana, in farm area.

Emi (ā'mē). **1** Town (pop. 2,963), Chiba prefecture, central Honshu, Japan, on SE coast of Chiba Peninsula, 12 mi. ENE of Tateyama; summer resort. **2** Town (pop. 5,723), Okayama prefecture, SW Honshu, Japan, 13 mi. ESE of Tsuyama; agr. center (rice, wheat, persimmons); raw silk, charcoal; livestock.

Emi (ĕ'mē), town (1945 pop. over 500), SE Tuva Autonomous Oblast, Russian SFSR, 20 mi. E of Chirgalandy, near Mongolian border.

Emigrant Gap, lumbering and resort village (pop. c.150), Placer co., E Calif., at a notch (Emigrant Gap) near summit of the Sierra Nevada, 35 mi. NE of Auburn; alt. 5,250 ft.; hunting, fishing. An emigrant trail passed here.

Emigrant Lake, Tuolumne co., E Calif., in the Sierra Nevada, c.85 mi. ENE of Stockton; c.2 mi. long.

Emigrant Pass, Nev.: see PALISADE.

Emigsville (ā'mĭgzvĭl, ĕ'–), village (1940 pop. 515), York co., S Pa., 4 mi. N of York; furniture.

Emi Koussi (āmē' kōōsē', ā'mē), extinct volcano (11,204 ft.), in Tebesti Massif, NW Chad territory, Fr. Equatorial Africa, 130 mi. NNW of Largeau (Faya); 20°N 18°30'E. Its huge crater is 12 mi. wide, c.4,000 ft. deep.

Emilchino, Ukrainian SSR: see YEMILCHINO.

Emilia, Italy: see EMILIA-ROMAGNA.

Emiliano Zapata (āmēlyä'nō säpä'tä). **1** Town (pop. 3,049), Michoacán, central Mexico, on central plateau, 26 mi. SSE of Ocotlán; cereals, sugar cane, fruit, livestock. **2** Town (pop. 1,630), Morelos, central Mexico, 18 mi. NE of Cuernavaca; sugar cane, cereals, fruit, livestock. **3** City (pop. 2,220), Tabasco, SE Mexico, on Usumacinta R. and 80 mi. ESE of Villahermosa; rubber, rice, tobacco, fruit, timber. Airfield.

Emilia-Romagna (ĕmē'lyä rômä'nyä), region (□ 8,542; pop. 3,338,721), N central Italy; ⊙ Bologna. Bordered by Lombardy and Veneto (N), Adriatic Sea (E), Tuscany and The Marches (S), Piedmont and Liguria (W); bet. 43°50'N and 45°8'N. Comprises 8 provs.: BOLOGNA, FERRARA, MODENA, PARMA, PIACENZA, and REGGIO NELL'EMILIA are in Emilia; FORLÌ and RAVENNA lie in historic ROMAGNA (E). Extends from the Adriatic almost across the peninsula, bet. the Po (N) and the Etruscan and Ligurian Apennines (S). Po R. plain prevails in E and Appenines in W. Area 15% forested. Drained by Trebbia, Taro, Secchia, and Panaro rivers (affluents of the lower Po) and by Reno, Montone, Ronco, and Savio rivers, which flow to the Adriatic. Continental type of climate in the interior, maritime along coast. Average annual rainfall ranges from 30.6 in. (E) to 33.5 in. (W); abundant in autumn. Agr. predominates, aided by irrigation in Po R. plain and by drainage of coastal marshes (Ferrara prov.). Chief producer of Italy's wheat, hemp, and tomatoes. Other major crops are sugar beets, vegetables (asparagus, onions, peas), fruit (grapes, apples, pears), and rice. Livestock raising (cattle, pigs) widespread. Fishing, tourism (Rimini, Riccione, Cattolica), and saltworks (Cervia, Comacchio) along coast. Leads Italy in petroleum output (Parma and Piacenza provs.); some important sulphur mines (Forlì prov.). Principal industries are food production (flour, sausage, beet sugar, cheese, canned tomatoes), alcohol distilling, fertilizer mfg., cement- and pottery making. Commerce aided by many Apennine passes (La Cisa, La Futa, Cerreto) and by adequate transportation facilities, including the Aemilian Way, which traverses region from Rimini (SE) to Piacenza (NW). Important under the Romans, Aemilia was conquered (5th cent.) by the Lombards. Most of present Romagna and Bologna fell under Byzantine rule in 6th cent. By 16th cent. region was included in several duchies and Papal States; in 1861 became part of Italy. Called Emilia until 1948.

Emílio Meyer (ĭmē'lyōō mĕyĕr'), town (pop. 538), E Rio Grande do Sul, Brazil, at N end of the Lagoa dos Patos, 45 mi. ESE of Pôrto Alegre; S terminus of railroad to Osório; sugar, tobacco. Until 1944, called Palmares.

Emily, Lake, Pope co., W Minn., 27 mi. SSW of Alexandria; 5 mi. long, 1 mi. wide. Drains into Chippewa R.

Eminabad (ā'mĭnäbäd"), town (pop. 8,679), Gujranwala dist., E Punjab, W Pakistan, 14 mi. SSE of Gujranwala; wheat, rice, gram.

Emine, Cape, Bulgaria: see YEMINE, CAPE.

Eminence. 1 City (pop. 1,462), Henry co., N Ky., 21 mi. NW of Frankfort, in Bluegrass region noted for breeding fine livestock, especially Hereford cattle. **2** Town (pop. 527), ⊙ Shannon co., S Mo., in the Ozarks, on Jacks Fork of Current R. and 35 mi. S of Salem. Resort; copper mines; lumber products. State park near by.

Emington or **Emmington,** village (pop. 150), Livingston co., E central Ill., 15 mi. ENE of Pontiac, in agr. and bituminous-coal area.

Eminonu (ĕmĭ'nûnü"), Turkish *Eminönü*, SE section (pop. 111,064) of Istanbul, Turkey in Europe, on the Bosporus at its opening on the Sea of Marmara.

Emin Pasha Gulf (ĕ'mĭn pä'shä), inlet of L. Victoria (S bank), NW Tanganyika, 60 mi. W of Mwanza.

Emirau, Bismarck Archipelago: see MUSSAU.

Emirdag (ĕmĭr'dä), Turkish *Emirdağ*, town (pop. 5,491), Afyonkarahisar prov., W central Turkey, 36 mi. NE of Afyonkarahisar, at NW foot of the mtn. Emir Dagi; wheat, barley, lentils; mohair goats. Formerly Aziziye.

Emir Dagi (ĕmĭr'däü"), Turkish *Emir Dağı*, peak (7,352 ft.), W central Turkey, 15 mi. NE of Bolvadin.

Emita, town, Tasmania, on W Flinders Isl. of Furneaux Isls., NW of Whitemark; sheep center.

Emlembe (ĕmlĕm'bŭ), village, N Swaziland, near Transvaal border, 25 mi. N of Mbabane.

Emlenton, borough (pop. 945), Venango co., W central Pa., 15 mi. SSE of Franklin and on Allegheny R.; oil wells and refineries; mfg. (tanks, cables, furnaces); bituminous coal.

Emley, former urban district (1931 pop. 1,637), West Riding, S Yorkshire, England, 7 mi. ESE of Huddersfield; coal mining. Inc. 1938 in Denby Dale.

Emlichheim (ĕm'lĭkh-hīm), village (pop. 2,946), in former Prussian prov. of Hanover, NW Germany, after 1945 in Lower Saxony, on the Vechte and 21 mi. NW of Lingen, near Dutch border; oil wells.

Emly, Gaelic *Imleach Iubhair*, town (pop. 178), W Co. Tipperary, Ireland, 8 mi. W of Tipperary; agr. market (dairying, cattle raising; potatoes, beets). Large cross is relic of bishopric (founded here in time of St. Patrick) amalgamated 1568 with see of Cashel.

Emma, Mount (7,698 ft.), NW Ariz., near Colorado R., c.80 mi. SW of Kanab, Utah.

Emmaboda (ĕ"mäbōō'dä), town (pop. 1,704), Kalmar co., SE Sweden, 30 mi. W of Kalmar; rail junction; glass and furniture mfg., stone quarrying.

Emmahaven, Indonesia: see PADANG.

Emmaljunga (ĕ"mälyōōng'ä), village (pop. 477), Kristianstad co., S Sweden, 17 mi. NNW of Hassleholm; grain, potatoes, stock.

Emmanouil Pappas or **Emmanuil Pappas,** Greece: see PAPPAS.

Emmasdale (ĕ'mŭzdāl), township (pop. 444), central Northern Rhodesia; residential suburb of Lusaka.

Emmastad (ĕ'mästät), town, E central Curaçao, Du. West Indies, on Schottegat harbor, just across (N) from Willemstad. Site of one of the world's largest oil refineries.

Emmaus (ĕmā'ŭs), anc. locality, central Palestine, after 1948 in W Jordan, on site of modern village of 'Imwas or Amwas, on W slope of Judaean Hills, 15 mi. WNW of Jerusalem. Not the Emmaus of the New Testament, it was scene (166 B.C.) of victory of Judas Maccabeus over Gorgias. As *Nicopolis* it was important in Roman times.

Emmaus (ĕmā'ŭs, ē'môs), borough (pop. 7,780), Lehigh co., E Pa., 5 mi. S of Allentown; commercial gas, rubber products, textiles. Settled by Moravians c.1740, inc. 1859. Formerly Emaus.

Emmaville, village (pop. 764), NE New South Wales, Australia, 170 mi. SSW of Brisbane; mining center (tin, silver-lead, arsenic ore).

Emmen (ĕ'mŭn), town (pop. 6,114), Drenthe prov., NE Netherlands, on the Hondsrug, 11 mi. NE of Coervorden; sheep market; mfg. (agr. machinery, cement), peat production. Market center for area of fen colonies. Prehistoric graves near by.

Emmen, industrial town (1950 pop. 11,024), Lucerne canton, central Switzerland, on Reuss R. and 2 mi. N of Lucerne. Includes part of EMMENBRÜCKE.

Emmenbrücke (ĕ'mŭnbrü'kŭ), industrial section of Emmen and Littau communes, Lucerne canton, central Switzerland, at confluence of Kleine Emme and Reuss rivers, NNW of Lucerne; aluminumware and other metal products, artificial silk, biscuits; woodworking.

Emmendingen (ĕ'mŭndĭng"ŭn), town (pop. 8,917), S Baden, Germany, at W foot of Black Forest, on canalized Elz R. and 8 mi. N of Freiburg; textile (silk, clothing) mfg.; leather-, metal-, and woodworking; paper milling, distilling. Tobacco. Has 16th–18th-cent. town hall.

Emmen River, Switzerland: see EMME RIVER.

Emmental or **Emmenthal** (ĕ'mŭntäl"), valley of upper Emme R., in Bern canton, W central Switzerland; farming, dairying, cattle breeding. Production of some of finest Swiss cheese; Langnau, on Ilfis R. (branch of Emme R.), is export center.

Emmerich (ĕ'mŭrĭkh), town (1939 pop. 16,381; 1946 pop. 7,311), in former Prussian Rhine Prov., W Germany, after 1945 in North Rhine-Westphalia, on right bank of the Rhine and 16 mi. W of Bocholt; customs port (accommodating ocean-going vessels) near Dutch border. Oil refining; mfg. of machinery, cables, metal nets, precision instruments, pharmaceuticals; paper milling, woodworking, printing; brickworks, potteries. First mentioned 697. Created (1233) free imperial city. Joined Hanseatic League in 14th cent. Passed to Cleves in 1402. Town was almost obliterated (destruction 97%) by frequent bombing in Second World War, and during heavy fighting following crossing (March, 1945) of the Rhine here by Canadians.

Emme River (ĕ'mŭ) or **Emmen River** (ĕ'mŭn), central Switzerland, rises 5 mi. NNE of Interlaken, flows 50 mi. NNW, through the Emmental, past Burgdorf, to the Aar E of Solothurn.

Emme River, Kleine (klī'nŭ–), central Switzerland, formed by 2 headstreams joining S of Schüpfheim; flows 36 mi. N and E, past Wolhusen, to the Reuss near Lucerne.

Emmersdorf (ĕ'mŭrsdôrf), town (pop. 2,223), Carinthia, S Austria, on Gail R. and 10 mi. W of Villach, summer resort, baths.

Emmerstedt (ĕ'mŭr-shtĕt), village (pop. 2,314), in Brunswick, NW Germany, after 1945 Lower Saxony, 2 mi. NW of Helmstedt; woodworking.

Emmerting (ĕ'mŭrtĭng), village (commune pop. 1,159), Upper Bavaria, Germany, 4 mi. ESE of Altötting; carbide, chlorine, and fertilizer mfg. at near-by Gendorf (pop. 301).

Emmet. 1 County (□ 395; pop. 14,102), NW Iowa, on Minn. line; ⊙ Estherville. Glaciated, rolling prairie region, dotted with small lakes and drained by East and West Des Moines rivers; includes Fort Defiance State Park. Agr. (cattle, hogs, poultry, corn, oats, soybeans); sand and gravel pits. Formed 1851. **2** County (□ 461; pop. 16,534), NW Mich.; ⊙ Petoskey. Bounded W by Little Traverse Bay and L. Michigan, N by the Straits of Mackinac; drained by small Maple R. Agr. (dairy products; livestock, potatoes, grain, fruit). Mfg. at Petoskey. Limestone quarries, sawmills, fisheries. Year-round resorts (hunting, fishing, camping, winter sports). Includes Walloon, Pickerel, Crooked, and Carp lakes, and state parks and forests. Organized 1853.

Emmet. 1 Town (pop. 482), Nevada co., SW Ark., 8 mi. NE of Hope. **2** Village (pop. 62), Holt co., N Nebr., 7 mi. W of O'Neill and on Elkhorn R.

Emmetsburg, city (pop. 3,760), ⊙ Palo Alto co., NW Iowa, resort on Medium L., 23 mi. E of Spencer, near West Des Moines R.; rail junction; mfg. (feed, dairy products, mattresses). Has a jr. col. Founded 1856.

Emmett. **1** City (pop. 3,067), ⊙ Gem co., W Idaho, on Payette R. and 25 mi. NW of Boise in agr. area (grain and fruit, especially cherries); fruit packing, lumber milling; feed, dairy products. Settled as trading post 1864, inc. as village 1900, as city 1909. Surrounding region lies within Boise irrigation project. Black Canyon Dam is near by. **2** City (pop. 143), Pottawatomie co., NE Kansas, 26 mi. NW of Topeka. **3** Village (pop. 230), St. Clair co., E Mich., 17 mi. W of Port Huron, in agr. area.

Emmiganur, India: see YEMMIGANUR.

Emmington, Ill.: see EMINGTON.

Emmitsburg, town (pop. 1,261), Frederick co., N Md., near Pa. line, 21 mi. NNE of Frederick, in agr. area (grain, dairy products); makes clothing. Seat of Mt. St. Mary's Col. (R.C.; for men) and St. Joseph's Col. (R.C.; for women). Elizabeth Bayley Seton, who founded R.C. Sisters of Charity here 1809, is buried in chapel of St. Joseph's. Area settled c.1734 as Poplar Fields; town inc. 1825.

Emmons, county (□ 1,546; pop. 9,715), S N.Dak., on S.Dak. line; ⊙ Linton; agr. area drained by Beaver Creek. Grain, livestock. Formed 1879.

Emmons, village (pop. 356), Freeborn co., S Minn., just N of Iowa line, 11 mi. SW of Albert Lea, in lake region; dairy products.

Emmons, Mount, Utah: see UINTA MOUNTAINS.

Emmons Glacier, Wash.: see MOUNT RAINIER NATIONAL PARK.

Emo (ē'mō), village (pop. estimate 700), W Ont., on Rainy R. and 20 mi. W of Fort Frances; dairying, mixed farming, lumbering.

Emöd (ĕ'mûd), Hung. *Emőd*, town (pop. 3,843), Borsod-Gömör co., NE Hungary, at S foot of Bükk Mts., 11 mi. S of Miskolc; vineyards, grain, tobacco; cattle.

Emory. **1** (ĕ'mùrē) or **Emory University,** residential village (1940 pop. 4,605), De Kalb co., NW central Ga., just NE of Atlanta. Seat of Emory Univ. **2** (ĕm'rē) Village (pop. 648), ⊙ Rains co., NE Texas, 28 mi. SE of Greenville; trade point in truck, cotton area; cotton gins, feed mills.

Emory, Lake, N.C.: see FRANKLIN, town.

Emory Peak, Texas: see CHISOS MOUNTAINS.

Empalme (ĕmpäl'mā), town (pop. 4,703), Sonora, NW Mexico, on Gulf of California, 5 mi. ENE of Guaymas; railroad workshops.

Empalme de González, Mexico: see EMPALME ESCOBEDO.

Empalme Escobedo (ĕskōbā'dō), town (pop. 1,937), Guanajuato, central Mexico, on railroad, on Laja R. and 11 mi. NE of Celaya; grain, alfalfa, sugar cane, fruit, livestock. Sometimes Empalme de González.

Empalme Villa Constitución (vē'yä kōnstētōōsyōn'), town (pop. estimate 1,800), SE Santa Fe prov., Argentina, 26 mi. SSE of Rosario; rail junction and agr. center (potatoes, corn, flax, livestock, poultry); sawmills.

Empangeni (ĕmpäng-gĕ'nē), town (pop. 3,179), Zululand, E Natal, U. of So. Afr., near Indian Ocean, 90 mi. NE of Durban; rail junction; sugar-milling center; in cotton, sugar, citrus-fruit region. Near by are govt. forestry plantations.

Empedrado (ĕmpädrä'dō), town (pop. 3,674), ⊙ Empedrado dept. (□ c.750; pop. 20,052), NW Corrientes prov., Argentina, port on Paraná R., on railroad and 35 mi. S of Corrientes. Farming center (cotton, rice, tobacco, citrus fruit, peas); stock raising and dairying. Sawmills.

Empedrado, village (1930 pop. 576), Maule prov., S central Chile, 25 mi. NNE of Cauquenes; grain, lentils, wine, sheep; lumbering.

Emperor Nicholas II Land, Russian SFSR: see SEVERNAYA ZEMLYA.

Empexa, Salar de (sälär' dā ĕmpāk'sä), salt flat in Potosí dept., W Bolivia, in the Altiplano, 105 mi. W of Uyuni, on Chile border; 30 mi. long, 10 mi. wide; alt. 12,270 ft.

Empire. **1** Village (pop. 1,448), Stanislaus co., central Calif., just E of Modesto. **2** Town (pop. 228), Clear Creek co., N central Colo., on headwater of Clear Creek, in Front Range, and 35 mi. W of Denver; alt. 8,603 ft. Mining point in natl.-forest area. Berthoud Pass near by. **3** Town (pop. 157), Dodge co., S central Ga., 12 mi. NW of Eastman. **4** Village (1940 pop. 558), Plaquemines parish, extreme SE La., on W bank (levee) of the Mississippi and 50 mi. SE of New Orleans, in the delta; hunting, fishing. Doullut Canal, with lock through the Mississippi levee here, connects river with waterways leading W into Gulf of Mexico and Barataria Bay. **5** Village (pop. 251), Leelanau co., NW Mich., 22 mi. WNW of Traverse City, on L. Michigan, in cherry-growing region. **6** Village (pop. 610), Jefferson co., E Ohio, 10 mi. N of Steubenville and on Ohio R.; clay products. **7** City (pop. 2,261), Coos co., SW Oregon, near North Bend, on Coos Bay; paper mill.

Empoli (ĕm'pôlē), town (pop. 12,534), Firenze prov., Tuscany, central Italy, on the Arno and 16 mi. WSW of Florence. Trade and industrial center; mfg. (glass, shoes, hosiery, wine, macaroni, paper, chemicals, matches, bicycles, agr. tools). Has church (founded 1093; largely rebuilt after Second World War) with paintings by Botticini and Della Robbia terra cottas. In Second World War suffered many air bombings, with destruction or heavy damage to over 700 houses.

Emporia (ĕmpô'rēü). **1** City (pop. 15,669), ⊙ Lyon co., E central Kansas, c.50 mi. SSW of Topeka, bet. Cottonwood and Neosho rivers; trade and rail center for extensive stock-raising and grain-growing area. Meat packing, flour milling, dairying; mfg. of mattresses, deodorants; railroad maintenance. Has Col. of Emporia (Presbyterian; 1882) and Kansas State Teachers Col. (1863). William Allen White, founder of Emporia *Gazette*, was b. here 1868. State park near by. Founded 1857, inc. 1870. Grew as trade center after arrival of railroad (1870). **2** Town (pop. 5,664), ⊙ Greensville co., S Va., on Meherrin R. and 38 mi. SSW of Petersburg, near N.C. line; shipping, processing center for agr. (cotton, peanuts, tobacco), timber area; cotton ginning; lumber; wood and foundry products. Inc. 1887. Co. courthouse dates from 1787. Textile milling at North Emporia (1940 pop. 865), just across river.

Emporiae or **Emporium,** Spain: see AMPURIAS.

Emporium, borough (pop. 3,646), ⊙ Cameron co., N central Pa., 65 mi. WNW of Williamsport and on Sinnemahoning Creek; electric equipment, explosives, leather; bituminous coal, timber. Settled 1810, laid out 1861, inc. 1864.

Empress, village (pop. 417), SE Alta., on Sask. border, on Red Deer R. and 70 mi. NNE of Medicine Hat; wheat, ranching.

Empress Augusta Bay, SW Bougainville, Solomon Isls., SW Pacific, bet. Cape Torokina and Mutupina Point; 15 mi. wide. Formerly Kaiserin Augusta Bay.

Empty Quarter, Arabia: see RUB' AL KHALI.

Em River, Swedish *Emån* (ām'ōn"), SE Sweden, rises SE of Nassjo, flows 120 mi. generally ESE to Kalmar Sound of Baltic 7 mi. S of Oskarshamn.

Ems or **Bad Ems,** town, Germany: see BAD EMS.

Ems, river, Germany see EMS RIVER.

Emsbüren (ĕms"bü'rùn), village (pop. 931), in former Prussian prov. of Hanover, NW Germany, after 1945 in Lower Saxony, 9 mi. S of Lingen; metalworking.

Emsdetten (ĕms'dĕ"tùn), town (pop. 21,735), in former Prussian prov. of Westphalia, NW Germany, after 1945 in North Rhine-Westphalia, near the Ems, 8 mi. SE of Rheine; a center of jute industry; cotton and linen weaving.

Em-sger, Wales: see BISHOP AND CLERKS.

Ems-Hunte Canal (ĕms'-hōōn'tù) or **Küsten Kanal** (kü'stùn känäl') [Ger.,=coastal canal], NW Germany, bet. Leer (on the Ems) and Oldenburg. Length 45 mi.; 9 locks; navigable for shallow-draught vessels. Utilizes lower course of Leda R. (affluent of the Ems). Beyond Oldenburg, canal connects with the Weser through canalized Hunte R.

Ems-Jade Canal (ĕms'-yä'dù), NW Germany, in East Friesland, connecting Emden (W) and Wilhelmshaven. Length 43 mi.; 6 locks; navigable for shallow-draught vessels. Built 1882–87.

Emsland (ĕms'länt), swampy region (□ 390) in NW Germany, bet. Ems R. (E) and Dutch border, W of Lingen and Meppen. Extensive drainage project (begun 1928) has considerably reduced moors and swamps. Oil fields (Emlichheim, Georgsdorf, Lingen) were developed here during 1940s; region now produces ⅓ of Germany's petroleum.

Ems River (ĕms), Du. *Eems*, NW Germany, rises 10 mi. N of Paderborn, meanders c.250 mi. E and N, past Rheine, to the North Sea, forming a 20-mi.-long estuary, of which the Dollart (near Emden) is a part. Below Münster it is paralleled by Dortmund-Ems Canal, which utilizes river's bed below Meppen.

Emst (āmst), village (pop. 343), Gelderland prov., E central Netherlands, 7 mi. N of Apeldoorn; mfg. of surgical bandages. Sometimes spelled Eemst.

Emstek (ĕms'tāk), village (commune pop. 6,728), in Oldenburg, NW Germany, after 1945 Lower Saxony, 5 mi. ESE of Cloppenburg; mfg. of building materials; brewing, distilling (brandy).

Ems-Vechte Canal, Germany, see VECHT RIVER.

Ems-Weser Canal (ĕms'-vā'zùr), NW Germany, part of Mittelland Canal, extends c.60 mi. E from Dortmund-Ems Canal (1 mi. NW of Bergeshövede; lock) to Minden (Weser crossing), where it connects with Weser-Elbe Canal. Navigable for 1,000-ton vessels. Eder R., a tributary of the Fulda, regulates canal's water supply.

Emsworth, England: see WARBLINGTON.

Emsworth, residential borough (pop. 3,128), Allegheny co., SW Pa., NW suburb of Pittsburgh, on Ohio R. Settled 1803, inc. 1897.

Emtsa, Russian SFSR: see YEMTSA.

Emukae (āmōōkä'ā) or **Emukai** (-ē), town (pop. 16,134), Nagasaki prefecture, NW Kyushu, Japan, on NW Hizen Peninsula, 11 mi. NW of Sasebo; commercial center in coal-mining area.

Emyrna or **Emyrne,** Madagascar: see IMERINA.

Emyvale, Gaelic *Sgairbh na gCaorach*, town (pop. 190), N Co. Monaghan, Ireland, 6 mi. N of Monaghan; shoe mfg.; agr. market (flax, oats, potatoes).

En [Arabic,=the], for Arabic names beginning thus and not found here: see under following part of the name.

Ena (ā'nä), town (pop. 10,345), Fukushima prefecture, central Honshu, Japan, on the Pacific, 7 mi. SE of Taira; fishing port.

Ena-, in Rus. names: see YENA-.

Enan, Korea: see YONAN.

Enare, lake and village, Finland: see INARI.

Enarea (ĕnärā'ä), mtn. district, in Kaffa prov., SW Ethiopia, bet. Omo and Dadessa rivers, N of Jimma. Drained by Gibbe R. Coffee gathering and exporting. Chief center, Saka.

Encamp (ăkā'), village (pop. c.500), Andorra, on headstream of Valira R. and 4 mi. NE of Andorra la Vella; livestock raising. The powerful Andorra radio station is just E, on L. Engolasters.

Encampment, town (pop. 288), Carbon co., S Wyo., on Encampment R., in the Sierra Madre, and 47 mi. SSE of Rawlins; alt. 7,306 ft. Once trade center of busy copper-mining area.

Encampment River, rises in Park Range, N Colo., flows 42 mi. N, past Encampment town, to N.Platte R. S of Saratoga.

Encantada, Cerro La, Mexico: see SAN PEDRO MÁRTIR, SIERRA.

Encantado (ĕngkäntä'dōō), city (pop. 1,321), NE Rio Grande do Sul, Brazil, on Taquari R. and 70 mi. NNW of Pôrto Alegre; hog slaughtering; wine-growing.

Encanto, Calif.: see SAN DIEGO, city.

Encanto, Cape (ĕngkän'tō), Quezon prov., central Luzon, Philippines, on E coast, at SE side of entrance to Baler Bay (inlet of Philippine Sea); 15°44'N 121°37'E.

Encarnación (ĕngkärnäsyōn'), town (pop. 422), Hidalgo, central Mexico, 8 mi. S of Jacala; iron deposits. Sometimes Ferrería de la Encarnación.

Encarnación, city (dist. pop. 19,062), ⊙ Itapúa dept., SE Paraguay, major Paraguayan port on Alto (upper) Paraná R., opposite Posadas (Argentina), and 185 mi. SE of Asunción. Rail terminus; commercial, lumbering, and agr. center (maté, tobacco, cotton, corn, rice, cattle). Trades also in hides and timber. Lumber mills; rice, corn, and maté mills; cotton gins; tanneries. Train ferry at adjoining (SE) Pacú-cuá (päkōō'-kwä') crosses the Paraná to Posadas. Founded 1632 as Jesuit mission of Itapúa. Severely damaged by 1926 tornado. Near by (N) are a number of Russian settlements.

Encarnación, La, Honduras: see LA ENCARNACIÓN.

Encarnación de Díaz (dā dē'äs), S city (pop. 5,987), Jalisco, central Mexico, on interior plateau, on railroad and 27 mi. S of Aguascalientes; alt. 6,135 ft.; corn, wheat, beans, chili, livestock.

Enchi (ĕn'chē), town (pop. 2,068), Western Prov., Gold Coast colony, 55 mi. NW of Prestea; cacao, cassava, corn. Gold placers along near-by Tano R.

Encinal (ĕn'sĭnăl), village (1940 pop. 1,071), La Salle co., SW Texas, 38 mi. N of Laredo; rail point in truck, cattle area.

Encinasola (ĕn-thēnäsō'lä), town (pop. 5,528), Huelva prov., SW Spain, in the Sierra Morena, near Badajoz prov. border, 12 mi. W of Fregenal de la Sierra; agr. center (olives, cereals, hogs, sheep). Alcohol and liquor distilling. Hunting.

Encinas Reales (ĕn-thē'näs rää'lĕs), town (pop. 2,907), Córdoba prov., S Spain, near Genil R., 10 mi. S of Lucena; olive-oil processing, flour milling. Cereals, melons, wine, aniseed; sheep, hogs.

Encinitas (ĕnsĭnē'tùs), village (1940 pop. 1,616), San Diego co., S Calif., on coast, 12 mi. SSE of Oceanside; floricultural center; also grows avocados, fruit, truck. Bathing beaches.

Encino (ĕnsē'nō). **1** Suburban section of LOS ANGELES city, Los Angeles co., S Calif., in San Fernando Valley, 9 mi. SSW of San Fernando; residential; large dairy farm. **2** Village (pop. 408), Torrance co., central N.Mex., 36 mi. ESE of Estancia; alt. 6,200 ft.; trade center in agr. and livestock region.

Encontrados (ĕngkōnträ'dōs), town (pop. 3,053), Zulia state, NW Venezuela, river port on Catatumbo R., in Maracaibo lowlands, 115 mi. SSW of Maracaibo; terminus of railroad from Cúcuta (Colombia). Outlet for coffeegrowing region on Colombian border; dairy industry.

Encounter Bay, inlet of Indian Ocean, SE South Australia, bet. Newland Head (W) and Murray R. mouth (E); 20 mi. E-W, 6 mi. N-S. Victor Harbor and Port Elliot on N shore.

Encrucijada (ĕngkrōōsēhä'dä), town (pop. 3,886), Las Villas prov., central Cuba, on railroad and 15 mi. NNE of Santa Clara; sugar-growing center; also tobacco, fruit, livestock. Sugar centrals near by.

Encruzilhada do Sul (ĕngkrōōzēlyä'dù dōō sōōl'), city (pop. 2,648), SE Rio Grande do Sul, Brazil, in hills of same name, 40 mi. SE of Cachoeira do Sul; road center; tobacco, fruit, livestock. Tungsten, tin, manganese deposits. Until 1944, called Encruzilhada.

Encs (ĕnch), town (pop. 1,766), Abauj co., NE Hungary, 21 mi. NE of Miskolc; wheat, rye, cattle, sheep.

Encuentros, Los, Guatemala: see LOS ENCUENTROS.

Encuolo, Ethiopia: see ENKWOLO, MOUNT.

Enda Medani Alem (ĕn'dä mĕdä'nē ä'lĕm), village (pop. 700), Tigre prov., N Ethiopia, on road and 34 mi. S of Makale; cereals, livestock.

Enda Selassié (ĕn′dä sĕlä′syä), town (pop. 1,530), Tigre Prov., N Ethiopia, on road and 40 mi. W of Aduwa; trade center.

Endau or **Bandar Endau** (bändär′ ĕndau′), town (pop. 1,466), NE Johore, Malaya, port on South China Sea at mouth of small Endau R. (Pahang border), 20 mi. NW of Mersing; fisheries, coconuts, rubber. **Endau Settlement** (pop. 1,472), 3 mi. SSE, has iron mines.

Ende or **Endeh** (ĕndĕ′), chief town (pop. 7,226) of Flores, Indonesia, on S coast of isl., port on inlet of Savu Sea; 8°50′S 121°38′E; exports copra, coffee, timber.

Endeavor, village (pop. 314), Marquette co., S central Wis., 11 mi. N of Portage, on Buffalo L.

Endeavour, Mount (9,300 ft.), NW B.C., near Alaska border, in Coast Mts., 75 mi. NNE of Wrangell; 57°25′N 131°30′W.

Endeavour Strait, channel of Torres Strait, N Queensland, Australia, bet. N coast of Cape York Peninsula and S shores of Prince of Wales and Horn isls.; opens into Gulf of Carpentaria (SW); 30 mi. long, 10 mi. wide.

Endeh, Indonesia: see ENDE.

Endelave (ĕ″nŭlä′vŭ), island (□ 5.1; pop. 510) in the Kattegat, Denmark, 10 mi. SE of mouth of Horsens Fjord, E Jutland; agr., fisheries. Endelave By, town.

Enderbury Island, uninhabited island (□ 2.2), Phoenix Isls., S Pacific, near CANTON ISLAND, c.2,000 naut. mi. SW of Honolulu; 3°8′S 171°5′W. Under Anglo-American condominium since 1939; historically similar to Canton.

Enderby (ĕn′dŭrbē), city (pop. 538), S B.C., on Shuswap R. and 21 mi. NNE of Vernon; dairying, lumbering, brick making.

Enderby, town and parish (pop. 3,040), central Leicester, England, 5 mi. SW of Leicester; hosiery, shoes, chemicals. Stone quarries near by.

Enderby Island, Australia: see DAMPIER ARCHIPELAGO.

Enderby Land, Antarctica, extends from Ice Bay to Edward VIII Bay, bet. 49°30′ and 57°20′E at c.66°50′S. Discovered 1831 by John Biscoe, Br. navigator.

Enderlin (ĕn′dŭrlĭn), city (pop. 1,504), Ransom co., SE N.Dak., 30 mi. SE of Valley City and on Maple R. Railroad junction; dairy products, grain, livestock. Inc. 1896.

Endicott. 1 Village (pop. 195), Jefferson co., SE Nebr., 5 mi. SE of Fairbury and on Little Blue R.; bricks. Near by is Quivera Park. **2** Industrial village (pop. 20,050), Broome co., S N.Y., on the Susquehanna, W of Binghamton and Johnson City, with which 2 towns it comprises the Triple Cities; large shoe industry (Endicott-Johnson Shoe Company). Also makes business machines, foundry products, stone and wood products. Settled c.1795, inc. 1906. Shoe mfg. began 1901. **3** Town (pop. 397), Whitman co., SE Wash., 18 mi. W of Colfax; wheat, oats, barley.

Endicott Mountains, N central Alaska, central part of Brooks Range, extends c.150 mi. E-W in lat. 68°N; rises to 8,800 ft.

Endicott River, SE Alaska, rises in Muir Glacier, near 58°50′N 135°44′W, flows 20 mi. SE to W side of Lynn Canal at 58°47′N 135°15′W.

Endingen (ĕn′dĭng-ŭn), village (pop. 2,988), S Baden, Germany, at N foot of the Kaiserstuhl, 7 mi. NNW of Emmendingen; tobacco mfg., leatherworking. Has remains of medieval walls; late-Gothic fountain; 16th-cent. town hall.

Endires, Turkey: see SUSEHRI.

Endless Caverns, Va.: see NEW MARKET.

En-dor or **Endor** (ĕn′dôr), Hebrew *Ein Dor*, Arabic *Indur*, biblical locality, Lower Galilee, N Palestine, S of Mt. Tabor, 6 mi. SE of Nazareth. In biblical history King Saul here consulted the witch. Modern Arab village of Indur abandoned 1948; Jewish settlement of Ein Dor established subsequently. Sometimes spelled Indor.

Endrick Water, river, Stirling, Scotland, rises in Campsie Fells 3 mi. E of Fintry, flows 29 mi. W, past Fintry, to S end of Loch Lomond. Just E of Fintry is the Loup of Fintry, 94-ft. waterfall.

Endröd (ĕn′drŭd), Hung. *Endrőd*, town (pop. 12,843), Bekes co., SE Hungary, on the Körös and 9 mi. SE of Mezötur; agr. (corn, wheat, tobacco), cattle raising near by.

Endwell, residential village (1940 pop. 3,436), Broome co., S N.Y., on the Susquehanna, between Endicott and Johnson City. Also called Hooper.

Endybalsk or **Endybal′sk** (ĕndĭbälsk′), village (1948 pop. over 500), N Yakut Autonomous SSR, Russian SFSR, in Verkhoyansk Range, 150 mi. SSW of Verkhoyansk; lead, zinc, molybdenum deposits.

′Eneiba, Egypt: see ′INEIBA.

Energy, village (pop. 503), Williamson co., S Ill., just S of Herrin, in coal-mining and agr. area.

Ene River, Peru: see APURÍMAC RIVER.

Enez, Turkey: see ENOS.

Enfidaville (ĕnfēdävēl′), village, Sousse dist., NE Tunisia, near the Gulf of Hammamet, on railroad and 25 mi. NNW of Sousse; road center; Fr. agr. settlement (olives, wine, cereals). Formerly named Dar-el-Bey. Near by are ruins of Roman *Aphrodisium.* Scene of heavy fighting in Tunisian campaign (April, 1943) of Second World War.

Enfield. 1 Municipality (pop. 17,231), E New South Wales, Australia, 8 mi. WSW of Sydney, in metropolitan area; mfg. center (rubber goods, bricks, tile). **2** Town (pop. 13,744), SE South Australia, 4 mi. N of Adelaide, in metropolitan area; agr.

Enfield, residential and industrial urban district (1931 pop. 67,874; 1951 census 110,458), Middlesex, England, 10 mi. N of London; site of royal small-arms factory (Enfield rifles); mfg. of metal products, wire, plastics. Has 13th-cent. church. Just W is district of Enfield Chase, for some years residence of Charles and Mary Lamb.

Enfield. 1 Town (pop. 15,464), Hartford co., N Conn., on the Connecticut, at Mass. line, and 15 mi. N of Hartford; dairy products, truck, tobacco. Includes mfg. villages of Thompsonville (pop. 9,633; carpets, hardware, tobacco, paper and wood products) and Hazardville (pop. 1,272; wood products, woolens). Town hall built 1775. Old site of Shaker settlement (c.1780–1915) is state prison farm. Settled c.1680. **2** Village (pop. 906), White co., SE Ill., 26 mi. NNE of Harrisburg, in agr. area. **3** Town (pop. 1,196), Penobscot co., central Maine, near the Penobscot, 33 mi. N of Bangor, in hunting, fishing, lumbering area. Inc. 1835. **4** Former town, Hampshire co., W central Mass.; inundated in 1937 by QUABBIN RESERVOIR. **5** Town (pop. 1,612), including Enfield village (pop. 1,111), Grafton co., W N.H., on Mascoma R. (water power) and Mascoma L. and 5 mi. E of Lebanon; textiles, lumber; fruit, truck, poultry, dairy products. Settled 1761. **6** Town (pop. 2,361), Halifax co., NE N.C., 18 mi. NNE of Rocky Mount; market and shipping center for (peanut and tobacco area). Settled before 1750.

Engadine (ĕng′gŭdēn, Fr. ăgädēn′), Ger. *Engadin* (ān′gädēn), Romansh *Engiadina* (ĕnjädē′nä), valley of upper Inn R. in Grisons canton, E Switzerland, bet. 2 chains of Rhaetian Alps. It extends from Maloja Pass 60 mi. NE to Austrian border; consists of Upper Engadine (SW) and Lower Engadine (NE). Bounded by mts., with Bernina Alps on S; noted for fine scenery, forests, and Alpine flowers. Pop. is largely Protestant and Romansh speaking. Has numerous health resorts and winter sports centers, as Sils, Silvaplana, St. Moritz, Pontresina, Celerina, Samaden, Vulpera, Bad Tarasp, Schuls. Swiss Natl. Park (□ 53, founded 1909), bet. Inn R. and Ofen Pass, is noted for its wildlife and rugged scenery.

Engadine (ĕng′ŭdīn), village, Mackinac co., SE Upper Peninsula, Mich., 16 mi. S of Newberry; supply point for resort area.

Engan, Norway: see OPDAL, Sor-Trondelag co.

En-gannim, Palestine: see JENIN.

Engano, Indonesia: see ENGGANO.

Engaño, Cape (ĕng-gä′nyō), easternmost tip of Hispaniola isl. and the Dominican Republic, on Mona Passage, 50 mi. ESE of Seibo; 18°36′N 68°19′W.

Engaño, Cape, Philippines: see PALAUI ISLAND.

Engaños, Río de los, Colombia: see YARÍ RIVER.

Engare Nanyuki or **Ngare Nanyuki** (both: ŭng-gä′rā nänyōō′kē), village, Northern Prov., NE Tanganyika, on NE slope of Mt. Meru, 20 mi. NNE of Arusha; coffee, corn, vegetables; livestock.

Engaru (ĕng-gä′rōō), town (pop. 14,862), W Hokkaido, Japan, 37 mi. W of Abashiri; lumbering, agr. (wheat, soybeans).

En-gedi, Engeddi (both: ĕngē′dē, –gĕ′dē, ĕn′gĕdē), or **Ein Gedi** (ān′ gĕdē′), locality, SE Israel, on W shore of Dead Sea, 17 mi. ESE of Hebron; 1,292 ft. below sea level. Hot springs noted since anc. times; health resort being developed here. In biblical history associated with story of Saul and David. Also spelled Engedi or En-geddi; in biblical history also called *Hazazon-Tamar.*

Engelberg (ĕng′ŭlbĕrk), town (pop. 2,409), Obwalden half-canton, central Switzerland, on Engelberger Aa and 9 mi. SE of Sarnen; winter, summer resort. Benedictine abbey (founded c.1120), 18th-cent. church. Obermatt hydroelectric plant is N.

Engelhard (ĕng′gŭlhärd″), village, Hyde co., E N.C., 35 mi. E of Belhaven, on Pamlico Sound; ships fish.

Engelhörner (ĕng′ŭlhûr″nŭr), group of peaks in Bernese Alps, S central Switzerland. Grosses Engelhorn (9,135 ft.), highest, is 3 mi. S of Meiringen.

Engels or **Engel's** (ĕn′gĭls), city (1939 pop. 73,279), central Saratov oblast, Russian SFSR, port on left bank of Volga R., opposite Saratov; industrial and agr. center; railroad-car building, meat packing (at S suburb of Privolzhski), flour milling; mfg. of chemicals, bonemeal, bricks, tiles. First settled 1747 by Ukrainians; until c.1932, called Pokrovsk. Was ⊙ German Volga Autonomous SSR (1923–41).

Engelsa, Imeni, or **Imeni Engel′sa** (ē′mĭnyē ĕn′gĭl-sŭ), town (1939 pop. over 500), SE Voroshilovgrad oblast, Ukrainian SSR, in the Donbas, W of Krasnodon; coal mines.

Engelsdorf (ĕng′ŭlsdôrf), town (pop. 8,956), Saxony, E central Germany, 4 mi. E of Leipzig; railroad workshops; mfg. of cardboard, dyes, laboratory equipment.

Engelskirchen (ĕng″ŭlskĭr′khŭn), village (pop. 5,759), in former Prussian Rhine prov., W Germany, after 1945 in North Rhine-Westphalia, 12 mi. E of Bergisch Gladbach; lead mining. Spinning mills.

Engen (ĕng′ŭn), town (pop. 2,627), S Baden, Germany, 7 mi. NNW of Singen; tobacco mfg. Summer resort (alt. 1,703 ft.). Has late-Romanesque church, renovated in baroque style; and 16th-cent. castle.

Enger (ĕng′ŭr), town (pop. 5,901), in former Prussian prov. of Westphalia, NW Germany, after 1945 in North Rhine-Westphalia, 5 mi. NW of Herford; cigar mfg. Has church containing tomb of Saxon chieftain Widukind.

Engerau, Czechoslovakia: see PETRZALKA.

Engers (ĕng′ŭrs), village (pop. 4,541), in former Prussian Rhine Prov., W Germany, after 1945 in Rhineland-Palatinate, on right bank of the Rhine and 3.5 mi. E of Neuwied; pumice-stone quarrying. Rail bridge across Rhine R. 1 mi. W.

Enggano or **Engano** (ĕng-gä′nō), island (□ 171; pop. 469, including 6 surrounding islets) in Indian Ocean off SW coast of Sumatra, Indonesia, 110 mi. S of Benkulen; 5°25′S 102°15′E; 22 mi. long, 10 mi. wide. Heavily wooded and hilly, rising to 922 ft. Timber, coconuts.

Enggor (ĕng″gōr′), village, N central Perak, Malaya, on railroad and 5 mi. NE of Kuala Kangsar; coal deposits.

Enghien (ăgyē′), Flemish *Edingen* (ā′dĭng-ŭn), town (pop. 4,427), Hainaut prov., SW central Belgium, 17 mi. SW of Brussels; mfg. (machines, electric lamps); linen weaving, lace making; butter market. Established in 11th cent.; was medieval trade and commercial center. Fr. possession until 1606.

Enghien-les-Bains (ăgyē′-lā-bē′), town (pop. 11,121), Seine-et-Oise dept., N central France, an outer NNW suburb of Paris, 8 mi. from Notre Dame Cathedral, on E shore of Enghien L.; spa (cold sulphur springs) and pleasure resort.

Engiabara, Ethiopia: see ENJABARA.

Engineer Mountain, peak (13,190 ft.) in San Juan Mts., at junction of Hinsdale, Ouray, and San Juan counties, SW Colo.

Engis (ăzhē′), town (pop. 3,466), Liége prov., E central Belgium, on Meuse R. and 8 mi. WSW of Liége; zinc and lead processing; limekilns.

Engizek Dag (ĕngĭzĕk′ dä), Turkish *Engizek Dağ*, peak (9,258 ft.), S Turkey, in the Taurus Mts., 20 mi. ENE of Maras.

England (ĭng′glŭnd, ĭng′lŭnd) [i.e., Angle-land], Lat. *Anglia*, S part and largest political division (□ 50,327; 1931 pop. 37,359,045; 1951 census pop. 41,147,938; with Monmouthshire: □ 50,873; 1931 pop. 37,794,003; 1951 census 42,611,354) of the isl. of Great Britain and of the UNITED KINGDOM OF GREAT BRITAIN AND NORTHERN IRELAND; ⊙ LONDON. Separated from France (S) by the English Channel and the narrow Strait of Dover, England is bounded by Wales (SW), the Irish Sea (NW), Scotland (N), and the North Sea (E). Rocky peninsula of Cornwall extends SW into the Atlantic; at its tip is Land's End, W extremity of Great Britain; near-by Lizard Head is its S extremity. Further W, in the Atlantic, are the Scilly Isls. S coast is indented by several large bays (St. Austell, Lyme, and Poole bays) and by inlet of Southampton Water and its approaches, Spithead and the Solent, protected by Isle of Wight. High chalk cliffs are prevalent on parts of S coast but there are good natural harbors at Southampton (principal British passenger port), Weymouth, Plymouth, and Falmouth, while small ports of Dover, Folkestone (both among the historical CINQUE PORTS), and Newhaven are manmade and chiefly serve cross-Channel traffic to France and Belgium. From S coast surface rises to fertile, low rolling hills (South Downs and North Downs), then slopes down to Thames valley. Bet. Thames estuary and The Wash (bay of North Sea, formed by mouths of several small rivers) is low, fertile agr. region of Norfolk and Suffolk, forming peninsula in North Sea and consisting partly of drained fenland; on coast are ports of Lowestoft and Yarmouth (England's chief herring-fishing centers), and Harwich (serving North Sea shipping to Belgium, the Netherlands, and Denmark). N of Thames valley, surface rises again to the Chilterns, Cotswolds, and other low chalk-hill ranges which slope N to important lowland basin of the Midlands, the industrial heart of England and Great Britain, centered on Birmingham and Wolverhampton. From N end of this basin the important central fold of the Pennines extends N to Scottish border. The Pennines are cut by 3 gaps (Aire, Tees, and Tyne dales or valleys); E of the range are high bleak moors, then the important YORKSHIRE coal-mining and industrial region slopes to low North Sea coast; to the W of the Pennines the equally important LANCASHIRE textile-milling region slopes to rocky Irish Sea coast. Cumbrian Mts., near Scottish border, are NW outcrop of the Pennines and rise to 3,210 ft. on Scafell Pike, highest peak of England; on SE slope of this range is the LAKE DISTRICT, with lakes Windermere, Ambleside, Ullswater, and others, noted for scenic beauty and associations with English poetry. Other distinctive regions of England include Lincolnshire (E), with bleak hill range near coast, and extensive sheep-raising and grain-growing lands further inland; Devon with high moors (Exmoor, Dartmoor) and noted dairying industry; and bleak mountainous Cumberland and Northumberland (with Cheviot Hills), on Scottish border. Natural harbors are formed by estuaries of larger English rivers; on Thames estuary (SE) are London and its many outports including Tilbury and Gravesend; on Humber estuary (E), created by confluence of the Trent and the Ouse, are Hull and fishing center of Grimsby; Newcastle is on Tyne estuary (NE); Liverpool and Birkenhead are near mouth of the Mersey (W); and Bristol Channel and Severn estuary (SW) serve Bristol, Avonmouth, and ports of S Wales. Very large British merchant fleet ranks 2d after that of the United States; it plays major role in world trade and forms one of the mainstays of British economy. Coal mining is the principal of England's basic industries; largest coal fields are those in counties of Northumberland and Durham (NE), Yorkshire (E), Nottingham and Derby (N central England), Lancashire and Staffordshire (W), Cumberland (NW), Warwick (central England), and Kent (SE). Iron deposits are worked in Cleveland region of Yorkshire, in Northampton region, in N Lancashire (near Barrow-in-Furness), and in W Cumberland. England's vastly important steel furnaces and mills are concentrated in co. Durham (NE), bet. Newcastle-upon-Tyne and Middlesbrough; in N Midlands (S Yorkshire, Derby, Nottingham, and Stafford); in N Lincolnshire (Scunthorpe region); in Leicester, Northampton, Shropshire (Wolverhampton region), S Lancashire, N Lancashire (Barrow-in-Furness), and on Cumberland coast. Steel mills supply a large number of major mfg. industries: shipbuilding (centered on Newcastle-upon-Tyne, Birkenhead, and Barrow-in-Furness); mfg. of machinery (chiefly in Yorkshire, Lancashire, the Midlands, and London region); automobiles and trucks (Coventry, Oxford, Bedford, Dagenham); locomotives; cutlery (Sheffield); and the metalworks centered on Birmingham. Internationally-known pottery industry of Staffordshire (centered on Stoke-on-Trent) uses local clay for earthenware, and china clay from Devon and Cornwall for porcelain mfg. Cotton mills of the vast English textile industry are concentrated in Lancashire; Yorkshire (especially Huddersfield, Bradford, and Leeds) is home of woolen milling. Leicester and Nottingham are knitting-mill centers; the latter is also noted for its lace. There are rayon mills in Lancashire, Norfolk, Suffolk, and in London region. Lancashire and Leeds region of Yorkshire have important clothing industry. Northampton, Leicester, and Norwich are shoe-mfg. centers. Large salt deposits in Cheshire have aided growth of heavy-chemicals industry there; co. Durham is another chemical-mfg. center. Port Sunlight (Cheshire) has major soapworks; Nottingham has important pharmaceuticals industry. Principal English oil refineries are at mouth of the Thames (Thameshaven, Shellhaven), on Manchester Ship Canal and on Mersey estuary, in Southampton region, and at Avonmouth. Large number of light industries have in recent years grown up in the metropolitan area of London, as well as in regions traditionally associated with heavy specialized industries that were hard hit by the depression of the 1930s (notably Tyneside, Manchester region, W Cumberland). Much of England's soil is utilized for grazing purposes; sheep raising is especially important in the Pennines, Lake District, North and South Downs, Wiltshire, Somerset, and Devonshire. Cattle are raised in most parts of S England; dairying is major industry in Berkshire, Wiltshire, and Devonshire. Fruitgrowing is important in Kent (also hop-growing center), Hampshire, and N Oxfordshire. Market gardens predominate in London region. Sugar-beet growing and sugar refining have developed rapidly in East Anglia in recent times, stimulated by protective tariffs and direct subsidies. Lincolnshire and Norfolk are important wheat and potato-growing regions; fruit and vegetables are grown and canned in Cambridgeshire. England has moist maritime climate; winter is tempered (especially on W and S coasts) by Gulf Stream. Prevailing wind direction is SW. There is abundant rainfall; winter rains predominate in W part, summer rains in E part of England. Winter fogs are frequent in SE England, especially in Thames estuary. Vacation travel is widespread in Britain, especially since introduction of paid vacations for industrial workers, and the numerous English seaside resorts attract vast numbers of summer visitors; since Second World War, great efforts have also been made to attract tourists from the United States. Most popular seaside resorts are on S coast and include Margate, Ramsgate, Deal, Hastings, Eastbourne, Brighton, Hove, Worthing, Bournemouth, Torquay, and Penzance; resorts on E and W coasts chiefly serve industrial pop. of the Midlands. Shakespeare's birthplace, Stratford-on-Avon, is among most popular attractions for overseas tourists. Principal cities of England are London, Birmingham, Liverpool, Manchester, South Shields, Sheffield, Leeds, Bristol, Hull, Newcastle-upon-Tyne, Bradford, Nottingham, Stoke-on-Trent, Leicester, Portsmouth, Coventry, Salford, Sunderland, Southampton, Bolton, Brighton, Wolverhampton, Derby, Southend, Norwich, Oldham, Blackpool, Huddersfield and Gateshead. English universities are at Cambridge, Oxford, London, Birmingham, Bristol, Durham, Leeds, Liverpool, Manchester, Reading, and Sheffield; among leading public schools are Eton, Harrow, Rugby, and Winchester. English history is closely associated with that of the other parts of the British Isles (Scotland, Wales, and Ireland). In earliest historic times all were settled by the Celts, a mixed people. Isl. was visited by Mediterranean trades in search of jet and pearls and of tin from Cornwall. In 55 B.C., Britain was invaded by Julius Caesar and later conquered and occupied (1st–5th cent. A.D.) by Romans. Roman period brought about conversion of Celts to Christianity, as well as many internal improvements, and bldg. of notable highways, still used in modern times. Parts of wall built by Hadrian on Scottish border are still visible. As decline of Rome led to withdrawal of her legions, Angles, Saxons, and Jutes began raids which developed (in 2d half of 5th cent.) into great invasions. Celt inhabitants fell back into Wales, Cornwall, and Brittany, while invaders established several kingdoms (Kent, Sussex, Essex, Wessex, East Anglia, Mercia, Deira, Bernicia). Bernicia and Deira were consolidated into Northumbria, but in 9th cent. Wessex gained hegemony over all the kingdoms. From 9th cent. onward Wessex was challenged by repeated Danish raids; these were repelled at first by Alfred the Great, but though his successors formed a united England, the entire country had come under rule of King Canute of Denmark by 1017. Edward the Confessor of the Wessex dynasty gained throne (1042), but upon his death (1066) crown was disputed by Harold the Saxon and William, duke of Normandy. With ensuing Norman conquest the important Anglo-Saxon period of cultural, economic, and political development came to an end. To Saxon economic feudalism and manorial system the Normans now added political and manorial feudalism, and, for the 1st time, attempted to establish a strong central govt. Accession (1154) of Henry II ended a period of anarchy and civil war, and opened era of constitutional and legal reform; at the same time English-held territory in France was expanded and 1st struggles bet. the countries began. Many new towns grew up in this period, and trade developed. Under King John, baronial wars bet. nobles and the king reached a climax; victory of the barons resulted (1215) in signing of the Magna Carta at Runnymede, which marked the inception of a parliamentary system that was steadily to grow in power. Baronial wars continued under Henry III, who was opposed by Simon de Montfort. Richard de Clare (Strongbow), earl of Pembroke, made 1st serious attempt (1169) to conquer Ireland; systematic conquest of Wales (1282) and of Scotland (1296) was undertaken by Edward I, who further reformed legal system. Hundred Years War with France began (1337) under Edward III; despite notable victories under Edward the Black Prince and Henry IV, England gained no tangible advantages. Outbreak (1348) of the Black Death led to drastic changes in English life by breaking down the manorial and feudal systems, and by leading to further growth of towns and trade. Radical thought spread at the same time and was symbolized by teachings of John Wyclif and by Wat Tyler's revolt. Richard II was deposed (1399) and succeeded by Henry IV (Bolingbroke), son of John of Gaunt. Under this 1st Lancastrian king war with France continued, while commerce, and especially woolen trade, continued to grow. Dynastic Wars of the Roses (c.1450–1485) bet. houses of Lancaster and York ended with accession of the Tudors in person of Henry VII. Under this dynasty, usually considered to mark beginning of modern English history, commercial expansion and overseas ventures brought England into conflict with Spain, culminating in defeat (1588) of the Spanish Armada. Henry VIII introduced (1531) the Reformation and strengthened English naval power; his work was completed by Edward VI and Elizabeth. Elizabethan period saw flowering of the Renaissance, especially in the field of literature. Succession to the throne was one of principal political questions in reigns of Edward VI, Mary I, and Elizabeth, whose chief rival was Mary Queen of Scots. Elizabeth's successor, James VI of Scotland, introduced (1603) the Stuart line as James I of England. During reigns of James and his son, Charles I, there developed a bitter struggle, led by the new bourgeois classes (generally identified with the Puritans in religion), to establish parliamentary supremacy over the king; in 1642 this struggle exploded into civil war. Parliamentarian victory was complete with execution (1649) of Charles I. Until his death (1658) Oliver Cromwell, as protector, was absolute ruler of England, but in 1660 the Stuarts, in the person of Charles II, regained the throne. Restoration period typified reaction against Puritanism; renewed prosperity and much political activity under Clarendon, Shaftesbury, and others marked this era. Overthrow (1688) of James II by the Bloodless Revolution and accession of William III and Mary (Mary II) symbolized the definite supremacy of Parliament. Under Queen Anne the Act of Union (1707) joined Scotland to England; name of the kingdom was henceforth Great Britain. Since the time of Elizabeth, English overseas expansion had developed, and mercantilist laws restricted commerce of the colonies; in 17th and 18th cent. England gained supremacy over Dutch in carrying trade, and engaged in active colonial rivalry with France. Ensuing wars of the Grand Alliance (1688–97) and of the Spanish succession (1701–14) resulted in consolidation of English overseas possessions. No long-term pacification of Ireland was achieved by conquests of that country undertaken by the Tudors, Stuarts, and by Cromwell. For later history of England after 1707, see GREAT BRITAIN. For the list of components of the BRITISH EMPIRE, see the article under that heading. For further information on England, see the separate articles on the cities, towns, physical features, and the individual counties. England is administratively divided into 40 counties (shires), some of which are subdivided so as to make 50 administrative divisions. The counties are: Bedfordshire (BEDFORD), BERKSHIRE, Buckinghamshire (BUCKINGHAM), Cambridgeshire (CAMBRIDGE), CHESHIRE, CORNWALL, CUMBERLAND, Derbyshire (DERBY), Devonshire (DEVON), Dorsetshire (DORSET), DURHAM, ESSEX, Gloucestershire (GLOUCESTER), HAMPSHIRE, Herefordshire (HEREFORD), Huntingdonshire (HUNTINGDON), KENT, LANCASHIRE, Lincolnshire (LINCOLN), the administrative co. of LONDON, MIDDLESEX, Monmouthshire (MONMOUTH; often included in Wales for administrative purposes), NORFOLK, Northamptonshire (NORTHAMPTON), NORTHUMBERLAND, Nottinghamshire (NOTTINGHAM), Oxfordshire (OXFORD), RUTLAND, SHROPSHIRE, SOMERSET, Staffordshire (STAFFORD), SUFFOLK, SURREY, SUSSEX, Warwickshire (WARWICK), WESTMORLAND, WILTSHIRE, Worcestershire (WORCESTER), Yorkshire (YORK).

England, city (pop. 2,136), Lonoke co., central Ark., 22 mi. SE of Little Rock, near Arkansas R.; agr. (cotton, truck, livestock); mfg. of lumber and building materials; cotton ginning.

Englefield, Cape, NW extremity of Melville Peninsula, SE Franklin Dist., Northwest Territories, on Gulf of Boothia, at W end of Fury and Hecla Strait; 69°51'N 85°39'W.

Englehart, town (pop. 1,262), E Ont., on Englehart R. and 29 mi. NNW of Haileybury; silver and cobalt mining; dairying.

Englewood, village (pop. estimate 150), SW B.C., on N Vancouver Isl., on Johnstone Strait, 3 mi. SE of Alert Bay; lumber-shipping port; sawmilling.

Englewood (ĕng'gŭlwŏŏd). **1** City (pop. 16,869), S suburb of Denver, Arapahoe co., N central Colo., on South Platte R.; alt. 5,200 ft. Trading point in irrigated agr. area; brooms, tools, dairy products. Greenhouses and fish hatcheries here. Inc. 1903. **2** Village (pop. 1,091), Lawrence co., S Ind., near Bedford. **3** City (pop. 341), Clark co., SW Kansas, near Okla. line, 45 mi. S of Dodge City; wheat, cattle. **4** Residential city (pop. 23,145), Bergen co., NE N.J., 12 mi. NNE of Jersey City; mfg. (leather goods, lighting fixtures, elevators, drugs, metal products); nurseries. Settled before Revolution, inc. 1899. **5** Village (pop. 678), Montgomery co., W Ohio, 10 mi. NW of Dayton and on Stillwater R.; makes machine tools, farm implements. Englewood Dam (4,700 ft. long, 125 ft. high) was completed in 1922 for flood control on the Stillwater. **6** Town (pop. 1,545), McMinn co., SE Tenn., 6 mi. ESE of Athens, in timber and farm area; makes clothing. Settled 1819; inc. 1919.

Englewood Cliffs, residential borough (pop. 966), Bergen co., NE N.J., on Hudson R. (ferry) just ESE of Englewood, on the Palisades.

Englewood Park, village (pop. 4,171, with adjacent Brownlee Park), Calhoun co., S Mich.

English, town (pop. 839), ⊙ Crawford co., S Ind., 36 mi. W of New Albany, in agr. and timber area; mfg. (wagon hubs and spokes, baskets); railroad shops.

English Bay or **Alexandrovsk** (ălŭksăn'drŏfsk), Kenai Indian village (pop. 75), S Alaska, W Kenai Peninsula, on Cook Inlet, 10 mi. SW of Seldovia; fishing. Has Russian Orthodox church.

English Bazar (bŭzär'), town (pop. 23,333), ⊙ Malda dist., NW West Bengal, India, on the Mahananda and 65 mi. N of Berhampore; trade center (rice, wheat, oilseeds, jute, barley, corn). Extensive mulberry growing. Sericulture station near by. Also called Angrezabad.

English Channel, Fr. *La Manche* (lä mäsh') [the sleeve], arm of the Atlantic bet. England and France, 350 mi. long. It is 112 mi. wide at W entrance, bet. Land's End and Ushant; greatest width, c.150 mi., bet. inner coast of Lyme Bay and inner coast of Gulf of Saint-Malo; narrowest, 21 mi., near Dover; □ 30,000; deepest 564 ft.; mean depth 175 ft. At E end, Strait of DOVER connects Channel with North Sea. Principal isls. are CHANNEL ISLANDS and Isle of WIGHT. Main inlets are: English coast—Mounts Bay, St. Austell Bay, Lyme Bay, the Solent, Spithead; Fr. coast—Gulf of Saint-Malo, Seine and Somme river estuaries. Major navigational landmarks and lighthouses are: England—Land's End, Lizard Head, Eddystone Rocks, Start Point, Bill of Portland,

St. Catherine's Point, Beachy Head, and Dungeness; France—Ushant and Batz isls., capes Fréhel, La Hague (at NW tip of Cotentin Peninsula), and La Hève. Regular cross-Channel shipping services bet. chief riparian ports: Southampton–Saint-Malo, Cherbourg–Le Havre, Newhaven–Dieppe. Other Br. ports: Plymouth, Exmouth, Portsmouth, Weymouth. Strait of Dover is crossed by ferries from Folkestone to Boulogne, and from Dover to Calais, Dunkirk, and Ostend. Fr. Channel coast has noted bathing resorts: Dinard, Saint-Malo, Deauville, Trouville, Dieppe, Le Touquet-Paris-Plage. Tourists visit the Mont-Saint-Michel and the invasion beaches (Utah, Omaha) of 1944. A Channel tunnel has been under consideration for several decades. Blanchard and Jeffries crossed channel by balloon in 1785. Matthew Webb 1st swam across it in 1875, and Blériot made 1st airplane crossing in 1909.

English Company's Islands, in Arafura Sea just N of Arnhem Bay; extend in 50-mi. chain parallel with NE coast of Arnhem Land, Northern Territory, Australia; comprise 4 rocky isls. and several islets. Inglis Isl. (15 mi. long, 4 mi. wide) is largest.

English Harbour, village and bay, S Antigua, B.W.I., 8 mi. SSE of St. John's. Has historic dockyard, where Nelson served 1784–87.

Englishman Bay, Washington co., E Maine, inlet of the Atlantic lying bet. Roque Isl. and Roque Bluffs; 4 mi. long, 2 mi. wide.

English River, W Ont., issues from Lac Seul, flows 330 mi. SW and W to Winnipeg R. just E of Man. border.

English River, SE Iowa, formed by forks rising in Poweshiek co. and joining W of Kalona; flows c.35 mi. generally E to Iowa R. 12 mi. S of Iowa City; 85 mi. long, including longest headstream.

Englishtown, fishing village, NE N.S., N Cape Breton Isl., on St. Ann's Bay, 20 mi. WNW of Sydney. First permanent white settlement on Cape Breton Isl., a French post was established here 1629, named St. Ann, for Anne of Austria. In 1713 Fort Dauphin and naval base were built. Fort was destroyed (1745) by Warren's fleet.

Englishtown, borough (pop. 1,004), Monmouth co., E N.J., 5 mi. NW of Freehold. American troops camped here just before the battle of Monmouth, 1778.

Engomer (ãgômâr'), village (pop. 238), Ariège dept., S France, in central Pyrenees, on the Lez (tributary of Salat R.) and 5 mi. SW of Saint-Girons; paper mill; hydroelectric plant.

Engstlenalp (ĕngst'lŭnälp"), mountain pasture (alt. 6,038 ft.) in the Alps, central Switzerland, 4 mi. SW of Engelberg. Engstlensee, a small lake, is near by.

Engteng (ĕng'dĕng'), Mandarin *Yungting* (yŏŏng'dĭng'), town (pop. 9,670), ⊙ Engteng co. (pop. 171,480), SW Fukien prov., China, near Kwangtung line, 60 mi. WNW of Lungki, and on tributary of Han R.; rice, wheat, sugar cane. Coal mines near by.

Enguera (ĕng'gĕrä), town (pop. 4,459), Valencia prov., E Spain, 10 mi. W of Játiva; woolen-textile center; olive-oil processing, paper and brandy mfg., lumbering; cereals, wine, raisins, fruit.

Enguídanos (ĕng-gē'dhänōs), town (pop. 1,811), Cuenca prov., E central Spain, near Cabriel R., 38 mi. SE of Cuenca; olives, grapes, truck produce, timber, livestock; apiculture. Limekiln; hydroelectric plant.

Enguinegatte, France: see GUINEGATTE.

Enham, England: see ANDOVER.

Enhaut (ĕn'hŏt), village (pop. c.2,000), Dauphin co., S central Pa., SE suburb of Harrisburg, near Susquehanna R.

Enhsien (ŭn'shyĕn'), town, ⊙ Enhsien co. (pop. 251,744), S Hopeh prov., China, near Pingyuan-Shantung line, 50 mi. NW of Tsinan; pear-growing center; cotton weaving; wheat, millet, kaoliang, peanuts. Until 1949 in Shantung prov.

Eni-, in Rus. names: see YENI-.

Enid (ē'nĭd). **1** Village (pop. 94), Tallahatchie co., NW central Miss., 11 mi. NE of Charleston. Near by is Enid Dam in Yocona R. **2** City (pop. 36,017), ⊙ Garfield co., N Okla., 65 mi. NNW of Oklahoma City; wholesale and distribution point (rail junction) and important wheat market and milling center, in area also producing livestock, poultry, dairy products, petroleum. Oil refineries; packed meat, poultry, and eggs; mfg. of steel products, oil-field equipment, building materials, aircraft, automotive parts, farm machinery, feed; railroad shops. Seat of Phillips Univ. Has also a state hosp., and Vance Air Force Base. Founded 1893 as tent village on site of a U.S. land office in the Cherokee Strip; inc. 1894.

Enid Dam, Miss.: see YOCONA RIVER.

Enid Reservoir, Miss.: see YOCONA RIVER.

Enigma, town (pop. 499), Berrien co., S Ga., 12 mi. E of Tifton.

Enilda (ĕnĭl'dŭ), village (pop. 350), W central Alta., 70 mi. SE of Peace River, 10 mi. W of Lesser Slave L.; lumbering, mixed farming.

Eningen or **Eningen unter Achalm** (ā'nĭng-ŭn ŏŏn'tŭr äkh'älm), E suburb (pop. 5,182) of Reutlingen, S Württemberg, Germany, at S foot of the Achalm. Inc. into Reutlingen in 1945.

Enipeus River or **Enipevs River** (both: ĕnĭpĕfs'), in central Thessaly, Greece, rises in N Orthrys Mts., flows 71 mi. N and NW to Peneus R. 18 mi. ESE of Larissa. Formerly called Chanarlis.

Enisei, in Rus. names: see YENISEI.

Eniseisk, Russian SFSR: see YENISEISK.

Eniwetok (ĕnĭwē'tŏk, ĕnē'wĕtôk), circular atoll (□ 2), Ralik Chain, Kwajalein dist., Marshall Isls., W central Pacific, 380 mi. WNW of Kwajalein; 11°30'N 162°15'E; c.50 mi. in circumference; 40 islets. In Second World War, Eniwetok was captured 1944 by U.S. forces. In 1948 installations for atomic bomb tests were established. Formerly Brown Atoll.

Enjabara (ĕn'jäbärä), Ital. *Engiabara,* town (pop. 3,500), Gojjam prov., NW Ethiopia, in Agaumdir dist., 20 mi. S of Dangila; stock raising (horses, mules).

Enka (ĕng'kŭ), company town (pop. 1,792), Buncombe co., W N.C., 7 mi. SW of Asheville; large rayon yarn plant.

Enkeldoorn (ĕng'kŭldōōrn), town (pop. 551), Gwelo dist., E central Southern Rhodesia, in Mashonaland, 85 mi. SSW of Salisbury; tobacco, wheat, dairy products, citrus fruit, livestock.

Enkenbach (ĕng'kŭnbäkh), village (pop. 2,492), Rhenish Palatinate, W Germany, 6 mi. NE of Kaiserslautern; rail junction; woodworking; tobacco products. Former Premonstratensian abbey (1150–1664) has Romanesque church.

Enkheim, Germany: see BERGEN-ENKHEIM.

Enkhuizen (ĕngk'hoizŭn), town (pop. 9,777) and port, North Holland prov., NW Netherlands, on the Ijsselmeer, 28 mi. NNE of Amsterdam, on clay land; center of vegetable-seed trade; shipbuilding; mfg. (cocoa, paper, cement). Communications center on Amsterdam-Friesland route; rail terminus; ferry to Stavoren. First Netherlands town to rebel (1572) against Spaniards; important fishing and commercial center in 17th cent. Scene of fighting (1940) in Second World War. Birthplace of Paul Potter.

Enkirch (ān'kĭrkh), village (pop. 2,200), in former Prussian Rhine Prov., W Germany, after 1945 in Rhineland-Palatinate, on the Mosel and 20 mi. NNW of Idar-Oberstein; noted for its wine.

Enkoping (ān'chû"pĭng), Swedish *Enköping,* city (1950 pop. 10,183), Uppsala co., E Sweden, 19 mi. E of Vasteras; rail junction; large metalworking industry. Long known for pepper grown here. Has 15th-cent. church and remains of 13th-cent. Franciscan monastery. In Middle Ages a trade center with port on arm (now silted up) of L. Malar.

Enkwolo, Mount (ĕng'kwōlō), Ital. *Encuolo,* peak (c.14,240 ft.), S central Ethiopia, in Arusi prov., E of L. Shala, at E edge of Great Rift Valley, 35 mi. SSE of Asselle; 7°22'N 39°20'E.

Enloe, town (pop. 186), Delta co., NE Texas, 16 mi. SSW of Paris, near North Fork of Sulphur R.; cotton gins, cannery.

Enlung, China: see TIENTUNG.

Enmore, village (pop. 3,171), ⊙ East Demerara dist., Demerara co., N Br. Guiana, near the Atlantic, on Georgetown-Rosignol RR and 13 mi. ESE of Georgetown; rice, sugar cane, stock.

Enna (ĕn'nä), province (□ 989; pop. 218,294), E central Sicily; ⊙ Enna. Hilly terrain, rising to 3,915 ft. in N; drained by Dittaino and Salso rivers. Agr. (wheat, grapes, olives, almonds). A major mining region (sulphur, gypsum, rock salt) of isl. Formed 1927.

Enna, city (pop. 21,261), ⊙ Enna prov., central Sicily, atop a steep hill (3,067 ft.), 13 mi. NE of Caltanissetta; 37°34'N 14°17'E. Numerous sulphur mines near by. Site of Gothic cathedral, ruins of 14th-cent. castle, 15th-cent. palaces, mus. Prehistoric artifacts found in vicinity. In anc. times dedicated to worship of Ceres. Small L. Pergusa is 4 mi. S; here Pluto was fabled to have seized Proserpine. Town was conquered by Saracens in 859, by Normans in 1087. Called Castrogiovanni until 1927. Scene of heavy fighting (1943) in Second World War.

Ennadai Lake (52 mi. long, 3–14 mi. wide), SW Keewatin Dist., Northwest Territories, near Mackenzie and Manitoba borders; 60°55'N 101°15'W. Drained N by Kazan R.

Ennazé, Syria: see NAZ'A, EL.

En Nebk, Syria: see NEBK, EN.

Ennedi Plateau (ĕnĕdē'), dissected area in SE Sahara, NE Chad territory, Fr. Equatorial Africa, near Anglo-Egyptian Sudan border; rises to 4,756 ft. Abundant wild game. First explored 1934.

Ennell, Lough (lŏkh ĕ'nŭl), lake (5 mi. long, 2 mi. wide), S Co. Westmeath, Ireland, 2 mi. SW of Mullingar; drained by Brosna R. Contains several wooded islets.

Ennenda (ĕnĕn'dä), town (pop. 2,804), Glarus canton, E central Switzerland, opposite Glarus, on Linth R.; woolen and cotton textiles (notably carpets), paper products.

Ennepe River (ĕ'nŭpŭ), W Germany, rises 1 mi. SE of Halver, flows c.25 mi. N and NW, past Gevelsberg, to the Ruhr at Hagen. Dammed in upper course.

Ennepetal (ĕ'nŭpŭtäl"), town (pop. 22,386), in former Prussian prov. of Westphalia, W Germany, after 1945 in North Rhine-Westphalia, in the Ruhr, on the Ennepe and 2 mi. SE of Gevelsberg; foundries, rolling mills; mfg. of agr. machinery and implements, tools, hardware, textiles, fireproof bricks. Formed (1949) through incorporation of Milspe (mĭl'spŭ) and Voerde (or Vörde) (fûr'dŭ). Hasper dam and reservoir c.2 mi. ESE.

Ennerdale Water, lake in the Lake District, SW Cumberland, England, 8 mi. ESE of Whitehaven; 2½ mi. long, ½ mi. wide. Fed by the Liza, drained by the Ehen.

Ennery (ĕnrē'), town (1950 census pop. 537), Artibonite dept., N central Haiti, 14 mi. E of Gonaïves, in agr. region (coffee, cotton, fruit).

Ennetbaden (ĕ'nĕtbä"dŭn), town (pop. 2,305), Aargau canton, N Switzerland, on Limmat R. opposite Baden; curative baths; leather, chemicals, metalworking.

Ennezat (ĕnzä'), agr. village (pop. 676), Puy-de-Dôme dept., central France, in the Limagne, 5 mi. E of Riom. Radio transmitter.

Ennigerloh (ĕ'nĭgŭrlō"), village (pop. 6,508), in former Prussian prov. of Westphalia, NW Germany, after 1945 in North Rhine-Westphalia, 7 mi. NE of Ahlen; grain, cattle.

Ennigloh (ĕ'nĭglō), village (pop. 6,982), in former Prussian prov. of Westphalia, NW Germany, after 1945 in North Rhine-Westphalia, 7 mi. NNW of Herford; grain.

Ennis (ĕ'nĭs), Gaelic *Inis,* urban district (pop. 5,871), ⊙ Co. Clare, Ireland, in center of co., on Fergus R. and 120 mi. WSW of Dublin; agr. market (grain, potatoes; dairying); rope and fishnet mfg. Site of R.C. cathedral of Killaloe diocese; has restored Franciscan abbey (founded 1242) and monuments to Daniel O'Connell and to the Manchester Martyrs. Near by are remains of Clare Abbey (1194) and Killone Abbey (1190).

Ennis. 1 Village (pop. c.350), Madison co., SW Mont., on Madison R. and 60 mi. SE of Butte. Near-by Ennis L. (artificial) is part of hydroelectric project. **2** City (pop. 7,815), Ellis co., N Texas, 32 mi. SSE of Dallas; market, processing point in rich blackland agr. region (cotton, grain, poultry, dairy products); railroad shops; cotton ginning, grain milling, poultry packing, mfg. of metal tags, oil-field equipment, paper goods. Settled c.1870, inc. 1893.

Enniscorthy (ĕ"nĭskôr'thē), Gaelic *Inis Córthaidh,* urban district (pop. 6,020), central Co. Wexford, Ireland, on Slaney R. and 13 mi. NNW of Wexford; agr. market (stock raising, dairying; potatoes); flour milling, iron founding, brewing, tobacco processing, bacon and ham curing, mfg. of electrical equipment, earthenware. Has keep of 12th-cent. Norman castle taken 1649 by Cromwell. St. Aidan's Cathedral (by Pugin) is seat of Ferns diocese. In 1798 town was sacked by United Irishmen, who attacked from near-by Vinegar Hill.

Enniskerry (ĕ"nĭskĕ'rē), Gaelic *Áth na Sgairbhe,* town (pop. 145), NE Co. Wicklow, Ireland, 11 mi. SSE of Dublin; agr. market (cattle, sheep; potatoes); resort.

Enniskillen (ĕ"nĭskĭ'lŭn), municipal borough (1937 pop. 4,880; 1951 census 6,318), ⊙ Co. Fermanagh, Northern Ireland, on isl. in river bet. Upper and Lower Lough Erne, 65 mi. WSW of Belfast; agr. market in potato-growing and cattle-raising region; cutlery mfg. Town was a stronghold of the Maguires. After Tyrone's rebellion English families were settled here. In 1689 forces of William III defeated those of James II here. Enniskillen became noted Protestant stronghold. Regimental barracks incorporate remains of anc. castle.

Ennistymon or **Ennistimon** (ĕ"nĭstĭ'mŭn), Gaelic *Inis Díomáin,* town (pop. 1,197), W Co. Clare, Ireland, near head of Liscannor Bay, 15 mi. WNW of Ennis; agr. market (dairying; grain, potatoes).

Ennore, India: see ENNUR.

Enns (ĕns), town (pop. 7,661), E Upper Austria, on the Enns, near its junction with the Danube, and 10 mi. SE of Linz; sugar refineries, breweries. One of Austria's oldest towns; established as a fortress in 9th cent.; chartered 1212, thus becoming Austria's 1st "city." Has Gothic church, mus. with Roman relics, and an old castle, the Ennsegg or Ennseck. Lorch (lôrkh), anc. *Laureacum,* inc. 1938 into Enns, is on site of Roman camp established c.170 A.D. by Marcus Aurelius.

Enns River (ĕns), central Austria, rises in the Niedere Tauern of Salzburg, 11 mi. S of Radstadt; flows E through Styria, through a gorge (Gesäuse) in Ennstal Alps thence N (at hydroelectric station of Hieflau) into Upper Austria, past Steyr (where it receives Steyr R.) and Enns, to the Danube 10 mi. SE of Linz. Length, 160 mi. Peat bogs in upper valley. Navigable below Steyr.

Ennstal Alps (ĕns'täl), range of Eastern Alps in Styria, central Austria, flanking Enns R. bet. Admont (W) and Hieflau (E). Highest peak, Hochtor (7,782 ft.). Enns R. gorge (followed by road and railroad) called the Gesäuse.

Ennur or **Ennore** (both: ĕnōōr'), village, Chingleput dist., E Madras, India; suburb (15 mi. N) of Madras; fishery research station (oysters, prawns). Motor-car assembly plant opened 1949.

Eno (ĕ'nō), village (commune pop. 10,443), Kuopio co., E Finland, on Pielinen R. and 17 mi. NE of Joensuu; lumbering. Quartz quarries near by.

Enoch, Loch (lŏkh ē'nŏk), lake (½ mi. long, ½ mi. wide) in NW Kirkcudbright, Scotland, 13 mi. N of Newton Stewart, at foot of Merrick mtn.

Enoggera (ĭnŏ'gŭrŭ), NW suburb (pop. 6,057) of Brisbane, SE Queensland, Australia; truck gardening.

Enola (ēnō'lŭ), village (pop. c.2,500), Cumberland co., S central Pa., 4 mi. NW of Harrisburg, across Susquehanna R.; railroad shops; mfg. of gases.

Enon (ē'nŏn), village (pop. 462), Clark co., W central Ohio, 7 mi. WSW of Springfield, in agr. area.

Enontekiö (ĕ'nōntĕ"kēü), Swedish *Enontekis* (ā'nôntä"kĭs), village (commune pop. 1,897), Lapi co., NW Finland, on L. Ounas, Finnish *Ounasjärvi* (ō'näsyăr"vē) (7 mi. long, 1–2 mi. wide), 95 mi. ENE of Kiruna; Lapp trade center.

Enon Valley (ē'nŭn), borough (pop. 392), Lawrence co., W Pa., 12 mi. SSW of New Castle.

Enoree (ĕ'nŭrē), village (pop. 1,045), Spartanburg co., NW S.C., on Enoree R. and 20 mi. S of Spartanburg; cotton mills.

Enoree River, NW S.C., rises in the Blue Ridge foothills N of Greenville, flows 85 mi. SE, past Enoree and Whitmire, to Broad R. 15 mi. NE of Newberry.

Enos (ē'nŭs), Turkish *Enez* (formerly *İnoz*) (ĕnĕz'), anc. *Aenos* or *Aenus*, modern Gr. *Ainos*, village (pop. 566), Adrianople prov., Turkey in Europe, on Gulf of Enos (inlet of Aegean Sea) at mouth of Maritsa R., 38 mi. NW of Gallipoli. Founded by Aeolian colonists, it was once an important port, supplanted (late 19th cent.) by Alexandroupolis.

Enosburg (ē'nŭsbûrg), town (pop. 2,101), Franklin co., NW Vt., 15 mi. NE of St. Albans and on Missisquoi R.; lumber, truck, dairy products. Chartered 1780. Its village of **Enosburg Falls** (pop. 1,289) makes patent medicines, textile equipment.

Eno-shima, Japan: see KATASE.

Enotah, Mount, Ga.: see BRASSTOWN BALD.

Enotayevka, Russian SFSR: see YENOTAYEVKA.

Énova (ā'nōvä), village (pop. 1,175), Valencia prov., E Spain, 5 mi. NE of Játiva; rice, oranges.

En-p'ing, China: see YANPING.

Enri, Formosa: see YÜANLI.

Enrick River, Scotland: see GLEN URQUHART.

Enriquillo (ĕnrēkē'yō), town (1950 pop. 2,160), Barahona prov., SW Dominican Republic, on the Caribbean, 24 mi. SSW of Barahona; coffee; hardwood.

Enriquillo, Lake, salt lake (□ c.75), Bahoruco prov., SW Dominican Republic; extends c.30 mi. W–E, up to 6 mi. wide, in a depression c.150 ft. below sea level. Surrounded by tropical forests, the lake abounds in iguanas and wild fowl. Hunting and fishing ground. In its center is Cabritos Isl. (c.5 mi. long). Near its shore are La Descubierta (N), Neiba (E), Duvergé (E).

Ensanche Colonia Sarmiento (ĕnsän'chā kōlō'nyä särmyĕn'tō), village (pop. estimate 300), central Comodoro Rivadavia military zone, Argentina, on Senguerr R. and 55 mi. NW of Sarmiento, in sheep-raising area. Until 1946 in Chubut natl. territory.

Enschede (ĕn'skhŭdā'), town (pop. 80,346; commune pop. 101,015), Overijssel prov., E Netherlands, on Twente Canal and 6 mi. SE of Hengelo; rail junction and customs station near Ger. border; Twente airport is 3 mi. N. A center of textile and textile-machinery industries; also mfg. of paper, plastics, chemicals, dairy products; egg market. Town, destroyed by fire in 1862, was completely rebuilt.

Ensdorf (ĕns'dôrf), town (pop. 5,390), SW Saar, on Saar R., just SE of Saarlouis; coal mining.

Ensenada (ĕnsānä'dä), town (pop. 18,042), NE Buenos Aires prov., Argentina, port on the Río de la Plata and suburb (5 mi. NE) of La Plata; meat-packing and fishing center; shipyards; mfg.: ceramics, hats, dairy products, fish oil. Ships grain, meat.

Ensenada, village (1930 pop. 113), Llanquihue prov., S central Chile, resort on E shore of L. Llanquihue, and 28 mi. NE of Puerto Montt, bet. Osorno and Calbuco volcanoes, on road to Argentina via Pérez Rosales Pass.

Ensenada, city (pop. 4,616), Northern Territory, Lower California, NW Mexico, port on Todos Santos Bay (Pacific), and 65 mi. SE of San Diego, Calif. Major fishing (tuna, corvina, barracuda, shrimps, oysters, lobsters), and fish-canning center, in irrigated valley (wheat, wine, beans); wineries, flour mills. Hot springs, and iron, kaolin, gypsum, onyx, and salt deposits near by.

Ensenada, village (pop. 4,730), SW Puerto Rico, on Guánica Bay, opposite Guánica, 21 mi. W of Ponce (linked by railroad); site of Guánica sugar mill, one of largest in the isl. Has fine harbor.

Ensenada Honda (ĕnsänä'dä ōn'dä), small, deep bay in E Puerto Rico, opposite Vieques Isl., 2 mi. S of Ceiba; surrounded by Roosevelt Roads, U.S. naval reservation. Fort Bundi is on N shore.

Ensheim (ĕns'hīm), town (pop. 3,065), S Saar, 6 mi. ESE of Saarbrücken; mfg. of steel products.

Enshih (ŭn'shŭ'), town (pop. 15,577), ⊙ Enshih co. (pop. 340,206), SW Hupeh prov., China, on Ching R. and 110 mi. WSW of Ichang, and on road to Szechwan; rice, wheat, beans, cotton. Iron deposits near by. Until 1912, Shihnan.

Ensign, city (pop. 227), Gray co., SW Kansas, 13 mi. SW of Dodge City, in grain region.

Ensisheim (āsēzĕm', Ger. ĕn'sĭs-hīm), town (pop. 3,212), Haut-Rhin dept., E France, on the Ill and 8 mi. N of Mulhouse; road center; potash mining. Its 16th-cent. town hall damaged in Second World War. Penitentiary.

Ensival (āsēväl'), town (pop. 5,584), Liége prov., E Belgium, on Vesdre R., just SW of Verviers; wool spinning and weaving.

Enso, Russian SFSR: see SVETOGORSK.

Ensui, Formosa: see YENSHUI.

Enta, Tibet: see NGEMDA.

Ent Air Force Base, Colo.: see COLORADO SPRINGS.

Entebbe (ĕntĕ'bŭ), town (pop. 7,933), ⊙ Uganda, in Buganda prov., port on NW shore of L. Victoria, 325 mi. WNW of Nairobi (Kenya); 0°4'N 32°28'E. Administrative center with fine residences of Br. officials. Has botanical gardens, recreation facilities; White Fathers mission, technical school. Airport (W). Kampala, Uganda's chief commercial center, is 19 mi. NNE.

Enterprise. 1 City (pop. 7,288), ⊙ Coffee co., SE Ala., 28 mi. WNW of Dothan; mfg., processing center for agr. area (peanuts, corn, cotton, livestock); work clothes, children's wear, peanut butter, peanut and vegetable oils, cotton, lumber; meat packing. Inc. 1899. Destruction of cotton crop (1910–15) by boll weevil led to successful conversion to peanut culture and diversified farming. Boll Weevil Monument (erected 1919) commemorates event. U.S. resettlement project was established near by in 1935. **2** City (pop. 795), Dickinson co., central Kansas, on Smoky Hill R. and 5 mi. ESE of Abilene; flour milling, metalworking. **3** Town (pop. 691), Clarke co., E Miss., 15 mi. SSW of Meridian and on Chickasawhay R. **4** City (pop. 1,718), ⊙ Wallowa co., NE Oregon, on Wallowa R., N of Wallowa L., and 40 mi. ENE of La Grande; alt. 3,757 ft.; trade center for near-by ranches; hq. for Wallowa Natl. Forest; lumber, dairy products. Inc. 1889. State fish hatchery here. **5** Town (pop. 790), Washington co., SW Utah, 33 mi. NNW of St. George; alt. 5,500 ft.; livestock.

Entfelden, Switzerland: see OBERENTFELDEN.

Entiat (ĕn'tēăt), town (pop. 420), Chelan co., central Wash., on the Columbia at mouth of the Entiat and 19 mi. N of Wenatchee.

Entiat Mountains, Wash.: see CASCADE RANGE.

Entiat River, central Wash., rises in the Cascades W of L. Chelan, flows c.50 mi. SE, bet. Chelan and Entiat ranges, to the Columbia at Entiat. Its narrow irrigated valley produces apples, and is gateway to mtn. recreational areas.

Enticcio (ĕntĭ'chō), village (pop. 1,130), Tigre prov., N Ethiopia, near Eritrean border, on Aduwa-Adigrat road; cereals, livestock.

Entlebuch (ĕnt'lŭbōōkh), district (pop. 18,375) and valley of upper Kleine Emme R., Lucerne canton, central Switzerland.

Entlebuch, town (pop. 3,190), Lucerne canton, central Switzerland, on Kleine Emme R., at mouth of Entlen R., and 13 mi. WSW of Lucerne; plywood, woolen textiles, foodstuffs.

Entotto, Ethiopia: see INTOTTO.

Entradas (ĕnträ'dŭsh), village (pop. 1,594), Beja dist., S Portugal, 18 mi. SSW of Beja; grain, sheep.

Entraigues-sur-la-Sorgue (ātrăg'-sür-lä-sôrg'), village (pop. 1,467), Vaucluse dept., SE France, 7 mi. NE of Avignon; ramie spinning, mfg. of condensers.

Entrammes (ātrăm'), village (pop. 371), Mayenne dept., W France, 6 mi. S of Laval; known for its cheese (*Port du Salut*).

Entraygues (ātrăg'), village (pop. 1,078), Aveyron dept., S France, on the Lot at mouth of the Truyère, 20 mi. N of Rodez; road center; tanning. Uranium ore mined near by.

Entrecasteaux (ātrŭkästō'), village (pop. 301), Var dept., SE France, 11 mi. W of Draguignan; wine-growing.

Entrecasteaux Islands, D', Territory of Papua: see D'ENTRECASTEAUX ISLANDS.

Entre-Deux, L' (lă'trŭ-dû), town and commune (pop. 3,806), S Réunion isl., on road and 6 mi. N of Saint-Pierre; cotton, coffee.

Entre-Deux-Guiers (ātrŭ-dû-gyâr'), village (pop. 626), Isère dept., SE France, at junction of 2 headstreams of Guiers R. and 17 mi. N of Grenoble, opposite Les Échelles (Savoie dept.); mfg. (paper, canes, furniture, leather straps).

Entre-deux-Mers (–mâr') [Fr.,=bet. 2 seas], region in Gironde dept., SW France, bet. Garonne R. (S) and Dordogne R. (N), extending E to Lot-et-Garonne dept. border. Its vineyards produce Bordeaux wines. Cereals, cattle.

Entre Douro e Minho (ĕn'trĭ dō'rōō ē mē'nyōō) [Port.,=bet. the Douro and the Minho], commonly abbreviated to **Minho**, former province (□ 2,749; 1940 pop. 1,679,798), northernmost Portugal; old ⊙ Braga. It contained Viana do Castelo, Braga, and Pôrto dists. Its Atlantic coastline extended from mouth of Minho R. (N) beyond that of the Douro (S). It was part of county of Portugal before Moors were expelled from territory S of the Douro. In 1936, prov. was divided bet. new Minho prov. and N portion of Douro Litoral prov. Sometimes called Entre Minho e Douro.

Entrego, El (ĕl ĕntrā'gō), village (pop. 1,836), Oviedo prov., NW Spain, 15 mi. SE of Oviedo; coal mining, lumbering.

Entre Minho e Douro, Portugal: see ENTRE DOURO E MINHO.

Entremont (ātrŭmō'), district (pop. 8,644), Valais canton, SW Switzerland; extends W and E of Val d'Entremont (valley watered by Drance R.). Includes, among others, communes of Bagnes and Orsières.

Entrena (ĕntrā'nä), town (pop. 1,075), Logroño prov., N Spain, 7 mi. SW of Logroño; cereals, wine, vegetables, livestock.

Entre Ríos (ĕn'trā rē'ōs) [Sp.,=bet. the rivers], province (□ 28,487; pop. 787,362), E Argentina, in MESOPOTAMIA; ⊙ Paraná. Located bet. Paraná R. (W) and Uruguay R. (E; Uruguay border). Low, swampy, fertile, alluvial area with temperate, humid subtropical climate. Principally a stock-raising and farming area; cattle (center, S, SE), horses (S), sheep (NW); hogs, goats, mules; poultry (mostly in E); alfalfa, wheat, corn, flax (S and center), citrus fruit and rice (E); also cotton, sunflowers, peanuts, oats, vegetables. Some clay, sandstone, lime, basalt, and iron deposits. Fisheries along Paraná and Uruguay rivers. Main river ports: Paraná, Bajada Grande, Concordia, Concepción del Uruguay. Rural industries: dairying, lumbering, quarrying, flour milling, tanning, food canning. Urban industries: meat packing (Colón, Paraná, Concordia, Gualeguaychú, Concepción del Uruguay); mfg. of cement, cider, ceramics, plaster, soap, matches, furniture, lard in Paraná. Major resorts: isls. in Paraná R. delta and the historic sites of La Paz, Concordia, and Concepción del Uruguay. Entre Ríos was set up as a province in 1814.

Entre Ríos, town (pop. c.2,900), ⊙ O'Connor (until 1906, Salinas) prov., Tarija dept., S Bolivia, 36 mi E of Tarija; corn. Until 1906, San Luis.

Entre Rios. 1 City, Mato Grosso, Brazil: see RIO BRILHANTE. **2** City, Minas Gerais, Brazil: see JOÃO RIBEIRO. **3** City, Rio de Janeiro, Brazil: see TRÊS RIOS.

Entre Rios (ĕn'trĭ rē'ōōsh), village, Niassa prov., N central Mozambique, on railroad and 130 mi. W of Nampula; corn, tobacco, beans. Formerly called Malema.

Entrevaux (ātrŭvō'), village (pop. 496), Basses-Alpes dept., SE France, on spur above the Var and 29 mi. NW of Nice, in Provence Alps; olive-oil mfg. Has old fortifications.

Entrevernes (ātrŭvârn'), commune (pop. 152), Haute-Savoie dept., SE France, near S tip of L. of Annecy, 8 mi. SSE of Annecy; anthracite mining, limestone quarrying.

Entre-Vesdre-et-Amblève (ā'trŭ-vĕz'drŭ-ā-āblĕv'), region of Liége prov., E central Belgium, bet. Vesdre R. (N) and Amblève R (S); dairying dist. stone quarries. Sprimont, main village.

Entrín or **Entrín Bajo** (ĕntrēn' bä'hō), town (pop. 875), Badajoz prov., W Spain, 17 mi. SE of Badajoz; cereals, livestock.

Entry Island (2 mi. long, 2 mi. wide), in Gulf of St. Lawrence, E Que., one of Magdalen Isls., 60 mi. NNE of Prince Edward Isl.; 47°17'N 61°42'W.

Entry Island, New Zealand: see KAPITI ISLAND.

Entwistle (ĕn'twĭsŭl), village (pop. estimate 200), central Alta., near Pembina R., 60 mi. W of Edmonton; mixed farming, lumbering.

Entzheim (ātsĕm', Ger. ĕnts'hīm), village (pop. 700), Bas-Rhin dept., E France, 7 mi. SW of Strasbourg. Has Strasbourg airport and meteorological station.

Enugu (ĕnōō'gōō), town (pop. 12,959), ⊙ Eastern Provinces, S Nigeria, in Onitsha prov., on railroad and 120 mi. NNE of Port Harcourt; alt. 750 ft. 6°27'N 7°28'E. W Africa's leading coal-mining center; trade in palm oil and kernels, yams, cassava, corn. Has technical school, hospitals.

Enugu Ngwo (ŭn-gwō'), town, Onitsha prov., Eastern Provinces, S Nigeria, on rail spur and 3 mi. WSW of Enugu; coal-mining center.

Enumclaw (ĕ'nŭmklô), town (pop. 2,789), King co., W central Wash., near White R., 22 mi. E of Tacoma, in foothills of Cascade Range. Timber, dairy products, poultry. Gateway to Mt. Rainier recreational area (SE). Founded 1885.

Envermeu (āvĕrmû'), agr. village (pop. 926), Seine-Inférieure dept., N France, 9 mi. ESE of Dieppe; dairying.

Envigado (ĕmvēgä'dō), town (pop. 4,253), Antioquia dept., NW central Colombia, in Cordillera Central, on railroad, on Porce R. and 6 mi. SSW of Medellín; alt. 5,272 ft. Textile milling; agr. products (coffee, corn, sugar cane, beans, yucca, potatoes, bananas).

Enying (ĕ'nyĭng), town (pop. 5,247), Veszprem co., W central Hungary, 20 mi. SSW of Szekesfehervar; wheat, rye, corn; dairy farming.

Enzan (ān'zā), town (pop. 15,199), Yamanashi prefecture, central Honshu, Japan, 10 mi. ENE of Kofu, in rice-growing area; raw silk.

Enza River (ĕn'tsä), N central Italy, rises in Etruscan Apennines 13 mi. ESE of Pontremoli, flows 50 mi. N, past Montechiarugolo and Sorbolo, to Po R. 6 mi. W of Guastalla. Forms Parma-Reggio nell'Emilia prov. boundary.

Enzeli, Iran: see PAHLEVI.
Enz River (ĕnts), S Germany, rises in the Black Forest 6 mi. W of Berneck, flows N, past Wildbad, to Pforzheim, then ENE to the Neckar at Besigheim. Length 65 mi. Receives the Nagold (right).
Eola (ēō'lū), village (1940 pop. 949), Avoyelles parish, E central La., on small Bayou Boeuf and 30 mi. SE of Alexandria, in Eola oil and natural-gas field; makes carbon black.
Eolus, Mount (14,079 ft.), SW Colo., in San Juan Mts., 12 mi. SSE of Silverton.
Eordaia (ĕôrdhä'ū), Lat. *Eordaea* (ēôrdē'ū), region of Greek Macedonia, in intermontane basin bet. Vermion (E) and Mouriki (W) massifs. Chief town, Ptolemais.
Eo River (ĕ'ō), in Lugo and Oviedo provs., NW Spain, rises in Cantabrian Mts. 12 mi. E of Lugo, flows 40 mi. NNE to Bay of Biscay at Ribadeo. Lower course along Lugo-Oviedo prov. border.
Eouo, Fr. Equatorial Africa: see EWO.
Epaktos, Greece: see NAUPAKTOS.
Epanome or **Epanomi** (both: ĕpŭnômē'), town (pop. 4,883), Salonika nome, Macedonia, Greece, on Chalcidice peninsula, 14 mi. S of Salonika; wheat, barley, oats; silk.
Epatlán (āpätlän'), officially San Juan Epatlán, town (pop. 920), Puebla, central Mexico, 7 mi. ENE of Matamoros; cereals, sugar cane, livestock.
Epazoyucan (āpäsoiōō'kän), town (pop. 1,546), Hidalgo, central Mexico, 10 mi. SE of Pachuca; corn, maguey, stock.
Epe (ā'pū), village (pop. 9,479), in former Prussian prov. of Westphalia, NW Germany, after 1945 in North Rhine-Westphalia, 3 mi. SSE of Gronau; grain, cattle.
Epe (ā'pū), town (pop. 3,654), Gelderland prov., E central Netherlands, 10 mi. N of Apeldoorn; egg and wooden-shoe market.
Epe (ĕ'pē), town (pop. 16,760), Nigeria colony, on coastal lagoon and 18 mi. SSE of Ijebu-Ode; trade center; cacao, palm oil and kernels. Bitumen deposits.
Epecuén, Lake (āpākwĕn') (□ 15), W Buenos Aires prov., Argentina, 110 mi. NNW of Bahía Blanca; 10 mi. long, 4 mi. wide. Its high salinity (38%) gives it therapeutic value. Carhué is on SE shore, health resort of Lago Epecuén on E shore. Salt and sodium sulphate are extracted.
Epeiros, Greece: see EPIRUS.
Epen (ā'pūn), town (pop. 384), Limburg prov., SE Netherlands, 11 mi. ESE of Maastricht, near Belg. border; resort.
Epéna (ĕpĕnä'), village, N Middle Congo territory, Fr. Equatorial Africa, on Likouala-aux-herbes R. and 40 mi. WSW of Impfondo; native market (palm kernels, copal, kola nuts, rubber); palm-oil milling, cacao plantations.
Eperjes, Czechoslovakia: see PRESOV.
Épernay (āpârnā'), town (pop. 18,716), Marne dept., N France, on left bank of the Marne and 15 mi. SSW of Rheims; a leading mfg. and shipping center of champagne wines grown in area, and hq. for some of oldest and best-known firms. Produces wine-processing and corking equipment, corks and casks. Wine is bottled, carbonated, and stored in labyrinthine caves (c.30 mi. long), which have been dug in surrounding chalk hills. Épernay was besieged by Henry IV in 1592 and bombarded during Ludendorff's "peace offensive" in 1918.
Épernon (āpĕrnõ'), village (pop. 1,765), Eure-et-Loir dept., N central France, 7 mi. WSW of Rambouillet; flour milling, grindstone mfg. Tourist resort. Damaged in Second World War.
Epes (ĕps), town (pop. 342), Sumter co., W Ala., on Tombigbee R. and 20 mi. NW of Demopolis.
Ephesus (ĕ'fūsūs), anc. Greek city of Asia Minor near mouth of the Cayster (modern Kucuk Menderes) in present-day W Asiatic Turkey, 32 mi. SSE of Smyrna. One of greatest of Ionian cities, whose wealth was proverbial. Passed from Lydian to Persian control. Its great temple to Artemis was burned down (4th cent. B.C.), but rebuilding began before Alexander the Great took Ephesus in 334 B.C. City passed (133 B.C.) to the Romans, under whom it was ⊙ prov. of Asia. Its great temple of Artemis (called temple of Diana by the Romans) was considered one of the Seven Wonders of the World. Ephesus became a center of Christianity and was visited by St. Paul, who addressed an epistle to the congregation. City was sacked (A.D. 262) by the Goths and temple destroyed; later somewhat restored. Seat of church council in 431. Harbor silted up and Ephesus was abandoned. Excavation (1869–74) of ruins of temple uncovered many artifacts, including sculptures by Phidias and Polycletus and a portrait of Alexander. Other ruins of interest include cathedral of St. John, which incorporated some materials from the old temple.
Ephraim (ē'frēūm). **1** City (pop. 1,987), Sanpete co., central Utah, in irrigated Sanpete Valley, just W of Wasatch Plateau, 60 mi. S of Provo; alt. 5,543 ft.; food processing (canned vegetables, cheese, flour, poultry); lumber. Jr. col. and mus. of Indian relics are here. Manti Natl. Forest just E. Settled 1854, inc. 1868. **2** Resort village (pop. 244), Door co., NE Wis., on Door Peninsula, on Green Bay, 24 mi. NE of Sturgeon Bay City. Annual regatta is held here. Founded 1853 as Moravian colony. Peninsula State Park is near by.
Ephraim, Hills of (ē'frūm), small range of low hills, NW Israel, extending c.15 mi. N–S bet. N edge of Plain of Sharon and Mt. Carmel, bounded by Mediterranean (W) and Plain of Jezreel (E). Rise to c.650 ft. Largest of several agr. settlements here is Zikhron Ya'aqov.
Ephrata (ĕfrä'tä), village (pop. 23), Commewijne dist., N Du. Guiana, landing on Cottica R. and 27 mi. E of Paramaribo; trading post in sugar- and coffeegrowing region.
Ephrata, Palestine: see BETHLEHEM.
Ephrata. 1 (ĕ'frūtū) Industrial borough (pop. 7,027), Lancaster co., SE Pa., 12 mi. NE of Lancaster, in rich agr. and stock-raising area; clothing, textiles, furniture, shoes, tobacco, metal products, paper boxes, fertilizer, bricks. Settled 1728–33 as communal religious community by German Seventh-day Baptists under leadership of Johann Conrad Beissel; established one of earliest printing presses in country. Their Ephrata Cloisters are now a state-maintained historical shrine. Inc. 1891. **2** (ēfrā'tū) Town (pop. 4,589), ⊙ Grant co., central Wash., 35 mi. E of Wenatchee, at S end of the Grand Coulee; wheat, alfalfa, apples. Airforce training base in Second World War. Inc. 1909.
Epi (ā'pē), volcanic island (□ 141; pop. c.2,000), New Hebrides, SW Pacific, 90 mi. SE of Espiritu Santo; c.27 mi. long, c.11 mi. wide; copra, cacao. Formerly Tasiko.
Epidamnus, Albania: see DURAZZO.
Epidaurus (ĕpĭdô'rūs), anc. town of Argolis, NE Peloponnesus, Greece, on Saronic Gulf, 20 mi. ENE of Nauplia. Here are ruins of anc. fortifications and temple of Artemis. Its fame lay in the sanctuary of Asclepius, of which there are remains of the celebrated temple, stadium, and theater. A trading and shipping city, Epidaurus colonized Aegina, Kos, Kalymnos, and Nisyros isls. It declined after loss of Aegina (580 B.C.). Just W of anc. site is modern village of Palaia Epidauros or Palaia Epidhavros [Gr.,=old Epidaurus] (pop. 926), formerly called Epidavra. NW of anc. site is modern town of Nea Epidauros or Nea Epidhavros [Gr.,=new Epidaurus] (pop. 1,333), formerly called Piada. Here Gr. independence was proclaimed (1822).
Epidaurus Limera, Greece: see MONEMVASIA.
Épierre (āpyâr'), village (pop. 421), Savoie dept., SE France, in Alpine Maurienne valley, on the Arc and 12 mi. NNW of Saint-Jean-de-Maurienne; electro-chemical works (phosphorus refining).
Epifan, Russian SFSR: see YEPIFAN.
Epilä (ĕ'pĭlä), suburb of Tampere, Häme co., SW Finland, on L. Pyhä, 3 mi. W of city center; tannery, dye works.
Epila (ā'pēlä), town (pop. 5,096), Saragossa prov., NE Spain, near Jalón R., 20 mi. WSW of Saragossa; sugar refineries, flour mills, alcohol distilleries; wine, cereals, fruit.
Épinac-les-Mines (āpēnäk'-lā-mēn'), village (pop. 1,368), Saône-et-Loire dept., E central France, 10 mi. ENE of Autun; coal mining since 1755.
Épinal (āpēnäl'), town (pop. 21,939), ⊙ Vosges dept., E France, on the Moselle (head of navigation) and 37 mi. SSE of Nancy; center of Vosges cotton-weaving industry. Produces lingerie, brushes, nougats, glucose. Hand embroidering and mineral oil processing. Known for its mfg. of popular colored pictures (*images d'Épinal*). Has 11th–14th-cent. church of Saint-Maurice. Founded (10th cent.) by bishops of Metz, it passed (1466) to duchy of Lorraine. It fell to Prussians in 1870 and was later fortified, remaining in Fr. hands during First World War. It suffered heavy damages during Second World War. U.S. military cemetery 2.5 mi. S.
Épinay-sur-Orge (āpēnā'-sür-ôrzh'), town (pop. 2,855), Seine-et-Oise dept., N central France, 12 mi. S of Paris. Insane asylum.
Épinay-sur-Seine (–sĕn'), town (pop. 16,198), Seine dept., N central France, a residential N suburb of Paris, 7 mi. from Notre Dame Cathedral, on right bank of the Seine, NW of Saint-Denis; forges, foundries; mfg. (chemicals, precision tools, glass, chocolate).
Épine, L', Marne dept., France: see LÉPINE.
Épine, Montagne de l' (mõtä'nyū dū lāpēn'), narrow limestone range in Savoie dept., SE France, extending c.10 mi. from the Grande-Chartreuse (S) to the Mont du Chat (N), and overlooking Chambéry trough (E). Rises to 4,700 ft.
Epiphania, Syria: see HAMA, city.
Epirus (ĕpī'rūs), Gr. *Epeirus* or *Ipiros* (both: ē'pĭrôs) [=mainland], NW division (□ 3,495; pop. 350,134) of Greece; ⊙ Ioannina. Bounded NW by Albania, W by Ionian Sea, S by Gulf of Arta, and E by main PINDUS system (which separates it from Macedonia and Thessaly), Epirus is a land of limestone ridges and valleys with a few alluvial plains drained by Thyamis, Acheron, Arachthos, and upper Aoos rivers and containing L. Ioannina. Located on the windward side of the Pindus, Epirus receives the heaviest annual rainfall (50 in.) of the Gr. mainland and has a relatively high annual temp. range. Traditionally known as a leading livestock-raising region, rearing mainly goats and sheep, it also produces hardy grains (barley), corn, fruit (pears, almonds), and in its sheltered areas olives and citrus fruit. Dairy and other livestock products are an important item. Fisheries along coast and in lagoons off Gulf of Arta. Main centers, Ioannina, Arta, and Preveza, are linked by highways. Epirus is divided administratively into the nomes of ARTA, IOANNINA, PREVEZA, and THESPROTIA. Modern Gr. Epirus occupies only the major S portion of anc. Epirus, a region that extended from the region of modern S Albania to the Acroceraunian promontory, where it bordered on Illyria. Its chief centers were Phoenice, Buthrotum, Dodona, and, later, Ambracia. The original Epirote tribes, apparently of Illyrian or Dorian stock, were barely known to the Greeks, who were, however, acquainted with the oracle at Dodona. The tribes were unified (after 4th cent. B.C.) under the hegemony of the Molossi, the most powerful Epirote group, whose chiefs became the paramount rulers. The Molossian kingdom reached its height under Pyrrhus (319–272 B.C.), whose costly victory over the Romans at Asculum (279 B.C.) was the original "Pyrrhic victory." The monarchy ended c.230 B.C. and a republic (the Epirote League) was set up with its ⊙ at Phoenice. Epirus sided with Macedon in the wars against Rome, was sacked 167 B.C. by Aemilius Paulus, and became a Roman prov., for which Octavian (Augustus) built (31 B.C.) a new capital at Nicopolis. The region was neglected in Byzantine times, when it was known as Epirus Vetus as opposed to Epirus Nova (central and N Albania). Following the conquest (1204) of Constantinople by the Crusaders, an independent despotat of Epirus was set up by Michael Angelus of the Comnenian line, lasting until 1318. After brief domination (middle 14th cent.) by the Serbs, Epirus passed to Turks following their capture of Ioannina (1430). Under Ottoman rule, Ali Pasha of Ioannina controlled (late 18th cent.) a semi-independent state in Epirus. Following Gr. independence, SE Epirus (E of Arachthos or Arta R.) passed to Greece in 1881, and SW Epirus followed in 1913 (confirmed 1919), N Epirus remaining part of Albania.
Episcopia (ĕpēskô'pyä), village (pop. 1,064), Potenza prov., Basilicata, S Italy, near Sinni R., 5 mi. W of Latronico; woolen mills.
Episcopia-Bihorului (ĕpēskô'pyä-bē'hôrōōlōōē), Hung. *Biharpüspoki* (bē'hŏrpü'spôkē), village (pop. 3,903), Bihor prov., W Rumania, 6 mi. N of Oradea; rail junction and frontier station near Hung. border; stone quarrying. In Hungary, 1940–45.
Episkopi (ĕpēskôpē'), village (pop. 1,236), Limassol dist., SW Cyprus, near Episkopi Bay, 7 mi. W of Limassol, in agr. region (grain, fruit, stock). Adjoined W by ruined city of CURIUM.
Episkopi Bay, small Mediterranean inlet of SW Cyprus, bounded E by Akrotiri Peninsula and Cape Zeughari. At its head is site of anc. Curium.
Epitácio Pessoa, Brazil: see PEDRO AVELINO.
Epitalion (ĕpĭtä'lēōn), village (pop. 2,548), Elis nome, W Peloponnesus, Greece, bet. Alpheus R. and N end of L. of Agoulinitsa, on railroad and 4 mi. SE of Pyrgos; livestock raising (cattle, sheep); olive oil, Zante currants, wheat. Formerly called Agoulinitsa or Agulinitsa.
Epitalion, Lake of, Greece: see AGOULINITSA, LAKE OF.
Epleny, Hungary: see OLASZFALU.
Epomanduodurum, France: see MANDEURE.
Eporedia, Italy: see IVREA.
Eport, Loch, Scotland: see NORTH UIST.
Eppan, Italy: see APPIANO.
Eppelborn (ĕ'pūlbôrn"), town (pop. 4,260), central Saar, 12 mi. N of Saarbrücken; agr. market (stock, grain).
Eppelheim (ĕ'pūlhīm), village (pop. 5,080), N Baden, Germany, after 1945 in Württemberg-Baden, 3 mi. W of Heidelberg; truck farming (vegetables, fruit); vineyards.
Eppendorf (ĕ'pūndôrf). **1** N district of Hamburg, NW Germany, on right bank of the Alster, opposite Winterhude dist., adjoining (S) Harvestehude dist.; site of Hamburg municipal hosp. **2** Village (pop. 4,643), Saxony, E central Germany, at N foot of the Erzgebirge, 10 mi. SW of Freiberg; cotton milling; mfg. of furniture, toys, cigars.
Eppeville (ĕpvĕl'), village (pop. 1,033), Somme dept., N France, on the Somme opposite Ham, and 13 mi. SW of Saint-Quentin; sugar milling, wire drawing.
Epping, residential urban district (1931 pop. 4,956; 1951 census 6,934), W Essex, England, 15 mi. NNE of London, at N edge of Epping Forest; agr. market. Has anc. church (probably 11th cent.). Epping Forest (the anc. royal Waltham Forest) originally included all Essex but was reduced to 5,600 acres when it became public park in 1882. Has numerous literary associations.
Epping. 1 Town (pop. 1,796), Rockingham co., SE N.H., 15 mi. W of Portsmouth and on Lamprey R.; mfg. (shoes, bricks). Early settlement, set off from Exeter 1741. **2** Village (pop. 158), Williams co., NW N.Dak., 16 mi. NE of Williston, near Epping–Spring Brook dam, large earthfill dam.

Eppingen (ĕp′pĭng-ŭn), town (pop. 4,836), N Baden, Germany, after 1945 in Württemberg-Baden, on the Elsenz and 14 mi. E of Bruchsal; tobacco, sugar beets; vineyards.

Epps, village (pop. 308), West Carroll parish, NE La., 37 mi. ENE of Monroe, in agr. area; cotton ginning, stave mfg.

Eppstein (ĕp′shtīn), village (pop. 1,530), Rhenish Palatinate, W Germany, 2 mi. SW of Frankenthal; wine. Has 12th-cent. castle, 15th-cent. church.

Epsom (ĕp′sŭm), residential town (1931 pop. 27,089) now in Epsom and Ewell municipal borough (1951 census pop. 68,049), N central Surrey, England, 14 mi. SW of London. Epsom Downs is scene of horse races, notably the Derby (founded 1780), named for the earl of Derby, and the "Oaks" named for his estate. Epsom Col. is school for sons of medical men. There are medicinal springs from which the name Epsom salts is derived.

Epsom, town (pop. 756), Merrimack co., S central N.H., on Suncook R. and 10 mi. E of Concord; agr. Includes Gossville village.

Epte River (ĕpt), NW France, rises E of Forges-les-Eaux (Seine-Inférieure dept.), flows 60 mi. S, past Gournay and Gisors, forming Eure-Oise and Eure–Seine-et-Oise dept. border, to the Seine above Vernon.

Epulu (ĕpōō′lōō), village, Eastern Prov., E Belgian Congo, 95 mi. W of Irumu, in cotton-growing region; tourist center, base for hunting expeditions and for excursions to Pygmy haunts in the forests of Ituri region.

Epureni (ĕpōōrān′), village (pop. 1,458), Barlad prov., E Rumania, 2 mi. NNW of Husi.

Epuyén (āpōōyĕn′), village (pop. estimate 600), NW Chubut natl. territory, Argentina, at E end of L. Epuyén, in the Andes, 45 mi. NNW of Esquel; alfalfa, oats, wheat, sheep, goats. Coal deposits near by.

Epuyén, Lake (□ 7; alt. 994 ft.), in the Andes, NW Chubut natl. territory, Argentina; 7 mi. long, 1–2 mi. wide.

Epworth, village and parish (pop. 1,795), Parts of Lindsey, NW Lincolnshire, England, 10 mi. N of Gainsborough, chief town of the Isle of AXHOLME; agr. market, with agr.-machinery works. John Wesley b. here.

Epworth, town (pop. 536), Dubuque co., E Iowa, 13 mi. WSW of Dubuque, in agr. area.

Eqlid, Iran: see IQLID.

Eqron, 'Eqron, or **Ekron** (all: ĕkrōn′), settlement (pop. 475), W Israel, in Judaean Plain, 3 mi. SSE of Rehovot; mixed farming. Founded 1883. Also called Mazkeret Batyah, Mazkereth Batya, or Matzkeret Batya (all: mätskĕrĕt′ bätyä′).

Equality, village (pop. 830), Gallatin co., SE Ill., on Saline R. and 10 mi. E of Harrisburg, in agr. area.

Equator, village, Rift Valley prov., W Kenya, at W rim of Great Rift Valley, on the equator, on railroad and 12 mi. SW of Eldama Ravine; alt. 8,716 ft. Coffee, wheat, corn.

Equatoria, province (□ 76,995; 1948 pop. estimate 620,344), southernmost Anglo-Egyptian Sudan; ⊙ Juba. Bordered by Belgian Congo and Uganda (S), Kenya (SE), and Ethiopia (E), it consists of lowland (N) and mtn. ranges (Imatong Mts., S). Drained by the Bahr el Jebel (White Nile); consists mainly of savanna and tropical woodlands (annual rainfall 45 in.). Agr. (cotton, peanuts, sesame, corn, durra), stock raising (cattle, sheep, goats). Main centers are Juba and Torit. Formerly called Mongalla prov., it was amalgamated (1935) with Bahr el Ghazal prov. to form Equatoria prov. and again separated in 1948.

Equatorial Current, surface drift current moving W in the oceans along the equator. Caused by the trade winds, it consists generally of a South Equatorial Current forming part of the counterclockwise circulation in the S hemisphere and a North Equatorial Current forming part of the clockwise circulation in the N hemisphere. These 2 currents are generally separated by a compensating Equatorial Countercurrent. The equatorial currents are best developed in the Atlantic and Pacific oceans, but are strongly affected by the monsoons in the Indian Ocean.

Equatorial Islands: see LINE ISLANDS.

Equator Province, Fr. *Equateur* (ākätûr′), province (□ 155,680; 1948 pop. 1,601,427), NW and W Belgian Congo; ⊙ Coquilhatville. Bordered by Fr. Equatorial Africa along Ubangi R. in N, NW, and W, and along Congo R. in SW. Lies almost entirely within Congo basin (mean alt. 1,200 ft.) and is covered with dense equatorial forest, save in N, where there are extensive savannas. Natives gather copal, palm kernels, palm oil, and cotton; Europeans have coffee, cacao, and rubber plantations. African food staples (manioc, yams, rice, plantains) are also grown. Some apiculture, fishing, stock raising. Cotton ginning, palm-oil milling, soap making. Navigable waterways are main means of transport; there are no railroads. Chief centers: Coquilhatville, Lisala, Boende, Basankusu. Prov. was called Coquilhatville, 1935–47.

Équeurdreville (ākûrdrüvēl′), residential W suburb (pop. 7,951) of Cherbourg, Manche dept., NW France, on N shore of Cotentin Peninsula.

Équihen-Plage (ākēā′-plăzh′), village (pop. 1,256), Pas-de-Calais dept., N France, small fishing port and beach resort on English Channel, 4 mi. SSW of Boulogne. Damaged in Second World War.

Equinox, textile-mill village (pop. 5,413, with adjacent Appleton Mills), Anderson co., NW S.C., near Anderson.

Equinox, Mount (3,816 ft.), SW Vt., highest peak of Taconic Mts., W of Manchester, in resort area. Road to summit.

Er [Arabic,=the], for Arabic names beginning thus: see under following part of the name.

Erabu-shima, Ryukyu Isls.: see OKINOERABU-SHIMA.

Eraclea, Sicily: see BIANCO, CAPE.

Eraclea Minoa, Sicily: see BIANCO, CAPE.

Erakhtur, Russian SFSR: see YERAKHTUR.

Eral (ā′rŭl), town (pop. 5,293), Tinnevelly dist., S Madras, India, on Tambraparni R. and 25 mi. ESE of Tinnevelly; palmyra, betel farms; bell-metal wares.

Eran (ā′rän), town (1939 pop. 2,273), on SW coast of Palawan, Philippines, on Eran Bay (inlet of S. China Sea).

Erandique (ärändē′kä), town (pop. 613), Lempira dept., W Honduras, in Sierra de Congolón, 20 mi. SSE of Gracias; alt. 4,153 ft. Commercial center; cotton weaving; wheat, livestock. Rich opal deposits near by were formerly exploited.

Erandol (ā′rŭndōl), town (pop. 15,098), East Khandesh dist., NE Bombay, India, 17 mi. SW of Jalgaon; road center; trades in cotton, millet, wheat, indigo, mangoes; cotton ginning.

Eraniel, India: see IRANIEL.

Erapuca (äräpōō′kä), highest peak (8,200 ft.) of W Honduras, at junction of Sierra del Merendón (S) and Sierra del Gallinero (N), 6 mi. WSW of La Unión; 14°39′N 88°59′W.

Era River (ā′rä), Tuscany, central Italy, rises in the Apennines 6 mi. E of Volterra, flows 33 mi. NW, past Capannoli, to Arno R. at Pontedera.

Erasmus, Mount (10,700 ft.), SW Alta., near B.C. border, in Rocky Mts., in Banff Natl. Park, 80 mi. NW of Banff; 51°57′N 116°55′W.

Erath (ē′răth), county (□ 1,085; pop. 18,434), N central Texas; ⊙ Stephenville. Drained by Bosque R. Rich diversified agr. area (peanuts, cotton, grain sorghums, wheat, corn, hay, pecans, fruit, truck, vetch seed); dairying, livestock (cattle, poultry, sheep, goats, hogs, horses). Oil, natural gas; coal deposits formerly worked. Formed 1856.

Erath, town (pop. 1,514), Vermilion parish, S La., 60 mi. SW of Baton Rouge, in the Acadian country; cotton ginning, sugar milling.

Erba (ĕr′bä), town (pop. 1,694), Como prov., Lombardy, N Italy, 7 mi. E of Como; silk and paper mills, foundries, nail factory; mfg. of automobile chassis.

Erbaa (ĕrbä′), town (pop. 6,185), Tokat prov., N central Turkey, on Kelkit R. and 26 mi. N of Tokat; tobacco, grain.

Erbach (ĕr′bäkh). **1** Town (pop. 5,099), S Hesse, W Germany, in former Starkenburg prov., in the Odenwald, on the Mümling and 15 mi. E of Heppenheim; textile mfg., woodworking. Has frequently renovated castle of counts of Erbach. **2** Village (pop. 2,328), N Württemberg, Germany, after 1945 in Württemberg-Baden, on the Danube and 7 mi. SW of Ulm; grain. Has 16th-cent. castle.

Erbendorf (ĕr′bündôrf), town (pop. 3,165), Upper Palatinate, NE Bavaria, Germany, in the Fichtelgebirge, on the Fichtelnab (a branch of the Nab) and 12 mi. NNW of Weiden; glass and textile mfg., woodworking. Coal, zinc, and lead mined in area.

Erbent, Turkmen SSR: see YERBENT.

Erbeskopf (ĕr′bŭskôpf), highest peak (2,677 ft.) of the Hunsrück, W Germany, 7 mi. NW of Birkenfeld.

Erbil or **Arbil** (ĕr′bĭl, ärbēl′), province (□ 6,364; pop. 240,273), N Iraq, in Kurdistan, bet. the Great Zab and the Little Zab and extending NE to the mts. on Iran border; ⊙ Erbil. Sesame, millet, corn, tobacco, grapes, oranges, apples; stock.

Erbil or **Arbil,** town (pop, 26,086), ⊙ Erbil prov., N Iraq, 50 mi. E of Mosul, at terminus of railroad from Kirkuk; agr. trade center (sesame, millet, corn, livestock), with roads leading to Iran, Turkey, and Syria. It is an anc. city, continuously inhabited from Assyrian times, from the founding in 3d millennium B.C. of the anc. town of Arbela (ärbē′lŭ), on whose mound the modern town stands. The battle of Gaugamela, also called the battle of Arbela, was fought on a tributary of the Great Zab R. c.30 mi. to WNW. In the battle Alexander the Great defeated the Persian hosts of Darius III in 331 B.C.

Erbisdorf, Germany: see BRAND-ERBISDORF.

Erbogachen, Russian SFSR: see YERBOGACHEN.

Ercegnovi, Yugoslavia: see HERCEG NOVI.

Ercek, Lake (ĕrchĕk′), Turkish *Erçek* (□ 39), E Turkey, in the mts. 12 mi. NE of Van; 10 mi. long, 6 mi. wide; alt. 6,200 ft. Connected with L. Van. Town of Ercek on E shore.

Erceldoune, Scotland: see EARLSTON.

Erchie (ĕr′kyĕ), town (pop. 4,201), Brindisi prov., Apulia, S Italy, 18 mi. SSW of Brindisi; wine, olive oil.

Ercildoune, Scotland: see EARLSTON.

Ercilla (ĕrsē′yä), town (pop. 1,274), Malleco prov., S central Chile, on railroad and 25 mi. SE of Angol; agr. center (wheat, oats, fruit, livestock); lumbering, flour milling.

Ercis (ĕrjĭsh′), Turkish *Erciş*, village (pop. 4,754), Van prov., SE Turkey, on N shore of L. Van, 35 mi. N of Van; wheat. Sometimes spelled Arjish.

Erciyas Dagi (ĕrjĭyäsh′ däŭ′), Turkish *Erciyaş Dağı*, anc. *Argaeus* (är′jēŭs), peak (12,848 ft.), central Turkey, in an offshoot of the Taurus Mts. in E Asia Minor, 12 mi. S of Kayseri. Extinct volcano. Formerly sometimes spelled Erjias.

Ercsi (ĕr′chē), market town (pop. 7,610), Fejer co., N central Hungary, on the Danube and 19 mi. S of Budapest; river port; sugar refinery, distilleries; sugar beets, corn, wheat; cattle, poultry.

Erd (ärd), Hung. *Érd*, town (pop. 13,062), Pest-Pilis-Solt-Kiskun co., N central Hungary, on the Danube and 12 mi. SW of Budapest; river port; brickworks; truck (dairy products, poultry, fruit). Ruins of Roman bridge near by.

Erdek (ĕrdĕk′), town (pop. 5,040), Balikesir prov., NW Turkey, on Kapidagi Peninsula, 10 mi. WNW of Bandirma, port on Gulf of Erdek, inlet of Sea of Marmara; olive and cereal dist. Formerly Artaki.

Erdely, Rumania: see TRANSYLVANIA.

Erdelyi-Havasok, Rumania: see TRANSYLVANIAN ALPS.

Erdeni Dzu, Mongolia: see KARAKORUM.

Erdevik (ĕr′dĕvēk), Hung. *Erdővég* (ĕr′dûvāg), village, Vojvodina, NW Serbia, Yugoslavia, 23 mi. WSW of Novi Sad, in the Srem.

Erdigg, Wales: see WREXHAM.

Erding (ĕr′dĭng), town (pop. 8,574), Upper Bavaria, Germany, 10 mi. SE of Freising; mfg. of agr. machinery, brewing, printing, tanning. Has late-Gothic church. Chartered 1341. Peat bogs in area.

Erdington (ûr′–), NE industrial suburb (pop. 70,762) of Birmingham, NW Warwick, England. Site of Oscott Col. Alfred Austin b. here.

Erdmannsdorf (ĕrt′mänsdôrf), village (pop. 3,202), Saxony, E central Germany, at N foot of the Erzgebirge, on Zschopau R. and 7 mi. E of Chemnitz; cotton milling, hosiery knitting.

Erdöbenye (ĕr′dûbänyĕ), Hung. *Erdőbénye*, town (pop. 3,116), Zemplen co., NE Hungary, in the Hegyalja, 16 mi. SW of Satoraljaujhely; vineyards, lentils, beans. Animal fossils here. Erdöbenyefürdö, with medicinal waters, near by.

Erdöcsokonya, Hungary: see CSOKONYAVISONTA.

Erdöd, Rumania: see ARDED.

Erdöszada, Rumania: see ARDUSAT.

Erdöszentgyörgy, Rumania: see SANGIORGIUL-DE-PADURE.

Erdötelek (ĕr′dûtĕlĕk), Hung. *Erdőtelek*, town (pop. 5,034), Heves co., N Hungary, 22 mi. NE of Jaszbereny; livestock.

Erdoveg, Yugoslavia: see ERDEVIK.

Erdre River (ĕr′drŭ), Loire-Inférieure dept., W France, rises 9 mi. E of Candé, flows W then S past Riaillé and Nort-sur-Erdre (below which it forms section of Brest-Nantes Canal), to Loire R. at Nantes; 65 mi. long. In its lower course the Erdre forms a series of lakes and traverses the city of Nantes in a tunnel.

Erebato River (ārābä′tō), Bolívar state, SE Venezuela, rises near Amazonas territory border, flows c.150 mi. N, through tropical forest country, to Caura R. at 6°14′N 64°29′W; not navigable.

Erebus, Mount (ĕ′rĭbŭs) (10,234 ft.), W Alta., near B.C. border, in Rocky Mts., in Jasper Natl. Park, 19 mi. SW of Jasper; 52°37′N 118°16′W.

Erebus, Mount, active volcano (13,202 ft.), on Ross Isl., just off Antarctica, in SW corner of Ross Sea; 77°35′S 167°10′E. Discovered 1841 by Sir James C. Ross.

Erebus Bay, SW Devon Isl., E central Franklin Dist., Northwest Territories, small inlet of Barrow Strait, at S end of Wellington Channel; 74°42′N 91°50′W. Contains Beechey Isl.

Erech (ē′rĕk, ĕ′rĕk) or **Uruk** (ōō′rōōk), anc. Sumerian city of Mesopotamia, whose site (present-day Warka) is in SE Iraq, in Muntafiq prov., near left bank of the Euphrates, 40 mi. WNW of Nasiriya, 13 mi. NW of site of Larsa, NW of site of Ur. Was one of most important early cities of S Mesopotamia; it was flourishing probably in 5th millennium B.C. and for long periods was ⊙ of what came to be Lower Babylonia. Excavations have revealed a ziggurat temple of Nana (equivalent of Ishtar), libraries with documents, and other finds. Erech in the Bible was one of the cities of Nimrod in Shinar.

Erechim (ĭrĭshēm′). **1** City (pop. 7,511), N Rio Grande do Sul, Brazil, in the Serra Geral, on railroad and 45 mi. N of Passo Fundo; center of agr. colony (grain, flax, hogs); distilling, meat processing. Also spelled Erexim. Originally named Boa Vista or Boa Vista do Erechim; then, José Bonifácio (1939-44). **2** City, Rio Grande do Sul, Brazil: see GETÚLIO VARGAS.

Eregli (ĕrā′lē), Turkish *Ereğli*. **1** Town (1950 pop. 18,480), Konya prov., S central Turkey, on railroad and 90 mi. ESE of Konya; cotton textile center; coal, charcoal; wheat. Sometimes called Konyaereglisi. **2** or **Marmara Eregli** (märmärä′-ĕrā′lē), anc. *Perinthus*, village (pop. 1,461),

Tekirdag prov., Turkey in Europe, port on Sea of Marmara 15 mi. SE of Corlu; grain market. Founded 600 B.C. by Samians. **3** anc. *Heraclea Pontica*, town (pop. 6,360), Zonguldak prov., N Turkey, port on Black Sea, 23 mi. SW of Zonguldak; important coal-mining center; also produces manganese and asbestos; grain, hemp, flax. Founded in 550 B.C. by colonists from Megara and Boeotia; destroyed by the Romans.

Ereikosa, Greece: see ERRIKOUSAI.

Erembodegem (ĕrŭmbō'dŭkhŭm), town (pop. 9,073), East Flanders prov., NW Belgium, on Dender R., just SSE of Alost; textile, leather, and shoe industries; market center for hop-growing area.

Eremokastron, Greece: see THESPIAI.

Eremomelos, Greece: see ANTIMELOS.

Erenler Dag (ĕrĕnlĕr'dä), Turkish *Erenler Dağ*, peak (7,608 ft.), W central Turkey, in Sultan Mts., 30 mi. WSW of Konya.

Erepecuru River (ĭrĭpĭkōōrōō') or **Cuminá River** (kōōmēnä'), N Pará, Brazil, rises in 2 branches in the Serra de Tumucumaque near Du. Guiana border, flows c.250 mi. S to the Trombetas (left tributary of the Amazon). Not navigable.

Ererti River (ĕrĕr'tē), Tigre prov., N Ethiopia, rises along W escarpment of Great Rift Valley near Debub, flows intermittently NE into Danakil desert and disappears in salt marshes 40 mi. NW of L. Egogi Bad; total length, c.100 mi.

Eres Fjord, Norway: see NAUSTE.

Eresfjord og Vistdal, canton, Norway: see NAUSTE.

Eresma River (ārĕ'zmä), in Segovia and Valladolid provs., central Spain, rises on NE slopes of the Sierra de Guadarrama, flows 105 mi. NW, past Segovia, to the Adaja 3 mi. above Valdestillas; the combined streams flow 10 mi. N and W to the Duero 7 mi. ENE of Tordesillas.

Eressos (ĕrĕsôs'), Lat. *Eresus* (ĕrē'sŭs), town (pop. 3,304), on W Lesbos isl., Greece, 33 mi. WNW of Mytilene; wheat, barley, wine, olive oil. The anc. Eresus was home of Sappho and Theophrastus. Excavations (1920s). Its landing on Aegean Sea is 2 mi. S.

Eretria (ĕrē'trēŭ), anc. city in W central Euboea, Greece, 11 mi. ESE of Chalcis, on S arm of Gulf of Euboea. The second city of Euboea in antiquity, it joined the Athenians in the Persian Wars, was destroyed (490 B.C.) by Darius I, and later rebuilt. The site of a school of philosophy and dialectics, it founded colonies in S Italy, Sicily, Chalcidice, and the Cyclades (Tenos, Kea). It fought in naval battles off Artemision and Salamis and at Plataea. Occupied by Romans (198 B.C.). Excavations have unearthed the theater, temples, and other ruins. On the site is modern town and port of Nea Psara (nä'ŭ psürä') [Gr.,=new Psara] (pop. 1,731), founded in 1820s by refugees from Psara; fisheries, wheat.

Eretria or **Eretreia** (both: ĕrä'trēŭ), village (1928 pop. 358), Larissa nome, SE Thessaly, Greece, 12 mi. E of Pharsala; chromite mining. Formerly called Tsagli or Chagli.

Erewash River (ĕ'riwŏsh), Nottingham and Derby, England, rises 2 mi. S of Sutton-in-Ashfield, flows 15 mi. S, past Ilkeston, to Trent R. just E of Long Eaton.

Erexim, Brazil: see ERECHIM.

Erfde (ĕrf'dŭ), village (pop. 2,692), in Schleswig-Holstein, NW Germany, 14 mi. W of Rendsburg; woodworking.

Erfoud (ĕrfōōd'), town (pop. 3,341), Meknès region, SE Fr. Morocco, on the Oued Ziz and 36 mi. SSE of Ksar-es-Souk; chief trade center of the TAFILALET oasis (dates, figs, barley, hard wheat, some vegetables). Handicraft industries (leather, wool, esparto articles).

Erft River (ĕrft), W Germany, rises on the Eifel 5 mi. SW of Münstereifel, flows c.65 mi. generally N, past Euskirchen, to the Rhine at NEUSS. Canalized in parts.

Erfurt (âr'fŏŏrt, -fûrt, Ger. ĕr'fŏŏrt), city (pop. 174,633), in former Prussian Saxony prov., central Germany, after 1945 in Thuringia, on Gera R. and 65 mi. WSW of Leipzig; 50°59'N 11°2'E. Rail and industrial center; mfg. of machinery, electrical equipment, office machines, glass, textiles, clothing, leather, shoes, furniture, tobacco products; metal- and woodworking, printing, distilling; center of important vegetable-producing and flower-seed-growing region. Airport (N). Has former Augustinian monastery (founded 13th cent.), where Luther took his vows; R.C. basilica (12th cent.); 13th-cent. church of St. Severus on site of church 1st mentioned 836; city mus.; 16th-cent. inn (Gustavus Adolphus' hq. during Thirty Years War); 16th-cent. bldgs. of former univ. (1392–1816), where Luther studied; numerous half-timbered houses. Former palace (18th cent.) was scene (1808) of Congress of Erfurt; 19th-cent. town hall contains many historical frescoes. One of oldest Ger. cities—it was mentioned by St. Boniface in 8th cent.—Erfurt grew as ford at Gera R. on important military highway, later became center for trade with Slavs. Chartered 1120. The center of Ger. trade in blue vegetable dyes, city was (14th and 15th cent.) member of Hanseatic League. Was under sovereignty of electors of Saxony and later (17th cent.) of electors of Mainz; passed to Prussia in 1802. Congress of Erfurt, attended by Napoleon, Alexander I of Russia, and several Ger. kings, is noted for Napoleon's meeting with Goethe and Talma's acting before a "parterre of kings." Erfurt's fortifications were razed 1873 to permit expansion of city. In 1891, Socialist congress here adopted the Erfurt Program. Bombed in Second World War; captured by U.S. troops in April, 1945; later occupied by Soviet forces. Just N is industrial suburb of Ilversgehofen.

Erg (ûrg), name given to a desert region of shifting sand dunes, especially in the Sahara of N Africa: the Great Western Erg [Fr. *Grand Erg Occidental*] in N central Algeria (Aïn-Sefra and Ghardaïa territories); the Great Eastern Erg [Fr. *Grand Erg Oriental*], in E Algeria and southernmost Tunisia, bet. Touggourt (NW), Ghadames (SE), and Fort Flatters (S), with dunes up to 650 ft. high; the Erg Iguidi, in SW Algeria and N Mauritania; the Erg Chech, in S Algeria, SW of the Touat oases; the Libyan Erg along Egypt-Cyrenaica border. The Saharan ergs are noted for complete absence of vegetation and lack of oases.

Ergani (ĕrgänē'), village (pop. 4,300), Diyarbakir prov., E Turkey, on the Tigris, on railroad and 36 mi. NW of Diyarbakir; rich deposits of copper, with some silver and chromium. Formerly Arghana and Ergani Osmaniye.

Erganimadeni, Turkey: see MADEN.

Ergasteria, Greece: see LAURION.

Ergene River (ĕrgĕnĕ'), anc. *Agrianes*, Turkey in Europe, rises in Istranca Mts. near Saray, flows 125 mi. W and SW, past Uzun Kopru, to the Maritsa 5 mi. NW of Ipsala. Formerly sometimes spelled Ergines, Ergeneh.

Ergeni Hills, Russian SFSR: see YERGENI HILLS.

Ergines River, Turkey: see ERGENE RIVER.

Ergolding (ĕr'gôl"dĭng), village (pop. 2,210), Lower Bavaria, Germany, 3 mi. NNE of Landshut; grain, livestock.

Ergoldsbach (ĕr'gôltsbäkh), village (pop. 3,480), Lower Bavaria, Germany, 11 mi. NNE of Landshut; pottery- and brickworks. Chartered 1444.

Ergolz River (ĕr'gôlts), N Switzerland, rises 4 mi. NW of Aarau, flows 17 mi. NW, past Sissach and Liestal, to the Rhine at Augst, 6 mi. ESE of Basel.

Ergué-Armel (ârgā'-ärmĕl'), SE suburb (pop. 6,464) of Quimper, Finistère dept., W France; tin-can mfg., woodworking.

Erhard, village (pop. 145), Otter Tail co., W Minn., 14 mi. N of Fergus Falls. Sometimes Erhart.

Erh-ch'iang, China: see CHARKHLIK.

Erh-chieh, Formosa: see ERHKIEH.

Erh Hai (ŭr'hī'), lake in NW Yunnan prov., China, 160 mi. WNW of Kunming; 25 mi. long, 6 mi. wide; drains into Mekong R.; alt. over 6,000 ft. Burma Road touches S end. Tali is on W shore; fisheries.

Erhkieh or **Erh-chieh** (both: ŭr'jyĕ'), Jap. *Niketsu* (nĕkä'tsōō), village, NE Formosa, on railroad and 2 mi. N of Lotung; sugar refinery, paper mill.

Erhlin (ŭr'lĭn'), Jap. *Nirin* (nē'rēn), town (1935 pop. 5,121), W central Formosa, near W coast, 25 mi. SW of Taichung and on railroad; sugar milling; rice, sugar cane, ramie, peanuts, livestock.

Erhshui (ŭr'shwā'), Jap. *Nisui* (nē'sōōē), village (1935 pop. 4,123), W central Formosa, 23 mi. SE of Taichung and on railroad; rice, sugar cane, tobacco, fruit; pineapple canning; timber.

Erhtaichan, Manchuria: see CHAOCHOW.

Erhyüan (ŭr'yüän'), town, ⊙ Erhyüan co. (pop. 42,720), NW Yunnan prov., China, 30 mi. NNW of Tali; timber, rice, wheat, millet, beans. Until 1913 called Langkiung.

Eriboll, Loch (lŏkh ĕ'rĭbŏl), sea inlet in NW Sutherland, Scotland, extends 8 mi. SSW from N coast of Scotland, SE of Durness; up to 2 mi. wide. Contains Chorrie Isl. (1 mi. long), and is notable for its scenery.

Eric Cove, Que.: see WOLSTENHOLME.

Erice (ĕrē'chĕ), until c.1935 **Monte San Giuliano** (môn'tĕ sän jōōlyä'nô), town (pop. 1,770), Trapani prov., W Sicily, 4 mi. NE of Trapani, in cereal-growing area. It is atop Monte San Giuliano (2,464 ft.), site of anc. Eryx, Elymian town, famous for its temple of Venus Erycina, which was taken by Romans in First Punic War. There are ruins of anc. walls, cathedral (14th cent.; restored 1865), medieval castle with remains of the temple, mus.

Ericeira (ĭrĕsā'rŭ), fishing village (pop. 2,379), Lisboa dist., central Portugal, on the Atlantic and 22 mi. NW of Lisbon; fish preserving. Bathing resort. Has old fort (1706).

Ericht, Loch (lŏkh ĕ'rĭkht), lake (14 mi. long, 1 mi. wide) in S Inverness and NW Perthshire, Scotland, extending SW-NE at foot of Ben Alder. Outlets: Ericht R. (SW) and Truim R. (NE). Forms part of Lochaber hydroelectric power system.

Ericht River. **1** In E Perthshire, Scotland, rises 13 mi. NW of Blairgowrie, flows 10 mi. SE, past Blairgowrie, to Isla R. 2 mi. NE of Coupar-Angus. **2** In NW Perthshire, Scotland, issues from SW end of Loch Ericht, flows 6 mi. S to Loch Rannoch.

Erick (ĕ'rĭk), city (pop. 1,579), Beckham co., W Okla., 30 mi. WSW of Elk City, near the Texas line, in agr. (cotton, corn, wheat) and stock-raising area; cotton ginning, feed milling, mattress mfg. Natural-gas field near by. Inc. 1903.

Ericson, village (pop. 186), Wheeler co., NE central Nebr., 10 mi. SW of Bartlett and on Cedar R.

Eridanus, Italy: see PO RIVER.

Eridio, Italy: see IDRO, LAGO D'.

Eridu (ā'rĭdōō), anc. Sumerian city of S Mesopotamia, whose site is in SE Iraq, in Muntafiq prov., c.15 mi. SW of Nasiriya, c.10 mi. S of the ruins of anc. Ur. Built originally near the Persian Gulf (now 130 mi. away), it is very old, dating perhaps from 8th millennium B.C. It was a center of worship of the water-god Ea. Excavations were made in mid-19th cent. and early 20th cent.

Erie, village, SE B.C., on Beaver Creek, at mouth of Erie Creek, 19 mi. ENE of Trail; mining (gold, silver, lead, zinc).

Erie. **1** County (□ 1,054; pop. 899,238), W N.Y.; ⊙ BUFFALO. Drained by Cattaraugus and Tonawanda creeks and small Buffalo and Cayuga creeks. Includes parts of Cattaraugus and Tonawanda Indian reservations. Extensive mfg.; stone and gypsum quarrying; agr. (dairy products; poultry, truck, fruit, potatoes, hay, beans, livestock). Formed 1821. **2** County (□ 264; pop. 52,565), N Ohio; ⊙ SANDUSKY. Bounded N by L. Erie; drained by Huron and Vermilion rivers and small Pipe Creek. Includes Kelleys Isl. Agr. area (wheat, corn, fruit, dairy products, livestock); mfg. at Sandusky, Huron, Vermilion. Limestone quarries; fisheries. Summer resorts. Formed 1838. **3** County (□ 812; pop. 219,388), NW Pa.; ⊙ Erie. Mfg. and agr. area bordered N by L. Erie; drained in S by tributaries of Allegheny R.; bounded NE by N.Y., W by Ohio. French forts built 1753 at Presque Isle and Le Boeuf (at Waterford) occupied 1760 by British. Claims to Erie Triangle ceded 1781–85 to U.S. govt. by N.Y. and Mass.; sold 1788 to Pa. Mfg. (machinery, metal and rubber products); agr. (grapes, cherries, cabbage, dairy products); sand. Formed 1800.

Erie. **1** Town (pop. 937), Weld co., N Colo., near South Platte R., 20 mi. N of Denver; alt. 5,000 ft.; diversified farming. Lignite mines near by. **2** Village (pop. 1,180), Whiteside co., NW Ill., near Rock R. (bridged here), 25 mi. ENE of Moline, in agr. area. Inc. 1872. **3** City (pop. 1,296), ⊙ Neosho co., SE Kansas, on Neosho R. and 14 mi. SE of Chanute; shipping and trading point in oil-producing and general-farming region. Oil and gas wells in vicinity. State park 5 mi. SE. Founded 1867, inc. 1870. **4** City (pop. 130,803), ⊙ Erie co., NW Pa., 80 mi. SW of Buffalo, N.Y., and on L. Erie; 42°8'N 80°5'W. Inland fishing and shipping center for lumber, coal, petroleum, grain, chemicals, iron, fish; only port in Pa. on Great Lakes. Port of entry. Electrical products, construction machinery, heaters, refrigerators, railroad equipment, paper, aluminum forgings, rubber products, clothing, chemicals; railroad shops. State soldiers' and sailors' home, Mercyhurst Col. here. PRESQUE ISLE peninsula encloses city's harbor (2 mi. long, 1 mi. wide). Gen. Anthony Wayne died here 1796. Fleet built here 1813 by Commodore Perry; his flagship (*Niagara*) in battle of Lake Erie reconstructed 1913. *Wolverine*, 1st all-iron warship (1843) on Great Lakes, now anchored here. Erie was stop on Underground Railroad. Laid out 1795, inc. as borough 1805, as city 1851.

Erie, Lake, in U.S. and Canada, 4th largest of the GREAT LAKES; 241 mi. long, 30–57 mi. wide, it lies c.572 ft. above sea level and covers □ 9,940, of which □ 5,094 are in Ont. (Canada). Lake also touches N.Y., Pa., and Ohio on its S, and a small portion of Mich. on W. The Detroit R. is its inlet from L. Huron, and Niagara R. is its outlet into L. Ontario. Navigation between lakes Huron and Erie follows a natural channel (St. Clair river and lake, and Detroit R.), but the Welland Canal bet. Erie and Ontario by-passes Niagara Falls. N.Y. State Barge Canal and the Hudson R. connect it with the Atlantic. Ice generally closes it to navigation from mid-December until about the end of March, and it is subject to violent storms. Principal U.S. ports are Buffalo and Dunkirk, N.Y.; Erie, Pa.; Conneaut, Ashtabula, Cleveland, Lorain, Sandusky, and Toledo, Ohio; and Detroit, on the lake's inlet. Main Canadian ports are Port Colborne, Port Dover, Port Stanley, and Leamington. A fruit belt (especially noted for grapes) lies along lake in W N.Y. and NE Ohio. Isls. include Bass and Kelleys isls. (Ohio), Pelee Isl. (Ont.). Probably the 1st white man to see L. Erie was Louis Jolliet in 1669. In the early 17th cent., forts and trading posts sprang up along its shore. The French and Indian Wars gave Great Britain control of the lake, which she retained even after the Revolution. At the close of the War of 1812, the British were defeated by Oliver H. Perry at Put-in-Bay, Sept., 1813, in the battle of Lake Erie. At the close of the war, the U.S.-Canadian boundary was established to run approximately through the lake's center.

Erieau (ĕr'ēō), village (pop. 288), S Ont., on L. Erie, 17 mi. SE of Chatham; dairying.

Erie Canal, N.Y., historic waterway more than 350 mi. long, extending from Albany (Hudson R.) to

Buffalo (L. Erie); has been improved and converted into N.Y. State Barge Canal. Authorized 1817 by state legislature; its middle section (Utica to Salina) was completed 1820, E section 1823, and entire canal opened 1827. Giving access to the interior from New York city, the canal opened eastern markets for the farm products of the Great Lakes region, carried a great stream of immigrants into the Middle West, created numerous large cities, and confirmed the commercial and financial leadership of New York. It functioned as a toll waterway until 1882; later, railroad competition (dating from 1850s), its inadequate navigability, and disclosure of a fraudulent canal administration brought about plans for its conversion, with its branches, into the present Barge Canal system.

Érieux River or **Eyrieux River** (both: ārēû'), Ardèche dept., S France, rises in the Monts du Vivarais near Saint-Agrève, flows c.40 mi. SE, past Saint-Martin-de-Valamas and Le Cheylard, to the Rhone above La Voulte-sur-Rhône.

Erieville, resort village, Madison co., central N.Y., 25 mi. SE of Syracuse. Lakes, reservoirs near by.

Erigavo (ĕrēgä'vō), town, NE Br. Somaliland, in Ogo highland, 240 mi. ENE of Hargeisa; stock-raising center. Hq. Erigavo dist.

Eriha, Palestine: see JERICHO.

Eriha or **Iriha** (ĭrē'hä), village, Aleppo prov., NW Syria, near Turkish border, 40 mi. SW of Aleppo; cotton, cereals.

Erikousa, Greece: see ERRIKOUSAI.

Eriksberg, Sweden: see EKEBY.

Erikub (ĕrēkōōb'), uninhabited atoll, Ratak Chain, Marshall Isls., W central Pacific, 175 mi. E of Kwajalein; c.20 mi. long; 14 islets. Formerly Chatham Isls.

Erimanthos, Greece: see ERYMANTHOS.

Erimo, Cape (ārē'mō), Jap. *Erimo-zaki*, S Hokkaido, Japan, in the Pacific; 41°55'N 143°15'E; lighthouse.

Erimomilos, Greece: see ANTIMELOS.

Erin: see IRELAND.

Erin (ĕ'rĭn), village (pop. 499), S Ont., 10 mi. S of Orangeville; dairying, lumbering; potatoes.

Erin, village (pop. 287), SW Trinidad, B.W.I., on the Serpent's Mouth, and 19 mi. SW of San Fernando; coconuts. Sometimes called San Francique. Erin Point is just SE.

Erin, town (pop. 858), ⊙ Houston co., NW Tenn., 23 mi. SW of Clarksville; makes work clothes; lumbering; poultry hatchery.

Erinpura (ā'rĭnpōōrŭ), town (pop., including cantonment area, 1,857), S Rajasthan, India, 21 mi. NNE of Sirohi; millet, corn, wheat.

Eris Fjord, Norway: see NAUSTE.

Eriskay (ĕ'rĭskā), island (pop. 420), Outer Hebrides, Inverness, Scotland, just S of South Uist, from which it is separated by the narrow Sound of Eriskay; 3 mi. long, 1½ mi. wide; rises to 609 ft. Prince Charles Edward, the Young Pretender, 1st landed on Scottish soil here in 1745.

Erith (ē'rĭth), municipal borough (1931 pop. 32,789; 1951 census 46,263), NW Kent, England, on the Thames and 9 mi. W of Gravesend; mfg. of chemicals, explosives, paper, cables, radios, lubricating oil, flour. Site (1216) of signing of peace treaty bet. the barons and King John. Has 13th-cent. church with Saxon parts. In the borough (W) is town of Belvedere, with chemical industry (borax products).

Erithrai, Greece: see ERYTHRAI.

Eritrea (ĕrĭtrē'ŭ), country (□ 45,754; 1948 pop. estimate 1,087,000, including c.26,000 Italians) of NE Africa, in federation with Ethiopia; ⊙ ASMARA. Separates N Ethiopia from the Red Sea, and is bounded N and W by Anglo-Egyptian Sudan, SE by Fr. Somaliland; its coastline extends from Cape Kasar (18°2'N) to a point (12°30'N) SE of Assab on Bab el Mandeb strait. Includes DAHLAK ARCHIPELAGO. SE Eritrea is an arid coastal strip c.40 mi. wide (part of DANAKIL desert extending into Ethiopia), with extinct volcanic cones; in NW Eritrea, a narrower coastal zone is bounded by steep escarpment of the central plateau (average alt. 3-7,000 ft.; rises to 9,885 ft. in Mt. Soira) which is a geological extension of N Ethiopia's highlands. In extreme NW, central plateau gradually descends to the Sudan desert. The climate is arid and excessively hot along the Red Sea, cooler and more humid in central uplands. Cereals (especially durum wheat), coffee, tobacco, fruits, and vegetables are upland crops. In W, cotton is intensively grown under irrigation near Tessenei (on Gash R.) and Karkabat (on Barka R.). Arid lowlands yield gum arabic, oil seeds, dates, fibers (agave); nomadic grazing. Pearl and mother-of-pearl fisheries off Massawa and in Dahlak Archipelago. Gold mined at Ugaro (W) and in Asmara area, where copper deposits are also worked. MASSAWA, country's chief port, is terminus of railroad to Asmara, Keren, Agordat, and Bisha (all on central plateau). Asmara (the center of Eritrea's industries) is a hub for roads to Kassala (Anglo-Egyptian Sudan), Aduwa and Addis Ababa (Ethiopia). ASSAB, the 2d port, has road to Addis Ababa via Dessye. Native pop. consists of Tigriña-speaking Coptic Christians, Tigré-speaking nomadic Moslems (in N), Arabic-speaking Moslems (mostly in coastal area), and pagan negroid tribes (in extreme SW). Italians numbered 60,000 just before Second World War. Eritrea was a tenuously-linked part of Ethiopia until 16th cent., when it fell to Ottoman Turks. Under petty chieftains 17th-19th cent.; territory was contested by Egypt, Ethiopia, and Italy after 1850s. Under Ital. influence after 1882, it became an Ital. colony in 1890, and a base for Ital. invasion of Ethiopia in 1896 and again in 1935–36. Became a "government" of Italian East Africa in 1936, its territory enlarged by incorporation of 3 adjacent Ethiopian provinces. Conquered (1941) by British during Second World War, after which it remained temporarily under Br. military administration. The United Nations decided (1950) that Eritrea was to be given its freedom in a federation with Ethiopia, effective 1952.

Erivan or **Erivan'** (ĕrĭvän', Rus. ĕrĭvän'yŭ), Armenian *Yerevan* (yĕrĕvän'), city (1926 pop. 64,613; 1939 pop. 200,031; 1946 pop. estimate 300,000), ⊙ Armenian SSR, on Zanga R. (bridged), on railroad and 110 mi. S of Tiflis, 1,100 mi. SSE of Moscow; alt. 3,419 ft.; 40°16'N 44°35'E. In picturesque orchard area, surrounded by mts. (N) and opening S on Aras R. valley at foot of Mt. Ararat. Industrial and cultural center; machine mfg. (auto and tractor parts, machine tools, electrical equipment, motors, textile and agr. machinery, cables), chemical industry (synthetic rubber, nitrate fertilizers, tires, carbide, caustic soda, paints, lacquers), light mfg. (watches, refractory bricks, window glass, woolens, shoes), food processing (wines, brandy, canned goods). Site of Armenian state univ. (1921), polytechnical school, agr., medical, and teachers (Armenian, Russian) colleges, conservatory, tropical research institute, Armenian state mus., public library (3,000,000 volumes). Has mus. of revolution, natl. mus., and many monuments. Situated largely on left bank of Zanga R., Erivan consists of modern central section with monumental govt. and public bldgs. (built mainly of volcanic tuff), surrounded by old labyrinthine quarters. Industrial sections (developed since c.1930) extend N to Arabkir (aluminum works based on Zaglik alunite; lined by tramway) and S to Shengavit (formerly a salt marsh; site of cable, hydroturbine, tire, and porcelain works) and are powered by hydroelectric stations along Zanga R. In N outskirts lie Matanderan govt. archives, depository of anc. Armenian MSS, formerly at Echmiadzin (Vagarshapat). Founded in 7th cent., Erivan became ⊙ Armenia under Persians, following downfall (15th cent.) of Tamerlane's empire. Changed hands frequently during Turkish-Persian struggles, until conquered (1827) by Russians. Ceded formally to Russia in 1828; became ⊙ Erivan govt. Once a major brandy-producing center; reached pop. of c.30,000 by First World War. Made ⊙ Armenian SSR in 1920. Name officially changed to Yerevan in 1936. Developed considerably after Second World War with influx of Armenians from abroad.

Eriz (ĕrēts'), mountainous commune (pop. 628), Bern canton, central Switzerland, 9 mi. ENE of Thun.

Erjias, Turkey: see ERCIYAS DAGI.

Erkelenz (ĕr'kŭlĕnts), town (pop. 6,402), in former Prussian Rhine Prov., W Germany, after 1945 in North Rhine-Westphalia, 23 mi. NNE of Aachen; textile mfg. Has 14th-cent. church.

Erkenschwick, Germany: see OER-ERKENSCHWICK.

Erken-Shakhar (ĕr'kyĭn-shŭkhär'), village (1939 pop. over 500), N Cherkess Autonomous Oblast, Stavropol Territory, Russian SFSR, on railroad and 10 mi. NNW of Cherkessk; wool washing, flour milling; cement plant.

Erkner (ĕrk'nŭr), village (pop. 6,459), Brandenburg, E Germany, on the Spree and 16 mi. ESE of Berlin, bet. 2 small lakes; market gardening; mfg. of coal-tar products, lime. Excursion resort.

Erkowit (ĕrkōwĕt'), village, Kassala prov., NE Anglo-Egyptian Sudan, in Red Sea hills, on road and 60 mi. S of Port Sudan; summer resort.

Erkrath (ĕrk'rät), village (pop. 7,616), in former Prussian Rhine Prov., W Germany, after 1945 in North Rhine-Westphalia, 6 mi. E of Düsseldorf; steelworks.

Erlaa (ĕr'lä), town (pop. 2,802), after 1938 in Liesing dist. of Vienna, Austria, 5 mi. SSW of city center; truck farming (poultry, fruit).

Erlach (ĕr'läkh), village (pop. 2,157), SE Lower Austria, on Pitten R. and 6 mi. S of Wiener Neustadt; corn, vineyards.

Erlach, Fr. *Cerlier* (sĕrlyā'), resort town (pop. 761), Bern canton, W Switzerland, just N of Ins, on L. Biel.

Erlangen (ĕr'läng"ŭn), city (1950 pop. 49,886), Middle Franconia, N central Bavaria, Germany, on Regnitz R. and Ludwig Canal, at mouth of Schwabach R., and 11 mi. NNE of Nuremberg; 49°36'N 11°E. Seat of Ger. electromedical industry (X-ray machines, hearing aids, electromedical and electrodental equipment). Other mfg.: cotton, gloves, musical instruments, cardboard, brushes, paint; leatherworking. Exports beer. Both old and new quarters of city are almost completely baroque in character, with late-17th-cent. church and early-18th-cent. city hall. A cultural center, it is site of Bavaria's only Protestant univ. (opened 1743), which has many scientific institutes; library contains over 450,000 volumes. Founded in 8th cent., Erlangen belonged to bishopric of Bamberg (1017–1361). Chartered in 14th cent. Property of the Hohenzollern (1402–1806); passed to Bavaria 1810. The settling here in 1686 of Huguenots resulted in building of town of Christian Erlang (united with Erlangen in 1824) and beginnings of industry. Old town completely rebuilt after disastrous fire of 1706. Georg Simon Ohm and Karl von Martius b. here; residence (1826–41) of poet Rückert.

Erlanger (ûr'lăng-ŭr). **1** Town (pop. 3,694), Kenton co., N Ky., a SW residential suburb of Covington; mfg. of concrete blocks, chemical toys, novelties; millwork. **2** Village (1940 pop. 1,359), Davidson co., central N.C., just N of Lexington; cotton mills.

Erlau, Hungary: see EGER.

Erlenbach (ĕr'lŭnbäkh), town (pop. 2,924), Zurich canton, N Switzerland, on L. of Zurich and 5 mi. SSE of Zurich; metalworking, printing.

Ermak-, in Rus. names: see YERMAK-.

Ermekeyevo, Russian SFSR: see YERMEKEYEVO.

Ermeland, Poland: see WARMIA.

Ermelo (ĕr'mŭlō), village (pop. 4,439), Gelderland prov., central Netherlands, 4 mi. S of Harderwijk, near the Ijsselmeer; egg market; duck breeding; resort. Sometimes spelled Ermeloo.

Ermelo, town (pop. 7,556), SE Transvaal, U. of So. Afr., 120 mi. E of Johannesburg; alt. 5,689 ft.; coal, gold, torbanite mining; in dairying, mealies, corn-growing region.

Ermenak (ĕrmĕnäk'), anc. *Germanicopolis*, town (pop. 6,713), Konya prov., S central Turkey, near Goksu R., 85 mi. SSE of Konya; barley, wheat, rye, sugar beets. Anc. remains.

Ermenonville (ĕrmnōvēl'), village (pop. 392), Oise dept., N France, 8 mi. SE of Senlis at SE edge of forest (□ c.20); sugar-beet processing. Has 18th-cent. château with fine park. Rousseau died here. Ruined 13th-cent. Cistercian abbey of Chaâlis is 2 mi. N.

Erment, Egypt: see ARMANT.

Ermera (ĕrmĕ'rŭ), town (pop. 117), ⊙ Ermera dist. (□ 766; pop. 86,282), Portuguese Timor, in central part of isl., 18 mi. SW of Dili; cinchona, copra, cinnamon.

Ermezinde (ĕrmĭzĕn'dĭ), village, Pôrto dist., N Portugal, 5 mi. NE of Oporto; rail junction; mfg. (knitwear, toys, pottery).

Ermidas (ĕrmē'dŭsh), village (pop. 1,823), Setúbal dist., S central Portugal, near Sado R., 15 mi. SE of Grândola; rail junction in heart of cork-producing region.

Ermihalyfalva, Rumania: see VALEA-LUI-MIHAI.

Ermine Street (ûr'mĭn), anc. Roman road in England, said to have linked *Londinium* (London) with *Lindum* (Lincoln). Exact length and route are disputed.

Ermington and Rydalmere (ûr'mĭngtŭn, rī'dŭlmēr), municipality (pop. 3,298), E New South Wales, Australia, 7 mi. WNW of Sydney, in metropolitan area; consists of 2 adjacent towns on N shore of Parramatta R.; industrial center; machinery, concrete pipes.

Ermioni, Greece: see HERMIONE.

Ermish, Russian SFSR: see YERMISH.

Ermland, Poland: see WARMIA.

Ermo-, in Rus. names: see YERMO-.

Ermont (ĕrmō'), town (pop. 9,291), Seine-et-Oise dept., N central France, an outer NNW suburb of Paris, 10 mi. from Notre Dame Cathedral, adjoining Eaubonne (E); rail junction. Mfg. (house furnishings, corks); truck gardening.

Ermoupolis, Greece: see HERMOUPOLIS.

Ermsleben (ĕrms'lā"bŭn), town (pop. 4,689), in former Prussian Saxony prov., central Germany, after 1945 in Saxony-Anhalt, at NE foot of the lower Harz, 6 mi. WSW of Aschersleben, in copper-slate mining region.

Ermua (ĕr'mwä), town (pop. 1,100), Vizcaya prov., N Spain, 6 mi. ENE of Durango; mfg. (firearms, electrical equipment); gold engraving. Mineral springs.

Ernakulam (ĕrnä'kōōlŭm), city (pop. 46,790), ⊙ Cochin administrative div., N Travancore-Cochin, India, on Arabian Sea, 110 mi. NNW of Trivandrum; connected by rail bridges via Willingdon Isl. (in harbor, W) with seaport of COCHIN. Industrial center; mfg. of coir mats and rope, copra, tiles, glycerin, perfume, soap, cooking oils; processing and tinning of kerosene, electroplating, sawmilling. Col. Linked with Quilon, 80 mi. SSE, by system of lagoons and canals.

Erne, Lough (lŏkh ûrn'), lake (40 mi. long, average width 5 mi., maximum depth 200 ft.) in Co. Fermanagh, Northern Ireland, consisting of Upper Lough Erne (SE) (10 mi. long, 3 mi. wide) and Lower Lough Erne (NW) (18 mi. long, 5 mi. wide), joined by 10-mi. strait (part of Erne R., which enters the lakes in SE and leaves them in NW). Both lakes contain numerous isls., including Boa, Devenish, and isl. on which Enniskillen is located. Fishing is carried on.

Ernée (ĕrnā'), town (pop. 3,561), Mayenne dept., W France, 13 mi. ESE of Fougères; road center;

mfg. (agr. machinery, footwear), tanning, cider milling. Has 17th-cent. church, built on site of medieval castle.

Erne River (ûrn), Ireland and Northern Ireland, rises in Lough Gowna, on border of cos. Longford and Cavan, flows 72 mi. NW, through cos. Cavan, Fermanagh, and Donegal, through Loughs Oughter and Erne, past Belturbet and Ballyshannon, to Donegal Bay of the Atlantic. Used for hydroelectric power.

Ernest, village (pop. 1,170), Indiana co., W central Pa., 4 mi. N of Indiana.

Ernest Sound, SE Alaska, bet. Cleveland Peninsula (SE) and Etolin Isl. (NW), N of Myers Chuck; opens S into Clarence Strait at 55°51'N 132°22'W.

Ernshof, Luxembourg: see BELVAL.

Ernstbrunn (ĕrnst'brŏŏn), town (pop. 2,546), N Lower Austria, 12 mi. NNE of Stockerau; rye, potatoes, cattle.

Ernstthal, Germany: see HOHENSTEIN-ERNSTTHAL.

Ernzen (ĕrnt'sůn), village (pop. 142), E central Luxembourg, 8 mi. SE of Ettelbruck; building-stone quarrying.

Ero-, in Rus. names: see YERO-.

Erode (ĕrōd'), city (pop. 39,483), Coimbatore dist., S central Madras, India, on Cauvery R. and 55 mi. ENE of Coimbatore; rail junction; trade center for cotton, rice, chili, tobacco, salt; rice mills. Pykara and Mettur hydroelectric systems linked here. Tuberculosis sanatorium 11 mi. WSW, at Perundurai.

Erongarícuaro (ārōng-gärē'kwärō), town (pop. 1,209), Michoacán, central Mexico, on W shore of L. Pátzcuaro, on railroad and 36 mi. WSW of Morelia; cereals, fruit, stock; timber.

Erongo Mountains (ĕrŏng'gō), W South-West Africa, extend 25 mi. E–W, 15 mi. NW of Karibib; rise to 7,710 ft. Tin, tungsten, tantalite mines.

Eros (ĕr'ůs), village (pop. 195), Jackson parish, N central La., 20 mi. WSW of Monroe, in agr. area.

Erpatak (ăr'pŏtŏk), Hung. *Érpatak*, town (pop. 3,144), Szabolcs co., NE Hungary, 10 mi. S of Nyiregyhaza; tobacco, corn, apples, pears; sheep, hogs.

Erpel (ĕr'půl), village (pop. 1,199), in former Prussian Rhine Prov., W Germany, after 1945 in Rhineland-Palatinate, on right bank of the Rhine (rail bridge), opposite Remagen. Has Romanesque church.

Erpeldange (ĕrpůldãzh'), village (pop. 215), SE Luxembourg, 10 mi. ESE of Luxembourg city; gypsum quarrying.

Erpelle-Cosina, Yugoslavia: see HERPELJE-KOZINA.

Erpfingen (ĕrp'fĭng-ůn), village (pop. 801), S Württemberg, Germany, after 1945 in Württemberg-Hohenzollern, in Swabian Jura, 9 mi. S of Reutlingen. Large stalactite cave near by.

Erpolzheim (ĕr'pôlts-hīm), village (pop. 696), Rhenish Palatinate, W Germany, 6 mi. SW of Frankenthal; wine.

Erquelinnes (ĕrkůlēn'), town (pop. 4,326), Hainaut prov., S Belgium, 12 mi. SSE of Mons; rail junction; station on Fr. border. Founded in 7th cent.

Erquy (ĕrkē'), village (pop. 1,451), Côtes-du-Nord dept., W France, fishing port on English Channel, 16 mi. ENE of Saint-Brieuc; resort with sheltered beach. Quartzite quarries near by.

Erraguntla, India: see PRODDATUR.

Errêgo (ĭră'gōō), village, Zambézia prov., central Mozambique, on road and 125 mi. N of Quelimane; cotton, peanuts, sesame, tobacco. Also Erêgo.

Errer (ĕ'rĕr), village, Harar prov., E central Ethiopia, in Great Rift Valley, on railroad and 30 mi. W of Diredawa, in agr. region (citrus fruit, bananas, coffee, figs, dates). Has hot mineral springs.

Errigal, Mount (ĕ'rĭgůl), mountain (2,466 ft.), NW Co. Donegal, Ireland, 12 mi. ENE of Dungloe; highest peak of Derryveach Mts.

Errikousai (ĕrĭkōō'sē), northernmost island (□ 1.5; pop. 552) in Ionian group, Greece, in Corfu nome, 7 mi. off NW Corfu isl.; 39°53'N 19°34'E; 2 mi. long, 1 mi. wide, rises to 430 ft. Fisheries. Sometimes Ereikosa or Erikousa; formerly Merlera.

Erris (ĕ'rĭs), district, NW Co. Mayo, Ireland, extending along coast bet. Benwee Head (W) and Downpatrick Head (E); interior is wild, desolate, and mountainous.

Erris Head, promontory on the Atlantic, NW Co. Mayo, Ireland, at N end of Mullet Peninsula and on W side of entrance to Broad Haven, 5 mi. N of Belmullet; 54°18'N 9°59'W.

Errol, agr. village and parish (pop. 1,891), SE Perthshire, Scotland, near Firth of Forth, 8 mi. E of Perth.

Errol, town (pop. 224), Coos co., N N.H., on Umbagog L. and Androscoggin R. and 22 mi. NNE of Berlin; agr., lumbering.

Erromanga (ĕrōmäng'ă), island (□ c.345; pop. 464), New Hebrides, SW Pacific, 240 mi. SE of Espiritu Santo; 35 mi. long, 25 mi. wide. Extinct volcanoes; savannas. Largest bay is Cook Bay, in E. Chief products: wool, sandalwood, copra. Martyrs' Memorial Church honors missionaries killed by natives.

Erronan, New Hebrides: see FUTUNA.

Ersakon (ĕrsůkôn'), village (1939 pop. over 500), N Cherkess Autonomous Oblast, Stavropol Territory, Russian SFSR, on Great Zelenchuk R. and 20 mi. NW of Cherkessk; grain, livestock.

Ersekë (ĕrsĕ'ků) or **Erseka** (ĕrsĕ'kä), town (1945 pop. 826), S Albania, at foot of the Grammos, 20 mi. S of Koritsa; lignite mining. Sometimes called Kolonjë or Kolonja, for the surrounding dist.

Ersekujvar, Czechoslovakia: see NOVE ZAMKY.

Ersekvadkert (ăr'shĕkvŏt"kĕrt), Hung. *Érsekvadkert*, town (pop. 3,722), Nograd-Hont co., N Hungary, 7 mi. SW of Balassagyarmat; flour mill, distilleries. Lignite deposits near by.

Ersh-, in Rus. names: see YERSH-.

Erskine, parish (pop. 2,129), NE Renfrew, Scotland. Includes agr. village of Bishopton, 5 mi. WNW of Renfrew.

Erskine (ûr'skĭn), village (pop. 608), Polk co., NW Minn., 29 mi. ESE of Crookston, in wheat, potato area; dairy products.

Erskineville, municipality (pop. 6,881), E New South Wales, Australia, 3 mi. SSW of Sydney, in metropolitan area; mfg. (furniture, shoes), brass foundries.

Erstein (ĕrstĕn', Ger. ĕr'shtīn), town (pop. 5,139), Bas-Rhin dept., E France, on the Ill and 12 mi. SSW of Strasbourg; sugar refining, wool spinning, metalworking, sauerkraut mfg.

Erstfeld (ĕrst'fĕlt), town (pop. 3,448), Uri canton, central Switzerland, on Reuss R. and 4 mi. S of Altdorf.

Ertarski, Russian SFSR: see YERTARSKI.

Ertil or **Ertil'** (ĕrtyĕl'), town (1948 pop. over 2,000), N Voronezh oblast, Russian SFSR, on rail spur from Mordovo and 55 mi. SE of Gryazi; sugar refinery. Developed 1937.

Ertvagoy (ărt'vôg-ûü), Nor. *Ertvågøy*, island (□ 47; pop. 1,098) in North Sea, More og Romsdal co., W Norway, bet. mainland and Tustna isl. (separated from both by narrow straits), 18 mi. ENE of Kristiansund; 13 mi. long, 8 mi. wide. Formerly spelled Ertvaagö.

Ertvelde (ĕrt'vĕldů), town (pop. 4,380), East Flanders prov., NW Belgium, near Ghent-Terneuzen Canal, 9 mi. N of Ghent; petroleum-refining center; mfg. (lubricating oil, grease, asphalt).

Eruh (ĕrōō'), village (pop. 1,004), Siirt prov., SE Turkey, 17 mi. SE of Siirt. Formerly Dih.

Eruslan River, Russian SFSR: see YERUSLAN RIVER.

Erval or **Herval** (ĕrväl'), city (pop. 1,225), SE Rio Grande do Sul, Brazil, 50 mi. WSW of Pelotas; breeding of cattle and race horses.

Erval, Serra do (sĕ'rů dōō), hilly area (c.600–c.1,600 ft.), S Rio Grande do Sul, Brazil, bet. Jacuí and Camaquã rivers. Copper, tin, tungsten, molybdenum deposits in vicinity of Camaquã, Caçapava do Sul, and Encruzilhada do Sul. Also spelled Serra do Herval.

Ervedosa do Douro (ĕrvĭdô'zů dōō dō'rōō), village (pop. 1,467), Viseu dist., N central Portugal, in Douro R. valley, 18 mi. ENE of Lamego; wine-growing (port wine); olives, figs, almonds, oranges.

Ervenice (ĕr'vyĕnyĭtsĕ), Czech *Ervěnice*, Ger. *Seestadl* (zä'shtädůl), village (pop. 3,491), NW Bohemia, Czechoslovakia, on railroad and 15 mi. SW of Teplice. Has major power plant (fed by Most coal field), which supplies electricity as far as Prague.

Ervidel (ĕrvēdĕl'), village (pop. 3,079), Beja dist., S Portugal, 12 mi. WSW of Beja; grain, sheep, timber.

Erving, town (pop. 1,322), Franklin co., NW Mass., on Millers R. and 10 mi. E of Greenfield; paper products. Settled 1801, inc. 1838. Includes part of MILLERS FALLS village.

Ervy-le-Châtel (ĕrvē'-lů-shätĕl'), village (pop. 907), Aube dept., NE central France, 19 mi. SSW of Troyes; building materials.

Erwin (ûr'wĭn). **1** Village (pop. 3,344), Harnett co., central N.C., 4 mi. WNW of Dunn; cotton milling. **2** Town (pop. 153), Kingsbury co., E central S.Dak., 9 mi. NE of De Smet. **3** Town (pop. 3,387), ⊙ Unicoi co., NE Tenn., on Nolichucky R. and 12 mi. S of Johnson City, near Bald Mts. and N.C. line; railroad shops; makes pottery, clothing, wood products. U.S. fish hatchery, mtn. recreation areas near by. Settled c.1775; inc. 1903.

Erwitte (ĕr'vĭ"tů), town (pop. 3,365), in former Prussian prov. of Westphalia, W Germany, after 1945 in North Rhine-Westphalia, 4 mi. S of Lippstadt. Has 12th–13th-cent. church.

Erymanthos or **Erimanthos** (both: ĕrĭ'mänthôs), Lat. *Erymanthus* (ĕrĭmăn'thůs), mountain massif in NW Peloponnesus, Greece, on border of Achæa and Elis; rises to 7,294 ft. 30 mi. NE of Pyrgos. In Gr. mythology it was the haunt of a boar killed by Hercules. Formerly called Olonos.

Erymanthos River or **Erimanthos River**, Lat. *Erymanthus*, in NW Peloponnesus, Greece, rises in Erymanthos mts., flows c.30 mi. SW and S, forming Elis-Arcadia border, to the Alpheus 9 mi. ESE of Olympia. Formerly Doana R.

Eryri, Wales: see SNOWDON.

Erythrae (ĕ'rĭthrē), anc. Greek city in Asia Minor, on Karaburun Peninsula opposite isl. of Chios, now in W Asiatic Turkey, 40 mi. W of Smyrna. Was one of the 12 Ionian cities and had a famous sybil and temple of Hercules.

Erythraean Sea: see RED SEA.

Erythrai or **Erithrai** (both: ĕrĭthrā'), town (pop. 3,495), Attica nome, E central Greece, on road to Thebes and 27 mi. NW of Athens; olive oil, wine; sheep and goat raising. Formerly called Kriekouki.

Eryx, Sicily: see ERICE.

Erzberg (ĕrts'bĕrk) [Ger.,=ore mountain], peak (c.5,000 ft.) of Eisenerz Alps in Styria, central Austria; has largest iron-ore deposits in Austria. In summer ore is mined at surface. Some of the mines have been in operation for over 1,000 years. City of EISENERZ at N foot.

Erzeni River, Albania: see ARZEN RIVER.

Erzerum, Turkey: see ERZURUM.

Erzgebirge (ârts'gůbĭr"gů) [Ger.,=Ore Mountains, a name for the range sometimes used in English], Czech *Krušné Hory* (krŏŏsh'nā hô'rĭ), mountain range on border of Bohemia (Czechoslovakia) and Saxony (Germany); extends c.100 mi. bet. the Fichtelgebirge (SSW) and the Elbe (NNE); rises to 4,080 ft. in Klinovec mtn. (Ger. *Keilberg*), in Czechoslovakia; second-highest peak is the Fichtelberg (3,983 ft.). The area has a wide variety of minerals; the mining of silver and iron was extensively carried on from 14th to 19th cent., notably at Jachymov; now the emphasis has shifted to nonferrous metals (tungsten, lead, tin, bismuth, arsenic, antimony, sulphur, and uranium). The chief mining centers are Annaberg, Freiberg, and Schneeberg. The uranium-ore deposits, developed since Second World War, are centered at Aue and Jachymov. Densely populated, the Erzgebirge is an important industrial area, particularly for metalworking and textile milling. Lumbering and the extraction of timber products are important too, and rye, oats, and potatoes are grown at high altitudes. There are numerous mineral springs; leading spas are Carlsbad and Teplice in Czechoslovakia, Brambach and Oberschlema in Germany. Forested slopes drop abruptly S toward valley of the Eger (lignite at Most and Sokolov); merge gently with highly industrialized Saxon foothills (N), where industry is centered at Chemnitz, Plauen, Zwickau, and in Oelsnitz-Lugau coal region. Embroidering and toy mfg. have long been traditional industries. Chemnitz-Chomutov line is main rail crossing. The SUDETENLAND dispute (1938) bet. Czechoslovakia and Germany resulted in transfer of Czech part of the Erzgebirge to Germany; it was returned to Czechoslovakia in 1945, and most of the German pop. was expelled.

Erzincan (ĕrzĭnjän'), province (□ 4,086; 1950 pop. 197,460), E central Turkey; ⊙ Erzincan. Bordered N by Erzincan Mts., S by Munzur and Mercan Mts. Drained by Euphrates R. Silver at Kemah. Fruit, grain. Sometimes Erzinjan and Erzingian.

Erzincan, town (1950 pop. 18,233), ⊙ Erzincan prov., E central Turkey, on Euphrates R. and railroad, 100 mi. WSW of Erzurum; makes vaccines; fruit, wheat, onions; mineral springs. Sometimes spelled Erzinjan and Erzingian. It was the Arsinga of Middle Ages.

Erzincan Mountains, E central Turkey, extend 60 mi. WNW–ESE just N of and parallel to Euphrates R.; rise to 11,604 ft. in Kesis Dag.

Erzingen (ĕr'tsĭng-ůn), village (pop. 1,633), S Baden, Germany, on S slope of Black Forest, 10 mi. ENE of Waldshut, on Swiss border; silk mfg.

Erzsebetbanya, Rumania: see BAIUT.

Erzsebetfalva, Hungary: see PESTSZENTERZSEBET.

Erzsebetvaros, Rumania: see DUMBRAVENI.

Erzurum or **Erzerum** (ĕrzŏŏrŏŏm'), prov. (□ 9,244; 1950 pop. 461,673), NE Turkey; ⊙ Erzurum. Bordered NW by Rize Mts.; drained by Euphrates, Aras, Oltu, and Coruh rivers. Cereals. Coal, lignite, some gold and silver.

Erzurum or **Erzerum**, anc. *Theodosiopolis*, city (1950 pop. 54,360), ⊙ Erzurum prov., Turkey, in Armenia, on railroad, near source of Euphrates and Aras rivers, 450 mi. E of Ankara, 110 mi. SE of Trebizond, on a high fertile plain; alt. 6,400 ft.; 39°50'N 41°20'E. Agr. trade center (wheat, barley, potatoes, onions). Has Pasteur Institute. Long a strategic fortress of Armenia, it figured prominently in the Russo-Turkish struggles of 19th cent. It no longer has its once-famous metalworking industry.

Es [Arabic,=the], for Arabic names beginning thus and not found here: see under following part of the name.

Esaki, Japan: see EZAKI.

Esan, Cape (ā'sä), Jap. *Esan-saki*, SW Hokkaido, Japan, at NE side of entrance to Tsugaru Strait; 41°49'N 141°11'E; lighthouse. Sometimes called Ezan and Yesan.

Esashi (äsä'shē), town (pop. 9,438), SW Hokkaido, Japan, on Sea of Japan, 32 mi. WNW of Hakodate; rail terminus; fishing, agr. (potatoes, grain). Gold rush here, 1899–1901.

Esaulovka, Ukrainian SSR: see YESAULOVKA.

Esbikesan, Turkey: see CIHANBEYLI.

Esbjerg (ĕs'byĕr), Dan. *Esbjærg*, city (1950 pop. 48,205) and port, in Ribe amt, SW Jutland, Denmark, on North Sea and 80 mi. SW of Aarhus. Important center of export trade; fisheries, dairy plant, margarine mfg. Airport. City developed with construction of harbor in 19th cent. FANO isl., opposite city, is resort suburb.

Esbly (ĕzblē'), town (pop. 2,325), Seine-et-Marne dept., N central France, river port on the Grand-Morin near its influx into the Marne, and 5 mi. SW of Meaux; building materials.

Esbo (ĕs'bōō, ĕs'bō), Finnish *Espoo* (ĕs'pō), village (commune pop. 21,496), Uusimaa co., S Finland, 10 mi. W of Helsinki; granite quarries. Has church (1458).

Esbon, city (pop. 278), Jewell co., N Kansas, 12 mi. WNW of Mankato, in grain and stock region.

Escaba (ĕskä'bä), village, SW Tucumán prov., Argentina, on Marapa R. and 70 mi. SW of Tucumán; dam and hydroelectric station.

Escacena del Campo (ĕskä-thā'nä dhĕl käm'pō), town (pop. 2,278), Huelva prov., SW Spain, 22 mi. W of Seville; chick-peas, cereals, olives, wine, hogs.

Escada (ĭshkä'dŭ), city (pop. 5,651), E Pernambuco, NE Brazil, on railroad and 32 mi. SW of Recife; sugar-milling center.

Escala, La (lä ĕskä'lä), town (pop. 2,349), Gerona prov., NE Spain, fishing port on the Mediterranean, and 18 mi. NE of Gerona; wine, cereals, vegetables.

Escalante (äskälän'tä), town (1939 pop. 4,477; 1948 municipality pop. 56,846), Negros Occidental prov., NE Negros isl., Philippines, at NW side of entrance to Tañon Strait, 45 mi. ENE of Bacolod; agr. center (rice, sugar cane). Sugar milling, sawmilling.

Escalante (ĕskŭlăn'tē), town (pop. 773), Garfield co., S Utah, on Kaiparowits Plateau, on Escalante R., and c.45 mi. E of Panguitch; alt. 5,303 ft.; trading point in cattle-grazing area. Settled 1875 by Mormons.

Escalante, Villa, Mexico: see VILLA ESCALANTE.

Escalante River, S Utah, rises in mtn. region W of Escalante, flows c.80 mi. SE to Colorado R. 8 mi. N of mouth of San Juan R.

Escalante River (ĕskälän'tä), Zulia state, W Venezuela, flows c.75 mi. N, through upper Maracaibo basin, past Santa Cruz and San Carlos, to L. Maracaibo 10 mi. S of Catatumbo R. mouth. Navigable for small craft. An oil pipe line follows its course.

Escalaplano (ĕskä"läplä'nô), village (pop. 2,338), Nuoro prov., SE Sardinia, 32 mi. NNE of Cagliari.

Escaldes, Les (lāz ĕskäld'), village (pop. c.500), Andorra, 1 mi. E of Andorra la Vella; alt. 3,629 ft. Tourist center with hot sulphur springs. Wool combing and spinning, tobacco processing. Hydroelectric plant. Sometimes called Las Escaldas.

Escalhão (ĭshkŭlyä'ō), village (pop. 1,750), Guarda dist., N central Portugal, near Sp. border, 35 mi. NNE of Guarda; olives, rye, potatoes, corn; livestock raising.

Escalier, L' (lĕskälyā'), village (pop. 2,074), SE Mauritius, on road and 7 mi. SW of Mahébourg, on the Rivière du Poste; sugar cane.

Escalón (ĕskälōn'), town (pop. 1,126), Chihuahua, N Mexico, 45 mi. SE of Jiménez; rail junction; cotton, grain, livestock.

Escalon (ĕ'skŭlŏn"), village (pop. 1,569), San Joaquin co., central Calif., 19 mi. SE of Stockton; wine, feed; ships fruit, hay.

Escalona (ĕskälō'nä), town (pop. 1,821), Toledo prov., central Spain, on Alberche R. and 29 mi. NW of Toledo; grapes, cereals, olives, sheep. Olive-oil presses, wineries, fisheries, potteries. Has ruins of castle, damaged during Peninsular War. The Castillejo cement plant is near by.

Escalona del Prado (dhĕl prä'dhō), town (pop. 1,186), Segovia prov., central Spain, 16 mi. N of Segovia; wheat, barley, rye, carobs.

Escalone, Palestine: see ASCALON.

Escalonilla (ĕskälōnē'lyä), village (pop. 2,966), Toledo prov., central Spain, 18 mi. WNW of Toledo; cereals, legumes, olives, grapes, wool, sheep, hogs; wine making, cheese processing, sawmilling.

Escalos de Baixo (ĭshkä'lōōsh dĭ bī'shōō), village (pop. 1,387), Castelo Branco dist., central Portugal, 7 mi. NE of Castelo Branco; olives, wheat, corn, beans.

Escambia (ĕskăm'bēŭ). **1** County (□ 962; pop. 31,443), S Ala.; ⊙ Brewton. Coastal plain bordering on Fla., drained by Conecuh (or Escambia) river. Cotton, truck, small fruit, poultry, dairy products. Formed 1868. **2** County (□ 663; pop. 112,706), extreme NW Fla.; ⊙ Pensacola. Bounded by Ala. line on W (here formed by Perdido R.) and N, Gulf of Mexico on S, Escambia R. on E. Rolling terrain in N, lowlands in S around Pensacola and Perdido bays. Dairying, farming (corn, peanuts, cotton, vegetables), forestry (lumber, naval stores), and fishing. Shipyards and other industry at Pensacola. Formed 1821.

Escambia Bay, N arm of Pensacola Bay, NW Fla.; 9 mi. long, 3–6 mi. wide; crossed by railroad bridge. Receives Escambia (Conecuh) R.

Escambia River, Fla.: see CONECUH RIVER.

Escanaba (ĕskŭnô'bŭ), city (pop. 15,170), ⊙ Delta co., S Upper Peninsula, Mich., c.55 mi. SSE of Marquette, on Little Bay De Noc. Important iron-ore shipping port; railroad and lumber-milling center; hardwood lumber, veneer, paper, foundry products, chemicals. Commercial and sport fishing. Agr. (truck, poultry; dairy products). Resorts. The Upper Peninsula State Fair is held here. Hiawatha Natl. Forest is NE. Settled 1852, inc. 1883.

Escanaba River, central Upper Peninsula, Mich., formed by junction of branches in SE Marquette co., flows c.40 mi. SE to Little Bay de Noc of Green Bay, 2 mi. N of Escanaba. Middle Branch rises NE of L. Michigamme, flows c.50 mi. SE. West Branch rises SE of Republic, flows c.30 mi. SE. East Branch rises SW of Ishpeming, flows c.35 mi. E and S to Middle Branch at Gwinn.

Escañuela (ĕskänūä'lä), town (pop. 1,948), Jaén prov., S Spain, 14 mi. NW of Jaén; olive oil, cereals.

Escarène, L' (lĕskärĕn'), village (pop. 726), Alpes-Maritimes dept., SE France, on the Paillon and 10 mi. NNE of Nice, on Nice-Turin RR; olive-oil pressing.

Escaro (ĕskärō'), village (pop. 259), Pyrénées-Orientales dept., S France, in CONFLENT valley, 8 mi. SW of Prades; iron mines.

Escarpada Point (äskärpä'dhä), extreme NE Luzon, Philippines, in Babuyan Channel, at tip of mountainous NE peninsula; 18°30'N 122°15'E.

Escarpelle, France: see ROOST-WARENDIN.

Escarpment, village, Central Prov., S central Kenya, at E edge of Great Rift Valley, on railroad and 24 mi. NW of Nairobi; alt. 7,390 ft.; hardwood industry; sisal, wheat, coffee, corn.

Escasú, Costa Rica: see ESCAZÚ.

Escatawpa River (ĕskŭtô'pŭ), in SW Ala. and SE Miss., rises in Washington co., Ala.; flows c.90 mi. S to Pascagoula Bay, Miss. Sometimes known as Dog R. Forms part of harbor of Pascagoula city at mouth.

Escatrón (ĕskätrōn'), town (pop. 1,906), Saragossa prov., NE Spain, on the Ebro and 15 mi. WNW of Caspe; olive-oil processing; sugar beets, cereals.

Escaudain (ĕskōdē'), town (pop. 5,713), Nord dept., N France, 3 mi. W of Denain; coal-mining center.

Escaudoeuvres (ĕskōdû'vrŭ), outer NE suburb (pop. 2,715) of Cambrai, Nord dept., N France, on the Escaut; sugar factory.

Escautpont (ĕskōpō'), town (pop. 3,550), Nord dept., N France, on the Escaut and 5 mi. NNE of Valenciennes; large glassworks.

Escaut River, France and Belgium: see SCHELDT RIVER.

Escazú (ĕskäsōō'), town (1950 pop. 1,430), San José prov., Costa Rica, on central plateau, 5 mi. WSW of San José; coffee, sugar cane, rice. Sometimes spelled Escasú.

Escazú, volcano (7,956 ft.), W central Costa Rica, 6 mi. SW of San José.

Esch, Luxembourg: see ESCH-SUR-ALZETTE.

Eschborn (ĕsh'bôrn), village (pop. 2,442), in former Prussian prov. of Hesse-Nassau, W Germany, after 1945 in Hesse, 6 mi. NW of Frankfurt city center; airport.

Eschen (ĕ'shŭn), village (pop. 1,022), N Liechtenstein, near the Rhine (Swiss border), 5 mi. N of Vaduz; stock raising. Mfg. of pottery.

Eschenbach (ĕ'shŭnbäkh). **1** Town, Middle Franconia, W Bavaria, Germany: see WOLFRAMS-ESCHENBACH. **2** or **Eschenbach in der Oberpfalz** (ĭn dĕr ō'bŭrpfälts"), town (pop. 3,009), Upper Palatinate, NE Bavaria, Germany, 18 mi. SE of Bayreuth; rye, barley, cattle, sheep. Has 15th-cent. church. Chartered c.1326.

Eschenbach (ĕ'shŭnbäkh), town (pop. 2,423), St. Gall canton, N Switzerland, near L. of Zurich, 5 mi. E of Rapperswil; metal products, cotton textiles.

Escher Canal (ĕ'shŭr), E central Switzerland; 3 mi. long Linth R. leaves its old bed at Mollis, flowing through canal to L. of Wallenstadt.

Eschershausen (ĕ"shŭrs-hou'zŭn), town (pop. 4,131), in former Prussian prov. of Hanover, NW Germany, after 1945 in Lower Saxony, 10 mi. NE of Holzminden; asphalt works; sawmilling, brewing, distilling. Novelist Raabe b. here. Until 1941 in Brunswick.

Eschikam (ĕ'shŭlkäm"), village (pop. 2,110), Lower Bavaria, Germany, in Bohemian Forest, on small Cham R. and 32 mi. N of Deggendorf; greenstone quarries. Chartered c.1330.

Escholtz Bay, Alaska: see ESCHSCHOLTZ BAY.

Escholtz Islands, Marshall Isls.: see BIKINI.

Escholzmatt (ĕ'shōltsmät"), town (pop. 3,518), Lucerne canton, central Switzerland, 23 mi. E of Bern; woolen textiles, foodstuffs.

Eschscholtz Bay (ĕ'shōlts) (30 mi. long, 7–16 mi. wide), NW Alaska, SE arm of Kotzebue Sound, NE Seward Peninsula, 50 mi. SE of Kotzebue; 66°20'N 161°25'W. Trapping and fishing; Elephant Point village on S shore. Contains Chamisso Isl. (2 mi. long), bird sanctuary. Sometimes spelled Escholtz.

Esch-sur-Alzette (ĕsh-sür-älzĕt') or **Esch,** town (pop. 26,851), S Luxembourg, on Alzette R. and 10 mi. SW of Luxembourg city; iron and ocher mining; steel center (blast furnaces, rolling mills), mfg. of steel products, railroad equipment, cement and tar products, synthetic fertilizer; beer brewing, liquor distilling; market center for barley, wheat, pulse, sugar-beet region.

Esch-sur-Sûre (-sür'), town (pop. 363), NW Luxembourg, on Sûre R. and 4 mi. S of Wiltz; woolen textiles, candles.

Eschwege (ĕsh'vā"gŭ), city (pop. 21,565), in former Prussian prov. of Hesse-Nassau, W Germany, after 1945 in Hesse, on the Werra and 25 mi. ESE of Kassel; 51°11'N 10°3'E. Rail junction; auto repair shops; mfg. of pharmaceuticals, textiles, shoes; metal- and woodworking, tanning. Has 11th- and 15th-cent. churches, 16th-cent. castle. First mentioned 974. Chartered 1249. Passed to Hesse in 1436.

Eschweiler (ĕsh'vī"lŭr), town (pop. 30,191), in former Prussian Rhine Prov., W Germany, after 1945 in North Rhine-Westphalia, 8 mi. ENE of Aachen (linked by tramway); 50°48'N 6°15'E. Rail junction; mining (coal, lignite) center; limestone quarries. Ironworks; steel construction; mfg. of tools, cables, chains, wire; leatherworking. Second World War damage included church of SS. Peter and Paul (Romanesque-Gothic, partly dating from 12th cent.; restored and enlarged 1880 and 1904), and noted Renaissance balcony of 13th-cent. ruined castle. First mentioned in 9th cent., town belonged to duchy of Jülich until French Revolutionary Wars. Passed to Prussia in 1815. Captured by U.S. troops in Nov., 1944, after heavy fighting.

Eschweiler, village (pop. 215), N Luxembourg, in the Ardennes, 3 mi. N of Wiltz; dairying.

Esclavos River (ĕsklä'vōs), Sp. *Río de los Esclavos,* S Guatemala, rises in highlands near Mataquescuintla, flows c.75 mi. generally S, past Santa Rosa, to the Pacific 37 mi. ESE of San José. Forms Santa Rosa–Jutiapa dept. border in lower course.

Esclusham Below (ĕsklōō'shăm), agr. and residential parish (pop. 2,366), E Denbigh, Wales, 2 mi. SW of Wrexham.

Escobal or **El Escobal** (ĕl ĕskōbäl'), village (pop. 597), Colón prov., central Panama, on Canal Zone border, road terminus on Gatun Lake, and 15 mi. SSW of Colón. Corn, rice, beans; stock raising, fishing.

Escobar (ĕskōbär'), town (pop. 4,021), NE Buenos Aires prov., Argentina, 28 mi. NW of Buenos Aires; mfg. of cigars, soap, tile, liquor; orchards. Sometimes called Belén.

Escobar, town (dist. pop. 5,462), Paraguarí dept., S Paraguay, on railroad and 50 mi. SE of Asunción; lumbering and agr. center (fruit, corn, livestock).

Escobedo (ĕskōbā'dō), town (pop. 999), Coahuila, N Mexico, in E outliers of Sierra Madre Oriental, 130 mi. NW of Monterrey; cereals, cattle, sheep.

Escobonal, El (ĕl ĕskōvōnäl'), village (pop. 2,061), Tenerife, Canary Isls., 15 mi. SW of Santa Cruz de Tenerife; cereals, potatoes, tomatoes, onions, bananas, livestock.

Escocesa Bay (ĕskōsä'sä), small inlet on N coast of Dominican Republic, bounded by Samaná Peninsula (SE). At its head is Matanzas.

Escoheag, R.I.: see WEST GREENWICH.

Escoma (ĕskō'mä), town (pop. c.8,700), La Paz dept., W Bolivia, near L. Titicaca and mouth of Suches R., 85 mi. NW of La Paz; alt. 12,516 ft.; trade center (barley, corn).

Escondida Point (ĕskōndē'dä), cape on Pacific coast of Guerrero, SW Mexico, 28 mi. SSW of Ometepec; 16°19'N 98°34'W.

Escondido (ĕskŭndē'dō), city (pop. 6,544), San Diego co., S Calif., 27 mi. N of San Diego, in agr. valley (grapes, citrus fruit, avocados, poultry; dairy products). Annual grape festival. SAN PASQUAL battlefield is E. Inc. 1888.

Escondido River (ĕskōndē'dō), SE Nicaragua, formed at Rama by union of Siquia, Mico, and Rama rivers; flows 60 mi. E, through hardwood and banana dist., to Bluefields Bay of Caribbean Sea at Bluefields. Banana, rubber, coconut shipping along entire course. Sometimes called Bluefields R.

Escorca (ĕskôr'kä), village (pop. 35), Majorca, Balearic Isls., in isl.'s most elevated section, 20 mi. NNE of Palma; olive growing, lumbering. Renowned Lluch monastery, with shrine to the Virgin, is 1½ mi. E.

Escorial or **Escurial** (ĕskô'rēŭl, –kū'–, Sp. ĕskōryäl', –kōō–), monastery and historic royal residence, Madrid prov., central Spain, in New Castile, at E slopes of the Sierra de Guadarrama, 26 mi. WNW of Madrid; adjoined N by the town of SAN LORENZO DEL ESCORIAL (formerly Escorial de Arriba) and E by El Escorial (formerly Escorial de Abajo). One of Europe's finest and largest edifices, built (1563–84) as a monastery (*Real Monasterio de San Lorenzo del Escorial*) for Hieronymite order by Philip II to commemorate victory over French at Saint-Quentin (1557). Constructed along pure classical lines of the late Renaissance, it was begun by Juan Bautista de Toledo and completed by his great pupil Juan de Herrera. The massive granite structure forms a quadrangle (675 by 528 ft.) of somber façades flanked by square towers. The magnificent twin-towered church is crowned by a dome. Inside the church are many art treasures, among them a crucifix by Benvenuto Cellini and baroque frescoes by Luca Giordano. The Escorial houses a famed collection of paintings—by Van der Weyden, Veronese, Titian, Bassano, Tintoretto, Claudio Coello, Ribera, El Greco, Velázquez, Goya, Mengs, and others. A large wing is taken up by the royal palace, mostly decorated in 18th-cent. style. The kings' Pantheon was added in 17th cent. The library has an invaluable collection of manuscripts. The Escorial was damaged by fire in 1671 and 1872, and suffered (1808) during Fr. invasion. Since 1885 the monastery has been inhabited by Augustinian monks. The town of **El Escorial** (pop. 2,597), on the Madrid–La Coruña

RR, is a tourist and summer resort; has hydroelectric station.

Escoriaza (ĕskōryä'thä), town (pop. 827), Guipúzcoa prov., N Spain, 32 mi. SW of San Sebastián, in agr. region (cereals, sugar beets, flax, fruit). Mfg. of soap, chocolate, linen. Has mineral springs and near-by ocher deposits. Believed to be of Roman origin. Devastated by fire in 1521.

Escouloubre (ĕskōōlōō'brü), village (pop. 216), Aude dept., S France, 22 mi. SSW of Limoux, near Aude R.; marble quarries. Mineral springs. Hydroelectric plant.

Escudo de Veraguas (ĕskōō'dō dä värä'gwäs), island in Mosquito Gulf of the Caribbean, W central Panama, 11 mi. off Bocas del Toro prov.; 2 mi. long, 1 mi. wide.

Escuinapa or **Escuinapa de Hidalgo** (ĕskwēnä'pä dā ēdäl'gō), city (pop. 5,864), Sinaloa, NW Mexico, in coastal lowland, on railroad to Mexico city and 45 mi. SE of Mazatlán; commercial and agr. center (corn, sugar cane, chick-peas, cotton, fruit, vegetables). Airport.

Escuintla (ĕskwēn'tlä), department (□ 1,693; 1950 pop. 124,761), S Guatemala, on the Pacific; ⊙ Escuintla. In Pacific piedmont, sloping S into coastal plain; drained by lower Nahualate, Madre Vieja, Guacalate, and Michatoya rivers. Includes Pacaya volcano (NE). Major sugar-cane dist. (mills at Pantaleón, El Baúl, Concepción, Salto); bananas (Tiquisate), coffee, corn, citronella, tropical fruit. Cattle raising in large fodder-grass areas. Chief centers (linked by rail) are Escuintla, Santa Lucía, Palín, and port of San José.

Escuintla, city (1950 pop. 9,822), ⊙ Escuintla dept., S Guatemala, in Pacific piedmont (alt. 1,109 ft.), near Guacalate R., 28 mi. SW of Guatemala, on railroad; 14°17'N 90°47'W. Commercial and agr. center in rich sugar-cane, cotton, and coffee dist.; citronella, lemongrass, tropical fruit (coconuts, pineapples, mangos); cotton gin. Sugar mills of Concepción and Salto near by. Winter resort (mineral baths). Flourished as political and indigo-trading center in 17th and 18th cent.

Escuintla, town (pop. 2,351), Chiapas, S Mexico, in Pacific lowland, on railroad and 38 mi. NW of Tapachula; sugar-cane center.

Escumains, Les (lāzĕskümē'), village (pop. estimate 800), E Que., on the St. Lawrence, at mouth of Escumains R., and 40 mi. NNE of Rivière du Loup; lumbering center.

Escuminac Bay (ĕskū'mĭnăk), tidal estuary (24 mi. long) of Restigouche R., N N.B., enters Chaleur Bay at Dalhousie. On S shore is Campbellton.

Escuminac Point, promontory on the Gulf of St. Lawrence, E N.B., at N entrance to Northumberland Strait, 30 mi. ENE of Chatham; 47°5'N 64°49'W.

Escuque (ĕskōō'kā), town (pop. 2,196), Trujillo state, W Venezuela, in Andean spur, 5 mi. W of Valera; alt. 3,380 ft. Resort in agr. region (coffee, grain, potatoes, sugar cane, cacao, tobacco). Petroleum wells near by.

Escurial (ĕskōōryäl'), town (pop. 2,096), Cáceres prov., W Spain, 20 mi. S of Trujillo; woolen-cloth mfg.; livestock, cereals, flax, olive oil.

Escurial, monastery and royal residence, Spain: see ESCORIAL.

Escurolles (ĕsküròl'), village (pop. 274), Allier dept., central France, in Limagne, 8 mi. W of Vichy; agr., poultry raising.

Escúzar (ĕskōō'thär), village (pop. 1,557), Granada prov., S Spain, 12 mi. SW of Granada; cereals, sugar beets, sheep.

Esdraelon, Plain of, Israel: see JEZREEL, PLAIN OF.

Eséka (ĕsä'kä), village, Sanaga-Maritime region, SW Fr. Cameroons, on railroad and 45 mi. ESE of Edéa; agr. center and native market; rice processing, palm-oil milling. Has R.C. and 2 Protestant missions, meteorological station.

Esel, Switzerland: see PILATUS.

Esenovichi, Russian SFSR: see YESENOVICHI.

Esens (ā'zŭns), town (pop. 3,673), in former Prussian prov. of Hanover, NW Germany, after 1945 in Lower Saxony, in East Friesland, near North Sea, 17 mi. W of Emden; woodworking, brewing.

Esera River (ēsä'rä), Huesca prov., NE Spain, rises in the central Pyrenees in the Maladetta massif at Fr. border, flows c.60 mi. SSW to Cinca R. 6 mi. NE of Barbastro. Feeds Aragon and Catalonia Canal. Hydroelectric plant (Seira) and irrigation reservoir (Barasona).

Esfahan, Iran: see ISFAHAN.

Esfarayen, Iran: see ISFARAIN.

Esgueira (ĕzhgā'rù), village (pop. 1,659), Aveiro dist., N central Portugal, 1 mi. ENE of Aveiro; brick mfg.

Esgueva River (ĕzgā'vä), Burgos and Valladolid provs., N central Spain, rises 20 mi. NE of Aranda de Duero, flows 76 mi. WSW, parallel to the Duero, to Pisuerga R. at Valladolid.

Esguevillas de Esgueva (ĕzgāvē'lyäs dhä ĕzgā'vä), town (pop. 1,020), Valladolid prov., N central Spain, 19 mi. ENE of Valladolid; sheep raising; cereals, vegetables, anise.

Esh [Arabic,=the], for Arabic names beginning thus and not found here: see under following part of the name.

Esher (ē'shŭr), formerly Esher and The Dittons, residential urban district (1931 pop. 17,076; 1951 census 51,217), NE Surrey, England, 15 mi. SW of London. Town of Esher has remains of 15th-cent. "Esher Place," founded by William of Waynefiete and occupied by Cardinal Wolsey; and of "Claremont," built 1768 by Lord Clive, residence of Princess Charlotte and of Louis Philippe. In urban dist. are Long Ditton and Thames Ditton, with automobile works and metal foundries. Just N of Esher is the well-known race course Sandown Park. East and West Molesey urban dist. was absorbed 1933.

Eshmunein, Egypt: see ASHMUNEIN, EL.

Eshowe (ĕ'shōwä), town (pop. 2,877), ⊙ Zululand, E Natal, U. of So. Afr., 70 mi. NNE of Durban; sugar-growing center; gold and chrome mining near by. Zircon deposits in region. In Zulu War, the town, held by small British detachment, was besieged for several months by large Zulu forces until relieved April 3, 1879.

Esh Sham, Syria: see DAMASCUS; SYRIA.

Esiama (ĕsyä'mä), town, Western Prov., SW Gold Coast colony, on Gulf of Guinea, 10 mi. W of Axim, in rice area; rice mill; fishing. Also spelled Essiama.

Esine (ĕ'zēnĕ), village (pop. 1,574), Brescia prov., Lombardy, N Italy, in Val Camonica, near Oglio R., 4 mi. SW of Breno; ironworks.

Esino River (ĕzē'nô), The Marches, central Italy, rises in the Apennines 6 mi. ESE of Gualdo Tadino, flows 55 mi. NE, past Matelica, to the Adriatic 7 mi. WNW of Ancona.

Esja (ĕs'yä), mountain (2,982 ft.), SW Iceland, 10 mi. NE of Reykjavik, overlooking Reykjavik harbor; 64°15'N 21°36'W.

Esk, river: see ESK RIVER.

Eska (ĕ'skä), village (pop. 55), S Alaska, in Matanuska Valley, on rail spur and 16 mi. NE of Matanuska village; coal mining.

Eskbank, village in Dalkeith parish, NE Midlothian, Scotland, on North Esk R.; carpet weaving.

Eskdale, village (1940 pop. 1,146), Kanawha co., W W.Va., 21 mi. SE of Charleston, in coal and agr. area.

Eskhar or **Eskhar'** (ĕskhär'), town (1939 pop. over 500), N central Kharkov oblast, Ukrainian SSR, 6 mi. W of Chuguyev, in Kharkov metropolitan area.

Eski Baba, Turkey: see BABAESKI.

Eski Dzhumaya, Bulgaria: see TARGOVISHTE.

Eskifjordur or **Eskifjordhur** (ĕ'skĭfyûr"dhür), Icelandic *Eskifjörður*, town (pop. 678), ⊙ Sudur-Mula co., E Iceland, on Reydar Fjord, 13 mi. S of Seydisfjordur; 65°4'N 14°W; fishing port; feldspar-quarrying region.

Eskije, Greece: see XANTHE.

Eski Krym, Russian SFSR: see STARY KRYM, Crimea.

Eskilstuna (ĕ'skĭlstü"nä), city (1950 pop. 53,577), Sodermanland co., E Sweden, on river draining L. Hjalmar into L. Malar, 50 mi. W of Stockholm; 59°22'N 16°31'E. Rail junction; industrial center, noted for its cutlery, hardware, and other steel products; steel-rolling mills, machinery works; mfg. of precision tools and instruments, electrical equipment. Site of technical col.; has 12th-cent. church. City, named for St. Eskil, became trade center in 12th cent.; chartered 1659. In 17th and 18th cent. iron and steel industry grew rapidly and soon rivaled that of Sheffield.

Eskimo, village (pop. 41), E central Alaska, near Fairbanks.

Eskimonaes, Greenland: see DANEBORG.

Eskimo Point, trading post, S Keewatin Dist., Northwest Territories, on Hudson Bay; 61°7'N 94°3'W; radio station, Royal Canadian Mounted Police post. Site of Anglican and R.C. mission.

Eskipazar (ĕskĭ'päzär"), village (pop. 825), Cankiri prov., N central Turkey, on railroad and 60 mi. WNW of Cankiri; grain, vetch; mohair goats. Formerly Mecidiye.

Eskisehir (ĕskĭ'shĕhĭr"), Turkish *Eskişehir*, province (□ 5,245; 1950 pop. 274,571), W central Turkey; ⊙ Eskisehir. Bordered N, E, SE by Sakarya R., W by Ulu Mts. Drained by Sakarya and Porsuk rivers. Resources include meerschaum, magnesite, and chromium in quantity; also potter's clay and asbestos. Sugar beets, wheat, oats; mohair goats, sheep, horses; poultry; long-staple cotton in N.

Eskisehir, Turkish *Eskişehir*, city (1950 pop. 88,459), ⊙ Eskisehir prov., W central Turkey, rail junction (repair shops) on Porsuk R., 125 mi. W of Ankara; 39°44'N 30°30'E. Known for its meerschaum, chromium, and magnesite, which it exports. Manufactures cotton goods and is center for cotton research. Trade and market center for grain and other agr. products; sugar refinery; silos and warehouses; aircraft assembly plant. Tiles have been made since Seljuk period. Long known for its hot mineral springs. City is perhaps on site of anc. Dorylaeum (dŏrĭlē'ŭm), where the crusaders defeated the Seljuk Turks in 1097; later became an early capital of the Ottoman Turks. Sometimes spelled Eski-Shehr or Eskishehir.

Eski Stambul, Bulgaria: see PRESLAV.

Eski-Zagra, Bulgaria: see STARA ZAGORA, city.

Eskridge, city (pop. 601), Wabaunsee co., E central Kansas, 26 mi. SW of Topeka; trade center for grain region. Coal mines in vicinity. State park near by.

Esk River, mostly in Cumberland, England, formed by confluence of 2 tributaries in Dumfriesshire, Scotland, 8 mi. NW of Langholm, flows SE, turns S and SW, past Longtown, to Solway Firth 8 mi. NNW of Carlisle; 20 mi. long.

Esk River, Midlothian, Scotland, formed just N of Dalkeith by the South Esk (rises in Moorfoot Hills, flows 19 mi. N past Dalkeith) and the North Esk (rises in Pentland Hills, flows 17 mi. NE past Penicuik), flows 4 mi. N past Inveresk to Firth of Forth at Musselburgh.

Esk River, Tasmania: see NORTH ESK RIVER; SOUTH ESK RIVER.

Eslam Qala, Afghanistan: see ISLAM QALA.

Esla River (ā'slä), in Leon and Zamora provs., NW Spain, chief tributary of the Duero or Douro; rises on S slopes of the Picos de Europa (Cantabrian Mts.), flows 175 mi. SSW to the Duero 16 mi. W of Zamora. Receives Bernesga and Órbigo rivers (right) and the Cea (left); middle course flanked by Esla irrigation canal. Dam and hydroelectric installations near Muelas del Pan (Zamora).

Eslarn (ĕs'lärn), village (pop. 3,385), Upper Palatinate, E Bavaria, Germany, in Bohemian Forest, 17 mi. ESE of Weiden; textile mfg., glass grinding, woodworking.

Eslida (äslē'dhä), town (pop. 1,125), Castellón de la Plana prov., E Spain, 15 mi. SW of Castellón de la Plana; cork-processing center; olive oil, cereals. Quicksilver mining. Summer resort.

Eslov (ās'lûv"), Swedish *Eslöv*, city (pop. 6,746), Malmohus co., S Sweden, 20 mi. NE of Malmo; rail junction; commercial center, with woolen mills and plants mfg. shoes, furniture, machinery, pianos; food canning.

Esme (ĕshmĕ'), Turkish *Eşme*, village (pop. 2,775), Manisa prov., W Turkey, on railroad and 85 mi. E of Manisa; valonia, wheat, barley, sesame, vetch, opium. Formerly Tokmak or Elvanlar.

Esmeralda (ĕzmäräl'dä), town (pop. 2,941), Camagüey prov., E Cuba, on railroad and 37 mi. NNW of Camagüey, in agr. region (sugar cane, coconuts, fruit, tobacco). Sometimes La Esmeralda. Sugar central of Jaronú is 13 mi. E.

Esmeralda or **La Esmeralda** (lä), town (pop. 916), Coahuila, N Mexico, on railroad and 125 mi. N of Torreón; silber, gold, copper, zinc mining.

Esmeralda, Nicaragua: see LA LIBERTAD.

Esmeralda (ĕz"mŭräl'dŭ), county (□ 3,570; pop. 614), S Nev.; ⊙ Goldfield. Mining and stock-grazing area bordering on Calif. Gold, silver. Silver Peak Mts. in W. Formed 1861.

Esmeralda (ĕzmäräl'dä), village, Amazonas territory, S Venezuela, landing on the Orinoco S of Cerro Duida and 215 mi. SE of Puerto Ayacucho, in tropical forest region (rubber, balata, vanilla); 3°10'N 65°33'W. Casiquiare R., linking the Orinoco with the Amazon, branches off 20 mi. W.

Esmeralda, La, Bolivia: see LA ESMERALDA.

Esmeraldas (ĕzmäräl'däs), province (□ 5,799; 1950 pop. 70,319), N Ecuador, on the Pacific; borders Colombia; ⊙ Esmeraldas. Its indented coastal lowlands rise E to the Andes. Watered by Esmeraldas and Santiago rivers. Just N of the equator, it has a tropical, humid climate of little seasonal changes (mean temp. c.75°F.); somewhat more arid along the coast, because of cool Humboldt Current. Gold washing along Santiago and Cayapas rivers. Almost entirely covered by dense rain forests yielding balsa wood, tagua nuts, rubber, and mangrove bark, which are exported. Agr. crops include cacao, tobacco, coconuts, rice, bananas. The city of Esmeraldas is its main seaport and trading center.

Esmeraldas, city (pop. 15,700), ⊙ Esmeraldas prov., NW Ecuador, Pacific port at mouth of Esmeraldas R., due E of Galápagos Isls., 120 mi. NW of Quito; 0°59'N 79°37'W. Seaport, reached by vessels from Guayaquil and Buenaventura (Colombia). Trading center in fertile agr. and lumbering region, producing cacao, tobacco, coconuts, rubber, tagua nuts, balsa wood. Sawmilling. Seat of import houses, customhouse, and airport. Just N is the little port and beach resort of Las Palmas, on the Pacific. Gold mines are near by.

Esmeraldas River, Esmeraldas prov., N Ecuador; formed c.50 mi. SE of its mouth by the Río Blanco and Guaillabamba R., it enters the Pacific 2 mi. N of Esmeraldas. Navigable. Some gold washing along its course.

Esmond. **1** Village (pop. 475), Benson co., N central N.Dak., 23 mi. W of Minnewaukan. **2** Village (1940 pop. 1,643) in Smithfield town, Providence co., NE R.I., on Woonasquatucket R. (bridged here) and 6 mi. NW of Providence. **3** Town (pop. 49), Kingsbury co., E central S.Dak., 13 mi. SW of De Smet.

Esna or **Esneh**, Egypt: see ISNA.

Esneux (ĕznû'), town (pop. 4,973), Liége prov., E Belgium, on Ourthe R. and 7 mi. S of Liége; tourist resort; quarrying.

Eso, island, Yugoslavia: see IZ ISLAND.

Esopus (ēsō'pŭs), village in Esopus town (1940 pop. 4,220), Ulster co., SE N.Y., on W bank of the Hudson and 7 mi. SSE of Kingston, in grape-growing and resort area. Seat of Mount St. Alphonsus Theological Seminary. John Burroughs lived near here. Town was formed in 1811, and was partly annexed by KINGSTON in 1818.

Esopus Creek, SE N.Y., rises in the Catskills in central Ulster co., flows N, then SE, to ASHOKAN RESERVOIR, whence it emerges from its S side and continues SE, then NE, to the Hudson at Saugerties; c.65 mi. long.

Espaillat (ĕspīyä'), province (□ 433; 1935 pop. 102,485; 1950 pop. 152,308), N Dominican Republic, on the coast; ⊙ Moca. Crossed by Cordillera Setentrional and including central section of Cibao region (La Vega Real). One of the most fertile and densely populated parts of the Republic. Main crops: coffee, cacao, tobacco, rice, corn. Served by Santiago-Sánchez RR. Through Moca also passes highway from Ciudad Trujillo. Other centers are Salcedo, Tenares, Veragua. Originally a part of La Vega prov., it was set up 1885.

Espalion (ĕspälyō'), town (pop. 2,806), Aveyron dept., S France, on the Lot and 15 mi. NE of Rodez; metalworks, glove factory; wool combing. Has 13th-cent. bridge.

Espaly-Saint-Marcel (ĕspälē'-sē-märsĕl'), village (pop. 1,442), Haute-Loire dept., S central France, 1 mi. W of Le Puy; lace mfg., paper milling.

España, Sp. name for SPAIN.

España or **Central España** (sĕnträl' ĕspä'nyä), sugar-mill village (pop. 1,292), Matanzas prov., W Cuba, on railroad and 40 mi. ESE of Matanzas.

Españita (ĕspänyē'tä), town (pop. 631), Tlaxcala, central Mexico, 16 mi. NW of Tlaxcala; maguey.

Espanola (ĕspŭnō'lŭ), village (pop. estimate 1,500), S central Ont., on Spanish R. and 40 mi. WSW of Sudbury; nickel, copper, gold mining; lumbering.

Espanola (ĕ"spănyō'lŭ), village (pop. 1,446), Rio Arriba co., N N.Mex., on Rio Grande and 24 mi. NNW of Santa Fe, in Santa Clara Pueblo land grant; alt. c.5,600 ft. Shipping point for fruit, livestock, wool; agr. (chili, vegetables), timber. San Juan and Santa Clara Pueblo Indian villages and Bandelier Natl. Monument are near by.

Española Island (ĕspänyō'lä) or **Hood Island** (□ 18), SE Galápagos Isls., Ecuador, in the Pacific, 35 mi. S of Puerto Baquerizo (San Cristóbal Isl.); 1°25'S 89°40'W.

Espardell (ĕspärdāl'), islet, Balearic Isls., bet. Iviza (N) and Formentera (S), 8 mi. SSE of Iviza; 38°48'N 1°29'E.

Espargo (ĭshpär'gō͝o), airfield, Cape Verde Isls., on SAL isl., c.450 mi. NW of Dakar (Fr. West Africa); 16°44'N 22°56'W. Inaugurated for trans-Atlantic flights in 1949.

Esparragalejo (ĕspärägälā'hō), town (pop. 1,736), Badajoz prov., W Spain, 5 mi. WNW of Mérida; cereals, chick-peas, stock.

Esparragosa de Lares (ĕspärägō'sä dhā lä'rĕs), town (pop. 2,276), Badajoz prov., W Spain, 1 mi. SW of Puebla de Alcocer; olives, cereals, livestock. Flour milling, olive-oil pressing; tile mfg.

Esparragosa de la Serena (lä sārā'nä), town (pop. 1,719), Badajoz prov., W Spain, 4 mi. SW of Castuera; cereals, olives, livestock.

Esparraguera (ĕspärägā'rä), town (pop. 4,048), Barcelona prov., NE Spain, 18 mi. NW of Barcelona, near Llobregat R.; cotton milling, chemical mfg.; lumbering; agr. trade. Near-by caves of Patracó have stalactites and stalagmites.

Esparta (ĕspär'tä), city (1950 pop. 1,925), Puntarenas, W Costa Rica, on Inter-American Highway and 12 mi. E of Puntarenas (linked by rail spur). Agr. and commercial center; stock raising; lumber industry. One of oldest cities of Costa Rica, it was founded 1574 and originally named Esparza. A Pacific outpost in colonial times, it was frequently attacked by pirates in 17th cent.

Espartel, Cape, NW Africa: see SPARTEL, CAPE.

Espartinas (ĕspärtē'näs), town (pop. 1,356), Seville prov., SW Spain, 7 mi. W of Seville; olives, vegetables, cereals, grapes.

Espe (ĕsp'ŭ), village in Ullensvang canton (pop. 2,441), Hordaland co., SW Norway, on Sor Fjord (a branch of Hardanger Fjord), 10 mi. N of Odda; wool milling. Farming, fruitgrowing near by. The 13th-cent. Ullensvang church is 8 mi. N; tourism.

Espeja (ĕspā'hä), village (pop. 1,040), Salamanca prov., W Spain, 10 mi. W of Ciudad Rodrigo; cereals, vegetables, livestock.

Espejo (ĕspā'hō), town (pop. 1,490), Santiago prov., central Chile, on railroad and 6 mi. S of Santiago; agr. center (grain, fruit, wine, livestock). Military air base.

Espejo, town (pop. 9,139), Córdoba prov., S Spain, on hill 19 mi. SE of Córdoba; olive-oil and meat processing, flour milling, wood turning, mfg. of footwear and plaster. Cereals, beans, hemp in area; stock raising. Gypsum quarries near by.

Espejo, Lake (□ 15; alt. 2,533 ft.), in the Andes, SW Neuquén natl. territory, Argentina, in the lake dist.; extends c.11 mi. SE from Chile border toward L. Nahuel Huapí.

Espeland (ĕsp'ülän), village (pop. 588) in Haus canton, Hordaland co., SW Norway, on railroad and 5 mi. E of Bergen; knit goods, hosiery.

Espelette (ĕspülĕt'), village (pop. 625), Basses-Pyrénées dept., SW France, in W Pyrenees, 10 mi. S of Bayonne; market; horse and sheep raising.

Espenberg, Cape (ĕ'spŭnbûrg), NW Alaska, N Seward Peninsula, on S side of entrance to Kotzebue Sound, 40 mi. SW of Kotzebue, on Arctic Circle; 66°32'N 163°47'W.

Espenhain (ĕ'spŭnhīn), village (pop. 2,205), Saxony, E central Germany, 11 mi. SSE of Leipzig; lignite mining. Power station.

Espera (ĕspā'rä), town (pop. 2,290), Cádiz prov., SW Spain, 36 mi. NE of Cádiz; agr. center (olives, cereals, chick-peas, livestock). Olive-oil processing. Sulphur springs. Has old castle and parish church.

Espera Feliz (ĭshpā'rŭ fēlēsh'), city (pop. 1,767), SE Minas Gerais, Brazil, near Espírito Santo border, 50 mi. WNW of Cachoeiro de Itapemirim; rail junction at S foot of the Pico da Bandeira; mica mining.

Esperança (ĭshpĭrā'sŭ), city (pop. 4,699), E central Paraíba, NE Brazil, 14 mi. N of Campina Grande, cotton-growing center; tobacco, beans, rice.

Esperança, Serra da (sĕ'rŭ dä), mountain range (alt. c.3,000 ft.) in central Paraná, Brazil, extends c.150 mi. N from Iguassú R. at União da Vitória toward Paranapanema R.

Esperance (ĕ'spŭrŭns), town (pop. 623), S Western Australia, on Esperance Bay, 215 mi. S of Kalgoorlie; terminus of railroad from Kalgoorlie; seaside resort. Exports gold. Saltworks.

Esperance, Mauritius: see POUDRE D'OR.

Esperance (ĕs'prŭnts), village (pop. 322), Schoharie co., E central N.Y., 16 mi. W of Schenectady.

Esperance, Cape (ĕ'spŭrŭns), N tip of Guadalcanal, Solomon Isls., SW Pacific; 9°16'S 159°43'E. In Second World War, naval battle of Cape Esperance (1943) was important U.S. victory.

Esperance, Port, Tasmania: see DOVER.

Esperance Bay, inlet of Indian Ocean, S Western Australia, W of Great Australian Bight; 19 mi. long, 10 mi. wide; contains several islets. Esperance town on NW shore.

Espérance Rock, L', New Zealand: see KERMADEC ISLANDS.

Esperantina (ĭshpĭrăntē'nŭ), city (pop. 1,683), N Piauí, Brazil, 90 mi. NNE of Teresina; cotton, babassu nuts, carnauba wax. Until 1944, called Boa Esperança.

Esperanza (ĕspārän'sä), town (pop. estimate 10,000), ⊙ Las Colonias dept. (□ 2,440; 1947 census 66,-365), central Santa Fe prov., Argentina, 17 mi. NW of Santa Fe. Mfg. and agr. center (wheat, flax, corn, oats, alfalfa, livestock). Vegetable-oil pressing, tanning, flour milling, sawmilling; mfg. of cardboard and wooden boxes, soap. Founded 1856 for European immigrants, largely German.

Esperanza, Bolivia: see CACHUELA ESPERANZA.

Esperanza, town (pop. 4,655), Las Villas prov., central Cuba, on railroad and 10 mi. W of Santa Clara; trading and agr. center (sugar cane, tobacco, fruit, livestock); mfg. of cigars and canned goods. Sugar centrals near by.

Esperanza, town (1950 pop. 536), Santiago prov., N Dominican Republic, in fertile Cibao valley, 26 mi. WNW of Santiago; cacao, coffee, tobacco, divi-divi, beeswax, hides.

Esperanza, town (pop. 3,002), Puebla, central Mexico, near S foot of Pico de Orizaba, 20 mi. W of Orizaba; alt. 8,064 ft. Rail junction; wheat- and corn-growing center. Airfield.

Esperanza or **Parada Esperanza** (pärä'dä), village (pop. 250), Paysandú dept., NW Uruguay, on railroad and 8 mi. ESE of Paysandú; wheat, cattle, sheep.

Esperanza, La, Argentina: see LA ESPERANZA.

Esperanza, La, Canary Isls.: see ROSARIO, EL.

Esperanza, La, Cuba: see PUERTO ESPERANZA.

Esperanza, La, Guatemala: see LA ESPERANZA.

Esperanza, La, Honduras: see LA ESPERANZA.

Esperanza, Sierra de (syĕ'rä dä ĕspärän'sä), mountain range of NE Honduras, near Caribbean Sea; extends c.70 mi. SW–NE bet. Aguán (N) and Sico (S) rivers; rises to c.4,000 ft.

Esperanza Inlet (ĕspŭrăn'zŭ) (22 mi. long), on W coast of Vancouver Isl., B.C., separates Nootka Isl. from Vancouver Isl.; at head of its Zeballos Arm (N) is ZEBALLOS, a gold-mining center. Hecate Channel (E) connects inlet with Tahsis Inlet of Nootka Sound.

Esperanzas, Las, Mexico: see LAS ESPERANZAS.

Espéraza (ĕspărăzä'), town (pop. 2,824), Aude dept., S France, on Aude R. and 8 mi. S of Limoux; felt-hat mfg. center. Plaster works. Has large Sp. pop.

Espergaerde (ĕ'spŭrgĕrdŭ), town (pop. 2,396), Frederiksborg amt, NE Zealand, Denmark, on the Oresund and 10 mi. ENE of Hillerod; fisheries.

Espicaya (ĕspēkī'ä), town (pop. c.3,300), Potosí dept., SW Bolivia, on Río Grande de San Juan and 12 mi. SSW of Tupiza; orchards, corn.

Espichel, Cape (ĭshpēshĕl'), steep headland on the Atlantic, on Portugal's W coast, 20 mi. WSW of Setúbal, commanding NW entrance to Sado estuary; 38°25'N 9°13'W; lighthouse.

Espiel (ĕspyĕl'), town (pop. 3,287), Córdoba prov., S Spain, 25 mi. NNW of Córdoba, in rich coal- and lead-mining dist. Olive-oil processing, soap mfg., flour milling. Cereals, livestock, honey, wine. Limestone quarries near by.

Espinal (ĕspēnäl'), town (pop. 5,666), Tolima dept., W central Colombia, in Magdalena valley, on railroad and 32 mi. SE of Ibagué. Resort; communication and tobacco-growing center; sugar cane, corn, bananas, cotton, stock; tobacco factories, pottery works, railroad shops.

Espinal, town (pop. 971), Veracruz, E Mexico, on Tecolutla R. and 15 mi. SSW of Papantla; corn, coffee, sugar cane.

Espinar, province, Peru: see YAURI.

Espinar, El (ĕl ĕspēnär'), town (pop. 2,149), Segovia prov., central Spain, at SW slopes of the Sierra de Guadarrama, 16 mi. SSW of Segovia. Resort. Also stock raising, lumbering, clay quarrying.

Espinardo (ĕspēnär'dō), NW suburb (pop. 4,425) of Murcia, Murcia prov., SE Spain; pepper-processing and -shipping center. Mfg. of fruit conserves, tin cans, knitwear, wax; silk spinning.

Espinhaço, Serra do (sĕ'rŭ dō͝o ĭshpēnyä'sō͝o), mountain range of E Brazil, extends S–N across central Minas Gerais and into S Bahia, where it merges with the Chapada Diamantina. Rises 1–2,000 ft. above central plateau; highest summits in spurs near Ouro Prêto (Itacolomi peak: 5,896 ft.) and Diamantina (Itambé: 6,155 ft.). Forms watershed bet. São Francisco R. basin (W) and streams draining directly E (Rio Doce, Jequitinhonha R.). In S, near Barbacena, it merges with the Serra da Mantiqueira. Brazil's major mineral storehouse, it has enormous iron reserves (notably at Itabira, Itabirito), and manganese, gold, diamond, and rock-crystal deposits. Chief towns in range are Ouro Prêto (former state ⊙), Counselheiro Lafaiete, Sabará, and Diamantina. Belo Horizonte is on W slope. Also called Serra Geral.

Espinho (ĭshpē'nyō͝o), town (pop. 7,914), Aveiro dist., N Portugal, on the Atlantic, on railroad and 10 mi. S of Oporto; sardine-fishing and canning center; bathing resort. Also makes knitwear, buttons, brooms, and rugs.

Espinillos, Argentina: see MARCOS JUÁREZ.

Espino, El, Nicaragua: see EL ESPINO.

Espinosa (ĭshpēnô'zŭ), city (pop. 1,003), N Minas Gerais, Brazil, near Bahia border, 130 mi. NNE of Montes Claros; cattle, sugar. Formerly spelled Espinoza.

Espinosa de Cerrato (ĕspēnō'sä dhā thĕrä'tō), town (pop. 1,036), Palencia prov., N central Spain, 30 mi. ESE of Palencia; cereals, potatoes, wine.

Espinosa de los Monteros (lōs mōntä'rōs), town (pop. 1,740), Burgos prov., N Spain, on railroad and 35 mi. WSW of Bilbao, in a region (Valle de Mena) which has affinity with Santander prov. and Basque Prov., rather than with central plateau. Stock raising, lumbering, and agr. (potatoes, cereals). Flour milling; mfg. of chocolate, dairy and meat products, pottery.

Espinoso del Rey (–sō dhĕl rā'), town (pop. 1,978), Toledo prov., central Spain, 23 mi. S of Talavera de la Reina; grapes, wheat, olives, livestock; lumbering, flour milling. Mineral springs.

Espinouse, Monts de l' (mō dŭ lĕspēnō͞oz'), granitic chain of S Massif Central, S France, in E Tarn and NW Hérault depts., bet. Mazamet (W) and Le Bousquet d'Orb (NE); c.40 mi. long. Rises to 3,694 ft. Sometimes spelled Espinouze.

Espira-de-l'Agly (ĕspērä'-dŭ-läglē'), village (pop. 1,222), Pyrénées-Orientales dept., S France, on Agly R. and 6 mi. NNW of Perpignan; wine-growing, sulphur refining.

Espírito Santo (ĭshpē'rētō͝o săn'tō͝o), coastal state (□ 15,780; 1940 pop. 750,107; 1950 census 870,-987) of E Brazil; ⊙ Vitória. Bounded by states of Bahia (N), Minas Gerais (W), Rio de Janeiro (S). Consists of coastal strip (c.250 mi. long, 75 mi. wide) rising in W toward great escarpment (Serra do Caparaó, Serra dos Aimorés). Drained by short coastal streams and by the Rio Doce, which gives access to mining region of Minas Gerais. State's low and marshy coast line has but one good harbor, Vitória, on Espírito Santo Bay. Coffee is chief agr. product; others are sugar, fruit (bananas, oranges), rice, manioc, and some cacao in N. Rosewood and monazitic sands are exported. Climate has been conducive to Eur. pioneer settlement in Santa Maria R. area. Principal towns are Vitória, which exports iron ore shipped by rail from Minas Gerais; and Cachoeiro de Itapemirim, with cement works and textile mills. A railroad links S part of state with Rio de Janeiro state. First settled in 1535, Espírito Santo became independent captaincy in 1799, prov. of Brazilian empire in 1824, and state of federal republic in 1889. The region of Serra dos Aimorés (□ 3,914, along NW border) is disputed by Espírito Santo and Minas Gerais.

Espírito Santo. 1 City (pop. 5,641), central Espírito Santo state, Brazil, on Espírito Santo Bay, 4 mi. E of Vitória; chocolate and candy factory. Dominated by a rocky height topped by convent of Our Lady of Penha (built in 16th cent.). Settled c.1535 as Villa Velha. **2** City, Paraíba, Brazil: see CRUZ DO ESPÍRITO SANTO. **3** City, Sergipe, Brazil: see INDIAROBA.

Espírito Santo Bay, inlet of the Atlantic on Espírito Santo coast, E Brazil, formed by mouth of Santa Maria R. Vitória is located on isl. near its head. Only sheltered natural harbor bet. Salvador and Rio de Janeiro city.

Espírito Santo do Pinhal, Brazil: see PINHAL.

Espíritu Santo (ĕspē'rētō͞o sän'tō), village, Cochabamba dept., central Bolivia, on N slopes of Cordillera de Cochabamba, 33 mi. NE of Sacaba, and on Cochabamba–Todos Santos road; coca plantations.

Espiritu Santo or **Santo,** volcanic island (□ 1,485; pop. c.4,000), largest, westernmost isl. of NEW HEBRIDES, SW Pacific; 15°15'S 166°55'E, Br. administrative hq. at Hog Harbour in NE and Fr. hq. at Segond Canal on S coast; c.75 mi. long, c.45 mi. wide, rises to 6,195 ft. St. Philip and St. James Bay is bet. Cape Cumberland and Cape Queiros in N; southernmost point is Cape Lisburn. Produces copra, coffee, cocoa. Discovered 1606 by Queiros. In Second World War, site of military base. Formerly Marina.

Espíritu Santo, Venezuela: see EL VALLE, Nueva Esparta state.

Espiritu Santo, Cape, NE Samar isl., Philippines, on Philippine Sea, opposite small Bacan Isl.; 12°33'N 125°11'E.

Espíritu Santo, Cape, on NE coast of Tierra del Fuego, at E entrance to Strait of Magellan, on Chile-Argentina line; 52°40'S 68°36'38"W.

Espíritu Santo, Sierra del (syĕ'rä dĕl), section of Sierra del Merendón, W Honduras; extends from area W of San Jerónimo 15 mi. NE to Santa Bárbara dept. border; rises to c.5,000 ft. in Elencia peak, 7 mi. NW of Florida.

Espíritu Santo Bay, inlet of Caribbean Sea in E coast of Yucatan Peninsula, Quintana Roo, SE Mexico, 10 mi. S of Ascensión Bay, 30 mi. SE of Felipe Carrillo Puerto.

Espiritu Santo Bay (ĕspĭ'rĭtōō săn'tō), S Texas, inlet sheltered from Gulf of Mexico by Matagorda Isl.; c.17 mi. long, 2–4 mi. wide. Joined by Gulf Intracoastal Waterway to Matagorda Bay (NE), San Antonio Bay (SW).

Espíritu Santo Island (□ 43), in Gulf of California, off E coast of Lower California, NW Mexico, 16 mi. N of La Paz; 7½ mi. long, 2–5 mi. wide; rises to 1,951 ft. Uninhabited. Of volcanic origin.

Espita (ĕspē'tä), town (pop. 4,504), Yucatan, SE Mexico, on railroad and 23 mi. NNW of Valladolid; agr. center (henequen, chicle, sugar cane, corn, fruit, wood).

Espluga de Francolí (ĕsplōō'gä dhä fräng-kōlē'), town (pop. 2,901), Tarragona prov., NE Spain, 5 mi. W of Montblanch; mfg. of cement, soap, alcohol, sparkling wine; olive-oil processing, sawmilling; agr. trade (cereals, potatoes, almonds, fruit). Mineral springs. Near by is famous Cistercian abbey of Poblet.

Esplugas (ĕsplōō'gäs), outer suburb (pop. 2,133) of Barcelona, Barcelona prov., NE Spain, 4 mi. W of city center; flour products, sparkling wine.

Espoo, Finland: see ESBO.

Esporlas (ĕspôr'läs), town (pop. 2,709), Majorca, Balearic Isls., 7 mi. NNW of Palma; carobs, olives, almonds, timber. Mfg. of woolen and cotton goods, cement, cardboard; sawmilling.

Esposende (ĭshpōōzān'dĭ), town (pop. 1,629), Braga dist., N Portugal, on Atlantic Ocean at mouth of Cávado R. and 20 mi. W of Braga; bathing resort; fisheries.

Espungabera (ĭshpōōng"gŭbĕ'rŭ), village, Manica and Sofala prov., S central Mozambique, on Southern Rhodesia border (opposite Mount Silinda), 140 mi. WSW of Beira; corn, beans. Also spelled Spungabera.

Espy (ĕ'spē), village (1940 pop. 773), Columbia co., E central Pa., on Susquehanna R. just E of Bloomsburg; mfg. (hosiery, fertilizer).

Esquel (ĕskĕl'), town (1947 pop. 5,548), ⊙ Futaleufú dept., W Chubut natl. territory, Argentina, in foothills of the Andes, 100 mi. S of San Carlos de Bariloche. Resort and agr. center (wheat, alfalfa, sheep, cattle). Lumbering, dairying, flour milling. Gold deposits. Has hydroelectric plant, seismographic station, airport. Cerro Esquel (N) rises to 7,020 ft.

Esquerdes (ĕskârd'), village (pop. 1,242), Pas-de-Calais dept., N France, on the Aa and 4 mi. SW of Saint-Omer; natl. explosives factory.

Esquiline Hill (ĕ'skwĭlīn, –lĭn), one of the 7 hills of Rome.

Esquimalt (ĕskwī'môlt), town, SW B.C., W suburb of Victoria, at SE end of Vancouver Isl., on Esquimalt Harbour (6 mi. long, 6 mi. wide at entrance), a bay of Juan de Fuca Strait; 48°26'N 126°26'W; naval base and port, with large drydock and ship-repair facilities. Harbor was 1st visited by Manuel de Quimper of the Spanish navy in 1790, and named Puerto de Cordova. Town came into being as naval station during the Crimean War, when Anglo-French fleet was based here for attack on Petropavlovsk, Kamchatka. Naval facilities were later expanded and permanent base was established here by the British govt.; taken over (1906) by Canada.

Esquina (ĕskē'nä), town (pop. 5,883), ⊙ Esquina dept. (□ c.1,500; pop. 29,483), SW Corrientes prov., Argentina, port at confluence of Corrientes and Paraná rivers, 105 mi. SW of Mercedes. Farming center (peas, rice, corn, cotton, tobacco, watermelons, stock). Tobacco processing. Has natl. col.

Esquipulas (ĕskēpōō'läs), town (1950 pop. 2,752), Chiquimula dept., E Guatemala, in highlands, near Honduras and Salvador borders, 20 mi. SE of Chiquimula; mecca of greatest religious pilgrimage, Indian and Ladino, in Central America. Spanish conquerers here commissioned carving, in dark-colored wood, of a figure of Christ which became known as the Black Christ of Esquipulas. Church dates from 1737.

Esquipulas, town (1950 pop. 1,549), Matagalpa dept., W central Nicaragua, 27 mi. S of Matagalpa, near Rio Grande; coffee, sugar cane, plantains; livestock.

Esquiri (ĕskē'rē), town (pop. c.3,400), Potosí dept., S central Bolivia, 15 mi. ENE of Puna; grain, potatoes, vegetables.

Esquivel (ĕskēvĕl'), village (pop. 1,739), Lima dept., W central Peru, on coastal plain, on railroad and 2 mi. WSW of Huaral; cotton-growing and -processing center.

Esquivias (ĕskē'vyäs), town (pop. 2,182), Toledo prov., central Spain, 22 mi. S of Madrid; olives, cereals, grapes, potatoes, onions, beans, tubers, melons; olive-oil pressing. Cervantes was married here and lived here for some time.

Esrum Lake (ĕs'rōōm) (5 mi. long, 2 mi. wide), NE Zealand, Denmark; bordered by forests on W and S. Esrum Canal (5.6 mi. long) connects lake with the Kattegat (N).

Es Salt, Jordan: see SALT.

Essarts, Les (lāzĕsär'), village (pop. 1,062), Vendée dept., W France, 12 mi. NE of La Roche-sur-Yon; fertilizer, small grains.

Esschen, Belgium: see ESSEN.

Esseg, Yugoslavia: see OSIJEK.

Essei, Russian SFSR: see YESSEI.

Essen (ĕ'sŭn), town (pop. 8,899), Antwerp prov., N Belgium, 18 mi. N of Antwerp; frontier station on Netherlands border; agr. market. Formerly spelled Esschen.

Essen (ĕ'sŭn). **1** Village (commune pop. 7,821), in Oldenburg, NW Germany, after 1945 in Lower Saxony, 10 mi. SW of Cloppenburg; rail junction; mfg. of building materials. **2** City (□ 73; 1939 pop. 666,743; 1946 pop. 524,728; 1950 pop. 605,-125), in former Prussian Rhine Prov., W Germany, after 1945 in North Rhine-Westphalia, bet. Ruhr R. (S) and Rhine-Herne Canal (N), 37 mi. N of Cologne; 51°26'N 7°E. Situated in a rich coal field, it is the industrial hub of the RUHR, a great steel-mfg. center (pig iron, steel, steel products). Other mfg.: chemicals, textiles (cloth, silk), glass, furniture. Coke ovens, cement- and brickworks. Brewing. Coal mined in suburbs, including BORBECK, KATERNBERG, KRAY, RÜTTENSCHEIDT, STEELE, and STOPPENBERG. Founded in 9th cent., but its importance dates only from 19th cent., when it had a rapid industrial rise after Friedrich Krupp built 1st steel plant here c.1810 and began to develop the coal field. Towards end of 19th cent., Krupp concern started building its model workers' colonies (at suburb of ALTENDORF) near the ever-expanding steel plant. Trunk lines were constructed to connect city with rest of the Ruhr. Essen boundaries reached Ruhr R. through incorporating suburbs of KUPFERDREH, RELLINGHAUSEN, and WERDEN; its port on Rhine-Herne Canal is at ALTENESSEN. A center of Ger. war industry, city was about 75% destroyed by Allied aerial attacks in Second World War; its ancient minster was damaged.

Essen, Bad, Germany: see BAD ESSEN.

Essendon, municipality (pop. 55,396), S Victoria, Australia, 6 mi. NW of Melbourne, in metropolitan area; commercial center for agr. region (oats, barley).

Essentuki, Russian SFSR: see YESSENTUKI.

Essequibo (ĕ"sŭkwē'bō), county (□ 65,215; pop. 58,439), Br. Guiana, on the Atlantic; chief town, Bartica. Covers about ¾ of the colony; bounded by Venezuela (W) and Brazil (SW and S). Traversed by Essequibo R., with its many affluents: Mazaruni, Cuyuni, Potaro, Rupununi. Main diamond- and gold-mining area. Includes famed Kaieteur Falls. Cattle are raised in S savanna; rice, sugar, and coconut plantations along the coast. First settled (1616) by the Dutch, it was a separate colony until united (1789) with Demerara and (1831) with Berbice. The co. (mainly of historical importance) comprises the administrative dists. of Essequibo proper (□ 2,035; pop. 23,000; ⊙ Suddie), Essequibo Isls. (NE), North West Dist. (NW), Mazaruni-Potaro dist. (center), and Rupununi dist. (S).

Essequibo Islands, district (□ 1,033; pop. 9,760), N Br. Guiana; ⊙ Leguan. Consists of Wakenaam, Leguan, Hog isls. in Essequibo R. estuary and of adjacent mainland, W of Georgetown on the Atlantic. Rice is grown.

Essequibo River, largest stream in Br. Guiana, draining more than half of the total area; rises in the Guiana Highlands on Brazil border at 1°12'N 58°47'W, flows c.600 mi. N, past Bartica and Parika, to the Atlantic in a 20-mi.-wide isl.-dotted estuary 13 mi. WNW of Georgetown. Lower course is navigable up to Bartica (c.50 mi.) for ocean-going vessels and another 12 mi. to Monkey Jump for small craft. Most of its course is interrupted by numerous rapids and falls, circumvented by railroad from Rockstone to Wismar on the Demerara. The river is still of great importance for carrying gold, diamonds, stone, and timber (greenheart), worked in the interior. Principal tributaries: Rupununi, Potaro, and Mazaruni-Cuyuni.

Essex, county (□ 707; pop. 174,230), S Ont., on L. Erie, L. St. Clair, and Mich. border; ⊙ Windsor.

Essex, town (pop. 1,935), S Ont., 14 mi. SE of Windsor, in fruitgrowing region; food canning, lumbering, mfg. of tools, bricks.

Essex, county (□ 1,527.7; 1931 pop. 1,755,459; 1951 census 2,043,574), SE England; ⊙ Chelmsford. Bounded by Middlesex and Hertford (E), Cambridge and Suffolk (N), North Sea (E), Thames R. (S), and London (SW). Drained by Thames, Roding, Blackwater, Chelmer, Colne, and Stour rivers. Undulating country, rising to low hills in NW; formerly covered by forest, of which only small part of Epping Forest remains. Agr. includes vegetables and fruit. Besides fisheries, there are noted oyster beds in river estuaries. Urban centers near London are mostly residential, and are part of London's suburban area. There are few important industries. Important towns are Tilbury and Harwich (ports), Southend-on-Sea (resort), Chelmsford, East Ham, West Ham, Colchester, and Waltham Holy Cross. Areas on Thames R. estuary were heavily bombed in Second World War.

Essex. 1 County (□ 500; pop. 522,384), NE Mass.; ⊙ Salem, Newburyport, Lawrence. On the coast, bounded N by N.H.; intersected by Merrimack and Ipswich rivers. Industrial centers (known for shoes,textiles, metal products) are Lynn, Lawrence, Haverhill, Newburyport. Resorts on coast include Gloucester and Cape Ann area, Manchester, Swampscott, Marblehead. Formed 1643. **2** County (□ 128; pop. 905,949), NE N.J., bounded W, N, and E by Passaic R., SE by Newark Bay; ⊙ NEWARK, state's largest city and industrial, commercial, transportation center. Includes many residential communities of N.Y.–N.J. metropolitan area. Varied mfg. (chiefly jewelry, radio and electronic equipment, pharmaceuticals, machinery, tools, metal products, clothing); nurseries, dairy and truck farms. Formed 1675. **3** County (□ 1,826; pop. 35,086), NE N.Y.; ⊙ Elizabethtown. Situated in the main Adirondack range; Mt. Marcy, highest peak (5,344 ft.) in state, is in co. Bounded E by L. Champlain; drained by Hudson R. (rising here), Ausable R., and other streams. Includes Lake Placid, Saranac Lake, and other noted resorts. Lumbering and agr. area (dairy products; potatoes, hay, livestock); some mfg.; iron and garnet deposits, granite quarries. Formed 1799. **4** County (□ 664; pop. 6,257), NE Vt., on Que. line, bounded E by Connecticut R.; ⊙ Guildhall. Mfg. (paper and wood products); agr., dairying; lumbering, hunting, and fishing. Drained by Moose, Nulhegan, and Clyde rivers. Formed 1792. **5** County (□ 250; pop. 6,530), E Va.; ⊙ Tappahannock. In tidewater region; bounded NE and E by the Rappahannock. Agr. (tobacco, corn, truck, peanuts, hay), livestock raising; lumber milling, vegetable canning. Formed 1692.

Essex. 1 Town (pop. 3,491), including Essex village (pop. 1,312), Middlesex co., S Conn., on the Connecticut and 20 mi. SE of Middletown; agr., mfg. (tools, electrical equipment, boats, wire goods, witch hazel). Summer resort (yachting). Includes Centerbrook and Ivoryton villages (combined pop. 1,372). Set off 1852. **2** Village (pop. 284), Kankakee co., NE Ill., 16 mi. WNW of Kankakee, in agr. area; ships grain. **3** Town (pop. 763), Page co., SW Iowa, near East Nishnabotna R., 5 mi. NE of Shenandoah; cement mfg., flour milling. **4** Suburban village (1940 pop. 4,999), Baltimore co., central Md., near Back R. 7 mi. E of downtown Baltimore; makes clothing, candles. **5** Town (pop. 1,794), Essex co., NE Mass., on tidewater inlet and 10 mi. NE of Salem; summer resort; boatbuilding, fishing. Settled 1634, inc. 1819. Includes village of South Essex. **6** City (pop. 549), Stoddard co., SE Mo., in Mississippi flood plain, 6 mi. E of Dexter. **7** Resort village, Essex co., NE N.Y., 28 mi. S of Plattsburg, on W shore of L. Champlain. Ferry to Charlotte, Vt. **8** Town (pop. 3,931), Chittenden co., NW Vt., just E of Burlington and on the Winooski. Includes Fort Ethan Allen (U.S. military reservation) and ESSEX JUNCTION village. Chartered 1763, settled 1783.

Essex Fells, borough (pop. 1,617), Essex co., NE N.J., 9 mi. NW of Newark; makes radar equipment. Inc. 1902.

Essex Junction, village (pop. 2,741) of Essex town, Chittenden co., NW Vt., just E of Burlington and on Winooski R.; railroad, highway focus. Brick, tile industry, dairy and maple products, truck, timber. Annual Champlain Valley Exposition here.

Essexvale, township (pop. 225), Bulawayo prov., SW Southern Rhodesia, in Matabeleland, on railroad and 25 mi. ESE of Bulawayo; alt. 3,828 ft. Tobacco, corn, dairy products. Gold deposits.

Essexville, city (pop. 3,167), Bay co., E Mich., 2 mi. NE of Bay City and on Saginaw R. near its mouth on Saginaw Bay; commercial fishing, cement mfg. Area was part of an Indian reservation, 1819–37. Inc. as village 1883, as city 1934.

Essey-lès-Nancy (ĕsā'-lā-näsē'), E suburb (pop. 2,378) of Nancy, Meurthe-et-Moselle dept., NE France; airport; chocolate mfg.; truck gardens.

Essiama, Gold Coast: see ESIAMA.

Essing (ĕ'sĭng), village (pop. 1,196), Lower Bavaria, Germany, on the Altmühl and 4 mi. WNW of Kelheim; grain, hogs.

Essingen (ĕ'sĭng-ūn), village (pop. 1,519), Rhenish Palatinate, W Germany, 3 mi. NW of Landau; wine; also tobacco, wheat.
Essington, village (1940 pop. 1,585), Delaware co., SE Pa., on Delaware R. just below Philadelphia. First white settlement in Pa. made 1643 by Swedes on Tinicum Isl. just offshore.
Essington, Port, Australia: see COBOURG PENINSULA.
Essling, town (pop. 3,964), after 1938 in Grossenzersdorf dist. of Vienna, Austria, 7 mi. E of city center. Near by, Archduke Charles defeated Napoleon, May 21–22, 1809.
Esslingen or **Esslingen am Neckar** (ĕs'lĭng-ūn äm nĕ'kär), city (1950 pop. 70,610), N Württemberg, Germany, after 1945 in Württemberg-Baden, on Neckar R. 6 mi. ESE of Stuttgart; 48°44'N 9°18'E. Noted for its wine, but also a mfg. center, with mfg. of machinery, locomotives, armatures, gears, tools, electrical goods, textiles (cotton, wool), furniture, vinegar; leatherworking. Has 13th-cent. castle, many noted Gothic churches, Gothic old city hall (chimes in tower), 18th-cent. new city hall; also teachers col., institute of technology. Founded 777; chartered 1219. Free imperial city until 1802.
Esso (ĕsô'), village, Kamchatka oblast, Khabarovsk Territory, Russian SFSR, in central mtn. range of Kamchatka Peninsula, 210 mi. N of Petropavlovsk; reindeer farms.
Essondale, village (pop. estimate 500), SW B.C., near lower Fraser R., 5 mi. ENE of New Westminster; lumbering, dairying, fruitgrowing.
Essonne River (ĕsôn'), in Loiret and Seine-et-Oise depts., N central France, rises in several headstreams in the Forest of Orléans, flows c.55 mi. N, past Malesherbes and La Ferté-Alais, to the Seine at Corbeil.
Essonnes, France: see CORBEIL.
Essoyes (ĕswä'), village (pop. 877), Aube dept., NE central France, on Ource R. and 14 mi. SW of Bar-sur-Aube; cheese.
Es Sukhne, Syria: see SUKHNE, ES.
Es Suweida, Syria: see SUWEIDA, ES.
Essvik (ĕs'vēk"), village (pop. 1,751), Vasternorrland co., NE Sweden, on small inlet of Gulf of Bothnia, at mouth of Ljunga R., 6 mi. SE of Sundsvall; pulp mills, sulphite works. Includes villages of Nyhamn (nü"hä'mūn) and Klampenborg (kläm'pūnbôr"yū).
Est, Canal de l' (känäl' dū lĕst'), N France, connects the Meuse with the Saône. Consists of 2 sections: N part is canalized Meuse R. from Belg. border at Givet, past Charleville-Mézières, Sedan, and Verdun to Troussey, where it is joined by MARNE-RHINE CANAL. S part extends from Toul along the Moselle to Golbey (2 mi. N of Épinal), whence it crosses Moselle-Saône watershed, and coincides with canalized Saône R. bet. Jussey and Port-sur-Saône (beyond which the Saône is naturally navigable). Total length, 280 mi. Wood and iron shipments.
Estacada (ĕ"stūkä'dū, stūkä'dū), city (pop. 950), Clackamas co., NW Oregon, 12 mi. ESE of Oregon City and on Clackamas R.; lumber milling.
Estaca Point or **Estaca de Vares Point** (ĕstä'kä dhä vä'rĕs), northernmost point of Spain, on Bay of Biscay, in La Coruña prov., Galicia, 46 mi. NE of La Coruña; 43°46'N 7°41'W. Lighthouse.
Estadilla (ĕstä-dhē'lyä), town (pop. 1,454), Huesca prov., NE Spain, near Cinca R., 6 mi. E of Barbastro; olive-oil processing; wine, fruit, cereals. Mineral springs.
Estados, Isla de los, Argentina: see STATEN ISLAND.
Estagel (ĕstäzhĕl'), town (pop. 2,037), Pyrénées-Orientales dept., S France, on the Agly and 11 mi. WNW of Perpignan; agr. market; wines, almonds. Physicist Arago b. here.
Estahbanat, Iran: see ISTAHBANAT.
Estaing (ĕstĕ'), village (pop. 627), Aveyron dept., S France, on the Lot and 15 mi. NNE of Rodez; wool spinning, slate quarrying. Has 15th-16th-cent. castle.
Estaires (ĕstâr'), town (pop. 4,259), Nord dept., N France, on the Lys and 9 mi. NNE of Béthune; textile-weaving center (chiefly linen).
Estakhr, Iran: see PERSEPOLIS.
Estância (ĭshtä'syū), city (pop. 10,324), S Sergipe, NE Brazil, head of navigation on Piauí R. (short coastal stream) and 37 mi. SW of Aracaju; textile mills, distilleries; mfg. of footwear, and oil, soap, and flour products.
Estancia (ästän'syä), town (1939 pop. 2,546; 1948 municipality pop. 8,781), Iloilo prov., NE Panay isl., Philippines, on Visayan Sea, 29 mi. ESE of Capiz; chief fishing town of Visayan Isls.; dried and canned fish.
Estancia (ĕstän'shū), town (pop. 916), ⊙ Torrance co., central N.Mex., 40 mi. SE of Albuquerque, in agr. and livestock region; alt. 6,100 ft.; wool, beans. Carbon-dioxide well near by. Cibola Natl. Forest and Manzano Range are W, Laguna del Perro just SE.
Estanislao del Campo (ĕstänēslou' dĕl käm'pō), town (pop. estimate 1,000), central Formosa natl. territory, Argentina, on railroad and 140 mi. NW of Formosa; agr. (cotton, corn, livestock).
Estanyó, Pic de l' (pēk dū lĕstänyō'), peak (alt. 9,554 ft.) of Andorra, in Central Pyrenees, 8 mi. NNE of Andorra le Vella, near Fr. border.
Estanzuela (ĕstänswä'lä), town (1950 pop. 1,938), Zacapa dept., E Guatemala, near Motagua R., 3 mi. NW of Zacapa; corn, beans, sugar cane; livestock.
Estanzuela, Mexico: see GARCÍA DE LA CADENA.
Estanzuela, village, Colonia dept., SW Uruguay, on railroad and 12 mi. NE of Colonia.
Estanzuelas (–läs), city (pop. 3,406), Usulután dept., E Salvador, in Lempa R. valley, near mouth of Sesori R.; grain, livestock and poultry raising.
Estaque, Chaîne de l' (shĕn dū lĕstäk'), barren limestone hill range of Bouches-du-Rhône dept., SE France, extending c.15 mi. E-W along peninsula separating the Étang de Berre (N) from the Gulf of Lion (S), and dominating the bay of Marseilles (SE). Average alt. 700 ft. Pierced by Arles-Marseilles RR tunnel and by sea-level ROVE Tunnel.
Estaque, L', NW suburb (pop. 1,969) of Marseilles, Bouches-du-Rhône dept., SE France, on N side of Marseilles bay; mfg. (chemicals, fertilizer, Portland cement). At SE entrance of ROVE Tunnel.
Estarreja (ĭshtūrä'zhū), town, Aveiro dist., N central Portugal, on railroad and 10 mi. NNE of Aveiro; mfg. of chemical fertilizer.
Estavayer-le-Lac (ĕstäväyā' lū läk'), Ger. *Stäffis* (shtĕ'fĭs), town (pop. 2,137), Fribourg canton, W Switzerland, on E shore of L. of Neuchâtel, 15 mi. W of Fribourg; flour, woodworking, printing. Medieval arcades and towers, 13th-cent. castle, 14th–15th-cent. church.
Estcourt, town (pop. 3,681), W Natal, U. of So. Afr., in Drakensberg range, on Bushmans R. and 50 mi. NW of Pietermaritzburg; alt. 3,833 ft.; rail junction; bacon processing, milk canning; in stock-raising region. Resort.
Este (ĕ'stĕ), anc. *Ateste*, town (pop. 7,413), Padova prov., Veneto, N Italy, at S foot of Euganean Hills, 17 mi. SW of Padua; mfg. (textile machinery, ceramics, furniture, soap, macaroni), beet-sugar refinery. Noted for its natl. mus. of antiquities. Has castle rebuilt in 14th cent. Trachyte quarries near by. An anc. center of civilization (10th to 2d cent. B.C.); seat (10th–13th cent. A.D.) of Este family; later (1405–1797) came under Venice.
Este, Pico del (pē'kō dĕl ĕ'stā), peak (3,448 ft.), NE Puerto Rico, in the Sierra de Luquillo, 27 mi. ESE of San Juan.
Esteban Echeverría, district, Argentina: see MONTE GRANDE.
Estelí (ĕstälē'), department (□ 770; 1950 pop. 43,506), W Nicaragua; ⊙ Estelí. On main continental divide; drained chiefly by Estelí R. Livestock raising; agr. (wheat, coffee, corn, beans, fodder grasses). Main towns (served by Inter-American Highway): Estelí, Condega.
Estelí, city (1950 pop. 5,525), ⊙ Estelí dept., W Nicaragua, on Inter-American Highway, on Estelí R. and 60 mi. N of Managua; agr. and commercial center; hat mfg., tanning, sawmilling.
Estelí River, NW Nicaragua, rises S of Estelí, flows c.50 mi. N, past Estelí, Condega, and Palacagüina, to Coco R. 5 mi. SE of Telpaneca.
Estella (ĕstĕ'lyä), city (pop. 6,992), Navarre prov., N Spain, on Ega R. and 22 mi. SW of Pamplona; industrial and agr. trade center. Woolen milling, tanning, meat packing; mfg. of knit goods, berets, cement, pottery, chocolate, brandy. Has medieval churches, convents, palaces. Flourished in Middle Ages as 2d city of kingdom of Navarre; was Don Carlos' stronghold in Carlist Wars (19th cent.). Benedictine monastery 2 mi. SW.
Estellénchs (ĕstĕlyĕnch'), town (pop. 613), Majorca, Balearic Isls., 10 mi. NW of Palma; fruit, olives, tomatoes. Bathing.
Estelline. 1 (ĕ'stūlīn) City (pop. 760), Hamlin co., E S.Dak., 25 mi. SSE of Watertown, near Big Sioux R.; dairy produce, livestock, poultry, grain. **2** (ĕ'stūlēn") Town (pop. 464), Hall co., NW Texas, 15 mi. NW of Childress, near Prairie Dog Town Fork of Red R.; retail center for cotton and cattle region.
Estell Manor, city (pop. 381), Atlantic co., S N.J., bet. Tuckahoe and Great Egg Harbor rivers, 18 mi. WSW of Atlantic City, in large rural area. Includes Estelville (or Estellville) village and a game preserve.
Estepa (ĕstā'pä), city (pop. 8,598), Seville prov., SW Spain, in NW foothills of the Cordillera Penibética, on highway to Seville, and 14 mi. ENE of Osuna. Processing and agr. center (olives, cereals, grapes, livestock). Sawmilling, flour milling, food canning; lime, stone, and gypsum quarrying; mfg. of furniture, ceramics, textile goods, chocolate; iron foundry. Called by Romans *Astapa*, when it was a stronghold in Second Punic War. Taken from the Moors by Ferdinand III in 1240.
Estepona (ĕstäpō'nä), town (pop. 10,091), Málaga prov., S Spain, in Andalusia, minor Mediterranean port at E foot of the Sierra Bermeja (spur of Cordillera Penibética), 25 mi. NNE of Gibraltar, 45 mi. SW of Málaga. Fishing and trading center in agr. region (grapes, figs, potatoes, lemons, oranges, cereals, vegetables, cork); timber; livestock. Fish canneries, saw mills, flour mills, iron and lead foundries. Has fine beaches.
Ester, village (pop. 73), in Tanana valley, central Alaska, 8 mi. W of Fairbanks; placer gold mining; farming.
Estérel (ĕstārĕl'), mtn. range of Provence Alps in Var and Alpes-Maritimes depts., SE France, forming steep and indented coastline on the Mediterranean; c.12 mi. long, 8 mi. wide. Traversed by mtn. road from Cannes to Fréjus and skirted by a shore railroad and scenic highway (*Corniche d'Or*). Heavily forested (cork oaks, pines). Rises to 2,021 ft. at Mont Vinaigre.
Esterhazy (ĕ'stūrhāzē), village (pop. 486), SE Sask., 40 mi. SSE of Yorkton; wheat, stock.
Esterias, Cape (ĕtĕ'ryäs), NW Fr. Equatorial Africa, 10 mi. NNW of Libreville; forms S point of Corisco Bay.
Esternay (ĕstĕrnā'), village (pop. 633), Marne dept., N France, on the Grand-Morin and 17 mi. N of Nogent-sur-Seine; rail junction. Porcelain factory.
Esternberg (ĕ'stūrnbĕrk), town (pop. 2,327), NW Upper Austria, near the Danube, 8 mi. ESE of Passau, Germany; vineyards, cattle.
Estero (ĕ'stūrō), village (pop. c.200), Lee co., SW Fla., 15 mi. S of Fort Myers, near Estero Bay, a lagoon (c.10 mi. long, 2 mi. wide) of the Gulf of Mexico partly enclosed by narrow Estero Isl. (c.7 mi. long; bathing beach). A religious community, founded 1894; grows citrus fruit, truck produce, and bamboo.
Estero Bay (ĕstā'rō), SW Calif., broad open bay of the Pacific, 12 mi. WNW of San Luis Obispo; vessels load oil from pipelines here. MORRO BAY is on an arm.
Estero Patiño, Argentina-Paraguay: see PATIÑO, ESTERO.
Estero Real (ĕstā'rō rääl'), river, W Nicaragua, rises 20 mi. NE of León, flows c.60 mi. WNW, past Puente Real and Puerto Morazán, to Gulf of Fonseca at NE base of Cosigüina Peninsula. Navigable in lower course, carrying grain and dairy products. Receives Villanueva R. (right).
Esterwegen (ĕs'tūrvā"gūn), village (pop. 2,369), in former Prussian prov. of Hanover, NW Germany, after 1945 in Lower Saxony, 12 mi. SE of Papenburg, in fen region. Site of concentration camp during Hitler regime.
Estes Park (ĕ'stēz), town (pop. 1,617), Larimer co., N Colo., in Front Range of Rocky Mts., on Thompson R. and 50 mi. NNW of Denver; alt. 7,500 ft. Noted resort; hq. for Rocky Mtn. Natl. Park (just W). Local mus. contains geological and botanical specimens from park. Near by are Horseshoe Falls, state fish hatchery, and NE entrance of park. In vicinity are 2 dams and power plants of Colo.-Big Thompson project. Settled 1859, inc. 1917.
Estevan (ĕ'stūvăn), town (pop. 3,120), SE Sask., on Souris R. at mouth of Long Creek, and 115 mi. SE of Regina, near N.Dak. border; lignite coal-mining center; briquette plant, flour mills, dairies, tree nurseries. Resort. Founded 1892. Electric power station supplies SE Sask.
Estevan Islands, W B.C., group (□ 51) of 7 isls. and several islets in Hecate Strait just S of Banks Isl.
Estherville (ĕs'tūr–), city (pop. 6,719), ⊙ Emmet co., NW Iowa, near Minn. line, on West Des Moines R. and 23 mi. NE of Spencer; mfg., trade, and shipping center, with meat packing and rendering plants, creameries, feed mills, bottling works, railroad shops; wood products, concrete, neon signs, fishing lines. Sand and gravel pits (S). Has jr. col. Just W is site of Fort Defiance (1862), preserved in a state park. Meteorite fell near by in 1879; large fragments are in museums in London, Vienna, and at Univ. of Minn. Settled 1857; inc. 1881 as town, 1894 as city.
Estherwood (ĕ'stūrwŏŏd), village (pop. 547), Acadia parish, S La., 6 mi. SW of Crowley; ships rice, other agr. products.
Esthonia: see ESTONIA.
Esthwaite Water, England: see HAWKSHEAD.
Estill (ĕ'stĭl), county (□ 260; pop. 14,677), E central Ky.; ⊙ Irvine. Drained by Kentucky and Red rivers and several creeks. Hilly agr. area (burley tobacco, corn, cattle, poultry, dairy products, truck); oil wells, timber. Includes part of Cumberland Natl. Forest Formed 1808.
Estill, town (pop. 1,659), Hampton co., SW S.C., 19 mi. S of Allendale, in tobacco, peanut, strawberry area; lumber mills.
Estill Springs, resort town (pop. 496), Franklin co., S Tenn., near Elk R., 7 mi. SE of Tullahoma; medicinal springs.
Estinnes-au-Val (ĕstēn'-ō-väl'), town, Hainaut prov., S Belgium, 8 mi. ESE of Mons; coal mining. Contiguous with village of Estinne-au-Mont (pop. 2,021).
Estique (ĕstē'kā), town (pop. 790), Tacna dept., S Peru, in Cordillera Occidental, 5 mi. S of Tarata.
Estissac (ĕstēsäk'), village (pop. 1,329), Aube dept., NE central France, 12 mi. W of Troyes; hosiery mfg., cabinetmaking.
Estiva, Brazil: see SÃO LUÍS ISLAND.
Estivella (ĕstēvĕ'lyä), village (pop. 1,220), Valencia prov., E Spain, 5 mi. WNW of Sagunto; mfg. of combs; olive-oil processing. Wine and oranges. Mineral springs.
Esto, town (pop. 217), Holmes co., NW Fla., near Ala. line, 14 mi. N of Bonifay, in agr. area.

Esto-Khaginka, Russian SFSR: see STEPNOYE, Rostov oblast.

Estômbar (ĭshtõm'bär), village (pop. 1,066), Faro dist., S Portugal, 5 mi. E of Portimão; figs, almonds, olives, carobs.

Eston, town (pop. 883), SW Sask., 75 mi. NW of Swift Current; grain, stock.

Eston, urban district (1931 pop. 31,341; 1951 census 33,315), North Riding, NE Yorkshire, England, on Tees R. estuary and 4 mi. E of Middlesbrough; iron-mining center at foot of Cleveland hills; has iron- and steelworks. In urban dist. are steel-milling towns of Grangetown (N; pop. 4,807), Normanby (W; pop. 4,122), and South Bank (NW; pop. 2,853).

Estonia (ĕstō'nēü, –nyü), Est. *Eesti* (ā'stē), Ger. *Estland,* Rus. *Estoniya,* northernmost of the Baltic States of NE Europe, since 1940 a constituent (Soviet Socialist) republic (□ 17,400; 1947 pop. estimate 1,000,000; 1934 pop. 1,126,413), of the USSR, but in 1951 still unrecognized as such by the U.S.; ⊙ Tallinn. Borders on Gulf of Finland (N), Latvia (S), Baltic Sea (W; with Gulf of Riga and isls. of SAARE, HIIUMAA, MUHU, and VORMSI), and Russian SFSR (with L. Peipus; E). Largely a lowland, with indented limestone cliffs on N coast; rises into glacial moraine ridges (1,040 ft.; S). Chiefly poor sandy, stony, glacial soils, except for some loam along watersheds; 20% forested. Principal lakes (Peipus, Vortsjarv) are linked by Ema R.; drain into Gulf of Finland via Narva R. (rapids). Moderate humid continental climate; mean temp., 18°–22°F. (Jan.), 59°–62°F. (July); yearly precipitation, 22 in. Pop. 90% Estonian (Ugro-Finnic group of Protestant religion), and 8% Russian. Administratively, Estonia falls (since 1950) into independent cities and raions. Chief mineral resource, besides phosphorite (at Maardu) and peat, is oil shale, which forms basis of a major distilling (gas, gasoline, asphalt, ash) industry (KOHTLA-JARVE, JOHVI, KIVIOLI, SILLAMAE). Other industries (textiles, matches, paper, furniture, agr. products) are centered on Tallinn (also shipbuilding, machine mfg.), Tartu, Narva, and Parnu. Fish (mainly anchovies and sprats) are processed along coast. PALDISKI is a major port and naval base. Agr. chiefly intensive dairy farming (butter) on basis of fodder grasses, root crops, and potatoes; also oats, rye, barley, and (in SE) fiber flax. Hogs and poultry also raised. Chief exports: butter, eggs, bacon, oil-shale products. Original Ugro-Finnic inhabitants of modern Estonia were Livs or Livonians (S; conquered in 13th cent. by Livonian Knights) and Esths or Estonians (N), ruled after early-13th cent. by Danes and also, after mid-14th cent., by Livonian Knights. After the knights lost their domain (1561), Estonia proper (N part) came under Swedish rule and the S part under Polish rule until 1629, when this also passed to Sweden. In 1710 Peter I of Russia conquered all Livonia, and Russian possession was confirmed in 1721. Modern Estonia (proclaimed 1918 an independent republic; recognized 1920 by USSR) was formed out of Rus. govts. of Estonia and N Livonia, as well as out of a portion of Pskov govt. (SE). Granting of military bases by Latvia to USSR in 1939 paved way for its annexation in 1940. After the Second World War (during which Germans occupied, 1941–44, Estonia), Estonia ceded c.1,000 sq. mi. of border territory to USSR; the extreme SE portion (mainly Rus. pop.) passed to Pskov oblast of Russian SFSR and the left bank of Narva R. (NE) to Leningrad oblast. Formerly spelled Esthonia.

Estor, El, Guatemala: see EL ESTOR.

Estoril (ĭshtōorēl'), town (pop. 2,935), Lisboa dist., W central Portugal, on the Atlantic, 13 mi. W of Lisbon (electric railroad); Portugal's most fashionable and best-known bathing and health resort along Port. Riviera. Equable winter climate attracts foreign tourists. Has fine waterfront hotels, casinos, and a modern thermal establishment. Just W is resort of Monte Estoril.

Estrada, La (lä ĕsträ'dhä), town (pop. 2,100), Pontevedra prov., NW Spain, agr. center 19 mi. NNE of Pontevedra. Lumbering, stock raising; cereals, fruit, wine in area.

Estrada Palma or **Central Estrada Palma** (sĕnträl', päl'mä), sugar-mill village (pop. 998), Oriente prov., E Cuba, 15 mi. SE of Manzanillo.

Estral Beach (ĕ'strŭl), village (pop. 188), Monroe co., extreme SE Mich., 9 mi. NE of Monroe, on L. Erie.

Estréchure, L', France: see SAINT-ANDRÉ-DE-VALBORGNE.

Estrée-Blanche (ĕsträ'-blãsh'), village (pop. 495), Pas-de-Calais dept., N France, 11 mi. SSE of Saint-Omer; coal mining, chemical mfg.

Estrées-Saint-Denis (ĕsträ'-sē-dünē'), village (pop. 1,597), Oise dept., N France, 8 mi. W of Compiègne; seed shipping.

Estreito (ĭshträ'tōō), town (pop. 117), SE Rio Grande do Sul, Brazil, on barrier beach bet. the Lagoa dos Patos and the Atlantic, 35 mi. E of Pelotas; tin deposits.

Estrêla (ĭshträ'lü), city (pop. 3,446), E central Rio Grande do Sul, Brazil, on Taquari R. and 60 mi. NW of Pôrto Alegre; stock raising, dairying, lard mfg., sugar growing. Founded in mid-19th cent. by German settlers. Old spelling, Estrella.

Estrêla, Serra da (sĕ'rü dä), range in central Rio de Janeiro state, Brazil, extending W from Petrópolis and overlooking Guanabara Bay (S). Forms part of great coastal escarpment (Serra do Mar). Rises to 4,500 ft. Formerly spelled Serra da Estrella.

Estrêla, Serra da, highest mountain range of Portugal, extending SW from Guarda along Castelo Branco–Guarda–Coimbra dist. border. Rises to 6,532 ft. at the Malhão da Estrêla. Constitutes westernmost outlier of Spanish Sierra de Guadarrama. Here rise Mondego and Zêzere rivers. Sheep pastures. Wool-milling center of Covilhã on SE slope. Noted tourist and winter-sports region. Formerly spelled Estrella.

Estrêla do Sul (dōō sōōl') [Port.,=southern star], city (pop. 1,546), W Minas Gerais, Brazil, in the Triângulo Mineiro, 40 mi. ENE of Uberlândia; alluvial diamond washings. Formerly spelled Estrella do Sul.

Estrella, Brazil: see ESTRÊLA.

Estrella, Chile: see LA ESTRELLA.

Estrella, La, Bolivia: see LA ESTRELLA.

Estrella, La, Costa Rica: see LA ESTRELLA.

Estrella, La (lä ĕstrĕ'lyä), village (pop. 1,624), Toledo prov., central Spain, 24 mi. SW of Talavera de la Reina; cereals, olives, horses, sheep.

Estrella do Sul, Brazil: see ESTRÊLA DO SUL.

Estremadura (ĕshtrĭmüdōō'rü), province (□ 2,064; 1940 pop. 1,379,533), central Portugal; ⊙ Lisbon. It includes most of Lisboa dist., S part of Leiria dist., and N part of Setúbal dist. Cities: Lisbon, Setúbal, Caldas da Rainha. It was formed 1936 from old Estremadura prov. (□ 6,941; 1940 pop. 2,114,658) which contained all of Leiria, Lisboa, Santarém, and Setúbal dists. Old Estremadura is bisected by the lower Tagus valley, one of Portugal's chief agr. regions. Grainfields alternate with orchards, vineyards, and truck gardens. There are rice fields and saltworks along Sado R. estuary above Setúbal, and cork forests further S. Industrial and commercial activity heavily concentrated in Lisbon area. The coastal area W of Lisbon (Port. Riviera) is noted for its mild climate and has fine resorts of Estoril and Cascais. Cintra and its beautiful surroundings also attract tourists. Estremadura was a Moslem prov. before Christian reconquest. Its history is largely that of its chief cities. Entire region was heavily damaged by 1755 earthquake. New provinces of Ribatejo, Beira Litoral, and Baixo Alentejo now contain parts of old Estremadura's territory.

Estremadura (ĕstrümüdōō'rü), Sp. *Extremadura* (ĕsträmä-dhōō'rä), historic region (□ 16,059; pop. 1,253,924), W Spain, bordering W on the Portuguese Estremadura. Now comprises CÁCERES and BADAJOZ provs., named for their chief cities. Separated by rugged Sierra de Gata and Sierra de Gredos from Leon and Old Castile (N), it rises gradually in E to the great central plateau (Meseta) of New Castile. The low Sierra Morena stretches along its S border with Andalusia. The N higher section (Cáceres prov.) is occasionally referred to as Upper Estremadura, in contrast to Lower Estremadura (Badajoz prov.). Mostly a monotonous tableland with some ranges and a few fertile plains, it is crossed E-W by the Tagus and Guadiana rivers. Spain's most backward region, it suffers from droughts, the effects of poor communication, absentee landlordism, and continuous emigration. Agr. and pasturage (sheep, hogs, goats, and some cattle) are its mainstay, and on them processing industries (olive oil, wine, flour, etc.) are based. Among the chief crops are olives, grapes, wheat, barley, chick-peas; cork, acorns. Rich phosphate mines at Logrosán (Cáceres). Lead, iron, zinc, tin, copper, and galena are also mined. Estremadura, first called Vetonia, formed part of the Roman prov. Lusitania. It was reconquered from the Moors in the 12th and 13th cent., and was frequently a battlefield in the Sp. wars with Portugal, and again in the Peninsular War (1808–14). Most of Estremadura was taken by the Nationalists during 1st year (1936) of the Sp. civil war. The conquistadors Pizarro and Cortés were b. here.

Estremera (ĕsträmä'rä), town (pop. 1,912), Madrid prov., central Spain, 35 mi. SE of Madrid; olives, cereals, grapes; olive-oil extracting, sawmilling, mfg. of esparto goods. Hydroelectric plant.

Estremoz (ĭshtrĭmôsh'), city (pop. 6,765), Évora dist., Alto Alentejo prov., S central Portugal, on railroad and 25 mi. NE of Évora; famous for its translucid white marble and for its pottery; olive oil and winemaking, cork processing, wool milling. Has noteworthy 13th-cent. castle and keep, built by King Diniz. In 17th cent., city was important in wars with Spain, Portuguese victories having been won at near-by Ameixial (1663) and Montes Claros (1665).

Estuaire, Fr. Equatorial Africa: see LIBREVILLE.

Esutoru, Russian SFSR: see UGLEGORSK.

Eszek, Yugoslavia: see OSIJEK.

Esztergom, county, Hungary: see KOMAROM-ESZTERGOM.

Esztergom (ĕs'tĕrgôm), Ger. *Gran* (grän), anc. *Strigonium,* city (pop. 22,171), ⊙ Komarom-Esztergom co., N Hungary, port on the Danube and 25 mi. NW of Budapest; rail terminus. Mfg. (machines, cognac, canes, pottery, brick, soap, candles); sawmills. Birthplace of St. Stephen; in 1198 became seat of Hungary's primate; dome-topped cathedral (19th cent.) overlooks the Danube. R.C. theological seminary, school of forestry, art gall. Warm springs (75°F.) are visited by many tourists. Coal and lignite mines, vineyards near by.

Et [Arabic,=the], for Arabic names beginning thus and not found here: see under following part of the name.

Eta (ā'tä) or **Eda** (ā'dä), town (pop. 4,133), Kumamoto prefecture, W Kyushu, Japan, 13 mi. NNW of Kumamoto; raw silk, rice, wheat.

Étables (ātä'blü), village (pop. 1,360), Côtes-du-Nord dept., W France, on English Channel, 8 mi. NNW of Saint-Brieuc; summer resort; tanning, biscuit mfg. Also called Étables-sur-Mer.

Etagala, Ceylon: see ELEPHANT ROCK.

Etah (ē'tä), Eskimo settlement, NW Greenland, in Prudhoe Land, on Smith Sound; 78°19'N 72°38'W. Discovered 1818 by John Ross, its Polar Eskimos or Arctic Highlanders have been studied by Peary, D. B. Macmillan, Knud Rasmussen, and others. Has been base for several arctic expeditions.

Etah (ā'tŭ), district (□ 1,719; pop. 984,760), W Uttar Pradesh, India; ⊙ Etah. On W Ganges Plain and Ganges-Jumna Doab; irrigated by Upper and Lower Ganges canals. Agr. (wheat, pearl millet, barley, corn, jowar, gram, cotton, mustard, sugar cane); small dhak jungle. Main towns: Kasganj, Etak, Soron, Jalesar. Present dist. formed 1856.

Etah, town (pop. 14,120), ⊙ Etah dist., W Uttar Pradesh, India, 50 mi. NE of Agra; road center; trades in grains, oilseeds, cotton, sugar cane. Large serais. Founded 14th cent.

Étain (ātē'), town (pop. 2,148), Meuse dept., NE France, on the Orne and 12 mi. ENE of Verdun; celluloid mfg. Shattered in First World War.

Etaiyapuram, India: see ETTAIYAPURAM.

Eta-jima, Japan: see NOMI-SHIMA.

Etal (ĕtäl'), atoll (pop. 244), Nomoi Isls., Truk dist., E Caroline Isls., W Pacific, c.5 mi. N of Satawan; 5°35'N 153°34'E; c.2 mi. long, 1 mi. wide; 15 low islets on reef.

Étampes (ātãp'), town (pop. 9,952), Seine-et-Oise dept., N central France, 31 mi. SSW of Paris; agr. trade center with truck gardens; metalworking (automobile and electrical equipment), canning, mfg. of chemicals. Has 12th-cent. church of Notre-Dame-du-Fort; 12th–16th-cent. church of St. Basil with Romanesque portal; a 12th-cent. keep; and 14th-cent. houses. Damaged in Second World War.

Étang (ātã') [Fr.,=pond, lagoon], for names beginning thus and not found here: see under following part of the name.

Étang du Nord or **L'Étang du Nord** (ātã' dü nôr', lātã'), village (pop. 3,928), E Que., on W Grindstone Isl., one of the Magdalen Isls.; 47°23'N 61°57'W; fishing port.

Étang-Salé or **Étang-Salé-les-Hauts** (–sälā'-lā-ō'), town (pop. 4,652, commune pop. 4,848), near SW coast of Réunion isl., 8 mi. NW of Saint-Pierre; sugar cane, beans. Beach resort of Étang-Salé-les-Bains (pop. 196) is on coast, 2.5 mi. W.

Étang Saumâtre, Haiti: see SAUMÂTRE, ÉTANG.

Étaples (ātä'plü), town (pop. 6,545), Pas-de-Calais dept., N France, fishing port at mouth of Canche R. on English Channel, 15 mi. S of Boulogne; mfg. of fishing equipment; limekilns. Has picturesque harbor. In 1492, Henry VII and Charles VIII signed a treaty here. Important Br. base in First World War. Heavily damaged in Second World War. Le TOUQUET-PARIS-PLAGE is 3 mi. W.

Etawa (ātä'vŭ), town (pop., including adjacent railway settlement of Bina, 8,979), Saugor dist., N Madhya Pradesh, India, 40 mi. NW of Saugor; rail junction (workshops); wheat, oilseeds, millet. Also called Bina-Etawa.

Etawah (ātä'vŭ), district (□ 1,669; pop. 883,264), W Uttar Pradesh, India; ⊙ Etawah. On W Ganges Plain and Ganges-Jumna Doab; drained by Chambal R.; irrigated by Upper and Lower Ganges canals. Agr. (pearl millet, wheat, barley, corn, gram, oilseeds, jowar, rice, sugar cane, cotton); dhak and babul groves. Main centers: Etawah, Auraiya, Jaswantnagar. Sometimes spelled Itawah.

Etawah, city (pop. 53,114), ⊙ Etawah dist., W Uttar Pradesh, India, on the Jumna, on railroad and 70 mi. ESE of Agra; road junction; hand-loom cotton-weaving center; oilseed milling, silk weaving. Has 15th-cent. mosque, Jain temple, ruins of 15th-cent. fort (built by Sultan of Jaunpur). Successively under Afghans, Rajputs, Moguls, nawabs of Farrukhabad and Oudh, Rohillas, and Mahrattas. Noted banking and commercial center in 17th cent. Sometimes spelled Itawa.

Etawah Branch, India: see GANGES CANALS.

Etawney Lake or **Etawnei Lake** (ĕtô'nē) (□ 546), N Man., 30 mi. N of Northern Indian L.

Etbai (ĕt'bī), narrow mountain range of NE Africa, fringing the Red Sea from the Gulf of Suez (N) to the Eritrea–Anglo-Egyptian Sudan border (S). Rises to 7,412 ft. at the Jebel Oda. Steep E slope to Red Sea rift valley; gentle W slope merges with Nubian Desert. Gold deposits at Gebeit (Anglo-Egyptian Sudan). Also called Red Sea Hills.

Etchemin River (ĕ'chŭmĭn, Fr. ĕchŭmē'), SE Que., issues from L. Etchemin (3 mi. long), 45 mi. SE of Quebec, flows 50 mi. NW to the St. Lawrence opposite Quebec.

Etchojoa (ĕchōhō'ä), town (pop. 1,505), Sonora, NW Mexico, in lowland near Gulf of California, on lower Mayo R. (irrigation) and 100 mi. SE of Guaymas. Agr. center (chick-peas, corn, rice, fruit, livestock).

Etchu (āt-chōō'), former province in central Honshu, Japan; now Toyama prefecture.

Étel (ātĕl'), town (pop. 2,580), Morbihan dept., W France, seaport on Étel R. (inlet of Bay of Biscay) and 9 mi. SE of Lorient; fish canning, oyster breeding, boatbuilding.

Eten (ātĕn'), town (pop. 5,139), Lambayeque dept., NW Peru, on coastal plain, on Eten R., just N of its port PUERTO ETEN, and 9 mi. S of Chiclayo. Rice mills, railroad shops; mfg. of straw hats, weaving of native textiles.

Eten River, Lambayeque dept., NW Peru, branches off from Lambayeque R. 4 mi. ENE of Pucalá, flows 30 mi. WSW, past Monsefú and Eten, to the Pacific, feeding numerous irrigation channels. Its upper course is also called the Reque (rā'kā).

Eterikan Strait (ĕtyĭrēkän'), in Russian SFSR, joins Laptev and E.Siberian seas of Arctic Ocean, at 73°45'N lat.; separates Maly Lyakhov and Bolshoi Lyakhov isls., off Yakut Autonomous SSR; 10 mi. wide.

Eternity Cape, SE central Que., on Saguenay R., 30 mi. above its mouth, 36 mi. ESE of Chicoutimi; 1,700 ft. high. Just WNW is Trinity Cape.

Etes (ĕ'tĕsh), town (pop. 2,917), Nograd-Hont co., N Hungary, 5 mi. W of Salgotarjan; grain; hogs.

Eth [Arabic,=the], for Arabic names beginning thus: see under following part of the name.

Ethan (ē'thŭn), town (pop. 319), Davison co., SE central S.Dak., 10 mi. S of Mitchell; dairy produce, grain.

Ethan Allen, Fort, Vt.: see ESSEX, town.

Ethel. 1 Town (pop. 723), Attala co., central Miss., on Yockanookany R. and 9 mi. ENE of Kosciusko; wood products. **2** Town (pop. 226), Macon co., N central Mo., near Chariton R., 18 mi. NW of Macon. **3** Village (pop. 1,032), Logan co., SW W.Va., 4 mi. ENE of Logan, in coal-mining region.

Ethete (ĕ'thŭtē), village (pop. c.150), Fremont co., W central Wyo., on branch of Popo Agie R., near Wind River Range, and 14 mi. N of Lander, in Wind River Indian Reservation; alt. c.5,500 ft. Episcopal mission school for Indian children and U.S. school here.

Ethiopia (ēthēō'pyŭ, -pēŭ), Amharic *Ityopya*, independent empire (□ 350,000–400,000; pop. estimates range from 8,000,000 to 15,500,000), E Africa; ⊙ Addis Ababa. The name Abyssinia (derived from Arabic *El Habesha*), although never official, has been widely used. Bounded N and NE by Eritrea, E by Fr. and Br. Somaliland, SE by Ital. Somaliland, S by Kenya, and W by Anglo-Egyptian Sudan. Lacking a seacoast, Ethiopia's principal outlet is the port of Djibouti (Fr. Somaliland) at terminus of country's only railroad, from Addis Ababa. Physiographically, Ethiopia is an almost isolated mtn. plateau rising steeply from the White Nile lowland in W. The highlands (rising to 15,158 ft. in Ras Dashan, N) are divided into a larger, higher NW section and a narrower SE range by the Great Rift Valley, a deep, steep-walled structural depression extending NE-SW across country from the Red Sea to L. Rudolf. The uplands SE of the rift valley descend gradually to the semi-arid OGADEN plateau which slopes toward the Indian Ocean. NE Ethiopia, where the escarpments enclosing the rift valley draw apart, is occupied by the DANAKIL desert, studded with salt pans. The rift valley proper is also marked by a chain of lakes (Zwai, Langana, Shala, Awusa, Abaya, Chamo, Stefanie), many of which are brackish. Ethiopia's N and W highlands, topped by extensive lava sheets, contribute their waters largely to the Nile basin. Here rise the Blue Nile (outlet of L. Tana, Ethiopia's largest lake) and its tributaries (Rahad, Dinder, Dadessa); the headstreams of the Sobat (which flows to the White Nile); and of the Atbara (the Nile's only important affluent below Khartoum). The Omo (flowing S to L. Rudolf) and the Awash (flowing NE through a section of the rift valley to the Danakil desert) also originate here. The SE ranges give rise to the Webi SHEBELI and to headstreams of the Juba (Ganale Dorya, Web, Dawa), all of which drain SE into Ital. Somaliland. Shorter streams (Jerer, Fafan), rising near Harar, lose themselves in the Ogaden. Three vertical climatic zones are usually distinguished: the *Kolla* (up to 5,500 ft.) is constantly hot (no month under 68°F.) and arid or semi-arid (as in Danakil and Ogaden regions, and in Great Rift Valley); the *Woina Dega* (5,500–8,000 ft.), with country's greatest pop. concentration, has yearly mean temp. of 62°F. (small annual range), cool nights, and rainfall (most of it in summer) ranging from 25 in. near Harar (E) to 80 in. in L. Tana dist. (NW); most of Ethiopia's crops are grown in this zone; the *Dega* (above 8,000 ft.), always cool, with warmest monthly mean just over 60°F., has extensive pasture lands, coniferous forests, and grows some grain in areas up to 11,000 ft. Ethiopia has a nearly self-contained agr. and pastoral economy. Chief crops are millet (durra), wheat, barley, tobacco, cotton, plantains, and coffee (especially long-berry Mocha in Harar area). Abyssinia coffee, gathered from a wild plant, grows in extensive upland forests, which also yield the landolphia rubber vine. Pastoralism is widespread; hardy, small horses and pack-mules are bred. Principal export products are coffee, beeswax, hides and skins (from cattle, goats, sheep, leopards, monkeys), grain. Gold (from placers in W streams and near Adola in S) and potash salts (from Danakir salt pans) are chief mineral products; platinum, copper, sulphur, and coal deposits remain unexploited. Petroleum prospecting under way (since Second World War) in the Ogaden. In addition to the 486-mi.-long railroad to Djibouti (427 mi. of which are in Ethiopia), Ethiopia is served by c.4,300 mi. of roads (largely dating from Ital. occupation) radiating from Addis Ababa to Asmara and Assab (in Eritrea) and to prov. capitals. Few rivers are navigable; Gambela (on Baro R.) is center for shipments to Khartoum. The larger towns are HARAR, Diredawa, Dessye, Gondar, Jimma, Aduwa. Aksum and Lalibala are major religious centers. The pop. pattern reveals a diversity of ethnic groups. The Amhara (ruling group) and Tigreans in N and center are of mixed Hamitic-Semitic origin and Coptic Christian religion. The Galla, of Hamitic origin, representing c.½ total pop., are either Christians, Moslems, or pagans. Pastoral Somalis (Moslems) live in SE, Nilotic Bantus in SW. The Falashas (Jews) are found N of L. Tana. Amharic is the official language. The origins of the Ethiopian state are unknown. Anciently it included a vaguely defined area S of Egypt, as it did in classical writings (where it appears as Aethiopia). Biblical references to Cush are mostly to what was then considered Ethiopia (largely the Anglo-Egyptian Sudan). The traditional account of the origin of the Ethiopian state is that the ruling line was founded c.1000 B.C. by Solomon's 1st son, whom the Queen of Sheba (identified with Ethiopia) is supposed to have borne. In the 1st cent. A.D., however, the earliest time for which there are authentic records, Ethiopia (with its capital at Aksum), was pagan. The country then probably comprised Tigre (present-day N Ethiopia), Nubia (S Anglo-Egyptian Sudan), and the coast of the Red Sea. In 4th cent. the Aksumite king was converted to Coptic Christianity by Frumentius, a bishop consecrated by the patriarch of Alexandria. Judaism was perhaps introduced from Yemen, across the Red Sea on the Arabian Peninsula. The rise of Islam in 7th cent. soon deprived Ethiopia of its outer territories (especially the Red Sea Coast). The restoration (c.1270) of the Solomonian dynasty, and a subsequent literary and architectural revival, led to the belief in medieval Europe that Ethiopia (confused with India) might be the land of Prester John. Portuguese embassies (in 16th cent.) and occasional explorers (notably James Bruce) later visited Ethiopia, but not until 19th cent. did the country enter the world scene. Theodore II, who after 1855 ruled most of Ethiopia, was defeated (1868) at Magdala by the British under Napier, after refusing to release a Br. diplomatic party. From the ensuing civil war, Menelik II emerged the sole ruler in 1889. When Italians (who had signed a treaty with Menelik in 1889) invaded Ethiopia in 1895, he defeated them decisively in the battle of Aduwa (1896), thus maintaining his country's independence. Renewed Ital. aspirations, fanned by a border clash (1934) at Walwal in Ogaden, led to the Italo-Ethiopian War (1935–36) and to Ital. occupation of Ethiopia, despite the threat of League of Nations sanctions. Ethiopia was amalgamated with Eritrea and Ital. Somaliland into Italian East Africa. In Second World War, it was a base (1940) for Italy's short-lived occupation of Br. Somaliland, but in 1941 was recaptured by British and Haile Selassie (emperor since 1930) was restored to his throne. After the war, Ethiopia repeatedly claimed former Ital. colonies (especially Eritrea) to gain an outlet to the sea, and in 1950 the United Nations decided to federate Eritrea with Ethiopia, the new relationship to become effective in 1952. Country is now governed by the emperor aided by a council of ministers and a parliament. Efforts have been undertaken to reduce illiteracy and to continue modernization of agr. and transportation begun by Italians. Administratively, Ethiopia is divided into 12 provinces (ARUSI, BEGEMDIR, GAMU-GOFA, GOJJAM, HARAR, ILUBABOR, KAFFA, SHOA, SIDAMO-BORANA, TIGRE, WALLAGA, WALLO), some of which bear the names of former kingdoms.

Etikoppaka, India: see YELLAMANCHILI.

Étival-Clairefontaine (ātēväl'-klârfōtĕn'), commune (pop. 2,083), Vosges dept., E France, on the Meurthe and 7 mi. NNW of Saint-Dié; paper milling.

Etive, Loch (lŏkh ĕ'tĭv), sea inlet in NW Argyll, Scotland, extending 18 mi. E and NE from the Firth of Lorne, NE of Oban; up to 1 mi. wide.

Etiwanda (ĕtĭwŏn'dŭ), village (1940 pop. 1,198), San Bernardino co., S Calif., 12 mi. W of San Bernardino, in the foothill citrus-fruit belt.

Etkul, Russian SFSR: see YETKUL.

Etla (āt'lä), officially San Pablo Etla, town (pop. 1,047), Oaxaca, S Mexico, on railroad, on Inter-American Highway and 11 mi. NNW of Oaxaca; alt. 5,384 ft. Cereals, coffee, tobacco, sugar cane, fruit, livestock. Market center. Onyx deposits near by. Place of pilgrimage (to sanctuary of Our Lord of the Mountain). Old Indian town; it has an anc. aqueduct. The surrounding valley was part of a land grant to Cortés.

Etna. 1 Town (pop. 649), Siskiyou co., N Calif., near Small Scott R., 22 mi. SW of Yreka, in a valley of Klamath Mts.; farming, hunting, fishing. **2** Town (pop. 458), Penobscot co., S central Maine, 16 mi. W of Bangor, in agr., recreational area. **3** Industrial borough (pop. 6,750), Allegheny co., SW Pa., on Allegheny R. opposite N Pittsburgh; iron, steel, and enameled products, oil, bronze, brass; agr. Ironmaking began 1832. Inc. 1868. **4** Village (pop. c.350), Lincoln co., W Wyo., on Salt R., near Idaho line, and 22 mi. N of Afton, in Star Valley; alt. c.5,600 ft. Dairy products, grain, livestock. Salt River Range just E. Rural electrification plant near by.

Etna, Mount (ĕt'nŭ), Sicilian *Mongibello* (mônjēbĕl'lō), anc. *Aetna*, highest active volcano (10,705 ft.) in Europe, in Catania prov., E Sicily, 18 mi. NNW of Catania; 37°44'N 15°E. Consists of inner cone, with main crater, and outer truncated cone, over 9,000 ft. high, on whose sides are over 200 subsidiary cones formed by lateral eruptions. On SE slope is large, precipitous cleft, the Valle del Bove, over 3 mi. wide, with walls 2–4,000 ft. high. To NW, at 9,652 ft., lies the observatory, approached by motor road (completed 1935; rises to 6,170 ft.) from Nicolosi, point of ascent for the mtn. Etna covers 460 sq. mi.; has base circumference of 90 mi. Its base, delineated by the Alcantara (N) and the Simeto (W and S), is encircled by a panoramic railroad. Has 4 vegetation zones: subtropical (up to 1,640 ft.), producing citrus fruit, olives, figs; temperate (to 4,260 ft.), devoted to vineyards and tree crops (almonds, hazelnuts, apples, pears); forest zone (to 6,880 ft.), with chestnut, pine, and birch woods and cereal growing; desert zone of lava and ashes, snow-covered 9 months of the year. Fertile, lower slopes (below 2,600 ft.) on E and S are among most densely populated agr. regions of world, especially in Catania-Nicolosi-Acireale triangle. Mt. Etna has had over 260 eruptions counted, ranging from 475 B.C. (described by Pindar and Aeschylus) to 1928 and 1947. Most destructive was that of 1669, which largely destroyed Catania. Nicolosi, 9 mi. NW of Catania, is starting point for the ascent.

Etna Green, town (pop. 444), Kosciusko co., N Ind., 30 mi. SSE of South Bend, in agr. area.

Étoile, Chaîne de l' (shĕn dŭ lätwäl'), barren limestone range of Bouches-du-Rhône dept., SE France, an outlier of Lower Provence Alps, forming semicircle (c.12 mi. long) around Marseilles. Rises to 2,600 ft.

Étoile du Congo, Belgian Congo: see STAR OF THE CONGO.

Etolin Island (ĕ'tōlĭn) (30 mi. long, 10–22 mi. wide), SE Alaska, in Alexander Archipelago, bet. Prince of Wales Isl. (W) and mainland (E), SW of Wrangell Isl.; 56°5'N 132°20'W; rises to 4,000 ft.; fishing.

Etolin Strait (60 mi. long, 30–50 mi. wide), W Alaska, bet. Nunivak Isl. (W) and Nelson Isl. and mainland (E), extends SE–NW bet. Kuskokwim Bay and Bering Sea.

Eton (ē'tŭn), urban district (1931 pop. 2,005; 1951 census 3,250), S Buckingham, England, on left bank of the Thames opposite Windsor. Site of Eton Col., largest and most famous English public school, founded (1440) by Henry VI. Has several bldgs. dating from 15th cent. Eton is closely connected with King's Col., Cambridge, with which it was founded.

Eton, town (pop. 297), Murray co., NW Ga., 13 mi. ENE of Dalton.

Etorofu-kaikyo, Russian SFSR: see FRIZ STRAIT.

Etorofu-to, Russian SFSR: see ITURUP ISLAND.

Etosha Pan (ĕtō'shŭ păn'), salt-water-filled depression (□ 1,404), N South-West Africa, in S part of Ovamboland, 40 mi. S of Ondangua; 18°50'S 16°20'E; 75 mi. long, 10–45 mi. wide. Has no outlet. Surrounded by game reserve.

Etowah (ĕ'tŭwä"), county (□ 555; pop. 93,892), NE Ala.; ⊙ Gadsden. Hilly region crossed by Coosa R. Mfg. (iron and steel products) at Gadsden and Attalla; cotton, truck. Deposits of coal, iron, limestone, fuller's earth, manganese, barites. Formed 1866.

Etowah, town (pop. 3,261), McMinn co., SE Tenn., 10 mi. SSE of Athens; farm-trade center; rail junction; lumber milling, mfg. of hosiery and clothing. Cherokee Natl. Forest near by.

Etowah River, NW Ga., rises in the Blue Ridge, flows 141 mi. SW, past Cartersville, to Rome where it unites with the Oostanaula to form Coosa R. Impounded E of Cartersville by ALLATOONA DAM.

Étrépagny (ātrāpänyē'), town (pop. 2,175), Eure dept., NW France, 10 mi. ENE of Les Andelys; cider distilling, sugar refining; mfg. of safety razors, furniture, brick.

Étrépilly (ātrāpēyē'), village (pop. 396), Seine-et-Marne dept., N central France, 6 mi. NNE of Meaux. First World War cemetery and memorial to Fr. defenders of Paris.

Étretat (ātrŭtä'), village (pop. 1,875), Seine-Inférieure dept., N France, on English Channel, 15 mi. NNE of Le Havre; fishing port and fashionable resort with small beach flanked by white cliffs.

Etropole, Bulgaria: see YETROPOLE.

Etruria (ātrōō'ryä), town (pop. estimate 2,000), S central Córdoba prov., Argentina, 35 mi. S of Villa María; grain, flax, stock.

Etruria (ĭtrōō'rēŭ), suburb in STOKE-ON-TRENT, NW Stafford, England, in the Potteries district; site of Wedgwood pottery factory.

Etruria (ĭtrōō'rēŭ), anc. country of W central Italy, now forming Tuscany and part of Umbria. This was territory of the Etruscans, a people of great artistic talents who probably immigrated from Asia Minor c.800 B.C. and in 6th cent. B.C. spread their civilization over much of Italy; they were later forced back and absorbed by Rome. Name was restored by Napoleon who set up (1801) kingdom of Etruria.

Etruscan Apennines (ētrŭ'skŭn ă'pĕnīnz) or **Tuscan Apennines** (tŭ'skŭn), division of N Apennines, N central Italy; extend c.170 mi. bet. passes of La Cisa (NW) and Bocca Serriola (SE). Form watershed bet. Po (N) and Arno and Tiber (S) rivers. Chief peaks: Monte Cimone (7,096 ft.), Monte Cusna (6,955 ft.), and Monte Prado (6,735 ft.). Crossed by various passes, including Passo di Cerreto, Passo dell'Abetone, Il Giogo, and La Futa. Include APUANE ALPS (NW).

Etsa, Egypt: see ITSA.

Etsch, Italy: see ADIGE RIVER.

Etsin Gol, Etzin Gol, or **Edsin Gol** (all: ĕtsēn' gōl'), river of NW China, formed at Tingsin in Kansu prov by union of Peita and Hei rivers, flows 200 mi. NNE, through Ningsia section of Inner Mongolia, to lake depression on Outer Mongolian border at 42°N 101°E. Also called Jo Shui. W of the Etsin Gol lives the West Mongol tribe of the Etsin Torgot.

Ettaiyapuram or **Etaiyapuram** (both: ātŭyä'pōōrŭm), town (pop. 9,130), Tinnevelly dist., S Madras, India, 26 mi. NNW of Tuticorin; cotton, jaggery.

Ettelbruck (ĕ'tŭlbrōōk), town (pop. 4,212), central Luxembourg, on Sûre R., at mouths of Alzette and Wark rivers, and 16 mi. N of Luxembourg city; rail junction; metal foundries; gravel quarries; mfg. (tanning fluid, furniture, tobacco), rose nurseries; market center for fruit (cherries, pears, apples, plums) and dairying region. Badly damaged in Second World War.

Et Tell el Abyad, El Tell el Abyad, or **Al-Tall al-Abyad** (all: ĕt-tĕl' ĕl-ăb'yăd), Fr. *Tell Abiad*, village, Euphrates prov., N Syria, on Turkish frontier, 100 mi. ENE of Aleppo; cereals. In vicinity (S) is an area rich in oil deposits.

Etten (ĕ'tŭn), village (pop. 4,019), North Brabant prov., SW Netherlands, 6 mi. WSW of Breda; stone quarrying; cigars, strawboard; agr.

Ettenheim (ĕ'tŭnhīm), town (pop. 3,116), S Baden, Germany, at W foot of Black Forest, 6 mi. SSW of Lahr; tobacco industry; paper milling, woodworking. Has rococo church.

Etter, Texas: see DUMAS.

Etterbeek (ĕ'tŭrbāk), E suburb (pop. 50,767) of Brussels, Brabant prov., central Belgium; woodworking, furniture mfg. Army barracks.

Ettingshall, England: see BILSTON.

Ettlingen (ĕt'lĭng-ŭn), town (pop. 14,993), N Baden, Germany, after 1945 in Württemberg-Baden, 4 mi. S of Karlsruhe (linked by tramway), textile milling (cotton spinning and weaving; velvet, clothing); mfg. of machinery, cellulose, paper, lumber milling. Has 18th-cent. castle and town hall.

Ettrick, agr. village and parish (pop. 308), SW Selkirk, Scotland, on Ettrick Water and 13 mi. ENE of Moffat. James Hogg b. and buried here.

Ettrick. 1 or **Ettricks**, village (pop. 3,030), Chesterfield co., E central Va., just NW of Petersburg, across Appomattox R. **2** Village (pop. 415), Trempealeau co., W Wis., on tributary of Black R. and 24 mi. N of La Crosse, in dairy and livestock area; woolen and flour mills.

Ettrick Forest, grazing area including Selkirkshire, Scotland, formerly part of extensive Caledonian Forest, covering part of SE Scotland. It was forfeited by Douglas family to the crown in 1455, became royal hunting ground, and was converted into sheep-grazing area in 16th cent.

Ettrick Pen, mountain (2,270 ft.) on Selkirk and Dumfries border, Scotland, 8 mi. ENE of Moffat.

Ettrick Water, river, Selkirk, Scotland, rises on Capel Fell, flows 33 mi. NE, past Ettrick and Selkirk, to the Tweed 3 mi. NE of Selkirk. Has high gradient; receives Yarrow Water 2 mi. SW of Selkirk.

Ettringham, England: see PRUDHOE.

Etyek (ĕ'tyĕk), town (pop. 4,033), Fejer co., N central Hungary, 14 mi. W of Budapest, corn, wheat, cattle.

Etymander, Afghanistan: see HELMAND RIVER.

Etzatlán (ĕtsätlän'), town (pop. 5,641), Jalisco, W Mexico, on interior plateau, near L. Magdalena, on railroad and 50 mi. W of Guadalajara; mining center (silver, gold, lead, zinc).

Etzenrot (ĕ'tsŭnrōt), village (pop. 870), N Baden, Germany, after 1945 in Württemberg-Baden, 3 mi. SE of Ettlingen; cotton spinning and weaving.

Etzina, China: see KARAKHOTO.

Etzin Gol, China: see ETSIN GOL.

Etzion Geber, Palestine: see EZION-GEBER.

Eu (û), town (pop. 5,118), Seine-Inférieure dept., N France, port on the Bresle near its mouth on the Channel, 18 mi. NE of Dieppe; road center; glassworks; copper and aluminum smelting, cider distilling, paper milling, brewing, barrel mfg. Has a 12th–13th-cent. Norman Gothic church and a recently restored castle (with park), once favorite residence of Louis-Philippe. Damaged in Second World War.

Eua (āōō'ä), island (□ 33; pop. 444), Tongatabu group, S Tonga, S Pacific; rises to c.1,000 ft.; 21°25'S 175°W. Formerly Middleburg Isl.

Eubank (ū'băngk), town (pop. 322), Pulaski co., S Ky., 14 mi. NNW of Somerset; buckwheat, hardwood lumber.

Euboea (ūbē'ŭ), Gr. *Evvoia* (ĕ'vēŭ), largest Greek island (□ 1,457; pop. c.162,800) in Aegean Sea, extending NW-SE off central Greece, separated from mainland by Oreos Channel (N) and gulfs of Euboea and Petalion (SW). It is part of a nome (□ c.1,480; pop. 166,251; ⊙ Chalcis) which includes its offshore PETALIA ISLANDS and STYRA in Gulf of Petalion, and isl. of SKYROS of the Northern Sporades, with its offshore isls. of SKYROPOULA and VALAXA. Euboea proper, 110 mi. long, up to 30 mi. wide, is mainly mountainous, rising to 5,718 ft. in the Dirphys. Its fertile valleys produce wheat, wine, olive oil; sheep, goats, and cattle. Important mineral products include lignite (Kyme, Aliverion, Psachna), magnesite (Limne, Chalcis, Mantoudion), marble (Karystos). Sulphur springs at Loutra Aidepsou. Fisheries along coast. In anc. times, leading cities were CHALCIS and ERETRIA. Originally independent, it was conquered (506 B.C.) by the Athenians, against which it rebelled unsuccessfully in 446 B.C.; fell 338 B.C. to Philip II of Macedon, and passed 191 B.C. under Roman rule. Transferred to Venetians (1204–1470), it became one of their main possessions in the Levant, until it came under Turkish rule (1470–1830). During the Middle Ages it was called Negropont, Ital. *Negroponte*, by the Venetians, Egripo or Euripos by the Greeks.

Euboea, Gulf of, or **Gulf of Evvoia**, arm of Aegean Sea, Greece, bet. Euboea (NE) and mainland of central Greece (SW); consists of N section (50 mi. long) and of S section (30 mi. long) joined by the narrow Euripos at CHALCIS. Connects N with Malian Gulf and Oreos Channel, S with Gulf of Petalion. Formerly called Talanti Channel or Atalante Channel in N section and Egripo Channel or Euripos Channel in S section.

Eucaliptus, Bolivia: see TOMÁS BARRÓN.

Eucla (ū'klŭ), village, SE Western Australia, near South Australia border, 440 mi. ESE of Kalgoorlie and on Great Australian Bight; anchorage.

Euclid (ū'klĭd), city (pop. 41,396), Cuyahoga co., N Ohio, just NE of Cleveland, on L. Erie; electrical goods, office machinery, metal products. Natl. American Shrine of Our Lady of Lourdes is here. Settled 1798.

Euclides da Cunha (ĕōōklē'dĭs dä kōō'nyŭ), city (pop. 809), NE Bahia, Brazil, 80 mi. E of Senhor do Bonfim; livestock, hides and skins, cotton. Until 1939, called Cumbe.

Euclid Heights (ū'klĭd), residential suburb (pop. 2,090), Garland co., central Ark., adjacent to Hot Springs.

Eudora (ūdō'rŭ). **1** Town (pop. 3,072), Chicot co., extreme SE Ark., 24 mi. SSW of Greenville (Miss.), near the Mississippi; cotton ginning and compressing, mfg. of hardwood-products. Inc. 1904. **2** City (pop. 929), Douglas co., E Kansas, on Kansas R. at mouth of Wakarusa R., and 8 mi. E of Lawrence; grain, potatoes.

Eudunda (ūdŭn'dŭ), town (pop. 735), SE South Australia, 60 mi. NE of Adelaide; wheat, fruit, dairy products.

Euenus River, Greece: see EVENOS RIVER.

Euerdorf (oi'ŭrdôrf), village (pop. 1,259), Lower Franconia, NW Bavaria, Germany, on the Franconian Saale and 4 mi. SW of Bad Kissingen; gypsum mfg., brewing, flour milling. Winegrowing.

Eufaula (ūfô'lŭ). **1** City (pop. 6,906), ⊙ Barbour co., SE Ala., on Chattahoochee R. (here forming Ga. line) and c.75 mi. SE of Montgomery; trade and shipping center, with boat connections, for cotton, peanut, and livestock area; cotton textiles and hosiery, lumber and lumber products, cottonseed and peanut oil, fertilizer. Settled in 1830s. Has many fine plantation homes. **2** City (pop. 2,540), ⊙ McIntosh co., E Okla., 34 mi. SSW of Muskogee, near confluence of Canadian and North Canadian rivers; cotton ginning, grain milling, mfg. of concrete blocks. Site of Eufaula Reservoir in the Canadian, a unit of Arkansas R. basin development plan, is E. Founded c.1872 near site of a Creek settlement. A U.S. school for Indian girls is here.

Euganean Hills (ūgā'nēŭn) (□ c.135), Ital. *Colli Euganei*, in Veneto, N Italy, 9 mi. SW of Padua; 11 mi. long N-S, c.10 mi. wide; rise to 1,978 ft. in Monte Venda. Trachyte and marble quarries. Volcanic in origin; many hot springs.

Eugene. 1 Town (pop. 180), Cole co., central Mo., near Osage R., 20 mi. SW of Jefferson City. **2** City (pop. 35,879), ⊙ Lane co., W Oregon, on the Willamette and 60 mi. S of Salem. Agr. trade and shipping center, with creameries, fruit and vegetable canneries; wool and lumber milling. Seat of Univ. of Oregon and Northwest Christian Col.; hq. Willamette Natl. Forest. Laid out 1852, inc. 1862.

Eugène-Étienne Hennaya (ûzhĕn'-ātyĕn' ĕnäyä'), village (pop. 2,795), Oran dept., NW Algeria, on railroad and 6 mi. NNW of Tlemcen; winegrowing; olive-oil processing. Also called Hennaya.

Eugenia Point (ĕōōhā'nyä), cape on Pacific coast of Lower California, NW Mexico, at SW entrance of Sebastián Vizcaíno Bay; 27°52'N 115°5'W.

Eugenópolis (ĕ"ōōzhĭnô'pōōlēs), city (pop. 1,267), SE Minas Gerais, Brazil, near Rio de Janeiro border, 12 mi. E of Muriaé; coffee. Until 1944, called São Manuel.

Eugowra (yōōgou'rŭ), town (pop. 714), E central New South Wales, Australia, 165 mi. WNW of Sydney; rail terminus; sheep and agr. center.

Eule, Czechoslovakia: see JILOVE.

Eulengebirge (oi'lŭngŭbĭr"gŭ) [Ger.,=owl mountains], Pol *Góry Sowie* (gōō'rĭ sô'vyĕ), range of the Sudetes in Lower Silesia, after 1945 in SW Poland, bet. upper Bystrzyca R. (NNW) and the Glatzer Neisse (SSE) opposite Bardo; c.30 mi. long. Highest point (3,327 ft.), the Hohe Eule, is 11 mi. S of Schweidnitz (Swidnica).

Euloeus, Iran: see KARUN RIVER.

Eumolpias, Bulgaria: see PLOVDIV, city.

Eunice (ū'nĭs). **1** Town (pop. 8,184), St. Landry parish, S central La., 20 mi. W of Opelousas; trade center for oil, cotton, and rice area. Cotton gins; cottonseed-oil, lumber, sugar, and rice mills; mfg. of soybean products, machine-shop products, mattresses, pumps. Has annual fair. Inc. 1895. **2** Town (pop. 2,352), Lea co., SE N.Mex., on Llano Estacado, near Texas line, 18 mi. S of Hobbs, in ranching region; carbon black. Oil wells and pipe lines near by. Settled 1909, platted 1927, inc. 1935.

Eunola (ūnō'lŭ), town (pop. 112), Geneva co., SE Ala.; suburb of Geneva.

Eupatoria, Russian SFSR: see YEVPATORIYA.

Eupen (Ger. oi'pŭn, Fl. û'pŭn, Fr. ûpĕn'), town (pop. 14,462), Liége prov., E Belgium, 20 mi. E of Liége, near Vesdre R.; wool spinning and weaving; cable mfg. Formerly in Germany; transferred (1919) to Belgium, after plebiscite under Treaty of Versailles.

Euphrates (ūfrā'tēz), Arabic *El Furat* or *Al Furat* (both: ĕl fōōrät'), province (□ 21,750; 1946 pop. 231,820), E Syria, in the Syrian Desert, on both sides of the Euphrates from the Turkish line (N) to Iraq (E and S); ⊙ DEIR EZ ZOR. Barren area, rich in oil deposits, especially near Deir ez Zor. Many sites of anc. cities, notably DURA and DIBSE.

Euphrates River, Arabic *Al Furat*, Turkish *Fırat* (fĭ'rät) or *Frat* (frät), a great river (c.1,700 mi. long) of SW Asia, formed in E central Turkey by 2 headstreams, the Euphrates proper (also called the Western Euphrates or the Kara Su) and the Murat. Both headstreams rise in the Turkish Armenian highlands bet. L. Van and the Black Sea; the Western Euphrates or Kara Su rises 14 mi. N of Erzurum and flows 285 mi. SW to its junction with the Murat 5 mi. NE of Kaban, WNW of Elazig; the Murat rises 40 mi. SW of Mt. Ararat and flows 380 mi. W to its junction with the W branch; the combined streams flow 305 mi. SW, past Keban and Birecik, to the Syrian line, making a total course of 685 mi. in Turkey. In the last part of its course in Turkey it comes to within 95 mi. of the Mediterranean coast before swinging S into Syria. It then flows SE across the Syrian Desert in E Syria, past Jarablus, Raqqa, and Deir ez Zor, and into Iraq, which it bisects, irrigating its date orchards, and flowing past Haditha, Hit, Habbaniyah, Al Falluja, Hindiya, Samawa, and Nasiriya, until it joins with the Tigris c.40 mi. NW of Basra to form the SHATT AL ARAB, a 120-mi. section of the joint stream which flows to the head of the Persian Gulf. The Turkish course of the Euphrates is through mountainous country, which feeds it with small streams, but in Syria it receives only the Belikh, the Khabur, and small wadis. Here begins the use of its waters for irrigation, as is also done in Iraq, but in neither country are the modern irrigation works as extensive as those of anc. times. The Euphrates is not usefully navigable, though certain shallow-draft craft can ascend it in Iraq. Bet. Hindiya and Samawa in central Iraq the Euphrates splits into 2 channels, the Shatt HINDIYA and the Shatt HILLA. The lower Euphrates and the Tigris water Mesopotamia, the birthplace of the great ancient civilizations, and along the Euphrates are the sites and ruins of great anc. cities: Sippar, Babylon, Erech, Larsa, Ur.

Eupora (ūpô'rŭ), town (pop. 1,338), Webster co., central Miss., c.50 mi. E of Greenwood, near Big

Black R., in agr., poultry, timber area. Sawmills, cotton gins. Settled 1887, inc. 1889.

Eurasia (yo͞orā′zhů, –shů), land mass comprising the continents of EUROPE and ASIA, in which Europe is geographically a W peninsula of Asia.

Eure (ûr), department (□ 2,331; pop. 315,902), in Normandy, NW France; ⊙ Évreux. Bounded by Seine R. estuary (NNW). Drained by the lower Seine (which separates bulk of dept. to S from the Vexin dist. along its right bank), its tributaries (Eure, Andelle, Epte), and the Risle. Primarily agr. (wheat, apples, sugar beets, flax, colza) and cattle-raising area. Large wooded tracts. Chief industries: textile milling (Bernay, Louviers, Thiberville), tanning and leather-working (Pont-Audemer, Pont-de-l'Arche, Beaumont-le-Roger), metalworking (Évreux, Verneuil, Rugles). Principal towns (Évreux, Louviers, Vernon, Les Andelys, Pont-Audemer) damaged during Ger. sweep across France (1940) and after Allied Normandy invasion (1944) in Second World War.

Eure, river, France: see EURE RIVER.

Eure-et-Loir (ûr-ā-lwär′), department (□ 2,293; pop. 258,110), NW France; ⊙ Chartres. Physically divided bet. the wheat-growing Beauce (E) and the stock-raising Perche hills (W). Primarily agr., with excellent wheat, oat, and barley yields, apple orchards, and dairying. Raises percheron horses, cattle, sheep. Some flour milling, tanning, mfg. of meat preserves, agr. machinery, and chemical fertilizer. Chief towns: Chartres (noted cathedral), Dreux, Nogent-le-Rotrou, Châteaudun.

Eureka (yo͞orē′ků), county (□ 4,182; pop. 896), N central Nev.; ⊙ Eureka. Mtn. region crossed in N by Humboldt R. Livestock; gold, silver, lead. Chief ranges are Diamond Mts. (in E, NE of Eureka) and Cortez Mts. (S of Humboldt R.). Part of Antelope Range is in S. Formed 1873.

Eureka. 1 City (pop. 23,058), ⊙ Humboldt co., NW Calif., port on HUMBOLDT BAY; largest Calif. city N of Sacramento (c.200 mi. SE); port of entry. Lumber-milling and commercial-fishing center in heart of redwood country; dairying, truck farming in region. Founded 1850, inc. 1856. U.S. Fort Humboldt here protected settlers from Indian attack during 1853–65. **2** Town (pop. 13), San Juan co., SW Colo., in San Juan Mts., 7 mi. NE of Silverton; alt. 9,800 ft.; silver mines. **3** City (pop. 2,367), ⊙ Woodford co., central Ill., 17 mi. E of Peoria; farm trade center, with cannery; corn, wheat, oats, soybeans, livestock, dairy products, poultry, truck. Seat of Eureka Col. Founded in 1830s, inc. 1859. **4** City (pop. 3,958), ⊙ Greenwood co., SE Kansas, on Fall R. and c.55 mi. E of Wichita; shipping and trade center for cattle-, grain-, and oil-producing region. Laid out 1867, inc. 1870. **5** Town (pop. 929), Lincoln co., NW Mont., on Tobacco R., near British Columbia line, and 60 mi. NW of Kalispell, in grain and dairying region; timber, berries. **6** Village (pop. c.500), ⊙ Eureka co., central Nev., 60 mi. WNW of Ely; alt. 6,837 ft. Gold, silver, lead; stock farms. Diamond Peak is 9 mi. NE. **7** Town (pop. 192), Wayne co., E central N.C., 12 mi. NNE of Goldsboro. **8** Village, Gallia co., Ohio: see CHAMBERSBURG. **9** Village, Chester co., S.C.: see HEMLOCK. **10** City (pop. 1,576), McPherson co., N S.Dak., 60 mi. WNW of Aberdeen; shipping center for grain and livestock; cement blocks; dairy produce, wheat, barley, oats. Agr. experiment station is here. Founded 1886. **11** City (pop. 1,318), Juab co., central Utah, SW of Utah L., 30 mi. SW of Provo in mtn. region; alt. 6,396 ft. Trade center for rich mining area (gold, silver, lead, zinc, copper). Settled 1870.

Eureka Sound, N Franklin Dist., Northwest Territories, arm (180 mi. long, 8-30 mi. wide) of the Arctic Ocean, bet. Axel Heiberg Isl. and Ellesmere Isl.; 79°N 87°W. Extends N from Norwegian Bay. Several arms radiate from it.

Eureka Springs, city (pop. 1,958), a ⊙ Carroll co., NW Ark., 33 mi. NE of Fayetteville, near Mo. line, in Ozark region; health resort, with mineral springs. Mfg. (lumber, stoves, fire-fighting apparatus). U.S. soil-conservation project near by. Settled 1879.

Eure River (ûr), Eure-et-Loir and Eure depts., NW France, rises in the Perche hills SW of La Ferté-Vidame, flows ESE to Chartres, thence N, past Maintenon and Louviers, to the Seine just above Pont-de-l'Arche; 140 mi. long. Receives Avre and Iton rivers (left).

Euripos or **Evripos** (yo͞orĭ′půs, Gr. ĕv′rĭpôs), Lat. *Euripus*, strait in Aegean Sea, Greece, bet. Euboea and mainland of central Greece, connects N and S sections of Gulf of Euboea; 5 mi. long, 130 ft. to 1 mi. wide. Chalcis is at narrowest point, site of drawbridge (built 1894) to the mainland. Strong tidal currents.

Euroa (yo͞orō′ů), town (pop. 2,175), N central Victoria, Australia, 80 mi. NNE of Melbourne in dairying area; livestock.

Europa, small volcanic islet, a dependency of Madagascar, in Mozambique Channel of Indian Ocean; 22°20′S 40°20′E.

Europa, Picos de (pē′kōs dhā ĕo͞orō′pä), highest massif of the Cantabrian Mts., N Spain, bet. New Castile, Asturias, and Leon; extends c.30 mi. E-W; rises in the Torre (or Peña) de Cerredo to 8,687 ft. Among other high peaks are the Peña Vieja (8,573 ft.), and the Torre de Llambrión (8,586 ft.). Largely calcareous and rich in magnesite deposits. Has some small glaciers.

Europa Point (yo͞orō′pů), southernmost point of Gibraltar; 36°6′20″N 5°20′45″W; lighthouse.

Europe, continent (with adjacent isls., □ c.3,700,000; 1950 pop. estimate 550,000,000), next to the island continent of Australia the world's smallest, and in area only slightly larger than the U.S. and Alaska combined. Actually a vast W peninsula of the great Eurasian land mass, it is separated from Asia rather by its diversity and cultural distinction than by any clear physiographic divide. Comprising only about 8% of the globe's land mass, it has approximately 25% of its population. Europe has been a pivotal area of world history for more than 2 millenniums because it bordered Asia, was close tc Africa, and fronted the Atlantic, across which led the westward expansion to the New World. Unlike the other continents, it is situated almost entirely in the Temperate Zone. Also favorable to economic and cultural activity is its extraordinarily indented coast line, so that most of it is close to the great maritime trade routes. It is washed in far N (Scandinavian Peninsula) and NE by the Arctic Sea (with embayments of the Barents Sea, White Sea, and Kara Sea), in W by the Atlantic Ocean (whose inlets, the Bay of Biscay, the English Channel, the Irish Sea, the North Sea, and Baltic Sea penetrate the coast), in S by the Mediterranean Sea (connecting W through narrow Strait of Gibraltar with the Atlantic and E, through the c.200-mi.-long waterway of the Dardanelles, Sea of Marmara, and Bosporus, with the Black Sea). Europe's E boundary lacks such a natural outline and has been variously defined, from the neighborhood of 65°E to 45°E. However, it is generally considered to follow a line marked by the low URAL MOUNTAINS, the small Kara R. NW of the Urals, and, SW of the Urals, the Ural R., the Caspian Sea, and the Manych Depression that intervenes bet. the Volga delta and the Greater CAUCASUS. The crest line of the Caucasus is the only clear-cut land border, across which, however, extend parts of the USSR (Transcaucasia). To the continent belong a host of isls., among them SPITSBERGEN and NOVAYA ZEMLYA off the N coast; GREAT BRITAIN, IRELAND, the HEBRIDES, ORKNEY ISLANDS, SHETLAND ISLANDS, CHANNEL ISLANDS, Isle of MAN, FAEROE ISLANDS, and ICELAND off the NW coast; numerous isls. in the Baltic; and the BALEARIC ISLANDS, CORSICA, SARDINIA, SICILY, CRETE, MALTA, and the Greek isls. in the Mediterranean. Europe extends some 4,000 mi. E–W. The extreme points of the mainland are: in the E, the NE Urals, at about 66°E; in the N, Cape Nordkyn, Norway, 71°8′1″N; in the W, Cape Roca, Portugal, 9°30′W; in the S, Point Marroquí, Spain, 36°N. Politically, Europe is divided into ALBANIA, ANDORRA, AUSTRIA, BELGIUM, BULGARIA, CZECHOSLOVAKIA, DENMARK, FINLAND, FRANCE, GERMANY, GREECE, HUNGARY, ICELAND, IRELAND, ITALY, LIECHTENSTEIN, LUXEMBOURG, MONACO, NETHERLANDS, NORWAY, POLAND, PORTUGAL, RUMANIA, SAAR, SAN MARINO, SPAIN, SWEDEN, SWITZERLAND, the Free Territory of TRIESTE, TURKEY in Europe, the European part of the UNION OF SOVIET SOCIALIST REPUBLICS (including European section of the RUSSIAN SOVIET FEDERATED SOCIALIST REPUBLIC, KARELIA, ESTONIA, LATVIA, LITHUANIA, BELORUSSIA, UKRAINE, and MOLDAVIA; in Transcaucasia—GEORGIA, ARMENIA, and AZERBAIJAN), the UNITED KINGDOM (ENGLAND, SCOTLAND, WALES, and NORTHERN IRELAND), VATICAN CITY, and YUGOSLAVIA; Britain's fortress GIBRALTAR is at S tip of Iberian Peninsula. (See articles on those countries for detailed geographic, economic, and historic information.) A huge mtn. chain, of which the Pyrenees, Jura, Apennines, Alps, Carpathians, Balkans, and the Caucasus are the principal parts, traverses the continent W–E. As intricate as Europe's coast line is its topography; the many broken mtn. systems departmentalize its area, fostering a strong regionalism. Above the continent's lowest section, the Manych Depression (c.75 ft. below sea level), tower its highest peaks in the Caucasus, among them Mt. Elbrus (18,481 ft.), Dykh-Tau (17,054 ft.), Mt. Kazbek (16,545 ft.), and others, which surpass Mont Blanc (15,781 ft.), culminating point of the ALPS, and occasionally held to be the highest elevation in Europe proper. Other well-known peaks include the Monte Rosa (15,203 ft.), Matterhorn (14,701 ft.), Finsteraarhorn (14,032 ft.), Jungfrau (13,653 ft.) in the Alps; the Pico de Aneto (11,168 ft.) of the Maladetta massif, highest in the PYRENEES, and the Mulhacén (11,411 ft.) of the SIERRA NEVADA in S Spain. Europe's average altitude is c.1,000 ft., since approximately half of the land lies below 600 ft., while in some parts, as in the Netherlands and along the Caspian Sea, it is below sea level. From N France and the Low Countries the Great Northern European Plain stretches eastward along the North Sea and Baltic Sea across Poland and Russia, whence it continues S into the Ukraine and far beyond the Urals into Siberia. More isolated, partly alluvial plains adjoin some of the larger rivers, particularly the Rhone-Saône valley in the PROVENCE, the Po valley in N Italy, the Arno valley of Tuscany, the Guadalquivir valley in Andalusia, the ALFÖLD in Hungary, the VOJVODINA in Yugoslavia, and the DOBRUJA near the Danube R. estuary; there are also the THRACIAN PLAIN and MACEDONIA in the Balkan Peninsula. These lowlands are the principal granaries. Though the agr. and pastoral output of Europe is enormous, increasing pop. and industrialization, as well as numerous destructive wars, have forced it to rely on imports of meat, cereals, and other foodstuffs. The continent's mtn. backbone is formed by young folded ranges of the later Tertiary and early Quaternary (Cenozoic). The entire formation owes its origin to the Alpine uplift contemporaneous and related to the Atlas in North Africa, the Himalayas of central Asia, and even the great Pacific ranges of the Americas. Layers of sedimentary stone occur in all the formerly submerged sections, including the N lowlands. Present volcanic activity (Mt. Vesuvius, Etna, Santorin, etc.) and earthquakes occur in the Mediterranean basin and in Iceland. An almost continuous belt of Tertiary folds guards the S flank of Europe, interrupted only at few key points, such as the Rhone furrow, the Morava-Vardar valley, and the low shore of the Black Sea. But there are good passes, used by transcontinental railroads, at all sections (e.g., Somport Pass and Col de Puymorens in the Pyrenees; Mont Cenis, Great St. Bernard Pass, Simplon Pass, St. Gotthard Pass, Brenner Pass in the Alps; Turnu-Rosu Pass and Predeal Pass in Rumanian Carpathians; Shipka Pass in the Balkan Mts.). Much lower than the Alps and greatly eroded are the older Hercynian ranges of Central Europe, such as the VOSGES, BLACK FOREST, HUNSRÜCK, EIFEL, and TAUNUS astride the Rhine, the ARDENNES, BOHEMIAN FOREST, ERZGEBIRGE, and SUDETES. Of probably similar Paleozoic origin are the MASSIF CENTRAL in the Auvergne of France (with many volcanic remains), the PENNINE CHAIN of England, and the Urals. These heavily forested ranges are in turn exceeded in age by the Caledonian system (folded in Silurian and Devonian ages) of Scandinavia and the Scottish Highlands, distinguished by the scenic fjords of Norway and the lochs and firths of Scotland. Also in N Europe lies the pre-Cambrian shield underlaying E Scandinavia, Finland, Karelia, and Kola Peninsula, a completely eroded mtn. stump, representing one of the world's oldest geological formations. The largest lakes—except for the saline Caspian Sea—are L. LADOGA and L. ONEGA in Russia, L. SAIMAA in lacustrine S Finland, and L. VATTER and L. VANER in S Sweden. Among other major lakes are L. BALATON in Hungary and L. of CONSTANCE on Austro-German-Swiss border. Europe is well served by a web of streams, most of them navigable, watering fertile alluvial lands, facilitating traffic, and furnishing hydroelectric power in their headstreams. By far the largest is the VOLGA RIVER, which, rising in the low Valdai Hills not far from the Baltic, flows E and S to the Caspian Sea. The DNIEPER RIVER, DON RIVER and DNIESTER RIVER flow into the Black Sea, as does the DANUBE RIVER, the only large European stream which flows E–W. Of the other Eastern European rivers, the Northern Dvina and the Pechora rivers drain into the Arctic Ocean; the Niemen, Vistula, and Oder into the Baltic Sea. Better known are the N and W European rivers, which have played an important part throughout history—the Elbe, Weser, Rhine, and Thames flowing to the North Sea; the Seine, Loire, Garonne, Douro, Tagus, and Guadalquivir to the Atlantic; the Ebro, Rhone, and Po to the Mediterranean. The major rivers are of good navigability and are interlaced by an intricate system of canals, e.g., MARNE-RHINE CANAL, RHONE-RHINE CANAL, LUDWIG CANAL (Rhine-Main-Danube), MITTELLAND CANAL (Rhine-Weser-Elbe-Oder), DANUBE-ODER CANAL, etc. The KIEL CANAL connects the Baltic Sea with the North Sea. Since Europe is open to the Gulf Stream and the North Atlantic Drift, its climate is unusually mild for those latitudes. Maritime influences, gradually decreasing towards the E, are still noticeable as far as the Urals, where conditions are, however, on the whole rigorous. Predominantly continental climate—i.e., long severe winters, hot summers—prevails also in more secluded area of the Balkan Peninsula and the MESETA (plateau) of central Spain. Nowhere in W Europe occur extremes in temp., and its ports are ice-free as far N as Narvik (Norway). The Mediterranean basin, shielded by mts. from arctic incursions, has a climate of its own, with mild rainy winters and dry, hot summers—rendering the region a famed resort area (e.g., French and Italian RIVIERA), also well suited for the growth of subtropical fruit. Similar conditions are enjoyed in the CRIMEA. Only the N sections of Scandinavia (LAPLAND), Finland, and Russia are subarctic. The quantity of rainfall on the continent is very variable, being largest in the oceanic and Mediterranean borderlands. The vegetation pattern corresponds closely to the climatic zones. Mixed forests once covered the greater part of Europe, but have now, except for the more mountainous regions, given way in most parts to fields and pastures. Scandinavia and Russia furnish large amounts of timber and wood pulp. Wide grassland belts are interspersed, particularly in the Hungarian and Balkan plains. Characteristic of the Mediterranean are pines, cork oaks, olive, and citrus trees. Of the hardy crops, barley is grown in Scandinavia above the Arctic Circle; the wheat line is not too far from the barley. Famous wines are grown in W and S Europe. The continent's fauna has close affinities with that of Asia and North Africa, but larger carnivorous animals are now rare. More distinctive animal types of Europe include the European bison (now restricted to Russia), the chamois, ibex, and marmot of the Alps and Pyrenees, and the elk of N Europe. The waters of Europe, particularly the North Sea and the Atlantic, are among the world's richest fishing grounds. Mineral resources are extensive and varied, and though they have been worked for centuries, Europe still leads in the production of coal and lignite (principally England; N and central France, Belgium, the Ruhr and Saar region, Silesia, Donetz Basin, Urals) and iron (N France, W Germany, Luxembourg, Sweden, Donetz Basin, N Spain). On coal and iron, which often occur near each other, are based the large-scale heavy industries associated with the Ruhr, Saar, the Midlands, Silesia, etc., situated in the most densely populated areas. Europe furnishes the bulk of potash (from Alsace) and about ⅔ of all mercury (Almadén, Istria). There are also important lead, copper, zinc, tungsten, antimony, bauxite, graphite, and phosphate resources. Russia is particularly rich in manganese and chromium. Major oil resources are encountered only in the Ploesti region of Rumania and in the Baku, Grozny, and Maikop fields of the USSR. Mineral springs and resorts of world fame abound. With the help of its manifold resources Europe—led by England and Western Europe—was entirely transformed by the Industrial Revolution of the 19th cent. European productivity is today only equaled by the U.S., to whose natural resources the people of Europe brought their skills. Though language has ceased to be here a reliable indicator of ethnic origin, the people of Europe are customarily classified along linguistic lines, i.e., Celtic (Irish, Gaelic, Welsh, Breton), Germanic (English, German, Dutch, Flemish, Danish, Norwegian, Swedish, Icelandic and Faeroese, Frisian), Romanic (French, Walloon, Italian, Romansh, Ladin or Friul, Sardinian, Spanish, Catalan, Portuguese, Gallegan, Rumanian), Greek, Albanian, Baltic (Lithuanian, Lettish), Slavic (Great Russian, Little Russian or Ukrainian, Belorussian or White Russian, Polish, Serbo-Croatian, Slovenian, Czech, Slovak, Bulgarian, Macedonian, Sorbian or Wendish). Non-Indo-European languages are used by the Basques of N Spain and SW France, the Maltese, and those E European peoples talking Finno-Ugric (Finnish, Estonian, Lappish, Karelian, Magyar, etc.) and Turkic-Tataric languages. Asiatic groups are scattered in Russia, especially in the Caucasus (e.g., Armenian). There are also minorities of Jews and Gypsies. Remains of prehistoric man and even of anthropoids are plentiful. Beginnings of civilization in Europe can be traced to the dawn of history, though antedated by Egypt and Mesopotamia. Europe was from earliest times swept by waves of immigrants from North Africa and Asia. After the 16th cent. the process was reversed, when the continent sent explorers and settlers to the four corners of the world, where they introduced their technological, political, and religious concepts. Empires of European nations came to occupy most of the other continents. Though Europe, like anc. Greece, was never a political reality, and though nationalism has for many years acted to accentuate the differences among its peoples, Europe has long been culturally and economically a unit. The disaster and ruin which accompanied Europe's centuries of wars and which were particularly persuasive in the Second World War, served, after 1945, to bring about some beginnings toward a movement for unity.

Europos or **Europus**, Syria: see Dura.

Eurotas River or **Evrotas River** (yŏŏrō'tŭs, Gr. ĕvrô'tŭs), in S Peloponnesus, Greece, rises in the Taygetus, flows 50 mi. SSE, past Sparta, to Gulf of Laconia, 8 mi. NE of Gytheion. Non-navigable. Formerly called Iri (ē'rē).

Eurville (ûrvēl'), village (pop. 1,134), Haute-Marne dept., NE France, on Marne R. and Marne-Saône Canal, 6 mi. SE of Saint-Dizier; forges, casting mill.

Eurymedon, river, Asia Minor: see Kopru River.

Eurytania, Evrytania, or **Evritania** (ūrĭtā'nēŭ, Gr. ĕvrĭtūnē'ŭ), nome (□ 854; pop. 53,474), central Greece; ⊙ Karpenesion. Bordered N by Thessaly, E by Phthiotis, S and W by Aetolia and Acarnania, it is one of the most mountainous nomes of Greece, including the Tymphrestos and the Chelidon. Livestock economy (sheep and goats); cheese produce tion. The anc. Eurytanes were subject to Aetolia.

Eusebio Ayala (ĕŏŏsā'byō īä'lä), town (dist. pop. 10,959), La Cordillera dept., S central Paraguay, in Cordillera de los Altos, 45 mi. E of Asunción; agr. center (tobacco, cotton, oranges, livestock). Processing of oil of petitgrain. Founded 1770. Formerly Barrero Grande.

Euskirchen (ois'kĭr"khŭn), town (pop. 14,206), in former Prussian Rhine Prov., W Germany, after 1945 in North Rhine-Westphalia, on the Erft and 14 mi. WSW of Bonn; rail junction; iron foundries; textile (cloth, woolens) mfg. Has 13th–14th-cent. church, 14th-cent. town hall.

Eustis (ū'stĭs). **1** City (pop. 4,005), Lake co., central Fla., 27 mi. NW of Orlando, on L. Eustis; resort; shipping center for citrus fruit and truck; packing houses, citrus-fruit canneries, creamery. Inc. 1925. **2** Town (pop. 763), Franklin co., W central Maine, on Dead R., in recreational, lumbering area, and 40 mi. NW of Farmington. Mfg. (tools, wood products) at Stratton village. **3** Village (pop. 413), Frontier co., S Nebr., 36 mi. WNW of Holdrege and on branch of Platte R.; silica; poultry and dairy produce, livestock, grain.

Eustis, Fort, Va.: see Lee Hall.

Eustis, Lake (c.5 mi. long, 3 mi. wide), Lake co., central Fla.; Eustis city is on E shore. Part of connected lake system (lakes Griffin, Harris, Dora, Apopka) drained by Oklawaha R.

Eutaw (ū'tô), town (pop. 2,348), ⊙ Greene co., W Ala., near Black Warrior R., c.30 mi. SW of Tuscaloosa, in cotton, corn, and potato area; lumber milling, cotton ginning. Settled 1818.

Eutaw Springs, S.C.: see Eutawville.

Eutawville (ū'tôvĭl), town (pop. 478), Orangeburg co., SE central S.C., 30 mi. ESE of Orangeburg, on L. Marion; lumber. Santee-Cooper hydroelectric and navigation development is E. Near by was fought the Revolutionary battle of Eutaw Springs (Sept. 8, 1781).

Eutin (oi'tĭn), town (pop. 19,115), in Schleswig-Holstein, NW Germany, on an isthmus formed by 2 small lakes, 19 mi. N of Lübeck; mfg. of agr. machinery, office equipment, electrical goods, paper products, chemicals, textiles); woodworking, food processing. Has moated castle; 13th-cent. church; Vosshaus, residence (1784–1802) of poet Voss. Chartered 1256. Became (c.1300) residence of bishops (later prince-bishops) of Lübeck, whose territory did not include city of Lübeck. In 1803 it became ⊙ secularized prince-bishopric and passed to Oldenburg. Went to Schleswig-Holstein in 1937. Carl Maria von Weber b. here.

Eutingen (oi'tĭng-ŭn), village (pop. 5,510), N Baden, Germany, after 1945 in Württemberg-Baden, on N slope of Black Forest, on the Enz and 2 mi. NE of Pforzheim; wine.

Eutritzsch (oi'trĭch), industrial N suburb of Leipzig, Saxony, E central Germany.

Eutsuk Lake (ōōt'sŭk), (□ 96; 48 mi. long, 1–8 mi. wide), W central B.C., in Coast Mts., in Tweedsmuir Park, 150 mi. WSW of Prince George; alt. 2,817 ft. Contains John Buchan and Lady Susan isls. Connected with Whitesail L. (NW). Drains E into Nechako R. through Tetachuck L.

Euville (ûvēl'), village (pop. 599), Meuse dept., NE France, on the Meuse and Canal de l'Est, 2 mi. SE of Commercy; stone quarries.

Euxine Sea: see Black Sea.

Euxton (ĕk'stŭn), residential village and parish (pop. 1,473), central Lancashire, England, 2 mi. NW of Chorley.

Evan (ĕ'vŭn), village (pop. 141), Brown co., SW Minn., near Minnesota R., 19 mi. W of New Ulm; dairy products.

Evandale, village (pop. 574), NE central Tasmania, 10 mi. SSE of Launceston and on S.Esk R.; sheep, orchards; flax mill.

Evangeline (ĭvăn'jŭlēn), parish (□ 672; pop. 31,629), S central La.; ⊙ Ville Platte. Agr. area, with rice as chief crop; also cotton, corn, sugar cane, truck, fruit, sweet potatoes, hay. Cotton ginning, rice and lumber milling, fruit and vegetable canning; mfg. of clay and concrete products, carbon black. Oil and gas wells; timber; sand and gravel. Includes Chicot State Park. Formed 1908.

Evangelist Island, Cuba: see Pines, Isle of.

Evangelist Islands or **Four Evangelists**, Sp. *Islas las Evangelistas*, group of 4 rocky islets and other detached rocks off coast of S Chile, at Pacific entrance to Strait of Magellan; 52°24'S 75°4'W. Formerly sometimes called Apostles Isls.

Evans (ĕ'vĭnz, ĭ'vĭnz), county (□ 186; pop. 6,653), E central Ga.; ⊙ Claxton. Coastal plain agr. (cotton, corn, tobacco, peanuts, livestock) and timber area drained by Canoochee R. Formed 1914.

Evans (ĕ'vĭnz), town (pop. 862), Weld co., N Colo., on S.Platte R. just S of Greeley, in irrigated agr. region; alt. 4,647 ft.

Evans, Mount (10,460 ft.), W Alta., near B.C. border, in Rocky Mts., in Jasper Natl. Park, 30 mi. S of Jasper; 52°27'N 118°8'W. Just S is Hooker Icefield.

Evans, Mount, NW Viti Levu, Fiji, SW Pacific; alt. 3,921 ft.

Evans, Mount (ĕ'vĭnz), peak (14,260 ft.) in Front Range, N central Colo., 35 mi. WSW of Denver. At summit, reached by highway, is Inter-University High Altitude Laboratory.

Evansburg, Pa.: see Evans City.

Evansburgh, village (pop. estimate 350), central Alta., on Pembina R. and 65 mi. W of Edmonton; coal mining, mixed farming, lumbering.

Evans City or **Evansburg**, residential borough (pop. 1,637), Butler co., W Pa., 10 mi. SW of Butler. Settled 1796, laid out 1836, inc. 1882.

Evansdale, town (pop. 3,571), Black Hawk co., E central Iowa, 5 mi. SE of Waterloo. Inc. after 1940.

Evans Mills, village (pop. 518), Jefferson co., N N.Y., 10 mi. NE of Watertown; powdered milk.

Evanston. 1 Residential city (pop. 73,641), Cook co., NE Ill., suburb just N of Chicago, on L. Michigan; some mfg. (radio equipment, agr. machinery, steel and glass products, brick, pharmaceuticals, screens and sashes, paint, sporting goods, toys). Seat of Northwestern Univ., Seabury-Western Theological Seminary, Evanston Collegiate Inst., Natl. Col. of Education, Evanston Township Community Col., Garrett Biblical Inst. The home of Frances E. Willard, city is the hq. of Women's Christian Temperance Union. Settled 1826, inc. 1892 as city. **2** Town (pop. 3,863), ⊙ Uinta co., extreme SW Wyo., on Bear R. and 50 mi. E of Ogden, Utah; alt. c.6,750 ft. Trade center, railroad div. point in farm and dairy region; coal, railroad ties, beverages. State hosp. for insane here. Settled 1869, inc. 1888. Developed with arrival of railroad.

Evansville. 1 Village (pop. 821), Randolph co., SW Ill., on Kaskaskia R. (bridged) and 38 mi. SSE of East St. Louis, in agr. and bituminous-coal area; shoe mfg. **2** City (pop. 128,636), ⊙ Vanderburgh co., SW Ind., on the Ohio and c.145 mi. SSW of Indianapolis; commercial, railroad, and mfg. center in agr. and bituminous-coal region; port of entry. Furniture, automobile, refrigerator factories; flour mills, meat-packing plants; mfg. also of farm and excavating machinery, tools, stoves, glassware, cigars, drugs, beer, chemicals, textiles. Large shipyards were active during Second World War. Evansville Col., and a state hosp. for the insane are here. Settled 1817; inc. as town in 1819, as city in 1847. **3** Village (pop. 478), Douglas co., W Minn., 18 mi. NW of Alexandria in lake region; ships dairy products. **4** City (pop. 2,531), Rock co., S Wis., 20 mi. S of Madison, in agr. area (tobacco, livestock, poultry; dairy products); mfg. of auto trailers, pumps, water-system equipment, canned foods; printing; tobacco warehouses. Seat of Wyler School for boys and Hallelujah Campgrounds. Settled 1839; inc. as village in 1866, as city in 1896. Theodore Robinson b. here. **5** Town (pop. 393), Natrona co., central Wyo., on N.Platte R. and just E of Casper; alt. c.5,200 ft. Sodium sulphate refined here.

Evanton, agr. village, E Ross and Cromarty, Scotland, on Glass R. near its mouth on Cromarty Firth, and 6 mi. NE of Dingwall. Just W is the Black Rock of Novar, narrow chasm, 100 ft. high, of Glass R. Evanton is site of airfield.

Evart (ĕ'vûrt), city (pop. 1,578), Osceola co., central Mich., 26 mi. SSW of Cadillac and on Muskegon R., in agr. area (dairy products; livestock, potatoes, corn, hay); mfg. (tools, powdered milk). Indian mounds near by. Inc. as village 1872, as city 1938.

Evarts (ĕ'vûrts), mining town (pop. 1,937), Harlan co., SE Ky., on Clover Fork of Cumberland R. and 35 mi. NE of Middlesboro, near Pine Mtn. in the Cumberlands; bituminous coal. Settled c.1800; inc. 1915.

Évaux or **Évaux-les-Bains** (āvō'-lā'bē') village (pop. 1,244), Creuse dept., central France, 13 mi. SSW of Montluçon; health resort with hot springs.

Evd-, in Rus. names: see Yevd-.

Eveleth (ĕ'vŭlĕth), city (pop. 5,872), St. Louis co., NE Minn., in Mesabi iron range, in region of lakes and woods, just S of Virginia; shipping point for iron ore; dairy products, beverages. Iron mines near by, Superior Natl. Forest N. City has junior col. and annual winter carnival. Settled 1892, inc. 1893. Growth dates from beginning of mining operations (c.1900).

Evenes, Norway: see Bogen.

Evening Shade, town (pop. 360), a ⊙ Sharp co., N Ark., 20 mi. N of Batesville, in agr. area.

Evenki National Okrug (ĕvyĕn'kē), administrative division (□ 285,900; pop. 25,000) of central Krasnoyarsk Territory, Russian SFSR, in central Siberia; ⊙ Tura. Bounded N by Taimyr Natl. Okrug, E by Yakut Autonomous SSR and Irkutsk oblast; drained by Lower Tunguska and Stony Tunguska rivers. Pop. is Evenki (Tungus). Forest area; fur trade, reindeer raising; fishing. Formed 1930.

Evenlode River, Gloucester and Oxfordshire, England, rises near Moreton-in-Marsh, Gloucester, flows 35 mi. SE, past Charlbury, to the Thames (Isis) 4 mi. NW of Oxford.

Evenos River or **Evinos River** (both: ĕ'vĭnôs), Lat. *Euenus*, in W central Greece, rises in Vardousia massif, flows 57 mi. SW to Gulf of Patras 6 mi. SE of Missolonghi. Hydroelectric plant. Formerly called Phidaris, Fidaris, Fidharis.

Evensk (ĕvyĕnsk'), village, N Khabarovsk territory, Russian SFSR, on Shelekhov Gulf of Sea of Okhotsk, at mouth of small Bolshaya Garmanda R., 40 mi. WSW of Gizhiga and 8 mi. E of Nayakhan; 61°50'N 159°15'E. Fisheries. Pop. of the village and near-by area are Eveny (Lamuts). Called Bolshaya Garmanda until 1951.

Evenvik, Norway: see Eivindvik.

Even Yehuda (ĕ'vĕn yŭhōōdä'), settlement (pop. 800), W Israel, in Plain of Sharon, 4 mi. SSE of Natanya; citriculture; poultry, vegetables. Has children's settlement. Founded 1932.

Even Yits-haq Ochberg, Israel: see RAMAT YITSHAQ OCHBERG.

Evêque, L' (lāvĕk'), peak (12,203 ft.) in the Alps, S Switzerland, 12 mi. WSW of Zermatt.

Everard, Cape (ĕ'vürärd), SE Victoria, Australia, in Tasman Sea; 37°48'S 149°16'E; alt. 538 ft. Site of monument in honor of Capt. Cook's 1st sighting (1770) of Australian coast.

Everard, Mount (3,850 ft.), N South Australia, just E of Musgrave Ranges.

Everard, Mount, low hill, Essequibo co., NW Br. Guiana, on right bank of Barima R. and 35 mi. SE of Morawhanna; starting place for launches to gold mines on Barima R.

Everbeek (ā'vürbāk), village (pop. 2,108), Hainaut prov., SW central Belgium, 4 mi. NNW of Lessines; agr., lumbering. Formerly spelled Everbecq.

Evercreech, agr. village and parish (pop. 1,145), E Somerset, England, 4 mi. SSE of Shepton Mallet. Horse and cattle markets held here. Has 15th-cent. church.

Évère (āvâr'), Flemish *Evere* (ā'vürü), residential town (pop. 15,460), Brabant prov., central Belgium, NE suburb of Brussels, on S edge of Haren airport. Has anc. church, restored in 18th cent.

Everek, Turkey: see DEVELI.

Everest, city (pop. 363), Brown co., extreme NE Kansas, 18 mi. WNW of Atchison, in grain, poultry and livestock region; dairying.

Everest, Mount (ĕ'vürĭst), highest point (29,002 ft.) of earth's surface, in NE Nepal Himalayas, on undefined Tibet-Nepal border, at 27°59'N 86°56'E. First observed 1849 by trigonometrical survey of India and named (c.1855) for a former surveyor-general (1830–43), Sir George Everest; preliminary height computations (1852) showed it to be the highest peak and these were confirmed in 1865. Summit composed of metamorphosed Permocarboniferous limestone, flanks of Permian to Jurassic sediments. Up to 1950, there had been 2 reconnaissances (1921, 1935) and 5 unsuccessful climbing expeditions, by C. G. Bruce (1922), E. F. Norton (1924), Hugh Ruttledge (1933, 1936), and H. W. Tilman (1938), all English. Highest point (28,126 ft.) was reached in 1924 by E. F. Norton, although Mallory and Irvine of same expedition may have exceeded that height before they were lost. The 1933 and 1938 expeditions reached approximately the height set in 1924. Mt. Everest is usually ascended along NE ridge from Rongbuk (Tibet). First aerial photographic survey made 1933. Although official Survey of India height is 29,002 ft., a commonly used unofficial reading is 29,141 ft. Tibetan name Chomolungma is sometimes attributed to Mt. Everest.

Everett (ĕv'rĭt, ĕ'vürĭt). **1** Residential city (pop. 45,982), Middlesex co., E Mass., 3 mi. N of Boston; also mfg. (iron and steel products, coke, shoes, petroleum products, chemicals, electrical apparatus, furniture, paints, paper and wood products). Settled before 1650, set off from Malden 1870, inc. as city 1892. **2** Borough (pop. 2,297), Bedford co., S Pa., 7 mi. E of Bedford and on Raystown Branch of Juniata R.; limestone; tile, clothing, lumber, feed, chemicals; agr. Laid out 1795, inc. 1873. **3** Port city (pop. 33,849), ⊙ Snohomish co., NW Wash., 25 mi. N of Seattle and on Puget Sound, at mouth of Snohomish R. Ships lumber, fish, dairy and paper products; port of entry; trade center for agr. region. A state home for girls is here; Tulalip Indian Reservation is near by. Settled c.1890 near spot where Capt. Vancouver landed in 1792.

Everett, Mount (2,624 ft.), extreme SW Mass., in the Berkshires, near N.Y. and Conn. lines, 7 mi. SSW of Great Barrington. Observation tower on summit. Surrounding peak is Mt. Everett State Reservation (1,000 acres), crossed by Appalachian Trail; has hiking and ski trails.

Everetts (ĕ'vürĭts), town, (pop. 244), Martin co., NE N.C., 6 mi. W of Williamston.

Evergem (ā'vür-khĕm), town (pop. 10,463), East Flanders prov., NW Belgium, 4 mi. N of Ghent; chemical industry.

Everglades, town (pop. 625), ⊙ Collier co., S Fla., c.65 mi. SSE of Fort Myers, on Gulf coast opposite Ten Thousand Isls.; rail terminus; resort and fishing port; sea-food canning.

Everglades, S Fla., swampy, subtropical region (c.100 mi. long, 50–75 mi. wide) of saw grass savannas and water dotted by island-like clumps of trees ("hammocks"). Covers greater part of Fla. peninsula S of L. Okeechobee; bounded E by slightly higher coastal strip (site of West Palm Beach and Miami), W by Big Cypress Swamp, S by mangrove swamps along Florida Bay and Gulf of Mexico. Occupies limestone plain sloping from 15 ft. (N) to sea level (S), surface of which is partly covered by muck and peat deposits, several feet deep in places. Rainfall averages more than 60 in. annually. Reclamation projects of state and federal governments include dike along S shore of L. Okeechobee, to prevent its periodic overflows into the Everglades, and thousands of miles of canals and ditches, draining more than 4,000,000 acres of land in and adjacent to the Everglades. Truck, sugar cane, and cattle-raising region has been developed adjacent to the lake. Overdrainage, rendering the muck and peat inflammable in dry years, caused great fires in lower Everglades in March, 1939. Part of S Everglades, judged unfit for cultivation, is now included in **Everglades National Park** (□ 1,719; established 1947). Park is S of Tamiami Trail, in Dade and Monroe counties, and includes much of Florida Bay, with its many keys; contains saw grass and water prairies, mangrove forests, sandy beaches, and rich variety of fauna and flora, much of it unique to this region; bird life (including herons, egrets, ibises, pelicans, and spoonbills) is especially notable. Seminole Indian reservation is W of lower Everglades.

Evergnicourt (āvĕrnyēkōōr'), village (pop. 511), Aisne dept., N France, on the Aisne and 14 mi. N of Rheims; paper mill.

Evergreen. **1** City (pop. 3,454), ⊙ Conecuh co., S Ala., 75 mi. SW of Montgomery; trading and shipping point in agr. area (cotton, peanuts, strawberries); lumber, wood and sheet-metal products, trailers, shirts. Settled c.1820. **2** Village (pop. c.1,500), Jefferson co., N central Colo., in Front Range, 20 mi. WSW of Denver; alt. 7,037 ft.; resort center. **3** Town (pop. 382), Avoyelles parish, E central La., 32 mi. SE of Alexandria, in cotton-growing area. **4** Town (pop. 245), Columbus co., SE N.C., 16 mi. SSE of Lumberton.

Evergreen Park, residential village (pop. 10,531), Cook co., NE Ill., suburb just SW of Chicago; truck farms. Inc. 1893.

Everlange (āvürläzh', ā'vürläng"ü), village (pop. 302), W central Luxembourg, 8 mi. SW of Ettelbruck; mfg. of agr. machinery; agr. (potatoes, wheat, rye, oats, sugar beets, pulse).

Everly (ĕ'vürlē), town (pop. 547), Clay co., NW Iowa, near Ocheyedan R., 9 mi. W of Spencer; feed milling.

Everman, town (pop. 451), Tarrant co., N Texas, just S of Fort Worth.

Eversberg (ā'fürsbĕrk), town (pop. 2,408), in former Prussian prov. of Westphalia, W Germany, after 1945 in North Rhine-Westphalia, near Ruhr R., 3 mi. ENE of Meschede; forestry.

Eversham (ĕ'vürshŭm), village (pop. 538), Berbice co., NE Br. Guiana, in Atlantic coastland, 23 mi. ESE of New Amsterdam; rice, sugar.

Everson (ĕ'vürsŭn). **1** Borough (pop. 1,520), Fayette co., SW Pa., just SE of Scottdale; metal products. Laid out 1874. **2** Town (pop. 345), Whatcom co., NW Wash., 12 mi. NE of Bellingham and on Nooksack R., in agr. region.

Everton, village (pop. 153), N Victoria, Australia, 130 mi. NE of Melbourne, near Beechworth; molybdenite mine.

Everton (ĕ'vürtŭn). **1** Town (pop. 198), Boone co., N Ark., 12 mi. ESE of Harrison; glass-sand mining. **2** City (pop. 306), Dade co., SW Mo., in Ozark region, on branch of Sac R., 25 mi. WNW of Springfield.

Evesham (ēv'shŭm, ē'shŭm, ē'sŭm), municipal borough (1931 pop. 8,799; 1951 census 12,066), SE Worcester, England, on Avon R. and 13 mi. SE of Worcester; market center, with canneries, for a beautiful and productive fruit- and vegetable-growing area; also metalworking, leather, pharmaceutical, and chemical industries. Has remains of early-8th-cent. Benedictine abbey, 14th-15th-cent. Church of All Saints, and St. Laurence Church, completed 1259. In 1265 Prince Edward (Edward I) defeated the barons under Simon de Montfort here.

Evg-, in Rus. names: see YEVG-.

Évian-les-Bains (āvyā'-lā-bē'), town (pop. 2,999), Haute-Savoie dept., SE France, on S shore of L. Geneva, 9 mi. SSW of Lausanne; fashionable health and summer resort. Its mineral water is bottled and exported. Resorts of Neuvecelle and Maxilly-sur-Léman near by.

Evilard, Switzerland: see BIEL.

Evinayong (āvēnäyōn'), town (pop. 870), continental Sp. Guinea, 65 mi. ESE of Bata; 1°28'N 10°39'E. Coffee, yucca, hardwoods. Also spelled Ebinayon.

Evington (ĕ'vĭng–), residential town and parish (pop. 1,802), central Leicester, England, just ESE of Leicester; shoes, typewriters. Has 14th-cent. church.

Évin-Malmaison (āvē'-mälmĕzō'), town (pop. 3,280), Pas-de-Calais dept., N France, 5 mi. NNW of Douai; coal mines.

Evinos River, Greece: see EVENOS RIVER.

Évisa (āvēzä'), village (pop. 781), W Corsica, 23 mi. N of Ajaccio; alt. 2,760 ft. Resort amidst chestnut forests.

Evitts Creek, in S Pa. and NW Md., rises in S Bedford co., Pa., flows c.30 mi. SW, bet. Evitts Mtn. (E) and Wills Mtn. (W), to North Branch of the Potomac just below Cumberland, Md. Dammed into two small reservoirs in Pa., c.9 mi. NE of Cumberland.

Evitts Mountain, S Pa., NE–SW ridge (2,000–2,400 ft.) of the Appalachian system, runs c.23 mi. NE from Md. border in S Bedford co.; quartzite.

Evje (ĕv'yü), village (pop. 571; canton pop. 1,682), Aust-Agder co., S Norway, on Otra R., on railroad and 35 mi. N of Kristiansand; nickel mining, refining; feldspar quarries. Uranium deposits.

Evkandzhinski, Russian SFSR: see YEVKANDZHINSKI.

Evlakh, Azerbaijan SSR: see YEVLAKH.

Evolène (āvôlĕn') or **Evolena** (āvōlā'nä), village (pop. 1,280), Valais canton, S Switzerland, on Borgne R. and 10 mi. SSE of Sion; resort (alt. 4,520 ft.).

Evonimos, Greece, see PERISTERA.

Evonymos, Greece: see PERISTERA.

Évora (ĕ'vōōrü), district (□ 2,853; pop. 207,952), in Alto Alentejo prov., S central Portugal; ⊙ Évora. Bounded E by Spain, part of frontier being formed by Guadiana R. Lies in fertile Alentejo lowland, with wheat fields and cork-oak forests. Main towns: Évora, Estremoz, Vila Viçosa, Borba.

Évora, anc. *Ebora* and *Liberalitas Julia,* city (pop. 21,851), ⊙ Évora dist. and Alto Alentejo prov., S central Portugal, 70 mi. ESE of Lisbon; commercial center of fertile Alentejo lowland (wheat, olive oil, cork, livestock); mfg. (cotton textiles, cordage, flour products, chocolate, metal products). Of great prominence ever since Roman times, it has ruins of a temple (2d or 3d cent. A.D., called temple of Diana), one of the best-preserved Roman structures in the Iberian Peninsula. Évora preserves the savor of the Middle Ages better than any other Portuguese city, and is strongly reminiscent of old Moorish towns of Andalusia. Its cathedral (archiepiscopal see since 1540) dates from 12th cent. and is adjoined by a 14th-cent. cloister. The univ., run by the Jesuits for 2 centuries after 1551, is now a high school. Évora had a bishopric by A.D. 300 and was important under the Visigoths and a great trade center under the Moors (c.715–1166). Recaptured by Portuguese under Gerald the Fearless, it changed hands several times in the wars with the Moors. After 1385, it was for many years the favorite seat of the Portuguese court. It was ⊙ of former Alentejo prov.

Évora Monte (mōn'tĭ), village (pop. 401), Évora dist., S central Portugal, on railroad and 15 mi. NE of Évora; cork and lumber industry. Has ruined castle (c.1300).

Evpatoriya, Russian SFSR: see YEVPATORIYA.

Évran (āvrā'), village (pop. 326), Côtes-du-Nord dept., W France, on Rance R. at NW end of Ille-Rance Canal, and 5 mi. SSE of Dinan; wool spinning.

Evrange (ĕvräzh'), Ger. *Ewringen* (ĕ'vrĭng-ŭn), village (pop. 92), Moselle dept., NE France, customs station on Luxembourg border opposite Frisange, 10 mi. N of Thionville.

Évrecy (āvrüsē'), village (pop. 198), Calvados dept., NW France, 8 mi. SW of Caen. Captured (Aug., 1944) by British after heavy fighting on near-by Hill 112.

Évreux (āvrû'), town (pop. 16,645), ⊙ Eure dept., NW France, on the Iton and 55 mi. WNW of Paris; agr. trade center; cider distilling, mfg. of optical glass, ticking, small metal products. In Second World War town center was heavily damaged, including 12th-17th-cent. cathedral (which has fine carved altar screens). Church of St. Taurin contains a 13th-cent. shrine. Roman town of *Mediolanum* was located 4 mi. ESE (present site of Le Vieil-Évreux). Bishopric since 4th cent. Became (10th cent.) seat of a county which changed hands frequently throughout Middle Ages and was abolished in French Revolution. Évreux was burned in 1119 and 1365.

Evripos, Greece, see EURIPOS.

Evritania, Greece, see EURYTANIA.

Évron (āvrō'), town (pop. 2,458), Mayenne dept., W France, 18 mi. ENE of Laval; road center; woodworking, cider milling, horse raising. Has noted 11th-14th-cent. Romanesque and Gothic church founded 648.

Evron or **'Evron** (ĕvrōn'), agr. settlement (pop. 250), Upper Galilee, NW Israel, near Mediterranean, 13 mi. NNW of Haifa, just S of Nahariya. Modern village founded 1945 on site of biblical locality of same name.

Evros, nome, Greece: see HEVROS.

Evros River, Bulgaria, Greece, Turkey: see MARITSA RIVER.

Evrotas River, Greece: see EUROTAS RIVER.

Evrykhou Valley (ĕvrēkhōō'), Nicosia dist., NW Cyprus, c.25 mi. W of Nicosia. Principal pyrite-mining region of the isl., with important Mavrovouni and Skouriotissa mines. Ore is crushed and shipped from KARAVOSTASI or Xeros on Morphou Bay. There are also copper-reducing plants at near-by LEFKA.

Evrytania, Greece: see EURYTANIA.

Evs-, in Rus. names: see YEVS-.

Evvoia, Greece: see EUBOEA.

Ewa (ā'vä, ā'wä), town (pop. 3,429), S Oahu, **T.H.,** 12 mi. WNW of Honolulu; sugar industry.

Ewab Islands, Indonesia: see KAI ISLANDS.

Ewald, Argentina: see AVELLANEDA.

Ewansville (ū'ünzvĭl), resort village, Burlington co., W N.J., on Rancocas Creek and 3 mi. ESE of Mt. Holly.

Ewarton (yōō'ŭrtŭn), town (pop. 2,900), St. Catherine parish, central Jamaica, at S foot of Mt. Diablo, 17 mi. NW of Spanish Town; rail terminus in agr. region. Processes and exports citrus fruit

Ewauna, Lake (ēwô'nů), S Oregon, small lake at Klamath Falls, S of Upper Klamath L. (connected by Link R.); drained by Klamath R.

Ewayong River, Nigeria: see BANSARA.

Ewe, Loch (lŏkh yōō'), inlet (8 mi. long, 4 mi. wide) on W coast of Ross and Cromarty, Scotland, connected at its head by short Ewe R. with Loch MAREE. In the inlet is Isle of Ewe (pop. 37), 2 mi. long, 1 mi. wide.

Ewell (yōō'ůl, -ĭl), residential town in Epsom and Ewell municipal borough, N central Surrey, England, just NE of Epsom; electrical appliance mfg.

Ewell, Md.: see SMITH ISLAND.

Ewen (ū'ůn), village (1940 pop. 537), Ontonagon co., NW Upper Peninsula, Mich., 24 mi. S of Ontonagon, in dairy area; sawmilling.

Ewijk, Netherlands: see SLIJK-EWIJK.

Ewing (ū'ĭng). **1** Village (pop. 330), Franklin co., S Ill., 16 mi. S of Mount Vernon, in bituminous-coal-mining and agr. area. **2** Town (pop. 316), Lewis co., NE Mo., near Middle Fabius R., 17 mi. WNW of Quincy, Ill. **3** Village (pop. 705), Holt co., N Nebr., 20 mi. SE of O'Neill and on Elkhorn R.; dairying; livestock, grain.

Ewingsville, village (pop. 1,156), Allegheny co., W Pa.

Ewloe, Wales: see BUCKLEY.

Ewo (ĕwō'), village, central Middle Congo territory, Fr. Equatorial Africa, 70 mi. SW of Fort-Rousset; trading post. Sometimes spelled Euoo.

Ewringen, France: see EVRANGE.

Ewst River, Latvia: see AIVIEKSTE RIVER.

Ewyk, Netherlands: see SLIJK-EWIJK.

Exaerde, Belgium: see EKSAARDE.

Exaltación (ĕksältäsyōn'). **1** Town (pop. c.2,700), Beni dept., N Bolivia, on Mamoré R. and 40 mi. NNE of Santa Ana, in the llanos; cattle. **2** Village (pop. c.1000), Pando dept., N Bolivia, on Beni R. and 45 mi. SSW of Riberalta; opposite Concepción; rubber.

Exaltación de la Cruz, district, Argentina: see CAPILLA DEL SEÑOR.

Excel, town (pop. 216), Monroe co., SW Ala., 8 mi. S of Monroeville.

Excelsior, town (pop. 1,447), S central Orange Free State, U. of So. Afr., 50 mi. ENE of Bloemfontein; alt. c.5,300 ft.; agr. center (grain, potatoes, apples, dairying, sheep, horses).

Excelsior, village (pop. 1,763), Hennepin co., E Minn., on S shore of L. Minnetonka and 16 mi. E of Minneapolis; resort in diversified-farming area; corn, fruit. Amusement park here. Experimental fruit farm near by.

Excelsior Mountain, peak (12,440 ft.) of the Sierra Nevada, on Mono-Tuolumne co. line, E Calif., 8 mi. W of Mono L.

Excelsior Mountains, in W Nev. and E Calif., S of Walker L., Nev., in Mono Natl. Forest; an E spur of Sierra Nevada. Rises to 8,766 ft.

Excelsior Springs, city (pop. 5,888), on Ray-Clay co. line, W Mo., 25 mi. NE of Kansas City. Health resort, mineral springs; coal mines; corn, oats, wheat. Founded 1880, inc. 1903. Jesse James b. near by.

Exchequer Dam; Exchequer Reservoir, Calif.: see MERCED RIVER.

Excideuil (ĕksēdû'ē), village (pop. 1,383), Dordogne dept., SW France, 19 mi. NE of Périgueux; food processing (truffles, *pâté de foie gras*, jam). Electrometallurgical plant.

Excursion Inlet, village (1939 pop. 23), SE Alaska, 30 mi. N of Hoonah; 58°25'N 135°27'W; fishing; cannery.

Exeland (ĕks'lůnd), village (pop. 211), Sawyer co., N Wis., 34 mi. ESE of Spooner, in cutover forest area; farming.

Exell, Texas: see AMARILLO.

Exe River (ĕks), Somerset and Devon, England, rises on Exmoor, flows 55 mi. SE and S, past Tiverton and Exeter, to the Channel at Exmouth.

Exeter (ĕk'sůtůr), village (pop. 1,589), S Ont., 30 mi. NNW of London; food canning, dairying, lumbering.

Exeter, county borough (1931 pop. 66,029; 1951 census 75,479) and city, ⊙ Devon, England, in E central part of co., on Exe R. and 37 mi. NW of Plymouth; 50°43'N 3°31'W. Port, rail center, and largest market town in SW England; mfg. of metal products, leather goods, wood products, agr. machinery, textiles, paper, paint, asphalt, pharmaceuticals, shoes, food products. Site of Roman fort of *Isca Damnoniorum;* has ruins of Saxon walls, Norman castle, and 14th-cent. priory. The noted cathedral (12th–14th cent.), with splendid transeptal towers and roof vaulting, contains the *Exeter Book.* Other notable bldgs.: old guildhall, 14th-cent. bishops' palace, Albert Memorial Mus. Site of Univ. Col. of the Southwest. Strategically located, Exeter was besieged in numerous wars from 9th to 17th cent. In Second World War cathedral was severely damaged and Elizabethan Bamfylde House destroyed by bombing.

Exeter. 1 City (pop. 4,078), Tulare co., S central Calif., in Sierra Nevada foothills near floor of San Joaquin Valley, 45 mi. SE of Fresno; shipping center for citrus- and deciduous-fruit dist.; also olives, alfalfa, cotton, livestock. Sequoia Natl. Park is c.20 mi. NE. Inc. 1911. **2** Village (pop. 107), Scott co., W central Ill., 13 mi. W of Jacksonville, in agr. area. **3** Town (pop. 734), Penobscot co., S central Maine, 20 mi. W of Old Town, in agr. region. **4** Town (pop. 355), Barry co., SW Mo., in the Ozarks, 4 mi. W of Cassville. **5** Village (pop. 747), Fillmore co., SE Nebr., 11 mi. NE of Geneva; dairy and poultry produce, livestock, grain. **6** Town (pop. 5,664), ⊙ Rockingham co., SE N.H., 10 mi. SW of Portsmouth and on Exeter R. at falls (site of early mills) of the Squamscott. Seat of Phillips Exeter Acad. (opened 1783). Mfg. (textiles, shoes, machinery, metal products); fruit, poultry, dairy products. Founded 1638 by John Wheelwright; noted in the Revolution for its patriot activities. Seat of N.H. govt. most of time from 1774 to 1784. **7** Borough (pop. 5,130), Luzerne co., NE central Pa., 6 mi. NNE of Wilkes-Barre and on Susquehanna R.; anthracite. Settled 1790, inc. 1884. **8** Town (pop. 1,870), Washington co., SW central R.I., on Queen R. and 18 mi. SSW of Providence; poultry, dairy products. Set off from North Kingston and inc. 1743.

Exeter River, Rockingham co., SE N.H., rises E of Manchester, flows 30 mi. E and NE, past Exeter, to Great Bay near Rockingham. Known as Squamscott R. below falls at Exeter.

Exhall, town and parish (pop. 4,426), N central Warwick, England, 4 mi. N of Coventry; coal mining. Has 13th-cent. church.

Exideuil (ĕksēdû'ē), village (pop. 231), Charente dept., W France, on Vienne R. and 9 mi. S of Confolens; paper mill.

Exin, Poland: see KCYNIA.

Exincourt (ĕgzĕkōōr'), E suburb (pop. 2,303) of Montbéliard, Doubs dept., E France, on Rhone-Rhine Canal; cotton spinning.

Exira (ĕksī'rů), town (pop. 1,129), Audubon co., W central Iowa, on East Nishnabotna R. and 14 mi. NNE of Atlantic; mfg. (prefabricated farm bldgs., dairy products). Settled 1852, laid out 1857, inc. 1880.

Exline, town (pop. 342), Appanoose co., S Iowa, near Mo. line, 6 mi. S of Centerville, in bituminous-coal-mining area.

Exmes (ĕm), village (pop. 348), Orne dept., NW France, 9 mi. E of Argentan; horse raising.

Exminster, town and parish (pop. 2,807), E central Devon, England, near Exe R., 3 mi. SE of Exeter; agr. market. Has 15th-cent. church; mental hosp.

Exmoor (ĕks'mōōr), plateau (□ 30), W Somerset and NE Devon, England, formerly forest, now moorland covered with bracken and grass. Much wild life (red deer and wild ponies). General height of over 1,200 ft. is broken by deep glens; highest point is Dunkery Beacon (1,708 ft.). Much frequented by sportsmen and tourists. It is background for Blackmore's *Lorna Doone.* Many prehistoric earthworks here.

Exmore, village (pop. 1,362), Northampton co., E Va., 20 mi. NE of Cape Charles town; cans and ships seafood, fruit, vegetables.

Exmouth (ĕks'mouth), urban district (1931 pop. 14,591; 1951 census 17,232), SE Devon, England, on the Channel, at mouth of Exe R. and 9 mi. SSE of Exeter; fishing port and seaside resort, with mild climate; agr. market. Major port in Middle Ages. Sir Walter Raleigh b. at near-by Hayes Barton.

Exmouth Gulf (ĕks'mouth), inlet of Indian Ocean, NW Western Australia; formed by peninsula (W) terminating in Northwest Cape; 55 mi. N–S, 30 mi. E–W. Onslow is near NE entrance.

Expanse, Lake, or Lac Simard (läk sēmär') (□ 59), SW Que., 90 mi. NNE of North Bay; 13 mi. long, 10 mi. wide; drained W by Ottawa R.

Experiment, village (pop. 4,265), Spalding co., W central Ga., just NW of Griffin.

Exploits, Bay of, inlet (30 mi. long, 2–6 mi. wide) of Notre Dame Bay, E N.F.; receives Exploits R. estuary 5 mi. S of Botwood, near head of bay. At entrance of bay is Thwart Isl.

Exploits River, N.F., rises as Lloyds R. in SW part of isl., flows ENE through King George IV L., Lloyds L., and Red Indian L., past Grand Falls (hydroelectric power) and Bishop's Falls, to Bay of Exploits 5 mi. S of Botwood; 200 mi. long. Receives Victoria R. in Red Indian L.

Exploring Islands, Fiji: see LAU.

Export, borough (pop. 1,690), Westmoreland co., SW central Pa., 19 mi. E of Pittsburgh; coal. Inc. 1911.

Extension, village, SW B.C., on SE Vancouver Isl., 4 mi. S of Naniamo; coal mining.

Extremadura, Spain: see ESTREMADURA.

Exuma (ĕksōō'mů, ĕgzōō'mů), islands and district (□ 100; pop. 3,784), central Bahama Isls., bet. Andros Isl. (W) and Eleuthera, Cat, and Long isls. (E); its northernmost cay is 38 mi. ESE of Nassau. The group extends 140 mi. NW–SE, traversed by the Tropic of Cancer. GREAT EXUMA ISLAND and LITTLE EXUMA ISLAND are in S. A U.S. naval base (granted in 1940) is at George Town on Great Exuma Isl.

Exuma Sound, deep Atlantic channel (c.100 mi. long NW–SE, c.40 mi. wide) in central Bahama Isls., bordered by Eleuthera Isl. (NE), Cat Isl. (E), Great Exuma Isl. (SW).

Eyak (ē'ăk, ī'-), village (1939 pop. 365), S Alaska, 4 mi. E of Cordova, on small L. Eyak; resort and residential dist. for Cordova.

Eyam (ēm, ē'ům), town and parish (pop. 1,065), NW Derby, England, 11 mi. SW of Sheffield; lead and fluorspar mining; shoe mfg. Has 17th-cent. Eyam Hall.

Eya River, Russian SFSR: see YEYA RIVER.

Eyasi, Lake (āyä'sē), N Tanganyika, 95 mi. W of Arusha; 45 mi. long, 10 mi. wide. Has salt and soda deposits. Sometimes called L. Njarasa. Fossil of *Africanthropus njarasensis* was found here in 1935.

Eychel (āshĕl'), village (pop. 338), Ariège dept., S France, on Salat R. and 2 mi. SE of Saint-Girons; cigarette-paper factory.

Eydehamn (ā'üdůhäm"ůn), village (pop. 1,191) in Stokken canton (pop. 2,187), Aust-Agder co., S Norway, on Tromoy Sound (inlet of the Skagerrak), 4 mi. NE of Arendal; mfg. of aluminum, electrodes. Formerly spelled Eydehavn.

Eydtkau, Russian SFSR: see CHERNYSHEVSKOYE.

Eydtkuhnen, Russian SFSR: see CHERNYSHEVSKOYE.

Eye (ī, ā). **1** Town and parish (pop. 1,531) in the Soke of Peterborough, NE Northampton, England, 4 mi. NE of Peterborough; brickworks. **2** Municipal borough (1931 pop. 1,733; 1951 census 1,631), N Suffolk, England, 18 mi. N of Ipswich; agr. market. Has ruins of Norman castle and of Benedictine priory (its 13th-cent. church still used). Roman and Br. remains found here.

Eye and Dunsden, England: see SONNING EYE.

Eyemouth (ī'můth), burgh (1931 pop. 2,231; 1951 census 2,269), E Berwick, Scotland, on North Sea at mouth of Eye Water, 8 mi. NNW of Berwick-on-Tweed; resort and herring-fishing port.

Eye Peninsula, Scotland: see LEWIS WITH HARRIS.

Eye Water, river, Berwick, Scotland, rises 8 mi. WNW of Ayton, flows 20 mi. NE and SE, past Reston and Ayton, to North Sea at Eyemouth.

Eygelshoven, Eigelshoven, or **Eijgelshoven** (all: īkh'ůls-hōvůn), town (pop. 4,499), Limburg prov., SE Netherlands, 4 mi. E of Heerlen, near Ger. border; coal-mining center.

Eyguières (ĕgyâr'), village (pop. 1,558), Bouches-du-Rhône dept., SE France, 20 mi. E of Arles; olives, fruits.

Eygurande or **Eygurande d' Ussel** (ĕgüräd' düsĕl'), village (pop. 449), Corrèze dept., S central France, 10 mi. NE of Ussel; cattle. Rail junction of Eygurande-Merlines 1 mi. S.

Eyjafjallajokull, Iceland: see MYRDALSJOKULL.

Eyjafjardar or **Eyjafjardhar** (ā'äfyär"dhär), Icelandic *Eyjafjarðar,* county [Icelandic *sýsla*] (pop. 4,394), N Iceland; ⊙ Akureyri. Extends along W shore of Eyja Fjord and inland to central plateau. Generally mountainous, cut by narrow valleys. Drained by Eyjafjard R. Cattle and sheep raising, fishing. Chief towns are Akureyri, Siglufjordur, Olafsfjordur (cities in, but independent of, co.), and Dalvik. Holar is historic locality.

Eyjafjardara or **Eyafjardhara** (ā'äfyär"dhärou'), Icelandic *Eyafjarðará,* river, N Iceland, rises on central plateau, flows 40 mi. N, past Holar, to Eyja Fjord 3 mi. SSE of Akureyri.

Eyja Fjord (ā'ä, ā'ů), Icelandic *Eyjafjörður* (ā'-äfyůr"dhůr), inlet (40 mi. long, 2–8 mi. wide) of Greenland Sea, N Iceland; 65°55'N 18°20'W. Contains Hrisley isl.; Akureyri city is near head.

Eylam, Iran: see ILAM.

Eylau, Russian SFSR: see BAGRATIONOVSK.

Eymet (ĕmĕ'), village (pop. 1,380), Dordogne dept., SW France, on Dropt R. and 13 mi. SSW of Bergerac; prune market; food preserving (*pâté de foie gras* and truffles). Has state agr. school.

Eymoutiers (ĕmōōtyā'), town (pop. 2,113), Haute-Vienne dept., W central France, in Monts du Limousin, on Vienne R. and 24 mi. ESE of Limoges; mfg. of ice-boxes, tanning. Hydroelectric plant 1 mi. downstream.

Eyne, Belgium: see EINE.

Eynesbury, England: see SAINT NEOTS.

Eynort, Loch, Scotland: see SOUTH UIST.

Eynsford (āns'fůrd), town and parish (pop. 2,353), NW Kent, England, on Darent R. and 5 mi. S of Dartford; paper milling. Church dates from Norman times. There is 15th-cent. bridge and ruins of Norman castle. Roman remains have been found in the area.

Eynsham (ĕn'shům, ān'-), town and parish (pop. 1,963), S central Oxfordshire, England, on the Thames and 6 mi. NW of Oxford; agr. market. Has 14th-cent. church.

Eyota (īō'tů), village (pop. 495), Olmsted co., SE Minn., 12 mi. E of Rochester; dairy products.

Eyrarbakki (ā'rärbä"kē), town (pop. 535), Arne co., SW Iceland, 30 mi. SE of Reykjavik; fishing port.

Eyre (âr), village, SE Western Australia, 305 mi. ESE of Kalgoorlie and on Great Australian Bight; sheep.

Eyre, New Zealand: see OHOKA.

Eyre, Lake (âr), shallow salt lake, NE central South Australia, 250 mi. N of Port Pirie. Nearly divided into 2 lakes: N part (□ 2.970; 90 mi. long, 40 mi. wide) and S part (□ 460; 38 mi. long, 16 mi. wide); 39 ft. below sea level. Occasionally dry. In wet seasons receives Neales, Macumba, and Barcoo rivers.

Eyrecourt (âr′kôrt), Gaelic *Dún an Ochta*, town (pop. 309), SE Co. Galway, Ireland, 6 mi. W of Banagher; agr. market (sheep; potatoes, beets).
Eyre Peninsula (âr), S South Australia, bet. Great Australian Bight (W) and Spencer Gulf (E), S of Gawler Ranges; 200 mi. N–S; rises to 1,000 ft.; triangular, with broad 250-mi. N base. Middleback Range (NE) contains iron. Irregular coastline. Chief ports: Port Augusta, Port Lincoln. Many offshore isls. Agr. and dairy products, livestock. Sometimes called Eyre's Peninsula.
Eyrieux River, France: see ÉRIEUX RIVER.
Eysden, Belgium: see EISDEN.
Eysden, Netherlands: see EIJSDEN.
Eyshishkes, Lithuania: see EISISKES.
Eysines (āsēn′), town (pop. 2,553), Gironde dept., SW France, 5 mi. NW of Bordeaux; vineyards, truck gardens.
Eysturoy, Faeroe Isls.: see OSTERO.
Eythorne, town and parish (pop. 1,699), E Kent, England, 5 mi. NNW of Dover; coal mining.
Eythra (ī′trä), village (pop. 3,237), Saxony, E central Germany, near the White Elster, 9 mi. SW of Leipzig city center; mfg. (machinery, bakery equipment).
Eyup (ĕyüp′), Turkish *Eyüp*, NW section (pop. 28,934) of Istanbul, Turkey in Europe.
Eyvan-e-Key, Iran: see AIVAN-I-KAI.
Eyzies, Les, officially **Les Eyzies-de-Tayac** (lāzāzē′-dŭ-täyäk′), village (pop. 497), Dordogne dept., SW France, on the Vézère and 10 mi. WNW of Sarlat; kaolin quarries near by. In near-by Cro-Magnon cave, skulls of a race dating from Aurignacian period were found 1868. In 1901, the caves of Combarelles and Font-de-Gaume revealed paleolithic paintings and carvings. In Le Moustier cave (on right bank of the Vézère above Les Eyzies) discovery of human skeleton and chipped flints has given name to Mousterian period of paleolithic culture. Tools and carvings found in near-by La Madeleine rock-shelter have led to the classification of the Magdalenian period.
Ez [Arabic,=the], for Arabic names beginning thus: see under following part of the name.
Ez-, in Rus. names: see YEZ-.
Ezaki (äzä′kē) or **Esaki** (āsä′kē), town (pop. 4,676), Yamaguchi prefecture, SW Honshu, Japan, on Sea of Japan, 21 mi. NE of Hagi; rice, wheat; sawmilling, fishing. Called Tamasaki until 1943.
Ezan, Cape, Japan: see ESAN, CAPE.
Ezcaray (ĕthkärī′), town (pop. 1,529), Logroño prov., N Spain, 30 mi. WSW of Logroño; terminus of branch railroad from Haro. Mfg. of woolen textiles, rugs, furniture, berets; cheese processing, rubber pressing. Agr. trade. Has fine Gothic church. Copper mining near by.
Èze (ĕz), Ital. *Eza*, old village (pop. 67), Alpes-Maritimes dept., SE France, 5 mi. ENE of Nice, on isolated rock near the Grande Corniche, overlooking the Mediterranean.
Ezeiza (āsā′sä), town (pop. estimate 2,500) in Greater Buenos Aires, Argentina, 18 mi. SSW of Buenos Aires; large international airport.
Ezel, Estonia: see SAARE.
Ezel (ēzĕl′), town (1940 pop. 147), Morgan co., E Ky., 31 mi. ESE of Mt. Sterling city, in coal and agr. area.
Ezine (ĕzĭnĕ′), town (pop. 6,702), Canakkale prov., NW Turkey, on Kucuk Menderes R. and 25 mi. SSW of Canakkale; copper deposits; cereals.
Ezion-geber (ē′zēŏn-gē′bûr), biblical port, S Palestine, at head of Gulf of Aqaba of the Red Sea, on site of modern Tell el Kheleifeh (tĕl′ ĕl khĕlā′fŭ), near ports of Elath and Aqaba. Naval base built here by King Solomon. Scene (1938) of excavations; anc. copper refinery was among the finds. Sometimes spelled Etzion Geber or Eziongeber.
Ezo, Japan: see HOKKAIDO.
Ezo-Fuji, Japan: see SHIRIBESHI-YAMA.
Ezpeleta (ĕspālā′tä), residential town (pop. estimate 2,000) in Greater Buenos Aires, Argentina, adjoining Quilmes, 11 mi. SE of Buenos Aires; glassware, gunpowder; horticulture.
Ezraa, Syria: see IZRA'.
Ezy-sur-Eure (ĕzē′-sür-ûr′), village (pop. 1,779), Eure dept., NW France, on Eure R., 16 mi. SE of Évreux; comb-mfg. center. Also Ézy-sur-Eure

F

Faaberg, Norway: see FABERG.
Faaborg (fô′bôr), city (pop. 4,699) and port, Svendborg amt, Denmark, on S coast of Fyn isl. and 21 mi. S of Odense; dairying, meat canning, mfg. of agr. machinery, shipbuilding.
Faal, Yugoslavia: see FALA.
Fabara (fävä′rä), town (pop. 1,817), Saragossa prov., NE Spain, 11 mi. ESE of Caspe; olive-oil processing; ships dried fruit (especially figs).
Fabbrico (fäb′brēkō), town (pop. 2,182), Reggio nell'Emilia prov., Emilia-Romagna, N central Italy, 15 mi. NE of Reggio nell'Emilia; mfg. (wine, agr. machinery, Diesel motors, metal tanks).
Fabens (fā′bĭnz), village (pop. 3,089), El Paso co., extreme W Texas, port of entry near the Rio Grande, 27 mi. SE of El Paso; shipping, processing center in irrigated farm area; cotton gin and compresses, cottonseed products.
Faberg (fô′bărg), Nor. *Fåberg*, village (pop. 393; canton pop. 8,896), Opland co., SE Norway, at foot of the Gudbrandsdal, on Lagen R. near its mouth on L. Mjosa, on railroad and 5 mi. NW of Lillehammer; agr., livestock. Sometimes spelled Faaberg.
Fabero (fävā′rō), village (pop. 1,329), Leon prov., NW Spain, 16 mi. N of Ponferrada; cereals, fruit, wine, lumber. Anthracite mines.
Faber's Lagoon, on Caribbean coast of Northern Dist., Br. Honduras, 15 mi. SSE of Corozal; 4 mi. wide, 7 mi. long.
Fabiansebestyen (fä′bĭän-shĕ″bĕsh-tyän), Hung. *Fábiánsebestyén*, town (pop. 1,558), Csongrad co., S Hungary, 7 mi. ENE of Szentes; wheat, flax, sheep.
Fabius (fā′bēŭs), village (pop. 369), Onondaga co., central N.Y., 16 mi. SE of Syracuse, in dairying area.
Fabius River, NE Mo., is formed by 3 branches, North, Middle, and South Fabius rivers. Main river, formed by junction of the North and the South Fabius just below Quincy, Ill., is 1 mi. long. North Fabius R. rises near Moulton, Iowa, flows c.130 mi. SE. Middle Fabius R. rises in Scotland co., flows c.90 mi. SE to the North Fabius. South Fabius R. rises in Knox co., flows c.100 mi. SE, N, and E.
Fabre (fä′brŭ), village (pop. estimate 500), W Que., near L. Timiskaming, 22 mi. SE of Haileybury; copper mining.
Fabriano (fäbrēä′nô), town (pop. 10,536), Ancona prov., The Marches, central Italy, 21 mi. SW of Iesi; rail junction. Noted for its paper industry since 12th cent.; mfg. (cement, automobile chassis, furniture, woolen textiles, soap, lubricating oils). Bishopric. Has cathedral (rebuilt 1617) and town hall (1255; restored) with picture gall. containing works of Allegretto Nuzi and Gentile da Fabriano. Badly damaged in Second World War by air and artillery bombing (1944).
Fabrica (fä′brĕkä), town (1939 pop. 9,760) in Sagay municipality, Negros Occidental prov., N Negros isl., Philippines, 32 mi. NE of Bacolod; agr. center (rice, sugar cane). Sugar milling, sawmilling.
Fábrica, La, Chile: see LA FÁBRICA.
Fábricas de San Juan de Alcaraz (fä′vrēkäs dhā sän hwän′ dhā älkäräth′), village (pop. 1,090), Albacete prov., SE central Spain, 42 mi. W of Hellín; metalworking (brass tubes, wires, cases). Zinc and copper mining near by.
Fabrichny or **Fabrichnyy** (fŭbrēch′nē), town (1948 pop. over 2,000), SW Alma-Ata oblast, Kazakh SSR, 30 mi. WSW of Alma-Ata.
Fabrizia (fäbrē′tsyä), village (pop. 3,897), Catanzaro prov., Calabria, S Italy, 17 mi. SE of Vibo Valentia; dairy products.
Fabyan House, N.H.: see CARROLL, town.
Facaeni (fŭkŭän′), Rum. *Făcăeni*, village (pop. 5,370), Ialomita prov., SE Rumania, on Borcea arm of the Danube and 13 mi. NE of Fetesti; fisheries.
Facatativá (fäkätätēvä′), town (pop. 9,779), Cundinamarca dept., central Colombia, in Sabana de Bogotá of Cordillera Oriental, on railroad and highway, and 25 mi. NW of Bogotá; alt. 8,576 ft. Rail junction; trading and flour-milling center in agr. region (wheat, corn, potatoes, fruit, livestock). Coal mines in vicinity. Founded 1543, it has old colonial bldgs. Carved stones with hieroglyphic inscriptions by the Chibchas are near by.
Fâches-Thumesnil (fäsh-tümänēl′), S suburban commune (pop. 7,875) of Lille, Nord dept., N France; flax spinning, meat processing, candy and biscuit mfg.
Fachi (fä′shē), village, E central Niger territory, Fr. West Africa, oasis in the Sahara, on desert road and 95 mi. WSW of Bilma; dates; salt.
Fachingen, Germany: see BIRLENBACH.
Fachow, China: see FAHSIEN.
Facit (fā′sĭt), town in Whitworth urban district, SE Lancashire, England, 4 mi. N of Rochdale; cotton milling.
Facsad, Rumania: see FAGET.
Factory Island, islet of the Los ISLANDS, Fr. Guinea, Fr. West Africa, off Atlantic coast, 3 mi. W of Conakry.
Factoryville, borough (pop. 1,005), Wyoming co., NE Pa., 12 mi. NNE of Scranton. Settled 1798.
Facundo Zuviría (fäkōōn′dō sōōvērē′ä), **Doctor Facundo Zuviría**, or **Zuviría**, town (pop. estimate 500), central Salta prov., Argentina, in Lerma Valley, on railroad and 20 mi. SSW of Salta, in tobacco and livestock area. Tobacco processing.
Fad, Loch (lŏkh), lake (2½ mi. long), S central part of Bute isl., Buteshire, Scotland, just S of Rothesay.
Fada (fä′dä, fädä′), village, N Chad territory, Fr. Equatorial Africa, on Ennedi Plateau, SE Sahara, 170 mi. ESE of Largeau; military outpost on caravan road to Libya.
Fada (fä′dä) or **Fada-N'Gourma** (fä″däng gōōr′mä), town (pop. c.4,100), SE Upper Volta, Fr. West Africa, 125 mi. E of Ouagadougou, linked by road. Exports shea nuts, kapok, peanuts, beeswax. Produces also millet, corn, beans, peas, potatoes, manioc; livestock. Meteorological station; R.C. and Protestant missions; airfield.
Fadama, Fr. Equatorial Africa: see BAKOUMA.
Fada-N'Gourma, Fr. West Africa: see FADA.
Fadd (fŏd), town (pop. 4,861), Tolna co., S central Hungary, on an arm of the Danube and 9 mi. NE of Szekszard; tobacco market; garden produce.
Faddei Island or **Faddey Island** (fŭdyā′) [Rus.,= Thaddeus], one of Anjou group of NEW SIBERIAN ISLANDS, off Yakut Autonomous SSR, Russian SFSR, bet. Kotelny and Novaya Sibir isls.; c.40 mi. in diameter. Discovered 1805 by Rus. explorer Sannikov.
Fades, France: see QUEUILLE.
Fadhili (fä′dhĭlē), oil field in Hasa, Saudi Arabia, 70 mi. NW of Dhahran; 26°57′N 49°15′E. Discovered 1949.
Fadhli (fädhlē′), sultanate and tribal area (pop. 25,000) of Western Aden Protectorate; ⊙ Shuqra. Extends 100 mi. along Gulf of Aden, just NE of Aden Colony, bet. Imad and Maqatin; pop. is pastoral (camel breeding; E) and agr. (ABYAN oasis). One of the original Nine Cantons, Fadhli 1st concluded a protectorate treaty in 1888. By a revised treaty (1944), closer relations were established and a British political officer was stationed in Abyan.
Fadiffolu Atoll (fŭdĭf′fōlōō), N central group (pop. 4,583) of Maldive Isls., in Indian Ocean, bet. 5°14′N and 5°34′N.
Faeno (fĕ′nŭ), Dan. *Fænø*, island (□ 1.5; pop. 77) in the Little Belt, Denmark, just SW of Middelfart; fertile, rolling terrain; wooded in N.
Faenza (fäĕn′zä), anc. *Faventia*, city (pop. 23,823), Ravenna prov., Emilia-Romagna, N central Italy, on Lamone R. and 18 mi. SW of Ravenna, on the Aemilian Way. Mfg. (automobile chassis, agr. machinery, furniture, textiles, soap, macaroni, pharmaceuticals). Noted for its anc. majolica (faïence) industry; has institute and international mus. (severely damaged) of ceramics. Bishopric. Possesses 15th-cent. cathedral, seminary, several palaces, library (badly damaged), art gall. Under the Manfredi in medieval times; passed to the papacy in 1501. It was heavily bombed (1944) in Second World War; some 4,000 bldgs. damaged or destroyed.
Faeroe Islands or **Faroe Islands** (both: fâ′rō), Dan. *Færøerne* (fârŭ′ûrnŭ), Faeroese *Fóroyar*, group of 21 volcanic islands (□ 540; pop. 29,178), of which 17 are populated, in N Atlantic Ocean, bet. Iceland and the Shetlands, and belonging to Denmark; 62°N 7°W; ⊙ THORSHAVN, on Stromo isl. High, rugged, and sparsely vegetated, they are subject to frequent storms and high winds, but their harbors —because of the warm North Atlantic Drift—are ice-free. Fishing, whaling, fowling, sheep raising are carried on. STROMO and OSTERO are largest isls. Colonized by Norsemen c.800, the isls. were Christianized in the 11th cent. and were ruled by Norway until 1380, when they were transferred to Denmark. Development of nationalism in 20th cent. led to recognition of the Faeroese language (an old Germanic speech akin to Icelandic) in 1912; and in 1948 the isls. were granted autonomy. The pop. nearly doubled in 20th cent.
Faesulae, Italy: see FIESOLE.
Faevik, Norway: see FEVIK.
Fafan River (fäfän′) or **Tug Fafan** (tŏŏg′ fäfän′), Harar prov., SE Ethiopia, rises in mts. at edge of Great Rift Valley, 20 mi. NE of Harar, flows intermittently SSE through the Ogaden, past Gabredarre and Gorrahei, and disappears in a marshy depression 35 mi. NE of Callafo (on the Webi Shebeli); c.350 mi. long. Receives Jerer R. at a point 20 mi. S of Sassabaneh.
Fafe (fä′fĭ), town (pop. 4,068), Braga dist., N Portugal, 14 mi. SE of Braga; branch railway terminus; textile center; lumbering, pottery mfg.
Fagagna (fägä′nyä), village (pop. 2,565), Udine prov., Friuli–Venezia Giulia, NE Italy, 8 mi. NW of Udine; tobacco warehouses.
Fagaras (fŭgŭräsh′), Rum. *Făgăraş*, Hung. *Fogaras* (fô′gŏrŏsh), town (1948 pop. 9,296), Sibiu prov., central Rumania, in Transylvania, on Olt R., on railroad and 115 mi. NW of Bucharest; trading center noted for its explosives mfg.; also produces furniture, bricks, tiles, rugs, salami. Greek-Catholic archbishopric, although the archbishop has resided since 1738 at BLAJ. Has 14th-cent. fortress now converted into barracks, 17th-cent. Greek-Catholic cathedral with beautiful frescoes. Founded c.12th cent. and considered the cradle of Walachian princes.

Fagaras Mountains, Rum. *Făgăraş,* highest range of the Transylvanian Alps, S central Rumania, partly in Transylvania, partly in Muntenia; extend for 35 mi. E–W between Turnu-Rosu Pass and upper Dambovita R.; rise to 8,361 ft. in Negoi and 8,344 ft. in Moldaveanu peaks.

Fagatogo (fäng'ätông'ō), village (pop. 1,157), E Tutuila, American Samoa.

Fagelfors (fō"gŭlfôrs', –fôsh'), Swedish *Fågelfors,* village (pop. 776), Kalmar co., SE Sweden, near Em R., 25 mi. W of Oskarshamn; woodworking.

Fagernes (fä'gŭrnās), village (pop. 887) in Nord-Aurdal canton (pop. 5,455), Opland co., S Norway, on Stranda Fjord (expansion of Begna R.), 40 mi. W of Lillehammer; rail terminus; center of Valdres region, with slate quarries. Has folk mus.

Fagersta (fä'gŭrstä"), city (1950 pop. 13,079), Vastmanland co., central Sweden, in Bergslag region, on Kolback R. 35 mi. NW of Vasteras; rail junction; steel-milling center, specializing in mfg. of high-speed tool steel; foundries, machinery and cement plants, woodworks. Inc. 1944 as city. Iron mines near by.

Fagervik (fä"gŭrvēk'), village (pop. 598), Vasternorrland co., NE Sweden, on Klinger Fjord (klĭng'-ŭr), Swedish *Klingerfjärden,* 10-mi.-long inlet of Gulf of Bothnia, 9 mi. NNE of Sundsvall; pulp mills, sulphite works.

Faget (fŭ'jĕt), Rum. *Făget,* Hung. *Facsád* (fŏ'chät), village (pop. 2,858), Timisoara prov., W Rumania, on Bega R., on railroad and 18 mi. NE of Lugoj; noted cattle market; flour milling; mfg. of liqueurs, brandy.

Fagnano, Lake (fänyä'nō), or **Lake Cami** (kä'mē) (□ 229; alt. 300 ft.), in S part of main isl. of Tierra del Fuego, mostly in Argentina, with small W part in Chile; extends 60 mi. W–E, 5 mi. wide. Mts. rise on its S shore.

Fagnano Castello (fänyä'nô kästĕl'lô), village (pop. 3,537), Cosenza prov., Calabria, S Italy, 22 mi. NNW of Cosenza; wine, olive oil, wood products.

Fagnano Olona (ôlô'nä), village (pop. 3,539), Varese prov., Lombardy, N Italy, near Olona R., 4 mi. NNE of Busto Arsizio; cotton and paper mills, mfg. of starch, floorwax, cement.

Fahaihil, Kuwait: see MENA AL AHMADI.

Fahlun, Sweden: see FALUN.

Fahraj, Fahrej, or **Fehraj** (all: färäj'), village, Eighth Prov., in Kerman, SE Iran, on highway to Zahidan, at S edge of the Dasht-i-Lut, and 33 mi. ESE of Bam. Sometimes called Iranshahr, it is commonly confused with another Fahraj or IRANSHAHR, 160 mi. SE, in Iranian Baluchistan.

Fahsien (Cantonese fä'yün'), Mandarin *Hua-hsien* (hwä'shyĕn'). **1** Town (pop. 8,820), ⊙ Fahsien co. (pop. 405,924), SW Kwangtung prov., China, on Foshan R. and 30 mi. NE of Chankiang; orange-peel production. Manganese deposits near by. Until 1912 called Fachow. **2** Town (pop. 93,399), ⊙ Fahsien co. (pop. 207,333), central Kwangtung prov., China, 25 mi. N of Canton, near Hankow-Canton RR; coal-mining center.

Faial Island (fīäl'), formerly **Fayal,** westernmost (□ 66; 1950 pop. 24,082) of the central Azores, in the Atlantic, separated from Pico Isl. (4 mi. E) by Faial Channel; HORTA (38°32'N 28°37'W), its chief city and port, is on SE shore. Isl. is 12 mi. long, up to 8 mi. wide. A perfectly shaped volcano (Pico Gordo, alt. 3,350 ft.), in central portion, is flanked by lesser cones. Faial is noted for its luxuriant flora (especially hortensias). Cereals, fruit, and wine are grown; cattle raising, dairying; whaling. Isl. was presented by Alfonso V to Isabella of Burgundy in 1466 and received numerous Flemish settlers. It suffered from repeated earthquakes, notably in 1760, 1862, and 1926. Administratively, it forms part of Horta dist.

Faid, Egypt: see FAYID.

Faidia or **Faydia** (fīdē'ä), village, W Cyrenaica, Libya, 10 mi. SSE of Cyrene, on the plateau Gebel el Akhdar; figs, nuts.

Faïd Pass (fäēd'), central Tunisia, 50 mi. E of Kasserine, near village of Sidi-bou-Zid. Scene of German break-through in Tunisian campaign (Feb., 1943) of Second World War. Recaptured by Americans April, 1943.

Faifo or **Faifoo** (fī'fō'), town, ⊙ Quangnam prov. (□ 4,800; 1943 pop. 1,001,600), central Vietnam, in Annam, South China Sea port, on railroad and 15 mi. SE of Tourane; trading center for agr. region (cinnamon, rice, corn, sugar cane, tea). In 17th cent. it was a leading center of trade with China.

Faiki (fīkī'), town (pop. 3,760), Zaria prov., Northern Provinces, N central Nigeria, 45 mi. NE of Zaria, on railroad; cotton, peanuts, ginger. Sometimes spelled Faki or Paki.

Failaka Island or **Faylakah Island** (fī'lăkŭ, fī'lĭchŭ) (□ 15; pop. 1,500), in Persian Gulf, belonging to Kuwait, 17 mi. E of Kuwait town; 8 mi. long, 2 mi. wide. Fishing, pearling; agr. (grain, melons, vegetables). Pop. is concentrated in village of Az Zor or Az Zaur, on NW point. Sometimes spelled Feilaka.

Failsworth (fālz'wûrth), urban district (1931 pop. 15,726; 1951 census 18,033), SE Lancashire, England, on Rochdale Canal and 5 mi. NE of Manchester; cotton spinning and weaving, coal mining, leather tanning, mfg. of aniline dyes and plastics.

Fains-les-Sources (fē-lā-sōōrs'), NW suburb (pop. 1,270) of Bar-le-Duc, Meuse dept., NE France, on Marne-Rhine Canal; glassworks.

Fairbank. 1 Town (pop. 653), on Buchanan-Fayette co. line, E Iowa, on Little Wapsipinicon R. and 7 mi. WSW of Oelwein; feed, wood products. Amish-Mennonite settlement. **2** Village, Talbot co., Md.: see TILGHMAN ISLAND. **3** Village (pop. 1,574, with adjacent Filbert), Fayette co., SW Pa., 7 mi. NW of Uniontown.

Fairbanks, town (pop. 5,771), E central Alaska, on Chena Slough, small tributary of Tanana R., and 250 mi. NNE of Anchorage; 64°50'N 147°45'W; commercial and supply center for interior of Alaska; port of entry. N terminus of Alaska RR and Alaska Highway; Steese and Elliott Highways radiate from here. Center of hydraulic gold-mining region; ore smelting, sawmilling, fur trading; agr. market. At COLLEGE, 3 mi. NW of town, is Univ. of Alaska, with agr. col., govt. agr. experiment station, and school of mines. Ladd Field air base and commercial airport is 5 mi. E of town; has regular air service to U.S. and all parts of Alaska. Eielson Air Force Base, 25 mi. SE of Fairbanks, was established after Second World War. Founded 1902, when gold was discovered in region, town was visited by heavy earthquake, 1912. Formerly W terminus of Yukon R. steamers from Whitehorse, Fairbanks expanded considerably after construction of Alaska RR (1923) and subsequent mechanization of mining operations. Canol Pipeline (closed at present), built during Second World War, runs to Whitehorse and Skagway.

Fair Bluff, town (pop. 1,056), Columbus co., SE N.C., on Lumber R. and 21 mi. S of Lumberton, near S.C. line, in agr. and lumber area.

Fairborn, city (pop. 7,847), Greene co., SW central Ohio, 10 mi. ENE of Dayton, in agr. area; cement, lumber; stone quarries. U.S. Wright-Patterson Air Force Base is near by. Formed by consolidation (1950) of former villages of Fairfield and Osborn.

Fairburn. 1 City (pop. 1,889), Fulton co., NW central Ga., 18 mi. SW of Atlanta, in agr. (cotton, corn, truck) area; lumber milling. Inc. as town 1854, as city 1925. **2** Town (pop. 80), Custer co., SW S.Dak., 20 mi. ESE of Custer and on French Creek.

Fairbury. 1 City (pop. 2,433), Livingston co., E central Ill., 30 mi. NE of Bloomington, in agr. and bituminous-coal-mining area; corn, wheat, soybeans, livestock, poultry; dairy products; mfg. of clothing, beverages. Gravel pits. Inc. 1895. **2** City (pop. 6,395), ⊙ Jefferson co., SE Nebr., 50 mi. SSW of Lincoln and on Little Blue R., near Kansas line; trade center for agr. area. Concrete and clay products, metal castings, windmills, flour; meat, poultry, and dairy products, livestock, grain. Municipal power plant and jr. col. here. Founded 1869.

Fairchance, borough (pop. 2,091), Fayette co., SW Pa., 6 mi. SSW of Uniontown; explosives.

Fairchild. 1 Locality, Spokane co., Wash.: see SPOKANE, city. **2** Village (pop. 592), Eau Claire co., W central Wis., 31 mi. SE of Eau Claire, in hilly stock-raising region.

Fairchild, Mount, Colo.: see MUMMY RANGE.

Fairdale, village (pop. 131), Walsh co., NE N.Dak., 39 mi. W of Grafton.

Fairfax, county (□ 415; pop. 98,557), N Va.; ⊙ Fairfax. Bounded SW and S by the Bull Run and Occoquan Creek, E and SE by the Potomac (Md. line); Arlington co. (E) separates it from Washington, D.C., whose suburbs (notably Falls Church) extend into Fairfax co. Chiefly residential; dairying, poultry raising, agr. (truck, corn, grains, fruit, hay). Includes MOUNT VERNON and other historic estates. Civil War engagements (notably battles of BULL RUN) were fought in W. Formed 1742.

Fairfax. 1 Village (pop. 2,717), Chambers co., E Ala., on Chattahoochee R. and 25 mi. NNW of Columbus, Ga.; cotton fabrics. **2** Residential town (pop. 4,078), Marin co., W Calif., adjacent to San Anselmo and 3 mi. W of San Rafael. Inc. 1931. **3** Town (pop. 335), Linn co., E Iowa, 8 mi. SW of Cedar Rapids; sausage. **4** Village (pop. 1,143), Renville co., S Minn., 19 mi. E of Redwood Falls in grain and livestock area; dairy products, beverages. **5** City (pop. 806), Atchison co., NW Mo., on Tarkio R. and 7 mi. S of Tarkio; corn, wheat, poultry, dairy products. **6** Town (pop. 2,017), Osage co., N Okla., near Arkansas R., 22 mi. WSW of Pawhuska, in oil area, also producing grain and livestock. Oil refineries; cotton ginning; mfg. of feed, metal cans, meat products. Founded c.1905, inc. 1909. **7** Town (pop. 1,567), Allendale co., SW S.C., 5 mi. SE of Allendale, in truck and livestock area; furniture, lumber. Settled 1876, inc. 1898. **8** Town (pop. 301), Gregory co., S S.Dak., 23 mi. ESE of Burke. **9** Rural town (pop. 1,129), Franklin co., NW Vt., 10 mi. SSE of St. Albans and on Lamoille R.; lumber, dairy products. Granted 1763, settled 1783. **10** Residential town (pop. 1,946), ⊙ Fairfax co., N Va., 15 mi. W of Washington, D.C., in agr. area. In co. courthouse (1800) are wills of George and Martha Washington. Inc. 1892.

Fairfield, municipality (pop. 15,987), E New South Wales, Australia, 15 mi. W of Sydney, in metropolitan area; mfg. (tile, terra cotta), wool scouring.

Fairfield, Derby, England: see BUXTON.

Fairfield. 1 County (□ 633; pop. 504,342), SW Conn., on Long Isl. Sound and N.Y. line, bounded E by Housatonic R.; ⊙ Bridgeport and Danbury. Many residential and resort communities lie within N.Y. City commuting radius; mfg. centers include Bridgeport (state's leading industrial city), Danbury, Fairfield, Stamford, and Stratford, producing chiefly electrical equipment, firearms, hats, tools, machinery, hardware, sewing machines, typewriters, clothing, textiles, chemicals, metal products, rubber, asbestos, paper, wood and glass products. Agr. (fruit, truck, dairy products); resorts on shore and L. Candlewood. Drained by Housatonic, Norwalk, Aspetuck, and Poquonock rivers. Constituted 1666. **2** County (□ 505; pop. 52,130), central Ohio; ⊙ LANCASTER. Drained by Hocking R. and small Rush and Little Walnut creeks; includes part of Buckeye L. (recreation). Agr. (livestock; dairy products; grain, fruit); mfg. at Lancaster and Bremen; oil wells, sand and gravel pits; timber. Formed 1800. **3** County (□ 699; pop. 21,780), N central S.C.; ⊙ Winnsboro. Bounded by Broad R. (W), Wateree Pond (E); includes part of Sumter Natl. Forest. Mainly agr. area (cotton, corn, beef); granite; timber. Textile milling. Formed 1785.

Fairfield. 1 City (pop. 13,177), SW industrial suburb of Birmingham, Jefferson co., N central Ala., in coal, iron, and limestone area; metalworking (nails and wire, sheet steel, tin plate), mfg. of coal-tar products, roofing and paving materials, industrial gases. Founded c.1910 (planned as steel-mfg. town), inc. 1919. **2** City (pop. 3,118), ⊙ Solano co., W central Calif., 15 mi. NE of Vallejo and adjoining Suisun City; trade and processing center for agr. area (fruit, sheep; dairy products). Travis (formerly Fairfield-Suisun) Air Forc Base is near by. Founded 1859; inc. as town i 1903, as city in 1938. **3** Industrial town (po 30,489), Fairfield co., SW Conn., on Long Is Sound, just SW of Bridgeport; aluminum, chem icals, explosives, machinery, furnaces, hardware, automobile accessories, metal and wire products, firearms; shore resort. Seat of Fairfield Univ. Includes Southport village, at mouth of small Mill R. (yachting). Scene of Indian battle (1637); burned by British (1779). Many Colonial houses, 18th-cent. town hall (restored 1937). Settled 1639. **4** Village (pop. 502), ⊙ Camas co., S Idaho, 25 mi. SW of Hailey in livestock and grain area; alt. 5,600 ft. Gold and silver mines near by. Boise Natl. Forest is N. **5** City (pop. 5,576), ⊙ Wayne co., SE Ill., 30 mi. E of Mount Vernon, in agr. area (livestock, grain, poultry, redtop seed; dairy products); mfg. (clothing, auto parts, paper boxes); oil wells. Settled c.1819, inc. 1840. **6** City (pop. 7,299), ⊙ Jefferson co., SE Iowa, 23 mi. E of Ottumwa; residential, trade, and mfg. center; produces washing machines, farm equipment, castings, chair cushions, gloves, feed, dairy products. Bituminous-coal mines near by. First annual Iowa State Fair held here in 1854. Has Parsons College (Presbyterian; coeducational; 1875) and Old Settlers' Park (with log cabin built in 1836). Inc. 1847. **7** Town (pop. 202), Nelson co., central Ky., 9 mi. NNE of Bardstown. **8** Mfg. town (pop. 5,811), including Fairfield village (pop. 3,776), Somerset co., S Maine, on the Kennebec just above Waterville. Pulp and woolen mills here and in village of Shawmut. Tuberculosis sanatorium, Good Will Homes and school here. Settled 1774, inc. 1788. **9** Town (pop. 693), Teton co., N central Mont., 35 mi. WNW of Great Falls and on branch of Sun R., just SE of Greenfield L. (reservoir of Sun R. irrigation system); trading point in grain and livestock region. **10** City (pop. 503), Clay co., S Nebr., 20 mi. SE of Hastings; livestock, grain. **11** Former village, Greene co., Ohio: see FAIRBORN. **12** Borough (pop. 451), Adams co., S Pa., 8 mi. SW of Gettysburg. **13** Town (pop. 1,742), ⊙ Freestone co., E central Texas, 32 mi. SE of Corsicana; highway junction in cattle, timber area; woodworking. Inc. 1933. **14** Town (pop. 1,428), Franklin co., NW Vt., 7 mi. E of St. Albans; maple sugar, dairy products, lumber, poultry. Chester A. Arthur b. here. Granted 1763, settled 1787. **15** Town (pop. 369), Spokane co., E Wash., 20 mi. SE of Spokane; wheat, peas, alfalfa.

Fairfield-Suisun Air Force Base, Calif.: see FAIRFIELD.

Fairford, town and parish (pop. 1,365), SE Gloucester, England, on Coln R. and 10 mi. N of Swindon; leather industry. Has 15th-cent. church. John Keble b. here. In parish, on the Thames and 4 mi. E of Fairford, is agr. market town of Lechlade (lĕch'lād), with 15th-cent. church.

Fairforest, village (1940 pop. 587), Spartanburg co., NW S.C., 4 mi. W of Spartanburg; foundry products.

Fairgrove, village (pop. 570), Tuscola co., E Mich., 21 mi. ENE of Saginaw, in agr. area.

Fair Harbor, N.Y.: see FIRE ISLAND.

Fair Haven. 1 Resort village (pop. c.1,500), St. Clair co., E Mich., 31 mi. NE of Detroit, on Anchor Bay; boat works. **2** Borough (pop. 3,560), Monmouth co., E N.J., on Navesink R. and 2 mi. NE of Red Bank. Inc. 1912. **3** Resort village (pop. 628), Cayuga co., W central N.Y., on Little Sodus Bay of L. Ontario, 14 mi. SW of Oswego. Near by is Fair Haven Beach State Park. **4** Town (pop. 2,286), including Fair Haven village (pop. 2,058), Rutland co., W Vt., 15 mi. W of Rutland and on Castleton R.; slate quarries (1st in Vt.; opened 1839); textiles; dairy products. Winter sports. Settled c.1780.

Fairhaven, town (pop. 12,764), Bristol co., SE Mass., at mouth of Acushnet R., on Buzzards Bay just E of New Bedford; resort; mfg. (tacks, small hardware, loom cranks); boatbuilding, shellfishery; dairying. Formerly whaling and shipbuilding center. Settled 1670, set off from New Bedford 1812.

Fair Head, Northern Ireland: see BENMORE.

Fair Hill, hamlet, Cecil co., NE Md., near Pa. line, 17 mi. E of Wilmington, Del. Annual Foxcatcher Natl. Cup Steeplechase is held here.

Fairhope. 1 Town (pop. 3,354), Baldwin co., SW Ala., on E shore of Mobile Bay, 13 mi. SE of Mobile; summer and winter resort (boating, fishing, hunting); lumber, dairy products, pecans. Founded 1894–95 by followers of Henry George, inc. 1908. Retained single tax until 1937. **2** Village (pop. 3,219, with adjacent Arnold City), Fayette co., SW Pa.

Fair Island (□ 1; pop. 282), E N.F., in Bonavista Bay, 40 mi. W of Gander; 48°58′N 53°45′W. Fishing.

Fair Isle, rocky island (pop. 108), most southerly of the Shetlands, Scotland, halfway bet. the Orkneys and main group of Shetland isls., 24 mi. SW of Sumburgh Head (on Mainland isl.) and 27 mi. ENE of North Ronaldsay isl.; 59°32′N 1°37′W; 3 mi. long, 2 mi. wide; rises to 712 ft. Isl. is navigational landmark, scene of many shipwrecks. Fair Isle is noted for knitted hosiery of many-colored design. Fishing, fish curing, and fish-oil production are chief industries; there are also sheep raising, oat growing, peat digging. Some copper ore is found. Isl. is noted bird-migration station.

Fairland, town (pop. 699), Ottawa co., extreme NE Okla., 8 mi. S of Miami, in agr. area (livestock, hay, grain). L. of the Cherokees (recreation) is just E.

Fair Lawn, borough (pop. 23,885), Bergen co., NE N.J., near Passaic R. just NE of Paterson; mfg. (dyes, airplanes, concrete products); nurseries. Includes planned community of Radburn (răd′-bûrn). Inc. 1924.

Fairlawn, village (pop. 1,621, with near-by Mallow), Alleghany co., W Va., near Covington. There is also a hamlet called Fairlawn in Montgomery co.

Fairlee. 1 (fâr′lē) Village, Kent co., E Md., 24 mi. E of Baltimore. Near by is St. Paul's Church (established 1672); present edifice dates from early 18th cent. **2** (fârlē′) Town (pop. 571), Orange co., E Vt., on the Connecticut and 25 mi. SE of Barre; dairying; near-by lakes Fairlee and Morey have resorts. Samuel Morey said to have built steamboat here, 1793.

Fairlee, Lake (fârlē′), E Vt., near Connecticut R., 24 mi. SE of Barre; c.2 mi. long; children's camp center.

Fairlie, township (pop. 957), ⊙ Mackenzie co. (□ 2,739; pop. 3,161), E central S.Isl., New Zealand, 100 mi. WSW of Christchurch; rail terminus in mtn. area; linen mill.

Fairlie (fâr′lē), town in Largs parish, N Ayrshire, Scotland, on Firth of Clyde, 3 mi. S of Largs; resort, with yacht-building yards. Site of ruins of Fairlie Castle (1521).

Fairmont. 1 Village (pop. 3,291, with adjacent South Lockport), Will co., NE Ill., just NNE of Joliet. **2** City (pop. 8,193), ⊙ Martin co., S Minn., on Middle Chain of Lakes, c.40 mi. SW of Mankato, near Iowa line. Resort; shipping point for grain, livestock, poultry area; food processing (dairy products, canned vegetables, flour, beverages, cattle feed); railroad maintenance equipment. Courthouse has pioneer relics. Platted 1857, inc. as village 1878, as city 1902. **3** City (pop. 729), Fillmore co., SE Nebr., 7 mi. N of Geneva; dairy and poultry produce, grain. **4** Town (pop. 2,319), Robeson co., S N.C., 10 mi. SSW of Lumberton; sawmilling. **5** Town (pop. 134), Garfield co., N Okla., 10 mi. ESE of Enid, in agr. area. **6** Textile village, Spartanburg co., NW S.C., on Tyger R. and 8 mi. WSW of Spartanburg. **7** City (pop. 29,346), ⊙ Marion co., N W.Va., on the Monongahela, at confluence of the West Fork and Tygart R., and 22 mi. NE of Clarksburg. Mining, industrial, and commercial center in rich bituminous-coal field; rail junction; mfg. of glass, sheet aluminum, mining machinery, fiberboard, chemicals, coke, coal by-products, clay products, tobacco products. Seat of Fairmont State Col. (a state teachers col.), state hosp. Scenic Valley Falls in gorge of Tygart R. are near. Founded 1843 as union of earlier communities.

Fairmont City, industrial village (pop. 2,284), St. Clair co., SW Ill., NE suburb of East St. Louis, within St. Louis metropolitan area; chemical, fertilizer, and zinc plants. Founded 1910, inc. 1914.

Fairmount. 1 City (pop. 573), Gordon co., NW Ga., 28 mi. ENE of Rome; slate mining, textile mfg. **2** Village (pop. 618), Vermilion co., E Ill., 12 mi. WSW of Danville, in agr. and bituminous-coal area. **3** Town (pop. 2,646), Grant co., E central Ind., 10 mi. S of Marion, in agr. area; mfg. (canned goods, flour, lumber); gas and oil wells. Natl. and state conferences of the Methodist Church are held here. **4** Village (pop. c.300), Somerset co., SE Md., on the Eastern Shore, near Big Annemessex R., 23 mi. SSW of Salisbury; fishing, truck farming. **5** Village (1940 pop. 1,127), Onondaga co., central N.Y., just W of Syracuse. **6** Village (pop. 660), Richland co., SE N.Dak., 14 mi. S of Wahpeton.

Fairmount Heights, town (pop. 2,097), Prince Georges co., central Md., E of Washington. Inc. 1927.

Fair Oak, agr. village and parish (pop. 1,167), S central Hampshire, England, 6 mi. NE of Southampton.

Fair Oaks. 1 Village (1940 pop. 1,812), Sacramento co., central Calif., on American R. and 12 mi. ENE of Sacramento; oranges, olives. **2** Village (pop. 2,788, with adjacent Grover City), San Luis Obispo co., SW Calif., 10 mi. S of San Luis Obispo. **3** Village (pop. 3,131), Cobb co., NW central Ga., just SE of Marietta. Also called Machinery City. **4** Locality, Henrico co., E central Va., near the Chickahominy, c.6 mi. E of Richmond; here was fought (May 31–June 1, 1862) an indecisive battle, sometimes called battle of Seven Pines, bet. McClellan and J. E. Johnston. Military cemetery.

Fair Plain, village (pop. 4,134), Berrien co., SW Mich., just S of Benton Harbor.

Fairplay, town (pop. 476), ⊙ Park co., central Colo., on South Platte R., in Rocky Mts., and 15 mi. E of Leadville; alt. 9,964 ft. Gold mines; livestock. Mt. Lincoln is 10 mi. NW.

Fair Play, city (pop. 383), Polk co., SW central Mo., in the Ozarks, 9 mi. W of Bolivar; grain products; dairy and poultry market.

Fairport. 1 Village (pop. c.200), Muscatine co., SE Iowa, on Mississippi R. and 7 mi. E of Muscatine. U.S. fish hatchery here. **2** Village (pop. 5,267), Monroe co., W N.Y., on the Barge Canal and 10 mi. SE of Rochester; mfg. (tin cans, chemicals, fruit pectin, canned foods, machinery, lenses); nurseries; agr. (apples, peaches, potatoes). Inc. 1867. **3** Village, Ohio: see FAIRPORT HARBOR.

Fairport Harbor or **Fairport,** village (pop. 4,519), Lake co., NE Ohio, on L. Erie at mouth of Grand R., 29 mi. NE of Cleveland; transships coal, iron ore. Resort; commercial fishing, truck gardening. Laid out 1810.

Fairton, village (pop. c.500), Cumberland co., SW N.J., on Cohansey Creek and 4 mi. S of Bridgeton; canned vegetables, hosiery.

Fairview, village (pop. 467), W Alta., 45 mi. WSW of Peace River; lumbering, mixed farming.

Fairview. 1 Village (pop. 398), Franklin co., SE Idaho, near Utah line, 5 mi. S of Preston. **2** Village (pop. 568), Fulton co., W central Ill., 8 mi. NW of Canton, in agr. and bituminous-coal-mining area; ships grain. **3** Village (pop. 1,524), St. Clair co., SW Ill., near East St. Louis. **4** City (pop. 336), Brown co., NE Kansas, 35 mi. WNW of Atchison; trading point in corn, dairy, livestock, and poultry region. **5** Village, Christian and Todd counties, SW Ky., 10 mi. E of Hopkinsville. Birthplace of Jefferson Davis, commemorated by Jefferson Davis State Monument in memorial park here. **6** Town (pop. 259), Newton co., SW Mo., in the Ozarks, 16 mi. E of Neosho. **7** Town (pop. 942), Richland co., NE Mont., on N.Dak. line and 10 mi. NNE of Sidney, near junction of Yellowstone R. with Missouri R.; lignite mines. **8** Borough (pop. 8,661), Bergen co., NE N.J., near Hudson R., 6 mi. NNE of Jersey City; mfg. (fireworks, food products, embroidery, clothing, lace); bleaching and dyeing works. Settled 1860, inc. 1894. There are also 2 small communities called Fairview in Burlington co. (near Medford and Riverside), and 1 each in Monmouth co. (near RIVER PLAZA) and Gloucester co. (near Sewell). **9** Village (pop. 1,721), Dutchess co., SE N.Y., just NE of Poughkeepsie. **10** City (pop. 9,311), Cuyahoga co., N Ohio, a W suburb of Cleveland. **11** Village (pop. 192), on Guernsey-Belmont co. line, E Ohio, 19 mi. E of Cambridge, in agr. and coal-mining area. **12** City (pop. 2,411), ⊙ Major co., NW Okla., 35 mi. WSW of Enid, in grain, livestock, and dairy area; dairy products, flour, feed. Settled 1893; inc. as town 1901, as city 1909. **13** Town (pop. 438), Multnomah co., NW Oregon, 7 mi. E of Portland; orchards. **14** Borough (pop. 259), Butler co., W Pa., 17 mi. NE of Butler. **15** Residential borough (pop. 697), Erie co., NW Pa., 10 mi. WSW of Erie, near L. Erie; baskets, tools. **16** Village, Northumberland co., E central Pa. **17** Town (pop. 155), Lincoln co., SE S.Dak., 8 mi. SSE of Canton and on Big Sioux R. **18** City (pop. 974), Sanpete co., central Utah, on San Pitch R. and 45 mi. SSE of Provo, in irrigated Sanpete Valley; alt. 6,023 ft. Settled 1859 by Mormons, inc. 1872. Dairying and agr. in vicinity. Wasatch Range near by. **19** Village (pop. 3,309), Yakima co., S Wash. There is also a Fairview in Snohomish co. **20** Town (pop. 775), Marion co., N W.Va., 10 mi. NW of Fairmont, in bituminous-coal area. **21** Village (pop. c.400), Lincoln co., W Wyo., on branch of Salt R., near Idaho line, and 3 mi. SW of Afton, in Star Valley; alt. c.6,000 ft. Dairy products, grain, livestock.

Fairview Park, town (pop. 902), Vermillion co., W Ind., near Wabash R., 17 mi. N of Terre Haute, in agr. and bituminous-coal area.

Fairview Shores, village (pop. 1,566), Orange co., central Fla.

Fairville, SW suburb (pop. estimate c.2,500) of St. John, SW N.B., on W bank of mouth of St. John R.

Fairwater, village (pop. 311), Fond du Lac co., E central Wis., on Grand R. and 20 mi. W of Fond du Lac, in farm area; cannery.

Fairway, city (pop. 1,816), Johnson co., E Kansas, a suburb of Kansas City. Inc. after 1950.

Fairway Rock, bare islet (1 mi. long), NW Alaska, in Bering Strait, near USSR line, 12 mi. SSE of Little Diomede Isl., 20 mi. W of Cape Prince of Wales; 65°37′N 168°44′W.

Fairweather, Cape, SE Alaska, on Gulf of Alaska, 85 mi. SE of Yakutat; 58°50′N 137°57′W.

Fairweather, Mount (15,300 ft.), on border bet. SE Alaska and B.C., in Fairweather Range of St. Elias Mts., 17 mi. NE of Cape Fairweather, 90 mi. SE of Yakutat, at SW end of Glacier Bay Natl. Monument; 58°54′N 137°32′W.

Fairweather Range, SE Alaska, S mountain group of St. Elias Mts., paralleling Gulf of Alaska for c.35 mi. from 59°N 137°30′W to 58°35′N 137°W; highest peak, Mt. Fairweather (15,300 ft.).

Fairy Stone State Park, S Va., recreational area (c.5,000 acres), 14 mi. WNW of Martinsville, on slope of Fairy Stone Mtn.; camping, bathing, boating, fishing. Here are found cross-shaped twinned crystals ("fairy stones").

Fais (fīs), coral island (pop. 250), Yap dist., W Caroline Isls., W Pacific, 60 mi. SE of Ulithi; 9°45′N 140°31′E; 1.5 mi. long, c.1 mi. wide; rises to 30 ft.; coconut palms.

Faisans, Île de, France and Spain: see BIDASSOA RIVER.

Faisi, Solomon Isls.: see SHORTLAND ISLANDS.

Faison (fā′sŭn), town (pop. 768), Duplin co., E central N.C., 20 mi. SSW of Goldsboro; cucumber market; ships local produce; pickle factory.

Faith. 1 Town (pop. 490), Rowan co., central N.C., 5 mi. S of Salisbury. **2** City (pop. 599), Meade co., W central S.Dak., 85 mi. NE of Sturgis; livestock-shipping point and trade center; animal fodder.

Faitsilong Archipelago (fā′sēlō), group of numerous isls. and islets of N Vietnam, in Gulf of Tonkin, off Quangyen prov., separated from mainland by Along and Faitsilong bays; main isls. are Catba Isl. and Île de la Table.

Faitsilong Bay, N Vietnam, arm of Gulf of Tonkin, bet. mainland and Faitsilong Archipelago, just E of Along Bay; c.20 mi. long, c.10 mi. wide. Strewn with numerous islets.

Faiyum, Fayum, Fayyum (all: fīyōōm′), or **Al-Fayyum** (ĕl–), province (□ 686; pop. 671,885), Upper Egypt, SW of Cairo; ⊙ Faiyum. A lowland, surrounded by desert and separated from the Nile (E) by a narrow strip of desert, it contains the lake BIRKET KARUN and owes its great fertility to the BAHR YUSUF. Cotton ginning, woolen and linen cloth mfg., dyeing; fishing; agr. (cereals, sugar cane, fruit, cotton). Main urban centers, besides Faiyum, are Ibshawai, Itsa, and Sinnuris. Served by railway from El Wasta, Beni Suef prov. In antiquity the Faiyum was the garden of Egypt. The region is rich in archaeological remains, the most important being the ruins of anc. Crocodilopolis, later Arsinoë, and the pyramid at Illahun.

Faiyum, Fayum, Fayyum, or **Al-Fayyum,** also **Medinet el Faiyum** or **Madinat al-Fayyum** (both: mĕdē′nĕt) [Arabic,=Faiyum city], city (pop. 72,465; with suburbs, 74,314), ⊙ Faiyum prov., Upper Egypt, 55 mi. SW of Cairo; 29°18′N 30°50′E. Important trading and rail center; cotton ginning, wool spinning and weaving, cotton-cloth dyeing, tanning, cigarette mfg. Site of the ruins of Crocodilopolis, later Arsinoë, the anc. capital of the Faiyum. Sometimes called Medina.

Faizabad or **Fayzabad** (fī′zŭbăd″, fī′zăbăd″), town (pop. 25,000), ⊙ Afghan Badakhshan, NE Afghanistan, on Kokcha R. and 195 mi. NNE of Kabul; oasis center (wheat, rice, beans, oilseed, cotton); rice and flour milling. Linked by auto highways with Mazar-i-Sharif (Afghan Turkestan) and Zebak. Pop. is chiefly Tadzhik. Coal and iron deposits near by. In ruins by 1830s, it was rebuilt in latter half of 19th cent.

Faizabad (fīzăbăd′), Chinese *Kiashi* or *Chia-shih* (jyä′shû′), town and oasis (pop. 148,989), W Sinkiang prov., China, 35 mi. E of Kashgar, and on highway S of the Tien Shan; wheat, rice, ramie, cotton; coal mines. Sometimes Paitzepa.

Faizabad, India: see FYZABAD.

Faizabad or **Feyzabad** (both: făz″ăbăd′), town, Ninth Prov., in Khurasan, NE Iran, 30 mi. SW of Turbat-i-Haidari.

Faizabad or **Fayzabad** (fīzŭbät′), village (1939 pop. over 500), NE Stalinabad oblast, Tadzhik SSR, 28 mi. E of Stalinabad; cotton, wheat; sericulture. Formerly Daragizy. Site of 1943 earthquake.

Faizpur (fīz′pōōr), town (pop. 11,663), East Khandesh dist., NE Bombay, India, near S foothills of Satpura Range, 22 mi. NE of Jalgaon; market center for cotton and timber (forests N); cotton ginning, handicraft cloth weaving, cloth and thread dyeing, oilseed pressing.

Fajami (făjă'mē), Fr. *Fadghami* or *Fadrhami*, town, Jezire prov., NE Syria, on Khabur R. and 40 mi. S of El Haseke.

Fajara (fäjä'rä), village (pop. 40), Gambia colony, in Kombo St. Mary dist., on the Atlantic, 8 mi. W of Bathurst (linked by road); resort.

Fajardo (fähär'dō), town (pop. 15,336), NE Puerto Rico, near the coast, on railroad and 32 mi. ESE of San Juan; trading and milling center for large sugar-growing region; port of entry; mfg. of cigars, soft drinks, furniture. Limekiln near by. Playa de Fajardo, its port, just E, is a fishing area and also ships sugar.

Fakahina, Tuamotu Isls.: see FANGAHINA.

Fakaofo (fäkou'fō), SE atoll (700 acres; pop. 570), TOKELAU, S Pacific, c.270 mi. N of Western Samoa; c.55 islets, some of which are privately owned; thick coconut groves. Site of chief village of group. Formerly Bowditch Isl.

Fakarava (fäkärä'vä), atoll (pop. 210), 2d largest but commercially most important of TUAMOTU ISLANDS, Fr. Oceania, S Pacific; 16°18'S 145°36'W. Its lagoon is 32 mi. long, 10 mi. wide; pearl-fishing center. Seat of Rotoava, former ⊙ Tuamotu Isls. Formerly Wittgenstein Isl.

Fakenham (fāk'nŭm), town and parish (pop. 2,843), N Norfolk, England, on Wensum R. and 23 mi. NW of Norwich; agr. market. Has 14th-15th-cent. church.

Fakfak or **Fak Fak** (fäk"fäk'), town (dist. pop. 4,849), Netherlands New Guinea, on Bombarai peninsula, 190 mi. SW of Manokwari; port on Ceram Sea, protected by Pandjang Isl. (10 mi. long, 1 mi. wide); trading center. Chief exports: copra, resin.

Faki, Nigeria: see FAIKI.

Fakiya River (fä'kēä), SE Bulgaria, rises near Turkish border 22 mi. E of Yelkhovo, flows 52 mi. NE, past Fakiya (pop. 1,828), to Mandra L.

Fakse (fäk'sŭ), town (pop. 1,924), Praesto amt, SE Zealand, Denmark, 33 mi. SSW of Copenhagen; limestone cutting, machinery mfg.

Fakse Bay, SE Zealand, Denmark, on Baltic Sea; average depth c.50 ft.; Praesto Fjord mouth (W).

Fakse Ladeplads (–lä'dhŭplăs), town (pop. 1,612) and port, Praesto amt, SE Zealand, Denmark, on Fakse Bay and 8 mi. NNE of Praesto; fisheries.

Faku or **Fa-k'u** (fä'kōō'), town, ⊙ Faku co. (pop. 279,130), E central Liaosi prov., Manchuria, 50 mi. N of Mukden; trades in cattle, horses, dairy products, soybean oil, wool, hides and skins. Formerly called Fakumen [=Faku gate], it was a major trade center at the Willow Palisade (Inner Mongolian line) until by-passed by railroad after 1900.

Fakumen, Manchuria: see FAKU.

Fal, river: see FAL RIVER.

Fala (fä'lä), Ger. *Faal* (fäl), village, NE Slovenia, Yugoslavia, on Drava R., on railroad and 10 mi. W of Maribor; powerful hydroelectric plant. Until 1918, in Styria.

Falaba (fälä'bä), town (pop. 1,329), Northern Prov., N Sierra Leone, near Fr. Guinea border, 25 mi. NE of Kabala, on road; peanuts, rice, hides, skins.

Falaise (fälĕz'), town (pop. 3,954), Calvados dept., NW France, 21 mi. SSE of Caen, bet. 2 rocky escarpments; hosiery mfg. Trade in horses and cattle. Almost leveled during Normandy campaign (1944) of Second World War, in which it was a key point (N lip of Falaise-Argentan pocket). Heavily damaged were its medieval castle (birthplace of William the Conqueror) of first dukes of Normandy, 11th-16th-cent. church of St. Gervais, and 13th-16th-cent. church of the Trinity.

Falakata (fäläkä'tŭ), village, Jalpaiguri dist., N West Bengal, India, 30 mi. E of Jalpaiguri; trades in rice, tea, mustard, tobacco. Tea garden just NE.

Falakron, Greece: see PHALAKRON.

Falam (fŭläm'), village, ⊙ N.Chin Hills dist., Upper Burma, on Manipur R. and 45 mi. WSW of Kalewa, near India border.

Falces (fäl'thĕs), town (pop. 3,287), Navarre prov., N Spain, on Arga R. and 11 mi. SSW of Tafalla; mfg. of brandy, plaster; sawmilling; trades in sugar beets, wine, fruit, cereals.

Falciu (fŭlch), Rum. *Fălciu*, town (1948 pop. 5,124), Barlad prov., E Rumania, on Prut R., on railroad and 25 mi. SSE of Husi; trading center (grain, wine, lumber, vegetables); brick mfg.

Falco, town (1940 pop. 80), Covington co., S Ala., 20 mi. SW of Andalusia, near Fla. line.

Falcon (făl'kŭn), town (pop. 245), Cumberland co., S central N.C., 15 mi. NE of Fayetteville.

Falcón (fälkōn'), state (□ 9,575; 1941 pop. 232,644; 1950 census 258,197), NW Venezuela, on the Caribbean, bordering on Gulf of Venezuela; ⊙ Coro. PARAGUANÁ PENINSULA is in N. Consists of N outliers of Andean spurs and coastal lowlands. Has hot, dry climate; some rains, especially E (Nov.–Feb.). Rich in petroleum; W oil fields, tributary to great Maracaibo oil region, are linked by pipe line with Altagracia (Zulia state); other oil deposits on Paraguaná Peninsula and at Pueblo Cumarebo. Coal mines near Coro and Pueblo Cumarebo; saltworks at Mitare. Fishing along coast, especially on Paraguaná Peninsula. Forests (E) yield divi-divi. Goats produced on large scale in arid region. In interior, notably around Churuguara, coffee, cacao, sugar cane, corn, and yuca are grown and cattle is raised. Capatárida (NW) is known for tobacco. State exports coffee, corn, goatskins, tobacco, petroleum, salted fish, fiber bags, and cheese, mostly to Dutch West Indies. Coro is its main commercial and distributing center. La Vela, Puerto Cumarebo, and Tucacas are leading ports.

Falcon, Cape (fälkō'), headland of Oran dept., NW Algeria, on the Mediterranean, forming W end of Oran Bay, 10 mi. NW of Oran city; 35°46'N 0°49'W. Lighthouse.

Falconara Marittima (fälkōnä'rä märēt'tēmä), town (pop. 4,279), Ancona prov., The Marches, central Italy, port on the Adriatic, 6 mi. W of Ancona. Rail junction; bathing resort; mfg. (machinery, machine tools, refrigerators, textiles, alcohol, wine).

Falconbridge, village (pop. estimate 500), SE central Ont., 10 mi. NE of Sudbury; nickel and copper mining.

Falcone, Cape (fälkô'nē), point on NW coast of Sardinia, opposite Asinara Isl.; 40°58'N 8°13'E.

Falcone, Point, northernmost point of Sardinia, on Strait of Bonifacio, opposite Corsica; 41°15'N 9°13'E.

Falconer (făl'kŭnŭr, fôl'–), village (pop. 3,292), Chautauqua co., extreme W N.Y., just NE of Jamestown; mfg. (metal cabinets, furniture; glass, metal, and stone products; textiles, feed). Settled 1807, inc. 1891.

Falcon Heights, village (pop. 3,884), Ramsey co., E Minn., NW suburb of St. Paul.

Falcon Island (8 mi. long, 4 mi. wide), W Ont., in L. of the Woods, just W of Aulneau Peninsula, 30 mi. SSW of Kenora.

Falcon Island, Tonga: see FONUAFOO.

Falda, La, Argentina: see LA FALDA.

Falémé River (fälä'mā), Fr. West Africa, rises NE of Fouta Djallon massif, flows c.250 mi. NNE, mostly along Fr. Sudan-Senegal border, past Satadougou and Kidira, to the Senegal 55 mi. WNW of Kayes. Interrupted by rapids, it is partly navigable July–Sept. Gold placers along its course.

Falenki (fä'lyĭnkē), village (1926 pop. 425), E Kirov oblast, Russian SFSR, on railroad and 70 mi. ESE of Kirov; flax processing.

Falerii, Italy: see CIVITA CASTELLANA.

Falerna (fälĕr'nä), village (pop. 2,140), Catanzaro prov., Calabria, S Italy, near Tyrrhenian Sea, 8 mi. WNW of Nicastro.

Falerone (fälĕrô'nĕ), village (pop. 663), Ascoli Piceno prov., The Marches, central Italy, 13 mi. WSW of Fermo; straw-hat mfg.

Faleshty (fŭlyĕsh'tē), Rum. *Fălești* (fŭlĕsht'), city (1941 pop. 4,869), W Moldavian SSR, 17 mi. SW of Beltsy, in orchard dist.; flour and oilseed milling, soap mfg.; trade in grain, fruit, livestock. Pop. largely Jewish until Second World War.

Falfurrias (fălfûr'ēŭs), city (pop. 6,712), ⊙ Brooks co., S Texas, 37 mi. S of Alice; shipping, trade center for rich truck, fruit, dairying area, with oil and natural-gas wells; creameries, packing plants, cotton gins, gas recycling plant; mfg. of gypsum products. Holds large annual rodeo. Inc. after 1940.

Falher, village (pop. 279), W Alta., 35 mi. S of Peace River; lumbering, mixed farming, wheat.

Faliron, Bay of, Greece: see PHALERON, BAY OF.

Falisolle (fälēzôl'), town (pop. 3,014), Namur prov., S central Belgium, 8 mi. E of Charleroi; coal.

Falkenau, Czechoslovakia: see SOKOLOV.

Falkenberg, France: see FAULQUEMONT.

Falkenberg (fäl'kŭnbĕrk), village (pop. 7,831), in former Prussian Saxony prov., central Germany, after 1945 in Saxony-Anhalt, 11 mi. E of Torgau; rail junction; agr. market (grain, sugar beets, potatoes, livestock).

Falkenberg, Poland: see NIEMODLIN.

Falkenberg (fäl'kŭnbĕr"yŭ), city (pop. 7,327), Halland co., SW Sweden, on the Kattegat at mouth of Atra R. (18th-cent. bridge), 20 mi. NW of Halmstad; metalworking, tanning, shoe mfg., brick making. Tourist resort; salmon fishing. Founded in 13th cent.

Falkenburg, Poland: see ZLOCIENIEC.

Falkensee (fäl'kŭnzā), residential town (pop. 28,275), Brandenburg, E Germany, 13 mi. WNW of Berlin; mfg. of electrical equipment, chemicals.

Falkenstein (fäl'kŭn-shtīn). **1** Village (pop. 2,276), Upper Palatinate, E Bavaria, Germany, in Bohemian Forest, 19 mi. ENE of Regensburg; metalworking; summer resort. **2** Town (pop. 13,888), Saxony, E central Germany, in the Erzgebirge, on Göltzsch R. and 11 mi. E of Plauen; curtain-making center; cotton, woolen, and paper milling, embroidering; mfg. of musical instruments, electrical appliances.

Falkirk (fôl'kŭrk), burgh (1931 pop. 36,566; 1951 census 37,528), E Stirling, Scotland, 11 mi. SE of Stirling, 23 mi. W of Edinburgh, near broad "carse" (fertile farm land) and center of mining and industrial region, with steel mills, chemical and leather industries. It was long famous for the "trysts of Falkirk," annual stock fairs. N, 2 mi., are well-known ironworks at CARRON, and 3 mi. ENE is Falkirk's port of GRANGEMOUTH. In 1st battle of Falkirk (1298) the English under Edward I defeated the Scots under Wallace; in 2d battle of Falkirk Prince Charles Edward, the Young Pretender, defeated (1746) General Hawley while retreating N. Wall of Antoninus passed Falkirk.

Falkland (fôk'lŭnd, fôlk'–), burgh (1931 pop. 791; 1951 census 1,037), W Fifeshire, Scotland, at foot of the Lomond Hills, 21 mi. N of Edinburgh; agr. market. Has 15th-cent. palace of the Stuarts, begun by James III, extended by James V. There are scanty remains of castle of earls (or thanes) of Fife, 1st mentioned in town's charter (1160); in the castle David, duke of Rothesay, was starved to death in 1402.

Falkland (fôk'lŭnd), town (pop. 174), Pitt co., E N.C., 10 mi. NW of Greenville, near Tar R.

Falkland Current, cold ocean current of South Atlantic Ocean, flowing N along E coast of Argentina to c.30°S, where it meets Brazil Current.

Falkland Islands, Sp. *Islas Malvinas* (ēs'läs mälvē'näs), island group (□ 4,618; 1948 pop. 2,268), a Br. crown colony in the South Atlantic, c.250 mi. off SE coast of Argentina, E of the Strait of Magellan; 51°–53°S 57°–62°W; ⊙ Stanley. Consists of 2 large isls.—East Falkland (with adjacent isls.: □ 2,580; pop. c.1,870) and West Falkland (with adjacent isls.: □ 2,038; pop. c.400)—separated by Falkland Sound (1½–20 mi. wide); and c.200 smaller isls., islets, and rocks. Also included in the colony are the so-called Falkland Island Dependencies, whose boundaries extend from the South Pole N to 58°S lat. bet. 50° and 80°W long. and to 50°S lat. bet. 20° and 50°W long. This area—which was formally annexed to the Br. crown in 1908—embraces SOUTH GEORGIA, SOUTH SANDWICH ISLANDS, SOUTH ORKNEY ISLANDS, SOUTH SHETLAND ISLANDS, and the part of ANTARCTICA containing Palmer Peninsula (Graham Land) and its offshore isls. The Falklands themselves—chiefly treeless and with hilly, windswept moorlands drenched by cold, drizzling rains (rain or snow falls c.250 days of the year, though it averages only 25–30 in.)—are bleak and inhospitable; mean annual temp. is c.42°F. East Falkland (90 mi. long, 55 mi. wide) rises to 2,245 ft., West Falkland (80 mi. long, 45 mi. wide) to 2,315 ft. Deep bays (Choiseul, Berkeley, King George, Queen Charlotte) indent its coast. It has many kinds of birds, but no native mammals. Sheep farming is the only industry: wool, skins, and tallow are exported. Peat, which abounds, is cut for local use. (In South Georgia, whaling is important, and the dependencies export whale and seal oil, and guano.) Stanley (pop. c.1,200), on NE East Falkland, is the only important town; it has a power plant and radio station and is connected by sea with Montevideo. Most of pop. are of Br. origin. A governor and executive and legislative councils rule the colony. The Br. claim to the Falklands is based on probable discovery by John Davis in 1592. But a colony was 1st established (1764) by the French under Bougainville at Port Louis, on East Falkland. (The old Fr. name for the isls., Îles Malouines—of which Malvinas is a Sp. variant—dates from this period.) The Fr. colony was transferred (1766) to Spain and renamed Soledad. John Byron took possession (1765) for Britain at Port Egmont (on West Falkland). A Br. colony was established (1766), taken by the Spanish (1770), restored (1771), and abandoned (1774) by the British. Soledad was also abandoned by the Spanish in 1811, but in 1820 was revived by the United Provs. of La Plata (Argentina). Seizure of a U.S. sealing vessel at Soledad in 1832 led to a U.S. punitive expedition. In 1832–33 the British occupied the isls. Argentina disputes Britain's claim to the Falklands, and both Argentina and Chile dispute her claim to the dependencies.

Falkland Sound, strait separating East and West Falkland Isls.; extends NE c.50 mi., 1½–20 mi. wide.

Falkner Island (fôk'nŭr), S Conn., islet in Long Island Sound, off Guilford, New Haven co.; lighthouse.

Falknov, Czechoslovakia: see SOKOLOV.

Falkoping (fäl'chŭ"pĭng), Swedish *Falköping*, city (1950 pop. 11,247), Skaraborg co., SW Sweden, 65 mi. ENE of Goteborg; rail junction; mfg. of paper, hosiery, wood products, shoes, leather goods. Has 12th-cent. church. Trade center since Middle Ages. Near by are prehistoric graves.

Falkville (fôk'vĭl), town (pop. 613), Morgan co., N Ala., 17 mi. SSE of Decatur.

Fallabón (fäyäbōn'), village, Petén dept., N Guatemala, on Br. Honduras border, 50 mi. ENE of Flores; lumbering, livestock raising.

Fallbrook, village (pop. 1,735), San Diego co., S Calif., near Santa Margarita R., 15 mi. NE of Oceanside; thermal belt here produces avocados, citrus fruit.

Fall Creek, village (pop. 584), Eau Claire co., W central Wis., 12 mi. ESE of Eau Claire; dairying, stock raising.

Fallen Leaf Lake, El Dorado co., E Calif., in the Sierra Nevada, just S of L. Tahoe; c.3 mi. long. Fallen Leaf (resort) is here.

Fallen Timbers State Park, Lucas co., NW Ohio, on Maumee R., near Maumee; marks site of battle of Fallen Timbers (1794), in which Anthony Wayne defeated the Indians and opened the area for settlement.

Fallersleben (fä'lŭrslā"bŭn), town (pop. 4,367), in former Prussian prov. of Hanover, NW Germany, after 1945 in Lower Saxony, on Weser-Elbe Canal and 13 mi. NE of Brunswick; building materials, tools; woodworking. Potash mining. Poet Hoffmann von Fallersleben b. here. Wolfsburg, with Volkswagen works, is 3.5 mi. ENE.

Fallingbostel (fä'lĭngbôs'tŭl), village (pop. 4,437), in former Prussian prov. of Hanover, NW Germany, after 1945 in Lower Saxony, 4 mi. E of Walsrode, in heath land; wood products, canned goods. Summer resort.

Falling Spring Dam, Va.: see JACKSON RIVER.

Falling Springs, W.Va.: see RENICK.

Fallis (fă'lĭs), town (pop. 105), Lincoln co., central Okla., 28 mi. NE of Oklahoma City, in agr. area.

Fall Lake, Lake co., NE Minn., in Superior Natl. Forest, just NE of Ely; 6 mi. long, 1 mi. wide. Fishing resorts. Village of Winton is at SW end of lake. Lake is fed and drained by Kawishiwi R.

Fall Line, in E U.S., zone at outer border of the PIEDMONT province where streams, passing from the more resistant rocks to softer coastal plain deposits, flow over rapids and waterfalls. As it marks head of navigation on rivers and good sites for industries needing water power, many cities (Trenton, N.J., Baltimore, Philadelphia, Washington, Richmond, Raleigh, N.C., Columbia, S.C., and Augusta, Macon, and Columbus, Ga.) have grown up along the Fall Line.

Fallon (fă'lŭn), county (□ 1,633; pop. 3,660), E Mont.; ⊙ Baker. Agr. region bordering on N.Dak. and S.Dak.; drained by O'Fallon Creek. Grain, livestock. Formed 1913.

Fallon. 1 Village (pop. c.200), Prairie co., E Mont., on Yellowstone R. and 10 mi. E of Terry; diversified farming. **2** City (pop. 2,400), ⊙ Churchill co., W Nev., on Carson R. and c.55 mi. E of Reno, near Carson L.; alt. 3,970 ft.; trade and processing center for dairying, livestock, and irrigated agr. area; dairy products, alfalfa meal. State fairgrounds and U.S. wildlife refuge here. Grew with development (1903–08) of Newlands irrigation project, supplied by TRUCKEE RIVER and CARSON RIVER. Inc. 1908.

Fall River, county (□ 1,748; pop. 10,439), SW S.Dak., on Wyo. and Nebr. lines; ⊙ Hot Springs. Agr. area drained by Cheyenne R. and numerous creeks; Fossil Cycad Natl. Monument and S extremity of Harney Natl. Forest in N. Sandstone quarries; dairy produce, livestock, alfalfa, corn, wheat. Formed 1883.

Fall River. 1 City (pop. 261), Greenwood co., SE Kansas, on Fall R. and 20 mi. SE of Eureka; cattle, grain; dairying. **2** Industrial city (pop. 111,963), a ⊙ Bristol co., SE Mass., on harbor on Mt. Hope Bay, at mouth of Taunton R., and 15 mi. SE of Providence, R.I. Its great cotton textile industry (begun 1811), stimulated by its fine harbor, water power, and damp climate, declined for time after 1929. Also makes rubber and paper products, refractories, brass, bronze, and silver products, gas ranges, hats, clothing. Port of entry. Port ships textiles, clothing; receives oil, rubber, mill supplies. Seat of Bradford Durfee Technical Inst. Settled 1656, set off from Freetown 1803, inc. as city 1854. **3** Village (pop. 479), Columbia co., S central Wis., on Crawfish R. and 23 mi. SE of Portage; agr.; cannery.

Fall River. 1 In NE Calif., rises in SW Plumas co., flows c.25 mi. SW to Middle Fork Feather R., 29 mi. NW of Nevada City. FEATHER FALLS on Fall R. is c.3 mi. from confluence of the rivers. Another Fall R., affluent of the Pit, is in Shasta co.; its waters are diverted through a tunnel to a hydroelectric plant on Pit R. near Fall River Mills. **2** In SE Kansas, formed by confluence of 2 headstreams in Greenwood co., flows c.90 mi. SE, past Eureka and Fall River city, to Verdigris R. just SE of Neodesha. Fall River Dam (94 ft. high, 6,455 ft. long, including earth-fill barrier and concrete spillway; completed 1949 by U.S. Army Engineers) is in stream at Fall River city; used for flood control and water supply; forms Fall River Reservoir (15 mi. long, max. width 1.5 mi.; capacity 263,000 acre-ft.).

Fall River Mills, village (pop. c.400), Shasta co., N Calif., on Fall R. at its junction with Pit R., and c.55 mi. NE of Redding; lumbering, dairying, farming.

Fall River Pass, Colo.: see ROCKY MOUNTAIN NATIONAL PARK.

Falls, county (□ 761; pop. 26,724), E central Texas; ⊙ Marlin. Mainly blackland prairies; drained by Brazos R. (falls here are recreation area). Agr. (cotton, corn, grain sorghums, alfalfa, oats, fruit, truck); cattle, poultry, hogs, horses; dairying. Clay mining; mfg., processing at Marlin (health resort, with mineral springs). Formed 1850.

Fallsburgh, resort village, Sullivan co., SE N.Y., 7 mi. NW of Monticello.

Falls Church, city (pop. 7,535), independent of any co., N Va., residential suburb 7 mi. W of Washington, D.C., across the Potomac. Truck, poultry; wood products, cut stone. The Falls Church, here, built 1767–69 on site of church built 1734. Inc. as town 1875, as city 1948, when it was separated from Fairfax co.

Falls City. 1 City (pop. 6,203), ⊙ Richardson co., extreme SE Nebr., 80 mi. SE of Lincoln and on Nemaha R., near Missouri R. and Kansas line. Railway div. point, trade center for agr. area; railroad repair shops; flour, cattle feed; dairy, meat, and poultry products, grain, livestock. Falls of Nemaha R. near by. Founded 1857, inc. 1858. **2** Town (pop. 853), Polk co., NW Oregon, 6 mi. SW of Dallas. **3** Town (pop. 422), Karnes co., S Texas, 7 mi. NE of Karnes City.

Falls Creek, borough (pop. 1,191), Jefferson and Clearfield counties, W central Pa., 3 mi. NW of Du Bois. Inc. 1900.

Falls River, in NW Wyo. and E Idaho, rises in SW corner of Yellowstone Natl. Park, Wyo.; flows c.50 mi. W and WSW to Henrys Fork 7 mi. SW of Ashton, Idaho. Bechler Falls are near junction in Yellowstone Natl. Park of Bechler R. branch with Falls R.

Fallston. 1 Village (pop. c.150), Harford co., NE Md., near Little Gunpowder Falls (stream), 19 mi. NNE of Baltimore; vegetable canneries, clothing factories. Little Falls Meeting House (Quaker) was erected 1773. **2** Borough (pop. 511), Beaver co., W Pa., on Beaver R. opposite New Brighton.

Falls View, village (pop. 1,038, with adjacent Charlton Heights), Fayette co., S central W.Va., on Kanawha R. and 25 mi. SE of Charleston.

Falls Village, Conn.: see CANAAN, town.

Falluja, Al, or **Al-Falludjah** (äl fäl-lōō'jü), village, Dulaim prov., central Iraq, on the Euphrates (here crossed by a bridge) and 35 mi. W of Baghdad; dates, sesame, millet, corn.

Falmouth (făl'mŭth), village, S Antigua, B.W.I., 7 mi. SE of St. John's, on fine bay. Was once a prosperous town.

Falmouth, village (pop. estimate 300), W central N.S., on Avon R., opposite Windsor; apples.

Falmouth, municipal borough (1931 pop. 13,492; 1951 census 17,036), SW Cornwall, England, on Falmouth Bay of the Channel, on Carrick Roads (estuarial section of Fal R.) and 45 mi. WSW of Plymouth; 50°9'N 5°3'W. Seaport, fishing town, and resort, with good harbor. Entrance is guarded by Pendennis Castle (W) and St. Mawes Castle (E), both 16th cent. Shipbuilding, metalworking; China clay shipped from here. In Civil War town was taken (1646) by Fairfax after 5-month siege. Formerly an important post for passengers and foreign mail, now popular because of its subtropical climate and gardens. Has 17th-cent. church.

Falmouth, town (pop. 2,561), ⊙ Trelawny parish, N Jamaica, seaport on N coast at mouth of small Martha Brae R., 17 mi. E of Montego Bay, 65 mi. NW of Kingston; 18°30'N 77°40'W. Trades in sugar, rum, coffee, ginger, pimento, bananas, honey, dyewood. Resort. In colonial times an important shipping point serving surrounding sugar estates.

Falmouth. 1 City (pop. 2,186), ⊙ Pendleton co., N Ky., on Licking R. at mouth of its South Fork, and 30 mi. SSE of Covington, in Bluegrass agr. area (dairy products, poultry, hay, corn, burley tobacco, honey). Mfg. of soft drinks, cheese, generators, shoes; flour milling. Pleistocene fossils found in vicinity. Settled 1776; town founded 1799. **2** Town (pop. 4,342), Cumberland co., SW Maine, on Presumpscot R. and Casco Bay and just NE of Portland. Includes villages of Falmouth Foreside (pop. 1,023) and West Falmouth. Old town of Falmouth, site of one of Maine's earliest settlements (c.1632), included Portland until 1786. Inc. 1718. **3** Town (pop. 8,662), including Falmouth village (pop. 2,713), Barnstable co., SE Mass., on SW point of Cape Cod, 17 mi. ESE of New Bedford, across Buzzards Bay; summer resort; agr. (truck, dairying, cranberries). U.S. Camp Edwards and Otis Air Force Base are near. Formerly active shipbuilding and whaling port. Has 18th-cent. buildings. Settled 1660, inc. 1686. Includes villages of Falmouth Heights, North Falmouth, East Falmouth (pop. 1,405), West Falmouth, Davisville, Hatchville, Mara Vista, Silver Beach, Teaticket, Waquoit (strawberries, asparagus), and WOODS HOLE. **4** Village (pop. 1,176), Stafford co., N Va., at falls of the Rappahannock (bridged) opposite Fredericksburg, in agr., dairying area. Founded 1727 as port; a thriving mfg. and trade center for almost a cent. Federal hq. here (1862) in Civil War battle of Fredericksburg.

Falmouth Bay (făl'mŭth), SW Cornwall, England, in the Channel NE of The Lizard; 5 mi. wide, it penetrates 5 mi. N. Overlooking its excellent harbor are St. Mawes Castle (E) and Pendennis Castle (W), built by Henry VIII.

Falmouth Heights, Mass.: see FALMOUTH.

Falougha, Lebanon: see FALUGHA.

Falq Al 'Ali, Trucial Oman: see UMM AL QAIWAIN.

Fal River (făl), W Cornwall, England, rises 2 mi. E of Roche, flows 25 mi. S to the Channel at Falmouth. Estuarial part is called Carrick Roads.

False Bay (20 mi. long, 18 mi. wide at mouth), SW Cape Prov., U. of So. Afr., inlet of the Atlantic, 12 mi. S of Cape Town. On W side of entrance is Cape Point, extremity of Cape of Good Hope; on E side is Cape Hangklip. Towns on bay include Simonstown (naval base), Muizenberg, and Strand. British forces landed here 1795.

False Cape, Nicaragua; Dominican Republic: see FALSO, CABO.

False Cape, W point of Sierra Leone Peninsula, W Sierra Leone, 5 mi. SW of Freetown; 8°26'N 13°18'W. Goderich is just NE.

False Cape Horn, headland in Tierra del Fuego, Chile, at S tip of Hardy Peninsula, 35 mi. NW of Cape Horn; 55°44'S 68°4'W. Has often been mistaken for Cape Horn, which it resembles.

False Divi Point (dĭ'vē), small promontory on Bay of Bengal, in Guntur dist., NE Madras, India, just W of Kistna R. mouth, 40 mi. SE of Masulipatam. False Point is 500 mi. NE, at Mahanadi R. mouth.

False Pass, village (pop. 42), on E shore of Unimak Isl., Aleutian Isls., SW Alaska.

False Point, small promontory in Bay of Bengal, in Cuttack dist., E Orissa, India, just N of Mahanadi R. mouth, 60 mi. E of Cuttack; 20°23'N 86°48'E. Lighthouse (S).

False Presque Isle (prĕsk ēl'), NE Mich., isl. in L. Huron 14 mi. NNE of Alpena; c.2 mi. long, 1½ mi. wide. Part of Presque Isle co.

False River, La.: see NEW ROADS.

Falset (fälsĕt'), city (pop. 2,287), Tarragona prov., NE Spain, 15 mi. W of Reus; center of rich wine-growing region; mfg. (alcohol, liqueur, lye); agr. trade (olive oil, wine, almonds, filberts, fruit). Lead deposits near by.

Falso, Cabo (kä'bō fäl'sō) [Sp.,=false cape], or **Point Agujas** (ägōō'häs), headland on Caribbean coast of SW Dominican Republic, 50 mi. SW of Barahona; 17°47'N 71°43'W.

Falso, Cabo, on Mosquito Coast of Nicaragua, on Caribbean Sea, 18 mi. NW of Cape Gracias a Dios; 15°12'N 83°22'W.

Falster (fäl'stûr), island (□ 198; pop. 45,665), Denmark, in Baltic Sea, separated from S Zealand by Storstrom strait; 28 mi. long (N–S), 15 mi. (N) to 3 mi. (S) wide. S tip, known as Gedser Odde, is Denmark's most southerly point; 25 mi. from Ger. coast. Highest point, 144 ft. Very fertile soil; forests in center and on E coast. Cities: Nykobing, Stubbekobing.

Falsterbo, town, Sweden: see SKANOR MED FALSTERBO.

Falsterbo Peninsula (fäl'stûrbōō"), S Sweden, sandy spit (5 mi. long, 1–4 mi. wide), on the Baltic, on SE side of mouth of Oresund, 15 mi. SSW of Malmo. At tip is Skanor med Falsterbo city. Narrow central part of peninsula is pierced by Falsterbo Canal (1.7 mi. long), completed in Second World War.

Falta, India: see DIAMOND HARBOUR.

Falterona, Monte (môn'tĕ fältĕrō'nä), peak (5,426 ft.) in Etruscan Apennines, central Italy, 22 mi. ENE of Florence. Source of Arno R.

Falticeni (fŭltĕchān'), Rum. *Fălticeni*, town (1948 pop. 10,563), Suceava prov., NE Rumania, in Moldavia, 65 mi. WNW of Jassy; rail terminus and trading center, noted for its woodworking industry (notably furniture mfg.); tanning. Founded in 18th cent. Jews form 25% of pop. Historic village of Baia, former residence of 1st ruler of Moldavia, is 5 mi. SW and has 2 old churches. Fortified monastery of Slatina is 16 mi. W.

Falugha (fălōō'gŭ), Fr. *Falougha*, village (pop. 1,492), central Lebanon, 14 mi. SSE of Beirut, surrounded by pine forests; alt. 4,000 ft.; resort; sericulture, cotton, cereals, tobacco, fruits.

Faluja (fălōō'jŭ), village, W Israel, at W foot of Judaean Hills, at N edge of the Negev, 30 mi. S of Tel Aviv, 25 mi. N of Beersheba. On one of main roads from coast to Hebron, it was scene (1948) of heavy fighting; Israeli forces isolated and defeated large Egyptian force in Faluja Gap.

Falun (fä'lŭn"), city (1950 pop. 16,858), ⊙ Kopparberg co., central Sweden, at N end of 10-mi. Runn L. (rŭn), 120 mi. NW of Stockholm; 60°36'N 15°39'E. Rail junction; sulphuric-ore and zinc mining; mfg. of railroad cars, machinery, electrical equipment, bricks. Hq. of one of Sweden's oldest and largest industrial corporations, which operated copper mines (now exhausted) here from 1230 onward, and now owns iron mines at Grangesberg, Dannemora, and in Lapland. Site of mining school; has industrial mus. An old spelling is Fahlun.

Famagusta (fämŭgōō'stŭ), district (□ 761; pop. 94,474), E Cyprus; ⊙ Famagusta. In N the KYRENIA MOUNTAINS continue through KARPAS PENINSULA, which juts SE into the Mediterranean. Predominantly lowland, irrigated by several reservoirs fed by PEDIAS RIVER. L. Paralimni, once isl.'s largest, has been drained. Agr. products include cereals, vetches, potatoes, cotton, citrus fruit, carobs, tobacco, olive oil. Stock raising (sheep, goats, hogs). Processing and cotton spinning centered at Famagusta, Cyprus' largest port, linked by rail with Nicosia. Among other towns are RIZOKARPASSO, AKANTHOU, and LEFKONIKO. Dist. has gypsum deposits.

Famagusta, Gr. *Ammochostos* (ämō'khôstôs), city (pop. 16,194), ⊙ Famagusta dist., E Cyprus, port on wide Famagusta Bay of the Mediterranean, 37 mi. E of Nicosia, linked by rail. Trades in citrus fruit (principal export), potatoes, carobs, raisins, olives, tobacco, wines, olives; mules, donkeys. Local industries include cotton spinning, brandy distilling, soap mfg. Fishing. Surrounded by medieval (27-ft. thick) walls. Has remains of numerous churches, of which the best preserved were converted into mosques. Among prominent edifices is Othello's Tower, 13th-cent. cathedral of St. Nicholas (now a mosque), and a Venetian palace. The modern S section of the town, inhabited by Greeks, is called Varosha. City is on site of anc. Arsinoë, built in 3d cent. B.C. by Ptolemy II. Annexed (1376) by the Genoese. Taken by Venetians in 1487, who made it seat of Cyprus governors. Surrendered (1571) to Turks after long siege. The extensive harbor installations, completed 1906, were enlarged 1932–33. A Br. naval base during Second World War, it was bombed by Axis aircraft. In near-by (N) camp "illegal" immigrants to Palestine were interned (1945–48). S of the city is one of isl.'s finest beaches, used for vacationing Br. Middle East forces. Almost ⅓ of pop. is Turkish.

Famaillá (fămīyä'), town (pop. estimate 2,500), ⊙ Famaillá dept. (□ c.600; 1947 pop. 55,593), central Tucumán prov., Argentina, 20 mi. SSW of Tucumán; rail junction and agr. center (sugar cane, rice, corn, livestock); flour milling, sugar refining, lumbering.

Famalicão (fămŭlĕkã'ō), village (pop. 1,629), Guarda dist., N central Portugal, in Serra da Estrêla, 8 mi. SW of Guarda; olive- and winegrowing.

Famanin or **Famenin** (both: fä"mĕnēn'), Fifth Prov., in Hamadan, W Iran, on the Qara Chai and 30 mi. NE of Hamadan, just off highway to Kazvin.

Famara Massif (fämä'rä), small basaltic range, N Lanzarote, Canary Isls., rising in Peñitas del Chache to isl.'s highest elevation (2,215 ft.).

Famars (fămär'), village (pop. 882), Nord dept., N France, 3 mi. S of Valenciennes; has remains of a Roman fortress.

Famatina (fämätē'nä), town (pop. estimate 800), ⊙ Famatina dept. (□ 1,795; 1947 pop. 6,043), N La Rioja prov., Argentina, in Famatina Valley, 50 mi. NW of La Rioja; fruit- and grain-growing center; also stock raising, lumbering. Ocher deposits. Gold, tungsten, and copper mines in Sierra de Famatina near by.

Famatina, Sierra de (syĕ'rä dā), subandean mountain range in N central La Rioja prov., Argentina, NW of Famatina; extends 45 mi. N–S from Catamarca prov. border; rises to 20,500 ft. in the Cumbre de la Mejicana. Rich in lead, copper, and other mineral deposits.

Famatina Valley, N central La Rioja prov., Argentina, bet. Sierra de Famatina and Sierra de Velasco; extends c.150 mi. N–S along fertile fruit and grain area. Main centers are Chilecito and Famatina. Lumbering and mining (copper, silver).

Famenin, Iran: see FAMANIN.

Familleureux (fămēürû'), town (pop. 2,062), Hainaut prov., SW central Belgium, 13 mi. ENE of Mons; glass blowing.

Fan, river, Albania: see FAN RIVER.

Fana (fänä'), village, S Fr. Sudan, Fr. West Africa, 75 mi. E of Bamako; peanuts, shea nuts, kapok.

Fana (fä'nä), canton (pop. 20,183), Hordaland co., SW Norway, just S of Bergen. Includes villages of FJOSANGER, FLESLAND, HOP, NESTTUN, STEND. Formerly spelled Fane.

Fanad Head (fă'nŭd), promontory on the Atlantic, N Co. Donegal, Ireland, on W side of entrance to Lough Swilly, 12 mi. NW of Buncrana; lighthouse (55°16'N 7°38'W).

Fanano (fänä'nô), village (pop. 893), Modena prov., Emilia-Romagna, N central Italy, 20 mi. NNW of Pistoia, near Monte Cimone; resort (alt. 2,100 ft.); woolen mill.

Fanar, Turkey: see PHANAR.

Fanarion, Greece: see PHANARION.

Fanchang or **Fan-ch'ang** (fän'chäng'), town, ⊙ Fanchang co. (pop. 138,979), S Anhwei prov., China, 25 mi. SW of Wuhu, near Yangtze R.; rice, wheat, rapeseed. Iron-mining center of TAOCHUNG is just W.

Fancheng or **Fan-ch'eng** (fän'chŭng'), town (1922 pop. estimate 65,000), NW Hupeh prov., China, on left bank of Han R., opposite Siangyang, and 165 mi. NW of Hankow; commercial center; cotton weaving, tung-oil processing, rice milling.

Fan-chih, China: see FANSZE.

Fancy Farm, town (pop. 419), Graves co., SW Ky., 10 mi. WNW of Mayfield, in agr. area.

Fand or **Fandi**, river, Albania: see FAN RIVER.

Fandrem, Norway: see FANNREM.

Fane, canton, Norway: see FANA.

Fane River, Ireland, rises in E Co. Monaghan, flows 24 mi. SE, past Castleblayney, through Lough Muckno and into Co. Louth, to Dundalk Bay 5 mi. SE of Dundalk.

Fan Fawr, Wales: see BLACK MOUNTAIN.

Fang (fäng'), village (1937 pop. 4,563), Chiangmai prov., N Thailand, 80 mi. NNE of Chiangmai, near Burma line; petroleum and asphalt deposits near by.

Fangahina (fäng'ähē'nä), atoll (pop. 101), central Tuamotu Isls., Fr. Oceania, S Pacific; 15°59'S 140°7'W. Sometimes spelled Fakahina.

Fangak (fäng'gäk), town, Upper Nile prov., S central Anglo-Egyptian Sudan, on right bank of the Bahr ez Zeraf, 60 mi. SW of Malakal in Sudd marshes.

Fangataufa (fäng'ätou'fä) or **Fangatou** (fäng'ätōō'), atoll (pop. 176), S Tuamotu Isls., Fr. Oceania, S Pacific; 22°15'S 138°45'W. Formerly Cockburn Isl.

Fangcheng. **1** or **Fang-ch'eng** (fäng'chŭng'), town, ⊙ Fangcheng co. (pop. 283,687), SW Honan prov., China, 30 mi. NE of Nanyang; pottery making; grain, sesame, beans. Until 1913 called Yuchow. **2** or **Fang-ch'eng** (fäng'chŭng'), Cantonese *Fongshing* (fông'shĭng'), town (pop. 6,853), ⊙ Fangcheng co. (pop. 207,229), SW Kwangtung prov., China, near Gulf of Tonkin and Vietnam border, 20 mi. SW of Yamhsien; rice, wheat, sugar cane. Manganese and antimony mines near by. **3** (fäng'jŭng') Town, ⊙ Fangcheng co. (pop. 95,000), W Sungkiang prov., Manchuria, China, 100 mi. SW of Kiamusze and on right bank of Sungari R.; beans, barley, rye; hog raising.

Fanghsien (fäng'shyĕn'), town (pop. 12,275), ⊙ Fanghsien co. (pop. 227,627), NW Hupeh prov., China, 50 mi. S of Yünhsien; rice, wheat, beans, millet.

Fangshan (fäng'shän'). **1** Town, ⊙ Fangshan co. (pop. 185,872), N Hopeh prov., China, 25 mi. SW of Peking, near Peking-Hankow RR; wheat, millet, kaoliang. Coal mining near by. **2** Town, ⊙ Fangshan co. (pop. 35,912), W Shansi prov., China, 35 mi. N of Lishih; beans, wheat, kaoliang, poultry, timber.

Fangtsun, China: see FATI.

Fangtze or **Fang-tzu** (both: fäng'dzŭ'), town, E central Shantung prov., China, on Tsingtao-Tsinan RR and 8 mi. SE of Weifang, in WEIFANG municipality; coal-mining center; tobacco processing; vegetable and wheat growing.

Fanhsien (fän'shyĕn'), town, ⊙ Fanhsien co. (pop 147,163), NE Pingyuan prov., China, on main road and 70 mi. E of Anyang; wheat, kaoliang, millet, beans. Until 1949 in Shantung prov. The name Fanhsien formerly was applied to a town 7 mi. SSE.

Fani River, Albania: see FAN RIVER.

Fanjeaux (fãzhō'), village (pop. 463), Aude dept., S France, 10 mi. SSE of Castelnaudary; cereals, livestock, wine. Has 13th-cent. church.

Fanne Fjord, Norway: see MOLDE FJORD.

Fannich, Loch (lŏkh fă'nĭkh), lake (7 mi. long, 1 mi. wide), in central Ross and Cromarty, Scotland; source of Conon R.

Fannin (fă'nĭn). **1** County (□ 396; pop. 15,192), N Ga., on Tenn. and N.C. lines; ⊙ Blue Ridge. In the Blue Ridge and partly (W) in Chattahoochee Natl. Forest. Farming (fruit, corn, hay, potatoes, livestock, dairy products), sawmilling, and resort area drained by Toccoa R. (forms L. Blue Ridge here). Pop. also works in copper mines of adjacent Polk co., Tenn. Formed 1854. **2** County (□ 906; pop. 31,253), NE Texas; ⊙ Bonham. Bounded N by Red R. (here the Okla. line); drained by South Sulphur and North Sulphur rivers. Rich prairie agr. area: cotton, corn, grains, alfalfa, legumes (especially peanuts), fruit, truck; livestock (cattle, hogs, sheep, poultry); extensive dairying. Timber, clay, limestone. Includes game preserve and reforestation project and artificial lakes Fannin, Coffee Mill, and Crockett. Co. formed 1837.

Fanning Island, atoll (□ 12.3; pop. 259), Line Isls., central Pacific, 155 mi. NW of Christmas Isl.; 3°52'N 159°19'W. Discovered 1798 by Americans; annexed 1888 by British; included 1916 in Br. Gilbert and Ellice Isls. colony. Cable relay station (1902) connects Canada and Suva, Fiji. Copra plantation with imported labor; no indigenous pop.

Fannrem (fän'rĕm), village in Orkdal (formerly Orkedalen) canton (pop. 4,126), Sor-Trondelag co., central Norway, on the Orkla, on railroad and 21 mi. SW of Trondheim; industrial center, producing copper matte, wood products, ground peat. Formerly spelled Fandrem.

Fanny Bay, village (pop. estimate 200), SW B.C., in E central Vancouver Isl., on Strait of Georgia, 14 mi. SE of Courtenay; lumber-shipping port.

Fano (fă'nû), Dan. *Fanø*, island (□ 22; pop. 2,575) of North Frisian group, Denmark, in North Sea off Esbjerg, SW Jutland, in Fano Bay; 10 mi. long, 2 mi. wide; resort. Odden (pop. 1,816), on NE coast, is main town.

Fano (fä'nô), anc. *Fanum Fortunae*, town (pop. 13,348), Pesaro e Urbino prov., The Marches, central Italy, port on the Adriatic, near mouth of Metauro R., 7 mi. SE of Pesaro; bathing resort. Mfg. (machinery, metal furniture, shoes, silk textiles). Bishopric. Has arch of Augustus, Malatesta palace (1413–21), and several churches, including a cathedral, all damaged in Second World War by Ger. demolition of their campaniles. First Ital. printing press in Arabic type set up here in 1514. An important Roman center; flourished in Middle Ages under the Malatesta of Rimini (1304–1463).

Fanos, Greece: see OTHONOI.

Fan River (fän) or **Fani River** (fä'nē), N Albania, formed by 2 headstreams, the greater Fan [Albanian *Fan i madh*] and the lesser Fan [Albanian *Fan i vogël*], which rise in the Mirdita highland, flow c.30 mi. in parallel courses (2 mi. apart in lower reaches), and after joining enter the Mat R. 8 mi. SE of Lesh. Chalcopyrite deposits along courses. Sometimes called Fand or Fandi.

Fanshaw, Cape, SE Alaska mainland, on Frederick Sound N of Kupreanof Isl.; 57°11'N 133°34'W; post office and cannery here.

Fansipan (fă'sēpă), mtn. range of N Vietnam, bet. Red River (N) and Black River (S); rises to 10,308 ft. in Fansipan peak, 17 mi. SW of Laokay. Crystalline and igneous formations.

Fan-ssu, China: see FANSZE.

Fansze or **Fan-ssu** (both: fän'sŭ'), town, ⊙ Fansze co. (pop. 111,171), NE Shansi prov., China, on upper Huto R. and 20 mi. NE of Taihsien, at foot of Wutai Mts.; rice, timber. Also written Fanchih.

Fantsing Mountain (fän'jĭng'), NE Kweichow prov., China, rises to over 4,500 ft. 35 mi. E of Szenan. Mercury deposits. Noted Taoist monastery.

Fantzetien or **Fan-tzu-t'ien** (both: fän'dzŭ'tyĕn), Jap. *Banshiden* (bän'shĭdän), village, W central Formosa, on railroad and 15 mi. NNE of Tainan; rail junction for Matow.

Fanum Fortunae, Italy: see FANO.

Fanwood, residential borough (pop. 3,228), Union co., NE N.J., 9 mi. WSW of Elizabeth; mfg. (paints, varnishes, cider). Settled before 1780, inc. 1895.

Fao or **Fa'w** (fä'ō, fä'-ōō), minor port, Basra prov., SE Iraq, on the Shatt al Arab just above its mouth on the Persian Gulf and 50 mi. SE of Basra; dates. Basra has taken its port trade since the clearing of the river channel here. Loading terminal for Zubair oil field (linked by pipe line).

Faou, Le (lū fōō'), village (pop. 1,075), Finistère dept., W France, 15 mi. ESE of Brest; fruit and vegetable preserving.

Faouët, Le (lū fōōā'), village (pop. 1,799), Morbihan dept., W France, 20 mi. N of Lorient; cattle market. Noted for its two 15th-cent. pilgrimage chapels, Sainte-Barbe and Saint-Fiacre.

Faqus (fă'kōōs), town (pop. 16,263), Sharqiya prov., Lower Egypt, on railroad and 20 mi. NE of Zagazig; cotton.

Fara, Iraq: see SHURUPPAK.

Fara or **Pharay** (both: fă'rŭ). **1** Islet (pop. 28) of the Orkneys, Scotland, just off SE coast of Hoy; 2 mi. long, 1 mi. wide. **2** Islet (pop. 40) of the Orkneys, Scotland, just off NW coast of EDAY; 3 mi. long. Good grazing land.

Farab (fŭräp'), town (1939 pop. over 500), E Chardzhou oblast, Turkmen SSR, on Trans-Caspian RR, near the Amu Darya, and 5 mi. NE of Chardzhou; cotton. Near by, on right bank of the Amu Darya opposite Chardzhou is port of Farab-Pristan or Farab-Pristan' (1939 pop. over 500).

Fara d'Adda, Italy: see FARA GERA D'ADDA.

Faradje (färä'jä), village, Eastern Prov., NE Belgian Congo, on Dungu R., on Congo Nile highway and 150 mi. N of Irumu, in cattle-raising area. Dominican mission. Coffee plantations in vicinity.

Farafangana (färäfäng-gä'nŭ), town (1948 pop. 6,783), Fianarantsoa prov., E Madagascar, 105 mi. SE of Fianarantsoa; cabotage port on Indian Ocean, head of Canal des Pangalanes; ships rice, manioc, arrowroot, coffee, vanilla, fibers, waxes, hides, wood. R.C. and Protestant missions, hosp. for Europeans, leprosarium.

Farafirah, Egypt: see FARAFRA.

Farafra or **Farafirah** (färä'fĭrŭ), small oasis (pop. 749) in Libyan Desert, W central Egypt, in Western Desert Prov., 300 mi. SSW of Alexandria. Caravan routes to Dakhla and Bahariya oases, and to Manfalut and Asyut, on the Nile. Chief village, Qasr Farafra.

Fara Gera d'Adda or **Fara d'Adda** (fä'rä jā'rä, däd'dä), village (pop. 3,240), Bergamo prov., Lombardy, N Italy, on Adda R. and 3 mi. NW of Treviglio.

Farah or **Farrah** (fŭ'rŭ, fŭrä'), province (□ 30,000; pop. 300,000), SW Afghanistan; ⊙ Farah. Bounded W by Iran and S by Baluchistan (Pakistan), it includes Afghan Seistan. It is largely desert traversed by rivers (Harut Rud, Farah Rud, Khash Rud, Helmand) draining into the Seistan lake depression. The few irrigated oases (Farah, Dilaram) lie in this depression and at the foot of the Hindu Kush outliers (NE) along the Kandahar-Farah highway. These oases contain most of pop. and agr. production and are settled predominantly by Durani Afghans. The S desert (Dasht-i-Margo) supports a sparse Baluch nomad pop., raising sheep and camels. Sometimes spelled Ferah or Ferrah.

Farah or **Farrah**, town (pop. 10,000), ⊙ Farah prov., W Afghanistan, on main highway and 135 mi. S of Herat, 220 mi. WNW of Kandahar, and on the Farah Rud (oasis); alt. 2,460 ft.; 32°24'N 62°7'E. On chief access route to Afghan Seistan, Farah was formerly one of chief agr. and commercial centers of Afghanistan. Usually identified with the anc. *Phra*, it flourished until destroyed by the Mongol raids (1221), revived and was again devastated (1837) by the Persian Nadir Shah, and remained long in ruins. Its modern importance dates from completion (1930s) of Kandahar-Herat auto road.

Farah (fŭr'ŭ), town (pop. 2,165), Muttra dist., W Uttar Pradesh, India, near the Jumna, 13 mi. SSE of Muttra; gram, jowar, grains, cotton, mustard.

Farahabad (färä"häbäd'), village, Second Prov., in E Mazanderan, N Iran, on Caspian Sea, 15 mi. N of Sari; site has been selected for development as a port.

Farah Rud or **Farrah Rud** (fŭ'rŭ rōōd', fŭrä'), river in Afghanistan, rises in central Afghanistan in outlier of the Hindu Kush 160 mi. N of Kandahar, flows 350 mi. SW, past Farah and Lash-Jawain, to the Hamun-i-Sabari, one of the lagoons of the Seistan depression on Iran border.

Faraján (färähän'), town (pop. 761), Málaga prov., S Spain, 8 mi. S of Ronda; acorns, chestnuts, corn, fruit, cork, livestock; charcoal burning, liquor distilling. Has mineral springs and unexploited copper and iron deposits.

Farallon de Medinilla, Marianas Isls.: see MEDINILLA.

Farallon de Pajaros, Marianas Isls.: see PAJAROS.

Farallon Islands (fâ'rŭlŏn) or **Farallones** (fârŭlō'nĕz), Calif., 2 groups of waterless rocky islets in the Pacific, 26 mi. W of the Golden Gate; part of San Francisco city and co. On Southeast Farallon (pop. 30), the only inhabited isl., are a lighthouse and a U.S. navy radio-beam compass and radar station. Isls. serve as a bird refuge and have seal herds. In early-19th cent., Russian sealers established a colony here.

Faramontanos de Tábara (färämōntä'nōs dhä tä'värä), village (pop. 1,022), Zamora prov., NW Spain, 16 mi. SW of Benavente; cereals, wine, livestock.

Faranah (färänä'), town (pop. c.2,550), central Fr. Guinea, Fr. West Africa, in interior highlands, 55 mi. SSE of Dabola; peanuts, rubber, tobacco, cattle.

Fara Novarese (fä'rä nôvärā'zĕ), village (pop. 2,407), Novara prov., Piedmont, N Italy, 11 mi. NW of Novara.

Faras (färäs'), village, Northern Prov., Anglo-Egyptian Sudan, on left bank of the Nile, on Egyptian border and 20 mi. N of Wadi Halfa; police and customs posts. Site of Meroitic remains (castle, temples) explored 1910–12.

Farasan Islands (färäsän'), low, sandy archipelago in Red Sea, off Asir coast, W of Qizan, belonging to Saudi Arabia. Consists of 2 large and many smaller isls.; the largest is 35 mi. long. Petroleum deposits. Once sought by Germany as a coaling station, they were occupied by British in First World War. Sometimes spelled Farsan and Farisan.

Fara San Martino (fä'rä sän märtē'nō), town (pop. 2,144), Chieti prov., Abruzzi e Molise, S central Italy, 14 mi. SSW of Lanciano; woolen mill, macaroni factory.

Farashdanga, India: see CHINSURA.

Faratsiho (färätsē'hōō), village, Tananarive prov., central Madagascar, in Ankaratra massif, 40 mi. SW of Tananarive; climatic resort (alt. 5,904 ft.); coffee, potatoes, sheep. R.C. and Protestant missions.

Faraulep (färou'lĕp), atoll (pop. 115), Yap dist., W Caroline Isls., W Pacific, 430 mi. E of Yap; 8°36'N 144°33'E; 2.25 mi. long, 1.5 mi. wide; 3 wooded islets on reef.

Farber, town (pop. 358), Audrain co., NE central Mo., near West Fork of Cuivre R., 18 mi. ENE of Mexico.

Farcet (fär'sĭt), town and parish (pop. 1,304), N Huntingdon, England, 3 mi. SSE of Peterborough; brickworks. Has Norman church.

Farciennes (färsyĕn'), town (pop. 11,041), Hainaut prov., S central Belgium, on Sambre R. and 5 mi. ENE of Charleroi; coal mining.

Far East, in the most restricted sense, term applied to the easternmost Asiatic countries along the Pacific Ocean, i.e., the Soviet Far East, Manchuria, Korea, China, and Japan. However, some or most of the countries of SE Asia (E of Afghanistan) and even central Asia are frequently included: Malay Archipelago (with Philippines and Indonesia), Malaya, Thailand, Indochina, Burma, India, Pakistan, Ceylon, Tibet, Bhutan, Nepal, Mongolia, and Eastern Siberia.

Far Eastern Territory, Rus. *Dal'ne-Vostochnyy Kray*, former administrative division of E Asiatic Russian SFSR, in the Soviet Far East (easternmost Siberia); ⊙ was Khabarovsk. Russian colonization of N part of region began in 17th cent. The left bank of the Amur, which had been ceded by Russia to China in 1689, was returned to Russia in 1858. The area bet. Ussuri R. and Sea of Japan was ceded by China in 1860. Following the Bolshevik revolution, much of the S part of the territory was occupied (1918) by U.S. and British troops (until 1920) and Japanese forces (until 1922) in connection with Allied intervention. Upon the withdrawal of the Japanese, the Far Eastern Republic, organized 1920 by local Bolsheviks and comprising Amur, Transbaikal, Kamchatka, and Maritime govts., joined the Russian SFSR as an oblast in 1922, was converted 1926 into a territory, and dissolved 1938 into Maritime and Khabarovsk territories.

Fareham (fâ'rŭm), urban district (1931 pop. 11,595; 1951 census 42,470), S Hampshire, England, at NW end of Portsmouth Harbour, 6 mi. NW of Portsmouth; railroad junction; agr. market, with leather tanneries, potteries, marine-equipment works, and flour mills.

Fareskur, Egypt: see FARISKUR.

Farewell, air base, S central Alaska, on N slope of Alaska Range, near Mt. McKinley Natl. Park, 160 mi. NW of Anchorage; 62°31'N 153°58'W.

Farewell, Cape, S extremity of Greenland, at S tip of Egger Isl. (17 mi. long, 13 mi. wide; rises to 2,900 ft.), one of the Cape Farewell Archipelago; 59°45'N 43°52'W.

Farewell, Cape, northwesternmost point of S.Isl., New Zealand; 40°30'S 172°48'E; lighthouse.

Farges-en-Septaine (färzh-ā-sĕptĕn'), village (pop. 359), Cher dept., central France, 12 mi. E of Bourges; has military camp and airport (Camp d'Avord).

Fargniers (färnyā'), residential town (pop. 3,628), Aisne dept., N France, at junction of Oise-Sambre Canal and Saint-Quentin Canal, opposite TERGNIER, and 13 mi. S of Saint-Quentin. Rebuilt in modern style after First World War.

Fargo (fär'gō). **1** Village (pop. c.275), Clinch co., S Ga., 26 mi. SSE of Homerville and on Suwannee R., at edge of Okefenokee Swamp; sawmilling. **2** City (pop. 38,256), ⊙ Cass co., E N.Dak., on Red River of the North and 190 mi. E of Bismarck; 46°53'N 96°45'W; alt. 900 ft.; largest city in state. Railroad junction and distribution center for automobiles, foodstuffs, farm machinery; manufactures include dairy products, fur coats, luggage, electrical apparatus, and steel, wool, and glass products. Seat of N.Dak. Agr. Col., Oak Grove Seminary, Concordia Conservatory of Music, a veterans' hosp., and St. Mary's Cathedral. Settled 1871, inc. 1875. **3** Town (pop. 318), Ellis co., NW Okla., 13 mi. WSW of Woodward, in livestock and grain area.

Fargues (färg), village (pop. 56), Gironde dept., SW France, 25 mi. SE of Bordeaux; sauterne wines. Also called Fargues-de-Langon.

Far Hills, borough (pop. 600), Somerset co., N central N.J., on North Branch of Raritan R. and 8 mi. N of Somerville, in country-estate area.

Faribault (fâ'rĭbō), county (□ 713; pop. 23,879), S Minn.; ⊙ Blue Earth. Agr. area drained by Blue Earth R. and bordering on Iowa. Corn, oats, barley, livestock, poultry. Food processing at Faribault. Formed 1855.

Faribault, city (pop. 16,028), ⊙ Rice co., SE Minn., on bluffs of Cannon and Straight rivers at their point of confluence, c.45 mi. S of St. Paul. Trade and industrial center for grain, livestock, and poultry area; food processing (dairy products, canned vegetables, flour, beverages); mfg. (agr. and household equipment, clothing, foundry products). State schools for feeble-minded and deaf and blind, 2 military academies, and girls' school are here. Fur-trading post established on site of city in 1826 by Alexander Faribault. Village platted 1854. Was early center for Episcopalian missionary activity.

Faridabad (fŭrē'däbäd), town (pop. 6,367), Gurgaon dist., SE Punjab, India, 18 mi. E of Gurgaon, 14 mi. SSE of New Delhi, near Agra Canal; local market for millet, wheat, sugar cane, cotton. Project to resettle refugees from W Pakistan and develop light consumer industries was begun in 1950.

Faridan, Iran: see DARAN.

Faridkot (fŭrēd'kōt), town (pop. 20,375), W Patiala and East Punjab States Union, India, 100 mi. WNW of Patiala; trades in gram, wheat, corn, cotton; mfg. of drugs and chemicals. Commercial col. Has 13th-cent. Rajput fort. Was ⊙ former princely state of Faridkot (□ 637; pop. 199,283) of Punjab States, since 1948 merged with Patiala and East Punjab States Union.

Faridnagar (fŭrēd'nŭgŭr), town (pop. 5,383), Meerut dist., NW Uttar Pradesh, India, 15 mi. SSW of Meerut; wheat, gram, jowar, sugar cane, oilseeds. Founded 16th cent.

Faridpur (fŭrēd'pŏŏr), district (□ 2,821; 1951 pop. 2,718,000), S central East Bengal, E Pakistan, in Ganges Delta; ⊙ Faridpur. Bounded N and NE by the Ganges (Padma R.), SE by Meghna R., W by Madhumati R.; drained by river arms of Ganges Delta. Alluvial soil (extensive marshes in S); rice, jute (trade center at Madaripur), oilseeds, sugar cane, wheat; date palms (N), betel palms (S). Goalundo (rice milling, ice and candle mfg.) is fish trade center. Oilseed milling, soap mfg., at Faridpur; cotton and oilcloth mfg., shipbuilding. Noted Moslem shrine at Faridpur. Figured in 17th-cent. revolt against Jahangir; invaded (17th–18th cent.) by Arakanese. Part of former Br. Bengal prov., India, until inc. 1947 into new Pakistan prov. of East Bengal, following creation of Pakistan.

Faridpur, town (pop. 10,480), Bareilly dist., N central Uttar Pradesh, India, 12 mi. SSE of Bareilly; sugar refining; wheat, rice, gram, sugar cane.

Faridpur, town (pop. 25,671), ⊙ Faridpur dist., S central East Bengal, E Pakistan, 31 mi. WSW of Dacca; rail terminus; oilseed milling; trades in rice, jute, oilseeds, sugar cane. Noted Moslem shrine.

Farila (fĕ'rĭlä"), Swedish *Färila*, village (pop. 979), Gavleborg co., E Sweden, on Ljusna R. and 7 mi. ESE of Ljusdal; grain, flax, potatoes, stock.

Farilhões Islands (fŭrēlyō'ĭsh), group of rocky islets in the Atlantic off coast of central Portugal, c.12 mi. NW of Peniche. Only Farilhão Grande (315 ft. high; lighthouse) is accessible; 39°29'N 9°33'W.

Farim (färēn'), town, N Port. Guinea, on Cacheu R. and 50 mi. NNE of Bissau; 12°21'N 13°35'W. Peanuts, coconuts, rubber, hardwoods; palm-oil mfg., tanning, cattle raising. Airfield. Binta, head of navigation (12 ft. draft), is 10 mi. downstream.

Fariman (färēmän'), town, Ninth Prov., in Khurasan, NE Iran, 40 mi. SSE of Meshed, on road to Afghan border.

Farina (fŭrī'nŭ), village, E central South Australia, 200 mi. N of Port Pirie, on Port Pirie–Alice Springs RR.; cattle.

Farina (fŭrī'nŭ), village (pop. 787), Fayette co., S central Ill., 20 mi. ESE of Vandalia, in agr. area; poultry, nursery products.

Faringdon (fă'-), town in Great Faringdon parish (pop. 2,702), NW Berkshire, England, near the Thames (13th-cent. bridge), 15 mi. WSW of Oxford in White Horse Vale; agr. market. Has 13th-cent. church, some Elizabethan inns, and 18th-cent. market hall. It was a residence of Saxon kings.

Farington, town and parish (pop. 2,860), W central Lancashire, England, 3 mi. S of Preston; cotton milling, agr. market in dairying, agr. region.

Farino (färēnō'), village (dist. pop. 288), W New Caledonia, 65 mi. NW of Nouméa; agr. products, livestock.

Fariones Point (färyō'nĕs), N cape of Lanzarote, Canary Isls., opposite Graciosa Isl.; 29°14'N 13°28'W.

Farisan Islands, Saudi Arabia: see FARASAN ISLANDS.

Farisita (fâ"rĭsē'tŭ), village (pop. c.125), Huerfano co., S Colo., on Huerfano R., in foothills of Sangre de Cristo Mts., and 17 mi. NW of Walsenburg; alt. 6,700 ft. Chapel of Penitentes near by.

Fariskur or **Fareskur** (fä'rĭskŏŏr), town (pop. 11,913; with suburbs 13,819), Daqahliya prov., Lower Egypt, on Damietta branch of the Nile just W of L. Manzala, on railroad, and 8 mi. SW of Damietta; fisheries.

Farjestaden (fĕr'yŭstä"dŭn), Swedish *Färjestaden*, village (pop. 572), Kalmar co., SE Sweden, W Oland isl., on Kalmar Sound of the Baltic, 4 mi. ESE of Kalmar (car ferry); port.

Farkasd (fär'käsht), Slovak *Farkašd*, town (pop. 5,038), S Slovakia, Czechoslovakia, near Vah R., on railroad and 19 mi. NNW of Komarno; agr. center (wheat, barley, sugar beets). Neded village is just SE.

Farkhad, Uzbek SSR: see BEGOVAT.

Farlam, village and parish (pop. 961), NE Cumberland, England, 10 mi. E of Carlisle; sheep grazing.

Farland Head, promontory on Firth of Forth, N Ayrshire, Scotland; 55°43'N 4°54'W.

Farley. 1 Town (pop. 745), Dubuque co., E Iowa, 17 mi. WSW of Dubuque; metal, leather, concrete, and dairy products; limestone quarries, gravel pit. **2** Town (pop. 98), Platte co., W Mo., on Missouri R. and 20 mi. NW of Kansas City.

Farlington, town and parish (pop. 5,672), SE Hampshire, England, on Langstone Harbour, 5 mi. NNE of Portsmouth; agr. market.

Farmer, town (pop. 114), Hanson co., SE S.Dak., 17 mi. E of Mitchell.

Farmer City, city (pop. 1,752), De Witt co., central Ill., 23 mi. SE of Bloomington, in agr. area; corn, wheat, soybeans, oats, livestock, poultry; dairy products; cheese factory. Inc. 1869.

Farmers, town (1940 pop. 236), Rowan co., NE Ky., on Licking R. and 39 mi. E of Paris; trade point in clay-mining and agr. area.

Farmers Branch, town (pop. 915), Dallas co., N Texas, just NW of Dallas.

Farmersburg. 1 Town (pop. 1,024), Sullivan co., SW Ind., 15 mi. S of Terre Haute; trading center in agr. (poultry, stock, grain), oil, and gas area; flour and lumber milling; bituminous-coal mining. Settled 1854, inc. 1871. **2** Town (pop. 263), Clayton co., NE Iowa, 8 mi. NNE of Elkader, in hog and dairying region; makes cheese.

Farmersville. 1 Village (1940 pop. 1,296), Tulare co., S central Calif., in San Joaquin Valley, just E of Visalia; orchards. **2** Village (pop. 485), Montgomery co., S central Ill., 23 mi. S of Springfield, in agr. and bituminous-coal area. **3** Village (pop. 587), Montgomery co., W Ohio, 13 mi. WSW of Dayton, in agr. area. **4** City (pop. 1,955), Collin co., N Texas, 36 mi. NE of Dallas; shipping, processing center in cotton area; candy making.

Farmerville, town (pop. 2,173), ⊙ Union parish, N La., 25 mi. NW of Monroe and on Bayou D'Arbonne (navigable); trade center for agr. area (cotton, corn); cotton gins, feed and lumber mills.

Farmingdale. 1 Town (pop. 1,449), Kennebec co., S Maine, on the Kennebec below Augusta, opposite Gardiner. Inc. 1852. **2** Borough (pop. 755), Monmouth co., E N.J., near Manasquan R., 7 mi. SE of Freehold; mfg. (musical instruments, concrete products, tomato products, condiments). **3** Village (pop. 4,492), Nassau co., SE N.Y., on W Long Isl., 10 mi. E of Mineola, in potato- and truck-growing area; aircraft factories; mfg. of clothing, food products, metal products, cement blocks, brick, life rafts. Seat of Long Isl. Agr. and Technical Inst. Bethpage State Park is just N. Settled 1695, inc. 1904.

Farmington. 1 Town (pop. 7,026), Hartford co., central Conn., on Farmington R. and 8 mi. WSW of Hartford. Includes Farmington village (1940 pop. 1,323) and industrial Unionville village (pop. 2,197), mfg. metal products, hardware, tools, felt, paper products, clothing. Many Colonial buildings, Miss Porter's school for girls here. State game sanctuary. Settled 1640. **2** Town (pop. 113), Kent co., W central Del., 4 mi. S of Harrington, in agr. area. **3** City (pop. 121), Oconee co., NE central Ga., 13 mi. S of Athens. **4** City (pop.

2,651), Fulton co., W central Ill., 21 mi. W of Peoria; bituminous-coal mines; agr. (grain, livestock); makes cement products. Laid out 1834, inc. 1857. **5** Town (pop. 899), Van Buren co., SE Iowa, near Mo. line, on Des Moines R. and 25 mi. NW of Keokuk; pickle processing. Coal mines, limestone quarries near by. State parks in vicinity. **6** Town (pop. 4,677), ⊙ Franklin co., W central Maine, on Sandy R. and 30 mi. NW of Augusta. Agr. trade center with canneries, light mfg. State teachers col. Birthplace (mus.) of Lillian Nordica here. Gateway to Rangeley Lakes and Dead R. areas. Settled 1781, inc. 1794. **7** City (pop. 2,325), Oakland co., SE Mich., 19 mi. NW of downtown Detroit and on the River Rouge. Residential; some mfg. (wines, dairy products, machine tools, cement blocks); fruit farming; nurseries. Settled 1824; inc. as village 1867, as city 1926. **8** Village (pop. 1,916), Dakota co., SE Minn., on small affluent of Mississippi R. and 20 mi. S of St. Paul; shipping point for dairy products in grain, potato, and livestock area; beverages. **9** City (pop. 4,490), ⊙ St. Francois co., E Mo., in the St. Francois Mts. near St. Francis R., 58 mi. S of St. Louis; flour mills, lead mines. State mental hosp. Settled 1799, laid out c.1822. **10** Town (pop. 3,454), including Farmington village (pop. 2,285), Strafford co., SE N.H., on Cocheco R. and 7 mi. NW of Rochester. Shoes (industry began 1835), metal products, monuments; agr.; resort. Henry Wilson b. here. Set off from Rochester 1797. **11** Town (pop. 3,637), San Juan co., NW N.Mex., on San Juan R., at mouth of Animas R., and 40 mi. SSW of Durango, Colo., in irrigated region; alt. c.5,300 ft. Oil-refining point; shipping center for near-by Navajo Indian Reservation; livestock, fruit, dairy products. Coal mines, gas and oil wells in vicinity. Aztec Ruins Natl. Monument is 13 mi. NE. Settled 1876, inc. 1901. **12** Village, Fayette co., SW Pa., 10 mi. SE of Uniontown. Just W is Fort Necessity Natl. Battlefield Site. **13** City (pop. 1,468), ⊙ Davis co., N Utah, on Great Salt L., 15 mi. N of Salt Lake City, just W of Wasatch Range in agr. area; alt. 4,302 ft. Settled 1848 by Mormons. Disastrous floods of 1923 and 1930 led to soil-conservation and reforestation project near by. **14** Town (pop. 239), Whitman co., SE Wash., 18 mi. NE of Colfax, near Idaho line; lumber, grain, fruit. **15** Town (pop. 824), Marion co., N W.Va., 17 mi. WNW of Fairmont, in agr., coal-mining, and oil-producing region.

Farmington River, coastal stream of W Liberia, flows c.75 mi. SSW, past Harbel, to the Atlantic at Marshall. Extensive rubber plantations on right bank. Navigable for 8 mi. below Harbel.

Farmington River, N Conn., formed at New Hartford by junction of West Branch (c.30 mi. long), rising in S Mass., and East Branch (c.14 mi. long); flows SE to Farmington, thence N and SE to the Connecticut above Hartford; c.40 mi. long. Water is supplied to Hartford and other places from Barkhamsted and East Branch reservoirs on East Branch and Nepaug Reservoir (c.3 mi. long), S of New Hartford on a short W tributary.

Farm Island (2 mi. long), S Ont., in St. Clair R., 7 mi. SW of Sarnia.

Farmland, town (pop. 943), Randolph co., E Ind., 13 mi. E of Muncie, in agr. area; mfg. (auto cranes, canned goods).

Farmoréah (färmôrā'ä), village, W Fr. Guinea, Fr. West Africa, near the Atlantic and Sierra Leone border, 45 mi. ESE of Conakry; bananas, palm oil, palm kernels.

Farmville. 1 Town (pop. 2,942), Pitt co., E N.C., 12 mi. W of Greenville; tobacco market, with warehouses and processing plants. Settled 1860; inc. 1872. **2** Town (pop. 4,375), ⊙ Prince Edward co., central Va., on Appomattox R. and 40 mi. E of Lynchburg; tobacco market; processing center for agr., timber area: lumber and grain milling, woodworking, dairying (butter), shoe and clothing mfg. Medicinal springs near by. Longwood Col. Hampden-Sydney Col. is 5 mi. SW, at Hampden Sydney. Inc. 1912.

Farnam, village (pop. 323), Dawson co., S central Nebr., 25 mi. WSW of Lexington; grain.

Farnams, Mass.: see CHESHIRE.

Farnborough (färn'bŭrŭ). **1** Urban district (1931 pop. 16,356; 1951 census 27,702), NE Hampshire, England, 8 mi. WNW of Guildford. Site of important aircraft research center and of Royal Air Force station; also includes part of Aldershot military camp. Here was home of Empress Eugenie of France, buried here with Napoleon III and the Prince Imperial, Louis, in crypt of church she built. Farnborough is also site of Benedictine Abbey of St. Michael. **2** Residential town and parish (pop. 4,373), NW Kent, England, 4 mi. SE of Bromley.

Farne Islands, Fearne Islands, Ferne Islands (all: färn), or **The Staples**, group of 26 islets, 2–5 mi. off NE coast of Northumberland, England, near Bamburgh. On principal isl., Farne Isl. (16 acres), St. Cuthbert and St. Aidan lived in 7th cent.; site of lighthouse (55°37'N 1°39'W). Longstone Isl. (NE) was scene of Grace Darling's heroism in the wreck of the *Forfarshire* in 1838, and is site of lighthouse (55°39'N 1°36'W).

Farneta (färnā'tä), village (pop. 318), Modena prov., Emilia-Romagna, N central Italy, near Dolo R., 3 mi. WSW of Montefiorino; hydroelectric plant.

Farnham (fär'nŭm), town (pop. 4,055), S Que., on Yamaska R. and 14 mi. E of St. Jean; railroad shops; mfg. of clothing, velvet, felt, industrial fabrics, linoleum; sugar refining, dairying. Site of tobacco experiment farm.

Farnham. 1 Town, Buckingham, England: see SLOUGH. **2** Residential urban district (1931 pop. 18,297; 1951 census 23,911), W Surrey, England, on the Wey and 10 mi. W of Guildford; agr. market in hop-growing region. Has 12th–17th-cent. castle of bishops of Winchester, 12th-cent. church, and several old inns. In urban dist. are Wrecclesham (SW), WAVERLEY (ESE). Aldershot is 3 mi. NE.

Farnham, village (pop. 396), Erie co., W N.Y., near L. Erie, 15 mi. NE of Dunkirk; canned foods.

Farnham, Mount (11,342 ft.), SE B.C., in Selkirk Mts., 65 mi. SW of Banff; 50°29'N 116°30'W.

Farnham Royal, residential town and parish (pop. 1,656), S Buckingham, England, 2 mi. NNW of Slough.

Farnhamville, town (pop. 399), Calhoun co., central Iowa, 20 mi. SW of Fort Dodge; feed.

Farningham, town and parish (pop. 1,579), NW Kent, England, on Darent R. and 5 mi. S of Dartford; paper milling. Has 13th-cent. church and ruins of manor house, residence of Capt. Bligh of the *Bounty*. Roman remains have been found here.

Farnley and Wortley (wûrt'lē), town (pop. 18,576) in Leeds county borough, West Riding, S central Yorkshire, England, on Aire R. and just SW of Leeds; woolen milling, leather tanning; mfg. of clothing, chemicals.

Farnley Tyas, England: see THURSTONLAND AND FARNLEY TYAS.

Farnumsville, Mass.: see GRAFTON.

Farnworth, municipal borough (1931 pop. 28,717; 1951 census 28,614), S Lancashire, England, just S of Bolton; cotton spinning and weaving; mfg. of chemicals, paint, soap, bottles, textile machinery. Has 14th-cent. church. Includes town of STONECLOUGH.

Faro (fä'rōō), city (pop. 844), westernmost Pará, Brazil, on left bank of Jamundá R. (Amazonas border) above its mouth on the Amazon, and 90 mi. W of Óbidos.

Faro (fä'rōō), district (□ 1,958; pop. 317,628), southernmost Portugal, coextensive with ALGARVE prov.; ⊙ Faro.

Faro, southernmost city (pop. 19,695) of Portugal, ⊙ Faro dist. and Algarve prov., on an inlet of the Atlantic, near Cape Santa Maria, and 135 mi. SSE of Lisbon; exports fruit (especially dried figs and almonds) and cork; tuna and sardine canning, cork processing, basketmaking, mfg. of flour products, olive oil, pottery, liqueur. Episcopal see since 1577. Recaptured from Moors by Alfonso III in 1249. Prosperous until 16th cent. Suffered severe earthquakes in 1722 and 1755.

Faro (fō'rū"), Swedish *Fårö*, island (□ 44; pop. 934), Gotland co., SE Sweden, in the Baltic just NE of Gotland isl., from which it is separated by 2-mi.-wide Farosund, 35 mi. NE of Visby; 57°56'N 19°10'E. Isl. is 10 mi. long, 2–8 mi. wide; with indented coastline. Agr. (rye, oats, potatoes); sheep raising. Faro village is on E coast. Lighthouse at NE extremity.

Faro, Punta del (pōōn'tä dĕl fä'rô), or **Cape Peloro** (pĕlô'rô), anc. *Pelorum* or *Peloris*, NE extremity of Sicily, E of Peloritani Mts., at NW end of Strait of Messina; 38°16'N 15°39'E. Near by is whirlpool of Garofalo, the supposed Charybdis of anc. legend.

Faroe Islands, N Atlantic: see FAEROE ISLANDS.

Faron, Mont (färō'), fortified hill (1,909 ft.) overlooking Toulon, Var dept., SE France, and its bay just S.

Farosund (fō"rüsŭnd'), Swedish *Fårösund*, village (pop. 1,321), Gotland co., SE Sweden, NE Gotland isl., on Farosund, a strait (6 mi. long, 1–2 mi. wide) of the Baltic, opposite Faro isl., 30 mi. ENE of Visby; stone quarrying; grain, flax, potatoes, sugar beets.

Farquhar Islands (fär'kûr, -kwûr), outlying dependency (pop. c.120) of the Seychelles, in Indian Ocean, 200 mi. NE of N tip of Madagascar and 525 mi. SE of Mahé Isl. (in Seychelles proper); 10°10'S 51°10'E. Copra; fisheries. Coral atoll, c.3 mi. long. Formerly a dependency of Mauritius, isls. were transferred (1922) to Seychelles. Near by are Cerf, Providence, and St. Pierre isls.

Farr, agr. village and parish (pop. 1,769), N Sutherland, Scotland, on the Atlantic, 10 mi. ENE of Tongue. Market town and tourist resort of Bettyhill is 2 mi. SW.

Farra d'Isonzo (fär'rä dēzōn'tsō), village (pop. 1,125), Gorizia prov., Friuli–Venezia Giulia, NE Italy, near Isonzo R., 5 mi. SW of Gorizia.

Farragut, town (pop. 495), Fremont co., SW Iowa, 7 mi. SW of Shenandoah, in agr. area (grain, livestock, poultry).

Farrah, Afghanistan: see FARAH.

Farrar (fă'rûr), town (pop. 30), Jasper co., central Ga., 12 mi. NNE of Monticello.

Farrar River, Scotland: see BEAULY RIVER.

Farrell (fă'rŭl), city (pop. 13,644), Mercer co., W Pa., on Shenango R. just S of Sharon; railroad and industrial center; steel. Inc. as borough 1901, as city 1932.

Farris Lake, Norway: see LARVIK.

Far Rockaway, SE N.Y., a shore-resort and residential section of S Queens borough of New York city, at base of Rockaway Peninsula.

Farroupilha (färōpē'lyŭ), city (pop. 1,642), NE Rio Grande do Sul, Brazil, on railroad and 10 mi. W of Caxias do Sul; winegrowing; flax. Colonized by Italians in 19th cent. Until 1934, Nova Vicenza.

Farrukhabad (fŭr"ŏŏkhäbäd'), district (□ 1,642; pop. 955,377), central Uttar Pradesh, India; ⊙ Fatehgarh. On Ganges Plain and Ganges-Jumna Doab (W); drained by the Ramganga; irrigated by Upper Ganges Canal and a distributary of Lower Ganges Canal. Agr. (wheat, gram, jowar, corn, barley, oilseeds, pearl millet, potatoes, sugar cane, tobacco, cotton); perfume mfg. Main centers: Farrukhabad (with Fatehpur), KANAUJ, Kaimganj.

Farrukhabad, city (pop., including joint municipality of FATEHGARH, 69,418), Farrukhabad dist., central Uttar Pradesh, India, near the Ganges, 80 mi. NW of Cawnpore; rail and road junction; trade center (grain, oilseeds, potatoes, sugar cane, tobacco, mangoes, cotton); mfg. of brassware and noted calico prints. Founded c.1714 by a nawab of Farrukhabad. Ruined tombs of nawabs just N. Anc. Buddhist ruins (including Asokan pillar capital) 19 mi. WSW, at village of Sankisa, anc. *Sankasya;* site of the Buddha's descent from heaven of the 33 gods; one of 8 great Buddhist pilgrimage sites.

Farrukhabad Branch, India: see GANGES CANALS.

Farrukhnagar (fŭr'ŏŏkhnŭg"ŭr). **1** Town (pop. 5,122), Gurgaon dist., SE Punjab, India, 13 mi. W of Gurgaon, near rail spur terminus; trades in salt, cotton, millet, oilseeds. Sometimes spelled Farukhnagar. **2** Town (pop. 2,754), Meerut dist., NW Uttar Pradesh, India, 10 mi. NE of Delhi; wheat, gram, jowar, sugar cane, oilseeds.

Fars (färs), anc. *Persis*, former province of S Iran; ⊙ was Shiraz. Situated on the Persian Gulf, it is bounded W by Khuzistan, N by Isfahan and Yezd, and E by Kerman; coextensive with ridge-and-valley section of central Zagros ranges, it includes Niriz L. basin and is watered by Kur and Pulvar rivers. Has 2 climatic belts, the hot coastal region and the cool mtn. section. Agr. in valleys and inland basins: grain, cotton, opium, dates, fruit, wine, saffron, gums; sheep raising. Sugar-beet cultivation and refining on Marvdasht plain. Main centers (carpet weaving, cotton and wool spinning) are Shiraz, Niriz, Kazerun, and Abadeh; the chief ports, Bushire and Lingeh. Pop. is largely tribal (Qashqai and Khamseh tribes). Known in anc. times as Persis, the region is commonly identified with the original home of the Persians and contained the early Persian capitals of PASARGADAE and PERSEPOLIS. It was formerly also called Farsistan. Since 1938, Fars and its SE subregion, Laristan, constitute Iran's Seventh Province (□ 75,476; pop. 1,403,586), to which the name Fars is commonly applied.

Farsala, Greece: see PHARSALA.

Farsan Islands, Saudi Arabia: see FARASAN ISLANDS.

Farshut (fär'shōōt'), town (pop. 15,721; with suburbs, 23,225), Qena prov., Upper Egypt, on railroad and 5 mi. W of Nag Hammadi; cereals, sugar, dates.

Farsistan, Iran: see FARS.

Farsley, former urban district (1931 pop. 6,158), West Riding, SW central Yorkshire, England, 4 mi. ENE of Bradford; woolen milling. Inc. 1937 in Pudsey.

Farso (fär'sû), Dan. *Farsø*, town (pop. 1,338), Aalborg amt, N Jutland, Denmark, 28 mi. SW of Aalborg; machinery mfg.

Farsund (fär'sōōn), town (pop. 1,820), Vest-Agder co., S Norway, port on inlet of North Sea, on SE Lista peninsula, 15 mi. SSE of Flekkefjord; exports salmon, mackerel, lobster, fish products; has tree nurseries. Active shipping center in early 19th cent.; rebuilt after fire in 1901.

Fartak, Ras (räs' färtăk'), cape of Eastern Aden Protectorate, on Arabian Sea, at entrance to Gulf of Aden; 15°38'N 52°14'E.

Farther Pomerania, region, Europe: see POMERANIA.

Fartura (färtōō'rŭ), city (pop. 1,809), S São Paulo, Brazil, near Paraná border, 35 mi. SE of Ourinhos; tobacco, coffee, cotton, grain.

Farum (fä'rōōm), town (pop. 1,430), Frederiksborg amt, Zealand, Denmark, 9 mi. SSE of Hillerod; pottery, cement.

Farwell. 1 Village (pop. 694), Clare co., central Mich., 17 mi. NNW of Mt. Pleasant and on Tobacco R., in lake and farm area; hunting, fishing. **2** Village (pop. 112), Pope co., W Minn., 13 mi. NW of Glenwood; dairy products. **3** Village, Howard co., Nebr.: see POSEN. **4** Village (pop. c.1,000), ⊙ Parmer co., NW Texas, on Llano Estacado, on state line contiguous to Texico, N.Mex., and 10 mi. E of Clovis, N.Mex.; market and shipping point in wheat and cattle region.

Fas, Fr. Morocco: see FEZ.

Fasa (fäsä'), town (1940 pop. 9,907), Seventh Prov., in Fars, S Iran, 85 mi. ESE of Shiraz; grain, sugar beets, cotton, opium, rice, tobacco.

Fasano (fäzä′nô), town (pop. 13,024), Brindisi prov., Apulia, S Italy, 8 mi. SSE of Monopoli; agr. trade (cereals, vegetables, wine, olive oil); soap mfg.

Fasher, El (ĕl fä′shur), town (pop. 23,650), ⊙ Darfur prov., W Anglo-Egyptian Sudan, 500 mi. WSW of Khartoum; 13°37′N 25°20′E. Caravan and trade center (gum arabic) on auto route from Khartoum to Ft. Lamy (Fr. Equatorial Africa). Airfield.

Fashn, El, or **Al-Fashn** (both: ĕl fäsh′ŭn), town (pop. 18,780; with suburbs, 21,314), Minya prov., Upper Egypt, on W bank of the Nile, on Ibrahimiya Canal, on railroad, and 50 mi. NNE of Minya; cotton ginning, woolen and sugar milling; cereals. Sometimes spelled Feshn.

Fashoda, Anglo-Egyptian Sudan: see KODOK.

Fasnia (fäs′nyä), town (pop. 1,605), Tenerife, Canary Isls., 20 mi. SW of Santa Cruz de Tenerife; cereals, tomatoes, grapes; flour milling.

Fast Castle, ruin of anc. fortress, E Berwick, Scotland, on North Sea, 3 mi. WNW of St. Abb's Head; former stronghold of earls of Home and of Logan of Restalrig. It is original of "Wolf's Crag" in Scott's *The Bride of Lammermoor.*

Fastnet Rock (făs′nĕt, făst′–, –nĭt), islet in the Atlantic, off SW Co. Cork, Ireland, 18 mi. SW of Skibbereen and 4 mi. SW of Cape Clear; site of 160-ft.-high lighthouse (51°23′N 9°36′W), most southerly point of Ireland.

Fastov (fä′stŭf), city (1926 pop. 14,208), W Kiev oblast, Ukrainian SSR, 35 mi. SW of Kiev; rail junction; machine mfg., woodworking. Destroyed in civil war (1919–20).

Fataki (fätä′kē), village, Eastern Prov., NE Belgian Congo, 70 mi. NE of Irumu, in gold-mining area; coffee plantations, vegetable farms, cinchona plantations in vicinity. R.C. mission with school for European children, hosp. for Europeans. Sanatorium.

Fatarella (fätärĕ′lyä), town (pop. 1,983), Tarragona prov., NE Spain, 8 mi. NNE of Gandesa; olive-oil processing, flour milling; almonds, wine.

Fate, city (pop. 141), Rockwall co., NE Texas, 25 mi. NE of Dallas, in agr. area.

Fatehabad (fŭtä′häbäd″), village, Eastern Prov., E Afghanistan, 14 mi. WSW of Jalalabad and on road to Kabul.

Fatehabad (fŭtā′häbäd). **1** Town, Hyderabad state, India: see DHARUR, Bir dist. **2** Village, W Madhya Bharat, India, 13 mi. SSW of Ujjain. Here Mogul army under Aurangzeb defeated Rajputs in 1658. Rail junction just S. **3** Village, Hissar dist., S Punjab, India, 29 mi. NNW of Hissar; millet, gram; leather goods. **4** Town (pop. 5,101), Agra dist., W Uttar Pradesh, India, 21 mi. SE of Agra; trades in pearl millet, gram, wheat, barley, oilseeds.

Fatehganj Sharki (fŭtā′gŭnj shär′kē) or **Fatehganj East**, town (pop. 2,406), Bareilly dist., N central Uttar Pradesh, India, on tributary of Ramganga and 23 mi. SSE of Bareilly; wheat, rice, gram, sugar cane, oilseeds.

Fatehgarh (fŭtā′gŭr), city (pop., including joint municipality of FARRUKHABAD and cantonment, 69,418), ⊙ Farrukhabad dist., central Uttar Pradesh, India, on the Ganges and 3 mi. ESE of Farrukhabad. Fort built c.1714 by a nawab of Farrukhabad; besieged by Mahrattas in 1751. Scene of Br. massacre in Sepoy Rebellion of 1857.

Fatehgarh Sahib (fŭtā′gŭr sŭhēb′), district, Patiala and East Punjab States Union, India.

Fatehjang (fŭtā′jŭng), town (pop. 5,919), Attock dist., NW Punjab, W Pakistan, 21 mi. SE of Campbellpur; local market center (wheat, cloth fabrics). Also spelled Fatahjang.

Fatehnagar (fŭtā′nŭgŭr), village, S Rajasthan, India, on railroad and 30 mi. NE of Udaipur; cotton ginning, match mfg.

Fatehpur (fŭtā′poor), district (□ 1,621; pop. 806,944), S Uttar Pradesh, India; ⊙ Fatehpur. On Ganges Plain and Ganges-Jumna Doab; irrigated by Lower Ganges Canal. Agr. (gram, barley, rice, jowar, wheat, oilseeds, sugar cane, pearl millet, cotton); mango and mahua groves. Main towns: Fatehpur, Bindki, Khaga.

Fatehpur. 1 Town (pop. 23,253), NE Rajasthan, India, 90 mi. NNW of Jaipur; rail spur terminus; market center (millet, wool, hides, salt); hand-loom weaving, pottery making. **2** Town (pop. 7,160), Bara Banki dist., central Uttar Pradesh, India, 17 mi. N of Nawabganj; hand-loom cotton weaving; trades in rice, gram, wheat, oilseeds, corn. Large imambarah. **3** Town (pop. 27,436), ⊙ Fatehpur dist., S Uttar Pradesh, India, 45 mi. SE of Cawnpore; road junction; trades in grains, oilseeds, ghee; mfg. of ornamental whips. Has 18th-cent. mosque and tomb. Large 18th-cent. *baradari* (Mogul summer mansion) 30 mi. WSW, at Kora village; flourished under Moguls.

Fatehpur Sikri (sē′krē), town (pop. 8,196), Agra dist., W Uttar Pradesh, India, 22 mi. WSW of Agra. Formerly an important city; founded by Akbar in 1569, it was ⊙ Mogul empire until 1584, when ⊙ was moved to Lahore. Some of most famous early Mogul buildings extant are here. Jami Masjid (Great Mosque), with ornate marble mausoleum of Salim Chishti (noted Moslem saint), is entered through the great Buland Darwaza (Gate of Victory). Other main buildings, N of the Jami Masjid, include palaces of Jodh Bai and Birbal, the Panch Mahal, the emperor's private audience hall, and a large serai. In 1527, Babar defeated Rajput confederacy just N of town.

Fatezh (fŭtyĕsh′), city (1926 pop. 4,534), NW Kursk oblast, Russian SFSR, 28 mi. NW of Kursk; hemp processing, flour milling. Orchards near by. Chartered 1779.

Fati (fä′dä′), Mandarin *Hua-ti* (hwä′dē′), SW suburb of Canton, Kwangtung prov., China, on right bank of Canton R., opposite W suburbs of Canton; terminus (Shekwaitong station) of Canton-Samshui RR; shipyards, coaling station. Has noted flower gardens. Sometimes called Fangtsun.

Fatick (fä′tĕk), town (pop. c.6,600), W Senegal, Fr. West Africa, on affluent of Saloum R. and 70 mi. ESE of Dakar; peanut-growing center.

Fatih (fätē′), SW section (pop. 181,025) of ISTANBUL, Turkey in Europe.

Fátima (fä′tĭmu, Port. fä′tēmu), village, Santarém dist., central Portugal, 13 mi. SE of Leiria. A place of pilgrimage, regarded as the "Lourdes of Portugal" since 1917.

Fatima, Wadi, or **Wadi Fatimah** (wä′dē fä′tĭmu), intermittent river valley in central Hejaz, Saudi Arabia, extends 100 mi. to Red Sea just S of Jidda; agr. development project.

Fatkong (fät′gông′), Mandarin *Fokang* (fŭ′gäng′), town (pop. 1,039), ⊙ Fatkong co. (pop. 78,912), central Kwangtung prov., China, 60 mi. N of Canton; tin-mining center. Also spelled Fukang.

Fatoto or **Fattoto** (fätō′tō), town (pop. 387), Upper River div., E Gambia, on left bank of Gambia R. (wharf and ferry) and 22 mi. ENE of Basse; fishing; peanuts, beeswax, hides and skins.

Fatra, mountains, Czechoslovakia: see GREATER FATRA; LESSER FATRA.

Fatsa (fätsä′), anc. *Phadisana*, village (pop. 3,888), Ordu prov., N Turkey, on Black Sea, 19 mi. W of Ordu; millet, corn.

Fatshan, China: see NAMHOI.

Fatsissio, Japan: see HACHIJO-JIMA.

Fatsizio, Japan: see HACHIJO-JIMA.

Fattatenda (fätätĕn′dä), village (pop. 17), Upper River div., E Gambia, on right bank of Gambia R. (wharf) and 15 mi. NE of Basse; peanuts, beeswax, hides and skins. A Br. trading post dating from early 18th cent.

Fatu Hiva or **Fatuhiva** (fä′tōō hē′vä), volcanic island (□ c.25; pop. 224), southernmost of Marquesas Isls., Fr. Oceania, S Pacific; 10°28′S 138°39′W; 8 mi. long. Fertile valleys; mtn. range with highest peak 3,675 ft. Oomoa is main harbor. Formerly Magdalena or Madeleine.

Fatu Huku or **Fatuhuku** (fä′tōō hōō′kōō), uninhabited rocky islet, Marquesas Isls., Fr. Oceania, S Pacific, 15 mi. N of Hiva Oa; rises to 1,180 ft. Formerly Hood Isl.

Fatwa (fŭt′wŭ), town (pop. 19,411), Patna dist., N central Bihar, India, on Ganges R. and 12 mi. SE of Patna; rail junction (spur to Islampur, 25 mi. SSW); rice, gram, wheat, oilseeds, barley; silk weaving.

Fau, Egypt: see FAW.

Faucigny (fōsēnyē′), valley of Arve R., Haute-Savoie dept., SE France, extending c.40 mi. SE from Geneva to the Sallanches basin. Separated from Chamonix valley (E) by Arve R. gorge at Servoz. Fertile agr. tracts (wine, fruits, cereals) threatened by floods. Watchmaking (Cluses and Annemasse). Historically, a prov. of Kingdom of Sardinia (⊙ Bonneville). Ruins of medieval castle of Faucigny at Contamine-sur-Arve.

Faucille, Col de la (kôl dù lä fōsē′), chief pass (alt. 4,340 ft.) of the E Jura, in Ain dept., E France, on the Geneva-Besançon road, 3 mi. NW of Gex; winter sports (hotels); splendid view of Mont Blanc (50 mi. SE) across L. Geneva.

Faucilles, Monts (mõ fōsē′), foothills of the Vosges, E France, forming an arc across Vosges dept., bet. Remiremont (E) and Lamarche (W); rise to 1,650 ft. Watershed bet. the Meuse and Moselle (draining N) and Saône R. (flowing S). Continued SW by Plateau of Langres. Numerous mineral springs (Plombières-les-Bains, Vittel, Contrexéville).

Faucogney (fōkônyā′), village (pop. 581), Haute-Saône dept., E France, at foot of the Vosges, 12 mi. NNE of Lure; cotton spinning; embroidery. Manganese mines near by.

Faugères (fōzhâr′), village (pop. 359), Hérault dept., S France, in Monts Garrigues, 16 mi. N of Béziers; distilling. Marble quarries.

Fauglia (fäōō′lyä), village (pop. 1,062), Pisa prov., Tuscany, central Italy, 10 mi. E of Leghorn, in grape- and olive-growing region.

Fauldhouse (fôld′hous), village in Whitburn parish, SW West Lothian, Scotland, 6 mi. WSW of West Calder; shale-oil mining.

Faulhorn (foul′hôrn), peak (8,806 ft.) in Bernese Alps, S central Switzerland, 7 mi. E of Interlaken.

Faulk (fôk), county (□ 997; pop. 4,752), N central S.Dak.; ⊙ Faulkton. Agr. area watered by artificial lakes and intermittent streams. Livestock, wheat. Formed 1873.

Faulkner (fôk′nŭr), county (□ 656; pop. 25,289), central Ark.; ⊙ Conway. Bounded SE by Arkansas R.; drained by small Cadron Creek. Agr. (cotton, livestock, poultry; dairy products); timber. Mfg. at Conway. Formed 1873.

Faulkton (fôk′tŭn), city (pop. 837), ⊙ Faulk co., N central S.Dak., 45 mi. SW of Aberdeen and on branch of James R.; livestock, grain. Near by is L. Faulkton, artificial lake used for recreation.

Faulquemont (fōkmõ′), Ger. *Falkenberg* (fäl′kŭnbĕrk), village (pop. 918), Moselle dept., NE France, on the Nied and 15 mi. SW of Forbach; coal.

Faunsdale, town (pop. 199), Marengo co., W Ala., 14 mi. ESE of Demopolis; farming.

Fauquembergues (fōkābârg′), agr. village (pop. 800), Pas-de-Calais dept., N France, on the Aa and 12 mi. SSW of Saint-Omer.

Fauquier (fôkēr′), county (□ 660; pop. 21,248), N Va.; ⊙ Warrenton. Mainly in the piedmont, with part of Blue Ridge in NW; bounded SW by Rappahannock R.; drained by Little R. Rich agr. area (wheat, forage crops, fruit, tobacco); noted for stock raising (notably horses, in Warrenton section) and dairying. Oak, hickory, pine timber. Formed 1759.

Faura (fou′rä), town (pop. 1,848), Valencia prov., E Spain, 3 mi. N of Sagunto; cereals, wine, oranges.

Faure (fô′rē), village, SW Cape Prov., U. of So. Afr., near False Bay, 20 mi. ESE of Cape Town; fruit, vegetables, viticulture. Just S is important Mohammedan shrine, tomb of Sheik Josef, 17th-cent. Javanese prince, exiled to Cape Town by the Dutch.

Faurei (fuŏorā′), Rum. *Făurei*, village (pop. 563), Galati prov., SE Rumania, 37 mi. SW of Braila; rail junction.

Fauresmith (four′smĭth), town (pop. 1,761), SW Orange Free State, U. of So. Afr., 70 mi. SW of Bloemfontein; alt. 4,538 ft.; stock, grain, feed crops. Site of govt. botanical reserve, scene of dry-farming experiments. Near by are Jagersfontein diamond and gold deposits.

Faurndau (fou′ŭrndou), village (pop. 3,680), Württemberg, Germany, after 1945 in Württemberg-Baden, on the Fils and 2 mi. W of Göppingen; grain, cattle. Has 13th-cent. church.

Fauro, Solomon Isls.: see SHORTLAND ISLANDS.

Fauske (fou′skù), agr. village (pop. 952; canton pop. 7,953), Nordland co., N central Norway, on Skjerstad Fjord, 25 mi. E of Bodo, in marble- and slate-quarrying region. In canton are SULITJELMA and FINNEID villages.

Faust (fôst), village, Franklin co., N N.Y., just NW of Tupper Lake village, on Raquette Pond, in resort region of the Adirondacks.

Fauville-en-Caux (fōvēl′-ā-kō′), village (pop. 1,141), Seine-Inférieure dept., N France, 24 mi. NE of Le Havre; flax, grain, cattle.

Favaios (fuvä′yoosh), agr. village (pop. 1,726), Vila Real dist., N Portugal, 13 mi. ESE of Vila Real; winegrowing.

Favara (fävä′rä), town (pop. 21,496), Agrigento prov., S Sicily, 4 mi. E of Agrigento; tanning extracts. Has late-13th-cent. castle. Many sulphur mines near by.

Favareta (fävärä′tä), village (pop. 1,403), Valencia prov., E Spain, 8 mi. ESE of Alcira; rice, oranges, olive oil, peanuts.

Faventia, Italy: see FAENZA.

Faverges (fävârzh′), village (pop. 1,832), Haute-Savoie dept., SE France, in the Bauges, 7 mi. NW of Albertville; mfg. (wax, cheese, silk fabrics), liqueur distilling.

Faverney (fävûrnā′), village (pop. 1,102), Haute-Saône dept., E France, 11 mi. NNW of Vesoul; tanning, hand embroidering. Its 13th-14th-cent. church was damaged in Second World War.

Faversham (fă′vûrshùm), municipal borough (1931 pop. 10,091; 1951 census 12,294), N Kent, England, 9 mi. WNW of Canterbury and on small, navigable inlet of The Swale. Has oyster fisheries, managed by anc. guild; agr. market, with breweries and brick and concrete works. Church contains tombs of King Stephen, his wife Mathilda, and son. There are remains of 12th-cent. abbey, founded by King Stephen. Town was a seat of Saxon kings; Æthelstan held a *witenagemot* here. James II was captured here on his 1st attempt to flee to France.

Favignana (fävēnyä′nä), anc. *Aegusa*, largest island (□ 7.5; pop. 4,763) of Egadi Isls., in Mediterranean Sea off W Sicily, 11 mi. SW of Trapani; 6 mi. long, 3 mi. wide; rises to 991 ft. Major tunny fisheries. Agr. (grapes, citrus fruit). Chief port, Favignana (pop. 4,455), on N coast; tunny canneries. Site of penal colony.

Favoriten (fävōrē′tùn), district (□ 8; pop. 104,947) of Vienna, Austria, 3 mi. S of city center; mfg. of locomotives.

Favourable Lake, village, NW Ont., in Patricia dist., near Favourable L. (16 mi. long, 4 mi. wide); 52°50′N 93°38′W; gold mining.

Faw or **Faw Qibli** (fou′ kĭb′lē), village (pop. 10,486), Qena prov., Upper Egypt, on railroad and 4 mi. WSW of Dishna; cereals, sugar, dates. Also Fau.

Fa'w, Iraq: see FAO.

Fawcett, Mount (6,213 ft.), on Alaska-B.C. border, in Coast Range, 35 mi. E of Wrangell; 56°33′N 131°28′W.

Fawley, town and parish (pop. 3,394), S Hampshire, England, on Southampton Water and 6 mi. SSE of Southampton; petroleum refinery, oil-storage tanks. Church dates from Norman times.

Fawn Grove, borough (pop. 397), York co., S Pa., 23 mi. SE of York, on Md. border.

Faxa Bay (fäk'sä), Icelandic *Faxaflói* (fäk'säflō"ē) or *Faxa Fjörður* (fyûr"dhür), inlet (30 mi. long, 50 mi. wide at mouth) of Atlantic, SW Iceland, bet. Snaefellsnes (N) and Reykjanes (S) peninsulas; 64°–64°49'N 21°23'–24°4'W. Reykjavik and Akranes are on SE shore. Bay extends 2 arms (E): Hval Fjord, Icelandic *Hvalfjörður* (hwäl'fyûr"-dhür) (20 mi. long), and Borgar Fjord, Icelandic *Borgarfjörður* (bôr'gärfyûr"dhür) (15 mi. long). Hval Fjord is site of several whale factories; was Allied naval station in Second World War. Faxa Bay banks are one of Iceland's best fishing grounds.

Faxina, Brazil: see ITAPEVA.

Faxon. 1 Town (pop. 135), Comanche co., SW Okla., 14 mi. SW of Lawton, in agr. area; cotton ginning. **2** Village (pop. 2,984, with adjacent Kenmar), Lycoming co., N central Pa.

Faya, Fr. Equatorial Africa: see LARGEAU.

Fayal Island, Azores: see FAIAL ISLAND.

Fayansovy or **Fayansovyy,** (fīän'sŭvē), town (1940 pop. over 500), SW Kaluga oblast, Russian SFSR, 2 mi. E of Kirov; rail junction; metalworks, porcelain mfg.

Faydia, Cyrenaica: see FAIDIA.

Fayence (fāyäs'), village (pop. 829), Var dept., SE France, 12 mi. WSW of Grasse, in flower-growing area; mfg. (corks, perfume essences, olive oil), winegrowing.

Fayet, Le, Haute-Savoie dept., France: see SAINT-GERVAIS-LES-BAINS.

Fayette (fāĕt', fā'ĭt). **1** County (□ 627; pop. 19,388), W Ala.; ⊙ Fayette. Agr. region drained by Sipsey and North rivers, crossed (N–S) by fall line. Cotton, corn, livestock; lumber milling. Deposits of coal, sandstone, fuller's earth. Formed 1824. **2** County (□ 199; pop. 7,978), W central Ga.; ⊙ Fayetteville. Bounded E by Flint R. Piedmont agr. (cotton, corn, truck, pecans, peaches), dairy, and livestock area. Formed 1821. **3** County (□ 718; pop. 24,582), S central Ill.; ⊙ Vandalia. Agr. area (corn, wheat; dairy products; poultry, livestock), with petroleum and natural-gas wells. Mfg. (shoes, roofing, brick); oil refineries. Drained by Kaskaskia R. Formed 1821. **4** County (□ 215; pop. 23,391), E Ind.; ⊙ Connersville. Agr. area (livestock, grain). Mfg. at Connersville. Drained by Whitewater R. Formed 1818. **5** County (□ 728; pop. 28,294), NE Iowa; ⊙ West Union. Prairie agr. area (hogs, cattle, poultry, corn, oats) drained by Volga, Maquoketa, and Turkey rivers, and by Buffalo Creek; limestone quarries, sand and gravel pits. Formed 1837. **6** County (□ 280; pop. 100,746), central Ky.; ⊙ LEXINGTON. Bounded S by Kentucky R.; drained by Elkhorn Creek and its North Branch and by several other creeks. Gently rolling upland agr. area, in heart of BLUEGRASS region; has many horse farms famous for their thoroughbred race and saddle horses. Agr. (burley tobacco, cattle, lambs, bluegrass seed, grain); limestone quarries. Mfg. at Lexington, an important commercial center. Formed 1780 from old Kentucky co. in Va. **7** County (□ 406; pop. 22,554), S central Ohio; ⊙ Washington Court House. Drained by Paint Creek, and small Sugar and Rattlesnake creeks. Agr. (livestock; dairy products; grain, fruit); mfg. at Washington Court House; limestone quarries. Formed 1810. **8** County (□ 800; pop. 189,899), SW Pa.; ⊙ UNIONTOWN. Coal-mining area; bounded W by Monongahela R.; drained by Youghiogheny R. Laurel Hill forms part of SE border; Chestnut Ridge crosses center of co. NE–SW. First settled 1752 by Virginians. Whisky Rebellion put down here in 1794. Home of Albert Gallatin at New Geneva. Cumberland Road passed through co. Bituminous coal, natural gas, limestone; mfg. (coke, whiskey, glass, chemicals, paper products); dairying. Formed 1783. **9** County (□ 704; pop. 27,535), SW Tenn.; ⊙ Somerville. Bounded S by Miss.; drained by Loosahatchie and Wolf rivers. Cotton, livestock, corn; lumber milling; wood products. Formed 1824. **10** County (□ 936; pop. 24,176), S central Texas; ⊙ La Grange. Drained by Colorado R. and headwaters of Lavaca and Navidad rivers. A leading Texas poultry-raising co.; livestock (cattle, horses, mules, sheep, goats), dairying, agr. (cotton, corn, grain sorghums, peanuts, fruit, truck). Some lumbering; oil wells. Formed 1837. **11** County (□ 659; pop. 82,443), S central W.Va.; ⊙ Fayetteville. On Allegheny Plateau; drained by Kanawha and Meadow rivers. Includes New R. Gorge, Babcock and Hawks Nest state parks. Bituminous-coal mining, agr. (livestock, dairy products, fruit, truck, tobacco); some timber. Formed 1831.

Fayette. 1 City (pop. 3,707), ⊙ Fayette co., NW Ala., on Sipsey R. and c.60 mi. WNW of Birmingham; lumber and cotton milling; dairy products, feed, fertilizer. Inc. 1821. **2** Town (pop. 1,469), Fayette co., NE Iowa, on Volga R. and 12 mi. NNE of Oelwein; feed milling. Limestone quarries near by. Seat of Upper Iowa Univ. (coeducational; 1857). **3** Town (pop. 397), Kennebec co., SW Maine, 16 mi. NW of Augusta, in resort area; agr., lumbering. **4** Town (pop. 1,498), ⊙ Jefferson co., SW Miss., 45 mi. SSW of Vicksburg; cotton, lumber. **5** City (pop. 3,144), ⊙ Howard co., central Mo., near Missouri R., 23 mi. NW of Columbia; agr. center. Seat of Central Col. Founded 1823. **6** Village (pop. 1,003), Fulton co., NW Ohio, c.40 mi. W of Toledo, near Mich. line; ships livestock, grain; makes transportation equipment; food canning. **7** Town (pop. 200), Sanpete co., central Utah, on Sevier Bridge Reservoir and 5 mi. N of Gunnison.

Fayette City, borough (pop. 1,404), Fayette co., SW Pa., 25 mi. S of Pittsburgh and on Monongahela R.; steel, coal. Settled 1794.

Fayetteville (fā'ĭtvĭl). **1** City (pop. 17,071), ⊙ Washington co., NW Ark., c.50 mi. NNE of Fort Smith, in the Ozarks. Seat of Univ. of Arkansas. Trade, distribution center for fruitgrowing, stock- and poultry-raising area. Mfg. of clothing, wood products; canneries, dairies, poultry-packing plants. Resort. U.S. veterans' hosp.; U.S. soil-conservation project and a recreational area are near. Several battles (including one at PEA RIDGE) took place near here in Civil War. Founded 1828, inc. 1836. **2** City (pop. 1,032), ⊙ Fayette co., W central Ga., 22 mi. SSW of Atlanta, in agr. area; cotton warehouse; sawmilling. **3** Town (pop. 245), St. Clair co., SW Ill., 26 mi. SE of East St. Louis, in bituminous-coal and agr. area. **4** Village (pop. 2,624), Onondaga co., central N.Y., 7 mi. E of Syracuse; mfg. (chemicals, cutting blocks, paper, furniture, machinery, metal products); agr. (dairy products; potatoes, apples, hay). Inc. 1844. **5** City (pop. 17,428), ⊙ Cumberland co., S central N.C., on Cape Fear R. (head of navigation) and 50 mi. SSW of Raleigh; trade center; textile and lumber mills. Has state teachers col. for Negroes. Fort Bragg (established 1918; a U.S. military reservation used principally as a field artillery center) and Pope Air Force Base are NE. Settled 1739 as Campbelltown by Scottish immigrants; inc. and named for Lafayette in 1783. Was state capital (1789–93); scene of state convention (1789) to ratify U.S. Constitution. In Civil War, occupied (1865) by Sherman and arsenal destroyed. **6** Village (pop. 401), Brown co., SW Ohio, 30 mi. E of Cincinnati and on East Fork of Little Miami R. **7** Village (1940 pop. 810), Franklin co., S Pa., 6 mi. E of Chambersburg, in agr. area. **8** Town (pop. 5,447), ⊙ Lincoln co., S Tenn., on Elk R. and 70 mi. SSE of Nashville, near Ala. line; shipping and trade center in timber, livestock, dairying, apple-growing region; mfg. of clothing, cotton yarn, dairy products, milk cans; flour and lumber milling. Old inn, here, dates from 1813. U.S. fish hatchery near by. **9** Town (pop. 462), Fayette co., S central Texas, 23 mi. SW of Brenham, in agr. area. **10** Town (pop. 1,952), ⊙ Fayette co., S central W.Va., near New R., 35 mi. SE of Charleston; bituminous-coal mining; agr. (livestock, dairy products, truck, fruit, tobacco); timber. New R. Gorge is near by. Settled 1818.

Fayid (fä'yĭd), village, Canal Governorate, NE Egypt, on Great Bitter L., part of Suez Canal, on Cairo-Suez RR, and 18 mi. S of Ismailia; coast-guard station. Sometimes spelled Faid.

Faylakah Island, Kuwait: see FAILAKA ISLAND.

Fayl-Billot or **Fays-Billot** (both: fā-bēyō'), village (pop. 1,410), Haute-Marne dept., NE France, 14 mi. ESE of Langres; produces wicker furniture. Basketmaking school.

Fay-le-Froid, France: see FAY-SUR-LIGNON.

Faymoreau (fāmôrō'), village (pop. 92), Vendée dept., W France, near Vendée R., 10 mi. NE of Fontenay-le-Comte; coal mining.

Fayón (fīōn'), village (pop. 1,252), Saragossa prov., NE Spain, on the Ebro and 20 mi. ENE of Caspe; olive-oil processing; ships almonds. Lignite mines near by.

Fays-Billot, France: see FAYL-BILLOT.

Fayston, town (pop. 172), Washington co., central Vt., in Green Mts., 10 mi. WSW of Montpelier.

Fay-sur-Lignon (fā-sür-lēnyō'), village (pop. 504), Haute-Loire dept., S central France, on N slope of Mont Mézenc, 12 mi. SSE of Yssingeaux; lacemaking, woodworking, cattle raising. Formerly Fay-le-Froid.

Fayt-lez-Manage (fāt-lā-mänäzh'), town (pop. 5,153), Hainaut prov., SW Belgium, 9 mi. NE of Mons, in coal-mining, steel-milling region.

Fayum, Egypt: see FAIYUM.

Fayyum, Egypt: see FAIYUM.

Fayzabad, Afghanistan: see FAIZABAD.

Fayzabad, Tadzhik SSR: see FAIZABAD.

Fazeley, town (pop. 2,886), SE Stafford, England, just S of Tamworth; cotton milling; agr. market.

Fazilka (fä'zĭlkŭ), town (pop. 28,262), Ferozepore dist., W Punjab, India, 50 mi. SW of Ferozepore; rail junction; wool market; trades in wheat, gram, oilseeds; woolen weaving, cotton ginning. Has col.

Fazughli (fäzōō'glē), village, Blue Nile prov., E Anglo-Egyptian Sudan, on the Blue Nile, near Ethiopian border and 50 mi. SSE of Roseires; 11°15'N 34°45'E. Region, inhabited by Nilotic tribes, is sometimes spelled Fazogli.

Feale River, Ireland, rises in NW extremity of Co. Cork, flows 37 mi. WNW, forming border bet. cos. Limerick and Kerry, past Abbeyfeale and Listowel, to the Shannon estuary 2 mi. SSW of Ballybunion. Its tidal estuary is called Cashen.

Fear, Cape, SE N.C., S tip of Smith Isl., in the Atlantic, 27 mi. S of Wilmington, near mouth of Cape Fear R. Lighthouse at 33°51'N 77°58'W; lightship stationed off dangerous Frying-Pan Shoals, which extend c.20 mi. S and SE from cape.

Fearn (fûrn), agr. village and parish (pop. 1,492), NE Ross and Cromarty, Scotland, 5 mi. SE of Tain. Has anc. church, part of former abbey established here 1338, transferred from Edderton.

Fearne Islands, England: see FARNE ISLANDS.

Feather Falls, N central Calif., waterfall (640-ft. drop) on Fall R., 18 mi. NE of Oroville (Butte co.).

Feather River, N central Calif., formed NE of Oroville, in foothills of the Sierra Nevada, by junction of South and Middle forks; flows SW to Oroville, then S through Sacramento Valley, past Marysville (head of shallow-draught navigation) and Yuba City, to Sacramento R. 16 mi. NW of Sacramento; c.80 mi. long. Just above Oroville, it receives North Fork (c.90 mi. long), which rises SE of Lassen Peak, flows SE to L. ALMANOR (impounded by power dam), thence SW to main stream; extensive private power developments along fork. The river's deep gorge (Feather River Canyon), followed by trans-sierra highway and railroad, is famed for its scenery. Middle Fork (c.80 mi. long) and South Fork (c.40 mi. long) both rise in the sierras, flow generally SW to their junction. Dredging (begun 1898) has taken much gold from river's basin. North Fork is contemplated site of Bidwell Bar Dam and reservoir of CENTRAL VALLEY project.

Featherston, county, New Zealand: see MARTINBOROUGH.

Featherston, borough (pop. 976), S N.Isl., New Zealand, 30 mi. NE of Wellington; agr. center.

Featherstone (fĕ'dhûrstŭn, –stōn), urban district (1931 pop. 14,955; 1950 census 13,925), West Riding, S central Yorkshire, England, 2 mi. W of Pontefract; coal-mining center. Just S is coal-mining center of South Featherstone.

Featherstone, village, Gwelo prov., E central Southern Rhodesia, in Mashonaland, 22 mi. NNW of Enkeldoorn; tobacco, wheat, citrus fruit, dairy products.

Feathertop, Mount (6,306 ft.), E central Victoria, Australia, in Australian Alps, 140 mi. NE of Melbourne.

Februarie 16, 1933, outer NW urban suburb (1948 pop. 11,861) of Bucharest, S Rumania, on left bank of Dambovita R.; agr. Until 1948, called Marele-Voevod-Mihai.

Fécamp (fākä'), town (pop. 16,072), Seine-Inférieure dept., N France, on English Channel, 22 mi. NNE of Le Havre; fishing port (cod fleets dispatched to Newfoundland and Iceland) and bathing resort, flanked by chalk cliffs; cod, herring, and mackerel curing and shipping, boatbuilding, mfg. (fishing equipment, cod-liver oil, clothing, cider). Famous for its Benedictine liqueur, 1st prepared here by Benedictine monks. Harbor installations, beach area, and fine 12th-cent. Norman Gothic abbey church damaged in Second World War (chiefly during Ger. retreat in 1944).

Fechenheim (fĕ'khŭnhīm), industrial suburb (pop. 10,134) of Frankfurt, W Germany, on right bank of the canalized Main and 4 mi. E of city center; mfg. of dyes.

Fecht River (fĕsht, Ger. fĕkht), Haut-Rhin dept., E France, rises in the Vosges at S foot of the Hohneck, flows c.30 mi. NE, through Munster valley (famous cheese), to the Ill above Sélestat.

Feckenham (fĕk'nŭm), town and parish (pop. 2,322), E Worcester, England, 4 mi. SSW of Redditch; agr. market. Has church dating from 14th-15th cent.

Feda (fā'dä), village (pop. 222; canton pop. 739), Vest-Agder co., S Norway, on Feda Fjord (14-mi. inlet of North Sea), 7 mi. ESE of Flekkefjord; electric plant, cement and carbide factories. Formerly spelled Fede or Fedde.

Fédala (fādälä'), city (pop. 15,813), Casablanca region, NW Fr. Morocco, on the Atlantic, 14 mi. NE of Casablanca; Morocco's chief petroleum-importing and storage center, an important fishing port, and a rapidly growing industrial city. A corsair refuge in 17th-18th cent., it was but a hamlet (pop. 250) in 1912. The new port (completed 1934), protected by 2 converging breakwaters, accommodates ships drawing up to 20 ft. Located on trunk railroad, Fédala is rapidly becoming Casablanca's outer mfg. suburb. Chief industries are fish and vegetable (peas, beans, spinach) canning, fruit preserving, meat packing, cork processing (including mfg. of bottle corks), oil refining, and brick mfg. There is a large modern cotton mill. Saltworks near by.

Fedan, Wadi, Jordan: see FIDAN, WADI.

Fedchenko, rail station, Uzbek SSR: see KUVA.

Fedchenko Glacier (fyĕ'chĭnkŭ), one of longest mountain glaciers of the world, in Pamir-Alai mtn. system, Tadzhik SSR; rises at 38°30'N 72°15'E, flows c.50 mi. N, parallel to Darvaza and Akademiya Nauk ranges, to 39°5'N (where it gives rise to the Muk-Su, left headstream of Surkhab R.). Site of meteorological observation post (alt. 14,800 ft.).

Fedde, Norway: see FEDA.

Fedderwarden (fĕ'dŭrvär"dŭn), village (commune pop. 5,421), in Oldenburg, NW Germany, after 1945 in Lower Saxony, in East Friesland, 4 mi. NW of Wilhelmshaven, in peat region. Commune is called Kniphausen (kŭnĭp-hou'zŭn).

Fede, Norway: see FEDA.

Federación (fādäräsyōn'), town (1947 census pop. 5,039), ⊙ Federación dept. (□ 1,405; 1947 census pop. 32,753), NE Entre Ríos prov., Argentina, port on Uruguay R. (Uruguay border), on railroad and 28 mi. NNE of Concordia; agr. and lumbering center. Sawmills, woodworking plants, tanneries, peanut- and sunflower-oil presses. Rice, corn, peanuts, flax; stock raising, poultry farming.

Federal, town (1940 pop. 78), St. Francois co., E Mo., in the Ozarks, near Big R., just S of Flat River.

Federal Capital Territory, Australia: see AUSTRALIAN CAPITAL TERRITORY.

Federal Dam, village (pop. 225), Cass co., N central Minn., on Leech Lake R., near Leech L. and Greater Leech Lake Indian Reservation, and 35 mi. ESE of Bemidji, in Chippewa Natl. Forest; grain, potatoes. Dam just W on Leech R.

Federal Heights, town (pop. 173), Adams co., N central Colo., near Denver.

Federalsburg, town (pop. 1,878), Caroline co., E Md., on Delmarva Peninsula 19 mi. ENE of Cambridge and on Marshyhope Creek, in agr. area; makes pearl and plastic buttons; vegetable canneries, poultry-dressing plants. Settled 1852.

Federated Malay States: see MALAYA.

Federated Shan States, Burma: see SHAN STATE.

Federation of Malaya: see MALAYA.

Federsee (fā'dŭrzā"), small lake (□ .5), S Württemberg, Germany, 6 mi. W of Biberach. Drained by Kanzach R., an affluent (right) of the Danube. Extensive remains of lake dwellings found in surrounding marshes.

Fedje (fĕd'yü), village in Austrheim canton (pop. 3,291), Hordaland co., SW Norway, on isl. (□ 3) of same name in North Sea, 34 mi. NNW of Bergen, 8 mi. off mainland; fishing, mfg. of cod-liver oil. Sometimes called Feje.

Fedjedj, Chott el (shôt' ĕl fĕjĕj'), saline lake in S Tunisia, forming an E arm of the larger Chott DJERID; c.60 mi. long; reaches to within 15 mi. of the Gulf of Gabès. Also spelled Fedjadj.

Fedj-M'Zala (fĕj'-mŭzälä'), village (pop. 1,482), Constantine dept., NE Algeria, 37 mi. W of Constantine; cereals.

Fedorovka (fyô'dŭrŭfkŭ). **1** Village (1926 pop. 3,338), NW Kustanai oblast, Kazakh SSR, on railroad (Dzharkul station) and 45 mi. NW of Kustanai; cattle raising; metalworking; quarrying. **2** Village (1939 pop. over 500), N West Kazakhstan oblast, Kazakh SSR, near railroad (Yaik station), 25 mi. E of Uralsk; cattle; metalworks. **3** Village (1948 pop. over 2,000), SW Bashkir Autonomous SSR, Russian SFSR, 45 mi. SW of Sterlitamak; lumbering; grain, livestock. **4** Village (1926 pop. 2,908), SW Rostov oblast, Russian SFSR, 28 mi. WNW of Taganrog; metalworks; wheat, sunflowers, cattle. **5** Village, Saratov oblast, Russian SFSR: see MOKROUS.

Feeding Hills, Mass.: see AGAWAM.

Fefan, Caroline Isls.: see TRUK.

Fegyvernek (fĕ'dyüvĕrnĕk), town (pop. 7,717), Jasz-Nagykun-Szolnok co., E central Hungary, on Tisza R. and 17 mi. ENE of Szolnok; sawmill.

Feher, Lake (fĕ'hār), Hung. *Fehér*, Csongrad co., S Hungary, 5 mi. N of Szeged; 3 mi. long, 2.5 mi. wide; carp and pike.

Fehergyarmat (fĕ'hār-dyŏrmŏt), Hung. *Fehérgyarmat*, town (pop. 5,779), Szatmar-Bereg co., NE Hungary, near the Szamos, 36 mi. E of Nyiregyhaza; brickworks; wheat, corn, rye, cattle, hogs.

Feher Karpatok, Czechoslovakia: see JAVORNIKY.

Feher Körös, Hungary and Rumania: see KÖRÖS RIVER.

Fehertemplom, Yugoslavia: see BELA CRKVA.

Fehervar, Hungary: see SZEKESFEHERVAR.

Fehmarn (fā'märn), Plattdeutsch *Femern* (fā'mŭrn), Baltic island (□ 71.4; 1939 pop. 10,037; 1946 pop. 21,252), Schleswig-Holstein, NW Germany, separated from mainland by Fehmarn Sound (c.1 mi. wide) and from Danish Lolland isl. by Fehmarn Belt (11-mi.-wide strait). Low in elevation (c.90 ft.), it is 10 mi. long (E-W), 7 mi. wide (N-S). Grain, potatoes, cabbage, beets. Main town: Burg.

Fehraj, Iran: see FAHRAJ.

Fehrbellin (fâr"bĕlēn'), town (pop. 3,875), Brandenburg, E Germany, on Rhin Canal and 35 mi. NW of Berlin; peat digging; woodworking. Scene (June, 1675) of victory of the elector Frederick William of Brandenburg over Swedes under Wrangel.

Fehring (fā'rĭng), village (pop. 1,366), Styria, SE Austria, near the Raab, 28 mi. ESE of Graz; rail junction; customs station near Hung. border; wheat, corn, vineyards.

Feia, Lagoa (lägō'ŭ fā'ŭ), lagoon (□ c.200), in E Rio de Janeiro state, Brazil, 10 mi. S of Campos, in marshy Paraíba R. delta. Connected by canal to the Atlantic at Macaé. Included in federal govt. project to drain the unhealthful Baixada Fluminense (coastal lowland).

Feicheng or **Fei-ch'eng** (both: fā'chŭng'), town, ⊙ Feicheng co. (pop. 341,747), W Shantung prov., China, 30 mi. SSW of Tsinan; peach-growing center; cotton, wheat, millet.

Feignies (fĕnyē'), town (pop. 2,292), Nord dept., N France, frontier station near Belg. border (opposite Quévy-le-Grand), 3 mi. NW of Maubeuge; tile-mfg. center; metalworks. MALPLAQUET is NW.

Fei-hsiang, China: see FEISIANG.

Feihsien (fā'shyĕn'), town, ⊙ Feihsien co. (pop. 446,526), S Shantung prov., China, 28 mi. NW of Lini; cotton weaving, tobacco processing; peanuts melons, grain.

Feijenoord, Netherlands: see ROTTERDAM.

Feijó (fā-zhô'), city (pop. 565), Acre territory, westernmost Brazil, hydroplane landing on a sub-affluent of the Juruá, on Amazonas line, and 200 mi. NW of Rio Branco; 8°25'S 70°25'W.

Feilaka Island, Kuwait: see FAILAKA ISLAND.

Feilding (fēl'dĭng), borough (pop. 5,001), ⊙ Oroua co. (□ 190; pop. 3,722), S N.Isl., New Zealand, 80 mi. NNE of Wellington; dairy plants, sheep ranches. In, but independent of, Oroua co.

Feilnbach (fī'lŭnbäkh), village (pop. 1,174), Upper Bavaria, Germany, on N slope of the Bavarian Alps, 7 mi. SW of Rosenheim; rail terminus; leather-working; peat cutting; resort (alt. 1,768 ft.) with mud baths.

Feira (fī'rŭ), township, Central Prov., Northern Rhodesia, on Zambezi R., at mouth of Luangwa R., opposite Zumbo (Mozambique), and 140 mi. E of Lusaka; tobacco, wheat, corn; livestock.

Feira or **Vila da Feira** (vē'lŭ dŭ fā'rŭ), town, Aveiro dist., N Portugal, 16 mi. S of Oporto; dairying, mfg. of soap, footwear. Has old castle, rebuilt by John I.

Feira de Santana (fā'rŭ dĭ săntä'nŭ), city (1950 pop. 27,285), Bahia, Brazil, 55 mi. N of Salvador; alt. 800 ft.; rail terminus; leading livestock center noted for its cattle fairs; also ships cotton, tobacco, beans. Has good climate, fine layout. Formerly spelled Feira de Sant'Anna.

Feisiang or **Fei-hsiang** (both: fā'shyäng'), town, ⊙ Feisiang co. (pop. 131,157), SW Hopeh prov., China, 40 mi. SSE of Singtai; cotton, rice, wheat, millet.

Feistritz, Windisch-, Yugoslavia: see BISTRICA.

Feistritz ob Bleiburg (fīs'trĭts ōp blī'bŏŏrk), town (pop. 2,064), Carinthia, S Austria, near Yugoslav border, 21 mi. ESE of Klagenfurt; grain, cattle.

Feistritz River, Styria, E Austria, rises in the Stuhleck of the Fischbach Alps, flows c.50 mi. S to the Lafnitz 4 mi. below Fürstenfeld.

Feje, Norway: see FEDJE.

Fejer (fĕ'yār), Hung. *Fejér*, Ger. *Stuhlweissenburg*, county (□1,494; pop. 224,504), W central Hungary; ⊙ SZEKESFEHERVAR. Vertes Mts. in NW, L. Velence in center; bounded E by the Danube. Agr. (grain, wine, potatoes, truck, beans, lentils), dairy farming, stock raising. Bauxite mines at Gant, Iszkaszentgyörgy; mfg. at Szekesfehervar, Velence, Ercsi.

Fejo (fī'ŭ), Dan. *Fejø*, island (□ 6.2; pop. 1,289), Denmark, in Smaalandsfarvand strait, 1.5 mi. N of Lolland isl.

Feke (fĕkĕ'), village (pop. 1,846), Seyhan prov., S Turkey, on Gok R. and 70 mi. NE of Adana; cereals.

Feketehalom, Rumania: see CODLEA.

Fekete Körös, Hungary and Rumania: see KÖRÖS RIVER.

Fekete River (fĕ'kĕtĕ), Hung. *Fekete víz*, S Hungary, rises S of Kadarkut, flows 75 mi. SE to the Drava 6 mi. SW of Siklos.

Feketic or **Feketich** (both: fĕk'ĕtĭch), Serbo-Croatian *Feketić*, Hung. *Bácsfeketehegy* (bäch'fĕk"-ĕtĕhĕdyü), village (pop. 5,638), Vojvodina, N Serbia, Yugoslavia, 7 mi. NNE of Vrbas, in the Backa.

Fela (fĕ'lä), village, Lake prov., NW Tanganyika, on railroad and 12 mi. SE of Mwanza; cotton, peanuts, rice, corn.

Felanitx (fälänēch'), city (pop. 7,403), Majorca, Balearic Isls., rail terminus 27 mi. ESE of Palma; agr. center at foot of San Salvador hill (with convent). Trades in cereals, vegetables, grapes, almonds, carobs, figs, olives, fruit. Alcohol and liquor distilling, wine making, flour milling, meat packing, textile milling, lumbering, wool processing; mfg. of cement articles, ceramics, apricot purée. Ruined Santueri castle (built by Moors), with subterranean vaults, is 2 mi. E.

Felchville, Vt.: see READING.

Feld am See (fĕlt' äm zā'), summer resort (pop. 872), Carinthia, S Austria, on small Brennsee or Feldsee, 12 mi. NNW of Villach.

Feldbach (fĕlt'bäkh), town (pop. 3,369), Styria, SE Austria, on the Raab and 23 mi. ESE of Graz; tannery, brewery, fruit and vegetable canning; summer resort. Riegersburg fortress near by.

Feldberg (fĕlt'bĕrk), town (pop. 2,862), Mecklenburg, N Germany, bet. 2 small lakes, 16 mi. E of Neustrelitz; sawmilling; granite quarrying. Health resort.

Feldberg, highest mountain (4,898 ft.) of the Black Forest, S Germany, 10 mi. SE of Freiburg. Noted winter-sports territory. Climatic health resort of Todtnau is at SW foot.

Feldberg, Grosser, Germany: see GROSSER FELDBERG.

Feldioara (fĕldyŏŏwä'rä), Ger. *Marienburg* (märē'-ŭnbŏŏrk), Hung. *Földvár* (fûld'vär), village (pop. 2,601), Stalin prov., central Rumania, on Olt R., on railroad and 12 mi. N of Stalin (Brasov); mfg. of furniture, oxygen, bricks, and tiles. Agr. school. Has remains of 13th-cent. Ger. fortress, ruins of 13th-cent. castle of Teutonic Knights, and 13th-cent. church. About 50% pop. are Germans.

Feldkirch (fĕlt'kĭrkh), city (pop. 15,313), Vorarlberg, W Austria, on Ill R., near the Rhine (Swiss border), 19 mi. SSW of Bregenz; rail center, customs station near Liechtenstein border; textile mills, breweries. Bishopric; large Jesuit acad.; castle built 1200, Gothic church 1478. Teachers col. at near-by Tisis.

Feldkirchen (fĕlt'kĭr"khŭn), town (pop. 3,218), Carinthia, S Austria, 12 mi. NW of Klagenfurt; market center; leather goods, brewery. Ironworks near by.

Feldkirchen (fĕlt'kĭr"khŭn), village (pop. 2,056), Upper Bavaria, Germany, 8 mi. E of Munich; paint mfg., metalworking.

Feldkirchen an der Donau (än dĕr dō'nou), town (pop. 2,973), N central Upper Austria, on left bank of the Danube and 15 mi. WNW of Linz; summer resort.

Feledince, Czechoslovakia: see JESENSKE.

Felegyhaza, Hungary: see KISKUNFELEGYHAZA.

Felek, Rumania: see AVRIG.

Felgueira, Viseu dist., Portugal: see CANAS DE SENHORIM.

Felgueiras (fĕlgā'rŭsh), agr. village (pop. 84), Pôrto dist., N Portugal, on branch railroad and 7 mi. SE of Guimarãis; biscuit mfg.

Felguera, La (lä fĕlgā'rä), town (pop. 6,983), Oviedo prov., NW Spain, in Asturias, on Nalón R. and 9 mi. ESE of Oviedo; chief center of Langreo mining basin (coal and iron); blast furnaces and steel mills (machinery, cables, hardware); chemical works (coal tar, nitrogen); coke industry.

Feliciano, department, Argentina: see SAN JOSÉ DE FELICIANO.

Feliciano River (fälēsyä'nō), NW Entre Ríos prov., Argentina, rises near Juan B. Arruabarrena, flows c.100 mi. SW, past San José de Feliciano, to Paraná R. 10 mi. NE of Hernandarías.

Felicitas Julia, Portugal: see LISBON.

Félicité Island (fälēsētā') (689 acres; pop., including The Sisters, 94), one of the Seychelles, in Indian Ocean, 2 mi. NE of La Digue Isl.; 4°19'S 55°50'E; copra, fisheries.

Felicity (fŭlĭ'sĭtē), village (pop. 716), Clermont co., SW Ohio, 29 mi. SE of Cincinnati, near Ohio R.

Felidu Atoll (fĕ'lĭdŏŏ), small central group (pop. 1,729) of Maldive Isls., in Indian Ocean, bet. 3°19'N and 3°41'N, just S of Male Atoll.

Felinfoel, Wales: see LLANELLY.

Felino (fĕlē'nô), town (pop. 1,553), Parma prov., Emilia-Romagna, N central Italy, 8 mi. SSW of Parma; sausage, canned foods.

Felipe Camarão (fĭlē'pĭ kămŭrā'ō), town (pop. 544), E Rio Grande do Norte, NE Brazil, on Potengi R. and 11 mi. W of Natal; saltworks; ships sugar and rice. Diatomite deposits. Until 1944, called São Gonçalo.

Felipe Carrillo Puerto (fälē'pä kärē'yō pwĕr'tō), town (pop. 652), Quintana Roo, SE Mexico, on E Yucatan Peninsula, 80 mi. NNE of Chetumal; terminus of strategic railroad to Vigía Chico on Caribbean Sea at Ascensión Bay, 33 mi. NE. Exports henequen, chicle, tropical hardwood. Former ⊙ territory. Santa Cruz de Bravo until 1935.

Felitto (fēlēt'tô), village (pop. 1,992), Salerno prov., Campania, S Italy, 5 mi. SSE of Rocca d'Aspide.

Félix (fā'lēks), town (pop. 1,376), Almería prov., S Spain, 11 mi. WNW of Almería; lead foundry. Olive-oil processing; ships grapes, almonds, esparto. Wine, cereals. Lead, sulphur mines in area.

Felix, Cape, N extremity of King William Isl., S Franklin Dist., Northwest Territories, on James Ross and Victoria straits; 69°55'N 97°50'W.

Felixburg, village, Gwelo prov., central Southern Rhodesia, in Mashonaland, 23 mi. SE of Umvuma; tobacco, wheat, dairy products, citrus fruit, livestock. Gold deposits.

Felixdorf (fā'lĭksdôrf), town (pop. 2,176), E Lower Austria, on Piesting R. and 4 mi. N of Wiener Neustadt; rail junction.

Felix Harbour, SE Boothia Peninsula, SE Franklin Dist., Northwest Territories, small bay of the Gulf of Boothia; 70°N 91°52'W. John Ross's *Victory* wintered here (1829–30 and 1830–31).

Felixstowe (fē'lĭkstō), urban district (1931 pop. 12,067; 1951 census 15,080), SE Suffolk, England, on North Sea bet. mouths of Deben R. and Orwell R., 11 mi. SE of Ipswich; 51°57'N 1°22'E. Fishing port and seaside resort. Site of seaplane base and naval radio station. Roman remains have been found here.

Felizzano (fĕlētsä'nô), village (pop. 1,826), Alessandria prov., Piedmont, N Italy, on Tanaro R. and 9 mi. W of Alessandria; bicycle mfg.

Felka, Czechoslovakia: see POPRAD.

Fellach bei Villach (fĕ'läkh bī fĭ'läkh), town (pop. 3,614), Carinthia, S Austria, near the Drau, 2 mi. NW of Villach; summer resort.

Fella River (fĕl'lä), NE Italy, rises in Carnic Alps 4 mi. WNW of Tarvisio, flows W, past Pontebba, S, and W to Tagliamento R. 6 mi. SE of Tolmezzo; 30 mi. long.

Fellbach (fĕl'bäkh), town (pop. 16,890), N Württemberg, Germany, after 1945 in Württemberg-Baden, 4 mi. E of Stuttgart (linked by tramway); foundries; mfg. of chassis, iron and steel goods; leatherworking. Brickworks. Vineyards.

Felletin (fĕltē'), town (pop. 2,035), Creuse dept., central France, on the Creuse and 5 mi. S of Aubusson; carpet mfg. center.

Fellin, Estonia: see VILJANDI.

Felling, urban district (1931 pop. 27,040; 1951 census 25,286), NE Durham, England, near Tyne R., 3 mi. SE of Newcastle-upon-Tyne; coal mining, metalworking. In urban dist. are towns of Pelaw (E; chemicals, paint) and Bill Quay (N; metalworking, glassworking).

Fellingsbro (fĕ"lĭngsbrōō'), village (pop. 748), Orebro co., S central Sweden, near Arboga R., 10 mi. WNW of Arboga; pulp, paper, and cardboard milling, metalworking, concrete-products mfg. Has medieval tower.

Fellowship, village (pop. including adjacent Den Amstel, 1,015), Demerara co., N Br. Guiana, near the Atlantic, 8 mi. WNW of Vreed-en-Hoop; sugar cane, rice.

Fellsmere, town (pop. 649), Indian River co., central Fla., 16 mi. NW of Vero Beach; sugar-milling center in large cane-growing area.

Felpham (fĕl'pùm), town and parish (pop. 2,827), SW Sussex, England, on the Channel just ENE of Bognor Regis; resort. Residence of Blake and Hayley, whose houses are preserved.

Fels, Luxembourg: see LAROCHETTE.

Felsberg (fĕls'bĕrk), town (pop. 2,021), in former Prussian prov. of Hesse-Nassau, W Germany, after 1945 in Hesse, on the Eder and 12.5 mi. SSW of Kassel; mfg. of machinery. Has ruined castle.

Felsenthal (fĕl'sùn-thôl"), town (1940 pop. 203), Union co., S Ark., 31 mi. ESE of El Dorado.

Felshtin, Ukrainian SSR: see GVARDEISKOYE.

Felsina, Italy: see BOLOGNA, city.

Felsöbanya, Rumania: see BAIA-SPRIE.

Felsödobsza (fĕl'shûdôpsŏ), Hung. *Felsődobsza,* town (pop. 1,471), Abauj co., NE Hungary, on Hernad R. and 16 mi. NE of Miskolc; grain, sheep. Prehistoric remains found.

Felsöfernezely, Rumania: see FIRIZA.

Felsögalla (fĕl'shûgŏl-lŏ), Hung. *Felsőgalla,* mining, industrial town (pop. 17,110), Komarom-Esztergom co., N Hungary, 30 mi. W of Budapest; rail center. Aluminum, cement, quicklime, carbide plants; brickworks. Lignite mines, limestone quarries near by.

Felsö-Hagi, Czechoslovakia: see VYSNE HAGY.

Felsömarosujvar, Rumania: see UIOARA-DE-SUS.

Felsöviso, Rumania: see VISEUL-DE-SUS.

Felsövizköz, Czechoslovakia: see SVIDNIK.

Felstead or **Felsted,** town and parish (pop. 1,845), central Essex, England, on Chelmer R. and 9 mi. NNW of Chelmsford; agr. market, with beet-sugar processing. Has public school, founded 1564, and church with Norman tower. Once center of Puritanism.

Felszerfalva, Austria: see HIRM.

Felten, Djebel, Algeria: see AÏN-SMARA.

Feltham (fĕl'tùm), residential and industrial urban district (1931 pop. 16,317; 1951 census 44,830), Middlesex, England, 13 mi. WSW of London; railroad workshops; mfg. of automobiles, aircraft, electrical equipment, cables. Site of airfield. In urban dist. (SE) are Hanworth, with electrical-equipment works; and Kempton Park, with racecourse; large waterworks supply NW London.

Felton (fäl'tōn), village (pop. 651), Oriente prov., E Cuba, on E inlet of Nipe Bay, and 45 mi. E of Holguín; refining of chromium and iron, mined in the Sierra de Nipe 15 mi. SSW.

Felton. 1 Resort village (pop. c.400), Santa Cruz co., W Calif., in Santa Cruz Mts., 6 mi. N of Santa Cruz. Redwood groves near by. **2** Town (pop. 455), Kent co., central Del., 10 mi. S of Dover; shipping point in agr. region; dairy products. **3** Village (pop. 258), Clay co., W Minn., 20 mi. NE of Fargo, N.Dak., in Red R. valley. **4** Borough (pop. 429), York co., S Pa., 12 mi. SE of York.

Feltre (fĕl'trĕ), anc. *Feltria,* town (pop. 6,098), Belluno prov., Veneto, N Italy, 17 mi. SW of Belluno, on hill (1,066 ft.) overlooking Piave R.; rail junction; mfg. (food products, furniture, floor wax, soap, lye, cement); foundry, woolen mill. Has cathedral, 12th-cent. church, seminary, mus., and 16th-cent. bldgs.

Femern, Germany: see FEHMARN.

Femés (fămās'), village (pop. 311), Lanzarote, Canary Isls., 13 mi. WSW of Arrecife; barley and wheat growing, stock raising. Exports fish. Has ruins of 1st cathedral built on the archipelago, later transferred to Las Palmas.

Femo (fā'mû), Dan. *Femø,* island (□ 4.4; pop. 602), Denmark, in Smaalandsfarvand strait, 7 mi. N of Lolland isl.

Femund Lake (fā'mōōn), Nor. *Femunden,* Hedmark co., E Norway, near Swedish border, 20 mi. SE of Roros; □ 78; 42 mi. long, 1–7 mi. wide, up to 426 ft. deep. Drained S by Trysil R., upper course of Klar R. Also called Femundsjo, Nor. *Femundsjø.*

Fen, river, China: see FEN RIVER.

Fen, Norway: see ULEFOSS.

Fenain (fünē'), residential town (pop. 4,590), Nord dept., N France, 10 mi. E of Douai, in coal-mining dist.

Fencheng or **Fen-ch'eng** (fŭn'chŭng'), town, ⊙ Fencheng co. (pop. 82,228), S Shansi prov., China, 25 mi. SSW of Linfen, near railroad; tobacco and vegetable-oil (sesame) processing; buckwheat, cotton. Until 1914 called Taiping.

Fenchow, China: see FENYANG.

Fenchuganj (fän'chōōgŭnj), village, Sylhet dist., E East Bengal, E Pakistan, on Kusiyara R. and 15 mi. SSE of Sylhet; rice, tea, oilseeds; general engineering factory. Tea processing near by.

Fen Ditton, agr. village and parish (pop. 1,056), S Cambridge, England, on Cam R. and 2 mi. NE of Cambridge; fruitgrowing. It is at the end of an anc. Br. earthwork. Has 13th–15th-cent. church. Scene of annual Cambridge Univ. boat races.

Fenelon Falls (fĕ'nùlŏn), village (pop. 1,158), S Ont., on Fenelon R., bet. Cameron L. (N) and Sturgeon L. (S), 12 mi. N of Lindsay, in Muskoka dist.; leather, woodworking; lumbering; resort.

Fener, Turkey: see PHANAR.

Fénérive or **Fénérive-Est** (fānārēv'-ĕst'), town, Tamatave prov., NE Madagascar, on coast, 50 mi. N of Tamatave; trading center for cloves, clove oil, coffee, vanilla; large coffee plantations. R.C. and several Protestant missions, hosp., school for Europeans. Airfield.

Fénétrange (fānātrāzh'), Ger. *Finstingen* (fĭn'stĭng-ùn), village (pop. 913), Moselle dept., NE France, on the Saar and 8 mi. N of Sarrebourg. Has 15th-cent. church.

Fengchen (fŭng'jŭn'), town (pop. 34,759), ⊙ Fengchen co. (pop. 277,632), E Suiyuan prov., China, 85 mi. ESE of Kweisui and on railroad, near the Great Wall (Chahar line); commercial center of Fengchen upland (alt. 4,500 ft.), a watershed grazing area of former lake basins. Flour milling, oilseed (sesame, rapeseed) pressing, wool and fur processing. In N Shansi until 1914, and in Chahar, 1914–28.

Fengcheng or **Feng-ch'eng** (fŭng'chŭng'). **1** Town (pop. 21,238), ⊙ Fengcheng co. (pop. 387,894), N central Kiangsi prov., China, on Kan R. and 32 mi. SSW of Nanchang, and on railroad; coal-mining center; wheat, cotton, rice, tobacco. **2** Town, ⊙ Fengcheng co. (pop. 368,500), S Liaotung prov., Manchuria, China, 30 mi. NW of Antung; railroad junction; lead mining; gold, copper, manganese, and coal deposits. Shipping point for agr. products. Until 1914 called Fenghwang or Fenghwangcheng.

Feng-chieh, China: see FENGKIEH.

Feng-ching, China: see FENGKING.

Feng-ch'iu, China: see FENGKIU.

Feng-ch'uan, Kwangtung prov., China: see FUNGCHÜN.

Fengchüan, Kweichow prov., China: see FENGKANG.

Feng-hsiang, China: see FENGSIANG.

Fenghsien (fŭng'shyĕn'). **1** Town, Kiangsu prov., China: see FENGSIEN. **2** Town (pop. 10,103), ⊙ Fenghsien co. (pop. 413,320), SW Shantung prov., China, near Pingyuan-Anhwei line, 45 mi. NW of Süchow; agr. center (beans, wheat, kaoliang, cotton). Until 1949 in Kiangsu. **3** Town (pop. 12,159), ⊙ Fenghsien co. (pop. 46,508), SW Shensi prov., China, near Kansu line, 45 mi. SW of Paoki, in mtn. region; millet, buckwheat, beans. Iron deposits near by.

Feng-hsin, China: see FENGSIN.

Fenghwa or **Feng-hua** (fŭng'hwä'), town (pop. 9,934), ⊙ Fenghwa co. (pop. 234,163), NE Chekiang prov., China, 18 mi. SW of Ningpo; rice, wheat, corn, peaches. Chiang Kai-shek was b. here in 1886.

Fenghwang or **Feng-huang** (both: fŭng'hwäng'). **1** Town, ⊙ Fenghwang co. (pop. 155,238), W Hunan prov., China, near Kweichow border, 35 mi. NNW of Chihkiang; rice, wheat, beans, corn. Mercury mining (NW). **2** or **Fenghwangcheng,** town, Liaotung prov., Manchuria, China: see FENGCHENG.

Feng-i, China: see FENGYI.

Fengjun (fŭng'rōōn'), town, ⊙ Fengjun co. (pop. 648,355), NE Hopeh prov., China, 15 mi. N of Tangshan; wheat, kaoliang.

Fengkang (fŭng'gäng'), town (pop. 2,568), ⊙ Fengkang co. (pop. 145,155), NE Kweichow prov., China, 40 mi. W of Szenan; cotton textiles; tea and lacquer processing; grain. Has noted monasteries. Until 1930 called Fengchüan.

Fengkieh or **Feng-chieh** (both: fŭng'jyĕ'), town (pop. 25,260), ⊙ Fengkieh co. (pop. 408,846), easternmost Szechwan prov., China, 70 mi. ENE of Wanhsien, and on left bank of Yangtze R. at W end of its gorges; distributing center near Hupeh border; rice, millet, sweet potatoes, cotton, tung oil, medicinal herbs. Iron and sulphur mines, coal deposits, saltworks near by. Until 1913 called Kweichow.

Fengking or **Feng-ching** (both: fŭng'jĭng'), town, SE Kiangsu prov., China, on Chekiang line, 40 mi. SW of Shanghai, and on Shanghai-Hangchow RR; commercial center.

Fengkiu or **Feng-ch'iu** (both: fŭng'chyō'), town, ⊙ Fengkiu co. (pop. 155,925), S Pingyuan prov., China, near Yellow R. (Honan line), 35 mi. SE of Sinsiang; cotton weaving; wheat, beans. Until 1949 in Honan prov.

Fenglin (fŭng'lĭn'), Jap. *Horin* (hō'rĕn), town (1935 pop. 4,370), E central Formosa, 19 mi. SW of Hwalien and on railroad; lumbering center; charcoal, camphor oil. Sugar cane, rice, tobacco, cattle.

Fenglingtu (fŭng'lĭng'dōō'), town, SW Shansi prov., China, on Yellow R., opposite Tungkwan, at Shensi-Honan line; terminus of railroad from Tatung.

Fengman (fŭng'män'), **Siaofengman,** or **Hsiao-fengman** (both: shyou'fŭng'män'), village, central Kirin prov., Manchuria, on Sungari R., on rail spur and 15 mi. SE of Kirin; site of Sungari R. dam (3,600 ft. long, 300 ft. high) and hydroelectric station (partly completed 1943), which supplies power to Fushun, Changchun, and Harbin.

Fengning (fŭng'nĭng'), town, ⊙ Fengning co. (pop. 89,369), SW Jehol prov., Manchuria, 45 mi. WNW of Chengteh; agr. center (millet, kaoliang, beans, medicinal herbs). Gold and oil-shale deposits.

Fengshan (fŭng'shän'). **1** Town, ⊙ Fengshan co. (pop. 72,705), NW Kwangsi prov., China, 60 mi. NE of Poseh; cotton textiles; rice, wheat, sweet potatoes. **2** Town, W Sungkiang prov., Manchuria, China, 40 mi. NW of Tungho, at Heilungkiang line.

Fengshan (fŭng'shän'), Jap. *Hozan* (hō'zän), since 1945 officially *Kaohiung* (gou'shyōōng'), town (1935 pop. 10,758), S Formosa, on railroad and 5 mi. E of Kaohiung city; pineapple canning, sugar milling; rice, peanuts. A military lease, it has airfields, army school, and radio station.

Fengshih (fŭng'shû'), town, SW Fukien prov., China, on Kwangtung line, 10 mi. WSW of Engteng, and on Ting R.; commercial center; exports paper, tobacco, timber.

Fengshun, China: see FUNGSHUN.

Fengsiang or **Feng-hsiang** (both: fŭng'shyäng'), town (pop. 10,100), ⊙ Fengsiang co. (pop. 192,-104), SW Shensi prov., China, 90 mi. WNW of Sian and on road to Lanchow; cotton weaving, paper mfg., winegrowing, tobacco processing; hides, sheepskins, wool.

Fengsien or **Fenghsien** (both: fŭng'shyĕn'), town, ⊙ Fengsien co. (1946 pop. 237,263), S Kiangsu prov., China, 22 mi. S of Shanghai and N of Hangchow Bay; agr. center (rice, wheat, beans, cotton); saltworks. The name Fengsien was applied until 1912 to a town now called Old Fengsien, 10 mi. E; present Fengsien was called Nankiao until it became co. ⊙ in 1912.

Fengsin (fĕng'sĭn') or **Feng-hsin** (fŭng'shĭn'), town (pop. 8,616), ⊙ Fengsin co. (pop. 98,011), NW Kiangsi prov., China, 24 mi. W of Nanchang; rice, wheat, beans.

Fengtai or **Feng-t'ai** (fŭng'tī'), town, ⊙ Fengtai co. (pop. 541,835), N Anhwei prov., China, 40 mi. WSW of Pengpu and on Hwai R.; rice, wheat, kaoliang, cotton, tobacco.

Fengtien, Manchuria: see MUKDEN.

Fengtu (fŭng'dōō'), town (pop. 14,287), ⊙ Fengtu co. (pop. 444,220), SE Szechwan prov., China, 27 mi. NE of Fowling and on left bank of Yangtze R.; exports tung oil; rice, kaoliang, indigo, wheat.

Fengyang (fŭng'yäng'), town, ⊙ Fengyang co. (pop. 166,282), N Anhwei prov., China, 10 mi. SE of Pengpu and on Tientsin-Pukow RR; tobacco-growing center; rice, wheat, kaoliang, corn. Home of the Ming dynasty (1368–1644); mausoleum near by. Sometimes spelled Fungyang.

Fengyi or **Feng-i** (both: fŭng'yē'), town (pop. 3,191), ⊙ Fengyi co. (pop. 45,700), NW Yunnan prov., China, on Burma Road, near the lake Erh Hai, 10 mi. SE of Tali; alt. 6,726 ft.; cotton textiles; tea, rice, wheat, beans. Arsenic mines, gold deposits near by. Until 1914, Chaochow.

Fengyüan (fŭng'yüän'), Jap. *Toyohara* (tōyō'härä), sometimes *Hogen* (hō'gän), town (1935 pop. 11,765), W central Formosa, 8 mi. N of Taichung and on railroad; agr. center; hemp processing (cloth, sacks), sawmilling, pineapple canning. Noted for its high-grade rice and tobacco. Formerly called Hulutun, Jap. *Koroton.*

Fenham, England: see NEWCASTLE-UPON-TYNE.

Fen-hsi, China: see FENSI.

Feni (fün'yē'), town (pop. 6,097), ⊙ Feni co. (pop. 74,511), W Kiangsi prov., China, on Yüan R. and 19 mi. E of Ichun, and on railroad; rice. Anthracite mines (N).

Feni, E Pakistan: see FENNY, town.

Feni Islands (fĕ'nē), volcanic group (□ c.45; pop. c.1,000), New Ireland dist., Bismarck Archipelago, Territory of New Guinea, SW Pacific; 4°5'S 153° 40'E; largest isls. are Ambitle (8 mi. long) and Babase (4 mi. long); coconuts. Also called Anir.

Feniscowles, England: see LIVESEY.

Fenit (fĕ'nĭt), Gaelic *Fiannait,* town (pop. 191), W Co. Kerry, Ireland, on Tralee Bay, 6 mi. W of Tralee; seaport for Tralee. St. Brendan b. here.

Fennimore (fĕ'nùmôr"), city (pop. 1,696), Grant co., extreme SW Wis., 26 mi. ESE of Prairie du Chien, in farm area (livestock, poultry, grain); dairy products, feed. Has hq. of a U.S. soil conservation project. Inc. 1919.

Fennville, village (pop. 639), Allegan co., SW Mich., 13 mi. WNW of Allegan, in fruitgrowing and dairying area; mfg. (canned goods, spray equipment, vinegar).

Fenny or **Feni** (fā'nē), town (pop. 5,421), Noakhali dist., SE East Bengal, E Pakistan, on left tributary of Fenny R. and 23 mi. NE of Noakhali; rail junction (spur to Belonia); rice, jute, oilseeds; perfume mfg.

Fenny River, on E Pakistan–Tripura (India) border, rises in N Chittagong Hills, flows 55 mi. SW, past Ramgarh, to Sandwip Channel 16 mi. S of Fenny.

Fenny Stratford, England: see BLETCHLEY.

Feno, Cap de (käp dü fěnō'), headland of W Corsica on the Mediterranean, 8 mi. WNW of Ajaccio; 41°58'N 8°33'E.

Fen River, Chinese *Fen Shui* (fŭn' shwā'), main stream of Shansi prov., China, rises in Luya Mts. SW of Ningwu, flows 430 mi. SSW, traversing entire prov., past Taiyüan, Hwohsien, Linfen, and Sinkiang (head of navigation), to Yellow R. (Shensi line) opposite Hancheng.

Fens, The, region of SE England, W and S of The Wash, covering parts of counties of Lincoln, Norfolk, Cambridge, Suffolk, and Huntingdon; c.70 mi. N–S, c.35 mi. E–W. Crossed by Witham, Welland, Nene, Ouse, and many other lesser rivers. Formed by gradual silting up of a large bay of North Sea of which The Wash is a relic. Romans 1st attempted drainage of The Fens, built roads here, and established stations in higher areas. Cornelius Vermuyden developed 1st effective drainage system after 1621; reclamation (in sections, or levels, e.g., BEDFORD LEVEL) was completed in 19th cent., and area is now under cultivation (fruit, vegetables, flowers); much small game. In anc. times The Fens were site of many hermits' cells, now marked by churches.

Fenshui (fŭn'shwā'), town (pop. 4,313), ⊙ Fenshui co. (pop. 43,114), NW Chekiang prov., China, 25 mi. N of Kienteh; rice, wheat, tea, tung oil.

Fen Shui, river, Shansi prov., China: see FEN RIVER.

Fensi or **Fen-hsi** (both: fŭn'shē'), town, ⊙ Fensi co. (pop. 51,446), S central Shansi prov., China, 40 mi. N of Linfen, near Fen R. and railroad; cattle raising; wheat, beans, kaoliang, millet. Coal mining near by.

Fentange (fĕntäzh'), village (pop. 224), S Luxembourg, 4 mi. SSE of Luxembourg city; farinaceous food products.

Fenton, town in the Potteries district, NW Stafford, England, since 1910 part of STOKE-ON-TRENT.

Fenton. **1** Town (pop. 446), Kossuth co., N Iowa, 14 mi. NW of Algona; dairy products, feed. **2** Village (pop. 4,226), Genesee co., SE central Mich., 15 mi. S of Flint and on Shiawassee R., in agr. area (dairy products; livestock, fruit, grain). Marl obtained from near-by lakes is used by cement works here. Also mfg. of tools, dies, castings. Lake resort. Settled 1834, inc. 1863. **3** Town (pop. 207), St. Louis co., E Mo., near Mississippi R., on the Meramec and just SW of St. Louis.

Fentress (fĕn'trĭs), county (□ 499; pop. 14,917), N Tenn.; ⊙ Jamestown. In the Cumberlands; drained by forks of Obey and Cumberland rivers. Includes part of Dale Hollow Reservoir. Lumbering (hardwoods), agr. (corn, tobacco, fruit, vegetables), dairying, livestock raising; bituminous-coal mines. Formed 1823.

Fentress, village (pop. c.250), Caldwell co., S central Texas, 11 mi. SW of Lockhart and on San Marcos R.

Fentsch, France: see FONTOY.

Fenua Iti, Cook Isls.: see TAKUTEA.

Fenua Ura, Society Isls.: see SCILLY ISLAND.

Fenwick (fĕ'nĭk), agr. village and parish (pop. 1,209), N Ayrshire, Scotland, 4 mi. NNE of Kilmarnock.

Fenwick, Conn.: see OLD SAYBROOK.

Fenwood, village (pop. 139), Marathon co., central Wis., 20 mi. WSW of Wausau; lumbering, dairying, stock raising.

Fenyang (fŭn'yäng'), town (1922 pop. estimate 65,000), ⊙ Fenyang co. (1946 pop. 149,160), central Shansi prov., China, on rail spur, on arm of Fen R. and 50 mi. SW of Taiyüan; winegrowing center; trades in tea, sugar, cotton cloth, wheat, tobacco. Until 1912 called Fenchow.

Feock (fē'ŭk), agr. village and parish (pop. 1,589), SW Cornwall, England, on Fal R. and 4 mi. S of Truro. Has 13th-cent. church.

Feodosiya (fēŭdō'shēŭ, -sēŭ, Rus. fă'ŭdô'sēŭ), anc. *Theodosia*, city (1926 pop. 28,656), E Crimea, Russian SFSR, major Black Sea port at W end of Feodosiya Gulf (20 mi. wide, 9 mi. long), 60 mi. WSW of Kerch; rail terminus; trade and food-processing center; tobacco, flour, wine, canned fish, alcohol, beer; metal- and brickworks. Exports mainly grain. Health resort with bathing beach, grape-cure establishments, and mud baths in bitter-salt lake of Adzhigol, 2 mi. N. Has picture gall. (1880), archaeological mus. (1811), meteorological institute, ruins of Genoese tower and walls. Founded (6th cent. B.C.) as Gr. colony trading in grain, hides, fish, salt; built in form of amphitheater. Called Caffa or Kaffa under Genoese; developed as flourishing trade port; passed (1475) to Turks; sacked (18th cent.) by Russians. Following construction of railroad and transfer of commercial port from Sevastopol, Feodosiya rallied again, but suffered during Bolshevik revolution and civil war. In Second World War, held (1941-44) by Germans, except for brief Soviet raid (1941-42).

Feodosiyevski, Russian SFSR: see ARTEMOVSKI, Irkutsk oblast.

Fer, Cap de (käp' dü fâr'), Arabic *Ras-el-Hadid*, rocky headland (alt. 1,578 ft.) of Constantine dept., NE Algeria, on the Mediterranean, bounding the Gulf of Philippeville on the E, 35 mi. WNW of Bône. It forms westernmost extremity of the Edough range; 37°5'N 7°11'E. Lighthouse.

Fer-à-Cheval, Cirque du, France: see SIXT.

Feragen Lake (fā'rägŭn) (□ 6), Sor-Trondelag co., central Norway, 17 mi. E of Roros; chromite mines NW.

Ferah, Afghanistan: see FARAH.

Ferbane (fûrbăn'), Gaelic *Féar Bán*, town (pop. 312), NW Co. Offaly, Ireland, on Brosna R. and on Grand Canal, 14 mi. W of Tullamore; agr. market (cattle; hops, barley, potatoes) and peat-digging center.

Ferch (fĕrkh), village (pop. 1,116), Brandenburg, E Germany, on Schwielow L., 9 mi. SW of Potsdam; mfg. of trucks, railroad equipment.

Ferdan, El, Egypt: see FIRDAN, EL.

Ferdinand, Bulgaria: see MIKHAILOVGRAD.

Ferdinand (fĕrdēnänd'), village (pop. 2,133), Severin prov., W Rumania, 10 mi. NE of Caransebes; metallurgical center; foundries, rolling mills.

Ferdinand. **1** Village (pop. 206), Idaho co., W Idaho, 10 mi. SW of Nezperce; livestock. **2** Town (pop. 1,252), Dubois co., SW Ind., c.45 mi. ENE of Evansville, in agr. area; mfg. (furniture, steam engines, farm and sawmill machinery); timber; stone quarries. Seat of Convent of Immaculate Conception. A state forest and small Ferdinand L. are NE.

Ferdinandov-vrakh, Bulgaria: see BOTEV PEAK.

Ferdows, Iran: see FIRDAUS.

Fère, La (lä fâr'), town (pop. 2,462), Aisne dept., N France, on braided Oise R. at mouth of the Serre, and 13 mi. SSE of Saint-Quentin, on Oise-Sambre Canal; agr. trade center. Arsenal (built 1616). Sugar-refining equipment made at near-by Charmes (pop. 1,612). A former fortress, La Fère was heavily damaged in First World War.

Fère-Champenoise (fâr-shäpŭnwäz'), town (pop. 2,119), Marne dept., N France, 22 mi. SW of Châlons-sur-Marne; agr. market. Brewery. Here Napoleon I was defeated by Allies in 1814; 1st battle of the Marne fought in area.

Feredjik, Greece: see PHERRAI.

Fère-en-Tardenois (fâr-ã-tärdnwä'), village (pop. 1,867), Aisne dept., N France, on the Ourcq and 12 mi. NNE of Château-Thierry; road junction; mfg. (footwear, railroad ties). Sand quarries near by. Battles of May-Aug., 1918, were fought in area. Oise-Aisne American Cemetery (6,012 graves) is 2 mi. E.

Ferejik, Greece: see PHERRAI.

Feren (fā'rŭn), town (pop. 2,464), in former Prussian prov. of Hanover, NW Germany, after 1945 in Lower Saxony, 10 mi. ESE of Lingen, in fen region.

Ferenc Jozsef Csucs, Czechoslovakia: see STALIN PEAK.

Ferentino (fĕrĕntē'nô), town (pop. 7,405), Frosinone prov., Latium, S central Italy, 6 mi. NW of Frosinone; wine, olive oil. Bishopric. Has cathedral with mosaic pavement (1116), pre-Roman and Roman ruins. Mineral baths near by.

Férez (fā'rĕth), town (pop. 1,478), Albacete prov., SE central Spain, 21 mi. SW of Hellín; olive-oil processing; wine, rice, esparto.

Ferfer (fĕrfĕr'), village (pop. 300), in the Mudugh, central Ital. Somaliland, on road and 24 mi. N of Belet Uen.

Fergana (fĕrgä'nŭ, Rus. fyĕrgŭnä'), oblast (□ 3,100; 1946 pop. estimate 600,000), E Uzbek SSR; ⊙ Fergana. In SW Fergana Valley. S part, irrigated by fan-shaped canal network of rivers descending from Alai Range (S), has extensive cotton growing and sericulture; in N, sheep raising in desert adjoining the Syr Darya. Cotton and silk milling at Fergana, Margelan, and Kokand, cement mfg. at Kuvasai, oil field at Chimion and refinery at Vannovski, chemical works at Shorsu. Crossed by railroad through Kokand and Andizhan, with spurs leading to Namangan and Kizyl-Kiya. Formed 1938, although an oblast, here, named Fergana and including a much larger area, existed 1876–1926.

Fergana, city (1932 pop. estimate 34,700), ⊙ Fergana oblast, Uzbek SSR, in Fergana Valley, on rail spur (stations Skobelevo I and II) and 5 mi. S of Margelan, 145 mi. ESE of Tashkent; 40°23'N 71°45'E. Industrial center; cotton ginning, silk spinning, cotton-textile milling, cottonseed-oil extraction, clothing mfg.; hydrolysis works, power plant. Teachers col. Founded 1876 by Russians following their conquest of Kokand khanate and named Novy Margelan [Rus.,=new Margelan]; later (1907) renamed Skobelev and, after Bolshevik revolution, Fergana.

Fergana Canal, Great, large irrigation trunk canal in Fergana Valley, Uzbek SSR; extends from Naryn R. at Uch-Kurgan generally WSW, past Stalino and Kokand, to Kanibadam; 170 mi. long. Built 1939.

Fergana Range, branch of Tien Shan mountain system, W Kirghiz SSR, lies bet. Osh and Dzhalal-Abad oblasts (W) and Tyan-Shan oblast (E); extends from China border c.125 mi. NW to Naryn R.; rises to 15,860 ft. Dense nut and almond woods on SW slope.

Fergana Valley, partly irrigated, mountain-enclosed steppe and desert of Soviet Central Asia, in Tien Shan mtn. system; bordered NW by Kurama and Chatkal ranges, NE by Fergana Range, S by Alai Range; drained by the Syr Darya and by many mtn. streams forming fan-shaped irrigation zones linked by Great FERGANA CANAL. Agr. (cotton, alfalfa, fruit, vineyards) and sericulture furnish basis of cotton, cottonseed-oil, soap-mfg. and fruit-processing industries. Oil fields and coal, mercury, and antimony mines along valley fringes are served by rail spurs branching off circular Fergana Valley RR, which links Kokand, Andizhan, and Namangan. Densely populated by Uzbeks, Tadzhiks, and Kirghiz. Divided politically into LENINABAD oblast (Tadzhik SSR), OSH and DZHALAL-ABAD oblasts (Kirghiz SSR), and ANDIZHAN, FERGANA, and NAMANGAN oblasts (Uzbek SSR). An anc. center of civilization, dominated successively by Turks, Persians, Arabs, Chinese, Mongols, and Uzbeks.

Fergoug, Oued (wĕd' fĕrgōōg'), short stream in Oran dept., NW Algeria, joining the Hammam 5 mi. S of Perrégaux. A dam at junction of streams stores water for irrigation of the Habra lowland N of Perrégaux.

Fergus, village (pop. 2,832), S Ont., on Grand R. and 13 mi. NNW of Guelph; mfg. of domestic appliances; fur farming; oats, peas, barley.

Fergus, county (□ 4,250; pop. 14,015), central Mont.; ⊙ Lewistown. Irrigated agr. region, mountainous in S; drained by Judith R., bounded N by Missouri R. Grain, livestock. Section of Lewis and Clark Natl. Forest in S. Formed 1885.

Fergus Falls, city (pop. 12,917), ⊙ Otter Tail co., W Minn., at falls of Otter Tail R., near mouth of Pelican R., c.50 mi. SE of Fargo, N.Dak.; trade center for grain, dairying, and poultry area; summer resort; food processing (dairy products, flour, beverages); wood and foundry products, woolens. State hosp. is here. City settled 1857, platted 1870, inc. 1872.

Ferguson. **1** Town (pop. 178), Marshall co., central Iowa, 8 mi. SSE of Marshalltown, in agr. area. **2** Town (pop. 550), Pulaski co., S Ky., in Cumberland foothills just S of Somerset. Before 1947, called Luretha. **3** City (pop. 11,573), St. Louis co., E Mo., near Mississippi R., suburb N of St. Louis; produces matches. Inc. 1894. **4** Village (pop. 1,741), Victoria co., S Texas.

Ferguson Park, suburb (pop. 5,203) of Newport News, Warwick co., SE Va.

Fergusson Island, volcanic island (□ 518), largest of D'Entrecasteaux Isls., Territory of Papua, SW Pacific, 30 mi. SE of New Guinea, across Ward Hunt Strait; 40 mi. long, 30 mi. wide; hot springs.

Feria (fā'ryä), town (pop. 4,089), Badajoz prov., W Spain, 33 mi. SE of Badajoz; agr. center (olives, cereals, hogs, sheep, goats). Copper and iron mining; olive-oil pressing.

Fériana (fāryänä'), town (pop. 4,192), Kasserine dist., W Tunisia, on railroad and 20 mi. SW of Kasserine; livestock and esparto market. Roman ruins at Thélepte, 3 mi. NE.

Ferintosh (fĕ'rĭntŏsh"), village (pop. 186), central Alta., 19 mi. SSW of Camrose; wheat, dairying.

Ferkéssédougou (fĕrkĕsĕdōō'gōō), town (pop. c.6,000), N Ivory Coast, Fr. West Africa, on railroad from Abidjan and 130 mi. N of Bouaké; trading, kapok-growing, stock-raising (sheep, goats) center. Meteorological station; R.C. mission.

Ferla (fĕr'lä), village (pop. 4,567), Siracusa prov., SE Sicily, near headwaters of Anapo R., 19 mi. WNW of Syracuse. Early Christian cemetery near by.

Ferlach (fĕr'läkh), Slovenian *Borovlje*, town (pop. 5,200), Carinthia, S Austria, near the Drau, 7 mi. S of Klagenfurt, near Yugoslav line; rail terminus; rolling mill, steelworks, mfg. (small arms, wire).

Ferland (fûr'lŭnd), village, NW Ont., near N shore of L. Nipigon, 200 mi. NNE of Port Arthur; 50°19'N 88°25'W; construction base for OGOKI RIVER project.

Fermanagh (fûrmă'nŭ), county (□ 653; 1937 pop. 54,569; 1951 census 53,040), Ulster, SW Northern Ireland; ⊙ Enniskillen. Bounded by cos. Cavan (S), Leitrim (SW), Donegal (NW), Monaghan (E), Ireland; and by Co. Tyrone (N). Drained by Erne R. Surface is hilly and broken; main feature of co. is the large Lough Erne, divided into upper and lower parts, linked by Erne R. Cuilcagh (2,188 ft.) is highest elevation. Marble, limestone, sandstone are quarried; there are some iron deposits. Potato growing, cattle raising, and lake fishing are main rural occupations. Leading industries are linen and woolen milling, and pottery mfg. (Belleek). Other towns are Lisbellow and Lisnaskea. Devenish isl., in Lough Erne, has famous round tower and ecclesiastical remains. There are other ruins of anc. castles, abbeys, and Danish raths.

Ferme Neuve (fârm nûv'), village (pop. 811), SW Que., in the Laurentians, on Lièvre R. and 11 mi. N of Mont Laurier, at foot of Mt. Sir Wilfrid; dairying, lumbering.

Fermentelos (fĕrmĕntĕ'lo͝osh), village (pop. 2,073), Aveiro dist., N central Portugal, 8 mi. SE of Aveiro; livestock, potatoes, beans.

Fermignano (fĕrmēnyä'nô), village (pop. 1,384), Pesaro e Urbino prov., The Marches, central Italy, on Metauro R. and 4 mi. S of Urbino; silk and woolen mills, cutlery mfg.

Fermin, Point (fûr'mĭn), promontory, W coast of Calif., just S of San Pedro; Los Angeles Harbor breakwater extends E from tip. U.S. Fort MacArthur is here.

Fermo (fĕr'mô), town (pop. 9,295), Ascoli Piceno prov., The Marches, central Italy, on hill 5 mi. W of the Adriatic, 17 mi. SE of Macerata; cotton mill, bell foundry; wineries, mfg. (vegetable oils, cutlery, agr. tools). Archbishopric. Has pre-Roman walls, Roman remains (arch, theater, reservoir), Gothic cathedral, and technical institute.

Fermoselle (fĕrmōsĕ'lyā), town (pop. 4,240), Zamora prov., NW Spain, near Port. border, bet. Duero and Tormes rivers, 38 mi. WSW of Zamora; brandy distilling, flour milling; agr. trade (wine, vegetables, fruit, potatoes). Has anc. castle.

Fermoy (fûrmoi'), Gaelic *Mainistir Fhear Muighe*, urban district (pop. 4,213), E Co. Cork, Ireland, on the Blackwater (bridged) and 19 mi. NNE of Cork; woolen and flour milling; agr. market in dairying region; fishing. Town was founded 1789; later large military station was established here. Has R.C. cathedral.

Fernáncaballero (fĕrnän'kävälyā"rō), town (pop. 2,350), Ciudad Real prov., S central Spain, on railroad and 9 mi. N of Ciudad Real; cereals, grapes, olives, potatoes, sheep, goats. Stone quarrying; alcohol distilling, olive-oil pressing.

Fernandes Pinheiro (fĕrnān'dĭs pēnyā'ro͝o), town (pop. 1,141), S central Paraná, Brazil, on railroad and 35 mi. SW of Ponta Grossa; woodworking, coffee processing; maté, timber.

Fernández (fĕrnän'dĕs), town (1947 pop. 3,048), ⊙ Robles dept. (□ 518; 1947 pop. 27,108), central Santiago del Estero prov., Argentina, on railroad and 25 mi. SE of Santiago del Estero; fruitgrowing center; cotton, sunflowers, livestock.

Fernández, Ciudad, Mexico: see CIUDAD FERNÁNDEZ.

Fernandina (fûrnăndē'nŭ), city (pop. 4,420), ⊙ Nassau co., extreme NE Fla., on Amelia Isl., near mouth of St. Marys R., 25 mi. NE of Jacksonville; port of entry; fishing (oysters, shrimp, menhaden) and pulp-milling center; mfg. of fish meal, oil; sea-food canning. Exports phosphate, lumber, naval stores, cottonseed. Became a free port in 1808 and developed rapidly as a resort of smugglers, slave traders, and pirates. Near by is Fort Clinch, built 1847–61, now a state park. Isl. was also site of a Spanish fort built in 1680s.

Fernandina Beach, town (pop. 554), Nassau co., extreme NE Fla., near Fernandina.

Fernandina Island (fĕrnändē'nä) or **Narborough Island** (när'bŭrŭ) (□ 245), W Galápagos Isls., Ecuador, in the Pacific, just W of Isabela Isl., 130 mi. WNW of Puerto Baquerizo (San Cristóbal Isl.). Circular in shape (c.20 mi. wide), it is of volcanic origin and rises to 3,720 ft. at 0°20'S 91°30'W.

Fernando de la Mora (fĕrnän'dō dā lä mō'rä), town (dist. pop. 9,931), Central dept., S Paraguay, on railroad and 4 mi. SE of Asunción; fruit; ceramics.

Fernando de Noronha (fĕrnăn'do͞o dĭ no͞orōn'yŭ), Brazilian island (□ 7; 1940 pop. 1,065; 1950 census pop. 648) in the South Atlantic, c.225 mi. NE of Cape São Roque on Brazilian bulge. With neighboring islets (□ 3.5), it constitutes (since 1942) a federal territory. Of volcanic origin, it has steep, rugged shore line. Semiarid climate (long dry season), influenced by SE trade winds. Scarcity of fresh water impedes agr. Has saltworks, limekiln, manioc flour mill; guano deposits. Pop. consists of penal colony (since 18th cent.), ex-convicts' settlement (Vila dos Remédios), and military contingent. Airfield. Given (1504) to Fernando de Noronha (its discoverer) as a hereditary captaincy; later became a dependency of Pernambuco. Coveted by several naval powers in 17th and 18th cent., it was successfully defended by Portuguese. Lighthouse on northernmost islet (3°49'S 32°23'W).

Fernando Po (fûrnăn'dō pō', fĕrnän'dō pō') Sp. *Fernando Póo*, Spanish island (□ 779; pop. 33,980) off W African coast, in the Gulf of Guinea (Bight of Biafra), forming (with Annobón isl.) insular part of Sp. Guinea, c.25 mi. S of Br. Cameroons coast and 100 mi. NW of continental Sp. Guinea (or Río Muni). Santa Isabel (3°46'N 8°46'W), its principal town and port on N coast, is ⊙ Sp. Guinea. Isl. is roughly rectangular, 35 mi. long, 20–25 mi. wide. Of volcanic origin, it rises to 9,350 ft. (or 9,449 ft.) in Santa Isabel Peak, a volcanic cone occupying isl.'s N half. Coast is steep and rocky. Only Santa Isabel and San Carlos have sheltered bays. Isl. has unhealthful climate (yearly mean temp. at sea level 82°F.), with rainy (May–Nov.) and dry seasons. Annual rainfall, increasing with alt., is over 80 in. Luxuriant tropical vegetation. While sugar cane was isl.'s 1st commercial crop in 19th cent., cacao is today its chief export. Other products are coffee, bananas, palm oil and kernels, copra, cinchona bark, kola nuts, and some citrus fruit. Cabinet woods are also exploited. The Bantu-speaking Bubi pop. (indigenous to Fernando Po) has mingled with Kru Negroes from neighboring continent. Discovered 1471 by Portuguese (among whom was Fernão do Po). Ceded to Spain 1778. Occupied 1827 by English who founded Clarencetown (now Santa Isabel). Reoccupied by Spain 1843.

Fernandópolis (fĕrnändô'po͝olēs), city, northwesternmost São Paulo, Brazil, 65 mi. NW of São José do Rio Prêto, in region of advancing agr. pioneer settlement; future railhead.

Fernando Prestes (fĕrnăn'do͞o prĕ'stĭs), city (pop. 1,138), N central São Paulo, Brazil, on railroad and 21 mi. SE of Catanduva; corn milling, coffee processing.

Fernán-Núñez (fĕrnän'-no͞o'nyĕth), town (pop. 10,583), Córdoba prov., S Spain, agr. trade center 15 mi. S of Córdoba; lime processing, flour milling. Olive oil, cereals, truck, wine; hog raising.

Fernan-Vaz (fĕrnã'-väz'), village, W Gabon, Fr. Equatorial Africa, on the Atlantic, on Fernan-Vaz lagoon (also called N'Komi lagoon), 70 mi. SSE of Port-Gentil; shipping point for a lumbering area noted for its mahogany and *okume* wood; palm-oil milling.

Ferndale. 1 Town (pop. 1,032), Humboldt co., NW Calif., 16 mi. SSW of Eureka; dairying center; truck, poultry farming. **2** Suburban village (pop. c.1,200), Anne Arundel co., central Md., 8 mi. S of downtown Baltimore. Friendship International Airport is near by. **3** City (pop. 29,675), Oakland co., SE Mich., just N of Detroit; mfg. (auto parts, paint, synthetic resins, metal products). Inc. as village 1919, as city 1927. **4** Resort village, Sullivan co., SE N.Y., 2 mi. S of Liberty. **5** Residential borough (pop. 2,619), Cambria co., SW central Pa., S suburb of Johnstown, on Stony Creek. Inc. 1896. **6** Village, Northumberland co., E central Pa. **7** Town (pop. 979), Whatcom co., NW Wash., 9 mi. NW of Bellingham and on Nooksack R.; dairy products, sugar beets.

Ferne Islands, England: see FARNE ISLANDS.

Ferney-Voltaire (fĕrnā'-vôltâr'), village (pop. 822), Ain dept., E France, on Swiss border, 4 mi. NNW of Geneva; customhouse; pottery, plastics. Known as the residence (1758–78) of Voltaire, whose castle and chapel still stand.

Fernhurst, agr. village and parish (pop. 1,576), NW Sussex, England, 3 mi. S of Haslemere. Has 13th-cent. church.

Fernie (fûr'nē), city (pop. 2,545), SE B.C., in Rocky Mts., on Elk R. and 120 mi. SSW of Calgary, at foot of Mt. Fernie (7,850 ft.); alt. 3,313 ft.; coal mining, coke making, lumbering. Tourist center.

Fern Lake, Ky. and Tenn.: see MIDDLESBORO, Ky.

Fernley, village (pop. c.450), Lyon co., W Nev., on Truckee Canal and 31 mi. E of Reno in irrigated agr. area; alt. 4,025 ft.; trading point and feeding base for livestock.

Ferno (fĕr'nô), village (pop. 2,059), Varese prov., Lombardy, N Italy, 5 mi. W of Busto Arsizio; textile mfg.

Fern Pass (fĕrn) (alt. 3,966 ft.), in Lechtal Alps, W Austria; highway over it runs from Innsbruck to Germany.

Fern Ridge Dam, Oregon: see LONG TOM RIVER.

Ferns, Gaelic *Fearna*, town (pop. 445), N Co. Wexford, Ireland, 7 mi. NNE of Enniscorthy; agr. market in dairying, agr. area (wheat, barley, potatoes, beets). Has 18th-cent. palace of bishops of Ferns, cathedral (1816), and ruins of Austin priory (founded c.1160) and of 12th-cent. castle. In anc. times town was ⊙ kingdom of Leinster; in 7th cent. St. Edan founded 1st monastery here; town subsequently suffered several Danish raids. Bishops of Ferns now live at Wexford; cathedral of diocese is at Enniscorthy.

Fernwood. 1 Village (1940 pop. 736), Pike co., SW Miss., 3 mi. S of McComb; lumber milling, plywood and veneer mfg. **2** Village, Delaware co., Pa.: see UPPER DARBY.

Ferokh (fĕrōk'), town (pop. 6,249), Malabar dist., SW Madras, India, near Beypore R. mouth, 6 mi. SE of Calicut; tile-, coffee-curing, and fertilizer works; sawmilling. Also spelled Ferok, Feroke. Fishing village of Beypore is 3 mi. W, across river; industrial school (coir products).

Ferolle Point (fĕ'rōl), promontory, NW N.F., at N edge of St. John Bay; 51°1'N 57°6'W.

Ferozepore (fĭrōz'po͝or), district (□ 4,085; pop. 1,423,076), W Punjab, India; ⊙ Ferozepore. Bordered by Sutlej R. (N, W), Pakistan Punjab and Bahawalpur state (W), Rajasthan (S); has enclave in Patiala and East Punjab States Union (E). Irrigated by several large canals; agr. (gram, wheat, cotton, oilseeds); hand-loom cotton and woolen weaving. Chief towns: Ferozepore, Fazilka, Moga, Muktsar. Scene (1845–46), of several battles in 1st Sikh war. Also spelled Firozpur.

Ferozepore, city (pop., including S cantonment area, 82,502), ⊙ Ferozepore dist., W Punjab, India, 50 mi. SSW of Amritsar. Rail junction; trade center; agr. market (wheat, gram, cotton, oilseeds); cotton ginning, hand-loom weaving, rice milling, mfg. of chemicals, confectioneries, flour, toys; engineering and enamel works; metalware. Large arsenal. Has col. Headworks of Sutlej valley irrigation system 4 mi. NW. Founded in time of Firoz Shah Tughluk, sultan of Delhi (1351–88). Occupied by British in 1835.

Ferozeshah (fĭrōz'shä), village, Ferozepore dist., W Punjab, India, 11 mi. ESE of Ferozepore. Here Sir Hugh Gough repulsed Sikhs (Dec., 1845) in 1st Sikh war.

Ferozpur, Kashmir: see GULMARG.

Ferozpur Jhirka, India: see FIROZPUR JHIRKA.

Ferques (fârk), village (pop. 1,250), Pas-de-Calais dept., N France, 9 mi. SSW of Calais; marble quarrying.

Ferragudo (fĕrŭgo͞o'do͞o), village (pop. 1,735), Faro dist., S Portugal, on the Atlantic 2 mi. SE of Portimão; fishing and canning (sardines).

Ferrah, Afghanistan: see FARAH.

Ferrai, Greece: see PHERRAI.

Ferrandina (fĕr-rändē'nä), town (pop. 7,625), Matera prov., Basilicata, S Italy, near Basento R., 9 mi. NNW of Pisticci; pottery, woolen cloth, wine, olive oil.

Ferrara (fŭrä'rŭ, It. fĕr-rä'rä), province (□ 1,015; pop. 381,299), Emilia-Romagna, N central Italy; ⊙Ferrara. Bounded by Po R. (N) and Adriatic Sea (E); low plain (average elevation 15 ft.) bordered by extensive lagoons, including Valli di COMACCHIO. Much of the land has been reclaimed, as around CODIGORO, and is traversed by numerous canals. Agr. (cereals, hemp, sugar beets); stock raising. Fishing and saltmaking at Comacchio; mfg. at Ferrara and Pontelagoscuro.

Ferrara, anc. *Forum Alieni*, city (pop. 58,187), ⊙ Ferrara prov., Emilia-Romagna, N central Italy, near Po R., 28 mi. NE of Bologna; 44°50'N 11°38' E. Agr. and mfg. center; beet sugar, macaroni, sausage, fertilizer, soap, candles, alcohol, pharmaceuticals, shoes, hemp products, glass, agr. machinery. Archbishopric. Has Romanesque-Gothic cathedral (begun 1135), moated castle (1385–1570), university (founded 1391), and many fine palaces, including Palazzo Schifanoia (1391–1471) and Palazzo dei Diamanti (1492–1565). In 13th cent. became a powerful principality and flourished as seat of Este family, patrons of arts and letters, whose court was famous throughout Europe. Inc. into Papal States in 1598. Residence of Ariosto and Tasso; Savonarola b. here. Severely bombed (1943–44) in Second World War, with destruction or heavy damage to some 2,300 houses.

Ferrat, Cape (fĕrä'), headland of Oran dept., NW Algeria, on the Mediterranean, 20 mi. NE of Oran; 35°54'N 0°22'W. It is overlooked by the Djebel Orousse (alt. 2,070 ft.).

Ferrat, Cape, France: see SAINT-JEAN-CAP-FERRAT.

Ferrato, Cape (fĕr-rä'tô), point on SE coast of Sardinia; 39°18'N 9°37'E.

Ferreira do Alentejo (fĕrā'rŭ do͞o älāntā'zho͞o), town (pop. 4,860), Beja dist., S Portugal, 14 mi. WNW of Beja; road center; grain milling, cheese mfg.

Ferreira do Zêzere (zā'zĭrĭ), town (pop. 381) Santarém dist., central Portugal, 9 mi. NE of Tomar; cheese mfg.

Ferreira Gomes (gō'mĭs), town, central Amapá territory, N Brazil, head of navigation on Araguari R. and 55 mi. N of Macapá; rubber, hardwood. Called Amapari, 1939–43.

Ferrel (fĕrĕl'), village (pop. 1,380), Leiria dist., W central Portugal, on the Atlantic, 3 mi. ENE of Peniche; sardine fisheries.

Ferrells Bridge Reservoir, Texas: see CYPRESS BAYOU.

Ferrelview, town (pop. 126), Platte co., W Mo., 16 mi. NNW of Kansas City.

Ferreñafe (fĕrānyä'fā), city (pop. 8,812), Lambayeque dept., NW Peru, on coastal plain, 9 mi. ENE of Lambayeque (connected by railroad), in area irrigated by Taimi Canal. Trading and milling center for important rice-producing region.

Ferrera Erbognone (fĕr-rā'rä ĕrbônyô'nĕ), village (pop. 1,334), Pavia prov., Lombardy, N Italy, 15 mi. WSW of Pavia; makes rice-mill machinery.

Ferreras de Abajo (fĕrā'räs dhā ävä'hō), village (pop. 1,008), Zamora prov., NW Spain, 23 mi. WSW of Benavente; potatoes, cereals, livestock.

Ferrería de la Encarnación, Mexico: see ENCARNACIÓN.

Ferrerías (fĕrārē'äs), town (pop. 1,153), Minorca, Balearic Isls., 15 mi. WNW of Mahón; cheese-processing center. Region raises cereals, cattle, sheep, goats, hogs, mules, horses. On adjacent (E) Santa Águeda mtn. are ruins of a Moorish castle. Near by are the gorge Barranco de Algendar and the beach Cala Galdaña.

Ferret, Cape (fĕrā'), on Bay of Biscay, Gironde dept., SW France, at S end of peninsula separating Arcachon Basin from the Atlantic, 37 mi. WSW of Bordeaux; lighthouse (44°38'N 1°15'W).

Ferret, Col de (kôl dŭ fĕrā'), Alpine pass (8,343 ft.) on Italo-Swiss border, near Great St. Bernard Pass, 16 mi. NW of Aosta; connects Dora Baltea (S) and Rhone valley (N). Crossed by mule path.

Ferrette (fĕrĕt'), Ger. *Pfirt* (pfĭrt), village (pop. 417), Haut-Rhin dept., E France, on N slopes of Jura Mts., near Swiss border, 10 mi. SSE of Altkirch; agr. school.

Ferriday, town (pop. 3,847), Concordia parish, E central La., 10 mi. NW of Natchez (Miss.), near Mississippi R., in agr. area (cotton, pecans, corn; dairy products; livestock); railroad shops, cotton gins and warehouses, lumber mills, gas-pumping plant. Founded 1903; inc. as village in 1905, as town in 1927.

Ferrier (fĕrēā'), town (1950 pop. 1,407), Nord dept., NE Haiti, 5 mi. SE of Fort Liberté, near Dominican Republic border; coffee, sisal, timber.

Ferriere (fĕr-rēā'rē), village (pop. 279), Piacenza prov., Emilia-Romagna, N central Italy, on Nure R. and 10 mi. SE of Bobbio; iron, copper mines.

Ferrière-aux-Étangs, La (lä fĕrēâr'-ōzātä'), village (pop. 321), Orne dept., NW France, 7 mi. NE of Domfront; iron mines.

Ferrière-la-Grande (–lä-grăd'), S suburb (pop. 3,982) of Maubeuge, Nord dept., N France; mfg. (furnaces, Diesel motors, gears).

Ferrières (fĕrēâr'). **1** or **Ferrières-en-Gâtinais** (–ā-gätēnā'), village (pop. 976), Loiret dept., N central France, near Loing R., 7 mi. NNE of Montargis; mfg. of optical glass and hosiery; tanning. **2** Village (pop. 345), Oise dept., N France, 5 mi. SSW of Montdidier; mfg. (agr. machinery, town clocks). **3** or **Ferrières-en-Brie** (–ā-brē'), village (pop. 584), Seine-et-Marne dept., N central France, 16 mi. ESE of Paris. Here Bismarck and Favre signed armistice of 1871.

Ferrières-en-Bray (–ā-brā'), village (pop. 912), Seine-Inférieure dept., N France, just E of Gournay; cheese and ceramics mfg., cider distilling.

Ferrières-en-Brie, France: see FERRIÈRES, Seine-et-Marne dept.

Ferrières-en-Gâtinais, France: see FERRIÈRES, Loiret dept.

Ferris. 1 Village (pop. 226), Hancock co., W Ill., 12 mi. ENE of Keokuk (Iowa), in agr. and bituminous-coal area. **2** Town (pop. 1,735), Ellis co., N Texas, 18 mi. SSE of Dallas; shipping point in rich blackland agr. area: cotton, grain, truck (especially onions). Brick mfg.; cotton ginning. Settled 1870, inc. 1874.

Ferrisburg, town (pop. 1,387), Addison co., W Vt., 18 mi. S of Burlington and on L. Champlain, at mouth of Otter Creek; lumber. Includes Basin Harbor (resort). Granted 1762, settled 1785.

Ferro, Canary Isls.: see HIERRO.

Ferrol, El, or **El Ferrol del Caudillo** (ĕl fĕrōl' dhĕl kou-dhē'lyō), city (pop. 40,664), La Coruña prov., NW Spain, in Galicia, chief Atlantic naval base on fortified Ferrol Bay (10 mi. long, ½–2 mi. wide), 12 mi. NE of La Coruña; 43°28'N 8°13'W. Harbor guarded by San Felipe (N) and Palma (S) forts; naval arsenal and dry docks for warship construction. Fishing, fish processing and shipping, boatbuilding; other mfg.: electrical equipment, furniture, pencils. Founded in 18th cent. when Charles III built an arsenal here. Has naval acad. Gen. Franco ("El Caudillo") b. here. In 1939 its name was officially changed from El Ferrol to El Ferrol del Caudillo.

Ferrol Bay, Peru: see CHIMBOTE.

Ferron (fĕ'rŭn), town (pop. 478), Emery co., central Utah, 11 mi. SW of Castle Dale, on Ferron Creek.

Ferros (fĕ'rōōs), city (pop. 1,676), E central Minas Gerais, Brazil, 75 mi. NE of Belo Horizonte; semiprecious stones and bismuth found here.

Ferru, Monte (môn'tĕ fĕr'rōō), extinct volcano (3,444 ft.), W Sardinia, 17 mi. N of Oristano.

Ferry, village (1939 pop. 31), central Alaska, on Nenana R. and 40 mi. S of Nenana, on Alaska RR; supply point for gold placers and quartz mines.

Ferry, county (□ 2,241; pop. 4,096), NE Wash., on British Columbia line; ⊙ Republic. Forested mtn. area watered by Columbia and Sanpoil rivers. Includes parts of Colville Indian Reservation and Colville Natl. Forest. Timber; gold, nickel, antimony, silver; hay, grain, livestock, dairy products. Formed 1899.

Ferry, village, Ferry co., NE Wash., port of entry at international line, 13 mi. WSW of Grand Forks, British Columbia.

Ferrybank, Gaelic *Sráid an Phuirt,* N suburb of Waterford, S Co. Kilkenny, Ireland, on Suir R.

Ferryden, fishing village in Montrose parish, NE Angus, Scotland, on South Esk R. near its mouth on the North Sea, opposite Montrose, with which it is linked by viaduct.

Ferry Frystone, town and parish (pop. 7,746), West Riding, S central Yorkshire, England, on Aire R. and 3 mi. N of Pontefract; coal-mining center.

Ferryhill, town and parish (pop. 10,397), central Durham, England, 6 mi. S of Durham; coal mining.

Ferryland, village (pop. 523), SE N.F., on SE coast of Avalon Peninsula, 40 mi. SSW of St. John's; fishing port; site of govt. bait depot. Lord Baltimore established settlement here 1624. In 1638 Sir David Kirke, count palatine of isl., established his ⊙ here. Settlement was raided 1673 by Dutch.

Ferryport-on-Craig, Scotland: see TAYPORT.

Ferrysburg, village (pop. 1,454), Ottawa co., SW Mich., opposite Grand Haven on Spring L. near its outlet to L. Michigan; makes boilers.

Ferryville (fĕrēvēl'), town (pop. 29,353), Bizerte dist., N Tunisia, on S shore of L. of Bizerte, 9 mi. SSW of Bizerte. Site of important Fr. naval base (Sidi Abdallah, just E), arsenal, and other military installations. Damaged in Second World War.

Ferryville, village (pop. 216), Crawford co., SW Wis., on the Mississippi and 32 mi. S of La Crosse, in livestock and dairy area; U.S. fish hatchery here.

Ferse River, Poland: see WIERZYCA RIVER.

Fershampenuaz (fyĕrshŭmpyĕnōōäs'), village (1929 pop. over 2,000), S central Chelyabinsk oblast, Russian SFSR, on left tributary of Ural R. and 30 mi. ENE of Magnitogorsk; grain, livestock. Gold placers near by.

Ferté-Alais, La (lä fĕrtā'-ālā'), village (pop. 958), Seine-et-Oise dept., N central France, on the Essonne and 11 mi. SSW of Corbeil. Has 12th-cent. church.

Ferté-Bernard, La (–bĕrnär'), town (pop. 5,074), Sarthe dept., W France, on Huisne R. and 12 mi. SW of Nogent-le-Rotrou; linen-mfg. center (cloth, bags), cattle and horse market; iron founding, cider and flour milling. Has 15th–16th-cent. church with fine stained-glass windows. Damaged in Second World War.

Ferté-Frênel, La (–frĕnĕl'), village (pop. 370), Orne dept., NW France, 24 mi. ENE of Argentan; cider distilling, sawmilling. Also spelled La Ferté-Fresnel.

Ferté-Gaucher, La (–gōshā'), village (pop. 1,835), Seine-et-Marne dept., N central France, on the Grand-Morin and 15 mi. N of Provins; agr. market. 1st battle of the Marne (1914) fought in area.

Ferté-Macé, La (–mäsā'), town (pop. 3,469), Orne dept., NW France, 23 mi. WNW of Alençon; textile center (cotton and linen fabrics); camera and cable mfg. Dairying.

Ferté-Milon, La (–mēlō'), village (pop. 1,573), Aisne dept., N France, on the Ourcq and 15 mi. NW of Château-Thierry; woodworking. Has ruins of 14th-cent. castle. Racine b. here.

Ferté-Saint-Aubin, La (–sē-tōbē'), town (pop. 3,139), Loiret dept., N central France, in the Sologne, 13 mi. S of Orléans; metalworking center (foundries, armament and edge-tool factories). Tree nurseries.

Ferté-sous-Jouarre, La (–sōō-zhwär'), town (pop. 3,866), Seine-et-Marne dept., N central France, on the Marne at influx of the Petit-Morin, and 11 mi. E of Meaux; millstone-mfg. center. Also makes rattan furniture, knitwear, agr. equipment. Has memorial to Br. soldiers killed here during 1st battle of the Marne (1914).

Ferté-Vidame, La (–vēdäm'), village (pop. 615), Eure-et-Loir dept., NW central France, in Perche hills, 17 mi. ENE of Mortagne; horse raising.

Fertile (fûr'tĭl). **1** Town (pop. 397), Worth co., N Iowa, on Lime Creek and 14 mi. NW of Mason City, in onion-growing region. **2** Resort village (pop. 890), Polk co., NW Minn., on small tributary of Red R. and 22 mi. SE of Crookston in diversified-farming area; dairy products, flour.

Fertörakos (fĕr'tûräkôsh), Hung. *Fertőrákos,* town (pop. 3,745), Sopron co., W Hungary, 4 mi. NE of Sopron; wheat, corn; cattle, ducks.

Fertöszentmiklos (fĕr'tûsĕntmĭklōsh), Hung. *Fertőszentmiklós,* town (pop. 3,640), Sopron co., W Hungary, 15 mi. SE of Sopron; wheat, corn, sugar beets; cattle, poultry.

Fertö to, Austria, Hungary: see NEUSIEDLER LAKE.

Ferwerd (fĕr'vûrt), village (pop. 1,476), Friesland prov., N Netherlands, near Waddenzee coast, 10 mi. N of Leeuwarden; cattle raising, dairying; potatoes.

Ferzikovo (fyĭrzyē'kŭvŭ), village (1939 pop. over 500), E Kaluga oblast, Russian SFSR, on railroad and 20 mi. E of Kaluga; rye, oats, potatoes.

Fès, Fr. Morocco: see FEZ.

Fesches-le-Châtel (fĕsh'-lù-shätĕl'), town (pop. 2,166), Doubs dept., E France, on Rhone-Rhine Canal and 5 mi. ENE of Montbéliard; hardware.

Feshi (fĕ'shē), village, Leopoldville prov., SW Belgian Congo, on Kwenge R. (tributary of Kwilu R.) and 75 mi. SW of Kikwit; native trade center.

Feshn, Egypt: see FASHN, EL.

Fessenden (fĕ'sùndùn), city (pop. 917), ⊙ Wells co., central N.Dak., 80 mi. NE of Bismarck; wheat, barley, rye. Seat of annual agr. exposition. Platted 1893.

Festenberg, Poland: see TWARDOGORA.

Festina (fĕstī'nù), village (pop. c.200), Winneshiek co., NE Iowa, 14 mi. SSW of Decorah; butter, feed.

Festiniog, Wales: see FFESTINIOG.

Festubert (fĕstübâr'), village (pop. 721), Pas-de-Calais dept., N France, 4 mi. ENE of Béthune. Captured (1914) by Germans. Scene of large-scale unsuccessful assault by British (1915) and of severe fighting in 1918.

Festus (fĕ'stùs), city (pop. 5,199), Jefferson co., E Mo., on Mississippi R. and 30 mi. S of St. Louis; shoes, textiles, grain products. Platted 1878.

Fetcham, residential town and parish (pop. 1,319), central Surrey, England, on Mole R. just W of Leatherhead.

Fetesti (fătĕsht'), Rum. *Fetești,* town (1948 pop. 11,946), Ialomita prov., SE Rumania, on Borcea arm of the Danube and 27 mi. NE of Calarasi; rail junction and agr. trading center. Has model farm, fruit-tree nurseries, agr. school.

Fethard, Gaelic *Fiodh Ârd,* town (pop. 1,024), S Co. Tipperary, Ireland, 9 mi. SE of Cashel; agr. (dairying, cattle raising; potatoes, beets). Has remains of anc. ramparts of Augustinian friary dating from time of King John, and of 14th-cent. church.

Fethiye (fĕtĭyĕ'), village (pop. 4,174), Mugla prov., SW Turkey, Mediterranean port 60 mi. SE of Mugla, 50 mi. ENE of Rhodes; rich chromium deposits, manganese, coal, lignite; tobacco, olives, cereals. Formerly Makri.

Fetlar (fĕt'lär), island (□ 15.5; pop. 217) of the Shetlands, Scotland, 3 mi. E of Yell isl. across Colgrave Sound; 6 mi. long, 4 mi. wide; rises to 522 ft. (N). Fetlar is noted for its ponies. Iron and kaolin are found here.

Feto, Cape (fā'tô), point on W coast of Sicily, W of Mazara del Vallo; 37°39'N 12°32'E.

Fettercairn, agr. village and parish (pop. 1,087), SW Kincardine, Scotland, 4 mi. WNW of Laurencekirk; malt distilling.

Fetters Springs or **Fetters Hot Springs,** village (pop. 2,391, with near-by Boyes Springs), Sonoma co., W Calif., 14 mi. SE of Santa Rosa.

Fetzara, Lake (fĕtzärä'), marshy lagoon (□ c.50) in Constantine dept., NE Algeria, just S of the coastal Edough range, 12 mi. SW of Bône. Drainage has been attempted. Also spelled Fezzara.

Feucht (foikht), village (pop. 4,319), Middle Franconia, N central Bavaria, Germany, 8 mi. SE of Nuremberg; rail junction; textile mfg., metal- and woodworking.

Feuchtwangen (foikht'väng"ùn), village (pop. 3,713), Middle Franconia, W Bavaria, Germany, 14 mi. SW of Ansbach; mfg. (furniture, precision instruments). Has Romanesque church. Was free imperial city until 1376.

Feuerbach (foi'ùrbäkh), industrial N suburb of Stuttgart, Germany.

Feuerkogel, Austria: see EBENSEE.

Feuerthalen (foi'ùrtä'lùn), town (pop. 2,602), Zurich canton, N Switzerland, on the Rhine opposite Schaffhausen; metalworking.

Feulen (foi'lùn), village, central Luxembourg, on Wark R. and 3 mi. W of Ettelbruck; chalk quarrying; tree nurseries. Consists of Oberfeulen (pop. 532) and Niederfeulen (pop. 291) villages.

Feuquières-en-Vimeu (fûkyâr'-ā-vēmû'), village (pop. 1,844), Somme dept., N France, 10 mi. WSW of Abbeville; locksmithing, metal founding.

Feurs (fûr), anc. *Forum Segusiavorum,* town (pop. 4,781), Loire dept., SE central France, in Forez Plain near the Loire, 12 mi. NE of Montbrison; agr. market, with processing plants; metalworking, paper milling, mfg. of glucose, fertilizer, and vegetable oils. Until 1441, seat of the counts of Forez and later (1793–1801) ⊙ Loire dept.

Fève, La, Palestine: see AFULA.

Fever River, Wis. and Ill.: see GALENA RIVER.

Fevig, Norway: see FEVIK.

Fevik (fā'vĭk, –vēk), village (pop. 453) in Fjaere canton, Aust-Agder co., S Norway, on the Skagerrak, 6 mi. SW of Arendal; shipbuilding. Formerly spelled Fevig and Faevik.

Fevzipasa (fĕvzĭ'pä-shä"), Turkish *Fevzipaşa,* village (pop. 2,484), Gaziantep prov., S Turkey, 6 mi N of Islahiye; rail junction. Just NE are ruins of anc. Hittite city of Senjirli.

Feyzabad, Iran: see FAIZABAD.

Feyzin (fāzē'), village (pop. 1,775), Isère dept., SE France, near left bank of the Rhone, 6 mi. S of Lyons; makes films, rubber bands.

Fez or **Fès** (both: fĕz), Arabic *Fas,* city (pop. 200,946), ⊙ Fez region (□ 15,602; pop. 1,081,765), N central French Morocco, on the Fez above its influx into the Sebou, and 150 mi. ENE of Casablanca; alt. 1,360 ft.; 34°3'N 4°59'W. Morocco's principal religious center, the sultan's traditional northern capital (Marrakesh having been his southern capital; Rabat has been his official residence since establishment of Fr. Protectorate), and the chief city of native handicraft industries and commerce. Strategically located at junction of roads from Tangier, Casablanca, Marrakesh, Algeria, and the trans-Atlas oases of S and SE Morocco, it is also on trunk railroad (electrified W of Fez) linking Fr. Morocco's Atlantic coast and Tangier with Algeria and Tunisia. Airfield just SE. Has textile mills (cotton, wool), oil-processing plant and soap factories, tanneries, flour mills (mfg. macaroni products); also processing of palm fibers, preserving of olives and other Mediterranean fruit grown in vicinity, mfg. of carpets and Morocco leather. Fez has given its name to the brimless cylindrical red felt hat, still a characteristic item of Mohammedan dress in many parts of the Islamic world. City has a Mediterranean subtropical climate, somewhat modified by Atlantic influences, with an annual average temp. of 64°F., excessively hot summers, and yearly rainfall of 22 inches (concentrated in winter months). City is an amalgam of 3 towns of different age and appearance. In the N, Fès el Bali (Old Fez), founded 808 by Idris I (whose shrine in the city is one of Morocco's holiest places of worship), is a medieval town crowded into the valley of the Fez wadi and served by a labyrinth of narrow alleys. Here are the picturesque market streets in which artisan guilds are still grouped by professions. Here also is the enormous Karaouine mosque with 14 gates (built 9th–11th cent.) which, as the seat of a famous Moslem univ. became the intellectual center of the Maghrib during the Middle Ages. Fès Djedid (New Fez), SW of old city, was founded in 1276 by the Merinid dynasty. Here are the sultan's palace and the Jewish quarter. S of the railroad station is modern

Fez, with administrative and residential dists. Fez was ⊙ of the Almohade and Merinide dynasties. It reached its greatest fame during 14th–15th cent. After 1547, it had to share its position with Marrakesh, and in 17th cent. Meknès became for 60 years the sultan's capital. In 1912, the Fr. protectorate over Morocco was recognized by the sultan at Fez. City's European pop. (1947) was 15,938.

Fezzan (fĕzăn'), SW division (□ c.280,000; 1947 pop. estimate 50,000) of LIBYA, in the Sahara S of Tripolitania; ⊙ Sebha. Has desert boundary with Tunisia (NW), Algeria (W), Niger territory of Fr. West Africa (S), and Cyrenaica (E). Pop. is concentrated in a string of oases extending SW from the Gebel es-Soda along Tripolitania line (Sebha, Murzuk, Brach, Gatrun), and in isolated oases (Ghadames, Ghat, Derg, Sinauen) along Tunisian and Algerian borders. Rainfall is almost nil. The Saharan expanse consists of hamadas (rock and gravel deserts) and ergs (sand dunes). Auto and caravan tracks link oases with Mediterranean coast at Misurata and Tripoli, with the S Algerian oases and the L. Chad region in the Sudan. All-Moslem pop. (Arabs, Tuaregs, Tibus) is ⅔ settled in oases, ⅓ nomadic and seminomadic. Agr. is entirely for local consumption; some dates and woven handicrafts are exported. An early focus of caravan routes, Fezzan was conquered by Rome (19 B.C.), by Arabs (7th cent. A.D.), by Bornu (13th cent.), and, after a bitter struggle, by Turkey in 1842. Acquired by Italy in 1912, it was not fully subjugated until 1930. Administratively, it formed part of Italy's Saharan military territory. During Second World War, it was traversed by Free French forces under Leclerc in 1942–43, and came under Fr. military administration in 1943. Under U.N. decision of 1949, Fezzan is one of the constituent units (Tripolitania and Cyrenaica are the others) of an independent federal kingdom of Libya established by 1952.

Ffestiniog or **Festiniog** (fĕstĭn'yôg), urban district (1931 pop. 9,078; 1951 census 6,923), NW Merioneth, Wales, 9 mi. ENE of Portmadoc; agr. market. Near by are zinc mines and noted waterfalls of CYNFAL RIVER. Urban dist. includes slate-mining center of BLAENAU-FFESTINIOG, and slate-mining towns of Congl-y-Wal (kŭng'ŭl-ŭ-wäl') (pop. 1,434) and Rhiwbryfdir (rēōōbrĭv'dĭr) (pop. 1,301).

Ffestiniog, Vale of, Wales: see DWYRYD RIVER.

Fforest Fawr, Wales: see BLACK MOUNTAIN.

Fiambalá (fyämbälä'), town (pop. estimate 500), S Catamarca prov., Argentina, on Abaucán R. and 37 mi. W of Belén; alt. c.5,500 ft.; grain-growing and stock-raising center; viticulture. Tin mines near by.

Fiambalá, Sierra de (syĕ'rä dā), subandean range in central Catamarca prov., Argentina, SE of Fiambalá, extends c.60 mi. NNE–SSW; rises to c.13,000 ft.; tin-mining area.

Fiambiro (fyämbē'rō), village (pop. 900), Harar prov., E central Ethiopia, in highlands 18 mi. ENE of Harar, in coffee- and durra-growing region.

Fianarantsoa (fyänäräntsōō'ŭ, –tsō'ŭ), province (□ 38,740; 1948 pop. 1,038,300), E and SE Madagascar; ⊙ Fianarantsoa. Fertile coastal plain; mountainous territory in W. Chief products are coffee, rice. Some copper, graphite, precious stones, and quartz mined. Waxes, honey, cloves, vanilla, arrowroot, hides, tobacco, rum, wild rubber, lumber are also exported. Food processing (notably beef canning, rice milling); woodworking, paper making. Transportation facilities include Manakara-Fianarantsoa railroad and Canal des Pangalanes. Principal centers are Fianarantsoa, Manakara, Farafangana, Mananjary, Nosy-Varika.

Fianarantsoa, town (1948 pop. 18,576), ⊙ Fianarantsoa prov., SE Madagascar, on highway and 180 mi. SSW of Tananarive; alt. 3,968 ft.; 21°25'S 47°5'E. Commercial and agr. center in noted rice and tobacco region; railroad to port of Manakara. Beef canning, rice processing, woodworking, printing; railroad workshops. Coffee plantations, vineyards. Cattle fairs held here. Has military camp, airport, racecourse, hosp., trade schools, teachers col., R.C. and Protestant missions. Seat of vicar apostolic.

Fianga (fyäng-gä'), village, W Chad territory, Fr. Equatorial Africa, in the Fianga swamps on Fr. Cameroons border, 30 mi. SW of Bongor; cotton ginning; millet, livestock.

Fianona, Yugoslavia: see PLOMIN.

Ficarazzi (fēkärä'tsē), village (pop. 2,668), Palermo prov., NW Sicily, near Gulf of Palermo, 6 mi. ESE of Palermo.

Ficarolo (fēkärō'lô), village (pop. 1,610), Rovigo prov., Veneto, N Italy, on Po R. and 12 mi. NW of Ferrara, in hemp- and peach-growing region.

Ficce, Ethiopia: see FICHE.

Fiche (fē'chä), Ital. *Ficce*, town, Shoa prov., central Ethiopia, on road and 50 mi. N of Addis Ababa, in cereal-growing region; trade center.

Fichtelberg (fĭkh'tŭlbĕrk), second-highest peak (3,983 ft.) of the Erzgebirge, E Germany, near Czechoslovak border, just NW of Oberwiesenthal (funicular railway).

Fichtelgebirge (fĭkh'tŭlgŭbĭr"gŭ), Czech *Smrčiny* (smûr'chĭnĭ), mountain knot on Czechoslovak-German border, at junction of Bohemian Forest (SE), the Erzgebirge (NE), Franconian Forest and Thuringian Forest (NW), and Franconian Jura (SW); rises to 3,448 ft. in the Schneeberg (W) and to 3,356 ft. in the Ochsenkopf. Of complex geologic structure, it has steep slopes except in upper basin of Eger R. (E); and is covered by spruce [Ger. *Fichte*] forests. Relatively densely populated; engaged in forestry, cattle breeding, porcelain and glass mfg. Main town, Wunsiedel. Red Main and White Main, Eger, and Saxonian Saale rivers rise here. Was mining center (silver, lead, copper, zinc, tin, and gold) in 14th and 15th cent.

Fichtelnab or **Fichtelnaab,** Germany: see NAB RIVER.

Fick, Syria: see FIQ.

Ficksburg, town (pop. 6,532), S Orange Free State, U. of So. Afr., on Basutoland border, on Caledon R. and 100 mi. E of Bloemfontein; alt. 5,347 ft.; trade center at one of main points of entry into Basutoland; agr. center (wheat, oats, rye, potatoes, malt, fruit); grain elevator; flour milling, fruit dehydrating, shoe mfg., sandstone quarrying.

Ficulle (fēkōōl'lĕ), village (pop. 939), Terni prov., Umbria, central Italy, 9 mi. NNW of Orvieto; ceramics industry.

Fidalgo, Port (fĭdăl'gō), S Alaska, bay (25 mi. long, 2 mi. wide) on E shore of Prince William Sound, 30 mi. NW of Cordova; 60°47'N 146°30'W.

Fidalgo Island, Skagit co., NW Wash., irregular isl. (c.8 mi. long) in Puget Sound, from whose E shore it is separated only by sloughs (bridged); site of Anacortes city. Bridge across Deception Pass connects S shore with Whidbey Isl.

Fidan, Wadi (wă'dē fĭdăn'), river valley in S central Jordan, extends from N of El Shobak 25 mi. NW to Wadi 'Araba 20 mi. S of Dead Sea. Sometimes spelled Wadi Fedan.

Fidaris River, Greece: see EVENOS RIVER.

Fidelity, village (pop. 157), Jersey co., W Ill., 18 mi. N of Alton; apples; bituminous coal.

Fidenza (fēdĕn'tsä), anc. *Fidentia*, town (pop. 8,000), Parma prov., Emilia-Romagna, N central Italy, 14 mi. WNW of Parma and on short Stirone R. (branch of Taro R.). Rail junction; agr. center; canned foods, wine, shoes, glass, insulators, fertilizer, furniture, cork products. Bishopric. Has fine Lombard-Romanesque cathedral (12th-13th-cent.) and remodeled 13th-cent. palace. Severely damaged by aerial bombing (1944) in Second World War. Called Borgo San Donnino until 1927.

Fidimin (fĭdē'mēn), village (pop. 12,347), Faiyum prov., Upper Egypt, 6 mi. NNW of Faiyum; cotton, cereals, sugar cane, fruits.

Fidra Island (fĭ'drŭ), rocky islet in Firth of Forth, N East Lothian, Scotland, 3 mi. WNW of North Berwick; lighthouse (56°4'N 2°47'W).

Fieberbrunn (fē'bûrbrōōn), town (pop. 2,725), Tyrol, W Austria, 7 mi. ENE of Kitzbühel; iron- and steelworks. Summer resort with mineral springs.

Field, village (pop. estimate 400), SE B.C., near Alta. border, in Rocky Mts., in Yoho Natl. Park, on Kicking Horse R. and 40 mi. WNW of Banff; alt. 4,075 ft.; silver, lead, zinc mining; lumbering; resort. Bet. this point and Hector the Canadian Pacific RR passes through the SPIRAL TUNNELS.

Fieldale (fēl'dāl"), industrial village (pop. 1,295), Henry co., S Va., in foothills of the Blue Ridge, on Smith R. and 4 mi. W of Martinsville; mfg. of towels, hosiery.

Fielden Peninsula, NE Ellesmere Isl., NE Franklin Dist., Northwest Territories, extends 10 mi. NE into Lincoln Sea of the Arctic Ocean; 82°50'N 64°W; 3–6 mi. wide. At NE extremity is Cape Joseph Henry.

Fielding, town (pop. 249), Box Elder co., N Utah, 16 mi. WNW of Logan, near Bear R.; alt. 4,400 ft.; agr., livestock.

Fieldon, village (pop. 250), Jersey co., W Ill., 23 mi. NW of Alton, in applegrowing area.

Field Place, England: see WARNHAM.

Fieldsboro, borough (pop. 589), Burlington co., W N.J., on Delaware R. and 6 mi. S of Trenton; brick mfg.

Fields Landing, village (pop. c.150), Humboldt co., NW Calif., on Humboldt Bay, 4 mi. S of Eureka; whale-processing plant.

Fiemme, Val di (väl dē fyĕm'mĕ), Ger. *Fleimser Tal*, valley of middle Avisio R., in the Dolomites, N Italy, SW of Marmolada peak. Agr., stock raising, and forestry. Chief centers: Cavalese, Predazzo.

Fieni (fyān'), village (pop. 1,935), Prahova prov., S central Rumania, on railroad and 13 mi. N of Targoviste; cementworks.

Fier (fē-ĕr') or **Fieri** (fē-ĕ'rē), town (1945 pop. 7,285), S central Albania, 20 mi. W of Berat near Seman R.; agr. center; cotton ginning; at S edge of Myzeqe plain. Pop. is largely Orthodox. Founded 1877 as Turkish estate. Ruins of anc. APOLLONIA are 5 mi. W.

Fierbinti (fyârbēnt'), Rum. *Fierbinți* or *Fierbinți-de-Jos* (–dā-jôs'), village (pop. 1,620), Bucharest prov., S Rumania, on Ialomita R. and 21 mi. NE of Bucharest. Also spelled Fierbintii-de-Jos.

Fier River (fyâr'), Haute-Savoie dept., SE France, rises in the Bornes (Savoy Pre-Alps), flows 41 mi. generally W, past Thônes, around N end of L. of Annecy, to the Rhone below Seyssel. Activates hydroelectric plants W of Annecy.

Fierro (fēĕ'rō), village (pop. c.500), Grant co., SW N.Mex., in Pinos Altos Mts., 12 mi. ENE of Silver City; alt. 6,658 ft. Iron-ore deposits near by.

Fierro-urcu (fyĕ'rō-ōōr'kōō), Andean peak (12,428 ft.), El Oro prov., S Ecuador, 14 mi. E of Zaruma.

Fiescherhörner (fē'shûrhûr"nûr), 2 groups of Alpine peaks, S central Switzerland: Grindelwalder Fiescherhörner, culminating in the Gross Fiescherhorn (13,294 ft.; 5 mi. S of Grindelwald); and Walliser Fiescherhörner, culminating in the Gross Wannehorn (12,825 ft.; 9 mi. S of Grindelwald).

Fiesole (fyā'zôlĕ), anc. *Faesulae*, town (pop. 2,647), Firenze prov., Tuscany, central Italy, 3 mi. NE of Florence. Resort (alt. 968 ft.) beautifully situated on hill overlooking Val d'Arno. Produces straw hats and soap. Bishopric. Has Romanesque cathedral (completed 1028; restored 1878–83), Franciscan church and convent (built on site of Roman acropolis), seminary, and mus. of antiquities. Near by is church of San Dominico with paintings by Fra Angelico. Once an Etruscan and later a Roman town; has portions of Etruscan town wall and well-preserved Roman theater and baths (excavated in 1873).

Fiesso d'Artico (fyĕs'sô där'tēkô), village (pop. 408), Venezia prov., Veneto, N Italy, near Brenta R., 8 mi. E of Padua; shoes, liquor.

Fiesso Umbertiano (ōōmbĕrtē'nô), village (pop. 1,478), Rovigo prov., Veneto, N Italy, 9 mi. N of Ferrara.

Fife or **Fifeshire** (–shĭr, –shûr), county (□ 504.7; 1931 pop. 276,368; 1951 census 306,855), E Scotland; ⊙ Cupar. Forms a peninsula in the North Sea, bet. firths of Tay and Forth, bounded by Clackmannan and Kinross (W) and Perthshire (NW). Drained by Eden and Leven rivers. Surface is hilly in W (rising to 1,713 ft. in West Lomond), leveling toward coasts; in center is fertile lowland of the Howe of Fife (Eden R. valley). Agr. is highly developed. There are extensive coal deposits (W and SW); limestone, oil shale, ironstone, and freestone are also worked. Industries include steel milling (Leven), iron founding, linen milling (Dunfermline), shipbuilding, mfg. of machinery, bricks, tiles, sails. Other towns are Kirkcaldy, Cowdenbeath, St. Andrews, Burntisland, Buckhaven, and Methil. At Rosyth is naval base, important in both world wars. There are numerous coastal resorts and fishing ports. Famous golfing resort is at St. Andrews, site of univ.

Fife-Keith, Scotland: see KEITH.

Fife Lake, village (pop. 347), Grand Traverse co., NW Mich., on small Fife L. and 18 mi. SE of Traverse City; fisheries. Deer, bird, rabbit hunting near by.

Fife Ness, promontory on North Sea, at mouth of the Firth of Forth, E Fifeshire, Scotland, 10 mi. SE of St. Andrews; 56°17'N 2°35'W. Just N, in North Sea, is dangerous reef of Carr Brigs or Carr Rocks, and North Carr Lightship, 2 mi. NE of Fife Ness.

Fifeshire, Scotland: see FIFE.

Fifield (fī'fēld), village (pop. c.400), Price co., N Wis., 4 mi. SSE of Park Falls, near Chequamegon Natl. Forest; ships Christmas trees.

Fifla (fē'flä), tiny islet of the Maltese Isls., in the Mediterranean, 2 mi. off Malta's S coast. Has remains of 17th-cent. chapel. Now uninhabited, it is used as gunnery target by Br. navy.

Fifteen Mile Falls Dam, Vt. and N.H.: see CONNECTICUT RIVER.

Fifty Lakes, village (pop. c.150), Crow Wing co., central Minn., 28 mi. NNE of Brainerd, near Whitefish L. Fishing, bathing resorts.

Figalia, Greece: see PHIGALIA.

Figeac (fēzhäk'), town (pop. 5,450), Lot dept., SW France, on the Célé and 31 mi. ENE of Cahors; road and market center; processing and shipping of *pâté de foie gras*, plums, dried prunes, walnuts, leather; wool spinning. Zinc, lead deposits and coal mines near by. Has two 12th-14th-cent. churches and many medieval houses. Figeac was a Huguenot stronghold. Champollion b. here.

Figeholm (fē'gŭhōlm"), town (pop. 785), Kalmar co., SE Sweden, on Baltic, at N end of Kalmar Sound, 7 mi. NNE of Oskarshamn; paper mills.

Figgjo, Norway: see GANDDAL.

Fighiera (fēgyä'rä), town (pop. estimate 1,000), SE Santa Fe prov., Argentina, 20 mi. SSE of Rosario; agr. center (potatoes, corn, flax, peas, livestock).

Fighting Island, islet, S Ont., in Detroit R., 7 mi. SW of Windsor.

Figline Valdarno (fēlyē'nĕ väldär'nô), town (pop. 5,007), Firenze prov., Tuscany, central Italy, near the Arno, 15 mi. SE of Florence; mfg. (agr. tools, pottery, shoes, macaroni, ammonia). Has church rebuilt in 13th cent.

Figtree, village, Bulawayo prov., SW Southern Rhodesia, in Matabeleland, on railroad and 22 mi. SW of Bulawayo; alt. 4,522 ft. Cattle-raising center; peanuts, corn.

Figueira, Brazil: see GOVERNADOR VALADARES.

Figueira da Foz (fēgā'rŭ dä fôzh'), city (pop. 10,299), Coimbra dist., Beira Litoral prov., N central Portugal, port at mouth of Mondego R. on the Atlantic, on railroad and 24 mi. W of Coimbra; leading bathing resort with fine beaches on both sides of Mondego estuary; fish-canning and distributing center. Ships salt (panned locally), olive oil, wine, oranges, timber, limestone; new cement factory; glass milling, pottery mfg. Fort Santa Catarina guards harbor entrance. Airfield.

Figueira de Castelo Rodrigo (dĭ kăshtä'lo͞o ro͞odrē'-go͞o), town (pop. 1,666), Guarda dist., N central Portugal, near Sp. border, 30 mi. NE of Guarda; flour milling, olive- and winegrowing. Near by is 13th-cent. frontier fortress of Castelo Rodrigo (site of Port. victory over Spaniards in 1664) and a 12th-cent. Cistercian convent.

Figueirô dos Vinhos (fēgärô' do͞ozh vē'nyo͞osh), town (pop. 1,226), Leiria dist., W central Portugal, 23 mi. SSE of Coimbra; resin extracting and processing; textile spinning and weaving. Has Renaissance church.

Figueras (fēgä'räs). **1** Fortified city (pop. 13,513), Gerona prov., NE Spain, in Catalonia, 20 mi. NNE of Gerona, 14 mi. S of Fr. border; road center and chief city of Ampurdán plain. Mfg. of textiles, chemicals, cement, explosives, bicycles, brandy; cork, meat, olive-oil processing. Trades in cereals. Has 18th-cent. fortress, now prison. In Sp. civil war was briefly seat of Loyalist govt. before it fell (1939) to the Nationalists. **2** Town (pop. 1,064), Oviedo prov., NW Spain, fishing port on Eo R. estuary, near Bay of Biscay, 2 mi. E of Ribadeo; fish processing.

Figueroa, department, Argentina: see LA CAÑADA.

Figuery (fĭgûrē'), village (pop. estimate 400), W Que., near Okikeska L., 7 mi. SSE of Amos; gold mining.

Figuier, Cape, Spain: see HIGUER, CAPE.

Figuig (fēgēg'), Saharan oasis (pop. 3,737), Oujda region, easternmost Fr. Morocco, on Algerian border, at E foot of the Djebel Grouz (spur of the Saharan Atlas), 65 mi. NE of Colomb-Béchar (Algeria); 32°12'N 1°14'W. Date palms. Reached by road from Béni-Ounif (4 mi. S), on Oran-Colomb-Béchar RR, and from Bou Arfa (50 mi. NW). Lead deposits in vicinity. Figuig was designated as part of Morocco in 1845.

Figurin Island, Russian SFSR: see NEW SIBERIAN ISLANDS.

Fiji (fē'jē), Melanesian island group (□ 7,056; pop. 259,638), SW Pacific, 2,000 mi. NE of Sydney; 16°35'–20°40'S 178°44'–179°17'E. Most important Br. colony in Pacific Ocean; comprises 250 isls., of which 80 are inhabited. Major volcanic isls. include VITI LEVU (largest isl. and seat of Suva, ⊙ colony), VANUA LEVU (2d largest), TAVEUNI, KANDAVU, KORO, NGAU, OVALAU. Koro Sea is in center of group. Minor coral and limestone isls. are in LAU group E of Koro Sea, and YASAWA and MAMANUTHA group W of Viti Levu. Larger isls. are mountainous. Dense forests on windward side of isls.; grassy plains and clumps of casuarina and pandanus on leeward side. The 2 largest isls. have central cores of plutonic rocks thought to be remnants of older continental mass. Hot springs in mtn. region. Fertile soil, rich in humic acid, yields sugar cane, taro, rice, cotton, pineapples. Mangrove forests on beaches and swampy delta lands. Limited fauna includes bats, rats, parrots, pigeons. Temp. ranges from 60° to 96°F.; annual rainfall, 60 in. (leeward side), 140 in. (windward side). Trade winds (May-Nov.); equatorial winds (Dec.-April). Chief ports, Suva and Lautoka on Viti Levu, export sugar, gold, copra, bananas, timber. Discovered 1643 by Tasman, ceded 1874 by native chiefs to Great Britain. Missionaries arrived 1835, helped to abolish cannibalism. Inhabitants: 50% Indian; 40% Fijian (Melanesian); remaining 10% are European, Chinese, Polynesian, Micronesian. Governed by Br. governor at Suva, who is also High Commissioner of Western Pacific. N of Vanua Levu is ROTUMA, dependency of Fiji. Formerly Viti.

Fika (fēkä'), town (pop. 4,872), Bornu prov., Northern Provinces, NE Nigeria, 38 mi. SSE of Potiskum; cassava, millet, durra. Diatomite quarrying.

Filabres, Sierra de los (fēlä'vrēs), Andalusian range in W central Almería prov., S Spain, S of Almanzora R. Important iron mines (Serón, Gérgal, Bédar).

Filabusi (fēläbo͞o'sē), township (pop. 95), Bulawayo prov., S central Southern Rhodesia, in Matabeleland, on Insiza R. (branch of Umzingwane R.) and 55 mi. ESE of Bulawayo; gold-mining center. Fred Mine is 4 mi. NE.

Filadelfia (fēlädĕl'fyä), village, Pando dept., NW Bolivia, on Tahuamanu R. and 22 mi. S of Cobija; rubber.

Filadelfia, town (pop. 1,595), Caldas dept., W central Colombia, in Cauca valley, 13 mi. N of Manizales; coffeegrowing, sericulture. Coal deposits near by.

Filadelfia, town (1950 pop. 886), ⊙ Carrillo canton, Guanacaste prov., NW Costa Rica, on Tempisque R. and 15 mi. SE of Liberia; trading center; stock raising, lumbering. Connected by road with river port of Bolsón. A cotton center in 19th cent.

Filadelfia (fēlädĕl'fyä), town (pop. 5,175), Catanzaro prov., Calabria, S Italy, 13 mi. NE of Vibo Valentia; bell foundry. Rebuilt after earthquake of 1783.

Filakovo (fĭ'lyäkôvô), Slovak *Fil'akovo,* Hung. *Fülek* (fü'lĕk), village (pop. 5,934), S Slovakia, Czechoslovakia, 45 mi. SE of Banska Bystrica; rail junction; mfg. (enamelware, agr. machinery), woodworking. Anthracite and lignite mining in vicinity.

Filandia (fēlän'dyä), town (pop. 3,580), Caldas dept., W central Colombia, on W slopes of Cordillera Central, 11 mi. SSE of Pereira; alt. 6,184 ft. Agr. center (coffee, sugar cane, cereals, yucca, fruit); sericulture. Coal deposits near by.

Filbert. 1 Village (pop. 1,574, with adjacent Fairbank), Fayette co., SW Pa., 7 mi. NW of Uniontown. **2** Coal-mining village (pop. 1,214), McDowell co., S W.Va., 8 mi. S of Welch.

Filehne, Poland: see WIELEN.

Filer, village (pop. 1,425), Twin Falls co., S Idaho, 9 mi. W of Twin Falls in irrigated agr. area noted for Idaho white beans; seed plants. Inc. 1909.

Filer City, village (pop. c.300), Manistee co., NW Mich., 3 mi. SE of Manistee and on Little Manistee R.; mfg. (paper pulp, chemicals).

Filettino (fēlĕt-tē'nô), village (pop. 1,834), Frosinone prov., Latium, S central Italy, in the Apennines, near source of Aniene R., 17 mi. N of Frosinone. Resort (alt. 3,484 ft.); alabaster quarries.

Filey, urban district (1931 pop. 3,733; 1951 census 4,764), East Riding, E Yorkshire, England, on North Sea at N end of Filey Bay, 7 mi. SE of Scarborough; seaside resort and fishing port. Just E is promontory of Filey Brigg. Has church dating from Norman times, rebuilt in 12th and 13th cent.

Filfila, Djebel (jĕ'bĕl fēlfēlä'), mountain in Constantine dept., NE Algeria, on Gulf of Philippeville, 10 mi. E of Philippeville; marble quarries.

Filiasi (fēlyäsh'), Rum. *Filiaşi,* village (pop. 4,689), Gorj prov., S Rumania, 21 mi. NW of Craiova; rail junction and lumbering center. Has 16th-cent. church; ruins of medieval city in vicinity.

Filiates, Greece: see PHILIATES.

Filiatra, Greece: see PHILIATRA.

Filibe, Bulgaria: see PLOVDIV, city.

Filicudi (fēlēko͞o'dē), anc. *Phoenicusa,* island (□ 3.5; pop. 1,047), one of Lipari Isls., in Tyrrhenian Sea off NE Sicily, W of Salina, 45 mi. NW of Milazzo; 3 mi. long, 2 mi. wide; rises to 2,536 ft. in center. Agr. (capers, wheat); fishing.

Filingué (fēlĭng'gā), town (pop. c.4,500), SW Niger territory, Fr. West Africa, c.100 mi. NE of Niamey. Experimental station for stock raising (cattle, astrakhan, etc.).

Filipestii-de-Padure (fēlēpĕsh'tĭ-dā-pŭ'do͞orĕ), Rum. *Filipeştii-de-Pădure,* village (1941 pop. 2,056), Prahova prov., S central Rumania, 13 mi. WNW of Ploesti; oil and natural-gas center; lignite mines.

Filipesti-Targ (fēlēpĕsh'tĭ-tûrg'), Rum. *Filipeşti-Târg,* town (1948 pop. 2,359), Prahova prov., S central Rumania, on Prahova R. and 11 mi. N of Ploesti; trading center (plum brandy, cheese, wool), with oil wells; also flour mills, cementworks. Has remains of a Cantacuzene palace and 17th-cent. chapel.

Filipovo (fēlē'pôvô), rail center, Plovdiv dist., S central Bulgaria, 4 mi. N of Plovdiv.

Filippias, Greece: see NEA PHILIPPIAS.

Filippine, Netherlands: see PHILIPPINE.

Filipsland, Sint, Netherlands: see SINT PHILIPSLAND.

Filipstad (fĭ'lĭpstäd"), city (pop. 6,066), Varmland co., W Sweden, in Bergslag region, bet. 2 small lakes, 30 mi. NE of Karlstad; rail junction; trade center in iron-mining region; mfg. of chemicals, crisp bread; metalworking, flour milling, brewing. Has 18th-cent. church. Founded 1611. John Ericsson b. here.

Filkino or **Fil'kino** (fĕl'kĭnŭ), village (1939 pop. over 500), N Sverdlovsk oblast, Russian SFSR, on right bank of Sosva R. (head of navigation) and 5 mi. E of Serov, on railroad; sawmilling. Charcoal burning just W, at Uglezhzheniye station.

Fillan River, Scotland: see DOCHART RIVER.

Filley, village (pop. 136), Gage co., SE Nebr., 10 mi. E of Beatrice, near Big Blue R.

Fillis, Greece: see PHYLLIS.

Fillmore, village (pop. 232), SE Sask., 24 mi. NE of Weyburn; mixed farming, dairying.

Fillmore. 1 County (□ 859; pop. 24,465), SE Minn.; ⊙ Preston. Agr. area watered by Root R. and bordering on Iowa. Livestock, dairy products, grain, potatoes, poultry; limestone. Formed 1853. **2** County (□ 577; pop. 9,610), SE Nebr.; ⊙ Geneva. Agr. region drained by branches of Big Blue R. Grain, livestock, dairy and poultry produce. Formed 1871.

Fillmore. 1 City (pop. 3,884), Ventura co., S Calif., 45 mi. NW of Los Angeles; oil refining. Citrus-fruit groves, oil fields near by. Inc. 1914. **2** Village (pop. 384), Montgomery co., S central Ill., 20 mi. ESE of Litchfield, in agr. and bituminous-coal area. **3** Town (pop. 284), Andrew co., NW Mo., near Nodaway R., 19 mi. NNW of St. Joseph. **4** Village (pop. 527), Allegany co., W N.Y., on Genesee R. and 20 mi. S of Warsaw, in agr. and timber area; feed, tile. **5** City (pop. 1,890), ⊙ Millard co., W central Utah, 60 mi. SSW of Nephi in livestock, poultry, and agr. area (alfalfa seed, wheat, potatoes); alt. 5,135 ft.; meat packing. Settled 1851. Capital of Utah Territory 1851–56. Pavant Mts. just E, in Fishlake Natl. Forest.

Fillmore Glen State Park (c.850 acres), Cayuga co., W central N.Y., in glen along small Fillmore Creek, near S end of Owasco L., c.18 mi. N of Ithaca. Waterfalls here. Camping, hiking, swimming, picnicking facilities.

Filomena Mata (fēlōmā'nä mä'tä), town (pop. 2,491), Veracruz, E Mexico, in Sierra Madre Oriental, on Puebla border, 30 mi. SW of Papantla; cereals, sugar cane, coffee, tobacco, fruit. Formerly Santo Domingo.

Filonovo, Russian SFSR: see NOVO-ANNENSKI.

Filottrano (fēlôt-trä'nô), town (pop. 1,920), Ancona prov., The Marches, central Italy, 15 mi. SW of Ancona; mfg. (harmoniums, harmonicas).

Fils River (fĭls), N Württemberg, Germany, rises in Swabian Jura just W of Wiesensteig, flows 40 mi. generally W, past Geislingen and Göppingen, to the Neckar at Plochingen.

Filton, town and parish (pop. 3,230), SW Gloucester, England, 4 mi. NNE of Bristol; aircraft works, airport.

Filyos River, Turkey: see YENICE RIVER.

Fimaina, Greece: see PHYMAINA.

Fimi River (fē'mē), right tributary of the Kasai in central and W Belgian Congo; rises as the Lukenie (lo͞okĕn'yä) just E of Katako Kombe, flows c.550 mi. W, past Lodja, Dekese, and Oshwe, to L. Leopold II, which it leaves, at Kutu, as the Fimi and flows W and SW to join the Kasai at Mushie. The Lukenie-Fimi is c.664 mi. long; navigable for 560 mi. below Lodja.

Finale Ligure (fēnä'lĕ lē'go͞orĕ), town (pop. 4,100), Savona prov., Liguria, NW Italy, port on Gulf of Genoa and 12 mi. SW of Savona, in agr., hemp, flax region. Resort known for its grottos. Airplane industry. Adjacent are villages of Finale Borgo (pop. 1,939; tannery) and Finale Pia (pop. 956). Limestone quarries near by. Until c.1940, Finalmarina or Finale Marina.

Finale nell'Emilia (nĕl-lĕmē'lyä), town (pop. 5,397), Modena prov., Emilia-Romagna, N central Italy, on Panaro R. and 22 mi. NE of Modena; rail terminus; hemp mill. Has 15th-cent. castle.

Finalmarina, Italy: see FINALE LIGURE.

Fiñana (fēnyä'nä), town (pop. 3,841), Almería prov., S Spain, 30 mi. NW of Almería; olive-oil processing, flour milling; stock raising. Ships grapes, almonds, sugar cane. Limestone quarries.

Fincastle (fĭn'kă"sŭl), town (pop. 405), ⊙ Botetourt co., W Va., 15 mi. N of Roanoke, in fruitgrowing, dairying, timber area. Rail station at Troutville, 5 mi. S.

Finch, village (pop. 397), SE Ont., 20 mi. NW of Cornwall; dairying, mixed farming.

Finchley, residential municipal borough (1931 pop. 58,964; 1951 census 69,990), Middlesex, England, 7 mi. NNW of London. Church dates from 12th cent. Finchley Common (now built up) was once notorious resort of highwaymen.

Finderne, N.J.: see MANVILLE.

Findhorn (fĭnd'hôrn), fishing village, NE Moray, Scotland, on Findhorn Bay of Moray Firth, at mouth of Findhorn R., 11 mi. W of Elgin. Two previous villages of same name and in this area were swept away by the sea, the last in 1701.

Findhorn River, Inverness, Nairn, and Moray, Scotland, rises in Monadhliath Mts., flows 62 mi. NE, past Forres, to Moray Firth at Findhorn.

Findlay (fĭn'lē, fĭnd'lē). **1** Village (pop. 680), Shelby co., central Ill., near Kaskaskia R., 24 mi. SSE of Decatur, in agr. and bituminous-coal area; ships grain. **2** City (pop. 23,845), ⊙ Hancock co., NW Ohio, c.40 mi. S of Toledo and on Blanchard R.; trade, rail, and mfg. center, in rich agr. area. Makes rubber tires and tubes, agr. machinery, pottery and porcelain, metal products; oil refining, beet-sugar processing. Findlay Col. is here. Laid out 1821; inc. as village in 1838, as city in 1887. Was a center of oil and gas production in 1880s.

Findlay, Mount (fĭn'lē), (10,780 ft.), SE B.C., in Selkirk Mts., 55 mi. NE of Nelson; 50°4'N 116°28'W.

Findlay Islands, group of 4 isls., NW Franklin Dist., Northwest Territories, in the Arctic Ocean, N of Bathurst Isl.; largest is LOUGHEED ISLAND.

Findley Lake, resort village (pop. c.300), Chautauqua co., extreme W N.Y., on small Findley L., 26 mi. W of Jamestown, in dairying area.

Findo, Norway: see FINNOY.

Findochty (fĭn'dŏkh-tē), burgh (1931 pop. 1,675; 1951 census 1,490), NW Banffshire, Scotland, on Moray Firth, and 3 mi. ENE of Buckie; fishing port.

Findon or **Finnan** (both: fĭ'nŭn), fishing village, NE Kincardine, Scotland, on North Sea, 6 mi. S of Aberdeen. It was formerly a noted haddock-fishing center which gave its name to smoked haddock —"finnan haddie."

Finedon (fĭn'dŭn), former urban district (1931 pop. 4,100), E Northampton, England, 3 mi. NE of Wellingborough; leather and shoe mfg.; ironstone mining, concrete mfg. Has 14th-cent. church. Inc. 1935 in Wellingborough.

Finestrat (fēnĕsträt'), town (pop. 1,335), Alicante prov., E Spain, 18 mi. SE of Alcoy; olive-oil processing, flour milling; wine, fruit.

Fingal (fĭng'gŭl), village (pop. 436), E Tasmania, 45 mi. ESE of Launceston and on S.Esk R.; coal-mining center; livestock, oats.

Fingal, village (pop. 210), Barnes co., SE N.Dak., 15 mi. SE of Valley City.

Fingal's Cave, Scotland: see STAFFA.

Finger Lake (20 mi. long, 7 mi. wide), Patricia dist., NW Ont.; 53°9'N 93°30'W. Drained by Severn R.

Finger Lakes, W central N.Y., group of long, narrow glacial lakes lying in N–S valleys, in scenic resort and agr. region lying bet. Geneseo (W) and vicinity of Syracuse (E). From W to E, they are CONESUS, HEMLOCK, CANADICE, HONEOYE, CANANDAIGUA, KEUKA, SENECA (□ c.67; largest of group), CAYUGA (38 mi. long; longest of group), OWASCO, SKANEATELES, and OTISCO lakes. Region is noted for its scenic beauty, and produces vegetables, grapes and wines, apples, wheat; many resorts and state parks.

Fingerville, mill village, Spartanburg co., NW N.C., near N.C. line, 13 mi. N of Spartanburg; cotton yarn.

Finglas (fĭn'glăs), Gaelic *Fionnghlas*, N suburb (pop. 1,093) of Dublin, Co. Dublin, Ireland. Has anc. cross and church founded by St. Patrick. In 1171 Anglo-Normans here defeated Roderick O'Connor.

Fingoé (fĕng-gwĕ'), village, Manica and Sofala prov., NW Mozambique, 130 mi. WNW of Tete; corn, beans. Gold washings near by. Also spelled Fingué.

Finhaut (fē-ō'), village (pop. 444), Valais canton, SW Switzerland, 5 mi. WSW of Martigny-Ville; resort (alt. 4,026 ft.). Barberine hydroelectric plant is SW.

Finiels, France: see LOZÈRE, MONT.

Finike (fĭnĭkĕ'), village (pop. 1,252), Antalya prov., SW Turkey, port on Gulf of Finike (Mediterranean Sea), 50 mi. SSW of Antalya; manganese; millet, wheat, sesame.

Finistère (fēnēstâr') [from Lat. *finis terrae*,=land's end], department (□ 2,714; pop. 724,735), W France, forming W tip of Brittany; ⊙ Quimper. Bounded N by English Channel, S and W by Atlantic Ocean. Its steep indented coastline has numerous promontories and natural harbors. Interior (with extensive livestock pastures) is traversed by 2 chains of old granitic mts. (Montagnes d'Arrée and the Montagnes Noires). In valleys of its numerous short streams early vegetables and fruits are intensively grown. Most of coastal population engaged in fishing and fish-preserving. Other industries: shipbuilding, iodine extracting, woodworking, food processing. Chief towns are Brest (commercial port and naval base), Quimper, Landerneau, Douarnenez, Concarneau, Morlaix. Tourists attracted by numerous small bathing resorts and by the characteristic Brittany countryside.

Finisterre (fēnēstĕ'rā), town (pop. 2,195), La Coruña prov., NW Spain, fishing port on inlet of the Atlantic, near Cape Finisterre, 36 mi. W of Santiago; fish processing, boatbuilding; ships lumber.

Finisterre, Cape, on Atlantic coast of Galicia, in La Coruña prov., NW Spain, 55 mi. SW of La Coruña; 42°53'N 9°18'W. Generally considered westernmost point of Spain, though Cape Toriñana (N) is at about same longitude.

Finisterre Range (fĭ'nĭstâr'), NE New Guinea, SE of Astrolabe Bay, extends into Huon Peninsula. Highest peaks: Mt. Sarawaket (13,454 ft.), Mt. Gladstone (11,400 ft.), Mt. Disraeli (11,000 ft.).

Finkenheerd, Germany: see BRIESKOW-FINKENHEERD.

Finkenstein (fĭng'kŭnshtīn), town (pop. 5,329), Carinthia, S Austria, near Gail R., 4 mi. SSE of Villach; bakery products.

Finland, Finnish *Suomi* (sōō'ômē), republic (□ 117,907; with water area, □ 130,091; pop. 3,958,778), N Europe; ⊙ HELSINKI. Bounded by Gulf of Finland (S), Gulf of Bothnia (W), Sweden (NW), Norway (N), and USSR (E). N Finland, crossed by the arctic circle, comprises central part of LAPLAND. Central and S parts of country consist of low plateau (c.500 ft. high), covered with numerous lakes; largest are Saimaa, Oulu, Päijänne, Pielinen, Kalla, and Keitele. Terrain rises toward Lapland and reaches 4,343 ft. in Mt. Haltia on Norwegian border. Also in Lapland is large L. Inari. Chief rivers of Finland are the Kemi, Oulu, Tornio (Torne), Muonio, Pats, Ounas, Kokemäki, Kymi, and Vuoksi (with large Imatra falls). Most rivers are important logging routes and abundant source of hydroelectric power. Finland's coast line is generally low, rocky, and indented by numerous small bays, protected by vast number of rocky islets and skerries. ALAND ISLANDS (bet. Baltic and Gulf of Bothnia) belong to Finland, but have entirely Swedish-speaking pop. and enjoy considerable autonomy. Over two-thirds of Finland is forested, and timber and wood products (mainly plywood, pulp, cellulose, paper, veneer, wallboard, spindles, bobbins, furniture) are mainstay of country's economy. Also important are textile milling, dairying, tanning, metalworking, mfg. of glass and ceramics. Minerals worked include red, gray, and black granite, limestone, copper (large mines at Outokumpu), iron, nickel, feldspar, asbestos, molybdenum, fossil meal, zinc, lead, silver, and gold. There are several steel mills and nonferrous-metal refineries. Finnish furniture, glass, ceramics, and handicrafts are noted for their modern design and high quality. Agr. (rye, oats, barley, potatoes, sugar beets), stock raising, and fishing are carried on. In Lapland, with pop. of partly nomadic, partly settled Lapps, reindeer raising and fishing are chief occupations. Tourist industry is important throughout the country. Considerable part of domestic trade and consumer-goods production is carried on through cooperatives. Finnish and Swedish are country's official languages; Swedish-speaking pop. (c.10 percent of total) forms majority in certain SW coastal regions. Lutheran religion predominates. There are universities at Helsinki (Finnish) and at TURKU (Finnish and Swedish), which is also seat of Lutheran primate of Finland. Administratively, country is divided into 10 counties [Finnish *lääni*]. Largest cities are Helsinki, Turku, Tampere, Lahti, Pori, Oulu, Vaasa, Kuopio, Jyväskylä, Kemi, Kotka, and Hämeenlinna. Climate is maritime in character and generally temperate, except in arctic regions. Conquered (before 8th cent. A.D.) by Finns from the Lapps, who retreated northward, country was conquered (12th cent.) and Christianized by Swedes under Eric IX. In 16th cent. it became a Swedish duchy and a royal appanage. From 14th cent. onward Finnish traders, especially from Pirkkala, pushed back country's N frontier by penetrating into Lapp territory. E border 1st defined (1323) by treaty bet. Sweden and Novgorod. Reformation officially adopted, 1593. In 17th cent. Swedish culture and language spread rapidly. Famine (1696) wiped out almost one-third of pop. In 1713 Peter I of Russia invaded Finland; under Treaty of Nystad (1721) Sweden ceded Vyborg (Viipuri) prov. to Russia. As Finland became repeated battleground for Swedes and Russians, Finnish separatist movements spread, especially in late 18th cent. In 1809 Finland passed to Russia under Treaty of Hamina, but it retained important autonomous rights as a grand duchy, united with Russia through the person of the tsar. Virtually a constitutional democracy, Finland's form of govt. differed greatly from that of Russia. In 19th cent. a great revival of Finnish nationalism and Finnish culture took place; notable expressions were Lönnrot's publication of sagas of the *Kalevala*, intensification of language struggle bet. Finns and Swedes, and, in late 19th and early 20th cent., the music of Sibelius. Finnish shipping and coastal towns suffered heavily during Crimean War, when Anglo-French fleet operated in Baltic. After mid-19th cent. country's industrialization proceeded rapidly. With accession (1894) of Nicholas II, Russian rule was tightened considerably and Finnish constitutional rights were infringed, leading (1905) to general strike and subsequently to declaration (1917) of Finnish independence. Until spring of 1918 the country was scene of civil war in which Finnish nationalists (Whites) under Mannerheim, with German aid, defeated Communist Red Guards. Among early measures taken by independent Finland were agrarian reform (1918–22) and introduction (1919) of prohibition (repealed 1931). Under Treaty of Tartu (1920) Russia recognized Finnish independence and ceded Pechenga (Petsamo) region. In the fall of 1939, Russia seized the opportunity, as Germany precipitated the West into the Second World War, to attack Finland. After the resulting Finnish-Russian War (Nov., 1939, to March, 1940), Finland was forced to cede considerable territory to Russia. In June, 1941, still rankling under the loss of territory to Russia, Finland joined Germany's attack on Russia, but was forced to capitulate (Sept., 1944) after large-scale Russian offensive. German troops in N Finland refused to surrender and had to be expelled by Finnish forces; in the ensuing warfare Finnish Lapland was laid waste. Peace treaty was signed (1947) in Paris bet. Finland and Allied powers (except for the United States, who had not declared war on Finland) under which Finland ceded the Vyborg (Viipuri) and Pechenga (Petsamo) regions to Russia and also agreed to $300,000,000 reparation payments to that country, and to virtual demilitarization. Finland also leased a coastal region (□ 152) surrounding Porkkala Peninsula to USSR for 50 years as naval base. In 1947 Finland further ceded small strip of territory on upper Pats R., with 2 important hydroelectric plants (since built by Finland as reparations), to the USSR. Prompt payment of Finnish reparations resulted in cancellation (1948) of 20% of total debt by USSR. In 1949 and 1950 Finland's political and economic stability was shaken by recurring Communist-led strikes.

Finland, Gulf of, E arm of Baltic Sea, bet. Finland (N) and USSR (including Estonia; E and S); 250 mi. long, up to 80 mi. wide. Narrowing E toward Leningrad (at mouth of Neva R.), the gulf contains the fortified isls. of Sursaari, Lavansaari, and Kotlin (with Kronstadt fortress). On N shore are the Finnish ports of Kotka, Helsinki, and the Soviet naval base of Porkkala. The other USSR ports are Vyborg, Leningrad, Tallinn, and the naval base of Paldiski. In addition to the Neva (outlet of L. Ladoga), the gulf receives the Saimaa Canal (outlet of Finnish Saimaa L. system) and Narva R. (outlet of L. Peipus). Generally shallow and of low salinity, the gulf freezes over 3–5 months in winter.

Finlay Mountains (fĭn'lē), Hudspeth co., extreme W Texas, NW–SE range c.25 mi. long, generally parallel to the Rio Grande (c.15 mi. away), and c.40 mi. SE of El Paso; rises to c.5,700 ft. Partly bounds Diablo Bolson (E).

Finlay River (fĭn'lē), N B.C., chief tributary of Peace R., rises in Stikine Mts. at about 57°30'N 126°30'W, flows 210 mi. SE to Finlay Forks (56°N 123°45'W), where it joins Parsnip R. to form Peace R.

Finlayson (fĭn'lēsŭn), resort village (pop. 195), Pine co., E Minn., 26 mi. N of Pine City; dairy products.

Finley, city (pop. 671), ⊙ Steele co., E N.Dak., 65 mi. NW of Fargo; dairy products, grain; livestock raising,

Finleyson, town (pop. 79), Pulaski co., S central Ga., 11 mi. S of Hawkinsville.

Finleyville, borough (pop. 684), Washington co., SW Pa., 13 mi. S of Pittsburgh; bituminous coal, lumber; agr.

Finnan, Scotland: see FINDON.

Finnan River (fĭ'nŭn), SW Inverness, Scotland, rises 5 mi. NE of head of Loch Shiel, flows 5 mi. S to head of Loch Shiel at Glenfinnan.

Finneid (fĭn'ād), village (pop. 475) in Fauske canton, Nordland co., N central Norway, at head of Skjerstad Fjord, 30 mi. E of Bodo; transshipment port for metals from Sulitjelma; outlet for Fauske canton marble and slate quarries.

Finneidfjord (-fyōr), village in Sor-Rana (Nor. *Sør-Rana*) canton (pop. 2,102), Nordland co., N central Norway, on Ran Fjord, on railroad and 13 mi. SW of Mo; oleomargarine factory.

Finney, county (□ 1,302; pop. 15,092), SW Kansas; ⊙ Garden City. Rolling prairie region. Wheat, livestock; sugar beets in irrigated area (S) along Arkansas R. Formed 1884.

Finniss, Cape, on W Eyre Peninsula, S South Australia; forms S end of Anxious Bay, 33°38'S 134°49'E.

Finnmark (fĭn'märk), county [Nor. *fylke*] (□ 18,799; pop. 58,790), N Norway, forming northernmost part of Scandinavian peninsula; ⊙ Vadso. Northernmost co. of Norway, it borders on Troms co. (SW), Norwegian Sea (NW), Barents Sea of the Arctic Ocean (N), the USSR (E), and Finland (S). Surface is low and undulating, drained by Alta, Tana, Pasvik, and other rivers. Offshore isls. are mountainous and partly glaciated; coast line is indented by deep fjords, including Alta, Porsang, Tana, and Varanger fjords. Relatively mild climate permits crop growing. During 2 summer months, region has continuous sunlight; sun is not visible at all during 2 winter months. Hammerfest is commercial center; Vadso and Vardo are other cities. Kirkenes village is center of important SOR-VARANGER iron mines. Some copper deposits near Alta and Varanger fjords. NORDKYN cape is northernmost point of European mainland; on Mageroy, an isl., are the North Cape and the Knivskjelodden, northernmost point of Europe. Co. has considerable aboriginal Lapp pop.; reindeer raising and fishing are their chief occupations; Kautokeino and Karasjok are Lapp centers. Another large section of pop. is of Finnish origin, here called *Kvener*. Fjords and adjacent sea areas abound in fish and support important fishing industry. Co. suffered heavily at close of Second World War when retreating Germans systematically laid it waste.

Finnmossen, Sweden: see NORDMARK-FINNMOSSEN.

Finnoy (fĭn'ûü), Nor. *Finnøy*, island (□ 10; pop. 1,206), Rogaland co., SW Norway, in Bokn Fjord, 11 mi. NNE of Stavanger. Fishing center; summer resort. Formerly spelled Findo and Finnö.

Finn River, Co. Donegal, Ireland, rises in Lough Finn (small lake) 17 mi. WSW of Letterkenny, flows 25 mi. E, past Ballybofey and Stranorlar, to confluence with Mourne R. at Lifford, forming Foyle R.

Finn River, Northern Ireland, flows c.30 mi. SW through cos. Fermanagh, Monaghan, and Cavan to upper Lough Erne 2 mi. N of Redhill.

Fino Mornasco (fē'nô môrnä'skô), village (pop. 2,670), Como prov., Lombardy, N Italy, 5 mi. SSW of Como; silk mills, foundry; furniture mfg.

Finow (fē'nō), town (pop. 9,616), Brandenburg, E Germany, on Finow Canal, near Hohenzollern Canal, and 4 mi. W of Eberswalde, 25 mi. NE of Berlin; foundries (steel, brass, light metals); chemical mfg. Power station. Airfield. Chartered 1935.

Finow Canal, E Germany, extends c.25 mi. E of Liebenwalde to HOHENZOLLERN CANAL 3 mi. NE of Niederfinow; 14 locks; navigable for barges up to 250 tons. Linked at Liebenwalde via 13-mi.-long Voss Canal to the Havel at Zehdenick. Built 1605–20; enlarged 1744–46; now superseded by Hohenzollern Canal.

Finowfurt (fē'nōfōōrt"), village (pop. 4,756), Brandenburg, E Germany, on Finow Canal and 6 mi. W of Eberswalde; metalworking.

Finsbury, metropolitan borough (1931 pop. 69,888; 1951 census 35,347) of London, England, N of the Thames, 1.5 mi. NE of Charing Cross; includes district of CLERKENWELL. Residential and business quarter. Here is Bunhill Fields cemetery, with graves of Bunyan, Blake, Defoe, Watts. Sadler's Wells Theatre (English ballet center), John Wesley's chapel, and the mint of the Bank of England are also here.

Finsbury Park, England: see HORNSEY.

Finschhafen (fĭnch'häfŭn), harbor, Huon Peninsula, NE New Guinea; contains 3 basins. Boatbuilding industry. In Second World War, Jap. air base (established 1942) was taken 1943 by Australian forces and became U.S. base. Sometimes called Finsch Harbour.

Finse (fĭn'sů), village in Ulvik canton, Hordaland co., SW Norway, on railroad and 75 mi. E of Bergen; highest station (4,009 ft.) bet. Oslo and Bergen. Skiing center and year-round resort in Hallingskarv mts., at foot of Hardanger Glacier (S).

Finsland (fĭns'län), village and canton (pop. 965), Vest-Agder co., S Norway, 19 mi. NW of Kristiansand; lumbering, mfg. of barrels; cattle raising, dairying. Archaeological findings from Stone Age made near by.

Finspang (fĭn'spông"), Swedish *Finspång*, town (pop. 11,902), Ostergotland co., SE Sweden, 16 mi. WNW of Norrkoping; steel mills, gun foundries (established in 16th cent.), turbine and machinery works. Has 17th-cent. castle and manor house. Remains of 15th-cent. castle near by.

Finsteraar Glacier, Switzerland: see AAR RIVER.

Finsteraarhorn (fĭn"stůrär'hôrn), peak (14,032 ft.), highest in Bernese Alps, S central Switzerland, 7 mi. SSE of Grindelwald, on border of Bern and Valais cantons. First climbed 1812. **Finsteraarjoch** (–yôkh), a pass (10,805 ft.), is N, and Finsteraarhorn Hütren (10,017 ft.) is S.

Finstermünz Pass (fĭn'stůrmünts), defile (alt. c.3,700 ft.) of the Inn, on Swiss-Austrian line, bet. Silvretta Group of Rhaetian Alps and Ötztal Alps, near Pfunds.

Finsterwalde (fĭn"stůrväl'dů), town (pop. 20,766), Brandenburg, E Germany, in Lower Lusatia, 30 mi. WSW of Cottbus, in lignite-mining region; woolen and paper milling, metalworking; mfg. of glass, furniture, machinery, tobacco and rubber products. Has 16th-cent. church, 17th-cent. palace. First mentioned 1288. Went to Saxony in 1635. Passed to Prussia in 1815.

Finstingen, France: see FÉNÉTRANGE.

Finthen (fĭn'tůn), village (pop. 4,245), Rhenish Hesse, W Germany, 4 mi. WSW of Mainz; fruit preserves.

Fintona (fĭn'tůnů), town (pop. 783), SW Co. Tyrone, Northern Ireland, 7 mi. S of Omagh; agr. market (potatoes, flax, oats; cattle). It is an anc. stronghold of the O'Neills.

Fintry, agr. village and parish (pop. 279), W Stirling, Scotland, on Endrick Water and 14 mi. N of Glasgow, at foot of Campsie Fells. Near by are remains of anc. Fintry Castle, stronghold of the Grahams. Just E is the Loup of Fintry, 94-ft. waterfall on Endrick Water.

Fiorano Modenese (fyôrä'nô môdĕnä'zē), village (pop. 1,444), Modena prov., Emilia-Romagna, N central Italy, 9 mi. SW of Modena; alcohol distillery, sausage factory.

Fiora River (fyô'rä), central Italy, rises at S foot of Monte Amiata, near Santa Fiora; flows 50 mi. S to Tyrrhenian Sea 11 mi. NW of Tarquinia. In lower course forms part of Tuscany-Latium boundary.

Fiord (fē'ôrd), county (□ 3,035; pop. 8), SW S.Isl., New Zealand; Puysegur Point is only settlement. Mountainous; indented by many sounds. Most of area is in Fiordland Natl. Park.

Fiordland National Park, largest park (□ 3,761) in New Zealand, on SW S.Isl.; contains many sounds, mts., rivers, and lakes, including L. MANAPOURI (deepest in New Zealand).

Fiorenzuola d'Arda (fyôrĕnzwô'lä där'dä), town (pop. 5,671), Piacenza prov., Emilia-Romagna, N central Italy, on Arda R. and 13 mi. SE of Piacenza. Agr. center; tomato cannery, sausage factory, tannery, petroleum refinery; foundry; paint and button works. Has Romanesque-Gothic church of 14th–15th cent.

Fiorito (fyōrē'tō), residential town (pop. estimate 2,000) in Greater Buenos Aires, Argentina, on Riachuelo R. and 7 mi. SW of Buenos Aires; chemical industry.

Fiq (fēk), Fr. *Fick*, town, Hauran prov., SW Syria, near Palestine and Jordan borders, 26 mi. NW of Der'a; cereals, wheat.

Firat River, Turkey: see EUPHRATES RIVER.

Fircrest, town (pop. 1,459), Pierce co., W central Wash., 2 mi. W of Tacoma.

Firdafylke, Norway: see SOGN OG FJORDANE.

Firdan, El, or **Al-Firdan** (both: ĕl fĭr'dăn), village, Canal Governorate, NE Egypt, on the Suez Canal, on railroad, and 11 mi. S of El Qantara. Sometimes spelled El Ferdan.

Firdaus or **Ferdows** (both: fĕrdōs'), town, Ninth Prov., in Khurasan, NE Iran, 175 mi. SSW of Meshed; center of irrigated fruitgrowing dist.; produces grain, silk, rugs. Antimony deposits near by. Founding is attributed to the Mongols (13th cent.). Until 1920s called Tun.

Firebaugh (fĭr'bô"), city (pop. 821), Fresno co., central Calif., 38 mi. WNW of Fresno and on San Joaquin R.; melons.

Fireco (fīrē'kō), village (1940 pop. 1,161), Raleigh co., S W.Va., 9 mi. S of Beckley, in coal-mining region.

Firehole River, NW Wyo., rises in SW corner of Yellowstone Natl. Park, flows 28 mi. N, through geyser area, joining Gibbon R. to form Madison R.

Fire Island or **Fire Island Beach,** SE N.Y., narrow barrier beach (c.30 mi. long) off S shore of Long Isl.; shelters Great South Bay and part of Moriches Bay from the Atlantic, and extends from point S of Babylon (W) to Moriches Inlet (E). Ferries from Bay Shore and Babylon. Has resort colonies of Saltaire (pop. 21), Fair Harbor, Point O'Woods, Ocean Beach (pop. 73), and Cherry Grove. At its W end are a state park and a lighthouse (built 1858). The 1938 hurricane and a storm in 1939 did much damage. Sometimes called Great South Beach.

Firenze (fērĕn'tsĕ), province (□ 1,498; pop. 853,032), Tuscany, central Italy; ⊙ Florence. Hill and mtn. terrain, including Etruscan Apennines (N); traversed by middle Arno R. valley. Watered by the Arno and its tributaries, Sieve, Elsa, and Pesa rivers. Extensive agr. (grapes, cereals, fruit, vegetables) and livestock raising in fertile valleys. Marble quarries at Montaione. Resorts (Fiesole, Vallombrosa). Amer. military cemetery at Castelfiorentino. Mfg. at Florence, Prato, Empoli, and Sesto Fiorentino. Area decreased 1927 to help form Pistoia prov.

Firenze, city, Italy: see FLORENCE.

Firenzuola (fērĕnzwô'lä), village (pop. 885), Firenze prov., Tuscany, central Italy, on Santerno R. and 24 mi. NNE of Florence; straw-hat mfg. Severely damaged (1944–45) in Second World War.

Firestone, town (pop. 297), Weld co., N Colo., near South Platte R., 25 mi. N of Denver; alt. 5,280 ft.

Firgas (fĭr'gäs), village (pop. 597), Grand Canary, Canary Isls., 9 mi. W of Las Palmas; cochineal, bananas, cereals, fruit. Mineral springs.

Firiza or **Firiza-de-Jos** (fērē'zä-dā-zhōs'), Hung. *Felsőfernezely* (fĕl'shûfĕr"nĕzĕl), village (pop. 1,214), Baia-Mare prov., NW Rumania, 7 mi. N of Baia-Mare; rail terminus and mining center (gold, silver, copper, lead, zinc, sulphur), with reduction works; mfg. of chemicals, and fertilizers. In Hungary, 1940–45.

Firmat (fērmät'), town (pop. estimate 3,000), S Santa Fe prov., Argentina, 60 mi. SW of Rosario; rail junction; agr. center (corn, wheat, flax, alfalfa, livestock).

Firminy (fērmēnē'), town (pop. 17,941), Loire dept., SE central France, on the Ondaine and 6 mi. SW of Saint-Étienne; major coal-mining center; iron and steel stamping, metalworking, aluminum reducing; mfg. of bricks, tiles, ribbons, elastic fabrics.

Firovo (fē'růvů), town (1939 pop. over 2,000), W Kalinin oblast, Russian SFSR, 32 mi. SSW of Bologoye; glassworks.

Firozabad, Delhi, India: see DELHI, state.

Firozabad (fīrō'zäbäd"), town (pop. 40,572), Agra dist., W Uttar Pradesh, India, 24 mi. E of Agra; major Indian glass-bangles mfg. center; cotton ginning; trades in pearl millet, gram, wheat, oilseeds, cotton.

Firoz Koh or **Firuz Kuh** (fērōz' kō), name sometimes applied to 2 W outliers of the Hindu Kush, in NW Afghanistan: the SAFED KOH (N) and the SIAH KOH (S). Inhabited largely by Persian-speaking Firoz-Kohi tribe.

Firozpur, India: see FEROZEPORE, district.

Firozpur, Kashmir: see GULMARG.

Firozpur Jhirka (fĭrōz'pŏŏr jĭr'kŭ), town (pop. 6,192), Gurgaon dist., SE Punjab, India, 45 mi. S of Gurgaon; agr. market center (millet, barley, gram, oilseeds); metalware; distillery. Sometimes spelled Ferozpur Jhirka.

First Connecticut Lake, N.H.: see CONNECTICUT LAKES.

First Eel Lake (□ 3; 3 mi. long, 2 mi. wide), SW N.B., near Maine border, 20 mi. SSW of Woodstock. Just S is Second Eel Lake (3 mi. long). Both drain into St. John R. by the short Eel R.

First Roach Pond, Piscataquis co., central Maine, 18 mi. NE of Greenville, in hunting, fishing area; 6 mi. long, 1.5 mi. wide. Formerly called Kokadjo L.

Firth. 1 Village (pop. 293), Bingham co., SE Idaho, 10 mi. NE of Blackfoot and on Snake R.; alt. 4,566 ft.; sugar beets, grain, potatoes, dairying. **2** Village (pop. 245), Lancaster co., SE Nebr., 20 mi. S of Lincoln and on N.Fork of Nemaha R.

Firthcliffe, industrial village (1940 pop. 644), Orange co., SE N.Y., 5 mi. SW of Newburgh; carpet mfg.

Firuzabad (fērōōz"äbäd'), town (1940 pop. 23,382), Seventh Prov., in Fars, S Iran, 55 mi. S of Shiraz; lumber, rice, grain. Attacked and ruined by Alexander the Great. Rebuilt by Sassanian dynasty.

Firuzkuh (fērōōz"kōō'), village (1940 pop. 3,041), Second Prov., in Teheran, N Iran, 75 mi. E of Teheran, and on Trans-Iranian RR and road to Mazanderan; road center in Firuz Kuh section (9,000 ft.) of Elburz mts.; grain, cotton, sheep raising; charcoal burning.

Firyuza (fēryōō'zŭ), health resort (1926 pop. 544), S Ashkhabad oblast, Turkmen SSR, on N slope of the Kopet-Dagh, 15 mi. WSW of Ashkhabad, near Iran border.

Fischamend (fĭsh'ämĕnt'), town (pop. 3,523), after 1938 in Schwechat dist. of Vienna, Austria, on Fischa R., near the Danube and 12.5 mi. ESE of city center; mfg. of motorcars. Includes Fischamend Dorf (pop. 807) and Fischamend Markt (pop. 2,716).

Fischa River (fĭsh'ä), SE Lower Austria, rises on the Schneeberg, flows 50 mi. NE to the Danube near Fischamend. Receives Piesting R. (left).

Fischbach Alps (fĭsh'bäkh), forested range of Eastern Alps, in Styria, E Austria, extending 27 mi. NE from Mur R., along Mürz R.; rise to 5,850 ft. in the Stuhleck, 5 mi. ESE of Mürzzuschlag.

Fischhausen, Russian SFSR: see PRIMORSK, Kaliningrad oblast.

Fisenge (fēsĕng'gā), township (pop. 57), Western Prov., N central Northern Rhodesia, on rail spur and c.15 mi. SW of Ndola, in copper belt.

Fisha Silim (fē'shä sĭlēm'), village (pop. 5,100), Gharbiya prov., Lower Egypt, 3 mi. SW of Tanta; cotton. The 13th-cent. saint Ahmad al-Badawi lived here.

Fish Creek, resort village (pop. c.200), Door co., NE Wis., on inlet of Green Bay, on Door Peninsula, 21 mi. NNE of Sturgeon Bay city; fishing and agr.

Fish Creek, central Mich., rises near Sheridan in Montcalm co., flows c.30 mi. E and S, past Carson City, to Maple R. just S of Hubbardston.

Fisher, county (□ 906; pop. 11,023), NW central Texas; ⊙ Roby. Rolling plains drained by Double Mtn. and Clear forks of Brazos R. Agr. and livestock region, producing some oil and natural gas; cotton, grain sorghums, grain, some fruit, truck; beef cattle, hogs, sheep, poultry; dairy products. Gypsum quarried. Formed 1876.

Fisher. 1 Town (pop. 289), Poinsett co., NE Ark., 29 mi. SSW of Jonesboro. **2** Village (pop. 894), Champaign co., E Ill., on the Sangamon (bridged here) and 14 mi. NNW of Champaign, in agr. area. **3** Village (pop. 302), Polk co., NW Minn., on Red Lake R. and 9 mi. W of Crookston, in grain and potato area.

Fisher, Mount (9,245 ft.), SE B.C., in Rocky Mts., 17 mi. ENE of Cranbrook, overlooking the Kootenay valley; 49°36'N 115°56'W.

Fisherman Island. 1 In Lincoln co., S Maine, narrow island (1 mi. long), 4 mi. SE of Boothbay Harbor. **2** In E Va., low island just off S tip of Cape Charles; c.1½ mi. long.

Fisherman Lake, coastal lagoon in W Liberia, on Atlantic Ocean, 35 mi. NW of Monrovia; 11 mi. long, 6 mi. wide. Outlet at Robertsport (W). Fisheries. An important Allied seaplane base during Second World War.

Fisherman Peninsula, Russian SFSR: see RYBACHI PENINSULA.

Fisher Peak (10,015 ft.), SW Alta., near B.C. border, in Rocky Mts., 35 mi. SE of Banff; 50°50'N 115°2'W.

Fishers or **Fishers Station,** town (pop. 219), Hamilton co., central Ind., 15 mi. NE of Indianapolis.

Fishers Hill, Va.: see STRASBURG.

Fishers Island, Suffolk co., SE N.Y., in E Long Island Sound, 11 mi. off NE tip of Long Isl. and 7 mi. SE of New London, Conn. (ferry connections); c.8 mi. long; average width c.1 mi. Separated from SE Conn. by Fishers Island Sound (2–3 mi. wide). Summer-resort and residential area. Fishers Island village (pop. 572) and Fort H. G. Wright, hq. of Long Isl. coast guard, are here. Discussions regarding isl.'s annexation to Conn. were held in the 1940s.

Fishers Lake (8 mi. long, 1 mi. wide), W N.S., 18 mi. ESE of Digby. Outlet: Mersey R.

Fishers Peak, Colo.: see RATON MOUNTAINS.

Fishers Station, Ind.: see FISHERS.

Fisherville, Mass.: see GRAFTON.

Fishguard, former urban district (1931 pop. 2,926) now in Fishguard and Goodwick urban dist. (1951 census 4,840), N Pembroke, Wales, on Fishguard Bay of Irish Sea, 13 mi. N of Haverfordwest; 51°59'N 5°W; passenger and fishing port, terminal of cross-channel service from Rosslare, Ireland. Site of radio station. In 1797 a French force under General Tate landed near by and was repulsed after 3 days. On St. George's Channel, 5 mi. NW, is promontory of Strumble Head, site of lighthouse (52°1'N 5°7'W).

Fish Hoek or **Fishhoek** (fĭsh' hŏŏk"), Afrikaans *Vis Hoek* or *Vishoek* (fĭs"hŏŏk'), town (pop. 3,126), SW Cape Prov., U. of So. Afr., on W side of False Bay of the Atlantic, 15 mi. S of Cape Town; popular seaside resort. In near-by Skildergat Cave prehistoric human remains have been found.

Fishhook, Alaska: see CHALKYITSIK.

Fish Hook Lake, Hubbard co., W Minn., just N of Park Rapids; 3 mi. long, 1 mi. wide. Fishing resorts. Drains through system of small streams into Crow Wing R.

Fish Hook River, rises in Becker co., W Minn., flows 40 mi. E and S, through Arago and Fish Hook lakes, to Straight R. 4 mi. S of Park Rapids. Fishing resorts on shore.

Fishing Bay, E Md., inlet (c.14 mi. long, 2–4 mi. wide) of Tangier Sound, indenting the Eastern Shore in S Dorchester co. Receives Blackwater and Transquaking rivers.

Fishing Creek, village, Md.: see HOOPER ISLANDS.

Fishing Creek, N N.C., rises 4 mi. NE of Henderson, flows c.75 mi. generally ESE to Tar R. 3 mi. N of Tarboro.

Fishing Islands, group of c.20 islets, S Ont., in L. Huron, just off foot of Saugeen Peninsula, 8 mi. W of Wiarton.

Fishing Lakes, group of 4 contiguous lakes in SE Sask., on Qu'Appelle R., 35 mi. NE of Regina. Total length 28 mi., average width 1 mi. Bet. the central lakes is Fort Qu'Appelle. Lakes are noted for whitefish.

Fishing River, W Mo., rises in Clay co., flows c.40 mi. NE and SE to the Missouri 25 mi. E of Kansas City.

Fishkill, village (pop. 841), Dutchess co., SE N.Y., on Fishkill Creek and 5 mi. ENE of Beacon, in potato-growing area; cider, lumber. Near-by village of Fishkill Landing joined Matteawan (1913) to form Beacon city.

Fishkill Creek, SE N.Y., rises in Dutchess co. E of Poughkeepsie, flows c.35 mi. SW to the Hudson just S of Beacon.

Fishkill Landing, N.Y.: see BEACON.

Fish Lake (5 mi. long, 1 mi. wide; alt. c.8,600 ft.), in Fish Lake Plateau, Sevier co., S central Utah, 37 mi. S of Richfield. Has fishing resorts.

Fish Lake Plateau, S central Utah, high tableland in Fishlake Natl. Forest, Sevier and Wayne counties. Watered by Fish L. and Fremont R. Reaches max. alt. in Mt. MARVINE (11,600 ft.). Other peaks are Mt. HILGARD (11,527 ft.) and Mt. TERRILL (11,530 ft.). Also known as Fish Lake Mts. Thousand Lake Mtn. (11,295 ft.) is in S outlier.

Fish River, intermittent stream, S South-West Africa, rises near 23°35'S 16°20'E, flows c.500 mi. S, past Mariental, Gibeon, and Seeheim, to Orange R. at 26°6'S 17°11'E.

Fish River, Aroostook co., N Maine, rises 35 mi. NW of Presque Isle, flows c.50 mi. SE, then N, connecting FISH RIVER LAKES, to St. John R. near Fort Kent.

Fish River Lakes, NE Maine, chain in NE Aroostook co., linked by Fish R.; includes Fish River L. (4 mi. long), Portage L. (4.5 mi. long), St. Froid L. (7 mi. long), Eagle L. (14 mi. long), Square L. (7 mi. long), Cross L. (5.5 mi. long), Long L. (11 mi. long); noted for excellent fishing, canoeing.

Fisht (fēsht), westernmost high peak (9,498 ft.) of the Greater Caucasus, Russian SFSR, in main range, 25 mi. NNE of Sochi.

Fishtown, village, Warri prov., Western Provinces, S Nigeria, on Gulf of Guinea, at mouth of Benin R., 55 mi. SW of Benin City; fishing center; salt making; coconuts, cassava, plantains.

Fish Village, village (1939 pop. 27), W Alaska, on Yukon R., near its mouth on Bering Sea, 23 mi. SE of Kwiguk; salmon fishing.

Fisk, town (pop. 542), Butler co., SE Mo., in Ozark region, on St. Francis R. and 11 mi. E of Poplar Bluff; ships rice.

Fiska, Norway: see JORPELAND.

Fiskars (fĭs'kärs, -käsh), Finnish *Fiskari* (fĭs'kärē), village in Pojo commune (pop. 6,507), Uusimaa co., S Finland, near head of Pojo Bay of Gulf of Finland, 50 mi. W of Helsinki; rail terminus; iron and steel mills, metalworks. Products shipped through port of Skuru.

Fiskdale, Mass.: see STURBRIDGE.

Fiskemfoss (fĭsk'ŭmfôs), waterfall (c.100 ft.) in Nord-Trondelag co., central Norway, on Nams R. and 10 mi. NNE of Grong; tourist attraction; hydroelectric plant.

Fiskenaesset (fĭ'skŭnĕ"sŭt), fishing settlement (pop. 154), Godthaab dist., SW Greenland, on Irkens Havn, small inlet of the Atlantic, 80 mi. SSE of Godthaab; 63°5'N 50°41'W. Radio station.

Fismes (fēm), town (pop. 2,751), Marne dept., N France, 16 mi. WNW of Rheims; furniture mfg., metalworking. A Ger. supply depot during First World War; captured (1918) by Americans. Bridge across the Vesle erected (1927) by state of Pennsylvania.

Fitch, Mount, Mass.: see GREYLOCK, MOUNT.

Fitch Bay, village (pop. estimate 300), S Que., on arm of L. Memphremagog, 10 mi. SSW of Magog; resort; dairying.

Fitchburg, city (pop. 42,691), a ⊙ Worcester co., N Mass., on N branch of Nashua R. and 22 mi. N of Worcester; woolens, paper and paper products, foundry and machine-shop products, electrical machinery, shoes, handbags, tools; granite quarries. State teachers col. Settled c.1730, inc. as town 1764, as city 1872.

Fitchville, Conn.: see BOZRAH.

Fitero (fētä'rō), town (pop. 2,848), Navarre prov., N Spain, 13 mi. W of Tudela; olive-oil processing; mfg. of soap, brandy, chocolate. Wine, cereals. Has radioactive mineral springs.

Fitful Head, broad headland at SW tip of Mainland isl., Shetlands, Scotland, rising to 928 ft., 5 mi. NW of Sumburgh Head; 59°54'N 1°23'W.

Fithian (fĭ'thēŭn), village (pop. 414), Vermilion co., E Ill., 12 mi. W of Danville, in agr. and bituminous-coal area.

Fitjar (fēt'yär), village and canton (pop. 3,036), Hordaland co., SW Norway, fishing port on NW shore of Stord isl., 32 mi. S of Bergen. Dates back at least to 961.

Fitri, Lake, Fr. Equatorial Africa: see FITTRI, LAKE.

Fittri, Lake (fētrē'), fresh-water lagoon (□ 20–40) in central Chad territory, Fr. Equatorial Africa, E of L. Chad and 75 mi. SW of Ati; c.12 mi. long, 10 mi. wide, 6–8 ft. deep; 13°N 17°30'E. Largely overgrown with reeds; it expands or contracts according to water supply. Receives Batha R. Sometimes spelled Fitri.

Fitz, agr. village and parish (pop. 241), central Shropshire, England, on Severn R. and 4 mi. NW of Shrewsbury; flour milling. Has Elizabethan manor house.

Fitzgerald, Alta.: see FORT FITZGERALD.

Fitzgerald, city (pop. 8,130), ⊙ Ben Hill co., S central Ga., c.50 mi. NE of Moultrie. Tobacco market and processing center for diversified farm area; mfg. of sheeting, clothing, naval stores, cottonseed oil, fertilizer; peanut milling, meat packing. Near by, where Davis was taken prisoner by Federal troops, is Jefferson Davis State Park. Settled 1895 by Union veterans. Inc. 1896.

Fitzmaurice River, NW Northern Territory, Australia, rises in hills 85 mi. WSW of Katherine, flows 100 mi. W to Joseph Bonaparte Gulf; widens at mouth to become Keyling Inlet (7 mi. N–S).

Fitz Roy (fēts roi'), village (pop. estimate 100), SE Comodoro Rivadavia military zone, Argentina, on railroad and 80 mi. NW of Puerto Deseado; sheep raising. Until 1946 in Santa Cruz natl. territory.

Fitzroy (fĭtsroi'), NE suburb (pop. 32,380) of Melbourne, S Victoria, Australia; mfg. center; engineering works.

Fitz Roy, Cerro (sĕ'rō fēts roi'), Patagonian peak (11,073 ft.) in the Andes, on Argentina-Chile border, 10 mi. NW of L. Viedma; 49°16'S. Sometimes called Chaltel.

Fitzroy Island, Chile: see CHONOS ARCHIPELAGO.

Fitzroy River (fĭtsroi'). **1** In E Queensland, Australia, formed by Dawson and Mackenzie rivers; flows N and SE, past Rockhampton, to Keppel Bay at Port Alma; 174 mi. long. Navigable for 49 mi. below Rockhampton by steamers carrying wool, gold, coal, copper, meat. **2** In NE Western Australia, rises in E King Leopold Ranges, flows 325 mi. SW and NW, through mountainous area, to King Sound near Derby. Margaret and Christmas rivers, main tributaries.

Fitzwilliam, resort town (pop. 872), Cheshire co., S N.H., 13 mi. SE of Keene, near Mass. line; granite quarries, wood products.

Fitzwilliam Island (8 mi. long, 4 mi. wide), S central Ont., one of the Manitoulin Isls., in L. Huron, just SE of Manitoulin Isl., separated from Saugeen Peninsula by 15-mi.-wide channel.

Fitzwilliam Strait, W Franklin Dist., Northwest Territories, arm (60 mi. long, 15–40 mi. wide) of the Arctic Ocean, bet. Melville Isl. and Prince Patrick Isl.; 76°10'–76°40'N 114°30'–117°30'W. At NE end is Emerald Isl. At SW end of Fitzwilliam Strait is Eglinton Isl., where strait divides into Crozier Channel (65 mi. long) and Kellett Strait (60 mi. long).

Fiuggi (fūd'jē), town (pop. 2,763), Frosinone prov., Latium, S central Italy, in the Appennines, 11 mi. SE of Subiaco. A major health resort (alt. 2,451 ft.) of Italy; lower part (alt. 2,037 ft.) of town has mineral baths.

Fiumalbo (fūmäl'bô), village (pop. 799), Modena prov., Emilia-Romagna, N central Italy, 22 mi. NW of Pistoia; woolen mill. Point of ascent for Monte Cimone.

Fiume, Yugoslavia: see RIJEKA.

Fiumefreddo Bruzio (fū"mĕfrĕd'dô brōō'tsyô), village (pop. 1,074), Cosenza prov., Calabria, S Italy, on Tyrrhenian Sea, 11 mi. WSW of Cosenza; wine, olive oil.

Fiumefreddo di Sicilia (dē sēchē'lyä), village (pop. 3,651) Catania prov., E Sicily, at NE foot of Mt. Etna, 13 mi. N of Acireale; fertilizer mfg.

Fiume Veneto (fū'mĕ vä'nĕtô), village (pop. 1,210), Udine prov., Friuli–Venezia Giulia, 4 mi. ESE of Pordenone.

Fiumicino (fūmēchē'nô). **1** Village (pop. 211), Forlì prov., Emilia-Romagna, N central Italy, on Rubicon R. and 10 mi. WNW of Rimini. **2** Town (pop. 2,983), Roma prov., Latium, central Italy, port on Tyrrhenian Sea, at N mouth of the Tiber, 15 mi. SW of Rome; bathing resort; glass mfg.

Fiumi Uniti (fū'mē ōōnē'tē), N central Italy, river formed by junction of Ronco and Montone rivers just S of Ravenna; flows 6 mi. E to the Adriatic.

Five Boroughs, Danish fortified towns in the English midlands, settled in the 9th cent. They were Derby, Leicester, Stamford, Nottingham, and Lincoln.

Five Forks. **1** Locality, Dinwiddie co., Va.: see DINWIDDIE, village. **2** Village (pop. 4,124, with near-by Arlington and Kenwood), Prince George co., E Va., a suburb of Hopewell.

Five Island Harbour, bay, W Antigua, B.W.I., 2 mi. WSW of St. John's.

Five Islands, village (pop. estimate 400), N central N.S., on Minas Basin, 30 mi. SSE of Amherst; dairying, mixed farming; port. Just offshore are several islets.

Five Islands or **Las Cotorras** (läs kōtô'räs), archipelago (319 acres) off NW Trinidad, B.W.I., in Gulf of Paria, c.7 mi. W of Port of Spain; consists, actually, of 6 tiny islets: Caledonia, Nelson, Lenagan, Rock, Pelican, and Craig (joined to Caledonia by narrow reef). Bathing and fishing resort.

Five Islands, village, Maine: see GEORGETOWN.

Five Islands, S La., name given to 5 salt domes scattered through coastal marshes of St. Mary and Iberia parishes; isls. contain large rock-salt mines, sulphur deposits, oil and gas wells. Include AVERY ISLAND (with noted bird sanctuary and gardens), BELLE ISLE, COTE BLANCHE ISLAND, JEFFERSON ISLAND, WEEKS ISLAND.

Fivemiletown, town (pop. 888), S Co. Tyrone, Northern Ireland, 14 mi. ENE of Enniskillen; frontier station on Irish border; agr. market (flax, potatoes, oats; cattle). Town was founded in reign of James I.

Five Points. **1** or **Fivepoints,** town (pop. 253), Chambers co., E Ala., 15 mi. NW of Lanett. **2** Village, Bernalillo co., N.Mex.: see ATRISCO.

Fives Lille (fē'vĕs lē'lā), town (pop. estimate 1,500), central Santa Fe prov., Argentina, on railroad and 55 mi. ENE of San Cristóbal; agr. center (corn, flax, sunflowers, wheat, livestock).

Five Towns, England: see STOKE-ON-TRENT; POTTERIES.

Fivizzano (fēvētsä'nô), town (pop. 1,394), Massa e Carrara prov., Tuscany, central Italy, 11 mi. N of Carrara; mfg. (macaroni, cement, paper, fertilizer, metal furniture, woolen textiles). Marble quarries near by.

Fixin (fēsē'), village (pop. 485), Côte-d'Or dept., E central France, on E slope of the Côte d'Or, 6 mi. SSW of Dijon; Burgundy wines.

Fizi (fē'zē), village, Kivu prov., E Belgian Congo, 120 mi. S of Costermansville, near NW shore of L. Tanganyika; alt. 4,097 ft. Trading center in cotton area.

Fjaere (fyăr'ŭ), village and canton (pop. 4,706), Aust-Agder co., S Norway, on the Skagerrak, on railroad and 10 mi. SW of Arendal. Has 13th-cent. church. Many archaeological findings from the Stone and Iron ages near by.

Fjaerlands Fjord (fyăr'läns), N arm of Sogne Fjord in Sogn og Fjordane co., W Norway; extends N c.15 mi. to Fjaerland village in Balestrand canton, 17 mi. NW of Sogndal, where arms of the Jostedalsbre glacier descend almost to water's edge.

Fjaler, Norway: see DALE, Sogn og Fjordane co.

Fjalkinge (fyĕl'kĭng-ŭ), Swedish *Fjälkinge,* village (pop. 692), Kristianstad co., S Sweden, 4 mi. E of Kristianstad; tobacco, grain, potatoes, stock.

Fjallbacka (fyĕl'bä"kä), Swedish *Fjällbacka,* fishing village (pop. 839), Goteborg och Bohus co., SW Sweden, on Skagerrak, 20 mi. N of Lysekil; seaside resort.

Fjelberg, Norway: see HALSNOY.

Fjeldsa, Fjeldse, or **Fjelsa,** Norway: see LOGA.

Fjerritslev (fyĕ'rĭtslĕv), town (pop. 1,811), Thisted amt, N Jutland, Denmark, 23 mi. ENE of Thisted; cement, machinery.

Fjordane, Norway: see SOGN OG FJORDANE.

Fjosanger (fyō'sängŭr), village in Fana canton, Hordaland co., SW Norway, 3 mi. S of Bergen. Has institute of scientific research and 11th-cent. Fanstoft stave church, moved here from Fortun.

Fjotland, Norway: see KNABEN.

Fjugesta (fyüyĕ'stä), village (pop. 965), Orebro co., S central Sweden, on Svart R. and 14 mi. WSW of Orebro; woodworking. Remains of anc. monastery near by.

Fkih-Bensalah (fkē-bĕnsälä'), town (pop. 3,580), Casablanca region, W central Fr. Morocco, near Béni Mellal.

Fla (flô), Nor. *Flå,* village and canton (pop. 1,509), Buskerud co., S Norway, on Hallingdal R., on railroad and 30 mi. NW of Honefoss; oats, barley, stock; lumbering. Sometimes spelled Flaa.

Flaa Lake, Norway: see FLA LAKE.

Flaamsdal, Norway: see FLAMSDAL.

Flachstöckheim (flăkh'shtŭk'hīm), SE district of WATENSTEDT-SALZGITTER, NW Germany; iron mining.

Flacq (fläk), town (pop. 758), E Mauritius, on railroad and 15 mi. E of Port Louis; sugar milling, alcohol distilling. Was ebony-trade center c.1700. Also called Central Flacq or Centre de Flacq.

Fladday, island (pop. 23), Inner Hebrides, Inverness, Scotland, just off N Raasay; 1½ mi. long, ½ mi. wide.

Fladstrand, Denmark: see FREDERIKSHAVN.

Flagey-Echézeaux (flăzhā'-āshāzō'), village (pop. 219), Côte-d'Or dept., E central France, 11 mi. SSW of Dijon; Burgundy wines.

Flagler (flă'glŭr), county (□ 483; pop. 3,367), NE Fla., on the Atlantic (E), and partly bounded W by Crescent L.; ⊙ Bunnell. Lowland agr. (corn, vegetables, citrus fruit, livestock) and forestry (lumber, naval stores) area, with swamps and small lakes. Formed 1917.

Flagler, town (pop. 793), Kit Carson co., E Colo., 43 mi. W of Burlington; alt. 4,920 ft. Flour, feed, livestock, dairy and poultry products.

Flagler, Fort, Wash.: see PORT TOWNSEND.

Flagler Beach, resort town (pop. 374), Flagler co., NE Fla., 30 mi. S of St. Augustine, on the Atlantic.

Flagstaff. **1** City (pop. 7,663), ⊙ Coconino co., N central Ariz., 65 mi. NE of Prescott, near San Francisco Peaks and Elden Mtn.; alt. 6,907 ft. Lumbering, stock raising and agr. (beans, potatoes, and oats) in vicinity; sawmills. Tourist center in scenic region (natl. parks, forests, Indian reservations). Seat of Lowell Observatory (1894) and state teachers col. Founded 1881. **2** Former plantation, Somerset co., W Maine, inundated 1949–50 by reservoir (Flagstaff L.) impounded by Long Falls Dam in Dead R.

Flagstaff Mountain (2,497 ft.), Somerset co., W Maine, near Flagstaff Pond (2.25 mi. long), 25 mi. NW of Bingham.

Flak Lake (fläk'), Nor. *Flaksvatn*, formerly *Flakksvand*, lake (□ 1) on Tovdal R. in Aust-Agder co., S Norway, 10 mi. NNE of Kristiansand. Terminus of 14-mi. railroad to Lillesand.

Flakstad (fläk'stä), village and canton (pop. 1,958), Nordland co., N Norway, on Flakstadoy (Nor. *Flakstadøy*), an isl. (□ 42; pop. 1,294) of the Lofoten Isls., in the North Sea, 35 mi. WSW of Svolvaer; cod-fishing center. Fisheries and summer resorts at Nusfjord (nōōs'fyōr) (sometimes spelled Nuss fjord) village, 5 mi. SSE, and at Sund (sōōn) village (pop. 120), 7 mi. SSW.

Fla Lake (flô), Nor. *Flåvatn*, Telemark co., S Norway, 30 mi. WNW of Skien; part of BANDAK-NORSJA CANAL; 10 mi. long, 2 mi. wide, 397 ft. deep. Sometimes spelled Flaa.

Flamanville (flämävēl'), village (pop. 259), Manche dept., NW France, near W coast of Cotentin Peninsula, 13 mi. SW of Cherbourg. Iron mines and granite quarries at Diélette (1 mi. N).

Flambeau Reservoir, Wis.: see FLAMBEAU RIVER.

Flambeau River (flăm'bō), N Wis., rises in lake region near Mich. line, flows NW, through large irregular Flambeau Reservoir (E of Butternut), then swiftly SW, past Park Falls and Ladysmith, to Chippewa R. 27 mi. NNE of Chippewa Falls; c.115 mi. long from head of longest branch, which is sometimes called North Fork in upper course. Receives South Fork (c.55 mi. long) near Rusk-Sawyer co. line. Has hydroelectric plants. Formerly important for logging.

Flamborough Head, chalk peninsula on North Sea, E Yorkshire, England, 5 mi. ENE of Bridlington, sheltering Bridlington Bay (S); 54°8'N 0°12'W. Its lighthouse is visible for 21 mi. Sea-carved chalk cliffs are inhabited by numerous sea fowl. An anc. earthwork (Danes' Dyke) crosses the peninsula. Off the coast here John Paul Jones won a victory in 1779.

Flambouron, Greece: see PIERIA.

Flamenco Island (flämĕng'kō) (□ 10), in Anegada Bay, SW Buenos Aires prov., Argentina, N of Gama Isl. and 50 mi. NE of Carmen de Patagones.

Flamenco Island, islet in Panama Bay of Panama Canal Zone guarding Pacific entrance of the Panama Canal, 3½ mi. SSE of Panama city. Joined to Perico Isl. and mainland by mole.

Flamingo Bay, village, Kassala prov., NE Anglo-Egyptian Sudan, minor port on Red Sea, on road and 3 mi. N of Port Sudan; sea-shell industry; sambuk building and repairing. It is also a customs station.

Flaminian Way (flŭmĭ'nēŭn), one of the principal anc. Roman roads, from Rome to Cisalpine Gaul, built 220 B.C. by Caius Flaminius; originally 209 mi. long, it was increased to 215 mi. when the course was changed for some 50 mi. The Aemilian Way was part of it.

Flamisell River (flämēsāl'), Lérida prov., NE Spain, rises in several headstreams N of Capdella in the central Pyrenees, flows c.25 mi. S to the Noguera Pallaresa at Pobla de Segur; 2 hydroelectric plants in upper course.

Flamsdal (flôms'däl), Nor. *Flåmsdal*, valley in Sogn og Fjordane co., W Norway; extends, as a continuation of Aurlands Fjord, c.10 mi. S to Myrdal in the Hardangerfjell. Following the valley are a remarkable zigzag road and a railway which passes through 20 tunnels bet. Myrdal and village (pop. 348) of Flam (Nor. *Flåm;* formerly called Fretheim), in Aurland canton; Flam is a tourist center at N end of valley. Sometimes spelled Flaamsdal.

Flanagan, village (pop. 672), Livingston co., N central Ill., 11 mi. W of Pontiac, in agr. and bituminous-coal area; grain, dairy products, poultry.

Flanders (flăn'dŭrz), Flemish *Vlaanderen* (vlän'dŭrŭn), Fr. *Flandre* (flã'drŭ), former county in the Low Countries, now divided bet. Belgium and France. Extending along the North Sea and W of the Scheldt (Escaut) river, it varied considerably in size in the course of its history, including at one time also Artois and parts of Picardy. In Belgian Flanders the Flemish language, a Low German dialect akin to Dutch, is spoken by the majority of the inhabitants; all the Flemish-speaking pop. of Belgium and France are, by extension, known as Flemings. A considerable part of N Flanders has been gained from the sea in past centuries. In 862 Baldwin Bras-de-Fer, a son-in-law of Emperor Charles II, became 1st count of Flanders. In the divisions (9th cent.) of the Carolingian empire, Flanders became a fief dependent on the French crown, but its powerful counts extended (11th cent.) their domains to the E; these additions, being held in fief to the Holy Roman Empire, became known as Imperial Flanders, in contrast to Crown Flanders, held from the French kings. The struggle for the succession to Flanders in the 12th cent. resulted in the loss of Artois and other dists. in W and S Flanders to the French crown. At the same time the Flemish cities—among which GHENT, BRUGES, YPRES, and COURTRAI were foremost—gained vast privileges. Their prosperity and the prosperity of Flanders depended on the growing cloth industry, which had been introduced in the 10th cent., and on the transit trade at such major ports as Bruges (later superseded by Antwerp) and Ghent. By 13th cent. the Flemish cloth industry was the foremost in Europe, and it has retained much of its importance. There followed in the 13th and 14th cent. a turbulent history. The French largely dominated the region, but they were thoroughly routed in the Battle of the Spurs (1302). The accession (1322) of the pro-French Louis of Nevers as count of Flanders threw the country into a civil war in which Bruges and Ypres sided against, and Ghent with, the count. The pro-French party emerged victorious. When Edward III of England, about to embark on the Hundred Years War with France, stopped English wool exports to Flanders, the Flemish cloth industry faced ruin. The Flemings united under the leadership of Ghent and allied themselves with England, taking part in Edward's great naval victory at Sluis (1340). In 1380 the weavers of Ghent rebelled once more. They took Bruges but were defeated (1382) by a French army at Roosebeke. The duke of Burgundy succeeded to Flanders in 1384. Under the Burgundian dynasty Flemish commerce and Flemish art reached their flower. The cloth industry, however, was in decline, and the political rights of the cities were curtailed. On the death (1477) of Charles the Bold, Mary of Burgundy restored the Flemish liberties in the Great Privilege. With Philip of Burgundy began (1482) the rule of the house of Hapsburg over Flanders and the rest of the Low Countries. Flanders joined (1576) in the revolt of the Netherlands against Philip II of Spain, but by 1584 the Spanish had recovered the county. It continued under Sp. rule until 1714, when the Peace of Utrecht awarded it to Austria. Parts of W Flanders, including Lille, were annexed to France bet. 1668 and 1678 and became known as French Flanders. Austria ceded the remainder of Flanders to France in the Treaty of Campo Formio (1797), but the Congress of Vienna awarded (1815) the former Austrian Flanders to the Netherlands. When Belgium gained (1830) independence, Flanders was divided into the provs. of EAST FLANDERS and WEST FLANDERS. Its strategic situation has made Flanders a major battleground since the Middle Ages. In First World War there was continuous fighting in French Flanders and West Flanders. In the Second World War the battle of Flanders began with the German invasion (May 10, 1940) of the Low Countries and ended with the surrender of the Belgian army and with the evacuation of the British at Dunkirk (May 26–June 4, 1940).

Flanders, French, region and former province of N France, bounded by North Sea (NW) and Belgium (NE and E), roughly coextensive with present NORD dept.; ⊙ Lille. Important coal-mining and industrial region. Chief cities are Lille, Roubaix, Tourcoing, Valenciennes, Douai, and seaport of Dunkirk. Flemish is still widely spoken in NW, bet. the Lys and North Sea. It shared history of county of FLANDERS until final incorporation (1662–78) into France by Louis XIV. Area has been battleground in almost every major European conflict.

Flanders Bay, N.Y.: see GREAT PECONIC BAY.

Flandes (flän'dĕs), town (pop. 4,644), Tolima dept., W central Colombia, landing on Magdalena R. opposite Girardot, on railroad to Bogotá, and 31 mi. ESE of Ibagué, in agr. region (yucca, bananas, cotton, tobacco); mfg. (cigars, chocolate).

Flandreau (flăn'drōō), city (pop. 2,193), ⊙ Moody co., E S.Dak., 35 mi. N of Sioux Falls and on Big Sioux R.; large cooperative creamery; grain, livestock, dairy products, poultry. Vocational high school for Indians is here. Permanently settled 1869.

Flandre Occidentale, Belgium: see WEST FLANDERS.

Flandre Orientale, Belgium: see EAST FLANDERS.

Flandria, Belgian Congo: see BOTEKE.

Flannan Isles or **Seven Hunters**, group of 7 uninhabited islets of the Outer Hebrides, Scotland, 20 mi. W of Lewis with Harris. Northernmost islet has lighthouse (58°16'N 6°38'W).

Flasher, village (pop. 413), Morton co., S N.Dak., 33 mi. SW of Bismarck and on Louise Creek.

Flat, village (pop. 91), W Alaska, near Iditarod R. and 60 mi. ENE of Holy Cross; 62°27'N 158°1'W; trading center for prospectors and trappers; placer gold mining. Airfield.

Flatanger, canton, Norway: see LAUVSNES.

Flat Brook, NW N.J., rises in NW Sussex co., flows c.20 mi. SW in the Appalachians, to the Delaware c.15 mi. above Delaware Water Gap; hunting, fishing in valley.

Flatbush, SE N.Y., a residential section of central Brooklyn borough of New York city. Has several 18th-cent. bldgs., including Reformed Protestant Dutch Church. Brooklyn Col. and Ebbets Field are here. Was a Dutch village in 17th cent. Kings County Hosp. and Brooklyn State Hosp. are in adjacent East Flatbush.

Flat Creek, village (pop. 1,520, with near-by Wegan), Walker co., NW central Ala., 20 mi. WNW of Birmingham.

Flatey (flät'ā"), islet, W Iceland, in Breidi Fjord, near S shore of Vestfjarda Peninsula; 65°22'N 22°55'W. The anc. "Book of Flatey," found here, is in Royal Library in Copenhagen; it describes early Viking voyages to Greenland and America.

Flateyri or **Flateyri i Onundarfirdi** (flät'ā"rē ē ŭ'nündärfĭr"dhē), Icelandic *Flateyri í Önundarfirði*, fishing village (pop. 431) Isafjardar co., NW Iceland, on Vestfjarda Peninsula, 10 mi. W of Isafjordur, on Onundar Fjord, Icelandic *Önundarfjörður*, 12-mi. inlet of Denmark Strait.

Flathead, county (□ 5,177; pop. 31,495), NW Mont.; ⊙ Kalispell. Agr. region bordering on British Columbia, bounded E by Continental Divide; drained by Flathead L. and Flathead R. Livestock, grain, timber, fruit. Sections of Flathead Natl. Forest in SE and N, part of Glacier Natl. Park in NE; ranges of Rocky Mts. throughout. Formed 1893.

Flathead Lake, NW Mont., 10 mi. SSE of Kalispell, just W of Mission Range, in fertile agr. valley of Flathead R., which enters (N), drains lake (S); of glacial origin, it is largest lake in state (□ 189; 30 mi. long, 15 mi. max. width, 220 ft. deep). Used for irrigation and hydroelectric power (dam at S end, at Polson). Biological station of state univ. on E side. Lake has many small isls.

Flathead Pass (alt. 6,769 ft.), in Bridger Range, S Mont., near Livingston.

Flathead Range, in Rocky Mts. of NW Mont., rises just N of Blackfoot R. in N Powell co.; extends NNW, bet. Swan R. and South Fork Flathead R., to L. McDonald in Glacier Natl. Park. Highest point, Swan Peak (9,255 ft.).

Flathead River, in Mont. and Canada, rises in SE British Columbia, flows S into NW Mont. just E of Whitefish Range, thence SSE, past Glacier Natl. Park, and S and W, past Kalispell and through FLATHEAD LAKE, to the Clark Fork near Paradise; c.240 mi. long; sometimes known in upper course as North Fork Flathead R. Principal tributaries: Middle Fork, rising near Continental Divide, flowing c.85 mi. NW to main stream N of Coram; South Fork, rising in SW corner of Flathead Natl. Forest, flowing c.80 mi. NNW, past Flathead Range, to Flathead R. SW of Coram. HUNGRY HORSE DAM is in South Fork 26 mi. NE of Kalispell. Flathead valley is diversified agr. (dairying, fruit growing), lumbering, mining, and resort region.

Flat Holme Island (hōm), Somerset, England, in Bristol Channel, 6 mi. WNW of Weston-super-Mare; ½ mi. long, ½ mi. wide; site of hosp., signal station, and lighthouse (51°22'N 3°7'W).

Flat Island (□ 1; pop. 347), in Placentia Bay, SE N.F., 20 mi. NE of Burin; 47°17'N 54°56'W; 2.5 mi. long. Fishing.

Flatlands, SE N.Y., a residential section of S Brooklyn borough of New York city, near W shore of Jamaica Bay; fishing, truck gardening.

Flat Mountain (9,200 ft.), peak in Continental Divide, in S part of Yellowstone Natl. Park, Wyo., S of Yellowstone L.

Flatonia (flŭtō'nēŭ), town (pop. 1,098), Fayette co., S central Texas, 28 mi. N of Yoakum; trade, shipping center in agr. area; fuller's earth, poultry-packing plants, cottonseed oil and grain mills. Founded 1874, inc. 1875.

Flatow, Poland: see ZLOTOW.

Flat River, city (pop. 5,308), St. Francois co., E Mo., in the St. Francois Mts. near Big R., 55 mi. S of St. Louis; lead-mining center. Has jr. col. Settled 1890, inc. as city 1934.

Flat River. 1 In central Mich., rises in N Montcalm co., flows c.60 mi. SSW, past Greenville and Belding, to Grand R. at Lowell. **2** In W central R.I., small stream (c.7 mi. long) in Coventry town; dammed to form Flat R. Reservoir (c.4 mi. long) E of Coventry village; reservoir drained from E by Southwest Branch of Pawtuxet R.

Flat Rock. 1 Village (pop. 558), Crawford co., SE Ill., 16 mi. NNW of Vincennes (Ind.), in agr. area (livestock, corn, wheat, poultry). **2** Industrial village (pop. 1,931), Wayne co., SE Mich., 20 mi. SW of Detroit, and on Huron R.; mfg. of auto lights, railroad shops, oil refineries. Settled 1824, inc. 1923. **3** Resort village, Henderson co., W N.C., in the Blue Ridge, 4 mi. S of Hendersonville; religious assembly center; has church built in 1832. Near by is Bonclarken, with church assembly grounds.

Flatrock Creek, E and central Ind., rises in NE Henry co., flows c.90 mi. SW and S to East Fork of White R. at Columbus.

Flattery, Cape, NE Queensland, Australia, in Coral Sea, 35 mi. N of Cooktown; 14°57'S 145°21'E. Rises to 859 ft.

Flattery, Cape, high promontory, NW Wash., at entrance to Juan de Fuca Strait; 48°23'N 124°43'W; discovered 1778 by Capt. James Cook. A lighthouse and meteorological station are here on tiny Tatoosh Isl.; Makah Indian Reservation is near by.

Flat Top, Va.: see OTTER, PEAKS OF.

Flatwoods. 1 Village (pop. 1,578, with adjacent Advance), Greenup co., extreme NE Ky., near Ohio R., 3 mi. W of Ironton, Ohio. **2** Town (pop. 288), Braxton co., central W.Va., 6 mi. NNE of Sutton.

Flaviac (flävyäk′), village (pop. 296), Ardèche dept., S France, 4 mi. E of Privas; silk spinning, mattress mfg.

Flawil (flä′vēl), town (pop. 5,753), St. Gall canton, NE Switzerland, 9 mi. W of St. Gall; cotton textiles (notably bandages), embroideries, knit goods.

Flawinne (fläwēn′), town (pop. 3,106), Namur prov., S central Belgium, on Sambre R. and 3 mi. W of Namur; coal-tar products.

Flaxton, city (pop. 436), Burke co., NW N.Dak., 10 mi. NW of Bowbells.

Flèche, La (lä flĕsh′)), town (pop. 8,103), Sarthe dept., W France, on Loir R. and 24 mi. SSW of Le Mans; commercial and road center; paper milling, tanning, footwear mfg. Ships poultry (especially pullets), grain, cheese. Noted for 17th-cent. col., the Prytanée, bestowed by Henry IV on the Jesuits and now a military school for officers' sons. The college's most famous pupil was Descartes.

Fleckney, town and parish (pop. 1,552), S central Leicester, England, 7 mi. NW of Market Harborough; hosiery.

Fleet, urban district (1931 pop. 4,526; 1951 census 9,018), NE Hampshire, England, 4 mi. NW of Aldershot; agr. market. Just NE is small lake of Fleet Pond.

Fleetwing, village (pop. 2,086, with adjacent Crystal Terrace), Bucks co., SE Pa.

Fleetwood, municipal borough (1931 pop. 23,001; 1951 census 27,525), W Lancashire, England, at mouth of the Wyre, on Irish Sea at entrance to Morecambe Bay, 17 mi. NW of Preston; fishing port (specializing in hake) and seaside resort, terminal of steamers to Belfast and Isle of Man; mfg. of leather products (industrial belting). Site of lighthouse. The tide deposits great quantities of gravel, commercially exploited. The port, named after its founder, Sir Peter Fleetwood, was built in early 19th cent.

Fleetwood, borough (pop. 2,338), Berks co., SE central Pa., 9 mi. NE of Reading. Founded 1800, inc. 1873.

Fleetwood Hill, Va.: see BRANDY.

Fleischmanns (flīsh′mŭnz), resort village (pop. 469), Delaware co., S N.Y., in the Catskills, 31 mi. WNW of Kingston.

Flekkefjord (flĕk′kŭfyōr), city (pop. 2,763), Vest-Agder co., S Norway, port at head of 4-mi. fjord (inlet of the North Sea), on railroad and 50 mi. W of Kristiansand; good harbor with narrow approaches. Mfg. (wood products, felt, wool products, leather); exports leather, lumber, agr., and fish products. Inc. 1771; important shipping and fishing center in early 19th cent.

Flekkeroy (flĕk′kŭr-ûü), Nor. *Flekkerøy*, island (□ 3; pop. 1,139), Vest-Agder co., S Norway, 4 mi. S of Kristiansand; coast resort, with good harbor. Has old fortress.

Flémalle-Grande (flāmäl′-grăd′), town (pop. 6,079), Liége prov., E Belgium, on Meuse R. and 4 mi. WSW of Liége; mfg. (steel tubing, tin plate, metalware). Flémalle-Haute (pop. 6,723) is 1 mi. WSW.

Fleming, town (pop. 221), SE Sask., on Man. border, 9 mi. SE of Moosomin; mixed farming.

Fleming, county (□ 350; pop. 11,962), NE Ky.; ⊙ Flemingsburg. Bounded W by Licking R., NE by its North Fork; drained by several creeks. Gently rolling upland agr. area, in outer Bluegrass region; burley tobacco, corn, alfalfa, livestock. Formed 1798.

Fleming. 1 Town (pop. 377), Logan co., NE Colo., near South Platte R., 20 mi. E of Sterling. **2** Town (pop. 943), Letcher co., SE Ky., in the Cumberlands, on North Fork of Kentucky R. and 3 mi. WNW of Jenkins. Bituminous-coal mining and agr. in region. **3** Borough, Centre co., Pa.: see UNIONVILLE.

Flemingsburg, town (pop. 1,502), ⊙ Fleming co., NE Ky., 16 mi. S of Maysville, in outer Bluegrass agr. region; millwork; flour and feed mills, chicken hatcheries. Summer resort on small lake near by. Settled c.1790.

Flemington, town in Cambuslang parish, N Lanark, Scotland, just ESE of Cambuslang; steel milling, coal mining.

Flemington. 1 Town (pop. 90), Liberty co., SE Ga., just SE of Hinesville. **2** Town (pop. 181), Polk co., SW Mo., 13 mi. NNW of Bolivar. **3** Borough (pop. 3,058), ⊙ Hunterdon co., W N.J., 20 mi. NNW of Trenton; farm market center (poultry, truck); mfg. (iron products, fur coats, rubber goods, pottery, chemicals). Agr. fairs held here since 1930. Scene (1935) of Hauptmann's trial for kidnaping and murder of Charles A. Lindbergh, Jr. Settled c.1730, inc. 1910. **4** Borough (pop. 1,446), Clinton co., N central Pa., just SW of Lock Haven. Inc. 1864. **5** Town (pop. 572), Taylor co., N W.Va., 7 mi. SW of Grafton.

Flen (flān), village (pop. 3,312), Sodermanland co., E Sweden, 20 mi. S of Eskilstuna; rail junction; metal- and woodworking. Has medieval church.

Flenige Lake, Denmark: see ARRESKOV LAKE.

Flensborg, city, Germany: see FLENSBURG.

Flensborg Fjord, Germany and Denmark: see FLENSBURG FIRTH.

Flensburg (flĕnz′bŭrg, Ger. flĕns′bŏŏrk), Danish *Flensborg* (flĕns′bôr), city (1939 pop. 70,871; 1946 pop. 101,577; 1950 pop. 102,045), in Schleswig-Holstein, NW Germany, port at W end of Flensburg Firth, 42 mi. NW of Kiel, at NW tip of the Angeln; 54°46′N 9°27′E. Rail junction and customs station near Danish border; airfield (W). Long noted for its rum and smoked eels; shipbuilding; copper- and brassworks. Mfg. of machinery, armatures, chemicals, optical instruments, glass and paper products; paper milling. Food processing (smoked fish, meat, chocolate, beverages). Has 12th- and 14th-cent. churches; teachers col.; city mus. N suburb Mürwick was site of naval station and acad. until 1945. Chartered 1284, it passed from Danish crown to Prussia in 1864. Was important Baltic trade center in 17th and 18th cent. Lost its large merchant fleet in Second World War. At near-by Glücksburg, German High Command capitulated (1945). Undamaged in Second World War; received a great influx of refugees after 1945.

Flensburg, village (pop. 281), Morrison co., central Minn., 8 mi. W of Little Falls, in grain and potato area.

Flensburg Firth, Danish *Flensborg Fjord* (flĕns′bôr fyôr′), Ger. *Flensburger Förde* (flĕns′bŏŏr″gŭr fûr′dŭ), Baltic estuarine inlet, c.30 mi. long, forming (since 1920) Danish-German border. Flensburg is at W end.

Flénu (flānü′), town (pop. 8,224), Hainaut prov., SW Belgium, 3 mi. WSW of Mons; coal mining.

Fléron (flārō′), town (pop. 3,668), Liége prov., E Belgium, 4 mi. E of Liége; coal mining.

Flers (flâr). **1** Village, Nord dept., France: see FLERS-EN-ESCREBIEUX. **2** or **Flers-de-l'Orne** (–dŭ-lôrn′), town (pop. 9,651), Orne dept., NW France, 31 mi. SSW of Caen; textile center (cotton and linen fabrics; shirts, corsets, hosiery). Other mfg.: rubber, asbestos, cartons; cider distilling, metalworking. Heavily damaged during battle of Falaise-Argentan pocket (Aug., 1944) in Second World War.

Flers-en-Escrebieux (–ãnĕskrŭbyû′), NNW suburb (pop. 1,469) of Douai, Nord dept., N France; coal mining, truck gardening. Until 1938, called Flers.

Flers-lez-Lille (–lā-lēl′), outer E suburb (pop. 7,283) of Lille, Nord dept., N France; mfg. of textile dyeing machinery, furniture; spinning of carded wool.

Flesberg (flās′bărg″, –băr″), village and canton (pop. 2,362), Buskerud co., S Norway, on Lagen R., on railroad and 30 mi. WNW of Drammen; lumbering.

Flesherton, village (pop. 431), S Ont., 23 mi. SW of Collingwood; woolen milling, lumbering; stock.

Flesland (flās′län), village (pop. 136) in Fana canton, Hordaland co., SW Norway, 7 mi. SW of Bergen, on a sound off North Sea; fishing, mfg. of fish meal and fish oil.

Fletcher. 1 Resort village (pop. c.500), Henderson co., W N.C., 12 mi. SSE of Asheville, in the Blue Ridge. **2** Village (pop. 515), Miami co., W Ohio, 6 mi. E of Piqua, in agr. area. **3** Town (pop. 875), Comanche co., SW Okla., 18 mi. NNE of Lawton; cotton ginning, broom mfg. **4** Town (pop. 485), Franklin co., NW Vt., 12 mi. SE of St. Albans, near Lamoille R.

Fletcher Islands, just off coast of Antarctica, in Bellingshausen Sea off Eights Coast; 72°5′S 95°20′W. Comprise McNamara and Dustin isls. Discovered 1940 by R. E. Byrd.

Fletchertown, England: see ALLHALLOWS.

Fletschhorn (flĕch′hôrn), peak (13,121 ft.) in Lepontine Alps, S Switzerland, 9 mi. S of Brig.

Fletton, England: see OLD FLETTON.

Fleurance (flûrãs′), town (pop. 2,965), Gers dept., SW France, on the Gers and 15 mi. N of Auch; agr. market; Armagnac brandy distilling, mfg. of dyes, sandals; horse breeding. A medieval stronghold, founded 1280.

Fleur-de-Lis, England: see MYNYDDISLWYN.

Fleurier (flûrēā′), town (pop. 3,357), Neuchâtel canton, W Switzerland, on Areuse R. and 17 mi. WSW of Neuchâtel, in the Jura; watches. Largest town in Val de Travers.

Fleurieu Peninsula (flûr′ēōō), name sometimes applied to peninsula S of Adelaide, SE South Australia, bet. Gulf St. Vincent (N) and Indian Ocean (SE), and jutting SW into Backstairs Passage at Cape Jervis; 33 mi. long, 22 mi. wide. Contains part of Mt. Lofty Ranges; fertile valleys and plains; dairy products, livestock. Resorts at Victor Harbor and Port Elliot.

Fleurus (flûrüs′), town (pop. 6,949), Hainaut prov., S central Belgium, 7 mi. NE of Charleroi. Rail junction; metal industry; jam and syrup processing; agr. market; coal mining. Scene of defeat of Spaniards by duke of Brunswick in 1622, of Germans and Dutch by French under Marshal Luxembourg in 1690, of Austrians under Prince of Coburg by French under Jourdan in 1794.

Fleury-les-Aubrais (flûrē′-lāzōbrā′), N suburban commune (pop. 6,321) of Orléans, Loiret dept., N central France; vinegar mfg., woodworking. Les Aubrais railroad station, junction of 5 major lines, is 1.5 mi. N of Orléans. Damaged in Second World War.

Fleury-sur-Andelle (–sür-ädĕl′), village (pop. 1,369), Eure dept., NW France, on the Andelle and 13 mi. SE of Rouen; textile and sawmilling.

Fleury-sur-Loire (–sür-lwär′), village (pop. 76), Nièvre dept., central France, on Loire Lateral Canal and 7 mi. W of Decize; stud farm. Kaolin quarries near by.

Fligely, Cape (flyē′gylē), northernmost point of Franz Josef Land, Russian SFSR, in Arctic Ocean, on NE Rudolf Isl.; 81°51′N 58°45′E.

Flimby, village and parish (pop. 2,199), W Cumberland, England, 2 mi. SSW of Maryport; coal mining; coal-tar chemicals.

Flims (flĭms), Romansh *Flem* (flĕm), village (pop. 1,060), Grisons canton, E Switzerland, 12 mi. W of Chur; health resort; alt. 3,510 ft.

Flinders, village (pop. 337; with naval depot, 873), S Victoria, Australia, at W side of entrance to Western Port, 45 mi. S of Melbourne. Site of naval base and Royal Australian Naval Col. (moved here in 1930 from Jervis Bay).

Flinders, Cape, NE Mackenzie Dist., Northwest Territories, on Coronation Gulf, at entrance of Bathurst Inlet, at W extremity of Kent Peninsula; 68°13′N 108°46′W.

Flinders Bay, inlet of Indian Ocean, SW Western Australia; Cape Leeuwin at W end; 24 mi. E-W, 8 mi. N-S.

Flinders Chase, Australia: see KANGAROO ISLAND.

Flinders Island. 1 Largest of Investigator Isls., in Great Australian Bight, 17 mi. off W coast of Eyre Peninsula, South Australia; 8 mi. long, 4 mi. wide; rises to 200 ft. Fertile; livestock. **2** Largest (□ 802; pop. 853) of Furneaux Isls., in Bass Strait, 33 mi. off NE coast of Tasmania; 39 mi. long, 20 mi. wide; rises to 2,550 ft. Indented by many bays; lagoons in E. Sheep, butter; tin. Chief town, Whitemark.

Flinders Passage, channel of Coral Sea, breaks through Great Barrier Reef off E coast of Queensland, Australia; leads into Cleveland Bay (site of Townsville); 21 mi. long, 7.5 mi. wide.

Flinders Ranges, E South Australia, extend from Gladstone 260 mi. NNE bet. lakes Torrens and Frome; rise to 3,900 ft. (St. Mary's Peak, 2d highest in state); lignite, copper, ochre, lead, radium, talc. Uranium-ore mine at Mt. Painter.

Flinders River, N Queensland, Australia, rises in Great Dividing Range W of Charters Towers, flows W past Hughenden and Richmond, thence NW and N to Gulf of Carpentaria; 520 mi. long. Saxby and Cloncurry rivers, main tributaries.

Flines-lès-Râches (flēn-lā-räsh′), town (pop. 3,317), Nord dept., N France, 6 mi. NE of Douai; woodworking; chicory.

Flin Flon, town (pop. estimate 7,500), W Man., 350 mi. NW of Winnipeg, on Sask. border; 54°45′N 101°53′W; mining and smelting center (copper, zinc, gold, silver, cadmium); lumbering, trapping.

Flinsberg, Poland: see SWIERADOW ZDROJ.

Flint. 1 Hamlet, Morgan co., N Ala., on inlet of Wheeler Reservoir (on Tennessee R.) and 6 mi. S of Decatur. Co. tuberculosis sanitarium here. **2** City (pop. 163,143), ⊙ Genesee co., SE central Mich., 50 mi. NW of Detroit, and on Flint R. Important automobile-mfg. center; produces finished vehicles, bodies and parts for assembly elsewhere, and replacement parts. Also mfg. of structural steel, foundry products, cement blocks, furniture, tents, awnings, chemicals, paints, varnish, dental supplies, beer, food products. Points of interest include the automobile plants, General Motors Inst. of Technology, the Flint Inst. of Arts, and Frederick Wright collection of antiques and curios. Flint Jr. Col. and a state school for the deaf are here. Settled 1819 as a fur-trading post on the site of an Indian village; platted 1835; inc. as city 1855. Fur trading and lumbering were succeeded in importance in late 19th cent. by mfg. of carts and carriages; after 1904, with establishment of its 1st auto plant, Flint became one of state's chief automobile centers.

Flint or **Flintshire** (–shĭr,–shŭr), county (□ 255.8; 1931 pop. 112,889; 1951 census 145,108), NE Wales, on the Irish Sea and the Dee estuary; ⊙ Mold. Bounded by Denbigh (W and S) and Cheshire (E), it also includes a detached portion to the SE (including Bangor-on-Dee and Overton) surrounded by Denbigh, Cheshire, and Shropshire. Drained by Dee R. and Clwyd R. Low terrain on coast and along Dee R. estuary, rising W toward Clwydian Hills. Chief industries are steel milling; mfg. of chemicals, artificial silk, pottery; metalworking; coal mining. Lead and copper are also mined. Besides Mold, other important towns are Buckley, Connah's Quay, Flint, Holywell, Sandycroft, Queensferry. Rhyl and Prestatyn are seaside resorts. There are many prehistoric monuments; vestiges of Roman and Saxon occupation; and anc. castles and monasteries. St. Asaph is of ecclesiastical importance. Co. is crossed by Offa's and Watt's dykes.

Flint, municipal borough (1931 pop. 7,655; 1951 census 14,257), Flintshire, Wales, on the Dee estuary and 10 mi. WNW of Chester; rayon-milling center, with coal and lead mines, alkali and paper works. Has ruins of castle, begun 1276 by Edward I, taken 1643 by Parliamentarians, and dismantled 1647. In 1399 Richard II here submitted to Bolingbroke. Flint was formerly large seaport. Municipal borough includes towns of Oakenholt, with paper mills, and Coleshill Fawr. Roman lead-smelting works have been excavated near by.

Flintbek (flĭnt'bāk), village (pop. 4,982), in Schleswig-Holstein, NW Germany, 5 mi. SW of Kiel; sugar refining.

Flint Creek, SW Mont., rises in Georgetown L., flows c.45 mi. N, past Philipsburg, bet. Flint Creek Range and Sapphire Mts., to the Clark Fork at Drummond.

Flint Creek Range, in Rocky Mts. of W Mont., rises in E Granite co. just S of the Clark Fork; extends c.25 mi. S toward Anaconda; elevations of 8-10,400 ft. Manganese, silver, and coal mined.

Flint Hills, in N Okla. and E Kansas, a low, hilly strip extending c.200 mi. bet. Arkansas R. (S) and Kansas R. (N), and rising 300–500 ft. above plain. Essentially an E-facing, limestone escarpment, capped by thin layer of flint gravel. Important grazing area.

Flint Island, uninhabited coral island, Line Isls., central Pacific, 125 mi. SW of Caroline Isl.; 11°25'S 151°48'W; 2.5 mi. long, .5 mi. wide. Claimed by U.S. under Guano Act (1856), worked for guano by the British, now abandoned.

Flintridge, unincorporated residential town, Los Angeles co., S Calif., in foothills of San Gabriel Mts., just NW of Pasadena.

Flint River. **1** In W Ga., rises S of Atlanta, flows 330 mi. generally S, past Albany (head of navigation) and Bainbridge, to Fla. line near Chattahoochee, where it unites with Chattahoochee R. to form the Apalachicola. Power dams at ALBANY and near WARWICK; another dam at source of Apalachicola R. to provide power and improve navigation. **2** In E central Mich., formed in Lapeer co. near Columbiaville by union of North (c.20 mi. long) and South (c.25 mi. long) branches, flows c.71 mi. SW to Flint, then NW, past Flushing, to Shiawassee R. just S of Saginaw and just above its junction with the Tittabawassee. **3** In S Tenn. and N Ala., rises in SE Lincoln co., Tenn., flows c.60 mi. S to Wheeler Reservoir, on Tennessee R., 16 mi. S of Huntsville, Ala.

Flintshire, Wales: see FLINT, county.

Flint Stone or **Flintstone,** village, Allegany co., W Md., in the Appalachians near Pa. line, and 11 mi. ENE of Cumberland. Gateway to small-game refuges and Green Ridge State Forest (c.17,000 acres; E). Hunting, fishing.

Flippin (flĭ'pĭn), town (pop. 646), Marion co., N Ark., 29 mi. E of Harrison, in the Ozarks.

Flirey (flērā'), village (pop. 138), Meurthe-et-Moselle dept., NE France, 14 mi. E of Saint-Mihiel.

Fliseryd (flē'sürüd), village (pop. 759), Kalmar co., SE Sweden, on Em R. and 12 mi. SW Oskarshamn; metalworking.

Flitsch, Yugoslavia: see BOVEC.

Flitwick, agr. village and parish (pop. 1,731), S central Bedford, England, 9 mi. S of Bedford. Has 15th-cent. church.

Flix (flēsh), town (pop. 2,859), Tarragona prov., NE Spain, on the Ebro and 14 mi. NNE of Gandesa; chemical works (nitrogen, sulphuric acid, soap); sericulture; olive-oil processing. Trades in wine, almonds, fruit, cereals.

Flixborough, town and parish (pop. 400), Parts of Lindsey, NW Lincolnshire, England, near Trent R., 3 mi. NW of Scunthorpe; steel milling, ironstone mining.

Flixecourt (flēks-kōōr'), town (pop. 2,929), Somme dept., N France, near the Somme, 13 mi. NW of Amiens; agr. market.

Flixton, residential town and parish (pop. 8,523), SE Lancashire, England, 7 mi. WSW of Manchester.

Flize (flēz), village (pop. 939), Ardennes dept., N France, on the Meuse (canalized) and 5 mi. SSE of Mézières; forges, brewery.

Flobecq (flôbĕk'), Flemish *Vloesberg* (vlōōz'bĕrkh), agr. village (pop. 3,476), Hainaut prov., SW central Belgium, 8 mi. N of Ath.

Floby (flōō'bü"), village (pop. 604), Skaraborg co., SW Sweden, 8 mi. WSW of Falkoping; hosiery knitting.

Flockton, former urban district (1931 pop. 1,471), West Riding, S Yorkshire, England, 7 mi. SW of Wakefield; coal mining. Inc. 1938 in Kirkburton.

Floda (flōō'dä"), village (pop. 835), Alvsborg co., SW Sweden, on Save R. and 15 mi. ENE of Goteborg; woodworking. Arts and crafts col. near by.

Flodden, small hill (228 ft.) in N Northumberland, England, 3 mi. SE of Coldstream, surrounded by Flodden Field, scene of battle (Sept. 9, 1513) in which James IV, King of the Scots, was defeated and killed by English under earl of Surrey. Battle is described in Scott's *Marmion*.

Flogny (flônyē'), village (pop. 370), Yonne dept., N central France, on Armançon R. and Burgundy Canal, and 8 mi. NW of Tonnerre; cheese mfg.

Flöha (flû'ä), town (pop. 6,876), Saxony, E central Germany, at N foot of the Erzgebirge, on Zschopau R. and 7 mi. ENE of Chemnitz; textile milling (cotton, rayon, silk), hosiery knitting; mfg. of glass, cardboard, storage batteries, boilers.

Floirac (fwäräk'), E industrial suburb (pop. 5,930) of Bordeaux, Gironde dept., SW France, near right bank of Garonne R.; chemical factories (soap, fats) and laboratories, forges, cementworks.

Floirli, Norway: see FLOYRLI.

Flomaton (flō'mùtùn), town (pop. 1,036), Escambia co., S Ala., on Fla. line, near Escambia R., 40 mi. N of Pensacola; meat curing, lumber milling; clothing.

Flône (flōn), village (pop. 331), Liége prov., E Belgium, on Meuse R. and 5 mi. ENE of Huy; zinc, lead processing.

Flood, village, S B.C., on Fraser R. and 25 mi. NE of Chilliwack; silver mining.

Floodwood, village (pop. 667), St. Louis co., NE central Minn., on St. Louis R. and c.40 mi. WNW of Duluth, in livestock and potato area; dairy, meat, poultry products, lumber.

Flora. **1** City (pop. 5,255), Clay co., S central Ill., 36 mi. ENE of Centralia; industrial and farmers' cooperative center, in agr., oil and natural-gas area; mfg. (shoes, food products, underwear, furniture); fruit, redtop seed, soybeans, peas, livestock, dairy products. Inc. 1867. **2** Town (pop. 1,657), Carroll co., W central Ind., 22 mi. ENE of Lafayette, in livestock and grain area; lumber, cement products, packed poultry, condensed milk; poultry hatchery; timber. Settled 1884, inc. 1898. **3** Town (pop. 655), Madison co., central Miss., 19 mi. NNW of Jackson.

Flora, Cape, W point of Northbrook Isl., Franz Josef Land, Russian SFSR, in Arctic Ocean; 79°57'N.

Florac (flôräk'), village (pop. 1,276), Lozère dept., S France, bet. Cévennes (E) and Causse Méjan (W), on the Tarnon near its mouth on the Tarn, and 14 mi. SSE of Mende; fruit- and winegrowing; chestnut trade.

Florala (flôră'lù), city (pop. 2,713), Covington co., S Ala., 23 mi. SSE of Andalusia, at Fla. line, near Conecuh Natl. Forest; lumber milling, mfg. (wood products, shirts and underwear, concrete blocks); peanut, soybean, and tung oil, cotton.

Floral City, village, Citrus co., central Fla., 13 mi. S of Inverness, near Tsala Apopka L.; citrus-fruit packing; phosphate quarrying.

Floral Park. **1** Village (pop. 5,128, with near-by Silver Bow Park), Silver Bow co., SW Mont., a suburb of Butte. **2** Residential village (pop. 14,582), Nassau co., SE N.Y., on W Long Isl., just E of Garden City; mfg. (slippers, photographic equipment, aircraft parts); flower growing. Inc. 1908.

Florange (flôrãzh'), Ger. *Flörchingen* (flûrkh'ĭng-ùn), town (pop. 5,267), Moselle dept., NE France, near the Moselle, 3 mi. SW of Thionville, in iron-mining dist.; metal- and woodworking. At Ebange (äbãzh'), 1 mi. E, are petroleum refinery, chemical works, steel mill.

Florânia (flŏŏrä'nyù), city (pop. 927), central Rio Grande do Norte, NE Brazil, 55 mi. SE of Açu; ships rice, cotton, fruit. Airfield. Until 1944, called Flores.

Flörchingen, France: see FLORANGE.

Flordell Hills, town (pop. 1,214), St. Louis co., E Mo., just NW of St. Louis.

Floreana (flōrĕä'nä), **Santa María Island** (sän'tä märē'ä), or **Charles Island** (□ 64; 1950 pop. 21), S Galápagos Isls., Ecuador, 60 mi. SW of Puerto Baquerizo (San Cristóbal Isl.); 1°20'S 90°25'W. Sparsely settled, it produces fruit, subsistence crops, cattle.

Floreffe (flôrĕf'), town (pop. 3,145), Namur prov., S central Belgium, on Sambre R. and 6 mi. WSW of Namur; glass mfg. Has 12th-cent. mill with noted 13th-cent. frescoes, and Premonstratensian abbey, founded 1121.

Florence, Ital. *Firenze* (fērĕn'tsē), anc. *Florentia*, city (pop. 271,975), ⊙ Tuscany and Firenze prov., central Italy, at S foot of Etruscan Apennines, on both banks of the Arno and 145 mi. NNW of Rome; 43°46'N 11°15'E. Industrial, agr., and transportation center; iron- and steelworks (automobile chassis, agr. machinery, refrigerators, motorcycles, bicycles), chemical plants, macaroni factories, food canneries, tanneries, textile and paper mills, mfg. of glass, furniture, silverware, straw hats, pharmaceuticals, shoes, soap, pottery, fertilizer, plastics, surgical instruments, candy. Market for wine, olive oil, flowers, fruit, and vegetables. Archbishopric. Florence was the cradle of the Ital. Renaissance and is one of the richest art cities of the world, with works by Michelangelo, Leonardo da Vinci, Raphael, Donatello, Verrocchio, Cellini, and others. Its many monuments date mostly from 13th to 15th cent. Gothic cathedral of Santa Maria del Fiore has a dome by Brunelleschi (1420–34). Near by is its campanile, designed by Giotto, and a baptistery with famous doors sculptured by Ghiberti. The church of Santa Croce (the pantheon of Florence) has frescoes by Giotto and fine works by the Della Robbia family and Rossellino. St. Mark's convent contains some of Fra Angelico's best works. Michelangelo's tombs of the Medici and many works by Donatello are in the Church of San Lorenzo. The imposing city hall, Palazzo della Signoria, has frescoes by Vasari; in the near-by Loggia is the Perseus by Cellini. One of the world's richest collections of paintings is in the gall. of 16th-cent. Uffizi palace (bldg. damaged in Second World War), which also houses Ital. natl. library (1,500,000 volumes) and state archives. Behind the Pitti palace (damaged), one-time residence of the Medici, are the Boboli gardens. Among its many medieval and Renaissance palaces, Or San Michele, Riccardi, Strozzi, and Rucellai deserve special mention. City is seat of several learned academies, including famous Accademia della Crusca, university, astronomical observatory, conservatories of music and art, and many museums (one with excellent Etruscan collection). An important town from Roman times; in 13th and 14th cent. center of struggle bet. Guelphs and Ghibellines, one result of which was banishment of Dante, who was b. here. Through frequent wars with its neighbors, particularly Pisa, it became seat of a strong, wealthy republic. The city's artistic and intellectual life reached its height in 14th-16th cent., greatly aided by the Medici family who gained control in 1st half of 15th cent. A revolution (1494–1512) placed Savonarola (martyred here in 1498) in power and employed Machiavelli on several missions. After the return of the Medici, Florence became capital (1569) of the grand duchy of Tuscany. From 1865 to 1870 it was capital of the kingdom of Italy. In Second World War badly damaged by air bombing (1943–44) and fighting (Aug., 1944). Most of the art treasures were spared, although many historic churches and palaces were hit and parts of its medieval quarters destroyed. All bridges across the Arno, except Ponte Vecchio, were blown up and destroyed.

Florence. **1** County (□ 805; pop. 79,710), E central S.C.; ⊙ Florence. Bounded E by Pee Dee R.; drained by Lynches R. Agr. area (tobacco, cotton, corn, pecans, truck), cattle; lumber. Mfg. center at Florence. Formed 1888. **2** County (□ 489; pop. 3,756), extreme NE Wis.; ⊙ Florence. Bounded N by Brule R. and E by Menominee R. (both on Mich. line). Contains section of Nicolet Natl. Forest, and several lakes. Lumbering, dairying, potato growing. Formed 1882.

Florence. **1** City (pop. 23,879), ⊙ Lauderdale co., NW Ala., on right bank of Tennessee R. and 100 mi. NNW of Birmingham. Mfg. center served by power from Wilson Dam (2.5 mi. E), in region yielding coal, iron, bauxite, and asphalt. Makes cotton fabrics, ranges, heaters; lumber milling, meat packing, dairying, bottling. Large Listerhill aluminum plant (built 1941) near by. Has a state teachers col. Laid out 1818, inc. 1826. Industries stimulated by construction of Wilson Dam and development of TVA. **2** Resort town (pop. 1,776), ⊙ Pinal co., S central Ariz., on Gila R. and 50 mi. SE of Phoenix in agr. area irrigated from San Carlos Reservoir of Coolidge Dam. State prison near by. Copper mines in vicinity. Founded 1866, inc. 1906. **3** Unincorporated town (pop. c.23,000), Los Angeles co., S Calif., residential and mfg. suburb 6 mi. S of downtown Los Angeles, in industrial dist. **4** City (pop. 2,773), Fremont co., S central Colo., on Arkansas R., just NE of Wet Mts., and 30 mi. WNW of Pueblo; alt. 5,187 ft. Dairy, truck, and poultry products, fruit, Oil wells and coal mines near by. Inc. 1887. **5** Village (pop. 107), Pike co., W Ill., on Illinois R. (bridged here) and 21 mi. WSW of Jacksonville, in agr. area. **6** City (pop. 1,009), Marion co., E central Kansas, on Cottonwood R. and 40 mi. NNE of Wichita, in grain and livestock region. Oil wells and stone quarries near by. State park in vicinity. Platted 1870, inc. 1872. **7** Town (pop. 1,325), Boone co., N Ky., 8 mi. SW of Covington, in outer Bluegrass agr. region. Big Bone Lick is near by. **8** Hosiery-producing village on Mill R., in NORTHAMPTON town, Hampshire co., W central Mass. Station on Underground Railroad until 1861. **9** Village (pop. 137), Lyon co., SW Minn., 20 mi. SW of Marshall, in corn, oat, barley area. **10** Village (pop. 313), Rankin co., central Miss., 10 mi. SSE of Jackson. **11** Village (pop. c.150), Ravalli co., W Mont., 15 mi. S of Missoula and on Bitterroot R., near Bitterroot Range and Idaho line; gold mine; dairy products. **12** Industrial village (pop. 6,785, with Roebling), Burlington co., W N.J., on the Delaware and 8 mi. S of Trenton; pipe foundry; mfg. of structural steel, munitions. **13** City (pop. 1,026), Lane co., W Oregon, 50 mi. W of Eugene and on Siuslaw R., near the coast; salmon fisheries; lumber, shingles. **14** City (pop. 22,513), ⊙ Florence co., E central S.C., 75 mi. ENE of Columbia. Rail junction and transfer point (with repair shops); mfg., trade, and shipping center for large agr. area (notably tobacco; also livestock, grain, truck, cotton); lumber milling, woodworking, printing; foundry and machine shops; fertilizer, bedding, naval stores. Near by are natl. cemetery, agr. experiment station, state industrial school for boys. City founded in 1850s as rail junction. **15** Town (pop. 226), Codington co., NE S.Dak., 15 mi. NW of Watertown. **16** Town (pop. 561), Williamson co., central Texas, c.40 mi. N of Austin; trade point in agr. area. **17** Village in Florence town (pop. 1,257), ⊙ Florence co., extreme NE Wis., 11 mi. NW of Iron Mountain (Mich.), in wooded area; dairying, stock raising; cabinetmaking.

Florence, Lake (4 mi. long), SE Alaska, on Admiralty Isl.; 57°48'N 134°38'W; fishing, hunting.

Florence Bay, Nyasaland: see LIVINGSTONIA.

Florence Lake, Fresno co., E central Calif., in the Sierra Nevada, c.60 mi. NE of Fresno; 3 mi. long. Impounded by Florence Lake Dam (154 ft. high, 3,106 ft. long; for power; completed 1926), on S fork of San Joaquin R. Tunnel carries water from lake to Huntington L. (12 mi. W).

Florenceville, village (pop. estimate 500), W N.B., on St. John R. and 20 mi. NNW of Woodstock; lumbering; potatoes.

Florencia (flōrĕn'syä), town (pop. 4,164), ⊙ Caquetá commissary, S Colombia, at E foot of Cordillera Oriental, on Orteguaza R. and 95 mi. SSW of Neiva (connected by road); 1°36'N 75°37'W. Agr. (rice, cattle) and trading center for region of dense tropical forests yielding rubber, balata gum, fine wood, medicinal plants, fibers, resins, cacao. Wild animals are hunted for furs and hides.

Florencia, La, Argentina: see LA FLORENCIA.

Florencio Varela (flōrĕn'syō värä'lä), town (pop. 5,433), ⊙ Florencio Varela dist. (□ 80; pop. 11,496), NE Buenos Aires prov., Argentina, 17 mi. SE of Buenos Aires; rail junction, airport. Agr. center (corn, alfalfa, grapes, livestock, poultry); mfg. of silk textiles, food preserves.

Florennes (flôrĕn'), town (pop. 3,034), Namur prov., S Belgium, 14 mi. W of Dinant; ceramics.

Florensac (flôrăsäk'), town (pop. 2,598), Hérault dept., S France, near the Hérault, 13 mi. ENE of Béziers; winegrowing, mfg. of equipment for viticulture.

Florentia, Italy: see FLORENCE.

Florentino Ameghino (flōrĕntē'nō āmägē'nō), department of SE Chubut natl. territory, Argentina; ⊙ was Camarones. In 1946 its S part was included in Comodoro Rivadavia military zone.

Florenville (flôrăvēl'), village (pop. 1,943), Luxembourg prov., SE Belgium, on Semois R. and 11 mi. SSW of Neufchâteau, in the Ardennes; pig market; quarrying.

Flores (flō'rĕs), W residential section of Buenos Aires, Argentina.

Flores (flō'rĭsh). **1** City, Maranhão, Brazil: see TIMON. **2** City (pop. 1,755), central Pernambuco, NE Brazil, near Paraíba border, 50 mi. WNW of Sertânia; manioc, cotton, livestock. **3** City, Rio Grande do Norte, Brazil: see FLORÂNIA.

Flores, canton, Costa Rica: see SAN JOAQUÍN.

Flores or **Ciudad Flores** (syōōdädh' flō'rĕs), city (1950 pop. 1,579), ⊙ Petén dept., N Guatemala, on isl. in S part of L. Petén, 160 mi. NNE of Guatemala; 16°56'N 89°53'W; alt. 449 ft. Trading center for towns in lake area; collection point for chicle, rubber, sugar cane, cacao. Once capital of Itzú Indians; came under Sp. rule in 17th cent.

Flores (flō'rĕs), island (□ 5,511), Lesser Sundas, Indonesia, bet. Flores Sea (N) and Savu Sea (S), just E of Sumbawa, 190 mi. S of Celebes; 8°3'–8°58'S 119°48'–123°2'E. Flores census div. (□ 6,627; pop. 626,684) includes near-by isls. of Solor, Rincha, and Komodo. Flores is 220 mi. long, 40 mi. wide. Mountainous, with many volcanic peaks, it rises to 7,874 ft. in central area. Unlike most Indonesian isls., Flores has dry climate. Fishing, agr. (coffee, rice), copra production, lumbering (sandalwood), stock raising. Malayan groups are predominant in W part of isl. and Papuans in E part: Flores thus represents a transitional area bet. Malayan-inhabited W Indonesia and Papuan-inhabited E Indonesia. Chief town and port is ENDE. Other centers: Larantuka or Larantoeka (both: lärăntōō'kŏŏ) at E tip of isl., and Maumere or Maoemere (both: moumĕ'rĕ) on NE coast. In late 16th cent., Port. missionaries were active here. The Dutch began trading with isl. in 1618 and gradually gained control over it. Until 1859 the Portuguese challenged Du. possession of E area.

Flores, department (□ 1,745; pop. 36,125), SW central Uruguay; ⊙ Trinidad. Bordered by Yí R. (N and NW), the Arroyo Grande (W). Crossed by Cuchilla Grande Inferior (E–W). Drained by Yí R. Sheep-raising area, producing wool. Agr. products: wheat, corn, linseed, oats, fruit; viticulture. Only populated center is Trinidad. Served by rail branch from Durazno and highway from Montevideo.

Flores, town, Uruguay: see LAS FLORES.

Flores, Arroyo de las (äroi'ō dā läs flō'rĕs), river in central Buenos Aires prov., Argentina, rises 30 mi. NW of Olavarría, flows c.110 mi. NE, past General Alvear, to the Salado 15 mi. SW of Monte.

Flores, Las, town, Argentina: see PIQUETE.

Flores, Villa, Mexico: see VILLA FLORES.

Flores de Ávila (dhā ä'vēlä), town (pop. 910), Ávila prov., central Spain, 29 mi. NW of Ávila; grain, wine; flour milling; stock raising.

Flores Head or **Kopondei Point** (kôpôndā'), promontory at NE tip of Flores, Indonesia, on Flores Sea; 8°3'S 122°52'E.

Floreshty (flŭryĕsh'tē), Rum. *Florești* (flôrĕsht'), city (1941 pop. 2,409), N Moldavian SSR, on railroad and 19 mi. NE of Beltsy; tobacco and flour-milling center; glassworks.

Flores Island (flō'rĭsh), westernmost (□ 55; 1950 pop. 7,845) of the Azores, in the Atlantic, forming, together with Corvo Isl. (12 mi. N), the archipelago's W group; Santa Cruz (39°27'N 31°9'W), its chief town, is on E coast. Of volcanic origin, rising to 3,087 ft. at the Morro Grande. There are crater lakes, hot springs, waterfalls. Noted for its luxuriant flora (especially hydrangeas). Cattle raising and dairying are chief occupations. The epic battle bet. the *Revenge* under Sir Richard Grenville and the Sp. fleet took place off Flores in 1591. Isl. is administratively part of Horta dist.

Flores Island, in Guanabara Bay, Rio de Janeiro state, Brazil, just off Neves (N suburb of Niterói), 5 mi. from Rio de Janeiro docks. Hq. of immigration service. Area, c.30 acres.

Flores Island (flô'rĭz) (□ 60), SW B.C., in Clayoquot Sound, just off W central Vancouver Isl., 10 mi. NW of Tofino; 49°20'N 126°8'W; 10 mi. long, 6 mi. wide; copper, gold, silver mining. On SE coast is village of Ahousat.

Flores Island, Indonesia: see FLORES.

Flores Island (flō'rĕs), S Uruguay, in the Río de la Plata, off coast of Canelones dept., 15 mi. E of Montevideo; 34°57'S 55°56'W. Really 3 small islets, under military jurisdiction, they have a quarantine station (for incoming vessels), hosp., observatory, radio station, and lighthouse. Discovered 1526 by Cabot.

Flores Sea, part of the Pacific, bet. Java Sea (W) and Banda Sea (E), bet. Celebes isl. in N and Flores and Sumbawa isls. in S, connected with Celebes Sea by Macassar Strait; c.150 mi. wide. Its N arm, Gulf of Bone, deeply indents S coast of Celebes. Contains numerous isls.

Floresta (flōōrĕ'stŭ), city (pop. 1,657), W Pernambuco, NE Brazil, 150 mi. W of Garanhuns; cotton, corn, tobacco.

Floresta (flôrĕ'stä), village (pop. 2,119), Messina prov., NE Sicily, in Nebrodi Mts., near head of Alcantara R., 8 mi. NNW of Randazzo; alt. c.4,150 ft.

Floresta, La, Uruguay: see LA FLORESTA.

Floresti, Moldavian SSR: see FLORESHTY.

Floresville (flô'rĭsvĭl), city (pop. 1,949), ⊙ Wilson co., S Texas, 29 mi. SE of San Antonio and on San Antonio R.; trade, shipping, processing center for agr. area (cotton, onions, peanuts, watermelons); cotton ginning, dairying.

Florham Park (flôr'ŭm), borough (pop. 2,385), Morris co., N N.J., 5 mi. E of Morristown. Settled 1655, inc. 1899.

Floriana (flōryä'nä), SW suburb (pop. 5,074) of Valletta, SE Malta, occupies base and S portion of narrow, heavily fortified Mt. Sceberras Peninsula, forming together with Valletta one imposing system of fortifications. Though founded c.1730 by the grand master Manoel de Vilhena, its walls and bastions were built earlier. Those suffered less during Second World War bombing than other bldgs., notably the parish church (1771), the monastery (founded 1588), and the civil hosp. The water tower, 18th-cent. seminary, and baroque Sarria church (1678) escaped severe damage.

Floriano (flōōryä'nōō), city (pop. 7,084), central Piauí, Brazil, head of regular navigation on right bank of Parnaíba R., opposite Barão de Grajaú (Maranhão), and 120 mi. S of Teresina; commercial center shipping livestock, hides and skins; rice milling, cotton ginning. Airport. Kaolin deposits near by.

Floriano Peixoto (pāshô'tōō), town (pop. 347), SW Amazonas, Brazil, on Acre R. (navigable) and 70 mi. NNE of Rio Branco; rubber, Brazil nuts, cacao, hides.

Florianópolis (flōōryŭnô'pōōlĭs), city (1950 pop. 49,290), ⊙ Santa Catarina, S Brazil, seaport on W coast of Santa Catarina Isl. and linked with the mainland by a huge steel bridge, and 450 mi. SW of Rio de Janeiro. State's chief commercial center, shipping output of rich agr. interior (sugar, coffee, tobacco, fruit, grapes, meat and dairy products); sugar refining, metalworking (hardware). The city's new section, built amidst numerous gardens on hill slopes surrounding the older harbor dist., presents a modern appearance. Most public bldgs. are in ornate 19th-cent. style. There are schools of law, pharmacy, and dentistry. Bishopric. Airport. Region 1st settled by colonists from São Paulo in 1675. Present city founded 1700 as Desterro; renamed (1893) for Floriano Peixoto.

Florida (flōrē'dä), industrial city (pop. 49,480) in N Greater Buenos Aires, Argentina, adjoining Vicente López. Textiles, chemicals, plastics, rubber, paper, lime, plaster, shoes, alcohol, dairy products, vegetable oils; meat packing, tanning.

Florida, province, Bolivia: see SAMAIPATA.

Florida, village (pop. 1,028), Concepción prov., S central Chile, 20 mi. E of Concepción; agr. (grain, vegetables, potatoes, livestock).

Florida, village (dist. pop. 240), Limón prov., E Costa Rica, on Reventazón R., on railroad and 4 mi. WSW of Siquirres; abacá, bananas, rubber; sawmill.

Florida (flô'rĭdŭ, Sp. flōrē'dä), town (pop. 7,030), Camagüey prov., E Cuba, on Central Highway and 23 mi. WNW of Camagüey; rail junction, trading and agr. center (sugar cane, oranges, cattle). Sugar mills in outskirts: the large **Central Florida** (pop. 2,660) is just N; the central Agramonte is S.

Florida (flōrē'dä), town (pop. 1,323), Copán dept., W Honduras, on Chamelecón R. and 18 mi. N of Santa Rosa; pottery making; sugar cane, livestock.

Florida or **Villa Florida** (vē'yä), town (dist. pop. 2,753), Misiones dept., S Paraguay, on Tebicuary R. and 85 mi. SE of Asunción; stock-raising center.

Florida, town (pop. 777), Amazonas dept., N Peru, on E Andean slopes, 29 mi. N of Chachapoyas; sugar cane; fruit. Formerly Pomacocha.

Florida, village, N Puerto Rico, 13 mi. SE of Arecibo; citrus-fruitgrowing center.

Florida, volcanic island, Solomon Isls., SW Pacific, c.15 mi. N of Guadalcanal; 20 mi. long, 10 mi. wide. Produces copra. Tulagi Harbor is formed by Gela on S coast of isl. and near-by TULAGI.

Florida, U. of So. Afr.: see ROODEPOORT-MARAISBURG.

Florida (flŏ'rĭdŭ), state (land □ 54,262; with inland waters □ 58,560; 1950 pop. 2,771,305; 1940 pop. 1,897,414), extreme SE U.S., bet. the Atlantic and the Gulf of Mexico, and across the Straits of Florida from Cuba; bordered N by Ga., NW by Ala.; 21st in area (including inland water), 20th in pop., admitted 1845 as the 27th state; ⊙ Tallahassee. Fla., the "Everglade State" or the "Peninsular State," is c.400 mi. long from the Ga. line (N) to Cape Sable (S), the southernmost point (25°7'N) of the U.S. mainland, within 135 mi. of Cuba. The E-W width averages c.125 mi. for the peninsula, and in the N, with the panhandle, is c.475 mi. wide. Geologically, Fla. is a slightly emerged portion of the shallow continental shelf. Coastal lowlands, frequently swampy, occupy most of the area. In the S are L. OKEECHOBEE, 2d largest fresh-water lake wholly in the U.S., the wet, black muck and peat lands of the EVERGLADES, and BIG CYPRESS SWAMP. Interior hills, rising in Walton co. to 345 ft., the highest point in the state, run from the Ga. and Ala. lines in the N, down the center of the peninsula to the Kissimmee Prairies above L. Okeechobee. Iron Mtn., near Lake Wales, is 325 ft. high. Below Starke, SW of Jacksonville, are thousands of small shallow lakes; some of the larger ones are Tsala Apopka, Apopka, Orange, and Harris. In N is OKEFENOKEE SWAMP. The SAINT JOHNS RIVER, longest (285 mi.) in the state, flows to the Atlantic, as does the St. Marys, which forms part of the Ga.-Fla. line. Rivers flowing to the Gulf include the Apalachicola, Suwannee, Peace, Withlacoochee. The Kissimmee flows to L. Okeechobee. Mainland Florida has a shore line of c.700 mi. The Atlantic coast is an almost straight beach, paralleled by barrier isls. enclosing Indian River and other lagoons, and broken only by Cape Canaveral, Biscayne Bay, and occasional inlets. The Florida Keys curve along the S tip of the peninsula to Key West, southernmost city of the U.S., 100 mi. from Havana. The Gulf Coast is characterized by more marshes, fewer barrier beaches, and a series of large indentations (Tampa, Apalachee, Choctawhatchee, St. Andrew, and Pensacola bays). Florida has a humid subtropical climate characterized by hot, rainy summers (July average temp. 85°F.) tempered by sea breezes, and mild, dry winters (Jan. average temp. 57°F.) with brief occasional frosts; hurricanes sometimes occur in the fall. In the cooler mainland, the growing season is 246–285 days; in the peninsula 285–350 days. The average annual rainfall is 50–55 in., largely concentrated in the summer and generally becoming heavier in the S; at Homestead (SW of Miami) it reaches 66 in. Forests, chiefly longleaf, slash, and loblolly pines, with some palmettos and hardwoods, cover much of Fla. Cypress is important in the Gulf coast marshes and in the swamps of the S peninsula (Big Cypress Swamp). Mangrove forests cover the SW shore of the peninsula below Cape Romano. North of L. Okeechobee, c.75% of the land is forested, c.10–15% is in farms, and the rest in marshes and prairies, notably the Kissimmee Prairies. South of the lake, c.55% of the area is forested, c.8% is cultivated or in pastures, and c.38% is occupied by the hammock-dotted wet savannas and waters of the EVERGLADES. Florida's principal source of income is tourism, accounting for ⅓ or more of the total income. The sandy beaches and barrier isls. of the Atlantic coast are especially popular in winter, notably Miami, Miami Beach, West Palm Beach, Palm Beach, Fort Lauderdale, Daytona Beach, and St. Augustine. Resorts are fewer along the Gulf coast, but some, such as St. Petersburg, Tampa, and Sarasota, are equally well-known. Another tourist area is the lake region (Orlando, Winter Haven, Lakeland). Next to tourism, the state's principal activity is the raising of truck products (more than 40% of the truck crop of the South and over 10% of that of the U.S.) and citrus fruit (notably oranges; it also leads U.S. in grapefruit, tangerines, limes). Outstanding truck centers (packing, canning) include Belle Glade, Pahokee, Plant City, Sanford, and Starke. A newer development is the L. Okeechobee sugar-cane dist. around Clewiston. The principal citrus-growing area is the central highlands (especially Polk, Orange, and Lake counties). Other important areas are the Indian River and Tampa Bay districts. Major citrus centers (packing, canning) include Auburndale, Lakeland, Orlando, Tampa, and Winter Haven. Frozen juices and by-products (citrus oils, citrus pulp for cattle feed) are becoming increasingly important. Bet. the truck and citrus areas are the chief cattle ranges of the state, the Kissimmee Prairies, centered on Kissimmee and Arcadia. Fla. ranks 2d in beef cattle among the states E of the Mississippi. The area N of the peninsula is characterized by general farming, chiefly on the clay soils of the interior highlands. Corn, which occupies more land than any other crop in the state, predominates here, and is grown along the Gulf coast N of Tampa. Cotton, peanuts, and tobacco (Gadsden co.) are also grown; nuts (tung, pecan) are the chief tree crops. Besides food processing, wood manufactures (lumber, paper and pulp, furniture, cigar boxes, fruit and vegetable crates, naval stores) are important; Pensacola, Tallahassee, Panama City, Port St. Joe, Marianna, Chattahoochee, Jacksonville, Tampa, Palatka, and Fernandina are wood-processing centers. Fla. ranks 2d in naval stores production (N, NW) and leads the U.S. in cigar mfg. (Tampa, Quincy, Jacksonville). The state supplies c.50% of the shrimp output (St. Augustine, New Smyrna, Apalachicola, Pensacola) and c.95% of the sponges (Tarpon Springs) of the U.S. Other commercially important fishes are red snapper (Pensacola), mullet, bluefish, and menhaden. Fernandina and Apalachicola are oyster centers. Shark fishing is carried on at Stuart. Commercial fishing is also done in Florida Keys. Game fishing in the Gulf Stream is a great tourist attraction. Fla. produces c.70% of the U.S. phosphate output, mined mostly in Polk co. (Bartow) and shipped through Tampa and South Boca Grande, and also leads in rutile and peat production. Limestone, sand, and gravel are other mineral products. There are large deposits of fuller's earth (mined in Gadsden co.) and clay. Oil is being produced at Sunniland in Big Cypress Swamp. Miami, Tampa, and Jacksonville are notable ports and international air centers. The Intracoastal Waterway and its connecting channels border the entire Atlantic coast and most of the Gulf coast of NW Fla. Also important is the Okeechobee Waterway across the S part of the peninsula. The state's institutions of higher learning include the Univ. of Florida (Gainesville), Univ. of Miami (Coral Gables), Florida State Univ. and Florida Agr. and Mechanical Col. (Tallahassee), Rollins Col. (Winter Park), Florida Southern Col. (Lakeland), John B. Stetson Univ. (De Land), Barry Col. (Miami), Bethune-Cookman Col. (Daytona Beach), and Univ. of Tampa. The region was discovered by Ponce de Leon in April, 1513, and named Florida probably because it was then the Easter season (*Pascua florida*) or because of the luxuriant plant life. Near the site of his landing Saint Augustine, oldest city in the U.S., was founded in 1565. Spain encouraged other settlements to protect the route of the treasure ships from Mexico and Peru and to prevent English and French encroachments. English colonists in Ga. and S.C. threatened E Fla., and the French, from the Mississippi valley, W Fla. As a result of Seven Years War, in which Spain sided with France against the British, Fla. came under British control (1763), which lasted until 1783. Influx of English settlers reached a peak during the American Revolution, when many Tories fled here from the colonies. Fla. was returned to Spain by Treaty of Paris in 1783. It was purchased by U.S. in 1821 and settlers poured in from neighboring states, especially into the area around the new capital of Tallahassee, founded 1824. Colonizers established an economy based on corn, cotton, and tobacco, similar to the rest of South. White expansion southward down the peninsula resulted in series of clashes with Seminole Indians, which culminated in the Seminole Wars (1818; 1835–42) and ended with forced removal to Oklahoma of most of the Indians. Some refused to leave and took refuge in the Everglades; here and in adjacent Big Cypress Swamp are several reservations today. During the Civil War, Fla. contributed to the South valuable supplies of cattle and salt. It suffered less than other southern states during Reconstruction days. During Spanish American War, Tampa was chief U.S. base. Development of peninsula was greatly furthered in the early 1900s by the railroad and hotel building efforts of Henry M. Flagler (along the E coast) and Henry B. Plant (along the W coast). Drainage work in N Everglades during this period also aided, as did the periodic land booms. Most famous of these booms started after First World War, reached peak in 1925, and collapsed in 1926. Development has been steadier since then, based upon large tourist trade, commercial farming, and increased mfg. In Second World War, Jacksonville and Pensacola were major military bases, and many training camps and air bases were est. See also articles on cities, towns, and geographic features, and the 67 counties: Alachua, Baker, Bay, Bradford, Brevard, Broward, Calhoun, Charlotte, Citrus, Clay, Collier, Columbia, Dade, De Soto, Dixie, Duval, Escambia, Flagler, Franklin, Gadsden, Gilchrist, Glades, Gulf, Hamilton, Hardee, Hendry, Hernando, Highlands, Hillsborough, Holmes, Indian River, Jackson, Jefferson, Lafayette, Lake, Lee, Leon, Levy, Liberty, Madison, Manatee, Marion, Martin, Monroe, Nassau, Okaloosa, Okeechobee, Orange, Osceola, Palm Beach, Pasco, Pinellas, Polk, Putnam, Saint Johns, Saint Lucie, Santa Rosa, Sarasota, Seminole, Sumter, Suwannee, Taylor, Union, Volusia, Wakulla, Walton, Washington.

Florida. 1 Town (pop. 479), Berkshire co., NW Mass., 21 mi. NNE of Pittsfield and on Deerfield R.; tourist trade. Includes village of Hoosac Tunnel, at E end of railroad tunnel through Hoosac Range. **2** Village (pop. c.200), Monroe co., NE central Mo., on Salt R. and 28 mi. SW of Hannibal. Mark Twain's birthplace; state park near by. **3** Village (pop. 1,376), Orange co., SE N.Y., 5 mi. SSW of Goshen, in onion-growing area. William H. Seward was b. here. **4** Village (pop. 227), Henry co., NW Ohio, on Maumee R. and 6 mi. SW of Napoleon.

Florida (flōrē'dä), department (□ 4,675; pop. 106,495), S central Uruguay; ⊙ Florida. Bounded by Yí R. (N), the Cuchilla Grande Principal and the Arroyo Casupá (E), Santa Lucía R. (S). The Cuchilla Grande Inferior crosses dept. E–W. Chiefly agr. area: wheat, corn, oats, linseed; major cattle- and sheep-raising region. Viticulture at La Cruz; dairy centers at 25 de Agosto and 25 de Mayo. Granite and limestone deposits at 25 de Mayo. Centers are Florida, Sarandí Grande, Casupá, Fray Marcos. Served by rail and highway net centering in Montevideo. Formed 1856.

Florida, city (pop. 16,000), ⊙ Florida dept., S central Uruguay, on the Arroyo Santa Lucía Chico, on railroad and highway, and 50 mi. N of Montevideo; 34°6'S 56°14'W. Flour milling, lumber milling; mfg. of stockings, textiles, mosaics. In agr. area (wheat, corn, oats, linseed). Has govt. bldg., public library, col. Founded 1809.

Florida, Cape, Fla.: see Key Biscayne.

Florida, La, Colombia: see La Florida.

Florida, Straits of (flŏ'rĭdů), passage (up to 90 mi. wide) bet. S tip of Fla. (Florida Keys) on the N, and Cuba and the Bahama Isls. on the S and SE; connects Gulf of Mexico with the Atlantic. Current passing through straits from the Gulf is the major component of the Florida Current, initial section of the Gulf Stream system.

Florida Bay, shallow body of water skirting S end of the Fla. peninsula, and partly sheltered S and E from the Atlantic by the Florida Keys; opens into Biscayne Bay (NE) and the Gulf of Mexico (NW). Bay has dredged navigation channels. Most of bay and its many small isls. are included in Everglades Natl. Park.

Floridablanca (flōrē'dābläng'kä), town (pop. 1,793), Santander dept., N central Colombia, 5 mi. SE of Bucaramanga; sugar cane, tobacco, coffee, fruit; liquor and perfume distilling; brewery.

Floridablanca, town (1939 pop. 2,071; 1948 municipality pop. 24,825), Pampanga prov., central Luzon, Philippines, on railroad and 12 mi. WSW of San Fernando; agr. center (sugar cane, rice).

Florida City (flŏ'rĭdů), town (pop. 1,547), Dade co., S Fla., 29 mi. SW of Miami; truck-produce shipping. Inc. 1913.

Florida Current, warm ocean current of North Atlantic Ocean, constituting initial section of Gulf Stream system. Formed by union of Antilles Current and of the major current component issuing from Gulf of Mexico through Straits of Florida, the Florida Current flows N along SE coast of U.S. to area of Cape Hatteras, where it becomes the Gulf Stream proper. It issues from the Gulf as dark indigo-blue water of c.80°F. moving at a surface velocity of 4–6 mi. per hour. The initial transport of 26,000,000 cu. mm per second rapidly increases and reaches its maximum in the Gulf Stream proper.

Florida Keys, S Fla., a chain (c.150 mi. long) of coral limestone isls. curving SW around tip of the Fla. peninsula from Virginia Key just S of Miami Beach, to Key West, c.100 mi. NNE of Havana; sometimes the name is extended to include the Marquesas Keys and Dry Tortugas farther W. The Florida Keys separate the shallow waters of Biscayne and Florida bays from the deep waters of the Straits of Florida. Mostly in Monroe co. and partly in Dade co., the keys are narrow and generally covered by dense growths of low trees and shrubs, with mangrove swamps on the landward side; their flora includes many plants typical of the West Indies. The isls., notably Key Largo (lär'gō) (the largest, 28½ mi. long) and Key West (site of Key West, southernmost city in U.S.), are best known for their commercial and sport fishing and as resorts; there is some citrus-fruit growing (mainly limes) and limestone quarrying. From Key Largo to Key West, the isls. are linked by a highway (123 mi. long; completed 1938 to replace railroad destroyed in 1935) which crosses to mainland at Key Largo. From NE to SW, principal isls. are: Virginia Key, Key Biscayne (bĭskān'), Sands Key, Elliott Key, Old Rhodes Key, Key Largo, Plantation Key; Upper Matecumbe Key (mătůkŭm'bē), site of Islamorada village (ī"slůmůrä'dů); Lower Matecumbe Key, site of Craig village; Long Key, Grassy Key; Vaca Key (vă'ků), site of Marathon village; Pigeon Key, West Summerland Key, Big Pine Key, Torch Keys, Ramrod Key, Summerland Key, Cudjoe Key (kŭ'jō), Sugarloaf Key, Saddlebunch Key, Boca Chica Key (bō'ků chē'ků), and Key West. In Sept., 1935, they were swept by a hurricane which took many lives and destroyed miles of highway and railroad.

Florida Mountains, SW N.Mex., extend N–S in Luna co. Chief peak, Arco del Diablo (7,400 ft.). Manganese deposits.

Floridia (flôrē'dyä), town (pop. 14,365), Siracusa prov., SE Sicily, near Anapo R., 7 mi. W of Syracuse, in cereal- and grape-growing region.

Florido River (flōrē'dō), N Mexico, rises in Sierra Madre Occidental SW of Hidalgo del Parral, on Durango–Chihuahua border; flows in semicircle of c.140 mi. N, past Villa Coronado, Villa López, and Jiménez, to Conchos R. at Camargo.

Floridsdorf (flō'rĭdzdôrf), outer NE district (□ 55; pop. 101,702) of Vienna, Austria, on left bank of the Danube; mfg. (locomotives, machinery, electrical goods); oil refining. Its former area (□ 19; pop. 86,782) was enlarged (1938) through incorporation of 10 towns, including Gerasdorf and Langenzersdorf.

Florin (flô'rĭn), village (pop. 1,319), Lancaster co., SE Pa., just W of Mount Joy.

Florina, Greece: see Phlorina.

Floris, town (pop. 215), Davis co., SE Iowa, 11 mi. SSE of Ottumwa, in bituminous-coal-mining and sheep-raising area.

Florissant (flô'rĭsůnt). **1** Town (pop. 53), Teller co., central Colo., on branch of South Platte R., in Rocky Mts., and 15 mi. NW of Pikes Peak, 25 mi. WNW of Colorado Springs; alt. c.8,180 ft. Tourist point. Dude ranches and petrified forest near by. **2** City (pop. 3,737), St. Louis co., E Mo., near Missouri R. just N of St. Louis. Settled by French c.1785, called St. Ferdinand by later Sp. settlers, present name made official 1939. Jesuit seminary near by.

Florli, Norway: see Floyrli.

Floro (flōr'ů), Nor. *Florø*, town (pop. 1,586), ⊙ Sogn og Fjordane co., W Norway, port on North Sea, 85 mi. N of Bergen; westernmost town of Norway; 61°35'N 5°1'E. Active fishing center, producing canned and frozen fish and fish products. Dates back to 1300.

Flörsheim (flûrs'hīm), village (pop. 8,132), in former Prussian prov. of Hesse-Nassau, W Germany, after 1945 in Hesse, on right bank of the canalized Main and 13 mi. WSW of Frankfurt; chemical mfg.

Floss (flôs), village (pop. 2,830), Upper Palatinate, NE Bavaria, Germany, 6 mi. NE of Weiden; textile mfg.

Flossmoor (flôs'môr), village (pop. 1,804), Cook co., NE Ill., S suburb of Chicago. Inc. 1924.

Flosta, canton, Norway: see Naresto.

Flosteroy, Norway: see Naresto.

Flotta (flŏ'tů), island (pop. 282) of the Orkneys, Scotland, bet. Hoy and South Ronaldsay; 3 mi. long, 2 mi. wide.

Flotte, La (lä flôt'), village (pop. 1,260), Charente-Maritime dept., W France, on NE shore of Île de Ré, 9 mi. WNW of La Rochelle; bathing resort; sardine fisheries, saltworks. Has 12th–15th-cent. church.

Flottum, Norway: see Singsas.

Floure (floor), village (pop. 162), Aude dept., S France, on Aude R. and 7 mi. ESE of Carcassonne; steel milling.

Flourtown, village, Montgomery co., SE Pa., NW residential suburb of Philadelphia.

Flovilla (flōvĭ'lů), town (pop. 315), Butts co., central Ga., 5 mi. ESE of Jackson. State park near by.

Flowerdale Forest, extensive mountainous deer forest (□ c.80) in W Ross and Cromarty, Scotland, SE of Gairloch. Rises to 2,869 ft. in the Baosbheinn, 8 mi. SE of Gairloch.

Flower Hill, village (pop. 1,948), Nassau co., SE N.Y., near N shore of W Long Isl., 5 mi. NNW of Mineola, in shore-resort area. Inc. 1931.

Flower Lake, N.Y.: see Saranac Lake, village.

Flowery Branch, town (pop. 610), Hall co., NE Ga., 9 mi. SW of Gainesville; mfg. (furniture, shoes, harnesses, rugs, bags), poultry processing.

Floyd. 1 County (□ 514; pop. 62,899), NW Ga., on Ala. line; ⊙ Rome. Valley and ridge area, including part of Chattahoochee Natl. Forest (N); drained by Coosa, Etowah, and Oostanaula rivers. Agr. (cotton, corn, hay, sweet potatoes, fruit, livestock, dairy products, poultry); textile mfg. Formed 1832. **2** County (□ 149; pop. 43,955), S Ind.; ⊙ New Albany. Hilly region, bounded S by Ohio R. (here forming Ky. line), and drained by small tributaries. Farming (grain, tobacco), stock raising, dairying; timber; sand, gravel. Extensive mfg. at New Albany. Formed 1819. **3** County (□ 503; pop. 21,505), N Iowa; ⊙ Charles City. Prairie agr. area (hogs, cattle, poultry, corn, soybeans, oats) drained by Shell Rock, Cedar, and Little Cedar rivers. Many limestone quarries, some gravel pits. Formed 1851. **4** County (□ 402; pop. 53,500), E Ky.; ⊙ Prestonsburg. In the Cumberlands; drained by Levisa Fork and several creeks. Bituminous-coal mining; oil and gas wells; some farms (poultry, dairy products, cattle, apples, corn, soybeans, white and sweet potatoes). Formed 1799. **5** County (□ 993; pop. 10,535), NW Texas; ⊙ Floydada. On Llano Estacado, with E-facing

Cap Rock escarpment; alt. 2,800–3,500 ft.; drained by White R. Agr. (partly irrigated) and livestock region; grain sorghums, wheat, cotton, alfalfa, some truck, fruit; cattle, hogs, sheep, poultry; dairying, beekeeping. Caliche quarries. Formed 1876. **6** County (□ 383; pop. 11,351), SW Va.; ⊙ Floyd. In the Blue Ridge; traversed by Appalachian Trail and Blue Ridge Parkway; drained by Little R. Agr., dairying, livestock raising, lumbering; flour milling, shirt mfg. at Floyd. Arsenopyrite deposits. Formed 1831.

Floyd. 1 Town (pop. 440), Floyd co., N Iowa, on Cedar R. and 5 mi. NNW of Charles City. Limestone quarries near by. **2** Town (pop. 493), ⊙ Floyd co., SW Va., 33 mi. SW of Roanoke; flour and lumber milling, mfg. of shirts.

Floydada (floidā'dů), town (pop. 3,210), ⊙ Floyd co., NW Texas, on Llano Estacado, 40 mi. NE of Lubbock, near White R.; market, shipping and processing center for agr. area (dairy products, grain sorghums, cotton, wheat, livestock, poultry); caliche quarries. Settled c.1889, inc. 1909.

Floyd Bennett Field, SE N.Y., airport in SE Brooklyn borough of New York city, on Jamaica Bay. A U.S. naval air station, it was formerly New York municipal airport.

Floyd Collins Crystal Cave, Ky.: see Cave City.

Floyd River, NW Iowa, rises near Sanborn in O'Brien co., flows 92 mi. generally SW, past Sheldon and Le Mars, to the Missouri at Sioux City. West Branch Floyd R. rises near Boyden, flows c.40 mi. SW to Floyd R. near Merrill.

Floyds Fork, stream, N Ky., rises in W Henry co., flows c.65 mi. SSW to Salt R. 2 mi. E of Shepherdsville.

Floyrli (flů'ürlē), Nor. *Fløyrli,* waterfall (2,400 ft.) in Rogaland co., SW Norway, on Floyrli R. (an affluent of Lyse Fjord) and 25 mi. E of Stavanger; site of hydroelectric station. Sometimes spelled Floirli or Florli.

Fluchthorn (flŏŏkht'hôrn), peak (11,165 ft.) in Silvretta Group of Rhaetian Alps, on Swiss-Austrian border, 7 mi. NNW of Schuls.

Fluchtkogel (flŏŏkht'kōgůl), peak (11,526 ft.) in Ötztal Alps of Tyrol, W Austria; SW of the Wildspitze.

Flüelen (flü'ůlůn), village (pop. 1,608), Uri canton, central Switzerland, on L. of Uri, near Reuss R. delta, and 1 mi. NNW of Altdorf; resort; woodworking. Has 14th-cent. castle.

Fluessen Lake, Du. *Fluessen Meer* (flü'sůn mār″), Friesland prov., N Netherlands, 6 mi. SSW of Sneek; 8 mi. long, 1 mi. wide. Water-sports center.

Flume, Mount, N.H.: see Franconia Mountains.

Flume, The, N.H.: see Franconia Notch.

Flumendosa River (flōōmĕndô'zä), SE Sardinia, rises in SE Monti del Gennargentu, flows W, turning SE near Gadoni, to Tyrrhenian Sea near Muravera; 79 mi. long. Forms artificial L. Alto del Flumendosa (hydroelectric station) in upper course; used for irrigation. Fishing in lower course.

Flumet (flümā'), village (pop. 283), Savoie dept., SE France, in Savoy Alps, on Arly R. and 11 mi. NNE of Albertville; mule-breeding station; sawmilling.

Fluminimaggiore (flōō″mēnēmäd-jô'rē), village (pop. 3,131), Cagliari prov., SW Sardinia, 9 mi. N of Iglesias; mining center (zinc, lead, silver, copper, barite).

Flumini Mannu River (flōō'mēnē män'nōō), S Sardinia, rises NE of Laconi, flows SSW, turning SSE near Samassi, through Campidano lowland, to Stagno di Cagliari; c.50 mi. long. Fisheries in lower course. Receives Cixerri (right) and Mannu (left) rivers. Also called Samassi R.

Flums (flōōms), town (pop. 4,649), St. Gall canton, E Switzerland, on Seez R. and 13 mi. ENE of Glarus; 3 hydroelectric plants; cotton textiles, calcium carbide. Just W is a mtn. resort area.

Flushing, Du. *Vlissingen* (vlĭ'sĭng-ůn), town (pop. 20,217) and port, Zeeland prov., SW Netherlands, at mouth of the Western Scheldt, on S coast of Walcheren isl. and 55 mi. SW of The Hague; terminus of cross-channel boats from Harwich (England); Netherlands and Belg. pilot station for Scheldt R. navigation. Oil refining, shipbuilding, mfg. of aircraft, engines, iron and steel products, asphalt; tin-coating plant. Has remains of 16th-cent. town gate, 18th-cent. town hall. Birthplace (1607) of Admiral de Ruyter. First city of the Netherlands to take sides (1572) with Prince of Orange against Spain.

Flushing. 1 Village (pop. 2,226), Genesee co., SE central Mich., 9 mi. WNW of Flint and on Flint R., in agr. area (dairy products; grain, beans); flour milling. Indian mounds near by. Settled 1833, inc. 1877. **2** A section of N Queens borough of New York city, SE N.Y., on Flushing Bay of East R.; residential, industrial (clothing, pharmaceuticals, electronic equipment, optical goods, machinery; stone, tar, and wood products; aircraft parts, boats). Seat of Queens Col. of City of New York. Bowne home (1661) and a Quaker meeting house (c.1696) are points of interest. Chartered to English settlers by Dutch West India Company (1645). Was noted for its gardens and nurseries in late-18th and early-19th cent. New York World's Fair (1939–40) was held at Flushing Meadow Park, which was later the temporary site of meetings of the United Nations. **3** Village (pop. 1,158), Belmont co., E Ohio, 20 mi. W of Wheeling (W.Va.), and on small Wheeling Creek, in coal-mining area. Settled 1809.

Flushing Bay, SE N.Y., shallow inlet of East R. in NW shore of Long Isl., in Queens borough, bet. Corona (W) and Flushing and College Point (E); c.1 mi. wide at entrance, 2 mi. long. On W shore is New York city municipal airport (La Guardia Field), with a seaplane base; on S shore is Flushing Meadow Park, scene of 1939–40 New York World's Fair, and later the temporary home of the United Nations.

Fluvanna (flōōvă'nů), county (□ 282; pop. 7,121), central Va.; ⊙ Palmyra. Bounded S by James R.; drained by Rivanna R. Agr. (especially tobacco), dairying, livestock; some timber; slate quarrying. Formed 1777.

Fluvanna, village (pop. c.300), Scurry co., NW central Texas, 15 mi. NW of Snyder; trade, shipping point for agr., cattle-ranching area.

Fluviá River (flōōvyä'), Gerona prov., NE Spain, rises near Olot, flows 52 mi. E to the Gulf of Rosas. Feeds canals irrigating Ampurdán plain.

Flying Fish, Cape, headland, Antarctica, at N extremity of Thurston Peninsula; 71°20'S 98°W. Discovered 1940 by R. E. Byrd.

Flying Point Neck, SW Maine, peninsula in Casco Bay, near Freeport; resort area.

Fly River, largest river of New Guinea, rises in Victor Emmanuel Range in central New Guinea, flows 650 mi. SE to Gulf of Papua; 50 mi. of its course forms boundary bet. Netherlands New Guinea and Territory of Papua. Navigable for 500 mi. from 50-mi.-wide mouth. Chief tributaries, Strickland and Tedi rivers.

Flys Peak, Ariz.: see Chiricahua Mountains.

Flysta (flü'stä″), residential village (pop. 1,789), Stockholm co., E Sweden, 6 mi. WNW of Stockholm city center.

Foa, La (lä fōä'), village (dist. pop. 924), W New Caledonia, 55 mi. NW of Nouméa; livestock, agr. products.

Foam Lake, town (pop. 564), SE central Sask., near Foam Lake (3 mi. long, 3 mi. wide), 55 mi. NW of Yorkton; railroad junction; woodworking, furniture mfg., flour milling, dairying. Site of Royal Canadian Mounted Police barracks.

Foard (fôrd), county (□ 676; pop. 4,216), N Texas; ⊙ Crowell. Bet. Pease R. (N), Wichita R. (S). Broken in W and SW (cattle ranches); agr. in E (wheat, cotton, alfalfa, truck, fruit); also produces horses, hogs, poultry; beekeeping. Oil, natural-gas wells; clay, gypsum, copper deposits. Formed 1891.

Foca (fôchä'), Turkish *Foça,* village (pop. 3,484), Smyrna prov., W Turkey, on Aegean Sea 27 mi. NW of Smyrna; tobacco, raisins; millstone grit. Near by are ruins of anc. Phocaea. Village was formerly known as Eskifoca [=old Foca] and Karafoca; sometimes spelled Focha and Fokia. NE, 7 mi., is Yenicefoca [=new Foca], a village (pop. 1,515) founded 1421 by Genoese.

Foca or **Focha** (both: fô'chä), Serbo-Croatian *Foča,* town (pop. 3,327), SE Bosnia, Yugoslavia, on Drina R., at Cotina R. mouth, and 28 mi. SSE of Sarajevo; rail branch terminus; trade and handicraft center. Numerous mosques. Important 15th-cent. caravan station on Dubrovnik-Nis road.

Foca Island (fō'kä), 1 mi. off Pacific coast of Piura dept., NW Peru, 10 mi. SW of Paita; 5°13'S 81°13'W; ½ mi. wide, 1 mi. long; guano deposits.

Focha, Turkey: see Foca.

Focha, Yugoslavia: see Foca.

Fochabers (fŏkh'ůbůrz), resort town, NE Moray, Scotland, on the Spey and 6 mi. SW of Buckie. Just N is Gordon Castle, dating from 15th cent. and later, seat of duke of Richmond.

Fockbek (fôk'bāk), village (pop. 3,043), in Schleswig-Holstein, NW Germany, 2 mi. W of Rendsburg; knitwear.

Focsani (fôk-shän',-shä'nē), Rum. *Focşani,* town (1948 pop. 27,960), ⊙ Putna prov., E Rumania, in Moldavia, 100 mi. NE of Bucharest; rail junction and commercial center. Trade in wine, lumber, grain; mfg. of cotton textiles, knitwear, clay products, soap, candles, pharmaceuticals; metalworking, flour milling, tanning. Has several 17th- and 18th-cent. churches. Founded at beginning of 15th cent. and soon split (1473–1859) bet. Moldavia and Walachia. Here Turks were defeated (1789) by Austro-Russian armies. Seat of commission for unification of Rumania (1859–62) and site of the signature of Rum.-Ger. truce (Dec., 1917). Was sometimes spelled Fokshani.

Fodderty, agr. village and parish (pop. 1,488), E Ross and Cromarty, Scotland, 2 mi. W of Dingwall. Parish includes Strathpeffer and Maryburgh.

Foëcy (fôĕsē'), village (pop. 1,135), Cher dept., central France, on Yèvre R. and Berry Canal, and 5 mi. SE of Vierzon; porcelain mfg. Also Foécy.

Foel, Wales: see Cwmavon.

Foel Cwmcerwyn, Wales: see Mynydd Prescelly.

Foel Fras (voil vräs'), mountain (3,091 ft.), N Caernarvon, Wales, 5 mi. E of Bethesda.

Fogaras, Rumania: see Fagaras.

Foggia (fôd'jä), province (□ 2,774; pop. 528,666), Apulia, S Italy, bordering on the Adriatic; ⊙ Foggia. Large central plain, enclosed on 3 sides by the Apennines and mountainous Gargano promontory. Includes Tremiti Isls. Watered by Candelaro, Carapelle, and Cervaro rivers. Agr. (cereals, olives, grapes, potatoes, citrus fruit). Sheep raising. Fishing (Manfredonia, Vieste, lakes of Varano and Lesina). Extensive saltworks at Margherita di Savoia. Bauxite mining, marble quarrying on Gargano promontory. Mfg. at Cerignola, Foggia, Lucera, Manfredonia.

Foggia, city (pop. 57,234), ⊙ Foggia prov., Apulia, S Italy, 75 mi. WNW of Bari; 41°28'N 15°33'E. In center of large plain (sheep raising, cereal growing); rail and road junction; major wheat and wool market of S Italy. Chief industries: flour milling, macaroni and cheese mfg., wine making, metalworking. Bishopric. Has 12th-cent. cathedral (much restored). Once a favorite residence of Frederick II. In Second World War, was chief German, and later, Allied air base in S Italy; badly damaged by air bombing.

Foglianise (fôlyänē'zē), village (pop. 2,029), Benevento prov., Campania, S Italy, 6 mi. WNW of Benevento; mfg. (woolen textiles, pharmaceuticals).

Foglia River (fô'lyä), The Marches, central Italy, rises in Etruscan Apennines SW of Sestino, flows 55 mi. ENE to the Adriatic at Pesaro.

Foglizzo (fôlyē'tsô), village (pop. 2,536), Torino prov., Piedmont, NW Italy, near Orco R., 16 mi. NNE of Turin; alcohol distilleries.

Fogo (fō'gōō), island (□ 184; 1940 pop. 22,914; 1950 pop. 16,705), one of Cape Verde Isls., in Leeward group, bet. São Tiago Isl. (35 mi. ENE) and Brava (12 mi. WSW), in the Atlantic. São Filipe (14°53'N 24°31'W), its chief town, is on W shore. Roughly circular (diameter 15 mi.), isl. has an active volcano, Cano Peak (alt. 9,281 ft.), the archipelago's highest mtn., with a symmetrical cone and a huge caldera (6 mi. wide). Last major eruption 1847. Castor beans, coffee, oranges, and tobacco are grown on N and W slopes.

Fogo Island (fō'gō) (□ 100; pop. 2,870), just off E N.F., near SE end of Notre Dame Bay, 20 mi. E of Twillingate; 15 mi. long, 10 mi. wide, rises to 382 ft. On NW coast is settlement of Fogo (pop. 1,036), fishing port with cod canneries and mink and fox farms; 49°44'N 54°15'W.

Fohai (fô'hī'), town (pop. 1,335), ⊙ Fohai co. (pop. 17,958), southernmost Yunnan prov., China, 85 mi. SW of Ningerh and on route to Thailand; alt. 4,003 ft.; tea-growing center; rice, timber, millet, beans, cotton. Until 1929, Menghai.

Fohnsdorf (fōns'dôrf), city (pop. 10,937), Styria, SE central Austria, near Mur R., 3 mi. N of Judenburg. Lignite mines near by.

Fohorem (fô-ô'rē), town, Portuguese Timor, in central Timor, 60 mi. SW of Dili; sandalwood. Formerly Vila Armindo Monteiro.

Föhr (fûr), North Sea island (□ 30; 1939 pop. 5,838; 1946 pop. 10,658) of North Frisian group, NW Germany, 4 mi. off Schleswig-Holstein coast; 7 mi. long (E–W), 5 mi. wide (N–S). Highly cultivated (grain, cattle). The resort of Wyk is the main town on the isl.

Foia, La (lä foi'ů), highest summit (2,960 ft.) in the Serra de Monchique, S Portugal.

Foiano della Chiana (fôyä'nô dĕl-lä kyä'nä), town (pop. 2,174), Arezzo prov., Tuscany, central Italy, in Val di Chiana, 15 mi. SSW of Arezzo; mfg. (metal furniture, agr. tools).

Foiano di Val Fortore (dē väl fôrtô'rē), village (pop. 2,303), Benevento prov., Campania, S Italy, 19 mi. NNE of Benevento; woolen mill.

Foinitsa, Yugoslavia: see Fojnica.

Foix (fwä), town (pop. 6,026), ⊙ Ariège dept., S France, at foot of the central Pyrenees, on Ariège R. and 45 mi. S of Toulouse; commercial center; dairy and livestock market; metalworking, felt and blanket mfg. Three towers (remains of a medieval castle) dominate the town from atop a rock 190 ft. high. Old ⊙ of the countship of Foix, which, after being united with the crownland in 1607, remained a prov. under jurisdiction of Toulouse parlement.

Fojnica, Foinitsa, or **Foynitsa** (all: foi'nētsä), village (pop. 2,036), S Bosnia, Yugoslavia, 27 mi. W of Sarajevo, near Sarajevo coal area; health resort with sulphur springs; gold mine; gold mill. Copper and pyrite deposits. Also Fojnica kod Kiseljaka.

Fokang, China: see Fatkong.

Foki (fô'kē), village (1939 pop. over 2,000), SW Molotov oblast, Russian SFSR, 27 mi. NE of Sarapul; flax retting; rye, oats, livestock.

Fokia, Turkey: see Foca.

Fokien, China: see Fukien.

Fokis, Greece: see Phocis.

Folarskarnuten, Norway: see Hallingskarv.

Folcroft (fŏl'krôft), borough (pop. 1,909), Delaware co., SE Pa., SW suburb of Philadelphia. Inc. 1927.

Folda (fôl'lä), fjord of the North Sea, in Nordland co., N Norway, 25 mi. NE of Bodo; 8 mi. wide at mouth; divides into North Folda (Nor. *Nordfolda*), 36 mi. long, and South Folda (Nor. *Sørfolda*), 24 mi. long. Herring fishing. Sometimes spelled Folla; sometimes called Foldenfjord.

Foldafoss, Norway: see Follafoss.

Földeak (fûl'dĕäk), Hung. *Földeák*, town (pop. 5,624), Csanad co., S Hungary, on Szaraz R. and 7 mi. N of Mako; grain, onions, paprika, hogs.
Foldenfjord, Norway: see FOLDA.
Földes (fûl'dĕsh), town (pop. 5,761), Hajdu co., E Hungary, 22 mi. SW of Debrecen; grain, potatoes; cattle, horses.
Földvar, Rumania: see FELDISARA.
Folegandros, Greece: see PHOLEGANDROS.
Folembray (fôläbrā'), village (pop. 1,476), Aisne dept., N France, near the Ailette, 12 mi. NNW of Soissons; glass-bottle works. Here treaty was signed (1596) bet. Henry IV and the duke of Mayenne, ending the Catholic League.
Foleshill, England: see COVENTRY.
Foley. 1 Town (pop. 1,301), Baldwin co., SW Ala., 25 mi. W of Pensacola, Fla.; naval stores, fertilizer. **2** Village (pop. 1,014), Taylor co., N Fla., c.55 mi. SE of Tallahassee; lumber-milling center. **3** Village (pop. 1,089), ⊙ Benton co., central Minn., 14 mi. NE of St. Cloud, in grain, livestock, truck-farming area; dairy products. **4** Town (pop. 203), Lincoln co., E Mo., near Mississippi R., 9 mi. S of Elsberry.
Folgaria (fôlgärē'ä), village (pop. 911), Trento prov., Trentino–Alto Adige, N Italy, 6 mi. ENE of Rovereto; resort (alt. 3,825 ft.).
Folgefonn (fôl'gûfôn), Nor. *Folgefonna* or *Folgefonni*, ice sheet (□ 110) in Hordaland co., SW Norway, 3d largest in Norway, lies on plateau in the Hardanger region S of Hardanger Fjord; extends from vicinity of Sor Fjord 22 mi. S, varying in width bet. 3-10 mi., and rising to 5,423 ft. Several arms descend from it, including the Buarbrae or Buarbre, which advances E to Sor Fjord. According to legend, 7 parishes are buried under the ice sheet. Formerly spelled Folgefond.
Folgoët, Le (lù fôlgôā'), village (pop. 424), Finistère dept., W France, 14 mi. NNE of Brest; dairying, horse breeding. Has fine 15th-cent. church with remarkable granite rood loft.
Folgoso de la Ribera, Spain: see TREMOR.
Foligno (fôlē'nyô), town (pop. 10,694), Perugia prov., Umbria, central Italy, 19 mi. SE of Perugia. Rail and road junction; industrial and commercial center; textiles (woolen, cotton), paper, machinery, metal furniture, soap, leather goods, wine, macaroni, fertilizer, wax, glass, matches. Bishopric. Has 12th-cent. Romanesque cathedral and several notable churches and palaces, including Palazzo Trinci (1389–1407; war damage restored) with archaeological mus. Seat of flourishing school of painting in 15th cent. In Second World War suffered much air bombing (1943–44) which destroyed or damaged half of its bldgs.
Folkestone (fōk'stùn), municipal borough (1931 pop. 35,889; 1951 census 45,200), SE Kent, England, on the Strait of Dover, 7 mi. WSW of Dover; 51°4'N 1°11'E; seaside resort and port for cross-Channel shipping, with services to Boulogne and Calais. Located at foot of chalk hills, it has parade of the Leas, along the cliffs. Traces of Roman occupation in vicinity. Has restored 11th-cent. church. Town was frequently bombed in Second World War. William Harvey b. here.
Folkingham, (fō'kĭng-ùm), agr. village and parish (pop. 446), Parts of Kesteven, S Lincolnshire, England, 10 mi. E of Grantham. Has church dating from 14th cent. and remains of a Norman castle.
Folkston, city (pop. 1,515), ⊙ Charlton co., SE Ga., 33 mi. SE of Waycross, near St. Marys R. (forms Fla. line here) and Okefenokee Swamp; sawmilling.
Folla, Norway: see FOLDA.
Follafoss (fôl'läfôs), village (pop. 558), in Verran canton (pop. 1,789), Nord-Trondelag co., central Norway, on Folla R. at its influx into Beitstad Fjord (an extension of Trondheim Fjord), 12 mi. WSW of Steinkjer; large wood-grinding plant powered by hydroelectric station at waterfall here. Formerly spelled Foldafoss.
Follansbee (fŏ'lùnzbē), steel-making town (pop. 4,435), Brooke co., W.Va., in Northern Panhandle, 3 mi. SE of Steubenville, Ohio, across the Ohio; coal mines, oil and gas wells; mfg. of chemicals, tar, tin products. Inc. 1906.
Folldal (fôl'däl), village (pop. 423; canton pop. 2,348), Hedmark co., E Norway, on E slope of the Dovrefjell, at head of the Folldal, on Folla R. (small tributary of Glomma R.) and 50 mi. SW of Roros; copper-pyrite mining center. Cable railroad to Alvdal.
Follett (fŏ'lĭt), town (pop. 540), Lipscomb co., extreme N Texas, in the Panhandle, 45 mi. W of Woodward, Okla., in wheat, cattle region.
Folligny (fôlēnyē'), village (pop. 102), Manche dept., NW France, 10 mi. N of Avranches; rail junction.
Follina (fôl-lē'nä), village (pop. 1,152), Treviso prov., Veneto, N Italy, 9 mi. WSW of Vittorio Veneto; alcohol distillery, woolen mill. Has 13th-cent. cloister.
Follinge (fû'lĭng-ù), Swedish *Föllinge*, village (pop. 601), Jamtland co., NW Sweden, on tributary of Indal R., 30 mi. N of Ostersund; dairying; lumber.
Follonica (fôl-lô'nēkä), town (pop. 4,836), Grosseto prov., Tuscany, central Italy, port on Tyrrhenian Sea, opposite Elba, 21 mi. NW of Grosseto. Industrial center; iron- and steelworks, cork industry, paper mill, macaroni factory.
Folly Beach, S.C.: see FOLLY ISLAND.
Folly Island, Charleston co., SE S.C., one of Sea Isls., 8 mi. S of Charleston, on the Atlantic; separated by Folly R. channel (W); c.6.5 mi. long. Highway bridged to James Isl. and mainland (N). On E shore is Folly Beach (resort); naval reservation is on NE end.
Folschviller (fôlshvēlâr'), Ger. *Folschweiler* (fôlsh'vīlùr), village (pop. 484), Moselle dept., NE France, 3 mi. SSW of Saint Avold; coal mining.
Folsom. 1 (fōl'sùm) City (pop. 1,690), Sacramento co., central Calif., 20 mi. ENE of Sacramento, and on American R., in general agr. and citrus-fruit area. Seat of a state prison. Folsom Dam is near by. First steam railroad in Calif. was built from here to Sacramento in 1856. Founded 1855 on road to the gold fields; inc. 1946. **2** (fŏl'sùm) Village (pop. 166), St. Tammany parish, SE La., 10 mi. N of Covington. **3** (fŏl'sùm) Borough (pop. 292), Atlantic co., S N.J., on Great Egg Harbor R. and 28 mi. NW of Atlantic City; canneries. **4** (fŏl'sùm) Village (pop. 206), Union co., NE N.Mex., on headstream of Cimarron R., near Colo. line, 29 mi. E of Raton; alt. c.6,450 ft. Shipping point for cattle and sheep. Capulin Mtn. Natl. Monument is 6 mi. SSW. Artifacts of Folsom culture have been found in vicinity.
Folsom Dam (fōl'sùm), central Calif., on American R. near Folsom; begun 1948 by U.S. army engineers, it will be 268 ft. high and will impound a reservoir of 1,000,000 acre-ft. capacity. As part of CENTRAL VALLEY development plan, it will serve for irrigation, power production, flood control.
Foltesti (fôltĕsht'), Rum. *Folteşti*, village (pop. 2,015), Galati prov., E Rumania, on railroad and 20 mi. N of Galati.
Fomboni (fōmbō'nē), chief town of Mohéli Isl., Comoro Isls., steamboat landing on N shore; 12°18'S 43°45'E. Numerous vanilla plantations in vicinity.
Fomento (fōmĕn'tō), town (pop. 6,038), Las Villas prov., central Cuba, on railroad and 27 mi. SE of Santa Clara; agr. center (sugar cane, tobacco, coffee, fruit, livestock). Sugar centrals of Isabel and Agabama in outskirts.
Fómeque (fō'mākā), town (pop. 1,039), Cundinamarca dept., central Colombia, in Cordillera Oriental, 15 mi. SE of Bogotá; alt. 6,342 ft.; cereals, coffee, fruit, cattle.
Fominki (fô'mĭnkē), village (1926 pop. 1,242), E Vladimir oblast, Russian SFSR, near Oka R., 22 mi. SE of Vyazniki; potatoes.
Fonafidin, Japan: see TORI-SHIMA.
Foncine-le-Haut (fōsēn-lù-ō'), village (pop. 320), Jura dept., E France, in the central Jura, 21 mi. NNE of Saint-Claude; diamond cutting, woodworking.
Fonda (fŏn'dù). **1** Town (pop. 1,120), Pocahontas co., N central Iowa, on Cedar Creek and 35 mi. W of Fort Dodge; machine shop, creamery; concrete products. **2** Village (pop. 1,026), ⊙ Montgomery co., E central N.Y., on Mohawk R. and the Barge Canal, and 10 mi. W of Amsterdam; freight transfer point; mfg. of gloves and textiles. Inc. 1850.
Fond-des-Blancs (fō-dā-blā'), town, Sud dept., SW Haiti, on Tiburon Peninsula, 23 mi. SW of Petit-Goâve; coffeegrowing.
Fond-des-Nègres (–nĕ'grù), village, Sud dept., SW Haiti, on Tiburon Peninsula, 18 mi. WSW of Petit-Goâve; coffeegrowing.
Fond du Lac (fŏn' dù lăk"), village, N Sask., near Northwest Territories border, at E end of L. Athabaska; 59°19'N 107°10'W; Hudson's Bay Co. trading post. In summer Hudson's Bay Co. steamers connect it with Fort Chipewyan; here begins canoe route to Churchill R. via Wollaston and Reindeer lakes. Formerly important fur-trading center.
Fond du Lac (fŏn' dù lăk", jŏŏ lăk"), county (□ 724; pop. 67,829), E Wis.; ⊙ Fond du Lac. Dairying and agr. area (vegetables, hemp, sugar beets). Diversified mfg. at Fond du Lac, Ripon, Waupun; also vegetable canning, processing of dairy products. S part of L. Winnebago (resorts) is in co. Drained by Milwaukee, Rock, Sheboygan, and Fond du Lac rivers. Formed 1836.
Fond du Lac, city (pop. 29,936), ⊙ Fond du Lac co., E Wis., at S end of L. Winnebago, 18 mi. SSE of Oshkosh; mfg. of precision tools, machinery, leather, refrigerators, caskets, automotive parts, clothing, beer, dairy products, textiles, wood and metal products; railroad shops; limestone quarries. Vacation resort. Settled c.1835 on site of late-18th-cent. French trading post; inc. 1852. Grew as lumbering town; industrialization followed coming of railroad. In 18th cent., name Fond du Lac was applied to many other regions around Great Lakes.
Fonde (fŏn'dē), mining village (pop. 1,478, with near-by Pruden), Bell co., SE Ky., in the Cumberlands at Tenn. line, 10 mi. W of Middlesboro; bituminous coal.
Fondi (fôn'dē), anc. *Fundi*, town (pop. 11,480), Latina prov., Latium, S central Italy, 13 mi. NW of Gaeta, in citrus-fruit region; canned foods, citrus extracts, matches. Town, including its Gothic cathedral (13th-14th cent.), palace (1466–77), 15th-cent. castle, and Dominican convent in which St. Thomas Aquinas taught, was badly damaged by air bombing (1943–44) in Second World War. L. Fondi (□ 2), a marshy, narrow coastal lake, used for fishing, is 4 mi. SW.
Fondo (fôn'dô), village (pop. 1,478), Trento prov. Trentino–Alto Adige, N Italy, 16 mi. WSW of Bolzano; resort (alt. 3,241 ft.).
Fondón (fōndōn'), town (pop. 1,278), Almería prov., S Spain, 11 mi. NE of Berja; olive oil, grapes, cereals. Iron and lead mines in near-by Sierra de Gádor.
Fondouk (fôndŏŏk'), village (pop. 1,606), Alger dept., N central Algeria, 17 mi. SE of Algiers, in E part of Mitidja plain irrigated by the Oued Hamiz (dam 3 mi. S, 148 ft. high); citrus groves, vineyards; perfume plants.
Fondouk-Djedid (–jĕdēd'), village, Grombalia dist., NE Tunisia, on railroad and 17 mi. SE of Tunis; winegrowing center. Olive groves. Camp-Servière (a military post) near by.
Fond-Parisien (fō-pärēzyē'), village, Ouest dept., S Haiti, on S shore of the Étang Saumâtre, 22 mi. E of Port-au-Prince; sugar cane, coffee, fruit.
Fonds-Saint-Denis (fō-sē-dùnē'), town (pop. 461), NW Martinique, 9 mi. NNW of Fort-de-France; rum distilling.
Fond-Verrettes (fō-vĕrĕt'), village (1950 pop. 480), Ouest dept., SE Haiti, near Dominican border, 30 mi. ESE of Port-au-Prince; coffeegrowing.
Fonelas (fōnā'läs), village (pop. 1,764), Granada prov., S Spain, 8 mi. NNW of Guadix; sugar beets, esparto, olive oil, cereals.
Fongshing, China: see FANGCHENG, Kwangtung.
Fonni (fôn'nē), village (pop. 4,844), Nuoro prov., central Sardinia, 15 mi. SSW of Nuoro. Numerous nuraghi near by.
Fonsagrada (fōnsägrä'dhä), town (pop. 887), Lugo prov., NW Spain, 26 mi. ENE of Lugo; flour mills; wine, fruit, lumber, livestock.
Fonseca (fōnsā'kä), town (pop. 1,722), Magdalena dept., N Colombia, at E foot of Sierra Nevada de Santa Marta, on Ranchería R. and 45 mi. S of Ríohacha; rice, stock. Copper deposits near by.
Fonseca, Gulf of, sheltered inlet (□ c.700) of the Pacific, in Central America, shared by Salvador, Honduras, and Nicaragua; 13°15'N 87°45'W; 20 mi. wide (at mouth) bet. Amapala and Cosigüina points. Receives Goascorán and Choluteca rivers, the Río Negro and the Estero Real. Low mangrove coasts. Main ports are La Unión (Salvador), Amapala (on Tigre Isl.; Honduras), and Puerto Morazán (on the Estero Real; Nicaragua). Discovered 1522.
Fontaine (fōtĕn'). **1** Agr. village (pop. 260), Territory of Belfort, E France, 7 mi. ENE of Belfort. **2** Outer W suburb (pop. 7,034) of Grenoble, Isère dept., SE France; leather tanning (for glove mfg.), mfg. of road-building machinery, saws, buttons, biscuits, and toothpaste. Iron foundries.
Fontainebleau (fŏn'tùnblō, Fr. fōtĕnblō'), town (pop. 13,498), Seine-et-Marne dept., N central France, near left bank of the Seine, 35 mi. SSE of Paris, in the midst of Forest of Fontainebleau; popular spring and autumn resort; cabinetmaking, metalworking, grape shipping. Has American art school. Long a royal residence (especially because of forest's excellent hunting grounds). Philip IV and Louis XIII b. here. Francis I built the magnificent Fr. Renaissance palace, later expanded by Henry IV. Abandoned as chief royal residence with construction of Versailles under Louis XIV, it still witnessed important historical events: here Louis XIV signed (1685) revocation of Edict of Nantes and Napoleon signed (1814) his first abdication. Pope Pius VII imprisoned here 1812–14. In 1949, it became military hq. of Western European Nations. The **Forest of Fontainebleau** (□ 66), bounded by the Seine (NE) and the Loing (E), extends 19 mi. from Melun (N) to Nemours (S), and is considered France's finest, with beautiful stands of oak and pine trees, and numerous odd-shaped sandstone outcroppings.
Fontaine-de-Vaucluse (fōtĕn'-dù-vōklüz'), village (pop. 556), Vaucluse dept., SE France, at W foot of Monts de Vaucluse, 16 mi. E of Avignon; paper mill. Known as the residence of Petrarch (mus.). The near-by "fountain," celebrated by him, is the source of Sorgue R. Until 1946, village was named Vaucluse.
Fontaine-Française (–frāsĕz'), agr. village (pop. 692), Côte-d'Or dept., E central France, 21 mi. NE of Dijon; dairying.
Fontaine-le-Dun (–lù-dū'), village (pop. 507), Seine-Inférieure dept., N France, 13 mi. SW of Dieppe; sugar-beet processing.
Fontaine-les-Grès (–lā-grĕ'), village (pop. 150), Aube dept., NE central France, 12 mi. NW of Troyes; hosiery mill.
Fontaine-lès-Luxeuil (–lā-lüksû'ē), village (pop. 1,308), Haute-Saône dept., E France, 14 mi. NW of Lure; paper mill, foundry.
Fontaine-l'Évêque (–lāvĕk'), town (pop. 8,443), Hainaut prov., S central Belgium, 6 mi. W of Charleroi; coal mining; mfg. (wire, nails).
Fontaines-sur-Saône (–sür-sōn'), village (pop. 1,592), Rhône dept., E central France, on the Saône and 6 mi. N of Lyons; textile printing and dyeing, chemical mfg.

Fontaine-Valmont (-välmõ'), village (pop. 937), Hainaut prov., S Belgium, on Sambre R. and 12 mi. SW of Charleroi; market center for sugar-beet area. Commune center of Sars-la-Buissière (pop. 808) is just N.

Fontana (fõntä'nä), town (pop. estimate 300), SE Chaco natl. territory, Argentina, on railroad and 5 mi. NW of Resistencia; agr. (cotton, peanuts, corn, citrus fruit); quebracho processing.

Fontana (fŏntă'nü). **1** Village (1940 pop. 4,523), San Bernardino co., S Calif., 9 mi. W of San Bernardino; large steel mill, including blast and open-hearth furnaces, hot strip and pipe mills. Fruit-packing plants, poultry hatcheries, winery. Has U.S. rabbit experiment station. Rabbit, poultry ranches. **2** City (pop. 168), Miami co., E Kansas, 10 mi. S of Paola, near Marais des Cygnes R., in stock-raising and general agr. region. **3** Resort village (pop. 726), Walworth co., SE Wis., at W end of L. Geneva, 23 mi. ESE of Janesville; boatbuilding.

Fontana, Lake (fõntä'nä) (□ 30.5; alt. 2,965 ft.), in the Andes, NW Comodoro Rivadavia military zone, Argentina, just N of 45°S, near Chile border; extends 15 mi. ESE (1–4 mi. wide) from Lago de la Plata, with which it is linked by 2-mi.-long channel. Outlet: Senguerr R.

Fontana Dam (fŏntă'nü), Graham and Swain counties, W N.C., in Little Tennessee R. above Cheoah Dam, 10 mi. N of Robbinsville. A major TVA dam (480 ft. high, 2,365 ft. long, for flood control and hydroelectric power, completed 1945). Impounds Fontana Reservoir (□ c.16.7; capacity 1,444,300 acre-feet), extending 22 mi. E to Bryson City; receives Nantahala and Tuckasegee rivers. On Graham co. side of dam is Fontana Dam village, also called Fontana Village, formerly the home of construction workers and now a popular resort.

Fontanafredda (fôntä"näfrĕd'dä), village (pop. 906), Udine prov., Friuli-Venezia Giulia, NE Italy, 3 mi. ENE of Sacile.

Fontanarejo (fõntänärä'hō), town (pop. 871), Ciudad Real prov., S central Spain, 35 mi. WNW of Ciudad Real; cereals; goats, cattle.

Fontanarosa (fôntä"närô'zä), village (pop. 2,347), Avellino prov., Campania, S Italy, 14 mi. NE of Avellino.

Fontana Village, N.C.: see FONTANA DAM.

Fontanella (fôntänĕl'lä), village (pop. 2,591), Bergamo prov., Lombardy, N Italy, 11 mi. SE of Treviglio; silk mill.

Fontanellato (fôntänĕl-lä'tô), village (pop. 1,092), Parma prov., Emilia-Romagna, N central Italy, 9 mi. WNW of Parma; canned foods. Has castle with frescoes by Parmigiano.

Fontanelle (fŏntünĕl'), town (pop. 812), Adair co., SW Iowa, 19 mi. NW of Creston; grain, poultry, livestock, dairy farms; feed milling.

Fontanetto da Po (fôntänĕt'tô dä pô'), village (pop. 2,078), Vercelli prov., Piedmont, N Italy, near Po R., 14 mi. SW of Vercelli. Also Fontanetto Po.

Fontarabie, Spain: see FUENTERRABÍA.

Fonte (fôn'tĕ), village (pop. 3,370), Treviso prov., Veneto, N Italy, 6 mi. E of Bassano; woolen mills, lye factory.

Fonte Boa (fõn'tĭ bō'ü), city (pop. 778), W central Amazonas, Brazil, steamer and hydroplane landing on right bank of the Amazon, and 400 mi. W of Manaus; rubber, Brazil nuts. Missionary settlement.

Fontenay-aux-Roses (fõtünā'-ō-rōz'), residential town (pop. 7,166), Seine dept., N central France, a SSW suburb of Paris, 5 mi. from Notre Dame Cathedral; truck and flower gardens; mfg. (clocks, combs). Teachers col.

Fontenay-le-Comte (-lü-kōt'), town (pop. 8,139), Vendée dept., W France, on Vendée R. and 19 mi. NW of Niort; road center; cloth bleaching and dyeing; woodworking. Has a 16th-cent. Renaissance castle and picturesque old houses. A prosperous town in 16th-17th cent., it figured prominently in Wars of Religion. Was ⊙ Vendée dept., 1790–1806.

Fontenay-sous-Bois (-sōō-bwä'), town (pop. 30,225), Seine dept., an E suburb of Paris, 6 mi. from Notre Dame Cathedral, just E of Vincennes; mfg. (furniture, electrical equipment, hardware, pharmaceuticals). Has flamboyant Gothic church with 13th-cent. tower.

Fontenoy (fõtünwä'), village (pop. 759), Hainaut prov., W Belgium, 5 mi. SE of Tournai. Monument commemorates famous battle here (1745), where, in War of the Austrian Succession, French under Marshal Saxe defeated British and their allies under duke of Cumberland.

Fontenoy (fŏn'tünoi, fõtünwä'), village (pop. 116), Yonne dept., N central France, 16 mi. SW of Auxerre. An obelisk commemorates victory (841) of Charles II of France and Louis the German over Emperor Lothair I, their elder brother. Sometimes referred to as battle of Fontenay, Fontanet, or Fontenailles.

Fontenoy-le-Château (fõtünwä'-lü-shätō'), village (pop. 839), Vosges dept., E France, on the Canal de l'Est and 18 mi. SW of Épinal; metalworking, brewing.

Fontes (fõn'tĭsh), hydroelectric plant, SW Rio de Janeiro state, Brazil, on the Ribeirão das Lajes, 5 mi. S of Piraí. Opened in 1907, it supplies Rio de Janeiro city and Volta Redonda with electricity. The Forçacava subterranean hydroelectric plants are near by.

Fontes (fõn'tĭsh), village (pop. 1,139), Vila Real dist., N Portugal, 6 mi. SW of Vila Real; vineyards (port wine).

Fontevivo (fôntĕvē'vô), village (pop. 615), Parma prov., Emilia-Romagna, N central Italy, 9 mi. WNW of Parma; fertilizer. Oil wells near by.

Fontevrault or **Fontevrault-l'Abbaye** (fõtüvrō'-läbā'), village (pop. 1,200), Maine-et-Loire dept., W France, 10 mi. SE of Saumur; vineyards. Site of a well-known Benedictine abbey founded in 1099 and noted for being the only mixed monastic community under the rule of a long line of abbesses. The 12th-cent. church contains remains of early Plantagenet kings. After Fr. Revolution the abbey became a penitentiary, but the historic sites have been preserved and restored.

Fontgombault (fõgōbō'), village (pop. 173), Indre dept., central France, on the Creuse and 4 mi. NW of Le Blanc, known for its 11th-cent. abbey, now occupied by a seminary. Has large 11th-12th-cent. Romanesque church.

Fonthill, village (pop. 1,000), S Ont., 5 mi. NNW of Welland; dairying, fruitgrowing.

Fontibón (fõntēbōn'), town (pop. 4,333), Cundinamarca dept., central Colombia, in Cordillera Oriental, 7 mi. NW of Bogotá, in agr. region (corn, wheat, potatoes, fruit, stock); alt. 8,451 ft. Techo airport near by serves Bogotá. Old colonial town.

Fontiveros (fõntēvā'rōs), town (pop. 1,382), Ávila prov., central Spain, 24 mi. NW of Ávila; wheat, barley, grapes, carobs, chick-peas, vetch, beans, sheep. Flour milling; limekilns. St. John of the Cross b. here (1542).

Fontoy (fõtwä'), Ger. *Fentsch* (fĕnch), town (pop. 1,910), Moselle dept., NE France, W of Thionville, in iron-mining dist.; blast furnaces, forges.

Font-Romeu (fõ-rômû'), winter-sports center, Pyrénées-Orientales dept., S France, in Cerdagne, 7 mi. NE of Puigcerdá; alt. 5,900 ft. Luxurious hotels, sanatorium.

Fontvieille (fõvyā'), village (pop. 1,764), Bouches-du-Rhône dept., SE France, at SW foot of the Alpines, 5 mi. NE of Arles; stone quarries and bauxite deposits near by. Here is the mill in which Alphonse Daudet wrote his *Lettres de mon moulin*.

Fonuafoo (fō'nōōäfōō') or **Falcon Island**, former volcanic island, Tonga, S Pacific; 20°19'S 171°25'W. Emerged 1885 as result of volcanic eruption, disappeared 1894, reappeared 1927, disappeared 1949.

Fonualei (fōnōōälā), uninhabited island, N Tonga, S Pacific; 40 mi. NW of Vavau; rises to 600 ft.; active volcano.

Fonyod (fô'nyōd), Hung. *Fonyód*, resort town (pop. 2,333), Somogy co., SW Hungary, on S shore of L. Balaton and 28 mi. NNW of Kaposvar.

Fonz (fōnth), town (pop. 1,510), Huesca prov., NE Spain, 7 mi. ESE of Barbastro; olive-oil processing; wine, sugar beets, cereals. Medieval castle.

Fonzaso (fôntsä'zô), village (pop. 2,388), Belluno prov., Veneto, N Italy, 22 mi. WSW of Belluno; alcohol distillery.

Foochow, Fuchow, or **Fu-chou** (all: fōō'chou', Mandarin fōō'jō'), city (1948 pop. 331,273), ⊙ Fukien prov., China, on left bank of Min R. 35 mi. from its mouth, and 380 mi. SSW of Shanghai; 26°7'N 119°20'E. Major commercial and industrial center; mfg. of bamboo, paper, leather, silk and cotton fabrics, lacquer ware; sugar milling. Exports timber, bamboo shoots, sugar cane, paper umbrellas, tea, camphor, fruit. Seat of Fukien Christian Univ. (1921), medical col., and col. for women. The walled city of Foochow lies 2 mi. from the river. Its commercial riverside suburb (S) is linked by the 440-yard-long Bridge of Ten Thousand Ages (on low granite pillars) with Nantai (or Nan-t'ai), the former foreign settlement and business center. Large vessels, barred by harbor silting, dock and transship their goods at the PAGODA anchorage, 15 mi. downstream. Near it is MAMOI naval base. In the near-by hills, surrounding Foochow as an amphitheater, are beautiful pagodas and monasteries, as well as the summer resort of KULIANG. The city dates from the Tang dynasty (A.D. 618–906); it was visited by Marco Polo on his return voyage and called Fugiu. Following the Opium War, it was one of the original ports opened (1842) to foreign trade and developed rapidly as China's leading tea-exporting center, shipping the noted black bohea tea. River silting and the decreasing demand for Fukien tea caused Foochow to decline. Although blockaded during the Sino-Japanese War, Foochow was one of the few Chinese ports not continuously held by the Japanese: it was briefly occupied in 1941 and again in 1944–45. Passed to Communists in 1949. It was known as Minhow (mĭn'hō'), 1934–43.

Foothills, village, W Alta., in Rocky Mts., near Jasper Natl. Park, 40 mi. SSW of Edson; coal mining.

Footscray (fŏŏts'krā'), municipality (pop. 53,459), S Victoria, Australia, 4 mi. W of Melbourne, in metropolitan area; ammunition plant. Also produces glucose, starch.

Foot's Cray, England: see SIDCUP.

Footville, village (pop. 562), Rock co., S Wis., 9 mi. W of Janesville; farm trade center; makes condensed milk.

Foping or **Fo-p'ing** (fŭ'pĭng'), town (pop. 503), ⊙ Foping co. (pop. 15,050), SW Shensi prov., China, 60 mi. NE of Nancheng, in Tsinling mtn. region; rice, wheat, beans, tea, cotton.

Forada (fôrā'dü, fü-), village (pop. 89), Douglas co., W Minn., 7 mi. S of Alexandria, in lake region; grain.

Foraker (fôr'ākür), town (pop. 105), Osage co., N Okla., 19 mi. NW of Pawhuska.

Foraker, Mount (fô'rükür) (17,280 ft.), S central Alaska, in Alaska Range, in Mt. McKinley Natl. Park, 130 mi. NNW of Anchorage; 62°57'N 151°27'W.

Forbach (fôrbäk', Ger. fôr'bäkh), town (pop. 7,897), Moselle dept., NE France, near Saar border, 33 mi. ENE of Metz, and 6 mi. SW of Saarbrücken; commercial center at S edge Saar coal basin. Mfg. (mining equipment, metal shoring, paper). Ruined feudal castle atop Schlossberg (c.1,000 ft.) overlooks town.

Forbach (fôr'bäkh), village (pop. 2,535), S Baden, Germany, in Black Forest, on the Murg and 14 mi. SSE of Rastatt; large hydroelectric station. Paper milling, woodworking. Climatic health resort (alt. 994 ft.) and tourist center.

Forbes, municipality (pop. 5,949), S central New South Wales, Australia, on Lachlan R. and 190 mi. WNW of Sydney; dairying center; wool, wheat, wine.

Forbes, village (pop. 204), Dickey co., S N.Dak., 11 mi. WSW of Ellendale, at S.Dak. line.

Forbes, Mount (11,902 ft.), SW Alta., near B.C. border, in Rocky Mts., in Banff Natl. Park, 75 mi. NW of Banff; 51°52'N 116°56'W.

Forbesganj (fôrbz'günj), town (pop. 8,787), Purnea dist., NE Bihar, India, 38 mi. NNW of Purnea, near Nepal border; frontier trade center (rice, jute, corn, tobacco, wheat, sugar cane).

Forbidden City, China: see PEKING.

Forbidden City, Tibet: see LHASA.

Forçacava (fōōrsükä'vü), 2 subterranean hydroelectric power plants, SW Rio de Janeiro state, Brazil, adjoining Fontes plant of Ribeirão das Lajes reservoir, 5 mi. S of Piraí. Fed by SANTANA reservoir via Vigário tunnel.

Forcados (fōrkä'dōs), town (pop. 3,001), Warri prov., Western Provinces, S Nigeria, port on Forcados R., near Bight of Benin, and 20 mi. WSW of Warri; palm-oil processing; hardwood, rubber, cacao. Has marine dockyard and hosp. Principal port of Nigeria until rise of Lagos after 1908.

Forcados River, W delta arm of Niger R., S Nigeria; leaves main course of the Niger near Patani, flows c.70 mi. W, past Patani, Burutu, and Forcados, through rich oil-palm area, to Gulf of Guinea 15 mi. below Forcados. Navigable for ocean-going ships in lower course.

Forcall (fôrkäl'), town (pop. 1,286), Castellón de la Plana prov., E Spain, 29 mi. S of Alcañiz; woolen milling; mfg. of dyes and sandals; lumbering.

Forcalquiers (fôrkälkyā'), village (pop. 1,712), Basses-Alpes dept., SE France, 25 mi. SW of Digne; road junction and rail branch terminus; agr. trade (cocoons, truffles, almonds, honey); lavender distilling. Has 12th–13th-cent. church (former cathedral).

Forchheim (fôrkh'hīm). **1** Village (pop. 3,646), N Baden, Germany, after 1945 in Württemberg-Baden, 4 mi. SW of Karlsruhe; textile mfg. Site of tobacco-research institute. **2** City (1950 pop. 16,533), Upper Franconia, N central Bavaria, Germany, on the Regnitz at mouth of Wiesent R., port on Ludwig Canal and 15 mi. SSE of Bamberg; rail junction; mfg. of lace trimmings, paper, chemicals; metalworking, tanning. Has Gothic church; former episcopal residence (after 2d half of 14th cent.) with local mus.; 14th–16th-cent. city hall; Nuremberg Gate (1698). First mentioned in 741; seat of numerous diets in 2d half of 9th cent. Louis the Child and Conrad I chosen king of Germany here. Belonged to bishop of Bamberg from 1007 until 1803. Three times unsuccessfully besieged by Swedes in Thirty Years War. Fortifications razed in 1838. Chartered 1889.

Forchies-la-Marche (fôrshē'-lä-märsh'), town (pop. 6,835), Hainaut prov., S central Belgium, 6 mi. WNW of Charleroi; coal mining.

Forchtenau (fôrkh'tünou), Hung. *Fraknó* (fräk'nô), village (pop. 1,256), Burgenland, E Austria, 12 mi. E of Neunkirchen; cherry and chestnut trees. Near by is castle Forchtenstein.

Forchtenberg (fôrkh'tünbĕrk), town (pop. 970), N Württemberg, Germany, after 1945 in Württemberg-Baden, on the Kocher and 18 mi. NE of Heilbronn; grain. Has medieval fortifications and castle.

Forclaz, Col de la (kôl dü lä fôrklä'), pass (5,020 ft.) in Pennine Alps, SW Switzerland, 4 mi. SW of Martigny-Ville; road over it leads from Martigny-Ville into France.

Ford, England: see SOUTH HYLTON.

Ford. **1** County (□ 488; pop. 15,901), E central Ill.; ⊙ Paxton. Agr. (corn, oats, soybeans, wheat, livestock, poultry); mfg. (cheese and other dairy products, canned foods, feed, clothing). Drained by Mackinaw R., North Fork of the Vermilion, and a headstream of the Sangamon. Formed 1859. **2** County (□ 1,083; pop. 19,670), SW Kansas; ⊙ Dodge City. Gently sloping prairie region, drained by Arkansas R. Grain, livestock. Formed 1873.

Ford, city (pop. 244), Ford co., SW Kansas, on Arkansas R. and 16 mi. ESE of Dodge City; grain, cattle.

Ford City. 1 Village (pop. 4,347), Kern co., S central Calif., just N of Taft, in oil fields. **2** Town (pop. 59), Gentry co., NW Mo., 32 mi. NE of St. Joseph. **3** Borough (pop. 5,352), Armstrong co., W central Pa., 4 mi. S of Kittanning and on Allegheny R.; glass products. Laid out 1871, inc. 1889.

Ford Cliff, borough (pop. 597), Armstrong co., W central Pa., 5 mi. S of Kittanning.

Forde (fûr'dù), Nor. *Førde*, village and canton (pop. 3,082), Sogn og Fjordane co., W Norway, at head of 15-mi. Forde Fjord (an inlet of North Sea), 28 mi. ESE of Floro. Agr. school near by. Copper mining in 18th cent.

Förderstedt (fûr'dùr-shtĕt), village (pop. 4,038), in former Prussian Saxony prov., central Germany, after 1945 in Saxony-Anhalt, 4 mi. NE of Stassfurt; lignite mining; cement mfg., lime processing.

Fordham, agr. village and parish (pop. 1,475), E Cambridge, England, 5 mi. N of Newmarket. Has 13th–14th-cent. church.

Fordham (fôr'dùm), SE N.Y., a W business district of the Bronx borough of New York city. Fordham Univ. is here.

Fordingbridge, town and parish (pop. 3,473), SW Hampshire, England, on Avon R. and 9 mi. S of Salisbury; agr. market. Has 13th–15th-cent. church.

Fordland, city (pop. 302), Webster co., S central Mo., in the Ozarks, 20 mi. E of Springfield; agr. (nuts).

Fordlândia (fôrdlăn'dyù), rubber plantation in W Pará, Brazil, on right bank of Tapajós R. and c.100 mi. SSW of Santarém. Original concession (□ 3,860) acquired by Ford in 1927. After poor initial results, part of concession was exchanged for BELTERRA (c.70 mi. N). Both plantations have now reverted to Brazilian ownership.

Fordon (fôr'dôn), town (pop. 3,514), Bydgoszcz prov., N central Poland, port on the Vistula, on railroad (here crosses river on 4,346-ft.-long bridge) and 7 mi. E of Bydgoszcz. Mfg. of paper, roofing materials, cement, tires; flour milling, sawmilling, spinning.

Fordongianus (fôrdônjä'nōōs), village (pop. 1,472), Cagliari prov., W central Sardinia, on Tirso R. and 13 mi. NE of Oristano. Thermal spring (140°F.), vast remains of anc. baths, amphitheater ruins here. Occupies site of Roman *Forum Traiani* (now 3 to 6 ft. below surface).

Fordoun (fŏrdōōn'), agr. village and parish (pop. 1,560), S central Kincardine, Scotland, 5 mi. N of Laurencekirk. Just N is market town of Auchinblae or Auchenblae (both: ŏkh"ùnblā'), with whisky distillery.

Ford River, SW Upper Peninsula, Mich., rises NE of Crystal Falls in Iron co., flows generally SE c.100 mi. to Green Bay 6 mi. SW of Escanaba.

Fords, industrial village in WOODBRIDGE township, Middlesex co., NE N.J., near Raritan R., 3 mi. NW of Perth Amboy; chemicals, plastics, bricks, metal products, clothing.

Fordsburg, W suburb of Johannesburg, S Transvaal, U. of So. Afr.

Fords Island, S Oahu, T.H., in Pearl Harbor; site of U.S. Luke Field (established 1919); bombed by Japanese (Dec. 7, 1941).

Fordson, Mich.: see DEARBORN.

Fordsville, town (pop. 533), Ohio co., W Ky., 24 mi. ESE of Owensboro, in agr., timber, coal area.

Fordville, village (pop. 376), Walsh co., NE N.Dak., 24 mi. SW of Grafton and on Forest R.; dairy and garden products, grain, poultry, potatoes.

Fordwick, industrial village, Augusta co., W Va., on Maury R. and 17 mi. WSW of Staunton; cement mfg.

Fordyce (fôrdīs', fôr'dīs), agr. village, N Banffshire, Scotland, near Moray Firth, 3 mi. SW of Portsoy.

Fordyce (fôr'dīs). **1** City (pop. 3,754), ⊙ Dallas co., S central Ark., 37 mi. SW of Pine Bluff. Railshipping and processing point for farm area (livestock, poultry, cotton, truck, fruit; dairy products); mfg. of wood products. **2** Village (pop. 165), Cedar co., NE Nebr., 7 mi. NW of Hartington, near Missouri R.

Forécariah (fōrākä'ryä), town (pop. c.4,350), W Fr. Guinea, Fr. West Africa, near coast, 40 mi. E of Conakry; bananas, rice, palm kernels, palm oil, copal gum, sesame, millet; cattle, sheep. Hematite deposits near by.

Forel, Mount (fōrĕl') (11,023 ft.), SE Greenland, near coast, at edge of inland icecap, near 66°55'N 36°45'W. Glacier de France extends 40 mi. SE to the sea.

Foreland. 1 Promontory, E point of Isle of Wight, Hampshire, England, on the Channel at entrance to the Spithead, 8 mi. S of Portsmouth; coastguard station. **2** Headlands of Kent, England: see NORTH FORELAND and SOUTH FORELAND.

Foreland Point, England: see LYNMOUTH.

Foreman, Ark.: see NEW ROCKY COMFORT.

Forenza (fôrĕn'tsä), town (pop. 5,360), Potenza prov., Basilicata, S Italy, 16 mi. N of Potenza, in agr. (cereals, grapes, olives) and livestock region.

Fore River, SW Maine, inlet of Casco Bay (with dredged channel) forming inner harbor and S boundary of Portland; receives Stroudwater R.; c.5 mi. long.

Forest (fôrā'), Flemish *Vorst* (vôrst), town (pop. 46,980), Brabant prov., central Belgium, 3 mi. SSW of Brussels; soap-mfg. center; cotton weaving.

Forest, town (pop. 1,570), S Ont., 22 mi. ENE of Sarnia; dairying, basket weaving, food canning, vinegar mfg.; fruit-, flax-growing region. Resort.

Forest, agr. village and parish (1931 pop. 1,117), Guernsey, Channel Isls., 3 mi. SW of St. Peter Port.

Forest, village (pop. 439), NW Tasmania, 105 mi. WNW of Launceston; dairying, sheep.

Forest. 1 County (□ 420; pop. 4,944), NW Pa.; ⊙ Tionesta. Forested region, drained by Allegheny R. (NW) and Clarion R. along part of S border. Settled by Moravian missionaries. Glass, leather, lumber; natural gas; recreation. Formed 1848. **2** County (□ 1,010; pop. 9,437), NE Wis., bounded partly N by Brule R. (on Mich. line); ⊙ Crandon. Most of co. is in Nicolet Natl. Forest, and contains Sugarbush Hill, highest point (1,951 ft.) in state, and many resort lakes. Lumbering, limited dairying and potato growing. There are 2 small Indian reservations. Formed 1885.

Forest. 1 Town (pop. 2,874), ⊙ Scott co., central Miss., 45 mi. W of Meridian, in Bienville Natl. Forest, with hq. here; pine and hardwood lumber, brooms, furniture; cotton ginning. **2** Village (pop. 1,114), Hardin co., W central Ohio, 12 mi. NNE of Kenton, in agr. area; farm equipment, motor vehicles, flour. Limestone quarry.

Forest Acres, town (pop. 3,240), Richland co., central S.C.; NE residential suburb of Columbia.

Forestburg, village (pop. 243), S central Alta., 45 mi. SE of Camrose; coal mining; agr.

Forest Cantons, Switzerland: see FOUR FOREST CANTONS, THE.

Forest City. 1 Village (pop. 278), Mason co., central Ill., 25 mi. SSW of Peoria, in agr. area. Mason State Forest is near by. **2** City (pop. 2,766), ⊙ Winnebago co., N Iowa, on Lime Creek and 23 mi. WNW of Mason City; canned foods (corn, pumpkin), packed poultry, meat products. Has Waldorf jr. col. State park near by. Platted 1856, inc. 1879. **3** Village, Washington co., E Maine, on Grand L. and 40 mi. NW of Calais; township (pop. 26) has hunting, fishing camps. **4** City (pop. 484), Holt co., NW Mo., on Missouri R. and 23 mi. NW of St. Joseph. **5** Town (pop. 4,971), Rutherford co., SW N.C., 18 mi. W of Shelby; cotton and lumber mills. Inc. 1895. **6** Borough (pop. 3,122), Susquehanna co., NE Pa., 6 mi. NNE of Carbondale and on Lackawanna R.; textiles, carpets; anthracite; agr. Laid out 1871. **7** Town (pop. c.350), Kitsap co., W Wash., just S of Port Orchard.

Forestdale. 1 Village, Barnstable co., Mass.: see SANDWICH. **2** Village, Providence co., R.I.: see NORTH SMITHFIELD.

Forester, town (pop. 818), Scott co., W Ark., c.45 mi. WNW of Hot Springs; sawmilling. U.S. wildlife preserve near by.

Forest Glen, residential village, Montgomery co., central Md., N suburb of Washington, on Rock Creek near D.C. line. A unit of Army Medical Center and a girls' school are here.

Forest Grove, city (pop. 4,343), Washington co., NW Oregon, 22 mi. W of Portland; lumber milling, dairying. Seat of Pacific Univ. Founded 1849, inc. 1872.

Forest Heights, town (pop. 1,125), Prince Georges co., central Md., S suburb of Washington, near the Potomac. Inc. 1949.

Forest Hill, residential town (pop. 11,757), S Ont., suburb of Toronto.

Forest Hill. 1 or **Forest Hills,** village (pop. 365), Rapides parish, central La., 19 mi. SW of Alexandria; lumber milling. Fishing, hunting near by. **2** Village (pop. 1,519), Tarrant co., N Texas, suburb just SE of Fort Worth. Inc. after 1940.

Forest Hills. 1 Village, Rapides parish, La.: see FOREST HILL. **2** A residential section of central Queens borough of New York city, SE N.Y. West Side Tennis Club here is scene of natl. and international matches. Some mfg. (leather and knit goods, stone products). **3** Borough (pop. 6,301), Allegheny co., SW Pa., E suburb of Pittsburgh. Inc. 1920.

Forestier Peninsula (fŏ'rùstyùr), SE Tasmania, in Tasman Sea, connected with Tasman Peninsula (S) by Eaglehawk Neck (narrow isthmus ¼ mi. long), with mainland (NW) by short neck of land; 12 mi. long, 9 mi. wide. Forms E and S shores of Blackman Bay and E shore of Norfolk Bay. Sawmills on W coast.

Forest Junction, village (pop. c.200), Calumet co., E Wis., 13 mi. ESE of Appleton; rail junction; barley growing.

Forest Lake, resort village (pop. 1,766), Washington co., E Minn., at W end of Forest L., 24 mi. NNE of St. Paul, in agr. area; dairy products, cattle feed, poultry.

Forest Lake, Washington co., E Minn., 24 mi. NNE of St. Paul; 4 mi. long, 1 mi. wide. Bathing and boating resorts.

Forest Lawn, village (pop. 646), S Alta., near Bow R., E suburb of Calgary.

Foreston (fŏ'rĭstùn). **1** Village (pop. 301), Mille Lacs co., central Minn., on branch of Rum R. and 25 mi. NE of St. Cloud; dairy products. **2** Town (1940 pop. 210), Clarendon co., E central S.C., 26 mi. SE of Sumter; turpentine.

Forest Park. 1 Town (pop. 2,653), Clayton co., N central Ga., 10 mi. S of Atlanta. **2** Residential village (pop. 14,969), Cook co., NE Ill., suburb just W of Chicago; some mfg. (Venetian blinds, file cabinets, cedar chests, burial vaults, feed, conduits); greenhouses. Veterans hosp. is near by. Inc. 1907. **3** Village (pop. 3,117), Will co., NE Ill.

Forest River, village (pop. 236), Walsh co., NE N.Dak., 15 mi. S of Grafton and on Forest R.

Forest River, NE N.Dak., rises in Walsh co., flows SE and E, past Minto, to Red River of the North; 90 mi. long.

Forest Row, town and parish (pop. 3,815), N Sussex, England, on Medway R. and 3 mi. SE of East Grinstead; agr. market.

Forest View, village (pop. 291), Cook co., NE Ill., W suburb of Chicago.

Forestville. 1 Village, Hartford co., Conn.: see BRISTOL. **2** Resort village (pop. 124), Sanilac co., E Mich., c.50 mi. N of Port Huron, on L. Huron. **3** Village (pop. 786), Chautauqua co., extreme W N.Y., 8 mi. E of Dunkirk; summer resort; canned foods, dairy products. **4** Village (pop. 2,197, with adjacent Primrose), Schuylkill co., E central Pa., 6 mi. W of Pottsville. **5** Village, Door co., NE Wis., on Door Peninsula, 11 mi. SSW of Sturgeon Bay, in dairying and fruitgrowing area.

Forêt, Baie de la (bĕ dù lä fôrĕ'), bay on Atlantic Ocean, Finistère dept., W France, c.10 mi. SE of Quimper; 3 mi. wide, 3 mi. long; shelters the port of Concarneau.

Forêt-lez-Chaudfontaine (fôrĕ'-lā-shōfōtĕn'), town (pop. 5,082), Liége prov., E Belgium, 4 mi. SE of Liége, near Vesdre R.; zinc smelting; chemical industry.

Forez (fōrā'), region and former county of SE central France, now in Loire and E Puy-de-Dôme depts.; ⊙ Feurs (until 1441), later Montbrison. It is wholly in the Massif Central. The **Monts du Forez** (W) extend c.45 mi. SSE–NNW along Puy-de-Dôme–Loire dept. border, from Vorey on the upper Loire to Saint-Just-en-Chevalet, where they merge with the BOIS NOIRS and the Montagnes de la MADELEINE. They rise to 5,380 ft. N of Ambert. The **Forez Plain,** a poorly drained oval-shaped Miocene lake bottom, lies E of Monts du Forez, bounded by Monts du Beaujolais (E) and Monts du Lyonnais (SE); 25 mi. long, 13 mi. wide; crossed S-N by Loire R. Recently drained, it has become a fertile agr. region (wheat, oats, sugar beets, wine, vegetables; pastures). Chief towns, located on periphery, are Montbrison, Feurs, Andrézieux (metalworks), Saint-Galmier, and Montrond-les-Bains (mineral springs).

Forfar, county, Scotland: see ANGUS.

Forfar (fôr'fûr), burgh (1931 pop. 9,659; 1951 census 9,981), ⊙ Angus, Scotland, in central part of co., 14 mi. NNE of Dundee, on E shore of small lake; agr. market, with jute and linen mills and biscuit factories. Town Cross (17th cent.) is on site of former royal castle taken by Robert the Bruce in 1308. Near by are remains of 12th-cent. Restenneth Priory, built by David I.

Forfarshire, Scotland: see ANGUS.

Forgan, parish (pop. 3,810, including NEWPORT burgh), NE Fifeshire, Scotland.

Forgan (fôr'gùn), town (pop. 410), Beaver co., extreme NW Okla., 6 mi. N of Beaver, in grain and livestock area.

Forgaria nel Friuli (fôgä'rēä nĕl frē'ōōlē), village (pop. 777), Udine prov., Friuli–Venezia Giulia, NE Italy, 16 mi. NW of Udine; hydraulic pumps. Formerly Forgaria.

Forges-les-Eaux (fôrzh-lāzō'), town (pop. 2,572), Seine-Inférieure dept., N France, 23 mi. NE of Rouen; resort with mineral springs. Important rail junction at Serqueux (1 mi. N).

Forges-lez-Chimay (–lā-shēmā'), village (pop. 929), Hainaut prov., S Belgium, 2 mi. S of Chimay; butter.

Forge Village, Mass.: see WESTFORD.

Forino (fôrē'nô), village (pop. 2,787), Avellino prov., Campania, S Italy, 5 mi. SW of Avellino.

Forio (fô'rēô), town (pop. 3,007), port on W coast of isl. of Ischia, Napoli prov., Campania, S Italy, 5 mi. W of Ischia. Resort with warm mineral baths.

Forked Deer River, W Tenn., formed 4 mi. SW of Dyersburg by junction of North and South forks; flows c.10 mi. SW to Obion R. near its mouth on the Mississippi. South Fork rises in McNairy co., flows c.100 mi. NW past Jackson, to join North Fork, which rises in Carroll co. and flows c.50 mi. W past Trenton and Dyersburg; receives Middle Fork (c.60 mi. long).

Forked Lake (fôr'kĭd) (□ c.2), N Hamilton co., NE central N.Y., irregularly shaped lake in resort region of the Adirondacks, just NE of Raquette L., to which it is joined by a stream.

Forked River (fôr′kĭd), village (1940 pop. 582), Ocean co., E N.J., near Barnegat Bay, 8 mi. S of Toms River village and on small Forked R. (navigable to village); boatbuilding; fishing. State yacht basin, ship-to-shore telephone receiving station here.

Forks, town (pop. 1,120), Clallam co., NW Wash., near Soleduck R. and Pacific coast, c.45 mi. WSW of Port Angeles. Inc. since 1940.

Fork Shoals, village, Greenville co., NW S.C., on Reedy R. and 16 mi. S of Greenville; textile milling.

Forksville, borough (pop. 145), Sullivan co., NE Pa., 30 mi. NE of Williamsport.

Fork Union, village, Fluvanna co., central Va., 22 mi. SSE of Charlottesville. Military acad. "Bremo" estate is just S, on the James near Bremo Bluff.

Forlì (fôrlē′), province (□ 1,126; pop. 444,528), Emilia-Romagna, N central Italy; ⊙ Forlì. Bordered by the Adriatic; largely mountainous, with fertile plain in N. Watered by Montone, Ronco, Savio, and Marecchia rivers. Historic Rubicon R. in E. Agr. (wheat, sugar beets, grapes, fruit); livestock raising. Fishing. Sulphur mining at Cesena, Mercato Saraceno, Perticara. Many bathing resorts (Rimini, Riccione, Cattolica, Cesenatico). Mfg. at Forlì, Rimini, Cesena.

Forlì, anc. *Forum Livii*, city (pop. 33,505), ⊙ Forlì prov., Emilia-Romagna, N central Italy, on Montone R. and 40 mi. SE of Bologna, on the Aemilian Way; 44°13′N 12°3′E. Agr. center; canned foods, wine, beet sugar; mfg. (shoes, felt, soap, majolica, paper); metal foundries. Bishopric. Has 14th-cent. citadel, cathedral, art gall., mus. Passed under papacy in 1504. Frequently bombed (1944) in Second World War, with destruction or heavy damage to over 700 houses and 15th-cent. church of San Biagio (destroyed).

Forlimpopoli (fôrlēmpô′pôlē), anc. *Forum Popilii*, town (pop. 2,353), Forlì prov., Emilia-Romagna, N central Italy, 5 mi. SE of Forlì; alcohol, fertilizer. Has 14th–15th-cent. castle.

Forlorn Point, Ireland: see CROSSFARNOGE POINT.

Forlovsholm (fûrlûfs′hôlm″), Swedish *Förlövsholm*, village (pop. 552), Kristianstad co., SW Sweden, near Skalder Bay of the Kattegat, 7 mi. N of Angelholm; grain, potatoes, stock.

Forman, town (pop. 466), ⊙ Sargent co., SE N.Dak., 23 mi. W of Lidgerwood.

Formby, residential urban district (1931 pop. 7,965; 1951 census 10,429), SW Lancashire, England, near the coast and Mersey R. estuary, 6 mi. SSW of Southport; market for dairying and agr. region. Has Formby Hall, a mansion of 14th-cent. origin. Here potatoes are said to have 1st been grown in England from seeds brought from America by Raleigh.

Formby, Tasmania: see DEVONPORT.

Formentera (fôrmĕntä′rä), islet (□ 37; pop. 3,392; 11 mi. long, up to 6 mi. wide) of the Balearic Isls., in the W Mediterranean, just S of Iviza. Flat in center; rolling terrain towards E, rising to 630 ft. Extensive saltworks in NW, based at San Francisco Javier. Also grows cereals, grapes, fruit; raises livestock. Partly covered by pine forests.

Formentor, Cape (fôrmĕntōr′), headland of N Majorca, Balearic Isls., at N entrance of Bay of Pollensa (Mediterranean), 40 mi. NE of Palma; 39°57′N 3°13′E. Lighthouse.

Formerie (fôrmürē′), village (pop. 1,197), Oise dept., N France, 22 mi. NW of Beauvais; market in butter-mfg. area.

Formia (fôr′myä), anc. *Formiae*, town (pop. 11,918), Latina prov., Latium, S central Italy, port on Gulf of Gaeta, 3 mi. NNE of Gaeta, in citrus-fruit region. Bathing resort; mfg. (agr. machinery, macaroni, wine, soap, matches, bricks). Has ruins of Roman villas. Severely damaged by air and naval bombing (1943–44) in Second World War. Formerly Mola di Gaeta.

Formiche, Punta delle (po͞on′tä dĕllĕ fôrmē′kĕ), point on SE tip of Sicily, 3 mi. SW of Pachino; 36°39′N 15°4′E.

Formiga (fo͝ormē′gů), city (pop. 9,010), S central Minas Gerais, Brazil, on railroad and 100 mi. WSW of Belo Horizonte; agr. trade center; flour milling, dairying; tobacco, cotton, and sugar processing.

Formigas Rocks (fo͝ormē′gůsh), group of rocks in Atlantic Ocean, projecting as much as 35 ft. from the sea in 37°16′N 24°46′W. They are the peaks of a submarine mtn. forming part of the Azores, 24 mi. NE of Santa Maria Isl.

Formigine (fōrmē′jēnĕ), town (pop. 1,924), Modena prov., Emilia-Romagna, N central Italy, 6 mi. SSW of Modena; wine, liquor, sausage, hats, tin boxes.

Formignana (fôrmēnyä′nä), village (pop. 371), Ferrara prov., Emilia-Romagna, N central Italy, 12 mi. E of Ferrara; canned fruit, liquor, hemp products.

Formigny (fôrmēnyē′), village (pop. 68), Calvados dept., NW France, 10 mi. WNW of Bayeux. Here French defeated (1450) British and drove them out of Normandy near end of Hundred Years' War.

Formigueiros (fōrmēgä′rōs), village (pop. 154), Lugo prov., NW Spain, 18 mi. NE of Monforte; iron mines.

Formosa (fōrmō′sä), national territory (□ 28,778; pop. 113,790), N Argentina, occupying the Chaco Central; ⊙ Formosa. Bounded by the parallel Pilcomayo (N) and Bermejo (S) rivers and by Paraguay R. (E). A hot, humid region with scrub forests yielding quebracho and other hardwoods. Some stock raising (cattle, horses, sheep) and agr. (cotton, corn, tobacco, sugar cane, peanuts, citrus fruit). Processing industries include meat packing, wine distilling, sugar refining, tanning, and lumbering, largely in the capital; also tannin extracting and dairying. A border dispute with Paraguay over the Estero Patiño (swamps along the Pilcomayo) was settled 1945, and a canalization program begun. Franciscans maintain several settlements in the territory.

Formosa, city (pop. 17,291), ⊙ Formosa natl. territory and Formosa dept. (□ c.2,300; pop. 30,859), Argentina, on Paraguay R., opposite Alberdi (Paraguay), on railroad and 575 mi. N of Buenos Aires, 70 mi. SSW of Asunción (Paraguay); 26°10′S 58°12′W. River port and agr. center for area producing tobacco, sugar cane, maté, livestock. Lumbering, tanning, meat packing, wine distilling, maté processing. Airport. Has administrative bldgs. and schools. Half the population is Indian.

Formosa (fo͝ormô′zů). **1** City (pop. 2,501), E Goiás, central Brazil, near Minas Gerais border, 110 mi. NE of Anápolis; cattle, hides, cotton, coffee, mangabeira rubber. Graphite deposits, gold placers. Airfield. **2** City, São Paulo, Brazil: see ILHABELA.

Formosa (fôrmō′sů) [Port.,=beautiful (island)], Chinese *Taiwan* or *T'ai-wan* (both: tī′wän′), Jap. *Taiwan* (tī′wän), island (□ 13,808) of Pacific Ocean, off SE China's Fukien coast (separated by Formosa Strait), forming with near-by islets, including the PESCADORES, a province (□ 13,886; 1950 pop. 7,617,753, including 160,000 aborigines) of China; ⊙ Taipei. Shaped like a tobacco leaf, Formosa extends 235 mi. N-S from Fukwei Point (25°18′N) to Cape Olwanpi (21°54′N) and 90 mi. E-W. It is traversed longitudinally by parallel slaty and schistose mtn. ranges, which occupy ⅔ of the total isl. area. Rising abruptly along the precipitous E coast, the mts. descend gradually toward the broad W alluvial coastal plain. The highest points are Mt. Morrison (13-14,000 ft.) and Mt. Sylvia (12,897 ft.), and there are about 70 peaks exceeding 10,000 ft. Rivers are precipitate in the upper mtn. gorges and sluggish in the coastal plain; the longest are Choshui, Tanshui, and Lower Tanshui rivers; the latter 2 are navigable in lower course. Jihyüeh (Sun-Moon) L. produces hydroelectric power. Situated astride the Tropic of Cancer, Formosa has a distinct tropical climate, with a hot, humid summer (April-Oct.) and a cooler, dry winter (Nov.-March). The isl. lies in the path of typhoons, which occur mainly during July-Sept. Formosa's coasts have few natural harbors, the best ones being Keelung, Kaohiung, and Suao. Reefs along the coasts render navigation difficult. Earthquakes are common. The extensive forests in the mtn. zone yield construction timber (oak, cypress, Japan cedar), camphor, and cork. Among the leading mineral resources are coal (mined near Keelung and Taipei), petroleum and natural gas (chief fields near Miaoli, Kinshui, and Chutung), gold and copper (Kinkwashih, Juifang), sulphur and salt. The isl. is an area of expanding agr. Rice, the dominant food crop, gives 2 harvests; sweet potatoes are another staple. Industrial crops, grown primarily for export, are sugar cane, bananas, pineapples, citrus fruit (oranges), and oolong tea. Formosa has a world monopoly in the production of natural camphor and camphor oil; jute and ramie are local fibers. Industry is concerned primarily with rice and sugar milling, pineapple canning, and other agr. processing. Cement (Kaohiung, Suao, Chutung) is exported. Metallurgical (mainly aluminum and ferroalloys) and chemical industries have developed in some of the larger industrial centers. Chief towns are, besides Taipei, the 2 main ports of Keelung and Kaohiung, and Tainan, Taichung, Kiayi, Sinchu, Changhwa, and Pingtung. Main towns on the less accessible E coast are Ilan, Lotung, Suao, Hwalien, and Taitung. The W coast centers are linked by 900 mi. of railroads and a dense network of sugar-plantation lines; on the E coast the only railroad links Hwalien and Taitung. The overwhelming majority of pop. is Chinese, speaking the Fukienese (Amoy) and Hakka dialects, and is settled primarily on the broad W plain where the highest pop. density (750 per sq. mi.) is found. About 70% of the pop. is engaged in agr. Primitive Malayan aborigines (2% of total pop.) inhabit the undeveloped mountainous interior. Earliest Chinese settlement of Formosa began in 7th cent., chiefly from the mainland provs. of Fukien and Kwangtung. The isl. was reached in 1590 by the Portuguese, who gave it its European name. In 1624, the Dutch founded forts in S at present Tainan and its Port, Anping, while the Spanish established bases in N at Tanshui and Keelung. The Dutch, however, succeeded in expelling the Spaniards in 1641, assuming control of the entire isl. They in turn were forced to abandon Formosa in 1662, when Koxinga, a general of China's Ming dynasty, fled here from the Manchus and established an independent kingdom. This fell to the Manchus in 1683. Chinese immigration increased and the Chinese soon outnumbered the aborigines, who were confined to the interior. The pop. had reached 3,500,000 when the isl. was ceded (1895) to Japan after the Sino-Japanese War. Under Japan's control the isl. was exploited for the benefit of the home economy, but was scarcely used for colonization by Japanese, who numbered 5% of the pop. at their peak influx. However, Formosa's economy was modernized and industrialized, railroads were built, and the large cities expanded. During the Second World War, Jap. air and naval bases (Keelung, Kaohiung, Kangshan) and industrial sites on Formosa were heavily bombed by U.S. planes. In accordance with the Cairo declaration of 1943 and the Potsdam Conference of 1945, Formosa was returned to China at the end of hostilities. In 1949, as the Chinese Communists gained complete control of the mainland, the Nationalist govt. of Chiang Kai-shek took refuge on the isl. The issue of Formosa's territorial status became a major issue among the great powers, further complicated (1950) by the intervention of China in the Korean war. Administratively, Formosa was divided (1945–50) into 11 cities (municipalities) and 8 counties; since 1950, it has 5 cities and 16 counties.

Formosa, Port. Guinea: see BIJAGÓS ISLANDS.

Formosa Strait, Chinese *T'ai-wan Hai-hsia* (hī′-shyä′), Jap. *Taiwan Kaikyo* (kī′kyō), arm of the Pacific Ocean, bet. China's Fukien coast and Formosa, and linking East and South China seas; 100 mi. wide at narrowest point. Chief ports are: Amoy, on mainland; and Tanshui, Anping (port of Tainan), and Kaohiung, on Formosa. Contains the Pescadores, and is situated in typhoon zone.

Formoso, city (pop. 271), Jewell co., N Kansas, 21 mi. NW of Concordia, in grain and stock area.

Fornacetta (fôrnächĕt′tä), village (pop. 894), Pisa prov., Tuscany, central Italy, near the Arno, 3 mi. W of Pontedera; machinery (agr., wine), nails.

Fornaka (fôrnäkä′), agr. village (pop. 703), Oran dept., NW Algeria, 12 mi. SSW of Mostaganem.

Fornalutx (fôrnälo͞och′), town (pop. 554), Majorca, Balearic Isls., 15 mi. NNE of Palma; olives, oranges, lemons, timber, sheep; flour milling, olive-oil pressing.

Fornebu (fôr′nůbo͞o), airport for Oslo, SE Norway, on Oslo Fjord, 5 mi. W of city center; 59°55′N 10°38′E. Chiefly used by short-distance services.

Fornells (fôrnāls′), village (pop. 548), Minorca, Balearic Isls., on spit of isl.'s N shore, 13 mi. NW of Mahón; lobster fishing.

Forney. 1 Mining town, Lemhi co., E Idaho, 26 mi. SW of Salmon, in Salmon River Mts.; copper and cobalt mining; ore shipped to refining plants at Garfield, Utah. **2** Town (pop. 1,425), Kaufman co., NE Texas, 17 mi. E of Dallas; trade point in agr. area (cotton, grains, poultry, truck). Settled 1872, inc. 1910.

Fornfelt, city (pop. 1,539), Scott co., SE Mo., near Mississippi R., 6 mi. S of Cape Girardeau, in agr. area.

Forno di Zoldo (fôr′nô dē zôl′dô), village (pop. 584), Belluno prov., Veneto, N Italy, 14 mi. N of Belluno; mfg. of agr. machinery.

Fornoli (fôr′nôlē), village (pop. 695), Lucca prov., Tuscany, central Italy, 1 mi. W of Bagni di Lucca; tanning extracts.

Fornos de Algodres (fôr′no͞osh dĭ älgō′drĭsh), town (pop. 1,188), Guarda dist., N central Portugal, near railroad, 21 mi. ESE of Viseu; agr. center in upper Mondego R. valley; dairying.

Fornosovo (fŭrnô′sůvů), town (1949 pop. over 500), central Leningrad oblast, Russian SFSR, on railroad (Novolisino station) and 12 mi. W of Tosno.

Fornovo di Taro (fôrnô′vô dē tä′rô), town (pop. 1,790), Parma prov., Emilia-Romagna, N central Italy, on Taro R., at mouth of Ceno R., and 13 mi. SW of Parma; rail junction; petroleum refinery. Oil wells near by. Has 11th-cent. Romanesque church.

Forres (fŏ′rĭz, –rĭs), burgh (1931 pop. 4,169; 1951 census 4,462), NE Moray, Scotland, on Findhorn R. and 12 mi. WSW of Elgin; agr. market; woolen milling, whisky distilling, fertilizer mfg. Town has many associations in history and legend. It was residence of several early Scottish kings, and is one of the places where Macbeth is reputed to have killed Duncan, whose palace was here. Forres was once notorious for witches; granite Witches' Stone marks site where they were burned. Sweno's Stone probably marks victory of Sweyn over Malcolm II. On near-by Cluny Hill is Nelson Tower (1807).

Forrest, county (□ 469; pop. 45,055), SE Miss.; ⊙ HATTIESBURG. Drained by Leaf R., Black Creek. Agr. (cotton, corn, truck), lumbering. Includes part of De Soto Natl. Forest. Formed 1908.

Forrest, village (pop. 1,040), Livingston co., E central Ill., 14 mi. SE of Pontiac, in agr. and bituminous-coal area.

Forrest City, city (pop. 7,607), ⊙ St. Francis co., E Ark., c.45 mi. WSW of Memphis, Tenn., at foot of Crowley's Ridge; trade and rail center for agr. area (peaches, cotton, sweet potatoes, corn, rice); timber. Cotton ginning and compressing, grist- and cottonseed milling, woodworking. U.S. soil-conservation project near by. Settled c.1868, inc. 1871.

Forrester Island (5 mi. long, 1 mi. wide), SE Alaska, in Alexander Archipelago, off SW Prince of Wales Isl., 50 mi. SSW of Craig; 54°48′N 133°32′W.

Forreston (fŏr′rŭstŭn), village (pop. 1,048), Ogle co., N Ill., 26 mi. WSW of Rockford, in rich agr. area; makes butter, cheese. Gravel pits.

Forrestville, village (pop. estimate 500), E Que., on the St. Lawrence, at mouth of Sault au Cochon R., and 32 mi. NW of Rimouski; lumbering, pulp milling, dairying. Airfield.

Forro (fôr′rō), Hung. *Forró,* town (pop. 1,508), Abauj co., NE Hungary, 20 mi. NE of Miskolc; distillery.

Fors (fôrs, fôsh), village (pop. 636), Kopparberg co., central Sweden, in Bergslag region, 5 mi. NE of Avesta; sulphuric-ore smelting.

Forsand, Norway: see DIRDAL.

Forsbacka (fôrs′bä″kä, fôsh′–), village (pop. 1,930), Gavleborg co., E Sweden, on Gavle R. and 4 mi. E of Sandviken; large iron- and steelworks.

Forserum (fôr′sürŭm″), village (pop. 1,783), Jonkoping co., S Sweden, 8 mi. SE of Jonkoping; stone quarrying, metal- and woodworking.

Forshaga (fôrs′hä″gä, fôsh′–), town (pop. 3,947), Varmland co., W Sweden, on Klar R. and 10 mi. N of Karlstad; paper mills, sulphite works, foundry.

Forssa (fōrs′sä), town (pop. 8,870), Häme co., SW Finland, 30 mi. WSW of Hameenlinna; rail terminus; cotton-milling center.

Forst, Czechoslovakia: see HOSTINNE.

Forst (fôrst). **1** Village (pop. 3,562), N Baden, Germany, after 1945 in Württemberg-Baden, 2 mi. NNW of Bruchsal; petroleum wells. Tobacco industry. **2** City (pop. 29,829), Brandenburg, E Germany, in Lower Lusatia, on left bank of the Lusatian Neisse and 75 mi. SE of Berlin, 14 mi. E of Cottbus; 51°44′N 14°40′E. Rail junction; woolen-milling center; mfg. of glass, machinery, chemicals; power station. Captured (April, 1945) by Soviet forces. A suburb, ZASIEKI, on right bank of the Lusatian Neisse was transferred (1945) to Polish administration. **3** Village (pop. 630), Rhenish Palatinate, W Germany, on E slope of Hardt Mts., 3 mi. SSE of Bad Dürkheim; wine.

Forstsee (fôrst′zā), small lake near NW shore of the Wörthersee, in Carinthia, S Austria, W of Klagenfurt. Higher by 525 ft. than the Wörthersee, its waters are used for hydroelectric works.

Forsvik (fôrs″vēk′, fôsh″–), village (pop. 616), Skaraborg co., S Sweden, on L. Bott, Swedish *Bottensjön* (bô′tŭn-shûn″) (5 mi. long, 2 mi. wide), on Gota Canal route, and 20 mi. W of Motala; pulp and lumber mills.

Forsyth (fôr′sīth, fôrsīth′). **1** County (□ 243; pop. 11,005), N Ga.; ⊙ Cumming. Bounded E by Chattahoochee R. Piedmont agr. (cotton, corn, hay, sweet potatoes, poultry) and lumber area. Formed 1832. **2** County (□ 424; pop. 146,135), N central N.C.; ⊙ Winston-Salem. In the piedmont; bounded W by Yadkin R. Largely agr. (tobacco, corn, hay, dairy products); timber (pine, oak). Mfg. at Winston-Salem and Kernersville; sawmilling. Formed 1849.

Forsyth. 1 City (pop. 3,125), ⊙ Monroe co., central Ga., 22 mi. NW of Macon, in farm area; mfg. of textiles, yarn, lumber; cotton ginning. Bessie Tift Col. here. Natl. wildlife refuge near by. Inc. 1822. **2** Town (pop. 354), ⊙ Taney co., S Mo., in the Ozarks, 8 mi. NE of Branson; resort, agr. Near by, Forsyth Dam in White R. impounds L. Taneycomo. **3** City (pop. 1,906), ⊙ Rosebud co., SE central Mont., on Yellowstone R. and 40 mi. WSW of Miles City; trading point for Tongue River Indian Reservation; livestock, grain, beets. Inc. 1904.

Forsyth Dam, Mo.: see WHITE RIVER.

Forsyth Island, Chile: see CHONOS ARCHIPELAGO.

Fort. For military posts not found here, see under following part of the name.

Fort, Czechoslovakia: see HOSTINNE.

Fort Abbas (ŭb-bäs′), town (pop. 1,167), Bahawalpur state, W Pakistan, in N Thar Desert, 70 mi. ESE of Bahawalpur, on rail spur; wheat; camel breeding.

Fort Adams, village, Wilkinson co., SW Miss., near the Mississippi, 33 mi. SSW of Natchez. Here were French mission (1698) and old Fort Adams (built 1798; traces remain).

Fort Albany, village, NE Ont., on small Albany Isl., in Albany R. near its mouth on James Bay; 52°14′N 81°37′W; Hudson's Bay Co. trading post. Established by the British before 1682, post alternated bet. Br. and Fr. possession until 1696; thereafter operated by Hudson's Bay Co.

Fort Aleksandrovski, Kazakh SSR: see FORT SHEVCHENKO.

Fortaleza (fôrtälä′sä), village, Pando dept., N Bolivia, on Beni R. and 90 mi. SW of Riberalta; rubber.

Fortaleza (fôrtŭlä′zŭ). **1** City (1950 pop. 213,604), ⊙ Ceará, NE Brazil, Atlantic port, 400 mi. NW of Recife; 3°44′S 38°32′W. Exports carnauba wax, oiticica oil, hides, cotton, coffee, sugar, castor beans, and rutile (mined in area). Industries include cotton milling, sugar refining, soap mfg. City is noted for handmade lace and carved woodwork. It is N terminus of railroad to Crato serving stock-raising interior; another railroad to Sobral (125 mi. W) is partially completed. Workshops. Airport. Open roadstead harbor (launch and lighter service bet. ships and mainland) now improved by new port works near Mucuripe Point (4 mi. E). Tropical climate with seasonal rainfall totaling 40 inches. City is modern, with wide avenues, park-like squares, and several skyscrapers. It has schools of law, pharmacy, business, and nursing, as well as a military institute, acad. of letters, historical and geographical society. Of several beaches, the Praia de Iracema is best known. Founded 1609 by the Portuguese as a fortress against Indian attacks. Occupied by Dutch (1637–54). Became ⊙ Ceará captaincy in 1810. Raised to status of city in 1823. Sometimes called Ceará by foreigners. **2** City, Minas Gerais, Brazil: see PEDRA AZUL.

Fort Amador (ă′mŭdōr), military reservation, Balboa dist., S Panama Canal Zone, S of Balboa on narrow peninsula flanking (E) Pacific entrance of the canal.

Fort Ancient State Memorial Park, SW Ohio, 6 mi. ESE of Lebanon and on Little Miami R. Includes Fort Ancient, large prehistoric earthwork fortification enclosing about 100 acres, containing burial mounds and village sites. Mound Builders Mus. contains pottery and other artifacts. Recreation facilities.

Fort Ann, village (pop. 463), Washington co., E N.Y., on Champlain division of the Barge Canal and 11 mi. NE of Glens Falls; makes athletic equipment.

Fort Apache (ŭpă′chē), town (pop. c.500), Navajo co., E central Ariz., in Fort Apache Indian Reservation, on White R. and 21 mi. SSW of McNary; Indian trading post, school, sanitarium. Established 1870 as military post.

Fort-Archambault (fôr′-ärshābō′), town, ⊙ Moyen-Chari region (□ 16,200; 1950 pop. 218,100), S Chad territory, Fr. Equatorial Africa, on Shari R. and 300 mi. SE of Fort-Lamy; foremost cotton center of Chad territory; cotton ginning, citrus plantations. Customs station. Has military camp, hosp., airport, R.C. and Protestant missions, trade school. Its vicinity is noted for abundance of wild game. Until 1946, in Ubangi-Shari colony.

Fort Atkinson. 1 Town (pop. 273), Winneshiek co., NE Iowa, on Turkey R. and 13 mi. SW of Decorah; creamery. In near-by state park is Fort Atkinson, built 1840–41 and partly restored. **2** City (pop. 6,280), Jefferson co., S Wis., on both banks of Rock R. and 30 mi. ESE of Madison; trade and shipping center for surrounding dairying area; mfg. (farm and creamery equipment, electrical fixtures, hosiery, canned foods, beer, sausage). L. Koshkonong is SW. Settled c.1836, inc. 1878. William D. Hoard began the *Hoard's Dairyman* here (1885).

Fort Augustus, agr. village, central Inverness, Scotland, at S end of Loch Ness, at mouth of Oich R., on Caledonian Canal, and 29 mi. SW of Inverness. A fort was established here 1716 for protection against the Highlanders after 1715 uprising, and reinforced 1730 by General Wade, who named it after William Augustus, duke of Cumberland. In 1876 bldgs. were occupied by Benedictine abbey.

Fort-Bayard, China: see SIYING.

Fort Bayard or **Bayard** (bī′ŭrd, bā′–), village (pop. 2,119), Grant co., SW N.Mex., in foothills of Pinos Altos Mts., 7 mi. E of Silver City; alt. c.6,100 ft. U.S. veterans hosp. here. Gold, silver, copper mines in vicinity. Pueblo ruins and Gila Natl. Forest near by. Inc. 1938.

Fort Beaufort (bō′fŭrt), town (pop. 8,024), SE Cape Prov., U. of So. Afr., on Kat R. and 40 mi. N of Grahamstown, at foot of Winterberg mts.; rail junction; agr. center (stock, dairying, citrus fruit). Has fort, built 1822, strategic center in Kaffir wars, 1837 and 1846.

Fort Bend, county (□ 867; pop. 31,056), S Texas; ⊙ Richmond. Drained by Brazos and San Bernard rivers. Large oil, natural-gas, sulphur production; agr. (cotton, rice, corn, truck, pecans, fruit); livestock (cattle, horses, sheep, hogs, goats, poultry). Formed 1837.

Fort Benning, Ga.: see COLUMBUS.

Fort Benton, city (pop. 1,522), ⊙ Chouteau co., N central Mont., on Missouri R. (at head of navigation) and 35 mi. NE of Great Falls; trade center in grain and livestock region. Founded as fur-trading post 1846, laid out 1865, inc. 1883. First reached by steamboat in 1859, it was supply point for gold prospectors and cattlemen; served during Indian wars, after 1870, as military outpost. Parts of trading post and blockhouse survive.

Fort Bidwell, village (pop. c.300), Modoc co., NE Calif., in Surprise Valley, 32 mi. NE of Alturas. Fort Bidwell Indian Reservation is here.

Fort Bragg, city (pop. 3,826), Mendocino co., NW Calif., on coast, c.140 mi. NNW of San Francisco; lumber milling (redwood); shipping point for dairy products, truck, fruit. Noyo (just S) is fishing port. Named for army post (established 1857) formerly here.

Fort Branch. 1 Town (pop. 1,944), Gibson co., SW Ind., 19 mi. N of Evansville, in agr. area; makes concrete blocks. **2** Village (1940 pop. 1,233), Logan co., SW W.Va., 3 mi. E of Logan, in coal-mining area.

Fort Bridger, village (pop. c.150), Uinta co., SW Wyo., on Blacks Fork and 30 mi. E of Evanston; alt. 6,657 ft. Original fort, now state park, here. Established as supply post (1843) by Jim Bridger, famous guide and trader; held by Mormons 1853–57. Later leased by Bridger to U.S. and used as fort until 1890.

Fort Calhoun (kălhōōn′), village (pop. 314), Washington co., E Nebr., 10 mi. N of Omaha and on Missouri R.; trade center for grain, livestock region. Stone monument in village park commemorates council held by Lewis and Clark with Indians.

Fort-Carnot (fôr′-kärnō′), town, Fianarantsoa prov., SE Madagascar, 40 mi. NW of Manakara; center of native trade; coffee plantations. Hosp.

Fort Caswell, summer resort, Brunswick co., SE N.C., on the Atlantic, at Cape Fear R. mouth, 2 mi. S of Southport.

Fort Charlet, Algeria: see DJANET.

Fort Charter, Southern Rhodesia: see CHARTER.

Fort Chimo (shēmō′), village, N Que., on Koksoak R., near its mouth on Ungava Bay; 58°9′N 68°18′W. A Hudson's Bay Co. post, it was 1st established here 1830. In region are rich iron deposits. Crystal I air base is 6 mi. SW.

Fort Chipewyan (chĭ″pŭwī′ŭn), trading post, NE Alta., on NW shore of L. Athabaska, opposite mouth of Athabaska R.; 58°43′N 111°9′W. Terminal of L. Athabaska navigation. Original Fort Chipewyan was built 1788 on SW shore of lake, 20 mi. ESE of site of present post, at instigation of Alexander Mackenzie, who made it the starting point of his voyages down Mackenzie R. to the Arctic Ocean (1789) and across the mts. to the Pacific (1792). Abandoned 1804 and replaced by present post, erected by the North West Co., operated by Hudson's Bay Co. since 1821. It became the trade and collecting center for the Mackenzie R. fur trade.

Fort Clayton, military reservation, Balboa dist., S Panama Canal Zone, on transisthmian railroad, near Miraflores locks, 4 mi. NW of Panama city.

Fort Cobb, town (pop. 665), Caddo co., W central Okla., 11 mi. W of Anadarko, and on Washita R., in farming area; cotton ginning, lumber milling.

Fort Collins, city (pop. 14,937), ⊙ Larimer co., N Colo., on Cache la Poudre R., E of Front Range, and 55 mi. N of Denver; alt. 5,100 ft. Trade and shipping center for livestock and irrigated sugar-beet region; mfg. (beet sugar, flour, dairy and meat products, bricks, tiles, woolen goods, machinery, beverages); fruit, grain, vegetables. City is hq. for Roosevelt Natl. Forest and seat of Colo. Agr. and Mechanical Col. Several diversion dams of Colorado–Big Thompson project in vicinity. Near-by are Fort Collins Mtn. Park and Lindenmier site, where prehistoric artifacts have been found. City settled (1864–1871) around military outpost, inc. 1883. Grew with growth of sugar-beet industry.

Fort Collinson, trading post, W Victoria Isl., SW Franklin Dist., Northwest Territories, on Walker Bay, inlet of Prince of Wales Strait; 71°35′N 117°49′W. At present unoccupied.

Fort Conger, locality, NE Ellesmere Isl., NE Franklin Dist., Northwest Territories, on Robeson Channel, opposite Greenland coast, at mouth of Lady Franklin Bay; 81°43′N 64°43′W; site of meteorological station established 1881–83 by A. W. Greely.

Fort Coulonge (kōōlōzh′), village (pop. 1,072), SW Que., on Ottawa R. at mouth of Coulonge R., and 18 mi. E of Pembroke; dairying, cattle raising. Founded 1680 as fur-trading post.

Fort Covington (kŏ′vĭngtŭn, kŭ′–), village (pop. 891), Franklin co., N N.Y., on Salmon R., at Que. line, and 14 mi. NW of Malone; port of entry.

Fort-Crampel (fôr′-krăpĕl′), village, central Ubangi-Shari, Fr. Equatorial Africa, on Gribingui R. and 80 mi. N of Fort-Sibut; cotton ginning. Has a trypanosomiasis center, R.C. and Protestant missions.

Fort Creve Coeur State Park, Ill.: see CREVE COEUR.

Fort-Dauphin (fôr′-dōfĕ′), town (1948 pop. 6,896), Tuléar prov., SE Madagascar, 240 mi. SE of Tuléar; 24°40′S 47°40′E. Seaport of S Madagascar, exporting mica, castor beans, sisal, waxes, construction and cabinet woods, rice, corn, beans, peanuts, cattle, dried fish. Has R.C. and 2 Protestant missions, meteorological station, hosp., prophylactic institute. Seat of vicar apostolic. Airport. The cradle of Fr. colonization of Madagascar, earliest settlement dating from 1528.

Fort Davis, military reservation, Cristobal dist., N Panama Canal Zone, near Gatun, 5 mi. S of Colón. Sometimes Fort William Davis.

Fort Davis, village (1940 pop. 989), ⊙ Jeff Davis co., extreme W Texas, in Davis Mts., 20 mi. SSW of Marfa; alt. c.5,000 ft. Tourist center, trading point in cattle-ranching area. Near by are ruins of old Fort Davis (frontier post 1854–91), Davis Mts. State Park recreation area, and McDonald Observatory on Mt. Locke (10 mi. NW).

Fort de Chartres State Park, Ill.: see PRAIRIE DU ROCHER.

Fort Defiance. 1 Village (1940 pop. 645), Apache co., E Ariz., in Navajo Indian Reservation, near N.Mex. line, 25 mi. NW of Gallup, N.Mex.; former military post. **2** Village, Augusta co., W Va., 7 mi. NNE of Staunton. Military acad.

Fort-de-France (fôr-dů-frãs'), city (pop. 48,576; commune pop. 66,006), ⊙ Martinique, Fr. West Indies, port on landlocked Fort-de-France Bay (□ c.15), on isl.'s W coast, 270 mi. N of Port of Spain, Trinidad, and 415 mi. SE of San Juan, Puerto Rico; 14°37'N 61°4'W. Since destruction (1902) of Saint-Pierre, it has been the principal commercial and shipping center of the isl.; it is on a beautiful deepwater bay, where ocean vessels can dock alongside. Ships sugar cane, cacao, and rum in large volume. Also a coaling station; base for Fr. fleet in the West Indies. A picturesque town backed by verdant hills. Has old fortification and Schoelcher Library. Statue of Empress Josephine is on main square. Thermal springs in environs. Formerly called Fort-Royal.

Fort de Kock, Indonesia: see BUKITTINGGI.

Fort-de-l'Eau (fôr'-dů-lō'), town (pop. 3,888), Alger dept., N central Algeria, on Algiers Bay, 8 mi. ESE of Algiers; bathing resort; truck gardening, wine-growing.

Fort Deposit, town (pop. 1,358), Lowndes co., S central Ala., 30 mi. SW of Montgomery, in the Black Belt; lumber. Grew around fort built here c.1813 by Andrew Jackson.

Fort-de-Possel (fôr'-dů-pôsĕl'), village, S Ubangi-Shari, Fr. Equatorial Africa, on Ubangi R. opposite Pandu (Belgian Congo), near mouth of Kemo R. and 65 mi. NE of Bangui; cotton ginning.

Fort Dodge, city (pop. 25,115), ⊙ Webster co., central Iowa, on Des Moines R. and c.70 mi. NNW of Des Moines; railroad and industrial center in mining and agr. area; gypsum mills (plaster, wall-board), brick- and tileworks, soybean-processing factory, meat-packing plant, creameries. Mfg. also of farm equipment, veterinary supplies, feed, canvas products. Valuable gypsum bed is here; bituminous coal and clay also mined. Has jr. col. and art gall. Fort Clarke was established here 1850, named Fort Dodge (for Henry Dodge) 1851, abandoned 1853. Town laid out 1854, inc. 1869.

Fort Donelson National Military Park (dŏ'nulsun) (102.5 acres; established 1928), N Tenn., along Cumberland R. just NW of Dover. In Civil War, Federals led by Grant and assisted by gunboats on the Cumberland captured fort (Feb., 1862), following capture of Confederate Fort Henry (8 mi. W) on banks of the Tennessee; victory was important factor in Union conquest of Ky. and W Tenn. Besides fort, earthworks, and mus., park includes a natl. cemetery (15.3 acres; established 1867).

Fort Duchesne (dōōshĕn', dŭshĕn'), village (pop. c.100), Uintah co., NE Utah, 20 mi. SW of Vernal; hq. for Uinta and Ouray, Kaibab, Kanosh, Paiute, and Shivwits Indian reservations.

Fort Dufferin, Burma: see MANDALAY.

Fort Dunlop, NE industrial suburb of Birmingham, NW Warwick, England; automobile-tire center.

Forteau Bay (fôrtō'), inlet (6 mi. long, 4 mi. wide at entrance) of Strait of Belle Isle, SE Labrador; 51°27'N 56°55'W. On NE side of entrance is Amour Point. On W shore of bay is fishing settlement of Forteau (pop. 163).

Forte dei Marmi (fôr'tĕ dā mär'mē), town (pop. 5,971), Lucca prov., Tuscany, central Italy, on Ligurian Sea, 5 mi. S of Massa; bathing resort.

Fort Edward, village (pop. 3,797), Washington co., E N.Y., on the Hudson at its junction with Champlain division of the Barge Canal, and 2 mi. S of Hudson Falls; paper milling; mfg. of clothing, electrical equipment, feed, cigars. Fort built here in 1755 to protect portage bet. the Hudson and L. Champlain; it was occupied by Burgoyne in 1777. Inc. 1849.

Forte Príncipe da Beira (fôr'tĭ prēn'sēpĭ dä bā'rů), town, SW Guaporé territory, W Brazil, on right bank of Guaporé R. (Bolivia border) and 250 mi. S of Pôrto Velho; airfield. Has old fort, built 1776–83 against Indians. Also called Príncipe da Beira.

Fort Erie, town (pop. 6,993), S Ont., on Niagara R., opposite Buffalo; steel milling, gold refining; mfg. of aircraft, automobile parts, buses, electrical equipment, chemicals, pharmaceuticals, paint. Many U.S. firms have branch works here. Airport. Established 1764 as military post, fort was taken from the British by American forces in War of 1812; Americans here withstood siege (1814), later abandoning and destroying fort. Just N of Fort Erie, on Niagara R., at W end of International Bridge from Buffalo, is suburb of Bridgeburg, former town, merged 1932 with Fort Erie.

Forte Roçadas, Angola: see ROÇADAS.

Fortescue (fôr'tĭskū), town (pop. 117), Holt co., NW Mo., on Missouri R., at mouth of Tarkio R., and 30 mi. NW of St. Joseph.

Fortescue Bay, inlet in Brunswick Peninsula, S Chile, a good anchorage on Strait of Magellan; 53°42'S 72°W.

Fortescue River (fôr'tĕskū), NW Western Australia, rises in hills 100 mi. SSW of Nullagine, flows 340 mi. NE and WNW, through mountainous region, to Indian Ocean 75 mi. WSW of Roebourne; intermittent.

Forteventura, Canary Isls.: see FUERTEVENTURA.

Fortezza (fôrtĕ'tsä), Ger *Franzenfeste*, village (pop. 721), Bolzano prov., Trentino–Alto Adige, N Italy, on Isarco R. and 5 mi. NNW of Bressanone; rail junction. Has fortress built 1833–38 to guard Brenner Pass.

Fort Fairfield, town (pop. 5,791), including Fort Fairfield village (pop. 2,521), Aroostook co., NE Maine, on Aroostook R. and 10 mi. NE of Presque Isle; port of entry at N.B. line. Potato-growing center. Settled 1816, inc. 1858.

Fort Fitzgerald or **Fitzgerald,** village, NE Alta., near Northwest Territories border, on Slave R., N of L. Athabaska, and 20 mi. SE of Fort Smith; 59°52'N 111°37'W; Hudson's Bay Co. trading post; transshipment point for Great Slave L., linked with Fort Smith by 2 portage roads, by-passing Slave R. rapids.

Fort Flatters (flätâr'), Saharan outpost and caravan station, Saharan Oases territory, E central Algeria, at S edge of the Great Eastern Erg, 280 mi. SSE of Ouargla; 28°6'N 6°48'E. Junction of desert tracks from Ouargla, Ghadames (Fezzan; NE), Djanet (SE), and Tamanrasset (S). Formerly called Temassinin.

Fort-Foureau (fôr'-fōōrō'), town, Nord-Cameroun region, N Fr. Cameroons, on left bank of Logone R. at its confluence with the Shari, opposite Fort-Lamy (Fr. Equatorial Africa) and 115 mi. NNE of Maroua; pottery making, experimental nurseries, fishing. Hosp. Final defeat (1900) of Rabah el Zobeir, sultan of Bornu, opened to the French the way to native kingdoms of Chad area. Also known as Kousseri (kōōsĕ'rē).

Fort Frances. 1 Town (pop. 5,897), ⊙ Rainy River dist., W Ont., on Rainy R. (bridge), near Rainy L., opposite International Falls, Minn.; paper, pulp, and lumber milling; in dairying, gold-mining region. Hunting and canoeing center. Hydroelectric station. Founded 1821 as Hudson's Bay Co. post; inc. 1903. **2** Trading post, Yukon: see FRANCES LAKE.

Fort Franklin, trading post, W Mackenzie Dist., Northwest Territories, on W shore of Great Bear L., at outlet of Great Bear R., 60 mi. ENE of Fort Norman; 65°11'N 123°28'W; established 1932 on site of fort built 1799 by the North West Co. Winter hq. of Franklin expedition, 1825–27.

Fort Fraser, village, central B.C., on Nechako R., near E end of Fraser L., 75 mi. W of Prince George; lumbering. Trading post, established here 1806 by Simon Fraser for the North West Co., was burned in 1817 and later rebuilt. Taken over by the Hudson's Bay Co., it was closed down c.1900.

Fort Frederica National Monument, Ga.: see SAINT SIMONS ISLAND.

Fort Fred Steele, village (pop. c.50), Carbon co., S Wyo., on N.Platte R. and 15 mi. E of Rawlins; alt. 6,515 ft. Includes original buildings of fort built 1868 to protect travelers on Overland stage route.

Fort Gaines, city (pop. 1,339), ⊙ Clay co., SW Ga., 19 mi. SW of Cuthbert, on Chattahoochee R. (bridged; forms Ala. line here); agr. trade center; peanut shelling, sawmilling. Inc. 1830.

Fort Garland, agr. village (1940 pop. 621), Costilla co., S Colo., on Trinchera Creek, in San Luis Valley just W of Sangre de Cristo Mts., and 24 mi. E of Alamosa; alt. 7,996 ft. Established 1858 as military post and commanded (1866–67) by Kit Carson. Part of original fort still standing.

Fort Garry, Man.: see WINNIPEG.

Fort Gay, town (pop. 714), Wayne co., W W.Va., on Big Sandy R. (bridged) opposite Louisa, Ky., and 20 mi. SSW of Huntington, in agr. and bituminous-coal region.

Fort George, B.C.: see PRINCE GEORGE.

Fort George, fort, N Inverness, Scotland, on promontory in Moray Firth, opposite Rosemarkie, 10 mi. NE of Inverness. Built 1784, it is now base depot of Seaforth Highlanders regiment.

Fort George Island, Mauritius: see PORT LOUIS.

Fort George River or **Big River,** central and W Que., issues from Nichicun L., on St. Lawrence-Hudson Bay watershed, flows 520 mi. W to James Bay. Also called Rivière la Grande (rēvyâr' lä grãd'). Near its mouth is Fort George (53°50'N 79°W), a Hudson's Bay Co. post.

Fort Gibson, town (pop. 1,496), Muskogee co., E Okla., at confluence of Arkansas, Neosho, and Verdigris rivers, 9 mi. E of Muskogee. One of oldest settlements in state, founded 1824 as army post in preparation for coming of the Five Civilized Tribes; served as chief military center for Indian Territory until 1857. Old bldgs. of the fort (abandoned 1890) have been restored. Fort Gibson Natl. Cemetery (established 1868) is here. FORT GIBSON DAM is near by.

Fort Gibson Dam, E Okla., in Neosho R. c.5 mi. N of Fort Gibson; begun 1946 by U.S. Corps of Engineers for flood control and power, dam is 110 ft. high, 2,850 ft. long. At floodtime, max. reservoir capacity is 922,000 acre-ft., and area is 51,200 acres.

Fort Good Hope, village (district pop. 351), W Mackenzie Dist., Northwest Territories, on Mackenzie R. at mouth of Hare Indian R., and 90 mi. NW of Norman Wells; 66°15'N 128°38'W; fur-trading post; govt. radio and meteorological station, Royal Canadian Mounted Police Post; site of R.C. mission. Established here 1821. Low temp. of –79°F. was recorded here Dec., 1910.

Fort Gouraud or **Fort-Gouraud** (fôr'-gōōrō'), **Idjil,** or **Ijil** (ējēl'), village, W Mauritania, Fr. West Africa, near Río de Oro border, in Adrar mtn. region, on caravan trail, and 150 mi. N of Atar. Saltworks at adjoining (W) Sebkra de Idjil pan. Landing field. Iron deposits in vicinity.

Fort Greene Park, SE N.Y., a residential section of NW Brooklyn borough of New York city, near Wallabout Bay. Monument commemorates Prison Ship Martyrs who died in British hulks here during the Revolution. Brooklyn Acad. of Music and Brooklyn Inst. of Arts and Sciences are here. Navy Yard is N.

Fort Griffin, village, Shackelford co., N central Texas, 14 mi. N of Albany and on Clear Fork of Brazos R. State park here (recreation) includes restored Fort Griffin (1867–81), once a famous frontier post.

Fort Gulick (gū'lĭk), military reservation, Cristobal dist., N Panama Canal Zone, on Bolivar highway and 3 mi. SSE of Colón.

Forth, Firth of, Scotland: see FORTH RIVER.

Fort Hall, town (pop. c.2,000), S central Kenya, on railroad and 45 mi. NNE of Nairobi; alt. 4,050 ft. Agr. center; coffee, sisal, wheat, corn; dairying. Near by is a hydroelectric plant serving Nairobi and Fort Hall.

Fort Hall, village (pop. c.150), Bingham co., SE Idaho, 11 mi. N of Pocatello in valley of Snake R.; alt. 4,444 ft.; agency hq. for Fort Hall Indian Reservation (irrigated agr. area). Original Fort Hall (built 1834; important post on Oregon Trail) was near by on Snake R.

Fort Hamilton, SE N.Y., a residential section of Brooklyn borough of New York city. Here is U.S. Fort Hamilton (1831), on the Narrows opposite Fort Wadsworth, Staten Isl.; on small reef offshore is Fort Lafayette (built 1822), a U.S. naval magazine.

Fort Hancock, village (pop. c.500), Hudspeth co., extreme W Texas, c.50 mi. SE of El Paso, near the Rio Grande; shipping point in irrigated farm region. Ruins of old Fort Hancock are near by.

Fort Hare, village (pop. 582), SE Cape Prov., U. of So. Afr., just N of Alice, 40 mi. NE of Grahamstown; site of South African Native Col., affiliated with Univ. of South Africa.

Fort Harrison, Burma: see SADON.

Fort Hertz, Burma: see PUTAO.

Fort Hill, village, Northern Prov., northernmost Nyasaland, on Northern Rhodesia border, 45 mi. WNW of Karonga, on road; corn, cassava. Customs post; airfield.

Fort Hill, Ohio: see SINKING SPRING.

Forth Mountain, hill (776 ft.), S central Co. Wexford, Ireland, 4 mi. WSW of Wexford.

Fort Howard, Md.: see NORTH POINT.

Forth River, in SE Scotland, is formed at Aberfoyle, Perthshire, by confluence of the Avondhu (ăvůndū') (12 mi. long) and Duchray Water (14 mi. long), which rise near Ben Lomond. The Forth then flows 65 mi. E, along Perthshire-Stirling border, past Stirling, along Stirling-Clackmannan border, to Alloa, where it begins to widen into the Firth of Forth; receives Teith, Devon, and other rivers. The Firth of Forth extends 51 mi. from Alloa to the North Sea, where its mouth is bounded by Fife Ness (N) and Dunbar (S), and is 1–19 mi. wide. At Kincardine, below Alloa, it is crossed by a road bridge (1936); at QUEENSFERRY it is spanned by the famous Forth Bridge. Just above Queensferry is naval base of Rosyth, with roadstead of St. Margaret's Hope, marked by lighthouse (56°2'N 3°29'W). In the firth are isls. of Inchkeith and Inchcolm; at its entrance are Bass Rock and Isle of May. The firth receives Leven, Esk, Almond, Avon, and Carron rivers. Chief riparian towns are: Kincardine, Grangemouth, Bo'ness, Burntisland, Edinburgh, Leith, Kirkcaldy, Leven, North Berwick, and Crail. It is connected with the Clyde by the Forth and Clyde Canal.

Forth River, N Tasmania, rises NNW of L. St. Clair, flows 52 mi. NNE to Bass Strait 5 mi. E of Ulverstone.

Fort Huachuca (wůchōō'ků), village (pop. c.1,800), Cochise co., SE Ariz., near Mex. line, 50 mi. WNW of Douglas; alt. 4,763 ft. U.S. military post near by.

Fortierville (fôr'tyävĭl"), village (pop. 413), S Que., near the St. Lawrence, 26 mi. ENE of Trois Rivières; lumbering, dairying, pig raising.

Fort Île-aux-Noix, Que.: see ÎLE-AUX-NOIX.

Fortín (fôrtēn') [Sp., =military post], in Latin American names: for names beginning thus and not found here, see under main part of name; e.g., for Fortín Roboré, see ROBORÉ.

Fortín, town (pop. 2,460), Veracruz, E Mexico, in Sierra Madre Oriental, on railroad and 5 mi. W of Córdoba; coffee-growing center. Famous for gardenias, orchids, camellias. Sometimes Fortín de las Flores.

Fortín Campero (kämpā'rō), village (pop. c.600), Tarija dept., S Bolivia, on Argentina border, on Tarija R., near confluence with Bermejo R., 95 mi. SSE of Tarija. Bermejo oil fields 10 mi. N.

Fortingall (fôr'tĭng-gŭl), town and parish (pop. 1,716), central Perthshire, Scotland, on Lyon R. and 8 mi. W of Aberfeldy; agr. market. Has remains of anc. earthworks, reputedly Roman.

Fortín General Bruguéz (fôrtēn' hānäräl' broo͞gĕs'), town (dist. pop. 600), Presidente Hayes dept., W Paraguay, in Chaco region, on Pilcomayo R. (Argentina border) and 85 mi. NW of Villa Hayes. Strategic outpost.

Fortín Puerto Heath, Bolivia: see PUERTO HEATH.

Fort Island (□ 1.7), Essequibo co., N Br. Guiana, in Essequibo R. estuary, E of Hog Isl., 23 mi. W of Georgetown. Site of one of earliest Du. settlements, former ⊙ Essequibo colony. An old massive fort, council chamber, and police hall (now a church) remain.

Fort James Island or **James Island,** in Gambia R., W Gambia, 17 mi. ESE of Bathurst. Discovered 1456 by sailors commissioned by Prince Henry the Navigator and named St. Andrew's Isl. Occupied by Courlanders (1651–61), it was then taken by British and renamed Fort James Isl. The fort was attacked repeatedly (1695–1708) by the French; abandoned (1816) following establishment of Bathurst settlement.

Fort Jameson, town (pop. 3,217), ⊙ Eastern Prov. (□ 23,000; pop. 320,000), E Northern Rhodesia, near Nyasaland border, 320 mi. ENE of Lusaka, on Great Road; 13°38'S 32°40'E. Tobacco center, producing flue-cured Virginia tobacco; corn, wheat; market gardening. Hunting in area. Has govt. school and European hosp. Airfield. Originally a military post; notorious for its slave trade in 19th cent. Became (1899) hq. of British South Africa Company's administration of North-Eastern Rhodesia. Was ⊙ former East Luangwa prov.

Fort Jefferson National Monument (land and water, □ 73.6; land only, 87 acres; established 1935), includes DRY TORTUGAS isl. group, in Gulf of Mexico c.65 mi. W of Key West, Fla. Old Fort Jefferson, never finished, was begun in 1846 on Garden Key (sometimes called Shark Isl.) for defense of Straits of Florida. Largest masonry fortification in Western Hemisphere, it is surrounded by high, thick walls and had moat 70 ft. wide, 30 ft. deep. Served as Federal prison during and after Civil War; a famous prisoner here was Dr. Samuel A. Mudd.

Fort Jennings, village (pop. 330), Putnam co., NW Ohio, 15 mi. NW of Lima and on Auglaize R.

Fort Johnson, village (pop. 930), Montgomery co., E central N.Y., on Mohawk R. and the Barge Canal, just W of Amsterdam. Here is Fort Johnson (1749), once home of Sir William Johnson, now a mus.

Fort Johnston, town (pop. 62), Southern Prov., Nyasaland, on Shire R., near its efflux from L. Nyasa, and 65 mi. N of Zomba; road center; tobacco, cotton, corn, peanuts. Has marine engineering shops, African hosp.

Fort Jones, town (pop. 525), Siskiyou co., N Calif., 13 mi. SW of Yreka, in a valley of Klamath Mts.

Fort Juliana, locality, E Ellesmere Isl., NE Franklin Dist., Northwest Territories, on Hayes Fjord, W arm (25 mi. long) of Hill Bay, an inlet of Buchanan Bay; 79°N 77°W. Site of hq. of Otto Sverdrup expedition, 1898–99.

Fort Keary, Burma: see HEIRNKUT.

Fort Kent, town (pop. 5,343), including Fort Kent village (pop. 3,001), Aroostook co., N Maine, on St. John R., at influx of Fish R., and 50 mi. NNW of Presque Isle; port of entry; trade center at N.B. line; potato-processing center; lumbering. Seat of a normal school. Terminus of U.S. Highway No. 1. Settled 1829 by Acadians, inc. 1869.

Fort Kobbe (kō'bē), military reservation, Balboa dist., S Panama Canal Zone, near the Pacific coast, 5 mi. SW of Panama city. Howard Field adjoins it W.

Fort Lallemand (fôr lälmã'), Saharan outpost, Saharan Oases territory, E central Algeria, at W edge of the Great Eastern Erg, 75 mi. SE of Ouargla; 31°17'N 6°18'E.

Fort-Lamy (fôr-lämē'), town (1950 pop. 23,500), ⊙ Chad territory and of Chari-Baguirmi region, W Chad, Fr. Equatorial Africa, at confluence of Shari R. and Logone R. opposite Fort-Foureau (Fr. Cameroons) and 1,120 mi. N of Brazzaville; 12°7'N 15°E. Commercial center, junction of caravan routes; trades in animal products; also markets salt, dates, millet; mfg. of tiles, bricks, carbonated drinks; food processing, fishing. Military camp, airport. Has veterinary centers, hosp., trade schools, R.C. and Protestant missions, large mosque. Founded 1900 by the French, it later became a strategic base for pacification (1903–12) of Negro kingdoms of central Sudan. Bombed by Italian planes, 1942.

Fort Langley, village (pop. estimate 500), SW B.C., on lower Fraser R. and 24 mi. ESE of Vancouver; lumbering, dairying, fruitgrowing. First Hudson's Bay Co. post in S B.C. was established here (1827) and played important part in securing British influence in the region; it was closed down c.1885. Site was provisionally chosen (1858) as ⊙ B.C.

Fort Laperrine, Algeria: see TAMANRASSET.

Fort Laramie (lă'rŭmē), town (pop. 300), Goshen co., SE Wyo., on N.Platte R., at mouth of Laramie R., and 20 mi. NW of Torrington, in fruit region; alt. 4,250 ft. **Fort Laramie National Monument** (214.4 acres; established 1938) is just W, on Laramie R.; includes buildings of fur-trading post (started 1834 as stockade, later rebuilt and enlarged) that was used (1849–90) as U.S. fort for protection of travelers on Oregon Trail.

Fort Lauderdale (lô'dûrdāl), city (pop. 36,328), ⊙ Broward co., S Fla., 25 mi. N of Miami, on the Atlantic coast; joined by navigable canals to L. Okeechobee (c.55 mi. NW). Noted resort, and trade and shipping center for a citrus-fruit and truck-produce region. Millwork; mfg. of prefabricated bldgs., furniture, concrete products; processing of feeds, fertilizers; canning; fishing. Port Everglades, a deepwater port and port of entry, is partly within the city (S). A Seminole Indian Reservation is near by. Settled around a fort built 1837 in Seminole War. Inc. 1911, and grew rapidly after 1920s.

Fort Lawn, agr. town (pop. 216), Chester co., N S.C., near Catawba R., 18 mi. E of Chester.

Fort Leavenworth, Kansas: see LEAVENWORTH.

Fort Lee, borough (pop. 11,648), Bergen co., NE N.J., on Hudson R. opposite upper Manhattan (George Washington bridge connection), on the Palisades; photographic film processing (Fort Lee was early center of moving-picture industry); mfg. (metal products, furniture, baby carriages); truck farming. Settled 1700, inc. 1904. Fort built here abandoned (1776) by General Greene after Fort Washington, on opposite shore, fell to British.

Fort Lennox, Que.: see ÎLE-AUX-NOIX.

Fort Liard (lē'ärd"), village (district pop. 216), SW Mackenzie Dist., Northwest Territories, near B.C. and Yukon borders, on Liard R., at mouth of Petitot R.; 60°14'N 123°28'W; trading post; radio station, Royal Canadian Mounted Police post; site of R.C. mission. Established c.1800.

Fort Liberté (fôr lēbĕrtā'), town (1950 census pop. 1,507), Nord dept., NE Haiti, port on small inlet of the Atlantic, 23 mi. E of Cap-Haïtien; ships sisal, logwood, coffee. Also tobacco growing.

Fort Lister, Nyasaland: see PALOMBE.

Fort Loramie (lô'rŭmē), village (pop. 508), Shelby co., W Ohio, 12 mi. WNW of Sidney, on L. Loramie. Fort Loramie built here (1794) by Anthony Wayne.

Fort Loudoun Dam (lou'dŭn), E Tenn., on Tennessee R., 20 mi. SW of Knoxville. Major TVA dam (122 ft. high, 4,190 ft. long; completed 1943); designed to aid navigation (has lock 360 ft. long, 60 ft. wide, providing max. lift of 80 ft.) and flood control and to supply hydroelectric power. Forms Fort Loudoun Reservoir (□ 22.7; 55 mi. long, capacity 386,500 acre-ft.; sometimes written Fort Loudon Reservoir).

Fort Lupton, town (pop. 1,907), Weld co., N Colo., on South Platte R. and 25 mi. NNE of Denver; alt. 4,906 ft. Trade center for grain and dairy region; beet sugar, canned vegetables; coal mines. Founded c.1872, inc. 1890. Site of Fort Lupton (1836–44), fur-trading post, is near by.

Fort Lyon, Colo.: see LAS ANIMAS.

Fort McHenry National Monument and Historic Shrine, Md.: see BALTIMORE.

Fort McKavett (mŭkă'vĭt), village (pop. c.150), Menard co., W central Texas, 20 mi. WSW of Menard and on San Saba R.; trade point in ranch area. Ruins of old Fort McKavett (1852) are here.

Fort McKenzie, village, N Que., near Kaniapiskau R.; 56°53'N 68°59'W; Hudson's Bay Co. post.

Fort Macleod, Alta., Canada: see MACLEOD, town.

Fort McLeod, B.C., Canada: see MCLEOD, FORT.

Fort MacMahon, Saharan outpost, Aïn-Sefra territory, central Algeria, at S edge of the Great Western Erg, on El-Goléa–Adrar auto track and 95 mi. SW of El-Goléa; 29°46'N 1°37'E.

Fort McMurray, village, NE Alta., on Athabaska R., at mouth of Clearwater R., and 160 mi. NE of Athabaska; 56°44'N 111°23'W. Hudson's Bay Co. fur-trading post. Erected 1790 as Fort of the Forks by the North West Co., it was taken over by the Hudson's Bay Co. in 1821; rebuilt and renamed 1875. Railroad terminal and site of airport serving the Far North. Adjacent is village of Waterways.

Fort Macon State Park, N.C.: see BOGUE ISLAND.

Fort McPherson, village (district pop. 325), NW Mackenzie Dist., Northwest Territories, near Yukon border, on Peel R., near its mouth on Mackenzie R., and 50 mi. S of Aklavik; 67°27'N 134°53'W; Hudson's Bay Co. fur-trading post; radio station, Royal Canadian Mounted Police summer post; site of Anglican and R.C. missions. Fort was established 1840.

Fort Madison, city (pop. 14,954), a ⊙ Lee co., extreme SE Iowa, on Mississippi R. (bridged here) and 17 mi. SW of Burlington; mfg. center: fountain pens, ink, mechanical pencils, farm tools, signal apparatus (flares, lamps), paint, paper, canned tomatoes, dairy products. State penitentiary is here. City was established as U.S. trading post in 1808; burned and abandoned in 1813 when besieged by Indians. Resettled 1833, inc. 1838. Formerly a river port.

Fort-Mahon-Plage (fôr-mäō'-plăzh'), village (pop. 819), Somme dept., N France, on English Channel, 20 mi. NW of Abbeville; bathing resort.

Fort Manning, town, Central Prov., Nyasaland, near Northern Rhodesia border, on road to Fort Jameson (20 mi. NW) and 60 mi. WNW of Lilongwe; alt. 4,200 ft. Customs station; tobacco, cotton, corn.

Fort Marion National Monument, Fla.: see SAINT AUGUSTINE.

Fort Massac State Park, Ill.: see METROPOLIS.

Fort Matanzas National Monument (mŭtăn'zŭs) (227.8 acres), NE Fla., on Atlantic coast at mouth of Matanzas R., and 15 mi. SSE of St. Augustine. Spaniards, led by Pedro Menéndez de Avilés, slaughtered 2 parties of Fr. Huguenots who surrendered (1565) near site of fort, and established Sp. supremacy in Fla. Fort was built 1736–42 by Spaniards for protection of St. Augustine. Ceded by treaty to English in 1763, to U.S. in 1821. Natl. monument established 1924.

Fort Meade, city (pop. 2,803), Polk co., central Fla., near Peace R., 10 mi. S of Bartow; trade center for citrus-fruit, truck, and phosphate-mining area. Settled around mid-19th-cent. fort.

Fort Mill, residential town (pop. 3,204), York co., N S.C., 7 mi. NE of Rock Hill, near the Catawba; textile mills.

Fort Miribel (fôr mērēbĕl'), Saharan outpost in Ghardaïa territory, central Algeria, on Laghouat-Zinder (Fr. West Africa) trans-Saharan auto track, and 80 mi. S of El-Goléa; 29°26'N 3°1'E.

Fort Mitchell, town (pop. 372), Kenton co., N Ky., SW residential suburb of Covington.

Fort Monroe, Va.: see OLD POINT COMFORT.

Fort Montgomery, village (1940 pop. 651), Orange co., SE N.Y., on W bank of the Hudson (crossed here by Bear Mountain Bridge) and 12 mi. S of Newburgh. Just S is Bear Mtn. section of Palisades Interstate Park.

Fort Morgan, city (pop. 5,315), ⊙ Morgan co., NE Colo., on South Platte R. and 70 mi. NE of Denver; alt. 4,240 ft. Trade center for sugar-beet, grain, and livestock region; oil refinery; beet sugar, canned vegetables, dairy products, automobile accessories. Established as military post on Overland Trail, named Fort Morgan 1866, inc. 1887.

Fort Morton, Burma: see SIMA.

Fort Munro (mŭnrō'), village, Dera Ghazi Khan dist., SW Punjab, W Pakistan, in S Sulaiman Range, 40 mi. WSW of Dera Ghazi Khan; hill resort (alt. 6,242 ft.); woolen handicrafts (blankets, saddlebags).

Fort Myer Heights, Va.: see ARLINGTON, co.

Fort Myers, city (pop. 13,195), ⊙ Lee co., SW Fla., on CALOOSAHATCHEE RIVER (bridged here), near the Gulf of Mexico, and c.95 mi. SSE of Tampa; shipping center for gladioli, citrus fruit, vegetables, and fish; citrus-fruit canning, boatbuilding, mfg. of shell novelties. Has fine beach on Estero Isl.; and many varieties of palm trees, some planted by Thomas A. Edison, who wintered and conducted botanical experiments here for many years. Grew around fort built 1841 in Seminole War and renamed 1850. Developed rapidly as a resort in 1920s.

Fort-National (fôr'-näsyônăl'), village (pop. 687), Alger dept., N central Algeria, in Great Kabylia, 10 mi. SE of Tizi-Ouzou. Founded in 1857 by French (originally named Fort-Napoléon) as a stronghold against insurgent Kabylian Berbers. Fine panorama of Djurdjura range from citadel (alt. 3,195 ft.).

Fort Necessity National Battlefield Site (2 acres; established 1931), SW Pa., 9 mi. SE of Uniontown; surrounded by state park (311 acres). Here occurred 1st battle (July 3, 1754) of Fr. and Indian War; colonial troops under George Washington were outnumbered by force of Fr. and Indians and obliged to surrender Fort Necessity (built in May, 1754). Reproduction of fort and Mt. Washington Tavern (c.1818; now state historical mus.) are here.

Fort Nelson, village (pop. estimate 150), NE B.C., at confluence of Muskwa R. and Sikanni Chief R., here forming Fort Nelson R., on branch of Alaska Highway; 58°49'N 122°32'W; Hudson's Bay Co. post; lumbering. Established c.1800, post was destroyed by Indians 1825, rebuilt 1865.

Fort Nelson River, NE B.C., formed at Fort Nelson by confluence of Muskwa and Sikanni Chief rivers, flows 100 mi. generally NW to Liard R. at Nelson Forks.

Fort Norman, village (district pop. 264), W Mackenzie Dist., Northwest Territories, on Mackenzie R., at mouth of Great Bear R., at foot of Franklin Mts.; 64°54'N 125°35'W; Hudson's Bay Co. fur-trading post; govt. radio and meteorological station, hosp., Royal Canadian Mounted Police Post. Site of R.C. mission. Transshipment point for waterborne traffic for Great Bear L. region. Fort was established 1810 by North West Co., taken over by Hudson's Bay Co. 1821. Oil center of Norman Wells is 45 mi. NW.

Fort Oglethorpe, town (pop. 692), Catoosa and Walker counties, extreme NW Ga., 7 mi. SE of Chattanooga, Tenn., and near U.S. Fort Oglethorpe.

Fort Opus, Yugoslavia: see OPUZEN.

Fortore River (fôrtô'rē), S Italy, rises in the Apennines in 2 headstreams, near Montefalcone di Valfortore (W) and Roseto Valfortore (E); flows 53 mi. N to the Adriatic 16 mi. ESE of Termoli. In upper course forms Campobasso-Foggia prov. boundary.

Fort Payne, city (pop. 6,226), ⊙ De Kalb co., NE Ala., on branch of Coosa R. and 34 mi. NE of Gadsden; trade center for cotton, poultry, and fruit area; clothing, hosiery, lumber, cotton, beverages, paper products. Deposits of clay, coal, iron, and fuller's earth in vicinity. Founded 1889. Site of Cherokee settlement near by.

Fort Peck, village (pop. 1,214), Valley co., NE Mont., on Fort Peck Reservoir and Missouri R. and 15 mi. SE of Glasgow. Built by govt. as permanent town for construction workers on near-by FORT PECK DAM. Prehistoric fossil collection here.

Fort Peck Dam, NE Mont., in Missouri R., 17 mi. SE of Glasgow; PWA project built (1933–40) to control floods, improve navigation, and provide hydroelectric power; one of largest earth-fill dams in world; 250 ft. high, c.4 mi. long. Fort Peck Reservoir (□ 383; capacity of 19,417,000 acre-ft.) is 2d largest in U.S.

Fort Phantom Hill, Lake, or **Fort Phantom Lake,** W central Texas, reservoir impounded by dam in a small S tributary of Clear Fork of the Brazos, c.7 mi. N of Abilene; area c.74,000 acre-ft.; fishing. Near by are ruins of Fort Phantom Hill, established 1851 as U.S. military post and later (1854–1880) as a frontier stage station.

Fort Pickens, Fla.: see SANTA ROSA ISLAND.

Fort Pierce, city (pop. 13,502), ⊙ St. Lucie co., SE Fla., c.55 mi. NNW of West Palm Beach; port on Indian R. lagoon (connected here with the Atlantic by Fort Pierce Inlet); major shipping center for citrus-fruit and vegetables, with large packing houses and canneries. Mfg. (millwork, fertilizer, concrete products). Shark fishing. Grew around fort built 1838 against Indians. Inc. 1909.

Fort Pierre (pēr), city (pop. 951), ⊙ Stanley co., central S.Dak., opposite Pierre, on the Missouri at mouth of Bad R.; grain and livestock. Founded 1817 as fur-trading post; known as Fort Pierre after 1832. Near by is bluff in which the Vérendryes buried a lead plate, in 1743, to claim surrounding territory for France.

Fort Pierre Bordes, Algeria: see TIN-ZAOUATENE.

Fort Plain, village (pop. 2,935), Montgomery co., E central N.Y., on Mohawk R. and the Barge Canal, and 23 mi. W of Amsterdam, in dairying and poultry area; mfg. (textiles, wood and paper products, clothing). Settled 1723, inc. 1832.

Fort Point, Maine: see JELLISON, CAPE.

Fort Polignac, Algeria: see POLIGNAC.

Fort Portal, town, Western Prov., Uganda, 90 mi. NNW of Mbarara; agr. trade center (tea, coffee, bananas, corn). Technical training school. Hotel. Hq. Toro dist., inhabited by Toro Bantus.

Fort Providence, village (district pop. 415), S Mackenzie Dist., Northwest Territories, on Mackenzie R., near W end of Great Slave L.; 61°21'N 117°39'W; trading post; airfield, govt. radio and meteorological station, Royal Canadian Mounted Police post; site of R.C. mission and boarding school. Established 1862.

Fort Pulaski National Monument, Ga.: see COCKSPUR ISLAND.

Fort Qu'Appelle (fôr käpĕl'), village (pop. 683), SE Sask., on Fishing Lakes 40 mi. ENE of Regina; mixed farming. Former post of the North West Co. and Hudson's Bay Co., established c.1800, discontinued 1880.

Fort Rae, Northwest Territories: see RAE.

Fort Raleigh National Historic Site, N.C.: see ROANOKE ISLAND.

Fort Randall Dam, SE S.Dak., in Missouri R. c.5 mi. S of Lake Andes, near Nebr. line. A major unit in Missouri R. Basin project for flood control, irrigation, and hydroelectric power, dam was authorized by Congress in 1944 and begun 1947; of earth-fill construction, it is one of largest (160 ft. high, 10,000 ft. long) of this type. Reservoir's projected capacity is 6,200,000 acre-ft.

Fort Randolph, military reservation, Cristobal dist., N Panama Canal Zone, on offshore Margarita Isl. of the Caribbean, 2 mi. NE of Colón.

Fort Recovery, village (pop. 1,231), Mercer co., W Ohio, 14 mi. SW of Celina and on Wabash R.; trading center for agr. area; dairy products, lumber, cigars. Oil wells. Fort Recovery was established here in 1791 by Anthony Wayne.

Fort Resolution, village (district pop. 635), S Mackenzie Dist., Northwest Territories, on S shore of Great Slave L., near mouth of Slave R.; 61°11'N 113°41'W; fur-trading center; airfield, govt. radio and meteorological station, Royal Canadian Mounted Police post; site of R.C. mission, hosp., and boarding school. Established c.1800 by the Hudson's Bay Co. Wood Buffalo Natl. Park extends S. At mouth of Slave R., 9 mi. NNE of fort, is Res-delta, a river-lake transshipment point for Yellowknife mining region.

Fortress, Aden Colony, administrative designation of ADEN township.

Fortress Monroe, Va.: see OLD POINT COMFORT.

Fortress Mountain, Wyo.: see ABSAROKA RANGE.

Fort Richardson, Alaska: see ANCHORAGE.

Fort Ripley, village (pop. 88), Crow Wing co., central Minn., on Mississippi R. and 15 mi. SW of Brainerd, in grain and potato area. Near by are Camp Ripley, used by Minn. Natl. Guard, and ruins of Old Fort Ripley (1850–78).

Fort Rixon (rĭk'sŭn), township (pop. 65), Bulawayo prov. SW central Southern Rhodesia, in Matabeleland, 45 mi. ENE of Bulawayo; road center; tobacco, corn; cattle, sheep, goats. A fortified station in 1896 Matabele rebellion.

Fortrose, burgh (1931 pop. 875; 1951 census 882), SE Ross and Cromarty, Scotland, on Moray Firth, on Black Isle, 8 mi. NE of Inverness; small port and seaside resort. In 6th cent. it was site of a monastery; in 1124 it became seat of bishops of Ross. Has ruins (mostly 14th cent.) of cathedral, whose stones were used by Cromwell to strengthen fortifications at Inverness.

Fort Rosebery, township (pop. 1,069), Western Prov., N Northern Rhodesia, near Belgian Congo border, 100 mi. NE of Elisabethville (road). Transferred 1947 from Northern Prov. Was ⊙ former Mweru-Luapula prov.

Fort Ross, trading post, SE Somerset Isl., central Franklin Dist., Northwest Territories, on Prince Regent Inlet; 72°N 94°7'W; radio and meteorological station; site of Anglican mission.

Fort Ross, historic site, Sonoma co., W Calif., on Pacific coast, 28 mi. W of Santa Rosa. In state park at site are restored bldgs. of Russian Fort Ross, a fur-trapping and trading post, 1812–41.

Fort-Rousset (fôr'-rōōsā'), town, ⊙ Likouala-Mossaka region (formed 1949; pop. 92,000), central Middle Congo territory, Fr. Equatorial Africa, 260 mi. N of Brazzaville; palm-oil products.

Fort-Royal, Martinique: see FORT-DE-FRANCE.

Fort Saint (Fr. fôr sē'), Saharan outpost, Southern Territories, southernmost Tunisia, near Fezzan and Algerian borders, 10 mi. NNE of Ghadames; 30°15'N 9°35'E.

Fort Saint David, India: see CUDDALORE.

Fort Saint George, India: see MADRAS, city.

Fort Saint James, village, central B.C., on E shore of Stuart L., 70 mi. NW of Prince George; Hudson's Bay Co. trading post; lumbering, stock raising. Established 1806 by North West Co., it was taken over 1821 by Hudson's Bay Co.

Fort Saint John, village (pop. estimate 500), E B.C., near Alta. border, near Peace R., on Alaska Highway (which crosses Peace R. on 2,275-ft. suspension bridge built 1943) and 40 mi. NW of Dawson Creek, 180 mi. NE of Prince George; fur trading, lumbering. Established 1805 by the North West Co., taken over 1821 by Hudson's Bay Co., fort was destroyed 1823 by Indians, rebuilt 1860. Near by are small coal mines.

Fort Sandeman, town (pop., including cantonment area, 9,353), ⊙ Zhob dist., NE Baluchistan, W Pakistan, near Zhob R., 165 mi. NE of Quetta; rail terminus; trade center (wheat, rice, felts, timber); handicrafts (woolen carpets, felts). Pine forests near by.

Fort San Lorenzo (săn lôrĕn'zō), ruined Sp. fortifications at Caribbean mouth of Chagres R., Cristobal dist., N Panama Canal Zone, 7 mi. WSW of Colón. Built 1575, it was taken by the buccaneer Morgan. Used by U.S. army in both World Wars.

Fort Saskatchewan (săskă'chuwŏn), town (pop. 921), central Alta., on North Saskatchewan R. and 15 mi. NE of Edmonton; coal mining; grain elevators, mixed farming, stock. First fort of the North West Mounted Police N of Calgary was established here.

Fort Scott, city (pop. 10,335), ⊙ Bourbon co., SE Kansas, on Marmaton R. and 28 mi. N of Pittsburg, near Mo. line; trade and shipping center for general agr. region; food processing (flour, condensed milk); mfg. of overalls, cement, foundry products; wood planing. Quarries (cement rock, flagstone) and coal mines near by. Has jr. col. City grew up around military post that was established in 1842, abandoned in 1855, and rebuilt during Civil War. Inc. 1860.

Fort Selkirk or **Selkirk,** trading post, SW Yukon, at confluence of Lewes and Pelly rivers, here forming Yukon R., 110 mi. SE of Dawson; 62°46'N 137°23'W; fur-trade center. Airfield, Royal Canadian Mounted Police post. Hudson's Bay Co. fort was established 1848, destroyed by Indians 1852. Hudson's Bay Co. re-established post in 1938.

Fort Severn (sĕ'vŭrn), village, NW Ont., on Hudson Bay, at mouth of Severn R.; 55°59'N 87°36'W; Hudson's Bay Co. post. Built by the British 1685, it was burned 1689 to prevent capture by the French. Fr. fort (1691) changed hands repeatedly, until handed over to Hudson's Bay Co. under Treaty of Utrecht (1713).

Fort Sherman, military reservation, Cristobal dist., N Panama Canal Zone, at NW entrance of Limon Bay (Caribbean) and 3 mi. W of Colón.

Fort Shevchenko (shĭfchĕn'kŭ), city (1948 pop. over 10,000), S Guryev oblast, Kazakh SSR, Caspian port on Mangyshlak Peninsula, 195 mi. SSW of Guryev; fishing center. Bautino, on coast just N, is a sealing base. Phosphorite deposits (S); manganese (SE). Founded 1846 in Rus. conquest of Kazakhstan; until 1939 called Fort Aleksandrovski (except, briefly in 1920s, Fort Uritskogo); was ⊙ former Adai dist. (1920–28).

Fort-Sibut (fôr'-sēbü'), town, ⊙ Kémo-Gribingui region (□ 17,375; 1950 pop. 82,300), central Ubangi-Shari, Fr. Equatorial Africa, 100 mi. NNE of Bangui; trading center for rubber, cotton, coffee; cotton ginning. Has Protestant mission, R.C. seminary.

Fort Sill, Okla.: see LAWTON.

Fort Simpson, village (district pop. 454), SW Mackenzie Dist., Northwest Territories, on small isl. in Mackenzie R., at mouth of Liard R.; 61°52'N 121°21'W; trading post; site of agr. experiment station, Anglican and R.C. missions and schools, airfield, govt. radio and meteorological station, hosp., Royal Canadian Mounted Police post. Oats, potatoes, barley, beets, vegetables are grown in vicinity of fort. Founded 1804 by North West Co. and named Fort of the Forks, it was renamed 1821, after being taken over by Hudson's Bay Co.

Fort Smith, village (pop. estimate 250; district pop. 531), administrative ⊙ Northwest Territories, in S Mackenzie Dist., on Alta. border, on Slave R. (head of navigation); 60°N 111°53'W; trading post; airfield, govt. radio and meteorological station, Royal Canadian Mounted Police post, public school. Site of many govt. offices; R.C. mission, hosp., and school; Anglican mission. Two portage roads connect it with Fort Fitzgerald, Alta., 20 mi. SE, by-passing Slave R. rapids. In Second World War it was U.S. Army supply base. Fort was founded 1870 by Hudson's Bay Co.

Fort Smith, city (pop. 47,942), a ⊙ Sebastian co., W Ark., c.125 mi. WNW of Little Rock and on Arkansas R., at Okla. line. Second-largest city of state and its chief mfg. center; furniture, glass, brick, textiles, tin cans, wood and paper products, bedding, cottonseed products, vehicle bodies, stoves, buckets; zinc smelting, petroleum and natural-gas processing. Mule market. Coal mines, hardwood timber in region. Has jr. col., a natl. Civil War cemetery, the Old Fort, and historical bldgs. U.S. Camp Chaffee and a state tuberculosis sanitarium near by. Founded as military post in 1817; became an important outfitting point in 1848 gold rush. Inc. 1842.

Fort Stanton, N.Mex.: see CAPITAN.

Fort Steele, village (pop. estimate 300), SE B.C., on Kootenay R., at mouth of St. Mary R., and 10 mi. NE of Cranbrook; ranching, fruitgrowing. In mining (gold, silver, copper, iron, lead) region.

Fort Stockton, city (pop. 4,444), ⊙ Pecos co., extreme W Texas, c.150 mi. WSW of San Angelo; trade, shipping center of cattle, sheep, and goat ranching, irrigated farm, and oil area; oil refineries, bottling works, cotton gins, machine shops; tourist resort. Old Fort Stockton (founded 1859; now in ruins) and Comanche Springs (Indian watering place; now used for irrigation) are near.

Fort Sumner, village (pop. 1,982), ⊙ De Baca co., E N.Mex., on Pecos R. and 60 mi. W of Clovis; trade and shipping point in livestock and irrigated agr. region (fruit, grain, potatoes). Near by are Alamogordo Dam, ruins of Fort Sumner (built 1862), and cemetery containing remains of Billy the Kid (William H. Bonney).

Fort Sumter National Monument, fortification on small sandbar in harbor of Charleston, S.C., 1 mi. E of Fort Moultrie (on Sullivans Isl.). Scene of opening engagement (April 12–13, 1861) of Civil War; seized by Confederates after heavy bombardment, it was later besieged by Federals for 20 months and finally evacuated (Feb. 17, 1865) when Sherman's troops began to advance on Charleston. Made a natl. monument (2.4 acres) in 1948.

Fort Supply or **Supply,** town (pop. 293), Woodward co., NW Okla., at mouth of Wolf Creek on North Canadian R., and 13 mi. NW of Woodward. Founded as U.S. Fort Supply in 1867. Fort Supply Dam is just S.

Fort Supply Dam, Woodward co., NW Okla., in Wolf Creek near its mouth on North Canadian R., just S of Fort Supply; 82 ft. high above streambed, 11,325 ft. long; for flood control and water supply; completed 1942. Impounds reservoir c.3½ mi. long.

Fort Ternan, village, Nyanza prov., W Kenya, on railroad and 18 mi. WSW of Londiani; sugar cane, coffee, sisal, corn.

Fort Thomas, residential city (pop. 10,870), Campbell co., N Ky., near left bank of the Ohio, just SE of Covington and Newport and within Cincinnati metropolitan dist.; dairy products, floral novelties, draperies; diamond cutting. Fort Thomas, a U.S. army post established 1887, is here.

Fort Thompson, village (1940 pop. 613), Buffalo co., central S.Dak., 50 mi. ESE of Pierre and on Missouri R.; hq. for Crow Creek and Lower Brule Indian reservations.

Fort Ticonderoga, N.Y.: see TICONDEROGA.

Fort Totten, village (pop. c.100), Benson co., NE central N.Dak., on Devils L. and 11 mi. SSW of Devils Lake city. Hq. of Devils L. Indian Reservation. Original fort still stands.

Fort Towson (tou'sŭn), town (pop. 713), Choctaw co., SE Okla., 14 mi. E of Hugo; trading point for farm area; cotton ginning. Ruins of old Fort Towson (1824) are near by.

Fort-Trinquet (fôr'-trĕkā'), airport, N Mauritania, Fr. West Africa, on Algiers-Dakar line, near Sp. Sahara border, 330 mi. NNE of Atar; 25°15'N 11°30'W.

Fortun, Norway: see SKJOLDEN.

Fortuna (fôrtōō'nä), village (pop. estimate 500), SE San Luis prov., Argentina, on railroad and 100 mi. S of Mercedes, in stock-raising and lumbering area.

Fortuna, town (pop. 2,975), Murcia prov., SE Spain, 14 mi. N of Murcia; olive-oil processing, basket mfg.; cereals, almonds, wine. The spa Baños de Fortuna is 3 mi. N.

Fortuna (fôrtōō'nŭ, –tū'–). **1** Town (pop. 1,762), Humboldt co., NW Calif., near coast, on Eel R. and c.15 mi. S of Eureka; lumbering, dairying, stock raising (sheep, cattle), farming. Inc. 1906. **2** Village (pop. 181), Divide co., NW N.Dak., port of entry 21 mi. W of Crosby.

Fortuna Ledge, Alaska: see MARSHALL.

Fortuna Strait (fŭrtōō'nŭ), in N main Kurile Isls. group, Russian SFSR, bet. Shiashkotan Isl. (N) and Lovushki Isls. (S); 12 mi. wide. Sometimes considered part of KRUZENSHTERN STRAIT.

Fortune, village (pop. 908), S N.F., on SE shore of Fortune Bay, near its entrance, 4 mi. WSW of Grand Bank; fishing port.

Fortune Bay, inlet (80 mi. long, 40 mi. wide at entrance) of the Atlantic, S N.F., 120 mi. WSW of St. John's, bounded SE by Burin Peninsula; 47°20'N 55°40'W. Near its entrance is Brunette Isl., beyond which are St. Pierre and Miquelon. It is cod, salmon, lobster fishing area; fish canning is carried on at settlements on shore. On SE shore is town of Grand Bank. In Jan., 1878, bay was scene of the "Fortune Bay Incident," a controversy over U.S. fishing rights.

Fortune Island, Bahama Isls.: see LONG CAY.

Fort Uritskogo, Kazakh SSR: see FORT SHEVCHENKO.

Fort Usher, village, Bulawayo prov., SW Southern Rhodesia, in Matabeleland, on road and 18 mi. S of Bulawayo; peanuts, corn; cattle, sheep, goats. Hosp. for Matabele natives. Hq. of Matobo dist.

Fort Valley, city (pop. 6,820), ⊙ Peach co., central Ga., 25 mi. SW of Macon; market, shipping, and canning center for peach-growing area; mfg. (truck bodies, agr. implements, yarn, feed, baskets). Fort Valley State Col. here. Settled c.1836, inc. 1856.

Fort Vancouver National Monument, Wash.: see VANCOUVER, city.

Fort Vermilion (vûrmĭl'yŭn), village (pop. estimate 350), N Alta., on Peace R. and 170 mi. W of L. Athabaska; 58°23'N 115°59'W. Hudson's Bay Co. trading post. Established on near-by site by North West Co. in 1798, it was taken over 1821 by Hudson's Bay Co.; later removed to present site. Vermilion Falls (25 ft. high) on Peace R. are 40 mi. E.

Fort Victoria, India: see BANKOT.

Fort Victoria, town (pop. 3,456), ⊙ Victoria prov., SE central Southern Rhodesia, in Mashonaland, 80 mi. SE of Gwelo; alt. 3,571 ft. Rail terminus; tourist center; tobacco, corn, peanuts, citrus fruit, dairy products. Asbestos and gold mining in dist. Historic fort. Noted Zimbabwe ruins are 15 mi. SSE. Sometimes called Victoria.

Fortville, town (pop. 1,786), Hancock co., central Ind., 20 mi. NE of Indianapolis, in agr. area (livestock, grain, vegetables); mfg. (chemicals, auto parts). Laid out 1849. Fort Benjamin Harrison is near by.

Fort Walton, resort town (pop. 2,463), Okaloosa co., NW Fla., 37 mi. E of Pensacola, near W end of Choctawhatchee Bay. Inc. 1941.

Fort Washakie (wŏ'shŭkē), village, Fremont co., W central Wyo., on branch of Popo Agie R. and 14 mi. NNW of Lander, near Wind River Range; alt. 5,502 ft. Hq. of Wind River Indian Reservation.

Fort Washington, village (pop. 1,864, with adjacent Ambler Highlands), Montgomery co., SE Pa., 13 mi. N of Philadelphia. Just S, along Wissahickon Creek, is Fort Washington State Park, with remains of Revolutionary fortifications.

Fort Wayne, city (pop. 133,607), ⊙ Allen co., NE Ind., at confluence of St. Marys and St. Joseph rivers here forming the Maumee, 105 mi. NE of Indianapolis; state's 3d-largest city; key railroad point, shipping and industrial center in rich farming, stock-raising, and dairying region. Has large plants producing electrical appliances, agr. and mining equipment, pumps and tanks, radio and electronic equipment, truck bodies; also makes tools, home appliances, paint, paper, clothing, textiles; meat packing, food processing. Seat of Concordia Col., St. Francis Col., Ind. Technical Col., Fort Wayne Art School and mus., and Fort Wayne Bible Inst. State school for feeble-minded here. Points of interest: co.-city historical mus.; Lincoln Mus.; McCulloch house (1838); R.C. cathedral; grave of Johnny Appleseed. Here, at portage bet. Great Lakes and Ohio R. waterways, the French founded a trading post after 1680 on site of chief village of Miami Indians. Fort Miami (one of earliest in Ind.), believed to have been established by the elder sieur de Vincennes, was built here in 1704. After figuring in Indian fighting, fort was occupied (1760) by the British, and taken by Indians in Pontiac's Rebellion. After subduing the Miami in 1794, Anthony Wayne built fort that gave city its name. Settlement grew as peaceful fur-trading center after end of Indian fighting in War of 1812. Inc. as town in 1829, as city in 1840. Coming of Wabash and Erie Canal in 1830s stimulated industrial growth.

Fort Wellington, village, Berbice co., NE Br. Guiana, on the coast, on Georgetown-Rosignol RR and 45 mi. SE of Georgetown; rice, sugar cane.

Fort White, village, N.Chin Hills dist., Upper Burma, on road and 33 mi. W of Kalewa. Junction of roads to Tiddim and Falam.

Fort White, town (pop. 329), Columbia co., N Fla., 19 mi. SSW of Lake City, in agr. area.

Fort Wilkins State Park, Mich.: see COPPER HARBOR.

Fort William, city (pop. 30,585), W Ont., on Thunder Bay, on NW shore of L. Superior, at mouth of Kaministikwia R., just S of its twin city of PORT ARTHUR and 200 mi. NE of Duluth. Major Great Lakes port, with a fine harbor, it is a grain-shipping center, with large grain elevators; site of important coal dock of the Canadian Pacific RR. Also terminal of Canadian Natl. RR. Transfer and bulk-breaking point for W Canada, it has paper, pulp, lumber, and flour mills, foundries, truck works, machine shops, shipyards. Hydroelectric power is supplied by near-by Kakabeka Falls. Founded 1678 as Fr. fur-trading post; Fort Kaministikwia (Kaministiquia) was built here 1717, abandoned to the British during Seven Years War. Fort William of the North West Co. was established 1801 after its original hq. at the Grand Portage was found to be on U.S. territory. Its importance declined in 19th cent. until coming of the railroad in 1885. Boat connection with Isle Royale Natl. Park (U.S.).

Fort William, India: see CALCUTTA.

Fort William, burgh (1931 pop. 2,524; 1951 census 2,661), SW Inverness, Scotland, on Loch Linnhe, at foot of Ben Nevis, 75 mi. NNW of Glasgow; tourist center for the Highlands. The fort was built by General Monck in 1655, rebuilt and renamed under William III in 1690, besieged by Jacobites, 1715 and 1745, and finally demolished in 1890. West Highland Mus. contains Jacobite relics. In 1940 town was damaged by a German plane. Just N, on Loch Linnhe, is Inverlochy, with important aluminum works and hydroelectric power station. Inverlochy Castle, 3 mi. NE of Fort William, dates mainly from 15th cent. and was scene (1645) of defeat of Covenanters by Montrose.

Fort Wingate, village (pop. c.150), McKinley co., NW N.Mex., in NW foothills of Zuni Mts., 12 mi. ESE of Gallup; alt. c.7,000 ft. Military installations and Navajo Indian School here. Part of Cibola Natl. Forest near by.

Fort Worth, city (1940 pop. 177,662; 1950 pop. 278,778), ⊙ Tarrant co., N Texas, 30 mi. W of Dallas at junction of Clear and West forks of Trinity R. Commercial, transportation (rail, air, highway), industrial center, with cattle-ranching plains to W, rich prairie agr. area to E; one of nation's most important grain, livestock markets, with huge stockyards, meat-packing plants, grain elevators and mills; an oil-refining center, at hub of great petroleum pipeline system; has administrative hq. of many oil companies. Aircraft, steel-fabricating plants, railroad shops; mfg. of chemicals, cottonseed products, processed foods (especially dried eggs, dairy products), oil-field and farm equipment, cement, vehicle bodies, furniture, textiles, leather goods, clothing, tire cord, boxes. Seat of Texas Christian Univ., Texas Wesleyan Col., and Southwestern Baptist Theological Seminary. U.S. Public Health Service hosp. is near by. To NW, reservoirs on West Fork of the Trinity (L. Bridgeport, Eagle Mtn. L., and L. Worth, with U.S. fish hatchery) supply water, recreation. City has noted botanic garden, many parks; holds annual Southwestern Exposition and Fat Stock Show. U.S. Carswell Air Force Base near. Settled 1843; Camp Worth (later Fort Worth) established here 1847 as an army post; grew to post-Civil War cow town; inc. 1873. Railroad, completed 1876 by citizens' efforts, aided growth of meat-packing industry; later, its industrial base was broadened by wheat growing and petroleum developments in region. In Second World War, new industries (notably aircraft making) were added.

Fort Wright, town (pop. 594), Kenton co., N Ky.

Fort Wrigley, Northwest Territories: see WRIGLEY.

Fort Yates, town (1940 pop. 1,152), ⊙ Sioux co., S N.Dak., on Missouri R. and 50 mi. S of Bismarck; livestock, poultry, grain. Indian agency hq.

Forty Fort, residential borough (pop. 6,173), Luzerne co., NE central Pa., 3 mi. NNE of Wilkes-Barre and on Susquehanna R. Settled 1772 on site of Colonial fort in the Wyoming Valley. Settlers made last stand here in Wyoming Valley massacre, 1778.

Forty Mile or **Fortymile**, village, W Yukon, near Alaska border, on Yukon R. at mouth of Fortymile R., and 40 mi. NW of Dawson; gold mining.

Fort Yukon (yōō'kŏn), village (pop. 475), NE Alaska, on Yukon R. at mouth of Porcupine R. and 140 mi. NE of Fairbanks, on the Yukon Flats, just N of Arctic Circle; 66°34'N 145°18'W; fur-trading center and supply base for trappers. Has hosp., schools, airfield. A post established here 1847 by Hudson's Bay Co., in agreement with Russians, was moved to Old Rampart House and later to British territory after U.S. purchase of Alaska.

Forumad (fōrōōmäd'), village, Ninth Prov., in Khurasan, NE Iran, 60 mi. WNW of Sabzawar, in small Jaghatai range; chromite mining.

Forum Alieni, Italy: see FERRARA, city.

Forum Cornelii, Italy: see IMOLA.

Forum Julii, France: see FRÉJUS.

Forum Julii, Italy: see CIVIDALE DEL FRIULI.

Forum Livii, Italy: see FORLÌ, city.

Forum Neronis, France: see LODÈVE.

Fos (fôs), village (pop. 647), Haute-Garonne dept. S France, on the Garonne and 9 mi. NE of Luchon; customhouse. Coal deposits near by. At Pont-du-Roy (2 mi. S) the Garonne enters France from Spain.

Fos, Gulf of, inlet of the Gulf of Lion, off coast of Bouches-du-Rhône dept., SE France; 6 mi. wide, 8 mi. long. W shore formed by Rhone delta (mouth of the Grand Rhône), E shore by limestone Chaîne de l'Estaque. Outlet of Étang de Bouc and Arles–Port-de-Bouc Canal terminate at Port-de-Bouc. Extensive saltworks near Fos-sur-Mer.

Fosdinovo (fôsdēnō'vô), village (pop. 561), Massa e Carrara prov., Tuscany, central Italy, 6 mi. NW of Carrara.

Fosen (fō'sŭn) or **Fosna** (fôs'nä), region (□ 2,027; pop. 44,168) in Sor-Trondelag co., central Norway, around Trondheim Fjord along North Sea coast; hilly, wooded, and indented by many fjords abounding in fish; some agr. and cattle raising. Bjugn and Orland are chief villages.

Fosforitny or **Fosforitnyy** (fôs'fŭrētnē), town (1939 pop. over 500), E central Moscow oblast, Russian SFSR, 3 mi. WSW of Yegoryevsk; phosphorite quarries.

Foshan (fŭ'shän'). **1** Town, ⊙ Foshan co. (pop. 6,500), ENE Heilungkiang prov., Manchuria, 130 mi. N of Kiamusze and on right bank of Amur River (USSR line); gold mining; corn, millet, kaoliang. The name Foshan formerly applied to Chaoyangchen, 20 mi. NNW and on Amur R., and also to another village, 28 mi. SSE and on Amur R. **2** City, Kwangtung prov., China: see NAMHOI.

Foshan River (fō'sän'), Mandarin *Fou-shan Shui*, SW Kwangtung prov., China, rises near Kwangsi-Kwangtung border, flows 100 mi. S, past Sunyi, Mowming, and Fahsien, to S.China Sea at Ngchün.

Fosna, Norway: see FOSEN.

Foso (fō'sō), town, Western Prov., S central Gold Coast colony, on railroad and 40 mi. N of Cape Coast (linked by road); cacao, cassava, corn. Gold deposits.

Foss, city (pop. 210), Washita co., W Okla., 13 mi. WSW of Clinton, in cotton and grain area; cotton ginning.

Fossacesia (fôs"sächā'zyä), village (pop. 1,954), Chieti prov., Abruzzi e Molise, S central Italy, 5 mi. ENE of Lanciano. Damaged by heavy fighting (1943–44) in Second World War.

Fossa Claudia, Italy: see CHIOGGIA.

Fossano (fôs-sä'nô), town (pop. 9,099), Cuneo prov., Piedmont, NW Italy, on Stura di Demonte and 14 mi. NNE of Cuneo; rail junction; textile and paper mills, tanneries, metallurgical works, mfg. of chemicals, fertilizers, machinery. Bishopric. Has anc. castle (1314), acad., mineral baths.

Fossanova (fôs"sänō'vä), village (pop. 146), Latina prov., Latium, S central Italy, 2 mi. SSE of Priverno. Has anc. Cistercian convent where St. Thomas Aquinas died in 1274.

Fossat, Le (lŭ fôsä'), agr. village (pop. 288), Ariège dept., S France, 11 mi. WNW of Pamiers.

Fosse-la-Ville (fôs-lä-vēl'), town (pop. 3,566), Namur prov., S central Belgium, 9 mi. SW of Namur, in fruitgrowing area.

Fosse-lez-Stavelot, Belgium: see TROIS-PONTS.

Fosse Way (fŏs' wā'), early Roman road in England, supposed to have gone from Isca Dumnoniorum (Exeter) NE past Aquae Solis (Bath), Corinum (Cirencester), and Ratae (Leicester) to Lindum (Lincoln). It intersected Watling Street.

Fossil, town (pop. 645), ⊙ Wheeler co., N Oregon, 17 mi. S of Condon; livestock. Prehistoric fossils discovered here.

Fossil Cycad National Monument (sī'kăd) (320 acres; established 1922), SW S.Dak., in Black Hills, 10 mi. WSW of Hot Springs. Preserves fossil remains of fernlike plants (cycads) dating from Mesozoic era.

Fossli (fôs'lē), village in Eidfjord canton, Hordaland co., SW Norway, 7 mi. ESE of Eidfjord village; tourist center on the Hardangervidda; road winds through many tunnels. Near by is the waterfall Voringfoss.

Fossombrone (fôs"sômbrō'nē), town (pop. 3,862), Pesaro e Urbino prov., central Italy, on Metauro R. and 16 mi. SW of Pesaro; silk-milling center. Bishopric. Has cathedral and ruined 15th-cent. castle. Near by is site of anc. *Forum Sempronii*.

Fossoway, agr. village and parish (pop. 1,092), Kinross, Scotland, 6 mi. W of Kinross.

Fossoy (fôswä'), village (pop. 207), Aisne dept., N France, 4 mi. E of Château-Thierry; winegrowing. Scene of an American victory in 1918.

Fosston, village (pop. 1,614), Polk co., NW Minn., on Poplar R., near White Earth Indian Reservation, and c.40 mi. WNW of Bemidji, in grain, livestock, potato area; dairy products. Settled 1884.

Fossum, Norway: see BORGESTAD.

Fos-sur-Mer (fôs-sür-mâr'), village (pop. 1,034), Bouches-du-Rhône dept., SE France, on Arles–

Port-de-Bouc Canal, near Gulf of Fos (Mediterranean Sea), 24 mi. WNW of Marseilles; saltworks. Carton and cement mfg. Damaged in Second World War.

Fostat, El, Egypt: see FUSTAT, EL.

Foster, village (pop. 354), S Que., on Centre Yamaska R., at N end of Brome L., 14 mi. SE of Granby; dairying.

Foster, county (□ 648; pop. 5,337), central N.Dak.; ⊙ Carrington; prairie drained by James R. Dairy products, livestock, wheat, poultry. Formed 1873.

Foster. 1 Town (pop. 108), Bracken co., N Ky., on the Ohio and 12 mi. W of Augusta. 2 Town (pop. 225), Bates co., W Mo., near Marais des Cygnes R., 12 mi. SW of Butler. 3 Village (pop. 114), Pierce co., NE Nebr., 8 mi. NW of Pierce and on branch of Elkhorn R. 4 Town (pop. 1,630), Providence co., W R.I., on Conn. line, on Ponaganset and Moosup rivers and 16 mi. W of Providence, in rural hilly area; Jerimoth Hill (812 ft.) is state's highest point. Timber, gravel pits, granite quarries. Set off from Scituate and inc. 1781.

Fosterdale, resort village, Sullivan co., SE N.Y., near Pa. line, 16 mi. WNW of Monticello.

Foster Peak (10,511 ft.), SE B.C., in Rocky Mts., on W edge of Kootenay Natl. Park, 27 mi. WSW of Banff; 51°4'N 116°10'W.

Fostoria (fŏstô'rēŭ). 1 Town (pop. 147), Clay co., NW Iowa, 7 mi. N of Spencer, in livestock and grain area. 2 City (pop. 14,351), on Seneca-Hancock co. line, N Ohio, 33 mi. SSE of Toledo and on East Branch of Portage R.; industrial, trade, and shipping center for agr. area. Mfg.: wood products, auto parts, carbon, wire, electrical goods, metal products, animal fats and oils, food products, fertilizer. Stockyards. Established 1854. 3 Village (1940 pop. 1,206), Montgomery co., E Texas, c.40 mi. NNE of Houston, in lumbering area.

Fot (fōt), Hung. *Fót*, town (pop. 6,403), Pest-Pilis-Solt-Kiskun co., N central Hungary, 9 mi. NE of Budapest. Has 19th-cent. R.C. church in Byzantine style.

Fotheringhay (fŏ'dhŭrĭng-gā), agr. village and parish (pop. 213), NE Northampton, England, on Nene R. and 9 mi. SW of Peterborough. Has remains of 12th-cent. Fotheringhay Castle, birthplace of Richard III and scene of imprisonment and execution of Mary Queen of Scots. The 15th-cent. church has memorial erected by Elizabeth to Edward (killed at Agincourt) and Richard, dukes of York.

Fotoba (fōtō'bä), village on N tip of Tamara Isl., one of the Los Isls. of Fr. Guinea, Fr. West Africa, 6 mi. W of Conakry.

Fotu La, pass, Kashmir: see LAMAYURU.

Fou-, for Chinese names beginning thus and not found here: see under Fow-.

Foucauld (fōōkō'), village, Casablanca region, W Fr. Morocco, 20 mi. NW of Settat, in wheat-growing area; livestock. Keradia iron deposits near by.

Fou Chiang, China: see FOW RIVER.

Fouday (fōōdā'), Ger. *Urbach* (ōōr'bäkh), village (pop. 257), Bas-Rhin dept., E France, in Bruche R. valley of the central Vosges, 16 mi. SW of Molsheim, at entrance of BAN-DE-LA-ROCHE valley; cotton milling.

Fouesnant (fōōänā'), village (pop. 719), Finistère dept., W France, 8 mi. SE of Quimper; cider making; fish preserving.

Foug (fōōg), village (pop. 1,319), Meurthe-et-Moselle dept., NE France, on Marne-Rhine Canal and 5 mi. W of Toul; foundries.

Fougamou (fōōgämōō'), village, W central Gabon, Fr. Equatorial Africa, on N'Gounié R. and 55 mi. NNW of Mouila, in gold-mining region.

Fougères (fōōzhâr'), town (pop. 18,599), Ille-et-Vilaine dept., W France, on Couesnon R. and 28 mi. NE of Rennes; shoe-mfg. center (especially ladies' and children's shoes). Also has glassworks, carton factory. Tin, wolfram, antimony deposits near by. Founded in Middle Ages, it has a noteworthy feudal castle, a 14th-cent. belfry, and the Gothic churches of Saint-Sulpice (14th-17th cent.) and Saint-Léonard (15th cent.). Heavily damaged in Second World War.

Fougerolles (fōōzhŭrôl'), village (pop. 1,493), Haute-Saône dept., E France, at foot of the Vosges, 15 mi. NNW of Lure; noted kirsch-distilling center. Barrel making, textile machinery mfg. Extensive cherry orchards in area.

Fou-hsin, Manchuria: see FUSIN.

Fouka (fōōkä'), village (pop. 1,699), Alger dept., N central Algeria, in the coastal region, 20 mi. SW of Algiers; truck gardens, vineyards.

Fouke (fōk), town (pop. 336), Miller co., extreme SW Ark., 16 mi. SE of Texarkana.

Foula (fōō'lä), island (□ 4; pop. 118), westernmost of the Shetlands, Scotland, 14 mi. W of Mainland isl.; 60°8'N 2°6'W; 3 mi. long, 2½ mi. wide. Mountainous in W, rising to 1,373 ft. Cod fishing and fowling are main industries; crofting, cattle and sheep raising, and potato growing are carried on. Hametoun is chief settlement.

Foulain (fōōlē'), village (pop. 412), Haute-Marne dept., NE France, on Marne R. and Marne-Saône Canal, and 6 mi. SSE of Chaumont; cutlery mfg.

Foul Bay, inlet of Red Sea, SE Egypt, just N of Tropic of Cancer; anc. BERENICE on W shore.

Fou-ling, China: see FOWLING.

Foulness Island (foul"nĕs'), (pop. 460), SE Essex, England, in the North Sea at mouth of the Crouch, N of the Thames estuary, 7 mi. NE of Shoeburyness; 5 mi. long, 3 mi. wide. Connected with mainland by road dam (W). At NE tip is promontory of Foulness Point.

Foul Point, headland of E Ceylon, on SE promontory of Koddiyar Bay, 6 mi. ESE of Trincomalee; lighthouse.

Foulpointe (fōōlpwĕt'), village, Tamatave prov., E Madagascar, on coast, 30 mi. N of Tamatave; N terminus of Canal des Pangalanes; lime mfg.

Foulridge, village and parish (pop. 1,358), NE Lancashire, England, just N of Colne; cotton milling.

Foulwind, Cape, at S end of Karamea Bight of Tasman Sea, NW S.Isl., New Zealand; 41°45'S 171°28'E.

Foumban (fōōmbän'), town, ⊙ Bamoun region, W Fr. Cameroons, 140 mi. NNW of Yaoundé, near Br. Cameroons border; native trade center with picturesque handicrafts (weaving, brass working, woodworking); large coffee plantations. Customs station. Has palace of Sultan of Foumbau, local mus., R.C. and Protestant missions.

Foumbot (fōōmbō'), village, Bamoun region, W Fr. Cameroons, 25 mi. SW of Foumban; alt. 3,280 ft.; agr. center with large coffee plantations.

Foum-el-Gueïss Dam, Algeria: see KHENCHELA.

Foum el Hassane (fōōm' ĕl häsän'), Saharan oasis and military outpost, Agadir frontier region, SW Fr. Morocco, 70 mi. SE of Tiznit, on desert track and caravan route to Fr. West Africa; 29°2'N 8°55'W.

Foum-Tatahouine (fōōm-tätähwēn'), town (pop. 2,016), Southern Territories, S Tunisia, 28 mi. S of Médenine; 32°55'N 10°27'E; road terminus, regional market, and military post; trade in dates, olives, wool, esparto products. Starting point for trans-Saharan caravans. Also spelled Foum-Tatahouïne, Tatahouine, or Tataouine.

Foum Zguid (fōōm' zgēd'), military post and small oasis in Marrakesh region, SW Fr. Morocco, in a wadi of the Djebel Bani, 60 mi. S of Ouarzazate; 30°5'N 6°53'W.

Foundiougne (fōōndyōō'nyŭ), town (pop. c.2,750), W Senegal, Fr. West Africa, port on Saloum R. delta (accessible to 6,000-ton vessels), on Foundiougne isl., and 75 mi. ESE of Dakar; peanut-trading center. Mission.

Fountain, county (□ 397; pop. 17,836), W Ind.; ⊙ Covington. Bounded W and N by Wabash R.; drained by small Coal Creek. Mfg. at Attica, Covington, and Veedersburg; bituminous-coal mining, dairying, farming (grain, livestock, truck, soybeans, fruit, poultry). Sand, gravel, clay pits. Formed 1825.

Fountain. 1 Town (pop. 713), El Paso co., central Colo., on Fountain Creek and 12 mi. SSE of Colorado Springs; alt. 5,500 ft. Shipping point in irrigated sugar-beet and alfalfa region. 2 Village (pop. 247), Mason co., W Mich., 15 mi. NE of Ludington and on small Lincoln R., in farm and resort area. 3 Village (pop. 312), Fillmore co., SE Minn., near Root R., 25 mi. SE of Rochester; dairy products. 4 Town (pop. 451), Pitt co., E N.C., 15 mi. ESE of Wilson.

Fountain City. 1 Town (pop. 588), Wayne co., E Ind., on a fork of Whitewater R. and 10 mi. N of Richmond, in livestock and grain area. 2 Village (1940 pop. 6,494), Knox co., E Tenn., N suburb of Knoxville. 3 City (pop. 934), Buffalo co., N Wis., on the Mississippi and 33 mi. NW of La Crosse, surrounded by bluffs; dairy, livestock farms; beer, dairy products. Merrick State Park near by.

Fountain Creek, central Colo., rises just N of Pikes Peak in Front Range, flows 22 mi. E and S to Colorado Springs, where it joins Monument Creek to form Fountain R.

Fountain Green, city (pop. 767), Sanpete co., central Utah, 12 mi. SE of Nephi; alt. 5,994 ft.; wool.

Fountain Hill. 1 Town (pop. 320), Ashley co., SE Ark., 19 mi. S of Monticello. 2 Borough (pop. 5,456), Lehigh co., E Pa., 4 mi. E of Allentown and on Lehigh R.

Fountain Inn, town (pop. 1,325), Greenville co., NW S.C., 16 mi. SE of Greenville, in agr. area; cotton textiles, knit goods, clothing, fertilizer.

Fountain River, formed through confluence of Fountain and Monument creeks in Colorado Springs, central Colo., flows 52 mi. SSE to Arkansas R. at Pueblo.

Fountain Run, town (pop. 218), Monroe co., S Ky., near Tenn. line, 20 mi. S of Glasgow.

Fountains Abbey, ruined Cistercian abbey in West Riding, central Yorkshire, England, 3 mi. SW of Ripon in Studley Park; built 1132. It is the largest monastic ruin in England.

Fou-p'ing, China: see FUPING.

Fouquières-lès-Lens (fōōkyâr'-lā-lä'), town (pop. 8,012), Pas-de-Calais dept., N France, 4 mi. E of Lens; coal mines; toy mfg.

Four Ashes, England: see BREWOOD.

Fouras-les-Bains (fōōrä'-lā-bē'), town (pop. 2,720), Charente-Maritime dept., W France, on the Pertuis d'Antioche of Bay of Biscay, near mouth of Charente R., 7 mi. NW of Rochefort; bathing resort on a wooded headland fortified by Vauban. Here Napoleon embarked for Île d'Aix and St. Helena in 1815. Until 1948, Fouras.

Fourchambault (fōōrshäbō'), town (pop. 4,899), Nièvre dept., central France, on right bank of Loire R. and 4 mi. NW of Nevers; industrial center mfg. electrical equipment, steel wire, cycle and auto accessories.

Fourche (fōōrsh, fôrsh), town (pop. 51), Perry co., central Ark., 12 mi. SW of Conway.

Fourche La Fave River (fōōrsh' lŭ fāv', fôrsh' lŭ fāv'), W Ark., rises in S Scott co. in the Ouachita Mts., flows 140 mi. ENE, past Perryville, to Arkansas R. 23 mi. NW of Little Rock. Nimrod Reservoir (c.22 mi. long) is impounded by Nimrod Dam (995 ft. long, 97 ft. high; for flood control), c.60 mi. above river's mouth.

Four Corners, village (pop. 1,284), Marion co., NW Oregon, a suburb of Salem.

Four Evangelists, Chile: see EVANGELIST ISLANDS.

Four Forest Cantons, the, Ger. *Die Vier Waldstätten* (dē fĕr' vält'shtĕtŭn), Switzerland; cantons of UNTERWALDEN, SCHWYZ, URI, and LUCERNE, 1st Swiss communities to win and maintain their freedom. They enclose the **Lake of the Four Forest Cantons**, for which see LUCERNE, LAKE OF.

Four Forest Cantons, Alps of the, Ger. *Vierwaldstätter Alpen*, N division of Central Alps, central Switzerland, bounded by the Reuss (E), by the Aar (W), and by Furka Pass (S). Main peaks are the Dammastock (11,922 ft.), Sustenhorn (11,507 ft.), and Titlis (10,639 ft.) S of L. of Lucerne. Pilatus (6,994 ft.) and Rigi (5,908 ft.) are outlying sub-Alpine mtn. masses overlooking L. of Lucerne.

Four Lakes, Dane co., S Wis., chain of lakes (MENDOTA, largest; MONONA, WAUBESA, and KEGONSA) linked by Yahara R. Madison is on isthmus bet. Mendota and Monona lakes.

Four League Bay, La.: see ATCHAFALAYA BAY.

Fourmies (fōōrmē'), town (pop. 11,805), Nord dept., N France, near Belg. border, 9 mi. SE of Avesnes; wool-spinning center; glassworks (bottles and flasks), metalworks; mfg. of hosiery, dyes and varnishes, cartons, spinning equipment.

Four Mountains, Islands of, group of 5 small uninhabited volcanic isls. of the Aleutians, SW Alaska, in N Pacific, W of Umnak Isl.; 52°50'N 170°W; consists of Chuginadak Island, rising to 5,680 ft., Carlisle Isl. (5,280 ft.), Herbert Isl. (4,235 ft.), Kagamil Isl. (2,920 ft.), and Uliaga Isl. (2,910 ft.). Group is noted for fog and strong sea currents. Aleuts on Uliaga Isl. were wiped out (1764) by Russians.

Fournels (fōōrnĕl'), village (pop. 243), Lozère dept., S France, 15 mi. S of Saint-Flour; sheep, cattle.

Fournoi, Greece: see PHOURNOI.

Four Oaks, town (pop. 942), Johnston co., central N.C., 14 mi. NE of Dunn; sawmilling.

Four Paths, town (pop. 1,070), Clarendon parish, S Jamaica, in Vere Plain, on Kingston-Montego Bay RR and 3 mi. E of May Pen; trades in citrus fruit.

Four Peaks, group of rocky points (7,691 ft., highest alt.), central Ariz., in S part of Mazatzal Mts., c.45 mi. ENE of Phoenix.

Four Roads, village, central Trinidad, B.W.I., 25 mi. SE of Port of Spain, in cacao-growing region.

Fours (fōōr), village (pop. 659), Nièvre dept., central France, 12 mi. E of Decize; horse breeding.

Fourseam, Ky.: see CHRISTOPHER.

Fourstones, England: see NEWBROUGH.

Fourteen Streams, village, NE Cape Prov., near Orange Free State and Transvaal borders, U. of So. Afr., on Vaal R. and 45 mi. N of Kimberley; rail junction; dairying. Important transportation center in pre-railroad days.

Fourth Lake, resort village, Herkimer co., N central N.Y., in the Adirondacks, on Fourth L. (□ c.3; part of FULTON CHAIN OF LAKES), c.50 mi. NNE of Utica.

Fourth Mile, tin-mining settlement (pop. 3,543), central Selangor, Malaya, 4 mi. SE of Kuala Lumpur, on road to Cheras.

Fousseret, Le (lŭ fōōsŭrĕ'), village (pop. 402), Haute-Garonne dept., S France, 21 mi. NE of Saint-Gaudens; horses, hogs.

Fouta Djallon or **Futa Jallon** (both: fōō'tä jälôn', jälō'), extensive massif of W Africa S of 13°N, mostly in N Fr. Guinea but with outliers in Liberia and Sierra Leone. Mean level is c.3,000 ft., though some peaks reach c.6,000 ft. A rolling country of crystalline origin with some deep valleys and picturesque scenery, it is known for its comparatively moderate, healthy climate and good pasturage (cattle). Towards Atlantic it falls in an escarpment. From it rise headstreams of the Niger, Senegal, and Gambia rivers. The region was annexed by France in 1881, though not pacified until 1906. Principal settlements: Labé, Dalaba, Pita, and Timbo. Sometimes spelled Fouta Djalon.

Foux, Cap à (kăp ä fōō'), westernmost headland of N peninsula of Haiti, on Windward Passage, 10 mi. SW of Môle-Saint-Nicolas; 19°42'N 73°27'W.

Foveaux Strait (fō'vō), New Zealand, bet. S tip of S.Isl. and Stewart Isl.; 20 mi. wide; large oyster beds. Bluff is on N shore.

Foveran, Scotland: see NEWBURGH, Aberdeen.

Fow, China: see FOW RIVER.

Fowcheng or **Fou-ch'eng** (both: fō'chŭng'), town, ⊙ Fowcheng co. (pop. 100,772), S Hopeh prov., China, 30 mi. NNW of Tehchow; wheat, kaoliang, millet.

Fowchow, China: see FOWLING.

Fowey (foi), municipal borough (1931 pop. 2,382; 1951 census 2,344), E Cornwall, England, on the Channel, at mouth of Fowey R., and 10 mi. SSE of Bodmin; port, resort, and pilchard-fishing center; exports kaolin. Has ruins of medieval St. Catherine's Fort. The church and Place House date from 15th cent. Fowey was of great maritime importance in 14th cent. Near by, at Pridmouth (W), are fossils and minerals of geological and archaeological interest. Castle Dore, 5 mi. NNW of Fowey, is believed to be castle of King Mark of Cornwall, and associated with legend of Tristram and Isolde.

Fowey River, Cornwall, England, rises in Bodmin Moor 5 mi. SE of Camelford, flows 30 mi. S, past Lostwithiel, to the Channel at Fowey. Navigable below Lostwithiel.

Fow Kiang, China: see FOW RIVER.

Fowler. 1 Town (pop. 1,857), Fresno co., central Calif., in San Joaquin Valley, 9 mi. SE of Fresno; packs and ships raisins, other fruit, nuts; winery. Inc. 1908. **2** Town (pop. 1,025), Otero co., SE central Colo., on Arkansas R. and 33 mi. ESE of Pueblo; alt. 4,300 ft. Shipping point in livestock, sugar-beet, and poultry region; canned goods, dairy and truck products, beans. **3** Town (pop. 2,117), ⊙ Benton co., W Ind., 27 mi. NW of Lafayette, in agr. area (grain, corn, oats, soybeans, livestock, poultry); poultry hatcheries, cannery. Laid out 1871. **4** City (pop. 778), Meade co., SW Kansas, on Crooked Creek and 26 mi. SSW of Dodge City; shipping point in cattle and grain region. Silica deposits. **5** Village (pop. 675), Clinton co., S central Mich., 21 mi. NNW of Lansing, in farm area.

Fowlers Bay, settlement, S South Australia, on W shore of Fowlers Bay of Great Australian Bight, 270 mi. NW of Port Lincoln; wheat, wool.

Fowlerton, town (pop. 292), Grant co., E central Ind., 18 mi. NNW of Muncie, in agr. area.

Fowlerville, village (pop. 1,466), Livingston co., SE Mich., 25 mi. ESE of Lansing and on Red Cedar R., in agr. area (grain, corn, poultry, livestock; dairy products); feed mill, creamery, nursery. Settled c.1836, inc. 1871.

Fowliang or **Fou-liang** (both: fō'lyäng'), town (1948 pop. 86,744), ⊙ Fowliang co. (1948 pop. 164,175), NE Kiangsi prov., China, on Chang R. (right headstream of Po R.) and 90 mi. NE of Nanchang, near E shore of Poyang L.; one of China's leading porcelain-mfg. centers, in kaolin-quarrying area. Coal mining near by. Established in 6th cent. A.D., it reached its greatest fame under the Northern Sung dynasty (c.1000), but declined following destruction during Taiping Rebellion. Was called Kingtehchen (or Ching-te-chen) until 1931, when Fowliang co. seat was moved here from a town 5 mi. N.

Fowling or **Fou-ling** (both: fō'lĭng'), town (pop. 32,291), ⊙ Fowling co. (pop. 829,496), SE Szechwan prov., China, on right bank of Yangtze R., at mouth of Kien R., and 50 mi. ENE of Chungking city; tung-oil trading center; match mfg.; produces hog bristles, rice, wheat, beans, rapeseed. Iron deposits near by. Once a leading opium market. Until 1913 called Fowchow.

Fowning or **Fou-ning** (both: fō'nĭng'), town (1935 pop. 62,144), ⊙ Fowning co. (1946 pop. 1,091,324), NE Kiangsu prov., China, 45 mi. ENE of Hwaiyin; rice, wheat, corn, beans, cotton.

Fow River (fō), Chinese *Fow Kiang* or *Fou Chiang* (both: jyäng), Szechwan prov., China, rises on Kansu border, flows c.350 mi. SE, past Pingwu, Changming (head of navigation), Santai, and Suining, to Kialing R. at Hochwan. Sometimes called Suining R.

Fowshan or **Fou-shan** (fō'shän'), town, ⊙ Fowshan co. (pop. 53,408), S Shansi prov., China, 20 mi. ESE of Linfen; kaoliang, corn, beans.

Fowsin, Manchuria: see FUSIN.

Fowyang or **Fou-yang** (fō'yäng'), town (1934 pop. estimate 50,000), ⊙ Fowyang co. (pop. 1,053,087), NW Anhwei prov., China, 110 mi. NW of Hofei and on Ying R.; commercial center; rice, wheat, beans, cotton, silk; winegrowing. Until 1912 called Yingchow.

Fox, village (pop. 2,453, with near-by Holt), Tuscaloosa co., W central Ala., 7 mi. ENE of Tuscaloosa.

Fox, Cape, SE Alaska, 10 mi. W of entrance to Pearse Canal; 54°46'N 130°51'W; southernmost cape of Alaska mainland.

Fox Bay, inlet at SW entrance of Falkland Sound, West Falkland Isl.; 52°S 60°W; port of entry.

Foxboro or **Foxborough,** town (pop. 7,030), including Foxboro village (pop. 2,774), Norfolk co., E Mass., 12 mi. W of Brockton; indicating and recording instruments, dyeing and finishing, electric furnaces, jewelers' tools. State mental hosp. here. Settled 1704, inc. 1778.

Foxburg, borough (pop. 422), Clarion co., W central Pa., 16 mi. WSW of Clarion and on Allegheny R.

Fox Chapel, borough (pop. 1,721), Allegheny co., SW Pa., N suburb of Pittsburgh. Inc. 1934.

Foxcroft, Maine: see DOVER-FOXCROFT.

Foxe Basin, SE Franklin Dist., Northwest Territories, arm (300 mi. long, 200–250 mi. wide) of the Atlantic, bet. Melville Peninsula and Baffin Isl.; 66°–70°N 73°30'–84°W. Connected S with Hudson Bay by Foxe Channel, NW with the Gulf of Boothia by Fury and Hecla Strait. In it are several isls., largest Jens Munk Isl. Basin is named after Luke Foxe, who explored it 1631.

Foxe Channel, SE Franklin Dist. and E Keewatin Dist., Northwest Territories, arm (200 mi. long, 90–200 mi. wide) of Hudson Bay, bet. Melville Peninsula and Southampton Isl. (W) and Foxe Peninsula of Baffin Isl. (E); 63°30'–66°N 78°–84°W. Connects Hudson Strait and Hudson Bay (S) with Foxe Basin (N).

Foxe Peninsula, SW Baffin Isl., SE Franklin Dist., Northwest Territories, extends 150 mi. W into Foxe Channel, bet. Foxe Basin and Hudson Strait; 50–100 mi. wide. W extremity is Cape Queen; 64°43'N 78°30'W. On SW coast is Cape Dorset trading post.

Foxford, Gaelic *Béal Easa*, town (pop. 741), NE Co. Mayo, Ireland, on Moy R. and 11 mi. NE of Castlebar; agr. market (cattle, sheep; potatoes); woolen milling.

Fox Glacier, W central S.Isl., New Zealand, in Tasman Natl. Park Southern Alps; rises near Mt. Tasman, flows c.10 mi. W to small Cook R.

Foxholes with Boythorpe, agr. parish (pop. 201), East Riding, E Yorkshire, England. Includes village of Foxholes, 10 mi. S of Scarborough; iron foundry, chalk quarries.

Foxhome, village (pop. 217), Wilkin co., W Minn., 11 mi. W of Fergus Falls, in grain area.

Fox Island, Jefferson co., N N.Y., in E part of L. Ontario, 6 mi. S of Cape Vincent; 1½ mi. long; max. width c.½ mi.

Fox Islands, easternmost group of the Aleutian Isls., SW Alaska, extending c.300 mi. SW from Alaska Peninsula. Largest isls. are UNIMAK, UNALASKA, and UMNAK. Fishing, fish canning, fur farming, sheep ranching. Discovered by Russian fur traders in mid-18th cent. Site of strategically important army and navy bases in Second World War.

Fox Islands, Mich., in L. Michigan 10 mi. SW of Beaver Isl. and c.40 mi. W of Petoskey; part of BEAVER ISLANDS archipelago. Include North Fox Isl. (2 mi. long, 1 mi. wide) and South Fox Isl. (c.5 mi. long, 1½ mi. wide; lighthouse). Gravel, timber; fisheries.

Fox Lake, Swedish *Foxen* (fōōk'sün) (8 mi. long, 1–2 mi. wide), W Sweden, on Norwegian border, 20 mi. NE of Halden. Connected (S) with Stora Le L. and (SE) with Lelang L., through which it drains into L. Vaner.

Fox Lake. 1 Village (pop. 2,238), Lake co., NE Ill., on Fox and Pistakee lakes of CHAIN-O'-LAKES, 17 mi. W of Waukegan; trade center in dairying, agr , and lake-resort area; mfg. (dairy products, beverages, bolts, cement blocks). State park near by. Inc. 1906. **2** City (pop. 1,153), Dodge co., S central Wis., bet. Fox and Beaverdam lakes, 8 mi. NNW of Beaver Dam, in dairying region. Settled 1838; inc. as village in 1893, as city in 1930.

Foxpark, village (pop. c.100), Albany co., SE Wyo., in Medicine Bow Mts., 33 mi. SW of Laramie; alt. c.9,100 ft. Supply point in timber region.

Fox Point, residential village (pop. 2,585), Milwaukee co., SE Wis., on L. Michigan, 7 mi. N of Milwaukee. Settled by Dutch c.1846; inc. 1926.

Fox River or **Rivière au Renard** (rēvyâr' ō rünär'), village (pop. estimate 900), E Que., on NE Gaspé Peninsula, on the St. Lawrence and 12 mi. NNE of Gaspé; fishing port; lumbering, dairying.

Fox River. 1 In SE Iowa and NE Mo., rises near Udell in Appanoose co., Iowa, flows c.85 mi. E and SE, into Mo., to the Mississippi 10 mi. SW of Keokuk. **2** In E central Wis., rises in lake region in Columbia co., flows WSW to within 1½ mi. of Portage (on the Wisconsin), thence flows generally NE, entering L. Winnebago at Oshkosh and draining it at Menasha (hydroelectric plant) and Neenah; continues to flow NE, past Appleton, Kaukauna, and De Pere, to Green Bay at Green Bay city; c.176 mi. long. At Portage, near its upper course, Portage Canal connects the Fox with the Wisconsin, forming a continuous waterway bet. the Great Lakes and the Mississippi. Rapids along its course furnish water power; principal tributary is Wolf R. Expands near Green L. to form L. Puckaway. The Fox was a well-known route for early explorers, missionaries, and traders; and forts, missions, and trading posts were established along its course. Louis Jolliet and Father Marquette were the 1st white men to reach (1673) the Mississippi by way of the Fox-Wisconsin portage. River is known as Upper Fox above L. Winnebago, and as Lower Fox below the lake. **3** In SE Wis. and N Ill., rises in Waukesha co., Wis., flows generally SSW, past Waukesha and Burlington, enters Ill., continuing SSW, past Elgin and Aurora, to Illinois R. at Ottawa; c.185 mi. long. Connects and drains Chain-O'-Lakes in Ill.

Fox River Grove, village (pop. 1,313), McHenry co., NE Ill., on Fox R. (bridged here) and 11 mi. NNE of Elgin, in agr. and resort area; mfg. (dairy products, beverages, bolts, cement blocks). Annual ski meet held here.

Fox River Heights, village (pop. 1,083), Kane co., NE Ill.

Foxton, borough (pop. 1,651), S N.Isl., New Zealand, 60 mi. NNE of Wellington, near mouth of Manawatu R.; agr. center at head of rail spur.

Fox Valley, village (pop. 382), SW Sask., 40 mi. N of Maple Creek; alt. 2,358 ft.; wheat, livestock.

Foxwarren, village (pop. 268), SW Man., 65 mi. SW of Dauphin; wheat, mixed farming.

Foxworth, village (1940 pop. 785), Marion co., S Miss., across Pearl R., just W of Columbia; lumber.

Foya (fō'yä), village, Western Prov., NW Liberia, on Sierra Leone border, 18 mi. W of Kolahun; palm oil and kernels, cotton, cassava, rice; cattle raising. Customs post.

Foyers, village, N central Inverness, Scotland, on Loch Ness at mouth of small Foyers R. (falls), 10 mi. NE of Fort Augustus; hydroelectric plant and aluminum works.

Foyil (foil), town (pop. 146), Rogers co., NE Okla., 32 mi. NE of Tulsa, in stock-raising and agr. area.

Foyle, Lough (lŏkh foil'), inlet of the Atlantic, bet. Co. Donegal, Ireland, and Co. Londonderry, Northern Ireland, extending 20 mi. inland from Inishowen Head. Receives Foyle R. below Londonderry. On lough are towns of Eglinton, Muff, and Moville.

Foyle River, Ireland, formed by confluence of Finn and Mourne rivers at Lifford (Co. Donegal, Ireland) and Strabane (Co. Tyrone, Northern Ireland), flows 16 mi. NE along Ireland–Northern Ireland border, past Londonderry, to head of Lough Foyle. Navigable below Londonderry for ships of 600 tons.

Foynes, Gaelic *Faing*, town (pop. 553), NW Co. Limerick, Ireland, on the Shannon (head of navigation for large vessels) and 21 mi. W of Limerick; 52°37'N 9°6'W; fishing port. From 1939 until end of Second World War town was European terminal of transatlantic flying boat services; now superseded by SHANNON AIRPORT. Just N, in the Shannon, is Foynes Isl., 1 mi. long and wide.

Foyn Island, Antarctica, in Weddell Sea off E coast of Palmer Peninsula; 66°30'S 62°30'W.

Foynitsa, Yugoslavia: see FOJNICA.

Foyos (foi'ōs), outer N suburb (pop. 2,839) of Valencia, Valencia prov., E Spain, in truck-farming area; burlap mfg.

Foz (fōth), town (pop. 1,212), Lugo prov., NW Spain, fishing port on inlet of Bay of Biscay, 12 mi. WNW of Ribadeo; fish processing (sardines), boatbuilding, flour milling; agr. trade.

Foz do Arelho (fôzh' dōō ărā'lyōō), village (pop. 1,100), Leiria dist., W central Portugal, on the Atlantic, 4 mi. NW of Caldas da Rainha; bathing resort. Fisheries.

Foz do Cunene (kōōnĕ'nĭ), town, Huíla prov., southwesternmost Angola, on the Atlantic, at mouth of Cunene R. (South-West Africa border), 150 mi. S of Mossâmedes; 17°14'S 11°46'E; fisheries.

Foz do Iguaçu (ēgwŏsōō'). city (pop. 1,432), southwesternmost Paraná, Brazil, on left bank of Paraná R. (navigable) 3 mi. above influx of the Iguassú (Brazil-Argentina-Paraguay borders), and 13 mi. NW of Iguassú Falls, 200 mi. E of Asunción, Paraguay; manioc, corn, rice. Airfield. Formerly spelled Foz do Iguassú. In Iguaçu territory, 1943–46.

Foz do Jordão (zhôrdã'ō), town, Acre territory, westernmost Brazil, near Peru border; 9°25'S 72°8'W Also Jordão.

Frackville, borough (pop. 6,541), Schuylkill co., E central Pa., 7 mi. NNW of Pottsville; anthracite; clothing mfg. Settled 1852, laid out 1861, inc. 1876.

Frade (frä'dĭ), city (pop. 404), E Ceará, Brazil, near the Jaguaribe, 40 mi. E of Senador Pompeu; irrigation agr. Formerly called Riacho do Sangue.

Frade, Ilha do (ē'lyŭ dōō), islet in Todos os Santos Bay, E Bahia, Brazil, 15 mi. NW of Salvador.

Fraga (frä'gä), city (pop. 6,414), Huesca prov., NE Spain, on the Cinca and 16 mi. SW of Lérida, in irrigated agr. area (olives, cereals, fruit); flour milling, soap mfg. Noted for its dried figs. Coal mines near by. Has Romanesque parochial church. Was long contested by Moors and Christians until taken (1149) by count of Barcelona.

Fragagnano (frägänyä'nô), village (pop. 4,167), Ionio prov., Apulia, S Italy, 13 mi. ESE of Taranto; wine making.

Fragneto Monforte (frănyā'tō mônfôr'tĕ), village (pop. 1,603), Benevento prov., Campania, S Italy, 8 mi. N of Benevento. Village (pop. 1,437) of **Fragneto l'Abate** (läbä'tĕ) is 2 mi. NE.

Fragoso, Cayo (kī'ō frägō'sō), long narrow key (25 mi. long, up to 3 mi. wide), off N central Cuba, 10 mi. N of Caibarién, just SE of the Sabana Archipelago. Broken into 3 parts. Lighthouse.

Fraidorf, Russian SFSR: see NOVOSELOVSKOYE.

Fraijanes (frīhä'nĕs), town (1950 pop. 1,480), Guatemala dept., S central Guatemala, on Inter-American Highway and 11 mi. SSE of Guatemala; alt. 5,670 ft.; grain; cattle raising, beekeeping.

Fraile, Cerro, or **Cerro El Fraile** (sĕ'rō ĕl frī'lā), Andean volcano (19,620 ft.) on Argentina-Chile border, 5 mi. W of Cerro Incahuasi; 27°3'S.

Fraile Muerto or **Frayle Muerto** (mwĕr′tō), town (pop. 4,100), Cerro Largo dept., NE Uruguay, on the Arroyo Fraile Muerto (a left affluent of the Río Negro), on railroad and 23 mi. WSW of Melo; trade center in cattle- and sheep-raising region; dairying; wheat, corn, linseed; orchards.

Fraile Pintado (pēntä′dō), town (pop. estimate 500), E Jujuy prov., Argentina, on railroad and 35 mi. NE of Jujuy, in irrigated area (sugar cane, bananas, citrus fruit, pepper, eggplant, livestock).

Frailes (frī′lĕs), town (pop. 2,662), Jaén prov., S Spain, 20 mi. SSW of Jaén; olive-oil processing; stock raising; cereals. Gypsum quarries. Mineral springs near by.

Frailes, Cordillera de los (kôrdĭyā′rä dā lōs), section of Eastern Cordillera of the Andes, W Bolivia; extends c.50 mi. S from S of Mt. Azanaque to SE of Río Mulato; rises to c.17,000 ft. Crossed by Río Mulato–Potosí RR at Cóndor Pass (15,813 ft.). Name sometimes also applied to Cordillera de Azanaques (N). Continued S by Cordillera de Chichas.

Frailes, Los (lōs), small uninhabited island group in the Caribbean, belonging to Venezuela, at NE tip of Margarita Isl.; guano deposits.

Frain, Czechoslovakia: see Vranov, Moravia.

Fraipont (frăpō′), town (pop. 1,478), Liége prov., E Belgium, on Vesdre R. and 9 mi. SE of Liége; metal industry.

Fraire (frâr), town (pop. 965), Namur prov., S Belgium, 5 mi. NNW of Philippeville; foundries; metal utensils.

Fraisse (frăs), residential town (pop. 3,375), Loire dept., SE central France, on the Ondaine and 7 mi. WSW of Saint-Étienne; aluminum plant. Sometimes spelled Fraisses.

Fraiture, Baraque, Belgium: see Baraque Fraiture.

Fraize (frăz), town (pop. 2,290), Vosges dept., E France, on the Meurthe and 7 mi. SSE of Saint-Dié; porcelain and cheese mfg., cotton milling. Tourist center for Vosges excursions.

Frakno, Austria: see Forchtenau.

Framby (frĕm′bü″), Swedish *Främby*, village (pop. 957), Kopparberg co., central Sweden, at N end of 10-mi.-long Runn L. (rŭn), just SE of Falun, in mining region (sulphuric ores, zinc). Includes Kallviken (chĕl′vē″kŭn), Swedish *Källviken*, village.

Frameries (främŭrē′), town (pop. 12,161), Hainaut prov., SW Belgium, 4 mi. SW of Mons; coke plants; mfg. (shoes, leather goods).

Framfield, agr. village and parish (pop. 1,667), E central Sussex, England, just ESE of Uckfield. Has Tudor church.

Fram Haven, small bay of Smith Sound, E Ellesmere Isl., NE Franklin Dist., Northwest Territories, just S of Cape Rutherford, at S entrance of Buchanan Bay; 78°47′N 75°W. Winter quarters of Otto Sverdrup's expedition, 1898–99.

Framingham (frā′mĭng-hăm″), town (pop. 28,086), Middlesex co., E central Mass., on Sudbury R. and 19 mi. WSW of Boston; automobile mfg. and assembly; mfg. (paper products, shoes, carpets, rubber and metal products); truck, dairying, poultry. State teachers col. here. Settled 1650, inc. 1700. Includes Saxonville village (1940 pop. 1,127).

Framlingham (frăm′lĭng-ŭm), town and parish (pop. 2,101), E central Suffolk, England, 15 mi. NNE of Ipswich; agr. market; flour mills. Has remains of medieval castle, refuge of Queen Mary after death of Edward VI, and former family seat of dukes of Norfolk. The 14th-15th-cent. church contains monuments to Howard family (dukes of Norfolk), including earl of Surrey.

Frammersbach (frä′mŭrsbäkh), village (pop. 3,297), Lower Franconia, NW Bavaria, Germany, on E slope of The Spessart, 7 mi. NW of Lohr; cider.

Frampton Cotterell (frămp′tŭn kŏt′rŭl), town and parish (pop. 2,081), SW Gloucester, England, 7 mi. NE of Bristol; agr. market. Has 15th-cent. church.

Framwellgate, industrial town (pop. 2,658) in Durham municipal borough, central Durham, England.

Framwellgate Moor, town and parish (pop. 2,587), central Durham, England, just N of Durham; coal mining.

Franca (frăng′kŭ), city (1950 pop. 27,715), NE São Paulo, Brazil, on railroad, 50 mi. NNE of Ribeirão Prêto, in coffeegrowing and extensive stock-raising region; mfg. (leather goods, furniture, cigarettes, dairy produce). Airfield. Diamond area near by.

Franca or **Villa Franca** (vē′yä fräng′kä), town (dist. pop. 1,967), Ñeembucú dept., S Paraguay, on Paraguay R. (Argentina border) and 75 mi. SSW of Asunción; minor port; cattle raising.

Française, Pointe (pwĕt frăsĕz′), on Atlantic coast of NW Fr. Guiana, at mouth of Maroni R., opposite Galibi Point; 5°45′N 53°58′W.

Francavilla al Mare (fräng″kävēl′lä äl mä′rĕ), town (pop. 4,108), Chieti prov., Abruzzi e Molise, S central Italy, on the Adriatic, 5 mi. SE of Pescara. Fishing center; bathing resort; mfg. (hosiery, wire, irrigation pumps). Largely destroyed (Dec., 1943) in Second World War by Ger. mines.

Francavilla Angitola (änjē′tôlä), village (pop. 2,098), Catanzaro prov., Calabria, S Italy, 12 mi. NE of Vibo Valentia.

Francavilla di Sicilia (dē sēchē′lyä), village (pop. 5,260), Messina prov., NE Sicily, near Alcantara R., 9 mi. WNW of Taormina.

Francavilla Fontana (fôntä′nä), town (pop. 19,630), Brindisi prov., Apulia, S Italy, 19 mi. ENE of Taranto; rail junction; agr. center (wine, olive oil, wheat, figs).

Francavilla Marittima (märēt′tēmä), village (pop. 2,113), Cosenza prov., Calabria, S Italy, 10 mi. E of Castrovillari; olive oil, dried figs.

France, republic (□ 212,659, including Corsica; pop. 40,502,513), W Europe, as Metropolitan France chief member of the French Union; ⊙ Paris. Administratively divided into 90 departments, which are further subdivided into *arrondissements*, cantons, and communes. It lies bet. 42°20′–51°5′N and 8°10′E–5°55′W. Washed in N by the English Channel and Strait of Dover, in W by the Atlantic Ocean with Bay of Biscay, and in S by the Mediterranean with Gulf of Lion. Apart from NE section, where it borders on Belgium, tiny Luxembourg, and the Saar, its international frontiers are physiographically well defined, accounting in part for the comparative stability of its area during last 300 years. It fronts on Germany in E along the Rhine. The Jura Mountains (E) form its national boundary with Switzerland, while the Alps from L. Geneva to the Mediterranean at Menton separate it from Italy. The Pyrenees in S are a forbidding barrier bet. France and Spain. Small, independent Monaco (SE), an enclave on the Mediterranean, and Andorra (S) in the Pyrenees, maintain, though independent, close contacts with France. The isl. of Corsica (□ 3,367), an integral part of Metropolitan France, lies in the Mediterranean, c.140 mi. SE of Nice. The long coast line of c.1,870 mi. has chalk cliffs in N, rocky indentations in Brittany, flat reaches in SW (the Landes) and along Mediterranean, lagoons in W, and Alpine spurs in SE. Because of W coast location and exposure to North Atlantic Drift, the climate is largely maritime (mild winters, cool summers), but influence of the sea decreases inland, climate becoming more continental (marked extremes) in the E. The S coast, with the famed Riviera, has an equable Mediterranean climate, one of the finest in Europe, though the cold *mistral* causes occasional damage in lower Rhone valley. Paris has an annual mean temp. of c.50°F., rainfall about 24 inches. France is just as much favored by its relief and soil. Its topography shows greatest variety, which, despite France's centralized government, helped to perpetuate the regional character of its old provs., such as Île-de-France at its historic center, surrounded by Champagne and Lorraine (E), Artois, Picardy, French Flanders, and Normandy (NW); Brittany, Maine, Anjou, and Poitou (W); Touraine, Orléanais, and Burgundy (S). Farther E are Franche-Comté, Savoy, and Dauphiné; in SE is the Provence; in S central the Auvergne; in S Guienne, Gascony, and Languedoc. France contains 7 major mtn. blocks. Geologically the oldest are the Ardennes (N), reaching into Belgium and Luxembourg; the wooded Vosges, facing the German Black Forest, with which they bound the Rhine valley; and the low hills of Brittany and Normandy (American Massif). The great Massif Central (highest peak Puy de Sancy, 6,187 ft.), in one of France's most backward regions, is an eroded, crystalline formation of little fertility, overlaid in some parts by young lava fields and so-called *puys* (volcanic cones), and flanked by SE escarpments (e.g., Cévennes). Far more imposing are the newer mtn. groups, especially the Alps, which occupy most of the country S and E of the Rhone valley and form several high subranges along international frontier—Maritime Alps, Cotian Alps, and Graian Alps. Through Mont Cenis tunnel and along the Riviera pass the international railroads to Italy. The Mont Blanc massif, highest elevation in the country, lies on Italian border SE of Geneva. Geologically related to the Alps are the parallel ranges of the Franco-Swiss Jura, a limestone formation, rising here to 5,652 ft. in Crêt de la Neige. The Pyrenees, which border Spain from the Atlantic to the Mediterranean, are almost as lofty as the Alps and resemble them in structure, but are an even more severe obstacle to traffic. Bet. these mtn. systems are valleys and saddles which link the main basins. The most important are the Saverne Gap in N Vosges, Col de Naurouze (SW) bet. Massif Central and the Pyrenees, Belfort Gap (E) bet. Vosges and Jura. Through the latter the Rhone-Saône corridor connects with the Rhine valley. These gates are key positions in rail, highway, and fluvial (canal) communications, frequently occupied by strategic trading towns, such as Toulouse, Belfort, Poitiers. France's 4 leading streams, the Seine (with its tributaries, the Oise, the Marne, and Yonne), the Loire (the longest), with the Allier, the Garonne (joined in Gironde estuary by Dordogne), and the Rhone (with its tributaries, the Saône, Doubs, and Isère), water the 3 great lowland sections, the Paris Basin, Aquitaine Basin, and Rhone-Saône corridor. The Moselle and Meuse belong to the Rhine system, which France shares with adjoining countries and the Netherlands. Of all major rivers only the Rhone drains into the Mediterranean. Navigability is best on the Seine, where Rouen and Paris have become great inland ports. Large-scale navigation, now handling about 10% of all traffic, has been made possible through a thick net of canalized arms and canals which spreads over all France and links the rivers and oceans, e.g., Canal du Midi from Garonne to the Mediterranean, Brest-Nantes canal, Rhone-Rhine canal, Burgundy canal. France's well-balanced economy is almost self-sufficient in agr. yields. Production varies with the regions, but the all-important Paris Basin leads in wheat and oats. Other food crops include potatoes, barley, rye, corn, tubers, and all kinds of fruit. The Paris Basin, with the great metropolis in its center (whence radiate all major airlines, railroads, and highways), is historically, socially, and economically the country's heartland. Made of several concave layers of limestone, covered by rich soil, its outer edges form concentric, partly forested ridges. Between those ridges and on slopes, truck gardening, fruit- and winegrowing, and grazing are carried on. Vegetable growing, stock raising, and dairying are the main activities of Brittany and Normandy. The Paris Basin extends SW beyond Orléans in the Loire valley (a highly productive land which is also renowned for its splendid *châteaux*) to the Aquitaine Basin, which centers chiefly around the Garonne to the Pyrenees piedmont. This region, intensively cultivated, is known for its vineyards, which are also conspicuous in the adjoining Mediterranean Languedoc. The sandy Atlantic strip (Landes) S of the Gironde, once a foremost sheep-grazing land, has been forested with pines that are now principal source for timber and naval stores. The alluvial Rhone valley is also productive in wine, olives, and fruit. Sericulture is on the decline. The Mediterranean section E of Marseilles, internationally known as the French Riviera or Côte d'Azur, with a string of glamorous resorts (Cannes, Antibes, Nice, Menton, etc.), supports a subtropical agr. of winter vegetables, citrus, and flowers for perfume (Grasse). France is celebrated for its wines, which are produced in most parts, except in N and NW, but especially in Burgundy, Champagne, and Languedoc, in Loire and Rhone valleys, and in the Bordeaux region. Though wines make up a substantial export item, the country imports ordinary wine for home consumption from Fr. North Africa. France's agr. productivity is matched by its industry, based on large iron and coal resources, which, however, do not fulfill all requirements of its great metallurgical output. Iron is mined principally in the Lorraine and in N Massif Central. The major coal fields, reaching into Belgium, are centered mainly S of Lille. Coal also occurs at scattered locations, especially in the Massif Central. The Saar, now economically within the orbit of France, supplies coking coal, taking iron for its steel mills in return. From these resources draw the steel and machine industries of Saint-Étienne, Le Creusot (munitions), Montbéliard, Thionville, Longwy, Vierzon, and Nancy. A great many hydroelectric plants, principally in the Alps, tap the enormous water power potential. On them thrive the aluminum works of Savoy, fed by ore from Languedoc, where bauxite was 1st mined near Les Baux (from which came the name of the ore). Other substantial mineral resources include salt (from sea and rocks); potash (Alsace), pyrites, gypsum (from which comes plaster of Paris), building material, and kaolin (utilized at Limoges and Sèvres porcelain factories). Not the least important of France's industrial products are the exquisite luxury and fashion articles made at Paris. Paris also has numerous consumer industries, notably chemical works and automobile plants. Lyons, the 3d city of France, at Rhone-Saône junction, excells in silk and rayon, and is known for its fairs. Textile centers are mainly in French Flanders (Lille, Roubaix, Valenciennes, Tourcoing), at Amiens and Roanne and in Alsace and Lorraine, where Strasbourg, Mulhouse, and Colmar are gateways to central Europe. Rheims (N), famous for its Gothic cathedral, is center of the champagne industry; Cognac (W) distills the brandy of that name; Besançon in the Jura manufactures clocks. Clermont-Ferrand is the rubber capital. There are a great number of local trading and mfg. towns. Countless small picturesque towns, spas, archaeological and historical sites cater to France's tourist trade. In addition to the Riviera resorts, there are Deauville, Trouville, Dinard, and Mont-Saint-Michel on English Channel, La Baule and Biarritz on Bay of Biscay, Chamonix, Annecy, and Aix-les-Bains in the Alps, Évian-les-Bains on L. Geneva, Versailles and Fontainebleau near Paris, Vichy in center, Carcassonne, Arles, Nîmes, and Avignon in the S. Lourdes in the Pyrenees is one of the most famed places of pilgrimage in Christendom. Nancy, Metz, Toul, Verdun, and Sedan are the traditional forts guarding the exposed E flank of the Paris Basin. Of France's transoceanic ports one of the most important is Marseilles, 2d city of the republic, dominating trade with North Africa and the Orient. Among Channel and Atlantic ports are Le Havre,

Cherbourg, Saint-Nazaire, Nantes, Bordeaux. Brest, Lorient, and Toulon (Mediterranean) are important naval bases. Most of the traffic with Great Britain passes through Dunkirk, Calais, Boulogne, Dieppe, and Le Havre. Saint-Malo and La Rochelle (old Huguenot stronghold) are among the many Atlantic fishing towns. Since France has been for centuries in the front rank of Western culture and a haven for scholars and artists, its museums, edifices, and educational institutions enjoy world repute. There are 16 universities, those of Aix-Marseilles, Besançon, Bordeaux, Caen, Clermont-Ferrand, Dijon, Grenoble, Lille, Lyons, Montpellier, Nancy, Paris, Poitiers, Rennes, Strasbourg, and Toulouse. The population of France is fairly stable, the number of deaths sometimes exceeding that of births. A majority lives in small towns and villages. Only some 20 French cities have more than 100,000 inhabitants, while Paris alone passes the million mark. The French are overwhelmingly R.C. Many foreigners have settled in France as industrial and agr. workers, notably Italians in the SE and Poles in N mining districts. Although the Latin cultural tradition has triumphed in all France, the N of France shows some Germanic admixture, in contrast with the distinctly Latin S. German dialect is spoken in Alsace and parts of Lorraine, and some Flemish in Fr. Flanders. In Celtic Brittany Breton is still cultivated, as is Basque in the Bayonne region. Some of Europe's earliest anthropological and archaeological remains have been found in France (e.g., Les Eyzies and Aurignac). The Mediterranean coast, especially Marseilles, had long been settled by Phoenician and Greek traders. Provence (Lat. *Gallia Narbonensis* or just *Provincia*) was colonized by Rome in 2d cent. B.C. But recorded history begins with Roman conquest (58–51 B.C.) under Julius Caesar, when the country was known as Gaul (Lat. *Gallia*) or Transalpine Gaul. It was then inhabited by Aquitanians (SW), Celts (center), and Belgae (N, NE). Christianity was introduced in 1st cent. Invaded by Germanic tribes (Visigoths, Franks, and Burgundi) in 5th cent. Clovis, king of Franks and founder of Merovingian dynasty, broke (486) Roman sway at Soissons, conquered S Gaul from the Visigoths, and extended his rule into Germany and beyond the Pyrenees. Kingdom split under his descendants into Neustria and Austrasia. Saracen invasions in 8th cent. were halted (732) by Charles Martel, whose son Pepin the Short became 1st Carolingian king, succeeded by Charlemagne, who was crowned Emperor in 800. Under him the Frankish realm expanded into central and NW Europe. An able administrator, he revived learning. The Treaty of Verdun (843), when his realm was partitioned among his grandsons, marks separate existence of France and Germany. At expense of monarchy, feudalism became a disrupting power, strengthening autonomy of the provinces (Aquitania, Burgundy, Flanders, Anjou, etc.). Norsemen from Scandinavia obtained (911) Normandy. Capetian kings, after 987, gradually re-established royal authority. Norman conquest (1066) of England led to loss of Normandy and, temporarily, other N territories to English crown. By 13th cent. France's culture, outstanding in architecture, poetry, manners, and scholastic learning, had become model for Europe. France took a leading part in the Crusades, notably under Louis IX, and crushed heretic Albigenses in the S. It was initially successful against English intrusions. The Valois succeeded to the throne in 1328, but their claim was disputed by English Crown. This provoked Hundred Years War (1337–1453), from which France, roused by Joan of Arc, finally emerged victorious; only Calais remained (until 1558) an English stronghold. Under Louis XI centralized royal regime began to emerge. The Italian Wars (1494–1559) ended with triumph of Hapsburg Spain. At the same time Reformation gained ground, bringing about ferocious religious conflicts (Massacre of St. Bartholomew's Day in 1572). Civil War involved the Guise against Protestant Henry of Navarre, who became as Henry IV first Bourbon king, embracing Catholicism upon entry (1594) into Paris. His assassination (1610) spelled the end of religious peace. Under his successors Louis XIII and Louis XIV (when a minor), the astute cardinals Richelieu and Mazarin shaped the destinies of the kingdom. France profited from Thirty Years War (1618–48). At home power of Huguenots was suppressed, and the nobles were overcome in Wars of the Fronde. Louis XIV, exalting royal splendor at Versailles, made centralization complete. Yet his costly wars (e.g., that of Spanish Succession, 1701–14), exhausted the country. Contributions to the downfall of the old regime were the excesses of Louis XV, the intolerable tax burdens of the peasantry, and the triumphs of the intellectual movement of the Enlightenment. The War of the Austrian Succession (1740–48) and the Seven Years War (1756–63) proved disastrous. France lost at Treaty of Paris an empire in India and North America. In 1788 the country was bankrupt and Louis XVI decided to convoke, for the 1st time since Henry IV, the States-General. Thus began (1789) the French Revolution, which led to execution of king, the Fr. Revolutionary Wars, the Reign of Terror, and the emergence of a military dictatorship under Napoleon Bonaparte, who established the 1st Empire (1804–15). After spectacular conquest of most of Europe, he was finally vanquished at Waterloo. Congress of Vienna (1814–15) gave France practically its present limits and restored the Bourbons under Louis XVIII. His successor, Charles X, champion of absolutism, antagonized the rising bourgeoisie and was ousted (1830) in the July Revolution. After Louis Philippe and the Revolution of 1848, emerged the Second Republic (1848–52), whose president, Louis Napoleon Bonaparte, became emperor as Napoleon III. The Second Empire went down in Franco-Prussian War (1870–71). Alsace and Lorraine were lost to Germany until 1918. During Third Republic (1871–1940) France made a quick recovery, survived the Commune of Paris, the ambitions of General Boulanger, and the crucial Dreyfus Affair. It expanded in Africa, though temporarily clashing with Great Britain (Fashoda Incident) and Germany (Moroccan Crisis). In First World War (1914–18) France under forceful leadership of Clemenceau shared the Allied victory, sealed by Treaty of Versailles. Occupied (1923–25) German Ruhr region. France was hard hit by the world-wide economic crisis of 1929. "Popular Front" coalition government, headed by Socialist Léon Blum, won 1936 election; it introduced social and economic reforms, but disastrously neglected rearmament. Signing of Munich Pact (1938) with Hitler could not delay outbreak (Sept., 1939) of Second World War, in which France was ignominiously overrun (May-June, 1940) by Germany. Marshal Pétain became chief of state in Vichy govt. of unoccupied S France, while General Charles de Gaulle formed in London the Free French movement to continue resistance against Germany. He was joined by some Fr. colonies. Allied invasion (Nov., 1942) of North Africa resulted in establishment of provisional government at Algiers and total German occupation of Metropolitan France. The Allies landed in France June 6, 1944, and in Aug., 1944, Paris was liberated. Peace returned in 1945. Through peace treaty (1947) with Italy, France acquired 4 small border districts (□ c.250; pop. c.5,000), with villages of Tende (Ital. *Tenda*) and Brigue (Ital. *Briga*). Post-war recovery was necessarily difficult, though aided by U.S. through European Recovery Plan. The Fourth Republic began officially in Dec., 1946. The new constitution reorganized the Fr. empire as the French Union, and established a parliament composed of a national assembly and of a weakened upper house. While Fr. economy was largely normalized by 1950, exceeding in production some of the pre-war figures, the troubled political life of the country was steered by precarious middle-of-the-road coalitions between the strong and demanding pressures of the extreme left and the extreme right. France became (1945) a member of the United Nations at San Francisco, entered (1948) an alliance with Great Britain, Belgium, Netherlands, and Luxembourg, and signed in the same year the North Atlantic Treaty. For information on Fr. overseas territories, see French Union and individual entries; for further information on France, see separate articles on towns, cities, physical features, provinces, and regions, and the following 90 departments: Ain, Aisne, Allier, Alpes-Maritimes, Ardèche, Ardennes, Ariège, Aube, Aude, Aveyron, Bas-Rhin, Basses-Alpes, Basses Pyrénées, Territory of Belfort, Bouches-du-Rhône, Calvados, Cantal, Charente, Charente-Maritime, Cher, Corrèze, Corsica, Côte-d'Or, Côtes-du-Nord, Creuse, Deux-Sèvres, Dordogne, Doubs, Drôme, Eure, Eure-et-Loir, Finistère, Gard, Gers, Gironde, Haute-Garonne, Haute-Loire, Haute-Marne, Hautes-Alpes, Haute-Saône, Haute-Savoie, Hautes-Pyrénées, Haute-Vienne, Haut-Rhin, Hérault, Ille-et-Vilaine, Indre, Indre-et-Loire, Isère, Jura, Landes, Loire, Loire-Inférieure, Loiret, Loir-et-Cher, Lot, Lot-et-Garonne, Lozère, Maine-et-Loire, Manche, Marne, Mayenne, Meurthe-et-Moselle, Meuse, Morbihan, Moselle, Nièvre, Nord, Oise, Orne, Pas-de-Calais, Puy-de-Dôme, Pyrénées-Orientales, Rhône, Saône-et-Loire, Sarthe, Savoie, Seine, Seine-et-Marne, Seine-et-Oise, Seine-Inférieure, Somme, Tarn, Tarn-et-Garonne, Var, Vaucluse, Vendée, Vienne, Vosges, Yonne.

France, Île de (ēl' dů frãs'), island (20 mi. long, 3–6 mi. wide) in Greenland Sea, off NE Greenland; 77°42'N 17°50'W. Almost entirely glaciated. Named (1905) by duke of Orléans.

France, Île de, island in Indian Ocean: see Mauritius.

France, Île-de-, France: see Île-de-France.

France Field, military reservation, Cristobal dist., N Panama Canal Zone, on Manzanillo Bay of the Caribbean, on transisthmian highway, and 1½ mi. ESE of Colón. U.S. army airfield.

Frances, village (pop. 112), SE South Australia, 185 mi. SE of Adelaide, near Victoria border, NE of Naracoorte; dairy products, livestock.

Francés, Cape (fränsěs'), SW Cuba, 40 mi. SW of Pinar del Río; 21°54'N 84°2'W. Lighthouse.

Francés, Cayo (kī'yō), key (3 mi. long, up to 1½ mi. wide), off N central Cuba, E of Cayo Fragoso, 13 mi. ENE of Caibarién. Lighthouse on W tip.

Frances, Lake, N Mont., in Pondera co., 25 mi. SW of Shelby; 5 mi. long, 3 mi. wide; fed by Marias R.; dammed at E end. Serves as reservoir of irrigation system. Town of Valier on N.

Francescas (frãsěskä'), village (pop. 297), Lot-et-Garonne dept., SW France, 6 mi. SE of Nérac; distilling; brickworks.

Frances Lake, trading post, SE Yukon, on Frances L. (27 mi. long, 1–2 mi. wide), 200 mi. E of Whitehorse; 61°16'N 129°18'W; Hudson's Bay Co. fur-trading post; radio station. Sometimes called Fort Frances. Frances R. (90 mi. long) drains the lake S to Liard R.

Francestown, town (pop. 405), Hillsboro co., S N.H., 19 mi. W of Manchester.

Francés Viejo, Cape (fränsěs' vyā'hō), headland, N Dominican Republic, 33 mi. NE of San Francisco de Macorís, 2 mi. NW of Cabrera; lighthouse (19°42'N 69°55'W).

Francesville, town (pop. 856), Pulaski co., NW Ind., near Big Monon Creek, 40 mi. N of Lafayette; flour, machine-shop products; ships milk, grain.

Franceville (frãsvēl'), town, ⊙ Haut-Ogooué region (□ 14,300; pop. 42,900), SE Gabon, Fr. Equatorial Africa, on Ogooué R. and 320 mi. ESE of Libreville; trading center in manganese- and gold-mining region. Has R.C. mission, hosp. for natives. Founded 1880 by de Brazza. Until 1946, Haut-Ogooué region was part of Middle Congo colony.

Franceville-Plage, France: see Merville-Franceville-Plage.

Franche-Comté (frãsh-kōtā') or **Free County of Burgundy,** region and former province of E France; ⊙ until 1676 was Dôle, later it was Besançon. Bounded by Switzerland (E), Burgundy (S and W) and the Vosges (N), it is now administratively divided into Jura, Doubs, and Haute-Saône depts. It is occupied by the central Jura and the lowland of upper Saône R., and traversed NE-SW by the Doubs. Stock-raising and cheese mfg. are chief agr. occupations, together with lumbering. Main industrial products are clocks, machines, and plastics. Principal towns are Besançon, Dôle, Lons-le-Saunier, Vesoul, and Pontarlier. Originally part of First Kingdom of Burgundy, it became Free County of Burgundy in 9th cent., and in 10th cent. a fief of kings of Arles. Passed (1034) to Holy Roman Empire. During following 6 centuries it was continually invaded and contested for by France, Germany, Burgundy, Switzerland, and Spain. Finally Louis XIV conquered Franche-Comté (1674) and obtained its cession from Spain in 1678. It was divided into present depts. in 1790.

Franchimont, Belgium: see Theux.

Francia (frän'syä), town, Río Negro dept., W central Uruguay, on railroad and 17 mi. NNW of Paso de los Toros, 105 mi. ENE of Fray Bentos; wheat, grain, cattle, sheep.

Francia, La, Argentina: see La Francia.

Francia, Peña de (pā'nyä dhā frän'thyä), mountain group of Salamanca prov., W Spain, a NE outlier of the Sierra de Gata. Highest point, 5,653 ft.

Francis, town (pop. 143), SE Sask., 40 mi. SE of Regina; grain elevators.

Francis. 1 Town (pop. 271), Pontotoc co., S central Okla., 8 mi. NNE of Ada, in agr. area. **2** Town (pop. 276), Summit co., N Utah, in Wasatch Mts., 12 mi. ESE of Park City; alt. c.6,500 ft.

Francis, Lake. 1 In Coos co., N N.H., formed by dam in Connecticut R. near Pittsburg, below First Connecticut L.; 5 mi. long. **2** In Okla.: see Illinois River, Ark. and Okla.

Francisco or **Central Francisco** (sěnträl' fränsē'skō), sugar-mill village (pop. 1,350), Camagüey prov., E Cuba, 45 mi. SSE of Camagüey.

Francisco (frănsĭ'skō), town (pop. 606), Gibson co., SW Ind., 7 mi. ESE of Princeton, in agr., gas and oil, and bituminous-coal area.

Francisco de Orellana, Peru: see Orellana, Loreto dept.

Francisco I. Madero (fränsē'skō ē' mädā'rō). **1** Town (pop. 2,679), Coahuila, N Mexico, near Nazas R., in irrigated Laguna Dist., on railroad and 20 mi. NE of Torreón; cotton, wine, vegetables, fruit, alfalfa, wheat. Formerly Chávez. **2** Town, Durango, Mexico: see Villa Madero.

Francisco León (lāōn'), town (pop. 516), Tabasco, S Mexico, in N outliers of Sierra Madre, 15 mi. N of Copainalá; cereals, fruit. Formerly Magdalena.

Francisco Morazán (mōräsän'), department (□ 3,870; 1950 pop. 220,409), S central Honduras; ⊙ Tegucigalpa. Astride continental divide; largely mountainous, including sierras de Comayagua (NW) and Lepaterique (center). Drained by headstreams of Sulaco R. (N), and by upper Choluteca (center) and upper Nacaome and Texíguat (S) rivers. Mainly agr. (corn, wheat, coffee, sugar cane, cotton, rice, plantains, fruit); dairying, poultry farming. Mfg. and processing industries concentrated at Tegucigalpa and Comayagüela. Pottery making, mat weaving, and tanning are local industries. Of the once important gold- and silver-mining centers (Cedros, Sabanagrande, Santa Lucía, Ojojona) only San Juancito remains in production. Iron mine at Agalteca; limestone quarrying. Main N-S road links centers of Tegucigalpa, Cedros, Talanga, and Sabanagrande. Called Tegucigalpa until 1943.

Francisco Portillo, Mexico: see AQUILES SERDÁN.

Francis E. Warren, Fort, Wyo.: see CHEYENNE.

Francistown, town, ⊙ TATI dist., E Bechuanaland Protectorate, near Southern Rhodesia border, 100 mi. SW of Bulawayo and on railroad; dairy plant; in mining region (gold, silver). Airfield; hosp.

Franck (frängk), village (pop. 1,000), E central Santa Fe prov., Argentina, 14 mi. WNW of Santa Fe; agr. center (alfalfa, flax, corn, livestock); dairying.

Franco da Rocha (frãng'kōō dä rô'shù), city (pop. 2,719), SE São Paulo, Brazil, on railroad and 17 mi. N of São Paulo.

Francoeur (frãkûr'), village (pop. 624), S Que., 45 mi. SW of Quebec; dairying; pigs, cattle.

Francofonte (fräng"kôfôn'tĕ), town (pop. 11,800), Siracusa prov., E Sicily, 7 mi. SW of Lentini, in citrus-fruit region.

François (frãswä'), town (pop. 2,329; commune pop. 11,923), E Martinique, port on the Atlantic, and 11 mi. E of Fort-de-France, in agr. region (bananas, sugar cane, cacao, coffee); rum distilling.

François Lake (□ 91), central B.C., 90 mi. W of Prince George; 68 mi. long, 2 mi. wide. Drains E into Fraser R. through Nechako R.

Franconia (frăngkō'nēù), Ger. *Franken* (fräng'kùn), historic region in S Germany, one of the basic duchies of medieval Germany, created a duchy in 9th cent. and named after the Franks, a Germanic tribe; included middle Rhine region, territory along both banks of Main R., and Hesse. Emperor Otto I dissolved and partitioned the duchy in 939, and vast territories passed to bishops of Würzburg and Bamberg and the abbot of Fulda. Two nominal duchies—Western or Rhenish Franconia and Eastern Franconia—emerged. The former soon broke up into several free cities, ecclesiastic states, and other territories; the title of the latter was assumed (15th cent.) by the bishop of Würzburg. Major part of Eastern Franconia passed to Bavaria bet. 1806 and 1815. In 1837, Louis I of Bavaria revived the name Franconia by creating the present administrative dists. of LOWER FRANCONIA, MIDDLE FRANCONIA, UPPER FRANCONIA.

Franconia, resort town (pop. 549), Grafton co., NW N.H., 30 mi. SW of Berlin, near Franconia Notch; skiing center.

Franconia Mountains, NW N.H., range of White Mts. in N Grafton co., SE of Franconia and E of FRANCONIA NOTCH. Principal peaks (N to S): North Twin Mtn. (4,769 ft.), South Twin Mtn. (4,926 ft.), Mt. Garfield (4,488 ft.), Mt. Lafayette (5,249 ft.; highest in range), Mt. Lincoln (5,108 ft.), Mt. Liberty (4,460 ft.), and Mt. Flume (4,327 ft.).

Franconian Forest, Ger. *Frankenwald* (fräng'-kùnvält), S outlier of the Thuringian Forest, Germany, extends 20 mi. bet. Rodach R. (NW) and the Fichtelgebirge (SE); rises to 2,608 ft. in the Döbraberg. Forested slopes; barley growing and cattle raising on plateaus.

Franconian Jura (jōō'rù, yōō'rù), Ger. *Fränkische Alb* (frĕng'kĭ-shù älp') or *Fränkischer Jura* (-shùr yōō'rä), plateau in central Bavaria, Germany, a continuation of the Swabian Jura, situated bet. Wörnitz (W), Danube (S), and Main (N) rivers; rises to 2,260 ft. in the Hesselberg. Wheat, barley, cattle; hops grown S of Nuremberg. Composed of Jurassic formations; numerous caves. Scenic N tip is called Franconian Switzerland, Ger. *Fränkische Schweiz* (shvīts').

Franconia Notch, Grafton co., NW N.H., pass in White Mts. W of FRANCONIA MOUNTAINS and just N of Woodstock; c.6 mi. long. Noted for scenic features, including: The Flume, narrow stream gorge 70 ft. deep entering the Notch from E; the Old Man of the Mountain, Great Stone Face, or Profile on PROFILE MOUNTAIN; and small Echo and Profile lakes (latter is source of Pemigewasset R.). Notch area made state forest in 1925.

Franconian Rezat, Ger. *Fränkische Rezat* (frĕng'kĭ-shù rä'tsät), river in Bavaria, Germany, rises S of Bergel, flows 37 mi. SE, past Ansbach and Spalt, to Georgensgmünd, where it joins the SWABIAN REZAT to form REDNITZ RIVER.

Franconian Saale, Germany: see SAALE RIVER.

Franconian Switzerland, Germany: see FRANCONIAN JURA.

Franconville (frãkõvēl'), town (pop. 6,130), Seine-et-Oise dept., N central France, 11 mi. NNW of Paris; truck.

Francs Peak, Wyo.: see ABSAROKA RANGE.

Franeker (frä'nùkùr), town (pop. 9,050), Friesland prov., N Netherlands, on the Harlinger Trekvaart and 11 mi. W of Leeuwarden; roofing tiles, bricks, stairs, synthetic fertilizer; dairying. Has 14th-cent. church, 16th-cent. town hall, 18th-cent. planetarium. Univ. here from 1585 to 1810.

Frangy (frãzhē'), village (pop. 619), Haute-Savoie dept., SE France, 12 mi. NW of Annecy; mfg. (drawing instruments, cheese).

Franière (frãnyâr'), town (pop. 1,411), Namur prov., S central Belgium, on Sambre R. and 6 mi. WSW of Namur; glassware, ceramics.

Frank, village (pop. 194), SW Alta., near B.C. border, in Rocky Mts., on Crowsnest R. and 5 mi. SE of Coleman; alt. 4,212 ft.; coal mining. Village was partly destroyed by landslide from Turtle Mtn., April 29, 1903.

Franken, Germany: see FRANCONIA.

Frankenau (fräng'kùnou), town (pop. 1,450), in former Prussian prov. of Hesse-Nassau, W Germany, after 1945 in Hesse, 21 mi. NNE of Marburg; grain.

Frankenberg (fräng'kùnbĕrk). **1** Town (pop. 6,944), in former Prussian prov. of Hesse-Nassau, W Germany, after 1945 in Hesse, on the Eder and 18 mi. N of Marburg; leatherworking. Has 13th–14th-cent. church. **2** Town (pop. 15,103), Saxony, E central Germany, on Zschopau R. and 8 mi. NE of Chemnitz; hosiery knitting, textile milling (cotton, wool, rayon, silk, carpets); mfg. of steel products, chemicals, cigars; printing. Towered over by old Sachsenburg castle.

Frankenburg (fräng'kùnbōōrk), town (pop. 4,683), SW central Upper Austria, in Hausruck Mts., 9 mi. NW of Vöcklabruck; metal products. Lignite mined in vicinity.

Frankeneck (fräng'kùnĕk), village (pop. 756), Rhenish Palatinate, W Germany, in Hardt Mts., 4 mi. WNW of Neustadt; paper milling.

Frankenhausen, Bad, Germany: see BAD FRANKENHAUSEN.

Frankenmarkt (fräng'kùnmärkt), town (pop. 2,788), SW Upper Austria, 11 mi. W of Vöcklabruck; market center; brewery.

Frankenmuth (frăng'kĭnmōōth), village (pop. 1,208), Saginaw co., E central Mich., 12 mi. SE of Saginaw and on Cass R., in farm area; mfg. (metal products, flour, cheese, beer, woolen goods, boxes). Settled 1845 by Germans; inc. 1904.

Frankenstein, Poland: see ZABKOWICE.

Frankenthal (fräng'kùntäl), city (1950 pop. 25,318), Rhenish Palatinate, W Germany, 7 mi. S of Worms, connected with the Rhine by 3-mi.-long canal (built 1777); 49°32'N 8°21'E. Second World War destruction (about 50%) completely eliminated sugar industry, and severely limited iron, chemical, and food industries. Other mfg.: furniture, barrels, beer. Has ruins of 12th-cent. church with beautifully carved portal; two 18th-cent. city gates. Founded by Franks; site of powerful monastery from 1119 to 1562, when it passed to Palatinate and was settled by Dutch Protestants. Chartered 1577. Completely destroyed by fire in 1689. Site (1755–94) of noted porcelain factory. Developed as industrial center after 1870.

Frankenwald, Germany: see FRANCONIAN FOREST.

Frankfield, town (pop. 2,260), Clarendon parish, central Jamaica, on Minho R. and 17 mi. NW of May Pen (linked by railroad), in agr. region (bananas, sugar cane, coffee, livestock).

Frankford, village (pop. 1,144), SE Ont., on Trent R. and 11 mi. WNW of Belleville; paper milling, food canning; hydroelectric station.

Frankford or **Kilcormac** (kĭlkôr'mùk), Gaelic *Cill Chormaic*, town (pop. 445), W Co. Offaly, Ireland, 12 mi. SW of Tullamore; agr. market (barley, potatoes; cattle) and peat-digging center.

Frankford. 1 Town (pop. 615), Sussex co., SE Del., 15 mi. SSE of Georgetown; canning, marketing center in agr. region (strawberries, truck). **2** City (pop. 449), Pike co., E Mo., near Mississippi and Salt rivers, 7 mi. SSE of New London. **3** NE industrial section of Philadelphia, Pa.; textiles, printing (magazines), ball bearings, radios; sugar refining. Annexed by Philadelphia 1845.

Frankfort, Germany: see FRANKFURT.

Frankfort. 1 Village (pop. 1,355), SE Cape Prov., U. of So. Afr., 11 mi. NNE of Kingwilliamstown; stock, grain; lumbering. **2** Town (pop. 3,635), NE Orange Free State, U. of So. Afr., on Wilge R. and 55 mi. SE of Vereeniging; alt. 5,131 ft.; agr. center (corn, cattle, sheep, horses); grain elevators.

Frankfort (frăngk'fùrt). **1** Village (pop. 685), Will co., NE Ill., 11 mi. E of Joliet, in agr. and bituminous-coal area. **2** City (pop. 15,028), ⊙ Clinton co., central Ind., 40 mi. NNW of Indianapolis; trading and distributing center in applegrowing and general farming region (grain, livestock). Mfg. of packed meat, foundry products, porcelain and enamelware, clothing, fertilizer, confections, brass fittings; railroad shops, oil refinery. Laid out 1830. **3** City (pop. 1,237), Marshall co., NE Kansas, on small affluent of Big Blue R. and 34 mi. NNE of Manhattan; trading center in grain area. Founded 1867, inc. 1875. **4** City (pop. 11,916), ⊙ Ky. and Franklin co., N central Ky., on both banks of Kentucky R. (bridged) and 50 mi. E of Louisville; 38°10'N 84°53'W; alt. 599 ft. Trade and shipping center in Bluegrass agr. (burley tobacco, livestock, dairy products, grain) and limestone-quarrying area; whisky-distilling center, mfg. of shoes, underwear, hemp twine, furniture, brooms, store fixtures, truck bodies, concrete pipes; sawmilling. Has airports. Places of interest include: present capitol (1909); old capitol (built 1827–30; Greek Revival), which houses mus. and library of state historical society; "Liberty Hall" (built 1796), said to have been designed by Thomas Jefferson; old cemetery with graves of Daniel and Rebecca Boone; state monument to Ky. heroes of all wars; monument to Daniel Boone. Has many fine old houses and gardens. Ky. State Col. for Negroes; state institute for feeble-minded (founded 1860) here. State penitentiary moved from here to La Grange in 1940. Near by are Stewart Home Training School for retarded children, U.S. lock in Kentucky R., and Dix Dam. Land here surveyed in 1773; squatters came 1774; settled 1779; organized 1786 by Gen. James Wilkinson; chosen ⊙ Ky. in 1792. Gen. Braxton Bragg's Confederates took Frankfort (1862) in Civil War, but promptly lost it again to the Union. **5** Town (pop. 578), Waldo co., S Maine, on the Penobscot and 14 mi. NNE of Belfast. Granite quarried at near-by Mt. Waldo. **6** City (pop. 1,858), Benzie co., NW Mich., 32 mi. WSW of Traverse City, on L. Michigan at mouth of Betsie R. Resort; fisheries, cannery; ships fruit. Has ferry service to Wis. and Upper Peninsula. Indian relics found near by. Settled 1870; inc. as village 1885, as city 1935. **7** Village (pop. 3,844), Herkimer co., central N.Y., on Mohawk R. and 9 mi. ESE of Utica; mfg. (farm tools, machinery, cheese). Summer resort. Settled 1723, inc. 1863. **8** Village (pop. 869), Ross co., S Ohio, 11 mi. WNW of Chillicothe and on small Paint Creek, in livestock and grain area. **9** City (pop. 331), Spink co., NE central S.Dak., 10 mi. E of Redfield and on James R.

Frankfort Heights, Ill.: see WEST FRANKFORT.

Frankfort on the Main, Germany: see FRANKFURT.

Frankfort Springs, borough (pop. 149), Beaver co., W Pa., 24 mi. W of Pittsburgh.

Frankfurt (frăngk'fùrt, Ger. frängk'fōōrt). **1** or **Frankfurt an der Oder** (än dĕr ō'dùr), also, in English, **Frankfort on the Oder** (frăngk'fùrt), city (1939 pop. 83,669; 1946 pop. 51,577), Brandenburg, E Germany, on left bank of the Oder and 50 mi. ESE of Berlin; 52°21'N 14°33'E. The section (1946 pop. 1,689) of the city on the E bank of the Oder, called Damm-Vorstadt in German, was placed under Polish administration in 1945 and is called SLUBICE by the Poles. Frankfurt is a rail junction (with workshops) and customs station, and commercial and agr. center (sugar refining, starch mfg., vegetable canning, and, notably, sausage making), mfg. also machinery, textiles, shoes, soap, ceramics, furniture, cigars. Founded in early Middle Ages by Frankish merchants; chartered 1253; important river crossing on trade route from Germany to Poland; joined Hanseatic League 1368. The univ. founded here 1506 was moved 1811 to Breslau. Heinrich von Kleist b. here. Frankfurt was besieged (1348) by Duke Waldemar and Emperor Charles IV, by the Hussites (1431–32), by Gustavus Adolphus (1631) in Thirty Years War, by Russians (1759) in Seven Years War, and by French (1806–08, 1812–13) in Napoleonic wars. In Second World War, captured (March 18, 1945) by Soviet forces after prolonged siege and heavy shelling (c.70% of city destroyed). **2** or **Frankfurt am Main** (äm mīn'), also, in English, **Frankfort** or **Frankfort on the Main** (frăngk'fùrt, mān'), city (□ 75; 1939 pop., including suburbs, 553,464; 1946 pop., including suburbs, 424,065; 1950 pop. 523,-923), Hesse, W Germany, port on the canalized Main and 100 mi. SE of Cologne, 260 mi. SW of Berlin; main city of Main-Taunus dist.; 50°6'N 8°40'E. A historic, cultural, and industrial center, it is a rail, river, road, and air (2 airports, one in NW and one in S outskirts) transportation hub and has long been known as a commercial and financial center, with trade fairs twice a year. Industry is concentrated in N and S suburbs, and at Höchst (W), the seat of the former I. G. Farben chemical cartel (basic chemicals, dyes, insecticides, pharmaceuticals, cosmetics, cleaning preparations). Building construction; heating, irrigation, drainage, and sanitation installations. Produces also heavy and light machinery, electrical equipment and appliances, precision instruments. Textile mfg., printing, food processing (meat, vegetable, and fruit preserves; flour products, candy, beer). Active river trade. Second World War destruction about 45%; the Old City (within 12th-cent. limits) was almost completely destroyed. Historic bldgs. include: the *Römer*, the old town hall; city archives, which housed the Golden Bull of 1356; Gothic church of St. Bartholomew (under reconstruction), where Holy Roman Emperors were elected and crowned; church of St. Paul (rebuilt), seat of Frankfurt Parliament (1848–49); the Goethe house (under reconstruction; furnishings were completely preserved), birthplace and home (1749–65) of the poet; and the ancestral home of the Rothschilds. Noted Städel art institute in S dist. of Sachsenhausen was destroyed. Modern administration bldg. of I. G. Farben chemical concern (W outskirts) remained virtually intact. Seat of univ., opened 1914. A Roman settlement, Frankfurt [Ger.,=ford of the Franks] was captured by the Franks in A.D. c.500. Charlemagne built a residence and convoked various assemblies here. Was ⊙ East Frankish Empire in 9th cent. First mention of the noted fairs was in 1240. Designated scene of election (1356) and coronation (1562) of Holy Roman Emperor. Was free imperial city (1372–1806). Accepted Reformation in 1530; joined Schmalkaldic League in 1536

Occupied many times in wars of 17th and 18th cent. Was ⊙ grand duchy of Frankfurt, created by Napoleon in 1810. Again created free city (1815); seat (1816–66) of Diet of German Confederation. Frankfurt Parliament met here in 1848–49 and drew up a constitution for a united Germany, but the whole scheme failed when Frederick William IV of Prussia refused to lead the proposed empire. Passed to Prussia in 1866 and was inc. into newly formed Prussian prov. of Hesse-Nassau. Treaty concluding Franco-Prussian War was signed here in 1871. After First World War, city was occupied for short time by Fr. troops. After its capture (March, 1945) by Americans, it became hq. of U.S. occupation forces and, in 1948, of bizonal (U.S.-British) administration.

Fränkische, for German names beginning thus, see under Franconian.

Fränkische Saale, Germany: see Saale River.

Frankleben (frängk'lā"bün), village (pop. 2,671), in former Prussian Saxony prov., central Germany, after 1945 in Saxony-Anhalt, 5 mi. SW of Merseburg; lignite mining; mfg. of steel products.

Franklin, village (1939 pop. 5), E Alaska, near Yukon border, 70 mi. W of Dawson; placer gold mining.

Franklin, district of Canada, a provisional administrative division (land area □ 541,753, total □ 549,253) of the Northwest Territories, almost coextensive with the Arctic Archipelago, the northernmost region of North America, bounded by Mackenzie and Keewatin dists. (S), the Arctic Ocean (W and N), and Greenland (E). Comprises isls. of Ellesmere, Baffin, Devon, Axel Heiberg, Ellef Ringnes, Amund Ringnes, Borden, Prince Patrick, Melville, Victoria, Bathurst, Cornwallis, Cornwall, Byam Martin, Bylot, Banks, Prince of Wales, Somerset, and King William, and numerous smaller isls.; also Melville and Boothia peninsulas of the mainland. Entire area constitutes a vast game preserve; fur trapping is chief occupation of Eskimo population. There are trading posts at Cambridge Bay, Repulse Bay, Cape Dorset, Lake Harbour, Frobisher Bay, Pangnirtung, Pond Inlet, Arctic Bay, and Craig Harbour. There are air bases on Frobisher Bay and Padloping Isl., and U.S.-Canadian weather stations are at Cambridge Bay, Axel Heiberg Isl., Cornwallis Isl., Ellesmere Isl., Isachsen Peninsula, Prince Patrick Isl., River Clyde, and Cape Christian. Dist. was created 1895, named after Sir John Franklin; boundaries defined 1897. Game preserve established 1926.

Franklin, village (pop. estimate 150), SW Man., 8 mi. E of Minnedosa; grain, mixed farming.

Franklin, New Zealand: see Pukekohe.

Franklin, town (pop. 788), SE Tasmania, 21 mi. SW of Hobart and on Huon R.; chief fruit-producing center of Tasmania; sawmills, coal mines.

Franklin. 1 County (□ 644; pop. 25,705), NW Ala.; ⊙ Russellville. Agr. and iron-mining region bordering on Miss., crossed (N–S) by fall line. Cotton, corn; deposits of coal, iron, limestone, bauxite. Part of Wm. B. Bankhead Natl. Forest in SE. Formed 1818. **2** County (□ 615; pop. 12,358), NW Ark.; ⊙ Charleston and Ozark. Intersected by Arkansas R.; drained by small Mulberry R.; situated in Ozark region. Agr. area (livestock, poultry, corn, cotton, peanuts). Coal mining; timber. Part of Ozark Natl. Forest and a game refuge are in co. Formed 1837. **3** County (□ 544; pop. 5,814), NW Fla., on the Gulf of Mexico (S), bet. Apalachicola (W) and Ochlockonee (E) rivers; ⊙ Apalachicola. Lowland area, partly swampy. Contains St. Vincent, St. George, and Dog isls., enclosing St. Vincent Sound, Apalachicola Bay, and St. George Sound. Fishing, forestry (lumber, naval stores), cattle raising. Formed 1832. **4** County (□ 269; pop. 14,446), NE Ga., on S.C. line; ⊙ Carnesville. Piedmont agr. area (cotton, corn, hay, sweet potatoes) drained by Broad R.; mfg. (textiles, lumber). Formed 1784. **5** County (□ 541; pop. 9,867), SE Idaho; ⊙ Preston. Agr. area (SW) along Bear R. Sugar beets, wheat, alfalfa, dairy, lumber. Formed 1913. **6** County (□ 434; pop. 48,685), S Ill.; ⊙ Benton. Bounded NW by Little Muddy R.; also drained by Big Muddy R. Bituminous-coal fields. Agr. (livestock, corn, wheat, poultry, fruit; dairy products). Mfg. (flour, metal products, leather goods). Formed 1818. **7** County (□ 394; pop. 16,034), SE Ind., bounded E by Ohio line; ⊙ Brookville. Agr. (tobacco, grain, livestock); some mfg. at Brookville. Drained by Whitewater R. and its East Fork. Formed 1810. **8** County (□ 586; pop. 16,268), N central Iowa; ⊙ Hampton. Rolling prairie agr. area (cattle, hogs, poultry, corn, oats, soybeans); limestone quarries. Formed 1855. **9** County (□ 577; pop. 19,928), E Kansas; ⊙ Ottawa. Rolling prairie region, drained by Marais des Cygnes R. Stock raising, corn growing and diversified agr. Oil and gas fields. Formed 1855. **10** County (□ 211; pop. 25,933), N central Ky.; ⊙ Frankfort (⊙ Ky.). Drained by Kentucky R. and by Elkhorn Creek and its North Branch. Gently rolling upland agr. area, in the Bluegrass; burley tobacco, cattle, hogs, sheep, dairy products, grain. Stone quarries, lead and zinc deposits. Mfg. at Frankfort. Formed 1794. **11** Parish (□ 648; pop. 29,376), NE La.; ⊙ Winnsboro. Bounded E by Tensas R. and Bayou Macon, W by Boeuf R. and Big Creek. Agr. (cotton, corn, hay, soybeans, sweet potatoes). Cotton ginning, lumber milling; mfg. of wood products, bricks. Part of oil and natural-gas field in N. Formed 1843. **12** County (□ 1,717; pop. 20,682), W Maine, bordering on Que.; ⊙ Farmington. Agr., recreational, lumbering region. Paper and pulp mills, canneries, wood products, shoe factories, textile mills; dairying. Hunting, fishing; resorts and camps center around Rangeley L. The Androscoggin, near S boundary, is chief river. Formed 1838. **13** County (□ 722; pop. 52,747), NW Mass.; ⊙ Greenfield. Predominantly rural; hilly in N. Bisected by Connecticut R.; drained by Deerfield and Millers rivers. Formed 1811. **14** County (□ 568; pop. 10,929), SW Miss.; ⊙ Meadville. Drained by Homochitto R. Agr. (cotton, corn); pine and hardwood timber; oil field. Includes part of Homochitto Natl. Forest. Formed 1809. **15** County (□ 932; pop. 36,046), E central Mo.; ⊙ Union. In Ozark region, on Missouri R.; drained by the Meramec. Agr. (wheat, corn, oats, hay), livestock; mfg., especially shoes, grain, lumber products; mining of copper, lead, zinc, barite, coal, silica, fire clay, limestone. Formed 1818. **16** County (□ 578; pop. 7,096), S Nebr.; ⊙ Franklin. Agr. region bounded S by Kansas; drained by Republican R. Grain, livestock, dairy and poultry produce. Formed 1871. **17** County (□ 1,685; pop. 44,830), NE N.Y.; ⊙ Malone. Bounded N by Que. line; S part is in the Adirondacks. Drained by Saranac, St. Regis, Salmon, Little Salmon, Chateaugay, and Raquette rivers. Includes many lakes and resorts (notably Saranac Lake, Tupper Lake), and part of St. Regis Indian Reservation. Dairying, some farming (potatoes, hay, hops, truck, fruit, poultry); timber. Hunting, fishing; canoe routes, hiking trails, ski trails. Formed 1808. **18** County (□ 494; pop. 31,341), N central N.C.; ⊙ Louisburg. Coastal plain area; drained by Tar R. Farming (tobacco especially; cotton); pine forests. Cotton ginning, textile mfg., sawmilling. Formed 1779. **19** County (□ 538; pop. 503,410), central Ohio; ⊙ Columbus. Intersected by Scioto and Olentangy rivers, and small Alum, Darby, and Big Walnut creeks. Agr. (livestock; dairy products; grain, fruit, truck); mfg. at Columbus; sand and gravel pits, limestone quarries. Formed 1803. **20** County (□ 754; pop. 75,927), S Pa.; ⊙ Chambersburg. Agr. and mfg. region; bounded S by Md. Tuscarora Mtn. along W border; part of Cove Mtn. lies in SW, part of South Mtn. in SE, part of Blue Mtn. in N. Drained by Conococheague Creek. Scene of many Indian massacres until end of Revolution; birthplace 1791 of James Buchanan (site now in state forest monument). Agr. (peaches, apples); mfg. (machinery, clothing, textiles, furniture); dairying; recreation. Formed 1784. **21** County (□ 561; pop. 25,431), S Tenn.; ⊙ Winchester. Bounded S by Ala.; drained by Elk R.; Cumberlands in E area, here rising to 1,800 ft. Livestock raising, dairying, agr. (corn, cotton, hay, potatoes). Timber tracts, coal mines. Formed 1807. **22** County (□ 293; pop. 6,257), NE Texas; ⊙ Mount Vernon. Bounded N by Sulphur R.; drained by White Oak and Cypress bayous. Dairying, lumbering, agr. (sorghums, cotton, corn, sweet potatoes, fruit, truck); some poultry, beef cattle, hogs, horses. Oil, natural-gas wells. Formed 1875. **23** County (□ 659; pop. 29,894), NW Vt., on Que. line and L. Champlain, rising to Green Mts. in E; ⊙ St. Albans. Mfg. (farm machinery, textile equipment, paper and wood products, medicines); dairy products, maple sugar; granite, lime; resorts. Drained by Missisquoi and Lamoille rivers. Formed 1792. **24** County (□ 718; pop. 24,560), S Va.; ⊙ Rocky Mount. Partly in the piedmont; rises to the Blue Ridge in NW; traversed by Appalachian Trail and Blue Ridge Parkway. Bounded NE by Roanoke R.; drained by Blackwater R. Agr. (especially tobacco; also wheat, corn). Mfg. of furniture, wood products, textiles at Rocky Mount. Lumbering; mica mining. Formed 1786. **25** County (□ 1,262; pop. 13,563), SE Wash., in Columbia basin agr. region; ⊙ Pasco. Watered by Columbia and Snake rivers. Wheat, alfalfa, fruit, truck, livestock. Formed 1883.

Franklin. 1 Town (pop. 100), Izard co., N Ark., 28 mi. NNW of Batesville. **2** Town (pop. 727), New London co., E Conn., on Yantic R. and 6 mi. NW of Norwich; dairy products, poultry. Includes part of Yantic village. **3** City (pop. 425), ⊙ Heard co., W Ga., 17 mi. NNW of La Grange, on Chattahoochee R.; tire-cord mfg. **4** Village (pop. 467), Franklin co., SE Idaho, near Utah line, just S of Preston in dairying and truck area; canned vegetables. First permanent settlement in Idaho; founded 1860 by Mormons, who introduced irrigation here. **5** Farming village (pop. 438), Morgan co., central Ill., 12 mi. SE of Jacksonville. **6** City (pop. 7,316), ⊙ Johnson co., central Ind., 20 mi. SSE of Indianapolis; trading center in agr. area; produces automobile parts, rayon, household appliances, furniture, lumber, glue, paint, metal articles, canned goods, flour, underwear. Seat of Franklin Col. Laid out 1822. **7** Town (pop. 146), Lee co., SE Iowa, 10 mi. WNW of Fort Madison. **8** Village (1940 pop. 540), Crawford co., SE Kansas, near Mo. line, 8 mi. N of Pittsburg, in coal-mining area. **9** City (pop. 4,343), ⊙ Simpson co., S Ky., 21 mi. SSW of Bowling Green, near Tenn. line; trade center and shipping point for timber and agr. (dark tobacco, strawberries, grain, livestock) area; mfg. of clothing, stone and concrete products, dairy products; lumber and flour mills. Founded 1820. **10** Town (pop. 6,144), ⊙ St. Mary parish, S La., 20 mi. NW of Morgan City and on navigable Bayou Teche; commercial and processing center of rich sugar-cane area; sugar and lumber milling. Has historic old houses. Founded 1800. **11** Town (pop. 709), Hancock co., S Maine, 30 mi. SE of Bangor, in recreational area; granite quarries. **12** Town (pop. 8,037), including Franklin village (pop. 5,348), Norfolk co., S Mass., 19 mi. N of Providence, R.I.; textiles, foundry products; poultry, dairying. Settled 1660, inc. 1778. **13** Village (pop. 546), Renville co., SW Minn., near Minnesota R., 12 mi. E of Redwood Falls, in grain, livestock, poultry area; dairy products. **14** Village (pop. 115), and NE suburb of Virginia, St. Louis co., NE Minn., in Mesabi iron range. **15** Town (pop. 324), Howard co., central Mo., just N of Boonville across the Missouri. **16** City (pop. 1,602), ⊙ Franklin co., S Nebr., 45 mi. SW of Hastings and on Republican R., near Kansas line; hog serum, feed; dairy, poultry, truck produce; grain, livestock. Inc. 1879. **17** City (pop. 6,552), Merrimack co., central N.H., at junction of Winnipesaukee R. and Pemigewasset R. (here forming the Merrimack), 17 mi. N of Concord. Water power developed its mills (paper, textiles, hosiery, machinery, metal products); dairy products, poultry. Daniel Webster b. here, in section then in Salisbury. Webster L. (2 mi. long) is near by (resort). Settled 1764; town inc. 1828, city 1895. **18** Borough (pop. 3,864), Sussex co., NW N.J., on Wallkill R. and 10 mi. NE of Newton, in hill and lake region; textiles, clothing; zinc mines (now depleted). Inc. 1913. **19** Resort village (pop. 558), Delaware co., S N.Y., in the Catskills, 9 mi. SW of Oneonta; farming, dairying. **20** Town (pop. 1,975), ⊙ Macon co., W N.C., on Little Tennessee R. and 55 mi. WSW of Asheville; mtn. resort; lumbering, mining (mica, corundum, kaolin), farming. Small L. Emory, formed by dam in river, is just N. Hq. for Nantahala Natl. Forest here. State game refuge near by. Inc. 1852. **21** City (pop. 5,388), Warren co., SW Ohio, 7 mi. NE of Middletown and on Great Miami R.; paper products, clothing, porcelain, roofing materials, furniture, electrical goods, printed matter. Laid out 1795. **22** Borough (pop. 1,833), Cambria co., SW central Pa., on Conemaugh R. just E of Johnstown. **23** City (pop. 10,006), ⊙ Venango co., NW central Pa., 7 mi. WSW of Oil City, at confluence of Allegheny R. and French Creek. Oil wells, refineries; mfg. (oil-well equipment, metal products); natural gas, bituminous coal. Site of Indian village and of early French, British, and American forts. Oil discovered 1860. Laid out 1795, inc. as borough 1828, as city 1868. **24** Town (pop. 5,475), ⊙ Williamson co., central Tenn., on Harpeth R. and 16 mi. SSW of Nashville, in farm, timber, phosphate-mining area; mfg. of stoves, overalls, cheese; lumber milling; tobacco warehouses. Civil War fighting here in 1864. Has Confederate cemetery. Area settled before 1800. **25** Town (pop. 1,209), ⊙ Robertson co., E central Texas, c.55 mi. SE of Waco; trade, shipping center for cotton, grain, truck area; cotton ginning, grain milling. Settled 1880, inc. 1912. **26** Town (pop. 878), Franklin co., NW Vt., 15 mi. NE of St. Albans, at Que. line; lumber. Includes L. Carmi, resort. Granted 1789 as Huntsburg, renamed 1817. **27** Town (pop. 4,670), Southampton co., SE Va., on Blackwater R. and 20 mi. W of Suffolk, in agr. area (peanuts, fruit, grain); lumber- and paper-milling center; peanut market. Inc. 1876. **28** Town (pop. 777), ⊙ Pendleton co., W.Va., in Eastern Panhandle, near South Branch of Potomac R., 33 mi. SE of Elkins; lumber milling, dairying; summer resort.

Franklin, Lake (30 mi. long, 2–10 mi. wide), N Keewatin Dist., Northwest Territories, just S of head of Chantrey Inlet, into which it is drained by Back R.; 67°N 96°15'W.

Franklin, Mount. 1 In N.H.: see Presidential Range. **2** In Texas: see Franklin Mountains.

Franklin, State of, in U.S., a govt. formed 1784 by inhabitants of Washington, Sullivan, and Greene counties in present E Tenn.; the state, then part of lands which N.C. ceded for a time to the U.S., elected officials, established a capital (1785) at Greeneville, and adopted a constitution; it passed out of existence in 1788, and its lands reverted temporarily to N.C.

Franklin Bay, NW Mackenzie Dist., Northwest Territories, inlet (30 mi. long, 25 mi. wide at mouth) of Amundsen Gulf, on W side of Parry Peninsula; 69°40'N 125°30'W. S part is called Langton Bay. Receives Horton R.

Franklin D. Roosevelt Lake, Wash.: see Grand Coulee Dam.

Franklin D. Roosevelt National Historic Site, N.Y.: see Hyde Park.

Franklin D. Roosevelt State Park, Ga.: see Warm Springs.

Franklin Falls Dam, N.H.: see PEMIGEWASSET RIVER.
Franklin Grove, village (pop. 741), Lee co., N Ill., 9 mi. E of Dixon, in rich agr. area.
Franklin Harbour, nearly landlocked inlet of Spencer Gulf, S South Australia, on E Eyre Peninsula; 8 mi. long, 4 mi. wide. Cowell town on N shore.
Franklin Island (12 naut. mi. long, 6 naut. mi. wide), just off Antarctica, 60 naut. mi. N of Ross Isl., in Ross Sea off Victoria Land; 76°7'S 168°20'E. Discovered 1841 by Sir James C. Ross.
Franklin Island, S Maine, lighthouse isl. in Muscongus Bay, 6 mi. SSW of Friendship.
Franklin Islands, Australia: see NUYTS ARCHIPELAGO.
Franklin Lake, NE Nev., shallow tule marsh in E Elko co., just E of Ruby Mts. Ruby L. is just S.
Franklin Lakes, borough (pop. 2,021), Bergen co., NE N.J., in lake region, 6 mi. NW of Paterson; includes Campgaw (kămp'gô), mfg. village (candy, Venetian blinds, textiles, feed). Inc. 1922.
Franklin Mountains, W Mackenzie Dist., Northwest Territories, extend c.300 mi. NW-SE along E bank of Mackenzie R., bet. Hare Indian R. (NW) and mouth of Liard R. (SE); highest peak, Mt. Clark (4,733 ft.), 50 mi. SE of Fort Norman.
Franklin Mountains, extreme W Texas, range extending N into Dona Ana co., N.Mex., from point just N of El Paso; highest point, Mt. Franklin (7,100 ft.).
Franklin Park, residential village (pop. 8,899), Cook co., NE Ill., suburb just WNW of Chicago; makes pipes, wire, cement blocks. Inc. 1892.
Franklin Roosevelt, Mount, Colo.: see WILSON, MOUNT.
Franklin Springs, city (pop. 182), Franklin co., NE Ga., 3 mi. W of Royston.
Franklin Square, residential village (1940 pop. 5,765), Nassau co., SE N.Y., on W Long Isl., just S of Garden City; mfg. (machinery, sweaters, cement blocks).
Franklin Strait, S Franklin Dist., Northwest Territories, arm (110 mi. long, 20–60 mi. wide) of the Arctic Ocean, bet. Boothia Peninsula and Prince of Wales Isl.; 72°N 97°W.
Franklinsville, N.C.: see FRANKLINVILLE.
Franklinton. 1 Town (pop. 2,342), ⊙ Washington parish, SE La., 62 mi. N of New Orleans and on the Bogue Chitto; trade and shipping center for timber, dairy, and agr. area (cotton, corn, sugar cane, vegetables). Cotton and cottonseed processing, lumber and sugar milling, vegetable canning, tung-oil extracting. Laid out 1821, chartered 1861. **2** Town (pop. 1,414), Franklin co., N central N.C., 24 mi. NNE of Raleigh; market and shipping center for tobacco and cotton area; textile mfg.; lumber mills.
Franklintown, borough (pop. 328), York co., S Pa., 15 mi. SW of Harrisburg.
Franklinville. 1 Village (1940 pop. 947), Gloucester co., SW N.J., on branch of Maurice R. and 6 mi. S of Glassboro; truck farming; basketmaking. Founded 1800. **2** Village (pop. 2,092), Cattaraugus co., W N.Y., on Ischua Creek and 17 mi. N of Olean; mfg. of dairy products, cutlery, tin cans, electrical machinery, feed, last blocks; printing; lumber milling. Grain growing. Settled 1806, inc. 1874. **3** or **Franklinsville,** town (pop. 778), Randolph co., central N.C., on Deep R. and 9 mi. ENE of Asheboro; textile and grain mills.
Franks Peak, Wyo.: see ABSAROKA RANGE.
Frankstadt, Czechoslovakia: see FRENSTAT POD RADHOSTEM.
Frankston, town (pop. 6,449), S Victoria, Australia, on E shore of Port Phillip Bay and 25 mi. SSE of Melbourne; summer resort; orchards. Produces ham, bacon.
Frankston, town (pop. 1,050), Anderson co., E Texas, 21 mi. NNE of Palestine, near Neches R.; lumber milling, woodworking; cans, ships vegetables, fruit.
Frankton, suburb (pop. 1,419) of Hamilton, W N.Isl., New Zealand, 70 mi. SSE of Auckland; rail junction.
Frankton, town (pop. 1,047), Madison co., E central Ind., on small Pipe Creek and 10 mi. NNW of Anderson, in agr. area.
Frankville, village (pop. c.200), Winneshiek co., NE Iowa, 12 mi. SE of Decorah; cheese factory.
Frannie, village (pop. c.75), Park co., NW Wyo., on branch of Shoshone R., near Mont. line, and 38 mi. NE of Cody; alt. c.4,220 ft. Supply point in oil region.
Frano (frōn'ū"), Swedish *Frånö,* village (pop. 1,748), Vasternorrland co., NE Sweden, on Angerman R. estuary, 18 mi. N of Harnosand; lumber and pulp milling, woodworking.
Franschhoek (fräns"hōōk') or **French Hoek** (hōōk), town (pop. 1,212), SW Cape Prov., U. of So. Afr., 15 mi. E of Stellenbosch; tobacco, viticulture, fruit. Founded in late-17th cent. by Huguenot settlers; scene (1739) of insurrection.
Frant, agr. village and parish (pop. 1,604), NE Sussex, England, 3 mi. S of Tunbridge Wells. Has 15th-cent. church.
Frantiskovy Lazne (frän'tyĭshkôvĭ läz'nyĕ), Czech *Františkovy Lázně,* Ger. *Franzensbad* (frän'tsūnsbät), village (2,283), W Bohemia, Czechoslovakia, 3 mi. N of Cheb. Rail junction; major health resort, with 27 alkaline, sulphate, and chalybeate springs. Extensive ferruginous peat deposits. First mentioned in 1406.
Franz (frăns), village, central Ont., on Hobon L. (4 mi. long), 130 mi. N of Sault Ste. Marie; rail junction; gold mining.
Franzburg (frănts'bōōrk), town (pop. 3,061), in former Prussian Pomerania prov., N Germany, after 1945 in Mecklenburg, 13 mi. SW of Stralsund; agr. market (grain, stock, sugar beets, potatoes); dairying, sawmilling.
Franz Canal, Yugoslavia: see DANUBE-TISZA CANAL.
Franzenfeste, Italy: see FORTEZZA.
Franzensbad, Czechoslovakia: see FRANTISKOVY LAZNE.
Franz Josef Fjord or **Franz Joseph Fjord** (frănts' jō'zŭf), Dan. *Kejser Franz Josephs Fjord,* inlet (125 mi. long, 1–20 mi. wide) of Greenland Sea, E Greenland; 73°10'N 22°–27°45'W. Near head it extends several arms to edge of inland icecap, which here discharges several glaciers; central arm reaches foot of Mt. Petermann. Fjord is connected S with King Oscar Fjord.
Franz Josef Land, Rus. *Zemlya Frantsa Iosifa,* archipelago (□ 8,000) of 85 isls., in Arctic Ocean; most northerly land of Eastern Hemisphere; part of Archangel oblast, Russian SFSR; bet. 79°45'N and 81°51'N, 42°10'E and 65°E. Consists of 3 sections separated by deep British Channel (W) and Austrian Sound (E); includes Aleksandra and George lands (W), Wilczek Land and Graham Bell Isl. (E), and main central section bet. Hooker (S) and Rudolf (N) isls., sites of govt. observation stations and permanent settlements on Tikhaya and Teplitz bays. Isls. are composed of basalt resting on Jurassic and Tertiary strata; covered 90% by glacier ice interspersed by poor lichen vegetation. Highest point (2,410 ft.) is on Wilczek Land. Annual mean temp., 6.5°F. Discovered 1873 by Weyprecht and Payer. Declared Soviet territory in 1926. Sometimes called Fridtjof Nansen Land, a name proposed 1930 by Soviet Acad. of Sciences, but never officially adopted.
Franz Josef Spitze, Czechoslovakia: see STALIN PEAK.
Franz Joseph Canal, Yugoslavia: see NOVI SAD-MALI STAPAR CANAL.
Franz Joseph Glacier, W central S.Isl., New Zealand, in Tasman Natl. Park Southern Alps; rises near Victoria Range, flows 8.5 mi. NW to small Waiho R.; airfield near by.
Frasca, Cape (frä'skä), point on W coast of Sardinia, at S end of Gulf of Oristano; 39°46'N 8°27'E. Tunny fishing.
Frascati (fräskä'tē), town (pop. 10,660), Roma prov., Latium, central Italy, in Alban Hills, 12 mi. SE of Rome; macaroni mfg. Summer resort (alt. 1,056 ft.); noted for its wine and its fine 16th- and 17th-cent. villas and gardens. Near by are ruins (theater, amphitheater) of anc. Tusculum, birthplace of Cato the Elder. The town and its villas, including the famous Villa Aldobrandini and Villa Torlonia, suffered severe damage in Second World War from repeated air bombings (1943–44).
Fraser (frā'zŭr). **1** Town (pop. 219), Boone co., central Iowa, on Des Moines R. and 6 mi. NW of Boone, in agr. and coal-mining area. State parks near by. **2** Village (pop. 1,379), Macomb co., SE Mich., 15 mi. NNE of downtown Detroit, near Clinton R. Inc. 1895. **3** City (pop. 134), St. Louis co., NE Minn., in Mesabi iron range, 6 mi. NE of Hibbing.
Fraserburg (frā'zŭrbûrg, –bûrkh), town (pop. 1,564), SW central Cape Prov., U. of So. Afr., 70 mi. WNW of Beaufort West, at foot of Nieuwveld Range; agr. center (sheep, grain, fruit).
Fraserburgh (frā'zŭrbûrŭ), burgh (1931 pop. 9,720; 1951 census 10,444), N Aberdeen, Scotland, on North Sea, 16 mi. NW of Peterhead; important herring-fishing center. Town was founded 1570 by Sir Alexander Fraser. Has 1736 market cross. Just N, on North Sea, is promontory of Kinnairds Head (kĭnârdz'), with remains of castle of the Frasers (1574); has lighthouse (57°42'N 2°W).
Fraser Island (frā'zŭr) or **Great Sandy Island** (□ 66), in Pacific Ocean just off SE coast of Queensland, Australia; forms E shore of Hervey Bay; 80 mi. long, 15 mi. wide; rises to 800 ft. Sandy, wooded; timber. Its northernmost point is Sandy Cape (24°41'S 153°17'E), forming E side of entrance to Hervey Bay.
Fraser Lake (12 mi. long, 3 mi. wide), central B.C., 75 mi. W of Prince George.
Fraser Mills, village (pop. estimate 450), SW B.C., on lower Fraser R. and 2 mi. NE of New Westminster; pulp and paper milling, lumbering.
Fraserpet (frā'zŭrpāt), town (pop. 1,339), N Coorg, India, on Cauvery R. and 15 mi. E of Mercara; rice, millet, tamarind. Limestone quarries near by.
Fraser River, chief river in B.C., rises on W slope of Yellowhead Pass in Rocky Mts., flows c.350 mi. NW through the Rocky Mtn. Trench to Prince George at NW end of the Cariboo Mts., turns sharply S for c.400 mi., passing Quesnel, Lillooet, and Yale, to Hope, where it turns W past Chilliwack, Mission, and New Westminster, and through a small delta to the Strait of Georgia 10 mi. S of Vancouver; 850 mi. long. Chief tributaries are the Nechako, Quesnel, Thompson, Chilcotin, Blackwater, and Lillooet rivers. Navigable below Yale. Above Yale it flows through spectacular scenery of the Canyon of the Fraser R., bet. mts. rising over 3,000 ft. Fraser R. was discovered 1793 by Sir Alexander Mackenzie, who traveled along its upper course on his way to the Pacific; in 1808 Simon Fraser explored river to its mouth and built several trading posts along its valley. Upper reaches of river were scene of 1858 gold rush and in 1859 gold was discovered in the Cariboo dist., further N along river valley; Cariboo Road was subsequently built from Kamloops. Lower course of river is followed by transcontinental routes of Canadian Pacific and Canadian National RRs.
Fraser River, N central Colo., formed by confluence of 2 forks just E of Vasquez Mts.; flows c.40 mi. NNW to Colorado R. just W of Granby.
Fraser's Hill, village (pop. 882), W Pahang, Malaya, in central Malayan range, on Selangor line, 40 mi. N of Kuala Lumpur; hill station (alt. 4,280 ft.) and experimental farm.
Frashër (frä'shûr) or **Fräsheri** (frä'shûrē), village (1930 pop. 302), S Albania, 10 mi. NNE of Përmet.
Frasne (frän), village (pop. 1,146), Doubs dept., E France, in the central Jura, 9 mi. WSW of Pontarlier; railroad junction; Gruyère cheese mfg. and shipping.
Frasnes-lez-Buissenal (–lā-bwēsnäl'), village (pop. 2,810), Hainaut prov., SW central Belgium, 11 mi. ENE of Tournai; beet-sugar refining, lumbering.
Frasnes-lez-Couvin (–lā-kōōvē'), village (pop. 1,062), Namur prov., S Belgium, 9 mi. S of Philippeville; chalk quarrying.
Frasnes-lez-Gosselies (–gôslē'), agr. village (pop. 2,429), Hainaut prov., S central Belgium, 5 mi. N of Gosselies.
Frassinoro (fräs-sēnô'rô), village (pop. 408), Modena prov., Emilia-Romagna, N central Italy, 5 mi. SSW of Montefiorino; foundry. Ruins of anc. abbey near by.
Frastak, Czechoslovakia: see HLOHOVEC.
Frastanz (frä'stänts), town (pop. 3,384), Vorarlberg, W Austria, on Ill R. and 2 mi. SE of Feldkirch; breweries; embroidery.
Frat River, Turkey: see EUPHRATES RIVER.
Frattamaggiore (frät"tämäd-jô'rē), town (pop. 19,168), Napoli prov., Campania, S Italy, 6 mi. N of Naples; hemp and cotton mills, dyeworks; foundry, rope factory.
Frattaminore (frät"tämēnô'rē), town (pop. 5,162), Napoli prov., Campania, S Italy, 1 mi. N of Frattamaggiore; shoe factory, flax mill.
Fratton, England: see PORTSMOUTH.
Frau, Switzerland: see BLÜMLISALP.
Frauenau (frou'ūnou), village (pop. 3,656), Lower Bavaria, Germany, in Bohemian Forest, 4 mi. ESE of Zwiesel; cut glass and furniture mfg. Has late-19th-cent. castle.
Frauenberg, Czechoslovakia: see HLUBOKA NAD VLTAVOU.
Frauenbreitungen, Germany: see BREITUNGEN.
Frauenburg, Latvia: see SALDUS.
Frauenburg (frou'ūnbōōrk) or **Frombork** (frôm'bôrk), village in East Prussia, after 1945 in Olsztyn prov., NE Poland, on Vistula Lagoon, 18 mi. NE of Elbing; fishing port; shipbuilding. Founded 1284; chartered 1310 (reverted to village status after 1945); passed 1466 to Poland. In 14th cent., one of largest cathedrals in Ermland built here. Copernicus, who lived here from 1510 until his death in 1543, is buried in the cathedral. Town passed 1772 to Prussia and became seat of bishop of Ermland. Ger. pop. left after Second World War.
Frauendorf (frou'ūndôrf), village (pop. 816), Styria, central Austria, on Mur R. and 11 mi. W of Judenburg. Ruins of castle Frauenburg, with alleged tomb of 13th-cent. minstrel Ulrich von Liechtenstein.
Frauenfeld (frou'ūnfĕlt"), town (1950 pop. 11,026), ⊙ Thurgau canton, N Switzerland, on Murg R., 21 mi. NE of Zurich; aluminumware, canned goods, pastry, silk and cotton textiles, chemicals; printing. Medieval castle, Thurgau Mus.
Frauenkirchen (frou'ūnkĭrkhūn), Hung. *Boldog Asszony* (bôl'dôg ŏs'sônyŭ), town (pop. 2,900), Burgenland, E Austria, 9 mi. SSE of Neusiedl; vineyards, sugar beets.
Frauenstadt, Poland: see WADOWICE.
Frauenstein (frou'ūn-shtīn), town (pop. 1,568), Saxony, E central Germany, in the Erzgebirge, 12 mi. SE of Freiberg, near Czechoslovak border; paper milling, woodworking, cigar mfg.; climatic health and winter-sports resort. Towered over by remains of anc. castle. Silver formerly mined here (from 1335).
Fraulautern, Saar: see SAARLOUIS.
Fraureuth (frou'roit), village (pop. 4,311), Thuringia, central Germany, 6 mi. W of Zwickau, in textile-milling region.
Fraustadt, Poland: see WSCHOWA.
Fray Bentos (frī bĕn'tōs), city (pop. 9,500), ⊙ Río Negro dept., W Uruguay, port on Uruguay R., on railroad and highway, and 170 mi. NW of Montevideo; 33°7'S 58°9'W. A busy port, reached by ocean-going vessels, it is an important meat-packing center, exporting the produce of a large stock-

raising region (cattle, hides, wool) and agr. area (wheat, corn, barley). Also has shipyards, machine shops, limekilns. Customhouse. Founded 1859 as Independencia; later renamed.

Frayle Muerto, Uruguay: see FRAILE MUERTO.

Fray Luis Beltrán (frī' lwēs' bĕlträn'), town (pop. estimate 800), N Mendoza prov., Argentina, in Mendoza R. valley (irrigation area), 14 mi. SE of Mendoza; rail junction and agr. center (wine, fruit, potatoes, goats, horses); wine making.

Fray Mamerto Esquiú, department, Argentina: see PIEDRA BLANCA.

Fray Marcos (frī mär'kōs), town (pop. 1,200), Florida dept., S central Uruguay, on railroad, on Santa Lucía R. and 45 mi. NNE of Montevideo; agr. center (wheat, corn, linseed); cattle raising; flour milling.

Frayser's Farm, Va.: see GLENDALE.

Frazee (frāzē'), village (pop. 1,021), Becker co., W Minn., on Otter Tail R., in lake resort region, and 9 mi. SE of Detroit Lakes; dairy products.

Frazer, village (pop. c.350), Valley co., NE Mont., on Missouri R. and 30 mi. ESE of Glasgow, in irrigated grain region.

Frazer Point, S extremity of Bathurst Isl., central Franklin Dist., Northwest Territories, on Barrow Strait; 75°N 98°50'W.

Frazeysburg, village (pop. 689), Muskingum co., central Ohio, 13 mi. NNW of Zanesville; plastics, lumber.

Frechen (frĕ'khŭn), town (pop. 18,269), in former Prussian Rhine Prov., W Germany, after 1945 in North Rhine-Westphalia, 6 mi. W of Cologne; lignite mining. Mfg. (briquettes, concrete pipes). Has 2 castles. Belonged to county, later duchy, of Jülich (1338 to French Revolution). Passed to Prussia 1816.

Freckenhorst (frĕ'kŭnhôrst), town (pop. 2,838), in former Prussian prov. of Westphalia, NW Germany, after 1945 in North Rhine-Westphalia, 3 mi. SSW of Warendorf; hog raising (ham). Has 12th-cent. church.

Freckleton, village and parish (pop. 1,541), W Lancashire, England, near Ribble R. estuary, 7 mi. W of Preston; cotton milling; agr. market for dairy farming, potato- and wheat-growing region.

Fredeburg (frā'dŏŏbŏŏrk), town (pop. 2,296), in former Prussian prov. of Westphalia, W Germany, after 1945 in North Rhine-Westphalia, 17 mi. SE of Arnsberg; slate quarries.

Fredensborg (frē'dŭnsbôr), town (pop., with adjacent town of Asminerod, 2,614), Frederiksborg amt, NE Zealand, Denmark, 5 mi. NE of Hillerod; mfg. (automobile bodies, margarine).

Frederic, village (pop. 893), Polk co., NW Wis., 37 mi. WNW of Rice Lake; butter, canned vegetables, woolen goods.

Frederica (frĕdŭrē'kŭ), town (pop. 675), Kent co., E Del., 10 mi. SSE of Dover and on Murderkill R., at head of navigation, in agr. area. Near by is Barratt's Chapel (c.1780) where annual services commemorate organization of Methodist Episcopal Church.

Frederica, Fort, Ga.: see SAINT SIMONS ISLAND.

Fredericia (frĕdh"ŭrē'shä), city (1950 pop. 25,981) and port, Vejle amt, E Jutland, Denmark, on the Little Belt 13 mi. SE of Vejle; rail junction; phosphate fertilizer works, tobacco factory, machine shops, metalworks, cotton mill; fisheries. Inc. in 17th cent. Has ruins of fortifications.

Frederick. 1 County (□ 664; pop. 62,287), N Md.; ⊙ Frederick. Bounded N by Pa. line, SW by the Potomac (Va. line), NE by Monocacy R.; also drained by Catoctin Creek. Rolling piedmont area, with extreme W in the Blue Ridge (locally called South and Catoctin mts.) and Middletown Valley. Rich agr. area (wheat, corn, hay, dairy products, apples, peaches, truck, poultry, livestock). Diversified industries, especially at Frederick. Mtn. resorts; black bass and trout fishing. Includes Sugar Loaf Mtn., part of abandoned Chesapeake and Ohio Canal, Gambrill State Park (W), and parts of Catoctin Recreational Demonstration Area, and Gathland and Washington Monument state parks. Formed 1748. **2** County (□ 432; pop. 17,537), N Va.; co. courthouse is at WINCHESTER, in but independent of co. Bounded (W, NE) by W.Va.; mainly in Shenandoah Valley, with mtn. ridges in W. Leading apple-growing co. of Va.; also grain, livestock, dairy products. Mfg., shipping, processing at Winchester. Formed 1738.

Frederick. 1 Town (pop. 599), Weld co., N Colo., near South Platte R., 25 mi. N of Denver, in grain and sugar-beet region; alt. 5,120 ft.; coal mines. **2** City (pop. 53), Rice co., central Kansas, 36 mi. NNW of Hutchinson, in wheat area. **3** City (pop. 18,142), ⊙ Frederick co., N Md., near Monocacy R., 23 mi. SE of Hagerstown; trade, distributing, and industrial center in prosperous agr. area; mfg. of clothing, brushes, electrical apparatus, pumps, household hardware, dairy products; railroad shops, vegetable canneries, grain mills, meat-packing plants, lime kiln; airport. Seat of Hood Col. (women) and state school for the deaf (1870). Here are Camp Detrick, U.S. Army chemical research station; Mt. Olivet Cemetery (with Francis Scott Key monument); Barbara Frietchie's home (reconstructed); home of Justice Roger Brooke Taney. Near by is Prospect Hall (built c.1732), home of Daniel Dulaney, city's founder. Frederick was held alternately by the Union and the Confederacy throughout the Civil War; near by was fought battle of Monocacy (July 9, 1864), in which Gen. Lew Wallace's Federals were defeated by Confederates under Gen. Jubal Early. Area settled by Palatine Germans; city laid out 1745, inc. 1817. **4** City (pop. 5,467), ⊙ Tillman co., SW Okla., 38 mi. WSW of Lawton; trade center for rich agr. area (wheat, cotton, alfalfa, livestock). Cotton ginning and compressing; mfg. of cottonseed oil, truck bodies, leather goods, wood products, mattresses, pottery, dairy products. Sand and gravel pits. Small Burts L. (fishing, swimming) is near by. **5** Town (pop. 408), Brown co., N S.Dak., 25 mi. N of Aberdeen and on Maple R.; trading point for agr. area; grain, livestock, poultry.

Frederick E. Hyde Fjord, inlet (120 mi. long, 2–10 mi. wide) of Arctic Ocean, N Greenland, in Peary Land region; 82°47'–83°15'N 25°20'–36°55'W. It is the E part of what was long thought to be PEARY CHANNEL.

Frederick Henry Bay, SE Tasmania, connects with Storm Bay of Tasman Sea (S) and with Norfolk Bay (E); 11 mi. long, 7 mi. wide. Opens N into Pitt Water, lagoon (7 mi. long, 2 mi. wide) with causeway linking Sorell with Bellerive peninsula.

Fredericksburg. 1 Town (pop. 211), Washington co., S Ind., on Blue R. and 22 mi. WNW of New Albany, in agr. area. **2** Town (pop. 701), Chickasaw co., NE Iowa, on branch of Wapsipinicon R. and 25 mi. ESE of Charles City; dairy and millwork products. **3** Village (pop. 517), Wayne co., N central Ohio, 9 mi. SSE of Wooster; pottery. **4** Village (pop. 1,149), Crawford co., NW Pa., just NW of Meadville. **5** Village (1940 pop. 563), Lebanon co., SE central Pa., 7 mi N of Lebanon, in poultry-raising area; mfg. of men's furnishings. **6** Town (pop. 3,854), Gillespie co., S central Texas; c.65 mi. W of Austin, in valley of Pedernales R. in hilly country of Edwards Plateau; ships wool, mohair, cattle, turkeys, granite (quarrying near by); cotton ginning, tanning, granite cutting, clothing mfg. Hunting, fishing attract visitors. Retains architecture, customs, language of Ger. settlers (1846); inc. 1928. **7** City (pop. 12,158), in but independent of Spotsylvania co., NE Va., on the Rappahannock (head of navigation) and 50 mi. N of Richmond. Tourist center, with historic bldgs.; highway and trade center in agr., dairying area; mfg. of clothing, footwear, food products, furniture, cellophane. Seat of Mary Washington Col. of Univ. of Va. Points of interest: Mary Washington's home (from 1774–89); "Kenmore," home of Washington's sister; Rising Sun Tavern (c.1760); James Monroe's law office; home of John Paul Jones. George Washington Birthplace Natl. Monument is 30 mi. ESE, in Westmoreland co.; Hill Military Reservation is 15 mi. SE, in Caroline co. City settled 1671, laid out 1727, inc. as town 1781, as city 1879. Grew as a port before the Revolution, in which it furnished munitions. Changed hands repeatedly in Civil War. Fredericksburg and Spotsylvania Co. Battlefields Memorial (□ 3.8; established 1927), a natl. military park, is W, with hq. in city; includes parts of 4 Civil War battlefields (Fredericksburg, CHANCELLORSVILLE, the WILDERNESS, SPOTSYLVANIA COURTHOUSE). In Battle of Fredericksburg (Dec., 1862), a major Confederate victory, Lee defeated Union forces under Burnside who attempted to cross the Rappahannock and advance on Richmond. In 2d battle of Fredericksburg (May 3, 1863), Confederates under Early were forced by Federals under Sedgwick to retreat in a rearguard action of battle of Chancellorsville. Park includes memorial shrine to Stonewall Jackson, killed in battle of Chancellorsville, and Fredericksburg Natl. Cemetery (12 acres; established 1865), with graves of more than 15,000 Federal dead.

Fredericksnagar, India: see SERAMPORE.

Frederick Sound, SE Alaska, bet. Kupreanof Isl. (S) and mainland, extends 50 mi. E-W; part of Inside Passage bet. Petersburg and Juneau.

Fredericktown. 1 Village, Cecil co., E Md., 17 mi. SE of Havre de Grace and on Sassafras R.; yachting; boatyards. Monument commemorates John Smith's exploration of region (1607–9). **2** City (pop. 3,696), ⊙ Madison co., SE Mo., in the St. Francois Mts., on branch of St. Francis R. and 75 mi. S of St. Louis. Agr.; mfg. (shoes, grain, lumber products); mining and processing of copper, nickel, cobalt and, especially, lead. Clark Natl. Forest near by. Founded 1819. **3** Village (pop. 1,467), Knox co., central Ohio, 7 mi. NNW of Mount Vernon and on Kokosing R.; foundry products, furniture, lamps, food products, asphalt. Laid out 1807. **4** Village (pop. 2,121, with adjacent Millsboro), Washington co., SW Pa., on the Monongahela and 17 mi. SE of Washington.

Fredericton, city (pop. 10,062), ⊙ New Brunswick prov. and York co., in S central part of prov., on St. John R. (bridge) and 55 mi. NW of St. John; 45°58'N 66°39'W; lumbering, woodworking, shoe and leather-goods mfg.; hunting and fishing center, in fruitgrowing and lumbering region. Near by are farms of Dominion Experimental Station. Public bldgs. include parliament house, govt. house, Anglican cathedral (seat of bishop), Univ. of New Brunswick (on hills in S part of city), Maritime Forest Ranger school, technical school. St. John R. is navigable for small sea-going vessels to this point, 84 mi. from Bay of Fundy. Village of St. Anne was settled here by Acadians in 1740; few traces remained when Fredericton was laid out by United Empire Loyalists in 1785 and renamed in honor of Prince Frederick, 2d son of George III. In 1787 it became ⊙ New Brunswick, supplanting St. John. Burpee Game Reserve is 10 mi. NE.

Frederika (frĕdrē'kŭ), town (pop. 210), Bremer co., NE Iowa, on Wapsipinicon R. (dammed here to form lake) and 26 mi. N of Waterloo; dairy products, feed. Limestone quarries near by.

Frederik Hendrik Island (frā'dŭrĭk hĕn'drĭk), Netherlands New Guinea, in Arafura Sea, nearly connected to S coast of isl., 130 mi. W of Merauke; c.110 mi. long, c.55 mi. wide; swampy.

Frederiksberg, Denmark: see COPENHAGEN, city.

Frederiksborg (frĭdh'rĭksbôr), amt (□ 519; 1950 pop. 147,695), NE Zealand, Denmark, on the Oresund (E) and the Kattegat (N); ⊙ Hillerod. Other cities: Helsingor, Frederikssund. Arreso, largest lake. Farming, machinery mfg., shipbuilding. Large wooded area in center.

Frederikshaab (frĭdh'rĭks-hôp"), Eskimo *Pamiut*, settlement (pop. 453), ⊙ Frederikshaab dist. (pop. 1,432), SW Greenland, on the coast at mouth of Kvane Fjord (30 mi. long); 62°N 49°38'W. Fishing port; seal hunting, sheep raising. Meteorological and radio station. Founded 1742. In dist. are important cryolite mines at Ivigtut.

Frederikshaab Glacier, Dan. *Frederikshaab Isblink*, outcrop of inland icecap, SW Greenland, on the Atlantic, 40 mi. NNW of Frederikshaab; 62°32'N 50°W. Important navigation landmark. Sometimes called Frederikshaab Ice Blink.

Frederikshald, Norway: see HALDEN.

Frederikshavn (–houn), city (1950 pop. 18,394) and port, Hjorring amt, N Jutland, Denmark, on the Kattegat and 20 mi. E of Hjorring. Fishing, commercial, seafaring center; shipbuilding, meat packing, machinery mfg. Long protected by Fladstrand Citadel, by which Frederikshavn was formerly known. Car ferry to Larvik, Norway; submarine cable to Sandefjord, Norway.

Frederiksoord (frād'ŭrĭksōrd), village (pop. 250), Drenthe prov., N central Netherlands, 11 mi. N of Meppel; colony for agr. rehabilitation of unemployed. Founded c.1818.

Frederikssund (frĭdh'rĭksŏŏn), city (pop. 3,557), and port, Frederiksborg amt, N Zealand, Denmark, on Roskilde Fjord and 22 mi. NW of Copenhagen; meat canning, machinery mfg., shipbuilding. Once port for Slangerup; grew after 1809 with decline of Slangerup as commercial center.

Frederiksted (frĕ'drĭkstĕd), city (pop. 1,897), St. Croix Isl., U.S. Virgin Isls., port on W shore of isl., 11 mi. WSW of Christiansted, 45 mi. S of Charlotte Amalie; 17°43'N 64°53'W. Has open roadstead, where ships anchor ¼ mi. offshore. Isl.'s main commercial center, handling about 80% of its imports; ships sugar. In picturesque setting with Romanesque churches and quaint bldgs. Locally called Westend.

Frederiksvaerk (frĭdh'rĭksvĕrk), city (pop. 3,029) and port, Frederiksborg amt, N Zealand, Denmark, near mouth of Roskilde Fjord, on canal bet. fjord and lake Arreso and 29 mi. NW of Copenhagen. Fisheries, steelworks. Founded during construction of canal, 1717–19.

Fredersdorf (frā'dŭrsdôrf), village (pop. 4,352), Brandenburg, E Germany, 15 mi. E of Berlin; mfg. of machinery; foundries.

Fred Mine, township (pop. 862), Bulawayo prov., S Southern Rhodesia, in Matabeleland, 4 mi. NE of Filabusi; gold mining.

Fredonia (frādō'nyä), town (pop. 3,853), Antioquia dept., NW central Colombia, on W slopes of Cordillera Central, 24 mi. SSW of Medellín; alt. 6,099 ft. Coffeegrowing center; sugar cane, bananas, cattle, hogs. Coal mines near by. Rail station is 3 mi. N.

Fredonia (frēdō'nēŭ). **1** Town, Prairie co., Ark.: see BISCOE. **2** Town (pop. 133), Louisa co., SE Iowa, at confluence of Iowa and Cedar rivers, 17 mi. WSW of Muscatine, in livestock area. **3** City (pop. 3,257), ⊙ Wilson co., SE Kansas, on Fall R. and 33 mi. NNW Coffeyville; trading center in agr. and oil-producing area; poultry packing, dairying; mfg. of cement, bricks, linseed oil. Founded 1868, inc. 1871. **4** Town (pop. 395), Caldwell co., W Ky., 31 mi. ENE of Paducah; stone quarries. **5** Village (pop. 7,095), Chautauqua co., extreme W N.Y., near L. Erie, just S of Dunkirk, in grape-growing area; summer resort. Mfg. (wine, grape juice, fruit products, toys, wood products, cement blocks); ships seed. A state teachers col. is here. Inc. 1829. **6** Village (pop. 268), Logan co., S N.Dak., 34 mi. ESE of Napoleon. **7** Borough (pop. 588), Mercer co., W Pa., 7 mi. N of Mercer. **8** Village (pop. 471), Ozaukee co., E Wis., on Milwaukee R. and 29 mi. N of Milwaukee, in farm area; mfg. (concrete mixers, truck bodies, iron castings).

Fredoy, Norway: see FREI.

Fredriksberg, Norway: see BERGEN.

Fredriksberg (frā'drĭksbĕr"yů), village (pop. 1,063), Kopparberg co., central Sweden, in Bergslag region, 20 mi. W of Grangesberg; sulphuric-ore smelting and refining. Ironworks (founded 1721) now closed.

Fredrikshald, Norway: see HALDEN.

Fredrikshamn, Finland: see HAMINA.

Fredrikssten, Norway: see HALDEN.

Fredrikstad (frĕd'rĭkstä), city (pop. 14,369), Ostfold co., SE Norway, on E shore of Oslo Fjord near its mouth on the Skagerrak, at mouth of Glomma R., on railroad and 50 mi. S of Oslo; lumber-milling center and fishing port, with canneries (fish, fruit, vegetables), fish-oil plants, shipyards, iron foundries, and paper, cardboard, and textile mills. Mfg. also of motors, plastics, leather goods, electrical equipment, construction materials; woodworking, brewing. Granite quarries near by. Has fortifications dating from founding (1567) of city by Frederick II; withstood siege (1716) by Charles XII of Sweden. Port entrance protected by Krakeroy (krô'kůr-ûü), Nor. *Krakerøy*, isl. (□ 7; pop. 4,092) in Oslo Fjord, just S of Fredrikstad; fish canneries, iron foundries. At locality of Hunn (hŏon) near by, iron implements dating from A.D. c.400 were excavated in 1950.

Fredriksvern, Norway: see STAVERN.

Freeborn (frē'bôrn), county (□ 702; pop. 34,517), S Minn.; ⊙ Albert Lea. Agr. area bordering on Iowa. Livestock, dairy products, grain, potatoes. Formed 1855.

Freeborn Lake, Freeborn co., S Minn., 11 mi. NW of Albert Lea; 3 mi. long, 1.5 mi. wide.

Freeburg. 1 Village (pop. 1,661), St. Clair co., SW Ill., 18 mi. SE of East St. Louis; mfg. (flour, electrical supplies); bituminous-coal mines; corn, wheat, dairy products, livestock, truck; timber. Inc. 1859. **2** Town (pop. 370), Osage co., central Mo., near Gasconade R., 23 mi. SE of Jefferson City. **3** Borough (pop. 506), Snyder co., central Pa., 11 mi. SW of Sunbury.

Freeburn, mining village (1940 pop. 1,281), Pike co., E Ky., in the Cumberlands, near Tug Fork, 11 mi. SE of Williamson, W.Va.; bituminous coal.

Free County of Burgundy, France: see FRANCHE-COMTÉ.

Freedom. 1 Village (pop. 2,765), Santa Cruz co., W Calif., just N of Watsonville; apple orchards. **2** Town (pop. 466), Waldo co., S Maine, 15 mi. NW of Belfast, in agr., recreational area. **3** Town (pop. 315), Carroll co., E N.H., on Ossipee R. and 30 mi. NE of Laconia, in recreational area; agr. **4** Town (pop. 332), Woods co., NW Okla., 25 mi. W of Alva, and on Cimarron R., in grain, livestock, and dairy area. **5** Borough (pop. 3,000), Beaver co., W Pa., on Ohio R., opposite Monaca, and 21 mi. NW of Pittsburgh; oil works, undertakers' supplies. Settled 1832, inc. 1838. **6** Village, Lincoln co., W Wyo., on Idaho line, on Salt R., and 18 mi. NNW of Afton, in Star Valley; alt. 5,556 ft. Dairy products, grain, livestock. Salt River Range just E.

Freehold, borough (pop. 7,550), ⊙ Monmouth co., E N.J., 26 mi. E of Trenton; trade center for truck-farming area; mfg. (rugs, textiles, tile, metal products); liquor distilleries. Monument (1884) commemorates battle of Monmouth (1778) fought near by. Has co. historical assn. collection, race track (opened 1873, reopened 1937), and 18th-cent. buildings. Settled before 1700; called Monmouth Courthouse 1715–1801; inc. as town 1867, as borough 1919. Philip Freneau lived here.

Freeland, borough (pop. 5,909), Luzerne co., E central Pa., 16 mi. S of Wilkes-Barre; clothing mfg.; anthracite; agr. Laid out 1868, inc. 1876.

Freelandville, village (1940 pop. 695), Knox co., SW Ind., 17 mi. NE of Vincennes, in agr. area.

Freeling, town (pop. 583), SE South Australia, 35 mi. NNE of Adelaide; wheat, fruit; wool, sheep, dairy products.

Freel Peak (10,900 ft.), E Calif., in the Sierra Nevada, just SE of L. Tahoe, on El Dorado-Alpine co. line.

Freels, Cape, on E coast of N.F., at N end of Bonavista Bay, 40 mi. NNW of Cape Bonavista; 49°14'N 53°29'W.

Freeman. 1 Township (pop. 185), Franklin co., W central Maine, 15 mi. N of Farmington. **2** Town (pop. 309), Cass co., W Mo., on South Grand R. and 9 mi. W of Harrisonville. **3** City (pop. 944), Hutchinson co., SE S.Dak., 40 mi. SE of Mitchell; cattle feed, sausages, dairy products, livestock, poultry, grain. Jr. col. and 2 parochial schools are here.

Freeman Lake, NW central Ind., resort lake (c.5 mi. long) impounded by power dam on Tippecanoe R. W of Yeoman.

Freeman Peak, Colo.: see TARRYALL MOUNTAINS.

Freemansburg, borough (pop. 1,739), Northampton co., E Pa., on Lehigh R. just below Bethlehem; zinc products. Settled c.1760, inc. 1856.

Freemans Peak, Colo.: see TARRYALL MOUNTAINS.

Freemanspur (frē'mŭnspûr"), village (pop. 451), on Franklin-Williamson co. line, S Ill., 4 mi. NNE of Herrin, in bituminous-coal-mining and agr. area.

Freemantle, England: see SOUTHAMPTON.

Freeport. 1 City (pop. 22,467), ⊙ Stephenson co., N Ill., on Pecatonica R. (bridged here) and 26 mi. W of Rockford; trade and industrial center in agr. area; mfg. (dairy and food products, especially cheese; toys, batteries, farm machinery, electrical equipment, patent medicines, toilet preparations, oil burners, windmills, gas engines, caskets, automobile bodies, hardware). Scene of an important Lincoln-Douglas debate (1858). Near by occurred a battle with Black Hawk's Indian forces. Settled 1835, inc. 1855. **2** City (pop. 30), Harper co., S Kansas, 40 mi. SW of Wichita, in wheat area. **3** Town (pop. 3,280), including Freeport village (pop. 1,622), Cumberland co., SW Maine, on Casco Bay 8 mi. SW of Brunswick; leather products, crabmeat packing. In 1820 papers were signed here preliminary to admission of Maine into the Union as a state. Desert of Maine, spreading dune area, near here. Settled c.1700, inc. 1789. **4** Village (pop. 452), Barry co., SW Mich., 23 mi. SE of Grand Rapids, in agr. area; makes rakes, wood products. **5** Village (pop. 558), Stearns co., central Minn., 25 mi. WNW of St. Cloud; dairy products. **6** Residential and resort village (pop. 24,680), Nassau co., SE N.Y., on inlets on S shore of Long Isl., 12 mi. ESE of Jamaica; fisheries; sport fishing. Mfg.: clothing, machinery, mattresses, furniture; wood, metal, and plastic products; toys, tile, marine propellers, aircraft and auto parts, boats. Settled c.1650, inc. 1892. **7** Village (pop. 566), Harrison co., E Ohio, 14 mi. WSW of Cadiz, and on Stillwater Creek, in agr. area; lumber, asphalt products. **8** Village, Wood co., Ohio: see WAYNE. **9** Borough (pop. 2,685), Armstrong co., W central Pa., 22 mi. NE of Pittsburgh and on Allegheny R., opposite mouth of Kiskiminetas R.; bituminous coal; brickmaking; fruit, dairying. Canal town in mid-19th cent. Settled c.1792, laid out c.1800. **10** City (pop. 6,012), Brazoria co., S Texas, c.55 mi. S of Houston; deep-water port and port of entry at mouth of the Brazos on Gulf of Mexico, and on Gulf Intracoastal Waterway. Center of Brazosport industrial area; mines and ships sulphur; magnesium extraction from sea water; chemical mfg. Fishing resort. A port since 1820s; grew after sulphur production began in 2d decade of 20th cent. and after port improvement and bldg. of chemical plants in Second World War. Chartered as city 1949.

Freer (frēr), city (pop. 2,280), Duval co., S Texas c.70 mi. W of Corpus Christi, in oil, natural-gas fields; cattle ranching in area. Inc. 1938.

Freesoil, village (pop. 208), Mason co., W Mich., 16 mi. NE of Ludington, near Big Sable R., in farm and resort area.

Freestone, county (□ 862; pop. 15,696), E central Texas; ⊙ Fairfield. Bounded NE and E by Trinity R. Agr. (cotton, corn, peanuts, grains, fruit, truck), livestock (cattle, hogs, poultry). Lumbering. Some oil, clay produced. Formed 1850.

Freetown, village (pop. estimate 300), central P.E.I., 9 mi. E of Summerside; mixed farming, dairying, potatoes.

Freetown, city (□ 4.8; pop. 64,576), ⊙ Sierra Leone, port on N shore of rocky SIERRA LEONE PENINSULA, 500 mi. SSE of Dakar, on the Atlantic; 8°29'N 13°13'W. Br. West Africa's best natural harbor (□ 7; minimum depth 30 ft.) and chief naval base and bunkering station on Sierra Leone R. estuary; exports palm oil and kernels, piassava, ginger, kola nuts, diamonds, platinum, gold, chromite. Fish processing, soap mfg.; ship repair works. Cline Town (adjoining E) is rail terminus of 2 lines from the interior of the protectorate, with railroad shops and chrome-loading docks. Kru Town (adjoining SW) is residential area of Kru tribe. City has Fourah Bay Col. (founded 1827; affiliated with Durham Univ.), Anglican St. George cathedral, Wesleyan Methodist mission, United Brethren in Christ mission, and R.C. mission, with associated secondary schools, and colonial hosp. (opened 1922). Rail branch leads to WILBERFORCE and Hill Station (pop. 155; alt. 900 ft.; 2 mi. SW), residential areas for govt. officials. Lungi airport is 8 mi. N, across the bay. Sir John Hawkins 1st landed here in 1562. Town was founded 1788 as a settlement for freed African slaves; sacked 1794 by Fr. revolutionaries. Became municipality in 1893. Administrative hq. for Sierra Leone Peninsula and offshore isls., which together form major part of colony.

Freetown, rural town (pop. 2,104), Bristol co., SE Mass., 8 mi. NE of Fall River. Settled 1675, inc. 1683. Includes villages of Assonet (1940 pop. 630) and East Freetown (lumber). Part of Long Pond is in NE.

Freeville, village (pop. 373), Tompkins co., W central N.Y., 10 mi. NE of Ithaca; seat of the George Junior Republic.

Freewater, city (pop. 1,489), Umatilla co., NE Oregon, contiguous to MILTON, 10 mi. SSW of Walla Walla, Wash.; flour and lumber milling, fruit packing.

Fregenal de la Sierra (frāgānäl' dhā lä syĕ'rä), city (pop. 10,265), Badajoz prov., W Spain, in Estremadura, at NW foot of the Sierra Morena, on railroad and 50 mi. SSE of Badajoz. Processing and agr. center in fertile valley (wheat, olives, potatoes, grapes, acorns, livestock); vegetable-oil and liquor distilling, tanning; mfg. of shoes, soap, and cork products. Galena deposits near by. The anc. town has Roman antiquities.

Fregeneda, La (lä frāhānä'dhä), town (pop. 1,314), Salamanca prov., W Spain, bet. Duero and Agueda rivers, 33 mi. NNW of Ciudad Rodrigo; Sp. customs station on railroad to Oporto, Portugal. Vegetables, fruit, olive oil, wine.

Fréhel, Cape (frāĕl'), on English Channel, Côtes-du-Nord dept., W France, 13 mi. WNW of Saint-Malo; 48°41'N 2°22'W; 236-ft. red granite cliffs attract tourists. Lighthouse destroyed in Second World War.

Frei (frā), island (□ 24; pop. 1,936) in North Sea, More og Romsdal co., W Norway, 3 mi. from mainland and S of Kristiansund; 12 mi. long, 4 mi. wide. Large peat bogs; agr. At village of Kvalvik (kväl'vĭk), at NE tip, is kelp factory. Road bridge joins isl. to Kristiansund. Isl. formerly called Fredoy (Nor. *Fredøy*) or Frej.

Freiberg, Czechoslovakia: see PRIBOR.

Freiberg (frī'bĕrk), town (pop. 42,303), Saxony, E central Germany, at N foot of the Erzgebirge, on the Freiberger Mulde and 20 mi. WSW of Dresden; textile milling; mining and smelting (lead, tin, zinc, nickel). Also mfg. of optical instruments, agr. machinery, electrical equipment, leather goods, glass, china; gold, silver, asbestos, and tobacco processing. Site of Radium Research Inst.; and noted mining col. (founded 1765). Has 15th-cent. basilica, with noted early-13th-cent. "golden gate" and with graves of dukes and electors of Saxony; 12th-cent. palace; 15th-cent. town hall. Settled c.1180 by miners from the Harz. Chartered c.1300; passed 1485 to house of Wettin. Henry the Pious introduced Reformation in 1536. Besieged 1642–43 by Swedes in Thirty Years War. In Seven Years War, Prussians here defeated (1762) Austrian forces. Silver mined here until 1913.

Freiberger Mulde (frī'bĕr"gůr mŏol'dů), river in E central Germany, rises in the Erzgebirge on Czechoslovak-German border 6 mi. SE of Frauenstein, flows c.65 mi. generally NW, past Freiberg and Döbeln, joining the ZWICKAUER MULDE 2 mi. N of Colditz to form MULDE RIVER. Receives Zschopau R. (left).

Freiburg (frī'bûrg, Ger. frī'bŏork). **1** or **Freiburg im Breisgau** (ĭm brīs'gou), city (1950 pop. 109,822), ⊙ (after 1945) South Baden, Germany, on W slope of Black Forest, on the Dreisam and 32 mi. NNE of Basel, 10 mi. E of the Rhine; 48°N 7°52'E. Cultural and tourist center (alt. 912 ft.), noted for its cathedral (12th–16th-cent.; built of red sandstone, with spire 384 ft. high) and univ. (founded 1457); rail junction, airport (NW outskirts). Mfg. of textiles, chemicals, machines, precision instruments, tobacco; synthetic fiber; woodworking, paper milling, printing, brewing. Trades in wine and timber. Second World War damage (about 50%) included almost complete destruction of the old part of the city; 16th-cent. city hall was heavily damaged. Has music acad. Seat of R.C. archbishop. Founded and chartered 1120. Property of dukes of Zähringen until 1218. Passed to Hapsburgs in 1368. Scene (1644) of Mercy's defeat by Condé and Turenne. Occupied by France, 1677–97. Ceded to Baden in 1805. Captured by Fr. troops in spring, 1945. **2** or **Freiburg an der Elbe** (än dĕr ĕl'bů), village (pop. 3,899), in former Prussian prov. of Hanover, NW Germany, after 1945 in Lower Saxony, near Elbe estuary, 17 mi. NNW of Stade; flour products, canned goods, building materials.

Freiburg, Poland: see SWIEBODZICE.

Freiburg, Switzerland: see FRIBOURG.

Freiburg an der Elbe, Germany: see FREIBURG, Hanover.

Freiburg im Breisgau, Germany: see FREIBURG, Baden.

Freienbach (frī'ůnbäkh"), town (pop. 3,384), Schwyz canton, NE central Switzerland, on L. of Zurich 15 mi. SE of Zurich. Etzel hydroelectric plant (E).

Freienhagen (frī'ůnhä'gůn), town (pop. 982), in former Prussian prov. of Hesse-Nassau, W Germany, after 1945 in Hesse, 8 mi. E of Korbach; lumber. Until 1929 in former Waldeck principality.

Freienwalde, Bad, Germany: see BAD FREIENWALDE.

Freienwalde in Pommern, Poland: see CHOCIWEL.

Freihung (frī'hŏong), village (pop. 1,122), Upper Palatinate, N central Bavaria, Germany, on the Vils and 12 mi. NNE of Amberg; lead and zinc mining.

Freila(frā'lä), town (pop. 1,637), Granada prov., S Spain, 7 mi. WNW of Baza; olive-oil processing, flour milling, basket mfg. Cereals, fruit, esparto, lumber.

Freilassing (frī'lä'sĭng), village (pop. 6,098), Upper Bavaria, Germany, on the Saalach and 4 mi. NW of Salzburg, on Austrian border; rail junction; textile mfg., food processing, lumber milling; summer resort (alt. 1,381 ft.).

Freimengen, France: see FREYMING.

Freinsheim (frīns'hīm), village (pop. 3,012), Rhenish Palatinate, W Germany, at NE foot of Hardt Mts., 7 mi. WSW of Frankenthal; fruit, wine.

Frei Paulo (frā pou'lŏo), city (pop. 1,757), W Sergipe, NE Brazil, 40 mi. NW of Aracaju; cotton, corn, dried meat. Until 1944, called São Paulo.

Freire, Argentina: see FREYRE.

Freire (frā'rā), town (pop. 2,202), Cautín prov., S central Chile, on railroad and 14 mi. S of Temuco; agr. center (wheat, barley, potatoes, livestock); lumbering, flour milling.

Freirina (frārē'nä), town (pop. 1,504), ⊙ Freirina dept. (□ 1,814; pop. 9,377), Atacama prov., N central Chile, on Huasco R., on railroad and 100 mi. N of La Serena, 20 mi. WNW of Vallenar. Trading, mining center. Silver, copper, gold, cobalt mines near by. Heavily damaged in 1922 earthquake.

Freising (frī'zĭng), city (1950 pop. 25,326), Upper Bavaria, Germany, on the Isar and 20 mi. NNE of Munich; 48°24'N 11°45'E. Metal products (Diesel motors, tractors, brewing machinery, aluminum articles), textiles (cloth, gloves), and chemicals (pharmaceuticals, cosmetics, soap); also printing, woodworking, brewing, flour milling. Has late-7th-cent. church; the cathedral was started in early 8th cent. Site of theological acad. See of Freising was founded by St. Corbinian in 724. Sacked by Magyars 955; captured 3 times in early Middle Ages. Secularized 1803; bishopric was re-established 1817; archbishop of Munich holds title. Near-by former Benedictine abbey of Weihenstephan has housed, since 1852, the Bavarian Acad. of Agr. and Brewing (founded 1804).

Freistadl, Czechoslovakia: see HLOHOVEC.

Freistadt (frī'shtät), town (pop. 5,542), NE Upper Austria, 18 mi. NNE of Linz, near Czechoslovak border, market center; breweries. Has 13th-cent. fortress.

Freistadt, Czechoslovakia: see KARVINA.

Freistatt (frī'stăd), town (pop. 135), Lawrence co., SW Mo., in the Ozarks, 7 mi. N of Monett.

Freistett (frī'shtĕt), village (pop. 2,748), S Baden, Germany, near the Rhine, 7.5 mi. NE of Kehl; woodworking; tobacco.

Freital (frī'täl), town (pop. 39,159), Saxony, E central Germany, on the Weisseritz and 4 mi. SW of Dresden; coal-mining center; woodworking; mfg. of musical instruments, cameras, glass, china, leather, sacking. Town created 1921 from former communes of Birkigt, Deuben, Niederhässlich, Potschappel, Zauckerode. Also includes Döhlen (W), with mfg. of steel products.

Freiwaldau, Czechoslovakia: see JESENIK.

Frei-Weinheim, Germany: see INGELHEIM.

Freixedas (frāshā'dŭsh), agr. village (pop. 1,338), Guarda dist., N central Portugal, 12 mi. NE of Guarda.

Freixo de Aspada-à-Cinta (frā'shōō dĭ äshpä'dŭ-ä-sēn'tŭ), town (pop. 2,703), Bragança dist., N Portugal, 50 mi. S of Bragança, near the Douro (Sp. border); agr. trade; mfg. of ceramics.

Frej, Norway: see FREI.

Fréjus (frāzhüs'), anc. *Forum Julii*, town (pop. 5,587), Var dept., SE France, near the Mediterranean at S foot of the Estérel, 16 mi. SW of Cannes; cork and olive processing, winegrowing, fruit (especially strawberry) shipping. Coal mining and fluorspar quarrying near by. Airport. Episcopal see. Founded by Caesar, and enlarged by Augustus who built harbor (since silted by alluvia deposited by Argens R.) now replaced by that of Saint-Raphaël (2 mi. ESE). Important Roman ruins include amphitheater of Septimius Severus, old town walls, thermae, and aqueduct. Early Gothic cathedral has a fine 5th-cent. baptistery. Captured day after Allied landings (Aug., 1944), Fréjus suffered damages in Second World War.

Fréjus, Pointe de (pwēt dŭ frā-zhüs'), Ital. *Punta del Fréjus* (pōōn'tä dĕl frā'ōōs), peak (9,659 ft.) of Cottian Alps, on Fr.-Ital. border 4.5 mi. S of Modane and 13 mi. SW of Mont Cenis pass. Pierced by famous Mont Cenis (or Fréjus) Tunnel (8.5 mi. long; built 1857–71; lengthened 1881) connecting Modane (France) and Bardonecchia (Italy). Tunnel is 4,163 ft. high at S end, 3,766 ft. high at N end, and is crossed by double-track Turin-Lyons RR. **Fréjus Pass** (alt. 8,370 ft.), just SW, crossed only by mule path.

Frelighsburg (frē'lĭgzbûrg), village (pop. 315), S Que., 10 mi. ESE of Bedford, near Vt.; dairying, pig raising.

Fremantle (frē'măntŭl, frĭ'–, frēmăn'tŭl), municipality (pop. 18,791) and chief port of Western Australia, 9 mi. SW of Perth, at mouth of Swan R.; 32°2'S 115°44'E. Terminus of Trans-Australian RR; superphosphate works, soap factories, flour mills, tannery. Bulk-wheat elevators on harbor. Exports wheat, wool, fruit, flour. Bathing beaches near by. Founded 1829. **Fremantle North** (pop. 2,946) and **Fremantle East** (pop. 6,197) are separate municipalities.

Fremington, agr. village and parish (pop. 1,172), N Devon, England, on Taw R. estuary and 3 mi. W of Barnstaple.

Fremont (frē'mŏnt). **1** County (□ 1,562; pop. 18,366), S central Colo.; ⊙ Canon City. Livestock-grazing and mining area, drained by Arkansas R. Coal, zinc, oil. Includes parts of Cochetopa and San Isabel natl. forests. Part of Sangre de Cristo Mts. in SW, of Wet Mts. in SE. Formed 1861. **2** County (□ 1,819; pop. 9,351), E Idaho; ⊙ St. Anthony. Mtn. area bordering on Mont. and Wyo. and drained by Henrys Fork and Teton R.; irrigation and dry farming in valleys. Wheat, oats, sugar beets, potatoes, dairy, lumber. Formed 1893. **3** county (□ 512; pop. 12,323), extreme SW Iowa, bounded by Mo. (S) and Nebr. (W; line here formed by Missouri R.); ⊙ Sidney. Prairie agr. area (cattle, hogs, poultry, grain, fruit, truck) with bituminous-coal deposits; drained by Nishnabotna R. Includes Waubonsie State Park. Formed 1847; annexed part of Otoe co., Nebr., in 1943. **4** County (□ 9,244; pop. 19,580), W central Wyo.; ⊙ Lander. Grain, livestock, sugar-beet region; watered by Sweetwater, Popo Agie, Wind, and Bighorn rivers. Coal, oil. Wind River Indian Reservation, Wind River Mts., and Washakie Natl. Forest in W. Formed 1884.

Fremont. 1 Town (pop. 947), Steuben co., extreme NE Ind., c.45 mi. N of Fort Wayne, near Mich. line; agr.; lumber milling. **2** Town (pop. 471), Mahaska co., S central Iowa, 13 mi. N of Ottumwa, in agr. area. **3** City (pop. 3,056), Newaygo co., W central Mich., 23 mi. NE of Muskegon, in dairying and fruitgrowing area; cannery (baby food). Indian village sites and mounds, and several small lakes are near by. Settled 1855; inc. as village 1875, as city 1911. **4** Town (pop. 207), Carter co., S Mo., in Ozark region, near Current R., 44 mi. NNW of Poplar Bluff. **5** City (pop. 14,762), ⊙ Dodge co., E Nebr., 30 mi. WNW of Omaha and on Platte R. Trade and distribution center in prairie region; grain, livestock; cement and tile products machine parts, beverages, refrigeration equipment, flour, feed; dairy and poultry produce, fruit. Midland Col., Fremont State Recreation Grounds, and Western Theological Seminary are here. Settled 1856, inc. 1858. **6** Town (pop. 698), Rockingham co., SE N.H., on Exeter R. and 19 mi. WSW of Portsmouth; agr. **7** Town (pop. 1,395), Wayne co., E central N.C., 11 mi. N of Goldsboro, in tobacco area. **8** City (pop. 16,537), ⊙ Sandusky co., N Ohio, on Sandusky R. and 30 mi. SE of Toledo; industrial and trade center for agr. area (grain, truck, sugar beets). Mfg. of auto parts, clothing, cutlery, electrical products, rubber goods; sugar refineries; nurseries. Home and tomb of Rutherford B. Hayes are in state park. Settled after War of 1812 as 2 towns: Crogansville and Lower Sandusky; united in 1829 as Lower Sandusky; renamed Fremont in 1849, and inc. as city in 1866. **9** Village (pop. 504), Waupaca co., E central Wis., on Wolf R. and 22 mi. NW of Oshkosh; lumbering, fishing; buttons mfg.

Fremont Island (7 mi. long, 2 mi. wide), in Great Salt L., NW Utah, just SE of Promontory Point, c.35 mi. NW of Salt Lake City.

Fremont Pass (11,318 ft.), central Colo., in Park Range, 10 mi. NE of Leadville. Crossed by highway. Village of Climax is here; Quandary Peak and Mt. Lincoln are near by.

Fremont Peak. 1 Peak in Ariz.: see SAN FRANCISCO PEAKS. **2** Peak (13,730 ft.) in Wind River Range, W central Wyo., c.50 mi. NW of Lander.

Frémont Peak State Park, Calif.: see GABILAN RANGE.

Fremont River, rises in small reservoir in Fish Lake Plateau, S central Utah, flows 60 mi. S and E, joining Muddy Creek in Wayne co., N of Henry Mts., to form Dirty Devil R., which flows to the Colorado.

French, village (pop. c.150), Colfax co., NE N.Mex., on Canadian R. at mouth of Vermejo R., and 30 mi. S of Raton; alt. c.5,800 ft. Trade and shipping point in irrigated agr. region; sugar beets, grain, fruit.

Frenchboro, Maine: see LONG ISLAND, plantation.

French Broad River, W N.C. and E Tenn., formed in the Blue Ridge, W N.C., by confluence of headstreams 10 mi. SW of Brevard; flows NE past Brevard, NNW past Asheville, Marshall, and Hot Springs, into Tenn., and generally W past Del Rio, joining Holston R. just above Knoxville to form Tennessee R.; 204 mi. long. Receives Pigeon (left) and Nolichucky (right) rivers. DOUGLAS DAM, E of Knoxville, forms Douglas Reservoir.

Frenchburg, town (pop. 268), ⊙ Menifee co., E central Ky., 31 mi. E of Winchester, in oil, timber, and farm area. Fishing near by.

French Cameroons: see CAMEROONS.

French Camp, village (pop. 162), Choctaw co., central Miss., 13 mi. W of Ackerman.

French Creek. 1 Village in French Creek town (pop. 694), Chautauqua co., extreme W N.Y., 25 mi. WSW of Jamestown. **2** Village, Upshur co., central W.Va., 8 mi. SSW of Buckhannon; state game farm.

French Creek 1. In SW N.Y. and NW Pa., rises in SW Chautauqua co., N.Y.; flows c.80 mi. SW and S, past Meadville, Pa., and SE to Allegheny R. at Franklin, Pa. Pioneer route from Great Lakes to interior. **2** In S.Dak., intermittent stream, rises near Custer in Black Hills, flows E 62 mi. to Cheyenne R.; gold, discovered here 1874, is still extracted.

French Equatorial Africa, group of 4 Fr. overseas territories (□ 971,833; 1950 pop. 4,406,600), W and N central Africa, bounded N by Libya, E by Anglo-Egyptian Sudan, S by Belgian Congo (along Ubangi and Congo rivers) and Cabinda (a detached part of Angola), W by the Atlantic Ocean, Sp. Guinea (Río Muni), Fr. Cameroons, Nigeria (along L. Chad), and Fr. West Africa; ⊙ Brazzaville. From a frontage of c.500 mi. on SE seaboard of the Gulf of Guinea, it stretches c.2,000 mi. NNE inland to the Sahara, where it culminates in the Tibesti Massif (11,204 ft.). GABON and MIDDLE CONGO are in S, UBANGI-SHARI in center, and CHAD in N. Except for the alluvial coast, dense tropical forest (□ c.300,000) covers all the littoral plain; the slopes of subcoastal highlands (Crystal Mts.) and the low, swampy regions (E) belong to Congo depression. High temperatures, with small annual range, and abundant rainfall characterize the forest belt; typical fauna includes gorillas, okapis, monkeys, leopards. In the center are open savannas with forest galleries along watercourses; here dry (Dec.-March) and wet seasons alternate; known for wild game (elephants, lions, buffaloes, birds, antelopes); also a stock-raising area. The semi-arid steppe and the sandy desert further N near L. Chad are marked by great heat and large diurnal changes. Ogooué, Kwilou-Niari, and Nyanga rivers drain directly to the Atlantic, while the Alima, Sanga, Likouala-Mossaka, Likouala-aux-herbes, and Koto flow to the Congo; Shari and Logone rivers flow to L. Chad. In the sparsely inhabited S, peopled by Bantu tribes and remnants of aboriginal pygmies, trypanosomiasis and leprosy still desolate much of the land. In N are people of Negroid-Hamitic stock (Fulahs, Saras, Tibbus), mostly Moslems. Arab nomads live in the desert. The non-natives (16,498 persons, including Europeans) are in main towns. Before 1940, the economy was based on forest products: hardwoods, *okume* logs, palm kernels, copal, kapok, wild rubber. After the Second World War it developed as the leading producer of cotton, diamonds, and gold in the Fr. Union. Exports also include cacao, coffee, peanuts, lead, zinc, hides, butter, ivory, beeswax. Rice and sisal have been introduced. Manioc, yams, plantains, sweet potatoes, corn, tobacco, red pepper are chief subsistence crops S of 7th parallel; in the drier interior millet, sesame, pulse are dominant. Communications facilities are bad. Until development of Pointe-Noire (completed 1946) no deep-water harbor existed along the seaboard, though lumber was commonly shipped from Libreville, Port-Gentil, Owendo, and, at favorable tides, from Fernan-Vaz and Setté-Cama. The only railroad (500 mi. long) runs bet. Pointe-Noire and Brazzaville, and roads are sparse and poor. Except for some sections of the Congo, Ubangi, Ogooué, and Sanga, natural waterways are navigable only intermittently. Some air facilities were established during Second World War. Abéché, the largest native town, was noted throughout 19th cent. for its caravan trade. The coast was discovered by Portuguese in 15th cent., but the whole region was long ignored. Fr. penetration began in Gabon (1839–49) and gradually extended to S. By 1894 Middle Congo boundaries were established after agreements with Congo Free State. Chad and Ubangi-Shari were effectively occupied only in 1903–13 and remained until 1920 under military rule. Previously (1888–1908) known as Fr. Congo colony, Fr. Equatorial Africa was organized in 1910 to embrace 3 colonies: Gabon, Middle Congo, Ubangi-Shari-Chad (Chad was later detached in 1920 to form a 4th colony). Following the Agadir crisis (1911), France ceded to Ger. Cameroons part of N Gabon and 2 tongue-like strips reaching to Congo R. and Ubangi R., while receiving from Germany a small area (*Bec-de-Canard*) bet. Logone and Shari rivers; the lost areas (□ c.100,000) France recovered by treaty of Versailles (1919). In Second World War, Fr. Equatorial Africa was the 1st of Fr. possessions to repudiate (1940) Vichy govt. By the new Fr. constitution (Oct., 1946), each of the 4 colonies became overseas territories within the French Union, with representation in Fr. parliament. Fr. Equatorial Africa is governed by a governor-general, each of the territories by a governor.

French Establishments in Oceania (ō"shē-ā'-nyŭ), Fr. *Établissements français de l'Océanie*, overseas territory (□ 1,554; pop. 55,734) of the French Union, constituting Fr. possessions in S Pacific; ⊙ Papeete on Tahiti, Society Isls. Until 1946 it was a colony, formed 1903 to embrace 105 isls. Its 5 principal archipelagoes are SOCIETY ISLANDS, MARQUESAS ISLANDS, TUBUAI ISLANDS, TUAMOTU ISLANDS, GAMBIER ISLANDS. These, in turn, are divided into administrative dists. Also called French Settlements of Oceania and, popularly French Oceania.

French Flanders, France: see FLANDERS, FRENCH.

French Frigate Shoal, T.H., crescent atoll comprising 13 sand islets and 1 rock islet (La Perouse Pinnacle alt. 120 ft.), N Pacific, c.480 mi. NW of Honolulu T.H.; 23°45'N 166°10'W; annexed 1895 by Republic of Hawaii. Site of radio beacon.

French Guiana: see GUIANA, FRENCH.

French Guinea (gĭ'nē), Fr. *Guinée française* (gēnā frăsĕz'), French overseas territory (□ c.95,350 pop. c.2,125,000), W Fr. West Africa, on the Atlantic; ⊙ CONAKRY. Bordered NW by Portuguese Guinea, N by Senegal and Fr. Sudan, SE by the Ivory Coast, and S by Liberia and Sierra Leone. Extends from indented, low coastal strip, fringed by reefs, to extensive mountainous hinterland of the Fouta Djallon massif (rising to c.6,000 ft.), the source of Gambia, Senegal, and Niger rivers. The E section merges with the Sudan. Its tropical climate is of the monsoon type, with rainfall and temp. highest along the coast. Conakry has mean annual temp. of 79°F. Dry season Nov.–April, during which period the harmattan blows from NE. Mineral resources—such as gold, iron, manganese, bauxite—are so far only of domestic importance. Chief source of income are bananas from extensive coastal plantations. Other exports include palm kernels, palm oil, rubber, copal gum, kola nuts, sesame, tobacco, pepper, pineapples, rice, millet, peanuts, honey. The interior forest region yields coffee. Cattle are pastured in Fouta Djallon mts., also a resort area because of its moderate climate. A W-E railroad links Conakry, the territory's major port, with the Niger basin. Intercolonial roads communicate with the other Fr. possessions. Among principal towns, apart from Conakry, are: Kankan, Kindia, Siguiri, Mamou, Kouroussa, and N'zérékoré. The French claimed the region in late 19th cent., when they set up (1882) the colony *Rivières du Sud* as dependency of Senegal. The Fouta Djallon highlands, though annexed in 1881, were not pacified until 1906. In early 1890s it became a separate colony as Fr. Guinea, which was proclaimed (1895) part of Fr. West Africa, and definitely organized in 1904. Now represented in French parliament.

French Harbour, village (pop. 406), on S coast of Roatán Isl., Bay Islands dept., N Honduras, 12 mi. ENE of Roatán; exports coconuts.

French Hoek, U. of So. Afr.: see FRANSCHHOEK.

French India, Fr. *Inde française* (ĕd' frāsĕz'), officially *Établissements français de* (or *dans*) *l'Inde* (ātāblĕsmā' frāsā' dü lĕd', dā), overseas territory (□ 193; pop. 317,259) of France, in India; ⊙ PONDICHERRY. Consists administratively of 4 separate areas, commonly known as settlements (Fr. *établissements*) and, after 1947, officially as free cities (Fr. *villes libres*) of KARIKAL, Pondicherry, and YANAM on E coast, and MAHÉ on W coast. Fr. influence in India spread following establishment (mid-17th cent.) of trading stations, until in 1740s, under La Bourdonnais and Dupleix, its sphere included most of Hyderabad and Madras; by 1817, Fr. territory was limited to these 4 settlements and CHANDERNAGORE (in Bengal). In 1947, France returned small plots of land (*loges;* sites of former trading posts) in Balasore, Calicut, Dacca, Cossimbazar, Masulipatam, Patna, and Surat to India and in 1948 agreed to hold plebiscites to determine question of accession of the 5 settlements to India; in June, 1949, Chandernagore voted to join India (actually merged in May, 1950).

French Indochina: see INDOCHINA.

French Island, uninhabited island in Western Port of Bass Strait, S Victoria, Australia, N of Phillip Isl.; fills N part of inlet; 11 mi. long E-W, 7.5 mi. wide N-S; low, marshy.

French Lake (7 mi. long, 5 mi. wide), S central N.B., 14 mi. E of Fredericton; drains into St. John R. through Maquapit and Grand lakes.

French Lick, resort town (pop. 1,946), Orange co., S Ind., 45 mi. WNW of New Albany, in agr. area (fruit, livestock, poultry); has noted mineral springs. Bituminous-coal mining; timber; stone quarries. It was a French trading post in the colonial period.

Frenchman Bay, Hancock co., S Maine, inlet of the Atlantic; extends inland c.20 mi. bet. Mt. Desert Isl. and Schoodic Peninsula.

Frenchman Creek, in Colo. and Nebr., rises in NE Colo., flows 151 mi. ESE, past Holyoke, Colo., and Wauneta and Palisade, S Nebr., to Republican R. near Culbertson. Dam (building begun 1947) near Wauneta.

Frenchman Flat, Nev.: see INDIAN SPRINGS.

Frenchman River, SW Sask. and NE Mont., rises in Cypress Hills, flows c.250 mi. SE, past Eastend and Val Marie, crossing into Mont., to Milk R. 30 mi. ENE of Malta.

Frenchmans Cay (kā, kē), islet (pop. 71), just off SW Tortola isl., Br. Virgin Isls., 5 mi. SW of Road Town; agr. (livestock, fruit, vegetables). Sometimes Frenchman Isl.

French Morocco, N Africa: see MOROCCO.

French Navarre, France: see LOWER NAVARRE.

French North Africa, general name for ALGERIA, French MOROCCO, and TUNISIA.

French Oceania: see FRENCH ESTABLISHMENTS IN OCEANIA.

Frenchpark, Gaelic *Dún Gar,* town (pop. 178), NW Co. Roscommon, Ireland, 9 mi. SW of Boyle; agr. market (cattle, sheep; potatoes). Has remains of 14th-cent. Dominican abbey church.

French River, S central Ont., issues from L. Nipissing, flows 50 mi. WSW to Georgian Bay 60 mi. NW of Parry Sound.

French Riviera, France: see RIVIERA.

French Rocks, town (pop. 4,271), Mandya dist., S central Mysore, India, 15 mi. WSW of Mandya, in sugar-cane area; rice milling. Fr. troops in service of Hyder Ali and Tippoo Sahib stationed here in 1780s. Also called Hirod. French Rocks rail station is 3 mi. S.

French Settlements of Oceania: see FRENCH ESTABLISHMENTS IN OCEANIA.

French Shore, part of N.F. coastline in which, under various treaties from 1713 to 1904, France had from Great Britain fishing rights. It 1st extended from Cape Bonavista N to Cape Norman, thence S to Point Riche; later it was extended S to Cape Ray.

French Somaliland (sōmä'lēlănd), Fr. *Côte française des Somalis,* Fr. overseas territory (□ c.8,500; 1946 pop. 45,867), E Africa, on Gulf of Aden and Bab el Mandeb strait (entrance to Red Sea); ⊙ DJIBOUTI, a free port. Bounded N by Eritrea, SE by Br. Somaliland, S and W by Ethiopia. The coast is deeply indented by the Gulf of Tadjoura, on which Djibouti, Ethiopia's principal outlet (at terminus of railroad from Addis Ababa) is situated. Largely a stony desert (extension of Ethiopia's Danakil desert), with isolated basaltic plateaus and highlands, territory is unproductive, except for small irrigated truck acreage. Nomadic pastoralism (sheep, goats). Climate is hot and torrid, with irregular, insufficient rainfall (2–10 in. per year). Salt, worked near Djibouti and in interior's salt lakes, is exported. Moslem pop. consists of Danakils (nomads), Issa Somalis, and Yemeni Arabs (the latter concentrated in Djibouti). French acquired Obock in 1862, but effective occupation dates from 1881. Djibouti founded c.1888; became ⊙ 1892. Colony assumed present name in 1896. Transit trade declined after Ital. conquest of Ethiopia (1936) and during Second World War. Became (1946) overseas territory of Fr. Union. Administered by a governor, assisted (since 1945) by a partially-elected council.

French Sudan (sōōdăn'), Fr. *Soudan,* French overseas territory (□ c.448,200; pop. c.3,080,000), Fr. West Africa; ⊙ BAMAKO. Crossed in N by the Tropic of Cancer. Entirely surrounded by Fr. possessions, it borders N on Algeria, W on Mauritania, SW on Senegal (Falémé R.), S on Fr. Guinea and Ivory Coast, SE on Upper Volta, and E on Niger territory. Comprises vast unpopulated tracts of the Sahara (N) and desolate savannas. Relatively high pop. density is found in S, in Sudan proper, along the Senegal and the large bend of the middle Niger, the latter a fertile lacustrine region, called Macina, used for irrigation. Increasing rainfall towards S. In the dry season (Nov.–June) blows the scorching harmattan. Gold from placers along Falémé R. and salt from Taoudéni (N) are exploited. There are also iron, mercury, arsenic, manganese, and phosphate deposits. Principal exports are peanuts, shea-nut butter, gum arabic, kapok, sisal, sesame, hides, wool, cattle. Subsistence crops include millet, corn, rice, cotton, manioc, cereals, melons. Some cotton and kapok ginning, rice milling, vegetable-oil extracting, native handicrafts. Railroad from Dakar to Koulikoro links the Senegal and Niger basins. A trans-Saharan road leads to Morocco. The Senegal is navigable to Kayes. Apart from Bamako, leading towns are Kayes, Ségou, Sikasso, Gao, Timbuktu, Goundam, Mopti. The population consists of Hamites (Tuaregs, Moors) and Negroid races. Fr. conquest of the region began (1855) under Faidherbe, but was not completed until end of 19th cent. Timbuktu was occupied 1893. Expansion led to dispute with Great Britain, but settlement was finally reached (1899). Out of the region called French Sudan the French set up in 1902 an area called Senegambia and Niger Territories; out of this, in turn, was established (1904) the colony of Upper Senegal and Niger, whose name was changed once more (1920) back to Fr. Sudan. Fr. Sudan is now represented by 3 deputies in the National Assembly of France. Mauritania obtained a W strip of the Fr. Sudan in 1945.

French Togoland: see TOGOLAND.

Frenchtown. 1 Village (pop. c.150), Missoula co., W Mont., on the Clark Fork and 15 mi. NW of Missoula, in irrigated agr. and mining region. Near-by small dam on the Clark Fork is unit in irrigation system. **2** Borough (pop. 1,305), Hunterdon co., W N.J., on Delaware R. and 10 mi. W of Flemington; mfg. (porcelain insulators, paper); hatcheries; poultry, fruit, grain; dairy and nursery products. Inc. 1867.

French Union, Fr. *Union française* (ünyō' frāsĕz'), (□ c.4,807,000; pop. c.117,427,000), name given in the French constitution of 1946 to the political organism composed of the French Republic and former Fr. colonies and other possessions. The French Republic consists of Metropolitan France (i.e., the 90 departments of continental France and CORSICA); of the Government General of ALGERIA (divided into the 3 departments of N Algeria and the Southern Territories); of the overseas departments of MARTINIQUE, GUADELOUPE, RÉUNION, and French GUIANA; of the overseas territories of FRENCH WEST AFRICA (DAHOMEY, FRENCH GUINEA, FRENCH SUDAN, IVORY COAST, MAURITANIA, NIGERIA, SENEGAL, UPPER VOLTA), FRENCH EQUATORIAL AFRICA (CHAD, GABON, MIDDLE CONGO, UBANGI-SHARI), MADAGASCAR and dependencies, COMORO ISLANDS, FRENCH SOMALILAND, FRENCH INDIA (i.e., PONDICHERRY, KARIKAL, MAHÉ, and YANAM), NEW CALEDONIA and dependencies; the FRENCH ESTABLISHMENTS IN OCEANIA, and SAINT PIERRE AND MIQUELON; of Fr. TOGOLAND and the Fr. CAMEROONS, held under U.N. trusteeship; and of the Anglo-French condominium of the NEW HEBRIDES. The associated states in the French Union are the protectorate of MOROCCO, the protectorate of TUNISIA, and, in Indo-China, VIETNAM, CAMBODIA, and LAOS. The president of the French Republic is also president of the French Union. He presides over the high council of the French Union, composed of representatives of the French government and of the associated states. The assembly of the French Union is a representative body; half of its members represents Metropolitan France, the other half represents the overseas departments and territories and the associated states.

Frenchville, agr. town (pop. 1,528), Aroostook co., N Maine, on St. John R. 8 mi. E of Fort Kent; potatoes shipped. Settled by Acadians, inc. 1869.

French West Africa, group of 8 Fr. overseas territories (□ c.1,805,200; pop. c.15,996,000); ⊙ DAKAR. Comprises DAHOMEY, FRENCH GUINEA, FRENCH SUDAN, IVORY COAST, MAURITANIA, NIGER, SENEGAL, and UPPER VOLTA. Embraces most of the great African bulge which protrudes into the Atlantic and is bounded S by the Gulf of Guinea. Lying bet. 4°N and 27° N, it borders in NW on Sp. West Africa, N on Algeria, NE on Libya, E on Fr. Equatorial Africa (Chad), SE on Nigeria. The Br. possessions of Gambia, Sierra Leone, and Gold Coast; Portuguese Guinea; and Liberia form enclaves along its coast. Generally a region of rolling plains with a few low ranges and plateaus (Fouta Djallon, Adrar des Iforas, Aïr), it extends N-S from the arid Sahara, through the savanna belt of the Sudan, to the torrid, equatorial rain forest of the Guinea coast. Principal rivers are the Senegal and Niger. Mineral resources (alluvial gold, diamonds, ilmenite, zircon, bauxite, iron, salt) are so far of little economic importance. The region is predominantly agr., producing chiefly, apart from subsistence crops, peanuts, palm kernels, palm oil, coffee, cacao, bananas, cotton, and sisal for export. Forests yield fine hardwood and gum. Cattle raising, impeded by the tsetse fly, is foremost in Fr. Sudan; sheep and goats are grazed extensively. Its few industries are devoted to processing (vegetable oil, palm fibers) and native handicrafts. The region is renowned for its big game. While the long-projected trans-Saharan RR has not been completed, communication is maintained by intercolonial routes, partial river navigation, and a few important railroads to the interior, such as the Dakar-Niger RR via Kayes and Bamako. Besides Dakar, hub of the entire region, are ports of Saint-Louis, Rufisque, Conakry, Abidjan (with Port-Bouet and Grand-Bassam), Porto-Novo, and Cotonou. Fr. West Africa was established by an 1895 decree and definitely constituted in 1904. After the fall of France (1940) it adhered to Vichy and quelled an unsuccessful de Gaullist coup, but peaceably joined the Allied forces in 1942. After the Second World War the territories were each given representation in the Fr. parliament. There are a large number of Berbers, Moors, and Tuaregs in N section, but bulk of the pop. is of Negro or dominantly Negro stock. Among leading Negro tribes, once organized in native kingdoms, are the Oulofs (Wolofs), Bambaras, Mandigos, Peuls (Fulbés), Mossi. See separate articles on the territorial divisions, towns, and physical features.

French West Indies: see WEST INDIES.

Frenda (frĕndä'), town (pop. 8,486), Oran dept., N Algeria, on wooded S slope of Saïda Mts., at edge of the High Plateaux, 26 mi. SW of Tiaret; alt. 3,600 ft. Trade center in region settled by European colonists growing wheat, wine, and vegetables. Woodworking, lace-making, tanning. Horse and sheep raising.

Freney (frünā'), village (pop. 155), Savoie dept., SE France, in Alpine Maurienne valley, on the Arc and 15 mi. ESE of Saint-Jean-de-Maurienne. Aluminum works at La Praz, 3 mi. W.

Freney-d'Oisans, Le (lů frünā'-dwäzā'), village (pop. 218), Isère dept., SE France, on upper Romanche R. and 5 mi. E of Le Bourg-d'Oisans; alt. c.3,000 ft. CHAMBON DAM is 1 mi. E.

Frensham (frĕn'shům, frŭn'–), residential town and parish (pop. 5,052), W Surrey, England, on the Wey and 3 mi. S of Farnham; agr. market. Has Norman church. Site of several large ponds. Near by are 3 natural mounds, named Devil's Jumps, of geological interest. In parish, 5 mi. SE, is market town of Hindhead, on a ridge (850 ft.). Near by is a deep gully known as Devil's Punch Bowl.

Frenstat pod Radhostem (frĕn'shtät pôd' rä'dhôstĕm), Czech *Frenštát pod Radhoštěm,* Ger. *Frankstadt* (frängk'shtät), town (pop. 6,412), NE Moravia, Czechoslovakia, at N foot of Radhost mtn., on railroad, and 20 mi. SSW of Ostrava. Woodworking (notably bentwood furniture), textile mfg. (cotton, woolen, linen). Popular summer and winter resort (skiing).

Fresh Creek or **Coakley Town,** town (pop. 156), W Bahama Isls., on E shore of Andros Isl., 40 mi. SW of Nassau; 24°42'N 77°45'W. Sponge fishing.

Freshfield, Mount (10,945 ft.), on Alta.-B.C. border, in Rocky Mts., on W edge of Banff Natl. Park, 70 mi. NW of Banff; 51°43'N 116°58'W.

Freshford, Gaelic *Achadh Úr,* town (pop. 474), NW Co. Kilkenny, Ireland, 8 mi. NW of Kilkenny; agr. market (cattle; barley, potatoes). Has church founded in 7th cent., rebuilt in 12th cent.

Freshwater, town and parish (pop. 3,124), W Isle of Wight, Hampshire, England, on Yar R. and 2 mi. SSW of Yarmouth; agr. market and resort. Was often visited by Tennyson, whose wife is buried here.

Freshwater, town (pop. 20), Park co., central Colo., on branch of Arkansas R., in Rocky Mts., and 40 mi. W of Colorado Springs; alt. c.9,000 ft. Formerly Guffey.

Fresia (frā'syä), village (1930 pop. 276), Llanquihue prov., S central Chile, 30 mi. NW of Puerto Montt, in agr. area (grain, flax, potatoes, livestock); dairying, lumbering.

Fresnaye-sur-Chédouet, La (lä frĕnā'sür-shādōōē'), village (pop. 233), Sarthe dept., W France, 8 mi. W of Alençon; woodworking.

Fresnay-sur-Sarthe (frĕnē'sür-särt'), town (pop. 2,155), Sarthe dept., W France, on Sarthe R. and 10 mi. SSW of Alençon; vegetable and fruit preserving; cider milling. Formerly named Fresnay-le-Vicomte and known as a textile-weaving center in 18th cent.

Fresneda, La (lä frĕsnā'dhä), town (pop. 1,179), Teruel prov., E Spain, 14 mi. SE of Alcañiz; olive-oil, fruit, truck produce.

Fresnes (frĕn). **1** Town, Nord dept., France: see FRESNES-SUR-ESCAUT. **2** Town (pop. 4,307), Seine dept., N central France, an outer S suburb of Paris, 7 mi. from Notre Dame Cathedral; woodworking. Penitentiary.

Fresne-Saint-Mamès (frĕn-sē-mämĕ'), village (pop. 461), Haute-Saône dept., E France, 15 mi. WSW of Vesoul; dairying.

Fresnes-en-Woëvre (frĕn-ã-vôĕ'vrů), village (pop. 443), Meuse dept., NE France, 12 mi. ESE of Verdun; horse raising.

Fresnes-sur-Escaut (-sür-ĕskō'), town (pop. 6,786), Nord dept., N France, on the Escaut and 6 mi. NNE of Valenciennes; coal mines; mfg. (cement, refractories, railroad equipment, beet sugar, chocolate). Until 1941, called Fresnes.

Fresnillo (frĕsnē'yō), officially Fresnillo de González Echeverría, city (pop. 24,614), Zacatecas, N central Mexico, on interior plateau, 33 mi. NW of Zacatecas; alt. 7,342 ft. Mining center (silver, copper; and gold, lead, zinc); foundries. Agr. market (cereals, vegetables, livestock). Has mining school, airfield. Founded 1554 by Francisco de Ibarra, it has been a rich source of silver since early colonial days. Its railroad station, 5 mi. NE, was inaugurated 1884 with linking of Mex. railway bet. El Paso (Texas) and Mexico City.

Fresno (frĕs'nō), town (pop. 3,985), Tolima dept., W central Colombia, in E foothills of Cordillera Central, on Manizales-Honda highway, 20 mi. WSW of Honda; coffeegrowing center; bananas, yucca, sugar cane, corn, cacao, tobacco, beans, livestock. Gold mines near by.

Fresno (frĕz'nō), county (□ 5,985; pop. 276,515), central Calif.; ⊙ Fresno. Stretches across San Joaquin Valley from Diablo Range (W) to crest of the Sierra Nevada (E), where there are peaks over 14,000 ft. Includes most of KINGS CANYON NATIONAL PARK and parts of Sierra and Sequoia natl. forests. Drained by Kings, San Joaquin, and Fresno rivers. FRIANT DAM is in co. Oil and natural-gas fields in W (Coalinga dist.). Rich irrigated valley section produces raisins (large part of U.S. crop), wine, and table grapes; cotton, figs, peaches, citrus fruit, nuts, truck, grain, alfalfa, sugar beets, rice, flax; also has dairying, stock and poultry raising. Extensive packing and processing industries (fruit drying, freezing, canning; wine making, distilling, dairying, lumber milling, cotton ginning); also diversified mfg. at Fresno. Sand and gravel, stone quarrying. Lumbering (pine, fir, cedar). Huntington, Shaver, Florence lakes (resorts); winter-sports areas; and hunting and fishing attract vacationers. Formed 1856.

Fresno, city (pop. 91,669), ⊙ Fresno co., central Calif., c.160 mi. SE of San Francisco, near geographical center of state; surrounded by huge acreages of irrigated vineyards and fig gardens, city is a railroad hub and processing, marketing, shipping, and mfg. center for a wide area of San Joaquin Valley. Fruit-packing plants (raisin plant here said to be world's largest), canneries, lumber mills, cottonseed- and olive-oil mills, foundries, brick and pottery plants; mfg. of farm equipment, machinery, clothing. Seat of Fresno State Col., a jr. col., and Pacific Bible Inst. of Fresno. Holds annual raisin festival and a dist. fair. Near by are Kearney Park (6 mi. W), an experimental farm of Univ. of Calif.; and Friant Dam (17 mi. N) of Central Valley Project. Sequoia and Kings Canyon natl. parks are c.50 mi. E. Founded 1872 on railroad in semiarid cattle-grazing region; grew with development of irrigated agr. (in 1870s) and winegrowing, which was soon succeeded in importance by raisin production. Inc. 1885.

Fresno Reservoir (frĕz'nō), in Hill co., N Mont., irrigation reservoir 20 mi. long; impounded in Milk R. 13 mi. WNW of Havre by Fresno Dam (111 ft. high, 2,070 ft. long; completed 1939).

Fresno River, central Calif., rises in NE Madera co., flows c.75 mi. generally SW and W, past Madera, into distributary channels flowing S to San Joaquin R. SW of Madera. Site of projected Hidden Reservoir of CENTRAL VALLEY project is on upper course.

Fresno de la Vega (frĕs'nō dhä lä vä'gä), town (pop. 1,202), Leon prov., NW Spain, 18 mi. S of Leon; cereals, wine, vegetables, cattle, sheep.

Fresno el Viejo (ĕl vyā'hō), town (pop. 1,707), Valladolid prov., N central Spain, 15 mi. SW of Medina del Campo; flour milling; stock raising; lumbering; cereals, vegetables, wine.

Fresnoy-le-Grand (frĕnwä-lů-grã'), town (pop. 2,448), Aisne dept., N France, 9 mi. NE of Saint-Quentin; textile-mfg. center (scarves, bedspreads, upholstery materials, curtains).

Fresquel River (frĕskĕl'), Aude dept., S France, rises just W of Castelnaudary, flows c.40 mi. ESE to the Aude below Carcassonne. Paralleled by the Canal du Midi.

Fressenneville (frĕsĕnvēl'), village (pop. 1,800), Somme dept., N France, 12 mi. WSW of Abbeville; locksmithing.

Fresser River (frĕsĕr'), Gerona prov., NE Spain, rises in the E Pyrenees near Fr. border, flows c.15 mi. S, past Ribas de Fresser, to the Ter at Ripoll. Hydroelectric stations.

Fresse-sur-Moselle (frĕs-sür-môzĕl'), town (pop. 2,025), Vosges dept., E France, on the Moselle and 14 mi. SE of Remiremont, in the S central Vosges; cotton milling.

Fret, Le (lů frā'), roadstead on Brest Roads, Finistère dept., W France, 8 mi. S of Brest on N shore of Crozon Peninsula.

Fréteval (frātväl'), village (pop. 552), Loir-et-Cher dept., N central France, on the Loir and 9 mi. NE of Vendôme; paper milling. Scene of Richard Cœur de Lion's victory over Philip Augustus (1194).

Fretheim, Norway: see FLAMSDAL.

Fretin (frůtē'), town (pop. 2,337), Nord dept., N France, 6 mi. SSE of Lille, in well-irrigated agr. area (sugar beets, potatoes, oats, forage crops); limekilns.

Fretum Gaditanum: see GIBRALTAR, STRAIT OF.

Fretum Gallicum: see DOVER, STRAIT OF.

Fretum Herculeum: see GIBRALTAR, STRAIT OF.

Fretum Siculum, Sicily: see MESSINA, STRAIT OF.

Freuchie (frōōkh'ē), agr. village, W Fifeshire, Scotland, 2 mi. E of Falkland.

Freudenberg (froi'důnbĕrk), town (pop. 1,828), N Baden, Germany, after 1945 in Württemberg-Baden, in the Odenwald, on the Main and 9 mi. WSW of Wertheim; fruit, grain.

Freudenstadt (froi'důn-shtät), town (pop. 9,634), S Württemberg, Germany, after 1945 in Württemberg-Hohenzollern, 29 mi. W of Tübingen; after Baden-Baden, the most frequented tourist center (alt. 2,388 ft.) of Black Forest; rail junction. Mfg. of cloth, clothing, machinery, pharmaceuticals; woodworking, dairying. Founded 1599 as refuge for Salzburg Protestants. Suffered heavy damage in Second World War.

Freudenthal, Czechoslovakia: see BRUNTAL.

Frêvent (frāvā'), town (pop. 3,504), Pas-de-Calais dept., N France, on Canche R. and 7 mi. S of Saint-Pol; mfg. of agr. machinery and building materials.

Frewsburg, village (pop. 1,383), Chautauqua co., extreme W N.Y., on Conewango Creek and 5 mi. SE of Jamestown; chemicals, furniture, lumber, canned foods; dairying.

Freyburg or **Freyburg an der Unstrut** (frī'bůrg, Ger. frī'bōōrk än dĕr ōōn'shtrōōt), town (pop. 5,856), in former Prussian Saxony prov., central Germany, after 1945 in Saxony-Anhalt, on the Unstrut and 5 mi. NNW of Naumburg; viticulture; fruitgrowing. Machinery mfg. Overlooked by 11th-cent. Neuenburg castle. Has 13th-cent. church. Frederick Ludwig Jahn lived and died here.

Freycinet Estuary, Australia: see SHARK BAY.

Freycinet Peninsula (frāsēnā'), E Tasmania, in Tasman Sea, just N of Schouten Isl.; forms E shore of Oyster Bay; 14 mi. long, 4 mi. wide; tin.

Freyming (frāmĕng'), Ger. *Freimengen* (frī'mĕng-ůn), town (pop. 6,831), Moselle dept., NE France, on Saar border, adjoining Merlebach (E) and 6 mi. SW of Forbach; coal mines.

Freyre or **Freire** (frā'rā), town (pop. 2,334), E Córdoba prov., Argentina, 20 mi. N of San Francisco; agr., stock raising, dairying; distilling.

Freystadt (frī'shtät), town (pop. 2,551), Upper Palatinate, central Bavaria, Germany, on small Schwarzach R. and 8 mi. SW of Neumarkt; grain, livestock. Has mid-18th-cent. church with early-14th-cent. tower. Just N is baroque pilgrimage church.

Freystadt. 1 Town, East Prussia: see KISIELICE, Olsztyn prov., Poland. **2** Town, Lower Silesia: see KOZUCHOW, Zielona Gora prov., Poland.

Freyung (frī'ōōng), village (pop. 3,846), Lower Bavaria, Germany, in Bohemian Forest, 17 mi. NNE of Passau; carbide and glass mfg., woodworking. Chartered 1354. Just NW is Wolfstein, site of late-16th-cent. castle.

Fria, Cape (frē'ů), or **Cape Frio** (frē'ō, frē'ōō), NW South-West Africa, on the Atlantic, 85 mi. SSE of mouth of Cunene R., S of Angola border; 18°26'S 12°E.

Friant (frē'ůnt, frī'–), village (1940 pop. 1,137), Fresno co., central Calif., 17 mi. NNE of Fresno. **Friant Dam** is on San Joaquin R. here. The dam, one of world's largest (3,430 ft. long, 320 ft. high; completed 1944) is a key irrigation and flood-control unit of CENTRAL VALLEY project. Forms Millerton L. (15 mi. long; site of natl. recreational area; fishing), from which Madera Canal and Friant-Kern Canal conduct water to irrigate the valley farms.

Friant-Kern Canal, S central Calif., a unit of CENTRAL VALLEY project, conducts water by gravity for 153 mi. from Friant Dam, along E side of San Joaquin Valley, to Kern R. near Bakersfield; irrigates large agr. acreages in Fresno, Tulare, Kern counties.

Friars Point, town (pop. 916), Coahoma co., NW Miss., 12 mi. NNW of Clarksdale, and on Mississippi R., in rich cotton, corn, and timber area; lumber milling, cotton ginning. Sometimes Friar Point.

Frías (frē'äs), town (1947 pop. 7,861), ⊙ Choya dept. (□ 5,400; pop. 23,769), SW Santiago del Estero prov., Argentina, at Catamarca prov. border, on small Albigasta R. and 50 mi. ESE of Catamarca. Rail junction; stock center (goats, horses, cattle); mfg. of cement, paper bags, furniture.

Frías, Bolivia: see POTOSÍ, city.

Frías, city (pop. 956), Piura dept., NW Peru, on W slopes of Cordillera Occidental, 25 mi. SW of Ayabaca; corn, sugar cane; cattle raising.

Frías, city (pop. 759), Burgos prov., N Spain, on La Bureba plain, on the Ebro and 36 mi. NE of Burgos; winegrowing, stock raising, flour milling. Has ruins of 15th-cent. castle.

Fribourg (frēbōōr'), Ger. *Freiburg* (frī'bōōrk), canton (□ 645; 1950 pop. 157,919), W Switzerland; ⊙ Fribourg. Pop. chiefly French speaking, Catholic. Agr. valleys; mts. in E and S. Noted for its cheese (particularly in GRUYÈRE dist.). Cereals, some sugar beets grown in N; SE part is largely pasture land (cattle raising, dairying). Several hydroelectric plants along Sarine R.

Fribourg, Ger. *Freiburg,* town (1950 pop. 28,767), ⊙ Fribourg canton, W Switzerland, on Sarine R. 1[illegible] mi. SW of Bern; chocolate, pastry, beer, flour, paper products; printing, metalworking (notably lamps); woodworking, tanning. Oelberg hydroelectric plant here. Fribourg was founded 1157 by a duke of Zähringen; joined Swiss Confederation in 1481. A bishop's see, it has a univ. Medieval architecture includes St. Nicolas cathedral (14th cent.), churches of Notre Dame (12th cent.) and St. Michel (17th cent.), Cordelier convent (13th cent.); several nunneries, Cantonal Mus. of Art and History and several other valuable collections; 7-arched Zähringen Bridge.

Friburgo, Brazil: see NOVA FRIBURGO.

Frickenhausen (frĭ'kůnhou'zůn), village (pop. 1,611), Lower Franconia, W Bavaria, Germany, on the Main (canalized) and 5 mi. SW of Kitzingen; winegrowing. Surrounded by 15th–16th-cent. walls; has late-Gothic town hall.

Friday Harbor, town (pop. 783), ⊙ San Juan co., NW Wash., on San Juan Isl. and 28 mi. SW of Bellingham; port of entry; salmon canneries; oceanographic laboratories.

Fridenfeld, Russian SFSR: see KOMSOMOLSKOYE, Saratov oblast.

Fridingen or **Fridingen an der Donau** (frē'dĭng-ůn än dĕr dō'nou), town (pop. 1,370), S Württemberg, Germany, after 1945 in Württemberg-Hohenzollern, in Swabian Jura, on the Danube and 6 mi. ENE of Tuttlingen; hydroelectric station. Cattle.

Fridley, village (pop. 3,796), Anoka co., E Minn., 8 mi. N of Minneapolis.

Fridtjof Nansen, Cape, Russian SFSR: see NANSEN CAPE.

Fridtjof Nansen, Mount (frĭ'jŏf năn'sĭn), peak (13,156 ft.), Antarctica, at head of Ross Shelf Ice; 85°26'S 167°W.

Fridtjof Nansen Island, Russian SFSR: see NANSEN ISLAND.

Fridtjof Nansen Land, Russian SFSR: see FRANZ JOSEF LAND.

Fridtjof Nansen Sound, Northwest Territories: see NANSEN SOUND.

Friedau, Yugoslavia: see ORMOZ.

Friedberg (frēd'bĕrk), village (pop. 1,629), Styria, Austria, on Pinka R. and 20 mi. S of Neunkirchen; rail junction; market, summer resort. Grain, vineyards; cattle, poultry.

Friedberg. 1 Town (pop. 8,697), Swabia, W central Bavaria, Germany, 4 mi. E of Augsburg; mfg. of machinery and precision instruments, woodworking. Has 13th-cent. castle and mid-17th-cent. town hall. Chartered 1404. **2** Town (pop. 13,743), central Hesse, W Germany, in former Upper Hesse prov., at E foot of the Taunus, 15 mi. NNE of Frankfurt; rail junction; sugar refining, mfg. of commercial chemicals. Has 13th-cent. fortress built on site of Roman camp. Friedberg was free imperial city, 1257–1802.

Friedeberg. 1 Town, Lower Silesia: see MIRSK, Wroclaw prov., Poland. **2** or **Friedeberg in Neumark,** Pomerania: see STRZELCE KRAJENSKIE, Zielona Gora prov., Poland.

Friedeck, Czechoslovakia: see FRYDEK.

Friedenfeld, Russian SFSR: see KOMSOMOLSKOYE, Saratov oblast.

Friedheim, Poland: see MIASTECZKO KRAINSKIE.

Friedland, Czechoslovakia: see FRYDLANT.

Friedland (frēt′länt). **1** Town (pop. 1,363), Brandenburg, E Germany, in Lower Lusatia, near Schwieloch L., 5 mi. S of Beeskow; forestry. **2** Town (pop. 8,357), Mecklenburg, N Germany, 15 mi. NE of Neubrandenburg; metalworking, sugar refining, brick and starch mfg., flour- and sawmilling; grain and cattle market. Has early-Gothic church and remains of old town walls and gates. Founded 1244 as fortified outpost by margraves of Brandenburg.

Friedland, Poland: see MIEROSZOW.

Friedland, Russian SFSR: see PRAVDINSK, Kaliningrad oblast.

Friedrichroda (frē″drĭkh-rō′dä), town (pop. 7,254), Thuringia, central Germany, on N slope of Thuringian Forest, 9 mi. SW of Gotha; climatic health and winter-sports resort; woodworking. Reinhardsbrunn palace (1827–35) incorporates remains of Benedictine monastery (founded 1085; destroyed 1525). Town founded 1035; chartered 1597. Bet. 17th and 19th cent. it had important textile-bleaching and iron-mining industries.

Friedrichsdorf (frē′drĭkhsdôrf), town (pop. 2,821), in former Prussian prov. of Hesse-Nassau, W Germany, after 1945 in Hesse, on S slope of the Taunus, 2 mi. N of Bad Homburg; mfg. (wool, stockings, biscuits). Founded 1687 by Huguenots.

Friedrichsfeld (–fĕlt), SE suburb of Mannheim, Germany.

Friedrichshafen (frē″drĭkhs-hä′fŭn), town (1939 pop. 24,041; 1946 pop. 15,356), S Württemberg, Germany, after 1945 in Württemberg-Hohenzollern, on N shore of L. of Constance, 11 mi. SSW of Ravensburg; rail junction; customs station (steamer connection to Switzerland). Railroad repair shops; mfg. of motors, cogwheels, precision instruments, textiles, household goods; leather- and woodworking. Has baroque ducal castle (formerly Benedictine monastery) and church. Formed 1811 through unification of former (1275–1802) free imperial city of Buchhorn and anc. former nunnery of Hofen. Became summer residence of kings of Württemberg in 1824. As home of the Zeppelin works and an airplane construction center, Friedrichshafen suffered severe destruction (about 80%) in Second World War.

Friedrichshain (–hīn), district (1939 pop. 346,264; 1946 pop. 193,115), E central Berlin, Germany, on the Spree. Mfg. (clothing, electrical equipment, food products). Called Horst Wessel Stadt during Hitler regime. After 1945 in Soviet sector.

Friedrichshall, Bad, Germany: see BAD FRIEDRICHSHALL.

Friedrichskoog (–kōk′), village (pop. 4,942), in Schleswig-Holstein, NW Germany, on small peninsula in the North Sea, 14 mi. SW of Heide, in the S Dithmarschen; cattle. Built on reclaimed (1854) polder land.

Friedrichsort (–ôrt), district (since 1922) of KIEL, NW Germany, harbor on W bank of Kiel Firth, 5 mi. N of city center; mfg. of machinery. Until 1945, site of secondary naval base.

Friedrichsruh (–rōō′), estate in Schleswig-Holstein, NW Germany, 14 mi. E of Hamburg city center. Was property and residence (1890–98) of Bismarck; contains his mausoleum.

Friedrichstadt (frē′drĭkh-shtät). **1** E suburb of Magdeburg, Saxony-Anhalt, central Germany, on the Elbe; site of Magdeburg airport. **2** Town (pop. 3,648), in Schleswig-Holstein, NW Germany, on the regulated Eider, at mouth of small Treene R., and 7 mi. S of Husum; market center for cattle- and horse-raising region. Has 17th-cent. church; many gabled houses. Founded 1619; was settled by Dutch merchants.

Friedrichstadt, Latvia: see JAUNJELGAVA.

Friedrichsthal (frē′drĭkhs-täl), town (pop. 14,660), S central Saar, 8 mi. NE of Saarbrücken; coal mining; steel industry; glass, shoe mfg.

Friedrich-Wilhelm Canal, Germany: see ODER-SPREE CANAL.

Friedrich-Wilhelmshafen, New Guinea: see MADANG.

Frielendorf (frē′lŭndôrf), village (pop. 2,195), in former Prussian prov. of Hesse-Nassau, W Germany, after 1945 in Hesse, 24 mi. SSW of Kassel; lignite mining.

Friemersheim, Germany: see RHEINHAUSEN.

Friend, city (pop. 1,148), Saline co., SE Nebr., 35 mi. WSW of Lincoln; flour, feed; dairy and poultry produce, grain, livestock. Founded c.1873.

Friendly, town (pop. 216), Tyler co., NW W.Va., on the Ohio and 8 mi. WNW of Middlebourne.

Friendly Islands: see TONGA.

Friendship, Br. Guiana: see BUXTON.

Friendship, village (pop. 332), Coronie dist., N Du. Guiana, in Atlantic coastland adjoining Totness, 80 mi. W of Paramaribo; coconut plantations.

Friendship. 1 Town (pop. 179), Hot Spring co., central Ark., 8 mi. NNE of Arkadelphia. **2** Resort and fishing town (pop. 772), Knox co., S Maine, on Muscongus Bay and SW of Rockland. **3** Village (pop. 1,344), Allegany co., W N.Y., 18 mi. NE of Olean; agr.; mfg. (hosiery, textiles, auto bodies, metal and wood products); timber. Inc. 1898. **4** Town (pop. 452), Crockett co., W Tenn., 11 mi SE of Dyersburg, in farm area. **5** Village (pop. 566), ⊙ Adams co., central Wis., on Little Roche a Cri Creek (tributary of the Wisconsin) and 29 mi. S of Wisconsin Rapids, in timber and dairying region.

Friendship International Airport, Md.: see BALTIMORE.

Friendship Island (□ c.¾), Knox co., S Maine, in Muscongus Bay, just S of Friendship.

Friends Lake, Warren co., E N.Y., resort lake (c.2 mi. long) in the Adirondacks 23 mi. NNW of Glens Falls; hotels, cottages, recreational facilities at community of Friends Lake.

Friendsville. 1 Town (pop. 607), Garrett co., extreme NW Md., in the Allegheny on Youghiogheny R., and 35 mi. W of Cumberland, in hunting, fishing, lumbering area. **2** Borough (pop. 65), Susquehanna co., NE Pa., 11 mi. WNW of Montrose.

Frier Fjord, Norway: see LANGESUND FJORD.

Friern Barnet (frī′ûrn bär′nĭt), residential urban district (1931 pop. 23,101; 1951 census 29,164), central Middlesex, England, 8 mi. N of London. Has Norman church. Just S is district of Colney Hatch (kō′nē), with large mental hosp.

Fries, Netherlands: see VRIES.

Fries (frēz), town (pop. 1,442), Grayson co., SW Va., in the Blue Ridge, on New R. and 3 mi. NW of Galax, in dairying, livestock, truck-farming area; cotton milling. Inc. 1901–02.

Friesach (frē′zäkh), town (pop. 3,509), Carinthia, S Austria, 19 mi. SW of Judenburg; resort (alt. 2,090 ft.); tannery. Surrounded by medieval moat and parts of 12th-cent. wall.

Friesack (frē′zäk), town (pop. 3,551), Brandenburg, E Germany, 14 mi. NE of Rathenow; woodworking, dairying, distilling; livestock market.

Friesenheim (frē′zŭnhīm), village (pop. 2,797), S Baden, Germany, at W foot of Black Forest, 2 mi. N of Lahr; tobacco industry; woodworking.

Friesische Wehde, Germany: see BOCKHORN.

Friesland, Germany: see JEVER.

Friesland (frēz′lănd, Du. frēs′länt), anc. *Frisia*, province (□ 1,248.8; pop. 459,361), N Netherlands; ⊙ Leeuwarden. Bounded by Groningen prov. (E), the Waddenzee (N), the Ijsselmeer (W), Overijssel prov. (S), Drenthe prov. (SE). Includes West Frisian Isls. of VLIELAND, AMELAND, and TERSCHELLING. Fertile and arable land near coastline, sandy heath and fenland farther inland; drained by numerous canals and by minor rivers flowing into the Ijsselmeer. Many picturesque lakes. Noted for its dairy industry and for cattle market at Leeuwarden; agr. (wheat, potatoes); mfg. (agr. machinery, reed products). Main towns: Leeuwarden, Sneek, Harlingen (chief port). Prior to 13th cent. Friesland covered area extending S to Scheldt R. and E to Weser R. In mid-15th cent. region E of Ems R. estuary became a county of the Holy Roman Empire. In 1498 area of present prov. came under Albert of Saxony; Frisian pop. revolted and region passed (1523) to Emperor Charles V. Subscribed (1579) to Union of Utrecht, but continued to appoint its own stadholders until 1748, when its stadholder, Prince William IV of Orange, became sole and hereditary stadholder of all the United Provinces of the Netherlands. Language of prov. is Frisian, which differs considerably from Dutch; has its own literature.

Friesland (frē′zlŭnd), village (pop. 311), Columbia co., S central Wis., 20 mi. ENE of Portage.

Friesoythe (frē′zoi″tŭ), town (pop. 5,952), in Oldenburg, NW Germany, after 1945 in Lower Saxony, 14 mi. NW of Cloppenburg, in peat region.

Friezenveen, Netherlands: see VRIEZENVEEN.

Frigate Island, easternmost (700 acres; pop. 118) of the Seychelles proper, in Indian Ocean, 35 mi. ENE of Victoria; 4°35′S 55°56′E; 1 mi. long, ½ mi. wide.

Frigento (frĕjĕn′tô), village (pop. 1,565), Avellino prov., Campania, S Italy, 10 mi. S of Ariano Irpino.

Frigid, Cape, E extremity of Keewatin Dist. mainland, Northwest Territories, on Roes Welcome Sound, at S entrance of Repulse Bay; 66°4′N 85°5′W.

Frigiliana (frēhēlyä′nä), town (pop. 1,955), Málaga prov., S Spain, in coastal hills, 30 mi. ENE of Málaga; sugar cane, raisins, olives, figs, potatoes, corn, truck produce. Flour- and sawmilling; mfg. of molasses, vinegar, olive oil.

Frignano (frēnyä′nô), commune (pop. 10,055), Caserta prov., Campania, S Italy, 2 mi. NW of Aversa. Comprises agr. towns of Frignano Maggiore (pop. 5,584) and Frignano Piccolo (pop. 4,471; after 1950 called Villa di Briano).

Friguiagbé (frēgyä′gbā), village, W Fr. Guinea, Fr. West Africa, on railroad and 55 mi. ENE of Conakry; banana growing.

Frijole (frēhō′lē), village, Culberson co., extreme W Texas, on E slope of Guadalupe Mts., in scenic region near N.Mex. line, c.100 mi. E of El Paso. Alt. 5,450 ft; one of highest communities in Texas.

Frijoles (frējō′lēs), town (pop. 118), Cristobal dist., central Panama Canal Zone, on transisthmian railroad, on E shore of the canal, and 14 mi. SE of Colón. Bananas, livestock.

Frimley, England: see CAMBERLEY.

Frimley and Camberley, England: see CAMBERLEY.

Frindsbury, England: see ROCHESTER.

Frinton-on-Sea, former urban district (1931 pop. 2,196) now in Frinton and Walton urban dist. (1951 census pop. 8,448), NE Essex, England, on North Sea, 8 mi. S of Harwich; seaside resort, with beach.

Frio (frē′ō), county (□ 1,116; pop. 10,357), SW Texas; ⊙ Pearsall. Drained by Frio R. Partly in irrigated Winter Garden truck and fruitgrowing area; also peanuts, corn, grain sorghums. Cattle ranching, dairying, poultry raising. Oil wells; clay, sand deposits. Formed 1858.

Frio, Cabo (kä′bōō frē′ōō), promontory on SE coast of Brazil, in Rio de Janeiro state, 75 mi. E of Rio. Cape proper with lighthouse (23°S 42°W) is at S tip of a rocky islet just offshore. Towns of Cabo Frio and Arraial do Cabo are on narrow peninsula (just N) bet. Araruama Lagoon (W) and the open Atlantic (E). Discovered 1503 by Amerigo Vespucci. Pirate stronghold in 16th cent.

Frio, Cape, South-West Africa: see FRIA, CAPE.

Frío, Río (rē′ō frē′ō), Alajuela prov., N Costa Rica, rises at E foot of the volcano Tenorio, flows 40 mi. N through Guatuso Lowland, past Los Chiles, to L. Nicaragua in Nicaragua at exit of San Juan R.

Frio Canyon, Texas: see FRIO RIVER.

Friockheim (frē′kĭm), village in Kirkden parish, E Angus, Scotland, on Lunan Water and 8 mi. E of Forfar; textile bleaching.

Friona (frēō′nŭ), city (pop. 1,202), Parmer co., NW Texas, on the Llano Estacado, 22 mi. SW of Hereford; shipping point for wheat and cattle area.

Frio River (frē′ō), Texas, rises on Edwards Plateau in Real co., flows S and SE c.220 mi. to receive Atascosa R. just before joining the Nueces below Three Rivers. Recreational areas at Frio Canyon N of Uvalde (Garner State Park here) and Frio State Park in Frio co.

Frisange (frēzãzh′), village (pop. 294), S Luxembourg, 7 mi. SSE of Luxembourg city, on Fr. border; rose-growing center.

Frische Nehrung, Poland and USSR: see VISTULA SPIT.

Frisches Haff, Poland and USSR: see VISTULA LAGOON.

Frisco. 1 Town (pop. 87), Summit co., central Colo., on headstream of Blue R., in Gore Range, and 7 mi. NNW of Breckenridge; alt. 9,097 ft. Small-scale gold and silver mining. **2** Village (pop. 1,501, with adjacent North Sewickley), Beaver co., W Pa., just SE of Ellwood City. **3** Town (pop. 736), Collin co., N Texas, 26 mi. N of Dallas, in agr. area (cotton, corn, cattle).

Frisco City, town (pop. 1,068), Monroe co., SW Ala., 7 mi. SW of Monroeville; woodworking.

Frisia, Netherlands: see FRIESLAND.

Frisian Islands (frĭ′zhŭn), island chain of the North Sea, extending along, and at distance of 3 to 20 mi. from, coasts of the Netherlands, Germany, and Denmark. Low in elevation, sea coast of isls. is subject to constant erosion by waves, while shore facing tidal waters is gradually being expanded (since 19th cent.) by diking. Heavy floods (especially 1362, 1570, 1634) throughout the centuries have altered the shape of most of the isls. and have greatly diminished the over-all land area of the group. Pop., predominantly Frisian, was engaged in shipping and fishing in Middle Ages; since early-19th cent., most of the isls. have been developed as health resorts. Chain is divided into 3 major groups. **West Frisian Islands,** belonging to the Netherlands, are offshore of Dutch provs. of North Holland, Friesland, and Groningen, and comprise inhabited isls. of TEXEL, VLIELAND, TERSCHELLING, AMELAND, and SCHIERMONNIKOOG, and 4 uninhabited isls. Sheep and cattle raising here. **East Frisian Islands,** belonging to Germany, and extending off German coast bet. the Dollart and Elbe R. estuary, consist of inhabited isls. of BALTRUM, BORKUM, JUIST, LANGEOOG, NORDERNEY, SPIKEROOG, and WANGEROOGE, all seaside resorts, and 4 uninhabited isls., including NEUWERK and SCHARHÖRN. **North Frisian Islands,** divided bet. Germany and Denmark, and extending along coast of Ger. Schleswig-Holstein and Danish Jutland, comprise inhabited isls. of AMRUM, FÖHR, SYLT, ROMO, FANO, and MANO, as well as several uninhabited isls. (including HELGOLAND and TRISCHEN), and HALLIG ISLANDS. Cattle grazing is the chief occupation.

Fristad (frē′städ″), village (pop. 903), Alvsborg co., SW Sweden, near Viska R., 7 mi. NNE of Boras; woodworking.

Fritsla (frĭt′slä″), village (pop. 2,311), Alvsborg co., SW Sweden, near Viska R., 12 mi. SSW of Boras; cotton milling, hosiery knitting.

Fritzlar (frĭts′lär), town (pop. 6,654), in former Prussian prov. of Hesse-Nassau, W Germany, after 1945 in Hesse, on the Eder and 15 mi. SW of Kassel. Developed around Benedictine abbey (with large, frequently remodeled church), founded by St. Boniface c.730. Henry I elected emperor here in 919. Passed to archbishopric of Mainz in 11th cent. Destroyed by war, 1078 and 1232. Peace of Lunéville gave it to Hesse-Darmstadt.

Friuli, province, Italy: see UDINE, province.

Friuli (frē'ōōlē), historical region bet. Carnic Alps and the Adriatic, now included in Friuli–Venezia-Giulia, NE Italy, and Slovenia, NW Yugoslavia; has fertile plain in S and part of Karst region in SE. Chief cities, Udine and Gorizia. After 1500 incorporated in Hapsburg possessions. Italy received W part in 1866 and E part in 1919, and included them in VENEZIA GIULIA. Italian peace treaty of 1947 gave E Friuli (but not Gorizia) to Yugoslavia.

Friuli-Venezia Giulia (–vĕnä'tsēä jū'lyä), region (□ 2,948; pop. 837,000), NE Italy; ⊙ Udine. Borders Austria (N), Yugoslavia (E), Veneto (W), Free Territory of Trieste (SE), and the Adriatic (S). Terrain ranges from Carnic Alps (N) to an extensive plain (S). Formed after Second World War to include prov. of UDINE (formerly part of Veneto), and part of GORIZIA prov. (from former region of VENEZIA GIULIA).

Friville-Escarbotin (frēvēl'-ĕskärbôtē'), commune (pop. 3,148), Somme dept., N France, 13 mi. W of Abbeville; iron founding, locksmithing, mfg. of plumbing fixtures.

Frizington, England: see ARLECDON AND FRIZINGTON.

Friz Strait or **Vries Strait** (both: frēs), Jap. *Etorofu-kaikyo* (ätō'rō'fōō-kīkyō'), in S Kuriles, Russian SFSR; separates Urup (N) and Iturup (S) isls.; 24 mi. wide. Named for 17th-cent. Du. navigator De Vries.

Fro, islands, Norway: see FRO ISLANDS.

Froan, Norway: see FRO ISLANDS.

Frobisher Bay (frō'bĭshŭr) or **Ward Inlet,** trading post, SE Baffin Isl., SE Franklin Dist., Northwest Territories, on Frobisher Bay, on S shore of Hall Peninsula; 63°30'N 67°30'W. Post was established 1914. Near by is Crystal II air base.

Frobisher Bay, inlet (150 mi. long, 20–40 mi. wide) of the Atlantic in SE Baffin Isl., SE Franklin Dist., Northwest Territories; 63°N 67°W. Discovered (1576) by Sir Martin Frobisher, it was believed to be a strait separating Baffin Isl. from another isl. until character as bay was established 1860.

Frobisher Lake (24 mi. long, 17 mi. wide), NW Sask., just N of Churchill L., into which it drains; 56°20'N 108°20'W; alt. 1,382 ft. Just N are Turnor and Wasekamio lakes.

Frodingham, England: see SCUNTHORPE.

Frodsham, market town and parish (pop. 3,025), N Cheshire, England, near mouth of Weaver R., on the Mersey, 11 mi. NE of Chester; mfg. of feed cakes. Has Norman church.

roeschwiller (frôshvēlâr'), Ger. *Fröschweiler* (frûsh'-vīlûr), village (pop. 445), Bas-Rhin dept., E France, 10 mi. NNW of Haguenau. Here French were defeated (1870) in Franco-Prussian War.

Froges (frôzh), village (pop. 323), Isère dept., SE France, on the Isère and 12 mi. NE of Grenoble, in GRÉSIVAUDAN valley; sheet aluminum works.

Frogmore, S.C.: see SAINT HELENA ISLAND.

Frognerseteren (frông'nûrsätrûn), suburban locality of Oslo, SE Norway, in hilly region 9 mi. NW of city center; alt. 1,539 ft. Manor house (18th cent.) now contains City Mus. Surrounded by Frogner Park (c.100 acres), of which Vigeland Park (founded 1931), with sculptures and large monolith by Vigeland, forms part. Near by is Ski Mus., containing polar equipment used by Nansen and Amundsen. Site of municipal home for undernourished children. Popular tourist resort. Until 1948, in Akershus co. Sometimes Frognersaeteren.

Frohavet (frō'hävů), section of the North Sea off coast of Norway bet. Fro Isls. (W) and the Fosen region in Sor-Trondelag co., N of entrance to Trondheim Fjord.

Frohburg (frō'bōōrk), town (pop. 4,880), Saxony, E central Germany, 6 mi. SE of Borna; metalworking, textile printing, hosiery knitting; mfg. of furniture, cardboard, toys, ceramics. Lignite mining. Has 16th-cent. castle.

Frohenbruck, Czechoslovakia: see VESELI NAD LUZNICI.

Frohna, town (pop. 208), Perry co., E Mo., 15 mi. SE of Perryville.

Frohnleiten (frōn'lītûn), village (pop. 2,345), Styria, SE Austria, on Mur R. and 14 mi. NNW of Graz; paper mills, lumberyards. Summer resort, with mineral springs. Castle Weiher (16th cent.) is S.

Froid (froid), town (pop. 555), Roosevelt co., NE Mont., near Medicine L. and Big Muddy Creek, 37 mi. NE of Poplar; livestock, dairy and poultry products, grain.

Froien, Norway: see FROYA.

Fro Islands (frō), Nor. *Froan* or *Frøyane*, group of tiny islands in North Sea, 20 mi. off W central coast of Norway, NE of Froya isl., extending c.20 mi. in a chain paralleling the coast; fishing. At N end (64°11'N 9°23'E) is the islet of Halten, 60 mi. NNW of Trondheim, with a lighthouse.

Froissy (frwäsē'), agr. village (pop. 433), Oise dept., N France, 11 mi. NE of Beauvais; hog raising.

Froland (frō'län), village and canton (pop. 2,601), Aust-Agder co., S Norway, on Nid R., on railroad and 7 mi. NW of Arendal; feldspar and quartz quarries. Lumber milling 3 mi. SW. Has historic church.

Froloyo (frô'luvŭ), city (1939 pop. over 10,000), central Stalingrad oblast, Russian SFSR, on railroad (Archeda station) and 80 mi. NNW of Stalingrad; flour-milling center; metal products. Limestone quarrying near-by. Archeda gas wells furnish natural gas to Stalingrad via pipe line.

Fromberg, town (pop. 442), Carbon co., S Mont., on Clarks Fork Yellowstone R. and 34 mi. SW of Billings; trading point; sugar beets, grain; bricks; coal.

Frombork, Poland: see FRAUENBURG.

Frome (frōōm), urban district (1931 pop. 10,739; 1951 census 11,116), E Somerset, England, on Frome R. and 11 mi. S of Bath; agr. market in dairying region; woolen mills, metalworks, brass and plastics works, flour mills. Near by is Selwood Forest; town is sometimes called Frome Selwood. Has 14th-cent. parish church containing remains of 10th-cent. church. Thomas Ken buried here.

Frome (frōm), town (pop. 1,950), Westmoreland parish, W Jamaica, 7 mi. NNW of Savanna-la-Mar; sugar cane, breadfruit, livestock. Has one of isl.'s largest sugar mills; exports unrefined sugar. Yeast factory near by.

Frome, Lake (□ 4.5), E South Australia, 160 mi. NE of Port Pirie; 4 mi. long, 2 mi. wide; 4–10 in. deep; usually dry.

Fromelennes (frômlĕn'), village (pop. 1,039), Ardennes dept., N France, on Belg. border 2 mi. ESE of Givet; copper smelting. Caves of Nichet (stalactites) are near by.

Fromentine, Goulet de (gōōlā' dů frômätēn'), strait in Bay of Biscay, off Vendée dept., W France, separating S end of Île de Noirmoutier from mainland; ½ mi. wide. It is in the process of silting up. Village of Fromentine on S shore is bathing resort.

Frome River (frōōm). **1** In Dorset, England, rises near NW border S of Yeovil, flows 35 mi. SE and E, past Dorchester, Wool, and Wareham, to Poole Harbour. **2** In central Gloucester, England, rises near Painswick, flows past Stroud to the Severn 7 mi. SW of Gloucester; 16 mi. long. **3** In S Gloucester, England, rises near Chipping Sodbury, flows 20 mi. to the Avon at Bristol. **4** In Hereford, England, rises 5 mi. N of Bromyard, flows 20 mi. S, past Bromyard, to the Lugg 3 mi. E of Hereford. **5** In E Somerset, England, rises 4 mi. NE of Bruton, flows 20 mi. NNE, past Frome, to the Avon 3 mi. SE of Bath.

Frômista (frō'mēstä), town (pop. 1,779), Palencia prov., N central Spain, on Canal of Castile and 16 mi. NNE of Palencia; cereals, vegetables, mules. Has 12th-cent. church.

Frommern (frô'mûrn), village (pop. 2,072), S Württemberg, Germany, after 1945 in Württemberg-Hohenzollern, in Swabian Jura, 2 mi. SE of Balingen; shale-oil processing, furniture mfg.

Fronberg (frōn'bĕrk), village (pop. 1,358), Upper Palatinate, E central Bavaria, Germany, on the Nab, just NE of Schwandorf; steel plant. Metal-working center since 15th cent.

Fröndenberg (frûn'důnbĕrk), village (pop. 7,091), in former Prussian prov. of Westphalia, W Germany, after 1945 in North Rhine-Westphalia, on the Ruhr and 5 mi. SE of Unna; rail junction.

Fronsac (frōsäk'), village (pop. 267), Gironde dept., SW France, on the Dordogne and 2 mi. W of Libourne; winegrowing.

Frontado, Villa, Venezuela: see VILLA FRONTADO.

Fronteira (frōntā'rů), town (pop. 3,279), Portalegre dist., central Portugal, 20 mi. SSW of Portalegre; terminus of rail spur from Estremoz; cheesemaking center; agr. trade (livestock, grain, olives); meat smoking, flour milling. At near-by Atoleiros, Portuguese defeated Spaniards in 1384.

Fronteiras (frōntā'rŭs), city (pop. 502), E Piauí, Brazil, near Ceará and Pernambuco borders, 17 mi. WSW of Campos Sales (Ceará). Until 1944, called Socorro.

Frontenac (frŏn'tůnăk). **1** County (□ 1,599; pop. 53,717), SE Ont., on L. Ontario and on the St. Lawrence; ⊙ Kingston. **2** County (□ 1,370; pop. 28,596), S Que., on Maine border, on Chaudière R.; ⊙ Megantic.

Frontenac. 1 City (pop. 1,569), Crawford co., SE Kansas, near Mo. line, just N of Pittsburg, in general agr. and coal-mining region. Laid out 1887, inc. 1895. **2** Town (pop. 1,099), St. Louis co., E Mo., just W of St. Louis.

Frontenac, Fort, Ont.: see KINGSTON, Ont.

Frontenay-Rohan-Rohan (frōtnĕ'-rôä'-rôä'), village (pop. 1,217), Deux-Sèvres dept., W France, 5 mi. SW of Niort; dairying; mfg. of wooden shoes. Anc. stronghold, and former fief of the Rohan family.

Frontenhausen (frôn"tůnhou'zůn), village (pop. 2,600), Lower Bavaria, Germany, on the Great Vils and 17 mi. E of Landshut; brickworks; brewing, tanning, flour and lumber milling. Has Gothic church. Chartered 1386.

Frontera, department, Argentina: see BERNARDO DE IRIGOYEN, Misiones natl. territory.

Frontera (frōntā'rä) or **Las Lapas** (läs lä'päs), village (pop. 150), Hierro, Canary Isls., 6 mi. SW of Valverde, in agr. region (cereals, potatoes, tomatoes, almonds, honey, grapes, figs); lumbering; stock raising; cheese processing, wine making.

Frontera. 1 Town, Coahuila, Mexico: see VILLA FRONTERA. **2** City, Tabasco, Mexico: see ALVARO OBREGÓN.

Frontera, La (lä frōntā'rä), town (pop. 807), Cuenca prov., E central Spain, 23 mi. N of Cuenca; cereals, grapes, saffron, livestock.

Frontera Comalapa (kōmälä'pä) or **Comalapa,** town (pop. 939), Chiapas, S Mexico, in Sierra Madre, 40 mi. S of Comitán; oranges, mangoes, lemons.

Frontera Hidalgo (ēdäl'gō), town (pop. 867), Chiapas, S Mexico, on Guatemala border, 8 mi. N of Suchiate; coffee.

Frontera Point, cape in Tabasco, SE Mexico, on Gulf of Campeche, at mouth of Grijalva and Usumacinta rivers, 7 mi. NNW of Alvaro Obregón; 18°37'N 92°28'W.

Fronteras (frōntā'räs), town (pop. 697), Sonora, NW Mexico, on railroad and 32 mi. S of Douglas, Ariz.; wheat, corn, alfalfa, cattle.

Frontier, county (□ 966; pop. 5,282), S Nebr.; ⊙ Stockville. Agr. region watered by Medicine Creek and other branches of Republican R. Grain, livestock. Formed 1872.

Frontier, village (1940 pop. 671), Lincoln co., SW Wyo., on Hams Fork just N of Kemmerer; alt. 6,954 ft.; coal mines. Silver-fox farm near by. Railroad station, North Kemmerer.

Frontier Illaqas, Kashmir: see GILGIT AGENCY.

Frontier Province, W Pakistan: see NORTH-WEST FRONTIER PROVINCE.

Frontignan (frōtēnyä'), town (pop. 4,416), Hérault dept., S France, on Rhone-Sète Canal and on lagoon of the Gulf of Lion, 4 mi. NE of Sète; winegrowing center, known for its muscatel; apéritif mfg., distilling, sulphur refining. Its Romanesque-Gothic church damaged in Second World War.

Frontino (frōntē'nō), town (pop. 2,145), Antioquia dept., NW central Colombia, in Cordillera Occidental, 27 mi. NW of Antioquia; alt. 4,032 ft.; gold mining; coffee, cotton, sugar cane, stock.

Frontino, Páramo (pä'rämō), Andean massif (13,385 ft.), Antioquia dept., NW central Colombia, in Cordillera Central, 40 mi. WNW of Medellín.

Fronton (frōtō'), village (pop. 1,233), Haute-Garonne dept., S France, 12 mi. S of Montauban; winegrowing, distilling.

Frontón Island, Peru: see SAN LORENZO ISLAND.

Front Range, in Rocky Mts. of Wyo. and Colo., extends c.300 mi. SE and S from Casper, E central Wyo., into Fremont co., S central Colo.; forms part of Continental Divide in Colo. Includes LARAMIE MOUNTAINS in Wyo., MEDICINE BOW MOUNTAINS in Wyo. and Colo., part of ROCKY MOUNTAIN NATIONAL PARK in N Colo., and PIKES PEAK in S end of range, near Colorado Springs. Headstreams of South Platte, Colorado, and Cache la Poudre rivers rise in Colo. The range lies largely within natl.-forest area. Prominent peaks in park part of range are Twin Sisters (11,435 ft.), Pagoda (13,491 ft.), Chief's Head (13,579 ft.), Mt. Meeker (13,911 ft.), Mt. BIERSTADT (14,048 ft.), and LONGS PEAK (14,255 ft.), highest point in park. Others in Colo. are Mt. Audubon (13,223 ft.), JAMES PEAK (13,260 ft.), Mt. McClellan (13,423 ft.), ARAPAHOE PEAK (13,506 ft.), Rosalie Peak (13,575 ft.), Mt. EVANS (14,260 ft.), TORREYS PEAK (14,264 ft.), and GRAYS PEAK (14,274 ft.). Chief passes in Colo. are BERTHOUD PASS (11,314 ft.) and LOVELAND PASS (11,992 ft.). Range is penetrated by MOFFAT TUNNEL and ALVA B. ADAMS TUNNEL. Gold, silver, coal, lead, and copper are mined throughout much of Colo. part of range.

Front Royal, town (pop. 8,115), ⊙ Warren co., N Va., near junction of South Fork and North Fork to form Shenandoah R., 19 mi. S of Winchester, at N end of Skyline Drive along crest of the Blue Ridge. Large viscose-rayon plant; mfg. of chemicals, preserves, apple brandy; food canning; limestone quarrying. Seat of Randolph-Macon Acad. Skyline Caverns, just SW, attract tourists. George Washington Natl. Forest is W. In Shenandoah Valley campaign of Civil War, Stonewall Jackson here defeated Union troops under Gen. N. P. Banks. Inc. 1788.

Frood Mine, town (pop. 70), SE central Ont., 3 mi. NW of Sudbury; nickel and copper mining.

Frooyane, Norway: see FRO ISLANDS.

Fröschweiler, France: see FROESCHWILLER.

Frose (frō'zů), village (pop. 3,349), in former Anhalt state, central Germany, after 1945 in Saxony-Anhalt, at N foot of the lower Harz, 5 mi. NW of Aschersleben; lignite mining. Has 12th-cent. church of former convent (founded in 10th cent.).

Frosinone (frôzēnô'nĕ), province (□ 1,251; pop. 445,607), Latium, S central Italy; ⊙ Frosinone. Mtn. and hill terrain, watered by Liri, Rapido, and Sacco rivers. Agr. (cereals, grapes, olives); livestock raising (sheep, goats, cattle). Asphalt mining (Castrocielo, Castro dei Volsci); alabaster quarrying (Filettino). Oil deposits at San Giovanni Incarico. Hydroelectric plants on Liri R. Contains abbey of MONTE CASSINO and resorts (Fiuggi, Guarcino). Mfg. at Isola del Liri and Sora. Formed 1926.

Frosinone, anc. *Frusino*, town (pop. 7,568) ⊙, Frosinone prov., Latium, S central Italy, in the Apennines, on branch of Sacco R. and 50 mi. ESE of Rome; 41°38'N 13°22'E. Agr. center; livestock market. Became ⊙ prov. in 1926. Severely damaged (1943–44) in Second World War air raids.

Froslev (frů'slĕv), Dan. *Frøslev*, town (pop. 1,742), Aabenraa-Sonderborg amt, S Jutland, Denmark, at Padborg station (Ger.-border station), 15 mi. S of Aabenraa, 4 mi. NW of Flensburg.

Froso, Swedish *Frösön* (frûs'ûn"), island (□ 16; pop. 5,891), in Stor L., Jamtland prov., N central Sweden, opposite Ostersund (bridge); 6 mi. long, 2–3 mi. wide. Hornsberg village (E) is tourist resort. Dairying.

Frosolone (frôzôlô'nĕ), village (pop. 2,015), Campobasso prov., Abruzzi e Molise, S central Italy, 12 mi. WNW of Campobasso; cutlery mfg.

Frost. 1 Village (pop. 326), Faribault co., S Minn., near Iowa line, 9 mi. ESE of Blue Earth; dairy products. **2** Town (pop. 585), Navarro co., E central Texas, 20 mi. W of Corsicana; trade point in agr. area (cotton, corn).

Frosta (frô'stä), agr. village and canton (pop. 3,174), Nord-Trondelag co., central Norway, 20 mi. SW of Levanger. Formerly spelled Frosten.

Frostburg, resort and trading town (pop. 6,876), Allegany co., W Md., in the Alleghenies, 9 mi. W of Cumberland; bituminous-coal and clay mining; makes firebrick, clothing. Seat of a state teachers col. and the Miners' Hosp. for tuberculosis. Big Savage Mtn. and Savage R. State Forest lie just W. Settled c.1812, inc. 1870.

Frosten, Norway: see FROSTA.

Frostproof, town (pop. 2,329), Polk co., central Fla., 13 mi. S of Lake Wales, near several lakes; cans and packs citrus fruit.

Frouard (frōōär'), town (pop. 5,028), Meurthe-et-Moselle dept., NE France, on the Moselle, at mouth of Meurthe R., on Marne-Rhine Canal and 5 mi. NNW of Nancy; rail junction; ironworks.

Frovi (frû'vē"), Swedish *Frövi*, village (pop. 997), Orebro co., S central Sweden, on L. Varing, Swedish *Varingen* (8-mi.-long expansion of Arboga R.), 15 mi. NE of Orebro; rail junction; lumber, pulp, and paper mills.

Froward Cape, southernmost point (1,200 ft. high) of American mainland, at tip of BRUNSWICK PENINSULA, Chile, on Strait of Magellan; 53°54'S 71°18'W.

Froya (frû'yä), Nor. *Frøya*, island (□ 57; pop. 4,113) in North Sea, Sor-Trondelag co., central Norway, 50 mi. WNW of Trondheim, separated by a 2-mi-wide channel from Hitra isl. (S); 18 mi. long, 9 mi. wide. Cod fishing, fish-oil refining, fish canning, notably at Titran village (pop. 526) in SW. Formerly spelled Froien or Froyen. The small Fro Isls. lie NE.

Frozen Strait, E Keewatin Dist., Northwest Territories, arm (50 mi. long, 12–20 mi. wide) of Foxe Channel, bet. Melville Peninsula and Southampton Isl.; 65°50'N 84°30'W. Connects Foxe Channel (SE) with Repulse Bay and Roes Welcome Sound.

Fructal, Brazil: see FRUTAL.

Frugères-les-Mines (früzhâr'-lā-mēn'), village (pop. 396), Haute-Loire dept., S central France, near Allier R., 7 mi. NNW of Brioude; coal mining.

Fruges (früzh), village (pop. 1,639), Pas-de-Calais dept., N France, 16 mi. ENE of Montreuil; tanning, shoe mfg. Agincourt is 3 mi. S.

Frühbuss, Czechoslovakia: see KRASLICE.

Fruita (frōō'tů), town (pop. 1,463), Mesa co., W Colo., on Colorado R., near Utah line, and 10 mi. NW of Grand Junction; alt. 4,512 ft. Trade center for irrigated sugar-beet and grain region; beans, pickles. Gas wells, coal and gold mines in vicinity. Colo. Natl. Monument near by. Inc. 1894.

Fruitdale. 1 Village (1940 pop. 757), Washington co., SW Ala., on Escatawpa R., near Miss. line, and 50 mi. NNW of Mobile; naval stores. **2** Town (pop. 70), Butte co., W S.Dak., 8 mi. E of Belle Fourche, just N of Black Hills, and on Belle Fourche R. **3** Town (pop. 876), Dallas co., N Texas, S suburb of Dallas.

Fruit Growers Dam, Colo.: see DELTA, city.

Fruit Heights, town (pop. 124), Davis co., N Utah, near Great Salt L., adjacent to Kaysville.

Fruithurst, town (pop. 318), Cleburne co., E Ala., 23 mi. ENE of Anniston, near Ga. line; lumbering.

Fruitland. 1 Town (pop. 573), Payette co., W Idaho, 6 mi. SE of Payette. **2** Town (pop. 1,028), Wicomico co., SE Md., 4 mi. SSW of Salisbury; ships truck; fruit and vegetable canneries, clothing factories, lumber mills. Inc. since 1940. **3** Village (pop. c.400), San Juan co., NW N.Mex., on San Juan R., near Colo. line, and 23 mi. WSW of Aztec, in irrigated fruitgrowing region; alt. 5,165 ft. Navajo Indian Reservation near by.

Fruitland Park, town (pop. 551), Lake co., central Fla., 4 mi. N of Leesburg, near L. Griffin, in citrus-fruitgrowing area.

"Fruitlands," Mass.: see HARVARD.

Fruitport, village (pop. 638), Muskegon co., SW Mich., 9 mi. SE of Muskegon, near Spring L.

Fruitvale, village (pop. estimate 200), S B.C., near Wash. border, on Beaver Creek and 8 mi. E of Trail; fruit, vegetables.

Fruitvale, village (pop. 3,654), Yakima co., S Wash., near Yakima.

Frumoasa (frōōmwä'sä), Hung. *Szépvis* (sāp'vēsh), village (pop. 3,466), Stalin prov., E central Rumania, 7 mi. NNE of Mercurea-Ciuc; agr. center; flour milling. In Hungary, 1940–45.

Fründenhorn (frün'důnhôrn"), peak (11,063 ft.) in Bernese Alps, S central Switzerland, 4 mi. ESE of Kandersteg.

Frunze (frōōn'zĕ), oblast (□ 6,000; 1946 pop. estimate 475,000), N Kirghiz SSR; ⊙ Frunze. Bounded by Kirghiz Range (S), Kungei Ala-Tau (E), and Kazakh SSR (N); drained by Chu R. and affluents. Includes fertile, irrigated Chu valley, producing sugar beets, fiber-bearing plants, wheat, fruit, essential oils. Cattle, pigs, horses raised. Industry (sugar refining, fiber processing, oil extraction) along branch of Turksib RR. Lead mine at Ak-Tyuz. Main cities: Frunze, Tokmak, Kant. Pop.: Russians, Ukrainians, Kirghiz. Formed 1939.

Frunze. 1 City (1926 pop. 36,610; 1939 pop. 92,659; 1948 pop. estimate 140,000), ⊙ Kirghiz SSR and Frunze oblast, in center of Chu valley, on branch of Turksib RR and 125 mi. WSW of Alma-Ata (linked by road), 1,900 mi. SE of Moscow; 42°54'N 74°35'E. Center of fertile irrigated area (sugar beets, fiber plants, essential oils). Agr. processing (meat, flour, tobacco, leather goods, wool); mfg. (tractor parts, machine tools, instruments, foundry goods, textiles). Has agr., teachers, and medical colleges, affiliate of USSR Acad. of Sciences, opera and ballet theater, Rus. and Kirghiz theaters, art gall., regional mus., botanical garden. Largely reconstructed since 1920s; surrounds parklike civic center (govt. bldgs., libraries, theaters) just N of railroad line. Founded 1873 as Rus. fortress of Pishpek; a small trading town until reached (1924) by railroad. Renamed (1925) for M. V. Frunze, Bolshevik leader (b. here 1885); became a leading economic center in 1930s. **2** or **Imeni M. V. Frunze,** town (1940 pop. over 500), N Osh oblast, Kirghiz SSR, in Fergana Valley, on Shakhimardan R. and 22 mi. S of Margelan; antimony-mining center. Until 1940, Kadamdzhai. **3** Town (1939 pop. over 500), SW Voroshilovgrad oblast, Ukrainian SSR, in the Donbas, on railroad (Sentyanovka junction) and 9 mi. NE of Kadiyevka; metalworks.

Frunzenski or **Frunzenskiy** (–zyĭnskē), NW suburb (1926 pop. 4,559) of Dnepropetrovsk, Dnepropetrovsk oblast, Ukrainian SSR, on left Dnieper R. bank and 7 mi. NW of city center. Until c.1935, called Kamenka.

Frunzenskoye (–skůyů), village, N central Osh oblast, Kirghiz SSR, in Fergana Valley, 20 mi. S of Margelan; wheat. Until 1940, Pulgan or Pulgon.

Frunzovka (frōōn'zůfků), village (1939 pop. over 2,000), W Odessa oblast, Ukrainian SSR, 40 mi. S of Balta; wheat, sunflowers. Until c.1935, Zakharovka.

Fruska Gora or **Frushka Gora** (both: frōō'shkä gô'rä), Serbo-Croatian *Fruška Gora*, mountain, Vojvodina, N Serbia, Yugoslavia, along right bank of the Danube; highest point (1,768 ft.) is 3 mi. S of Beocin, in the Srem. Covered with forests and vineyards. Coal mining at VRDNIK, CEREVIC, and near BEOCIN; cement plant at Beocin. Deer and wild-boar hunting. Orthodox Eastern monasteries (17th–18th cent.), here, noted for fine iconostases.

Frutal (frōōtäl'), city (pop. 2,106), westernmost Minas Gerais, Brazil, in the Triângulo Mineiro, near São Paulo border, 70 mi. SW of Uberaba; cattle. Formerly spelled Fructal.

Frutigen (frōō'tēgůn), town (pop. 5,115), Bern canton, SW central Switzerland, 12 mi. SW of Interlaken; watches, matches. Mtn. climbing.

Frutillar (frōōtēyär'), town (1930 pop. 1,317), Llanquihue prov., S central Chile, on W bank of L. Llanquihue, on railroad and 25 mi. NNW of Puerto Montt; tourist resort; dairying, lumbering.

Fryanovo (fryä'nůvů), town (1926 pop. 2,582), E Moscow oblast, Russian SFSR, 20 mi. N of Noginsk; woolen mill.

Fryatt, Mount (frī'ůt) (11,026 ft.), W Alta., near B.C. border, in Rocky Mts., in Jasper Natl. Park, 24 mi. SSE of Jasper; 52°34'N 117°56'W.

Fryazino (–zēnů), town (1939 pop. over 500), E Moscow oblast, Russian SFSR, 9 mi. S of Noginsk; rail junction.

Frydek (frē'dĕk), Czech *Frýdek*, Ger. *Friedeck* (frē'dĕk), town (pop. 11,628), E Silesia, Czechoslovakia, on right bank of Ostravice R. opposite MISTEK, and 11 mi. SSE of Ostrava; part of commune of Frydek-Mistek (pop. 26,573). Rail junction; base for excursions into the Beskids; specializes in dyeing and mfg. of cotton textiles. Has 13th-cent. church, 18th-cent. pilgrimage center. Coal and iron deposits in vicinity.

Frydlad, Poland: see DEBRZNO.

Frydland, Poland: see MIEROSZOW.

Frydlant (frēd'länt), Czech *Frýdlant*, Ger. *Friedland* (frēd'länt), town (pop. 4,308), N Bohemia, Czechoslovakia, at N foot of the Sudetes, 11 mi. N of Liberec; rail junction; textile industry (mainly linen and jute). Noted for high-lying Wallenstein castle (now a mus.), old fortifications, Gothic church. Title of duke of Friedland awarded to Wallenstein, here, in 1625.

Frydlant nad Ostravici (näd' ôsträvĭ"tsē), Czech *Frýdlant nad Ostravicí*, town (pop. 4,031), NE Moravia, Czechoslovakia, on Ostravice R. and 17 mi. SSE of Ostrava; rail junction; aluminum- and ironworks.

Fryeburg (frī'bûrg), town (pop. 1,926), including Fryeburg village (pop. 1,023), Oxford co., W Maine, on the Saco and 36 mi. WSW of Auburn, near N.H. line. Year-round resort center, mfg. (wood and leather products, canned foods). Fryeburg Acad. here. Settled 1762, inc. 1777.

Fryerning, England: see INGATESTONE AND FRYERNING.

Frying-Pan Shoals, N.C.: see FEAR, CAPE.

Fryk, Lake, Swedish *Fryken* (frü'kůn) (□ 39), W Sweden, near Norwegian border, in the Fryksdal, 10 mi. NW of Karlstad; 43 mi. long (N–S), 1 mi. wide. Drains S into L. Vaner by Nor R. Narrows divide lake into Upper L. Fryk, Swedish *Övre Fryken* (N), Central L. Fryk, Swedish *Mellan Fryken*, and Lower L. Fryk, Swedish *Nedre Fryken* (S). **Fryksdal,** Swedish *Fryksdalen* (früks'dä"lůn), valley formed by L. Fryk, is noted for scenic beauty and is locale of several works by Selma Lagerlof.

Fryksta, Sweden: see KIL.

Frystat, Czechoslovakia: see KARVINA.

Fryvaldov, Czechoslovakia: see JESENIK.

Fsinj, Yugoslavia: see SINJ, S Croatia.

Fthiotis, Greece: see PHTHIOTIS.

Fu, China: see FU RIVER.

Fua Mulaku Island (fōō'ä mōō'lŭkōō), small S island (pop. 2,525) of Maldive Isls., in Indian Ocean, 24 mi. NE of Addu Atoll; 0°17'S 73°26'E; coconuts; fishing, palm-mat weaving.

Fuan (fōō'än'), town (pop. 10,802), ⊙ Fuan co. (pop. 224,997), NE Fukien prov., China, near Chekiang line, 70 mi. NNE of Foochow; rice, sweet potatoes, wheat, sugar cane.

Fuan, Korea: see PUAN.

Fubine (fōōbē'nĕ), village (pop. 1,631), Alessandria prov., Piedmont, N Italy, 10 mi. NW of Alessandria.

Fucecchio (fōōchĕk'kyô), town (pop. 3,737), Firenze prov., Tuscany, central Italy, near the Arno, 23 mi. W of Florence; agr. trade center; mfg. (shoes, hosiery, brooms, matches, bicycles, motorcycles).

Fu-chien, China: see FUKIEN.

Fuchin (fōō'jĭn'), town, ⊙ Fuchin co. (pop. 225,000), NE Sungkiang prov., Manchuria, 80 mi. ENE of Kiamusze and on right bank of Sungari R.; rye, soybeans, kaoliang, millet, hemp, tobacco; hog bristles.

Fu-ch'ing, China: see FUTSING.

Fuchow or **Fu-chou** (fōō'chou', Mandarin fōō'jō'). **1** City, Fukien prov., China: see FOOCHOW. **2** City (1948 pop. 17,545), ⊙, but independent of, Linchwan (Lin-ch'uan) co. (1948 pop. 306,212), N central Kiangsi prov., China, 50 mi. SE of Nanchang and on Fu R.; commercial center; ramie, rice, cotton, hemp; exports indigo. Barite and rock-crystal deposits. Warm springs, 10 mi. E. Became independent municipality in 1949. **3** Town, Liaotung prov., Manchuria, China: see FUHSIEN. **4** Town, Yunnan prov., China: see FUNING.

Fuchskauten (fŏŏks'kou"tůn), highest peak (2,155 ft.) of the Westerwald, W Germany, 10 mi. SW of Dillenburg.

Fuchsstadt (fŏŏks'shtät), village (pop. 658), Lower Franconia, W Bavaria, Germany, 6 mi. SSE of Würzburg; wheat, barley, beets, cattle. Has church dating from 2d half of 18th cent.

Fuchu (fōōchōō'). **1** Town (pop. 27,250), Greater Tokyo, central Honshu, Japan, 5 mi. ESE of Tachikawa; rice, wheat, raw silk. **2** Town (pop. 14,058), Hiroshima prefecture, SW Honshu, Japan, 10 mi. NW of Fukuyama; mfg. center; spinning and textile mills. Produces *koto* (Jap. harps). **3** Town (pop. 11,142), Hiroshima prefecture, SW Honshu, Japan, just E of Hiroshima; agr. and livestock center; rice, wheat, charcoal, sake. **4** Town, Toyama prefecture, Japan: see NENAKA.

Fu-ch'uan, China: see FUCHWAN.

Fuchun River, China: see TSIENTANG RIVER.

Fuchwan or **Fu-ch'uan** (both: fōō'chwän'), town, ⊙ Fuchwan co. (pop. 111,477), NE Kwangsi prov., China, 65 mi. SE of Kweilin, near Hunan line; mat-weaving center; wheat, tobacco, tea. Tin, coal mines near by.

Fucino, Lago (lä'gô fōōchē'nô), anc. *Fucinus Lacus*, former lake, in the Apennines, Aquila prov., Abruzzi e Molise, S central Italy, E of Avezzano. Had average area of 60 sq. mi. and was c.12 mi. long. Its W outlet to Liri R. near CAPISTRELLO, originally constructed (A.D. 52) by Emperor Claudius, was restored and lake drained (1854–75) by Prince Torlonia. Reclaimed land (40,789 acres) is intensively cultivated in cereals, potatoes, sugar beets, grapes, and fruit. Formerly also Lago di Celano.

Fud, El (ĕl fōōd'), village, Harar prov., SE Ethiopia, in the Ogaden, 80 mi. SW of Dagahbur, in arid pastoral region (camels, sheep).

Fudooka (fōōdō'ōkä), town (pop. 4,536), Saitama prefecture, central Honshu, Japan, 11 mi. E of Kumagaya; rice, raw silk.

Fuego (fwā'gō), active volcano (12,582 ft.; alt. of crater, 11,854 ft.), S central Guatemala, on Sacatepéquez-Chimaltenango dept. border, 12 mi. SW of Antigua. In full activity at the coming of the Spaniards in 16th cent.; has undergone over 20 major recorded eruptions. Its eruption of 1773 caused earthquakes destroying ANTIGUA city.

Fuego, Tierra del, Chile–Argentina: see TIERRA DEL FUEGO.

Fuencaliente (fwĕng-kälyĕn'tā), town (pop. 3,158), Ciudad Real prov., S central Spain, noted spa in Sierra Morena, near Córdoba-Jaén prov. border, 45 mi. SW of Ciudad Real. Region raises fruit, olives, potatoes, livestock. Lumbering, olive-oil pressing; mfg. of cork articles, tiles.

Fuencaliente de la Palma (dhā lä päl′mä), village (pop. 612), Palma, Canary Isls., 14 mi. SSW of Santa Cruz de la Palma; grapes, figs, potatoes, cereals, cochineal, timber. Cheese processing, wine making.

Fuencaliente Point, S extremity of Palma, Canary Isls., 16 mi. SSW of Santa Cruz de la Palma; 28°28′N 17°49′W. Lighthouse.

Fuencarral (fwĕng-käräl′), town (pop. 3,376), Madrid prov., central Spain, on railroad and 6 mi. N of Madrid, in agr. region (cereals, truck produce, grapes, stock); mfg. of lace, soap.

Fuendejalón (fwĕndähälōn′), village (pop. 1,387), Saragossa prov., NE Spain, 18 mi. SE of Tarazona; olive oil, wine, cereals.

Fuengirola (fwĕng-hērō′lä), town (pop. 4,052), Málaga prov., S Spain, minor port and fishing center on the Mediterranean, 16 mi. SW of Málaga (linked by rail), in agr. region (grapes, olives, wheat, figs, raisins, beans, livestock). Has fish canneries (mainly tuna), textile plants; marble and agate quarries; and near-by saltworks. Beaches. Over the town towers an anc. castle of Roman origin.

Fuenlabrada (fwĕnlävrä′dhä), town (pop. 1,655), Madrid prov., central Spain, on railroad and 10 mi. SSW of Madrid; grain growing; mfg. of woolen goods, artificial flowers, sweets.

Fuenlabrada de los Montes (dhā lōs mōn′tĕs), town (pop. 2,877), Badajoz prov., W Spain, near Ciudad Real prov. border, 5 mi. SE of Herrera del Duque; olives, cereals, grapes, honey, livestock.

Fuenllana (fwĕnlyä′nä), town (pop. 980), Ciudad Real prov., S central Spain, 23 mi. E of Valdepeñas; cereals, chick-peas, grapes, sheep, goats. Lumbering; gypsum quarrying.

Fuenmayor (fwĕmīōr′), town (pop. 2,033), Logroño prov., N Spain, near the Ebro, 5 mi. W of Logroño; wine-production center; flour mills; fruit, vegetables, cereals, olive oil. Has 17th-cent. church and many old mansions.

Fuensalida (fwĕnsälē′dhä), town (pop. 4,178), Toledo prov., central Spain, 17 mi. NW of Toledo; winegrowing, sheep-raising center. Limekilns; mfg. of soap, chocolate. Palace of dukes of Frías.

Fuensanta de Martos (fwĕnsän′tä dhā mär′tōs), town (pop. 3,894), Jaén prov., S Spain, 11 mi. SW of Jaén; olive-oil processing, flour milling; cereals, livestock. Gypsum and limestone quarries.

Fuente (fwĕn′tā), town (pop. 1,152), Coahuila, N Mexico; SE suburb of Piedras Negras; stock raising; foundries.

Fuente, La, Spain: see FUENTE DEL MAESTRE.

Fuente-Alamo (fwĕn′tā-ä′lämō), town (pop. 2,553), Albacete prov., SE central Spain, 20 mi. NE of Hellín; saffron, cereals, olive oil, wine.

Fuentealbilla (fwĕntä-älvē′lyä), town (pop. 1,969), Albacete prov., SE central Spain, 25 mi. NE of Albacete; alcohol distilling, flour milling; saffron, cereals, wine. Saltworks and gypsum quarries near by.

Fuentecén (fwĕntā-thĕn′), town (pop. 1,359), Burgos prov., N Spain, 9 mi. WSW of Aranda de Duero; cereals, potatoes, sugar beets, grapes, sheep.

Fuente de Cantos (fwĕn′tā dhā kän′tōs), town (pop. 10,642), Badajoz prov., W Spain, in Estremadura, 55 mi. SE of Badajoz; agr. center, chiefly for cereals and livestock, also grapes, olives. Iron foundries, olive-oil presses, liquor distilleries, flour mills. Region has galena deposits. Prehistoric and Roman remains near by. Zurbarán b. here (1598).

Fuente del Arco (dhĕl är′kō), town (pop. 1,804), Badajoz prov., W Spain, on railroad and 9 mi. SE of Llerena.

Fuente del Maestre (mäĕ′strā) or **La Fuente,** city (pop. 8,145), Badajoz prov., W Spain, in Estremadura, in fertile Tierra de Barros, 32 mi. SE of Badajoz; processing, lumbering, and agr. center (cereals, olives, grapes, livestock); mfg. of olive oil, liquor, chocolate, tiles; limekilns.

Fuente de Pedro Naharro (dhā pā′dhrō nä-ä′rō), town (pop. 2,509), Cuenca prov., E central Spain, 50 mi. SE of Madrid; grain- and winegrowing; stock (sheep, goats) raising.

Fuente de Piedra (pyā′dhrä), town (pop. 1,874), Málaga prov., S Spain, at S foot of the Sierra de Yeguas, 12 mi. NW of Antequera; sugar beets, olives, corn; stone quarrying; saltworks.

Fuente de San Estebân, La (sän′ ĕstävän′, lä), village (pop. 1,727), Salamanca prov., W Spain, 21 mi. NE of Ciudad Rodrigo; flour mills.

Fuente de Santa Cruz (sän′tä krōōth′), town (pop. 724), Segovia prov., central Spain, 30 mi. S of Valladolid; cereals, grapes; flour milling, liquor distilling.

Fuente el Fresno (ĕl frĕ′snō), town (pop. 4,142), Ciudad Real prov., S central Spain, 19 mi. NNE of Ciudad Real; agr. center (olives, grapes, cereals, livestock); olive-oil pressing, charcoal burning.

Fuente el Saz (säth′), town (pop. 740), Madrid prov., central Spain, 17 mi. NE of Madrid; cereals, grapes, sheep.

Fuente-Encarroz (–ĕng-kärōth′), town (pop. 2,910), Valencia prov., E Spain, 4 mi. S of Gandía; flour milling; shipping of oranges; olive oil, vegetables. Marble and stone quarries. Ruins of Rebollet castle near by.

Fuenteguinaldo (fwĕn″tāgēnäl′dō), town (pop. 2,451), Salamanca prov., W Spain, 13 mi. SW of Ciudad Rodrigo; cement mfg., flour milling; cereals, vegetables, lumber. Limestone quarries. Was hq. of Wellington in 1812.

Fuenteheridos (fwĕn″tā-ārē′dhōs), town (pop. 1,184), Huelva prov., SW Spain, in Sierra Morena, 5 mi. W of Aracena; timber, chestnuts, fruit, olives.

Fuente la Higuera (fwĕn′tā lä ēgā′rä), town (pop. 2,634), Valencia prov., E Spain, 23 mi. SW of Játiva; olive-oil processing, flour milling, alcohol and brandy distilling. Wine and cereals.

Fuentelapeña (fwĕntäläpā′nyä), town (pop. 2,035), Zamora prov., NW Spain, 19 mi. S of Toro; meat processing; wine, cereals, livestock, lumber.

Fuentelcésped (–thĕ′spĕdh), town (pop. 815), Burgos prov., N Spain, 5 mi. SE of Aranda de Duero; winegrowing; flour milling.

Fuentelencina (–lĕn-thē′nä), town (pop. 750), Guadalajara prov., central Spain, 20 mi. ESE of Guadalajara; cereals, olives, beans, potatoes, sheep; flour milling, olive-oil pressing.

Fuentelespino de Moya (–läspē′nō dhä moi′ä), village (pop. 653), Cuenca prov., E central Spain, 37 mi. ESE of Cuenca; cereals, saffron, potatoes, livestock. Potteries.

Fuentelmonje (fwĕn″tĕlmōn′hā), village (pop. 610), Soria prov., N central Spain, 28 mi. SE of Soria; cereals, grapes, livestock. Gypsum quarrying. Near by is a large irrigation reservoir.

Fuenteovejuna or **Fuente Obejuna** (both: fwĕn″tā ōvähōō′nä), town (pop. 5,688), Córdoba prov., S Spain, in Andalusia, 8 mi. WSW of Peñarroya-Pueblonuevo; olive-oil processing, flour- and sawmilling. Stock raising; lumbering; honey, cereals, wine, vegetables. Important coal and silver-bearing lead mines in area; limestone and clay quarries. Scene of drama *Fuenteovejuna* by Lope de Vega. In 1430, town was given to Knights of Calatrava; palace of the Knights, formerly a Moorish castle, is now the parish church.

Fuente-Palmera (fwĕn″tā-pälmā′rä), town (pop. 1,784), Córdoba prov., S Spain, 23 mi. WSW of Córdoba; olive-oil and cheese processing. Cereals, lumber, livestock.

Fuentepelayo (fwĕn″tāpälī′ō), town (pop. 1,604), Segovia prov., central Spain, 19 mi. NNW of Segovia; cereals, carobs, chick-peas, potatoes, livestock. Flour milling; lumbering; mfg. of naval stores and textile goods.

Fuenterrabía (fwĕntärävē′ä), Fr. *Fontarabie* (fōtäräbē′), Basque city (pop. 1,193), Guipúzcoa prov., N Spain, on Bay of Biscay at mouth of Bidassoa R. (Fr. border), opposite Hendaye (France); fishing, fish canning, boatbuilding; cement mfg., rubber processing. The medieval town on hill has anc. walls, Gothic church, and castle (12th–16th cent.); the new town (just N; pop. 1,766) is popular seabathing resort. Fuenterrabía, formerly a fortress, was repeatedly attacked by the French, notably by Condé in 1638, without success.

Fuenterrebollo (–rävō′lyō), town (pop. 1,244), Segovia prov., central Spain, 27 mi. NNE of Segovia; grain, hemp, livestock, resins; woolen goods.

Fuenterrobles (–rō′vlĕs), town (pop. 1,321), Valencia prov., E Spain, 16 mi. NW of Requena; wine, olive oil, saffron, livestock.

Fuentes (fwĕn′tĕs), town (pop. 1,051), Cuenca prov., E central Spain, in Serranía de Cuenca, 9 mi. SE of Cuenca; cereals, saffron; sheep, goats; dairying. Gypsum, alabaster quarrying.

Fuentesaúco (fwĕntäsäōō′kō), town (pop. 2,993), Zamora prov., NW Spain, 23 mi. SSE of Zamora; breweries, brandy distilleries, flour mills; chick-peas, cereals, wine, livestock.

Fuentes Claras (fwĕn′tĕs klä′räs), village (pop. 1,462), Teruel prov., E Spain, on the Jiloca and 18 mi. SSE of Daroca; wine, saffron, sugar beets.

Fuentes de Andalucía (dhā ändälōō-thē′ä), town (pop. 9,320), Seville prov., SW Spain, on railroad and 36 mi. E of Seville; stock-raising (hogs, goats, horses, mules, cattle) and agr. center (cereals, olives).

Fuentes de Béjar (bā′här), village (pop. 1,289), Salamanca prov., W Spain, 10 mi. NE of Béjar; wool-trade center. Meat processing; cereals, wine.

Fuentes de Ebro (ā′vrō), town (pop. 2,305), Saragossa prov., NE Spain, near the Ebro, 16 mi. SE of Saragossa; produces sugar beets, cereals, fruit, onions. NW, c.4 mi., is terminus of Imperial Canal.

Fuentes de León (lāōn′), town (pop. 4,923), Badajoz prov., W Spain, in the Sierra Morena, near Huelva prov. border, 21 mi. SE of Jerez de los Caballeros; agr. center (olives, grapes, livestock); liquor distilling, flour- and sawmilling, meat salting, charcoal burning.

Fuentes de Nava (nä′vä), town (pop. 1,875), Palencia prov., N central Spain, near Canal of Castile, 14 mi. WNW of Palencia; brewery; livestock, cereals, wine.

Fuentes de Oñoro (ōnyō′rō), village (pop. 789), Salamanca prov., W Spain, 15 mi. W of Ciudad Rodrigo; Sp. customs station opposite Vilar Formoso (Portugal), and on railroad to Lisbon. After a 3-day battle fought here (1811) bet. Wellington and Masséna, the French were forced to retire.

Fuentes de Ropel (rōpĕl′), town (pop. 1,338), Zamora prov., NW Spain, 7 mi. E of Benavente; cereals, vegetables, wine, livestock.

Fuentes Georginas, Guatemala: see ZUNIL, town.

Fuente-Tójar (fwĕn′tā-tō′här), town (pop. 1,609), Córdoba prov., S Spain, 12 mi. SE of Baena; olive oil processing, flour milling; sheep and hog raising; lumbering.

Fuente Vaqueros (väkā′rōs), village (pop. 2,534), Granada prov., S Spain, near Genil R., 10 mi. WNW of Granada; cement mfg. Cereals, sugar beets, tobacco, lumber.

Fuerte, El, Mexico: see EL FUERTE.

Fuerte, Río del (rē′ō dĕl fwĕr′tä), river, NW Mexico; formed in Chihuahua by Río Verde and Urique R., flows W into Sinaloa, then SW, past El Fuerte, San Blas, and Ahome, to Gulf of California 27 mi. W of Los Mochis, at Lechuguilla Isl.; c.175 mi. long; c.350 mi. long with Río Verde.

Fuerte del Rey (fwĕr′tā dhĕl rā′), town (pop 2,596), Jaén prov., S Spain, 9 mi. NW of Jaén; olive-oil processing; stock raising; cereals and wine. Red earth quarries.

Fuerte General Roca (hānäräl′ rō′kä), town (pop. 7,416), ⊙ General Roca dept. (pop. 52,618), N Río Negro natl. territory, Argentina, in Río Negro valley (irrigation area), on railroad and 28 mi. ESE of Neuquén; processing center in fruitgrowing area. Wine making, dried-fruit processing, food canning, alcohol distilling, lumbering. Agr. products: fruit, wine, alfalfa. Gypsum deposits. Has agr. school and research station. Sometimes called General Roca.

Fuerte Island, in the Caribbean, off coast of Bolívar dept., N Colombia, 85 mi. SW of Cartagena; 9°23′N 76°12′W.

Fuerte Olimpo or **Olimpo** (ōlēm′pō), town (dist. pop. 3,078), ⊙ Olimpo dept., N Paraguay, in the Chaco, inland port on Paraguay R. (Brazil border) and 30 mi. N of Asunción; trading and stock-raising center; tanneries, tileworks. Radio station. Founded 1792 as Borbón, old colonial fort.

Fuerteventura (fwĕr″tāvĕntōō′rä), second largest island (□ 666; pop. 13,173) of the Canary Isls., in Las Palmas prov., Spain, in the Atlantic; chief town and port, Puerto de Cabras. It is closest to African continent, 65 mi. W of Cape Juby on coast of Sp. Morocco. Lanzarote is just across La Bocayna channel. Isl. is 60 mi. long NE–SW, bet. Punta Gorda (28°45′N 13°55′W) and Jandía Point (28°3′N 14°30′W). On Jandía Peninsula (SW) is isl.'s highest elevation (2,648 ft.). Mostly comprised of arid rolling plains, it has a number of volcanic peaks bet. which lie the more fertile sections (alfalfa, wheat, barley, corn, potatoes, tomatoes, fruit, cochineal). Camels, sheep, and goats are raised. The isl., exposed to African winds, suffers from great drought. There are a few artesian wells. Alfalfa, lime, gypsum, and cochineal are the principal exports. Fishing (tuna) along the coast. Sometimes spelled Forteventura.

Fufeng (fōō′fŭng′), town, ⊙ Fufeng co. (pop. 127,272), SW Shensi prov., China, 60 mi. W of Sian, near Lunghai RR; cotton weaving; grain.

Fuga Island (fōō′gä) (13 mi. long, 4 mi. wide; 193[illegible] pop. 536), in Babuyan Isls., Cagayan prov., c.2[illegible] mi. N of Luzon, Philippines, in Luzon Strait, forming N boundary of Babuyan Channel; long, narrow, rises to 625 ft.; rice growing, fishing.

Fügen (fü′gŭn), village (pop. 1,746), Tyrol, W Austria, 6 mi. E of Schwaz, in the Zillertal; summer resort.

Fuglnes (fōōl′nās), cape on Soroy Sound (inlet of Norwegian Sea in W Kvaloy isl.), Finnmark co., N Norway, 2 mi. WNW of Hammerfest; 70°40′11″N 23°40′20″E. Cairn marks N extremity of meridian arc surveyed (1816–52; again in 1929) to S extremity at Izmail (Ismail), on Danube delta, by Russians and Scandinavians.

Fuglo (fōōl′ŭ, Dan. *Fuglø*, Faeroese *Fugloy*, island (□ 5; pop. 201) of the NE Faeroe Isls., separated from Svino by Fuglo Fjord; highest point c.2,00[illegible] ft. Fishing, sheep raising.

Fuhai, China: see BULUN TOKHOI.

Fuhlsbüttel (fōōls′bü″tŭl), outer district of Hamburg, NW Germany, on right bank of the Alster and 5 mi. N of city center; site of Hamburg airport.

Fuhrberg (fōōr′bĕrk), village (pop. 1,434), in former Prussian prov. of Hanover, NW Germany, after 1945 in Lower Saxony, 10 mi. SW of Celle, in old dist.; sawmilling.

Fuhsien (fōō′shyĕn′). **1** Town (1938 pop. 19,991), ⊙ Fuhsien co. (1946 pop. 646,532), S Liaotung prov., Manchuria, China, on South Manchuria RR and 55 mi. NNE of Dairen, on Liaotung peninsula; chicken farming. Coal mining and kaolin quarrying at Wuhutsui, 25 mi. SW, on Fuchow inlet of Gulf of Liaotung. The name Fuhsien was applied 1913–31 to a town 18 mi. WNW, called Fuchow until 1913. Present Fuhsien was called Wafangtien until 1931; it developed rapidly after building of railroad in 1900s. **2** Town, ⊙ Fuhsien co. (pop. 31,296), N Shensi prov., China, on Lo R. and 40 mi. SSW of Yenan, in mtn. region; cotton weaving; wheat, millet, beans. Graphite deposits near by.

Fu-hsin, Manchuria: see FUSIN.

Fujaira or **Fujayrah** (fōōjī′rŭ), independent Arab sheikdom (□ 500; pop. 4,000) in Trucial Oman without treaty relations with Britain; situated on Gulf of Oman coast of Oman Promontory bet. Khor Kalba (S) and Dibba (N), corresponding t[illegible]

Shumailiya (Shamailiya) coastal dist. Main town, Fujaira (pop. 1,000), is on coast, 60 mi. ESE of Sharja across Oman Promontory; pearling, agr. Sheikdom was formerly under suzerainty of Sharja.

Fuji (fo͞o'jē), town (pop. 21,049), Shizuoka prefecture, central Honshu, Japan, 20 mi. NE of Shizuoka; commercial center for fruitgrowing area; paper milling.

Fuji, Mount, Japan: see FUJIYAMA.

Fujieda (fo͝ojē'ädä), town (pop. 14,730), Shizuoka prefecture, central Honshu, Japan, 10 mi. SW of Shizuoka; agr. center (citrus fruit, tea, pears, sweet potatoes).

Fuji-Hakone National Park (fo͞o'jē-häkō'nä) (□278), central Honshu, Japan, in Kanagawa, Shizuoka, and Yamanashi prefectures, in mountainous region; hot springs, virgin forests, scenic lakes. Its central feature is Fujiyama.

Fujiidera (fo͝ojē'dărä), town (pop. 9,589), Osaka prefecture, S Honshu, Japan, 9 mi. SE of Osaka, in agr. area (rice, wheat), poultry; raw silk.

Fujikawa (fo͝ojē'käwä), town (pop. 9,380), Shizuoka prefecture, central Honshu, Japan, 12 mi. NE of Shimizu; fruitgrowing center (citrus fruit, pears); paper milling.

Fujikoto (fo͝ojē'kō'tō), village (pop. 5,714), Akita prefecture, N Honshu, Japan, 14 mi. ENE of Noshiro; mining (lead, gold, silver, copper); agr.

Fujimiya (fo͝ojē'mēä), city (pop. 40,904), Shizuoka prefecture, central Honshu, Japan, 22 mi. NE of Shizuoka, in agr. area (rice, tea, mulberry fields); textiles. Has 16th-cent. shrine, prefectural agr. school. Formed in early 1940s by combining Omiya (1940 pop. 26,049) and Tomioka (1940 pop. 5,474). Sometimes called Fujinomiya.

Fujinomiya, Japan: see FUJIMIYA.

Fujioka (fo͝ojē'ōkä). **1** Town (pop. 14,429), Gumma prefecture, central Honshu, Japan, 6 mi. SE of Takasaki, in agr. area (rice, wheat); silk cocoons, soy sauce. **2** Town (pop. 6,313), Tochigi prefecture, central Honshu, Japan, 10 mi. SW of Tochigi; rice, raw silk.

Fuji River, Jap. *Fuji-gawa,* central Honshu, Japan, in Yamanashi and Shizuoka prefectures; rises in mts. c.25 mi. NW of Kofu, flows 100 mi. generally S, past villages near W foothills of Fujiyama, to Suruga Bay at Kambara. Hydroelectric plants on its small tributaries.

Fujisaki (fo͝ojē'säkē), town (pop. 7,364), Aomori prefecture, N Honshu, Japan, 4 mi. NNE of Hirosaki; rice.

Fuji-san, Japan: see FUJIYAMA.

Fujisawa (fo͝ojē'säwŭ). **1** Town (1947 pop. 4,815), Iwate prefecture, N Honshu, Japan, 12 mi. ESE of Ichinoseki; agr., sheep raising, raw-silk culture. Gold and silver formerly mined here. **2** City (1940 pop. 36,769; 1947 pop. 78,759), Kanagawa prefecture, central Honshu, Japan, on N shore of Sagami Bay, 11 mi. SW of Yokohama; agr. center (potatoes, wheat). Has 14th-cent. Buddhist temple. Sometimes spelled Fuzisawa.

Fujishima (fo͝ojē'shĭmä), town (pop. 5,002), Yamagata prefecture, N Honshu, Japan, 5 mi. NE of Tsuruoka; rice growing.

Fujita (fo͝ojē'tä), town (pop. 5,075), Fukushima prefecture, N Honshu, Japan, 9 mi. NNE of Fukushima; silk cocoons, rice, peaches.

Fujiwara (fo͝ojē'wärä), town (pop. 7,782), Tochigi prefecture, central Honshu, Japan, 10 mi. NE of Nikko; mining (gold, silver, copper).

Fujiyama, Fuji-yama (fo͞o"jē-yä'mä, fo͝ojē'yämä), **Mount Fuji,** or **Fuji-san** (-sä), highest peak (12,389 ft.) of Japan, in Shizuoka prefecture, central Honshu, 55 mi. WSW of Tokyo, in Fuji-Hakone Natl. Park. An extinct volcano known for its beautiful cone-like symmetry. Its summit crater is roughly circular, c.2,000 ft. in diameter. Snow-capped; upper part of mtn. is barren; lower slopes are wooded. At mtn. base (65 mi. in circumference) are 5 lakes; L. Kawaguchi (3 mi. long, 1 mi. wide) is largest. Summer and winter sports in foothills; mtn. climbing (July-Aug.). Fujiyama last erupted in 1707. Sacred since anc. times; until Meiji Restoration (1868), no woman was allowed to climb it. Another form: Fuji-no-yama.

Fujoska (fü'yōskou"), Icelandic *Fujóskå,* river, N Iceland, rises on central plateau, flows 70 mi. N to Eyja Fjord 15 mi. N of Akureyri.

Fuka (fo͞o'kŭ), village, N Egypt, on coastal railroad 45 mi. ESE of Matruh.

Fukae (fo͝okä'ā) or **Fukue** (fo͝oko͞o'ā), town (pop. 15,047) on Fukae-shima of isl. group Goto-retto, Nagasaki prefecture, Japan, 7 mi. NE of Tomie, on E coast; agr. center (sweet potatoes, wheat, soybeans). Sometimes spelled Fukaye.

Fukae-shima (fo͝okä'āshĭma), largest and southernmost island (□ 129; pop. 72,249 including offshore islets) of isl. group Goto-retto, Nagasaki prefecture, Japan, in E.China Sea, 50 mi. W of Kyushu; 32° 40'N 128°40'E; 14 mi. long, 13 mi. wide; several large bays. Whaling, fishing; wheat, soybeans. Chief town, Tomie. Sometimes spelled Hukaesima, Fukaye Shima, and Fukai.

Fukagawa (fo͝okä'gäwŭ), town (pop. 12,811), W central Hokkaido, Japan, on Ishikari R. and 17 mi. WSW of Asahigawa; rail junction; agr. (rice, potatoes, sugar beets, soybeans), livestock raising.

Fukai, Japan: see FUKAE-SHIMA.

Fukang. 1 or **Fu-k'ang** (fo͞o'käng'), town and oasis (pop. 12,474), central Sinkiang prov., China, 20 mi. NE of Urumchi and on highway N of the Tien Shan; wine center; livestock, wheat, kaoliang. **2** Town, Kwangtung prov., China: see FATKONG.

Fukaura (fo͝okä'o͝orä), town (pop. 6,618), Aomori prefecture, N Honshu, Japan, on Sea of Japan, 28 mi. W of Hirosaki; fishing, rice growing.

Fukawa (fo͝okä'wä). **1** Town (pop. 3,104), Ibaraki prefecture, central Honshu, Japan, on Tone R. and 4 mi. SW of Ryugasaki; rice, silk cocoons. **2** Town (pop. 13,294), Yamaguchi prefecture, SW Honshu, Japan, on Sea of Japan, 13 mi. WSW of Hagi. Rail junction; mining (gold, silver, copper, coal) and agr. (rice, wheat, fruit, raw silk) center; mfg. (pottery, sake). Fishing port. Hot springs near by.

Fukaya (fo͝okä'yä), town (pop. 19,314), Saitama prefecture, central Honshu, Japan, 7 mi. NW of Kumagaya; raw-silk center; tile mfg., spinning.

Fukaye, Japan: see FUKAE.

Fukaye Shima, Japan: see FUKAE-SHIMA.

Fuke (fo͞o'kā), town (pop. 6,763), Osaka prefecture, S Honshu, Japan, on Osaka Bay, 7 mi. NNW of Wakayama; rice, poultry, cotton textiles; fishing.

Fukiage (fo͝okē'ägä), town (pop. 6,053), Saitama prefecture, central Honshu, Japan, 5 mi. SE of Kumagaya; rice, wheat.

Fukiang, China: see KANKU.

Fukien or **Fu-chien** (both: fo͞o'kyĕn', Mandarin fo͞o'jyĕn'), province (□ 45,000; pop. 11,000,000) of SE China, on Formosa Strait; ⊙ Foochow. Bounded N by Chekiang, W by Kiangsi, and SW by Kwangtung, mountainous Fukien prov. is traversed by parallel, eroded granite and porphyry ranges (alt. to 3,000 ft. and over) extending generally SW–NE bet. the Bohea Hills on the Kiangsi border and the rocky, isl.-strewn coast. The short, swift rivers flow in the SW–NE structural depressions and join the main streams at right angles. These are the Min, the natural gateway to Fukien, draining the greater N part of the prov.; and the lesser Lung. Both are associated with river-mouth cities (Foochow, Amoy), which are Fukien's leading ports. The climate is largely subtropical, and has mild temperatures, China's heaviest rainfall (60–70 inches annually), and occasional typhoons. Agr. is restricted to the river valleys and deltas. Fukien grows 2 crops of rice, as well as sweet potatoes, wheat, beans, rapeseed, and vegetables. Among the chief export products are bamboo shoots, sugar cane, tobacco, mushrooms, fruit (longans, litchi nuts, oranges, pomelos). Fukien has long been one of China's leading tea producers, noted for its black bohea tea, grown in the Bohea Hills. Its timber resources are important, yielding pine, fir, camphor, and bamboo woods for export; and fisheries are a major source of livelihood along the indented coast. Mining is of secondary importance, coal, kaolin, manganese, and lead-zinc being the chief minerals. In addition to its 2 large ports, Foochow and Amoy, industry is found in Nanping, Kienow (former Kienning), Tsinkiang, and Lungki. From the point of view of transportation, the prov. is oriented toward the sea and has poor roads linking it with neighboring provs. As a result of its overland isolation from the rest of China, Fukien's pop. has maintained its own dialects: the N Fukienese or Foochow dialect, spoken throughout Min R. basin; and the S Fukienese (Hoklo) or Amoy dialect, spoken in Lung R. area. There are some Hakka in the extreme SW on the Kiangsi-Kwangtung line near Changting, and a few aborigines. Fukien's orientation toward the sea brought about large-scale overseas emigration. Traditionally called Min, the region passed (2d cent. A.D.) to China in the later Han dynasties. It received its present name (derived from the cities of Foochow and Kienning) during the Sung dynasty (960–1280) and maintained a flourishing camphor and sugar trade under the Mongols (13th cent.). The prov.'s 1st European contacts were in 16th cent., and it passed to Manchu control in 1646. In late-17th cent. began Fukienese emigration, 1st to Formosa and Hainan, and in 19th cent. to countries of SE Asia. During Sino-Japanese War, Jap. occupation of Fukien was restricted to the coast. The prov. passed to Communist control in 1949. Formerly spelled Fokien.

Fuki-kaku, Formosa: see FUKWEI POINT.

Fukiya (fo͝okē'yä), town (pop. 2,861), Okayama prefecture, SW Honshu, Japan, 30 mi. NW of Okayama; copper mining; rice, wheat, sake, raw silk, charcoal, persimmons.

Fukow or **Fu-kou** (fo͞o'gō'), town, ⊙ Fukow co. (pop. 46,363), NE central Honan prov., China, 55 mi. S of Kaifeng; cotton weaving; rice, wheat, beans.

Fuku (fo͞o'go͞o'), town, ⊙ Fuku co. (pop. 113,338), northernmost Shensi prov., China, on Yellow R. (Shansi line), opposite Paoteh, and 90 mi. NE of Yülin; kaoliang, millet, wheat.

Fukuchiyama (fo͝oko͞och'yämŭ), city (1940 pop. 31,848; 1947 pop. 38,325), Kyoto prefecture, S Honshu, Japan, 40 mi. NW of Kyoto; mfg. center (rubber goods, cotton textiles, Western-style clothing), wood- and metalworking; sake, soy sauce, raw silk. Sometimes spelled Fukutiyama.

Fukude (fo͝oko͞o'dā) or **Fukuda** (-dä), town (pop. 7,665), Shizuoka prefecture, central Honshu, Japan, on Philippine Sea, 9 mi. ESE of Hamamatsu; rice, watermelons.

Fukue (fo͝oko͞o'ā). **1** Town (pop. 15,529), Aichi prefecture, central Honshu, Japan, on NW Atsumi Peninsula, port on Atsumi Bay, 19 mi. WSW of Toyohashi; fishing center (hatcheries); rice, raw silk. Exports fish. Sometimes spelled Hukue. **2** Town, Nagasaki prefecture, Japan: see FUKAE.

Fu-kuei Chiao, Formosa: see FUKWEI POINT.

Fukugawa, Japan: see TOKUYAMA.

Fukui (fo͝oko͞o'ē), prefecture [Jap. *ken*] (□ 1,647; 1940 pop. 643,904; 1947 pop. 726,264), S Honshu, Japan; ⊙ Fukui. Bounded W by Wakasa Bay and Sea of Japan. Chief port, TSURUGA. Generally mountainous, with wide coastal plain; drained by small streams. Chief agr. products: rice, sweet potatoes, tobacco. Extensive poultry raising; also fishing, raw-silk production, mfg. (textiles, lacquer ware, paper, sake, soy sauce).

Fukui, city (1940 pop. 94,595; 1947 pop. 77,320), ⊙ Fukui prefecture, S Honshu, Japan, 28 mi. NNE of Kyoto; major textile center (silk, rayon); woodworking, mfg. (paper, leather goods, sake, soy sauce). Bombed (1945) in Second World War; heavily damaged by earthquake in 1948. Sometimes spelled Hukui.

Fukuji, Japan: see SHIRAISHI.

Fukum, Aden: see LITTLE ADEN.

Fukuma (fo͝oko͞o'mä), town (pop. 6,008), Fukuoka prefecture, N Kyushu, Japan, on Genkai Sea, 12 mi. NNE of Fukuoka; agr. center (rice, wheat, barley); fishery.

Fukumitsu (fo͝oko͞o'mĭtso͞o), town (pop. 6,542), Toyama prefecture, central Honshu, Japan, 12 mi. E of Kanazawa; silk textiles.

Fukung (fo͞o'go͝ong'), village, ⊙ Fukung dist. (pop. 14,862), NW Yunnan prov., China, near Burma line, 100 mi. N of Paoshan, in watershed bet. Salween and Mekong rivers; rice, wheat, beans, rapeseed, timber; saltworks. Until 1935, Shangpo.

Fukuno (fo͝oko͞o'nō), town (pop. 12,334), Toyama prefecture, central Honshu, Japan, 15 mi. E of Kanazawa; cotton-textile center.

Fukuoka (fo͞o"ko͞o-ō'kä, fo͝oko͞o'ōkä), prefecture, [Jap. *ken*] (□ 1,907; 1940 pop. 3,094,132; 1947 pop. 3,178,134), N Kyushu, Japan; ⊙ Fukuoka. Bounded N by Genkai Sea, Hibiki Sea, and Shimonoseki Strait, E by Suo Sea (W section of Inland Sea), SW by the Ariakeno-umi. Principal port, MOJI. Generally mountainous; drained by many small streams and Chikugo R. Tallow trees (*sapium sebiferum*) and mulberry trees. Chikuho, largest coal field in Japan, comprises major part of N interior. Chikugo R. valley is chief agr. area, producing rice, wheat, barley, tobacco. On N coast are major industrial centers of YAWATA, WAKAMATSU, KOKURA. Principal mfg. center is Fukuoka (W), seat of Kyushu Imperial Univ.

Fukuoka. 1 Town (pop. 5,101), Aichi prefecture, central Honshu, Japan, 4 mi. S of Okazaki; cotton milling; rice, herbs. **2** City (1940 pop. 306,763; 1947 pop. 328,548), ⊙ Fukuoka prefecture, N Kyushu, Japan, port on SE shore of Hakata Bay, 550 mi. WSW of Tokyo; 33°35'N 130°24'E. Short Naka R. divides city into 2 sections, with business center on W shore, and Fukuoka port (known as Hakata) on E shore. Cultural and mfg. center of prefecture; textiles, pottery, paper, cotton and metal goods; known for dolls. Exports machinery, plate glass, porcelain, bamboo and paper products. Seat of Kyushu Imperial Univ. (1910) and Fukuoka Products Mus. Has 2 coal mines. Hakata area was scene of battles during Mongol invasions (1274–81); opened 1899 to foreign trade. Fukuoka was ⊙ feudal prov. of Chikuzen. Includes (since early 1940s) former town of Hakozaki. Heavily bombed (1945) in Second World War. Sometimes spelled Hukuoka. **3** Town (pop. 6,729), Iwate prefecture, N Honshu, Japan, 20 mi. SW of Hachinohe; silk cocoons, soybeans; rabbit furs. **4** Town (pop. 6,095), Toyama prefecture, central Honshu, Japan, 5 mi. WSW of Takaoka; agr. center; textiles.

Fukura (fo͝oko͞o'rä), town (pop. 9,886), on Awajishima, Hyogo prefecture, Japan, 12 mi. WSW of Sumoto, on strait bet. Harima Sea and Kii Channel; terminus of railroad from Sumoto; agr. (rice, fruit, vegetables), poultry; woodworking, pottery making, raw silk.

Fukuroi (fo͝oko͞o'rōē), town (pop. 12,182), Shizuoka prefecture, central Honshu, Japan, 11 mi. ENE of Hamamatsu; agr. center (tea, watermelons).

Fukushima (fo͞o"ko͞oshē'mŭ, Jap. fo͝oko͞o'shĭmä), prefecture [Jap. *ken*] (□ 5,321; 1940 pop.1,625,521; 1947 pop. 1,992,460), N and central Honshu, Japan; ⊙ Fukushima. Bounded E by the Pacific; partly mountainous, with volcanic Bandai-san near L. Inawashiro, in hot-springs area. Abukuma R. drains fertile plains producing rice, soybeans, fruit, tobacco. Part of Joban coal field in S. Fishing, raw-silk culture, horse breeding, lumbering, mfg. (textiles, pottery). Principal centers: Fukushima, WAKAMATSU, KORIYAMA, TAIRA.

Fukushima, sometimes spelled Fukusima. **1** Town (pop. 10,127), Fukuoka prefecture, N central Kyushu, Japan, 15 mi. E of Saga; rail terminus; agr. center (rice, barley, wheat). Site of feudal castle. **2** City (1940 pop. 48,287; 1947 pop. 86,763), ⊙ Fukushima prefecture, N Honshu, Japan, 150 mi. NNE of Tokyo and on Abukuma R.; 37°45'N 140°28'E. Silk-textile center. **3** Town (pop. 4,941), Gumma prefecture, central Honshu, Japan, 7 mi. SW of Takasaki; rice, wheat, raw silk. **4** Town (pop. 12,920), Miyazaki prefecture, SE Kyushu, Japan, 33 mi. SSW of Miyazaki; commercial center for area producing rice, wheat, lumber, livestock. **5** Town (pop. 8,683), Nagano prefecture, central Honshu, Japan, 24 mi. NNW of Iida; horse breeding, lumbering.

Fuku-shima (fo͝okoo'shĭmä), island (□ 6; pop. 8,730), Nagasaki prefecture, Japan, in inlet of Genkai Sea, 6 mi. NNW of Imari; 4 mi. long, 3 mi. wide. Rice growing, horse breeding.

Fukusima, Japan: see FUKUSHIMA.

Fukutiyama, Japan: see FUKUCHIYAMA.

Fukuwatari (fo͝oko͞owä'tä'rē), town (pop. 3,037), Okayama prefecture, SW Honshu, Japan, 15 mi. N of Okayama, in agr. area (rice, wheat, peppermint, pears); sake, charcoal, raw silk.

Fukuyama (fo͞o'ko͞oyä'mo͝o, Jap. fo͝oko͞o'yämä). **1** Town (pop. 9,389), Fukushima prefecture, central Honshu, Japan, just N of Koriyama; rice, soybeans, silk cocoons. **2** Town (1940 pop. 56,653; 1947 pop. 59,576), Hiroshima prefecture, SW Honshu, Japan, port on Hiuchi Sea, on delta mouth of short Ashida R., 53 mi. ENE of Hiroshima; mfg. center (dyestuff, rubber goods, cotton textiles, sake). Exports textiles, floor mats, sugar, fertilizer. Bombed in Second World War. **3** Town, Hokkaido, Japan: see MATSUMAE. **4** Town (pop. 11,720), Kagoshima prefecture, S Kyushu, Japan, on NE shore of Kagoshima Bay, 17 mi. ENE of Kagoshima; commercial center in agr. area (rice, wheat); raw silk. Fisheries.

Fukuzaki (fo͝oko͞o'zäkē), town (pop. 7,223), Hyogo prefecture, S Honshu, Japan, 9 mi. NNE of Himeji, in agr. area (rice, wheat, fruit, flowers); woodworking, processed tea, floor mats, sake, raw silk.

Fukwei Point (fo͞o'gwā'), Chinese *Fu-kuei Chiao* (jyou), Jap. *Fuki-kaku* (fo͝okē'käko͞o), northernmost point of Formosa, on E.China Sea; 25°18'N 121°32'E. Steep, rocky promontory; lighthouse.

Fulacunda (fo͞oläko͞on'do͞o), village, W Port. Guinea, 30 mi. E of Bissau; almonds, rubber, rice.

Fulah (fo͞o'lä), name referring to a former native empire in W Africa inhabited by the predominantly Moslem Fulah or Fulani. Region is now included in N Nigeria and adjacent territories of Fr. West Africa. The Fulah conquered the Hausa states early in 19th cent. and were in turn subjugated by the British.

Fularki or **Fu-la-erh-chi** (both: fo͞o'lär'jē'), town, W central Heilungkiang prov., Manchuria, 15 mi. SW of Tsitsihar, at crossing of Nonni R. and Chinese Eastern RR; transshipment point.

Fulbeck, town and parish (pop. 577), Parts of Kesteven, W Lincolnshire, England, 10 mi. N of Grantham; ironstone quarrying.

Fulbourn, town and parish (pop. 2,022), S Cambridge, England, 5 mi. ESE of Cambridge; agr. market. Church dates from 13th cent.

Fulda (fo͝ol'dä), city (1950 pop. 42,244), in former Prussian prov. of Hesse-Nassau, W Germany, after 1945 in Hesse, on the Fulda and 54 mi. S of Kassel; 50°33'N 9°40'E. Historic and cultural center; bishopric (since 1752) and scene of annual conference of Ger. R.C. bishops. Rail junction; mfg. of textiles (canvas, cloth, felt, raincoats), chemicals, rubber, tires, dyes, polish, soap, agr. machinery, roller bearings; metal- and woodworking. Large enameling plant. Agr. market center. Most noteworthy bldgs., including the cathedral (with crypt containing tomb of St. Boniface), the castle, and the library, are baroque. Church of St. Michael (9th cent.) is in Carolingian style. Has theological seminary. Was seat of univ. 1734–1803. Developed around Benedictine abbey (founded 744 by St. Boniface), which became Christianizing center of central Germany and was long a seat of culture. The abbots were powerful princes of the Holy Roman Empire and ruled over a large territory until the abbey was secularized in 1803. Fulda was chartered in 12th cent. Passed 1815 to Hesse-Kassel. Captured by U.S. troops in April, 1945.

Fulda (fo͝ol'do͞o), village (pop. 1,149), Murray co., SW Minn., 11 mi. SE of Slayton, in grain area; dairy products.

Fulda River, W Germany, rises on the Wasserkuppe, flows 95 mi. N, past Fulda, Hersfeld, and Kassel, to Münden, where it joins WERRA RIVER to form WESER RIVER. Navigable for small craft below Hersfeld. Receives the Eder (left).

Fülek, Czechoslovakia: see FILAKOVO.

Fuleli Canal (fo͝olā'lē), irrigation channel in Hyderabad dist., S Sind, W Pakistan; flows c.100 mi. SSE from left bank of Indus R. 3 mi. NW of Hyderabad, past Tando Muhammad Khan, to just N of Rann of Cutch. Waters fields of rice, millet, cotton, and wheat.

Fulford, Fla.: see NORTH MIAMI BEACH.

Fulford Harbour, village, SW B.C., on SE Saltspring Isl., 11 mi. E of Duncan; fishing port; lumbering, dairying; poultry, sheep, fruit.

Fulham (fo͝o'lŭm), residential metropolitan borough (1931 pop. 150,928; 1951 census 122,047) of London, England, on N bank of the Thames (here crossed by Putney Bridge), 5 mi. SW of Charing Cross. The 16th-cent. Fulham Palace is country residence of bishops of London, many of whom are buried in cemetery of parish church.

Fuliola (fo͞olyō'lä), village (pop. 1,014), Lérida prov., NE Spain, 14 mi. WNW of Cervera, in irrigated agr. area (olive oil, wine, cereals, sugar beets); hog raising.

Fullarton, village (pop. 707), SW Trinidad, B.W.I., on the Gulf of Paria, 20 mi. SW of San Fernando, in coconut-growing region.

Fullersta (fŭ'lŭrstä"), residential village (pop. 2,593), Stockholm co., E Sweden, 6 mi. SW of Stockholm city center.

Fullerton (fo͝o'lŭrtŭn). **1** City (pop. 13,958), Orange co., S Calif., 22 mi. SE of Los Angeles and just N of Anaheim; fruit-packing, processing, canning plants (citrus fruit, vegetables, walnuts, avocados); oil-field center; mfg. of cans, glass products, machinery. Has jr. col. Inc. 1904. **2** Village (pop. 1,501), Greenup co., NE Ky., on Ohio R. just above Portsmouth, Ohio, in fruitgrowing area. On site of part of Lower Shawneetown, one of last Indian settlements in Ky., built c.1729, deserted c.1753. **3** City (pop. 1,520), ⊙ Nance co., E central Nebr., 32 mi. W of Columbus and on Loup R., in prairie region; dairying, grain. Platted 1878. **4** Village (pop. 206), Dickey co., SE N.Dak., 16 mi. W of Oakes. **5** Village (pop. c.3,000), Lehigh co., E Pa., on Lehigh R. just N of Allentown; furniture, textiles, castings.

Fullerton, Cape, E Keewatin Dist., Northwest Territories, on Hudson Bay, at S end of Roes Welcome Sound; 63°58'N 88°47'W.

Fullerville, town (pop. 529), Carroll co., W Ga., 15 mi. NNE of Carrollton.

Fully (fülē'), town (pop. 2,729), Valais canton, SW Switzerland, on the Rhone and 3 mi. NE of Martigny-Ville; farming.

Fulnek (fo͝ol'nĕk), town (pop. 1,544), S central Silesia, Czechoslovakia, 19 mi. WSW of Ostrava; rail terminus; mfg. of footwear, woolen textiles. Former center of the United Brethren. J. A. Comenius taught here.

Fülöpszallas (fü'lûpsäl-läsh), Hung. *Fülöpszállás,* town (pop. 6,483), Pest-Pilis-Solt-Kiskun co., central Hungary, 22 mi. WSW of Kecskemet; rail junction; flour mills.

Fulpmes (fo͝olp'mĕs), town (pop. 2,079), Tyrol, W Austria, 8 mi. SSW of Innsbruck; rail terminus; metalworking (tools, hardware). Summer resort; winter sports; main town of beautiful Stubai Valley.

Fulstone, England: see NEW MILL.

Fulton (fo͝ol'tŭn). **1** County (□ 611; pop. 9,187), N Ark.; ⊙ Salem. Bounded N by Mo. line; drained by Spring and Strawberry rivers. Agr. (cotton, truck, corn, feed crops; livestock, poultry; dairy products); hardwood timber. Ships moss. Formed 1842. **2** County (□ 523; pop. 473,572), NW central Ga.; ⊙ Atlanta. Bounded NW by Chattahoochee R. Includes major part of Atlanta metropolitan area. Piedmont mfg., commercial, and agr. (cotton, corn, truck, fruit, livestock, dairy products, poultry) area. Formed 1853. **3** County (□ 874; pop. 43,716), W central Ill.; ⊙ Lewistown. Bounded SE by Illinois R.; drained by Spoon R.; includes group of bayou lakes (resorts) along Illinois R. Agr. (livestock, corn, wheat, soybeans, poultry; dairy products). Bituminous-coal mining. Mfg. (feed, farm machinery, wood products, overalls, cement products, tractor parts). Clay deposits; timber. Formed 1823. **4** County (□ 367; pop. 16,565), N Ind.; ⊙ Rochester. Agr. (truck, poultry, soybeans, livestock; dairy products); some mfg. at Rochester and Akron; timber. Lake resorts. Drained by Tippecanoe R. Formed 1835. **5** County (□ 205; pop. 13,668), extreme SW Ky.; ⊙ Hickman. Bounded W by the Mississippi (Mo. line), S by Tenn.; drained by Obion Creek and Bayou de Chien. Has exclave (□ c.10; within Mississippi R. bend) in Mo., separated from Ky. by meander of river, which forms state line here. Agr. area (cotton, corn, livestock, dark tobacco), timber. Formed 1845. **6** County (□ 497; pop. 51,021), E central N.Y.; ⊙ Johnstown. Situated in the Adirondacks; drained by East Canada Creek and Sacandaga R. Includes Sacandaga Reservoir and several lakes (resorts). Dairying, poultry raising, farming. Has large glovemaking industry (mainly at Gloversville, Johnstown), and other mfg. Formed 1838. **7** County (□ 407; pop. 25,580), NW Ohio; ⊙ Wauseon. Bounded N by Mich. line; drained by Tiffin R. Stock raising, farming (wheat, sugar beets, corn, oats, hay, tomatoes); diversified mfg. Formed 1850. **8** County (□ 435; pop. 10,387), S Pa.; ⊙ McConnellsburg. Mountainous agr. region, with Tuscarora Mtn. along E, Sideling Hill along W borders. Settled in 1740s by Scotch-Irish. Bituminous coal, limestone; buckwheat, livestock, gristmill products. Formed 1850.

Fulton. **1** Town (pop. 696), Clarke co., SW Ala., 60 mi. SW of Selma; lumber. **2** Town (pop. 385), Hempstead co., SW Ark., 18 mi. NE of Texarkana and on Red R. near mouth of Little R. Site of flood-control dam on Little R. is c.10 mi. NW. **3** City (pop. 2,706), Whiteside co., NW Ill., on the Mississippi (bridged here), just NNE of Clinton, Iowa; trade and shipping center in agr. area (corn, wheat, truck, livestock, poultry; dairy products); mfg. (pickles, novelties, tanks, boilers). Inc. 1859. **4** Town (pop. 366), Fulton co., N Ind., 15 mi. NN[E] of Logansport, in agr. area. **5** City (pop. 243), Bourbon co., SE Kansas, near Mo. line, 10 mi. N of Fort Scott, in stock-raising, dairying, and general agr. region. **6** City (pop. 5,516), Fulton co., SW Ky., at Tenn. line, contiguous to SOUTH FULTON, Tenn., and 24 mi. SW of Mayfield, Ky., in agr. area (corn, dark tobacco, sweet potatoes, cotton), with oak timber. Rail junction; mfg. of clothing, food products, butane gas, concrete blocks; feed and lumber mills, cotton gin. Settled 1860; inc. 1874. **7** Village, Keweenaw co., Mich.: see MOHAWK. **8** Town (pop. 1,343), ⊙ Itawamba co., NE Miss., near the Tombigbee, 18 mi. E of Tupelo, in agr. area (cotton, corn, sorghum); lumber milling, mfg. of clothing. Settled 1848, inc. 1850. **9** City (pop. 10,052), ⊙ Callaway co., central Mo., 22 mi. NE of Jefferson City. Agr. center; mfg. (flour, fire-clay products, shoes); coal. Westminster Col., William Woods Col., state institutions for deaf and insane. Inc. 1859. **10** City (pop. 13,922), Oswego co., N central N.Y., on Oswego R. (water power) and the Barge Canal, and 10 mi. SSE of Oswego; mfg. (confectionery, textiles, paper and aluminum products, firearms, machinery, cutlery, canned foods); sand and gravel. Ships dairy products, fruit, truck, poultry. State park near by. Inc. as village in 1835, as city in 1902. **11** Village (pop. 269), Morrow co., central Ohio, 18 mi. ESE of Marion. **12** Town (pop. 139), Hanson co., SE central S.Dak., 10 mi. E of Mitchell.

Fulton Chain of Lakes, N central N.Y., group of small lakes in the Adirondacks, extending SW from vicinity of Raquette L.; lakes are connected by streams, and drained by Middle Branch of Moose R. Fourth L. (□ c.3) is largest of group. Noted canoe route through hunting, fishing, and resort region. Old Forge, Inlet, and other resorts are here.

Fultondale, town (pop. 1,304), Jefferson co., N central Ala., a N suburb of Birmingham. Also called Lewisburg. Inc. since 1940.

Fultonville, village (pop. 840), Montgomery co., [E] central N.Y., on Mohawk R. (bridged), opposite Fonda, and 10 mi. W of Amsterdam; mfg. (gloves, textiles, wringers).

Fults (fŭlts), village (pop. 120), Monroe co., SW Ill., 30 mi. S of East St. Louis, in agr. area.

Fulwood (fo͝ol'–), urban district (1931 pop. 7,387; 1951 census 13,087), W central Lancashire, England, just N of Preston; cotton milling, metalworking.

Fuma (fo͞o'mä), town (pop. 4,143), Chiba prefecture, central Honshu, Japan, 9 mi. SE of Sawara; rice, raw silk, poultry.

Fumaiolo, Monte (môn'tĕ fo͞omä-yô'lô), peak (4,61[?] ft.) in Etruscan Apennines, N central Italy, 6 mi. ESE of Bagno di Romagna. Source of Tiber R.

Fuman, Iran: see FUMEN.

Fumay (fümā'), town (pop. 3,626), Ardennes dept., N France, near Belg. border, in the Ardennes, [1]1 mi. N of Mézières, on loop of entrenched Meuse R.; major slate-quarrying center. Makes heating equipment.

Fumba (fo͞om'bä), town, on W coast of Zanzibar, 1[?] mi. SSE of Zanzibar town; fishing.

Fumel (fümĕl'), town (pop. 3,812), Lot-et-Garonne dept., SW France, on the Lot and 14 mi. ENE of Villeneuve-sur-Lot; iron and steel foundries, cement works. Mfg. of refractories at Libos (1 mi. SW). Iron ore mined near by (chiefly at Cuzorn).

Fumen or **Fuman** (both: fo͞omän'), town (1940 pop. 4,934), First Prov., in Gilan, N Iran, 18 mi. WSW of Resht; tobacco, rice, silk, honey; charcoal burning; sheep raising. Was an administrative center until 16th cent.

Fumin (fo͞o'mĭn'), town, ⊙ Fumin co. (pop. 34,148), E central Yunnan prov., China, 15 mi. NW of Kunming; alt. 5,675 ft.; rice, wheat, millet, beans, fruit. Coal mines and saltworks near by.

Fu Mun, China: see BOCA TIGRIS.

Funabashi (fo͝onä'bä'shē), city (1940 pop. 50,90[?]; 1947 pop. 78,996), Chiba prefecture, central Honshu, Japan, at NW base of Chiba Peninsula, on shore of Tokyo Bay, adjacent to Ichikawa (W), 13 mi E of Tokyo; fish hatcheries. Mfg. of fountain pens, woodworking, flour milling. Includes (since 1937) former town of Katsushika. Sometimes spelled Hunabasi.

Funabiki, Japan: see FUNEHIKI.

Funafuti (fo͞o"näfo͞o'tē), atoll (□ 1; pop. 528), ⊙ and port of entry of ELLICE ISLANDS, SW Pacific; 8°30'S 179°8'W; 30 islets on reef c.13 mi. long. Coconut, palm trees; sandy, unfertile soil. Main village is on largest islet (also called Funafuti), on E side of atoll. Discovered 1819 by Capt. De Peyster, included 1915 in Br. colony of Gilbert and Ellice Isls. Site of Sir Edgeworth David's test (1897) which proved Darwinian theory of atoll formation. In Second World War, U.S. forces occupied it (1943) and established (1945) bases.

Funagawaminato, Japan: see FUNAKAWAMINATO.

Funahiki, Japan: see FUNEHIKI.

Funaho (fo͝onä'hō), town (pop. 7,050), Okayama prefecture, SW Honshu, Japan, just W of Kurashiki, in agr. area (rice, wheat, pears); raw sil[k].

Funakata, Japan: see TATEYAMA.

Funakawaminato (fo͞onä'käwä-mēnä'tō) or **Funagawaminato** (–gäwä–), town (pop. 15,475), Akita prefecture, N Honshu, Japan, on S Oga Peninsula, port on Sea of Japan, 19 mi. NW of Akita; rail terminus; rice, charcoal; fishing. Exports rice, oil, lumber, sake. Sometimes called Funakawa; sometimes spelled Hunakawaminato.

Funaki (fo͞onä'kē), town (pop. 7,771), Yamaguchi prefecture, SW Honshu, Japan, 5 mi. N of Ube; agr. center (rice, wheat); combs, raw silk. Coal mine near by.

Funakoshi (fo͞onä'kō'shē). **1** Town (pop. 4,327), Akita prefecture, N Honshu, Japan, at S base of Oga Peninsula, on S shore of Hachiro-gata; agr., fishing. **2** Town (pop. 10,710), Hiroshima prefecture, SW Honshu, Japan, just E of Hiroshima, on Hiroshima Bay; sake, soy sauce, canned food; truck gardening.

Funami (fo͞onä'mē), town (pop. 2,388), Toyama prefecture, central Honshu, Japan, 10 mi. NE of Uozu; rice, watermelons.

Funan (fo͞o'nän'), town, ⊙ Funan co. (pop. 79,619), SW Kwangsi prov., China, on Li R., on railroad and 28 mi. WSW of Nanning; peanut-processing center. Until 1914 called Sinning.

Funaoka (fo͞onä'ōkä), town (pop. 10,614), Miyagi prefecture, N Honshu, Japan, 16 mi. SSW of Sendai; rice, silk cocoons.

Funatsu (fo͞onä'tso͞o), town (pop. 11,922), Gifu prefecture, central Honshu, Japan, 25 mi. SSE of Toyama; lead-mining center.

Funchal (fo͞onshäl'), district (□ 302; pop. 250,124) of Portugal, coextensive with Madeira isls., of which only MADEIRA and PÔRTO SANTO ISLAND are inhabited; ⊙ Funchal.

Funchal, city (pop. 54,856), ⊙ Funchal dist., Madeira, port on SE shore of MADEIRA isl., 650 mi. SW of Lisbon; 32°38'N 16°54'W. Third largest Portuguese city and internationally-known resort, noted for its beautiful setting (on steep slopes rising sharply from the sea) and balmy climate. Exports famed Madeira wines, embroidery, wickerwork, fruit, dairy produce, fish. Industries include sugar milling and distilling; mfg. of tobacco products, soap, flour products, slaked lime; canning. Episcopal see since 1514. Has late-15th-cent. cathedral, the convent church of Santa Clara (containing Zarco's tomb), and 3 forts (remains of fortifications dating from 1572–1637). Funchal is a submarine cable station and busy port-of-call. Founded 1421 by João Gonçalves Zarco. Sacked 1566 by French privateers. Under Sp. domination 1580–1640. Temporarily occupied by British (1801, 1807).

Funcheira (fo͞onshā'rŭ), village, Beja dist., S Portugal, 32 mi. SW of Beja; rail junction.

Fundación (fo͞ondäsyōn'), town (pop. 6,905), Magdalena dept., N Colombia, at W foot of Sierra Nevada de Santa Marta, 50 mi. S of Santa Marta; terminus of railroad from Santa Marta; banana growing.

Fundão (fo͞ondã'ō), city (pop. 704), central Espírito Santo, Brazil, on railroad and 28 mi. N of Vitória; sweet potatoes.

Fundão, town (pop. 3,346), Castelo Branco dist., central Portugal, on N slope of Serra da Guardunha, on railroad and 11 mi. S of Covilhã; center of wood industry (sawmilling, cork processing, furniture mfg.). Vineyards and olive groves in area. Tungsten deposits in mts. (W).

Fundi, Italy: see FONDI.

Fundición de Avalos, Mexico: see AVALOS.

Fundición de Tinyahuarco (fo͞ondēsyōn' dā tēnyäwär'kō), town (pop. 714), Pasco dept., central Peru, in Nudo de Pasco of the Andes, on railroad and 6 mi. S of Cerro de Pasco. In early 20th cent. the smelter for Cerro de Pasco mines, it was later replaced by the La Oroya smelter.

Funding Fjord, Faeroe Isls.: see OSTERO.

Fundul-Moldovei (fo͞on'do͝ol-môldô'vā), village (pop. 3,604), Suceava prov., N Rumania, in the Moldavian Carpathians, on Moldova R. and 9 mi. W of Campulung; rail terminus, with large limestone quarries, pyrite mine. Pojorata rail junction and summer resort is 4 mi. SE.

Fundy, Bay of (fŭn'dē), inlet (extends 100 mi. NE inland, 60 mi. wide at entrance) of the Atlantic, bet. NE Maine, S N.B., and NW N.S.; 44°15'–45°30'N 64°56'–67°30'W. Its chief arms are Passamaquoddy Bay (NW), Chignecto Bay (NE), and Minas Channel (E). On N shore, at mouth of St. John R., is St. John; other towns on bay are Eastport, St. Andrews, and Digby. Tides, rising up to 70 ft., are among highest in the world.

Fundy National Park (□ 79.5), S N.B., on Bay of Fundy, at mouth of Chignecto Bay, 50 mi. ENE of St. John. Established 1949.

Funehiki (fo͞onā'hēkē), town (pop. 7,217), Fukushima prefecture, N central Honshu, Japan, 11 mi. ENE of Koriyama; agr. (tobacco, rice, wheat), horse breeding. Sometimes called Funabiki and Funahiki.

Fünen, Denmark: see FYN.

Funeral Mountains, Calif.: see AMARGOSA RANGE.

Funes (fo͞o'nĕs), town (pop. estimate 1,000), SE Santa Fe prov., Argentina, 9 mi. W of Rosario, in agr. area (alfalfa, corn, flax, livestock).

Funes, town (pop. 1,707), Nariño dept., SW Colombia, in the Andes, 17 mi. NE of Ipiales; coffee, wheat, corn, potatoes, cacao, sugar cane, livestock.

Funes, town (pop. 1,490), Navarre prov., N Spain, on Arga R. and 20 mi. NNW of Tudela; sugar-beet center; gypsum quarries.

Fünfhaus (fünf'hous), district (□ 1; pop. 98,934) of Vienna, Austria, 3 mi. W of city center.

Fünfkirchen, Hungary: see PECS.

Fung or **El Fung** (ĕl fo͞ong'), former province, Anglo-Egyptian Sudan, now a dist. in Blue Nile prov. with hq. at Singa. Also a native kingdom 15th–19th cent., with ⊙ at Old Sennar (now in ruins).

Fungchün (fo͞ong'chün'), Mandarin *Feng-ch'uan* (fŭng'chwän'), town (pop. 9,063), ⊙ Fungchün co. (pop. 101,023), W Kwangtung prov., China, on West R. and 12 mi. ESE of Wuchow; rice, wheat, beans. Sometimes spelled Fungtsun, Fungchwan.

Fungshun (fo͞ong'so͞on'), Mandarin *Fengshun* (fŭng'-sho͞on'), town (pop. 3,788), ⊙ Fungshun co. (pop. 192,830), E Kwangtung prov., China, 25 mi. SSE of Meihsien; grain. Tin mining.

Fungtsun, China: see FUNGCHÜN.

Fungurume (fo͞ong-go͞oro͞o'mā), village, Katanga prov., SE Belgian Congo, on railroad and 30 mi. NW of Jadotville; copper mining; agr. (manioc, peas, beans).

Fungyang, China: see FENGYANG.

Funing (fo͞o'nĭng'). **1** Town, Fukien prov., China: see SIAPU. **2** Town, ⊙ Funing co. (pop. 266,314), NE Hopeh prov., China, 60 mi. ENE of Tangshan; rice, pears; fisheries. **3** Town (pop. 5,401), ⊙ Funing co. (pop. 39,164), southeasternmost Yunnan prov., China, 70 mi. ENE of Wenshan and on road to Kwangsi prov.; rice, millet, beans, cotton. Until 1927 called Fuchow.

Funiu Mountains, Chinese *Funiu Shan* (fo͞o'nyō' shän'), E outlier of the Kunlun system, in W Honan prov., China, bet. upper Sha and Pai rivers; rises to 7,874 ft. NW of Nanchao. Wild silk growing.

Funk, village (pop. 123), Phelps co., S Nebr., 7 mi. E of Holdrege and on branch of Platte R.

Funkia, Sierra Leone: see GODERICH.

Funk Island, islet in the Atlantic, off E N.F., 37 mi. E of Fogo Isl.; 49°45'N 53°14'W. Together with Two Islets, just W, it was one of the last breeding grounds of the now extinct great auk.

Funkley, village (pop. 28), Beltrami co., N Minn., 30 mi. NE of Bemidji, in grain and potato area.

Funkstown, town (pop. 879), Washington co., W Md., on Antietam Creek just SSE of Hagerstown.

Funshion River (fŭn'shŭn), Co. Cork, Ireland, rises in Galty Mts., flows WSW, then curves SE, past Kildorrery, to the Blackwater 2 mi. ENE of Fermoy; 27 mi. long.

Funston, town (pop. 233), Colquitt co., S Ga., 5 mi. W of Moultrie.

Funston, Fort, Calif.: see SAN FRANCISCO.

Funtana Raminosa, Sardinia: see GADONI.

Funter (fŭn'tŭr), fishing village, SE Alaska, on N Admiralty Isl., on Icy Strait 20 mi. W of Juneau.

Funtua (fo͞ontwä'), town (pop. 6,923), Katsina prov., Northern Provinces, N Nigeria, on railroad and 45 mi. NW of Zaria; road junction; peanuts, cotton; cattle, skins. Also Funtuwa.

Funza (fo͞on'sä), town (pop. 1,368), Cundinamarca dept., central Colombia, 13 mi. NW of Bogotá; wheat, potatoes, fruit, livestock.

Funza River, Colombia: see BOGOTÁ RIVER.

Fuping, **1** or **Fou-p'ing** (fō'pĭng'), town, ⊙ Fuping co. (pop. 93,908), W Hopeh prov., China, 70 mi. W of Paoting, in Taihang Mts., near Chahar-Shansi line; mica and graphite mining. **2** or **Fu-p'ing** (fo͞o'pĭng'), town (pop. 13,798), ⊙ Fuping co. (pop. 201,224), central Shensi prov., China, 35 mi. NNE of Sian and on railroad; cotton weaving; beans, millet.

Fuquay Springs (fo͞o'kwā), town (pop. 1,992), Wake co., central N.C., 16 mi. SSW of Raleigh; tobacco market; lumber mills.

Fúquene, Laguna de (lägo͞o'nä dā fo͞o'kānā), lake (□ 15; alt. 8,464 ft.) in Cundinamarca dept., central Colombia, in Cordillera Oriental, bordering on Boyacá dept., 60 mi. NNE of Bogotá; c.5 mi. long. Popular resort, noted for fishing, duck hunting.

Fur, Denmark: see FUUR.

Furadouro (fo͞orŭdō'ro͞o), fishing village (pop. 405), Aveiro dist., N central Portugal, on the Atlantic, 16 mi. N of Aveiro; bathing resort.

Furancungo (fo͞oräko͞ong'gō), village, Manica and Sofala prov., NW Mozambique, on road and 90 mi. NNW of Tete, near Nyasaland border; gold placers.

Furano (fo͞orä'nō), town (pop. 19,655), central Hokkaido, Japan, 30 mi. S of Asahigawa, in agr. area; rail junction; flour, hemp cloth.

Furcy (fürsē'), village, Ouest dept., S Haiti, mtn. resort 10 mi. SSE of Port-au-Prince.

Füred, Hungary: see BALATONFÜRED.

Fure Lake, Dan. *Furesø* (fo͞o'rŭsû"), (2 mi. long), deepest (124 ft.) in Denmark, NE Zealand, c.10 mi. NW of Copenhagen; forest borders S shore.

Furens River (fürä'), Loire dept., SE central France, rises at Mont Pilat, flows 22 mi. NW, past Saint-Étienne and Saint-Priest-en-Jarez, to the Loire at Andrézieux. It crosses the Saint-Étienne coal field and industrial dist.

Fures, France: see TULLINS.

Fürfeld (für'fĕlt"), village (pop. 692), N Württemberg, Germany, after 1945 in Württemberg-Baden, 9 mi. NW of Heilbronn; cigar mfg.

Fürigen, Switzerland: see STANSSTADT.

Fu River, Chinese *Fu Shui* (fo͞o' shwā'), E Kiangsi prov., China, rises in Bohea Hills on Fukien line S of Kwangchang, flows 180 mi. generally N, past Nanfeng, Nancheng, and Fuchow, to Poyang L. E of Nanchang, forming common delta with Kan R.

Furka Pass (fo͞or'kä) (7,971 ft.), in the Alps, S central Switzerland, on border of Uri and Valais cantons; crossed by Furka Road, leading from Gletsch to Andermatt. **Furka Tunnel** (1 mi. long), under the pass, is used by Furka Railway, which forms part of rail line connecting W with E Switzerland.

Furland, Denmark: see FUUR.

Furlo Pass (fo͞or'lō), tunnel (alt. 581 ft.) in Apennine hills, The Marches, central Italy, 7 mi. SE of Urbino. Built A.D. c.77 by Emperor Vespasian to give access to the Flaminian Way; 120 ft. long, 17 ft. wide, 14 ft. high. Crossed by road bet. Fossombrone and Acqualagna.

Furman, town (pop. 293), Hampton co., SW S.C., 45 mi. N of Savannah, Ga., in tobacco area.

Furmanov (fo͞or'mŭnŭf), city (1938 pop. 33,600), NW Ivanovo oblast, Russian SFSR, 17 mi. NNE of Ivanovo; cotton-milling center. Chartered 1918; until c.1941, Sereda.

Furmanovo (–nŭvŭ), village (1939 pop. over 500), W West Kazakhstan oblast, Kazakh SSR, on Greater Uzen R. and 135 mi. SW of Uralsk; cattle, sheep, horses. Formerly Slomikhino.

Furna (fo͞or'nŭ), village, Cape Verde Isls., small port on NE shore of Brava isl., 2 mi. NE of Nova Sintra; fishing.

Furna (fürnä'), village, Tunis dist., N Tunisia, 19 mi. WSW of Tunis; cereals, wine, cattle.

Furnace Creek, Calif.: see DEATH VALLEY NATIONAL MONUMENT.

Furnas (fo͞or'nŭsh), village (pop. 3,021), Ponta Delgada dist., E Azores, on São Miguel Isl., 20 mi. E of Ponta Delgada; noted spa with mineral springs (including hot geysers). Luxuriant vegetation (hydrangeas, rhododendrons, palm trees); fine hotel. Lagoa das Furnas (1 mi. diameter) is a crater lake just SW. Mineral springs date from 1630 volcanic eruption.

Furnas, Brazil: see APIAÍ.

Furnas (fûr'nŭs), county (□ 722; pop. 9,385), S Nebr.; ⊙ Beaver City. Agr. region drained by Republican R. and Beaver and Sappa creeks; bounded S by Kansas. Livestock, grain. Formed 1873.

Furneaux Island, Tuamotu Isls.: see MARUTEA.

Furneaux Islands (fûr'nō), group in Bass Strait, 13 mi. off NE coast of Tasmania; 40°S 148°E. Comprise FLINDERS ISLAND (largest), CAPE BARREN ISLAND, CLARKE ISLAND, and many smaller isls. Mountainous, fertile; rugged coast line. Sheep, dairy products; tin. Chief town, Whitemark on Flinders Isl. Discovered 1773 by Tobias Furneaux, Br. navigator.

Furnes (fürn), Flemish *Veurne* (vûr'nŭ), town (pop. 7,569), West Flanders prov., W Belgium, at E end of Dunkirk-Furnes Canal, 6 mi. WSW of Nieuport, at junction of several small canals; mfg. (bricks, tiles); agr. market. Has 13th-cent. church of St. Walpurga, 15th-cent. church of St. Nicholas, 17th-cent. town hall and palace of justice.

Furnes, Norway: see BRUMUNDDAL.

Furness (fûr'nĭs, –nĕs), hilly peninsula, N Lancashire, England, bet. Duddon estuary and Morecambe Bay; has iron mines in SW. Chief industrial centers are BARROW-IN-FURNESS and DALTON-IN-FURNESS. N portion of Furness is part of the Lake District.

Furni, Greece: see PHOURNOI.

Fürstenau (für'stŭnou), town (pop. 3,573), in former Prussian prov. of Hanover, NW Germany, after 1945 in Lower Saxony, 15 mi. E of Lingen; grain, cattle.

Fürstenberg (für'stŭnbĕrk). **1** or **Fürstenberg an der Oder** (än dĕr ō'dŭr), town (pop. 5,259), Brandenburg, E Germany, on left bank of the Oder and 15 mi. SSE of Frankfurt, in lignite-mining region; port at E terminus of Oder-Spree Canal (locks); steel milling, shipbuilding, glass mfg., basket weaving. **2** Village (pop. 1,411), in former Prussian prov. of Hanover, NW Germany, after 1945 in Lower Saxony, on right bank of the Weser and 7 mi. SSW of Holzminden; porcelain factory (founded 1747). Until 1941 in Brunswick. **3** Town (pop. 444), in former Prussian prov. of Hesse-Nassau, W Germany, after 1945 in Hesse, 7 mi. SSW of Korbach; lumber. Until 1929 in former Waldeck principality. **4** Town (pop. 6,601), Mecklenburg, N Germany, on the Havel and 13 mi. SSE of Neustrelitz; popular summer and excursion resort. Lumber trade; flour- and sawmilling. Has former grand-ducal palace. Destroyed by fire in 1797 and 1807. During Napoleonic Wars, was hq. (1806) of Marshal Bernadotte. Just N was site of notorious Nazi concentration camp of Ravensbrück.

Fürstenfeld (für'stŭnfĕlt), town (pop. 6,956), Styria, SE Austria, on Feistritz R. and 30 mi. E of Graz; market center; tobacco mfg. Hop growing.

Fürstenfeldbruck (für"stŭnfĕlt'bro͝ok), town (pop. 11,258), Upper Bavaria, Germany, on the Amper and 14 mi. WNW of Munich; brewing, tanning; summer resort. Former Cistercian abbey (founded 1263) has church dating from 1st half of 18th cent. Town chartered c.1305.

Fürstenfelde, Poland: see BOLESZKOWICE.

Fürstenwalde (für″stŭnväl′dŭ), town (pop. 21,782), E Germany, on Spree R. and Oder-Spree Canal, and 30 mi. ESE of Berlin; woolen milling, metalworking; mfg. of machinery, electrical equipment, chemicals, shoes, ceramics, food products, musical instruments. Tuberculosis sanitariums near by. Has 15th-cent. church, 16th-cent. town hall. Chartered 1285; seat of bishops of Lebus from 1371 until late-16th cent. Under Treaty of Fürstenwalde (1373), Margrave Otto of Wittelsbach ceded Brandenburg to Wenceslaus, eldest son of Emperor Charles IV.

Fürstenzell (für′stŭntsĕl″), village (pop. 3,075), Lower Bavaria, Germany, 7 mi. SW of Passau; mfg. of chemicals, bricks, tiles; brewing. Has Cistercian monastery (founded in late 13th cent.; secularized 1803). Granite quarrying in area.

Fürta (fŏŏr′tŏ), town (pop. 2,358), Bihar co., E Hungary, 7 mi. SW of Berettyoujfalu; tobacco, hemp, hogs.

Furtei (fōōrtā′), village (pop. 1,367), Cagliari prov., S Sardinia, on Flumini Mannu R. and 25 mi. NNW of Cagliari. Kaolin mine near by.

Fürth (fürt), city (1950 pop. 99,503), Middle Franconia, Bavaria, Germany, on the Rednitz where it joins the Pegnitz to form the Regnitz, almost adjacent (NW) to Nuremberg, and on Ludwig Canal; 49°28′N 11°E. Rail and road junction; airport (N outskirts). Industrial center; has noted glass (especially mirrors) and toy industries. Other mfg.: machines, precision and optical instruments, textiles, chemicals (bronze color), radios, furniture, paper; leather-, metal-, and woodworking; printing, brewing. Has 14th-cent. church, 19th-cent. city hall. Founded 793. Development began only when Jews, denied entrance into Nuremberg, settled here (14th cent.). Passed to Bavaria and was chartered 1806. First Ger. railroad opened (1835) bet. here and Nuremberg. Captured by U.S. troops in April, 1945.

Furth or **Furth im Wald** (fŏŏrt′ ĭm vält′), town (pop. 9,678), Upper Palatinate, E Bavaria, Germany, in Bohemian Forest, on small Cham R. and 32 mi. NNE of Straubing, near Czechoslovak border; glass and textile mfg., tanning, woodworking. Summer resort. Has 17th-cent. church. Chartered 1332. Furth railroad pass (1,540 ft.) across Bohemian Forest is c.3 mi. N.

Furtwangen (fŏŏrt′väng″ŭn), town (pop. 5,036), S Baden, Germany, in Black Forest, on the Breg and 12 mi. W of Villingen; rail terminus; a center of Black Forest watch industry; mfg. of machinery and precision instruments, metal- and woodworking, lumber milling. Climatic health resort and winter-sports center (alt. 2,755 ft.). Has school for watchmakers, wood carvers, and straw-plaiters.

Furubira (fŏŏrōō′bĕrä) or **Furuhira** (–hĕrä), town (pop. 8,741), SW Hokkaido, Japan, on Sea of Japan, 19 mi. WNW of Otaru; fishing port.

Furuichi (fŏŏrōō′ēchē). **1** Town (pop. 4,853), Hiroshima prefecture, SW Honshu, Japan, just N of Hiroshima; rice, persimmons. **2** Town (pop. 8,262), Osaka prefecture, S Honshu, Japan, 9 mi. SE of Osaka; rice, wheat, raw silk; poultry.

Furukamappu, Russian SFSR: see YUZHNO-KURILSK.

Furukawa (fŏŏrōō′käwä). **1** Town (pop. 8,657), Gifu prefecture, central Honshu, Japan, 8 mi. NW of Takayama; lumbering; charcoal, raw silk, sake, bamboo shoots. **2** Town (pop. 17,639), Miyagi prefecture, N Honshu, Japan, 22 mi. NNE of Sendai; rice-collection center; horse trading.

Furulund, Norway: see SULITJELMA, village.

Furulund (fü′rülŭnd″), village (pop. 1,064), Malmohus co., S Sweden, 7 mi. NNW of Lund; woolen milling, sheep raising, grain growing.

Furuogrund (fü′rüŭ″grŭnd″), Swedish *Furuögrund*, village (pop. 286), Vasterbotten co., N Sweden, on Gulf of Bothnia, 14 mi. NNE of Skelleftea; sawmilling, woodworking.

Fury and Hecla Strait, SE Franklin Dist., Northwest Territories, arm (100 mi. long, 10–20 mi. wide) of the Arctic Ocean, bet. Baffin Isl. and Melville Peninsula; 69°55′N 81°30′–86°W. Connects Foxe Basin (E) with Gulf of Boothia. Contains many small isls. Strait is on route from Hudson Bay to the Arctic Archipelago, but because of year-round ice it is rarely navigable. Discovered 1822 by Sir William Parry; named after ships of his expedition.

Fury Point, cape, SE Somerset Isl., E Franklin Dist., Northwest Territories, on Prince Regent Inlet, on NE side of Creswell Bay; 72°45′N 91°52′W.

Fusa (fōō′sä), town (pop. 4,261), Chiba prefecture, central Honshu, Japan, 7 mi. E of Abiko; rice, wheat, raw silk, poultry.

Fusa, Norway: see EIKELANDSOSEN.

Fusagasugá (fōōsägäsōōgä′), town (pop. 4,886), Cundinamarca dept., central Colombia, in Cordillera Oriental, on Pan-American Highway and 26 mi. SW of Bogotá; alt. 5,728 ft. Trading center and summer resort in agr. region (wheat, fruit, coffee, vegetables, cattle).

Fusan, Korea: see PUSAN.

Fusaro (fōōzä′rô), coastal lake (□ .4), Campania, S Italy, in Phlegraean Fields, 11 mi. W of Naples; 1 mi. long. Connected with Tyrrhenian Sea by 2 artificial canals. Used for oyster culture. On its banks is a fishing school.

Fuscaldo (fōōskäl′dô), town (pop. 2,636), Cosenza prov., Calabria, S Italy, near Tyrrhenian Sea, 15 mi. NW of Cosenza, in fruitgrowing region.

Fusch an der Grossglocknerstrasse (fŏŏsh′ än dĕr grōsglôk′nŭrshträsŭ), village (pop. 729), Salzburg, W central Austria, 22 mi. SW of Bischofshofen; summer resort (alt. 2,320 ft.), with radioactive springs.

Fuse (fōō′sā), city (1940 pop. 134,724; 1947 pop. 133,934), Osaka prefecture, S Honshu, Japan, just E of Osaka; industrial center; engineering works, chemical plants; mfg. (celluloid, metalwork, rubber goods, pottery, drugs). Since 1937, includes former towns of Kosaka and Kusune.

Fusen-ko, Korea: see PUCHON RIVER.

Fushan (fōō′shän′), town, ⊙ Fushan co. (pop. 215,689), NE Shantung prov., China, near Shantung peninsula's N coast, 8 mi. SW of Chefoo; pongee, straw plait; beans. Fisheries, saltworks on coast near by.

Fushih, China: see YENAN.

Fushiki, Japan: see TAKAOKA, Toyama prefecture.

Fu Shui, China: see FU RIVER.

Fushun (fōō′shōōn′). **1** City (1940 pop. 279,604) in, but independent of, Liaotung prov., Manchuria, China, on railroad spur from Sukiatun, and 28 mi. ENE of Mukden; leading coal-mining and oil-shale-mining center of Manchuria and China. Mfg. of cement, firebrick, mining equipment; coking, oil-shale distilling and cracking; aluminum reduction (based on alunite from Yentai and Niusintai). Power plant (fed by coal dust). City consists of old town (SW), adjoining vast open-cut mine; and new town (NE), adjoining rail station. Large-scale coal mining began here in 1902, in connection with railroad construction; oil-shale mining was begun in 1929. **2** Town (pop. 23,471), ⊙ Fushun co. (pop. 774,116), SW Szechwan prov., China, 35 mi. NW of Luhsien and on To R.; sugar-milling center; match mfg.; rice, wheat, sweet potatoes, millet, beans. Coal and oil deposits, saltworks near by.

Fusien, Lake (fōō′shyĕn′), Chinese *Fusien Hu* or *Fu-hsien Hu*, E central Yunnan prov., China, 30 mi. SSE of Kunming; 20 mi. long, 5 mi. wide; alt. over 4,000 ft. On shores are Chengkiang (N), Kiangchwan (W). Sometimes L. Chengkiang.

Fusignano (fōōzēnyä′nô), village (pop. 1,452), Ravenna prov., Emilia-Romagna, N central Italy, on Senio R. and 4 mi. NNE of Lugo.

Fusin or **Fu-hsin** (fōō′shĭn′), city, ⊙ but independent of Fusin co. (pop. 118,490), W central Liaosi prov., Manchuria, on railroad and 75 mi. NNE of Chinchow; major coal-mining center, in agr. dist. (kaoliang, buckwheat, soybeans). In former Mongol area; agr. colonization and mining began c.1900. Part of Jehol prov. until 1934, and again during 1946–49. Sometimes written Fowsin or Fou-hsin.

Fussa (fōōs′sä), town (pop. 14,066), Greater Tokyo, central Honshu, Japan, 5 mi. NW of Tachikawa; raw silk.

Füssen (fü′sŭn), town (pop. 9,643), Swabia, SW Bavaria, Germany, at E foot of Allgäu Alps, on the Lech and 21 mi. SE of Kempten, near Austrian border; customs station; rail terminus; tourist center. Mfg. of textiles, cordage, leather products, paper; brewing. Summer and winter resort (alt. 2,614 ft.). Near by are sulphur springs and 2 small lakes. Town has former Benedictine abbey (founded 628), with early-18th-cent. baroque church (built on old Romanesque foundations) and 10th-11th-cent. crypt. The early-14th-cent. castle was renovated during 1st half of 19th cent. Town chartered c.1294. Here, in 1745, a treaty, concluded bet. Austria and Bavaria, resulted in the latter's withdrawal from the War of the Austrian Succession.

Fustat, El, Al-Fustat, or **El Fostat** (ĕl fōōstät′), anc. city of Egypt, founded by Arabs in 7th cent. A.D. on the Nile near site of modern Cairo. Also called Old Cairo [Arabic *Masr al-Qadimah*], its site is today SW section of Cairo, opposite Roda Isl.

Fustiñana (fōōstēnyä′nä), town (pop. 2,257), Navarre prov., N Spain, on Tauste Canal and 7 mi. ESE of Tudela; sugar beets, pepper, cereals.

Fusung (fōō′sōōng′), town, ⊙ Fusung co. (pop. 59,953), NE Liaotung prov., Manchuria, 85 mi. NE of Tunghwa, at W foot of Changpai mtn., on Towtao R. (left headstream of the Sungari).

Futa, La (lä fōō′tä), pass (alt. 2,963 ft.), N central Italy, in Etruscan Apennines, on watershed bet. Santerno (E) and Sieve (W) rivers, 5 mi. WSW of Firenzuola. Crossed by road bet. Florence and Bologna.

Futae (fōōtä′ā), town (pop. 5,470), on Shimo-jima of Amakusa Isls., Kumamoto prefecture, Japan, on N coast of isl., 24 mi. NNE of Ushibuka; rice, sweet potatoes.

Futagawa (fōōtä′gäwä), town (pop. 14,753), Aichi prefecture, central Honshu, Japan, 4 mi. SE of Toyohashi; agr. center (rice, sweet potatoes); spinning mills. Sometimes spelled Hutagawa.

Futa Jallon, Fr. West Africa: see FOUTA DJALLON.

Futak, Yugoslavia: see FUTOG.

Futalaufquén, Lake (fōōtäloufkĕn′) (□ 25; alt. 1,903 ft.), in the Andes, W Chubut natl. territory, Argentina, N of 43°S; c.12 mi. long, 1–3 mi. wide. L. Menéndez (NW) is linked to it by short river.

Futaleufú, department, Argentina: see ESQUEL.

Futaleufú (fōōtälĕōōfōō′), village (1930 pop. 573), Chiloé prov., S Chile, in the Andes, on Futaleufú R. (inlet of L. Yelcho) and 115 mi. SE of Castro, on Argentina border; sheep raising, lumbering.

Futamata (fōōtä′mätŭ), town (pop. 10,336), Shizuoka prefecture, central Honshu, Japan, on Tenryu R. and 12 mi. NNE of Hamamatsu; transportation center.

Futami (fōōtä′mē). **1** Town (pop. 9,980), Hyogo prefecture, S Honshu, Japan, on Harima Sea, 7 mi. NW of Akashi, in agr. area (rice, wheat, flowers, market produce); floor mats, soy sauce, malt; woodworking, fish canning. **2** Town (pop. 7,782), Mie prefecture, S Honshu, Japan, on SW shore of Ise Bay, 4 mi. ENE of Uji-yamada, in rice-growing area; home industries (floor mats, agr. implements). Near by, in Ise Bay, are 2 rocks (called Wedded Rocks) joined by a rope, with a *torii* on the larger rock. These are likened to the 2 gods who, in Jap. mythology, created Japan.

Futase (fōōtä′sä), town (pop. 21,346), Fukuoka prefecture, N Kyushu, Japan, 16 mi. E of Fukuoka; commercial center in coal-mining and agr. area; rice, tobacco, raw silk.

Futatsui (fōōtä′tsōōē), town (pop. 4,399), Akita prefecture, N Honshu, Japan, 11 mi. E of Noshiro; rice, charcoal.

Futing (fōō′dĭng′), town (pop. 12,645), ⊙ Futing co. (pop. 209,185), NW Fukien prov., China, on Chekiang line, 33 mi. NNE of Siapu, on Nankwan Bay (inlet of E.China Sea); center of sweet-potato and sugar-cane production; wheat, rice.

Futog (fōō′tôk), Hung. *Futak* (fōō′tŏk), village (pop. 5,356), Vojvodina, N Serbia, Yugoslavia, on the Danube and 6 mi. W of Novi Sad, in the Backa. Consists of larger old Futog, Serbo-Croatian *Stari Futog*, Hung. *Ófutak* (E; largely Serbian pop.) and new Futog (W; Ger. pop.). Serbo-Croatian *Novi Futog*, Hung. *Újfutak*.

Futrono (fōōtrō′nō), village (1930 pop. 287), Valdivia prov., S central Chile, on N bank of L. Ranco, in Chilean lake dist., 50 mi. SE of Valdivia; resort.

Futsing or **Fu-ch'ing** (both: fōō′chĭng′), Fukienese *Hokkiang* (hōk′chyäng′), town (pop. 24,690), ⊙ Futsing co. (pop. 331,380), E Fukien prov., China, 25 mi. SSE of Foochow, on Futsing (or Haitan) Bay of Formosa Strait; rice, wheat, peanuts, beans.

Futsukaichi (fōōtsōōkī′chē), town (pop. 10,132), Fukuoka prefecture, N Kyushu, Japan, 9 mi. SE of Fukuoka; agr. center (rice, wheat, barley).

Futtsu (fōōt′tsōō), town (pop. 7,280), Chiba prefecture, central Honshu, Japan, on W Chiba Peninsula, on Tokyo Bay, 8 mi. SW of Kisarazu; agr. (rice, fruit), fishing.

Futuna (fōōtōō′nä), island (pop. 304), New Hebrides, SW Pacific, 45 mi. E of Tanna; c.3 mi. long; copra. Also called Erronan.

Futuna, volcanic island (pop. 2,005), Hoorn Isls., WALLIS AND FUTUNA ISLANDS protectorate, SW Pacific, 120 mi. SW of Wallis Isls.; 8 mi. long, 5 mi. wide; rises to 2,500 ft. Only inhabited isl. of group. Coconuts, breadfruit, timber. Polynesian natives.

Futun River (fōō′tōōn′), Chinese *Futun Ki* or *Fu-t'un Chi*, W headstream of Min R., in Fukien prov., China, rises in Bohea Hills on Kiangsi line, flows 100 mi. SE, past Shaowu (for which it is sometimes named Shaowu R.) and Shunchang, to Min R. above Nanping.

Fuur, Fur, or **Furland** (fōōr′lăn), island (□ 8.6; pop. 1,427) in Lim Fjord, N Jutland, Denmark, 5 mi. E of Mors isl., 1 mi. N of Salling peninsula; highest point c.250 ft. Agr.; small fishing harbor on SW coast.

Fuveau (füvō′), village (pop. 1,504), Bouches-du-Rhône dept., SE France, near the Arc, 8 mi. SE of Aix-en-Provence, in lignite-mining region.

Fuwa or **Fuwah** (fōō′wŭ), village, Quaiti state, Eastern Aden Protectorate, on Mukalla Bay of Gulf of Aden, 7 mi. SW of Mukalla; airfield.

Fuwa or **Fuwah** (fōō′wŭ), town (pop. 18,975; with suburbs, 21,352), Gharbiya prov., Lower Egypt, on Rosetta branch of the Nile and 12 mi. NNE of Damanhur; cotton ginning, wool spinning, rug weaving; cotton, rice, cereals, fruits.

Fuwei, Formosa: see HUWEI.

Fuyang (fōō′yäng′), town (pop. 6,032), ⊙ Fuyang co. (pop. 178,208), N Chekiang prov., China, 20 mi. SW of Hangchow and on Tsientang R.; papermaking, brick and tile mfg.; rice, wheat, fruit, cotton.

Fuyi, China: see LINTSEH.

Fuyo, Korea: see PUYO.

Fuyü (fōō′yü′). **1** Town, ⊙ Fuyü co. (pop. 59,518), W Heilungkiang prov., Manchuria, 40 mi. NE of Tsitsihar; soybeans, wheat, corn, millet, kaoliang. **2** Town, ⊙ Fuyü co. (pop. 446,202), NW Kirin prov., Manchuria, 90 mi. NNW of Changchun, and on right bank of Sungari R., above Nonni R. mouth; flour-milling center; woolen-cloth weaving, lumber milling. Prior to the railroad era (c.1900), the town was a leading Manchurian trade center on the border of Inner Mongolia; called Petuna, Chinese *Hsincheng*, until 1914.

Fuyüan (fōō'yüän'). **1** Town, Sinkiang prov., China: see JIMASA. **2** Town, ⊙ Fuyüan co. (pop. 20,000), northeasternmost Sungkiang prov., Manchuria, China, 35 mi. WSW of Khabarovsk, and on right bank of Amur R., at junction of Ussuri R. arm (USSR line); granite quarrying; soybeans, wheat, kaoliang, tobacco. Called Suiyüan until 1929.

Fuyün (fōō'yün'), town, ⊙ Fuyün co. (pop. 6,245), N Sinkiang prov., China, in the Altai Mts., 50 mi. SE of Sharasume, in region of upper reaches of the Black Irtysh; cattle raising; grain. Gold and tungsten mines.

Füzesabony (fü'zĕ-shŏbônyŭ), town (pop. 6,133), Heves co., N Hungary, on Eger R. and 11 mi. S of Eger; brickworks.

Füzesgyarmat (fü'zĕsh-dyŏrmŏt), town (pop. 8,829), Bekes co., SE Hungary, 30 mi. N of Bekescsaba; flour mills, brickworks; grain, sheep.

Fuzeta (fōōzā'tŭ), town (pop. 2,313), Faro dist., S Portugal, on railroad and 11 mi. ENE of Faro, on the Atlantic (S coast); winegrowing center; fisheries.

Füzfő or **Füzfögyartelep** (füz'fŭjär"tĕlĕp), Hung. *Fűzfőgyártelep*, town (pop. 1,006), Veszprem co., NW central Hungary, 6 mi. ESE of Veszprem, near Balatonfüzfő (pop. 1,010), on NE shore of L. Balaton; paper-milling center.

Fuzisawa, Japan: see FUJISAWA, Kanagawa prefecture.

Fyen, Denmark: see FYN.

Fyn (fün), Ger. *Fünen*, island (□ 1,149; pop. 338,013), 2d largest of Denmark, bet. S Jutland and Zealand; bounded by Little Belt (W) and Great Belt (E). N part is in Odense amt, S part in Svendborg amt. Largest lake, Arreskov L.; drained by Odense R. Chief cities: Odense, Svendborg, Nyborg. Mostly lowland with fertile soil; agr. (grain, sugar beets), dairy farming, cattle breeding. Sometimes spelled Fyen.

Fyne, Loch (lŏkh fīn), arm of the Firth of Clyde, S Argyll, Scotland, extends 40 mi. N and NE from Kilbrannan Sound and Sound of Bute; 1 to 5 mi. wide. Shore is picturesque and is indented by several small lochs, including Gilp and East Tarbert, and many glens. Near its head is Inveraray. At Ardrishaig the Crinan Canal connects loch with the Sound of Jura. Loch Fyne is noted for its herring fisheries; cod, haddock, ling, and whiting are also caught.

Fynnhyttan, Sweden: see DALA-FYNNHYTTAN.

Fyre Lake (fü'rŭ), Nor. *Fyresvatn*, Telemark co., S Norway, 55 mi. W of Skien; 16 mi. long, 2 mi. wide, 430 ft. deep; alt. 895 ft. Drains into the Nid. Fisheries.

Fyresdal (fü'rŭsdäl), village and canton (pop. 1,759), Telemark co., S Norway, on Fyre L. and 55 mi. W of Skien, in lake region; fishing, cattle raising. Copper mines are N.

Fyris River, Swedish *Fyrisån* (fü'rĭsôn"), E Sweden, rises W of Osthammar, flows 50 mi. in winding course generally S, past Orbyhus and Uppsala, to NE arm of L. Malar 5 mi. S of Uppsala.

Fyvie (fī'vē), town and parish (pop. 3,180), N Aberdeen, Scotland, on Ythan R. and 7 mi. NNW of Old Meldrum; agr. market. Fyvie Castle dates from 15th cent.

Fyzabad, since 1948 officially **Faizabad** (both: fī'zäbäd"), district (□ 1,710; pop. 1,319,425), E central Uttar Pradesh, India; ⊙ Fyzabad. On Ganges Plain; bounded N by the Gogra. Agr. (rice, wheat, gram, sugar cane, oilseeds, barley, corn, jowar); hand-loom cotton weaving, sugar milling. Main centers: Fyzabad, Tanda, Akbarpur, Jalalpur.

Fyzabad, since 1948 officially **Faizabad**, city (pop., including E suburb of AJODHYA and cantonment, 57,632), ⊙ Fyzabad dist., E central Uttar Pradesh, India, on right bank of the Gogra and 75 mi. E of Lucknow; rail and road junction; sugar processing, oilseed milling; trades in grains, oilseeds, sugar cane. Veterinary col. The mausoleums of Shuja-ud-daula (died 1775), a nawab of Oudh, and of his widow (died 1816) are notable. There is a late-18th-cent. fort built over river. In Guptar Park are mus. (built 1871) and library. Was ⊙ Oudh kingdom, 1724–75, until ⊙ was moved to Lucknow. Hydroelectric plant 10 mi. W, near village of Sohwal.

Fyzabad (fī'zŭbăd), village (pop. 2,649), SW Trinidad, B.W.I., 8 mi. SSW of San Fernando; oil wells. Formerly an East Indian settlement.

G

Gaarden, Germany: see KIEL.

Gaasbeek (gäs'bāk), agr. village (pop. 359), Brabant prov., central Belgium, 9 mi. WSW of Brussels. Has 13th-cent. church. Formerly spelled Gaesbeek.

Gaastra (gă'strŭ), city (pop. 575), Iron co., SW Upper Peninsula, Mich., 2 mi. SE of Iron River city.

Gaaton or **Ga'aton** (both: gä-ätōn'), agr. settlement, Upper Galilee, NW Israel, near Mediterranean, 13 mi. NNW of Haifa, just S of Nahariya. Modern village founded 1948 on site of biblical locality of same name.

Gabarret (gäbärā'), village (pop. 960), Landes dept., SW France, 26 mi. ENE of Mont-de-Marsan; distilling.

Gabarus Bay (găbŭrōōs'), inlet (8 mi. long, 5 mi. wide at entrance), E N.S., on SE coast of Cape Breton Isl., SW of Louisburg; 45°50'N 60°6'W.

Gabas (gäbäs'), village, Basses-Pyrénées dept., SW France, in Ossau valley at the foot of Pic du Midi d'Ossau, 22 mi. SSE of Oloron-Sainte-Marie; alt. 3,346 ft.; spa and winter-sports station. Cable car to Artouste L. (alt. 6,444 ft.) near Sp. border. Hydroelectric plant near by.

Gabbro Lake, Minn.: see BALD EAGLE LAKE.

Gabela (găbĕ'lä), town (pop. 4,996), Benguela prov., W Angola, 35 mi. ESE of Pôrto Amboim (linked by rail); coffee-growing center in foothills of central plateau. Also ships cotton, palm oil, wheat, corn. Pottery mfg., woodworking. Govt. technical school.

Gabela (gä'bĕlä), village, W Herzegovina, Yugoslavia, on Neretva R., on railroad and 2 mi. ENE of Metkovic, on Dalmatia border.

Gaberones (găbĕrō'nĕs), town, ⊙ Gaberones dist. (pop. 12,312), SE Bechuanaland Protectorate, 90 mi. NNE of Mafeking, on railroad; livestock. Hq. of Batlokwa tribe. Airfield; hosp. Dist. includes Bamalete (1909) and Batlokwa (1933) reserves.

Gabès (gä'bĕs, Fr. gäbĕs'), anc. *Tacapae*, town (pop. 22,512), ⊙ Gabès dist. (□ 1,744; pop. 92,261), SE Tunisia, fishing port on the Gulf of Gabès, 200 mi. S of Tunis; railroad terminus. Airfield. Center of a coastal oasis (8 mi. long, 5 mi. wide). Trade in dates, olives, wine, hides, and wool. Tunny and sponge fisheries. Handicraft textile mfg.; plaster works. On site of a Phoenician settlement. In Second World War captured from the Germans by the Allies in March, 1943, after successful flanking of Mareth Line.

Gabès, Gulf of, anc. *Syrtis Minor*, inlet of the central Mediterranean, in E and SE Tunisia, bounded by the Kerkennah isls. (NE) and by Djerba (SE); 60 mi. long, 60 mi. wide. On its shores are Sfax (N) and Gabès (W). Sponge and tunny fisheries.

Gabia la Grande (gä'vyä lä grän'dä), outer SW suburb (pop. 3,831) of Granada, S Spain; agr. trade center (cereals, sugar beets, hemp, tobacco). Olive pressing, flour- and sawmilling. Gypsum and limestone quarries. Granada airport near by.

Gabian (gäbyä'), village (pop. 893), Hérault dept., S France, 12 mi. N of Béziers; oil wells. Winegrowing.

Gabii (gā'bēī), anc. town of Latium, 12 mi. E of Rome on road to Praeneste (Palestrina). Legend says that Romulus was raised here. One of the most important of the Latin cities, it supposedly resisted a siege by Lucius Tarquinius Superbus, but it was early overshadowed by Rome and, though it had lost all importance even in the days of the republic, it was still a bishopric in 9th cent. Only a temple (3d cent. B.C.) remains on the site, now the village of Castiglione.

Gabilan Range (gă'bĭlăn), one of the Coast Ranges, W Calif., extends c.35 mi. SE from Pajaro R. at S end of Santa Cruz Mts. to juncture with Diablo Range E of Soledad; rises to 3,453 ft. in S. Gabilan Peak (3,169 ft.) is included in Frémont Peak State Park (c.300 acres) S of San Juan Bautista.

Gabin (gō'bēn), Pol. *Gąbin*, Rus. *Gombin* (gôm'bēn), town (pop. 3,108), Warszawa prov., central Poland, 55 mi. WNW of Warsaw; flour milling, tanning, brick mfg., peat cutting.

Gabino Mendoza, Bolivia: see NOVIEMBRE, 27 DE.

Gabiro (găbē'rō), village, NE Ruanda-Urundi, in Ruanda, 35 mi. NE of Kigali; administrative center of Kagera Natl. Park.

Gable Island (□ 7.6), Tierra del Fuego natl. territory, Argentina, in Beagle Channel bet. the main isl. of Tierra del Fuego and Navarino Isl., 32 mi. E of Ushuaia; 5 mi. long.

Gablenz (gä'blĕnts), E industrial suburb of Chemnitz, Saxony, E central Germany.

Gablonz, Czechoslovakia: see JABLONEC NAD NISOU.

Gabo Island, uninhabited granite island in Tasman Sea, just off SE coast of Victoria, Australia, near Cape Howe; 1½ mi. long, ½ mi. wide; generally barren; lighthouse.

Gabon (găbō') or **Gabun** (gŭbōōn'), overseas territory (□ 103,089; 1950 pop. 408,800), W Fr. Equatorial Africa; ⊙ Libreville. Bordered SW and W by the Gulf of Guinea, NW by Spanish Guinea (Río Muni), N by Fr. Cameroons; adjoined E and S by Middle Congo territory. Region consists of Gabon estuary and the delta and basin of Ogooué R. Astride the equator; has tropical climate, with up to 100 in. of rainfall. From the dense equatorial forest which covers most of the area come mahogany, ebony, Gabon walnut, and *okume* wood—Gabon's chief exports. Some gold mining in S. Fishing; also shark and whale processing. European cacao and rubber plantations are mainly in N. Wild rubber, kapok, waxes, and kola nuts are gathered and African staples (manioc, sweet potatoes, corn, plantains) are raised. Save for the lower Ogooué R., Gabon's streams are navigable only intermittently. Principal centers: Libreville, Port-Gentil, Franceville. Gabon coast was discovered by Portuguese in 15th cent. and its ports soon became noted as centers of slave trade. In 1839–42, French obtained rights in Gabon estuary; Cape Lopez was ceded to France 1862. Gabon was practically abandoned after Franco-Prussian War (1870). Du Chaillu and de Brazza explored the area. In 1888–1908 it was united with Middle Congo as the French Congo. Made separate colony in 1910 and a territory in 1946 (when some frontier adjustments were carried out in Franceville area), with representation in Fr. parliament. Sometimes Gaboon.

Gabon River or **Gabon Estuary**, great estuary, tributary to Gulf of Guinea in W Gabon, Fr. Equatorial Africa, c.100 mi. NE of Port-Gentil and just N of the equator; 40 mi. long, 9 mi. wide (at its mouth). Fed by several minor streams rising in Crystal Mts. Libreville and Owendo are on NW shore. Discovered by Portuguese in 15th cent., it was long considered the finest harbor of W African coast. Also spelled Gabun.

Gaboury (găbōōrē'), village, W Que., 16 mi. ESE of Haileybury; gold mining.

Gabredarre (găbrĕdä'rä), village (pop. 200), Harar prov., SE Ethiopia, in the Ogaden, on Fafan R., on road, and 110 mi. SE of Dagahbur. Has mosque. Occupied in Italo-Ethiopian War by Italians (1935), and in Second World War by British, who made it their hq. in the Ogaden.

Gabriel (găbrĕĕl'), town (pop. 1,063), Havana prov., W Cuba, 24 mi. SSW of Havana; tobacco, fruit, vegetables. Also El Gabriel.

Gabriel, Mount, hill (1,339 ft.), SW Co. Cork, Ireland, near Roaringwater Bay, just N of Schull.

Gabriel Channel, narrow strait in central Tierra del Fuego, Chile, connecting Admiralty Sound and Strait of Magellan, bet. Dawson Isl. and SW coast of main isl. of Tierra del Fuego; 30 mi. long. Famous for its heavy squalls.

Gabriels (gā'brēŭlz), resort village, Franklin co., NE N.Y., in the Adirondacks, 10 mi. N of Saranac Lake village. Several lakes are near by.

Gabriola Island (găbrēō'lŭ) (□ 20), Gulf Isls., SW B.C., in Strait of Georgia just off Vancouver Isl., 3 mi. E of Nanaimo; 9 mi. long, 2 mi. wide; mixed farming. Village of Gabriola is at W tip.

Gabro Lake, Minn.: see BALD EAGLE LAKE.

Gabrovo (gä'brôvô), city (pop. 21,268), Gorna Oryakhovitsa dist., N central Bulgaria, on Yantra R. and 50 mi. SE of Pleven, on N slope of central Balkan Mts.; rail terminus; linked with Kazanlik (S) through Shipka Pass; major mfg. center; woolen, cotton, and linen textiles, knitwear, metalware, gunpowder, furniture, leather goods, shoes; flour and sawmilling, woodworking. Fruitgrowing near by. Has technical high school, old monastery. Center of Bulg. culture under Turkish rule; developed as important industrial town following its liberation (1877).

Gabú, Port. Guinea: see NOVA LAMEGO.

Gabun, Fr. Equatorial Africa: see GABON.

Gacé (gäsā'), village (pop. 1,371), Orne dept., NW France, on the Touques and 15 mi. ENE of Argentan; road junction; textile waste processing, distilling, dairying.

Gachalá (gächälä'), town (pop. 1,134), Cundinamarca dept., central Colombia, in Cordillera Oriental, 40 mi. E of Bogotá; alt. 5,768 ft.; coffee, wheat, potatoes, livestock. Sulphur deposits near by.

Gachetá (gächātä'), town (pop. 1,065), Cundinamarca dept., central Colombia, in Cordillera Oriental, 37 mi. ENE of Bogotá; alt. 5,892 ft.; coffee, wheat, stock.

Gach Saran (gäch' särän'), oil town, Sixth Prov., in Khuzistan, SW Iran, 150 mi. E of Abadan (linked by pipeline) and 40 mi. ESE of Behbehan; oil field opened 1941.

Gacilly, La (lä gäsēyē'), village (pop. 605), Morbihan dept., W France, 8 mi. NNW of Redon. Menhirs near by.

Gacka River (gäts'kä), W Croatia, Yugoslavia, rises 8 mi. SE of Otocac, flows c.30 mi. NW, past Otocac, disappearing underground into the Karst 7 mi. WNW of Otocac.

Gackle, village (pop. 604), Logan co., S N.Dak., 30 mi. SW of Jamestown.

Gacko or **Gatsko** (both: gäts'kô), village (pop. 1,393), E Herzegovina, Yugoslavia, 38 mi. ESE of Mostar, near Montenegro border; road junction; local trade center.

Gadag (gŭd'ŭg), city (pop., including N industrial area of Betigeri, 56,283), Dharwar dist., S Bombay, India, 33 mi. E of Hubli; rail and road junction; trades in cotton and silk fabrics, millet, wheat;

cotton milling, hand-loom weaving, oilseed pressing, tanning, mfg. of chemical disinfectants, biris, metal goods. Other spellings of Betigeri: Bettigeri, Betgeri, Bettegeri.

Gadaladeniya (gŭdŭlŭdä'nĭyŭ), village (pop., including near-by villages, 1,077), Central Prov., Ceylon, on Kandy Plateau, 6 mi. WSW of Kandy. Noted 14th-cent. Buddhist vihara (monastery). Anc. Buddhist temple at Lankatilaka, 1.5 mi. SSE, regarded as most beautiful example of Kandy-type temples.

Gadame or **Gidami** (both: gŭdä'mē), Ital. *Ghidami*, village, Wallaga prov., W central Ethiopia, near source of Dabus R., 34 mi. NW of Saio; 9°N 34°38'E.

Gadames, Fezzan: see GHADAMES.

Gadara (gă'dŭrŭ), anc. city of Palestine, a city of the Decapolis. Vespasian destroyed it, and its ruins are probably those at a site in Jordan c.5 mi. SE of Sea of Galilee.

Gadarwara (gä'dŭrvärŭ), town (pop. 10,146), Hoshangabad dist., NW Madhya Pradesh, India, 70 mi. E of Hoshangabad; flour and dal milling; pottery. Coal deposits 12 mi. S, near Mohpani. Rail station (just S) spelled Gadarvada.

Gaddede (yĕ'dŭdŭ), Swedish *Gäddede*, village (pop. 473), Jamtland co., NW Sweden, in mtn. region, on upper Angerman R. and 65 mi. W of Lycksele; customs point on Norwegian border; tourist and fishing resort.

Gadderbaum (gä'dŭrboum), village (pop. 8,918), in former Prussian prov. of Westphalia, NW Germany, after 1945 in North Rhine-Westphalia, in Teutoburg Forest, just SW of Bielefeld.

Gadebusch (gä'dŭbōōsh), town (pop. 5,135), Mecklenburg, N Germany, 13 mi. WNW of Schwerin; agr. market (grain, potatoes, stock); agr.-implement mfg. Has 13th–15th-cent. church, 16th-cent. former grand-ducal castle, 17th-cent. town hall. First mentioned in 12th cent. Scene (Dec., 1712) of Swedish victory over Danes and Saxonians.

Gaden, Tibet: see GANDEN.

Gadenstedt (gä'dŭn-shtĕt), village (pop. 3,317), in former Prussian prov. of Hanover, NW Germany, after 1945 in Lower Saxony, 5 mi. S of Peine; limonite mines, oil wells.

Gade River, Hertford, England, rises 4 mi. NNE of Great Berkhampstead, flows 16 mi. SE and S, past Hemel Hempstead, to Colne R. at Rickmansworth.

Gades, Spain: see CÁDIZ, city.

Gadhada (gŭd'ŭdŭ), town (pop. 6,785), E Saurashtra, India, 39 mi. WNW of Bhaunagar; rail spur terminus; markets millet, wheat, cotton, oilseeds; handicraft cloth weaving, wood carving. Center of Hindu reform sect (founded 1804). Sometimes called Gadhada Swaminarayan.

Gad-Hinglaj (gŭd'hĭng'glŭj), town (pop. 9,017), Kolhapur dist., S Bombay, India, 34 mi. SSE of Kolhapur; market center for rice, chili, tobacco; oilseed milling. Sometimes written Gadhinglaj.

Gadilam River (gŭdĭlŭm'), South Arcot dist., SE Madras, India, rises E of Kalrayan Hills, flows SE and E through fertile agr. valley, past Panruti, to Bay of Bengal S of Cuddalore; 50 mi. long. In middle course, linked with Ponnaiyar R. (N).

Gadlys (găd'lĭs), town (pop. 8,165) in Aberdare urban dist., NE Glamorgan, Wales, on Cynon R.; coal mining.

Gadoni (gädô'nē), village (pop. 1,239), Nuoro prov., central Sardinia, 29 mi. SSW of Nuoro. Chalcopyrite mines 3 mi. S, near Funtana Raminosa.

Gádor (gä'dhōr), town (pop. 1,757), Almería prov., S Spain, 8 mi. N of Almería; ships oranges, grapes, esparto. Rich lead and sulphur deposits, mined since Phoenician times.

Gádor, Sierra de (syĕ'rä dhā), range in Almería prov., S Spain, NE of Berja; silver-bearing lead, and sulphur and zinc mines.

Gadoros (gä'dôrôsh), Hung. *Gádoros*, town (pop. 4,824), Bekes co., SE Hungary, 16 mi. E of Szentes; flour mills; wheat, tobacco, hogs.

Gadres, Palestine: see GAZA.

Gadrut (gŭdrōōt'), village (1926 pop. 1,929), S Nagorno-Karabakh Autonomous oblast, Azerbaijan SSR, 25 mi. SSE of Stepanakert; sericulture.

Gadsby, village (pop. 120), S central Alta., 15 mi. E of Stettler; coal mining, dairying, wheat growing.

Gadsden (gădz'dŭn), county (□ 508; pop. 36,457), NW Fla.; ⊙ Quincy. Bounded N by Ga., E and S by Ochlockonee R. and L. Talquin, W by Apalachicola R. Rolling agr. area (corn, peanuts, tobacco, vegetables; dairy products; poultry, hogs). Mfg. (food products, lumber, naval stores, cigars, brick). Large deposits of fuller's earth (mined near Quincy); also clay, sand, and gravel pits. Formed 1823.

Gadsden. 1 City (pop. 55,725), ⊙ Etowah co., NE Ala., on Coosa R. and c.60 mi. NE of Birmingham. Industrial center in iron, coal, manganese, and limestone area; mfg. of rubber tires and tubes, cotton hosiery, fabrics, and yarn, tractors, wire mesh, ranges and heaters; metalworking (pig iron, sheet steel, reinforcing bars), dairying, lumber milling. Founded c.1845, inc. 1871. Grew with exploitation of mineral resources in vicinity. Alabama City was annexed 1932. Noccalula Falls are just NW. **2** Town (pop. 255), Crockett co., W Tenn., 5 mi. SW of Humboldt.

Gadshill (gădz'hĭl), agr. village, N Kent, England, 3 mi. NW of Rochester. The low hill here is noted as scene of Falstaff's robberies in Shakespeare's *Henry IV*. "Gadshill Place" was home of Charles Dickens from 1856 until his death in 1870.

Gadurra (gŭdhōō'rŭ), airport of Rhodes, Greece, just NW of Lindos, on E coast; 36°8'N 28°4'E.

Gadwal (gŭdväl'), town (pop. 14,716), Raichur dist., S Hyderabad state, India, near Kistna R., 30 mi. E of Raichur; millet, sugar cane; rice and oilseed milling, cotton ginning; noted hand-woven silk textiles. Cattle market.

Gadyach (gŭdyäch'), city (1926 pop. 10,215), N Poltava oblast, Ukrainian SSR, on Psel R. and 60 mi. NNW of Poltava; rail terminus; metalworking, light mfg., flour milling, tanning.

Gadzema (gädzĕ'mä), township (pop. 663), Salisbury prov., central Southern Rhodesia, in Mashonaland, on railroad and 7 mi. N of Hartley; alt. 3,804 ft. Gold-mining center.

Gadzhi-Gasan or **Khadzhi-Gasan** (gŭjē"-gŭsän', khŭ–), town (1939 pop. over 500) in Kirov dist. of Greater Baku, Azerbaijan SSR, 4 mi. NW of Baku; oil wells (developed 1939).

Gadzin Han or **Gadzhin Khan** (both: gä'jĭn khän), Serbo-Croatian *Gadžin Han*, village, S Serbia, Yugoslavia, 10 mi. SE of Nis.

Gaekwar's Dominions, India: see BARODA, former princely state.

Gaesbeek, Belgium: see GAASBEEK.

Gaesti (gŭyĕsht'), Rum. *Găeşti*, town (1948 pop. 7,726), Arges prov., S central Rumania, in Walachia, on railroad and 16 mi. SSW of Targoviste; flour milling, furniture mfg., tobacco processing; active trade. Extensive tobacco plantations.

Gaeta (gäă'tä), town (pop. 4,967), Latina prov., Latium, S central Italy, port on promontory on N shore of Gulf of Gaeta, 45 mi. NW of Naples. Bathing resort; fishing and glass-mfg. center. Archbishopric. The coast bet. Gaeta and Formia was a favorite resort of anc. Romans. A prosperous duchy from 9th to 12th cent., when it fell to Normans and later to Kingdom of Naples. Its port and citadel were strongly fortified by the Bourbons, whose defeat here, after a long siege (1860–61) by Ital. troops, marked the end of the Kingdom of the Two Sicilies. The town, including its cathedral and other medieval bldgs., suffered heavy damage from air and naval bombing (1943–44) in Second World War.

Gaeta, Gulf of, inlet of Tyrrhenian Sea, S central Italy, bet. Monte Circeo (NW) and Cape Miseno (SE); 65 mi. long, 20 mi. wide. Receives Volturno and Liri (here called Garigliano) rivers. Chief ports: Gaeta, Formia, Terracina.

Gafanha da Boa Hora (gŭfä'nyŭ dŭ bō'ŭ ô'rŭ), agr. village (pop. 1,585), Aveiro dist., N central Portugal, 9 mi. SW of Aveiro, in reclaimed coastal region.

Gafanha da Encarnação (ĕng-kärnäsä'ō), agr. village (pop. 2,133), Aveiro dist., N central Portugal, 2 mi. WSW of Aveiro; in coastal region reclaimed from Aveiro lagoon; boatbuilding.

Ga'fariya, El, or **Al-Ja'fariyah** (both: ĕl găfärē'yŭ, jä–), village (pop. 5,863), Gharbiya prov., Lower Egypt, on the Bahr Shibin and 9 mi. SE of Tanta; cotton.

Gaferut (gä'fĕrōōt), coral island, Yap dist., W Caroline Isls., W Pacific, 60 mi. NE of Faraulep; 9°14'N 145°23'E; ¾ mi. long, ½ mi. wide; mangrove trees, phosphate deposits.

Gáfete (gä'fĭtĭ), village (pop. 1,629), Portalegre dist., central Portugal, 16 mi. NW of Portalegre; grain, corn, olives, cork; sheep and goat raising.

Gaffney, city (pop. 8,123), ⊙ Cherokee co., N S.C., 18 mi. NE of Spartanburg, near N.C. line; farm trade, mfg., shipping center; textiles, clothing, foundry and machine-shop products, mill equipment, food products, gloves, bricks; limestone quarry. Seat of Limestone Col. Inc. 1875.

Gaff Topsail, mountain (1,477 ft.), W central N.F., 20 mi. E of NE end of Grand L., 49°9'N 56°38'W.

Gafle, Sweden: see GAVLE.

Gaflenz (gä'flĕnts), village (pop. 1,515), SE Upper Austria, 17 mi. SE of Steyr; foundry.

Gafour (găfōōr'), village, Teboursouk dist., N central Tunisia, on Siliana R. and 10 mi. SSE of Teboursouk; railroad yards; silos.

Gafsa (găf'sŭ, găfsä'), anc. *Capsa*, town (pop. 11,320), ⊙ Gafsa dist. (□ 4,290; pop. 150,211), S central Tunisia, on Sfax-Tozeur mining railroad and 180 mi. SSW of Tunis; 34°25'N 8°47'E. Largest town in Tunisia's phosphate-mining area. Mines are at M'Dilla (10 mi. S), Metlaoui (22 mi. WSW), Moularès (28 mi. W), and Redeyef (35 mi. W). Town lies in fertile oasis growing dates, olives, apricots, figs, citrus fruit, and grapes. Native handicraft (woolen blankets, rugs). Airfield. Thermal springs. There is a large mosque and remains of Roman thermae. Important settlement since Numidian times. Prehistoric discoveries made in area have given town's name to a paleolithic culture (Capsian) of North Africa. In Second World War, Gafsa area was scene of some of 1st engagements bet. Americans and Germans in Tunisian campaign (Feb., 1943).

Gage, county (□ 858; pop. 28,052), SE Nebr.; ⊙ Beatrice. Agr. region drained by Big Blue R.; bounded S by Kansas. Grain, livestock, dairy and poultry produce. Formed 1857.

Gage, city (pop. 648), Ellis co., NW Okla., 22 mi. SW of Woodward, and on Wolf Creek, in grain, livestock, and poultry area.

Gagetown, village (pop. estimate c.300), ⊙ Queens co., S N.B., on St. John R. and 25 mi. ESE of Fredericton, in apple-growing and farming region.

Gagetown, village (pop. 401), Tuscola co., E Mich., 32 mi. ENE of Bay City.

Gaggenau (gä'gŭnou), town (pop. 6,256), S Baden, Germany, on W slope of Black Forest, on the Murg and 6 mi. SE of Rastatt; mfg. of vehicles (cars, trucks, buses, bicycles), Diesel motors, machinery, gas stoves; food processing, paper milling; glassworks. Second World War destruction c.50%.

Gagino (gä'gēnŭ), village (1948 pop. over 2,000), SE Gorki oblast, Russian SFSR, on Pyana R. and 25 mi. NE of Lukoyanov; hemp processing.

Gagliano Castelferrato (gälyä'nô kästĕl"fĕr-rä'tô), village (pop. 4,374), Enna prov., E central Sicily, 18 mi. NE of Enna.

Gagliano del Capo (dĕl kä'pô), village (pop. 3,003), Lecce prov., Apulia, S Italy, 6 mi. S of Tricase.

Gagnoa (gänyō'ä), town (pop. c.2,150), S Ivory Coast, Fr. West Africa, 145 mi. WNW of Abidjan; agr. center (coffee, cacao, tobacco, bananas, manioc, yams). Experiment (cacao) and climatological stations. R.C. and Protestant missions. Sawmill near by.

Gagny (gänyē'), town (pop. 7,219), Seine-et-Oise dept., N central France, outer ENE suburb of Paris, 8 mi. from Notre Dame Cathedral; plaster works; mfg. of electric carillons.

Gago Coutinho (gä'gōō kōtēn'yōō), town (pop. 1,411), Bié prov., SE Angola, near Northern Rhodesia border, on road and 190 mi. SE of Vila Luso.

Gagraun (gä'groun), noted Rajput fort, SE Rajasthan, India, on Kali Sindh R., at mouth of tributary, and 2 mi. N of Brijnagar. Very strongly fortified; withstood siege by Ala-ud-din in 1300; surrendered 1562 to Akbar.

Gagry (gä'grē), city (1926 pop. 3,656, 1940 estimate 12,000), NW Abkhaz Autonomous SSR, Georgian SSR, port on Black Sea, on coastal railroad and 45 mi. NW of Sukhumi; subtropical health resort; tobacco, citrus fruit; distilling, sawmilling, metalworking. Coast guard station. A Gr. colony in antiquity; passed (1810) from Turkey to Russia.

Gagry Range, a 25-mi. spur of the W Greater Caucasus, extends to Black Sea just N of Gagry.

Gahanna (gŭhă'nŭ), village (pop. 596), Franklin co., central Ohio, 7 mi. NE of Columbus.

Gahmar (gŭ'hŭmŭr), town (pop. 11,593), Ghazipur dist., E Uttar Pradesh, India, on the Ganges and 15 mi. ESE of Ghazipur; rice, gram, barley, oilseeds, sugar cane. Also spelled Ghahmar.

Gaiarine (gäyärē'nē), village (pop. 1,154), Treviso prov., Veneto, N Italy, 7 mi. N of Oderzo; alcohol distillery.

Gaiba, Lake (gī'bä), on Bolivia-Brazil border, 80 mi. N of Puerto Suárez (Bolivia); 8 mi. long, 4 mi. wide. Receives Pando R. or Canal Pedro II and another affluent (outlets of L. UBERABA). Connected with Paraguay R. by NE outlet. Small Bolivian lake port of La Gaiba or Puerto Quijarro (pop. c.300) is on SW shore.

Gaibanda (gībän'dŭ), town (pop. 11,128), Rangpur dist., N East Bengal, E Pakistan, near main course of the Brahmaputra, 34 mi. SE of Rangpur; rice, oilseed, and flour milling, soap mfg.; trades in rice, jute, tobacco, oilseeds, sugar cane. Also spelled Gaibandha.

Gaidaro (gī'dhŭrô), northernmost island of the Dodecanese, Greece; 37°28'N 26°58'E.

Gaidaros, Greece: see PATROKLOU.

Gaïdouronesi, Greece: see PATROKLOU.

Gaiduk or **Gayduk** (gīdōōk'), town (1939 pop. over 2,000), W Krasnodar Territory, Russian SFSR, in NW outlier of the Greater Caucasus, on railroad and 5 mi. NW of Novorossisk; cement making.

Gaigetsu, Korea: see AEWOL.

Gaighata (gīgä'tŭ), village, 24-Parganas dist., E West Bengal, India, on upper Jamuna (Ichamati) R. and 35 mi. NE of Calcutta; rice, jute, linseed, tobacco. Until 1947, in Jessore dist. of Br. Bengal prov.

Gaika, Southern Rhodesia: see CHICAGO-GAIKA.

Gaikwar's Dominions, India: see BARODA, former princely state.

Gail, town (pop. c.200), ⊙ Borden co., NW Texas, just below Cap Rock escarpment of Llano Estacado, 30 mi. W of Snyder, near Colorado R.; trading center for cattle-ranching area.

Gaildorf (gīl'dôrf), town (pop. 2,893), N Württemberg, Germany, after 1945 in Württemberg-Baden, on the Kocher and 8 mi. S of Schwäbisch Hall; cattle.

Gailingen (gī'lĭng-ŭn), village (pop. 1,487), S Baden, Germany, on the Rhine (Swiss border; bridge) and 5 mi. E of Schaffhausen; fruit.

Gailitz River (gī'lĭts), N Italy and S Austria, rises in Julian Alps S of Tarvisio, flows c.20 mi. N bet. Carnic Alps (W) and Karawanken (E) to Gail R. near Arnoldstein, Carinthia.

Gaillac (gäyäk'), town (pop. 6,253), Tarn dept., S France, on the Tarn and 13 mi. W of Albi; commercial and road center known for its sparkling wines; flour milling, vegetable shipping, macaroni mfg. Hydroelectric plants near by.

Gaillard (gäyär'), town (pop. 2,900), Haute-Savoie dept., SE France, on the Arve, just SW of Annemasse, and 3 mi. ESE of Geneva on Swiss border; precision instruments, vermouth mfg.

Gaillard, Lake (gĭl"yärd', gĭlärd'), S Conn., reservoir (2.5 mi. long) in North Branford town; dam at S end; drained by Branford R.

Gaillard Cut (găl'yärd"), formerly **Culebra Cut** (kŭlā'brŭ, kū–, –lĕb'–), Panama Canal Zone, now occupied by S section of the Panama Canal, it was dug through the low continental divide to link Chagres R. valley (N) with that of the Rio Grande (SE). It is approximately 8 mi. long, 300 ft. wide at bottom, and 45 ft. deep, joining artificial lakes Gatun and Miraflores (at Pedro Miguel locks). Has to be constantly dredged. Renamed 1913 for the engineer who made this difficult section of the canal.

Gaillon (gäyõ'), town (pop. 1,947), Eure dept., NW France, near left bank of the Seine, 7 mi. SSW of Les Andelys; agr. market; starch mfg. Former residence of archbishops of Rouen.

Gail River (gīl), S Austria, rises in Carnic Alps, flows 75 mi. E to Drau R. E of Villach. Narrow upper valley is called the Lesachtal; middle stretch is a swampy region; grain grown in broad lower valley.

Gailtal Alps (gĭl'täl), S Austria, extend 55 mi. E-W bet. Carnic Alps (S) and Drau R. (N). Highest peak, the Sandspitze (9,391 ft.), is in its W group, the Lienz Dolomites.

Gaimán (gīmän'), town (pop. estimate 2,000), ⊙ Gaimán dept., E Chubut natl. territory, Argentina, on railroad, on Chubut R. (irrigation) and 20 mi. W of Rawson; agr. (alfalfa, potatoes, peas, fruit, sheep, cattle, poultry), lumbering, dairying.

Gaina, Rumania: see HALMAGIU.

Gaines, county (□ 1,479; pop. 8,909), NW Texas; ⊙ Seminole. Bounded W by N.Mex.; on the Llano Estacado; alt. c.3,000 ft. Cattle ranching; natural-gas fields; agr. (grain sorghums, some truck, cotton, corn, hay, poultry, dairy products); hogs, mules, goats, sheep. Salt, potash deposits. Formed 1876.

Gaines, village (pop. 352), Genesee co., SE central Mich., 14 mi. SW of Flint.

Gaines, Fort, Ala.: see DAUPHIN ISLAND.

Gainesboro, town (pop. 992), ⊙ Jackson co., N central Tenn., on Cumberland R. and 65 mi. ENE of Nashville; trade point in hilly region producing oil, timber, farm products (corn, tobacco); makes work shirts. Center Hill and Dale Hollow dams near by. Cordell Hull practiced law here.

Gaines Cotton Mill, Ga.: see GAINESVILLE COTTON MILLS.

Gaines's Mill, Va.: see COLD HARBOR.

Gainesville. 1 Town (pop. 319), Sumter co., W Ala., on Tombigbee R. and 45 mi. SW of Tuscaloosa; wood products. **2** City (pop. 26,861), ⊙ Alachua co., N Fla., c.65 mi. WSW of St. Augustine; rail junction; resort; processing and shipping center, dealing in lumber, treated-wood products, boxes, naval stores, concrete blocks, tung oil, vegetables. Seat of Univ. of Florida. City founded c.1854 on site of a trading post (established 1830) and inc. 1869. Near by are Newmans L. and Paynes Prairie, a large marsh. **3** City (pop. 11,936), ⊙ Hall co., NE central Ga., near Chattahoochee R., c.50 mi. NE of Atlanta; textile mfg. and poultry-processing center; surgical gauze, tobacco and print cloth, hosiery, yarns, overalls, lumber, chairs, harness; has many hatcheries. Brenau Col. and hq. of Chattahoochee Natl. Forest here; Riverside Military Acad. near by. City severely damaged by tornado in 1936. **4** Town (pop. 309), ⊙ Ozark co., S Mo., in the Ozarks, 33 mi. WSW of West Plains; lumber products; cotton gins. **5** Village (pop. 314), Wyoming co., W N.Y., 9 mi. S of Warsaw, in potato-growing area. Belva Ann Lockwood, suffragette leader and 1st woman candidate for President, was b. near by. **6** City (pop. 11,246), ⊙ Cooke co., N Texas, c.60 mi. NNW of Dallas and on Elm Fork of Trinity R.; trade, shipping, processing center for oil, agr., dairying, timber region; oil refinery, flour and cottonseed-oil mills, railroad shops; mfg. of leather goods, brooms, fishing tackle, wood products, clothing, dairy products. Seat of a jr. col. and a state training school for delinquent girls. Holds annual Community Circus. Founded 1850 on the California Trail, inc. 1873.

Gainesville Cotton Mills, village (pop. 1,708), Hall co., N Ga., near Gainesville. Also called Gaines Cotton Mill.

Gainfarn (gīn'färn), town (pop. 2,999), E Lower Austria, 4 mi. SSW of Baden.

Gainsborough, village (pop. 307), SE Sask., near Man. and N.Dak. borders, 70 mi. E of Estevan; mixed farming.

Gainsborough, urban district (1931 pop. 18,689; 1951 census 17,509), Parts of Lindsey, NW Lincolnshire, England, on Trent R. and 14 mi. NW of Lincoln; shipbuilding (barges and coastal vessels), steel milling, mfg. of boilers, agr. machinery; agr. market. The Old Hall, supposed to have been built by John of Gaunt, was rebuilt 1480–1500. Congregational Church was built in memory of John Robinson, pastor of the Pilgrim Fathers in Holland, b. in a near-by village. Gainsborough is the St. Ogg's of George Eliot's *Mill on the Floss.* It was established by the Danish king Sweyn, who made it his capital and died here.

Gainy or **Gayny** (gīnē'), village (1948 pop. over 2,000), N central Komi-Pemyak Natl. Okrug, Molotov oblast, Russian SFSR, on Kama R. (landing) 90 mi. NNW of Kudymkar; lumber, livestock.

Gaiole in Chianti (gäyô'lĕ ēn kyän'tē), village (pop. 599), Siena prov., Tuscany, central Italy, 11 mi. NE of Siena; wine making and exporting.

Gaira (gī'rä), town (pop. 3,371), Magdalena dept., NE Colombia, minor port on Caribbean Sea, on railroad and 4 mi. S of Santa Marta; sugar cane, bananas. Marble deposits near by.

Gairdner, Lake (gârd'nŭr), shallow salt lake (□ 1,840), S South Australia, near base of Eyre Peninsula, 160 mi. N of Port Lincoln; 96 mi. long, 30 mi. wide; partly dry in summer.

Gairloch (gâr'lŏkh), town and parish (pop. 2,376), W Ross and Cromarty, Scotland, at head of the Gairloch, 30 mi. N of Kyle; fishing port and seaside resort, at edge of Flowerdale Forest. An inlet, Gairloch, extends 5 mi. inland from The Minch; up to 3½ mi. wide. At mouth of loch is Longa Isl.

Gairsay, island (pop. 5) of the Orkneys, Scotland, just off NE coast of Pomona; 1 mi. long; rises to 334 ft.

Gais (gīs), town (pop. 2,254), Appenzell Ausser Rhoden half-canton, NE Switzerland, 3 mi. NE of Appenzell, at foot of Gäbris mtn.; alt. 3,014 ft.; cotton textiles, embroideries.

Gaisberg (gīs'bĕrk), W Austria, peak (4,219 ft.) just E of Salzburg ascended by cogwheel railway; excellent view.

Gaiselberg (gī'zŭlbĕrk), village (pop. 346), NE Lower Austria, 27 mi. NNE of Vienna; oil well.

Gaiserwald (gī'zŭrvält"), town (pop. 2,173), St. Gall canton, NE Switzerland, 2 mi. NW of St. Gall; embroideries.

Gaisin or **Gaysin** (gī'sēn), city (1926 pop. 15,330), E Vinnitsa oblast, Ukrainian SSR, 50 mi. SE of Vinnitsa; sugar refining, distilling, fruit canning, flour milling.

Gaisstein, Austria: see KITZBÜHEL ALPS.

Gaithersburg (gā'thŭrzbûrg), town (pop. 1,755), Montgomery co., central Md., 20 mi. NNW of Washington, in dairying area; vegetable cannery, feed mill. Seat of an international latitude observatory supervised by U.S. Coast and Geodetic Survey. Game refuge near by.

Gaivoron or **Gayvoron** (gī'vŭrŭn), city (1948 pop. over 2,000), N Odessa oblast, Ukrainian SSR, on the Southern Bug and 50 mi. WNW of Pervomaisk; narrow-gauge rail junction; flour mill, metalworks.

Gaizin or **Gayzin'** (gī'zēn), Lettish *Gaiziņ*, highest point (1,017 ft.) of Latvia, in central Vidzeme hills, 10 mi. W of Madona.

Gakhar, W Pakistan: see GHAKKAR.

Gakona (gŭkō'nŭ), village (pop. 48), S Alaska, on Copper R. and 90 mi. NNE of Valdez, on Tok Cut-off; supply point for trappers and prospectors.

Gakona River, S central Alaska, rises in SE foothills of Alaska Range near 63°9'N 145°12'W, flows 70 mi. S to Copper R. at Gakona.

Gakuch (gä'kŏŏch), village, Punial state, Gilgit Agency, NW Kashmir, on Gilgit R. and 35 mi. NW of Gilgit.

Gala (gä'lä), village, Nyanza prov., W Kenya, on railroad and 10 mi. SSE of Butere; cotton, peanuts, sesame, corn.

Gala-Assiya (gŭlä"-ŭsē'ŭ), village, S Bukhara oblast, Uzbek SSR, on Bukhara-Vabkent road and 6 mi. NNE of Bukhara; cotton.

Galabets Pass (gäläbĕts') (alt. 5,216 ft.), W central Bulgaria, in SW Teteven Mts., 12 mi. W of Zlatitsa, on highway bet. Zlatitsa and Sofia.

Galadi or **Galladi** (gä'lädē), village (pop. 500), Harar prov., SE Ethiopia, near Ital. Somaliland border, in the Ogaden, 75 mi. E of Wardere, in arid pastoral region; water hole and market.

Galahad, village (pop. 166), SE Alta., 50 mi. WSW of Wainwright; grain; farming, dairying.

Galaico, Macizo, Spain: see GALICIAN MOUNTAINS.

Galan (gälä'), village (pop. 350), Hautes-Pyrénées dept., SW France, on Lannemezan Plateau, 16 mi. E of Tarbes; winegrowing, sheep raising.

Galán, Cerro (sĕ'rō gälän'), peak (15,400 ft.) in the Andes, W Jujuy prov., Argentina, 25 mi. SW of Rinconada; rich tin deposits.

Galana River, Kenya: see ATHI RIVER.

Galana Sagan (gä'länä sägän') or **Sagan River,** S Ethiopia, rises E of L. CHAMO, flows 150 mi. S, W, and S to L. Stefanie.

Galang (gäläng'), island (□ c.40; 7 mi. long), Riouw Archipelago, Indonesia, 40 mi. SE of Singapore, just S of Rempang; lumbering, fishing.

Galanta (gä'läntä), town (pop. 3,707), NW Slovakia, Czechoslovakia, 28 mi. E of Bratislava; rail junction; agr. center (wheat, barley, rye).

Galapa (gälä'pä), town (pop. 2,982), Atlántico dept., N Colombia, in Caribbean lowlands, 9 mi. SW of Barranquilla; cotton, corn, livestock.

Galapagar (gäläpägär'), town (pop. 1,186), Madrid prov., central Spain, 20 mi. NW of Madrid; cereals, carobs, timber, livestock; flour milling.

Galápagos Islands (gälä'pägōs) [Sp.,=tortoises], officially **Archipiélago de Colón** (ärchēpyā'lägō dā kōlōn'), group (□ 2,966; 1950 pop. 1,346) and territory of Ecuador, administered as part of Guayas prov., in the Pacific, c.650 mi. W of Ecuador mainland and c.1,000 mi. SW of the Panama Canal; chief town, Puerto Baquerizo. Crossed by the equator, the isls. are situated roughly bet. 1°N–1°30'S and 89°–92°W. Group consists of 13 large and many smaller isls. of volcanic origin, the largest being E-W, SAN CRISTÓBAL ISLAND (Chatham Isl.), CHAVES ISLAND or Santa Cruz Isl. (Indefatigable Isl.), SANTIAGO ISLAND or San Salvador Isl. (James Isl.), ISABELA ISLAND (Albemarle Isl.), and FERNANDINA ISLAND (Narborough Isl.). The isls.—except for Isabela, the largest—are roughly circular in shape, with high craters (some rising to c.5,000 ft.) in their centers. The climate is tempered by the cool Peru or Humboldt Current. Largely desolate lava piles, the isls. have little vegetation along the narrow coast, but the high volcanic mts. cause heavy rains which have mantled the slopes with dense jungles. Though little exploited, some sugar cane, coffee, yucca, maguey, and cattle are raised. Excellent fishing grounds (lobster, tuna, corvina). Some hides, lizard skins, salt, sulphur, and fish are exported. The isls. owe their fame to the peculiar fauna and flora, which point to their long isolation from the continental mainland. The giant tortoises, some about 400 years old, are considered the oldest living animals on earth. In this naturalists' paradise, now a protected sanctuary, there are sea and land iguanas, flightless cormorants, and many other strange land and sea creatures, some now on the verge of extinction. The group, originally known as Encantadas, was discovered (1535) by the Sp. navigator Tomás de Berlanga. During the colonial epoch the isls. were visited by whalers and buccaneers, from whom stem the English names, and who did much to disturb the primal nature of the isls. Ecuador occupied them in 1832. The Galápagos were visited (1835) by Darwin during the famous voyage of the *Beagle.* His observation of the wildlife furnished some important proofs for the theory of evolution. Since then the isls. have frequently been visited by scientific expeditions because of their geological and biological interest. During the Second World War they served as a vital air base. Ecuador maintains a penal settlement at Villamil on Isabela Isl.

Galaroza (gälärō'thä), town (pop. 2,367), Huelva prov., SW Spain, 9 mi. WNW of Aracena; chestnuts, pears, apricots, olives, walnuts, timber.

Galarza or **General Galarza** (hānäräl' gälär'sä), town (pop. estimate 1,300), S Entre Ríos prov., Argentina, on railroad and 30 mi. N of Gualeguay; grain, livestock, poultry center.

Galashiels (gălŭ-shēlz'), burgh (1931 pop. 13,102; 1951 census 12,496), NE Selkirk, Scotland, on Gala Water and 28 mi. SE of Edinburgh; woolen (tweed) milling and knitting center; also tanning, textile printing, and mfg. of textile machinery, pharmaceuticals, wax polishes. Has 14th-cent. Manor House, 17th-cent. market cross, and 18th-cent. Manufacturers' Cloth Hall. Near by is anc. Pictish earthwork.

Galata, Bulgaria: see STALIN GULF.

Galata (gälä'tä), village (pop. 728), Nicosia dist., W central Cyprus, on N slopes of Olympus Mts., 28 mi. WSW of Nicosia. Has deciduous-fruit experiment station.

Galata (gä'lätä), commercial section (pop. 48,748) of Istanbul, Turkey, originally a Genoese settlement, on N side of the Golden Horn.

Galata (gŭlā'tŭ), village (pop. c.100), Toole co., N Mont., 25 mi. E of Shelby; trading and livestock-shipping point.

Galati or **Galatz** (both: gäläts'), Rum. *Galaţi*, city (1948 pop. 80,411), ⊙ Galati prov., E Rumania, in Moldavia, on lower Danube bet. the mouths of Prut R. (E) and Siret R. (W), on SW shore of L. Brates, and 120 mi. NE of Bucharest; 45°28'N 28°4'E. Important inland port and fishing center, shipping large quantities of lumber and wheat. Main base of Rumanian Danube flotilla, naval base, and rail junction. Harbor installations include shipyards and dockyards, arsenal, grain elevators, cold-storage plants for fish, extensive lumber yards and gasworks. Produces cotton textiles, hosiery, boots, hardware, clay products, dyes, varnishes, chemicals, soap, candles, confectionery, printed matter; processes foods and refines petroleum. City is built in terraces around a hill. It has an airport and was made seat of International Danube Commission in 1856. Orthodox bishopric. There are several old churches, notably 16th-cent. St. George church with sepulcher of hetman Mazeppa. Of legendary foundation, the town became an international trading center in 16th cent. and later a free port (1834–83). Modern development began at the unification of Rumania (1861). Galati was formerly known for its large Jewish pop., now much reduced. Harbor works greatly damaged by retreating Germans in 1944.

Galatia (gŭlā'shŭ) [from Gr.,=Gaul], anc. territory of N central Asia Minor, in present Turkey (around Ankara). So called from the Gauls who had invaded and conquered it in 3d cent. B.C. Originally composed of parts of Phrygia and Cappadocia, the territory of the Gauls increased until it extended from Bithynia and Pontus (N) to Pamphylia (S). About 230 B.C., Attalus I of Pergamus checked the Gauls and reduced limits of Galatia. Became subject to Romans in 189 B.C. and made a Roman prov. in 25 B.C. Chief city was Ancyra (modern Ankara); other cities were Pessinus and Gordium.

Galatia. 1 Village (pop. 933), Saline co., SE Ill., 8 mi. NNW of Harrisburg, in bituminous-coal mining and agr. region. 2 City (pop. 89), Barton co., central Kansas, 22 mi. NNW of Great Bend; wheat.

Galatina (gälätē'nä), town (pop. 16,081), Lecce prov., Apulia, S Italy, 12 mi. S of Lecce; agr. center; wine making, food canning, tanning. Has 14th-cent. church.

Galatista, Greece: see ANTHEMOUS.

Galatone (gälä'tônĕ), town (pop. 10,998), Lecce prov., Apulia, S Italy, 15 mi. SSW of Lecce; agr. center (cereals, grapes, olives, tobacco); alcohol distilling.

Galatro (gä'lätrô), village (pop. 2,769), Reggio di Calabria prov., Calabria, S Italy, 3 mi. N of Cinquefrondi, in olive- and grape-growing region. Has hot mineral baths.

Gala Water (gä'lů), river in Midlothian, Selkirk, and Roxburgh, Scotland, rises in Moorfoot Hills, flows 21 mi. SSE, past Stow and Galashiels, to the Tweed just SE of Galashiels.

Galax (gā'lăks), town (pop. 5,248), Carroll and Grayson counties, SW Va., in the Blue Ridge, 65 mi. SW of Roanoke, near N.C. line; mfg. center in agr. area; furniture, caskets, glass products, hosiery, textiles, dairy products; lumber and flour milling. Ships evergreens (galax). Founded 1903; inc. 1906.

Galaxeidion or **Galaxidhion** (both: găluksĭ'dhēôn), town (pop. 2,240) Phocis nome, W central Greece, port on W shore of Bay of Crisa (or Galaxeidion), an inlet of Gulf of Corinth, 10 mi. S of Amphissa; fisheries; trade in olive oil, wine, livestock. On site of anc. Oeanthea; important commercial port (shipbuilding) during Middle Ages; destroyed by pirates in 1660, by the Turkish navy in 1821. Rebuilt 1835. Also spelled Galaxidi and Galaxidion.

Galciana (gälchä'nä), village (pop. 2,242), Firenze prov., Tuscany, central Italy, 2 mi. W of Prato; dyes, paint.

Gáldar (gäl'där), city (pop. 5,337), Grand Canary, Canary Isls., 13 mi. WNW of Las Palmas; agr. center and minor port on isl.'s N shore; bananas, tomatoes, potatoes, onions, cochineal, cereals, livestock. Granite quarries; limekilns, flour mills. Mfg. of cheese.

Galdhopiggen, Norway: see JOTUNHEIM MOUNTAINS.

Galeana (gälää'nä). 1 Town (pop. 797), Chihuahua, N Mexico, in Sierra Madre Occidental, on Santa María R. and 135 mi. SW of Ciudad Juárez; cereals, fruit, vegetables, cattle. Noted for white marble deposits said to be the equal of Carrara. 2 City (pop. 1,782), Nuevo León, N Mexico, in Sierra Madre Oriental, 60 mi. SSE of Monterrey, in wheat-growing area; alt. 5,426 ft.

Galeata (gälĕä'tä), village (pop. 1,235), Forlì prov., Emilia-Romagna, N central Italy, on Ronco R. and 17 mi. SSW of Forlì.

Galena (gůlē'nů), village (pop. 172), W Alaska, on Yukon R. and 140 mi. W of Tanana; 64°45'N 156°56'W; trapping; supply point. Airfield, refueling base on Fairbanks-Nome air line. School. Founded c.1919 as supply point for Galena prospectors.

Galena (gůlē'nů) or **Spillimacheen** (spĭlĭmůkēn'), village, SE B.C., on Columbia R. and 40 mi. SW of Banff, on slope of Rocky Mts.; silver, lead, zinc mining.

Galena. 1 City (pop. 4,648), ⊙ Jo Daviess co., extreme NW Ill., on Galena R. (bridged here), near the Mississippi, and 12 mi. ESE of Dubuque, Iowa; trade and shipping point in dairying region containing lead and zinc deposits; mfg. (dairy products, beverages, gloves and mittens, foundry products, stoves, mining machinery, lubricating oil, thermometers). Lead mined here since early-18th cent. Settled c.1820 after the U.S. placed mines under govt. protection (1807); laid out and named in 1826; inc. 1835. Until 1860s, Galena was active center of the lead-mining areas of NW Ill. and SW Wis. and one of the busiest steamboat ports on the upper Mississippi. Ulysses S. Grant lived here before and after Civil War; his home is a state mus. There are also a mus. of history and art and many old and beautiful bldgs. 2 City (pop. 4,029), Cherokee co., extreme SE Kansas, near Okla. line, 7 mi. W of Joplin (Mo.), in mining and agr. area; lead, zinc smelting; makes mining equipment. Founded in 1870s, when lead was discovered near by; inc. 1877. 3 Town (pop. 259), Kent co., E Md., near Sassafras R., 23 mi. NW of Dover, Del. 4 Town (pop. 439), ⊙ Stone co., SW Mo., in the Ozarks, on James R. and 30 mi. SSW of Springfield; tomatoes, corn, wheat; canning factories. 5 Village (pop. 424), Delaware co., central Ohio, 18 mi. NNE of Columbus.

Galena Mountain, peak (13,300 ft.) in San Juan Mts., San Juan co., SW Colo.

Galena Park, city (pop. 7,186), Harris co., S Texas, E suburb of Houston, absorbed 1948 by Houston.

Galena River, in Wis. and Ill., rises in extreme SW Wis., flows c.25 mi. generally SW, past Galena (Ill.), to the Mississippi 2 mi. SW of Galena. Formerly Fever R.

Galenstock (gäl'ůnshtôk"), peak (11,749 ft.) in the Alps, S central Switzerland, S of the Rhonestock, NE of Rhone Glacier. The Galengrat (a mtn. ridge) and the Galensattel (a mtn. saddle) are near by.

Galeota Point (gălēō'tů), headland on SE coast of Trinidad, B.W.I., 50 mi. SE of Port of Spain; 10°8'N 60°59'W. First point of the isl. sighted by Columbus (July 31, 1498).

Galera (gälā'rä), town (pop. 3,057), Granada prov., S Spain, 22 mi. NE of Baza; hemp processing, flour milling; lumbering; stock raising. Wine, cereals, vegetables.

Galera, Cerro (sĕ'rō gůlē'rů), highest peak (c.1,205 ft.) of the Panama Canal Zone, 6 mi. WSW of Panama city, in jungle country.

Galera, La (lä), town (pop. 1,145), Tarragona prov., NE Spain, 10 mi. SSW of Tortosa; olive-oil processing; sheep, wine, vegetables.

Galera Point, Pacific cape in Valdivia prov., S central Chile, 28 mi. SW of Valdivia; 40°S 73°46'W. Lighthouse.

Galera Point, headland on Pacific coast of Esmeraldas prov., NW Ecuador, 28 mi. WSW of Esmeraldas; 0°51'N 80°6'W.

Galera Point (gůlĕr'ů), cape on NE coast of Trinidad, B.W.I., 45 mi. ENE of Port of Spain; 10°50'N 60°54'W. Lighthouse.

Galeras Volcano (gälä'räs), active Andean volcano (13,996 ft.) in Nariño dept., SW Colombia, near Ecuador border, just W of Pasto. Sometimes Pasto Volcano.

Galesburg. 1 City (pop. 31,425), ⊙ Knox co., NW central Ill., c.45 mi. WNW of Peoria; important rail center (with railroad shops); livestock market. Mfg. (brick, iron and steel products, farm tools, clothing, outboard motors, washing machines, hardware, paint, sanitary supplies, candy). Coal mines, clay and gravel pits. Seat of Knox Col. Town and col. founded 1836 by Presbyterians from Mohawk valley, N.Y., under George Washington Gale; Galesburg was inc. as town in 1841, and grew rapidly with the coming of the railroad (1854); inc. as city in 1876. Was an important Underground Railroad station and scene of a Lincoln-Douglas debate. Carl Sandburg b. here. 2 City (pop. 189), Neosho co., SE Kansas, 15 mi. SSE of Chanute; livestock, grain, poultry; dairying. 3 City (pop. 1,200), Kalamazoo co., SW Mich., 8 mi. E of Kalamazoo and on Kalamazoo R., in agr. area (grain, fruit, livestock). A seedhouse ships seeds, plants. Settled 1829; inc. as village 1869, as city 1931. 4 Village (pop. 169), Traill co., E N.Dak., 30 mi. NW of Fargo.

Gales Ferry, Conn.: see LEDYARD.

Galesville, city (pop. 1,193), Trempealeau co., W Wis., on tributary of Black R. and 19 mi. NNW of La Crosse, in dairy, timber, and applegrowing area; dairy products, feed, canned food; limestone quarries. Near-by L. Marinuka is a resort. Settled 1854; inc. as village in 1887, as city in 1942.

Galeton (gāl'tůn), borough (pop. 1,646), Potter co., N Pa., in the Alleghenies, on Pine Creek and 19 mi. E of Coudersport; gloves, metal and wood products; railroad yards. Resort center for hunting, fishing region. Inc. 1896.

Galetta (gůlĕ'tů), village (pop. estimate 200), SE Ont., on Mississippi R., near its mouth on L. des Chats, and 27 mi. W of Ottawa; lead and zinc mining; hydroelectric power.

Galga River (gŏl'gŏ), N Hungary, rises in Cserhat Mts., flows c.35 mi. SE to the Zagyva near Jaszfenyszaru.

Galgate (găl'gāt), village, N Lancashire, England, 4 mi. S of Lancaster and in parish of Ellel (pop. 1,904); silk spinning and weaving.

Galgau (gůl'gůōō), Rum. *Gâlgău*, Hung. *Galgó* (gŏl'gō), village (pop. 972), Cluj prov., N Rumania, near Somes R., on railroad and 13 mi. NW of Dej. In Hungary, 1940–45.

Galgenen (gäl'gĕnůn), town (pop. 2,178), Schwyz canton, NE central Switzerland, 15 mi. NE of Schwyz. Siebnen hydroelectric plant is E.

Galgo, Rumania: see GALGAU.

Galgo, Bahía del, Fr. West Africa: see LÉVRIER BAY.

Galgoc, Czechoslovakia: see HLOHOVEC.

Gali (gä'lyē), city (1939 pop. over 2,000), S Abkhaz Autonomous SSR, Georgian SSR, on railroad and 40 mi. SE of Sukhumi; agr. center; tea, citrus fruit.

Gália (gä'lyů), city (pop. 3,124), W central São Paulo, Brazil, on railroad and 31 mi. W of Bauru; coffee, cotton, and rice processing; pottery mfg. Formerly Gallia.

Galiakot (gůlyä'kōt), town (pop. 4,247), S Rajasthan, India, on Mahi R. and 29 mi. SE of Dungarpur; millet, corn. Annual religious fair. Was ⊙ early rulers of former Dungarpur state.

Galiano Island (gălĭä'nō) (□ 22), SW B.C., Gulf Isls., in Strait of Georgia off SE Vancouver Isl., bet. Valdes Isl. and Mayne Isl., 25 mi. SW of Vancouver; 16 mi. long, 1–3 mi. wide. Mixed farming, lumbering. Galiano village on S coast.

Galibier, Col du (kôl dü gälēbyā'), pass (alt. 8,507 ft.) bet. Cottian Alps (E) and Dauphiné Alps (W), on Savoie–Hautes-Alpes dept. border, SE France, 2.5 mi. N of Col du LAUTARET. On scenic road from Saint-Michel (in Maurienne valley) to Briancon and upper Oisans valley. Tunnel under crest of pass.

Galibi Point (gälē'bē), on Atlantic coast of NE Du. Guiana, on left bank of Marowijne or Maroni R., opposite Pointe Française; 5°45'N 54°2'W.

Galich, peak, Poland: see HALICZ.

Galich (gä'lyĭch). 1 City (1939 pop. over 10,000), W central Kostroma oblast, Russian SFSR, on L. Galich (10 mi. long, 4 mi. wide), 65 mi. NE of Kostroma (linked since c.1950 by direct railroad); woodworking, distilling, clothing mfg. Dates from 1237. 2 Pol. *Halicz* (hä'lyēch), city (1931 pop. 4,386), N Stanislav oblast, Ukrainian SSR, on the Dniester and 13 mi. N of Stanislav; agr. processing (cereals, vegetable oils); dairying, truck gardening. Has several old churches with medieval relics. Ruins of fortress near by. An old Ruthenian settlement; became (c.1134) ⊙ duchy of Przemysl; later ⊙ duchy of Galich, which disintegrated in 1340. City passed to Poland in c.1366, to Austria in 1772; scene of Russo-Ger. battles during First World War. Reverted to Poland (1919); ceded to USSR in 1945. Rail junction Galich is just NNE.

Galiche (gä'lĭchĕ), village (pop. 5,465), Vratsa dist., NW Bulgaria, on Skat R. and 12 mi. SSW of Oryakhovo; flour milling; winegrowing, grain, livestock.

Galichitsa, mountain, Yugoslavia: see GALICICA.

Galichnik, Yugoslavia: see GALICNIK.

Galicia (gůlĭ'shů), Pol. *Galicja*, Ger. *Galizien*, Rus. *Galitsiya*, region, SE Poland and NW Ukrainian SSR. Borders S on Czechoslovakia, extends from the Carpathians into the Vistula valley (N); drained by Vistula, Raba, Dunajec, Wisloka, San, and Dniester rivers. Principal cities are Cracow, Tarnow, Rzeszow, Przemysl, and Nowy Sacz, in Poland; and Lvov, Stanislav, Drogobych, Borislav, Stryy, and Kolomiya, in Ukrainian SSR. E part of region is rich in oil and natural gas, with centers at Jaslo and Krosno, Poland, and Drogobych and Borislav, Ukrainian SSR. Gas pipe lines supply other industrial cities. Lumbering, wood- and metalworking are important throughout the region; hydroelectric power is abundant. Rye, oats, potatoes, barley, wheat, and sugar beets are chief crops; stock raising. Pol. part of region included in Krakow and Rzeszow provs.; Ukrainian SSR part covers Lvov, Drogobych, and Stanislav oblasts. Until 1919 Galicia was an Austro-Hungarian crownland (□ 30,309; 1910 pop. 8,025,675); ⊙ Lvov (Lemberg). Originally the Rus. duchy of Galich (Pol. *Halicz*), united after 1188 with that of Vladimir, it came to Poland in 14th cent. Most of Galicia passed (1772) to Austria with 1st partition of Poland. In 1846, after abortive Pol. rising, Austria annexed Cracow, an independent republic since 1815. In 1848 Cracow and Lvov were centers of revolutionary activity. Galicia obtained (1861) limited autonomy and representation in Austrian parliament; Polish, spoken in section W of San R., and Ukrainian, spoken E of river, became official languages, along with German. Though Polish, as well as Ukrainian, nationalism grew considerably, a Pol. legion was organized in Galicia in First World War and fought on Austrian side until 1917. During war entire region was scene of heavy fighting. In 1918 the newly-proclaimed Poland drove Austrians out of W part of Galicia and fought troops of newly established Ukrainian republic and expelled them from E Galicia. Paris Peace Conference (1919) assigned all of Galicia to Poland, its E part being subject to a plebiscite scheduled for 1944. Poland, however, obtained full title to E Galicia in treaty (1920) with the Ukraine, confirmed (1921) by Polish-Soviet Treaty of Riga. Under Polish-Soviet Treaty of 1945 most of E Galicia was awarded to Ukrainian SSR.

Galicia (gůlĭ'shů, Sp. gälē'thyä), anc. *Gallaecia*, region (□ 10,984; pop. 2,495,860) and former kingdom, NW Spain, occupying NW corner of Iberian Peninsula, and comprising the provs. of LA CORUÑA, LUGO, ORENSE, and PONTEVEDRA; chief city, La Coruña. Bounded by Bay of Biscay (N), the Atlantic (W), Portugal (S), and Asturias and Leon (E). Covered by moderately elevated mts. and by plateaus of Lugo and Orense, cut by deep valleys. Drained by the Miño (forming border with Portugal in lower course) and several short rivers (e.g., Lerez, Ulla), which reach the coast in deep inlets (*rías*) formed by their drowned valleys. High, rocky, deeply indented coast line, reaching here westernmost (Cape Toriñana and Cape Finisterre) and northernmost (Estaca Point) points of Spain. Densely populated coast has several excellent harbors. Pleasant climate, with greatest rainfall in Spain. Extensive forests and pastures; cattle and hog raising is important. Agr. products: corn, rye, potatoes, vegetables, fruit. Vineyards in Miño, Sil, Ulla valleys. Leads Spain in fishing industry (especially sardines); processed fish extensively exported. Mineral deposits (tin, tungsten, iron), known to the Romans, are now little exploited. Granite, clay, slate quarries; mineral springs. Other industries: boatbuilding, tanning, dairy-products and meat processing, brandy distilling, lumbering; mfg. of cotton and linen cloth, chemicals, candy. Poor communications in interior. Chief cities: Vigo and La Coruña, trading ports and industrial centers; El Ferrol, naval base; Santiago de Compostela, a great pilgrimage center. Galicia was invaded by Celts (6th cent. B.C.); conquered by Romans (3d-2d cent. B.C.); formed kingdom of Suevi (5th-6th cent. A.D.); taken by Visigoths (6th-8th cent.). Soon after Moorish invasion, it was freed (8th cent.) by Asturians, who made it part of their kingdom; briefly (1063–73) was independent; was inc. again in kingdom of Asturias and Leon, later of Castile. Scene of bitter fighting in Peninsular War (1808–14). Galicians are simple and poor but industrious people, deeply attached to their customs and traditions.

Galician Mountains (gŭlĭ'shŭn), Sp. *Montes de Galicia* (mōn'tĕs dhā gälē'thyä) or *Macizo Galaico* (mä-thē'thō gälī'kō), range in Galicia, NW Spain, continuing the Cantabrian Mts. (of which they are sometimes considered a spur) westward to the Atlantic (Cape Finisterre). Irregular, highly eroded formation, rising in the Cabeza de Manzaneda to 5,833 ft. Mineral deposits, which include tin, tungsten, iron, lignite, are now little exploited. Largely wooded; range has fine pastures, favored by abundant rainfall. Drained by Miño R. flowing SW to Portugal border. Among its subranges is the Sierra (Serra) de Gerez, which branches off SW to Portugal.

Galicica or **Galichitsa** (both: gä'lēchētsä), Serbo-Croatian *Galičica*, Albanian *Galiçicë*, mountain in Macedonia, Yugoslavia, bet. L. Ochrida and L. Prespa. Highest point (7,397 ft.) is on Albania border, 12 mi. S of Ochrida.

Galicnik or **Galichnik** (both: gä'lēchnĭk), Serbo-Croatian *Galičnik*, village, W Macedonia, Yugoslavia, near Radika R., 8 mi. NE of Debar; cheese making.

Galien (gŭlēn'), village (pop. 610), Berrien co., extreme SW Mich., 16 mi. NW of South Bend (Ind.), in agr. area (grain, sugar beets, truck, peppermint, honey; dairy products). Has farmers' cooperative exchange.

Galilee (gă'lĭlē), Hebrew *Hagalil*, mountainous region, N Israel, bounded by Plain of Jezreel (S), Zebulun Valley and Mediterranean (W), Lebanese border (N), Syrian border, Sea of Galilee, and the Jordan (E). Lower Galilee (S) is centered on Nazareth and Tiberias; rises to 1,929 ft. on Mt. Tabor. Upper Galilee (N) is centered on Safad; includes L. Hula and swamp region near headwaters of the Jordan; highest elevations are Jebel Jarmaq (3,963 ft.) and Jebel Heidar (3,435 ft.). Hill farming (grain, fruit, stock, poultry; dairying) is chief occupation. Fisheries in Sea of Galilee and L. Hula. In biblical history Galilee is closely associated with ministry of Jesus. After fall (A.D. 70) of Jerusalem it became a center of Jewish culture. Border areas were scene (1948) of fierce fighting during Arab invasion of Israel.

Galilee, Lake, or **Jochmus Lake** (□ 80), E central Queensland, Australia, 210 mi. SSW of Townsville; 19 mi. long, 10 mi. wide; frequently dry.

Galilee, Sea of, or **Lake Tiberias** (tībē'rēŭs), freshwater lake (□ 64; 13 mi. long, 3–7 mi. wide), N Palestine, on Israel-Jordan border; through it flows the Jordan R. It is 696 ft. below sea level, lying in part of the GREAT RIFT VALLEY. It appears in the Old Testament as the Sea of Chinnereth or Chinneroth (whence modern Heb. *Yam Kinneret*), and in the New Testament it is variously named from near-by geographical features—Galilee, Gennesaret, or Tiberias (from the last comes the Arabic *Bahret Tabariya* or *Tabariyeh*). In time of Jesus there were 9 flourishing towns on its shores, among them Magdala, Capernaum, Tabigha, and TIBERIAS, of which only the last remains.

Galina Point (gŭlē'nŭ), cape on N coast of Jamaica, 3 mi. N of Port Maria; 18°25'N 76°54'W.

Galinduste (gälēndōō'stä), village (pop. 1,503), Salamanca prov., W Spain, 22 mi. SSE of Salamanca; cereals.

Galion (găl'yŭn), city (pop. 9,952), Crawford co., N central Ohio, 13 mi. W of Mansfield and on Olentangy R.; road machinery, motor vehicles, communications equipment, electrical goods, clothing, metal products. Settled 1831.

Galisteo (gälēstā'ō), town (pop. 1,193), Cáceres prov., W Spain, 10 mi. WSW of Plasencia; cereals, vegetables, pepper. Has remains of fortified walls.

Galite, La (lä gälēt'), island (□ 3; pop. c.170), in the central Mediterranean, off N coast of Tunisia, 55 mi. WNW of Bizerte; 37°22'N 8°56'E; of volcanic origin; rises to 1,109 ft. Lobster fishing; goats.

Galiuro Mountains (gälēōō'rō), Graham co., SE Ariz., NE of Tucson; extend c.55 mi. SE-NW along right bank of San Pedro R. in section of Crook Natl. Forest. Chief peaks are KENNEDY PEAK (7,540 ft.) and BASSETT PEAK (7,650 ft.).

Galizien, Poland and Ukrainian SSR: see GALICIA.

Galkayu (gälkä'yōō), town (pop. 500), in the Mudugh, central Ital. Somaliland, 130 mi. NW of Obbia; 6°46'N 47°26'E; road junction; livestock center. Has native fort. Called Rocca Littorio by Italians.

Galkino (gäl'kēnŭ). **1** Village, Pavlodar oblast, Kazakh SSR, 55 mi. E of Pavlodar, in wooded area. **2** Village (1948 pop. over 2,000), W Kurgan oblast, Russian SFSR, 30 mi. N of Shchuchye; flour mill.

Gallabat (gălă'băt), village, Kassala prov., NE Anglo-Egyptian Sudan, on Ethiopian border opposite Metemma, 90 mi. SE of Gedaref.

Galladi, Ethiopia: see GALADI.

Gallarate (gäl-lärä'tĕ), town (pop. 12,546), Varese prov., Lombardy, N Italy, 11 mi. SSW of Varese. Rail junction; cotton-milling center; mfg. (embroidery, rayon, textile machinery, scales), alcohol distilling, cheese making; printing. Has 12th-cent. church, cathedral (1856–70), mus., technical school.

Gallareta, La, Argentina: see LA GALLARETA.

Gallarta, Spain: see ABANTO Y CIÉRVANA.

Gallatin (gă'lŭtĭn). **1** County (□ 328; pop. 9,818), SE Ill.; ⊙ Shawneetown. Bounded NE by Wabash R. and SE by the Ohio; drained by Saline R. SW corner is in Ill. Ozarks. Corn, wheat, livestock, dairy products, poultry. Bituminous-coal mining. Includes part of Shawnee Natl. Forest. Formed 1812. **2** County (□ 100; pop. 3,969), N Ky.; ⊙ Warsaw. Bounded N by Ohio R. (Ind. line), S by Eagle Creek. Gently rolling upland agr. area (burley tobacco, corn, livestock), in outer Bluegrass region. Some mfg. (especially wood products) at Warsaw. Formed 1798. **3** County (□ 2,517; pop. 21,902), SW Mont.; ⊙ Bozeman. Agr. area bordering on Idaho (S) and Yellowstone Natl. Park; drained by Gallatin R. and Hebgen L. Livestock, grain. Missouri R. formed in NW, near Three Forks, by junction of Gallatin R. with Jefferson and Madison rivers. Parts of Gallatin Natl. Forest in S and NE. Gallatin Range extends N into co. from Yellowstone Natl. Park; includes Mt. Blackmore (10,196 ft.). Formed 1865.

Gallatin. **1** City (pop. 1,634), ⊙ Daviess co., NW Mo., on Grand R. and 23 mi. WNW of Chillicothe; agr. (corn, wheat, hay, oats). Near by is site of a Mormon settlement of 1830s. Laid out 1837. **2** City (pop. 5,107), ⊙ Sumner co., N Tenn., near Cumberland R., 24 mi. NE of Nashville; tobacco and livestock market; makes shoes, tobacco and wood products, cheese. Several fine ante-bellum houses near by. In Civil War, Union garrison here was captured (1862) by Gen. John H. Morgan. Founded 1802.

Gallatin Gateway, village (pop. c.150), Gallatin co., SW Mont., on Gallatin R. and 10 mi. SW of Bozeman; tourist trade. Just S are Gallatin Canyon and Gallatin Natl. Forest. Yellowstone Natl. Park is 35 mi. S.

Gallatin Range, in Rocky Mts., of NW Wyo. and SW Mont., rises S of Bozeman, Mont.; extends c.45 mi. S, bet. Gallatin and Yellowstone rivers, into NW corner of Yellowstone Natl. Park, Wyo. Prominent peaks: Mt. Holmes (10,300 ft.; in Wyo.); Mt. Blackmore (10,196 ft.; in Mont.); Electric Peak (11,155 ft.; in Mont. and Yellowstone Natl. Park), highest point in range.

Gallatin River, in SW Mont. and NW Wyo., rises in Gallatin Range in NW corner of Yellowstone Natl. Park, Wyo.; flows 120 mi. N, forming deep canyon bet. Madison and Gallatin ranges in SW Mont., to point just NE of Three Forks, where it joins the Madison and Jefferson rivers to form the Missouri. Used for irrigation.

Gallatown, Scotland: see DYSART.

Galle (gäl, gŭl), Singhalese *gala* [=rock], city (□ 7; pop. 49,038), ⊙ Southern Prov. and Galle dist. (□ 631; pop., including estate pop., 459,682), Ceylon, on SW coast, overlooking a large but treacherous harbor, 65 mi. SSE of Colombo; coastal road and trade (vegetables, rice, rubber, tea, coconuts, cinnamon) center. A famous emporium of the East in anc. times; revived under Port. rule (1507–c.1640) to become the main port of Ceylon; following completion of Colombo harbor in 1885 it again declined. Older part of city lies S, within 17th-cent. Du. fort situated on a promontory (lighthouse at end). Was ⊙ Ceylon (1640–56) under Dutch, until ⊙ transferred to Colombo; city was formally ceded to English by Dutch in 1802. Formerly called Point de Galle.

Gállego River (gä'lyägō), in Huesca and Saragossa provs., NE Spain, in Aragon, rises near Pourtalet pass in the central Pyrenees on Fr. border, flows c.130 mi. SW and S to the Ebro near Saragossa. Hydroelectric plants (Biescas, Anzánigo, Peña reservoir); irrigation.

Gallegos, town, Argentina: see RÍO GALLEGOS.

Gallegos de Argañán (gälyä'gōs dhā ärgänyän'), village (pop. 1,333), Salamanca prov., W Spain, 9 mi. WNW of Ciudad Rodrigo; cereals.

Gallegos River (gäyä'gōs), Patagonian stream in S Santa Cruz natl. territory, Argentina, rises at Chile border, flows E to the Atlantic at town of Río Gallegos. Length, with its main headstream (Turbio River), c.200 mi. Estuary is called Puerto Gallegos.

Galley Head, promontory on the Atlantic, S Co. Cork, Ireland, 8 mi. SSW of Clonakilty; lighthouse (51°32'N 8°57'W). Ruins of anc. Dundeady Castle.

Galley Hill, locality, Swanscombe parish, Kent, England, 3 mi. W of Gravesend; skeleton of prehistoric man found here 1888.

Gallia, Brazil: see GÁLIA.

Gallia: see GAUL; FRANCE.

Gallia (gă'lēŭ), county (□ 471; pop. 24,910), S Ohio; ⊙ Gallipolis. Bounded E by Ohio R., here forming W.Va. line; intersected by Raccoon Creek and small Symmes and Campaign creeks. Agr. (livestock, grain, tobacco, fruit); mfg. at Gallipolis; coal mines; limestone, sand, gravel. Formed 1803.

Gallia Narbonensis, Latin name for the Roman colony of Provincia (Provence) in S France.

Galliate (gälyä'tĕ), town (pop. 10,284) Novara prov., Piedmont, N Italy, near junction of Cavour Canal with Ticino R., 4 mi. ENE of Novara; cotton and linen textiles, machinery, glucose.

Gallicano (gäl-lēkä'nō), village (pop. 2,070), Lucca prov., Tuscany, central Italy, near Serchio R., 4 mi. S of Castelnuovo di Garfagnana; explosives.

Galliera Veneta (gäl-lyä'rä vä'nĕtä), village (pop. 1,638), Padova prov., Veneto, N Italy, 17 mi. N of Padua; silk mills, macaroni factory.

Gallikos River, Greece: see ECHEDOROS RIVER.

Gallina Mountains (gīē'nŭ, gŭlē'nŭ), W N.Mex., extend c.30 mi. E-W in N Catron and Socorro counties; rise to 9,560 ft.

Gallinaria (gäl-lēnä'rēä), islet in Gulf of Genoa, Liguria, NW Italy, 2 mi. SE of Albenga; 5,032 ft. in circumference, 285 ft. high. Has ruined Benedictine abbey (founded 1169; now a private house).

Gallina River, Sierra Leone: see MOA RIVER.

Gallinas, Point (gäyē'näs), Caribbean cape on Guajira peninsula, N Colombia, the northernmost point of the South American mainland; 12°28'N 71°40'W.

Gallinas Peak (gīē'nŭs, gŭlē'nŭs) (9,798 ft.), central N.Mex., rises from high tableland in Lincoln Natl. Forest, 10 mi. W of Corona.

Gallinas River, N central N.Mex., rises in S Sangre de Cristo Mts., flows c.70 mi. SE, past Las Vegas, to Pecos R. 21 mi. NW of Santa Rosa. Known in upper course, to point just below Las Vegas, as Gallinas Creek.

Gallinero, Sierra del (syĕ'rä dĕl gäyēnā'rō), N continuation of Sierra del Merendón, in Copán dept., W Honduras; extends from ERAPUCA peak (8,200 ft.) c.25 mi. N to area W of San Jerónimo. The name Gallinero is sometimes applied to Sierra del Espíritu Santo.

Gallipoli (gŭlĭ'pŭlē, It. gäl-lē'pôlē), anc. *Anxa* and *Callipolis*, town (pop. 12,818), Lecce prov., Apulia, S Italy, port on rocky isl. in Gulf of Taranto, 23 mi. SW of Lecce; connected by bridge with its suburb on the mainland. Produces wine and olive oil (exported in considerable quantities); mfg. (toys, hosiery); foundries. Bishopric. Has 13th-17th-cent. castle, 17th-cent. cathedral.

Gallipoli (gŭlĭ'pŭlē), Turkish *Gelibolu* (gĕlĭ'bôlōō"), anc. *Callipolis*, modern Gr. *Kallipolis*, town (pop. 16,496), Canakkale prov., Turkey in Europe, port on S shore of Gallipoli Peninsula, at E end of the Dardanelles where it opens on the Sea of Marmara, 22 mi. NE of Canakkale and 130 mi. WSW of Istanbul. Commercial and agr. center (wheat, barley, oats, rye); important bean market. Occupied by the Ottoman Turks in 1354 (their 1st conquest in Europe), it has always been a strategic point in the defense of Constantinople.

Gallipoli Peninsula, Turkish *Gelibolu*, anc. *Chersonesus Thracica* (Thracian Chersonese), Turkey in Europe, extends 55–60 mi. SW bet. the Gulf of Saros of the Aegean (NW) and the Dardanelles (SE); 3½–13 mi. wide. Chief cities: Gallipoli, Eceabat. In 1915 the peninsula was scene of a costly and futile expedition by the British to force the Dardanelles. It was part of the demilitarized zone of the straits, 1920–36.

Gallipolis (gă"lŭpŭlēs'), city (pop. 7,871), ⊙ Gallia co., S Ohio, on the Ohio and c.40 mi. E of Portsmouth, in agr. area (corn, tobacco, fruit, livestock); furniture, meat and dairy products, stoves, boilers, brooms. State hosp. for epileptics is near by. Large roller-gate dam is on the Ohio near city. Settled 1790; inc. 1865 as city.

Gallitzin (gŭlĭt'sĭn), borough (pop. 3,102), Cambria co., SW central Pa., 7 mi. W of Altoona; clothing mfg.; bituminous coal. Settled c.1796.

Gallivare (yĕ'lĭvä"rŭ), Swedish *Gällivare*, village (pop. 3,222), Norrbotten co., N Sweden, 50 mi. SSE of Kiruna; rail junction; center of major iron-mining region. Ore shipped by rail to Lulea or Narvik. Has old Lapp church. Mining begun 1704, abandoned 1735; modern operations begun 1893. Formerly spelled Gellivare.

Gallman, village (pop. 170), Copiah co., SW Miss., 4 mi. SSW of Crystal Springs.

Gallneukirchen (gäl"noi'kĭrkhŭn), town (pop. 2,431), N Upper Austria, 6 mi. NE of Linz, N of the Danube; rye, wheat; cattle.

Gallo (yĕl'ŭ"), Swedish *Gällö*, village (pop. 518), Jamtland co., N central Sweden, on Revsund L., Swedish *Revsundsjön* (räv'sŭnd"shŭn") (15 mi. long, 1–6 mi. wide), 25 mi. SE of Ostersund; sawmills, brickworks. Has 17th-cent. fort.

Gallo, Cape, Greece: see AKRITAS, CAPE.

Gallo, Cape (gäl'lô), point on NW coast of Sicily, at NW end of Gulf of Palermo, 8 mi. NNW of Palermo; 38°13'N 13°19'E.

Galloo Island (gŭlōō'), Jefferson co., N N.Y., in E part of L. Ontario, 12 mi. W of Sackets Harbor village; 4 mi. long, ½–1¼ mi. wide. Lighthouse here.

Gallopolis, Brazil: see GALÓPOLIS.
Gallo River (gä'lyō), Guadalajara prov., central Spain, in New Castile, rises in spur (Sierra Menera) of the Cordillera Ibérica near Alustante, flows c.60 mi. NW and W, past Molina, to the Tagus 4 mi. NE of Zaorejas.
Galloway (gă'lōwā, -lůwā), district of SW Scotland, comprising counties of Wigtown and Kirkcudbright. Region is known for black, hornless Galloway cattle; dairying is chief industry. Main towns: Kirkcudbright, Castle Douglas, Wigtown, Newton Stewart, Portpatrick, and Stranraer. Galloway is not a political or administrative division. W Wigtown is a rocky double peninsula (called the Rhinns, or Rinns, of Galloway) which juts into the North Channel of the Irish Sea and is indented NE by Loch Ryan and SE by Luce Bay. It is 28 mi. long and is linked with mainland by a 6-mi.-wide isthmus, on which is Stranraer. At N end is Corsewall Point (55°2'N 5°10'W); at S end is the headland called the Mull of Galloway (54°39'N 4°52'W), the most southerly point of Scotland.
Gallspach (gäls'päkh), village (pop. 1,933), central Upper Austria, 10 mi. WNW of Wels.
Gallup (gă'lŭp), town (pop. 9,133), ⊙ McKinley co., NW NMex., on branch of Little Colorado R., near Ariz. line, and c.125 mi. WNW of Albuquerque; alt. 6,503 ft. Trade center and railroad div. point in stock-raising and coal-mining region. Ships wool and cattle; serves as distribution point for near-by Navajo and Zuni Indian reservations. Intertribal Indian ceremonial (held annually in Aug.) is occasion for trade and demonstration of native arts among Navajo, Apache, and Pueblo Indians. U.S. ordnance depot is S. Zuni Mts. near by. Founded c.1879, inc. 1891.
Gallups Island, E Mass., in outer Boston Bay, 6 mi. SE of downtown Boston; c.½ mi. long.
Gallur (gälyōōr'), town (pop. 3,702), Saragossa prov., NE Spain, bet. the Ebro and the Imperial Canal, 28 mi. NW of Saragossa, in fertile agr. area (fruit, pepper, alfalfa, sugar beets); sugar refinery; meat processing.
Galluzzo (gäl-lōō'tsō), village (pop. 2,116), Firenze prov., Tuscany, central Italy, 2 mi. SW of Florence; pottery, liquor. Has Carthusian monastery (founded 1342) with Della Robbia terra cottas.
Gallya-Aral (gŭlyä"-ŭräl'), village (1948 pop. over 500), E Samarkand oblast, Uzbek SSR, on Trans-Caspian RR and 40 mi. NE of Samarkand; wheat; metalworks. Formerly called Milyutinskaya.
Galofalo, Sicily: see GAROFALO.
Galo Fjord, Swedish *Gålöfjärden* (gōl'û"fyĕr"dûn), inlet (27 mi. long, 1–10 mi. wide) of the Baltic, E Sweden. At head is Sodertalje; short Sodertalje Canal here connects fjord with arm of L. Malar.
Gal-On (gäl'-ōn'), settlement (pop. 150), W Israel, at W foot of Judaean Hills, at N edge of the Negev, 18 mi. S of Rehovot; mixed farming. Founded 1946; withstood heavy Arab attacks, 1948. Also spelled Gal On or Gal-on.
Galop Island (gă'lŭp), St. Lawrence co., N N.Y., in the St. Lawrence amid the Galops Rapids, at Ont. line, c.1 mi. SW of Cardinal, Ont.; c.1½ mi. long.
Galópolis (gŏŏlô'pōōlēs), town (pop. 1,621), NE Rio Grande do Sul, Brazil, 4 mi. S of Caxias do Sul; winegrowing. Formerly spelled Gallopolis.
Galops Rapids, N.Y. and Ont.: see GALOP ISLAND.
Galoya (gŭlō'yŭ), village, North Central Prov., Ceylon, 34 mi. ESE of Anuradhapura; rail junction; sawmilling.
Gal Oya (gäl' ō'yŭ), river, Ceylon, rises in E Ceylon Hill Country, E of Badulla; flows N and E, past Inginiyagala, to Indian Ocean 10 mi. S of Kalmunai; 62 mi. long. Dam and irrigation project under construction at INGINIYAGALA.
Galpón, Argentina: see EL GALPÓN.
Galsi (gŭl'sē), village, Burdwan dist., W West Bengal, India, 12 mi. WNW of Burdwan; river research laboratory for Damodar Valley project.
Galston (gôls'tŭn), burgh (1931 pop. 4,601; 1951 census 4,560), N central Ayrshire, Scotland, on Irvine R. and 5 mi. E of Kilmarnock; lace-mfg. center; bacon and ham curing. Near by are coal mines. Just N is 15th-cent. Loudon Castle, with modern additions.
Galszecs, Czechoslovakia: see SECOVCE.
Galt (gôlt), city (pop. 15,346), S Ont., on Grand R. and 24 mi. WNW of Hamilton; silk milling, textile knitting, woodworking; mfg. of clothing, shoes, machinery, tools, hardware. Founded 1816.
Galt. 1 City (pop. 1,333), Sacramento co., central Calif., 25 mi. SSE of Sacramento; condensed milk, poultry, wine. Inc. 1946. **2** Town (pop. 117), Wright co., N central Iowa, 7 mi. ESE of Clarion; livestock, grain. **3** City (pop. 409), Grundy co., N Mo., 13 mi. ENE of Trenton.
Galty Mountains or **Galtee Mountains** (both: gôl'tē), range, SE Co. Limerick and SW Co. Tipperary, Ireland, extending 15 mi. E–W; rises to 3,018 ft. on Galty More, 8 mi. S of Tipperary.
Galva (găl'vŭ). **1** City (pop. 2,886), Henry co., NW Ill., 23 mi. NE of Galesburg; trade and industrial center in agr. and bituminous-coal area; mfg. (farm machinery, hardware, boilers, pumps, tools). Small L. Calhoun (resort) is S. Near by is BISHOP HILL village. Founded 1854, inc. 1867. **2** Town (pop. 492), Ida co., W Iowa, near Maple R., 18 mi. SSE of Cherokee; rendering plant. **3** City (pop. 426), McPherson co., central Kansas, 7 mi. E of McPherson, in wheat region. Oil field here.
Galván, Argentina: see PUERTO GALVÁN.
Galvarino (gälvärē'nō), town (pop. 1,209), Cautín prov., S central Chile, 27 mi. NW of Temuco; wheat-growing center; oats, potatoes, peas, livestock; lumbering.
Galveias (gŭlvā'ŭsh), village (pop. 2,190), Portalegre dist., central Portugal, 32 mi. WSW of Portalegre; flour milling, beekeeping, pottery mfg.
Galveston (găl'vŭstŭn), county (□ 430; pop. 113,066), S Texas; ⊙ GALVESTON, port, industrial center, coast resort. Bounded E by Galveston Bay, S by Gulf of Mexico and West Bay; includes Bolivar Peninsula and Galveston Isl. (site of Galveston). Sulphur, chemical, oil-refining industries; processing and shipping of cotton, wheat, metals, agr. products. Some agr. (truck, fruit, rice, cotton, pecans), livestock raising. Oil, natural-gas fields. Fisheries; shrimping; sport fishing. Formed 1838.
Galveston. 1 Town (pop. 905), Cass co., N central Ind., 8 mi. NW of Kokomo, in agr. area; makes cheese. **2** City (pop. 66,568), ⊙ Galveston co., S Texas, 45 mi. SE of Houston, on fine harbor near NE end of Galveston Isl. (c.30 mi. long, 1–3 mi. wide; 2 causeways to mainland), lying across entrance to Galveston Bay, an arm of Gulf of Mexico. A leading U.S. port, with deepwater channel from the Gulf to its large harbor, and channels leading thence to Texas City (N) and Houston (NW); also on Gulf Intracoastal Waterway. Port of entry; huge exports of sulphur, cotton, wheat, flour; also handles metals, sugar, rice, cottonseed and lumber products; large drydocks, shipyards. A terminus for 6 railroads. Has huge grain elevators and cotton compresses; also machine shops, flour and rice mills, meat-packing plants, breweries, and plants producing chemicals, steel, iron, tin, bronze, and copper products, hardware, petroleum products. Large fishing and shrimping fleet. City's situation on long beach, its equable climate, the fishing, and its subtropical plantings (especially oleanders) have made it a popular resort. Seat of Univ. of Texas medical school and a group of hospitals. Here are Fort Travis (est. 1898) and Fort Crockett (est. 1897–99), active in Second World War, and Fort San Jacinto (NE of city). Region was known early to Sp. explorers; it was probably here that Cabeza de Vaca was shipwrecked in 1528. After exploration of bay in late 18th cent., isl., with a good natural harbor, became outlaw country and hq. for adventurers, revolutionists, and buccaneers, notably Jean Lafitte, who renamed the place Campeachy and made it home port, 1817–21, for pirate forays against Sp. shipping. Settlement gained importance in 1830s; in Texas Revolution it was a naval base, and later became a gateway for immigrants and goods entering the new Republic. Despite yellow fever, hurricanes, and a Union blockade and brief occupation (1862) in Civil War, growth as a cotton port continued; harbor improvements completed 1896 made it a deepwater port. In 1900 a hurricane leveled the city, killing thousands; in rebuilding, the city adopted a commission government (1st of its kind in U.S.), constructed massive seawall along the Gulf, and raised the ground level of city by several ft.
Galveston Bay, S Texas, inlet of Gulf of Mexico c.20 mi. SE of Houston, with its entrance bet. tip of Bolivar Peninsula and NE end of Galveston Isl.; c.35 mi. long NE–SW; max. width c.19 mi. With deepwater channels from the Gulf to harbors of Galveston, Texas City, Houston, and other cities, and crossed by Gulf Intracoastal Waterway, bay is center of one of most important U.S. port and industrial regions. Bay supplies oyster shell for cement. In NE arm (Trinity Bay), receives Trinity R.; in NW arm (San Jacinto Bay) receives San Jacinto R., followed in part by Houston Ship Channel. In E, it is divided by reefs from East Bay (c.22 mi. long, 2–5 mi. wide), lying NW of Bolivar Peninsula; in SW, connected by passages to West Bay (c.20 mi. long, 3–6 mi. wide), lying bet. Galveston Isl. and coast.
Galveston Island, Texas: see GALVESTON.
Gálvez (gäl'vĕs), town (pop. estimate 5,000), S central Santa Fe prov., Argentina, 75 mi. NNW of Rosario; agr. center (wheat, flax, oats, barley, sunflowers, livestock); mfg. of wire nets, furniture, dairy products. Plant nurseries. Has theater.
Gálvez (gäl'vĕth), town (pop. 4,403), Toledo prov., central Spain, 17 mi. SW of Toledo; agr. center (cereals, vegetables, olives, grapes, livestock). Makes olive oil, cheese, flour.
Galway (gôl'wā), Gaelic *na Gaillimhe*, county (□ 2,293.2; pop. 165,201), Connacht, W Ireland; ⊙ Galway. On the Atlantic bordered by cos. Clare (S), Mayo (N), Roscommon (N and E), and Offaly and Tipperary (SE). Drained by the Shannon and Suck rivers and their tributaries. Of the many lakes, loughs Corrib and Derg are largest. Surface is barren and mountainous in W; rises to 2,395 ft. on Benbaun. Connemara is lake and moorland region in NW. In E surface is level, with fertile soil. Coastline is deeply indented; main inlet, Galway Bay. There are numerous isls. on Atlantic coast; ARAN ISLANDS and Inishbofin are largest. Limestone, marble, copper, lead are worked. Sea and lake fisheries (herring, salmon, lobster) are important. Stock raising (cattle, sheep), agr. (potatoes, beets). Industries include woolen milling, sugar refining, mfg. of fish nets, rope, furniture, agr. implements, cattle feed, fertilizer. Peat is exploited industrially at Attymon. Besides Galway, other towns are Tuam, Ballinasloe, Oughterard, Athenry, Clifden, Loughrea, and Portumna. Aughrim or Aghrim was scene of important battle (1691). There are numerous monastic ruins (Inishmore isl., Clonfert), raths, anc. stone monuments, and other traces of early occupation.
Galway, Gaelic *Gaillimh*, urban district (pop. 20,370), ⊙ Co. Galway, Ireland, at head of Galway Bay, at mouth of Lough Corrib, 115 mi. W of Dublin; 53°16'N 9°3'W; seaport and fishing center (herring, salmon), with dock installations. Chief exports are herring, salmon, woolens, marble, agr. produce. Industries include mfg. of fish nets, rope, agr. implements, furniture, hosiery, cattle feed, fertilizer. Features of town are fragmentary remains of 13th-cent. town walls, including Spanish Arch; Church of St. Nicholas (1320); 1342 bridge; University Col. (constituent of Natl. Univ. of Ireland), founded 1849 as successor to 16th-cent. col. that made Galway an intellectual center and stronghold of Gaelic language; Lynch's Stone, in Lynch's mansion, commemorating execution of a mayor's son; remains of 1296 Franciscan friary; and the Claddagh, fishermen's quarter. A fort built here 1124 by the men of Connaught was taken (1232) by Richard de Burgh, who colonized district. Galway later became important center of trade with Spain. Town was taken 1652 by Ludlow; it surrendered 1691 to General Ginkel after battle of Aughrim. Since 1922 port has again grown in importance.
Galway, village (pop. 188), Saratoga co., E N.Y., 10 mi. NE of Amsterdam, in dairying area.
Galway Bay, inlet (30 mi. long, 23 mi. wide at entrance) of the Atlantic, bet. Co. Galway and Co. Clare, Ireland. Entrance is protected by Aran Isls. At head of bay is Galway.
Galyatetö (gŏ'yŏtĕtû), Hung. *Galyatető*, village, Heves co., N Hungary, 8 mi. N of Gyöngyös; climatic resort (alt. 3,166 ft.) in Matra Mts.
Gamaches (gämäsh'), town (pop. 2,769), Somme dept., N France, on the Bresle and 15 mi. SW of Abbeville; metal- and glassworks. Has 12th-15th-cent. church.
Gamagori (gämä'gōrē), town (pop. 23,357), Aichi prefecture, central Honshu, Japan, on Atsumi Bay, 10 mi. WNW of Toyohashi; summer resort; fishery.
Gama Island (gä'mä) (□ 7), in Anegada Bay, SW Buenos Aires prov., Argentina, 45 mi. NE of Carmen de Patagones.
Gamaliya, El, or **Al-Jamaliyah** (ĕl gămälē'yů, jă–), village (pop. 17,364), Daqahliya prov., Lower Egypt, on El Bahr el Saghir and 4 mi. WNW of Manzala; cotton, cereals.
Gamarra (gämä'rä), town (pop. 1,963), Magdalena dept., N Colombia, on Magdalena R. and 50 mi. SSE of El Banco; livestock. Cableway to Ocaña and Cúcuta is E.
Gamarri, Lake (gämä'rē), in salt marshes of Aussa dist., NE Ethiopia, near Fr. Somaliland border, 15 mi. NE of L. Abbé; c.5 mi. long.
Gamas (gŏ'mäsh), Hung. *Gamás*, town (pop. 2,452), Somogy co., SW Hungary, 18 mi. N of Kaposvar; wheat, corn.
Gambaga (gämbä'gä), town (pop. 1,949), Northern Territories, NE Gold Coast, on road and 80 mi. NNE of Tamale; millet, durra, yams, cattle. Hq. Mamprusi dist.
Gambang (gäm'bäng), village (pop. 508), E Pahang, Malaya, on road and 18 mi. WSW of Kuantan; tin mining.
Gambara (gäm'bärä), village (pop. 2,992), Brescia prov., Lombardy, N Italy, 16 mi. NE of Cremona; silk mill.
Gambassi (gämbäs'sē), village (pop. 1,407), Firenze prov., Tuscany, central Italy, 22 mi. SW of Florence; cementworks.
Gambat (gŭm'bŭt), town (pop. 4,893), Khairpur state, W Pakistan, 18 mi. SW of Khairpur; millet, wheat, cotton; handicraft cloth weaving (sheets), pottery mfg.; lacquer work.
Gambatesa (gämbätä'zä), village (pop. 3,241), Campobasso prov., Abruzzi e Molise, S central Italy, 14 mi. ESE of Campobasso.
Gambela or **Gambeila** (both: gämbā'lä), Sudanese trading station (pop. 500), Wallaga prov., W central Ethiopia, on Baro R. and 65 mi. W of Gore; 8°15'N 34°34'E; road junction. Commercial center and transshipment point at head of navigation on Baro-Sobat-White Nile river system to Khartoum, 860 mi. away. Situated on chief communication route bet. Ethiopia and Anglo-Egyptian Sudan. Exports coffee, beeswax, hides; imports salt, liquor, cotton and canned goods. In vicinity are alluvial gold deposits. Administered as part of Upper Nile prov. of Anglo-Egyptian Sudan after it was leased (1907) from Ethiopia.
Gambell (găm'bůl), village (pop. 310), on NW St. Lawrence Isl., W Alaska, c.200 mi. W of Nome; whaling, fox trapping. Cooperative store. Site of Presbyterian mission. Air landing-strip.

Gambellara (gămbĕl-lä'rä), village (pop. 2,061), Vicenza prov., Veneto, N Italy, 11 mi. SW of Vicenza, in grape- and tobacco-growing region; alcohol distilleries. Basalt quarries near by.

Gambhira, India: see BIJAIGARH.

Gambia (găm'bēŭ), British colony and protectorate (□ c.4,000; 1949 pop. estimate 268,000), W Africa; ⊙ BATHURST. It is a 15- to 30-mi.-wide, wedge-like enclave in Senegal (Fr. West Africa), bordering both banks of Gambia R. for almost 300 mi. of its lower course; its narrow Atlantic Ocean frontage coincides with Gambia R. estuary. The colony (□ 69) consists of SAINT MARY'S ISLAND (site of Bathurst) and KOMBO SAINT MARY (mainland dist. just SW of Bathurst). Several other small areas (Ceded Mile, Albreda, Brefet, Bajana, MacCarthy Isl.) are historically in Gambia colony, but are administered (since 1946) as part of the protectorate, which represents the bulk of Gambia (□ 3,964). Near the coast, climate is pleasant bet. Dec. and May (dry season). Precipitation (30–50 in. per year) is heaviest June–Oct. Upriver dists. are excessively hot. Health conditions are poor because of inadequate drainage near river banks and shortage of housing. Peanuts are by far the leading export crop. For their cultivation c.10,000 "strange farmers" enter Gambia as seasonal labor from neighboring Fr. and Port. territories. Palm kernels, hides, and beeswax are minor exports. Millet, rice, and corn are subsistence crops. In 1948, a large-scale poultry farm was established at Yundum for chicken and egg shipments to England, but by 1951 the scheme had largely failed. Shark fisheries. Industry is limited to peanut-oil mfg., handicraft spinning and weaving, bamboo working, mat and pottery mfg. Yundum airport (SW of Bathurst) was developed during Second World War. There is little overland transport, the Gambia R. being the chief trade artery. Native pop. consists of Mohammedan Mandingoes (⅗ of total), Wollofs (mainly at Bathurst), and Serahulis, and of pagan Fulas and Jolas. The Gambia was discovered by early Portuguese navigators. The British became dominant in early 17th cent. and were never permanently dislodged despite repeated French and Dutch assaults. Governed as part of Sierra Leone until 1843, and as one of the West African Settlements 1866–88. The colony received a separate govt. in 1888, and by 1902 the protectorate had been established within present boundaries. For administration the protectorate is divided into 4 divisions: Western (⊙ Brikama), Central (⊙ Kerewan), MACCARTHY ISLAND (⊙ Georgetown), and UPPER RIVER (⊙ Basse).

Gambia River, Fr. *Gambie,* in Fr. West Africa and Gambia, rises near town of Labé (Fr. Guinea) in Fouta Djallon mts., flows c.700 mi. W, entering Gambia at Koina and passing Basse, Georgetown, Kuntaur, and Kaur, to the Atlantic at Bathurst. Navigable for ocean-going vessels (13-ft. draught) below Georgetown, 175 mi. upstream, and for flat-bottom vessels below Koina, 292 mi. upstream. An important trade artery, it carries peanuts, beeswax, hides, skins.

Gambier (găm'bēr, gămbēr'), village (pop. 1,037), Knox co., central Ohio, 5 mi. E of Mount Vernon and on Kokosing R. Seat of Kenyon Col.

Gambier, Mount, Australia: see MOUNT GAMBIER.

Gambier Island (găm'bēr) (□ 27), SW B.C., in Howe Sound, 17 mi. NW of Vancouver; 6 mi. long, 5 mi. wide. S part is deeply indented. On E coast is New Brighton village; lumbering.

Gambier Islands, at entrance to Spencer Gulf, 22 mi. W of Yorke Peninsula, South Australia. Comprise Wedge Isl. (3 mi. long, 1 mi. wide) and 4 islets. Limestone; sheep run.

Gambier Islands, Fr. *Archipel des Gambier,* or **Mangareva** (măng"ärä'vä), coral group, Fr. Oceania, S Pacific; 23°10'S 135°W. Comprise 4 isls. and many uninhabited islets within reef with 40-mi. circumference. Mangareva, largest and only important isl. (pop. 553), is 5 mi. long; rises to 1,400 ft.; chief village is Rikitea, ⊙ Gambier Isls. Mangareva was discovered 1797 by British; annexed 1881 by France. Isls. have copra and coffee plantations, many pearl fisheries. Polynesian natives. The administrative div. (□ c.12; pop. 6,696) of FRENCH ESTABLISHMENTS IN OCEANIA which embraces the Gambiers also includes 23 atolls of the Tuamotu group.

Gambiraopet or **Ghambiraopet** (both: gŭmbĭrou'-pät), town (pop. 5,394), Karimnagar dist., E central Hyderabad state, India, 39 mi. WSW of Karimnagar; rice, millet, oilseeds.

Gambo (gămbō'), village, S Ubangi-Shari, Fr. Equatorial Africa, 35 mi. WSW of Bangassou; experimental cotton plantations.

Gamboa or **North Gamboa** (gămbō'ŭ), Sp. *Gamboa Norte* (gämbō'ä nôr'tā), town (pop. 3,082), Balboa dist., S Panama Canal Zone, on Chagres R., at N end of Gaillard Cut, on transisthmian railroad, and 16 mi. NW of Panama city. Radio tower, emergency port. Region produces corn, rice, oranges; livestock. South Gamboa adjoins SE.

Gambo Lake (□ 8), E N.F., 20 mi. SE of Gander; 20 mi. long; drains into Bonavista Bay.

Gambolò (gämbôlô'), town (pop. 4,162), Pavia prov., Lombardy, N Italy, on Terdoppio R. and 15 mi. NW of Pavia, in cereal-growing region; piano factory.

Gamboma (gămbōmä'), village, central Middle Congo territory, Fr. Equatorial Africa, 100 mi. NE of Djambala; native market and medical center (notably for trypanosomiasis treatment).

Gambut (gămbōōt'), village, E Cyrenaica, Libya, 33 mi. ESE of Tobruk. Scene of fighting (1941–42) bet. Axis and British in Second World War.

Gamela, Greece: see TYMPHE.

Gameleira (gŭmĭlā'rŭ), city (pop. 3,010), E Pernambuco, NE Brazil, on railroad and 50 mi. SW of Recife, in sugar-growing region. Formerly spelled Gamelleira.

Gamelleira, Brazil: see GAMELEIRA.

Gamelleira do Assuruá, Brazil: see SANTO INÁCIO.

Gamerco (gă'mûrkō, gŭmâr'kō), village (pop. c.400), McKinley co., NW N.Mex., just N of Gallup, near Ariz. line; alt. 6,750 ft.; coal mining. Pueblo ruins near by.

Gamila, Greece: see TYMPHE.

Gaming (gä'mĭng), town (pop. 4,421), SW Lower Austria, 15 mi. ESE of Waidhofen an der Ybbs; mfg. (machinery, small agr. tools). Ruins of Carthusian convent.

Gamka River (găm'kŭ), S Cape Prov., U. of So. Afr., rises in Nieuwveld Range, N of Beaufort West, flows 160 mi. SSW, past Beaufort West and Calitzdorp, to confluence with Olifants R. 10 mi. S of Calitzdorp, forming Gouritz R.

Gamlakarleby, Finland: see KOKKOLA.

Gamla Uppsala (gäm'lä ŭp'sä"lä) [=Old Uppsala], village (pop. 789), Uppsala co., E Sweden, on Fyris R. and 2 mi. NNE of UPPSALA. In pagan times ⊙ Sweden, it lost its importance in 13th cent., when kings moved their residence to Stockholm. Has several stone monuments and mounds, dating from 4th–6th cent.

Gamleby (gäm'lŭbü"), town (pop. 836), Kalmar co., SE Sweden, on Gamleby Bay, Swedish *Gamlebyviken,* 15-mi.-long inlet of Baltic, 13 mi. NW of Vastervik; port; sawmilling, fruit canning; mfg. of bricks, furniture. Site of agr. school.

Gamlingay, town and parish (pop. 1,408), SW Cambridge, England, 14 mi. W of Cambridge; agr. market. Has 14th–15th-cent. church.

Gamlitz (gäm'lĭts), town (pop. 3,231), Styria, SE Austria, 4 mi. S of Leibnitz; vineyards, wheat, potatoes, poultry.

Gammelstad (gä'mŭlstäd"), village (pop. 544) Norrbotten co., N Sweden, on Lule R. and 5 mi. NW of Lulea; flour milling, woodworking. Has 15th-cent. church.

Gamo, Japan: see KAMO, Kagoshima prefecture.

Gamonal (gämōnäl'), village (pop. 1,522), Toledo prov., central Spain, 6 mi. W of Talavera de la Reina; cereals, olives, livestock; meat products.

Gamonal de Ríopico (dhā rē'ōpē"kō), town (pop. 1,057), Burgos prov., N Spain, 2 mi. E of Burgos; cereals, vegetables; liquor distilling, flour milling.

Gampaha (gŭm'pŭhŭ), town (pop. 2,883), Western Prov., Ceylon, 16 mi. NE of Colombo; trades in coconuts, rice, cinnamon, vegetables. Govt. Botanic and Experiment Garden (opened 1876); here 1st Para rubber trees were introduced into Ceylon; has caoutchouc shrubs, ipecac plants, and part of original jungle of Ceylonese low country.

Gampel (gäm'pŭl), village (pop. 768), Valais canton, S Switzerland, on the Rhone, at mouth of Lonza R., and 5 mi. E of Leuk.

Gampola (gŭmpō'lŭ), anc. *Gangasiripura* [Singhalese,=royal city on the river], town (pop. 9,194), Central Prov., Ceylon, on Kandy Plateau, on the Mahaweli Ganga and 10 mi. SSW of Kandy; trade center (tea, rubber, rice, vegetables). Anc. Hindu temple; annual religious festival. Founded 1347 and became (for c.30 years) ⊙ Ceylon.

Gamprin (gämprēn'), village (pop. 390), N Liechtenstein, on the Rhine (Swiss border) and 5 mi. N of Vaduz. Cattle raising. Has near-by prehistoric remains.

Gamrie, agr. village, NE Banffshire, Scotland, near Moray Firth, 7 mi. E of Banff.

Gamu-Gofa (gä'mōō-gō'fä), province (□ 15,000), S Ethiopia, bordering on Kenya; ⊙ Chancha. Situated bet. Galana Sagan (E) and Omo (W) rivers; includes L. Chamo, part of lakes Abaya and Stefanie, and N tip of L. Rudolf, in Great Rift Valley. Mostly mountainous (more than 5,000 ft. high), and forested, rising to c.13,780 ft. in Mt. Gughe, with hilly plateau in S. Agr. (cereals, plantain, cotton, tobacco) and stock raising. Chief centers: Gardula and Bako. Prov. formed c.1941.

Gamvik (gäm'vĭk, -vēk), fishing village (pop. 461; canton pop. 1,610), Finnmark co., N Norway, on Barents Sea of Arctic Ocean, 80 mi. NW of Vardo, 13 mi. ESE of Nordkyn cape; 71°4'N 28°16'E; northernmost village on European mainland.

Gan (gã), village (pop. 774), Basses-Pyrénées dept., SW France, 5 mi. S of Pau; mfg. of berets, bricks and tiles. Vineyards. Marble quarried near by.

Ganado. 1 (gŭnä'dō) Village (1940 pop. 963), Apache co., NE Ariz., in Navajo Indian Reservation, 47 mi. WNW of Gallup, N.Mex.; alt. 6,400 ft.; trading post. Presbyterian hosp. and mission here. **2** (gŭnā'dŭ) Town (pop. 1,258), Jackson co., S Texas, 34 mi. NE of Victoria; rail, trade point in agr. area. Founded 1883.

Ganale Dorya (gä'nälā dō'ryä), Ital. *Ganale Doria'* river in S Ethiopia, rises on Mt. Guramba near source of Webi Shebeli (E edge of Great Rift Valley), flows c.380 mi. S, E, and S to Dolo, where it unites with Dawa R. to form Juba R. Interrupted by Baratieri Falls. Receives Web R. near Dolo. Forms boundary bet. Harar and Sidamo-Borana provs.

Gananoque (gănŭnō'kwē, -kwŭ), town (pop. 4,044), SE Ont., on the St. Lawrence, at mouth of Gananoque R., near the Thousand Isls., and 18 mi. ENE of Kingston; metalworking (steel, copper), mfg. of automobile parts; dairying; resort. Founded 1798.

Gananoque River, SE Ont., issues from Gananoque L. (6 mi. long), 8 mi. NNE of Gananoque, flows 15 mi. SSW to the St. Lawrence at Gananoque.

Ganaweh, Bandar, Iran: see BANDAR GANAWEH.

Gancheshty, Moldavian SSR: see KOTOVSKOYE.

Ganchi (gän'chē), village (1926 pop. 1,284), central Leninabad oblast, Tadzhik SSR, 8 mi. ENE of Ura-Tyube; wheat, sericulture.

Ganciova (gûnchô'vä), Rum. *Gânciova,* village (pop. 3,362), Dolj prov., S Rumania, 28 mi. S of Craiova.

Gand, Belgium: see GHENT.

Ganda, Angola: see VILA MARIANO MACHADO.

Gandajika (gändäjē'kä), village, Kasai prov., S Belgian Congo, 50 mi. SW of Kabinda; has agr. research station notably for cotton; cotton ginning.

Gandak River (gŭn'dŭk), left tributary of the Ganges, in S Nepal and NW Bihar, India, formed 55 mi. W of Katmandu (Nepal) by junction of KALI GANDAKI RIVER and TRISULI RIVER, which drain area bet. Dhaulagiri and Gosainthan peaks; flows SW (here called Narayani or Sapt Gandaki) into India, and SE, forming part of Uttar Pradesh–Bihar border, through fertile Ganges Plain of NW Bihar, to the Ganges opposite Patna; total length, including Kali Gandaki R., c.420 mi. Dam on India–Nepal border serves Tribeni Canal. Also called Great Gandak in India. Formerly spelled Gunduk. In Bihar another tributary of the Ganges, BURHI GANDAK RIVER, flows E of the Gandak's lower course.

Gandamak (gŭn'dŭmŭk), village (pop. over 2,000), Eastern Prov., Afghanistan, 26 mi. WSW of Jalalabad and on highway to Kabul. Scene of British massacre (1842) by Afghans. By the treaty of Gandamak (1879), in 2d Afghan War, the Afghan emir ceded Kurram, Pishin, and Sibi areas to Britain, which also obtained control over the Khyber Pass.

Gandara (gŭn'dŭrŭ), village (pop. 4,342), Southern Prov., Ceylon, on S coast, 5 mi. E of Matara; fishing center; vegetables, rice.

Gandava (gŭndä'vŭ), village, Kalat state, E Baluchistan, W Pakistan, 70 mi. SSW of Sibi, on Kachhi plain; markets wheat, millet, cotton goods. Sometimes spelled Gandawa.

Ganddal (gän'däl), village (pop. 214) in Hoyland (Nor. *Høyland*) canton (pop. 11,191), Rogaland co., SW Norway, 10 mi. S of Stavanger; rail junction; furniture mfg. Woolen-milling village (pop. 351) of Figgjo (fĭg'yô) is 4 mi. SE.

Gandefjord, Norway: see GANDS FJORD.

Ganden (gän'dĕn) or **Gaden** (gä'dĕn), Chinese *Kateng Ssu* (gä'dŭng sŭ'), lamasery, S Tibet, on the Kyi Chu and 25 mi. ENE of Lhasa. One of the 3 great lamaseries of Tibet (the others are Drepung and Sera). Founded 1409 by Tsong-kha-pa, founder of *Gelukpa* [Yellow Hat] sect of Lamaism, it is oldest lamasery of *gelukpas;* has mausoleum of Tsong-kha-pa.

Gander, town (pop. 293, not including airport personnel; total pop. estimated at 3,000), E N.F., near Gander L., 50 mi. E of Grand Falls; 48°57'N 54°32'W; site of major transatlantic airport. Begun 1936 for experimental transport flights, field was completed in 1939. During Second World War it was considerably expanded and became major Allied base. After the war it became main North American terminal for air services to all parts of Europe. Though subject to heavy snowfalls, Gander is relatively fog free.

Ganderkesee (gän'dŭrkŭzā"), village (commune pop. 15,034), in Oldenburg, NW Germany, after 1945 in Lower Saxony, 4 mi. WSW of Delmenhorst; mfg. of building materials.

Gander Lake (□ 46.5; 30 mi. long, up to 3 mi. wide), E N.F., 35 mi. E of Grand Falls, at confluence of Northwest Gander R. and Southwest Gander R., which here form Gander R.

Gander River, E N.F., rises as Northwest Gander R. on Partridgeberry Hill, S of Grand Falls, flows NE to Gander L., where it receives Southwest Gander R., thence flows NE to Gander Bay of the Atlantic, 25 mi. N of Gander; 110 mi. long.

Gandersheim, Bad, Germany: see BAD GANDERSHEIM.

Gandesa (gändā'sä), city (pop. 2,771), Tarragona prov., NE Spain, 17 mi. NNW of Tortosa, in hilly region of olive groves and vineyards; trades in almonds, filberts, fruit, cereals. Gypsum and alabaster quarries in vicinity. Has Romanesque church (12th–16th cent.). Mineral springs at Font Calda monastery near by.

Gandevi (gŭndä'vē), town (pop. 8,688), Surat dist., N Bombay, India, 28 mi. SSE of Surat; trades in cotton, millet, molasses, ghee, castor oil; sugar mfg., distilling, hand cloth weaving, dyeing, and printing; pottery works.

Gandhara (gŭndä'rŭ), anc. region of NW India, astride middle Indus R.; main cities were Peshawar and Taxila. Originally a prov. of the Persian Empire, it was reached (326 B.C.) by Alexander the Great. Under Bactrian rule (3d cent.–1st cent. B.C.), it developed noted Greco-Bactrian school of sculpture, consisting mainly of images of Buddha and reliefs representing scenes from Buddhist texts. The region continued to flourish under the Kushans (1st cent. A.D.), but was raided (early 6th cent.) by Huns.

Gandi (gän'dē), town (pop. 8,078), Sokoto prov., Northern Provinces, NW Nigeria, on Sokoto R. and 35 mi. ESE of Sokoto; rice, millet, cotton; cattle, skins.

Gandía (gändē'ä), city (pop. 16,795), Valencia prov., E Spain, 38 mi. SSE of Valencia; its Mediterranean port, El Grao de Gandía (pop. 2,600; 2.5 mi. NE), exports large quantities of oranges. Center of rich truck-farming area. Tanning, silk spinning, sawmilling, olive-oil processing, canning (fruit, vegetables); other mfg.: orange extracts and beverages, brandy and liqueur, candy, tiles, felt hats, shoes. Has Gothic collegiate church, baroque palace of Borja family (now Jesuit col.), and Colegio de Escuela Pia founded (16th cent.) by St. Francis Borja, b. here. City probably of Greek origin; occupied (8th–13th cent.) by Moors. Duchy of Gandía belonged (1483–1740) to Borja or Borgia family.

Gandino (gändē'nō), village (pop. 3,548), Bergamo prov., Lombardy, N Italy, 14 mi. NE of Bergamo; woolen mills, dyeworks.

Gandiole or **Gandiol** (both: gändyôl'), NW Senegal, Fr. West Africa, on coast just S of Senegal R. mouth, 8 mi. S of Saint-Louis; salt raking, peanut growing, fishing.

Gandi River, Nigeria: see Sokoto River.

Gandjur, Manchuria: see Ganjur.

Gando (gän'dō), village (pop. 692), Grand Canary, Canary Isls., 13 mi. S of Las Palmas. Beach resort and airport with seaplane base. Adjoining is Point Gando (27°56'N 15°21'W).

Gando, Nigeria: see Gwandu.

Gandoca (gändō'kä), village, Limón prov., E Costa Rica, on Caribbean Sea, at mouth of small Gandoca R., 40 mi. SE of Limón; bananas.

Gands Fjord (gäns), Nor. *Gandefjord* or *Gandsfjord*, S branch of Bokn Fjord, Rogaland co., SW Norway, just E of Stavanger; extends S 8 mi. to Sandnes.

Gandy, village (pop. 88), Logan co., central Nebr., 3 mi. E of Stapleton, near S.Loup R.

Gandzha, Azerbaijan SSR: see Kirovabad, city.

Ganga, river, India: see Ganges River.

Ganga Chu, Tibet: see Manasarowar Lake.

Gangadhar River, India: see Sankosh River.

Gangadwara, India: see Hardwar.

Gangaikondapuram, India: see Jayankondacholapuram.

Gangakher (gŭng'gäkär), town (pop. 7,698), Parbhani dist., NW Hyderabad state, India, on Godavari R. and 22 mi. S of Parbhani; millet, oilseeds; cotton ginning. Also spelled Gangakhed.

Gangala na Bodio (gäng-gä'lä nä bōd'yō), village, Eastern Prov., NE Belgian Congo, on Dungu R., a headstream of the Uele, at SW extremity of Garamba Natl. Park, 295 mi. ENE of Buta; noted elephant taming and training center established in 1927. Sometimes spelled Gangara na Bodio.

Gangán (gäng-gän'), village (pop. estimate 200), N Chubut natl. territory, Argentina, 170 mi. NW of Rawson; sheep-raising center.

Ganganagar, India: see Sri Ganganagar.

Gangapur (gŭng'gäpŏŏr). **1** Village (pop. 4,769), Aurangabad dist., NW Hyderabad state, India, 25 mi. SW of Aurangabad; millet, wheat, oilseeds; cotton ginning. **2** Town (pop. 11,050), E Rajasthan, India, 65 mi. SE of Jaipur; local trade in millet, gram, barley, wheat; handicraft cotton weaving. **3** Town (pop. 5,357), S Rajasthan, India, 25 mi. WSW of Bhilwara; millet, cotton, wheat; cotton ginning. Formerly in enclave of Gwalior state. **4** Town (pop. 2,336), Benares dist., SE Uttar Pradesh, India, 9 mi. W of Benares city center; rice, barley, gram, wheat, sugar cane.

Ganga River, India: see Ganges River.

Gangasiripura, Ceylon: see Gampola.

Gangavati, India: see Gangawati.

Gangaw (gäng-gô'), village, Pakokku dist., Upper Burma, on Myittha R. and 85 mi. NW of Pakokku, on road to Kalemyo. In Second World War, scene of fighting.

Gangawati (gŭng-gä'vŭtē), town (pop. 7,613), Raichur dist., SW Hyderabad state, India, on Tungabhadra R. and 26 mi. ENE of Koppal; millet, rice, sugar cane; cotton ginning, oilseed milling. Also spelled Gangavati.

Gang Canal (gŭng) or **Bikaner Canal** (bē'kŭnär), important irrigation channel in W Punjab and N Rajasthan, India; from left bank of Sutlej R., just NW of Ferozepore, flows c.170 mi. SSW to 7 mi. ESE of Anupgarh (Rajasthan). From headworks for distance of 84 mi. lined with concrete. Has several distributaries. Opened 1927. Sometimes called Bikaner-Gang Canal.

Gangchhendzönga, India: see Kanchenjunga.

Ganges (găn'jēz), village (pop. estimate 500), SW B.C., on E Saltspring Isl., 11 mi. ENE of Duncan; fishing port; lumbering, dairying; poultry, sheep.

Ganges (gãzh), town (pop. 3,743), Hérault dept., S France, in the Cévennes, on Hérault R. and 24 mi. NNW of Montpellier; silk-hosiery mfg. center. Metalworking, olive-oil pressing.

Ganges Canals (găn'jēz), important irrigation system in Uttar Pradesh, India, in Ganges-Jumna Doab; comprise Upper and Lower Ganges canals. **Upper Ganges Canal** (opened 1855–56) leaves right bank of the Ganges at Hardwar (headworks), runs W and SE, paralleling river and forming Anupshahr Branch (E) and Mal Branch (W) distributaries; thence S, splitting SE of Aligarh into Cawnpore (E) and Etawah (W) branches. Total length of main canal and distributaries, c.5,950 mi. **Lower Ganges Canal** (opened 1879–80) leaves right bank of the Ganges 5 mi. E of Dibai (headworks at Naraura), runs SSE and S, splitting into Farrukhabad and Bewar branches (E) and Bhognipur Branch (W) distributaries; latter branch crosses Cawnpore and Etawah branches of Upper Ganges Canal; Etawah Branch continues ESE as Lower Ganges Canal, dividing into various distributaries in SE end of Ganges-Jumna Doab; total length of main canal and distributaries, c.5,120 mi. Entire system irrigates over □ 1,700 and also furnishes hydroelectric power.

Ganges Delta, NE India and E Pakistan, area formed by mouths of the Ganges; bounded N by Padma R., E by Meghna R. estuary mouth, S by Bay of Bengal, W by Bhagirathi R. (Hooghly R. in lower course). Radial slope of delta is SE. In S area lie the Sundarbans, a region of half-reclaimed isls. and tidal creeks. There appears to be no appreciable land accretion, except at ends of delta face, since 18th cent. Dists. within delta: 24-Parganas, Khulna, Bakargunj, Noakhali (isls. only), Faridpur, Jessore, Kushtia, Murshidabad (area E of the Bhagirathi), and Nadia. Main distributaries: Madhumati, Jamuna, Jalangi, and Arial Khan rivers.

Ganges-Jumna Doab (-jŏŏm'nŭ dō'äb) [Hindi *Doab*=two waters], a rich alluvial tract in Uttar Pradesh, India, bet. Ganges (E) and Jumna (W) rivers; from Siwalik Range extends SSE to confluence of 2 rivers at Allahabad. Largest wheat-producing area in Uttar Pradesh.; other crops include barley, gram, millet, corn, sugar cane, cotton. Irrigated by Ganges Canals system and by Eastern Jumna Canal. The word *Doab* is applied to land bet. any 2 confluent rivers in India, but when unqualified it refers to tract bet. Jumna and Ganges rivers.

Ganges Plain, low alluvial region, in N India and E Pakistan, formed by the Ganges and its tributaries; comprises greater part of Uttar Pradesh, large part of Bihar, and most of East and West Bengal. One of most heavily populated and cultivated areas in Asia. Extensive canal irrigation system in Uttar Pradesh.

Ganges River, Sanskrit and Hindi *Ganga* (gŭng'gŭ), sacred river of the Hindus in N India and E Pakistan; formed in W Kumaun Himalayas by junction of headstreams (Bhagirathi River and Alaknanda R.) at Devaprayag, Uttar Pradesh, at 30°9'N 78°37'E. Flows W through Siwalik Range, S onto Ganges Plain at Hardwar (headworks of Upper Ganges Canal), past Anupshahr, and SE past Farrukhabad, Kanauj, Cawnpore, Allahabad (here receives Jumna R., forming one of most sacred confluences in India), thence E past the holy city of Benares, past Ghazipur and Ballia, into Bihar, past Patna, Monghyr, Bhagalpur, and Sahibganj, and SE into West Bengal, bifurcating (5 mi. NE of Jangipur) into Padma River (its main channel) and Bhagirathi River (lower course becomes Hooghly River). As the Padma, it continues SE through East Bengal (E Pakistan), past Rajshahi, receiving Jamuna R. (main bed of the Brahmaputra) 20 mi. NNW of Faridpur; combined streams continue SE, joining Meghna River NW of Chandpur and emptying (as the Meghna) into Bay of Bengal through 4 main mouths. Total length, from source of the upper Bhagirathi to junction with the Meghna, c.1,560 mi. Principal left tributaries rise in the Himalayas; include (NW to SE) Ramganga, Gumti, Gogra, Gandak, Kosi, and Mahananda rivers; right tributaries include Jumna and Son rivers. Used extensively as a trade artery. Regarded since Puranic times as one of most sacred Hindu rivers in India, although according to prophecy its sanctity should have passed to the Narbada in early-20th cent. Large melas held at Hardwar and Allahabad.

Gangi (gän'jē), town (pop. 9,890), Palermo prov., N central Sicily, in Madonie Mts., 20 mi. SSE of Cefalù; cheese. Has 16th-cent. cathedral.

Gangkofen (gäng'kō"fŭn), village (pop. 2,575), Lower Bavaria, Germany, 9 mi. NW of Eggenfelden; mfg. of chemicals, brewing, woodworking. Chartered 1450.

Gangoh (gŭng'gō), town (pop. 16,266), Saharanpur dist., N Uttar Pradesh, India, 21 mi. SW of Saharanpur; wheat, rice, rape and mustard, grain. Has 2 mosques, built by Akbar and Jahangir, and mausoleum built 1537 by Humayun.

Gangoli, India: see Coondapoor.

Gangotri (gŭnggō'trē), noted Hindu mountain shrine, Tehri dist., N Uttar Pradesh, India, in W Kumaun Himalayas, on the Bhagirathi and 50 mi. NE of Tehri; pilgrimage center. Has square temples (closed in winter), built in 18th cent. by Gurkha commander. N terminus of Gangotri glacier lies 10 mi. SE; source of Bhagirathi R. **Gangotri Peak** (21,700 ft.) is 9 mi. SSW.

Gangpur (gäng'pŏŏr), former princely state (□ 2,477; pop. 398,171) in Orissa States, India; ⊙ was Sundargarh. Inc. 1949 into newly-created dist. of Sundargarh, Orissa.

Gangra, Turkey: see Cankiri, town.

Gang Rimpoche, Tibet: see Kailas, peak.

Gangtok (gäng'tôk), town, ⊙ Sikkim, India, in SW Assam Himalayas, 28 mi. NE of Darjeeling; trades in corn, rice, pulse, oranges. Maharaja of Sikkim's palace here. Buddhist monastery of Rumtek or Rhumtek 4 mi. SW.

Ganguli, India: see Coondapoor.

Gangviken (gông'vē"kŭn), Swedish *Gångviken*, village (pop. 698), Vasternorrland co., NE Sweden, on small inlet of Gulf of Bothnia, 5 mi. N of Sundsvall, opposite Alno isl.; seaside resort.

Gan Hashomron (gän' häshōmrōn'), settlement (pop. 200), W Israel, in Plain of Sharon, 5 mi. ENE of Hadera; farming, citriculture. Founded 1934.

Ganhrai Bay (gä'nyŭrī'), inlet of South China Sea, S Vietnam, at mouths of Dongnai R., W of Cape Saint-Jacques; 5 mi. wide.

Ganja, Azerbaijan SSR: see Kirovabad, city.

Ganjam (gŭn'jäm), district (□ 6,888; pop. 1,768,485), SE Orissa, India; ⊙ Chatrapur. Bounded E by Bay of Bengal, S by Madras; larger W section crossed (NE–SW) by Eastern Ghats, in which lie The Maliahs (hilly tribal area); drained by Rushikulya R. Agr. (rice, oilseeds, millet) in E plains; forests yield sal, bamboo. Hand-loom weaving, fishing (pomfrets, sardines, seerfish, mackerel), salt panning; some mica mined. Chief towns: Berhampur, Parlakimedi, Aska, Russellkonda. Formerly a dist. of Madras; in 1936, major portion transferred to newly-created Orissa prov.; in 1949, territory (□ 7,688; pop. 1,855,264) was reduced by inc. of NW subdivision into new Baudh dist.

Ganjam. **1** Suburb, Mysore, India: see Seringapatam. **2** Village, Ganjam dist., SE Orissa, India, on Bay of Bengal, at mouth of Rushikulya R., 18 mi. ENE of Berhampur; chief port and town of dist. until outbreak of fever epidemic in early-19th cent. Salt pans (N).

Ganj Daranagar, India: see Daranagar, Uttar Pradesh.

Ganj Dundwara, India: see Dundwaraganj.

Ganj Tirwa, India: see Tirwa.

Ganjur or **Gandjur** (gänjŏŏr'), Chinese *Kanchumiao* (gän'jōō'myou'), lamasery in N Inner Mongolian Autonomous Region, Manchuria, 95 mi. SW of Hailar; religious and trading center of the Barga steppe; holds annual fair.

Gann, village (pop. 177), Knox co., central Ohio, 14 mi. ENE of Mount Vernon.

Gannat (gänä'), town (pop. 4,255), Allier dept., central France, in Limagne, 11 mi. W of Vichy; agr. trade center (wheat, barley, malt, wine, mushrooms, potatoes, dairy products). Has 12th–15th-cent. Gothic church of Sainte-Croix.

Gannavaram (gŭ'nŭvŭrŭm), village, Kistna dist., NE Madras, India, in Kistna R. delta, 12 mi. E of Bezwada; rice, sugar cane, tobacco.

Gannett, Mount (9,620 ft.), S Alaska, in Chugach Mts., 60 mi. E of Anchorage; 61°13'N 148°11'W.

Gannett Peak (gă'nĭt) (13,785 ft.), in Wind River Range, W central Wyo., c.50 mi. NW of Lander; highest point in state.

Gannvalley, village (pop. c.200), ⊙ Buffalo co., central S.Dak., 70 mi. ESE of Pierre; farm trading point; wheat.

Ganovce, Czechoslovakia: see Poprad.

Gänserndorf (gĕn'zŭrndôrf), town (pop. 3,513), E Lower Austria, 18 mi. NE of Vienna; rail junction; wine.

Gan Shlomo (gän' shlōmō'). **1** Settlement (pop. 250) W Israel, in Judaean Plain, just SW of Rehovot; citriculture; processing of preserves, fruit juices. Founded 1927. **2** Agr. settlement, W Israel, in Plain of Sharon, 5 mi. NNE of Herzliya. Both also spelled Gan Shelomo.

Gan Shmuel (shmōō-ĕl'), settlement (pop. 400), W Israel, in Plain of Sharon, on railroad and 2 mi. NE of Hadera; mixed farming, citriculture. Founded 1896. Also spelled Gan Shemuel.

Ganshoren (gäns'hōrŭn), residential town (pop. 9,188), Brabant prov., central Belgium, N suburb of Brussels; site of deaf-and-dumb institute.

Ganso Azul, Peru: see Agua Caliente.

Gant (gänt), Hung. *Gánt*, town (pop. 1,946), Fejer co., N central Hungary, in Vertes Mts., 13 mi. N of Szekesfehervar; bauxite mine near by.

Ganta (gän'tä), town, Central Prov., N Liberia, on Fr. Guinea border, 140 mi. NE of Monrovia (linked by road); trade in cacao, palm oil and kernels, kola nuts; brickworks.

Ganthier (gätyā'), agr. town (1950 census pop. 871), Ouest dept., S Haiti, on the Cul-de-Sac plain, 18 mi. E of Port-au-Prince; cotton, sugar are grown.

Gantsevichi (gŭntsyĕ'vēchē), Pol. *Hancewicze* (hänts ĕvĕ'chĕ), town (1931 pop. 3,000), N Pinsk oblast, Belorussian SSR, 32 mi. SE of Baranovichi; flour milling, sawmilling, glassworking.

Gantts Quarry, town (pop. 426), Talladega co., central Ala., near Sylacauga; marble and limestone quarrying.

Gan Yavne (gän' yäv'nä), settlement (pop. 450), W Israel, in Judaean Plain, 9 mi. SW of Rehovot; mixed farming. Founded 1931; heavily attacked by Arabs, 1948.

Ganyushkino (gŭnyōō'shkēnŭ), village, NW Guryev oblast, Kazakh SSR, on Caspian Sea, near Volga R. delta, 55 mi. E of Astrakhan; fishing center.

Ganzur (găn'zōōr) or **Janzur** (jăn'–), village (pop. 9,533), Minufiya prov., Lower Egypt, 10 mi. N of Shibin el Kom; cereals, cotton, flax.

Gao (gou), town (pop. c.7,600), E Fr. Sudan, Fr. West Africa, on trans-Saharan road, on left bank of the Niger, and 240 mi. NW of Niamey (Niger territory); 16°17'N 3°W. Linked by river boat with Timbuktu, 200 mi. WNW. Airport and trading center, exporting butter, hides, wool, livestock. Region also produces rice, millet, potatoes, beans.

Gaoua (gä'wä), town (pop. c.2,600), SW Upper Volta, Fr. West Africa, near Gold Coast border, 90 mi. SE of Bobo-Dioulasso; shea nuts, peanuts, rubber, millet, corn, rice, livestock. Copper mines and gold deposits near by.

Gaoua, New Hebrides: see GAUA.

Gaoual (gäwäl'), town (pop. c.4,600), N Fr. Guinea, Fr. West Africa, in Fouta Djallon massif, on Dakar-Abidjan road and 155 mi. NNE of Conakry; peanuts, rubber, cattle. Hospital, customhouse.

Gap (găp), anc. *Vapincum*, town (pop. 11,086), ⊙ Hautes-Alpes dept., SE France, in arid S Dauphiné Alps, 50 mi. SSE of Grenoble; alt. 2,424 ft. Regional commercial and road center on Veynes-Briançon branch railroad. Important cattle and lumber trade. Mfg. (furniture, crates, pharmaceuticals), flour milling, liqueur distilling, fruit preserving. Episcopal see. Notre-Dame-du-Laus (5 mi. SE) is pilgrimage center. A Gallo-Roman city. Medieval ⊙ Gapençais dist. which joined Dauphiné in 1512. Town suffered (1630) from plague and, after 1685, from revocation of Edict of Nantes.

Gap, village (1940 pop. 738), Lancaster co., SE Pa., 15 mi. E of Lancaster. Nickel deposits (formerly mined) are SW.

Gap, The, Malaya: see SEMANGKO GAP.

Gapan (gäpän'), town (1939 pop. 6,107; 1948 municipality pop. 25,719), Nueva Ecija prov., central Luzon, Philippines, on railroad and 50 mi. N of Manila; agr. center (rice, corn, tobacco).

Gar or **Gar Gunsa** (gär' gōōn'sä), Chinese *K'o-erh-k'u-sha* (kŭr'kōō'shä'), town [Tibetan *dzong*], W Tibet, in W Kailas Range, on Gartang R. (left tributary of upper Indus R.) and 38 mi. NNW of Gartok, on main Leh-Gartok trade route; alt. 14,-060 ft. Barley grown near by.

Gara (gä'rä) [Bulg.,=rail station]: for names in Bulgaria beginning thus and not found here, see under following part of the name.

Gara (gŏ'rŏ), town (pop. 4,473), Bacs-Bodrog co., S Hungary, 11 mi. SSE of Baja; flour mill.

Gara, Lough (lŏkh gă'rù), lake (5 mi. long, 4 mi. wide), on borders of Co. Sligo and Co. Roscommon, Ireland, 5 mi. W of Boyle; drained NE by Boyle R. Contains numerous islets.

Garabit, France: see RUINES.

Garachico (gärächē'kō), town (pop. 1,821), Tenerife, Canary Isls., minor port 32 mi. WSW of Santa Cruz de Tenerife; potatoes, wheat, corn, rye, bananas, tomatoes, beans, livestock; timber; sulphur and pumice. Severely damaged during 1705 volcanic eruption.

Garachiné (gärächēnā'), village (pop. 1,158), Darién prov., E Panama, on Garachiné Bay of the Pacific, 27 mi. SW of La Palma; plantains, corn, rice, livestock; lumbering.

Garad (gäräd'), village, in the Mugdugh, central Ital. Somaliland, on Indian Ocean, 120 mi. NE of Obbia.

Garadu (gä'rädōō) or **Jaradu** (jä'–), village (pop. 8,854), Faiyum prov., Upper Egypt, 7 mi. W of Faiyum; cotton, cereals, sugar cane, fruits.

Garafía (gäräfē'ä) or **Santo Domingo** (sän'tō dōmĭng'gō), town (pop. 549), Palma, Canary Isls., 15 mi. NW of Santa Cruz de la Palma; tobacco, cereals, potatoes, almonds, onions, lentils, garlic, livestock; timber. Charcoal burning, flour milling, cheese processing, wine making.

Garagoa (gärägō'ä), town (pop. 1,249), Boyacá dept., central Colombia, in valley of Cordillera Oriental, 32 mi. S of Tunja; alt. 5,676 ft. Coffee, sugar cane, cereals, stock; flour and textile milling. Emerald mines near by.

Garai River, E Pakistan: see MADHUMATI RIVER.

Garajonay, Alto de (äl'tō dhā gärähōnī'), small volcanic massif in W Gomera, Canary Isls., rises to highest elevation (c.4,860 ft.) of the isl.

Garamba National Park (gäräm'bä) (□ 1,937; established 1938), NE Belgian Congo, on Anglo-Egyptian Sudan border and bet. Aka, Dungu, and Garamba rivers, headstreams of the Uele. Former hunting reserve, it is covered with high-grass savanna with occasional forest galleries and is noted as home of the white rhinoceros, eland, and giraffe. In specially reserved sectors elephants are captured for taming at GANGALA NA BODIO, administrative center of park.

Garam River, Czechoslovakia: see HRON RIVER.

Garanbi, Cape, Formosa: see OLWANPI, CAPE.

Garango (gäräng'gō), village, S central Upper Volta, Fr. West Africa, 15 mi. W of Tenkodogo; shea nuts, peanuts, livestock. Dispensary, mission.

Garanhuns (gùrùnyōōns'), city (pop. 16,279), E central Pernambuco, NE Brazil, 120 mi. SW of Recife; W terminus of rail spur connecting with Recife-Maceió line; commercial center of the interior (coffee, cotton, castor beans, manioc, tobacco, cattle); leatherwork. Has historic church of Our Lady of Prazeres. Ilmenite deposits near by.

Garapan, Marianas Isls.: see SAIPAN.

Gararu (gùrùrōō'), city (pop. 832), N Sergipe, NE Brazil, on right bank of navigable São Francisco R. (Alagoas border) and 26 mi. NW of Propriá; rice, cotton.

Garautha (gŭrou'tŭ), village, Jhansi dist., S Uttar Pradesh, India, on tributary of the Dhasan and 45 mi. ENE of Jhansi; jowar, oilseeds, gram.

Garay, Argentina: see HELVECIA.

Garbagnate Milanese (gärbänyä'tĕ mēlänā'zĕ), village (pop. 2,884), Milano prov., Lombardy, N Italy, 9 mi. NNW of Milan; machinery mfg.

Garbayuela (gärvīwā'lä), town (pop. 984), Badajoz prov., W Spain, near Ciudad Real prov. border, 8 mi. S of Herrera del Duque; olives, cereals, fruit, livestock.

Garber. 1 Town (pop. 153), Clayton co., NE Iowa, at confluence of Turkey and Volga rivers, 8 mi. WSW of Guttenberg; creamery. **2** or **Garber City,** city (pop. 957), Garfield co., N Okla., 16 mi. E of Enid, in wheat, livestock, and dairy area; oil wells and refineries; farm machinery, flour, feed, packed meat. Inc. as town 1901, as city 1920.

Garbikaraagae, Turkey: see ACIPAYAM.

Garbou (gûr'bō), Rum. *Gârbou*, Hung. *Csákigorbó* (chä'kēgôr"bō), village (pop 1,375), Cluj prov., N Rumania, 23 mi. W of Dej. In Hungary, 1940–45.

Garça (gär'sù), city (pop. 7,669), W central São Paulo, Brazil, on railroad and 32 mi. W of Bauru, in pioneer agr. zone; coffee and cotton processing, rice milling, mfg. of macaroni, alcohol distilling.

Garças River (gär'sùs), E Mato Grosso, Brazil, left tributary of Araguaia R., which it enters at Barra do Garças after a northeastward course of 160 mi. Important diamond washings.

Garches (gärsh), town (pop. 7,795), Seine-et-Oise dept., N central France, a W residential suburb of Paris, 7 mi. from Notre Dame Cathedral, just W of Saint-Cloud; mfg. of perfumes and pharmaceuticals; textile printing. Golf course.

García (gärsē'ä). **1** or **Villa García,** or **Villa de García** (vē'yä dā), town (pop. 2,209), Nuevo León, N Mexico, in foothills of Sierra Madre Oriental, on railroad and 20 mi. WNW of Monterrey; alt. 2,277 ft. Mining (silver, lead, zinc) and agr. center (tomatoes, barley, livestock). **2** or **Ciudad García** (syōōdädh'), city (pop. 8,775), Zacatecas, N central Mexico, on interior plateau, 30 mi. WSW of Zacatecas; alt. 6,830 ft. Mining (tin, mercury) and agr. center (cereals, vegetables, sugar cane, livestock); tanning. Formerly Jerez.

García de la Cadena (gärsē'ä dā lä kädā'nä), town (pop. 1,503), Zacatecas, N central Mexico, 40 mi. SSW of Tlaltenango; alt. 5,575 ft. Formerly Estanzuela.

Garcia-Hernandez (–ĕrnän'dās), town (1939 pop. 2,009; 1948 municipality pop. 13,690), S Bohol isl., Philippines, on Mindanao Sea, 30 mi. E of Tagbilaran; agr. center (rice, coconuts).

Garciaz (gär-thēäth'), town (pop. 2,442), Cáceres prov., W Spain, 12 mi. SE of Trujillo; flour milling; stock raising; cereals, wine, vegetables.

Garcinarro (gär-thēnä'rō), town (pop. 1,204), Cuenca prov., E central Spain, 50 mi. ESE of Madrid; olives, cereals, grapes, sheep.

Gard (gär), department (□ 2,271; pop. 393,279), in Languedoc, S France; ⊙ NÎMES. Bounded by the Gulf of Lion (S), the lower Rhone and its delta (E), and the CÉVENNES (NW). Traversed SW–NE by the limestone Monts Garrigues. Drained by short streams which rise in the Cévennes and empty either into the Mediterranean (Vidourle R.) or into the Rhone (Gard R., Cèze R.). Diversified agr. ranges from wine, fruit, and cereal growing in lowlands to olive growing and sericulture on slopes of Cévennes. Dept. has important mines: coal (La Grand' Combe, Bessèges), asphalt (Saint-Ambroix), and scattered iron, lead, zinc, and copper mines. Industry is concentrated in Alès area (metallurgy, chemicals, textiles), in the silk-spinning towns of the Cévennes (Le Vigan, Saint-Hippolyte-du-Fort, Sumène), and in Nîmes (shoes, clothing, upholstery).

Gard, river, France: see GARD RIVER.

Garda (gär'dä), village (pop. 1,501), Verona prov., Veneto, N Italy, port on SE shore of Lago di Garda, 17 mi. NW of Verona, in lemon- and olive-growing region; resort. Has fish hatchery. Marble quarries near by.

Garda, Lago di (lä'gô dē), or **Benaco** (bĕnä'kô), anc. *Lacus Benacus*, largest lake (□ 143) of Italy, on Lombardy-Veneto border, 65 mi. E of Milan, in provs. of Trento (N), Verona (E), and Brescia (W); separated from Adige R. valley by Monte Baldo; 32 mi. long, 2–11 mi. wide, alt. 213 ft., max. depth 1,135 ft. Fishing (carp, trout, eels). Receives Sarca R. (N), leaving it (SE) as Mincio R. On its picturesque banks, amid vineyards and groves of olives and citrus fruits, are Riva, Gargnano, Salò, Desenzano del Garda, and Peschiera del Garda. Small steamers ply bet. them. Until 1919 extreme N end of lake belonged to Austria.

Gardabani (gŭrdùbä'nyē), village (1932 pop. estimate 1,350), S Georgian SSR, on railroad and 20 mi. SSE of Tiflis, near Kura R.; truck produce, livestock. Until 1947, Karayazy.

Gardanne (gärdän'), town (pop. 4,086), Bouches-du-Rhône dept., SE France, 12 mi. NNE of Marseilles; electrochemical works; mfg. (tiles, bristles, candied fruit).

Gardar, Greenland: see IGALIKO.

Garde, Cap de (käp' dù gärd'), headland, NE Algeria, on the Mediterranean, at E extremity of coastal Edough range, sheltering port of Bône (just S); 36°58'N 7°46'E. Lighthouse.

Garde, La (lä gärd'), village (pop. 38), Isère dept., SE France, in Oisans valley, on S slopes of the Grandes-Rousses range, 1 mi. NNE of Le Bourg-d'Oisans; talc quarries.

Garde-Freinet, La (–frĕnā'), village (pop. 932), Var dept., SE France, on crest of Monts des Maures, 9 mi. WNW of Saint-Tropez; chestnuts, cork. Moorish stronghold (10th cent.).

Gardelegen (gär'dùlā'gùn), town (pop. 12,322), in former Prussian Saxony prov., central Germany, after 1945 in Saxony-Anhalt, 20 mi. WSW of Stendal; center of asparagus-, hop-, and malt-growing region; button and brick mfg. Has 13th-cent. church, 16th-cent. town hall.

Garden, county (□ 1,685; pop. 4,114), W Nebr.; ⊙ Oshkosh. Agr. area watered by N.Platte R.; U.S. migratory waterfowl refuge in N. Livestock, grain, sugar beets. Formed 1910.

Garden, village (pop. 399), Delta co., S Upper Peninsula, Mich., 25 mi. E of Escanaba, on E shore of Big Bay De Noc.

Gardena (gärdē'nù). **1** City (pop. 14,405), Los Angeles co., S Calif., suburb 10 mi. S of downtown Los Angeles; truck, fruit, poultry farms; residential; some mfg. Inc. 1930. **2** Village (pop. 116), Bottineau co., N N.Dak., 10 mi. S of Bottineau, in farm and forest area.

Gardena, Val (väl gärdä'nä), Ger. *Grödnertal*, picturesque valley (15 mi. long) in the Dolomites, N Italy, NW of Marmolada peak. Traversed E–W by Gardena R. (branch of Isarco R.). Noted as resort (Ortisei) and wood-carving (toys, religious articles) area.

Garden City. 1 Town (pop. 534), Cullman co., N central Ala., on Mulberry Fork and 35 mi. N of Birmingham; cooperage. **2** S suburb (pop. 104) of Greeley, Weld co., N Colo.; alt. 4,650 ft. **3** Town (pop. 1,557), Chatham co., SE Ga., a suburb of Savannah. **4** Village (pop. 764), Ada co., SW Idaho, just W of Boise. **5** City (pop. 10,905), ⊙ Finney co., SW Kansas, on Arkansas R. and 46 mi. WNW of Dodge City; trade center for irrigated agr. region; beet sugar, alfalfa meal, dairy products. Has agr. experiment station and jr. col. Founded 1878, inc. 1887. **6** City (pop. 9,012), Wayne co., SE Mich., 15 mi. W of downtown Detroit; residential; truck farming. Inc. as village 1927, as city 1934. **7** City (pop. 590), Cass co., W Mo., 10 mi. SE of Harrisonville; grain, livestock. **8** Village (pop. 14,486), Nassau co., SE N.Y., on W Long Isl., just N of Hempstead; has large publishing industry; also produces greases, aerial and marine instruments, beverages. Episcopal cathedral here. Seat of Adelphi Col. (women), Cathedral School of St. Mary for girls, and St. Paul's School for boys. Mitchel Air Force Base is near by. Founded c.1869, inc. 1919. **9** Town (pop. 763), Tulsa co., NE Okla., just S of Tulsa, and on Arkansas R. Inc. 1925. **10** Town (pop. 282), Clark co., E central S.Dak., 10 mi. NE of Clark; potato-shipping point; grain, livestock. **11** Village (pop. c.200), ⊙ Glasscock co., W Texas, 25 mi. S of Big Spring; market for livestock-ranching area. **12** Town (pop. 164), Rich co., N Utah, on W shore of Bear L., 22 mi. NW of Randolph, near Idaho line; alt. 5,924 ft.; irrigated farming.

Garden Grove. 1 Village (pop. 3,768), Orange co., S Calif., just NW of Santa Ana; citrus fruit, truck, walnuts. **2** Town (pop. 417), Decatur co., S Iowa, near Weldon R., 10 mi. ENE of Leon, in livestock and grain area. Settled 1846 by Mormons.

Garden Island, village (pop. 39), E central Alaska, near Fairbanks.

Garden Island, in Indian Ocean, 1.5 mi. N of Cape Peron, SW Western Australia; forms W shore of Cockburn Sound; 5.5 mi. long, 1 mi. wide; hilly, grassy. Quarantine station.

Garden Island Bay, Mich.: see BEAVER ISLANDS.

Garden Island Bay, extreme SE La., a bay at tip of Mississippi R. delta; along its marshy shores a rich sulphur deposit was found in 1951.

Garden Key, Fla.: see FORT JEFFERSON NATIONAL MONUMENT.

Garden Oaks, residential village (1940 pop. 797), Harris co., S Texas, NW suburb of Houston.

Garden of the Gods, just NW of Colorado Springs, central Colo.; area of curiously eroded sandstone formations that have been fancifully identified by such names as Bear and Seal, Siamese Twins, Punch and Judy, etc. Popular tourist resort.

Garden Peninsula, Mich., irregular neck of land extending c.20 mi. S from the Upper Peninsula into L. Michigan SW of Manistique; shelters Big Bay De Noc on E. Max. width, c.9 mi. Point Detour is at its tip.

Garden Plain, city (pop. 323), Sedgwick co., S Kansas, 18 mi. W of Wichita, in wheat region.

Garden Reach, town (pop. 85,188), 24-Parganas dist., SE West Bengal, India, on Hooghly R. and 4 mi. WSW of Calcutta city center; jute milling, cotton milling, ginning, and baling; tannery; large power station. In E area is King George's Dock (opened 1928; water area 190 acres, depth 56 ft.), equipped with 35 berths; dry docks. Town was residence of last nawab of Oudh. Fort taken 1756 by Clive, during recapture of Calcutta.

Garden View, village (pop. 2,024), Lycoming co., N central Pa.

Gardenville, village (1940 pop. 851), Erie co., W N.Y., 3 mi. SE of Buffalo; wood products, chemicals.

Gardermoen (gär'dürmöün), village (pop. 472) in Ullensaker canton (pop. 8,457), Akershus co., SE Norway, 20 mi. NE of Oslo; 60°11'N 11°6'E. Site of Oslo international airport.

Gardez or **Gardiz** (gŭrdäz'), town (pop. 15,000), ⊙ Southern Prov., E Afghanistan, 60 mi. S of Kabul (linked by highway); alt. 7,511 ft.; road and trade center for lumbering area. Fort. Trade route leads across Paiwar Pass to Parachinar (Pakistan).

Gardinas, Belorussian SSR: see GRODNO, city.

Gardiner (gärd'nŭr). **1** City (pop. 6,649), Kennebec co., S Maine, on the Kennebec just below Augusta. Mfg. (shoes, textiles, paper, wood products) here and at South Gardiner. Founded 1760, town inc. 1803, city 1850. **2** Village (1940 pop. 602), Park co., S Mont., on Yellowstone R., at N boundary of Yellowstone Natl. Park, and 44 mi. S of Livingston. Roosevelt Arch, just S, is N entrance to park. **3** Resort village, Ulster co., SE N.Y., on Small Wallkill R. and 12 mi. W of Poughkeepsie. A 17th-cent. gristmill is here.

Gardiner, Mount (12,903 ft.), E Calif., in the Sierra Nevada, 15 mi. W of Independence.

Gardiner River, in NW Wyo. and S Mont., rises in Gallatin Range in NW corner of Yellowstone Natl. Park, Wyo.; flows SE and N, past Mammoth Hot Springs, to Yellowstone R. at Gardiner, Mont.; 20 mi. long.

Gardiners Bay, SE N.Y., inlet (c.10 mi. long E-W, 8 mi. wide) of Block Island Sound, bet. N and S peninsulas of Long Isl., and bet. Gardiners Isl. (E), Shelter Isl. (W). Connected by channels to Little Peconic and Great Peconic bays (W). Oyster beds; fishing; yachting.

Gardiners Island (3,000 acres), SE N.Y., bet. flukes of E Long Isl., 11 mi. E of Greenport. Bought 1639 by Lion Gardiner, isl. was site of 1st permanent English settlement in present N.Y. state; it was owned for 300 years by Gardiner's descendants; now it is a private game preserve. On Gardiners Point, a 14-acre isl. just N, is old Fort Tyler (1898; abandoned).

Garding (gär'dĭng), town (pop. 3,015), in Schleswig-Holstein, NW Germany, on Eiderstedt peninsula, 15 mi. SW of Husum; weaving, woodworking. Cattle, horses. Has late-Romanesque church. Chartered 1590. Theodor Mommsen b. here.

Gardiz, Afghanistan: see GARDEZ.

Gardner. 1 Village (pop. c.250), Huerfano co., S Colo., on Huerfano R. and 24 mi. WNW of Walsenburg; alt. 7,000 ft. Outfitting point for excursions into near-by Sangre de Cristo Mts. **2** Town (pop. 981), Grundy co., NE Ill., 27 mi. SSW of Joliet in bituminous-coal-mining and agr. area; makes clothing; grain, dairy products. **3** City (pop. 676), Johnson co., E Kansas, 27 mi. SW of Kansas City, Kansas; trading point in grain and livestock area; mfg. of chemicals. Santa Fe and Oregon trails branched off here from their shared route from Independence, Mo. State park near by. **4** City (pop. 19,581), Worcester co., N Mass., 9 mi. W of Fitchburg; principally furniture mfg.; also machinery, silverware, stoves and heaters, foundry and machine-shop products. Settled 1764, inc. as town 1785, as city 1923. Includes village of Otter River. **5** Village (pop. 136), Cass co., E N.Dak., 20 mi. NNW of Fargo.

Gardner Island, triangular atoll (□ 1.5; pop. 79), Phoenix Isls., S Pacific, 230 mi. S of Canton Isl.; 4°40'S 174°31'W; 4 mi. long. Discovered 1828 by Americans; included 1937 in Br. colony of Gilbert and Ellice Isls. Produces some copra. Sometimes called Nikumaroro. Formerly Kemins Isl.

Gardner Lake. 1 In SE Conn., resort lake (c.2 mi. long) 6 mi. W of Norwich, near Salem; has Minnie Isl. state park. **2** In Washington co., E Maine, 6 mi. NE of Machias; 7 mi. long.

Gardner Pinnacles, island (alt. 170 ft.) in Hawaiian Isls., N Pacific, c.590 mi. NNW of Honolulu, T.H.; 25°N 168°W; discovered 1820 by American traders.

Gardnerville, village (1940 pop. 536), Douglas co., W Nev., near Minden, on East Carson R.; gold, silver, tungsten, barium; grain, cattle.

Gardo (gär'dō), town (pop. 300), in the Mijirtein, N Ital. Somaliland, near Br. Somaliland border, on road and 165 mi. SW of Hordio; 9°30'N 49°5'E; alt. 2,657 ft. Trade center, with native fort. Formerly called El Lagodei.

Gardon d'Alès River (gärdõ dälĕ'), in Lozère and Gard depts., S France, rises in the Cévennes, S of Mont Lozère, flows c.30 mi. SE, past La Grand' Combe and Alès, joining the Gardon d'Anduze near Vézénobres to form GARD RIVER.

Gardon d'Anduze River (dãdüz'), in Gard dept., S France, has several headstreams (all named Gardon) which descend from the Cévennes; flows c.30 mi. SE, past Anduze, joining the Gardon d'Alès near Vézénobres to form GARD RIVER.

Gardone Riviera (gärdô'nĕ rēvyä'rä), commune (pop. 2,432), Brescia prov., Lombardy, N Italy, on W shore of Lago di Garda, 18 mi. ENE of Brescia, in winter-resort region. Comprises Gardone Sopra (commune seat; pop. 540) and several near-by villages.

Gardone Val Trompia (gärdô'nĕ väl trôm'pyä), town (pop. 3,669), Brescia prov., Lombardy, N Italy, on Oglio R. and 10 mi. N of Brescia; firearms, ammunition, wire. Has church built 1442.

Gard River (gär), Gard dept., S France, formed by confluence of the GARDON D'ALÈS and the GARDON D'ANDUZE, flows c.35 mi. SE to the Rhone 4 mi. above Beaucaire. Near Remoulins it is spanned by the PONT DU GARD, anc. Roman aqueduct.

Gards Kopinge (yĕrts' chû'pĭng-ù), Swedish *Gärds Köpinge*, village (pop. 754), Kristianstad co., S Sweden, 5 mi. S of Kristianstad; grain, potatoes, sugar beets, stock.

Gardula (gärdōō'lä), Ital. *Gardulla*, town (pop. 4,000), Gamu-Gofa prov., S Ethiopia, near L. Chamo, 150 mi. SSE of Jimma, in agr. region (durra, maize, barley, cotton, tobacco); 5°37'N 37°29'E; cotton weaving, pottery making.

Gareg Lwyd, Wales: see BLACK MOUNTAIN.

Gare Loch (gâr' lŏkh'), sheltered inlet of Firth of Clyde, W Dumbarton, Scotland, extends 7 mi. NNW from the Clyde at Helensburgh to Garelochhead; 1 mi. wide. Good anchorage; testing ground for Clyde-built ships.

Garelochhead (gâr"lŏkh-hĕd'), village in Rhu parish, W Dumbarton, Scotland, at head of Gare Loch, 6 mi. NW of Helensburgh; yachting resort.

Gareloi Island (gâr'ùloi) (6 mi. long, 5 mi. wide), largest of Delarof Isls., Aleutian Isls., SW Alaska; 51°47'N 178°52'W. In center rises active volcano of Mt. Gareloi, 5,334 ft. high.

Garenne-Colombes, La (lä gärĕn'-kôlõb'), town (pop. 24,022), Seine dept., N central France, a NW suburb of Paris, 6 mi. from Notre Dame Cathedral, within N bend of the Seine, just N of Courbevoie; automobile plant; mfg. (electrical and photographic equipment, rugs, pharmaceuticals).

Garesnica (gä'rĕshnētsä), Serbo-Croatian *Garešnica*, village (pop. 3,005), N Croatia, Yugoslavia, on Ilova R. and 23 mi. S of Bjelovar, in Slavonia; rail terminus; local trade center.

Garessio (gärĕs'syô), town (pop. 6,409), Cuneo prov., Piedmont, NW Italy, near Tanaro R., 17 mi. SSE of Mondovì; chemicals (perfume, dyes), glass, furniture.

Garfagnana (gärfänyä'nä), mountain district (□ 240) in Lucca prov., Tuscany, central Italy, ENE of Apuane Alps; watered by upper Serchio R. Livestock raising (cattle, sheep), agr. (grapes, olives, fruit); forestry (lumber; paper milling; chestnuts). Chief town, Castelnuovo di Garfagnana.

Garfield. 1 County (□ 2,994; pop. 11,625), W Colo.; ⊙ Glenwood Springs. A plateau area, bordering on Utah; drained by Colorado R. Livestock, grain. Includes parts of Grand Mesa, Holy Cross, and White R. natl. forests. U.S. oil-shale reserve is near Grand Valley town. Formed 1883. **2** County (□ 4,793; pop. 2,172), E central Mont.; ⊙ Jordan. Agr. area, bounded N by Missouri R. and Fort Peck Reservoir. Livestock. Fort Peck Game Reservation in N. Formed 1919. **3** County (□ 570; pop. 2,912), central Nebr.; ⊙ Burwell. Agr. area watered by Cedar, N.Loup, and Calamus rivers. Livestock, grain. Formed 1884. **4** County (□ 1,054; pop. 52,820), N Okla.; ⊙ Enid. Drained by tributaries of Cimarron R. and by the Salt Fork of Arkansas R. Agr. area (mainly wheat; also corn, oats, barley, alfalfa, livestock, poultry; dairy products). Grain milling, diversified mfg. at Enid. Oil and gas wells; refineries, gasoline plants. Waterfowl hunting. Formed 1893. **5** County (□ 5,217; pop. 4,151), S Utah; ⊙ Panguitch. Mtn. area bounded E by Colorado R. and crossed by Sevier, East Fork Sevier, and Escalante rivers. Livestock, grain. Henry Mts. in NE; Paunsaugunt Plateau in W, including part of Bryce Canyon Natl. Park and lying in Dixie Natl. Forest. Formed 1882. **6** County (□ 714; pop. 3,204), SE Wash.; ⊙ Pomeroy. Rolling plateaus bounded N by Snake R. and rising to Blue Mts. in S. Wheat, livestock, truck, fruit. Formed 1881.

Garfield. 1 Town (pop. 83), Benton co., extreme NW Ark., 29 mi. NNE of Fayetteville, in the Ozarks. **2** Town (pop. 213), Emanuel co., E central Ga., 14 mi. ENE of Swainsboro, in agr. area. **3** City (pop. 297), Pawnee co., SW central Kansas, on Arkansas R. and 11 mi. SW of Larned; grain, livestock. **4** Village (pop. 244), Douglas co., W Minn., 7 mi. WNW of Alexandria, in lake region; dairy products. **5** Industrial city (pop. 27,550), Bergen co., NE N.J., on Passaic R. just ENE of Passaic; mfg. (machinery and mechanical equipment, chemicals, pharmaceuticals, rubber goods, textiles, clothing, ice cream, paper products, embroidery). Inc. as borough 1898, as city 1917. **6** Village (pop. 2,079), Salt Lake co., N Utah, near Great Salt L., 15 mi. W of Salt Lake City, at N tip of Oquirrh Mts.; alt. 4,240 ft.; copper mining and smelting; cobalt refining. **7** Town (pop. 674), Whitman co., SE Wash., 13 mi. NE of Colfax, near Idaho line; wheat, peas, oats.

Garfield, Mount, N.H.: see FRANCONIA MOUNTAINS.

Garfield Heights, city (pop. 21,662), Cuyahoga co., N Ohio, a SE residential suburb of Cleveland. Founded 1904.

Garfield Mountain, Mont.: see BITTERROOT RANGE.

Garforth, urban district (1931 pop. 3,774; 1951 census 12,357), West Riding, S central Yorkshire, England, 7 mi. E of Leeds; coal mining.

Gargalianoi (gärgŭlēä'nē), city (pop. 8,926), Messenia nome, SW Peloponnesus, Greece, 27 mi. W of Kalamata; agr. center; olives, wheat, livestock. Also spelled Gargaliani and Gharghaliani.

Gargano or **Monte Gargano** (môn'tĕ gärgä'nô), mountain promontory (□ 778), Foggia prov., S Italy; extends from Candelaro R. c.35 mi. E into the Adriatic; rises to 3,465 ft. in Monte Calvo. On N coast are lakes of Lesina and Varano; Gulf of Manfredonia is S. Karst region, used for sheep raising and agr. (olives, grapes). Bauxite mining (San Giovanni Rotondo), marble quarrying (San Marco in Lamis).

Garganta, La (lä gärgän'tä), village (pop. 1,493), Cáceres prov., W Spain, 5 mi. SW of Béjar; chestnuts, nuts, wine, fruit. Mineral springs. Summer resort.

Garganta la Olla (ō'lyä), town (pop. 2,047), Cáceres prov., W Spain, 17 mi. ENE of Plasencia; olive-oil processing, sawmilling; stock raising; wine, fruit, honey. Trout fishing.

Gargantilla (gärgäntē'lyä), village (pop. 1,015), Cáceres prov., W Spain, 18 mi. NE of Plasencia; olive-oil processing; stock raising; fruit, pepper, lumber.

Gargaon, India: see NAZIRA.

Gargarus, Mount, Turkey: see IDA MOUNTAINS.

Gargas (gärgä'), village (pop. 14), Vaucluse dept., SE France, 3 mi. NW of Apt; ocher quarries.

Gargathy Inlet, Va.: see ASSAWAMAN ISLAND.

Gargnano (gärnyä'nô), resort village (pop. 878), Brescia prov., Lombardy, N Italy, port on W shore of Lago di Garda, 9 mi. NNE of Salò; alcohol distillery. Has 13th-cent. convent.

Gárgoles de Abajo (gär'gōlĕs dhä ävä'hō), town (pop. 508), Guadalajara prov., central Spain, near the Tagus, 29 mi. ENE of Guadalajara; cereals, grapes, potatoes, beans, olives. Paper milling.

Gargrave, village and parish (pop. 1,232), West Riding, W Yorkshire, England, on Aire R. and 4 mi. WNW of Skipton; cotton milling.

Gar Gunsa, Tibet: see GAR.

Garhakota (gŭrhä'kōtŭ), town (pop. 7,888), Saugor dist., N Madhya Pradesh, India, on Sonar R. and 27 mi. E of Saugor; wheat, oilseeds; cattle market.

Garhchiroli (gŭrchĭrō'lē), village, Chanda dist., S Madhya Pradesh, India, near Wainganga R., 40 mi. ENE of Chanda; rice, millet, flax. Hematite deposits near by. Ruins of 10th-cent. Hindu temples 15 mi. SSW, at village of Markandi.

Garhgaon, India: see NAZIRA.

Garh Gazali, E Pakistan: see MADHUPUR JUNGLE.

Garhi Habibullah (gŭr'hē hŭbē'bōōl-lŭ), village, Hazara dist., NE North-West Frontier Prov., W Pakistan, 18 mi. NNE of Abbottabad, near Kashmir border; corn, barley; match mfg., woolen-blanket weaving, mule breeding. Also called Garhi Habibullah Khan.

Garhi Ikhtiar Khan (ĭktyär' khän'), town (pop. 1,350), Bahawalpur state, W Pakistan, 8 mi. WNW of Khanpur; trades in dates.

Garhi Khairo (khī'rō), village, Upper Sind Frontier dist., N Sind, W Pakistan, 32 mi. SW of Jacobabad; local market for millet, wheat, gram. Sometimes spelled Garhi Khairah.

Garhi Yasin (yä'sĭn), town (pop. 8,397), Sukkur dist., NE Sind, W Pakistan, 25 mi. NW of Sukkur; market center (wheat, millet, rice, oilseeds); handicrafts (cloth weaving, metalwork).

Garhmuktesar (gŭrmōōktā'sŭr), town (pop. 5,950), Meerut dist., NW Uttar Pradesh, India, on the Ganges and 28 mi. ESE of Meerut; trades in timber and bamboo. Large Hindu temple (consists of 4 principal shrines) dedicated to goddess Ganga; a sacred well near by, surrounded by 80 pillars. Mosque built in 1283. Anc. Hindu fort. Large annual religious mela.

Garhshankar (gŭr'shŭngkŭr), town (pop. 6,885), Hoshiarpur dist., N central Punjab, India, 25 mi. SSE of Hoshiarpur; local trade in wheat, gram, corn, sugar, timber; hand-loom weaving.

Garhwa, India: see GARWA.

Garhwal (gŭrväl'), district (□ 5,628; pop. 602,115), Kumaun div., N Uttar Pradesh, India; ⊙ Pauri. In central Kumaun Himalayas (Siwalik Range is

S); bounded (N, NE) by Tibet (border undefined); drained by Alaknanda R. Agr. (wheat, barley, rice, rape and mustard, corn, chili, turmeric, tea); extensive sal, chir, oak, and rhododendron forests. Main towns: Lansdowne, Srinagar, Pauri. Noted pilgrimage centers at Badrinath and Kedarnath. Dist. contains Himalayan peaks NANDA DEVI and KAMET.

Gari (gŭrē'), village (1939 pop. over 500), N central Sverdlovsk oblast, Russian SFSR, on Sosva R. (landing) and 27 mi. NE of Sosva; lumbering.

Garian (gärēyăn'), town, W Tripolitania, Libya, on the plateau Gebel Nefusa, on main road and 50 mi. S of Tripoli; alt. 2,352 ft.; railroad terminus; power station; olive-oil pressing, flour milling, weaving (carpets, barracans). Has 18th-cent. Turkish fort, mosque. Jewish community which had lived in troglodyte dwellings departed for Israel in 1950.

Garibaldi (gărĭbôl'dē, Port. gŭrēbäl'dē), city (pop. 2,321), NE Rio Grande do Sul, Brazil, on S slope of the Serra Geral, on railroad and 24 mi. WSW of Caxias do Sul; winegrowing and -shipping center; also ships dairy produce, wheat, lard, fruit. City is one of earliest Italian settlements in state.

Garibaldi (gärēbäl'dē), village (pop. 2,000), Tripolitania, Libya, near Mediterranean Sea, on main road and 13 mi. W of Misurata; agr. settlement (cereals, dates, olives, livestock) founded 1938–39 by Italians.

Garibaldi (gărŭbôl'dē), town (pop. 1,249), Tillamook co., NW Oregon, on Tillamook Bay (off Pacific Ocean) and c.60 mi. W of Portland in dairying and agr. area; lumber milling. Inc. 1946.

Garibaldi, Mount (8,787 ft.), SW B.C., in Coast Mts., in Garibaldi Park, 40 mi. N of Vancouver.

Garibaldi Park (□ 973), provincial park, SW B.C., in Coast Mts., 40 mi. N of Vancouver. Mtn. region; includes Mt. Weart (9,300 ft.), Wedge Mtn. (9,484 ft.), Mt. Garibaldi (8,787 ft.).

Garigliano River, Italy: see LIRI RIVER.

Garioch (gâ'rēŏkh), lowland district (□ c.150) in central Aberdeen, Scotland. Chief town, Inverurie. Noted for its cattle and fertility of its soil, it is called the "granary of Aberdeen."

Garissa (gärē'sä), village, Northern Frontier Prov., E Kenya, on Tana R. (ferry), on road and 150 mi. NW of Lamu; 0°26'S 39°33'E; rice. Airfield.

Garitz (gä'rĭts), village (pop. 2,132), Lower Franconia, NW Bavaria, Germany, just SW of Bad Kissingen; pottery, glass.

Garividi, India: see VIZIANAGARAM.

Garko or **Gerko** (gä'rkō), town (pop. 5,121), Kano prov., Northern Provinces, N Nigeria, 30 mi. SE of Kano; cotton, peanuts, millet; cattle, skins.

Garla (gŭr'lŭ), town (pop. 5,848), Warangal dist., E Hyderabad state, India, 50 mi. SE of Warangal; rice milling.

Garland, county (□ 721; pop. 47,102), central Ark.; ⊙ HOT SPRINGS. Intersected by OUACHITA RIVER. Agr. (cotton, truck, livestock). Health and pleasure resorts. Novaculite quarrying. Hot Springs Natl. Park and part of Ouachita Natl. Forest are in co. Formed 1873.

Garland. 1 Town (pop. 351), Miller co., extreme SW Ark., 18 mi. ESE of Texarkana, near Red R.; cotton, livestock. **2** Town (pop. 581), Penobscot co., central Maine, 22 mi. NW of Bangor, in agr. region. **3** Village (pop. 184), Seward co., SE Nebr., 20 mi. NW of Lincoln. **4** Town (pop. 539), Sampson co., SE central N.C., 15 mi. SSW of Clinton; ships berries; lumber milling. **5** Town (pop. 157), Tipton co., W Tenn., 5 mi. WNW of Covington. **6** Town (pop. 10,571), Dallas co., N Texas, industrial suburb c.12 mi. NE of downtown Dallas; makes aircraft, seismic instruments, bus bodies, heaters. **7** City (pop. 1,008), Box Elder co., N Utah, 18 mi. W of Logan; alt. 4,344 ft. Trade center for agr. area (grain, sugar beets); beet sugar, flour.

Garlasco (gärlä'skô), town (pop. 5,462), Pavia prov., Lombardy, N Italy, 11 mi. W of Pavia; mfg. (agr. machinery, turbines, shoes).

Garlieston or **Garliestown** (gär'lēstŭn), small port in Sorbie parish, SE Wigtown, Scotland, on Wigtown Bay, 6 mi. SE of Wigtown. Near by are remains of Eggerness and Cruggleton castles.

Garlin (gärlē'), village (pop. 482), Basses-Pyrénées dept., SW France, 19 mi. NNE of Pau; wine, corn, cattle. A medieval stronghold built 1305.

Garlitos (gärlē'tōs), town (pop. 1,309), Badajoz prov., W Spain, 13 mi. SE of Puebla de Alcocer; olive-oil pressing, flour milling; livestock.

Garm (gärm), oblast (□ 7,600; 1946 pop. estimate 200,000), central Tadzhik SSR; ⊙ Novabad. Bounded N by Kirghiz SSR, S by Afghanistan (Panj R.); mtn. region, including Trans-Alai Range (N), Peter the First Range (center), Darvaza Range (S, SE); drained by Surkhab R. Wheat in mtn. valleys, goat and sheep raising on mtn. slopes. Gold placers along rivers. Pop. mainly Tadzhik; some Kirghiz. Formed 1939.

Garm, town (1926 pop. 604), central Garm oblast, Tadzhik SSR, on Surkhab R. and 90 mi. NE of Stalinabad; 39°2'N 70°22'E. Wheat, sericulture, livestock. Was ⊙ Karategin div. of former Bukhara khanate and ⊙ Garm oblast until 1950.

Garmisch-Partenkirchen (gär'mĭsh-pär"tŭn-kĭr'-khŭn, –pär'tŭn-kĭr"khŭn), town (pop. 24,624), Upper Bavaria, Germany, at S foot of the Wettersteingebirge, on the Loisach and 20 mi. NW of Innsbruck, 50 mi. SSW of Munich; alt. 2,323 ft. Metal- and woodworking, printing, brewing. Climatic summer resort, and winter-sports center; starting point for ascent of the Wettersteingebirge. Has Romanesque church, and mid-18th-cent. pilgrimage church. Site of mtn. ornithological observatory. Rack-and-pinion railroad leads to the ZUGSPITZE. Originally 2 separate villages, which were united and chartered 1935. Scene of Olympic Winter Games of 1936.

Garmo Peak, Tadzhik SSR: see STALIN PEAK.

Garmouth, fishing village, NE Moray, Scotland, on Spey Bay of Moray Firth, at mouth of the Spey, 8 mi. ENE of Elgin. In 1650 Charles II landed here after signing Covenants.

Garmrud, Iran: see MIANEH.

Garmsar (gärmsär'), town, Second Prov., in Teheran, N Iran, on highway and 50 mi. ESE of Teheran; railroad junction for lines to Bandar Shah (on Caspian Sea) and Meshed. Formerly called Qishlaq.

Garmsel or **Garmser**, Afghanistan: see LANDI MUHAMMAD AMIN KHAN.

Garnacha, Ensenada de (ĕnsänä'dä dā gärnä'chä), sheltered inlet, W Cuba, on the Gulf of Guanahacabibes, 45 mi. WSW of Pinar del Río.

Garnavillo (gärnŭvĭ'lō), town (pop. 581), Clayton co., NE Iowa, near the Mississippi, 8 mi. NW of Guttenberg, in corn, hog, and dairy region.

Garner (gär'nŭr). **1** Town (pop. 1,696), ⊙ Hancock co., N Iowa, on East Branch Iowa R. and 20 mi. W of Mason City; rail junction; feed, wood and metal products. Peat beds near by. Inc. 1881. **2** Town (pop. 1,180), Wake co., central N.C., 5 mi. SSE of Raleigh.

Garnerville, village (pop. c.1,400), Rockland co., SE N.Y., 2 mi. NW of Haverstraw; fur dyeing; mfg. of clothing, textiles, machinery, hardware.

Garnet, Calif.: see DESERT HOT SPRINGS.

Garnet Lake, resort village, Warren co., E N.Y., on small Garnet L. in the Adirondacks, 25 mi. NW of Glens Falls.

Garnett (gär'nĕt), city (pop. 2,693), ⊙ Anderson co., E Kansas, 23 mi. S of Ottawa; trade center for livestock, grain, poultry, and dairy region; woodworking. Oil wells in vicinity. Edgar Lee Masters b. here. State park near by. Founded 1856; inc. as town 1861, as city 1870.

Garnkirk (gärnkûrk'), village in Cadder parish, N Lanark, Scotland, 7 mi. ENE of Glasgow; has fireclay works.

Garnock River, Ayrshire, Scotland, rises 6 mi. NE of Largs, flows 21 mi. S, past Kilbirnie, Dalry, and Kilwinning, to Firth of Clyde just WSW of Irvine.

Garobadha (gŭrō'bädŭ), village, Garo Hills dist., W Assam, India, 16 mi. WNW of Tura; trades in rice, cotton, mustard, jute.

Garoe (gär'wä), village (pop. 200), in the Mudugh, N central Ital. Somaliland, near Br. Somaliland border, 85 mi. SW of Gardo; road junction.

Garoet, Indonesia: see GARUT.

Garofalo (gärô'fälō), whirlpool in Strait of Messina, near Punta del Faro, just off NE Sicily; the supposed Charybdis of anc. legend. Opposite it, on Ital. coast, is rock of Scylla. Sometimes spelled Galofalo.

Garo Hills (gä'rō), autonomous district (□ 3,152; pop. 233,569), W Assam, India; ⊙ Tura. Bounded E by Khasi Hills, S and SW of E Pakistan; coextensive with Garo Hills (rise to c.4,630 ft. in Nokrek Peak), at extreme W of Assam Range; drained by tributaries of the Brahmaputra. Sal and bamboo tracts; lac growing; coal deposits (NW); agr. (rice, cotton, mustard, jute, sugar cane, tobacco). Main villages: Tura, Garobadha, Phulbari. Projected railroad to service coal area. Present dist. formed 1869; obtained special status (1950) in accordance with Indian constitution. Pop. 88% Animist tribes (including Garos), 6% Hindu, 4% Moslem.

Garonne, Haute-, France: see HAUTE-GARONNE.

Garonne Lateral Canal (gŭrōn', gärôn'), in SW France, parallels Garonne R. from Castets (Gironde dept.) to Toulouse (Haute-Garonne dept.), where it joins the Canal du Midi; 120 mi. long. Used for wine, cereal, and fruit shipments.

Garonne River, anc. *Garumna*, SW France, rises in the Val d'Aran (central Pyrenees) just inside Spain, flows 402 mi. generally NW, past Toulouse, Agen, Marmande, and Bordeaux, to the Bec d'AMBÈS, where it is joined by the Dordogne to form the GIRONDE estuary. With its tributaries (Neste, Save, Gers, Baïse—from the left; Salat, Ariège, Tarn, Lot—from the right) it drains the AQUITAINE BASIN. Ocean-going ships ascend to Bordeaux. Because of river's irregular regime the Garonne Lateral Canal follows it from Castets (above Bordeaux) to Toulouse. In Gironde dept. noted wines are produced along its banks.

Garoua or **Garua** (gärōō'ä), town, ⊙ Benoué region, N Fr. Cameroons, on right bank of Benue R. and 400 mi. NNE of Yaoundé, near Br. Cameroons border; 9°17'N 13°21'E. Peanut- and cotton- (from Fr. Equatorial Africa) shipping port and native market. Cotton plantations; mechanized peanut cultivation. Customs station; airfield; jr. col.

Garove, Bismarck Archipelago: see VITU ISLANDS.

Garpenberg (gär'pŭnbĕr"yŭ), village and commune (pop. 1,983), Kopparberg co., central Sweden, in Bergslag region, 12 mi. NNE of Avesta; mining center (copper, zinc, lead, iron).

Garphyttan (gärp"hü'tän), village (pop. 655), Orebro co., S central Sweden, 10 mi. WNW of Orebro; steel wire, linen. Just SW is small natl. park.

Garrard (gă'rŭrd, gâr'ŭd), county (□ 234; pop. 11,029), central Ky.; ⊙ Lancaster. Bounded N by Kentucky R., W by Herrington L. (impounded by dam in Dix R.). Gently rolling upland agr. area (burley tobacco, corn, wheat, hay), in Bluegrass region. Formed 1796.

Garrauli (gŭr-rou'lē), village, N Vindhya Pradesh, India, on Dhasan R. and 6 mi. W of Nowgong. Was ⊙ former petty state of Garrauli (□ 39; pop. 5,827) of Central India agency, since 1948 merged with Vindhya Pradesh.

Garraway (gă'rŭwā), town, Maryland co., SE Liberia, on Atlantic Ocean 18 mi. WNW of Harper; copra, cassava, rice; cattle raising. Mission station.

Garraway Stream, village (pop. 353), Essequibo co., central Br. Guiana, on Potaro R. (crossed here by suspension bridge), on road from Bartica to Kaieteur Falls, and 80 mi. SSW of Bartica. Sometimes called Potaro or Potaro Landing.

Garray (gärī'), village (pop. 369), Soria prov., N central Spain, on the Duero (Douro) and 3 mi. N of Soria, in agr. region (grain, stock). Just S is the ruined city of NUMANTIA.

Garrel (gä'rŭl), village (commune pop. 6,225), in Oldenburg, NW Germany, after 1945 in Lower Saxony, 7 mi. N of Cloppenburg; cattle.

Garretson, city (pop. 745), Minnehaha co., E S.Dak., 16 mi. NE of Sioux Falls and on branch of Big Sioux R., near Minn. line; dairy products, poultry, grain.

Garrett (gă'rĭt), county (□ 668; pop. 21,259), extreme W Md.; ⊙ Oakland. Bounded SE by North Branch of the Potomac (forms W.Va. line here), W by W.Va. line, N by Pa. line; drained by Youghiogheny, Casselman, Savage rivers. Area of the Allegheny, with Backbone Mtn., highest point in Md. Known for excellent hunting and fishing, co. includes Savage R., Swallow Falls, and Potomac state forests, and Deep Creek L. Mining (bituminous coal, fireclay); lumbering; agr. (truck, dairy products, grain, livestock); maple sugar and syrup. Formed 1872.

Garrett. 1 Village (pop. 213), Douglas co., E central Ill., 23 mi. E of Decatur, in agr. area. **2** City (pop. 4,291), De Kalb co., NE Ind., 20 mi. N of Fort Wayne; trading center in agr. area (grain, livestock, soybeans); mfg. of wood products, artificial bait, underwear, dairy products; railroad shops. **3** Town (1940 pop. 938), Floyd co., E Ky., in Cumberland foothills, 17 mi. W of Pikeville, in bituminous-coal, timber, oil, and gas area. **4** Borough (pop. 761), Somerset co., SW Pa., 10 mi. S of Somerset and on Casselman R.; bituminous coal.

Garrett Hill, village (1940 pop. 3,101, with adjacent ROSEMONT), Delaware co., SE Pa., W residential suburb of Philadelphia.

Garrett Park, town (pop. 524), Montgomery co., central Md., NW suburb of Washington, on Rock Creek. Georgetown Preparatory School (for boys; founded 1789 by Jesuits) is near by.

Garrettsville, village (pop. 1,504), Portage co., NE Ohio, 25 mi. ENE of Akron and on small Eagle Creek; rubber goods, baskets, lumber, grain products.

Garriga, La (lä gärē'gä), village (pop. 3,139), Barcelona prov., NE Spain, 5 mi. N of Granollers; mfg. of cotton fabrics, laces, leather belts, furniture, tiles; tanning, lumbering. Trades in wine, olive oil, livestock. Mineral springs.

Garrigues, Monts (mõ gärēg'), limestone foothills of the Cévennes, S France, extending NE across Hérault and Gard depts., from the Étang de Thau (S) to the Rhone near Pont-Saint-Esprit (N). The most prominent hills overlook Montpellier and Nîmes. Average alt. 700–800 ft. Winegrowing on SE slopes.

Garrison. 1 Town (pop. 457), Benton co., E central Iowa, 27 mi. WNW of Cedar Rapids; brick and tile plant, creamery. Limestone quarries near by. **2** Village (1940 pop. 570), Baltimore co., N Md., 11 mi. NW of downtown Baltimore. Near by is "The Caves" (1730), home of Charles Carroll. **3** Village (pop. 150), Crow Wing co., central Minn., on Mille Lacs L., 19 mi. ESE of Brainerd; summer resort. **4** Village (pop. c.100), Powell co., W central Mont., on the Clark Fork and 10 mi. NNW of Deer Lodge; phosphate fertilizer. **5** Village (pop. 88), Butler co., E Nebr., 35 mi. NW of Lincoln and on branch of Big Blue R. **6** Village (1940 pop. 594), Putnam co., SE N.Y., on E bank of the Hudson and 8 mi. S of Beacon. **7** City (pop. 1,890), McLean co., N central N.Dak., 65 mi. NNW of Bismarck; lignite mines; grain, dairy products, turkeys. Garrison Dam in Missouri R. is near. Inc. 1920. **8** Town (pop. 699), Nacogdoches co., E Texas, near Atoyac Bayou, 17 mi. NNE of Nacogdoches, in cotton, lumber, cattle area; creosoted lumber, brick, tile.

Garrison Dam, central N.Dak., in Missouri R. near Garrison. A major unit in Missouri R. Basin project for flood control, irrigation, hydroelectric power and navigation, dam was begun 1947; of earth-fill construction (one of largest of this type), it is 210 ft. high, 12,000 ft. long. Projected reservoir capacity is 23,000,000 acre-ft.

Garristown, Gaelic *Baile Uí Gháirigh*, town (pop. 92), W Co. Dublin, Ireland, 9 mi. WSW of Balbriggan; agr. market (cattle; grain, potatoes).

Garrobo, El (ĕl gärō'vō), town (pop. 741), Seville prov., SW Spain, in outliers of the Sierra Morena, 16 mi. NNW of Seville; cereals, cork, livestock; mfg. of brooms.

Garrogue River, Co. Sligo, Ireland, issues from N end of Lough Gill, flows 3 mi. NW to Sligo Bay at Sligo.

Garron Point (gă'rŭn), promontory on the North Channel, E Co. Antrim, Northern Ireland, 15 mi. NNW of Larne; 55°2'N 5°59'W.

Garrovilla, La (lä gärōvē'lyä), town (pop. 2,108), Badajoz prov., W Spain, on railroad and 7 mi. W of Mérida; cereals, olives, hogs, sheep.

Garrovillas or **Garrovillas de Alconétar** (gärōvē'lyäs dhā älkōnā'tär), town (pop. 6,117), Cáceres prov., W Spain, in Estremadura, near the Tagus, 20 mi. NNW of Cáceres; meat processing, flour milling; mfg. of wool textiles, footwear, chocolate; stock raising, lumbering; cereals, vegetables, olive oil, wine. Roman bridge (1st cent. A.D.) across Tagus near by.

Garrucha (gärōō'chä), town (pop. 2,771), Almería prov., S Spain, port on the Mediterranean, and 16 mi. SE of Huércal-Overa; terminus of mining railroad from Bédar. Exports lead and iron, fruit (grapes, oranges, almonds), esparto. Fishing, fish processing, boatbuilding. Iron foundry. Petroleum wells near by.

Garry, Cape, SE Somerset Isl., E Franklin Dist., Northwest Territories, on Prince Regent Inlet, on SE side of Creswell Bay; 72°16'N 93°23'W. Sometimes called Cape Clara.

Garry, Lake (□ 980), NW Keewatin Dist., Northwest Territories, near Mackenzie Dist. boundary, just E of L. Pelly, 66°N 100°W; 60 mi. long, 2–38 mi. wide. Drained E by Back R.

Garry, Loch, Scotland: see GLENGARRY.

Garry Island (5 mi. long, 4 mi. wide), NW Mackenzie Dist., Northwest Territories, in Beaufort Sea of the Arctic Ocean, off mouth of Mackenzie R. delta; 69°19'N 135°40'W.

Garry River. 1 In Inverness, Scotland: see GLENGARRY. **2** In Perthshire, Scotland, rises 16 mi. W of Blair-Atholl, flows 20 mi. NE, E, and SE, through Loch Garry (3 mi long), past Blair-Atholl, to Tummel R. 2 mi. NW of Pitlochry.

Gars (gärs), village (pop. 591), Upper Bavaria, Germany, on the Inn and 13 mi. SW of Mühldorf; hydroelectric plant; site of former Augustinian abbey (founded in 11th cent.).

Garsdon, England: see MALMESBURY.

Garsen, town, Coast Prov., SE Kenya, on right bank of Tana R., on road and 35 mi. NW of Kipini; rice, sugar cane, copra.

Garson, village (pop. estimate 1,000), SE central Ont., 5 mi. N of Sudbury; nickel, copper mining.

Garson Quarry, village (pop. 255), SE Man., 23 mi. NE of Winnipeg; grain, dairying.

Garstang, village and parish (pop. 999), W Lancashire, England, on Lancaster Canal and 10 mi. NNW of Preston; cotton milling, paper mfg. Has ruins of 15th-cent. Greenhalgh Castle, built by 1st earl of Derby.

Garstedt (gär'shtĕt), village (pop. 8,313), in Schleswig-Holstein, NW Germany, 9 mi. NNW of Hamburg city center; mfg. (chemicals, precision instruments, furniture).

Garsten (gär'stŭn), town (pop. 5,489), E Upper Austria, on the Enns, just S of Steyr. Its former Benedictine abbey now a penal colony.

Garston, town (pop. 17,262) in Liverpool borough, SW Lancashire, England, on Mersey R.; metallurgical and nonferrous-metal industry; leather tanning, mfg. of glassware, concrete, metal products.

Gartempe River (gärtãp'), in Haute-Vienne and Vienne depts., central France, rises in Plateau of Millevaches 7 mi. S of Guéret, flows W then N, past Montmorillon and Saint-Savin, to the Creuse near La Roche-Posay; 120 mi. long.

Garth, Wales: see MAESTEG.

Garthby, village (pop. estimate 500), S Que., on L. Aylmer, 30 mi. NW of Megantic; asbestos, chrome mining; dairying, cattle raising, potato growing.

Gartok (gär'tŏk, -tŏk), Chinese *K'a-ta-k'o* (kä'dä'-kŭ'), town, W Tibet, in W Kailas Range, 650 mi. WNW of Lhasa, 240 mi. SE of Leh, at junction of India-Lhasa trade route (via Shipki Pass) with main Leh-Lhasa trade route; alt. 15,100 ft.; 31°44'N 80°20'E. Main trade center (wool, barley, yak tails, salt, musk, borax, rice, vegetables) of W Tibet; large annual fair. Opened 1904 to trade. Also called Garyarsa.

Gartsherrie (gärt-shĕ'rē), N suburb of Coatbridge, N Lanark, Scotland; known for its ironworks.

Gartz or **Gartz an der Oder** (gärts" än dĕr ō'dŭr), town (pop. 3,672) in former Prussian Pomerania prov., E Germany, after 1945 in Mecklenburg, on the West Oder (Berlin-Stettin Canal) and 18 mi. SSW of Stettin; agr. market (tobacco, grain, sugar beets, potatoes, livestock); sawmilling; river fisheries. Has Gothic church and remains of old town walls.

Garua, Fr. Cameroons: see GAROUA.

Garulia (gä'rōōlyŭ), town (pop. 20,150), 24-Parganas dist., SE West Bengal, India, on Hooghly R. and 17 mi. N of Calcutta city center; jute and cotton milling; iron- and steel-rolling works. Syamnagar, NE suburb, has Sanskrit col., 18th-cent. fort ruins.

Garumna, France: see GARONNE RIVER.

Garus (gärōōs'), former province of W Iran, in the Kurd country; main town, Bijar. Bounded W by Kurdistan, N by Azerbaijan, and E by Khamseh and Hamadan, it joined AZERBAIJAN in 1938 to form Iran's Fourth Prov.

Garut or **Garoet** (both: gärōōt'), town (pop. 24,219), W Java, Indonesia, in Preanger region, 30 mi. SE of Bandung; alt. 2,336 ft.; vacation resort and trade center for agr. area (tea, rice, tobacco, cinchona bark); cotton milling, soap mfg.

Garvagh (gär'vŭ), town (pop. 876), E Co. Londonderry, Northern Ireland, 10 mi. S of Coleraine; agr. market (potatoes, flax, oats).

Garvani, peak, Yugoslavia and Greece: see VARNOUS.

Garvão (gärvã'ō), village (pop. 1,451), Beja dist., S Portugal, on railroad and 35 mi. SW of Beja; grain, cork, livestock. Has 16th-cent. church.

Garve Water (gärv) or **Blackwater,** river, Ross and Cromarty, Scotland, rises 16 mi. SE of Ullapool, flows 25 mi. SE, through Loch Garve (2 mi. long) and past Contin, to Conon R. 2 mi. SE of Contin. Its upper course is called Glasoarnoch R. Near Contin are the picturesque Falls of Rogie.

Garvin, county (□ 814; pop. 29,500), S central Okla.; ⊙ Pauls Valley. Intersected by Washita R., and by small Rush and Wildhorse creeks. Agr. (cotton, broomcorn, oats, fruit, corn, livestock, poultry, alfalfa, pecans). Farm-products processing, some mfg. at Pauls Valley, Wynnewood, and Lindsay. Oil wells; oil refining. Formed 1907.

Garvin. 1 Village (pop. 264), Lyon co., SW Minn., near L. Shetek, 16 mi. S of Marshall; dairy products. **2** Town (pop. 155), McCurtain co., extreme SE Okla., 9 mi. WNW of Idabel, in farm area.

Garvolin, Poland: see GARWOLIN.

Garw, town, Wales: see OGMORE AND GARW.

Garwa or **Garhwa** (both: gŭr'vŭ), town (pop. 8,712), Palamau dist., W Bihar, India, 19 mi. WNW of Daltonganj; road junction; trade center (rice, corn, gram, barley, oilseeds, wheat). Lac growing, shellac mfg. near by.

Garwin, town (pop. 518), Tama co., central Iowa, 12 mi. ENE of Marshalltown; feed, wood products.

Garwolin (gärvô'lēn), Rus. *Garvolin* (gärvô'lēn), town (pop. 5,315), Warszawa prov., E central Poland, 35 mi. SSE of Warsaw; mfg. of agr. machinery, fleece clothes, cement, bricks, flour.

Garwood, industrial borough (pop. 4,622), Union co., NE N.J., 6 mi. W of Elizabeth; mfg. (metal products, cleansers, paper and rubber products). Inc. 1903.

Garw River (gă'rōō), Glamorgan, Wales, rises just N of Blaengarw, flows 7 mi. S, past Blaengarw and Pontycymmar, to Ogwr R. 3 mi. N of Bridgend.

Gary (gâ'rē). **1** Industrial city (pop. 133,911), Lake co., extreme NW Ind., at S end of L. Michigan, c.25 mi. SE of downtown Chicago, of whose metropolitan area it is a part. One of world's greatest steel-producing centers and heart of heavily industrialized CALUMET region; second-largest city in state; port facilities on Grand Calumet and Little Calumet rivers. Here are coke and by-products plants, 12 blast furnaces, more than 50 open-hearth furnaces, and rolling, rail, plate, wheel, and axle mills, and mills producing structural shapes, tin plate, and many other metal products. City also makes cement, chemicals, automotive accessories, and clothing, and refines oil. Contains several parks, including a lake-front dunes area, and a well-planned system of boulevards. Has a jr. col.; city's platoon school system is noted. Built on land purchased in 1905 by U.S. Steel Corporation, which chose site because of its midway position bet. iron regions of the Northwest and coal mines of East and Northeast. Named for Elbert H. Gary in 1906; inc. 1909. **2** Village (pop. 278), Norman co., NW Minn., 13 mi. ENE of Ada, in agr. area; dairy products. **3** City (pop. 558), Deuel co., E S.Dak., 12 mi. ENE of Clear Lake, on Minn. line; trading point for agr. area; dairy products, livestock, grain. State school for blind is here. **4** Village (pop. 2,858, with adjacent Ream), McDowell co., S W.Va., 5 mi. S of Welch; coal.

Garyarsa, Tibet: see GARTOK.

Garysburg, town (pop. 344), Northampton co., NE N.C., 6 mi. E of Roanoke Rapids, near Roanoke R.

Garyton, village (pop. 2,146), Porter co., NW Ind., 5 mi. ESE of Gary.

Garyville, village (pop. 1,850), St. John the Baptist parish, SE La., 32 mi. WNW of New Orleans and on E bank (levee) of the Mississippi; lumber.

Garz or **Garz auf Rügen** (gärts' ouf rü'gŭn), town (pop. 3,365), in former Prussian Pomerania prov., N Germany, after 1945 in Mecklenburg, on S Rügen isl., 11 mi. E of Stralsund; agr. market (grain, potatoes, stock). Site of earthwork remains of anc. Wendish fortress of Charenza, destroyed 1168 by Danes. Poet Arndt b. near by.

Garza (gär'sä), village (pop. estimate 800), ⊙ Sarmiento dept. (□ 575; 1947 pop. 5,511), central Santiago del Estero prov., Argentina, on railroad and 50 mi. SE of Santiago del Estero; agr. center (cotton, wheat, alfalfa, sheep).

Garza (gär'zŭ), county (□ 914; pop. 6,281), NW Texas; ⊙ Post. Rolling plains at foot of Cap Rock escarpment (in W); alt. 2,500–3,000 ft. Drained by Salt and Double Mtn. forks of Brazos R. Cattle ranching (in lower plains); agr. (cotton, grain sorghums, corn, wheat, some truck and fruit) on high plains above Cap Rock; also some dairying, stock raising (hogs, sheep, goats). Oil, natural-gas wells; clay, gypsum, lignite deposits. Formed 1876.

Garza Dam, Texas: see TRINITY RIVER.

Garza García (gärsē'ä), town (pop. 1,655), Nuevo León, N Mexico, in foothills of Sierra Madre Oriental, 6 mi. W of Monterrey; chick-peas, grain, stock.

Garza-Little Elm Reservoir, Texas: see TRINITY RIVER.

Garzan River (gärzän'), SE Turkey, rises in Bitlis Mts. 12 mi. SE of Mus, flows 65 mi. S, past Besiri, to Tigris R. 22 mi. SW of Siirt.

Garzas (gär'säs), reservoir and hydroelectric project, W central Puerto Rico, in Cordillera Central, c.10 mi. NW of Ponce. Completed 1943.

Garzas, Las, Argentina: see LAS GARZAS.

Garz auf Rügen, Germany: see GARZ.

Garzón (gärsōn'), town (pop. 4,367), Huila dept., S central Colombia, in upper Magdalena valley, 55 mi. SSW of Neiva; agr. center (rice, cotton, cacao, coffee, cattle). Airfield. Founded 1782. Cathedral town with bishopric. Asphalt mines, where mastodon fossils have been excavated, are near by.

Garzón, Lake, fresh-water coastal lagoon (7 mi. long, c.3 mi. wide), Maldonado dept., S Uruguay, on Rocha dept. border, 20 mi. ENE of Maldonado.

Gas, city (pop. 294), Allen co., SE Kansas, 3 mi. E of Iola, in livestock, grain, and dairy region. Gas fields here.

Gasa or **Ghasa** (gä'sä), fortified village [Bhutanese *dzong*], NW Bhutan, on upper Sankosh R. and 26 mi. NW of Punakha.

Gasan-Kuli (gŭsän"-kōōlyē'), town (1926 pop. 3,471), SW Ashkhabad oblast, Turkmen SSR, port on Caspian Sea, near Iran border, 240 mi. WSW of Ashkhabad; fish canning, rug weaving.

Gaschurn (gä'shōōrn), town (pop. 2,610), Vorarlberg, W Austria, on Ill R., in Montafon valley, and 26 mi. SE of Feldkirch; tourist center (alt. 3,162 ft.). Waterfall near by.

Gas City, city (pop. 3,787), Grant co., E central Ind., 5 mi. SSE of Marion, in agr. area (livestock, grain, dairy, poultry farms); mfg. (glass, barrels, concrete products). Grew after a natural-gas boom in 1887.

Gascogne, Golfe de, France: see BISCAY, BAY OF.

Gasconade (găskŭnād'), county (□ 520; pop. 12,342), E central Mo.; ⊙ Hermann. In Ozark region, bounded N by Missouri R.; drained by Gasconade and Bourbeuse rivers. Agr. (corn, wheat, livestock); mfg. (grain products, lumber products, shoes); timber; flint, fire-clay, diaspore, zinc, lead mines. Formed 1820.

Gasconade, town (pop. 448), Gasconade co., E central Mo., at confluence of Missouri and Gasconade rivers, 8 mi. W of Hermann.

Gasconade River, central Mo., rises in the Ozarks in Wright co., flows c.265 mi. NE to Missouri R. near Gasconade. Navigable for 40 mi., March 1–Nov. 30; dams at Richland and Vienna.

Gascony (gă'skŭnē), Fr. *Gascogne* (gäskô'nyŭ), region and old province, SW France; ⊙ Auch. Bounded by the Bay of Biscay (W), the Pyrenees (S), and roughly by the Garonne (N and E), it lies in the AQUITAINE BASIN and includes the LANDES, the LANNEMEZAN PLATEAU, and the hilly ARMAGNAC dist. Chief towns are Tarbes, Bayonne, Auch, Biarritz, Dax, and Lourdes. Under the Romans Gascony was known 1st as *Aquitania Propia*, later as *Novempopulana*. It has been inhabited by the Vascones or Basques since paleolithic period, but the Basque language and customs have persisted only in the region surrounding Bayonne. Conquered by Visigoths (5th cent.) and by Franks (6th cent.), and again by Basque-speaking peoples from S of Pyrenees, who in 601 set up the duchy of Vasconia or Gascony. Fighting with Visigoths, Franks, and Arabs resulted in anarchy until in 1058 the dukes of Aquitaine absorbed all of Gascony except Lower Navarre and Béarn. It passed under English domination (12th–15th cent.), and was finally united with the royal domain by Henry IV in 1607. In 1790 Gascony was broken up administratively into Landes, Gers, and Hautes-Pyrénées depts. and parts of Basses-Pyrénées, Lot-et-Garonne, Tarn-et-Garonne, and Haute-Garonne depts.

Gascony, Gulf of, France: see BISCAY, BAY OF.

Gascoyne (gă'skoin), village (pop. 76), Bowman co., SW N.Dak., 16 mi. E of Bowman.

Gascoyne River (gă'skoin), W Western Australia, rises in NE Robinson Ranges, flows 475 mi. W to Shark Bay of Indian Ocean at Carnarvon; intermittent flow. Lyons R. (225 mi. long) is the main tributary.

Gasc River, Eritrea and Anglo-Egyptian Sudan: see GASH RIVER.

Gascueña (gäskwā'nyä), town (pop. 1,254), Cuenca prov., E central Spain, 26 mi. NW of Cuenca; olives, wheat, grapes, sheep; flour, olive oil.

Gashaka (gäshä'kä), town (pop. 1,088), S Br. Cameroons, administered as part of Adamawa prov. of Nigeria, on headstream of Temba R. and 145 mi. SSW of Yola; 7°22'N 11°28'E. Trade center; peanuts, sesame, hemp, rice, cotton; cattle.

Gasherbrum I (gŭ'shûrbrōōm) or **Hidden Peak** (26,470 ft.), peak in main range of Karakoram mtn. system, N Kashmir, at 35°44'N 76°42'E. Climbing attempts made by 2d Dyhrenfurth Himalayan expedition (1934) and Fr. expedition (1936). **Gasherbrum II** (26,360 ft.) lies just NW, at 35° 46'N 76°39'E.

Gash River (gäsh), Ital. *Gasc*, in NE Africa, rises 15 mi. SW of Asmara (Eritrea), flows generally WNW, forming section of Eritrea-Ethiopia border, enters Anglo-Egyptian Sudan near Kassala and loses itself in Sudan desert in direction of Atbara R. Length, c.300 mi. Seasonally dry; its waters reach the Atbara in flood period. Used for irrigation at Tessenei (Eritrea) and Kassala. Called Mareb R. in upper course.

Gasmata (gäsmä'tä), town, S New Britain, Bismarck Archipelago, Territory of New Guinea, SW Pacific, 200 mi. SW of Rabaul. In Second World War, site of Jap. air base.

Gaspar (gŭspär'), city (pop. 1,186), NE Santa Catarina, Brazil, on Itajaí Açu R. and 10 mi. E of Blumenau; molybdenum deposits.

Gaspar Grande (gă'spûr grăn'dē) or **Gasparee** (găspûrē'), islet (319 acres) off SW Trinidad, B.W.I., outside Chaguaramas Bay, 9 mi. W of Port of Spain; bathing and fishing resort. Gasparillo or Little Gasparee isl. is off N coast.

Gaspar Hernández (gäspär' ĕrnän'dĕs), town (1950 pop. 742), Espaillat prov., N Dominican Republic, near coast, 30 mi. ENE of Santiago; cacao, rice, coffee, corn.

Gasparilla Island (găspûrĭ'lŭ), SW Fla., narrow barrier island (c.6 mi. long) in the Gulf of Mexico, at entrance to Charlotte Harbor (W), S of Gasparilla Pass (inlet connecting small Gasparilla Sound and the Gulf); lighthouse at 26°43'N 83°15'W. Contains villages of Gasparilla (ferry to mainland), in N, and Boca Grande (bō'kŭ grănd') (resort, port of entry, and fishing station) and South Boca Grande, in S. Railroad bridge to mainland at isl.'s N end; railroad extends to South Boca Grande, important shipping port for phosphate rock.

Gasparillo (găspûrĭ'lō), village (pop. 2,647), W Trinidad, B.W.I., 22 mi. SSE of Port of Spain; sugar cane, coconuts. Small, uninhabited Gasparillo or Little Gasparee isl. is just N of Gaspar Grande isl., 7 mi. W of Port of Spain.

Gaspé (găspā', găs'pā, găs'pē), village (pop. 924), E Que., on Gaspé Bay, near E extremity of Gaspé Peninsula; market center in lumbering, vegetable-growing region; tourist resort. Site of govt. salmon and trout hatchery. Cartier landed here (1534) and claimed Canadian mainland for France.

Gaspé, Cape, E extremity of Gaspé Peninsula, E Que., on the Gulf of St. Lawrence, bet. mouth of the St. Lawrence (N) and Gaspé Bay (S), 16 mi. ESE of Gaspé; 48°45'N 64°10'W; lighthouse.

Gaspé Bay, inlet (22 mi. long, 6 mi. wide at mouth) of the Gulf of St. Lawrence, E Que., at E end of Gaspé Peninsula. Near its head is Gaspé.

Gaspé East, county (□ 2,348; pop. 33,871), E Que., at E end of Gaspé Peninsula, bet. the St. Lawrence (N) and Chaleur Bay (S); ⊙ Percé.

Gaspee Point (găs"pē'), promontory in Warwick town, Kent co., E R.I., on Providence R. c.5 mi. S of Providence; bathing beaches. Br. sloop *Gaspee* burned here by patriots, 1772.

Gaspé Peninsula (găspā', găs'pā, găs'pē), broad tongue of land, E Que., extends E into the Gulf of St. Lawrence, bet. the St. Lawrence (N) and Chaleur Bay (S); 150 mi. long bet. Matapedia R. (W), at its base, and Point St. Peter, its E extremity; 60–90 mi. wide. Interior is heavily wooded, mountainous, and uninhabited, with many lakes and streams. Backbone of peninsula is the Shickshock Mts., outcrop of the Appalachian system, rising to 4,160 ft. in Mt. Jacques Cartier or Tabletop, and having several other peaks over 3,000 ft. high. Region is drained by Cascapedia, St. John, York, Grand, and Grand Pabos rivers. Coastal settlements are inhabited by French-Canadians (N); S part of peninsula is inhabited by people of French-Canadian, Acadian, Scotch, Irish, and English stock. Fishing (cod), lumbering, pulp milling are chief industries. There are numerous resorts; with opening of highway (1928) that circles entire peninsula, tourism became important. Chief towns: Gaspé, Matane, Percé, Chandler, New Carlisle.

Gaspereau, Lake (gă'spûrō, găspûrō') (8 mi. long, 4 mi. wide), W central N.S., 20 mi. W of Windsor; drains into Minas Basin.

Gasperina (găspĕrē'nä), village (pop. 3,175), Catanzaro prov., Calabria, S Italy, near Ionian Sea, 12 mi. SSW of Catanzaro; wine, olive oil.

Gaspé West, county (□ 2,198; pop. 12,397), E Que., on N side of Gaspé Peninsula, on the St. Lawrence; ⊙ Ste. Anne des Monts.

Gaspoltshofen (gäs'pōlts-hōfŭn), town (pop. 3,486), central Upper Austria, 13 mi. W of Wels; potatoes, cattle.

Gasport, village (1940 pop. 788), Niagara co., W N.Y., on the Barge Canal and 25 mi. NNE of Buffalo; makes cider, vinegar, baskets, machinery. Limestone quarry.

Gaspra (gŭsprä'), town (1939 pop. over 500), S Crimea, Russian SFSR, Black Sea resort, adjoining (E) Koreiz, 5 mi. SW of Yalta. Has Gothic palace (1820s), now a sanatorium. Tolstoy lived here, 1901–02.

Gassaway, town (pop. 1,306), Braxton co., central W.Va., on Elk R. and 4 mi. W of Sutton, in agr. area; railroad shops. Founded 1904.

Gasselternijveen or **Gasselternijeveen** (both: khä'sŭltĕr'nīvān"), town (pop. 1,267), Drenthe prov., NE Netherlands, 12 mi. E of Assen; potato-flour milling. Sometimes spelled Gasselternyveen.

Gassen, Poland: see JASIEN.

Gassino Torinese (gäs'sēnō tôrēnā'sĕ), village (pop. 2,742), Torino prov., Piedmont, NW Italy, near Po R., 7 mi. NE of Turin; alcohol distillery. Until c.1936 called Gassino.

Gassville (găs'vĭl), town (pop. 273), Baxter co., N Ark., 35 mi. E of Harrison, in the Ozarks.

Gastein, town, Austria: see BAD GASTEIN.

Gasteiner Ache (gä'stīnûr ä'khŭ), river, Salzburg, central Austria; rises on the Ankogel; flows 25 mi. N, through GASTEIN VALLEY, past BAD GASTEIN and BAD HOFGASTEIN, to the Salzach near Lend. Forms 2 waterfalls in Bad Gastein.

Gastein Valley (gä'stīn), in Salzburg, W central Austria, on N slope of the Hohe Tauern, 35–55 mi. S of Salzburg; popular and beautiful resort area (with thermal springs) traversed by the Gasteiner Ache and Tauern RR; baths at BAD GASTEIN and BAD HOFGASTEIN. Some gold and silver has been mined. Hydroelectric station near Lend.

Gastel, Oud-, Netherlands: see OUD-GASTEL.

Gastello (gŭstyĕ'lŭ), town (1940 pop. 4,266), S Sakhalin, Russian SFSR, on E coast railroad and 11 mi. SW of Poronaisk; rail junction; coal mining. Under Jap. rule (1905–45), called Nairo (nī'rō).

Gaster (gä'stûr), lowland of Linth Canal, NE Switzerland; Gaster dist. (pop. 8,767), St. Gall canton, extends to E.

Gastineau Channel (găs'tĭnō), SE Alaska, bet. Douglas Isl. and mainland; navigable. On it are Thane, Douglas, and Juneau. It is 20 mi. long and has a 16-ft. tide.

Gaston (gă'stŭn), county (□ 358; pop. 110,836), S N.C.; ⊙ Gastonia. In piedmont region; bounded S by S.C., E by Catawba R. (Mountain Isl. and Catawba lakes); drained by its South Fork. Largely agr. (cotton, wheat, hay, poultry, dairying); timber (pine, oak). Produces much of combed cotton yarn made in U.S., with textile center at Gastonia; sawmilling. Formed 1846.

Gaston. 1 Town (pop. 729), Delaware co., E central Ind., 12 mi. NNW of Muncie; livestock, grain, tomatoes; cannery. **2** Town (pop. 1,218), Northampton co., NE N.C., near Va. line, 2 mi. N of Roanoke Rapids. Inc. 1950. **3** Town (pop. 368), Washington co., NW Oregon, 25 mi. WSW of Portland.

Gastona (gästō'nä), town (pop. estimate 500), S Tucumán prov., Argentina, near Gastona R., 40 mi. SSW of Tucumán; stock raising.

Gastona River (gästō'nä), S Tucumán prov., Argentina, rises as Solco R. at S foot of Nevado del Aconquija, flows 65 mi. ESE, past Concepción, to the Salí R. 8 mi. NW of Río Hondo.

Gastonia (găstō'nēŭ), city (pop. 23,069), ⊙ Gaston co., S N.C., 19 mi. W of Charlotte, in the piedmont, near S.C. line. Major textile-milling center, noted for its fine-combed cotton yarn; also mfg. of thread, tire fabric, textile machinery; cotton warehouses. State orthopedic hosp. and Kings Mtn. battlefield near by. Inc. 1877.

Gastonville (găstōvēl'), village (pop. 693), Constantine dept., NE Algeria, on the Oued Saf-Saf and 13 mi. S of Philippeville; wine, cereals, olives.

Gastor, El (ĕl găstôr'), town (pop. 1,985), Cádiz prov., SW Spain, 11 mi. NW of Ronda; cereals, olives, almonds. Has mineral springs.

Gastoune or **Gastouni** (both: gästōō'nē), town (pop. 4,248), Elis nome, W Peloponnesus, Greece, on railroad and 15 mi. NW of Pyrgos; livestock-trading center; trades in Zante currants, wheat. Ruins of Franco-Byzantine church. Founded (13th cent.) under the French, it became commercial center and ⊙ Elis under Turks. Site of battles of Gr. war of independence. Sometimes spelled Gastuni and Ghastouni.

Gastouni River, Greece: see PENEUS RIVER.

Gastourion (gŭstōō'rēōn), village (pop. 1,120), central Corfu isl., Greece, 4 mi. S of Corfu city. Site of the Achilleion villa, built 1890–91 for Elizabeth of Austria and bought by William II of Germany. Also spelled Gasturi.

Gastre or **Gastres** (gä'strā, –strĕs), village (pop. estimate 300), ⊙ Gastre dept. (pop. 3,389), N Chubut natl. territory, Argentina, 110 mi. NE of Esquel; stock raising (sheep, goats), lead mining.

Gastrikland (yĕs'trĭklănd"), Swedish *Gästrikland*, province [Swedish *landskap*] (□ 1,768; pop. 120,-657), E Sweden, on Gulf of Bothnia. Included in SE part of Gavleborg co. Formerly spelled Gestrikland.

Gastuni, town, Greece: see GASTOUNE.

Gastuni River, Greece: see PENEUS RIVER.

Gasturi, Greece: see GASTOURION.

Gat, Fezzan: see GHAT.

Gat, Israel: see GATH.

Gata (gä'tä), town (pop. 2,441), Cáceres prov., W Spain, 25 mi. S of Ciudad Rodrigo; mfg. of textiles, flour milling, olive-oil processing; honey, lumber, livestock.

Gata (gä'tä), village, NW Bosnia, Yugoslavia, 8 mi. N of Bihac, on Croatia line; hot sulphur baths.

Gata, Cape (gä'tä), S Cyprus, on Mediterranean Sea, at SE end of Akrotiri Peninsula; 34°33'N 33°3'E. Lighthouse.

Gata, Cape, Sp. *Cabo de Gata*, on the Mediterranean coast of Andalusia, S Spain, 18 mi. ESE of Almería, at E edge of Gulf of Almería; 36°43'N 2°12'W. Lighthouse. Salt marshes near by.

Gata, Sierra de (syĕ'rä dhā gä'tä). **1** Westernmost range of the central mountain system of Spain, bet. Tagus and Douro (or Duero) valleys, separating Leon from Estremadura. Extends NE from Portugal to upper Alagón R. valley. Highest point, Jálama peak (5,577 ft.). Tungsten deposits. **2** Range in Almería prov., S Spain, extending along the Mediterranean NE from Cape Gata. Gold, silver, platinum, lead mines.

Gata de Gorgos (gä'tä dhā gôr'gōs), village (pop. 4,101), Alicante prov., E Spain, 20 mi. SE of Gandía; vegetable-fiber processing (baskets, hats, mats), rush-furniture mfg., olive pressing. Raisins, cereals, almonds, sheep in area.

Gataia (gŭtä'yä), Rum. *Gătaia*, Hung. *Gátalja* (gä'tŏlyŏ), village (pop. 3,398), Timisoara prov., W Rumania, 24 mi. SSE of Timisoara; rail junction, agr. center.

Gatbo (gät'bō), village (1939 pop. 1,240) in Bacon municipality, Sorsogon prov., extreme SE Luzon, on Sugot Bay (small inlet of Albay Gulf), 7 mi. ENE of Sorsogon; sulphur mining. Near by are coal mines.

Gatchina (gä'chēnŭ), city (1926 pop. 18,589), W central Leningrad oblast, Russian SFSR, on Izhora R. and 25 mi. SSW of Leningrad; rail junction; metalworking, lumber milling. Peat works near by. City developed around palace (built 1766–70; now a mus.) 1st used as summer residence by Paul I. City chartered 1795. Scene of severe civil war battles (1917–19) in defense of Petrograd. Named Trotsk (1923–29) and Krasnogvardeisk (1929–44). During Second World War, held (1941–44) by Germans in siege of Leningrad.

Gate, town (pop. 197), Beaver co., extreme NW Okla., 27 mi. E of Beaver, in grain-growing area; ships silica.

Gate City, town (pop. 2,126), ⊙ Scott co., SW Va., near North Fork of Holston R., 35 mi. WSW of Abingdon, near Tenn. line; trade center for agr., timber, livestock region; shirts, wood products, limestone. Natural Tunnel is W; a pass across Clinch Mtn. is just E. Settled in late-18th cent.; inc. 1892.

Gatehouse of Fleet, burgh (1931 pop. 888; 1951 census 877), S Kirkcudbright, Scotland, 6 mi. NW of Kirkcudbright; agr. market.

Gates, county (□ 343; pop. 9,555), NE N.C.; ⊙ Gatesville. Coastal plain; bounded N by Va., S by Chowan R.; Dismal Swamp in E. Agr. (peanuts, cotton, corn, soybeans); timber (gum, pine, cypress). Sawmilling, some fishing. Formed 1778.

Gates, town (pop. 234), Lauderdale co., W Tenn., 13 mi. S of Dyersburg, in timber and farm region.

Gates Center, village (1940 pop. 799), Monroe co., W N.Y., just W of Rochester; chemicals, stone products.

Gateshead (gāts'hĕd), county borough (1931 pop. 122,447; 1951 census 115,017), N Durham, England, on Tyne R. just S of Newcastle-upon-Tyne (connected by bridges); coal mining, shipbuilding, locomotive and railroad car shops, metalworking, mfg. of chemicals, pharmaceuticals, glass, aluminum products, cables. Grindstone quarries at hill of Gateshead Fell (S; 512 ft.). Parish church dates from c.12th cent.; rebuilt. In county borough are industrial suburbs of Dunston (W) and Heworth (E), with quarries and coal mines, and Low Fell (SW), site of Team Valley Trading Estate with small-scale industries, set up in 1930s to provide alternative employment for coal miners.

Gateside, Scotland: see STRATHMIGLO.

Gates Mills, village (pop. 1,056), Cuyahoga co., N Ohio, 15 mi. E of Cleveland and on Chagrin R.

Gatesville. 1 Town (pop. 323), ⊙ Gates co., NE N.C., 30 mi. WNW of Elizabeth City, in agr. and timber area; hunting, fishing. **2** City (pop. 3,856), ⊙ Coryell co., central Texas, on Leon R. and 37 mi. W of Waco; trade, processing center for agr., livestock area; cotton ginning, poultry packing, dairying, grain milling. State training school for delinquent boys. U.S. Camp Hood is S. Ruins of Fort Gates (est. 1849) are near.

Gateway. 1 Town (pop. 97), Benton co., extreme NW Ark., 33 mi. NNE of Fayetteville. **2** Resort village (pop. c.50), Mesa co., W Colo., on Dolores R., near Utah line, and 35 mi. SW of Grand Junction; alt. 5,478 ft. Uncompahgre Natl. Forest near.

Gath or **Gat** (both: gät), settlement (pop. 300), W Israel, at W foot of Judaean Hills, near N edge of the Negev, 18 mi. S of Rehovot; feed crops, vegetables; woodworking. Modern settlement founded 1942; withstood heavy Arab attacks, 1948. In vicinity is site of biblical city of Gath.

Gath Mine, township (pop. 1,862), Victoria prov., SE central Southern Rhodesia, in Mashonaland, 2 mi. ENE of Mashaba; asbestos-mining center.

Gathright Dam, Va.: see JACKSON RIVER.

Gatico (gätē'kō), village (1930 pop. 1,005), Antofagasta prov., N Chile, port on the Pacific, 30 mi. S of Tocopilla; nitrate production. Copper deposits near by.

Gatico, Cordillera de (kôrdĭyä'rä dā), W spur of the Andes, N Chile, 70 mi. E of Iquique; extends c.70 mi. NNW-SSE, bounding the Pampa del Tamarugal E; rises to over 16,000 ft.

Gâtinais (gätēnā'), region and old district of N central France, in Loiret, Yonne, and Seine-et-Marne depts. Historical ⊙ was Montargis. Drained by Loing R. Poultry and cattle raising; small grains. Noted for its honey.

Gâtine (gätēn'), district of W France, now part of Deux-Sèvres dept., crossed by the Gâtine hills (rising to 750 ft.) and centered on Parthenay. Region noted for its hedgerows. Extensive livestock raising.

Gatineau (gă'tĭnō, Fr. gätēnō'), county (□ 2,432; pop. 29,754), SW Que., on Ont. border, on Ottawa and Gatineau rivers; ⊙ Maniwaki.

Gatineau, village (pop. 2,822), SW Que., on Ottawa R. and 6 mi. NE of Hull; dairying, cattle raising.

Gatineau Point, Que.: see POINTE GATINEAU.

Gatineau River, SW Que., rises in the Laurentians N of Baskatong L., flows 230 mi. S, through Baskatong L., past Maniwaki, to Ottawa R. at Hull, opposite Ottawa. There are several rapids; hydroelectric power.

Gatley, England: see CHEADLE AND GATLEY.

Gatliff, village (1940 pop. 1,210), Whitley co., SE Ky., near Pine Mtn. in the Cumberlands, 19 mi. WNW of Middlesboro; bituminous-coal mining. Fish hatchery here.

Gatlinburg, resort city (pop. 1,301), Sevier co., E Tenn., 30 mi. SE of Knoxville, in Great Smoky Mts. Natl. Park (hq. near by); handicraft workshops (pottery, wood). Has several museums, settlement school. Mt. Le Conte is just SE. Inc. 1945.

Gato, El, Chile: see RÍO GATO.

Gatooma (gŏŏtōō'mŏŏ), city (pop. 3,343; including suburbs, 3,441), Salisbury prov., central Southern Rhodesia, in Mashonaland, on railroad, 85 mi. SW of Salisbury; alt. 3,814 ft. Agr. and cotton-milling center; engineering works; brick- and woodworking, mineral-water bottling. Tobacco, cotton, peanuts, citrus fruit grown near by. Hq. of native commissioner; police post; airfield. Has experimental cotton-farm research station. Gold-mining center of Eiffel Flats is 5 mi. ENE. Golden Valley mine is 12 mi. NW.

Gátova (gä'tōvä), village (pop. 1,210), Castellón de la Plana prov., E Spain, 15 mi. WNW of Sagunto; olive-oil processing; cereals, almonds, figs, wine. Summer resort.

Gatow (gä'tō), residential section of Spandau dist., W Berlin, Germany, on the Havel and 10 mi. WSW of city center; 52°28'N 13°9'E. After 1945, chief airport in British sector; a terminus of Western Allied air lift during Soviet blockade of West Berlin, 1948–49.

Gat Rimmon or **Gat Rimon** (both: gät' rēmōn'), settlement (pop. 200), W Israel, in Plain of Sharon, just S of Petah Tiqva; mixed farming, citriculture. Founded 1926.

Gatrun or **Gatroun** (gätrōōn'), village (pop. 699), S Fezzan, Libya, on caravan route and 80 mi. SE of Murzuk, in a Saharan oasis; date growing, basket weaving.

Gatsko, Yugoslavia: see GACKO.

Gattinara (gät-tēnä'rä), town (pop. 5,541), Vercelli prov., Piedmont, N Italy, near Sesia R., 17 mi. NW of Novara, in grape-growing region; wine, textiles.

Gattman, village (pop. 150), Monroe co., E Miss., near Ala. line and Buttahatchie R., 19 mi. ENE of Aberdeen.

Gatton, town (pop. 1,581), SE Queensland, Australia, 45 mi. W of Brisbane; agr. center (corn, sugar cane).

Gatumba (gätōōm'bä), village, NW Ruanda Urundi, in Ruanda, on Nyawarongo R. and 27 mi. W of Kigali; center of tin-mining area; also columbite, tantalite, and wolfram mining.

Gatun (gŏŏtnōōn'), Sp. *Gatún* (gä–), town (pop. 2,276), Cristobal dist., N Panama Canal Zone, on Gatun L., at N efflux of Chagres R., on transisthmian railroad, and 6 mi. S of Colón. Lighthouse; naval reservation and radio station. Site of **Gatun Dam** (115 ft. high, 7,700 ft. long; completed 1912) and the 2 sets of Gatun Locks which raise (and lower) vessels in 3 steps to (and from) 85-ft. level of Gatun L. A hydroelectric station near dam's spillway supplies current to canal works and the towns of the zone. The dam impounds **Gatun Lake** (□ 163.38; 85 ft. above sea level; capacity 4,407,000 acre-feet), part of the canal route, which crosses it NW-SE bet. Juan Gallegos and Barro Colorado isls. The **Gatún River,** formerly an affluent of Chagres R., flows c.20 mi. SW to NE arm of the lake.

Gau, Fiji: see NGAU.

Gaua (gäōō'ä), Fr. *Gaoua* (gäwä'), volcanic island (pop. 210), southernmost and 2d largest of Banks Isls., New Hebrides, SW Pacific, 45 mi. NE of Espiritu Santo; circular, c.10 mi. in circumference. Sometimes called Santa Maria.

Gau-Algesheim (gou'-äl'gŭs-hīm), town (pop. 3,841), Rhenish Hesse, W Germany, 5 mi. E of Bingen; rail junction; mfg. of chemicals. Has ruins of 15th-cent. castle.

Gauani (gäwä'nē), village, Harar prov., E central Ethiopia, in Great Rift Valley, near Awash R., 90 mi. WNW of Diredawa.

Gauchy (gōshē'), SSW suburb (pop. 2,616) of Saint-Quentin, Aisne dept., N France; rayon milling, graphite processing.

Gaucín (gou-thēn'), town (pop. 2,844), Málaga prov., S Spain, on S slopes of the Sierra de Ronda, 27 mi. N of Gibraltar; trades in agr. produce (cereals, tubers, olives, olive oil, almonds, fruit, cork, dairy products). Noted for its wines. Has ruins of Moorish castle. Mineral waters near by. Hydroelectric plant on gorge of Guadiaro R. 5 mi. W.

Gaud (gō), village (pop. 306), Haute-Garonne dept., S France, 9 mi. NNE of Luchon; metal furniture factory.

Gaudan (goudän'), village, S Ashkhabad oblast, Turkmen SSR, 20 mi. S of Ashkhabad (connected by highway); USSR-Iran border station.

Gaud-i-Zirreh or **Gawd-i-Zirrah** (goud'ĕ-zērä'), salt tract in Farah prov., southwesternmost Afghanistan, near Pakistan line; 60 mi. long, 15 mi. wide. Receives seasonal overflow of Seistan lake depression via Shelagh R.

Gaugamela: see ERBIL, town.

Gauhati (gouhä'tē), town (pop. 29,598), ⊙ Kamrup dist., W Assam, India, on Brahmaputra R. and 42 mi. N of Shillong; airport; trade center (rice, mustard, jute, cotton, lac); tea processing, cotton ginning, flour, rice, and oilseed milling, soap mfg. Has Univ. of Gauhati (since 1948 an affiliating body for all Assam cols.), Earle Law Col. Gauhati (anc. *Pragjyotishapura*) was ⊙ anc. Hindu kingdom of Kamarupa and of late-18th-cent. Ahom kingdom. Ruins of 10th-cent. Hindu temple near by. Sivaite temple (pilgrimage center) 2 mi. WSW, at village of Kamakhya.

Gauja River or **Gauya River** (gou'yä), Ger. *Aa* or *Livländische Aa* [=Livonian Aa], also *Treider Aa,* longest river (260 mi.) of Latvia, in Vidzeme, rises in Vidzeme hills, 23 mi. SE of Cesis, flows in winding course, ENE, NNW, and SW, past Strenci, Valmiera, Cesis, and Sigulda, to Gulf of Riga 15 mi. NNE of Riga. Connected near its mouth with Western Dvina R. via system of lakes. Nonnavigable; timber floating.

Gaul (gôl), Latin *Gallia* (gă'lēŭ), anc. designation for the land S and W of the Rhine, W of the Alps, and N of the Pyrenees—roughly the area of modern France. The name was extended by the Romans to include Italy from Lucca and Rimini northwards, excluding Liguria. This extension of the name is derived from its settlers of 4th and 3d cent. B.C.—invading Celts, who were called Gauls by the Romans. The Gaul in Italy was called Cisalpine Gaul [on this side the Alps], in distinction to Transalpine Gaul; Cisalpine Gaul was divided into Cispadane Gaul [on this side the Po] and Transpadane Gaul. By 100 B.C., Rome had acquired S Transalpine Gaul, and by the time of Julius Caesar it had been pacified. It was usually called the Province (*Provincia,* hence modern Provence), and it included a strip 100 mi. wide along the sea from the E Pyrenees northeastward and up the Rhone valley nearly to Lyons. Julius Caesar conquered Gaul in the Gallic Wars (58 B.C.–51 B.C.). He is the best anc. source on anc. Gaul, and he has immortalized its ethnic divisions, Aquitania (S of the Garonne), Gaul proper (modern central France), and Belgica (very roughly Belgium).

Gaula River (gou'lä), Sor-Trondelag co., central Norway, rises c.10 mi. N of Roros, flows NW, through pyrite-mining dist. to Storen, where it is joined by the Sokna, and then N to an inlet of Trondheim Fjord 8 mi. SSW of Trondheim. Length, 90 mi. Roros-Trondheim RR follows its valley. Sometimes spelled Gula.

Gauldal (goul'däl), valley of the Gaula in Sor-Trondelag co., central Norway; a region (□ 2,187; pop. 23,684) extending from Trondheim Fjord S to Roros. Pyrite mining near Alen. Sometimes spelled Guldal.

Gauley Bridge, village (pop. 1,134), Fayette co., S central W.Va., on Kanawha R. (here formed by confluence of Gauley and New rivers) and 25 mi. ESE of Charleston. Near by (SE) are Hawks Nest State Park (road to Hawks Nest Lookout; mus.) and 3-mi.-long Hawks Nest Tunnel, which diverts New R. waters (impounded here by Hawks Nest Dam) to a hydroelectric plant. In Civil War, Gen. Rosecrans defeated a Confederate force here in 1861.

Gauley Mountain, W.Va.: see BIG SPRUCE KNOB.

Gauley River, SE W.Va., rises in the Alleghenies in W Pocahontas co., NW of Marlinton; flows 104 mi. generally WSW, joining New R. at Gauley Bridge to form Kanawha R. Carnifex Ferry State Park (275 acres) is on its banks, 7 mi. SW of Summerville; marks scene of Civil War engagement (1861) won by Union troops.

Gaultois Island (gôl'tŭs) or **Long Island** (□ 34; pop. 427), in Hermitage Bay, S N.F.; 47°40'N 56'W; 10 mi. long, 2–7 mi. wide; rises to 725 ft. (W). Gaultois (pop. 199), on E coast, is fishing settlement.

Gaur (gour), ruined city, Malda dist., NW West Bengal, India, on tributary of the Mahananda and 4 mi. S of English Bazar. Was ⊙ Bengal under rule of Sen kingdom and Afghans (12th cent.). In 1198 it was taken by the Moslem sultanate of Delhi and became a center of Moslem culture until it passed (16th cent.) to the Afghans. Abandoned 1575 because of the plague. There are several reminders of the old Moslem splendor, including three 16th-cent. mosques; most striking are Golden Mosque and a mosque built over the imprint of a foot said to be that of Mohammed. Called by the Sens Lakshmanavati and Laknauti, by early Moslems Jannatabad, Fatehabad, Husainabad, Nusratabad.

Gaura-Barhaj, India: see BARHAJ.

Gaurdak (gourdäk'), town (1939 pop. over 2,000), SE Chardzhou oblast, Turkmen SSR, on SW spur of the Baisun-Tau, 50 mi. E of Kerki, on rail spur from Mukry; extensive sulphur mines; chemical industry (sulphuric acid, superphosphates).

Gaurhati (gourhä'tē), Fr. *Goretti* or *Goretty* (gōrĕtē'), S suburb of CHANDERNAGORE, Hooghly dist., S central West Bengal, India, on Hooghly R.; jute milling. Became Fr. trading post in early-18th cent., attached administratively to Chandernagore. Returned 1950 to India.

Gaurihar (gou'rĭhär), village, N Vindhya Pradesh, India, 39 mi. N of Panna. Was ⊙ former petty state of Gaurihar (□ 72; pop. 10,481) of Central India agency, since 1948 merged with Vindhya Pradesh.

Gauri Phanta (gou'rē pŭn'tŭ), village, Kheri dist., N Uttar Pradesh, India, 18 mi. N of Palia, on Nepal border; rail spur terminus; trades in rice, jute, oilseeds, potatoes, and sabai grass from Nepal.

Gauripur (gou'rĭpŏŏr), town (pop. 5,783), Goalpara dist., W Assam, India, on right tributary of the Brahmaputra and 5 mi. NNW of Dhubri; trades in rice, mustard, jute, tobacco, cotton.

Gauripur, E Pakistan: see GOURIPUR.

Gauri Sankar (gou'rē sŭng'kŭr), peak (23,440 ft.) in NE Nepal Himalayas, on undefined Nepal-Tibet border, 35 mi. W of Mt. Everest, at 27°58'N 86°20'E.

Gause (gôz), village (pop. c.750), Milam co., central Texas, 22 mi. WNW of Bryan, in cotton, corn, truck area.

Gausta (gou'stä), mountain (6,178 ft.) in Telemark co., S Norway, just S of Rjukan.

Gausvik (gous'vĭk, –vēk), village (pop. 380) in Sandtorg canton (pop. 5,072), on E Hinnoy of the Vesteralen group, Troms co., N Norway, 12 mi. S of Harstad; textile milling.

Gautami Godavari River, India: see GODAVARI RIVER.

Gautampura (gou'tŭmpŏŏrŭ), village, W central Madhya Bharat, India, near Chambal R., 28 mi. NW of Indore; local market (wheat, cotton); handicraft cloth weaving and printing.

Gauting (gou'tĭng), village (pop. 7,528), Upper Bavaria, Germany, on Würm R. and 9 mi. SW of Munich; cattle. Has Gothic church.

Gauya River, Latvia: see GAUJA RIVER.

Gava (gä'vŏ), Hung. *Gáva,* town (pop. 3,210), Szabolcs co., NE Hungary, 15 mi. NNW of Nyiregyhaza; corn, wheat, vineyards; cattle.

Gavá (gävä'), village (pop. 6,012), Barcelona prov., NE Spain, 10 mi. SW of Barcelona, on fertile Llobregat coastal plain; mfg. (electric heaters, iron pipes); agr. trade (fruit, asparagus, hazelnuts, wine). Medieval castle of Ampruñá near by.

Gavana, Rumania: see PITESTI.

Gavardo (gävär'dô), town (pop. 3,194), Brescia prov., Lombardy, N Italy, on Chiese R. and 11 mi. ENE of Brescia; alcohol distillery.

Gavarnie (gävärnē'), village (pop. 186), Hautes-Pyrénées dept., SW France, in central Pyrenees, on Gave de Pau R. and 19 mi. SSE of Argelès-Gazost; alt. 4,497 ft. The **Cirque de Gavarnie** (sērk'dŭ–) (3 mi. S), the most popular tourist site of the Pyrenees, is a natural amphitheater rising 4,000 ft. in terraces above its base (alt. 5,740 ft.). Its snow-covered crest forms Franco-Sp. border. Here rises the Gave de Pau in a spectacular waterfall (1,385 ft. high). The BRÈCHE-DE-ROLAND leads into cirque from Spain.

Gavdos or **Gavdhos** (both: gäv'dhôs), Greek island (□ 13; pop. 278), in Mediterranean Sea off S coast of Crete, 39 mi. SSE of Canea; 34°50'N 24°6'E; 7 mi. long, 4 mi. wide. Identified with biblical Clauda (klô'dŭ) (Acts 27.16).

Gave, in France: for names beginning thus see under following part of the name; e.g., for Gave de Pau, see PAU, GAVE DE.

Gávea, Pedra da (pā'drŭ dä gä'vĭŭ), granitic peak (2,762 ft.) in Federal Dist. of Brazil, near the Atlantic, 9 mi. SW of center of Rio de Janeiro. Overlooks Rio's fashionable residential dists.

Gavello (gävĕl'lô), village (pop. 549), Rovigo prov., Veneto, N Italy, 7 mi. ESE of Rovigo.

Gavet, France: see Livet-et-Gavet.

Gavi (gä'vē), village (pop. 1,995), Alessandria prov., Piedmont, N Italy, 5 mi. S of Novi Ligure.

Gavia, Passo di (päs'sô dē gä'vyä), pass (8,599 ft.), N Italy, at S end of Ortles mtn. group, W of Corno dei Tre Signori. Crossed by road bet. Ponte di Legno and Bormio.

Gavião (gŭvyã'ō), town (pop. 1,695), Portalegre dist., central Portugal, near Tagus R., 14 mi. E of Abrantes; pottery mfg., leather working. Fruit and winegrowing.

Gavião River, S central Bahia, Brazil, rises in N Serra do Espinhaço near Minas Gerais border, flows 150 mi. generally NE, past Condeúba, to the Rio de Contas near 14°S 41°W.

Gavilanes (gävēlä'nĕs), town (pop. 1,247), Ávila prov., central Spain, on S slopes of the Sierra de Gredos, 22 mi. N of Talavera de la Reina; forage, chestnuts, grapes, olives, vegetables, cereals; stock raising, flour milling, olive-oil pressing, lumbering.

Gaviota (găvēō'tŭ), hamlet, Santa Barbara co., SW Calif., on Santa Barbara Channel, 29 mi. W of Santa Barbara; vessels load oil from offshore pipelines here. Gaviota Pass crosses Santa Ynez Mts. to N.

Gaviota Island (gävyō'tä), off coast of Coquimbo prov., N central Chile, just E of Choros Isls., 45 mi. NNW of La Serena; 1½ mi. long; 29°16'S.

Gavirate (gävērä'tē), village (pop. 2,496), Varese prov., Lombardy, N Italy, near L. of Varese, 6 mi. NW of Varese; cotton mills, sausage factories.

Gavkhaneh or **Gavkhuni**, Iran: see Zaindeh River.

Gavle (yĕv'lŭ), Swedish *Gävle*, city (1950 pop. 46,894), ⊙ Gavleborg co., E Sweden, on small Gavle Bay (*Gävlebukten*), inlet of Gulf of Bothnia, at mouth of Gavle R., 100 mi. NNW of Stockholm; 60°40'N 17°10'E. Seaport (ice-bound during 3 winter months), shipping iron from Kopparberg co., also timber, pulp, paper, steel; imports coal, coke, oil, fertilizer. Rail junction. Shipyards; lumber, pulp, paper, and textile mills, fish canneries; mfg. of chemicals, porcelain, leather goods, tobacco products. Modern in character, it has 16th-cent. castle, 17th-cent. church, and 18th-cent. courthouse. First mentioned in 8th cent.; chartered 1446. S of city is Viking burial ground. Sometimes spelled Gafle (Swedish *Gäfle*), Gevle, or Gefle.

Gavleborg (-bôr"yŭ), county [Swedish *län*] (□ 7,608; 1950 pop. 284,993), E Sweden; ⊙ Gavle. On Gulf of Bothnia, it comprises Gastrikland prov. (S), most of Halsingland prov. (N), and small part of Dalarna prov. (NE). Low and level along coast, rises inland toward wooded highland; drained by Ljusna, Voxna, Jardra, Gavle, and Dal rivers. Lumbering, sawmilling, agr. (grain, flax, potatoes), and stock raising are important. Chief industries are steel milling (Sandviken), paper and pulp milling, wood- and metalworking, sulphite mfg. Cities are Gavle, Sandviken, Soderhamn, Bollnas, and Hudiksvall. Sometimes spelled Gevleborg, Gafleborg (Swedish *Gäfleborg*), or Gefleborg.

Gavle River, Swedish *Gävleån* (yĕv'lŭōn"), E Sweden, issues from Stor L., flows 30 mi. E to Gavle Bay of Gulf of Bothnia at Gavle.

Gavorrano (gävōr-rä'nō), town (pop. 1,541), Grosseto prov., Tuscany, central Italy, 16 mi. NW of Grosseto; mining (iron pyrites, lignite).

Gavray (gävrā'), village (pop. 784), Manche dept., NW France, on the Sienne and 11 mi. SSE of Coutances; horse raising.

Gavre, Forêt du (fôrĕ' dü gä'vrŭ) (□ 16), Loire-Inférieure dept., W France, N of Blain; Brittany's largest domanial forest.

Gavrilovka (gŭvrē'lŭfkŭ). **1** Town (1942 pop. over 500), W Gorki oblast, Russian SFSR, 9 mi. E of Dzerzhinsk; peat works. **2** Town (1939 pop. over 500), N central Kharkov oblast, Ukrainian SSR, on railroad (Shpakovka station) and 9 mi. W of Kharkov.

Gavrilovka Vtoraya (ftŭrī'ŭ) [Rus.,=Gavrilovka No. 2], village (1926 pop. 2,502), E Tambov oblast, Russian SFSR, 14 mi. N of Kirsanov; wheat, legumes.

Gavrilov-Posad (gŭvrē'lŭf-pŭsät'), city (1926 pop. 2,237), SW Ivanovo oblast, Russian SFSR, 45 mi. SW of Ivanovo; cotton milling, food processing (potatoes, wheat, chicory). Chartered 1789.

Gavrilovski Zavod, Ukrainian SSR: see Druzhkovka.

Gavrilov-Yam (gŭvrē'lŭf-yäm"), city (1939 pop. over 10,000), E Yaroslavl oblast, Russian SFSR, on Kotorosl R. and 21 mi. S of Yaroslavl; linen-milling center; tobacco, potato processing. Became city in 1938.

Gavur Mountains, Turkey: see Amanos Mountains.

Gawan (gŭvän'), town (pop. 2,722), Budaun dist., N central Uttar Pradesh, India, on tributary of the Ganges and 14 mi. NNW of Gunnaur; wheat, pearl millet, mustard, barley, gram.

Gawd-i-Zirrah, Afghanistan: see Gaud-i-Zirreh.

Gawler, town (pop. 4,436), SE South Australia, 24 mi. NNE of Adelaide; rail junction; agr.; dairy products.

Gawler Ranges, S South Australia, extend 100 mi. E-W across base of Eyre Peninsula; rise to 1,550 ft. in Nukey Bluff; feldspar.

Gay. 1 Town (pop. 241), Meriwether co., W Ga., 26 mi. E of La Grange. **2** Village, Logan co., W.Va.: see Mount Gay.

Gaya, Czechoslovakia: see Kyjov.

Gaya (gä'yä), town (pop. c.3,100), SW Niger territory, Fr. West Africa, on left bank of the Niger, near Dahomey border, on intercolonial route and 140 mi. SE of Niamey; peanuts, kapok; goats. Airfield.

Gaya (gī'ŭ, gŭ'yŭ), district (□ 4,766; pop. 2,775,361), W central Bihar, India; ⊙ Gaya. On Ganges Plain; spurs of Chota Nagpur Plateau in S; bounded W by Son R.; drained by tributaries of Son and Ganges rivers. Irrigated by Patna Canal (W); steamer service. Mainly alluvial soil; rice, gram, wheat, barley, oilseeds, sugar cane, corn, rape and mustard; mahua and lac growing in forest areas. Saltpeter extraction; stone quarrying, mica mining. Mfg. of shellac, pottery, brass implements; silk-cloth weaving; saltworks. Gaya is industrial and pilgrimage center. Famous Bo tree and temple at Buddh Gaya. Hindu temple and Asokan cave carvings on Barabar Hill.

Gaya, city (pop. 105,223), ⊙ Gaya dist., central Bihar, India, on tributary of the Ganges and 55 mi. S of Patna; rail and road junction; airport; trade center (rice, gram, oilseeds, wheat, sugar cane, corn, wool); shellac mfg. Noted Vishnuite temple; Hindu pilgrimage center. Silk-cloth weaving near by. Stone quarries 18 mi. NE, at Pathalkati. Extensive Buddhist sculptures 14 mi. E, at Punawan.

Gaya (gä'yä'), town (pop. 3,382), Kano prov., Northern Provinces, N Nigeria, 35 mi. ESE of Kano; road junction; cotton, peanuts, millet; cattle, skins.

Gayduk, Russian SFSR: see Gaiduk.

Gay Head, W tip of Martha's Vineyard, in **Gay Head** town (pop. 88), Dukes co., SE Mass., 15 mi. WSW of Edgartown; cranberries; fishing, pottery making. Lighthouse on colorful clay cliffs here since 1799. Settled 1669, inc. 1870.

Gayle or **Gayle Village** (gāl), town (pop. 1,080), St. Mary parish, N Jamaica, 8 mi. SW of Port Maria; tropical fruit.

Gaylesville (gālz'vĭl), farming town (pop. 194), Cherokee co., NE Ala., on Chattooga R., near Ga. line, and 10 mi. NE of Centre.

Gaylord (gā'lŭrd). **1** City (pop. 231), Smith co., N Kansas, on North Fork Solomon R. and 9 mi. SSW of Smith Center; grain, livestock. **2** City (pop. 2,271), ⊙ Otsego co., N Mich., 27 mi. SE of Petoskey; trade center for agr. and lake resort area; potatoes, fruit, livestock, hardwood timber. A tuberculosis sanitarium and Dearborn Colony, a "back-to-the-land" movement begun 1932, are near by. Inc. as village 1881, as city 1922. **3** Village (pop. 1,229), ⊙ Sibley co., S Minn., c.55 mi. SW of Minneapolis; trade point in grain, livestock, poultry area; dairy products. Platted 1881.

Gaylordsville, Conn.: see New Milford.

Gayndah (găn'dä), town (pop. 1,039), E Queensland, Australia, on Burnett R. and 175 mi. NW of Brisbane; agr. center (sugar cane, cotton).

Gayny, Russian SFSR: see Gainy.

Gays, village (pop. 261), Moultrie co., central Ill., 6 mi. WSW of Mattoon, in agr. area.

Gaysin, Ukrainian SSR: see Gaisin.

Gays Mills, village (pop. 662), Crawford co., SW Wis., on Kickapoo R. and 24 mi. NE of Prairie du Chien, in farm area (apples, poultry); butter and other dairy products, flour, feed.

Gayville, town (pop. 271), Yankton co., SE S.Dak., 11 mi. E of Yankton; small trading point for agr. area.

Gayvoron, Ukrainian SSR: see Gaivoron.

Gaywood, England: see King's Lynn.

Gayzin', Latvia: see Gaizin.

Gaza (gä'zŭ), Arabic *Ghazze*, town (1946 pop. estimate 37,820), SW Palestine, at NW edge of the Negev, near Mediterranean, on railroad and 40 mi. SSW of Tel Aviv. Has anc. mosque of Hashim, remains of 5th-cent. church of St. Porphyry, and traces of anc. gates. Of great antiquity, Gaza is repeatedly mentioned in the Bible (here sometimes called *Azzah*), notably in connection with story of Samson. It was one of chief cities of Philistines; among its later captors were Alexander the Great, the Maccabees, and Romans. As Gadres it was fortified by Crusaders. In First World War successfully besieged (1917) by British, who established large military cemetery here. Important Allied army camp in Second World War. It is the center of a rectangular coastal strip of land (□ c. 135)—designated as Arab in the U.N.'s partition (1947) of Palestine—occupied by Egypt in 1948.

Gazala, El (ĕl gäzä'lä), or **Ain el Gazala** (īn), village, E Cyrenaica, Libya, 38 mi. W of Tobruk, on Mediterranean coast. Scene of fighting (1941–42) bet. Axis and British in Second World War.

Gazalkent (gŭzŭlkyĕnt'), town (1948 pop. over 2,000), SE South Kazakhstan oblast, Kazakh SSR, on Chirchik R. and 30 mi. NE of Tashkent; cotton, fruit.

Gazelle Peninsula, NE New Britain, Bismarck Archipelago, SW Pacific; 50 mi. wide; separated from rest of isl. by isthmus c.20 mi. wide. Many crater mts. N of Blanche Bay (NE). Rabaul and Kokopo on Blanche Bay. Hot springs.

Gazi (gä'zē), village, Eastern Prov., N Belgian Congo, 60 mi. NW of Stanleyville; experimental plantations (rubber, cacao, coffee); palm oil.

Gazi (gä'zē), village (pop. c.2,500), SE Kenya, in coastal protectorate, minor port on Indian Ocean, 28 mi. SSW of Mombasa; copra center; sugar cane, fruits.

Gaziantep (gäzēän'tĕp), prov. (□ 3,268; 1950 pop. 328,082), S Turkey; ⊙ Gaziantep. Borders E on Euphrates R., S on Syrian frontier. Grain, pistachios, olives, tobacco. Formerly Antep (Ayntab, Aintab).

Gaziantep, city (1950 pop. 72,743), ⊙ Gaziantep prov., S Turkey, 115 mi. ENE of Adana, bet. Taurus Mts. and the Euphrates, 25 mi. from Syria; 37°4'N 37°25'E. Mfg. of cotton goods; agr. trade (grain, lentils, pistachios). A strategic place in the Crusades, it was taken (1183) by Saladin. Center of Turkish resistance (1920–21) to Fr. occupation of Syria; surrendered to France after 6-month siege, was returned to Turkey late 1921. Formerly Aintab, Antep, or Ayntab.

Gazimur River (gŭzēmōōr'), E Chita oblast, Russian SFSR, rises in Nerchinsk Range, flows 250 mi. NNE, past Aleksandrovski Zavod, Gazimurski Zavod, and Kurleya, to Argun R. 65 mi. above its mouth. Banks abound in silver-lead ores.

Gazimurski Zavod or **Gazimurskiy Zavod** (gŭzēmōōr"skē zŭvôt'), village (1948 pop. over 2,000), SE Chita oblast, Russian SFSR, on Gazimur R. and 50 mi. SSE of Sretensk; lead and zinc mines. Former silver-mining center.

Gazir, Lebanon: see Ghazir.

Gazulapalle, India: see Nandyal.

Gazzada (gätsä'dä), village (pop. 1,367), Varese prov., Lombardy, N Italy, 3 mi. S of Varese; mfg. (celluloid, textile machinery, cotton goods).

Gazzaniga (gätsänē'gä), village (pop. 3,810), Bergamo prov., Lombardy, N Italy, on Serio R. and 10 mi. NE of Bergamo; cotton and woolen mills.

Gbangbaia (gŭbängbī'ä), village (pop. 327), South-Western Prov., SW Sierra Leone, on branch of Bagru R. and 20 mi. NNE of Bonthe; palm oil and kernels, piassava, rice.

Gbap (gŭbäp'), town (pop. 340), South-Western Prov., S Sierra Leone, on Kittam R. (tidal inlet) and 20 mi. ESE of Bonthe; fishing; cassava, corn.

Gbarnga (gŭbäng'gä), town, Central Prov., N central Liberia, 105 mi. NE of Monrovia; palm oil and kernels, cassava, rice. Also spelled Gbanga.

Gbekebo (bākā'bō), town, Ondo prov., Western Provinces, S Nigeria, river port on coastal channel, 13 mi. SSE of Okitipupa; palm oil and kernels, rubber, timber.

Gbely (ŭgbĕ'lĭ), Hung. *Egbeli* (ĕg'bĕlē), village (pop. 3,687), W Slovakia, Czechoslovakia, on railroad and 11 mi. ESE of Breclav; natural-gas and oil processing. First deep well sunk here in 1913.

Gboko (bō'kō), town, Benue prov., Northern Provinces, E central Nigeria, 45 mi. SE of Makurdi; shea nuts, sesame, cassava, durra, yams.

Gbolobo (gŭbō'lōbō), village, Maryland co., SE Liberia, on Cavalla R. (Fr. Ivory Coast border) and 16 mi. NE of Harper (linked by road); hq. of rubber plantation.

Gdansk (gŭdä'nyŭsk), Pol. *Gdańsk*, province [Pol. *województwo*] (□ 4,141; pop. 732,150), N Poland; ⊙ Danzig (Gdansk). Borders N on the Baltic; low level coast line includes W half of Gulf of Danzig, Hel Peninsula, and W parts of Vistula Lagoon and Vistula Spit. Inland is agr. region of low rolling hills. Drained by the lower Vistula. Shipping, shipbuilding, fishing are principal industries, concentrated in port cities of Danzig, Gdynia, and Elbing (Elblag); other towns are Zoppot (Sopot; noted seaside resort), Tczew, Starogard (Stargard), Wejherowo, Lebork (Lauenburg), and Marienburg (Malbork). Principal crops are rye, potatoes, oats, wheat; livestock. Prov. created 1945 from former free city of Danzig and parts of East Prussia, Ger. Pomerania prov., and N part of former Pol. Pomorze prov.

Gdansk, city, Poland: see Danzig.

Gdanska, Zatoka, Poland: see Danzig, Gulf of.

Gdanskaya Bukhta, Poland: see Danzig, Gulf of.

Gdingen, Poland: see Gdynia.

Gdov (ŭgdôf'), city (1948 pop. over 10,000), N Pskov oblast, Russian SFSR, port on E shore of L. Peipus, 65 mi. NNW of Pskov; flour milling, light mfg. Chartered 1431.

Gdynia (gŭdĭ'nēŭ, Pol. gŭdĭ'nyä), Ger. *Gdingen* (gŭdĭng'ŭn), Baltic coast city (1946 census pop. 77,829; 1950 pop. estimate c.117,700), Gdansk prov., N Poland, on Gulf of Danzig, 12 mi. NNW of Danzig; 54°38'N 18°35'E. Major seaport; rail junction; exports include coal, lumber, sugar, bacon, eggs; imports iron ore, artificial fertilizers, rice, fruits, herrings, cotton. Brick making, rice milling, sawmilling. Has inner and outer ports, the latter separated from the sea by a mole. Navigation school. Several resorts near by. The construction of Gdynia, 1st Polish-controlled seaport since 18th cent., was begun 1921 on a selected site of the seacoast to end dependence of Poland on Danzig as its only major outlet on the Baltic. By 1934, Gdynia handled more freight than Danzig and was a leading Baltic port; became Poland's main naval base and shipbuilding center. Its 1937 pop. was 83,806. During Second World War, Gdynia (only 4 mi. from border of German-annexed free city of Danzig) was evacuated by its Pol. pop., annexed to Germany, and renamed Gotenhafen. Although a battlefield in 1939 and 1945 and its harbor partly destroyed, Gdynia suffered relatively little damage.

Géant, Aiguille du, France: see AIGUILLE DU GÉANT.

Géant, Col du (kôl dü zhā-ā′), Ital. *Colle di Gigante*, pass (alt. 11,056 ft.) in Mont Blanc Massif, on Fr.-Ital. border, 4 mi. ENE of Mont Blanc, on trail from Chamonix to Courmayeur. Refuge.

Gearhart, city (pop. 568), Clatsop co., NW Oregon, 12 mi. SSW of Astoria and on Pacific Ocean; beach resort.

Geary (gēr′ē), county (□ 399; pop. 21,671), E central Kansas; ⊙ Junction City. Region of low hills drained in W by Smoky Hill and Republican rivers, which join at Junction City to form Kansas R. Livestock, grain. Limestone deposits. Formed 1889.

Geary (gâr′ē, gēr′ē), city (pop. 1,614), on Blaine-Canadian co. line, central Okla., c.45 mi. WNW of Oklahoma City; trade and processing center for cotton, wheat, livestock, and dairy area. U.S. soil conservation camp near by. Founded 1898.

Geauga (jēô′gů), county (□ 407; pop. 26,646), NE Ohio; ⊙ Chardon. Drained by Cuyahoga, Chagrin, and Grand rivers; includes several small lakes. Agr. area (dairy products, grain, fruit, poultry, truck); maple syrup and sugar; mfg. at Chardon and Middlefield. Formed 1805.

Geaune (zhōn), village (pop. 406), Landes dept., SW France, 18 mi. SSE of Mont-de-Marsan; corn, cattle, poultry.

Geba (zhĕ′bä), village, central Port. Guinea, on right bank of Geba R. and 6 mi. W of Bafatá; almonds, palm oil. R.C. mission.

Gebal, Lebanon: see BYBLOS.

Geba River (zhĕ′bä), principal watercourse of Port. Guinea, rises just inside Fr. Guinea, traverses section of S Senegal, then flows SW, past Bafatá (head of navigation), and forms a deep estuary (50 mi. long, 5 mi. wide) on the Atlantic; 200 mi. long. Bissau is on estuary's N bank. Chief tributary, the Corubal, enters estuary from SE.

Gebeit (gĕbāt′), village, Kassala prov., NE Anglo-Egyptian Sudan, on road, 110 mi. NNW of Port Sudan; gold-mining center, connected by road with its Red Sea port, Muhammad Ghul. A rail station named Gebeit is 50 mi. SSW of Port Sudan.

Gebel [Arabic,=mountain, hill], for all names beginning thus: see under following proper noun.

Gebel, Bahr el, Anglo-Egyptian Sudan: see BAHR EL JEBEL.

Gebesee (gā′bůzā″), town (pop. 3,378), in former Prussian Saxony prov., central Germany, after 1945 in Thuringia, on Gera R. near its mouth on the Unstrut, and 11 mi. NNW of Erfurt; grain, sugar beets, potatoes, stock.

Gebhardshagen (gĕp′härts-hä″gůn), W district of WATENSTEDT-SALZGITTER, NW Germany; iron mining.

Gebhard Woods State Park, Ill.: see MORRIS.

Gebo (jē′bō), village (pop. c.175), Hot Springs co., N central Wyo., near Bighorn R., 10 mi. N of Thermopolis; alt. 4,570 ft.; coal mines.

Gebweiler, France: see GUEBWILLER.

Gebze (gĕbzĕ′), village (pop. 4,238), Kocaeli prov., NW Turkey, on railroad and 28 mi. SE of Istanbul, near Gulf of Izmit; cereals, vetch. Ruins of anc. Libyssa just E.

Gedaref (gĕdärĕf′), town (pop. 23,000), Kassala prov., NE Anglo-Egyptian Sudan, on railroad and 120 mi. SSW of Kassala; trade center; agr. (cotton, wheat, barley, corn, fruits); livestock. Road leads SE to Gallabat on Ethiopian border.

Geddes (gĕ′dēz), city (pop. 502), Charles Mix co., S S.Dak., 10 mi. NW of Lake Andes; business center for agr. area.

Geddes, Mount (gĕ′dĭs) (11,000 ft.), SW B.C., in Coast Mts., 180 mi. NW of Vancouver; 51°27′N 125°20′W.

Geddington (gĕ′–), agr. village and parish (pop. 995), NE central Northampton, England, on Ise R. and 3 mi. NNE of Kettering. Site of an Eleanor Cross (1290). Has church of Saxon and Norman origin.

Gedeh, Mount (gůdĕ′), volcanic peak (9,705 ft.), W Java, Indonesia, in Preanger region, 18 mi. SE of Bogor; sometimes spelled Gede. Its twin peak (9,905 ft.) is Mt. Pangrango (päng-räng′ō); also spelled Pangerango.

Gede Point, Indonesia: see JAVA HEAD.

Gedera (gĕdē′rů, gĕdĕrä′), settlement (pop. 1,600), W Israel, in Judaean Plain, 17 mi. S of Tel Aviv; health resort; grain, citrus fruit, grapes. Founded 1884.

Gediz (gĕdĭz′), town (pop. 5,866), Kutahya prov., W Turkey, on Gediz R. and 40 mi. SW of Kutahya; carpets; valonia, raisins, figs, wheat, barley; iron and lignite in dist. Formerly Hermus.

Gediz River, anc. *Hermus*, W Turkey, rises in Murat Dag 15 mi. E of Gediz, flows 215 mi. SW and W, past Salihli, Manisa, and Menemen, to Gulf of Smyrna 6 mi. SE of Foca. Formerly sometimes called Sarabat.

Gedling, town and parish (pop. 2,822), S Nottingham, England, 3 mi. ENE of Nottingham; coal mining. Church dates from c.1250.

Gedo (gĕ′dō), Ital. *Ghedo*, town (pop. 2,000), Shoa prov., central Ethiopia, on road and 95 mi. W of Addis Ababa; 9°N 37°24′E.

Gedrosia, Iran and Pakistan: see BALUCHISTAN.

Gedser (gĕ′sůr), town (pop. 1,184) and port, Maribo amt, Denmark, on S tip of Falster isl. The tip of Falster, called Gedser Odde. is most southerly point of Denmark.

Gee Cross, England: see HYDE.

Geel or **Gheel** (khāl), town (pop. 22,711), Antwerp prov., N Belgium, 25 mi. ESE of Antwerp. Site of a large colony of insane patients, living in private families, and dating from the 14th cent. Tradition links town with 6th-cent. Irish martyr St. Dymphna, at whose shrine insane persons are said to have been cured.

Geelong (jēlông′, –lŏng′), city and port (pop. 18,740; metropolitan Geelong 44,561), S Victoria, Australia, on Corio Bay (W arm of Port Phillip Bay) and 42 mi. SW of Melbourne; rail junction; 2d city and port of Victoria. Industrial center for agr. and dairying area; woolen mills, meat-packing plants, automobile plants. Exports wool, wheat, meat, hides. Gold discovered 1851 in vicinity. Includes suburbs of West Geelong (pop. 15,763), and Newton and Chilwell (pop. 10,058).

Geelvink Bay (khāl′vĭngk), deep inlet of the Pacific, Netherlands New Guinea, bounded W by Vogelkop peninsula; 200 mi. E–W, 200 mi. N–S; contains Japen Isls. and numerous islets. Schouten Isls. are at entrance, Manokwari at W side of entrance.

Geelvink Channel, strait of Indian Ocean bet. Houtman Abrolhos and W coast of Western Australia; 70 mi. long, 30 mi. wide. Its SE inlet, Champion Bay, is site of Geraldton.

Geeraardsbergen, Belgium: see GRAMMONT.

Geertruidenberg (khār′troidůnbĕrkh), town (pop. 3,344), North Brabant prov., SW Netherlands, 9 mi. NNE of Breda and on Donge R.; machine shops; shipbuilding; container mfg. Electric-power station, here, supplies all of North Brabant prov. (except Tilburg) and parts of Zeeland prov. Has 15th-cent. church. Besieged (1592) by Maurice of Nassau, having been surrendered 2 years before to Spain by English. Sometimes called Den Berg.

Geestemünde, Germany: see BREMERHAVEN.

Geesthacht (gāst′häkht), town (pop. 19,591), in Schleswig-Holstein, NW Germany, harbor on right bank of the Elbe and 18 mi. ESE of Hamburg; building of river and coastal ships; mfg. of railroad cars, optical goods, wood products. Formerly munitions center (gunpowder, dynamite). Has tuberculosis sanatorium and research station. Was joint possession of Hamburg and Lübeck, 1420–1868; in Hamburg, 1868–1937. Chartered 1924.

Geeveston (jēvs′tůn), town (pop. 1,360), SE Tasmania, 28 mi. SW of Hobart, near Huon R. estuary; sawmills, orchards; iron.

Gefara or **Jefara** (jĕfä′rä), arid, sandy plain in W Tripolitania, Libya, bet. fertile coastal strip (N) and the plateau Gebel Nefusa (S). Has arid torrid climate; annual rainfall 2 in. (W) to 16 in. (E). Chief center Azizia. Predominantly pastoral (goats, sheep); agr. settlements (Bianchi, Giordani) in E. Crossed (N–S) by roads and railroad.

Gefell (gůfĕl′), town (pop. 1,802), in former Prussian Saxony prov. exclave, central Germany, after 1945 in Thuringia, 9 mi. NNW of Hof; woodworking; ocher mining.

Gefle, Sweden: see GAVLE.

Gefrees (gůfrās′), town (pop. 2,968), Upper Franconia, NE Bavaria, Germany, on W slope of the Fichtelgebirge, 7 mi. SSW of Münchberg; mfg. of heavy machinery, textiles, dyes; brewing, tanning. Has Gothic church. Granite quarries in area.

Gegechkori (gyĕgyĭchkō′rē), village (1939 pop. over 2,000), W Georgian SSR, 20 mi. NW of Kutaisi; corn, tea, soybeans, livestock. Formerly Martvili.

Gehlenburg, Poland: see BIALA, Olsztyn prov.

Gehrden (gĕr′důn), town (pop. 3,939), in former Prussian prov. of Hanover, W Germany, after 1945 in Lower Saxony, 7 mi. SW of Hanover.

Gehren (gā′růn), town (pop. 4,264), Thuringia, central Germany, on N slope of Thuringian Forest, 5 mi. SE of Ilmenau; china and lacquer mfg. Has Renaissance palace.

Geidam (gē′däm, gī′däm), town (pop. 3,562), Bornu prov., Northern Provinces, NE Nigeria, on the Komadugu Yobe and 110 mi. NW of Maiduguri, near Fr. West Africa border; agr. trade center; cassava, millet, durra; cattle, skins.

Geiersberg, Germany: see GEYERSBERG.

Geiger (gī′gůr, gē′gůr), town (pop. 133), Sumter co., W Ala., near Miss. line, 50 mi. SW of Tuscaloosa.

Geilenkirchen (gī″lůn-kĭr′khůn), town (pop. 5,736), in former Prussian Rhine Prov., W Germany, after 1945 in North Rhine-Westphalia, 6 mi. NNW of Alsdorf; rail junction; potteries.

Geilo (yä′lō), village (pop. 417) in Hol canton, Buskerud co., S Norway, in Hallingskarv mts., at head of the Hallingdal, on railroad and 75 mi. WNW of Honefoss; alt. 2,605 ft. Popular summer and winter-sports resort; tool mfg.; agr.

Geiranger (gā′rängůr), village in Sunnylven canton, More og Romsdal co., W Norway, at head of Geiranger Fjord, 45 mi. SE of Alesund; tourist center. Until 1940, called Maraak, Meraak, or Merok. N section of village is now called Marak.

Geiranger Fjord, an E arm of Sunnylven Fjord (branch of Stor Fjord) in More og Romsdal co., W Norway, winding E c.15 mi. to Geiranger; famous scenic area, noted for Seven Sisters (Nor. *Syv Søstre*) and Bridal Veil (Nor. *Brudeslør*) waterfalls on N shore, c.10 mi. W of Geiranger, and for the Pulpit (Nor. *Prækestolen*), a rock promontory on S shore. Formerly spelled Gejranger.

Geisa (gī′zä), town (pop. 2,067), Thuringia, central Germany, in Rhön Mts., 17 mi. NE of Fulda; grain, potatoes, livestock; weaving. First mentioned in 8th cent.

Geiselhöring (gī″zůlhů′rĭng), village (pop. 3,805), Lower Bavaria, Germany, on Kleine Laaber R. and 9 mi. WSW of Straubing; brewing, tanning; wheat, cattle. Has rococo church.

Geisenfeld (gī′zůnfĕlt), village (pop. 3,291), Upper Bavaria, Germany, on Ilm R. and 10 mi. SE of Ingolstadt; grain, livestock. Has Renaissance church. Chartered 1362.

Geisenhausen (gī″zůnhou′zůn), village (pop. 3,459), Lower Bavaria, Germany, 5 mi. NW of Vilsbiburg; textile mfg., brewing, tanning. Chartered 1453.

Geisenheim (gī′zůnhīm), town (pop. 6,420), in former Prussian prov. of Hesse-Nassau, W Germany, after 1945 in Hesse, in the Rheingau, on right bank of the Rhine (landing) and 14 mi. WSW of Wiesbaden; noted for its wine. Machinery mfg., kaolin works. Has late-Gothic church. Site of viticultural, pomological, and horticultural acad. (founded 1870–73).

Geising (gī′zĭng), town (pop. 2,156), Saxony, E central Germany, in the Erzgebirge, 16 mi. SSW of Pirna, near Czechoslovak border, in mining region (bismuth, tungsten;) woodworking. Climatic health resort and winter-sports center.

Geislautern, Saar: see VÖLKLINGEN.

Geislingen or **Geislingen an der Steige** (gīs′lĭngůr än dĕr shtī′gů), town (pop. 20,478), N Württemberg, Germany, after 1945 in Württemberg-Baden, on the Fils and 10 mi. SE of Göppingen; 48°37′N 9°50′E. Rail junction; mfg. of foundry products, silicon-steel household goods, silverware, silver-plated hollow ware, precision machines and instruments, tools, copper wire; also cut glass costume jewelry, cotton. Iron mining in vicinity Has late-Gothic church. Founded and chartered in 13th cent. Sold to Ulm in 1396. Part of Bavaria 1802–10.

Geismar (gīs′mär), village (pop. 4,052), in former Prussian prov. of Hanover, W Germany, after 1945 in Lower Saxony, 2 mi. SE of Göttingen; metal working, flour milling.

Geispolsheim (gĕspôlzĕm′, Ger. gīs′pôls-hīm), town (pop. 1,997), Bas-Rhin dept., E France, 7 mi. SW of Strasbourg; sauerkraut and cheese mfg.; tobacco and corn growing.

Geissan (gās′săn) or **Qeissan** (kās′–), village, Blue Nile prov., E central Anglo-Egyptian Sudan, on Ethiopian border, on road and 80 mi. SSE of Roseires. Police post.

Geistingen, Germany: see HENNEF.

Geistown (gīs′toun), borough (pop. 2,148), Cambria co., SW central Pa., 3 mi. SE of Johnstown.

Geita (gā′tä), town (pop. c.3,000), NW Tanganyika 55 mi. WSW of Mwanza, on road; gold-mining and processing center. Airfield.

Geithain (gīt′hīn), town (pop. 5,825), Saxony, E central Germany, 18 mi. NW of Chemnitz; rail junction; hosiery knitting, cotton milling; mfg. of enamelware; brickworks. Has 12th-cent. church Stone quarries near by.

Geithus (yāt′hōōs), village (pop. 1,537) in Modum canton (pop. 11,309), Buskerud co., SE Norway on Drammen R., on railroad and 16 mi. NNW of Drammen; wood-pulp, paper, and textile milling wood cracking; mfg. of dyes, furniture, leather fire-fighting equipment, cement; metalworking Zinc mining. Sometimes spelled Gjeithus. Industrial village (pop. 1,128) of Amot (ô′môt), Nor. *Åmot*, is 3 mi. SW; resort (pop. 1,292) of Vikersund (vē′kůrsōōn), with mineral springs, is 3 mi. NE.

Gejranger Fjord, Norway: see GEIRANGER FJORD.

Gela (jä′lä), town (pop. 31,918), Caltanissetta prov. S Sicily, port on Mediterranean Sea, 60 mi. W of Syracuse, in cotton-growing region. The Greek colony of Gela was founded (688–687 B.C.) by Rhodes. Colonists from Gela founded Agrigent 580–579 B.C. Reached its zenith under Hippocrates (498 B.C.). Aeschylus died here, 456 B.C. Near by are Greek necropolises, remains of Doric temple. Refounded 1233 by Frederick II and called Terranova di Sicilia until 1928. In Second World War, one of initial landing points in Allied invasion of Sicily, July 9–10, 1943.

Gelai, Tanganyika: see NATRON, LAKE.

Gelchsheim (gĕlkhs′hīm), village (pop. 978), Lower Franconia, W Bavaria, Germany, 13 mi. SW of Kitzingen; grain.

Geldenaken, Belgium: see JODOIGNE.

Gelderland, Guelderland (both: gĕl′důrlănd, Du. khĕl′důrlänt), or **Guelders,** province (□ 1,921.5; pop. 1,028,127), E and central Netherlands;

Arnhem. Bounded by the Ijsselmeer (NW), Utrecht prov. (W), Maas R. (S), Germany (E), Overijssel prov. (E,NE). Drained by Ijssel R., and by Waal and Lower Rhine rivers, which enclose the BETUWE, a fertile lowland (SW); in N, near the Ijsselmeer, is the Veluwe, an unproductive, hilly heathland. Fruit (Tiel area), grain, flax, tobacco; poultry, mfg. (bricks, textiles, leather goods, machinery, electrical apparatus, chemicals). Chief cities: Arnham, Nijmegen, Apeldoorn, Zutphen. In 16th cent. ceded by dukes of Gelderland to Emperor Charles V; part of Hapsburg dominions until it subscribed (1579) to Union of Utrecht. In 1715 E part of the area, including ducal ⊙ Geldern, was ceded to Prussia. Center of combat in Second World War, suffering heavy damage.

eldermalsen (khĕl'dŭrmälsŭn), town (pop. 1,752), Gelderland prov., central Netherlands, 16 mi. SSE of Utrecht; beet-sugar refining, mfg. (electrical appliances, furniture, fireproof bricks).

eldern (gĕl'dŭrn), town (pop. 5,776), in former Prussian Rhine Prov., W Germany, after 1945 in North Rhine-Westphalia, in the Ruhr, on the Niers and 13 mi. SE of Goch; rail junction. Has 18th-cent. town hall. Was ⊙ GELDERLAND until 1715.

eldrop (khĕl'drŏp), town (pop. 6,833), North Brabant prov., SE Netherlands, 4 mi. E of Eindhoven; textiles (wool, cotton, linen), bicycles.

eleen (khŭlān'), town (pop. 10,802), Limburg prov., SE Netherlands, 11 mi. NE of Maastricht; chemicals; iron-, stone-, and woodworking.

elememi Dag (gĕlĕmĕ'mĭ dä"), Turkish *Gelememi Dağ*, peak (10,560 ft.), SE Turkey, in Hakari Mts., 15 mi. WSW of Beytussebap.

elenau or **Gelenau im Erzgebirge** (gĕ'lŭnou ĭm ĕrts'gûbĭr"gŭ), village (pop. 6,850), Saxony, E central Germany, in the Erzgebirge, 9 mi. SSE of Chemnitz; cotton milling, hosiery knitting.

elendzhik (gyĕlyĭnjĕk'), city (1948 pop. over 10,000), W Krasnodar Territory, Russian SFSR, port on small, oval bay of Black Sea, at S foot of the Greater Caucasus, 19 mi. SE of Novorossisk; climatic health resort; dairying; vineyards, orchards. Became city in 1853. Across bay (W) lies resort of Solntsedar (1948 pop. over 500), founded 1908; wine making.

elib (gĕlēb'), town (pop. 2,000), in the Benadir, S Ital. Somaliland, on Juba R. and 60 mi. NE of Kismayu, in agr. region (sesame, corn, durra). Has hosp. and leprosarium.

elibolu, Turkey: see GALLIPOLI.

élida (hā'lē-dhä), village (pop. 1,656), Barcelona prov., NE Spain, 16 mi. WNW of Barcelona, in winegrowing area; knitwear mfg.; wine, wheat, fruit.

elidonya, Cape (gĕlĭ'dônyä"), on SW coast of Asia Minor, on the Mediterranean, at entrance of Gulf of Antalya (Adalia); 36°12'N 30°24'E. Formerly also Khelidonia. Just S are tiny Besadalar isls., just E small Sulu or Granbusa Isl.

élise River (zhälēz'), Gers and Lot-et-Garonne depts., SW France, rises in Armagnac hills near Aignan, flows 59 mi. NNE, past Mézin, to the Baïse at Lavardac.

Gellert, Mount (gĕl'lārt), or **Mount Gerhardus** (gĕr'hŏrdo͞osh), Hung. *Gellérthegy*, Ger. *Blocksberg*, N central Hungary, in Buda Mts., on right bank of the Danube, overlooking Budapest; alt. 770 ft. Budapest municipal baths (thermal springs) on E slope. Illuminated cross marks altar of St. Gellert, 11th-cent. missionary. Royal palace on small hill to N.

Gelli, Wales: see RHONDDA.

Gelligaer (gĕth-lĭgär'), urban district (1931 pop. 41,043; 1951 census 36,159), E Glamorgan, Wales, 6 mi. NE of Pontypridd; coal-mining center.

Gellivare, Sweden: see GALLIVARE.

Gelmyazov or **Gel'myazov** (gĭlmyä'zŭf), village (1926 pop. 7,064), W Poltava oblast, Ukrainian SSR, 14 mi. NW of Zolotonosha; metalworks.

Gelnhausen (gĕln'hou"zŭn), town (pop. 6,918), in former Prussian prov. of Hesse-Nassau, W Germany, after 1945 in Hesse, on the Kinzig and 12 mi. ENE of Hanau; mfg. (pharmaceuticals, rubber products, armatures, lace, shoes, faïence); tobacco industry. Has ruins of 12th-cent. imperial castle; 12th–13th-cent. church. Created free imperial city in 1170. Novelist Grimmelshausen b. here.

Gelnica (gĕl'nyĭtsä), Hung. *Gölnicbánya* (gûl'nĭts-bä"nyŏ), town (pop. 3,240), E central Slovakia, Czechoslovakia, on railroad and 17 mi. NW of Kosice; iron and copper mining. Mercury mining in vicinity. Health resort of Thurzo (to͞or'zô) (alt. 1,875 ft.) is just NW.

Gelo River, Ethiopia: see GILA RIVER.

Gelos (zhŭlō'), S suburb (pop. 1,990) of Pau, Basses-Pyrénées dept., SW France, on the Gave de Pau; produces chemicals and sabots; meat processing, horse breeding. Also spelled Gélos.

Gelsa (hĕl'sä), town (pop. 1,982), Saragossa prov., NE Spain, on the Ebro and 28 mi. SE of Saragossa; olive oil, wine, fruit.

Gelsa, Yugoslavia: see JELSA.

Gelsenkirchen (gĕl"zŭn-kĭr'khŭn), city (□ 40; 1939 pop. 317,568; 1946 pop. 265,793; 1950 pop. 310,108), in former Prussian prov. of Westphalia, W Germany, after 1945 in North Rhine-Westphalia, port on Lippe Lateral Canal, adjoining (N) Essen; major coal-mining center of the Ruhr; blast furnaces, foundries, steel-rolling and wire mills, coke works; extraction of coal-tar products. Mfg. of machinery, stoves, cables, armatures, screws, rivets, radios. A center of Ger. glass industry (especially windowpanes). Rapid development of garment industry since 1945. Has 3 castles. Second World War destruction about 50%. Was small peasant community with c.1,000 inhabitants in 1850. Impetus toward industrialization came with opening (1853) of 1st coal mine. Chartered 1875. In 1928 it inc. neighboring towns of BUER and Horst (NW).

Gelterkinden (gĕl'tŭrkĭn'dŭn), town (pop. 2,707), Basel-Land half-canton, N Switzerland, on Ergolz R. and 14 mi. SE of Basel; shoes, silk textiles.

Gelting (gĕl'tĭng), village (pop. 2,539), in Schleswig-Holstein, NW Germany, near Flensburg Firth, 18 mi. E of Flensburg, in the Angeln; metal- and woodworking, food processing. Has 18th-cent. estate.

Geluwe (khā'lüwŭ), town (pop. 5,808), West Flanders prov., W Belgium, 2 mi. WNW of Menin; textile industry; market center for tobacco-growing area. Destroyed in First World War; since rebuilt. Formerly spelled Gheluwe.

Gelves (hĕl'vĕs), town (pop. 2,213), Seville prov., SW Spain, near the Guadalquivir, 4 mi. SW of Seville; olives, olive oil.

Gem, county (□ 555; pop. 8,730), W Idaho; ⊙ Emmett. Agr., lumbering area irrigated along Payette R. Hay, sugar beets, fruit, truck, dairy products. Mts. in N. Formed 1915.

Gem, city (pop. 118), Thomas co., NW Kansas, on Prairie Dog Creek and 7 mi. ENE of Colby; agr., stock raising.

Gemas (gĕmäs'), town (pop. 2,849), E Negri Sembilan, Malaya, 45 mi. ESE of Seremban; rail junction at fork of E coast and W coast lines, in rubber-growing area.

Gembloux (zhāblo͞o'), town (pop. 5,404), Namur prov., central Belgium, 11 mi. NW of Namur; rail junction; cutlery center; mfg. (locks, tools, agr. machinery); sugar refining. Agr. col., housed in old abbey; old town walls.

Gemen (gā'mŭn), town (pop. 2,147), in former Prussian prov. of Westphalia, W Germany, after 1945 in North Rhine-Westphalia, 1 mi. N of Borken; linen weaving. Has 17th-cent. castle.

Gemena (gĕmĕ'nä), village, Equator Prov., NW Belgian Congo, 150 mi. WNW of Lisala; cotton ginning.

Gemert (khā'mŭrt), town (pop. 5,212), North Brabant prov., E Netherlands, 5 mi. N of Helmond; textiles (cotton, wool, linen), blanket weaving.

Gemlik (gĕmlĭk'), town (pop. 7,104), Bursa prov., NW Turkey, port on Gulf of Gemlik of Sea of Marmara, 17 mi. NNE of Bursa; artificial-silk factory; olive-growing center; small chromium deposits. Sometimes spelled Ghemlik. Formerly called Kiye or Ghio.

Gemmi Pass (gĕ'mē) (7,609 ft.), in Bernese Alps, S Switzerland; road over the pass leads from Kandersteg (Bern canton) to Leukerbad (Valais canton).

Gemona del Friuli (jĕmô'nä dĕl frē'o͞olē), town (pop. 3,036), Udine prov., Friuli-Venezia Giulia, NE Italy, 15 mi. NNW of Udine, near Tagliamento R. Rail junction; mfg. (alcohol, paper, silk textiles, agr. machinery), dairy products. Has Romanesque-Gothic cathedral (13th–14th cent.), palace (1502), and church with a Madonna by G. B. Cima.

Gémozac (zhāmôzäk'), village (pop. 957), Charente-Maritime dept., W France, 12 mi. S of Saintes; brandy distilling.

Gemsa (gĕm'sŭ) or **Jimsah** (jĭm'sŭ), town, E Egypt, on the Red Sea at entrance to Gulf of Suez, 65 mi. NNW of Safaga; its oil wells are abandoned.

Gemsbok Pan, Bechuanaland Protectorate: see GHANZI.

Gemünd (gŭmünt'), town (pop. 2,559), in former Prussian Rhine Prov., W Germany, after 1945 in North Rhine-Westphalia, on Urft R. and 14 mi. WSW of Euskirchen; metalworking.

Gemünden (gŭmün'dŭn). **1** Town (pop. 3,013), Lower Franconia, NW Bavaria, Germany, at junction of the Main (canalized) and the Franconian Saale, 21 mi. NNW of Würzburg; rail junction; woodworking. Has late-Gothic church, late-16th-cent. town hall. On near-by hill (E) are ruins of castle with 14th-cent. watchtower. **2** Town, Rhine Prov., W Germany: see DAUN-GEMÜNDEN.

Genabum, France: see ORLÉANS.

Genadendaal (khŭnä"dŭndäl'), town (pop. 2,626), SW Cape Prov., U. of So. Afr., 30 mi. SSE of Worcester. Moravian mission station, established 1737, with grain mills, printing works.

Genale (jĕnä'lā), town (pop. 500), in the Benadir, S Ital. Somaliland, on the Webi Shebeli (dammed here 1924–26 for irrigation) and 8 mi. NW of Merca; center of major agr. area (66,500 acres) developed by Italians after 1912. Chief banana-producing region of Ital. Somaliland (exports via Merca); other crops are cotton, corn, castor beans, tobacco, peanuts, sugar cane, tropical fruit. Processing plants at Vittorio d'Africa, 7 mi. SW.

Genalguacil (hānälgwä-thēl'), town (pop. 902), Málaga prov., S Spain, at NW slopes of the Sierra Bermeja, 15 mi. S of Ronda; olives, cork, chestnuts, wine; mfg. of liquor and olive oil.

Genappe (zhŭnäp'), Flemish *Genepien* (gā'nŭpēn), town (pop. 1,829), Brabant prov., central Belgium, on Dyle R. and 6 mi. E of Nivelles; agr. market; beet-sugar refining. Just S is battlefield of Quatre-Bras where (1815) Wellington defeated Marshal Ney in an important battle of Waterloo campaign.

Genarp (yā'närp"), village (pop. 755), Malmohus co., S Sweden, 11 mi. SE of Lund; grain, stock. Has 16th-cent. church.

Génave (hā'nävā), town (pop. 1,756), Jaén prov., S Spain, 30 mi. NE of Villacarrillo; olive-oil processing; wine, cereals, livestock.

Genay (zhŭnā'), village (pop. 1,072), Ain dept., E France, near Saône R., 10 mi. N of Lyons; surgical dressing mfg.

Genazzano (jĕnätsä'nô), town (pop. 4,225), Roma prov., Latium, central Italy, 18 mi. SE of Tivoli. Has noted pilgrimage chapel.

Genc, province, Turkey: see BINGOL, province.

Genc (gĕnch), Turkish *Genç*, village (pop. 795), Bingol prov., E central Turkey, on Murat R. and 11 mi. SSE of Bingol; grain. Formerly Darahini.

Gençay (zhãsā'), agr. village (pop. 911), Vienne dept., W central France, 14 mi. SSE of Poitiers; mule raising. Has ruins of 13th–14th-cent. castle.

Genck, Belgium: see GENK.

Gendorf, Germany: see EMMERTING.

Gendrey (zhãdrā'), village (pop. 317), Jura dept., E France, 12 mi. NE of Dôle; horse breeding.

Gendringen (khĕn'drĭng-ŭn), town (pop. 1,750), Gelderland prov., E Netherlands, on Old Ijssel R. and 21 mi. ESE of Arnhem, near Ger. border; door- and window-frame mfg., wooden shoes, carpets.

Gendt or **Gent** (both: khĕnt), town (pop. 206), Gelderland prov., E Netherlands, near Waal R., 5 mi. ENE of Nijmegen; shipbuilding; public-works construction.

Gene Autry (ô'trē), town (pop. 170), Carter co., S Okla., 8 mi. NE of Ardmore, in farm area. Formerly Berwyn (bûr'wĭn).

Geneffa, Egypt: see GINEIFA.

Geneina or **El Geneina** (ĕl gĕnā'nŭ), town, Darfur prov., W Anglo-Egyptian Sudan, near Fr. Equatorial Africa border, frontier post on road and 200 mi. W of El Fasher; 13°29'N 22°27'E. Commercial and agr. center; gum arabic, sesame, corn, durra; livestock. Airfield. Chief center of Dar Masalit sultanate.

Génelard (zhãnŭlär'), village (pop. 892), Saône-et-Loire dept., E central France, on Bourbince R. and Canal du Centre, 10 mi. NNW of Charolles; mining equipment, refractories.

Genemuiden (khā'nŭmoi'dŭn), village (pop. 3,553), Overijssel prov., N central Netherlands, on the Zwartewater and 8 mi. NNW of Zwolle; mat weaving, dairying, agr., cattle raising.

Genepien, Belgium: see GENAPPE.

General, El, Costa Rica: see EL GENERAL.

General Acha (hānäräl' ä'chä), town (1947 pop. 5,207), ⊙ Utracán dept. (pop. 10,252), central La Pampa prov., Argentina, on railroad and 55 mi. SSW of Santa Rosa; agr. and lumbering center. Rye, wheat, alfalfa, livestock; dairying. Airport. Former territorial capital.

General Alvarado, district, Argentina: see MIRAMAR.

General Alvarado (älvärä'dō) or **Alvarado**, town (pop. estimate 500), central Salta prov., Argentina, in Lerma Valley, on railroad and 5 mi. SSW of Salta. Agr. center (alfalfa, tobacco, potatoes, livestock).

General Alvear (älvāär'). **1** Town (pop. 2,660), ⊙ General Alvear dist. (□ 1,306; pop. 8,763), central Buenos Aires prov., Argentina, 50 mi. W of Las Flores; grain and livestock center. **2** Town (pop. estimate 2,500), ⊙ General Alvear dept. (□ 7,550; 1947 pop. 21,557), E central Mendoza prov., Argentina, on railroad (Colonia Alvear station), on Atuel R. and 45 mi. SE of San Rafael; agr. center (alfalfa, wine, fruit, grain, livestock; apiculture); food canning.

General Anaya (änī'ä), SE section of Mexico city, central Mexico; residential and industrial suburb (textile goods, plastics, rubber products, pencils, wood products).

General Aquino, Paraguay: see GENERAL E. AQUINO.

General Arenales (äränä'lĕs), town (pop. 2,487), ⊙ General Arenales dist. (□ 572; pop. 23,169), N Buenos Aires prov., Argentina, at Arenales station, 30 mi. NW of Junín, in agr. region (wheat, flax, livestock).

General Artigas (ärtē'gäs), town (dist. pop. 11,045), Itapúa dept., SE Paraguay, on railroad and 40 mi. NW of Encarnación; lumbering and agr. center (maté, fruit, livestock); apiculture; sawmilling. Formerly Cangó or Bobí.

General Belgrano, for Argentine names not found here: see under BELGRANO.

General Belgrano. 1 Department, Córdoba prov., Argentina: see OLIVA. **2** Department, La Rioja prov., Argentina: see OLTA.

General Belgrano (bĕlgrä'nō), town (pop. 7,660), ⊙ General Belgrano dist. (□ 715; pop. 12,094), E Buenos Aires prov., Argentina, on the Río Salado and 80 mi. S of Buenos Aires. Agr. center (flax, sunflowers, grain, livestock); dairying, flour milling.

General Bilbao, Bolivia: see ARAMPAMPA.

General Bravo (brä'vō), town (pop. 1,225), Nuevo León, N Mexico, on San Juan R. (irrigation) and 70 mi. ENE of Monterrey; cotton, sugar cane, cereals, cactus fibers.

General Cabrera (käbrā'rä) or **Cabrera,** town (pop. 4,111), S central Córdoba prov., Argentina, 45 mi. SW of Villa María; grain, alfalfa, sunflowers; stock raising, dairying, flour milling.

General Câmara (zhĭnĭräl' kä'märŭ), city (pop. 2,352), E Rio Grande do Sul, Brazil, on Jacuí R., on railroad and 45 mi. W of Pôrto Alegre; rice, hides, lard. Coal mined in near-by São Jerônimo area. Until 1938, called Santo Amaro.

General Campos (hānäräl' käm'pōs), town (pop. estimate 2,000), E central Entre Ríos prov., Argentina, on railroad and 25 mi. WSW of Concordia; stock raising, rice growing.

General Capdevila (käpdävē'lä), village (pop. estimate 400), ⊙ Campo del Cielo dept. (pop. 64,157), SW Chaco prov., Argentina, on railroad and 80 mi. SW of Presidencia Roque Sáenz Peña; agr. center (corn, sunflowers, spurge); stock raising, dairying, lumbering.

General Cepeda (sāpā'dä), town (pop. 3,383), Coahuila, N Mexico, in Sierra Madre Oriental, on railroad and 30 mi. W of Saltillo; alt. 4,967 ft. Agr. center (corn, beans, alfalfa, istle fibers, candelilla wax, cattle).

General Cerri or **General Daniel Cerri** (dänyĕl' sĕ'rē), town (pop. 2,398), SW Buenos Aires prov., Argentina, port on mouth of Sauce Chico R. and 5 mi. W of Bahía Blanca; meat-packing center; winegrowing. Exports meat. Formerly Cuatreros.

General Conesa (kōnā'sä). **1** Town (pop. estimate 1,000), ⊙ Tordillo dist. (□ 500; pop. 2,325), E Buenos Aires prov., Argentina, 23 mi. SE of Dolores; stock-raising center. **2** Village (pop. estimate 1,000), ⊙ Conesa dept., E Río Negro natl. territory, Argentina, inland port on navigable Río Negro and 90 mi. NW of Viedma; stock raising, fruitgrowing.

General Daniel Cerri, Argentina: see GENERAL CERRI.

General Deheza (dā-ā'sä) or **Deheza,** town (pop. estimate 1,000), S central Córdoba prov., Argentina, 38 mi. SW of Villa María; wheat, flax, alfalfa, rye, livestock; dairying, flour milling.

General Delgado (dĕlgä'dō), town (dist. pop. 4,972), Itapúa dept., SE Paraguay, 40 mi. WNW of Encarnación; sugar-cane center; alcohol and liquor distilling. Sometimes Colonia General Delgado.

General Díaz (dē'äs), town (dist. pop. 2,752), Ñeembucú dept., S Paraguay, near Paraná R., 25 mi. S of Pilar, in fruit and cattle area.

General E. Aquino or **General Aquino** (ä'kē'nō), town (dist. pop. 7,885), San Pedro dept., central Paraguay, 75 mi. NE of Asunción; maté, oranges.

General Elizalde, Ecuador: see BUCAY.

General Enrique Martínez (ĕnrē'kä märtē'nĕs), town (pop. 1,000), Treinta y Tres dept., E central Uruguay, port on Cebollatí R., on highway, and 33 mi. ENE of Treinta y Tres; shipping point for agr. products (wheat, corn, linseed), cattle, sheep. Customhouse. Rice plantations at confluence of Olimar and Cebollatí rivers (6 mi. SW). Until early 1930s called La Charqueada.

General Escobedo (ĕskōbā'dō), town (pop. 429), Nuevo León, N Mexico, on railroad and 10 mi. N of Monterrey; grain, livestock.

General Galarza, Argentina: see GALARZA.

General Grant Grove; General Grant National Park, Calif.: see KINGS CANYON NATIONAL PARK.

General Güemes (gwä'mĕs) or **Güemes,** town (1947 pop. 5,584), central Salta prov., Argentina, 25 mi. NE of Salta. Rail junction; lumbering and agr. center (rice, sugar cane, vegetables, citrus fruit, livestock); sawmills, sugar refineries. Airport.

General Guido (gē'dō), town (pop. estimate 1,800), ⊙ General Guido dist. (□ 1,176; pop. 4,947), E Buenos Aires prov., Argentina, 25 mi. SSW of Dolores; agr. center (grain, flax, livestock).

General Gutiérrez (gōōtyĕr'ĕs), town (pop. estimate 700), N Mendoza prov., Argentina, in Mendoza R. valley (irrigation area), 9 mi. SE of Mendoza; rail junction; agr. center (wine, fruit, potatoes); wine making, alcohol distilling.

General José Ballivián, Bolivia: see REYES.

General José F. Uriburu, Argentina: see ZÁRATE.

General Juan Madariaga, Argentina: see GENERAL MADARIAGA.

General Lagos (lä'gōs), town (pop. estimate 500), SE Santa Fe prov., Argentina, near Paraná R., 12 mi. SSE of Rosario; agr. center (corn, potatoes, flax, goats, horses).

General Lagos (lä'gōs), village (pop. 73), Tarapacá prov., N Chile, in the Andes, on Bolivia border, 85 mi. NE of Arica; last Chilean stop on international railroad (Arica-La Paz). Sulphur mined near by.

General Lamadrid, department, Argentina: see VILLA CASTELLI.

General Lamadrid (lämädrēdh'). **1** Town (pop. 3,636), ⊙ General Lamadrid dist. (□ 1,911; pop. 13,835), W central Buenos Aires prov., Argentina, 60 mi. WSW of Olavarría; rail junction; grain, livestock; dairying. **2** Town, Tucumán prov., Argentina: see LA MADRID.

General Las Heras (läs ā'räs), town (pop. 2,707), ⊙ General Las Heras dist. (□ 280; pop. 6,234), NE Buenos Aires prov., Argentina, 38 mi. SW of Buenos Aires; agr. center (alfalfa, grain, livestock).

General Lavalle, department, Argentina: see VILLA UNIÓN.

General Lavalle (lävä'yä). **1** Town (pop. 2,223), ⊙ Lavalle dist. (□ 1,110; pop. 5,605), E Buenos Aires prov., Argentina, 40 mi. W of Dolores, near Samborombón Bay; cattle- and sheep-raising center; fishing (lobsters, shrimps, anchovies). **2** Town (pop. 2,891), S Córdoba prov., Argentina, 66 mi. SSE of Río Cuarto; cereals, flax, alfalfa, sunflowers, livestock; dairying.

General López, department, Argentina: see SAN URBANO.

General Luna (lōō'nä), town (1939 pop. 1,842; 1948 municipality pop. 5,719), on Siargao Isl., Surigao prov., Philippines, just off NE tip of Mindanao; coconuts.

General Machado, Cuba: see GENERAL PERAZA.

General Madariaga or **General Juan Madariaga** (hwän' mädäryä'gä), town (pop. 7,685), ⊙ General Madariaga dist. (□ 1,240; pop. 13,232), E Buenos Aires prov., Argentina, 75 mi. NNE of Mar del Plata; agr. center (flax, potatoes, corn, livestock); dairying.

General Magdaleno Cedillo, Mexico: see CIUDAD DEL MAÍZ.

General Manuel Campos (mänwĕl' käm'pōs), village (pop. estimate 500), E La Pampa natl. territory, Argentina, on railroad and 70 mi. SE of Santa Rosa; grain and livestock center; salt mining.

General Mitre, department, Argentina: see UNIÓN.

General Mitre. 1 Town, Córdoba prov., Argentina: see VILLA GENERAL MITRE. **2** Town, Santiago del Estero prov., Argentina: see PINTO.

General Nikolayevo (gänäräl' nĭkôlī'ŭvô), village (pop. 5,478), Plovdiv dist., S central Bulgaria, 15 mi. NE of Plovdiv; flour milling; fruit, truck. Formerly Kalachlii.

General Obligado, department, Argentina: see RECONQUISTA.

General O'Brien or **O'Brien,** town (pop. 2,978), N central Buenos Aires prov., Argentina, 23 mi. NW of Bragado; agr. center (corn, alfalfa, livestock).

General Ocampo, department, Argentina: see CATUNA.

General Ortega (hānäräl' ôrtā'gä), town (pop. estimate 300), N Mendoza prov., Argentina, in Mendoza R. valley (irrigation area), on railroad and 10 mi. SE of Maipú, in wine and fruit area; wine making, alcohol distilling, dried-fruit processing.

General Pacheco (pächā'kō), village (pop. estimate 700) in Greater Buenos Aires, Argentina, 13 mi. NW of Buenos Aires; international airport; radio station.

General Paz, district, Argentina: see RANCHOS.

General Paz (päs'), town (pop. estimate 2,000), ⊙ General Paz dept. (□ c.1,100; pop. 17,535), N Corrientes prov., Argentina, 80 mi. ESE of Corrientes, rail terminus and agr. center (cotton, tobacco, oranges, livestock); textile milling, dairying. Formerly Caa-Catí.

General Paz, Lake (alt. c.3,000 ft.), in the Andes, 40 mi. SW of Tecka (Argentina); 23 mi. W-E, 1–5 mi. wide. The Chile-Argentina boundary cuts it, N-S, into 2 equal parts. Also called L. General Vinter or L. General Winter.

General Pedernera, Argentina: see MERCEDES, San Juan prov.

General Pedro Antonio Santos (pā'drō äntō'nyō sän'tōs) or **Ciudad Santos** (syōōdädh' sän'tōs), city (pop. 1,358), San Luis Potosí, E Mexico, in E foothills of Sierra Madre Oriental, 28 mi. SSE of Valles; agr. center (cotton, sugar cane, tobacco, fruit, livestock). Formerly Tancanhuitz.

General Peraza (pārä'sä), town (pop. 2,347), Havana prov., W Cuba, 9 mi. S of Havana; dairying, mfg. of paint. Has Inst. of Technology and Rancho Boyeros airport. Originally called Lutgardita, and, later, General Machado until 1934.

General Pico (pē'kō), city (1947 pop. 12,546), ⊙ Maracó dept. (pop. 16,208), N La Pampa prov., Argentina, 70 mi. NW of Santa Rosa. Rail junction (Pico station); trading and farming center (wheat, rye, barley, alfalfa, livestock). Meat packing, flour milling, dairying; sawmills, grain elevator, railroad shops. Has agr. research station (mainly for cereals).

General Pinedo (pēnā'dō), town (pop. estimate 1,500), S Chaco natl. territory, Argentina, on railroad and 65 mi. SW of Presidencia Roque Sáenz Peña; lumbering, agr. (corn, cotton, sunflowers, spurge), stock raising, dairying.

General Pinto (pēn'tō). **1** Town (pop. 3,734), ⊙ General Pinto dist. (□ 1,680; pop. 21,309), NW Buenos Aires prov., Argentina, 21 mi. WNW of Lincoln, in farming area (wheat, corn, livestock). **2** Town, Santiago del Estero prov., Argentina: see PINTO.

General Pueyrredón, district, Argentina: see MAR DEL PLATA.

General River, Costa Rica: see DIQUÍS RIVER.

General Roca. 1 Department, Córdoba prov., Argentina: see VILLA HUIDOBRO. **2** Department, La Rioja prov., Argentina: see CHEPES.

General Roca (rō'kä). **1** Town (pop. estimat 1,000), E Córdoba prov., Argentina, 12 mi. ESI of Marcos Juárez; wheat, corn, flax, alfalfa, live stock. **2** Town, Río Negro natl. territory, Argen tina: see FUERTE GENERAL ROCA.

General Rodríguez (rōdrē'gĕs), town (pop. 4,691) ⊙ General Rodríguez dist. (□ 139; pop. 8,613), NI Buenos Aires prov., Argentina, 9 mi. ESE o Luján; agr. center (flax, corn, oats, cattle, sheep)

General Saavedra (sävā'drä), town (pop. c.2,800) Santa Cruz dept., central Bolivia, 8 mi. NE o Montero; rice, sugar cane. Formerly Bibosi.

General Salgado (zhĭnĭräl' sälgä'dōō), city (pop 731), NW São Paulo, Brazil, 70 mi. WNW of Sã José do Rio Prêto; grain, coffee, cotton, fruit.

General Sánchez Cerro, province, Peru: see OMATE

General San Martín. 1 Department, Córdoba prov. Argentina: see VILLA MARÍA. **2** Department Corrientes prov., Argentina: see LA CRUZ. **3** De partment, La Rioja prov., Argentina: see ULAPES

General San Martín (hānäräl' sän' märtēn'). **1** City Buenos Aires prov., Argentina: see SAN MARTÍN **2** Town (pop. estimate 1,000), SE La Pampa natl territory, Argentina, on railroad and 70 mi. SE o General Acha. Agr. center (barley, wheat, oats livestock). Mining of salt and sodium sulphate Formerly Villa Alba. **3** Town, Mendoza prov. Argentina: see SAN MARTÍN.

General Sarmiento. 1 District, Buenos Aires prov. Argentina: see SAN MIGUEL. **2** Department, L Rioja prov., Argentina: see VINCHINA.

General Simón Bolívar (sēmōn' bōlē'vär), villag (pop. 836), Durango, N Mexico, on affluent o Aguanaval R. and 60 mi. SSE of Torreón; antimon mining; silver, gold, lead deposits. Formerly Sa Bartolo.

General Taboada, Argentina: see AÑATUYA.

General Terán (tärän'), town (pop. 2,348), Nuev León, N Mexico, 45 mi. SE of Monterrey; agr center (fruit, grain, cactus fibers, livestock).

General Toshevo (gänäräl' tôshĕ'vô), village (pop 2,102), Stalin dist., NE Bulgaria, in S Dobruja 12 mi. NE of Tolbukhin; grain, sheep, flax. I Rumania (1913–40) called Casim.

General Treviño (hānäräl' trävē'nyō), town (pop 1,674), Nuevo León, N Mexico, in lowland, 65 mi NE of Monterrey; corn, cotton, sugar cane, cactu fibers.

General Trías (trē'äs), town (pop. 375), Chihuahua N Mexico, at W foot of Sierra Madre Occidental on railroad and 28 mi. SW of Chihuahua; alt. 5,29 ft. Corn, fruit, beans, cattle. Formerly Sant Isabel.

General Trias (trē'äs), town (1939 pop. 3,781; 194 municipality pop. 15,963), Cavite prov., S Luzon Philippines, 17 mi. SSW of Manila; agr. cente (rice, fruit, coconuts).

General Uriburu, Argentina: see ZÁRATE.

General Vargas (zhĭnĭräl' vär'gŭs), city (pop 1,069), W central Rio Grande do Sul, Brazil, nea Ibicuí R., 65 mi. E of Alegrete; corn, rice, cereals cattle. Until 1944, São Vicente.

General Vedia (hānäräl' vādh'yä), town (pop. estimate 700), E Chaco natl. territory, Argentina, 4 mi. NNE of Resistencia, near Paraguay R.; agr (corn, cotton, livestock).

General Viamonte, district, Argentina: see LOS TOLDOS.

General Vicente Guerrero, Mexico: see VILLA VICENTE GUERRERO.

General Villegas (vīyā'gäs), town (pop. 4,723), ⊙ General Villegas dist. (□ 2,791; pop. 28,409), NW Buenos Aires prov., Argentina, 120 mi. WSW of Junín, in agr. area (wheat, corn, livestock); dairying.

General Vinter, Lake, Argentina-Chile: see GENERAL PAZ, LAKE.

General Winter, Lake, Argentina-Chile: see GENERAL PAZ, LAKE.

General Zuazua (swä'swä), town (pop. 2,077), Nuevo León, N Mexico, on Pesquería R. and 20 mi. NE of Monterrey; grain, cotton, sugar cane, livestock.

Generoso Ponce, Brazil: see JACI-PARANÁ.

Genesaia or **Yenisaia** (both: yĕnĭsä'yŭ), village (1928 pop. 1,795), Xanthe nome, W Thrace, Greece, 6 mi. SE of Xanthe. A flourishing tobacco center under Turkish rule, known as Yenije (Yenidje) or Yenije-i-Karasu, it was supplanted (1890s) by rail town of Xanthe.

Genesee (jĕ'nŭsē", jĕnŭsē'). **1** County (□ 644; pop. 270,963), SE central Mich.; ⊙ FLINT. Drained by Flint and Shiawassee rivers. Agr. dairy products; livestock, poultry, fruit, grain, hay, truck, beans, sugar beets. Mfg. at Flint. Summer resorts. Marl deposits. Organized 1836. **2** County (□ 501; pop. 47,584), W N.Y.; ⊙ Batavia. Drained by Tonawanda and Oak Orchard creeks. Agr. area (dairy products, poultry, fruit, wheat, potatoes, hay, truck); diversified mfg. at Batavia. Timber; sand and gravel; gypsum quarries. Includes part of Tonawanda Indian Reservation. County formed 1802.

Genesee. 1 City (pop. 552), Latah co., W Idaho, 12 mi. SSE of Moscow; agr. (potatoes, grain, peas). **2** Village (pop. c.500), Potter co., N Pa., 16 mi. NNE of Coudersport, near N.Y. line; chemicals; dairy products.

Genesee Depot (dē'pō), village, Waukesha co., SE Wis., 23 mi. WSW of Milwaukee, in agr. area.

Genesee River, in Pa. and N.Y., rises in the Alleghenies in Potter co., Pa., flows c.158 mi. generally N, crossing the Barge Canal S of Rochester, N.Y., to L. Ontario at Rochester, where falls supply power. Flood-control dam at Mount Morris. Its valley is noted for beauty and fertility. In Wyoming and Livingston counties (N.Y.) is Letchworth State Park (c.10,000 acres), which extends for c.13 mi. along the Genesee and includes part of its gorge (c.350 ft. deep). Here, in park, are 3 scenic waterfalls, campgrounds, a noted arboretum, a Seneca council house, and mus. of Indian and pioneer relics.

Geneseo. 1 (jĕnúsē'ō, jĕ'nùsōō) City (pop. 4,325), Henry co., NW Ill., on old Illinois and Mississippi Canal and 20 mi. E of Moline; farm trade center in agr. (corn, oats, wheat, livestock, poultry, truck) and bituminous-coal area. Mfg. (dairy and canned foods, bandages). State fish hatchery near by. Settled 1836, inc. 1855. **2** (jĕnùsē'ō) City (pop. 660), Rice co., central Kansas, 34 mi. NNW of Hutchinson, in wheat area; oil refining. Oil and gas wells near by. **3** (jĕnùsē'ō) Village (pop. 2,838); ⊙ Livingston co., W central N.Y., on Genesee R. and 28 mi. SSW of Rochester; trade center in agr. area (peas, corn, fruit); summer resort; mfg. (soap, meal, canned foods). Salt deposits. Seat of a state teachers col. Settled c.1790, inc. 1832.

Genest, Le (lù zhùnĕ'), village (pop. 203), Mayenne dept., W France, 6 mi. WNW of Laval; anthracite mines. Gold and antimony mining at near-by La Lucette.

Genêts (zhùnā'), village (pop. 479), Manche dept., NW France, on Bay of Saint-Michel of English Channel, 5 mi. W of Avranches; mineral springs. Mont-Saint-Michel and Tombelaine isls. accessible from here across sands at low tide.

Geneva (jùnē'vù), Fr. *Genève* (zhùnĕv'), canton (□ 109; 1950 pop. 201,505), SW Switzerland, bet. the Jura and the Alps, almost surrounded by Fr. territory; ⊙ Geneva. Consists mainly of city of Geneva which, with its suburbs, accounts for 144,423 of cantonal pop. Its rural areas produce fruits, vegetables, wine. Industry concentrated in the capital. Pop. is French speaking of Protestant (majority) and Catholic faiths.

Geneva, Fr. *Genève,* Ger. *Genf* (gĕnf), Ital. *Ginevra* (jēnĕv'rä), city (1950 pop. 144,422), ⊙ Geneva canton, SW Switzerland, on L. Geneva, at efflux of Rhone R.; largely surrounded by Fr. territory; 46°12'N 6°10'E; alt. 1,237 ft. An anc. settlement (*Genava*) of the Allobroges, Geneva was included in Roman Gaul and became an episcopal see under the Roman empire. It later passed successively to Burgundians, Franks, Transjurane Burgundy, and the Holy Roman Empire. In 16th cent. it became focal point of the Reformation and later (especially in 18th cent.) a cosmopolitan and intellectual center. Annexed to France from 1798 to 1814, it became (1815) ⊙ the newly admitted canton. Geneva was a residence of Calvin and Voltaire, and birthplace of Rousseau, de Saussure, and Necker. Seat of International Red Cross since 1864, League of Nations (1920–46), International Labor Organization, and other international bodies; it is also a noted tourist center. Mfg. (watches, clothes, aluminumware, bicycles, motorcycles, sewing machines, scales, flour, biscuits, tobacco, pencils, chemicals); printing. Geneva is divided by the Rhone into the Old Town (left bank; seat of government and center of traffic), with suburbs of Plainpalais (SW) and Eaux Vives (E), and the residential *Quartier St. Gervais,* with suburb of Pâquis. There are 7 bridges, numerous parks, monuments, and old bldgs. Points of interest: Cathedral of St. Pierre (12th–14th cent.; on a hill and on site of a Roman temple), 16th-cent. town hall (now cantonal offices), univ. (originally Calvin's academy) with its noted library and mus., Mus. of Art and History, Palace of the League of Nations, Palace of Justice, the observatory, zoological and botanic gardens.

Geneva, county (□ 578; pop. 25,899), SE Ala.; ⊙ Geneva. Coastal plain bordering on Fla., drained by Pea and Choctawhatchee rivers. Cotton, bees. Formed 1868.

Geneva. 1 Town (pop. 3,579), ⊙ Geneva co., SE Ala., at confluence of Choctawhatchee and Pea rivers, 42 mi. SE of Andalusia, near Fla. line; clothing, cotton fabric, lumber. Settled 1836, inc. 1872. **2** Town (pop. 209), Talbot co., W Ga., 27 mi. ENE of Columbus. **3** City (pop. 5,139), ⊙ Kane co., NE Ill., on Fox R. (bridged here) and 35 mi. W of Chicago, in agr. area (grain, livestock; dairy products); mfg. (timing devices, flour, feed, radio and kitchen cabinets, metal products, auto parts, screens, heaters). Seat of state training school for girls. Founded c.1833, inc. 1867. **4** Town (pop. 999), Adams co., E Ind., on the Wabash and 35 mi. NE of Muncie, in agr. area. Gene Stratton Porter lived here. **5** Town (pop. 242), Franklin co., N central Iowa, 6 mi. SE of Hampton; livestock, grain. **6** Village (pop. 332), Freeborn co., S Minn., on small lake and 14 mi. NNE of Albert Lea; dairy products. **7** City (pop. 2,031), ⊙ Fillmore co., SE Nebr., 50 mi. WSW of Lincoln and on branch of Big Blue R.; trade, cattle-shipping center; paint, oil, flour, feed; dairy and poultry produce, grain. Reform school for girls. Platted 1858. **8** City (pop. 17,144), Ontario co., W central N.Y., in Finger Lakes region, at N end of Seneca L., 35 mi. SE of Rochester; trade center for a fruit- and vegetable-growing region. Mfg.: canned foods, machinery, boilers, furnaces, ranges, radiators, optical goods, flour, cutlery, canvas goods. Nurseries. Seat of Colleges of the Seneca (Hobart and William Smith colleges), and a state agr. experiment station connected with Cornell Univ. Sampson Col. is at near-by SAMPSON. Settled 1788; inc. as village in 1812, as city in 1898. **9** Village (pop. 4,718), Ashtabula co., extreme NE Ohio, 8 mi. WSW of Ashtabula; metal products, tools, wheels, floor mops; wineries, greenhouses, apiaries. Lake resort. Settled 1802; inc. 1867. **10** Town, Utah co., Utah: see PROVO.

Geneva, Lake, or **Lake Leman** (lē'mùn), Fr. *Lac Léman* (läk lāmā'), Ger. *Genfersee* (gĕn'fùrzā"), anc. *Lemanus* or *Lemannus,* bet. SW Switzerland and Haute-Savoie, France; c.45 mi. long, 8 mi. wide at widest point, □ 224, alt. 1,220 ft., max. depth 1,017 ft. It extends as a crescent generally E-W; N part (□ 134) is Swiss, S part (□ 90) French. The Rhone traverses lake from E to W, leaving at Geneva. The Alps (E and S) and the Jura (W and N) create a mountainous background. Its water, deep blue and remarkably transparent, is subject to the so-called *seiches,* i.e. fluctuations similar to ocean tides and probably caused by changes in atmospheric pressure; there are 21 species of fish. The beauty of the lake has been a topic of many writers (e.g., Byron, Voltaire, Rousseau, Dumas). Its shores are dotted with resorts: MONTREUX and VEVEY in Switzerland, THONON-LES-BAINS and EVIAN-LES-BAINS in France. GENEVA and LAUSANNE are its large cities.

Geneva, Lake, Walworth co., SE Wis., near Ill. line; resort lake (c.8 mi. long, c.1 mi. wide). Lake Geneva city, on NE shore, is largest resort; others are Fontana and Williams Bay. Fishing, year-round lake sports. Drained by White R.

Genevad (yā'nùväd"), village (pop. 433), Halland co., SW Sweden, near Laholm Bay of the Kattegat, 7 mi. SE of Halmstad; cotton milling.

Geneva-on-the-Lake (jùnē'vù), resort village (pop. 388), Ashtabula co., extreme NE Ohio, just N of Geneva and 8 mi. W of Ashtabula, on L. Erie.

Genevia (jùnē'vēù) or **College Station,** village (pop. c.1,000), Pulaski co., central Ark., 5 mi. SE of Little Rock.

Genf, Switzerland: see GENEVA, city.

Genfersee, Switzerland: see GENEVA, LAKE.

Gengenbach (gĕng'ùnbäkh), town (pop. 3,692), S Baden, Germany, on W slope of Black Forest, on the Kinzig and 5 mi. SW of Offenburg; metal- and woodworking, paper and lumber milling, printing. A former free imperial city, it is still surrounded by medieval walls. Former Benedictine abbey (founded in 8th cent.) has 12th-cent. church.

Genichesk (gĕnyēchĕsk'), city (1932 pop. estimate 13,340), SE Kherson oblast, Ukrainian SSR, port on Sea of Azov, 55 mi. SW of Melitopol, on rail spur; flour milling, cotton ginning, fish canning; saltworks.

Genichesk Strait, narrow channel off NE Crimea, USSR, connecting Sea of Azov (E) and Sivash lagoon (W); separates Genichesk city (N) from tip of Arabat Tongue (S).

Genil River (hānēl'), Andalusia, S Spain, rises from glacier in the Veleta peak of the Sierra Nevada, flows c.150 mi. WNW through rich and fertile valley, past Granada, Puente-Genil, and Écija, to the Guadalquivir near Palma del Río. Feeds several irrigation canals.

Génissiat (zhānēsyä'), village (pop. 1,327), Ain dept., E France, on the Rhone, at foot of the Jura, and 19 mi. SW of Geneva, 3 mi. S of Bellegarde. Site of Génissiat dam (338 ft. high, 656 ft. long, 335 ft. wide at base) and hydroelectric plant (inside dam; begun 1937, inaugurated 1948). The project, largest in France, is part of program (somewhat like that of the Tennessee Valley Authority) to make the Rhone navigable from Geneva to Marseilles, and to build several power plants in its upper course across the Jura.

Genitsa, Greece: see GIANNITSA.

Genízaro Lagoon, Nicaragua: see TISMA LAGOON.

Genk (gĕngk), town (pop. 39,103), Limburg prov., NE Belgium, 8 mi. ENE of Hasselt; market center. Formerly spelled Genck. Coal-mining town of Winterslag (wĭn'tùrslàkh) is 2 mi. N; town of Winterslag-Cité (–sētā'), residential area for Winterslag miners, is 1.5 mi. NW.

Genkai Sea (gān'kī), Jap. *Genkai-nada,* NE arm of E.China Sea, bet. N coast of Kyushu, Japan (E), and isls. (W) which form E boundary of Tsushima Strait; merges with Hibiki Sea (NE); 36 mi. E-W, 28 mi. N-S. Fukuoka city is on SE inlet (Hakata Bay).

Genlis (zhālēs'), village (pop. 1,311), Côte-d'Or dept., E central France, 10 mi. SE of Dijon; glassworks, distilleries. Osier trade.

Gennargentu, Monti del (môn'tē dĕl jĕn-närjĕn'tōō), highest mountain mass in Sardinia, near center of isl.; extends 15 mi. N from Flumendosa R.; rises to 6,016 ft. at Punta Lamarmora, to 6,000 ft. at Bruncu Spina. Chestnut forests in W.

Gennep (khĕ'nĕp), town (pop. 3,676), Limburg prov., E Netherlands, on Maas R. and 11 mi. SSE of Nijmegen, near Ger. frontier; rail junction and border station; railroad shops, clay kilns, sawmills; furniture mfg.

Gennes (zhĕn), village (pop. 691), Maine-et-Loire dept., W France, on Loire R. and 9 mi. NW of Saumur; mushroom and fruit preserving, wine-growing. Remains of 6th-cent. Benedictine abbey near by.

Gennesaret, Lake of, Palestine: see GALILEE, SEA OF.

Gennevilliers (zhĕnvēyā'), industrial town (pop. 25,159), Seine dept., N central France, a NNW suburb of Paris, 6 mi. from Notre Dame Cathedral, within N loop of the Seine, adjoining Asnières (S); mfg. (aircraft parts, electric bulbs, radio tubes, special steel molds, rubber, films). Truck gardens fertilized by discharge of Paris sewers.

Genoa (jĕ'nōù, jùnō'ù), Ital. *Genova* (jĕ'nôvä), anc. *Genua,* city (pop. 512,313, pop. Greater Genoa 634,646), ⊙ Liguria and GENOVA prov., N Italy, fortified port at head of Gulf of Genoa, at center of Ital. Riviera, 80 mi. S of Milan; 44°25'N 8°55'E. Rail center; 5th largest city and chief port of Italy; rivals Marseilles as leading Mediterranean seaport; provides a major S outlet for Central Europe. The modernized harbor is hq. of principal Ital. lines. Exports olive oil, wine, silks, velvets, flowers, soap, motor cars. Imports coal, coke, mineral oils, chemicals, machinery. Next to its commerce, shipbuilding predominates. Other chief industries: iron- and steelworks (damaged in Second World War); mfg. of automobile chassis, airplane motors; refineries (beet sugar, oil seed, olive oil, sulphur), food canneries, breweries, distilleries (wine, ethyl alcohol), tanneries; refrigerator, chemical, and munition plants; fertilizer and rope works; textile and paper mills. Produces 25% of Italy's soap. Archbishopric. Has many notable churches, including cathedral of San Lorenzo (consecrated 1118; slightly damaged in Second World War), medieval church of San Donato (damaged), 16th-cent. churches of the Annunciation (damaged) and St. Ambrose. Its famous palaces include the municipal palace (1564; with mus. containing Paganini's violin and letters of Columbus), Bianco (1565; severely damaged), Rosso (1677; severely damaged), ducal palace (former residence of the doges). Has acad. of fine arts (severely damaged), famous Carlo Felice theater (1826–28; severely damaged), corn and stock exchanges, schools of commerce and navigation, and university (1812), originally a Jesuit col. (1623). Famous citizens have included Columbus, Mazzini, Paganini. A chief port of the Ligurians, Genoa came under Roman rule in 3d cent. B.C. After fall of Roman Empire, it was invaded by Lombards (7th cent.) and Saracens (936). In succeeding 2 cent., Genoa developed as a great maritime republic, promoting the Crusades, colonizing Levant, winning Corsica, and finally vanquishing her former ally, Pisa, in 1284. During 14th cent., rivalry with Venice ended in defeat (1378–80). Continued civil strife and intervention, especially by the French, gradually caused the dogedom (established 1339) to lose all its outlying possessions. Corsica, the last, was ceded to France 1768. Genoa was inc. 1797 by Napoleon into Ligurian Republic, which was annexed 1805 to French Empire. In 1815, Genoa united with kingdom of Sardinia. Greater Genoa was established 1926, with addition to Genoa commune of 19 near-by communes extending 6 mi. N to PONTEDECIMO, and 15 mi. along sea bet. NERVI (E) and VOLTRI (W), and including SAN PIER D'ARENA, RIVAROLO LIGURE, and SESTRI PONENTE. In Second World War, suffered one naval (1941) and numerous air bombings (especially 1942–44), which caused severe destruction to the harbor and to industrial and commercial dists.

Genoa (jùnō'ù). **1** Town (pop. 257), Lincoln co., E central Colo., 10 mi. E of Limon; alt. 5,598 ft. **2** City (pop. 1,690), De Kalb co., N Ill., on South Branch of Kishwaukee R. (bridged here) and 21 mi. WNW of Elgin, in rich agr. area; mfg. (electric motors, telephone equipment, hair clippers). Inc. 1911. **3** Village (pop. 1,026), Nance co., E central Nebr., 20 mi. W of Columbus and on Loup R.; dairy produce, grain. Pawnee Indian village excavated near by. Diversion dam on Loup R. Settled 1857. **4** Village (pop. c.150), Douglas co., extreme W Nev., 12 mi. SSW of Carson City, bet. Carson Range and Carson R.; alt. c.4,800 ft. Founded c.1849 as Mormon Station, renamed 1855. First permanent settlement in state. Was ⊙ Douglas co. 1861–1916. **5** Village (pop. c.450), Cayuga co., W central N.Y., in Finger Lakes region, 19 mi. S of Auburn; cheese. **6** Village (pop. 1,723), Ottawa co., N Ohio, 13 mi. SE of Toledo; limestone products. Settled 1835 as Stony Ridge Station. **7** Village, Harris co., S Texas, 12 mi. SE of Houston, in truck-farm area. Here is U.S. Ellington Air Force Base, military air base in both world wars. **8** Village (pop. 340), Vernon co., SW Wis., on the Mississippi and 17 mi. S of La Crosse; fishing. Navigation dam on the Mississippi here.

Genoa, Gulf of (jĕ'nōū, jŭnō'ū), Italy, N portion of LIGURIAN SEA, enclosed by RIVIERA DI LEVANTE and RIVIERA DI PONENTE. Receives Magra, Roya, Centa, Taggia, rivers. Major inlets: gulfs of Spezia and Rapallo. Chief ports: Genoa, Savona, Imperia.

Genoa City (jŭnō'ū), village (pop. 866), Walworth co., SE Wis., on Ill. line, near small L. Elizabeth, 8 mi. SE of Lake Geneva city, in dairy-farm area; mfg. (furnaces, food products).

Genoa River (hā'nōä), in Patagonia, Argentina, in Chubut natl. territory and Comodoro Rivadavia military zone, rises in Andean foothills S of L. General Paz, flows E to José de San Martín, then SSE to Senguerr R. 20 mi. N of Ensanche Colonia Sarmiento; c.120 mi. long.

Genola (jŭnō'lŭ). **1** Village (pop. 79), Morrison co., central Minn., 13 mi. E of Little Falls, in agr. area. **2** Town (pop. 314), Utah co., N central Utah, 25 mi. N of Nephi.

Génolhac (zhānōlăk'), village (pop. 541), Gard dept., S France, on E slope of Mont Lozère, 17 mi. NNW of Alès; tanning extracts.

Genossar (gĕnōsär'), **Ginneisar** (gēnĕsär'), or **Ginossar** (gēnō-), settlement (pop. 300), Lower Galilee, NE Israel, on W shore of Sea of Galilee, 4 mi. NNW of Tiberias; fishing; bananas, grapes, feed crops, vegetables, poultry. Possibly site of biblical locality of *Chinnereth*.

Génova (hā'nōvä), town (pop. 2,403), Caldas dept., W central Colombia, at W foot of Cordillera Central, 16 mi. SW of Armenia; coffee, corn, rice, bananas, yucca, sugar cane.

Génova, town (1950 pop. 565), Quezaltenango dept., SW Guatemala, in coastal plain, 6 mi. SSE of Coatepeque, on railroad; coffee, sugar cane, grain, livestock.

Genova (jĕ'nôvä), province (□ 700; pop. 867,608), Liguria, N Italy; ⊙ Genoa. Comprises central and W RIVIERA DI LEVANTE, enclosed by Ligurian Apennines; drained by upper Scrivia and Trebbia and various small rivers. Area is half forest, with the rest in pastures, orchards, vineyards, and farms. Agr. (olives, grapes, peaches, vegetables, flowers); cattle raising; fishing. Slate quarries (Lavagna, Cicagna, Uscio). Copper mine (Libiola). Has notable shipbuilding and heavy industry concentrated within Greater Genoa and at Chiavari. Resorts (Rapallo, Santa Margherita Ligure) on the Riviera. Area greatly reduced to form La Spezia (1923) and Savona (1927) provs.

Genova, city, Italy: see GENOA.

Genovés (hānōvās'), village (pop. 1,322), Valencia prov., E Spain, 3 mi. E of Játiva; olive oil, wine, rice, oranges. Gypsum quarries.

Genovesa Island (hānōvā'sä) or **Tower Island** (□ 5), NE Galápagos Isls., Ecuador, in the Pacific, 90 mi. NNW of Puerto Baquerizo; 0°20'N 89°55'W.

-ensan, Korea: see WONSAN.

Genshu, Korea: see WONJU.

Gent, Belgium: see GHENT.

Gent, Netherlands: see GENDT.

Gent, Sas van, Netherlands: see SAS VAN GENT.

Gentbrugge (gĕnt'brŭ'gŭ), town (pop. 17,883), East Flanders prov., NW Belgium, 2 mi. E of Ghent; steel wire, nails.

Genthin (gĕntēn'), town (pop. 17,776), in former Prussian Saxony prov., central Germany, after 1945 in Saxony-Anhalt, on Plaue Canal and 17 mi. W of Brandenburg; paper milling, lumbering, sugar refining; mfg. of soap, dyes, bricks.

Gentilly (zhãtēyē'), village (pop. 489), S Que., on the St. Lawrence and 14 mi. ENE of Trois Rivières; dairying, pig raising, lumbering.

Gentilly, town (pop. 16,256), Seine dept., N central France, just S of Paris, 3 mi. from Notre Dame Cathedral, bet. Montrouge (W) and Le Kremlin-Bicêtre (E); tanning, distilling, mfg. of precision instruments, varnishes, chicory. Just N is the Cité Universitaire (within Paris city limits).

Gentio do Ouro (zhĕntē'ōō dōō ō'rōō), town (pop. 2,821), W central Bahia, Brazil, in the Serra do Açuruá, 45 mi. SE of Barra; gold, black-diamond mining.

Gentioux (zhätyōō'), village (pop. 206), Creuse dept., central France, 15 mi. SW of Aubusson; peat extracting.

Gentioux, Plateau of, barren tableland of Massif Central, in Creuse dept., central France, bet. Royère and Gentioux.

Gentofte (gĕn'tôftŭ), residential N suburb (pop. 82,113) of Copenhagen, Denmark.

Gentry (jĕn'trē), county (□ 488; pop. 11,036), NW Mo.; ⊙ Albany. Drained by Grand R.; agr. (corn, wheat, oats), livestock, poultry, bluegrass seed. Formed 1841.

Gentry. 1 or **Gentry City,** town (pop. 729), Benton co., extreme NW Ark., 22 mi. NW of Fayetteville, in the Ozarks; livestock, poultry, fruit; railroad ties. **2** Town (pop. 159), Gentry co., NW Mo., on Middle Fork of Grand R. and 45 mi. NE of St. Joseph.

Gentryville (jĕn'trēvĭl), town (pop. 234), Spencer co., SW Ind., on small Little Pigeon Creek and 32 mi. ENE of Evansville.

Genua, Italy: see GENOA, city.

Genval (zhăväl'), town (pop. 4,354), Brabant prov., central Belgium, 10 mi. SSE of Brussels; paper mfg.

Genzan, Korea: see WONSAN.

Genzano di Lucania (jĕntsä'nō dē lōōkä'nyä), town (pop. 7,153), Potenza prov., Basilicata, S Italy, 19 mi. NE of Potenza, in agr. region (wheat, legumes, grapes); hosiery mfg.

Genzano di Roma (rô'mä), town (pop. 8,541), Roma prov., Latium, central Italy, in Alban Hills, near L. Nemi, 7 mi. S of Frascati; summer resort; alcohol distillery. Damaged in Second World War.

Geoagiu (jwäj'), Hung. *Algyógyalfalu* (ŏl'dyōdyŏlfō" lōō), village (pop. 2,445), Hunedoara prov., W central Rumania, near Mures R., 18 mi. ENE of Deva; thermal mineral and radioactive springs near by.

Geographe Bay (jēō'grŭfē), inlet of Indian Ocean, SW Western Australia, bet. Bunbury (NE) and Cape Naturaliste (NW); 40 mi. across mouth, 10 mi. N–S. Busselton near S shore.

Geographe Channel, strait of Indian Ocean, bet. W coast of Western Australia and Bernier Isl.; forms NW entrance to Shark Bay; 50 mi. long, 21 mi. wide.

Geographical Society Island (55 mi. long, 6–20 mi. wide), in King Oscar Archipelago, E Greenland, in Greenland Sea, at mouth of Franz Josef Fjord; 72°55'N 23°5'W. Rises 5,674 ft. at W extremity. Separated by narrow channels from Ymer Isl. (N) and Traill Isl. (S).

Geokchai or **Geokchay** (gēŭkchī'), city (1944 pop. over 10,000), central Azerbaijan SSR, 30 mi. E of Yevlakh; road center; metalworks, distillery; cotton, vineyards, sericulture. Rail station (SSW) is Udzhary.

Geokmaly (gēŭkmä'lē), town (1939 pop. over 500) in Kirov dist. of Greater Baku, Azerbaijan SSR, 6 mi. NW of Baku; oil fields.

Geok-Tepe (gēŏk"-tyĭpyĕ', gŭk'tĕpä'), town (1948 pop. over 2,000), S Ashkhabad oblast, Turkmen SSR, on Trans-Caspian RR and 28 mi. WNW of Ashkhabad, near Iran border, in orchard area; woolen milling, wine making, rug weaving. On site of fortress Dengil-Tepe, occupied by Russians after month-long siege (1880–81).

Georai, India: see GEVRAI.

George, town (pop. 11,993), S Cape Prov., U. of So. Afr., near Indian Ocean, at foot of Outeniqua Mts., 200 mi. W of Port Elizabeth, 25 mi. NE of Mossel Bay; rail junction; shoe mfg., sawmilling; stock, fruit. Site of industrial and forestry schools, experimental hop farm. Has Anglican cathedral. Airport. First town established (1811) after British occupation of the Cape. Montagu Pass over Outenitqua Mts. is 5 mi. N.

George, county (□ 481; pop. 10,012), SE Miss.; ⊙ Lucedale. Bordered E by Ala.; drained by Pascagoula and Escatawpa rivers and Black and Red creeks. Agr. (cotton, corn, truck; tung groves); lumbering. Includes part of De Soto Natl. Forest. Formed 1910.

George, town (pop. 1,210), Lyon co., NW Iowa, near Little Rock R., 38 mi. NNE of Le Mars; leather and metal products. Inc. 1889.

George, Cape, on Northumberland Strait, NE N.S., on W of entrance to George Bay, 18 mi. NNE of Antigonish; 45°53'N 61°54'W.

George, Cape, SW headland (800 ft. high) of Cambridge Isl., off W coast of S Chile, at entrance to Nelson Strait on the Pacific; 51°37'S 75°18'W.

George, Lake (□ 60), SE New South Wales, Australia, 17 mi. NE of Canberra; 15 mi. long, 6 mi. wide; usually dry.

George, Lake (□ 2.75; 3 mi. long, 2 mi. wide), SW N.B., 20 mi. WSW of Fredericton; drains into St. John R. Antimony is mined near by.

George, Lake, SW Uganda, in W branch of Great Rift Valley, NE of L. Edward (connected by Kazinga Channel); 18 mi. long, 10 mi. wide; alt. 2,997 ft. Swampy papyrus shores; fish.

George, Lake. 1 In N Fla., a widening of St. Johns R., 19 mi. S of Palatka; c.11 mi. long, 5–7 mi. wide. **2** In extreme NW Ind., just W of Hobart; c.3 mi. long; swimming, boating, fishing. Impounded by power dam on short Deep R. **3** In S central Ont. and E Upper Peninsula, Mich., a widening of St. Marys R., 10 mi. E of Sault Ste. Marie and E of Sugar Isl.; c.11 mi. long, 2–5 mi. wide; traversed by international line. **4** In NE N.Y., long narrow lake (33 mi. long, 1–3 mi. wide) in foothills of the Adirondacks, S of L. Champlain, into which it drains through short outlet; its beautiful scenery and many isls. make it center of resort area. Lake George village is at S end, and Bolton Landing is on W shore; there are several state camp sites. Area was a battleground in the French and Indian War and in the Revolution; vestiges of Fort George (1759), in Lake George Battleground Park, and of Fort William Henry (1755) are at S end.

George Air Force Base, Calif.: see VICTORVILLE.

George Bay, inlet (20 mi. long, 20 mi. wide at entrance) of the Gulf of St. Lawrence, NE N.S., at E end of Northumberland Strait, forming SW shore of Cape Breton Isl. Strait of Canso connects it with the Atlantic.

George Bay, Tasmania: see SAINT HELEN'S.

George Bryan Coast, Antarctica, along S shore of Bellingshausen Sea, bet. 78° and 85°W. Discovered 1940 by U.S. expedition.

George V Coast, Antarctica, extends bet. 142°20'E and 153° E. Discovered by Sir Douglas Mawson, leader of 1911–14 expedition, who called it King George V Land. The South Magnetic Pole has been placed here at 70°S 148°E.

George Hill, summit (3,004 ft.) of the Alleghenies, in Garrett co., extreme NW Md., just SE of Accident.

George Land, island in W Franz Josef Land, Russian SFSR, W of British Channel; 80 mi. long, 15–30 mi. wide; deeply indented coast; 80°30'N 48°–50°E. Formerly Prince George Land.

Georgenberg, Poland: see MIASTECZKO.

Georgensgmünd (gäōr'gŭnsgŭmünt'), village (pop. 2,853), Middle Franconia, W central Bavaria, Germany, on the Franconian Rezat where it joins the Swabian Rezat to form the Rednitz, and 4 mi. ENE of Spalt; grain, livestock.

Georgenswalde, Russian SFSR: see OTRADNOYE, Kaliningrad oblast.

Georgenthal (gäōr'gŭntäl"). **1** Village, Saxony, E central Germany: see SACHSENBERG-GEORGENTHAL. **2** Village (pop. 2,582), Thuringia, central Germany, in Thuringian Forest, 8 mi. SSW of Gotha; china mfg., wood carving. Site of institute of medical physics and technology. Climatic health resort. Has remains of 12th-cent. Cistercian monastery, destroyed 1525 in Peasants' War.

George Richards, Cape, N extremity of Melville Isl., W central Franklin Dist., Northwest Territories, on Hazen Strait; 76°50'N 109°10'W.

George River, N Que., rises N of Michikamau L., on Labrador border, flows 365 mi. NW, through Indian House L., to Ungava Bay 80 mi. NE of Fort Chimo.

Georges Clemenceau (zhôrzh' klŭmäsō'), village (pop. 620), Oran dept., NW Algeria, 8 mi. SSW of Mostaganem; vineyards.

Georges Islands, Knox co., S Maine, group in Muscongus Bay, SW of Port Clyde; include Allen (1.5 mi. long, .5 mi. wide), Burnt (.75 mi. in diameter), and smaller Benner, Davis, and Thompson isls.

George VI Sound, Antarctica, separates Alexander I Isl. from base of Palmer Peninsula, in 72°S 68°W. Discovered 1935 by Lincoln Ellsworth, and explored 1936–37 by Br. expedition, which named it.

Georges Mills, resort village, Sullivan co., W N.H., in Sunapee town, at N end of L. Sunapee, 22 mi. W of Franklin.

Georges Run, village (pop. 1,261, with adjacent Deandale), Jefferson co., E Ohio, on the Mississippi, 4 mi. S of Steubenville.

Georgetown, principal settlement of ASCENSION ISLAND, dependency of St. Helena colony in S Atlantic; minor port on Clarence Bay (W shore). International cable station; has naval installations.

Georgetown. 1 Village (pop. 124), N Queensland, Australia, 175 mi. SW of Cairns; cattle. Former gold-mining center. **2** Village (pop. 298), S South Australia, 25 mi. ESE of Port Pirie; wheat, fruit; livestock.

George Town, town (pop. 445), central Bahama Isls., on E Great Exuma Isl., just above Tropic of Cancer, 140 mi. SE of Nassau; 23°30'N 75°47'W. Stock raising (sheep, goats, hogs). Has sheltered harbor. U.S. naval base was granted here 1940.

Georgetown, largest city (pop. 73,509) and ⊙ Br. Guiana and Demerara co., on the coast, on right bank of Demerara R. mouth, 200 mi. WNW of Paramaribo (Du. Guiana); 6°49'N 58°10'W. Chief port of the colony, with 1/5 of country's pop.; handles bulk of all trade. Commanding a good harbor (with dry dock) for ocean vessels, it is also a major communication center for coastal and river shipping; terminus for railroad to Rosignol (55 mi. SE); connected by ferry with Vreed-en-Hoop across Demerara R. Has a local and international airport. It exports the agr. produce of the fertile, irrigated surrounding plains (sugar, rice, tropical fruit) and the rich produce of the hinterland (timber, balata, bauxite, gold, diamonds). There are large sugar mills. A clean, well-laid-out city, with wide, tree-lined streets and intersected by many canals. Has notable Botanic Gardens. Among its fine public bldgs. are town hall, law courts, Anglican and R.C. cathedrals, mus., and library. Fort William Frederick is an old Du. fort. Tropical climate (mean temp. c.80°F.), with 2 rainy seasons, April to mid-Aug., and mid-Nov. to end of Jan. Founded by the British in 1781 and named for George III, it was largely built by the French in the 3 following years, and was then held by the Dutch, who called it Stabroek. When the British occupied the colony during Napoleonic Wars, the original name was restored (1812). East Indians, introduced as plantation workers, now form almost half of its pop. Sometimes called Demerara. With its environs, the city forms the Georgetown and East Bank dist. (□ 5.5; pop. 94,035).

Georgetown. 1 Town (pop. 2,562), S Ont., 25 mi. W of Toronto; paper milling; mfg. of electrical equipment, shoes, stockings, furniture; in dairying, sandstone-quarrying region. **2** Town (pop. 769), ⊙ Kings co., E P.E.I., on Cardigan Bay, on railroad and 30 mi. E of Charlottetown; 46°11'N 62°32'W; fishing port, with fish canneries; also ships agr. produce.

Georgetown, town (pop. 841), ⊙ MacCarthy Isl. div., E central Gambia, on MACCARTHY ISLAND in

Gambia R. (wharf and ferry), and 125 mi. E of Bathurst; peanuts, palm oil and kernels, rice. Site of prison and school.

George Town, India: see MADRAS, city.

Georgetown, town (pop. 1,462), ⊙ CAYMAN ISLANDS, dependency of Jamaica, B.W.I., on W end of Grand Cayman isl., 210 mi. WNW of Montego Bay (Jamaica); 19°17′N 81°23′W. Exports tortoise shells, sharkskins, rope, mahogany, cedar, dyewood. Caribbean meteorological station, erected in 1935.

George Town, city coextensive with **Penang** (pēnăng′) municipality (pop. 189,068), ⊙ PENANG settlement, NW Malaya, on NE Penang isl., linked by ferry services with BUTTERWORTH and PRAI, on mainland across Penang Channel; 5°25′N 100°20′E. Leading port of Federation of Malaya, exporting tin, rubber, copra; seat of resident commissioner; industry (in S suburbs) includes tin smelting, rice and coconut-oil milling, mfg. of soap, rattan and bamboo articles. Has govt. buildings, banks, European and Chinese residential sections. Pop. is 70% Chinese, 15% Indian, 10% Malay. Founded 1786, it succeeded Malacca as the leading trading center of Malay Peninsula, but declined (middle 19th cent.) in favor of Singapore, after transfer there (1836) of Straits Settlements capital. Penang harbor was raided (1915) by Ger. cruiser *Emden* and captured (Jan., 1942) by Jap. forces in Second World War.

Georgetown, town (pop. 1,119), E St. Vincent, B.W.I., 10 mi. NE of Kingstown, in agr. region (sugar cane, cotton, arrowroot); sugar mill; also mfg. of rum and molasses.

George Town, town (pop. 292), N Tasmania, 30 mi. NW of Launceston and on E shore of Tamar R. estuary; resort.

Georgetown, Tobago, B.W.I.: see MOUNT SAINT GEORGE.

Georgetown, county (□ 813; pop. 31,762), E S.C.; ⊙ Georgetown. On the coast; bounded NE by Pee Dee R., S by Santee R.; watered by Waccamaw and Black rivers; Winyah Bay in S. Formerly a region of great plantations; economy is now based on timber, agr. (grain, tobacco), dairying, fishing, tourist trade. Formed 1798.

Georgetown. 1 Mining village (pop. c.600), El Dorado co., E Calif., in the Sierra Nevada, 12 mi. N of Placerville. Was thriving gold camp in 1850s. **2** Town (pop. 329), ⊙ Clear Creek co., N central Colo., on headstream of Clear Creek, in Front Range, and 40 mi. W of Denver; alt. 8,640 ft. Gold, silver, lead, copper mines. Prior to 1878 one of most important silver camps in Colo. **3** Village (1940 pop. 1,241), Fairfield co., SW Conn., on Norwalk R. and 10 mi. N of Norwalk; wire-screen mill. Partly in Redding, Weston, and Wilton towns. **4** Town (pop. 1,923), ⊙ Sussex co., S Del., 33 mi. S of Dover; market center for farm region; sawmills. Has historic bldgs. State school for feeble-minded near by. Inc. 1869. **5** A former city of D.C., part (since 1895) of WASHINGTON, D.C. **6** Village (pop. 550), ⊙ Quitman co., SW Ga., on Chattahoochee R. and 20 mi. WNW of Cuthbert; sawmilling. **7** Village (pop. 404), Bear Lake co. SE Idaho, 18 mi. N of Paris and on Bear R.; alt. 6,006 ft.; center of agr. area. **8** City (pop. 3,294), Vermilion co., E Ill., 10 mi. S of Danville; bituminous-coal mines; agr. (corn, wheat, soybeans, truck, livestock, poultry; dairy products). Laid out 1827, inc. 1869. **9** Town (pop. 449), Floyd co., S Ind., 8 mi. W of New Albany, in agr. area. **10** City (pop. 5,516), ⊙ Scott co., N Ky., on North Branch of Elkhorn Creek and 12 mi. N of Lexington; processing center in Bluegrass agr. (burley tobacco, corn, wheat) area; limestone quarries; produces canned tomatoes, dairy products, flour, meat products, cleaned seeds; mfg. of pencils, precision tools; distillery. Seat of Georgetown Col. (Baptist; 1829). Has many fine old houses. Settled 1776 as McClelland's Station; renamed Georgetown and inc. 1790. **11** Village (pop. 355), Grant parish, central La., 30 mi. N of Alexandria. **12** Resort town (pop. 510), Sagadahoc co., SW Maine, on several isls. at mouth of the Kennebec; farming, fishing. Includes Five Islands and Robinhood villages. **13** Town (pop. 2,411), including Georgetown village (pop. 1,578), Essex co., NE Mass., 9 mi. E of Lawrence; shoe mfg. Settled 1639, inc. 1838. **14** Village (pop. 192), Clay co., W Minn., on Red R. at mouth of Buffalo R., and 14 mi. N of Fargo, N.Dak., in grain area. **15** Town (pop. 327), Copiah co., SW Miss., 30 mi. S of Jackson, near Pearl R., in agr. and timber area. **16** Village (pop. 2,200), ⊙ Brown co., SW Ohio, 36 mi. SE of Cincinnati and on small White Oak Creek; trade center for agr. area (tobacco); makes shoes, monuments, flour. Laid out 1819. Boyhood home of Ulysses S. Grant is here; his birthplace (at POINT PLEASANT) is W. **17** Borough (pop. 246), Beaver co., W Pa., on Ohio R. and 4 mi. E of East Liverpool, Ohio. **18** Village (1940 pop. 5,085), Luzerne co., NE central Pa., just S of Wilkes-Barre, in anthracite region. **19** City (pop. 6,004), ⊙ Georgetown co., E S.C., 55 mi. NE of Charleston, at head of Winyah Bay (c.15 mi. from the Atlantic), where 4 rivers (Pee Dee, Waccamaw, Black, and Sampit) enter the bay. Year-round resort (yachting), port of entry, and lumber-shipping port; mills process lumber, pulp, paper, chemicals; fishing, dairying. Settled in early 18th cent.; flourished for a time as exporter of rice, indigo, and naval stores to Great Britain and the West Indies. Has church dating from 1740s and other fine old bldgs. **20** City (pop. 4,951), ⊙ Williamson co., central Texas, at junction of North and South forks to form San Gabriel R., and 25 mi. N of Austin; market for ranches to W (wool, mohair), farms to S and E (cotton, grain, dairy products, poultry); cottonseed-oil, feed, cheese, packed poultry. Seat of Southwestern Univ. Founded 1848, inc. 1871.

Georgetown Lake, SW Mont., in Granite and Deer Lodge counties, 15 mi. WNW of Anaconda; artificial lake (3 mi. long, 3 mi. max. width) fed by Flint Creek. Fish hatchery here.

George Washington Birthplace National Monument (393.7 acres; established 1930), in Westmoreland co., E Va., on Potomac R. and c.30 mi. ESE of Fredericksburg. Memorial bldg. (completed 1931) on site of "Wakefield" (Washington's birthplace and early childhood home, destroyed by fire c.1779) is designed and furnished in style of 18th-cent. plantation home. Property includes period garden and burial ground of Washington's family.

George Washington Bridge, SE N.Y., vehicular suspension bridge over the Hudson bet. upper Manhattan borough of New York city and Fort Lee, N.J. Constructed 1927–31, improved 1939–40; main span is 3,500 ft. long and 250 ft. above the water. Noted for its beauty, it is one of longest of its type.

George Washington Memorial Parkway, Md. and Va.: see NATIONAL CAPITAL PARKS.

George West, city (pop. 1,533), ⊙ Live Oak co., S Texas, on Nueces R. and 24 mi. W of Beeville, in cotton, grain, cattle area. Mfg. (tile, solvents). Inc. after 1940.

George Wright, Fort, Wash.: see SPOKANE, city.

Georgia or **Georgian Soviet Socialist Republic,** Armenian *Vrastan* (vrä′stän), Georgian *Sakartvelo* (säkärt′vĕlô), Rus. *Gruziya* (grōō′zēŭ), Turkish *Gürcistan* (gür′jĕstän″), constituent republic (□ 29,-400; 1947 pop. estimate 3,555,000) of the USSR, in W Transcaucasia; ⊙ Tiflis (Tbilisi). Bounded by Black Sea (W), Turkey and Armenia (S), Azerbaijan (E), Russian SFSR (N). Includes Abkhaz and Adzhar Autonomous SSRs and South Ossetian Autonomous Oblast. Since 1944, it extends across the main Caucasus crest to Klukhori and Akhalkhevi. Situated largely on S slopes of the Greater Caucasus, on the Lesser Caucasus, and in the intervening Rion and Kura valleys (separated by Surami Range); includes a great variety of natural regions, ranging from humid, subtropical Black Sea lowland to dry E Kura steppes. Principal rivers, fed by high rainfall and by Caucasus snow and glaciers, and activating major hydroelectric stations (in italics), are: Gumista (*Sukhumges*), Kodor, Ingur, Rion (*Rionges*), and Adzharis-Tskhali (*Atsges*) rivers (in Black Sea drainage area) and Kura (*Zages*) and Khram (*Khramges*) rivers (in Caspian drainage area). Irrigation schemes exist in dry Alazan, Iora, and Kura river valleys. Although well forested in higher altitudes (mainly W), Georgia does not have an important lumber industry (except paper milling at Zugdidi). Mineral wealth includes manganese (leading USSR mines at Chiatura; ferromanganese plant at Zestafoni), bituminous coal (Tkibuli, Tkvarcheli), lignite (Akhaltsikhe), petroleum (Mirzaani), barite, andesite, Glauber's salt, rare metals, and building stone. Major industries are ferrous metallurgy (pig iron, ingot and rolled steel products and tubing at Rustavi), mfg. (automobiles, machines for coal-mining and agr.-processing industries), cement (Kaspi). Numerous health resorts (Borzhomi, Abastumani, Tskhaltubo, Teberda). Main economic regions are: humid subtropical Black Sea lowland (COLCHIS), with yearly rainfall of over 100 in. and red lateritic soils (citrus and other fruit, tea; tung, camphor, eucalyptus, and essential oils; ramie, tobacco, silk); Imeretia, with coal and manganese mines; Kakhetia, chief Georgian wine dist. The republic's exports (manganese, petroleum products, tobacco, citrus fruit, wine, tea) are shipped via Batum, Poti, and Sukhumi, main ports on Black Sea. Communications with rest of USSR are by Black Sea coastal railroad via Sukhumi, by rail via Baku, and by Georgian (bus service), Ossetian, and Sukhumi military roads across the Greater Caucasian crest. Principal cities are Tiflis (mfg. and educational center), Kutaisi, Batum, Rustavi, Gori, Poti, Chiatura, and Sukhumi. Pop. is ⅔ Georgian; minorities are Armenians (mainly in Tiflis), Azerbaijani Turks, Ossetians, Russians, Adzhar, Abkhaz, and Greeks. Georgia is divided administratively into independent cities and *raions* (*rayons*). Known by Greeks and Romans as Colchis (W) and Iberia (E), Georgia developed as a kingdom around Kartlia and Kakhetia as a nucleus, including at various times Abkhazia, Svanetia, Mingrelia, Imeretia, and Guria. Had (12th–13th cent.) its greatest expansion; after the Mongol conquest, fell apart (15th cent.) into its constituent principalities, which were vassals (until 18th cent.) of Persia and Turkey. E Georgia (Kartlia and Kakhetia) and W Georgia passed to Russia in 1800–01 and 1803–10 respectively. Until Bolshevik revolution, Georgia was divided into Tiflis and Kutais govts. and into Kars govt. (annexed 1829, 1878 from Turkey; returned 1921). Following civil war (1917–21), Georgian SSR was constituted (1921), joined (1922) the USSR as a member of Transcaucasian SFSR; became (1936) a separate constituent republic. Stalin, a native of Georgia, was born in Gori.

Georgia, state (land only □ 58,518; with inland waters □ 58,876; 1950 pop. 3,444,578; 1940 pop. 3,123,723), SE U.S., bordered by N.C. and Tenn. (N), S.C. (E), Atlantic Ocean (SE), Fla. (S), and Ala. (W); 20th in area, 13th in pop.; one of the original 13 colonies, the 1st southern state to ratify the Constitution; ⊙ Atlanta. Ga. is the largest state (320 mi. long N–S; 254 mi. wide E–W) E of the Mississippi. It rises gradually from the Atlantic to the Appalachians in broad steps: the low coastal plain (c.60% of the area), the hilly piedmont (c.30% of the area; 500–1,500 ft. high), and the mountain region (c.10% of the area), rising to 4,784 ft. in BRASSTOWN BALD (NE), highest point in the state. The coastal plain is largely covered by pine forests, with a flat, swampy and sparsely settled tidewater area in the E where oak, cypress, palmetto, and magnolia trees are found, and OKEFENOKEE SWAMP in the SE. The estuary-indented shore line (c.100 mi. long) is bordered by the SEA ISLANDS, which enclose narrow channels traversed by the Intracoastal Waterway. Bet. the coastal plain and the piedmont is the fall line, crossing the state from Augusta (E) to Columbus (W). Below the fall line is a narrow sand-hill belt. In the piedmont are STONE MOUNTAIN (1,686 ft.) and Kennesaw Mtn. (1,809 ft.), near Atlanta, and here are red clay and sandy loam soils, and pine and hardwood (oak, gum, hickory, beech) forests. The mtn. region, largely in Chattahoochee Natl. Forest, contains the E Appalachian chain in the NE (the Blue Ridge terminates here at Mt. Oglethorpe); part of the Great Appalachian Valley in the NW; and a small portion of the Cumberland Plateau (Lookout and Sand mts.) in the extreme NW. The Blue Ridge has here an average elevation of 3,000 ft. Its narrow river valleys are characterized by many falls, including AMICALOLA FALLS. The area is heavily forested (oak, poplar, hickory, beech, pine, hemlock). The valley and ridge area of the Great Appalachian Valley and the adjacent Cumberland Plateau area are mainly forested in pines. Of the state's many rivers, the Savannah, Ogeechee, Altamaha, Saint Marys, and Satilla flow to the Atlantic; the Alapaha, Chattahoochee, Flint, and Etowah flow S and SW into systems entering the Gulf of Mexico; and the Nottely and Hiwassee flow NW into the Tennessee R. system. With few exceptions, state's lakes (mostly in mts. and piedmont) are formed by power dams; they include lakes Chatuge, Nottely, Burton, Rabun, Blue Ridge, Allatoona, Clark Hill, and Lloyd Shoals. WARM SPRINGS is the state's most famous mineral spring. Ga. has a humid subtropical climate characterized by hot summers (average temp. 78°F.) and mild winters (average temp. 44°F.), with only a few inches of snowfall in the mountains and piedmont. The annual precipitation, highest (up to c.75 inches) in the extreme NE Blue Ridge, averages c.50 inches, with spring and fall relatively dry. There is a long growing season, ranging (N to S) from 200 to 250 days, except in the mts. (c.180 days). Farming and mfg. are the primary bases of the state's economy. Erosion (especially in the piedmont) and soil depletion (necessitating much fertilizer) are major problems; 17% of the state's area is severely eroded. Corn (a major food staple) occupies the largest acreage, but cotton, peanuts, and tobacco are the chief cash crops. Ga. leads the U.S. in peanut and pecan production and ranks high in peaches and some truck crops (watermelons, pimento peppers, velvet beans, sweet potatoes). Grains (oats, barley), hay, and apples are also grown. Corn and cotton are raised throughout much of the state; tobacco, peanuts, pecans, and some truck crops come chiefly from the coastal plain. Livestock raising (hogs, cattle, poultry) is widespread. Principal industries are cotton milling (cloth, tire cord fabric, yarn, thread, clothing, hosiery, bedspreads) and wood processing (lumber, paper and pulp, furniture, boxes, naval stores); forests, chiefly pine, cover c.⅔ of the state. Ga. produces c.75% of U.S. naval stores (c.50% of world production) and tire cord. Other important industries are food processing (pimento and sea food canning, meat packing, dairying), metal fabricating (machinery, motor vehicles, foundry products), fertilizer mixing, brick and tile mfg., and mining. Ga. is nation's chief producer of kaolin (c.70% of U.S. total) and fuller's earth, and ranks 2d in granite and barite; other important minerals are marble and bauxite. Iron and coal are mined in small quantities. Atlanta is the South's chief rail center. The piedmont is the principal mfg. area, with numerous textile mills (at Atlanta, Athens, La Grange,

Gainesville, Griffin, Monroe, and Newman), metal-working and food-processing plants, and lumber mills. The state's chief granite belt is here, extending from Elbert co. on the S.C. line (E) to the Ala. line (W), with Elberton and Lithonia the major centers. Along the fall line the major cities—AUGUSTA, COLUMBUS, MACON, and MILLEDGEVILLE—are cotton-milling, clay-mining, and brick and tile mfg. centers. The coastal plain is the center of the naval-stores industry and an important lumbering and agr. area. The principal towns of the upper coastal plain—Waycross, Valdosta, Moultrie, Fitzgerald, Thomasville, Cordele, Americus, and Dublin—are tobacco markets and wood- and peanut-processing centers. Albany and Dawson are major peanut and pecan markets. Bauxite is mined at Andersonville. On coast, Savannah, the chief naval-stores market in the world, and Brunswick are seaports and industrial and fishing centers. In the Blue Ridge the principal towns are Toccoa (industrial), Clayton and Blue Ridge (resorts), Tate (marble quarrying), and Dahlonega (gold mining). In the valley and ridge area are Rome (industrial), Cartersville (barite mining and textile mfg.), Dalton, Cedartown, Calhoun, Canton, and Lafayette. The state's institutions of higher learning include the Univ. of Georgia (at Athens), Georgia Institute of Technology and Emory Univ. (at Atlanta), and Mercer Univ. (at Macon). Ga. was crossed by Hernando De Soto in 1540, and the Spanish later established missions and garrisons in the Sea Isls. The English, under James Oglethorpe, founded Savannah, the 1st town, in 1733. He ended the long rivalry for the region bet. the Spanish and English by winning the battle of Bloody Marsh on SAINT SIMONS ISLAND in 1742. By 1754 Ga. became a royal colony; it exported rice, indigo, skins, lumber, naval stores, and meat to England. During the Revolution the British took most of the important towns. In 1802, Ga. assumed its present boundaries and in the 1830s the Creek and Cherokee Indians were moved out of the state. The widespread adoption of the cotton gin, invented here in 1793 by Eli Whitney, greatly increased the demand for Negro slaves, and strengthened the plantation system. In the Civil War, the state suffered great devastation during Sherman's march from Atlanta to Savannah. After the war, the breakdown of the plantation system brought a widespread system of farm tenancy. By the turn of the century, agr. still presented many problems, but mfg. had become well established in the piedmont. The coming of the cotton boll weevil after the First World War resulted in needed crop diversification, which firmly established such important crops as tobacco, peanuts, and peaches, and promoted livestock raising. In the Second World War, Fort Benning (near Columbus) was a major military training center and many new camps were established. In 1945 a new constitution was adopted; it confirmed earlier reforms, notably those concerning the notorious penal system. In 1946 thousands of Negroes (c.⅓ of the pop.) voted (on the strength of a U.S. Supreme Court decision) for the 1st time in the Democratic primary. See also the articles on the cities, towns, geographic features, and 159 counties: APPLING, ATKINSON, BACON, BAKER, BALDWIN, BANKS, BARROW, BARTOW, BEN HILL, BERRIEN, BIBB, BLECKLEY, BRANTLEY, BROOKS, BRYAN, BULLOCH, BURKE, BUTTS, CALHOUN, CAMDEN, CANDLER, CARROLL, CATOOSA, CHARLTON, CHATHAM, CHATTAHOOCHEE, CHATTOOGA, CHEROKEE, CLARKE, CLAY, CLAYTON, CLINCH, COBB, COFFEE, COLQUITT, COLUMBIA, COOK, COWETA, CRAWFORD, CRISP, DADE, DAWSON, DECATUR, DE KALB, DODGE, DOOLY, DOUGHERTY, DOUGLAS, EARLY, ECHOLS, EFFINGHAM, ELBERT, EMANUEL, EVANS, FANNIN, FAYETTE, FLOYD, FORSYTH, FRANKLIN, FULTON, GILMER, GLASCOCK, GLYNN, GORDON, GRADY, GREENE, GWINNETT, HABERSHAM, HALL, HANCOCK, HARALSON, HARRIS, HART, HEARD, HENRY, HOUSTON, IRWIN, JACKSON, JASPER, JEFF DAVIS, JEFFERSON, JENKINS, JOHNSON, JONES, LAMAR, LANIER, LAURENS, LEE, LIBERTY, LINCOLN, LONG, LOWNDES, LUMPKIN, MCDUFFIE, MCINTOSH, MACON, MADISON, MARION, MERIWETHER, MILLER, MITCHELL, MONROE, MONTGOMERY, MORGAN, MURRAY, MUSCOGEE, NEWTON, OCONEE, OGLETHORPE, PAULDING, PEACH, PICKENS, PIERCE, PIKE, POLK, PULASKI, PUTNAM, QUITMAN, RABUN, RANDOLPH, RICHMOND, ROCKDALE, SCHLEY, SCREVEN, SEMINOLE, SPALDING, STEPHENS, STEWART, SUMTER, TALBOT, TALIAFERRO, TATTNALL, TAYLOR, TELFAIR, TERRELL, THOMAS, TIFT, TOOMBS, TOWNS, TREUTLEN, TROUP, TURNER, TWIGGS, UNION, UPSON, WALKER, WALTON, WARE, WARREN, WASHINGTON, WAYNE, WEBSTER, WHEELER, WHITE, WHITFIELD, WILCOX, WILKES, WILKINSON, WORTH.

Georgia, town (pop. 1,055), Franklin co., NW Vt., just S of St. Albans, on L. Champlain; agr. Chartered 1763.

Georgia, Strait of, channel (150 mi. long, 20–40 mi. wide) bet. mainland of British Columbia and Vancouver Isl., connecting Queen Charlotte Sound (via Discovery Passage and Johnstone Strait) with Puget Sound and Juan de Fuca Strait. Forms part of the inland water route to Alaska. Contains numerous isls., notably Texada and Gulf Isls. The mainland is deeply indented with inlets and sounds. Much fishing in the strait. Locally called The Gulf.

Georgiana, town (pop. 1,596), Butler co., S central Ala., 15 mi. SSW of Greenville, in cotton and truck area; lumber milling. Settled 1824, inc. 1869.

Georgian Bay, NE arm (120 mi. long, 65 mi. wide) of L. Huron, S central Ont., separated from main part of lake by Saugeen Peninsula and Manitoulin Isl. Coastline is indented by Owen Sound, Parry Sound, Nottawasaga Bay, and other inlets. On SE shore are numerous summer resorts. Bay is joined with L. Ontario by inland water route via Severn R., L. Simcoe, and Trent Canal.

Georgian Bay Islands National Park (□ 5.37), S central Ont., comprises 30 small isls. in Georgian Bay, NE of Midland; recreational area. Noted limestone formations and caves. Established 1929.

Georgian Military Road, 133-mi. automobile highway across the Greater Caucasus, linking Tiflis (Georgia) and Dzaudzhikau (Russian SFSR). Follows Terek and Aragva river valleys, passing through Daryal Gorge and crossing the Caucasian crest at Pass of the Cross at 7,815 ft. Main way stations are Kazbeg (at E foot of Mt. Kazbek), Pasanauri, and Mtskheta.

Georgiaville, R.I.: see SMITHFIELD.

Georgiye-Osetinskoye, Russian SFSR: see KOSTA-KHETAGUROVO, Stavropol Territory.

Georgiyevka (gēôr'gēŭfkŭ). **1** Village (1948 pop. over 2,000), SE Dzhambul oblast, Kazakh SSR, on Chu R., near Kirghiz SSR border, and 10 mi. N of Frunze; irrigated agr. (wheat, tobacco); limestone quarrying; cement mfg. Just SE, on Chu R., is Chumysh Dam, head of Atbashi (left) and Georgiyevka irrigation canals. **2** Village (1939 pop. over 2,000), E Semipalatinsk oblast, Kazakh SSR, 16 mi. NE of Zhangis-Tobe. **3** Village (1939 pop. over 500), S South Kazakhstan oblast, Kazakh SSR, 20 mi. ESE of Chimkent; cotton; orchards. **4** Town (pop. over 2,000), S Voroshilovgrad oblast, Ukrainian SSR, in the Donbas, 10 mi. SSW of Voroshilovgrad; coal mines.

Georgiyevsk (gēôr'gēŭfsk), city (1926 pop. 22,597), S Stavropol Territory, Russian SFSR, on Podkumok R. and 85 mi. SE of Stavropol, in N foothills of the Greater Caucasus. Rail (freight yards) and agr. center; junction of railroad to Budennovsk; produces flour, sunflower oil, meat, dairy and canned goods; machine mfg. (armatures). Founded 1777 as Rus. fortress. By agreement signed here (1783) Georgia became vassal of Russia.

Georgiyevskoye (–skŭyŭ), village (1926 pop. 483), E central Kostroma oblast, Russian SFSR, 28 mi. NNE of Manturovo; flax.

Georgsdorf (gāôrks'dôrf), village (pop. 742), in former Prussian prov. of Hanover, NW Germany, after 1945 in Lower Saxony, at junction of Süd-Nord and Coevorden-Piccardie canals, 9 mi. N of Nordhorn; oil wells.

Georgsmarienhütte (gāôrks'mär'ē'ünhü"tŭ), village (pop. 5,760), in former Prussian prov. of Hanover, NW Germany, after 1945 in Lower Saxony, on N slope of Teutoburg Forest, 5 mi. S of Osnabrück; foundries. Until 1937, Georgs Marien Hütte.

Georgswalde, Czechoslovakia: see JIRIKOV.

Ger, Pic de (pēk dü zhâr'), summit (8,569 ft.) of central Pyrenees, Basses-Pyrénées dept., SW France, 5 mi. SE of Laruns; winter sports area. At its foot lies Les Eaux-Bonnes.

Gera (gā'rä), city (pop. 89,212), Thuringia, central Germany, on the White Elster and 35 mi. SSW of Leipzig; 50°53'N 12°6'E. Rail junction; woolen-milling center; textile dyeing and printing, metal- and woodworking; mfg. of carpets, machinery, chemicals, pharmaceuticals, glass, paper, leather, furniture. Has 16th-cent. town hall; Trinity Church (1611); Osterstein palace (1686–1735), on site of earlier fortress; old orphanage (1738), now mus. Airfield (N). First mentioned 995; chartered 1224. Largely destroyed by fire in 1780. Was ⊙ principality of Reuss Younger Line until 1918.

Geraardsbergen, Belgium: see GRAMMONT.

Geraberg (gā'räbĕrk"), village (pop. 3,674), Thuringia, central Germany, on N slope of Thuringian Forest, on Gera R. and 4 mi. NW of Ilmenau; glass mfg., woodworking. Has 18th-cent. church.

Gerabronn (gā'räbrôn"), town (pop. 2,254), N Württemberg, Germany, after 1945 in Württemberg-Baden, 10 mi. NW of Crailsheim; grain.

Gerace (jĕrä'chĕ), town (pop. 2,675), Reggio di Calabria prov., Calabria, S Italy, 4 mi. NW of Locri; olive oil, wine, raw silk. Hot mineral baths near by. Bishopric. Has cathedral consecrated 1045 (restored). Damaged by earthquakes of 1783, 1907, 1908. Formerly Gerace Superiore.

Gerace Marina, Italy: see LOCRI.

Gerace Superiore, Italy: see GERACE.

Geraci Siculo (jĕrä'chē sē'kōōlō), village (pop. 3,737), Palermo prov., N central Sicily, in Madonie Mts., 14 mi. SSE of Cefalù; agr. tools, macaroni.

Gerakine or **Yerakini** (both: yĕrŭkēnē'), village (1928 pop. 303), Chalcidice nome, Macedonia, Greece, 7 mi. S of Polygyros, at head of Toronic Gulf of Aegean Sea; magnesite and chrome mining.

Gerakovouni, Greece: see OTHRYS.

Geral, Serra (sĕ'rŭ zhĭräl'). **1** In S Brazil, name given to the S and E edge of the unbroken Paraná plateau. It is a diabase cuesta extending E-W across N central Rio Grande do Sul, abutting on the Serra do Mar (coastal escarpment) in SE Santa Catarina, then stretching generally NNW across central Paraná and into São Paulo (where it is known as the Serra de Botucatu). Its numerous ramifications provide the principal relief features of the interior of the S states. **2** Range, in Piauí and Ceará, NE Brazil: see GRANDE, SERRA.

Gerald, town (pop. 429), Franklin co., E central Mo., in Ozark region, 20 mi. SW of Washington; grain products, livestock; fire-clay pits.

Gerald, Ostrov, or **Ostrov Geral'da,** Russian SFSR: see HERALD ISLAND.

Geral de Goiás, Serra (sĕ'rŭ zhĭräl' dĭ goi-äs'), mtn. range of central Brazil, forms Goiás-Bahia border for 300 mi. bet. 10°30'S and 15°S, and divides drainage basins of Tocantins R. (W) and São Francisco R. (E). Max. alt. 3,000 ft. Component ranges are, N-S: Serra do Duro, Serra Taguatinga, and Serra de São Domingos. Some gold deposits.

Geraldine, borough (pop. 924), ⊙ Geraldine co. (□ 690; pop. 5,255), E S.Isl., New Zealand, 80 mi. SW of Christchurch; agr. center; dairy; linen mill.

Geraldine, town (pop. 374), Chouteau co., N central Mont., 50 mi. E of Great Falls; grain, livestock.

Geraldton, municipality and port (pop. 5,972), W Western Australia, 230 mi. NNW of Perth and on Champion Bay of Geelvink Channel; 28°47'S 114°37'E. Port for Murchison Goldfield; rail center; superphosphate works, brewery, crayfish cannery. Subtropical tourist resort.

Geraldton, town (pop. 2,979), W central Ont., 140 mi. NE of Port Arthur; lumbering. Inc. 1937.

Geraneia or **Yerania** (both: yĕrä'nēŭ), mountain on Megaris Peninsula, E central Greece, rises to 4,431 ft. 12 mi. NE of Corinth. Formerly Makryplagi.

Gérardmer (zhārärmā'), town (pop. 3,368), Vosges dept., E France, at E end of L. of Gérardmer (1½ mi. long, ½ mi. wide), 14 mi. SSW of Saint-Dié, in the Vosges; alt. 2,200 ft. Linen-milling center (table cloths, handkerchiefs), also known for its *Gérомé* cheese. Sawmilling, brush and felt mfg. A noted tourist center, it was almost completely destroyed in Second World War. Bet. Gérardmer and the Col de la SCHLUCHT are smaller lakes of Longemer and Retournemer.

Gera River (gā'rä), central Germany, rises in Thuringian Forest WSW of Ilmenau, flows 40 mi. generally N, past Geraberg, Arnstadt, and Erfurt, to the Unstrut 11 mi. NNW of Erfurt.

Gerasa, Jordan: see JERASH.

Gerasdorf (gā'räsdôrf), town (pop. 2,802), after 1938 in Floridsdorf dist. of Vienna, Austria, 7.5 mi. NE of city center; orchards, vegetables.

Gerash, Jordan: see JERASH.

Gerba, Tunisia, see DJERBA.

Gerber (gûr'bŭr), village (1940 pop. 508), Tehama co., N Calif., 10 mi. SSE of Red Bluff, in stock-raising and farming area; railroad shops.

Gerbéviller (zhĕrbāvēlâr'), agr. village (pop. 999), Meurthe-et-Moselle dept., NE France, on Mortagne R. and 7 mi. S of Lunéville. Completely destroyed in Aug., 1914.

Gerbier de Jonc, Mont (mõ zhĕrbyā' dŭ zhõ'), extinct volcano (5,089 ft.) in Monts du Vivarais, Ardèche dept., S France, 7 mi. N of Burzet; here rises the Loire. Sometimes spelled Gerbier de Joncs.

Gerbstedt (gĕrp'shtĕt), town (pop. 6,326), in former Prussian Saxony prov., central Germany, after 1945 in Saxony-Anhalt, 8 mi. NNE of Eisleben; copper-slate mining; mfg. of agr. machinery.

Gerce (gĕr'tsĕ), Hung. *Gérce*, town (pop. 2,002), Vas co., W Hungary, 18 mi. E of Szombathely; wine, honey, plums.

Gercus (gĕrjüsh'), Turkish *Gercüş*, village (pop. 2,328), Mardin prov., SE Turkey, 40 mi. NE of Mardin; cotton, grain.

Gerdauen, Russian SFSR; see ZHELEZNODOROZHNY, Kaliningrad oblast.

Gerdine, Mount (jûrdīn') (12,600 ft.), S Alaska, in Alaska Range, 90 mi. WNW of Anchorage; 61°35'N 152°29'W.

Gerecse Mountains (gĕ'rĕ-chĕ), N Hungary, extend from Tata 16 mi. E along the Danube; average alt. 1,800 ft.; forested slopes; quarries of red marble and basalt; lignite deposits.

Gerede (gĕrĕdĕ'), village (pop. 4,012), Bolu prov., NW Turkey, 31 mi. ENE of Bolu; grain, flax, mohair goats.

Gerede River, Turkey: see YENICE RIVER.

Geremoabo, Brazil: see JEREMOABO.

Gerena (hārā'nä), town (pop. 3,801), Seville prov., SW Spain, on railroad and 12 mi. NW of Seville; agr. (cereals, chick-peas, tubers, alfalfa, olives, acorns, livestock). Apiculture; sawmilling.

Geresik, Indonesia: see GRESIK.

Gérgal (hĕr'gäl), town (pop. 1,816), Almería prov., S Spain, 20 mi. N of Almería; olive-oil processing, flour milling; wine, esparto, grapes and other fruit. Lead mines in dist. (aerial tramway). Has Moorish castle.

Gergebil or **Gergebil'** (gyĕrgyĭbēl'), village (1939 pop. over 500), central Dagestan Autonomous SSR, Russian SFSR, in the E Greater Caucasus, on right affluent (Kara Koisu; hydroelectric station) of the Avar Koisu and 23 mi. S of Buinaksk, in fruit-growing area; fruit canning. Limestone quarrying. Pop. largely Avar.

Gergei (jĕrjä′), village (pop. 1,925), Nuoro prov., S central Sardinia, 34 mi. N of Cagliari. Nuraghe near by.

Gergovie, Plateau (plätō″ zhĕrgōvē′), volcanic terrace in the Monts Dôme, Puy-de-Dôme dept., central France, overlooking the Limagne, 4 mi. SSE of Clermont-Ferrand. Here, during siege (53 B.C.) of the Gaulish oppidum of Gergovia, Vercingetorix succeeded in fighting off Caesar's army.

Gergy (zhĕrzhē′), village (pop. 678), Saône-et-Loire dept., E central France, on Saône R. and 8 mi. NE of Chalon-sur-Saône; wood and metal engraving.

Gerhardus, Mount, Hungary: see Gellert, Mount.

Gerihun (gĕrēhōōn′), village (pop. 1,038), South-Western Prov., S central Sierra Leone, on railroad and 10 mi. E of Bo; palm oil and kernels, cacao, coffee.

Gerindote (hārĭndō′tā), town (pop. 2,000), Toledo prov., central Spain, 16 mi. WNW of Toledo; olive-oil pressing. Exports wool.

Gering (gēr′ĭng), city (pop. 3,842), ⊙ Scotts Bluff co., W Nebr., just S of Scottsbluff across N. Platte R. Railroad div. point, trade center for irrigated agr. area. Bricks and tiles, beet sugar; dairy, meat, and poultry products, grain. Oregon Trail Days, pageant celebrating movement W of pioneers, held here annually. Scotts Bluff Natl. Monument near by. Founded 1887, inc. 1890.

Geringswalde (gä″rĭngsväl′dů), town (pop. 4,910), Saxony, E central Germany, 10 mi. WSW of Döbeln; hosiery and glove knitting; mfg. of furniture, tools, cosmetics.

Gerizim, Mount (gĕ′rĭzĭm, gērī′zĭm), Arabic *Jebel et Tur* or *Jebel et Tor*, peak (2,890 ft.) of Palestine, after 1948 in W Jordan, in Samarian Hills, just SE of Nablus. Here are remains of anc. temple destroyed (c.130 B.C.) by Maccabeans, of castle built by Justinian, and of 5th-cent. Byzantine church. Summit was scene of traditional Samaritan Passover rites.

Gerko, Nigeria: see Garko.

Gerlach or **Gerlachovka,** peak, Czechoslovakia: see Stalin Peak.

Gerlach (gûr′lăk, –läk), village (pop. c.500), Washoe co., NW Nev., in SW tip of Black Rock Desert, 80 mi. NNE of Reno; railroad division point; gypsum products.

Gerlafingen (gĕr′läfĭng-ůn), town (pop. 3,230), Solothurn canton, NW Switzerland, on Emme R. and 3 mi. SSE of Solothurn; metal products.

Gerlan, Wales: see Bethesda.

Gerli (hĕr′lē), industrial town (pop. estimate 25,000) in Greater Buenos Aires, Argentina, adjoining Lanús, 4 mi. S of Buenos Aires; machinery, textiles, paper, lime; sawmills.

Gerlingen (gĕr′lĭng-ůn), village (pop. 4,631), N Württemberg, Germany, after 1945 in Württemberg-Baden, 5 mi. WNW of Stuttgart; grain, cattle.

Gerlogubi (gĕr′lōgōōbē), Ital. *Gherlogubi,* village, Harar prov., SE Ethiopia, in the Ogaden, 20 mi. WSW of Wardere; nomadic stock raising (camels, sheep).

Gerlos Pass (gĕr′lōs) (alt. 4,874 ft.), W Austria, bet. Kitzbühel and Zillertal Alps, connects Tyrol and Salzburg provinces. Small hydroelectric station near by on short Gerlos R.

Gerlsdorfer Spitze, Czechoslovakia: see Stalin Peak.

Germa or **Djerma** (jĕr′mä), village (pop. 118), central Fezzan, Libya, 70 mi. NW of Murzuk, in an oasis (dates). Has Roman ruins (fort, walls, mausoleum).

German East Africa: see Tanganyika.

Germania (hĕrmä′nyä), village (dist. pop. 1,029), Limón prov., E Costa Rica, 5 mi. NW of Siquirres, on railroad; rubber, abacá, bananas. Pop. is largely Negro.

Germania Land, ice-free peninsula, NE Greenland; extends 40 mi. E into Greenland Sea; 77°7′N 19°40′W. Forms N shore of Dove Bay.

Germán Jordan, Bolivia: see Cliza.

German New Guinea: see New Guinea, Territory of.

Germannsdorf (gĕr′mänsdôrf′), village (pop. 1,622), Lower Bavaria, Germany, in Bohemian Forest, 10 mi. ENE of Passau; graphite mining.

German Ocean: see North Sea.

Germanton, town (pop. 118), Stokes co., N N.C., 10 mi. N of Winston-Salem.

Germantown. 1 Village (pop. 811), Clinton co., SW Ill., 21 mi. W of Centralia, in agr. area. **2** Town (pop. 260), Bracken and Mason counties, N Ky., 11 mi. W of Maysville, in outer Bluegrass region. Annual (Aug.) fair and horse show dates from 1854. **3** Suburb of Annapolis, Anne Arundel co., central Md. There is also a village called Germantown in Montgomery co. **4** Village (pop. 2,478), Montgomery co., W Ohio, 12 mi. SW of Dayton and on small Twin Creek; tobacco market. Rendering plant; mfg. of millwork, machinery, tobacco boxes. Laid out 1814. **5** NW residential section of Philadelphia, Pa. Settled by Germans c.1683, laid out 1684, inc. 1689, annexed by Philadelphia 1854. It was an early center of printing and publishing. Washington defeated here, 1777. Howe House and several other colonial buildings are standing. **6** Town (pop. 408), Shelby co., SW Tenn., 12 mi. E of Memphis. **7** Village (pop. 357), Washington co., SE Wis., near Menomonee R. 16 mi. NNW of Milwaukee; dairy products, canned vegetables.

German Valley, village (pop. 206), Stephenson co., N Ill., 9 mi. SE of Freeport, in agr. area; nursery.

German Volga Autonomous Soviet Socialist Republic, Rus. *Nemtsev Povolzhya ASSR,* former administrative division (□ 10,900; 1939 pop. 605,542) of S European Russian SFSR, on the lower Volga; ⊙ was Engels. Constituted in 1919 as a workers' commune and later, in 1923, as an autonomous republic, on basis of Ger. pop. descended from colonists who settled here under Catherine II. Was part of Lower Volga Territory (1928–34) and in Saratov Territory (1934–36). Unit dissolved (1941) and Ger. pop. resettled elsewhere in USSR; territory divided bet. Saratov and Stalingrad oblasts.

Germany, Ger. *Deutschland* (doich′länt), country, N central Europe, on the North Sea and the Baltic, bordered by the Netherlands, Belgium, and Luxembourg (W), France (SW), Switzerland and Austria (S), Czechoslovakia (SE, E center), Poland and the USSR (E), and Denmark (N center); largest city is Berlin. For border changes and political administration after Second World War see latter part of article. Its post-First World War area (□ 180,999; 1933 pop. 65,218,461), increased by incorporation of the Saar in 1935, Austria and the Sudetenland in 1938, and Memel in 1939 (when total area of Greater Germany was □ 226,174; 1939 pop. 79,509,315), shrank after Second World War to the region (□ 136,462; 1946 pop. 65,151,019) W of the Oder-Neisse line and excluding the Saar. Germany may be divided into 3 distinct physiographic regions: ranges of the Central Alps and uplands (S), the Hercynian massif (center), and lowlands (N). The climate is temperate maritime in W and S, humid continental in E and central sections. Temperature range increases W-E, but N-S differences are almost negligible because of greater elevation in S. Mean annual temperature is 48°F., average rainfall 27 in.; warmest region is upper Rhine plain. Almost ⅔ of the country's extensive forests are coniferous; among the broadleafs, beech predominates. Germany is predominantly industrial, with rich natural resources (especially coal, lignite, salt, peat); however, both the metal and textile industries depend largely on foreign raw materials. The 4 major industrial regions (Rhine-Main, Rhenish-Westphalian, central German, Saxonian) are located in the Hercynian massif. The extensive use of fertilizer (made predominantly from local potash supplies) and the govt.'s vigorous encouragement of the use of scientific farming methods have resulted in large yields per acre from the generally poor soil. Before Second World War Germany was c.80% self-sufficient in agr. produce. Among the major rivers only the Danube, draining the S uplands, flows SE (to Black Sea); the Rhine, Ems, Weser, and Elbe flow N into the North Sea, the Oder into the Baltic. An extensive canal system (e.g., Mittelland Canal, Berlin-Stettin Canal) covers N Germany, connecting the natural N-S trade routes in E-W direction, thus linking the rest of Germany with the major ports. The rail net is most dense in North Rhine–Westphalia, in Saxony, and in and around Berlin. As of 1933 about 64% of the Germans were Lutheran Protestants, most of the rest being Roman Catholics. Catholicism is strongest in Bavaria (S) and in the Rhineland (W). The southernmost physiographic region, the S uplands, presents a predominantly agr. picture. It is bordered E by the Bohemian Forest and S by the Allgäu Alps and the Bavarian Alps (rising to 9,719 ft. in the Zugspitze, Germany's highest peak). These ranges are fronted by a plateau of very recent geologic origin, which descends gradually towards the narrow valley of the Danube. Cattle raising and dairying are the chief occupations in the Allgäu and in Upper Bavaria; tourism is also an important industry (Berchtesgaden, Garmisch-Partenkirchen, Oberammergau; numerous lakes, including the Ammersee, the Chiemsee, and the Königssee). Lower Bavaria is a major wheat-growing area of Germany; the whole state of Bavaria is Germany's major hop producer and center of the brewing industry. There are lignite mines in the Alpine foothills and also in the Upper Palatinate, whose kaolin quarries supply the noted Rosenthal porcelain factories at Kronach and Selb; large salt deposits at Berchtesgaden and Bad Reichenhall. The leading cities of the region are Aschaffenburg, Augsburg, Bamberg, Bayreuth, Constance, Fürth, Munich, Nuremberg, Regensburg, and Würzburg. Germany's central physiographic region consists of the low ranges (mostly of Mesozoic origin) which extend from the L. of Constance and the great Rhine bend at Basel (SW) to the Elbe in the E and the Mittelland Canal in the N, occupying over ⅓ of the country's area. Rye, oats, and potatoes are grown in the hilly regions; stock raising concentrates on beef cattle and hogs. Extensive viticulture on the steep slopes of the rivers (Neckar, Main, Nahe, Mosel, Ahr) in SW and W and in the mild Rhine plain (to mouth of Main R. opposite Mainz), where tobacco, corn, sugar beets, and fruit are also cultivated. The scenic Black Forest, with watch-making and wood-carving industries and tourism (Baden-Baden, Freudenstadt, Wildbad), generally follows the Rhine plain N, terminating near Pforzheim (a noted jewelry center); it is separated by the Triassic depression of the picturesque Neckar River valley from the raw Swabian Jura, which extends NE over most of Württemberg and continues beyond Ulm as the Franconian Jura in central and N Bavaria. Stuttgart, a major transportation hub and publishing center of Germany, and many smaller towns engaged in secondary industries are located bet. the 2 ranges. Further N, the densely-forested Hardt Mountains cover central section of Rhenish Palatinate; W of the Rhine the Odenwald and the Spessart occupy most of S Hesse. Here, due to the good natural transportation routes afforded by the Rhine and the Main, developed the Rhine-Main or Middle Rhine industrial region, concentrating on the mfg. of chemicals. The smallest of Germany's 4 major industrial regions, it is located bet. Karlsruhe (S) and Mainz and Frankfurt (N); includes industrial centers of Mannheim, Ludwigshafen, Offenbach, and Darmstadt, and the historic cities of Heidelberg, Speyer, and Worms. Astride the Rhine's most picturesque section, bet. Mainz and Bonn, are the Rhenish Slate Mountains, consisting primarily of folded Devonian slate. The Hunsrück and the bleak volcanic Eifel with its crater lakes, separated by Mosel R., comprise W section; E of the Rhine gorge, extending in NE direction, are the Taunus, rich in mineral springs (Wiesbaden, Bad Nauheim, Bad Homburg), the Rheingau Mountains (noted wine region), the Westerwald (iron deposits in Lahn R. and Sieg R. valleys), and the Rothaargebirge. Along the N rim of the Rhenish Slate Mts. extends Germany's major mfg. zone, the Rhenish-Westphalian industrial region. Located on both sides of the Rhine, it includes the industrial belt E and W of Düsseldorf and the Ruhr region; Aachen (SW tip) is main entry point into Germany from W Europe. W of the Rhine are the lignite fields of Cologne (the metropolis of the Rhineland), Stolberg (brass industry), and the textile centers of Krefeld, München Gladbach, and Rheydt. The Wupper, on whose middle course are Remscheid (tool mfg.), Solingen (cutlery), and Wuppertal (textiles), enters the Rhine at Leverkusen (chemicals). In the huge coal fields of the Ruhr region concentrates most of the country's steel production, with centers at Dortmund (also iron-ore mining), Duisburg (head of Rhine deep-sea navigation), and Essen. The Teutoburg Forest borders the noted Westphalian linen dist. (Bielefeld, Rheine). Central Germany (E of the Rhenish Slate Mts.) is covered by the Rhön Mountains (SW), the Hessian and Thuringian highlands (center), the Wesser Mountains (NW), the Harz (NE), and the Thuringian Forest (SE). The central German industrial region developed around the rich mines of this area. There are extensive lignite fields (NE Hesse, Halle-Merseburg-Weissenfels region), coal is mined in the Deister and near Osnabrück, large copper-slate deposits around Mansfeld, Stassfurt is major potash-mining center; exploitation of the rich iron-ore deposits of Watenstedt-Salzgitter was started in 1937. Mfg. of chemicals predominates in this region (leading industrial centers are Bitterfeld, Erfurt, Halle, Hanover, Leuna, Magdeburg), but there are also highly specialized local industries (optical instruments at Jena, locomotives at Kassel, noted Thuringian toys and glassware). Many sugar refineries bet. Brunswick and Magdeburg. The densely populated Saxonian industrial region is the 4th major mfg. zone of the country. It is located in the foothills of the highly mineralized Erzgebirge, and produces c.½ of Germany's textiles (Chemnitz, Plauen, Zittau, Zwickau). Other mfg. centers are Aue, Dresden (precision and optical instruments), Glauchau, Görlitz (railroad cars), Meissen (porcelain), and Riesa (steel). Leipzig is a seat of the publishing industry. Extensive lignite deposits S of Leipzig (Borna); coal mines around Zwickau and Dresden (Freital). E of the Elbe, separated from the Erzegebirge by the Saxonian Switzerland, are the Sudetes with the Riesengebirge. The N German lowlands, covering most of N Germany and forming part of the North European Plain, constitute the northernmost physiographic region of Germany. Predominantly agr., they are dissected in general N-S direction by Weser, Elbe, and Oder rivers. Sandy morainic soil (resulting from extensive glaciation of area during Ice Age) covers most of the lowlands, yielding large crops of potatoes (utilized to great extent in mfg. of synthetics) and sugar beets (especially E of the Elbe); extensive forests in E; lake region N of Berlin (Kummerow, Müritz, Schwerin, Werbellin). The country's best soil is in the Magdeburg basin (wheat, barley, sugar beets). Heath (Lüneburg Heath) and moors (peat-cutting) form a central belt, which is fronted by fertile coastal strip (polders along the North Sea); cattle raising (East Friesland, North Friesland) and dairying; rye and oats; truck produce along Elbe R. estuary; horse-breeding in Baltic regions. There are oil wells in the Emsland (W) and in Celle-Peine region, large salines at Lüneburg and Stade. The shallow irregular North Sea coast is fronted by the East and North Frisian Islands; strong wave action has made diking imperative. Off the Baltic coast is an isl. group including Fehmarn, Rügen, and Usedom. With the exception of Kiel, Emden, and Wilhelmshaven all major Ger. ports have outer ports: Bremerhaven below Bremen, Cuxhaven below Hamburg, Travemünde below Lübeck, and Warnemünde below Rostock. Kiel Canal is major link bet. Baltic and North Sea ports. Fishing is an important industry in most of the coastal towns. For the history of Germany before 1871 see articles on Prussia and other member-states of the German Empire: Anhalt, Baden, Bavaria, Bremen, Brunswick, Hamburg, Hesse-Darmstadt, Lippe, Lübeck, Mecklenburg-Strelitz, Oldenburg, Saxony, Schaumburg-Lippe, Waldeck, and Württemberg. Prussia's long struggle for hegemony in Germany was realized after the Franco-Prussian War (1870–71); the Ger. states were united in the newly created German Empire [Ger. *Deutsches Reich*], of which King William I of Prussia was proclaimed emperor. At the peace treaty with France Germany received Alsace and Lorraine and emerged as the leading power of continental Europe. Chancellor Bismarck, who had been the leading single force in the unification of Germany, now sought to consolidate the new state and to establish peaceful relations with its neighbors. He allied the country with Austria-Hungary (1879) and Italy (1882) in the Triple Alliance, and kept alive the Three Emperors' League of Germany, Austria-Hungary, and Russia. Bismarck was dismissed (1890) by William II (1888–1918), whose aggressive foreign policy, in conjunction with the intensive remilitarization of the empire, soon became a threat to peace. The Triple Entente (England, France, Russia) faced Germany and her allies in the First World War (1914–18), and in 1918 exhausted Germany had to accept the Allied armistice terms and, later, the peace terms of Versailles (1919). William II fled and abdicated (Nov., 1918) after the outbreak of a Social Democratic revolution which swept the rulers of the Ger. states off their thrones. At the peace conference of Versailles Germany lost all her colonies: Caroline Isls., Marianas Isls., Marshall Isls., Nauru, present Territory of New Guinea, and Western Samoa (Pacific possessions); Cameroons, Ruanda-Urundi, South-West Africa, Tanganyika, and Togoland (African possessions). Alsace and Lorraine were returned to France, West Prussia (including Poznan and Danzig) and parts of Upper Silesia were given to Poland. Plebiscites provided for in the peace terms resulted in the transfer of Eupen, Malmedy, and Moresnet to Belgium, and of N Schleswig to Denmark. The Saar was placed under Fr. administration for 15 years; Germany was demilitarized and the Rhineland occupied by Allied forces. The 1st few years of the newly formed federal Weimar Republic were marked by internal political unrest, mass unemployment, and extreme currency inflation. Among the political parties the extremes soon emerged dominant, with the chauvinist elements merged in Adolf Hitler's National Socialist party. A semblance of normalcy returned in the mid-twenties, when Allied reparation demands were eased and the republic joined (1926) the League of Nations. The economic disaster of 1929 paved the way for the Nazi *coup d'état* of 1933. Within a year Hitler's dictatorship had become absolute; centralization of every aspect of Ger. life and a complete cultural blackout, accompanied by a reign of terror, enforced by the notorious Gestapo and concentrating on the extermination of political opponents and the Jews, marked the internal policy of the Third Reich. Intensive remilitarization, despite Versailles restrictions, and an aggressive foreign policy (formation of the "Axis," annexation of Austria, the Sudetenland, and Memel, creation of protectorates of Bohemia and Moravia) inevitably led towards war, whose outbreak was precipitated by the invasion (Sept. 1, 1939) of Poland. The fortunes of war turned against the victorious Ger. army in 1943; by the spring of 1945 nearly all Germany was occupied by Allied troops and most major Ger. cities lay in ruins. Hitler was dead by April, 1945, and on May 7–8 the Ger. govt., headed by Admiral Doenitz, signed an unconditional surrender; this govt. was dissolved shortly afterwards and its functions were taken over by the military commanders in Germany. The Allied plan for Germany, sketched at the Yalta Conference (Feb., 1945), was implemented at the Potsdam Conference (Aug., 1945). The region E of the Oder and the Lusatian Neisse rivers (part of Brandenburg and most of Pomerania and Silesia) was placed under Polish administration, as was the part of East Prussia S of the Braniewo (Braunsberg)-Goldap line; the N section of East Prussia was transferred to the USSR and became Kaliningrad oblast of the Russian SFSR. The rest of Germany was divided into 4 zones, and the 17 states of pre-war Germany were redistributed and reconstituted into 16 new states. The Br. zone (□ 37,698; 1946 pop. 22,304,509; 1950 pop. 24,114,144) was composed of the former Prussian provs. of Hanover, Schleswig-Holstein, and Westphalia, N portion of former Prussian Rhine Province, and of the former states of Brunswick, Hamburg, Lippe, Oldenburg, and Schaumburg-Lippe; these were reconstituted into the new states of Hamburg, Lower Saxony, North Rhine-Westphalia, and Schleswig-Holstein. The S portion of former Prussian Rhine Prov., small W section (see Montabaur) of former Prussian Hesse-Nassau prov., Rhenish Hesse, the Bavarian Rhenish Palatinate, S Baden, S Württemberg, former Prussian Hohenzollern prov., and Lindau were put into the Fr. occupation zone (□ 15,520; 1946 pop. 5,077,816; 1950 pop. 5,568,697) and reconstituted as the new states of Baden, Rhineland-Palatinate, and Württemberg-Hohenzollern. The U.S. zone (□ 41,490; 1946 pop. 17,254,945; 1950 pop. 17,875,085) was composed of Bavaria, N Baden and N Württemberg (constituted into Württemberg-Baden), Bremen (enclave in Br. zone), Hesse state (the pre-1918 Hesse-Darmstadt), and major portion of former Prussian Hesse-Nassau prov. (constituted into new state of Hesse). The Russian zone (□ 41,379; 1946 pop. 17,313,734) was composed of former Prussian Saxony prov., larger part of former Prussian Brandenburg prov., and of Anhalt, Mecklenburg, Saxony (state), and Thuringia; these were reconstituted into the new states of Brandenburg, Mecklenburg, Saxony-Anhalt, and Thuringia. Berlin was divided into 4 zones separately occupied by the 4 powers. In 1949 the states of W Germany combined into the German Federal Republic [Ger. *Deutsche Bundesrepublik* or *Bundesrepublik Deutschland*] (□ 94,707; 1950 pop. 47,557,926), with provisional ⊙ at Bonn; the sovietized E Ger. states formed the German Democratic Republic [Ger. *Deutsche Demokratische Republik*], with ⊙ in East Berlin.

Germein Bay, inlet of Spencer Gulf, at base of Yorke Peninsula, South Australia; 9 mi. N-S, 5 mi. E-W. Port Pirie on S inlet.

Germersheim (gĕr'mŏrs-hīm), town (pop. 4,848), Rhenish Palatinate, W Germany, on the Rhine at mouth of the Queich, and 7 mi. SSW of Speyer; rail junction; brewing, metal- and woodworking. Founded by Romans. Was residence of Frankish kings. Chartered 1276.

Germfask (jûrm'făsk", –făst"), village, Schoolcraft co., S Upper Peninsula, Mich., on Manistique R. and 25 mi. NE of Manistique, near Manistique L. Seney Natl. Wildlife Refuge is adjacent. Fishing.

Germigny-des-Prés (zhĕrmēnyē'-dā-prā'), village (pop. 130), Loiret dept., N central France, near right bank of Loire R., 17 mi. ESE of Orléans; has noted Carolingian church (9th–11th cent.) with fine 9th-cent. mosaic.

Germiston (jûr'mĭstŭn), city (pop. 104,306; including suburbs 131,618), S Transvaal, U. of So. Afr., on Witwatersrand, 8 mi. ESE of Johannesburg; alt. 5,479 ft.; rail center with extensive workshops; gold-mining, smelting, refining center. Other industries are cotton ginning, mfg. of explosives, chemicals, steel products, cutlery, agr. implements, matches, clothing, soap, starch, glucose, oil cake. Important power station. Rand airport 3 mi. SW.

Germoe (gûr'mō), village and parish (pop. 313), W Cornwall, England, 5 mi. WNW of Helston; tin mining. Has 15th-cent. church.

Gernrode (gĕrn'rō"dŭ), town (pop. 6,033), in former Anhalt state, central Germany, after 1945 in Saxony-Anhalt, in the lower Harz, 5 mi. S of Quedlinburg; climatic health resort; wood- and metalworking. Has noted 10th-cent. church of former monastery (founded 960).

Gernsbach (gĕrns'băkh), town (pop. 4,776), S Baden, Germany, in Black Forest, on the Murg and 8 mi. SE of Rastatt; mfg. of cigarette paper, woodworking. Climatic health resort (alt. 525 ft.) and tourist center. Has late-Gothic church, Renaissance town hall.

Gernsheim (gĕrns'hīm), town (pop. 5,983), S Hesse, W Germany, in former Starkenburg prov., on the Rhine and 11 mi. SW of Darmstadt; malting. Peter Schöffer b. here.

Gero (gā'rō), town (pop. 6,177), Gifu prefecture, central Honshu, Japan, 23 mi. S of Takayama. Hot springs.

Geroldsgrün (gā'rôltsgrün"), village (pop. 2,192), Upper Franconia, NE Bavaria, Germany, in Franconian Forest, 14 mi. W of Hof; mfg. of slide rules and pencils; woodworking, brewing. Slate quarries in area.

Gerolstein (gā'rôl-shtīn"), village (pop. 2,566), in former Prussian Rhine Prov., W Germany, after 1945 in Rhineland-Palatinate, in the Eifel, 32 mi. NNE of Trier; rail junction; resort with mineral springs. Numerous fossils of middle Devonian period found here.

Gerolzhofen (gā"rôlts-hō'fŭn), town (pop. 4,566), Lower Franconia, NW Bavaria, Germany, on small Volkach R. and 12 mi. SSE of Schweinfurt; brickworks; tanning, brewing, lumber and flour milling. Has late-Gothic town hall and church.

Gerona (hārō'nä), town (1939 pop. 2,004; 1948 municipality pop. 26,763), Tarlac prov., central Luzon, Philippines, 8 mi. N of Tarlac; agr. center (coconuts, rice, sugar).

Gerona (hārō'nä), northeasternmost province (□ 2,272; pop. 322,360) of Spain, in Catalonia; ⊙ Gerona. Bounded by France (N; frontier along crest of E Pyrenees) and the Mediterranean (E). Occupied by S slopes and spurs of the Pyrenees and by fertile Ampurdán plain. Drained by the Ter (hydroelectric plants) and the Fluviá. Has rocky and indented coast line (Cape Creus, Gulf of Rosas) with numerous bathing resorts. Predominantly agr.: wheat, corn, potatoes, wine, olive oil, fruit. Extensive stock raising (cattle, sheep, pigs). Large forested tracts. Chief industry: cork processing. Other mfg.: textiles, cement, paper, ceramics; tanning, meat packing. Chief towns: Gerona, Figueras, Olot, Palamós, San Felíu de Guixols.

Gerona, city (pop. 28,752), ⊙ Gerona prov., NE Spain, 50 mi. NE of Barcelona, and on Ter R. at mouth of the Oñar; 41°59'N 2°49'E. Communications and trade center; cotton spinning and weaving, tanning; mfg. of cement, paper, buttons, artificial stones, mosaics; printing; cork, wine, and olive oil processing. Dominated by fortified height of Montjuich, city is surrounded by anc. fortifications. Episcopal see since 3d cent. Has Gothic cathedral (14th–16th cent.) with 73-ft.-wide single nave, Romanesque church of San Pedro (with prov. mus. in cloisters), and 14th-cent. church of San Felíu. Dating from pre-Roman times, Gerona was captured by Moors (c.712), by Charlemagne (785), again by Moors (795). After liberation (1015) by Christians, became ⊙ Gerona county and shared history of Catalonia. In the Peninsular War it heroically, but unsuccessfully, resisted the French, 1808–09.

Geronimo (jŭrŏ'nĭmō), town (pop. 103), Comanche co., SW Okla., 8 mi. S of Lawton, in agr. area.

Gerpinnes (zhĕrpēn'), village (pop. 2,084), Hainaut prov., S central Belgium, 6 mi. SSE of Charleroi; marble quarrying.

Gerpir (gĕr'pĭr), cape, E extremity of Iceland, 65°5'N 13°28'W.

Gerrard's Cross (jĕ'rŭrdz), town and parish (pop. 2,942), SE Buckingham, England, 9 mi. E of High Wycombe; soap industry.

Gerrer River, Ethiopia: see Jerer River.

Gerresheim (gĕ'rŭs-hīm), suburb of Düsseldorf, W Germany, 3.5 mi. E of city center; glassworks (bottles). Has 13th-cent. church.

Gerringong, municipality (pop. 881), E New South Wales, Australia, on coast, 65 mi. S of Sydney; dairying center.

Gerry (gĕ'rē), resort village, Chautauqua co., extreme W N.Y., 6 mi. N of Jamestown and c.6 mi. from Chautauqua L. (SW).

Gers (zhâr), department (□ 2,429; pop. 190,431), in Gascony, SW France, at foot of the Pyrenees; ⊙ Auch. A dissected upland (Armagnac hills) sloping S–N from Lannemezan Plateau, bounded roughly by Garonne valley (E and N) and by the Landes (W). Drained by the Save, Gimone, Gers, Baïse (tributaries of the Garonne), and the Adour. Grows corn, wheat, forage crops, wine, fruit; raises poultry (mainly turkeys and geese) and cattle. Noted for its Armagnac brandy. Has some food processing industries. Chief towns are Auch (former ⊙ Gascony) and Condom (brandy-distilling center).

Gersau (gĕr'sou), village (pop. 1,878), Schwyz canton, central Switzerland, on L. of Lucerne, 6 mi. WSW of Schwyz; health resort; silk textiles.

Gersdorf (gĕrs'dôrf), village (pop. 8,465), Saxony, E central Germany, 11 mi. WSW of Chemnitz; coal mining; hosiery knitting, cotton milling.

Gersfeld (gĕrs'fĕlt), town (pop. 2,361), in former Prussian prov. of Hesse-Nassau, W Germany, after 1945 in Hesse, in the Hohe Rhön, on the Fulda and 13 mi. SW of Fulda; popular summer and winter resort.

Gers-Nazik, Lake (gĕrs"näzĭk') (□ 12), E Turkey, 40 mi. E of Mus; 6 mi. long, 3 mi. wide; alt. 6,1[illegible] ft. Sometimes called Nazik.

Gersoppa Falls (gĕrsŏ'pŭ) or **Jog Falls** (jō[illegible]), cataract of Sharavati R., in Western Ghats, on Bombay-Mysore border, India, 26 mi. ESE of Honavar; one of most spectacular natural beauties in India. River falls in 4 cascades; highest, c.8[illegible] ft. Tourist bungalows on each side of river. Hydroelectric works at Jog, 1.5 mi. E (downstream) do not impair falls' beauty. Gersoppa village is [illegible] mi. WNW of falls.

Gersprenz River (gĕr-shprĕnts'), W Germany, rises in the Odenwald 4 mi. SE of Lindenfels, flows [illegible] mi. N and E to the canalized Main, 3 mi. W of Aschaffenburg.

Gers River (zhâr), Hautes-Pyrénées, Gers, and Lot-et-Garonne depts., SW France, rises in Lannemezan Plateau, flows 110 mi. N, past Auch and Lectoure, to the Garonne 5 mi. above Agen.

Gerster, town (pop. 47), St. Clair co., W Mo., 12 mi. SSE of Osceola.

Gerstetten (gĕr'shtĕ"tŭn), village (pop. 3,314), Württemberg, Germany, after 1945 in Württemberg-Baden, 7 mi. SW of Heidenheim; grain.

Gerstheim (gĕrstĕm', Ger. gĕrst'hīm), village (pop. 1,614), Bas-Rhin dept., E France, on Rhone-Rh[illegible]

Canal, 4 mi. SE of Erstein; customhouse near Rhine R. bridge (Ger. border), opposite Ottenheim; tobacco mfg.

Gersthofen (gĕrst'hō"fŭn), town (pop. 5,928), Swabia, W Bavaria, Germany, on the Lech and 4 mi. N of Augsburg; hydroelectric plant; mfg. (machinery, chlorine, leather products).

Gerstungen (gĕr'shtōōng"ŭn), village (pop. 3,433), Thuringia, central Germany, in Thuringian Forest, on the Werra and 11 mi. W of Eisenach, opposite Obersuhl; furniture mfg., woodworking, linen milling. After 1945, traffic check point bet. East and West Germany.

Gersweiler (gĕrs'vī"lŭr), town (pop. 7,661), S Saar, near Fr. border, on Saar R. and 2.5 mi. W of Saarbrücken; coal mining; metal- and woodworking.

Gertsa (gyĕr'tsŭ), Rum. *Herța* (hĕr'tsä), city (1941 pop. 5,741), S Chernovtsy oblast, Ukrainian SSR, in N Bukovina, near Prut R., 17 mi. SE of Chernovtsy, on Rum. border; agr. center (grain, livestock). Has 18th-cent. church. Formerly in Dorohoi dept. of Rumania; Gertsa dist. (□ c.150; 1941 pop. 28,313) was ceded (1940), with N Bukovina, to USSR.

Gertwiller (gĕrt"vĕlâr'), Ger. *Gertweiler* (gĕrt'vīlŭr), village (pop. 600), Bas-Rhin dept., E France, 1 mi. E of Barr; winegrowing, olive-oil pressing, gingerbread mfg.

Gerty (gûr'tē), town (pop. 155), Hughes co., central Okla., 19 mi. SSE of Holdenville; cotton ginning.

Gervais (jûr'văs), town (pop. 457), Marion co., NW Oregon, 12 mi. NNE of Salem in Willamette valley.

Géryville (zhārēvēl'), town (pop. 7,210), Aïn-Sefra territory, NW central Algeria, in the Saharan Atlas (Djebel Amour), 95 mi. SE of Saïda (linked by road); 33°40'N 1°1'E. Trade center (barley, esparto, wool). Carpet mfg. Established as military post 1852.

Gerzat (zhĕrzä'), town (pop. 2,393), Puy-de-Dôme dept., central France, in the Limagne, 4 mi. NE of Clermont-Ferrand; flour and dairy products.

Gerze (gĕrzĕ'), anc. *Carusa*, village (pop. 4,272), Sinop prov., N Turkey, on Black Sea, 15 mi. S of Sinop; spelt, tobacco, olives.

Gesäuse, Austria: see ENNSTAL ALPS.

Geschriebenstein (gŭshrēb'ŭnshtīn), highest peak (2,897 ft.) of Burgenland, E Austria, on Austro-Hung. border and 12 mi. NW of Szombathely, Hungary.

Geschwenda (gŭ-shvĕn'dä), village (pop. 3,387), Thuringia, central Germany, on N slope of Thuringian Forest, 5 mi. NW of Ilmenau; china and glass mfg., woodworking.

Geseke (gā'zŭkŭ), town (pop. 10,657), in former Prussian prov. of Westphalia, W Germany, after 1945 in North Rhine-Westphalia, 7 mi. ESE of Lippstadt; metalworking.

Geserich Lake, Poland: see JEZIORAK, LAKE.

Gesher (gĕ'shĕr), settlement (pop. 180), Lower Galilee, NE Israel, on Jordan border, on right bank of the Jordan (bridge), on railroad and 11 mi. S of Tiberias; mixed farming. Founded 1939. Resisted heavy Arab attacks, 1948.

Gesoriacum, France: see BOULOGNE.

Gessenay, Switzerland: see SAANEN.

Gessopalena (jĕs"sôpälā'nä), town (pop. 1,808), Chieti prov., Abruzzi e Molise, S central Italy, 14 mi. SSE of Chieti; cement-making center.

Gest, Wales: see PORTMADOC.

Gestalgar (hĕstälgär'), town (pop. 1,493), Valencia prov., E Spain, on Turia R. and 12 mi. WSW of Liria; olive oil, wine, beans; lumbering.

Gestrikland, Sweden: see GASTRIKLAND.

Gestro, Uebi, Ethiopia: see WEB RIVER.

Gesualdo (jĕswäl'dô), village (pop. 2,870), Avellino prov., Campania, S Italy, 16 mi. ENE of Avellino.

Geta (yā'tä), fishing village (commune pop. 827), Aland co., SW Finland, on N Aland isl., 20 mi. N of Mariehamn; tourist resort.

Getafe (hātä'fā), town (pop. 8,965), Madrid prov., central Spain, in New Castile, 8 mi. S of Madrid. Industrial center situated on a wide plain (cereals, truck produce, olives, grapes) flanked E by Los Angeles hill (with Heart of Jesus monument), considered geographical center of Spain. Makes radio and electrical equipment, telephones, airplanes, pharmaceuticals, cardboard boxes, brushes, alcohol, liquor, flour. Among notable bldgs. are parochial church of Santa María Magdalena and a Piarist seminary. Getafe is a hq. for military aviation.

Geteina or **El Geteina** (ĕl gĕtā'nŭ), town, Blue Nile prov., E central Anglo-Egyptian Sudan, in Gezira Plain on right bank of the White Nile, on road and 50 mi. SSW of Khartoum; cotton, wheat, barley, corn, fruits, durra; livestock.

Gethsemane (gĕthsĕ'mŭnē), village, Nelson co., central Ky., 17 mi. ESE of Elizabethtown; distillery. At near-by Trappist is a Trappist monastery, Abbey of Our Lady of Gethsemani, where port du salut cheese is made.

Geti (gĕ'tē), village, Eastern Prov., NE Belgian Congo, 20 mi. SE of Irumu; tourist center in region of L. Albert, near Uganda border. R.C. mission.

Getinge (yā'tĭng-ŭ), village (pop. 344), Halland co., SW Sweden, near the Kattegat, 10 mi. NNW of Halmstad; mfg. of windmill generators.

Getsubi-to, Korea: see CHEMULPO.

Gettorf (gĕ'tôrf), village (pop. 3,931), in Schleswig-Holstein, NW Germany, 8 mi. NW of Kiel; seed-selection station; potteries. Woodworking, flour milling, dairying. Has Gothic church. First mentioned 1259; place of pilgrimage in Middle Ages.

Gettysburg (gĕ'tēzbûrg). **1** Village (pop. 451), Darke co., W Ohio, 7 mi. E of Greenville and on Greenville Creek. **2** Borough (pop. 7,046), ⊙ Adams co., S Pa., 36 mi. SW of Harrisburg; mfg. of furniture, clothing; wheat, corn, apples; tourist center. Gettysburg Col., Lutheran Theological Seminary here. Gettysburg Natl. Military Park (□ c.4; established 1895) includes battlefield where turning point of Civil War came with repulse of Lee's 2d attempted invasion of the North. Much of 1st fighting in battle of Gettysburg (June 30–July 4, 1863), bet. Army of the Potomac under Meade and Lee's Army of Northern Virginia, took place on Cemetery Hill and Culp's Hill, eminences near N end of low Cemetery Ridge, S of Gettysburg; toward battle's end, Federal defenses farther S on ridge, notably at Round Top, repulsed the gallant but unsuccessful charge spearheaded by Pickett's division; the battle and campaign were ended with orderly retreat of Confederates into Va. Gettysburg Natl. Cemetery (15.6 acres; dedicated 1863 by Lincoln in his most famous address) is in park. **3** City (pop. 1,555), ⊙ Potter co., N central S.Dak., 50 mi. NNE of Pierre; trade center for agr. region; flour mill, oil-compounding plant; dairy products, livestock, poultry, wheat, corn, potatoes. Founded 1881.

Getúlina (zhĭtōōlē'nŭ), city (pop. 2,280), W central São Paulo, Brazil, 15 mi. SW of Lins; coffee processing, pottery mfg.; agr. (coffee, cotton, sugar cane).

Getúlio Vargas (zhĭtōō'lyōō vär'gŭs), city (pop. 1,768), N Rio Grande do Sul, Brazil, in the Serra Geral, near railroad, 26 mi. N of Passo Fundo; grain, hogs. Until 1934, Erechim.

Getz Shelf Ice, shelf ice in Antarctica, on the South Pacific, along shore of Marie Byrd Land, in 74°30'S 131°W. Discovered 1940 by U.S. expedition.

Geuda Springs (gū'dŭ), city (pop. 245), on Cowley-Sumner co. line, S Kansas, on Arkansas R. and 40 mi. S of Wichita; grain, livestock. Oil fields.

Geulim (gĕ-ōōlēm'), settlement (pop. 150), W Israel, in Plain of Sharon, 5 mi. ESE of Natanya; mixed farming, citriculture. Founded 1945 after settlement attempt in 1937 had failed.

Geul River (khûl), Limburg prov., SE Netherlands, rises 7 mi. W of Aachen (Germany), flows 20 mi. NW to Maas R. near Bunde, 4 mi. NNE of Maastricht.

Geva (gĕvä'), settlement (pop. 400), NE Israel, in SE part of Plain of Jezreel, near railroad, 6 mi. ESE of Afula; mixed farming. School serves surrounding region.

Gevar, Turkey: see YUKSEKOVA.

Gevaram, Gevar'am, or **Gvar Am** (all: gvär'-äm'), settlement (pop. 250), SW Israel, in Judaean Plain, at NW edge of the Negev, near border of Egyptian-held Palestine, 11 mi. NE of Gaza; mixed farming. Founded 1942; formerly called Kibbutz Mahar or Qibbuts Mahar (both: kēbōōts' mähär').

Gevas (gĕvăsh'), Turkish *Gevaş*, village (pop. 2,238), Van prov., SE Turkey, on SE shore of L. Van, 19 mi. SW of Van; wheat. Formerly Vastan.

Gevat, Israel: see GVAT.

Gévaudan (zhāvōdā'), region, formerly in Languedoc prov., S France, now in Lozère dept. Occupied by the Montagnes de la Margeride, Monts d'Aubrac, and part of the CAUSSES. It was ruled by the powerful bishops of Mende.

Gevelsberg (gā'fŭlsbĕrk), town (pop. 25,432), in former Prussian prov. of Westphalia, W Germany, after 1945 in North Rhine-Westphalia, in the Ruhr, on the Ennepe and 6 mi. WSW of Hagen; foundries, enameling works; mfg. of agr. implements, bicycles, sewing machines, refrigerators, stoves, ovens, electric irons and plates, screws, locks, lamps, glass, ceramics. Active trade. Developed around Cistercian abbey (founded 1230).

Gevgeli; Gevgelija, Yugoslavia: see DJEVDJELIJA.

Gevizli Dag (gĕvĭzlĭ'dä), Turkish *Gevizli Dağ*, peak (4,400 ft.), W Turkey, in Aydin Mts., 8 mi. NNE of Aydin.

Gevle, Sweden: see GAVLE.

Gevrai (gäv'rī), town (pop. 7,220), Bir dist., NW Hyderabad state, India, 18 mi. N of Bir; millet, wheat; cotton ginning. Also spelled Georai.

Gevray-Chambertin (zhŭvrā'-shābĕrtē'), village (pop. 1,473), Côte-d'Or dept., E central France, on E slope of the Côte d'Or, 7 mi. SSW of Dijon; noted Burgundy vintage wines.

Gevulot, Gevuloth, or **Gvulot** (all: gvōōlōt'), settlement (pop. 75), SW Israel, in the Negev, 20 mi. W of Beersheba; mixed farming, fruitgrowing. On Negev water pipe line. Founded 1943.

Gex (zhā), village (pop. 1,231), Ain dept., E France, near Swiss border, 10 mi. NNW of Geneva, below the Col de la FAUCILLE; alt. 2,123 ft.; blue cheese mfg., tanning, diamond cutting. Splendid view of the Alps (SE) across Switzerland. The territory of Gex (*pays de Gex*), along E slopes of the Jura and Swiss border, bet. Gex (N) and Collonges (S), passed from medieval counts of Geneva to dukes of Savoy, was conquered (1536) by the Swiss, and ceded to France in 1601. Since 1815 it has been a neutral customs zone.

Geyer (gī'ŭr), town (pop. 6,085), Saxony, E central Germany, in the Erzgebirge, 14 mi. S of Chemnitz; textile knitting, lace and ribbon making, metalworking, shoe mfg. Winter-sports center.

Geyersberg (gī'ŭrsbĕrk), highest elevation (1,918 ft.) of The Spessart, W Germany, 12 mi. SE of Aschaffenburg. Sometimes spelled Geiersberg.

Geyik Dag (gĕvĭk' dä), Turkish *Geyik Dağ*, peak (9,480 ft.), S Turkey, in Taurus Mts., 3 mi. E of Gundogmus.

Geylang Serai (gălăng' sŭrī'), NE suburb (pop. 10,817) of Singapore, Singapore isl., on city line, 3 mi. NE of city center. Pop. is 70% Malay.

Geysers, The, Calif.: see GEYSERVILLE.

Geyserville (gī'zŭrvĭl), village (pop. c.600), Sonoma co., W Calif., in Russian R. valley, 22 mi. NNW of Santa Rosa; ships fruit. Trade center for region of mineral and hot springs (health resorts). The Geysers (or Big Geysers) are 8 mi. NE.

Geysir or **Great Geysir** (gā'sĭr), hot springs, SW Iceland, near S foot of Langjokull, 50 mi. E of Reykjavik, near 64°16'N 20°15'W. Inactive since an eruption (1913–14) of Hekla volcano. Near by are c.50 active hot springs.

Geyve (gāvĕ'), village (pop. 2,413), Kocaeli prov., NW Turkey, on railroad, on Sakarya R., and 19 mi. S of Adapazari; tobacco, chick-peas, sesame; coal and lignite near by.

Gezer (gē'zŭr) or **Hadassah-Gezer** (hädäsä'-gĕ'zĕr), agr. settlement (pop. 150), W Israel, at W foot of Judaean Hills, 6 mi. SSW of Lydda. Modern village founded 1945; repelled heavy Arab attacks, 1948. Just SE is village of Abu Shusha (ä'bōō shōōshä'), site of biblical locality of Gezer (gē'zŭr), scene of important excavations. Finds include noted Gezer Calendar (c.925 B.C.). Here is the Mont Gisard of the Crusades, where Baldwin IV defeated (1177) Saladin. The site, a natural fortress, has long been a key to the strategic road which passes here.

Gezira, prov., Anglo-Egyptian Sudan: see BLUE NILE.

Gezira (jŭzē'rŭ), irrigated mesopotamia in E central Anglo-Egyptian Sudan, S of Khartoum, bet. White Nile and Blue Nile and bounded S by Sennar-Kosti RR; 80 mi. wide, 150 mi. long. The Gezira gravity-flow irrigation scheme (begun 1925) is fed by SENNAR dam. Long-staple cotton is rotated with durra and hyacinth beans (food and forage crops). Small areas are under peanuts and vegetables. Main centers are Wad Medani (agr. research station) and Hasiheisa.

Gezira or **Geziret** (both: jŭzē'rŭ) [Arabic,=island], island in the Nile, Lower Egypt, a part of Cairo opposite the Bulak quarter, with which it is connected by a bridge built 1909. Residential area; has racecourse, hotels, aquarium, 19th-cent. palace. Sometimes called Bulak Isl.

Geziret Shandawil (shăn'dăwēl) or **Jazirat Shandawil** (jă–), village (pop. 14,667), Girga prov., central Upper Egypt, on railroad and 6 mi. NNW of Sohag; cotton, cereals, dates, sugar cane.

Ghab, El, or **Al-Ghab** (both: ĕl-găb'), valley (c.30 mi. long, 5 mi. wide), Latakia prov., W Syria, bordering on Aleppo and Homs provs., 30 mi. E of Latakia. Watered by the Orontes.

Ghabaghib (găbă'gĭb). **1** Village, Euphrates prov., E central Syria, 30 mi. SW of Deir ez Zor. **2** Village, Hauran prov., SW Syria, 23 mi. S of Damascus.

Ghabat el Arab, Anglo-Egyptian Sudan: see WANKAI.

Ghadames or **Rhadames** (both: gŭdä'mĕs, gädämĕs'), Fr. *Ghadamès*, Ital. *Gadames*, anc. *Cydamus*, town (pop. 2,405), N Fezzan, Libya, near Tunisian and Algerian borders, in a walled Saharan oasis; 30°9'N 9°30'E. Caravan center and road junction; artisan industries (leather goods, carpets, slippers, baskets). Has mosque and fort. Placed under Tunisian administration in 1948.

Ghafsaï or **Rhafsaï** (both: gäfsī'), village (pop. 388), Fez region, N Fr. Morocco, on S slope of Rif Mts., near Sp. Morocco border, 20 mi. N of Fez; olive- and winegrowing.

Ghaggar River (gŭg'gŭr), stream mostly in Punjab and in Patiala and East Punjab States Union, India; rises in Siwalik Range in Himachal Pradesh c.20 mi. NW of Nahan, flows c.215 mi. generally SW to village 9 mi. WSW of Sirsa (Hissar dist.). Here it feeds 2 irrigation canals which extend W into N Rajasthan, to points just SW of Hanumangarh. Seasonal. Probably once an affluent of the Indus; most of its old bed in Rajasthan (India) and Bahawalpur state (W Pakistan) is still traceable.

Ghahmar, India: see GAHMAR.

Ghaidha, Gheidha, or **Ghaydah** (gā'dŭ), village and oasis, Quaiti state, Eastern Aden Protectorate, 30 mi. ENE of Shihr. Site of airfield, also known as Haifif.

Ghail, for names in Aden Protectorate beginning thus: see under GHEIL.

Ghakkhar (gŭk'kŭr), town (pop. 6,929), Gujranwala dist., E Punjab, W Pakistan, 10 mi. NNW of Gujranwala; wheat, rice, gram; rice and oilseed milling. Also spelled Ghakhar and Gakhar.

Ghambiraopet, India: see GAMBIRAOPET.

Ghanadha, Khor al, or **Khawr al-Ghanadah** (both: khōr ăl gănā'dŭ), coastal creek on Trucial Coast of Persian Gulf, separating sheikdoms of Abu Dhabi (W) and Dibai (E); 24°50'N 54°47'E.

Ghansis, Bechuanaland Protectorate: see GHANZI.

Ghantanji, India: see GHATANJI.

Ghantila (gŭn'tĭlŭ), village, N Saurashtra, India, 24 mi. NNE of Morvi; local market for salt, millet, cotton; cotton ginning.

Ghanzi (gän'zē) or **Khanzi** (khän'zē), town, ⊙ Ghanzi dist. (pop. 5,183), W Bechuanaland Protectorate, at N edge of Kalahari Desert, near South-West Africa border, 300 mi. ENE of Windhoek; 21°34'S 21°47'E; dairying. Airfield. Dist. includes the Ghanzi Farms, tract allocated (1898) to Boer farmers by Cecil Rhodes; now crown land. Sometimes spelled Ghansis. Dist. sometimes called Gemsbok Pan.

Gharandal (gärän'dăl), village, S Jordan, 32 mi. WSW of Ma'an; fruit; sheep, goat raising.

Gharapuri, island, India: see ELEPHANTA.

Gharaunda (gŭroun'dŭ), town (pop. 7,287), Karnal dist., E Punjab, India, 11 mi. S of Karnal; local trade in grain, cotton.

Gharb, Fr. Morocco: see RHARB.

Gharbi, Chott el (shôt' ĕl gärbē') [Arabic,=western shott], marshy saline lake or salt flat, NW Algeria, near Fr. Morocco border in the High Plateaus (interior drainage), S of El-Aricha.

Gharbi, Jebel el, Lebanon: see LEBANON, mts.

Gharbiya or **Al-Gharbiyah** (ĕl gärbē'yŭ), largest province (□ 2,711; pop. 2,334,287) of Egypt, in Nile Delta; ⊙ TANTA. Bounded S by Minufiya prov., E by Damietta branch of the Nile, N by L. Burullus and Mediterranean Sea, W by Rosetta branch of the Nile. Industries: cotton ginning, rice husking, mfg. of straw mats and pottery. Agr.: cotton, cereals, rice, fruits. El MAHALLA EL KUBRA is the major textile center of Egypt. Served by main railroads, by the Damietta and Rosetta branches of the Nile, and by the Bahr Shibin and other canals. Sites of antiquity: BAHBIT EL HIGARA (anc. Iseum), Sa el Hajar (anc. SAIS), SEBENNYTOS.

Ghardaïa (gärdäyä'), military territory (□ 50,264; 1948 pop. 219,473) of central Algeria, one of the SOUTHERN TERRITORIES, in the Sahara; ⊙ Laghouat. Bounded by Alger (N) and Oran (NW) depts., with which it is linked by road. Djelfa (territory's northernmost town) is S terminus of railroad from Algiers. Other towns, all Saharan oases, are Laghouat, Ghardaïa (center of the Mzab oases), and El Goléa, on the trans-Saharan auto track to Zinder (Fr. West Africa). Principal export products are dates and wool.

Ghardaïa, town (pop. 17,537), Ghardaïa territory, central Algeria, in the Sahara, 300 mi. S of Algiers; 32°29'N 3°42'E. Commercial and religious center of the MZAB oases, reached by desert road from Djelfa (N) and Touggourt (NE). Grows date palms, subsistence crops (cereals, vegetables) entirely irrigated by subterranean waters. Handicraft industries (woolens, carpets, leather and pottery articles, jewelry). Town is built in the shape of a pyramid, its superimposed arcaded dwellings resembling a beehive. The market square is the scene of picturesque activity. Town is dominated by a mosque (height of minaret, 300 ft.) and is surrounded by walls. A Fr. section, with hosp. and military quarters, has grown just S of Ghardaïa since 1880s.

Ghardaqah, Al-, Egypt: see HURGHADA.

Ghardawat or **Ghardhawat,** Kuria Muria Isls.: see GHARZAUT.

Ghardimaou (gärdēmou'), town (pop. 1,321), Souk-el-Arba dist., NW Tunisia, on the Medjerda and on railroad, 23 mi. NW of Le Kef; custom station on Algerian border. Lumbering, cork-oak shipping. Zinc, lead, and mercury mines near by.

Gharghaliani, Greece: see GARGALIANOI.

Gharraf, Shatt al (shät' äl gär-räf'), river, SE Iraq, an offshoot (c.70 mi. long) of the Tigris, which it leaves (as the Shatt Hai or Hay) at Kut al Imara, and flows S, reaching the Euphrates through a series of smaller arms or canals. It is important for irrigation, a certain amount of control being obtained from a barrage S of Kut al Imara.

Ghar Rouban, Algeria: see MARNIA.

Gharzaut (gärzout'), **Ghardhawat,** or **Ghardawat** (gärdhäwăt'), rock islet in the Kuria Muria group, off SE Oman, just N of Qibliya isl.

Ghasa, Bhutan: see GASA.

Ghastouni, Greece: see GASTOUNE.

Ghat or **Rhat** (both: gät), Ital. *Gat,* walled town (pop. 2,056), SW Fezzan, Libya, near Algerian border, on road and 240 mi. WSW of Murzuk, in a Saharan oasis (cereals, dates, vegetables); 24°58'N 10°11'E. Caravan center; artisan industries (carpets, leather goods, baskets). Has fort and old mosques. Natron extracting near by. Placed under Algerian administration c.1945.

Ghatal (gä'täl), town (pop. 17,226), Midnapore dist., SW West Bengal, India, on tributary of the Rupnarayan and 31 mi. NE of Midnapore; metalware mfg.; trades in rice, pulse, potatoes, jute. Site of former Dutch factory.

Ghatampur (gä'tŭmpŏŏr), village, Cawnpore dist., S Uttar Pradesh, India, 24 mi. SSW of Cawnpore; gram, wheat, jowar, barley, mustard.

Ghatanji (gŭtŭn'jē), town (pop. 4,426), Yeotmal dist., SW Madhya Pradesh, India, on tributary of Penganga R. and 21 mi. SSE of Yeotmal; millet, oilseeds; cotton ginning. Sometimes spelled Ghantanji.

Ghatkopar (gät'kōpŭr), town (pop. 18,176), Bombay Suburban dist., W Bombay, India, on Salsette Isl., 11 mi. NNE of Bombay city center; mfg. of machinery, textiles, matches, ink, binding tape; local ghee trade; mango gardening; lithographic printing presses. Sometimes Ghatkopar-Kird.

Ghatprabha River (gät'prŭbŭ), S Bombay, India, rises in Western Ghats 15 mi. NE of Savantvadi, flows 140 mi. ENE, past Gokak, Mudhol, and Bagalkot, to Kistna R. 16 mi. NE of Bagalkot. Hydroelectric plant at 180-ft. falls, 13½ mi. NW of Gokak; dam (2 mi. above falls) supplies irrigation canal which extends 14 mi. E from dam, rejoining Ghatprabha R. 10 mi. NE of Gokak.

Ghats (gôts, gäts) [Hindi *ghat*=step], 2 mountain systems of peninsular India, forming E and W edges of Deccan Plateau and running, respectively, roughly parallel to Bay of Bengal and Arabian Sea coasts. Actually, *ghats* are stairs leading to a river, such as those used by Hindu pilgrims at Benares and Muttra; word was applied to various passes through the mts. and then to the ranges themselves, which, in places, have a steplike appearance. **Eastern Ghats** extend from Mahanadi R. c.875 mi. SW, S, and WSW, crossing S Orissa, NE and central Madras, SE Hyderabad, and SE Mysore states, to junction with Western Ghats in NILGIRI HILLS. Consist of series of disconnected hills with average height of 2,000 ft., rising to peaks of 4–5,000 ft. at N and S ends; Dodabetta peak, in the Nilgiris, is 8,640 ft. high. Main S outliers are JAVADI HILLS, SHEVAROY HILLS, and CHALK HILLS. Range overlooks low, fertile coastal plain (30–100 mi. wide, N to S), watered by deltas of the Godavari, Kistna, Penner, Palar, and Cauvery rivers which, breaking through the Ghats from the W, flow to Bay of Bengal. Eastern Ghats give rise to some smaller, E-flowing streams, including Rushikulya and Vamsadhara rivers (N). Rainfall varies from 30–40 in. in S to 50–80 in. in N section. Forests are usually sparse, but contain valuable sal, teak, and red sandalwood trees. Cauvery R. has important power and irrigation works at METTUR and power plant near Sivasamudram; projected power dams on Godavari R. and on Machkund R. (left tributary of the Godavari). Remote hill areas, such as the MALIAHS in Orissa, are inhabited by primitive tribes. **Western Ghats,** Sanskrit *Sahyadri,* extend c.1,000 mi. generally NNW–SSE in an almost continuous chain bet. Tapti R. valley (N) and Cape Comorin (S tip of India). From its N limit near Nandurbar, in N Bombay, range runs SSW to a point E of Bombay city, whence it continues SSE for the rest of its length, traversing Bombay, W Mysore, Coorg, and W Madras, where it merges with Eastern Ghats in Nilgiri Hills. Just S of the Nilgiris, the Ghats are interrupted by PALGHAT GAP (c.20 mi. wide), but rise again in ANAIMALAI HILLS and CARDAMOM HILLS along Madras and Travancore-Cochin border; terminate c.10 mi. N of Cape Comorin. Ajanta Hills are a NE spur. Bet. Western Ghats and Arabian Sea is a 10–35-mi.-wide coastal strip, broken in places, as in the Konkan and Kanara regions, by rugged spurs of the Ghats which reach almost to the sea. In the N, where it has a general height of 3,000 ft., the range rises to 5,400 ft. in Kalsubai Peak; S of Mahabaleshwar (4,719 ft.) height diminishes, but increases again S of Mysore line, where peaks rise to 5–7,000 ft.; the WYNAAD section culminates in Camel's Hump (7,673 ft.) and the Nilgiris in Dodabetta peak; in Travancore, the Ghats reach their highest point in Anai Mudi peak (8,841 ft.). Geologically the Ghats consist, in the N, of Deccan trap, sometimes capped by laterite soils, and, in the S, of gneissic rock formations; range was probably uplifted in early-Tertiary era. Western Ghats are main watershed of peninsular India, giving rise to such large rivers as the Godavari, Bhima, Kistna, Tungabhadra, and Cauvery, which flow E across Deccan Plateau to Bay of Bengal, while from its steep W face numerous short streams drain into Arabian Sea. By robbing SW monsoon of its moisture, the Ghats exert important climatic influence: annual rainfall averages 100 in. along coast, up to 200 in.—in places c.400 in.—in the hills, but only to 20–40 in. in the Deccan and S Madras. Almost everywhere slopes are covered with dense tropical evergreen and deciduous forests; at higher altitudes, as in the Nilgiris and Anaimalais, subtropical and temperate-climate trees occur. Bamboo, teak, blackwood, sandalwood, and ebony are commercially exploited. Cultivation is confined to S sections, where tea, coffee, cinchona, pepper, cardamom, and rubber grow on large estates. Elephants, bison, and tigers are common. Although the Ghats are crossed by 3 rail lines (Bombay-Nasik, Bombay-Poona, Mormugão-Dharwar), aside from line through Palghat Gap, they have generally proved an effective barrier to travel. Hill streams provide an important water-power resource: chief hydroelectric plants include 3 in KOLABA dist., Bombay, which supply power to Bombay city area, one at JOG in Mysore, and the MUNNAR works in Travancore; PERIYAR LAKE, in Travancore, is a large irrigation reservoir. Several popular hill resorts are situated throughout the Western Ghats, notably Matheran, MAHABALESHWAR, OOTACAMUND in the Nilgiris, and KODAIKANAL in PALNI HILLS. Among many sites of historical interest are Trimbak (pilgrimage center near source of Godavari R.), Shivner fort (near Junnar), where Sivaji was born, the Karli cave temples, and Panhala hill fortress.

Ghatsila, India: see MOSABONI.

Ghaudex or **Ghaudesh,** Maltese Isls.: see Gozo.

Ghauspur (gous'pŏŏr), town (pop. 1,232), Bahawalpur state, W Pakistan, 15 mi. NNW of Khanpur; wheat, millet.

Ghaydah, Aden: see GHAIDHA.

Ghayl, for names in Aden Protectorate beginning thus: see under GHEIL.

Ghazal, Bahr el, Anglo-Egyptian Sudan: see BAHR EL GHAZAL.

Ghazal, Bahr el, Fr. Equatorial Africa: see BAHR EL GHAZAL.

Ghaziabad (gä'zēäbäd"), town (pop. 23,834), Meerut dist., NW Uttar Pradesh, India, 12 mi. E of Delhi; rail junction; road center; trades in wheat, millet, sugar cane, oilseeds, leather; iron and steel rolling mill; hand-loom cotton weaving, mfg. of glass, acids. Founded 1740.

Ghazian (gäzēän'), village, First Prov., in Gilan, N Iran, on Caspian Sea, 15 mi. NNW of Resht, on spit of Murdab Lagoon, opposite Pahlevi across shallow access channel; customhouse.

Ghazipur (gä'zēpŏŏr), district (□ 1,306; pop. 985,380), E Uttar Pradesh, India; ⊙ Ghazipur. On Ganges Plain, bounded S by the Ganges. Agr. (rice, barley, gram, oilseeds, wheat, millet, sugar cane, corn); a major Indian center of legal opium-poppy cultivation. Main towns: Ghazipur, Reotipur, Gahmar, Sherpur.

Ghazipur, town (pop. 31,326), ⊙ Ghazipur dist., E Uttar Pradesh, India, on the Ganges and 40 mi. ENE of Benares; road junction; trade center (grain, oilseeds, sugar cane, cotton, hides); govt. opium factory (only one of its kind in India); perfume mfg. Has tomb of Lord Cornwallis (died here 1805). There are 14th-cent. Afghan palace and tomb ruins. Founded c.1330.

Ghazir (gäzēr'), Fr. *Rhazir* or *Gazir,* village (pop. 2,648), central Lebanon, near the coast, 14 mi. NE of Beirut; summer resort. Silkworm breeding and silk spinning. Also cereals, lemons.

Ghazni (gŭz'nē, gäz'nē), town (pop. 25,000), Kabul prov., E Afghanistan, on Ghazni R. and 75 mi. SSW of Kabul, on highway to Kandahar; alt. 7,279 ft.; 33°44'N 68°18'E. Agr. and commercial center; sheepskin mfg., silk weaving; irrigated agr. (grain, opium; orchards, vineyards). Livestock trade. An unattractive walled town, it is dominated by 13th-cent. citadel on a rock rising 150 ft. above the plain. Ruins of old Ghazni (NE; destroyed 1153) include tomb of Mahmud of Ghazni (ruled 997–1030) and two 100-ft.-high minarets. Ghazni was one of the great strongholds (10th–12th cent.) of Afghanistan and is noted as the capital of the Ghaznevids, the country's 1st Moslem dynasty. It flourished under Mahmud, the greatest of the Ghaznevids, who ruled an empire extending from W Persia to the Punjab; had 1st Afghan univ. Old Ghazni was razed 1153 by the Ghorids. It was held by British troops in 1st Afghan War (1839–42) and has revived recently as main town on Kabul-Kandahar auto road.

Ghazni River, E Afghanistan, rises N of Ghazni in outliers of the Hindu Kush, flows 100 mi. S, past Ghazni, to the salt lake Ab-i-Istada.

Ghazze, Palestine: see GAZA.

Ghedem (gĕdĕm'), mountain (3,035 ft.) in Eritrea, near Gulf of Zula, 15 mi. SE of Massawa; low-grade iron and manganese deposits.

Ghedi (gä'dē), town (pop. 5,167), Brescia prov., Lombardy, N Italy, 10 mi. SSE of Brescia, in cereal-, tobacco-growing region; cutlery; cheese.

Ghedo, Ethiopia: see GEDO.

Gheel, Belgium: see GEEL.

Gheidha, Aden: see GHAIDHA.

Gheil Ba Wazir, Ghail Ba Wazir, or **Ghayl Ba Wazir** (gāl' bă' wäzēr'), town and oasis (1946 pop. 12,000), Quaiti state, Eastern Aden Protectorate, 23 mi. NE of Mukalla; major tobacco-growing center, noted for its hookah tobacco; also grows bananas, citrus fruit.

Gheil Ba Yamin, Ghail Ba Yamin, or **Ghayl Ba Yamin** (yămēn'), town (pop. 407), Eastern Aden Protectorate, 60 mi. NNW of Shihr; hq. of Hamumi tribe, under Kathiri control. Airfield; radio station. Also called Gheil Bin Yomein (Yumein) and known as Laijun or Leijun.

Ghelar, Rumania: see HUNEDOARA, town.

Ghelemso (gĕlĕm'sō), village (pop. 1,000), Harar prov., E central Ethiopia, in Chercher Mts., 27 mi. NE of Harar; coffee, cereals, cattle.

Gheluwe, Belgium: see GELUWE.

Ghemines (gĕmēnĕs'), village (pop. 1,900), W Cyrenaica, Libya, near Gulf of Sidra, on coastal road and 30 mi. S of Benghazi; agr. market (barley, fruit, vegetables, livestock). Has mosque and Berber fort.

Ghemme (gĕm'mĕ), village (pop. 3,948), Novara prov., Piedmont, N Italy, near Sesia R., 14 mi. NW of Novara; cotton mill.

Ghent (gĕnt), Flemish *Gent* (khĕnt), Fr. *Gand* (gã), city (pop. 166,797; with suburbs 228,798), ⊙ East Flanders prov., NW Belgium, on Scheldt R. at mouth of Lys R., at S end of Ghent-Terneuzen Canal, and 31 mi. NW of Brussels; 51°4'N 3°42'E. The second largest port and chief textile center of Belgium, an episcopal see, and an education and art center. It imports cotton, linen, coal, petroleum products, and makes cotton, linen, and jute textiles, heavy electrical equipment; flour milling, beer brewing; flower market. Has univ. founded 1816 by William I, Gothic cathedral of St. Bavon (begun in 13th cent.; completed 1531), 13th-cent. church of St. Nicholas, 12th-cent. Romanesque church of St. James, remains of 7th-cent. abbey of St. Bavon, 14th-cent. belfry containing a celebrated carillon, 15th-cent. cloth hall, town hall (begun in 16th cent.), 12th-cent. castle of counts of Flanders, art mus., archaeological mus., mus. of decorative arts, and many old private houses. One of the oldest cities and the historic ⊙ of Flanders, town is on site of two 7th-cent. monasteries and grew around a fortress established several centuries later on a small island. The town soon spread to near-by islets, still connected by numerous bridges. It was a major cloth-weaving center by 13th cent., when Ghent won its independence. Survived many temporary rulers and retained considerable independence until establishment of Spanish regime at end of 15th cent. There were many religious struggles in 16th cent., culminating in signature of Pacification of Ghent (1576; an attempt to secure religious freedom and expel Spaniards from the Netherlands). Again taken by Spaniards in 1584 and remained under the Hapsburgs until the French Revolution. Ghent suffered no serious damage in either World War. Flemish painting flourished at Ghent under the Burgundian dynasty (15th cent.); Hugo van der Goes worked here most of his life and Huybrecht and Jan van Eyck's masterpiece, the *Adoration of the Lamb*, is the altar piece of the Cathedral of St. Bavon. The Treaty of Ghent, ending war bet. U.S. and Great Britain and establishing principle of freedom of the seas, was signed here in 1814. In 1900 Ghent introduced municipal unemployment insurance system subsequently known as the Ghent system.

Ghent. 1 (jĕnt) Town (pop. 368), Carroll co., N Ky., on Ohio R. opposite Vevay, Ohio, and 45 mi. SW of Cincinnati. **2** (gĕnt) Village (pop. 336), Lyon co., SW Minn., on branch of Redwood R. and 7 mi. NW of Marshall, in grain area.

Ghent-Terneuzen Canal (–ternû'zûn), NW Belgium and Zeeland prov., SW Netherlands; runs 32 mi. N-S, bet. Ghent (Belgium) and the Western Scheldt at Terneuzen (Netherlands); enters the Netherlands from Belgium 1.5 mi. S of Sas van Gent; 28 ft. deep, 315 ft. wide. Serves Wondelgem and Zelzate (Belgium), San van Gent and Sluiskil (Netherlands); carries Belg. traffic using port of Terneuzen.

Gheorgheni (gyôrgän'), Hung. *Gyergyószentmiklós* (dyĕr'dyōsĕntmē"klōsh), town (1948 pop. 10,031), Mures prov., E central Rumania, in Transylvania, in W foothills of the Moldavian Carpathians, on railroad and 26 mi. NNW of Mercurea-Ciuc; lumbering center with large sawmills; mfg. of bricks, distilling. Over 90% pop. are Magyars (Szeklers). Sometimes spelled Gheorghieni. In Hungary, 1940–45. Noted resort area of Lacul-Rosu (lä'kōōl-rôs'), Rum. *Lacul-Roşu* [=red lake], is c.15 mi. ENE (alt. 3,215 ft.).

Ghergani (gĕrgän'), village (pop. 776), Bucharest prov., S central Rumania, on railroad and 24 mi. SSE of Targoviste; orchards.

Ghéris, Oued (wĕd' gărēs'), desert stream in SE Fr. Morocco, rises in the High Atlas, flows SE and S, past Goulmina, into the Sahara, skirting the Tafilalet oasis (E), and joins the Oued Ziz to form the Oued ed Daoura, which loses itself in the Algerian Sahara near lat. 29°N. Length, c.170 mi. Also spelled Oued Rhéris.

Gherla (gĕr'lä), Ger. *Armenierstadt* (ärmā'nēūr-shtät"), Hung. *Szamosújvar* (sŏ'môshōōvŏr), town (1948 pop. 6,663), Cluj prov., N Rumania, in Transylvania, on Little Somes R., on railroad and 7 mi. S of Dej; livestock-shipping center; mfg. of edible oils, alcohol, bricks, oriental rugs and cloth. Has a 16th-cent. citadel (now a reformatory). Armenian-Catholic bishopric. Was settled in 17th cent. by Armenians who have since become Magyarized and number ⅓ of total pop. In Hungary, 1940–45.

Gherlogubi, Ethiopia: see Gerlogubi.

Gheva River (gĕ'vä), Tigre prov., N Ethiopia, rises near Adigrat, flows c.125 mi. S and W to Takkaze R. 25 mi. W of Abi Addi.

Ghiannitsa, Greece: see Giannitsa.

Ghidami, Ethiopia: see Gadame.

Ghigner, Ethiopia: see Ginir.

Ghilan, Iran: see Gilan.

Ghilarza (gēlär'tsä), village (pop. 3,258), Cagliari prov., W central Sardinia, 10 mi. S of Macomer, in cork area.

Ghimbi, Ethiopia: see Gimbi.

Ghimes Pass (gē'mĕsh), Rum. *Ghimeş*, pass (alt. 3,081 ft.), in the Moldavian Carpathians, E central Rumania, in Transylvania, 17 mi. NE of Mercurea-Ciuc; highway corridor. Lumbering center of Ghimes-Faget (gē'mĕsh-fû'jĕt), Rum. *Ghimeş-Făget*, is at its N end.

Ghimir, Ethiopia: see Ginir.

Ghimpati (gēmpäts'), Rum. *Ghimpaţi*, village (pop. 2,207), Bucharest prov., S Rumania, 23 mi. NNW of Giurgiu; tobacco processing.

Ghinda (gĕn'dä), town (pop. 1,250), Massawa div., central Eritrea, on railroad and 12 mi. NE of Asmara; cereals, agave, citrus fruit, tobacco.

Ghingiabiet (gĭn'jäbyĕt), village, Gojjam prov., NW Ethiopia, 20 mi. WNW of Bure in horse-raising and irrigated agr. (peaches, lemons, limes) region.

Ghinir, Ethiopia: see Ginir.

Ghio, Turkey: see Gemlik.

Ghiona, Greece: see Giona.

Ghioroc (gyôrôk'), Hung. *Gyorok* (dyô'rôk), village (pop. 1,811), Arad prov., W Rumania, on railroad and 12 mi. E of Arad; noted for its red and white wines and large peach orchards; also sawmills and bell foundries.

Ghirizat, El, or **Al-Ghirizat** (both: ĕl gĭrē'zăt), village (pop. 8,329), Girga prov., central Upper Egypt, 12 mi. WNW of Sohag; cotton, cereals, dates, sugar cane.

Ghisoni (gēzônē'), village (pop. 889), central Corsica, 14 mi. SSE of Corte; lumber, skins.

Ghistelles, Belgium: see Gistel.

Ghizar, Kashmir: see Kuh Ghizar.

Ghizar River, Kashmir: see Gilgit River.

Ghlin (glē), town (pop. 6,452), Hainaut prov., SW Belgium, 3 mi. WNW of Mons; coal mining, lumbering; agr. market.

Ghom, Iran: see Qum.

Ghoom, India: see Darjeeling, town.

Ghor (gōr'), **Ghor-i-Taiwara** (–ĭ-tĭwä'rû), or **Taiwara,** town (pop. over 500), Herat prov., W central Afghanistan, 130 mi. E of Sabzawar, and on tributary of the Farah Rud, in valley bet. 2 outliers of the Hindu Kush; chief town of Ghorat dist., inhabited by Persian-speaking Taimani nomads. Near by are ruins of anc. Ghor, celebrated as seat of the Afghan family, the Ghorids, who overthrew the Ghazni dynasty in 1153 and ruled until c.1210. The greatest of the Ghorids was Mohammed (ruled 1173–1206), who conquered N India and founded the sultanate of Delhi. Sometimes spelled Ghur.

Ghor, The (gōr), Arabic *El Ghor*, great depression of Palestine, in W Jordan and E Israel, forming lower part of Jordan valley, extends 65 mi. N-S bet. Sea of Galilee (696 ft. below sea level) and the Dead Sea (1,292 ft. below sea level); 1–12 mi. wide. S of the Dead Sea it is continued by the depression called Araba to the Gulf of Aqaba.

Ghoraghat (gō'rägät), village, Dinajpur dist., NW East Bengal, E Pakistan, 48 mi. SE of Dinajpur; rice, jute, sugar cane. Hindu ruins. Moslem outpost at end of 15th cent.

Ghorak (gō'rŭk), town (pop. over 2,000), Kandahar prov., S central Afghanistan, 40 mi. NE of Girishk, in outliers of the Hindu Kush.

Ghorat, Afghanistan: see Ghor.

Ghorawal (gō'rŭvŭl), town (pop. 1,122), Mirzapur dist., SE Uttar Pradesh, India, 30 mi. SSE of Mirzapur; rice, gram, barley, wheat, oilseeds. Also spelled Ghurawal.

Ghorband (gōr'bŭnd), town, Kabul prov., E Afghanistan, 45 mi. NW of Kabul, in picturesque valley of Ghorband R. (right tributary of the Panjshir); 35°N 68°40'E. Iron ore mined in valley.

Ghorian, Afghanistan: see Ghurian.

Ghor-i-Taiwara, Afghanistan: see Ghor.

Ghosi (gō'sē), village, Azamgarh dist., E Uttar Pradesh, India, 22 mi. ENE of Azamgarh; rice, barley, wheat, sugar cane.

Ghost Mountain (10,512 ft.), SE B.C., near Alta. border, in Rocky Mts., in Hamber Provincial Park, 40 mi. SSE of Jasper, on edge of the Chaba Icefield; 52°18'N 117°53'W.

Ghotki (gōt'kē), town (pop. 5,236), Sukkur dist., NE Sind, W Pakistan, 36 mi. NE of Sukkur; market center (wheat, millet, rice, wool, sugar cane); handicrafts (pipe bowls, snuff boxes, scissors, cooking pots); cloth weaving. Mangoes grown near by.

Ghoumenitsa, Greece: see Goumenissa.

Ghoumrassen (gōōmräsĕn'), tribal village, Southern Territories, S Tunisia, in the N Sahara, 11 mi. NW of Foum-Tatahouine; olives, sheep, camels. Also spelled Ghoumerassen or Ghomrassen.

Ghouta, Syria: see Ghuta.

Ghoy (gwä), agr. village (pop. 1,175), Hainaut prov., SW central Belgium, 2 mi. NW of Lessines.

Ghrib Dam, Algeria: see Chéliff River.

Ghubaishiya or **Ghubayshiyah** (gōōbīshē'yû), town, Muntafiq prov., SE Iraq, on the lake Hor al Hammar, on Baghdad-Basra RR and 50 mi. ESE of Nasiriya; dates.

Ghum, India: see Darjeeling, town.

Ghumli (gōōm'lē), ruined site, W Saurashtra, India, 45 mi. SSW of Jamnagar; was ⊙ Jethwa Rajputs from 7th to early-14th cent.

Ghur, Afghanistan: see Ghor.

Ghuraf, Al (ăl gōōräf'), village (1946 pop. 530), Kathiri state, Eastern Aden Protectorate, in the Wadi Hadhramaut, 3 mi. S of Tarim; airfield.

Ghurawal, India: see Ghorawal.

Ghurfa, Al, or **Al Ghurfah** (ăl gōōr'fû), town (1946 pop. 3,579), Kathiri state, Eastern Aden Protectorate, in the Wadi Hadhramaut, 3 mi. SW of Seiyun; date groves.

Ghurian or **Ghorian** (gōōryän'), town (pop. 7,000), Herat prov., NW Afghanistan, halfway to Iran border, 40 mi. W of Herat, near left bank of the Hari Rud at W end of its irrigated valley; alt. 2,680 ft.; agr. processing center.

Ghusuri (gōōs'ōōrē), N suburb of Howrah city, Howrah dist., S West Bengal, India, on the Hooghly and 2.5 mi. NNE of Hooghly, 3 mi. N of Calcutta city center; jute milling and pressing, cotton and oilseed milling, mfg. of glass, cigarettes, hosiery, rope; iron- and steel-rolling works, tannery. Has Tibetan monastery, built 1775.

Ghuta or **Ghutah** (gōō'tû), Fr. *Ghouta*, fertile valley in SW Syria, extending E from Damascus. Watered by the Barada and the A'waj, which supply the irrigation system. Apricots, pears, nuts, olives, berries, cereals, grapes. Dairy cattle.

Ghythion, Greece: see Gytheion.

Giadinh (zhä'dĭng'), town (1936 pop. 7,059), ⊙ Gindinh prov. (□ 460; 1943 pop. 364,900), S Vietnam, in Cochin China, 2 mi. N of Saigon. Intensive rice cultivation; rubber, sugar cane, fruit. Coconut-oil extraction, tile mfg.; stockyard. Schools of applied arts and photography.

Giado (jä'dō), village (pop. 1,150), W Tripolitania, Libya, on the plateau Gebel Nefusa, 30 mi. WSW of Jefren, in agr. (olives, cereals) and livestock (sheep, goats) region; alt. c.2,160 ft.; road junction; barracans, prayer rugs, terra-cotta vases. Has power station.

Giaginskaya (gēä'gĭnskīŭ), village (1926 pop. 13,170), SE Adyge Autonomous Oblast, Krasnodar Territory, Russian SFSR, on railroad and 17 mi. N of Maikop; flour mill, metalworks; wheat, sunflowers.

Gialam (zhä'läm'), town, Bacninh prov., N Vietnam, on left bank of Red R., opposite Hanoi (linked by Doumer Bridge); airport of Hanoi; mfg. (paints).

Gialo or **Jalo** (both: jä'lō), town (pop. 2,700), W Cyrenaica, Libya, 145 mi. SE of Agedabia, in an oasis (c.9 mi. long) at N end of Libyan Desert; dates, figs, olives, barley; goats.

Giamda or **Gyamda** (gyäm'dä), Chinese *Chiang-ta* (jyäng'dä), after 1913 *Taichao* or *T'ai-chao* (tī'-jou'), town [Tibetan *dzong*], E Tibet, in Kham prov., on road to Chamdo and 120 mi. ENE of Lhasa, on Giamda R. (left tributary of Brahmaputra R.); rice growing; gold mining.

Giangthanh (zhäng'tä'nyû), town, Hatien prov., S Vietnam, on Cambodia line, 13 mi. NE of Hatien, on Vinhte Canal.

Giannitsa or **Yiannitsa** (both: yĕnĭtsä'), city (pop. 16,401), Pella nome, Macedonia, Greece, on highway and 30 mi. WNW of Salonika, N of former L. Giannitsa (drained in 1930s); trade center for Giannitsa lowland; grain, rice, cotton, silk, tobacco; poultry, cattle. Known as Yenije-i-Vardar under Turkish rule. Also spelled Ghiannitsa; formerly Genitsa, Yenitsa, or Janitza.

Giannutri (jän-nōō'trē), island (□ 1) in Tuscan Archipelago, in Tyrrhenian Sea, Italy, in Grossato prov., 7 mi. S of Monte Argentario; 1.5 mi. long; rises to 272 ft. (N). Has ruins of Roman villa (1st cent. A.D.).

Giant, industrial village, Contra Costa co., W Calif., on San Pablo Bay, NE of Richmond; explosives.

Giant City State Park, Ill.: see Carbondale.

Giant Mountain (4,622 ft.), Essex co., NE N.Y., in the Adirondacks, E of Keene Valley and 10 mi. ENE of Mt. Marcy.

Giant Mountains, Poland and Czechoslovakia: see Riesengebirge.

Giant's Castle, peak (10,868 ft.), in the Drakensberg, W Natal, U. of So. Afr., on Basutoland border, 65 mi. SSW of Ladysmith.

Giant's Causeway, headland on N coast of Co. Antrim, Northern Ireland, terminating in promontory of Benbane Head, 11 mi. NE of Coleraine; extends 3 mi. along coast, 7 mi. ENE of Portrush. It consists of many thousands of small basaltic columns (usually 15–20 inches in diameter) of volcanic origin, forming 3 natural platforms (Little, Middle, and Grand Causeway), with several large caves and rock formations which have been given imaginative names (e.g., Giant's Amphitheater, Giant's Chair, Giant's Chimney, Giant's Organ). According to legend, the Causeway was built by or for giants to travel across to Scotland; similar basaltic formations are found on some isls. of the Hebrides. A ship of the Armada was wrecked in Spanish Bay here.

Giant's Tank, Ceylon: see Madhu Road.

Giarabub, Cyrenaica: see Jarabub.

Giarai (zhä'rī'), town, Baclieu prov., S Vietnam, 18 mi. SW of Baclieu, in well-irrigated area (canals); rice-growing center.

Giardini (järdē'nē), village (pop. 4,641), Messina prov., E Sicily, port on Ionian Sea, 1 mi. S of Taormina; chemical industry.

Giarratana (jär-rätä'nä), village (pop. 3,821), Ragusa prov., SE Sicily, near Irminio R., 9 mi. NNE of Ragusa.

Giarre (jär'rĕ), town (pop. 9,194), Catania prov., E Sicily, at E foot of Mt. Etna, 8 mi. N of Acireale; wine, soap fertilizer industries.

Giarso (jär'sō), town (pop. 2,000), Gamu-Gofa prov., S Ethiopia, near the Galana Sagan, 26 mi. S of Gardula; trade center; weaving.

Giat (zhēä'), village (pop. 791), Puy-de-Dôme dept., central France, 19 mi. NNE of Ussel; brewing.

Giaveno (jävā'nō), village (pop. 3,414), Torino prov., Piedmont, NW Italy, 17 mi. W of Turin, in fruitgrowing region; cotton and paper mills.

Gibara (hēbä'rä), town (pop. 8,045), Oriente prov., E Cuba, port on N coast (Gibara Bay), 18 mi. NNE of Holguín (linked by rail). Seaside resort and trading center in agr. region (sugar cane, tobacco, corn, bananas, cattle); mfg. of cigars, lumbering. Gold, copper, and lead deposits in vicinity. Here the Sp. troops embarked after Spanish-American War. The town was disputed during 1933 revolution. Near by, at Gibara Bay, Columbus made his 1st landing on the isl. (1492).

Gibara River, Oriente prov., E Cuba, flows 20 mi. N to Gibara Bay (Atlantic) SE of Gibara. Lower course navigable for small vessels.

Gibbe River (gĭ'bā), Kaffa prov., SW Ethiopia, rises 15 mi. W of Jimma, flows c.100 mi. E and NE, through Enarea dist., to Omo R. 20 mi. SSE of Nonno.

Gibbeton or **Gibton** (both: gēbtōn'), settlement (pop. 270), W Israel, in Judaean Plain, just W of Rehovot; farming, citriculture. Founded 1933.

Gibbon (gĭ'bŭn). **1** Village (pop. 830), Sibley co., S Minn., 15 mi. W of Gaylord, in agr. area; dairy products. **2** Village (pop. 1,063), Buffalo co., S Nebr., 13 mi. ENE of Kearney and on Wood R.; flour, canned goods, feed.

Gibbon River, NW Wyo., rises in Washburn Range, Yellowstone Natl. Park, flows 37 mi. SW, through geyser region, joining Firehole R. to form Madison R. in W part of park.

Gibbs (gĭbz), town (pop. 144), Adair co., N Mo., near Salt R., 10 mi. SE of Kirksville.

Gibbsboro (gĭbz'–), borough (pop. 906), Camden co., SW N.J., 11 mi. SE of Camden; paint mfg.

Gibb's Hill (gĭbz), highest point (240 ft.) of Bermuda, in Southampton parish, 4 mi. WSW of Hamilton; lighthouse.

Gibbs Island (7 naut. mi. long, 1–1½ naut. mi. wide), E South Shetland Isls., off Palmer Peninsula, Antarctica; 61°30'S 55°35'W.

Gibbstown (gĭbz'–), village (pop. 2,546), Gloucester co., SW N.J., near the Delaware, 7 mi. W of Woodbury; explosives factory.

Gibellina (jēbĕl-lē'nä), village (pop. 6,664), Trapani prov., W Sicily, 13 mi. S of Alcamo, in cereal- and olive-growing region. Anc. castle. Numerous remains of cave dwellers near by.

Gibeon (gĭ'bēŭn), town, S central South-West Africa, 100 mi. NNW of Keetmanshoop; sheep.

Gibraleón (hēvrälāōn'), town (pop. 5,614), Huelva prov., SW Spain, in Andalusia, near Odiel R., 8 mi. N of Huelva, in fertile agr. region (cereals, vegetables, wine, olives, figs, almonds, timber); olive-oil extracting, alcohol distilling, flour milling; mfg. of tiles and soap. Old historic town with ducal palace.

Gibraltar (jĭbrôl'tŭr), Sp. *Jibraltar*, anc. *Calpe*, British crown colony (□ 2¼; 1948 pop. estimate 28,460, including a garrison of 4,760), SW Europe, at S tip of Spain. Heavily fortified naval base at NE gate of the Strait of Gibraltar, occupying narrow peninsula (2¾ mi. long, ¾ mi. wide) that juts S from Cádiz prov., Spain, and is linked to mainland by low isthmus (c.1 mi. long, ½ mi. wide), part of which is neutral ground. Strategically placed opposite Ceuta in North Africa (16 mi. S); near Ceuta is Point Almina, on which is Mt. ACHO, which, with Gibraltar, was one of the anc. PILLARS OF HERCULES. Tangier is 37 mi. SW. ALGECIRAS BAY or Gibraltar Bay (W) is a good anchorage. Gibraltar terminates in the 100-ft. cliffs of Europa Point (36°6'N 5°21'W). From the sandy plain—generally called North Front—it rises abruptly in the Rock of Gibraltar to 1,396 ft. Steep precipices are on the E side, while it falls more gradually towards W, where the city and port of Gibraltar nestle. The rock is made of Jurassic limestone and contains extensive caves in which some valuable archaeological finds have been made. It is now honeycombed by largely invisible defense works and arsenals. A tunnel permits communication bet. E and W side. Slopes are covered by Mediterranean shrubs. The climate is generally temperate, though occasionally quite hot in summer months. Temp. ranges bet. 45°–65°F. in winter and 55°–85°F. in summer. Rainy season lasts from Dec. to May, with an annual rainfall of about 21 inches. Precarious water supply depends on shallow wells in N isthmus and 38 acres of catchment area, feeding to reservoirs in the Rock which hold 14,000,000 gallons. There are neither forests nor industries, though construction of a sardine and olive cannery has been proposed. It serves, however, as an important coaling station for transoceanic shipping, and has a free port. Artificial harbor of c.440 acres is bounded by 2 long moles with a detached mole acting as breakwater. There are modern loading and repair facilities and 3 large graving docks. Since the town is a fortress, most of the area is taken up with military installations, including barracks and hospitals. The civilian pop., which is kept low, lives in the so-called South Town around Rosia Bay, but many of the laborers reside in the thriving Sp. border town LA LÍNEA. The Northern Town—or just Town—climbs up the slope to 250 ft. It contains the business section, mus., remains of anc. Moorish castle, R.C. cathedral, governor's residence, called the Convent (former Franciscan monastery), and Arengo's palace. Bet. these 2 sections lies picturesque Alameda Park. On NE side of the Rock is small village of CATALAN BAY, inhabited by fishermen of Genoese origin. An airfield was built during Second World War on N isthmus, which is now also cut by a moat. There is a highway along the W base of the Rock. The pop. is predominantly of Sp. descent and R.C. denomination. Both English, the official language, and Spanish are spoken. Administrative power is vested in a governor, who also commands the fortress. He is assisted by an executive council. Formation of a legislative council was announced in 1948. Known to the ancients as Calpe, Gibraltar has been in turn occupied by Phoenicians, Carthaginians, Romans, and Visigoths. Its present name derives from Arabic Jebel-al-Tarik [mount of Tarik], which dates from the capture of the peninsula by the Moorish conqueror Tarik in 711. The Moors were the 1st to fortify the Rock. Temporarily held 1309–33 by the Spanish, who regained it from the Moors in 1462. The English have maintained possession of the peninsula since 1704, when it was taken by combined English-Dutch fleet under Admiral Sir George Rooke during War of Spanish Succession; officially transferred (1713) to Great Britain by Treaty of Utrecht. Gibraltar was subjected to several unsuccessful sieges by the Spanish and French, notably in the "Great Siege" (Sept. 13, 1779, to March 12, 1783). Key point for anti-submarine campaign in First World War. In Sp. civil war (1936–39) many refugees fled here. Most of the civilian pop. was evacuated to England and elsewhere during the Second World War, when the naval base played an important part in the Allied Mediterranean defense. Fortifications were then strengthened. It was frequently raided by Axis planes, but no severe damage was caused. After Second World War, Spain renewed its claims to Gibraltar.

Gibraltar, village (1940 pop. 607), Berks co., SE central Pa., near Schuylkill R., 5 mi. SE of Reading.

Gibraltar (hēbrältär'), town (pop. 517), Zulia state, NW Venezuela, on SE shore of L. Maracaibo, 4 mi. NE of Bobures; sugar cane, cacao. Founded 1597. Sacked by the buccaneer Henry Morgan.

Gibraltar, Strait of (jĭbrôl'tŭr), anc. *Fretum Herculeum* and *Fretum Gaditanum*, passage, c.36 mi. long, connecting the Atlantic and the Mediterranean, bet. southernmost Spain and northwesternmost Africa. Its W limits are Cape Trafalgar (Spain) and Cape Spartel (International Zone of Tangier); its E limits Gibraltar and Point Almina (just E of Ceuta, NW Africa). Width ranges from 8 mi. off Point Marroquí to 27 mi. at W entrance. Average depth, c.1,200 ft. Surface current from the Atlantic flows E at 2.5 mi. per hour. A counter-current flows at greater depth. The 2 promontories at E entrance are the classical Pillars of Hercules.

Gibraltar Dam, Calif: see SANTA YNEZ RIVER.

Gibsland, town (pop. 1,085), Bienville parish, NW La., 40 mi. E of Shreveport; shipping center for truck-farming area. Has training school for Negroes. Founded c.1885.

Gibson. **1** County (□ 499; pop. 30,720), SW Ind.; ⊙ Princeton. Bounded W by Wabash R. (here forming Ill. line) and N by White R.; also drained by Patoka R., small Black R. and Pigeon Creek. Agr. area (grain, livestock, poultry, truck, fruit); mfg. (concrete blocks, food products, oil-well supplies, electric clocks). Bituminous-coal mines; natural-gas and oil wells; timber. Formed 1813. **2** County (□ 607; pop. 48,132), NW Tenn.; ⊙ Trenton. Bounded NE by South Fork of Obion R., SW by Middle Fork of Forked Deer R. Fertile agr. area (cotton, corn, strawberries, vegetables, livestock). Mfg. at Humboldt. Timber tracts, marble and granite deposits. Formed 1823.

Gibson. **1** Town (pop. 460), ⊙ Glascock co., E Ga., 37 mi. WSW of Augusta; sawmilling. Cotton area. **2** City, Ford co., Ill.: see GIBSON CITY. **3** Town (pop. 117), Dunklin co., extreme SE Mo., near St. Francis R., 14 mi. N of Kennett. **4** Town (pop. 609), Scotland co., S N.C., 9 mi. WSW of Laurinburg, near S.C. line. **5** Town (pop. 308), Gibson co., NW Tenn., 5 mi. NE of Humboldt.

Gibsonburg, village (pop. 2,281), Sandusky co., N Ohio, 11 mi. W of Fremont; limestone quarries; dairy products, livestock, grain. Founded 1871.

Gibson City or **Gibson,** city (pop. 3,029), Ford co., E central Ill., 24 mi. NNW of Champaign; trade and processing center in rich agr. area (corn, oats, wheat, soybeans, livestock, poultry); canned foods; cheese, feed. Inc. 1894.

Gibson Dam, Mont.: see SUN RIVER.

Gibson Desert, central belt of Western Australian desert, E of Murchison Goldfield and bet. Great Sandy Desert (N) and Victoria Desert (S); sand dunes, scrub, salt marshes.

Gibson Island, resort village, Anne Arundel co., central Md., on narrow neck bet. Chesapeake Bay and Magothy R., 14 mi. NNE of Annapolis; known for yachting. Near by is Fort Smallwood Park (owned by Baltimore), around fortification which was active 1896–1926.

Gibsons Landing, village (pop. 262), SW B.C., on Thornbrough Channel of Howe Sound, 20 mi. WNW of Vancouver; resort. Opposite Keats Isl.

Gibsonville, town (pop. 1,866), Guilford and Alamance counties, N central N.C., 13 mi. E of Greensboro, in agr. area; hosiery mills

Gibton, Israel: see GIBBETON.

Gidami, Ethiopia: see GADAME.

Giddalur (gĭdŭlōōr'), town (pop. 5,219), Kurnool dist., N Madras, India, in Eastern Ghats, 65 mi. SE of Kurnool; sawmilling; millet, turmeric, mangoes. Timber, bamboo, fibers in near-by forests. Sometimes spelled Giddalore.

Giddarbaha (gĭd"dŭrbä'hŭ), town (pop. 6,317), Ferozepore dist., W Punjab, India, 50 mi. S of Ferozepore; gram, wheat, oilseeds; cotton ginning. Sometimes called Mandi Giddarbaha.

Giddings (gĭ'dĭngz), city (pop. 2,532), ⊙ Lee co., S central Texas, c.45 mi. E of Austin; trade, shipping center in agr. area (cotton, truck, peanuts, poultry, dairy products); turkey packing, cottonseed-oil milling, peanut shelling. Founded 1872 by Wends from near-by Serbin (just SW), 1st Wendish settlement in state, settled 1855.

Gideon (gĭ'dēŭn), city (pop. 1,754), New Madrid co., extreme SE Mo., in Mississippi flood plain, 8 mi. SSE of Malden. Inc. 1909.

Gidida, El (gĭdē'dŭ), or **Al-Jadidah** (jă–), village (pop. 2,797) in Dakhla oasis, S central Egypt, 8 mi. SSW of El Qasr; dates, oranges, wheat, barley.

Gidrotorf (gēdrŭtôrf'), town (1926 pop. 2,800), W Gorki oblast, Russian SFSR, 3 mi. WSW of Balakhna; has large power station fed by local peat deposits.

Gidzhduvan, Uzbek SSR: see GIZHDUVAN.

Giebelstadt (gē'bŭl-shtät), village (pop. 1,316), Lower Franconia, W Bavaria, Germany, 9 mi. S of Würzburg; grain, cattle.

Giebichenstein (gē"bĭkhŭn-shtīn'), N suburb of Halle, Saxony-Anhalt, central Germany. Has remains of 10th-cent. castle, until 15th cent. a residence of archbishops of Magdeburg; destroyed (1636) in Thirty Years War by Swedes.

Gieboldehausen (gēbôl'dŭhou"zŭn), village (pop. 3,104), in former Prussian prov. of Hanover, W Germany, after 1945 in Lower Saxony, 13 mi. NE of Göttingen; woodworking.

Gielkhola, India: see KALIMPONG.

Gien (zhēē'), town (pop. 6,168), Loiret dept., N central France, on right bank of the Loire and 37 mi. ESE of Orléans; opaque faïence mfg. center. Wine trade. Suffered considerable damage in Second World War (15th-cent. church and Renaissance houses destroyed). The 15th-cent. castle (now courthouse) has been preserved.

Giengen or **Giengen an der Brenz** (gĕng'ŭn än dĕr brĕnts'), town (pop. 5,615), N Württemberg, Germany, after 1945 in Württemberg-Baden, 6 mi. SE of Heidenheim; grain, cattle. Has Gothic-baroque church.

Giens Peninsula (zhēē'), Var dept., SE France, on the Mediterranean, bet. Gulf of Giens (W) and Rade d'Hyères (E). Consists of a former rocky isl. (4 mi. long; once part of the Hyères isl. group) connected with mainland S of Hyères by 2 sandy tombolos separated by lagoon. Saltworks near base.

Gierlach, peak, Czechoslovakia: see STALIN PEAK.

Gier River (zhēā'), Loire and Rhône depts., E central France, rises on N slope of Mont Pilat 6 mi. ENE of Saint-Genest-Malifaux, flows 27 mi. NE, through E part of Saint-Étienne coal basin and industrial dist., past Saint-Chamond and Rive-de-Gier, to the Rhone at Givors.

Giessbach (gēs'bäkh), stream in Bernese Alps, S central Switzerland; flows to L. of Brienz opposite Brienz; noted for its 7 cascades totaling 980 ft. in height.

Giessen (gē'sŭn), city (1946 pop. 31,601, including suburbs 39,709; 1950 pop. 46,701), central Hesse, W Germany, ⊙ former Upper Hesse prov., on the Lahn (head of navigation) and 31 mi. N of Frankfurt; 50°36'N 8°41'E. Rail junction; mfg. of machine tools, fittings, cash registers, clothing, mirror glass, soap, tobacco, cigars; food processing. Manganiferous iron ore mined just S. Site (1607–1945) of Protestant univ., now converted into agr. and veterinary col.; and of acad. for medical research (founded 1949). Second World War destruction (67%) resulted in heavy damage to all noteworthy bldgs. Chartered 1248. Passed to Hesse in 1265. Belonged (1567–1604) to independent Hessen-Marburg; then went to HESSE-DARMSTADT.

Giesshübel-Sauerbrunn, Czechoslovakia: see CARLSBAD.

Giessübel (gēs'ü"bŭl), village (pop. 1,270), Thuringia, central Germany, in Thuringian Forest, 10 mi. S of Ilmenau; popular health and winter-sports resort; glass mfg., woodworking.

Gieten (khē'tŭn), town (pop. 1,805), Drenthe prov., NE Netherlands, on the Hondsrug, 8 mi. E of Assen; meat packing; vegetable growing. Prehistoric graves near by.

Gievedal, Norway: see GJOVDAL.

Giffard (zhē'făr), village (pop. 4,909), S central Que., on the St. Lawrence and 3 mi. NE of Quebec; dairying; vegetables, poultry.

Gifford, agr. village in Yester parish, central East Lothian, Scotland, 4 mi. SSE of Haddington. Has ruins of 13th-cent. Yester Castle.

Gifford. 1 Village (pop. 1,459), Indian River co., E Fla., just N of Vero Beach. **2** Town (pop. 16), Macon co., N central Mo., on Chariton R. and 23 mi. NNW of Macon. **3** Village, Hampton co., SW S.C., 12 mi. SSE of Allendale; lumber, vegetable seeds.

Giffordgate, Scotland: see HADDINGTON.

Giffre River (zhē'frü), Haute-Savoie dept., SE France, rises in the Chablais, near Swiss border, flows 22 mi. generally W, past Sixt, Samoëns and Taninges, to the Arve below Marignier where it activates hydroelectric and electrochemical plant.

Gifhorn (gĭf'hôrn), town (pop. 8,767), in former Prussian prov. of Hanover, NW Germany, after 1945 in Lower Saxony, on the Aller and 15 mi. N of Brunswick; mfg. of machinery, chemicals, furniture; food processing (canned goods, flour products, beverages), sawmilling. Has 16th-cent. castle.

Gifu (gē'fōō), prefecture [Jap. *ken*] (□ 4,052; 1940 pop. 1,265,024; 1947 pop. 1,493,644), central Honshu, Japan; ⊙ Gifu. Bounded S by Kiso R.; largely mountainous, with fertile plain near Nagoya area. Agr. (rice, persimmons, herbs), extensive sawmilling and charcoal production; mfg. (textiles, pottery, cutlery, paper products, sake), woodworking. Lead mined at Funatsu, lignite at Mitake. Principal centers: Gifu, OGAKI, SEKI.

Gifu, city (1940 pop. 172,340; 1947 pop. 166,995), ⊙ Gifu prefecture, central Honshu, Japan, on Nagara R. and 20 mi. NNW of Nagoya; rail junction; mfg. center (textiles, paper products). Fishing (with cormorants) on Nagara R. Site of Nawa Entomological Inst. (1896). Hq. of Oda Nobunaga (16th cent.). City reconstructed after earthquake of 1891. Sometimes called Gihu.

Gigant (gēgänt'), town (1939 pop. over 2,000), S Rostov oblast, Russian SFSR, on railroad and 10 mi. W of Salsk; metalworks; wheat, cotton, livestock. In 1930s, center of one of largest state farms of USSR.

Giganta, La (lä hēgän'tä), peak (9,631 ft.), Guanajuato, central Mexico, in Sierra Madre Occidental, 9 mi. NNW of Guanajuato.

Giganta, Sierra de la (syĕ'rä dā), range in S Lower California, NW Mexico, extends c.180 mi. SE along coast of Gulf of California, from Concepción Bay to La Paz Bay; rises to 5,794 ft. in Cerro de la Giganta, NW of Loreto.

Gigante (hēgän'tä), town (pop. 2,068), Huila, S central Colombia, in upper Magdalena valley, on highway, and 40 mi. SSW of Neiva; rice, cacao, coffee, livestock. Owes its name to giant mastodon fossils found here.

Gigante, Cerro (sĕ'rō) (7,645 ft.), mountain in center of the Sierra Grande, W Córdoba prov., Argentina, 35 mi. W of Córdoba; granite quarries.

Gigante, Colle di, Italy and France: see GÉANT, COL DU.

Gigaquit (hēgä'kēt, hēgäkēt'), town (1939 pop. 1,929; 1948 municipality pop. 14,431), Surigao prov., on NE coast of Mindanao, Philippines, 20 mi. SE of Surigao; copra; mining.

Gigen (gēgĕn'), village (pop. 5,631), Pleven dist., N Bulgaria, near influx of Iskar R. into the Danube, 21 mi. W of Nikopol; flour milling; livestock, truck. Has ruins of anc. Roman town of Oescus.

Gigena (hēhā'nä), town (pop. 2,391), W Córdoba prov., Argentina, 26 mi. N of Río Cuarto; cereals, flax, sunflowers, livestock.

Giggiga, Ethiopia: see JIJIGA.

Giggleswick, agr. village and parish (pop. 786), West Riding, W Yorkshire, England, on Ribble R. just WNW of Settle. Has grammar school founded in 1512 and 16th-cent. church.

Gigha (gī'ŭ), island (□ 6, including Cara isl.; pop. 240), S Argyll, Scotland, separated from Kintyre peninsula by 3-mi.-wide Sound of Gigha; 6 mi. long, 2 mi. wide; rises to 331 ft. Chief occupation is cod and ling fishing.

Gig Harbor, town (pop. 803), Pierce co., W Wash., across arm of Puget Sound NW of Tacoma; fishing and ferry base; ships berries, eggs, lumber, evergreens. Inc. after 1940.

Gight Castle, Scotland: see METHLICK.

Giglio (jē'lyô), island (□ 8; pop. 2,141) in Tuscan Archipelago, in Tyrrhenian Sea, Italy, in Grosseto prov., 10 mi. W of Monte Argentario; 5.5 mi. long, 3 mi. wide; mountainous, rising to 1,634 ft. (center). Has village of Giglio Castello (N) and its port, Giglio Porto, on E coast. Vineyards; granite quarries; iron pyrites deposits.

Gignac (zhēnyäk'), town (pop. 2,021), Hérault dept., S France, on Hérault R. and 16 mi. W of Montpellier; winegrowing, olive preserving, barrel mfg.

Gigüela River (hēgwā'lä), New Castile, central Spain, rises W of Cuenca, flows c.125 mi. SW to swamps NE of Ciudad Real, where the Guadiana emerges. Its lower course (c.25 mi.), after joining the Záncara, is sometimes called Záncara.

Giheina, Gihena (both: gĭhā'nü), or **Juhaynah** (jōōhā'nü), town (pop. 40,427), Girga prov., central Upper Egypt, 7 mi. S of Tahta; cotton ginning, pottery making; cotton, cereals, dates, sugar cane. In vicinity are large Mohammedan and Christian cemeteries. Also spelled Guhena and Gohana.

Gihu, Japan: see GIFU, city.

Gijo, Korea: see UISONG.

Gijón (hēhōn'), town (pop. 72,053), Oviedo prov., NW Spain, largest city and principal seaport of Asturias, on Bay of Biscay, 15 mi. NE of Oviedo; industrial and commercial center exporting coal and iron in large quantity. Extends along 2 bays separated by rocky promontory; excellent new harbor El Musel (ocean-going vessels) and shipyards at NW end of W bay. Iron and steel industries (tubes, mining equipment and other machinery, hardware); chemical works (fertilizers, oxygen, acetic acid); oil refinery, tobacco factory, brewery, sugar mills; glass and cement mfg.; fish and meat processing. Has 15th-cent. church, some 17th-cent. mansions, and naval acad. Beach of San Lorenzo (E bay) is popular summer resort. Probably of Roman origin, Gijón was one of the 1st towns recaptured (722) from the Moors by the Christians; it flourished under Pelayo, 1st king of Asturias; ⊙ kingdom until 791. Was refuge (1588) of remnants of the Invincible Armada after defeat by English. In the Sp. civil war, it was last N Sp. port to fall (1937) to Insurgents.

Gila (hē'lü), county (□ 4,750; pop. 24,158), E central Ariz.; ⊙ Globe. Bounded by San Carlos, Gila, and Verde rivers. Chief ranges are Sierra Ancha and Pinal Mts. Roosevelt Dam and Reservoir on Salt R. and Coolidge Dam and San Carlos Reservoir on Gila R. provide water for irrigation. Co. includes parts of Tonto Natl. Forest and San Carlos and Fort Apache Indian reservations. Copper, gold, silver, asbestos, vanadium are mined. Formed 1881.

Gila, village (pop. c.200), Grant co., SW N.Mex., on Gila R., just S of Mogollon Mts., and 23 mi. NW of Silver City; alt. c.4,300 ft. Supply point for camping trips. Gila Wilderness Area is near by in Gila Natl. Forest. Gila Cliff Dwellings Natl. Monument is 25 mi. NE.

Gila Bend, village (1940 pop. 582), Maricopa co., SW Ariz., near Gila R., 50 mi. SW of Phoenix; center of cotton and livestock area. Gila Indian Reservation is across river.

Gila Bend Mountains, Maricopa co., SW Ariz., near Gila R., SW of Phoenix; rise to c.3,000 ft.

Gila Cliff Dwellings National Monument (160 acres; established 1907), SW N.Mex., on branch of Gila R., in Gila Natl. Forest, and 32 mi. N of Silver City. Consists of 4 well-preserved cave dwellings in face of overhanging cliff which were occupied by Pueblo Indians who migrated into area c.1,000 years ago. They practiced irrigated agr. and made superior pottery.

Gila Mountains. 1 In Graham co., SE Ariz., near Safford; extend SE–NW along right bank of Gila R.; rise to c.7,000 ft. **2** In Yuma co., SW Ariz., E of Yuma Desert, ESE of Yuma; extend N from Tinajas Altas Mts. to Gila R.; rise to 3,150 ft. in S.

Gilan (gēlän'), former province of N Iran, on SW shore of Caspian Sea, astride the lower Sefid Rud; main center, Resht. Bordered S by Elburz chain, it has a humid subtropical climate, favoring some of Iran's richest commercial crops, but also inducing malarial conditions. Silk (85% of Iran's total production), rice, tea (Lahijan), fruit, olives (Manjil, Rudbar) are the leading products. Main centers are Resht and its port Pahlevi, Fumen, and Lahijan. Pop. speaks Gilaki, an Iranian tongue. Noted throughout the Middle Ages as a silk region, Gilan was among the Caspian provs. that were, during 1723–32, under Russian control. In 1938, the prov. was joined with W Mazanderan, Khamseh, Kazvin, and Arak to form Iran's First Province (□ 30,000; 1940 pop. 2,367,537), to which the name Gilan (sometimes spelled Ghilan) is commonly applied.

Gilan or **Gilan-Gharb** (gärb) [Persian,=West Gilan], town (1942 pop. estimate 1,500), Fifth Prov., in Kermanshah, W Iran, near Iraq line, 70 mi. WSW of Kermanshah; center of Bavandpur agr. dist. (grain, cotton, tobacco).

Gila River (gē'lä) or **Gelo River** (gĕ'lō), Ital. *Ghila* or *Ghelo*, in Ilubabor prov., SW Ethiopia, rises S of Gore, flows c.170 mi. WNW, through plain infested by malaria and tsetse fly, to Pibor R. 28 mi. NNE of Akobo on Anglo-Egyptian Sudan border.

Gila River (hē'lü), intermittent stream, rising in SW N.Mex., flows c.650 mi. generally SW, across Ariz., to Colorado R. near Yuma. Receives San Francisco, San Pedro, Santa Cruz, Salt, and Agua Fria rivers; drains □ 58,100. Coolidge Dam irrigates extensive area in which alfalfa, cotton, corn, and fruit are raised. Valley was once inhabited by early American Indians, of whose dwellings and implements there are many remains. Buckeye, Florence, and Hayden, Ariz., are on river, which passes San Carlos, Gila River, and Gila Bend Indian reservations, and Casa Grande and Gila Cliff Dwellings natl. monuments. Gila Natl. Forest and govt.-preserved Gila Wilderness Area (entered via Silver City, N.Mex.) are in headwater region.

Gilau (jē'lŭōō), Rum. *Gilău*, Hung. *Gyalu* (dyŏ'lōō), village (pop. 3,404), Cluj prov., W central Rumania, on Little Somes R., in NE foothills of the Apuseni Mts., 10 mi. W of Cluj; lumbering center; wood cracking. Has 16th-cent. castle. In Hungary, 1940–45.

Gilawia, El, or **Al-Jilawiyah** (both: ĕl gĭlă'wĭyü, jĭ-), village (pop. 8,078), Girga prov., central Upper Egypt, 8 mi. ESE of Tahta; cotton, cereals, dates, sugar cane.

Gilbert, town (pop. estimate 1,000), S central Entre Ríos prov., Argentina, on railroad and 40 mi. W of Concepción del Uruguay; agr. center (wheat, flax, oats, corn, livestock).

Gilbert. 1 Town (pop. 1,114), Maricopa co., S central Ariz., 18 mi. ESE of Phoenix; cotton gin; alfalfa, wheat, cotton, flax. **2** Town (pop. 51), Searcy co., N Ark., 27 mi. SE of Harrison and on Buffalo R. **3** Town (pop. 297), Story co., central Iowa, 6 mi. N of Ames; livestock, grain. **4** Village (pop. 452), Franklin parish, NE La., 41 mi. SE of Monroe, in agr. area; cotton ginning. **5** Village (pop. 2,247), St. Louis co., NE Minn., in Mesabi iron range, just SE of Virginia, in mining and agr. area (livestock, poultry, potatoes). Founded 1907, inc. 1909. **6** Town (pop. 172), Lexington co., central S.C., 20 mi. W of Columbia; canning, lumber milling. **7** Town (pop. 722), Mingo co., SW W.Va., 23 mi. E of Williamson; bituminous coal.

Gilbert, Mount (10,200 ft.), SW B.C., in Coast Mts., 120 mi. NNW of Vancouver; 50°50′N 124°17′W.

Gilbert and Ellice Islands (ĕl'ĭs), Br. colony (□ 375; pop. 36,000), W central and SW Pacific; established 1915, placed under Western Pacific High Commission at Suva, Fiji; include GILBERT ISLANDS, ELLICE ISLANDS, OCEAN ISLAND, FANNING ISLAND, WASHINGTON ISLAND, CHRISTMAS ISLAND, PHOENIX ISLANDS; ⊙ Tarawa, in Gilbert Isls. All are atolls except Ocean Isl., ⊙ colony before Second World War. Colony's chief exports: copra, phosphate. Natives are Micronesians, Polynesians.

Gilbert Islands, small group in Tierra del Fuego, Chile, on the Pacific bet. Stewart Isl. and Londonderry Isl.; 55°S 71°15′W.

Gilbert Islands, group of atolls (□ 144; pop. 27,824), in Br. colony of GILBERT AND ELLICE ISLANDS, W central Pacific; 3°17′N–2°38′S 172°58′–176°49′E. Include 10 isls. N of equator: LITTLE MAKIN, MAKIN, MARAKEI, ABAIANG, NIKUNAU, TARAWA, MAIANA, ABEMAMA, KURIA, ARANUKA; and 6 isls. of Kingsmill Group S of equator: NONOUTI, TABITEUEA, BERU, ONOTOA, TAMANA, ARORAE. Tarawa ⊙ and port of colony. Rainfall ranges from 150 in. on N isls. to 15 in. on S isls.; periodic droughts on dryer isls. Coconut, palm trees; no livestock. Taro is only agricultural product; some copra is exported. Natives are Micronesians. Discovered 1764 by Capt. Byron, included 1915 in Gilbert and Ellice Isls. colony. In Second World War, Makin, Abaiang, Marakei, Tarawa, and Abemama were occupied 1941 by Japanese. Regained 1943 by U.S. forces, they became bases for attacking Marshall Isls.

Gilbert Lake, Otsego co., central N.Y., 12 mi. NNW of Oneonta; c.½ mi. long. State park here; camping, hiking.

Gilberton (gĭl'bûrtŭn), borough (pop. 2,641), Schuylkill co., E central Pa., 8 mi. NNW of Pottsville; anthracite. Inc. 1873.

Gilbertown, town (pop. 413), Choctaw co., SW Ala., 16 mi. SSW of Butler.

Gilbert Peak, Utah: see UINTA MOUNTAINS.

Gilbert Plains, village (pop. 810), W Man., on Valley R. and 19 mi. W of Dauphin; dairying, lumbering; grain, stock; brick making, clay and marl quarrying; grain elevators.

Gilbert River, N Queensland, Australia, rises near junction of Gregory Range with Great Dividing Range; flows 312 mi. NW, through cattle-raising region, to Gulf of Carpentaria. Einasleigh R., main tributary.

Gilberts, village (pop. 183), Kane co., NE Ill., 7 mi. NW of Elgin, in agr. area (dairy products; livestock).

Gilbertsville, village (pop. 456), Otsego co., central N.Y., 11 mi. W of Oneonta, in dairying and grain-growing area.

Gilbertville. 1 Town (pop. 399), Black Hawk co., E central Iowa, on Cedar R. and 8 mi. SE of Waterloo; feed milling. **2** Village, Worcester co., Mass.: see HARDWICK.

Gilboa (gĭlbō'ŭ), agr. settlement, N Israel, at SE end of Plain of Jezreel, at NW foot of Mt. Gilboa, 6 mi. SE of Afula. Modern settlement founded 1948 on site of village of Zera'im (zĕrä-ēm'), abandoned by Arab pop. In biblical history scene of Saul's defeat and death at hands of Philistines. The Well of Harod, Gideon's hq. prior to battle on Hill of Moreh, was in immediate vicinity; as *Ain Jalud* it was scene (1260) of defeat of Mongol garrison of Syria by Crusaders and Egyptian Mameluks.

Gilboa (gĭlbō'ŭ). **1** (also gĭl'boi) Village, Schoharie co., E central N.Y., in the Catskills, 40 mi. SW of Albany. Gilboa Dam here impounds Schoharie

Reservoir in SCHOHARIE CREEK. 2 Village (pop. 181), Putnam co., NW Ohio, 15 mi. W of Findlay and on Blanchard R.; limestone quarry.

Gilboa, Mount, hill range, NE Israel, on Jordan border, extends c.10 mi. NW–SE bet. Jordan valley and SE edge of Plain of Jezreel; rises to 1,630 ft. 6 mi. W of Beisan. In biblical history Saul was defeated and killed by Philistines at NW foot of range, near present-day settlement of Gilboa.

Gilbués (zhĕlbwĕs'), city (pop. 431), S Piauí, Brazil, 220 mi. SW of Floriano; cattle raising. Formerly spelled Gilboés.

Gilchrist (gĭl'krĭst), county (□ 339; pop. 3,499), N Fla., bounded by Santa Fe (N) and Suwannee (W) rivers; ⊙ Trenton. Flatwoods area with many small lakes. Farming (corn, vegetables, peanuts), cattle raising, lumbering. Formed 1925.

Gilchrist, summer resort, Galveston co., S Texas, on Gulf of Mexico shore of Bolivar Peninsula, 28 mi. NE of Galveston.

Gilcrest (gĭl'krĕst), town (pop. 429), Weld co., N Colo., near South Platte R., 40 mi. NNE of Denver, in irrigated sugar-beet and garden-truck area; alt. 4,752 ft.

Gildersleeve, Conn.: see PORTLAND.

Gildersome (gĭl'dûrsûm), former urban district (1931 pop. 3,044), West Riding, SW central Yorkshire, England, 5 mi. SW of Leeds; woolen milling, mfg. of textile machinery. A colony of cloth weavers from Gelderland, Netherlands, settled here in 1571. Inc. 1937 in Morley.

Gildessa, Ethiopia: see JALDESSA.

Gildford, village (pop. c.200), Hill co., N Mont., 29 mi. W of Havre; storage and shipping point for livestock, grain.

Gilead (gĭ'lēûd, –ăd), mountainous region of anc. Palestine, E of Jordan R., bet. Sea of Galilee and the Dead Sea. Mt. Gilead (3,597 ft.) rises just N of modern Salt (Jordan).

Gilead. 1 Village, Tolland co., Conn.: see HEBRON. **2** Town (pop. 140), Oxford co., W Maine, on the Androscoggin and 23 mi. SW of Rumford, partly in White Mtn. Natl. Forest. **3** Village (pop. 109), Thayer co., SE Nebr., 10 mi. E of Hebron, near Little Blue R.

Gilena (hēlā'nä), town (pop. 4,081), Seville prov., SW Spain, 11 mi. E of Osuna; agr. center (olives, cereals). Liquor distilling, flour milling; stone quarrying.

Gileppe, Barrage de la, Belgium: see BARRAGE DE LA GILEPPE.

Giles (jīlz). **1** County (□ 619; pop. 26,961), S Tenn.; ⊙ Pulaski. Bounded S by Ala.; drained by Elk R. and small Richland Creek. In fertile bluegrass region; produces dairy products, livestock, cotton, tobacco, truck crops; phosphate mining. Formed 1809. **2** County (□ 356; pop. 18,956), SW Va.; ⊙ Pearisburg. In the Alleghenies; bounded NW, N by W.Va.; lies entirely within Jefferson Natl. Forest. Drained by New R. Agr. (corn, wheat, apples), dairying, livestock and poultry raising. Lumbering, lumber milling; mfg. (especially rayon), leather tanning. Some coal mining. Includes Mountain Lake (resort village). Formed 1806.

Gilford, town (pop. 832), NW Co. Down, Northern Ireland, on Bann R. and 4 mi. WNW of Banbridge; linen, thread.

Gilford (gĭl'fûrd), town (pop. 1,251), Belknap co., central N.H., on L. Winnipesaukee just NE of Laconia; summer and winter resort.

Gilford Island (□ 159), SW B.C., at E end of Queen Charlotte Strait, 15 mi. ENE of Alert Bay; 21 mi. long, 4–12 mi. wide. NE part of isl. rises to 4,820 ft. on Mt. Read.

Gilgandra (gĭlgăn'drû), town (pop. 2,231), E central New South Wales, Australia, on Castlereagh R. and 210 mi. NW of Sydney; sheep and agr. center.

Gilgenburg, Poland: see DABROWNO.

Gilgil (gĭl'gĭl), town, Rift Valley prov., W central Kenya, in Great Rift Valley, 18 mi. NNW of Naivasha; rail junction for Thomson's Falls; alt. 6,581 ft.; 0°30'S 36°20'E; center of stock-raising dist.; corn, barley, oats; dairy farming. Airfield. Diatomite mined near by.

Gilgilchai or **Gil'gil'chay** (gĭlgĭlchī'), town (1945 pop. over 500), NE Azerbaijan SSR, on railroad and 5 mi. SE of Divichi, near Caspian Sea coast; fisheries; orchards.

Gilgit (gĭl'gĭt), leased area (□ 1,480; pop. 22,495), NW Kashmir; ⊙ Gilgit. In trans-Indus extension of N Punjab Himalayas; bounded S by Indus R.; drained by Gilgit and Hunza rivers. Agr. (wheat, corn, pulse, barley, rice). Only town, Gilgit. Was part of former Gilgit dist., divided (1934) into Gilgit leased area and Gilgit Wazarat; until 1947, leased by British from maharaja of Jammu and Kashmir for administrative purposes. Held after 1948 by Pakistan. Prevailing mother tongue, Shina.

Gilgit, town (pop. 4,671), ⊙ Gilgit leased area and Gilgit Agency, NW Kashmir, in trans-Indus extension of N Punjab Himalayas, on Gilgit R. and 130 mi. NNW of Srinagar; wheat, corn, pulse. Fort. Anc. Buddhist center; now an important frontier station for surrounding tribal areas.

Gilgit Agency, former administrative division (□ 14,680; pop. 76,526) of NW Kashmir, under British Political Agent, with hq. at Gilgit. Bordered W by North-West Frontier Prov. (now part of W Pakistan), NE by Sinkiang (China). Comprised feudatory states of Chilsa, Ghizar, Hunza, Ishkuman, Kuh, Nagar, Punial, and Yasin. Extremely mountainous area at junction of Hindu Kush and Karakoram ranges; crossed S by W Punjab Himalayas; dominated by Distaghil (25,868 ft.), Rakaposhi (25,550 ft.), and, on S border, Nanga Parbat (26,660 ft.) peaks; drained by Gilgit, Hunza, and, in S, Indus rivers. Agency 1st established 1878, abolished, and re-established 1889. Although these 8 princely states acknowledged the suzerainty of Kashmir, they were never actually part of its territory; they were formerly called Frontier Illaqas. In 1947, upon Br. withdrawal from India, agency was transferred to Kashmir govt.; states, however, refused to submit to Kashmir control and opted in favor of Pakistan. Pop. (87% Moslem) speaks mostly Shina and Burushaski.

Gilgit River, in N Kashmir, rises from a glacier in trans-Indus extension of Punjab Himalayas, at 35°55'N 72°35'E; flows N, E past Gupis, and SE past Sher Qila and Gilgit, to Indus R. 7 mi. N of Bunji; c.150 mi. long. In upper course called Ghizar. Receives Hunza R. below Gilgit.

Gilgit Wazarat, Kashmir: see ASTOR, district.

Gil Island (□ 89; 16 mi. long, 4–8 mi. wide), W B.C., in Hecate Strait bet. Pitt and Princess Royal isls.

Gill (gĭl). **1** Town (1940 pop. 24), Meriwether co., W Ga., 24 mi. SW of Griffin. **2** Agr. town (pop. 1,070), Franklin co., NW Mass., on Connecticut R. and 7 mi. NE of Greenfield. Inc. 1793. Includes village of Riverside.

Gill, Lough (lŏkh gĭl'), lake (5 mi. long, 2 mi. wide), NE Co. Sligo, Ireland, just SE of Sligo. In it is the tiny isl. of Innisfree, celebrated in Yeats's poem. Outlet: Garrogue R.

Gillean Island, Scotland: see KYLE.

Gilleleje (gĭ'lŭlī"ŭ), town (pop. 1,890), Frederiksborg amt, N Zealand, Denmark, on N tip of isl., on the Kattegat and 13 mi. N of Hillerod; fishing, shipbuilding.

Gillespie (gĭlĕ'spē), county (□ 1,055; pop. 10,520), S central Texas; ⊙ Fredericksburg. In scenic hill country of Edwards Plateau; alt. c.1,000–2,000 ft.; drained by Pedernales R. and several creeks. Ranching (goats, sheep, beef cattle); wool, mohair marketed; also some poultry, dairying. Agr. (corn, wheat, peanuts, grain sorghums, fruit, truck). Hunting, fishing attracts visitors. Granite quarrying. Formed 1848.

Gillespie (gûlĭ'spē), city (pop. 4,105), Macoupin co., SW Ill., 25 mi. NE of Alton; bituminous-coal mining; agr. (dairy products; livestock, grain). Inc. 1869.

Gillett. 1 (jûlĕt') Town (pop. 774), Arkansas co., E central Ark., 26 mi. SSE of Stuttgart; rice and lumber milling; ships pecans. **2** (jĭ'lĭt, –lĕt) City (pop. 1,410), Oconto co., NE Wis., 30 mi. NW of Green Bay city; woodworking, cheese making, vegetable canning. Inc. as village in 1900, as city in 1944.

Gillette (jĭlĕt'), town (pop. 2,191), ⊙ Campbell co., NE Wyo., 80 mi. ESE of Sheridan; alt. 4,544 ft. Trade center in grain, livestock, and mining region; flour, dairy products. Near by are agr. experiment station of state univ. and large strip mine from which coal is taken.

Gillham (gĭ'lûm), town (pop. 207), Sevier co., SW Ark., 9 mi. N of De Queen, near Okla. line.

Gilliam (gĭl'yûm), county (□ 1,211; pop. 2,817), N Oregon; ⊙ Condon. Bounded N by Columbia R. and W by John Day R. Wheat, wool, lumber, livestock. Formed 1885.

Gilliam. 1 (gĭl'yûm) Village (pop. c.475), Caddo parish, NW La., 22 mi. N of Shreveport, near Red R.; cotton ginning. Natural-gas field near by. **2** (gĭ'lûm) Town (pop. 306), Saline co., central Mo., near Missouri R., 13 mi. NE of Marshall.

Gillingham. 1 (gĭ'lĭng-ûm) Town and parish (pop. 3,274), N Dorset, England, on Stour R. and 4 mi. NW of Shaftesbury; agr. market in dairying region; flour mills. Has 15th-cent. church, 16th-cent. grammar school, and some remains of "The Castle" built by Saxon or Norman chieftain. In 1042 Edward the Confessor was elected king by witenagemot meeting here. **2** (jĭl'ĭng-ûm) Residential municipal borough (1931 pop. 61,536; 1951 census 68,099), N Kent, England, on Medway R. estuary just NE of Chatham; industry and trade is based on the Chatham dockyards, the mfg. of brick and concrete, and the surrounding fruitgrowing region. Site of Royal Naval Hosp. There are 15th-cent. church and remains of former palace of archbishops of Canterbury. Municipal borough includes district of Brompton (W) and agr. market town of Rainham (ESE), with limestone quarries.

Gills Rock, northernmost village of Door Peninsula, NE Wis., in Door co., on Green Bay, 36 mi. NE of Sturgeon Bay city; fishing. A U.S. bird sanctuary is here. Ferry service to Washington Isl.

Gillsville (gĭlz'vĭl), town (pop. 152), Hall and Banks counties, NE Ga., 9 mi. E of Gainesville; pottery.

Gilly (zhēlē'), town (pop. 24,048), Hainaut prov., S central Belgium, 2 mi. ENE of Charleroi; coal mining, metal industry; mfg. (cables, glassware). Has 11th-cent. Cistercian abbey.

Gilman (gĭl'mûn). **1** Village (pop. c.300), Eagle co., W central Colo., on Eagle R., in Gore Range, and 20 mi. N of Leadville; alt. 9,000 ft. Gold, silver, lead, zinc, and copper mining. Mt. of the Holy Cross is 7 mi. SW. **2** Village, New London co., Conn.: see BOZRAH. **3** City (pop. 1,602), Iroquois co., E Ill., 25 mi. SSW of Kankakee, in agr. area (corn, oats, wheat, soybeans, livestock, poultry; dairy products); mfg. (clothing, monuments). Inc. 1867. **4** Town (pop. 508), Marshall co., central Iowa, 14 mi. SSE of Marshalltown; corn cannery. **5** Village, Essex co., Vt.: see LUNENBURG. **6** Village (pop. 402), Taylor co., N central Wis., on Yellow R. and 40 mi. NE of Eau Claire; dairy products, lumber.

Gilman City, agr. city (pop. 450), Harrison co., NW Mo., 12 mi. SE of Bethany.

Gilman Hot Springs, Calif.: see SAN JACINTO.

Gilmanton (gĭl'mûntûn), town (pop. 754), Belknap co., central N.H., 8 mi. SSE of Laconia, in farming, resort area. Iron formerly mined at Gilmanton Iron Works village.

Gilmer (gĭl'mûr). **1** County (□ 439; pop. 9,963), N Ga.; ⊙ Ellijay. In the Blue Ridge and partly (N) in Chattahoochee Natl. Forest; drained by Coosawattee R. Farming (fruit, potatoes, corn, hay, livestock), sawmilling, and resort area; textile mfg. at Ellijay. Formed 1832. **2** County (□ 339; pop. 9,746), central W.Va.; ⊙ Glenville. On Allegheny Plateau; drained by Little Kanawha R. and tributaries. Oil and gas wells, coal mines; agr. (livestock, fruit, tobacco, potatoes, corn); timber. Some industry (glass, lumber) at Glenville. Formed 1845.

Gilmer. 1 Village (pop. 1,371), Orange co., SE Texas. **2** City (pop. 4,096), ⊙ Upshur co., NE Texas, near Little Cypress Bayou, 36 mi. WNW of Marshall; trade center for agr., lumber, oil area; oil refining, lumber and cottonseed-oil milling. Settled 1858, inc. 1902.

Gilmerton (gĭlmûr'tûn), SE suburb of Edinburgh, Midlothian, Scotland. Former limestone-quarrying center.

Gilmore City, town (pop. 746), on Humboldt-Pocahontas co. line, N central Iowa, 21 mi. NW of Fort Dodge; livestock, grain.

Giloca River, Spain: see JILOCA RIVER.

Gilolo, Indonesia: see HALMAHERA.

Gilp, Loch, Scotland: see LOCHGILPHEAD.

Gilpin (gĭl'pĭn), county (□ 149; pop. 850), N central Colo.; ⊙ Central City. Mining and livestock-grazing region; gold, silver, lead, copper, zinc. Includes parts of Arapaho and Roosevelt natl. forests and of Front Range in W. Formed 1861.

Gilroy (gĭl'roi), city (pop. 4,951), Santa Clara co., W Calif., in Santa Clara Valley, 28 mi. SE of San Jose; cattle, canned and dried fruit, vegetables, wine; oil refinery. Chartered 1870. Gilroy Hot Springs (resort) is 8 mi. NE, in Diablo Range.

Gilsdorf (gĭls'dôrf), village (pop. 542), E central Luxembourg, just E of Diekirch, near Sûre R.; building-stone quarrying.

Gilsum (gĭl'sûm), town (pop. 578), Cheshire co., SW N.H., on Ashuelot R. (water power) and 9 mi. N of Keene; textiles, mining (feldspar, mica).

Giltner, village (pop. 284), Hamilton co., SE central Nebr., 15 mi. SE of Grand Island; dairying; grain, livestock.

Gilze, Netherlands: see RIJEN.

Gimbi (gĭm'bē), Ital. *Ghimbi*, town (pop. 6,000), Wallaga prov., W central Ethiopia, 50 mi. W of Nakamti, on plateau bet. Dadessa and Birbir rivers; 9°6'N 35°46'E; road junction. Trade center (hides, coffee, beeswax, gold).

Gimborn (gĭm'bôrn), village (pop. 5,789), in former Prussian Rhine Prov., W Germany, after 1945 in North Rhine-Westphalia, 5 mi. NW of Gummersbach; ironworks.

Gimbsheim (gĭmps'hīm), village (pop. 3,031), Rhenish Hesse, W Germany, near the Rhine, 10 mi. N of Worms; brickworks; basket weaving. Sugar beets.

Gimco City (jĭm'kō), town (pop. 13), Madison co., E central Ind., 3 mi. SE of Alexandria.

Gimie, Morne (môrn" zhēmē'), highest peak (3,145 ft.) of St. Lucia, B.W.I., 10 mi. S of Castries.

Gimigliano (jēmēlyä'nô), town (pop. 3,339), Catanzaro prov., Calabria, S Italy, on S slope of La Sila mts., 6 mi. NW of Catanzaro; marble quarrying.

Gimir, Ethiopia: see GINIR.

Gimli (gĭm'lē), village (pop. 1,045), SE Man., on L. Winnipeg, 50 mi. N of Winnipeg; lumbering, mixed farming; resort. First Icelandic settlement in Man., it was established 1875.

Gimma, Ethiopia: see JIMMA.

Gimo (yē'mō"), village (pop. 1,051), Uppsala co., E Sweden, 9 mi. SW of Osthammar; rail junction; ironworks (founded in 17th cent.), hosiery mills; woodworking. Has 13th-cent. church, 18th-cent. castle.

Gimoly (gĭmô'lĭ), village (1939 pop. under 500), S central Karelo-Finnish SSR, 110 mi. NW of Petrozavodsk, on N shore of Gimoly L. (15 mi. long); magnetite deposits.

Gimone River (zhēmôn'), Gers and Tarn-et-Garonne depts., SW France, rises in Lannemezan Plateau near Boulogne (Haute-Garonne dept.), flows 83 mi. NNE, past Gimont and Beaumont-de-Lomagne, to the Garonne 3 mi. S of Castelsarrasin.

Gimont (zhĕmō′), village (pop. 1,692), Gers dept., SW France, on the Gimone and 14 mi. E of Auch; agr. market; orchards.

Gimry (gĭmrē′), village (1939 pop. over 500), central Dagestan Autonomous SSR, Russian SFSR, at NW end of Gimry Range, near confluence of Avar Koisu and Andi Koisu rivers (here forming Sulak R.), 15 mi. WSW of Buinaksk, in fruitgrowing area; fruit canning, wine making. Pop. largely Avar. Shamil, leader of Caucasian rebellions, b. here 1798.

Gimry Range, outlier of the E Greater Caucasus, in central Dagestan Autonomous SSR, Russian SFSR; extends from Gimry c.50 mi. SE; rises to 6,900 ft. Forms divide bet. Avar Koisu (river) and coastal drainage area.

Gindi River, Nigeria: see ZAMFARA RIVER.

Ginegar, Israel: see GINNEIGAR.

Gineifa or **Jinayfah** (gĭnā′fü, jĭ-), village, Suez Governorate, NE Egypt, on Suez fresh-water canal, on Cairo-Suez RR, and 18 mi. NNW of Suez.

Gines (hē′nĕs), town (pop. 1,729), Seville prov., SW Spain, 6 mi. W of Seville; olives, cereals, grapes.

Ginestar (hĕnĕstär′), town (pop. 1,419), Tarragona prov., NE Spain, 10 mi. E of Gandesa; olive-oil processing; almonds, fruit, cereals, wine.

Ginestas (zhĕnüstä′), village (pop. 747), Aude dept., S France, near the Canal du Midi, 9 mi. NW of Narbonne; winegrowing.

Gineta, La (lä hĕnā′tä), town (pop. 3,975), Albacete prov., SE central Spain, 12 mi. NW of Albacete; sandal mfg., brandy distilling, flour milling; wine, saffron, cereals.

Gin Ganga (gĭn′ gŭng′gŭ), river, SW Ceylon, rises in S Sabaragamuwa Hill Country, E of Deniyaya; flows W and generally SSW, past Baddegama, to Indian Ocean at Gintota; 70 mi. long.

Gingee (gĭn′jē), village (pop. 5,989), South Arcot dist., E central Madras, India, 15 mi. W of Tindivanam. Noted rock fortress just W, constructed by Vijayanagar kings in early-16th cent.; it comprises 3 fortified hills connected by stone ramparts; bridges lead over deep ravines to citadel on summit of highest hill (c.600 ft.); was scene of numerous sieges by Indian powers, French, and English until surrendered to English by Hyder Ali in 1780.

Gingerbread Ground, reef, NW Bahama Isls., on N Great Bahama Bank, halfway bet. Grand Bahama Isl. (N) and the Biminis (S), at 26°N.

Ginger Island, islet, Br. Virgin Isls., 3 mi. SSW of Virgin Gorda isl., W of Cooper Isl.

Gingerland, village, SE Nevis, B.W.I., 4 mi. E of Charlestown; sea-island cotton, sugar cane.

Gingin, town (pop. 275), SW Western Australia, 40 mi. N of Perth; orchards; cattle.

Gingoog (hēngō′ōg), town (1939 pop. 3,879; 1948 municipality pop. 30,699), Misamis Oriental prov., N Mindanao, Philippines, on Gingoog Bay (22 mi. long, 15 mi. wide), 39 mi. NE of Cagayan; agr. center (corn, coconuts); sawmilling.

Ginir (gĭnēr′) or **Gimir** (gĭmēr′), Ital. *Ghinir, Ghimir*, or *Ghigner*, town (pop. 3,500), Harar prov., S central Ethiopia, near Web R., 180 mi. SW of Harar; 7°9′N 40°42′E; alt. 6,516 ft. Major commercial center (hides, cereals, wax, honey, salt, cotton goods). Airfield.

Ginkgo Petrified Forest State Park, Wash.: see ELLENSBURG.

Ginneigar or **Ginegar** (both: gēnĕgär′), agr. settlement (pop. 400), N Israel, at N edge of Plain of Jezreel, 4 mi. SW of Nazareth. Near by is extensive Balfour Forest. Modern village founded 1922 on site of biblical locality of same name.

Ginneisar, Israel: see GENOSSAR.

Ginneken (khĭ′nükün), town (pop. 13,915), North Brabant prov., SW Netherlands, S suburb of Breda, on Mark R.

Ginosa (jēnô′zä), anc. *Genusium*, town (pop. 12,552), Ionio prov., Apulia, S Italy, 10 mi. SE of Matera; wine, olive oil, ink.

Ginossar, Israel: see GENOSSAR.

Ginsburg, Turkmen SSR: see KAAKHKA.

Ginsheim (gĭns′hīm), former suburb (pop., including Gustavsburg, 8,105) of MAINZ, after 1945 in Hesse, W Germany, on right bank of the Rhine and 4 mi. SE of Mainz; steel construction, repair of watercraft; mfg. of machinery, vehicles, heating equipment. United after 1945 with Gustavsburg.

Gintota (gĭntō′tŭ), anc. *Gimhatittha*, village, Southern Prov., Ceylon, on SW coast, at mouth of the Gin Ganga, 3 mi. WNW of Galle; plywood and coir-rope mfg.

Ginzo de Limia (hēn′thō dhä lē′myä), town (pop. 1,992), Orense prov., NW Spain, 20 mi. SSE of Orense; agr. trade (corn, fruit); lumbering.

Gioda (jō′dä), village (1950 pop. 2,000), Tripolitania, Libya, near Gulf of Sidra, on highway and 17 mi. S of Misurata, in fertile, irrigated region. Agr. settlement (cereals, olives, fodder, vegetables) founded by Italians in1938.

Giof, El (ĕl jōf′), largest oasis (1950 pop. 2,200), in the Kufra group of oases, S Cyrenaica, Libya, 350 mi. SSE of Gialo. Also spelled Jof.

Giofra or **Jofra** (jō′frä), group of Saharan oases in SE Tripolitania, Libya, 150 mi. SSW of Sirte, at N foot of Gebel es-Soda range. Chief oases are Hun, Sokna, and Uaddan. Linked by road with Misurata. Dates.

Giogo, Il (ēl jô′gô), pass (alt. 2,894 ft.), N central Italy, in Etruscan Apennines, on watershed bet. Santerno (E) and Sieve (W) rivers, 4 mi. NNE of Scarperia. Crossed by road bet. Florence and Firenzuola.

Gioia, Gulf of (jô′yä), inlet of Tyrrhenian Sea, S Italy, bet. Cape Vaticano (N) and Strait of Messina (S); 25 mi. long, 10 mi. wide. Chief ports: Gioia Tauro, Palmi, Bagnara Calabra.

Gioia dei Marsi (dā mär′sē), village (pop. 1,777), Aquila prov., Abruzzi e Molise, S central Italy, near reclaimed Lago Fucino area, 15 mi. SE of Avezzano. Rebuilt after earthquake (1915).

Gioia del Colle (dĕl kôl′lĕ), town (pop. 20,067), Bari prov., Apulia, S Italy, 23 mi. SSE of Bari; mfg. (agr. machinery, woolen textiles); alcohol distilling, cheese making. Has anc. castle.

Gioia Tauro (tou′rô), town (pop. 8,832), Reggio di Calabria prov., Calabria, S Italy, port on Gulf of Gioia, 26 mi. NNE of Reggio di Calabria. Industrial center; olive oil refining, sawmilling; mfg. (machinery, soap, bricks), wine making; fishing. Rebuilt after earthquake of 1783.

Gioiosa Ionica (jôyô′zä yô′nēkä), town (pop. 4,796), Reggio di Calabria prov., Calabria, S Italy, 5 mi. N of Siderno Marina, in agr. region (olives, wheat, citrus fruit); pottery mfg. Has Roman theater excavated 1925–26.

Gioiosa Marea (märā′ä), village (pop. 1,824), Messina Prov., NE Sicily, port on Tyrrhenian Sea, 5 mi. NW of Patti.

Gion (gē′ō), town (pop. 13,134), Hiroshima prefecture, SW Honshu, Japan, just N of Hiroshima; rice, wheat, persimmons.

Giona (gēō′nü), highest massif of central Greece, in Phocis nome; rises to 8,236 ft. 11 mi. NW of Amphissa. Also spelled Ghiona.

Giongrieng (zhông′ryĕng′), town, Rachgia prov., S Vietnam, 15 mi. ESE of Rachgia, in highly irrigated area; rice-growing center.

Giordani (jôrdä′nē), village (1950 pop. 1,500), W Tripolitania, Libya, on road and 25 mi. SW of Tripoli, in the Gefara plain. Agr. settlement (grain, lucerne, olives, almonds, citrus fruit) founded 1938–39 by Italians.

Giornico (jôr′nēkô), town (pop. 696), Ticino canton, S Switzerland, on the Ticino and 16 mi. NNW of Bellinzona.

Gioura or **Yioura** (both: yē͞oo′rü), uninhabited Aegean island (□ 4.8) in Northern Sporades, Magnesia nome, Greece, 45 mi. off Thessalian mainland; 39°24′N 24°11′E; 4 mi. long, 1.5 mi. wide.

Giovinazzo (jôvēnä′tsô), anc. *Natiolum*, town (pop. 12,416), Bari prov., Apulia, S Italy, port on the Adriatic, 11 mi. WNW of Bari. Agr. center (citrus fruit, vegetables, olives, grapes, almonds); fishing; netmaking, ironworking. Bishopric. Has 13th-cent. cathedral.

Giovi Pass (jô′vē) (alt. 1,548 ft.), in Ligurian Apennines, N Italy, 10 mi. N of Genoa. Crossed by road (built 1815–24) bet. Genoa and Novi Ligure; penetrated by railroad tunnel 5 mi. long, opened 1854).

Gi-Paraná River (zhē′-pürünä′), Guaporé territory, W Brazil, rises in the Serra dos Parecis, flows N and then NW to the Madeira (right bank) near Amazonas border. Length, c.400 mi. Not navigable. Lower course also called Machado R. Formerly spelled Gy-Paraná.

Gipping River, England: see ORWELL RIVER.

Gippsland (gĭps′lănd), rural district (□ 13,655), SE Victoria, Australia, E of Melbourne, bet. Australian Alps and SE coast. Partly mountainous and forested, with fertile plains producing corn, oats, sugar beets. Contains coal, gold, bauxite. Chief town, SALE.

Gir (gēr), hilly tract on S Kathiawar peninsula, India, SE of Junagarh; consists of wild, rugged country, densely forested (teak, blackwood); noted for its big game. Last refuge of Indian lion.

Giraglia, Corsica: see CORSE, CAPE.

Giraltovce (gĭ′rältôftsĕ), Hung. *Girált* (gĭ′rält), town (pop. 1,353), E Slovakia, Czechoslovakia, on Topla R. and 15 mi. NE of Presov; tanning; potato trade.

Giran, Formosa: see ILAN.

Girang, Tibet: see KYERONG.

Girão, Cape (zhĕrā′ō), rugged headland of Madeira isl., 6 mi. W of Funchal. Rises to 2,000 ft. in a sheer cliff; 32°39′N 17°W.

Girard (jĭrärd′). **1** Community, Los Angeles co., Calif.: see WOODLAND HILLS. **2** Village (pop. 244), Burke co., E Ga., 19 mi. E of Waynesboro. **3** City (pop. 1,740), Macoupin co., SW central Ill., 25 mi. SSW of Springfield, in agr. and bituminous-coal area; ships grain. Inc. 1855. **4** City (pop. 2,426), ⊙ Crawford co., extreme SE Kansas, 11 mi. NW of Pittsburg; trade center for grain region; metal products, soap, ointment. Founded 1868; inc. as town 1869, as city 1871. **5** City (pop. 10,113), Trumbull co., NE Ohio, just NW of Youngstown and on Mahoning R.; steel milling; also makes leather goods, metal products, heating apparatus. Settled c.1800. **6** Residential borough (pop. 2,141), Erie co., NW Pa., 15 mi. SW of Erie; trading center; potatoes, fruit; wood and metal products, leather. Settled c.1800, inc. 1846.

Girardot (hērärdôt′), city (pop. 22,557), Cundinamarca dept., central Colombia, river port on right bank of upper Magdalena R., opposite Flandes (Tolima dept.), on Neiva-Bogotá RR and 55 mi. WSW of Bogotá. Trading, communication, and processing center in coffeegrowing region; exports coffee, cattle, hides, tropical produce. Mfg. of textile goods, nonalcoholic beverages, tobacco products; tanning, coffee roasting. Airport. Steel bridge across the Magdalena.

Girardota (hērärdō′tä), town (pop. 2,038), Antioquia dept., NW central Colombia, on Porce R., on railroad and 12 mi. NE of Medellín; alt. 4,816 ft.; sugar cane, corn, beans, yucca, coffee.

Girardville (jĭrärd′vĭl), borough (pop. 3,864), Schuylkill co., E central Pa., 9 mi. NNW of Pottsville; anthracite. Settled c.1832, inc. 1872.

Giraumont (zhĕrōmō′), village (pop. 69), Meurthe-et-Moselle dept., NE France, 6 mi. S of Briey; iron mining.

Gird Gwalior (gĭrd′ gwä′lyōr), district, N Madhya Bharat, India; ⊙ Lashkar.

Girdle Ness, promontory on North Sea, NE Kincardine, Scotland, 2 mi. ESE of Aberdeen, just S of mouth of the Dee; site of Girdleness Lighthouse (57°2′N 2°3′W).

Girdletree (gûr′dŭltrē), village (pop. c.500), Worcester co., SE Md., near Chincoteague Bay, 22 mi. SSE of Salisbury; rail-shipping point for truck, seafood.

Girdwood, village (pop. 79), S Alaska, on Turnagain Arm of Cook Inlet, 30 mi. SE of Anchorage.

Gireis or **Jirays** (gĭrās′, jĭ-), village (pop. 7,636), Minufiya prov., Lower Egypt, on Rosetta branch of the Nile and 3 mi. NW of Ashmun; cereals, cotton, flax.

Giresun (gērüsōōn′) or **Kerasun** (kĕräsōōn′), prov. (□ 2,630; 1950 pop. 299,243), N Turkey, on Black Sea; ⊙ Giresun. Drained by Kelkit and Harsit rivers. Copper and zinc near coast. Hazelnuts, filberts, corn. Heavily forested.

Giresun or **Kerasun,** anc. *Cerasus*, town (1950 pop. 12,367), ⊙ Giresun prov., N Turkey, port on Black Sea 110 mi. NE of Sivas, 70 mi. W of Trebizond; market for hazelnuts, corn. Copper deposits are W. From here Lucullus is said to have introduced the cherry into Italy in 1st cent. B.C.; the word cherry is derived from its name. Sometimes spelled Kiresun, Kerasund, and Kerasunt.

Giresun Mountains, NE Turkey, extend 60 mi. E from point 10 mi. NE of Mesudiye, N of Kelkit R.; rise to 10,154 ft. in Kiliclar Dag. Gumusane Mts. adjoin E. Town of Alucra on S slope.

Girga (gĭr′gă) or **Jirja** (jĭr′jă), province (□ 609; pop. 1,288,425), central Upper Egypt, in Nile valley; ⊙ SOHAG. Bounded S by Qena prov., E by Arabian Desert, N by Asyut prov., W by Libyan Desert. Industries: cotton ginning, silk and cotton weaving, pottery making, sugar milling, dairying; agr. (cotton, cereals, dates, sugar cane). Main urban centers: Sohag, AKHMIM, El Balyana, Giheina, TAHTA, Tema, Girga, El Manshah. Ruins of anc. Abydos are near present-day ARABA EL MADFUNA.

Girga or **Jirja,** town (pop. 32,438), Girga prov., central Upper Egypt, on W bank of the Nile, on railroad, and 53 mi. WNW of Qena, 19 mi. SE of Sohag; cotton ginning, pottery making, dairying; cotton, cereals, dates, sugar cane. Has old Coptic convent.

Girgenti, Sicily: see AGRIGENTO.

Giridih (gērē′dē), town (pop. 25,326), Hazaribagh dist., E central Bihar, India, 60 mi. ENE of Hazaribagh; rail spur terminus; coal-mining and trade (rice, rape and mustard, oilseeds, corn, sugar cane, barley) center. Extensive mica mining 50 mi. WNW, at Kodarma.

Girifalco (jērēfäl′kô), town (pop. 6,118), Catanzaro prov., Calabria, S Italy, 11 mi. WSW of Catanzaro; wine, olive oil, silk. Severely damaged by earthquake in 1626.

Giri Raj, India: see GOBARDHAN.

Giri River (gē′rē) or **N'giri River** (ŭng-gē′rē), NW Belgian Congo, rises 30 mi. NNW of Budjala, flows c.225 mi. S and SW to Ubangi R. at Giri landing, 70 mi. above the confluence Ubangi-Congo. Extensive swamps and flooded expanses of tropical forest in its lower course. Navigable for 110 mi. downstream from Monianga.

Girishk (gĭrĭshk′), town (pop. 8,000), Kandahar prov., S Afghanistan, on Helmand R. and 70 mi. WNW of Kandahar, on highway to Farah; alt. 3,641 ft.; center of irrigated oasis. Diversion dam (completed 1949) here feeds Boghra Canal. Formerly located on right bank around anc. fort, the town has been rebuilt on left bank. Fort was held by British in 1st and 2d Afghan Wars.

Girnar (gĭrnär′), noted hill on S central Kathiawar peninsula, India, just E of Junagarh; has several peaks up to c.2,000 ft.; rises to 3,666 ft. in center. Sacred site of the Jains, visited annually by numerous pilgrims. Has many interesting temples; Neminath is largest. Leper asylum. At W foot of hill is large granite rock with inscribed edicts of Asoka (c.250 B.C.) and later epigraphical records.

Girna River (gĭr′nŭ), N central Bombay, India, rises in N Western Ghats, W of Kalvan, flows E past Malegaon, NE past Bhadgaon, and WNW to Tapti R. 7 mi. S of Chopda; c.200 mi. long. Headworks of Girna irrigation canal are 5 mi. S of Satana; extends 27 mi. ENE to just N of Malegaon.

Jamda irrigation system (headworks at Jamda village, 8 mi. NNW of Chalisgaon) waters large sugar-growing area.

Giromagny (zhērômänyē'), town (pop. 2,569), Territory of Belfort, E France, at foot of the S Vosges, 8 mi. N of Belfort; textile-milling center (berets, hosiery). Metalworks.

Girón (hērōn'), town (pop. 2,134), Santander dept., N central Colombia, on W slopes of Cordillera Oriental, 4 mi. SW of Bucaramanga. Tobacco-growing center; also cacao, rice, coffee, sugar cane. A shrine is site of annual pilgrimage.

Girón, town (1950 pop. 1,623), Azuay, S Ecuador, in the Andes, 22 mi. SSW of Cuenca, on highway; agr. center (cereals, livestock); dairying.

Gironcourt-sur-Vraine (zhērōkōōr'-sür-vrĕn'), village (pop. 398), Vosges dept., E France, 12 mi. ESE of Neufchâteau; produces bottles for VITTEL mineral waters.

Gironde (jĭrŏnd', Fr. zhērōd'), department (□ 4,141; pop. 858,381), in former Guienne prov., SW France; ⊙ Bordeaux. Lies in Aquitaine Basin, bounded by the Bay of Biscay (W), and drained by Garonne and Dordogne rivers which join to form the Gironde estuary. Largest dept. of France. BORDELAIS (N and center) contains some of France's finest vineyards (Château-Latour, Château Lafite, Château-Margaux in MÉDOC, Saint-Émilion, and Sauternes). The infertile LANDES (S and W) are covered with pine forests and produce some livestock. The dept. also grows cereals, tobacco, vegetables, fruits. Industry (processing of local produce and of imported minerals and raw materials) is heavily concentrated in BORDEAUX area. Other important towns are Libourne (wine trade), Arcachon (bathing resort and fishing port), and Coutras.

Gironde, estuary on the Bay of Biscay, SW France, formed by confluence of Garonne and Dordogne rivers; extends c.45 mi. SSE-NNW from the Bec d'Ambès (c.14 mi. N of Bordeaux) to the Pointe de Grave, opposite Royan; 2 to 7 mi. wide. Bounded by Gironde dept. (W and SE) and Charente-Maritime dept. (NW). Along its W shore are some of France's finest vineyards (MÉDOC). Navigable, despite sandbanks and a treacherous tide, to ocean-going ships which ascend to Bordeaux and Libourne. Its mouth, bet. Pointe de la Coubre (N) and Pointe de Grave (S), is commanded by Cordouan lighthouse.

Gironella (hērōnĕ'lyä), town (pop. 2,552), Barcelona prov., NE Spain, on Llobregat R. and 5 mi. SSE of Berga; cotton milling; agr. trade (wheat, potatoes, corn).

Girouard, Mount (jŭrärd') (9,825 ft.), SW Alta., near B.C. border, in Rocky Mts., in Banff Natl. Park, 8 mi. ENE of Banff, overlooking L. Minnewanka; 51°14'N 115°24'W.

Girthon (gûr'thŭn), agr. village and parish (pop. 1,015, including part of Gatehouse of Fleet burgh), S Kirkcudbright, Scotland, just S of Gatehouse of Fleet. Has ruins of 12th-13th-cent. church.

Girton (gûr'tŭn), residential town and parish (pop. 1,112), S Cambridge, England, just NW of Cambridge. Site of Girton Col., 1st of the Cambridge Univ. women's colleges. Has 15th-cent. church.

Girvan (gûr'vŭn), burgh (1931 pop. 5,292; 1951 census 5,990), S Ayrshire, Scotland, on Firth of Clyde at mouth of Girvan Water, 18 mi. SW of Ayr, opposite Ailsa Craig; fishing port and resort. Its woolen mills were formerly important.

Girvan Water, river, Ayrshire, Scotland, rises 5 mi. W of Loch Doon, flows 35 mi. NW and SW, past Straiton and Dailly, to Firth of Clyde at Girvan.

Girwa River, Nepal and India: see GOGRA RIVER.

Gisard, Mont, Palestine: see GEZER.

Gisborne, land district, New Zealand: see HAWKE'S BAY.

Gisborne (gĭz'bôrn), borough and port (pop. 14,765; metropolitan Gisborne 16,984), ⊙ Cook co. (□ 791; pop. 6,918), E N.Isl., New Zealand, on Poverty Bay and 85 mi. NE of Napier. Summer resort. Exports wool, frozen meat, dairy products. Gisborne is in, but independent of, Cook co.

Gisburn Lake (gĭz'–) (□ 9), S N.F., N of Fortune Bay; 8 mi. long, up to 3 mi. wide; 47°48'N 54°51'W.

Gischala (gĭ'skūlŭ), anc. locality, Upper Galilee, N Palestine, near Lebanese border, at NW foot of Mt. Jarmaq, 5 mi. NW of Safad. On site is modern Jish, village abandoned (1948) by Arab pop. In Roman times, a fortified town, noted for its olive oil, it was home of Johanan of Gischala, leader of Jewish rising (A.D. 66) against Romans.

Giseifu, Korea: see UIJONGBU.

Gishu, Korea: see UIJU.

Gisikon (gē'zēkōn), village (pop. 198), Lucerne canton, central Switzerland, on Reuss R. and 7 mi. NE of Lucerne. Separatist Sonderbund forces were defeated here (1847) by Federal Swiss troops. Formerly spelled Gislikon.

Giske (yĭsk'ŭ), village and canton (pop. 2,424), More og Romsdal co., W Norway, on Giske isl. (□ 1; pop. 564), 4 mi. NW of Alesund; fishing, fish-oil refining. Has medieval stave church.

Gislaved (yĭs'lävād"), village (pop. 2,526), Jonkoping co., S Sweden, on Nissa R. and 20 mi. WNW of Varnamo; mfg. of rubber shoes; metalworking.

Gislikon, Switzerland: see GISIKON.

Gisors (zhēzôr'), town (pop. 4,572), Eure dept., NW France, on the Epte and 17 mi. SW of Beauvais; communications center; tanning, textile dyeing, furniture mfg. In horse-raising area. Has noted 13th–16th-cent. church with Renaissance façade (heavily damaged 1939–45), and extensive ruins of feudal castle (built in 12th cent. and scene of century-long strife bet. English and French). Town hall and numerous old houses destroyed in Second World War. Old ⊙ Vexin Normand.

Gissar (gēsär'), village (1926 pop. 920), NW Stalinabad oblast, Tadzhik SSR, on railroad (Khanaka station) and 12 mi. WSW of Stalinabad, on Gissar Canal (joining Kafirnigan R. and the Surkhan Darya); cotton; metalworks. Dist. is noted for Gissar (Hissar) sheep.

Gissar Range, branch of Tien Shan mountain system in W Tadzhik SSR; extends just S of and parallel to Zeravshan Range; rises to c.20,000 ft. Crossed by Leninabad-Stalinabad highway. Mineral deposits include coal, phosphorites, and tungsten. Sometimes considered part of Pamir-Alai system. **Gissar Valley** extends along Stalinabad-Termez RR from Kafirnigan R. to the Surkhan Darya; drained by Gissar Canal (built 1940–42); cotton, subtropical crops.

Gissi (jēs'sē), town (pop. 3,187), Chieti prov., Abruzzi e Molise, S central Italy, 11 mi. SW of Vasto; cementworks.

Gistel (khĭs'tŭl), town (pop. 5,317), West Flanders prov., NW Belgium, 5 mi. SSE of Ostend; agr. market. Formerly spelled Ghistelles.

Giswil (gĭs'vēl), town (pop. 2,437), Obwalden half-canton, central Switzerland, near L. of Sarnen, 5 mi. SSW of Sarnen.

Gitschin, Czechoslovakia: see JICIN.

Gittelde (gĭ'tĕl"dŭ), village (pop. 2,697), in Brunswick, NW Germany, after 1945 Lower Saxony, 6 mi. NW of Osterode; sawmilling, brewing.

Giuba River, Ital. Somaliland: see JUBA RIVER.

Giubiasco (jōōbēä'skô), town (pop. 2,932), Ticino canton, S Switzerland, near Ticino R., 1 mi. SW of Bellinzona; linoleum, metal products.

Giudecca (jūdĕk'kä), one of islands forming S quarter of Venice, N Italy.

Giuliana (jūlyä'nä), village (pop. 3,219), Palermo prov., SW central Sicily, 12 mi. SSW of Corleone.

Giuliano in Campania (jūlyä'nō ēn kämpä'nyä), town (pop. 19,646), Napoli prov., Campania, S Italy, 3 mi. S of Aversa; hosiery mfg.

Giulianova (jūlyänō'vä), town (pop. 4,082), Teramo prov., Abruzzi e Molise, S central Italy, port on the Adriatic, 15 mi. ENE of Teramo; bathing resort; mfg. (agr. machinery, cement, jewelry, hats, alcohol, soap). Renaissance cathedral.

Giulie, Alpi, Italy and Yugoslavia: see JULIAN ALPS.

Giulietti, lake, Ethiopia: see EGOGI BAD.

Giulvaz (jōōl'vŭz), Rum. *Giulvăz,* Hung. *Torontálgyülvész* (tô'rôntäldyül"vās), village (pop. 1,467), Timisoara prov., W Rumania, on railroad and 19 mi. SW of Timisoara; mineral springs near by.

Giumbo (jōōm'bō), town (pop. 1,000), in the Benadir, S Ital. Somaliland, near mouth of Juba R. on Indian Ocean opposite Gobuen.

Giuncarico (jōōngkä'rēkô), village (pop. 857), Grosseto prov., Tuscany, central Italy, 12 mi. NNW of Grosseto; macaroni.

Giuppana, island, Yugoslavia: see SIPAN ISLAND.

Giurgiu (jōōr'jōō), Bulg. *Giurgevo* (jōōr'jāvô), anc. *Theodorapolis,* town (1948 pop. 30,197), Bucharest prov., S Rumania, in Walachia, 40 mi. SSW of Bucharest; busy inland port on left bank of the Danube opposite Ruse (Bulgaria). Rail junction and terminus of 4 oil pipe lines from Ploesti. Ships petroleum and grain and has general trade with Bulgaria (ferry service). Has major sugar refinery, breweries, flour mills, textile mills, sawmills, brick kilns. A Roman town was established here A.D. 483–563, but the city was founded in 14th cent. by Genoese merchants, who called it San Giorgio. It was important in Walacho-Turkish (16th cent.) and Russo-Turkish wars. Bombed and burned in First World War.

Giussano (jūs-sä'nô), village (pop. 4,180), Milano prov., Lombardy, N Italy, 17 mi. N of Milan; textile mfg. (silk, cotton, linen).

Givat Ada or **Giv'at Ada** (gēv-ät' ädä'), settlement (pop. 200), W Israel, in Plain of Sharon, 7 mi. NE of Hadera; mixed farming. Founded 1903; suffered Arab attacks, 1936–39 and 1948.

Givatayim or **Givataim** (both: gēvätĭm'), residential suburb (1949 pop. 11,000) of Tel Aviv, W Israel, in Plain of Sharon, 3 mi. E of city center; printing, tile and toy mfg., honey processing. Founded 1922. Sometimes spelled Giva'at Ayim.

Givat Brenner or **Giv'at Brenner** (both: gēv-ät' brĕ'nĕr), settlement (pop. 1,400), W Israel, in Judaean Plain, 2 mi. SSW of Rehovot, 14 mi. S of Tel Aviv; industrial center; mfg. of sprinklers, essential oils, preserves; fruit- and vegetable-juice canning; mixed farming. Health resort; sanitarium. Founded 1928. Also spelled Giva'at Brenner.

Givat Hayim or **Giv'at Haiyim** (hä'yēm), settlement (pop. 900), W Israel, in Plain of Sharon, 3 mi. SSE of Hadera; food canning (preserves, vegetables, fruit), barrel mfg.; mixed farming, horse breeding. Sports center. Founded 1932 on reclaimed swamp land. Sometimes spelled Givat Haim.

Givat Hen or **Giv'at Hen** (hĕn), settlement (pop. 200), W Israel, in Plain of Sharon, 2 mi. E of Herzliya; mixed farming. Founded 1933.

Give (gē'vŭ), town (pop. 1,585), Vejle amt, central Jutland, Denmark, 15 mi. NW of Vejle; peat, furniture, chemicals.

Givenchy-en-Gohelle (zhēväshē'-ā-gôĕl'), village (pop. 1,244), Pas-de-Calais dept., N France, 7 mi. N of Arras, at NW end of Vimy Ridge. Scene of heavy fighting (1915, 1918) in First World War.

Givenchy-lès-Labassée (–lā-läbäsā'), village (pop. 354), Pas-de-Calais dept., N France, on Aire–La Bassée Canal and 5 mi. E of Béthune. A pivot position of Br. front during First World War.

Givet (zhēvā'), town (pop. 5,319), Ardennes dept., N France, on the Meuse and 26 mi. NNE of Mézières, bounded on 3 sides by Belg. territory; customs station. Mfg. of rayon, sandstone pipes, pencils, chemicals; brewing, tanning. Its old fortifications include 18th-cent. Charlemont citadel (ruined in First World War). Town damaged in Second World War.

Givhans Ferry State Park (gĭ'vŭnz) (1,235 acres), SE S.C., recreational area along bluffs of Edisto R., c.30 mi. NW of Charleston.

Giving, Norway: see DYPVAG.

Givors (zhēvôr'), town (pop. 12,653), Rhône dept., E central France, on right bank of Rhone R., at mouth of the Gier, and 12 mi. S of Lyons; industrial and transportation center; metallurgy (blast furnaces, foundries); brick- and glassworks. Produces electrical equipment, chinaware, cement pipes, hardware, and rayon. Fruit preserving and shipping. Important freight yards at junction of Saint-Étienne and Rhone valley rail lines. The 18th-cent. Givors canal (9 mi. long) to Rive-de-Gier, formerly used for coal shipments, has lost most of its economic significance. Town was heavily damaged during Second World War.

Givry or **Givry-près-l'Orbize** (zhēvrē'-prĕ-lôrbēz'), village (pop. 1,393), Saône-et-Loire dept., E central France, 5 mi. W of Chalon-sur-Saône; vineyards; wine making.

Giza, Gizeh, El Giza, or **Al-Jizah** (ĕl gē'zŭ, jē'–), province (□ 392; pop. 820,241), Upper Egypt, in Nile valley; ⊙ GIZA. Bounded S by Beni Suef prov., E by Arabian Desert, N by Cairo governorate, and W by Libyan Desert. Sugar refining, mfg. of bricks and clay piping; agr. (cotton, corn, sugar cane). Main urban centers are Giza, Helwan, Ausim. The prov. is rich in archaeological remains, with the great pyramids at Giza and at SAKKARA and ruins of anc. MEMPHIS.

Giza, Gizeh, El Giza, or **Al-Jizah,** town (pop. 66,213; with suburbs, 68,520), ⊙ Giza prov., Upper Egypt, on W bank of the Nile and 3 mi. SW of Cairo city center; 30°1'N 31°13'E. Five mi. SW are the 3 famous pyramids of Cheops or Khufu, Khafra, and Mankara, and the Sphinx. The pyramid (c.2900 B.C.) of Cheops (also called the Great Pyramid) was one of the Seven Wonders of the World and the largest pyramid ever built, covering 13 acres, and in the original state was 768 ft. square and 482 ft. high. The modern town of Giza is a corn market and has a large cigarette factory.

Gizai or **Jizay** (gĭzā', jĭ–), village (pop. 6,447), Minufiya prov., Lower Egypt, on Rosetta branch of the Nile and 5 mi. W of Minuf; cereals, cotton.

Gizan, Saudi Arabia: see QIZAN.

Gizeh, Egypt: see GIZA.

Gizel or **Gizel'** (gēzyĕl'), village (1926 pop. 2,345), E North Ossetian Autonomous SSR, Russian SFSR, on Gizeldon R. (left tributary of the Terek) and 6 mi. WNW of Dzaudzhikau; wheat, corn, truck, livestock. Upstream, on Gizeldon R. and 12 mi. SW of Dzaudzhikau, is village of Koban, site of Gizeldon hydroelectric station.

Gizhduvan (gēzhdōōvän'), city (1932 pop. estimate 4,900), S Bukhara oblast, Uzbek SSR, 26 mi. NE of Bukhara; food processing, metalworking, cotton milling. Formerly spelled Gidzhduvan; briefly known (c.1935–37) as Akmal-Abad.

Gizhiga (gēzhĭgä'), village, NW Koryak Natl. Okrug, Kamchatka oblast, Khabarovsk Territory, Russian SFSR, port on Gizhiga Bay of Sea of Okhotsk, at mouth of Gizhiga R., 200 mi. N of Palana. Fishing center; trading point (furs, fish); lignite mines. Founded 1753.

Gizhiga Bay, NW arm of Shelekhov Gulf of Sea of Okhotsk, NE Siberian Russian SFSR; separated from Penzhina Bay by Taigonos Peninsula; 160 mi. wide, 90 mi. long; frozen Nov.–May. In extreme NE at Gizhiga, it receives **Gizhiga River** (160 mi. long), rising in Kolyma Range.

Gizo (gē'zō), volcanic island, New Georgia group, Solomon Isls., SW Pacific, 20 mi. W of New Georgia isl.; c.5 mi. long, c.2 mi. wide; small port.

Gizycko (gē-zhĭts'kô), Pol. *Giżycko,* Ger. *Lötzen* (lŭ'tsŭn), town (1939 pop. 16,288; 1946 pop. 4,534) in East Prussia, after 1945 in Olsztyn prov., NE Poland, in Masurian Lakes region, at N end of L. Niegocinskie, 40 mi. S of Chernyakhovsk (Insterburg; now in Kaliningrad oblast); cattle and grain market; sawmilling. Near-by castle built 1335 by Teutonic Knights. In First World War, town was (1915) Ger. army hq. After Second World War, when it was c.50% destroyed, it was evacuated by its Ger. pop.

Gizzeria (jētsĕrē'ä), village (pop. 3,794), Catanzaro prov., Calabria, S Italy, near Tyrrhenian Sea, 6 mi. W of Nicastro; wine, olive oil, dried figs.

Gjaevedal, Norway: see GJOVDAL.

Gjeithus, Norway: see GEITHUS.

Gjerestad, Norway: see GJERSTAD.

Gjerpen, Norway: see BORGESTAD.

Gjerstad (yăr'stä), village and canton (pop. 2,617), Aust-Agder co., S Norway, on railroad and 30 mi. NNE of Arendal; wood-pulp factory. Formerly spelled Gjerestad.

Gjersvika (yărs'vēkä), village in Royrvik (Nor. *Røyrvik*) canton (pop. 463), Nord-Trondelag co., central Norway, at NW tip of Limingen L., 48 mi. NE of Grong; pyrite mining (Grong Mines). Mining also at Skorovas, 17 mi. SSE, on Tunn L.

Gjesdal or **Gjestal,** Norway: see ALGARD.

Gjevedal, Norway: see GJOVDAL.

Gjevgjelija, Yugoslavia: see DJEVDJELIJA.

Gjeving, Norway: see DYPVAG.

Gjinokastër or **Gjinokastra,** Albania: see ARGYROKASTRON.

Gjoa Haven, Northwest Territories: see PETERSON BAY.

Gjorgucat or **Gjorgucati,** Albania: see JERGUCAT.

Gjovdal (yûv'däl), Nor. *Gjøvdal,* village and canton (pop. 426), Aust-Agder co., S Norway, 34 mi. NNW of Arendal, in a long, narrow river valley, surrounded by high peaks; timber, cattle, fish. Formerly spelled Gjevedal, Gjaevedal, or Gievedal.

Gjovik (yû'vĭk, –vēk), Nor. *Gjøvik,* city (pop. 5,723), Opland co., SE Norway, on NW shore of L. Mjosa, 60 mi. N of Oslo; rail terminus; mfg. of motors, snowplows, wallboard; flour milling, dairying; agr. market.

Gjurgjevac, Yugoslavia: see DJURDJEVAC.

Glaama River, Norway: see GLOMMA RIVER.

Glaamfjord, Norway: see GLOMFJORD.

Glace Bay (glās), town (pop. 25,147), NE N.S., on E coast of Cape Breton Isl., 12 mi. ENE of Sydney; coal-mining center; site of radio-transmitting station. Just SW is mining suburb of Caledonia Mines; just N that of New Aberdeen.

Glacier, resort village, SE B.C., in Rocky Mts., 35 mi. NE of Revelstoke, in Glacier Natl. Park, at foot of Mt. Bonney (10,194 ft.); alt. 3,817 ft. Just NE, on Canadian Pacific RR transcontinental main line, is the Connaught Tunnel.

Glacier, county (□ 2,974; pop. 9,645), N Mont.; ⊙ Cut Bank. Agr. area bordering on Alta.; drained by Milk and Marias rivers and Lower St. Mary L. Livestock, grain; petroleum, natural gas. Blackfeet Indian Reservation, part of Glacier Natl. Park, and ranges of Continental Divide in W. Formed 1919.

Glacier Bay National Monument (□ 3,590.2), SE Alaska, on B.C. border, at SE end of St. Elias Mts., 75 WNW of Juneau. Includes SE part of Fairweather Range S of Mt. Fairweather; upper part of Glacier Bay, inlet (65 mi. long, 2–15 mi. wide) of Icy Straight and Cross Sound, 60 mi. W of Juneau; and Muir Glacier. High peaks include Bertha, Crillon, La Perouse mts. Established 1925. Region explored (1794) by Vancouver.

Glacier Highway, scenic road, SE Alaska, extends from Thane c.35 mi. NW, through Juneau and Tee Harbor, to foot of Mendenhall Glacier.

Glacier Island (9 mi. long, 2–5 mi. wide), S Alaska, in Prince William Sound, 35 mi. WSW of Valdez; 60°53'N 147°12'W; rises to 1,648 ft.

Glacier Mountain (12,438 ft.), in Rocky Mts., in Summit county, central Colo.

Glacier National Park (□ 521), SE B.C., in Selkirk Mts., centered on Glacier. High peaks include mts. Rogers, Bonney, Dawson, and Grand Mtn. Established 1886.

Glacier National Park (□ 1,560), NW Mont., c.40 mi. NE of Kalispell, in Rocky Mts.; bounded W by Flathead R., SW by its Middle Fork, and N by Canadian border, separating it from Waterton Lakes Natl. Park in Alta. Scenic, glacier-carved region astride Continental Divide (here following LEWIS RANGE); includes some of most spectacular peaks of the Rockies, more than 60 glaciers and 200 lakes, numerous streams and waterfalls, extensive forests, and colorful wildflower fields. Park hq. at West Glacier, on W boundary. Highest peak is Mt. Cleveland (10,448 ft.), near Alta. line. Going-to-the-Sun Highway (c.50 mi. long), passing near Going-to-the-Sun Mtn. (9,604 ft.), is famous scenic route connecting E and W park boundaries and crossing Continental Divide at Logan Pass (6,664 ft.). Principal lakes: L. McDonald (10 mi. long, 1 mi. wide; alt. 3,154 ft.), near W boundary; Waterton L. (11 mi. long, ½ mi. wide; alt. 4,196 ft.), straddling Alta. line; and St. Mary L. (9½ mi. long, 1 mi. wide; alt. 4,482 ft.), on E boundary and connecting with Lower St. Mary L. (6 mi. long, 1 mi. wide; alt. 4,470 ft.), in Glacier co. Blackfoot Glacier (□ 10; alt. c.7,500 ft.) is SW of St. Mary L. and near Mt. Jackson (10,033 ft.). Park was established 1910; joined (1932) to Waterton Lakes Natl. Park (Canada) under name of Waterton-Glacier International Peace Park. Park administrations, though separate, cooperate closely.

Glacier Park, Mont.: see EAST GLACIER PARK.

Glacier Peak (10,436 ft.), NW Wash., in Cascade Range, c.50 mi. ENE of Everett.

Glacis (gläsē'), village on W coast of Mahé Isl., Seychelles, on North West Bay (inlet of Indian Ocean), 2½ mi. NW of Victoria; copra, essential oils; fisheries.

Gladbach, Germany: see BERGISCH GLADBACH; MÜNCHEN GLADBACH.

Gladbach-Rheydt, Germany: see MÜNCHEN GLADBACH; RHEYDT.

Gladbeck (glät'bĕk), city (1950 pop. 71,689), in former Prussian prov. of Westphalia, W Germany, after 1945 in North Rhine-Westphalia, in the Ruhr, bet. Bottrop (W), Essen (S), and Gelsenkirchen (E); mfg. of pipes, metalware, textiles, devotional articles; sawmilling, food processing (cheese). Coal mining. Second World War destruction c.40%. First mentioned in 9th cent. Chartered 1919.

Gladbrook, town (pop. 862), Tama co., central Iowa, on Wolf Creek and 14 mi. NE of Marshalltown; feed; dairy, concrete, and metal products.

Glade, city (pop. 107), Phillips co., N Kansas, 4 mi. S of Phillipsburg.

Gladenbach (glä'dùnbäkh), town (pop. 2,971), in former Prussian prov. of Hesse-Nassau, W Germany, after 1945 in Hesse, in the Westerwald, 8 mi. WSW of Marburg; metal- and woodworking.

Glade Park, village (pop. c.125), Mesa co., W Colo., near Utah line, 10 mi. WSW of Grand Junction; alt. 6,496 ft.; grain, potatoes, beans.

Glades, county (□ 746; pop. 2,199), S Fla., bounded E by L. Okeechobee; ⊙ Moore Haven. Everglades cattle-raising area, with some truck farming and fishing. Crossed by Caloosahatchee R. Includes Seminole Indian Reservation. Formed 1921.

Glade Spring, town (pop. 827), Washington co., SW Va., 12 mi. NE of Abingdon.

Gladewater (glăd'wô"tùr), city (pop. 5,305), Gregg and Upshur counties, E Texas, near Sabine R., 12 mi. W of Longview, in East Texas oil field; oil, gasoline refining. Settled 1870, inc. 1931; boomed after oil discovery, 1930.

Gladsmuir (glădz'mūr), village and parish (pop. 1,779), W East Lothian, Scotland, 4 mi. W of Haddington; coal mining. William Robertson was minister here for 15 years.

Gladstone. **1** Town and port (pop. 5,244), E Queensland, Australia, on Port Curtis (inlet of Pacific Ocean) and 60 mi. SE of Rockhampton; cotton-producing center; exports coal. **2** Town (pop. 887), S South Australia, 21 mi. ESE of Port Pirie; rail junction; wheat, wine; wool, dairy products; timber. **3** Village, W Western Australia, 200 mi. N of Geraldton and on Hamelin Pool of Shark Bay; sheep.

Gladstone, town (pop. 699), S Man., on Whitemud R. and 35 mi. WNW of Portage la Prairie; grain elevators; dairying; stock, poultry.

Gladstone, village (pop. 227), NE Tasmania, 55 mi. NE of Launceston, on Ringarooma R.; sheep; tin.

Gladstone (glăd'stōn). **1** Village (pop. 340), Henderson co., W Ill., 8 mi. ENE of Burlington, Iowa; ships grain; limestone quarries. **2** City (pop. 4,831), Delta co., S Upper Peninsula, Mich., 8 mi. NNE of Escanaba, on Little Bay De Noc. Shipping point for grain; mfg. (wood products, sporting equipment, trailer parts); fisheries. Agr. (potatoes, strawberries, fruit). Resort. Founded 1887, inc. 1889. **3** Village (pop. 224), Stark co., W N.Dak., 10 mi. E of Dickinson and on Heart R. **4** Residential city (pop. 2,434), Clackamas co., NW Oregon, near Oregon City, on Clackamas R. Inc. 1911.

Gladstone, Mount, New Guinea: see FINISTERRE RANGE.

Gladwin, county (□ 503; pop. 9,451), E central Mich.; ⊙ Gladwin. Drained by Tittabawassee and Tobacco rivers and small Cedar R. Agr. (livestock, grain, seed, potatoes); dairy products; oil wells; farm-products processing. Many small lakes (resorts); hunting, fishing. Has state forest, game refuge, and park. Organized 1875.

Gladwin, city (pop. 1,878), ⊙ Gladwin co., E central Mich., 40 mi. NW of Bay City, and on small Cedar R., in livestock and dairy area; oil wells. A dist. office of Mich. Conservation Dept. and Gladwin State Park on small Cedar R. here. Hunting and fishing near by. Settled 1865; inc. as village 1885, as city 1893.

Gladwyne, Pa.: see LOWER MERION.

Glaeno (glĕ'nû), Dan. *Glænø,* low island (□ 2; pop. 121) in Smaalandsfarvand strait, Denmark, just S of Zealand.

Glaf Fjord, Swedish *Glafsfjorden* (gläfs'-fyōōr"dùn), lake (□ 39), W Sweden, near Norwegian border, extends SE from Arvika; 25 mi. long, 1–4 mi. wide. Drains S into L. Vaner by By R.

Glageon (gläzhō'), village (pop. 1,705), Nord dept., N France, 8 mi. SE of Avesnes; wool spinning, tanning.

Glain (glē), town (pop. 3,798), Liége prov., E Belgium, W suburb of Liége.

Glalluz, peak, Yugoslavia: see JALOVEC.

Glama River, Norway; see GLOMMA RIVER.

Glamfjord, Norway: see GLOMFJORD.

Glamis (glämz; in Shakespeare glä'mĭs), agr. village and parish (pop. 985), W Angus, Scotland, at foot of Sidlaw Hills, 6 mi. SW of Forfar. In 1034 Malcolm II died in this vicinity; a sculptured cross in the village is known as Malcolm's Gravestone. Macbeth was thane of Glamis, and Glamis Castle, present structure of which dates from 17th cent., is one of the places erroneously claimed to be scene of murder of Duncan. Elizabeth, queen consort of George VI, b. here.

Glamoc or **Glamoch** (both: glä'môch), Serbo-Croatian *Glamoč,* village (pop. 3,912), SW Bosnia, Yugoslavia, 55 mi. SSW of Banja Luka.

Glamorgan, coal-mining village (pop. c.500), Wise co., SW Va., just N of Wise.

Glamorgan or **Glamorganshire** (glùmôr'gùn,–shĭr), county (□ 813.2; 1931 pop. 1,225,717; 1951 census 1,201,989), SE Wales, on Bristol Channel; ⊙ Cardiff. Bounded by Carmarthen (NE), Brecknock (N), and Monmouth (E). Drained by Taff, Tawe, Rhondda, Rhymney, Loughor, Ogmore, Garw, and Neath rivers. Mountainous in N, leveling toward S and SW (Gower peninsula). Economically most important Welsh co., with large coal resources, and center of British steel-rolling and tinplate-mfg. industry (copper, tin, spelter). In S is fertile agr. land (cattle and sheep grazing, dairying). Besides Cardiff, other important towns are ports of Swansea (tinplate center), Port Talbot, Barry, and Penarth; coal-mining centers of Merthyr Tydfil, Rhondda, Aberdare, Llwchwr, and Mountain Ash; and industrial towns of Pontypridd, Caerphilly, Neath, and Maesteg. There are vestiges of Roman occupation, and remains of anc. castles (Cardiff, Caerphilly). Industrial rise of co. was rapid in 19th cent.; it was severely affected by economic depression in 1930s. Efforts were made to introduce new light industries (now centered on Treforest) to lessen unemployment in coal mining.

Glamsbjaerg (gläms'byĕr), town (pop. 1,471), Odense amt, Denmark, on Fyn isl. and 14 mi. SW of Odense; machinery, furniture, margarine.

Glan (glän), town (1939 pop. 956) in Cotabato municipality, Cotabato prov., W Mindanao, Philippines; copra, abacá.

Glanadda, Wales: see BANGOR.

Glanamman, Wales: see CWMAMMAN.

Glandore (glăndôr'), Gaelic *Cuan Dor,* village (pop. 82), S Co. Cork, Ireland, on small inlet of the Atlantic, 8 mi. E of Skibbereen; fishing port, seaside resort, noted for mild climate.

Glandorf, village (pop. 479), Putnam co., NW Ohio, c.22 mi. W of Findlay and on Blanchard R.; tile factory.

Glanerbrug (khlä'nùrbrûkh), village (pop. 7,883), Overijssel prov., E Netherlands, 3 mi. E of Enschede; frontier station on Ger. border.

Glanmire (glănmīr'), Gaelic *Gleann Maghair,* village (pop. 215), SE Co. Cork, Ireland, 4 mi. ENE of Cork; woolen milling.

Glan River (glän), Carinthia, S Austria, rises E of the Ossiachersee, flows 25 mi. E, then S at Sankt Veit, through the ZOLLFELD, thence E again at Klagenfurt to Drau R. 3 mi. E of Grafenstein; length, c.50 mi.

Glan River (glän), W Germany, rises just N of Waldmohr, flows 50 mi. NE to the Nahe, 3 mi. E of Sobernheim. Receives the Lauter (right).

Glanruddery Mountains (glănrŭ'dùrē), range, NE Co. Kerry, Ireland, extending 10 mi. N from Castleisland; rises to 1,097 ft.

Glanworth, Gaelic *Gleannabhair,* village (pop. 189), NE Co. Cork, Ireland, on Funshion R. (bridge) and 5 mi. NW of Fermoy; woolen milling. Has 13th-cent. church of Dominican abbey, founded by the Roches, and ruins of castle of Roche family.

Glapwell, village and parish (pop. 319), NE Derby, England, 5 mi. NW of Mansfield; coal mining.

Glarentza, Greece: see KYLLENE.

Glaris, Switzerland: see GLARUS.

Glarner Alpen, Switzerland: see GLARUS ALPS.

Glärnisch (glĕr'nĭsh), mountain in Glarus Alps, E central Switzerland, 1 to 5 mi. SW of Glarus; culminates in Vorder-Glärnisch (7,660 ft.), Mittler-Glärnisch or Bächistock (9,572 ft.), and Hinter-Glärnisch or Rüchen (9,529 ft.).

Glarus (glâ'rŭs, glä'rōōs), Fr. *Glaris* (glärēs'), canton (□ 264; 1950 pop. 37,674), E central Switzerland; ⊙ Glarus. Pop. German speaking, largely Protestant. In basin of Linth R., and almost surrounded by high mts., with meadows and forests in the valleys; pastures (cattle raising, dairying) cover lower mtn. slopes, which rise to peaks and glaciers of Glarus Alps; cultivation is limited to extreme N. Hydroelectric plants along the Linth; main industry, woolen and cotton textiles. L. of Wallenstadt is in N, Tödi mts. in S.

Glarus, Fr. *Glaris,* town (1950 pop. 5,695), ⊙ Glarus canton, E Switzerland, on Linth R. and 19 mi. W of Liechtenstein border; surrounded by mts.; woodworking, printing; cotton textiles, flour, pastry, tobacco.

Glarus Alps, Ger. *Glarner Alpen,* N division of Central Alps, chiefly in Glarus canton, E central Switzerland; bounded S by the Vorderrhein, E by the Rhine, and N by Seeztal, L. of Wallenstadt, and Linth Canal. Highest peak, Tödi (11,886 ft.). Penetrated by valleys of Linth (Linthal) and upper Seez (Weisstannental) rivers. Crossed by Klausen Pass.

Glasco. **1** City (pop. 803), Cloud co., N central Kansas, on Solomon R. and 35 mi. NNW of Salina; flour, dairy products. **2** Village (pop. c.1,000),

Ulster co., SE N.Y., on W bank of the Hudson and 8 mi. above Kingston; mfg. (clothing, brick).

Glascock, county (□ 142; pop. 3,579), E Ga.; ⊙ Gibson. Bounded W by Ogeechee R. Coastal plain agr. (cotton, corn, peanuts, vegetables, fruit) and sawmilling area, with kaolin deposits. Formed 1857.

Glascote, town in parish of Bolehall and Glascote (pop. 4,847), N Warwick, England, just SE of Tamworth; coal mining. Just W is coal-mining village of Bolehall.

Glasford, Scotland: see GLASSFORD.

Glasford, village (pop. 922), Peoria co., central Ill., 13 mi. SW of Peoria; agr.; bituminous-coal mines; timber; feed, wood products.

Glasgo, Conn.: see GRISWOLD.

Glasgow (glăs'gō, glăz'–; glăs'kō), burgh (1931 pop. 1,088,461; 1951 census 1,089,555), city, and county in itself, Lanarkshire, Scotland, on the Clyde, at mouth of Kelvin R., and 42 mi. W of Edinburgh; 55°51'N 4°16'W. It is largest city of Scotland and 2d in size of Great Britain; major port, with huge shipyards and dock installations extending along the Clyde to Dumbarton and Greenock; commercial and industrial center. Industries, besides shipbuilding, include tanning; milling of woolens, cotton, silk, and rayon; locomotive building, metal founding; mfg. of chemicals, paper, paint, soap, tobacco and food products, machinery, machine tools, domestic appliances, typewriters, whisky. Although the Clyde is navigable for ocean shipping to Glasgow, Greenock is main passenger port for the city. PRESTWICK is the international and RENFREW the local airport for Glasgow. While the city is wealthy, it has notorious slum areas, especially in the Gorbals district (S). Among city's noted features are: Buchanan and Sauchiehall streets, shopping and commercial centers; 12th-cent. cathedral (St. Mungos); Corporation Art Galleries; Institute of Fine Arts; Mitchell Library; and extensive Kelvingrove Park. There are few bldgs. of historic interest. Glasgow Univ. was founded in 1450 by Bishop Turnbull; present bldgs. were begun in 1870; there are faculties of arts, science, engineering, medicine, law, and theology. The "Glasgow School" of art dates from late 19th cent.; Sir John Lavery was its leader and chief exponent. Site of city was early occupied; Stone and Bronze Age implements have been excavated here. In 6th cent. St. Mungo reputedly founded a bishopric here, which was restored in 1115 by David I, and c.1180 William the Lion granted a charter to town, then called *Gleschu.* In 1300 fortified 13th-cent. palace of the bishops was taken by Wallace in battle of "Bell o' the Brae." Glasgow was taken by Montrose in 1645 and by Prince Charles Edward in 1745. In 1740 construction of harbor works was begun. In 1941 the city and especially the shipyards were heavily bombed. Although mostly in Lanarkshire, city limits extend into Dumbartonshire (N) and Renfrewshire (W). Among main suburbs of Glasgow are GOVAN, Langside (site of 1568 battle in which the Regent Moray defeated troops of Mary Queen of Scots; site marked by memorial), Provan, POLLOKSHAWS, Pollokshields, Cathcart, CALTON, CAMLACHIE, DALMARNOCK, MARYHILL, Kelvinside, PARTICK, and Rutherglen.

Glasgow (glăs'gō, –kō). **1** Village (pop. 158), Scott co., W central Ill., 17 mi. SW of Jacksonville, in agr. area. **2** City (pop. 7,025), ⊙ Barren co., S Ky., 29 mi. E of Bowling Green; trade center for agr. area (burley tobacco, corn, dairy products, livestock, and fruit); oil wells, hardwood timber; stone quarries; mfg. of clothing, dairy products, soft drinks, concrete blocks, mattresses; lumber, flour, and feed mills, tobacco warehouses; airport. State fish hatchery near by. Named 1799. **3** City (pop. 1,440), Howard co., central Mo., on Missouri R. and 10 mi. NW of Fayette; ships grain, cattle; canning factory. Lewis Col. here. Laid out 1836, inc. 1845. **4** City (pop. 3,821), ⊙ Valley co., NE Mont., 145 mi. ESE of Havre and on Milk R., near Fort Peck Reservoir and Dam, in extensively irrigated region. Shipping point for grain, sugar beets, livestock; gas wells; flour, beverages; poultry and truck produce. Growth of city stimulated by construction of dam. Founded 1887, platted 1888. **5** or **Smiths Ferry,** borough (pop. 214), Beaver co., W Pa., on Ohio R. just above East Liverpool, Ohio. **6** Town (pop. 810), Rockbridge co., W Va., in the Blue Ridge, on North R. near its mouth on the James and 22 mi. NW of Lynchburg; large carpet mill; brick mfg. Natural Bridge is 5 mi. W. **7** Town (pop. 881), Kanawha co., W W.Va., on the Kanawha and 14 mi. SE of Charleston, in coal-mining region.

Glasgow Junction, Ky.: see PARK CITY.

Glashütte (gläs'hü"tŭ), town (pop. 4,007), Saxony, E central Germany, in the Erzgebirge, 13 mi. S of Dresden; watchmaking center; mfg. of office machinery, machine tools, paper.

Glasinac or **Glasinats** (both: glä'sĭnäts), region (alt. c.3,000 ft.) in Dinaric Alps, SE Bosnia, Yugoslavia; extends c.10 mi. N-S, along E foot of Romanija Mts.; partly within Sarajevo coal area. Chief village, Sokolac (pop. 1,315), is 20 mi. E of Sarajevo.

Glaslough, Ireland: see GLASSLOUGH.

Glasnevin (glăsnĕ'vĭn), Gaelic *Glas Naoidhean,* N suburb (pop. 8,934) of Dublin, Co. Dublin, Ireland; site of famous botanical gardens, founded 1790 by Royal Dublin Society. Cemetery here has graves of Curran, Parnell, Michael Collins.

Glasoarnoch River, Scotland: see GARVE WATER.

Glassboro, borough (pop. 5,867), Gloucester co., SW N.J., 16 mi. S of Camden; agr. trade center (fruit, truck); mfg. (glass products, vinegar, clothing, baskets). State teachers col. (1923.) Settled 1775, inc. 1920.

Glasscock, county (□ 864; pop. 1,089), W Texas; ⊙ Garden City. Rolling prairies and woodlands, drained by tributaries of Colorado R.; alt. 2,100–2,500 ft. Ranching region (sheep, goats, beef cattle); agr. (grain sorghums, corn, oats, cotton). Some oil, natural gas. Formed 1887.

Glassford or **Glasford,** town and parish (pop. 1,177), N Lanark, Scotland, 5 mi. S of Hamilton; coal mining.

Glass Houghton (hou'tŭn), town and parish (pop. 8,602), West Riding, S central Yorkshire, England, 2 mi. NNW of Pontefract; coal-mining center.

Glasslough or **Glaslough** (both: glăslŏkh'), Gaelic *Baile Glaslocha,* town (pop. 132), N Co. Monaghan, Ireland, 6 mi. NNE of Monaghan; flax, oats, potatoes; flax-scutching center.

Glass Mountains, extreme W Texas, in Brewster and Pecos counties; range extends c.25 mi. ENE from point c.13 mi. E of Alpine; rises to 6,523 ft.

Glassport, industrial borough (pop. 8,707), Allegheny co., SW Pa., on Monongahela R., opposite Clairton, and 10 mi. SSE of Pittsburgh; glass, steel, refined oil. Inc. 1902.

Glass River. 1 In Inverness, Scotland: see BEAULY RIVER. **2** In Ross and Cromarty, Scotland, issues from SE end of Loch Glass (4 mi. long), 5 mi. WNW of Evanton, flows 7 mi. ESE, past Evanton, to Cromarty Firth just SE of Evanton.

Glastenbury (glă'stŭnbĕ"rē, glă'sŭn–), town (pop. 1), Bennington co., SW Vt., in the Green Mts. 10 mi. NE of Bennington.

Glastonbury (glă'stŭnbŭrē), municipal borough (1931 pop. 4,514; 1951 census 5,081), central Somerset, England, on Brue R. and 5 mi. SW of Wells; agr. market in dairying region; leather and shoe industry. Traditionally place where St. Joseph of Arimathea founded 1st Christian church in England, also identified through legend with Isle of Avalon, where King Arthur and Queen Guinevere are buried. According to tradition, 1st Glastonbury thorn was St. Joseph's staff, which took root where he rested it on Wearyall Hill, and which blossomed annually on Christmas Eve, until almost destroyed by Puritans. The Saxon king Ine founded Glastonbury abbey in 8th cent. Abbey refounded by St. Dunstan in 946, burned in 1184, rebuilt by Henry II, and suppressed by Henry VIII. Medieval center of learning and pilgrimage. Abbot's kitchen and parts of chapel remain. Lake village remains found near by; mus. of antiquities here.

Glastonbury (glă'stŭnbĕ"rē, glă'sŭn–), town (pop. 8,818), Hartford co., central Conn., on the Connecticut and 5 mi. SE of Hartford; agr. (tobacco, peaches); mfg. (textiles, leather, silverware, metal products). Includes South Glastonbury village (1940 pop. 779). Settled c.1650, inc. 1690.

Glatt River (glät), N Switzerland, outlet of the Greifensee, flows 22 mi. NNW, past NE suburbs of Zurich, to the Rhine 3 mi. W of Eglisau.

Glatz (gläts) or **Klodzko** (kwôts'kô), Pol. *Kłodzko,* town (1939 pop. 22,000; 1946 pop. 22,814) in Lower Silesia, after 1945 in Wroclaw prov., SW Poland, at S foot of the Eulengebirge, on the Glatzer Neisse and 50 mi. SSW of Breslau (Wroclaw); rail junction; cotton, linen, and paper milling, metalworking, sugar refining, machinery mfg., jam making; fruit gardens. Has 15th-cent. church, castle (1st mentioned 981), fortress walls, medieval houses. Founded 10th cent. by Bohemian princes; became (1462) ⊙ Glatz co. Heavily damaged in Thirty Years War; captured 1741 by Frederick the Great, who fortified it; withstood Fr. siege in 1807.

Glatzer Neisse River, Poland: see NEISSE RIVER.

Glatzer Schneegebirge, Czechoslovakia: see KRALICKY SNEZNIK.

Glauchau (glou'khou), town (pop. 34,906), Saxony, E central Germany, on the Zwickauer Mulde and 7 mi. NNE of Zwickau; textile center (cotton, wool, rayon, silk; synthetic-fiber milling and knitting); metalworking; mfg. of machinery, musical instruments, leather goods, hats. Captured by Hussites in 1430. Georg Agricola b. here.

Glazier Lake, Maine and N.B., on international line 19 mi. W of Fort Kent; 5 mi. long.

Glazmanka, Latvia: see GOSTINI.

Glazok (glŭzôk'), village (1926 pop. 7,306), W Tambov oblast, Russian SFSR, on right headstream of Voronezh R. and 15 mi. NNE of Michurinsk; grain, tobacco.

Glazov (glä'zŭf), city (1939 pop. over 10,000), N Udmurt Autonomous SSR, Russian SFSR, on Cheptsa R. (landing), on railroad and 90 mi. NNE of Izhevsk; flax- and food-processing center; glass-working. Teachers col. City chartered 1780.

Glazunovka (glŭzōōnôf'kŭ), village (1939 pop. over 500), S Orel oblast, Russian SFSR, 31 mi. SSE of Orel; fruit and vegetable canning, hemp milling.

Gleann a Chapaill, Ireland: see GLEN OF THE HORSE.

Gleason, town (pop. 1,063), Weakley co., NW Tenn., 28 mi. SE of Union City, in corn, cotton, livestock, tobacco area.

Glebe (glēb), municipality (pop. 20,510), E New South Wales, Australia, on S shore of Port Jackson, just SW of Sydney, in metropolitan area; industrial center; brass foundries, flour mills, shoe factories, chemical plant.

Glebokie, Belorussian SSR: see GLUBOKOYE, Polotsk oblast.

Gleichen (glē'chŭn), town (pop. 477), S Alta., near Bow R., 45 mi. ESE of Calgary; coal mining; wheat elevators, ranching.

Gleichenberg, Austria: see BAD GLEICHENBERG.

Gleisdorf (glīs'dôrf), town (pop. 4,472), Styria, SE Austria, on Raab R. and 12 mi. E of Graz; rail junction; leather goods. Fruit shipped; vineyards.

Gleisweiler (glīs'vī"lŭr), climatic resort (pop. 584), Rhenish Palatinate, W Germany, on E slope of Hardt Mts., 3 mi. NW of Landau; grape cure.

Gleiwitz (glī'vĭts) or **Gliwice** (glēvē'tsĕ), industrial city (1939 pop. 117,250; 1946 census pop. 95,980; 1950 pop. estimate 128,200) in Upper Silesia, after 1945 in Katowice prov., S Poland, port at E end of Gliwice Canal, on Klodnica R., and 17 mi. W of Katowice; 50°18'N 18°40'E. Coal-mining and steel-milling center; mfg. of machinery, chemicals, refractory bricks. Technical col.; radio station. Founded in Middle Ages; chartered 1276. Passed 1742 to Prussia. First large foundry set up in late-18th cent. Heavily damaged in Second World War.

Gleiwitz Canal or **Gliwice Canal,** Pol. *Kanał Gliwicki* (kä'nou glēvēts'kē), in Upper Silesia, after 1945 in SW Poland, bet. the Oder (W; 2 mi. N of Kozle) and Gleiwitz (Gliwice; E), paralleling Klodnica R.; 25 mi. long. Replaces earlier Klodnitz Canal, built 1792–1822.

Gleize, La (lä glāz'), village (pop. 1,067), Liége prov., E Belgium, on Amblève R. and 19 mi. SE of Liége; agr., lumbering. Has 12th-cent. Romanesque church. Sanitarium near by.

Glemsford, former urban district (1931 pop. 1,261), SW Suffolk, England, 5 mi. NNW of Sudbury; agr. market; mfg. of horse-hair products.

Glen, village, W Orange Free State, U. of So. Afr., on Modder R. and 13 mi. NE of Bloemfontein, in stock-raising region; alt. 4,272 ft. Site of govt. agr. col. and experimental farm, established 1919.

Glen, N.H.: see BARTLETT.

Glen, Mount (7,512 ft.), SE Ariz., highest peak in Dragoon Mts., 17 mi. N of Tombstone.

Glena (glĕ'nŭ), bay and wooded valley, central Co. Kerry, Ireland, at S end of Lough Leane, 4 mi. S of Killarney.

Glen Afton, village (pop. 461), W N.Isl., New Zealand, 55 mi. SSE of Auckland; coal mine; rail terminus.

Glen Albyn, Scotland: see GREAT GLEN OF SCOTLAND.

Glenallen, town (pop. 107), Bollinger co., SE Mo., 20 mi. WSW of Jackson.

Glenalmond (glĕnă'mŭnd), valley of Almond R., in central and SE Perthshire, Scotland, noted for its scenic beauty, celebrated by Wordsworth. Section of valley called Sma' Glen, 6 mi. NNE of Crieff, is traditional site of grave of Ossian. Episcopal Trinity Col., a public school founded 1841, is 4 mi. WNW of Methven.

Glen Alpine. 1 Resort village, El Dorado co., E Calif., in the Sierra Nevada, just S of L. Tahoe. Fallen Leaf L. is near by. **2** Town (pop. 695), Burke co., W central N.C., 5 mi. W of Morganton; hosiery mfg.

Glénans, Les (lā glānä'), or **Îles-Glénans** (ēl–), group of rocky islands in Bay of Biscay, off coast of Finistère dept., W France, 12 mi. SSW of Concarneau; oyster fishing.

Glenarden or **Glen Arden,** town (pop. 492), Prince Georges co., central Md., E of Washington.

Glenarm (glĕnärm'), town (pop. 853), E Co. Antrim, Northern Ireland, on the North Channel, 10 mi. NW of Larne; seaport; ships bauxite (mined near by), iron, limestone. Glenarm Castle dates from 1636. There are remains of 15th-cent. Franciscan monastery.

Glenavon (glĕnă'vŭn), village (pop. 216), SE Sask., 33 mi. SE of Indian Head; mixed farming.

Glenavy (glĕnă'vē), agr. village (district pop. 1,311), S Co. Antrim, Northern Ireland, on the short Glenavy R., near its mouth on Lough Neagh, and 11 mi. W of Belfast; flax, potatoes, cattle.

Glenbarry (glĕnbă'rē), agr. village, NE Banffshire, Scotland, 10 mi. SW of Banff, at foot of Knock Hill (1,409 ft.).

Glenbervie (glĕnbûr'vē), agr. village and parish (pop. 644), central Kincardine, Scotland, on Bervie Water and 7 mi. WSW of Stonehaven. Parish includes Drumlithie, agr. village 2 mi. E of Glenbervie.

Glenbeulah (glĕn"bū'lŭ), village (pop. 384), Sheboygan co., E Wis., on small Mullet R. and 17 mi. WNW of Sheboygan, in dairy and grain area.

Glenboro, village (pop. estimate 650), SW Man., 35 mi. SE of Brandon; grain elevators.

Glenbrook. 1 Village, Fairfield co., Conn.: see STAMFORD. **2** Resort, Douglas co., W Nev., on E shore of L. Tahoe, 10 mi. SW of Carson City.

Glenburn. 1 Town (pop. 694), Penobscot co., S Maine, just NW of Bangor, in agr., recreational region. **2** Village (pop. 281), Renville co., N central N.Dak., 20 mi. N of Minot.

Glen Burnie, residential suburb, Anne Arundel co., central Md., 10 mi. S of downtown Baltimore. State training school for Negro girls. Friendship International Airport is near by.

Glencairn, Dumfries, Scotland: see MONIAIVE.

Glen Campbell, borough (pop. 510), Indiana co., W central Pa., 22 mi. NE of Indiana.

Glen Carbon, village (pop. 1,176), Madison co., SW Ill., 12 mi. NE of East St. Louis, in bituminous-coal and agr. area. Inc. 1892.

Glencliff, N.H.: see WARREN.

Glencoe (glĕnkō′), village (pop. 636), SE South Australia, 225 mi. SSE of Adelaide, 15 mi. NW of Mt. Gambier; rail terminus; acacia timber.

Glencoe (glĕn′kō), village (pop. 836), S Ont., 30 mi. SW of London; beet and tobacco growing, dairying, woodworking, oil production.

Glencoe (glĕnkō′), valley of Coe R., N Argyll, Scotland, in Appin district, extending c.10 mi. from its mouth on Loch Leven. The glen is overhung by several high mts., now property of the National Trust; among them (S) is a group named The Sisters of Glencoe, rising to 3,497 ft. In the glen is a cleft named Ossian's Cave. In 1692 the glen was scene of massacre of the Macdonald clan by their traditional enemies, the Campbells, and English soldiers by order of Sir John Dalrymple, secretary of state to William III.

Glencoe, town (pop. 3,606), NW Natal, U. of So. Afr., 35 mi. NE of Ladysmith; rail junction; coal-mining center.

Glencoe (glĕn′kō). **1** Town (pop. 1,466), Etowah co., NE Ala., 5 mi. SE of Gadsden; limestone. Inc. 1939. **2** Residential village (pop. 6,980), Cook co., NE Ill., N suburb of Chicago, on L. Michigan, 7 mi. NW of Evanston; truck, poultry. Settled 1836, inc. 1869. **3** City (pop. 2,801), ⊙ McLeod co., S central Minn., on Buffalo Creek and c.45 mi. WSW of Minneapolis; farm trade and livestock-shipping point in grain, sugar-beet, and poultry area; dairy products, flour, beverages. Platted 1855. **4** Town (pop. 309), Payne co., N central Okla., 11 mi. NE of Stillwater, in agr. area; cotton ginning.

Glencorse, town and parish (pop. 1,277), central Midlothian, Scotland, 8 mi. S of Edinburgh; agr. market. Site of base depot of Royal Scots regiment. Near by is an Edinburgh reservoir.

Glen Cove, city (pop. 15,130), Nassau co., SE N.Y., on N shore of W Long Isl., 8 mi. N of Mineola, at entrance to Hempstead Harbor; trade center for summer resort area. Mfg.: office supplies, clothing, radios, wood products, photoengraving equipment, hardware. Seat of Webb Inst. of Naval Architecture. Settled 1668, inc. 1918.

Glendale, village, Salisbury prov., NE Southern Rhodesia, in Mashonaland, on railroad and 18 mi. WSW of Bindura; alt. 3,849 ft. Tobacco, corn, dairy products. Gold deposits.

Glendale. 1 City (pop. 8,179), Maricopa co., S central Ariz., 8 mi. NW of Phoenix, in Salt R. valley; agr. trading point in diversified farming area; cotton ginning, fruit and vegetable packing; dairy products. Settled in 1890s, inc. 1910. **2** City (pop. 95,702), Los Angeles co., S Calif., N suburb of Los Angeles, in SE San Fernando Valley, on slope of Verdugo Hills (foothills of San Gabriel Mts.); residential and industrial (aircraft, petroleum products, machinery, cement, chemicals, auto parts, pottery, glass). Airport; large civic auditorium. Seat of Glendale Col. and Cal-Aero Technical Inst. Here are Brand Park (c.600 acres); Casa Adobe (adobe bldg. dating from 1860s); Forest Lawn Memorial Park, a cemetery containing reproductions of great works of art and Wee Kirk O' the Heather, a reproduction of Scotland's church of Annie Laurie. Laid out 1886 on site of 1st Spanish land grant (1784) in Calif.; inc. 1906. **3** Village, Berkshire co., Mass.: see STOCKBRIDGE. **4** City (pop. 4,930), St. Louis co., E Mo., W of St. Louis. **5** A section of W Queens borough of New York city, SE N.Y.; mfg. (clothing, candles, soap, electrical equipment; wood, glass, paper, and stone products; dies, thermometers). **6** Suburban residential village (pop. 2,402), Hamilton co., extreme SW Ohio, 11 mi. N of downtown Cincinnati. Laid out 1852, inc. 1855. **7** City (pop. 871), Douglas co., SW Oregon, 21 mi. NNW of Grants Pass; lumber. **8** Village (1940 pop. 3,828), Allegheny co., SW Pa., 6 mi. SW of Pittsburgh. **9** Village, Providence co., R.I.: see BURRILLVILLE. **10** Textile village (pop. 1,244), Spartanburg co., NW S.C., 4 mi. E of Spartanburg; cotton milling. **11** Town (pop. 226), Kane co., S Utah, 18 mi. N of Kanab and on Virgin R.; alt. 5,824 ft.; coal. **12** Hamlet, Henrico co., E central Va., 12 mi. SE of Richmond. Here was fought (June 30, 1862) an inconclusive engagement (also called battle of Frayser's Farm) of Seven Days Battles. **13** Residential town (pop. 1,467), Marshall co., NW W. Va., in Northern Panhandle, near the Ohio, 10 mi. SSW of Wheeling; makes toys. Reynolds Memorial Hosp. here. Inc. 1924.

Glendalough (glĕn′dŭlŏkh″), wooded valley, E central Co. Wicklow, Ireland, 10 mi. W of Wicklow. Site of noted ruins of the "Seven Churches" (ecclesiastical establishment founded in 6th cent. by St. Kevin), a round tower, and Kevin's Cross (granite monolith). Cave at foot of vale is legendary retreat of St. Kevin.

Glendive (glĕn′dīv), city (pop. 5,254), ⊙ Dawson co., E Mont., on Yellowstone R., at head of navigation, and 70 mi. NE of Miles City. Trading and shipping point in irrigated grain and sugar-beet region; railway div. point with repair shops; livestock, poultry. Lignite mines near by; gas wells 20 mi. S. Laid out 1880, inc. 1902.

Glendo, town (pop. 215), Platte co., E Wyo., near N.Platte R., 31 mi. N of Wheatland; alt. 4,718 ft. Supply point in ranching region.

Glendon, village (pop. estimate 300), E Alta., 65 mi. N of Vermilion; mixed farming, lumbering.

Glendon, borough (pop. 601), Northampton co., E Pa., on Lehigh R. just SW of Easton.

Glendora (glĕndô′rŭ). **1** Residential city (pop. 3,988), Los Angeles co., S Calif., 22 mi. ENE of downtown Los Angeles, in foothill citrus-fruit belt; citrus-fruit packing. Founded 1887, inc. 1911. **2** Village (pop. 178), Tallahatchie co., NW central Miss., on Tallahatchie R. and 23 mi. NNW of Greenwood.

Glen Echo, residential town (pop. 356), Montgomery co., central Md., NW suburb of Washington, on the Potomac. Amusement park. Near by is the house built 1897 for Clara Barton. Near village of **Glen Echo Heights** (1940 pop. 797), just SE, is hq. of Army Map Service.

Glen Echo Park, town (pop. 217), St. Louis co., E Mo., NW of St. Louis.

Glen Elder, city (pop. 582), Mitchell co., N Kansas, on Solomon R. and 11 mi. WNW of Beloit; grain, livestock, poultry; dairying. Mineral springs.

Glenelg (glĕnĕlg′), town (pop. 13,867), SE South Australia, on coast of Gulf St. Vincent and 6 mi. SW of Adelaide, in metropolitan area; summer resort. Colony of South Australia proclaimed here, 1836.

Glenelg, fishing village and parish (pop. 1,690), W Inverness, Scotland, on the Sound of Sleat, 6 mi. SE of Kyle, opposite Skye. Near by are several anc. brochs.

Glenelg River, SW Victoria, Australia, rises in the Grampians W of Mt. William, flows generally W and S, past Casterton, to Discovery Bay at South Australia border; 280 mi. long; frequently dry. Wannon R., main tributary.

Glen Ellis Falls, N.H.: see ELLIS RIVER.

Glen Ellyn, residential village (pop. 9,524), Du Page co., NE Ill., W suburb of Chicago, just E of Wheaton. Platted 1851, inc. 1892.

Glen Ferris, industrial village, Fayette co., S central W.Va., on the Kanawha (power dam) and 25 mi. SE of Charleston; ferrochrome-alloy plant.

Glenfield, borough (pop. 870), Allegheny co., SW Pa., 9 mi. NW of Pittsburgh and on Ohio R., opposite Coraopolis.

Glenfinnan, Scotland: see SHIEL, LOCH.

Glen Flora. 1 Village (pop. c.700), Wharton co., S Texas, on Colorado R. 6 mi. NW of Wharton; trade point in oil, agr. area. **2** Village (pop. 91), Rusk co., N Wis., 11 mi. ENE of Ladysmith; dairying.

Glenford, village (pop. 180), Perry co., central Ohio, 16 mi. W of Zanesville.

Glen Forrest, town (pop. 430), SW Western Australia, 15 mi. E of Perth; firebrick.

Glen Gardner, borough (pop. 654), Hunterdon co., W N.J., 12 mi. E of Phillipsburg. State tuberculosis sanatorium near by.

Glengariff (glĕn-gă′rĭf), Gaelic *Gleann Garbh*, village (district pop. 764), SW Co. Cork, Ireland, on Glengariff Harbour, inlet of Bantry Bay, 7 mi. NW of Bantry; fishing port and seaside resort, noted for its scenic beauty and mild climate, celebrated by Thackeray. Near by is Sugarloaf mtn.

Glengarnock, Scotland: see KILBIRNIE.

Glengarry (glĕn-gă′rē), county (□ 478; pop. 18,732), SE Ont., on the St. Lawrence and on Que. border; ⊙ Cornwall.

Glengarry, valley of Garry R. in central Inverness, Scotland, noted for scenic beauty. For centuries, the home of the Macdonnells. Garry River rises in Loch Quoich, flows 15 mi. E through Loch Garry (5 mi. long, ¾ mi. wide), past INVERGARRY, to Loch Oich.

Glen Grey, U. of So. Afr.: see LADY FRERE.

Glenham (glĕ′nŭm), town (pop. 168), Walworth co., N S.Dak., 8 mi. E of Mobridge, near Missouri R.

Glen Haven, village, Leelanau co., NW Mich., 22 mi. NW of Traverse City, bet. Glen L. (c.5 mi. long) and L. Michigan. Has state park. Fishing, hunting. Near by is Sleeping Bear Point, with large sand dunes. A sand dune, c.600 ft. above the level of the lake, is moving c.6 ft. a year toward Glen L.

Glen Head, village (1940 pop. 1,262), Nassau co., SE N.Y., on N shore of W Long Isl., just S of Glen Cove.

Glen Hedrick (hĕ′drĭk), village (pop. 1,484), Raleigh co., S W.Va., 3 mi. SE of Beckley, in coal region.

Glenhope, village (pop. 40), N S.Isl., New Zealand, 45 mi. SW of Nelson; rail terminus; deer hunting.

Glen Hope or **Glenhope,** borough (pop. 199), Clearfield co., central Pa., 20 mi. NNW of Altoona.

Glenida, Lake, N.Y.: see CARMEL.

Glen Innes (glĕn ĭ′nĭs), municipality (pop. 5,453), NE New South Wales, Australia, 180 mi. SSW of Brisbane; mining (tin, bismuth).

Glen Jean, village (pop. 2,459, with near by Scarbro and Hilltop), Fayette co., S central W.Va., 10 mi. N of Beckley, in coal region.

Glen Lake, Mich.: see GLEN HAVEN.

Glenlivet (glĕnlĭ′vŭt), valley of Livet Water, 8-mi.-long river, in S Banffshire, Scotland. Noted for its whisky distilleries, which operated illicitly before 1824. In 1594 the Catholics here defeated the Protestants.

Glenluce (glĕnlōōs′), town in Old Luce parish, central Wigtown, Scotland, near Luce Bay, 9 mi. ESE of Stranraer; agr. market. Near by are ruins of Glenluce or Luce Abbey, founded 1190.

Glen Lyn (glĕn″ lĭn′), town (pop. 240), Giles co., SW Va., in the Alleghenies, on New R. and 21 mi. ENE of Bluefield, at W.Va. line; large hydroelectric plant.

Glen Lyon (glĕn lī′ŭn), 28-mi.-long mountain valley of Lyon R., SW Perthshire, Scotland, noted for its scenic beauty.

Glen Lyon, village (pop. 3,921), Luzerne co., E central Pa., near Susquehanna R., 5 mi. WSW of Nanticoke; corsets.

Glenmont, village (pop. 242), Holmes co., central Ohio, 28 mi. SE of Mansfield.

Glenmora, town (pop. 1,556), Rapides parish, central La., 24 mi. SW of Alexandria; agr. (truck, poultry, fruit, livestock, cotton, corn, sugar cane, potatoes); lumber mills, cotton gins. Settled 1898, inc. 1913.

Glen More, Scotland: see GREAT GLEN OF SCOTLAND.

Glenmorgan (glĕnmôr′gŭn), village (pop. 127), S Queensland, Australia, 210 mi. W of Brisbane; rail terminus; cattle, wheat.

Glenn, county (□ 1,317; pop. 15,448), N central Calif.; ⊙ Willows. E part is in Sacramento Valley; rises in W to Coast Ranges, where highest point in co. (Black Butte) is 7,450 ft. Includes part of Mendocino Natl. Forest (W). Watered by Sacramento R.; on a tributary (Stony Creek) are irrigation reservoirs of Orland reclamation project. Part of Sacramento Natl. Wildlife Refuge is in SE. Stock raising (beef cattle, sheep, poultry), irrigated farming (alfalfa, sugar beets, rice, barley, olives, almonds, prunes, pears, apricots, citrus fruit). Waterfowl, pheasant, deer hunting. Formed 1891.

Glenn, village, Allegan co., SW Mich., 19 mi. W of Allegan, near L. Michigan; resort.

Glennallen, village (pop. 142), SE Alaska, 15 mi. NNW of Copper Center.

Glen Nevis, Scotland: see BEN NEVIS.

Glenn Highway, S Alaska, extends 189 mi. ENE from Anchorage to Copper R., where it joins Richardson Highway (to Fairbanks) 10 mi. NNW of Copper Center. Follows course of Matanuska and Tazlina rivers along NW slope of Chugach Mts.; serves Eklutna, Palmer, Chickaloon, Sutton, and other localities in fertile MatanuskaValley.

Glenns Ferry, village (pop. 1,515), Elmore co., SW Idaho, on Snake R. and 25 mi. SE of Mountain Home; railroad div. point in irrigated agr. area (potatoes, onions, grain). Laid out 1883 on site of ferry station established 1865.

Glenn Springs, town (1940 pop. 134), Spartanburg co., NW S.C., 11 mi. SSE of Spartanburg.

Glennville, city (pop. 2,327), Tattnall co., E central Ga., 35 mi. SSW of Statesboro, in farm area; vegetable canning, sawmilling, cotton ginning.

Glen of the Horse or **Gleann a Chapaill,** ravine (2 mi. long) on N side of Mangerton Mtn., SE central Co. Kerry, Ireland, 5 mi. S of Killarney.

Glenolden (glĕnōl′dŭn), borough (pop. 6,450), Delaware co., SE Pa., SW suburb of Philadelphia; pharmaceutical supplies. Settled c.1654, inc. 1894.

Glenora (glĕnô′rŭ), village (pop. 144), SE Tasmania, 25 mi. NW of Hobart, near Derwent R.; fruit, hops.

Glenorchy (glĕnôr′kē), township (pop. 114), S central S.Isl., New Zealand, on NE shore of L. Wakatipu and 125 mi. WNW of Dunedin; reached by steamer from Kingston; tourist center. Mt. Earnslaw near by. Tungsten mines; gold.

Glenorchy (glĕnôr′kē), town (pop. 2,752), SE Tasmania, 1 mi. N of Hobart and on Derwent R.; collection center for wool, sheepskin, hides, furs.

Glen Park, village (pop. 516), Jefferson co., N N.Y., on Black R., just NW of Watertown.

Glen Parva, town and parish (pop. 749), central Leicester, England, 4 mi. S of Leicester; chemical works.

Glenpool, town (pop. 280), Tulsa co., NE Okla., 14 mi. S of Tulsa, in agr. area.

Glen Raven, village (pop. c.400), Alamance co., N central N.C., just NW of Burlington; cotton mill.

Glen Ridge. 1 Town (pop. 126), Palm Beach co., SE Fla. **2** Residential borough (pop. 7,620), Essex co., NE N.J., 5 mi. NW of Newark; mfg. (medicines, metal polish); commercial printing. Settled in early 19th cent., inc. 1895.

Glen Robertson, village (pop. estimate 500), SE Ont., 25 mi. NNE of Cornwall; dairying, mixed farming.

Glen Rock. 1 Borough (pop. 7,145), Bergen co., NE N.J., 3 mi. N of Paterson; mfg. (cement, chemicals, steam shovels); mineral water. Settled c.1710, inc. 1896. **2** Borough (pop. 1,477), York co., S Pa., 12 mi. S of York; furniture, machinery, clothing. Inc. 1860.

Glenrock, town (pop. 1,110), Converse co., E central Wyo., on N Platte R. and 23 mi. E of Casper, in sheep and cattle region; alt. c.5,000 ft.; oil refining. Oil wells, coal and vermiculite mines in vicinity. Near by is site of Deer Creek Station, military post established 1861 on Oregon Trail.

Glen Rogers, village (pop. 1,593), Wyoming co., S W.Va., 13 mi. WSW of Beckley, in coal region.

Glen Rose, city (pop. 1,254), ⊙ Somervell co., N central Texas, near junction of Paluxy Creek with Brazos R., 23 mi. WSW of Cleburne. Health and vacation resort, with mineral springs; bathing, fishing. Trade center for agr. area. Inc. 1926.

Glen Roy, valley of S Inverness, Scotland, along Roy R. (8 mi. long) N of Roy Bridge. The Parallel Roads of Glen Roy, a series of terraces on each side of the valley, represent, according to one theory, the water levels of anc. lakes.

Glens Falls, city (pop. 19,610), Warren co., E N.Y., on the Hudson (water power) and 18 mi. NNE of Saratoga Springs, near Adirondack foothills (W); paper and lumber milling; mfg. of clothing, food products, metal products, cement, brick, chemicals, machinery. Limestone quarries. Charles Evans Hughes was b. here. Settled 1763; inc. as village in 1839, as city in 1908.

Glenshaw, Pa.: see SHALER.

Glenside, Pa.: see ABINGTON.

Glen Tanar or **Glen Tanner,** Scotland: see ABOYNE.

Glenties (glĕntēz'), Gaelic *Gleanntaigh,* town (pop. 535), SW Co. Donegal, Ireland, on Owenea R. and 13 mi. NW of Donegal; peat-digging center; mfg. of clothing, knitted goods.

Glentilt (–tĭlt'), valley of Tilt R., Perthshire, Scotland, extending 16 mi. SW from Loch Tilt to Blair Atholl, overlooked by the Grampians. Marble is found here.

Glen Ullin (ŭ'lĭn), city (pop. 1,324), Morton co., S central N.Dak., 45 mi. W of Mandan. Airport.

Glen Urquhart (glĕn ûr'khûrt), valley of Enrick R., in N central Inverness, Scotland. Enrick R. rises 12 mi. ESE of Strone, flows 18 mi. N and E to Loch Ness at Strone.

Glenview, residential village (pop. 6,142), Cook co., NE Ill., NW suburb of Chicago, just W of Wilmette; makes tools, brick; nurseries. Naval air station. Inc. 1899.

Glenvil or **Glenville,** village (pop. 281), Clay co., SE Nebr., on branch of Little Blue R. and 10 mi. SE of Hastings.

Glenville. 1 Village, Fairfield co., Conn.: see GREENWICH. **2** Village (pop. 672), Freeborn co., S Minn., on Shell Rock R., near Iowa line, and 6 mi. SE of Albert Lea, in livestock, poultry, truck-farming area; dairy products. **3** Village, Clay co., Nebr.: see GLENVIL. **4** Town (pop. 1,789), ⊙ Gilmer co., central W.Va., on the Little Kanawha and 21 mi. WSW of Weston, in agr. region; glass mfg., lumber milling. Seat of Glenville State Col.

Glenville Dam, N.C.: see TUCKASEGEE RIVER.

Glen White, village (1940 pop. 1,026), Raleigh co., S W.Va., 5 mi. SW of Beckley, in agr., coal mining area.

Glenwillow, village (pop. 257), Cuyahoga co., N Ohio, 15 mi. SE of downtown Cleveland.

Glen Wills, settlement, E central Victoria, Australia, in Australian Alps, 155 mi. NE of Melbourne; gold mine.

Glenwood. 1 Town (pop. 413), Crenshaw co., S Ala., near Conecuh R., 15 mi. SW of Troy. **2** Town (pop. 843), Pike co., SW Ark., 31 mi. WSW of Hot Springs; peaches, strawberries, cotton, pine pulpwood; manganese, cinnabar, slate deposits near. **3** Town (pop. 684), Wheeler co., SE central Ga., 15 mi. W of Vidalia; mfg. (naval stores). **4** Village (pop. 762), Cook co., NE Ill., S suburb of Chicago. **5** Town (pop. 412), on Rush-Fayette co. line, E Ind., 8 mi. W of Connersville, in agr. area. **6** City (pop. 4,664), ⊙ Mills co., SW Iowa, on Keg Creek and 17 mi. SSE of Council Bluffs, in grain and livestock area; meat packing. Seat of state institution for feeble-minded children (1876). Founded by Mormons as Rushville; renamed Coonsville in 1852 and Glenwood in 1853; inc. 1857. **7** Plantation (pop. 53), Aroostook co., E Maine, 26 mi. SW of Houlton, in wilderness recreational area. **8** City (pop. 2,666), ⊙ Pope co., W Minn., on L. Minnewaska and 17 mi. S of Alexandria; resort in agr. area; dairy products, cattle feed, bottled spring water. Platted 1866, inc. as village 1881, inc. as city 1912. **9** Town (pop. 258), Schuyler co., N Mo., near Chariton R., 3 mi. W of Lancaster. **10** Village (pop. c.100), Catron co., SW N.Mex., on San Francisco R., just W of Mogollon Mts., and 29 mi. SSW of Reserve, in hunting and fishing region; alt. 4,745 ft. Prehistoric artifacts, thought to mark beginning of Mogollon culture, found near by. Village is in Gila Natl. Forest. **11** Town (1940 pop. 176), McDowell co., W N.C., 5 mi. SSE of Marion. **12** Town (pop. 338), Sevier co., central Utah, 5 mi. E of Richfield. **13** Village (pop. 1,913), Pittsylvania co., S Va., near Chatham.

Glenwood City, city (pop. 778), St. Croix co., W Wis., 17 mi. NW of Menomonie; dairy products, poultry, cement.

Glenwood Landing, village (1940 pop. 1,343), Nassau co., SE N.Y., on N shore of W Long Isl., overlooking Hempstead Harbor and just SW of Glen Cove, in resort and agr. area; boat repairing. Large power station.

Glenwood Springs, city (pop. 2,412), ⊙ Garfield co., W central Colo., on Colorado R., at mouth of Roaring Fork R., N of Elk Mts., and 75 mi. NE of Grand Junction; alt. 5,823 ft. Resort, with hot mineral springs; hq. of White R. Natl. Forest. Dairy products, potatoes. Oil-shale deposits in vicinity. Hydroelectric plant just NE receives water from dam and diversion tunnel on Colorado R.; supplies power to Denver. Near by is scenic Glenwood Canyon, 1,000 ft. deep in places, extending 15 mi. along Colorado R. City laid out 1883, inc. 1885.

Gleschendorf (glĕ'shŭndôrf), village (pop. 10,296), in Schleswig-Holstein, NW Germany, 12 mi. N of Lübeck; grain, cattle. Until 1937 in Oldenburg.

Gletsch, hamlet, Valais canton, S central Switzerland, on the Rhone, at foot of Rhone Glacier, and 12 mi. SSE of Innertkirchen; alt. 5,784 ft. Junction of Furka Pass, Grimsel Pass, and Rhone valley roads. Hotel.

Gletscherhorn (glĕ'chŭrhôrn"), peak (13,064 ft.) in Bernese Alps, S central Switzerland, 13 mi. SSE of Interlaken.

Glevum, England: see GLOUCESTER, city.

Glewe, Germany, see NEUSTADT-GLEWE.

Glicério (glēsĕ'ryŏŏ), city (pop. 1,230), NW São Paulo, Brazil, on railroad and 18 mi. SE of Araçatuba; butter and cheese processing, distilling; agr. (coffee, cotton). Formerly Glycerio.

Glidden. 1 Town (pop. 996), Carroll co., W central Iowa, near Middle Raccoon R., 7 mi. E of Carroll; dairy products. **2** Mining village, Harlan co., SE Ky., in the Cumberlands c.5 mi. SE of Harlan; bituminous coal. **3** Village (1940 pop. 799), Ashland co., N Wis., 34 mi. SSE of Ashland, in submarginal farm area; dairy products, lumber.

Glienicke (glē'nĭkŭ), village (pop. 5,232), Brandenburg, E Germany, 9 mi. NW of Berlin city center; market gardening.

Glifadha, Greece: see GLYPHADA.

Glimakra (glē'mōkrä"), Swedish *Glimåkra,* village (pop. 949), Kristianstad co., S Sweden, 19 mi. N of Kristianstad; granite quarrying; glass, furniture.

Glimmingehus (glĭ'mĭng-ŭhüs"), castle, Kristianstad co., S Sweden, 6 mi. SW of Simrishamn. Built in 1490, it was one of Skane's strongest fortresses. Closely associated with Selma Lagerlöf's *The Wonderful Adventures of Nils.*

Glin, Gaelic *Gleann Chorbraighe,* town (pop. 573), NW Co. Limerick, Ireland, on the Shannon estuary, 28 mi. WSW of Limerick; fishing port. Has 13th-cent. castle.

Glina (glē'nä), village (pop. 2,543), N Croatia, Yugoslavia, on Glina R., on railroad and 18 mi. SW of Sisak; trade center in plum-growing region.

Glina River, N Croatia, Yugoslavia, rises 3 mi. N of Slunj, flows E and NNE, past Topusko and Glina, to Kupa R. 7 mi. W of Petrinja; c.60 mi. long.

Glinde (glĭn'dŭ), village (pop. 4,956), in Schleswig-Holstein, NW Germany, 8 mi. E of Hamburg city center; woodworking.

Glindenberg (glĭn'dŭnbĕrk), village (pop. 1,324), in former Prussian Saxony prov., central Germany, after 1945 in Saxony-Anhalt, near the Elbe, 8 mi. N of Magdeburg; site of frost-research station. Just S of village, the Weser-Elbe Canal divides into 2 branches: S branch extends 3 mi. to the Elbe at Rothensee, N suburb of Magdeburg; E branch extends 2 mi. to Ihle Canal at Hohenwarthe (Elbe crossing).

Glindow (glĭn'dō), village (pop. 4,296), Brandenburg, E Germany, 7 mi. WSW of Potsdam, on Glindow L. (3-mi.-long expansion of the Havel); tile mfg.; excursion resort.

Glines Canyon Dam, Wash.: see ELWHA RIVER.

Gliniany, Ukrainian SSR: see GLINYANY.

Glinka (glyēn'kŭ), village (1939 pop. over 500), central Smolensk oblast, Russian SFSR, 13 mi. WNW of Yelnya; dairying, flax processing.

Glinki (glēn'kē), Ger. *Stolzenhagen* (shtôl"tsŭnhä'gŭn), suburb of Stettin, Szczecin prov., NW Poland, near W shore of Damm L., 6 mi. N of city center; steel milling.

Glinnoye (glyē'nŭyŭ), village (1926 pop. 6,250), SE Moldavian SSR, on left bank of Dniester R. and 15 mi. SE of Tiraspol, in fruitgrowing dist.; winemaking and canning center.

Glinsk (glyēnsk), village (1926 pop. 3,508), SW Sumy oblast, Ukrainian SSR, near Sula R., 12 mi. SW of Romny; wheat.

Glinyany (glyē'nyŭnē), Pol. *Gliniany* (glyēnyä'nē), town (1931 pop. 4,391), central Lvov oblast, Ukrainian SSR, 20 mi. E of Lvov; agr. (cereals, potatoes), carpet mfg. Has ruins of old castle.

Glion, Switzerland: see MONTREUX.

Glittertind: Norway: see JOTUNHEIM MOUNTAINS.

Gliwice, city, Poland: see GLEIWITZ.

Gliwicki, Kanal, Poland: see GLEIWITZ CANAL.

Globe, city (pop. 6,419), ⊙ Gila co., SE central Ariz., 75 mi. E of Phoenix, near Pinal Mts. (S and W), in mining and ranching area. Settled 1876 as silver-mining center, developed as one of largest copper-producing centers in U.S. After 1918 copper production dropped. Copper, silver, gold, asbestos, mercury mines in vicinity. San Carlos Indian Reservation is just E.

Globe and Phoenix, N gold-mining suburb (pop. 1,725) of Que Que, Gwelo prov., central Southern Rhodesia.

Globino (glô'bēnŭ), town (1926 pop. 8,206), S Poltava oblast, Ukrainian SSR, 21 mi. NNW of Kremenchug; sugar mill; dairying.

Glocester (glŏ'stŭr), town (pop. 2,682), Providence co., NW R.I., on Conn. line, on Chepachet R. (bridged at Chepachet village) and 15 mi. WNW of Providence; woolen mills; dairying. Set off from Providence and inc. 1731.

Glockner, Austria: see GROSSGLOCKNER.

Glocknerstrasse or **Grossglocknerstrasse,** Austria: see HOHE TAUERN.

Glodeni (glôdān'), village (pop. 2,343), Prahova prov., S central Rumania, 6 mi. N of Targoviste; oil and natural-gas center.

Glodyany (glŭdyä'nē), Rum. *Glodeni* (glôdĕn'), village (1941 pop. 3,250), NW Moldavian SSR, 20 mi. WNW of Beltsy; agr. center: corn, wheat, sugar beets.

Glodzhovo (glô'jôvô), village (pop. 4,839), Ruse dist., NE Bulgaria, 21 mi. ESE of Ruse; wheat, rye, sunflowers.

Glogau (glō'gou) or **Glogow** (gwô'gōōf), Pol. *Głogów,* town (1939 pop. 33,495; 1946 pop. 1,681) in Lower Silesia, after 1945 in Zielona Gora prov., W Poland, port on the Oder and 55 mi. NW of Breslau (Wroclaw); rail junction; sugar refining, shipbuilding; power station. After Second World War, when it was virtually obliterated, its Ger. pop. left; present pop. is entirely Polish. Of many fine medieval bldgs., 13th-cent. parish church (heavily damaged) remains. First mentioned in early 11th cent.; chartered 1250. Was (1252–1506) ⊙ principality, later duchy, under branch of Pol. Piast dynasty. In Thirty Years War, captured 1642 by Swedes under Torstensson. As result of War of Austrian Succession it passed (1745) to Prussia. Under Fr. occupation, 1806–14.

Gloggnitz (glôg'nĭts), town (pop. 6,990), SE Lower Austria, on Schwarza R. and 7 mi. SW of Neunkirchen; E terminus of Semmering RR; resort (alt. 1,440 ft.). One of its 2 castles was Benedictine abbey until 1803.

Glogow (gwô'gōōf), Pol. *Głogów.* **1** Town (pop. 1,870), Rzeszow prov., SE Poland, 10 mi. N of Rzeszow; tanning, spinning, flour milling, sawmilling; brickworks. Also called Glogow Malopolski, Pol. *Głogów Małopolski.* **2** Town, Zielona Gora prov., Poland: see GLOGAU.

Glogowek (gwôgōō'vĕk), Pol. *Głogówek,* Ger. *Oberglogau* (ō'bûrglō'gou), town (1939 pop. 7,581; 1946 pop. 4,532) in Upper Silesia, after 1945 in Opole prov., S Poland, near Czechoslovak border, 20 mi. S of Oppeln (Opole); sugar refining, flax processing; cattle market. Has 17th-cent. palace and town hall, remains of medieval fortifications.

Glomach Falls (glŏ'mŭkh), SW Ross and Cromarty, Scotland, on a headstream of the Elchaig; drops 370 ft.

Glomawr (glō'mär), mining village (1940 pop. 1,050), Perry co., SE Ky., in Cumberland foothills, on North Fork Kentucky R. and 3 mi. SE of Hazard; bituminous coal.

Glomfjord (glôm'fyōr), village (pop. 418) in Meloy canton, Nordland co., N Norway, 35 mi. N of Mo; aluminum and ammonia works. Rock sculpture attracts tourists. Formerly spelled Glaamfjord, Nor. *Glåmfjord.*

Glomma River (glôm'mä) or **Glama River** (glô'mä), Nor. *Glomma* or *Glåma,* SE Norway, issues from small Rien L. 20 mi. NE of Roros, flows 185 mi. in a winding course generally S, past Roros, Tynset, Alvdal, Rena, Elverum, and Kongsvinger, through Oyeren L., past Sarpsborg and Sandesund (head of sea navigation), to the Skagerrak at Fredrikstad. Rena R. (left) is chief tributary. Longest river in Scandinavia, it is one of Norway's chief lumber-carrying waterways. Sometimes spelled Glaama.

Glommerstrask (glô'mûrstrĕsk"), Swedish *Glommersträsk,* village (pop. 662), Norrbotten co., N Sweden, 50 mi. W of Pitea; lumbering, tar mfg.

Glonn (glôn), village (pop. 2,877), Upper Bavaria, Germany, 18 mi. SE of Munich; rye, cattle. Has rococo church.

Gloppen, Norway: see VEREIDE.

Glorenza (glôrĕn'tsä), Ger. *Glurns,* village (pop. 732), Bolzano prov., Trentino–Alto Adige, N Italy, in Val Venosta, on Adige R. and 29 mi. W of Merano. Has 16th-cent. walls and church dating from 1481.

Gloria, La, Colombia: see LA GLORIA.

Glória do Goitá (glô'ryŭ dŏŏ goitä'), city (pop. 1,346), E Pernambuco, NE Brazil, 27 mi. W of Recife; sugar, cotton.

Gloria Glens Park, resort village (pop. 98), Medina co., N Ohio, on small Chippewa L., 7 mi. SW of Medina.

Gloriana, village (pop. 1,612, with adjacent Ragsdale), Dougherty co., SW Ga.

Glorieta, village (pop. c.500), Santa Fe co., N central N.Mex., 12 mi. SE of Santa Fe, near Pecos R., in Sangre de Cristo Mts.; alt. c.7,430 ft. Trading point and railroad loading station in Santa Fe Natl. Forest.

Glorioso Islands (glōrēō'zō), Fr. *Îles Glorieuses* (ēl' glôryûz'), group of islets (pop. c.25), dependency of Madagascar, in Indian Ocean at NE extremity of Mozambique Channel, 125 mi. WNW of N tip of Madagascar; 11°33'S 47°20'E. Consists of Île Glorieuse, the largest, Île de Lys, and Île Verte, linked by a sand bar which emerges at low tide. Coconuts, guano, corn; turtle fishing. Claimed by France 1892.

Glösa (glû'zä), village (pop. 4,871), Saxony, E central Germany, at N foot of the Erzgebirge, 3 mi. N of Chemnitz; hosiery knitting.

Glossa, Cape, Albania: see LINGUETTA, CAPE.

Glossop (glŏ'sŭp), municipal borough (1931 pop. 19,509; 1951 census 18,014), NW Derby, England, 13 mi. E of Manchester, at edge of The Peak; chief cotton-milling center of Derby; also woolen milling, paper mfg., metalworking. Has 19th-cent. Glossop Hall, now a school. In municipal borough are towns of: Hadfield (NW; pop. 5,778), with leatherworking, shoe mfg., silk and woolen milling; and Dinting (W), with cotton milling.

Gloster (glŏ'stûr), town (pop. 1,467), Amite co., SW Miss., 34 mi. SE of Natchez, in timber and agr. region, near La. line; lumber milling. Inc. 1884.

Glostrup (glô'strōōp), town (pop. 8,361), Copenhagen amt, NE Zealand, Denmark, 6 mi. W of Copenhagen; bicycles, engines, furniture, chemicals.

Glotovka (glô'tŭfkŭ), town (1948 pop. over 2,000), W Ulyanovsk oblast, Russian SFSR, 14 mi. ENE of Inza; sawmilling.

Gloucester (glŏ'stûr, glô'–), town (pop. 1,702), E New South Wales, Australia, 65 mi. N of Newcastle; gold-mining center; dairy products.

Gloucester (glŏ'stûr), county (□ 1,854; pop.49,913), NE N.B., on Chaleur Bay and Gulf of St. Lawrence; ⊙ Bathurst. Includes Shippigan and Miscou isls.

Gloucester or **Gloucestershire** (glŏ'stûr–, glô'–, –shĭr), county (□ 1,257.2; 1931 pop. 786,000; 1951 census 938,618), W England; ⊙ Gloucester. Bounded by Monmouth (W), Hereford (NW), Worcester (N), Warwick (NE), Oxford (E), Wiltshire (S), and Somerset (SW). Drained by Severn, Avon, Frome, and Wye rivers. Has 3 distinct regions: Cotswold Hills (E), Severn valley (center), and Forest of Dean (W). Dairy farming and cheese making; sheep raising in Cotswolds; fruitgrowing. There are coal fields in Forest of Dean and near Bristol. Chief industries are mfg. of leather, shoes, glassware, tobacco, chocolate (all centered on Bristol), aircraft, bricks and tiles; petroleum refining (Avonmouth), woolen milling (Stroud). Chief commercial and industrial center is Bristol; other important towns are Cheltenham, Tewkesbury, Cirencester, Stroud. There are noted cathedrals and churches at Bristol, Gloucester, Tewkesbury, and Cirencester. Traces of Roman occupation are found in many parts of the co.

Gloucester, county borough (1931 pop. 52,937; 1951 census 67,268), ⊙ Gloucestershire, England, in N central part of co., on the Severn near the Cotswolds and the Forest of Dean, 31 mi. NE of Bristol; 51°51'N 2°15'W; industrial and shipping city, with railroad shops and mfg. of chemicals, agr. machinery, cutlery, electrical equipment, cordage. There are also shipyards and breweries. It is a port, connected by GLOUCESTER AND BERKELEY SHIP CANAL with port installations at SHARPNESS, on the Severn. As *Glevum* and, later, *Claudia Castra,* it was an important Roman station. Its famous 11th-cent. cathedral, with 225-ft. tower built c.1450, is on site of an abbey founded 681 by Osric and contains tomb of Edward II. With Worcester and Hereford it is scene of annual festival of the Three Choirs. Other features are New Inn (1450), 12th-cent. church of St. Mary-de-Crypt, 11th-13th-cent. Abbot's House, and Spa Pump Room (chalybeate springs). Near by are remains of 12th-cent. Llanthony Abbey. Just N is suburb of Wotton, in parish of Wotton St. Mary Without (pop. 2,471).

Gloucester, village (1931 pop. 457), Sierra Leone colony, on Sierra Leone Peninsula, 4 mi. ESE of Freetown; road junction; cassava, corn.

Gloucester. **1** County (□ 329; pop. 91,727), SW N.J., bounded W by Delaware R.; ⊙ Woodbury. Mfg. (petroleum and coal products, chemicals, soap, clothing, glassware, canned goods, building materials, explosives); agr. (truck, fruit). Drained by Maurice R. and Big Timber Creek. Formed 1686. **2** County (□ 225; pop. 10,343), E Va.; ⊙ Gloucester. In tidewater region; bounded W and S by York R., E by Mobjack Bay; many tidal inlets. Agr. (especially truck; also grain, tobacco, livestock); bulb growing; fisheries (oysters, fish). Formed 1651.

Gloucester. **1** City (pop. 25,167), Essex co., NE Mass., on Cape Ann and 29 mi. NE of Boston; fishing port and summer resort. At head of excellent Gloucester Harbor (protected by breakwater built out from Eastern Point; lighthouse), which for over 3 centuries has been used by fishing ships. Fish processing; mfg. (glue, sails, isinglass, nets, oilskins); boatbuilding. Port has some commerce, and is a port of entry. The bronze *Fisherman* is a memorial to Gloucestermen lost at sea. Developed as summer resort and artists' center in late 19th cent. Colonists landed 1623; inc. as town 1642, as city 1873. Resort villages include Annisquam (ăn'ĭskwäm), Bay View, Lanesville (all on N shore), Bass Rocks, Magnolia, Riverdale, West Gloucester. **2** City (pop. 14,357), Camden co., SW N.J., on Delaware R. just below Camden; mfg. (asbestos, cork, and paper products, chemicals, structural steel, lumber, textiles, gas heaters); nursery products, truck. Site of Fort Nassau (built 1623). Settled by Friends 1682, laid out 1687, inc. 1868. **3** Village (pop. c.350), ⊙ Gloucester co., E Va., near Chesapeake Bay, 55 mi. E of Richmond; mfg. of winches; fishing. Courthouse (1766) and old debtors' prison here. Founded 1769.

Gloucester, Cape, E Queensland, Australia, in Coral Sea; forms E side of entrance to Edgecumbe Bay; 20°2'S 148°27'E. Gloucester Isl. off N end.

Gloucester, Cape, W New Britain, Bismarck Archipelago, SW Pacific. In Second World War, site of Jap. air base taken 1943 by U.S. forces.

Gloucester and Berkeley Ship Canal (bärk'lē), in Gloucester, England, extends 16 mi. NE–SW bet. Gloucester and the Severn at port of Sharpness; navigable for seagoing ships.

Gloucester Point, hamlet, Gloucester co., E Va., on peninsula in Chesapeake Bay, at York R. mouth; ferry to Yorktown (S).

Gloucestershire, England: see GLOUCESTER, county.

Glouster (glou'stûr), village (pop. 2,327), Athens co., SE Ohio, 12 mi. N of Athens, and on small Sunday Creek, in coal mining area.

Glover (glŭ'vûr), town (pop. 727), including villages of Glover (pop. 228) and West Glover (pop. 58), Orleans co., N Vt., on Barton R. and 16 mi. S of Newport; agr.

Glover Island, N.F.: see GRAND LAKE.

Gloversville (glŭ'vûrzvĭl), city (pop. 23,634), Fulton co., E central N.Y., 11 mi. NW of Amsterdam; important glove-mfg. center (since early-19th cent.); also makes leather coats, handbags, knit goods, textiles, lumber, wood and paper products, cement blocks, machinery. Inc. 1890.

Glowno (gwôv'nô), Pol. *Głowno,* Rus. *Glovno* (glôv'nô), town (pop. 8,344), Lodz prov., central Poland, 18 mi. NNE of Lodz; copper-rolling mill; flour milling; grain trade.

Glozhene (glô'zhĕnĕ), village (pop. 3,605), Vratsa dist., NW Bulgaria, 8 mi. WSW of Oryakhovo; vineyards, grain, livestock.

Glubczyce (gwōōp-chĭ'tsĕ), Pol. *Głubczyce,* Ger. *Leobschütz* (lā'ôp-shüts), town (1939 pop. 13,505; 1946 pop. 5,020) in Upper Silesia, after 1945 in Opole prov., S Poland, near Czechoslovak border, 20 mi. WNW of Ratibor (Raciborz); rail junction; woolen milling, sugar refining; livestock market. Stone Age graves found near by. First mentioned 1107. Until 1742, part of Bohemian principality of Jägerndorf. Considerably damaged in Second World War.

Gluboki or **Glubokiy** (glōōbô'kē), town (1939 pop. over 10,000), W Rostov oblast, Russian SFSR, 14 mi. NNE of Kamensk; machine mfg., flour milling.

Glubokoye (glōōbô'kŭyŭ). **1** Town (1948 pop. over 500), NW East Kazakhstan oblast, Kazakh SSR, on Irtysh R., on railroad (Glubochanka station) and 20 mi. NW of Ust-Kamenogorsk; Irtysh copper refinery; lumber mill; power plant. **2** Pol. *Głębokie* (gwĕbô'kyĕ), city (1931 pop. 7,544), S central Polotsk oblast, Belorussian SSR, 50 mi. SW of Polotsk; flax-trading center; mfg. (cement, furniture), fruit canning, tanning, flour milling. Scene of defeat (1661) of Swedes by Pol. hetman Stephen Czarnecki. Passed (1793) from Poland to Russia; reverted (1921) to Poland; ceded to USSR in 1945. **3** Town, Sverdlovsk oblast, Russian SFSR: see MALOMALSK.

Glucholazy (gwōō"khôwä'zĭ), Pol. *Głuchołazy,* Ger. *Ziegenhals* (tsē'gŭnhäls), town (1939 pop. 9,772; 1946 pop. 7,658) in Upper Silesia, after 1945 in Opole prov., S Poland, at N foot of the Jeseniky, 35 mi. SW of Oppeln (Opole). Frontier station on Czechoslovak border, opposite Jesenik; health resort; paper milling, metalworking, glove mfg.

Gluck (glŭk), village (pop. 1,634), Anderson co., NW S.C., 4 mi. S of Anderson.

Glücksburg (glüks'bŏŏrk), town (pop. 5,172), in Schleswig-Holstein, NW Germany, 6 mi. NE of Flensburg, in the Angeln; Baltic seaside resort on Flensburg Firth; mfg. (electrotechnical and optical goods, wood products). Has 16th-cent. moated castle; German High Command capitulated here in May, 1945.

Glückstadt (glük'shtät), town (pop. 12,427), in Schleswig-Holstein, NW Germany, port on Elbe estuary, and 28 mi. NW of Hamburg; railroad repair shops; mfg. of chemicals, textiles, paper and wood products. Herring fleet. Trades in wood and vegetables of vicinity. Founded 1616 by Christian IV of Denmark to rival Hamburg in Elbe trade.

Glukhov (glōō'khŭf), city (1926 pop. 16,000), NE Sumy oblast, Ukrainian SSR, 65 mi. NNW of Sumy; sawmilling, woodworking, hemp processing; dairying, fruit canning, flour milling. Teachers col.

Glukhovo, Russian SFSR: see NOGINSK, Moscow oblast.

Glurns, Italy: see GLORENZA.

Glusha (glōōshä'), town (1926 pop. 791), E central Bobruisk oblast, Belorussian SSR, 16 mi. W of Bobruisk; glass, peat works.

Glushkovo (glōōshkô'vŭ), village (1926 pop. 7,632), W Kursk oblast, Russian SFSR, on Seim R. and 14 mi. S of Rylsk; woolen mill.

Glussk (glōōsk), town (1926 pop. 4,414), central Bobruisk oblast, Belorussian SSR, on Ptich R. and 28 mi. SW of Bobruisk; woodworking; clothing mill. Also spelled Glusk.

Glyadyanskoye (glyŭdyän'skŭyŭ), village (1926 pop. 1,633), S Kurgan oblast, Russian SFSR, on Tobol R. and 35 mi. S of Kurgan, in agr. area.

Glyboka (glĭbô'kŭ), Ger. *Hliboka* (hlĭbô'kä), Rum. *Adâncata* (ädûn'kätä), village (1941 pop. 4,619), S Chernovtsy oblast, Ukrainian SSR, in N Bukovina, 13 mi. S of Chernovtsy, near Rum. border; major rail junction (Adynkata station); dairying.

Glycerio, Brazil: see GLICÉRIO.

Glyder Fawr (glĭ'dûr vour'), mountain (3,279 ft.), central Caernarvon, Wales, 6 mi. S of Bethesda. Just E is peak of Glyder Fach (väkh') (3,262 ft.).

Glyde River, cos. Monaghan and Louth, Ireland, rises 5 mi. W of Carrickmacross, flows 35 mi. SE to Dundalk Bay at Castlebellingham, conjointly with Dee R.

Glyncorwg or **Glyncorrwg** (glĭnkô'rōōg), urban district (1931 pop. 10,203; 1951 census 9,236), N central Glamorgan, Wales, 8 mi. E of Neath; coal mining. Urban dist. includes towns of ABERGWYNFI AND BLAENGWYNFI and CYMMER.

Glyndebourne (glīn'bôrn, glīn'dŭbûrn), agr. village in Glynde parish (pop. 257), S Sussex, England, 2 mi. E of Lewes. Has Tudor mansion and park, converted into open-air opera stage; scene of annual Glyndebourne Opera Festival (opened 1934), specializing in Mozart operas. Just S is village of Glynde, with limestone quarries. Lord Wolseley lived here.

Glyndon (glĭn'dŭn). **1** Village (pop. c.500), Baltimore co., N Md., 17 mi. NW of Baltimore, in area of dairy farms and country estates. Near by are Sagamore Farms (thoroughbred stables) and course of Md. Hunt Cup race, run annually in April. **2** Village (pop. 411), Clay co., W Minn., on Buffalo R. and 10 mi. E of Fargo, N.Dak., in Red R. valley; grain.

Glynn (glĭn), fishing village (district pop. 1,535), SE Co. Antrim, Northern Ireland, on Larne Lough, 2 mi. S of Larne.

Glynn, county (□ 423; pop. 29,046), SE Ga.; ⊙ Brunswick. Bounded E by the Atlantic, NE by Altamaha R., SW by Little Satilla R.; includes St. Simons and Jekyll isls. Coastal plain fishing (shrimp, crabs), forestry (lumber, naval stores), and farming (poultry, livestock, dairy products, truck) area; mfg. at BRUNSWICK. Formed 1777.

Glyntaff, Wales: see PONTYPRIDD.

Glyntawe (glĭntou'ē), village in parish of Ystradgynlais Higher (ŭstrădgun'lĭs) (pop. 1,779), SW Brecknock, Wales, 15 mi. SW of Brecknock; stone quarrying; brick mfg.

Glyphada or **Glifadha** (both: glĭfä'dhŭ), seaside resort (pop. 3,148), 8 mi. SSE of Athens, Greece, on Saronic Gulf.

Gmelinka (ŭgmyĕ'lyĭnkŭ), village (1948 pop. over 2,000), NE Stalingrad oblast, Russian SFSR, on railroad (Gmelinskaya station) and 40 mi. S of Krasny Kut, near Kazakh SSR border; metalworks; wheat.

Gmünd (gŭmünt'). **1** Village (pop. 1,890), Carinthia, S Austria, 8 mi. N of Spittal an der Drau; tourist center and summer resort (alt. 2,401 ft.); mfg. (agr. implements), lumber and cotton mills, tannery, brewery. **2** Town (pop. 6,664), NW Lower Austria, 26 mi. SE of Budweis and on Luznice R. (Czechoslovak border) opposite CESKE VELENICE (rail junction); mfg. of glass, textiles, machines, and pottery.

Gmund or **Gmund am Tegernsee** (gŭmōōnt' äm tā'gŭrnzā"), village (pop. 3,246), Upper Bavaria, Germany, in Bavarian Alps, at NE tip of the lake Tegernsee, 8 mi. E of Bad Tölz; paper milling; resort (alt. 2,425 ft.).

Gmünd, Schwäbisch, Germany: see SCHWÄBISCH GMÜND.

Gmund am Tegernsee, Germany: see GMUND.

Gmunden (gŭmōōnd'ŭn), city (pop. 13,892) in the Salzkammergut, S central Upper Austria, on N shore of L. TRAUN, at efflux of Traun R., and 35 mi. SW of Linz; summer resort (alt. 1,395 ft.); breweries, wood carving.

Gmundner See, Austria: see TRAUN, LAKE.

Gnadau (gŭnä'dou), village (pop. 1,106), in former Prussian Saxony prov., central Germany, after 1945 in Saxony-Anhalt, 4 mi. SSE of Schönebeck. Moravian Brothers' settlement, with school, teachers col., and publishing plant, was established here in 1767. Noted for pretzels baked here.

Gnadenburg, Russian SFSR: see VINOGRADNOYE.

Gnadenflyur, Russian SFSR: see PERVOMAISKOYE, Saratov oblast.

Gnadenhutten (jĭnā'dŭnhŭ"tŭn), village (pop. 895), Tuscarawas co., E Ohio, 9 mi. S of New Philadelphia and on Tuscarawas R. State memorial park marks site of massacre (1782) of 96 Christian Indians by white men.

Gnaden See, Germany: see UNTERSEE.

Gnarrenburg (gŭnä'rŭnbōōrk), village (pop. 1,972), in former Prussian prov. of Hanover, NW Germany, after 1945 in Lower Saxony, 9 mi. SW of Bremervörde; glassworks.

Gnesen, Poland: see GNIEZNO.

Gnesta (gŭnā'stä"), village (pop. 1,385), Södermanland co., E Sweden, on Klemming L., Swedish *Klemmingen* (klĕ'mĭng-ŭn) (12 mi. long, 1 mi. wide), 14 mi. SW of Sodertalje; paper mills. Has medieval church.

Gnidus, Turkey: see CNIDUS.

Gniew (gŭnyĕf'), Ger. *Mewe* (mā'vŭ), town (1946 pop. 3,120), Gdansk prov., N Poland, port on the Vistula, at Wierzyca R. mouth, and 37 mi. SSE of Danzig; rail spur terminus; lumbering, flour milling, mfg. of machinery, furniture; brewing.

Gniewkowo (gŭnyĕfkô'vô), Ger. *Argenau* (är'gŭnou), town (pop. 3,819), Bydgoszcz prov., central Poland, on railroad and 9 mi. NE of Inowroclaw; mfg. of machinery, soap, candles, mustard; flour milling, sawmilling.

Gniezno (gŭnyĕz'nô) or **Gnesen** (gŭnā'zŭn), city (1946 pop. 30,292), Poznan prov., W central Poland, 30 mi. ENE of Poznan, at W end of the Kujawy, in lake region. Rail junction; trade center; mfg. of machinery, arms, chemicals, cement, bricks, furniture, liqueur, beer; tanning, sugar and flour milling, sawmilling. Has noted 10th-cent. cathedral. One of the oldest Pol. cities and legendary cradle of Pol. nation; was first ⊙ Poland. Metropolitan see of Poland established here, 1000, at Congress of Gniezno; according to some historians, Boleslav I was recognized as king of Poland by Emperor Otto III. City passed to Prussia in 1793 and again in 1815. In 1821, archiepiscopal see transferred to Poznan. Returned to Poland in 1919. In Second World War, in Ger. Wartheland; suffered no damage.

Gnila Lipa River, Ukrainian SSR: see GNILAYA LIPA RIVER.

Gnilaya Lipa River (gnyĭlī'ŭ lyē'pŭ), Pol. *Gnila Lipa,* in W Ukrainian SSR, rises in the Gologory, ENE of Bobrka; flows 50 mi. SSE, past Peremyshlyany, Rogatin, Burshtyn, and Bolshovtsy, to Dniester R. 2 mi. N of Galich.

Gniloaksaiskaya, Russian SFSR: see AKSAI, village.

Gnivan or **Gnivan'** (gnyē'vŭnyŭ), town (1926 pop. 2,019), W Vinnitsa oblast, Ukrainian SSR, 11 mi. SW of Vinnitsa; sugar refinery.

Gnjilane or **Gnyilane** (both: gŭnyē'länĕ), village (pop. 8,287), S Serbia, Yugoslavia, 20 mi. SE of Pristina, in the Kosovo; hemp growing.

Gnoien (gŭnoi'ŭn), town (pop. 5,368), Mecklenburg, N Germany, 14 mi. WNW of Demmin; agr. market (grain, sugar beets, potatoes, stock). Has early-Gothic church.

Gnosjo (gŭnōō'shŭ"), Swedish *Gnosjö,* village (pop. 1,034), Jonkoping co., S Sweden, 17 mi. NW of Varnamo; metalworking, furniture mfg.

Gnyilane, Yugoslavia: see GNJILANE.

Goa (gō'ä), town (1939 pop. 3,019; 1948 municipality pop. 13,487), Camarines Sur prov., SE Luzon, Philippines, 45 mi. NNW of Legaspi, at foot of Mt. Isarog; lumbering and agr. center (rice, abacá, corn).

Goa (gō'ŭ), district (□ 1,348; pop. 540,925), PORTUGUESE INDIA; ⊙ Pangim, the ⊙ Port. India. At S end of the Konkan; bounded W by Arabian Sea, N, E, and S by S Bombay state; includes ANGEDIVA ISLAND (S); crossed E by Western Ghats; drained by several mtn. streams. Mostly hilly country (several peaks rise to nearly 4,000 ft.), with cultivated coastal strip. Rice is chief crop; also cashew and betel nuts, coconuts, mangoes. Fish (mackerel, sardines) caught and cured. Salt drying, palm-mat weaving, manganese mining (E of Mormugão and at Sanguém), sugar milling (at Sigao); coir work. Teak, blackwood, bamboo from E forests. Mormugão and Pangim are important ports and trade centers. Area under Vijayanagar kingdom from c.1370 to 1470; part of Bijapur sultanate when in 1510 small section around town of Goa (Old Goa) was captured by Portuguese under Affonso de Albuquerque. Early missionary labors of St. Francis Xavier here (1542–52) were mainly responsible for Goa's present large (c.50%) R.C. pop. Fortification and colonization led to further acquisitions of territory and growth of Goa as a major trade and missionary center at end of 16th cent. Period of decay soon followed and seat of govt. moved (c.1760) to new town of PANGIM. Mahratta invasions repulsed during 18th cent. Present boundaries acquired in mid-19th cent.

Goa or **Old Goa,** Port. *Velha Goa* (vä'lyŭ gō'ŭ) or *Goa Velha,* town (pop. 2,707), W Goa dist., Port. India, on N Tissuari Isl., 5 mi. E of Pangim. Captured by Portuguese in 1510; soon became leading emporium in India, reaching peak of prosperity in late-16th cent. Ecclesiastical importance continued long after commercial and military decline; governor-general moved c.1760 to PANGIM (New Goa). Now mostly in ruins, but surviving bldgs. include churches of St. Francis of Assisi (a converted mosque) and Bom Jesus (with tomb of St. Francis Xavier). A Buddhist relic (Buddha's tooth) is believed to have been taken from Jaffna (Ceylon) by Portuguese and destroyed here in 1560.

Goajira, Colombia: see GUAJIRA.

Goalpara (gōäl'pärŭ), district (□ 3,979; pop. 1,014,285), W Assam, India; ⊙ Dhubri. Mainly in Brahmaputra valley; EASTERN DUARS (N), spurs of Garo Hills (S); bounded N by Bhutan, W by Gangadhar (Sankosh) R. and West Bengal (India), SW by East Bengal (Pakistan), E by Manas R.; traversed by Brahmaputra R. and drained by its tributaries; swamp lakes (E central, SE). Mainly alluvial soil; rice, mustard, jute, tobacco, cotton, tea; jute trade at Dhubri and Patamari. Sal timbering (center at Bilasipara) and lac growing in dispersed forest areas; tea processing, cotton ginning and baling. Present dist. was part of 17th-cent. Mogul empire. Pop. 46% Moslem, 30% Hindu, 23% Animist tribes (including Garos and Mechs).

Goalpara, town (pop. 7,793), Goalpara dist., W Assam, India, on Brahmaputra R. and 42 mi. ENE of Dhubri; road center; trades in rice, mustard, jute, lac; cotton ginning. Former frontier station of East India Company's territories.

Goalundo (gōŭlōōn'dō), village, Faridpur dist., S central East Bengal, E Pakistan, on the Padma (Ganges), just below Jamuna R. (Brahmaputra) mouth, and 10 mi. NNW of Faridpur; rail spur terminus; fish trade center; rice milling, ice and candle mfg.; rice, jute, oilseeds, sugar cane.

Goascarán (gwäskärän'), town (pop. 1,408), Valle dept., S Honduras, on Goascarán R. (Salvador border), on Inter-American Highway (bridge) and 18 mi. WNW of Nacaome; customs station; agr. Limestone quarry.

Goascarán River, on Salvador-Honduras border, rises in several branches in SE Sierra de Guajiquiro, flows c.75 mi. S, along international frontier, past Goascorán (Inter-American Highway bridge), to La Unión Bay of Gulf of Fonseca. Called San Juan R. in upper course.

Goaso (gōä'sō), town, Ashanti, W Gold Coast, 60 mi. W of Kumasi; kola-nut center; cacao, hardwood, rubber.

Goat Island. 1 Small lighthouse island, SW Maine, ½ mi. off Kennebunkport. **2** Island, N.Y.: see NIAGARA FALLS. **3** Small island in Newport harbor, SE R.I.; site of U.S. naval torpedo station.

Goat Islands, off S coast of Jamaica, in Old Harbour Bay, 18 mi. WSW of Kingston; consist of Great Goat Isl. (3 mi. long) and tiny Little Goat Isls.; leased to U.S. for 99 years in 1940.

Goat Rock Dam, Ga. and Ala.: see CHATTAHOOCHEE RIVER.

Goba or **Gobba** (gō'bä), town (pop. 3,000), Harar prov., S central Ethiopia, near source of Web R., at foot of Mt. Bale, 50 mi. WSW of Ginir, in forested region; 7°N 40°E; alt. c.8,200 ft. Market center (hides, wax, honey). Near by are hot mineral springs. Was ⊙ former Bale prov.

Goba (gō'bä), village, Sul do Save prov., S Mozambique, on Swaziland border, on Umbeluzi R. and 35 mi. SW of Lourenço Marques (linked by rail); citrus, corn, beans.

Gobabis (gōbä'bĭs), town (pop. 2,055), E South-West Africa, near Bechuanaland Protectorate border, on edge of Kalahari Desert, 120 mi. E of Windhoek; rail terminus; cattle-raising center. Airfield. Epukiro Reserve (□ c.4,000), of Herero and Bechuana tribes, is 50 mi. NNE.

Gobacchien (gô'bäk'kyĕn), town, Tanan prov., S Vietnam, in the Plaine de Joncs, on West Vaico R. (head of navigation) and 50 mi. W of Saigon.

Gobad (gōbäd'), plain of S Fr. Somaliland, E of L. Abbé; watered by the Oued Gobad; agr. experiment station.

Gobannium, England: see ABERGAVENNY.

Gobardanga (gōbŭrdäng'gŭ), town (pop. 5,544), 24-Parganas dist., SE West Bengal, India, on tributary of upper Jamuna (Ichamati) R. and 34 mi. NE of Calcutta city center; trades in rice, jute, pulse, betel nuts, coconuts, potatoes.

Gobardhan (gō'bŭrdŭn), since 1948 officially **Govardhan** (gō'vŭrdŭn), town (pop. 6,019), Muttra dist., W Uttar Pradesh, India, 13 mi. W of Muttra. Pilgrimage center, built around a tank, lying within a recess of sacred hill of Giri Raj (4–5 mi. long; alt. c.100 ft.). Noted temple of Hari Deva; 3 cenotaphs.

Gobba, Ethiopia: see GOBA.

Göbelsberg, Austria: see HAUSRUCK MOUNTAINS.

Gobernador Benegas (gōbĕrnädōr' bānā'gäs), town (pop. estimate 700), N Mendoza prov., Argentina, 5 mi. S of Mendoza; rail junction, winegrowing center.

Gobernador Crespo (krĕ'spō) or **Crespo,** town (pop. estimate 1,200), central Santa Fe prov., Argentina, on railroad and 50 mi. E of San Cristóbal; agr. center (flax, corn, sunflowers, livestock); dairying, flour milling, lumbering.

Gobernador Garmendia (gärmĕn'dyä), town (pop. estimate 500), NE Tucumán prov., Argentina, on railroad and 45 mi. NE of Tucumán; stock-raising and lumbering center; sawmills.

Gobernador Gordillo, Argentina: see CHAMICAL.

Gobernador Ingeniero Valentín Virasoro, Argentina: see GOBERNADOR VIRASORO.

Gobernador Mansilla, Argentina: see MANSILLA.

Gobernador Piedrabuena (pyädräbwā'nä), village (pop. estimate 500), E Tucumán prov., Argentina, on railroad and 32 mi. ENE of Tucumán; stock-raising and lumbering center.

Gobernador Virasoro or **Gobernador Ingeniero Valentín Virasoro** (ĕnhānyā'rō välĕntēn' vērāsō'rō), town (pop. estimate 1,000), NE Corrientes prov., Argentina, on railroad and 50 mi. SSW of Posadas; farming center (rice, maté, livestock). Formerly called Vuelta del Ombú.

Gobi or **Gobi Desert** (gō'bē), Chinese *Han Hai* (hän' hī') [=dry sea], sometimes *Shamo* (shä'mô') [=sandy desert], vast stretch of desert country in central Asia, extending from the Pamir to Manchuria and from the Altai and Sayan mts. to the Nan Shan; more specifically the name is applied to the E part of this region, the W section being known as the TAKLAMAKAN DESERT and situated in the Tarim basin. The Gobi proper (□ c.500,000) is a gravelly and sandy desert plateau (average alt.: 3–5,000 ft.; c.1,000 mi. long, c.500 mi. wide), with some scanty pasture land and treeless short-grass steppe on its periphery. It is situated partly in S and SE Mongolian People's Republic (¼ of desert's area) and in China's Kansu, Ningsia, and Suiyuan provs. and the Inner Mongolian Autonomous Region. Sparsely inhabited by a Mongolian nomadic pop., the Gobi is crossed by the Kalgan–Ulan Bator highway.

Gobi Altai or **Gobi Altay** (both: ăltī', ăl'tī), aimak (□ 49,900; pop. 45,000), SW Mongolian People's Republic; ⊙ Yusun Bulak. Bounded S by China's Sinkiang prov., it is traversed by the Gobi section of the Altai Mts., and consists largely of semi-desert and desert. Very sparsely populated; grazing economy.

Gobi Altai, mountains, Mongolia: see ALTAI MOUNTAINS.

Gobichettipalaiyam, India: see GOPICHETTIPALAIYAM.

Gobi Desert, Mongolia: see GOBI.

Goble, city (pop. 73), Columbia co., NW Oregon, 35 mi. N of Portland and on Columbia R.

Gobler, town (pop. 116), Pemiscot co., extreme SE Mo., 16 mi. W of Caruthersville.

Gobles (gō'bŭlz), village (pop. 622), Van Buren co., SW Mich., 16 mi. WNW of Kalamazoo, in agr. area (fruit, potatoes, corn).

Gobo (gō'bō), town (pop. 15,648), Wakayama prefecture, S Honshu, Japan, on W coast of Kii Peninsula, 23 mi. S of Wakayama, in rice-growing, lumbering area; textile mills.

Gobo (gō'bō), village, Gwelo prov., central Southern Rhodesia, in Mashonaland, on railroad and 11 mi. W of Umvuma; alt. 4,499 ft. Iron deposits.

Gobuen (gōbwĕn'), town (pop. 2,000), in the Benadir, S Ital. Somaliland, port near mouth of Juba R. on Indian Ocean opposite Giumbo, 9 mi. NE of Kismayu; commercial center.

Goc or **Goch** (gōch), Serbo-Croatian *Goč,* mountain (3,687 ft.), S central Serbia, Yugoslavia, 5 mi. SSW of Vrnjci.

Goceano, Catena del (kätā'nä dĕl gôchĕä'nô), mountain chain, N central Sardinia; extends 20 mi. SW from Mannu d'Oschiri R.; rises to 4,130 ft. at Monte Rasu.

Goch (gôkh), town (pop. 11,469), in former Prussian Rhine Prov., W Germany, after 1945 in North Rhine-Westphalia, on the Niers and 7 mi. S of Cleves; rail junction; food processing (preserves, dried vegetables). Mfg. of shoes, brushes, cigars; plush weaving, tanning, woodworking. Chartered c.1240. Part of GELDERLAND until 1715. Scene (Feb., 1945) of heavy fighting in Second World War; town about 70% destroyed.

Goch, mountain, Yugoslavia: see GOC.

Gochenée (gôshnā'), village (pop. 333), Namur prov., S Belgium, 9 mi. SW of Dinant; marble quarrying.

Gochsheim (gôks'hīm). **1** Town (pop. 1,547), N Baden, Germany, after 1945 in Württemberg-Baden, on the Kraichbach and 7 mi. E of Bruchsal; tobacco, wine. **2** Village (pop. 3,285), Lower Franconia, NW Bavaria, Germany, 3 mi. SE of Schweinfurt; barley.

Goclaw, Poland: see JASIEN.

Gocong (gô'kông'), town, ⊙ Gocong prov. (□ 230; 1943 pop. 119,800), S Vietnam, 25 mi. S of Saigon, in alluvial plain bet. Vaico R. mouth and Mekong delta; rice-growing and trading center.

Godabawa (gōōdä'bä'wä), town (pop. 6,993), Sokoto prov., Northern Provinces, NW Nigeria, 25 mi. N of Sokoto; agr. trade center (cotton, millet, tobacco, cattle, skins). Sometimes spelled Gwadabawa.

Godagari (gōdä'gärĭ), village, Rajshahi dist., W East Bengal, E Pakistan, on Padma R., at Mahananda R. mouth, and 19 mi. WNW of Rajshahi; river trade center; rice milling; jute, oilseeds, wheat. Rail spur terminus 2 mi. SE, at Godagari Ghat.

Godall (gōdäl'), village (pop. 1,445), Tarragona prov., NE Spain, 12 mi. S of Tortosa; olive-oil processing; wine, wheat, figs.

Godalming (gŏ'dŭlmĭng), municipal borough (1931 pop. 10,401; 1951 census 14,239), SW Surrey,

England, on the Wey and 4 mi. SW of Guildford; agr. market, with leather, paper, and hosiery industries. Site of Charterhouse public school, founded 1611 in London, removed 1872 to Godalming. Has Norman church, 17th-cent. almshouses, and several old inns.

Godarpura (gō'dŭrpŏŏrŭ) or **Mandhata** (mändä'tŭ), village, Nimar dist., W Madhya Pradesh, India, on Narbada R., on Madhya Bharat–Madhya Pradesh border and 31 mi. NNW of Khandwa; annual pilgrimage center. Has noted Sivaite, Vishnuite, and Jain temples (mostly 14th and 18th cent.); largest temple (Sivaite) is on small Mandhata isl., just N.

Godauha (gō'dou'hä'), town, Tayninh prov., S Vietnam, on Saigon-Pnompenh highway and 35 mi. NW of Saigon, on East Vaico R.; peanut center.

Godavari, district, India: see EAST GODAVARI; WEST GODAVARI.

Godavari, rail station, India: see RAJAHMUNDRY.

Godavari, Nepal: see PATAN.

Godavari River (gōdä'vŭrē), central India, rises in Western Ghats WSW of Nasik, in Bombay; flows SE past Nasik, along Bombay-Hyderabad border, E across N Hyderabad, past Paithan and Nander, SE along Hyderabad's E border (separates Madhya Pradesh and Madras), entering Madras through steep gorge in Eastern Ghats, and SSE past Rajamundry, to Bay of Bengal in 2 main mouths, Gautami Godavari (N) and Vasishta Godavari (S); 900 mi. long. Forms wide alluvial delta with extensive navigable irrigation-canal system (headworks at Dowlaiswaram), linked with that of Kistna delta (S). Receives (left) Purna, Pranhita, Indravati, and Sabari rivers; chief right tributary, Manjra R. Main stream navigable by coracle in central course. Construction of dam c.20 mi. above Rajahmundry begun 1948 as part of irrigation and hydroelectric project. Sacred river to Hindus; its several pilgrimage centers include Trimbak, Bhadrachalam, and Rajahmundry.

Goddard, village, SE Alaska, on W coast of Baranof Isl., 13 mi. S of Sitka; hot springs resort.

Goddard, city (pop. 274), Sedgwick co., S Kansas, 14 mi. W of Wichita, in wheat region.

Goddelau (gô'dùlou), village (pop. 4,164), S Hesse, W Germany, in former Starkenburg prov., near an arm of the Rhine, 7 mi. WSW of Darmstadt; rail junction.

Godeanu or **Godeanul** (gôdyä'nŏŏ, –l), mountain group in W Transylvanian Alps, SW Rumania, c.25 mi. WSW of Lupeni, SE of the Tarcu and SW of the Retezat.

Godega di Sant'Urbano (gô'dĕgä dē säntōōrbä'nô), village (pop. 855), Treviso prov., Veneto, N Italy, 5 mi. NE of Conegliano; shoe factory.

Godella (gō-dhĕ'lyä), outer NW suburb (pop. 4,472) of Valencia, Valencia prov., E Spain; sawmilling, plaster mfg.; cereals.

Godelleta (gō-dhĕlyā'tä), village (pop. 1,588), Valencia prov., E Spain, 17 mi. WSW of Valencia; wine, olive oil, beans.

Goderich (gŏd'rĭch, gŏd'–), town (pop. 4,557), ⊙ Huron co., S Ont., on L. Huron, at mouth of Maitland R., and 60 mi. NNW of London; major lake port, with grain elevators, saltworks, flour and lumber mills; mfg. of machinery, brass products, chemicals. Also a resort and market in fruitgrowing, farming, fishing region.

Goderich, village (1931 pop. 992), Sierra Leone colony, minor port on Atlantic Ocean, on Sierra Leone Peninsula, just NE of False Cape, and 5 mi. SW of Freetown; fishing. Formerly called Funkia.

Goderville (gōdârvēl'), village (pop. 1,278), Seine-Inférieure dept., N France, 15 mi. NE of Le Havre; grain, flax, cattle.

Godesberg, Bad, Germany: see BAD GODESBERG.

Godewaersvelde (gōdvârsvĕld', Fl. khō'dùwärsfĕldù), village (pop. 837), Nord dept., N France, near Belg. border, 7 mi. NE of Hazebrouck; textile weaving, cheese mfg. Just E is the Mont des Cats (518 ft.), one of the few hills dominating Flanders plain and First World War battlefield. Atop hill is a Trappist monastery.

Godfrey. 1 Village (pop. 168), Morgan co., N central Ga., 10 mi. SSW of Madison. **2** Village (pop. 1,438), Madison co., SW Ill., just N of Alton.

Godhavn (gōdh'houn"), town (pop. 319), W Greenland, ⊙ North Greenland prov. and Godhavn dist. (pop. 553), at S tip of Disko isl., on Davis Strait, at mouth of Disko Bay; 69°15'N 53°32'W. Seaport in fishing, sealing, hunting, and fowling region. Has hosp., radio station, magnetic observatory (established 1926), biological research station.

Godhra (gō'drŭ), town (pop. 41,986), ⊙ Panch Mahals dist., N Bombay, India, 65 mi. ESE of Ahmadabad; rail and road junction; trades in timber (forests near by), firewood, corn, cotton, peanuts; oilseed pressing, tanning, flour milling, glass mfg.

Godínez (gōdē'nĕs), town (pop. 45), Sololá dept., SW central Guatemala, on Inter-American Highway and 7 mi. ESE of Sololá; alt. 7,139 ft. Road junction near E end of L. Atitlán; corn, beans.

Göding, Czechoslovakia: see HODONIN.

Godinne (gôdēn'), village (pop. 690), Namur prov., S Belgium, on Meuse R. and 8 mi. S of Namur; tourist resort; fruitgrowing. Small Gothic church.

Godley. 1 Village (pop. 102), on Grundy-Will co. line, NE Ill., 22 mi. SSW of Joliet, in agr. and bituminous-coal area. **2** Town (pop. 424), Johnson co., N central Texas, 10 mi. NW of Cleburne, in agr. area.

Godley Glacier, W central S.Isl., New Zealand, in Tasman Natl. Park Southern Alps; rises near Sealy Pass, flows 8 mi. S to Godley R.

Godman Air Force Base, Ky.: see KNOX, FORT.

Godmanchester (gŏd'mŭnchĕstŭr, gŏn'shĭstŭr), municipal borough (1931 pop. 1,993; 1951 census 2,499), S central Huntingdon, England, on Ouse R. just S of Huntingdon; agr. market. Has church dating from 14th cent. and many old houses. Said to be site of the Roman *Durolipons*.

Godna, India: see REVELGANJ.

Godo (gō'dō), town (pop. 5,348), Gifu prefecture, central Honshu, Japan, 9 mi. W of Gifu, in rice-growing area.

Godoi Point (gōdoi'), headland on the Pacific coast of Llanquihue prov., S central Chile, on Coronados Gulf, 20 mi. N of Ancud; 41°34'S 73°48'W.

Gödöllö (gû'dûl-lû), Hung. *Gödöllő*, resort town (pop. 11,824), Pest-Pilis-Solt-Kiskun co., N central Hungary, 14 mi. NE of Budapest; rail junction; electrical apparatus plant. Agr. experiment station, R.C. acad., château here.

Godolphin (gùdŏl'fĭn), agr. village, W Cornwall, England, 4 mi. NW of Helston; China-clay quarrying. Plymouth china 1st made here.

Godoy (gōdoi'), town (pop. estimate 2,000), SE Santa Fe prov., Argentina, 30 mi. SSE of Rosario; agr. center (corn, potatoes, flax, wheat, sunflowers).

Godoy Cruz (krōōs'), city, ⊙ Godoy Cruz dept. (□ 13; 1947 census pop. 39,741), N Mendoza prov., Argentina, on railroad, just S of Mendoza; agr. and mfg. center. Wine making, food canning, meat packing, alcohol distilling, brewing, flour milling, sawmilling, textile milling, tanning, oil refining; mfg. of sweets, vinegar, matches. Agr. products: wine, fruit, potatoes, alfalfa. Hydroelectric station near by.

Godoysund, Norway: see TYSNESOY.

Godramstein (gō'dräm-shtīn"), village (pop. 1,956), Rhenish Palatinate, W Germany, on the Queich and 2 mi. NW of Landau; wine; also wheat, tobacco.

Godshill, agr. village and parish (pop. 1,008), on Isle of Wight, Hampshire, England, 4 mi. W of Shanklin. Has 14th-cent. church.

Gods Lake (□ 432), NE Man.; 60 mi. long, 18 mi. wide; 54°30'N 94°W. Drained N by Gods R.

Gods River, NE Man., issues from Gods L., flows 200 mi. N and NW to Hayes R. 50 mi. SSW of York Factory. Numerous rapids.

Godstone, residential town and parish (pop. 3,303), E Surrey, England, 6 mi. E of Reigate. Church (partly 13th cent.) was rebuilt by Sir Gilbert Scott. Has 16th-cent. inn.

Godthaab (gôt'hôp"), Eskimo *Nuk*, town (pop. 970), SW Greenland, ⊙ South Greenland prov. and Godthaab dist. (pop. 1,962), on Godthaab Fjord, near its mouth on Davis Strait; 64°11'N 51°44'W. Seaport, in fishing, sheep-raising, hunting, fowling region. Has hosp., teachers col., radio station, govt. sheep-raising station, fox-fur farm. Here are U. S. and Canadian consulates in Greenland. Hans Egede landed here (1721) to begin modern colonization of Greenland; settlement founded 1727. In Second World War, during occupation of Denmark, it was seat of Greenland administration. Near by are remains of 10th-cent. Norse settlement.

Godthaab Fjord, inlet (70 mi. long, 2–20 mi. wide) of Davis Strait, SW Greenland; 64°30'N 51°W. Extends in an arc NE and SE to edge of inland ice-cap. On S shore, near mouth, is Godthaab town. In widest part, NE of Godthaab, are several isls.; largest, Stor Isl., rises to 5,351 ft.

Godwin (gŏd'wĭn), town (pop. 145), Cumberland co., SE central N.C., 15 mi. NE of Fayetteville.

Godwin Austen, Mount, Kashmir: see K².

Goé (gôā'), Flemish *Gulke* (gûl'kù), town (pop. 892), Liége prov., E Belgium, on Vesdre R. and 5 mi. E of Verviers; wool spinning and weaving.

Goebelsmühle (gû'bùlsmülù), village, N central Luxembourg, on Sûre R., at mouth of Wiltz R., and 6 mi. NNW of Ettelbruck; oats, potatoes; cattle raising, dairying. Just SSE is agr. commune center of Bourscheid (pop. 271).

Goede Hoop, Kaap van, Netherlands New Guinea: see GOOD HOPE, CAPE OF.

Goedereede (khōō"dùrā'dù) or **Goeree** (khōōrā'), town (pop. 1,148), South Holland prov., SW Netherlands, on NW end of Goeree-Overflakkee isl., 7 mi. W of Hellevoetsluis; chicory drying. Lighthouse. Was important port; now silted up.

Goedgegun (gōōd'gāgŭn"), village, S Swaziland, 60 mi. S of Mbabane and on main E–W road, in tobacco-growing region.

Goehner (gō'nùr), village (pop. 67), Seward co., SE Nebr., 27 mi. W of Lincoln.

Goëland, Lac (läk gôēlā'), lake (20 mi. long, 12 mi. wide), W Que., 120 mi. NNE of Val d'Or.

Goenoeng Api, Indonesia: see GUNUNG API.

Goenoengsitoli, Indonesia: see GUNUNGSITOLI.

Goeree (khōōrā'), island, South Holland prov., SW Netherlands; bounded by North Sea (W, N), the Grevelingen (S), the Haringvliet (NE), Overflakkee isl. (E), with which it forms isl. of Goeree-Overflakkee. Chief town is Goedereede, name sometimes given to isl. as well. Isl. was flooded in Second World War.

Goeree-Overflakkee, Netherlands: see GOEREE; OVERFLAKKEE.

Goes (khōōs), town (pop. 12,762), Zeeland prov., SW Netherlands, on South Beveland isl. and 14 mi. ENE of Flushing; agr. market center; mfg. (paints, organ mechanisms). Has 15th-cent. church, remains of 15th-cent. castle. Sometimes Ter Goes.

Goethals Bridge (gō'thùlz), bridge over Arthur Kill bet. Staten Isl., N.Y., and Elizabeth, N.J.; cantilever structure 8,600 ft. long, with a main span 672 ft. long and 135 ft. above water. Opened 1928.

Goetzenbruck (gĕtsĕnbrük'), Ger. *Götzenbrück* (gû'tsùnbrük), village (pop. 1,599), Moselle dept., NE France, in the N Vosges, 17 mi. SE of Sarreguemines; optical-glass mfg.

Goff, city (pop. 315), Nemaha co., NE Kansas, 40 mi. NNW of Topeka; livestock, grain.

Goffstown, town (pop. 5,638), including Goffstown village (pop. 1,336), Hillsboro co., S N.H., 7 mi. WNW of Manchester and on Piscataquog R. above Glen L. (formed by dam; hydroelectric power). Wood products, poultry, fruit; summer resort. Site of Hillsboro County Farm, at Grasmere village. First granted (1734) by Mass. as Narragansett No. 4, regranted 1748, inc. 1761.

Gofitskoye (gô'fētskŭyù), village (1939 pop. over 2,000), central Stavropol Territory, Russian SFSR, on Stavropol Plateau, 50 mi. E of Stavropol; flour mill; wheat, cotton. Formerly Medvedka.

Gogeb, river, Ethiopia: see GOJAB RIVER.

Gogebic (gōgē'bĭk), county (□ 1,112; pop. 27,053), W Upper Peninsula, Mich.; ⊙ Bessemer. Bounded NW by L. Superior, S and SW by Wis.; drained by Montreal, Presque Isle, and Ontonagon rivers. Much of co. is in Ottawa Natl. Forest. Gogebic L. is NE. Gogebic Range (iron mining) crosses co. Also lumbering, agr. (potatoes, truck, grain, hay, fruit, livestock), dairying. Some mfg. at Ironwood. Resorts (hunting, fishing). Many small lakes and waterfalls. Organized 1887.

Gogebic Lake, W Upper Peninsula, Mich., 21 mi. E of Bessemer, in Ottawa Natl. Forest; c.15 mi. long, 2 mi. wide. Contains resorts, 2 parks. Drained by West Branch of Ontonagon R.

Gogebic Range, in N Wis. and Upper Peninsula of Mich., extends c.80 mi. W from Wakefield in E Gogebic co. (Mich.) across Wis. line into Iron and Ashland counties, and terminates in Bayfield co.; c.½–1 mi. wide; rises to 1,823 ft. W of Ironwood. Known for rich iron deposits; principal mining centers are Ironwood (Mich.) and Hurley (Wis.). Iron was discovered here in 1848; 1st shipment of ore from Ashland, Wis. (port for mining area) was made in 1884. Sometimes called Penokee-Gogebic Range (pĭnō'kē–). The name Penokee Range is sometimes given to westernmost end (in Wis.), sometimes to the whole section in Wis.

Göggingen (gû'gĭng-ùn), SW suburb (pop. 9,283) of Augsburg, Swabia, W Bavaria, Germany, near the Wertach; mfg. of textiles, machinery, precision instruments, chemicals; printing.

Gogha (gō'gŭ), village (pop. 4,705), Amreli dist., N Bombay, India, on Gulf of Cambay, 10 mi. SE of Bhaunagar; roadstead, with shipyards for coastal steamers; cotton weaving. Lighthouse just N. Harbor sheltered by Piram Isl. (5 mi. SE), an offshore sand bar, in 13th cent. a pirate stronghold. Until 1949, Gogha was in Ahmadabad dist. Sometimes spelled Gogo.

Gogmagog Hills or **Gog Magog Hills** (gŏg'-mā'gŏg), low chalk elevations, S Cambridge, England, 4 mi. SE of Cambridge.

Gogo, India: see GOGHA.

Gogola (gōgō'lù), village, Diu dist., Portuguese India, 1 mi. N of Diu, across arm of Arabian Sea (Chassi R.), in small enclave on S tip of Kathiawar peninsula, W India; fishing.

Gogo-shima (gōgō'shĭma), island (□ 4; pop. 6,621), Ehime prefecture, Japan, in Iyo Sea (SW section of Inland Sea), just off NW coast of Shikoku, near Matsuyama; 4 mi. long, 1.5 mi. wide; hilly. Grows sweet potatoes. Fishing.

Gogra River (gō'grŭ), major left tributary of the Ganges, in Tibet, Nepal, and India, rises (as Karnali R.) in the Himalayas W of Rakas L., Tibet, at c.30°40'N 81°E; flows SE into Nepal, SSW, W, and ESE through Nepal Himalayas, and S, cutting across Siwalik Range in a deep gorge and splitting into 2 arms, Kauriala (right) and Girwa (left), rejoining in India 8 mi. SSE of Kauriala Ghat to form Gogra R. proper. As the Gogra, flows generally SE past Fyzabad, Ajodhya, Tanda, Barhaj, and Revelganj to the Ganges below Chapra; total length, c.640 mi. Commonly called Kauriala in India above mouth of its right affluent, Sarda R. Main tributaries in Nepal (as the Karnali) are Seti (right) and Bheri (left) rivers; in India (as the Gogra) receives Sarda (right) and Rapti (left) rivers. Navigable by river steamers below Ajodhya; extensive river trade (grain, timber, spices, vegetables, molasses, ghee, dal).

Gogrial (gōgrēäl'), village (pop. 400), Bahr el Ghazal prov., S Anglo-Egyptian Sudan, on Jur R., on road, and 60 mi. N of Wau; cotton, corn, durra; livestock raising.

Gohad (gō′hŭd), town (pop. 6,734), NE Madhya Bharat, India, 23 mi. NE of Lashkar; agr. market (millet, gram, wheat).

Gohana, Egypt: see GIHEINA.

Gohana (gōhä′nŭ), town (pop. 6,818), Rohtak dist., SE Punjab, India, 17 mi. NNE of Rohtak; agr. market (millet, wheat, gram, sugar cane).

Gohfeld (gō′fĕlt), village (pop. 13,367), in former Prussian prov. of Westphalia, NW Germany, after 1945 in North Rhine-Westphalia, on the Werre and 6 mi. NE of Herford; cigar mfg., woodworking.

Gohilwad (gō′hĭlvŭd), district, E Saurashtra, India; ⊙ Bhaunagar.

Gohlis (gō′lĭs), N suburb of Leipzig, Saxony, E central Germany. Schiller resided here, 1785.

Göhren (gû′rún), village (pop. 2,624), in former Prussian Pomerania prov., N Germany, after 1945 in Mecklenburg, on SE Rügen isl., on the Baltic, 14 mi. ESE of Bergen; seaside resort.

Gohyakkoku, Japan: see OYAMA, Toyama prefecture.

Goi (gō′ē), town (pop. 12,080), Chiba prefecture, central Honshu, Japan, on Chiba Peninsula, on Tokyo Bay, 6 mi. SSW of Chiba; rail junction; agr., fishing.

Goiana (goi-ä′nŭ), city (pop. 9,681), E Pernambuco, NE Brazil, head of navigation on tidal Goiana R. and 37 mi. NNW of Recife (steam-launch service); ships sugar, tobacco, cotton; sugar milling, alcohol distilling. Manganese deposits. Airfield. Formerly spelled Goyana or Goyanna.

Goiandira (goiändē′rŭ), city (pop. 1,787), SE Goiás, central Brazil, 125 mi. SE of Goiânia; here railroad from Anápolis divides into 2 branches (one to Belo Horizonte and Rio de Janeiro, the other to Uberaba and São Paulo). Formerly Goyandira.

Goiânia (goi-ä′nyŭ), city (1950 pop. 41,584), ⊙ Goiás, central Brazil, on plateau (alt. 2,500 ft.), 570 mi. NW of Rio de Janeiro, 40 mi. SW of Anápolis (railhead); 16°40′S 49°19′W. Built along ultramodern lines (patterned on Belo Horizonte), to replace unhealthful Goiás city (70 mi. NW) as state ⊙. First planned in 1933, it became the seat of govt. in 1937 (while still under construction), and was officially inaugurated in 1942. Accessible by air, and by road from Anápolis. Although primarily an administrative center, city has gained in economic importance as the heart of a pioneer zone noted for its livestock and mineral deposits (quartz crystals, diamonds, nickel, titanium, chromium). Has faculties of law, pharmacy, and dentistry.

Goianinha (goi-ŭnē′nyŭ), city (pop. 1,176), E Rio Grande do Norte, NE Brazil, on railroad and 30 mi. S of Natal; sugar, cotton, cereals. Formerly spelled Goyaninha.

Goiás (goi-äs′), state (□ 240,333; 1940 pop. 826,414; 1950 pop. 1,234,740), central Brazil; ⊙ Goiânia. Extending from 5°S to 19°S lat., it is landlocked; bounded E by the Serra Geral de Goiás (Bahia and Minas Gerais border) and W by Araguaia R. (Mato Grosso and Pará border). Lies in interior highland (average alt. 2,500 ft.), crossed by several short mtn. ranges (Serra dos Pireneus, Chapada dos Veadeiros, Serra dos Cristais). From a central divide, tributaries of the Amazon (Tocantins, Araguaia) drain northward, tributaries of the Paranaíba (headstream of the Paraná) southward. Savanna vegetation in S supports extensive livestock industry. Chief crops are tobacco, coffee, rice, corn, and cotton. Heavily wooded N region remains largely unoccupied except for backward Indian tribes. State contains important, but for the most part unexploited, mineral deposits, especially quartz crystals (near Cristalina), diamonds, titanium, nickel (at Niquelândia), and chromium (at Piracanjuba). Goiás is penetrated by 2 rail lines (from São Paulo and Rio de Janeiro) which join at Goiandira, and have terminus at Anápolis. Tocantins and Araguaia rivers are navigable bet. rapids by small craft. State is served by several airfields. Exports include jerked beef, hides, lard, minerals. Chief cities are Goiânia (⊙ since 1937), Goiás (former ⊙), Anápolis, Ipameri, and Catalão. First visited by prospectors from São Paulo in mid-17th cent. Scene of extensive gold washings in 18th cent. Became captaincy-general in 1744, prov. of Brazilian empire in 1820s, and state of federal republic in 1889. Future ⊙ Brazil (federal dist.) is to be located in Goiás state c.100 mi. NE of Goiânia. Formerly spelled Goyaz and Goiaz.

Goiás, city (pop. 5,905), S central Goiás, central Brazil, on the Rio Vermelho and 70 mi. NW of Goiânia; cattle center; ships tobacco, coffee, sugar, vanilla. Emeralds found near by. Airfield. A gold-rush town in 18th cent. (then named Villa Boa), it was ⊙ Goiás state until superseded (1937) by newly planned and healthier Goiânia. Old spelling, Goyaz and Goiaz.

Goiatuba (goi-ŭtōō′bŭ), city (pop. 997), S Goiás, central Brazil, 100 mi. S of Goiânia; stock raising.

Goiaz, Brazil: see GOIÁS.

Goicoechea, canton, Costa Rica: see GUADALUPE.

Goil, Loch (lŏkh goil′), 6-mi.-long inlet of Loch Long, SE Argyll, Scotland; 1 mi. wide. At head is village of Lochgoilhead.

Goilo (goi′lô), petroleum and natural-gas field, N Croatia, Yugoslavia, 5 mi. E of Kutina, in Slavonia. First wells drilled in 1938 (natural gas) and 1941 (petroleum). Natural-gas pipe line to carbon-black plant at Kutina.

Going-to-the-Sun Highway; Going-to-the-Sun Mountain, Mont.: see GLACIER NATIONAL PARK.

Goirle or **Goorle** (khōr′lŭ), town (pop. 6,121), North Brabant prov., S Netherlands, 3 mi. S of Tilburg; linen and blanket weaving, jute spinning; mfg. of radio parts.

Góis (gô′ēsh), town (pop. 698), Coimbra dist., N central Portugal, 18 mi. ESE of Coimbra; paper milling. Has interesting old church.

Goisern (goi′zŭrn), town (pop. 6,405) in the Salzkammergut, S Upper Austria, 5 mi. S of Bad Ischl; resort (alt. 1,640 ft.) with mineral springs; wood carving.

Goitacazes (goitŭkä′zĭs), town (pop. 1,266), NE Rio de Janeiro state, Brazil, on railroad and 5 mi. SSE of Campos; sugar milling.

Goito (goi′tô), village (pop. 944), Mantova prov., Lombardy, N Italy, on Mincio R. and 9 mi. NW of Mantua; paper, macaroni; limekilns.

Gojab River (gōjäb′), Ital. *Gogeb*, Kaffa prov., SW Ethiopia, rises 50 mi. SE of Gore, flows c.140 mi. ESE to Omo R. 12 mi. NW of Waka.

Gójar (gō′här), village (pop. 1,431), Granada prov., S Spain, 5 mi. S of Granada; olive-oil processing; cereals, wine, sugar beets.

Gojharia (gōjär′yŭ), town (pop. 5,446), Mehsana dist., N Bombay, India, 12 mi. SSE of Mehsana; millet, pulse, wheat; tanning. Also spelled Gojaria.

Gojjam (gō′jäm), province (□ c.24,300), NW Ethiopia, bordering on Anglo-Egyptian Sudan; ⊙ Debra Markos. Largely a forested mtn. plateau region rising to 13,625 ft. in Choke Mts. (E) and descending to grassy plain (W); includes AGAUMDIR dist. Lies bet. Blue Nile and Dinder rivers; contains small part of L. Tana (N). Pop. largely Amhara. Agr. (cereals, coffee, honey) and stock raising (horses, mules, cattle, sheep). Gold deposits near Qubba (W). Trade centers: Debra Markos, Bure, Dangila, Dambacha. Formerly part of Amhara prov.

Gojo (gōjō′), town (pop. 12,584), Nara prefecture, S Honshu, Japan, on W central Kii Peninsula, 24 mi. SSE of Osaka; agr. center (rice, mulberry trees); makes sake, chopsticks.

Gojonome (gōjō′nōmä), town (pop. 7,934), Akita prefecture, N Honshu, Japan, 7 mi. NNE of Showa; sake brewing, woodworking.

Gojra (gōj′rŭ), town (pop. 12,964), Lyallpur dist., SE central Punjab, W Pakistan, 29 mi. SW of Lyallpur; trade center for wheat, gram, cotton, gur; cotton ginning, flour milling, mfg. of fruit drinks, chutneys.

Gokak (gō′käk), town (pop. 13,826), Belgaum dist., S Bombay, India, on Ghatprabha R. and 29 mi. NE of Belgaum; trades in cotton, jaggery, chili, millet; hand-loom weaving, wooden-toy mfg. Hydroelectric plant (3½ mi. NW; 180 ft.) at falls of Ghatprabha R. powers near-by cotton mills.

Gokarn (gō′kŭrn), town (pop. 10,082), Kanara dist., S Bombay, India, on Arabian Sea, 22 mi. SSE of Karwar; betel farming; rice. Sivaite temple (scene of annual festival fair). Sanikatta, its port (3 mi. E; on sheltered inlet), has saltworks.

Gokase River (gōkä′sä), Jap. *Gokase-gawa*, E Kyushu, Japan, rises in mts. in Miyazaki prefecture, 31 mi. W of Nobeoka; flows ESE, past Mamihara, and SE to Hyuga Sea (N arm of Philippine Sea) at Nobeoka; 83 mi. long.

Gokasho (gōkä′shō), town (pop. 3,922), Mie prefecture, S Honshu, Japan, port on inlet of Kumano Sea, 10 mi. S of Uji-yamada; lumber, charcoal, rye, sweet potatoes. Exports fish.

Gokcha, Armenian SSR: see SEVAN, LAKE.

Gok Irmak (gûk′ ĭrmäk″) or **Gok River**, Turkish *Gök*, N Turkey, rises in Kure Mts. 10 mi. W of Daday, flows 120 mi. E, past Daday, Taskopru, and Boyabat, to the Kizil Irmak 18 mi. ESE of Boyabat.

Gok River, Turkey: see GOK IRMAK; GOKSU.

Gokstad (gōk′stä), village in Sander canton, Vestfold co., SE Norway, just ENE of Sandefjord; scene (1880) of excavation of well-preserved anc. viking ship and utensils, now in Oslo mus.

Goksu (gûksü′) or **Gok River**, Turkish *Göksü*. **1** anc. *Calycadnus*, river, S Turkey, rises in Taurus Mts., flows 150 mi. SE, past Silifke, to Mediterranean Sea. Frederick Barbarossa drowned in it while on a crusade. **2** River, S central Turkey, rises 20 mi. ESE of Pinarbasi, flows 115 mi. SSW, past Feke, to Seyhan R. 17 mi. NW of Kozan. **3** River, S Turkey, rises in Maras Mts. at Engizek Dag 25 mi. NNE of Maras, flows 90 mi. E and SE to Euphrates R. 11 mi. WNW of Yaylak.

Goksun (gûksōōn′), Turkish *Göksun*, village (pop. 2,529), Maras prov., S central Turkey, 38 mi. NW of Maras; rye, hemp.

Gokul (gō′kōōl), town (pop. 2,700), Muttra dist., W Uttar Pradesh, India, on the Jumna and 5 mi. SSE of Muttra; pilgrimage center. Hq. of Vallabhacharya sect (Gosains). Traditionally the site where Vishnu 1st appeared as Krishna.

Gokwe (gō′kwā), village, Gwelo prov., N Southern Rhodesia, in Matabeleland, 80 mi. NW of Que Que; cattle, sheep, goats. Hq. of native commissioner for Sebungwe dist. Police post.

Gol (gōl), village and canton (pop. 2,763), Buskerud co., S Norway, in the Hallingdal, on railroad and 60 mi. NW of Honefoss; agr., stock raising, lumbering. Has church dating from c.1200. Sanitarium 10 mi. N.

Gola (gō′lŭ). **1** Town (pop. 4,592), Gorakhpur dist., NE Uttar Pradesh, India, on the Gogra and 28 mi. S of Gorakhpur; rice, wheat, potatoes, barley, oilseeds. Also called Gola Bazar and Gola urf Madri. **2** Town (pop. 7,679), Kheri dist., N Uttar Pradesh, India, 21 mi. WNW of Lakhimpur; sugar processing; trades in rice, wheat, gram, corn, oilseeds. Noted Sivaite temple of Gokarannath, Gosain monasteries. Also called Gola Gokarannath or Gola Gokaran Nath.

Gola (gō′lŭ), island (424 acres; 1½ mi. long) off NW Co. Donegal, Ireland, 4 mi. SW of Bloody Foreland.

Golaghat (gō′lägät), town (pop. 5,470), Sibsagar dist., E central Assam, India, on tributary (navigable for part of year) of the Brahmaputra and 23 mi. SW of Jorhat; trades in tea, rice, rape and mustard, sugar cane, jute, cotton; tea processing. Extensive tea gardens near by.

Gola Gokarnnath, India: see GOLA, Uttar Pradesh.

Golakganj (gō′lŭkgŭnj), village, Goalpara dist., W Assam, India, on Gangadhar (Sankosh) R. and 11 mi. WNW of Dhubri; rail junction, with spur to Dhubri; rice, mustard, jute.

Golancz (gôwä′nyŭch), Pol. *Gołańcz*, Ger. *Gollantsch* (gô′länch), town (1946 pop. 1,382), Poznan prov., W central Poland, 40 mi. NNE of Poznan; rail junction; cattle market.

Golaya Pristan or **Golaya Pristan′** (gô′lĭŭ prē′-stŭnyŭ), town (1926 pop. 5,709), SW Kherson oblast, Ukrainian SSR, on Dnieper R. (landing) and 8 mi. SSW of Kherson; health resort; also has peat bogs.

Golaya Snova, Russian SFSR: see GOLOSNOVKA.

Golbahar, Afghanistan: see GULBAHAR.

Golbey (gōlbā′), N suburb (pop. 3,855) of Épinal, Vosges dept., E France, at influx of Canal de l'Est into Moselle R.; tool making, cotton weaving, nougat and margarine mfg.

Golborne (gōl′bŭrn), urban district (1931 pop. 7,321; 1951 census 16,876), S Lancashire, England, 6 mi. N of Warrington; rayon spinning, heavy engineering (colliery equipment), fruit packing.

Golcar (gō′kŭr), former urban district (1931 pop. 9,812), West Riding, SW Yorkshire, England, on Colne R. and 3 mi. W of Huddersfield; woolen and shoddy milling. Inc. 1937 in Colne Valley.

Golchikha or **Gol′chikha** (gŭlchē′khŭ), village (1948 pop. over 500), NW Taimyr Natl. Okrug, Krasnoyarsk Territory, Russian SFSR, N of Arctic Circle, on S Yenisei Gulf, 165 mi. NNW of Dudinka; govt. observation post.

Golconda (gŏlkŏn′dŭ), old fort and city, Atraf-i-Balda dist., central Hyderabad state, India, 5 mi. W of Hyderabad. Seat of Moslem kingdom of Golconda from early-16th cent. until annexed to Mogul empire by Aurangzeb in 1687; was treasury and market for diamonds mined at several places along Kistna R. and cut and polished near Golconda. Several royal tombs near by. Sometimes spelled Golkunda.

Golconda. **1** Town (pop. 1,066), ⊙ Pope co., extreme SE Ill., on Ohio R. and 25 mi. S of Harrisburg, in rich agr. area (fruit, corn, wheat, livestock); wood products; fluorspar mines. Inc. 1845. **2** Village (pop. c.300), Humboldt co., N Nev., on Humboldt R. and 13 mi. E of Winnemucca; ships livestock. Tungsten deposits.

Golcuk (gûljük′), Turkish *Gölcük*, village (pop. 8,834), Kocaeli prov., NW Turkey, on Gulf of Izmit, 7 mi. WSW of Izmit; shipyards, naval base; trade in cereals.

Golcuk, Lake, Turkish *Gölcük*, or **Lake Hazar** (häzär′), lake (□ 27), E central Turkey, 15 mi. SE of Elazig; 13 mi. long, 3 mi. wide; alt. 3,790 ft. Tigris R. rises here.

Golcuv Jenikov (gôl′chōōf yĕ′nyĕkôf), Czech *Golčův Jeníkov*, Ger. *Goltsch-Jenikau* (gôlch″-yä′nēkou), village (pop. 1,734), E Bohemia, Czechoslovakia, on railroad and 7 mi. S of Caslav; agr. center (sugar beets, potatoes).

Goldach (gôl′däkh), town (pop. 3,480), St. Gall canton, NE Switzerland, 5 mi. NE of St. Gall, near L. Constance; textiles (silk, cotton), embroideries, flour, chemicals.

Goldap (gô′ŏŏdäp), Pol. *Goldap*, Ger. *Goldap* (gôl′däp), town (1939 pop. 12,786; 1946 pop. 632) in East Prussia, after 1945 in Bialystok prov., NE Poland, on Goldap R. and 30 mi. SE of Chernyakhovsk (Insterburg; now in Kaliningrad oblast). Frontier station near USSR border, 14 mi. ESE of Ozersk; rail junction. In First World War, heavily damaged (1914) by Russians; virtually obliterated in Second World War, after which its Ger. pop. was expelled.

Goldap River, Pol. *Goldap*, in East Prussia, after 1945 in NE Poland, rises SE of Goldap, flows 35 mi. generally NW in a winding course, past Goldap, to Angerapp R. 8 mi. NE of Wegorzewo.

Goldau, Switzerland: see ARTH.

Goldbach (gôlt′bäkh), village (pop. 4,936), Lower Franconia, NW Bavaria, Germany, 2 mi. NE of Aschaffenburg; woodworking, paper milling.

Gold Bar, town (pop. 305), Snohomish co., NW Wash., 25 mi. ESE of Everett, in agr., lumbering region.

Gold Beach, village (pop. 677), ⊙ Curry co., SW Oregon, 55 mi. W of Grants Pass, at mouth of Rogue R. on Pacific Ocean; fishing resort. Siskiyou Natl. Forest near by. Inc. 1945.

Goldberg (gôlt'bĕrk), town (pop. 5,507), Mecklenburg, N Germany, on small Goldberg L., 15 mi. SSW of Güstrow; spa; agr. market (grain, sugar beets, potatoes, stock).

Goldberg, Poland: see ZLOTORYJA.

Gold Bridge, village (pop. estimate 400), SW B.C., in Coast Mts., on Bridge R. and 120 mi. N of Vancouver; gold and silver mining.

Gold Coast, British colony and protectorates (□ 91,690; pop. 4,095,276 including Br. Togoland), W Africa, on Gulf of Guinea; ⊙ Accra. Consists of Gold Coast colony (coastal belt 40–100 mi. wide; □ 23,490; pop. 2,194,466; ⊙ Cape Coast), and of the inland protectorates of ASHANTI and NORTHERN TERRITORIES. The part of TOGOLAND under Br. trusteeship (□ 13,040; pop. 378,666) is administratively included in Gold Coast. Rectangular in shape, with a coast line of 334 mi., Gold Coast is surrounded on 3 sides by Fr. possessions: Ivory Coast (W), Upper Volta (N), and Fr. Togoland (E). From a sandy, often marshy coastal scrub zone, rain forests extend northward to the Ashanti uplands (2,000–2,500 ft.). N Ashanti and Northern Territories are an extensive savanna and park-savanna plain. The VOLTA RIVER, which combines the waters of the White and the Black Volta, is the territory's master stream, crossing it from NW to SE; shorter rivers flowing S from the Ashanti uplands are the Tano, Ankobra, Pra, and Densu. Gold Coast has a monsoon-type tropical climate marked by 2 rainy seasons (March–July, Sept.–Nov.); precipitation varies in 4 main climatic regions: the coastal belt (except extreme SW) is driest (30 in. rainfall per year at Accra); Axim, in SW corner, receives over 80 in., the forest zone 55–65 in., and the N savanna 40–55 in. Influence of the Saharan harmattan is felt during Dec.–Jan., especially in N. Cacao is by far the ranking commercial crop; grown by natives on small holdings throughout the forest zone of the colony and of Ashanti, it is exported via TAKORADI and ACCRA. Gold Coast normally supplies 30% of the world's cacao beans; the spread of a blight (called the "swollen shoot") has been checked as the result of experiments conducted by the West Africa Cocoa Research Inst. at Tafo. Among secondary export crops are palm oil, copra, kola nuts, coffee, and rubber. Rice, cassava, corn, plantains, and yams are principal local food crops. The production of tobacco and cotton (as yet on a small scale) is being encouraged. Limes are a specialty crop near coast (Abakrampa, Asebo). Only land suitable for livestock raising is in Northern Territories and along coast E of Accra. Timber (especially mahogany) is shipped from the forest zone of the interior. Gold Coast has a wealth of mineral resources. Gold, mined and dredged at widely scattered points in the colony (Bibiani, Tarkwa, Prestea, Kibi) and in Ashanti (Obuasi, Konongo, Juaso), is still the most valuable mineral export item. The important manganese mine at Nsuta supplies over 20% of U.S. manganese needs. Bauxite has been mined since Second World War at Awaso and Mpraeso; construction of an alumina reduction plant is planned, together with a hydroelectric plant at Ajena on lower Volta R. Diamonds are found at Oda, Kade, and Kibi in the colony. Industry is limited to agr. processing and native handicrafts. Takoradi has a modern cocoa-butter factory, Accra a new brewery. Two rail lines (length, 536 mi., including spurs) penetrate the hinterland from Accra and Takoradi-Secondi respectively, joining at Kumasi (⊙ Ashanti and largest inland market). Thence, all-weather roads (c.3,000 mi.) serve Northern Territories and radiate to surrounding Fr. territories. Harbor facilities are excellent at Takoradi (modern harbor opened 1928); elsewhere lighterage is necessary. There are airfields at Accra, Takoradi, Kumasi, and Tamale. Gold Coast has numerous govt. and mission schools, including technical training centers and agr. experiment stations; Univ. Col. and Achimota Teachers Col. are at Achimota, 6 mi. N of Accra. The chief native languages are Akan (in Ashanti and the colony), Ewe, Ga, Mole (chiefly in Northern Territories), and Hausa. Among Akan peoples (Fanti, Ashanti) fetishism is still prevalent. The Moslem influence (especially in Northern Territories) was spread by Hausa immigrants from N Nigeria. The Gold Coast was 1st visited by Portuguese gold and slave traders who founded Elmina in 1471. In 17th–18th cent. slave trade was carried on by rival Dutch, British, and Danish companies, all of which established posts along the coast; the Danes withdrew in 1850, the Dutch in 1871–72. Br. holdings, administered as part of Sierra Leone, were constituted as Gold Coast colony in 1874, and included Lagos until 1886. Protectorate over Ashanti and Northern Territories established 1901. Gold Coast is ruled by an appointed governor aided by an executive and a legislative council. Under constitution of 1946, it has 1st Br. govt. in Africa with an unofficial majority of Africans. For administration, the governor is represented by chief commissioners at Cape Coast for the colony (divided into Eastern and Western provinces), at Kumasi (Ashanti), and at Tamale (Northern Territories).

Gold Coast, name applied to a section of the W African shore line on Gulf of Guinea, off Gold Coast colony. It is flanked by Ivory Coast (W) and Slave Coast (E). Named for gold deposits found in coastal region by 1st European navigators (after 1471).

Gold Creek or **Goldcreek,** village (pop. c.50), Powell co., W central Mont., on the Clark Fork, at mouth of small Gold Creek, and 16 mi. NW of Deer Lodge. Gold is dredged mechanically from Gold Creek, near source of which, in Flint Creek Range, gold was 1st discovered (c.1856) in Mont.

Golden, village (pop. estimate 750), SE B.C., on Columbia R., at mouth of Kicking Horse R., and 60 mi. ENE of Revelstoke, on slope of Rocky Mts.; alt. 2,583 ft.; dairying, sheep-raising center, in mining (silver, gold, lead, barites, zinc), fruit growing, and lumbering region.

Golden, Gaelic *Gabhail in,* town (pop. 140), central Co. Tipperary, Ireland, on Suir R. and 4 mi. WSW of Cashel; agr. market (dairying; potatoes, beets). Near by are ruins of 12th-cent. Athassel Priory.

Golden. **1** City (pop. 5,238), ⊙ Jefferson co., N central Colo., on Clear Creek, just E of Front Range, and 10 mi. W of Denver; alt. 5,680 ft. Resort and trading point in livestock and poultry region; truck, dairy products, beverages, pottery, firebrick. Coal and gold mines in vicinity. Colo. School of Mines and state industrial school for boys here. Grave of William F. Cody (Buffalo Bill) on Lookout Mtn., and Rocky Mtn. Natl. Park near by. City founded 1859 as mining town, served as territorial ⊙ 1862–67, inc. 1886. **2** Village (pop. 512), Adams co., W Ill., 24 mi. ENE of Quincy, in agr. area (corn, wheat, oats, livestock); makes seed sowers. **3** Village (pop. 206), Tishomingo co., extreme NE Miss., 33 mi. ENE of Tupelo, in agr. and timber area; sawmills.

Golden Bay, inlet of Tasman Sea, extreme N S.Isl., New Zealand, bet. Cape Farewell and Separation Point; 20 mi. wide. Takaka near SE shore. Visited 1642 by Tasman. Sometimes called Massacre Bay.

Golden Beach, resort town (pop. 156), Dade co., S Fla., on Atlantic coast, 14 mi. NNE of Miami.

Golden Chersonese: see MALAY PENINSULA.

Golden City, city (pop. 839), Barton co., SW Mo., 20 mi. NE of Carthage; agr.; coal.

Goldendale, town (pop. 1,907), ⊙ Klickitat co., S Wash., on Klickitat R. and 55 mi. SSW of Yakima; lumber, wheat, alfalfa, dairy products, livestock. Settled c.1863.

Goldene Aue (gôl'dùnù ou'ù), fertile region in central Germany, bet. the Harz (N) and the Kyffhäuser (S), extending c.30 mi. bet. Nordhausen (W) and Sangerhausen (E); drained by Helme R.

Golden Gate, village (pop. 199), Wayne co., SE Ill., 37 mi. E of Mount Vernon, in agr. area.

Golden Gate, strait (5 mi. long, 1–2 mi. wide), W Calif., bet. SAN FRANCISCO BAY and the Pacific. **Golden Gate Bridge** (built 1933–37) extends across the strait from San Francisco to Marin co. It is longest (4,200 ft. bet. towers) single-span suspension bridge in world; over-all length is 9,266 ft., and center span is 220 ft. above water.

Golden Hinde, mountain (7,219 ft.), SW B.C., on central Vancouver Isl.; highest peak in Strathcona Provincial Park, 30 mi. W of Courtenay; 49°40'N 125°45'W.

Golden Horn, narrow inlet of the Bosporus, Turkey, forming harbor of Istanbul, separating Galata and Pera from the city proper.

Golden Horn Bay, Rus. *Bukhta Zolotoi Rog* (bōōkh'tŭ zŭlŭtoi" rôk'), narrow, sheltered inlet of Eastern Bosphorus strait; harbor of Vladivostok, SW Maritime Territory, Russian SFSR; extends 4 mi. NE and E into Muravyev-Amurski Peninsula. Year-round navigation; during freezing period (Dec.–March) ice-breakers keep harbor open for shipping.

Golden Meadow, fishing village (pop. 2,820), Lafourche parish, SE La., on Bayou Lafourche (navigable) and 40 mi. SSW of New Orleans; fish- and shellfish-packing center. Duck hunting, fur trapping near by.

Golden Prairie, village (pop. 246), SW Sask., 22 mi. NNW of Maple Creek; wheat.

Golden Rock, town (pop. 16,412), Trichinopoly dist., S Madras, India; SE suburb of Trichinopoly; locomotive and railway-car works. Created during 1920s on modern town-planning principles.

Goldens Bridge, village (1940 pop. 509), Westchester co., SE N.Y., on reservoir in Croton R., 7 mi. NNE of Mount Kisco; rail junction; mfg. of sweaters.

Goldenstedt (gôl'dùn-shtĕt), village (commune pop. 5,415), in Oldenburg, NW Germany, after 1945 in Lower Saxony, 7 mi. NE of Vechta; mfg. of agr. machinery and cigars.

Golden Valley, town (pop. 577), Salisbury prov., central Southern Rhodesia, in Mashonaland, 12 mi. NW of Gatooma; gold-mining center.

Golden Valley. **1** County (□ 1,178; pop. 1,337), central Mont.; ⊙ Ryegate. Agr. area drained by Musselshell R. Livestock, grain. Part of Lewis and Clark Natl. Forest in NW. Formed 1920. **2** County (□ 1,014; pop. 3,499), W N.Dak., on Mont. line; ⊙ Beach. Fertile agr. and grazing area; lignite mines; stock raising, wheat, grain. Organized 1912.

Golden Valley, village (pop. 5,551), W suburb of Minneapolis, Hennepin co., E Minn.

Goldenvalley or **Golden Valley,** village (pop. 339), Mercer co., central N.Dak., 70 mi. NW of Bismarck and on Spring Creek.

Goldenville, village (pop. estimate 800), E N.S., on St. Mary R. and 30 mi. SW of Guysborough; gold mining.

Golders Green, England: see HENDON.

Goldfield. **1** City (pop. 81), Teller co., central Colo., in Rocky Mts. 9 mi. SSW of Pikes Peak, 20 mi. WSW of Colorado Springs; alt. 9,882 ft. Former shipping point in Cripple Creek gold dist., with pop. of 3,000 in 1890s. **2** Town (pop. 665), Wright co., N central Iowa, near Boone R., 5 mi. N of Eagle Grove; rail junction; dairy products, feed. **3** Village (1940 pop. 530), ⊙ Esmeralda co., S Nev., 25 mi. S of Tonopah; alt. 5,684 ft. Famous old gold town, once remarkable for its boomtime elegance; gold was discovered 1902 and peak production reached in 1910. Old Goldfield Hotel is extant.

Goldfields, village (1946 pop. 8; 1941 pop. 276), NW Sask., on N shore of L. Athabaska, near Alta. border; 59°27'N 108°29'W. Until 1943 gold was mined here; pitchblende mining was begun here later.

Gold Hill. **1** Village (pop. c.100), Boulder co., N central Colo., in E foothills of Front Range, 7 mi. NW of Boulder; alt. c.8,550 ft. Summer resort and gold-mining point. Miners' Hotel (1872) preserves old-time furnishings and decorations. **2** Old mining camp, Storey co., W Nev., near Virginia City; once a rich gold town, near Comstock Lode. **3** Town (1940 pop. 249), Rowan co., central N.C., 13 mi. SSE of Salisbury. **4** Town (pop. 619), Jackson co., SW Oregon, 11 mi. NW of Medford and on Rogue R.; gypsum products; cement mfg.

Goldingen, Latvia: see KULDIGA.

Goldington, residential town and parish (pop. 1,440), N central Bedford, England, on Ouse R. and 2 mi. ENE of Bedford. Has 14th-cent. church and ruins of 13th-cent. Newenham Priory.

Goldkronach (gôlt"krō'näkh), town (pop. 1,145), Upper Franconia, NE Bavaria, Germany, at W foot of the Fichtelgebirge, 7 mi. NE of Bayreuth; woodworking. Known in 14th and 15th cent. for its rich gold mines.

Gold Lake, NE Calif., in the Sierra Nevada, 12 mi. SW of Portola; c.1½ mi. long. Fishing and vacation resort.

Goldonna (gōldŏ'nù), village (pop. 364), Natchitoches parish, NW central La., 20 mi. NE of Natchitoches and on Saline Bayou. Saltworks near by.

Goldpines, village, NW Ont., on Chukuni R., at NW end of L. Seul, and 70 mi. NW of Sioux Lookout; hydroelectric power center on the Ear Falls.

Gold Point, town (pop. 132), Martin co., E N.C., 10 mi. W of Williamston.

Goldroad, village (1940 pop. 718), in Black Mts., W Ariz., 20 mi. SW of Kingman; alt., 5,225 ft. Gold mines near by.

Goldsboro. **1** Town (pop. 198), Caroline co., E Md., 16 mi. WSW of Dover, Del.; ships truck; vegetable cannery. **2** City (pop. 21,454), ⊙ Wayne co., E central N.C., near Neuse R., 45 mi. SE of Raleigh, on the coastal plain. Bright-leaf tobacco market; trade and shipping center (tobacco, cotton, truck); mfg. of textiles, cotton yarn, furniture, boxes, farm implements, electric-light bulbs, fertilizer, feed, cottonseed oil. State hosp. for insane, orphans' home. Settled c.1840, inc. 1847. **3** Borough (pop. 558), York co., S Pa., 9 mi. SE of Harrisburg and on Susquehanna R.

Goldston (gōl'stùn), town (pop. 372), Chatham co., central N.C., 12 mi. NW of Sanford; lumber milling.

Goldthwaite (gōld'thwāt), town (pop. 1,566), ⊙ Mills co., central Texas, 30 mi. SE of Brownwood; market, shipping center for diversified agr., ranching area (cattle, sheep, goats, poultry, dairy products, cotton, grain, peanuts, fruit).

Goldville, textile village (pop. 1,730), Laurens co., NW central S.C., 12 mi. ESE of Laurens; fabrics, yarn.

Gole (gûlĕ'), Turkish *Göle,* village (pop. 2,545), Kars prov., NE Turkey, 28 mi. WNW of Kars; barley. Formerly Merdenik.

Goléa, El- (ĕl-gôlāä'), town (pop. 6,279) and Saharan oasis, Ghardaïa territory, central Algeria, at E edge of the Great Western Erg, on Djelfa–In-Salah auto track, and 140 mi. SSW of Ghardaïa; 30°35'N 2°53'E. Date palms. Has old citadel and tomb of Father de Foucauld. Military post occupied by Fr. since 1891.

Golegã (gōōlĭgā'), town (pop. 4,661), Santarém dist., central Portugal, 16 mi. NE of Santarém; trade center of rich winegrowing region also producing olives and grain; cord mfg. Has fine Manueline 16th-cent. church.

Golema Reka, river, Yugoslavia: see TRESKA RIVER.

Goleniow (gôlĕn'yōōf), Pol. *Goleniów*, Ger. *Gollnow* (gôl'nō), town (1939 pop. 13,740; 1946 pop. 1,713) in Pomerania, after 1945 in Szczecin prov., NW Poland, on Ihna R. and 15 mi. NE of Stettin; woolen and cotton milling, metalworking, furniture mfg.; limestone quarrying. After 1945, briefly called Golonog, Pol. *Gołonóg*. Its Ger. pop. left after Second World War.

Golesnica or **Goleshnitsa** (both: gô'lĕshnĭtsä), Serbo-Croatian *Golešnica*, mountain, Macedonia, Yugoslavia; highest point (6,927 ft.) is 15 mi. W of Titov Veles.

Golesti (gôlĕsht'), Rum. *Goleşti*, village (pop. 1,537), Arges prov., S central Rumania, 19 mi. S of Campulung; rail junction. See also SCHITU-GOLESTI.

Goleta (gōlē'tů), village (1940 pop. 1,317), Santa Barbara co., SW Calif., on the coast, 8 mi. W of Santa Barbara; citrus fruit, walnuts, truck. Oil, natural-gas fields near by.

Golf, village (pop. 258), Cook co., NE Ill., N suburb of Chicago, 6 mi. W of Evanston.

Golfe-Juan (gōlf-zhüä'), town (pop. 3,228), Alpes-Maritimes dept., SE France, on sheltered Juan Gulf (fleet anchorage) of the Mediterranean, 3 mi. ENE of Cannes; resort on Fr. Riviera. Essential-oil distilling, artistic pottery and furniture mfg. Here Napoleon landed in 1815 on his return from Elba (commemorative column).

Golfete, Guatemala: see DULCE, Río.

Golfito (gōlfē'tō), town (1950 pop. 4,256), Puntarenas, S Costa Rica, Pacific port on sheltered inlet (El Golfito) of the Golfo Dulce, and 40 mi. SE of Puerto Cortés and El Palmar (linked by rail); 8°38'N 83°13'W. Leading banana port of Costa Rica. Developed in 1930s, it supplanted (with Quepos) the port of Limón in banana exports.

Golf Manor, village (pop. 3,603), Hamilton co., extreme SW Ohio, suburb c.6 mi. N of downtown Cincinnati. Inc. 1947.

Golfo degli Aranci (gôl'fô dĕlyärän'chē), village (pop. 412), Sassari prov., NE Sardinia, port on Gulf of Terranova, 60 mi. NE of Sassari; rail terminus; lobster fishing. Sometimes called Golfo Aranci.

Golftyn, Wales: see CONNAH'S QUAY.

Golfview, town (pop. 84), Palm Beach co., SE Fla., near Palm Beach.

Goliad (gō'lēăd), county (□ 871; pop. 6,219), S Texas; ⊙ Goliad, one of state's oldest cities. Drained by San Antonio R. Cattle ranching, agr. (corn, cotton, grain sorghums, flax, broomcorn, fruit, truck); livestock (horses, hogs, poultry), dairying. Oil, natural-gas wells. Includes state park at Goliad. Formed 1836.

Goliad, historic city (pop. 1,584), ⊙ Goliad co., S Texas, 85 mi. SE of San Antonio, near San Antonio R. Market, trade, shipping point in agr., petroleum-producing area. Sp. mission and presidio established here 1749; known as La Bahia, settlement was captured and held briefly by filibustering expedition from U.S. in 1812 and 1821. Seized by Texans at beginning of Texas Revolution; in 1836, when Mex. advance began, Col. J. W. Fannin and more than 300 men were shot here a week after their capture during attempted retreat. The massacre thus contributed to the Texans' battle cry at San Jacinto, "Remember the Alamo! Remember Goliad!" The mission (restored), ruins of the fort, and a memorial shaft are in a state park; ruins of another mission (1754) are near.

Golija or **Goliya** (gô'lēyä). **1** Mountain in Dinaric Alps, W Montenegro, Yugoslavia, along left bank of the Piva; highest point (6,498 ft.) is 14 mi. W of Savnik. **2** Mountain in Dinaric Alps, W Serbia, Yugoslavia; highest point (6,012 ft.) is 12 mi. NW of Novi Pazar.

Golima River (gō'lēmä), NE Ethiopia, rises on escarpment of Great Rift Valley near Kobbo, flows intermittently c.100 mi. E and NE, into Danakil desert, and disappears c.50 mi. SW of L. Egogi Bad.

Golina (gôlē'nä), town (pop. 1,769), Poznan prov., W central Poland, 7 mi. WNW of Konin; flour milling, brick mfg.

Golintsi (gô'lĭntsē), village (pop. 3,646), Vidin dist., NW Bulgaria, 2 mi. ESE of Lom; vineyards, grain, hemp, truck.

Golitsino (gŭlyē'tsĭnŭ), village (1926 pop. 4,033), N Penza oblast, Russian SFSR, on Moksha R. and 45 mi. NW of Penza, in hemp area. Sometimes spelled Golitsyno.

Golitsyno (gŭlyē'tsĭnŭ). **1** Village (1926 pop. 1,500), central Moscow oblast, Russian SFSR, 25 mi. WSW of Moscow; furniture mfg., metalworking. **2** Village, Penza oblast, Russian SFSR: see GOLITSINO.

Goliya, mountain, Yugoslavia: see GOLIJA.

Golkoy (gûlkû'ē), Turkish *Gölköy*, village (pop. 2,767), Ordu prov., N Turkey, 24 mi. WSW of Ordu; grain. Formerly Kusluyan.

Golkunda, India: see GOLCONDA.

Gollantsch, Poland: see GOLANCZ.

Gollel (gŏ'lĕl), village, SE Swaziland, on Natal border, 85 mi. SE of Mbabane.

Göllersdorf (gû'lûrsdôrf), village (pop. 1,293), NE Lower Austria, 9 mi. NW of Stockerau. Has 15th-cent. château.

Göllheim (gûl'hīm), village (pop. 1,742), Rhenish Palatinate, W Germany, 15 mi. WNW of Frankenthal; noted for battle fought here in 1298, in which German king, Adolf of Nassau, was defeated and slain by forces of his rival, Albert of Hapsburg.

Golling (gō'lĭng), town (pop. 2,873), Salzburg, W Austria, near the Salzach, 7 mi. SSE of Hallein; summer resort; gypsum quarries. Golling falls (200 ft. high) are near by.

Gollnow, Poland: see GOLENIOW.

Gollub, Poland: see GOLUB.

Golmés (gōlmās'), village (pop. 1,377), Lérida prov., NE Spain, 16 mi. E of Lérida, in irrigated area (olive oil, wine, sugar beets, cherries).

Golmovski or **Gol'movskiy** (gŭlmôf'skē), town (1939 pop. over 500), central Stalino oblast, Ukrainian SSR, in the Donbas, c.10 mi. NE of Gorlovka.

Gölnicbanya, Czechoslovakia: see GELNICA.

Goloby (gô'lůbē), Pol. *Hołoby* (hôwô'bē), village (1931 pop. 1,460), central Volyn oblast, Ukrainian SSR, 16 mi. SE of Kovel; flour milling; bricks.

Golodayevka (gŭlůdī'ůfkŭ). **1** Village, SW Rostov oblast, Russian SFSR, near Taganrog: see KUIBYSHEVO. **2** Village, N central Rostov oblast, Russian SFSR, near Millerovo: see PERVOMAISKOYE.

Golodnaya Step, town, Uzbek SSR: see MIRZACHUL.

Golodnaya Step or **Golodnaya Step'** (gŭlôd"nīŭ styĕp') [Rus.,=hunger steppe]. **1** In S central Kazakh SSR: see BET-PAK-DALA. **2** Irrigated loess plain, SW South Kazakhstan oblast, Kazakh SSR, W of the Syr-Darya; bounded NW by desert Kyzyl-Kum; intensive cotton growing. Main town, Ilich (cotton-ginning center).

Gologory (gŭlůgô'rē), Pol. *Gologóry* (gôwôgōō'rē), mountains in Volyn-Podolian Upland, W Ukrainian SSR; extend c.35 mi. bet. Lvov (W) to Zolochev (E); average alt. 1,500 ft.

Golo Island (gō'lō) (9 mi. long, 1.5 mi. wide; 1939 pop. 750), one of the Lubang Isls., Mindoro prov., Philippines, in S.China Sea, just SE of Lubang Isl., 6 mi. off NW coast of Mindoro isl.; rises to 958 ft. Rice growing.

Golonog, Poland: see GOLENIOW.

Golo River (gōlō'), longest in Corsica, rises S of Monte Cinto, flows c.45 mi. NE through narrow mtn. valley, to Tyrrhenian Sea 12 mi. SSE of Bastia, forming marshy delta. Followed by Ajaccio-Bastia RR in lower course.

Golosnovka (gŭlůsnôf'kŭ), village (1939 pop. over 2,000), NW Voronezh oblast, Russian SFSR, 35 mi. NW of Voronezh; wheat. Until c.1938, Golaya Snova.

Golovanevsk (gŭlůvä'nyĭfsk), village (1926 pop. 4,050), N Odessa oblast, Ukrainian SSR, 30 mi. NW of Pervomaisk; light mfg.

Golovin (gŏ'lůvĭn), village (pop. 86), NW Alaska, on S Seward Peninsula, on Golovnin Lagoon, N arm (25 mi. long) of Norton Sound, 70 mi. E of Nome; fishing, gold mining; supply center for rich gold-mining region; fish-salting, cold-storage plant. Has territorial school. Sometimes called Cheenik.

Golovinshchino (gŭlůvēn'shchĭnŭ), village (1926 pop. 2,882), central Penza oblast, Russian SFSR, 40 mi. W of Penza; wheat, sugar beets. Sometimes spelled Golovinshchina.

Golovita, Lake, Rumania: see RAZELM, LAKE.

Golovnino (gŭlůvnyē'nů), village (1948 pop. over 2,000), on S Kunashir Isl., S Kuriles, Russian SFSR, port on Nemuro Strait, 25 mi. SW of Yuzhno-Kurilsk, at S foot of Golovnin volcano (1,778 ft.); oyster beds; fisheries. Under Jap. rule (until 1945), called Tomari (tōmä'rē).

Golovnin Strait (gŭlůvnyēn'), Jap. *Matsuwa-Kaikyo* or *Koronin-kaikyo*, in central main Kurile Isls. group, Russian SFSR; separates Raikoke (N) and Matua (S) isls.; 11 mi. wide.

Golovno (gŭlôv'nů), Pol. *Holowno* (hôwôv'nô), village (1939 pop. over 500), W Volyn oblast, Ukrainian SSR, near source of Pripet R., 28 mi. WNW of Kovel; wheat, rye, potatoes.

Golpa (gôl'pä), village (pop. 1,332), in former Prussian Saxony prov., central Germany, after 1945 in Saxony-Anhalt, 8 mi. NNE of Bitterfeld; lignite mining. Major power station, located bet. Golpa and Zschornewitz (2 mi. E), supplies Berlin and Leipzig; completed 1918.

Golpayegan, Iran: see GULPAIGAN.

Golpazari (gûl"päzärŭ'), Turkish *Gölpazarı*, village (pop. 2,006), Bilecik prov., NW Turkey, 13 mi. E of Bozuyuk; cereals.

Golran, Afghanistan: see GULRAN.

Gols (gōls), town (pop. 3,077), Burgenland, E Austria, near E shore of Neusiedler L., 20 mi. NE of Sopron, Hungary; vineyards, sugar beets.

Golshan, Iran: see TABAS.

Golspie (gŏl'spē), town and parish (pop. 1,392), SE Sutherland, Scotland, on Dornoch Firth, 7 mi. NNE of Dornoch; fishing port. Just N is Dunrobin Castle, noted seat of dukes of Sutherland, begun c.1275.

Golssen (gôl'sůn), town (pop. 2,327), Brandenburg, E Germany, in Lower Lusatia, near Spree Forest, on Dahme R. and 13 mi. W of Lübben; vegetables, stock.

Goltry (gōl'trē), town (pop. 277), Alfalfa co., N Okla., 18 mi. WNW of Enid, in grain-producing area.

Göltzsch River (gûlch), E central Germany, rises in the Erzgebirge 3 mi. S of Falkenstein, flows c.20 mi. N and NE, past Auerbach, Rodewisch, and Lengenfeld, to the White Elster at Greiz.

Golub (gô'lōōp), Ger. *Gollub* (gô'lōōp), town (pop. 6,017), Bydgoszcz prov., N central Poland, on Drweca R., on railroad and 20 mi. ENE of Torun; sawmilling, flour milling, mfg. of mineral water. Castle ruins. Includes town of Dobrzyn nad Drweca, across river.

Golubac or **Golubats** (both: gô'lōōbäts), village, E Serbia, Yugoslavia, on the Danube (Rum. border) and 60 mi. E of Belgrade. Ruins of medieval fortress with 9 towers.

Golubovci or **Golubovtsi** (both: gô'lōōbôftsē), village (pop. 5,326), S Montenegro, Yugoslavia, in Zeta lowland, 7 mi. S of Titograd.

Golubovka (gŭlōōbôf'kŭ), town (1939 pop. over 10,000), SW Voroshilovgrad oblast, Ukrainian SSR, in the Donbas, 6 mi. N of Kadiyevka; coal mines. Formerly Golubovski Rudnik.

Golumet or **Golumet'** (gŭlōōmĕt'yů), village (1926 pop. 3,122), S Irkutsk oblast, Russian SFSR, 30 mi. WSW of Cheremkhovo, in agr. area.

Golva (gŏl'vů), village (pop. 174), Golden Valley co., W N.Dak., 24 mi. SW of Medora.

Golyama Kamchiya River (gôlyä'mä käm'chēä), E Bulgaria, rises NW of Kotel in Lisa Mts., flows c.80 mi. generally E, past Tsar Krum, to Rakla, here joining Luda Kamchiya R. to form Kamchiya R. Receives Vrana R. (left) at Tsar Krum. Also called Golyama Ticha R.

Golyama Kutlovitsa, Bulgaria: see MIKHAILOVGRAD.

Golyama Ticha River, Bulgaria: see GOLYAMA KAMCHIYA RIVER.

Golyamo Konare (–mô kônä'rĕ), village (pop. 7,153), Plovdiv dist., S central Bulgaria, in Plovdiv Basin, 12 mi. NE of Pazardzhik; flour milling; livestock, rice, fruit, truck.

Golyamo Shivachevo (shēvä'chĕvô), village (pop., 3,236), Yambol dist., E central Bulgaria, on S slope of central Balkan Mts., 15 mi. W of Sliven; sheep raising. Lignite mining (N). Formerly Iztochno Shivachevo.

Goly Karamysh, Russian SFSR: see KRASNOARMEISK, Saratov oblast.

Golyshi (gŭlĭshē'), town (1939 pop. over 500), E Kostroma oblast, Russian SFSR, on Vetluga R. and 3 mi. NW of Sharya; sawmilling.

Golyshmanovo (gŭlĭsh'mŭnůvů), town (1939 pop. over 2,000), S Tyumen oblast, Russian SFSR, on Trans-Siberian RR and 40 mi. WNW of Ishim; metalworking, dairying. Until 1948, Katyshka.

Gölzau, Germany: see WEISSANDT-GÖLZAU.

Goma (gō'mä), town, Kivu prov., E Belgian Congo, on N shore of L. Kivu, 33 mi. NNE of Costermansville; trading and tourist center at S foot of the Virunga range; communications hub (air, road, lake) near Ruanda-Urundi and Uganda borders. Airfield. Coffee and banana plantations in vicinity. Goma was seat of Intercolonial Soil Conservation Conference in 1948. Kibati, 9 mi. N, has cemetery of First World War; Ger. East African troops were defeated here (1914).

Gomal Pass, Afghanistan and W Pakistan: see GUMAL PASS.

Gomara, territory, Sp. Morocco: see XAUEN.

Gómara (gō'märä), town (pop. 869), Soria prov., N central Spain, 16 mi. SE of Soria; stock raising; chocolate mfg.

Gomastapur (gō'mŭstäpōōr), village, Rajshahi dist., W East Bengal, E Pakistan, on Mahananda R. and 13 mi. N of Nawabganj; rice, wheat, oilseed, jute. Formerly spelled Gumastapur.

Gomba (gōōmbä'), town (pop. 1,160), Sokoto prov., Northern Provinces, NW Nigeria, on Niger R., at mouth of Kebbi R., and 70 mi. S of Birnin Kebbi; cassava, durra, millet. Sometimes spelled Gwomba.

Gombari (gōmbä'rē), village, Eastern Prov., NE Belgian Congo, on Bomokandi R. and 110 mi. NNW of Irumu; trading post in palm- and rice-growing region; palm-oil milling, rice processing. Has Protestant mission and military camp. Remnants of Pygmy tribes are still to be found here and in vicinity.

Gombasek, Czechoslovakia: see ROZNAVA.

Gombe (gŭm'bĕ), town (pop. 3,243), Bauchi prov., Northern Provinces, E central Nigeria, 85 mi. E of Bauchi; agr. center; cassava, millet, durra.

Gombe Lutete (gōm'bā lōōtĕ'tā), village, Leopoldville prov., W Belgian Congo, on left bank of Congo R. and 115 mi. NE of Boma; fibers, palm products. Baptist mission.

Gombe Matadi (mätä'dē), village, Leopoldville prov., W Belgian Congo, 120 mi. NE of Boma; trading center in fiber-growing region. R.C. missions, schools.

Gombin, Poland: see GABIN.

Gombrun, Iran: see BANDAR ABBAS.

Gomel or **Gomel'** (gō'mĕl, –mŭl, Rus. gô'mĭl), oblast (□ 6,100; 1946 pop. estimate 800,000), SE Belorussian SSR; ⊙ Gomel. In Dnieper Lowland; drained by Dnieper and Sozh rivers. Chiefly agr. (flax, potatoes, rye), livestock raising (pigs, dairy cattle), lumbering (SW); truck gardens and orchards near Gomel. Mfg. (agr. machinery, glass, paper), lumbering, at Gomel, Dobrush, Rechitsa, Zhlobin, Rogachev. Chief transportation centers: Gomel, Zhlobin. Formed 1938.

Gomel or **Gomel'**, city (1939 pop. 144,169), ⊙ Gomel oblast, Belorussian SSR, on high right bank of Sozh R., near mouth of the Iput, and 175 mi. SE of Minsk; 52°25'N 31°E. Industrial and transportation center; mfg. (agr. implements, lathes, electrical goods, textiles, glass); railroad shops; woodworking, food processing. Glassworks at Kostyukovka (N), paper mill at Dobrush (E). Has early-19th-cent. palace, cathedral, art and historical mus.; teachers col., lumber and agr. institutes. Includes left-bank suburb of Novo-Belitsa (match works). Dates from 12th cent.; acquired by Russia (1772); city developed rapidly in 19th cent. Scene of pogroms after 1905. Pop. 40% Jewish until Second World War, when city was held (1941–43) by Germans. Formerly also known as Homel.

Gomen (gō'mān), town (pop. 1,781), Kochi prefecture, S Shikoku, Japan, 6 mi. E of Kochi; tea; mulberry groves.

Gomera (gōmä'rä), anc. *Herenessus* and *Junonia Minor*, island (□ 146; pop. 28,571) of the Canary Isls., 20 mi. W of Tenerife, in Santa Cruz de Tenerife prov., Spain; 16 mi. long, 11 mi. wide. Chief town and port, San Sebastián or San Sebastián de la Gomera. Volcanic isl. with high, rugged coast line and mountainous interior, rising to c.4,860 ft. (Alto de Garajonay). Has year-round mild, subtropical climate. Water, however, is scarce. Among chief crops for export are: potatoes, tomatoes, bananas, grapes, cereals, tobacco, figs, almonds, sugar cane, chick-peas. Some fishing, stock raising, and lumbering. Gomera was conquered (1404–05) for Spain by Jean de Béthencourt.

Gomera, La, Guatemala: see LA GOMERA.

Gomersal, England: see SPENBOROUGH.

Gomeshan, Iran: see GUMISHAN.

Gometra (gōmĕ'trů), island (pop. 37) of the Inner Hebrides, Argyll, Scotland, just W of Ulva; 2 mi. long, 1½ mi. wide; rises to 503 ft. Fishing. There are basaltic columns.

Gómez, Lake (gō'mĕs), N Buenos Aires prov., Argentina, 12 mi. W of Junín, S of Mar Chiquita; 9 mi. long, c.2 mi. wide.

Gómez Farías (färē'äs). **1** Town (pop. 2,330), Jalisco, central Mexico, on railroad and 6 mi. N of Guzmán; alfalfa, cotton, sugar cane, grain, fruit, stock. Formerly San Sebastián. **2** Town (pop. 565), Tamaulipas, NE Mexico, 45 mi. S of Ciudad Victoria; cereals, henequen, stock.

Gómez Island, on Caribbean coast of Magdalena dept., N Colombia, in alluvial Magdalena R. delta, just W of Salamanca Isl., immediately N of Barranquilla.

Gómez Palacio (pälä'syō), city (pop. 25,588), Durango, N Mexico, in fertile irrigated Laguna Dist., 3 mi. NW of Torreón across Nazas R. Rail junction; processing and agr. center (cotton, corn, wheat, barley, wine, fruit, sugar cane, tobacco, vegetables). Wine and liquor distilling, vegetable-oil pressing, cotton ginning, flour and textile milling, tanning; iron and steel foundries; mfg. of agr. implements, explosives, chemicals, soap, clothing.

Gómez Plata (plä'tä), town (pop. 2,305), Antioquia dept., NW central Colombia, in Cordillera Central, 38 mi. NE of Medellín; alt. 6,119 ft. Gold-mining center in agr. region (coffee, bananas, corn, yucca, sugar cane, cacao, tobacco, cattle); food canning. At Guadalupe Falls, 7 mi. N, is important hydroelectric plant.

Gomezserracín (gōmĕth-sĕrä-thēn'), town (pop. 821), Segovia prov., central Spain, 25 mi. NNW of Segovia; cereals, carobs; timber, resins.

Gomishan, Iran: see GUMISHAN.

Gommern (gô'můrn), town (pop. 6,227), in former Prussian Saxony prov., central Germany, after 1945 in Saxony-Anhalt, 9 mi. ESE of Magdeburg; sugar refining, shoe mfg.; quartzite quarrying. Tuberculosis sanitarium.

Gömör-Szepesi Erchegyseg, Czechoslovakia: see SLOVAK ORE MOUNTAINS.

Gompel (gôm'půl), town, Antwerp prov., N Belgium, 2 mi. ENE of Mol; window-glass mfg.

Goms (gōs), district (pop. 4,518), NE Valais canton, S Switzerland. Rhone R. rises in its NE sect.

Gona (gō'nů), town, Territory of Papua, NE New Guinea, 100 mi. NE of Port Moresby. In Second World War, scene of bloody fighting.

Gonabad (gŏn"äbäd'), town (1941 pop. 2,775), Ninth Prov., in Khurasan, NE Iran, 145 mi. SSW of Meshed and on Meshed-Zahidan road; agr. and road center; grain, opium. Sometimes called Juimand, Juymand, or Joveymand for small village just N. Also spelled Gunabad.

Gonaïves (gônäēv'), city (1950 census pop. 13,534), ⊙ Artibonite dept. (□ c.2,600; 1950 pop. 568,666), W Haiti, port on NE shore of the Gulf of Gonaïves, 70 mi. NNW of Port-au-Prince; 19°27'N 72°41'W. Its fine harbor, together with that of Saint-Marc (23 mi. S), exports agr. products of the fertile Artibonite Plain (coffee, bananas, cotton, sugar cane, rice); also ships precious wood (lignum vitae, mahogany), beeswax, hides, skins, castor beans. Fishing and rice milling. Airfield. A historic town of Indian origin. On its Place d'Armes, Dessalines proclaimed (1804) Republic of Haiti. Toussaint L'Ouverture, hero of struggle for independence, was captured near by.

Gonaïves, Gulf of, on W coast of Haiti, E of Windward Passage, bet. the 2 peninsulas; c.75 mi. wide. On it are Gonaïves, Saint-Marc, and Port-au-Prince. Receives Artibonite R. In S is the Île de la Gonâve; the passage S of the isl. is called Canal de la Gonâve (Gonâve Channel) or Canal du Sud (Southern Channel).

Gonars (gônärs'), village (pop. 2,167), Udine prov., Friuli–Venezia Giulia, NE Italy, 12 mi. S of Udine; lye mfg.

Gonâve, Île de la (ēl dů lä gônäv'), long narrow island (□ 254; 1950 pop. 26,894), belonging to Haiti, in the Gulf of Gonaïves, 32 mi. WNW of Port-au-Prince; 35 mi. long, c.8 mi. wide; rises to 2,303 ft. Cotton, cattle, and subsistence crops are raised. Largely covered by forests. Good fishing grounds. The channel S of it is called Canal de la Gonâve or Canal du Sud.

Gonaveh, Bandar, Iran: see BANDAR GANAWEH.

Gonbad-e-Qavos, Iran: see GUNBAD-I-QAWUS.

Gönc (gûnts), town (pop. 3,306), Abauj co., NE Hungary, 33 mi. NE of Miskolc. Has 15th-cent. church.

Goncali (gônjälŭ'), Turkish *Goncalı*, village (pop. 493), Denizli prov., SW Turkey, 6 mi. N of Denizli; rail junction.

Goncelin (gōslĕ'), village (pop. 695), Isère dept., SE France, on the Isère and 16 mi. NE of Grenoble, in GRÉSIVAUDAN valley; ships fruit, vegetables.

Gonda (gōn'dů), district (□ 2,827; pop. 1,719,644), N Uttar Pradesh, India; ⊙ Gonda. Bounded N by W Nepal Himalaya foothills (Nepal border), S by Gogra R.; drained by the Rapti. Agr. (rice, wheat, corn, gram, oilseeds, barley, sugar cane); extensive sal jungle (N). Main towns: Balrampur, Gonda, Utraula, Colonelganj. Noted Buddhist archaeological site at Set Mahet.

Gonda, town (pop. 21,567), ⊙ Gonda dist., NE Uttar Pradesh, India, 27 mi. NNW of Fyzabad; rail and road junction; sugar and rice milling; trades in grains, oilseeds. Founded 16th cent.

Gondal (gōn'důl), town (pop. 30,553), central Saurashtra, India, on Kathiawar peninsula, 23 mi. S of Rajkot; road junction; trade center (oilseeds, cotton, millet, cattle); mfg. of matches, soap; oilseed milling, cotton ginning, handicraft cloth-weaving and embroidering. Girasia Col. Has several fine temples. Was ⊙ former princely state of Gondal (□ 1,024; pop. 244,514) of Western India States agency; established in 17th cent. by Jadeja Rajputs; merged 1948 with Saurashtra.

Gondar (gŏn'dŭr), town (pop. 15,000), ⊙ Begemdir prov., NW Ethiopia, in highlands N of L. Tana, 250 mi. NNW of Addis Ababa; 12°35'N 37°30'E; alt. c.7,500 ft.; connected by road (435 mi.) with Massawa (Eritrea) and Gallabat (Anglo-Egyptian Sudan). Commercial center (coffee, honey, butter, cereals, livestock); artisan industries (metalworking, leatherworking). Has notable remains of palaces (resembling European medieval fortresses) and churches of 17th-18th cent. Capital of Ethiopia, 17th–19th cent. Suffered greatly from civil wars in 18th–19th cent. when it was burned and sacked several times, most recently in 1867 by Theodore and in 1887 by Mahdist troops. Occupied 1936 by the Italians, it was the last outpost of Italian East Africa to fall (1941) to the British in the Second World War.

Gondia (gōnd'yů), town (pop. 20,120), Bhandara dist., central Madhya Pradesh, India, 75 mi. ENE of Nagpur; rail junction; trade center in agr. area; rice and oilseed milling; glass and tile works; shellac mfg. Game hunting in near-by forests.

Gondo, Switzerland: see SIMPLON PASS.

Gondokoro (gōndō'kōrō), village, Equatoria prov., S Anglo-Egyptian Sudan, on right bank of the Bahr el Jebel (White Nile) and 5 mi. N of Juba; cotton, peanuts, sesame, corn, durra; livestock. A noted slave- and ivory-trading center until suppressed by Sir Samuel Baker and Col. Charles Gordon in 1870s.

Gondomar (gōndōōmär'), town, Pôrto dist., N Portugal, on right bank of Douro R. and 5 mi. SE of Oporto; clock and watchmaking, gold filigreeing, textile milling.

Gond-Pontouvre, Le (lů gō-pōtōō'vrů), town (pop. 3,220), Charente dept., W France, on the Touvre near its mouth into the Charente and 2 mi. NNE of Angoulême; felt processing (for pulp), cement-working.

Gondrecourt-le-Château (gōdrůkōōr'-lů-shätō') or **Gondrecourt**, village (pop. 1,106), Meuse dept., NE France, on the Ornain and 18 mi. SSW of Commercy; rail junction; cheese mfg., sawmilling, granite quarrying.

Gondreville (gōdrůvēl'), village (pop. 913), Meurthe-et-Moselle dept., NE France, on Moselle R. and 4 mi. ENE of Toul; woolen milling.

Gondrin (gōdrĕ'), village (pop. 576), Gers dept., SW France, 8 mi. SW of Condom; white wines and Armagnac brandy.

Gondwana (gōndvä'nů), historical region comprising greater part (E and N) of Madhya Pradesh, India. Name is derived from Dravidian tribe of Gonds, now inhabiting large jungle and hill tracts of central India, who ruled the region from late-14th cent. until overthrown by Mahrattas in early-18th cent. Region gives its name to Gondwana land, a hypothetical Paleozoic continent believed to have existed in S Indian Ocean.

Gonen (gûnĕn'), Turkish *Gönen*, town (pop. 9,930), Balikesir prov., NW Turkey, on Gonen R. and 33 mi. NNW of Balikesir; wheat, barley, spelt, corn, tobacco.

Gonen River, Turkish *Gönen*, anc. *Aesepus*, NW Turkey, rises 10 mi. WSW of Yenice, flows 70 mi. NNE, past Yenice and Gonen, to Gulf of Erdek 22 mi. ENE of Biga.

Gonesse (gônĕs'), town (pop. 3,968), Seine-et-Oise dept., N central France, an outer NNE suburb of Paris, 10 mi. from Notre Dame Cathedral; mfg. of haberdashery supplies, batteries; sauerkraut preserving.

Gonfaron (gōfärō'), village (pop. 1,525), Var dept., SE France, on N slope of Monts des Maures, 22 mi. NE of Toulon; mfg. (corks, olive oil).

Gonfreville-l'Orcher (gōfrůvēl'-lôrshā'), commune (pop. 4,476), Seine-Inférieure dept., N France, on Seine R. estuary and 5 mi. E of Le Havre; petroleum refinery, cannon foundry. Includes metalworking town of Mayville (pop. 2,243).

Gongala Peak, Ceylon: see RAKWANA HILL COUNTRY.

Gongkar, Tibet: see KONGKA.

Gongola River (gông-gō'lä), NE Nigeria, rises on E slopes of Bauchi Plateau, 20 mi. E of Leri, flows NE and E past Nafada, and S past Shellen, to Benue R. at Numan; length, c.300 mi. Receives Hawal R. (left) 8 mi. N of Shellen. Navigable (Aug.-Sept.) below Nafada.

Gongolona (gông-gōlō'nä), village, Guanacaste prov., NW Costa Rica, on Abangares R. and 5 mi. NE of Las Juntas gold mines.

Goñi (gō'nyē), village (pop. 550), Florida dept., S central Uruguay, in the Cuchilla Grande Inferior, on highway and railroad, and 45 mi. NNW of Florida; cigar mfg.; wheat, cattle, sheep.

Goniadz (gôn'yäts), Pol. *Goniądz*, Rus. *Goniondz* (gôn'yônts), town (pop. 1,863), Bialystok prov., NE Poland, on Biebrza R. and 30 mi. NNW of Bialystok; flour milling.

Goniana (gōnyä'nů), village, W Patiala and East Punjab States Union, India, 25 mi. SSE of Faridkot; cotton ginning, flour milling.

Gonic, N.H.: see ROCHESTER.

Goniondz, Poland: see GONIADZ.

Gonja, Gold Coast: see SALAGA.

Gonjo (gôn'jō), Chinese *Kung-chüeh* (gōōng'jüĕ') or *Kung-chiao* (–jyou'), after 1913 *Kunghsien* (–shyĕn'), town, E Tibet, in Kham prov., 75 mi. SE of Chamdo; alt. 11,830 ft. Oil deposits.

Gonnesa (gôn-nä'zä), village (pop. 3,382), Cagliari prov., SW Sardinia, 5 mi. SW of Iglesias; lignite distillation plant. Lignite mines of Bacu Abis and Terras Collu near by (□ 15.5; 50,000 tons yearly production). Nuraghe village (100 houses) is SW.

Gonnos (gôn'ôs), town (pop. 2,949), Larissa nome, NE Thessaly, Greece, 16 mi. NNE of Larissa, at S foot of Lower Olympus, near Peneus R. Site of former fortress guarding Vale of Tempe. Formerly called Dereli.

Gonnosfanadiga (gôn"nôsfänä'dēgä), village (pop. 5,822), Cagliari prov., SW Sardinia, 14 mi. NE of Iglesias. Molybdenum and lead mines, iron deposits near by.

Gonobitz, Yugoslavia: see KONJICE.

Gonohe (gōnō'hā), town (pop. 10,433), Aomori prefecture, N Honshu, Japan, 11 mi. W of Hachinohe; rice growing, stock raising, lumbering.

Gonsenheim (gôn'zůnhīm), W suburb of Mainz, W Germany; mfg. (shoes, fruit preserves).

Gonvick (gŏn'vĭk), village (pop. 375), Clearwater co., NW Minn., 15 mi. NNW of Bagley, in grain and livestock area; dairy products.

Gonzaga (gônzä'gä), village (pop. 1,652), Mantova prov., Lombardy, N Italy, 14 mi. S of Mantua. Agr. center; dairy products, livestock, silk cocoons, cereals, sugar beets; furniture making, distilleries. Ancestral home of Gonzaga family, who ruled Mantua for 380 years.

Gonzales (gŭnză'lĭs), county (□ 1,058; pop. 21,164), S central Texas; ⊙ Gonzales. Drained by Guadalupe and San Marcos rivers. An important poultry-raising area (chickens, turkeys); also agr. (corn, grain sorghums, cotton, hay, potatoes, fruit, truck); cattle, hogs, horses, mules; dairying, beekeeping. Clay and kaolin mining; mineral springs (health resorts). Power dams impound lakes (recreation) in Guadalupe R. Includes Palmetto State Park and Gonzales State Park (site of 1st battle of Texas Revolution). Formed 1836.

Gonzales. **1** (gŭnză'lĭs) City (pop. 1,821), Monterey co., W Calif., in Salinas valley, 17 mi. SE of Salinas; milk processing, vegetable packing and shipping. Inc. 1947. **2** (gŭnză'lŭs) Village (pop. 1,642), Ascension parish, SE La., 21 mi. SE of Baton Rouge, in agr. area (truck, sugar cane, strawberries); oil wells. **3** (gŭnză'lĭs) City (pop. 5,659), ⊙ Gonzales co., S central Texas, c.65 mi. E of San Antonio, near mouth of San Marcos R. on the Guadalupe; poultry-shipping and hatching center in livestock and agr. area (cotton, truck, pecans, dairy products); mfg. (cotton goods, feed, cottonseed products). Near by are Palmetto State Park (NW), lakes impounded by dams in Guadalupe R. (power, recreation). Founded 1825. Near here in 1835 was fought 1st battle of Texas Revolution; park at COST (6 mi. SW) encloses battlefield.

González (gōnsä'lĕs), town (pop. 1,126), Tamaulipas, NE Mexico, on Gulf plains, on railroad and 55 mi. NW of Tampico; corn, henequen, fruit, livestock.
Gonzalez (gŏnză'lŭs, –zä'–), village, Escambia co., NW Fla., 12 mi. NNW of Pensacola; farm trade center. Clay pit near by.
González (gōnsä'lĕs), town, San José dept., S Uruguay, on railroad and 12 mi. NW of San José; creaels, cattle, sheep.
González, Ciudad, Mexico: see DOCTOR HERNÁNDEZ ALVAREZ.
González Chaves (chä'vĕs), town (pop. 6,777), ⊙ González Chaves dist. (□ 1,590; pop. 13,464), S Buenos Aires prov., Argentina, 27 mi. NNE of Tres Arroyos; agr. center (oats, wheat, cattle).
González River, Mexico: see NUEVO, Río.
Gonzalo River, Cuba: see HATIGUANICO RIVER.
Gonzanamá (gōnsänämä'), town (1950 pop. 1,232), Loja prov., S Ecuador, in the Andes, on Pan-American Highway, 20 mi. SW of Loja; alt. 7,329 ft. Cereals, potatoes, livestock. Mfg. of woolen goods (blankets, carpets).
Goochland, county (□ 289; pop. 8,934), central Va.; ⊙ Goochland. Bounded S by James R. Agr. (tobacco, wheat, corn, hay), some dairying, livestock; timber; coal deposits. Has fine old estates. State penal farms are in co. Formed 1727.
Goochland, village (pop. c.100), ⊙ Goochland co., central Va., near the James, 25 mi. WNW of Richmond. State penal farms near by. Rail station at Maidens, 1 mi. S.
Goode, Mount (10,600 ft.), S Alaska, in Chugach Mts., 65 mi. E of Anchorage; 61°20'N 148°W.
Goodell (gŏŏdĕl'), town (pop. 242), Hancock co., N Iowa, 26 mi. SW of Mason City; livestock, grain.
Goodenough, Cape, headland on Wilkes Land, Antarctica, on Norths Coast; 66°5'S 127°5'E. Discovered 1931 by Sir Douglas Mawson.
Goodenough Island, volcanic island, D'Entrecasteaux Isls., Territory of Papua, SW Pacific, 20 mi. SE of New Guinea, across Ward Hunt Strait; 20 mi. long, 15 mi. wide. Formerly Morata.
Goodeve, village (pop. 272), SE Sask., in the Beaver Hills, 33 mi. WSW of Yorkton; mixed farming.
Goodfellow Air Force Base, Texas: see SAN ANGELO.
Goodfellow-Terrace, town (pop. 503), St. Louis co., E Mo.
Good Friday Gulf, N Franklin Dist., Northwest Territories, arm (70 mi. long, 35–60 mi. wide) of the Arctic Ocean, bet. Amund Ringnes Isl. and Axel Heiberg Isl.; 78°N 94°W.
Good Ground, N.Y.: see HAMPTON BAYS.
Good Hope. 1 Town (pop. 189), Walton co., N central Ga., 7 mi. E of Monroe. **2** Village (pop. 392), McDonough co., W Ill., 6 mi. N of Macomb, in agr. and bituminous-coal area; ships grain.
Goodhope, village (pop. 3,366, with adjacent Narco), St. Charles parish, SE La., 15 mi. W of New Orleans.
Good Hope, Cape of, Du. *Kaap van Goede Hoop* (käp' vän khōō'dù hōp'), promontory on the Pacific, northernmost point of New Guinea, on Vogelkop peninsula; 0°21'S 132°25'E. Also called Tanjung Yamursba and Tandjung Jamursba.
Good Hope, Cape of, Afrikaans *Kaap de Goede Hoop* (käp dù khōō'dù hōp'), SW Cape Prov., U. of So. Afr., on the Atlantic, on W side of entrance of False Bay, 30 mi. S of Cape Town and at extremity of Cape Peninsula. Terminates in Cape Point (34°21'S 18°29'E), sheer cliff rising to 840 ft. on Vasco da Gama Peak. On cape is Cape of Good Hope Nature Reserve, established 1939. The cape was 1st rounded (1486) by Bartholomew Diaz, who erected commemorative pillar (of which there are some remains), followed (1497) by Vasco da Gama. The extreme S point of Africa is Cape AGULHAS, c.100 mi. ESE.
Goodhope, Mount (10,670 ft.), SW B.C., in Coast Mts., 140 mi. NNW of Vancouver, overlooking Chilko L.; 51°8'N 124°11'W.
Goodhue, county (□ 758; pop. 32,118), SE Minn.; ⊙ Red Wing. Agr. area drained by Cannon R. and bounded NE by Mississippi R. and Wis. Dairy products, livestock, poultry, corn, oats, barley. Sioux Indian reservation in NE. Co. formed 1853.
Goodhue, village (pop. 489), Goodhue co., SE Minn., near Mississippi R., 12 mi. SSW of Red Wing; dairy products.
Gooding, county (□ 722; pop. 11,101), S Idaho; ⊙ Gooding. Agr. and stock-raising area bounded S by Snake R. Irrigated region around Gooding produces potatoes, dry beans, sugar beets, fruit, alfalfa. Tableland in N slopes to Snake River Plain in S. Co. formed 1913.
Gooding, city (pop. 3,099), ⊙ Gooding co., S Idaho, on Big Wood R. and 16 mi. W of Shoshone in irrigated agr. area (livestock, poultry, fruit, grain). State school for deaf and blind is here. Founded 1883 as Toponis, renamed 1896.
Goodland. 1 Town (pop. 337), Collier co., S Fla., c.50 mi. S of Fort Myers, on Marco Isl. (c.5 mi. long); connected by road with near-by mainland; fishing, clamming; resort. Formerly called Marco, then Collier City. **2** Town (pop. 1,218), Newton co., NW Ind., 32 mi. NW of Lafayette, in agr. area; dairy products; stone quarrying. **3** City (pop. 4,690), ⊙ Sherman co., NW Kansas, 105 mi. NNW of Garden City, in agr. area (grain, livestock, poultry; dairying); railroad maintenance. Fossils have been found in vicinity. Inc. 1887.
Goodlands, village (pop. 4,238), N Mauritius, 6 mi. NNW of Rivière du Rempart; sugar cane.
Goodlettsville, village (pop. 1,590), Davidson co., N central Tenn., 13 mi. N of Nashville.
Goodman. 1 Town (pop. 878), Holmes co., central Miss., c.50 mi. NNE of Jackson, near Big Black R. Has dist. jr. col. **2** Town (pop. 477), McDonald co., extreme SW Mo., in the Ozarks, 10 mi. S of Neosho. **3** Village (1940 pop. 761), Marinette co., NE Wis., 20 mi. SW of Iron Mountain, Mich.; sawmilling, woodworking.
Goodna (gŏŏd'nù), town (pop. 1,159), SE Queensland, Australia, 15 mi. WSW of Brisbane; corn, sugar cane, bananas.
Goodnews or **Goodnews Bay,** village (1939 pop. 48), SW Alaska, on N side of Goodnews Bay, 110 mi. S of Bethel; mining (platinum, gold, osmiridium); trapping.
Goodnews Bay, SW Alaska, inlet (10 mi. long, 1–6 mi. wide) of Kuskokwim Bay, NW of Bristol Bay; 59°5'N 161°40'W. Platinum village at mouth. Region is rich in platinum and osmiridium placers.
Goodnight, (gŏŏd'nīt), village (pop. c.300), Armstrong co., extreme N Texas, on edge of high plains of the Panhandle, 20 mi. WNW of Clarendon; retail center in cattle and grain area.
Goodrich, village (pop. 448), Sheridan co., central N.Dak., 15 mi. E of McClusky.
Goodridge, village (pop. 144), Pennington co., NW Minn., 17 mi. E of Thief River Falls; dairy products.
Goodsir, Mount (11,686 ft.), SE B.C., in Rocky Mts., on S edge of Yoho Natl. Park, 35 mi. W of Banff; 51°12'N 116°23'W.
Goodsonville, N.C.: see BOGER CITY.
Goodsprings, village (1940 pop. 564), Walker co., NW central Ala., 26 mi. WNW of Birmingham.
Good Thunder, village (pop. 476), Blue Earth co., S Minn., on Maple R. and 12 mi. S of Mankato; dairy products.
Goodview, village (pop. 777), Winona co., SW Minn., on Mississippi R. just NW of Winona.
Good Water, town (pop. 1,227), Coosa co., E central Ala., 10 mi. NW of Alexander city; woodworking. Talladega Natl. Forest near by. Inc. 1875.
Goodwell, town (pop. 714), Texas co., extreme NW Okla., 11 mi. SW of Guymon; livestock, grain. Seat of Panhandle Agr. and Mechanical Col.
Goodwick, former urban district (1931 pop. 2,314) now in Fishguard and Goodwick urban dist. (1948 pop. estimate 4,773), N Pembroke, Wales, on Fishguard Bay of Irish Sea; fishing port and resort.
Goodwin, town (pop. 141), Deuel co., E S.Dak., 13 mi. E of Watertown.
Goodwin Sands, a 10-mi. stretch of shoals and sand bars off Channel coast of Kent, England, forming a breakwater E of The Downs roadstead; marked by several lightships and numerous buoys. They have been scene of frequent shipwrecks and constitute major danger to navigation. The Sands are reputed to be remains of isl. of Lomea, property of Earl Godwin.
Goodwood, village, W Sussex, England, 3 mi. NE of Chichester; site of Goodwood House, seat of dukes of Richmond. Surrounding park has racecourse, scene of annual races.
Goodwood, residential town (pop. 33,590), SW Cape Prov., U. of So. Afr., 6 mi. E of Cape Town.
Goodyear. 1 Company town (pop. 1,254), Maricopa co., S central Ariz., 20 mi. SE of Phoenix, in cotton area. Inc. since 1940. **2** Village, Windham co., Conn.: see KILLINGLY.
Goodyear Lake, Otsego co., central N.Y., 5 mi. NE of Oneonta; c.2 mi. long. Resort.
Goole (gōōl), port and municipal borough (1931 pop. 20,239; 1951 census 19,227), West Riding, SE Yorkshire, England, 24 mi. SW of Hull and on Ouse R. at mouth of Don R., with shipyards and a good harbor; 53°42'N 0°55'W. Engages in shipbuilding, metalworking, and mfg. of machinery, chemicals, sugar, flour. Chief exports: woolens, coal, cotton; chief imports: dyes, foodstuffs, timber, raw wool, linen. Terminal of several passenger lines to the Continent.
Goolwa, village (pop. 552), SE South Australia, 40 mi. SSE of Adelaide, near Murray R. mouth; dairy products, livestock.
Goomsur, India: see RUSSELLKONDA.
Goona, India: see GUNA.
Goondiwindi (gŭndùwĭn'dē), town (pop. 2,467), S Queensland, Australia, near New South Wales border, 180 mi. WSW of Brisbane; wheat-raising center.
Goor (khōr), town (pop. 4,996), Overijssel prov., E Netherlands, 9 mi. WSW of Hengelo, near Twente Canal; textile center (cotton mfg., lace and net weaving, bleaching); mfg. of crates, boxes; building stone.
Goorle, Netherlands: see GOIRLE.
Goose Bay, village (1939 pop. 40), S Alaska, on W side of Knik Arm, 13 mi. N of Anchorage; has docks and air landing strip.
Goose Bay, village, SE Labrador, on Goose Bay, inlet of L. Melville, at mouth of Hamilton R.; 53°19'N 60°25'W. The large air base and radio station, built here in Second World War as military and ferrying base, is now used by Canadian commercial aircraft on transatlantic routes. Lumbering.
Gooseberry Island (2 mi. long, 1 mi. wide), in Bonavista Bay, E N.F., 40 mi. E of Gander; 48°53'N 53°38'W.
Goose Creek, former city, Harris co., S Texas; now part of BAYTOWN.
Goose Creek. 1 In Nev. and Idaho, rises in Elko co., NE Nev., flows 70 mi. N, into Cassia co., S Idaho, entering Snake R. near Burley. Dam, 4 mi. SSW of OAKLEY, forms Goose Creek Reservoir. **2** In N Wyo., rises in Bighorn Mts., flows c.40 mi. generally NE, past Sheridan (here receiving Little Goose Creek), to Tongue R. near Mont. line.
Goose Island, Que.: see OIES, ÎLE AUX.
Goose Island (4 mi. long), in S Tierra del Fuego, Chile, at SE entrance of Christmas Sound off Hoste Isl.; 55°22'S 69°50'W.
Goose Lake, town (pop. 148), Clinton co., E Iowa, 13 mi. NW of Clinton; concrete blocks. Limestone quarry near by.
Goose Lake. 1 In Ill.: see BANNER. **2** In S Oregon and N Calif., receding body of water extending N-S across state line in Lake co., Oregon, and Modoc co., Calif.; 28 mi. long, 9 mi. wide.
Goose Land, Rus. *Gusinaya Zemlya* (gōōsē'nĭŭ zĭmlyä'), peninsula on W coast of S isl. of Novaya Zemlya, Russian SFSR; 50 mi. wide, 20 mi. long; 71°45'N 52°E. Belushya Guba is on S coast.
Goose River, E N.Dak., rises in Nelson, Steele, and Grand Forks counties; flows SE, past Mayville and Hillsboro, to Red River of the North near Caledonia; 90 mi. long, including longest branch.
Goosnargh (gōōs'nùr), village and parish (pop. 1,144), central Lancashire, England, 5 mi. NNE of Preston; cattle raising, dairy farming.
Goosport, village (pop. 8,318), Calcasieu parish, SW La., near Lake Charles.
Gooty (gōō'tē), town (pop. 12,333), Anantapur dist., NW Madras, India, 30 mi. N of Anantapur; road junction; grain trade center; cotton ginning; tannery. Noted 11th-cent. fortress on hill (c.2,000 ft.) just E. Granite quarries near by.
Gopalganj (gō'pälgŭnj), village, Faridpur dist., S central East Bengal, E Pakistan, on Madhumati R. and 26 mi. WSW of Madaripur; road terminus; rice milling; rice, jute, oilseeds, sugar cane. Extensive swamps near by.
Gopalpur (gō'pälpŏŏr), village, Ganjam dist., SE Orissa, India, on Bay of Bengal, 9 mi. ESE of Berhampur; small port (open roadstead); seaside resort; exports rice, oilseeds, fish, forest produce; imports vegetable oil, piece goods, kerosene, oil, matches. Lighthouse.
Gopalpur, E Pakistan: see NATOR.
Gopeng (gōpĕng'), town (pop. 3,717), central Perak, Malaya, on W slopes of central Malayan range, 10 mi. SE of Ipoh; a tin-mining center of Kinta Valley.
Gopichettipalaiyam (gōpĭchĕ'tĭpälĭyŭm) or **Gobichettipalaiyam** (gōbĭ-), town (pop. 16,140), Coimbatore dist., S central Madras, India, near Bhavani R., 45 mi. NE of Coimbatore; tobacco, rice, millet. Corundum mined near by. Also spelled Gobichettipalayam and Gobichettipalyam.
Gopiganj (gō'pēgŭnj), town (pop. 4,159), Benares dist., SE Uttar Pradesh, India, 36 mi. W of Benares; rice, barley, gram, wheat, millet. Carpet mfg. 8 mi. E, at village of Aunrai (also called Aurai).
Goplo, Lake (gôp'wô), Pol. *Gopło*, Ger. *Goplosee* (gôp'lōzā") (□ 9), W central Poland, 9 mi. SSE of Inowroclaw; long, narrow; max. depth 52 ft.; forms part of Notec R. course. Known in early times as *Mare Polonosum.*
Göppingen (gŭ'pĭng-ùn), city (pop. 35,784), N Württemberg, Germany, after 1945 in Württemberg-Baden, at N foot of Swabian Jura, on the Fils and 22 mi. ESE of Stuttgart; 48°43'N 9°39'E. Rail junction; transshipment point; noted for its mineral water (exported). Produces agr. and textile machinery, tractors, machine tools, precision instruments (watches, dental equipment), industrial chemicals, pharmaceuticals, textiles (cotton, linen, knit goods, bandages, clothing). Other mfg.: construction togs, ceramics, furniture; leather- and woodworking, printing; glassworks. Has 15th-cent. church, 16th-cent. castle. Chartered 1029. Almost completely destroyed by fire in 1425 and 1782. Hohenstaufen castle is near by.
Gopuri, India: see SEVAGRAM.
Goquao (gō'kwou'), town, Rachgia prov., S Vietnam, 23 mi. SE of Rachgia; rice.
Gor (gôr), town (pop. 1,721), Granada prov., S Spain, 11 mi. NE of Guadix; flour milling, footwear mfg. Olive oil, esparto, sugar beets, aromatic plants; sheep raising.
Gora (gōō'rä), Pol. *Góra*, Ger. *Guhrau* (gōō'rou), town (1939 pop. 5,650; 1946 pop. 3,526) in Lower Silesia, after 1945 in Wroclaw prov., W Poland, 13 mi. S of Leszno; sugar refining, brewing.
Goradiz (gŭrŭdyĕs'), town (1939 pop. over 500), S Azerbaijan SSR, near Aras R. (Iran border), 45 mi. SSE of Agdam; cotton, wheat, sericulture.
Goragorski or **Goragorskiy** (gŭrŭgôr'skē), town (1939 pop. over 500), SW Grozny oblast, Russian SFSR, in Terek Range, 34 mi. WNW of Grozny (linked by oil pipe line); petroleum-production cen-

ter. Developed in late 1930s. Sometimes called Gorski.

Gora Kalwaria (gōō'rä kälvär'yä), Pol. *Góra Kalwaria*, Rus. *Gora-Kalvariya* or *Gora-Kal'variya* (both: gô'rŭ-kŭlvä'rēŭ), town (pop. 3,687), Warszawa prov., E central Poland, on the Vistula and 19 mi. SSE of Warsaw. Rail spur terminus; mfg. of vegetable oil, flour milling, sawmilling. Formerly spelled Gora Kalwarja.

Gorakhpur (gō'rŭkpōōr), district (□ 4,524; pop. 3,963,574), E Uttar Pradesh, India; ⊙ Gorakhpur. Bounded N by Nepal, E by Bihar, S by the Gogra; drained by Rapti R. Agr. (rice, wheat, barley, oilseeds, gram, sugar cane, corn); extensive sal jungle (N). Leading sugar-milling dist. in India. Main centers: Gorakhpur, Barhaj, Padrauna, Deoria. Buddhist remains near KASIA. Formerly spelled Goruckpur.

Gorakhpur, city (pop., including rail colony, 98,977), ⊙ Gorakhpur dist., NE Uttar Pradesh, India, on Rapti R. and 130 mi. NE of Allahabad; rail junction (workshops); road and trade (grains, oilseeds, sugar cane) center; hand-loom cotton weaving; sugar milling. Former recruiting center for Ghurka regiments. Damaged by earthquake in 1934. Founded c.1400; named for Hindu saint. Formerly spelled Goruckpur.

Goram Islands (gôräm') or **Gorong Islands** (gôrōōng'), group of 3 isls., S Moluccas, Indonesia, in Banda Sea 30 mi. SE of Ceram; 4°7'S 131°20'E. Comprise Manawoka (mänäwō'kŭ; 11 mi. long, 2 mi. wide), Goram (8 mi. long, 3 mi. wide), and Panjang (pänjäng'; 7 mi. long, 2 mi. wide). Isls. are wooded and hilly; lumbering.

Gorance or **Gorantse** (both: gô'räntsĕ), hamlet, S Serbia, Yugoslavia, 6 mi. SSW of Kacanik, near Lepenac R. (Macedonia border), in the Kosovo; chromium mine.

Goransko (gô'ränskô), village, N Montenegro, Yugoslavia, on Piva R. and 15 mi. ESE of Gacko. The Durmitor rises 11 mi. E.

Gorazde or **Gorazhde** (both: gô'räzhdĕ), Serbo-Croatian *Goražde*, village (pop. 2,543), SE Bosnia, Yugoslavia, on the Drina, on railroad and 30 mi. ESE of Sarajevo, in fruit- and tobacco-growing area. Serbian printing plant, here, in 16th cent.

Gorbals, Scotland: see GLASGOW.

Gorbatov (gŭrbä'tŭf), city (1926 pop. 3,267), W Gorki oblast, Russian SFSR, on Oka R. and 12 mi. N of Pavlovo; hemp-milling center; rope mfg. Chartered 1779.

Gorbatovka (–kŭ), town (1942 pop. over 500), W Gorki oblast, Russian SFSR, 10 mi. E of Dzerzhinsk; peat works.

Gorbea (gōrbā'ä), town (pop. 2,910), Cautín prov., S central Chile, on railroad and 26 mi. S of Temuco; agr. center (wheat, barley, potatoes, vegetables, livestock); flour milling, lumbering.

Gorbitsa River (gôr'bētsŭ), NE Chita oblast, Russian SFSR, left tributary of Shilka R., which it joins 30 mi. below Ust-Karsk; 45 mi. long. Part of Russo-Chinese frontier from 1689 to 1858.

Gorbunovo, Russian SFSR: see NIZHNI TAGIL.

Gorce (gôr'tsĕ), mountain group in W Beskids, in Krakow prov., S Poland, bet. upper Raba and Dunajec rivers. Highest point (4,301 ft.), the Turbacz, is 6 mi. NE of Nowy Targ.

Gorchakovo, Stantsiya (stän'tsēŭ gŭrchŭkô'vŭ) [Rus., =Gorchakovo station], town (1926 pop. 563), E Fergana oblast, Uzbek SSR, just S of Margelan, on Kokand-Andizhan RR; junction of rail spur to Fergana and Kizyl-Kiya; cotton ginning.

Gorchen, Poland: see MIEJSKA GORKA.

Gorcum, Netherlands: see GORINCHEM.

Gorcy (gôrsē'), village (pop. 860), Meurthe-et-Moselle dept., NE France, on Belg. border, 4 mi. WNW of Longwy; iron founding, steel-wire mfg.

Gorda, Punta (pōōn'tä gôr'dhä), N point of Fuerteventura, Canary Isls., 18 mi. NNW of Puerto de Cabras; 28°45'N 13°55'W.

Gorda, Sierra (syĕ'rä), E range of Sierra Madre Occidental, in Guanajuato, central Mexico, 15 mi. E of San Luis de la Paz; rises to 8,300 ft.

Gordes (gôrd), village (pop. 193), Vaucluse dept., SE France, on S slope of Monts de Vaucluse, 10 mi. WNW of Apt; stone quarries. Cistercian abbey near by.

Gordes (gûrdĕs'), Turkish *Gördes*, village (pop. 3,095), Manisa prov., W Turkey, 50 mi. ENE of Manisa; carpets; wheat, barley, vetch, tobacco; mica and emery near by. Sometimes spelled Gordus.

Gordeyevka (gŭrdyā'ŭfkŭ), village (1926 pop. 1,884), W Bryansk oblast, Russian SFSR, 18 mi. NW of Klintsy; distilling. Also called Gordeyevo.

Gordium (gôr'dēŭm), anc. ⊙ Phrygia, central Asia Minor; its site is c.50 mi. WSW of Ankara, Turkey, just W of Polatli. Here Alexander the Great cut the Gordian knot.

Gordo, town (pop. 952), Pickens co., W Ala., 22 mi. NW of Tuscaloosa; sawmills.

Gordo, Cerro (sĕ'rō gôr'dō), Andean peak (17,500 ft.) on Salta-Catamarca prov. border, NW Argentina, in central Sierra de Aguas Calientes, 32 mi. WSW of Molinos.

Gordo, El (ĕl), town (pop. 1,569), Cáceres prov., W Spain, 28 mi. WSW of Talavera de la Reina; wool-cloth mfg., olive-oil processing; cereals, fruit, wine, livestock.

Gordo, Pico, Azores: see FAIAL ISLAND.

Gordon, Eskimo settlement and trading post (1939 pop. 25), NE Alaska, near Yukon border, on Demarcation Bay of Beaufort Sea, just SE of Demarcation Point; 69°40'N 141°12'W.

Gordon, town (pop. 4,485), E New South Wales, Australia, 8 mi. NNW of Sydney, in metropolitan area; coal-mining center.

Gordon, county (□ 358; pop. 18,922), NW Ga.; ⊙ Calhoun. Valley and ridge area drained by Oostanaula, Conasauga, and Coosawattee rivers. Agr. (cotton, corn, sweet potatoes, hay, fruit, livestock); textile mfg. at Calhoun. Part of Chattahoochee Natl. Forest and New Echota Marker Natl. Monument in W. Formed 1850.

Gordon. 1 Town (pop. 275), Houston co., SE Ala., on Chattahoochee R. (here forming Georgia line) and 18 mi. ESE of Dothan; naval stores. **2** Town (pop. 1,761), Wilkinson co., central Ga., 18 mi. ENE of Macon; clay-mining center. **3** City (pop. 2,058), Sheridan co., NW Nebr., 40 mi. E of Chadron and on branch of Niobrara R. near S.Dak. line; trade and shipping point for agr. region; flour; dairy and poultry produce, grain, livestock. Inc. 1921. **4** Village (pop. 197), Darke co., W Ohio, 14 mi. SSE of Greenville, in agr. area. **5** Borough (pop. 1,039), Schuylkill co., E central Pa., 9 mi. NW of Pottsville; anthracite. Settled 1856, inc. 1891. **6** Town (pop. 404), Palo Pinto co., N central Texas, c.60 mi. WSW of Fort Worth; rail point in agr. area. **7** Village, Douglas co., NW Wis., 31 mi. SSE of Superior, in lake region. A reforestation state nursery is here.

Gordon, Camp, Ga.: see AUGUSTA.

Gordoncillo (gôr-dhōn-thē'lyō), town (pop. 1,336), Leon prov., NW Spain, 34 mi. S of Leon; cereals, wine.

Gordonhorne Peak (9,562 ft.), SE B.C., 60 mi. NNW of Revelstoke; 51°47'N 118°50'W.

Gordon Island (30 mi. long), in Tierra del Fuego, Chile, at Pacific end of Beagle Channel, bet. Hoste Isl. (S) and the main isl. of Tierra del Fuego (N); 55°S 69°30'W.

Gordon River, W Tasmania, rises in King William Range, flows 90 mi. S, W, and NNW, through wild, uninhabited area, to Macquarie Harbour of Indian Ocean; receives Franklin R.

Gordons Bay, Afrikaans *Gordonsbaai* (khôr"dônsbī'), village (pop. 1,021), SW Cape Prov., U. of So. Afr., on E side of False Bay, 30 mi. SE of Cape Town; popular seaside resort; fishing port.

Gordonsburg, town (1940 pop. 315), Lewis co., central Tenn., 22 mi. W of Columbia.

Gordonstoun or **Gordonstown,** agr. village, N Moray, Scotland, 5 mi. NNW of Elgin. The castle, former seat of the Gordon-Cummings, is now site of noted public school.

Gordonsville. 1 Town (pop. 304), Smith co., N central Tenn., 20 mi. E of Lebanon, near Center Hill Dam. **2** Town (pop. 1,118), Orange co., N central Va., 18 mi. NE of Charlottesville; rail junction; trade point in country-estate and agr. area; hosiery mfg. Zachary Taylor's birthplace near by.

Gordon Town, village, SE Jamaica, mtn. resort (alt. c.2,000 ft.) 7 mi. NE of Kingston.

Gordonvale, town (pop. 2,239), NE Queensland, Australia, 15 mi. S of Cairns; agr. center; sugar mill.

Gordonville, city (pop. 130), Cape Girardeau co., SE Mo., near Mississippi R., 8 mi. W of Cape Girardeau.

Gore (gō'rā), town (pop. 25,000), ⊙ Ilubabor prov., SW Ethiopia, on road and 95 mi. WNW of Jimma; 8°9'N 35°33'E; alt. c.6,580 ft. Collecting center for much of coffee exported to Anglo-Egyptian Sudan via Gambela. Airfield. Founded 1910–13.

Gore (gôr), borough (pop. 5,000), S S.Isl., New Zealand, 35 mi. NE of Invercargill and on Mataura R.; rail junction; wool, grain, flour; coal.

Gore, town (pop. 387), Sequoyah co., E Okla., 21 mi. SE of Muskogee, and on Arkansas R.

Gore, Point, S Alaska, cape on Gulf of Alaska at S tip of Kenai Peninsula, 30 mi. SE of Seldovia; 59°12'N 150°58'W.

Gore Bay, town (pop. 702), ⊙ Manitoulin dist., S central Ont., on N Manitoulin Isl., on North Channel of L. Huron, 90 mi. SW of Sudbury; fishing port, with freezing plant, lumber mills; resort.

Gorée (gôrā'), island (c.1,000 yards long, 300 yards wide) and village, W Senegal, Fr. West Africa, on SE tip of Cape Verde peninsula, c.2 mi. E of Dakar, from which extend jetties. Site of govt. school and printing press. Fortified isl. was 1st stronghold of the French who seized it from Dutch in 1677. Became center of slave trade. The French were dislodged several times, last during Napoleonic Wars; returned 1817. With ascendance of Dakar all commercial activity ceased.

Goree (gōrē'), town (pop. 640), Knox co., N Texas, c.65 mi. WSW of Wichita Falls; trade, ginning point in cotton, grain, cattle area.

Goregaon (gō'rāgoun). **1** Village, Bombay Suburban dist., W Bombay, India, on Salsette Isl., 16 mi. N of Bombay city center; rice; chemical mfg., vegetable-oil milling, palmyra-tree tapping. **2** Village, Kolaba dist., Bombay, India: see MANGAON.

Gorele (gûrĕlĕ'), Turkish *Görele*, village (pop. 1,983), Giresun prov., N Turkey, on Black Sea, 32 mi. ENE of Giresun; hazelnuts; copper. Formerly Elevi.

Gorelki (gŭryĕl'kē), town (1948 pop. over 500), N Tula oblast, Russian SFSR, 4 mi. N of Tula.

Goreloye (gŭryĕ'lŭyŭ), village (1926 pop. 6,217), central Tambov oblast, Russian SFSR, on Tsna R. (locks) and 13 mi. N of Tambov; potatoes.

Gore Mountain, N.Y.: see NORTH CREEK.

Gorenji Logatec, Yugoslavia: see DOLENJI LOGATEC.

Gore Pass (9,000 ft.), N Colo., in Park Range at N end of Gore Range, W of Kremmling. Crossed by highway.

Gore Range, part of Park Range in N central Colo.; extends SSE from Kremmling to Breckenridge, bet. Eagle and Blue rivers. Chief peaks: Red Peak (13,183 ft.), Blue River Peak (13,000 ft.), Mt. Powell (13,398 ft.). Crossed in S by Shrine Pass (11,075 ft.) and Vail Pass (10,603 ft.). Occupies natl. forest area.

Goresbridge (gôrzbrĭj'), Gaelic *Crosaire na Ghúlaigh*, town (pop. 291), E Co. Kilkenny, Ireland, on Barrow R. and 11 mi. E of Kilkenny; agr. market (cattle; barley, potatoes).

Goretti, India: see GAURHATI.

Goreville, village (pop. 581), Johnson co., S Ill., 17 mi. S of Herrin, in fruitgrowing region of Ill. Ozarks.

Gorey, fishing village, Jersey, Channel Isls., on E coast of isl., 4 mi. ENE of St. Helier; lighthouse (49°12'N 2°1'W). Near by is Mont Orgueil Castle, dating from 12th cent.

Gorey, Gaelic *Guaire*, town (pop. 2,687), NE Co. Wexford, Ireland, 17 mi. NE of Enniscorthy; agr. market (dairying; wheat, barley, potatoes, beets); tanneries.

Gorgan, Iran: see GURGAN.

Gorgany Mountains (gŭrgä'nē), section of the Carpathians in SW Ukrainian SSR; extend 70 mi. SE-NW, bet. Veretski and Yablonitsa passes; rise to 6,023 ft. in Syvulya peak; thick forests cover 80% of area (oak and beech on lower slopes; conifers at higher alt.); sheep grazing in subalpine meadows.

Gorgas (gôr'gŭs), village (1940 pop. 895), Walker co., NW central Ala., on Mulberry Fork and 25 mi. WNW of Birmingham. There are 2 power plants near by, on Black Warrior R.

Görgenyszentimbre, Rumania: see GURGHIU.

Gorgol River (gôrgôl'), principal Senegal R. affluent in Mauritania, Fr. West Africa, formed by union of Gorgol Blanc (right) and Gorgol Noir (left) which rise W of Kiffa and join 40 mi. E of Kaédi, its mouth on the Senegal. The combined stream is navigable for canoes bet. Aug. and Oct.

Gorgona (gôrgô'nä), northernmost island (□ .8; pop. 138) of Tuscan Archipelago, in Tyrrhenian Sea, Italy, in Livorno prov., 22 mi. WSW of Leghorn; 1 mi. long; rises to 689 ft. (W). Contains agr. penal colony.

Gorgona Island (gôrgō'nä), off Pacific coast of SW Colombia, 32 mi. NW of Guapi (Cauca dept.); 3°N 78°12'W; 6 mi. long, c.2 mi. wide.

Gorgonzola (gôr"gŭnzō'lŭ, It. gôrgônzô'lä), town (pop. 4,754), Milano prov., Lombardy, N Italy, 11 mi. ENE of Milan. Noted for its pressed-milk cheese; mfg. (silk textiles, hosiery, bicycles, sausage).

Gorgora (gōr'gōrä), village, Begemdir prov., NW Ethiopia, on N shore of L. Tana, 28 mi. SW of Gondar, in cereal-growing and stock-raising (cattle, sheep) region; road terminus.

Gorgue, La (lä gôrg'), town (pop. 2,039), Nord dept., N France, on the Lys and 8 mi. NNE of Béthune; textile weaving (chiefly linen), metal-working, vegetable preserving.

Gorham (gô'rŭm). **1** Village (pop. 447), Jackson co., SW Ill., 25 mi. WSW of Herrin, in agr. region. **2** City (pop. 375), Russell co., central Kansas, 8 mi. W of Russell. **3** Agr. town (pop. 4,742), including Gorham village (pop. 1,911), Cumberland co., SW Maine, just W of Portland. Seat of a state teachers col. Includes part of South Windham village. Settled on land grant of 1728, inc. 1764. **4** Town (pop. 2,639), including Gorham village (pop. 1,739), Coos co., NE N.H., on the Androscoggin just below Berlin, at mouth of Peabody R.; surrounded by peaks of Presidential Range; paper milling; resort center, with annual winter carnival. Settled c.1805, inc. 1836.

Gori (gô'rē), city (1926 pop. 10,547, 1939 pop. 15,000), central Georgian SSR, in Kartlia region, on Kura R., on railroad and 38 mi. WNW of Tiflis. Road center; junction of railroad to Stalinir; industrial hub in orchard and truck-garden dist.; cotton milling, fruit and vegetable canning, sawmilling; wineries, glassworks. Teachers col. First mentioned as fortress in 12th cent.; passed (1801) to Russia. Destructive earthquake here in 1920. Stalin b. here.

Goribidnur (gō'rĭbĭdnōōr), town (pop. 5,162), Kolar dist., E Mysore, India, on Penner R. and 45 mi. N of Bengalore; match mfg., oilseed milling; handicrafts (wickerwork, biris, woolen blankets).

Gorica, Italy: see GORIZIA, city.

Gorica, oblast, Yugoslavia: see NOVA GORICA.

Gorin, Mo.: see SOUTH GORIN.

Gorinchem or **Gorkum** (both: khôr'kŭm), town (pop. 15,321), South Holland prov., SW Netherlands, on Upper Merwede R. and 13 mi. E of Dordrecht; rail junction; mfg. of steel and copper wire, machinery, cement, shoes; shipbuilding, sugar refining, fish canning; gasoline storage tanks; dairy products. Has 15th-cent. church, 16th-cent. Bethlehem House (now site of Old Gorinchem Mus.). Town mentioned in 13th. cent.; became a major trade center in 15th. cent.; captured by Beggars of the Sea in 1572. Sometimes spelled Gorcum.

Goring, residential town and parish (pop. 1,929), S Oxfordshire, England, on the Thames and 5 mi. S of Wallingford. Has 12th-cent. church. Also called Goring-on-Thames.

Goring-by-Sea, England: see WORTHING.

Goring Tso, Tibet: see ZILLING TSO.

Goris (gô'rēs), city (1926 pop. 2,960), SE Armenian SSR, in Karabakh Upland, 55 mi. ENE of Nakhichevan; sericulture, tobacco; rug weaving. Formerly Geryusy.

Goritsy (gŭrē'tsē), village (1926 pop. 505), SE Kalinin oblast, Russian SFSR, 30 mi. NW of Kimry; flax.

Göritz, Poland: see GORZYCA.

Gorizia (gōrī'tsēŭ, It. gôrē'tsyä), province (□ 181; pop. 115,252), FRIULI–VENEZIA GIULIA, NE Italy; ⊙ Gorizia. Borders on Yugoslavia, Free Territory of Trieste, and the Adriatic; largely plain, enclosed by hills on N and E. Watered by lower Isonzo river. Agr. (cereals, fruit, vegetables); cattle raising. Mfg. at Gorizia and Monfalcone. By 1947 treaty of peace, Gorizia lost territory (□ 871; pop. 84,900) in N and E to Yugoslavia.

Gorizia, Ger. *Görz* (gûrts), Slovenian *Gorica,* city (pop. 30,265), ⊙ Gorizia prov., Friuli–Venezia Giulia, NE Italy, on Yugoslav border, on Isonzo R. and 21 mi. NNW of Trieste; 45°56'N 12°37'E. Road, rail, and industrial center; mfg. (textile machinery, electrical equipment, agr. tools, organs, canned foods, paper, soap, tar, dyes, shoes, hosiery). Archbishopric. Has 14th-cent. cathedral (frequently remodeled), baroque church (1680–1725), old castle, and palace (1745) with mus. Was ⊙, with Gradisca, of former Austrian crownland of Görz-Gradisca (□ 1,127; 1910 pop. 256,471), annexed by Italy in 1919. During First World War, region was scene of heavy fighting bet. Austrians and Italians; city suffered severe damage. By 1947 treaty of peace, Yugoslavia received E outskirts where new Yugoslav city of NOVA GORICA was built.

Gorj, Rumania: see TARGU-JIU.

Gorjanci, mountains, Yugoslavia: see ZUMBERAK MOUNTAINS.

Görkau, Czechoslovakia: see JIRKOV.

Gorkha, Nepal: see GURKHA.

Gorki, Gorky, or **Gor'kiy** (gôr'kē), oblast (□ 29,100; 1946 pop. estimate 3,600,000) in central European Russian SFSR; ⊙ Gorki. Drained by Volga and lower Oka rivers. Industrialized lower Oka R. valley (SW) has largest urban centers; metal handicraft industries (Pavlovo), and metallurgical works (Vyksa, Tashino, Kulebaki); wooded steppe (SE) has grain agr.; extensive forested region (N) has flax and potatoe agr. Mfg. (ships, railway stock, locomotives, automobiles, paper-making machinery, machine tools). Lumbering, with wood cracking (Vakhtan) and paper milling (Pravdinsk). Chemical industry (Dzerzhinsk) uses phosphorites, peat, limestone, and gypsum. Also petroleum refining at Gorki, shoe and leather industry at Bogorodsk, hemp milling (ropes, fishnets) at Reshetikha and Gorbatov. Power furnished by local peat (Gidrotorf) and by lumber, Baku oil, and Donbas coal. Volga and Oka rivers carry half of freight, with good rail network (S); N served by Gorki-Kirov line. Formed 1929 as a territory (Rus. *krai* or *kray*) which included Chuvash Autonomous SSR, Mari and Udmurt Autonomous Oblasts; became an oblast in 1936. Called Nizhegorod (a contracted form of Nizhni Novgorod) until 1932.

Gorki. 1 City (1939 pop. over 10,000), NE Mogilev oblast, Belorussian SSR, on Pronya R. and 28 mi. SE of Orsha; mfg. (starch, molasses, clothing), lumber milling. Agr. col., agr. experiment station. Power plant. **2** or **Gorky** or **Gor'kiy,** city (1926 pop. 222,356; 1939 pop. 644,116; 1946 estimate 900,000), ⊙ Gorki oblast, Russian SFSR, on right bank of Volga R. (below Gorki dam at GORODETS), at mouth of the Oka, and 260 mi. E of Moscow; 56°20'N 44°E. Major transportation and industrial center and (after Second World War) 4th-largest city of USSR; junction of 3 rail lines and Volga-Oka river traffic. Mfg. (rolling stock, locomotives, automobiles, ships, airplanes, oil-drilling machinery, bridging equipment, generators, machine tools, metal goods, Diesel motors, radio, telephone, and electrical equipment, glass products, shoes); chemicals (oil gas, acids, petroleum products); sawmilling, woodworking, woolen and flour milling, dairying. Oldest section, on high right bank of Oka R., is site of 13th-cent. turreted kremlin with palace (now oblast administration seat) and two 13th-cent. cathedrals, Rus. baroque Stroganov church (1719), university, medical, agr., chemical, river transportation, and machine-building institutes, regional and art mus. Across Oka R. (bridged) lies industrial dist. of Kanavino, with site of former fairs and Molotov auto plant. Six mi. WNW of kremlin, on Volga R., lies Sormovo, site of noted shipyards and rolling-stock and locomotive works (founded 1848); inc. (c.1928) into Gorki city, which extends 10 mi. along right Volga R. bank and 10 mi. along lower Oka R. Founded (1221) by Vladimir princes as outpost against Mordvinians and Volga Bulgars, and named Nizhni Novgorod. Became important trading center and (1350) ⊙ principality, which fell (1393) to Moscow. Proximity of fairs at MAKARYEV turned city into most flourishing 17th-cent. city of Moscow domain. Center of resistance against Poles (1611–12). Became famous for its fairs, held yearly after 1817, except during revolution and civil war; the fairs were dissolved in 1930. Balakirev, 19th-cent. composer, and Maxim Gorki, for whom it was renamed (1932), b. here. Damaged by Ger. air raids during Second World War. **3** or **Gorki Leninskoye** (lyĕ'nyĭnskŭyŭ), village, central Moscow oblast, Russian SFSR, 17 mi. SSE of Moscow, 8 mi. SSE of Lenino. Former country home of V. I. Lenin, who died here; memorial mus.

Gorki-Pavlovy, Russian SFSR: see KAMINSKI.

Gorkovskoye or **Gor'kovskoye** (gôr'kŭfskŭyŭ), village (1939 pop. over 2,000), E Omsk oblast, Russian SFSR, 27 mi. NNW of Kalachinsk; dairy farming; metalworking. Formerly Ikonnikovo.

Gorkum, Netherlands: see GORINCHEM.

Gorlago (gôrlä'gô), village (pop. 1,923), Bergamo prov., Lombardy, N Italy, 7 mi. ESE of Bergamo; button factories.

Gorleston, England: see YARMOUTH.

Gorlev (gûr'lĕv), Dan. *Gørlev,* town (pop. 1,285), Holbaek amt, W Zealand, Denmark, 22 mi. WSW of Holbaek; sugar refinery.

Gorlice (gôrlē'tsē), town (pop. 6,100), Rzeszow prov., SE Poland, 20 mi. E of Nowy Sacz; rail spur terminus; petroleum refinery; mfg. of fertilizer, boilers, ceramic products.

Görlitz (gûr'lĭts), city (pop. 85,686) in former Prussian Lower Silesia prov., E Germany, after 1945 in Saxony, on left bank of the Lusatian (Görlitzer) Neisse and 55 mi. E of Dresden, 90 mi. W of Breslau; 51°10'N 14°59'E. Following 1945 div. along the Neisse, section on right bank of river came under Pol. administration and is now called ZGORZELEC by Poles. Görlitz is chief city of Upper Lusatia, in important lignite-mining region; rail junction; woolen and linen milling, metal working, brewing, mfg. of railroad cars, machinery, glass, electric lamps, chemicals, leather goods. Lutheran bishopric. Has 15th-cent. church, 16th-cent. reproduction of the Holy Sepulchre, remains of 14th-cent. castle, many 16th-cent. houses. Jakob Boehme lived here. Bohemian town of Görlitz was founded c.1200 near Slav village of Gorlice (1st mentioned 1071); passed (1253) to margraves of Brandenburg; returned 1323 to Bohemia. Joined Lusatian League in 1346; was (1377–96) ⊙ duchy of Görlitz; withstood Hussite attack in 1429. Passed 1526 to Hapsburgs; later joined Schmalkaldic League. Devastated during Thirty Years War; transferred 1635 to Saxony under Treaty of Prague; passed 1815 to Prussia. Damaged by artillery fire in Second World War; captured (May 8, 1945) by Soviet troops.

Görlitzer Neisse River, Germany: see NEISSE RIVER.

Gorlovka (gôr'lŭfkŭ), city (1926 pop. 23,125; 1939 pop. 108,693), central Stalino oblast, Ukrainian SSR, in the Donbas, 25 mi. NNE of Stalino; rail junction; major coal-mining and industrial center; mfg. of coal-mining machines; coke, nitrate fertilizers. Suburbs include Nikitovka, Kalininsk, Komsomolsk.

Gorlovo (gôr'lŭvŭ), village (1926 pop. 5,154), W Ryazan oblast, Russian SFSR, near railroad (Millionaya station), 21 mi. W of Skopin; wheat.

Gorman, city (pop. 1,317), Eastland co., N central Texas, 38 mi. NNE of Brownwood; rail, market point in peanut-producing area. Founded 1890, inc. 1902.

Gormanston or **Gormanstown** (gôr'mŭnstŭn), Gaelic *Rinn Mhic Gormáin,* fishing village, E Co. Meath, Ireland, on the Irish Sea, 3 mi. NW of Balbriggan.

Gormanston (gôr'mŭnztŭn), town (pop. 493), W Tasmania, 90 mi. WSW of Launceston. Zinc-lead mines near by.

Gorna-banya (gôr'nä-bä'nyä), village (pop. 3,729), Sofia dist., W Bulgaria, W suburb of Sofia; health resort (thermal springs); fruit, truck, livestock. Formerly Yukari-banya.

Gorna Dzhumaya (jōō'mī'ä) [Bulg.,=upper Dzhumaya], after 1950 called **Blagoyevgrad** (blägô'yĕvgrät), city (pop. 14,066), ⊙ Gorna Dzhumaya dist. (formed 1949), SW Bulgaria, near Struma R., 50 mi. S of Sofia. Health resort and watering place; commercial center; tobacco processing. Has ruins of anc. Roman settlement. The chief center of Bulg. Macedonia, it was renamed 1950. Sometimes spelled Gorna Jumaya. Lower Dzhumaya (Gr. *Kato Tzoumagia*) is a Gr. Macedonian town now called HERAKLEIA.

Gorna Gnoinitsa or **Gorna Gnoynitsa** (gnoinē'tsä), village (pop. 3,226), Vidin dist., NW Bulgaria, 20 mi. SE of Lom; grain, legumes.

Gorna Jumaya, Bulgaria: see GORNA DZHUMAYA.

Gorna Mitropoliya (mĕtrôpôlē'ä), village (pop. 3,407), Pleven dist., N Bulgaria, 9 mi. WNW of Pleven; grain, oil-bearing plants, legumes, sugar beets.

Gorna Oryakhovitsa (ôryä'khôvĕtsä), city (pop. 10,303), ⊙ Gorna Oryakhovitsa dist. (formed 1949), N Bulgaria, near Yantra R., 60 mi. ESE o[f] Pleven; major rail junction; cattle market, grape-exporting center; sugar and flour milling, tanning mfg. of chemical fertilizers, distilling, winemaking fruit canning, vegetable-oil extracting. Has schoo[l] of horticulture. Developed following building o[f] Sofia-Stalin RR.

Gornaya Shoriya (gôr'nĭŭ shô'rēŭ), mountainou[s] region (□ 8,300) at SW end of Kuznetsk Ala-Tau in S Kemerovo oblast, Russian SFSR, just S o[f] Kuznetsk Basin; heavily forested. Inhabited b[y] Shors, a Tatar group who engage in fur trapping semi-nomadic livestock raising, lumbering. Chiefl[y] important for extensive iron deposits (TELBES TEMIR-TAU, TASHTAGOL), manganese reserve[s] (USA RIVER), limestone, dolomite, quartz (Chu gunash), fireproof clays.

Gornergrat (gôr'nŭrgrät"), sharp, rocky ridg[e] (10,283 ft.), part of the Rifflehorn, in Pennin[e] Alps, S Switzerland, 3 mi. SSE of Zermatt, wit[h] which it is connected by rack-and-pinion railway Below is Gorner Glacier (c.5 mi. long). Gornergra[t] is noted for its extraordinary view of the Mont[e] Rosa–Breithorn–Matterhorn group of mts.

Gorni Dabnik (gôr'nē dŭbnēk'), village (pop. 3,847) Pleven dist., N Bulgaria, 14 mi. WSW of Pleven grain, oil-bearing plants, legumes. Sometime[s] spelled Dubnik.

Gornja Lendava, Yugoslavia: see LENDAVA, village

Gornja Radgona (gôrn'yä räd'gônä), Ger. *Oberrad kersburg* (ō'bŭrrä"tkûrs-bŏŏrk), village (pop 1,880), NE Slovenia, Yugoslavia, on Mura R opposite Radkersburg (Austria), on railroad an[d] 20 mi. NE of Maribor, at E foot of the Slovensk[e] Gorice. Trade center for winegrowing region champagne. Until 1918, in Styria.

Gornja Stubica, Yugoslavia: see DONJA STUBICA.

Gornji Grad (gôr'nyē grät'), Ger. *Oberburg* (ō'bŭr bŏŏrk"), village, N Slovenia, Yugoslavia, 22 mi NE of Ljubljana, at E foot of Savinja Alps; summe[r] resort; lumbering. Former monastery, with churc[h] and castle of bishops of Ljubljana. Until 1918 in Styria.

Gornji Lapac, Yugoslavia: see DONJI LAPAC.

Gornji Milanovac, Yugoslavia: see MILANOVAC central Serbia.

Gornji Vakuf or **Gornyi Vakuf** (fä'kŏŏf), village, [S] Bosnia, Yugoslavia, on Vrbas R. and 40 mi. W o[f] Sarajevo. Alluvial gold deposits near by. Coppe[r] mine at Mracaj, Serbo-Croatian *Mračaj,* 4 mi. SS[E] of town.

Gorno Ablanovo (gôr'nô äblä'nôvô), village (pop 3,650), Ruse dist., NE Bulgaria, 17 mi. SW of Ruse wheat, rye, sunflowers.

Gorno-Altai Autonomous Oblast or **Gorno-Alta[i] Autonomous Oblast** (gôr"nŭ-ŭltī') [Rus.,=moun tainous Altai], administrative division (□ 35,800 1939 pop. 161,431) of SE Altai Territory, in SW Siberian Russian SFSR; ⊙ Gorno-Altaisk. I[n] ALTAI MOUNTAINS, on Mongolian border; draine[d] by Biya and Katun rivers. Continental climate Has many mineral resources, chiefly gold, man ganese, and mercury; over ½ of area is foreste[d] (mainly NE). Pop. 52% Russian, 37% Altai tribes (Oirots, Telenget, Teleut). Agr. and dair[y] farming (cheese, butter) in NE river valleys; live stock raising (sheep, cattle, maral); hunting, lum bering, fishing; furniture making, mfg. of fel[t] boots. Chuya highway to Mongolia passes alon[g] Katun and Chuya rivers; serves popular touris[t] area. Formed 1922; called Oirot or Oyrot (Oira or Oyrat, until 1936) Autonomous Oblast unt[il] 1948.

Gorno-Altaisk or **Gorno-Altaysk** (–ŭltīsk'), cit[y] (1939 pop. 23,573), ⊙ Gorno-Altai Autonomou[s] Oblast, Altai Territory, Russian SFSR, nea[r] Katun R. (head of navigation), 130 mi. SE o[f] Barnaul; 51°58'N 85°55'E. Agr. center; dairying sawmilling, tanning; brickworks. Originally Ulala known as Oirot-Tura or Oyrot-Tura, 1936–48.

Gorno-Badakhshan Autonomous Oblast (–bŭdŭkh shän') [Rus.,=mountain Badakhshan], administra tive division (□ 23,600; 1946 pop. estimate 50,000 of SE Tadzhik SSR; ⊙ Khorog. In the PAMIR bounded E by China, S and W by Afghanistan separated by 10-mi.-wide land tongue from Paki stan. E section has high plateau character (11,500 13,000 ft.), W section has deep valleys and hig[h] ranges oriented E–W; drained by affluents of Pan[j] R., which forms USSR-Afghanistan border. In cludes many lakes (Kara-Kul, Sarez L., Yashil-Kul Zor-Kul). Mainly livestock raising (cattle, sheep goats, yak); some wheat grown in low valleys Gold placers (Rang-Kul) and salt deposits. Im portant Osh-Khorog mtn. highway forms mai[n] transportation route. Pop. mainly Tadzhik tribe[s] (W); some Kirghiz (E). Formed 1927.

Gornostayevka (gŭrnŭstī'ŭfkŭ), village (1926 pop 4,257), central Kherson oblast, Ukrainian SSR near Dnieper R., 55 mi. NE of Kherson; metal works.

Gornozavodsk (gôr"nŭzŭvôtsk'), city (1940 pop 10,345), on W coast of S Sakhalin, Russian SFSR 7 mi. S of Nevelsk; S rail terminus of W coast railroad; coal-mining center; tar works. Under Jap rule (1905–45), called Naihoro (nīhō'rō).

Gorny or **Gornyy** (gôr'nē), town (1939 pop. over 2,000), E central Saratov oblast, Russian SFSR, on rail spur and 10 mi. SW of Rukopol; oil-shale mining center. Developed in late 1930s, N of Savelyevka village.

Gornya, in Yugoslav names: see GORNJA.

Gornyak (gŭrnyäk'). **1** Town (1946 pop. over 500), SW Altai Territory, Russian SFSR, on railroad and 30 mi. S of Rubtsovsk; lead-zinc mine. Until 1946, called Zolotushino mine. **2** Town, Chelyabinsk oblast, Russian SFSR: see KOPEISK.

Gornyatski or **Gornyatskiy** (gŭrnyät'skē), town (1946 pop. over 500), NE Komi Autonomous SSR, Russian SFSR; NE suburb of Vorkuta; coal mines.

Gorny Balyklei or **Gornyy Balykley** (gôr'nē bŭlĭklyā'), village (1926 pop. 4,963), E central Stalingrad oblast, Russian SFSR, on right bank of Volga R. (landing) and 40 mi. SSW of Kamyshin, in melon dist.; wheat, cattle. Formerly called Balyklei. Verkhni Balyklei, village (1926 pop. 3,539), is across river.

Gornyi, in Yugoslav names: see GORNJI.

Goroblagodatskaya, Russian SFSR: see KUSHVA; BLAGODAT.

Gorodenka (gŭrŭdyĕn'kŭ), Pol. *Horodenka* (hôrô-dĕn'kä), city (1931 pop. 12,303), E Stanislav oblast, Ukrainian SSR, on right tributary of the Dniester and 23 mi. NE of Kolomyya; agr. center; food processing (grain, tobacco, flax, hops, fruit, vegetables), sugar refining; stone quarrying. Has ruins of 15th-cent. castle. Passed from Poland to Austria (1772); reverted to Poland (1919); ceded to USSR in 1945.

Gorodets (gŭrŭdyĕts'), city (1926 pop. 11,336), W Gorki oblast, Russian SFSR, on Volga R., at Gorki dam, and 30 mi. NW of Gorki; shipbuilding, light mfg. Has several old churches, remains of old earthen wall. Former center of Old Believers. Dates from 1152; became E border fortress of Rostov-Suzdal principality; passed (1393) to Moscow. Alexander Nevski died here, 1263. Gorki dam (8 mi. long) across the Volga is designed to create on right Volga bank a storage reservoir (□ c.600), linked by ship canal with the river at Gorodets. New city, opposite Gorodets, is site of hydroelectric station, linked by rail with Pravdinsk.

Gorodeya (gŭrŭdyā'ŭ), Pol. *Horodziej* (hôrô'dzyā), town (1939 pop. over 500), E Baranovichi oblast, Belorussian SSR, 23 mi. NE of Baranovichi; rye, oats, potatoes.

Gorodishche (gŭrŭdyēsh'chĭ). **1** Pol. *Horodyszcze* (hôrôdĭsh'chĕ), town (1931 pop. 1,020), central Baranovichi oblast, Belorussian SSR, 14 mi. N of Baranovichi; cement mfg., tanning, flour milling. Has ruins of 10th-cent. fortress. **2** Pol. *Horodyszcze,* village (1939 pop. over 500), S Pinsk oblast, Belorussian SSR, in Pripet Marshes, on Yaselda R., at mouth of the Pina, 9 mi. NE of Pinsk; woodworking, veneering. Has 17th-cent. church and nunnery. **3** City (1926 pop. 4,934), E central Penza oblast, Russian SFSR, 29 mi. ENE of Penza, in grain area; distilling, flour milling, match mfg. Chartered 1783. **4** Village (1926 pop. 2,261), S central Stalingrad oblast, Russian SFSR, near N branch of Stalingrad circular railroad, 5 mi. N of Stalingrad; truck produce. **5** City, Dnepropetrovsk oblast, Ukrainian SSR: see MARGANETS. **6** Town (1926 pop. 13,520), SE Kiev oblast, Ukrainian SSR, 30 mi. WSW of Cherkassy; sugar-refining center. Called (c.1935–44) Imeni G. I. Petrovskogo.

Gorodishchi (–chē), town (1926 pop. 2,917), W Vladimir oblast, Russian SFSR, on Klyazma R., on railroad (Usad station) and 6 mi. NE of Orekhovo-Zuyevo; cotton-milling center.

Gorodnitsa (gŭrŭdnyē'tsŭ), town (1926 pop. 2,721), W Zhitomir oblast, Ukrainian SSR, on Sluch R. and 20 mi. NW of Novograd-Volynski; rail terminus; ceramics (feldspar quarries); sawmill.

Gorodnya (gŭrôd'nyŭ), town (1926 pop. 4,992), NW Chernigov oblast, Ukrainian SSR, 31 mi. NNE of Chernigov; metalworking, dairying; peat cutting.

Gorodok (gŭrŭdôk'). **1** City (1926 pop. 5,508), N Vitebsk oblast, Belorussian SSR, 20 mi. NNW of Vitebsk; mfg. of transportation equipment; sawmilling, food products. **2** City (1939 pop. over 2,000), SW Buryat-Mongol Autonomous SSR, Russian SFSR, on Dzhida R. and 210 mi. SW of Ulan-Ude, 10 mi. from Mongolian frontier. Center of molybdenum- and tungsten-mining area along upper Dzhida R.; developed in late 1930s. **3** Town (1926 pop. 7,787), W Kamenets-Podolski oblast, Ukrainian SSR, 25 mi. SW of Proskurov; sugar refining, machine mfg. Also called Gorodok-Proskurovski. **4** Pol. *Gródek Jagielloński* (grōō'dĕk yägyĕlôn'yŭskē), city (1931 pop. 12,942), SW Lvov oblast, Ukrainian SSR, 16 mi. WSW of Lvov; agr. processing (grain, flax, vegetables). Fisheries along small Vereshitsa L. (N). Has monument to Pol. king Wladislaw Jagiello. Under Austrian rule (1772–1918); reverted to Poland (1919); ceded to USSR in 1945.

Goroka (gōrōkä'), town, Territory of New Guinea, 110 mi. WNW of Lae, in central highlands; govt. station.

Goroken (gō'rōkĕn), peak (10,748 ft.) in highlands of central Ethiopia, N of Omo R. source, 45 mi. ENE of Nakamti.

Gorokhov (gŭrô'khŭf), Pol. *Horochów* (hôrô'khōōf), city (1931 pop. 5,991), S Volyn oblast, Ukrainian SSR, on left tributary of Styr R. and 30 mi. SW of Lutsk; tanning, flour milling, brick mfg. Has old church, ruins of medieval palace. Passed from Poland to Russia (1795); reverted to Poland (1921); ceded to USSR in 1945.

Gorokhovets (gŭrô'khŭvyĭts), city (1926 pop. 3,957), NE Vladimir oblast, Russian SFSR, on Klyazma R. and 21 mi. E of Vyazniki; metalworking center; boatbuilding, paper milling. Has 1643 Nikolski monastery, 17th-cent. cathedral. Founded 1239.

Görömbölytapolca, Hungary: see TAPOLCA.

Goromna, Ireland: see GORUMNA.

Goromonzi (gōrōmōn'zē), village, Salisbury prov., NE central Southern Rhodesia, in Mashonaland, 22 mi. E of Salisbury; tobacco, wheat, corn, citrus fruit, dairy products. Police post. Has native secondary school.

Gorong Islands, Indonesia: see GORAM ISLANDS.

Gorontalo (gôrôntä'lō), town (pop. 15,603), N Celebes, Indonesia, port on islet of Gulf of Tomini, 140 mi. WSW of Manado; 0°31'N 123°3'E; trade center, shipping timber, resin, rattan, kapok, copra, hides.

Gorontalo, Gulf of, Indonesia; see TOMINI, GULF OF.

Goroshki, Ukrainian SSR: see VOLODARSK-VOLYNSKI.

Gorowo Ilaweckie (gōōrô'wô ēwävĕts'kyĕ), Pol. *Górowo Iławeckie,* Ger. *Landsberg* (länts'bĕrk), town (1939 pop. 3,120; 1946 pop. 939) in East Prussia, after 1945 in Olsztyn prov., NE Poland, 30 mi. S of Kaliningrad, near USSR border; grain and cattle market. After 1945 briefly called Gorowo Pruskie, Pol. *Górowo Pruskie.*

Gorrahei (gō'rähā), village (pop. 200), Harar prov., SE Ethiopia, in the Ogaden, on Fafan R., on road, and 125 mi. SE of Dagahbur. Occupied by Italians (1935) after aerial bombardment in Italo-Ethiopian War and by British (1941) in Second World War. Sometimes spelled Gorrahai.

Gorredijk (khô"rŭdĭk'), town (pop. 3,063), Friesland prov., N Netherlands, 6 mi. ENE of Heerenveen; limekilns; boat building; mfg. (dairy machinery, milk cans, baby carriages); cattle market. Sometimes spelled Gorredyk.

Gorrie, village (pop. estimate 500), S Ont., on Maitland R. and 30 mi. ENE of Goderich; dairying, mixed farming.

Gorriti Island (gôrē'tē), small islet off coast of Maldonado dept., S Uruguay, just W of Punta del Este, guarding the port of Maldonado city.

Gorron (gôrō'), village (pop. 1,654), Mayenne dept., W France, 11 mi. NW of Mayenne; makes military footwear.

Gorseinon (gôrsī'nŭn), town (pop. 4,546) in Llwchwr urban dist., W Glamorgan, Wales, 5 mi. NW of Swansea; coal mining, tinplate mfg.

Gorshechnoye (gŭrshĕch'nŭyŭ), village (1926 pop. 2,391), E Kursk oblast, Russian SFSR, 17 mi. NNE of Stary Oskol; wheat.

Gorskaya Autonomous Soviet Socialist Republic, Russian SFSR: see MOUNTAIN AUTONOMOUS SOVIET SOCIALIST REPUBLIC.

Gorski, Russian SFSR: see GORAGORSKI.

Gorski Izvor (gôr'skē ĕz'vôr), village (pop. 3,575), Khaskovo dist., S central Bulgaria, 9 mi. NW of Khaskovo; cotton, tobacco, vineyards. Formerly Kuru-cheshme.

Gorski Kotar (kô'tär) [Serbo-Croatian, =mountainous district], region in NW Croatia, Yugoslavia, in Dinaric Alps. Highest peak, Veliki Risnjak (5,012 ft.), is 12 mi. NE of Rijeka (Fiume). Large pine forests; tourist area.

Gorsko-Ivanovskoye, Ukrainian SSR: see GORSKOYE, Voroshilovgrad oblast.

Gorsko Slivovo (gôr'skô slē'vôvô), village (pop. 3,615), Gorna Oryakhovitsa dist., N Bulgaria, 12 mi. N of Sevliyevo; horticulture, grain, livestock. Formerly Daa Slivovo.

Gorskoye (gôr'skŭyŭ). **1** City (1939 pop. over 2,000), W Voroshilovgrad oblast, Ukrainian SSR, in the Donbas, 10 mi. NNE of Popasnaya; coal-mining center. Until c.1940, Gorsko-Ivanovskoye. **2** Village (1939 pop. over 500), W Fergana oblast, Uzbek SSR, on railroad and 8 mi. W of Kokand; cotton.

Gort, Gaelic *Gort Inse Guaire,* town (pop. 1,046), S Co. Galway, Ireland, 17 mi. SE of Galway; agr. market (sheep; potatoes, beets). Coole Park (N) was home of Lady Gregory. Near-by Ballylea Castle was residence of W. B. Yeats.

Gorton, SE suburb (pop. 50,127) of Manchester, SE Lancashire, England; mfg. of cotton textiles, leather, chemicals, locomotives. Site of 2 Manchester reservoirs.

Gortyna (gôrtī'nŭ), anc. town in central Crete, 30 mi. SSW of Candia. Flourished under the Romans until Byzantine times as the chief town of Crete. Destroyed (8th cent. A.D.) by the Saracens. Excavations (1884) revealed the Acropolis, a theater, temples, several statues, and legal MSS.

Goruckpur, India: see GORAKHPUR.

Gorumahisani (gō"rōōmŭhĭsä'nē), village, Mayurbhanj dist., NE Orissa, India, 39 mi. NNW of Baripada; rail spur terminus. Important iron-ore deposits near by; ore mined and shipped by rail to iron- and steelworks at Jamshedpur, 32 mi. N.

Gorumna (gôrŭm'nŭ), island (5,908 acres; 4 mi. long, 3 mi. wide) at entrance to Kilkieran Bay, near N shore of Galway Bay, SW Co. Galway, Ireland, 25 mi. W of Galway, separated by narrow channels from mainland (E) and Lettermullen isl. (W). Sometimes spelled Goromna. Just N is Lettermore isl.

Goryacheistochnenskaya (gŭryä"chĕ-ēstôch'nyĭnskīŭ) [Rus.,=hot spring], village (1939 pop. over 2,000), SE Grozny oblast, Russian SFSR, in E Terek Range, 9 mi. NE of Grozny; health resort (dry steppe climate); hot springs. Until c.1940, Goryachevodsk [Rus.,=hot water].

Goryachevodskaya (gŭryä"chĭvôt'skīŭ), village (1926 pop. 8,306), S Stavropol Territory, Russian SFSR, just SE of Pyatigorsk, across Podkumok R.; flour mill; truck produce.

Goryachi Klyuch or **Goryachiy Klyuch** (gŭryä"chē klyōōch') [Rus.,=hot spring], town (1932 pop. estimate 3,830), S central Krasnodar Territory, Russian SFSR, at N foot of the Greater Caucasus, 25 mi. SSE of Krasnodar; climatic health resort. Sulphur, salt, and ferruginous springs near by.

Goryachinsk (gŭryŭchēnsk'), village (1948 pop. over 500), W Buryat-Mongol Autonomous SSR, Russian SFSR, on E shore of L. Baikal, 85 mi. NNE of Ulan-Ude; health resort with hot springs.

Goryn River or **Goryn' River** (gŭrĭn'yŭ), Pol. *Horyń* (hôrĭn'yŭ), in W European USSR, rises in Volyn-Podolian Upland NE of Zalozhtsy (Ukrainian SSR), flows ENE past Izyaslav and Slavuta, NNW past Ostrov, and N past Dubrovitsa, into Belorussian SSR, past Stolin (head of navigation) and David-Gorodok, to Pripet R. 7 mi. NNE of David-Gorodok; 404 mi. long. Receives Sluch R.

Görz, Italy: see GORIZIA, city.

Gorzano, Monte (môn'tĕ gôrtsä'nô), chief peak (8,040 ft.) of Monti della Laga, S central Italy, 6 mi. ESE of Amatrice.

Gorze (gôrz), village (pop. 564), Moselle dept., NE France, 9 mi. SW of Metz.

Gorzno (gōōzh'nô), Pol. *Górzno,* town (pop. 1,694), Bydgoszcz prov., N central Poland, 45 mi. ENE of Torun; mfg. of chemicals, mineral-water bottling, flour milling.

Gorzow. **1** or **Gorzow Slaski** (gô'zōōf shlō'skē), Pol. *Gorzów Śląski,* Ger. *Landsberg in Oberschlesien* (länts'bĕrk ĭn ō"bŭr-shlā'zyŭn), town (1939 pop. 3,049; 1946 pop. 2,435) in Upper Silesia, after 1945 in Opole prov., S Poland, on Prosna R. and 35 mi. NE of Oppeln (Opole); agr. market (grain, potatoes, livestock). Until 1939, Ger. frontier station on Pol. border, opposite Praszka. **2** or **Gorzow Wielkopolski,** town, Brandenburg: see LANDSBERG or LANDSBERG AN DER WARTHE, Zielona Gora prov., Poland.

Gorzyca (gōō-zhĭ'tsä), Pol. *Górzyca,* Ger. *Göritz* (gû'rĭts), town (1939 pop. 1,974; 1946 pop. 182) in Brandenburg, after 1945 in Zielona Gora prov., W Poland, near the Oder, 12 mi. NNE of Frankfurt an der Oder.

Gosaba (gōsä'bŭ), village, 24-Parganas dist., West Bengal, India, 14 mi. SE of Port Canning; model land-reclamation project for Sunderbans area.

Gosainganj (gō'sīngŭnj) or **Goshainganj** (gō'shīn–). **1** Town (pop. 2,951), Fyzabad dist., E central Uttar Pradesh, India, 20 mi. SE of Fyzabad; trades in rice, wheat, gram, sugar cane. **2** Town (pop. 2,881), Lucknow dist., central Uttar Pradesh, India, 12 mi. ESE of Lucknow; wheat, rice, gram, millet.

Gosainkund (gō'sīnkōōnd) or **Gosainthan** (–tän), village, N Nepal, 45 mi. ENE of Gurkha, 35 mi. SW of Gosainthan peak; Hindu pilgrimage center; annual (July) mela. Group of c.20 sacred lakes near by.

Gosainthan (gōsīn'tän), Tibetan *Shisha Pangma* (shēshä' pängmä'), peak (26,291 ft.) in NE Nepal Himalayas, S Tibet, at 28°21'N 85°47'E. Up to 1950, unattempted by climbers.

Gosau (gō'zou), village (pop. 1,807) in the Salzkammergut, S Upper Austria, 10 mi. SSW of Bad Ischl; wood carving. Hydroelectric station S.

Göschenen, Switzerland: see SAINT GOTTHARD.

Gose (gō'sā), town (pop. 8,654), Nara prefecture, S Honshu, Japan, on N Kii Peninsula, 19 mi. SE of Osaka, in rice-growing area; produces drugs. Agr. and industrial schools.

Gosei, Formosa: see WUSI.

Gosen (gō'sān), town (pop. 18,485), Niigata prefecture, central Honshu, Japan, 14 mi. SE of Niigata; textile center.

Gosford (gŏs'fôrd), municipality (pop. 4,410), E New South Wales, Australia, 32 mi. NNE of Sydney and on N inlet of Broken Bay; summer resort; citrus-fruit center.

Gosforth. **1** Village and parish (pop. 799), SW Cumberland, England, near Wastwater, 11 mi. SE of Whitehaven; sheep raising, agr. Has well-known Viking cross (14½ ft. high), dating probably from 7th cent. **2** Urban district (1931 pop. 18,044; 1951 census 24,424), SE Northumberland, England, 3 mi. N of Newcastle-upon-Tyne; coal-mining center. On the racecourse George Stephenson built his 1st locomotive in 1814. In urban dist. (W) is coal-mining town of Coxlodge.

Gösgen, Switzerland: see NIEDERGÖSGEN.

Goshainganj, India: see GOSAINGANJ.

Goshcha (gôsh'chŭ), Pol. *Hoszcza* (hôsh'chä), village (1931 pop. 1,340), SE Rovno oblast, Ukrainian SSR, on Goryn R. and 16 mi. E of Rovno; flour milling; sugar beets, truck.

Goshen (gō'shŭn), county (□ 2,230; pop. 12,634), SE Wyo.; ⊙ Torrington. Agr. area bordering on Nebr.; watered by N.Platte R. Sugar beets, grain, beans, livestock. Formed 1911.

Goshen. 1 Town (pop. 286), Pike co., SE Ala., on Conecuh R. and 10 mi. SW of Troy. **2** Town (pop. 940), Litchfield co., NW Conn., in Litchfield Hills, just W of Torrington; dairying; childrens' camps. Produced cheese commercially after 1792. State park, state forest. Asaph Hall b. here. **3** City (pop. 13,003), ⊙ Elkhart co., N Ind., on Elkhart R. and 24 mi. ESE of South Bend; distribution center in agr. area (livestock; dairy products; soybeans, grain). Mfg.: steel products, hydraulic presses, batteries, tanks, burlap bags, furniture, veneer and other wood products, condensed milk, rubber products, underwear, radios, phonographs, refrigerators, special production machinery. Timber. Settled c.1830, inc. 1868. Has a large Mennonite pop.; Goshen Col. (Mennonite) is here. **4** Agr. town (pop. 321), Hampshire co., NW Mass., 13 mi. NW of Northampton; maple sugar. **5** Town (pop. 356), Sullivan co., SW N.H., 7 mi. S of Newport. **6** Village (pop. c.400), Cape May co., S N.J., near Delaware Bay, 4 mi. N of Cape May Court House; agr., fishing. **7** Village (pop. 3,311), ⊙ Orange co., SE N.Y., 6 mi. SE of Middletown, in dairying and truck-farming area; mfg. (pipe fittings, machinery, chemicals, clothing). Resort, with lakes near by. Good Time and Historic (or Harriman) harness-racing tracks are here; and the Hambletonian race is held here. Settled during 18th cent.; inc. 1809. **8** Town (pop. 525), Utah co., central Utah, 12 mi. E of Eureka; alt. 4,530 ft.; agr., livestock. **9** Town (pop. 94), Addison co., W central Vt., in Green Mts., 16 mi. N of Rutland. **10** Town (pop. 124), Rockbridge co., W Va., on Calfpasture R. and 19 mi. NNW of Buena Vista; textile milling. Goshen Pass is just SE; a 4-mi. river gap (followed by highway) cut through a mtn. ridge.

Goshen Hole, lowland region (c.40 mi. N-S, 120 mi. E-W) of Great Plains, in E Wyo. and W Nebr., drained by North Platte R.; consists of mesas, buttes, and badland topography as well as irrigated agr. dists. (sugar beets, grain, potatoes; dairy products). Scottsbluff, Torrington, Mitchell are chief towns. Crossed by Oregon Trail (mid-19th cent.).

Goshen Pass, Va.: see GOSHEN.

Goshogawara (gōshōgä'wärä), town (pop. 11,049), Aomori prefecture, N Honshu, Japan, 16 mi. W of Aomori; rice collection.

Gosier (gôzyā'), town (commune pop. 8,784), SW Grande-Terre, Guadeloupe, on the Petit Cul de Sac, 3½ mi. SE of Pointe-à-Pitre, in sugar-growing region. Sometimes called Le Gosier.

Goskopi, Russian SFSR: see KOPEISK.

Goslar (gôs'lär), city (1950 pop. 40,735), in Brunswick, NW Germany, after 1945 in Lower Saxony, at NW foot of the upper Harz, 25 mi. SSW of Brunswick; rail junction; mining center (copper, lead, zinc, iron, and sulphur mines in the Rammelsberg, just SE). Foundries; mfg. of machinery, office equipment, chemicals, pharmaceuticals, textiles, garments, knitwear, suspenders, furniture, wood products; food processing; glassworks. Major tourist center for Harz excursions. Goslar has completely preserved its medieval appearance. Remains of powerful fortifications include the Zwinger, a 16th-cent. round tower. The Kaiserhaus, Germany's largest extant Romanesque palace, was built (mid-11th cent.) by Emperor Henry III. City has several Romanesque-Gothic churches; Gothic town hall; many half-timbered houses, including the noted Brusttuch (1526). Founded in 10th cent. to protect rich silver mines in vicinity. A favorite residence of the early emperors, Goslar was a free imperial city (until 1802), and a prosperous member of the Hanseatic League. Until 1941 it was in former Prussian prov. of Hanover.

Gosnold (gŏz'nŭld), town (pop. 56), Dukes co., SE Mass.; comprises ELIZABETH ISLANDS, extending 15 mi. SW from Cape Cod, bet. Buzzards Bay and Vineyard Sound, SE of New Bedford; fishing community; summer resorts. Cuttyhunk, on westernmost isl., is only village. Settled 1641, inc. 1864.

Gosper, county (□ 466; pop. 2,734), S Nebr.; ⊙ Elwood; agr. region. Grain, livestock. Formed 1873.

Gospic (gôs'pēch), Serbo-Croatian *Gospić*, town (pop. 5,287), W Croatia, Yugoslavia, on railroad and 70 mi. SSE of Rijeka (Fiume); chief town of the Lika; local trade center.

Gosport (gŏs'–), municipal borough (1931 pop. 38,338; 1951 census 58,246), SE Hampshire, England, on the Spithead and on Portsmouth Harbour opposite Portsmouth; 50°48'N 1°8'W; port and naval base, with naval barracks, royal victualing yard, and naval hosp.; yacht-building center. Holy Trinity Church (1696) has organ on which Handel is said to have played. In municipal borough (S) is town of Alverstoke (pop. 5,211), and, on The Solent 3 mi. W, the bathing resort of Lee-on-the-Solent (pop. 2,715).

Gosport (gŏz'pôrt, gŏs'–), town (pop. 672), Owen co., SW central Ind., on West Fork of White R. and 40 mi. SW of Indianapolis, in agr. area (hogs, cattle, corn); mfg. of cement products.

Göss, Austria: see LEOBEN.

Gossamu-lez-Paulis, Belgian Congo: see PAULIS.

Gossas (gô'säs), town (pop. c.4,700), W Senegal, Fr. West Africa, on railroad to Niger and 90 mi. E of Dakar; trading post in peanut-growing region.

Gossau (gô'sou). **1** Town (pop. 7,512), St. Gall canton, NE Switzerland, 6 mi. W of St. Gall; textiles (woolen, cotton), embroideries, chemicals; metalworking. **2** Town (pop. 2,387), Zurich canton, N Switzerland, 11 mi. ESE of Zurich; metalworking, silk textiles.

Gosselies (gôslē'), town (pop. 10,171), Hainaut prov., S central Belgium, on Charleroi-Brussels Canal and 4 mi. NNW of Charleroi; coal mining; mfg. of metal products.

Gössenheim (gû'sunhīm), village (pop. 920), Lower Franconia, NW Bavaria, Germany, on small Wern R. and 20 mi. W of Schweinfurt; cabbage, cattle, hogs. NE (½ mi.) are remains of castle Homburg, one of Franconia's most spectacular ruins; main bldgs. date from 11th cent., outer works from 13th cent.

Gössnitz (gûs'nĭts), town (pop. 8,202), Thuringia, central Germany, on the Pleisse and 7 mi. S of Altenburg; woolen milling; mfg. of machinery, buttons, lacquer.

Gossolengo (gôs-sôlĕng'gô), village (pop. 491), Piacenza prov., Emilia-Romagna, N central Italy, near Trebbia R., 5 mi. SW of Piacenza; paper mill.

Gossville, N.H.: see EPSOM.

Gössweinstein (gûs"vīn'shtīn), village (pop. 1,378), Upper Franconia, N Bavaria, Germany, in the Franconian Switzerland, on the Wiesent and 9 mi. WNW of Pegnitz; grain, livestock. Has mid-18th-cent. pilgrimage church and parish house (formerly a summer residence of bishops of Bamberg).

Gostimë (gôstē'mù) or **Gostima** (gôstē'mä), village (1930 pop. 149), central Albania, 8 mi. SW of Elbasan; road junction.

Gostingen, Poland: see GOSTYN.

Gostini or **Gostyni** (gō'stēnē), Lettish *Gostiņi*, Rus. (until 1917) *Glazmanka*, city (pop. 993), S central Latvia, in Latgale, on right bank of the Western Dvina, at mouth of Aiviekste R., and 10 mi. NNW of Jekabpils; sugar beets. Until 1920, in Rus. Vitebsk govt.

Gostinopolye, Russian SFSR: see VOLKHOV.

Gostishchevo (gŭstyēsh'chĭvŭ), village (1926 pop. 2,003), S Kursk oblast, Russian SFSR, 13 mi. N of Belgorod; sugar beets.

Gostivar (gô'stēvär), village (pop. 7,561), NW Macedonia, Yugoslavia, on Vardar R., on narrow-gauge railroad and 30 mi. SW of Skoplje; trade center of the upper Polog (cattle, wood, fruit, wheat); handicraft. First mentioned in 14th cent.

Gostomel or **Gostomel'** (gŭstô'mĭl), town (1926 pop. 2,507), N central Kiev oblast, Ukrainian SSR, 15 mi. NW of Kiev, N of Bucha; ceramics.

Gostyn (gô'stĭnyù), Pol. *Gostyń*, town (1946 pop. 8,021), Poznan prov., W Poland, 37 mi. SSE of Poznan; rail junction; mfg. of glass, bricks, machinery, metalware, furniture, liqueur, mineral water; sugar milling, woodworking. In Second World War, under Ger. rule, called Gostingen.

Gostyni, Latvia: see GOSTINI.

Gostynin (gôstĭ'nēn), town (pop. 7,357), Warszawa prov., central Poland, on railroad and 14 mi. SW of Plock; brick mfg., flour milling, sawmilling.

Gota (gō'tä), village (pop. 350), Harar prov., E central Ethiopia, in Great Rift Valley, on railroad and 33 mi. W of Diredawa.

Gota (yû'tä"), Swedish *Göta*, village (pop. 535), Alvsborg co., SW Sweden, on Gota R. and 13 mi. SSW of Trollhattan; pulp mills, sulphite works.

Gota Canal (yû'tä"), Swedish *Göta kanal*, S Sweden. Name is applied to waterway bet. the Kattegat at Goteborg (W) and the Baltic, E of Soderkoping; includes Gota R. and lakes Vaner, Vatter, Bor, and Rox. Entire route is 240 mi. long, of which 55 mi. consist of canals. W section uses Gota R. bet. Goteborg and L. Vaner at Vanersborg; short canals by-pass falls at Trollhattan and lake outlet at Vanersborg. Route then crosses L. Vaner to its E shore at Sjotorp; thence central canal section extends SE, through several small lakes, to L. Vatter at Karlsborg. From opposite shore of L. Vatter, at Motala, E canal section extends (E) through L. Rox, to Slat Bay, Swedish *Slätbaken*, of Baltic, 3 mi. E of Soderkoping. Waterway serves a large number of major industrial towns of S Sweden; tourist steamers ply on Gota Canal bet. Goteborg and Stockholm. Canal sections of waterway are 47 ft. wide, 10 ft. deep; there are 58 locks. Completed 1832.

Gotafors (yû"täfôrs', –fôsh'), Swedish *Götafors*, village (pop. 651), Jonkoping co., S Sweden, on Laga R. and 20 mi. S of Jonkoping; sulphite works.

Gotaland, Sweden: see SWEDEN.

Gotarike, Sweden: see SWEDEN.

Gota River, Swedish *Göta älv* (yû"tä ĕlv'), SW Sweden, issues from SW end of L. Vaner at Vanersborg, flows 60 mi. SW, past Trollhattan (falls; major power station), to the Kattegat at Goteborg. Apart from short stretches at outflow from L. Vaner and at the Trollhattan, both by-passed by canals, entire length is navigable and forms W section of Gota Canal route. Just E of Kungalv the Nordre R., Swedish *Nordre älv* (nōōr"drù ĕlv'), leaves Gota R., flows 12 mi. SW, past Kungalv, to the Skagerrak 8 mi. NW of Goteborg.

Gotebo (gō'tùbō), town (pop. 574), Kiowa co., SW Okla., 13 mi. ENE of Hobart, in cotton and wheat area; cotton ginning, flour milling; oil wells.

Goteborg (yûtùbôr'yù) or **Gothenburg** (gŏ'thŭnbûrg, gŏ'tŭn–), Swedish *Göteborg*, city (1950 pop. 353,991), ⊙ Goteborg och Bohus co., SW Sweden, on the Kattegat opposite N tip of Denmark, at mouth of Gota R. (W terminus of Gota Canal route), 240 mi. W of Stockholm; 57°42'N 11°58'E. Second-largest city of Sweden and its chief seaport, ice-free the year round, with shipping services to all parts of the world. It is largest Scandinavian shipbuilding center, with extensive yards, dry-dock, marine-engine works, and auxiliary services. Railroad center; airport at Torslanda (WNW). Among its many industries are mfg. of ball bearings, automobiles and trucks, machinery, china; cotton milling, sugar refining, metal- and woodworking, brewing. Large fish catches are landed here and shipped by rail to the Continent. Free port established 1922. Seat of Lutheran bishop; site of univ. (1891), technical and medical col., navigation school, ship-testing laboratory, and Oceanographic Institute. Scene of annual trade and industries fair. Originally planned by Dutch architects, city retains old canals and many of its early stately bldgs., besides numerous modern residential and public bldgs. Has 17th-cent. royal residence, large Slottskogen park, botanical gardens; maritime mus., and museums of natural history, cultural history, and art. At port entrance is New Alvsborg fortress (1647); of other old fortifications a moat, surrounding old part of city, and Carolus Rex Bastion remain. Founded 1619 by Gustavus Adolphus on site of earlier settlement the town's commercial importance grew rapidly after mid-18th cent. and further increased during Napoleon's continental blockade, when city became a center of British trade with Europe. Goteborg liquor-licensing system originated here (1865) and became basis of Swedish liquor laws. Introduction of steam in 1870s gave further impetus to Goteborg's development as port. An old spelling is Gottenburg.

Goteborg och Bohus (yûtùbôr'yù ō bōō'hüs"), Swed *Göteborg och Bohus*, county [Swed. *län*] (□ 1,980 1950 pop. 557,238), SW Sweden; ⊙ Goteborg. On the Kattegat and the Skagerrak, it forms part of Bohuslan and of Vastergotland provs. Coast line is indented by numerous small fjords; offshore are many small isls. and skerries. Orust and Tjorn are largest isls. Fishing (herring, anchovy) and fish canning are main occupation; other industries are stone quarrying, paper and textile milling, wood and metalworking, shipbuilding. There are numerous seaside resorts. Cities are Goteborg Uddevalla, Molndal, Kungalv, Lysekil, Stromstad and Marstrand.

Gotegaon, India: see CHHINDWARA, town.

Gotemba (gōtäm'bä), town (pop. 13,061), Shizuoka prefecture, central Honshu, Japan, 15 mi. NNE of Numazu; commercial center in agr. area (rice, tea)

Gotene (yû'tùnù), Swedish *Götene*, village (pop 1,824), Skaraborg co., SW Sweden, 12 mi. E of Lidkoping; foundries, limestone quarries; wood and metalworking. Has medieval church.

Gotenhafen, Poland: see GDYNIA.

Gotera, Salvador: see SAN FRANCISCO.

Gotha (gō'thù, –tù, Ger. gō'tä), city (pop. 57,639) Thuringia, central Germany, 15 mi. W of Erfurt 50°57'N 10°43'E. Rail junction; mfg. of railroad cars, machinery, electrical equipment, precision instruments, textiles, synthetic chemicals, soap rubber products, musical instruments, glass, china bricks, tobacco products, and food products (notably sausages). Has former ducal palace of Friedenstein (1643–57), 18th-cent. Friedrichsta Palace, early-15th-cent. church, 16th-cent. town hall, remains of 13th-cent. Augustine monastery Leina Canal, built 1366–69, supplies water to city from near-by Thuringian Forest. Gotha was a residence of Charlemagne. First mentioned as town in 1189, it passed in 1440 to electors of Saxony, in 1485 to the Ernestine line, and in 1640 to Ernest the Pious, 1st duke of Gotha. Was C duchy of Saxe-Coburg-Gotha, 1826–1918. From late-18th cent. until Second World War, it was a center of geographic research and publishing; well known house of Justus Perthes published *Almanac de Gotha* here from 1764. It was also seat of many insurance companies. At congress here (1875) Ger. socialist groups formulated party program Second World War destruction about 20%.

Gotham (gŏ'tùm), village and parish (pop. 1,344) S Nottingham, England, 7 mi. SSW of Nottingham; gypsum mining. The inhabitants early acquired a reputation for doing ridiculous things (such as trying to drown an eel), possibly rooted in ingenious efforts to appear to be fools in order to prevent King John from residing here o establishing a highway through it. Has 13th-14th-cent. church.

Gotham (gŏ'thŭm), a name for New York city, SE N.Y., first used by Washington Irving and others in the *Salmagundi Papers*.

Goth Chani, W Pakistan: see CHANIGOT.

Gothenburg, Sweden: see GOTEBORG.

Gothenburg (gŏth'ŭnbûrg), city (pop. 2,977), Dawson co., S central Nebr., 35 mi. ESE of North Platte and on Platte R.; dairying; livestock, grain. Fur-trading post, built 1854, was moved here (1931) from near-by Oregon Trail. Settled 1882, inc. 1884.

Gothic Mountain (gŏ'thĭk). **1** Peak (12,646 ft.) in Rocky Mts., Gunnison co., W central Colo. **2** Peak (4,738 ft.) in Essex co., NE N.Y., in the Adirondacks, c.3 mi. ENE of Mt. Marcy and c.9 mi. SSE of Lake Placid village.

Gothland, island, Sweden: see GOTLAND.

Gotland (gŏt'lŭnd, Swed. gôt'länd), island (□ 1,167; 1950 pop. 59,054), comprising most of Gotland co. [Swed. *län*] (□ 1,224; pop. 59,505), SE Sweden, in Baltic Sea, 60 mi. E of Oskarshamn, 100 mi. NW of Liepaja (Latvia). Gotland county, coextensive with the historical province [Swedish *landskap*] of Gotland, includes isls. of Gotland, Faro, and Gotska Sando; ⊙ Visby. The isl. (56°54'–57°56'N 18°6'–19°7'E) is 75 mi. long (NE–SW), 2–28 mi. wide. Several wide bays indent low coast line; undulating surface rises to 272 ft. Tourist traffic is important. Chief produce: rye, oats, sugar beets, flax, potatoes; sheep raising. Industries include quarrying (limestone, marble, sandstone), sugar refining, lumbering. Chief centers are VISBY and Slite. Archaeological remains indicate that Gotland, inhabited since Stone Age, was nearly depopulated by a climatic change to intense cold bet. 600 and 300 B.C. Anc. Roman, Arabic, and Anglo-Saxon coins demonstrate early wide commercial activity. In 12th cent. German merchants settled at Visby (Wisby), which became one of the chief towns of the Hanseatic League. The conflicts over trading privileges bet. the city's merchants and the peasant-traders of the isl. left Gotland open to conquest (1280) by the Swedish king, Magnus I. Its trade decreased, fires and plagues in 14th cent. reduced its pop., and it was devastated (1361) and conquered (1362) by Waldemar IV of Denmark; returned to Hanseatic League 1370. Became pirate base. In 1570 Gotland passed to Denmark, in 1645 regained by Sweden. Old customs and the ruins of anc. churches and castles are reminders of the isl.'s important role in the past. Old spellings include Gothland and Gottland.

Gotnya, Russian SFSR: see PROLETARSKI, Kursk oblast.

Goto-retto (gōtō-rĕt'tō), island group (□ 249; pop. 154,207), Nagasaki prefecture, Japan, in E.China Sea, 25 mi. W of Kyushu; 32°53'N 129°E. A 60-mi. chain comprising FUKAE-SHIMA (largest isl.), NAKADORI-SHIMA, HISAGA-SHIMA, NARU-SHIMA, WAKAMATSU-SHIMA, UKU-SHIMA, OJIKA-SHIMA, and many scattered islets. Generally mountainous, fertile (rice, sweet potatoes); ornamental coral. Whaling, fishing. Sometimes Anglicized as Goto Isls.

Gotska Sando, Swedish *Gotska Sandön* (gôt'skä sänd'ŭn"), island (□ 14; pop. 21), Gotland co., SE Sweden, in the Baltic, 60 mi. NE of Visby; 58°22'N 19°16'E. Isl. is 5 mi. long, 1–4 mi. wide; rises to 138 ft. Has 3 lighthouses and radio beacons. Part of isl. is natl. park.

Gotsu (gō'tsōō), town (pop. 12,950), Shimane prefecture, SW Honshu, Japan, port on Sea of Japan, at mouth of short Gono R., and 12 mi. NE of Hamada; rail junction; cattle-raising, rice-growing center; raw silk. Exports charcoal. Sometimes called Iwami-gotsu.

Gottenburg, Sweden: see GOTEBORG.

Gottesberg, Poland: see BOGUSZOW.

Gottesgab, Czechoslovakia: see BOZI DAR.

Gotteszell (gô'tŭstsĕl"), village (pop. 1,745), Lower Bavaria, Germany, in Bohemian Forest, 9 mi. N of Deggendorf; granite and quartz quarrying; brewing. Has Cistercian abbey (founded in 13th cent.; secularized 1803) with Romanesque basilica.

Göttingen (gû'tĭng-ŭn), city (1950 pop. 78,438), in former Prussian prov. of Hanover, W Germany, after 1945 in Lower Saxony, on the Leine and 24 mi. NE of Kassel; 51°32'N 9°56'E. A famous university city, it is also a rail junction and a center for mfg. of optical and precision instruments; also mfg. of machinery, electrical goods, aluminum ware, industrial chemicals, pharmaceuticals, cosmetics, textiles, paper products, furniture; printing, food processing (canned goods, beer, spirits). Göttingen, 1st mentioned in 953, was chartered c.1200, became a member of the Hanseatic League, and was active in cloth mfg. The univ., founded 1737 by Elector George Augustus (later George II of England), 1st specialized in history and political science. When, in 1837, the king revoked the constitution of Hanover, 7 professors (including the brothers Grimm and other notable scholars) of the univ. issued a strong protest and were summarily dismissed. This celebrated incident led to the decline of the university's reputation until it was revived at end of 19th cent. by strong mathematics and physics departments. The univ. of Helmstedt was absorbed in 1810. The city, virtually undamaged in Second World War, has the typical quiet and pleasant character of a Ger. univ. town and has preserved much of its medieval architecture, including 14th- and 15th-cent. churches, 14th-cent. town hall, and many half-timbered houses.

Gottland, island, Sweden: see GOTLAND.

Gottleuba, Bad, Germany: see BAD GOTTLEUBA.

Gottmadingen (gôt'mä'dĭng-ŭn), village (pop. 2,977), S Baden, Germany, 3 mi. SW of Singen, near Swiss border; mfg. of agr. machinery, brewing.

Gottolengo (gôt-tōlĕng'gô), village (pop. 3,280), Brescia prov., Lombardy, N Italy, 17 mi. S of Brescia; marmalade mfg.

Gottorp (gô'tôrp), castle in Schleswig-Holstein, NW Germany: see SCHLESWIG, town.

Gott Peak (9,700 ft.), S B.C., in Coast Mts., 80 mi. NNE of Vancouver; 50°22'N 122°17'W.

Gottschee, Yugoslavia: see KOCEVJE.

Gottwaldov (gôt'väldôf), city (pop. 45,737), ⊙ Gottwaldov prov. (□ 1,972; pop. 593,576), E Moravia, Czechoslovakia, on railroad and 48 mi. ENE of Brno; 49°13'N 17°40'E. Industrial center, famous for leather and rubber works; mfg. of shoes, boots, hosiery, machinery, machine tools. Organized as an almost self-sufficient factory community, it has many consumers' industries and broad educational facilities for workers. Though chartered in 1497, it had no economic importance until creation of world-wide shoe export industry by Thomas Bata in 1913. Considerably damaged in Second World War; captured by USSR in 1945. Until 1948, known as Zlin (zlĭn), Czech *Zlín*. Auxiliary works and municipal airport at OTROKOVICE.

Götzenbrück, France: see GOETZENBRUCK.

Götzis (gût'sĭs), town (pop. 5,163), Vorarlberg, W Austria, near the Rhine, 7 mi. SW of Dornbirn; textiles (lace, embroidery); mineral springs. Ruins of castle near by.

Gouarec (gwärĕk'), village (pop. 547), Côtes-du-Nord dept., W France, port on Blavet R. and Brest-Nantes Canal, and 23 mi. S of Guingamp; dairying; cider milling.

Gouaux-de-Luchon (gwō-dŭ-lüshō'), village (pop. 130), Haute-Garonne dept., S France, 5 mi. N of Luchon; iron mining.

Goubellat (gōōbĕlät'), village, Medjez-el-Bab dist., N central Tunisia, 33 mi. SW of Tunis; French agr. settlement; cereals, vegetables, livestock, poultry. Zinc mine near by. Hit in Second World War.

Gouda (gou'dä, Du. khou'dä), town (pop. 37,283), South Holland prov., W Netherlands, near Hollandsche IJssel R., 12 mi. ENE of Rotterdam; rail junction; mfg. of pottery, clay pipes, candles, soap, white lead, explosives, yarn, clothing, furniture, cigars; machine shops, liquor distilleries; important cheese market (Gouda cheese). Intersected by many canals. Has 15th-cent. Gothic town hall, 16th-cent. church (*Sint Janskerk* or *Groote Kerk*), town mus. Town chartered in 1272; center of medieval cloth trade. Erasmus received his schooling here prior to 1475; later (1486–87) worked in near-by monastery. Town taken (1572) by Beggars of the Sea. Formerly also known as Ter Gouw.

Gouda Mountains (gōō'dä), forested basalt range of Fr. Somaliland, on N coast of Gulf of Tadjoura, 40 mi. WNW of Djibouti; rise to over 5,700 ft.

Goudge, town (pop. estimate 800), E central Mendoza prov., Argentina, on railroad, on arm of Diamante R. (irrigation) and 13 mi. ESE of San Rafael; fruit and stock center; dried-fruit processing.

Goudhurst (goud'–), town and parish (pop. 2,722), S Kent, England, 11 mi. S of Maidstone; agr. market. Has 15th-cent. church and 15th-cent. timbered inn.

Goudiry (gōōdē'rē), town (pop. c.500), E Senegal, Fr. West Africa, on Dakar-Niger RR and 65 mi. ENE of Tambacounda; peanuts, hardwoods, essential oils.

Goudreau (gōōdrō'), village (pop. estimate 150), central Ont., 120 mi. N of Sault Ste. Marie; gold, iron mining.

Gough Island (gŏf) or **Diego Alvarez Island** (dyā'gō älvä'rĕz), uninhabited volcanic islet (8 mi. long, 4 mi. wide) of Tristan da Cunha group, dependency (since 1938) of St. Helena colony, in the S Atlantic 250 mi. SSE of Tristan da Cunha; 40°20'S 10°W. Large guano deposits. Held by the British since 1816.

Gougnies (gōōnyē'), village (pop. 711), Hainaut prov., S central Belgium, 7 mi. ESE of Charleroi; marble quarrying and processing.

Gouhenans (gōōŭnä'), village (pop. 472), Haute-Saône dept., E France, 6 mi. S of Lure; chemicals.

Gouin Reservoir (gōōē') (50 mi. long, 30 mi. wide), central Que., W of L. St. John; collective name of series of interconnected lakes with deeply indented shoreline, containing numerous isls. Drained by St. Maurice R.

Goulburn (gōl'bŭrn), municipality (pop. 15,991), SE New South Wales, Australia, on Hawkesbury R. and 50 mi. NE of Canberra; rail junction; iron-mining center; woolen mills, granite quarries. Has R.C. cathedral. Founded 1820. Wombeyan limestone caves near by.

Goulburn Islands, small group in Arafura Sea, 1 mi. off N coast of Northern Territory, Australia. Comprise N.Goulburn Isl. (□ 14; 10 mi. long), S.Goulburn Isl. (□ 30; 20 mi. long), and several islets; sandy. Wild cotton, pearl shell. Aboriginal reservation.

Goulburn River, central Victoria, Australia, rises in Great Dividing Range SE of Woods Point, flows generally NW, past Eildon Weir (reservoir), Alexandra, Yea, and Seymour, thence N, past Nagambie, Murchison, and Shepparton (hydroelectric plant), and WNW to Murray R. 7 mi. NE of Echuca, at New South Wales border; 280 mi. long; used for irrigation.

Gould (gōōld). **1** Town (pop. 1,076), Lincoln co., SE Ark., 32 mi. ESE of Pine Bluff, in cotton-growing area. **2** Town (pop. 303), Harmon co., SW Okla., 26 mi. W of Altus, near Texas line, in agr. area (cotton, grain, sweet potatoes); cotton ginning.

Goulding, village, Escambia co., extreme NW Fla., NW of Pensacola.

Goulds (gōōldz), village (1940 pop. 920), Dade co., S Fla., 10 mi. SW of Miami; truck-produce shipping.

Gouldsboro or **Gouldsborough** (gōōlz'–, gōōldz'–), resort town (pop. 1,168), Hancock co., S Maine, on peninsula across Frenchman Bay from Bar Harbor. Inc. 1739.

Goulette, La (lä gōōlĕt'), town (pop. 14,949), Tunis dist., N Tunisia, outport for TUNIS city (6 mi. WSW), on a sand bar bet. L. of Tunis (W) and Gulf of Tunis (E), at lake's outlet. Linked with Tunis by a deep-sea channel (for ships drawing 20 ft.) and by a causeway (electric trolley) across lake. Sheltered anchorage; fishing port and iron-ore shipping center. A favorite summer resort of Tunis residents. Villages of Khéreddine (seaplane base) and Le Kram are just N, near base of sand bar. Captured by Spaniards, La Goulette was fortified by Charles V. Taken by Turks in 1574 after a memorable siege. French citizens and Italians made up over half of town's 1946 pop.

Goulimine (gōōlēmēn'), Saharan military outpost, Agadir frontier region, southwesternmost Fr. Morocco, near Ifni enclave (Spanish), 55 mi. SSW of Tiznit; 28°59'N 10°4'W.

Goulmina (gōōlmēnä'), town (pop. 2,390), Meknès region, S central Fr. Morocco, oasis on the Oued Ghéris, at S foot of the High Atlas, 35 mi. SW of Ksar-es-Souk; date palms.

Goumbo-Guéoul, Fr. West Africa: see GUÉOUL.

Goumenissa (gōōmĕ'nĭsŭ), town (pop. 4,927), Kilkis nome, Macedonia, Greece, 23 mi. W of Kilkis, at E foot of the Paikon; trading center for silk, cotton, wine, red peppers. Formerly called Goumenitsa or Ghoumenitsa.

Goundam (gōōndäm'), town (pop. c.6,400), central Fr. Sudan, Fr. West Africa, in mid-Niger basin, 50 mi. WSW of Timbuktu; exports gum and hides. Region also produces millet, rice, wheat, corn, peanuts, beans. Marble deposits near by.

Gourara (gōōrärä'), group of c.20 small Saharan oases, in Aïn-Sefra territory, W central Algeria, at S edge of the Great Western Erg. Fed by artesian waters, they are strung out along El-Goléa-Adrar auto track. Chief oasis, Timimoun. Export: dates.

Gouraya (gōōräyä'), village (pop. 1,243), Alger dept., N central Algeria, on the Mediterranean, 16 mi. WSW of Cherchel; winegrowing. Iron mined in vicinity.

Gouraya, Djebel, Algeria: see BOUGIE.

Gourbeyre (gōōrbâr'), town (commune pop. 4,011), S Basse-Terre, Guadeloupe, 2 mi. ESE of Basse-Terre; coffee and cacao growing. Popular excursion point, with near-by thermal springs.

Gourdan-Polignan (gōōrdä'-pōlēnyä'), village (pop. 360), Haute-Garonne dept., S France, on the Garonne at the mouth of Neste R. and 8 mi. WSW of Saint-Gaudens; mfg. of tanning extracts. Limekilns.

Gourdon (gōōrdō'), town (pop. 2,090), Lot dept., SW France, 20 mi. N of Cahors; market center (truffles, walnuts); food canning and shipping, wool spinning.

Gourdon (gôr'dŭn), fishing village in Bervie parish, SE Kincardine, Scotland, on North Sea, 2 mi. S of Inverbervie.

Gouré (gōō'rā), town (pop. c.800), S Niger territory, Fr. West Africa, near Nigeria border and 85 mi. E of Zinder; trades in gum, peanuts, cotton; livestock; salt, sodium sulphate, natron. Subsistence crops from irrigated area: millet, wheat, potatoes, tomatoes, beans. Airstrip.

Gourgouvitsa, Greece: see LOUTRA AIDEPSOU.

Gourin (gōōrē'), town (pop. 2,612), Morbihan dept., W France, on S slope of Montagnes Noires, 28 mi. NNW of Lorient; slate-quarrying center. Iron deposits near by. Yearly religious festival followed by horse races and wrestling matches.

Gouripur, West Bengal, India: see NAIHATI.

Gouripur or **Gauripur** (both: gou'rĭpōōr), town (pop. 7,781), Mymensingh dist., central East Bengal, E Pakistan, 11 mi. E of Mymensingh; rice, jute, oilseeds; rice and oilseed milling.

Gouritz River (gou'rĭts), S Cape Prov., U. of So. Afr., formed by confluence of Gamka R. and Olifants R. 10 mi. S of Calitzdorp, flows 80 mi. S to the Indian Ocean 20 mi. SW of Mossel Bay. Receives Groot R. Valley separates Langeberg range (W) from Outeniqua Mts. (E).

Gourma-Rharous (go͞ormä″-rärо͞os′), town (pop. c.1,250), central Fr. Sudan, Fr. West Africa, on left bank of the Niger and 70 mi. E of Timbuktu; gum, rice, millet; livestock, hides. Dispensary.

Gournay or **Gournay-en-Bray** (go͞ornā′-ā-brā′), town (pop. 3,490), Seine-Inférieure dept., N France, on the Epte and 17 mi. WNW of Beauvais; dairying center noted for its cream cheese; meat preserving, footwear mfg. Town center damaged in Second World War.

Gourock (go͝o′rŭk), burgh (1931 pop. 8,845; 1951 census 9,107), NW Renfrew, Scotland, on the Clyde estuary, 24 mi. WNW of Glasgow; port, yachting center, and seaside resort. Promontory of Cloch Point, 3 mi. WSW, on Firth of Clyde, is site of lighthouse (55°57′N 4°51′W).

Gourrama (go͞orämä′), village, Meknès region, S central Fr. Morocco, on S slope of the High Atlas, 35 mi. NE of Ksar-es-Souk; asbestos mine.

Gousany (gŭo͞osä′nē), town (1939 pop. over 2,000) in Ordzhonikidze dist. of Greater Baku, Azerbaijan SSR, on S shore of Apsheron Peninsula, 13 mi. E of Baku.

Goussainville (go͞osĕvēl′), town (pop. 6,789), Seine-et-Oise dept., N central France, outermost NNE suburb of Paris, 12 mi. from Notre Dame Cathedral; sugar milling.

Goûter, Dôme du (dōm dü go͞otā′), peak (14,121 ft.) of Mont-Blanc massif, on Fr.-Ital. border, just W of Mont Blanc.

Gouveia (gōvā′ŭ), town (pop. 3,534), Guarda dist., N central Portugal, on NW slope of Serra da Estrêla, 21 mi. SE of Viseu; cheese mfg., woodworking. Has old castle.

Gouverneur (gŭ″vŭrno͝or′, go͞o″–), resort village (pop. 4,916), St. Lawrence co., N N.Y., on Oswegatchie R. and 25 mi. S of Ogdensburg; mfg. of textiles, clothing, paper, cheese, feed. Zinc and lead mines; talc, marble, and limestone quarries; talc mills. Dairying. Iron mines near by. Named for Gouverneur Morris, whose mansion still stands. Laid out 1787, inc. 1850.

Gouvieux (go͞ovyû′), town (pop. 2,241), Oise dept., N France, near the Oise, 8 mi. W of Senlis; wall-paper mfg., mushroom shipping. Sand quarries.

Gouvy (go͞ovē′), town, Luxembourg prov., E Belgium, in the Ardennes, near Ourthe R., 7 mi. S of Vielsalm, near border of grand duchy of Luxembourg; pig market. Commune center of Limerlé (lēmĕrlā′) (pop. 1,872), is 2 mi. SSW.

Gouw, Ter, Netherlands: see GOUDA.

Gouyave (go͞oyäv′), town (pop. 2,003), W Grenada, B.W.I., 7 mi. N of St. George's; cacao growing, fishing. Sometimes called Charlotte Town.

Gouy-lez-Piéton (gwē-lā-pyātō′), town (pop. 3,311), Hainaut prov., S central Belgium, 9 mi. NW of Charleroi, near Charleroi-Brussels Canal; metal industry; agr. market.

Gouzeaucourt (go͞ozōko͞or′), village (pop. 1,077), Nord dept., N France, 10 mi. SSW of Cambrai; weaving. Briefly captured by Germans, Nov., 1918.

Govan (gō′vŭn), town (pop. 350), S Sask., near Last Mountain L., 60 mi. NNW of Regina; resort.

Govan (gŭ′vŭn), industrial suburb (pop. 364,801) of Glasgow, Lanark, Scotland, on S shore of the Clyde; important shipyards; mfg. of machinery, machine tools, chemicals, asbestos.

Govan (gō′văn′), town (pop. 109), Bamberg co., S central S.C., 9 mi. SW of Bamberg.

Govap (gō′văp′), town, Giadinh prov., S Vietnam, on railroad and 3 mi. N of Saigon; rice and oilseed milling. Sometimes called Hanhthongxa.

Govardhan, India: see GOBARDHAN.

Gove, county (□ 1,070; pop. 4,447), W central Kansas; ⊙ Gove. Level to sloping area, drained in S by Smoky Hill R. Wheat, livestock. Formed 1886.

Gove or **Gove City,** city (pop. 206), ⊙ Gove co., W Kansas, on affluent of Smoky Hill R. and 23 mi. ESE of Oakley; grain, livestock, poultry area.

Goverla or **Goverlya** (gŭvyĕr′lŭ,–lyŭ), Czech *Hoverla,* Pol. *Howerla,* highest peak (6,752 ft.) in Chernagora section of the Carpathians, SW Ukrainian SSR, 12 mi. W of Zhabye. Prut R. rises at E foot.

Governador Island (go͞ovĕrnŭdōr′), largest island (□ 12; 7 mi. long) in Guanabara Bay, SE Brazil, 7 mi. N of center of Rio de Janeiro (ferry service), and in Federal Dist. Has Galeão international airport, naval air station, shipyards. Retains many colonial residences. Many of its c.40,000 inhabitants commute to Rio. Formerly called Maracajá; renamed for Rio's 1st governor, Correio de Sá.

Governador Portela (pôrtĕ′lŭ), town (pop. 3,352), W central Rio de Janeiro state, Brazil, in the Serra do Mar, 35 mi. NNW of Rio; rail junction; dairying, coffeegrowing.

Governador Valadares (vŭlŭdä′rĭs), city (1950 pop. 20,864), E Minas Gerais, Brazil, head of navigation on the Rio Doce, on railroad and 150 mi. NE of Belo Horizonte; commercial center on Rio de Janeiro–Bahia highway. Experienced short-lived boom in Second World War when it became center of mica extraction for export to U.S. Airfield. Until 1939, called Figueira.

Government Hill, Malaya: see PENANG HILL.

Government Village, Mont.: see HUNGRY HORSE.

Governor's Bay, village (pop. 148), ⊙ Mt. Herbert co. (□ 66; pop. 488), E S.Isl., New Zealand, 9 mi. S of Christchurch, on Lyttelton harbor; summer resort; orchards.

Governor's Harbour, town (pop. 516), central Bahama Isls., on small cay off central Eleuthera Isl., 70 mi. E of Nassau; 25°10′N 76°13′W. Trading point; grows tomatoes, pineapples.

Governors Island (2 mi. long, 1 mi. wide), W N.F., on S side of the Bay of Islands, 20 mi. WNW of Corner Brook; 49°5′N 58°22′W; lobster canning.

Governors Island (173 acres), SE N.Y., in Upper New York Bay just S of the Battery of Manhattan (ferry connections). A U.S. military reservation, it is site of historic Fort Jay (early 19th cent.), and old Castle Williams, a military prison built 1807–11. After purchase (1637) from the Indians by Wouter Van Twiller, it was long the home of colonial governors.

Govindgarh (gō′vĭndgŭr). **1** Town (pop. 3,028), E Rajasthan, India, 24 mi. ESE of Alwar; millet, gram, barley. **2** Town (pop. 3,787), E Vindhya Pradesh, India, near Kaimur Hills, 11 mi. S of Rewa; markets corn, millet, timber.

Govone (gôvô′nĕ), village (pop. 1,037), Cuneo prov., Piedmont, NW Italy, near Tanaro R., 8 mi. NNE of Alba.

Govora or **Baile-Govora** (bŭ′ēlā-gô′vôrä), Rum. *Băile-Govora,* town (1948 pop. 1,156), Valcea prov., S central Rumania, on railroad and 8 mi. SW of Ramnicu-Valcea; noted health and summer resort (alt. 1,181 ft.) with iodine, sulphurous, and ferruginous springs. The 15th-cent. Govora monastery (2 mi. SE) was an important printing center in 17th cent.

Gowanda (gōwŏn′dŭ, gŭ–), village (pop. 3,289), on Cattaraugus-Erie co. line, W N.Y., on Cattaraugus Creek and 20 mi. E of Dunkirk, in dairying area; mfg. (leather, glue, beverages, vinegar, cheese, maple syrup, chemicals, metal products). Natural-gas wells; sand and gravel. Near by are: Cattaraugus Indian Reservation, and Gowanda State Homeopathic Hosp. for mental disorders. Settled 1810, inc. 1848.

Gowanus, N.Y.: see SOUTH BROOKLYN.

Gowbarrow, England: see ULLSWATER.

Gowen (gou′ŭn), village (pop. c.500), Latimer co., SE Okla., 10 mi. WSW of Wilburton, in coal-mining area.

Gower (gou′ŭr), town (pop. 350), Clinton co., NW Mo., 16 mi. SE of St. Joseph.

Gower (gou′ŭr), Welsh *Gwyr* (gwĭr), peninsula, SW Glamorgan, Wales, bet. Loughor R. estuary and Bristol Channel; 15 mi. long, 5 mi. wide. There are several caves. Brandy Cove, on Bristol Channel 6 mi. SW of Swansea, is a former smugglers' haunt. Prehistoric relics have been found here. At W extremity is promontory of WORMS HEAD.

Gowerton, town (pop. 3,075), in Llwchwr urban dist., W Glamorgan, Wales, 4 mi. WNW of Swansea; steel milling.

Gowganda (gougăn′dŭ), village (pop. estimate 250), E Ont., on Gowganda L., 60 mi. SSE of Timmins; silver and cobalt mining.

Gowganda Lake (6 mi. long, 1 mi. wide), E Ont., 80 mi. N of Sudbury; drains N into Montreal R.

Gowran (gou′rŭn), Gaelic *Gabhrán,* town (pop. 368), E Co. Kilkenny, Ireland, 8 mi. ESE of Kilkenny; agr. market (cattle; barley, potatoes). Has anc. collegiate church.

Gowrie (gou′rē), town (pop. 1,052), Webster co., central Iowa, 16 mi. SSW of Fort Dodge; rail junction; dairy products. Inc. 1870.

Goya (goi′ä), town (pop. 22,099), ⊙ Goya dept. (□ c.1,700; pop. 32,395), W Corrientes prov., Argentina, port on Paraná R. and 120 mi. SSW of Corrientes. Rail terminus; processing and agr. center. Sawmills, flour mills, tanneries, meat-packing plants; dairy products, ceramics. Ships citrus fruit, tobacco, cotton, flax, rice, corn, livestock. Airport. Has tobacco research station, natl. col.

Goya Gate, India: see BARODA, city.

Goyana, Brazil: see GOIANA.

Goyaninha, Brazil: see GOIANINHA.

Goyave (gôyäv′), town (commune pop. 1,695), E Basse-Terre isl., Guadeloupe, 12 mi. NE of Basse-Terre; agr. center (cacao, coffee, sugar cane); lumbering, sugar milling, liquor distilling.

Goyaz, Brazil: see GOIÁS.

Goyllarisquizga (goiyärēskēs′gä), town (pop. 2,955), Pasco dept., central Peru, in Nudo de Pasco of the Andes, 16 mi. NNW of Cerro de Pasco (connected by railroad); alt. 13,983 ft. Major coal-mining center, shipping ore to LA OROYA smelter. Also Goyllarisquisga.

Goynuk (gûēnük′), Turkish *Göynük,* village (pop. 1,627), Bolu prov., NW Turkey, 33 mi. SE of Adapazari; grain, flax, mohair goats.

Goyomai Strait (gōyō′mī), small channel bet. Cape Noshappu of Nemuro peninsula, E Hokkaido, Japan, and Shuishio Isl. of lesser Kurile Isls., Russian SFSR; connects SE Nemuro Strait with the Pacific; 5 mi. wide.

Goyu (gō′yо͞o), town (pop. 2,602), Aichi prefecture, central Honshu, Japan, 7 mi. NW of Toyohashi; rice, raw silk.

Goz-Beida (gôz-bādä′), village, E Chad territory, Fr. Equatorial Africa, 120 mi. SSE of Abéché; customs station near Anglo-Egyptian Sudan border; leather handicrafts; vegetables, fruit.

Gozo (gŏt′sō), anc. *Gaulus* or *Gaulos,* Maltese *Ghaudex* or *Ghaudesh* (both: gou′dĕsh), 2d largest island (□ 25.89; pop. 27,612) of the Maltese Isls., in the Mediterranean, c.2 mi. off NW tip of Malta and 13 mi. NW of Valletta; principal town, VICTORIA. It is about 9 mi. long, 3 mi. wide. Has a steep coast; rises to 638 ft. Imjar landing is SE. Considered more fertile than Malta, isl. produces fruit, vegetables, grapes, livestock. Fishing. Mfg. of native embroidery. Impressive megalithic ruins 1½ mi. E of Victoria. Also noteworthy is 18th-cent. Fort Chambray, 3½ mi. SE of Victoria. In isl.'s center is a decaying citadel (c.1600), which encloses a cathedral and remains of medieval architecture. Isl. was a stronghold of the Knights Hospitalers. A legend holds it to be Ogygia isl., where Odysseus met Calypso.

Goz Ragab or **Goz Regeb** (both: gōz′ rĕgĕb′), town, Kassala prov., NE Anglo-Egyptian Sudan, on right bank of Atbara R., on road and 70 mi. NW of Kassala. Police post.

Gozzano (gôtsä′nô), village (pop. 3,307), Novara prov., Piedmont, N Italy, near S end of L. of Orta, 23 mi. NNW of Novara; rayon industry.

Graaff Reinet (gräf″ rīnĕt′, Afrik. khräf), town (pop. 13,905), SE central Cape Prov., U. of So. Afr., on Sundays R. and 135 mi. NNW of Port Elizabeth, on the Great Karroo; center of important agr. region (fruit, flowers, viticulture, wool, mohair, cattle); scene of agr. fairs. Site of teachers' training col. Resort. Airfield. Founded 1786; a short-lived republic was proclaimed here 1795.

Graal-Müritz or **Ostseebad Graal-Müritz** (ôst′zābät′ gräl′-mü′rĭts), village (pop. 3,875), Mecklenburg, N Germany, on the Baltic, 13 mi. NNE of Rostock; seaside resort. Created 1938 through incorporation of Graal and Bad Müritz.

Graasten (grô′stŭn), town (pop. 2,283), Aabenraa-Sonderborg amt, S Jutland, Denmark, 11 mi. SE of Aabenraa; mfg. of chemicals; machine shops, ship-building.

Graben (grä′bŭn), village (pop. 3,258), N Baden Germany, after 1945 in Württemberg-Baden, on the Pfinz and 5 mi. WNW of Bruchsal; rail junction; asparagus, strawberries, tobacco.

Grabill (grā′bĭl″), town (pop. 370), Allen co., NE Ind., 13 mi. NE of Fort Wayne, in agr. area.

Grabow (grä′bō), town (pop. 8,708), Mecklenburg N Germany, on regulated Elde R. and 21 mi. NNW of Wittenberge; woodworking, brewing; mfg. of leather products, barrels, gingerbread.

Grabow or **Grabow nad Prosna** (grä′bо͞of näd prôs′nō), Pol. *Grabów nad Prosną,* town (1946 pop. 1,548), Poznan prov., SW Poland, on Prosna R. and 18 mi. S of Kalisz; flour milling, sawmilling. Before First World War, in Prussia, on Rus. Poland border.

Grabs (gräps), town (pop. 4,292), St. Gall canton, NE Switzerland, 2 mi. W of the Rhine, near Liechtenstein border, 4 mi. NW of Vaduz, Liechtenstein embroideries, shoes.

Grabusa, Cape, Crete: see VOUXA, CAPE.

Gracac (grä′chäts), Serbo-Croatian *Gračac,* village (pop. 2,581), W Croatia, Yugoslavia, on railroad and 32 mi. ENE of Zadar, at SE foot of Velebit Mts.; local trade center.

Gracanica or **Grachanitsa** (both: grä′chänĭtsä), Serbo-Croatian *Gračanica,* village (pop. 5,651), NE Bosnia, Yugoslavia, on Spreca R., on railroad and 20 mi. NW of Tuzla; center of plum and sugar-beet area.

Gracanica, monastery, Yugoslavia: see PRISTINA.

Graçay (gräsā′), village (pop. 1,288), Cher dept. central France, 12 mi. WSW of Vierzon; livestock market; sheet mfg. Megaliths near by.

Grace, village (pop. 761), Caribou co., SE Idaho, 10 mi. SW of Soda Springs and on Bear R.; alt. 5,226 ft.; dairy (cheese), cattle.

Grâce-Berleur (gräs-bĕrlûr′), town (pop. 7,756) Liége prov., E Belgium, 3 mi. W of Liége; mfg. of boilers.

Gracefield, village (pop. 537), SW Que., on Gatineau R. and 50 mi. NNW of Ottawa; dairying, cattle raising.

Gracehill or **Ballykennedy** (bă″lēkĕ′nŭdē), agr. village, W central Co. Antrim, Northern Ireland, 2 mi. WSW of Ballymena; cattle; flax, potatoes. A Moravian settlement, founded 1746.

Gracemont, town (pop. 301), Caddo co., W central Okla., 8 mi. N of Anadarko, in agr. area.

Graceville. **1** City (pop. 1,638), Jackson co., NW Fla., near Ala. line and Holmes Creek, 21 mi. NW of Marianna; rail terminus; peanut shelling, lumber milling. **2** Village (pop. 962), Big Stone co., W Minn., 18 mi. N of Ortonville in diversified-farming area; dairy products. State park near by.

Gracey, town (1940 pop. 234), Christian co., SW Ky., 11 mi. W of Hopkinsville, in agr. area.

Grachanitsa, Yugoslavia: see GRACANICA.

Grachevka (grŭchôf′kŭ). **1** Village (1926 pop. 2,876), W Chkalov oblast, Russian SFSR, on Tok R. and 25 mi. NE of Buzuluk; metalworking; wheat, sunflowers, livestock. **2** Village (1926 pop. 3,422), NW Voronezh oblast, Russian SFSR, 12 mi. ENE of Usman; grain, tobacco.

Gracia (grä'thyä), large W section of Barcelona, Barcelona prov., NE Spain, at S foot of the Pelada.

Gracias, department, Honduras: see LEMPIRA.

Gracias (grä'syäs), city (pop. 1,521), ⊙ Lempira dept., W Honduras, near Mejocote R. (right affluent of Jicatuyo R.), 18 mi. SE of Santa Rosa de Copán; 14°34'N 88°38'W; alt. 2,352 ft. Commercial center in agr. area (corn, wheat, rice, potatoes, coffee). Has col., airfield. One of oldest cities (founded c.1530) of Honduras; flourished (16th–17th cent.) as mining and colonial administrative center; declined after 18th cent. Destroyed 1915 by earthquake; later rebuilt.

Gracias a Dios, Cabo, Nicaragua: see CABO GRACIAS A DIOS.

Graciosa Island (grŭsyô'zů), northernmost (□ 23; 1950 pop. 9,525) of the central Azores, in the Atlantic, c.35 mi. NW of Terceira Isl.; 8 mi. long, 4 mi. wide. Santa Cruz (39°5'N 28°1'W), its chief port, is on N shore. Of volcanic origin, it rises to 1,338 ft. at the Caldeira do Enxôfre; steep coast. Fertile lava soil supports luxuriant vegetation. Agr. (wine, fruit, cereals), cattle raising. Administratively part of Angra do Heroísmo dist.

Graciosa Island (grä-thyō'sä), uninhabited islet (□ 10½; 5 mi. long, up to 2 mi. wide), Canary Isls., just N of Lanzarote across narrow El Río channel; of volcanic origin; rises to over 800 ft. Isl. now largely overlaid by sands from Sahara.

Gradac or **Gradac Dalmatinski** (grä'däts däl'-mätĭnskē), Ital. *Grado* (grä'dô), village, S Croatia, Yugoslavia, on Adriatic Sea, 45 mi. ESE of Split, in Dalmatia; seaside resort.

Gradacac or **Gradachats** (both: grä'dächäts), Serbo-Croatian *Gradačac,* town (pop. 4,282), NE Bosnia, Yugoslavia, 25 mi. NNW of Tuzla; local trade center.

Gradets (grä'děts), village (pop. 4,081), Vidin dist., NW Bulgaria, 6 mi. WNW of Vidin; vineyards, truck, sunflowers. Formerly Gartsi.

Gradisca d'Isonzo (grädē'skä dēzôn'tsô), town (pop. 886), Gorizia prov., Friuli–Venezia Giulia, NE Italy, on Isonzo R. and 6 mi. SW of Gorizia; mfg. (hosiery, agr. tools, brushes). Archbishopric. Has cathedral and old castle. Was ⊙, with Gorizia, of former Austrian crownland of Görz-Gradisca.

Gradishte (grädē'shtě), village (pop. 3,363), Gorna Oryakhovitsa dist., N Bulgaria, 20 mi. NNE of Sevliyevo; horticulture, grain, livestock. Formerly Osma Gradishte.

Gradiska, Gradishka, Bosanska Gradiska, or **Bosanska Gradishka** (bô'sänskä grä'dĭshkä), Serbo-Croatian *Bosanska Gradiška,* village (pop. 5,573), N Bosnia, Yugoslavia, on Sava R., opposite Stara Gradiska (Croatia), and 26 mi. N of Banja Luka; trade center. Fortified and called Berbir under Turkish rule.

Gradiste or **Gradishte** (both: grä'dĭshtě). **1** or **Backo Gradiste** or **Bachko Gradishte** (both: bäch'kô), Serbo-Croatian *Bačko Gradište,* Hung. *Bácsföldvár* (bäch'fůldvär), village (pop. 6,033), Vojvodina, N Serbia, Yugoslavia, on arm of the Tisa and 6 mi. S of Becej, in the Backa. **2** or **Veliko Gradiste** or **Veliko Gradishte** (vě'lĭkô), Serbo-Croatian *Veliko Gradište,* village, (pop. 2,762), E Serbia, Yugoslavia, on the Danube (Rum. border) and 50 mi. E of Belgrade; fishing. Hydroelectric plant.

Gradistea (grŭdēsh'tyä), Rum. *Grădiştea,* village (pop. 583), Valcea prov., S central Rumania, 28 mi. SW of Ramnicu-Valcea; orchards.

Gradizhsk (grŭdyē'zhŭsk), town (1926 pop. 11,967), S Poltava oblast, Ukrainian SSR, near Dnieper R., 17 mi. WNW of Kremenchug; lumber, flour, clothing industries.

Grado (grä'dô), town (pop. 5,831), Gorizia prov., Friuli–Venezia Giulia, NE Italy, on isl. in Adriatic Sea, 26 mi. SSE of Udine; connected with mainland by causeway across Grado Lagoon (3 mi. wide). One of most fashionable bathing resorts of the Adriatic. Has 6th-cent. cathedral with mosaic floor.

Grado (grä'dhō), town (pop. 2,850), Oviedo prov., NW Spain, 11 mi. WNW of Oviedo; shoe mfg., flour milling; corn, potatoes, fruit. Iron mines near by.

Grado, Yugoslavia: see GRADAC.

Gradoli (grä'dôlē), village (pop. 2,159), Viterbo prov., Latium, central Italy, near L. Bolsena, 20 mi. NW of Viterbo. Has 16th-cent. Farnese palace.

Gradski Umet or **Gradskiy Umet** (grät"skē ōōmyôt'), village (1939 pop. over 500), E Tambov oblast, Russian SFSR, 13 mi. SE of Kirsanov; grain, sugar beets. Also called Grad-Umet.

Gradsko (gräd'skô), village, Macedonia, Yugoslavia, on Vardar R., near the Crna Reka mouth, on railroad and 13 mi. SSE of Titov Veles. Excavations of anc. structures at near-by site of Stobi, an important city of late Roman Empire.

Grad-Umet, Russian SFSR: see GRADSKI UMET.

Grady (grā'dē). **1** County (□ 355; pop. 18,928), SW Ga.; ⊙ Newton. Bounded S by Fla. line. Coastal plain area drained by Ochlockonee R. Agr. (sugar cane, tobacco, corn, truck, peanuts, pecans, tung nuts, livestock) and forestry (lumber, naval stores); mfg. at Cairo. Formed 1905. **2** County (□ 1,092; pop. 34,872), central Okla.; ⊙ Chickasha. Bounded N by Canadian R.; intersected by Washita R.; and drained also by small Rush Creek and Little Washita R. Diversified agr. (cotton, broomcorn, wheat, oats, hay, watermelons, tomatoes, alfalfa), stock raising, dairying. Mfg. at Chickasha. Oil wells; oil refining. Formed 1907.

Grady. 1 Town (pop. 517), Lincoln co., SE Ark., 20 mi. ESE of Pine Bluff. **2** Village (pop. 130), Curry co., E N.Mex., near Texas line, 30 mi. NNW of Clovis.

Graemsay (grām'sā), island (pop. 114) of the Orkneys, Scotland, in the Sound of Hoy, bet. Hoy and Pomona; 2 mi. long, 1 mi. wide; rises to 205 ft.

Graettinger (grě'tĭnjůr), town (pop. 1,016), Palo Alto co., NW Iowa, near West Des Moines R., 10 mi. NNW of Emmetsburg; mfg. (feed, dairy products, concrete blocks). Sand and gravel pits near by.

Graf, town (pop. 44), Dubuque co., E Iowa, 10 mi. W of Dubuque.

Gräfelfing (grä'fůlfĭng"), village (pop. 8,128), Upper Bavaria, Germany, on Würm R. and 6 mi. W of Munich; mfg. of precision instruments, textiles, paper; tanning.

Grafenau (grä'fůnou), town (pop. 3,975), Lower Bavaria, Germany, in Bohemian Forest, 19 mi. NNW of Passau; textile mfg., woodworking, brewing. Has 17th-cent. town hall. Chartered 1376.

Gräfenberg (grā'fůnběrk), town (pop. 1,763), Upper Franconia, N central Bavaria, Germany, 16 mi. NE of Nuremberg; tanning, brewing, flour and lumber milling. Summer resort. Chartered 1378.

Gräfenberg, hill near Kiedrich, in the Rheingau, W Germany; noted vineyards on slopes.

Gräfenberk or **Gräfenberg,** Czechoslovakia: see JESENIK.

Gräfendorf (grā'fůndôrf), village (pop. 1,069), Lower Franconia, NW Bavaria, Germany, on the Franconian Saale and 16 mi. WSW of Bad Kissingen; hydroelectric station; cabbage, hogs.

Gräfenhainichen (grā'fůnhī'nĭchůn), town (pop. 6,503), in former Prussian Saxony prov., central Germany, after 1945 in Saxony-Anhalt, 11 mi. NE of Bitterfeld; lignite mining; mfg. of chemicals. Poet Gerhardt b. here.

Grafenhausen (grä"fůnhou'zůn), village (pop. 1,225), S Baden, Germany, in Black Forest, 10 mi. SSE of Neustadt; summer resort (alt. 2,936 ft.).

Gräfenroda (grā"fůnrō'dä), town (pop. 4,799), Thuringia, central Germany, on N slope of Thuringian Forest, 8 mi. SW of Arnstadt; mfg. of china, glass, optical and precision instruments; woodworking.

Grafenstein (grä'fůnshtīn), town (pop. 2,205), Carinthia, S Austria, near the Drau, 7 mi. E of Klagenfurt; summer resort.

Gräfenthal (grā'fůntäl"), town (pop. 3,380), Thuringia, central Germany, in Thuringian Forest, 9 mi. SW of Saalfeld; china and wire-netting mfg.; slate quarrying; climatic health resort. Towered over by remains of Wespenstein castle, seat (1438–1599) of marshals of Pappenheim.

Gräfentonna (grā"fůntô'nä), village (pop. 2,365), Thuringia, central Germany, 4 mi. ESE of Langensalza; tufaceous-limestone and gypsum quarrying. Has old Kettenburg castle, now prison.

Grafenwöhr (grä'fůnvûr"), town (pop. 4,590), Upper Palatinate, NE Bavaria, Germany, 12 mi. WNW of Weiden; brewing, dairying. Chartered bet. 1366 and 1427. Peat bogs in area.

Graffignano (gräf-fēnyä'nô), village (pop. 900), Viterbo prov., Latium, central Italy, near the Tiber, 12 mi. NNE of Viterbo; mfg. (watch parts, glass).

Graford (grā'fůrd), town (pop. 655), Palo Pinto co., N central Texas, c.55 mi. WNW of Fort Worth, near the Brazos; trade point in cattle, agr. area.

Gräfrath (grāf'rät"), suburb (1925 pop. 10,582) of Solingen, W Germany, 2.5 mi. N of city center. Inc. 1929 into Solingen.

Grafskaya, Russian SFSR: see KRASNOLESNY.

Grafton, municipality and river port (pop. 8,283), NE New South Wales, Australia, on Clarence R. and 160 mi. S of Brisbane; dairying and agr. center. Exports sugar, bananas, timber. Anglican cathedral. Hydroelectric plant near by. S. Grafton, on Clarence R. opposite Grafton, is separate municipality.

Grafton, village (pop. estimate 450), SE Ont., near L. Ontario, 8 mi. ENE of Cobourg; dairying, fruitgrowing.

Grafton, county (□ 1,717; pop. 47,923), central and W N.H.; ⊙ Woodsville. Summer and winter resort region, including large area of White Mts. and White Mtn. Natl. Forest. Lumbering, agr. (fruit, poultry, dairy products), mica quarrying, mfg. (textiles, wood products). Drained by Connecticut, Ammonoosuc, Pemigewasset, Mascoma, Baker rivers. Formed 1769.

Grafton. 1 City (pop. 1,117), Jersey co., W Ill., at junction of Illinois and Mississippi rivers, 14 mi. WNW of Alton, in agr. area. Inc. 1853. Pere Marquette State Park (c.5,000 acres; recreational area) is W, along Illinois R. **2** Town (pop. 278), Worth co., N Iowa, 14 mi. NNE of Mason City; livestock, grain. **3** Town (pop. 8,281), Worcester co., S central Mass., 8 mi. ESE of Worcester; leather, abrasives, worsteds. Settled 1718, inc. 1735. Includes villages of North Grafton (1940 pop. 1,062), Farnumsville (1940 pop. 878), Fisherville (1940 pop. 1,264), Saundersville, and Wilkinsonville (1940 pop. 564), on Blackstone R. and partly in Sutton town. **4** Village (pop. 159), Fillmore co., SE Nebr., 9 mi. NW of Geneva. **5** Town (pop. 442), Grafton co., W central N.H., on Mascoma R. and 35 mi. NW of Concord; mica quarries. **6** Resort village, Rensselaer co., E N.Y., 13 mi. ENE of Troy. Small lakes near by. **7** City (pop. 4,901), ⊙ Walsh co., NE N.Dak., 38 mi. NNW of Grand Forks and on Park R. Center of rich agr. area and important shipping point; dairy products, livestock, grain, potatoes. Seat of state school for feeble-minded. Inc. 1883. **8** Village (pop. 1,194), Lorain co., N Ohio, 6 mi. SSE of Elyria and on East Branch of Black R.; foundry products, grain and dairy products, electrical goods, lumber. **9** Town (pop. 422), Windham co., SE Vt., 10 mi. WNW of Bellows Falls and on Saxtons R. Grafton State Forest here. **10** City (pop. 7,365), ⊙ Taylor co., N W.Va., on Tygart R. and 12 mi. SSE of Fairmont, in coal-mining, timber, and agr. area. Rail junction (repair shops, yards); mfg. of glass, china, foundry products; granite works. Natl. cemetery here. Just S is Tygart R. Reservoir. Settled 1852. **11** Village (pop. 1,489), Ozaukee co., E Wis., on Milwaukee R. and 19 mi. N of Milwaukee, in farm area; mfg. (iron castings, welders, saws, stoves, yarn). Inc. 1896.

Grafton, Cape, NE Queensland, Australia, in Coral Sea; forms SE end of Trinity Bay; 16°52'S 145°56'E. Rises to 1,230 ft.

Grafton, Mount (10,983 ft.), E Nev., 40 mi. SSE of Ely, in outlying section of Egan and Shell Creek ranges.

Graglia, Santuario di, Italy: see BIELLA.

Gragnana (gränyä'nä), village (pop. 2,107), Massa e Carrara prov., Tuscany, central Italy, 2 mi. N of Carrara; paper mill.

Gragnano (gränyä'nô), town (pop. 10,529), Napoli prov., Campania, S Italy, 2 mi. E of Castellammare di Stabia; macaroni mfg. center; wine, packing boxes.

Gragnano Trebbiense (trěb-byěn'sē), village (pop. 696), Piacenza prov., Emilia-Romagna, N central Italy, near Trebbia R., 6 mi. WSW of Piacenza; tomato cannery.

Graham (grā'ům). **1** County (□ 4,610; pop. 12,985), SE Ariz.; ⊙ Safford. Chief ranges are Gila, Pinaleno, and Galiuro mts. Gila and San Carlos rivers and San Carlos Reservoir supply water for irrigation. San Carlos Indian Reservation is in N; parts of Crook Natl. Forest are in SW. Cotton, alfalfa, citrus fruits, truck products; cotton ginning. Formed 1909. **2** County (□ 891; pop. 5,020), NW Kansas; ⊙ Hill City. Rolling prairie region, drained by South Fork Solomon R. Wheat, livestock. Formed 1880. **3** County (□ 295; pop. 6,886), extreme W N.C.; ⊙ Robbinsville. Bounded W by Tenn., E by Nantahala R., N by Little Tennessee R.; Unicoi Mts. in W, Snowbird Mts. in S; included in Nantahala Natl. Forest; drained by Cheoah R. Farming (corn, potatoes, tobacco), cattle raising, lumbering; resort area. Hydroelectric plants at Fontana and Cheoah dams in Little Tennessee R., and at Santeetlah Dam in Cheoah R. Formed 1872.

Graham. 1 Town (pop. 160), Appling co., SE central Ga., 10 mi. WNW of Baxley. **2** Mining village (1940 pop. 1,063), Muhlenberg co., W Ky., 13 mi. ESE of Madisonville; bituminous coal. **3** Town (pop. 311), Nodaway co., NW Mo., on Nodaway R. and 13 mi. SW of Maryville. **4** Town (pop. 5,026), ⊙ Alamance co., N central N.C., 22 mi. E of Greensboro; textile milling center (hosiery, fabrics, yarn); sawmilling. Established 1849. **5** City (pop. 6,742), ⊙ Young co., N Texas, c.55 mi. S of Wichita Falls; commercial, processing center for cattle, agr., oil area; oil refining, meat packing, grain and cottonseed-oil milling, mfg. of carbon black, saddles. Possum Kingdom L. (state park; recreation) is c.5 mi. SE. Founded 1872. **6** Town, Tazewell co., Va.: see BLUEFIELD, W.Va. and Va.

Graham, Mount, highest peak (10,713 ft.) in Pinaleno Mts., SE Ariz., 13 mi. SW of Safford.

Graham Beach, N.Y.: see SOUTH BEACH.

Graham Bell Island, easternmost island of Franz Josef Land, Russian SFSR, in Arctic Ocean; 45 mi. long, 25 mi. wide; 81°N 64°E. Terminates NE in Cape Kohlsaat. Discovered 1898–99 by U.S. Wellman expedition.

Graham Island. 1 Largest (□ 2,485) of the Queen Charlotte Isls., W B.C., in the Pacific 60 mi. WSW of Prince Rupert, separated from Alaska by Dixon Entrance, from B.C. mainland by Hecate Strait, and from Moresby Isl. (S) by Skidegate Inlet and Channel. It is 70 mi. long, 20–55 mi. wide. Queen Charlotte Mts. extend along SW coast, rising to 4,100 ft. on Mt. Needham. Inlets include Masset Sound, expanding into Masset Inlet in center of isl., and Naden Harbour. Lumbering, fishing, fish canning, stock raising are main occupations of the people, who are mainly Haida Indians. Chief villages are Massett, Queen Charlotte, and Skidegate. Large anthracite deposits are undeveloped. **2** Island (c.15 mi. long, 3–7 mi. wide), NE Franklin Dist., Northwest Territories, in Norwegian Bay of the Arctic Ocean, W of Ellesmere Isl.; 77°15'N 90°50'W.

Graham Lake, Hancock co., S Maine, just N of Ellsworth, in hunting, fishing area; 13 mi. long.

Graham Land, Antarctica: see PALMER PENINSULA.

Grahamstad, U. of So. Afr.: see GRAHAMSTOWN.

Grahamstown, Afrikaans *Grahamstad* (–stät), town (pop. 22,993), S Cape Prov., U. of So. Afr., 70 mi. NE of Port Elizabeth; judicial center of E Cape Prov. and shipping center for dairying, wool-producing, fruitgrowing region. Site of Rhodes Univ. Col. (1904), constituent col. of Univ. of South Africa; Natl. Library for the Blind. Features include Albany Mus. (1855) and Fine Arts Association gallery. Has Anglican cathedral and R.C. pro-cathedral. Airfield. Founded 1812 as outpost in Kaffir territory; attacked by Kaffirs in 1819, 1834, 1846, and 1849.

Grahn (grän), village (1940 pop. 679), Carter co., NE Ky., 27 mi. WSW of Ashland; makes firebrick.

Grahovo or **Grakhovo** (grä'khôvô). **1** or **Bosansko Grahovo** or **Bosansko Grakhovo** (bô'sänskô), village (pop. 1,307), W Bosnia, Yugoslavia, 12 mi. NNE of Knin, near Croatia border; local trade center. **2** Village, W Montenegro, Yugoslavia, 14 mi. SW of Niksic.

Graian Alps (grā'yůn), Fr. *Alpes Grées* or *Alpes Graies*, Ital. *Alpi Graie*, N division of Western Alps, on Fr.-Ital. border; extend in an arc from Cottian Alps at Mont Cenis (SW) to Little St. Bernard Pass (N) and Dora Baltea valley (NE). Bounded W by Isère and Arc R. valleys. Highest peak, Gran Paradiso (13,323 ft.). Contain many glaciers. Just N is Mont Blanc group. Savoy Alps are NW offshoots.

Graïba (grībä'), village, Sfax dist., E Tunisia, 34 mi. WSW of Sfax; junction of Tunis-Gabès and Sfax-Tozeur RR lines. Olive groves.

Graie, Alpi, or **Alpes Graies:** see GRAIAN ALPS.

Graig, England: see ROGERSTONE.

Graigue (grāg), village, Co. Laoighis, Ireland, on the Barrow opposite Carlow.

Graiguenamanagh (grāg"nůmä'nů), Gaelic *Gráig na Manach*, town (pop. 1,064), E Co. Kilkenny, Ireland, on Barrow R. and 10 mi. N of New Ross, at foot of Mt. Brandon; agr. market (cattle; barley, potatoes). Has remains of Abbey of Duiske (1212).

Grain, Arabia: see KUWAIT.

Grain, Isle of, island (□ 4.9; pop. 550) bet. the Thames and the Medway, N Kent, England, opposite Sheerness and separated from mainland by narrow Yantlet Creek; 2 mi. wide, 3 mi. long.

Grain Coast, name formerly frequently applied to the littoral of Liberia, W Africa, bet. 4° and 6°N; sometimes also included section of Sierra Leone coast. Named for its former trade in "grains of paradise" or Malaguetta pepper.

Grainfield, city (pop. 371), Gove co., NW Kansas, 21 mi. E of Oakley.

Grainger (grān'jůr), county (□ 310; pop. 13,086), E Tenn.; ⊙ Rutledge. Traversed SW-NE by Clinch Mtn.; bounded N by Clinch R., E and S by Holston R. Includes part of Cherokee Reservoir. Farm and timber region; livestock, dairy products, corn, tobacco. Lumbering, marble quarrying. Mineral springs (resorts). Formed 1796.

Graingers (grān'jůrz), town (pop. 168), Lenoir co., E central N.C., 5 mi. NE of Kinston, near Neuse R.

Grainola, town (pop. 79), Osage co., N Okla., 26 mi. NW of Pawhuska, near Kansas line.

Grainton, village (pop. 91), Perkins co., SW central Nebr., 35 mi. SW of North Platte.

Grain Valley, town (pop. 348), Jackson co., W Mo., 22 mi. E of Kansas City.

Graisivaudan, France: see GRÉSIVAUDAN.

Graissessac (grāsůsäk'), town (pop. 2,318), Hérault dept., S France, in the Monts de l'Espinouse, 12 mi. WSW of Lodève; coal-mining center.

Graivoron or **Grayvoron** (grī'vůrůn), city (1926 pop. 8,905), SW Kursk oblast, Russian SFSR, on Vorskla R. and 39 mi. WSW of Belgorod; metalworks. Chartered 1838.

Grajahú, Brazil: see GRAJAÚ.

Grajal de Campos (grähäl' dhä käm'pōs), town (pop. 1,203), Leon prov., NW Spain, 35 mi. SE of Leon; cereals, wine, vegetables; sheep raising. Has anc. palace and ruins of 15th-cent. castle.

Grajaú (grůzhäōō'), city (pop. 2,463), W central Maranhão, Brazil, head of navigation on Grajaú R. and 260 mi. SW of São Luís; stock-raising center (horses, mules); ships copaiba oil, hides. Airfield. Copper, manganese, and gypsum deposits near by. Formerly spelled Grajahú.

Grajaú River, Maranhão, NE Brazil, rises near 6°50'S 46°45'W, flows c.300 mi. NNE, past Grajaú (head of navigation), to Mearim R. in lake dist. 15 mi. S of Baixo Mearim. Formerly spelled Grajahú.

Grajera (grähā'rä), town (pop. 211), Segovia prov., central Spain, 40 mi. NW of Segovia; cereals, carobs, vetch, livestock. Airport (service to Madrid, Burgos, and Vitoria).

Grajewo (gräyě'vô), Rus. *Grayevo* (grůyä'vō), town (pop. 6,171), Bialystok prov., NE Poland, on railroad and 45 mi. NW of Bialystok; glass works. Before Second World War, pop. over 50% Jewish; during war, under administration of East Prussia.

Grakhovo (grä'khůvů), village (1926 pop. 871), SW Udmurt Autonomous SSR, Russian SFSR, 30 mi. SSE of Mozhga; rye, oats, flax, livestock.

Grakhovo, Yugoslavia: see GRAHOVO.

Gram or **Gramby** (gräm'bü), town (pop. 1,588), Haderslev amt, S Jutland, Denmark, 17 mi. WNW of Haderslev; rug mfg.

Grama, Brazil: see SÃO SEBASTIÃO DA GRAMA.

Gramada (grämä'dä), village (pop. 4,662), Vidin dist., NW Bulgaria, 8 mi. ESE of Kula; grain, livestock, truck.

Gramalote (grämälō'tā), town (pop. 2,378), Norte de Santander dept., N Colombia, on slopes of Cordillera Oriental, 19 mi. W of Cúcuta; alt. 3,346 ft.; coffee, cacao, fique fibers.

Gramastetten (grä'mäshtĕtůn), village (pop. 2,203), N Upper Austria, 7 mi. NNW of Linz, N of the Danube; rye, potatoes.

Gramat (grämä'), village (pop. 1,783), Lot dept., SW France, in the Causse de Gramat, 27 mi. NE of Cahors; tanning, cheese making, food canning, mfg. of clothing. Tourists visit near-by karstlike formations, stalactite caverns, and subterranean stream of Padirac (5 mi. N).

Gramat, Causse de, France: see CAUSSES.

Gramatneusiedl (grä"mätnoi'zēdůl), town (pop. 2,141), after 1938 in Schwechat dist., of Vienna, Austria, 13 mi. SSE of city center; rail junction.

Grambow (gräm'bō), village (pop. 640) in former Prussian Pomerania prov., E Germany, after 1945 in Mecklenburg; frontier station on Pol. border, 8 mi. WNW of Stettin.

Gramby, Denmark: see GRAM.

Gramercy (gră'můrsē), village (pop. 1,184), St. James parish, SE central La., 36 mi. WNW of New Orleans and on E bank (levee) of the Mississippi; sugar milling. Inc. since 1940.

Gramercy Park, SE N.Y., a residential district of S central Manhattan borough of New York city, S of 23d St. and E of 4th Ave., and centering on small Gramercy Park.

Gramilla (grämē'yä), village (pop. estimate 500), ⊙ Jiménez dept. (□ 2,200; 1947 pop. 11,398), W Santiago del Estero prov., Argentina, on railroad and 40 mi. NW of Santiago del Estero, in agr. (alfalfa, corn) and lumbering area; hides.

Gramisdale, Scotland: see BENBECULA.

Grammichele (gräm-mēkā'lě), town (pop. 13,772), Catania prov., SE central Sicily, 7 mi. E of Caltagirone, in cereal- and grape-growing region; canned vegetables. Rebuilt near its old site following destruction by earthquake of 1693.

Grammont (grämō'), Flemish *Geraardsbergen* (formerly *Geeraardsbergen*) (khā'rärdzběr'khůn), town (pop. 11,283), East Flanders prov., W central Belgium, on Dender R. and 8 mi. SW of Ninove; textile center; match mfg. Has 15th-cent. Gothic town hall. Its charter, granted in 1068, is called the "*Magna Carta*" of Flanders.

Grammos (grä'môs), Albanian *Gramos* or *Gramosi*, section of main Pindus mtn. system on Albanian-Greek border, SW of L. Prespa; rises to 8,268 ft. in Mt. Grammos [Albanian *Mal i Qukapesit*], 18 mi. S of Koritsa. Scene of military operations (1947–49) against Greek guerrillas. The name Grammos is often applied to the Voion section of the Pindus system, adjoining SE.

Gramos or **Gramosi,** Albania-Greece: see GRAMMOS.

Grampian (grăm'pēůn), borough (pop. 589), Clearfield co., W central Pa., 5 mi. W of Curwensville; bituminous coal; agr.

Grampian Mountains (grăm'pyůn), extensive range in Scotland, extending SW–NE across the country, dividing the Lowlands from the Highlands; rises to 4,406 ft. in BEN NEVIS, highest peak in Great Britain. S slope is gentle, with large deer forests; N slope is precipitous, with noted wild scenery. The CAIRNGORM MOUNTAINS form part of the range and include some of the highest peaks, including Ben Macdhui, Cairntoul, and Cairngorm. The Grampians are source of the headwaters of the Dee, Don, Spey, Findhorn, Esk, Tay, and Forth rivers.

Grampians (grăm'pēůnz, –pyůnz), mountain range in SW central Victoria, Australia, SW spur of Great Dividing Range; extend c.40 mi. NW from Ararat; rise to 3,828 ft. at Mt. William; gold deposits.

Grampound, agr. village and parish (pop. 419), W central Cornwall, England, on Fal R. (fine stone bridge) and 6 mi. WSW of St. Austell; tanneries.

Gramsh (grämsh) or **Gramshi** (gräm'shē), village (1930 pop. 368), central Albania, on Devoll R. and 18 mi. SSE of Elbasan.

Gramvousa, Cape, Crete: see VOUXA, CAPE.

Gran, Hungary: see ESZTERGOM.

Graña, La (lä grä'nyä), suburb (pop. 1,364) of El Ferrol, La Coruña prov., NW Spain, on Ferrol Bay opposite El Ferrol; shipyards.

Granada (grůnä'dů, Sp. gränä'dhä), department (□ 540; 1950 pop. 48,990), SW Nicaragua, on NW shore of L. Nicaragua; ⊙ Granada. Largely level; extends from Malacatoya R. (N) nearly to the Pacific (SW); includes Zapatera Isl. in L. Nicaragua, volcano Mombacho, and Tisma and Genízaro lagoons of Tipitapa R. Important agr. region: coffee (on Mombacho slopes), cacao and sugar cane (Nandaime), grain (Diriá and Diriomo), fruit, tobacco, vegetables, plantains; livestock. Lumbering (N). Industry is based on agr. (coffee processing, alcohol distilling, sugar milling). Mfg. in Granada. Dept. served by Inter-American Highway, railroad from Managua, and lake shipping. Main centers: Granada, Nandaime.

Granada, city (1950 pop. 21,743), ⊙ Granada dept., SW Nicaragua, on L. Nicaragua, at NE foot of volcano Mombacho, and 27 mi. SE of Managua; 11°55'N 85°58'W. Rail terminus; industrial and commercial center; shipbuilding, lumber and sugar milling, distilling, mfg. (clothing, furniture, ice, soap). Agr. (coffee, sugar cane). Has cathedral (seat of bishop), Jesuit col. (N of city), and old fort (hq. of Natl. Guard). Its univ. (1846) was transferred 1951 to Natl. Univ. at León. Founded 1524; became one of most important cities of colonial Nicaragua; attacked repeatedly (17th–18th cent.) by pirates. Early center of independence movement. The filibuster William Walker sacked city in 1856.

Granada, town (1939 pop. 8,868), in metropolitan Bacolod, Negros Occidental prov., W Negros isl., Philippines, 6 mi. E of Bacolod proper; agr. center (rice, sugar cane).

Granada, province (□ 4,838; pop. 737,690), S Spain, in Andalusia; ⊙ Granada. Bounded S by the Mediterranean; crossed by several mtn. ranges including (W to E) the Sierra Nevada, rising here to highest peak in Spain (Mulhacén, 11,411 ft.); drained by Genil R. and its tributaries. Straight, rocky coast has no good ports. The mountainous areas have fertile hills and valleys, giving way to high plains and a luxuriant coastal tract. Alpujarras mtn. dist. in SW. Iron, copper, mercury, lead mines (Sierra Nevada); marble, gypsum, and limestone quarries; mineral springs. Essentially agr.; cereals, sugar beets, sugar cane, olive oil, tobacco (40% of Sp. production), wine, fruit and vegetables, hemp and esparto; some tropical plants (pineapples, bananas, coffee, cotton) along coast; sericulture. Sugar production is chief industry; also olive-oil processing, flour milling, brandy distilling; some mfg. of textiles, soap, footwear, pottery. Tourist industry. Trade hampered by poor communications; Granada connected with coastal town of Motril partly by secondary railway, partly by aerial tramway. Chief cities: Granada, Guadix, Motril, Baza, Loja.

Granada, anc. *Illiberis*, city (pop. 140,941), ⊙ Granada prov., S Spain, in Andalusia, on Genil R., at foot of the Sierra Nevada, and 225 mi. S of Madrid; 37°11'N 3°35'W. Its beautiful location and great art treasures make it one of most visited tourist resorts of Spain. Industrial, commercial, and road center in fertile dist. producing cereals, sugar cane and sugar beets, olive oil, wine, truck produce, and hemp; sericulture. Has govt. munitions factory, and brewery, sugar mills, tanneries, alcohol and brandy distilleries, chemical works. Other mfg.: textiles, knit goods, hats, footwear, essential oils, artificial flowers, soap, and candy. Of special importance for export are art objects (iron-, copper-, and leatherwork; tapestries, rugs) made here since Moorish times. The Darro R., flowing here into the Genil, divides the city into 2 sections: on right bank, Albaicín hill (once quarter of Moorish aristocracy, now home of gypsies) and modern town below; on left bank, Alhambra hill (crowned by Moorish fort, walls, and towers, by Moorish palace, and palace of Charles V), which dominates Antequeruela quarter (built in 15th cent.). The magnificent Alhambra palace (13th–14th cent.), once residence of Moorish kings, is greatest monument of Moorish art in Spain, with graceful patios (of Lions, of Myrtles, of Daraxa) and richly ornamented halls and apartments (of the Ambassadors, of the Two Sisters). The imposing palace of Charles V (started 1526) is still unfinished. On near-by hill is Generalife, royal summer pleasure resort, celebrated for its gardens. Also notable are Renaissance cathedral (1523–1703); the adjoining Gothic royal chapel, burial place of Ferdinand and Isabella; the 16th-cent. old chancery; the Cartuja (1516), a secularized Carthusian convent; and fine Moorish and Renaissance mansions. A univ. was founded in 16th cent. The old quarters have narrow, crooked streets with Arabian-style houses. The city was an old Roman colony which suffered under the Visigoths and rose to prominence under the Moors, when it became ⊙ independent kingdom (1031–90); it fell in 12th cent. to the Almoravides and then to the Almohades. In 1238 it became ⊙ Moorish kingdom of Granada (which included Málaga and Almería and parts of Jaén and Cádiz), achieving great prosperity as trade and art center. It was the last stronghold of Moorish power in Spain and was conquered (Jan., 1492) by the Catholic Kings, Ferdinand and Isabella, after defeat of Boabdil. Became an archiepiscopal see. It declined after expulsion (1609) of the Moriscos. Has observatory and military airport.

Granada (grůnä'dů). **1** Town (pop. 551), Prowers co., SE Colo., on Arkansas R., near Kansas line, and 17 mi. E of Lamar; trading point in grain and sugar-beet area. **2** Village (pop. 403), Martin co., S Minn., on small affluent of Blue Earth R. and 6 mi. ENE of Fairmont, in grain, potato, and livestock area.

Granada de Río Tinto, La (lä gränä'dhä dhä rē'ōtēn'tō), town (pop. 361), Huelva prov., SW Spain, in Sierra Morena, 9 mi. SSE of Aracena; acorns, cork, olives, timber, stock. Manganese deposits.

Granadella (gränä-dhä'lyä), town (pop. 1,456), Lérida prov., NE Spain, 18 mi. S of Lérida; agr. trade (olive oil, wine, almonds, cereals); sheep.

Granadilla de Abona (gränä-dhē'lyä dhä ävō'nä), town (pop. 1,690), Tenerife, Canary Isls., 32 mi. SW of Santa Cruz de Tenerife; cereals, tomatoes, grapes, oranges, potatoes, fruit, livestock. Fishing, lumbering; flour milling, cheese processing. Its port Puerto Abona is 8 mi. E.

Granado, El (ĕl gränä'dhō), town (pop. 785), Huelva prov., SW Spain, near Port. border, 20 mi. N of Ayamonte; cereals, sheep, goats, hogs.

Granados (gränä'dhōs), town (pop. 1,142), Sonora, NW Mexico, on Bavispe R. and 115 mi. NE of Hermosillo; livestock, grain.

Granaglione (gränälyō'nĕ), village (pop. 375), Bologna prov., Emilia-Romagna, N central Italy, on Reno R. and 3 mi. S of Poretta Terme; foundry.

Granard (gră'nŭrd), Gaelic *Gránárd*, urban district (pop. 1,197), E Co. Longford, Ireland, 13 mi. ENE of Longford; agr. market (dairying; potatoes).

Granarolo (gränärô'lô), village (pop. 691), Ravenna prov., Emilia-Romagna, N central Italy, 5 mi. NNE of Faenza; rail junction; foundry.

Granarolo dell'Emilia (dĕlĕmē'lyä), village (pop. 441), Bologna prov., Emilia-Romagna, N central Italy, 6 mi. ENE of Bologna; hemp mill.

Granátula or **Granátula de Calatrava** (gränä'tŏŏlä dhä käläträ'vä), town (pop. 3,311), Ciudad Real prov., S central Spain, on railroad and 15 mi. SE of Ciudad Real. Iron and manganese mining. Region raises olives, grapes, livestock. Alcohol distilling; mfg. of plaited goods and brooms.

Gran Banco de Buena Esperanza (grän' băng'kō dä bwä'nä ĕspärän'sä), bank and reefs in center of Gulf of Guacanayabo, off Oriente prov., E Cuba, c.20 mi. W of Manzanillo.

Granbury, city (pop. 1,683), ⊙ Hood co., N central Texas, 34 mi. SW of Fort Worth and on Brazos R.; shipping point in agr. area; poultry hatchery; cottonseed-oil mill. Settled c.1860, inc. 1873.

Granbusa Island, Turkey: see SULU ISLAND.

Granby (grăn'bē, grăm'–), city (pop. 14,197), S Que., on North Yamaska R. and 40 mi. E of Montreal; woolen and silk milling, tobacco processing; mfg. of rubber products, hosiery, plastics, furniture; market in apple-growing, dairying area; fox-fur farms.

Granby. 1 Town (pop. 463), Grand co., N Colo., on Frazer R., near its mouth in Colorado R., and 55 mi. NW of Denver; alt. 7,935 ft.; vegetables. Just NE, on Colorado R., is Granby Dam (begun 1942; important unit in Colorado–Big Thompson project of Bureau of Reclamation). Dam is 300 ft. high, 930 ft. long; from Granby Reservoir (expected capacity 550,000 acre-ft.), water will be pumped into Shadow Mountain L. and Grand L., then conducted through ALVA B. ADAMS TUNNEL to E slope of Continental Divide and used for irrigation and power. **2** Town (pop. 2,693) Hartford co., N Conn., on Mass. line and 15 mi. NW of Hartford; agr. (tobacco). Includes part of McLean Game Refuge. Settled c.1664, inc. 1786. **3** Town (pop. 1,861), Hampshire co., S central Mass., 6 mi. NE of Holyoke. Settled 1727, inc. 1768. **4** City (pop. 1,670), Newton co., SW Mo., in the Ozarks, 18 mi. SE of Joplin; agr. center; zinc, lead mines. Settled 1850s. **5** Town (pop. 74), Essex co., NE Vt., 16 mi. NE of St. Johnsbury; hunting, fishing.

Gran Canaria, Canary Isls.: see GRAND CANARY.

Grancey-le-Château (gräsā'-lŭ-shätō'), agr. village (pop. 270), Côte-d'Or dept., E central France, on the Plateau of Langres, 24 mi. N of Dijon; has 17th–18th-cent. castle.

Gran Chaco, South America: see CHACO.

Gran Chaco, province, Bolivia: see YACUIBA.

Gran Couva (grän″ kōō'vä'), village (pop. 223), W central Trinidad, B.W.I., at W foot of Montserrat Hills, 19 mi. SE of Port of Spain; cacao growing.

Grand (grã), village (pop. 558), Vosges dept., E France, 10 mi. W of Neufchâteau; furniture mfg.

Grand. 1 County (□ 1,867; pop. 3,963), N Colo.; ⊙ Hot Sulphur Springs. Livestock-grazing and truck-farming area, bounded E by Front Range; drained by Colorado R. Includes parts of Arapaho and Routt natl. forests and of Rocky Mtn. Natl. Park in NE. Formed 1874. **2** County (□ 3,692; pop. 1,903), E Utah; ⊙ Moab. Stock-grazing area bordering on Colo., bounded W by Green R., drained by Colorado R. Mineral deposits (vanadium, uranium) near Moab, copper in La Sal Mts. (SE). Includes much of East Tavaputs Plateau and Book Cliffs. Arches Natl. Monument is N of Moab. Co. formed 1890.

Grand' Aldée, Fr. India: see TIRUMALARAJANPATNAM.

Grand Anicut (ă'nĭkŭt″), control works for Mettur irrigation system, Tanjore dist., SE Madras, India, 9 mi. E of Trichinopoly; prevents reunion of Cauvery R. with its arm, the Coleroon, at E end of Srirangem Isl., dividing their waters to supply and control Cauvery R. delta; 1,000 ft. long. System was originally (c.11th cent.) constructed by Chola kings. The 19th-cent. regulating dams (just W of main dam at bifurcation point of Cauvery and Vennar rivers) and shutters (constructed in 1920s) on Grand Anicut further control division of water supply bet. the 2 rivers and feed **Grand Anicut Canal**, which extends from right bank of Cauvery R. at the Grand Anicut E past Tanjore, and S through SW non-deltaic tract of Tanjore dist. (rice, sugar cane, millet, peanuts), to point 12 mi. SSW of Pattukkottai; c.60 mi. long. Total length, including numerous distributaries, c.700 mi. Shorter Vadavar Canal serves area N and E. Total area irrigated by both, c.300,000 acres. Also called Mettur Canal.

Grand Anse (grănd ăns'), village (pop. estimate c.400), NE N.B., on Chaleur Bay, 30 mi. NE of Bathurst; fishing port (herring, mackerel, clams, smelt).

Grand Atlas, Fr. Morocco: see ATLAS MOUNTAINS.

Grand Bahama Island (bŭhä'mŭ, bŭhä'mŭ), island (75 mi. long W–E, up to 15 mi. wide) and district (□ 430; pop. 2,333), NW Bahama Isls., just W of Great Abaco Isl., 60 mi. E of West Palm Beach, Fla., and 110 mi. NNW of Nassau. Chief settlement is West End on its W tip. Eight-Mile Rock, on picturesque Hawksbill Creek, is 27 mi. SE of West End, linked by road. Main activities are timber cutting and fishing (turtles, sponge, deep-sea fish). Some subsistence crops. Isl. was permanently settled in 1806. Sometimes called Great Bahama Isl.

Grand Ballon, France: see GUEBWILLER, BALLON DE.

Grand Bank, town (pop. 2,331), S N.F., on SE shore of Fortune Bay, on Burin Peninsula, 150 mi. WSW of St. John's; 47°5′N 55°46′W; important base for Grand Banks fisheries. Site of govt. bait depot, govt. hosp., and radio station. Near by, lobster and salmon canning and lumbering are carried on.

Grand Banks, submarine plateau off SE Newfoundland, extends 420 mi. E–W and 350 mi. N–S; 42°52′–48°40′N 47°26′–53°31′W. Depth ranges from 22 to 100 fathoms, with several shoals in the 2–10 fathom range. Mostly in Labrador Current, E edge of Banks lies along path of the Gulf Stream. As a result of meeting of the streams the Banks are a major fishing ground and one of the world's most important cod-fishing regions, visited by fishermen from the United States, Canada, Great Britain, Scandinavia, and France. NE part of the Banks is one of world's most important fog fields, and icebergs are carried along by the Labrador Current, reaching their greatest frequency in April.

Grand Bassa (bă'sŭ), county, S Liberia, on Atlantic coast; ⊙ Buchanan. Bounded E by Sangwin R., W by Farmington R.; drained by lower St. John and Cess rivers; extends c.40 mi. inland. Agr. (palm oil and kernels, cassava, rice). Main centers: Buchanan, River Cess, Trade Town.

Grand Bassa, town, Liberia: see BUCHANAN.

Grand-Bassam (bäsäm') or **Bassam**, town (pop. c.4,650), SE Ivory Coast, Fr. West Africa, Atlantic port on spit at entrance to Ebrié Lagoon, at mouth of Comoé R., 18 mi. E of Abidjan, joined by inland waterway. Exports coffee, cacao, bananas, palm kernels, rubber, timber. Sawmilling, mfg. of furniture. Seat of department of justice, R.C. and Protestant missions, customhouse. It was ⊙ Ivory Coast until replaced (1900) by Bingerville.

Grand Bay or **Grand Baie**, village (pop. 1,157), N Mauritius, on the Grand Bay (inlet of Indian Ocean), 9 mi. NW of Rivière du Rempart; sugar.

Grand Beach, village (pop. 105), Berrien co., extreme SW Mich., on L. Michigan, at Ind. line, 28 mi. SW of Benton Harbor.

Grand Blanc (grănd″ blăngk'), residential city (pop. 998), Genesee co., SE central Mich., 7 mi. SSE of Flint, in agr. area (livestock, grain, beans, alfalfa; dairy products). Settled 1823, inc. 1930.

Grand-Bois, Haiti: see CORNILLON.

Grand-Bois, village (pop. 2,498), on S coast of Réunion isl., 4 mi. E of Saint-Pierre; sugar mill.

Grand-Bornand, Le (lŭ grã-bôrnä'), village (pop. 488), Haute-Savoie dept., SE France, in the Bornes (Savoy Pre-Alps), 15 mi. ENE of Annecy; alt. 3,054 ft. Winter sports.

Grand-Bourg (grã-bōōr'), town (commune pop. 13,833), SW Marie-Galante isl., Guadeloupe, 19 mi. ESE of Basse-Terre; minor port in sugar-growing region; sugar milling, alcohol distilling.

Grand-Bourg, Le (lŭ), agr. village (pop. 492), Creuse dept., central France, near Gartempe R., 11 mi. W of Guéret; horse raising.

Grand Buëch River, France: see BUËCH RIVER.

Grand Caicos, island, Turks and Caicos Isls.: see MIDDLE CAICOS.

Grand Caillou, Bayou (kăyōō', kălōō'), navigable waterway in SE La., extends from N Terrebonne parish c.35 mi. generally S to Caillou Bay, an arm of the Gulf of Mexico; partly canalized. Linked by connecting waterways to Gulf Intracoastal Waterway, Caillou L., and other navigable bayous.

Grand Calumet River, Ill. and Ind.: see CALUMET RIVER.

Grandcamp-les-Bains (grãkã-lā-bē'), village (pop. 1,438), Calvados dept., NW France, fishing port on English Channel, 17 mi. NW of Bayeux. American troops landed just E of here (Omaha Beach) on June 6, 1944, in Second World War.

Grand Canal, Chinese *Yün Ho* [transit river], longest canal of China, c.1,000 mi. long, constituting main N–S waterway of N China plain. Extending from Pai R. at Tientsin (N) to Tsientang R. at Hangchow (S), it falls into 3 sections. The S section (built 605–17) extends from Hangchow, through S Kiangsu, past Kashing, Soochow, Wusih, and Changchow, to Chinkiang, on S bank of Yangtze R. The central section, the oldest, believed to date from 6th cent. B.C., extends from N bank of the Yangtze R. at Kwachow, through N Kiangsu, past Yangchow and along E shore of Kaoyü L. to Hwaiyin, which was on an arm of Yellow R. when the canal was built. The N section, built 1280–83 by Kublai Khan, extends from Hwaiyin through Shantung and Hopeh, past Tsining, Lintsing, and Tehchow, to Tientsin. Although navigable for shallow-draught vessels, the canal has lost much of its former importance through widespread silting.

Grand Canal, Ireland, extends 80 mi. E-W bet. Dublin and the Shannon at Shannon Harbour, serving Tullamore. It was begun 1755.

Grand Canary, Sp. *Gran Canaria* (grän' känä'ryä), island (□ 592; pop. 279,875) of the Canary Isls., in Las Palmas prov., Spain, bet. Tenerife (W) and Fuerteventura (E); ⊙ Las Palmas. Almost circular in shape (28 mi. in diameter), with its center at about 28°N 15°35′W. Most populous and important of the entire archipelago, Grand Canary has enchanting landscape and exceedingly mild climate, which attract many tourists, particularly in winter. Extinct volcanic peaks rise, toward isl.'s center, to c.6,400 ft. (Los Pechos). The shore line is generally steep, enclosing fine harbors and beaches. Fertile soil yields bananas, sugar cane, tobacco, citrus fruit, tomatoes, coffee, potatoes, cereals, which are exported, chiefly through Puerto de la Luz, which is the port of Las Palmas as well as an important fueling and communications center for transatlantic shipping. Industries are restricted to processing of local produce, fish salting and canning ranking 1st.

Grand Cane, village (pop. 286), De Soto parish, NW La., 29 mi. S of Shreveport, in farming area; cotton ginning.

Grand Canyon, village (1940 pop. 595), Coconino co., in Grand Canyon Natl. Park, N Ariz., 65 mi. NW of Flagstaff; alt. 6,866 ft.; hq. for park.

Grand Canyon, NW Ariz., enormous gorge (217 mi. long, 4–18 mi. wide from rim to rim, 1 mi. deep, from N rim) of Colorado R., extending E-W through high plateau region (5,000–9,000 ft.), from mouth of Little Colorado R. (E) to L. Mead. One of earth's most awe-inspiring spectacles, canyon reveals in its rock strata exposed by erosion the record of long geologic change that began in Archeozoic era and proceeded as sequence of uplift, erosion, submergence in sea, deposition of sediment on sea floor, followed again by uplift and a repeated cycle, which is still at work on materials of canyon. The varicolored strata, the steep and embayed rims, and the isolated towers, "temples," mesas, and other eroded rock forms in the chasm catch the light of sun and shadow and glow with changing hues of intense, air-filling beauty. Park hq. at Grand Canyon village, on S rim 65 mi. NW of Flagstaff. Most scenic of trails giving access to bottom of gorge are Bright Angel Trail and Kaibab Trail, which crosses canyon by means of 440-ft. suspension bridge. Excellent views are obtained from Yavapai Point on S rim and Point Imperial on N rim. Tourist accommodations on both rims. García López de Cárdenas was 1st white man to see canyon (1540); John W. Powell conducted 1st boat trip through it (1869). Part of Canyon in Coconino co. was established (1908) as natl. monument and expanded (1919) into Grand Canyon Natl. Park (□ 1,008.2; includes 105 mi. of gorge). Adjacent area (just W, in Mohave co.) was set aside in 1932 as Grand Canyon Natl. Monument (□ 306.3; includes Toroweap Point, with fine view of inner gorge of Colorado R.). Havasupai Indian Reservation (pop. 200) is in Havasu Canyon, at W end of park; Navajo and Hopi Indian reservations are E of park.

Grand Canyon of Santa Helena, Texas: see BIG BEND NATIONAL PARK.

Grand Canyon of the Arkansas, Colo.: see ROYAL GORGE.

Grand Canyon of the Snake River, Idaho: see SNAKE RIVER.

Grand Canyon of the Tuolumne, Calif.: see YOSEMITE NATIONAL PARK.

Grand Canyon of the Yellowstone, Wyo.: see YELLOWSTONE NATIONAL PARK.

Grand Cape Mount, county, W Liberia, on Atlantic coast; ⊙ Robertsport. Bounded E by Lofa R., W by Mano R. (Sierra Leone frontier); contains Fisherman L.; extends c.40 mi. inland. Agr. (palm oil and kernels, kola nuts, coffee, cassava, rice); fisheries. Main center, Robertsport. Sometimes called Cape Mount.

Grand Cascapedia (kă″skŭpē'dēŭ), **Cascapedia**, or **Cascapédia** (käskäpädēä'), village (pop. estimate 500), E Que., S Gaspé Peninsula, on Cascapedia R., near its mouth on Chaleur Bay, and 26 mi. NE of Dalhousie; dairying, lumbering.

Grand Caverns, Va.: see GROTTOES.

Grand Cayman (kā'mŭn, kīmăn'), island (□ 70.72; pop. 5,311), Cayman Isls., dependency of Jamaica, B.W.I., westernmost and largest of the Cayman group, 190 mi. WNW of Jamaica; 17 mi. long, 4–7 mi. wide, surrounded by coral reefs. Chief settlements are Georgetown (pop. 1,462), ⊙ Cayman Isls., situated in W at 19°17′N 81°23′W; also Bodden Town (pop. 618), West Bay (pop. 1,866), Prospect (pop. 414), and East End (pop. 564). Exports tropical fruit, mahogany, cedar, dyewood, tortoise shells, sharkskins, thatch rope.

Grand Cess, town, Maryland co., SE Liberia, port on Atlantic Ocean, at mouth of Grand Cess R. (80 mi. long; rises in Niete Mts.), 38 mi. WNW of Harper; copra, cassava, rice; fishing. Formerly Grand Sesters.

Grand Chain, Ill.: see New Grand Chain.

Grand-Champ (grã-shã′), agr. village (pop. 709), Morbihan dept., W France, 8 mi. NNW of Vannes. Menhirs and dolmens near by.

Grand Codroy River, SW N.F., rises in Anguille Mts., flows 30 mi. SW to Cabot Strait 6 mi. SE of Cape Anguille. Valley is one of most fertile regions of N.F.; sheep; potatoes, buckwheat, hay.

Grand Colombier (grã-kôlôbyā′), mountain (5,033 ft.) of the S Jura, Ain dept., E France, overlooking the Rhone and the L. of Bourget (7 mi. SSE). At its foot are Culoz (S) and Seyssel (NE).

Grand' Combe, La (lä grã kōb′), town (pop. 9,689), Gard dept., S France, on the Gardon d'Alès and 7 mi. NNW of Alès; coal-, lignite-mining center.

Grand Combin, Switzerland: see Combin, Grand.

Grand Cornier (grã kôrnyā′), peak (13,008 ft.) in Pennine Alps, S Switzerland, 7 mi. WNW of Zermatt.

Grand Coteau (grăng′ kŭtō″), village (pop. 1,103), St. Landry parish, S central La., 9 mi. S of Opelousas; agr. Seat of Col. of Sacred Heart (for women).

Grand Coulee (kōō′lē), city (pop. 2,741), Grant co., NE central Wash., 75 mi. WNW of Spokane and on Columbia R. Inc. 1935; includes 3 communities established during construction (1933–41) of **Grand Coulee Dam,** 1 of world's largest dams (550 ft. high; 4,300 ft. long), built at point where the Columbia diverges from head of the Grand Coulee, its dry prehistoric channel (c.50 mi. long), now site of equalizing reservoir in project harnessing the Columbia for power, irrigation, and flood control. Franklin D. Roosevelt Lake (151 mi. long), behind the dam, is recreational area.

Grand-Couronne (grã-kōōrôn′), town (pop. 2,980), Seine-Inférieure dept., N France, on left bank of Seine R. and 7 mi. SSW of Rouen; paper milling.

Grand-Croix, La (lä grã-krwä′), town (pop. 3,130), Loire dept., SE central France, in the Jarez 10 mi. NE of Saint-Étienne; metallurgy, silk weaving, toy making.

Grand Cul de Sac (grã küdsäk′), bay in N Guadeloupe, Fr. West Indies, bet. Basse-Terre and Grand-Terre, and linked by 4-mi.-long Rivière Salée with Petit Cul de Sac.

Grand Detour, village (pop. c.300), Ogle co., N Ill., on Rock R. and 32 mi. SW of Rockford. Founded 1835 by Leonard Andrus. In 1837, John Deere built 1st Grand Detour steel plow here; he established with Andrus state's 1st plow industry, which remained in village until 1869 despite Deere's withdrawal and establishment (1847) of factory at Moline.

Grande, Arroyo (äroi′ō grän′dā). **1** River, SW Uruguay, on Flores-Soriano dept. border, rises in the Cuchilla Grande Inferior 10 mi. WNW of Arroyo Grande town, flows c.65 mi. N to the Río Negro 2 mi. below confluence of Yí R. **2** River, Río Negro dept., W central Uruguay, rises in the Cuchilla de Haedo ESE of Guichón, flows 55 mi. SSW to the Río Negro just above mouth of the Arroyo Don Esteban.

Grande, Bahía (bäē′ä grän′dā), broad inlet of the S Atlantic in SE Santa Cruz natl. territory, Argentina, bet. Río Chico estuary (N) and Point Dungeness (S); 140 mi. N–S, c.45 mi. W–E. Receives estuaries of Santa Cruz R., Coyle R., and the Río Chico.

Grande, Boca (bō′kä grän′dā), or **Boca de Navíos** (bō′kä dā nävē′ōs), largest mouth of Orinoco R. delta, Delta Amacuro territory, NE Venezuela, on the Atlantic; 40 mi. long, up to 6 mi. wide. Receives the Orinoco arms Río Grande and Brazo Imataca, near Curiapo. Good navigability.

Grande, Ilha (ē′lyŭ grän′dĭ). **1** or **Ilha das Sete Quedas** (däs sĕ′tĭ kā′dŭs), long narrow island in Paraná R., Brazil, bet. Paraná (E) and Mato Grosso (W) states; extends 45 mi. upstream from Pôrto Guaíra; hardwood. **2** Island, Rio de Janeiro, Brazil: see Ilha Grande Bay.

Grande, Río, (rē′ō grän′dā). **1** River, Jujuy prov., Argentina: see Grande de Jujuy, Río. **2** River, Mendoza prov., Argentina, rises in the Andes near Planchón peak, flows c.180 mi. SE and S, joining Barrancas R. at Neuquén line above Buta Ranquil to form the Río Colorado. **3** Small river (25 mi. long) in E central Tierra del Fuego natl. territory, Argentina, entering the Atlantic at village of Río Grande. Its sands carry some gold.

Grande, Río, river in central Bolivia, formed by confluence of Caine River and Chayanta River at Pucara (Potosí dept.); flows 510 mi. generally E, N, and NW, through Santa Cruz dept., past Cabezas and Ingeniero Montero Hoyos, to the Mamoré 40 mi. S of Loreto. Receives Mizque and Piray rivers (left), Azero R. (right). Forms in upper course Chuquisaca-Cochabamba border. Navigable for c.100 mi. above mouth. Also called the Guapay (gwäpī′) in its lower part, below mouth of Azero R.

Grande, Rio (rē′ōō grän′dĭ). **1** One of the headstreams of the Paraná, in SE central Brazil, rises in S Minas Gerais near Rio de Janeiro border on N slope of the Serra da Mantiqueira, flows tortuously WNW, and in its lower half forms Minas Gerais-São Paulo border up to its confluence with Paranaíba R. at Mato Grosso line, where the Paraná is formed; over 650 mi. long. Maribondo Falls (35 mi. N of São José do Rio Prêto) are to be harnessed for hydroelectric power. River navigable for c.130 mi. above falls. Receives the Sapucaí-Gauçu and the Rio Pardo (left). **2** River in W Bahia, Brazil, rises in the Serra Geral de Goiás on Goiás border, flows 300 mi. NE to the São Francisco (left bank) at Barra. Receives the Rio Prêto (left). Regular navigation below Barreiras is part of São Francisco navigation system.

Grande, Río (rē′ō grän′dä), or **Catamayo River** (kätämī′ō), Loja prov., S Ecuador, rises at S foot of Cordillera de Zamora, flows c.100 mi. W to join Macará R., forming the Chira 20 mi. SW of Celica at Peru border. Copper and kaolin deposits along its course.

Grande, Río, Guatemala: see Motagua River.

Grande, Rio (rē″ō grănd′), river in Portland parish, E Jamaica, rises in E Blue Mts., flows c.25 mi. NW, past Moore Town, to the N coast W of Port Antonio.

Grande, Río, Mexico: see Aguanaval River; Rio Grande.

Grande, Río, or **Río Grande de Matagalpa** (rē′ō grän′dā dā mätägäl′pä), river in central Nicaragua, rises 25 mi. SW of Matagalpa, on Güisisil mtn., flows over 200 mi. E, past Esquipulas and La Cruz, to Caribbean Sea at Río Grande village. Navigable in lower course. Receives Tuma R. (left).

Grande, Río, river in Coclé prov., central Panama, rises in continental divide 20 mi. NW of Penonomé, flows 30 mi. SSE to Parita Gulf of the Pacific below Puerto Posada (port of Penonomé).

Grande, Río, river, Ica dept., SW Peru, rises in Cordillera Occidental E of Ica, flows 120 mi. S and SW to the Pacific 14 mi. NW of San Nicolás; used for irrigation.

Grande, Rio (rē′ōō grän′dĭ), estuarine inlet of the Atlantic, in W Port. Guinea, extending c.30 mi. inland from Bolama, at its mouth. Formerly navigated by slave traders. Also called Bolola R. and Rio Grande de Buba.

Grande, Río (rē′ō grän′dā), river, W Salvador, rises in coastal range near Juayúa, flows c.25 mi. S, past Juayúa, Nahuizalco, and Sonsonate, to the Pacific near Acajutla.

Grande, Río, U.S. and Mexico: see Rio Grande.

Grande, Río, main arm of Orinoco R. delta, Delta Amacuro territory, NE Venezuela; branches off E of Barrancas (Monagas state), flows c.100 mi. E to the Atlantic at Boca Grande (or Boca de Navíos) 3 mi. NNE of Curiapo; navigable.

Grande, Rivière la, Que.: see Fort George River.

Grande, Salar (sälär′ grän′dā), salt flat (alt. 2,180 ft.) in Atacama Desert of N Chile, 40 mi. S of Iquique; extends 35 mi. NNW–SSE (2–5 mi. wide); supplies most of Chile's salt; has borax.

Grande, Salina, Argentina: see Salina Grande.

Grande, Salto, Argentina-Uruguay: see Salto Grande.

Grande, Serra (sĕ′rŭ grän′dĭ), **Serra Geral** (zhĭräl′), or **Serra Ibiapaba** (ēbyäpä′bŭ), northernmost range of NE Brazilian highlands, on Piauí-Ceará border, extending c.200 mi. S–N to within 50 mi. of the Atlantic coast. Rises to 3,000 ft. Presents uninterrupted front except for Poti R. gorge (followed by Crateús-Oiticica RR) near lat. 5°S. Name of Ibiapaba sometimes only given to N part of range.

Grande, Sierra (syĕ′rä grän′dā), pampean mountain range in W Córdoba prov., Argentina, a central ridge of the Sierra de Córdoba, extends c.40 mi. N–S, W of Alta Gracia; Cerro Gigante rises to 7,645 ft.

Grande Aldée, Fr. India: see Tirumalarajanpatnam.

Grande-Anse (grăd-ăs′), village, SW Désirade isl., Guadeloupe dept., Fr. West Indies, 30 mi. E of Pointe-à-Pitre; sisal, cotton; fishing.

Grande Baie (grănd bā′) or **Saint Alexis de la Grande Baie** (sĕtälĕksēs′ dŭ lä), village (pop. 2,230), S central Que., on Ha Ha Bay of the Saguenay, at mouth of Ha Ha R., and 13 mi. SE of Chicoutimi; dairying, lumbering center.

Grande-Brière, La (lä grăd-brēĕr′), peat bog (□ 27), Loire-Inférieure dept., W France, N of Saint-Nazaire; former lagoon intersected by drainage canals. Pop. is clustered on higher ground and has monopoly on turf cutting; duck hunting.

Grande-Casse (grăd-käs′), peak (12,668 ft.) of Massif de la Vanoise (Savoy Alps), Savoie dept., SE France, 9 mi. ESE of Bozel; glaciers.

Grande Cayemite Island, Haiti: see Cayemites Islands.

Grande Chartreuse (grăd shärtrŭz′), Jurassic limestone massif of the Dauphiné Pre-Alps, Isère dept., SE France; a compact formation (average alt. 5,000 ft.), difficult of access; c.25 mi. long (N–S) and 15 mi. wide (E–W), with abrupt outward slopes, bounded by the Isère R. valley (S and E) and by the Chambéry depression (N). Rises to 6,847 ft. at Chamechaude peak. Grenoble lies at foot of its southernmost spur. Aromatic herbs found here flavor celebrated liqueur, originated by monks of **Monastery of La Grande Chartreuse,** located in high valley (alt. 3,205 ft.), 12 mi. NNE of Grenoble. Founded c.1084 by St. Bruno, it was principal seat of Carthusians until 1903, when order was expelled and established itself at Tarragona, Spain. Convent was several times destroyed; present bldgs. (mus.) date mainly from 17th cent.

Grande Comore Island (grăd′ kômôr′) (□ 442; pop. c.81,000), largest and westernmost of Comoro Isls., in Mozambique Channel of Indian Ocean c.200 mi. off Mozambique coast, off NW Madagascar; 36 mi. long, 20 mi. wide. Rises to 7,904 ft. in volcanic cone. Has dry, healthy climate. Produces vanilla, cacao, cloves, copra fibers; also rice, manioc, sweet potatoes, pulse, oilseeds. Sawmilling; mfg. of edible oils, soap. Handicrafts include mfg. of pottery, rug weaving, wood carving. Pop. consists mainly of Moslemized Makwas and Arabs. Chief town is Moroni on SW coast. Formerly composed of 7 independent sultanates; placed under Fr. protectorate 1886.

Grande de Añasco, Río, Puerto Rico: see Añasco River.

Grande de Arecibo, Río, Puerto Rico: see Arecibo River.

Grande de Chiapa, Río, Mexico: see Grijalva River.

Grande de Jujuy, Río (rē′ō grän′dā dā hōōhōō′ē), or **Río Grande,** river in Jujuy prov., N Argentina, rises as the Quebrada de Humahuaca, flows S and SE past Tilcara, Tumbaya, and Jujuy, then NE, past San Pedro, to join Lavayén R., forming the San Francisco; 150 mi. long. Used for irrigation and hydroelectric power. Sometimes called the Jujuy.

Grande del Durazno, Cuchilla (kōōchē′yä grän′dā dĕl dōōrä′snō), hill range, Durazno dept., central Uruguay, branches off from the Cuchilla Grande Principal at source of the Yí, 2 mi. W of Cerro Chato; extends 115 mi. W, across Durazno dept., to confluence of Yí R. and the Río Negro. Rises to c.850 ft.

Grande de Lípez, Río (rē′ō grän′dā dā lē′pĕs), river in Potosí dept., SW Bolivia; rises on W slopes of Cordillera de Lípez 20 mi. S of Quetena; flows 125 mi. N, past Quetena, to Salar de Uyuni 33 mi. SW of Uyuni. Called Quetena R. in upper course.

Grande de Loíza, Río, Puerto Rico: see Loíza River.

Grande de Manatí, Río, Puerto Rico: see Manatí River.

Grande de Matagalpa, Río, Nicaragua: see Grande, Río.

Grande de Moa, Cayo (kī′ō grän′dā dā mō′ä), small reef (2 mi. long, ½ mi. wide) off NE Cuba, Oriente prov., 35 mi. NW of Baracoa; 20°42′N 74°54′W.

Grande de Otoro, Río, Honduras: see Ulúa River.

Grande de San Juan, Río, Bolivia: see San Juan River.

Grande de San Miguel, Río (dā sän′ mēgĕl′), river, E Salvador, rises N of San Francisco, flows S, past San Francisco and San Miguel, and SW to Jiquilisco Bay of the Pacific W of Jucuarán; c.45 mi. long.

Grande de Santiago, Río, Mexico: see Santiago River.

Grande de Tárcoles, Río, Costa Rica: see Tárcoles River.

Grande de Térraba, Río, Costa Rica: see Diquís River.

Grande Ecaille, Lake, La.: see Port Sulphur.

Grande Inferior, Cuchilla (kōōchē′yä grän′dā ēnfāryōr′), hill range, W outlier of Cuchilla Grande Principal, S central Uruguay, extends c.120 mi. across Florida and Flores depts.; at Cardona it branches off into the cuchillas del Bizcocho and San Salvador. Rises to 820 ft. Crossed by rail from Florida to Durazno and Sarandí del Yí.

Grande-Motte (grăd-môt′), peak (12,018 ft.) of Massif de la Vanoise (Savoy Alps), Savoie dept., SE France, 9 mi. N of Lanslebourg. Glacier on N slope. Also called Aiguille de la Grande-Motte.

Grande Nèthe River (grăd nĕt′), Flemish *Groote Nete* (grō′tŭ nā′tŭ), N Belgium, rises 10 mi. ESE of Mol, flows 41 mi. W, past Meerhout, Westerloo, and Berlaar, joining Petite Nèthe at Lierre to form Nèthe River.

Grande Prairie (grănd prâ′rē, Fr. grăd prârē′), town (pop. 2,267), W Alta., near B.C. border, on Bear R., near its mouth on Wapiti R., and 250 mi. NW of Edmonton, 110 W of Lesser Slave L.; 55°10′N 118°48′W. Distributing center for farming region; coal mining, lumbering; wheat. Settlement began 1910.

Grande Principal, Cuchilla (kōōchē′yä grän′dā prēnsēpäl′), hill range, E Uruguay, extends from SE of Aceguá, on Uruguay-Brazil border, c.200 mi. SW, SE, and W across Cerro Largo dept. and along dept. borders bet. Tacuarembó, Durazno, and Florida (W), and Treinta y Tres and Lavalleja (E), to 20 mi. W of Minas. Rises to 1,600 ft. Major outliers are the cuchillas Grande del Durazno and Grande Inferior. Crossed by Montevideo-Melo RR.

Grand Erg, Algeria: see ERG.

Grande River (grän'dĕ) or **Imera Settentrionale** (ē'mĕrä sĕt-tĕntrēōnä'lĕ), anc. *Himera Septentrionalis,* N Sicily, rises in Madonie Mts. SW of Polizzi Generosa, flows 20 mi. NNW to Tyrrhenian Sea near ruins of Himera.

Grande Rivière (grãd rēvyâr'), village (pop. 630), E Que., on E Gaspé Peninsula, on Gulf of St. Lawrence, at mouth of Grand R., 30 mi. S of Gaspé; fishing center; lumbering, dairying. Site of fishery research station of Laval Univ.

Grande-Rivière-du-Nord (–dü-nôr'), town (1950 census pop. 3,270), Nord dept., N Haiti, in foothills of the Massif du Nord, on the Grande Rivière du Nord (50 mi. long), on railroad and 13 mi. S of Cap-Haïtien; coffee- and fruitgrowing. Has colonial church. Birthplace of Jean Jacques Dessalines, Haiti's liberator. Gold, lead, zinc, silver deposits near by.

Grande Rivière Sud Est, Mauritius: see GRAND RIVER SOUTH EAST.

Grande Ronde River (grănd rŏnd'), NE Oregon–SE Wash., rises in Blue Mts., flows c.180 mi. NE, past La Grande, to the Snake in SE corner of Wash.

Grandes, Salinas, Argentina: see SALINAS GRANDES.

Grande-Saline (grãd-sälēn'), town (1950 census pop. 807), Artibonite dept., W central Haiti, at mouth of Artibonite R. on Gulf of Gonaïves, 15 mi. SSW of Gonaïves, in salt marshes.

Grande-Sassière (–säsyâr'), peak (12,333 ft.) of Graian Alps, on Fr.-Ital. border, 3 mi. NE of Tignes (Savoie dept., France). Glaciers. Also called Aiguille de la Grande-Sassière.

Grandes Bergeronnes (grãd bĕrzhĕrôn'), village (pop. 503), E Que., on the St. Lawrence and 30 mi. N of Rivière du Loup, in mica-mining region; lumbering, dairying, blueberry canning.

Grandes-Dalles, Les, France: see SAINT-PIERRE-EN-PORT.

Grandes Jorasses (grãd zhôräs'), peak (13,799 ft.) of Mont Blanc massif, on Fr.-Ital. border, 7 mi. SE of Chamonix.

Grande Soufrière, La, Basse-Terre, Guadeloupe: see SOUFRIÈRE.

Grandes-Rousses (grãd-rōōs'), range of Dauphiné Alps, in Isère and Savoie depts., SE France, bet. Belledonne range (W), Oisans valley (S), and upper Maurienne valley (N). Rises to 11,394 ft.

Grand Étang (grănd" ätăng'), lake (2½-mi. circumference; alt. 1,740 ft.), central Grenada, B.W.I. 5 mi. NE of St. George's, in crater of an extinct volcano. On it are a resthouse and sanatorium.

Grande-Terre (grãd-târ'), island (□ 218.63; pop. 131,423), E half of GUADELOUPE isl., Fr. West Indies, separated from Basse-Terre by narrow Rivière Salée channel; c.25 mi. long. It is of a low-lying limestone formation; water is scarce. Sugar cane is its principal product. Pointe-à-Pitre, leading port and commercial center of Guadeloupe, is on SW coast.

Grandeza, La, Mexico: see LA GRANDEZA.

Grand Falls. 1 Town (pop. 1,806), ⊙ Victoria co., NW N.B., on St. John R. and 90 mi. NW of Fredericton, near Maine border; lumbering center and agr. market in potato region. Just NW are 74-ft. falls of St. John R., site of hydroelectric station. **2** Town (pop. 4,505), central N.F., on Exploits R., on railroad, and 165 mi. NW of St. John's; 48°56'N 55°40'W; newsprint-milling center; important hydroelectric plant. Lumbering and subsistence farming in the region. Newsprint is shipped via Botwood.

Grand Falls. 1 Spectacular waterfalls of upper Hamilton R., W Labrador, 25 mi. SW of Michikamau L., near 53°34'N 64°25'W. River here narrows to 200 ft., negotiates series of rapids over distance of 4 mi., then falls 245 ft., leaping inland plateau into McLean Canyon, from which sheer cliffs rise several hundred feet on either side. It then flows 12 mi. through the canyon over a further series of rapids. Total fall from rapids above main falls to end of McLean Canyon is 1,038 ft. Discovered (1839) by John McLean of Hudson's Bay Co., the falls were forgotten until rediscovered by 2 expeditions under Bryant, Kenaston, Carey, and Crole; surveyed 1894. Sometimes called Great Falls. **2** In central Ont., waterfalls (150 ft. high) of the Mississagi R., 30 mi. NW of Blind River.

Grand Falls, plantation (pop. 22), Penobscot co., S central Maine, 12 mi. NE of Old Town.

Grandfalls, town (pop. 995), Ward co., extreme W Texas, in the Pecos valley, 38 mi. E of Pecos; trade point in irrigated fruit and truck region.

Grandfather Mountain (5,964 ft.), NW N.C., in the Blue Ridge, 16 mi. SW of Boone.

Grand-Ferrand, France: see DÉVOLUY.

Grandfield, town (pop. 1,232), Tillman co., SW Okla., near Red R., 25 mi. NNW of Wichita Falls (Texas), in agr. area; oil refineries and pipe lines; cotton ginning, feed and flour milling. Inc. 1909.

Grand Forks, city (pop. 1,259), S B.C., on Wash. border, on Granby R. and 35 mi. W of Trail; fruit- and vegetable-growing center, with canneries and seed nurseries, in irrigated farming region; lumbering. Former mining center.

Grand Forks, county (□ 1,438; pop. 39,443), E N.Dak.; ⊙ Grand Forks. Wheat-producing area bordered E by Red River of the North, watered by Goose R. and Turtle R. Agr. produce; mfg. at Grand Forks. Formed 1873.

Grand Forks, city (pop. 26,836), ⊙ Grand Forks co., E N.Dak., 75 mi. N of Fargo, at confluence of Red River of the North and Red Lake R.; 2d largest city of N.Dak.; 47°55'N 97°2'W. Railroad junction and distribution center; grain refining and meat packing; dairy products, poultry, wheat, livestock, sugar beets, candy. Seat of Univ. of N.Dak. and Wesley Col. Settled 1871, inc. 1881.

Grand-Fort-Philippe (grã-fôr-fēlēp'), town (pop. 3,792), Nord dept., N France, fishing port on North Sea at mouth of Aa R. and 12 mi. WSW of Dunkirk; fish packing.

Grand-Fougeray or **Le Grand-Fougeray** (lü grã-fōōzhürā'), agr. village (pop. 1,041), Ille-et-Vilaine dept., W France, 17 mi. ENE of Redon. Formerly called Fougeray.

Grand-Gallargues (grã-gälärg'), village (pop. 1,165), Gard dept., S France, near the Vidourle, 13 mi. SW of Nîmes; winegrowing; barrels, fertilizer.

Grand Gaube (grã' gōb'), village (pop. 2,328), N Mauritius, on N coast, 7 mi. NNW of Rivière du Rempart; sugar cane. Founded after 1835 by freed slaves.

Grand-Goâve (grã-gwäv'), town (1950 census pop. 1,862), Ouest dept., S Haiti, on NE coast of Tiburon Peninsula, 23 mi. WSW of Port-au-Prince; sugar cane, bananas.

Grand Gorge, village (pop. c.500), Delaware co., S N.Y., in the Catskills, c.40 mi. NW of Kingston, in resort and dairying area.

Grand-Gosier (grã-gōzyā'), town (1950 census pop. 532), Ouest dept., SE Haiti, minor port on the Caribbean, 38 mi. SE of Port-au-Prince; coffee, construction wood.

Grand Harbour, fishing village, chief settlement of Grand Manan Isl., SW N.B., on E coast of isl., 30 mi. SE of St. Andrews.

Grand Harbour, small inlet, E Malta, washing E shore of peninsula on which Valletta is built. Serves as harbor for Valletta and the "Three Cities" (SENGLEA, COSPICUA, VITTORIOSA). It is lined by dockyards and naval installations. Its entrance is guarded by the old forts St. Elmo and Ricasoli.

Grand Haven, city (pop. 9,536), ⊙ Ottawa co., SW Mich., 11 mi. SSE of Muskegon, on outlet of Spring L. (here receiving Grand R.) to L. Michigan. Important port, fishing, and mfg. center (printing presses, tools, plumbing fixtures, auto parts, marine engines, pianos, leather gloves, clothing); oil refineries. Ships grapes, celery, potatoes. Resort. Has U.S. coast guard station. State park near by. Inc. 1867.

Grandin (grăn'dĭn). **1** Town (pop. 263), Carter co., S Mo., in the Ozarks, near Current R., 24 mi. W of Poplar Bluff; lumber. **2** Agr. village (pop. 156), Cass co., E N.Dak., 27 mi. NNW of Fargo, near Elm R.

Grand Island. 1 City (pop. 22,682), ⊙ Hall co., SE central Nebr., 85 mi. W of Lincoln and on Wood R., near Platte R.; 40°55'N 98°23'W; alt. 1,864 ft. Railroad, mfg., and shipping center for livestock, agr., and dairy area. Has railroad repair shops. Horse, mule, and cattle market; distribution center for area's grain, fruit, and farm products. Produces beet sugar, flour, agr. appliances, dairy and poultry products. Cathedral (R.C.), hosp., and airport here. State park and U.S. Central Monitoring Station, checking point for radio broadcasts, near by. Settled 1857, laid out 1866 by the Union Pacific, inc. 1871. **2** Town (1940 pop. 1,055), Erie co., W N.Y., comprising Grand Isl. (7½ mi. long, 1–6½ mi. wide) and adjacent small isls. in Niagara R. bet. N.Y. and Ont., just NW of Buffalo; linked by bridges to N.Y. and Ont. Buckhorn Island State Park is on Grand Isl.'s N shore and small Buckhorn Isl.; Beaver Island State Park is on its S shore and adjacent Beaver Isl. Grand Island village is near S tip.

Grand Island. 1 Island (c.2 mi. long), SE La., in Gulf of Mexico, in passage connecting L. Borgne (W) and Mississippi Sound (E). Grand Isl. Pass, to N, is principal deepwater navigation channel bet. sound and lake. **2** Island, Alger co., N Mich., in L. Superior off the Upper Peninsula, 3 mi. N of Munising; one of largest Mich. isls. (c.13,000 acres). Wooded area, with game refuge; resort.

Grand Isle (grănd" īl'), county (□ 77; pop. 3,406), NW Vt., on a peninsula and several isls. in L. Champlain; ⊙ North Hero. Dairying, fruit, marble, lumber; resorts. Includes North Hero Isl., Grand Isle, and Isle La Motte, site of state's 1st white settlement (c.1665). Organized 1802.

Grand Isle, agr. town (pop. 1,230), Aroostook co., NE Maine, on St. John R. and 20 mi. E of Fort Kent. Inc. 1869.

Grand Isle. 1 Island (pop. 1,190) in Jefferson parish, extreme SE La., c.50 mi. S of New Orleans, bet. Gulf of Mexico (S) and Caminada Bay (NW) and Barataria Bay (NE); c.7 mi. long, 1½ mi. wide; W end bridged to mainland. Commercial and sport fishing, truck farming. La. State Univ. marine laboratory is here. Isl. was hq. for Lafitte's pirates in early-19th cent. **2** Island (c.13 mi. long) and town (pop. 735), Grand Isle co., NW Vt., in L. Champlain, 12 mi. SW of St. Albans; fruit, dairy products, lumber; resort. Oldest Vt. log cabin here. Isl. includes SOUTH HERO town (S); bridged to North Hero Isl. and to mainland.

Grand Junction. 1 City (pop. 14,504), ⊙ Mesa co., W Colo., on Colorado R., at mouth of Gunnison R., near Utah line, and c.200 mi. WSW of Denver; alt. 4,587 ft. Resort; rail and industrial center in Grand Valley (irrigated agr. and livestock area); packing and canning of fruits and vegetables; beet sugar, meat and dairy products, flour, bricks, metal appliances, beverages. Jr. col. and hq. of Grand Mesa Natl. Forest here. Near by are Colo. Natl. Monument and Grand Mesa Natl. Forest. Founded 1881, inc. 1882. Development stimulated by arrival of railroads (large workshops and yards are here) and irrigation of surrounding countryside. **2** Town (pop. 1,036), Greene co., central Iowa, 18 mi. W of Boone; rail junction; concrete products. Sand pits near by. Inc. 1873. **3** Town (pop. 477), Hardeman co., SW Tenn., near Miss. border, 45 mi. E of Memphis, in cotton, corn, livestock area.

Grand Laget (grã läzhā'), peak (10,282 ft.) in Pennine Alps, SW Switzerland, 11 mi. SE of Martigny-Ville.

Grand-Lahou (grã-läōō'), town (pop. c.4,700), S Ivory Coast, Fr. West Africa, Atlantic port at mouth of Bandama R., 70 mi. W of Abidjan. Ships cacao, coffee, palm oil, palm kernels, rubber, hardwood. Sawmilling. Customhouse. R.C. and Protestant missions.

Grand Lake, locality, central N.S., on Shubenacadie L., 17 mi. N of Halifax; quartzite mining. Gold formerly mined.

Grand Lake. 1 Lake (□ 67; 20 mi. long, 7 mi. wide), S central N.B., 30 mi. E of Fredericton; drains into St. John R. (S) by the short Jemseg stream. Short streams drain into it from several smaller lakes near by. Along N and W shore are important coal fields, whence coal was 1st shipped to New England in 1643. At N end of lake is hydroelectric power station. There are shad and alewife fisheries. In Fr. period, called Lac Freneuse. **2** Lake (□ 129; 60 mi. long, 6 mi. wide), W N.F., 15 mi. SE of Corner Brook. Connected N with Sandy L. by narrow channel and with Deer L. by the Newfoundland Canal. In S part of lake is uninhabited Glover Isl. (□ 74; 25 mi. long, 3 mi. wide).

Grand Lake, town (pop. 309), Grand co., N Colo., on N fork of Colorado R., in Front Range, and 20 mi. E of Hot Sulphur Springs; alt. 8,369 ft. Fishing and boating resort on Grand L., small storage reservoir (continuous with Shadow Mountain L., just SW) in Colorado–Big Thompson project. Town is W entrance to Rocky Mtn. Natl. Park.

Grand Lake. 1 Lake in Cameron parish, SW La., a widening of MERMENTAU RIVER. **2** Lake in Iberia, St. Martin, and St. Mary parishes, S La., a widening of ATCHAFALAYA RIVER. **3** Lake in W Washington co., E Maine, 21 mi. WNW of Calais; 8 mi. long. **4** Largest of CHIPUTNETICOOK LAKES, E Maine and N.B.; 17 mi. long. **5** Lake in Piscataquis and Penobscot counties, N central Maine, 33 mi. NNW of Millinocket; 8 mi. long. Source of East Branch of Penobscot R. **6** Lake in Presque Isle co., NE Mich., 13 mi. N of Alpena. Separated from L. Huron (E) by narrow strip of land with Presque Isle village (resort) on it; c.8 mi. long, 1.5 mi. wide; fishing. **7** Lake (9 mi. long, 3 mi. wide) in Mercer and Auglaize counties, W Ohio; formed 1845 by damming Wabash R. S of Celina. Resort; fishing, duck hunting; state park. Formerly L. St. Marys. Sometimes also called Grand Reservoir. **8** Lake in Okla.: see GRAND RIVER DAM.

Grand Lake Stream, plantation (pop. 294), Washington co., E Maine, near Grand L., 25 mi. W of Calais.

Grand Lake Victoria (32 mi. long, 3 mi. wide), SW Que., 120 mi. NE of North Bay; alt. 1,051 ft. Source of Ottawa R.

Grand Ledge, city (pop. 4,506), Eaton co., S central Mich., 10 mi. WNW of Lansing and on Grand R., in agr. area (livestock, grain, beans, hay; dairy products); mfg. (clay products, furniture). Sandstone (commercially worked) and coal deposits. Settled c.1848; inc. as village 1871, as city 1893.

Grand-Lemps, Le (lü grã-lã'), village (pop. 1,635), Isère dept., SE France, 12 mi. S of La Tour-du-Pin; textile printing, mfg. of silk fabrics and footwear.

Grand-Lieu, Lake of (grã-lyû') (□ 27), in Loire-Inférieure dept., W France, c.7 mi. SW of Nantes; empties into Loire R. It is shallow and marshy; fishing, duck hunting. Village of Saint-Philbert-de-Grand-Lieu near S end.

Grand-Lucé, Le (lü grã-lüsā'), agr. village (pop. 942), Sarthe dept., W France, 16 mi. SE of Le Mans.

Grand Manan Island (mŭnăn'), island (pop. 2,457; 16 mi. long, 7 mi. wide) in the Bay of Fundy, SW N.B., near entrance to Passamaquoddy Bay, 23 mi. SE of St. Andrews, off Maine coast 15 mi. SE of

Eastport; 44°45'N 66°48'W. Popular resort, known for its bold cliffs, 200–400 ft. high, on W and S sides. Sardine, cod, haddock, hake, pollock, lobster fisheries. On E coast is chief village. First mentioned in Hakluyt's account of Stephen Bellinger's voyage in 1583, isl. was visited by Champlain in 1605. After Revolutionary War it was settled by United Empire Loyalists; until 1817 its possession was disputed by the U.S. Off coast are many islets.

Grand Marais (mûrā'). **1** Fishing and resort village (1940 pop. 535), Alger co., N Upper Peninsula, Mich., 37 mi. NE of Munising, on harbor on L. Superior. **2** Village (pop. 1,078), ⊙ Cook co., NE Minn., on L. Superior, in Superior Natl. Forest, and c.110 mi. NE of Duluth; resort in grain and dairying area. Cascade State Park is recreational area near by.

Grand Meadow, village (pop. 766), Mower co., SE Minn., 20 mi. E of Austin, in grain and livestock area; dairy products. Limestone quarry near by.

Grand'Mère (grā'mĕr'), city (pop. 8,608), S central Que., on St. Maurice R. (waterfalls) and 20 mi. NNW of Trois Rivières; paper and woolen milling, lumbering, mfg. of clothing, bricks. Hydroelectric station.

Grand Mesa (mā'sù) (□ c.50; alt. 10,000 ft.), flat-topped mountain in Delta and Mesa counties, W Colo.; lies within part of Grand Mesa Natl. Forest. Deposits of coal and oil shale.

Grand Monadnock, N.H.: see MONADNOCK, MOUNT.

Grand-Morin River (grā-môrē'), Marne and Seine-et-Marne depts., N central France, rises in Marshes of Saint-Gond, flows c.50 mi. WNW, past Esternay and Coulommiers, to the Marne 7 mi. below Meaux.

Grand Mound, town (pop. 526), Clinton co., E Iowa, 23 mi. W of Clinton; metal products.

Grand Mountain (10,842 ft.), SE B.C., in Selkirk Mts., in Glacier Natl. Park, 35 mi. SE of Revelstoke; 51°4'N 117°23'W.

Grand Muveran, Switzerland: see MUVERAN, GRAND.

Grand Narrows, resort village (pop. estimate 100), NE N.S., central Cape Breton Isl., on Barra Strait (ferry), bet. Bras d'Or L. and Great Bras d'Or, 30 mi. WSW of Sydney.

Grândola (grăn'dōōlŭ), town (pop. 3,067), Setúbal dist., S central Portugal, on railroad and 30 mi. SE of Setúbal; cork-processing center; trade in grain, olive oil, honey.

Grand Paradis, Italy: see GRAN PARADISO.

Grand Pass, town (pop. 124), Saline co., central Mo., near Missouri R., 14 mi. NW of Marshall.

Grand Pauvre, Grenada, B.W.I.: see VICTORIA.

Grand-Pont (grā-pō'), town, ⊙ Haute-Mana and Haute-Approuague dist. (pop. 792), Inini territory, S Fr. Guiana, on affluent of upper Mana R.; 3°44'N 53°20'W. Gold placer mines in vicinity.

Grand-Popo (grănd'-pō'pō, Fr. grā'-pôpō'), town (pop. 3,100), S Dahomey, Fr. West Africa, minor port on Gulf of Guinea, at Mono R. mouth, near Fr. Togoland border, on railroad and 55 mi. W of Porto-Novo; palm kernel, palm-oil center. Customhouse; R.C. and Protestant missions.

Grand Portage, Indian village (pop. c.400), Cook co., extreme NE Minn., on L. Superior, near Mich. line, in Grand Portage Indian Reservation, and 140 mi. NE of Duluth. Fishing center. Was busy fur-trading point in 18th cent. and central depot for North West Company. It was E terminus of the Grand Portage, 9-mi. overland link bet. L. Superior and Pigeon R.; the route of the old trail, long used by Indians, explorers, and traders, was dedicated 1951 as a natl. historic site.

Grand Port Range, E Mauritius, rises to 2,093 ft. in Mt. Lagrave, 8 mi. NW of Mahébourg.

Grand Prairie, city (1940 pop. 1,595; 1950 pop. 14,594), Dallas co., N Texas, industrial suburb 12 mi. WSW of downtown Dallas. Large aircraft plant was established here 1948–49. Also mfg. of truck bodies, brooms, rubber goods. U.S. Hensley Field is near. Annexed Dalworth Park in 1943.

Grand Pré (grăn prā', Fr. grā prā'), agr. village (pop. estimate 250), central N.S., on Minas Basin, 3 mi. ENE of Wolfville. The old village (founded c.1675), which stood near the present site, was famous as an early home of the Acadians and of Evangeline, heroine of Longfellow's poem.

Grandpré (grāprā'), village (pop. 575), Ardennes dept., N France, on the Aire (which cuts gap through the Argonne here) and 9 mi. SE of Vouziers. Scene of heavy fighting during American advance (Oct., 1918) in First World War.

Grand-Pressigny, Le (lù grā-prĕsēnyē'), village (pop. 696), Indre-et-Loire dept., W central France, on Claise R. and 14 mi. NE of Châtellerault; dairying, fertilizer mfg. Has neolithic remains and 12th-cent. keep of a ruined castle.

Grand-Quevilly, Le (lù grā-kùvēyē'), outer SW suburb (pop. 9,718) of Rouen, Seine-Inférieure dept., N France, on left bank of Seine R.; blast furnaces, forges, shipbuilding yards; chemical fertilizer mfg., paper milling.

Grand Rapids. 1 City (pop. 176,515), ⊙ Kent co., SW Mich., c.60 mi. WNW of Lansing, at rapids (head of navigation) on Grand R.; 2d largest city in state, and nation's best-known furniture-making and -marketing center. Also an important rail, wholesale, and distribution center for fruitgrowing and dairying region. In addition to large furniture factories and wholesale showrooms, city has plants producing railroad equipment, foundry and machine-shop products, refrigerators, auto parts, plumbing supplies, phonographs, radios, chemicals, paint, varnish, flour, cereals, paper products. Gypsum mining and processing; oil refining. Lake resorts. The city has an art gall., public mus., furniture mus., Aquinas Col., Calvin Col. and Theological Seminary, and a jr. col. Site of several Indian villages and a trading post before 1824. Logs were floated down the river and milled here during lumber-boom period; city's huge furniture industry was outgrowth of lumbering. By end of 19th cent., it had become largest U.S. producer of furniture. City has retained leadership in furniture styling, despite rise of rivals in production. Inc. as village 1838, as city 1850. **2** Village (pop. 6,019), ⊙ Itasca co., N central Minn., on Mississippi R., near Pokegama and Bass lakes, and c.75 mi. NW of Duluth; paper, dairy products, rutabagas, beverages. School of agr., experiment station of state univ., and co. fairgrounds are here. State forests and numerous lakes in vicinity. Settled 1877, inc. 1891. **3** Village and township (pop. 198), La Moure co., SE central N.Dak., on James R. and 7 mi. NNW of La Moure; ⊙ until 1886. **4** Village (pop. 657), Wood co., NW Ohio, 11 mi. WNW of Bowling Green and on Maumee R.; grain, milk, apples; natural-gas wells. **5** City, Wood co., Wis.: see WISCONSIN RAPIDS.

Grand-Rechain, Belgium: see PETIT-RECHAIN.

Grand Reservoir, Ohio: see GRAND LAKE.

Grand Rhône, France: see RHONE RIVER.

Grand Ridge, village (pop. 530), La Salle co., N Ill., 7 mi. S of Ottawa, in agr. and bituminous coal area.

Grandrieu (grārēû'), village (pop. 325), Lozère dept., S France, 19 mi. NNE of Mende; furniture making, dairying.

Grandris (grārē'), village (pop. 745), Rhône dept., E central France, in the Monts du Beaujolais, 12 mi. WNW of Villefranche; mfg. of cotton goods.

Grand River, S Ont., rises NW of Orangeville, flows S past Fergus, Kitchener, Galt, and Brantford, thence SE past Dunnville to L. Erie at Port Maitland; 165 mi. long; navigable for 70 mi.

Grand River. 1 Town (pop. 350), Decatur co., S Iowa, near Thompson R., 18 mi. SW of Osceola, in livestock and grain area. Limestone quarries near by. **2** Village (pop. 448), Lake co., NE Ohio, just W of Painesville; processes fats and oils. Formerly Richmond.

Grand River. 1 In Colo. and Utah, a former name for the COLORADO RIVER above the mouth of Green R. **2** In S Iowa and NW Mo., rises near Creston, Iowa; meanders c.215 mi. SE to Missouri R. just below Brunswick, Mo. Receives Locust and Medicine creeks. **3** In S central La., fed by network of waterways in low swampy region bet. Atchafalaya R. and Mississippi R., SW of Baton Rouge; winds c.50 mi. generally S to L. Palourde NW of Morgan City. Partly navigable; formerly part of Plaquemine–Morgan City Waterway, it is now an alternate route. **4** In S and SW Mich., rises near Jackson in Jackson co., flows N to Lansing, then NW and W, past Portland, Ionia and Grand Rapids (head of navigation), to Spring L., which empties through short outlet to L. Michigan at Grand Haven; c.260 mi. long. Supplies power. **5** In NE Ohio, rises in SE Geauga co., flows NE to West Farmington, then N and W, past Painesville, to L. Erie at Fairport Harbor; c.75 mi. long. **6** In Okla., name for NEOSHO RIVER. **7** In S.Dak., formed by confluence of N and S forks in Perkins co., NW S.Dak., flows 209 mi. ESE to Missouri R. near Mobridge. The site of Shadehill Dam (begun 1948), unit in Bureau of Reclamation plan for development of Missouri R. basin, is in upper course, in Perkins co. **8** In E central Wis., rises in Fond du Lac co., flows generally SW, past Markesan, then NW to Fox R. near Montello; c.35 mi. long.

Grand River Dam, NE Okla., 13 mi. SE of Vinita, on Neosho R. (locally called Grand R.); 6,565 ft. long, 152 ft. high above stream bed; built for power and flood control; completed 1940. Sometimes called Pensacola Dam. Impounds L. of the Cherokees or Grand L. (recreation), which extends c.55 mi. upstream to vicinity of Miami, near Kansas and Mo. borders.

Grand Rivers, town (pop. 234), Livingston co., SW Ky., on Kentucky Reservoir (Tennessee R.), 22 mi. ESE of Paducah, near Kentucky Dam. Kentucky Dam State Park is W.

Grand River South East or **Grande Rivière Sud Est** (grād' rēvyâr' südĕst'), village (pop. 173), E Mauritius, on Indian Ocean at mouth of the Grand River South East (25 mi. long), 7 mi. SSE of Flacq; railhead for rich sugar-growing region; ships sugar, alcohol.

Grand'Rivière (grā rēvyâr'), town (pop. 490), N Martinique, at N foot of Mont Pelée, 20 mi. NNW of Fort-de-France; banana and cacao growing; rum distilling.

Grand Saline (sùlēn', sā'līn), city (pop. 1,810), Van Zandt co., NE Texas, near Sabine R., 32 mi. NW of Tyler; salt mining, processing center, with one of largest U.S. salt mines. Oil fields near by.

Grand Sentinel Dome, Calif.: see KINGS CANYON NATIONAL PARK.

Grand-Serre, Le (lù grā-sâr'), agr. village (pop. 370), Drôme dept., SE France, 21 mi. SE of Vienne; esparto processing.

Grands Mulets (grā mülā'), rocky ledge (alt. 10,010 ft.) on N slope of Mont Blanc, Haute-Savoie dept., SE France, on customary line of ascent from Chamonix, with hotel and observatories.

Grandson or **Granson** (both: grāsō'), Ger. *Grandsee* (gränt'zā), town (pop. 1,726), Vaud canton, W Switzerland, on L. of Neuchâtel and 2 mi. N of Yverdon, in Grandson dist. (pop. 12,233). Here Swiss Confederates defeated Charles the Bold of Burgundy in 1476.

Grand Terre Island (grănd' târ'), Jefferson parish, extreme SE La., irregularly shaped island (c.6 mi. long) c.45 mi. SSE of New Orleans, bet. Barataria Bay (N) and Gulf of Mexico (S). Barataria Bay lighthouse (29°16'N 89°57'W) is at SW end, near old Fort Livingston (abandoned 1893).

Grand Teton National Park (tē'tŏn, tē'tŭn) (□ 465; established 1929), NW Wyo., just S of Yellowstone Natl. Park, near Idaho line. Magnificent glaciated mtn. region, including most scenic section of N– TETON RANGE; Grand Teton (13,766 ft.) is highest peak in park and 2d highest in Wyo. Other summits are Mt. Owen (12,922 ft.), Middle Teton (12,798 ft.), Mt. Moran (12,594 ft.), South Teton (12,505 ft.), Teewinot (tē'wĭnŏt) (12,317 ft. Cloudveil Dome (12,026 ft.). In E, includes part of scenic JACKSON HOLE country, including Jackson L. Park has other glacial lakes (Leigh, Jenny, Phelps), many streams, 2 glaciers (on Grand Teton), coniferous forests, abundant wildlife (including moose, elk, bighorn sheep), hiking and riding trails, campgrounds, lodges and guest ranches. The difficult Teton peaks attract mtn. climbers. Region first known to white men early in 19th cent.; visited by Astorians in 1811 and later much frequented by furtrappers. Established as natl. park (□ 148.3) in 1929; enlarged (1950) to include most of former Jackson Hole Natl. Monument.

Grand Tower, city (pop. 963), Jackson co., SW Ill., on the Mississippi and 27 mi. WSW of Herrin, in agr. region. Named for 60-ft. rock in Mississippi R. here. Inc. 1872.

Grand Traverse (tră'vûrs), county (□ 464; pop. 28,598), NW Mich.; ⊙ Traverse City. Grand Traverse Bay is in N. Drained by Boardman and Betsie rivers. Fruit growing (especially cherries). Agr. (truck, corn, potatoes, livestock; dairy products). Mfg. at Traverse City. Fisheries. Resorts. Natl. High School Orchestra and Band Camp at Interlochen. Contains state forest and park; and Green, Duck, and Long lakes. Organized 1851.

Grand Traverse Bay, NW Mich., an arm of L. Michigan deeply indenting NW shore of the Lower Peninsula, c.25 mi. SW of Petoskey; c.22 mi. long N–S, 12 mi. wide. Bounded W by Leelanau Peninsula; divided into East and West arms by Old Mission Peninsula (17 mi. long, 3 mi. wide). Traverse City is at S end of West Arm. Known for deepwater trout trolling, boating, ice fishing. Its shores are an important resort and cherry-growing area.

Grand Trianon, France: see TRIANON.

Grand Trunk Road, noted highway of N India and NW Pakistan, extending some 1,450 mi. bet. Calcutta (E) and Peshawar (W) and traversing India states of West Bengal, Bihar, Uttar Pradesh, Delhi, Punjab, and Patiala and East Punjab States Union, and Pakistani provs. of Punjab and North-West Frontier Prov. From Calcutta it runs through Asansol, Benares, Allahabad, Cawnpore (Kanpur), Aligarh, Delhi, Ambala, Ludhiana, Jullundur, Amritsar, Lahore, and Rawalpindi, to Peshawar. Roughly follows route of old Northern Road (Sanskrit *Uttarapatha*) of anc. Aryan India and of the road bet. the Indus and Sonargaon in Bengal built (1540s) by Afghan emperor Sher Shah. Present road partly built by Moguls; greatly extended by British in mid-19th cent.

Grand Turk, town and island (□ 9.4; 6½ mi. long, 2 mi. wide; pop. 1,668), ⊙ TURKS AND CAICOS ISLANDS, dependency of Jamaica, B.W.I., 135 mi. NNW of Cap-Haïtien (Haiti); 21°30'N 71°10'W. Cable station; salt panning, sponge fishing, lobster canning.

Grand Valley, village (pop. 622), S Ont., on Grand R. and 11 mi. W of Orangeville; dairying, lumber milling.

Grand Valley, town (pop. 296), Garfield co., W Colo., on Colorado R. and 40 mi. W of Glenwood Springs, in irrigated fruit, grain, and livestock region; alt. 5,095 ft. Power plant here. U.S. oil shale reserve and deposits of ammonium sulphate in vicinity. Grand Valley Dam, unit in Grand Valley irrigation project, is 27 mi. SW.

Grand Valley, fertile fruitgrowing region in Mesa co., W Colo., extending c.50 mi. along Colorado R. from Palisade almost to Utah line. Grand Valley project, 14 mi. SSW of De Beque, with dam on Colorado R. that diverts water into 55-mi. canal, irrigates more than 40,000 acres. Chief crop, peaches. Grand Junction is marketing and shipping center.

Grand-Veymont, France: see VERCORS.

Grandview, town (pop. 847), W Man., on Valley R. and 28 mi. W of Dauphin; grain elevators, stockyards; lumbering, dairying, mixed farming.

Grandview. 1 Village (pop. 1,349), Sangamon co., central Ill., just NE of Springfield, in agr. and bituminous-coal area. Inc. 1939. **2** Town (pop. 664), Spencer co., SW Ind., on Ohio R. and 33 mi. E of Evansville, in agr. area. **3** Town (pop. 311), Louisa co., SE Iowa, 12 mi. SW of Muscatine, in livestock area. **4** City (pop. 1,556), Jackson co., W Mo., 15 mi. S of Kansas City; apples, dairy products; feed mill. In 1951, Grandview Airport was designated as site of U.S. Continental Air Command Hq. **5** City (pop. 886), Johnson co., N central Texas, 35 mi. SSE of Fort Worth; trade point in cotton, grain, dairy area. **6** City (pop. 2,503), Yakima co., S Wash., 35 mi. SE of Yakima; fruit, lumber, truck, dairy products, potatoes. Founded 1905, inc. 1919.

Grandview Heights, city (pop. 7,659), Franklin co., central Ohio, a W suburb of Columbus.

Grand View-on-Hudson or **Grandview,** village (pop. 302), Rockland co., SE N.Y., on W bank of the Hudson and 2 mi. S of Nyack. Near by is a section of Palisades Interstate Park.

Grandvillars (grävēlär'), town (pop. 2,580), Territory of Belfort, E France, in Belfort Gap, 9 mi. SE of Belfort; barbed wire and hardware mfg.

Grandville, city (pop. 2,022), Kent co., SW Mich., 6 mi. SW of Grand Rapids, near Grand R., in farm area (celery, peaches, grain); mfg. (refrigerator parts, plaster, stucco). Inc. as village 1887, as city 1933.

Grandvilliers (grävēyā'), village (pop. 1,212), Oise dept., N France, 17 mi. NNW of Beauvais; hosiery mfg.

Grand Wash Cliffs (1–2,000 ft.), in Mohave co., NW Ariz., extending N from point near Music Mtn. to lat. 36°30'N; bisected by Grand Canyon of Colorado R. In N, above L. Mead, form W escarpment of Shivwits Plateau.

Grane, Arabia: see KUWAIT.

Graneros (grănā'rōs), town (pop. estimate 700), ⊙ Graneros dept. (□ c.1,000; 1947 pop. 20,699), S Tucumán prov., Argentina, on railroad, on Marapa R. and 60 mi. SSW of Tucumán; agr. (corn, wheat, sugar cane, cotton, livestock) and lumbering center.

Graneros, town (pop. 3,494), O'Higgins prov., central Chile, on railroad and 8 mi. N of Rancagua; agr. center (grain, alfalfa, beans, potatoes, fruit, livestock); makes condensed milk.

Grange, Australia: see HENLEY AND GRANGE.

Grange, urban district (1931 pop. 2,648; 1951 census 3,070), N Lancashire, England, on Morecambe Bay and 8 mi. E of Ulverston; seaside resort.

Grange, agr. village and parish (pop. 1,154), N Banffshire, Scotland, on Isla R. and 4 mi. E of Keith.

Grange, hamlet, W St. Croix Isl., U.S. Virgin Isls., just N of Frederiksted. Alexander Hamilton's mother is buried here.

Grange Hill, village, Westmoreland parish, W Jamaica, 8 mi. NNW of Savanna-la-Mar; sugar cane, fruit, stock.

Grangemouth (grānj'mŭth), burgh (1931 pop. 11,799; 1951 census 15,305), E Stirling, Scotland, on the Forth estuary at mouth of Carron R., at E end of Forth and Clyde Canal, and 3 mi. ENE of Falkirk; 56°1'N 3°44'W; port, with extensive docks and shipyards, important oil refinery, and soap-works. Early experiments in steam navigation were made here; in 1802 the *Charlotte Dundas* was launched at Grangemouth for service on Forth and Clyde Canal.

Granger (grān'jŭr). **1** Town (pop. 300), Dallas co., central Iowa, 16 mi. NW of Des Moines, in agr. area. **2** Town (pop. 122), Scotland co., NE Mo., bet. North and South Wyaconda rivers, 10 mi. E of Memphis. **3** City (pop. 1,637), Williamson co., central Texas, 37 mi. NNE of Austin; trade center in cotton, corn, truck area; cotton ginning, feed milling. **4** City (pop. 1,164), Yakima co., S Wash., 22 mi. SE of Yakima, near Yakima R.; alfalfa. **5** Town (pop. 122), Sweetwater co., SW Wyo., on Blacks Fork, at mouth of Hams Fork, and 26 mi. W of Green River town; alt. 6,240 ft.; livestock.

Granges, Switzerland: see GRENCHEN.

Grangesberg (grĕn'yūsbĕr"yū), Swedish *Grängesberg*, village (pop. 5,471), Kopparberg co., central Sweden, in Bergslag region, 30 mi. W of Fagersta; rail junction; center of one of richest Swedish iron-mining regions. Other ores mined include wolfram, molybdenum, zinc, lead. Mfg. of firearms, explosives. Mines operated since 16th cent. Ores shipped by rail to port of Oxelosund, on the Baltic. Includes mining village of Bjorkasen (byōōr"kō'sūn), Swedish *Björkåsen*.

Granges-sur-Vologne (gräzh-sür-vôlôny'), town (pop. 2,244), Vosges dept., E France, on small Vologne R. and 12 mi. SW of Saint-Dié; cotton milling, coffee roasting.

Grangetown, England: see ESTON.

Grangetown, Wales: see CARDIFF.

Grangeville (grānj'vĭl), city (pop. 2,544), ⊙ Idaho co., central Idaho, 22 mi. S of Nezperce, in fertile valley of Salmon R.; trading point for wheat and livestock region, hq. for Nezperce Natl. Forest; lumber milling. Settled 1876, inc. 1897. Growth stimulated by discovery of gold (1898) near by.

Gränichen (grĕ'nĭkh-ŭn), town (pop. 3,543), Aargau canton, N Switzerland, 3 mi. SE of Aarau; metal products.

Granicus (grŭnī'kŭs), Turkish *Kocabaş* (kôjäbäsh'), small river (45 mi. long) of anc. Mysia, NW Turkey, rising 13 mi. W of Can and flowing NE, past Biga, to Sea of Marmara (Propontis). Site of Alexander the Great's victory over Darius' Persian army in 334 B.C.

Granite (gră'nĭt), county (□ 1,717; pop. 2,273), W Mont.; ⊙ Philipsburg. Mining and agr. region, drained N by the Clark Fork. Manganese, silver, coal; livestock. Deerlodge Natl. Forest and Flint Creek Range in E. Formed 1893.

Granite. 1 Village (pop. c.100), Chaffee co., central Colo., on Arkansas R., just E of Sawatch Mts., and 14 mi. S of Leadville; alt. c.8,940. Scene of early gold discoveries. Gold is still dredged. **2** Village (pop. c.500), Baltimore co., N Md., near Patapsco R., 14 mi. WNW of downtown Baltimore; granite quarries. **3** City (pop. 1,096), Greer co., SW Okla., 9 mi. NE of Mangum, near North Fork of Red R.; red-granite quarrying; monument mfg., cotton ginning, meat and vegetable processing. Seat of a state reformatory. Settled and inc. 1900. **4** Town (pop. 40), Grant co., NE Oregon, 40 mi. SSW of La Grande and on a headstream of John Day R.

Granite City, industrial city (pop. 29,465), Madison co., SW Ill., on the Mississippi and 6 mi. N of East St. Louis, within St. Louis metropolitan area; railroad and mfg. center (steel and iron products, railway equipment, chemicals, beverages, roofing material, enamelware, lubricants, food products, starch). U.S. army supply depot here. Horseshoe L. (E) is state game preserve, fishing resort. Inc. 1896. Developed after establishment of steel industry in 1892–93.

Granite Creek Desert, Nev.: see BLACK ROCK DESERT.

Granite Falls. 1 City (pop. 2,511), Chippewa and Yellow Medicine counties, ⊙ Yellow Medicine co., SW Minn., at falls of Minnesota R., 13 mi. SE of Montevideo; trade center in grain, livestock, poultry area; dairy products. Hydroelectric plant here. Platted 1872, inc. as village 1879, as city 1889. Sioux Indian reservation is near by. **2** Town (pop. 2,286), Caldwell co., W central N.C., 7 mi. NW of Hickory; textile center; mfg. of cotton yarn, hosiery, twine, furniture, machinery. Power dams in near-by Catawba R. **3** Town (pop. 635), Snohomish co., NW Wash., 15 mi. NE of Everett; lumber, dairy products, truck, potatoes. About 1½ mi. E, South Fork of Stillaguamish R. drops over 350-ft. Granite Falls.

Granite Mountain (7,700 ft.), central Ariz., highest peak in the Sierra Prieta, 7 mi. NW of Prescott.

Granite Peak. 1 Peak (12,850 ft.) in S Mont., highest point in Mont., in Beartooth Range c.50 mi. SE of Livingston, near Yellowstone Natl. Park. **2** Peak in N.Mex.: see MOGOLLON MOUNTAINS.

Granite Quarry, town (pop. 591), Rowan co., central N.C., 4 mi. SSE of Salisbury; granite quarrying, clothing mfg.

Granite Range. 1 In Mont.: see BEARTOOTH RANGE. **2** In NW Nev., in Washoe co., N of Smoke Creek Desert. Rises to 8,990 ft. in Granite Peak, 11 mi. NNW of Gerlach.

Graniteville. 1 Village, Middlesex co., Mass.: see WESTFORD. **2** Village, Iron co., SE central Mo., 20 mi. SSE of Potosi; company town for large granite quarry. **3** A section of Richmond borough of New York city, SE N.Y., on N Staten Isl.; makes fireworks. **4** Village (pop. 3,362) Aiken co., W S.C., 5 mi. W of Aiken; textile and dye plants. Founded 1846 as one of 1st mill towns in the South. **5** Village, Washington co., Vt.: see BARRE.

Granitola, Cape (grănētô'lä), point on W coast of Sicily, SW of Castelvetrano; 37°33'N 12°41'E; tunny fishing.

Granja (gră'zhŭ), city (pop. 3,275), N Ceará, Brazil, on railroad and 12 mi. S of Camocim; decadent port on small Camocim R.; saltworks; ships cotton, carnauba wax, hides. Has 18th-cent. church.

Granja. 1 Village (pop. 1,524), Évora dist., S central Portugal, near Sp. border, 15 mi. NE of Moura. **2** Village (pop. 282), Pôrto dist., N Portugal, on railroad and 7 mi. SSW of Oporto; suburban seaside resort of Oporto.

Granja, La, Spain: see SAN ILDEFONSO.

Granja de Rocamora (grän'hä dhä rōkämō'rä), village (pop. 1,241), Alicante prov., E Spain, on fertile plain, 6 mi. NE of Orihuela; olive oil, cereals, truck produce, hemp.

Granja de Torrehermosa (tôräĕrmō'sä), town (pop. 7,911), Badajoz prov., W Spain, near Córdoba border, on railroad and 10 mi. WNW of Fuenteovejuna; agr. center (cereals, chick-peas, livestock); lumbering, sawmilling.

Granki (grän'kē), town (1948 pop. over 500), W Smolensk oblast, Russian SFSR, 22 mi. WNW of Smolensk; peat works.

Grankulla (grän"kŭ'lä), Finnish *Kauniainen* (kou'nĕĭ"nĕn), residential town (pop. 2,279), Uusimaa co., S Finland, 8 mi. WNW of Helsinki. Site of sanitarium.

Gran Meseta Central (grän' măsā'tä sĕnträl'), Patagonian plateau in central Santa Cruz natl. territory, Argentina, N of the upper Río Chico; alt. 1,600–2,000 ft.

Gran Morelos (grän mōrā'lōs), town (pop. 1,244), Chihuahua, N Mexico, 37 mi. SW of Chihuahua; corn, livestock. Formerly San Nicolás de Carretas, or San Nicolás.

Granna (grĕn'ä"), Swedish *Gränna*, city (pop. 1,313), Jonkoping co., S Sweden, on SE shore of L. Vatter, 20 mi. NE of Jonkoping; fruitgrowing center, especially noted for its pears; tourist resort. Founded 1652; chartered 1693.

Grannis (gră'nĭs), town (pop. 193), Polk co., W Ark., 24 mi. SSW of Mena, near Okla. line.

Grano, village (pop. 27), Renville co., N N.Dak., 30 mi. NNW of Minot, near Souris R.

Granollers (grănōlyĕrs'), Catalan *Granollérs*, city (pop. 13,114), Barcelona prov., NE Spain, in Catalonia, 17 mi. NE of Barcelona; communications and mfg. center. Produces chemicals (fertilizers, acetic acid, glycerin), vegetable oils, cement, liqueur, alcohol, sparkling wine, cheese; cotton spinning and weaving, flour- and sawmilling, vegetable canning. Trades in dried fruit, truffles, hemp, livestock. Has 14th-cent. church.

Grañón (grănyōn'), town (pop. 1,042), Logroño prov., N Spain, 30 mi. W of Logroño; cereals, potatoes, sugar beets, lumber, livestock.

Granon (grän'ŭn"), Swedish *Granön*, village (pop. 495), Vasterbotten co., N Sweden, on Ume R. and 40 mi. NW of Umea; sawmills, brickworks.

Gran Pajonal (grän pähōnäl'), highlands (c.5,000 ft.) in Pasco and Junín depts., E central Peru, E outliers of the Andes along Tambo R. bend and upper Ucayali R., S of the Pampa del Sacramento.

Gran Paradiso (grän pärädē'zô), Fr. *Grand Paradis* (grā pärädē'), NW Italy, highest peak (13,323 ft.) in Graian Alps, 16 mi. SSE of Aosta. Site of natl. park established 1922.

Gran Piedra (grän' pyā'drä), mountain (3,710 ft.), Oriente prov., E Cuba, near S coast, 15 mi. E of Santiago de Cuba.

Gran Pilastro, peak, Austro-Italian border: see HOCHFEILER.

Gran Quivira National Monument (grăn kĭvēr'ŭ) (450.9 acres; established 1909), central N.Mex., 20 mi. SSE of Mountainair, just E of Chupadera Mesa. Ruins of 17th-cent. Sp. mission (including church and living quarters) and 18 Pueblo Indian dwellings, abandoned bet. 1672 and 1678 because of drought and Apache raids. Earliest Indian settlement on site was made c.1300.

Gran River, Czechoslovakia: see HRON RIVER.

Gran Sasso d'Italia (grän säs'sô dētä'lyä), highest mountain group in the Apennines, S central Italy, bet. upper Vomano and Pescara rivers; extends c.20 mi. WNW-ESE; rises to 9,560 ft. in Monte CORNO.

Gransee (grän'zā"), town (pop. 6,092), Brandenburg, E Germany, 16 mi. ENE of Neuruppin; mfg. (cement, tiles, starch); market gardening. Has 15th-cent. church, remains of 15th-cent. town walls.

Granson, Switzerland: see GRANDSON.

Grant. 1 County (□ 631; pop. 9,024), central Ark.; ⊙ Sheridan. Drained by Saline R. Agr. (cotton, corn, peanuts, livestock); cotton ginning, lumber milling. Formed 1869. **2** County (□ 421; pop. 62,156), E central Ind.; ⊙ Marion. Agr. area (livestock, grain, poultry, fruit, truck; dairy products). Diversified mfg. at Marion. Natural-gas and oil wells. Drained by Mississinewa R. Formed 1831. **3** County (□ 568; pop. 4,638), SW Kansas; ⊙ Ulysses. Gently rolling wheat area, drained by Cimarron R. (in S) and its North Fork. Small natural-gas fields. Formed 1888. **4** County (□ 250; pop. 9,809), N Ky.; ⊙ Williamstown. Drained by Eagle Creek. Gently rolling upland agr. area (burley tobacco, corn, hay, livestock, poultry, dairy products), in Bluegrass region. Formed 1820. **5** Parish (□ 670; pop. 14,263), central La.; ⊙ Colfax. Bounded E by Little R., W and SW by Red R. Agr. (cotton, corn, hay, peanuts, sweet potatoes, truck, pecans, watermelons). Some mfg. at Colfax. Oil, timber, sand, gravel. Includes part of Kisatchie Natl. Forest; and lakes Iatt and Nantaches. Formed 1869. **6** County (□ 557; pop. 9,542), W Minn.; ⊙ Elbow Lake. Agr. area drained by Mustinka and Pomme de Terre rivers. Grain, livestock. Formed 1868. **7** County (□ 762; pop. 1,057), W central Nebr.; ⊙ Hyannis; agr. region; livestock. Formed 1887. **8** County (□ 3,970; pop. 21,649), SW N.Mex.; ⊙ Silver City. Livestock-grazing, copper- and silver-mining area; watered by Gila R.; borders on Ariz. Includes Pinos Altos Mts. in NE, Big Burro and Little Burro Mts. near Tyrone, and parts of Gila Natl. Forest. Formed 1868. **9** County (□ 1,672; pop. 7,114), S N.Dak.; ⊙ Carson. Agr. area watered by Heart and Cannonball rivers. Stock raising; dairy products, poultry, grain, wheat. Formed 1916. **10** County (□ 999; pop. 10,461), N Okla.; ⊙ Medford. Bounded N by Kansas line; intersected by Salt Fork of Arkansas R. Agr. area (wheat, oats, alfalfa, corn, barley, watermelons, cattle, hogs; dairy products). Some mfg. at Medford and Pond Creek. Oil and natural-gas wells. Formed 1893. **11** County (□ 4,532; pop. 8,329), E central Oregon; ⊙ Canyon City. Mtn. area crossed by John Day R. Livestock grazing, logging, quicksilver mining. Parts of Whitman and Malheur natl. forests are in N, in Blue Mts. Part of Malheur Natl. Forest is in SE, in Strawberry Mts. Formed 1864. **12** County (□ 684; pop. 10,233), NE S.Dak., on Minn. line; ⊙ Milbank. Agr. area watered by intermittent streams; part of Sisseton Indian Reservation in NW. Dairy products, wheat, corn, sorghum, alfalfa, soybeans. Formed 1873. **13** County (□ 2,777; pop. 24,346), E central Wash., in Columbia basin agr. region; ⊙ Ephrata. Grand Coulee Dam on Columbia R. is at NE corner; the Grand Coulee is along NW border. Fruit, grain, livestock, alfalfa. Health resorts on Soap L. Formed 1909. **14** County (□ 477; pop. 8,756), W.Va., in Eastern Panhandle; ⊙ Petersburg. Bounded NW by North Branch of the Potomac (Md. line); drained by South Branch of the Potomac and Patterson Creek. Traversed by Allegheny Front (in W), and by Knobly and Patterson Creek mts. Includes part of Monongahela Natl. Forest. Agr. (livestock, fruit, tobacco, grain, truck), timber. Some small industries at Petersburg. Formed 1866. **15** County (□ 1,168; pop. 41,460), extreme SW Wis.; ⊙ Lancaster. Bounded S by Ill. line, N by Wisconsin R., W by the Mississippi (here forming Iowa line); drained by Platte and Blue rivers, small Grant R. Farming, dairying, stock raising; mining (zinc, lead); some mfg. Contains Wyalusing State Park. Formed 1836.

Grant. 1 Town (pop. 191), Marshall co., NE Ala., 12 mi. N of Guntersville, near Guntersville Reservoir. **2** Town (pop. 237), Montgomery co., SW Iowa, on West Nodaway R. and 18 mi. S of Atlantic. Bituminous-coal mines near by. **3** Village (pop. 646), Newaygo co., W central Mich., 24 mi. ENE of Muskegon, in dairy, truck and poultry region. **4** Village (pop. 1,091), ⊙ Perkins co., SW central Nebr., 55 mi. WSW of North Platte; flour; dairying; livestock. **5** Town (pop. 351), Choctaw co., E Okla., 5 mi. S of Hugo, near Red R., in farm area.

Grant, Camp, Ill.: see ROCKFORD.

Grant, Mount. 1 Peak (11,247 ft.), Churchill co., W central Nev., 53 mi. ENE of Fallon; highest in Clan Alpine Mts. **2** Peak (11,303 ft.), Mineral co., W Nev., 10 mi. WNW of Hawthorne; highest in Wassuk Range.

Gran Tarajal (grän' tärähäl'), village (pop. 521), Fuerteventura, Canary Isls., 22 mi. SSW of Puerto de Cabras; minor port; ships alfalfa.

Granta River, England: see CAM RIVER.

Grantchester, agr. village and parish (pop. 546), S Cambridge, England, on Cam R. and 2 mi. SW of Cambridge. Has church dating from 14th cent. Village is subject of poems by Tennyson and Rupert Brooke. Brooke lived at its Old Vicarage.

Grant City. 1 City (pop. 1,184), ⊙ Worth co., NW Mo., near Middle Fork of Grand R., 26 mi. ENE of Maryville; livestock, poultry. Settled 1864. **2** A section of Richmond borough of New York city, SE N.Y., on E Staten Isl.

Grantfork, village (pop. 162), Madison co., SW Ill., 30 mi. ENE of East St. Louis, in agr. area.

Grantham (grăn'tŭm, grăn'thŭm), municipal borough (1931 pop. 19,711; 1951 census 23,405), Parts of Kesteven, SW Lincolnshire, England, on Witham R. and 23 mi. SSW of Lincoln; railroad center with locomotive works; machinery, boilers, electrical equipment. Agr. market. Has 13th-cent. parish church of St. Wulfram (280-ft. steeple); medieval Angel Inn where Richard III condemned the duke of Buckingham to death (1483); and statue of Sir Isaac Newton, who attended King's School here. Site of an Eleanor Cross, re-erected in 1910. There are 2 libraries with valuable books. Site of 1st victory of Cromwell over the Royalists (1643). Grantham is on the anc. Ermine Street.

Grantham, town (pop. 359), Sullivan co., W N.H., 9 mi. N of Newport.

Grant Land, NE Franklin Dist., Northwest Territories, N part of ELLESMERE ISLAND, bet. the Arctic Ocean (N), Nansen Sound (W), Greely Fjord (S), and Robeson Channel and Lady Franklin Bay (E). It is crossed by United States Range, rising to c.11,000 ft.

Granton, fishing village in Edinburgh, Scotland, just N on the Firth of Forth.

Granton, village (pop. 299), Clark co., central Wis., 16 mi. WSW of Marshfield, in dairying and lumbering region.

Grantorto (grăntôr'tô), village (pop. 1,072), Padova prov., Veneto, N Italy, near Brenta R., 10 mi. NE of Vicenza; alcohol distillery.

Grantown-on-Spey (grăn'toun-ŏn-spā'), burgh (1931 pop. 1,577; 1951 census 1,541), S Moray, Scotland, on the Spey and 20 mi. S of Forres; resort in pine-wood region; agr. market. Founded 1776 by Sir James Grant.

Grant Park, village (pop. 564), Kankakee co., NE Ill., 13 mi. ENE of Kankakee, in agr. area.

Grant Point, cape, NW Adelaide Peninsula, N Keewatin Dist., Northwest Territories, on Queen Maud Gulf, at entrance of Simpson Strait; 68°20'N 98°54'W.

Grant Range, E Nev., in NE corner of Nye co., SSW of Ely, S of White Pine Mts. Troy Peak (11,263 ft.) and Timber Mtn. (10,280 ft.) are at S end in sec. of Nevada Natl. Forest.

Grants, village (pop. 2,251), Valencia co., W N.Mex., on San Jose R., near San Mateo Mts., 70 mi. W of Albuquerque; alt. 6,458 ft. Trade and shipping point in ranching and agr. region (truck, fruit); sawmill. Parts of Cibola Natl. Forest near by, Mt. Taylor 15 mi. ENE.

Grantsburg, village (pop. 931), ⊙ Burnett co., NW Wis., 26 mi. N of St. Croix Falls; dairy products, poultry.

Grants Pass, city (pop. 8,116), ⊙ Josephine co., SW Oregon, on Rogue R. in Klamath Mts. and 25 mi. WNW of Medford, in irrigated fruitgrowing and farming area; trade center; hq. for near-by Siskiyou Natl. Forest; lumbering, dairying, canning; fishing resort (salmon). Gold mines in vicinity. Oregon Caves Natl. Monument 25 mi. S. Inc. 1887.

Grant's Pass, channel (c.3 mi. wide) bet. Dauphin Isl. and Mobile co., SW Ala.; leads from Mississippi Sound of Gulf of Mexico to Mobile Bay.

Grant's Town, S suburb of Nassau, New Providence Isl., Bahamas; fruit and vegetable market.

Grantsville. 1 Town (pop. 461), Garrett co., W Md., in the Alleghenies near Casselman R. and Pa. line, 22 mi. W of Cumberland; bituminous coal and fire-clay mining; dairying. **2** City (pop. 1,537), Tooele co., NW Utah, just S of Great Salt L., 10 mi. NW of Tooele; alt. 4,304 ft. Grain, alfalfa, livestock, turkeys. Settled 1850 by Mormons, inc. 1867. **3** Town (pop. 959), ⊙ Calhoun co., central W.Va., on Little Kanawha R. and 35 mi. SE of Parkersburg, in agr. region (livestock, fruit, tobacco, grain); natural-gas and oil wells, timber. Laid out 1866.

Grant Town, village (pop. 1,273), Marion co., N W.Va., 4 mi. N of Fairmont, in coal-mining area.

Grantville, town (pop. 1,359), Coweta co., W Ga., 9 mi. SW of Newman, in farm area; yarn mfg.

Grantwood, town (pop. 133), St. Louis co., E Mo., SW of St. Louis.

Granum (grā'nŭm), town (pop. 238), S Alta., at foot of Porcupine Hills, 32 mi. WNW of Lethbridge; wheat, ranching.

Granville, municipality (pop. 26,942), E New South Wales, Australia, 12 mi. W of Sydney, in metropolitan area; industrial center; iron foundries, furniture mfg., flour mills.

Granville, village, W Yukon, 35 mi. SE of Dawson; gold mining.

Granville (grāvēl'), town (pop. 9,937), Manche dept., NW France, bathing resort and port with sheltered harbor at foot of narrow, rocky promontory projecting into the Channel, 15 mi. NW of Avranches; mfg. (fishing equipment, fertilizer, biscuits); processes imported coal; codfish processing. Old town, atop rocky ledge, has 18th-cent. fortifications. From Cape Lihou (headland's W tip) is view of Chausey Isls. (c.10 mi. WNW).

Granville (grăn'vĭl), county (□ 543; pop. 31,793), N N.C., on Va. line; ⊙ Oxford. In piedmont area; drained by Tar R. Farming (especially tobacco; corn); timber. Industry at Oxford; sawmilling. Formed 1746.

Granville. 1 Village (pop. 978), Putnam co., N central Ill., near the great bend of Illinois R., 5 mi. S of Spring Valley; bituminous-coal mines; wood products; corn, oats, wheat, livestock, dairy products, poultry. Inc. 1861. **2** Town (pop. 350), Sioux co., NW Iowa, 20 mi. NE of Le Mars; livestock, grain. **3** Town (pop. 740), Hampden co., SW Mass., 15 mi. W of Springfield; small wood products. Includes state forest and village of Granville Center. **4** Village (pop. 2,826), Washington co., E N.Y., near Vt. line, 20 mi. ENE of Glens Falls; slate quarrying; mfg. (roofing materials, furniture, gloves, feed, machinery). Summer resort. Settled 1870, inc. 1885. **5** City (pop. 404), McHenry co., central N.Dak., 24 mi. E of Minot; dairy produce, grain, livestock. **6** Village (pop. 2,653), Licking co., central Ohio, 7 mi. W of Newark, and on Raccoon Creek, in diversified-farming area. Seat of Denison Univ. Settled 1805, inc. 1832. **7** Village (pop. 2,157), Washington co., SW Pa., 19 mi. ESE of Washington. **8** Town (pop. 213), Addison co., central Vt., on White R. and 24 mi. SW of Montpelier, in Green Mts.; wood products. **9** Town (pop. 1,004), Monongalia co., N W.Va., on the Monongahela and 2 mi. NW of Morgantown. Inc. after 1940.

Granville Ferry, village (pop. estimate 350), W N.S., on Annapolis Basin, opposite Annapolis; dairying; apples.

Granvin (grän'vĭn), village and canton (pop. 1,190), Hordaland co., SW Norway, on a branch of Hardanger Fjord, 50 mi. ENE of Bergen; summer resort at terminus of railroad to Voss and of ferry across Hardanger Fjord to Kinsarvik.

Gran Zebrù (grän zĕbrōō'), glacier-topped peak (12,661 ft.) in Ortles mtn. group, N Italy. N of Monte Cevedale.

Grao, El, Spain: see VILLANUEVA DEL GRAO.

Grao de Gandía, El, Spain: see GANDÍA.

Grao de Valencia, Spain: see VILLANUEVA DEL GRAO.

Grão Mogol (grā'ō mōōgôl'), city (pop. 846), N Minas Gerais, Brazil, in the Serra do Espinhaço, 60 mi. E of Montes Claros; diamonds found here.

Grapeland, town (pop. 1,358), Houston co., E Texas, 12 mi. N of Crockett; trade, shipping point in oil, agr., lumber area; oil refineries, recycling plants; sawmills; canning plants. Inc. 1924.

Grapeville, village (pop. 1,563), Westmoreland co., SW Pa., just E of Jeannette; glassmaking.

Grapevine, city (pop. 1,824), Tarrant co., N Texas, 19 mi. NE of Fort Worth; trade point in cotton, truck area; oil refinery; cottonseed-oil mill. Settled 1854, inc. 1907.

Grapevine Mountains, Calif.: see AMARGOSA RANGE.

Grapevine Peak, Calif. and Nev.: see AMARGOSA RANGE.

Grapevine Reservoir, Texas: see TRINITY RIVER.

Grappa, Monte (môn'tĕ grăp'pä), mountain group (17 mi. long, 14 mi. wide) in Veneto, N Italy, bet. Piave (E) and Brenta (W) rivers; rises to 5,827 ft. in Monte Grappa, 8 mi. NNE of Bassano. Scene of heavy fighting (1917–18) bet. Austrians and Italians in First World War.

Grappenhall, town and parish (pop. 2,449), N Cheshire, England, on Manchester Ship Canal and 3 mi. SE of Warrington; leather-tanning center. Has 15th-cent. church and 16th-cent. and 17th-cent. houses.

Gras, Lac de (läk dŭ grä'), lake (□ 345), central Mackenzie Dist., Northwest Territories; 64°30'N 110°30'W; 40 mi. long, 3–18 mi. wide. Drains N through Contwoyto L. into Bathurst Inlet by Burnside R.

Gras, Les (lā grä'), village (pop. 330), Doubs dept., E France, near Swiss border, 11 mi. NE of Pontarlier; watchmaking tools.

Grasberg (grĕs'bĕr"yŭ), Swedish *Gräsberg*, village (pop. 620), Kopparberg co., central Sweden, in Bergslag region, 6 mi. NNE of Ludvika; iron mining.

Grasleben (gräs'lā"bŭn), village (pop. 3,228), in Brunswick, NW Germany, after 1945 in Lower Saxony, 5 mi. N of Helmstedt, opposite Weferlingen; chemicals, paper products, beer.

Graslitz, Czechoslovakia: see KRASLICE.

Grasmere (grăs'mēr), former urban district (1931 pop. 988), W Westmorland, England, 4 mi. WNW of Ambleside, on beautiful Grasmere, a lake 1 mi. long, ½ mi. wide; tourist resort in sheep-raising country. Site of grave of the poet Wordsworth and his sister Dorothy, and of mus. in Wordsworth's house. De Quincy and Samuel Taylor Coleridge also lived in Grasmere. Urban dist. was included (1935) in new urban dist. of The Lakes.

Grasmere. 1 Village, Hillsboro co., N.H.: see GOFFSTOWN. **2** A section of Richmond borough of New York city, SE N.Y., on NE Staten Isl.; mfg. (paints, furniture, hardware).

Graso, Swedish *Gräsö* (grĕs'ū"), island (□ 47; pop. 1,062), E Sweden, in Gulf of Bothnia, just NE of Oregrund, across narrow channel; 16 mi. long, 2–3 mi. wide. Tourist resort.

Grasonville (grā'sŭnvĭl), village (1940 pop. 987), Queen Annes co., E Md., on the Eastern Shore, bet. inlets of Eastern Bay and Chester R.; trade center for fruitgrowing area.

Grassano (gräs-sä'nô), town (pop. 7,252), Matera prov., Basilicata, S Italy, 17 mi. WSW of Matera; wine, olive oil, cheese.

Grasse (gräs), town (pop. 13,731), Alpes-Maritimes dept., SE France, 17 mi. WSW of Nice, on slopes of Roquevignon hi., overlooking the Mediterranean (8 mi. SE); alt. 700–1,380 ft. Health resort noted for its mild winter climate and a leading center of Fr. perfume industry, surrounded by extensive flower (chiefly rose) gardens, orange and olive groves. Principal activity is distilling of variegated essences. An old town with steep and winding streets and an early Gothic cathedral. Razed 1536 by Francis I. Fragonard b. here.

Grasselli, N.J.: see LINDEN.

Grassflat or **Grass Flat,** village (1940 pop. 914), Clearfield co., central Pa., 9 mi. NE of Philipsburg.

Grassina (gräs'sēnä), village (pop. 2,097), Firenze prov., Tuscany, central Italy, 4 mi. SSE of Florence; soap mfg.

Grass Lake, village (pop. 878), Jackson co., S Mich., 10 mi. E of Jackson, on small Grass lake, in agr. and dairy area.

Grass Lake, lake, Ill.: see CHAIN-O'-LAKES.

Grassrange or **Grass Range,** town (pop. 234), Fergus co., central Mont., on branch of Musselshell R. and 30 mi. E of Lewistown, in ranching region; livestock, grain.

Grass River, NE N.Y., formed just S of Canton by small tributaries, flows c.60 mi. generally NE, past Massena, to the St. Lawrence 12 mi. NE of Massena.

Grasston, village (pop. 154), Kanabec co., E Minn., on Snake R. and c.55 mi. N of Minneapolis; dairy products.

Grass Valley. 1 City (pop. 5,283), Nevada co., E central Calif., 50 mi. NE of Sacramento, on W slope of the Sierra Nevada; alt. c.2,400 ft. Center of gold-mining area (mines producing since 1850). Lumber, fruit. Home of Lola Montez, who lived here (1852–54), is preserved. Inc. 1861. **2** City (pop. 195), Sherman co., N Oregon, 10 mi. S of Moro; grain.

Grassy, village (pop. 352), SE King Isl., Tasmania, 14 mi. SE of Currie; tungsten mines.

Grassy Key, Fla.: see FLORIDA KEYS.

Grassy Mountain, Ga.: see OGLETHORPE, MOUNT.

Grassy Park, residential town (pop. 6,142), SW Cape Prov., U. of So. Afr., 7 mi. S of Cape Town.

Grassy Sound, S N.J., inlet of the Atlantic, bet. Cape May Peninsula and a barrier isl., W of North Wildwood; c.1 mi. in diameter. Crossed by Intracoastal Waterway channel.

Grastorp (grĕs'tôrp"), Swedish *Grästorp*, town (pop. 1,191), Skaraborg co., SW Sweden, 14 mi. WSW of Vanersborg; grain, stock.

Gratianopolis, France: see GRENOBLE.

Gratiot (grā'shēut, grā'–), county (□ 566; pop. 33,429), central Mich.; ⊙ Ithaca. Drained by Maple, Pine, and Bad rivers. Agr. (livestock, poultry, fruit, grain, sugar beets, beans, corn; dairy products). Mfg. at Alma, Ithaca, and St. Louis. Oil wells, refineries; mineral springs (health resorts). State game area in SE. Organized 1855.

Gratiot. 1 (grā'shēut, grā'–) Village (pop. 187), on Licking-Muskingum co. line, central Ohio, 11 mi. W of Zanesville. **2** (grā'shŭt) Village (pop. 323), Lafayette co., S Wis., on Pecatonica R. and 18 mi. W of Monroe, in livestock and dairy area.

Gratis (grā'tĭs). **1** Town (pop. 70), Walton co., N central Ga., 17 mi. WSW of Athens. **2** Village (pop. 575), Preble co., W Ohio, 21 mi. WSW of Dayton and on small Twin Creek.

Gratkorn (grät'kôrn), town (pop. 4,759), Styria, SE Austria, on Mur R. and 6 mi. NNW of Graz; grain, potatoes, poultry.

Gratwein (grät'vīn), town (pop. 2,025), Styria, SE Austria, on Mur R. and 7 mi. NNW of Graz; paper mills, mfg. (cellulose, leather goods); summer resort. Vineyards.

Grätz, Poland: see GRODZISK, Poznan prov.

Gratz, borough (pop. 653), Dauphin co., S central Pa., 17 mi. SSE of Sunbury.

Gratzen, Czechoslovakia: see NOVE HRADY.

Grau, province, Peru: see CHUQUIBAMBILLA.

Graua (grä'wä), town (pop. 3,000), Harar prov., E central Ethiopia, 28 mi. SW of Harar, in highlands amid coniferous and eucalyptus trees; coffee, cereals.

Graubünden, Switzerland: see GRISONS.

Graudenz, Poland: see GRUDZIADZ.

Grau-du-Roi, Le (lŭ grō-dü-rwä'), village (pop. 1,372), Gard dept., S France, port on Gulf of Aigues-Mortes, 14 mi. ESE of Montpellier, at S end of AIGUES-MORTES maritime canal; fishing. Bathing resort. Damaged in Second World War.

Grauehörner (grou'ühûr'nŭr), group of peaks in Glarus Alps, E Switzerland; highest is Piz Sol (9,342 ft.), 10 mi. NW of Chur.

Grauhorn (grou'hôrn), peak (10,695 ft.) in Rhaetian Alps, SE central Switzerland, 10 mi. NNE of Biasca.

Graulhet (grōlā'), town (pop. 6,049), Tarn dept., S France, on Dadou R. and 14 mi. SW of Albi; leather-working center (tanning, tawing, mfg. of morocco leather and glue).

Graupen, Czechoslovakia: see KRUPKA.

Graus (grous), town (pop. 2,431), Huesca prov., NE Spain, on the Esera and 38 mi. E of Huesca; mfg. of sandals, rope, silk fabrics, nougats; olive-oil processing, flour- and sawmilling. Trades in livestock, almonds, cereals. Has remains of medieval walls. Sanctuary of La Peña near by.

Grauves (grōv), village (pop. 340), Marne dept., N France, 5 mi. S of Épernay; winegrowing (champagne).

Gravarne (gräv'är"nŭ), fishing village (pop. 1,939), Goteborg och Bohus co., SW Sweden, on the Skagerrak, 8 mi. NW of Lysekil; fish canning, stone quarrying.

Gravatá (grŭvŭtä'), city (pop. 8,676), E Pernambuco, NE Brazil, on railroad and 50 mi. WSW of Recife; ships coffee, sugar, and manioc. Kaolin and white marble deposits near by.

Gravataí (grŭvŭtäē'), city (pop. 2,799), E Rio Grande do Sul, Brazil, on Gravataí R. (short tributary of the Jacuí) and 15 mi. ENE of Pôrto Alegre; manioc flour, fruit. Gravataí airport is just N of Pôrto Alegre. Formerly spelled Gravatahy.

Grave (khrä'vŭ), town (pop. 2,658), North Brabant prov., E Netherlands, on Maas R. and 19 mi. ENE of 's Hertogenbosch; cigar mfg. Old fortress of dukes of Brabant here.

Grave, La, or **La Grave-en-Oisans** (lä gräv'-ãnwäzã'), Alpine village (pop. 181), Hautes-Alpes dept., SE France, on upper Romanche R. and 19 mi. NW of Briançon, just W of Col du Lautaret; alt. 5,006 ft. Lead mines. Alpinism, winter sports.

Grave, Pointe de (pwĕt dŭ gräv'), N tip of Médoc, Gironde dept., SW France, on Bay of Biscay at mouth of the Gironde opposite Royan (ferryboat), 55 mi. NNW of Bordeaux; 45°34'N 1°4'W. Has monument commemorating Lafayette's embarkation for America (1777) and arrival of U.S. troops in 1917.

Gravedona (grävĕdô'nä), village (pop. 1,557), Como prov., Lombardy, N Italy, port on NNW shore of L. Como, 27 mi. NNE of Como; paper mills; hydroelectric plant. Has 12th-cent. baptistery, 16th-cent. palace.

Grave-en-Oisans, La, Hautes-Alpes dept., France: see GRAVE, LA.

Gravelbourg (grä'vŭlbûrg), town (pop. 1,079), S Sask., on Wood R. and 55 mi. SW of Moose Jaw; grain elevators, flour and lumber mills; silver-fox farming. Site of R.C. cathedral and Gravelbourg Col. (1918), affiliated with Univ. of Ottawa.

Gravelines (grävlēn'), Flemish *Gravelinghe* (grä'vŭlĭng-gŭ), town (pop. 1,788), Nord dept., N France, 12 mi. WSW of Dunkirk, seaport on canalized Aa R. near its mouth on North Sea; fish salting, salt refining, fertilizer and chicory mfg. Has 16th-17th-cent. fortifications. Here, in 1558, Spaniards under Egmont defeated French. Petit-Fort-Philippe (pop. 1,377) is small fishing village (2 mi. NNW) opposite Grand-Fort-Philippe.

Gravellona (grävĕl-lô'nä), village (pop. 1,914), Pavia prov., Lombardy, N Italy, 4 mi. WNW of Vigevano; cotton mills.

Gravellona Toce (tô'chĕ), village (pop. 2,869), Novara prov., Piedmont, N Italy, near Toce R., 15 mi. SSE of Domodossola; mfg. (aluminum, cotton textiles, sausage).

Gravelly Range, in Rocky Mts. of SW Mont., rises E of Ruby R., near Idaho line; extends c.40 mi. N to Virginia City. Largely within Beaverhead Natl. Forest. Highest peaks: Old Baldy (9,572 ft.), Cascade Mtn. (9,900 ft.), Black Butte (bŭt) (10,546 ft.).

Gravelotte (grävŭlôt'), village (pop. 266), Moselle dept., NE France, 7 mi. W of Metz. Scene of decisive battle (also known as battle of Saint-Privat), in which Germans defeated French during Franco-Prussian War (1870).

Gravenbrakel, 's, Belgium: see BRAINE-LE-COMTE.

Gravendeel, 's, Netherlands: see 's GRAVENDEEL.

Gravenhage, 's, Netherlands: see HAGUE, THE.

Gravenhurst (grā'vŭnhûrst), town (pop. 2,122), S Ont., at S end of Muskoka L., 90 mi. N of Toronto; diatomite mining, dairying, boatbuilding, brush making. Resort; has 3 sanatoria.

Gravenmoer, 's, Netherlands: see 's GRAVENMOER.

Gravenzande, 's, Netherlands: see 's GRAVENZANDE.

Graves (gräv), winegrowing region in Gironde dept., SW France, extending SE from Bordeaux to Langon along left bank of Garonne R. Chief centers: Pessac (Château-Haut-Brion vineyards), Léognan, Cérons, Barsac, Preignac. Adjoining (SE) is the Sauternes dist.

Graves, county (□ 560; pop. 31,364), SW Ky.; ⊙ MAYFIELD. Bounded S by Tenn.; drained by West Fork Clarks R., Mayfield and Obion creeks, and Bayou de Chien. Gently rolling agr. area (dark tobacco, grain); clay pits; timber. Some mfg. at Mayfield. Formed 1821.

Gravesend (grāvz'ĕnd'), municipal borough (1931 pop. 35,495; 1951 census 45,043), NW Kent, England, on the Thames, opposite Tilbury, and 20 mi. E of London; 51°26'N 0°23'E; port, with extensive docks, forming part of London port system; pilot station. Industries: shipbuilding, metal casting, fishing, market gardening, mfg. of soap, leather, paper. For centuries the place for official reception of distinguished visitors to London, and the starting point of many expeditions, including those of Frobisher and Cabot. There are recreational gardens on foundations of fort built by King Alfred, extended by Henry VIII and Elizabeth. St. George's church contains tomb of Pocahontas and memorial windows donated by ladies of Virginia. In municipal borough (E) is district of Milton-next-Gravesend (pop. 20,988).

Gravesend (grāvz'ĕnd"), SE N.Y., a residential section of SW Brooklyn borough of New York city, on Gravesend Bay (an arm of Lower New York Bay). Settled in 1643 by Lady Deborah Moody and her followers in search for religious freedom.

Gravette (gră'vĭt), town (pop. 894), Benton co., extreme NW Ark., 30 mi. NNW of Fayetteville, in the Ozarks; ships apples, dairy products, grain.

Gravigny (grävēnyē'), village (pop. 1,140), Eure dept., NW France, on the Iton and 2 mi. N of Évreux; iron founding, wool weaving.

Gravina, Port (grŭvē'nŭ), S Alaska, bay (15 mi. long) on E shore of Prince William Sound, 20 mi. NW of Cordova; 60°42'N 146°18'W.

Gravina di Puglia (grävē'nä dē pōō'lyä), town (pop. 21,909), Bari prov., Apulia, S Italy, 7 mi. W of Altamura, in cereal-growing, stock-raising area; rail junction; cheese, wine, soap. Bishopric. Has cathedral, convent, ruins of castle.

Gravina Island (grŭvē'nŭ) (20 mi. long, 3–9 mi. wide; 1939 pop. 56), SE Alaska, one of Gravina Isls., Alexander Archipelago, just W of Ketchikan; 55°15'N 131°45'W; rises to 2,740 ft.; fishing, trapping.

Gravina Islands, part of Alexander Archipelago, SE Alaska, bet. Clarence Strait (W) and Revillagigedo Channel (E), S of Ketchikan. Largest isls. (N–S) are Gravina, Annette, and Duke. Largest settlement is Metlakahtla on Annette Isl. Fishing, fish processing, lumbering.

Gravity, town (pop. 369), Taylor co., SW Iowa, 6 mi. N of Bedford; livestock, grain.

Gravosa, Yugoslavia: see DUBROVNIK.

Grawn, village, Grand Traverse co., NW Mich., 7 mi. SSW of Traverse City; pulpwood market; ships farm produce, especially potatoes.

Gray, town (pop. 5,310), Haute-Saône dept., E France, port on left bank of Saône R., opposite Arc, and 27 mi. ENE of Dijon; commercial and railroad center, handling grains, wines, iron, and lumber; meat processing, cotton milling. Has 16th-cent. town hall. Damaged in Second World War.

Gray. 1 County (□ 869; pop. 4,894), SW Kansas; ⊙ Cimarron. Rolling plain region, drained by Arkansas R. Grain, livestock. Formed 1887. **2** County (□ 937; pop. 24,728), extreme N Texas; ⊙ Pampa. In the Panhandle; alt. 2,800–3,250 ft.; drained by North Fork of Red R. and McClellan Creek. One of state's most productive oil and natural-gas counties, lying in huge Panhandle field; refineries, mfg. (carbon black, oil-well equipment and supplies, chemicals); cattle and wheat ranching, agr. (fruit, hay, cotton, truck); clay and caliche deposits. Hunting, fishing in L. McClellan region (park here). Formed 1876.

Gray. 1 Town (pop. 866), ⊙ Jones co., central Ga., 14 mi. NNE of Macon, in farm area. **2** Town (pop. 183), Audubon co., W central Iowa, 30 mi. N of Atlantic, in agr. area; feed. **3** or **Grays,** village (pop. c.500), Knox co., SE Ky., in Cumberland foothills, 5 mi. E of Corbin, in bituminous-coal region. **4** Town (pop. 1,631), Cumberland co., SW Maine, 14 mi. N of Portland; farm trade center. Dry Mills village has large fish hatchery and game farm. Settled c.1750, inc. 1778.

Gray Air Force Base, Texas: see KILLEEN.

Gray Court, town (pop. 479), Laurens co., NW S.C., 25 mi. SE of Greenville.

Grayevo, Poland: see GRAJEWO.

Grayling, city (pop. 2,066), ⊙ Crawford co., N central Mich., c.45 mi. ESE of Traverse City and on Middle Branch of Au Sable R., in lake-resort, timber, and farm area; lumber milling. Winter-sports center. A Natl. Guard training camp, state fish hatchery, and Hartwick Pines State Park (c.8,500 acres) are near by. Inc. as village 1903, as city 1934.

Graymont, Ga.: see TWIN CITY.

Grays. 1 Town (1940 pop. 47), Woodruff co., E central Ark., 8 mi. ESE of Augusta. **2** Village, Knox co., Ky.: see GRAY.

Grays Harbor, county (□ 1,905; pop. 53,644), W Wash.; ⊙ Montesano. Rolling hills, rising to Olympic Mts. in E; bounded W by Pacific Ocean and Grays Harbor. Includes Chehalis Indian Reservation and parts of Olympic Natl. Forest and Quinault Indian Reservation. Drained by Chehalis R. Produces lumber, wood products, fish, shellfish, dairy products, truck. Formed as Chehalis co. 1854, renamed 1915.

Grays Harbor, W Wash., an inlet of Pacific Ocean at mouth of Chehalis R.; c.15 mi. long, 2–13 mi. wide. Lumber-shipping port; Aberdeen and Hoquiam are on N shore.

Grays Knob, mining village (1940 pop. 602), Harlan co., SE Ky., in the Cumberlands, 26 mi. NE of Middlesboro; bituminous coal.

Grays Lake or **Grayslake,** village (pop. 1,970), Lake co., extreme NE Ill., 11 mi. W of Waukegan, in dairying, agr., and lake-resort area. Small Grays L. is here. Mfg. (dairy products, canned foods, cement and wood products, gelatin). Inc. 1895.

Grayson, village (pop. 332), SE Sask., 16 mi. SSE of Melville; mixed farming, stock.

Grayson. 1 County (□ 514; pop. 17,063), W central Ky.; ⊙ Leitchfield. Bounded N by Rough R., SE by Nolin R.; drained by Bear Creek. Rolling agr. area (dairy products, poultry, burley tobacco, corn, hay). Asphalt mining (co. ranks 2d in production in Ky.); bituminous-coal mines, stone quarries. Formed 1810. **2** County (□ 984; pop. 70,467), N Texas; ⊙ Sherman. Bounded N by Red R. and L. Texoma, here forming the Okla. line. Rich diversified agr., cattle, and dairying area (cotton, corn, grains, peanuts, pecans, fruit, truck); also hogs, poultry, sheep. Some oil, timber produced. Mfg., farm-products processing at Sherman and Denison. Formed 1846. **3** County (□ 451; pop. 21,379), SW Va.; ⊙ Independence. Bounded S by N.C.; Iron Mts. (including White Top Mtn. and Mt. Rogers, highest peak in Va.) are along N and W borders; part of Blue Ridge in SE corner. Drained by New R. Includes part of Jefferson Natl. Forest and a section of Appalachian Trail. Agr. (fruit, potatoes, truck), livestock and poultry raising, dairying; mfg. (especially of textiles and wood products) at towns of Galax and Fries. Formed 1778.

Grayson. 1 Town (pop. 227), Gwinnett co., N central Ga., 25 mi. ENE of Atlanta. **2** Town (pop. 1,383), ⊙ Carter co., NE Ky., on Little Sandy R. and 20 mi. WSW of Ashland; trade center in iron-mining and agr. (dairy products, livestock, poultry, tobacco, corn, wheat) area; clay pits, coal mines, timber; brickworks, feed and lumber mills. Seat of Ky. Christian Col. Carter and Cascade limestone caves near by. **3** Village (pop. 455), Caldwell parish, NE central La., 32 mi. S of Monroe; lumber milling. **4** Town (pop. 64), Clinton co., NW Mo., 21 mi. SE of St. Joseph.

Grays Peak (14,274 ft.), N central Colo., in Front Range, bet. Clear Creek and Summit counties, 45 mi. W of Denver.

Grays Thurrock, residential former urban district (1931 pop. 18,173), S Essex, England, on the Thames and 20 mi. E of London; mfg. of concrete, chemicals, soap; chalk quarrying. In the near-by chalkpits remains have been found of extinct animals and fine examples of anc. excavations known as deneholes. There are traces of Roman occupation. Grays Thurrock was inc. (1936) in THURROCK.

Graysville. 1 Town (pop. 879), Jefferson co., N central Ala., 12 mi. NW of Birmingham. **2** Town (pop. 120), Catoosa co., NW Ga., 17 mi. NW of Dalton, on Tenn. line, in agr. area. **3** Village (pop. 138), Monroe co., E Ohio, 23 mi. NE of Marietta, in agr. area. **4** Town (pop. 820), Rhea co., E Tenn., 30 mi. NNE of Chattanooga, in coal, timber, fruit area; makes hosiery.

Grayville, city (pop. 2,461), on Edwards-White co. line, SE Ill., on Wabash R. at mouth of Bonpas Creek, and 16 mi. SW of Mount Carmel; agr. (corn, wheat, livestock, fruit, poultry); mfg. (clothing, buttons, wood products); fisheries. Inc. 1851.

Grayvoron, Russian SFSR: see Graivoron.

Graz (gräts), city (1951 pop. 226,271), ⊙ Styria, Austria, on Mur R. and 80 mi. SW of Vienna; 2d largest city of Austria; rail, industrial, and cultural center. Hydroelectric plant; iron- and steelworks; mfg. (bicycles, motorcycles, machines, linen, cotton, furniture, glass, matches, leather goods, soap); paper mills, breweries. Built around the Schlossberg (1,558 ft.), with its well-known Uhrturm (Clock Tower) and ruins of 15th-cent. fortress, blown up by French in 1809. Points of interest: Univ. (1890–95), Johanneum Mus. (founded 1811; 1 of finest in Austria), opera house (built 1899), Gothic cathedral (1449–62), 13th- and 15th-cent. churches, Renaissance Rathaus, 16th-cent. Landhaus, Mausoleum of Ferdinand II, who was b. here. Graz is also a summer resort and spa. Eggenberg (ĕg'ŭnbĕrk), W suburb, now inc. into Graz.

Grazalema (grä-thälā'mä), town (pop. 2,045), Cádiz prov., S Spain, in spur of the Cordillera Penibética, at foot of the Pinar mtn., 11 mi. W of Ronda, in one of Andalusia's rainiest regions. Produces olive oil, cereals, grapes, vegetables, fruit, timber, livestock. Flour milling, sawmilling, dairying; mfg. of woolen goods. Copper deposits near by.

Grazhdanovka (grŭzhdä'nŭfkŭ), village (1939 pop. over 2,000), E Tambov oblast, Russian SFSR, 33 mi. NE of Tambov; wheat.

Grazhdanskaya, Russian SFSR: see Novo-Malorossiskaya.

Grdelica or **Grdelitsa** (both: gûrdĕ'lĭtsä), village (pop. 5,881), SE Serbia, Yugoslavia, on the Southern Morava, on railroad and 9 mi. SSE of Leskovac; mfg. of woolen textiles.

Greaaker, Norway: see Greaker.

Greaca, Lake (grĕä'kä) (□ 35.5), in Bucharest prov., S Rumania, W of Oltenita; fishing area, part of swamps along left shore of the Danube.

Greaker (grā'ôkûr), Nor. *Greåker*, village (pop. 2,006) in Tune canton (pop. 9,723), Ostfold co., SE Norway, on Glomma R., on railroad and 4 mi. NE of Fredrikstad; shipbuilding, lumbering, paper and cellulose milling, woodworking. Sometimes spelled Greaaker.

Greasbrough (grēz'brŭ), former urban district (1931 pop. 3,599), West Riding, S Yorkshire, England, 2 mi. NNW of Rotherham; coal mining. Inc. 1936 in Rotherham.

Greasley (grēz'lē), town and parish (pop. 6,427), W Nottingham, England, 7 mi. NW of Nottingham; coal mining. Has 14th-cent. fortified manor house.

Great, for names beginning thus and not found here: see under Greater.

Great, in Rus. names: see also Bolshaya, Bolshe-, Bolshiye, Bolshoi, Bolshoye; Velikaya, Veliki, Velikiye, Veliko-, Velikoye.

Great Abaco Island (ă'bŭkō), constituting most of Abaco (or Abaco and Cays) (kāz, kēz) dist. (including Little Abaco and Cays, □ 776; pop. 3,461), N Bahama Isls., E of Grand Bahama Isl., 33 mi. N of Nassau; forms roughly a right angle c.100 mi. long, up to 14 mi. wide. It is adjoined NW by Little Abaco Isl. and is surrounded by many small cays. Has several fine harbors. Largely wooded. Main products are timber, fish, sponge, fruit. Principal settlements: Hope Town (on E cay), Cherokee Sound and Marsh Harbour (E central), Green Turtle Cay (NE), Sandy Point (SW). The isl. was settled (1783) by loyalists from New York City. At SE end, where Northeast and Northwest Providence channels join, is the "Hole in the Wall," a widely known perforated rock, now site of a lighthouse.

Great American Desert, in SW U.S. and NW Mexico, name formerly given to vast arid and semiarid region lying bet. W base of the Rockies and E base of the Sierra Nevada and the Cascades S of central Oregon; included parts of the Great Basin and Colorado Plateau provinces, and the deserts (Colorado, Yuma, Mojave, and Sonoran) of SE Calif., SW Ariz., and N Sonora, Mexico.

Great Amwell, residential town and parish (pop. 2,104), E Hertford, England, just SSE of Ware. Church dates from 13th-cent.

Great Andaman Islands: see Andaman Islands.

Great Appalachian Valley or **Great Valley,** E N.America, longitudinal chain of lowlands of the Appalachian Mountains; extends from Canada on NE to Ala. on SW. Represented from NE to SW by the great St. Lawrence R. lowland, Richelieu R. valley, L. Champlain lowland, and the valley of the Hudson R. bet. the L. Champlain region and the point near Kingston, N.Y., where the Wallkill R. valley extends SW to meet the Kittatinny Valley of N N.J.; from Kittatinny Valley, it is continued by the Lebanon valley (Pa.), Cumberland Valley (Pa. and Md.), Shenandoah Valley in Va., the Valley of E Tenn. (drained by Tennessee R.) in Tenn., and Coosa R. valley of Ala., where the lowland meets the Gulf coastal plain. It contains rich agr. land, notably in the Cumberland and Shenandoah valleys.

Great Arber, Ger. *Grosser Arber* (grō'sŭr är'bŭr), Czech *Javor* (yä'vôr), highest peak (4,780 ft.) of the Bohemian Forest, in Bavaria, near German-Czechoslovak border, 9 mi. N of Regen. White Regen R. rises on NW slope.

Great Atlas, Fr. Morocco: see Atlas Mountains.

Great Australian Bight, wide bay of Indian Ocean indenting S coast of Australia, bet. Cape Pasley (W) of Western Australia and Cape Carnot (E) of Eyre Peninsula, South Australia; 720 mi. E–W, 220 mi. N–S. Contains part of Recherche Archipelago, Nuyts Archipelago, Investigator and Whidbey isls.

Great Averill Lake (ā'vŭrŭl), NE Vt., near Que. line, 8 mi. W of Canaan, in hunting, fishing area; 2 mi. long.

Great Backbone Mountain, Md.: see Backbone Mountain.

Great Baddow (bă'dō), town and parish (pop. 3,652), central Essex, England, 2 mi. SE of Chelmsford; agr. market. Has 14th-cent. church. Prehistoric artifacts found here.

Great Badminton or **Badminton** (băd'–), agr. village and parish (pop. 356), SW Gloucester, England, 15 mi. ENE of Bristol; seat of duke of Beaufort. Game of Badminton derives its name from village.

Great Bahama Bank (bŭhā'mŭ, bŭhä'mŭ), large shoal in the Bahamas, SE of Florida, and S of Little Bahama Bank, from which it is separated by Northwest Providence Channel. Extends from just E of Miami (across Straits of Florida) c.350 mi. SE bet. Cuba and Andros Isl.

Great Bahama Island, Bahama Isls.: see Grand Bahama Island.

Great Barrier Island, volcanic island and county (□ 110; pop. 191) of New Zealand, 55 mi. NE of Auckland; forms breakwater for Hauraki Gulf; 25 mi. long, 13 mi. wide; mountainous. Sheep farms, gold and silver mines; summer resort. Tryphena is ⊙ Great Barrier Isl. co.

Great Barrier Reef, largest coral reef in world, in Coral Sea; forms natural breakwater for E coast of Queensland, Australia; extends 1,250 mi. SE from New Guinea coast on Torres Strait to Swains Reef near Tropic of Capricorn. Separated from Queensland coast by generally shallow, treacherous channel 10–100 mi. wide. Consists of detached coral reefs (10–90 mi. wide), shoals, and islets. Broken by many passages, including Great Northeast Channel, Flinders Passage, and Trinity Opening. Isls. contained within reef include Northumberland, Cumberland, and Palm groups, and Whitsunday and Hinchinbrook isls.; coral gardens; tourist resorts.

Great Barrington (bă'rĭngtŭn), town (pop. 6,712), including Great Barrington village (pop. 3,913), Berkshire co., SW Mass., on Housatonic R. and 18 mi. SSW of Pittsfield, in the Berkshires; summer resort; ski center. Mfg. (paper, cotton goods); dairying, poultry; timber. Has fine old houses. Settled 1726, set off from Sheffield 1761. Includes state forest, villages of Housatonic (pop. 1,601), and Van Deusenville.

Great Basin, W U.S., vast interior region (more than □ 200,000) lying bet. the Sierra Nevada and S Cascades on the W and the Wasatch Range (Rocky Mts.) and W face of Colorado Plateau on the E and SE; extends N to meet the high lava plain (Columbia Plateau) of central Oregon and S Wash., and S to merge with the deserts of SW Ariz., SE Calif., and N Sonora, Mexico. Almost triangular in shape, it covers parts of Oregon and Idaho, most of Nevada, W Utah, and part of SE Calif.; it is sometimes considered to include the interior area bet. the drainage basins of the Columbia, Colorado, and Rio Grande rivers. Its surface is characterized by rugged, N–S mtn. ranges (many of them raised by faulting), typically 7–10,000 ft. high (3–5,000 ft. above their bases), separating c.100 basins of interior drainage; entire region is semiarid in climate and its few streams (largest are Humboldt and Carson rivers) enter saline lakes or sinks. Lakes vary in size with seasonal rainfall; largest are Great Salt, Utah, Sevier, Pyramid, Winnemucca, and Walker lakes, remnants of enormous prehistoric lakes Bonneville and Lahontan, which covered much of present area of the Basin. It includes several deserts—Great Salt Lake Desert, Black Rock Desert, Smoke Creek Desert, Carson Sink, Mojave Desert, Death Valley (containing lowest point in N.America), and Colorado Desert (including irrigated Imperial Valley, and Salton Sink). Agr. is possible only under irrigation; region's scanty timber (juniper, pine) is found only at higher alts., and minerals and grazing lands are the chief resource. J. C. Frémont explored part of the region (1843–45) and gave it its name. The name Great American Desert was formerly applied to its most arid portion. Physiographically the Great Basin is called the Basin and Range province.

Great Basses, Singhalese *Maha Ravana Kotuw* [=Great Ravana's Rocks], small group of rocks of SE coast of Ceylon; 6°11'N 81°29'E; lighthouse.

Great Bay. 1 Inland tidal bay in SE N.H., receive Exeter, Lamprey, Oyster, and Bellamy rivers opens through Little Bay into Piscataqua R., bet Dover and Portsmouth; 6 mi. long, 4 mi. wide **2** Inlet of the Atlantic in SE N.J., at mouth o navigable Mullica R., 9 mi. NNE of Atlantic City c.5 mi. in diameter. Entered from Atlantic b Little Egg Inlet; traversed by Intracoastal Water way channel.

Great Bear Lake (□ 12,000), central Mackenzi Dist., Northwest Territories, on the Arctic Circle 64°47'–67°2'N 117°27'–125°6'W. Irregular i shape, it is 200 mi. long, 25–110 mi. wide, and ex tends several arms. Contains many small isls Drained (SW) by Great Bear R. (c.100 mi. long into Mackenzie R. On E shore, on Labine Point is Port Radium, radium- and uranium-mining cen ter. Fort Franklin, on SW shore, at outlet of Grea Bear R., was Sir John Franklin's winter quarter 1825–27; NE extremity of lake was site of Fort Confidence, Franklin's winter quarters, 1837. Be cause of heavy icing, lake is navigable only months in the year. Discovered before 1800 b traders of North West Co., who established pos (1799) on site of Fort Franklin.

Great Bedwyn, town and parish (pop. 789), E Wilt shire, England, 4 mi. WSW of Hungerford; agr market. Has 13th-cent. church.

Great Belt, Dan. *Store Bælt*, Denmark, strai (c.40 mi. long, c.10 mi. wide) connecting the Katte gat (through Samso Belt, N) with Baltic Se (through Langeland Belt, S), bet. Fyn and Lange land isls. (W) and Zealand and Lolland isls. (E) S of Zealand it branches into Smaalandsfarvan strait (E).

Great Bend. 1 City (pop. 12,665), ⊙ Barton co. central Kansas, on Arkansas R., near mouth o Walnut Creek, and c.50 mi. NW of Hutchinson trade center for wheat and oil region; flour milling produce packing, oil refining. Settled 1871, inc 1872. Grew as railhead and cattle town on Chis holm Trail. Industries stimulated in 1930s by de velopment of oil and gas fields in vicinity. **2** Vil lage (pop. c.400), Jefferson co., N N.Y., on Blac R. and 10 mi. ENE of Watertown. Camp Drun (formerly Pine Camp) is near by. **3** Village (pop 169), Richland co., SE N.Dak., 12 mi. SW o Wahpeton and on Wild Rice R. **4** Residential bor ough (pop. 751), Susquehanna co., NE Pa., on Sus quehanna R. and 12 mi. SE of Binghamton, N.Y. cheese factory, sawmill; agr.

Great Berg River (bûrg, Afrik. bĕrkh), SW Cap Prov., U. of So. Afr., rises E of Stellenbosch, flow 140 mi. generally NW, past Paarl, Wellington, an Hopefield, to St. Helena Bay of the Atlantic 20 mi NE of Saldanha.

Great Berkhampstead, Berkhampstead, or **Berk hamsted** (all: bûr'kŭmstĭd), residential urban dis trict (1931 pop. 8,052; 1951 census 10,777), SW Hertford, England, 10 mi. W of St. Albans. Site o 11th-cent royal castle, where Edgar Atheling sub mitted to William the Conqueror, Thomas à Becket and Chaucer lived, and Henry II held court After Poitiers, John II of France was imprisone here. Castle was pulled down in 16th cent. and re placed by Berkhamsted House, boyhood residence of Charles I. Has 16th-cent. grammar school an 13th-cent. church. William Cowper b. here.

Great Bernera (bûr'nŭrŭ), island, Outer Hebrides Ross and Cromarty, Scotland, in Loch Roag, on W coast of Lewis with Harris; 6 mi. long, up to 3 mi wide; rises to 265 ft. Just N of Great Bernera i Little Bernera, 1 mi. long, ½ mi. wide. Pop. o 2 isls., 514.

Great Bitter Lake, Egypt: see Bitter Lakes.

Great Blasket Island, Ireland: see Blasket Islands.

Great Boars Head, SE N.H., promontory (.5 mi long) on coast N of Hampton Beach; Little Boar Head is 3 mi. N.

Great Bookham, residential town and parish (pop 3,068), central Surrey, England, 2 mi. SW o Leatherhead. Has Norman church.

Great Brak River (brăk), Afrikaans *Grootbrakrivie* (khrŏŏtbräk"rĭfĕr'), town (pop. 2,436), S Cap Prov., U. of So. Afr., on Great Brak R., just abov its mouth on the Indian Ocean, 11 mi. NE of Mos sel Bay; leather, shoe-mfg. center; resort.

Great Bras d'Or, N.S.: see Bras d'Or Lake.

Great Brewster Island, Mass.: see Brewster Islands.

Great Britain, principal island (□ 88,745; 193 pop. 44,795,357; 1951 census 48,840,893) of th United Kingdom of Great Britain and North ern Ireland; ⊙ London. Its political and geo graphical divisions are England, Scotland, an Wales. Isl. is 595 mi. long bet. Lizard Point (S and Cape Wrath (N); width varies from 26 mi. bet head of Loch Broom (W) and head of Dornoc Firth (E) in Scotland, to 320 mi. bet. Land's En (W) and North Foreland (E) in S England. Isl. i bounded by English Channel and narrow Strait o Dover (S) which separate it from the Continent North Sea (E), Atlantic (N, NW, and SW) an North Channel, Irish Sea, and St. George's Chan nel (W), which separate it from Ireland. Administratively, Great Britain includes Isle of Wight (S), Scilly Isls. (SW), the Hebrides (NW), and Orkney and Shetland isls. (N), but not Isle of Man and Channel Isls. It is sometimes called Britain. As a political unit, Great Britain came into being (1707) under Queen Anne, through Act of Union, which joined Scotland to England. With accession (1714) of Hanoverian dynasty came the beginning of the present-day cabinet system and full development of party govt. The 18th cent. saw rapid British colonial and mercantile expansion, coupled with a period of internal stability and of great literary and artistic progress. The Seven Years War, ended (1763) by Treaty of Paris, established British control of the seas, as well as in North America and India. American Revolution caused serious loss to the empire, but was soon made up by settlement of Australia and New Zealand. Great Britain's part in French Revolutionary Wars and in defeat of Napoleon further improved her lines of empire communication, especially those to India. Irish rebellion (1798), caused by British denial of parliamentary reform, resulted in Ireland being united with Great Britain, with Irish representation in British Parliament. With accession (1837) of Victoria, throne of Hanover was separated from that of Great Britain; her reign saw development of the industrial revolution, which brought with it a wide range of new social problems and inequities. Though legislation to remedy these came slowly, British intellectual climate was favorable to social and political reforms throughout the 19th and early 20th cent. Industrial and trade development was accompanied by imperial expansion in Africa and by consolidation of possessions elsewhere. In later part of the century, trade-union power began to increase; education was developed along national lines; and a regular civil service was founded. In the years before outbreak of First World War social legislation included provisions for old-age pensions and child welfare; universal suffrage was introduced. First World War resulted in heavy losses in men and was followed by serious economic dislocation. The Statute of Westminster granted status of equality to self-governing dominions and created concept of the BRITISH COMMONWEALTH OF NATIONS. In Second World War Great Britain suffered heavy air attacks on its cities, while entire adult pop. was directly involved in the war through the armed services, home defense, or war production. An ineffectual Labor Party govt. had been formed (1924) under MacDonald, but 1st govt. with clear mandate to implement Labor program was elected 1945. The years after the war saw vast improvements in social and educational services; notable was introduction (1948) of National Health Service. Major economic crisis developed shortly after the war. At the same time the British withdrew (1948) from India and Pakistan. A program of progressive nationalization of means of production and transportation was pursued. American aid, in the form of direct loans and through the European Recovery Program, as well as devaluation of British currency, eventually helped to turn the tide of Great Britain's economic crisis. The official title of United Kingdom of Great Britain and Ireland came into being with union bet. Great Britain and Ireland. No change was made after creation (1922) of Irish Free State, but in 1927 the kingdom's official title became United Kingdom of Great Britain and Northern Ireland. It did not, however, gain widespread usage until after Second World War. The overseas components of the BRITISH EMPIRE are listed under that heading.

Great Broughton, England: see BROUGHTON.

Great Budworth, village and parish (pop. 447), N central Cheshire, England, 2 mi. N of Northwich; mfg. of chemicals. Has 14th-cent. church and many Tudor houses. Just S is the lake of Budworth Mere.

Great Burnt Lake, N.F.: see CROOKED LAKE.

Great Burstead, agr. village and parish (pop. 3,690), S central Essex, England, just S of Billericay. Has Norman church.

Great Cacapon (kŭkā'pŏn), village (1940 pop. 1,052), Morgan co., W.Va., in Eastern Panhandle, on the Potomac, at Cacapon R. mouth, and 21 mi. NW of Martinsburg; glass-sand quarries.

Great Captain Island, SW Conn., isl. (.4 mi. long) in Long Isl. Sound, 3 mi. offshore, S of Greenwich; lighthouse here since early 19th cent. Little Captain Isl. is E.

Great Cedar Swamp, N.J.: see DENNISVILLE.

Great Central Lake (□ 20), SW B.C., in central Vancouver Isl., just S of Strathcona Park, in fishing, lumbering area 11 mi. NW of Port Alberni; Great Central village, at E end, at head of rail spur, saws and ships lumber.

Great Channel, seaway connecting Indian Ocean with Andaman Sea (NE) and Strait of Malacca (SE), bet. Nicobar Isls. and isls. off NW Sumatra (c.110 mi. apart); lies on Colombo-Singapore shipping lane.

Great Chazy River (shā"zē'), NE N.Y., issues from Chazy L., flows c.40 mi. NE and E, past Champlain, to L. Champlain 4 mi. S of Rouses Point.

Great Chebeague Island (shĭbēg'), SW Maine, resort and residential isl. (c.2,000 acres) in Casco Bay. Chebeague Island village is on E shore.

Great Clifton, village and parish (pop. 1,259), W Cumberland, England, 3 mi. E of Workington; coal mining.

Great Cloche Island (klōsh) (10 mi. long, 4 mi. wide), S central Ont., one of the Manitoulin Isls., in the North Channel of L. Huron, just off Little Current, Manitoulin Isl. Has railroad connection with mainland and Little Current.

Great Coggeshall, England: see COGGESHALL.

Great Colinet Island (kôlĕnā') (□ 5; pop. 174), in St. Mary's Bay, SE N.F., 25 mi. SE of Argentia; 5 mi. long, 2 mi. wide; 46°59'N 53°42'W. Fishing. Little Colinet Isl. (2 mi. long) is 2 mi. N.

Great Corby, England: see WETHERAL.

Great Cranberry Island, Maine: see CRANBERRY ISLES.

Great Crosby, Lancashire, England: see CROSBY.

Great Cumbrae (kŭmbrā'), island (□ 5.5, including Little Cumbrae isl.; pop. 2,144), Buteshire, Scotland, in the Firth of Clyde, bet. S part of Bute isl. (W) and mainland of Ayrshire (E), just W of Largs; 4 mi. long, 2 mi. wide; rises to 417 ft. On S coast is town of MILLPORT. Main occupations are fishing and agr. (grain, vegetables).

Great Diamond Island, SW Maine, resort isl. (369 acres) in Casco Bay off Portland; site of Fort McKinley. Sand spit connects with Little Diamond Isl.

Great Dismal Swamp, Va. and N.C.: see DISMAL SWAMP.

Great Divide, North America: see CONTINENTAL DIVIDE.

Great Dividing Range, general name for mts. and plateaus roughly paralleling E and SE coasts of Australia; forms watershed bet. rivers flowing to Coral and Tasman seas and those flowing to Gulf of Carpentaria and Indian Ocean. Subdivisions of the range include AUSTRALIAN ALPS, containing Mt. Kosciusko (7,305 ft.; highest peak of Australia), MCPHERSON RANGE, NEW ENGLAND RANGE, BLUE MOUNTAINS, the GRAMPIANS.

Great Driffield, England: see DRIFFIELD.

Great Duck Island (5 mi. long, 2 mi. wide), S central Ont., one of the Manitoulin Isls., in L. Huron 8 mi. S of Manitoulin Isl. Just SE is Outer Duck Isl. (2 mi. long).

Great Duck Island, Maine: see LONG ISLAND, plantation.

Great Dunmow, England: see DUNMOW.

Great East Pond, Maine and N.H., on state line just E of Wakefield, N.H.; c.4 mi. long.

Great Egg Harbor Bay, SE N.J., inlet of the Atlantic (c.5 mi. long) 8 mi. SW of Atlantic City; entered from Atlantic by Great Egg Harbor Inlet (bridged) N of Ocean City, which is on Peck Beach bet. bay and ocean. Bay traversed by Intracoastal Waterway channel. Sometimes called Great Egg Bay. Receives from W TUCKAHOE RIVER, from NW **Great Egg Harbor River,** rising SE of Camden, flowing c.50 mi. SE, past Mays Landing (head of navigation), to head of Great Egg Harbor Bay near Somers Point city. Sometimes called Great Egg R.

Great End, England: see SCAFELL.

Greater, for names beginning thus and not found here: see under GREAT.

Greater, in Rus. names: see also BOLSHAYA, BOLSHIYE, BOLSHOI, BOLSHOYE.

Greater Antilles, West Indies: see ANTILLES.

Greater Anyui River, Russian SFSR: see ANYUI.

Greater Balkhan Range, Turkmen SSR: see BALKHAN.

Greater Cheremshan River (chĕrĭmshän'), Rus. *Bolshoi Cheremshan,* in E central European Russian SFSR, rises c.15 mi. S of Shugurovo, flows NW past Cheremshan, and generally SW past Nikolskoye (Ulyanovsk oblast), to Volga R. 15 mi. SE of Sengilei; 245 mi. long. Lumber floating for 45 mi. in lower course. Lesser Cheremshan R., Rus. *Maly Cheremshan,* is chief tributary (right); 65 mi. long.

Greater Fatra or **Greater Fatra Mountains** (făt'rä), Slovak *Vel'ká Fatra* (vĕl'kä), Hung. *Nagy Fatra* (nŏ'dyŭ fŏ'trŏ), mountain range of the Carpathians, W central Slovakia, Czechoslovakia; extend c.25 mi. S from Vah R. near Ruzomberok; rise to 5,218 ft. in the Ostrodok. Site of numerous health resorts with mineral springs. Woodworking communities on E, N, and W edges. S offspurs formerly noted for their precious-metal mines; small-scale mining of silver and gold still carried on at Kremnica and Banska Bystrica.

Greater Hesse, Germany: see HESSE.

Greater Ik River (ĕk), Rus. *Bolshoi Ik,* in SE European Russian SFSR, rises in the S Urals 35 mi. E of Mrakovo, flows W, past Mrakovo, and S, past Isyangulovo (head of navigation) to Sakmara R. opposite Saratak; 135 mi. long.

Greater Irgiz River: see IRGIZ RIVER, Russian SFSR.

Greater Kas River, Russian SFSR: see KAS RIVER.

Greater Kemin River, Kirghiz SSR: see KEMIN.

Greater Kinel River (kēnyĕl'), Rus. *Bolshoi Kinel,* SE European Russian SFSR, rises in W foothills of the S Urals 13 mi. S of Ponomarevka, flows WNW past Asekeyevo, Buguruslan, and Pokhvistnevo, and WSW past Podbelskaya, Kinel-Cherkassy, and Timashevo, to Samara R. 3 mi. E of Kinel; 190 mi. long. Lumber floating. Receives Lesser Kinel R., Rus. *Maly Kinel* (80 mi. long), and Kutuluk R. (left).

Greater Kokshaga River (kŭkshŭgä'), Rus. *Bolshaya Kokshaga,* central European Russian SFSR, rises 25 mi. NW of Yaransk, flows 135 mi. generally S, past Sanchursk, to the Volga 3 mi. ENE of (opposite) Mariinski Posad; lumber floating. Receives Greater Kundysh R. (right). Also called Kokshaga.

Greater Kundysh River (kōōndĭsh'), Rus. *Bolshoi Kundysh,* central European Russian SFSR, rises 15 mi. ESE of Tonkino, flows c.70 mi. generally SSE, past Kilemary, to Greater Kokshaga R. 23 mi. SW of Ioshkar-Ola; lumber floating. Also called Upper Kundysh, Rus. *Verkhni Kundysh,* or simply Kundysh.

Greater Sundas, Indonesia: see SUNDA ISLANDS.

Greater Tsivil River, Russian SFSR: see TSIVIL, rivers.

Greater Uzen River, Russian SFSR: see UZEN, rivers.

Greater Walachia, Rumania: see WALACHIA.

Greater Yenisei River, Russian SFSR: see YENISEI RIVER.

Great Exuma Island (ĕksōō'mŭ, ĕgzōō'mŭ), main island (c.40 mi. long, 1–2 mi. wide) of the Exuma isls., central Bahama Isls., adjoined SE by Little Exuma Isl., 120 mi. SE of Nassau. Fringed by numerous cays, and good harbors. Main activity is stock raising (sheep, goats, pigs). Among the settlements are George Town (E), Moss Town (center), Rolleville (N). Originally settled by refugees from Europe, South Carolina, and E Florida, who planted cotton. A U.S. naval base (granted in 1940) is at George Town.

Great Falls, village (pop. 101), SE Man., on Winnipeg R. (waterfalls) and 60 mi. NE of Winnipeg; hydroelectric-power center.

Great Falls, falls, Labrador: see GRAND FALLS.

Great Falls. 1 City (pop. 39,214), ⊙ Cascade co., W central Mont., on Missouri R., at mouth of Sun R., near falls for which city was named, and 75 mi. NNE of Helena; 47°31'N 111°18'W; alt. 3,330 ft. Largest city in state, port of entry, and industrial and commercial center for irrigated agr. and mining region; copper and zinc reduction plants, railroad shops, oil refinery; copper wire and cable, electrical equipment, bricks, furs, flour, feed, beverages, dairy products. R.C. cathedral, Presbyterian church, hosp., state school for deaf and blind, fish hatchery, airport, U.S. Air Force base here. Four hydroelectric plants and coal mines near by. Giant Springs, scenic and recreation point, on outskirts of city. Founded 1883, inc. 1888. **2** Village (pop. 3,533), Chester co., N S.C., on the Catawba and 22 mi. ESE of Chester; textile mills. Power plants here generate electricity for towns and cities in wide area.

Great Falls Dam, central Tenn., on Caney Fork of Cumberland R., 11 mi. NE of McMinnville, upstream from Center Hill Dam. Privately-built power dam (92 ft. high, 800 ft. long; completed 1916), now owned by TVA. Forms small reservoir (□ 3.5; capacity 54,500 acre-ft.).

Great Falls of the Potomac (pŭtō'mŭk), in Potomac R. (here forming state line bet. Md. and Va.), c.15 mi. WNW of Washington. Series of cascades (greatest drop 35 ft.) and rapids in 200-ft. gorge. Sometimes known as Great Falls. Power dam here. Great Falls Park (140 acres) is recreational area on both banks of river; section on Md. side is crossed by old Chesapeake and Ohio Canal (now recreational waterway) and includes parts of iron foundry and mill once owned by George Washington.

Great Faringdon, England: see FARINGDON.

Great Fish Bay, Angola: see TIGRES BAY.

Great Fish River, Canada: see BACK RIVER.

Great Fish River, SE Cape Prov., U. of So. Afr., rises NE of Graaff Reinet, flows 400 mi. in winding course generally SE, past Cradock and Cookhouse, to the Indian Ocean 15 mi. ENE of Port Alfred. Forms S boundary of former prov. of British Kaffraria. Receives Little Fish R.

Great Gandak River, India: see GANDAK RIVER.

Great Geysir, Iceland: see GEYSIR.

Great Glen of Scotland, Glen More, or **Glen Albyn,** depression extending 60 mi. NE–SW across Scotland along an anc. fault, bet. Moray Firth at Inverness and Loch Linnhe at Fort William, dividing central from NW Highlands. It contains lochs Ness, Oich, and Lochy, and is traversed by the CALEDONIAN CANAL.

Great Goat Island, Jamaica: see GOAT ISLANDS.

Great Gott Island, Hancock co., S Maine, isl. (c.1 mi. wide) at entrance to Blue Hill Bay, just S of Mt. Desert Isl.

Great Guana Cay (gwä"nŭ kā', kē'), long narrow islet (c.9 mi. long), Bahama Isls., in center of Exuma isls., 90 mi. SE of Nassau; 24°5'N 76°20'W.

Great Gull Island, N.Y.: see GULL ISLANDS.

Great Hanwood, village and parish (pop. 311), central Shropshire, England, 4 mi. SW of Shrewsbury; coal and barite mines.

Great Harwood, urban district (1931 pop. 12,789; 1951 census 10,738), E central Lancashire, England, 4 mi. NE of Blackburn; cotton milling, coal mining. Birthplace (1791) of John Mercer, inventor of processes for mercerizing textiles and mfg. parchment paper. Has 16th-cent. church.

Great Haseley, town and parish (pop. 486), S Oxfordshire, England, 5 mi. WSW of Thame; ironworks. Has church partly dating from 12th cent.

Great Horton, England: see BRADFORD.

Great Hucklow, agr. village and parish (pop. 128), NW Derby, England, 8 mi. ENE of Buxton; former lead-mining center.

Great Hungarian Plain: see ALFÖLD.

Great Inagua Island or **Inagua Island** (ĭnä'gwŭ), island and district (including Little Inagua Isl., □ 560; pop. 890), Bahama Isls., southernmost isl. of the Bahamas and one of the largest, 55 mi. NE of Cape Maisí (E Cuba), 350 mi. SE of Nassau; in lat. 21°N. Chief settlement is Matthew Town on its W tip. The isl. has a large, shallow lake in its center, which abounds in bird wildlife. Salt panning is the principal activity. Little Inagua Isl. adjoins NE.

Great Isaac, cay, NW Bahama Isls., 20 mi. NE of the Biminis, 65 mi. ENE of Miami, Fla.; 26°2'N 79°6'W. Lighthouse. Sometimes called Great Isaacs.

Great Island (□ 20.5; 5 mi. long, 4 mi. wide), in Cork Harbour, Co. Cork, Ireland. On S shore is CÓBH.

Great Island, Maine: see HARPSWELL.

Great Kai, Indonesia: see NUHU CHUT.

Great Karimun, Indonesia: see KARIMUN ISLANDS.

Great Karroo or **Central Karroo** (kŭrōō'), plateau region, S central Cape Prov., U. of So. Afr., bounded by Wittebergen, Swartberg, and Witteberge ranges (S), Cold Bokkeveld and Middelberg ranges (W), the Northern Karroo (N), and SW extension of Drakensberg range (E). Arid semidesert region, fertile where irrigated. Stock raising, principally sheep and goats, and citrus-fruit and grain growing are important. Average elevation 2–3,000 ft.; numerous mts. up to 5,000 ft. high dot plateau. Principal towns are Beaufort West, Graaff Reinet, and Prince Albert.

Great Kei River (kā), SE Cape Prov., U. of So. Afr.; formed 35 mi. ESE of Queenstown by confluence of Swart Kei R. (120 mi. long) and White Kei R. (90 mi. long), it flows 140 mi. in winding course generally ESE to the Indian Ocean 35 mi. NE of East London. Forms S boundary of the Transkeian Territories.

Great Khingan Mountains, Manchuria: see KHINGAN MOUNTAINS.

Great Kills, SE N.Y., a section of Richmond borough of New York city, on SE Staten Isl.; boatbuilding.

Great Koldewey (kô'lŭvā), Dan. *Store Koldewey,* island (55 mi. long, 2–5 mi. wide) in Greenland Sea, NE Greenland, at mouth of Dove Bay; 75°56'–76°44'N 18°55'W. Rises to 3,186 ft. Just off NE coast is Little Koldewey, Dan. *Lille Koldewey,* 10 mi. long; 76°40'N 18°50'W; during Second World War site of German weather station, captured by U.S. forces.

Great Laaber River, Ger. *Grosse Laaber* (grō'sŭ lä'bŭr), Bavaria, Germany, rises 5 mi. ESE of Mainburg, flows 43 mi. NE to the Danube, 5 mi. NW of Straubing.

Great Lake, Cambodia: see TONLE SAP.

Great Lake, largest lake in Tasmania, on wide, central plateau (alt. 4,000 ft.) and 65 mi. NNW of Hobart; □ 44; 12 mi. long, 7 mi. wide, 40 ft. deep; contains several islets. Tourist resort known for trout fishing. Miena dam on S shore.

Great Lakes, in central N.America, largest group of fresh-water lakes in world, on U.S.-Canada border; bounded N by Ont. (Canada), W and S by Minn., Wis., Ill., Ind., Mich., Ohio, Pa., and N.Y. They include L. SUPERIOR (2d in size among inland waters only to the saline Caspian Sea), L. HURON, L. MICHIGAN (only one entirely in U.S.), L. ERIE, and L. ONTARIO. Their water surface is □ c.94,710, of which □ c.33,695 are in Canada. The international line passes approximately through the center of all except L. Michigan. Connected by navigable straits and canals (St. Marys R. and SAULT SAINTE MARIE CANALS, Straits of MACKINAC, St. Clair river and lake, Detroit R., Niagara R., Welland Canal), the lakes form a continuous waterway c.1,160 mi. long from Duluth, Minn., at W end of L. Superior, to the E end of L. Ontario, whence the St. Lawrence R. (navigable for medium drafts) flows to the Atlantic; their ports are also connected with tidewater by 2 other routes for limited drafts: the N.Y. State Barge Canal system and the Hudson R., and the Illinois Waterway system, which links L. Michigan with the Mississippi and thence to the Gulf of Mexico (Great Lakes-to-Gulf Waterway, c.1,630 mi. long). The Great Lakes-St. Lawrence seaway and power project, long under discussion by the U.S. and Canada, would deepen the canals by-passing rapids in the St. Lawrence bet. Montreal and L. Ontario, provide for the passage of ocean-going vessels to head of lake system, and supply additional hydroelectric power. The lakes carry enormous commerce during their navigation season (generally 7–8 months); ice (which closes some of the ports entirely) and violent storms almost eliminate winter navigation. Chief cargoes are iron ore (from L. Superior region), grain from Can. and U.S. ports, coal, limestone, steel, and countless manufactured articles. Most important ports and industrial cities include Duluth, Minn.; Superior and Milwaukee, Wis.; Chicago, Ill.; Gary, Ind.; Detroit, Mich.; Windsor, Hamilton, Toronto, and Kingston, Ont.; Toledo and Cleveland, Ohio; Erie, Pa.; Buffalo and Rochester, N.Y. Fisheries, despite depletion, remain important, and there are many resort dists. Isle Royale (L. Superior) is a natl. park, and many other isls. attract summer visitors. French traders were the first white men to see the Great Lakes; possibly Étienne Brulé visited L. Huron c.1612 or earlier, and in 1615 Samuel de Champlain voyaged on lakes Huron and Ontario. La Salle sailed his *Griffon* from L. Erie to Green Bay (arm of L. Michigan) in 1679. This region, rich in furs, was a prize for which the English and French struggled for many years; contest for the lakes' possession was finally ended only at the close of the War of 1812. Settlement thereafter was rapid; the opening in 1820s of the Erie Canal accelerated immigration and commerce and was the early impetus for the growth (later stimulated by railroads) of farms and cities (notably Chicago) of the lake region. Ease of transportation and accessibility of raw materials (especially L. Superior iron ore and Appalachian coal) for mfg. have made the Great Lakes region the heavy-industry heartland of N.America; in addition, the buying power of its workers and the farm pop. of the Middle West supports enormously diversified consumer goods industries.

Great Lakes Naval Training Station, Ill.: see NORTH CHICAGO.

Great Lyakhov Island, Russian SFSR: see BOLSHOI LYAKHOV ISLAND.

Great Machipongo Inlet, Va.: see HOG ISLAND.

Great Malvern, England: see MALVERN.

Great Manich Lake, Russian SFSR: see MANYCH-GUDILO, LAKE.

Great Marlow, England: see MARLOW.

Great Marton, England: see MARTON.

Great Meadows, Pa.: see FORT NECESSITY NATIONAL BATTLEFIELD SITE.

Great Miami River or **Miami River** (mīă'mŭ, –ē), SW Ohio, formed in Logan co. by outlet of Indian L. and small Wolf Creek, flows generally SW for c.160 mi., past Sidney, Piqua, Dayton, and Hamilton, to Ohio R. in extreme SW Ohio. After severe flood of 1913, retarding basins were built in its valley. Chief tributaries are Stillwater, Mad, and Whitewater rivers.

Great Misery Island or **Misery Island** (98 acres), NE Mass., in the Atlantic, c.5 mi. ENE of Salem; with near-by Little Misery Isl., comprises state reservation.

Great Missenden (mĭ'sŭndŭn), residential town and parish (pop. 3,289), S central Buckingham, England, 5 mi. NNE of High Wycombe; agr. market. Has 14th-cent. church and remains of 13th-cent. abbey.

Great Morava River, Yugoslavia: see MORAVA RIVER.

Great Moshier Island (mō'zhŭr), SW Maine, in Casco Bay off Yarmouth; ¾ mi. long.

Great Moss, England: see BILLINGE AND WINSTANLEY.

Great Nafud, Arabia: see NAFUD.

Great Namaqualand or **Great Namaland,** South-West Africa: see NAMAQUALAND.

Great Nansei, Ryukyu Isls.: see OKINAWA.

Great Natuna (nätōō'nä), **Bunguran,** or **Boengoeran** (both: bōōng-ōōrän'), largest island (40 mi. long, 25 mi. wide) of NATUNA ISLANDS, Indonesia, in S.China Sea, 140 mi. NW of Cape Datu, Borneo; 3°55'N 108°14'E. Rises to 3,046 ft.; surrounded by many islets. Timber, coconuts.

Great Neck, residential village (pop. 7,759), Nassau co., SE N.Y., on N shore of W Long Isl., on Great Neck peninsula (c.3 mi. long) bet. Little Neck and Manhasset bays, c.8 mi. NNE of Jamaica; business center for summer-estate area. Mfg.: wood boxes, metal products, musical instruments. Inc. 1921.

Great Neck Estates, residential village (pop. 2,464), Nassau co., SE N.Y., on N shore of W Long Isl., just S of Great Neck. Inc. 1911.

Great Neck Plaza (plä'zŭ), residential village (pop. 4,246), Nassau co., SE N.Y., on N shore of W Long Isl., just S of Great Neck. Inc. 1930.

Great Nicobar Island: see NICOBAR ISLANDS.

Great Northeast Channel, passage of Coral Sea connecting Torres Strait (SW) with Gulf of Papua (NE), bet. S coast of New Guinea and northernmost part of Great Barrier Reef; c.100 mi. long, 20 mi. wide; contains Darnley Isl.

Great Northern Peninsula or **Petit Nord Peninsula** (pŭtē' nôr'), N part of Newfoundland, extending 170 mi. NNE from Bonne Bay (SW) and head of White Bay (SE) to Cape Norman and Cape Bauld, at N extremity of isl. Long Range Mts. extend along W coast, rising to 2,666 ft. on Gros Morne. St. Anthony (NE) is largest town of region. On shores are numerous fishing settlements.

Great Oasis, The, Egypt: see KHARGA.

Great Onyx Cave, Ky.: see CAVE CITY.

Great Ormes Head, Welsh *Pen Gogarth* (pĕn gō'gärth), N promontory of Caernarvon, Wales, projecting into Irish Sea, 2 mi. NW of Llandudno, 679 ft. high; site of lighthouse (53°21'N 3°52'W).

Great Ouse River, England: see OUSE RIVER.

Great Palm Island, largest (□ 21) of Palm Isls., in Coral Sea, 15 mi. off E coast of Queensland, Australia, at entrance to Halifax Bay; 8.5 mi. long, 4.5 mi. wide; rises to 1,818 ft. Contains largest native settlement in Australia. Produces peanuts, pineapples, sugar cane.

Great Paternoster Islands, Indonesia: see TENGA ISLANDS.

Great Peconic Bay (pēkŏ'nĭk, pĭ–), SE N.Y., bet. N and S peninsulas of E Long Isl. and near their bases, just E of Riverhead; c.6 mi. in diameter. Receives Peconic R. in Flanders Bay, its W arm; Shinnecock Canal joins it to Shinnecock Bay (S). Connected by channels to Little Peconic Bay (E), thence to Gardiners Bay and Block Island Sound. Sometimes Peconic Bay.

Great Pedro Bluff (pĕ'drō), headland, St. Elizabeth parish, S Jamaica, 60 mi. WSW of Kingston; 17°51'N 77°44'W.

Great Pee Dee River, N.C. and S.C.: see PEE DEE RIVER.

Great Plains, W North America, a sloping plateau generally c.400 mi. wide, bordering E base of the Rocky Mts. from Alta. (Canada) on the N to the Llano Estacado in E N.Mex. and W Texas. Inner margin is generally c.6,000 ft. high, and the E boundary with the Central (or Interior) Plains is usually considered to be the 2,000-ft. elev. line. In Canada, Great Plains include parts of Alta. and Sask.; in U.S., the E parts of Mont., Wyo., Colo., and N.Mex., and the W parts of the Dakotas, Nebr., Kansas, Okla., and Texas. Generally characterized by rainfall under 20 in., vegetation limited to short grass for the most part, large level tracts (such as the LLAMO ESTACADO), although there are areas of highlands (Black Hills), badlands (S.Dak.), sand hills (Nebr.), and lowlands (Goshen Hole). Stock grazing and grain growing are of chief importance, although dry farming on unsuitable land and overpasturing led to the drought-year dust storms which created the DUST BOWL; irrigation is practiced in limited areas. Drained by headwaters of the Missouri and by the Platte, Republican, Arkansas, Kansas, and Canadian rivers. Mineral resources are petroleum and natural gas (Sask., Alta., N.Dak., Mont., Wyo., Kansas, Okla., Texas), coal (SE Colo.), gold, silver, lead (Black Hills); there are large reserves of lignite and sub-bituminous coal in N portion of the Plains.

Great Pocomoke Swamp (pō'kŭmōk), in S Del. and SE Md., freshwater swamp covering □ c.50, mainly in S Sussex co., Del.; Pocomoke R. rises here. Once yielded much cypress timber, including peat-preserved logs; lumbering and disastrous peat fire (1930) destroyed much vegetation. Also called Big Cypress Swamp.

Great Point, Mass.: see NANTUCKET ISLAND.

Great Quittacas Pond (kwĭ'tŭkŭs), Plymouth co., SE Mass., 11 mi. N of New Bedford; c.3.5 mi. long. Joined by streams of Assawompsett Pond (NW) and Snipatuit Pond (SE).

Great Ragged Island or **Ragged Island,** islet (c.4 mi. long, up to 1½ mi. wide), S Bahama Isls., in part of the archipelago usually called Ragged Isl. and Cays or Jumento Cays; adjoined S by Little Ragged Isl., and situated 70 mi. N of Cuba and 225 mi. SE of Nassau. Principal activity is salt panning; the surrounding sea abounds in fish. Chief settlement, Duncan Town (22°12'N 75°44'W).

Great Rhos, Wales: see RADNOR FOREST.

Great Rift Valley or **Rift Valley,** a great depression of the Near East and E Africa, traceable N–S over ⅙ of the earth's circumference, and extending from Syria (35°N lat.) to Mozambique (20°S lat.) in SE Africa. Although it is not a continuous trench over this vast distance—plateaus, even mts., interrupt its path—its course is dramatically traceable by the lakes and seas which fill its elongated pockets. In Asia are the Sea of Galilee, the Jordan Valley, the Dead Sea, and the Gulf of Aqaba, leading to the Red Sea. Fom the Red Sea and the Gulf of Aden the trough cuts into Africa through the lowland bet. the Ethiopian highlands and the Somaliland ranges. It deepens and narrows in S central Ethiopia, holding a series of brackish lakes (Zawi, Abaya, Chamo, Stefanie) and at the Kenya line holding L. Rudolf; from here the massive valley continues S where it will ultimately meet, N of L. Nyasa, a western branch of the rift which begins c.300 mi. SW of L. Rudolf in Uganda. The E branch is deep (1,500–3,000 ft. below the E African plateau) and wide (30–50 mi.) in Kenya, and holds the alkaline lakes Baringo, Nakuru, Naivasha, and Magadi (soda deposits); here numerous land forms (eruptive cones, lava flows) attest to recent volcanic activity. The E branch in Tanganyika is somewhat broken until the deeply entrenched shores of L. Nyasa are reached in S. The W branch (also called the Albertine Rift) of the Great Rift Valley borders the Congo basin, and, overlooked by the towering peaks of Ruwenzori and Virunga Mts., holds the lakes Albert, Edward, Kivu, and Tanganyika. Bet. the 2 branches, atop a plateau, is L. Victoria.

The rift, now combined once more, is filled by L. Nyasa for 360 mi.; its outlet, Shire R., follows the valley to the Zambezi, and the rift valley disappears in the Mozambique coastal lowlands bet. Beira and the Zambezi delta on the Indian Ocean. The floor of the valley is not only many hundreds of feet below sea level (such as the floor of the Dead Sea,–2,600 ft., and the bottom of L. Tanganyika, –c.2,200 ft.), but is also often thousands of feet high, as in central Tanganyika and Ruanda-Urundi, where it is level with the E African plateau. The origin of the rift valley has captured both the imagination and the serious study of geologists for years. Among the theories are: that the trough resulted from the collapse of a great crustal arch which had been upfolded over E Africa during Cretaceous and early Tertiary times; and that the great fissure was due to the tensional pull of great land masses in motion.

Great Rowsley, England: see ROWSLEY.

Great Ruaha River, Tanganyika: see RUFIJI RIVER.

Great Saimaa, Finland: see SAIMAA.

Great Saint Bernard Pass (bûrnärd'), Fr. *Grand-Saint-Bernard* (grä-sē-bĕrnär'), Ital. *Gran San Bernardo* (grän sän bĕrnär'dô), Alpine pass (alt. 8,110) on Italo-Swiss border, in SW Pennine Alps E of Mont Blanc group, on road bet. Martigny-Ville (16 mi. NNW) and Aosta (12 mi. SE), connecting Rhone valley (Switzerland) with Val d'Aosta (Italy). Hospice founded 11th cent. by St. Bernard of Menthon; present bldgs. 1st built in 16th cent., often enlarged. Hospice is run by Augustinian monks famed for their rescue (with the aid of St. Bernard dogs) of snowbound travelers. The pass, known to Gauls and Romans, was crossed (1800) by Napoleon I with 40,000 men.

Great Saint Lawrence, N.F.: see SAINT LAWRENCE.

Great Salt Lake, NW Utah, just NW of Salt Lake City, bet. Wasatch Range and Great Salt Lake Desert. Large inland salt lake (75 mi. long, 50 mi. wide; max. depth 35 ft., average depth 13 ft.; alt. 4,197 ft.) fed by Jordan, Weber, and Bear rivers. Has no outlet and fluctuates greatly in size: □ c.2,300 (1873), □ 2,203 (1877), □ 1,078 (1940; smallest on record), □ 1,469 (1950). Chief islands are ANTELOPE ISLAND and FREMONT ISLAND; longest peninsula is PROMONTORY POINT, extending S from N shore and forming Bear River Bay in NE. Brine shrimps occur extensively in lake. Its water (20–27% salinity) contains more than 6,000,000,000 tons of salt (chiefly sodium chloride—common salt—extracted for commercial use) and is several times more saline than ocean water. Was explored by James Bridger (1825), John C. Frémont (c.1843), and Howard Stansbury (1849–50). Now has resorts on S shore and is crossed by railroad cutoff (completed 1903) that extends W from Ogden and passes through S tip of Promontory Point. Lake is remnant of enormous, prehistoric body of water known as L. BONNEVILLE.

Great Salt Lake Desert, arid region in NW Utah, just W of Great Salt Lake, extending c.110 mi. S from Grouse Creek Mts. and bordering on Nev. Long an obstacle to W migration, now crossed by highway and railroad. Extremely level stretch in W, near Nev. line is known as Bonneville Speedway or Bonneville Salt Flats. World speed records for automobiles were established on it by Sir Malcolm Campbell (1935), Captain George E. T. Eyston (1938), and John Cobb (1939).

Great Saltpeter Caves, Ky.: see MOUNT VERNON.

Great Salt Plains Dam, Okla.: see SALT FORK OF ARKANSAS RIVER.

Great Salt Pond, R.I.: see BLOCK ISLAND.

Great Sand Dunes National Monument (□ 56.1; established 1932), S Colo., at E edge of San Luis valley, 20 mi. NE of Alamosa. Area of enormous, shifting sand dunes more than 800 ft. high, paralleling W base of Sangre de Cristo Mts.; formed by action of wind on light, sandy soil of valley floor.

Great Sandy Desert, N belt of Western Australian desert, S of Kimberley Goldfield and E of Pilbara Goldfield; sand dunes, scrub, salt marshes.

Great Sandy Desert, arid region (150 mi. long, 30–50 mi. wide) in S Oregon, extending roughly NW–SE and occupying parts of Lake and Harney counties. Area largely volcanic, on foundation of porous mantle rock into which surface waters disappear. Grazing in E near Harney and Malheur lakes.

Great Sandy Island, Australia: see FRASER ISLAND.

Great Sankey, residential village and parish (pop. 2,097), S Lancashire, England, 2 mi. W of Warrington.

Great Scarcies River (skär'sēz), W Africa, largely in Sierra Leone, rises N of Kindia in W Fr. Guinea, flows c.160 mi. SW along Sierra Leone–Fr. Guinea border and into Sierra Leone, past Kambia, and forms common estuary with Little Scarcies 25 mi. N of Freetown. Navigable c.30 mi. from mouth to area of Kambia. Also called Kolenté R. (kōlĕn'tā).

Great Schütt, Czechoslovakia: see SCHÜTT.

Great Shelford, town and parish (pop. 1,864), S Cambridge, England, on Cam R. and 4 mi. S of Cambridge; agr. market; flour mills. Has church built 1307. Just S is agr. parish (pop. 503) of Little Shelford, with 13th–14th-cent. church.

Great Sitkin Island (12 mi. long, 8 mi. wide), Andreanof Isls., Aleutian Isls., SW Alaska, 20 mi. NE of Adak Isl.; 52°3'N 176°7'W; active volcano (5,740 ft.) in center.

Great Skellig, Ireland: see SKELLIGS, THE.

Great Slave Lake (□ 11,170; also estimated as c.13,000), S Mackenzie Dist., Northwest Territories, near Alta. border; 60°50'–62°47'N 108°55'–117°W. It is 300 mi. long, 30–140 mi. wide; North Arm extends 80 mi. NW from main body of lake; at E extremity of lake is McLeod Bay (80 mi. long). Lake contains numerous isls.; its W shore is wooded, E and N parts are in tundra-like muskeg country. Drained W by Mackenzie R.; receives Yellowknife R. (N), Slave R. (S), and Hay R. (SW). Yellowknife town (N) is gold-mining center and largest town of Northwest Territories, scene (1934) of gold discoveries. Other villages are Hay River (SW), Fort Resolution (S), Reliance (E), and Rae (NW). Fort Providence is on Mackenzie R. near its outlet from Great Slave L. Lake was discovered 1771 by Samuel Hearne but was not completely surveyed until 1921–25. Named after the Slave (Dogrib) Indians.

Great Slave River, Canada: see SLAVE RIVER.

Great Smoky Mountains, W N.C. and E Tenn., part of the Appalachian system, and sometimes considered a range of UNAKA MOUNTAINS; lie bet. Asheville (E) and Knoxville (W), and meet Bald Mts. (NE) and Unicoi Mts. (SW). The Great Smokies are W escarpment of the Appalachians here, and merge on E into the BLUE RIDGE escarpment. Highest section has been set aside in **Great Smoky Mountains National Park** (□ 789.3; established 1930, dedicated 1940), through which crest of main range (here the N.C.-Tenn. line) zigzags for 71 mi.; area in N.C., c.□ 427.7; in Tenn., c.□ 361.6. Park extends 54 mi. bet. Pigeon R. (NE) and Little Tennessee R. (SW), and is c.20 mi. wide. Peaks over 6,000 ft. include CLINGMANS DOME (6,642 ft.), highest point in Tenn.; Mt. GUYOT (6,621 ft.), Mt. LE CONTE (6,593 ft.), Mt. Chapman (6,430 ft.), Mt. Collins (6,188 ft.), and Mt. Kephart (6,100 ft.). Almost unbroken forestland (130 tree species), 40% of it virgin growth; there are notable displays of mtn. laurel, rhododendron, and wildflowers; animal life is varied and plentiful; 600 mi. of streams afford fishing. Park hq. at Gatlinburg; typical mtn. communities are within park, and Cherokee Indian reservation (near Cherokee, N.C.) adjoins. Transmountain highway from Gatlinburg to Cherokee passes through Newfound Gap (5,048 ft.); Blue Ridge Parkway terminates in park. A favorite resort area, with lodges, hotels, campgrounds; hiking trails (including Appalachian Trail along crest of range), museums of Indian and pioneer handicraft. Great Smoky Mts. were explored in mid-19th cent. by Thomas L. Clingman and Arnold Guyot, geologists. Name of range and park is derived from deep blue haze characteristic of region.

Great Snow Mountain (9,500 ft.), N central B.C., in Rocky Mts.; 57°27'N 124°1'W.

Great Somes River, Rumania: see SOMES RIVER.

Great Sound, sheltered lagoon (6 mi. long, 4 mi. wide), W Bermuda. Its brilliantly clear waters are dotted with small islets. Hamilton is on E shore.

Great Sound, S N.J., inlet (c.4 mi. long) of the Atlantic, just E of Cape May Court House; sheltered from ocean by Seven Mile Beach isl., site of Avalon and Stone Harbor resort boroughs. Crossed by Intracoastal Waterway channel.

Great South Bay, SE N.Y., an arm of the Atlantic, bet. S shore of W Long Isl. and a barrier beach (pierced by several inlets); extends from inlet near Rockaway Beach (W) c.45 mi. to Moriches Bay (E). Long Beach (resort), Jones Beach and other state parks (connected by causeways to Long Isl.), and Fire Isl. (resorts) are on the dunes of the outer barrier; there are many marshy isls. in bay. Amityville, Lindenhurst, Babylon, Bay Shore, Sayville, Patchogue, and other resort and residential communities are on Long Isl. shore. The noted Blue Point oysters are grown here.

Great South Beach, N.Y.: see FIRE ISLAND.

Great Spruce Head Island, Maine: see DEER ISLAND, Hancock co.

Great Stone Face, N.H.: see PROFILE MOUNTAIN.

Great Stour River or **Stour River** (stou'ŭr), Kent, England, rises 6 mi. ESE of Ashford, flows 40 mi. NW and NE, past Ashford, Canterbury, and Sandwich, to Pegwell Bay of the Channel 3 mi. N of Sandwich. Receives short Little Stour R. 5 mi. NW of Sandwich; called Stour R. below this point. With a short N arm it cuts off Isle of Thanet. Navigable below Canterbury.

Great Sugar Loaf, mountain (1,659 ft.), NE Co. Wicklow, Ireland, 5 mi. SW of Bray.

Great Swartberg, U. of So. Afr.: see SWARTBERG.

Great Tenasserim River, Burma: see TENASSERIM RIVER.

Great Thatch Island, uninhabited islet, Br. Virgin Isls., just W of Tortola and just N of St. John.

Great Torrington, municipal borough (1931 pop. 2,913; 1951 census 2,872), N Devon, England, on Torridge R. and 5 mi. SSE of Bideford; agr. market; dairying, glove mfg. Cardinal Wolsey was rector here. There is a medieval church.

Great Urswick, England: see URSWICK.

Great Valley, village (pop. c.200), Cattaraugus co., W N.Y., 6 mi. NE of Salamanca; wooden containers, lumber.

Great Valley. 1 In E U.S.: see GREAT APPALACHIAN VALLEY. **2** In Calif.: see CENTRAL VALLEY.

Great Victoria Desert, Australia: see VICTORIA DESERT.

Great Village, village (pop. estimate 650), central N.S., near Cobequid Bay, 16 mi. W of Truro; dairying, mixed farming.

Great Vils River or **Vils River,** Ger. *Grosse Vils* (grō'sŭ fĭls'), Bavaria, Germany, rises 5 mi. WNW of Dorfen, flows 78 mi. ENE to the Danube at Vilshofen. Receives Kleine Vils R. (left).

Great Wakering, town and parish (pop. 2,258), SE Essex, England, near the Thames estuary, 5 mi. ENE of Southend-on-Sea; agr. market.

Great Wall, monumental wall in N China, extending c.1,500 mi. from Kansu E to Gulf of Chihli of Yellow Sea at Shanhaikwan (Hopeh). It is 20 ft. wide at base and narrows to 12 ft. at the top; its height varies from 15 to 30 ft.; at intervals of 200 yards are towers c.40 ft. high. It is solidly built of earth and stone faced with brick in E reaches, where it is fairly well preserved. The W portions, however, consisting merely of an earthen mound, have greatly deteriorated. The Great Wall's principal gateways are at Shanhaikwan (at E end), Kalgan, Yenmen, and Kiayükwan (at W end). Built by Shih Hwangti (246–209 B.C.) of the Ch'in dynasty as a defense against the Huns, the Great Wall was restored under the Ming emperor Hsien-tung (1465–87). It was, however, never of great military utility in preventing invasions. Although it serves mainly as a geographical boundary separating areas of Chinese and Mongol settlement, Chinese colonization has penetrated to some extent beyond the Great Wall, notably in Jehol and in Inner Mongolia.

Great Walsingham, England: see LITTLE WALSINGHAM.

Great Waltham (wôl'thŭm, wôl'tŭm), town and parish (pop. 1,941), central Essex, England, on Chelmer R. and 5 mi. N of Chelmsford; agr. market. Has Norman church.

Great Warley, residential town and parish (pop. 2,676), SW Essex, England, 2 mi. SSW of Brentwood.

Great Wass Island, Washington co., E Maine, off Jonesport; 5 mi. long, .5–1.5 mi. wide. Coast Guard station.

Great Whale River, N Que., rises E of L. Bienville, flows 365 mi. W, through L. Bienville, to Hudson Bay. At its mouth is Great Whale River (55°17'N 77°47'W), Hudson's Bay Co. trading post.

Great Whernside (whûrn'-), mountain (2,310 ft.) in the Pennines, W Yorkshire, England, 13 mi. NE of Settle. On its slopes are coal mines, now abandoned, and lead mines. Nidd R. rises here.

Great Wilne, England: see SHARDLOW WITH GREAT WILNE.

Great Works, Maine: see OLD TOWN.

Great Works River, SW Maine, rises in central York co., flows c.27 mi. generally S to Salmon Falls R. 8 mi. below Berwick.

Great Yarmouth, England: see YARMOUTH.

Great Yegorlyk River, Russian SFSR: see YEGORLYK RIVER.

Great Zab, Iraq and Turkey: see ZAB, GREAT.

Great Zelenchuk River, Russian SFSR: see ZELENCHUK.

Grebbestad (grĕ'bŭstäd''), town (pop. 731), Goteborg och Bohus co., SW Sweden, on the Skagerrak, 17 mi. S of Stromstad; fishing port and seaside resort; fish canning, stone quarrying. In region are numerous rocks and caves with prehistoric drawings. Just N is locality of Greby (grā'bü''), site of Iron Age burial ground.

Grebenki (grĭbyôn'kē), village (1926 pop. 4,737), W Kiev oblast, Ukrainian SSR, 35 mi. SSW of Kiev; metalworks. Sugar refinery near by.

Grebenkovski or **Grebenkovskiy** (grĕbyĭnkôf'skē), town (1926 pop. 1,100), NW Poltava oblast, Ukrainian SSR, 25 mi. WNW of Lubny; rail junction; metalworking, food processing. Also called Grebenka.

Grebenstein (grā'bŭn-shtīn), town (pop. 4,422), in former Prussian prov. of Hesse-Nassau, W Germany, after 1945 in Hesse, 9 mi. NNW of Kassel; lumber.

Greby, Sweden: see GREBBESTAD.

Grecia (grā'syä), city (1950 pop. 2,824), Alajuela prov., W Costa Rica, on central plateau, on Inter-American Highway and 7 mi. NW of Alajuela; agr. and commercial center; processing of sugar cane, coffee, corn, manioc.

Grecia, Nicaragua: see LIMAY.

Greco, Cape (grĕ'kō), anc. *Pedalium*, E promontory of Cyprus, at S gate of Famagusta Bay; 34°56'N 34°6'E. Lighthouse.

Greding (grā'dĭng), village (pop. 1,905), Middle Franconia, central Bavaria, Germany, 13 mi. NE of Eichstätt; brewing, flour and lumber milling. Surrounded by medieval wall; has Romanesque church. Limestone quarries in area.

Gredos, Sierra de (syĕ'rä dhä grā'dhōs), range in central Spain, separating Old Castile (N) from New Castile and Estremadura (S), continuing SW the Sierra de Guadarrama, and 25 mi. W of Madrid. Extends c.70 mi. E-W, rising in the Plaza del Moro Almanzor or Plaza de Almanzor to 8,504 ft., highest point on central plateau (Meseta). Heavily forested (timber, naval stores) and with fine scenery, the range is a favorite tourist site. Known for its mtn. goats.

Greece, Gr. *Hellas* (hĕ'lŭs) or *Ellas* (modern Gr. ĕläs'), kingdom (□ 51,182, of which 9,854 sq. mi. are isls.; pop. 7,460,203; all figures, based on 1940 census, are adjusted to include the Dodecanese, added to Greece in 1947; 1951 census, including the Dodecanese, is 7,602,900), SE Europe; ⊙ ATHENS. Occupies southernmost part of the Balkan Peninsula and numerous isls. in the Ionian and Aegean seas of the Mediterranean, which washes the indented, irregular mainland in W, E, and S. The isl. of CRETE, farther S, is in Mediterranean Sea proper, 160 mi. N of Libya, North Africa. Greece's N land frontier touches on Albania, Yugoslavia, and Bulgaria. European Turkey borders NE along Maritsa or Evros R. In E, across the Aegean Sea, lies Asiatic Turkey, along whose coast are scattered the DODECANESE isls., notably RHODES, as well as the AEGEAN ISLANDS of CHIOS, SAMOS, and LESBOS. The W coast, fringed by IONIAN ISLANDS (among them CORFU, LEUKAS, CEPHALONIA, ZANTE), is separated from S Italy by the Ionian Sea. Other Greek isls. include EUBOEA off the coast of Attica and Boeotia, THASOS off E Macedonia, SALAMIS and AEGINA near Athens, the CYCLADES (NAXOS, ANDROS, PAROS, TENOS, MELOS, KEA, AMORGOS, Ios, etc.) and Northern SPORADES in the Aegean. Mainland Greece is split by the Isthmus of CORINTH (4 mi. at its narrowest), where a canal cuts off the PELOPONNESUS sub-peninsula that juts its numerous headlands southward into the sea, terminating in Cape Matapan (36°23'N 22°29'E). In the N in the Aegean is the 3-pronged CHALCIDICE peninsula of Macedonia; on its E prong lies autonomous MOUNT ATHOS with its 20 Greek Orthodox monasteries. The rocky coast of Greece is deeply penetrated by gulfs, such as the gulfs of MESSENIA, LACONIA, and ARGOLIS in S Peloponnesus, those of PATRAS and CORINTH bet. central Greece and the Peloponnesus, the SARONIC GULF off W Attica, and the Gulf of SALONIKA in N, at whose head is the major port of Salonika. Greece is predominantly mountainous, dissected by small, rapid rivers and enclosing a few isolated basins. Lowlands are few, mainly in MACEDONIA, THRACE, and THESSALY, which, together with EPIRUS, are the main agr. areas. Principal ranges continue the Dinaric Alps of Albania and Yugoslavia, paralleling the coast and crossing Macedonia and Euboea. They pass through the Peloponnesus and the isls.—which represent drowned ridges, though some are volcanic—and are deflected into Asia Minor. The PINDUS MOUNTAINS roughly separate N Greece into E and W halves. Spurs include the OTHRYS mts. and Mt. OLYMPUS, the country's highest peak (9,570 ft.), famed as legendary seat of the anc. gods. PARNASSUS massif (8,062 ft.) towers over the Gulf of Corinth. Outliers of the RHODOPE mts. enter Thrace from Bulgaria. Near the S extremity of the Peloponnesus are the TAYGETUS mts. (7,895 ft.). Caverns, subterranean passages, and other karst formations are numerous in the limestone regions. Most of the rivers run dry during the summer. None are navigable for commercial shipping. Larger rivers are in the NE, foremost the VARDAR RIVER, whose valley connects with the Morava of Yugoslavia. Other rivers in Macedonia are Struma, Mesta, and Aliakmon; Achelous, Evinos, Spercheios in central Greece; Thyamis, Acheron, Arachthos in Epirus; Peneus in Thessaly; Eurotas and Alpheus in the Peloponnesus. There are several small lakes, such as L. COPAIS in Boeotia, now drained, and L. VOIVEIS in Thessaly. The climate is on the whole Mediterranean, especially on the coast and in the isls., where all the larger settlements are. The lowlands have little frost or snow, which occurs in the inhospitable highlands. Rainfall is heaviest in W (c.50 in.), decreasing towards E. Athens has c.20 in., with mean Jan. temp. of 47°F., July 80°F. Dry summers make irrigation necessary. The isls. are frequently visited by earthquakes. Greece is moderately rich in minerals. There are a variety of deposits, of which iron ore, iron pyrite, magnesite, chromite, and emery are exported. Other resources include lignite, bauxite, copper, zinc, lead, silver, antimony, nickel, molybdenum, sulphur, Santorin earth, limestone, gypsum. The silver mines of LAURION in Attica, now yielding lead-zinc and iron, were well known in antiquity. So were the many marble deposits: KARYSTOS on Euboea, PENTELIKON and HYMETTUS massif. Coal and petroleum have to be imported. The great hydroelectric potential is so far little developed. Forests, though largely depleted, still cover about 1/5 of the area (spruce, pine), yielding some resins, turpentine, charcoal, and timber. The country is in an advanced stage of soil erosion, and the ungrateful interior uplands are—apart from some fertile pockets—only suited to sheep and goat grazing. While about 60% of all the people gain their livelihood from the land, the agr. output has to be supplemented by grain imports. Farming methods are antiquated; since little fertilizer is used, the yield is generally low. Only an estimated 1/5 of the area is under cultivation. Of this a greater part is still devoted to cereals, but more lucrative commercial crops are pushed, chiefly tobacco (Macedonia), raisins (Zante) and currants from Peloponnesus and central Greece. The former accounts for c.45%, the latter for c.12½% of all exports. Other agr. products include olives and olive oil, grapes and wines, figs, oranges, lemons, vegetables, rice, cotton, hemp, sesame, apples, pears, almonds, carobs. On these products are based various processing industries: tobacco factories, wineries, flour mills, olive presses, soapworks, canneries. Industries suffer from lack of power resources and capital. The Second World War and civil war aftermath had a disastrous effect on the entire economy, but American assistance contributed toward a slow recovery. In 1949 88% of pre-war level in mfg. was reached. Leading industries are textiles and chemicals; also metallurgy (iron and steel, aluminum, copper), shipbuilding, tanning, brewing; mfg. of building materials, machinery, foodstuffs, electric power. Most (60-70%) of all the plants are located in the ATHENS-PIRAEUS dist. (comprising more than 1,000,000 people) which turns out all kinds of consumer goods. Through Piraeus passes the bulk of foreign trade. Salonika and environs form another industrial nucleus (food, tobacco, leather, machinery); it is an important terminus of trade route from Danube basin. Both Piraeus and Salonika have free zones. Transit and tourist traffic somewhat compensate for the unfavorable trade balance. The country possesses a large merchant marine. Sponge fishing is carried on extensively. Compared to the many illustrious place names of anc. Greece, there are few cities of importance. Among them are KAVALLA in Macedonia, a tobacco center; TRIKKALA and LARISSA in fertile Thessalian lowlands; VOLOS, a wheat port with textile and metal factories; CORINTH and PATRAS on the Peloponnesus, shipping raisins and currants; KALAMATA, processing center and port in S Peloponnesus, surrounded by orchards; HERMOPOLIS on Syros isl., an Aegean trade center; CANDIA and CANEA, chief towns of Crete; CORFU on isl. of that name, a renowned winter resort. Communication is impeded by the rugged relief. A standard-gauge railroad links Athens-Piraeus with Salonika and ALEXANDROUPOLIS and joins Salonika with Yugoslavia. Narrow-gauge lines connect Athens with the Peloponnesus and chief centers of Thessaly. There are also connections to Turkey and Bulgaria. International airlines call at ELLENIKON airport near Athens. Illiteracy was 27% in 1940. Athens and Salonika have universities. The overwhelming majority of the people are Greek Orthodox; the Greek primate is the archbishop of Athens, who recognizes the Eastern Patriarch of Constantinople. Though present-day Greeks are racially and culturally far removed from their country's remarkable anc. inhabitants, the pop. is now quite homogeneous, and modern Greek is almost universally spoken. Scattered communities retain Albanian dialects in W and on Peloponnesus. There are also small Bulgarian and Turkish minorities in NE. Nordic, Mongol, Slav, Turk, and Albanian migrations have left their imprint. In Greece flourished some of the oldest civilizations of Europe, foremost those of Minos (on Crete) and Mycenae. These cultures disappeared by 1100 B.C. Waves of Greek immigrants arrived before 1000 B.C.—Achaeans, Aeolians, and Ionians probably preceding the Dorians. The Ionians settled on the Ionian Isls. and the shores of Asia Minor. Diverse geography favored development of city-states (*polis*). From 8th cent. B.C. onward, colonies were founded all over the Mediterranean, Sicily and MAGNA GRAECIA in S Italy becoming the most prominent. Recorded history is generally considered to begin with initiation of the Olympic Games in 776 B.C. The Persian Wars (499–449) were concluded successfully, despite the Greeks' unwillingness to unite. During the 5th cent. Greek civilization reached its peak. That era, known as the Age of Pericles, equally creative in sculpture, architecture, poetry, drama, and philosophy, was to become the fountainhead of Western culture. Athens, which was the principal political and intellectual center of Greece, succumbed in Peloponnesian War (431–404) to militaristic SPARTA, which in turn lost hegemony to Corinth and THEBES. Philip II of Macedon won (338 B.C.) Greece through battle of Chaeronea, paving way for the conquests of his son, Alexander the Great, who spread Greek civilization over the known world. By 146 B.C. all of Greece was conquered by the Romans, who themselves became Hellenized. The glory of Greece from then on was of all countries, while the political history of Greece itself went the turbulent way of the other Balkan regions. Greece remained a part of the East Roman (Byzantine) Empire from its formation (A.D. 395) until its conquest by the Turks in 15th cent. (Constantinople fell 1453), completed in 1756. Venetians held large sections—Crete until 1669, Ionian Isls. until 1797. Turkish inroads had, however, begun much earlier, in the footsteps of Visigoths, Huns, Avars, Slavs, and Bulgars. In 1821 Greek war of independence was started under leadership of Alexander and Demetrios Ypsilanti, assisted by Greek foreign minister of Alexander I of Russia, Capo d'Istria. The revolution was hailed by European liberals and sentimentalists, among whom was Lord Byron, who died at MISSOLONGHI. Defeated Turkey recognized (1829) Greece, in Treaty of Adrianople, as an autonomous principality. In 1832 a Bavarian prince was chosen king as Otto I. He was deposed in 1862, when a democratic constitution was introduced, and a Danish prince appointed (1863) king as George I. Britain ceded (1864) the Ionian Isls. Thessaly and part of Epirus were acquired in 1881. Dispute over Crete led to Greco-Turkish War (1896–97), in which Greece was defeated, though Crete was declared independent and later incorporated (1913) into Greece. In Balkan Wars (1912–13) Greece obtained SE Macedonia and W Thrace, also sections of Epirus, which, however, are still claimed by Albania. During First World War Greece was torn bet. pro-Allied Venizelos and the neutral factions headed by King Constantine, who abdicated in 1917. At peace conference Greece was rewarded with a Bulgarian strip on the Aegean coast and with European Turkey except the Zone of the Straits. Greek invasion (1921–22) of Asia Minor proved disastrous. Conference of Lausanne (1923) established Maritsa R. as Greco-Turkish frontier. Under League of Nations supervision 2,000,000 Greeks from Asia Minor were resettled in Greece, and about 800,000 Turks and 80,000 Bulgarians left the country. During Second World War Italy invaded (Oct., 1940) Greece, which resisted successfully until German attack in April, 1941. Rightist and leftist guerilla groups held most of the country after the German defeat. The war left the country in political and economic chaos. In Sept., 1946, a plebiscite called for the return of the monarch, George II, while in N mts. leftists, who set up a rival govt., waged an occasionally successful campaign until beaten in 1949. The Dodecanese was ceded by Italy in 1947. For further information see individual articles on cities, towns, islands, physical features, and the following nomes (Gr. *nomoi*=administrative divisions), listed here according to respective regions: Aegean Isls.—Chios, Lesbos, Samos; central Greece—AETOLIA AND ACARNANIA (divided 1950 into 2 nomes, Aetolia, Acarnania), ATTICA, BOEOTIA, Euboea, EURYTANIA, PHOCIS, PHTHIETIS; Crete—CANEA, HERAKLEION, LASETHI, RETHYMNE; Dodecanese; Epirus—ARTA, IOANNINA, PREVEZA, THESPROTIA; Ionian Isls.—Cephalonia, Corfu, Leukas, Zante; Macedonia—Chalcidice (with autonomous Mount Athos), DRAMA, HEMATHEIA, KASTORIA, KAVALLA, KILKIS, KOZANE, PELLA, PIERIA, PHLORINA, SALONIKA, SERRAI; Peloponnesus—ACHAEA, ARCADIA, ARGOLIS AND CORINTHIA (divided 1950 into 2 nomes, Argolis, Corinthia), ELIS, LACONIA, MESSENIA; Thessaly—KARDITSA, LARISSA, MAGNESIA, TRIKKALA; Thrace—HEVROS, RHODOPE, XANTHE.

Greeley. 1 County (□ 783; pop. 2,010), W Kansas; ⊙ Tribune. Agr. and stock-raising area, bordering W on Colo. Formed 1887. **2** County (□ 570; pop. 5,575), E central Nebr.; ⊙ Greeley. Agr. area drained by Cedar and N.Loup rivers. Livestock, grain, dairy products. Formed 1872.

Greeley. 1 City (pop. 20,354), ⊙ Weld co., N Colo., in irrigated grain and sugar-beet area, bet. Cache la Poudre and South Platte rivers, 50 mi. NNE of Denver; alt. 4,637 ft. Rail center; food-processing (beet sugar, flour, canned vegetables, beverages). Colo. State Col. of Education, Meeker Mus. here. Near by are Fort Vasquez and Rocky Mtn. Natl. Park. City founded as cooperative settlement (1870) by Nathan C. Meeker, agent of Horace Greeley, who sponsored settlement; inc. 1885. Grew with development of beet-sugar industry. **2** Town (pop. 360), Delaware co., E Iowa, 9 mi. NE of Manchester; concrete blocks, feed, butter. Limestone quarries near by. **3** City (pop. 436), Anderson co., E Kansas, on Pottawatomie Creek and 19 mi. SSE of Ottawa; livestock, grain; dairying. **4** Village (pop. 787), ⊙ Greeley co., E central Nebr., 45 mi. N of Grand Island; dairy products.

Greeleyville, town (pop. 600), Williamsburg co., E central S.C., 11 mi. WSW of Kingstree. Formerly Greelyville.

Greely Fjord, W Ellesmere Isl., NE Franklin Dist., Northwest Territories, arm (130 mi. long, 1–15 mi. wide) of the Arctic Ocean, extending E from junction of Eureka and Nansen sounds, opposite Axel Heiberg Isl.; 80°26'–81°3'N 75–86°20'W.

Greelyville, S.C.: see GREELEYVILLE.

Green. 1 County (□ 282; pop. 11,261), central Ky.; ⊙ Greensburg. Drained by Green R. and Russell Creek. Rolling agr. area (livestock, grain, burley tobacco); cedar timber. Some industry at Greensburg. Formed 1792. **2** County (□ 586; pop. 24,172), S Wis.; ⊙ Monroe. Generally hilly area, bounded S by Ill. line, drained by Sugar and Pecatonica rivers; includes New Glarus Woods State Park. Dairying region, with mfg. (cheese, wood products, feed, hardware). Formed 1836.

Green, city (pop. 219), Clay co., N Kansas, 7 mi. ENE of Clay Center, in livestock and grain region.

Green Acres or **Greenacres,** village (pop. 1,287), Spokane co., E Wash.
Greenacres City, town (pop. 531), Palm Beach co., SE Fla., 8 mi. SSW of West Palm Beach.
Green Bay, city (pop. 52,735), ⊙ Brown co., E Wis., port of entry at mouth of Fox R., at head of Green Bay, c.100 mi. N of Milwaukee; railroad, distribution, and industrial center. Its harbor (icebound Dec.–April) is one of the finest on the Great Lakes. Chief industries are cheese processing and paper milling. There are ironworks, machine shops, woodworking and clothing factories, limestone quarries, and fisheries. Has mus. containing historical relics. A trading post was established here in 1634 by Jean Nicolet, and a mission by Father Allouez in 1669. Others visiting the region were Nicolas Perrot, Louis Jolliet, and Father Marquette. Here the 1st permanent settlement of Wis. was made in 1701; Augustin de Langlade built (1745) a trading post. The French erected (1717) a fort which was occupied in 1761 by the British. After War of 1812, the U.S. established (1816) Fort Howard at Green Bay; in early-19th cent., the American Fur Company set up hq. on the site and dominated fur trade of the region. After opening (1825) of Erie Canal, Green Bay became a lumbering and agr. center. Inc. 1854.
Green Bay, arm of L. Michigan extending SW from N end of the lake, forming SE boundary of Upper Peninsula, Mich., and sheltered by Door Peninsula, Wis.; c.100 mi. long, 10–20 mi. wide. Its N arms are BIG BAY DE NOC and LITTLE BAY DE NOC. At its head is the port Green Bay; on W shore are Marinette and Menominee. The bay is connected to L. Michigan by canal cutting across Door Peninsula at Sturgeon Bay.
Greenbelt, town (pop. 7,074), Prince Georges co., central Md., Washington suburb 11 mi. NE of the White House. Garden city surrounded by broad belt of park; planned and built by the Federal Resettlement Administration as experimental model community for moderate-income families; services and businesses are owned cooperatively. Inc. 1937.
Greenbrier, county (□ 1,026; pop. 39,295), SE W.Va.; ⊙ Lewisburg. Bounded E by Va.; partly on Allegheny Plateau, with Allegheny Mtn. along SE border, Grassy Knob and other summits are in NW; drained by Greenbrier and Meadow rivers. Resort region, with mineral springs (notably WHITE SULPHUR SPRINGS); partly in Monongahela Natl. Forest; includes Blue Bend Recreation Area. Coal mining, lumbering, limestone quarrying; agr. (livestock, dairy products, fruit, tobacco). Formed 1778.
Greenbrier, town (pop. 375), Faulkner co., central Ark., 10 mi. N of Conway.
Green Brier, town (pop. 890), Robertson co., N Tenn., 18 mi. N of Nashville, in tobacco-growing region.
Greenbrier River, E W.Va., formed by junction of 2 headstreams just S of Durbin, in NE Pocahontas co.; flows c.165 mi. generally SSW, past Marlinton, Ronceverte, and Alderson, to New R. just S of Hinton.
Greenbury Point, Md.: see SEVERN RIVER.
Greenbush. 1 Town (pop. 477), Penobscot co., S central Maine, on the Penobscot and 9 mi. above Old Town; hunting, fishing area. Includes Olamon (ōlĕ'mŭn) village. **2** Village, Plymouth co., Mass.: see SCITUATE. **3** Village (pop. 713), Roseau co., NW Minn., on fork of Two Rivers and 22 mi. SW of Roseau, in grain, potato, poultry area; dairy products.
Green Camp, village (pop. 388), Marion co., central Ohio, 5 mi. SW of Marion and on Scioto R.
Green Cape, SE New South Wales, Australia, forms N point of entrance to Disaster Bay of Tasman Sea; 37°15'S 150°4'E; lighthouse.
Greencastle, Gaelic *Teampall Maoil,* fishing village (district pop. 992), NE Co. Donegal, Ireland, on W shore of Lough Foyle, 3 mi. ENE of Moville. Has castle built 1305.
Greencastle, fishing village (district pop. 754), S Co. Down, Northern Ireland, on N shore of Carlingford Lough, near its mouth, 4 mi. WSW of Kilkeel. Has large Norman keep.
Green Castle, city (pop. 287), Sullivan co., N Mo., 16 mi. WNW of Kirksville.
Greencastle. 1 City (pop. 6,888), ⊙ Putnam co., W central Ind., near Eel R., c.40 mi. WSW of Indianapolis; rail, trade, and distribution center for livestock, grain, and dairy area; produces zinc, lumber, crushed stone, cement. Timber; stone quarries. Seat of De Pauw Univ. Laid out 1822. **2** Borough (pop. 2,661), Franklin co., S Pa., 10 mi. SSW of Chambersburg; clothing, canned and frozen foods, metal products. Laid out 1784, inc. 1805.
Green Cay (kā, kē), islet, S central Bahama Isls., E of Andros Isl., 75 mi. S of Nassau; 24°1'N 77°20'W.
Green City, city (pop. 673), Sullivan co., N Mo., 20 mi. WNW of Kirksville; agr.
Green Cove Springs, town (pop. 3,291), ⊙ Clay co., NE Fla., on St. Johns R. and 23 mi. S of Jacksonville; trade center and resort with mineral springs, in stock-raising, farming, and lumbering area. Settled 1830.
Greendale. 1 Town (pop. 2,018), Dearborn co., SE Ind., near Ohio R., just N of Lawrenceburg, in agr. area; distills whisky. **2** Village (pop. 2,752), Milwaukee co., SE Wis., on Root R. and 8 mi. SSW of Milwaukee. Founded as a garden city by Federal Resettlement Administration; inc. 1938.
Greene (grā'nŭ), village (pop. 2,356), in Brunswick, NW Germany, after 1945 in Lower Saxony, on the Leine and 4 mi. W of Bad Gandersheim; knitwear.
Greene. 1 County (□ 645; pop. 16,482), W Ala.; ⊙ Eutaw. Bounded N by the Sipsey, W by Tombigbee, E by Black Warrior rivers; in the Black Belt. Cotton, cattle, pecans, corn, timber, potatoes. Formed 1819. **2** County (□ 579; pop. 29,149), NE Ark.; ⊙ PARAGOULD. Bounded E by St. Francis R.; drained by Cache R.; intersected by Crowley's Ridge. Agr. (cotton, corn, hay, livestock); timber; gravel. Mfg. at Paragould. Includes Crowley's Ridge State Park (recreation). Formed 1833. **3** County (□ 404; pop. 12,843), NE central Ga.; ⊙ Greensboro. Piedmont area drained by Oconee, Ogeechee, and Apalachee rivers. Agr. (cotton, corn, grain, fruit, livestock); textile mfg., sawmilling. Formed 1786. **4** County (□ 543; pop. 18,852), SW central Ill.; ⊙ Carrollton. Bounded W by Illinois R.; drained by Macoupin and Apple creeks. Agr. (livestock, corn, wheat, oats, poultry, fruit; dairy products). Bituminous-coal mining; potter's clay. Mfg. (tile, bricks, pottery, sewer pipes, food products, clothing, stationery). Formed 1821. **5** County (□ 549; pop. 27,886), SW Ind.; ⊙ Bloomfield. Drained by West Fork of White R. and Eel R. Agr. area (grain, fruit, livestock), with bituminous-coal mines, timber. Mfg. at Bloomfield, Jasonville, Linton. Formed 1821. **6** County (□ 501; pop. 15,544), central Iowa; ⊙ Jefferson. Prairie agr. area (hogs, cattle, poultry, corn, soybeans) drained by Raccoon R., and with bituminous-coal deposits; also has sand and gravel pits. Formed 1851. **7** County (□ 728; pop. 8,215), SE Miss.; ⊙ Leakesville. Bordered E by Ala.; drained by Leaf and Chickasawhay rivers. Agr. (cotton, corn, livestock); lumbering. Includes part of De Soto and Chickasawhay natl. forests. Formed 1811. **8** County (□ 677; pop. 104,823), SW Mo.; ⊙ SPRINGFIELD. In the Ozarks; drained by James, Sac, Little Sac, and Pomme de Terre rivers. Agr. (grain, apples, strawberries, grapes, tomatoes), livestock; mfg. at Springfield; iron, lead, limestone. Formed 1833. **9** County (□ 653; pop. 28,745), SE N.Y.; ⊙ Catskill. Mtn.-resort area, with small lakes, situated mainly in the Catskills; bounded E by the Hudson, and drained by Schoharie and Catskill creeks. Farming (clover, fruit, truck, poultry), dairying; some timber. Includes part of Catskill State Park. Formed 1800. **10** County (□ 269; pop. 18,024), E central N.C.; ⊙ Snow Hill. On coastal plain; drained by small Contentnea Creek. Agr. (especially tobacco; corn), timber (pine, gum) area; sawmilling. Formed 1799. **11** County (□ 416; pop. 58,892), SW central Ohio; ⊙ Xenia. Intersected by Little Miami and Mad rivers and small Caesar Creek. Agr. area (livestock, grain, truck, poultry); mfg. at Xenia, Yellow Springs, Fairborn. Sand and gravel pits, mineral springs. Formed 1803. **12** County (□ 577; pop. 45,394), SW Pa.; ⊙ Waynesburg. Coal-mining and agr. area; bounded S and W by W.Va., E by Monongahela R. In dispute bet. Pa. and Va. until 1784. Largest sheep-raising co. in Pa.; dairying, grain; bituminous coal, gas, oil, limestone, sandstone, clay, shale, sand. Formed 1796. **13** County (□ 617; pop. 41,048), NE Tenn.; ⊙ Greenville. Bounded SE by N.C., with Bald Mts. along border (rise to 4,889 ft. in Big Butt); drained by Nolichucky R. Includes part of Cherokee Natl. Forest. Agr. (tobacco, fruit, corn, hay), livestock raising, dairying; lumbering (oak, pine). Mfg. at Greeneville. Formed 1783. **14** County (□ 153; pop. 4,745), N central Va.; ⊙ Stanardsville. Bounded NW by the Blue Ridge, NE by Rapidan R. and its Conway R. branch; includes part of Shenandoah Natl. Forest. Diversified agr. (grain, hay, tobacco, fruit), livestock (cattle, hogs, sheep, poultry); dairying. Timber (oak, pine). Formed 1838.
Greene. 1 Town (pop. 1,347), Butler co., N central Iowa, on Shell Rock R. and 27 mi. SE of Mason City; feed, butter, concrete blocks. Limestone quarries, sand pits near by. Inc. 1879. **2** Agr. town (pop. 974), Androscoggin co., SW Maine, on the Androscoggin just above Lewiston. **3** Village (pop. 1,628), Chenango co., S central N.Y., on Chenango R. and 17 mi. NNE of Binghamton, in dairying area; mfg. (silk textiles, furniture, machinery, metal products). Settled 1792, inc. 1842. **4** Village, Kent co., R.I.: see COVENTRY.
Greeneville, town (pop. 8,721), ⊙ Greene co., NE Tenn., 60 mi. ENE of Knoxville; burley tobacco market; trade center for rich agr. and timber area; mfg. of tobacco, wood products, hosiery, fertilizer, evaporated milk, leather goods, radios, lumber and flour milling. In 1785, succeeded Jonesboro as ⊙ short-lived State of Franklin; site of capitol is marked. Morgan Monument honors Gen. John H. Morgan, killed in Greeneville during Civil War. Home, grave, and tailor shop of Andrew Johnson are here; now included in Andrew Johnson Natl. Monument, established (1942) to commemorate Johnson's rise from humble origin to presidency. Tusculum Col., tobacco experiment station of Univ. of Tenn. Col. of Agr. near by.
Greenfield, England: see SADDLEWORTH.
Greenfield. 1 City (pop. 1,309), Monterey co., W Calif., in Salinas valley, 10 mi. NW of King City; berries, alfalfa. Inc. 1947. **2** City (pop. 987), Greene co., SW central Ill., 26 mi. S of Jacksonville, in bituminous-coal-mining and agr. area; canned foods; corn, wheat, oats, livestock, dairy products, poultry. Inc. 1867. **3** City (pop. 6,159), ⊙ Hancock co., central Ind., on small Brandywine Creek and 21 mi. E of Indianapolis, in agr. area (livestock, grain, vegetables); mfg. (underwear, canned goods). James Whitcomb Riley was b. here. Settled 1828, inc. 1850. **4** Town (pop. 2,102), ⊙ Adair co., SW Iowa, near Middle Nodaway R. (hydroelectric plant), c.50 mi. WSW of Des Moines; trade and shipping center for livestock, grain, and poultry region; mfg. (butter, tools, farm-machinery parts). Settled 1841, inc. 1876. **5** Town (pop. 88), Penobscot co., S central Maine, 10 mi. NE of Old Town, in hunting, fishing area. **6** Town (pop. 17,349), including Greenfield village (pop. 15,075), ⊙ Franklin co., NW Mass., on Connecticut R., near mouth of Deerfield R., and 19 mi. N of Northampton; mfg. (machine parts, tools, machinery), printing; dairying, apples, potatoes. E terminus of Mohawk Trail. Settled 1686, set off from Deerfield 1753. **7** City (pop. 1,213), ⊙ Dade co., SW Mo., near Sac R., 33 mi. WNW of Springfield; agr. Settled 1841. **8** Town (pop. 430), Hillsboro co., S N.H., 21 mi. WSW of Manchester. Ski trails. **9** Village (pop. 4,862), Highland co., SW Ohio, 22 mi. W of Chillicothe, and on Paint Creek, in agr. area; mfg. of footwear, harnesses, sporting goods, bags, store fixtures. Stone quarries. Platted 1798, inc. 1841. **10** Town (pop. 191), Blaine co., W central Okla., 8 mi. S of Watonga, near North Canadian R., in agr. area. Inc. 1930. **11** Town (pop. 1,706), Weakley co., NW Tenn., 22 mi. SSE of Union City; ships fruit, vegetables.
Greenfield, Wales: see HOLYWELL.
Greenfield Lake, N central Mont., in Teton co., just W of Fairfield and 35 mi. WNW of Great Falls; 4 mi. long, 1 mi. wide, fed by branches of Sun R. Used as reservoir of Sun R. irrigation system.
Greenfield Park, residential town (pop. 1,819), S Que., 8 mi. E of Montreal.
Greenfield Park, resort village, Ulster co., SE N.Y., in the Catskills, 5 mi. W of Ellenville.
Greenfield Village, in Dearborn, Mich., a reproduction of an early Amer. village, established in 1933 by Henry Ford as a part of Edison Inst. Included are historical bldgs., some original bldgs. moved here, others reproductions; Edison's Menlo Park workshop and Fort Myers laboratory, the birthplaces of Noah Webster and Luther Burbank, Stephen Foster's home, and the Wright brothers' cycle shop and home; a group of shepherds' cottages (17th cent.) from the Cotswolds; ande arly Amer. homes, public bldgs., a school (functioning), and craft shops.
Greenford, England: see EALING.
Green Forest, town (pop. 738), Carroll co., NW Ark., 20 mi. WNW of Harrison, in the Ozarks; tomato canneries.
Green Harbor, Mass.: see MARSHFIELD.
Greenhills or **Green Hills,** village (pop. 3,005), Hamilton co., extreme SW Ohio, a N suburb of Cincinnati. Established 1938 by Federal Resettlement Administration as experimental model community; inc. as village in 1939.
Green Hills, village (pop. 1,734, with adjacent Southside), Maury co., central Tenn.
Greenhithe, England: see SWANSCOMBE.
Greenhorn, town (1940 pop. 5), Baker co., E Oregon, 35 mi. W of Baker.
Greenhorn Mountain, peak (12,334 ft.) in Wet Mts., S Colo., 22 mi. NW of Walsenburg.
Green Island, Que.: see VERTE, ÎLE.
Green Island, town, Hanover parish, W Jamaica, 24 mi. WSW of Montego Bay; banana port. Tiny Green Isl. is just off coast.
Green Island, borough (pop. 2,697), SE S.Isl., New Zealand, 4 mi. SW of Dunedin; coal mines, flour mills.
Green Island. 1 Town (pop. 120), Jackson co., E Iowa, 31 mi. SE of Dubuque, in agr. area. **2** Industrial village (pop. 4,016), Albany co., E N.Y., on Green Isl. (2 mi. long) in the Hudson, bet. Troy and Watervliet (bridges to both cities); food products, machinery, boilers, textiles, paper. Inc. 1869.
Green Island. 1 Island in Knox co., S Maine, in entrance to Penobscot Bay and 11 mi. SSE of South Thomaston; .6 mi. long. **2** Island in Knox co., S Maine, just SW of Vinalhaven Isl.; 1.5 mi. long; lighthouse at S end.
Green Isle, village (pop. 332), Sibley co., S Minn., c.40 mi. SW of Minneapolis, in farming area; dairy products.
Green Lake, county (□ 355; pop. 14,749), central Wis.; ⊙ Green Lake. Predominantly dairying and farming area (vegetables, poultry). Mfg. in Berlin; canneries, creameries, fur farms. Intersected by Fox and Grand rivers. Includes Green L. and L. Puckaway (resorts). Formed 1858.

Green Lake, village (pop. 728), ⊙ Green Lake co., central Wis., on Green L., 26 mi. W of Fond du Lac, in dairying region; butter, boats, knit goods; summer resort.

Green Lake. 1 In Hancock co., S Maine, 6 mi. NW of Ellsworth, in hunting, fishing area; 6 mi. long. **2** In Grand Traverse co., NW Mich., just S of Interlochen, in resort area; c.3 mi. long, 1 mi. wide. Joined by passage to Duck L. (E). **3** In Kandiyohi co., SW central Minn., 10 mi. NE of Willmar; 4 mi. long, 2.5 mi. wide. **4** In SE Texas, lake (c.3 mi. long), 12 mi. SW of Port Lavaca in marshy coastal region just N of San Antonio Bay. **5** In Green Lake co., central Wis., 25 mi. W of Fond du Lac; c.8 mi. long, 2 mi. wide; summer homes on shores.

Greenland, Dan. *Grønland* (grŭn'länt), Danish colony (□ 840,000; pop. 21,412) off NE North America, an island, the largest in the world (if Australia is considered a continent), bounded N by Arctic Ocean, E by Greenland Sea, SE by Denmark Strait (which separates it from Iceland, c.175 mi. away), S by the Atlantic, and W by Davis Strait and Baffin Bay (which separate it from Baffin Isl.). Greenland is 1,660 mi. long from Cape Farewell (59°45'N) to Cape Morris Jesup (83°39'N; world's northernmost point of land, 440 mi. from the North Pole); max. width, 750 mi., bet. 11°40'W and 73°8'W. Geologically part of the Canadian shield, Greenland is 85% covered with an icecap c.7,000 ft. thick (over 8,000 ft. thick, according to some measurements), a basin surrounded by a chain of coastal mts. which rise to 12,139 ft. in Mt. Gunnbjorn (SE) and generally 4–8,000 ft. high. Only some 132,000 sq. mi. of coastland is ice-free. The extreme northern peninsula (Peary Land) has no icecap. Numerous glaciers flow from the icecap to the many fjords that indent coast line; Humboldt and Petermann glaciers are among the largest. Many glaciers "calve" tremendous icebergs; those on E coast are carried S by the cold East Greenland current and reach Atlantic shipping lanes; on W coast icebergs are carried into Davis Strait but usually melt in the warm West Greenland current. Cold winds from the interior make the weather uncertain and foggy. Representative mean temp. ranges are: at Ivigtut, 21°F. (Feb.) to 50°F. (July), with average annual rainfall of 45.7 inches; at Upernavik, –9°F. (Feb.) to 41°F. (July), with average annual rainfall of 9 inches. Extreme temperatures recorded at Thule range from –70°F. (Feb.) to 57°F. (July). Among Greenland's largest fjords and bays are Sondre Strom Fjord, Disko Bay (containing large DISKO isl.), Umanak Fjord, and Melville Bay, and St. George, Victoria, Frederick E. Hyde, Independence, Danmark, and Franz Josef fjords, and Scoresby Sound. On NW are Kane Basin and Hall Basin. Cryolite, mined at IVIGTUT, is Greenland's most important mineral; lignite is mined on Disko isl.; graphite, telluric iron, and some copper are also found. Marble quarries at MARMORILIK. Agr. and grazing are very limited, but there is some grazing land in SW part of isl., where sheep are raised. Vegetation in Peary Land, at N extremity of isl., supports herds of musk oxen; also found among Greenland fauna are the arctic hare, lemming, polar bear, white and blue fox, white wolf, ermine. While whaling has declined in importance, cod and halibut fisheries have developed rapidly in recent years; seals and walruses are hunted. The entire trade of Greenland is a state monopoly, and only vessels (Danish and foreign alike) having special permission may enter Greenland ports. Greenland is Danish crown colony, administered by a board of governors in Copenhagen. Isl. is divided into provinces of South Greenland (pop. 10,882; ⊙ GODTHAAB) and North Greenland (pop. 8,836; ⊙ GODHAVN). East Greenland (pop. 1,372) and Thule colony (pop. 322) form separate administrative entities. Other important settlements are Julianehaab, Frederikshaab, Holsteinsborg, Egedesminde, Sukkertoppen, Christianshaab, Jakobshavn, Umanak, Upernavik, Thule, Angmagssalik, Scoresbysund, and Nanortalik. The pop., over 90% of which live on W coast, includes only 580 Danes; the remainder, native Greenlanders, are of mixed Eskimo and Danish ancestry; pure Eskimos are found only in the THULE and ETAH regions, which have been subject of extensive anthropological study. Greenland was discovered (c.982) by Eric the Red; settlement began (985) with foundation of Brattahlid (near present Julianehaab), followed by other villages. From here Leif Ericson sailed to North America and c.1000 introduced Christianity here. In early 11th cent. there were 2 settlement groups: the Eastern Settlement, Norse *Østerbygd*, and the Western Settlement, Norse *Vesterbygd*, both on SW coast of isl. Greenland became a bishopric (1126) at Gardar, the modern Igaliko; in 1261 isl. came under Norwegian rule. By 15th cent. colony had declined and its people died out. Searchers for the NORTHWEST PASSAGE subsequently charted the coast. Frobisher sighted (1576) the coast, and when Davis landed (1587) at Sanderson's Hope (now KAERSORSSUAK), he found no Norsemen. Hudson sighted (1607) E coast and named Cape Hold with Hope. In 1721 the missionary Hans Egede, sponsored by king of Denmark, landed at Godthaab and opened modern phase of Greenland's colonization. In 17th and 18th cent. whaling was carried on extensively along E coast, chiefly by the Dutch and British. Trade with the colony was declared Danish govt. monopoly c.1775. By end of 18th cent. most of the larger W coast settlements were established. Eskimo settlement on E coast began in 1894, when Angmagssalik was founded. In 1815, at the Congress of Vienna, Denmark retained the colony through an oversight of the delegates, who detached Norway from Denmark, but forgot to mention the outlying Norwegian possessions. In 19th cent. exploration activity reached peak with expeditions by Kane, Hall, Ross, Peary (who reached Cape Morris Jesup, 1892), Nordenskjöld, Scoresby, and Nansen (who was 1st to cross the icecap, 1888). In 20th cent. noted expeditions were undertaken by Rasmussen (who led the 5 Thule expeditions), Nansen, Mylius-Erichsen, Koch, Courtauld, MacMillan, Freuchen, Wegener, the duke of Orléans, Charcot, Univ. of Michigan, and Cambridge Univ. E coast was annexed (1931) by Norway, but awarded (1933) to Denmark by International Court of Justice. During Second World War the U.S. established (1940) a consulate at Godthaab and was allowed to establish military bases and weather stations. Shortly after 1941 several German weather stations on E coast were captured.

Greenland. 1 Town (pop. 164), Washington co., NW Ark., 4 mi. S of Fayetteville, in the Ozarks. **2** Town (pop. 719), Rockingham co., SE N.H., on Great Bay just E of Portsmouth; agr. Site of Weeks House (c.1638; one of state's oldest).

Greenland Sea, S part of Arctic Ocean, off NE Greenland and N of Iceland. Cold East Greenland Current carries much ice; polar drift ice is prevalent in other parts of the sea.

Greenlane, borough (pop. 550), Montgomery co., SE Pa., 29 mi. NW of Philadelphia.

Greenlaw, town and parish (pop. 889), S Berwick, Scotland, on Blackadder Water and 7 mi. SW of Duns; agr. market. Has 17th-cent. parish cross. Formerly ⊙ Berwick, and scene of border warfare. S, 3 mi., are 13th-cent. ruins of Hume Castle (former seat of earls of Hume), taken 1650 by Cromwell.

Greenlawn, residential village (pop. 1,000), Suffolk co., SE N.Y., on N shore of W Long Isl., 3 mi. E of Huntington, in dairying and truck-farming area; packs sauerkraut.

Greenleaf, city (pop. 614), Washington co., N Kansas, c.40 mi. NNW of Manhattan; grain, livestock, poultry; dairying.

Greenlee, county (□ 1,874; pop. 12,805), SE Ariz.; ⊙ Clifton. Mtn. region drained by Blue, Gila, and San Francisco rivers. Some irrigation near Duncan. Morenci is mining center. Parts of Crook and Apache natl. forests here. Mining (copper, silver), cattle and sheep ranching; truck products, cotton, alfalfa. Formed 1909.

Green Lowther, Scotland: see LOWTHER HILLS.

Greenly Island, islet, E Que., near Labrador border, in the Gulf of St. Lawrence, at SW end of Belle Isle Strait; 51°22'N 57°12'W; fishing settlement. Col. Bernt Balchen here rescued (1927) crew of catapult mail plane of the liner *Bremen*.

Greenmount, village (pop. c.150), Carroll co., N Md., 27 mi. NW of Baltimore; canned vegetables; vehicle bodies.

Green Mountain Dam, Colo.: see BLUE RIVER.

Green Mountain Falls, town (pop. 106), El Paso and Teller counties, central Colo., on Fountain Creek and 10 mi. NW of Colorado Springs, near Pikes Peak; alt. 7,694 ft. Near-by cascades are of scenic interest.

Green Mountains, Vt., range of the Appalachians extending N–S through center of state from Mass. to Que.; generally low (2–3,000 ft.). Range rises to 4,393 ft. in Mt. Mansfield; includes Killington Peak (4,241 ft.), Lincoln Mtn. (4,135 ft.), Camels Hump (4,083 ft.). Missisquoi, Lamoille, and Winooski rivers cut range from E to W; many smaller streams and fertile valleys. Noted for scenic beauty, with many resorts. Marble, granite, talc, and asbestos mined. Large areas are included in Green Mtn. Natl. Forest; the Long Trail (260 mi. long; in part identical with Appalachian Trail; built for hikers) extends along full length of range. In NW Mass., Green Mts. continue as Hoosac Range.

Greenock (grĭ'nŭk), burgh (1931 pop. 78,949; 1951 census 76,299), NW Renfrew, Scotland, on the Clyde estuary at head of Firth of Clyde, and 21 mi. WNW of Glasgow; 55°58'N 4°45'W; a major port of Scotland with extensive docks (improved, beginning 1707). There are important shipyards and sugar refineries; also woolen milling, tanning, mfg. of machinery, aluminum products, boilers, chemicals. Greenock is noted for unusually heavy rainfall. North Kirk, built 1591, was removed from original site to NW suburb of Seafield to make way for shipyards; it contains windows by William Morris, Burne-Jones, Rossetti, and Fort Madox Brown. At West Kirk cemetery is grave of Burns's "Highland Mary." James Watt (commemorated by Watt Inst. and statue by Chantrey) and Capt. Kidd b. here. In Second World War Greenock was important debarkation port for American troops and supplies.

Greenock (grē'nŏk), village (1940 pop. 585), Allegheny co., SW Pa., on Youghiogheny R. and 4 mi. SE of McKeesport.

Greenore (grĕnôr'), Gaelic *Grianphort*, town (pop. 231), NE Co. Louth, Ireland, on SW shore of Carlingford Lough, 11 mi. E of Dundalk; 54°1'N 6°8'W; seaport with dock installations, exporting beef, cattle, agr. produce; seaside resort.

Greenore Point (grĕnôr'), promontory on St. George's Channel, SE Co. Wexford, Ireland, 4 mi. SE of Rosslare; 52°14'N 6°19'W.

Greenpoint, SE N.Y., a residential and industrial section of N Brooklyn borough of New York city.

Green Pond, village (pop. c.300), Colleton co., S S.C., 12 mi. S of Walterboro; rail junction.

Greenport, summer-resort village (pop. 3,028), Suffolk co., SE N.Y., on N fluke of E Long Isl., 20 mi. NE of Riverhead; mfg. of awnings, barrels; boatbuilding; fisheries (especially oysters). A terminus of Long Isl. RR. Inc. 1838.

Green Ridge, town (pop. 335), Pettis co., central Mo., 11 mi. SW of Sedalia; agr.

Green Ridge State Forest, Md.: see FLINT STONE.

Green River. 1 City (pop. 583), Emery co., E Utah, 55 mi. SE of Price and on Green R.; alt. 4,079 ft.; melons. **2** Town (pop. 3,187), ⊙ Sweetwater co., SW Wyo., on Green R., near mouth of Bitter Creek, and 13 mi. WSW of Rock Springs; alt. c.6,100 ft. Railroad div. point; shipping center for sheep and cattle in forest and agr. area. Founded 1868 near Overland stage route, inc. 1891. Developed with arrival of railroad.

Green River. 1 In N and NW Ill., rises NW of Shabbona, flows c.110 mi. generally WSW, past Amboy, to Rock R. E of Moline. **2** In central Ky., rises in Lincoln co. SSW of Danville, flows SSW, W past Greensburg and Munfordville, through Mammoth Cave Natl. Park, past Brownsville and Morgantown, generally NW past Livermore, and N to Ohio R. 7 mi. SE of Evansville, Ind.; 370 mi. long; drains □ 9,430. Main tributaries: Russell Creek, and Barren, Mud, and Pond (left) and Nolin and Rough (right) rivers. Navigable by means of locks for 198 mi., to Mammoth Cave. **3** In Vt. and Mass., rises on E slope of Green Mts. in Windham co., SE Vt., flows c.30 mi. SSE to Deerfield R. just S of Greenfield, Mass. **4** In W Wash., rises in Cascade Range NE of Mt. Rainier, flows 60 mi. NW and W to junction with White R., forming Duwamish R. S of Seattle. **5** In Wyo., Colo., and Utah, flows generally S from Wind River Range through W Wyo. and E Utah (with loop in NW Colo.) to Colorado R. (of which it is largest tributary) in SE Utah. Rises near Fremont Peak, passes Green River town, Wyo., flows through Canyon of Lodore in Dinosaur Natl. Monument (NW Colo. and NE Utah), and enters Colorado R. SW of Moab; 730 mi. long; drains □ 44,400. Traverses rugged mtn. region throughout most of course. Tributaries: Blacks Fork (Wyo.), Yampa R. (Colo.), Duchesne, Price, and San Rafael rivers (Utah). Main stream unnavigable; hydroelectric developments planned.

Green River Pass, Wyo.: see WIND RIVER RANGE.

Greensboro. 1 Town (pop. 2,217), ⊙ Hale co., W Ala., 35 mi. S of Tuscaloosa, in Black Belt cotton area; woodworking, food processing, cotton ginning. Settled c.1816, inc. 1823. **2** Town (pop. 565), Gadsden co., NW Fla., 29 mi. WNW of Tallahassee, in agr. area. **3** City (pop. 2,688), ⊙ Greene co., NE central Ga., 29 mi. SSE of Athens; mfg. (sheeting, bedspreads, lumber); cotton ginning. Laid out 1786, inc. 1803. **4** Town (pop. 241), Henry co., E central Ind., near Big Blue R., 6 mi. SW of New Castle, in agr. area. **5** Town (pop. 1,181), Caroline co., E Md., 20 mi. SW of Dover, Del., at head of navigation on Choptank R., in truck-farm area; vegetable canneries; mfg. of leather goods, evaporated milk. Laid out 1732. **6** City (pop. 74,389), ⊙ Guilford co., N central N.C., 25 mi. E of Winston-Salem, in piedmont area. Rail junction (shops); insurance, educational, distribution, and textile (cotton, rayon, nylon) center; mfg. of work clothes, hosiery, machinery, stoves, clay products, chemicals, fertilizer, cigars; lumbering. Seat of Greensboro Col. (Methodist; women; 1838), Bennett Col. (Negro; Methodist; women; 1873), Woman's Col. of Univ. of N.C., Agr. and Technical Col. of N.C., and Immanuel Lutheran Col. (Negro; coeducational). O. Henry b. here. Guilford College village (seat of Guilford Col.) and Guilford Courthouse Natl. Military Park are near by. Settled 1749; laid out 1808. **7** Borough (pop. 651), Greene co., SW Pa., 13 mi. SW of Uniontown and on Monongahela R. **8** Town (pop. 737), Orleans co., N Vt., 18 mi. NW of St. Johnsbury; lumbering, dairying; winter sports. Caspian L. is resort.

Greensburg. 1 City (pop. 6,619), ⊙ Decatur co., SE central Ind., c.45 mi. SSE of Indianapolis; trade center for agr., oil, and gas area; ships tobacco; some mfg. (food products, wire fences, hardware, shirts, fertilizer, brooms); stone quarries. Settled 1822, inc. 1859. **2** City (pop. 1,723), ⊙ Kiowa co., S Kansas, 30 mi. W of Pratt, in grain and livestock region. Inc. 1886. **3** Town (pop.

1,032), ⊙ Green co., central Ky., on Green R. and 37 mi. SE of Elizabethtown, in agr. (burley tobacco, grain) and cedar timber area; mfg. of quilted articles, office supplies, soft drinks, staves; feed, flour, and lumber mills, tobacco warehouse. Courthouse, here, built 1799. Settled c.1780 as Glovers Station. **4** Town (pop. 423), ⊙ St. Helena parish, SE La., near Tickfaw R., 40 mi. NE of Baton Rouge; agr. **5** City (pop. 16,923), ⊙ Westmoreland co., SW central Pa., 25 mi. ESE of Pittsburgh; plumbing supplies, metal products, coke, beverages, glass, bricks, clothing; oil, gas; agr. Seton Hill Col. here. Settled 1782, inc. 1799.

Greens Farms, Conn.: see WESTPORT.

Greensfork, town (pop. 413), Wayne co., E Ind., on a fork of Whitewater R. and 9 mi. NW of Richmond, in agr. area.

Greens Peak (10,115 ft.), E Ariz., in White Mts., 16 mi. ENE of McNary.

Greenspond Island (2 mi. long, 2 mi. wide), E N.F., on N side of Bonavista Bay, 45 mi. W of Gander; 49°4'N 53°36'W. On S shore is fishing port of Greenspond (pop. 790).

Green Springs, village (pop. 1,082), on Seneca-Sandusky co. line, N Ohio, 8 mi. SSE of Fremont and on small Green Creek; health resort, with mineral springs.

Greensville, county (□ 301; pop. 16,319), S Va.; ⊙ Emporia. Bounded S by N.C., N by Nottoway R.; drained by Meherrin R. and its Fontaine Creek branch. Agr. (especially peanuts; also cotton, tobacco), livestock (cattle, hogs); lumber milling; mfg., processing of farm products at Emporia. Formed 1781.

Greentop, town (pop. 281), Schuyler co., N Mo., on Salt R. and 10 mi. N of Kirksville; agr.; coal.

Greentown, residential town (pop. 1,160), Howard co., central Ind., on Wildcat Creek and 9 mi. E of Kokomo, in agr. area (livestock, grain, poultry); cannery. Founded 1848.

Green Tree, town (pop. 373), Lincoln co., S central N.Mex., 14 mi. SW of Lincoln. Sometimes Palo Verde.

Greentree, borough (pop. 2,818), Allegheny co., SW Pa., adjacent to SW Pittsburgh. Inc. 1885.

Green Turtle Cay, islet and town (pop. 294), N Bahama Isls., just off NE Great Abaco Isl., 35 mi. NW of Hope Town, 125 mi. N of Nassau; 26°50'N 77°23'W. Fishing, some fruitgrowing (pineapples). Town is sometimes called New Plymouth.

Greenup (grē'nŭp), county (□ 350; pop. 24,887), extreme NE Ky.; ⊙ Greenup. Bounded N and E by Ohio R. (Ohio line); drained by Little Sandy R. and Tygarts Creek. In E is part of Huntington (W.Va.)-Ashland metropolitan dist. Hilly agr. area (corn, tobacco, apples, cattle, truck); iron deposits. Some industry at Russell. Formed 1803.

Greenup. 1 Village (pop. 1,360), Cumberland co., SE central Ill., 19 mi. SSE of Mattoon, in fruit-growing area; shoe, broom factories. Founded 1836, inc. 1855. **2** Town (pop. 1,276), ⊙ Greenup co., NE Ky., on the Ohio, at Little Sandy R. mouth, and 14 mi. SSE of Portsmouth, Ohio, in agr. area (truck, grain); makes flour, caskets. Co. courthouse, here, built 1811. Race track near by.

Greenvale, residential village (1940 pop. 1,006), Nassau co., SE N.Y., on W Long Isl., 5 mi. N of Mineola.

Green Valley, village (pop. 503), Tazewell co., central Ill., 10 mi. S of Pekin, in agr. and bituminous-coal area.

Greenview, village (pop. 795), Menard co., central Ill., 19 mi. N of Springfield; grain, livestock, dairy products, poultry; bituminous-coal mining.

Greenville, town, ⊙ Sinoe co., SE Liberia, port on Atlantic Ocean, at mouth of Sinoe R., 155 mi. SE of Monrovia; copra, palm oil and kernels, raffia. Formerly called Sino or Sinoe.

Greenville, county (□ 789; pop. 168,152), NW S.C.; ⊙ Greenville. Bounded N by N.C. line, W by Saluda R.; drained by Enoree and Reedy rivers. Mfg. (especially cotton textiles) in Greenville and its surrounding mill villages; agr. (cotton, corn), dairying; vermiculite mining. Summer-resort area, with part of the Blue Ridge in N. Formed 1786.

Greenville. 1 City (pop. 6,781), ⊙ Butler co., S Ala., 42 mi. SSW of Montgomery; processing center for cotton and truck area; mfg. of clothing, wood products; lumber milling, cotton ginning; pecans, fertilizer. Settled 1819. **2** Village (pop. 1,153), Plumas co., NE Calif., 14 mi. N of Quincy, in the Sierra Nevada; lumbering, gold mining; summer resort. L. Almanor is 7 mi. NW. **3** Town (pop. 1,163), Madison co., N Fla., c.40 mi. E of Tallahassee; plywood mfg. Founded in mid-19th cent. **4** City (pop. 733), ⊙ Meriwether co., W Ga., 18 mi. E of La Grange, in a truck and cotton area; mfg. of lumber products. **5** City (pop. 4,069), ⊙ Bond co., SW central Ill., on East Fork of Shoal Creek and 40 mi. E of Alton, in agr. area (corn, wheat; dairy products; alfalfa); evaporated milk, clothing, steel products. Bituminous-coal mines, natural-gas wells. Seat of Greenville Col. Settled 1815, inc. 1855. **6** Town (pop. 298), Floyd co., S Ind., 11 mi. NW of New Albany, in agr. area. **7** Town (pop. 173), Clay co., NW Iowa, 9 mi. S of Spencer. **8** City (pop. 2,661), ⊙ Muhlenberg co., W Ky., 19 mi. ESE of Madisonville. Trade and processing center for bituminous-coal-mining, agr. (corn, hogs, tobacco), oil-well, clay-pit, and timber area; mfg. of tobacco and clay products; lumber, flour, and feed mills, oil refinery. **9** Town (pop. 1,889), Piscataquis co., central Maine, at S end of Moosehead L.; hq. for hunting, fishing, camping area. Wood products, canoes. Settled 1824, inc. 1836. **10** City (pop. 6,668), Montcalm co., central Mich., 27 mi. NE of Grand Rapids, and on Flat R. Potato market; mfg. (refrigerators, farm implements, machinery, foundry products, gloves). Resort. Inc. as village 1867, as city 1871. **11** City (pop. 29,936), ⊙ Washington co., W Miss., on the Mississippi and 50 mi. W of Greenwood; river port; trade, processing, and shipping center for rich cotton-growing area of the Mississippi-Yazoo delta. Mfg. (insulating board, boxes, cottonseed-oil products, bricks, chemicals). After destructive 1927 flood, higher levees were built and L. Ferguson was created by a cutoff of river. Inc. 1870. **12** City (pop. 270), ⊙ Wayne co., SE Mo., in Ozark region, on St. Francis R. and 24 mi. N of Poplar Bluff; agr.; lumber. **13** Town (pop. 1,280), Hillsboro co., S N.H., on the Souhegan (water-power) and 18 mi. W of Nashua; textiles. Set off from Mason 1872. **14** Resort village, Greene co., SE N.Y., in foothills of the Catskills, 21 mi. SW of Albany. **15** Residential village (1940 pop. 2,645), Westchester co., SE N.Y., bet. Scarsdale (SE) and Dobbs Ferry (W). **16** Town (pop. 16,724), ⊙ Pitt co., E N.C., 33 mi. SE of Rocky Mount and on Tar R.; important market and processing center for bright-leaf tobacco. Seat of East Carolina Teachers Col. Founded 1786. **17** City (pop. 8,859), ⊙ Darke co., W Ohio, 33 mi. NW of Dayton and on Greenville Creek; trade center for rich agr. area (corn, tobacco, wheat); mfg. of electrical appliances, clothing, stoves, food and dairy products, machinery, tile; meat-packing plant, poultry hatcheries; gravel pits. Laid out 1808, inc. 1838. In 1793, Gen. Anthony Wayne built Fort Greenville here (marker on site); after his victory at Fallen Timbers, a treaty in which Indians ceded much of Northwest Territory was signed here in 1795. **18** Borough (pop. 9,210), Mercer co., NW Pa., 14 mi. NNE of Sharon, and on Shenango R.; trading center in agr. area; metal products, dairy products; railroad shops; sandstone. Thiel Col. here. Settled c.1796, laid out 1798, inc. 1837. **19** Village, Providence co., R.I.: see SMITHFIELD. **20** City (pop. 58,161), ⊙ Greenville co., NW S.C., 95 mi. NW of Columbia, in piedmont region near the Blue Ridge, and on Reedy R., near the Saluda. One of principal industrial and commercial centers of the Southeast, with many textile mills, food-processing and packing plants, foundries, chemical and woodworking plants, machinery shops, and other mfg. Center of industrial region of mill towns. Has biennial Southern Textile Exposition and S.C. Singing Convention. Seat of Furman Univ. (with which Greenville Woman's Col. is merged), and Bob Jones Univ. Air force base. City site was colonial plantation until 1797, when village of Pleasantburg was laid out; renamed Greenville 1831. Annexed West Greenville town in 1948. **21** City (pop. 14,727), ⊙ Hunt co., NE Texas, on Sabine R. and c.45 mi. NE of Dallas; commercial, trade, processing, shipping center for rich blackland agr. region(cotton); has large cotton compress, grain and cottonseed mills, oil refinery, railroad shops; mfg. of clothing, furniture, food products. A U.S. cottonseed-improvement station is near. Settled 1846, inc. 1874.

Greenville Creek, SW Ohio, rises in E Ind. near Ohio line, flows NE and E, into Ohio, past Greenville and Gettysburg, to Stillwater R. at Covington; c.40 mi. long.

Greenwald, village (pop. 207), Stearns co., central Minn., 34 mi. W of St. Cloud; dairy products.

Greenway, town (pop. 288), Clay co., extreme NE Ark., 24 mi. NE of Paragould, near Mo. line.

Greenwich (grĭ'nĭj), residential metropolitan borough (1931 pop. 100,924; 1951 census 91,492) of London, England, on S bank of the Thames, 6 mi. ESE of Charing Cross. Here are Royal Naval Col. and Greenwich Hosp., on site of royal palace (built 1433), where Henry VIII, Mary, and Elizabeth were b., and where Edward VI died. Greenwich was scene of "whitebait dinners," held until 1890 at the close of sessions of Parliament for cabinet members. Until 1946 a 180-ft. hill in Greenwich Park (185 acres) was site of the Royal Greenwich Observatory (51°28'38.1"N 0° long.). Site for the observatory was chosen and the 1st bldgs. designed by Wren in 1675; present bldgs. completed 1899. Observatory, controlled by British Admiralty, has made regular meteorological and magnetic observations since 1838 and almost daily photographs of the sun since 1873. Due to interference from London bldgs. the magnetic observation station was transferred (1923) to Abinger, Surrey. After Second World War it was decided (1946) to move observatory to Hurstmonceux Castle, Sussex, because of interference from glare of London street lights and neon signs, the move to be completed by 1953. The original site at Greenwich continues, however, to be the official point from which longitude is reckoned; was accepted for nautical and international calculations by Washington Meridian Conference in 1884. In 1937 Natl. Maritime Mus. was opened in Greenwich. Pedestrian tunnel links Greenwich with the Isle of Dogs on N bank of the Thames.

Greenwich. 1 (grĕ'nĭch, grĭ'nĭch, grēn'wĭch) Residential, resort town (pop. 40,835), Fairfield co., extreme SW Conn., on N.Y. line and Long Isl. Sound, just W of Stamford. Printing and publishing, mfg. (textiles, vacuum cleaners, metal products, boats and marine engines, furniture). Includes villages of Cos Cob (kŏs'kŏb') (on Cos Cob Harbor), Riverside, Glenville, Old Greenwich, and East Port Chester. Area purchased from Indians (1640); town raided by British (1779). Bruce Mus., Edgewood School (1910; pioneer progressive coeducational school), Rosemary Hall School for girls (1890). Audubon Nature Center (400 acres), a wildlife sanctuary, was opened in 1943. **2** (grēn'-wĭch) Village in Greenwich township (pop. 966), Cumberland co., SW N.J., on Cohansey Creek and 7 mi. SW of Bridgeton; canneries. Seaport in 18th cent. Monument (1908) commemorates scene of tea-burning "party," 1774. **3** (grēn'wĭch) Industrial village (pop. 2,212), Washington co., E N.Y., on Batten Kill and 14 mi. E of Saratoga Springs, in farming and dairying area; mfg. (clothing, textiles, paper, machinery, feed). Inc. 1809. **4** (grēn'wĭch) Village (pop. 1,204), Huron co., N Ohio, 19 mi. N of Mansfield; dairy, livestock, poultry farms. Makes tractors, electric products. Inc. 1879. **5** Town, Kent co., R.I.: see EAST GREENWICH, WEST GREENWICH.

Greenwich Bay (grĕ'nĭch, grĭ-), E central R.I., arm of Narragansett Bay just S of Warwick; c.5 mi. long, 3.5 mi. wide; center of resort and summer-home area, with several state parks.

Greenwich Island (16 naut. mi. long, ½-7 naut. mi. wide), South Shetland Isls., off Palmer Peninsula, Antarctica; 62°30'S 59°50'W. Chile garrisoned the isl. (1947), disputing Britain's claim, established a base (Arturo Prat Base), and renamed the isl. for President González Videla.

Greenwich Village (grĕ'nĭch, grĭ'-, grēn'wĭch), SE N.Y., a section of lower Manhattan borough of New York city, lying approximately bet. 14th St. (N), Houston St. (S), Washington Square (E), and the Hudson (W). Settled as a separate village in colonial days, and later successively an exclusive residential section, a tenement dist., and (after 1910) the home and workshop of nonconformist artists, writers, and theater people. Its narrow streets, old houses, and deliberately picturesque restaurants, shops and night clubs, together with its lingering aura of bohemianism, attract tourists. Outdoor art exhibits are held semiannually near Washington Square.

Greenwood, city (pop. 363), S B.C., near Wash. border, on Border Creek and 45 mi. W of Trail; silver, lead, zinc mining.

Greenwood. 1 County (□ 1,150; pop. 13,574), SE Kansas; ⊙ Eureka. Rolling to hilly area, drained by Fall R. Livestock, grain. Extensive oil and natural-gas fields. Formed 1862. **2** County (□ 458; pop. 41,628), W S.C.; ⊙ Greenwood. Bounded NE by Saluda R., dammed in SE by Buzzard Roost Dam to form L. Greenwood. Includes part of Sumter Natl. Forest. Has considerable mfg. (chiefly textiles) and fertile agr. land (cotton, corn, truck, fruit, lespedeza hay); dairying. Formed 1897.

Greenwood. 1 Village (pop. 2,421), Macon co., E Ala. There is also a Greenwood in Jefferson co., S of Bessemer. **2** Town (pop. 1,634), a ⊙ Sebastian co., W Ark., 14 mi. SSE of Fort Smith; coal-shipping point; planing mill; dairy, poultry, cotton farming. **3** Town (pop. 746), Sussex co., SW Del., 25 mi. SSW of Dover; shipping point for farm products; dye works. **4** Town (1940 pop. 293), Jackson co., NW Fla., 7 mi. NE of Marianna; ships peanuts. **5** Town (pop. 3,066), Johnson co., central Ind., 12 mi. S of Indianapolis; mfg. (household appliances, canned goods, automobile parts, livestock remedies). **6** Town (pop. 604), Oxford co., W Maine, 16 mi. SSW of Rumford, in summer resort area. Includes Locke Mills village. Settled 1802, inc. 1816. **7** Village, Middlesex co., Mass.: see WAKEFIELD. **8** City (pop. 18,061), ⊙ Leflore co., W central Miss., on Yazoo R. and 50 mi. E of Greenville, in cotton-growing area; cotton-marketing, -shipping, and -processing center; cottonseed products, packed meat, electronic-testing instruments, lumber, trailers. Settled 1834, inc. 1844. **9** Village (pop. 364), Cass co., SE Nebr., 15 mi. NE of Lincoln and on Salt Creek of Platte R. **10** City (pop. 13,806), ⊙ Greenwood co., W S.C., 65 mi. WNW of Columbia, near L. Greenwood. Rail and road junction; mfg., trade, shipping center for agr. area (cotton, truck, corn, fruits); surrounded by mill villages. Textile and lumber mills, machine shops, foundries, food-processing and canning plants; printing. Seat of Lander Col., Brewer Normal Inst. (Negro), orphanage. State park near by; Buzzard Roost hydroelectric development is on the Saluda. Settled 1824, inc. as town 1857, as city 1927. **11** City (pop. 956), Clark co., central Wis., on Black R. and 50 mi. WSW of Wausau, in dairying, lumbering, and farming area; makes cheese, butter; vegetable canning, sawmilling.

Greenwood, Lake, W central S.C., reservoir (c.20 mi. long) formed on Saluda R. by Buzzard Roost Dam, 14 mi. E of Greenwood; a N arm receives Reedy R. Used for hydroelectric power. Bordered by Greenwood State Park (c.1,100 acres).

Greenwood Lake, in SE N.Y. and N N.J., resort lake (c.7 mi. long) bisected by state line, c.20 mi. NW of Paterson, N.J., in mtn. resort area; fishing, winter sports. Greenwood Lake village (pop. 819), Orange co., N.Y., at N end.

Greer, county (□ 637; pop. 11,749), SW Okla.; ⊙ Mangum. Bounded E by North Fork of Red R. (with ALTUS DAM in SE); drained also by the Elm and Salt forks of Red R. Includes a state park. Agr. (cotton, wheat, corn), stock raising, dairying. Mfg. at Mangum. Granite quarries. Formed 1907.

Greer, town (pop. 5,050), Greenville and Spartanburg counties, NW S.C., 11 mi. NE of Greenville; peach-shipping center; textile mills; canned foods, grain and cottonseed products.

Greers Ferry Dam, Ark.; see LITTLE RED RIVER.

Grées, Alpes, France and Italy: see GRAIAN ALPS.

Greetland, former urban district (1931 pop. 4,299), West Riding, SW Yorkshire, England, 2 mi. S of Halifax; woolen and cotton milling; mfg. of textile machinery. Inc. 1937 in Elland.

Greetwell, England: see LINCOLN, city.

Grefrath (grāf'rät), village (pop. 5,917), in former Prussian Rhine Prov., W Germany, after 1945 in North Rhine-Westphalia, near the Niers, 4 mi. N of Süchteln; textile mfg.

Gregg, county (□ 284; pop. 61,258), E Texas; ⊙ Longview. Drained by Sabine R. In huge East Texas oil field (discovered 1930); a leading oil-producing co. of Texas. Also natural gas, iron, lignite, clay. Some lumbering, agr. (cotton, corn, sweet potatoes, fruit, truck), livestock (cattle, hogs, poultry), dairying. Longview, Kilgore, Gladewater are industrial centers. Formed 1873.

Gregg River, village, W Alta., in Rocky Mts., near E side of Jasper Natl. Park, 30 mi. ENE of Jasper; coal mining. Formerly Kaydee.

Greggton, village (pop. 2,168), Gregg co., E Texas, 4 mi. W of Longview; oil-field supply point.

Gregory, county (□ 1,023; pop. 8,556), S S.Dak., on Nebr. line; ⊙ Burke. Agr. and stock-raising region watered by intermittent streams and bounded E by Missouri R. Livestock, dairy products, poultry, grain. Formed 1862.

Gregory, city (pop. 1,375), Gregory co., S S.Dak., 90 mi. SSE of Pierre; trading point for livestock and agr. region; dairy products, livestock, grain.

Gregory, Lake, San Bernardino co., S Calif., in San Bernardino Mts., near L. Arrowhead, 10 mi. N of San Bernardino; c.1 mi. long. Crestline and other mtn. resorts are nearby.

Gregory Park, village, St. Catherine parish, S Jamaica, on Cobre R., on railroad and 5 mi. WNW of Kingston.

Gregory Range, plateau, N central Queensland, Australia, W spur of Great Dividing Range; extends 170 mi. SE from Croydon; alt. 1,000 ft.; gold deposits.

Gregory Town, town (pop. 303), central Bahama Isls., on N Eleuthera Isl., 25 mi. NW of Governor's Harbour, 55 mi. ENE of Nassau: 25°24'N 76°35'W. Pineapples, tomatoes.

Greifenberg, Poland: see GRYFICE.

Greifenburg (grī'fůnbo͝ork), village (pop. 1,453), Carinthia, S Austria, near the Drau, 23 mi. ESE of Lienz; tannery, paper mills; summer resort with mineral springs. Ruins of old castles near by.

Greifenhagen, Poland: see GRYFINO.

Greifensee (grī'fůnzā″), lake (□ 3), Zurich canton, N Switzerland. Inlet (S): Aa R., outlet (N): Glatt R. Greifensee village (pop. 266), on it, has old castle and church.

Greifenstein (grī'fůnshtīn), village (pop. 341), central Lower Austria, on the Danube and 9 mi. NNW of Vienna; large sandstone quarries. Ruins of 12th-cent. fortress.

Greiffenberg (grī'fůnběrk), town (pop. 1,626), Brandenburg, E Germany, 6 mi. NNW of Angermünde; grain, tobacco, sugar beets; dairying.

Greiffenberg, Poland: see GRYFOW SLASKI.

Greifswald (grīfs'vält″), city (pop. 43,590), in former Prussian Pomerania prov., N Germany, after 1945 in Mecklenburg, on small Ryck R. near its mouth on Greifswalder Bodden bay of the Baltic, and 65 mi. NW of Stettin, 20 mi. SE of Stralsund; 54°5'N 13°23'E. Cultural center with noted univ. (founded 1456). Rail junction; fish preserving, chalk processing, brewing; mfg. of machinery, chemicals; grain and wood trade. Spa. Site of observatory. Lutheran bishopric. Has 13th-cent. church and many late-Gothic gabled houses. Founded 1241; chartered c.1250; joined Hanseatic League in 1278. In Thirty Years War it was allied with the Swedes; passed to Sweden in 1648. Occupied by French, 1807–10; passed to Prussia in 1815.

Greifswalder Bodden (grīfs'väl″důr bô'důn), Baltic bay, N Germany, bet. Rügen isl. and mainland; 15 mi. long, 7–17 mi. wide. At W end it forms BODDEN strait.

Greifswalder Oie (oi'ů), Baltic islet (124 acres), N Germany, 15 mi. NNE of Wolgast; 54°15'N 13°55'E. Lighthouse.

Grein (grīn), town (pop. 2,632), E Upper Austria, on left bank of the Danube and 25 mi. E of Linz; summer resort. Greinburg, castle, here.

Greinerville (grěnârvěl'), village, Katanga prov., E Belgian Congo, on railroad and 8 mi. W of Albertville. Its low-grade coal deposits are intermittently exploited. Also called Makala.

Greiveldange (grī'vůldäng″ů), village (pop. 381), SE Luxembourg, 10 mi. E of Luxembourg city; near Moselle R. and Ger. border; grape-growing center.

Greiz (grīts), city (pop. 45,410), Thuringia, central Germany, on the White Elster, at mouth of Göltzsch R., and 12 mi. NNE of Plauen; 50°39'N 12°12'E. Woolen-milling center; mfg. of machinery, chemicals, paper, leather. Has 2 palaces (the older dating from 16th cent.). Until 1918, ⊙ principality of Reuss Older Line.

Grejsdal (grīs'dhäl), town (pop. 1,860), Vejle amt, E Jutland, Denmark, 3 mi. N of Vejle; mfg. (cork, brick); orchards.

Grembergen (grěm'běr-khůn), town (pop. 4,797), East Flanders prov., N Belgium, on Scheldt R. and 2 mi. N of Dendermonde; textile industry; agr. market.

Gremikha (grěmē'khů), village, NE Murmansk oblast, Russian SFSR, port on Barents Sea, on Kola Peninsula, 175 mi. ESE of Murmansk; fisheries. Pop. largely Lapp (Saami).

Gremsmühlen, Germany: see MALENTE.

Gremyach (grĭmyäch'), village (1939 pop. over 500), NE Chernigov oblast, Ukrainian SSR, near Desna R., 22 mi. N of Novgorod-Severski; hemp, potatoes.

Gremyacheye (grĭmyä'chāyĭ), village (1939 pop. over 2,000), S Moscow oblast, Russian SFSR, 17 mi. ENE of Stalinogorsk; wheat.

Gremyachinsk (grĭmyä'chĭnsk), city (1949 pop. over 10,000), E central Molotov oblast, Russian SFSR, on railroad (Baskaya station) and 22 mi. N of Chusovoi; a major mining center in Kizel bituminous-coal basin. Developed in early 1940s; became city in 1949.

Gremyachye or **Gremach'ye** (grĭmyä'chyĭ), village (1939 pop. over 2,000), W central Voronezh oblast, Russian SFSR, on Don R. and 15 mi. SW of Voronezh; garden fruit and vegetables.

Grenaa (grĕ'nô), city (pop. 7,251) with adjacent port, Randers amt, E Jutland, Denmark, 31 mi. NE of Aarhus, at E tip of Djursland peninsula; textile mill, meat packing, fisheries, shipbuilding.

Grenaa Peninsula, Denmark: see DJURSLAND.

Grenada (grůnā'dů), island (□ c.120; pop. 65,618), southernmost of the Windward Isls., B.W.I., adjoined N by the Grenadines, 85 mi. N of Port of Spain, Trinidad; ⊙ St. George's. Situated bet. 11°58'–12°14'N and 61°36'–61°48'W; c.21 mi. long, 12 mi. wide. Mean annual temp. c.79°F.; rainfall varies with alt., from 30–140 inches. Largely covered by rugged, forested mts., it rises in Mt. St. Catherine to 2,749 ft. The picturesque isl. abounds in streams, springs, and crater lakes. Ridges crossing from central range toward E and W coast enclose fertile valleys. Principal staples for export are cacao, nutmeg, mace, coconuts; also sugar cane, bananas, spices, cotton, limes. Processing industries include rum distilleries, sugar mills, cotton gins; mfg. of lime juice and lime oil. Its trading center and port is St. George's, also ⊙ Windward Isls. Grenada is said to have been discovered (1498) by Columbus, who named it Concepción. The native Caribs resisted an early English attempt (1609) to settle the isl., but the French gained a foothold in 1650. The British controlled the isl., 1762–79, and have held it continuously since 1783. About 2% of the pop. is white, the remainder Negro. English is generally spoken, though some of the peasantry still speak a Fr. patois. Grenada isl. constitutes the main section of **Grenada** colony (□ 133; pop. 72,387), which includes the S Grenadines, among them Carriacou. Though belonging to the Br. Windward Isls. colony, it has a local govt. and legislative council of its own.

Grenada (grĭnä'dů), county (□ 447; pop. 18,830), NW central Miss.; ⊙ Grenada. Drained by Yalobusha and Skuna rivers. Agr. (mainly cotton; also corn, livestock; dairy products); timber. Formed 1870.

Grenada, city (pop. 7,388), ⊙ Grenada co., NW central Miss., on Yalobusha R. and 28 mi. NE of Greenwood, in agr. (cotton, corn), dairying, and timber area; mfg. of hosiery, boxes, cottonseed products, creosoted-wood products, mirrors; lumber milling. Near by is Grenada Dam (flood control) in Yalobusha R. Settled in early 1830s, inc. 1836.

Grenada Dam; Grenada Reservoir, Miss.: see YALOBUSHA RIVER.

Grenade (grůnäd'). **1** or **Grenade-sur-Garonne** (–sür-gärôn'), village (pop. 1,883), Haute-Garonne dept., S France, near influx of the Save into Garonne R., 14 mi. NNW of Toulouse; hosiery mfg., cucumber pickling, dairying, horse raising. **2** or **Grenade-sur-l'Adour** (–sür-lädo͞or'), village (pop. 676), Landes dept., SW France, on Adour R. and 9 mi. SSE of Mont-de-Marsan; cementworks; poultry market.

Grenadier Island (5 mi. long, 1 mi. wide), SE Ont., one of the Thousand Isls., in the St. Lawrence, 15 mi. SW of Brockville.

Grenadier Island, Jefferson co., N N.Y., in E part of L. Ontario, 5 mi. SSW of Cape Vincent; 2¼ mi. long, ¼–1¼ mi. wide.

Grenadines (grěnůdēnz', grě'nůdēnz), archipelago, the S part of the Windward Isls., B.W.I., a chain of islets extending 60 mi. bet. St. Vincent (N) and Grenada (SSW), whose dependencies they are. Chief isls. are Bequia, Mustique, Cannouan, belonging to St. Vincent; and Carriacou, the largest of the group, belonging to Grenada. Sea-island cotton is their staple crop. Also limes and livestock. The isls. have excellent beaches and enjoy continuous breezes, but so far have attracted few tourists.

Grenay (grůnā'), town (pop. 8,776), Pas-de-Calais dept., N France, 4.5 mi. WNW of Lens, in coal-mining dist.; rail junction.

Grenchen (grěn'khůn), Fr. *Granges* (gräzh), town (1950 pop. 12,630), Solothurn canton, NW Switzerland, 6 mi. W of Solothurn; watches, metal products, rubber goods.

Grenchenberg Tunnel (grěn'khůnběrk″) (5 mi. long), in the Jura, NW Switzerland, under the Grenchenberg; used by railway leading from Moutier to Grenchen.

Grenelle (grůněl'), a SW quarter of Paris, France, on left bank of the Seine, comprised in 15th *arrondissement*. Noted for its deep artesian well.

Grenell Island (grěněl'), Jefferson co., N N.Y., one of the Thousand Isls., c.7 mi. SW of Alexandria Bay; c.½ mi. long. Grenell village is here.

Grenfell, municipality (pop. 2,425), SE central New South Wales, Australia, 110 mi. NNW of Canberra; rail terminus; sheep, agr. center. Gold mines near by.

Grenfell, town (pop. 856), SE Sask., 34 mi. E of Indian Head; grain elevators. Resort.

Grenier Air Force Base, N.H.: see MANCHESTER.

Grenloch (grěn'lŏk), village (1940 pop. 559), Camden co., SW N.J., on Big Timber Creek and 11 mi. S of Camden; hosiery, metal and plastic products.

Grenoble (grůnô'blů), anc. *Cularo*, later *Gratianopolis*, city (pop. 97,287), ⊙ Isère dept., SW France, in Alpine GRÉSIVAUDAN valley, at S foot of the Grande Chartreuse, 60 mi. SE of Lyons, on left bank of Isère R. just above influx of the Drac; 45°12'N 5°43'E. Industrial and cultural (univ.) center, and a leading tourist gateway to the Dauphiné Alps. Has France's most important kid-glove manufactures (more than 70 factories). Local hydroelectric plants, intensively developed since 1885, power metalworks (ferro-alloys, turbines and various power-plant machinery, machine tools, industrial plumbing fixtures, electrical transmission equipment, edge-tools), numerous cementworks and paper mills. Grenoble also produces metal accessories (snap fasteners, zippers, etc.) for textile and glove industry. Other mfg.: underwear, straw hats, flour products (2 large factories), candy, chocolate, and beer. Has fine art mus.; Renaissance palace of the dauphins (now courthouse); 12th-13th-cent. cathedral; and church of St. André (13th-14th cent.) containing tomb of Bayard. Overlooking town from atop southernmost spur of the Grande Chartreuse is old Fort de la Bastille (cable car; panorama). Celebrated Monastery of La Grande Chartreuse is 12 mi. NNE. One of France's most scenically located cities, Grenoble was spared major damage in Second World War. Gaulish *Cularo* was raised (c.380) to rank of town by emperor Gratian. Became ⊙ Dauphiné, passing to France in 1341. Its famous univ. was founded 1339. In 1815, it was first Fr. stronghold which openly received Napoleon I on his return from Elba. Stendhal b. here.

Grenola (grěnō'lů), city (pop. 380), Elk co., SE Kansas, on Caney R. and 30 mi. WNW of Winfield; livestock, grain.

Grenora, city (pop. 525), Williams co., NW N.Dak., 36 mi. NNW of Williston, near Mont. line. Deposits of Glauber's salts near by.

Grense-Jakobselv (grěn'sů-yä'kôpsělv″), Lapp fishing village in Sor-Varanger canton, Finnmark co., NE Norway, on USSR border, on Barents Sea of Arctic Ocean, at mouth of small Jakobs R. 19 mi. ENE of Kirkenes, 18 mi. NW of Pechenga.

Grenville, county (□ 463; pop. 15,989), SE Ont., on the St. Lawrence and on N.Y border; ⊙ Brockville (in Leeds co.); chief town, Prescott.

Grenville, village (pop. 737), S Que., on Ottawa R., opposite Hawkesbury; mining (magnesite, feldspar, graphite), limestone quarrying; dairying.

Grenville, town (pop. 1,194), E Grenada, B.W.I., 9 mi. NE of St. George's, on Grenville Bay; cacao, coconuts. Also called La Baye.

Grenville. 1 Village (pop. 102), Union co., NE N.Mex., on headstream of North Canadian R. and 26 mi. WNW of Clayton; alt. c.6,000 ft. Shipping point for ranch and farm products. Grenville Caves near by. **2** Town (pop. 207), Day co., NE S.Dak., 11 mi. NNE of Webster, near Waubay L.; trade center of agr. community.

Grenville, Cape, on NE coast of Cape York Peninsula, N Queensland, Australia, in Coral Sea; forms N tip of entrance to Temple Bay; 11°58'S

143°15'E. Joined to mainland by low, swampy isthmus.

Grenville, Mount (10,200 ft.), SW B.C., in Coast Mtns., 120 mi. NNW of Vancouver; 50°51'N 124°16'W.

Grenville Channel (55 mi. long, 1 mi. wide), W B.C., separating Pitt Isl. from mainland.

Grenzach (grĕnts'äkh), village (pop. 2,762), S Baden, Germany, at S foot of Black Forest, on the Rhine (Swiss border) and 4 mi. S of Lörrach; mfg. (chemicals, paper, textiles). Winegrowing. Has mineral spring.

Grenzhausen, Germany: see HÖHR-GRENZHAUSEN.

Grenzmark Posen–West Prussia (grĕnts'märk pō'zŏn), Ger. *Grenzmark Posen–Westpreussen*, former province (□ 2,978; pop. 332,485) of NE Prussia, Germany; ⊙ Schneidemühl. Established 1922, it covered those sections of former provs. of Posen and West Prussia remaining in Germany after 1919. Reduced 1937 to dist. status and inc. in Pomerania.

Gréoux-les-Bains (grāōō'-lā-bē'), village (pop. 650), Basses-Alpes dept., SE France, on Verdon R. and 29 mi. SW of Digne; thermal resort.

Greppin (grĕ'pĭn), village (pop. 9,937), in former Prussian Saxony prov., central Germany, after 1945 in Saxony-Anhalt, 3 mi. N of Bitterfeld; lignite mining; aniline-dye mfg.

Gresford, town and parish (pop. 1,502), E Denbigh, Wales, 3 mi. NNE of Wrexham; coal. Has 15th-cent. church.

Gresham (grĕ'shŭm). **1** Village (pop. 267), York co., SE central Nebr., 15 mi. NE of York; dairying, livestock, grain. **2** Town (pop. 3,049), Multnomah co., NW Oregon, 10 mi. E of Portland, near Columbia R. in fruitgrowing region; dairying, fruit packing. Inc. 1905. Has co. fair. **3** Village (pop. 427), Shawano co., E central Wis., 10 mi. NW of Shawano; lumbering, agr.

Gresik (grĕsĕk') or **Grisee** (grĭsē'), town (pop. 25,621), NE Java, Indonesia, on Madura Strait, opposite Madura, 8 mi. NW of Surabaya; fishing center. Tanning, textile milling, shipbuilding, sawmilling, rattan weaving. Noted for its mfg. of silver and gold ornaments. Oil fields near by. Chinese colony was established here in early 14th cent. Gresik was important port during 15th and 16th cent. An early Moslem center, town has grave (1419) of one of first Moslem preachers in Indonesia. Also spelled Grissee, Grise, and Geresik.

Grésivaudan or **Graisivaudan** (both: gräzēvōdā'), Alpine glacial trough in Isère dept., SE France, forming section of Isère R. valley, bet. Chambéry trough (N) and Grenoble (S), bordered by the Grande Chartreuse (W) and Belledonne (E) ranges; c.30 mi. long, 2–4 mi. wide. Intensive agr. (tobacco, corn, wheat, wine, truck; peaches and chestnuts). Industry powered by hydroelectric power in Villard-Bonnot area (metallurgy, chemical works, paper mills) and at GRENOBLE. Towns, roads and railroad built along valley slopes to avoid flash floods. Lower Isère R. valley bet. Grenoble and Voiron sometimes called Bas-Grésivaudan.

Gressenich (grĕ'sŭnĭkh), village (pop. 5,879), in former Prussian Rhine Prov., W Germany, after 1945 in North Rhine-Westphalia, 3 mi. E of Stolberg. Lead and zinc mined near by.

Gressier (grĕsyā'), village (1950 pop. 401), Ouest dept., S Haiti, on Gonâve Channel, 10 mi. W of Port-au-Prince; sugar cane, bananas.

Gressk (gryĕsk), village (1939 pop. over 500), NW Bobruisk oblast, Belorussian SSR, 11 mi. NNW of Slutsk; grain, potatoes.

Gressoney (grĕsônā'), Alpine valley, Val d'Aosta region, NW Italy; extends 22 mi. S from slopes of Monte Rosa to Val d'Aosta; watered by LYS RIVER. Contains resort villages of Gressoney-Saint-Jean (pop. 135) and Gressoney-la-Trinité (pop. 43; hydroelectric plant; gold mines).

Gresten (grĕ'stŭn), village (pop. 1,257), SW Lower Austria, 12 mi. E of Waidhofen an der Ybbs; rail terminus; power station; mfg. (cutlery, scythes).

Grésy-sur-Isère (gräzē'-sür-ēzâr'), agr. village (pop. 461), Savoie dept., SE France, in Isère R. valley and 9 mi. SW of Albertville, on S slope of the Bauges.

Greta (grē'tŭ), town (pop. 1,135), E New South Wales, Australia, 25 mi. NW of Newcastle; coal-mining center.

Gretna, village (pop. 482), SE Man., 65 mi. SSW of Winnipeg, on N. Dak. border; grain elevators, flour mills.

Gretna, Scotland: see GRETNA GREEN.

Gretna (grĕt'nŭ), village (pop. 330), SE Tasmania, 22 mi. NW of Hobart and on Derwent R.; cattle, oats, legumes.

Gretna. **1** Town (pop. 385), Gadsden co., NW Fla., 6 mi. WNW of Quincy. **2** City (pop. 13,813), ⊙ Jefferson parish, SE La., on W bank of the Mississippi, opposite New Orleans (ferries); industrial and residential suburb; mfg. (cottonseed oil, alcohol, wood and petroleum products, insecticides, fertilizer). Founded in early-19th cent. as Mechanicsham; merged 1913 with McDonoghville. **3** Village (pop. 438), Sarpy co., E Nebr., 17 mi. WSW of Omaha; flour; livestock, grain, dairy produce. **4** Town (pop. 803), Pittsylvania co., S Va., 12 mi. S of Altavista; trading point in tobacco-growing area; grain milling.

Gretna Green, agr. village in Gretna parish (pop. 2,857), S Dumfries, Scotland, on Sark R. near its mouth on Solway Firth, and 8 mi. E of Annan, on English border. Famous for many years as place for runaway marriages, performed in Old Blacksmith's Shop, Gretna Hall, and Old Toll Bar. After 1856, however, law required 21-day residence in Scotland by one of parties before marriage license was issued. Just S, on English border, is town of Gretna, established as munitions center in First World War.

Greussen (groi'sŭn), town (pop. 5,004), Thuringia, central Germany, 10 mi. SSE of Sondershausen, in sugar-beet-growing and market-gardening region; sugar refining, brewing; mfg. of agr. machinery, ceramics, sausages.

Greve (grā'vĕ), town (pop. 1,650), Firenze prov., Tuscany, central Italy, on Greve R. (small affluent of the Arno) and 14 mi. S of Florence; wine making.

Greveldiun-Capelle, 's, Netherlands: see 's GREVELDUIN-CAPELLE.

Grevelingen, Netherlands: see KRAMMER.

Greven (grā'vŭn), village (pop. 8,460), in former Prussian prov. of Westphalia, NW Germany, after 1945 in North Rhine-Westphalia, on the Ems and 10 mi. N of Münster; textile mfg.

Grevena (grĕvĕnä'), town (pop. 4,392), Kozane nome, Macedonia, Greece, on right tributary of the Aliakmon and 24 mi. SW of Kozane; road center; wheat, tobacco; dairy products; timber, charcoal. Also spelled Ghrevena.

Grevenbroich (grā"vŭnbroikh'), town (pop. 13,066), in former Prussian Rhine Prov., W Germany, after 1945 in North Rhine-Westphalia, on the Erft and 8 mi. SE of Rheydt; rail junction; coal-powered aluminum plant.

Grevenmacher (grā'vŭnmäkh"ŭr), old town (pop. 2,503), ⊙ Grevenmacher dist., E Luxembourg, on Moselle R. and 15 mi. ENE of Luxembourg city, on Ger. border; vineyards; sawmills; market center for agr. (wheat, pulse) region; dolomite quarrying.

Grevesmühlen (grā'vŭsmü"lŭn), town (pop. 10,670), Mecklenburg, N Germany, 12 mi. W of Wismar; grain market; sawmilling, malting, cement mfg., distilling.

Grey, county (□ 1,708; pop. 57,160), S Ont., on Georgian Bay of L. Huron; ⊙ Owen Sound.

Grey, New Zealand: see GREYMOUTH.

Greyabbey or **Grey Abbey** (grā ă'bē), agr. village (district pop. 1,361), NE Co. Down, Northern Ireland, on E shore of Strangford Lough, 7 mi. ESE of Newtownards; flax, oats; sheep. There are remains of abbey founded 1193.

Greybull (grā'bŏŏl), town (pop. 2,262), Big Horn co., N Wyo., on Bighorn R., at mouth of Greybull R., just W of Bighorn Mts., and 7 mi. N of Basin; oil-refining point in livestock and irrigated agr. region; sugar beets, beans, dairy products, flour, timber. Settled 1904, inc. 1912.

Greybull River, NW Wyo., rises in Absaroka Range, flows c.70 mi. NE, past Meeteetse, to Bighorn R. at Greybull.

Grey Eagle, village (pop. 400), Todd co., central Minn., 12 mi. SE of Long Prairie, in lake region; resort; dairy products.

Greyerz, Switzerland: see GRUYÈRE.

Grey Islands, group of 2 islands off NE N.F., in the Atlantic. Largest isl. is Bell Isl. or Grey Isl. South (□ 34; pop. 52), 50 mi. N of Cape St. John; 50°44'N 55°35'W; 10 mi. long, 7 mi. wide; site of lighthouse (SW) and radio station. N of Bell Isl., 7 mi., is Groais Isl. (grā) or Grey Isl. North (□ 16); 7 mi. long, 4 mi. wide; site of radio station. Both isls. are hilly, rising to over 500 ft.

Greylock, Mount (3,491 ft.), highest point in Mass., in the Berkshires, 5 mi. SSW of North Adams. Has 2 roads to summit, where there are a lodge and a war memorial beacon. Crossed by Appalachian Trail. The surrounding Mt. Greylock State Reservation (8,400 acres) has noted ski trails and campgrounds; includes Saddle Ball mtn. (3,300 ft.), Mt. Fitch (3,140 ft.), and Mt. Williams (2,900 ft.).

Greymouth (grā'mŭth), borough (pop. 8,375) and port, ⊙ Grey co. (□ 1,579; pop. 4,706), on W coast of S.Isl., New Zealand, at mouth of Grey R., and 20 mi. NNE of Hokitika. Exports coal, gold, timber. Nationalized coal mines. Greymouth borough is in, but independent of, Grey co.

Grey River, W S.Isl., New Zealand, rises in Spenser Mts., flows 75 mi. SW, past Ngahere, to Tasman Sea at Greymouth.

Greys River, W Wyo., rises in E Lincoln co., flows N bet. Salt River and Wyoming ranges, and W to Snake R. just E of Idaho line; c.60 mi. long.

Greystone, village, Bulawayo prov., S central Southern Rhodesia, in Matabeleland, 60 mi. E of Bulawayo; tobacco, corn; livestock.

Greystones, Gaelic *Cloch Liath*, town (pop. 1,640), NE Co. Wicklow, Ireland, on the Irish Sea, 4 mi. SSE of Bray; fishing port and popular resort.

Greytown, borough (pop. 1,176), S N.Isl., New Zealand, 40 mi. NE of Wellington; sawmills, dairy plants, fruit canneries.

Greytown, Nicaragua: see SAN JUAN DEL NORTE, town.

Greytown, town (pop. 4,661), S central Natal, U. of So. Afr., on Umvoti R. and 40 mi. NNE of Pietermaritzburg; agr. center (cattle, sheep, wattle bark). Louis Botha b. near by.

Grez-en-Bouère (grĕz'-ā-bwâr'), village (pop. 509), Mayenne dept., W France, 18 mi. SE of Laval; flour milling; tile mfg.

Grezzana (grĕtsä'nä), village (pop. 1,223), Verona prov., Veneto, N Italy, in Monti Lessini, 5 mi. N of Verona; wine making. Marble quarries near by.

Gribbell Island (□ 96; 16 mi. long, 2-10 mi. wide), W B.C., in Douglas Channel (N arm of Hecate Strait) just N of Princess Royal Isl.

Gribingui River (grēbĭng-gē'), headstream of Shari R. in central and N Ubangi-Shari territory, Fr. Equatorial Africa, rises 60 mi. ENE of Dekoua, flows c.175 mi. WNW and N, past Fort-Crampel, to join Bamingui R. 100 mi. W of N'Délé, forming the Shari.

Gridley. **1** City (pop. 3,054), Butte co., N central Calif., in Sacramento Valley, 17 mi. N of Yuba City; ships fruit, grain, livestock; fruit canning, rice milling. Inc. 1905. **2** Village (pop. 817), McLean co., central Ill., 18 mi. NNE of Bloomington, in agr. area; makes cheese. **3** City (pop. 360), Coffey co., SE Kansas, 25 mi. SSE of Emporia, in livestock and grain region. Oil fields near by.

Griekwastad, U. of So. Afr.: see GRIQUATOWN.

Gries (grēs), suburb of Bolzano, Bolzano prov., Trentino-Alto Adige, N Italy; health resort.

Griesbach (grēs'bäkh), village (pop. 2,026), Lower Bavaria, Germany, 15 mi. SW of Passau; brewing, flour and lumber milling, tanning.

Griesbach, Bad, Germany: see BAD GRIESBACH.

Griesheim (grēs'hīm). **1** Town (pop. 8,035), S Hesse, W Germany, in former Starkenburg prov., 4 mi. W of Darmstadt; mfg. of iron, steel, and metal goods, and of chemicals; brickmaking. **2** W industrial district (pop., including settlement of Neufeld, 12,565) of Frankfurt, Hesse, W Germany, on right bank of the canalized Main; mfg. (chemicals, machinery).

Grieskirchen (grēs'kĭrkhŭn), town (pop. 4,221), central Upper Austria, 22 mi. WSW of Linz; market center (grain); breweries. Old city hall.

Gries Pass (grēs), minor crossing (8,080 ft.) on Swiss-Italian border, in Lepontine Alps, 6 mi. ESE of Münster; 46°27'N. Links upper Rhone valley of Valais and upper Toce valley of Piedmont.

Griessen Pass, Austria: see HOCHFILZEN.

Griffen, town (pop. 3,241), Carinthia, S Austria, 20 mi. ENE of Klagenfurt; wheat, potatoes, fruit.

Griffeth Mountain, peak (11,500 ft.) in Front Range, Clear Creek co., N central Colo.

Griffin. **1** City (pop. 13,982), ⊙ Spalding co., W central Ga., 35 mi. SSE of Atlanta, in fertile agr. area (cotton, truck, fruit). Textile mfg. center (broadcloth, corduroy, velveteen, towels, hosiery, underwear, uniforms); canning (vegetables, peaches), sawmilling. State agr. experiment station near by. Laid out 1840, inc. 1843. **2** Town (pop. 249), Posey co., SW Ind., near the Wabash, 25 mi. NW of Evansville, in agr. and petroleum area.

Griffin, Lake (c.9 mi. long, 2 mi. wide), Lake co., central Fla.; linked by canal with near-by L. Eustis, it is part of lake system drained by Oklawaha R.

Griffing Park, town (pop. 2,096), Jefferson co., SE Texas, N suburb of Port Arthur. Inc. 1929.

Griffiss Air Force Base, N.Y.: see ROME.

Griffith, town (pop. 5,727), S central New South Wales, Australia, 310 mi. SE of Broken Hill; rail junction; agr. center (grapes, rice, citrus fruit).

Griffith, town (pop. 4,470), Lake co., extreme NW Ind., 8 mi. SW of Gary, near Ill. line; castings, paper products, photographic specialties. Settled 1891, inc. 1904.

Griffith Island (11 mi. long, 7 mi. wide), central Franklin Dist., Northwest Territories, in Barrow Strait, off S Cornwallis Isl.; 74°35'N 95°25'W.

Griffithstown, England: see PANTEG.

Griffithville, town (pop. 207), White co., central Ark., 11 mi. SSE of Searcy.

Grifte (grĭf'tŭ), village (pop. 1,675), in former Prussian prov. of Hesse-Nassau, W Germany, after 1945 in Hesse, near confluence of Eder and Fulda rivers, 7 mi. SSW of Kassel; flour products.

Grifton (grĭf'tŭn), town (pop. 510), Pitt co., E N.C., 17 mi. S of Greenville.

Grigan, Marianas Isls.: see AGRIHAN.

Griggs, county (□ 714; pop. 5,460), E central N.Dak.; ⊙ Cooperstown. Wheat-growing area drained by Sheyenne R.; machinery, livestock, dairy products, grain. Formed 1881.

Griggsville, city (pop. 1,119), Pike co., W Ill., 26 mi. W of Jacksonville, in agr. area (corn, wheat, livestock, poultry; dairy products). Inc. 1878.

Grignan (grēnyä'), village (pop. 604), Drôme dept., SE France, near the Lez, 12 mi. WNW of Nyons; brickworks. Has 16th-cent. castle (recently restored) of counts of Grignan. Mme. de Sévigné buried here.

Grignano Polesine (grēnyä'nô pôlä'zēnĕ), village (pop. 1,579), Rovigo prov., Veneto, N Italy, 3 mi. SW of Rovigo.

Grignasco (grēnyä'skô), village (pop. 2,012), Novara prov., Piedmont, N Italy, near Sesia R., 22 mi. NW of Novara, in grape-growing region; rail junction; furniture, ceramics.

Grigno (grē'nyō), village (pop. 978), Trento prov., Trentino-Alto Adige, N Italy, 9 mi. ESE of Borgo, in Valsugana.

Grignols (grēnyôl'), village (pop. 878), Gironde dept., SW France, in the Landes, 12 mi. SW of Marmande; lumber, cattle.

Grignon, France: see THIVERVAL.

Grigny (grēnyē'), town (pop. 3,861), Rhône dept., E central France, on right bank of Rhone R. and 10 mi. S of Lyons; mfg. of chemicals, soap, chinaware, and macaroni.

Grigoriopol or **Grigoriopol'** (grēgŭrēô'pŭl), town (1926 pop. 8,876), E Moldavian SSR, on left bank of Dniester R. and 23 mi. ENE of Kishinev; wine center; flour milling.

Grijalva River (grēhäl'vä), S Mexico, rises in headstreams (including Cuilco R.) in Sierra Madre of W Guatemala, flows c.400 mi. NW and N, through Chiapas and Tabasco, to Gulf of Campeche 6 mi. NNW of Alvaro Obregón, after converging with main arm of Usumacinta R. Navigable for c.60 mi. upstream and for large inland stretches; serves, with its branches, as main line of communication in the forested plains. Sometimes called Río Grande de Chiapa, Chiapa R., or Mezcalapa R. (měskälä'pä) in its middle course. Named for Juan de Grijalva, who discovered it in 1518.

Grijota (grēhō'tä), town (pop. 1,225), Palencia prov., N central Spain, on Canal of Castile and 4 mi. NW of Palencia; cereals, wine, sheep.

Grijpskerk (khrīps'kĕrk), town (pop. 1,349), Groningen prov., N Netherlands, 11 mi. WNW of Groningen; dairying; summer resort. Former site of Reitsema and Aikema castles. Dutch defeated here (1581) by Spaniards. Sometimes Grypskerk.

Grik (grēk), town (pop. 1,212), N Perak, Malaya, near upper Perak R., 45 mi. NE of Taiping; road terminus in forested dist.; rice, rubber.

Grillby (grĭl'bü"), village (pop. 396), Uppsala co., E Sweden, 5 mi. E of Enkoping; grain, potatoes, stock.

Grim, Cape, NW Tasmania, in Indian Ocean, near Hunter Isls. in Bass Strait; 40°41'S 144°43'E.

Grimailov or **Grimaylov** (grēmī'lŭf), Pol. *Grzymałów* (gzhĭmä'wōof), village (1931 pop. 4,084), E Ternopol oblast, Ukrainian SSR, on right tributary of Zbruch R. and 13 mi. ENE of Terebovlya; rail spur terminus; flour milling, brick mfg., distilling. Has old palace.

Grimaldi (grēmäl'dē). **1** Town (pop. 2,229), Cosenza prov., Calabria, S Italy, 10 mi. SSW of Cosenza; wine, olive oil. **2** Resort village (pop. 319), Imperia prov., Liguria, NW Italy, on the Riviera, 4 mi. W of Ventimiglia, just across the border from Menton, France. Near by are famous caverns, inhabited in Paleolithic times, where remains of Cro-Magnon man and of a Negroid type were found in 1901–02. The caverns and the prehistoric mus., where part of the abundant archaeological finds (fossilized fauna, artifacts, steatite statuettes) were deposited, were damaged in the Second World War.

Grimari (grēmärē'), village, central Ubangi-Shari, Fr. Equatorial Africa, 40 mi. W of Bambari; cotton weaving. Has agr. school and experimental cotton plantations. Quarantine station, R.C. and Protestant missions.

Grimaud (grēmō'), village (pop. 580), Var dept., SE France, at E foot of Monts des Maures, 6 mi. W of Saint-Tropez, near the Mediterranean; winegrowing. Feldspar quarries. Has Romanesque church and ruined castle.

Grimaylov, Ukrainian SSR: see GRIMAILOV.

Grimbergen (grĭm'bĕr-khŭn), agr. village (pop. 7,496), Brabant prov., central Belgium, 6 mi. N of Brussels. Premonstratensian abbey; mental institution. Formerly spelled Grimberghen.

Grimes, county (□ 801; pop. 15,135), E central Texas; ⊙ Anderson. Bounded W by Navasota and Brazos rivers. Diversified agr. (cotton, corn, grain, watermelons, other fruit and truck); cattle, hogs, sheep, goats; extensive dairying. Timber (mainly pine), hunting, fishing. Includes game preserve. Formed 1846.

Grimes, town (pop. 582), Polk co., central Iowa, 12 mi. NW of Des Moines; canning (corn, beans, pumpkin).

Grimesland (grīmz'lŭnd), town (pop. 414), Pitt co., E N.C., near Tar R., 11 mi. ESE of Greenville.

Grimisay, Scotland: see GRIMSAY.

Grimm, Russian SFSR: see KAMENSKI.

Grimma (grĭ'mä), town (pop. 14,310), Saxony, E central Germany, on the Mulde and 16 mi. ESE of Leipzig; rail junction; metalworking, paper milling, machinery mfg. Has 13th-cent. church; school founded 1550. Porphyry quarries near by. Just SE are ruins of Nimbschen convent where Katharina von Bora was a nun prior to her marriage to Luther.

Grimmen (grĭ'mŭn), town (pop. 8,298), in former Prussian Pomerania prov., N Germany, after 1945 in Mecklenburg, 14 mi. S of Stralsund; agr. market (grain, sugar beets, potatoes, stock). Has early-Gothic church and old town gates.

Grimnitz Lake (grĭm'nĭts), Brandenburg, E Germany, just N of Joachimsthal; 3 mi. long.

Grimsaker (grĭms"ō'kûr), Swedish *Grimsåker*, village (pop. 1,124), Kopparberg co., central Sweden, on West Dal R. and 60 mi. W of Falun; tanning, stock raising. Includes Myckelbyn (mü'kŭlbün") village.

Grimsay or **Grimisay** (both: grĭm'sā), island (pop. 278), Outer Hebrides, Inverness, Scotland, bet. North Uist and Benbecula; 3½ mi. long, 1½ mi. wide.

Grimsby (grĭmz'bē), town (pop. 2,331), S Ont., on L. Ontario, 15 mi. ESE of Hamilton; mfg. of electrical equipment, stoves, furniture, leather; fruit canning, distilling, basket weaving, dairying; in fruitgrowing region. Resort.

Grimsby, county borough (1931 pop. 92,459; 1951 census 94,527), Parts of Lindsey, N Lincolnshire, England, on Humber R. near its mouth and 15 mi. SE of Hull; 53°35'N 0°4'W; largest Br. fishing port, with extensive docks begun 1849; terminal of passenger services to the Continent. Shipbuilding, metalworking, brewing, and industries allied with the fishing industry. The port handles mainly fish, coal, and timber. Has 13th-cent. parish church. Richard I held a parliament here. In county borough (W) is paper-milling town of West Marsh.

Grimsel Lake (grĭm'zŭl), Ger. *Grimselsee* (grĭm'zŭlzā"), in Bernese Alps, S central Switzerland, 11 mi. SSE of Innertkirchen; □ 1, alt. 6,262 ft., max. depth 328 ft. Formed by 2 dams on upper Aar R., which supply water to Oberhasli hydroelectric works. Grimsel Road passes Grimsel Hospice (NE), follows lake's E shore, and crosses **Grimsel Pass** (7,159 ft.; on border of Bern and Valais cantons), long a route bet. upper Aar and Rhone valleys.

Grimsey (grēms'ā"), Icelandic *Grímsey*, island (3 mi. long), N Iceland, in Greenland Sea, within Arctic Circle; 66°33'N 18°W. Fisheries.

Grimshaw, village (pop. 287), W Alta., near Peace R., 13 mi. W of Peace River; lumbering, mixed farming, dairying, wheat.

Grimstad (grĭm'stä), city (pop. 2,336), Aust-Agder co., S Norway, port on the Skagerrak, on railroad and 26 mi. NE of Kristiansand. Has excellent, well-protected harbor, site in 19th cent. of timber exporting and shipbuilding, and home of a large fleet before steamship era. Fruitgrowing center; production of wines, juices, preserves. Ibsen wrote his 1st play, *Catilina*, here.

Grimsvotn (grēms'vû"tŭn), Icelandic *Grímsvötn*, volcanic region, SE Iceland, in W part of Vatnajokull; 64°27'N 17°20'W; rises to 5,659 ft. Craters are filled with water; eruptions are accompanied by floods.

Grindavik (grĭn'tävēk"), Icelandic *Grindavík*, officially *Járngerðarstaðahverfi í Grindavík*, fishing village (pop. 330), Gullbringu og Kjosar co., SW Iceland, on S coast of Reykjanes Peninsula, 25 mi. SW of Reykjavik.

Grindelwald (grĭn'dŭlvält"), town (pop. 2,916), Bern canton, S central Switzerland, at foot of the Schreckhorn and Wetterhorn, on Black Lütschine R. and 9 mi. ESE of Interlaken; year-round resort noted for mtn. climbing; alt. 3,400 ft. The Upper and Lower Grindelwald glaciers are SE.

Grindheim (grĭn'hām), village and canton (pop. 774), Vest-Agder co., SW Norway, 30 mi. NW of Kristiansand; molybdenite mines. Sometimes called Grindum.

Grindsted (grĭns'dĕdh), town (pop. 2,989), Ribe amt, central Jutland, Denmark, 27 mi. NE of Esbjerg; chemical plant.

Grindstone. **1** Village, Jefferson co., N.Y.: see GRINDSTONE ISLAND. **2** Village (pop. 1,366), Fayette co., SW Pa., 10 mi. NNW of Uniontown.

Grindstone Island (5 mi. long, 4 mi. wide), in the Gulf of St. Lawrence, E Que., one of the Magdalen Isls., 60 mi. N of Prince Edward Isl.; 47°23'N 61°55'W. Étang du Nord (W) is chief town. Fisheries. Wolf Isl., narrow spit of land, extends NE to Grosse Isl.

Grindstone Island, Jefferson co., N N.Y., one of largest of the Thousand Isls., in the St. Lawrence, at Ont. line, just N of Clayton, N.Y.; c.6 mi. long, 1–2½ mi. wide. Grindstone village (resort), and Canoe Point and Picnic Point state parks are here.

Grindum, Norway: see GRINDHEIM.

Gringley-on-the-Hill, village and parish (pop. 724), N Nottingham, England, 12 mi. NE of Worksop; brick- and tileworks. Has 15th-cent. church.

Grinnell (grĭnĕl'). **1** City (pop. 6,828), Poweshiek co., central Iowa, 50 mi.ENE of Des Moines; corn cannery, shoe and glove factories; dairy products, packed poultry, cosmetics, concrete blocks, wood and metal products. Seat of Grinnell Col. (founded 1855; coeducational; nonsectarian). Founded 1854 by Josiah Bushnell Grinnell, and inc. 1865. **2** City (pop. 364), Gove co., NW Kansas, 12 mi. E of Oakley, in grain and cattle area.

Grinnell, Cape (grĭnĕl'), SW Devon Isl., E Franklin Dist., Northwest Territories, on Wellington Channel; 75°10'N 92°15'W.

Grinnell Island, Northwest Territories: see DEVON ISLAND.

Grinnell Land, NE Franklin Dist., Northwest Territories, NE part of ELLESMERE ISLAND, bet. Grant Land (N), Greely Fjord, (W), Ellesmere Land (S), and Kennedy Channel and Kane Basin (E).

Grinnell Peninsula, Northwest Territories: see DEVON ISLAND.

Griñón (grēnyōn'), town (pop. 852), Madrid prov., central Spain, on railroad and 16 mi. SSW of Madrid; cereals, truck produce, grapes.

Grinsdale, village and parish (pop. 161), NW Cumberland, England, on Eden R. and 3 mi. NW of Carlisle; mfg. of synthetic fertilizer; dairy farming.

Grintavec, peak, Yugoslavia: see SAVINJA ALPS.

Grintouz, Yugoslavia: see SAVINJA ALPS.

Grinzing (grĭnt'sĭng), section of Döbling dist. of Vienna, Austria, at S foot of the Wiener Wald, 4 mi. N of city center.

Grip (grēp), village and canton (pop. 224), More og Romsdal co., W Norway, on a tiny isl. in North Sea, 10 mi. NW of Kristiansund; fisheries.

Gripsholm (grĭps-hôlm'), castle, Sodermanland co., E Sweden, on S shore of L. Malar, 30 mi. WSW of Stockholm, just S of Mariefred. Built in 14th cent., it was rebuilt (16th cent.) by Gustav Vasa and became a favorite royal residence. Has noted collection of paintings.

Griqualand East (grē'kwŭlănd, grĭ'kwŭ–), district (□ 6,602; total pop. 360,775; native pop. 347,085) of the TRANSKEIAN TERRITORIES, E Cape Prov., U. of So. Afr., bounded by Tembuland (S), Pondoland (SE), Natal Prov. (NE), and Basutoland (N); center near 30°40'S 29°E; ⊙ Kokstad. Drakensberg range extends along NW border of dist. Dairying, stock raising, wool production are chief occupations. Largely a Native Reserve, dist. is under administration of United Transkeian Territories General Council.

Griqualand West, district (□ 15,077; pop. 144,725), NE Cape Prov., U. of So. Afr., S of Bechuanaland, bounded by Orange R. (S), Langeberg range (W), and Orange Free State border (E); ⊙ Kimberley. Other towns are Griquatown, Delport's Hope, Postmasburg, Barkly West, Douglas, and Warrenton. Bisected by Vaal R.; W part of dist. lies on Kaap Plateau. Mining (diamonds, manganese, galena) and agr. (stock, grain, fruit, dairying). Formerly the territory of Griqua chief Waterboer, it became crown colony 1873; annexed to Cape Colony 1880.

Griquatown, Afrikaans *Griekwastad* (khrē'kwästät"), town (pop. 1,822), N central Cape Prov., U. of So. Afr., in Asbestos Mts., 95 mi. W of Kimberley, in Griqualand West; alt. 3,960 ft.; in mining (diamonds, asbestos, galena) and agr. (wool, mohair, grain) region. Has remains of fort; scene of siege of British troops in Griqua War. Griqua chief Waterboer buried here. Airfield. In South African War town changed hands several times.

Grise, Indonesia: see GRESIK.

Grisek (grēsĕk'), village (pop. 742), NW Johore, Malaya, on Muar R. and 15 mi. NE of Bandar Maharani; rubber plantations.

Grishino, Ukrainian SSR: see KRASNOARMEISKOYE, Stalino oblast.

Grishkovtsy (grĕshkôf'tsē), town (1939 pop. over 500), S Zhitomir oblast, Ukrainian SSR, 5 mi. NE of Berdichev.

Grisignana (grēzēnyä'nä), Slovenian *Grožnjan* (grôzh'nyän), village (pop. 1,537), S Free Territory of Trieste, 4 mi. SE of Buie. Placed 1947 under Yugoslav administration.

Gris-Nez, Cape (grē-nā') [Fr.,=gray nose], anc. *Itium Promontorium*, headland of N France (Pas-de-Calais dept.), on narrowest part of Strait of Dover (21 mi. SSE of South Foreland; closest Fr. point to English coast), 13 mi. SW of Calais; 50°52'N 1°35'E. Lighthouse atop cliff (c.160 ft. high).

Grisolia (grēzô'lyä), village (pop. 2,449), Cosenza prov., Calabria, S Italy, 7 mi. SSE of Scalea; wine.

Grisolles (grēzôl'), village (pop. 1,497), Tarn-et-Garonne dept., SW France, on the Garonne Lateral Canal and 14 mi. SSW of Montauban; produces brooms, brushes, hosiery.

Grisons (grēzō'), Ger. *Graubünden* (grou'bündŭn), Ital. *Grigioni* (grējō'nē), Romansh *Grishun* (grē'-shōōn), canton (□ 2,746; 1950 pop. 136,050), E Switzerland; largest canton; ⊙ CHUR. German, Italian, and Romansh are spoken. Contains, or is bordered by, peaks and glaciers of the Rhaetian, Lepontine, and Glarus Alps. Pastures and forests in the highlands; meadows, cultivated fields, and some orchards (N) and vineyards (S) in the valleys; maize (N) and other cereals grown. Hydroelectric system is well developed along Poschiavino R. and in the Prätigau. Numerous resorts in the ENGADINE and elsewhere (notably DAVOS and AROSA). Swiss Natl. Park is near Ital. border (E). Industry is comparatively insignificant and diversified. Once part of Roman Rhaetia, Grisons had a turbulent history. Its name was derived from the Gray League, one of 3 medieval factions which became allied as the Swiss Confederation; later (1803) it became a Swiss canton.

Grissee, Indonesia: see GRESIK.

Griswold (grĭz'wōld), village (pop. estimate 200), SW Man., near Assiniboine R., 24 mi. WSW of Brandon; grain, stock.

Griswold (grĭz'wŭld). **1** Town (pop. 5,728), including Jewett City borough (pop. 3,702), New London co.; SE Conn., on Quinebaug R. and 7 mi. NE of Norwich; textiles, agr. (poultry, fruit, truck). Includes villages of Glasgo (glăs'gō) and Pachaug (pă'chŏg"), on Pachaug Pond (3 mi. long). State forest here. Settled c.1690, inc. 1815; Jewett City inc. 1895. **2** Town (pop. 1,149), Cass co., SW Iowa, 14 mi. SSW of Atlantic; shipping center for corn and livestock area; mfg. (feed, oil burners). State park near by. Inc. 1880.

Griswoldville, Mass.: see COLRAIN.

Grita, La, Venezuela: see LA GRITA.

Grita, Sierra de la (syĕ'rä dā lä grē'tä), section of Sierra del Merendón in Santa Bárbara dept., W Honduras; extends c.40 mi. SW-NE parallel to Guatemala border; forms divide bet. Motagua and Chamelecón rivers; rises to 4,495 ft.

Gritsev (grē'tsyĭf), town (1926 pop. 4,247), NE Kamenets-Podolski oblast, Ukrainian SSR, 15 mi. SSE of Shepetovka; sugar beets, wheat.

Griva (grē'vä), Lettish *Grīva,* Ger. *Griwa,* city (pop. 5,546), SE Latvia, in Zemgale, on left bank of the Western Dvina, opposite Daugavpils; flour milling, oilcloth mfg.

Grivegnée (grēvùnyā'), town (pop. 18,970), Liége prov., E Belgium, on Ourthe R. and 2 mi. SSE of Liége; blast furnaces, metal foundries; textiles.

Grivita (grē'vētsä), Rum. *Grivița,* outer NW urban suburb (1948 pop. 39,917) of Bucharest, S Rumania; industrial establishments, notably vegetable and fruit canneries. Major railroad repair and construction shops.

Griwa, Latvia: see GRIVA.

Grizebeck, England: see KIRKBY IRELETH.

Grizzana (grētsä'nä), village (pop. 307), Bologna prov., Emilia-Romagna, N central Italy, 19 mi. SSE of Bologna; marble working.

Grizzly Mountain, Colo.: see SAWATCH MOUNTAINS.

Grizzly Peak (13,738 ft.), SW Colo., in San Juan Mts., bet. Dolores and San Juan counties.

Grmec Mountains or **Grmech Mountains** (both: gùrmĕch'), Serbo-Croatian *Grmeč Planina,* in Dinaric Alps, NW Bosnia, Yugoslavia; extend c.35 mi. NW-SE, bet. Una and Sana rivers. Highest point, Crni Vrh [Serbo-Croatian,=black peak] (5,261 ft.) is 8 mi. ENE of Bosanski Petrovac.

Groais Island, N.F.: see GREY ISLANDS.

Grobbendonk (grô'bùndôngk), town (pop. 4,140), Antwerp prov., NE Belgium, on Little Nethe R. and 15 mi. E of Antwerp; market gardening. Has remains of 17th-cent. castle; parts of Roman villa and camp have been excavated here.

Grobina or **Grobinya** (grō'bēnyä), Lettish *Grobiņa,* Ger. *Grobin,* city (pop. 1,074), W Latvia, in Kurzeme, 6 mi. E of Liepaja; sugar beets, potatoes; flour milling. Has castle ruins. Chartered 1695.

Groby, agr. village and parish (pop. 1,122), central Leicester, England, 5 mi. WNW of Leicester; granite quarrying and processing. Just NW is Bradgate Park, with ruins of old mansion. Lady Jane Grey b. here.

Gröbzig (grûp'tsĭkh), town (pop. 3,155), in former Anhalt state, central Germany, after 1945 in Saxony-Anhalt, 7 mi. SW of Köthen, in coal-mining region.

Grochow (grô'khōōf), Pol. *Grochów,* suburb of Warsaw, Warszawa prov., E central Poland, on right bank of the Vistula and 5 mi. E of city center. Scene (1831) of Rus. victory over Pol. insurgents.

Grocka or **Grotska** (both: grôts'kä), village, N central Serbia, Yugoslavia, on the Danube and 16 mi. SE of Belgrade.

Grodek, Poland: see RADKOW.

Grodek Jagiellonski, Ukrainian SSR: see GORODOK, Lvov oblast.

Grodekovo (grŭdyĭkô'vŭ), town (1926 pop. 4,066), SW Maritime Territory, Russian SFSR, on branch of Trans-Siberian RR and 50 mi. NNW of Voroshilov; USSR-China frontier station, near Manchurian border; metalworks, flour mill; grain, soybeans, rice.

Grödig (grû'dĭkh), town (pop. 2,906), Salzburg, W Austria, 5 mi. S of Salzburg; cement works, brewery.

Gröditz (grû'dĭts), town (pop. 5,406), Saxony, E central Germany, 10 mi. NE of Riesa, in lignite-mining region; mfg. of steel products.

Grodkow (grôt'kōōf), Pol. *Grodków,* Ger. *Grottkau* (grôt'kou), town (1939 pop. 4,867; 1946 pop. 2,953) in Upper Silesia, after 1945 in Opole prov., SW Poland, 16 mi. N of Neisse (Nysa); agr. market (grain, sugar beets, potatoes, livestock); woodworking, brick mfg. Gothic church.

Grödnertal, Italy: see GARDENA, VAL.

Grodno (grôd'nù), oblast (□ 5,000; 1946 pop. estimate 800,000), W Belorussian SSR; ⊙ Grodno. In lowland on Pol. border (W); drained by Neman R. Humid continental climate (short summers). Extensive agr. (rye, oats, barley, potatoes, flax); livestock. Coniferous and deciduous forests. Industries based on agr. (sugar refining at Skidel, food processing and preserving, tanning, distilling, woolen weaving) and timber (sawmilling, veneering). Mfg. in main urban centers (Grodno, Lida, Volkovysk). Formed (1944) out of W part of Belostok oblast.

Grodno, Lith. *Gardinas* (gärdĭ'näs), city (1931 pop. 49,818), ⊙ Grodno oblast, W Belorussian SSR, on Neman R. (landing) and 155 mi. W of Minsk, 85 mi. SW of Vilna, near Pol. border; 53°42'N 25°51'E. Rail junction; lumber- and grain-trading center; mfg. (agr. machinery, motorcycles, bicycles, fine cloth, leather goods, cigarettes, paper, tarboard, matches, glass, pottery, bricks), agr. processing (grain, flax, vegetables, hops, tobacco), sawmilling; chalk quarrying. Phosphorite deposits near by (SW). Has teachers col., ruins of 14th-cent. castle, and several old churches. Old Rus. settlement, known in 12th cent. Successively captured by Lithuanians, Teutonic Knights, and Poles. Was ⊙ Lithuania in 14th cent.; developed as trading center in 16th cent.; 2d partition of Poland signed here in 1793. Passed (1795) from Poland to Russia; was ⊙ Grodno govt. until it reverted (1921) to Poland. During Second World War, under administration of East Prussia; ceded to USSR in 1945. Jewish pop. largely exterminated during Second World War.

Grodovka (grô'dùfkŭ), town (1926 pop. 1,776), central Stalino oblast, Ukrainian SSR, in the Donbas, on railroad and 7 mi. SE of Krasnoarmeiskoye; coal mining. Village of Grodovka (1926 pop. 3,244) is 4 mi. NE.

Grodzisk (grô'jĭsk). **1** or **Grodzisk Wielkopolski** (vyĕlkôpôl'skē), Ger. *Grätz* (grĕts), town (1946 pop. 6,015), Poznan prov., W Poland, 26 mi. WSW of Poznan; rail junction; machinery mfg., brewing, distilling, sawmilling. **2** or **Grodzisk Mazowiecki** (mäzôvyĕts'kē), Rus. *Grodisk* (grô'dyĭsk), town (pop. 14,610), Warszawa prov., E central Poland, on railroad and 19 mi. WSW of Warsaw; chemical, metal (notably aluminum), textile, and leather industries; flour milling; brickworks. Large radio station.

Grodzyanka (grŭdzyän'kŭ), town (1939 pop. over 500), NE Bobruisk oblast, Belorussian SSR, 17 mi. NNE of Osipovichi; sawmilling; peat.

Groede (khrōō'dù), town (pop. 1,105), Zeeland prov., SW Netherlands, on Flanders mainland, 2 mi. WSW of Breskens; wood products, roofing and ornamental tiles.

Groenlo (khrōōn'lō), town (pop. 5,182), Gelderland prov., E Netherlands, 7 mi. NW of Winterswijk; tanneries, textile mills, knitting mills; shoes, beer, bricks. Coal deposits near by. Also Groenloo.

Groesbeck (grōs'bĕk), city (pop. 2,182), ⊙ Limestone co., E central Texas, near Navasota R., 36 mi. E of Waco; market, trade center in cotton, grain, poultry, dairying area; cotton ginning; brick, lumber. State park, with old Fort Parker (restored), is just N.

Groesbeek (khrōōz'bāk), village (pop. 4,674), Gelderland prov., E Netherlands, 5 mi. SE of Nijmegen; border station near Ger. frontier. Much damaged (1944–45) in Second World War.

Groitsy, Poland: see GROJEC.

Groitzsch (groich), town (pop. 7,213), Saxony, E central Germany, on Schnauder R., near its mouth on the White Elster, and 14 mi. SSW of Leipzig; mfg. of machinery, shoes, plastics, cardboard; metalworking.

Groix (grwä), island (pop. 4,334) in Bay of Biscay, off Brittany coast (Morbihan dept.), W France, 8 mi. SSW of Lorient (ferry); 5 mi. long, 2 mi. wide; tuna fishing and canning. Megalithic monuments and sea caves on rugged S shore. Groix village (pop. 644) and Port-Tudy on N shore.

Grojec (grōō'yĕts), Pol. *Grójec,* Rus. *Groitsy* (groi'tsē), town (pop. 6,841), Warszawa prov., E central Poland, 26 mi. SSW of Warsaw; mfg. (cement, tiles, agr. tools, linen, flour). Before Second World War, pop. was 50% Jewish.

Grombalia (grômbälyä'), town (pop. 5,043), ⊙ Grombalia or Cape Bon dist. (□ 1,115; pop. 211,434), NE Tunisia, near base of Cape Bon Peninsula, on Tunis-Gabès RR and 22 mi. SE of Tunis; winegrowing center and agr. market (livestock, fruits, wine); mfg. (flour paste, olive oil, building materials).

Grömitz (grû'mĭts), village (pop. 4,381), in Schleswig-Holstein, NW Germany, on Lübeck Bay, 6 mi. NE of Neustadt; Baltic seaside resort.

Gronau (grō'nou). **1** Town (pop. 5,172), in former Prussian prov. of Hanover, NW Germany, after 1945 in Lower Saxony, on the Leine and 8 mi. SW of Hildesheim; food processing (canned goods, dairy products, beer, spirits); mfg. of chemicals, toys, leather goods. **2** Town (pop. 20,455), in former Prussian prov. of Westphalia, NW Germany, after 1945 in North Rhine-Westphalia, 18 mi. W of Rheine; rail junction and customs station on Dutch border; textile center (linen, cotton, garments). First mentioned 1365. Chartered 1898.

Grondines or **Saint Charles des Grondines** (sē shärl dā grōdēn'), village (pop. 435), S central Que., on the St. Lawrence and 16 mi. WSW of Donnacona; dairying; stock raising.

Grone (grō'nù), village (pop. 4,142), in former Prussian prov. of Hanover, W Germany, after 1945 in Lower Saxony, just W of Göttingen; printing.

Grönenbach (grû'nùnbäkh), village (pop. 3,265), Swabia, SW Bavaria, Germany, 8 mi. SSE of Memmingen; textile mfg.; summer resort. Has Gothic church with Romanesque crypt, and 16th-cent. castle.

Grong (grông), village (pop. 334; canton pop. 1,979), Nord-Trondelag co., central Norway, on Nams R. and 25 mi. E of Namsos; railroad junction for Nordland railway and branch line to Namsos. Lumbering, fresh-water fishing, hunting near by. Slate quarry. Grong Mines are located on Tunn L., 45 mi. NE, at Gjersvika. Niobium deposits in region.

Grongar Hill (grōn'gär), elevation (c.400 ft.), central Carmarthen, Wales, near Towy R., 4 mi. W of Llandilo; celebrated in poem by John Dyer, who lived near by.

Groningen (grō'nĭng-ùn), town (pop. 144), ⊙ Saramacca dist. (□ 9,873; pop. 13,437), N Du. Guiana, on left bank of Saramacca R. and 21 mi. W of Paramaribo; cacao, coffee, rice.

Gröningen (grû'nĭng-ùn), town (pop. 4,269), in former Prussian Saxony prov., central Germany, after 1945 in Saxony-Anhalt, on the Bode and 8 mi. ENE of Halberstadt; paper milling; agr. market (sugar beets, grain, vegetables).

Groningen (grō'nĭng-ùn, Du. khrō'nĭng-ùn), province (□ 866.7; pop. 449,862), N Netherlands; ⊙ Groningen. Bounded by North Sea (N), Eems R. estuary (NE), Germany (E), Drenthe prov. (S), Friesland prov. (W). Belt of fertile soil near coast; reclaimed fenland area and peat bogs inland. Drained by numerous canals, including Eems Canal, the Hoendiep, and the Winschoter Diep. Cattle raising, dairying; agr. (potatoes, vegetables, mustard seeds, sugar beets). Mfg. of agr. machinery, potato flour (centered on Ter Apel area). Chief towns: Groningen, Winschoten, Delfzijl (port). In 1040, came into possession of bishops of Utrecht; constant struggles thereafter bet. citizens and their rulers. Prov. subscribed (1579) to Union of Utrecht.

Groningen, city (pop. 132,021), ⊙ Groningen prov., N Netherlands, at junction of Eems Canal and the Hoendiep, 34 mi. E of Leeuwarden; 53°13'N 6°34'E. Rail junction; airport at Eelde, 6 mi. S. Grain and cattle market; sugar-refining center; mfg. (chemicals, synthetic fertilizer, paints, leather, textiles, packaging materials, furniture, potato flour). Univ. (founded 1614), 15th-cent church (*Martinikerk*), 16th-cent. guardhouse, 17th-cent. church (*Nieuwe Kerk*), mus. Painters Jozef Israëls and Hendrik Willem Mesdag b. here. Site (A.D. 48) of a Roman camp; a major city in 12th cent., providing ships for the Crusades; joined Hanseatic League in 1284; subscribed (1579) to Union of Utrecht. Taken (1580) by Spaniards; recaptured (1594) for States-General by Maurice of Nassau; besieged (1672) by Bishop von Galen of Münster in behalf of Louis XIV.

Gronnedal (grû'nùdäl), Dan. *Grønnedal,* naval base in S Greenland, on W coast, near Ivigtut; 61°15'N 48°7'W.

Gronsund (grûn'sōōn), Dan. *Grønsund,* strait (min. width ½ mi.), Denmark, bet. Moen and Bogo (N) and Falster (S) isls., joining Smaalandsfarvand strait to Baltic Sea.

Gronvollfoss (grûn'vôlfôs), Nor. *Grønvollfoss,* falls (72 ft.) on Tinne R. in Telemark co., S Norway, 8 mi. N of Notodden; hydroelectric plant.

Groom, town (pop. 678), Carson co., extreme N Texas, in the Panhandle, c.40 mi. E of Amarillo; trade center for agr., livestock, dairying area.

Groomsport (grōōmz'pôrt), fishing village (district pop. 1,773), NE Co. Down, Northern Ireland, on the Irish Sea at mouth of Belfast Lough, 3 mi. ENE of Bangor.

Grootbrakrivier, U. of So. Afr.: see GREAT BRAK RIVER.

Groote Eylandt (grōōtĭ'lùnd), largest island (□ 950) in Gulf of Carpentaria, 25 mi. off NE coast of Northern Territory, Australia; 38 mi. long, 25 mi. wide; rises to 600 ft. Barren, rocky. Mission station, aboriginal reservation.

Groote Nete, Belgium: see GRANDE NÈTHE RIVER.

Groote Schuur (krōō'tù skür') [Afrikaans,=great barn], estate, SW Cape Prov., U. of So. Afr., on SSE outskirts of Cape Town, near Rondebosch. Formerly residence of Cecil Rhodes, it is official residence of Union premier. On estate, presented to Union by Rhodes, are bldgs. of Univ. of Cape Town and Rhodes Memorial.

Grootfontein (grōōtfōntān'), town (pop. 1,550), N South-West Africa, 220 mi. NNE of Windhoek; 19°34'S 18°7'E; alt. 4,792 ft.; rail terminus; agr. center; in mining region (copper, lead, zinc, vanadium). Airfield. Hoba West farm, 12 mi. W, is site (19°35'S 17°56'E) of largest known meteorite (c.60 tons), discovered 1920, now national monument. E of town is Okavango Native Territory, a reserve (□ c.12,300) set aside for the use of several tribes.

Groot Fortuin, Indonesia: see SIBERUT.

Groot-Scheepvaart Canal, Netherlands: see EEMS CANAL.

Gropello Cairoli (grôpĕl'lô kīrô'lē), village (pop. 2,860), Pavia prov., Lombardy, N Italy, 8 mi. W of Pavia; saws.

Grosio (grô'zyô), village (pop. 2,667), Sondrio prov., Lombardy, N Italy, in the Valtellina, on Adda R. and 21 mi. ENE of Sondrio, in stock-raising region. Bell foundry; hydroelectric plant.

Gros Islet (grōs), fishing village (pop. 730), NW St. Lucia, B.W.I., 6 mi. NNE of Castries, on fertile plain (limes, tropical fruit, sugar). Adjoining S, at Gros Islet Bay, site was leased (1940) for 99 years to U.S. as naval air base.

Groslay (grōlā′), town (pop. 3,573), Seine-et-Oise dept., N central France, an outer N suburb of Paris, just E of Montmorency, 9 mi. from Notre Dame Cathedral; truck-gardening center (supplies Paris). Mfg. of agr. implements.

Gros Morne (grō môrn′), mountain (2,666 ft.), in Long Range Mts., W N.F., near Bonne Bay, 45 mi. N of Corner Brook; 49°36′N 57°48′W; highest point in Newfoundland.

Gros-Morne, town (1950 census pop. 2,254), Artibonite dept., N Haiti, 16 mi. N of Gonaïves; coffee- and fruitgrowing. Manganese deposits near.

Gros-Morne, town (pop. 1,252), N central Martinique, 8 mi. NNE of Fort-de-France; sugar-cane and pineapple growing; rum distilling, fruit canning.

Grosne River (grōn), Saône-et-Loire dept., E central France, rises in the Monts du Beaujolais near Monsol, flows c.40 mi. NNE, past Cluny, to the Saône 7 mi. SE of Chalon-sur-Saône.

Grosnez Point (grō′nā), promontory at NW extremity of Jersey, Channel Isls., 8 mi. NW of St. Helier; 49°15′N 2°14′W. Site of ruins of 14th-cent. Grosnez Castle.

Gros Pate, mountain (2,115 ft.), in Long Range Mts., NW N.F., 35 mi. S of Point Riche.

Gros Piton, St. Lucia, B.W.I.: see PITONS, THE.

Gross, Grosse, Grosser, Grosses, in German names: for features beginning thus and not found here, see under main part of name; e.g., for Gross Lauteraarhorn, see LAUTERAARHORN, GROSS.

Gross, village (pop. 29), Boyd co., N Nebr., 14 mi. E of Butte, near S.Dak. line and Missouri R.

Grossa, Isola, Yugoslavia: see DUGI OTOK.

Grossachsenheim (grōs″säk′sŭnhīm), town (pop. 2,345), N Württemberg, Germany, after 1945 in Württemberg-Baden, 3 mi. W of Bietigheim; wine. Has 15th-cent. church, 15th–16th-cent. castle.

Grossalmerode (grōs′äl″mürō′dŭ), village (pop. 4,579), in former Prussian prov. of Hesse-Nassau, W Germany, after 1945 in Hesse, 12 mi. ESE of Kassel; mfg. of melting pots. Fire clay quarried near by.

Grossalsleben (grōs″äls′lā″bŭn), town (pop. 1,841), in former Anhalt exclave, central Germany, after 1945 in Saxony-Anhalt, 4 mi. S of Oschersleben; sugar beets, grain, vegetables.

Grossandelfingen, Switzerland: see ANDELFINGEN.

Grossarl (grōs′ärl), town (pop. 2,273), Salzburg, W central Austria, on N slope of Hohe Tauern, 12 mi. S of Bischofshofen; summer resort (alt. 3,018 ft.).

Grossauheim (grōs″ou′hīm), village (pop. 9,573), in former Prussian prov. of Hesse-Nassau, W Germany, after 1945 in Hesse, on right bank of the canalized Main and 2 mi. S of Hanau; mfg. of electrical goods.

Gross Aulowönen, Russian SFSR: see KALINOVKA.

Gross Beeren (grōs″ bā′rŭn), village (pop. 2,459), Brandenburg, E Germany, 12 mi. SSW of Berlin city center. Scene (Aug., 1813) of victory of Prussians under Bülow over Napoleon's forces under Oudinot.

Gross-Bitesch, Czechoslovakia: see VELKA BITES.

Grossbliederstroff (grōsblēdĕrstrôf′), Ger. *Grossblittersdorf* (grōs′blĭtŭrs-dôrf), town (pop. 2,190), Moselle dept., NE France, on left bank of Saar R., 6 mi. SE of Forbach, on Saar border; cattle shipping.

Grossbottwar (grōs″bôt′vär), town (pop. 2,796), N Württemberg, Germany, after 1945 in Württemberg-Baden, 8 mi. NE of Ludwigsburg; wine.

Grossbreitenbach (grōs″brī′tŭnbäkh), town (pop. 4,361), Thuringia, central Germany, in Thuringian Forest, 9 mi. SE of Ilmenau; mfg. of china, glass, light bulbs, optical and precision instruments; woodworking.

Gross Bülten (grōs″ bül′tŭn), village (pop. 2,436), in former Prussian prov. of Hanover, NW Germany, after 1945 in Lower Saxony, 4 mi. SSW of Peine; limonite mining.

Grossdeuben (grōs″doi′bŭn), village (pop. 3,598), Saxony, E central Germany, on the Pleisse and 7 mi. S of Leipzig, in lignite-mining region.

Gross Dirschkeim, Russian SFSR: see DONSKOYE.

Grosse Île (grōs ēl′), island (2 mi. long), S Que., in the St. Lawrence, 30 mi. ENE of Que.; quarantine station.

Grosse Island (grōs) (3 mi. long, 2 mi. wide), in the Gulf of St. Lawrence, E Que., one of the Magdalen Isls., 80 mi. NNE of Prince Edward Isl.; 47°37′N 61°31′W. Wolfe Isl., narrow spit of land, extends SW to Grindstone Isl.

Grosse Isle (grōs″ ēl′), Wayne co., SE Mich., isl. in Detroit R. just S of Wyandotte; c.8 mi. long, 1½ mi. wide; bridges to Mich. bank. Residential area. Has U.S. naval base and an airport. Post office name is Grosse Ile.

Grosseislingen, Germany: see EISLINGEN.

Grosse Karras Mountains (grō′sŭ kä′räs), S South-West Africa, extend 40 mi. NE-SW, 50 mi. SE of Keetmanshoop; rise to 7,224 ft. on Schroffenstein. Also called Karas Mts.

Grosse Laaber, Germany: see GREAT LAABER RIVER.

Grosse Mühl River (grō′sŭ mül′), mostly in N Upper Austria, rises in the Bohemian Forest in SE Germany, flows c.30 mi. SE and S, past Aigen and Rohrbach, to the Danube just below hydroelectric station at Partenstein.

Grossenehrich (grō″sŭnā′rĭkh), town (pop. 1,433), Thuringia, central Germany, 9 mi. SSW of Sondershausen; grain, tobacco, sugar beets, fruit.

Grossenhain (grō′sŭnhīn), town (pop. 17,708), Saxony, E central Germany, 20 mi. NW of Dresden; woolen and paper milling; mfg. of agr. machinery, glass.

Grossenkneten (grō″sŭn-kŭnā′tŭn), village (commune pop. 8,459), in Oldenburg, NW Germany, after 1945 in Lower Saxony, 14 mi. S of Oldenburg city; mfg. of building materials.

Grossenmeer (grō′sŭnmâr″), village (commune pop. 7,477), in Oldenburg, NW Germany, after 1945 in Lower Saxony, 9 mi. NNE of Oldenburg city, in peat region. Commune is called Moorriem (mōr′rēm″).

Grossenzersdorf (grōsĕnt′sŭrsdôrf), outer E district (□ 83; pop. 29,573) of Vienna, Austria, on left bank of the Danube. Formed (1938) through incorporation of 19 towns, including Aspern, Breitenlee, Essling, and Grossenzersdorf (pop. 2,594; 8 mi. E of city center; wine).

Grosse Pointe (grōs point′), city (pop. 6,283), Wayne co., SE Mich., 9 mi. NE of downtown Detroit, on L. St. Clair; residential suburb. Inc. as village 1879, as city 1934.

Grosse Pointe Farms, residential city (pop. 9,410), Wayne co., SE Mich., suburb 10 mi. NE of downtown Detroit, on L. St. Clair. Alger House, a branch of Detroit Inst. of Arts, is here. Inc. as village 1893, as city 1949.

Grosse Pointe Park, residential village (pop. 13,075), Wayne co., SE Mich., 8 mi. NE of downtown Detroit, on L. St. Clair. Inc. 1907.

Grosse Pointe Shores, village (pop. 1,032), Wayne and Macomb counties, SE Mich., 11 mi. NE of Detroit, on L. St. Clair. Inc. 1911.

Grosse Pointe Woods, residential village (pop. 10,381), Wayne co., SE Mich., 11 mi. NE of downtown Detroit, near L. St. Clair. Inc. 1926 as Lochmoor; name was changed 1939.

Grosser Arber, Germany: see GREAT ARBER.

Grosser Beerberg, Germany: see BEERBERG.

Grosser Belchen, France: see GUEBWILLER, BALLON DE.

Grosser Burgberg, Germany: see BAD HARZBURG.

Grosser Ettersberg (grō′sŭr ĕ′tŭrsbĕrk), mountain (1,558 ft.), Thuringia, central Germany, 5 mi. NW of Weimar. It was site of Buchenwald, notorious Nazi concentration camp. Ettersburg castle (N slope) was scene (1779) of 1st performance of original version of Goethe's *Iphigenie auf Tauris.*

Grosser Feldberg (fĕlt′bĕrk), highest peak (2,887 ft.) of the Taunus, W Germany, 6 mi. WNW of Oberursel.

Grosser Ölberg, Germany: see SIEBENGEBIRGE.

Grosser Priel, Austria: see TOTES GEBIRGE.

Grosse Tete (grōs″ tĕt′), village (pop. 548), Iberville parish, SE central La., 15 mi. W of Baton Rouge.

Grossetete, Bayou (bī′ō), SE central La., rises in Pointe Coupee parish, flows SE c.36 mi. to Bayou Plaquemine 8 mi. below Plaquemine; navigable.

Grosseto (grôs-sā′tô), province (□ 1,738; pop. 185,-801), Tuscany, central Italy, bordering on Tyrrhenian Sea; ⊙ Grosseto. Comprises most (90%) of the MAREMMA.

Grosseto, town (pop. 15,988), ⊙ Grosseto prov., Tuscany, central Italy, near Ombrone R., 40 mi. SSW of Siena; 42°46′N 11°7′E. Agr. center (cereals, wine, olive oil, wool) on reclaimed land, which until mid-19th cent. was a malarial swamp. Mfg. (agr. machinery, pumps, refrigerators, straw hats). Bishopric. Has cathedral and palace (severely damaged) with archaeological mus. Near by are hot mineral springs of Bagno Roselle and ruined walls of anc. Etruscan city of Russellae. Badly damaged by heavy air bombing (1943–44) in Second World War.

Grossevichi (grô′syĭvĕchē), village (1939 pop. over 500), S Khabarovsk Territory, Russian SFSR, port on Sea of Japan, 75 mi. S of Sovetskaya Gavan; fish canning.

Grosse Vils, Germany: see GREAT VILS RIVER.

Grossgartach (grōs″gär′täkh), village (pop. 3,458), N Württemberg, Germany, after 1945 in Württemberg-Baden, 4 mi. W of Heilbronn; wine.

Gross-Gerau (grōs″-gā′rou), town (pop. 8,292), S Hesse, W Germany, in former Starkenburg prov., 8 mi. NW of Darmstadt; rail junction; mfg. of machinery, vehicles, textiles; metal- and woodworking, sugar refining, food processing.

Gross Gleidingen (grōs″ glī′dĭng-ŭn), village (pop. 601), in Brunswick, NW Germany, after 1945 in Lower Saxony, 4 mi. SW of Brunswick; rail junction.

Grossglockner (grōs′glôknŭr) or **Glockner,** highest peak (12,460 ft.) of Austria and of the Hohe Tauern, near borders of Carinthia, Salzburg, and East Tyrol provinces. First ascended 1800. Feeds great PASTERZE glacier.

Gross Görschen (grōs″ gûr′shŭn), village (pop. 731), in former Prussian Saxony prov., central Germany, after 1945 in Saxony-Anhalt, 13 mi. SW of Leipzig, 4 mi. SE of Lützen. Scene (May, 1813) of battle in which Napoleon defeated Prusso-Russian forces. Scharnhorst killed here. Action sometimes called battle of Lützen.

Grosshansdorf-Schmalenbeck (grōs″häns′dôrf-shmä′lŭnbĕk), village (pop. 5,328), in Schleswig-Holstein, NW Germany, 14 mi. NE of Hamburg city center; flour milling.

Grossheidekrug, Russian SFSR: see VZMORYE, Kaliningrad oblast.

Gross-Hessen, Germany: see HESSE.

Gross Hettingen, France: see HETTANGE-GRANDE.

Grosshorn (grōs′hôrn), peak (12,353 ft.) in Bernese Alps, S central Switzerland, 5 mi. S of Mürren.

Gross Ilsede (grōs″ ĭl′zŭdŭ), village (pop. 2,746), in former Prussian prov. of Hanover, NW Germany, after 1945 in Lower Saxony, 3 mi. S of Peine; in limonite-mining and oil region.

Grosskamsdorf, Germany: see KAMSDORF.

Grosskayna (grōs″kī′nä), village (pop. 4,122), in former Prussian Saxony prov., central Germany, after 1945 in Saxony-Anhalt, 6 mi. SW of Merseburg; lignite mining. Power station.

Grosskorbetha (grōs″kôr′bā″thä), village (pop. 3,434), in former Prussian Saxony prov., central Germany, after 1945 in Saxony-Anhalt, on the Saxonian Saale and 5 mi. NE of Weissenfels; rail junction; quartzite mining. Formerly called Corbetha.

Gross Lafferde (grōs″ lä′fŭrdŭ), village (pop. 3,491), in former Prussian prov. of Hanover, NW Germany, after 1945 in Lower Saxony, 6 mi. S of Peine, in limonite-mining region.

Grosslaufenburg, Switzerland: see LAUFENBURG.

Gross-Meseritsch, Czechoslovakia: see VELKE MEZIRICI.

Grossmoyeuvre, France: see MOYEUVRE-GRANDE.

Grossörner (grōs″ûr′nŭr), village (pop. 5,874), in former Prussian Saxony prov., central Germany, after 1945 in Saxony-Anhalt, at E foot of the lower Harz, on the Wipper and 3 mi. SW of Hettstedt; copper-slate mining and smelting; copper and brass processing.

Grossostheim (grōs″ōst′hīm), village (pop. 5,557), Lower Franconia, NW Bavaria, Germany, 5 mi. SW of Aschaffenburg; textile and pottery mfg.

Gross Ottersleben (grōs″ ō′tŭrslā″bŭn), residential town (pop. 16,009), in former Prussian Saxony prov., central Germany, after 1945 in Saxony-Anhalt, 4 mi. SW of Magdeburg.

Grossotto (grôs-sôt′tô), town (pop. 2,066), Sondrio prov., Lombardy, N Italy, in the Valtellina, on Adda R. and 20 mi. ENE of Sondrio; hydroelectric plant.

Grosspetersdorf (grōs″pā′tŭrsdôrf), village (pop. 1,797), Burgenland, E Austria, 14 mi. W of Szombathely, Hungary; grain, vineyards.

Grossraming (grōs′rämĭng), town (pop. 3,244), E Upper Austria, on the Enns and 12 mi. SE of Steyr; scythes.

Gross Räschen (grōs″ rĕ′shŭn), town (pop. 11,895), Brandenburg, E Germany, in Lower Lusatia, 18 mi. SW of Cottbus; lignite mining; mfg. (electrical equipment, glass, tiles).

Gross Reken (grōs″ rā′kŭn), village (pop. 5,556), in former Prussian prov. of Westphalia, NW Germany, after 1945 in North Rhine-Westphalia, 8 mi. ESE of Borken; cattle.

Grossröhrsdorf (grōs″rûrs′dôrf), town (pop. 8,285), Saxony, E central Germany, in Upper Lusatia, 15 mi. NE of Dresden; textile milling (cotton, linen, ribbon); mfg. of plastics.

Grossrosseln (grōs″rô′sŭln), town (pop. 4,372), SW Saar, on Rossel R. (Fr. border), opposite Petite-Rosselle, in the Warndt, 3 mi. S of Völklingen; coal mining.

Gross Salze, Poland: see WIELICZKA.

Gross-Schlatten, Rumania: see ABRUD.

Gross Schönau (grōs″ shû′nou), town (pop. 8,299), Saxony, E central Germany, in Upper Lusatia, 7 mi. W of Zittau; frontier station on Czechoslovak border, opposite Varnsdorf; textile center (cotton, wool, linen, silk); machinery mfg. Noted for table linen made here.

Gross Siegharts (grōs′ zēg′härts), town (pop. 2,694), NW Lower Austria, 27 mi. NNW of Krems; textiles (linens, rugs).

Gross Sittensen (grōs″ zĭ′tŭnzŭn), village (pop. 1,897), in former Prussian prov. of Hanover, NW Germany, after 1945 in Lower Saxony, on the Oste and 9 mi. E of Zeven; weaving, sawmilling.

Gross Skaisgirren, Russian SFSR: see BOLSHAKOVO.

Gross Strehlitz, Poland: see STRZELCE.

Gross-Umstadt (grōs″-ōōm′shtät), town (pop. 5,-313), S Hesse, W Germany, in former Starkenburg prov., on N slope of the Odenwald, 12 mi. E of Darmstadt; woodworking.

Grossvenediger (grōs″fŭnā′dĭgŭr), second-highest peak (12,008 ft.) of the HOHE TAUERN, S Austria, on Salzburg–East Tyrol border, 16 mi. W of the Grossglockner. Deposits of precious stones in Habach Valley on N slope. The Kleinvenediger (klīn′–) is 11,420 ft. high.

Grosswangen (grōs′väng″ŭn), agr. town (pop. 2,332), Lucerne canton, central Switzerland, 13 mi. WNW of Lucerne.

Grosswardein, Rumania: see ORADEA.

Gross Wartenberg, Poland: see SYCOW.

Grossweil (grōs′vīl), village (pop. 500), Upper Bavaria, Germany, at N foot of the Bavarian Alps, near the Kochelsee, 13 mi. SSE of Weilheim; lignite mining.

Gross-Zimmern (grōs″-tsĭ′mŭrn), village (pop. 5,807), S Hesse, W Germany, in former Starkenburg prov., on the Gersprenz and 8 mi. E of Darmstadt; grain.

Grostenquin (grōtăkē′), village (pop. 99), Moselle dept., NE France, 9 mi. S of Saint-Avold.

Grosulovo, Ukraine: see VELIKAYA MIKHAILOVKA.

Grosuplje (grô′so͞oplyĕ), village (pop. 1,924), central Slovenia, Yugoslavia, 10 mi. SSE of Ljubljana; rail junction. Until 1918, in Carniola.

Grosvenor Dale, Conn.: see THOMPSON.

Gros Ventre Range (grō vĕn′tŭr), in Rocky Mts. of NW Wyo., just E of Snake R. and Jackson Hole. Prominent points: Triangle Peak (11,525 ft.), Darwin Peak (11,645 ft.), Doubletop Peak (11,715 ft., highest in range). Includes part of Teton Natl. Forest.

Groton (grô′–, grō′–), agr. village and parish (pop. 318), S Suffolk, England, 4 mi. W of Hadleigh. John Winthrop, early governor of Connecticut, b. here. Just W is village of Edwardstone where the elder John Winthrop, governor of Massachusetts, was born.

Groton. 1 (grŏ′tŭn) Town (pop. 21,896), including Groton borough (pop. 7,036), New London co., SE Conn., on Long Isl. Sound, opposite New London, bet. Mystic R. (E) and the Thames (bridged here to New London, 1943). Builds submarines; mfg. (thread, wood and paper products), agr., fishing; resorts. U.S. submarine base, coast guard school on the Thames N of borough. Includes villages of West Mystic (pop. 2,362), where, in 1637, English defeated Pequot Indians, Noank (nō′ăngk) (pop. 1,149), and Old Mystic (partly in Stonington town). State school for deaf near by. Monument marks site of Fort Griswold (1775), lost to British in Revolution. Settled c.1650, inc. as town 1704, borough inc. 1903. **2** (grŏ′tŭn) Town (pop. 2,889), Middlesex co., N Mass., 14 mi. WSW of Lowell; paper, wood products, lumber; apples, dairying, poultry. Seat of famous Groton preparatory school. Settled and inc. 1655; destroyed in King Philip's War and later rebuilt. **3** (grŏ′tŭn) Town (pop. 105), Grafton co., W central N.H., 24 mi. NNW of Franklin; mica products. **4** (grŏ′tŭn, grô′–) Village (pop. 2,150), Tompkins co., W central N.Y., in Finger Lakes region, 12 mi. NE of Ithaca; mfg. (typewriters, wood and food products); agr. (dairy products; truck, hay). Inc. 1860. **5** (grō′tŭn) City (pop. 1,084), Brown co., NE S.Dak., 20 mi. E of Aberdeen; trade center for rich agr. area; dairy products, livestock, poultry, grain. Settled 1881, inc. 1886. **6** (grŏ′tŭn) Town (pop. 712), including Groton village (pop. 435), Caledonia co., NE Vt., on Wells R. and 16 mi. SW of St. Johnsbury; lumber, granite; dairy products. Winter sports. Groton Pond (2.5 mi. long), in Groton State Forest, is resort.

Grotska, Yugoslavia: see GROCKA.

Grottaferrata (grôt″tăfĕr-rä′tä), village (pop. 2,089), Roma prov., Latium, central Italy, in Alban Hills, 2 mi. SW of Frascati; wine making, alcohol distilling, paper mfg. Noted for its Basilian monastery, founded 1004 and now a natl. monument.

Grottaglie (grôt-tä′lyĕ), town (pop. 14,457), Ionio prov., Apulia, S Italy, 11 mi. ENE of Taranto; pottery, wine, olive oil. Has school of ceramics.

Grottaminarda (grôt″tămēnär′dä), town (pop. 3,165), Avellino prov., Campania, S Italy, 18 mi. NE of Avellino.

Grottammare (–mä′rĕ), town (pop. 2,951), Ascoli Piceno prov., The Marches, central Italy, port on the Adriatic, 14 mi. SSE of Fermo; bathing resort; woolen mill. Pope Sixtus V b. here.

Grottau, Czechoslovakia: see HRADEK NAD NISOU.

Grotte (grôt′tĕ), town (pop. 8,704), Agrigento prov., S Sicily, 9 mi. NNE of Agrigento, in major sulphur-mining region. Many anc. grottoes near by.

Grotte di Castro (dē kä′strô), village (pop. 3,899), Viterbo prov., Latium, central Italy, near L. Bolsena, 13 mi. WSW of Orvieto.

Grotteria (grôt-tĕrē′ä), town (pop. 3,573), Reggio di Calabria prov., Calabria, S Italy, 7 mi. NNW of Siderno Marina, in agr. region (grapes, olives, citrus fruit).

Grottkau, Poland: see GRODKOW.

Grottoes, town (pop. 908), Augusta and Rockingham cos., NW Va., in S Shenandoah Valley, 15 mi. NE of Staunton; rayon and nylon mfg. Grand Caverns and other caves near by. Just E is Shenandoah Natl. Park.

Grottole (grôt′tôlĕ), village (pop. 3,188), Matera prov., Basilicata, S Italy, 13 mi. WSW of Matera, in agr. region (cereals, grapes, olives).

Grötzingen (grû′tsĭng-ŭn). **1** Village (pop. 5,045), N Baden, Germany, after 1945 in Württemberg-Baden, on the Pfinz and 4 mi. E of Karlsruhe; rail junction; mfg. of chemicals. Small petroleum well. Has 16th–17th-cent. castle. **2** Town (pop. 1,239), N Württemberg, Germany, after 1945 in Württemberg-Baden, 3.5 mi. W of Nürtingen; grain.

Grouin, Pointe du (pwĕt dü gro͞oē′), headland on the Gulf of Saint-Malo of the English Channel, in Ille-et-Vilaine dept., W France, 9 mi. NNE of Saint-Malo; 48°43′N 1°50′W. Oyster beds.

Grouse Creek Mountains (6–8,000 ft.), Box Elder co., NW Utah, near Nev. line; extend 30 mi. S from Raft River Mts.

Grouville (gro͞o′vĭl), agr. village and parish (1945 pop. 2,040), Jersey, Channel Isls., near Grouville Bay on E coast of isl., 3 mi. E of St. Helier.

Grouw (khrou), town (pop. 2,445), Friesland prov., N Netherlands, on Grouw Canal and 8 mi. S of Leeuwarden, on a small lake; mfg. (lumber products, oleomargarine); water-sports center.

Grouw Canal, Friesland prov., N Netherlands; extends 18 mi. SW-NE, bet. the WIJDE EE at Fonejacht (6 mi. ESE of Leeuwarden) and Sneek; crosses Sneek L. to connect with Scharster-Rhine Canal. Serves Grouw.

Grouz, Djebel (jĕ′bĕl gro͞oz′), mtn. range in easternmost Fr. Morocco, extending c.50 mi. W from Figuig oasis along Algerian border. Rises to 6,000 ft. Forms W outlier of Algeria's Saharan Atlas.

Grove (grō′vä), town (pop. 4,716), Pontevedra prov., NW Spain, in Galicia, fishing port on Arosa Bay, and 12 mi. WNW of Pontevedra; fish processing and shipping (shellfish), boatbuilding; cereals, wine.

Grove, town (pop. 928), Delaware co., NE Okla., 22 mi. E of Vinita, near L. of the Cherokees (W) and Mo. line (E); trade center and shipping point for agr. area (grain, corn, fruit); mfg. (flour, leather products, feed); timber.

Grove City. 1 Village (pop. 481), Meeker co., S central Minn., 8 mi. W of Litchfield; dairy products. **2** Village (pop. 2,339), Franklin co., central Ohio, 7 mi. SW of Columbus, in truck-gardening area. Beulah Park (horse racing) is here. **3** Borough (pop. 7,411), Mercer co., W Pa., 27 mi. E of Youngstown, Ohio; mfg. (engines, aluminum and steel products); bituminous coal, limestone. Grove City Col. is here. Settled 1798, laid out 1844, inc. 1883.

Grove Hill, farming town (pop. 1,443), ⊙ Clarke co., SW Ala., bet. Tombigbee and Alabama rivers, 65 mi. SW of Selma; woodworking, cotton ginning.

Groveland. 1 Village (pop. c.300), Tuolumne co., central Calif., in resort region of the Sierra Nevada, c.60 mi. ESE of Stockton. Founded in gold rush, when it was known as First Garrote. **2** Town (pop. 1,028), Lake co., central Fla., 29 mi. W of Orlando; citrus-fruit packing and canning. Inc. 1922. **3** Residential town (pop. 2,340), including Groveland village (pop. 1,230), Essex co., NE Mass., on Merrimack R. opposite Haverhill. Settled c.1639, inc. 1850.

Grovemont, N.C.: see SWANNANOA.

Grove Place, agr. station, Manchester parish, central Jamaica, on Kingston–Montego Bay RR and 50 mi. WNW of Kingston. Govt. maintains here an agr. school.

Groveport, village (pop. 1,165), Franklin co., central Ohio, 9 mi. SE of Columbus, in agr. area.

Grover. 1 Town (pop. 146), Weld co., NE Colo., on Crow Creek, near Wyo. line, and 40 mi. NE of Greeley; alt. 5,000 ft. Sugar beets, beans, wheat. **2** Town (pop. 535), Cleveland co., S N.C., 9 mi. SSE of Shelby, at S.C. line; mfg. of cotton goods. **3** Village, Jefferson co., Ohio: see TILTONSVILLE. **4** Village (pop. c.300), Lincoln co., W Wyo., near Salt R. and Idaho line, just W of Salt River Range, 5 mi. N of Afton; alt. 6,167 ft. Dairy products, grain, livestock.

Grover City, village (pop. 2,788, with adjacent Fair Oaks), San Luis Obispo co., SW Calif., on the Pacific, 8 mi. S of San Luis Obispo.

Grover Hill, village (pop. 463), Paulding co., NW Ohio, 18 mi. SSW of Defiance, in agr. area.

Groves, village (1940 pop. 2,474), Jefferson co., SE Texas; N suburb of Port Arthur.

Grovespring, town (pop. 104), Wright co., S central Mo., in the Ozarks, 40 mi. ENE of Springfield.

Groveton. 1 Village, Coos co., N.H.: see NORTHUMBERLAND. **2** City (pop. 805), ⊙ Trinity co., E Texas, c.30 mi. SW of Lufkin; trade, shipping point in agr., lumber, cattle area.

Groveville, village (pop. c.600), Mercer co., W N.J., on Crosswicks Creek and 5 mi. SE of Trenton; yarn, textiles, baskets.

Growler Mountains, Pima co., SW Ariz., W of Ajo; rise to 3,000 ft. in N half; extend into Organ Pipe Cactus Natl. Monument (S).

Groznjan, Free Territory of Trieste: see GRISIGNANA.

Grozny or **Groznyy** (grôz′nē), oblast (□ 12,700; 1946 pop. estimate 600,000) in S European Russian SFSR; ⊙ Grozny. On N slopes of the central Greater Caucasus; includes (from S to N) mtn. section cut by deep river gorges, fertile Sunzha R. plain (main agr. dist.), oil-bearing Sunzha and Terek ranges in dry watershed area, and dry Caspian steppe (N). Main economic asset of region is Grozny oil fields, with producing centers at Grozny, Goragorski, and Novogroznenski. Refining and mfg. of oil-drilling equipment at Grozny. Corn, winter wheat, fodder crops; orchards, vineyards, garden crops (canning at Grozny); soybeans and cotton along Terek R. Hog and dairy farming in lowlands, sheep and goat raising in mts. Main centers: Grozny, Kizlyar. Formed 1944 out of greater part of abrogated Chechen-Ingush Autonomous SSR and Kizlyar area. Pop. largely Russian and Ukrainian (S), Nogai Tatar (N).

Grozny or **Groznyy,** city (1939 pop. 172,468), ⊙ Grozny oblast, Russian SFSR, at N foot of the central Greater Caucasus, on Sunzha R. and 300 mi. NW of Baku, 900 mi. SSE of Moscow; 43°18′N 45°42′E. Center of major petroleum dist.; oil refining and cracking (production of gasoline, paraffin), mfg. of oil-drilling equipment, machinery, iron smelting, woodworking. Has oil-fed power station, petroleum research institute, teachers col. Petroleum fields 5 mi. NW of city in operation since 1893, those 4 mi. SE since 1913. Grozny is linked by oil pipe lines with Makhachkala, Goragorski, Tuapse, and Trudovaya (in Donets Basin). Founded 1818 as Rus. fortress in Caucasus conquest; became city in 1870. In Second World War, an objective of Ger. army, which was stopped, however, 50 mi. W.

Grozon (grôzō′), village (pop. 353), Jura dept., E France, 16 mi. NNE of Lons-le-Saunier; plaster works, cheese factory.

Grubbs (grŭbz). **1** Town (pop. 313), Jackson co., NE Ark., 12 mi. ENE of Newport and on Cache R. **2** Village, New Castle co., Del.: see ARDEN.

Grubeshov, Poland: see HRUBIESZOW.

Grubisno Polje (gro͞o′bĭshnô pô′lyĕ), Serbo-Croatian *Grubišno Polje*, village (pop. 2,780), N Croatia, Yugoslavia, 8 mi. N of Daruvar, at S foot of Bilo Gora, in Slavonia; rail terminus; local trade center.

Grudziadz (gro͞o′jōts), Pol. *Grudziądz*, Ger. *Graudenz* (grou′dĕnts), city (pop. 36,805), Bydgoszcz prov., N Poland, port on the Vistula and 40 mi. NE of Bydgoszcz. Rail junction; trade center; mfg. of chemicals, ceramics, bricks, glass, roofing materials, candy; sawmilling, flour milling, tanning, brewing, distilling, mineral-water bottling. Has castle, built by Teutonic Knights. Passed 1772 to Prussia; its fortress, built by Frederick II, was defended (1807) by Prussian general Courbière against Napoleon. City grew in 2d half of 19th cent., following building (1879) of railroad bridge over the Vistula. Grudziadz reverted to Poland in 1919. In Second World War, a battlefield in 1939; suffered relatively heavy damage.

Grues, Île aux (ēl ō grü′), or **Crane Island** (5 mi. long, 1 mi. wide), in the St. Lawrence, S Que., 35 mi. ENE of Quebec. Just NE is Île aux Oies.

Grugliasco (gro͞olyä′skô), village (3,195), Torino prov., Piedmont, NW Italy, 5 mi. W of Turin; woodworking tools, vermouth.

Gruinard Bay (grĭn′yŭrd), inlet of the Atlantic, NW Ross and Cromarty, Scotland, 10 mi. W of Ullapool; 5 mi. wide at mouth, extends 4 mi. inland. In it is Gruinard Isl., 1½ mi. long, c.1 mi. wide, rising to 345 ft.

Gruinart, Loch, Scotland: see ISLAY.

Gruissan (grüēsā′), village (pop. 1,095), Aude dept., S France, near the coast, 7 mi. SSE of Narbonne; fishing, winegrowing. Saltworks.

Grukhi, Russian SFSR: see LESOZAVODSKI, Kirov oblast.

Grulich, Czechoslovakia: see KRALIKY.

Grulla (grü′lü), village (pop. 1,013), Starr co., extreme S Texas, c.75 mi. WNW of Brownsville and on the Rio Grande; trade point in rich irrigated agr. area.

Grullo, El, Mexico: see EL GRULLO.

Grullo Bayou, Texas: see BAFFIN BAY.

Grumant City (gro͞o′mänt), Nor. *Grumantbyen* (–bü″ŭn), coal-mining settlement and port, W West Spitsbergen, Spitsbergen group, on S shore of Is Fjord, 11 mi. SW of Longyear City; 78°9′N 15°5′E. Mines operated by USSR; pop. (entirely Russian) in winter 1948–49 was c.350. In Second World War, settlement was destroyed (July, 1943) by German navy; later rebuilt.

Grumbkowkeiten; Grumbkowsfelde, Russian SFSR: see PRAVDINO.

Grumello del Monte (gro͞omĕl′lô dĕl môn′tĕ), village (pop. 2,188), Bergamo prov., Lombardy, N Italy, near Oglio R., 11 mi. SE of Bergamo; cement, buttons, wine. Has agr. school.

Grumo Appula (gro͞o′mô äp′po͞olä), town (pop. 9,987), Bari prov., Apulia, S Italy, 11 mi. SW of Bari; rail junction; flour.

Grumo Nevano (nĕvä′nô), town (pop. 8,146), Napoli prov., Campania, S Italy, adjacent to Frattamaggiore; mfg. (hosiery, packing boxes).

Grums (grŭms), village (pop. 2,268), Varmland co., W Sweden, on NW shore of L. Vaner, 14 mi. W of Karlstad; ironworks. Near by are Iron Age graves.

Grun or **Grun′** (gro͞on′yŭ), village (1926 pop. 5,456), SE Sumy oblast, Ukrainian SSR, 13 mi. WSW of Akhtyrka; wheat.

Grüna (grü′nä), village (pop. 7,990), Saxony, E central Germany, 6 mi. W of Chemnitz; hosiery and glove knitting, machinery mfg.

Gruna, Scotland: see OUT SKERRIES.

Grünau (grü′nou), town (pop. 2,379), S Upper Austria, 9 mi. SE of Gmunden; rail terminus; scythes.

Grünaue, Poland: see JANKAU.

Grunay, Scotland: see OUT SKERRIES.

Grünbach am Schneeberge (grün′bäkh äm shnā′bĕrgŭ), town (pop. 2,575), SE Lower Austria, 7 mi. NW of Neunkirchen; lignite mined near by.

Grünberg (grün′bĕrk), town (pop. 3,318), central Hesse, W Germany, in former Upper Hesse prov., 12 mi. E of Giessen; textile mfg., lumber milling.

Grünberg (grün′bĕrk) or **Zielona Gora** (zhĕlô′nä go͞o′rä), Pol. *Zielona Góra*, town (1939 pop. 26,076; 1946 pop. 15,738) in Lower Silesia, after 1945 ⊙

Zielona Gora prov., W Poland, 50 mi. SE of Frankfurt, 70 mi. WSW of Poznan; 51°56'N 15°30'E. Rail junction; lignite mining; woolen milling, railroad-car mfg., construction industry; grape- and fruitgrowing. Power station. Founded early-13th cent.; chartered 1315. Has 13th-cent. church, 14th-cent. town hall. Became important as staging point on trade route from Berlin to Upper Silesia; at peak of commercial importance in 15th cent.

Grünburg (grün'bo͝ork), town (pop. 3,725), E Upper Austria, on Steyr R. and 9 mi. SW of Steyr; cutlery. Castle and ruined fortress Leonstein near by.

Grund, Bad, Germany: see BAD GRUND.

Grundlsee (gro͞on'dŭlzā), resort (pop. 1,426), Styria, central Austria, 11 mi. SE of Bad Ischl, on Grundlsee, a small lake (□ 1.5, 4 mi. long, 22 ft. deep, alt. 2,325 ft.) in the Salzkammergut, at S foot of the Totes Gebirge.

Grundsund (grŭnd'sŭnd"), fishing village (pop. 965), Goteborg och Bohus co., SW Sweden, on SW coast of Skaftoland isl., on the Skagerrak, 4 mi. S of Lysekil; fish canning, oilskin-clothing mfg.

Grundy. 1 County (□ 432; pop. 19,217), NE Ill.; ⊙ Morris. Agr. (corn, oats, soybeans, wheat, livestock, poultry; dairy products). Bituminous coal, clay, limestone. Mfg.: clay products, clothing, machinery; wire, leather, paper, and food products. Drained by Illinois, Des Plaines, and Kankakee rivers. Includes Gebhard Woods State Park on the Illinois and Michigan Canal Parkway. Formed 1841. **2** County (□ 501; pop. 13,722), central Iowa; ⊙ Grundy Center. Rolling prairie agr. area (hogs, cattle, corn, soybeans, oats) drained by Wolf Creek. Formed 1851. **3** County (□ 435; pop. 13,220), N Mo.; ⊙ Trenton. Drained by Thompson and Weldon rivers; grain, livestock, coal. Formed 1841. **4** County (□ 358; pop. 12,558), SE central Tenn.; ⊙ Altamount. In the Cumberlands; drained by Elk R., and small Collins and Little Sequatchie rivers. Coal mining, lumbering; some agr. Formed 1844.

Grundy, town (pop. 1,947), ⊙ Buchanan co., SW Va., on Levisa Fork and 50 mi. W of Bluefield, near Ky. and W.Va. lines; bituminous-coal-mining center; lumber milling; foundry products, electrical equipment.

Grundy Center, town (pop. 2,135), ⊙ Grundy co., central Iowa, 24 mi. WSW of Waterloo; agr. trade center with corn cannery. Inc. 1877.

Grünendeich (grü'nŭndīkh"), village (pop. 2,205), in former Prussian prov. of Hanover, NW Germany, after 1945 in Lower Saxony, near Elbe estuary, 5 mi. SE of Stade; cherries.

Grünenplan (grü'nŭnplän"), village (pop. 3,366), in former Prussian prov. of Hanover, NW Germany, after 1945 in Lower Saxony, 4 mi. SW of Alfeld; glassworks; canary-bird farming. Summer resort. Until 1941 in Brunswick.

Grünfelde (grün'fĕl"dŭ), Pol. *Grunwald* (gro͞on'vält), village in East Prussia, after 1945 in Olsztyn prov., NE Poland, 25 mi. SW of Allenstein (Olsztyn), 5 mi. NNE of Dabrowno. Teutonic Knights were decisively defeated here, 1410, by Poles and Lithuanians under Wladislaw Jagiello; often called battle of Tannenberg (a village 3 mi. ENE).

Grünhain (grün'hīn), town (pop. 3,243), Saxony, E central Germany, in the Erzgebirge, 5 mi. E of Aue, near Czechoslovak border, in uranium-mining region; metal- and woodworking, hosiery knitting, cutlery mfg.

Grünhainichen (grün"hī'nĭ-khŭn), village (pop. 2,204), Saxony, E central Germany, at N foot of the Erzgebirge, 11 mi. ESE of Chemnitz; toy mfg., hosiery knitting.

Grünheide, Russian SFSR: see KALUZHSKOYE.

Grünhorn or **Gross Grünhorn** (grōs' grün'hôrn), peak (13,277 ft.) in Bernese Alps, S central Switzerland, 7 mi. S of Grindelwald. Klein Grünhorn (12,849 ft.) is N.

Grünsfeld (grüns'fĕlt), town (pop. 2,090), N Baden, Germany, after 1945 in Württemberg-Baden, 15 mi. SE of Wertheim; grain, strawberries. Has 16th-cent. town hall.

Grünstadt (grün'shtät), town (pop. 5,564), Rhenish Palatinate, W Germany, on N slope of Hardt Mts., 9 mi. WNW of Frankenthal; stoneware; wine.

Grunwald, Poland: see GRÜNFELDE.

Grushka (gro͞osh'kŭ), village (1926 pop. 2,794), N Odessa oblast, Ukrainian SSR, 35 mi. NW of Pervomaisk. Just NW is Ulyanovka (1926 pop. 912), with large sugar refinery.

Grütli, Switzerland: see RÜTLI.

Gruver. 1 Town (pop. 135), Emmet co., NW Iowa, 7 mi. E of Estherville; livestock, grain. **2** Town (pop. 813), Hansford co., extreme N Texas, in high plains of the Panhandle, 80 mi. NNE of Amarillo; ships wheat, cattle.

Gruvgarden, Sweden: see DALA-FYNNHYTTAN.

Gruyère (grüyâr'), Ger. *Greyerz* (grī'ŭrts), district (pop. 26,107) in upper Saane valley, Fribourg canton, W Switzerland, noted for its cheese and its cattle breeding. Natives speak Gruérien dialect. Main town, Bulle. Village of Gruyères (pop. 1,356) is on high hill overlooking the valley.

Gruz, Yugoslavia: see DUBROVNIK.

Gruzino (gro͞ozē'nŭ), town (1926 pop. 2,433), N Novgorod oblast, Russian SFSR, 7 mi. E of Chudovo, across Volkhov R.; match mfg.

Gruziya, USSR: see GEORGIA.

Gruzsko-Zoryanskoye (gro͞os'kŭ-zŭryän'skŭyŭ), town (1939 pop. over 500), central Stalino oblast, Ukrainian SSR, in the Donbas, on railroad (Ryasnoye station) and 6 mi. SE of Makeyevka; coal mines.

Gryazi (gryä'zē), city (1939 pop. over 10,000), NW Voronezh oblast, Russian SFSR, 65 mi. NNE of Voronezh; rail junction; railroad shops; food processing, distilling, woodworking; limestone.

Gryaznoye (gryäz'nŭyŭ), village (1926 pop. 809), W Ryazan oblast, Russian SFSR, 15 mi. SSE of Mikhailov; distilling; wheat.

Gryaznukha (gryŭzno͞o'khŭ), village (1939 pop. over 2,000), central Altai Territory, Russian SFSR, 18 mi. SSE of Bisk, in agr. area.

Gryazovets (gryŭzô'vyĭts), city (1926 pop. 5,229), S Vologda oblast, Russian SFSR, 28 mi. SSE of Vologda; flax retting. Ferruginous springs near by. Chartered 1780.

Grybow (grĭ'bo͞of), Pol. *Grybów*, town (pop. 2,198), Krakow prov., SE Poland, on Biala R. and 11 mi. E of Nowy Sacz; lumbering, brewing, tanning, distilling.

Grycksbo (grüks'bo͞o"), village (pop. 1,655), Kopparberg co., central Sweden, 7 mi. NW of Falun; paper mills, specializing in mfg. of filter paper.

Gryfice (grĭfē'tsĕ), Ger. *Greifenberg* (grī'fŭnbĕrk), town (1939 pop. 10,817; 1946 pop. 4,898) in Pomerania, after 1945 in Szczecin prov., NW Poland, on the Rega and 45 mi. NE of Stettin; sugar refining, fruit processing, flour milling, mfg. of furniture, bricks, tiles. In Second World War, c.50% destroyed.

Gryfino (grĭfē'nô), Ger. *Greifenhagen* (grīfŭnhä'gŭn), town (1939 pop. 9,858; 1946 pop. 1,347) in Pomerania, after 1945 in Szczecin prov., NW Poland, on E arm of Oder R. and 13 mi. SSW of Stettin; woolen milling, wood cracking, tanning, fruit processing, soap mfg.; grain and cattle market. In Second World War, c.90% destroyed.

Gryfow Slaski (grĭ'fo͞of shlô'skē), Pol. *Gryfów Śląski*, Ger. *Greiffenberg* (grī'fŭnbĕrk), town (1939 pop. 4,349; 1946 pop. 4,053) in Lower Silesia, after 1945 in Wroclaw prov., SW Poland, on Kwisa R. and 20 mi. ESE of Görlitz; linen milling, woodworking, tanning, fertilizer mfg.

Grygla (grē'glä), village (pop. 216), Marshall co., NW Minn., on tributary of Thief R. and 29 mi. NE of Thief River Falls; dairy products.

Grypskerk, Netherlands: see GRIJPSKERK.

Grytgol (grüt"yûl'), Swedish *Grytgöl*, village (pop. 450), Ostergotland co., SE Sweden, 9 mi. NW of Finspang; mfg. of wire and nails.

Grythyttan (grüt'hü"tän), village (pop. 792), Orebro co., S central Sweden, in Bergslag region, on L. Torrvarp, Swedish *Torrvarpen* (tôr'vär"pŭn) (7 mi. long), 13 mi. E of Filipstad; limestone and slate quarrying, sawmilling, wood- and metalworking. In 17th cent. a center of iron industry.

Grytten, Norway: see ANDALSNES.

Grytviken, Falkland Isls. Dependencies: see SOUTH GEORGIA.

Grzymalow, Ukrainian SSR: see GRIMAILOV.

Gspaltenhorn (kshpäl'tŭnhôrn"), peak (11,287 ft.) in Bernese Alps, S central Switzerland, 5 mi. SW of Mürren.

Gstaad (kshtät), resort (alt. 3,450 ft.), Bern canton, SW central Switzerland, on Saane R. and 17 mi. NNW of Sion. Has 15th-cent. chapel.

Gsteig or **Gsteig bei Gstaad** (kshtīk' bī kshtät'), resort village (alt. 3,936 ft.), Bern canton, SW central Switzerland, 11 mi. NNW of Sion and on Saane R.

Gsür (ksür), peak (8,897 ft.) in Bernese Alps, SW central Switzerland, 2 mi. WNW of Adelboden.

Gua, India: see NOAMUNDI.

Guabas, Las, Panama: see LAS GUABAS.

Guabito (gwäbē'tō), village (pop. 796), Bocas del Toro prov., W Panama, on Sixaola R. (opposite Sixaola, Costa Rica), on railroad and 26 mi. NW of Bocas del Toro. Bananas, cacao, abacá, tobacco, coffee, rubber; stock raising, lumbering. Sometimes called Sixaola.

Guacalate River (gwäkälä'tā), S Guatemala, rises near Chimaltenango, flows c.50 mi. S, bet. Fuego and Agua volcanoes, past Alotenango and Masagua, to the Pacific 6 mi. W of San José.

Guacanayabo, Gulf of (gwäkänīä'bō), shallow inlet of Caribbean S coast of Cuba, in Oriente and Camagüey provs., N of Cape Cruz; horseshoe-shaped, c.60 mi. wide N-S, 60 mi. long. Dotted by coral reefs, with the Gran Banco de Buena Esperanza in its center. At its head is port of Manzanillo. Receives Cauto R.

Guacara (gwäkä'rä), town (pop. 4,246), Carabobo state, N Venezuela, near NW shore of L. Valencia, 9 mi. ENE of Valencia; agr. center (cotton, sugar cane, cacao, corn, fruit, stock).

Guacarí (gwäkärē'), town (pop. 2,516), Valle del Cauca dept., W Colombia, in Cauca valley, on railroad and 25 mi. NE of Cali; tobacco, sugar cane, coffee, corn, bananas, cacao, stock. Silver, gold, and platinum deposits near by.

Guachalla (gwächä'yä), town (pop. c.3,900), La Paz dept., W Bolivia, in Cordillera Real, 3 mi. S of Sorata; *oca*, potatoes, barley. Until c.1945, Ilabaya.

Guácharo, cavern, Venezuela: see CARIPE.

Guácharos Caves, Colombia: see PITALITO.

Gua Chempedak or **Guar Chempedak** (go͞oä'chĕmpĕ'däk), village (pop. 810), W central Kedah, Malaya, on railroad and 19 mi. SSE of Alor Star; tea, rice, rubber.

Guachinango (gwächēnäng'gō), town (pop. 1,166), Jalisco, W Mexico, 23 mi. W of Ameca; silver, lead, copper mining.

Guachipas (gwächē'päs), village (pop. estimate 500), ⊙ Guachipas dept. (□ 715; 1947 pop. 2,958), S Salta prov., Argentina, on Guachipas R. and 50 mi. S of Salta, in stock-raising area; flour milling.

Guachipas River, NW Argentina, formed by confluence of Calchaquí R. and Santa María or Cajón R. in S Salta prov. 10 mi. E of Cafayate, flows N 125 mi. to join Toro R. just E of Coronel Moldes, forming the Pasaje or Juramento, the upper part of the Río Salado.

Guacimal or **Planta de Guacimal** (plän'tä dā gwäsēmäl'), village (dist. pop. 2,646), Puntarenas prov., W Costa Rica, on Guacimal R. (small coastal stream) and 7 mi. NNW of Puntarenas; corn, rice, beans, livestock.

Guácimo (gwä'sēmō), village, Limón prov., E Costa Rica, rail junction on Guácimo R. (an affluent of Parismina R.) and 7 mi. E of Guápiles; bananas, rubber.

Guacoca, Honduras: see SAN FRANCISCO DE LA PAZ.

Guaçuí (gwŭswē'), city (pop. 3,828), S Espírito Santo, Brazil, on railroad, 35 mi. W of Cachoeiro de Itapemirim; coffee hulling. Until 1944, called Siqueira Campos.

Guadahortuna (gwä"dhäôrto͞o'nä), town (pop. 2,913), Granada prov., S Spain, 22 mi. NW of Guadix; agr. trade center (cereals, potatoes, sugar beets, tobacco); brandy distilling; stock raising.

Guadaira River (gwä-dhī'rä), Seville prov., SW Spain, rises in W spur of the Cordillera Penibética near Cádiz prov. border, flows c.60 mi. NW to the Guadalquivir just S of Seville.

Guadajoz River (gwädhähōs'), Andalusia, S Spain, rises in spur of the Cordillera Penibética near Alcalá la Real, flows c.125 mi. WNW, past Castro del Río, to the Guadalquivir just SSW of Córdoba.

Guadalajara (gwä"dŭlŭhä'rŭ, gwŏ–, Sp. gwä-dhälähä'rä), city (pop. 229,235), ⊙ Jalisco, W central Mexico, on central plateau, near left bank of Santiago (Lerma) R., 290 mi. NW of Mexico city; 20°40'N 103°21'W; alt. 5,069 ft. Second largest city in Mexico, it is an important commercial center and a road and rail hub, and is highly regarded as a resort because of its beautiful mtn. setting and mild, clear, dry climate. Situated in rich agr. region (wheat, corn, beans, peanuts, fruit, livestock). Major industries: flour and textile milling, tanning, brewing, metal founding, mfg. of shoes, bricks, cement, vegetable oils, matches, soap, hosiery. Famous for artistic glassware and pottery. Receives power from hydroelectric plant at falls of Juanacatlán, on the Santiago near by. Airport. An old colonial town, it is laid out in rectangular style with a central plaza on which border the 16th–17th-cent. cathedral (containing an *Assumption of the Blessed Virgin* by Murillo), governor's palace (begun 1643) with murals by Orozco, and other public bldgs. Guadalajara has a univ., state mus., theaters, a number of baroque churches, and beautiful parks. Founded in 1530 or 1531 by Cristóbal de Oñate upon the order of Nuño de Guzmán, it was named after the latter's birthplace in Spain. Because of Indian raids it had to be moved twice and was finally established 1542 at the present site, then becoming the capital of Nueva Galicia and seat of the bishopric of W Mexico. Battle of Calderón Bridge (Jan. 17, 1811), in which Hidalgo y Costilla, an early leader of the independence movement, was defeated, took place on the Santiago (Lerma) R. E of city.

Guadalajara, province (□ 4,709; pop. 205,726), central Spain, in New Castile; ⊙ Guadalajara. Situated on great central plateau (Meseta); borders W on Madrid prov., NW on Segovia prov., N on Soria prov., NE on Saragossa prov., E on Teruel prov., S on Cuenca prov. Watered by the Tagus and its tributaries—Gallo, Tajuña, and Henares rivers. Spurs of the Sierra de Guadarrama and Cordillera Ibérica are in N and NE. Fertile Alcarria plain is in S central and SW section, chiefly along Henares R. Climate, depending on alt., is of rigorous continental type (hot summers, cold winters). Molina (NE) is considered coldest city in Spain. The plains and valleys are much warmer and support semitropical crops, such as olives. Widely grown also are wheat, barley, rye, grapes, hemp, aromatic plants, beans, chick-peas, forage, fruit. Considerable apiculture and stock raising (goats, sheep). Extensive forests yield timber and naval stores. Minerals are also of economic importance. Through saltworks near Imón, Guadalajara prov. ranks among leading salt producers of Spain. Iron is mined at Setiles. Silver was formerly worked at Hiendelaencina. Other resources include gypsum, lime, slate, aragonite, marble; mineral springs. Copper, gold, silver, lead, sulphur, lignite occur, but are little exploited. Some textile milling (woolen goods). Though Guadalajara is the most populous city, Sigüenza is its bishopric. Brihuega trades in agr. produce. Prov. is served by the Madrid-Saragossa RR. Heavily disputed during Sp. civil war (1936–39), most of the region remained in Loyalist hands until close of hostilities. The battle of Guadalajara (March, 1937) was fought near Brihuega.

Guadalajara, anc. *Arriaca*, city (pop. 21,466, with suburbs 23,503), ⊙ Guadalajara prov., central Spain, in New Castile, on left bank of Henares R. and 30 mi. NE of Madrid (linked by railroad and highway); 40°38′N 3°11′W. Situated in an agr. region which produces cereals, vegetables, forage, olives, grapes, and fruit. Chiefly known for its history and institutions, it has some minor industries, such as flour milling, tanning, dairying, olive-oil pressing, meat packing, sawmilling; mfg. of cement products, aromatic essences, soap, textile goods, tiles. Guadalajara has an acad. for army engineers, natl. institute, and military airport. The city, modernized in 19th cent., has only a few outstanding bldgs. (mostly damaged during 1936–39 civil war), notably the old mansion of the Mendoza family, the Infantado Palace (begun 1461, partly destroyed 1936, rebuilt since 1947) with Gothic, Mudejar, and Renaissance features. There are several notable churches. A fine bridge of Roman foundation crosses the Henares. Of Celtiberian origin, Guadalajara flourished as a Roman colony. It was held by the Moors from 712 to end of 11th cent. The famed civil war battle of Guadalajara (March, 1937), in which Italian contingents were crushingly defeated by the Loyalists, was actually fought near Brihuega, 18 mi. NE.

Guadalaviar River, Spain: see TURIA RIVER.

Guadalcacín, Lake (gwä-dhälkä-thēn′), artificial lake (5 mi. long, up to 2 mi. wide), Cádiz prov., SW Spain, formed by Majaceite R. 5 mi. S of Arcos de la Frontera.

Guadalcanal (gwä′dŭlkŭnăl′, gwŏ′–), volcanic island (□ 2,500; pop. c.14,000), Solomon Isls., SW Pacific; 9°37′S 160°15′E; 90 mi. long, 35 mi. wide; seat of HONIARA, ⊙ Br. protectorate. Mountainous, Mt. Popomansiu (c.8,000 ft.) highest peak. Coconut plantations; some gold. In Second World War, Guadalcanal (occupied early 1942 by Japanese) was scene (Aug. 7, 1942) of 1st Allied invasion northward. Fighting centered around the airfield named by U.S. forces Henderson Field. There was heavy naval fighting in the surrounding waters, notably at SANTA CRUZ ISLANDS and off Cape ESPERANCE and Lunga Point. Isl. was finally conquered by Feb., 1943, and became an important U.S. base.

Guadalcanal (gwä-dhälkänäl′), town (pop. 6,354), Seville prov., SW Spain, in the Sierra Morena, on railroad and 50 mi. NNE of Seville. Old mining center (barite, copper, silver, iron, coal) in agr. region (olives, potatoes, grapes, stock, timber). Liquor distilling, flour milling, olive-oil pressing.

Guadalcázar (gwä-dhälkä′sär), city (pop. 998), San Luis Potosí, N central Mexico, on interior plateau, 50 mi. NE of San Luis Potosí; alt. 5,489 ft. Silver-mining center; gold, lead, arsenic deposits.

Guadalcázar (–kä′thär), town (pop. 1,577), Córdoba prov., S Spain, 13 mi. SW of Córdoba; olive oil, cereals, livestock.

Guadalete River (–lā′tā), Cádiz prov., SW Spain, rises in spur of the Cordillera Penibética near Málaga prov. border, flows c.85 mi. SW in wide curve, past Villamartín and Arcos de la Frontera, to the Atlantic at Bay of Cádiz opposite Cádiz. Not navigable. Main affluent, Majaceite R. The decisive battle (711) in which Roderick was defeated by Tarik is believed to have taken place at the Laguna de JANDA, though it has long been known as the "battle of Guadalete."

Guadalhorce River (–lôr′thā), Málaga prov., S Spain, in Andalusia, rises in spur of the Cordillera Penibética in Granada prov., flows c.75 mi. in large curve W, S, and E, through El CHORRO gorge and past Álora, to the Mediterranean 3 mi. SW of Málaga. Used for hydroelectric power and irrigation. Its valley serves as communication line to Guadalquivir valley and is followed by railroad to Málaga.

Guadalimar River (–lēmär′), in Albacete and Jaén provs., S Spain, rises near prov. border, flows 80 mi. generally WSW to Guadalquivir R. 10 mi. SW of Linares. Falls along its course used for hydroelectric power.

Guadalix de la Sierra (–lēks′ dhā lä syĕ′rä), town (pop. 1,287), Madrid prov., central Spain, on E slopes of the Sierra de Guadarrama, 25 mi. N of Madrid; cattle and sheep grazing; flour milling, cheese processing; stone quarrying.

Guadalmedina River (gwä-dhälmä-dhē′nä), Málaga prov., S Spain, rises N of Colmenar, flows c.25 mi. S to the Mediterranean at Málaga, dividing city in two.

Guadalmez (–māth′), village (pop. 1,534), Ciudad Real prov., S central Spain, in Sierra Morena, near Guadalmez R., 7 mi. WSW of Almadén; cereals, vegetables, stock. Hunting, fishing.

Guadalmez River, S Spain, rises in Sierra Morena, flows c.60 mi. NW, partly along Córdoba–Ciudad Real border, to Zújar R. 13 mi. W of Almadén.

Guadalope River (–lō′pā), in Teruel and Saragossa provs., E Spain, rises NE of Teruel, flows c.120 mi. N, past Alcañiz, to the Ebro near Caspe.

Guadalquivir River, Bolivia: see TARIJA RIVER.

Guadalquivir River (gwä-dhälkēvēr′), anc. *Baetis*, Arabic *Vad-el-kebir* [=large river], largest stream of Andalusia, S Spain, rises in the Sierra de Cazorla in Jaén prov. at c.4,500 ft., flows swiftly W, past Andújar and Montoro, to Córdoba, where it becomes navigable for small vessels, and its valley widens into the fertile Andalusian plain bet. the Sierra Morena (N) and the Cordillera Penibética (S). From there on it flows slowly SW, past Seville, its head of navigation for ocean vessels, turning S while crossing extensive marshes and branching off into several arms, to the Atlantic near Sanlúcar de Barrameda; c.350–400 mi. long. Extensively used for irrigation, particularly bet. Seville and Córdoba, a populous agr. region, which yields grapes, olives, grain, sugar beets, fruit, vegetables, and cotton. Canals below Seville circumvent its windings, rendered hazardous by incoming tides. Several hydroelectric plants along its course. Main tributaries are: right—Guadalimar and Guadiato; left—Guadiana Menor, Guadajoz, and Genil.

Guadalupe (gwä″dŭlōōp′, gwŏ″–, gô–, Sp. gwä-dhälōō′pä, wä–), village (pop. estimate 1,000), E Santa Fe prov., Argentina, on L. Guadalupe (a bayou lake of the Paraná) and 3 mi. NNE of Santa Fe, in agr. area (corn, wheat, flax; citrus nurseries).

Guadalupe, town (pop. c.6,200), Santa Cruz dept., central Bolivia, on road and 4 mi. SSE of Valle Grande; corn, potatoes, barley.

Guadalupe (gwŭdŭlōō′pĭ), city (pop. 536), W Piauí, Brazil, on right bank of Parnaíba R. (Maranhão border) and 50 mi. W of Floriano; babassu nuts. Until 1944, called Pôrto Seguro.

Guadalupe (gwä″dŭlōōp′, gwŏ″–, gô–, Sp. gwä-dhälōō′pä, wä–), town (pop. 1,596), Huila dept., S central Colombia, on affluent of upper Magdalena R. and 15 mi. SW of Garzón; rice, cacao, coffee, stock.

Guadalupe, town (1950 pop. 8,452), ⊙ Goicoechea canton, San José prov., Costa Rica, on central plateau, 2 mi. NE of San José (linked by tramway); coffee, grain, truck produce.

Guadalupe, town (pop. 1,138), Camagüey prov., E Cuba, in hills, 20 mi. W of Morón; cattle, tobacco. Has sulphurous springs. Copper deposits near by.

Guadalupe. 1 Town, Chihuahua, Mexico, near Ciudad Juárez: see GUADALUPE BRAVOS. **2** Town, Chihuahua, Mexico, near Chihuahua: see GUADALUPE VICTORIA. **3** Village (pop. 265), Northern Territory, Lower California, NW Mexico, 14 mi. N of Ensenada; Russian agr. settlement in small irrigated valley (wheat, fruit, livestock). **4** Town (pop. 2,371), Nuevo León, N Mexico, 3 mi. E of Monterrey; chick-peas, grain, livestock. **5** Town (pop. 1,601), Puebla, central Mexico, 9 mi. SW of Acatlán; sugar cane, corn, fruit, livestock. Ruins near by. **6** Town (pop. 974), San Luis Potosí, N central Mexico, 21 mi. SW of Matehuala; maguey, corn, livestock. Magdalenas thermal springs 6 mi. NW. **7** Town (pop. 4,133), Zacatecas, N central Mexico, on interior plateau, 4 mi. ESE of Zacatecas; alt. 7644 ft. Rail junction; agr. center (cereals, sugar cane, vegetables, livestock). Has old cathedral and Jesuit col.

Guadalupe. 1 Town (pop. 1,436), Ica dept., SW Peru, on Pisco–Ica RR and highway, and 6 mi. NNW of Ica; cotton, grapes. **2** City (pop. 4,708), Libertad dept., NW Peru, on coastal plain, terminus of railroad from Pacasmayo, on Pan American Highway and 13 mi. N of San Pedro, in irrigated agr. area (rice, sugar cane, cotton); rice milling, cotton ginning.

Guadalupe. 1 NW suburb (1939 pop. 7,160) of Cebu city, on Cebu isl., Philippines; corn, coconuts. **2** Town (1939 pop. 5,788) in Carcar municipality, central Cebu isl., Philippines, 24 mi. SW of Cebu city; agr. center (corn, coconuts).

Guadalupe, city (pop. 2,425), San Vicente dept., S central Salvador, on W slope of volcano San Vicente, 6 mi. SW of San Vicente; coffee-growing center.

Guadalupe, town (pop. 3,597), Cáceres prov., W Spain, in Estremadura, in the Sierra de Guadalupe, 31 mi. E of Trujillo; olive-oil processing, lumbering; cork, fruit. Has noted 14th-cent. Hieronymite monastery (now Franciscan), containing shrine of Our Lady of Guadalupe, whose worship was transferred (16th cent.) to Guadalupe Hidalgo (Mexico). Town's imposing Gothic church has two cloisters (Moorish and Gothic).

Guadalupe. 1 County (□ 2,998; pop. 6,772), E central N.Mex.; ⊙ Santa Rosa. Stock-grazing, grain area; watered by Pecos R. Plateau (5–6,000 ft.) in W. Formed 1891. **2** County (□ 715; pop. 25,392), S central Texas; ⊙ Seguin. Drained by San Marcos and Guadalupe rivers and Cibolo Creek. Power dams form lakes (recreational areas). Agr. (cotton, corn, peanuts, grain sorghums, pecans, vegetables, fruit); livestock raising (cattle, sheep, hogs, poultry); dairying, beekeeping. Oil, natural gas; clay mining. Mfg., processing of farm products at Seguin. Hunting, fishing. Formed 1846.

Guadalupe. 1 or **Guadalupe Village**, Yaqui Indian village, Maricopa co., S central Ariz., 8 mi. SE of Phoenix. Easter ceremonies attract visitors. **2** City (pop. 2,429), Santa Barbara co., SW Calif., 8 mi. W of Santa Maria and on Santa Maria R.; dairying, farming. Inc. 1946.

Guadalupe, Uruguay: see CANELONES, city.

Guadalupe, Lake, bayou lake (□ 25) in Paraná R. basin, E central Santa Fe prov., Argentina, just NE of Santa Fe; c.20 mi. long.

Guadalupe, Sierra de (syĕ′rä dhā gwä-dhälōō′pä), mountain range of Cáceres prov., W Spain, bet. Tagus and Guadiana rivers; extends c.30 mi. W from the border of Toledo prov. to the vicinity of Trujillo. Highest point, 5,121 ft.

Guadalupe Bravos (brä′vōs), town (pop. 1,214), Chihuahua, N Mexico, on Rio Grande and 32 mi. SE of Ciudad Juárez; cotton, cereals, cattle. Sometimes Guadalupe.

Guadalupe de los Reyes (dhā lōs rā′ĕs), town (pop. 1,459), Sinaloa, NW Mexico, in W outliers of Sierra Madre Occidental, 70 mi. SE of Culiacán; silver and gold mining; corn, sugar cane.

Guadalupe Falls, Colombia: see GÓMEZ PLATA.

Guadalupe Hidalgo (ēdäl′gō), former town, now part (pop. c.10,000) of Gustavo A. Madero, Federal Dist., central Mexico, 2½ mi. N of Mexico city. It has the basilica of Guadalupe, containing the shrine of Our Lady of Guadalupe, one of the principal shrines of Christendom and the focal point of the greatest pilgrimage in the Western Hemisphere. In 1531 Juan Diego, an Indian, reported to Archbishop Zumágarraga his miraculous visions of the Virgin on the hill of Tepeyacac; the site was renamed Guadalupe in honor of the shrine of Our Lady of Guadalupe (Spain). To this was added later the name of Hidalgo y Costilla, the revolutionary priest of 1810, who adopted her banner as his standard. She is the patroness of Mexico, especially beloved by Mex. Indians. The Treaty of Guadalupe Hidalgo, signed here Feb. 2, 1848, ended the Mexican War.

Guadalupe Island (□ 102), in the Pacific, c.150 mi. off coast of Lower California, NW Mexico; 29°11′N 118°17′W; 23 mi. long, c.7 mi. wide. Rises to 4,500 ft. Goat grazing.

Guadalupe Mountains, range of Sacramento Mts., in S N.Mex. and W Texas. Its highest peak, Guadalupe Peak (8,751 ft.), is highest point in Texas. Other peaks in Texas part of range: El Capitan (8,078 ft.) and Bush Mtn. (8,676 ft.). Just S of Guadalupe Pass, in Texas, are Delaware Mts. In N.Mex. are Carlsbad Cavern Natl. Park and part of Lincoln Natl. Forest.

Guadalupe Pass (5,426 ft.), W Texas, highway pass bet. Guadalupe and Delaware mts., c.100 mi. E of El Paso.

Guadalupe Peak (8,751 ft.), W Texas, in Guadalupe Mts., c.100 mi. E of El Paso. Highest point in Guadalupe Mts. and in Texas. Salt lakes and flats are just W; Guadalupe Pass just S.

Guadalupe River, Texas, rises in springs in Kerr co. on Edwards Plateau, flows generally SE c.458 mi., past Kerrville, New Braunfels, Seguin, Gonzales, and Victoria, to head of San Antonio Bay. Receives Comal and San Marcos rivers in upper course, San Antonio R. near its mouth. Hydroelectric plants; also used for irrigation.

Guadalupe Victoria (vēktōr′yä). **1** or **Guadalupe**, town (pop. 1,304), Chihuahua, N Mexico, in Conchos R. valley, 45 mi. SE of Chihuahua; cotton, cereals, cattle. **2** Town (pop. 4,336), Durango, N Mexico, on interior plateau, on railroad and 45 mi. NE of Durango; agr. center (corn, wheat, cotton, fruit, livestock). **3** or **Nuevo Saltillo** (nwā′vō sältē′yō), town (pop. 2,230), Puebla, central Mexico, 25 mi. N of Serdán; cereals, fruit, maguey.

Guadalupe y Calvo (ē käl′vō), town (pop. 1,343), Chihuahua, N Mexico, in Sierra Madre Occidental, 95 mi. NNE of Culiacán; alt. 7,145 ft.; silver, gold, copper mining.

Guadamur (gwä-dhämōōr′), town (pop. 1,477), Toledo prov., central Spain, 7 mi. WSW of Toledo; olives, cereals, grapes, esparto, sheep, goats; olive-oil pressing. Has old castle.

Guadarrama (gwä-dhärä′mä), town (pop. 1,176), Madrid prov., central Spain, on E slopes of the Sierra de Guadarrama, on railroad and 28 mi. NW of Madrid; cattle, sheep, goat grazing. Resin processing. Medicinal spring; sanatoriums. The Guadarrama Pass on highway to Segovia and Valladolid is 3 mi. NW.

Guadarrama, Sierra de (syĕ′rä dhā), mountain range in central Spain, NW of Madrid, rises from central plateau and extends c.120 mi. NE roughly bet. Tagus and Douro (Duero) rivers, separating Old Castile from New Castile. The rugged, frequently snow-capped range rises in the Peñalara to 7,972 ft. The sierra is crossed by several passes, such as the Guadarrama and NAVACERRADA, which link Madrid with Segovia. Largely forested, it yields fine timber and naval stores. There are several resorts, sanatoriums, and skiing chalets on its slopes. Among its subranges is the Sierra de Ayllón (NE). The Sierra de Guadarrama is considered to form part of the Cordillera Carpeto-Vetónica.

Guadarrama River, New Castile, central Spain, rises in the Sierra de Guadarrama NW of Madrid, flows c.90 mi. S, through Madrid and Toledo provs., to the Tagus 7 mi. W of Toledo.

Guadasuar (–swär′), town (pop. 3,904), Valencia prov., E Spain, 3 mi. NW of Alcira, in rich truck-farming area; peanut-oil processing, flour milling. Also rice, wine, lumber, sheep.

Guadazaón River (–thäōn'), Cuenca prov., central Spain, rises in the Serranía de Cuenca NW of Cañete, flows c.50 mi. S and SE to Cabriel R. 2 mi. N of Enguídanos.

Guadeloupe (gôdŏolōop', gwŏdŏolōop', Fr. gwädŏolōop'), overseas department (□ 687.26; pop. 278,864) of France, in the Leeward Isls., West Indies, consisting of the twin isl. of Guadeloupe (□ 583; pop. 235,195), and the dependencies MARIE-GALANTE (SE), DÉSIRADE (E), Les SAINTES (SW), SAINT-BARTHÉLEMY, and northern half of SAINT MARTIN (NW); ⊙ BASSE-TERRE. Of the 2 isls. forming Guadeloupe itself, rugged Basse-Terre (sometimes called Guadeloupe proper) is W, low-lying GRANDE-TERRE is E, separated by narrow Rivière Salée channel. They lie halfway bet. Montserrat (NNW) and Dominica (SSE), c.300 mi. ESE of San Juan, Puerto Rico, and 80 mi. NNW of Martinique; 15°57'–16°3'N 61°10'–61°48'W. The climate, generally healthful and tempered by trade winds, varies greatly in different sections. Hurricanes occur occasionally. Grande-Terre, made of coral limestone, is much drier, whereas Basse-Terre, rising in the dormant volcano Soufrière to 4,869 ft., receives considerable rainfall, increasing with alt. The latter is watered by numerous streams; its forested mts. are intersected by deep ravines. Basse-Terre is settled almost entirely along its coast; grows bananas, cacao, coffee, vanilla, bay leaves, sugar cane. The picturesque isl. has several thermal springs. On Grande-Terre, sugar cane is cultivated almost exclusively. There are many sugar mills and rum distilleries, centered at POINTE-À-PITRE, the dept.'s leading port and commercial center. Of the dependencies, only Marie-Galante has some economic importance as sugar-growing isl. Guadeloupe was discovered (1493) by Columbus, who named it for a monastery in Estremadura. After the Spaniards abandoned it in 1604, without undertaking colonization, the French started settlements, in 1635. The isls. were frequently attacked and captured by the British, but have been since 1816 continuously under Fr. sovereignty. In Second World War, after France's capitulation (1940), Guadeloupe adhered to the Vichy govt., but came to an agreement with the U.S. in 1943. In 1946 it became an overseas dept. of France, headed by a prefect. It is administratively divided into 2 *arrondissements*. The pop., having shifted in colonial times from a majority of Indians, then Europeans, and then Negroes, is now largely mulatto. The Les Saintes isls. are inhabited by Bretons. While French is the official language, a Fr. patois is generally spoken. Most of the dept.'s exports go to France.

Guadeloupe Passage, channel (c.35 mi. wide) in Leeward Isls., West Indies, bounded by Montserrat and Antigua (N) and Guadeloupe (S).

Guadiana, Ensenada de (ĕnsänä'dä dä gwädyä'nä), sheltered bay, W Cuba, 35 mi. ENE of Cape San Antonio, the E extension of the Gulf of Guanahacabibes; c.13 mi. long, 10 mi. wide.

Guadiana Menor River (gwä-dhyä'nä mänôr'), Granada and Jaén provs., S Spain, rises near Guadix, flows 110 mi. NW to the Guadalquivir 7 mi. SE of Úbeda.

Guadiana River (Sp. gwä-dhyä'na; Port. gwŏo-dhyä'nŏo), anc. *Anas*, S central Spain and SE Portugal, one of the longest (c.510 mi.) rivers of the Iberian Peninsula. It has several headstreams, all converging in a swampy lake region (Ojos del Guadiana) NE of Ciudad Real out of which flows the Guadiana proper. The Alto Guadiana, rising in the La Mancha plateau, flows NW to a point just above the Ojos del Guadiana, where it joins the combined Záncara-Gigüela, also considered a headstream of the Guadiana. The Guadiana flows generally W through S New Castile and Estremadura, past Mérida, to Badajoz, where it turns S and follows the Port. line (except for a swing into Portugal of c.100 mi.) to the Gulf of Cádiz of the Atlantic at Vila Real de Santo António (Portugal) just below Ayamonte (Spain). Of limited navigability (Mértola in Portugal is head of navigation), it transports copper ore from Pomarão, the river port for Mina de São Domingos. Compared with other large Iberian streams, the Guadiana's economic importance is negligible. Possessing little water volume, it crosses a sparsely populated region, but irrigates the fertile Mérida area. There are a number of hydroelectric plants. Receives Jabalón, Zújar, and Chanza rivers on left.

Guadiaro River (gwä-dhyä'rō), Andalusia, S Spain, chiefly in Málaga prov., rises N of Ronda in the Sierra de Ronda, flows c.55 mi. SSW and SSE, partly along Cádiz prov. border in lower course, to the Mediterranean 10 mi. NNE of Gibraltar. Used for hydroelectric power.

Guadiato River (–tō), Córdoba prov., S Spain, rises on S slopes of the Sierra Morena near Fuenteovejuna, flows SE, then SW, to the Guadalquivir near Posadas; 75 mi. long. Upper course traverses coal- and lead-mining dist.

Guadibeca River, Spain: see BARBATE RIVER.

Guadiela River (gwä-dhyä'lä), Cuenca prov., New Castile, central Spain, rises near Guadalajara prov. border in the Serranía de Cuenca, flows c.70 mi. SW and W, past La Isabela, to the Tagus 4 mi. W of Buendía, near Bolarque Falls and hydroelectric plant.

Guadix (gwä-dhēsh', –ēks'), anc. *Acci*, city (pop. 18,318), Granada prov., S Spain, in Andalusia, railroad junction at foot of the Sierra Nevada, 28 mi. ENE of Granada; sugar and flour milling, olive-oil processing; mfg. of soap, tiles, chocolate, woolen and cotton cloth. Cereals, vegetables, sugar beets, tobacco in area. Iron mines in vicinity. Episcopal see since Visigothic times. Gypsies still live in cave dwellings, dug out in hillsides. Has baroque cathedral (18th cent.) and remains of Moorish fort (*alcazaba*). Founded by Romans; flourished (8th-15th cent.) under Moors; liberated (1489) by the Catholic Kings.

Guadualito (gwä-dhwälē'tō), town (pop. 3,118), Apure state, W central Venezuela, on Sarare R., in llanos, and 11 mi. N of Arauca (Colombia); trading and cattle-raising center. Airport.

Guaduas (gwä'dhwäs), town (pop. 2,011), Cundinamarca dept., central Colombia, on W slopes of Cordillera Oriental above Magdalena R., 13 mi. SE of Honda; alt. 3,304 ft. Sugar cane, tobacco, coffee, fruit, livestock.

Guafo Gulf (gwä'fō, wä'fō), inlet of the Pacific in Chiloé prov., S Chile, connects the Pacific and the Gulf of Corcovado, separating Chiloé Isl. (N) and Guaitecas Isls. (S); 30 mi. wide. Guafo Isl. is off its entrance (W).

Guafo Island or **Huafo Island** (□ 65; pop. 8), in the Pacific, 20 mi. off SW coast of Chiloé Isl., Chiloé prov., S Chile, at mouth of Guafo Gulf; 43°35'S 74°45'W; 13 mi. long, 9 mi. wide. Stock raising (cattle, sheep, goats).

Guagnano (gwänyä'nô), village (pop. 3,961), Lecce prov., Apulia, S Italy, 12 mi. WNW of Lecce; wine, olive oil.

Guagno (gwä'nyô), village (pop. 1,018), W central Corsica, 20 mi. NNE of Ajaccio; mineral springs 3 mi. W.

Guagua (gwä'gwä), town (1939 pop. 4,497; 1948 municipality pop. 34,738), Pampanga prov., central Luzon, Philippines, on railroad and 6 mi. SW of San Fernando; meat packing, fish canning.

Guahyba, Brazil: see GUAÍBA.

Guahyra, Brazil: see PÔRTO GUAÍRA.

Guaíba (gwäē'bŏo), city (pop. 2,860), E Rio Grande do Sul, Brazil, on right bank of Guaíba R. diagonally opposite Pôrto Alegre; cattle, hides, rice, grain. Kaolin deposits. Old spelling, Guahyba. Until c.1925, called Pedras Brancas.

Guaíba River, N inlet of the Lagoa dos Patos, E Rio Grande do Sul, Brazil; 30 mi. long, up to 10 mi. wide. Formed at Pôrto Alegre by confluence of Jacuí, Caí, Sinos, and Gravataí rivers, for which it becomes an estuary. Its silted channel is dredged to permit ships to reach Pôrto Alegre. Old spelling, Guahyba R.

Guaiçara (gwīsä'rŏo), town (pop. 1,387), W central São Paulo, Brazil, on railroad and 5 mi. NNW of Lins; coffee, lumber. Formerly Guayçara.

Guaico (gwī'kō), village (pop. 1,225), N Trinidad, B.W.I., on railroad and 25 mi. ESE of Port of Spain, in cacao-growing region; adjoins U.S. army base Fort Read (W).

Guaicuí (gwīkwē'), town (pop. 212), N central Minas Gerais, Brazil, at influx of the Rio das Velhas into the São Francisco, 14 mi. NE of Pirapora. Formerly spelled Guaicuhy.

Guaillabamba (gwī-yäbäm'bä), village, Pichincha prov., N central Ecuador, in the Andes, near Guaillabamba R., on Pan American Highway and 15 mi. NE of Quito; tropical fruit, sugar cane, livestock.

Guaillabamba River, in Pichincha and Esmeraldas provs., N Ecuador, rises in the Andes W and N of the Cotopaxi, flows c.130 mi. N and W to join the Río Blanco, forming the Esmeraldas at 0°28'N 79°25'W.

Guaimaca (gwīmä'kä), town (pop. 852), Francisco Morazán dept., central Honduras, on Jalán R. and 38 mi. NE of Tegucigalpa, on road; livestock; wheat, corn, coffee. Airfield.

Guáimaro (gwī'märō), town (pop. 4,737), Camagüey prov., E Cuba, on Central Highway and 40 mi. ESE of Camagüey. Lumbering and agr. center (fruit, sugar cane, cattle); mfg. of dairy and meat products; sawmilling.

Guainía River, Colombia and Venezuela: see NEGRO, RIO.

Guaíra (gwäē'rŏo). **1** Village, Paraná, Brazil: see PÔRTO GUAÍRA. **2** City (pop. 2,564), N São Paulo, Brazil, 24 mi. NE of Barretos; rice processing, distilling; cattle raising. Formerly Guayra.

Guairá (gwīrä'), department (□ 1,236; pop. 91,702), S Paraguay; ⊙ Villarrica. Drained by the Tebicuary-mi, a branch of the Tebicuary. Fertile lowlands with mild, subtropical climate. Lumbering and agr. area producing principally sugar cane; also maté, cotton, tobacco, oranges, wine, livestock. Processing concentrated at Villarrica. Independencia is a wine-making center.

Guaira, La, Venezuela: see LA GUAIRA.

Guaíra Falls (gwäē'rŏo) or **Sete Quedas Falls** (sĕ'tĭ kä'dŏos), Sp. *Guairá* (gwīrä'), cataract on Alto Paraná R. at Brazil-Paraguay border, just below Pôrto Guaíra (Brazil) and 220 mi. ENE of Asuncion (Paraguay); 24°5'S 54°17'W. Formed at point where the resistant Serra de Maracaju is crossed by Paraná R., resulting in narrowing of river bed (4 mi. wide at Pôrto Guaíra) into a gorge c.200 ft. wide. Although the Port. name refers to 7 falls, there are actually 18, the largest c.100 ft. high. Because of river's volume, the falls are spectacular (especially on Braz. side) and have enormous hydroelectric potential. The falls and river gorge are circumvented by a Braz. railroad from Pôrto Guaíra to Pôrto Mendes. Formerly spelled Guayra.

Guaire River (gwī'rä), in Federal Dist. and Miranda state, N Venezuela, rises W of Los Teques in the coastal range, flows NE, past Antímano, to Caracas, then ESE, past Petare and Santa Lucía, to Tuy R. and Santa Teresa; c.50 mi. long. It waters the Caracas Valley.

Guaitará River, Colombia: see CARCHI RIVER.

Guaitarilla (gwītärī'yä), town (pop. 1,787), Nariño dept., SW Colombia, in the Andes at W foot of Galeras Volcano, 18 mi. WSW of Pasto; alt. 8,704 ft. Corn, wheat, coffee, potatoes, sugar cane, cacao, livestock.

Guaitecas Islands (gwītā'käs), Chiloé prov., S Chile, archipelago just N of Chonos Archipelago (of which it is sometimes considered a part), bet. 43°47'S and 44°10'S, separated from Chiloé Isl. (N) by Guafo Gulf. Consists of a number of sparsely inhabited isls., including: Guaiteca, Ascensión (□ 21; pop. 451), Clotilde, Manzano, Leucayec or Leucallec. Main village is Melinka or Puerto Melinka, on Ascensión.

Guaiúba (gwīōō'bŏo), town (pop. 1,475), N Ceará, Brazil, on Fortaleza-Crato RR and 23 mi. SSW of Fortaleza; irrigation agr. Formerly Guayuba.

Guajaba, Cayo (kī'ō gwähä'bä), coral island (12 mi. long, c.4 mi. wide), off E Cuba, in Old Bahama Channel, bet. Cayo Romano (NW) and Cayo Sabinal (SE), 22 mi. NW of Nuevitas; charcoal burning, fishing. Part of Camagüey Archipelago.

Guajará Mirim (gwŏozhärä' mērēn'), city (pop. 1,306), W Guaporé territory, W Brazil, port on right bank of Mamoré R. (Bolivia border), opposite Guayaramerín (Bolivia), and 170 mi. SSW of Pôrto Velho; S terminus of Madeira-Mamoré RR. Rubber-shipping point and trade center for imports from Bolivia. Customs station. Airfield.

Guajará River, Brazil: see ACARÁ RIVER.

Guájar-Faragüit (gwä'här-färägwēt'), town (pop. 1,190), Granada prov., S Spain, 7 mi. NW of Motril; olive-oil processing, flour milling; almonds, esparto, corn.

Guájaro, Ciénaga de (syä'nägä dä gwä'härō), lake in Atlántico dept., N Colombia, in marshy Caribbean lowlands, 32 mi. SW of Barranquilla; 9 mi. long, 1–3 mi. wide.

Guajataca River (gwähätä'kä), NW Puerto Rico, rises just S of Lares, flows c.30 mi. N, past Lares and through L. Guajataca, to the Atlantic 1½ mi. NW of Quebradillas. The artificial L. Guajataca (2½ mi. long), along its mid-course 5 mi. S of Quebradillas, serves irrigation system of the NW. On a canal is Isabela hydroelectric project.

Guajay, Cuba: see WAJAY.

Guaje, El, Mexico: see VILLAGRAN, Guanajuato.

Guaje, Llano del (yä'nō dĕl gwä'hä), arid depression in N outliers of Sierra Madre Oriental of Coahuila, N Mexico, NE of the Bolsón de Mapimí; alt. c.3,000 ft.

Guajiquiro (gwähēkē'rō), town (pop. 147), La Paz dept., SW Honduras, in Sierra de Guajiquiro, 5 mi. NE of Opatoro; coffee, wheat.

Guajiquiro, Sierra de (syĕ'rä dā), part of main Andean divide in SW Honduras; extends c.20 mi. SW–NE bet. Marcala and Opatoro; rises to over 7,000 ft. Forms watershed bet. upper Ulúa (NW) and Goascorán (SE) rivers. Also called Sierra de Opatoro.

Guajira or **La Guajira** (lä gwähē'rä), commissary (□ 4,726; 1938 pop. 53,409; 1950 estimate 53,990), N Colombia, on Caribbean Sea, the northernmost part of Colombia and of the S. Amer. continent; ⊙ Uribia. It is a peninsula situated NE of Sierra Nevada de Santa Marta, and separated by Ranchería R. (SW) from Magdalena dept. and by the Montes de Oca (S) from Venezuela. Apart from low outliers of the Cordillera Oriental, it consists of arid plains, having a desert aspect and high tropical temperatures. On indented coast are rich pearl banks, and marine salt is also worked there. Its mineral resources, thus far little exploited, include gold, copper, phosphates, gypsum, petroleum, coal. Most important crop is divi-divi bark, used for tanning purposes; some stock grazing (goats, sheep, cattle). At W foot of Montes de Oca, corn, beans, yucca, and coconuts are grown and cattle is raised. Hides and livestock are exported to Venezuela. The primitive Indian pop. manufactures hammocks and native textile goods. Sometimes spelled Goajira. Uribia, the main town, was built c.1930.

Gualaca (gwälä'kä), village (pop. 934), Chiriquí prov., W Panama, in Chiriquí R. valley, 10 mi. NE of David; road terminus; coffee, bananas, cacao, livestock.

Gualaceo (gwäläsĕ'ō), town (1950 pop. 2,735), Azuay prov., S Ecuador, in the Andes, 13 mi. ENE of Cuenca; alt. 7,611 ft. Agr. center (sugar cane, semitropical fruit, grain); mfg. of straw hats and textiles. Gold washing. Mercury deposits near by.

Gualaco (gwälä'kō), town (pop. 408), Olancho dept., E central Honduras, on N slope of Sierra de Agalta, on upper Sico R. and 30 mi. NE of Juticalpa, in livestock area; sugar milling; coffee, sugar, rice.

Gualaihué, Chile: see HUALAIHUÉ.

Gualán (gwälän'), town (1950 pop. 2,933), Zacapa dept., E Guatemala, on Motagua R. and 15 mi. NE of Zacapa, on railroad; agr. center; corn, wheat, coffee, sugar cane, livestock. Important port for small craft before founding of Puerto Barrios.

Gualaquiza (gwäläkē'sä), village, Santiago-Zamora prov., SE Ecuador, on E slopes of the Andes, 60 mi. SE of Cuenca (connected by road). A Salesian mission known for its straw plaiting.

Gualchos (gwäl'chōs), town (pop. 1,085), Granada prov., S Spain, 7 mi. E of Motril; cereals, wine, fruit. Its small fishing port of Castell de Ferro (pop. 1,205) is on Mediterranean 2 mi. ESE.

Gualdácano (gwäl-dhä'känō), suburban commune (pop. 7,101) SE of Bilbao, Vizcaya prov., N Spain; chemical works (explosives), sawmills. Chief village, La Cruz (pop. 2,661).

Gualdo Tadino (gwäl'dô tädē'nô), town (pop. 3,667), Perugia prov., Umbria, central Italy, 22 mi. ENE of Perugia. Noted for its ceramic industry; soap, perfume, wine, paint, leather goods. Bishopric. Has 13th-cent. cathedral. Near here Narses defeated and slew Totila in 552.

Gualeguay (gwälägwī'), city (pop. 23,237), ⊙ Gualeguay dept. (□ 2,385; 1947 pop. 42,065), S Entre Ríos prov., Argentina, on Gualeguay R., on railroad and 115 mi. NNW of Buenos Aires; cattle and agr. center. Slaughter houses, dairy plants, flour mills, tobacco factories. Trade in livestock, wheat, oats, flax, corn, fruit, olives, poultry. Airport. Has teachers col., theaters. Its port is Puerto Ruiz, 6 mi. SW.

Gualeguaychú (gwälägwīchōō'), city (pop. 36,911), ⊙ Gualeguaychú dept. (□ c.4,000; pop. estimate 95,000), SE Entre Ríos prov., Argentina, on Gualeguaychú R. near its mouth (7 mi. SE) on Uruguay R. and opposite Fray Bentos (Uruguay), 110 mi. N of Buenos Aires. Railhead; meat-packing center in area producing cattle, grain, and poultry. Also has sawmills. Heavy trade with Uruguay. Has natl. col., mus. of natural history and fine arts.

Gualeguaychú River, E Entre Ríos prov., Argentina, rises ENE of Villaguay, flows c.80 mi. S, past Gualeguaychú, to Uruguay R. opposite Fray Bentos (Uruguay), 7 mi. ESE of Gualeguaychú.

Gualeguay River, Entre Ríos prov., Argentina, rises 20 mi. WNW of Chajarí, flows c.220 mi. S, past Gualeguay, to Paraná Ibicuy R, an arm of Paraná R. in its delta, 22 mi. SW of Gualeguay.

Gualleco (gwäyä'kō), village (1930 pop. 244), Talca prov., central Chile, 23 mi. NW of Talca, in agr. area (wheat, barley, wine, livestock).

Gualpatanta (gwälpätän'tä), village, Colón dept., E Honduras, in Mosquitia, on Patuca R. and 65 mi. SE of Iriona; 15°11'N 84°38'W. Lumbering; livestock. Also spelled Wualpatanta.

Gualqui, Chile: see HUALQUI.

Gualtieri (gwältyä'rē), town (pop. 2,637), Reggio nell'Emilia prov., Emilia-Romagna, N central Italy, near Po R., 14 mi. N of Reggio nell'Emilia; foundry; wine making.

Guam (gwäm), island (□ 216; 1940 pop. 22,290; 1950 pop. 58,754), belonging to U.S., largest, most populous, and southernmost of MARIANAS ISLANDS, in W Pacific; c.30 mi. long, 4–10 mi. wide; 13°27'N 144°47'E. Mountainous in S, rising to 1,334 ft.; fertile valleys. Cultivates rice, coconuts, coffee, cacao, tobacco, pineapples, indigo; principal export, copra. APRA HARBOR, on W coast, is only good port. Inhabitants of Guam are chiefly Chamorros. Isl. was discovered 1521 by Magellan; belonged after 1668 to Spain; was taken 1898 by U.S. in Spanish-American War. Placed (1917) under Navy Dept.; granted (1950) local self govt. under civilian rule of Dept. of Interior. Guam is divided into 15 municipalities. It became an air-line base on the transpacific route in 1935. After much delay, appropriations were approved (1941) for improvement of Guam as an advance naval base, but before this could be accomplished Japan attacked (Dec. 7, 1941) and Guam fell on Dec. 9. Americans landed on Guam July 20, 1944, and after a bloody fight regained control of the isl. It became a major base for air and sea operations for the rest of the war.

Guamá (gwŭmä'), city (pop. 684), E Pará, Brazil, on Guamá R. and 80 mi. ESE of Belém; cacao, rubber. Until 1944, São Miguel do Guamá.

Guama (gwä'mä), town (pop. 2,097), Yaracuy state, N Venezuela, 7 mi. SW of San Felipe; cacao, coffee, sugar, corn, fruit.

Guamal (gwämäl'), town (pop. 1,994), Magdalena dept., N Colombia, on Magdalena R. and 20 mi. WNW of El Banco; yucca, livestock.

Guamaní River (gwämänē'), rivulet, SE Puerto Rico, flows c.10 mi. S, past Guayama, to the Caribbean. Its source is linked through artificial tunnel with L. Carite (on the La Plata), where water is diverted to feed the 3 Carite hydroelectric plants and irrigation channels.

Guamá River (gwŭmä'), E Pará, Brazil, rises near 3° S 47°W, flows N and then W to the Pará (Amazon delta) at Belém. Length, c.200 mi. Navigable to Ourém. Receives Capim R. (left) and joins the Guajará opposite Belém.

Guamblin Island (gwämblēn', wäm–) or **Socorro Island** (sōkō'rō), off coast of Aysén prov., S Chile, just N of 45°S and separated from Chonos Archipelago by Adventure Bay; 13 mi. long, c.5 mi. wide. Rises to 715 ft.

Guaminí (gwämēnē'), town (pop. 2,367), ⊙ Guaminí dist. (□ 1,864; pop. 16,239), W Buenos Aires prov., Argentina, 120 mi. N of Bahía Blanca, on Laguna del Monte; agr. area (alfalfa, grain, livestock); resort.

Guamo. 1 or **El Guamo** (ĕl gwä'mō), town (pop. 2,450), Bolívar dept., N Colombia, in Magdalena basin, 45 mi. SE of Cartagena; cotton, rice, corn, cattle. **2** Town (pop. 3,226), Tolima dept., W central Colombia, in Magdalena valley, on railroad and 23 mi. SSW of Girardot; agr. center (tobacco, yucca, bananas, rice, corn, cotton, cattle, hogs). Coal deposits near by.

Guamote (gwämō'tā), town (1950 pop. 2,567), Chimborazo prov., S central Ecuador, in high Andean valley, on Pan American Highway, on Guayaquil-Quito RR and 19 mi. SSW of Riobamba; cereals, potatoes, sheep, cattle. Native woolen goods. Trade with coast. Heavily damaged by 1949 earthquake.

Guamúchil (gwämōō'chēl), town (pop. 4,526), Sinaloa, NW Mexico, on Mocorito R., on railroad and 60 mi. NW of Culiacán; agr. center (chick-peas, sugar cane, tomatoes, fruit). Tropical forests (dyewood, rubber) near by.

Gua Musang (gōōä' mōōsäng'), village (pop. 357), S Kelantan, Malaya, 90 mi. S of Kota Bharu, on E coast railroad (dismantled during Second World War); jelutong factory.

Guamutas (gwämōō'täs), town (pop. 1,237), Matanzas prov., W Cuba, 23 mi. SE of Cárdenas; sugar cane, fruit, sisal.

Guanabacoa (gwänäbäkō'ä), city (pop. 30,287), Havana prov., W Cuba, 3 mi. E of Havana across Havana Harbor; mfg. of furniture, soft drinks, preserves, cigars, dairy products, tiles, pharmaceutical products; poultry farming. Mineral springs, copper deposits, stone quarries near by. An old colonial town with fine churches, administrative bldgs., theater, monasteries.

Guanabara Bay (gwŭnŭbä'rŭ), deep inlet of the Atlantic, in SE Brazil; city of RIO DE JANEIRO is on SW shore flanked by granitic peaks. It is 1 mi. wide at entrance (guarded on W by sheer SUGAR LOAF MOUNTAIN, and by forts), c.18 mi. long, up to 12 mi. wide. Contains numerous isls., notably Governador, Paquetá, Villegaignon, and Lage (which lies athwart entrance). Bay is sufficiently deep for large vessels to come alongside Rio wharves. W shore and most of isls. are in Federal Dist. Niterói, on E Shore opposite Rio, is ⊙ Rio de Janeiro state. N shore, fringed by BAIXADA FLUMINENSE coastal plain, is low and marshy. A federal reclamation project has been under way here since 1935. Also called Rio de Janeiro Bay.

Guanacache, Argentina: see HUANACACHE.

Guanacaste (gwänäkä'stä), province (□ 4,000; 1950 pop. 88,190) of NW Costa Rica, on the Pacific; ⊙ Liberia. Bounded N by Nicaragua and E by the Cordillera de Guanacaste, it includes greater part of Nicoya Peninsula (S) and is drained by Tempisque R. Mainly a stock-raising region, it also produces corn, beans, rice, sugar cane, hardwood; coffee on mtn. slopes. Gold mining along Abangares R. Served by Inter-American Highway and navigation on Tempisque R. Main centers are Liberia, Nicoya, and Santa Cruz.

Guanacaste, Cordillera de (kôrdĭyä'rä dā), section of continental divide in NW Costa Rica, extends 70 mi. NW-SE; rises to 6,627 ft. in the volcano Miravalles. Other heights are Orosi, Rincón de la Vieja, and Tenorio.

Guanaceví (gwänäsävē'), mining settlement (pop. 2,512), Durango, N Mexico, on E slopes of Sierra Madre Occidental, 70 mi. SSW of Hidalgo del Parral; mining center (gold, silver, lead, copper).

Guanaco (gwänä'kō), mining settlement (1930 pop. 120), Antofagasta prov., N Chile, on Andean plateau, on railroad and 65 mi. NE of Taltal; silver and gold mining.

Guanagazapa (gwänägäsä'pä), town (1950 pop. 508), Escuintla dept., S Guatemala, in Pacific piedmont, 11 mi. ESE of Escuintla; coffee, sugar cane, grain; livestock.

Guanaguana (gwänägwä'nä), town (pop. 609), Monagas state, NE Venezuela, 38 mi. NW of Maturín; tobacco growing.

Guanahacabibes Peninsula (gwänä-äkäbē'bĕs), Pinar del Río prov., W Cuba, westernmost part of the isl., facing Yucatan; extends c.45 mi. E from Cape San Antonio. The region is unhealthful and sparsely populated.

Guanahani, island, Bahama Isls.: see SAN SALVADOR ISLAND.

Guanaja Island (gwänä'hä), easternmost island (pop. 1,847) in Bay Islands dept., N Honduras, in Caribbean Sea, 34 mi. N of Trujillo; 10 mi. long, 3 mi. wide; rises to 1,200 ft. Coconuts, bananas, fruit, cacao. Main town, Guanaja (pop. 1,086), is on Sheen Cay and Hog Cay, 2 islets off SE coast, linked by bridge. Formerly called Bonacca. Sighted (1502) by Columbus.

Guanajay (gwänähī'), city (pop. 10,527), Pinar del Río prov., W Cuba, on Central Highway, on railroad and 25 mi. SW of Havana, in agr. region (sugar cane, tobacco, fruit); mfg. of cigars.

Guanajibo River (gwänähē'bō), SW Puerto Rico, flows c.25 mi. S and WNW, past San Germán, to Mona Passage 3 mi. SW of Mayagüez.

Guanajuato (gwänä-whä'tō), state (□ 11,805; 1940 pop. 1,046,490; 1950 pop. 1,317,629), central Mexico, on the central plateau; ⊙ Guanajuato. Bounded by San Luis Potosí (N), Jalisco (W), Michoacán (S), and Querétaro (E). It is a mountainous region (average alt. c.6,000 ft.), traversed by ranges (rising to c.11,000 ft.) of the Sierra Madre Occidental. Drained by Lerma R. and its affluents (the Río Turbio and Laja R.); the artificial L. Yuriria is in S. The climate, subtropical but moderately cool, varies with alt.; there are summer rains. Among the leading mining states of Mexico, it is fabulously rich in minerals, especially silver; also contains gold, lead, copper, zinc, tin, mercury, opals; mining is centered at Guanajuato, Irapuato, Xichú. Possesses many mineral springs. Fertile, well-irrigated plateaus and valleys produce corn, wheat, barley, alfalfa, rice, beans, chick-peas, potatoes, chili, sugar cane, tobacco, cotton, coffee, canary seed, peaches, pears; oranges in NE. Stock raising on considerable scale. Textile and flour mills, tanneries; liquor, alcohol, and wine distilleries; mfg. of straw hats, leather goods, shawls, glassware, ceramics; food-preserves industry concentrated at León, Guanajuato, Celaya, Irapuato, Salamanca, Acámbaro, and Valle de Santiago. Area was conquered by Spanish in 1526. Heavily disputed (1810) during early struggle for independence under Miguel Hidalgo y Costilla. Formed Sp. intendancy with Querétaro until 1824.

Guanajuato, city (pop. 23,521), ⊙ Guanajuato, central Mexico, in Sierra Madre Occidental, 80 mi. SSW of San Luis Potosí, 175 mi. NW of Mexico city; alt. 6,837 ft.; 21°1'N 101°15'W. Mining center (principally silver and gold; but also lead, copper, mercury). Has agr. trade (cereals, vegetables, sugar cane, fruit, livestock). Mfg. (gold-, silver-, and ironworks); potteries, cotton and silk mills, tanneries); dairy industry. Airport. Picturesque colonial city, founded 1554. Situated in a precipitous gorge (Cañada de Marfil, "ivory ravine"), it has steep, winding streets, and is a popular tourist spot. Has a state col. and a number of lavish old churches. The famed Alhóndiga de Granaditas (formerly a public granary, now a prison) was besieged and captured (1810) by Hidalgo y Costilla in the struggle for independence, for which Guanajuato was a principal center. La Valenciana church, built by the enormous riches of the now defunct La Valenciana silver mines, is in city outskirts.

Guañape (gwänyä'pä), village (pop. 42), Libertad dept., NW Peru, minor port on the Pacific, 12 mi. W of Virú; salt deposits.

Guanape (gwänä'pä), town (pop. 524), Anzoátegui state, NE Venezuela, 55 mi. WSW of Barcelona; cotton, corn, cattle.

Guañape Islands (gwänyä'pä), group of small islands (pop. 1,328), 7 mi. off Pacific coast of Libertad dept., NW Peru, 23 mi. S of Salaverry; 8°35'S 78°57'W; guano deposits; lighthouse.

Guanare (gwänä'rā), city (1941 pop. 3,650; 1950 census 8,062), ⊙ Portuguesa state, N Venezuela, in llanos, on highway to Barquisimeto (75 mi. NNE, direct) and 210 mi. WSW of Caracas; 9°3'N 69°45'W. Agr. region (cotton, coffee, cacao, sugar cane, corn, cattle). Iron deposits near by. Through its port Guerrilandia (S), on Guanare R., it is reached by river boat from Ciudad Bolívar and other towns on Orinoco and Apure rivers. Airfield. Known for natl. shrine to Our Lady of Coromoto, patron saint of Venezuela. In Andean foothills (NW) are the Santa Ana thermal springs.

Guanare River, W Venezuela, rises in Andean spur S of Tocuyo (Lara state), flows c.200 mi. E through llanos of Portuguesa and Bolívar states, past Biscucuy, Guerrilandia, Guanarito, and Arismendi, to Portuguesa R. at La Unión. W of Guanarito a 110-mi.-long arm, the Guanare Viejo, leaves the Guanare, forms part of Portuguesa-Barinas border, and rejoins the main stream 28 mi. from its mouth. Navigable.

Guanarito (gwänärē'tō), town (pop. 382), Portuguesa state, W Venezuela, in llanos, landing on Guanare R. and 45 mi. ESE of Guanare; cotton, cattle.

Guanay (gwänī'), town (pop. c.1,000), La Paz dept. W Bolivia, on Mapiri R., at mouth of the Tipuani, and 60 mi. NE of Sorata; cacao, sugar cane, rubber. Formerly also Huanay.

Guancha, La (lä gwän'chä), village (pop. 1,028), Tenerife, Canary Isls., 26 mi. WSW of Santa Cruz de Tenerife; corn, potatoes, wheat, grapes; mfg. of embroidery.

Guandacol (gwändäkōl'), village (pop. estimate 500), W La Rioja prov., Argentina, 110 mi. W of La Rioja. Mining and farming center (wheat, grapes, anise); zinc and lead mines; flour milling.

It is in a fertile subandean valley of a tributary of the Bermejo.

Guandu River (gwăndōō′), coastal stream of Rio de Janeiro state, Brazil, rises in the Serra do Mar, flows c.30 mi. S to Sepetiba Bay of the Atlantic near Itaguaí. In lower course it forms W border of Federal Dist. Receives (right) the Ribeirão das Lages.

Guane (gwä′nā), town (pop. 2,248), Pinar del Río prov., W Cuba, on Cuyaguateje R. and 28 mi. SW of Pinar del Río; rail terminus and agr. center (sugar, tobacco, beeswax, honey); lumbering.

Guane River, Cuba: see Cuyaguateje River.

Guanhães (gwŭnyä′ĭs), city (pop. 2,445), E central Minas Gerais, Brazil, 55 mi. SE of Diamantina; coffee, dairy products. Beryl mining.

Guánica (gwä′nēkä), town (pop. 4,833), SW Puerto Rico, on well-protected Guánica Bay, on railroad and 20 mi. W of Ponce; sugar-milling, -refining, and -shipping center. Port of entry. Originally settled 1510. Site of 1st landing of U.S. troops (1898). The large Guánica sugar mill is 2½ mi. W at Ensenada.

Guánica Lagoon (c.3 mi. long), SW Puerto Rico, near the coast, 2 mi. N of Ensenada, and linked with the Caribbean. Known for wild fowl.

Guaniguanico, archipelago, Cuba: see Colorados, Los.

Guaniguanico, Serranía de (sĕrānē′ä dā gwänēgwänē′kō), low hilly range, Pinar del Río prov., W Cuba, extends c.40 mi. NW from Mantua, forms outliers of the Sierra de los Órganos. Rugged limestone formation. Sometimes, as Cordillera de Guaniguanico, it is considered to include the entire W range of the isl. with the Sierra de los Órganos and Sierra del Rosario.

Guanillos (gwänĭ′yōs), abandoned village, Tarapacá prov., N Chile, former port on the Pacific, and 9 mi. W of Salar Grande (salt flat), 75 mi. S of Iquique; exported guano. Copper, silver deposits near by.

Guanipa River (gwänē′pä), NE Venezuela, rises on low tableland NE of Pariaguán (Anzoátegui state), flows c.175 mi. ENE, through lowland marshes, to Gulf of Paria 13 mi. W of Pedernales. Partly navigable. Receives Amaná R.

Guano (gwä′nō), town (1950 pop. 4,477), Chimborazo prov., Ecuador, in high Andean valley, 6 mi. N of Riobamba. Noted for mfg. of woolen goods (yarns, carpets, blankets, etc.); sisal-hemp industry uses henequen grown in vicinity. Thermal springs near by. Heavily damaged by 1949 earthquake. Also called La Matriz.

Guanoco (gwänō′kō), asphalt lake in Sucre state, NE Venezuela, in Gulf of Paria lowlands, 37 mi. NE of Maturín; considered to contain largest deposits in the world. Linked by local railroad with village of Guanoco, 4 mi. SW. Petroleum deposits near by.

Guanta (gwän′tä), town (pop. 1,699), Anzoátegui state, NE Venezuela, port on the Caribbean, serving Barcelona (10 mi. SW), with which it is linked by rail and highway; ships cattle, hides, lumber, coffee, petroleum. Excellent natural harbor. Lignite and semibituminous coal deposits near by.

Guantajaya or **Huantajaya** (both: wäntī′ä), former mining settlement, Tarapacá prov., N Chile, 5 mi. E of Iquique; silver deposits, famed in colonial period, are now abandoned.

Guantánamo (gwäntä′nämō), city (pop. 42,423), Oriente prov., E Cuba, on railroad and 40 mi. ENE of Santiago de Cuba. Served by ports Caimanera and Boquerón (11 mi. SSE) on sheltered Guantánamo Bay, where U.S. maintains a naval reserve. Important trading and processing center for rich agr. region (sugar cane, molasses, coffee, cacao, corn, onions, potatoes, honey, beeswax, cattle). Coffee roasting, sugar milling, tanning, sawmilling; mfg. of chocolate, liqueurs, vermicelli, salt. Several sugar centrals are near by. Has airfield; and fine administrative bldgs., theater.

Guantánamo Bay, sheltered Caribbean inlet (12 mi. long, up to 5 mi. wide), Oriente prov., SE Cuba, 8 mi. S of Guantánamo, which is served by ports Caimanera (W) and Boquerón (E), opposite each other on central narrows. The S basin with adjoining shore line is site of the U.S. naval reserve and includes airfields (McCalla Field) and fortifications. Called Cumberland Harbor by the English when they landed (1741) here under Admiral Vernon and Gen. Wentworth. U.S. troops disembarked on the beach in Spanish-American War.

Guantánamo River, Oriente prov., E Cuba, rises E of Santiago de Cuba, flows c.50 mi. E and SSE to Guantánamo Bay near Caimanera. Navigable for small vessels in lower course.

Guap, Caroline Isls.: see Yap.

Guapi (gwä′pē, gwäpē′), town (pop. 1,348), Cauca dept., SW Colombia, minor port on the Pacific, at mouth of small Guapi R., 90 mi. W of Popayán; 2°36′N 77°53′W. Pearl fisheries. Airport. Sometimes Guapí.

Guapi Island. 1 Island in the coastal lagoon Laguna del Budi, Cautín prov., S central Chile, 40 mi. SW of Temuco; c.4 mi. long. Cereals, livestock. **2** Island in L. Ranco, Valdivia prov., S central Chile, 35 mi. E of La Unión; 3 mi. long, 2 mi. wide. Resort.

Guápiles (gwä′pēlĕs), town (dist. pop. 2,766), Limón prov., E Costa Rica, at N foot of the volcano Turrialba, 55 mi. NNW of Limón. Agr. center (corn, livestock). Formerly an important banana center.

Guapimirim (gwŭpēmērēn′), town (pop. 1,821), central Rio de Janeiro state, Brazil, on railroad and 32 mi. NNE of Rio; fruit. Formerly spelled Guapy-Mirim.

Guapó (gwŭpô′), city (pop. 901), S Goiás, central Brazil, 18 mi. WSW of Goiânia. Until 1944, called Ribeirão.

Guapo (gwä′pō), village, SW Trinidad, B.W.I., on N shore of SW peninsula, 14 mi. WSW of San Fernando. Petroleum wells near by.

Guapo, Venezuela: see El Guapo.

Guaporé (gwŭpōōrĕ′), federal territory (□ 98,132; 1950 census pop. 37,438), W Brazil; ⊙ Pôrto Velho. Bounded S and W by Guaporé, Mamoré, and Madeira rivers (which form Bolivia border), and N by Amazonas and E by Mato Grosso states. Crossed NW-SE by low mtn. range (westernmost spur of the Serra dos Parecis) which merges in N with the Amazon lowland. Drained by the Madeira and its tributaries. Collecting of latex, Brazil nuts, and copaiba is chief occupation of sparse pop. Valuable lumber is also shipped. Large tracts are uninhabited and unexplored. Chief towns are Pôrto Velho and Guajará Mirim at either terminus of Madeira-Mamoré RR (227 mi. long), completed around the rapids on Madeira and Mamoré rivers in 1913. Region prospered during short rubber boom in early 20th cent. Guaporé territory was carved out of parts of Amazonas and Mato Grosso in 1943.

Guaporé, city (pop. 2,691), NE Rio Grande do Sul, Brazil, in the Serra Geral, 90 mi. NW of Pôrto Alegre; winegrowing, meat processing, dairying.

Guaporé River or **Iténez River** (ētā′nēs), central S America, rises in the Serra dos Parecis (Mato Grosso, Brazil) near 14°40′S 59°0′W, flows c.750 mi. NW, past Mato Grosso city (head of barge navigation), through empty tropical rain forest, forming Brazil-Bolivia border from 14°S to its influx into the Mamoré. Rubber is gathered along its shores. Chief tributaries are the Rio Verde, Río Blanco, Itonamas, Paraguá (left). Guaporé is the Braz. name, Iténez the Bolivian name.

Guápulo (gwä′pōōlō), village, Pichincha prov., N central Ecuador, in the Andes, 3 mi. ENE of Quito; a beautiful resort. Has notable art treasures in the 1st church built on Ecuadorian soil.

Guaqui (gwä′kē), town (pop. c.11,300), La Paz dept., W Bolivia, on Gulf of Taraco of L. Titicaca, near Peru border, and 50 mi. W of La Paz; alt. 12,506 ft. Chief Bolivian port on L. Titicaca (steamer service to Puno, Peru) and terminus of rail line from La Paz. Founded 1900; succeeded Puerto Pérez as main Titicaca port. Formerly also spelled Huaqui.

Guará (gwŭrä′), city (pop. 2,411), NE São Paulo, Brazil, on railroad and 50 mi. N of Ribeirão Prêto; sugar milling, distilling, pottery mfg., tanning, rice and coffee processing.

Guara (gwä′rä), town (pop. 1,114), Havana prov., W Cuba, on railroad and 25 mi. SSE of Havana, in sugar-growing region.

Guarabira (gwŭrŭbē′rŭ), city (pop. 6,184), E Paraíba, NE Brazil, on railroad (junction of spur to Bananeiras) and 45 mi. NW of João Pessoa; cotton ginning, processing of agave fibers; livestock. Formerly called Independência.

Guarachita, Mexico: see Villamar.

Guaraci (gwŭrŭsē′), city (pop. 1,652), N São Paulo, Brazil, 25 mi. W of Barretos; coffee, sugar cane, rice, tobacco.

Guarajambala River (gwärähämbä′lä), SW Honduras, formed 13 mi. ESE of Candelaria by union of San Juan R. (right) and shorter Río Negro (left); flows 13 mi. SW to Lempa R. 12 mi. SSE of Candelaria; length (including San Juan R.), c.50 mi.

Guarambaré (gwärämbärā′), town (dist. pop. 7,216), Central dept., S Paraguay, 20 mi. SE of Asunción; processing center; sugar refineries, alcohol distilleries, cotton gins, rice mills. Agr. products: rice, tobacco, cotton, fruit; cattle. Founded near by in 1538, moved to present site in 1673.

Guaranda (–rän′dä), city (1950 pop. 7,287), ⊙ Bolívar prov., central Ecuador, in the Andes, on headstream of Chimbo R. and 105 mi. SSW of Quito, 70 mi. NE of Guayaquil, towered over by the snow-capped Chimborazo (NE); 1°37′S 79°W; alt. 8,720 ft. Pleasant temperate climate. Agr. center, producing and trading in cinchona, cereals, timber, cattle. Tanning. Salt and mercury deposits near by. Before construction of Andean railroad it was an important transshipment point bet. Guayaquil and Quito.

Guaranda, Cordillera de (kōrdĭ-yä′rä dā), W Andean range, central Ecuador, on Bolívar–Los Ríos prov. border, running parallel (N-S) to main cordilleras, just W of Guaranda; c.30 mi. long. Rises to over 9,500 ft.

Guaranésia (gwŭrŭnĕ′zyŭ), city (pop. 4,453), SW Minas Gerais, Brazil, near São Paulo border, on railroad and 6 mi. W of Guaxupé; ships coffee, sugar, cereals, fruit, tobacco.

Guaraní, Argentina: see Monteagudo.

Guarani (gwŭrŭnē′). **1** City, Ceará, Brazil: see Pacajús. **2** City (pop. 2,242), S Minas Gerais, Brazil, on railroad and 35 mi. NE of Juiz de Fora; coffee, tobacco, sugar, butter. Formerly spelled Guarany.

Guarantã (gwŭrŭntã′), city (pop. 1,510), W central São Paulo, on railroad and 45 mi. NW of Bauru; coffee, sugar, tobacco.

Guarapari (gwŭrŭpŭrē′), city (pop. 1,635), S central Espírito Santo, Brazil, port on the Atlantic, 28 mi. SW of Vitória; exploits monazitic sands. Formerly spelled Guarapary.

Guarapiche River (gwäräpē′chā), Monagas state, NE Venezuela, rises in coastal range SW of San Antonio, flows c.100 mi. generally E in a semicircle, past Maturín, to San Juan R. near its mouth on the Gulf of Paria. Navigable for small craft.

Guarapo (gwärä′pō), naval reservation, Cristobal dist., N Panama Canal Zone, on tiny Guarapo Isl. in Gatun L., 7 mi. SSW of Colón.

Guarapuava (gwŭrŭpwä′vŭ), city (pop. 3,698), S central Paraná, Brazil, 140 mi. W of Curitiba; stock-raising center; processes hides, maté, corn, animal fats; sawmilling. Airfield.

Guararapes (gwŭrŭrä′pĭs), city (pop. 4,664), NW São Paulo, Brazil, on railroad and 15 mi. W of Araçatuba; coffee and rice processing, distilling, pottery mfg.

Guararé (gwärärā′), town (pop. 828), Los Santos prov., S central Panama, in Pacific lowland, on branch of Inter-American Highway and 4 mi. N of Las Tablas; sugar cane, livestock.

Guararema (gwŭrŭrā′mŭ), city (pop. 1,321), SE São Paulo, Brazil, on great bend of Paraíba R. (which here is nearest São Paulo), on railroad and 40 mi. ENE of São Paulo; rum distilling; agr. (beans, rice, corn).

Guaratinguetá (gwŭrŭtĕng-gĭtä′), city (1950 pop. 21,480), SE São Paulo, Brazil, on Paraíba R., on railroad and 100 mi. NE of São Paulo; dairying center; meat packing, textile milling (woolens); agr. (rice, fruit, coffee).

Guaratuba (gwŭrŭtōō′bŭ), city (pop. 566), SE Paraná, Brazil, port on Guaratuba Bay (sheltered 10-mi. inlet of the Atlantic), 25 mi. S of Paranaguá; timber, rice, sugar. Kaolin deposits.

Guaraúna (gwŭrŭōō′nŭ), town (pop. 426), SE central Paraná, Brazil, on railroad and 18 mi. SSW of Ponta Grossa; manganese deposits. Until 1944, called Valinhos.

Guaraúnos (gwäräōō′nōs), town (pop. 655), Sucre state, NE Venezuela, 12 mi. SE of Carúpano; cacao growing.

Guar Chempedak, Malaya: see Gua Chempedak.

Guarcino (gwärchē′nō), town (pop. 2,727), Frosinone prov., Latium, S central Italy, in the Apennines, on branch of Sacco R. and 11 mi. NNW of Frosinone. Resort (alt. 2,050 ft.); paper mills, foundry.

Guarco, El, canton, Costa Rica: see Tejar.

Guarco Valley (gwär′kō), E section of central plateau of Costa Rica, in Cartago prov. Separated from San José area (W) by Ochomogo Pass, it lies bet. Irazú volcano (NE) and the Cordillera de Talamanca (SW); 10 mi. long, 4 mi. wide; alt. 3,600–4,800 ft. Agr.: potatoes, grain, truck produce, livestock. Main centers are Cartago, Tejar, San Rafael, Paraíso.

Guarda (gwär′dŭ), district (□ 2,122; pop. 294,166), in Beira Alta prov., N central Portugal; ⊙ Guarda. Bounded by Spain (E) and the Douro (N). Traversed in SW by the Serra da Estrêla which here rises to 6,532 ft. Sheep raising is chief occupation; agr., including winegrowing in upper Mondêgo and Douro river valleys. Some dairying and textile milling.

Guarda, city (pop. 6,556), ⊙ Guarda dist., Beira Alta prov., N central Portugal, near NE extremity of Serra da Estrêla, 85 mi. SE of Oporto; alt. 3,450 ft. Rail junction; agr. trade center; leatherworking, distilling. Episcopal see. Has 15th–16th-cent. cathedral, and large sanatorium. Founded 1197 as a fortress against the Moors.

Guardafui, Cape (gwärdäfōō′ē, –fwē′), Arabic *Ras Assir*, anc. *Aromata*, easternmost point of Africa after near-by Ras Hafun, in Ital. Somaliland, at tip of E Africa's "horn," on Indian Ocean; 11°49′N 51°17′E. Forms S entrance of Gulf of Aden. Socotra isl. is 145 mi. ENE. Lighthouse.

Guardamar del Segura (gwärdhämär′ dhĕl sägōō′rä), town (pop. 3,645), Alicante prov., E Spain, near the Mediterranean, S of mouth of Segura R., 20 mi. SSW of Alicante; sweet potatoes, corn, peppers, watermelons.

Guardavalle (gwär″däväl′lĕ), town (pop. 4,944), Catanzaro prov., Calabria, S Italy, near Gulf of Squillace, 28 mi. S of Catanzaro; wine, olive oil, silk.

Guard Bridge, Scotland: see Leuchars.

Guardia, La (lä gwär′dhyä). **1** Town (pop. 3,031), Pontevedra prov., NW Spain, in Galicia, 24 mi. SSW of Vigo, seaport on the Atlantic near Miño R. estuary (Port. border); fishing and fish processing, lobster shipping, boatbuilding; embarkation point for emigrants. Has Jesuit col. Tourist resort. **2** Town (pop. 3,364), Toledo prov., central Spain, 19 mi. SSE of Aranjuez; agr. center (cereals, grapes). Lumbering, flour milling, dairying. Hydroelectric plant.

Guardia de Jaén, La (dhä hä'ĕn'), town (pop. 2,843), Jaén prov., S Spain, 6 mi. ESE of Jaén; olive-oil processing; cereals, esparto, fruit. On slope of hill crowned by ruins of anc. fort.

Guardia Escolta (ĕskōl'tä), village (pop. estimate 1,000), SE Santiago del Estero prov., Argentina, on railroad and 55 mi. SE of Añatuya; agr. center (flax, corn, alfalfa, livestock); dairying; experimental farm.

Guardiagrele (gwärdyägrā'lĕ), town (pop. 4,015), Chieti prov., Abruzzi e Molise, S central Italy, 12 mi. S of Chieti; woolen textiles, wrought-iron products. Severely damaged in Second World War.

Guardia Lombardi (gwär'dyä lômbär'dē), village (pop. 1,619), Avellino prov., Campania, S Italy, 22 mi. ENE of Avellino; macaroni mfg.

Guardia Sanframondo (sänfrämôn'dô), town (pop. 5,852), Benevento prov., Campania, S Italy, 13 mi. NW of Benevento; wine, olive oil. Has medieval castle.

Guardo (gwär'dhō), town (pop. 2,267), Palencia prov., N central Spain, on Carrión R. and 42 mi. ENE of Leon; livestock, potatoes, cereals. Anthracite and bituminous-coal mines near by.

Guardunha, Serra da (sĕ'rŭ dŭ gwärdōō'nyŭ), mtn. range in Castelo Branco dist., central Portugal, just S of Fundão; rises to 4,012 ft.

Guare (gwä'rā), village, Los Ríos prov., W central Ecuador, in tropical lowlands, on tributary of the Guayas system, and 15 mi. WNW of Babahoyo, in fertile agr. region (cacao, sugar cane, rice, tropical fruit and woods); rice milling.

Guareí (gwŭrĭ-ē'), city (pop. 1,028), S central São Paulo, Brazil, 17 mi. NNW of Itapetininga; coffee, cotton, rice. Bituminous schist deposits near by.

Guareña (gwärā'nyä), town (pop. 7,870), Badajoz prov., W Spain, 14 mi. ESE of Mérida; processing and agr. center (olives, chick-peas, tubers, cereals, grapes, livestock); wine, vinegar, vermouth distilling; mfg. of shoes, soap.

Guarenas (gwärā'näs), town (pop. 3,093), Miranda state, N Venezuela, in valley of coastal range, 20 mi. E of Caracas; agr. center (coffee, corn, cacao, sugar cane, fruit); sugar milling.

Guariba (gwŭrē'bŭ), city (pop. 1,845), N central São Paulo, Brazil, on railroad and 30 mi. SW of Ribeirão Prêto, in coffee region; furniture mfg.

Guárico (gwä'rēkō), state (□ 25,640; 1941 pop. 135,089; 1950 census 163,505), central Venezuela; ⊙ San Juan de los Morros. Bordered N by outliers of the coastal range, S by Orinoco R. and its tributaries, the Apure and Portuguesa. Entirely a llano region, with tropical climate. Primarily a cattle-raising area. Agr. crops include coffee, cacao, sugar cane in N; corn, cotton, tobacco along the rivers. Main industry is dairying; some coal mining. Valle de la Pascua is its trading center. San Juan de los Morros is a popular health resort.

Guárico, town (pop. 1,546), Lara state, NW Venezuela, in N Andean spur, on transandine highway and 45 mi. SW of Barquisimeto; alt. 3,546 ft. Coffee, cereals, sugar cane, tobacco, fruit, livestock.

Guarico, Cape (gwärē'kō), headland, Oriente prov., E Cuba, 24 mi. NW of Baracoa; 20°22'N 74°29'W.

Guárico River (gwä'rēkō), in N and central Venezuela, rises W of Belén (Carabobo state), flows c.300 mi. E and S, past Barbacoas (Aragua state), El Sombrero and Calabozo (Guárico state), to N arm of Apure R. 15 mi. ESE of San Fernando. Navigable for small craft. Receives Orituco R.

Guariquén (gwärēkĕn'), town (pop. 634), Sucre state, NE Venezuela, on narrow inlet of Gulf of Paria, 39 mi. NNE of Maturín; rice, coconuts.

Guar Island (gwär) (□ 13.5; pop. 2,207), S central Chile, in Reloncaví Sound, 13 mi. S of Puerto Montt; 41°41'S 72°57'W; 6 mi. long, 4 mi. wide. Chief village, Quetrulauquén.

Guarita (gwärē'tä), town (pop. 825), Lempira dept., W Honduras, near Sumpul R. (Salvador border), 21 mi. SSW of Gracias; commercial center; indigo, grain, livestock.

Guaro (gwä'rō), town (pop. 956), Oriente prov., E Cuba, 9 mi. W of Mayarí, near Nipe Bay; agr. settlement (sugar cane).

Guaro (gwä'rō), town (pop. 2,555), Málaga prov., S Spain, 23 mi. W of Málaga; olives, figs, raisins.

Guarromán (gwärōmän'), town (pop. 2,426), Jaén prov., S Spain, 7 mi. NNW of Linares; olive-oil processing; cereals, wine. Lead mines.

Guarujá (gwŭrōōzhä'), city (pop. 5,397), SE São Paulo, Brazil, on S coast of Santo Amaro Isl., 5 mi. SE of Santos (linked by rail). State's leading bathing resort (with casino) on the open Atlantic; shipyards. New tourist playground at adjoining Praia Pernambuco.

Guarulhos (gwŭrōō'lyōōs). **1** Town, Rio de Janeiro, Brazil: see GUARUS. **2** City (pop. 6,660), SE São Paulo state, Brazil, outer NE suburb of São Paulo, 10 mi. from city center, near Tietê R. Major airport. Mfg. (cotton and silk textiles, leather goods, lace, pottery); truck gardens, vineyards. Founded 1560. Has old cathedral.

Guarus (gwŭrōōs'), town (pop. 6,368), NE Rio de Janeiro state, Brazil, in Paraíba R. delta, on railroad and 4 mi. N of Campos; sugar growing and milling. Until 1943, called Guarulhos.

Guasapampa, Sierra de (syĕ'rä dā gwäsäpäm'pä), pampean mountain range in W Córdoba prov., Argentina, W ridge of Sierra de Córdoba, extends c.45 mi. S from the Salinas Grandes; rises to c.4,500 ft.

Guasave (gwäsä'vä), town (pop. 4,997), Sinaloa, NW Mexico, on Sinaloa R. (irrigation) and 85 mi. NW of Culiacán; agr. center (chick-peas, corn, sugar cane, tomatoes, fruit).

Guasayán, department, Argentina: see SAN PEDRO, Santiago del Estero prov.

Guasayán, Sierra de (syĕ'rä dā gwäsäyän'), pampean mountain range in W Santiago del Estero prov., Argentina, extends c.50 mi. S from the area 10 mi. S of Río Hondo to La Punta; rises to c.2,000 ft. Rich in minerals: lime, granite, gypsum, sand, quartzite, copper, manganese; petroleum wells.

Guasca (gwäs'kä), village (pop. 761), Cundinamarca dept., central Colombia, 24 mi. NE of Bogotá; alt. 8,914 ft.; mfg. of textile goods.

Guascama Point (gwäskä'mä), Pacific headland on coast of Nariño dept., SW Colombia, 60 mi. NNE of Tumaco; 2°38'N 78°30'W.

Guasco, town, Chile: see HUASCO.

Guasco River, Chile: see HUASCO RIVER.

Guasila (gwäzē'lä), village (pop. 2,538), Cagliari prov., S Sardinia, 23 mi. N of Cagliari.

Guasimal (gwäsēmäl'), town (pop. 1,721), Las Villas prov., central Cuba, on railroad and 13 mi. S of Sancti-Spíritus; tobacco, sugar cane, stock.

Guasipati (gwäsēpä'tē), town (pop. 1,678), Bolívar state, E Venezuela, 10 mi. NW of El Callao, 130 mi. ESE of Ciudad Bolívar; gold mining; diamond market. Airfield.

Guaso River (gwä'sō), Oriente prov., E Cuba, rises 5 mi. NNW of Jamaica, flows 20 mi. S, past Guantánamo, to Guantánamo Bay 4 mi. N of Caimanera. Navigable below Guantánamo for small boats.

Guastalla (gwästäl'lä), town (pop. 3,934), Reggio nell'Emilia prov., Emilia-Romagna, N central Italy, near Po R., 15 mi. N of Reggio nell'Emilia; mfg. (agr. machinery, furnaces, pumps, packing boxes, insecticides). Bishopric. Has 16th-cent. cathedral.

Guasti (gwŏ'stē), village (pop. c.650), San Bernardino co., S Calif., just E of Ontario; wine-growing.

Guatacondo (gwätäkōn'dō), village (pop. 178), Tarapacá prov., N Chile, on W slope of the Andes, 85 mi. SE of Iquique; copper-mining center.

Guatajiagua (gwätähyä'gwä), city (pop. 3,812), Morazán dept., E Salvador, 6 mi. W of San Francisco; pottery making; coffee, sugar cane, grain.

Guatapé (gwätäpā'), town (pop. 2,427), Antioquia dept., NW central Colombia, in Cordillera Central, 28 mi. E of Medellín; alt. 6,299 ft.; corn, yucca, cattle, stock.

Guatavita (gwätävē'tä), town (pop. 1,043), Cundinamarca dept., central Colombia, in Cordillera Oriental, 28 mi. NE of Bogotá; alt. 8,583 ft. Cereals, potatoes, fruit, stock; mfg. of textile goods. L. Guatavita, 5 mi. NE, was held sacred by anc. Chibchas.

Guatemala (gwätŭmä'lŭ), republic (□ 42,042; 1950 pop. 2,786,403), northernmost and most populous country of Central America; ⊙ Guatemala. Extends c.170 mi. bet. the Caribbean Sea (Gulf of Honduras) on NE and Pacific Ocean on S. Bounded N and W (partly along SUCHIATE RIVER and USUMACINTA RIVER) by Mexico, E and SE by Honduras and Salvador (Río de la Paz), while the N isolated lowland of Petén dept. reaching into YUCATAN PENINSULA has British Honduras on E. Situated approximately bet. 13°45'–17°50'N and 88°15'–92°10'W, Guatemala is of diverse topography and great scenic beauty, popular with American tourists. Traversed E–W by the main cordillera of Central America, which continues into Mexico as Sierra Madre. This formidable chain, rising in the Tajumulco (13,816 ft.) to highest elevation in Central America, is flanked for its entire length on the Pacific side by a string of volcanoes, such as Tacaná (13,333 ft.) on Mexican border, Acatenango (12,992 ft.), Agua (12,310 ft.), Atitlán (11,565 ft.), Fuego (12,582 ft.), and Santa María (12,362 ft.); the last 2 are active. At their highest near the narrow Pacific coast line, towards which they fall steeply, the mts. descend more gently toward the N interior and the Caribbean. There are several spurs, such as Sierra de Santa Cruz, Sierra de Chamá, Sierra de las Minas, and the Chuchumatanes massif, which cut across the principal centers of colonization, enclosing high plateaus (generally above 4,000 ft.). Violent earthquakes are a frequent occurrence. There are numerous rivers, short torrents on the Pacific side, longer ones emptying into the Caribbean. Tributary to the Caribbean are SASTOON RIVER (on Br. Honduras border) and MONTAGUA RIVER. The POLOCHIC RIVER flows through large L. IZABAL, whose outlet is the navigable Río DULCE. Among the picturesque mtn. lakes of the interior are L. ATITLÁN, surrounded by volcanic cones, and L. AMATITLÁN. L. PETÉN lies in midst of N jungle. The climate of the country—geographically within the tropics—varies greatly. The coastal plains and Petén dept. are hot and humid, constituting, as in most Latin American countries, the tropical *tierra caliente* zone up to 1,500 ft. This area, rich in hardwoods, medicinal plants, chicle, bananas, and abacá plantations, is the region of luxuriant rain forests and savannas. The *tierra templada* of the uplands (c.3,500 ft.–10,000 ft.), with a climate from subtropical to temperate, yields the principal crops and supports livestock. Above this zone extends the cool *tierra fría*, suitable for wheat, potato, and apple growing, and sheep raising. A rainy season, called winter, lasts approximately from May to Oct. Annual rainfall is about 45 inches on the plateau, but reaches 200 inches in some lowland sections. The mid-Motagua valley is arid. Mineral resources are so far of little economic importance. Some lead and silver (Huehuetenango dept.), chromite (Jalapa dept.), sulphur, and salt is mined. There are a few unimportant gold placers, and also non-exploited petroleum deposits in Petén and Izabal depts. While the country is predominantly agricultural, only about 10% of the area is cultivated. Forests cover an estimated 60%, principally in the plains. They are rich in mahogany, cedar, dyewoods, lignum vitae, rubber, balsa, cinchona, etc., and furnish chicle, a substantial export, which is flown out by plane from the Petén area. The leading tropical crop from the lowlands is bananas. These were formerly grown in Montagua and Caribbean basin, where, because of plant disease, bananas have been largely superseded by abacá. Most of the banana crop is now produced near the Pacific coast, particularly near TIQUISATE. By far the leading crop is coffee, a "mild" variety, raised on mtn. slopes of the Pacific depts. and in the interior of Verapaz dept. Coffee alone averages 60% of all exports, followed by bananas, c.30%. The other agr. exports are abacá, essential oils (from citronella and lemon grass), coconuts, hides, and honey. Subsistence crops include corn (grown in all parts), beans, sugar, rice, cotton, tobacco, cacao. In 1949 the U.S. took 92% of entire exports, and supplied 74% of the imports (petroleum products, pharmaceuticals, textiles, cotton, flour, paper, machinery, vehicles, metal goods). Foreign trade passes principally through Caribbean port of PUERTO BARRIOS; lesser ports are LÍVINGSTON and, on the Pacific, Ocós, CHAMPERICO, and SAN JOSÉ. Chief trading center is the capital, Guatemala city (alt. 4,872 ft.), largest city of Central America, seat of famous San Carlos Univ. Here are textile mills (leading industry) and a cement plant. The few domestic industries process the primary products and turn out consumer goods such as leather ware, furniture, soap, matches, cigarettes, rubber goods. Trading and mfg. centers, most of them located in the highlands, are, apart from the capital, ANTIGUA (the old, once flourishing capital, destroyed by 1773 earthquake), COBÁN, ESCUINTLA, MAZATENANGO, QUEZALTENANGO (focus of pre-Spanish settlements), RETALHULEU, TOTONICAPÁN, ZACAPA. The country is crossed by the Inter-American Highway. Railroads communicate with Mexico and Salvador and link the capital (also a hub for natl. and international air lines) with the Caribbean and Pacific ports. The native Indians (c.65% of the people) follow, except in large urban centers, their own mode of life, distinctive in old craft and folklore. Most of them own their fields but also work the large plantations, owned by the Creole governing class and, formerly, by German immigrants (dispossessed during Second World War). A few Caribs and Negroes live on the NE coast. In Guatemala originated the great Maya-Quiché civilizations, to which testify the fabulous ruins of QUIRIGUÁ (Izabal dept.), TIKAL, and UAXACTÚN (Petén dept.). These people were defeated (1523–24) by the Sp. conquistador Pedro de Alvarado, head of captaincy general of Guatemala, which included most of Central America, and whose capital became Antigua. Independence of Central America was declared (1821) at Guatemala city. Guatemala was briefly annexed to Mexican Empire under Iturbide. It was also the nucleus of the Central American Federation (1823–38), but seceded in 1839. Then forceful leaders, the conservatives Rafael Carrera, Manuel Estrada Cabrera, and the liberal Justo Rufino Barrios attempted to dominate Central American affairs in 19th and early 20th cent. Boundary dispute with Honduras was settled 1933; Guatemala still claims Br. Honduras. Social reforms were introduced (1936) by Jorge Ubico. Guatemala sided with the Allies in the 2 World Wars. The Guatemalan people are predominantly R.C. While Spanish is the official and most widely used language, a large minority still speaks several Indian dialects. For further information see separate articles on towns, cities, physical features, and the following 22 depts.: CHIMALTENANGO, CHIQUIMULA, EL PROGRESO, ESCUINTLA, GUATEMALA, HUEHUETENANGO, IZABAL, JALAPA, JUTIAPA, PETÉN, QUEZALTENANGO, QUICHÉ, RETALHULEU, SACATEPÉQUEZ, SAN MARCOS, SANTA ROSA, SOLOLÁ, SUCHITEPÉQUEZ, TOTONICAPÁN, ALTA VERAPAZ, BAJA VERAPAZ, ZACAPA.

Guatemala, department (□ 821; 1950 pop. 439,611), S central Guatemala; ⊙ Guatemala. In central highlands; bounded N by Motagua R.; includes L. Amatitlán (S). Mainly agr. (corn, black beans, coffee, fodder grasses, sugar cane); cattle and hog raising. Home industries produce pottery, textiles.

Chief cities, Guatemala (center of mfg. industries) and Amatitlán (summer resort), are linked by railroad crossing dept. NE–SW.

Guatemala or **Guatemala City,** city (1950 pop. 283,100), ⊙ Guatemala and Guatemala dept., in broad valley of central highlands, on Inter-American Highway, on railroad, and 150 mi. SW of Puerto Barrios, its Caribbean port; 14°35′N 90°32′ W; alt. 4,872 ft. Largest city of Central America; connected by rail with the ports of Puerto Barrios, San José, and Champerico, and with Mexico City and San Salvador; also served by international and local airlines. A major commercial center for exporting and importing activities; handles most of Guatemala's coffee trade. Mfg.: cement, furniture, leather goods, soap, textiles, cigars, beer, and food products. Laid out in checkerboard fashion, Guatemala centers on Parque Central (formerly called Plaza de Armas), which has Natl. Palace (completed 1943; N), cathedral (built 1782–1815; E), and city hall (SW). Business district (S) is adjoined by railroad station, yards, and small-scale industries. Residential areas terminate N in Minerva Park (with noted relief map of the country) and S in La Aurora Park (airport, zoological garden, archaeological mus., observatory, and race track). Guatemala is seat of Univ. of San Carlos, one of the outstanding institutions of higher learning in Central America. There are also: technical school (military academy; founded 1873), library, mus. of history and fine arts, botanical garden, and general archives. Campo de Marte (SE) is popular parade ground. To the Central Market (behind cathedral) come products of near-by agr. area and native handicrafts and textiles. The 3d permanent capital of Guatemala, city was founded 1776 following destruction by earthquake (1773) of former capital of ANTIGUA. It was itself destroyed by earthquake in 1917–18, but rebuilt on same site in modern fashion. The climate is equable the year round.

Guateque (gwätā′kā), town (pop. 2,103), Boyacá dept., central Colombia, in valley of Cordillera Oriental, 37 mi. S of Tunja; alt. 6,235 ft. Oranges, wheat, corn, silk, cattle; flour milling. Site of anc. Indian village. Iron and coal deposits near by.

Guática (gwä′tēkä), town (pop. 1,597), Caldas dept., W central Colombia, on E slopes of Cordillera Occidental, 24 mi. NW of Manizales; alt. 6,217 ft.; coffeegrowing.

Guatiquía River (gwätēkē′ä), central Colombia, a headstream of Meta R., rises in Cordillera Central E of Bogotá, flows c.100 mi. S and E, past Villavicencio, joining Metica R. (lower Guayuriba R.) to form the Meta 50 mi. E of Villavicencio.

Guatire (gwätē′rā), town (pop. 3,225), Miranda state, N Venezuela, on E slopes of coastal range, 25 mi. E of Caracas, in agr. region (coffee, cacao, sugar cane, corn, fruit); sawmilling, sugar milling.

Guatiza (gwätē′thä), village (pop. 882), Lanzarote, Canary Isls., 10 mi. NNE of Arrecife; cereals, fruit, vegetables; flour milling.

Guatraché (gwäträchā′), town (pop. estimate 1,000), ⊙ Guatraché dept. (pop. 9,446), E La Pampa prov., Argentina, 85 mi. SE of Santa Rosa; rail junction, agr. center (wheat, alfalfa, flax, grapes, livestock). A salt lake is near by.

Guatulame (gwätōōlä′mā), village (1930 pop. 497), Coquimbo prov., N central Chile, on railroad and 20 mi. SW of Ovalle; grain, fruit, livestock. Copper and gold deposits near by.

Guatuso Lowland (gwätōō′sō), tropical plain in N Costa Rica, bet. the Cordillera de Guanacaste (S) and L. Nicaragua (N); drained by the Río Frío. Largely inhabited by Guatuso Indians. Main settlements are Los Chiles, San Rafael, and Upala. Stock raising, lumbering; cacao.

Guaviare River (gwävyä′rä), central and E Colombia, rises as Guayabero R. (gwäyäbā′rō) in Cordillera Oriental 30 mi. SE of Purificación (Tolima dept.), flows E in llano lowlands to Orinoco R. (Venezuela border) at San Fernando de Atabapo (Venezuela); total length, c.650 mi. The entire river is sometimes called Guayabero. Because of obstructions, navigable only for short distances. Considered dividing line bet. N llanos (low grasslands) and S selvas (dense tropical forests).

Guaviyú (gwävĭyōō′), village, Paysandú dept., NW Uruguay, on railroad and 33 mi. NNE of Paysandú; model cattle farm.

Guaxindiba (gwŭshēndē′bŭ), village, S central Rio de Janeiro state, on railroad and 10 mi. NE of Niterói; cement mill.

Guaxupé (gwŭshōōpĕ′), city (pop. 8,563), SW Minas Gerais, Brazil, near São Paulo border, 70 mi. E of Ribeirão Prêto; rail junction; important coffee-growing center.

Guayabal or **San José Guayabal** (sän hōsā′ gwīäbäl′), town (pop. 1,795), Cuscatlán dept., central Salvador, 14 mi. NE of San Salvador; road junction; rice, beans, sugar cane.

Guayabal, town (pop. 517), Guárico state, central Venezuela, landing on Guárico R. and 65 mi. S of Calabozo; cattle raising.

Guayabal, Lake, artificial reservoir, S Puerto Rico, in Cordillera Central, 2½ mi. N of Juana Díaz. A 2,800-ft. tunnel diverts water into Toro Negro and Doña Juana rivers.

Guayabero River, Colombia: see GUAVIARE RIVER.

Guayacán (gwīäkän′), town (pop. 1,219), Coquimbo prov., N central Chile, on small inlet of the Pacific, 2 mi. S of Coquimbo; beach resort; copper smelting and explosives mfg. Ships iron ore from Romeral to Huachipato.

Guayaguayare (gwī″ŭgwīä′rē), village (pop. 559), SE Trinidad, B.W.I., on fine beach, 3 mi. W of Galeota Point, 45 mi. SE of Port of Spain; coconuts, cacao. Oil fields near by.

Guayama (gwīä′mä), town (pop. 19,408), S Puerto Rico, near the coast, on railroad and 33 mi. S of San Juan; 17°59′N 66°7′W. Trading, sugar milling, and dairying center in agr. region (principally sugar cane, but also tobacco, coffee, corn, fruit); mfg. of needlework. Ships through Arroyo and Puerto Jobos. Seat of a senatorial dist. Founded 1736. Has fine colonial bldgs., San Antonio church, city hall. Adjoining E is a U.S. military reservation.

Guayambre River (gwīäm′brā), SE Honduras, rises in Sierra de Dipilto (Nicaragua border) in several branches joining 14 mi. ENE of Danlí; flows c.50 mi. NE, joining Guayape R. 23 mi. SE of Juticalpa to form PATUCA RIVER.

Guayamouc River (gwäyämōōk′), central and E Haiti, rises in the Massif du Nord NW of Saint-Michel-de-l'Atalaye, flows c.70 mi. SE, through fertile plain, past Hinche, to the Artibonite at Dominican Republic border. Not navigable.

Guayaneco Islands (gwīänā′kō), off coast of Aysén prov., S Chile, on S shore of Gulf of Peñas, N of Juan Stuven Isl.; 47°45′S 75°W. Consists of several uninhabited isls., principally Byron Isl. (W) and Wager Isl. (E), separated by Rundle Passage. Wager rises to 1,834 ft.

Guayanilla (gwīänē′yä), town (pop. 3,113), S Puerto Rico, on railroad and 10 mi. W of Ponce; sugar-milling and -trading center. Oil refinery. Its port Playa de Guayanilla is 1½ mi. SE. Serves near-by San Francisco (SW) and Rufina (S) sugar mills. Port of entry. First settled 1511.

Guayape (gwīä′pā), town (pop. 393), Olancho dept., central Honduras, on upper Guayape R. and 18 mi. WSW of Salamá; sugar cane, grain.

Guayape River, E central Honduras, rises NW of Guayape, flows c.150 mi. SE, past Guayape, ENE, through Olancho Valley, and S, joining Guayambre R. 23 mi. SE of Juticalpa to form PATUCA RIVER. Gold placers in upper course. Receives Jalán R. (right).

Guayaquil (gwīäkēl′), city (1950 pop. 262,624), ⊙ Guayas prov., W Ecuador, Pacific port on right bank of Guayas R. (45 mi. inland from Gulf of Guayaquil), in equatorial lowlands, and 170 mi. SW of Quito; 2°12′S 79°52′W. The largest city of Ecuador, it is its principal seaport and a processing and trade center, outlet for Ecuador's most fertile agr. area. Through it passes most of the country's exports and imports. It is connected by rail with Quito (though the cost of this transport over the Andes is almost prohibitive) and with the oil fields of Santa Elena Peninsula (W). Has a tropical climate with average temp. bet. 75°–85°F.; a healthier dry season lasts May–Dec. Among the exports are cacao (Ecuador's chief source of revenue), coffee, cotton, rubber, tropical fruit, tagua nuts, balsa wood, wool, hides, Panama hats. Industries include: tanneries, shoe factories, distilleries, soap and candle factories, chemical plants, foundries, sawmills, machine shops, shipyards, textile mills, sugar mills, breweries; a large cement plant is in W outskirts. Mercury deposits are near by. Guayaquil is served by an international airport. It is a bishopric, and seat of a notable univ., cathedral; and has several theaters, colonial bldgs., modern hotels, and large shipping offices and warehouses along the 2½ mi. river front. Founded 1536 by Benalcázar, Guayaquil was often subjected in the 17th cent. to attacks by buccaneers and was frequently destroyed by fires and scourged by plagues (yellow fever was a constant evil until the sanitation work of Gorgas in the 20th cent.). It rose against Spain in 1820, being occupied by patriot forces under Sucre in 1821. Here in 1822 took place the historic meeting bet. Bolívar and San Martín. Guayaquil was severely damaged by the 1942 earthquake.

Guayaquil, Gulf of, Pacific bay in Guayas prov., SW Ecuador, S of Santa Elena Peninsula. One of the largest inlets of the W coast of South America, it is c.110 mi. wide at its mouth and drives a wedge c.50 mi. inland to Puná Isl. and the wide estuary of Guayas R.

Guayaramerín (gwäyärämärēn′) or **Puerto Sucre** (pwĕr′tō sōō′krā), town (pop. c.1,600), Beni dept., N Bolivia, port on Mamoré R. and 50 mi. ENE of Riberalta, on Brazil border opposite Guajará Mirim (terminus of Madeira-Mamoré RR), Brazil; rubber export point; trade center for Brazilian imports and local merchandise; customs station. Military post; airfield.

Guayas (gwī′äs), province (□ 8,270; 1950 pop. 547,443), W Ecuador; ⊙ GUAYAQUIL. Largest and most populous prov. of Ecuador. Its lowlands, on the Gulf of Guayaquil and bordered E by steep Andes, are watered by Guayas R., a large network of navigable streams to which the Vinces, Daule, Babahoyo, and Chimbo (or Yaguachi) are tributary. Climate is tropical, averaging 80°F., with rainy season Dec.–May. Santa Elena Peninsula, a more arid area, has petroleum- and saltworks, and also gold, platinum, and sulphur deposits; mercury deposits are near Guayaquil. Guayas, in the most fertile region of Ecuador, is essentially agr. and a leading producer of cacao; other crops are sugar cane, coffee, tobacco, cotton, rice, mangoes, bananas, pineapples. Some cattle raising. Fishing on the coast and in inland streams. The forests yield balsa wood, tagua nuts, rubber, *toquilla* straw (from which Panama hats are made), and fine timber. Guayaquil, a major seaport and the largest city of the country, also controls most of the export and import trade, and is an important mfg. center. Other river ports and trading centers are Yaguachi, Daule, Balzar, Santa Flena, and Milagro. Salinas, seaside resort on Santa Elena Peninsula, has oil refineries and saltworks. Petroleum refining also at La Libertad. The Galápagos Isls., forming a separate territory, are administered by Guayas prov.

Guayas River, Guayas prov., W central Ecuador, formed by many navigable affluents rising on W slopes of the Andes S of the equator and joining above Guayaquil, among them the Daule, Vinces, Chimbo (or Yaguachi), and Babahoyo; it enters Gulf of Guayaquil in wide estuary, forming an interlaced delta. From Guayaquil, where river is 2 mi. wide and is navigable for ocean-going vessels, it flows c.40 mi. S to its mouth opposite Puná Isl. Its length, including the Babahoyo, one of its headstreams, is c.100 mi. The Guayas is one of the largest river systems on W coast of South America. During rainy season smaller steamers can reach Zapotal, 90 mi. SW of Quito. It waters one of most fertile regions of Ecuador (cacao, rice, sugar cane, coffee, tobacco, cotton, tagua nuts, balsa wood, stock).

Guayatayoc, Lake of (gwīätīōk′), salt lake (□ 90; alt. c.12,000 ft.) in central Jujuy prov., Argentina, at foot of Sierra de Aguilar; 25 mi. long, 3–5 mi. wide. Receives small Miraflores R.

Guayçara, Brazil: see GUAIÇARA.

Guaycurú (gwīkōōrōō′), railroad station, San José dept., S Uruguay, 27 mi. NW of San José. Blue-granite deposits in vicinity.

Guaymallén, Argentina: see VILLA NUEVA, Mendoza prov.

Guaymas (gwī′mäs), city (pop. 8,796), Sonora, NW Mexico, port on Gulf of California, near mouth of Yaqui R., 80 mi. S of Hermosillo, for which it is the port; 27°56′N 110°54′W. Rail terminus; shipping, trading, and fishing center. Exports ores (gold, silver), hides, cotton, tobacco, cereals, pearls. Machine shop, lumberyard, tanneries, cold-storage plants; shark-liver-oil extracting. The area also produces cereals, winter vegetables, fruit. Graphite deposits near by. Famed as a fisherman's paradise for centuries, the city is a popular resort.

Guaynabo (gwīnä′bō), town (pop. 2,159), N Puerto Rico, 6 mi. S of San Juan; dairy and sugar industry; cement- and glassworks.

Guayos (gwī′ōs), town (pop. 3,617), Las Villas prov., central Cuba, on railroad and 10 mi. NNW of Sancti-Spíritus; tobacco, sugar cane, cattle.

Guayquerías del Tunuyán, Sierra (syĕ′rä gwīkārē′äs dĕl tōōnōōyän′), pampean range in N central Mendoza prov., Argentina, E of Tunuyán; extends c.40 mi. N–S; rises to c.3,500 ft. Sometimes called Sierra del Tunuyán.

Guayquiraró River (gwīkērärō′), S Corrientes prov., Argentina, rises SW of Curuzú-Cuatiá, flows c.80 mi. SW and W, along Corrientes–Entre Ríos prov. border, to Paraná R. 25 mi. S of Esquina.

Guayra. 1 Village, Paraná, Brazil: see PÔRTO GUAÍRA. **2** City, São Paulo, Brazil: see GUAÍRA.

Guayra, La, Panama: see LA GUAYRA.

Guayra Falls, Brazil and Paraguay: see GUAÍRA FALLS.

Guayubín (gwīōōbēn′), town (1950 pop. 775), Monte Cristi prov., NW Dominican Republic, on the Yaque del Norte and 20 mi. SE of Monte Cristi, in fertile agr. region (tobacco, coffee, cacao, divi-divi, cotton, fine hardwood, hides); mfg. of cheese and sweets.

Guayuriba River (gwäyōōrē′bä), central Colombia, a headstream of Meta R., rises in Cordillera Oriental S of Bogotá, flows c.150 mi. SE, E, and NNE, through llano grasslands, joining Guatiquía R. to form the Meta. Its lower course is called Metica R.

Guazacapán (gwäsäkäpän′), town (1950 pop. 3,184), Santa Rosa dept., S Guatemala, in coastal plain, 3 mi. WSW of Chiquimulilla; livestock-raising center; coffee, sugar cane, grain.

Guazapa (gwäsä′pä), city (pop. 2,267), San Salvador dept., W central Salvador, on railroad and 10 mi. N of San Salvador, at SW foot of volcano Guazapa; market center; grain, sugar cane.

Guazapa, extinct volcano (4,629 ft.), Cuscatlán dept., W central Salvador, 15 mi. NNE of San Salvador. Guazapa city is at SW, Suchitoto at NE foot.

Guazapares (gwäsäpä′rĕs), mining settlement (pop. 317), Chihuahua, N Mexico, in Sierra Madre Occidental, 160 mi. SW of Chihuahua; silver, gold, copper deposits.

Guazú-cuá (gwäsōō'-kwä'), town (dist. pop. 3,041), Ñeembucú dept., S Paraguay, 25 mi. E of Pilar; stock-raising and tanning center.

Guba (gōō'bä), village, Katanga prov., SE Belgian Congo, on railroad and 35 mi. NW of Jadotville; agr.; salt extracting. Benedictine mission.

Gubakha (gōōbä'khŭ), city (1926 pop. 6,805; 1946 pop. estimate 50,000), E central Molotov oblast, Russian SFSR, on Kosva R. and 12 mi. S of Kizel, on railroad; major coke-producing center, based on Kizel and Kuzbas coal; bituminous-coal mining, metalworking, sawmilling, food processing. An old coal town which developed on right bank of Kosva R. prior to First World War; became a city in 1941, when it absorbed left-bank town of Krzhizhanovsk (1936 pop. estimate 18,100) which had developed in early 1930s around coking and coal-mining installations and had originally been called Kizelstroi.

Guban (gōōbän'), coastal region of NW Br. Somaliland, on the Gulf of Aden, bet. Zeila and Berbera.

Gubat (gōō'bät, gōōbät'), town (1939 pop. 5,992; 1948 municipality pop. 29,245), Sorsogon prov., extreme SE Luzon, Philippines, on Philippine Sea, 30 mi. ESE of Legaspi; port for inter-isl. shipping. Exports abacá, copra.

Gubba, Ethiopia: see QUBBA.

Gubba (gōōb'bä), village (pop. 770), Cyrenaica, Libya, on coastal road and 20 mi. W of Derna, on the plateau Gebel el Ahkdar; flour mill. Agr. settlement (olives, vegetables, livestock) founded here 1933 by Italians was called Berta.

Gubbi (gōō'bē), town (pop. 6,129), Tumkur dist., central Mysore, India, on Shimsha R. and 11 mi. W of Tumkur; local agr. trade center (rice, millet, coconuts, tamarind); rice and oilseed milling, handloom cotton and silk weaving, mfg. of country carts.

Gubbio (gōōb'byō), anc. *Iguvium*, town (pop. 7,432), Perugia prov., Umbria, central Italy, 19 mi. NE of Perugia. Produces majolica, for which it was noted in 16th cent., metalware, cement. Bishopric. Medieval in appearance; has old cathedral, fine ducal palace, and mid-14th-cent. palace of the consuls with mus. containing famous bronze Iguvine Tables found 1444 near ruins of Roman theater.

Guben (gōō'bŭn), city (pop. 25,297), Brandenburg, E Germany, in Lower Lusatia, on left bank of the Lusatian Neisse and 70 mi. SE of Berlin; 51°57'N 14°45'E. Rail junction; lignite mining; woolen milling, brewing, mfg. of hats, hosiery, belting, machinery, cardboard; fruit and vegetable market. Airfield (N). Has remains of old town walls. Originally Wendish settlement, 1st mentioned c.1000; chartered 1235. Commercial and winegrowing center in early Middle Ages; passed 1304 to Brandenburg, 1368 to Bohemia, 1635 to Saxony, 1815 to Prussia. In Second World War, c.60% destroyed. Following 1945 div. of E Germany along the Oder, a small section (pop. c.3,000) of the city on right bank of river came under Pol. administration and is now called GUBIN; has hydroelectric plant.

Guberlya Mountains (gōōbĕrlyŭ'), low, southernmost section of the Urals, Russian SFSR, in Ural R. bend, NW of Orsk; rise to 1,437 ft. A highly mineralized region, it has deposits of iron, chrome and nickel ores at Khalilovo and quality-steel mill at Novo-Troitsk.

Gubin (gōō'bēn), town (1946 pop. 3,040), Zielona Gora prov., W Poland, before 1945 part of GUBEN, E Germany, on right bank of the Lusatian Neisse; hydroelectric power station. Chartered after 1945.

Gubkin (gōōp'kĭn), town (1939 pop. over 500), E Kursk oblast, Russian SFSR, 12 mi. W of Stary Oskol; metalworks. Iron mine, opened 1939, in iron-ore dist. of Kursk magnetic anomaly. Until 1939, Korobkovo.

Guca or **Gucha** (both: gōō'chä), Serbo-Croatian *Guča*, village (pop. 583), W Serbia, Yugoslavia, 10 mi. SW of Cacak.

Güchenbach, Saar: see RIEGELSBERG.

Guchkovo, Russian SFSR: see DEDOVSK.

Gudalur (gōō'dŭlōōr). **1** Town (pop. 17,398), Madura dist., S Madras, India, 4 mi. SW of Cumbum, in Kambam Valley; teak, bamboo, turmeric from Cardamom Hills (W); lumbering (railway sleepers). **2** Village, Nilgiri dist., SW Madras, India, 15 mi. WNW of Ootacamund; road center in the Wynaad; rice, bamboo, teak, blackwood. Mica quarries near by. Cinchona, tea, and coffee estates in area. Tea processing 5 mi. NW, at village of Devarshola.

Gudauty (gōōdŭōō'tē), city (1926 pop. 3,601), NW Abkhaz Autonomous SSR, Georgian SSR, port on Black Sea, on railroad and 20 mi. WNW of Sukhumi; wines, tobacco, citrus fruit. Iron foundry, alabaster works; tanning.

Gudbrandsdal (gŏŏd'bränsdäl), valley (c.100 mi. long) of Lagen R., Opland co., S central Norway, extends from the Dovrefjell (where it connects with the Romsdal) SE to L. Mjosa at Lillehammer, its chief town. It lies bet. the Jotunheim (W) and Rondane (E) mts. Main villages of valley are Dombas, Dovre, Otta, Vinstra, and Ringebu. Valley is traversed by Dovre RR (Oslo-Trondheim and Kristiansand), opened 1921. There are slate quarries. Agr., stock raising, and dairying are chief occupations; Gudbrandsdal horses are noted. Important trade route since prehistoric times, valley is site of many anc. graves and is connected with several sagas and legends, notably with that of Peer Gynt. Many old folk customs and dialects have been preserved here; also several stave churches and wooden houses with elaborate carvings. Gudbrandsdal folk mus. has been established at Maihaugen, suburb of Lillehammer. In literature, the valley is associated with Bjornson, Undset, and Hamsun. In Second World War the entire Gudbrandsdal was scene (April, 1940) of heavy fighting bet. Anglo-Norwegian and German forces.

Gudebrandslagen River, Norway: see LAGEN RIVER.

Guden River, Dan. *Gudenaa* (gōō'dhŭnô), longest (98 mi.) in Denmark. Rises 14 mi. NNW of Vejle, E Jutland, flows generally N through Himmelbjaerget hills, traversing Mos L. (in this region sometimes called Bredvads R. or Vorvads R.), Jul L., and smaller lakes, past Silkeborg, thence N and NE, past Randers, to Randers Fjord. Navigable in lower course. Randers is chief port. Salmon fishing.

Gudensberg (gōō'dŭnsbĕrk), town (pop. 3,643), in former Prussian prov. of Hesse-Nassau, W Germany, after 1945 in Hesse, 11 mi. SSW of Kassel; lumber.

Gudermes (gōō'dyĭrmyĭs), city (1926 pop. 2,976), S Grozny oblast, Russian SFSR, 22 mi. E of Grozny; rail junction on Rostov-Baku RR; railroad repair and machine shops; fruit and vegetable canning. Oil deposits near by. Became city in 1941.

Gudgeri (gōōdgä'rē), town (pop. 4,157), Dharwar dist., S Bombay, India, 33 mi. SE of Dharwar; agr. market (cotton, peanuts, wheat); handicraft cloth weaving.

Gudhjem (gōōdh'hyĕm), town (pop. 820), Bornholm amt, Denmark, on NE shore of Bornholm isl. and 13 mi. NE of Ronne; fisheries; granite quarry.

Gudia (gōō'dyä) or **Gudja** (gōō'jä), village (parish pop. 1,486), E Malta, 3 mi. S of Valletta. Has old and new parish churches (1436, 1656), 18th-cent. Dorell Palace. Damaged in Second World War.

Gudibanda (gōōdĭbŭn'dŭ), town (pop. 2,914), Kolar dist., E Mysore, India, 45 mi. NW of Kolar; tile mfg., tobacco curing.

Güdingen (gü'dĭng-ŭn), town (pop. 5,037), S Saar, on Saar R. and 3 mi. SE of Saarbrücken; metalworking, chemical mfg.

Gudivada (gōōdĭvä'dŭ), city (pop. 23,919), Kistna dist., NE Madras, India, in Kistna R. delta, 20 mi. NNW of Masulipatam; rail junction (spur to Masulipatam); rice milling; sugar cane, oilseeds, tobacco.

Gudiyattam or **Gudiyatam** (gōōdĭyä'tŭm), city (pop. 32,671), North Arcot dist., central Madras, India, 18 mi. W of Vellore, in agr. valley of Palar R.; cotton-milling and trade center; hides and skins; ceramics, electrical supplies. Sugar-cane research. Sometimes spelled Gudiyatham.

Gudja, Malta: see GUDIA.

Gudron, Russian SFSR: see ORSK.

Gudur (gōō'dōōr). **1** or **Guduru** (gōōdōō'rōō), town (pop. 7,060), Kurnool dist., N Madras, India, 12 mi. WSW of Kurnool; rice and oilseed (peanut) milling; tamarind, mangoes. Saltworks near by. **2** Town (pop. 12,105), Nellore dist., E Madras, India, 22 mi. SSW of Nellore; rail junction; ceramics; rice and oilseed milling. Important mica quarries near by.

Gudvangen, Norway: see NAEROY FJORD.

Guebwiller (gĕbvēlâr'), Ger. *Gebweiler* (gĕp'vīlŭr), town (pop. 9,695), Haut-Rhin dept., E France, in narrow, winegrowing valley of SE Vosges Mts., 13 mi. NNW of Mulhouse, overlooked by the Ballon de Guebwiller; industrial center mfg. cotton goods, textile machinery, furniture, parquetry, varnishes and lacquer. Has 14th–15th-cent. former Dominican church and 16th-cent. town hall. Murbach (3 mi. WNW) has fine remains of Romanesque abbatial church.

Guebwiller, Ballon de (bälō dŭ), or **Grand Ballon** (grā bälō'), Ger. *Grosser Belchen* (grō'sŭr bĕl'-khŭn) or *Sulzer Belchen* (zōōl'tsŭr), highest summit (4,672 ft.) of the Vosges, in Haut-Rhin dept., E France, 5 mi. W of Guebwiller, on a spur E of the principal Vosges range. Accessible by "crest" road from Cernay, 7 mi. SE. Winter sports. Held by French in First World War.

Guecho (gä'chō), outer suburban commune (pop. 17,795) NW of Bilbao, Vizcaya prov., N Spain, on Bilbao Bay (an inlet of Bay of Biscay). Includes villages of ALGORTA and Las ARENAS.

Gueckedou (gĕkĕ'dōō), town (pop. c.1,700), S Fr. Guinea, Fr. West Africa, near Liberia border, 135 mi. SSW of Kankan; rice, palm kernels, coffee, kola; cattle. Has agr. school, R.C. mission, customhouse, sleeping-sickness clinic.

Gué-de-Constantine (gā'-dŭ-kōstātēn'), village, Alger dept., N central Algeria, an outer SE suburb of Algiers, adjoining Kouba; mfg. of electric cables, sulphur refining.

Güéjar-Sierra (gwā'här-syĕ'rä), village (pop. 2,944), Granada prov., S Spain, on Genil R., at foot of Sierra Nevada, and 10 mi. E of Granada; olive-oil processing, lumbering, stock raising. Cereals, almonds, chestnuts. Marble quarries.

Guelderland, Netherlands: see GELDERLAND.

Guelders, Netherlands: see GELDERLAND.

Guellala (gĕlälä'), village, SE Tunisia, on S shore of Djerba isl., 9 mi. S of Houmt-Souk; noted for its pottery.

Guelma (gĕlmä'), anc. *Calama*, town (pop. 12,673), Constantine dept., NE Algeria, in the Constantine Mts., on railroad and 45 mi. ENE of Constantine; road center and important cattle market; olive-oil milling, tanning, mfg. of flour products. Calamine and sulphur mined at near-by Héliopolis. Among Roman ruins are thermae and a theater. Town also preserves part of Byzantine walls. There is an agr. school for natives. Noted spa of Hammam-Meskoutine is 9 mi. W.

Guelph (gwĕlf), city (pop. 23,273), ⊙ Wellington co., S Ont., on Speed R. (30-ft. falls) and 27 mi. NW of Hamilton; knitting mills; meat packing, paper milling, woodworking; mfg. of machinery, domestic appliances, carpets, clothing, yarns, hats, rubber products, leather, shoes, electrical equipment, automobile parts. Center of agr. region. Near by are gypsum and limestone quarries. Hydroelectric station. Site of Ontario Agr. Col., Ontario Veterinary Col., Trent Inst., and Loretto Acad. Scene of annual prov. fair and stock show. Founded 1827 by John Galt; inc. 1879.

Guelta Zemmur (gwĕl'tä thāmōōr'), Saharan outpost and well, NW Río de Oro, Sp. West Africa; 25°4'N 12°9'W.

Guémar (gāmär'), Saharan village, Touggourt territory, E Algeria, one of the Souf oases, 10 mi. NNW of El-Oued; Deglet Nur dates, tobacco.

Guéméné or **Guéméné-sur-Scorff** (gāmānā'-sür-skôrf'), town (pop. 2,116), Morbihan dept., W France on Scorff R. and 11 mi. W of Pontivy; agr. market; horse raising. Noted for distinctive female costumes.

Guéméné-Penfao (pĕnfou'), village (pop. 1,375), Loire-Inférieure dept., W France, on Don R. and 22 mi. WSW of Châteaubriant; sawmilling. Formerly named Guéméné.

Güemes, Argentina: see GENERAL GÜEMES.

Güémez (gwā'mĕs), town (pop. 663), Tamaulipas, NE Mexico, 16 mi. NE of Ciudad Victoria; silver, lead, copper mining.

Guened, France: see VANNES.

Guenguel, Meseta de (māsā'tä dā gĕng-gĕl'), Patagonian plateau in W Comodoro Rivadavia military zone, Argentina, extends c.20 mi. E from Chile border, N of L. Buenos Aires; rises to c.4,800 ft.

Guéoul or **Goumbo-Guéoul** (gōōm'bō-gāōōl'), village, W Senegal, Fr. West Africa, on Dakar–Saint-Louis RR and 38 mi. S of Saint-Louis, in peanut-growing region.

Güepi or **Güeppi** (gōōĕ'pē), military post (pop. 152), Loreto dept., N Peru, on Putumayo R. (Colombia line) at mouth of small Güepi R. (Ecuador border); 0°7'S 75°15'W; airfield.

Guer (gâr), village (pop. 1,182), Morbihan dept., W France, 13 mi. E of Ploërmel; apple orchards. Near-by Coëtquidan camp is temporary site of Saint-Cyr military acad.

Güera, Río de Oro: see AGÜERA, LA.

Güer Aike, Argentina: see RÍO GALLEGOS.

Guérande (gārād'), town (pop. 2,504), Loire-Inférieure dept., W France, 11 mi. WNW of Saint-Nazaire; market center for saltworkers and peat cutters from surrounding marshes and bogs. Has 12th–16th-cent. church of Saint-Aubin, a 15th-cent. castle and well-preserved medieval walls and towers.

Guerche-de-Bretagne, La (lä gârsh-dŭ-brŭtä'nyŭ), town (pop. 2,798), Ille-et-Vilaine dept., W France, 17 mi. NNE of Châteaubriant; mfg. (footwear, agr. machinery). Has 13th-cent. church and medieval wooden houses.

Guerche-sur-l'Aubois, La (–sür-lōbwä'), village (pop. 1,726), Cher dept., central France, on Aubois R. and Berry Canal, and 10 mi. WSW of Nevers; cattle-fattening center; mfg. (electrical equipment, cartons, bricks). Horse training school.

Guercif (gĕrsēf'), town (pop. 2,994), Fez region, NE Fr. Morocco, on railroad and 37 mi. E of Taza; market center in semi-arid Moulouya valley. Truck gardens. Smectic clay quarries (NE).

Guéret (gārā'), town (pop. 8,239), ⊙ Creuse dept., central France, 38 mi. NE of Limoges; transportation and market center (livestock, dairy produce, potatoes); mfg. (furniture, tires, musical instruments). Built (7th cent.) around an abbey, it became ⊙ countship of Marche.

Guérigny (gārēnyē'), town (pop. 2,613), Nièvre dept., central France, on Nièvre R. and 7 mi. N of Nevers; blast furnaces and forges mfg. naval equipment.

Guerlédan, France: see MÛR.

Guerneville (gûrn'vĭl), resort village (1940 pop. 1,089), Sonoma co., W Calif., 17 mi. W of Santa Rosa and on Russian R. Applegrowing, dairying, quicksilver mining, redwood lumbering in area. Armstrong Redwoods State Park is NW.

Guernewood Park, resort village, Sonoma co., W Calif., on Russian R. and 17 mi. W of Santa Rosa.

Guernica or **Guernica y Luno** (gĕrnē'kä ē lōō'nō, sometimes in English gûr'nĭkŭ), town (pop. 1,977), Vizcaya prov., N Spain, in the Basque Provs., near head of inlet of Bay of Biscay, 12 mi. ENE of Bilbao. Metalworking (ammunitions and firearms, hardware), furniture mfg., food processing. The old oak tree under which the diet of Vizcaya met from the Middle Ages to the 19th cent. is a symbol of the lost liberties of the Basques. In April, 1937, German planes, sent to aid the Insurgents in the Sp. civil war, bombed and destroyed Guernica. The indiscriminate bombing of women and children became a symbol of Fascist brutality. The event inspired one of Picasso's most celebrated paintings.

Guernsey (gûrn′zē), anc. *Sarnia*, island (□ 24.5; 1951 pop. 43,546), 2d-largest of Channel Isls., 16 mi. NW of Jersey and 28 mi. W of Normandy coast of France; ⊙ SAINT PETER PORT. It is 8 mi. long and 5 mi. wide with low beach in N and rocky cliffs on S coast. Isl. is famous for its fine cattle; chief industries are cattle breeding, dairying, growing of fruit and flowers (mostly under glass), and quarrying of blue granite. Climate is moderate (mean temperature is 43°F for February, 60.5°F for July; mean annual rainfall is 38 inches). Victor Hugo lived in St. Peter Port for over 15 years. In 1940 isl. was occupied by Germans, held until 1945. Part of pop. had previously been evacuated to England.

Guernsey, county (□ 529; pop. 38,452), E Ohio; ⊙ Cambridge. Drained by Wills Creek. Agr. (livestock; dairy products; fruit, grain); mfg. at Cambridge; coal and clay mining, limestone quarrying. Formed 1810.

Guernsey. 1 Town (pop. 113), Poweshiek co., central Iowa, 30 mi. NNE of Oskaloosa, in agr. area. **2** Town (pop. 721), Platte co., SE Wyo., on N. Platte R. and 18 mi. NE of Wheatland; alt. 4,361 ft. Supply station; iron-ore shipping point. Limestone quarries. Guernsey Dam and powerhouse, units in North Platte project, are just W.

Guernsey Dam, SE Wyo., on N.Platte R. and 2 mi. W of Guernsey; rock and earthfill dam 105 ft. high, 560 ft. long; completed 1927 as unit in North Platte project. Used for hydroelectric power and irrigation; forms Guernsey Reservoir (capacity 46,000 acre-ft.).

Guernsey Island (1 mi. long, 1 mi. wide), W N.F., in the Bay of Islands, 25 mi. NW of Corner Brook; 49°12′N 58°23′W.

Guéroulde, La (lä gärōōd′), village (pop. 188), Eure dept., NW France, on Iton R. and 19 mi. SW of Évreux; agr. tools.

Guerrara (gĕrärä′), Saharan village, Ghardaïa territory, central Algeria, one of the Mzab oases, 50 mi. NE of Ghardaïa, on road to Touggourt; date palms. Founded in 16th cent.

Guerrero (gĕrā′rō), state (□ 24,887; 1940 pop. 732,910; 1950 pop. 917,719), SW Mexico, on the Pacific; ⊙ Chilpancingo. Bounded by Michoacán (NW), Mexico and Morelos (N), Puebla (NE), Oaxaca (E and SE). Largely mountainous; traversed E-W by the Sierra Madre del Sur, culminating in the Cerro Teotepec (12,149 ft.). It has a fertile coastal strip with a good harbor at the resort Acapulco, and contains fertile, densely wooded valleys in the mts., especially in the valley of the Río de las Balsas, which crosses the state E-W. Climate varies: cool in sierras, subtropical in uplands, humid-tropical in coastal lowlands and lower Río de las Balsas valley. Potentially one of the richest mining states in the republic; its mineral wealth is thus far of secondary importance, though some gold, lead, copper, zinc, and mercury are mined at Taxco, Iguala, Huitzuco, and San Miguel Totolapan. Immense forests supply fine construction wood, rubber, resins, dyes, vanilla, tanning extracts. Agr. is the chief industry: corn, rice, wheat, sugar cane, coffee, cacao, bananas, limes, chile, tobacco, cotton, and other tropical fruit and vegetables, grown mostly in coastal regions. Rural industries: lumbering, mining, flour milling, cotton ginning, vegetable-oil extracting, native handicrafts. Processing industries (lumber mills, foundries, cigar factories, distilleries, tanneries) concentrated at Acapulco, Chilpancingo, Iguala, Taxco; Taxco is especially famous for silverware. Set up 1849, the state was named for Vicente Guerrero, hero of the revolutionary wars.

Guerrero. 1 or **Ciudad Guerrero** (syōōdädh′ gĕrā′rō), city (pop. 1,023), Chihuahua, N Mexico, in Sierra Madre Occidental, 85 mi. W of Chihuahua; alt. 6,560 ft.; silver, gold, lead, copper mining. Airfield. **2** Town (pop. 1,337), Coahuila, N Mexico, near the Rio Grande (Texas border), 25 mi. SSW of Piedras Negras; grain and cattle center. **3** Officially Villa de Guerrero, town (pop. 1,407), San Luis Potosí, E Mexico, in fertile Gulf plain, 60 mi. WSW of Tampico. Rail junction; agr. center (coffee, tobacco, sugar cane, rice, fruit, cattle); copra production. **4** City (pop. 1,786), Tamaulipas, N Mexico, on Río Salado, near its mouth on Rio Grande (Texas border), and 50 mi. SSE of Nuevo Laredo; agr. center (cotton, sugar cane, corn, cattle).

Guerrilandia, Venezuela: see GUANARE.

Guesnain (gānē′), residential town (pop. 3,564), Nord dept., N France, 4 mi. ESE of Douai, in coal-mining dist.

Guetaria (gātä′ryä), town (pop. 1,361), Guipúzcoa prov., N Spain, fishing port on Bay of Biscay, 11 mi. W of San Sebastián; fish processing, boatbuilding; lumbering. Has 13th-cent. Gothic church. Harbor protected by fortified isl. of San Antón.

Guettar, El (ĕl gĕtär′), village, Gafsa dist., S central Tunisia, 10 mi. SE of Gafsa; palm and olive trees. Scene of a battle during Tunisian campaign (Feb.-Mar., 1943) in Second World War.

Gueugnon (gûnyō′), town (pop. 4,871), Saône-et-Loire dept., E central France, on the Arroux and 22 mi. SW of Le Creusot; blast furnaces, forges. Construction materials.

Gueydan (gādän′, gā′dŭn), town (pop. 2,041), Vermilion parish, S La., 45 mi. ESE of Lake Charles city; rice, sugar cane, cotton; rice milling. Inc. 1899.

Güferhorn (gü′fŭrhôrn″), peak (11,103 ft.) in the Alps, SE Switzerland, 11 mi. NNE of Biasca, in the Adula group.

Guffey, Colo.: see FRESHWATER.

Gugand (gügã′), village (pop. 733), Vendée dept., W France, 17 mi. W of Cholet; textile weaving.

Guggisberg (gŏŏ′gĭsbĕrk″), town (pop. 2,516), Bern canton, W central Switzerland, 9 mi. ESE of Fribourg; farming.

Gughe, Mount (gōō′gā), S Ethiopia, peak (c.13,780 ft.) in mts. forming edge of Great Rift Valley W of lakes Abaya and Chamo, in Gamu-Gofa prov., 45 mi. N of Gardula.

Guglielmo, Monte (môn′tĕ gōōlyĕl′mô), mountain (6,394 ft.) in Brescia prov., Lombardy, N Italy, bet. Lago d'Iseo and Val Trompia, 15 mi. N of Brescia.

Güglingen (gü′glĭng-ŭn), town (pop. 1,728), N Württemberg, Germany, after 1945 in Württemberg-Baden, 11 mi. SW of Heilbronn; wine.

Guglionesi (gōōlyônā′zē), town (pop. 5,977), Campobasso prov., Abruzzi e Molise, S central Italy, near Biferno R., 8 mi. SSW of Termoli; pottery making. Gypsum, ochre, kaolin quarries near by.

Guguan (gōōgwän′), uninhabited volcanic island (□ 2), Saipan dist., N Marianas Isls., W Pacific, 250 mi. NNE of Guam; 1.5 mi. long, 1 mi. wide; rises to 988 ft.; active volcano.

Gugu Mountains (gōō′gōō), forested highland region in E central Ethiopia, on border bet. Arusi and Harar provs., at edge of Great Rift Valley, SW of Chercher Mts.; rise to 11,886 ft. in Mt. Gugu, 95 mi. SE of Addis Ababa. Coffee-growing area.

Guhena, Egypt: see GIHEINA.

Guhrau, Poland: see GORA.

Guía de Gran Canaria (gē′ä dhā grän′ känä′ryä), city (pop. 2,495), Grand Canary, Canary Isls., 15 mi. W of Las Palmas, on isl.'s N shore; agr. center (bananas, cereals, fruit, tomatoes, livestock). Known for its cheese.

Guía de Isora (ēsō′rä), village (pop. 1,419), Tenerife, Canary Isls., 38 mi. WSW of Santa Cruz de Tenerife; cochineal, cereals, fruit, tomatoes, livestock. Sometimes Guía de Izora.

Guía de Izora, Canary Isls.: see GUÍA DE ISORA.

Guiana (gēä′nŭ, gēä′-), Sp. *Guayana*, region of NE South America, just N of the equator. In general it is considered to be an area entirely surrounded by water—Orinoco R. (N), the Casiquiare (W), the Río Negro and the Amazon (S), and the Atlantic (N and E)—and including SE Venezuela, part of N Brazil, and British, Dutch, and French Guiana. The 3 European possessions are, in a narrower sense, called Guiana. Throughout the region the same physical characteristics prevail. A low, alluvial coastal belt, varying in width from 5–30 mi., constitutes its only cultivated part (rice, sugar cane, cacao, coffee, tropical fruit). On it borders a wide, intermediate, somewhat higher area containing the main mineral (bauxite, gold, diamonds) and forest (balata, rubber, hardwood) resources. The vast mountainous hinterland is made up of the GUIANA HIGHLANDS (mostly in Venezuela) and its outliers (Pacaraima, Kanuku, Acaraí, and Tumuc-Humac ranges), which include little-explored, densely wooded plateaus and occasional savannas. Descending from these mts. in rapids and gigantic waterfalls (such as ANGEL FALL and KAIETEUR FALLS) are many streams which, though navigable for larger vessels only near the coast, form the main lines of communication; among them are the Essequibo, Berbice, Courantyne or Corantijn, Saramacca, Surinam, Maroni or Marowijne, and Oyapock rivers. Climate is tropical and humid with 2 wet seasons (April–mid-Aug. and mid-Nov.–end of Jan.), less pronounced in the interior, and relieved by trade winds from NE bet. Oct. and July. The region is sparsely populated; all towns—apart from some mining establishments—are near the coast. Its polyglot pop. includes only a small percentage of Europeans and native Indians; East Indians, introduced during 19th cent. as agr. laborers, now form the most prominent element (about 40%) together with so-called Bush Negroes, who resumed their tribal life in the interior. The Guiana coast was discovered (1498) by Columbus, who, however, did not make a landing here. Among its early explorers were Amerigo Vespucci and Alonso de Ojeda. European freebooters were attracted by the legend of El Dorado, to which Sir Walter Raleigh (1595 and 1617), its 1st propagator, fell a victim. The Dutch were the first to settle (1613) on the coast of present-day Br. Guiana, the British and French following suit, but the status of each nation's colony was to change many times.

Guiana, British, British crown colony (□ 83,000; pop. 375,701), NE South America, on the Atlantic, bordering W on Venezuela, E on Du. Guiana (Courantyne or Corantijn R.), S on Brazil (Serra Acaraí); ⊙ Georgetown. The only Br. colony on the South American mainland and the most prosperous of the 3 colonial Guianas, it extends bet. 1°–9°N and 57°–61°W, with a coast line about 270 mi. long. Has a tropical, humid climate with mean temp. of 80.3°F. Includes Pakaraima Mts. (W central) and Kanuku Mts. (S). Drained by the Essequibo (with Cuyuni and Mazaruni tributaries), Demerara, Berbice, Barima, Barama, Potaro, and Waini rivers, which also serve as its main lines of communication, though their mid- and upper-courses are interrupted by many falls and rapids, such as the majestic Kaieteur Falls on the Potaro. The large mineral resources of the interior are its main source of income. Alluvial gold is mined along most of the rivers, notably the Mahdia, Cuyuni (Aurora mine), Essequibo (Omai mine). The diamond fields on the Mazaruni rank next to those in South Africa. The bauxite industry is centered at Mackenzie up Demerara R., where the ore is loaded in ocean-going vessels. Forests, covering 87% of the colony, yield fine cabinet wood, dyewood, balata, rubber. Only about 200 sq. mi along alluvial coastal plain are under cultivation main crops are sugar cane and rice, also coconuts coffee, cacao, corn, livestock; cattle are raised on interior savannas of the Rupununi dist. and driven along a trail (Rupununi cattle trail) to the coast Main industries: rice milling, sugar refining, rum and molasses distilling, coconut-oil pressing. Apart from gold, diamonds, and bauxite, Br. Guiana exports timber, charcoal, balata, hides, sugar, rum molasses, rice. Georgetown and New Amsterdam are the leading ports and trading centers. A coasta railroad joins Vreed-en-Hoop with Rosignol Bartica is head of navigation for Essequibo R and terminal of inland roads to mining regions an Kaieteur Falls. First European settlements were made by the Dutch West India Company in early 17th cent., resulting in 3 separate colonies: Es sequibo, Demerara, and Berbice. Generally held by Holland during the next 200 years, the area wa invaded by French, Portuguese, and British severa times during 18th cent., and the British held the colonies from 1796 to 1802. They were finally ceded to England in 1815 and merged (1831) a counties into one unit; and the Dutch were con firmed in their possession of Surinam, the forme Br. colony. Gold was 1st discovered here in 1884 In 1940, U.S. acquired 99-year leases to military and naval bases near Bartica and Hyde Park The colony's pop. is about 3% white and 3% native Indian, about 42% East Indian, 38% Negro, and the rest of varied stock.

Guiana, Dutch, or **Surinam** (sōō′rĭnăm, sōōrĭnăm′) Du. *Suriname* (sürēnä′mŭ), territory (□ 55,143 pop. 211,804) of the Netherlands, NE South America, on the Atlantic, bordered W by Br Guiana (Courantyne or Corantijn R.), E by Fr Guiana (Maroni or Marowijne R.), S by Brazi (Tumuc-Humac Mts.); ⊙ Paramaribo. Extend bet. 2°–6°N and 54°–58°W, with a coast line c.22 mi. long. Includes outliers of the Guiana High lands (Wilhelmina and Oranje Mts.) and is draine by the Nickerie, Coppename, Saramacca, Surinam and Cottica rivers, most of them, in their lowe courses, of good navigability. Among its valuabl mineral resources is bauxite, worked and shippe at Paranam and Moengo; also alluvial gold, no tably along Saramacca and Lawa rivers. The a most impenetrable tropical forests of the interio yield hardwood (greenheart, teak, mahogany, etc.) balata, and dyewood. Of the fertile, canalize coastland only about 150 sq. mi. are cultivated its principal crops being rice (mainly in Nickeri dist.), sugar cane, coffee, cacao, corn, coconuts bananas. Lumbering, sugar and rice milling, rur distilling, and mining are its leading industrie Exports include: bauxite, gold, timber, balata, rum molasses, fruit. Apart from Paramaribo (the terr tory's trading and shipping center), Nieuw Amste dam and Nieuw Nickerie have some importanc as local ports. Mariënburg has large sugar refiner Railroad inland to Dam serves the gold-minin region near Lawa R. In early 17th cent. th Dutch, British, and French landed here in turn but the only successful settlement was undertake (1650) by Lord Willoughby, to whom the colon was awarded by Charles II. At the Peace of Bred (1667), it was granted to the Dutch in exchange fo New Netherlands (now New York). The Britis reoccupied Du. Guiana from 1799 to 1802 and agai in 1804. It was finally given to the Dutch after th Congress of Vienna (1815); the British obtaine the former Du. colony, now Br. Guiana. Aft 1922 Du. Guiana became a part of the Netherlan kingdom, and was confirmed as a self-governin member within the Union of the Netherlands. I 1927 it was divided into the 7 dists.: Paramarib (coextensive with Paramaribo city), Nickeri Coronie, Saramacca, Surinam, Commewijne, an Marowijne. Its present pop. is about ½ Negr and mulatto, ¼ Br. Indian, the rest being native Indians and Chinese, Europeans, and Americans. It is sometimes called Netherlands Guiana.

Guiana, French, Fr. *Guyane française,* overseas department (□ c.34,740; pop. 28,537) of France, NE South America, on the Atlantic; ⊙ Cayenne. The easternmost of the European possessions in Guiana, bounded W by Du. Guiana (Maroni or Marowijne R.), E and S by Brazil (Oyapock R. and Tumuc-Humac Mts.). Divided administratively into a 25-mi.-wide coastal strip of Fr. Guiana proper (□ c.4,440; pop. 23,513) and the interior territory of ININI. Extends bet. 1°25′–5°45′ N and 51°40′–54°30′W. Has coast line c.200 mi. long. An almost undeveloped region, ill-famed because of its penal settlements. Fr. Guiana includes a number of rocky islets along its coast, among them DEVILS ISLAND, one of the Îles du Salut. Intersected by many rivers: Mana, Sinnamary, Comté, Approuague. Although rich in all kinds of minerals (iron, copper, silver, lead, mercury, platinum, diamonds), only alluvial gold is produced on large scale (St-Élie, À Dieu Vat placers). In the little-explored, forested interior are rosewood, hardwood, and balata. The cultivated areas (c.15 sq. mi.) of the swampy coastland grow sugar cane, coffee, cacao, rice, cassava, corn, spices, and tropical fruit. Gold, balata, rosewood extract, hides, fish glue are exported. Main ports: Cayenne, St-Georges, St-Laurent. The 1st important Fr. settlement was founded at Cayenne in 1643. In the Dutch Wars of Louis XIV, Cayenne was captured (1676) by the Dutch but then retaken. During the Napoleonic Wars, Cayenne was occupied (1808–17) by the Portuguese, although the Congress of Vienna had restored the colony to France in 1815. Political prisoners were sent here in 1798 and an official penal colony was established in 1854. Until 1935 convicts were shipped to Fr. Guiana. A decree of 1944 called for the closing of all penal colonies, and by 1946 most of them were dissolved. In the same year Fr. Guiana became (March 19, 1946) an overseas dept. of France, consisting of 13 communes. The territory of Inini, set up as a separate unit in 1930, was reunited with Fr. Guiana proper as a dependency in 1946.

Guiana Highlands, mountainous tableland, mainly in S and SE Venezuela, and extending into Br. Guiana and Brazil. A thickly forested plateau of great geological antiquity, it covers half the area of Venezuela. Highlands extend from right bank of Orinoco R. to Brazilian border ranges of Parima and Pacaraima, reaching their highest point in Mt. Roraima (9,219 ft.). Consist of crystalline rocks with sandstone and lava caps. The vast plateaus are separated by deep valleys and have a number of magnificent waterfalls, such as ANGEL FALL, considered the highest in the world. Vegetation ranges from savannas to semi-deciduous forests, making region an enormously rich storehouse for fine cabinet woods (cedar, mahogany), rubber, balata, chicle, vanilla, divi-divi, oil-bearing and medicinal plants. The highlands contain large resources of minerals and precious stones; thus far only gold (at El Callao, Tumeremo, Guasipati) and diamonds have been mined. The Sierra Imataca (NE) has extensive iron deposits. Inaccessibility has retarded exploration and development.

Guiard (gēär′), village (pop. 1,763), Oran dept., NW Algeria, 7 mi. SW of Aïn-Témouchent; olive- and winegrowing.

Güicán (gwēkän′), town (pop. 1,628), Boyacá dept., central Colombia, at W foot of Sierra Nevada de Cocuy, 65 mi. NE of Sogamoso; alt. 9,721 ft.; wheat, corn, potatoes, silk.

Guiche, La (lä gēsh′), village (pop. 385), Saône-et-Loire dept., E central France, in Monts du Charollais, 11 mi. NE of Charolles; cattle.

Guichen (gēshē′), village (pop. 568), Ille-et-Vilaine dept., W France, 10 mi. SSW of Rennes; tanning; cattle.

Guichón (gwēchōn′), town (pop. 2,700), Paysandú dept., NW Uruguay, in N foothills of Cuchilla de Haedo, on railroad and 55 mi. E of Paysandú; trade center; grain, cattle.

Guidder (gēdĕr′), village, Benoué region, N Fr. Cameroons, 60 mi. NE of Garoua, near Fr. Equatorial Africa border; horses, cattle; limestone quarrying near by.

Guide, England: see BLACKBURN.

Guide Rock, village (pop. 676), Webster co., S Nebr., 10 mi. E of Red Cloud and on Republican R. near Kansas line; livestock, grain. Fish hatchery is here.

Guidonia (gwēdô′nyä), village (pop. 1,500), Roma prov., Latium, central Italy, 15 mi. NE of Rome. Formerly chief Ital. center of aeronautical studies (established in 1935); severely damaged in Second World War.

Guienne, Fr. *Guyenne* (both: gyĕn), former province of SW France, corresponding roughly to N Aquitaine Basin, bet. Garonne R. (S) and Massif Central (NE); ⊙ Bordeaux. Its name derives from AQUITAINE with which it was synonymous until the Hundred Years' War. A rich agr. and wine-growing area drained by the Garonne, the Dordogne, and their tributaries, it now covers Gironde, Dordogne, Lot, Aveyron, and part of Tarn-et-Garonne and Lot-et-Garonne depts. The prov. passed to England (1154) and was reconquered by France in 1453. Its main components were the Bordelais, PÉRIGORD, Agenais, QUERCY, and ROUERGUE. Guienne had its own *parlement* at Bordeaux. It was broken up into present depts. in 1790.

Guiglo (gē′lyō), village, W Ivory Coast, Fr. West Africa, 145 mi. NW of Sassandra; coffee, rice, kola nuts.

Güigüe (gwē′gwā), town (pop. 2,949), Carabobo state, N Venezuela, near S shore of L. Valencia, 16 mi. ESE of Valencia; agr. center (cotton, corn, sugar cane, cacao, fruit, stock).

Guigues (gēg), village (pop. estimate 500), W Que., near L. Timiskaming, 9 mi. E of Haileybury; quartz, silica mining.

Guihulñgan (gēhōōl″nyōōgän′), town (1939 pop. 3,967; 1948 municipality pop. 89,745), Negros Oriental prov., E Negros isl., Philippines, on Tañon Strait, 29 mi. E of Binalbagan; agr. center (corn, coconuts, tobacco).

Guijá, Mozambique: see CANIÇADO.

Güija, Lake (gwē′hä), on Salvador-Guatemala border, 40 mi. NW of San Salvador; 20 mi. long, 6 mi. wide, 150 ft. deep; 80% in Salvador; alt. 2,000 ft. Summer resort area. Receives Ostúa R. (W). Its outlet, Desagüe R., flows c.10 mi. SE to Lempa R. Its large isl. has ruins of anc. Indian town.

Guijo de Granadilla (gē′hō dhā gränä-dhē′lyä), village (pop. 1,121), Cáceres prov., W Spain, 12 mi. NNW of Plasencia; cereals, livestock, cork.

Guijo de Santa Bárbara (sän′tä bär′värä), town (pop. 1,013), Cáceres prov., W Spain, 24 mi. ENE of Plasencia; fruit, olive oil, livestock. Summer resort.

Guijuelo (gēhwā′lō), town (pop. 3,024), Salamanca prov., W Spain, 12 mi. NNE of Béjar; meat and cheese processing, soap and footwear mfg.; cereals, vegetables, livestock.

Guilarte, Mount (gēlär′tā) (3,953 ft.), SW central Puerto Rico, in Cordillera Central, 13 mi. NW of Ponce.

Guild, N.H.: see NEWPORT.

Guilden Sutton (gĭl′dŭn sŭ′tŭn), village and parish (pop. 404), W Cheshire, England, 3 mi. ENE of Chester; dairy farming.

Guildford (gĭl′fŭrd), municipality (pop. 2,217), SW Western Australia, NE residential suburb of Perth; fruit, grain.

Guildford, municipal borough (1931 pop. 30,754; 1951 census 47,484), ⊙ Surrey, England, in W central part of co., on the Wey and 27 mi. SW of London; agr. market (sheep and cattle fairs), with knitting mills, milk-canning works, and mfg. of machine tools and paint. Has 17th-cent. guildhall, church of St. Mary (partly Norman), Abbot's Hosp. (old-age home, founded 1619 by Archbishop Abbot), cathedral founded 1927, and grammar school (1509). Ruins of Norman castle stand on a mound. Lewis Carroll buried here. In Malory's *Morte d'Arthur*, Astolat, home of Elaine, is identified with Guildford. In municipal borough are towns of Stoke and Stoughton.

Guildhall (gĭld′hôl), town (pop. 270), ⊙ Essex co., NE Vt., on the Connecticut and 24 mi. NE of St. Johnsbury. Town hall dates from 1795. Settled 1764.

Guilford (gĭl′fŭrd), county (□ 651; pop. 191,057), N central N.C.; ⊙ GREENSBORO. In piedmont region; drained by Haw and Deep rivers. Agr. (tobacco, corn, dairy products, poultry); timber (pine, oak). Mfg. centers (textiles, furniture) at Greensboro and High Point; sawmilling. Formed 1770.

Guilford. 1 Town (pop. 5,092), including Guilford village (1940 pop. 1,986), New Haven co., S Conn., on Long Isl. Sound and 13 mi. E of New Haven; agr. (dairy products, poultry, apples, tomatoes), mfg. (furniture, metal products, cutlery, tools, boats, leather products, canned foods); seafood (oysters, lobsters); resorts. Has some of state's oldest houses, including stone Whitfield house (1639–40; restored 1936; now a mus.). Includes villages of North Guilford (fine early-19th-cent. churches), Sachem Head (resort, yachting center), and Leete's Island (resort colony in coastal area). Settled 1639. **2** Industrial town (pop. 1,842), including Guilford village (pop. 1,431), Piscataquis co., central Maine, on the Piscataquis and 8 mi. W of Dover-Foxcroft; textiles, wood products. Settled 1803, inc. 1816. **3** Town (pop. 164), Nodaway co., NW Mo., on Little Platte R. and 14 mi. SSE of Maryville. **4** Village in Guilford town (1940 pop. 1,884), Chenango co., S central N.Y., 30 mi. NE of Binghamton. **5** Town (pop. 796), Windham co., SE Vt., just SE of Brattleboro; agr.; resorts.

Guilford College, village (1940 pop. 661), Guilford co., N central N.C., 5 mi. W of Greensboro. Seat of Guilford Col. (Friends; coeducational; 1834). Near by is Guilford Courthouse Natl. Military Park (148.8 acres; established 1917), scene of important battle (1781) of Revolutionary War bet. Amer. troops under Gen. Nathanael Greene and British led by Lord Cornwallis; Americans, though forced to retreat, inflicted heavy losses that led to final defeat of British at Yorktown.

Guillaume, Le (lŭ gēyōm′), village (pop. 4,472), W Réunion isl., on road and 4 mi. SE of Saint-Paul; sugar cane, tobacco.

Guillaumes (gēyōm′), village (pop. 405), Alpes-Maritimes dept., SE France, on the Var and 23 mi. SSE of Barcelonnette, in Provence Alps. Dairying, olive-oil pressing. Near by is Valberg (alt. 5,475 ft.), a winter sports resort.

Guillelmo, Lake (gīyĕl′mō) (□ 6), SW Río Negro natl. territory, Argentina, in Nahuel Huapí natl. park, in glacial valley among high peaks, S of L. Mascardi (with which it is linked), 20 mi. SW of San Carlos de Bariloche; 4 mi. long; alt. c.3,000 ft.

Guillena (gēlyā′nä), town (pop. 3,265), Seville prov., SW Spain, on affluent of the Guadalquivir, on railroad and 10 mi. NNW of Seville; agr. center (cereals, corn, oranges, olives, timber, livestock); apiculture; sawmilling.

Guillestre (gēyĕ′strŭ), Alpine village (pop. 942), Hautes-Alpes dept., SE France, near the upper Durance, in Queyras valley, 16 mi. S of Briançon; road junction on *route des Alpes;* sawmilling, cheese mfg. Has 16th-cent. red-marble church.

Guillon (gēyō′), village (pop. 290), Yonne dept., N central France, on Serein R. and 9 mi. E of Avallon.

Guil River (gēl), in Hautes-Alpes dept., SE France, rises on Fr. slope of Monte Viso, in Cottian Alps, flows 30 mi. generally WSW through deep Queyras valley to the Durance just W of Mont-Dauphin.

Guilsfield, Wales: see WELSHPOOL.

Guilvinec (gēlvēnĕk′), town (pop. 4,417), Finistère dept., W France, fishing port on Bay of Biscay, 18 mi. SW of Quimper; sardine and lobster canning, lace mfg.

Güimar (gwēmär′), town (pop. 6,646), Tenerife, Canary Isls., 14 mi. SW of Santa Cruz de Tenerife; agr. center in fertile Güimar valley (potatoes, tomatoes, grapes, onions, wheat, figs, bananas; goats, hogs). Has medicinal waters. Hydroelectric plant. Its port is 2½ mi. SE.

Guimarães (gēmŏorā′ĭsh), city (pop. 1,266), N Maranhão, Brazil, on Cumã Bay of the Atlantic, and 40 mi. NW of São Luís; manioc, corn, sugar. Bituminous schist deposits.

Guimarãis or **Guimarães** (both: gēmŏorā′ĭsh), fortified city (pop. 12,568), Braga dist., Minho prov., N Portugal, on branch railroad and 10 mi. SE of Braga; textile center (cotton, linen goods), with important cutlery and shoe industry. Preserves feudal castle (rebuilt c.1100) with 9 towers, medieval collegiate church, and other ecclesiastical bldgs. Afonso Henriques, 1st monarch of Portugal, b. here c.1110.

Guimaras Island (gēmäräs′) (□ 223; 1939 pop. 37,797), Iloilo prov., Philippines, off SE coast of Panay isl. across Iloilo Strait, 7 mi. W of Negros isl. across Guimaras Strait; 26 mi. long, 12 mi. wide. Generally low, rising in central area to 825 ft. Rice, coconuts. Chief center is Jordan (1939 pop. 1,660; 1948 municipality pop. 15,677) on NW coast, opposite Iloilo city on Panay isl.

Guimaras Strait, channel bet. Visayan Sea and Panay Gulf, Philippines, bounded W by Panay isl. and Guimaras Isl., E by Negros isl.; c.80 mi. long, 7–16 mi. wide. The narrows (1½–4 mi. wide) bet. SE coast of Panay and Guimaras Isl. is called Iloilo Strait.

Guimba (gēm′bä, gēmbä′), town (1939 pop. 3,655; 1948 municipality pop. 33,029), Nueva Ecija prov., central Luzon, Philippines, 17 mi. NE of Tarlac; agr. center (rice, corn).

Guimbal (gēmbäl′), town (1939 pop. 3,737; 1948 municipality pop. 11,862), Iloilo prov., S Panay isl., Philippines, on Panay Gulf, 17 mi. W of Iloilo; rice-growing center.

Guimerá (gēmärä′), town (pop. 1,155), Lérida prov., NE Spain, 8 mi. SSW of Cervera; agr. trade (livestock, cereals, olive oil, wine).

Guimiliau (gēmēlyō′), village (pop. 284), Finistère dept., W France, 10 mi. SW of Morlaix. Has 16th-cent. calvary (finest in Brittany) and 16th–17th-cent. church with sculptured porch.

Guin, Switzerland: see DÜDINGEN.

Guin (gwĭn), town (pop. 1,137), Marion co., NW Ala., 70 mi. NW of Birmingham; woodworking center.

Guinayangan (gēnäyäng′än), town (1939 pop. 2,018; 1948 municipality pop. 8,390), Quezon prov., S Luzon, Philippines, port on Ragay Gulf, 55 mi. E of Lucena; fishing, agr. (coconuts, rice).

Guindulman (gēndōōlmän′), town (1939 pop. 2,229; 1948 municipality pop. 18,597), SE Bohol isl., Philippines, 45 mi. ENE of Tagbilaran; agr. center (rice, coconuts). Manganese deposits.

Guindy, India: see SAIDAPET.

Guinea (gĭ′nē), Fr. *Guinée,* Port. *Guiné,* Sp. *Guinea,* now little used term for W coast of central Africa along Gulf of Guinea and northward partly along the W coast of the great African bulge approximately bet. 15°N and 16°S. While the concept has varied, Guinea is generally considered to include the shore of all the Br., Fr., and Port. equatorial possessions from Senegal to Angola, divided by Niger delta into Upper Guinea and Lower Guinea. Guinea in a narrower sense lies entirely N of the line, and includes the littoral of S SENEGAL (Casamance area), PORTUGUESE GUINEA, FRENCH GUINEA, SIERRA LEONE, LIBERIA, IVORY COAST, GOLD COAST, TOGOLAND, DAHOMEY, and NIGERIA. Parts of this coast bear distinctive names, derived from early colonial trade: GRAIN COAST, Ivory Coast, Gold Coast, SLAVE COAST. The region is on the whole characterized by a monsoon climate with heavy rainfall, covered largely by tropical forests. The name is sometimes believed to derive from the old town of Djenné or Jenné in Fr. Sudan.

Guinea, hamlet (formerly Guinea Station), Caroline co., E Va., 11 mi. S of Fredericksburg. House where Stonewall Jackson died after battle of Chancellorsville is preserved as a shrine.

Guinea, Gulf of, wide inlet of the Atlantic off W African coast just S of that continent's great bulge. Considered to extend from Cape Palmas (4°22'N 7°43'W) on Liberian coast to Fr. Equatorial Africa at c.10°E. Contains isls. of Fernando Po and Annobón (Spain), São Tomé and Príncipe (Portugal). Flanking the huge Niger delta near head of Gulf of Guinea are the bights of Benin (W) and Biafra (E). Lesser streams flowing to the gulf are the Volta, Cameroon, and Ogooué.

Guinea Current, warm ocean current of North Atlantic Ocean, flowing E in Gulf of Guinea along Guinea coast of W Africa.

Guinea Station, Va.: see GUINEA.

Guinegate (gĭn'gāt), modern Fr. *Enginegatte* (ãzhēgāt'), agr. village (pop. 430), Pas-de-Calais dept., N France, 10 mi. S of Saint-Omer. Here French were defeated by the Flemish under Maximilian (1479) and again by the English and Maximilian (1513) in the Battle of the Spurs.

Güines (gwē'nĕs), city (pop. 22,669), Havana prov., W Cuba, 28 mi. SE of Havana; rail junction, processing and trading center in irrigated agr. region (sugar cane, tobacco, vegetables, fruit, cattle); cigar making, textile milling, canning. Sugar centrals in outskirts.

Guînes (gēn), town (pop. 3,359), Pas-de-Calais dept., N France, 6 mi. S of Calais, in fertile truck-gardening area. The celebrated meeting of the "Field of the Cloth of Gold" (1520) bet. Henry VIII and Francis I was held at Balinghem (3 mi. E).

Guingamp (gĕgã'), town (pop. 6,905), Côtes-du-Nord dept., W France, on Trieux R. and 18 mi. WNW of Saint-Brieuc; road and rail center; tanning, woodworking, mfg. (hosiery and agr. equipment). Has 14th-cent. church of Notre-Dame-de-Bon-Secours, where religious festivals are held.

Guinguinéo (gĭng-gēnā'ō), village, W Senegal, Fr. West Africa, rail junction 100 mi. ESE of Dakar; peanut growing.

Guinobatan (gēnōbätän'), town (1939 pop. 4,697; 1948 municipality pop. 32,280), Albay prov., SE Luzon, Philippines, on railroad and 10 mi. WNW of Legaspi; agr. center (abacá, rice, coconuts).

Güinope (gwēnō'pā), town (pop. 1,762), El Paraíso dept., S Honduras, 10 mi. SW of Yuscarán; coffee-growing center; plantains, sugar cane, fruit (oranges), grain. Airfield.

Guintinua Island, Philippines: see CALAGUA ISLANDS.

Guion (gī'ŭn), town (pop. 219), Izard co., N Ark., 19 mi. WNW of Batesville and on White R.

Guipúzcoa (gēpōōth'kwä), province (□ 771; pop. 331,753), N Spain, one of the Basque Provs., and the smallest of Spain; ⊙ San Sebastián. Bounded by Bay of Biscay (N) and France (NE); covered by W spurs of the Pyrenees sloping to sea; drained by the Bidassoa (Fr. border) and other short rivers. Has high, rocky coast with few natural harbors (Pasajes, San Sebastián). Abundant rainfall. Agr.: vegetables, potatoes, corn, apples, sour *chacolí* wine. Extensive cattle, sheep, and hog raising. Important fishing and fish processing (Pasajes, Fuenterrabía). Limestone and marble quarries. Prov. is essentially industrial. Metallurgy, chief industry, generally carried on in small plants: armaments (Placencia), rolling stock (Beasaín, Irún), machinery and hardware (Tolosa, Eibar), precision instruments (Eibar), electrical equipment (San Sebastián, Rentería). Other mfg.: paper (Tolosa, Rentería), textiles (Vergara, Andoain), chemicals, (San Sebastián, Rentería), furniture, flour products. Good communications. Its language is one of Basque dialects.

Guir, Cape, or **Cape Rhir** (both: gēr), headland of SW Fr. Morocco, on the Atlantic, 20 mi. NW of Agadir; 30°38'N 9°53'W. Lighthouse. Rising to 1,165 ft. above the coastal road, it constitutes SW extremity of the High Atlas.

Guir, Oued (wĕd' gēr'), desert stream in SE Fr. Morocco, rises in the High Atlas above Gourrama, flows generally SE, past Boudenib and Abadla (Aïn-Sefra territory, W Algeria), to the Oued Saoura near Igli. Length, over 200 mi. Lower course is a dry wadi most of the year.

Güira or **Güira de Macurijes** (gwē'rä dā mäkōōrē'hĕs), town (pop. 1,166), Matanzas prov., W Cuba, 23 mi. SE of Matanzas; rail junction and spa in agr. region (sugar cane, fruit).

Güira de Melena (mālā'nä), town (pop. 8,824), Havana prov., W Cuba, on railroad and 25 mi. SSW of Havana, in agr. region (tobacco, bananas, potatoes, pineapples, livestock); mfg. of cigars, dairying.

Guiratinga (gērŏtēng'gŭ), city (pop. 2,307), E Mato Grosso, Brazil, 170 mi. ESE of Cuiabá; diamond washings in near-by Garças R. Until 1939, called Santa Rita do Araguaia; and, 1939–43, Lajeado.

Güiria (gwē'ryä), town (pop. 5,885), Sucre state, NE Venezuela, on S coast of Paria Peninsula, on Gulf of Paria and 65 mi. E of Carúpano; exports cacao, coffee, petroleum. Airport. Iron-ore shipping station of PUERTO DE HIERRO is 13 mi. ENE.

Guisa (gē'sä), town (pop. 1,339), Oriente prov., E Cuba, at N foot of the Sierra Maestra, 10 mi. SE of Bayamo; cattle raising, dairying.

Guisambourg (gēzäbōōr'), village, NE Fr. Guiana, landing on Approuague R. estuary near the coast, and 50 mi. SE of Cayenne; tropical fruit, rubber. Also called Approuague.

Guisando (gēsän'dō), town (pop. 850), Ávila prov., central Spain, on S slopes of the Sierra de Gredos, 25 mi. NW of Talavera de la Reina; olives, cereals, fruit, livestock. Olive-oil pressing, lumbering. Hydroelectric station. In vicinity are celebrated monolithic sculptures of Celtiberian origin. Ruins of Hieronymite monastery Toros de Guisando are 30 mi. E; here Castilian nobles designated (1468) Isabella as heiress to throne.

Guisane River (gēzän'), Hautes-Alpes dept., SE France, rises at the Col du Lautaret, flows 18 mi. SE in deep valley bet. Massif du Pelvoux (W) and Cottian Alps (E), past Le Monêtier-les-Bains, to the Durance at Briançon. Followed by Grenoble-Briançon road.

Guisborough (gĭz'bŭrŭ), urban district (1931 pop. 6,306; 1951 census 8,609), North Riding, NE Yorkshire, England, 8 mi. ESE of Middlesbrough, at foot of Cleveland hills; iron mining; agr. market. Has ruins of old priory and of 14th-cent. church.

Guiscard (gēskär'), agr. village (pop. 751), Oise dept., N France, 6 mi. NNE of Noyon.

Guiscriff (gēskrēf'), village (pop. 1,388), Morbihan dept., W France, 25 mi. NW of Lorient; kaolin quarries.

Guise (gēz, gwēz), town (pop. 5,947), Aisne dept., N France, on the Oise and 16 mi. ENE of Saint-Quentin; industrial center with large ironworks (founded 1859 as a cooperative venture by Godin, a disciple of Fourier). Mfg. (leather belts, electrical equipment). Has ruins of ancestral castle of house of Guise. Town damaged in both world wars.

Guiseley (gīz'lē), former urban district (1931 pop. 5,607), West Riding, central Yorkshire, England, 6 mi. NNE of Bradford; woolen milling, bleaching, and printing; mfg. of steel and aluminum products, electrical equipment, asbestos. Inc. 1937 in Ilkley.

Güisisil (gwēsēsēl'), mountain (3,346 ft.) in SW Nicaragua, on Managua-Matagalpa dept. border, 10 mi. SW of Ciudad Darío.

Guisona (gēsō'nä), town (pop. 1,661), Lérida prov., NE Spain, 8 mi. N of Cervera; cementworks; olive-oil and wine processing, flour milling.

Guitinguitin, Mount, Philippines: see SIBUYAN ISLAND.

Guîtres (gē'trŭ), village (pop. 932), Gironde dept., SW France, on Isle R. and 9 mi. NNE of Libourne; wheat growing, sawmilling, barrelmaking. Has 12th–13th-cent. church.

Guiuan (gēwän', gē'wän), town (1939 pop. 4,067; 1948 municipality pop. 27,202), SE Samar isl., Philippines, at tip of narrow SE peninsula, on Leyte Gulf, sheltered by Tubabao Isl., near Calicoan Isl., 80 mi. SE of Catbalogan; coconut-growing center. Naval base here was retained by U.S. by terms of U.S.-Philippines pact of 1947.

Gujan-Mestras (güzhã'-mĕsträ'), town (pop. 3,318), Gironde dept., SW France, on SE shore of Arcachon Basin at mouth of Leyre R., 26 mi. SW of Bordeaux; ostreiculture, fish canning. School of pisciculture. Bathing beach.

Gujarat (gōōjŭrät'), fertile plain in N Bombay, India, generally considered to extend bet. S extremity of Aravalli Range (N) and Narbada R. (S), and bet. Rann of Cutch (NW) and Satpura and Vindhya ranges (SE); lies partly on E Kathiawar peninsula; drained by Sabarmati and Mahi rivers. Crops include cotton, millet, rice, wheat, and tobacco. Ahmadabad, Baroda, and Sidhpur are large cotton-milling centers. Name also applied to larger surrounding area where Gujarati is spoken. A part of 4th-cent. A.D. Gupta empire; later (15th–16th cent.) prospered as an independent sultanate; annexed to Mogul empire in 1570s, conquered by Mahrattas in early-18th cent. Other spellings: Gujerat, Guzerat.

Gujarat States, group of former princely states (total □ 7,493; pop. 1,458,702) situated within N and central Bombay, India. Comprised Balasinor, Bansda, Bariya, Cambay, Chota Udaipur, Dharampur, Jawhar, Lunavada, Rajpipla, Sachin, Sunth (Sant), Surgana, and numerous petty states, including those of old Rewa Kantha Agency (Dangs, Pandu Mewas, and Sankheda Mewas). Following breakup (1818) of Mahratta empire, they entered into various relations with Br. administration. In 1933, all were placed in a political agency (Gujarat States Agency), with hq. at Baroda, under govt. of India. In 1944, merged with Baroda and Western India States into 1 large agency. By Aug., 1949, all states inc. into various dists. of Bombay.

Gujar Khan (gōō'jŭr khän'), village, Rawalpindi dist., N Punjab, W Pakistan, 26 mi. SSE of Rawalpindi; local market for grain, cloth fabrics; metal products.

Gujerat, India: see GUJARAT.

Gujranwala (gōōjrän'välŭ), dist. (□ 2,311; 1951 pop. 1,044,000), Punjab, Pakistan; ⊙ Gujranwala. In Rechna Doab; bounded W by Chenab R.; irrigated by Upper and Lower Chenab canal systems. Very flat country; wheat, rice, millet, sugar cane are chief crops. Metal products; hand-loom weaving, rice milling. Trade centers: Gujranwala, Wazirabad, Hafizabad.

Gujranwala, city (1951 pop. 124,000), ⊙ Gujranwala dist., NE Punjab, W Pakistan, 40 mi. NNW of Lahore; center for wheat, rice, millet, cotton, sugar cane, cloth fabrics, metal products; rice milling, match and crayon mfg., cotton ginning, oilseed pressing, tanning; engineering and metalworks (iron, aluminum); woolen mills. Well-known iron-safe and brassware handicraft industries; also glazed pottery, ivory bangles, cotton cloth, tools, jewelry. Orange groves near by. Has col. Famous Sikh ruler, Ranjit Singh, b. here, 1780.

Gujrat (-jrät'), dist. (□ 2,266; 1951 pop. 1,157,000), NE Punjab, W Pakistan; ⊙ Gujrat. In N Chaj Doab, bet. Jhelum R. (W) and Chenab R. (E); bordered N by Kashmir. Fairly level alluvial tract, with wheat, millet, cotton, rice, and sugar-cane crops; hand-loom weaving; metalwork. Chief towns: Gujrat, Jalalpur Jattan, Mandi Bahauddin, Lala Musa. Formed part of kingdom of Porus in 4th cent. B.C.; site of battle of Hydaspes placed opposite Jalalpur (Jhelum dist.) by some, opposite Jhelum by others. Scene of final struggle bet. Sikhs and British (1848–49) for control of Punjab.

Gujrat, town (1941 pop. 30,899), ⊙ Gujrat dist., NE Punjab, W Pakistan, 70 mi. NNW of Lahore; trade center; agr. market (wheat, millet, cotton, rice, sugar cane); metalworks; furniture mfg., hand-loom weaving, handicrafts (pottery, iron- and brassware, shoes). Col. Site of Br. victory over Sikhs (Feb., 1849), which led to end of Sikh power in Punjab, is near by.

Gukasyan (gōōkŭsyän'), village (1939 pop. over 500), NW Armenian SSR, in the Lesser Caucasus, 16 mi. N of Leninakan; livestock, wheat, barley.

Gukovo (gōō'kŭvŭ), town (1939 pop. over 500), W Rostov oblast, Russian SFSR, in Donets Basin, on railroad and 12 mi. NNW of Krasny Sulin; coal-mining center.

Gukunsi, Bechuanaland Protectorate: see HUKUNTSI.

Gulaothi (gōōlou'tē), town (pop. 7,901), Bulandshahr dist., W Uttar Pradesh, India, 10 mi. NNW of Bulandshahr; trades in wheat, oilseeds, barley, cotton, jowar, corn.

Gula River, Norway: see GAULA RIVER.

Gulbahar or **Golbahar** (gōōlbŭhär'), village, Kabul prov., E Afghanistan, on Panjshir R. and 10 mi. NNE of Charikar, at foot of the Hindu Kush; summer resort.

Gulbarga (gōōlbŭr'gŭ), district (□ 6,975; pop. 1,312,055), W Hyderabad state, India, on Deccan Plateau; ⊙ Gulbarga. Bounded S by Kistna R.; mainly lowland except for N forested hills (teak, ebony, bamboo, sandalwood); drained by Bhima R. and its tributary, the Kagna. Mainly sandy red soil with small black-soil area (W); millet, oilseeds (chiefly peanuts, flax), cotton, wheat, rice. Oilseed, flour, and rice milling, cotton ginning, limestone quarrying and dressing, match mfg.; cattle raising. Main towns: Gulbarga (cotton-milling and trade center; archaeological landmarks), Shahabad (cement-mfg. center). Wadi is a major rail junction. Became part of Hyderabad during state's formation in 18th cent. Pop. 78% Hindu, 17% Moslem.

Gulbarga, city (pop. 53,551), ⊙ Gulbarga dist., W Hyderabad state, India, 110 mi. W of Hyderabad; cotton-milling and agr. trade (chiefly millet, wheat) center; flour and oilseed milling. Numerous architectural landmarks include 13th-cent. mosque modeled after that in Córdoba, Spain; its entire area (over 35,000 sq. ft.) covered with roof.

Gulbene (gōōl'bānā), Ger. *Alt-Schwanenburg*, city (pop. 3,819), NE Latvia, in Vidzeme, 100 mi. ENE of Riga; rail junction; brewing, distilling, flour milling. Village of Jaungulbene or Yaungulbene (both: youn'gōōl"bānā) [Lettish,=new Gulbene; Ger. *Neu-Schwanenburg*] is 10 mi. SW.

Gulcha or **Gul'cha** (gōōl'chŭ), village (1939 pop. over 500), E Osh oblast, Kirghiz SSR, on N slope of Alai Range, on Osh-Khorog highway and 38 mi. SE of Osh; wheat, cattle. Copper deposits near by. Until 1938, Gulcha-Guzar.

Guldal, Norway: see GAULDAL.

Guldborg (gōōl'bôr), town (pop. 539), Maribo amt, Denmark, on Lolland isl., on Guldborg Sound and 12 mi. NE of Maribo; ferry.

Guldborg Sound, strait (20 mi. long; min. width ½ mi.), Denmark, bet. Lolland and Falster isls.

Guldsmedshyttan (gŭld'smäts"hü'tän), village (pop. 1,705), Orebro co., S central Sweden, at NW end of L. Rasval, Swedish *Råsvalen* (rōs'vä"lŭn) (6 mi. long), 9 mi. NW of Lindesberg; iron, manganese, and lead mines and smelters; foundries. Hydroelectric station. Founded in 16th cent.; silver formerly mined here. Includes villages of Stripa (strē'pä") and Stora (stōōr'ō"), Swedish *Storå*.

Guldsmedvik, Norway: see GULLSMEDVIK.

Guledgarh (gōōlād'gŭr), town (pop. 18,307), Bijapur dist., S Bombay, India, 10 mi. SE of Bagalkot; agr. market (peanuts, cotton, wheat); handicraft cloth weaving. Limestone quarries near by. Also spelled Guledgud or Guledgudd.

Gulek Bogaz, Turkey: see CILICIAN GATES.

Gulen, Norway: see EIVINDVIK.

Gulf, county (□ 557; pop. 7,460), NW Fla., on Gulf of Mexico (S, W) and bounded E by Apalachicola R.; ⊙ Wewahitchka. Swampy lowland area, bordered by long sandspit enclosing St. Joseph Bay; contains L. WIMICO and part of Dead L. Forestry (naval stores, lumber, paper), cattle raising, fishing, and some farming (corn, peanuts). Formed 1925.

Gulf, village, Matagorda co., S Texas, near Matagorda Bay, 17 mi. S of Bay City; large sulphur deposits.

Gulf Intracoastal Waterway, U.S.: see INTRACOASTAL WATERWAY.

Gulf Islands, SW B.C., group in Strait of Georgia, bet. mainland and SE Vancouver Isl. Include Saltspring, Galiano, Valdes, Gabriola, Mayne, Saturna, and Pender isls. Lumbering, mixed farming, fishing.

Gulfport. 1 Town (pop. 3,702), Pinellas co., W Fla., suburb of St. Petersburg. Settled 1843, inc. 1913. **2** Village (pop. 232), Henderson co., W Ill., on the Mississippi (bridged here), opposite Burlington, Iowa. **3** City (pop. 22,659), ⊙ Harrison co., SE Miss., 12 mi. W of Biloxi, on deepwater harbor on Mississippi Sound; seaport, port of entry, and summer and winter resort. Imports bauxite, other minerals; ships lumber, cotton. Processes sea food, naval stores, lumber, tung oil, cotton; mfg. of milk of magnesia, clothing. A large veterans hosp. is here. Gulf Park Col. is at near-by Long Beach. Settled in 1891; inc. as town in 1898, as city in 1904. Grew as lumber port after opening (1902) of artificial harbor.

Gulf Stream, largest of the oceanic warm current systems, in North Atlantic Ocean, consisting of the FLORIDA CURRENT, the Gulf Stream proper, and the NORTH ATLANTIC CURRENT, to all of which the name Gulf Stream is popularly applied. Formed by the junction of the Antilles Current and the current issuing from the Gulf of Mexico through the Straits of Florida, the system flows NE along the SE coast of the U.S., and veers E along 40°N, merging with the North Atlantic Current, which has considerable influence on the climate of W and NW Europe. The term Gulf Stream is properly applied to the middle section of the system bet. Cape Hatteras and the GRAND BANKS SE of Newfoundland. Here, on Grand Banks, the Gulf Stream meets the cold Labrador Current and continues E as the North Atlantic Current. In the Gulf Stream proper, the system reaches its maximum transport of 90,000,000 cu. mm per second, with a surface temp. of 65–70°F. and moving at 4 mi. per hour. Characterized by high salinity and a deep-blue color, the Gulf Stream was 1st observed in 1513 by Ponce de León.

Gulf Stream, resort town (pop. 163), Palm Beach co., SE Fla., 16 mi. S of West Palm Beach, on Atlantic coast.

Gulgong (gŭlgŏng'), town (pop. 1,580), E central New South Wales, Australia, 145 mi. NW of Sydney; gold-mining center.

Gulhek or **Qolhak** (both: kōlhäk'), town, Second Prov., in Teheran, N Iran, 7 mi. N of Teheran, at foot of Elburz mts.; summer resort with noted gardens; summer residence of foreign legations and embassies. Near by is main Teheran radio station.

Gulistan (gōōlĭstän'), village, Quetta-Pishin dist., NE Baluchistan, W Pakistan, in Toba-Kakar Range, 36 mi. NW of Quetta.

Gulistan (gōō'lĭstän"), Rus. *Gyulistan* (gyōōlyĭstän'), village, W central Azerbaijan SSR, 4 mi. SSE of Shaumyanovsk. By treaty signed here (1813) Persia ceded N Azerbaijan khanates to Russia.

Gulkana (gŭlkă'nŭ), village (pop. 38), S Alaska, on Copper R. and 50 mi. NNE of Valdez, on Richardson Highway, just S of junction with Tok Cut-off; supply and trading point; gold mining.

Gulkana River, S Alaska, rises in foothills of Alaska Range near 62°49'N 145°50'W, flows 70 mi. S to enter Copper R. 3 mi. S of Gulkana. Passes through placer gold-mining region.

Gulke, Belgium: see GOÉ.

Gulkevichi or **Gul'kevichi** (gōōlkyĕ'vēchē), village (1926 pop. 6,242), E Krasnodar Territory, Russian SFSR, on railroad and 7 mi. SE of Kropotkin; flour milling, metalworking; wheat, sunflowers, sugar beets.

Gullanget (gŭl'ĕng"ŭt), Swedish *Gullänget*, village (pop. 1,613), Vasternorrland co., NE Sweden, 2 mi. NW of Ornskoldsvik; lumber and paper mills.

Gullbringu og Kjosar (gü'tŭlbrĭng"gü ô kyō'sär), Icelandic *Gullbringu og Kjósar*, county [Icelandic *sýsla*] (pop. 6,178), SW Iceland, on S shore of Faxa Bay; ⊙ Hafnarfjordur. Includes Reykjanes Peninsula. Keflavik is largest town; cities of Reykjavik and Hafnarfjordur are in but independent of co. Generally hilly, with large lava fields. Fishing, agr.

Gullegem (khŭ'lŭ-khĕm), town (pop. 6,758), West Flanders prov., W Belgium, 3 mi. WNW of Courtrai; textile industry; agr. market. Formerly spelled Gulleghem.

Gullfoot Lake or **Gull Lake** (6 mi. long, 1 mi. wide), S Ont., 45 mi. NW of Peterborough; drains S by Gull R. into Balsam L. and Trent R. Minden is near N end.

Gullfoss (gü'tŭlfôs"), waterfall (c.100 ft. high) of the Hvita, SW Iceland, 55 mi. ENE of Reykjavik.

Gullholmen (gŭl'hôl"mŭn), fishing village (pop. 428), Goteborg och Bohus co., SW Sweden, at N end of Harmano (här'mänû"), Swedish *Harmanö*, isl. (□ 3) in the Skagerrak, 6 mi. S of Lysekil; seaside resort.

Gull Island, Mich.: see BEAVER ISLANDS.

Gull Islands, SE N.Y., 2 small islands in E entrance to Long Island Sound, 10 mi. S of New London, Conn. On Great Gull Isl. (c.½ mi. long) is U.S. Fort Michie. Little Gull Isl. (just NE) has lighthouse (41°12'N 72°6'W).

Gull Lake, town (pop. 730), SW Sask., in the Cypress Hills, 35 mi. WSW of Swift Current; alt. 2,568 ft.; grain elevators, lumbering, stock.

Gull Lake. 1 Lake (15 mi. long, 4 mi. wide), S central Alta., 15 mi. NNW of Red Deer. Drains SW into Red Deer R. through Blindman R. **2** Lake, Ont.: see GULLFOOT LAKE.

Gull Lake. 1 Lake in Kalamazoo and Barry counties, SW Mich., c.12 mi. NE of Kalamazoo; c.4.5 mi. long, 1 mi. wide. **2** Lake (□ 21) in Cass and Crow Wing counties, central Minn., 8 mi. WNW of Brainerd; 9 mi. long, 3 mi. wide. Fishing, bathing, and boating resorts. Drains into Crow Wing R. Fed in N by Upper Gull L. (3 mi. long, 1 mi. wide). Used as reservoir. Dam on E outlet.

Gullsmedvik (gōōls'mĕdvēk), N suburb of Mo, Nordland co., N central Norway, on Ran Fjord; iron mine. Formerly spelled Guldsmedvik.

Gullspang (gŭl'spông"), Swedish *Gullspång*, village (pop. 494), Skaraborg co., S central Sweden, on Gullspang R., Swedish *Gullspångsälven* (10 mi. long), bet. L. Skager (E) and L. Vaner (W), 20 mi. NE of Mariestad; hydroelectric station, foundry, fish hatchery.

Gullui (gōōl'lwē), village (pop. 400), Agordat div., W Eritrea, 26 mi. S of Tessenei; cotton, grain, gum arabic.

Gulluk or **Kulluk** (gülük', kü–), Turkish *Güllük* or *Küllük*, village (pop. 826), Mugla prov., SW Turkey, small port on Gulf of Mandalya of the Aegean, 42 mi. W of Mugla.

Gully, village (pop. 183), Polk co., NW Minn., c.40 mi. NW of Bemidji; dairy products.

Gulmarg (gōōl'mŭrg), village, Baramula dist., W central Kashmir, in Pir Panjal Range, 25 mi. W of Srinagar; alt. 8,500 ft. Resort and recreation (skiing, golf, polo) center. Nanga Parbat mtn., 80 mi. NNE, is visible. Road terminus at Tangmarg, 2 mi. E. At Ferozpur or Firozpur, 3 mi. E, are anc. temple ruins similar to those near Awantipur; was anc. customs and watch station.

Gulnar (gülnär'), Turkish *Gülnar*, village (pop. 1,228), Icel prov., S Turkey, 75 mi. WSW of Mersin; wheat, barley, potatoes, sugar beets. Formerly Anaypazari.

Gulpaigan or **Golpayegan** (both: gōlpĭgän'), town (1942 pop. 20,844), Sixth Prov., W central Iran, 60 mi. SE of Arak and on highway to Isfahan; ⊙ former Gulpaigan prov.; agr. center (grain, cotton, opium, fruit). Wood carving, wool weaving. Gulpaigan prov. was inc. 1938 into Iran's Sixth Prov. (see KHUZISTAN).

Gulpen (khŭl'pŭn), town (pop. 2,186), Limburg prov., SE Netherlands, 9 mi. ESE of Maastricht; candy, sugar products, beer, clay products.

Gulran or **Golran** (gōōlrän'), town (pop. over 2,000), Herat prov., NW Afghanistan, 60 mi. NW of Herat and 20–30 mi. from Iran and USSR borders. Pop. is largely Jamshidi.

Gulripshi or **Gul'ripshi** (gōōlrĭpshē'), village (1939 pop. over 2,000), W Abkhaz Autonomous SSR, Georgian SSR, on Black Sea, 7 mi. SE of Sukhumi; health resort; essential oils; citrus fruit.

Gulsehir, Turkey: see ARAPSUN.

Gulu (gōō'lōō), town, ⊙ Northern Prov. (□ 33,607; pop. 945,104), N Uganda, 170 mi. N of Kampala; agr. trade center (cotton, peanuts, sesame). Has hosp., wireless station. Hq. Acholi dist. inhabited by Nilotic Acholi tribe.

Gulwe (gōōl'wā), town, Central Prov., E central Tanganyika, on railroad and 50 mi. SE of Dodoma; cotton, gum arabic. Station for Mpwapwa, 8 mi. NE.

Gulyai-Pole or **Gulyay-Pole** (gōōlyī'-pô"lyĭ), city (1926 pop. 12,027), NE Zaporozhe oblast, Ukrainian SSR, 50 mi. ESE of Zaporozh; leather products, flour, chemicals, metalworks.

Gulyantsi (gōōlyän'tsē), village (pop. 4,741), Pleven dist., N Bulgaria, on Vit R. and 12 mi. WSW of Nikopol; grain, livestock, truck.

Guma or **Guma Bazar** (gōōmä' bäzär'), Chinese *Pishan* or *P'i-shan* (both: pē'shän'), town and oasis (pop. 95,760), SW Sinkiang prov., China, 90 mi. WNW of Khotan, and on highway skirting SW edge of Taklamakan Desert; silk textiles, carpets; cotton, wheat, melon, fruit, cattle.

Guma (gōōm'ŭ), village, N central Himachal Pradesh, India, 18 mi. NNW of Mandi; rice, corn. Rock salt worked near by.

Gumaca (gōōmä'kä), town (1939 pop. 3,640; 1948 municipality pop. 19,131), Quezon prov., S Luzon, Philippines, on Lopez Bay, 33 mi. E of Lucena; fishing and agr. center (coconuts, rice).

Gumal Pass (gōō'mŭl) (alt. c.5,000 ft.), at junction of borders of Afghanistan and of Baluchistan and North-West Frontier Prov., W Pakistan, c.40 mi. N of Fort Sandeman. An important trade route for Afghan traveling merchants. Name also applied to entire course of **Gumal River,** which rises in E Afghanistan, W of Urgun, flows SSE to Pakistan border, and ENE, skirting N end of Toba-Kakar Range, through N Sulaiman Range, to plain SW of Tank; length, c.150 mi. Reaches the Indus only when flooded. Receives Zhob R. (right) in Sulaiman Range. Used for irrigation in Dera Ismail Khan dist. Pass and river also spelled Gomal.

Gumastapur, E Pakistan: see GOMASTAPUR.

Gumba (gōōm'bä) or **Gumba-Mobeka** (–mōbĕ'kä), village, Equator Prov., NW Belgian Congo, on Congo R. at mouth of Mongala R., and 120 mi. W of Lisala; steamboat landing and agr. center, with palm-oil mills at Mobeka.

Gumbinnen, Russian SFSR: see GUSEV.

Gumbum, China: see KUMBUM.

Gumel (gōōmĕl'), town (pop. 5,203), Kano prov., Northern Provinces, N Nigeria, near Fr. West Africa border, 75 mi. NE of Kano; agr. trade center; cotton, peanuts, millet, durra; honey; cattle, skins.

Gumeracha, village (pop. 431), SE South Australia, 18 mi. ENE of Adelaide; dairy products, livestock.

Gumeshevski Zavod, Russian SFSR: see POLEVSKOI.

Gumgum, Turkey: see VARTO.

Gumi, Nigeria: see GUMMI.

Gumiel de Hizán or **Gumiel de Izán** (both: gōōmyĕl' dhä ē-thän'), town (pop. 2,016), Burgos prov., N Spain, 7 mi. N of Aranda de Duero; agr. center (grapes, potatoes, cereals, livestock). Retains its old walls, and ruins of convent.

Gumiel del Mercado (dhĕl mĕrkä'dhō), town (pop. 1,525), Burgos prov., N Spain, 8 mi. NW of Aranda de Duero; wheat- and winegrowing; sheep raising; flour milling, liquor distilling. Lime kiln.

Gumishan, Gomeshan, or **Gomishan** (all: gōmĕshän'), town, Second Prov., in Gurgan, NE Iran, on Caspian Sea, 25 mi. NW of Gurgan, near USSR border; cotton; sheep raising. Formerly called Gumish Tepe or Gumish Tappeh.

Gumish Tappeh or **Gumish Tepe,** Iran: see GUMISHAN.

Gumista River (gōōmē'stŭ), coastal stream in Abkhaz Autonomous SSR, Georgian SSR, rises in E and W branches in Bzyb Range, flows c.25 mi. S to Black Sea W of Sukhumi. On it is Sukhumi hydroelectric station(*Sukhumges*), 7 mi. N of Sukhumi.

Gumma (gōōm'mä), prefecture (□ 2,446; 1940 pop. 1,299,027; 1947 pop. 1,572,787), central Honshu, Japan; ⊙ MAEBASHI. Generally mountainous terrain, with mtn. range (including Mt. Asama) along W border; hot springs in W area. Drained by upper Tone R. Large production of raw silk; agr. (rice, wheat). Textile mfg. at principal center (Maebashi, TAKASAKI, KIRYU, ISEZAKI). Sometimes spelled Gunma.

Gummersbach (gōō'mŭrsbäkh), town (pop. 28,705), in former Prussian Rhine Prov., W Germany, after 1945 in North Rhine-Westphalia, 27 mi. E of Cologne; 51°2'N 7°33'E. Mfg. of boilers, tools, electrical goods, textiles; leatherworking, lumber and paper milling (wallpaper), tanning. Chartered 1857.

Gummfluh (gōōm'flōō), cliff (8,075 ft.) in the Alps, SW Switzerland, 5 mi. WSW of Gstaad.

Gummi (gōōmē'), town (pop. 15,039), Sokoto prov., Northern Provinces, NW Nigeria, on Zamfara R. and 65 mi. S of Sokoto; cotton, millet; cattle, skins. Sometimes spelled Gumi.

Gumpolds, Czechoslovakia: see HUMPOLEC.

Gumpoldskirchen (gōōm'pôltskĭr"khŭn), town (pop. 3,209), after 1938 in Mödling dist. of Vienna, Austria, 12 mi. SSW of city center; noted for its wine.

Gumri, Armenian SSR: see LENINAKAN, city.

Gumsur, India: see RUSSELLKONDA.

Gumti River (gōōm'tē). **1** In central Uttar Pradesh, India, rises in forest and swamp land in N Pilibhit dist., flows c.500 mi. generally SE, past Nimkhar, Lucknow, Sultanpur, Jaunpur, and Kirakat, to the Ganges 3 mi. WSW of Saidpur. Seasonal flow for 35 mi. below source; navigable in part of lower course. **2** In Tripura (India) and Pakistan Bengal, rises in E Tripura, flows S and generally W, past Radhakishorepur and Comilla, to Meghna R. 23 mi. SE of Dacca; c.120 mi. long.

Gumuldjina or **Gumuljina,** Greece: see KOMOTINE.

Gumurdjina or **Gumurjina,** Greece: see KOMOTINE.

Gumusane (gümü'shänĕ"), Turkish *Gümüşane*, prov. (□ 3,884; 1950 pop. 203,474), NE Turkey; ⊙ Gumusane. Bordered N by Trebizond and Rize Mts., S by Erzincan Mts. Drained by Harsit, Kelkit, and Coruh rivers. Forested; copper in NW. Grain. Sometimes spelled Gumush-Hane.

Gumuszne, Turkish *Gümüşane*, village (1950 pop. 4,173), ⊙ Gumusane prov., Turkey, on Harsit R. 105 mi. WNW of Erzurum, 40 mi. SSW of Trebizond; potatoes, grain. Sometimes Gumush-Hane.

Gumusane Mountains, Turkish *Gümüşane*, NE Turkey, extend 25 mi. W from Gumusane, N of Kelkit R.; rise to 10,319 ft. Giresun Mts. adjoin W. Copper in E.

Gumushacikoy (gümüsh'häjŭkû"ē), Turkish *Gümüşhacıköy*, town (pop. 7,383), Amasya prov., N central Turkey, 35 mi. WNW of Amasya; lead mines also yield some silver and gold; grain, tobacco, hemp. Formerly Gumuskane.

Guna (gōō'nä), peak (13,881 ft.) in highlands of Begemdir prov., NW Ethiopia, 20 mi. SE of Debra Tabor.

Guna (gŏŏn'ŭ), town (pop., including cantonment area, 15,328), ⊙ Guna dist., N Madhya Bharat, India, 115 mi. SSW of Lashkar; trades in wheat, millet, oilseeds, gram, corn; cotton ginning, oilseed milling, hand-loom weaving. Sometimes spelled Goona.

Gunabad, Iran: see GONABAD.

Gunbad-i-Qawus or **Gonbad-e-Qavos** (both: gōnbäd'ĕkävōs'), town (1940 pop. 9,637), Second Prov., in Gurgan, NE Iran, on Gurgan R. and 50 mi. NE of Gurgan; agr. center; cotton, tobacco; sheep raising. Also called Gunbad-i-Qabus.

Gun Cay (kā, kē), islet, NW Bahama Isls., in Cat Cays (S Biminis); 24°34'N 79°18'W. Lighthouse.

Gunchu (gōōn'chōō), town (pop. 15,074), Ehime prefecture, W Shikoku, Japan, 14 mi. SW of Matsuyama, on Iyo Sea; commercial center in agr. area; sake, pottery, soy sauce; fishing.

Gund, Kashmir: see BANIHAL.

Gundagai (gŭn'dùgī), village (pop. 1,355), SE New South Wales, Australia, 60 mi. WNW of Canberra and on Murrumbidgee R.; gold-mining center; chromite.

Gundalpet, India: see GUNDLUPET.

Gunda Road, India: see HOSPET.

Gundelen (gōōndyĭlyĕn'), village (1926 pop. 3,677), W central Kabardian Autonomous SSR, Russian SFSR, on N slope of the central Greater Caucasus, 25 mi. WNW of Nalchik; dairying; grain.

Gundelfingen (gŏŏn'dùlfĭng"ùn), town (pop. 4,588), Swabia, W Bavaria, Germany, 6 mi. WSW of Dillingen; stove mfg., dairying; cabbage, cattle, sheep. Has Gothic church. Chartered 1278.

Gundelsheim (gŏŏn'dùls-hīm), town (pop. 2,749), N Württemberg, Germany, after 1945 in Württemberg-Baden, on the canalized Neckar and 10 mi. N of Heilbronn; cigar mfg., food processing. Has medieval walls and towers, and 2 castles.

Gundlakamma River (gōōndlŭkŭm'mŭ), NE Madras, India, rises in Eastern Ghats, E of Nandyal, flows NE past Cumbum (reservoir) and Markapur, and SE past Addanki to Coromandel Coast of Bay of Bengal 12 mi. E of Ongole; c.140 mi. long.

Gundlupet (gōōnd'lōōpĕt), town (pop. 6,237), Mysore dist., S Mysore, India, 35 mi. S of Mysore, on main road to Ootacamund; biri mfg., hand-loom silk weaving; cattle raising. Teak, sandalwood in forested hills (S). Formerly spelled Gundalpet.

Gundogmus (gündōmōōsh') or **Eksere** (ĕksĕrĕ'), Turkish *Gündoğmuş*, village (pop. 934), Antalya prov., SW Turkey, 80 mi. E of Antalya; grain.

Gundorovka (gōōndùrôf'kŭ), town (1946 pop. over 500), W Rostov oblast, Russian SFSR, in Donets Basin, near Northern Donets R., 12 mi. W of Kamensk; coal-mining center.

Gunduk River, India: see GANDAK RIVER.

Guneyce (günäjĕ'), Turkish *Güneyce*, town (pop. 1,611), Rize prov., NE Turkey, 10 mi. S of Rize; corn; zinc.

Gunflint Lake, NE Minn. and W Ont., in chain of lakes on Can. line, partly in Cook co., Minn., 30 mi. NW of Grand Marais; 8 mi. long, 1 mi. wide. Fishing resorts.

Gunge (gōōng'gā), town (pop. 3,710), on Awajishima, Hyogo prefecture, Japan, on Harima Sea, 10 mi. NNW of Sumoto; commercial center in agr. area (rice, wheat); straw goods, poultry.

Gungu (gōōng'gōō), village, Leopoldville prov., SW Belgian Congo, on Kwilu R. and 55 mi. SE of Kikwit; palm-oil and rice processing; coffee growing.

Gunib (gōōnyēp'), village (1926 pop. 387), central Dagestan Autonomous SSR, Russian SFSR, in the E Greater Caucasus, on the Kara Koisu (right affluent of the Avar Koisu) and 32 mi. SSW of Buinaksk; alt. 7,736 ft.; orchards. Pop. largely Avar. A strong natural fortress in Caucasian wars. Here Shamil, leader of anti-Rus. independence movement, made last stand and was captured (1859).

Gunja (gōō'nyä), village, NE Croatia, Yugoslavia, on Sava R. (Bosnia border) opposite Brcko, on railroad, in Slavonia.

Gun Lake, in Barry and Allegan counties, SW Mich., 10 mi. WSW of Hastings, in onion-growing area; c.3 mi. long, 2 mi. wide. Drained by Gun R., which flows c.15 mi. SW to Kalamazoo R. at Otsego.

Gunma, Japan: see GUMMA.

Gunn, town (1940 pop. 36), Sweetwater co., SW Wyo., near Bitter Creek, 5 mi. NE of Rock Springs; alt. c.6,650 ft.

Gunnarstorp (gŭ'närstôrp"), village (pop. 726), Malmohus co., S Sweden, 10 mi. ENE of Halsingborg; coal mining.

Gunnaur (gŏŏn'nour), town (pop. 7,259), Budaun dist., N central Uttar Pradesh, India, 45 mi. WNW of Budaun; trades in wheat, pearl millet, mustard, barley, gram, jowar.

Gunnbjorn, Mount (gŏŏn'byôrn), Dan. *Gunnbjørns Fjæld*, highest known peak (12,139 ft.) of Greenland, in SE part of isl., near Blosseville Coast; 68°54'N 29°49'W. Extends large glaciers to Denmark Strait.

Gunn City, town (pop. 57), Cass co., W Mo., 10 mi. E of Harrisonville.

Günne (gü'nù), village (pop. 749), in former Prussian prov. of Westphalia, W Germany, after 1945 in North Rhine-Westphalia, on the Möhne and 5 mi. SW of Soest. Site of dam for large Möhne reservoir (completed 1913), which constitutes major water and power supply of Ruhr region. Dam was damaged by aerial attacks in May, 1943.

Gunnebo (gŭ'nùbōō") or **Gunnebobruk** (gŭ"nùbōō-brük'), village (pop. 854), Kalmar co., SE Sweden, on Verkeback Bay (vĕr'kùbäk"), Swedish *Verkebäcksviken*, 8-mi.-long inlet of Baltic, 4 mi. WSW of Vastervik; ironworks (founded 1764).

Gunnedah (gŭ'nùdä), municipality (pop. 4,314), E central New South Wales, Australia, on Namoi R. and 160 mi. NW of Newcastle; coal-mining center.

Gunnersbury, England: see BRENTFORD AND CHISWICK.

Gunning, village (pop. 661), E New South Wales, Australia, 35 mi. N of Canberra; copper-mining center; granite quarries.

Gunnison, county (□ 3,242; pop. 5,716), W central Colo.; ⊙ Gunnison. Livestock-grazing and coal-mining region, drained by Gunnison R. Taylor Park reservoir and dam are part of irrigation system in E. Co. includes ranges of Rocky Mts. and parts of Grand Mesa, Cochetopa, Holy Cross, and Uncompahgre natl. forests. Formed 1877.

Gunnison. 1 Town (pop. 2,770), ⊙ Gunnison co., W central Colo., on Gunnison R., just N of San Juan Mts., and 95 mi. SE of Grand Junction; alt. 7,683 ft. Resort and trade center in well-irrigated valley; dairy products, livestock. Hq. for Gunnison Natl. Forest. Western State Col. of Colo. is here. Coal, gold, silver mines near by. Laid out as silver-mining town 1879, inc. 1880. **2** Town (pop. 453), Bolivar co., NW Miss., 8 mi. NE of Rosedale near Mississippi R., in cotton-growing area. **3** City (pop. 1,144), Sanpete co., central Utah, bet. Wasatch Range and Sevier R., 13 mi. SW of Manti in irrigated sugar-beet area; alt. 5,215 ft.; flour, poultry. Founded 1860, inc. 1893.

Gunnison, Mount (12,714 ft.), W Colo., in West Elk Mts., 12 mi. ESE of Paonia.

Gunnison River, W central Colo., formed by confluence of Slate and Taylor rivers above Gunnison; flows c.180 mi. W and NW to Colorado R at Grand Junction. Uncompahgre R. is tributary. Gunnison Tunnel (5.8 mi. long; completed 1909 as unit in Uncompahgre reclamation project) diverts water from Gunnison R. into Uncompahgre valley. River course W of Sapinero lies in spectacular canyon, part of which has been set aside as BLACK CANYON OF THE GUNNISON NATIONAL MONUMENT.

Gunong (gōōnōōng') [Malay,=mountain]. For Malayan names beginning thus and not found here, see under following part of the name.

Gunong Semanggol (sĕmäng"gōl'), village (pop. 665), NW Perak, Malaya, 9 mi. NW of Taiping, in Krian rice dist.

Gunpowder Falls, stream, N Md., rises in NE Carroll co., near Pa. line, winds c.60 mi. generally SE, through Baltimore co., to Gunpowder R. c.15 mi. ENE of Baltimore. PRETTYBOY DAM, LOCH RAVEN DAM impound water-supply reservoirs.

Gunpowder River, N Md., estuary (c.9 mi. long) receiving Gunpowder Falls and Little Gunpowder Falls (streams); enters Chesapeake Bay in Aberdeen Proving Ground, c.15 mi. ENE of Baltimore.

Gun River, Mich.: see GUN LAKE.

Güns, Hungary: see KÖSZEG.

Guns Island, islet in the Irish Sea, near entrance to Strangford Lough, Co. Down, Northern Ireland, 4 mi. NE of Ardglass.

Gunskirchen (gōōns'kĭrkhùn), town (pop. 3,097), central Upper Austria, 4 mi. WSW of Wels; wheat, cattle.

Guntakal (gōōn'tŭkŭl), town (pop., including, adjacent railway settlement of Timmancherla, 20,414), Anantapur dist., NW Madras, India, 36 mi. NNW of Anantapur; major rail junction (workshops); cotton ginning; grain trade.

Gunten (gōōn'tùn), resort, Bern canton, central Switzerland, on L. of Thun, 5 mi. SE of Thun.

Gunter (gŭn'tùr), town (pop. 463), Grayson co., N Texas, 16 mi. SSW of Sherman, in agr. area.

Gunter Air Force Base, Ala.: see MONTGOMERY city.

Güntersberge (gün'tùrsbĕr"gù), town (pop. 1,358), in former Anhalt state, central Germany, after 1945 in Saxony-Anhalt, in the lower Harz, 12 mi. SW of Quedlinburg; tourist resort; dairying.

Guntersblum (gōōn'tùrsblōōm"), village (pop. 3,051), Rhenish Hesse, W Germany, 11 mi. N of Worms; wine.

Guntersdorf (gōōn'tùrsdôrf), village (pop. 1,135), NE Lower Austria, 20 mi. NNW of Stockerau; rye, potatoes, wine.

Guntersville (gŭn'–), city (pop. 5,253), ⊙ Marshall co., NE Ala., on Guntersville Reservoir (on Tennessee R.) and 27 mi. NW of Gadsden; river port, processing center for cotton area; textiles, lumber. Settled c.1818, named Marshall 1838, renamed 1848. Industries stimulated by construction of Guntersville Dam (7 mi. NW) and development of TVA.

Guntersville Dam, NE Ala., on Tennessee R., 7 mi. NW of Guntersville, upstream from Wheeler Dam. Major TVA dam (94 ft. high, 3,979 ft. long) completed 1939; concrete construction, earthfill wings; designed to aid navigation (has lock) and flood control and to supply power. Forms Guntersville Reservoir (□ 108; 82 mi. long, 1–4 mi. wide; capacity 1,018,700 acre-ft.; sometimes called Guntersville L.) in Marshall and Jackson counties.

Guntown, town (pop. 299), Lee co., NE Miss., 13 mi. N of Tupelo, in agr. and timber area.

Guntramsdorf (gōōn'trämsdôrf), town (pop. 5,143), after 1938 in Mödling dist. of Vienna, Austria, 11 mi. SSW of city center; wine.

Gunt River (gōōnt), Tadzhik SSR, in the Pamir, rises in Yashil-Kul (lake), flows c.80 mi. WSW, past Shugnan, to Panj R. at Khorog.

Guntur (gōōntōōr'), district (□ 5,795; pop. 2,277,283), NE Madras, India; ⊙ Guntur. Lies bet. Eastern Ghats (N) and Coromandel Coast of Bay of Bengal (S); SE portion is in Kistna R. delta. Agr.: millet, rice, tobacco (dist. is main tobacco area of state), oilseeds (chiefly peanuts), cotton, chili. Steatite mines in several dispersed outcrops. Main towns: Guntur, Tenali, Chirala. Noted Buddhist archaeological remains at Amaravati.

Guntur, city (pop. 83,599), ⊙ Guntur dist., NE Madras, India, in Kistna R. delta, 220 mi. N of Madras; rail junction (spurs to Tenali and Macherla); road and trade (cotton, tobacco) center; tobacco curing, paper, rice, and oilseed milling, ghee processing, mfg. of cotton cloth, cement, tin containers; tannery. Has several cols. affiliated with Andhra Univ., whose main cols. were moved here from Waltair, suburb of VIZAGAPATAM, during Second World War; agr. research station. City founded (mid-18th cent.) by French; cession to English (1788) confirmed in 1823. Ruined 12th-cent. hill fortress 12 mi. WSW, at village of Kondavid.

Gunung Api or **Goenoeng Api** (gōōnōōng' ä'pē), island (□ 8), Banda Isls., S Moluccas, Indonesia, in Banda Sea, just W of Bandalontar; roughly circular, 3 mi. in diameter. Has active volcano, 2,159 ft. high. Fishing.

Gunungsitoli or **Goenoengsitoli** (both: gōōnōōng" sĕtō'lē), town (pop. 3,124) on E coast of Nias isl., Indonesia, off W Sumatra, port on Indian Ocean, 85 mi. WSW of Sibolga; 1°17'N 97°37'E; ships copra and nutmeg. Lighthouse.

Gunupur (gōōn'ōōpōōr), town (pop. 7,416), Koraput dist., S Orissa, India, on Vamsadhara R. and 28 mi. NW of Parlakimedi; rail spur terminus; exports rice, timber; distillery.

Gunzan, Korea: see KUNSAN.

Günzburg (günts'bōōrk), town (1950 pop. 10,201), Swabia, W Bavaria, Germany, at confluence of the Danube and the Günz, 14 mi. ENE of Ulm; rail junction; mfg. of cotton, agr. machinery, paper; brewing. Has Gothic church, Renaissance castle, town mus. with large collection of prehistoric finds. A former Roman settlement, Günzburg was chartered c.1346.

Gunzenhausen (gōōn"tsùnhou'zùn), town (pop. 8,377), Middle Franconia, W Bavaria, Germany, on the Wörnitz and 15 mi. SE of Ansbach; rail junction; mfg. of machines, precision instruments, textiles; woodworking, printing, brewing. Has late-Gothic church. Chartered 1472. Osiander b. here.

Günz River (günts), Bavaria, Germany, formed 8 mi. NE of Memmingen by Östliche Günz R. (20 mi. long) and Westliche Günz R. (19 mi. long), flows 35 mi. N to the Danube at Günzburg.

Gupis (gōōpĭs'), village, ⊙ Kuh Ghizar governorship, Gilgit Agency, NW Kashmir, on Gilgit (Ghizar) R. and 55 mi. WNW of Gilgit. Fort.

Gur, Lough (lŏkh gûr'), lake (1 mi. long, 1 mi. wide), NE Co. Limerick, Ireland, 11 mi. SSE of Limerick. On shore are noted Druidical remains.

Gura (gōō'rä), town, Adi Caieh div., central Eritrea, on plateau, 5 mi. S of Decamere. Marble quarry near by. Its airport was Italian air force hq. in Ethiopian campaign (1935–36) and Allied air base in Second World War.

Gurabo (gōōrä'bō), town (pop. 4,419), E Puerto Rico, on Loíza R. and 17 mi. SSE of San Juan; sugar and tobacco growing; tobacco stripping.

Gura-Dimieni (gōō'rä-dēmyăn'), village (pop. 979), Buzau prov., SE central Rumania, 18 mi. NNW of Buzau; petroleum production.

Gurafarda (gōō'räfär"dä), Ital. *Gurrafarda*, village, Ilubabor prov., SW Ethiopia, 55 mi. NW of Maji, in mtn. region N of Akobo R. District considerably depopulated by slave trade which persisted until recent times.

Gurage (gōōrä'gä), fertile mountainous district in Shoa and Arusi provs., central Ethiopia, bet. Awash R., Omo R., and L. Zwai; source of Billate R. Rises to 11,345 ft. (N). Agr. (bananas, cereals, coffee, tobacco), stock raising, and pottery making. Annexed by Ethiopia in 1889.

Gurahont (gōō"rähônts'), Rum. *Gurahonț*, Hung. *Honctő* (hôn'tsû), village (pop. 960), Arad prov., W Rumania, on White Körös R., on railroad and 45 mi. E of Arad; cementworks.

Gura-Humorului (gōō'rä-hōōmô'rōōlwē), town (1948 pop. 4,573), Suceava prov., N Rumania, on E slopes of the Moldavian Carpathians, on railroad and 16 mi. E of Campulung; summer resort and trading center; sawmilling, tanning, mfg. of pottery and bricks. Jews compose 25% of pop. Former Voronet (Rum. *Voroneț*,) monastery, famous for its 15th-cent. church with its exterior Byzantine frescoes, is 3 mi. S. Humorului 16th-cent. monastery is 3 mi. N.

Guramba, Mount (gōōräm'bä) (11,045 ft.), in Sidamo-Borana prov., S Ethiopia, in highlands SE of L. Awusa, 160 mi. S of Addis Ababa; 6°45'N 38°41'E. Source of Webi Shebeli (here called Wabi) and Ganale Dorya rivers.

Gura-Ocnitei (gōō'rä-ôk'nētsä), Rum. *Gura-Ocniței*, village (pop. 2,928), Prahova prov., S central Rumania, 5 mi. ENE of Targoviste; oil and natural-gas center.

Gurban Saikhan or **Gurban Sayhan** (gōōr'bän sī'-khän), mountain range of the E Gobi Altai, in S Mongolian People's Republic, in Gobi desert, extending c.70 mi. WNW from Dalan Dzadagad; rises to 9,396 ft. Archaeological remains and traces of anc. men were discovered here (1925) by R. C. Andrews.

Gurdaspur (gōōr'däspōōr), district (□ 1,359; pop. 862,006), NW Punjab, India; ⊙ Gurdaspur. Largely in N Bari Doab, bet. Ravi R. (W) and Beas R. (SE), with NE section in foothills of Punjab Himalayas; bordered W by Pakistan Punjab; has 2 small enclaves (including Dalhousie hill resort) in Himachal Pradesh (NE). Irrigated by Upper Bari Doab Canal (headworks at Madhopur); wheat, gram, corn, sugar cane, rice, and oilseeds grown; hand-loom woolen weaving. Chief towns: Batala, Dhariwal. Original dist. (□ 1,846; pop. 1,153,511) was reduced (1947) by inc. of W portion into Sialkot dist., Pakistan Punjab.

Gurdaspur, town (pop. 16,641), ⊙ Gurdaspur dist., NW Punjab, India, 41 mi. NE of Amritsar; agr. market center (wheat, gram, corn, rice, sugar cane); hand-loom weaving.

Gurdon (gûr'dŭn), city (pop. 2,390), Clark co., S central Ark., 15 mi. SSW of Arkadelphia, in cotton- and corn-growing area; railroad shops, lumber mills, cotton gins.

Gurdzhaani (gōōrjüä'nyē), city (1926 pop. 6,410), E Georgian SSR, 25 mi. E of Tiflis (linked by railroad); rail junction; wine center in Kakhetian wine region.

Gurev-, in Rus. names: see GURYEV-.

Gurgan (gōōrgän') or **Gorgan** (gôr–), town (1940 pop. 21,376), Second Prov., NE Iran, 185 mi. ENE of Teheran, at N foot of Elburz mts., 20 mi. from SE corner of Caspian Sea; alt. 377 ft. Main center of former Gurgan prov., in fertile agr. area; cotton, tobacco, flax, sesame, rice, citrus fruit; rug weaving. Its Caspian Sea port was formerly Bandar Gaz, since 1930s supplanted by Bandar Shah. Dating from 8th cent., it was destroyed (14th cent.) by Tamerlane. Flourished c.1800 during rise of Kajar dynasty, which originated here. Until 1930s called Astarabad, Asterabad, or Astrabad. **Gurgan** prov., bounded E by Khurasan, S by Shahrud and Samnan, E by Mazanderan and Caspian Sea, and N by Turkmen SSR (USSR), was included (1938) in Iran's Second Prov. (see TEHERAN).

Gurgan Lagoon, inlet of SE Caspian Sea, in NE Iran, nearly closed off by Miyan Kaleh Peninsula and Ashuradeh Isls.; 45 mi. long, 7 mi. wide. On it are the ports of Bandar Gaz (partly silted) and Bandar Shah.

Gurgan River, NE Iran, rises in the Ala Dagh W of Bujnurd, flows 150 mi. W, past Gunbad-i-Qawus and Pahlevi Dezh, to SE corner of Caspian Sea. Used for irrigation.

Gurgaon (gōōr'goun), district (□ 2,287; pop. 872,978), SE Punjab, India; ⊙ Gurgaon. Bordered E by Jumna R., NW by Patiala and East Punjab States Union; N outliers of Aravalli Range in S. Has enclaves in Rajasthan (S). Agr. (millet, gram, barley, wheat, oilseeds); hand-loom weaving. Chief towns: Rewari, Palwal, Gurgaon. Original dist. (□ 2,234; pop. 851,458) was enlarged (1948) by inc. of former Punjab state of Pataudi.

Gurgaon, town (pop. 9,935), ⊙ Gurgaon dist., SE Punjab, India, 15 mi. SW of Delhi; local trade center for grain, cotton, salt, oilseeds; hand-loom weaving, dyeing. Sometimes called Hidayatpur and Hidayatpur Chauni.

Gurghiu (gōōr'gēōō), Hung. *Görgényszentimbre* (gûr'-gän-sĕntĕm'brĕ), village (pop. 1,498), Mures prov., central Rumania, 21 mi. NE of Targu-Mures; pottery making. Forestry school. Has remains of a Rakoczy fortress destroyed (1708) by Austrians. In Hungary, 1940–45.

Gurgueia, Serra da (sĕ'rŭ dä gōōrzhä'ŭ), range of NE Brazilian highlands, on Piauí-Bahia border, separating drainage of the Parnaíba and São Francisco basins. Alt., 2–3,000 ft. Continued by Serra da Tabatinga (W) and Serra do Piauí (NE). Gurgueia R. rises on N slope.

Gurgueia River, S Piauí, Brazil, rises near Bahia border, flows c.250 mi. NNE, past Bom Jesus and Jerumenha, to the Parnaíba above Floriano. One of its headstreams, the Paraim, rises in the Serra da Gurgueia and traverses L. Parnaguá. Navigable.

Guria (gōō'ryŭ), Rus. *Guriya* (gōō'rēŭ), region of W Georgian SSR, on Black Sea, S of lower Rion R. Tea, citrus fruit, tung oil. Main towns: Poti, Makharadze. Passed (1804) to Russia.

Guriev-, in Rus. names: see GURYEV-.

Gurk (gōōrk), village (pop. 1,160), Carinthia, S Austria, on Gurk R. and 17 mi. N of Klagenfurt; paper mill. Formerly seat of bishop; has 11th-cent. cathedral. Place of pilgrimage and summer resort (alt. 2,171 ft.).

Gurkfeld, Yugoslavia: see KRSKO.

Gurkha or **Gorkha** (gōōr'kŭ), town, central Nepal, 50 mi. NW of Katmandu; rice, barley, corn, wheat, millet, vegetables. Gorakhnath shrine, regarded by Gurkhas as most sacred shrine of their race, here. An early independent petty kingdom and ancestral home of ruling dynasty of Nepal; became ⊙ Gurkhas after its capture (1559) by Drabya Sah, who laid foundations for future Gurkha power. In 1769, after a 4-year war, Gurkha king Prithwi Narayan defeated Newar kingdom in Nepal Valley; moved Gurkha ⊙ to Katmandu, where it has remained up to the present.

Gurk River (gōōrk), Carinthia, S Austria, rises in Gurktal Alps; flows 40 mi. generally E, then S above Althofen, through the Krappfeld, to Glan R. 5 mi. E of Klagenfurt; length, 65 mi.

Gurktal Alps (gōōrk'täl), W range of the Noric Alps, S Austria, along Salzburg-Carinthia-Styria border; extend c.30 mi. E from Katschberg Pass, rising to 8,008 ft. in the Eisenhut; forested slopes; pastures.

Gurla Mandhata (gōōr'lŭ mändä'tŭ), Tibetan *Memo Nani*, peak (25,355 ft.) in the Himalayas, SW Tibet, near Nepal border, S of Manasarowar L., 105 mi. SSE of Gartok.

Gurlen (gōōrlyĕn'), village (1926 pop. 2,035), N Khorezm oblast, Uzbek SSR, in Khiva oasis, on railroad and 24 mi. NNW of Urgench; cotton ginning.

Gurley, village (pop. 219), Cheyenne co., W Nebr., 12 mi. N of Sidney and on branch of N.Platte R.

Gurleyville, Conn.: see MANSFIELD.

Gurmatkal (gōōrmŭtkäl'), town (pop. 9,045), Gulbarga dist., SW central Hyderabad state, India, 18 mi. ENE of Yadgir; millet, cotton, oilseeds, tobacco. Cattle raising in near-by hills. Sometimes spelled Gurmatkol.

Gurnee (gûrnē'), village (pop. 1,097), Lake co., extreme NE Ill., on Des Plaines R. (bridged here), just W of Waukegan.

Gurnet Point, Mass.: see PLYMOUTH BAY.

Gurnigel (gōōr'nēgŭl), peak (5,062 ft.) in Bernese Alps, W central Switzerland, 7 mi. W of Thun; resort of **Gurnigelbad** (alt. 3,800 ft.) on NW slope.

Gurpinar (gürpŭnär'), Turkish *Gürpınar*, village (pop. 436), Van prov., SE Turkey, 27 mi. SSE of Van; grain. Also called Kasrik.

Gurrea de Gállego (gōōrā'ä dhā gä'lyāgō), town (pop. 1,147), Huesca prov., NE Spain, on Gállego R. and 20 mi. SW of Huesca; mfg. (paper, tiles); sugar beets, cereals, fruit.

Gursarai (gōōr'sŭrī), town (pop. 4,029), Jhansi dist., S Uttar Pradesh, India, 40 mi. ENE of Jhansi; jowar, oilseeds, wheat, gram.

Gurskoy (gōōrsk'ûü), Nor. *Gurskøy*, island (□ 53; pop. 3,346) in North Sea, More og Romsdal co., W Norway, one of the Sor Isls., separated from mainland by a narrow strait, 16 mi. SW of Alesund; 9 mi. long, 9 mi. wide. Joined to Hareid Isl. by a road bridge.

Guruè (gōō'rwā), village, Zambézia prov., N central Mozambique, in Namuli Mts., 165 mi. N of Quelimane; tea plantation.

Guru Har Sahai (gōōr'ōō hŭr' sŭhī'), town (pop. 2,311), Ferozepore dist., W Punjab, India, 21 mi. SSW of Ferozepore; wheat, gram. Sometimes called Mandi Guru Har Sahae.

Gurun (gōōrōōn'), village (pop. 1,869), W central Kedah, Malaya, on railroad and 22 mi. SSE of Alor Star; rubber, tea.

Gurun (gürün'), Turkish *Gürün*, village (pop. 4,556), Sivas prov., central Turkey, on Tohma R. and 75 mi. SSE of Sivas; alt. 4,100 ft.; wheat. Hittite inscriptions found here.

Gurupá (gōōrōōpä'), city (pop. 255), E central Pará, Brazil, on right bank of the Amazon and 220 mi. W of Belém, opposite Gurupá Isl. (□ c.1,900), which divides lower Amazon into 2 branches. Hydroplane landing. Formerly Santo Antônio de Gurupá.

Gurupá Island (□ c.1,900), in Amazon delta, E Pará, Brazil, 220 mi. W of Belém, and W of Marajó Isl. Also called Ilha Grande de Gurupá.

Gurupi River (gōōrōōpē'), N Brazil, forms Pará-Maranhão border throughout its course (NNE) of c.300 mi. to the Atlantic, which it enters below Viseu. Gold washing in lower course. Bauxite deposits recently discovered near its mouth. Formerly spelled Gurupy.

Guru Sikhar, peak, India: see ABU.

Guruzala or **Gurzala** (both: gōōr'zŭlŭ), town (pop. 7,243), Guntur dist., NE Madras, India, on rail spur and 55 mi. WNW of Guntur; cotton ginning, sheep raising; chili, peanuts, rice. Experimental farm (cotton research). Extensive 2d–3d-cent. A.D. Buddhist ruins (stupas, monasteries) 23 mi. W, near Kistna R., on hill called Nagarjunakonda or Nagarjuna Durgam; discovered 1926.

Guryev or **Gur'yev** (gōōr'yĭf), oblast (□ 98,600; 1946 pop. estimate 300,000), W Kazakh SSR; ⊙ Guryev. On NE Caspian Sea; includes below-sea-level depression (N drained by lower Ural and Emba rivers) and, in S, waterless Mangyshlak and Buzachi peninsulas and Ust-Urt plateau. Contains Emba oil field, one of chief USSR petroleum areas, centered at DOSSOR, MAKAT, and KOSCHAGYL. Pipe lines link Dossor, Guryev, Orsk, and Koschagyl. Natural-gas fields NW of Guryev. Extensive borax deposits (Inderborski). Fishing (carp, herring) is important; centered at Ganyushkino, Guryev (canning plant), Fort Shevchenko. Coal, manganese, oil, and phosphorites found on Mangyshlak Peninsula. Raising of sheep, cattle, camels. Guryev-Kandagach RR passes through NE. Pop.: Kazakhs, Russians. Formed 1938.

Guryev or **Gur'yev**, city (1939 pop. over 30,000), ⊙ Guryev oblast, Kazakh SSR, on Ural R., 10 mi. from Caspian Sea and 410 mi. SE of Orsk, 1,250 mi. NW of Alma-Ata; 47°15'N 51°52'E. Terminus of railroad from Kandagach and of oil pipe lines from Emba oil field; oil refinery; center of fishing industry; canning, metalworking, fur and leather processing. Founded early 17th cent. on right bank of Ural R.; expanded in 1930s to left bank, site of oil refinery and installations.

Guryevka or **Gur'yevka** (–kŭ), town (1939 pop. over 2,000), W central Ulyanovsk oblast, Russian SFSR, 2 mi. SSE of Barysh; woolen milling.

Guryevsk or **Gur'yevsk** (gōōr'yĭfsk). **1** Residential town (1939 pop. 4,198), W Kaliningrad oblast, Russian SFSR, 6 mi. NE of Kaliningrad. Until 1945, in East Prussia and called Neuhausen (noi'houzŭn). **2** City (1939 pop. over 10,000), W Kemerovo oblast, Russian SFSR, on railroad and 70 mi. S of Kemerovo, in Kuznetsk Basin. Founded 1726 as silver smelter; converted 1919 to iron- and steel-works.

Gurzuf (gōōrzōōf'), town (1926 pop. 2,798), S Crimea, Russian SFSR, port on Black Sea, 7 mi. NE of Yalta; climatic and beach resort; winegrowing center. Sanatoriums (mainly for army-navy personnel) in shore park, over 1 mi. long. Ruins of 6th-cent. fortress, built under Justinian I and later used by Genoese. Pushkin lived here, 1820.

Gusar (gōōsär'), village (1939 pop. over 500), SW Leninabad oblast, Tadzhik SSR, near Pendzhikent, in Zeravshan R. valley; wheat, fruit.

Gusau (gōōzou'), town (pop. 14,878), Sokoto prov., Northern Provinces, NW Nigeria, on Sokoto R., on railroad and 30 mi. SSE of Kaura Namoda. Agr. trade center (millet, cattle, skins); cotton-shipping point; timber. Site of hosp., leper settlement. Airfield. Gold mining, diamond deposits near by.

Gusbat, El, Tripolitania: see CUSSABAT.

Gusev (gōō'syĭf), city (1939 pop. 24,534), E Kaliningrad oblast, Russian SFSR, on the Pissa, on railroad and 70 mi. E of Kaliningrad; flour-milling center and cattle market; mfg. (agr. implements, textiles); trade in agr. produce, cattle, horses. Founded 1724 by Frederic William I as resettlement center for area devastated by epidemic. Until 1945, in East Prussia and called Gumbinnen (gōōmbĭ'nŭn).

Gusevski or **Gusevskiy** (gōō'syĭfskē), town (1949 pop. over 500), S Vladimir oblast, Russian SFSR, near Gus-Khrustalny; peat works.

Gushantsi (gōōshän'tsē), village (pop. 3,734), Vratsa dist., NW Bulgaria, 8 mi. NE of Berkovitsa; livestock, grain.

Gusinaya Zemlya, Russian SFSR: see GOOSE LAND.

Gusinje or **Gusinye** (both: gōō'sĭnyĕ), village (pop. 5,777), E Montenegro, Yugoslavia, 30 mi. ENE of Titograd, near Albania border, in North Albanian Alps. Long contested bet. Montenegro and Albania.

Gusinoye Ozero (gōōsē'nŭyŭ ô'zyĭrŭ) [Rus.,=goose lake], town (1941 pop. over 500), S Buryat-Mongol Autonomous SSR, Russian SFSR, on lake Gusinoye Ozero (□ 64), 13 mi. NNW of Novo-Selenginsk, on Ulan-Ude–Naushki RR. Large lignite deposits and underground coal-gas plant here. Developed after 1941.

Gus-Khrustalny or **Gus'-Khrustal'nyy** (gōōs"-khrōō-stäl'nē), city (1926 pop. 17,941), S Vladimir oblast, Russian SFSR, 37 mi. SSE of Vladimir; glass- and crystal-working center; mfg. (cotton textiles, washing machines); peat working. Raised to status of a city in 1931.

Gusmar (gōōs'mär) or **Gusmari** (gōōs'märē), village (1930 pop. 138), S Albania, 9 mi. SW of Tepelenë, in Kurvelesh hills; coal mining. Sometimes called Kurvelesh or Kurveleshi.

Guspini (gōōspē'nē), town (pop. 8,061), Cagliari prov., SW Sardinia, 16 mi. NNE of Iglesias; mining industry. Lead-zinc-silver mines near by, including that of MONTEVECCHIO.

Gussago (gōōs-sä'gô), village (pop. 987), Brescia prov., Lombardy, N Italy, 5 mi. NW of Brescia; foundry.

Gussenbakh, Russian SFSR: see MEDVEDITSA, village.

Güssing (gü'sĭng), Hung. *Németújvár* (nā'mĕt-ōō"ēvär), town (pop. 2,815), Burgenland, E Austria, 18 mi. SW of Szombathely.

Gussola (gōōs-sô'lä), village (pop. 2,715), Cremona prov., Lombardy, N Italy, near Po R., 18 mi. SE of Cremona.

Gusswerk (gōōs'vĕrk), town (pop. 2,806), Styria, E central Austria, on Salza R. and 28 mi. NNE of Leoben; paper mills; abandoned ironworks.

Gustanj (gōō'shtänyü), Slovenian *Guštanj*, Ger. *Gutenstein* (gōō'tünshtīn), village, N Slovenia, Yugoslavia, on Meza R., on railroad and 32 mi. W of Maribor, near Austrian border. Has steel mill (one of oldest in Europe; high-grade steel) with 2 Bessemer converters and steel foundry. Includes hamlet of Ravne (NW). Until 1918, in Styria.

Gustavia (güstävyä'), town, W Saint-Barthélemy, Fr. West Indies, 150 mi. NNW of Basse-Terre, Guadeloupe; 17°54'N 62°52'W. Agr. (cotton, tropical fruit, livestock) and fishing. Has a good harbor.

Gustavo A. Madero or **Villa Gustavo A. Madero** (vē'yä gōōstä'vō ä' mädā'rō), town (pop. 25,929), Federal Dist., central Mexico, 2½ mi. N of Mexico city; mfg. center (flour and textile milling, soapmaking). GUADALUPE HIDALGO now forms part of Gustavo A. Madero. Mineral springs and stone quarries are near by.

Gustavsberg (gŭs'täfsbĕr"yü). **1** Village (pop. 2,175), Stockholm co., E Sweden, on Varmdo isl., on bay of the Baltic, 13 mi. E of Stockholm; porcelain, pottery, and tile mfg. center (since 1827). **2** Village (pop. 539), Vasternorrland co., NE Sweden, on Alno isl., 4 mi. ENE of Sundsvall; sawmills. Includes Strand (stränd) village.

Gustavsburg (gōō'stäfsbōōrk), former suburb (1939 pop. 2,719) of MAINZ, after 1945 in Hesse, W Germany, near junction of Rhine and canalized Main rivers. After 1945, part of GINSHEIM.

Gustavus (gŭstā'vŭs), village (pop. 69), SE Alaska, on Icy Strait, 50 mi. W of Juneau, near Glacier Bay Natl. Monument; gold mining and milling.

Güsten (gü'stŭn), town (pop. 8,160), in former Anhalt State, central Germany, after 1945 in Saxony-Anhalt, on the Wipper and 6 mi. W of Bernburg; rail junction; machinery mfg., woodworking.

Gustine. **1** (gŭ"stēn') City (pop. 1,984), Merced co., central Calif., in San Joaquin Valley, 25 mi. S of Modesto; irrigated farming, fruitgrowing, dairying; condensed-milk plant. Inc. 1915. **2** (gŭs'tēn") Town (pop. 421), Comanche co., central Texas, near Leon R., 33 mi. ENE of Brownwood; rail point in agr. area.

Guston, town and parish (pop. 1,597), E Kent, England, 2 mi. N of Dover; agr. market.

Güstrow (gü'strō), city (pop. 32,899), Mecklenburg, N Germany, 20 mi. S of Rostock; 53°48'N 12°11'E. Rail center; metal- and woodworking; mfg. of machinery, food products; wool market. Has 13th-cent. basilica and 16th-cent. former ducal palace. On site of anc. Wendish fort; chartered 1228. Was ⊙ (1520–1695) small duchy of Mecklenburg-Güstrow. During Thirty Years War it was ⊙ (1628–29) Wallenstein's duchy of Mecklenburg.

Gusukube (gōōsōō'kōō"bä), town (1950 pop. 16,519), on E point of Miyako-shima, in the S Ryukyus, 8 mi. SE of Hirara.

Gusum (gü'sŭm"), village (pop. 1,378), Ostergotland co., SE Sweden, 5 mi. NW of Valdemarsvik; foundry (established 1653), slide-fastener mfg.

Gusyatin (gōōsyä'tyĭn), Pol. *Husiatyn* (hōōsyä'tĭn), village (1931 pop. 2,639), E Ternopol oblast, Ukrainian SSR, on Zbruch R. and 18 mi. ENE of Chortkov; stone-quarrying center; brickworking. Soviet-Polish frontier station (1921–39).

Gus-Zhelezny or **Gus'-Zheleznyy** (gōōs"-zhĭlyĕz'nē), village (1939 pop. over 500), N Ryazan oblast, Russian SFSR, on Gus R. (left tributary of Oka R.), near its mouth, and 10 mi. WNW of Kasimov; metalworking.

Guta (gōō'tä), Hung. *Gúta* (gōō'tŏ), village (pop. 11,718), W Slovakia, Czechoslovakia, on Great Schütt isl., at junction of Little Danube and Vah rivers; rail terminus; major agr. center (barley, wheat, corn, sugar beets).

Gutach River, Germany: see WUTACH RIVER.

Gutai or **Gutay** (gōōtī'), town (1944 pop. over 500), SW Chita oblast, Russian SFSR, on Chikoi R. and 95 mi. S of Petrovsk; gold and molybdenum mining.

Gutau (gōō'tou), town (pop. 2,120), NE Upper Austria, 15 mi. NE of Linz, N of the Danube; summer resort (alt. 1,915 ft.).

Gutay, Russian SFSR: see GUTAI.

Gutenfürst (gōō'tünfürst"), village (pop. 232), Saxony, E central Germany, 10 mi. SW of Plauen, 8 mi. N of Hof; grain, livestock. After 1945, traffic check point bet. East and West Germany.

Gutenstein (gōō'tünshtīn), village (pop. 1,819), E Lower Austria, 11 mi. WSW of Berndorf; rail terminus; ruined castle. Pilgrimage church of Mariahilfberg near by.

Gutenstein, Yugoslavia: see GUSTANJ.

Gütersloh (gü'turslō), town (pop. 35,968), in former Prussian prov. of Westphalia, NW Germany, after 1945 in North Rhine-Westphalia, 10 mi. SW of Bielefeld; mfg. of bicycles, washing machines, cables, chains, furniture, plywood; silk and cotton spinning, food processing (ham, sausage, pumpernickel). Chartered 1825.

Guthrie (gŭ'thrē), county (□ 596; pop. 15,197), W central Iowa; ⊙ Guthrie Center. Prairie agr. area (hogs, cattle, poultry, corn, oats), drained by Middle Raccoon and South Raccoon rivers and by Middle R. Bituminous-coal mines, sand and gravel pits. Has state park. Formed 1851.

Guthrie. **1** City (pop. 1,253), Todd co., S Ky., at Tenn. line, 23 mi. SE of Hopkinsville, in agr. and timber area; rail junction; produces creosoted railroad ties; sawmilling. Settled 1860; inc. 1867. **2** City (pop. 10,113), Logan co., central Okla., 28 mi. N of Oklahoma City, near Cimarron R.; processing and commercial center for oil-producing, dairying, and agr. area. Mfg. of dairy products, machinery, feed, flour, cottonseed products, furniture, oil-field equipment, sheet-metal and glass products; railroad shops; poultry hatcheries; greenhouses. Seat of Benedictine Heights Col. Mineral Wells Park is near by. Founded 1889, inc. 1890; it was territorial capital until 1907, then state capital until 1910. **3** Village (pop. c.100), ⊙ King co., NW Texas, c.85 mi. E of Lubbock; trading point for ranching region, and hq. for large 6666 Ranch.

Guthrie Center, town (pop. 2,042), ⊙ Guthrie co., W central Iowa, on South Raccoon R. and c.45 mi. WNW of Des Moines; milling (flour, cereals, feed). Coal mines near by. State park is N. Inc. 1880.

Gutiérrez, province, Bolivia: see PORTACHUELO.

Gutiérrez (gōōtyĕ'rĕs), town (pop. c.2,700), Santa Cruz dept., E central Bolivia, on road from Santa Cruz and 20 mi. NNE of Lagunillas; agr. products (corn, vegetables).

Gutiérrez, Lake (□ 7; alt. 2,600 ft.), SW Río Negro natl. territory, Argentina, in Nahuel Huapí natl. park, 5 mi. WSW of San Carlos de Bariloche; 7 mi. long.

Gutiérrez Zamora (sämō'rä), town (pop. 3,849), Veracruz, E Mexico, on Tecolutla R., 5 mi. from its mouth on the Gulf, and 15 mi. E of Papantla; tobacco-growing center.

Guttaring (gōō'tärĭng), town (pop. 2,292), Carinthia, S Austria, 20 mi. NNE of Klagenfurt; summer resort; leather goods. Meteorological station; pilgrimage church of Mariahilf.

Guttenberg (gŭ'tünbûrg). **1** Town (pop. 1,912), Clayton co., NE Iowa, on the Mississippi (dam and locks here) and 30 mi. NW of Dubuque; cannery (corn, tomatoes), pearl-button factory; mfg. of boxes, railroad ties, farm tools, beverages. Lead and zinc deposits; timber. First settled in 1834 as Prairie la Porte; colonized and named by German immigrants 1845; inc. 1851. **2** (also gōō'tŭnbûrg) Town (pop. 5,566), Hudson co., NE N.J., near Hudson R., 5 mi. NNE of Jersey City; mfg. (embroideries, textiles, clothing, knit goods, metal products, vegetable oils). Inc. 1859.

Guttentag, Poland: see DOBRODZIEN.

Guttstadt, Poland: see DOBRE MIASTO.

Gutu (gōō'tōō), rural township (pop. 199), Victoria prov., E central Southern Rhodesia, in Mashonaland, 36 mi. NE of Fort Victoria; tobacco, wheat, corn; livestock. Hq. of native commissioner for Gutu dist. Police post.

Guty (gōō'tē), town (1926 pop. 2,097), NW Kharkov oblast, Ukrainian SSR, 8 mi. WSW of Bogodukhov; sugar refining.

Gützkow (güts'kō), town (pop. 3,870), in former Prussian Pomerania prov., N Germany, after 1945 in Mecklenburg, near the Peene, 11 mi. S of Greifswald; agr. market (grain, potatoes, sugar beets, stock).

Gutzlaff Island (gŭts'lăf), in N Chusan Archipelago of E.China Sea, Kiangsu prov., China, 50 mi. SE of Shanghai; 30°49'N 122°10'E; 500 yds. across. Lighthouse; telegraph station.

Guyandot River (gī'ŭndŏt"), SW W.Va., rises in Raleigh co. SSW of Beckley, flows SW, W, and NNW past Gilbert, Logan, and Barboursville, to Ohio R. at Huntington; 166 mi. long.

Guyenne, France: see GUIENNE.

Guyhirne, England: see WISBECH SAINT MARY.

Guymon (gī'mŭn), city (pop. 4,718), ⊙ Texas co., extreme NW Okla., on high plains of the Panhandle, near North Canadian R., c.105 mi. N of Amarillo (Texas); trade center for wheat, livestock, and dairy area. Oil and gas wells. Mfg. (carbon black, gasoline, farm machinery, metal products). U.S. soil conservation station is near by. Inc. 1905.

Guyot, Mount. **1** (gēō') Peak (13,370 ft.) in Rocky Mts., central Colo., bet. Park and Summit counties. **2** (gē'ō) Peak (6,621 ft.) in Great Smoky Mts., on Tenn.-N.C. line, 40 mi. ESE of Knoxville.

Guyot Glacier (gē'ō), SE Alaska, W arm of Malaspina Glacier, in St. Elias Mts., drains into Icy Bay c.70 mi. E of Yakutat; 60°N 141°22'W.

Guyotville (güyōvēl'), town (pop. 5,142), Alger dept., N central Algeria, on the Mediterranean, 8 mi. WNW of Algiers, and 5 mi. NE of Cape Sidi-Ferruch; truck-gardening center, also supplying Algiers with grapes, citrus fruit. Beach resort.

Guyra (gī'rŭ), town (pop. 1,407), NE New South Wales, Australia, 185 mi. N of Newcastle; sheep and agr. center.

Guysborough (gīz'bŭrŭ), county (□ 1,611; pop. 15,461), S central N.S., on the Atlantic; ⊙ Guysborough.

Guysborough, village (pop. estimate 800), ⊙ Guysborough co., E central N.S., at head of Chedabucto Bay, 30 mi. SE of Antigonish; fishing port; ships pulpwood. Site of French fort, established 1636.

Guy's Cliffe, village and parish (pop. 11), central Warwick, England, on Avon R. just N of Warwick; site of cave where, according to legend, Guy, earl of Warwick, lived and died.

Guy's Hill (gīz), village, St. Mary parish, E central Jamaica, 25 mi. NW of Kingston; tropical fruit, coffee, spices.

Guyton (gī'tŭn), town (pop. 633), Effingham co., E Ga., 25 mi. NW of Savannah.

Guyzance, village and parish (pop. 150), E Northumberland, England, 6 mi. SSE of Alnwick; chemical works.

Guzar (gōōzär'), village (1939 pop. over 2,000), SW Kashka-Darya oblast, Uzbek SSR, on railroad and 30 mi. SE of Karshi; metalworking, processing of agr. products.

Guzerat, India: see GUJARAT.

Guzmán or **Ciudad Guzmán** (syōōdädh' gōōsmän'), city (pop. 22,170), Jalisco, W Mexico, in W outliers of Sierra Madre Occidental, on railroad and 70 mi. S of Guadalajara; alt. 4,988 ft. Agr. processing center (cereals, alfalfa, vegetables, sugar cane, fruit, livestock); mfg. of shoes, wire, soap, furniture, chocolate; sawmills, flour mills, tanneries. Mercury mining near by. Starting point for ascent of the volcanic Colima peaks, c.15 mi. SW. Formerly Zapotlán el Grande.

Guzmán, Lake (□ 56), Chihuahua, N Mexico, 60 mi. SW of Ciudad Juárez; 12 mi. long, 3–6 mi. wide. Receives Casas Grandes R.

Gvar Am, Israel: see GEVARAM.

Gvardeisk or **Gvardeysk** (gvŭrdyäsk'), city (1939 pop. 9,272), W central Kaliningrad oblast, Russian SFSR, on Pregel R. and 23 mi. E of Kaliningrad; trade center (wood, agr. produce). Founded 1280–90 as fortress of Teutonic Knights. Until 1945, in East Prussia and called Tapiau (tä'pēou).

Gvardeiskoye or **Gvardeyskoye** (gvŭrdyä'skŭyü), village (1926 pop. 2,337), W Kamenets-Podolsk oblast, Ukrainian SSR, 13 mi. WSW of Proskurov; peat bogs. Until 1946, Felshtin.

Gvat (gvät), settlement (pop. 700), NW Israel, in NW part of Plain of Jezreel, 5 mi. WSW of Nazareth; mixed farming. Founded 1926. Also spelled Gevat.

Gvozdets (gvŭzdyĕts'), Pol. *Gwoździec* (gvōōzh'dzyĕts), town (1939 pop. over 500), E Stanislav oblast, Ukrainian SSR, on left tributary of the Prut and 11 mi. ENE of Kolomyya; flour milling, brick mfg. Has old monastery and church.

Gvulot, Israel: see GEVULOT.

Gwa (gwä), village, Sandoway dist., Lower Burma, on Arakan coast, at mouth of minor Gwa R. and 6 mi. S of Sandoway (linked by road); harbor has 10-ft. channel.

Gwaai (gwä-ī'), village, Bulawayo prov., W central Southern Rhodesia, in Matabeleland, near Gwaai R., on railroad and 85 mi. NW of Bulawayo; alt. 3,270 ft. Tobacco, peanuts, corn; livestock.

Gwaai River, W Southern Rhodesia, rises near Fig tree, flows 260 mi. NW, past Gwaai, to Zambezi R. 65 mi. E of Victoria Falls. Receives Umguza and Shangani rivers (right).

Gwadabawa, Nigeria: see GODABAWA.

Gwadar or **Gwadur** (gwô'dŭr), town and port on the Arabian Sea coast of Baluchistan, constituting with surrounding enclave (□ 300) a dependency of Oman, on promontory, 290 mi. W of Karachi, near Iran border; coastal trade; fisheries (catfish); salt pans. Attacked and burned in 1581 by the Portuguese, it was ceded (late-18th cent.) by Kalat to Oman.

Gwalior (gwäl'yôr), former princely state (□ 26,008; pop. 4,006,159), central India; ⊙ was Lashkar. Consisted of large main body and numerous enclaves (SW). House of Gwalior founded by Ranoji Sindhia, a Mahratta chief who became independent of the peshwa (hereditary Mahratta ruler; hq. at Poona) in mid-18th cent. Early ⊙ was (c.1750–1810) Ujjain. Taking advantage of widespread disorders, the Gwalior forces soon overran much of central India, until checked by British in early 19th cent. In 1948, state was merged with Madhya Bharat. Sometimes called Sindhia's Dominions.

Gwalior, town (pop. 34,488), NE Madhya Bharat, India, 2 mi. N of LASHKAR. Lies at foot of Gwalior Fort (S), celebrated medieval stronghold approached through 6 imposing gateways and surrounded by battlemented walls; fort area stands on sandstone hill c.300 ft. above city; c.1¾ mi. long (N–S), ½ mi. wide. Among many bldgs. of historical interest in fort are elaborately ornamented palaces, temples, and shrines, while just below walls are remarkable 15th-cent. rock sculptures. Town has pottery works, cotton, flour, and oilseed mills, ice and match factories; handicraft cloth weaving and stone carving. Airport. Held in 6th-cent. A.D. by White Huns, from 10th to 12th cent. by Kachwaha Rajputs; taken by Kutb-ud-din in 1196, by Altamsh in 1232. During Rajput occupation in 15th cent. attained fame as cultural center (Tan Sen attended singing school; tomb is SE). Under Moguls in 16th and 17th cent.; since 18th cent. a Mahratta stronghold, although captured by British in 1780, 1843, and 1858 (after Sepoy uprising). Name of Gwalior commonly applied to combined area of Gwalior and Lashkar.

Gwalior Residency, group (□ 27,869; pop. 4,954,75–) of former princely states in political relations with govt. of India; hq. were at Lashkar. Established 1782; included Gwalior, Khaniadhana (1888), Rampur (1936), and Benares (1936).

Gwanda, village (pop. 788), Bulawayo prov., S Southern Rhodesia, in Matabeleland, on railroad and 60 mi. SSE of Bulawayo; livestock center (cattle, sheep, goats); corn. Hq. of native commissioner; police post. Gold, arsenic, nickel mined near by.
Gwandu (gän'dōō), town (pop. 7,469), Sokoto prov., Northern Provinces, NW Nigeria, 55 mi. SW of Sokoto; agr. trade center (cotton, millet, cattle, skins). Originally in Sokoto or Fulah empire; became (1817) seat of semi-independent emirate (Gando or Gandu) which included parts of what is now Fr. West Africa.
Gwaram (gäräm'), town (pop. 2,909), Kano prov., Northern Provinces, N Nigeria, 110 mi. SE of Kano; road center in tin-mining area; cassava, millet, durra.
Gwashki, W Pakistan: see ZIARAT.
Gwatar (gwô'tûr), Persian *Gvater* (gvätĕr'), town, Eighth Prov., in Makran, southeasternmost Iran, minor port on Gwatar Bay, 55 mi. E of Chahbahar, at Pakistan line; customs, quarantine, police post.
Gwatar Bay (gwŭ'tûr), inlet of Arabian Sea, at S end of Iran-Pakistan border; 20 mi. long (E–W), 10 mi. wide. Seaplane base at Cape Jiwani (E).
Gwato (gä'tō), village, Benin prov., Western Provinces, S Nigeria, on Benin R. opposite Koko and 22 mi. SSW of Benin City; hardwood, rubber, palm oil and kernels. A major port (16th–19th cent.) in European slave trade, serving Benin City.
Gweedore (gwēdôr'), Gaelic *Gaoth Dobhair*, fishing village, NW Co. Donegal, Ireland, on small inlet 7 mi. NNE of Dungloe; tourist resort, founded in 19th cent. by Lord George Hill. It is in the picturesque Gweedore highland dist., extending c.7 mi. along the coast.
Gwelo (gwĕ'lō), province (□ 30,429; pop. c.433,000), central Southern Rhodesia; ⊙ Gwelo. A central ridge of high veld (4–6,000 ft.) forms watershed for streams flowing SE (Nuanetsi, Lundi, Sabi) and NW (Shangani) across lower middle veld. Chief crops: tobacco, corn, wheat, cotton, peanuts, citrus fruit. Extensive livestock raising and dairying. A rich mining region yielding gold (Que Que area), asbestos (Shabani), chrome (Selukwe), iron. Principal towns (Gwelo, Que Que) and European settlements along railroad in high veld. European pop. (1946), 10,066. Prov. formed c.1948.
Gwelo, city (pop. 8,364; including suburbs, 9,578), ⊙ Gwelo prov., central Southern Rhodesia, in Matabeleland, 95 mi. NE of Bulawayo; alt. 4,694 ft. Major rail and cattle center in important mining dist. (gold, iron, chromite); tanning, woodworking, corn milling, dairying. Has secondary schools. Airfield.
Gwembe (gwĕm'bä), administrative center, ⊙ Gwembe dist., Southern Prov., Northern Rhodesia, 10 mi. ESE of Chisekesi.
Gwennap, town and parish (pop. 4,866), W Cornwall, England, 3 mi. SE of Redruth; tin mining. Site of Gwennap Pit (large amphitheater), center of Cornish Methodism and scene of sermons by Wesley. Has 15th-cent. church. In parish (N) is agr. village of St. Day, former tin-mining center.
Gwersyllt, Wales: see MOSS.
Gwese (gwĕ'sä), village, Kivu prov., E Belgian Congo, 19 mi. SW of Costermansville. European agr. center (notably coffee plantations). R.C. mission with native school for medical assistants.
Gwinn, village (1940 pop. 918), Marquette co., NW Upper Peninsula, Mich., 19 mi. SSW of Marquette, at junction of Middle and East branches of Escanaba R., in agr. area. Co. park near by (camping, bathing, fishing).
Gwinner, village (pop. 197), Sargent co., SE N.Dak., 20 mi. ENE of Oakes.
Gwinnett (gwĭnĕt'), county (□ 437; pop. 32,320), N central Ga.; ⊙ Lawrenceville. Piedmont area bounded NW by Chattahoochee R. and drained by Apalachee and Yellow rivers. Agr. (cotton, corn, hay, fruit, livestock, poultry); mfg. at Buford and Lawrenceville. Formed 1818.
Gwomba, Nigeria: see GOMBA.
Gwoza (gōzä'), town (pop. 1,020), N Br. Cameroons, administered as part of Bornu prov. of Nigeria, 30 mi. S of Bama; road junction; peanuts, millet, cotton; cattle, skins.
Gwozdziec, Ukrainian SSR: see GVOZDETS.
Gwy, Wales. see WYE RIVER.
Gwyddelwern (gwĭdh-ĕl'wĕrn), village and parish (pop. 702), NE Merioneth, Wales, 2 mi. N of Corwen; granite quarrying.
Gwydir River (gwī'dûr), N New South Wales, Australia, rises in Great Dividing Range near Uralla, flows 415 mi. NW, past Moree, and W to Darling or Barwon R. 8 mi. NE of Collarenebri.
Gwynn Island, Mathews co., E Va., just offshore (causeway connection) in Chesapeake Bay, 5 mi. N of Mathews; c.3 mi. long. Site of Gwynn village; fisheries.
Gwyr, Wales: see GOWER.
Gy (zhē), village (pop. 940), Haute-Saône dept., E France, 11 mi. ESE of Gray; dairying; wine.
Gyaing River (jīng), in Tenasserim, Lower Burma, formed at Kyondo (head of navigation) by union of 2 headstreams, flows 42 mi. W to Salween R. at Moulmein.
Gyalu, Rumania: see GILAU.
Gyamda, Tibet: see GIAMDA.
Gyangtse or **Gyantse** (both: gyän'tsĕ'), Chinese *Chiang-tzu* (jyäng'dzŭ'), town [Tibetan *dzong*], S Tibet, near the Nyang Chu, 100 mi. SW of Lhasa, at junction of main Leh-Lhasa trade route and route S to Kalimpong; alt. 12,895 ft. Trade center (wool, barley, salt, borax, furs, musk, yak tails, cotton goods, sugar, tea); noted hand-loom woolen cloth- and carpetmaking; barley, mustard, peas, wheat. Has large Yellow Hat lamasery of Palkhor Choide. Indian trade agency and post and telegraph office after 1904.
Gyanpur (gyän'pŏŏr), town (pop. 1,126), Benares dist., SE Uttar Pradesh, India, 30 mi. W of Benares; rice, barley, gram, wheat, millet.
Gyanyima (gyänyē'mä), village, SW Tibet, on a Tanakpur-Gartok trade route, 70 mi. SSE of Gartok; trades in wool and barley. Has fort. Also called Kharkho.
Gyaraspur (gyä'rŭspŏŏr), village, SE Madhya Bharat, India, 21 mi. NE of Bhilsa; wheat. Medieval temple ruins.
Gyaros or **Yiaros** (yēä'rôs), Lat. *Gyarus* (jīä'rŭs), Aegean island (□ 7; pop. 31) in the Cyclades, Greece, NW of Syros isl.; 37°38'N 24°44'E; 4 mi. long, 2.5 mi. wide; fisheries.
Gyatsa (gyä'tsä), town [Tibetan *dzong*], S Tibet, on the Brahmaputra and 100 mi. ESE of Lhasa.
Gyda, village, Russian SFSR: see GYDY.
Gyda Bay (gĭ'dŭ), SW arm of Yenisei Gulf of Kara Sea, on Tyumen oblast–Krasnoyarsk Territory border, Russian SFSR, bet. Yavai (W) and Mamont (E) peninsulas; 60 mi. long, up to 20 mi. wide, c.15 ft. deep; low tundra shores.
Gydan, Russian SFSR: see KOLYMA RANGE.
Gyda Peninsula (gĭ'dŭ), NW Siberian Russian SFSR, in Tyumen oblast and Krasnoyarsk Territory, bet. mouths of Taz and Yenisei rivers; bounded by Ob Bay (W) and Yenisei Gulf (NE). In N, divided by Gyda Bay into Yavai Peninsula (W) and Mamont Peninsula (E); largely tundra-covered.
Gydy (gĭdē'), village (1948 pop. over 500), NE Yamal-Nenets Natl. Okrug, Tyumen oblast, Russian SFSR, N of Arctic Circle, on Gyda Bay, 425 mi. NE of Salekhard; trading post. Also called Gyda or Gydoyamo.
Gyekenyes (dyä'kā-nyĕsh), Hung. *Gyékényes*, town (pop. 2,205), Somogy co., SW Hungary, 15 mi. S of Nagykanizsa, on Yugoslav line; rail junction.
Gyergyoalfalu, Rumania: see JOSENI.
Gyergyoszentmiklos, Rumania: see GHEORGHENI.
Gyergyotölgyes, Rumania: see TULGHES.
Gyldenloves Height, Denmark: see ZEALAND.
Gyllenfors (yü"lŭnfôrs', –fôsh'), village (pop. 1,476), Jonkoping co., S Sweden, on Nissa R. and 20 mi. WNW of Varnamo; metalworking.
Gympie (gĭm'pē), city (pop. 8,413), SE Queensland, Australia, on Mary R. and 90 mi. N of Brisbane; dairying, agr. center (bananas, sugar cane). Silver mine, limestone quarry near by. Former goldmining center.
Gyobingauk (jō'bĭng-gouk'), town (pop. 7,675), Tharrawaddy dist., Lower Burma, 50 mi. SSE of Prome, on railroad to Rangoon.
Gyochi, Formosa: see YÜCHIH.
Gyoma (dyô'mŏ), town (pop. 12,242), Bekes co., SE Hungary, on the Körös and 11 mi. SE of Mezötur; trade, agr. center; rail junction. Flour mills, brickworks, distilleries, pottery; printing.
Gyömber, peak, Czechoslovakia: see DUMBIER.
Gyömrö (dyûm'rû), Hung. *Gyömrő*, town (pop. 7,654), Pest-Pilis-Solt-Kiskun co., N central Hungary, 15 mi. ESE of Budapest; flour mills; wheat, potatoes; cattle, horses, hogs.
Gyöngyös (dyûn'dyûsh), city (pop. 24,086), Heves co., N Hungary, at S foot of Matra Mts., 44 mi. NE of Budapest; rail, trade center for agr. (grain, livestock, fruit) region; textiles, brickworks, pottery, copper products. Large Franciscan col. Poultry; wine, toys, wooden ornaments made in vicinity. Coal mines, sulphuric mineral springs near by.
Gyöngyöspata (dyûn'dyûshpŏ"tŏ), town (pop. 3,359), Heves co., N Hungary, 6 mi. WNW of Gyöngyös; sugar beets.
Gyönk (dyûngk), town (pop. 3,074), Tolna co., SW central Hungary, 18 mi. NW of Szekszard; shoe mfg.; wheat, potatoes. Ger. settlements near by.
Gyoo-to, Pescadores: see YÜWENG ISLAND.
Gyoparosfürdö, Hungary: see OROSHAZA.
Györ (dyûr), Hung. *Győr*, Ger. *Raab*, Latin *Arrabona*, city (pop. 57,192), ⊙ but independent of Györ-Moson co., NW Hungary, at confluence of Raba R., Repce R., and an arm of the Danube, 66 mi. WNW of Budapest. One of Hungary's foremost industrial and rail centers; river port. Has steel mills; machine mfg., 2d in importance only to Budapest, produces vehicles and railroad cars. It is Hungary's textile center (linen, silk, artificial silk, wool). Large distilleries; leads in vegetable-oil mfg.; brickworks; linoleum, soap, watches, salami, grain products, chocolate, candy mfg. Built on site of Roman camp; became bishopric in 11th cent. Under Turkish rule, 1594–98; made a free royal town in 1743. Captured 1809 by Napoleon; occupied for several months by the French. Hungarians decisively defeated 1849 by Haynau near by. Has baroque city hall, Carmelite convent, and church. An excellent breed of horses is raised in the vicinity.
Györköny (dyûr'kûnyû), town (pop. 3,478), Tolna co., W central Hungary, 7 mi. W of Paks; wheat, corn, potatoes.
Györ-Moson (dyûr'-mô-shôn), Hung. *Győr-Moson*, county (□ 876; pop. 156,800), N Hungary; ⊙ GYÖR. In level Little Alföld; bounded N by the Danube, drained by Raba R. One of Hungary's best-developed agr. regions; grain, potatoes, sugar beets, cattle, hogs, horses, poultry. Industry centers at Györ; also at Mosonmagyarovar (breweries, distilleries, flour mills) and Mosonszentjanos (brickworks). Peat is cut in the HANSAG. In 1920 Györ combined with what was left of co. of MOSON, Ger. *Wieselburg*. Small bridgehead section of co., S of Bratislava, was ceded 1947 to Czechoslovakia.
Gyorok, Rumania: see GHIOROC.
Györszentivan (dyûr'sĕntĭvän), Hung. *Győrszentiván*, town (pop. 6,056), Györ-Moson co., NW Hungary, 4 mi. E of Györ; distilleries; grain, sugar beets, horses.
Györszentmarton (dyûr'sĕntmär"tôn), Hung. *Győrszentmárton*, Ger. *Martinsberg*, town (pop. 3,125), Györ-Moson co., NW Hungary, 10 mi. SE of Györ; brickworks. Benedictine abbey, located on nearby hill (Hung. *Pannonhalma*), established in 980; center of Benedictine order in Hungary; library has c.100,000 vols., collection of archives.
Gyotaishin, Korea: see ODAEJIN.
Gyotoku (gyō'tōkōō), town (pop. 11,266), Chiba prefecture, central Honshu, Japan, on Tokyo Bay just S of Ichikawa; small port near mouth of Edo R. Exports salt.
Gy-Paraná River, Brazil: see GI-PARANÁ RIVER.
Gyppeswyk, England: see IPSWICH.
Gypsum (jĭp'sŭm). **1** Town (pop. 345), Eagle co., W central Colo., on Eagle R., just N of Sawatch Mts., and 6 mi. W of Eagle; alt. 6,325 ft. **2** City (pop. 523), Saline co., central Kansas, 13 mi. SE of Salina, in wheat and livestock region; flour milling, woodworking. **3** Village, Ottawa co., N Ohio, 9 mi. WNW of Sandusky across Sandusky Bay; gypsum quarrying and processing.
Gypsumville, village (pop. estimate 200), central Man., near NE end of L. Manitoba, 150 mi. NNW of Winnipeg; gypsum quarrying.
Gytheion, Gythion, or **Yithion** (all: yē'thēôn), Lat. *Gythium* (jĭ'thēŭm), town (pop. 7,893), Laconia nome, S Peloponnesus, Greece, port on Gulf of Laconia and 23 mi. SSE of Sparta; chief port of Laconia; fisheries; exports citrus and dried fruits, olive oil, cotton. Includes Marathonisi isl. (E). Has ruins of anc. city. Developed by Phoenicians, became chief port of Sparta; sacked 455 B.C. by Athenians. Called Marathonisi during Turkish occupation. Also spelled Ghythion.
Gyttorp (yüt'tôrp"), village (pop. 511), Orebro co., S central Sweden, 3 mi. W of Nora; rail junction; mfg. of explosives, ammunition.
Gyula (dyōō'lŏ), city (pop. 25,169), ⊙ Bekes co., SE Hungary, on the White Körös and 9 mi. ESE of Bekescsaba; trade and market center; mfg. (woolens, chemicals, matches, sausage, shoes, cognac, bricks, flour). Wheat, tobacco; dairy farming. Has fine château.
Gyulafehervar, Rumania: see ALBA IULIA.
Gyulaj (dyōō'loi), town (pop. 2,758), Tolna co., W central Hungary, 22 mi. NW of Szekszard; wheat, wine, cattle.
Gyulavari (dyōō'lŏvärĭ), Hung. *Gyulavári*, town (pop. 4,389), Bekes co., SE Hungary, on the White Körös and 7 mi. SSW of Sarkad; distilleries, brickworks; grain, tobacco.
Gyulbakht or **Gyul'bakht** (gyōōlbäkht'), town, (1945 pop. over 500) in Molotov dist. of Greater Baku, Azerbaijan SSR, 16 mi. WSW of Baku; oil.
Gyulistan, Azerbaijan SSR: see GULISTAN.
Gyumush (gyōōmōōsh'), village, central Armenian SSR, on Zanga R. and 15 mi. NNE of Erivan; large hydroelectric station and reservoir.
Gyumyurdzhina, Greece: see KOMOTINE.
Gyuyeshevo (gyōōyĕ'shĕvô), village (pop. 1,005), Sofia dist., W Bulgaria, on E slope of Osogov Mts., 9 mi. WSW of Kyustendil; rail terminus on Yugoslav border (customhouse). Linked with Kriva Palanka (Yugoslavia) by road through Velbazh Pass.
Gyuzdek (gyōōzdyĕk'), town (1939 pop. over 500) in Molotov dist. of Greater Baku, Azerbaijan SSR, 8 mi. W of Baku; oil wells.
Gzhatsk (ŭgzhätsk'), city (1939 pop. over 10,000), NE Smolensk oblast, Russian SFSR, 100 mi. WSW of Moscow; flour milling, garment mfg. Veterinary institute. Founded in early 18th cent. as grain river port; chartered 1776. During Second World War, held (1941–43) by Germans.
Gzira (gzē'rä), Maltese *Gżira*, tiny island (c.1½ mi. long, ¼ mi. wide) and town (pop. 6,295) off E Malta, in Marsamuscetto Harbour, just NW of Valletta. At islet's E tip is baroque Fort Manoel (built 1726), severely battered during Second World War, when it was occupied by Br. navy. Has quarantine station.

H

Ha or **Ha Dzong** (hä'dzông'), fortified town [Bhutanese *dzong*], W Bhutan, on right tributary of the Raidak and 40 mi. WSW of Punakha, on main Yatung (Tibet)-Punakha route. Buddhist monasteries near by. Formerly spelled Hah.

Haabai, Haapai, or **Hapai** (all: hä'pī), island group (pop. 7,483), central Tonga, S Pacific; 19°42'S 174°29'W; comprises c.30 small coral isls. of which Lifuka, seat of Pangai (⊙ Haabai group), is most important.

Haacht (häkht), village (pop. 3,532), Brabant prov., central Belgium, 7 mi. NNW of Louvain; brewing; agr. Formerly spelled Haecht.

Haad Yai, Thailand: see HAT YAI.

Haag (häk). **1** Town (pop. 4,553), W Lower Austria, 8 mi. NE of Steyr; cutlery. **2** or **Haag am Hausruck** (äm hous'ro͝ok), town (pop. 2,356), W central Upper Austria, 7 mi. ESE of Ried im Innkreis, in Hausruck Mts. Starhemberg castle is here.

Haag or **Haag in Oberbayern** (ĭn ō'bŭrbī"ŭrn), village (pop. 2,134), Upper Bavaria, Germany, 16 mi. WSW of Mühldorf; beer; woodworking. Has 13th-cent. watchtower. Chartered 1324.

Haag, Den, Netherlands: see HAGUE, THE.

Haag am Hausruck, Austria: see HAAG.

Haag in Oberbayern, Germany: see HAAG.

Haakon (hä'kŭn), county (□ 1,815; pop. 3,167), central S.Dak.; ⊙ Philip. Agr. and cattle-raising region drained in S by Bad R. and bounded N by Cheyenne R. Dairying, ranching; livestock, poultry, grain. Formed 1914.

Haaksbergen (häks'bĕr-khŭn), town (pop. 4,785), Overijssel prov., E Netherlands, 8 mi. SSW of Hengelo, near Ger. border; textiles (cotton weaving, bleaching, dyeing), cable mfg.

Haalsnoy, Norway: see HALSNOY.

Haaltert (häl'tŭrt), town (pop. 5,779), East Flanders prov., N central Belgium, 3 mi. SSW of Alost; cotton weaving, lace making; agr. market. Formerly spelled Haeltert.

Haamstede (häm'stēdŭ), town (pop. 1,137), Zeeland prov., SW Netherlands, on Schouwen isl. and 8 mi. WNW of Zierikzee; bulb growing, flax; chicory drying. Airfield. Has 17th-cent. castle. Village of Burgh is 1 mi. SW.

Haan (hän), town (pop. 13,138), in former Prussian Rhine Prov., W Germany, after 1945 in North Rhine-Westphalia, just NW of Solingen; metal-working.

Haapai, Tonga: see HAABAI.

Haapajärvi (hä'päyăr"vē), village (commune pop. 9,215), Oulu co., W central Finland, on Kala R. and 65 mi. E of Kokkola; rail junction; fossil-meal quarrying.

Haapakoski (hä'päkōs"kē), village in Pieksämäki rural commune (pop. 8,268), Mikkeli co., SE central Finland, in Saimaa lake region, 35 mi. SSW of Kuopio; metalworks, machine shops.

Haapamäki (hä'pămă"kē), village in Keuruu commune (pop. 11,321), Vaasa co., W Finland, 40 mi. W of Jyväskylä; important rail junction, in lumbering region.

Haapaniemi (hä'pänē"ĕmē), S suburb of Kuopio city, Kuopio co., S central Finland, on L. Kalla; large bobbin mills.

Haapsalu or **Khaapsalu** (häp'sälo͞o), Ger. *Hapsal*, city (pop. 4,649), W Estonia, shallow port on Baltic Sea inlet, 55 mi. SW of Tallinn; rail terminus; meat packing, fisheries, ship repair, home industries, truck farming. Summer resort (bathing beach, mud baths). Has ruins of 13th-cent. episcopal castle. Was summer home of Rus. imperial family. Founded 1228 by Danes; passed in 1346 to Livonian Knights, in 1561 to Sweden; occupied 1710 by Russia.

Haar (här), village (pop. 7,592), Upper Bavaria, Germany, 8 mi. ESE of Munich; mfg. of chemicals, metalworking. Has 13th-cent. church.

Haardt (härt), village (pop. 1,735), Rhenish Palatinate, W Germany, on E slope of Hardt Mts., just N of Neustadt; wine; apricots, peaches.

Haardt Mountains, Germany: see HARDT MOUNTAINS.

Haarlem (här'lŭm), city (pop. 156,856), ⊙ North Holland prov., W Netherlands, 11 mi. W of Amsterdam, 4.5 mi. from North Sea coast; 52°20'N 4°36'E. Rail junction; shipbuilding; machinery, chemical, and textile industries; foundries; railroad repair shops; cocoa and chocolate mfg. center; printing industry. Center of chief Dutch flower-bulb-growing area, exporting bulbs (particularly tulips) to all parts of the world. Seat of R.C. bishop. Famous for medieval gabled houses; has City Hall (*Stadhuis*), begun 1250, and 15th-cent. church (Groote Kerk of St. Bavo). Chartered 1245 by William, Count of Holland. Spanish siege (1572–73), followed by a massacre. Lourens Koster is said to have printed from movable type, here, in medieval times. In 17th cent. center of artistic activity of Frans Hals, Jacob van Ruisdael, and Adriaen van Ostade. Formerly also Harlem.

Haarlemmermeer (här'lŭmŭrmär) [Du.,=Haarlem lake], **fenland** area (□ 71.5), formerly a shallow body of water, North Holland prov., W Netherlands, SE of Haarlem, bet. Amsterdam and Leiden; crossed and surrounded by numerous drainage canals, including the Ringvaart, and supplemented by mechanical drainage plants. Formed by destructive flood (16th cent.); completely drained by 1852. Agr. area, growing wheat, vegetables, flax; stud-farming center. Commune (pop. 36,059) of Haarlemmermeer is coextensive with drained area; at its center is village of Hoofddorp or Hoofddorp-Haarlemmermeer (pop. 3,392), 6 mi. SSE of Haarlem.

Haarlev (hôr'lĕv), town (pop. 537), Praesto amt, Zealand, Denmark, 17 mi. NNE of Praesto; rail junction.

Haarsteeg (här'stākh), village (pop. 1,909), North Brabant prov., S central Netherlands, 5 mi. WNW of 's Hertogenbosch; leather tanning, shoe mfg.

Haase River or **Hase River** (both: hä'zŭ), NW Germany, rises in Teutoburg Forest NW of Borgholzhausen, flows 80 mi. N and W, past Osnabrück and Quackenbrück (head of navigation), to Dortmund-Ems Canal at Meppen. Canalized in lower course.

Haastrecht (häs'trĕkht), village (pop. 1,340), South Holland prov., W Netherlands, on Hollandsche Ijssel R. and 3 mi. E of Gouda; cigar mfg., laundering, dairying.

Haast River (häst), W S.Isl., New Zealand, rises in Southern Alps S of Mt. Sefton, flows 60 mi. SW to Tasman Sea 22 mi. NE of Jackson's Bay.

Haba, La (lä ä'vä), town (pop. 3,112), Badajoz prov., W Spain, 30 mi. E of Mérida; cereals, chick-peas, tubers, melons, olives, livestock.

Habana, La, Cuba: see HAVANA.

Habay-la-Neuve (äbā'-lä-nûv'), village (pop. 2,011), Luxembourg prov., SE Belgium, in the Ardennes, 8 mi. WNW of Arlon; agr., lumbering.

Habay-la-Vieille (–vyā'), agr. village (pop. 886), Luxembourg prov., SE Belgium, in the Ardennes, 9 mi. WNW of Arlon. Has 18th-cent. castle.

Habban (häb-băn'), town (pop. 1,000), Wahidi sultanate of Balhaf, Eastern Aden Protectorate, on the Wadi Meifa'a and 75 mi. WNW of Balhaf, 15 mi. E of Yeshbum; agr. oasis. Formerly a separate Wahidi sultanate.

Habbaniya or **Habbaniyah** (häb-bänē'yŭ), town, Dulaim prov., central Iraq, on the Euphrates and 45 mi. W of Baghdad, on NE shore of L. Habbaniya; British military and air base. Seaplane base.

Habbaniya, Lake, salt lake (□ 54), Dulaim prov., central Iraq, just S of the Euphrates in a natural depression bet. Al Falluja and Ramadi, 50 mi. W of Baghdad; 15 mi. long, 8 mi. wide. Since 1911 attempts have been made to use it as flood-control and storage reservoir; canals and regulating apparatus were completed after Second World War.

Habelschwerdt, town, Poland: see BYSTRZYCA KLODZKA.

Habelschwerdt Mountains (hä'bŭl-shvĕrt"), Ger. *Habelschwerdter Gebirge* (hä'bŭl-shvĕr'tŭr gŭbĭr'-gŭ), Pol. *Góry Bystrzyckie* (go͞o'rĭ bĭs-chĭts'kyĕ), range of the Sudetes along Lower Silesia (after 1945, SW Poland) and Czechoslovakia border; extend c.20 mi. bet. Polanica Zdroj (NW) and Miedzylesie (SE); rise to 3,205 ft. 5 mi. SW of Bystrzyca Klodzka. Largely in Czechoslovakia, and separated from Habelschwerdt Mts. by upper Divocha Orlicka R., lie the parallel ADLERGEBIRGE.

Habersham (hă'bŭrshŭm), county (□ 283; pop. 16,553), NE Ga. on S.C. line; ⊙ Clarkesville. Blue Ridge (N) and piedmont (S) area. Farming (cotton, hay, sweet potatoes, apples, peaches, poultry) lumbering, and textile mfg. Part of Chattahoochee Natl. Forest in N. Formed 1818.

Habiganj (hŭb'ĭgŭnj), town (pop. 11,856), Sylhet dist., E East Bengal, E Pakistan, in Surma Valley, on branch of Kusiyara R. and 45 mi. SW of Sylhet; trades in rice, tea, oilseeds, hides. Rice research station. Tea processing near by. Rail station 7 mi. SSE, at Shaistaganj.

Habo (hä'bo͞o"), village (pop. 1,040), Skaraborg co., S Sweden, near S end of L. Vatter, 8 mi. NNW of Jonkoping; cotton milling, metal- and woodworking. Has 17th-cent. church.

Habomai (häbō'mī"), village, E Hokkaido, Japan, on narrow peninsula, 8 mi. E of Nemuro. The **Habomai Islands** (E) are the westernmost isls. of the non-volcanic Kurile chain, including Shuishio and Shibotsu isls.

Habor, river, Syria: see KHABUR RIVER.

Haboro (häbō'rō), town (pop. 13,635), W Hokkaido, Japan, on Sea of Japan, 55 mi. NW of Asahigawa; rice, soybeans, potatoes, stock raising; fishing.

Habra (äbrä'), irrigated lowland in Oran dept., NW Algeria, bet. Perrégaux (S) and the Gulf of Arzew (N); water supplied by the Oued Hammam, dammed S of Perrétaux. Grows citrus fruit, cotton, and vegetables.

Hab River (hŭb), in SE Baluchistan, W Pakistan, rises in N Pab Range S of Khuzdar, flows SSE, just W of Kirthar Range, and SSW, along Sind border, to Arabian Sea N of Cape Monze; c.250 mi. long.

Habry (hä'brĭ), town (pop. 1,155), E Bohemia, Czechoslovakia, 11 mi. SSE of Caslav; sugar beets, potatoes.

Habsburg or **Hapsburg** (both: häps'bo͝ork), village (pop. 148), Aargau canton, N Switzerland, near Aar R., just SW of Brugg. Its castle (built c.1020) was, in 12th and 13th cent., seat of counts of Hapsburg.

Habsheim (äbzĕm', Ger. häps'hīm), town (pop. 2,015), Haut-Rhin dept., E France, 4 mi. ESE of Mulhouse; hosiery and silk mfg.

Habu (hä'bo͞o), largest town (pop. 12,705) on Innoshima, Hiroshima prefecture, Japan, on S coast of isl.; shipyards, ironworks. Produces insect powder, citrus fruit.

Habunsha, Formosa: see KIAOPANSHAN.

Haccourt (äko͞or'), village (pop. 2,721), Liége prov., E Belgium, near Liége-Maastricht Canal, just W of Visé; Portland-cement mfg.

Hachado Pass, Argentina-Chile: see PINO HACHADO PASS.

Hachenburg (hä'khŭnbo͝ork), town (pop. 2,618), in former Prussian prov. of Hesse-Nassau, W Germany, after 1945 in Rhineland-Palatinate, 17 mi. SW of Siegen; has 17th-cent. castle.

Hachibama (hä"chē'bämä) or **Hachihama** (–hämä), town (pop. 4,665), Okayama prefecture, SW Honshu, Japan, on inlet of Inland Sea, just S of Okayama; rice, wheat, pears, raw silk; sake brewing.

Hachijo-jima (hä"chējō'-jĭmä), second largest island (□ 27; pop. 12,038) of isl. group Izu-shichito, Greater Tokyo, Japan, in Philippine Sea, 110 mi. SSE of O-shima; 33°6'N 139°48'E; 8 mi. long, 5 mi. wide. Mountainous; rises to 2,812 ft. Has 2 active volcanoes. Dairying, fishing, weaving. Ogago is chief center. Formerly penal colony for political prisoners. Sometimes spelled Hatizyo-sima; formerly called Fatsizio, Fatsissio.

Hachiman (hä"chē'mä). **1** Town (pop. 9,982), Gifu prefecture, central Honshu, Japan, 26 mi. NNE of Gifu; raw silk, cotton. **2** Town (pop. 14,509), Shiga prefecture, S Honshu, Japan, near E shore of L. Biwa, 21 mi. ENE of Kyoto; textile-collecting center; mfg. (sailcloth, sake, peppermint camphor). Sometimes spelled Hatiman.

Hachinohe (hä"chē'nōhā), city (1940 pop. 73,494; 1947 pop. 91,405), Aomori prefecture, N Honshu, Japan, on the Pacific, 45 mi. SE of Aomori; mfg. (cement, chemicals, textiles), food processing, fishing. Sometimes spelled Hachinoe and Hatinoe.

Hachioji (hächēō'jē), city (1940 pop. 75,186; 1947 pop. 72,947), Greater Tokyo, central Honshu, Japan, 25 mi. W of Tokyo; rail center; mfg. (textiles, machinery, sake), woodworking; poultry farms. Bombed (1945) in Second World War. Includes (since early 1940s) former town of Komiya (1940 pop. 12,907). Sometimes spelled Hatiozi.

Hachiro-gata (hächērō'gätä), lagoon (□ 87), Akita prefecture, N Honshu, Japan, at base of Oga Peninsula, 11 mi. NNW of Akita; connected (S) with Sea of Japan; 16 mi. long, 8 mi. wide.

Hachiya (hächē'yä), town (pop. 12,632), Fukuoka prefecture, N Kyushu, Japan, 25 mi. SE of Yawata, on Suo Sea; rail junction; commercial center in coal-mining area; grain.

Hachy (äshē'), Flemish *Hertzig* (hĕrt'sĭkh), agr. village (pop. 1,544), Luxembourg prov., SE Belgium, in the Ardennes, 6 mi. W of Arlon.

Hacialbaz Dag (häjŭ"älbäz' dä), Turkish *Hacıalbaz Dağ*, peak (7,562 ft.), Sultan Mts., W central Turkey, 9 mi. NNE of Yalvac.

Hacin, Turkey: see SAIMBEYLI.

Hackensack (hă'kĭnsăk). **1** Resort village (pop. 272), Cass co., central Minn., 12 mi. SSE of Walker in region of woods and lakes; grain, potatoes. **2** City (pop. 29,219), ⊙ Bergen co., NE N.J., on Hackensack R. and 10 mi. N of Jersey City; residential, industrial suburb; mfg. (pumps, metal products, glass, furniture, clothing, chemicals, slippers, paper and food products). Has first Dutch Reformed church (1696; later rebuilt and enlarged), co. buildings, several pre-Revolutionary dwellings. Settled 1639 by Dutch, city inc. 1921. Several Revolutionary engagements fought here. Samuel Cooper, Confederate general, b. here.

Hackensack River, SE N.Y. and NE N.J., rises in Rockland co., N.Y.; flows c.45 mi. S, past Oradell, N.J. (dammed here to form Oradell Reservoir, c.3.5 mi. long) and Hackensack, through marshy Hackensack Meadows (□ c.50), to Newark Bay W of Jersey City. Tidal and navigable to New Milford. Principal freight; coal and coke.

Hacketstown, Gaelic *Baile an Droichid*, town (pop. 317), NE Co. Carlow, Ireland, 16 mi. E of Carlow; agr. market (sheep; wheat, beets, potatoes).

Hackett, city (pop. 440), Sebastian co., W Ark., 13 mi. S of Fort Smith, near Okla. line.

Hackettstown, town (pop. 3,894), Warren co., NW N.J., in fertile Musconetcong valley, 14 mi. W of Dover; leather, metal products, machinery, clothing, fireworks, toys; truck, dairy products. Centenary Jr. Col. for girls here. Inc. 1853.

Hacking, Port, inlet of Pacific Ocean, E New South Wales, Australia, just S of Botany Bay, bet. Cape Baily and Big Jibbon Point; 4 mi. wide at mouth, 4 mi. long; semi-circular. Cronulla, resort town, on W shore; bathing beach.

Hackleburg, town (pop. 534), Marion co., NW Ala., 32 mi. SSW of Tuscumbia; lumber, cotton. Wm. B. Bankhead Natl. Forest is E.

Hackney, residential and industrial metropolitan borough (1931 pop. 215,333; 1951 census 171,-337) of London, England, N of the Thames, 4 mi. NE of Charing Cross; once exclusive residential dist. Parish church has 16th-cent. tower. Hackney Marshes, now public park (c.300 acres), were once resort of highwaymen.

Hacoi (hä'koi'), town, Haininh prov., N Vietnam, on Gulf of Tonkin, 15 mi. WSW of Moncay.

Hacres Dag, Turkey: see Kurtik Dag.

Hadagalli (hŭ'dŭgŭlē) or **Huvvinahadagalli** (hŭvĭnŭ–), town (pop. 6,095), Bellary dist., NW Madras, India, 35 mi. SW of Hospet; peanut milling; date palms. Also spelled Huvinahadgalli.

Hadali (hŭdä'lē), town (pop. 5,203), Shahpur dist., W central Punjab, W Pakistan, 31 mi. WNW of Sargodha; wheat, cotton, oilseeds.

Hadama (hä'däma) or **Adama** (ä'dämä), town, Shoa prov., central Ethiopia, on railroad and 50 mi. SE of Addis Ababa. Trade center (coffee, hides, beeswax).

Hadamar (hä'dämär), town (pop. 5,426), in former Prussian prov. of Hesse-Nassau, W Germany, after 1945 in Hesse, 4 mi. N of Limburg. Has 17th-cent. town hall and former castle. Site of concentration camp during Hitler regime.

Hadano (hä"dä'nō), town (pop. 15,993), Kanagawa prefecture, central Honshu, Japan, 9 mi. NE of Odawara, in agr. area (tobacco, sweet potatoes, soybeans); mfg. (textiles, sake, soy sauce).

Hadar (hädär'), settlement (pop. 500), W Israel, in Plain of Sharon, 3 mi. ESE of Herzliya; citriculture, mixed farming. Founded 1929.

Hadar (hā'där), village (pop. 129), Pierce co., NE Nebr., 7 mi. SSE of Pierce and on branch of Elkhorn R.

Hadarba, Ras (räs' hädär'bä), headland of NE Anglo-Egyptian Sudan on the Red Sea, 170 mi. N of Port Sudan. Also called Ras Elba.

Hadar Hacarmel (hädär' häkärmĕl'), SW residential suburb of Haifa, NW Israel, on N slope of Mt. Carmel, overlooking Bay of Acre of the Mediterranean. Site of technical col., Haifa municipal bldgs., and law courts. Founded 1912.

Hadd, Bahrein: see Muharraq.

Hadd (hăd, häd), village, E Oman, 110 mi. SE of Muscat, on Ras al Hadd (E cape of Arabian Peninsula); 22°33'N 59°48'E. Airfield.

Hadda or **Hadda Sharif** (hŭ'dŭ shŭrēf'), village, Eastern Prov., Afghanistan, 6 mi. S of Jalalabad; archaeological site; excavations (1920s) have uncovered Buddhist monasteries and sculpture of the Greco-Buddhist school of Gandhara.

Hadda or **Haddah** (häd'dŭ), village, central Hejaz, Saudi Arabia, in the Wadi Fatima, 17 mi. W of Mecca and on highway to Jidda. Frontier bet. Jordan and Saudi Arabia was partly defined here in 1925 by the British and Ibn Saud.

Haddam (hă'dŭm). **1** Town (pop. 2,636), Middlesex co., S Conn., bisected by the Connecticut (here bridged), just below Middletown; agr., mfg. (plastic and wire products, nails, farm implements). Includes Higganum, mfg. village. State forest. Settled 1662, inc. 1668. **2** City (pop. 375), Washington co., N Kansas, on small affluent of Little Blue R. and 25 mi. NE of Concordia; grain, livestock.

Haddenham. 1 Agr. village and parish (pop. 1,361), central Buckingham, England, 6 mi. SW of Aylesbury. Has 13th-cent. church. **2** Town and parish (pop. 1,733), in Isle of Ely, N Cambridge, England, 6 mi. SW of Ely; agr. market. Has 13th-cent. church, built on site of a church founded 673.

Haddington, county, Scotland: see East Lothian.

Haddington, burgh (1931 pop. 4,405; 1951 census 4,497), ⊙ East Lothian, Scotland, in central part of co., on Tyne R. (15th-cent. bridge) and 16 mi. E of Edinburgh; woolen milling, hosiery knitting; agr. market. The 12th- or 13th-cent. parish church of St. Mary contains grave of Carlyle's wife, Jane Welsh (b. here), and is called the "Lamp of the Lothians." S suburb of Giffordgate is birthplace of John Knox (commemorated by Knox Inst.).

Haddingtonshire, Scotland: see East Lothian.

Haddonfield, residential borough (pop. 10,495), Camden co., SW N.J., 5 mi. SE of Camden. Indian King Tavern was site of meeting of 1st state legislature, 1777. British and Hessians camped here in Revolution. Settled 1682, inc. 1875.

Haddon Hall, mansion in parish of Nether Haddon (pop. 28), N central Derby, England, on Wye R. and 2 mi. SE of Bakewell. Built in 14th cent., it is seat of duke of Rutland.

Haddon Heights, residential borough (pop. 7,287), Camden co., SW N.J., 5 mi. SE of Camden. Laid out c.1891, inc. 1904.

Haddummati Atoll (hŭd-dŏŏm'mŭtē), S central group (pop. 3,646) of Maldive Isls., in Indian Ocean, bet. 1°46'N and 2°8'N; coconuts, breadfruit.

Hadejia (ädäjä'), town (pop. 5,143), Kano prov., Northern Provinces, N Nigeria, on Hadejia R. (branch of the Komadugu Yobe) and 110 mi. NE of Kano; agr. trade center; cotton, peanuts, millet, durra. Sometimes spelled Hadeija.

Hadele Gubo (hä'dĕlä gōō'bō), village (pop. 250), Wallo prov., NE Ethiopia, in Aussa dist., near L. Gamarri, 27 mi. SE of Sardo.

Hademarschen, Germany: see Hanerau-Hademarschen.

Hadera (hŭdä'rŭ), settlement (1949 pop. 12,500), W Israel, in Plain of Sharon, near Mediterranean, 25 mi. NNE of Tel Aviv; orange-growing center; mfg. of machinery, bldg. materials, tiles, aluminum brushes, paper; vegetable canning. Cement plant. Technical school. Founded 1890 in marsh region which was subsequently drained. Railroad from Tel Aviv under construction (1950). Near by are noted eucalyptus groves.

Haderslev (hădh'ŭrslĕv), amt (□ 518; pop. 69,118), SE Jutland, Denmark, on the Little Belt; ⊙ Haderslev. Agr., livestock. After 1864 region was in Germany until 1920 plebiscite.

Haderslev, Ger. *Hadersleben,* city (1950 pop. 18,276), ⊙ Haderslev amt, SE Jutland, Denmark, port on Haderslev Fjord and 37 mi. WSW of Odense; machine shops, breweries, lumber mill, tanneries. Cathedral, theological seminary, teachers' seminary. City flourished in Middle Ages. After 1864 in Germany until 1920 plebiscite.

Haderslev Fjord (13 mi. long), narrow inlet of the Little Belt, S Jutland, Denmark. Haderslev city and port are on it.

Hadfield, England: see Glossop.

Hadgaon (hŭd'goun), village (pop. 3,677), Nander dist., N Hyderabad state, India, 32 mi. NE of Nander; millet, cotton, wheat.

Hadhal, Mongolia: see Khadkhal.

Hadhr, Al, or **Al-Hadr** (äl hä'dŭr), anc. *Hatra,* village, Mosul prov., N Iraq, 55 mi. SW of Mosul. Conquered A.D. 115 by Trajan, its ruins constitute some of the few remaining stone monuments of Iraq.

Hadhramaut or **Hadramawt** (hädrämout'), region on S coast of Arabian Peninsula, on the Arabian Sea, corresponding in its broadest application to the Eastern Aden Protectorate, bet. the Western Aden Protectorate and the Oman sultanate. Politically, the name refers to the Hadhramaut states, a collective term for the Quaiti and Kathiri sultanates. In the most restricted sense, Hadhramaut refers to the **Wadi Hadhramaut,** the longest intermittent river valley of Aden Protectorate. Beginning in area of Husn al 'Abr, it extends 350 mi. E, past Shibam, Seiyun, and Tarim, and SE to the Arabian Sea near Seihut. The Wadi Duan (right) is the chief tributary. Under Quaiti control, except for Kathiri-ruled central section and the Mahri mouth, the Wadi Hadhramaut is a major agr. dist. in its middle reaches, producing dates, grain, sesame.

Hadhrami or **Hadrami** (both: hadh'rämē), sectional Upper Yafa sheikdom, Western Aden Protectorate; ⊙ Ash Shibr. Protectorate treaty concluded in 1903.

Hadibu (hä'dĭbōō), **Tamrida,** or **Tamridah** (tăm'rĭdŭ), town, ⊙ Socotra and of entire Mahri sultanate of Qishn and Socotra, on isl.'s N coast; 12°39'N 54°1'E. Residence of senior Mahri sultan; fisheries. Airfield. Sometimes Tamarida.

Hadim (hädŭm'), Turkish *Hadım,* village (pop. 2,584), Konya prov., S central Turkey, 60 mi. S of Konya; cereals.

Haditha or **Hadithah** (hädē'thŭ), town, Dulaim prov., NW central Iraq, on the Euphrates and 70 mi. NW of Ramadi; oil refinery; dates, livestock. Just W, the oil pipe line from the Kirkuk oilfields divides, 2 branches leading to Haifa (Israel), and 2 to Tripoli (Lebanon).

Hadja, Yemen: see Hajja.

Hadjeb-el-Aïoun (häjĕb'-ĕl-äyōōn'), town (pop. 1,763), Kairouan dist., central Tunisia, on Sousse-Tozeur RR and 36 mi. SW of Kairouan; sheep market, esparto, olives. Lead mines near by. Military post.

Had Kourt (häd' kōōrt'), village, Rabat region, N Fr. Morocco, in Rharb lowland, 16 mi. ESE of Souk el Arba du Rharb; livestock.

Hadleigh (hăd'lē). **1** Town, Essex, England: see Benfleet. **2** Urban district (1931 pop. 2,951; 1951 census 3,089), S Suffolk, England, 9 mi. W of Ipswich; agr. market. Has 14th-cent. church, 15th-cent. guildhall, and many old houses.

Hadley. 1 Suburb, Hertford, England: see East Barnet Valley. **2** Town and parish (pop. 3,278), central Shropshire, England, 2 mi. E of Wellington; iron- and steelworks; tile- and brickworks.

Hadley. 1 Town (pop. 2,639), Hampshire co., W central Mass., on Connecticut R. opposite Northampton; paper mills. Settled 1659, inc. 1661. **2** Village (pop. 139), Murray co., SW Minn., near Des Moines R., 5 mi. W of Slayton; dairy products.

Hadlow (–lō), town and parish (pop. 2,563), W Kent, England, 4 mi. NE of Tonbridge; agr. market in hop-growing region. Site of modern castle.

Hadlyme, Conn.: see Lyme.

Hadmersleben (hät'mŭrslā"bŭn), town (pop. 3,842), in former Prussian Saxony prov., central Germany, after 1945 in Saxony-Anhalt, 4 mi. SE of Oschersleben; lignite and potash mining.

Hadong (hä'dŏng'), Jap. *Kato,* town (1949 pop. 16,179), S.Kyongsang prov., S Korea, on Somjin R. and 20 mi. WSW of Chinju; agr. center (rice, barley, soy beans, hemp, fruit).

Hadong (hä'dông'), town, ⊙ Hadong prov. (□ 650; 1943 pop. 964,400), N Vietnam, in Tonkin, 5 mi. S of Hanoi; silk-spinning and trading center; mfg. (walking sticks, lace, embroidery, fans).

Hadr, Al, Iraq: see Hadhr, Al.

Hadramawt, Aden: see Hadhramaut.

Hadrami, Aden: see Hadhrami.

Hadranum, Sicily: see Adrano.

Hadres (hä'drās), village (pop. 1,320), N Lower Austria, on Pulkau R. and 22 mi. N of Stockerau, near Czechoslovak border; vineyards, corn.

Hadri, Bahr al, Oman: see Masira Bay.

Hadria, Italy: see Adria.

Hadrianopolis, Turkey: see Adrianople, city.

Hadrumetum, Tunisia: see Sousse.

Hadsel, canton, Norway: see Melbu.

Hadseloy (hät'sŭl-ûü), Nor. *Hadseløy,* island (□ 39; pop. 4,564) in North Sea, Nordland co., N Norway, in the Vesteralen group, bet. Langoy (N), Hinnoy (E), and Austvagoy (S), 20 mi. NNE of Svolvaer; 10 mi. long (E–W), 5 mi. wide; rises to 1,683 ft. On it are Melbu (S) and Stokkmarknes (N) villages. Highway circles isl. Hadsel church (W) is tourist attraction. Many Viking relics found here.

Hadsten (häs'dŭn), town (pop. 1,943), Aarhus and Randers amts, E Jutland, Denmark, 13 mi. NNW of Aarhus; meat packing.

Hadsund (hä'sōōn), town (pop. 3,058), Aalborg amt, N Jutland, Denmark, on Mariager Fjord and 23 mi. SSE of Aalborg; cement, limestone; meat packing.

Had Yai, Thailand: see Hat Yai.

Ha Dzong, Bhutan: see Ha.

Haecht, Belgium: see Haacht.

Haedo or **Mariano J. Haedo** (märyä'nō hō'tä ä-ā'dhō), industrial town (pop. estimate 5,000, with suburbs, 15,000) in Greater Buenos Aires, Argentina, adjoining Ramos Mejía, 12 mi. W of Buenos Aires. Products: alcohol, insecticides, electrical accessories, liqueurs; sawmills, railroad shops. Hospitals.

Haedo, Cuchilla de (kōōchē'yä dä), hill range, N Uruguay, extends c.200 mi. S and SW from the Brazil border 30 mi. SW of Rivera; rises to 1,000 ft.

Haegebostad, canton, Norway: see Snartemo.

Haegebostad Tunnel, Norway: see Kvineshei Tunnel.

Haeju (hă'jōō'), Jap. *Kaishu* or *Kaisyu* (both: kī'shōō'), city (1944 pop. 82,135), ⊙ Hwanghae prov., central Korea, fishing port on inlet of Yellow Sea, 65 mi. S of Pyongyang; 38°2'N 125°42'E; commercial center for gold-mining and agr. area; gold refining. Sometimes spelled Haiju.

Haelen, Belgium: see Halen.

Haeltert, Belgium: see Haaltert.

Haemus, Bulgaria: see Balkan Mountains.

Haenam (hă'năm'), Jap. *Kainan,* township (1946 pop. 14,507), S.Cholla prov., SW Korea, 20 mi. SE of Mokpo; rice, barley, soy beans.

Ha-erh-pin, Manchuria: see Harbin.

Hafat (häfät'), village on Mahri coast, Eastern Aden Protectorate, on Arabian Sea, 6 mi. ENE of Qishn; exports frankincense.

Hafelekar (hä"fŭlŭkär'), peak (7,657 ft.) of the Nordkette (Bavarian Alps), in Tyrol, W Austria, overlooking Innsbruck (just S). Reached by cable and aerial railway.

Hafenlohr (hä'fŭnlōr), village (pop. 996), Lower Franconia, NW Bavaria, Germany, on the Main (canalized) and 16 mi. WNW of Würzburg; furniture mfg., woodworking, lumber milling.

Haffe or **Haffah** (häf'fŭ), town, Latakia prov., W Syria, 15 mi. ENE of Latakia; tobacco, cereals. Just S is the citadel of Sahyun.

Hafford, village (pop. 291), central Sask., 50 mi. NW of Saskatoon, near Redberry L. (9 mi. long, 6 mi. wide); wheat.

Hafik (häfĭk'), village (pop. 1,881), Sivas prov., central Turkey, on the Kizil Irmak and 21 mi. ENE of Sivas; wheat, barley. Formerly Kochisar.

Hafizabad (hä'fĭzäbäd"), town (pop. 17,093), Gujranwala dist., E Punjab, W Pakistan, 30 mi. WSW of Gujranwala; trade center; agr. storehouse (wheat, rice, millet); rice, oilseed, and flour milling, cotton ginning.

Haflong (hä'flŭng), town (pop. 1,471), ⊙ North Cachar Hills dist., central Assam, India, in Barail Range, 27 mi. NNE of Silchar; trades in rice, cotton, sugar cane, tobacco. Silk growing near by. Also spelled Haflang.

Hafnarfjordur or **Hafnarfjordhur** (häp'närfyûr"-dhûr), Icelandic *Hafnarfjörður,* city (pop. 4,904), ⊙ and in but independent of Gullbringu og Kjosar co., SW Iceland, on Faxa Bay, 5 mi. S of Reykjavik; 64°4'N 21°57'W; fishing center. Extensive lava deposits near by.

Hafnerzell, Germany: see Obernzell.

Hafrs Fjord (häfsh, häfs), inlet of North Sea, in Rogaland co., SW Norway, near Stavanger. Scene of naval battle (872) when Harold I won the victory which gave him kingship over all Norway. Sometimes spelled Hafs Fjord.

Hafslo (häfs'lô), village and canton (pop. 2,872), Sogn og Fjordane co., W Norway, on E shore of Luster Fjord (an arm of Sogne Fjord), 6 mi. NE of Sogndal. Cattle raising, lumbering near by. Glaciers from the Jostedalsbre descend almost to water's edge. Ornes is in canton.

Hafslund, Norway: see SARPSBORG.
Haft Kel (häft' kĕl'), oil town, Sixth Prov., in Khuzistan, SW Iran, 50 mi. ENE of Ahwaz; pipe line to Abadan refinery; oil field opened 1928.
Hafun (häfo͞on'), peninsula of N Ital. Somaliland, on Indian Ocean, 90 mi. S of Cape Guardafui. Ras Hafun, at its E tip, is Africa's easternmost headland (10°27'N 51°23'30"E). Peninsula consists of a rocky isl. (17 mi. long, 13 mi. wide, 390 ft. high), linked to mainland by sandy isthmus (19 mi. long, 25 mi. wide). Encloses bay (N), largely transformed by Italians into an extensive evaporation basin for salt. Hordio, on mainland, and Hafun (pop. 5,000), on peninsula's N shore, are linked by aerial cable (15 mi. long) for salt hauling. Town of Hafun was renamed Dante by Italians.
Haga (hä'gä"), village (pop. 650), Kalmar co., SE Sweden, on N Oland isl., 15 mi. NNE of Borgholm; brick mfg.
Hag Abdalla or **Hag Abdullah** (hăg' äbdo͝ol'lä), town, Blue Nile prov., E central Anglo-Egyptian Sudan, in the Gezira, on left bank of the Blue Nile S of influx of Dinder R., on railroad, and 30 mi. S of Wad Medani; cotton, wheat, barley, corn, fruits, durra; livestock.
Hagaman (hā'gùmùn), village (pop. 1,114), Montgomery co., E central N.Y., 2 mi. N of Amsterdam; tanning.
Hagan (hā'gĭn), city (pop. 525), Evans co., E central Ga., 3 mi. W of Claxton.
Hagari, India: see BELLARY, city.
Hagari River (hŭ'gùrē) or **Vedavati River** (vādä'-vùtē), in Mysore and NW Madras, India, rises in Baba Budan Range in 2 headstreams joining SE of Kadur, flows (as the Vedavati) c.100 mi. NE, past Hiriyur, and (here becoming the Hagari) c.170 mi. generally N to Tungabhadra R. 25 mi. WNW of Adoni, on Madras-Hyderabad border. Dammed 10 mi. SW of Hiriyur to form irrigation reservoir. Sometimes spelled Hagary or Haggari.
Hagastrom (hä'gästrûm"), Swedish *Hagaström*, village (pop. 935), Gavleborg co., E Sweden, on Gavle R. and 3 mi. W of Gavle; rail junction; paper mills.
Hagelstadt (hä'gùl-shtät), village (pop. 1,164), Upper Palatinate, E Bavaria, Germany, 10 mi. SE of Regensburg; brick- and tileworks.
Hagen or **Hagen in Westfalen** (hä'gùn ĭn vĕst"-fä'lùn), city (□ 34; 1939 pop. 151,760; 1946 pop. 126,516; 1950 pop. 146,099), in former Prussian prov. of Westphalia, W Germany, after 1945 in North Rhine-Westphalia, on Ennepe R. and 10 mi. S of Dortmund city center; 51°22'N 7°27'E. An important rail hub of the Ruhr, and a steel-mfg. center; mfg. of machinery, metalware, agr. implements, chemicals, rubber and leather goods, textiles, paper. Sawmilling, woodworking, food processing. Has institute of technology. Chartered 1746. Rapid industrial development started after 1870. Second World War destruction 50–75%.
Hagenau, France: see HAGUENAU.
Hagenbach (hä'gùnbäkh). **1** Village (pop. 2,202), Rhenish Palatinate, W Germany, near the Rhine, 6 mi. W of Karlsruhe; grain, tobacco, sugar beets. **2** Village, N Württemberg, Germany: see BAD FRIEDRICHSHALL.
Hagendingen, France: see HAGONDANGE.
Hagengebirge (hä'gùngùbĭr'gù), small range of Salzburg Alps, extending c.15 mi. S of Hallein, Austria, along Austro-Ger. border, W of the Salzach; rises (N) to 7,275 ft. in the Hoher Göll (hō'ùr gûl'). Königssee (in Germany) is at W foot.
Hagen in Westfalen, Germany: see HAGEN.
Hagenow (hä'gùnō), town (pop. 9,443), Mecklenburg, N Germany, 17 mi. SW of Schwerin; rail junction; agr. market (stock, grain, potatoes).
Hagen Range (hä'gùn), E central New Guinea, SW Pacific; alt. c.13,000 ft.
Hagerman (hā'gùrmùn). **1** Village (pop. 520), Gooding co., S Idaho, 15 mi. SW of Gooding and on Snake R.; melons. U.S. fish hatchery. **2** Village (pop. 1,024), Chaves co., SE N.Mex., near Pecos R., 23 mi. SSE of Roswell, in cotton and alfalfa region. Sanitarium here. **3** Village (pop. 1,605, with adjacent North Bellport), Suffolk co., SE N.Y., just E of Patchogue.
Hagerman Pass, Colo.: see SAWATCH MOUNTAINS.
Hagerstown (hā'gùrztoun). **1** town (pop. 1,694), Wayne co., E Ind., on a fork of Whitewater R. and 16 mi. WNW of Richmond; trading center in livestock and grain area; mfg. (machinery, piston rings, fertilizer). **2** City (pop. 36,260), ⊙ Washington co., W Md., in Cumberland Valley (locally Hagerstown Valley), c.55 mi. E of Cumberland. Trade, rail, and highway center for NW Md., a rich agr. area with slate and stone quarries. Mfg. (pipe organs, aircraft, dust-control equipment, dairy equipment, sheet metal and foundry products, clothing, shoes, leather goods, silk ribbon, fertilizer, millwork, dairy products, feed); printing and publishing plants, railroad shops, airport. Has a jr. col. After Civil War battles of Antietam and South Mtn., c.5,000 Confederate soldiers were buried at Hagerstown. Near by is state reformatory for men. Settled c.1740 on land granted to Jonathan Hager 1737; laid out 1762 as Elizabeth Town; renamed and inc. 1813.
Hagerstown Valley, Md.: name locally given to S part of CUMBERLAND VALLEY.
Hagersville (hā'gùrzvĭl), village (pop. 1,455), S Ont., 22 mi. SW of Hamilton; dairying, grain and seed milling, stone quarrying, natural-gas wells.
Hagetmau (äzhĕtmō'), village (pop. 1,686), Landes dept., SW France, 17 mi. SSW of Mont-de-Marsan; woodworking, distilling, ribbon weaving.
Hagfors (häg"fôrs',-fōsh'), village (pop. 5,150), Varmland co., W Sweden, in Bergslag region, on small tributary of Klar R., 25 mi. NW of Filipstad; iron-smelting center in iron-mining region.
Haggari River, India: see HAGARI RIVER.
Haggate, England: see BRIERCLIFFE.
Hagi (hä'gē), city (1940 pop. 32,270; 1947 pop. 41,579), Yamaguchi prefecture, SW Honshu, Japan, 16 mi. NNW of Yamaguchi, port on Sea of Japan, at delta mouth of Abu R.; industrial center; ironworks, chemical plants; sake, pottery, woodworking. Exports grain, lumber, canned fish, limestone. Known as former seat of Mori clan.
Hagia or **Ayia** (both: äyē'ù), town (pop. 2,910), Larissa nome, E Thessaly, Greece, near Aegean Sea, 18 mi. ENE of Larissa, in valley bet. Ossa and Pelion mts.; olives, almonds, livestock (goat, sheep); dairy products. Also spelled Aghia.
Hagia Galene or **Ayia Galini** (both: äyē'ù gùlē'nē), village (pop. 460), Rethymnon nome, central Crete, small S coast port on Gulf of Mesara, 22 mi. SE of Rethymnon (linked by road).
Hagia Laura, Greece: see KALAVRYTA.
Hagiang (hä'zhäng'), town, ⊙ Hagiang prov. (□ 3,200; 1943 pop. 109,300), N Vietnam, in Tonkin, near China border, on Clear R. and 135 mi. NNW of Hanoi (linked by road); cardamoms. Cinnabar deposits.
Hagia Paraskeve or **Ayia Paraskevi** (both: äyē'ù pùrùskivē'), town (pop. 4,357), on N central Lesbos isl., Greece, 18 mi. NW of Mytilene; wheat, barley, citrus fruits, figs. Also spelled Aghia Paraskevi.
Hagiassos or **Ayiassos** (both: äyēä'sôs), town (pop. 6,066), SE Lesbos isl., Greece, 9 mi. W of Mytilene; olive oil, wine. Also spelled Aghiassos.
Hagihara, Japan: see HAGIWARA, Gifu prefecture.
Hagion Oros or **Ayion Oros** (both: ä'yēōn ô'rôs) [Gr., =holy mountain], Ital. *Monte Santo* (mōn'tä sän'tō), Greece; the name of a mountain (Mt. ATHOS), a Greek political division (MOUNT ATHOS), a cape (AKRATHOS), and a gulf (SINGITIC GULF).
Hagion Pneuma or **Ayion Pnevma** (both: pnĕv'mù), town (pop. 2,996), Serrai nome, Macedonia, Greece, 7 mi. ENE of Serrai; cotton, corn, barley, potatoes. Formerly Veznikon; later, until 1930s, Monoikon.
Hagios, Greece: see LOUTRA AIDEPSOU.
Hagios Athanasios or **Ayios Athanasios** (both: ä'yôs ùthùnä'sēôs). **1** Town (pop. 4,301), Drama nome, Macedonia, Greece, 7 mi. SE of Drama; tobacco, corn. Formerly called Boriane or Boriani. Sometimes spelled Aghios Athanassios. **2** Village (pop. 2,865), Salonika nome, Macedonia, Greece, on railroad and 12 mi. NW of Salonika. Formerly called Kavakli; also Aghios Athanassios.
Hagios Demetrios or **Ayios Dhimitrios** (both: dhĭmē'trēôs), S suburb (pop. 14,608), of Athens, Greece, 3 mi. from city center. Formerly called Brachami.
Hagios Elias or **Ayios Ilias** (both: ä'yôs ēlyē'ùs) [Gr., =Saint Elias], name of several peaks in Greece. **1** The highest (7,895 ft.) is the main peak of the Taygetus, in S Peloponnesus, 10 mi. SW of Sparta. **2** In Euboea, Greece: see OCHE.
Hagios Eustratios or **Ayios Evstratios** (both: ĕfsträ'-tēôs), Greek Aegean island (□ 16.1; pop. 1,131), in Lesbos nome, S of Lemnos; 39°30'N 25°4'E; 8 mi. long, 4 mi. wide, rises to 3,074 ft.; wheat, wine; fisheries. Main town, Hagios Eustratios, on NW shore. Sometimes called Hagiostrati and Aistratis.
Hagios Georgios, town, Peloponnesus, Greece: see NEMEA.
Hagios Georgios or **Ayios Yeoryios** (both: yôr'yôs) [Gr., =Saint George], anc. *Belbina*, uninhabited island (□ 2.2) in Aegean Sea, Attica nome, Greece, off mouth of Saronic Gulf, 12 mi. SSW of Cape Sounion; 37°29'N 23°57'E; 3 mi. long, 1.5 mi. wide. Sometimes Hagios Gheorghios; formerly Velvina.
Hagios Georgios Keratsiniou or **Ayios Yeoryios Keratsiniou** (kĕrùtsĭnē'o͞o), SW suburb (pop. 36,591) of Athens, Greece, just NW of Piraeus; site of large coal-fed power plant supplying Athens and Piraeus. Also called Keratsinion.
Hagios Kyrikos or **Ayios Kirikos** (both: kē'rĭkôs), town (pop. 3,023), main town of Icaria isl., Greece, on E shore; charcoal; figs; fisheries. Sulphur springs near by. Also spelled Hagios Kerykos or Aghios Kirykos.
Hagios Nikolaos or **Ayios Nikolaos** (nĭkō'läôs), town (pop. 2,558), ⊙ Lasethi nome, E Crete, port on Gulf of Mirabella, 33 mi. ESE of Candia; trades in olive oil; raisins, carobs, wheat, citrus fruits.
Hagiostrati, Greece: see HAGIOS EUSTRATIOS.
Hagiwara (hägē'wärä). **1** Town (pop. 9,551), Aichi prefecture, central Honshu, Japan, 3 mi. SW of Ichinomiya; agr. center (rice, wheat); raw silk. **2** or **Hagihara** (-härä), town (pop. 6,164), Gifu prefecture, central Honshu, Japan, 18 mi. S of Takayama; rice, wheat, raw silk, charcoal.
Hagley, village (pop. 320), N Tasmania, 15 mi. WSW of Launceston; flax mill.
Hagondange (ägōdäzh'), Ger. *Hagendingen* (hä'gùn-dĭng-ùn), town (pop. 8,114), Moselle dept., NE France, near left bank of Moselle R., 10 mi. N of Metz, in iron-mining dist.; steel milling, Portland cement mfg.
Hagonoy (hägōnoi', ägō–), town (1939 pop. 2,118; 1948 municipality pop. 37,532), Bulacan prov., S central Luzon, Philippines, 23 mi. NW of Manila, on Pampanga delta; agr. center (rice, sugar, corn).
Hag's Head, cape on the Atlantic, W Co. Clare, Ireland, 8 mi. W of Ennistymon; 52°57'N 9°29'W. Site of ruined O'Brien's Tower, built 1835.
Hague, village (pop. 295), central Sask., 30 mi. NNE of Saskatoon; mixed farming, dairying.
Hague (hāg). **1** Resort village (1940 pop. 632), Warren co., E N.Y., in the Adirondacks, on W shore of L. George, 8 mi. SSW of Ticonderoga. **2** Farming village (pop. 328), Emmons co., S N.Dak. 20 mi. SSE of Linton. **3** Village, Westmoreland co. E Va., 50 mi. ESE of Fredericksburg. Near by is Yeocomico Church, originally built 1655; rebuilt 1706.
Hague, La, (lä äg'), cape of Manche dept., NW France, forming NW extremity of Cotentin Peninsula, on English Channel, separated from Alderney (10 mi. W) by Race of Alderney, and 15 mi. WNW of Cherbourg; 49°43'N 1°57'W. Lighthouse.
Hague, The (hāg'), Du. *'s Gravenhage* (skrä'vùnhä'khù) or *Den Haag* (dùn häkh'), Fr. *La Haye* (lä ä') city (pop. 532,998), de facto ⊙ the Netherlands and ⊙ South Holland prov., W Netherlands, 30 mi. SW of Amsterdam, 4 mi. from North Sea; 52°4'N 4° 19'E. One of most beautiful cities of Europe, with fine streets, handsome public buildings, and numerous picturesque waterways. Residence of the royal court, seat of the legislature, supreme court of justice, and International Court of Justice (since 1945) under the U.N. Almost wholly residential; some trade and mfg. (wood and rubber products, clothing); hq. of some business houses. Site of the Binnenhof, inner court of palace originally built in 13th cent., now housing both chambers of the legislature, and including 13th-cent. Hall of Knights (*Ridderzaal*), where many historic meetings have been held. Near-by Prisoners' Gate (*Gevangenenpoort*), 14th-cent. prison, was site of murder of Jan and Cornelius de Witt (1672). The 17th-cent. Renaissance Mauritshuis, originally a private residence of Maurice of Nassau, now houses a noted picture gallery containing some of the greatest works of Rembrandt. The beautiful Peace Palace (*Vredespaleis*), completed in 1913, housed Permanent Court of Arbitration set up by 1899 Peace Conference; after 1922 it housed Permanent Cour of International Justice and, since 1945, International Court of Justice. Other notable buildings Royal Library, Mus. of Anc. Art, 15th–16th-cent Gothic Groote Kerk, New Church (containing tomb of Spinoza), and 16th-cent. town hall. Center of city is the Plein, a square flanked by ministerial buildings. The Hague is birthplace of William III, stadholder and later king of England. In 13th cent. The Hague was site of a hunting lodge of Counts of Holland ('s Gravenhage means count hedge or wood, hence Haag and Hague). In 125 Count William began building a palace, complete by his son Floris V. In 14th and 15th cent. a settlement grew around the palace; in 1586, States General were convened to meet in The Hague. I became residence of the stadholders and ⊙ 17th cent. republic which ended (1672) with murder o the de Witts. In 18th cent. The Hague was one o the chief diplomatic and intellectual centers of Eur ope and scene of many peace conferences. Receive its town charter from Louis Napoleon in early 19t cent., after seat of government had been remove to Amsterdam. From 1815 to 1830 was alternativ meeting place, with Brussels, of United Nether lands legislature. Since 1830 it has been de fact ⊙ the Netherlands; in mid-19th cent. was consid erably expanded and improved by efforts of Wi liam II. In 1899 The Hague was site of Peace Con ference called by Nicholas II of Russia; signing o The Hague Convention followed. In 1907 the 2 Peace Conference was held here. During latte part of Second World War, The Hague was chi launching point of German rocket weapons, an some city blocks were destroyed by air bombin Near by is popular North Sea resort of SCHEVENINGEN.
Haguenau (ägnō'), Ger. *Hagenau* (hä'gùnou), tow (pop. 15,103), Bas-Rhin dept., E France, on th Moder and 16 mi. N of Strasbourg; commercial cen ter (Alsatian hops); mfg. (footwear, woolens, ca pets, furniture, pharmaceuticals, water meters Oil drilled near by. Has large military barrack Heavily damaged in Second World War (includin 12th-cent. church of St. George and 13th-cen church of St. Nicholas). Just N, Forest of Hagu nau (□ 50), largest in Alsace, was scene of heav fighting (1945).
Hague's Peak, Colo.: see MUMMY RANGE.
Hagui (hägo͞o'ē) or **Hakui** (häko͞o'ē), town (po 6,853), Ishikawa prefecture, central Honshu, Ja pan, on W Noto Peninsula, on Sea of Japan, 24 m NNE of Kanazawa, in agr. area (rice, vegetables silk textiles.
Hah, Bhutan: see HA.

Ha Ha Bay, inlet (7 mi. long, 3 mi. wide) of the Saguenay R., S central Que., 12 mi. ESE of Chicoutimi. At its head are Bagotville, Port Alfred, and Grande Baie.

Haha-jima (hähä'jē'mä), volcanic island (□ 8; pop. 1,905), northernmost of Bailey Isls., Bonin Isls., W Pacific, 32 mi. ESE of Chichi-jima; 9 mi. long, 1.5 mi. wide; rises to 1,000 ft. Sugar refinery. In Second World War, site of Jap. air base. Formerly Coffin Isl.

Haha-jima-retto, Bonin Isls.: see BAILEY ISLANDS.

Hahira (hähī'rū, hū-), town (pop. 1,010), Lowndes co., S Ga., 12 mi. NNW of Valdosta; tobacco market.

Hahnenkamm, Austria: see KITZBÜHEL.

Hahnenmoos (hä'nŭmōs"), pass (6,431 ft.) in Bernese Alps, SW central Switzerland; road leads from Lenk to Adelboden.

Hahnville (hän'vĭl), village (pop. c.300), ⊙ St. Charles parish, SE La., on the Mississippi and 19 mi. W of New Orleans; sugar cane, rice, truck. Oil and gas refining near by.

Hahot (hŏ'hōt), Hung. *Hahót*, town (pop. 2,550), Zala co., W Hungary, 14 mi. S of Zalaegerszeg; potatoes, wheat, rye, hogs.

Hai, China: see PAI RIVER, Hopeh prov.

Hai, Shatt al, Iraq: see GHARRAF, SHATT AL.

Haian (hī'än'). **1** Town, N Kiangsu prov., China, 12 mi. NNW of Jukao; agr. center (rice, cotton, wheat). **2** Village, Kwangtung prov., China: see HOION.

Haibak or **Aibak** (ī'bŭk), town (pop. 10,000), Mazar-i-Sharif prov., N Afghanistan, in Afghan Turkestan, on highway from Kabul and 37 mi. SE of Tashkurghan, on Khulm R.; irrigated agr. The Takht-i-Rustam (5 mi. SSW) is a collection of Buddhist stupas and other archaeological remains.

Haibara (hī'bärä), town (pop. 7,852), Nara prefecture, S Honshu, Japan, 13 mi. SE of Nara; agr. center (rice, raw silk).

Haicheng or **Hai-ch'eng** (hī'chŭng'). **1** Town, Fukien prov., China: see HAITENG. **2** Town, Kansu prov., China: see HAIYÜAN. **3** Town, ⊙ Haicheng co. (1946 pop. 823,330), SW Liaotung prov., Manchuria, China, 80 mi. SW of Mukden and on South Manchuria RR; magnesite mining; limestone quarry; brick and tile plant. Wild silk, raw cotton.

Haichow, China: see SINHAI, Shantung prov.

Haid, Czechoslovakia: see BOR.

Haida, Czechoslovakia: see NOVY BOR.

Haidarabad, India, Pakistan: see HYDERABAD.

Haidargarh (hī'dŭrgŭr), village, Bara Banki dist., central Uttar Pradesh, India, on branch of Sarda Canal and 25 mi. SSE of Bara Banki; rice, gram, wheat, oilseeds.

Haidarnagar, India: see NAGAR, Mysore.

Haidar Pasha, Turkey: see HAYDARPASA.

Haidenschaft, Yugoslavia: see AJDOVSCINA.

Haidershofen (hī'dŭrs-hō"fŭn), village (pop. 2,124), W Lower Austria, on the Enns and 3 mi. NNE of Steyr; wheat, cattle.

Haidhof, Germany: see MESSNERSKREITH.

Haidmühle (hīt'mü"lŭ), village (pop. 1,714), Lower Bavaria, Germany, in Bohemian Forest, 22 mi. NE of Passau, on Czechoslovak border; rye, potatoes.

Haïdra (īdrä'), anc. *Ammoedara*, village, Kasserine dist., W Tunisia, in Tebessa Mts., 33 mi. NW of Kasserine; rail junction and customhouse near Algerian border. Lumber, esparto grass. Important Roman ruins (1st cent. A.D.) include a triumphal arch, a temple, a theater, and mausoleums. There is also a Byzantine citadel.

Haiduong (hī'zwŭng), city (1936 pop. 13,000), ⊙ Haiduong prov. (□ 900; 1943 pop. 843,500), N Vietnam, in Tonkin, on Thaibinh R., on Hanoi-Haiphong RR and 30 mi. ESE of Hanoi, in intensive agr. (rice, tobacco, corn) area; distilling, silk-spinning. Kaolin and stone quarrying.

Haifa (hī'fä), city (1946 pop. estimate 145,430; 1950 pop. estimate 130,000), NW Israel, on Bay of Acre of the Mediterranean, at mouth of Kishon R., at foot of Mt. Carmel, 55 mi. NNE of Tel Aviv; 32°49'N 35°E. Chief seaport of Israel; rail junction; industrial center, with oil refinery at terminus of pipe line from Kirkuk, Iraq; textile mills, foundries, mfg. of bldg. materials, cables, radios, chemicals, fertilizer, electrical equipment, plastics, rubber products, machinery, glass, pottery; processing of food products, especially olive oil. Auto-assembly plant. Site of technical col. (at Hadar Hacarmel), nautical school; has hosp., municipal mus. Airfield (NE). Known in biblical times as Sycaminum. As Caiphas or Caiffa it was important fortress during the Crusades; destroyed (1191) by Saladin. Captured (1799) by Napoleon and (1839) by Ibrahim Pasha. At close of British regime (May, 1948) evacuated by Arab pop. Chief residential suburbs include Hadar Hacarmel (SW), Ya'arot ha Carmel (S), Neve Shaanan (SE), and Bat Galim (NW). Zebulun Valley (E and NE) forms part of city's industrial and residential zone.

Haifeng. 1 Town, Kwangtung prov., China: see HOIFUNG. **2** Town, Shantung prov., China: see WUTI.

Haifif, Aden: see GHAIDHA.

Haifung, China: see HOIFUNG.

Haiger (hī'gŭr), town (pop. 3,331), in former Prussian prov. of Hesse-Nassau, W Germany, after 1945 in Hesse, in the Westerwald, on the Dill and 3 mi. W of Dillenburg; machinery mfg. Has late-Gothic church.

Haigler, village (pop. 398), Dundy co., S Nebr., 20 mi. W of Benkelman and on Republican R., at Kansas line, near Colo. line; livestock, grain, poultry produce.

Hai Ho, China: see PAI RIVER, Hopeh prov.

Haiju, Korea: see HAEJU.

Haik, Lake (hīk), Wallo prov., NE Ethiopia, near L. Ardibbo, 17 mi. NE of Dessye; alt. 6,660 ft.; 4 mi. long, 3 mi. wide.

Hai-k'ang, China: see HOIHONG.

Haiki, Japan: see SASEBO.

Hai-k'ou, China: see HOIHOW.

Haikow or **Hai-k'ou** (both: hī'kō'), Jap. *Kaiko* (kī'kō), village (1935 pop. 3,984), W central Formosa, on W coast, 15 mi. W of Huwei; trade with Pescadores during SW monsoon (March–Sept.).

Hail (hīl), **Ha'il** (hä'ĭl), or **Hayel** (häyĕl'), town (pop. 15,000), ⊙ Jebel Shammar prov., N Nejd, Saudi Arabia, 370 mi. NW of Riyadh and on caravan route bet. Medina and Iraq; 27°30'N 42°E. Caravan trade with Iraq; agr. (dates, fruit, grain); handicrafts; stock raising. Was seat of Rashid dynasty of Jebel Shammar until captured in 1921 by Ibn Saud.

Hailakandi (hīlä'kändē), town (pop. 3,084), Cachar dist., S Assam, India, in Surma Valley, on tributary of Barak (Surma) R. and 17 mi. WSW of Silchar; trades in rice, tea, sugar cane, rape and mustard; tea processing. Extensive tea gardens near by. Rail spur terminus 10 mi. SSE, at Lalaghat.

Hailar (hī'lär'), Chinese *Hailaerh*, formerly *Hulun* (hōō'lōōn'), city (pop. 16,140), N Inner Mongolian Autonomous Region, Manchuria, on Chinese Eastern RR and 400 mi. NW of Harbin, and on Hailar (Argun) R.; leading transportation center of the Barga region; trades in horses and hides. Wool washing, flour milling, tanning, food canning. Airport. Consists of the old Chinese and new industrial towns (S) and railroad settlement (N). Founded 1734 as a Chinese fort, it developed greatly after construction (1903) of railroad. In Manchukuo, it was ⊙ North Hsingan prov.; and later (1946–49), ⊙ Hsingan prov. Called Hulun by Chinese until it became an independent municipality in 1947.

Hailar River, Manchuria: see ARGUN RIVER.

Haile, village and parish (pop. 799), W Cumberland, England, 7 mi. SSE of Whitehaven; iron mining. Church dates from 10th cent.

Hailey, agr. village and parish (pop. 1,024), W Oxfordshire, England, 2 mi. N of Witney.

Hailey, city (pop. 1,464), ⊙ Blaine co., S central Idaho, on Big Wood R. and c.100 mi. E of Boise; alt. 5,342 ft.; trade center for mining (silver, lead) and livestock area; summer resort, hq. for Sawtooth Natl. Forest; lumber milling. Has hot springs. Sawtooth Mts. are N. Laid out 1881, inc. as village 1903, as city 1909.

Haileybury, town (pop. 2,268), ⊙ Timiskaming dist., E Ont., on L. Timiskaming, 80 mi. N of North Bay; distributing and residential center for rich mining region, with pulp, lumber milling; ski resort. Airfield. Silver, gold, cobalt are mined in immediate vicinity. Site of mining school. Developed after discovery (1903) of silver at near-by COBALT; inc. 1905. Town was almost wholly destroyed (1922) by fire.

Haileyville, city (pop. 1,107), Pittsburg co., SE Okla., 12 mi. ESE of McAlester and contiguous to HARTSHORNE, in coal-mining, lumbering, stock-raising area. Settled c.1890.

Hailin (hī'lĭn'), town, ⊙ Hailin co., S Sungkiang prov., Manchuria, 10 mi. W of Mutankiang and on railroad; lumbering center.

Haillicourt (āyĕkōōr'), town (pop. 2,632), Pas-de-Calais dept., N France, 5 mi. SSW of Béthune; coal mines.

Hailsham (hāl'shŭm), town and parish (pop. 5,420), SE Sussex, England, 7 mi. N of Eastbourne; agr. market. Has 15th-cent. church.

Hailun (hī'lōōn'), town (pop. c.50,000), ⊙ Hailun co. (pop. 393,304), E central Heilungkiang prov., Manchuria, on railroad and 120 mi. N of Harbin; major agr. center, in wheat-growing area; flour milling, oilseed pressing, distilling, knitting (hosiery). Formerly called Tungken.

Hailung (hī'lōōng'), town, ⊙ Hailung co. (pop. 262,365), NE Liaotung prov., Manchuria, on railroad and 65 mi. N of Tunghwa, at Sungari reservoir; grain-producing center; timber, hemp, tobacco. Formerly called Hweipeh.

Hailuoto (hī'lōō-ōtō), Swedish *Karlö* (kärl'û"), island (□ 68; pop. 1,696) in Gulf of Bothnia, Oulu co., W Finland, 12 mi. W of Oulu; 14 mi. long (E-W), 1–9 mi. wide. Hailuoto fishing village (S). The isl.'s isolated position makes it of ethnographical interest.

Haimen (hī'mŭn'). **1** Town, E Chekiang prov., China, outer port (20 mi. SE) of Linhai, on E. China Sea, at mouth of Ling R. **2** Town (pop. 95,218), ⊙ Haimen co. (pop. 512,499), N Kiangsu prov., China, 50 mi. NNW of Shanghai, across estuary of Yangtze R. (N); cotton spinning; cotton, beans, rice, hemp, wheat.

Haïmer, Oued el, Fr. Morocco: see BOU BEKER.

Hainan (hī'nän'), second largest island (□ 13,000; pop. 2,500,000) off China coast, in S.China Sea, E of Gulf of Tonkin, forming part of Kwangtung prov.; main town, Kiungshan. Separated from Luichow Peninsula of the mainland by Hainan Strait (10–15 mi. wide), the isl. is 185 mi. long (SW-NE) and 100 mi. wide, and rises to 5,118 ft. in the densely forested Wuchi Mts. (S center). It has a tropical monsoon climate, favoring the cultivation of coffee, rubber, rice, tobacco, and sugar cane in the coastal lowland. The isl. yields tropical wood and coconuts along the S shore. Its interior is rich in minerals, including tin, tungsten, and gold-copper ores and, above all, high-grade iron deposits mined at Tientu and Shekluk (Shihlu). Hainan is circled by an all-weather highway linking the chief coastal towns. Principal ports are Hoihow (port for Kiungshan on Hainan Strait) and Yülin (S), connected by railroad with the iron mines. The majority of the Chinese pop., in coastal lowland, is Hoklo. Aborigines are the Li, in interior mts., and the Yaos, near N coast. Under Chinese control since 110 B.C., Hainan was fully inc. into China under Mongol Yüan dynasty (1280–1368) and became part of Kwangtung upon its creation in late-14th cent. Chinese colonization developed later from Fukien prov. During Sino-Japanese War, the isl. was occupied (1939–45) by the Japanese, who developed the new port and naval base of Yülin, the railroads, and the mines. After the war, plans were being made to constitute Hainan a separate prov. as the isl. passed (1950) to Chinese Communist control.

Hainan Strait, in S.China Sea, China, joins Gulf of Tonkin (W) and S.China Sea proper (E), separating Luichow Peninsula (N) and Hainan isl. (S); 10–15 mi. wide, 50 mi. long. Hoihow is on S shore. Main shipping route bet. Hong Kong and Haiphong. Also called Kiungchow Strait.

Hainasch, Latvia: see AINAZI.

Hainaut (ĕnō'), Flemish *Henegouwen* (hā'nŭkh-ou"ŭn), province (□ 1,437; pop. 1,247,299), SW Belgium; ⊙ Mons. Bounded by Brabant and East Flanders provs. (N), West Flanders prov. (NW), France (W, S), Namur prov. (E). Drained by Scheldt, Dender, and Sambre rivers and Charleroi-Brussels Canal. Cattle raising and dairying in S. Includes the great coal-mining area called the Borinage. Chief cities: Mons and Charleroi, with machine mfg. and metal industries. Other important industrial towns: Châtelet, Carnières, Ath, Châtelineau, Gilly, Jumet, Montignies-sur-Sambre, Quaregnon. Greater part of prov. is French-speaking, with N area Flemish-speaking.

Hainburg or **Hainburg an der Donau** (hīn'bōōrk än dĕr dō'nou), town (pop. 7,155), E Lower Austria, 8 mi. W of Bratislava, Czechoslovakia; tobacco mfg. Old Roman outpost.

Haindorf, Czechoslovakia: see HEJNICE.

Haine River (ĕn), SW Belgium and N France, rises near Anderlues, flows 40 mi. N and W, through Hainault coal-mining area, past St-Ghislain, to Scheldt R. at Condé-sur-l'Escaut.

Haines, village (pop. 336), SE Alaska, on Chilkoot Inlet, arm of Lynn Canal, and 75 mi. NNW of Juneau, 15 mi. SSW of Skagway; outlet for Porcupine gold-mining district. Fishing, fish processing, fur farming. During Second World War a highway, the HAINES CUT-OFF, was built connecting Haines with the Alaska Highway at Haines Junction, Canada. Docks are at Chilkoot Barracks, just S, formerly site of Fort William H. Seward, U.S. army post.

Haines, town (pop. 321), Baker co., NE Oregon, 10 mi. NNW of Baker; alt. 3,333 ft.

Haine-Saint-Pierre (ĕn-sē-pyâr'), town (pop. 6,844), Hainaut prov., S Belgium, 11 mi. W of Charleroi; coal mining; coke plants; mfg. of railroad rolling stock, pottery. Just W is commune center of Haine-Saint-Paul (-pôl) (pop. 7, 198).

Haines City, city (pop. 5,630), Polk co., central Fla., c.50 mi. ENE of Tampa; citrus-fruit shipping center, with packing houses and canneries; mfg. of fertilizer, citrus oil and pulp feed. A military institute is here.

Haines Cut-off, SE Alaska, NW B.C., and SW Yukon, branch (150 mi. long) of the Alaska Highway; extends N from Haines, Alaska, via Chilkat Pass, B.C., to junction with Alaska Highway at Haines Junction, Yukon. Alaska Highway outlet to Gulf of Alaska and SE Alaska towns on the Alaska Panhandle.

Haines Falls, resort village, Greene co., SE N.Y., in the Catskills, at upper end of Kaaterskill Clove, 12 mi. W of Catskill. Scenic waterfall here. North L. is E.

Haines Junction, locality, SW Yukon, 120 mi. NW of Skagway, and on Alaska Highway, at junction with Haines Cut-off, road to Haines, Alaska; 60°45'N 137°32'W.

Haines Landing, Maine: see RANGELEY.

Hainesport, village (pop. 1,130), Burlington co., W N.J., 2 mi. W of Mt. Holly.

Hainesville. 1 Village (pop. 154), Lake co., NE Ill., 10 mi. W of Waukegan. **2** Village (pop. c.200), Sussex co., NW N.J., 2 mi. E of the Delaware and 14 mi. N of Newton, in hilly region; dairying center.

Hainfeld (hīn'fĕlt), town (pop. 3,456), central Lower Austria, 13 mi. SE of Sankt Pölten; grain, cattle, fruit.

Hainichen (hī'nĭ-khŭn), town (pop. 8,875), Saxony, E central Germany, 13 mi. NE of Chemnitz; woolen milling, tanning; mfg. of machinery, needles. Poet Gellert b. here.

Haining (hī'nĭng'), town (pop. 5,149), ⊙ Haining co. (pop. 321,943), N Chekiang prov., China, 25 mi. ENE of Hangchow, on Hangchow Bay; rice, tea, watermelons, silk. Offers good view of Hangchow bore (see HANGCHOW BAY).

Haininh, province, Vietnam: see MONCAY.

Hainsberg (hīns'bĕrk), town (pop. 5,525), Saxony, E central Germany, on the Weisseritz and 5 mi. SW of Dresden; coal mining; metalworking, glass mfg.

Hainspach, Czechoslovakia: see LIPOVA.

Hainuzuka (hīnōō'zōōkä) or **Hainutsuka** (–tsōōkä), town (pop. 13,435), Fukuoka prefecture, W Kyushu, Japan, 12 mi. E of Saga; mulberry groves. Agr. experiment station.

Haiphong (hī'fông'), city (1943 pop. 65,400; 1948 pop., with suburbs, 142,956) and main port of N Vietnam, in Tonkin, in Kienan prov., on arm of Thaibinh R. delta near Gulf of Tonkin and 55 mi. ESE of Hanoi (linked by railroad); 20°52'N 106°41'E. Industrial center; mfg. of cement, glass, china, cotton textiles, buttons, candles, oxygen; tin smelting, shipbuilding, rice and oilseed milling. A naval station, it also exports rice, corn, zinc, tin, silk, and cotton, and, via its subsidiary ports of Port Redon, Quangyen, Hongay, and Campha, the coal of the Quangyen basin. Situated 18 mi. from the open sea, it consists of industrial W suburbs, a native quarter, and the European section and docks (E). It developed after 1874 on the site of a Fr. concession and rapidly became a leading port and industrial center, handicapped, however, by heavy silting in its access channels.

Hai River, China: see PAI RIVER, Hopeh prov.

Haironville (īrōvēl'), village (pop. 374), Meuse dept., NE France, on the Saulx and 7 mi. SW of Bar-le-Duc; forges.

Hairy Hill, village (pop. 235), central Alta., 19 mi. NNE of Vegreville; tanning, dairying, mixed farming, grain.

Hais, Br. Somaliland: see HEIS.

Hais or **Hays** (hīs'), town (pop. 3,500), Hodeida prov., W Yemen, on Tihama coastal plain, 70 mi. SE of Hodeida and on road to Taiz; noted pottery-mfg. center; jewelry mfg., sheepskin tanning. Sometimes also spelled Heis, Heys, or Hes.

Haitan Island or **Hai-t'an Island** (hī'tän') (pop. 99,460), off NE Fukien prov., China, in E.China Sea, at N entrance to Formosa Strait, 50 mi. SE of Foochow; 17 mi. long, 10 mi. wide. Sweet potatoes, wheat. Chief town is Pingtan or P'ing-t'an (pop. 5,382), fishing port on W coast. The isl. shelters (W) Haitan Bay (or Futsing Bay), which provides a deep anchorage.

Haiteng (hī'tĕng') or **Hai-ch'eng** (hī'chŭng'), town (pop. 4,946), ⊙ Haiteng co. (pop. 119,096), S Fukien prov., China, 13 mi. W of Amoy, on Lung R. estuary; sweet potatoes.

Haiterbach (hī'tŭrbäkh), town (pop. 1,607), S Württemberg, Germany, after 1945 in Württemberg-Hohenzollern, in Black Forest, 4 mi. SW of Nagold; lumbering.

Haiti (hā'tē), Fr. *Haïti* (äētē'), island republic (□ c.10,700; 1950 census pop. 3,111,973), West Indies, occupying the W third of HISPANIOLA isl.; ⊙ Port-au-Prince. Bordered E by Dominican Republic, bounded N by the Atlantic, S by the Caribbean, bet. 18°–20°N and 71°35'–74°30'W. Consists largely of 2 peninsulas (the longer, Tiburon Peninsula, SW) jutting W into Windward Passage and enclosing the Gulf of Gonaïves, in which is the Île de la Gonâve. Tortuga Isl. is off Haiti's NW coast. About 4/5 of its area is covered by wooded ranges such as the Massif du Nord (N), Massif de la Selle (SE; with highest point 8,793 ft.), and Massif de la Hotte (SW). Bet. the ranges lie the fertile, densely populated plains: Plaine du Nord (N), Artibonite (W), Central (center), Cul-de-Sac (S). Watered by many streams, the only important one being the Artibonite, largest of the isl. Has equable, tropical climate with little seasonal change, relieved by NE trade winds; cooler in mts. Temp. in the lowlands ranges bet. 70° and 85°F.; main rainy periods: April-June, Oct.-Nov. Though Haiti is one of the most densely populated regions of the Americas (it has an estimated 280 persons per sq. mi.), approximately 90% of its pop. is rural. Main agr. crops—coffee, cotton, sugar—make up, respectively, 50%, 15%, and 11% of its exports. Also grown: for foreign trade—sisal, bananas, cacao; for domestic consumption—corn, sweet potatoes, beans, peas, rice, manioc, fruit. The forests yield fine timber, (mahogany, cedar, rosewood, lignum vitae, fir, oak). Other exports include goatskins, castor beans, oil cake, honey, beeswax, cashew nuts, rum, molasses, sisal bags, and mahogany articles. Deep-sea fishing along the coast. While the country is rich in a variety of minerals (silver, copper, iron, sulphur, iridium, manganese, kaolin, gypsum, limestone), these deposits are almost untapped; however, a bauxite concession has been granted. Apart from some processing plants (sugar milling, cotton ginning, alcohol and rum distilling, vegetable-oil extracting, sawmilling), its industries are negligible. Main towns are the 5 departmental capitals, Port-au-Prince, Gonaïves, Cap-Haïtien, Port-de-Paix, and Les Cayes, also the country's leading ports. Railroad links Port-au-Prince with Saint-Marc and Artibonite Plain. Haiti is increasingly visited by foreign tourists. Inhabited by Arawak Indians when Columbus discovered Hispaniola isl.; he landed here Dec. 6, 1492, near Cape Saint Nicolas, and built a fort, La Navidad, near the present Cap-Haïtien. Neglected by the Spaniards during early colonial era, the region was subjected to incursions in the 17th cent. by Fr. and Br. privateers based on Tortuga Isl. The Treaty of Ryswick (1697) recognized Fr. authority over the W third of the isl. The prosperous colony, depending on Negro slave labor, came to be known as Saint-Domingue, producing sugar, indigo, cotton, and coffee. Many slaves were introduced each year and by 1789 its society was stratified into 3 distinct classes: whites, free mulattoes and free Negroes, and Negro slaves. The outbreak of the French Revolution had immediate repercussions. There were several uprisings, which gained momentum under Toussaint L'Ouverture, who was subsequently named governor. In 1795 Spain ceded its part of the isl., Santo Domingo, to France, and in 1801 Toussaint conquered it. Napoleon's Gen. Leclerc led an expedition which captured Toussaint, but Leclerc was unable to conquer the interior. The French were forced to withdraw and Haiti—readopting the anc. Indian name—became the 2d free republic of the Americas, proclaiming its independence at Gonaïves in 1804. Dessalines, its 1st president, took the title of emperor soon after, but was assassinated in 1806. Internal strife has persisted through most of the country's history. After the death of Dessalines, Haiti was divided bet. Henri Christophe and Pétion. The former founded a kingdom in the North (1811–20). After Christophe's death, the constitutionally elected president of the South, Boyer, unified the country and also for a time brought Santo Domingo under Haitian control (1822–44). U.S. held a customs receivership, 1905–41, and marines occupied Haiti 1915–34. It is ruled by a small mulatto class, which clings to the Fr. cultural tradition. The impoverished Negroes (95% of the pop.) speak a patois, called Creole, and retain some of the anc. African folklore, though their magic vodun rites (commonly called voodoo) have been overemphasized by observers. The republic's principal problem is its overpopulation. Haitians have filtered into the Dominican Republic, and border clashes have resulted, the worst in 1937, when Dominican troops entered Haitian territory and massacred more than 10,000 Haitians. A United Nations mission of technical assistance to the republic was undertaken in 1948.

Haiti, island, West Indies: see HISPANIOLA.

Haiwee Reservoirs, Calif.: see OWENS RIVER.

Haiya Junction (hī'yä), village, Kassala prov., NE Anglo-Egyptian Sudan, 110 mi. SSW of Port Sudan. Here railroad from Port Sudan branches to Atbara (W) and Kassala (S).

Haiyang (hī'yäng'). **1** Town, Hopeh prov., China: see LINYÜ. **2** Town, ⊙ Haiyang co. (pop. 479,842), NE Shantung prov., China, port on S coast of Shantung peninsula, on Yellow Sea, 65 mi. NE of Tsingtao; on pongee; grain, melons.

Haiyen (hī'yĕn'). **1** Town (pop. 9,073), ⊙ Haiyen co. (pop. 186,449), NE Chekiang prov., China, 50 mi. ENE of Hangchow, on Hangchow Bay; silk, cotton, rice, wheat. **2** Town, ⊙ Haiyen co. (pop. 5,242), NE Tsinghai prov., China, on upper Sining R. and 60 mi. NW of Sining, near the lake Koko Nor; cattle raising. Until 1943 called Sankiocheng.

Haiyüan (hī'yüän'), town, ⊙ Haiyüan co. (pop. 47,712), SE Kansu prov., China, 105 mi. ENE of Lanchow, in mtn. region; kaoliang, millet, beans. Pop. is largely Moslem. Until 1914, Haicheng.

Hajar or **Hajr** (hä'jŭr), coastal hill country of Oman, extending 300 mi. along Gulf of Oman bet. Oman Promontory and Ras al Hadd. Consisting of a series of limestone ridges and tablelands (rising to 9,900 ft. in the Jabal Akhdar), the Hajar country is divided by the Wadi Sama'il into the Western Hajar and Eastern Hajar. The Western Hajar is separated from the Gulf of Oman by the fertile, populous Batina coastal plain, while the Eastern Hajar's limestone formations hug the coast bet. Muscat and Ras al Hadd.

Hajdu (hoi'dōō), county (□ 998; pop. 197,653), E Hungary; ⊙ DEBRECEN. Includes the HORTOBAGY (NW; part of the Alföld); drained by Kösely and Hortobagy rivers. Level agr. region (grain, potatoes, paprika, wine); cattle, sheep; garden products (spices, honey, fruit). Extensive flour milling; home industries. Industrial centers at Debrecen, Balmazujvaros, Hajduböszörmeny.

Hajdubagos (hoi'dōōbŏgôsh), town (pop. 2,472), Bihar co., E Hungary, 10 mi. S of Debrecen; wheat, corn, hogs, poultry.

Hajduböszörmeny (hoi'dōōbû"sûrmānyŭ), Hung. *Hajdúböszörmény*, city (pop. 30,409), Hajdu co., E Hungary, 12 mi. NNW of Debrecen; market center for agr., livestock area; mfg. (stockings); brickworks.

Hajdudorog (hoi'dōōdôrôg), town (pop. 11,779), Hajdu co., E Hungary, 10 mi. N of Hajduböszörmeny; market center; home industries. Center of Hungarian Greek-Orthodox Church.

Hajduhadhaz (hoi'dōōhôt"häz), Hung. *Hajdúhadház*, town (pop. 12,450), Hajdu co., E Hungary, 10 mi. N of Debrecen; market center; wheat, paprika, cattle.

Hajduki Wielkie, Poland: see CHORZOW.

Hajdunanas (hoi'dōōnä"näsh), Hung. *Hajdúnánás*, city (pop. 18,770), Hajdu co., E Hungary, 15 mi. SW of Nyiregyhaza; market center for agr. (wheat, tobacco, corn), cattle region; exports straw hats.

Hajdusamson (hoi'dōō-shäm"shôn), Hung. *Hajdúsámson*, town (pop. 7,320), Hajdu co., E Hungary, 7 mi. NE of Debrecen; wheat, corn, cattle, hogs.

Hajduszoboszlo (hoi'dōōsô"bôslō), Hung. *Hajdúszoboszló*, city (pop. 17,669), Hajdu co., E Hungary, on Kösely R. and 12 mi. SW of Debrecen; grain, tobacco, cattle. Mineral springs, natural gas near by.

Hajduszovat (hoi'dōōsôvät), Hung. *Hajdúszovát*, town (pop. 4,101), Hajdu co., E Hungary, on Kösely R. and 12 mi. SW of Debrecen; grain, potatoes, hogs, sheep.

Hajeb, El (ĕl häjĕb'), town (pop. 4,926), Meknès region, N central Fr. Morocco, on N slope of the Middle Atlas, 18 mi. SE of Meknès; alt. 3,445 ft. Palm-fiber processing; corn, barley, sheep.

Hajika (hä"jē'kä), town (pop. 4,518), Tochigi prefecture, central Honshu, Japan, 4 mi. SE of Kiryu, in agr. area; textiles.

Hajipur (hä'jēpōōr), town (pop. 21,963), Muzaffarpur dist., N Bihar, India, on Ganges R. at Gandak R. mouth, and 7 mi. N of Patna; rail and road junction; trade center (rice, wheat, barley, corn, sugar cane, tobacco); rice and sugar milling. Important in late-16th-cent. struggle bet. Akbar and Afghan governors of Bengal.

Hajja or **Hajjah** (häj'jŭ), town (pop. 2,500), ⊙ Hajja prov. (pop. 380,000), N central Yemen, in maritime range, 50 mi. NW of Sana; trade center. Sometimes spelled Hadja.

Hajmasker (hoi'mäsh-kĕr), Hung. *Hajmáskér*, town (pop. 4,711), Veszprem co., NW central Hungary, 6 mi. NE of Veszprem; rail junction; potatoes, corn, hogs.

Hajo (hä'jō), village, Kamrup dist., W Assam, India, near the Brahmaputra, 15 mi. WNW of Gauhati; rice, mustard, jute. Pilgrimage center. Has 16th-cent. Vishnuite temple (erection consecrated by human sacrifice).

Hajos (hoi'ōsh), Hung. *Hajós*, town (pop. 5,311), Pest-Pilis-Solt-Kiskun co., S central Hungary, 16 mi. NNE of Baja; corn, tobacco; hogs, horses. Shrine of St. George.

Hajr, Oman: see HAJAR.

Hajr, Wadi (wä'dē hä'jŭr), intermittent coastal river of Eastern Aden Protectorate, forms border bet. Wahidi sultanate of Bir Ali and the Quaiti state, flows 60 mi. SE to Gulf of Aden at Meifa. Irrigates Hajr prov. (⊙ Kanina) of Quaiti state, one of chief agr. areas of protectorate.

Haka (hăkä'), village, N.Chin Hills dist., Upper Burma, 20 mi. SSW of Falam, near India border.

Hakalau (häkälä'ōō), coast village (pop. 689), E Hawaii, T.H., 12 mi. N of Hilo; sugar mill.

Hakari (häkyärē'), Turkish *Hakâri*, province (□ 3,722; 1950 pop. 44,204), SE Turkey; ⊙ Hakari. Bordered E by Iran, S by Iraq. Drained by Great Zab (Zap) R. Produces naphtha; mountainous and unproductive. Sometimes spelled Hakkari.

Hakari, Turkish *Hakâri*, village (1950 pop. 2,664), ⊙ Hakari prov., SE Turkey, near Great Zab R., 200 mi. E of Diyarbakir, 24 mi. from Iraq line and 36 mi. from Iran line; grain. Sometimes spelled Hakkari. Formerly Colemerik (Turkish *Çölemerik*) or Julamerk.

Hakari Mountains, Turkish *Hakâri*, SE Turkey, cover area 100 mi. by 50 mi., with Iranian frontier on E, Iraq frontier on S, and Buhtan R. on N; rise to 13,675 ft. in Cilo Dag.

Hakata, port, Japan: see FUKUOKA, city, Fukuoka prefecture.

Hakata Bay (hä"kä'tä), SE inlet of Genkai Sea, N Kyushu, Japan, bet. Cape Nishiura (W) and Shigano-shima (E); 12 mi. long E-W, 4 mi. wide N-S; contains small isl. Nakano-shima. Fukuoka is on SE shore.

Hakata-shima (häkä"tä'shĭmä), island (□ 8; pop. 12,421), Ehime prefecture, Japan, in Hiuchi Sea (central section of Inland Sea), 8 mi. off N coast of Shikoku, just NE of O-shima; 5 mi. long, 2.5 mi. wide. Mountainous, fertile; sweet potatoes, tobacco, oranges, melons. Some fishing.

Hakgala (hŭkgä'lŭ), peak (7,127 ft.) in Piduru Ridges, central Ceylon, 5 mi. SE of Nuwara Eliya; last 1,600 ft. rises in bare rock. Noted Hakgala botanical gardens on NE slope; meteorological observatory.

Haki (hä'kē), town (pop. 4,470), Fukuoka prefecture, N central Kyushu, Japan, on Chikugo R. and 18 mi. E of Kurume; rice, wheat, barley, tobacco, raw silk.

Hakin, Wales: see MILFORD HAVEN, urban district.

Hakirya (häkĕryä') or **Kirya** (kēryä'), E residential suburb of Tel Aviv, W Israel, in Plain of Sharon.

Formerly colony of Sarona (zärō'nä), founded 1871 by Germans, it was renamed 1948 when it became provisional ⊙ Israel. While Jerusalem became ⊙ early in 1950, some govt. offices remain in Hakirya. Also spelled Hakiryah or Kiryah.

Hakkari, Turkey: see HAKARI.

Hakluyt Island (hăk'lo͞ot) (3 mi. long, 1 mi. wide), off NW Greenland, in N Baffin Bay, at mouth of Inglefield Gulf; 77°24'N 72°35'W. Northernmost point reached (1616) by Baffin.

Hakodate (häkō'dä'tä), city (1940 pop. 203,862; 1947 pop. 211,441), SW Hokkaido, Japan, on small peninsula in Tsugaru Strait, 70 mi. N of Aomori (on Honshu); 41°46'N 140°44'E. Chief port of isl., major fishing center; industrial center (ironworks, shipyards, woodworking factories). Exports canned and salted fish, rice, lumber. Yunokawa hot springs are just E of city. Port opened 1854 to Amer. ships and 1857 to general foreign trade. Formerly sometimes Hakodadi.

Hakone (hä"kō'nä), town (pop. 662), Kanagawa prefecture, central Honshu, Japan, 9 mi. WSW of Odawara, on small lake; tourist inns.

Hakone, Mount, Jap. *Hakone-yama,* extinct volcano in central Honshu, Japan, near Hakone; has 6 central cones (highest is c.4,700 ft.) and a crater (c.8 mi. long, c.4 mi. wide). It is part of high volcanic range cutting across central Honshu. During period of Tokugawa shogunate, there was a gate (at S end of crater) forming the barrier to Hakone Pass connecting Tokyo and Kyoto.

Hakozaki, Japan: see FUKUOKA, city, Fukuoka prefecture.

Haksberg (hōks'bĕr"yŭ), Swedish *Håksberg,* village (pop. 582), Kopparberg co., central Sweden, in Bergslag region, 2 mi. NNE of Ludvika; iron and lead mining.

Hakui, Japan: see HAGUI.

Hakurei-to, Korea: see PAENGNYONG ISLAND.

Hakusa-to, Pescadores: see PAISHA ISLAND.

Hakusen, Korea: see PAKCHON.

Hakuto-san, Korea and Manchuria: see CHANGPAI MOUNTAINS.

Hal (äl), Flemish *Halle* (hä'lù), town (pop. 17,564), Brabant prov., central Belgium, 10 mi. SSW of Brussels, on Charleroi-Brussels Canal; textile center; shoe mfg.; market center for cherry, potato, chicory area. Has 14th-cent. Gothic church which attracts many pilgrims.

Ha La (hä'lä'), pass (alt. 13,975 ft.) in W Assam Himalayas, Bhutan, 10 mi. WNW of Ha, on main Yatung (Tibet)-Punakha route.

Hala (hä'lŭ), town (pop. 7,964), Hyderabad dist., central Sind, W Pakistan, near Indus R., 28 mi. N of Hyderabad; trades in grain, cloth fabrics, ghee, tobacco, sugar; hand-loom weaving (wearing apparel), mfg. of glazed pottery, tiles; fruitgrowing (mangoes, dates, plantains).

Halab, Syria, see ALEPPO.

Halabja or **Halabdjah** (häläb'jä), town, Sulaimaniya prov., NE Iraq, in the mts. of Kurdistan, near Iran border, 35 mi. SE of Sulaimaniya; tobacco, fruit, livestock. Chief town of the Jaf Kurds. Also spelled Alabja.

Halachar, China: see TINGYÜANYING.

Halachó (äläсhō'), town (pop. 4,112), Yucatan, SE Mexico, on railroad and 45 mi. SW of Mérida; agr. center (henequen, sugar cane, corn, fruit); tropical wood.

Halaib (hälä-ēb'), village, Kassala prov., NE Anglo-Egyptian Sudan, minor port on Red Sea, on road and 185 mi. NNW of Port Sudan; fishing.

Halanzy (äläzē'), town (pop. 2,781), Luxembourg prov., SE Belgium, 9 mi. SSW of Arlon, on Fr. border; blast furnaces.

Halar (hä'lär), district, W Saurashtra, India; ⊙ Jamnagar.

Halas, Hungary: see KISKUNHALAS.

Halba (hälbă'), town, N Lebanon, near Syrian border, 15 mi. ENE of Tripoli; sericulture, cereals, oranges.

Halberry Head, Scotland: see CLYTH NESS.

Halberstadt (häl'bùr-shtät), city (pop. 47,652), in former Prussian Saxony prov., central Germany, after 1945 in Saxony-Anhalt, near N foot of the lower Harz, on the Holtemme and 30 mi. SW of Magdeburg; 51°53'N 11°4'E. Rail junction; paper and textile milling, sugar refining; mfg. of basic chemicals, machinery, leather and rubber goods, gloves, sausages, chocolate. Heavily bombed in Second World War (destruction about 55%); the 13th–17th-cent. cathedral was severely damaged. Other noted bldgs. include 12th-cent. Church of Our Lady (*Liebfrauenkirche*) and 14th-cent. town hall. Founded as bishopric in 814. City was burned (1179) by Henry the Lion. Annexed (1648) by Brandenburg. A city judge here published (c.1230) the Sachsenspiegel, important collection of early German laws.

Halberton (hôl'bùrtùn, hô'–), village and parish (pop. 1,202), E Devon, England, 3 mi. E of Tiverton. Has 15th-cent. church.

Halbturn (hälp'to͞orn), village (pop. 1,951), Burgenland, E Austria, near Hung. border, 37 mi. SE of Vienna; wine.

Halbur (hăl'bùr), town (pop. 235), Carroll co., W central Iowa, 7 mi. SW of Carroll, in agr. area.

Halcon, Mount (hälkōn', äl–), highest peak (8,484 ft.) of Mindoro isl., Philippines, in N part of isl., 16 mi. SW of Calapan.

Halcott, Mount (hôl'kŭt) (3,537 ft.), Greene co., SE N.Y., in the Catskills, 28 mi. NW of Kingston.

Haldaur (hŭl'dour), town (pop. 6,014), Bijnor dist., N Uttar Pradesh, India, 11 mi. SE of Bijnor; rice, wheat, gram, sugar cane.

Haldefjall, Finland: see HALTIA, MOUNT.

Haldeman (hôl'dĭmùn), village (1940 pop. 511), Rowan co., NE Ky., in Cumberland Natl. Forest, 40 mi. WSW of Ashland; makes firebricks.

Halden (häl'dùn, häl'lùn), city (pop. 9,419), Ostfold co., SE Norway, on Swedish border, on railroad and 60 mi. ESE of Oslo, on Idde Fjord (ĭd'dù), 17-mi.-long arm of the Skagerrak, at mouth of small Tista R.; industrial center. Its mills process cellulose, paper, cardboard, textiles; mfg. of leather goods, shoes, matches, butter; brewing. Granite and marble quarries near by. Overlooked by Fredrikssten fortress, built 1661–71, demilitarized 1905 under Treaty of Karlstad. Halden, called Frederikshald or Fredrikshald from 1665 to 1927, was important border fortress and withstood several Swedish sieges. During a siege in 1718, Charles XII of Sweden received his fatal wound. City rebuilt after major fire in 1826.

Haldensleben (häl'dùnslā"bùn), town (pop. 22,010), in former Prussian Saxony prov., central Germany, after 1945 in Saxony-Anhalt, on Weser-Elbe Canal and 14 mi. NW of Magdeburg; rock-salt mining; sugar refining; mfg. of pottery, gloves. Has late-Gothic church, remains of medieval town walls. Formed 1938 by union of towns of Neuhaldensleben and Althaldensleben.

Haldibari (hŭldē'bärē), town (pop. 1,568), Cooch Behar dist., NE West Bengal, India, 42 mi. W of Cooch Behar; jute trade center; rice, tobacco, oilseeds, sugar cane.

Haldimand (hôl'dĭmùnd), county (□ 488; pop. 21,854), S Ont., on L. Erie and on Grand R.; ⊙ Cayuga.

Haldi River, India: see KASAI RIVER.

Haldummulla (hŭl"do͞om-mo͝ol'lŭ), town (pop. 906), Uva Prov., S central Ceylon, in Ceylon Hill Country, 20 mi. SSW of Badulla; tea, rice, vegetables.

Haldwani (hŭldvä'nē), town (pop., including Kathgodam and Ranibagh, 17,976), Naini Tal dist., N Uttar Pradesh, India, 12 mi. SSE of Naini Tal, at foot of Siwalik Range; match mfg., sugar milling; trade center for hill goods, rice, wheat, oilseeds. Founded 1834. Rail spur terminus 4 mi. N, at Kathgodam.

Hale, urban district (1931 pop. 10,667; 1951 census 12,155), N Cheshire, England, just S of Altrincham; metalworking.

Hale. 1 County (□ 663; pop. 20,832), W central Ala.; ⊙ Greensboro. In Black Belt; bounded on W by Black Warrior R. Cotton, livestock, grain, timber. Formed 1867. **2** County (□ 979; pop. 28,211), NW Texas; ⊙ Plainview. On the Llano Estacado; alt. 3,250–3,375 ft.; drained by White R. A leading Texas agr. co., with large irrigated acreage; grain sorghums, alfalfa, potatoes, sugar beets, fruit, truck; dairying; poultry (especially turkeys); beef cattle, sheep, hogs; beekeeping. Oil, clay deposits. Has small lakes (waterfowl hunting). Formed 1876.

Hale, city (pop. 452), Carroll co., NW central Mo., near Grand R., 17 mi. SE of Chillicothe; grain, livestock, coal.

Haleakala (hä'läăkälä'), mountain (10,032 ft.), E Maui, T.H., part of Hawaii Natl. Park; largest inactive crater (□ 19) in the world; 2,000 ft. deep, 7.5 mi. long, 2.4 mi. wide, 20 mi. in circumference. Rare silver sword plants grow here.

Haleb, Syria: see ALEPPO.

Halebid, India: see BELUR, Mysore.

Haleburg, town (pop. 93), Henry co., SE Ala., near Chattahoochee R., 19 mi. NE of Dothan.

Hale Center, town (pop. 1,626), Hale co., NW Texas, on the Llano Estacado, 10 mi. SW of Plainview; trading point for livestock and agr. area. Established 1893, inc. 1921.

Haledon (hăl'dùn), borough (pop. 6,204), Passaic co., NE N.J., just NW of Paterson; mfg. (textiles, labels, ribbons, pharmaceuticals, beeswax). Inc. 1908.

Haleiwa (hä'lāē'wä, –ē'vä), village (pop. 2,141), Oahu, T.H., on NW coast; coral gardens; tourism.

Halemaumau (hä'lämä'o͞omä'o͞o), fiery pit in KILAUEA crater of Mauna Loa, S central Hawaii, T.H.; 250 ft. wide, 400 ft. long, with floor covering 95 acres; fluctuating level of molten lava, c.740 ft. below rim of pit.

Halen (hä'lùn), agr. village (pop. 3,054), Limburg prov., NE Belgium, 4 mi. SE of Diest. Formerly spelled Haelen.

Hales Bar Dam, S Tenn., in Tennessee R., 15 mi. W of Chattanooga, below Chickamauga Dam, near Ala.-Ga.-Tenn. border. Privately built power dam (112 ft. high, 2,315 ft. long; completed 1913), now owned by TVA. Has navigation lock (265 ft. long, 60 ft. wide) providing max. lift of 41 ft. Forms long, narrow reservoir (□ 10; capacity 154,200 acre-ft.).

Hales Corners, village (1940 pop. 841), Milwaukee co., SE Wis., 10 mi. SW of Milwaukee, in dairy and farm area; fox farm.

Halesite (hāl'sīt"), village (1940 pop. 553), Suffolk co., SE N.Y., on Huntington Harbor on N shore of W Long Isl., just N of Huntington, in summer-resort area.

Halesowen (hālz'ōwùn), municipal borough (1931 pop. 31,059; 1951 census 39,884), N Worcester, England, 7 mi. W of Birmingham; machinery and machine-tool works; foundries. Has ruins of early 13th-cent. Halesowen Abbey and of 12th-cent. Norman church with 15th-cent. tower.

Halesworth (hālz'wûrth), urban district (1931 pop. 2,024; 1951 census 2,154), NE Suffolk, England, on Blyth R. and 15 mi. SW of Lowestoft; agr. market; shoe mfg., milk canning. Has 15th-cent. church and several old houses.

Halethorpe, Md.: see ARBUTUS.

Halewood, residential village and parish (pop. 1,175), SW Lancashire, England, 7 mi. ESE of Liverpool; truck gardening.

Haley's Island, Maine: see ISLES OF SHOALS.

Haleyville, city (pop. 3,331), Winston co., NW Ala., c.65 mi. NW of Birmingham, in Wm. B. Bankhead Natl. Forest; lumber milling, cotton ginning.

Halfa, former province, Anglo-Egyptian Sudan: see WADI HALFA.

Half Assini (äsē'nē), town, Western Prov., SW Gold Coast colony, on Gulf of Guinea, 45 mi. WNW of Axim; fishing center; rice, cassava.

Halfaya Pass or **Halfayah Pass** (hălfä'yù), in coastal hills of NW Egypt, 5 mi. SSE of Salum, near Libyan border. Scene of heavy fighting (1941–42) in Second World War.

Half Dome, Calif.: see YOSEMITE NATIONAL PARK.

Half-moon Bay, New Zealand: see OBAN.

Half Moon Bay, village (pop. 1,168), San Mateo co., W Calif., c.20 mi. S of San Francisco, on picturesque Half Moon Bay, which is sheltered on N by Pillar Point; artichoke growing and shipping; fishing; vegetable canning.

Halfway. 1 Village (pop. 2,153), Washington co., W Md., just SW of Hagerstown. **2** Town (pop. 312), Baker co., NE Oregon, near Idaho line, 36 mi. ENE of Baker.

Halfway Mountain, (1,400 ft.), W central N.F., 8 mi. SW of Buchans, near N shore of Red Indian L.

Halfway Rock Light, SW Maine, small lighthouse isl. midway bet. Portland Head and Seguin Isl. Light, Casco Bay; completed 1871.

Half Way Tree, N suburb of Kingston, ⊙ St. Andrew parish, SE Jamaica, in Liguanea Plain, c.3½ mi. N of Kingston, in agr. region (mangoes, vegetables, coffee, cattle); mfg. of cigars and cigarettes; dairying. Has old parish church. In N outskirts is King's House, since 1872 the official residence of governor of Jamaica.

Halfweg (hä'lùvā), hamlet (pop. 1,673), North Holland prov., W Netherlands, on the Ringvaart and 7 mi. W of Amsterdam; has old town hall. Sugar refinery near by.

Halhal (hälhäl'), village, Keren div., N Eritrea, 20 mi. NW of Keren; fruit, vegetables, grain.

Haliacmon River, Greece: see ALIAKMON RIVER.

Haliartus (hălēär'tùs), anc. town of Boeotia, E central Greece, on S edge of drained L. Copais, 12 mi. W of Thebes. Here the Spartan general Lysander was killed in battle (395 B.C.) against Thebes. Haliartus was destroyed (171 B.C.) by Romans. On site is modern village of Haliartos or Aliartos (1928 pop. 371), formerly called Krimpas.

Haliburton, county (□ 1,486; pop. 6,695), S Ont., on Burnt R.; ⊙ Minden.

Haliburton, village (pop. estimate 1,000), S Ont., near N end of Kashagawigamog L., 50 mi. NNE of Lindsay; corundum mining, lumbering.

Halibut Cove, fishing settlement, S Alaska, SW Kenai Peninsula, on Kachemak Bay, 19 mi. NE of Seldovia.

Halicarnassus (hă"lĭkärnă'sùs), anc. city of Caria, SW Asia Minor, on the Ceramic Gulf (Gulf of Kos or Kerme), on the Aegean opposite Kos isl.; BODRUM, Mugla prov., Turkey, is on the site. The anc. place was founded by Dorians and for a time was one of the cities of the Dorian Hexapolis. It later came under the Persians and became a residence of Carian kings, the most famous of whom was Mausolus; on his death was built (c.352 B.C.) the magnificent tomb called the Mausoleum, one of the Seven Wonders of the World. The Mausoleum was desecrated in Middle Ages by the Knights Hospitalers; some slight remains are in the British Museum. The city was conquered by Alexander c.334 B.C. Herodotus and Dionysius b. here.

Halicz (hä'lēch), Rus. *Galich* (gä'lĭch), peak (4,380 ft.) in the Carpathians, SE Poland, 13 mi. SW of Turka, Ukrainian SSR, near USSR border.

Halicz, Ukrainian SSR: see GALICH, Stanislav oblast.

Halidon Hill (hă'lĭdùn), elevation (537 ft.) in N Northumberland, England, 2 mi. NW of Berwick-upon-Tweed, overlooking the Tweed; here the English under Edward III defeated the Scots under Archibald Douglas, July 19, 1333.

Halifax, county (□ 2,063; pop. 122,656), S N.S., on the Atlantic; ⊙ Halifax. Largest co. of prov.

Halifax, city (pop. 70,488), ⊙ and largest city of Nova Scotia, on S coast of prov., on Halifax Harbour, a fine sheltered bay on the Atlantic; 44°40'N 63°7'W. Seaport and commercial center, with dock installations, grain elevators, cold-storage plants; fishing center. Ice-free the year round, Halifax is chief Canadian winter terminal of transatlantic shipping lines, and the E terminal of Canadian National and Canadian Pacific railroads. Industries include oil refining (at near-by IMPEROYAL), shipbuilding, meat packing, sugar refining, mfg. of clothing, furniture, food products. It exports fish, lobsters, and the produce brought by the rail lines. Site of Dalhousie Univ., King's Col., St. Mary's Col., Nova Scotia Technical Col., Nova Scotia Col. of Art, and Dominion Fisheries Experimental Station. The Citadel, a massive old fortress on hill overlooking town and harbor, was built 1794–97. Other features are St. Paul's Church (1750), oldest Anglican church in Canada, donated by George II; Government House (1800); Province Bldg. (1818); Point Pleasant Park. Founded 1749, Halifax became naval base for 1758 expedition against Louisburg, and for British operations in American Revolution and the War of 1812. Until 1906 a British garrison was stationed here. In both world wars Halifax was naval base, convoy terminal, and port of embarkation. In 1917 a vessel carrying explosives was rammed in the harbor, causing many casualties and major damage; and in 1945 an explosion of the naval arsenal rocked the city. The *Halifax Gazette* (1752), 1st Canadian newspaper, continues as the *Nova Scotia Royal Gazette*. Halifax was inc. 1842 as city.

Halifax, county borough (1931 pop. 98,115; 1951 census 98,376), West Riding, SW Yorkshire, England, near Calder R. and 15 mi. WSW of Leeds; woolen-, worsted-, and cotton-milling center; carpet, machinery, leather, and chemical industries. Has 15th-cent. church; grammar school founded 1585; Piece Hall built 1779; Akroyd mus. and art gall.; and Renaissance town hall designed by Sir Charles Barry. Defoe is supposed to have written part of *Robinson Crusoe* at the Rose and Crown Inn. Just E of Halifax is 15th-cent. mansion of Shibden Hall, now owned by city. In county borough are mfg. suburbs of Copley (pop. 3,784), Ovenden (pop. 9,070), and Northowram (pop. 3,154).

Halifax. 1 County (□ 722; pop. 58,377), NE N.C.; ⊙ Halifax. Bounded N and E by Roanoke R., S by Fishing Creek. In piedmont agr. (tobacco, peanuts, cotton, corn) and timber area; industry at Roanoke Rapids, Scotland Neck, and Weldon. Formed 1758. **2** County (□ 808; pop. 41,442), S Va.; ⊙ Halifax. Bounded S by N.C., N and E by Roanoke R.; drained by Dan, Banister, and Hyco rivers (hydroelectric plants). A leading Va. tobacco-growing co.; also wheat, corn, livestock. Mfg. at South Boston and Halifax. Formed 1752.

Halifax. 1 Rural town (pop. 944), Plymouth co., SE Mass., 10 mi. WNW of Plymouth. Settled c.1670, inc. 1734. **2** Town (pop. 346), ⊙ Halifax co., NE N.C., 28 mi. NNE of Rocky Mount and on Roanoke R. Site of 1st N.C. constitutional convention (1776). Settled c.1750. **3** Borough (pop. 822), Dauphin co., S central Pa., 14 mi. NNW of Harrisburg and on Susquehanna R.; shoes. **4** Town (pop. 343), Windham co., SE Vt., on Mass. line, 11 mi. SW of Brattleboro. **5** Town (pop. 791), ⊙ Halifax co., S Va., on Banister R. (hydroelectric dam) and 28 mi. ENE of Danville, in agr. area (tobacco, wheat, hay); woolen milling, shoe mfg. Inc. 1875.

Halifax Bay, inlet of Coral Sea, E Queensland, Australia, bet. Lucinda Point (NW) and Magnetic Isl. (SE); 50 mi. long, 15 mi. wide. Palm Isls. at N entrance.

Halifax Harbour, inlet (15 mi. long, 6 mi. wide at entrance) of the Atlantic, S N.S. On W shore is Halifax; on E is Dartmouth. N part of inlet is called Bedford Basin.

Halifax River, narrow lagoon (c.25 mi. long) in Volusia co., NE Fla., sheltered from the Atlantic by barrier beach (site of Daytona Beach and other resorts); extends N from Ponce de Leon Inlet (at N end of Hillsborough R. lagoon). Followed by Intracoastal Waterway.

Halil River (hälēl'), SE Iran, rises in one of Zagros ranges S of Kerman, flows 200 mi. SE, past Sabzawaran, to Jaz Murian salt-lake depression.

Halin (hälēn'), village, SE Br. Somaliland, near Ital. Somaliland border, 100 mi. NE of Las Anod; stock raising.

Halisahar (hä'lĭsŭhŭr), town (pop. 25,804), 24-Parganas dist., SE West Bengal, India, on Hooghly R. and 25 mi. N of Calcutta city center; paper milling. Formerly called Kumarhata.

Haliyal (hŭl'ĭyăl, hŭl'yäl), town (pop. 6,448), Kanara dist., S Bombay, India, 19 mi. WSW of Dharwar; trades in teak, blackwood, bamboo, rice. Br. frontier post in 18th cent. Also spelled Halyal.

Halkett, Cape, N Alaska, on Arctic Ocean, 110 mi. ESE of Barrow; 70°47'N 152°5'W. Eskimo trading post of Cape Halkett is 10 mi. WNW.

Halkirk (hăl'kûrk), village (pop. 121), S central Alta., 23 mi. E of Stettler; coal mining, mixed farming, dairying, wheat.

Halkirk (hôl'kûrk), agr. village and parish (pop. 1,725), N Caithness, Scotland, on Thurso R. and 6 mi. S of Thurso. There are ruins of anc. Brawl Castle, adjoining modern structure.

Halkyn (häl'kĭn), agr. village and parish (pop. 1,288), Flint, Wales, 3 mi. WSW of Flint.

Hall, Austria. **1** City in Tyrol: see SOLBAD HALL IN TIROL. **2** Town in Upper Austria: see BAD HALL.

Hall. 1 County (□ 426; pop. 40,113), NE Ga.; ⊙ Gainesville. Piedmont area drained by Chattahoochee and Oconee rivers. Farming (cotton, corn, hay, sweet potatoes, poultry) and mfg. (textiles, furniture). Formed 1818. **2** County (□ 540; pop. 32,186), S central Nebr.; ⊙ GRAND ISLAND. Agr. and industrial region drained by Platte R. and its branches. Mfg. at Grand Island; grain, livestock, dairy and poultry produce. Formed 1859. **3** County (□ 896; pop. 10,930), NW Texas; ⊙ Memphis. In plains region below Cap Rock escarpment of Llano Estacado; alt. c.1,700 ft.; crossed by Prairie Dog Town Fork of Red R. Agr., chiefly cotton; also grain and sweet sorghums, wheat, potatoes, alfalfa, some fruit and truck; beef and dairy cattle, hogs, sheep, poultry. Formed 1876.

Hall, village (pop. c.150), Granite co., W Mont., on Flint Creek and 55 mi. W of Helena; ships livestock.

Hall, Schwäbisch, Germany: see SCHWÄBISCH HALL.

Halla, Mount (häl'lä'), Korean *Halla-san*, Jap. *Kanra-san*, volcanic peak (6,398 ft.), central Cheju Isl., Korea, 10 mi. S of Cheju; highest peak of isl.; sacred to Buddhists. Formerly sometimes called Mt. Auckland.

Hallabrottet (hĕ'läbrô"tŭt), Swedish *Hällabrottet*, village (pop. 1,043), Orebro co., S central Sweden, 10 mi. S of Orebro; marble and limestone quarries, limeworks.

Halladale, river, Sutherland, Scotland, rises 18 mi. NW of Helmsdale, flows 22 mi. N to the Atlantic 3 mi. E of Strathy.

Hallam. 1 Village (pop. 172), Lancaster co., SE Nebr., 18 mi. S of Lincoln. **2** Borough, Pa.: see HELLAM.

Hallam Peak (10,560 ft.), SE B.C., near Hamber Provincial Park, 55 mi. SW of Jasper: 52°11'N 118°46'W.

Hallamshire (hă'lŭmshĭr), anc. lordship in West Riding, S Yorkshire, England. The boundaries are unknown, but it included the towns of Sheffield and Ecclesfield.

Halland (hä'länd), county [Swedish *län*] (□ 1,901; 1950 pop. 163,363), SW Sweden, on the Kattegat; ⊙ Halmstad. Coextensive with the historical province [Swed. *landskap*] of Halland, conquered from Denmark by Charles X of Sweden in 1658. Low and undulating, drained by Laga, Nissa, and Atra rivers. Fishing, especially for salmon. Rye, oats, flax, and sugar beets are grown. Metalworking industries. Cities are Halmstad, Laholm, Falkenberg, and Varberg.

Hallandale (hă'lŭndāl), town (pop. 3,886), Broward co., S Fla., 15 mi. N of Miami, on Atlantic coast; vegetable-packing houses. Inc. 1927.

Hallaniya or **Hallaniyah** (hăl"lănē'yŭ, häl"–), chief island (□ 22; 1947 pop. c.70) of the Kuria Muria group, off SE Oman; 7½ mi. long, 3½ mi. wide; rises to 1,647 ft.; 17°31'N 56°5'E. Fishing, goat raising. Telegraph station operated here temporarily (1859–60).

Hallaton, agr. village and parish (pop. 423), SE Leicester, England, 7 mi. NNE of Market Harborough. Has church dating from 13th cent. Near by are remains of anc. Br. earthwork called Hallaton Castle.

Hall Basin, channel (40 mi. long, 30 mi. wide) in the Arctic, bet. NE Ellesmere Isl. (Canada) and NW Greenland, joining Robeson Channel (N) with Kennedy Channel (S); part of passage bet. the Atlantic and Lincoln Sea of the Arctic Ocean; 81°30'N 62°30'W.

Hallby (hĕl'bü"), Swedish *Hällby*, residential village (pop. 1,037), Sodermanland co., E Sweden, 3 mi. WNW of Eskilstuna.

Halle, Belgium: see HAL.

Halle (hä'lŭ). **1** or **Halle an der Saale** (än dĕr zä'lŭ), city (pop. 222,505), in former Prussian Saxony prov., central Germany, after 1945 ⊙ Saxony-Anhalt, on the Saxonian Saale and 22 mi. NW of Leipzig, 95 mi. SW of Berlin; 51°29'N 11°59'E. Rail hub; airport (at Schkeuditz, SE). Center of potash-, salt-, and lignite-mining region; sugar refining, paper milling, metalworking, brewing; mfg. of machinery, chemicals, pharmaceuticals, soap, clothing, leather, glass, stationery, chocolate. Has important sugar trade. Power station. Noted univ. (founded 1694) absorbed (1817) Univ. of Wittenberg. Seat of provincial col. of drama and music; and Academia Leopoldina, society for natural sciences. Has 15th-cent. cathedral, 16th-cent. Red Tower, and remains of 15th-cent. Moritzburg, former archiepiscopal castle. N suburb of Giebichenstein has remains of 10th-cent. castle, until 15th cent. a residence of archbishops of Magdeburg; destroyed (1636) in Thirty Years War by Swedes. First of the Francke Institutes (1695) and 1st Bible Society (1710) were founded here. Originally mentioned as Frankish outpost, Halle was given 968 by Otto I to archbishops of Magdeburg, who frequently resided here. Its saline springs contributed to city's rapid commercial growth; was member of Hanseatic League (1281–1478). Passed to Brandenburg under Treaty of Westphalia (1648). Handel b. here. **2** or **Halle in Westfalen** (ĭn vĕst"fä'lŭn), town (pop. 5,204), in former Prussian prov. of Westphalia, NW Germany, after 1945 in North Rhine-Westphalia, on S slope of Teutoburg Forest, 8 mi. NW of Bielefeld; woodworking.

Hallefors (hĕ"lŭfôrs', –fôsh'), Swedish *Hällefors*, village (pop. 3,649), Orebro co., S central Sweden, in Bergslag region, 13 mi. ENE of Filipstad; iron mines, steel mills; lumbering.

Halleforsnas (hĕ"lŭfôrs"nĕs'), Swedish *Hälleforsnäs* village (pop. 1,890), Sodermanland co., E Sweden, 15 mi. S of Eskilstuna; ironworks, foundries.

Hallein (hä'līn), city (pop. 15,319), Salzburg, W Austria, near Ger. border, on river Salzach and 9 mi. S of Salzburg; saltworks, mfg. (tobacco, chemicals, cellulose, textiles), tanneries, breweries; spa. Mus. contains Celtic and Roman antiquities. Has 18th-cent. church of pilgrimage. Salt mines at near-by Dürnberg.

Halle in Westfalen, Germany: see HALLE, Westphalia.

Halle-Merseburg, Germany: see SAXONY, province.

Hallenberg (hä'lŭnbĕrk). **1** Town, Saxony, central Germany: see STEINBACH-HALLENBERG. **2** Town (pop. 2,472), in former Prussian prov. of Westphalia, W Germany, after 1945 in North Rhine-Westphalia, 22 mi. N of Marburg; forestry.

Hallencourt (äläko͞or'), village (pop. 1,214), Somme dept., N France, 8 mi. SSE of Abbeville; jute and linen weaving. Phosphatic limestone working.

Hallett (hă'lĭt), town (pop. 120), Pawnee co., N Okla., 14 mi. ESE of Pawnee; agr. trade center.

Hallettsville (hă'lĭtsvĭl), city (pop. 2,000), ⊙ Lavaca co., S Texas, on Lavaca R. and 17 mi. NE of Yoakum; trade, shipping point in agr. area (poultry, cotton, tomatoes, corn); large poultry-packing plant; cotton gins, cottonseed-oil mill; soft drinks, sheet-metal products.

Hallevik (hĕ"lŭvēk'), Swedish *Hällevik*, fishing village (pop. 636), Blekinge co., S Sweden, on S shore of Listerland peninsula, on the Baltic, 4 mi. SE of Solvesborg; seaside resort.

Halleviksstrand (hĕ"lŭvēks"stränd'), Swedish *Hälleviksstrand*, fishing village (pop. 302), Goteborg och Bohus co., SW Sweden, on W coast of Orust isl., on the Skagerrak, 10 mi. S of Lysekil; seaside resort.

Halley (hă'lē), town (pop. 149), Desha co., SE Ark., 6 mi. E of Dermott, near Mississippi R.

Halliday, village (pop. 477), Dunn co., W central N.Dak., 38 mi. NNE of Dickinson and on Spring Creek.

Hallig Islands (hä'lĭg), Ger. *Die Halligen* (dē hä'lĭgŭn), island group of the North Frisian group, NW Germany, in the North Sea, off Schleswig-Holstein coast. There are 11 isls., including NORDSTRAND, PELLWORM, Nordmarsch-Langeness, and Hooge. Rising barely above sea level, and often submerged during storms, isls. are noted for excellent pastures. Houses are built on piles.

Hallikhed, India: see ALIKHER.

Halling (hô'lĭng), town and parish (pop. 2,173), N Kent, England, on Medway R. and 4 mi. SW of Rochester; agr. market. Has 13th-cent. church. An Ice Age human skeleton found here, is of anthropological interest.

Hallingdal (häl'lĭngdäl), valley (70 mi. long) of Hallingdal R., upper course of DRAMMEN RIVER, Buskerud co., S Norway; extends ENE from S slope of Hallingskarv mts. to Gol, then SSE to the lake Kroderen. The Hardangervidda rises on W side of valley. Important barley- and oat-growing region; stock raising, lumbering. Main villages are Nesbyen, Geilo, Hol, Al, Gol, and Fla. There are several anc. stave churches. Valley is noted for its peasants' customs and dances.

Hallingskarv (häl'lĭngskärv), Nor. *Hallingskarvet*, mountain range in Buskerud, Hordaland, and Sogn og Fjordane counties, S Norway; forms NE section of the Hardangerfjell; extends E–W c.60 mi.; rises to 6,342 ft. in the Folarskarnuten, 10 mi. E of Finse. Tourist area.

Hall Island (6 mi. long, 2 mi. wide), W Alaska, in Bering Sea, 3 mi. NW of St. Matthew Isl., 180 mi. WNW of Nunivak Isl.; 60°33'N 172°42'W. Rugged and uninhabited, isl. rises to 1,500 ft.

Hall Island. 1 In SE Franklin Dist., Northwest Territories, in the Gulf of Boothia, near W entrance of Fury and Hecla Strait, off NW Baffin Isl.; 70°N 87°W; 40 mi. long, 6 mi. wide. **2** In SE Franklin Dist., Northwest Territories, in the Atlantic, off Hall Peninsula, SE Baffin Isl.; 62°32'N 64°10'W; 6 mi. long.

Hall Island, Gilbert Isls.: see MAIANA.

Hall Island, in S Franz Josef Land, Russian SFSR, in Arctic Ocean, E of MacClintock Isl.; separated from Wilczek Land (NE) by Austrian Sound; 25 mi. long, 25 mi. wide.

Hall Islands, group, E Caroline Isls., W Pacific, c. 70 mi. N of Truk; include NOMWIN and MURILO atolls.

Hall Lake, N.Mex.: see ELEPHANT BUTTE DAM.

Hall Land, region, NW Greenland, on Hall Basin, opposite Ellesmere Isl.; 81°30'N 61°W. Covered by inland icecap except for coastal strip 3–25 mi. wide; includes Petermann Glacier (S). On coast is POLARIS BAY.

Hallmundarhraun, Iceland: see EIRIKSJOKULL.

Hallnas (hĕl'nĕs"), Swedish *Hällnäs*, village (pop. 585), Vasterbotten co., N Sweden, on Vindel R. and 40 mi. NW of Umea; rail junction; stock raising, dairying. Site of sanitarium.

Hallock, village (pop. 1,552), ⊙ Kittson co., extreme NW Minn., on Two Rivers, near Man. line, and c.60 mi. N of Grand Forks, N.Dak., in grain, potato, and livestock area; dairy products. Hunting and fishing in vicinity. Platted 1879, inc. 1887.

Hallouf, Djebel, Tunisia: see SOUK-EL-KHEMIS.

Hallowell (hŏl'ōwĕl, -lùwùl), city (pop. 3,404), Kennebec co., S Maine, on the Kennebec just below Augusta. Boatbuilding, mfg. (shoes, wood and metal products); Hallowell granite used for state capitol. Settled c.1754; town inc. 1771, including present Augusta; city inc. 1850.

Hall Peninsula, SE Baffin Isl., SE Franklin Dist., Northwest Territories, extends 150 mi. SE into Davis Strait, bet. Cumberland Sound and Frobisher Bay; 100 mi. wide at base. SE extremity is Blunt Peninsula; 62°40'N 65°10'W. Frobisher Bay trading post on S shore.

Halls, town (pop. 1,808), Lauderdale co., W Tenn., 10 mi. S of Dyersburg; shipping point for timber and cotton-growing area.

Hallsberg (häls'bĕr"yù), town (pop. 3,575), Orebro co., S central Sweden, 14 mi. SSW of Orebro; rail junction; metalworking, tanning, shoe mfg.

Hallsboro, lumber-milling village, Columbus co., SE N.C., 6 mi. E of Whiteville, near L. Waccamaw.

Halls Corners, village (pop. 254), Trumbull co., NE Ohio.

Hall's Creek, village, NE Western Australia, 190 mi. S of Wyndham; mining center of Kimberley Goldfield.

Hall's Stream, N.H., Vt., and Que., rises in NW N.H., flows c.20 mi. SSW to the Connecticut at Canaan, Vt.; forms international line above Beecher Falls, Vt.

Hallsta, Sweden: see NORRLAND.

Hallstahammar (häl"stähä'mär), town (pop. 6,324), Vastmanland co., central Sweden, on Kolback R. and 10 mi. W of Vasteras; steel milling; mfg. of machine tools, electrical equipment, bricks.

Hallstatt (häl'shtät), village (pop. 1,494), S Upper Austria, in the Salzkammergut, on SW shore of L. of Hallstatt and 10 mi. S of Bad Ischl; saltworks (mines near by); wood carving. In mid-19th cent. a near-by cemetery yielded prehistoric, perhaps Celtic, remains which have given its name to the Hallstatt epoch of the Iron Age.

Hallstatt, Lake of, Ger. *Hallstättersee* (häl'shtĕtùrzā"), S Upper Austria, in the Salzkammergut, 7 mi. S of Bad Ischl; 5 mi. long, 1 mi. wide, max. depth 410 ft., alt. 1,620 ft.; beautiful alpine scenery. Hallstatt on SW, Steeg on NW shore.

Hallstavik-Haverodal (häl"stävēk'-hē"vùrû"däl'), Swedish *Hallstavik-Häverödal*, village (pop. 2,822), Stockholm co., E Sweden, on small bay of Gulf of Bothnia, 35 mi. ENE of Uppsala; seaport; pulp and paper-milling center. Has 13th-cent. church.

Hallstead, residential borough (pop. 1,445), Susquehanna co., NE Pa., on Susquehanna R. and 13 mi. SE of Binghamton, N.Y.; furnaces, boxes, meat products. Founded 1787, inc. 1874.

Hallsville. **1** Town (pop. 225), Boone co., central Mo., 13 mi. NNE of Columbia. **2** Town (pop. 617), Harrison co., E Texas, 12 mi. W of Marshall, near Sabine R.; rail point in agr. area.

Halltown, town (pop. 99), Lawrence co., SW Mo., in the Ozarks, 18 mi. W of Springfield; state park near by.

Halluin (älwĕ'), town (pop. 10,340), Nord dept., N France, customs station on Belg. border opposite Menin, 5 mi. NNW of Tourcoing near Lys R.; important textile center (linen and cotton cloth, rugs). Other mfg. (chemicals, beer, furniture, cement, wallpaper, biscuits).

Hallwilersee (häl'vēlùrzä"), lake, N Switzerland, bordering on Lucerne and Aargau cantons, traversed by Aa R.; 5 mi. long, □ 4, alt. 1,473 ft., max. depth 145 ft. Hallwil hamlet and castle (9th cent.) are N.

Hallwood, village (pop. c.400), Accomack co., E Va., 13 mi. S of Pocomoke City, Md., in truck-farm area; vegetable canning.

Halma, village (pop. 177), Kittson co., NW Minn., 18 mi. SE of Hallock, in Red R. valley; dairy products.

Halmagiu (hûl'mäjōō), Rum. *Hălmagiu*, Hung. *Nagyhalmágy* (nŏ'dyùhŏl"mädyù), village (pop. 1,146), Arad prov., W Rumania, on White Körös R., on railroad and 60 mi. ENE of Arad; lumbering and agr. center. Near-by Gaina (gû'ēnä) is noted for picturesque peasant costumes, as well as for traditional yearly fairs at which marriageable girls of the district offer themselves for bids to prospective husbands.

Halmahera (hälmùhĕ'rù), largest island (□ c.6,870; pop. 75,910) of the Moluccas, Indonesia, c.150 mi. E of Celebes across Molucca Passage; 2°14'N–0°56'S 127°21'–128°53'E. Shaped roughly like Celebes Isl. Consists of 4 peninsulas (largest being c.100 mi. long, c.40 mi. wide) separated by 3 deep bays. Largely wooded and mountainous, rising to 4,948 ft., with narrow coastal plain. Has several active volcanoes. Chief products: nutmeg, ironwood, resin, sago, rice, tobacco, coconuts. Its outport is Ternate on small TERNATE isl. just off W coast. There are anchorages at Jailolo or Djailolo (jīlō'lō), on W coast, and at Weda on SE coast. Halmahera accepted Du. sovereignty in 1683. In Second World War isl. was Jap. air base; after Allied conquest of New Guinea it was heavily bombed (1944), forcing Jap. withdrawal. Also spelled Halmaheira or Halmahaira; also called Jailolo, Djailolo, Jilolo, or Gilolo.

Halmeu (häl'mĕōō), Hung. *Halmi* (hŏl'mē), village (pop. 4,051), Baia-Mare prov., N Rumania, customs station on USSR border, on railroad and 12 mi. NNE of Satu-Mare; mfg. of alcohol, yeast, flour. In Hungary, 1940–45.

Halmstad (hälm'städ"), city (1950 pop. 35,276), ⊙ Halland co., SW Sweden, on Laholm Bay (Kattegat), at mouth of Nissa R., 70 mi. SSE of Goteborg; 56°41'N 12°52'E; seaport, rail junction, and industrial center, with textile, pulp, and paper mills; mfg. of machinery, bicycles, gloves. Stone quarries near by. Has 14th-cent. church, 15th-cent. castle, and several museums. Chartered 1322; medieval fortifications demolished in 18th cent. Bathing beach near by.

Halmundarhraun, Iceland: see EIRIKSJOKULL.

Halmyros or **Almiros** (both: älmĭrôs'), town (pop. 7,073), Magnesia nome, SE Thessaly, Greece, near Gulf of Volos, 16 mi. SW of Volos; trades in tobacco, almonds, olives. Chromite mining 10 mi. NW. Also spelled Almyros.

Halogaland, Norway: see HELGELAND.

Halol (hä'lōl), town (pop. 6,308), Panch Mahals dist., N Bombay, India, 20 mi. SSW of Godhra; trades in grain, timber, hardware, tobacco, cotton cloth; markets corn, wheat, millet; sawmills; cotton ginning.

Halong Bay, Tonkin: see ALONG BAY.

Halonnesos or **Alonnisos** (both: ülô'nĭsôs), Aegean island (□ 24; pop. 1,386), in the Northern Sporades, Magnesia nome, Greece, 26 mi. off Thessalian mainland, separated from Skopelos isl. (W) by Strait of Halonnesos; 39°14'N 23°54'E; 12 mi. long, 2 mi. wide. Fisheries; sheep and goat raising. Town and port of Halonnesos is at SW end. Sometimes spelled Halonnisos. Isl. is also called Chiliodromia (Khiliodhromia) and Iliodromia (Iliodhromia).

Hals (häls), town (pop. 1,496) and port, Aalborg amt, N Jutland, Denmark, at E entrance of Lim Fjord, 15 mi. E of Aalborg; fisheries, meat packing.

Halsa (häl'sä), village and canton (pop. 1,307), More og Romsdal co., W Norway, near mouth of Halse Fjord, 16 mi. E of Kristiansund. Tannery, sawmills near by. Formerly spelled Halse.

Halsall (hôl'sùl), agr. village and parish (pop. 1,774), SW Lancashire, England, 5 mi. SSE of Southport.

Halsbrücke (häls'brü"kù), village (pop. 2,353), Saxony, E central Germany, at N foot of the Erzgebirge, 3 mi. N of Freiberg; mining (lead, tin, zinc, nickel).

Halse, village, Norway: see HALSA.

Halse Fjord (häl'sù), inlet of North Sea, in More og Romsdal co., W Norway, E of Kristiansund, and extending SE c.30 mi. to Todalen. On it are Halsa and Stangvik.

Halsenoy, Norway: see HALSNOY.

Halsey (hôl'sē), city (pop. 388), Linn co., W Oregon, 17 mi. S of Albany, near Willamette R. in dairying, livestock, and agr. area (grain, fruit).

Halsingborg (hĕl"sĭngbôr'yù), Swedish *Hälsingborg*, city (1950 pop. 71,718), Malmohus co., S Sweden, port on the Oresund, 30 mi. NNW of Malmo; 56°3'N 12°42'E. Terminus of train ferry to Helsingor, Denmark (Oslo-Copenhagen main line). Commercial and industrial center, with shipyards and copper, machinery, brick, and fertilizer works; woolen and paper mills, sugar refineries, breweries. Has 13th-cent. church; 12th-cent. tower is sole remains of anc. fortifications. Founded in early Middle Ages, city was ceded 1658 to Sweden by Denmark, seized and plundered by Danes 1676, regained by Sweden 1710. To NE is coal-mining region; clay found near by is used in local potteries. Formerly also spelled Helsingborg.

Halsingland (hĕl'sĭng-länd"), Swed. *Hälsingland*, historic province [Swed. *landskap*] (□ 5,933; pop. 155,006), E central Sweden, included largely in Gavleborg co.

Halsnoy (häl'sùn-ûi), Nor. *Halsnøy*, island (□ 15; pop. 1,486) in Hardanger Fjord, Hordaland co., SW Norway, 30 mi. NNE of Haugesund; 9 mi. long, 5 mi. wide. Fisheries and canneries at villages of Saebovik (sä'bùvĭk) (Nor. *Sæbøvik*) in W, and Toftevag (tôf'tùvôg) (Nor. *Toftevåg*) in N, both in Fjelberg canton (pop. 2,115). On a NW peninsula are remains of medieval Augustinian abbey. Formerly spelled Halsenoy or Haalsnoy.

Halso (häls'û), Swedish *Halsö*, fishing village (pop. 568), Goteborg och Bohus co., SW Sweden, on isl. (309 acres) of Halso in the Skagerrak, 12 mi. WNW of Goteborg; shipbuilding.

Halstad (hŏl'städ"), village (pop. 635), Norman co., NW Minn., on Red R. and 32 mi. N of Fargo, N. Dak., in agr. area (grain, potatoes, livestock poultry); dairy products.

Halstead (hôl'-, hăl'-), urban district (1931 pop. 5,883; 1951 census 5,995), N Essex, England, on Colne R. and 12 mi. WNW of Colchester; agr. market, with tanneries, artificial-silk mills, flour mills. Has 15th-cent. church.

Halstead (hôl'stĭd), city (pop. 1,328), Harvey co., S central Kansas, on Little Arkansas R. and 23 mi. NNW of Wichita; market and shipping point for wheat and livestock region; flour milling. Founded 1873, inc. 1877.

Halstenbek (häl'stùnbāk), village (pop. 6,080), in Schleswig-Holstein, NW Germany, 2 mi. SE of Pinneberg, in region noted for tree nurseries; rubber mfg., woodworking.

Halsteren (häl'stùrùn), village (pop. 1,706), North Brabant prov., SW Netherlands, 2.5 mi. NNW of Bergen op Zoom; mfg. of drainage pipes; agr.

Halswell (hălz'wùl), village (pop. 1,008), ⊙ Halswell co. (□ 40; pop. 2,056), E S.Isl., New Zealand, 7 mi. SW of Christchurch; limestone quarry.

Haltdalen (hält'dälùn), village and canton (pop. 1,069), Sor-Trondelag co., central Norway, on Gaula R., on railroad and 42 mi. SE of Trondheim; cattle raising, lumbering; sawmilling. Formerly spelled Holtaalen. Originally called Holtdalr.

Haltemprice (hô'tùmprīz), urban district (1951 census 35,649), East Riding, Yorkshire, England, 4 mi. NW of Hull; residential and industrial suburb.

Halten, Norway: see FRO ISLANDS.

Haltern (häl'tùrn), town (pop. 10,003), in former Prussian prov. of Westphalia, W Germany, after 1945 in North Rhine-Westphalia, in the Ruhr, on canalized Lippe R. and 9 mi. N of Recklinghausen; rail junction; metalworking.

Haltia, Mount, Finnish *Haltiatunturi* (häl'tēätōōn"-tōōrē), Swedish *Haldefjäll* (häl'dùfyĕl"), Nor. *Reisduoddarhaldde* (rās'dwôdärhäl"dù), highest peak (4,343 ft.) of Finland, at NW extremity of country, in Lapland, on Norwegian border; 69°17'N 21°15'E.

Haltom City, town (pop. 5,760), Tarrant co., N Texas, NE suburb of Fort Worth. Inc. after 1940.

Halton, county (□ 363; pop. 28,515), S Ont., on L. Ontario; ⊙ Milton West.

Halton (hôl'tùn). **1** Town and parish (pop. 3,332), central Buckingham, England, 4 mi. SE of Aylesbury; agr. market. Site of Royal Air Force station. **2** Town (pop. 2,968) in Runcorn urban dist., N Cheshire, England; leather tanning.

Haltwhistle, town and parish (pop. 4,193), SW Northumberland, England, on South Tyne R. and 14 mi. W of Hexham; coal mining; paint works; agr. market. Near by are Featherstonehaugh Castle and Unthank Hall (Bishop Ridley b. here).

Halun-Arshan, Manchuria: see WENCHÜAN.

Halutsa (hälōō'tsä), agr. settlement, S Israel, in the Negev, 16 mi. S of Beersheba. On Negev water pipe line. Formerly called Bir 'Asluj (bĕr'äslōōj'), it was evacuated by Arab pop., 1948, and became Egyptian army base. In Byzantine times site of a church.

Halvad (hŭl'vŭd), town (pop. 7,091), N Saurashtra, India, 38 mi. NW of Wadhwan; rail terminus; local market for cotton, millet, salt; hand-loom weaving. Has fine palace built on small lake.

Halver (häl'vùr), town (pop. 11,989), in former Prussian prov. of Westphalia, W Germany, after 1945 in North Rhine-Westphalia, 6 mi. WSW of Lüdenscheid; ironworks.

Halyal, India: see HALIYAL.

Halycus, Sicily: see PLATANI RIVER.

Halycyae, Sicily: see SALEMI.

Halys River, Turkey: see KIZIL IRMAK.

Ham. **1** Cities, Essex, England: see EAST HAM and WEST HAM. **2** Residential former urban district (1931 pop. 2,206), N Surrey, England, 2 mi. NW of Kingston-on-Thames; automobile works. Near by is a 16th-cent. mansion. Inc. 1933 in Richmond.

Ham (häm), town (pop. 3,077), Somme dept., N France, on the Somme (canalized) and 12 mi. SW of Saint-Quentin; road center. Metalworking (wire drawing, mfg. of bakery equipment and metal plumbing fixtures), sugar milling, canning. Its 15th-cent. castle (state prison famed for detention and escape [1846] of Louis Napoleon) is now in ruins. Ham changed hands several times in First World War, was rebuilt and again damaged in 1939–45.

Hama (hä'mä). **1** Town, Kumamoto prefecture, Japan: see HAMA-MACHI. **2** Town (pop. 5,541), Saga prefecture, NW Kyushu, Japan, on E Hizen Peninsula, on Ariakeno-umi and 15 mi. SW of Saga; agr. center; mulberry trees.

Hama or **Hamah** (hä'mä, hämä'), province (□ 2,314; 1946 pop. 167,714), W Syria; ⊙ HAMA. Mainly desert except for the area in the vicinity of Hama which is irrigated by the Orontes; cotton, corn, millet, oranges, apples, pears, apricots. Main urban centers: Hama, Kafr Behum, Qumkhane, Selemiya.

Hama or **Hamah**, town (pop. c.70,000), ⊙ Hama prov., W Syria, bisected by the Orontes, on railroad, and 115 mi. NNE of Damascus; alt. 1,100 ft. Agr. center (cotton, cereals, fruit); tanning, weaving. Famed for its beautiful gardens irrigated by huge water wheels (90 ft. in diameter). A very old city, it was a center of the Hittites. As *Hamath*, it is mentioned often in the Bible and is called N boundary of Israel. Passed to Assyrians (9th cent. B.C.), Persians, Alexander the Great, and the

Seleucids. Renamed *Epiphania* by Antiochus IV (Antiochus Epiphanes), Hama was later under Rome and Byzantine Empire, and in 7th cent. was taken by the Arabs. Crusaders held it briefly; later passed to Turks. The learned prince Abu-l-Fida ruled it early in 14th cent. Despite Islamic rule, Christianity persisted in the city. Hama was formerly known for its silk, woolen, and cotton goods.

Hamaapil, Israel: see HAM MAAPIL.

Hamad, SW Asia: see SYRIAN DESERT.

Hamada (hä″mä′dä), city (1940 pop. 32,230; 1947 pop. 39,585), Shimane prefecture, SW Honshu, Japan, on Sea of Japan, 40 mi. NW of Hiroshima; major fishing port; fish canneries, spinning and textile mills; charcoal. Site of feudal castle.

Hamada el Homra, Libya: see HAMMADA EL HAMRA.

Hamadan (hă′mŭdăn, Persian hämädän′), city (1940 pop. 103,874), Fifth Prov., W Iran, 175 mi. WSW of Teheran, and on highway to Kermanshah, at N foot of the Alwand; alt. 6,000 ft.; 34°47′N 48°21′E. Major trade center of W Iran and chief city of former Hamadan prov.; leather goods, rugs, matches, wool, flour, alcohol. Noted for its copper work. Among its notable bldgs. are the tomb of Avicenna (died here 1037), the reputed sepulchers of Esther and Mordecai, and the great mosque Masjid-i-Jama adjoining the large market square. In S outskirts is the hill Musallah, with citadel (ruined in 18th cent.) and a large overturned stone lion, remainder of 10th-cent. gate. Pop. is Turkish, Persian, Jewish, and Armenian. The biblical *Achmetha* and anc. *Ecbatana,* it was ⊙ Media and, after its capture (550 B.C.) by Cyrus, the summer residence of the Achaemenian Persian Empire. Its royal treasury was plundered by Alexander the Great, who captured city in 330 B.C., and later by Seleucus and Antiochus III. The city passed to the Arabs in A.D. 645. It was stormed by Tamerlane; and Agha Mohammed Khan, founder of the Kajar dynasty, destroyed all anc. remains in late-18th cent. The small prov. of Hamadan became part (1938) of Iran's Fifth Prov. (see KERMANSHAH).

Hamadera, Japan: see SAKAI, Osaka prefecture.

Hamajima (hämä′jĭmä) or **Hamashima** (–shĭmä), town (pop. 6,353), Mie prefecture, S Honshu, Japan, port on Ago Bay, 14 mi. S of Uji-yamada; fishing; rice, tea, poultry, raw silk.

Hamam, Turkey: see HAYMANA.

Hama-machi (hä′mä-mächē) or **Hama,** town (pop. 6,561), Kumamoto prefecture, W central Kyushu, Japan, 18 mi. SE of Kumamoto; commercial center in agr. area; sake, tea.

Hamamatsu (hämä′mätsōō), city (1940 pop. 166,-346; 1947 pop. 125,767), Shizuoka prefecture, central Honshu, Japan, on Philippine Sea, 42 mi. WSW of Shizuoka; transportation center; mfg. (textiles, musical instruments, woodwork); chemical plants. Bombed (1945) in Second World War.

Hamana, Lake (hä″mä′nä), Jap. *Hamana-ko,* lagoon (□ 28), Shizuoka prefecture, central Honshu, Japan, 5 mi. W of Hamamatsu; connected with Philippine Sea by narrow, shallow outlet; 8 mi. long, 5 mi. wide; many small coves. Fish hatcheries and resorts on shores. Excursion boats.

Hamanaka (hämä′näkä). **1** Fishing village (pop. 9,822), SE Hokkaido, Japan, on the Pacific, 27 mi. WSW of Nemuro. **2** Town, Wakayama prefecture, Japan: see SHIMOTSU.

Hamar (hä′mär), city (pop. 10,183), ⊙ Hedmark co., SE Norway, on E shore of L. Mjosa and 60 mi. N of Oslo; 60°47′N 11°4′E. Rail junction and center of one of Norway's richest agr. regions. Mfg. of locomotives, agr. machinery, building materials, condensed milk, shoes, leather goods, soap; metalworking. Site of Norwegian state archives. Has folk mus., railroad mus., and remains of 12th-cent. cathedral and bishops' palace. Hamar was founded 1152 by Nicholas Breakspear (later Pope Adrian IV) and is now a Lutheran see. City was destroyed by Swedes in 1567; the modern city dates from 1848.

Hamarat el Sheikh, Anglo-Egyptian Sudan: see HAMRA ESH SHEIKH.

Hamasa, Indonesia: see TANAHMASA.

Hamasaka (hämä′säkä), town (pop. 7,455), Hyogo prefecture, S Honshu, Japan, on Sea of Japan, 15 mi. NE of Tottori, in agr. area (rice, wheat, fruit, flowers); woodworking; straw products.

Hamasaki (hämä′säkē), town (pop. 6,716), Saga prefecture, NW Kyushu, Japan, on N Hizen Peninsula, on Genkai Sea, 20 mi. NW of Saga; agr. center (rice, wheat); raw silk.

Hamashima, Japan: see HAMAJIMA.

Hamasien, Eritrea: see ASMARA.

Hambach (häm′bäkh), village (pop. 3,274), Rhenish Palatinate, W Germany, on E slope of Hardt Mts., 1.5 mi. S of Neustadt; chestnuts. Ruins of 11th-cent. castle were scene (1832) of Ger. Liberal meeting known as Hambacher Fest.

Hambantota (hŭmbŭntō′tŭ), town (pop. 3,966), ⊙ Hambantota dist. (□ 1,013; pop., including estate pop., 149,848), Southern Prov., Ceylon, on S coast, 65 mi. E of Galle; coconut palms. Meteorological observatory. Major govt. salterns of Ceylon, consisting of natural depressions called *lewayas,* here. Pop. largely Malays. Cotton growing has been successfully introduced into dist.

Hamberg, village (pop. 124), Wells co., central N.Dak., 10 mi. NNE of Fessenden.

Hambergen (häm′bĕr″gŭn), village (pop. 3,626), in former Prussian prov. of Hanover, NW Germany, after 1945 in Lower Saxony, 15 mi. N of Bremen; flour milling.

Hamber Provincial Park (□ 3,800), SE B.C., on Alta. border, in the Rocky and Selkirk mts., NE of Revelstoke; extends along upper reaches of the Columbia R. and borders on Jasper and Banff natl. parks. Peaks over 10,000 ft. high include mts. Sir Sanford, Laussedat, Mummery, Bryce, Shackleton, Iconoclast, Adamant, Ghost. Numerous small headwaters of Columbia R. rise here.

Hamble, town in parish of Hamble-le-Rice (pop. 1,203), S Hampshire, England, on Southampton Water at mouth of Hamble R. estuary, 5 mi. SE of Southampton; aircraft works. Site of marine training school. Has 14th-15th-cent. church.

Hambleden (hăm′bŏldŭn), agr. village and parish (pop. 1,331), SW Buckingham, England, near the Thames, 3 mi. NNE of Henley-on-Thames; flour milling. Has 14th-cent. church.

Hambledon. 1 Town and parish (pop. 2,288), SE Hampshire, England, 10 mi. N of Portsmouth; agr. market. Church dates from 13th cent. **2** Agr. village and parish (pop. 1,156), SW Surrey, England, 7 mi. SSW of Guildford. Large sanitarium here.

Hamblen (hăm′blĭn), county (□ 174; pop. 23,976), NE Tenn.; ⊙ Morristown. In Great Appalachian Valley region; Bays Mtn. along SE border. Bounded N by Cherokee Reservoir (Holston R.), S by Nolichucky R. Agr. (tobacco, corn, potatoes, truck, poultry, dairy products, livestock). Mfg. at Morristown. Formed 1870.

Hamble River, Hampshire, England, rises 5 mi. N of Fareham, flows 9 mi. SSW, past Botley and Hamble, to Southampton Water just S of Hamble.

Hambleton, town (pop. 283), Tucker co., NE W. Va., just SE of Parsons.

Hamborn (häm′bôrn), industrial outer suburb (1925 pop. 126,618) of DUISBURG, W Germany, on right bank of the Rhine and 5 mi. N of city center, adjoining (N) Ruhrort and Meiderich; blast furnaces, steel mills; zinc refining; coal mining. Commune until 1911, when it inc. numerous suburbs and was chartered. Inc. 1929 into Duisburg, which was subsequently called Duisburg-Hamborn until 1935.

Hamburg (hăm′bûrg), officially the "free Hansa city of Hamburg," in Ger. *Hansestadt Hamburg* (hän′zŭ-shtät häm′bŏŏrk), city and state (□ 288; 1939 pop. 1,711,877; 1946 pop. 1,424,136; 1950 pop. 1,604,600), NW Germany, 150 mi. NW of Berlin, surrounded by Lower Saxony and Schleswig-Holstein; 53°33′N 10°E. Germany's largest port and 2d-largest city, at head of Elbe R. estuary, 55 mi. SE of its mouth on the North Sea, at meeting point of ocean-going and inland navigation. The Elbe here divides into 2 arms: the Norderelbe (on which Hamburg proper is situated) and the Süderelbe, connected by several canals; maze of isls. bet. the arms is occupied primarily by docks and shipyards. Harbor installations extend 6 mi. W from mouth of Bille R., covering an area of 27 sq. mi., with c.160 mi. of shore line; outer port at CUXHAVEN. Overseas traffic is concentrated in large free-port area, opposite SANKT PAULI dist. and connected with city by tunnel under the Norderelbe; area is bordered by basins devoted to inland navigation. Oldest harbor basins, devoted to inter-European ocean trade, are on right bank of the Norderelbe, bet. mouths of Alster (W) and Bille (E) rivers, bordering oldest part of Hamburg. Imports and exports are highly diversified; Harburg (on left bank of the Süderelbe) deals primarily in raw materials; ALTONA is fishing harbor. The Kiel Canal, entering Elbe R. estuary c.40 mi. NW, and Elbe-Trave Canal, entering the Elbe 25 mi. ESE, afford direct water connection with Baltic ports of Kiel and Lübeck, respectively. As an industrial center, Hamburg concentrates on the production of semifinished goods, which are shipped both overseas and to city's vast hinterland. Leading industries are shipbuilding (greatly curtailed after Second World War), food processing, metal smelting (especially copper); also mfg. of rubber (at HARBURG-WILHELMSBURG), tobacco products, chemicals, and textiles. Intensive truck farming is carried on in outer rural dists. (VIERLANDE). Until early-19th cent., Hamburg city consisted of historic Old City (E) and 17th-cent. New City (W), separated by canalized ALSTER RIVER and surrounded by fortifications. The disastrous fire of 1842, which destroyed about ⅓ of the inner city, and consequent rebuilding according to modern plans account for the lack of historic bldgs. and medieval architecture. The only 2 churches to survive the great fire—the 14th-cent. St. Katharinen and St. Jacobi—were heavily damaged in Second World War, as were the churches of St. Michaelis (1st built 1648–58), St. Petri (founded in 12th cent.), and St. Nicolai (founded c.1200), and the 19th-cent. Exchange. The imposing town hall (1886–97) and the noted Chilehaus (20th-cent. office bldg.) are intact. Inner city is the commercial quarter; fashionable life centers around Binnenalster basin of dammed Alster R. After the fortifications were razed (1820–33) and replaced by tree-lined avenues along which many public bldgs. (court houses, marine observatory, central post office and railroad station, concert hall) are located, Hamburg rapidly expanded. Residential dists. developed around the Aussenalster basin (N) and towards the NE: BARMBECK, EPPENDORF, HARVESTEHUDE, ROTHERBAUM (site of univ.), WINTERHUDE; EILBECK (E) and EIMSBÜTTEL (W) were absorbed in 1894, BLANKENESE in 1929. Airport at N outer dist. of FUHLSBÜTTEL; central cemetery at OHLSDORF (NNE); Stellingen (NW) is site of world-renowned Hagenbeck zoo. Sailors' dist. of Sankt Pauli (adjoining the New City) crowded against Altona (W) until the latter, together with BERGEDORF (E), Harburg-Wilhelmsburg (S), WANDSBEK (NE), and other communities, was inc. 1938 into city, and Greater Hamburg emerged. In early-9th cent., Charlemagne captured the castle Hammaburg, where, in 831, Louis the Pious founded a bishopric. Raised in 834 to archbishopric, see was transferred to Bremen in 845. A duke of Holstein gave impetus to the secular development of Hamburg by founding (1188) a town next to the old cathedral (razed 1805). In 1241, Hamburg concluded a protective commercial treaty with Lübeck, out of which the powerful Hanseatic League grew. With the discovery of America and the opening of sea routes to India, the balance of trade shifted from Lübeck to Hamburg, which was created a free imperial city in 1510 and soon afterward accepted the Reformation. The 1st Ger. exchange was opened here in 1558; the arrival of English cloth merchants (expelled from Antwerp), Dutch Protestants, and Portuguese Jews added to the city's prosperity. In early-17th cent., Hamburg was surrounded by a new ring of fortifications, and for over a century successfully defended its trading supremacy against Denmark. The Napoleonic Wars and the ensuing Continental Blockade dealt a severe blow to ocean trade, but after 1815 Hamburg's development as an international port began. Razing of the fortifications was begun in 1820; in 1847 the HAPAG shipping company was founded; bet. 1870–90 lines were opened to all parts of the world and the building of a free port was started. The "free and Hansa city" of Hamburg joined (1871) the German Empire and later the Weimar Republic. A univ. was founded in 1919. The treaties following the First World War arrested Hamburg's continuing growth for only a short time; in the 1930s the city was one of the 5 leading ports of the world, with huge shipyards lining the Elbe shores. The law creating Greater Hamburg was passed 1937 (operative 1938), and Cuxhaven and 7 villages were given up in exchange for over 30 Prussian communities. Heavily damaged in Second World War (destruction about 50%), with much loss of life. Hamburg was occupied by Br. troops in May, 1945. It was inc. as a state into Br. occupation zone and joined (1949) the German Federal Republic (the West German state). Brahms and Felix Mendelssohn b. here.

Hamburg. 1 Town (pop. 2,655), ⊙ Ashley co., SE Ark., c.50 mi. E of El Dorado, in lumbering (pine, oak) and agr. area (cotton, corn, hay); sawmilling, cotton ginning. State game refuge near by. **2** Village, Conn.: see LYME. **3** Village (pop. 225), Calhoun co., W Ill., on the Mississippi (ferry) and 35 mi. NW of Alton; apple growing. **4** City (pop. 2,086), Fremont co., extreme SW Iowa, on Nishnabotna R., near Mo. line, and 18 mi. SW of Shenandoah; mfg. (beverages, feed, brick); has large nursery. Inc. 1867. **5** Village (pop. 184), Carver co., S Minn., c.40 mi. WSW of Minneapolis; dairy products. **6** Village (1940 pop. 102), Franklin co., SW Miss., 20 mi. E of Natchez. **7** Borough (pop. 1,305), Sussex co., NW N.J., on Wallkill R. just N of Franklin; mfg. (wire, paper); dairying. "Gingerbread Castle" here has scenes from various fairy tales. Inc. 1920. **8** Industrial village (pop. 6,938), Erie co., W N.Y., 12 mi. S of Buffalo, near L. Erie, in truck-farming region; mfg. (baskets, canned foods, metal and wood products, lenses, aircraft parts). Summer resort. Holds annual co. fair. Settled c.1808 by Germans; inc. 1874. **9** Borough (pop. 3,805), Berks co., E central Pa., 15 mi. NNW of Reading and on Schuylkill R.; mfg. (clothing, metal products); agr. Founded 1779, inc. 1837. **10** Village, Aiken co., W S.C., on Savannah R. opposite Augusta, Ga. Founded as W terminus of state's 1st railroad, completed 1833 to Charleston. **11** Village (pop. c.100), Marathon co., central Wis., 14 mi. NW of Wausau; silver-fox ranch.

Hambye (äbē′), village (pop. 322), Manche dept., NW France, 10 mi. SE of Coutances; livestock. Has ruins of Benedictine abbey founded c.1145.

Hamden. 1 Town (pop. 29,715), New Haven co., S Conn., just N of New Haven. Residential, with mfg. (hardware, lighting fixtures, firearms, fishing tackle, furniture, tools, metal and wire products, brick, tile, concrete blocks, elastic webbing), agr. (fruit, truck). Includes Mount Carmel (kär′mŭl) village, near Sleeping Giant or Mt. Carmel, in Sleeping Giant State Park. Site of Eli Whitney's arms factory is marked, and his model barn (1816) is preserved. Settled c.1664, set off from New

Haven 1786. **2** Village (pop. 951), Vinton co., S Ohio, 27 mi. ESE of Chillicothe, in agr. area.

Hamdh, Wadi, or **Wadi Hamd** (wă'dē hämd'), largest wadi of Hejaz, Saudi Arabia, extending c.300 mi. from area of Medina to the Red Sea S of Wejh.

Häme (hă'mā), Swedish *Tavastehus* (tävä'stühüs"), county [Finnish *lääni*] (□ 7,118; including water surface, □ 8,357; pop. 538,854), S central Finland; ⊙ Hämeenlinna. Low and undulating, interspersed with numerous lakes; L. Päijänne forms E boundary of co. Lumbering and timber-processing industries are important; agr. (rye, oats, barley, potatoes), stock raising, dairying. Mfg. of furniture, machinery, glass (Riihimäki), leather and rubber products. Cities are Tampere, Lahti, and Hämeenlinna.

Hämeenkyrö (hă'mān-kü"rû), Swedish *Tavastkyro* (tävästkü'rō), village (commune pop. 10,056), Turku-Pori co., SW Finland, in lake region, 20 mi. NW of Tampere; lumbering.

Hämeenlinna (hă'mānlĭn"nä), Swedish *Tavastehus* (tävä'stühüs"), city (pop. 21,199), ⊙ Häme co., S Finland, on small L. Vanaja, Finnish *Vanajavesi* (vä'näyävĕ"sē), 60 mi. NNW of Helsinki; 61°N 24°27'E. Textile, plywood, and spool mills, tanneries, rubber works. Site of teachers' seminary. Has Häme Castle (N), 1st mentioned 1308; its oldest parts reputedly date from c.1250. City, inc. 1639, was originally built N of castle; moved 1779 to present site. Terminus (1862) of 1st Finnish railroad, from Helsinki. Sibelius b. here. Aulanko recreation area, near by.

Hamel, Le (lû ämĕl'), village (pop. 428), Somme dept., N France, near the Somme, 12 mi. E of Amiens; velvet mfg. Devastated March-June, 1918, in First World War, and captured by Australians and Americans.

Hamelin, Germany: see HAMELN.

Hamelin Pool, Australia: see SHARK BAY.

Hameln (hä'mùln) or **Hamelin** (hă'mùlĭn), city (1950 pop. 48,086), in former Prussian prov. of Hanover, W Germany, after 1945 in Lower Saxony, port on the Weser and 24 mi. SW of Hanover. It is chiefly known as the scene of the legend of the Pied Piper of Hamelin, an event allegedly occurring here in 1284. It is a rail and mfg. center, with foundries and rolling mills, and mfg. of pharmaceuticals, furniture, rugs, blankets, ceramics, pottery; food processing (soup concentrates, flour, yeast). Salmon fisheries. Trade in potash, asphalt, coal, wood, grain. An anc. Saxon settlement, Hameln became a missionary outpost c.750, received city rights c.1200, and, while frequently changing hands, acquired considerable independence. Became a member of the Hanseatic League (1426–1572). Though somewhat damaged in Second World War, it retained many historic bldgs., notably the Rattenkrug (built 1568), the museum (1569), and the Widding House (1612–13). Frescoes illustrating the old legend adorn the so-called Ratcatcher's House (built 1602–3).

Hamelwörden (hä"mùlvûr'dùn), village (pop. 3,960), in former Prussian prov. of Hanover, NW Germany, after 1945 in Lower Saxony, near Elbe estuary, 14 mi. NNW of Stade; cattle.

Hamersley Range (hă'mùrzlē), N Western Australia, S of Fortescue R.; extends 160 mi. ESE from Robe R. Highest peak (2,798 ft.), Mt. Margaret; asbestos.

Hamersville (hă'mùrzvĭl), village (pop. 380), Brown co., SW Ohio, 32 mi. ESE of Cincinnati, in agr. area.

Hamgyong-namdo, Korea: see SOUTH HAMGYONG.

Hamgyong-pukdo, Korea: see NORTH HAMGYONG.

Hamhung (häm'hoong'), Jap. *Kanko*, city (1944 pop. 112,184), ⊙ S.Hamgyong prov., N Korea, on Tongsongchon R. and 115 mi. NE of Pyongyang; commercial center in agr. area (rice, soy beans, potatoes). Sake brewing, metalworking, cotton weaving. Near by are coal mines. City was important during 15th cent.; the founder of the Li dynasty (the last imperial line) was born here. Heavily damaged in Korean war (1950–51). Formerly sometimes spelled Hamheung.

Hami (hämē'), village, Quaiti state, Eastern Aden Protectorate, 14 mi. ENE of Shihr, on Gulf of Aden.

Hami (hä'mē'), Uigur *Kumul* (*Qumul*) or *Komul* (*Qomul*) (all: kōmōōl'), town and oasis (pop. 39,141), E Sinkiang prov., China, in oasis, 300 mi. ESE of Urumchi, and on Silk Road; 42°48'N 93°27'E. Melon-growing center; airport. Trades in wool, cotton and silk textiles, grapes; produces wheat, beans, fruit, cattle. Coal, gold, and lead mines. Saltworks near by.

Hamidiya or **Hamidiyah** (hähĭdē'yù), Fr. *Hamidié* or *Hamidiyé*. **1** Town, Aleppo prov., NW Syria, on railroad and 17 mi. S of Aleppo; cotton, cereals. **2** Town, Latakia prov., W Syria, on the Mediterranean, near Lebanese line, 55 mi. S of Latakia; sericulture, cereals.

Hamidiye. 1 Village, Ordu prov., Turkey: see MESUDIYE. **2** Town, Seyhan prov., Turkey: see CEYHAN, town. **3** Village, Zonguldak prov., Turkey: see DEVREK.

Hamill Peak (10,640 ft.), SE B.C., in Selkirk Mts., 60 mi. NE of Nelson; 50°13'N 116°38'W.

Hamilton, village (pop. 43), W Alaska, on arm of Yukon R. delta, 70 mi. SW of St. Michael; fur-trading post, supply point, steamer landing. School. Sometimes called Old Hamilton. New Fort Hamilton village is 10 mi. S.

Hamilton. 1 W suburb of Newcastle, E New South Wales, Australia; mfg. (electric bulbs). Horse racing. **2** Town (pop. 7,180), SW Victoria, Australia, 160 mi. W of Melbourne; rail junction; dairying and agr. center.

Hamilton, city (1949 pop. estimate c.3,000), chief port and ⊙ Bermuda, on Bermuda Isl., at head of sheltered Great Sound; 32°18'N 64°42'W. Focus of Bermuda's governmental, commercial, and social life. Laid out in rectangular fashion, it stretches for a mile along coast. Has mus., fort, hotels, parks, a cathedral. Inc. 1790; succeeded (1815) St. George as ⊙. Flourishing tourist trade. Hamilton parish (1939 pop. 1,863) is in E Bermuda, surrounding Harrington Sound.

Hamilton, city (pop. 166,337), ⊙ Wentworth co., S Ont., on Hamilton Harbour, at head of L. Ontario, 36 mi. SW of Toronto and 60 mi. NW of Buffalo, at foot of high bluff and of the Niagara escarpment. Lake port, rail hub, and industrial center, it has important steel, cotton, and knitting mills, automobile plants, railroad shops. Other industries include mfg. of clothing, felt, hardware, glass, soap, farm implements, cans, wire, domestic appliances, typewriters; tobacco processing. Surrounding country is noted fruitgrowing region. Airport. Site of McMaster Univ., technical school, collegiate institute. Has R.C. and Anglican cathedrals, and notable court house and city hall. Dundurn Castle, in Dundurn Park, is mus. of Wentworth Historical Society. Hamilton was laid out 1813 by George Hamilton; in same year it was scene of battle of Stony Creek. Battlefield is preserved as public park. Hamilton Harbour (5 mi. long, 4 mi. wide at mouth), formerly called Burlington Bay, is separated from L. Ontario by sand bar; entrance channel was cut 1823–32.

Hamilton, borough (pop. 21,982; metropolitan Hamilton 26,401), ⊙ Waikato co. (□ 648; pop. 14,321), N N.Isl., New Zealand, 70 mi. SSE of Auckland and on Waikato R.; dairy products, timber. Hamilton is in, but independent of, Waikato co.

Hamilton, burgh (1931 pop. 37,862; 1951 census 40,173), N Lanark, Scotland, on Avon Water near its mouth on the Clyde, and 10 mi. SE of Glasgow; coal mining, steel milling, woolen milling; machinery mfg. Hamilton Palace, seat of dukes of Hamilton, was pulled down in 1919, endangered by coal mines. In May, 1941, Rudolf Hess landed on near-by Hamilton estate after his flight from Germany.

Hamilton, village (1931 pop. 128), Sierra Leone colony, minor port on Atlantic Ocean, on Sierra Leone Peninsula and 7 mi. SSW of Freetown; fishing. Platinum mining (E).

Hamilton, village (pop. 231), S central Tasmania, 32 mi. NW of Hobart; coal mines; sheep.

Hamilton. 1 County (□ 514; pop. 8,981), N Fla., on Ga. line (N), bounded by Suwannee R. (S, E) and Withlacoochee R. (W); ⊙ Jasper. Flatwoods area with swamps in E; drained by Alapaha R. Farming (corn, peanuts, cotton, tobacco, vegetables), stock raising (hogs, cattle), and lumbering. Formed 1827. **2** County (□ 435; pop. 12,256), SE Ill.; ⊙ McLeansboro. Agr. (livestock, poultry, fruit, wheat, corn, redtop seed). Mfg. (clothing, dairy and food products, wood products). Drained by North Fork of Saline R. Formed 1821. **3** County (□ 403; pop. 28,491), central Ind.; ⊙ Noblesville. Diversified mfg., including the processing of farm products, at Noblesville and Sheridan; grain, dairy products, livestock (especially draft horses). Drained by West Fork of White R., and by Cicero, and small Prairie and Duck creeks. Formed 1823. **4** County (□ 577; pop. 19,660), central Iowa; ⊙ Webster City. Prairie agr. area (hogs, poultry, cattle, corn, soybeans, oats) drained by Boone and Skunk rivers; bituminous-coal deposits. Formed 1856. **5** County (□ 992; pop. 3,696), SW Kansas; ⊙ Syracuse. Prairie region, bordered W by Colo.; drained by Arkansas R. Wheat, livestock. Formed 1886. **6** County (□ 541; pop. 8,778), SE central Nebr.; ⊙ Aurora. Agr. region bounded N and NW by Platte R. Livestock, grain. Formed 1870. **7** County (□ 1,747; pop. 4,105), NE central N.Y.; ⊙ Lake Pleasant. Situated entirely in the Adirondacks; drained by tributaries of the Hudson and by Raquette, Black, and Sacandaga rivers. Well-known resorts on Indian, Long, Raquette, Piseco, and Pleasant lakes, and Fulton Chain of Lakes; many skiing areas; hunting, fishing. Some agr. (dairy products; poultry, hay, grain, livestock). Formed 1816. **8** County (□ 414; pop. 723,952), extreme SW Ohio; ⊙ CINCINNATI. Bounded W by Ind. line, S by Ohio R. (here forming Ky. line); drained by Great Miami, Little Miami, and Whitewater rivers and by small Mill Creek. Entirely within metropolitan dist. of Cincinnati; its agr. areas produce dairy products, truck, poultry, livestock. Gravel pits. Formed 1790. **9** County (□ 576; pop. 208,255), SE Tenn.; ⊙ CHATTANOOGA. Bounded S by Ga.; crossed N-S by Tennessee R. Includes parts of Hales Bar and Chickamauga reservoirs. Walden Ridge is in W and NW, parts of Lookout Mtn. and of Chickamauga and Chattanooga Natl. Military Park in S. Fertile farm lands (livestock, corn, hay, fruit, tobacco); coal and iron deposits, timber tracts. Mfg. at Chattanooga. Formed 1819; absorbed James co. (former □ 160) in 1919. **10** County (□ 844; pop. 10,660), central Texas; ⊙ Hamilton. Mainly prairies; drained by Leon, Bosque, and Lampasas rivers. Livestock, especially poultry; also cattle, sheep, goats (wool, mohair marketed), hogs, horses; agr. (cotton, grain, hay, peanuts, fruit, potatoes). Natural-gas field. Formed 1842.

Hamilton. 1 Town (pop. 1,623), ⊙ Marion co., NW Ala., 80 mi. NW of Birmingham, near Miss. line; lumber, cotton. Settled c.1818. **2** City (pop. 449), ⊙ Harris co., W Ga., 21 mi. NNE of Columbus, in agr. area; sawmilling. Summer resort. **3** City (pop. 1,776), Hancock co., W Ill., on the Mississippi, opposite Keokuk (Iowa; connected by bridge); trade and shipping center in agr. area (corn, wheat, soybeans, livestock, poultry, fruit; dairy products); mfg. (clothing, beekeepers' equipment). Stone quarry. Near by is L. Keokuk or L. Cooper, formed by Keokuk Dam in Mississippi R., with recreational and resort facilities. Inc. 1859. **4** Town (pop. 376), Steuben co., NE Ind., on small Hamilton L., 34 mi. NNE of Fort Wayne, in agr. and resort area; sawmills. **5** Town (pop. 245), Marion co., S central Iowa, near Cedar Creek, 27 mi. WNW of Ottumwa, in bituminous-coal-mining and agr. area. **6** City (pop. 456), Greenwood co., SE Kansas, 27 mi. S of Emporia, in stock-raising, dairying, and grain-growing region. **7** Rural town (pop. 2,764), Essex co., NE Mass., 9 mi. W of Gloucester. Settled 1638, inc. 1793. **8** City (pop. 1,728), Caldwell co., NW Mo., 24 mi. W of Chillicothe; lumber, grain, and livestock center. Founded 1855, inc. 1868. **9** City (pop. 2,678), ⊙ Ravalli co., W Mont., 45 mi. S of Missoula and on Bitterroot R., near Bitterroot Range and Idaho line; trading point for irrigated agr. and mining region; gold, silver, lead, zinc mines; lumber mills; dairy products, livestock. Fish hatchery and laboratory operated by U.S. Public Health Service here. Inc. 1894. **10** Ghost mining town, White Pine co., E Nev., in White Pine Mts., c.35 mi. W of Ely. During its silver boom (c.1865–73), its pop. reached c.10,000. **11** Village (pop. 3,507), Madison co., central N.Y., 25 mi. SW of Utica, in dairying and truck-farming region. Seat of Colgate Univ. Settled 1795, inc. 1816. **12** Town (pop. 514), Martin co., E N.C., on Roanoke R. (head of navigation) and 18 mi. ENE of Tarboro; sawmilling. **13** Village (pop. 241), Pembina co., NE N.Dak., 9 mi. E of Cavalier. Seat of co. fair. **14** City (pop. 57,951), ⊙ Butler co., extreme SW Ohio, 18 mi. N of Cincinnati and on Great Miami R.; trade and industrial center for agr. area. Mfg.: paper products, paper-mill machinery, steel and iron products, furnaces, safes, Diesel engines, woolens. Gravel pits. Settled on site of Fort Hamilton (built by Arthur St. Clair, in 1791); inc. 1810. **15** Village, R.I.: see NORTH KINGSTOWN. **16** City (pop. 3,077), ⊙ Hamilton co., central Texas, c.60 mi. W of Waco; trade, shipping center in poultry-raising, agr. area; flour and feed milling, poultry packing and hatching. A natural-gas field is W. **17** Town (pop. 351), Loudoun co., N Va., 6 mi. W of Leesburg, in E foothills of the Blue Ridge. **18** Town (pop. 294), Skagit co., NW Wash., on Skagit R. and 18 mi. ENE of Mt. Vernon, in agr., lumbering region.

Hamilton, Cape, SW Victoria Isl., SW Franklin Dist., Northwest Territories, on W coast of Wollaston Peninsula; 69°31'N 116°25'W.

Hamilton, Fort, N.Y.: see FORT HAMILTON.

Hamilton, Lake. 1 In W central Ark., 5 mi. S of Hot Springs; largest lake in Ark., created in OUACHITA RIVER by Carpenter Dam; c.25 mi. long. **2** In Fla.: see LAKE HAMILTON. **3** In Texas: see DEVILS RIVER.

Hamilton, Mount. 1 Peak (4,372 ft.), W Calif., in Mount Hamilton Range (part of Diablo Range), c.50 mi. SE of San Francisco. On summit is Lick Observatory of Univ. of Calif. **2** Peak, Nev.: see WHITE PINE MOUNTAINS.

Hamilton Acres, village (pop. 214), W Alaska, near Yukon R. delta.

Hamilton Air Force Base, Calif.: see SAN RAFAEL.

Hamilton Beach, village, S Ont., W suburb of Hamilton, on narrow spit bet. Hamilton Bay and L. Ontario; resort.

Hamilton City, village (1940 pop. 703), Glenn co., N central Calif., 19 mi. NE of Willows and on Sacramento R.; beet-sugar refining; ships fruit.

Hamilton Cove or **Sainte Anne de Portneuf** (sĕt än dû pôrnûf'), village (pop. estimate 800), E Que., on the St. Lawrence and 30 mi. WNW of Rimouski; lumbering center.

Hamilton Dam, Texas: see BUCHANAN DAM.

Hamilton Field, Calif.: see SAN RAFAEL.

Hamilton Inlet, bay (50 mi. long, 25 mi. wide at entrance) of the Atlantic, SE Labrador, the outlet of L. Melville; 54°20'N 58°W. At head of bay is settlement of Rigolet.

Hamilton Lakes, town (pop. 882), Guilford co., N central N.C., W residential suburb of Greensboro.

Hamilton River, S Labrador, issues as Ashuanipi R. from Ashuanipi L., on Que. border, flows in a great arc N and then SE, through a series of lakes, to the GRAND FALLS, where it becomes the Hamilton R. At the Grand Falls it drops 1,038 ft. over a distance of 16 mi., with main fall of 245 ft. Below the Grand Falls it flows SE and then ENE, through L. Melville, past Rigolet, to Hamilton Inlet of the Atlantic. Total length, 600 mi.

Hamilton Square, village (pop. c.2,000), Mercer co., W N.J., 5 mi. E of Trenton; pottery, rubber goods, radiators.

Hamina (hä'mĭnä), Swedish *Fredrikshamn* (frā"drĭks-hä'mŭn), city (pop. 6,468), Kymi co., SE Finland, on Gulf of Finland, 10 mi. NE of Kotka; seaport, shipping timber and wood products; rail terminus. Has medieval church, town hall (1798), and remains of 18th-cent. fortifications. Founded in 14th cent., chartered 1653, it was originally called Vehkalahti. Destroyed (early 18th cent.) by Russians; rebuilt and renamed after 1721. Came to Russia 1743. Under Treaty of Hamina (1809) Sweden ceded all of Finland to Russia.

Hamiota (hămĭō'tŭ), village (pop. 546), SW Man., 36 mi. NW of Brandon; lumbering; wheat.

Hamira (hŭmē'rŭ), village, N Patiala and East Punjab States Union, India, 6 mi. NNE of Kapurthala; sugar milling, liquor distilling, mfg. of agr. implements, chemicals.

Hamirpur (hŭmĕr'pŏŏr), district (□ c.2,515; pop. c.591,900), S Uttar Pradesh, India; ⊙ Hamirpur. Bounded NE by the Jumna; drained by Betwa R. Agr. (gram, jowar, wheat, sesame, pearl millet, barley, cotton). Main towns: Charkhari, MAHOBA, Rath, Maudaha, Hamirpur. Formerly part of Br. Bundelkhand. Original dist. (□ 2,443; 1939 pop. 575,538) was enlarged 1950 by inc. of several former petty states.

Hamirpur. 1 Village, Kangra dist., N Punjab, India, 38 mi. SSE of Dharmsala; wheat, corn; leather goods. **2** Town (pop. 8,144), ⊙ Hamirpur dist., S Uttar Pradesh, India, on Jumna R., just above Betwa R. mouth, and 37 mi. WSW of Cawnpore; trades in gram, jowar, wheat, sesame, pearl millet. Has 11th-cent. Rajput fort ruins. Founded 11th cent. by a Karchuli Rajput.

Hamitabat, Turkey: see ISPARTA, town.

Hamiz Dam, Algeria: see FONDOUK.

Hamjong (häm'jŭng'), Jap. *Kanju,* township (1944 pop. 11,824), S.Pyongan prov., N Korea, 22 mi. W of Pyongyang; cotton weaving.

Hamler, village (pop. 490), Henry co., NW Ohio, 12 mi. SSE of Napoleon.

Hamlet. 1 Town (pop. 659), Starke co., NW Ind., 27 mi. SW of South Bend; ships farm produce. **2** Village (pop. 154), Hayes co., S Nebr., 35 mi. WNW of McCook and on Frenchman Creek. **3** Village, Chautauqua co., extreme W N.Y., 13 mi. SE of Dunkirk. **4** Town (pop. 5,061), Richmond co., S N.C., 5 mi. SE of Rockingham, near S.C. line; rail junction (shops); trade and shipping center for fruit-growing area; mfg. of ice cream, beverages; lumbering.

Hamletsburg, village (pop. 131), Pope co., extreme SE Ill., on Ohio R. and 10 mi. ENE of Paducah, Ky.

Hamley Bridge, town (pop. 579), S South Australia, 40 mi. N of Adelaide and on Light R.; rail junction; agr. center.

Hamlin, county (□ 520; pop. 7,058), E S.Dak.; ⊙ Hayti. Dairying and livestock area drained by Big Sioux R. and several lakes. Grain, poultry, potatoes. Formed 1873.

Hamlin. 1 City (pop. 118), Brown co., NE Kansas, 6 mi. NW of Hiawatha, near Nebr. line; corn, livestock, poultry; dairying. **2** Plantation (pop. 430), Aroostook co., NE Maine, on St. John R. and 29 mi. NE of Presque Isle. **3** City (pop. 3,569), on Fisher-Jones co. line, W central Texas, 37 mi. NNW of Abilene; railroad division point; processing center in cotton area, also yielding oil, gypsum, sand, gravel; mfg. (gypsum products, cottonseed oil, feed); cotton gins and compresses. Inc. 1907. **4** Town (pop. 841), ⊙ Lincoln co., W W.Va., on Mud R. and 20 mi. ESE of Huntington, in coal, natural-gas, and oil region.

Hamlin Lake, Mich.: see BIG SABLE RIVER.

Hamm or **Hamm in Westfalen** (häm' ĭn vĕst"fä'lŭn), city (1950 pop. 59,372), in former Prussian prov. of Westphalia, W Germany, after 1945 in North Rhine-Westphalia, in the Ruhr, port at E head of Lippe Lateral Canal, 19 mi. NE of Dortmund, and on Lippe R.; transshipment center; wire mills; mfg. of machinery, stoves, ovens. Coal mining. Second World War destruction (c.55%) included the noted 14th- and 16th-cent. churches, and the Gothic town hall. Founded 1226 as ⊙ county of Mark. Hot saline springs near by.

Hamm (häm), agr. village, S Luxembourg, on Alzette R. and 3 mi. E of Luxembourg city. Site of U.S. military cemetery; Gen. George S. Patton buried here.

Hamma, El- (ĕl-häm-mä'), anc. *Aquae Tacapitanae,* town (pop. 7,227), Gabès dist., SE central Tunisia, 17 mi. W of Gabès; oasis with date palms and olive trees. Mineral springs and remains of Roman thermae. Captured by Allies in Second World War, after flanking of Mareth Line.

Ham Maapil, Ham Ma'apil, or **Hama'apil** (hämääpēl'), settlement (pop. 150), W Israel, in Plain of Sharon, 6 mi. SE of Hadera; mixed farming. Founded 1945.

Hammad, SW Asia: see SYRIAN DESERT.

Hammada el Hamra or **Hamada el Homra** (both: hämä'dä ĕl häm'rä) [Arabic,=red desert], desolate rocky region (□ c.19,300) of the Sahara in Libya, mostly in N Fezzan and partly in Tripolitania, bet. 28°N and 30°30'N; c.170 mi. long, 160 mi. wide. Rises in the Gebel es-Soda (E) to c.2,700 ft.

Hamma-Djerid, El- (ĕl-häm-mä'-jĕrēd'), village, Tozeur dist., SW Tunisia, in the Bled-el-Djerid oasis, at SE edge of the Chott el Rharsa, 6 mi. NNE of Tozeur; date-palms. Roman thermae.

Hammam or **Hammam 'Ali** (häm-măm' ălē'), village, Sana prov., central Yemen, 45 mi. S of Sana and on motor road to Hodeida; hot-springs resort.

Hammam, El, or **Al-Hammam** (both: ĕl häm'măm), village (pop. 5,511), Western Desert prov., N Egypt, on coastal railroad and 35 mi. SW of Alexandria.

Hammam, El, or **Al-Hammam. 1** Town, Aleppo prov., NW Syria, on Turkish border, 34 mi. WNW of Aleppo; cotton, cereals. **2** Town, Euphrates prov., N central Syria, on right bank of Euphrates R. and 90 mi. WNW of Deir ez Zor. Oil deposits near by.

Hammam, Oued (wĕd' häm-mäm'), stream in Oran dept., NW Algeria, rises in several headstreams in High Plateaus, flows c.160 mi. N, past Perrégaux, to the Habra lowland (adjoining the Gulf of Arzew) which its waters irrigate. Storage and flood-control dams at Bou-Hanifia (177 ft. high; 20 mi. SSW of Perrégaux) and at influx of Oued Fergoug.

Hammam-bou-Hadjar (bōō-ăjär'), town (pop. 7,041), Oran dept., NW Algeria, 29 mi. SW of Oran; rail-spur terminus, health resort; vineyards.

Hammamet (häm-mämĕt'), town (pop. 7,778), Grombalia dist., NE Tunisia, port on the Gulf of Hammamet, 36 mi. SE of Tunis; citrus-growing center (chiefly lemons). Fisheries.

Hammamet, Gulf of, inlet of the central Mediterranean, off NE coast of Tunisia, bet. Cape Bon Peninsula (N) and Monastir (S); 25 mi. long, 50 mi. wide. On it are towns of Sousse, Hammamet, and Nabeul. Tunny and anchovy fisheries.

Hammam-Lif (häm-mäm'-lēf'), anc. *Naro,* town (pop. 20,187), Tunis dist., N Tunisia, on S shore of Gulf of Tunis, 10 mi. ESE of Tunis; bathing and health resort (hot springs). Cement- and brickworks. Vineyards. Winter residence of bey of Tunis.

Hammam-Mélouane, Algeria: see ROVIGO.

Hammam-Meskoutine (-mĕskōōtēn'), village, Constantine dept., NE Algeria, in Constantine Mts., on railroad and 9 mi. W of Guelma; noted spa with hot springs (160°-205°F.). Olive-oil milling.

Hammam-Rirha (-rēgä'), village, Alger dept., N central Algeria, 11 mi. NE of Miliana; spa and winter resort in coastal range of Tell Atlas (alt. 1,700 ft.), amidst Aleppo pine forests; noted for its curative waters. Ruins of Roman *Aquae Calidae.* Also spelled Hammam-Righa.

Hamma-Plaisance (häm-mä'-plăzäs'), village (pop. 2,492), Constantine dept., NE Algeria, near the Oued Rhumel, 4 mi. N of Constantine; thermal springs; paper and flour milling.

Hammar, Hor al, or **Hur al-Hammar** (both: hōōr äl häm-mär'), lake (□ c.750; c.70 mi. long, c.15 mi. wide), SE Iraq, NW of Basra, just S of junction of the Euphrates with the Tigris, both of which feed it. Largely surrounded by marshes.

Hammarby (hä'märbü"), village (pop. 959), Gavleborg co., E Sweden, on small lake, 8 mi. SW of Sandviken; sulphite works. Has old manor house.

Hammar Island, Swedish *Hammarö* (hä'märû") (□ 21; pop. 6,607), Varmland co., W Sweden, in N part of L. Vaner, 4 mi. S of Karlstad; 7 mi. long, 1-5 mi. wide. On NW coast is Skoghall-Vidon village, with paper and lumber milling industry. On E shore is 14th-cent. church.

Hammarland (hä'märländ"), fishing village (commune pop. 1,596), Aland co., SW Finland, on W shore of Aland isl., opposite Eckero isl., 12 mi. NW of Mariehamn.

Hammarstrand (hä'märstränd"), village (pop. 452), Jamtland co., N central Sweden, on Indal R. (falls) and 30 mi. W of Sollefteа; tourist resort; hydroelectric station. Has 13th-cent. church.

Hamme (hä'mŭ), town (pop. 16,463), East Flanders prov., NW Belgium, on branch of Scheldt R. and 5 mi. N of Dendermonde; textiles (cotton).

Hammel (hä'mŭl), town (pop. 2,029), Skanderborg amt, E central Jutland, Denmark, 15 mi. N of Skanderborg; cement works, machine shops, meat canneries.

Hammelburg (hä'mŭlbŏŏrk), town (pop. 5,703), Lower Franconia, NW Bavaria, Germany, on the Franconian Saale and 10 mi. SW of Bad Kissingen; printing, brewing, distilling, tanning, lumber and flour milling; winegrowing. Has 14th-cent. church. Johann Froben, printer, b. here.

Hammels or **Hammel,** SE N.Y., a section of S Queens borough of New York city, on Rockaway Peninsula.

Hammenhog (hä"mŭnhûg'), Swedish *Hammenhög,* village (pop. 602), Kristianstad co., S Sweden, 9 mi. WSW of Simrishamn; grain, potatoes, sugar beets, stock.

Hammerdal (hä'mŭrdäl"), village (pop. 634), Jamtland co., N central Sweden, on Hammerdal L. (5 mi. long), 35 mi. NE of Ostersund; woodworking, lumbering.

Hammerfest (häm'mŭrfĕst), city (pop. 3,538), Finnmark co., N Norway, on W coast of the isl. Kvaloy, on Soroy Sound (inlet of Norwegian Sea), 130 mi. NE of Tromso; 70°40'N 23°43'E. World's northernmost city (though other villages are farther N); fishing, sealing, and whaling center, with port ice-free the year round; fish-oil processing. Seaplane base. Climate is unusually mild due to influence of North Atlantic Drift; there is continuous sunlight from May 13th until July 29th, while sun is not visible bet. Nov. 21st and Jan. 23d. Inc. 1789. Bombarded (1809) by British; destroyed by fire in 1890. In Second World War used as submarine base by Germans, who destroyed city upon their retreat, 1944–45. FUGLNES cape, 2 mi. WNW, is site of meridian cairn.

Hamme River (hä'mŭ), NW Germany, rises 10 mi. NW of Osterholz-Scharmbeck, flows c.30 mi. S and SW to the Weser at Vegesack.

Hämmern, Germany: see MENGERSGEREUTH-HÄMMERN.

Hammersmith, residential metropolitan borough (1931 pop. 135,523; 1951 census 119,317) of London, England, on N bank of the Thames, 5 mi. W of Charing Cross. It is site of St. Paul's School, noted public school founded 1509 by John Colet and attended by Milton and Pepys. Olympia is large exhibition bldg. Here also were Kelmscott Press of William Morris and Doves Press of Cobden-Sanderson.

Hammerstein, Poland: see CZARNE.

Hammerum (hä'mŭrōōm), town (pop. 1,001), Ringkobing amt, W Jutland, Denmark, 32 mi. E of Ringkobing; textiles.

Hamm in Westfalen, Germany: see HAMM.

Hammon (hă'mŭn), town (pop. 621), Roger Mills co., W Okla., 15 mi. N of Elk City, in stock raising, dairying, agr. area (wheat, cotton); cotton ginning.

Hammonasset Point (hămŭnă'sĭt), S Conn., peninsula (c.2 mi. long) on Long Isl. Sound near Madison. Here are Hammonasset Beach State Park and mouth of **Hammonasset River** (c.20 mi. long), which rises S of Middletown, flows SSE to Clinton Harbor just E of Hammonasset Point.

Hammond, B.C.: see PORT HAMMOND.

Hammond (hă'mŭnd). **1** Village (pop. 405), Piatt co., central Ill., 18 mi. E of Decatur, in grain and soybean area. **2** Industrial city (pop. 87,594), Lake co., extreme NW Ind., near L. Michigan, on Ill. line and on Grand Calumet R., bet. Gary and Chicago; important industrial center in CALUMET region. Mfg. of railroad cars and accessories, steel, machinery, petroleum products, tanks, agr. implements, surgical instruments and supplies, furniture, pianos, corn starch and other corn products, clothing, soap; printing and publishing. Settled 1851, inc. 1884. **3** City (pop. 8,010), Tangipahoa parish, SE La., c.45 mi. E of Baton Rouge; called "strawberry capital of America"; truck, dairy, poultry, peppers, sweet potatoes. Mfg. (crates, clothing, brick, building materials). Seat of Southeastern Louisiana Col. and an agr. experiment station. Settled 1855, inc. 1888. **4** Plantation (pop. 120), Aroostook co., E Maine, just NW of Houlton, in agr. area. **5** Village (pop. 192), Wabasha co., SE Minn., on Zumbro R. and 15 mi. NNE of Rochester, in grain and potato area. **6** Resort village (pop. 329), St. Lawrence co., N N.Y., bet. Black L. and St. Lawrence R., 19 mi. SW of Ogdensburg; timber; agr. (grain, hay, potatoes). **7** Town (pop. 522), Clatsop co., NW Oregon, 5 mi. W of Astoria and on Columbia R. **8** Village (pop. 554), St. Croix co., W Wis., 16 mi. E of Hudson; dairying.

Hammondsport, village (pop. 1,190), Steuben co., S N.Y., at S end of Keuka L., 20 mi. NNW of Corning, in grape-growing area; wine-making center; mfg. of electrical machinery, metal products, aircraft parts, canned foods. Summer resort. Birthplace of Glenn Curtiss, who made aviation experiments here. Inc. 1871.

Hammondville, town (pop. 94), De Kalb co., NE Ala., near Valley Head, c.10 mi. NE of Fort Payne.

Hammonia, Brazil: see IBIRAMA.

Hammonton, town (pop. 8,411), Atlantic co., S N.J., 27 mi. SE of Camden; trade, market center for fruit-growing, agr. region (poultry, truck); mfg. (fruit products, canned foods, clothing, cut glass). Settled in 1850s, inc. 1866.

Hamoir (ämwär'), village (pop. 1,257), Liége prov., E Belgium, 14 mi. S of Liége; dairying center; tourist resort.

Hamônia, Brazil: see IBIRAMA.

Hamont (ämõ'), village (pop. 5,246), Limbourg prov., NE Belgium, 15 mi. S of Eindhoven, near Netherlands line.

Hamor, Lake (hä'môr), Hung. *Hámor,* NE Hungary, in Bükk Mts., 7 mi. W of Miskolc; 1 mi. long, 360 ft. wide. Town of Hamor (pop. 1,030) and resort of LILLAFÜRED on its shore.

Hampden, borough (pop. 243), E coast of S.Isl., New Zealand, 40 mi. NNE of Dunedin; resort.

Hampden (hăm′dŭn, hămp–), county (□ 621; pop. 367,971), SW Mass., bordering on Conn.; ⊙ Springfield. Bisected by Connecticut river, which supplies power to its industrial cities. Metal products, food products, plastics, wood and paper products. Tobacco, dairying, truck. Formed 1812.

Hampden. 1 Town (pop. 3,608), Penobscot co., S Maine, on the Penobscot just below Bangor, in agr. area. Park commemorates Dorothea Dix, b. here. Settled 1767, inc. 1794. **2** Town (pop. 1,322), Hampden co., S Mass., 8 mi. ESE of Springfield; dairying, truck. Settled c.1740, inc. 1878. **3** Village (pop. 203), Ramsey co., NE N.Dak., 30 mi. NNE of Devils Lake.

Hampden Sydney, Va.: see FARMVILLE.

Hampi (hŭm′pē), village, Bellary dist., NW Madras, India, on right bank of Tungabhadra R. and 33 mi. NW of Bellary. Site of famous ruined city of Vijayanagar [Hindi,=city of victory]; flourished from 1336 until sacked 1565 by Deccan sultans after battle of Talikota. Ruins of city's main ramparts (□ c.9) enclose remains of several palaces, Sivaite and Vishnuite temples, and other granite monuments, providing notable panorama of Dravidian architecture. Tourists' bungalow just S, at village of Kamalapuram.

Hampreston, agr. village and parish (pop. 2,500), SE Dorset, England, on Stour R. and 3 mi. ESE of Wimborne Minster.

Hampshire (hămp′shĭr, –shŭr), county (□ 1,649.7; 1931 pop. 1,102,770; 1951 census 1,292,211), S England; ⊙ Winchester. Includes administrative cos. of Southampton or Southamptonshire (mainland part; □ 1,502.6; 1931 pop. 1,014,316; 1951 census 1,196,617) and the Isle of WIGHT. Bounded by Dorset and Wiltshire (W), Berkshire (N), Surrey and Sussex (E), and English Channel (S). Drained by Itchen, Test, Avon, and Wey rivers. Undulating country, crossed by North and South Downs, with partly wooded New Forest in SW noted for its beauty. Sheep and hog raising. Main industries are at large commercial port of Southampton and naval port of Portsmouth. Besides Winchester, other important towns are Eastleigh (railroad workshops), Bournemouth, Christchurch (resorts), Gosport, Basingstoke, and Aldershot (military center). There are several resorts on Isle of Wight. Shortened form of Hampshire is Hants.

Hampshire. 1 County (□ 537; pop. 87,594), W central Mass.; ⊙ Northampton. Bisected by Connecticut R.; drained by Westfield R. and other small streams. The Berkshires touch W sec.; Mt. Tom and Mt. Holyoke are near the Connecticut. Generally agr. and forested. Formed 1662. **2** County (□ 639; pop. 12,577), NE W.Va., in Eastern Panhandle; ⊙ Romney. Bounded N by Potomac R. (Md. line), E by Va.; drained by South Branch of the Potomac and Cacapon R. Traversed by valleys and ridges of the Appalachians. Agr. (livestock, dairy products, fruit); some mfg.; limestone quarrying, timber. Formed 1753.

Hampshire, village (pop. 970), Kane co., NE Ill., c.45 mi. WNW of Chicago, in agr. area (dairy products; livestock, grain).

Hampstead (hămp′stĭd, hăm′–), village (pop. estimate c.200), S N.B., on St. John R. (ferry) and 24 mi. N of St. John; granite quarrying.

Hampstead, residential metropolitan borough (1931 pop. 88,947; 1951 census 95,073) of London, England, N of the Thames, 4 mi. NNW of Charing Cross. Popular with artists and writers, it was residence of Keats, Joanna Baillie, Constable, Du Maurier, and Kate Greenaway. On N side of borough, on hill, is Hampstead Heath, a public common, once resort of highwaymen. Here was the inn where the Kit-Cat Club (including Pope, Addison, Steele) met. Annual fair held on the heath.

Hampstead. 1 Town (pop. 677), Carroll co., N Md., 25 mi. NW of Baltimore; clothing factories, vegetable cannery. **2** Town (pop. 902), Rockingham co., SE N.H., 8 mi. NNW of Haverhill, Mass. Near-by Island Pond (2 mi. long) has summer colony.

Hampton (hămp′tŭn, hăm′–), village (pop. estimate c.550), ⊙ Kings co., S N.B., on Kennebecasis R. and 20 mi. NE of St. John, in dairying and farming region. Popular summer residence for St. John.

Hampton, residential former urban district (1931 pop. 13,061), Middlesex, England, on the Thames and 12 mi. SW of London. Here is Hampton Court Palace, one of largest royal residences, built 1515 by Cardinal Wolsey. It became property of Henry VIII in 1526, was partly rebuilt under William III after plans by Wren, and was occupied by sovereigns until time of George II. Scene (1604) of Hampton Court Conference of clergy. Hampton also residence of Garrick, Wren, and Sir Richard Steele. Inc. (1937) in Twickenham.

Hampton, county (□ 562; pop. 18,027), S S.C.; ⊙ Hampton. Bounded SW by Savannah R.; drained by the Coosawhatchie. Hunting grounds, timberland, farms (tobacco, peanuts, strawberries, potatoes, cotton). Formed 1878.

Hampton. 1 Town (pop. 838), ⊙ Calhoun co., S Ark., 21 mi. E of Camden, in agr. area; cotton ginning, sawmilling. **2** Farming town (pop. 672), Windham co., E Conn., on Little R. and 9 mi. NE of Willimantic, in hilly region; dairy products. Has 18th- and 19th-cent. houses, part of state forest. **3** City (pop. 386), Bradford co., N Fla., 18 mi. NE of Gainesville; rail junction. **4** City (pop. 864), Henry co., N central Ga., 9 mi. N of Griffin, in agr. area. **5** Village (pop. 706), Rock Island co., NW Ill., on the Mississippi just above Moline. **6** City (pop. 4,432), ⊙ Franklin co., N central Iowa, 29 mi. S of Mason City; railroad junction; agr. trade and processing center (canned corn, packed poultry, feed); wood, metal, stone, and concrete products; nursery. Limestone quarries, sand and gravel pits near by. Beeds Lake State Park is NW. Founded 1856, inc. 1870. **7** Village (pop. 275), Dakota co., SE Minn., 24 mi. S of St. Paul in grain, potato, livestock area. **8** Village (pop. 289), Hamilton co., SE central Nebr., 5 mi. E of Aurora. **9** Town (pop. 2,847), including Hampton village (pop. 1,614), Rockingham co., SE N.H., 10 mi. S of Portsmouth. Mfg. (shoes, wood products); fruit, truck, dairy products. Henry Dearborn b. here. Hampton Beach, on coast, is a resort. NORTH HAMPTON and HAMPTON FALLS were formerly in Hampton. Settled 1638, inc. 1639. **10** Borough (pop. 975), Hunterdon co., W N.J., near Musconetcong R., 13 mi. E of Phillipsburg. **11** Town, N.C.: see RUTH. **12** Town (pop. 2,007), ⊙ Hampton co., SW S.C., 55 mi. N of Savannah, Ga., in agr. area (cotton, corn, potatoes); wood products, naval stores, beverages. **13** Village (pop. 1,164), Carter co., NE Tenn., 5 mi. SE of Elizabethtown. **14** City (pop. 5,966), in but independent of Elizabeth City co., SE Va., port on HAMPTON ROADS opposite Norfolk (ferry), near Newport News. Large fisheries; packs and ships seafood; mfg. of building materials, metal products, fertilizer. Co. courthouse here. Near by are U.S. Fort Monroe (at OLD POINT COMFORT) and Langley Air Force Base (opened 1917 as Langley Field). Seat of Syms-Eaton Acad., continuation of one of 1st free public schools in America, and of Hampton Inst. Settled 1610, it is one of oldest continuous English settlements in country; laid out 1680, inc. as town 1849, as city 1908. Sacked by British in 1813, burned by Confederates in 1861.

Hampton Bays, summer-resort village (pop. 1,269), Suffolk co., SE N.Y., on shore of SE Long Isl., 7 mi. W of Southampton, in diversified-farming area; boat yards. Formerly called Good Ground.

Hampton Beach, N.H.: see HAMPTON.

Hampton Falls, town (pop. 629), Rockingham co., SE N.H., 11 mi. SSW of Portsmouth. Set off from Hampton 1726.

Hampton Harbor, SE N.H., small bay (1 mi. long, ½ mi. wide) S of Hampton, near Mass. line; receives 2 tidal streams.

Hampton National Historic Site, Md.: see TOWSON.

Hampton Roads, great roadstead, SE Va., bet. Old Point Comfort (N) and Sewall Point (S), through which James, Nansemond, and Elizabeth rivers enter Chesapeake Bay; c.4 mi. long. One of world's finest natural harbors, accommodating vessels of any draft. On it are port cities of NEWPORT NEWS (N) and NORFOLK and PORTSMOUTH (S), together constituting Port of Hampton Roads, one of busiest U.S. seaports, administered by a state port authority. Newport News is a major shipbuilding center. Hampton is also on N shore. Since colonial days an important naval base; site of U.S. Atlantic Fleet hq. (at Norfolk) and Norfolk Navy Yard (at Portsmouth). In Civil War, at battle of Hampton Roads (March, 1862), the ironclads *Monitor* and *Merrimac* met in their famous engagement.

Hampton Wick, residential former urban district (1931 pop. 2,960), Middlesex, England, on the Thames and 11 mi. SW of London; metal foundries. Inc. 1937 in Twickenham.

Hamra, El, or **Al-Hamra** (both: ĕl hämrä′), village, Hama prov., W Syria, 22 mi. NE of Hama; cotton, cereals. Sometimes called Houmeiré or Al-Humayrah.

Hamra, Jazirat al (jăzē′rät ăl häm′rŭ), island off Trucial Coast, in Persian Gulf, belonging to Ras al Khaima sheikdom; 25°43′N 55°47′E.

Hamra esh Sheikh or **Hamarat el Sheikh** (both: hăm′rŭ ĕsh shāk′), village, Kordofan prov., central Anglo-Egyptian Sudan, at S edge of Libyan desert, 180 mi. NW of El Obeid; gum arabic, livestock.

Hamrange (häm′rông″ŭ), Swedish *Hamrånge*, village (pop. 1,241), Gavleborg co., E Sweden, near Gulf of Bothnia, 18 mi. N of Gavle; grain, flax, potatoes, stock.

Hamrong (häm′rông′), industrial town, Thanhhoa prov., N central Vietnam, 3 mi. NE of Thanhhoa; sawmilling, paper and match mfg.

Hamrun (hämrōōn′), Maltese *Hamrun*, industrial town (pop. 17,124), E Malta, 1½ mi. SW of Valletta. Adjoined (NE) by Floriana at base of Mt. Sceberras Peninsula. Mfg. of buttons, bricks, tiles, candles, mirrors, beer. Though many houses were wrecked during Second World War air raids, its monuments have suffered little. Among them are 16th-cent. church, Augustinian monastery (founded 1617), 18th-cent. church, and grand master de Wignacourt's water tower.

Hamry, Czechoslovakia: see HLINSKO.

Hams Fork, river, SW Wyo., rises in S tip of Salt River Range, flows c.100 mi. S, past Kemmerer, and E, past Opal, to Blacks Fork of Green R. at Granger.

Ham Sud (hăm süd′), village (pop. estimate), ⊙ Wolfe co., S Que., at foot of Ham Mtn. (2,325 ft.), 30 mi. NE of Sherbrooke; dairying, cattle raising, potato growing.

Ham-sur-Sambre (hã-sür-sã′brŭ), town (pop. 2,927), Namur prov., S central Belgium, on Sambre R. and 9 mi. W of Namur; glassblowing center.

Hamta Pass (hŭm′tŭ) (alt. c.14,050 ft.), in SE Pir Panjal Range of Punjab Himalayas, in Kangra dist., NE India, 60 mi. E of Dharmsala. Also spelled Hamtah.

Hamtramck (hămtră′mĭk), city (pop. 43,355), Wayne co., SE Mich., entirely surrounded by Detroit. Factories here produce automobiles, alloys and metal products, machinery, electrical supplies, roofing, paint, varnish. Its pop. is largely of Polish descent. Inc. as village 1901, as city 1922; grew after coming (c.1910) of automobile industry. Its public school system, reorganized in 1923, undertook a notable plan of education for democracy.

Hamun, Iran and Afghanistan: see SEISTAN.

Hamun-i-Helmand, Iran and Afghanistan: see SEISTAN.

Hamun-i-Lora (hä′mōōn-ē-lō′rŭ), closed salt-marsh depression in Chagai dist., N Baluchistan, W Pakistan; 36 mi. long (N–S), 3–10 mi. wide. Receives the Pishin Lora (SE) and drainage of Chagai Hills (W); dry for most of year.

Hamun-i-Mashkel (–mŭsh′kăl), closed salt-marsh depression in Chagai dist., W Baluchistan, W Pakistan, just W of Sandy Desert; 55 mi. long (E-W), 8–20 mi. wide. Receives Mashkel R. (E) and drainage of hills (N); dry for most of year. Thick deposits of brine salt worked.

Hamun-i-Puzak, Afghanistan: see SEISTAN.

Hamun-i-Sabari, Iran and Afghanistan: see SEISTAN.

Hamurre, El (ĕl hämŏŏr′rā), village, in the Mudugh, central Ital. Somaliland, 80 mi. SW of Eil; road junction. Also called Geriban.

Hamza or **Hamzah** (häm′zŭ), town, Diwaniya prov., SE central Iraq, on the Hilla (branch of the Euphrates) and 17 mi. S of Diwaniya; rice, dates, corn, millet, sesame.

Hamzoren, Bulgaria: see BEZMER.

Han, river: see HAN RIVER.

Hana (hä′nä), Czech *Hánà*, fertile agr. region of undulating lowlands (alt. 632–832 ft.), central Moravia, Czechoslovakia; noted for its strong ethnographic and agr. characteristics; lies approximately bet. Olomouc (N), Prerov (E), Prostejov (W), and Kojetin (S). Chief industries: sugar milling, brewing, dairying; grows well-known malt and barley. Drained by Morava R.

Hana (hä′nä), village (pop. 548), E Maui, T.H., principal E coast port.

Hanábana River (änä′bänä), W Cuba, flows c.50 mi. along Matanzas–Las Villas prov. border, emptying into the Zapata marshes. Formerly Amarillas.

Hanabanilla River (änäbänē′yä), central Cuba, small affluent (c.20 mi. long) of the Arimao, which it joins 15 mi. E of Cienfuegos. Known for its waterfall.

Hanaford, village (pop. 280), Franklin co., S Ill., 7 mi. NE of West Frankfort, in bituminous-coal and agr. area. Also called Logan.

Hanagita Peak (hănŭgē′tŭ) (8,520 ft.), S Alaska, in Chugach Mts., 80 mi. ENE of Cordova; 61°5′N 143°43′W.

Hanakpinar, Turkey: see CINAR.

Hanalei (hä′nälā′ē), village (pop. 366), N Kauai, T.H., near head of **Hanalei Bay** and Ahukini Harbor.

Hanam, province, Vietnam: see PHULY.

Hanamaki (hänä′mäkē), town (pop. 20,955), Iwate prefecture, N Honshu, Japan, on Kitakami R. and 22 mi. S of Morioka, in rice-growing, stock-raising area; silk textiles, paper goods. Hot springs near.

Hanamaulu (hä′nämä-ōō′lōō), village (pop. 1,032), SE Kauai, T.H.; sugar-producing village 2 mi. N of Lihue and on **Hanamaulu Bay,** a good landing.

Hanamkonda, India: see WARANGAL, city.

Hanamsagar (hŭnŭmsä′gŭr), town (pop. 5,102), Raichur dist., SW Hyderabad state, India, 45 mi. NW of Gangawati; millet, oilseeds.

Hanaoka (hänä′ōkä). **1** Town (pop. 9,561), Akita prefecture, N Honshu, Japan, 4 mi. NNW of Odate; rice; copper mining. **2** Town (pop. 6,843), Mie prefecture, S Honshu, Japan, just W of Matsuzaka; rice, wheat, raw silk.

Hanapepe (hä′näpā′pā), coast village (pop. 1,266), S Kauai, T.H. Port Allen is near by.

Hanau (hä′nou), city (1939 pop. 42,191; 1946 pop. 22,067; 1950 pop. 30,625), in former Prussian prov. of Hesse-Nassau, W Germany, after 1945 in Hesse, port on right bank of the canalized Main, at mouth of Kinzig R., and 10 mi. E of Frankfurt; 50°8′N 8°56′E. Rail junction; a center of jewelry industry (smelting of precious metals; diamond polishing); produces rubber goods (tires, shoes). Other mfg.: sun lamps, corrugated cardboard; leather- and woodworking. Lumber trade. Second World War destruction (about 75%) included most noteworthy bldgs. Has school for precious metal-working. Old town developed around castle of counts of Hanau. Chartered 1303. New town founded at end of 16th cent. by Protestant Dutch refugees. Passed to Hesse-Kassel in 1736, and with it to Prussia in 1866. Old and new town were united 1833. Brothers Grimm and composer Hindemith b. here. Near by, in 1813, Napoleon defeated Austrian and Bavarian forces after the battle of Leipzig.

Hanawa (hä″nä′wä), town (pop. 12,288), Akita prefecture, N Honshu, Japan, 40 mi. E of Noshiro; rice, charcoal, dyes.

Hancesti, Moldavian SSR: see KOTOVSKOYE.

Hanceville, town (pop. 775), Cullman co., N central Ala., 10 mi. SE of Cullman; farm shipping center.

Hancewicze, Belorussian SSR: see GANTSEVICHI.

Hancheng or **Han-ch'eng** (hän′chŭng′), town, ⊙ Hancheng co. (pop. 115,041), E Shensi prov., China, 120 mi. NE of Sian and on Yellow R. (Shansi line); coal-mining center.

Han-chiang, town, China: see HANKONG.

Han Chiang, river, China: see HAN RIVER.

Hanchon (hän′chŭn′), Jap. *Kansen,* township (1944 pop. 11,412), S.Pyongan prov., N Korea, on Korea Bay, 22 mi. NW of Pyongyang, in agr. area.

Hanchow, China: see KWANGHAN.

Han-ch'uan, China: see HANCHWAN.

Hanchung, China: see NANCHENG, Shensi prov.

Hanchwan or **Han-ch'uan** (hän′chwän′), town (pop. 21,361), ⊙ Hanchwan co. (pop. 364,941), E central Hupeh prov., 30 mi. W of Hankow and on Han R.; silkgrowing center; cotton weaving, bean-cake processing; wheat, peanuts.

Hancock. 1 County (□ 485; pop. 11,052), E central Ga.; ⊙ Sparta. Bounded E by Ogeechee R., W by Oconee R. Intersected by fall line. Agr. (cotton, corn, forage, pecans, livestock), sawmilling. Formed 1793. **2** County (□ 797; pop. 25,790), W Ill.; ⊙ Carthage. Bounded W by the Mississippi, here dammed into L. Keokuk; drained by La Moine R. and Bear Creek. Agr. area (corn, wheat, soybeans, fruit; dairy products; livestock, poultry). Bituminous-coal mining; limestone quarries, sand pits; commercial fisheries. Some mfg. Formed 1825. **3** County (□ 305; pop. 20,332), central Ind.; ⊙ Greenfield. Drained by Sugar Creek, small Brandywine Creek, and Big Blue R. Agr. area (livestock, grain, vegetables). Some mfg. and canning at Greenfield and Fortville. Formed 1827. **4** County (□ 570; pop. 15,077), N Iowa; ⊙ Garner. Prairie agr. area (cattle, hogs, poultry, corn, oats, sugar beets) drained by branches of Iowa R. and Lime Creek. Contains small lakes; peat beds, sand and gravel pits; state parks. Formed 1851. **5** County (□ 187; pop. 6,009), NW Ky.; ⊙ Hawesville. Bounded N and NE by Ohio R. (Ind. line); drained by headstreams of Panther Creek. Agr. area (burley tobacco, livestock, corn, grain, truck); coal mines, oil wells. Formed 1829. **6** County (□ 1,542; pop. 32,105), S and SE Maine; ⊙ Ellsworth, gateway to Mt. Desert Isl. and Acadia Natl. Park. Mfg. (wood and paper products, machinery), agr., dairying, granite quarrying, hunting, fishing. Bays, isls., and inland lakes are resort sites. Drained by Penobscot R. **7** County (□ 485; pop. 11,891), SE Miss.; ⊙ Bay St. Louis. Borders on Mississippi Sound (S); Pearl R. separates it from La. (W). Agr. (corn, truck, pecans, livestock, poultry); lumbering; sea-food shipping. Shore resorts. Formed 1812. **8** County (□ 532; pop. 44,280), NW Ohio; ⊙ Findlay. Intersected by Blanchard R. Livestock, grain; diversified mfg., especially at Findlay; limestone quarries. Includes Van Buren State Park. Formed 1820. **9** County (□ 231; pop. 9,116), NE Tenn.; ⊙ Sneedville. Borders N on Va.; traversed by Powell Mtn. and other ridges of the Appalachians; drained by Clinch and Powell rivers. Agr. (livestock, tobacco, fruit). Formed 1844. **10** County (□ 82; pop. 34,388), W.Va., at tip of Northern Panhandle; ⊙ New Cumberland. Bounded N and W by Ohio R. (Ohio line), E by Pa. Industrial region; steel milling (especially at Weirton), mfg. of clay products, chemicals, cement, metal alloys, fabricated products (at Weirton, New Cumberland, Chester). Coal mines, clay and glass-sand pits. Some agr., especially fruit. Includes Tomlinson Run State Park. Formed 1848.

Hancock. 1 Town (pop. 264), Pottawattamie co., SW Iowa, 26 mi. ENE of Council Bluffs. **2** Resort town (pop. 755), Hancock co., S Maine, on Frenchman Bay N of Mt. Desert Isl. and 8 mi. E of Ellsworth. **3** Town (pop. 963), Washington co., W Md., on the Potomac (bridged) and 25 mi. W of Hagerstown, at narrowest point of Md. (c.2 mi. wide); center for agr., timber, and sand-mining area. Hunting preserves near. **4** Town (pop. 445), Berkshire co., NW Mass., 7 mi. NNW of Pittsfield, near N.Y. line; resort; dairying. **5** City (pop. 5,223), Houghton co., NW Upper Peninsula, Mich., opposite Houghton, on Keweenaw Waterway (port facilities), in copper-mining region. Mfg. (foundry products, machinery, wood products); lumber milling, commercial fishing. Resort. Seat of Suomi Col. and Theological Seminary. Platted 1859; inc. as village 1875, as city 1903. **6** Village (pop. 852), Stevens co., W Minn., 9 mi. SE of Morris, in grain, stock, poultry area; dairy products. **7** Resort town (pop. 612), Hillsboro co., S N.H., 28 mi. W of Manchester. **8** Summer-resort village (pop. 1,560), Delaware co., S N.Y., in the Catskills, at junction of East and West branches here forming the Delaware, 35 mi. ESE of Binghamton; mfg. (wood alcohol, wood products, textiles). Inc. 1888. **9** Town (pop. 391), Addison co., central Vt., on White R. and 27 mi. SW of Montpelier, in Green Mts.; wood products; winter sports. **10** Village (pop. 449), Waushara co., central Wis., 24 mi. SE of Wisconsin Rapids, in dairying and farming area. State experimental farm near by.

Hancock, Fort, N.J.: see SANDY HOOK.

Hancock, Lake, Polk co., central Fla., 3 mi. N of Bartow; c.4 mi. long, 3 mi. wide; source of Peace R.

Hancock, Mount. 1 Peak (4,430 ft.), White Mts., Grafton co., N central N.H., NE of North Woodstock. **2** Peak (10,100 ft.), Rocky Mts., in S Yellowstone Natl. Park, NW Wyo., 10 mi. S of Yellowstone L.

Hancocks Bridge, village, Salem co., SW N.J., on Alloway Creek and 5 mi. S of Salem; muskrat trapping. Hancock House (1734), site of massacre of Revolutionary troops by Tories, here.

Hand, county (□ 1,436; pop. 7,149), central S.Dak.; ⊙ Miller. Level agr. region watered by numerous intermittent streams and artificial lakes. Dairy products, livestock, wheat, oats, rye, barley, corn. Formed 1873.

Handa (hän′dä). **1** City (1940 pop. 49,153; 1947 pop. 59,819), Aichi prefecture, central Honshu, Japan, on E Chita Peninsula, on Chita Bay, 18 mi. S of Nagoya; mfg. center (soy sauce, sake, cotton textiles). Includes (since 1937) former towns of Kamesaki and Narawa. **2** Town (1947 pop. 8,383), Tokushima prefecture, E central Shikoku, Japan, 30 mi. W of Tokushima; rice, wheat; raw silk.

Handawor (hŭn′dŭvôr) or **Handwara** (hŭn′dvŭrŭ), village, Baramula dist., W Kashmir, 14 mi. NNW of Baramula; rice, corn, wheat, oilseeds.

Handegg (hän′dĕk), hamlet, Bern canton, S central Switzerland, on Aar R. and 9 mi. SSE of Meiringen; waterfall (150 ft. high); hydroelectric plant. Also known as Handeck.

Handen (hän′dŭn), village (pop. 1,037), Stockholm co., E Sweden, 10 mi. SSE of Stockholm; paper mills.

Handeni (händĕ′nē), town, Tanga prov., NE Tanganyika, on road and 80 mi. WSW of Tanga; sisal, corn, cotton. Also called Chanika.

Handforth, former urban district (1931 pop. 1,031), NE Cheshire, England, 5 mi. SW of Stockport; cotton milling. Has Handforth Hall, a 16th-cent. mansion. Inc. 1936 in Wilmslow.

Handia (hŭnd′yŭ), village, Allahabad dist., SE Uttar Pradesh, India, 22 mi. ESE of Allahabad; rice, gram, barley, wheat, oilseeds, sugar cane.

Handies Peak (14,013 ft.), SW Colo., in San Juan Mts., 11 mi. NE of Silverton.

Handley. 1 Village (1940 pop. 4,284), Tarrant co., N Texas, E suburb of Fort Worth. **2** Village (pop. 1,007), Kanawha co., W W.Va., on Kanawha R. and 17 mi. SE of Charleston.

Handlova (händ′lôvä), Slovak *Handlová,* Hung. *Nyitrabánya* (nyĭ′trŏbä′nyô), town (pop. 8,863), W central Slovakia, Czechoslovakia, 35 mi. ESE of Trencin; rail terminus; important lignite mines.

Handol (hän′dŭl″), Swedish *Handöl,* village (pop. 245), Jamtland co., NW Sweden, in mts. near Norwegian border, on a small lake, 12 mi. ESE of Storlien; talc quarrying.

Handsboro, village (pop. 3,400, with adjacent Mississippi City), Harrison co., SE Miss., 8 mi. W of Biloxi, on Mississippi Sound, in shore-resort area.

Handsworth. 1 NW industrial suburb (pop. 26,980) of Birmingham, NW Warwick, England. Site of the Soho ironworks of Boulton and Watt. Its 15th-cent. church has tombs of Boulton and Watt. **2** Town (pop. 17,472) in Sheffield county borough, West Riding, S Yorkshire, England, 3 mi. ESE of Sheffield; steel-milling center.

Handwara, Kashmir: see HANDAWOR.

Handzame (händ′zämŭ), village (pop. 3,274), West Flanders prov., W Belgium, 6 mi. E of Dixmude; agr., cattle raising. Destroyed in First World War; later rebuilt. Formerly spelled Handzaeme.

Haneda (hänĕ′dä′), airport for Tokyo, Japan, in central Honshu, 10 mi. S of Tokyo city center, on Tokyo Bay.

Hanerau-Hademarschen (hä′nŭrou-hä′dŭmär″-shŭn), village (pop. 4,210), in Schleswig-Holstein, NW Germany, 14 mi. SE of Heide; sawmilling. Hademarschen was residence (1879–88) of Theodor Storm.

Haney, village (pop. estimate 1,000), SW B.C., on Fraser R. and 22 mi. E of Vancouver; lumbering, dairying; fruit, vegetables; canning, brick mfg.

Hanford. 1 City (pop. 10,028), ⊙ Kings co., S central Calif., in San Joaquin Valley, 30 mi. S of Fresno; trade, shipping, and processing center in rich farming (grain, fruit, cotton), stock-raising, and dairying region; rail and highway center. Flour, feed, condensed milk, canned foods, petroleum products. Inc. 1891. **2** Village (pop. 922), Franklin co., central Ohio, just ESE of Columbus.

Hanford Works, Wash.: see RICHLAND.

Hangal (hän′gŭl), town (pop. 6,895), Dharwar dist., S Bombay, India, 50 mi. S of Dharwar; rice, millet, betel leaf, cotton. Irrigation canal near by.

Hangam or **Hengam** (both: hăng-gäm′), Arabic *Hanjam* or *Henjam* (both: hănjăm′), Persian Gulf island (1940 pop. estimate 1,000) of SE Iran, in Strait of Hormuz, just off S coast of Qishm isl.; 26°38′N 55°55′E; 6 mi. long, 4 mi. wide. Site of British naval base during First World War; after 1934, Iranian naval and quarantine station.

Hangay Mountains, Mongolia: see KHANGAI MOUNTAINS.

Hangchow or **Hang-chou** (both: hăng′chou′, Chinese häng′jō′), city (1944 pop. 606,136; 1948 pop. 517,559), ⊙ Chekiang prov., China, on left bank of Tsientang R. at head of Hangchow Bay, on railroad and 100 mi. SW of Shanghai; 30°15′N 120°12′E. Commercial and cultural center; mfg. (silk and satin goods, paper fans, joss paper, matches, soap). Seat of Chekiang univ. and Hangchow Christian Col. The S terminus of the Grand Canal, Hangchow's port, not accessible to ocean-going vessels, is restricted to coastal and inland trade, and ships silk, tea, paper fans. Hangchow's charming natural setting on the shore of scenic WEST LAKE and at the foot of high wooded hills attracts many visitors. Outside the NW Wulin gate, on rail spur, is former Japanese foreign settlement of Kungchenkiao, established 1896. Founded A.D. 606, Hangchow was ⊙ Wu-Yüeh kings (907–960). Most of its picturesque monasteries and shrines date from this period. As Linan, ⊙ late Sung dynasty (1127–80), it experienced a flourishing literary period, which produced the philosopher Chu Hsi (Chu Hi). It was visited by Marco Polo, who called it Kinsai or Quinsay [for the Chinese *Kingshih* or *Ching-shih,* = capital city]. City was devastated 1861 in the Taiping Rebellion and rebuilt along modern lines. During Sino-Japanese War, it was occupied (1937–45) by the Japanese. It passed in 1949 to Communist control. In 1927 it became a municipality under provincial jurisdiction. Hangchow is ⊙, but independent of, Hanghsien co. (1944 pop. 372,594).

Hangchow Bay, inlet of E.China Sea, in Chekiang prov., China, forming estuary of Tsientang R. E of Hangchow; 100 mi. long, 70 mi. wide at mouth. Along its shores, protected by sea walls, are Haiyen and Haining (N), and Siaoshan, Tzeki, and Chinhai (S). Chusan Archipelago lies across its mouth. Noted for spectacular tidal phenomenon, known as the Hangchow bore, which is best viewed from Haining. The bore, the strength of the current, and shallow water render the bay unusable for ocean-going vessels.

Hangelar (häng′ulär), village (pop. 2,228), in former Prussian Rhine Prov., W Germany, after 1945 in North Rhine-Westphalia, 3 mi. ENE of Bonn; airport.

Hangha (häng′hä), village (pop. 931), South-Eastern Prov., E Sierra Leone, on railroad and 7 mi. NNE of Kenema; chromite-mining center. Asbestos deposits (N).

Hanghsien, China: see HANGCHOW.

Hanging Hills, S central Conn., small trap ridge just NW of Meriden, rising to 1,024 ft. in West Peak; area is state park, with recreational facilities.

Hanging Rock, village (pop. 465), Lawrence co., S Ohio, on Ohio R. and 4 mi. NW of Ironton, in coal-mining area.

Hangklip, Cape, SW Cape Prov., U. of So. Afr., on the Atlantic, bet. False Bay (W) and Walker Bay (E), 35 mi. SE of Cape Town, 20 mi. E of Cape of Good Hope; 34°24′S 18°49′E.

Hango (häng′ŭ″), Swedish *Hangö,* Finnish *Hanko* (häng′kō), city (pop. 6,778), Uusimaa co., SW Finland, on 15-mi.-long peninsula of same name on the Baltic at mouth of Gulf of Finland, 50 mi. SE of Turku; 59°50′N 22°58′E. Seaport, kept ice-free the year round; herring-fishing center; rail terminus. Exports butter, fish, timber, pulp. Mfg. of margarine, biscuits; granite processing (quarries near by). Seaside resort. Pop. predominantly Swedish-speaking. Offshore are remains of fortress (1789). City inc. 1874. After Russo-Finnish War of 1939–40 surrounding region (□ 45) was leased to USSR for 30 years as naval base (evacuated by Russians Dec., 1941), but in Russo-Finnish armistice of 1944 the USSR exchanged it for 50-year lease on Porkkala region (confirmed by Treaty of Paris, 1947).

Hangtang or **Hang-t'ang,** China: see SINGTANG.

Han Hai, Mongolia: see GOBI.

Hanham, town in parish of Hanham Abbots (pop. 1,258), SW Gloucester, England, 3 mi. E of Bristol; shoe industry.

Hanhthongxa, Vietnam: see GOVAP.

Hanifa, Wadi, or **Wadi Hanifah** (wă′dē hănē′fŭ), one of chief wadies of Arabian Peninsula, in Nejd, extending c.200 mi. E-W S of Riyadh.

Hänigsen (hĕ′nĭksŭn), village (pop. 3,777), in former Prussian prov. of Hanover, NW Germany, after 1945 in Lower Saxony, 9 mi. S of Celle; oil.

Hanish Islands (hänēsh′), archipelago in Red Sea, 70 mi. SSW of Hodeida, and belonging to Yemen. Includes the larger Hanish Kabir (12 mi. long) and the Hanish Saghir (4 mi. long).

Hanita (hänētä′), settlement (pop. 250), W Galilee, NW Israel, on Lebanese border, 20 mi. NNE of Haifa; precision-instrument mfg.; stock raising, bee keeping, horticulture; poultry. Modern village founded 1938 on site of anc. locality of same name. Withstood Arab attacks, 1948.

Hanjam, Iran: see HANGAM.

Hanka, Lake, Manchuria and USSR: see KHANKA, LAKE.

Hankiang, town, China: see HANKONG.

Han Kiang, river, China: see HAN RIVER.

Hankins, resort village, Sullivan co., SE N.Y., on the Delaware (here forming Pa. line) and 17 mi. W of Liberty.

Hankinson, city (pop. 1,409), Richland co., SE N.Dak., 20 mi. SW of Wahpeton; dairy products, livestock, grain. Site of convent and acad. of Sisters of St. Francis. Inc. 1912.

Hanko, Finland: see HANGO.

Hankong (hän'gông'), Mandarin *Hankiang* or *Hanchiang* (both: -jyäng'), town, E Fukien prov., China, 3 mi. SE of Putien, on Hinghwa Bay; saltworks.

Hankow or **Han-k'ou** (hăng'kou', Chinese hän'kō'), large city (1947 pop. 641,513 or 749,952), in but independent of Hupeh prov., China, port on left bank of Yangtze R. at Han R. confluence, and 420 mi. W of Shanghai, 670 mi. S of Peking; 30°32'N 114°19'E. Largest of the WUHAN tri-cities, Hankow is the foremost mfg. and commercial center of central China, producing machinery, chemicals, cement, and cotton and silk goods. Its excellent location at the junction of China's leading navigable river (the Yangtze) and the important Peking-Hankow-Canton RR (with river ferry here) has earned it the title of "Chicago of China." Its port, though 600 river miles from the E.China Sea, is accessible to ocean-going ships. Hankow is the country's leading tea market, and also exports cotton and egg products. Situated on the central Yangtze plain, in the midst of Hupeh's lake region, Hankow extends 8 mi. along Han R., and past the confluence down the Yangtze. It consists of a Chinese city (SW on the Han), and the former foreign concessions, where the city's mfg., commercial, and banking interests are concentrated. City airport is in W outskirts. Hankow's phenomenal development as the metropolis of central China dates from 1858, when it became one of the first inland cities opened to foreign trade by the Treaty of Tientsin. The foreign concessions were granted to the Germans (until 1917), the Russians (until 1920), the British (until 1927), the Japanese and French (until 1938). During the Sino-Japanese War, the city was held (1938–45) by the Japanese. It passed to Communist control in 1949. Hankow became a municipality under provincial jurisdiction in 1931 and under the central govt. in 1947.

Hanks, village (pop. 115), Williams co., NW N.Dak., 33 mi. NNW of Williston; small-scale ranching in vicinity.

Hanley, town (pop. 359), S central Sask., 35 mi. SSE of Saskatoon; grain elevators, dairying.

Hanley, town in the Potteries district, NW Stafford, England, since 1910 part of STOKE-ON-TRENT. Arnold Bennett b. here.

Hanley Falls, village (pop. 320), Yellow Medicine co., SW Minn., on Yellow Medicine R. and 9 mi. SW of Granite Falls, in corn, oat, barley area.

Hanley Hills, town (pop. 2,219), St. Louis co., E Mo., just W of St. Louis.

Hanlontown, town (pop. 257), Worth co., N Iowa, near Lime Creek, 13 mi. NW of Mason City; peat mining and processing.

Hann (hän), village, W Senegal, Fr. West Africa, on Hann Bay, on railroad, and 3 mi. NE of Dakar. Beach resort; botanic and zoological gardens.

Hanna, town (pop. 1,756), SE central Alta., 35 mi. ENE of Drumheller; coal mining, dairying, mixed farming, flour milling.

Hanna. 1 Town (pop. 325), McIntosh co., E Okla., 20 mi. NNW of McAlester, in agr. area; cotton ginning. **2** Town (pop. 1,326), Carbon co., S Wyo., 35 mi. E of Rawlins; alt. c.6,770 ft.; coal mines. Near by is site of Fort Halleck, military post established 1862 on Overland stage route. Settled 1887, inc. 1936.

Hanna City, village (pop. 671), Peoria co., central Ill., 11 mi. W of Peoria, in agr. and bituminous-coal mining area.

Hannaford, village (pop. 313), Griggs co., E central N.Dak., 10 mi. S of Cooperstown and on branch of Sheyenne R.

Hannah, village (pop. 257), Cavalier co., N N.Dak., port of entry 21 mi. NW of Langdon, near Can. line.

Hannastown, village (1940 pop. 809), Westmoreland co., SW Pa., 5 mi. NE of Greensburg; coal, coke. Pre-Revolutionary co. seat and center of dispute bet. Pa. and Va. over possession of Westmoreland territory, resolved 1779 by extension of Mason-Dixon line westward. Destroyed 1782 by Indian raid.

Hannibal (hă'nĭbŭl). **1** City (pop. 20,444), on Marion-Ralls co. line, NE Mo., on Mississippi R. (bridged here) 18 mi. below Quincy, Ill., and 100 mi. NW of St. Louis; industrial, rail, and trade center. Mfg.: shoes, cigars, cement; steel, lumber, and metal products. Grain, dairying center. Important river port in early 19th cent. Hannibal-LaGrange Col. here. Boyhood home of Mark Twain is preserved; a mus., statue, lighthouse, and bridge commemorate him. Founded 1819. **2** Village (pop. 501), Oswego co., N central N.Y., 10 mi. SW of Oswego, in dairy and fruit area.

Hanno (hän-nō'), town (pop. 34,151), Saitama prefecture, central Honshu, Japan, 23 mi. WNW of Kawaguchi; textiles (silk, cotton), raw silk.

Hannover, Germany: see HANOVER.

Hannoversch-Münden, Germany: see MÜNDEN.

Hannut (änü'), Flemish *Hannuit* (hä'noit), town (pop. 2,583), Liége prov., E central Belgium, 13 mi. NW of Huy; market center.

Hano (hō'nō, hä'nō), Indian pueblo, NE Ariz., atop a mesa in Hopi Indian Reservation, c.65 mi. NNE of Winslow; alt. c.6,200 ft. Founded in 17th cent. by immigrant Tewa-speaking Indians who have since adopted Hopi customs.

Hano Bay, Swedish *Hanöbukten* (hän'û"bŭk"tŭn), inlet (35 mi. long, 15 mi. wide) of Baltic, S Sweden. Chief ports are Simrishamn (at S end) and Ahus. Receives Helge R.

Hanoi (hä'noi, hä'noi'), city (1943 pop. 119,700; 1948 pop., with suburbs, 237,146), ⊙ Tonkin, now North Vietnam, in (but independent of) Hadong prov., on right bank of Red R., 55 mi. WNW of Haiphong, its port on Gulf of Tonkin; 21°2'N 105°50'E. River port, railroad and industrial center, accessible to barges and small vessels; linked by railroad to Haiphong, Saigon, Kunming (Yunnan prov., China), and Dongdang and Nacham (near Kwangsi prov. border, China). Rice milling, distilling, brewing, mfg. of cotton and silk textiles, woolen rugs, ceramics (china, bricks, tile), matches, explosives, leather goods, buttons. Has univ., school and mus. of Far East studies, museums of industry and commerce, geology, and mines; botanic gardens. Situated on S shore of the Great Lake (deltaic arm of Red R.), Hanoi is linked by Doumer road and rail bridge (1 mi. long; completed 1902) across Red R. with left bank suburb of Gialam (rail shops, airport). City is divided by railroad viaduct into the administrative city on site of demolished 19th-cent. fortress (NW on shore of Great Lake), with military barracks, official residences, and 11th-cent. Great Buddha pagoda; the Annamese native quarter (NE) with tortuous streets, temples, pagodas; and the Fr. concession (SE), the modern European-style business and residential section, with univ., museums, and the 15th-cent literary temple of Vanmieu, dedicated to Confucius. Hanoi was 1st mentioned (7th cent.) as seat of Chinese command, was invested and destroyed repeatedly by Chinese and Annamese armies until it became (1428–1788) seat of Lê dynasty of N Annam. One of its Annamese names, Dongkinh, was corrupted (16th cent.) by Europeans into Tonkin. After the reunion (1802) of Annam, it remained ⊙ Tonkin, was occupied by the French briefly in 1873 and again 1882; from 1902 until the end of the Second World War, it was ⊙ Union of Indochina. After Aug., 1945, it was briefly ⊙ Vietnam under the Vietminh, until recaptured Dec., 1946, by the French.

Hanoura (hänō'rä), town (pop. 7,579), Tokushima prefecture, E Shikoku, Japan, 8 mi. SE of Tokushima; rice-growing center; wheat, raw silk; mats.

Hanover, town (pop. 3,290), S Ont., on Saugeen R. and 28 mi. S of Owen Sound; woodworking, dairying, silk milling; mfg. of stockings, furniture.

Hanover (hă'nōvûr), Ger. *Hannover* (hänō'vûr, -fûr), former Prussian province (□ 14,959; 1939 pop. 3,457,477), NW Germany, after 1945 included in the new state of Lower Saxony, in zone of British occupation; ⊙ was Hanover. In W portion of North German lowlands, it extended from the Netherlands and the North Sea in NW to Harz mts. in SE, bounded by former Prussian provs. of Westphalia (S, SW) and Hesse-Nassau (S), Thuringia (S), former Prussian Saxony prov. (E), Mecklenburg and Schleswig-Holstein (NE); Oldenburg and Bremen (N) formed complete enclave, Brunswick (S) and Hamburg (NE) partial enclaves. Drained by navigable Ems, Weser, Aller, and Elbe rivers. Hanover, Osnabrück, Hildesheim, Emden, Lüneburg, Celle, and Göttingen are principal cities. Most of its area is agr. lowland producing grain, potatoes, and sugar beets. Stock raising is important. Some oil, potash, and coal are mined. Most of the area was originally included in Guelph holdings of BRUNSWICK. In 1692, Duke Ernest Augustus of Brunswick-Lüneburg was raised to rank of elector and chose Hanover as his capital; his lands were known henceforth as electorate of Hanover. He was the husband of Sophia, granddaughter of James I of England; their son, Elector George Louis, ascended English throne as George I. Personal union of Great Britain and Hanover continued until accession (1837) of Queen Victoria, when Salic law placed nearest male heir (Ernest Augustus, son of George III) on throne of Hanover, which had become a kingdom in 1815. For siding with Austria in Austro-Prussian War, Hanover was annexed as a prov. by Prussia. After capture (1945) by British, Canadian, and U.S. troops, Hanover was inc. into new state of Lower Saxony in Br. occupation zone.

Hanover, Ger. *Hannover*, city (1939 pop. 470,950; 1946 pop. 354,955; 1950 pop. 441,615), was ⊙ former Prussian prov. of Hanover, W Germany, after 1945 ⊙ Lower Saxony, port on the Leine (head of navigation), on Weser-Elbe Canal, and 60 mi. SE of Bremen; 52°23'N 9°44'E. Major transshipment point and industrial center; mfg. of machinery, machine tools, vehicles, precision and optical instruments, electrical equipment, rubber, asbestos, synthetic chemicals, textiles; petroleum refining. Food (chocolate, biscuits, beer) and tobacco processing. Seat of Lutheran bishop. Hanover's core, the Altstadt (old town), on right bank of the Leine, suffered greatest damage in Second World War. Completely destroyed were: the old palace, birthplace of Queen Louise of Prussia; Leibniz House, residence (1676–1716) of the philosopher; most of the half-timbered Renaissance bldgs. which gave Hanover its distinctive character. Gutted were: the Gothic old town hall; 17th–18th-cent. Leine castle with burial vault containing tombs of Electress Sophia and George I of England; and splendid 19th-cent. opera. Hanover was 1st mentioned 1163, chartered 1241, passed to Brunswick 1369, joined Hanseatic League 1386. Was chosen (1692) ⊙ newly created electorate (after 1815, kingdom; after 1866, prov.) of Hanover. Just S is the Neustadt (new town), 1st mentioned in 1283 and separately administered until 1824; has 17th-cent. church (gutted) with grave of Leibniz. Ägidien-Neustadt (developed after 1750) is SE, with new town hall and several museums. E residential dist. is site of veterinary col. (founded 1887), large zoo, race track. Noted institute of technology is in NE dist., near large castle of Herrenhausen (completely destroyed), which once was a favorite residence of kings of England. Industry is concentrated in N and S outskirts of the city and in the W district of Linden.

Hanover, parish (□ 177.08; pop. 51,684), Cornwall co., NW Jamaica, on W promontory of the isl.; ⊙ Lucea. Principal agr. crops: rice, bananas, lime, yams, breadfruit. Lucea and Green Island ship bananas. Near Lucea are phosphate deposits.

Hanover. 1 Town (pop. 1,543), E central Cape Prov., U. of So. Afr., 40 mi. SE of De Aar; sheep, feed crops, fruit; alt. 4,500 ft. **2** Village (pop. 429), SE Cape Prov., U. of So. Afr., 6 mi. NE of King-williamstown; stock, grain; lumbering.

Hanover, county (□ 466; pop. 21,985), E central Va.; ⊙ Hanover. Partly in the piedmont (W), with coastal plain (E); bounded N, E, SE by North Anna and Pamunkey rivers, S by the Chickahominy; drained by South Anna R. Agr., especially truck farming for market of near-by Richmond; also tobacco, livestock, peanuts, hay. Co. saw much fighting (at Cold Harbor, Gaines's Mill, Mechanicsville) in Civil War. Formed 1720.

Hanover. 1 Village, New London co., Conn.: see SPRAGUE. **2** Village (pop. 1,643), Jo Daviess co., NW Ill., on Apple R. (bridged here) and 25 mi. SE of Dubuque (Iowa), in agr. area; mfg. (flour, feed, wool cloth). **3** Town (pop. 1,060), Jefferson co., SE Ind., near Ohio R., 5 mi. WSW of Madison, in agr. area. Seat of Hanover Col. **4** City (pop. 854), Washington co., NE Kansas, on Little Blue R. and 11 mi. NW of Marysville; poultry and egg packing, bottling. **5** Town (pop. 211), Oxford co., W Maine, on the Androscoggin and 11 mi. WSW of Rumford; winter sports. **6** Town (pop. 3,389), Plymouth co., E Mass., on North R. and 20 mi. SE of Boston; mfg. (tacks and other metal products); dairying, poultry. Settled 1649, inc. 1727. **7** Village (pop. 377), Jackson co., S Mich., 13 mi. SW of Jackson, in diversified farming area. **8** Village (pop. 228), Hennepin and Wright counties, E Minn., on Crow R. and 24 mi. WNW of Minneapolis, in grain, livestock, poultry area. **9** Village (pop. c.150), Fergus co., central Mont., on branch of Judith R. and 7 mi. NW of Lewistown; plaster. **10** Town (pop. 6,259), including Hanover village (pop. 4,999), Grafton co., W N.H., on the Connecticut just above Lebanon; sports equipment, dairy products. Seat of Dartmouth Col. Winter sports center. Granted 1761, settled shortly thereafter. **11** Village (pop. c.1,500), Grant co., SW N.Mex., in foothills of Pinos Altos Mts., 11 mi. ENE of Silver City; alt. c.6,400 ft. Gold, silver, copper mines in vicinity. Black Peak is 8 mi. NNW, Gila Natl. Forest near by. **12** Village (pop. 308), Licking co., central Ohio, 8 mi. E of Newark. **13** Urban township (pop. 15,051), Luzerne co., NE central Pa., on Susquehanna R., in Wyoming Valley, bet. Nanticoke and Wilkes-Barre, in anthracite region. **14** Borough (pop. 14,048), York co., S Pa., 17 mi. SW of York; shoes, furniture, clothing, cigars, wall paper, pretzels. Harness-racing horses bred near by. First Civil War battle N of Mason-Dixon line fought here 1863. Inc. 1815. **15** or **Hanover Court House,** village (pop. c.100), ⊙ Hanover co., E central Va., near Pamunkey R., 15 mi. N of Richmond. Patrick Henry lived here and pleaded (1763) his 1st important case in the co. courthouse (c.1735; extant). Near by is hamlet of Hanovertown, which in 1751 nearly became ⊙ Va.

Hanover Island, off coast of S Chile, bet. Jorge Montt Isl. (S) and Chatham Isl. (NE), 95 mi. NW of Puerto Natales; 40 mi. long, 5–22 mi. wide; 51°S 74°40'W. Uninhabited.

Hanover Junction, N.Mex.: see VANADIUM.

Hanoverton (hănō′vûrtŭn), village (pop. 344), Columbiana co., E Ohio, 23 mi. E of Canton.
Hanovertown, Va.: see HANOVER, village.
Han Pijesak or **Khan Piyesak** (both: khän pēyĕ′-säk), village, E Bosnia, Yugoslavia, on railroad and 7 mi. S of Vlasenica, bet. Visocnik mtn. (WSW) and Javor Mts. (N).
Han River. 1 Chinese *Han Kiang* or *Han Chiang* (both: hän′ jyäng′), river in S China, rises on Fukien-Kiangsi prov. border near Changting, flows 210 mi. S, past Shanghang, Fengshih, into Kwangtung prov., past Taipu and Chaoan, to S. China Sea, forming delta in area of Swatow and Tenghai. Receives Mei R. (right). Navigable below Taipu, 100 mi. above mouth. Called Ting R., Chinese *Ting Kiang* or *Ting Chiang,* in upper course. **2** Chinese *Han Shui* (hän′shwā′), river in Shensi and Hupeh provs., China, rises in area of Nancheng (Shensi prov.), flows 750 mi. ESE, through S Shensi, bet. the Tsinling Mts. (N) and Tapa Shan, past Ankang, and into Hupeh prov., past Yünhsien, Künhsien, Kwanghwa (Laohokow), Fancheng, Icheng, and Hanchwan, to Yangtze R. at the Wuhan cities. Navigable for junks below Nancheng in summer floods; regular year-round navigation begins at Kwanghwa (Laohokow). Flowing through deep gorges in S Shensi, the Han rises 20 ft. in flood (beginning in April-May), inundating its lower valley. It receives the Tan, and the joint Pai and Tang rivers (left), from Honan prov.
Han River (hän), Korean *Han-gang,* Jap. *Kan-ko,* central Korea, rises in mts. c.100 mi. E of Seoul, flows SW, and turns generally NW past Chungju, Yoju, and Seoul to Yellow Sea at Kanghwa Isl. (nearly connected to mainland); 292 mi. long; navigable 185 mi. by small craft. Has hydroelectric plant in upper course; drains large agr. area. It was an important defense line in the seesaw fighting (1950–51) of the Korean war. Principal tributary, called Pukhan R. (Anglicized as North Han), is c.110 mi. long.
Hansa, Brazil: see CORUPÁ.
Hansag (hŏn′shäg), Hung. *Hanság,* central swampy district (□ 218) of the Little Alföld, NW Hungary; 34 mi. long, 11 mi. wide; fed by Ikva and Repce rivers, drained by Fertö Canal; peat cutting.
Hansboro, village (pop. 134), Towner co., N N.Dak., port of entry 33 mi. N of Cando, near Can. border. U.S. customhouse here.
Hansell (hăn′sŭl), town (pop. 190), Franklin co., N central Iowa, 5 mi. E of Hampton; livestock, grain.
Hansen, village (pop. 463), Twin Falls co., S Idaho, 8 mi. E of Twin Falls and on Snake R.; alt. 4,000 ft.; beets, hay, fruit, grain, cattle.
Hansen Dam, Calif.: see TUJUNGA CREEK.
Hansford, county (□ 907; pop. 4,202), extreme N Texas; ⊙ Spearman. Bounded N by Okla. line; in high grassy plains of the Panhandle; alt. 3,000–3,800 ft. Wheat-producing area; also grain sorghums, seed wheat; beef cattle, some sheep, poultry, hogs; some dairying. Natural-gas wells. Formed 1876.
Hanshan (hän′shän′), town, ⊙ Hanshan co. (pop. 206,461), E Anhwei prov., China, near Kiangsu line, 45 mi. WSW of Nanking; rice, wheat, corn, kaoliang.
Hanshow or **Han-shou** (both: hän′shō′), town, ⊙ Hanshow co. (pop. 333,859), N Hunan prov., China, on Tungting L., at delta of Yüan R., 25 mi. ESE of Changteh; rice, wheat, beans, cotton. Until 1912 called Lungyang.
Han Shui, China: see HAN RIVER.
Hansi (hän′sē), town (pop. 22,590), Hissar dist., S Punjab, India, 14 mi. ESE of Hissar; trades in cotton, oilseeds, salt, grain; cotton ginning, handloom weaving; metalwork. Captured 1192 by Kutb-ud-din, general of Muhammad Ghori; at end of 18th cent. held for short time by George Thomas, noted adventurer.
Hansjo (hän′shû″), Swedish *Hansjö,* residential village (pop. 1,110), Kopparberg co., central Sweden, near N end of L. Orsa, 10 mi. NNE of Morastrand; grain, stock.
Hanska, village (pop. 473), Brown co., S Minn., near L. Hanska, 12 mi. S of New Ulm, in grain, livestock, poultry area; dairy products.
Hanska, Lake, Brown co., S Minn., 28 mi. W of Mankato; 7.5 mi. long, .5 mi. wide. Drains into Minnesota R.
Hans Lollik Islands (hănz″ lŏ′lĭk), 2 islets and several rocks just off N St. Thomas Isl., U.S. Virgin Isls., 4 mi. NNE of Charlotte Amalie. Hans Lollik Isl. proper (489 acres; alt. 713 ft.) is at 18°24′ 64°54′; Little Hans Lollik is just N.
Hanslope, agr. village and parish (pop. 1,161), N Buckingham, England, 4 mi. N of Wolverton. Has 15th-cent. church.
Hanson, county (□ 431; pop. 4,896), SE central N.Dak.; ⊙ Alexandria. Agr. and livestock-raising region drained by James R. Dairy products, corn, wheat. Formed 1871.
Hanson. 1 Town (pop. 393), Hopkins co., W Ky., 7 mi. N of Madisonville, in coal-mining and agr. area. **2** Residential town (pop. 3,264), Plymouth co., E Mass., 25 mi. SSE of Boston; cranberries. Settled 1632, set off from Pembroke 1820.
Hansot (hän′sōt), town (pop. 5,808), Broach dist., N Bombay, India, 13 mi. SW of Broach; local market for wheat, millet, fish.
Hanspach, Czechoslovakia: see LIPOVA.
Hanston, city (pop. 286), Hodgeman co., SW central Kansas, on small affluent of Pawnee R. and 31 mi. W of Larned; grain, livestock.
Han-sur-Lesse (hã-sür-lĕs′), village (pop. 581), Namur prov., SE Belgium, on Lesse R. and 15 mi. SE of Dinant; tourist resort. Here river flows through series of limestone caves.
Hansweert or **Hansweerd** (both: hän′svärt), town (pop. 1,835), Zeeland prov., SW Netherlands, on South Beveland isl. 6 mi. SE of Goes, on the Western Scheldt at S end of South Beveland Canal; mfg. (synthetic fertilizer, machinery, sails).
Hantan (hän′dän′), town, ⊙ Hantan co. (pop. 170,282), SW Hopeh prov., China, on Peking-Hankow RR and 35 mi. S of Singtai, at highway crossing; cotton center; kaoliang, corn, millet.
Hanthawaddy (hăn″thŭwŏd′ē, hän′thäwŭdē″), southernmost district (□ 1,927; 1941 pop. 459,522) of Pegu div., Lower Burma, on Gulf of Martaban; ⊙ Rangoon. Split by RANGOON RIVER; drained by numerous creeks; mud flats, scrub vegetation on coast. Intensive rice-growing area; fisheries; forests (govt. reserves) in W. Served by Thongwa-Pegu RR and TWANTE CANAL. Separated 1879 from Rangoon dist.
Hants, county (□ 1,229; pop. 22,034), central N.S., on the Bay of Fundy; ⊙ Windsor.
Hants, England: see HAMPSHIRE.
Hantsport, town (pop. estimate 1,000), W central N.S., on Avon R., near its mouth on the Minas Basin, and 5 mi. NNW of Windsor; paper mfg., gypsum quarrying, fruit packing.
Hantsun, China: see HWANGHWA.
Hanumangarh (hŭnŏŏmän′gŭr), town (pop. 5,027), N Rajasthan, India, 125 mi. NNE of Bikaner, in canal-irrigated area; market center for millet, wheat, gram, wool, cattle; hand-loom cotton and woolen weaving. Rail junction just NW. Has noted fort. Formerly called Bhatnair.
Hanumannagar (hŭnŏŏmän′nŭgŭr), town, SE Nepal, in the Terai, 60 mi. NW of Purnea (India); rice, jute, corn, oilseeds. Annual fair.
Hanwell, England: see EALING.
Hanworth, England: see FELTHAM.
Hanyang (hän′yäng′), town (1947 pop. 69,483), ⊙ Hanyang co. (1947 pop. 488,968), E central Hupeh prov., China, on left bank of the Yangtze opposite Wuchang, at mouth of Han R. opposite Hankow; one of the WUHAN tri-cities; metallurgical center (iron, steel), based on Tayeh iron ore and Pingsiang coking coal. Arsenal. An old monastery town, Hanyang was industrialized after establishment in 1891 of steelworks.
Hanyin (hän′yĭng′), town (pop. 5,597), ⊙ Hanyin co. (pop. 112,184), S Shensi prov., China, 32 mi. NW of Ankang; rice, wheat, beans, millet.
Hanyu (hänyōō′), town (pop. 11,831), Saitama prefecture, central Honshu, Japan, 9 mi. E of Kumagaya; mfg. (*tabi,* rubber goods).
Hanyüan (hän′yüän′), town, ⊙ Hanyüan co. (pop. 123,177), E Sikang prov., China, near Szechwan line, 50 mi. SE of Kangting, and on highway; bamboo shoots, pepper, rice, wheat. Lead-zinc mines. Called Tsingki until 1914. Until 1938 in Szechwan.
Hanzinne (häzēn′), village (pop. 632), Namur prov., S central Belgium, 9 mi. SSE of Charleroi; pottery.
Hao (hou), atoll (pop. 190), central Tuamotu Isls., Fr. Oceania, S Pacific; 18°13′S 140°54′W. Formerly Bow Isl. Also called Harp Isl.
Hao-ch'ing, China: see HOKING.
Haofeng, China: see HOFENG, Hupeh prov.
Haoli or **Haolikang,** Manchuria: see HINGSHAN, Sungkiang prov.
Haophel, Palestine: see AFULA.
Haoshan, China: see HOKSHAN.
Haouz (houz), lowland of SW Fr. Morocco, just N of the High Atlas, surrounding Marrakesh. A former saline lake, it was filled by alluvium and is drained by the Tensift. Olive groves, vineyards, date palms irrigated from Oued N'Fis dam (25 mi. SSW of Marrakesh).
Hapaho, China: see KHABAKHE.
Hapai, Tonga: see HAABAI.
Haparanda (hä″pärän′dä), city (pop. 2,940), Norrbotten co., NE Sweden, on Gulf of Bothnia, at mouth of Torne R., 60 mi. ENE of Lulea; 65°51′N 24°6′E; frontier station on Finnish border, opposite Tornio. Rail junction; seaport, shipping lumber, tar, fish, Lapp products. Shipbuilding. Site of meteorological observatory. Annual temp. ranges from 14°F. (Jan.) to 60°F. (July); average annual rainfall 20 inches. Inc. as town 1827; as city 1842. In both World Wars it was important as reception station for refugees, wounded, and prisoners of war.
Hapeville (hāp′vĭl), city (pop. 8,560), Fulton co., NW central Ga., 7 mi. SSW of Atlanta; auto-assembly and airplane-rebuilding plants; sawmilling. Inc. 1891.
Happisburgh (hăz′brŭ, hăz′bŭrŭ), village and parish (pop. 534), NE Norfolk, England, on North Sea, 17 mi. NE of Norwich; seaside resort and small fishing port. Has 15th-cent. church.
Happy, town (pop. 690), on Randall-Swisher co. line, NW Texas, on Llano Estacado, c.40 mi. N of Plainview; trading center in wheat, cattle, dairying, poultry area.
Hapsal, Estonia: see HAAPSALU.
Hapsburg, Switzerland: see HABSBURG.
Hapton, village and parish (pop. 1,970), E Lancashire, England, 3 mi. W of Burnley; mfg. of chemicals for textile, tanning, and paper industries.
Hapur (hä′pŏŏr), town (pop. 33,756), Meerut dist., NW Uttar Pradesh, India, 18 mi. SSE of Meerut; rail and road junction; trades in wheat, millet, sugar cane, oilseeds, cotton, bamboo; cotton ginning, mfg. of chemical fertilizer. Has 17th-cent. mosque.
Haputale (hŭp′ōōtŭlā), village, Uva Prov., S central Ceylon, in Uva Basin, 18 mi. SE of Nuwara Eliya; tea transport center; tea processing. Just W is scenic Haputale Gap (alt. 4,583 ft.).
Haquira (äkē′rä), town (pop. 929), Apurímac dept., S central Peru, in the Andes, 65 mi. SE of Abancay; alt. 11,975 ft.; gold mining.
Hara (hä′rä). **1** Town, Fukushima prefecture, Japan: see HARANOMACHI. **2** Town (pop. 5,267), Gumma prefecture, central Honshu, Japan, just SW of Nakanojo; rice, wheat. **3** Town (pop. 9,659), Shizuoka prefecture, central Honshu, Japan, on N shore of Suruga Bay, 4 mi. NW of Numazu; agr. center (pears, peaches, rice, tea); paper milling.
Hara, river, Mongolia: see KHARA GOL.
Haradh or **Harad** (härädh′), oil field in Hasa, Saudi Arabia, 160 mi. SSW of Dhahran and on railroad to Riyadh; discovered 1949.
Haradh or **Harad,** village, Hodeida prov., NW Yemen, 15 mi. E of Midi, at Asir border.
Hara Gol, Mongolia: see KHARA GOL.
Harahan (hă′rŭhăn), village (pop. 3,394), Jefferson parish, SE La., on the Mississippi, just W of New Orleans, in farming and dairying area; lumber, veneer. Huey P. Long Bridge is near by.
Hara Hira, Mongolia: see KHARKHIRA.
Hara Hoto, China: see KARAKHOTO.
Haraichi (härī′chē). **1** Town (pop. 6,675), Gumma prefecture, central Honshu, Japan, 8 mi. W of Takasaki; rice, wheat, raw silk. **2** Town (pop. 3,892), Saitama prefecture, central Honshu, Japan, 5 mi. N of Omiya; rice, wheat, sake.
Haraiya (hŭrī′yŭ), village, Basti dist., NE Uttar Pradesh, India, 17 mi. W of Basti; rice, wheat, barley, sugar cane. Sometimes spelled Harraiya.
Haraldshaugen, Norway: see HAUGESUND.
Haralson (hă′rŭlsŭn), county (□ 285; pop. 14,663), NW Ga.; ⊙ Buchanan. Bounded W by Ala. line. Piedmont area drained by Tallapoosa R. Agr. (cotton, corn, grain, fruit, livestock), textile mfg., and sawmilling. Formed 1856.
Haralson, town (pop. 142), Coweta co., W Ga., 16 mi. SE of Newnan.
Haram (hä′räm), canton (pop. 4,182), More og Romsdal co., W Norway, N of Alesund. In it are some of Nord Isls., including HARAMSOY, and part of mainland, including BRATTVAG village.
Haramachi, Japan: see HARANOMACHI.
Haramosh Range, Kashmir: see KAILAS-KARAKORAM RANGE.
Haramsoy (hä′räms-ûü), Nor. *Haramsøy,* island (□ 5; pop. 808) in North Sea, More og Romsdal co., W Norway, one of the Nord Isls., 12 mi. NNE of Alesund; c.5 mi. long, 2 mi. wide. Fisheries; piano and organ factory; processing of fish meal, guano, fish oil.
Haramukh (hŭ′rŭmŏŏk), peak (c.16,000 ft.) of W Punjab Himalayas, W central Kashmir, 22 mi. N of Srinagar.
Haran or **Harran** (härän′), anc. *Carrhae* or *Carrae* (kă′rē), village (pop. 748), Urfa prov., S Turkey, 24 mi. SSE of Urfa (anc. Edessa); wheat, barley. Anc. Haran (Charran), frequently mentioned in the Bible, was home of Abraham's family after the migration from Ur. At the battle of Carrhae (53 B.C.) the Romans were defeated and Crassus killed by the Parthians.
Haranhalli (hä′rŭnhŭlē), town (pop. 2,433), Hassan dist., W central Mysore, India, 5 mi. SSW of Arsikere; cotton ginning. Kaolin workings near by. Also spelled Harnahalli.
Haranomachi (hä′rä-nō-mä″chē), town (pop. 16,691), Fukushima prefecture, N Honshu, Japan, on the Pacific, 28 mi. ESE of Fukushima; agr. and livestock raising center; spinning. Until 1897, called Haramachi; sometimes called Hara.
Hara Nuur, Mongolia: see KHARA NOR.
Haraoti (hărou′tē), the country of the Haras, a tribe of Chauhan Rajputs, situated in SE Rajasthan, India; comprises area of former Rajputana states of Bundi, Kotah, and Jhalawar.
Harappa (hŭrŭp′pŭ), village, Montgomery dist., SE Punjab, W Pakistan, on old bed of Ravi R. (S of present course) and 13 mi. W of Montgomery. Noted site of several successive cities of Indus Civilization, bet. 4000 and 2000 B.C. Prehistoric nature established in early 1920s; excavations have uncovered brick walls and dwellings, cemetery, copper and bronze implements, pictographic seals, many terra-cotta objects; antiquities in near-by mus.
Harar (hä′rŭr), province (□ 156,000), SE Ethiopia; ⊙ Harar. Borders on Fr., Br., and Ital. Somaliland. The largest prov. of Ethiopia, occupying c.40% of country's area, it extends c.500 mi. S from Awash

R. and c.600 mi. E from the Ganale Dorya. Pop. largely Somali and Galla. Consists of fertile, temperate, highland core (5–10,000 ft. high) extending WSW-ENE along edge of Great Rift Valley; AUSSA desert lowland (N); arid Ogaden plateau (S). Has forests (oleaster, cedar, acacia, euphorbia candelabra) in highlands. Watered by Webi Shebeli, Web, Fafan, and Jerer rivers. Agr. (coffee, millet, wheat, barley, maize, durra) and cattle raising chiefly in highlands. Nomadic grazing (camels, sheep, goats) in the OGADEN. Chief products: coffee, grown especially around Harar and in the CHERCHER highland, hides, and wax. Gold deposits near Harar. Commercial centers: Diredawa, Harar, Jijiga, Ginir. Crossed by Djibuti-Addis Ababa railroad. Main road, paralleling railroad, is joined by roads from Berbera (Br. Somaliland) and Mogadishu (Ital. Somaliland). Formerly also spelled Harrar.

Harar, city (pop. 40,000), ⊙ Harar prov., E central Ethiopia, on an affluent of the Wabi, on road and 225 mi. E of Addis Ababa, in highlands at edge of Great Rift Valley; alt. c.6,000 ft.; 9°21′N 42°1′E. Commercial center with road to Diredawa (26 mi. NW on railroad); coffee, hides, cereals, cotton, tobacco, fruit; oilseed pressing, Sansevieria fiber processing. Gold deposits near by. Has leprosarium. An anc. walled city, it was long the capital of an emirate. Held by Egypt 1875–85; incorporated into Ethiopia 1887. Has remained a Moslem center. Bombed and occupied by Italians in 1936 in Italo-Ethiopian War. Taken (1941) by British in Second World War. Formerly also Harrar.

Harardera (härärdĕ′rä), village (pop. 700), in the Mudugh, central Ital. Somaliland, near Indian Ocean, 65 mi. SW of Obbia; cattle water hole; wood carving. Has native forts.

Harasta or **Harastah** (härä′stŭ), village (pop. c.5,000), Damascus prov., SW Syria, on Damascus-Homs road and 5 mi. NE of Damascus, in the fertile Ghuta valley; melons, olives, grapes.

Harat, Afghanistan: see HERAT.

Harau or **Harauabad,** Iran: see KHALKHAL.

Haraucourt (ärōkōōr′), village (pop. 808), Ardennes dept., N France, 5 mi. S of Sedan; iron founding.

Hara Usa, Mongolia: see KHARA USU.

Harazé (häräzā′), military outpost, central Chad territory, Fr. Equatorial Africa, 90 mi. NE of Ati.

Harbel (här′bĕl), town, Marshall territory, W Liberia, on Farmington R. and 32 mi. E of Monrovia; hq. of extensive rubber plantations. Agr. research station. Rubber is exported via Marshall, and also, since 1950, via free port of Monrovia.

Harbertôn, Argentina: see PUERTO HARBERTÓN.

Harberton, village and parish (pop. 1,041), S Devon, England, 2 mi. SW of Totnes; market center. Fine medieval church; 16th-cent. inn.

Harbin (här′bĭn, här′bēn′), Chinese *Ha-erh-pin* (här′bĭn′), Rus. *Kharbin* (khärbyēn′), city (1941 pop. 637,573; 1947 estimate 760,000), ⊙ Sungkiang prov., Manchuria, port on right bank of Sungari R. and 320 mi. NNE of Mukden, near Hulan R. mouth, 45°47′N 126°39′E. Economic center and transportation hub of N Manchuria, at junction of the Chinese Eastern and South Manchuria railroads, and of lines to Aigun (N) and Kirin (S). Harbin is Manchuria's leading food-processing center, with a vast complex of flour mills, tobacco- and soybean-processing plants, and distilleries; it also has extensive railroad shops, boatbuilding yards, steel foundry, auto assembly plant, sawmills; and it manufactures chemicals and explosives, leather, brick and glass, cement, and agr. implements. Harbin's main exports are soybean products (oil and cake) and wheat flour. Of marked Russian appearance, Harbin has long had an important Russian minority, estimated in 1945 at 40,000. The city consists of several sections, sharply differentiated in their functions. Along the Sungari bank (opposite the left-bank winter harbor) is the commercial Pristan dist., the industrial and port dist. at the foot of the Sungari bridge, and the old Chinese residential section of Fukiatien (with many consumer industries). Farther inland and adjoining these riverside sections are the new city of Harbin (administrative and business offices) and the modern residential section of Machiakow (radio and power stations, airport). On the left bank, below the winter harbor, is the industrial suburb of Sungpu. Founded 1897 by the Russians as a construction settlement on the Chinese Eastern RR, Harbin had been selected as the junction of Manchuria's trunk rail lines. It boomed as a supply base during Russo-Japanese War, reaching pop. of 100,000 in 1905, but declining later. The city's real development came, however, only during and after First World War, when pop. increased eightfold from 1911 to 1931. Its meteoric rise was primarily the result of foreign capital, introduced after the city had been opened (1905) to foreign trade. In Manchukuo, Harbin was officially renamed Pinkiang (bĭn′jyäng′) as ⊙ Pinkiang prov (□ 24,655; 1940 pop. 4,234,206) during 1934–45. Under Nationalist rule (1946–49), city was an independent municipality under the central govt. Became ⊙ Sungkiang prov. in 1949.

Harbine (här′bīn″), village (pop. 85), Jefferson co., SE Nebr., 13 mi. WSW of Beatrice.

Harbke (härp′kŭ), village (pop. 1,730), in former Prussian Saxony prov., central Germany, after 1945 in Saxony-Anhalt, 3 mi. SE of Helmstedt; lignite mining. Power station.

Harbledown, village and parish (pop. 900), E Kent, England, just W of Canterbury. It is the "Little Town" of Chaucer's *Canterbury Tales.* Anc. hosp. for lepers, founded in Norman times by Lanfranc, is now almshouse attached to Norman church.

Harbonnières (ärbônyâr′), village (pop. 1,222), Somme dept., N France, 13 mi. SW of Péronne; chemical plant. Captured by Australians (1918) in First World War.

Harbor Beach, city (pop. 2,349), Huron co., E Mich., 17 mi. E of Bad Axe, on L. Huron; commercial fishing and resort center; mfg. (butter, corn and wheat products). Settled 1837; inc. as village 1882, as city 1909.

Harbor City, S industrial section of Los ANGELES city, Los Angeles co., S Calif., just NW of Wilmington, in harbor dist.

Harbord (här′bŭrd), town (pop. 3,618), E New South Wales, Australia, 8 mi. NNE of Sydney, on coast, in metropolitan area; seaside resort.

Harbor Island, Bahama Isls.: see HARBOUR ISLAND.

Harbor Island, Texas: see ARANSAS PASS, city.

Harborne, SW industrial suburb (pop. 21,769) of Birmingham, NW Warwick, England. The church has 15th-cent. tower.

Harbor Springs, resort city (pop. 1,626), Emmet co., NW Mich., on Little Traverse Bay of L. Michigan, and 4 mi. NNW of Petoskey; hardwood lumber; boat yards, fisheries; agr. (potatoes, fruit). Inc. as village 1881, as city 1932.

Harbor View, village (pop. 392), Lucas co., NW Ohio, on Maumee Bay, E of Toledo across Maumee R.

Harbour au Bouche, N.S.: see HAVRE BOUCHER.

Harbour Buffet (bŭ′fĭt), fishing village (pop. 391), SE N.F., on SE coast of Long Isl., in Placentia Bay, 17 mi. NNW of Argentia; 47°32′N 54°4′W.

Harbour Grace, town (pop. 2,414, including Harbour Grace South Side), SE N.F., on NE coast of Avalon Peninsula, on Conception Bay, on railroad and 26 mi. WNW of St. John's; fishing port, with fish-freezing and -smoking installations, and cod-liver-oil processing plant. Also mfg. of shoes, clothing, paper bags. Has cathedral, see of R. C. bishop. Town is hq. of mobile tuberculosis clinic, serving Avalon Peninsula. Airfield was starting point of several early transatlantic flights.

Harbour Island or **Harbor Island,** islet and district (□ 1½; pop. 769), central Bahama Isls., off NE tip of Eleuthera Isl., 33 mi. NE of Nassau; 25°30′N 76°38′W. The small isl. is one of the most densely populated in the archipelago; produces tomatoes, pineapples, coconuts. The chief settlement, Dunmore Town, has a fine harbor. Harbour Isl. was one of the 1st in the Bahamas to be settled by buccaneers. Its fine beaches attract many tourists.

Harbour Island (1 mi. long), largest of Penguin Isls., just off S N.F.; 47°23′N 56°59′W.

Harburg (här′bŏŏrk), town (pop. 2,472), Swabia, W Bavaria, Germany, on the Wörnitz and 6 mi. NW of Donauwörth; cement and pottery works. Chartered c.1250. On near-by hill is a 17th-cent. castle with 13th-cent. watchtower. Limestone quarries in area.

Harburg-Wilhelmsburg (–vĭl′hĕlmsbŏŏrk), S district (1933 pop. 112,593) of Hamburg, NW Germany; inc. into Hamburg in 1938, it was formed in 1927 by the combining of Harburg (1925 pop. 72,905) and Wilhelmsburg (1925 pop. 32,517), separated by the Süderelbe. Harburg is industrial port on left bank of the Süderelbe, handling primarily raw materials (petroleum, phosphates, pyrites, coal); site of noted rubber factories and petroleum refineries; mfg. of machinery, chemicals, vegetable fats, textiles. Wilhelmsburg (N) is situated on diked, partly rural, Wilhelmsburg isl., bet. the Norderelbe and the Süderelbe; it has metal smelters, petroleum refineries, wool-carding mills, shipyards, power plants. Both Harburg and Wilhelmsburg came to Hanover in 1705. Heavily damaged in Second World War.

Harbury, town and parish (pop. 1,246), SE central Warwick, England, 5 mi. SE of Leamington; agr. market, with cementworks. Has 13th-cent. church.

Harby, agr. village and parish (pop. 608), NE Leicester, England, 8 mi. N of Melton Mowbray; cheese making.

Harchies (ärshē′), town (pop. 3,125), Hainaut prov., SW Belgium, 11 mi. W of Mons; coal mining.

Harchoka, India: see BHARATPUR, village.

Harcourt, village (pop. 600), central Victoria, Australia, 105 mi. NW of Melbourne, near Castlemaine, in fruitgrowing area; granite quarries.

Harcourt, town (pop. 303), Webster co., central Iowa, 16 mi. S of Fort Dodge, in agr. area.

Harcuvar Mountains (härkōō′vär), in Yuma and Maricopa counties, W Ariz., W of Wickenburg; rise to c.5,000 ft.

Hard (härt), town (pop. 4,281), Vorarlberg, W Austria, on L. of Constance, at mouth of the Rhine, and 3 mi. W of Bregenz; textiles (silk, velvet); shipyards.

Harda (hŭr′dŭ), town (pop. 15,120), Hoshangabad dist., W Madhya Pradesh, India, in fertile Narbada valley, 50 mi. SW of Hoshangabad; agr. trade center (wheat, millet, cotton, oilseeds); brassware.

Hardangerfjell (härdäng′ŭrfyĕl), mountains in SW Norway, bet. Sogne Fjord (N) and Hardanger Fjord (S), rising to 6,155 ft. in the **Hardangerjokel** (–yû″kŭl), Nor. *Hardangerjøkel,* formerly *Hardangerjøkull,* 4 mi. SW of Finse. There are numerous waterfalls. To S is the great **Hardangervidda** (–vĭd″dä) or **Hardanger Plateau,** sometimes called simply the Vidda, in Hordaland and Buskerud counties, SW Norway, a barren bedrock area (□ c.2,500), the largest in Europe, extending c.100 mi. bet. head of Hardanger Fjord and the Hallingdal; average elevation c.3,500 ft. Grooved by deep, steep-sided valleys; contains numerous lakes; traversed by Oslo-Bergen RR and E-W highway. On the coast it is indented by Hardanger Fjord and its branches. Winter-sports and tourist area, especially the fjords and the FOLGEFONN glacier.

Hardanger Fjord, inlet (c.80 mi. long) of North Sea, Hordaland co., SW Norway, extends NE into Hardanger highland region to Eidsfjord. Its mouth, 35 mi. NNE of Haugesund, is protected by Stord, Bomlo, and several other isls. SOR FJORD is a S arm. Brisling and salmon fishing; tourist traffic.

Hardburly, mining village (1940 pop. 1,412), Perry co., SE Ky., in Cumberland foothills, 5 mi. NE of Hazard; bituminous coal.

Hardee (här′dē), county (□ 630; pop. 10,073), central Fla.; ⊙ Wauchula. Rolling terrain, partly swampy, with many small lakes; drained by Peace R. Citrus-fruit, truck, and strawberry region, with cattle and poultry raising. Formed 1921.

Hardeeville (här′dēvĭl), town (pop. 546), Beaufort and Jasper counties, S S.C., 15 mi. N of Savannah, Ga.; sawmills.

Hardegsen (här′dĕksŭn), town (pop. 2,722), in former Prussian prov. of Hanover, W Germany, after 1945 in Lower Saxony, 9 mi. NNW of Göttingen; sawmilling. Has remains of anc. castle.

Hardelot or **Hardelot-Plage** (ärdŭlō′-pläzh′), small bathing resort, Pas-de-Calais dept., N France, on English Channel, 6 mi. S of Boulogne.

Hardeman (här′dŭmŭn). **1** County (□ 655; pop. 23,311), SW Tenn.; ⊙ Bolivar. Bounded S by Miss.; drained by Hatchie R. Cotton, corn, fruit, truck, livestock; timber; some lumbering. Formed 1823. **2** County (□ 685; pop. 10,212), N Texas; ⊙ Quanah. Bet. Pease R. (S) and Prairie Dog Town Fork of Red R. (here forming Okla. line) on N. Wheat, cotton, cattle; also grain sorghums, poultry, dairy products. Gypsum mining; some oil production; clay deposits. Includes L. Pauline (hunting, fishing). Formed 1858.

Harden, England: see BINGLEY.

Hardenberg. 1 Village, Hanover, W Germany: see NÖRTEN-HARDENBERG. **2** Town, Rhine Prov., W Germany: see NEVIGES.

Hardenberg (här′dŭnbĕrkh), town (pop. 1,957), Overijssel prov., E Netherlands, on Vecht R., near Overijssel Canal, and 16 mi. N of Almelo; clothing mfg., meat packing, dairying. Sometimes spelled Hardenbergh.

Harderwijk (här′dŭrvīk), town (pop. 7,947) and port, Gelderland prov., central Netherlands, on the Ijsselmeer, 17 mi. NW of Apeldoorn; mfg. (soap, furniture, cigars, limestone); fishing, fish curing, duck raising; egg market. Botanical gardens. Chartered in 1231; in Middle Ages a Hanseatic city; from 1647 to 1811, seat of provincial univ. where Linnaeus once taught. Sometimes spelled Harderwyk.

Hardesty, town (pop. 201), Texas co., extreme NW Okla., 16 mi. E of Guymon.

Hardheim (härt′hīm), village (pop. 3,663), N Baden, Germany, after 1945 in Württemberg-Baden, on E slope of the Odenwald, 11 mi. S of Wertheim; metal- and woodworking, food processing. Has 16th-cent. castle, keep of 15th-cent. castle.

Hardhorn with Newton, agr. parish (pop. 1,036), W Lancashire, England, just ENE of Blackpool; dairy farming, wheat, potato, and barley growing.

Hardin. 1 County (□ 183; pop. 7,530), extreme SE Ill.; ⊙ Elizabethtown. Bounded S and E by Ohio R.; drained by short Big Creek. NW corner lies in Ill. Ozarks. Agr. (wheat, corn; dairy products; poultry, livestock). Mining (lead, zinc, fluorspar). Includes part of Shawnee Natl. Forest, and Cave in Rock State Park. Formed 1839. **2** County (□ 574; pop. 22,218), central Iowa; ⊙ Eldora. Prairie agr. area (hogs, cattle, poultry, corn, oats, soybeans) drained by Iowa R. Limestone quarries, sand and gravel pits, coal deposits. Has several state parks. Formed 1851. **3** County (□ 616; pop. 50,312), central and N Ky.; ⊙ Elizabethtown. Bounded N by Ohio R. (Ind. line), E by Salt R. and Rolling Fork; drained by Rough and Nolin rivers. Gently rolling agr. area (livestock, burley tobacco, corn, wheat); limestone quarries, sand pits, asphalt deposits. Some mfg. at Elizabethtown. Includes U.S. Fort KNOX. Formed 1792. **4** County (□ 467; pop. 28,673), W central Ohio; ⊙ Kenton. Intersected by Scioto, Blanchard, and Ottawa rivers. Agr. area (livestock, onions, grain, dairy products, peppermint, poultry); mfg. at Kenton, Ada, and Forest; limestone quarries, gravel pits. Formed 1833. **5** County (□ 595; pop. 16,908), SW Tenn.; ⊙ Savannah. Bounded S by Miss. and Ala., NE by Tennessee R. Timber and agr. (livestock, cotton, corn, hay) area; limestone deposits. Mfg. at Savannah. Includes Pickwick Landing Dam and part of Pickwick Landing Reservoir in S, Shiloh Natl. Military Park in SW. Formed 1819. **6** County (□ 895; pop. 19,535), E Texas; ⊙ Kountze. Bounded E by Neches R. and drained by its tributaries. S part on Gulf coastal plains; rolling, wooded in N (lumbering). Agr. (especially truck; also corn, potatoes); livestock raising. Oil, natural-gas fields. Formed 1858.

Hardin. 1 Village (pop. 928), ⊙ Calhoun co., W Ill., on Illinois R. and 30 mi. NW of Alton; center of apple- and grain-growing dist.; vinegar factory. **2** Town (pop. 324), Marshall co., SW Ky., near East Fork Clarks R., 17 mi. E of Mayfield. **3** City (pop. 747), Ray co., NW Mo., near Missouri R., 8 mi. E of Richmond; agr. (corn, wheat, oats); grain elevators. **4** City (pop. 2,306), ⊙ Big Horn co., S Mont., on Bighorn R., at mouth of Little Bighorn R., and 45 mi. E of Billings; trading point for Crow Indian Reservation; beet sugar, dairy products, livestock; gas wells, stone quarries. Inc. 1911.

Harding. 1 County (□ 2,136; pop. 3,013), NE N.Mex.; ⊙ Mosquero. Livestock-grazing and grain area; watered by branches of Canadian R. Formed 1921. **2** County (□ 2,683; pop. 2,289), NW S.Dak., bounded W by Mont., N by N.Dak.; ⊙ Buffalo. Cattle-raising area watered by Little Missouri R. Large deposits of lignite coal; numerous small ranches. Cave Hills, East and West Short Pines, and Slim Buttes are limestone ridges in N, SW, and E; part of Custer Natl. Forest near each. Formed 1908.

Harding, village (pop. 124), Morrison co., central Minn., near Platte R., 20 mi. NE of Little Falls, in agr. area. Inc. 1938.

Hardingstone, England: see NORTHAMPTON, city.

Hardinsburg. 1 Town (pop. 247), Washington co., S Ind., 28 mi. WNW of New Albany, in agr. area. **2** Town (pop. 902), ⊙ Breckinridge co., NW Ky., 35 mi. E of Owensboro, in agr. (burley tobacco, corn, wheat) and hardwood-timber area; cottage industries (quilted articles, boudoir novelties); textiles, beverages; flour and feed mills.

Hardinxveld or **Hardingsveld** (both: här'dĭngks-fĕlt), town (pop. 7,535), South Holland prov., SW Netherlands, on Upper Merwede R. (here forming Lower Merwede and New Merwede rivers) and 5 mi. W of Gorinchem; shipbuilding; mfg. (building machinery, iron products, woven mats); fishing.

Hardisty, town (pop. 494), E Alta., on Battle R. and 22 mi. SW of Wainwright; grain elevators, stockyards, mixed farming.

Hardman, town (pop. 58), Morrow co., N Oregon, 15 mi. SSW of Heppner; wheat.

Hardo Daska, W Pakistan: see DASKA.

Hardoi (hŭr'dōē), district (□ 2,320; pop. 1,239,279), central Uttar Pradesh, India; ⊙ Hardoi. On Ganges Plain; bounded SW by Ganges, E by Gumti rivers; drained by the Ramganga; irrigated by Sarda Canal system. Agr. (wheat, gram, barley, pearl millet, rice, oilseeds, jowar, sugar cane, corn); a major Indian sugar-processing dist.; cotton weaving. Main towns: Hardoi, Shahabad, Sandila, Mallanwan.

Hardoi, town (pop. 24,252), ⊙ Hardoi dist., central Uttar Pradesh, India, 35 mi. SSE of Shahjahanpur; road and trade (grains, oilseeds) center; sugar milling, woodworking, saltpeter processing.

Hardt Mountains or **Haardt Mountains** (both: härt), range in Rhenish Palatinate, W Germany, extends c.25 mi. N of Queich R.; rises to 2,240 ft. in the Kalmit; densely forested (broadleaf); orchards and vineyards on E slopes. Geologically, range is a continuation of the Vosges.

Hardtner, city (pop. 373), Barber co., S Kansas, 9 mi. W of Kiowa, near Okla. line; cattle, wheat.

Harduaganj (hŭrdwä'gŭnj), town (pop. 4,042), Aligarh dist., W Uttar Pradesh, India, near Upper Ganges Canal, 6 mi. NE of Aligarh; wheat, barley, pearl millet, gram, cotton. Hydroelectric plant.

Hardwar (hŭr'dvär), town (pop. 40,823), Saharanpur dist., N Uttar Pradesh, India, at foot of Siwalik Range, on the Ganges (headworks of Ganges Canal system) and 105 mi. NE of Delhi. Regarded as one of 7 most sacred Hindu centers in India. Principal object of pilgrimage is temple of Gangadwara and adjoining bathing ghat (*Hari-ke-charan*, = Vishnu's footprint); other Vishnuite and Sivaite temples. Duodecennial gathering (Kumbh mela) attended by great numbers of pilgrims. Sacked (1399) by Tamerlane. Called Gangadwara by Moslem historians. Hydroelectric station near Pathri, 7 mi. SSW, and another at Bahadrabad, 7 mi. WSW.

Hardwick. 1 Village (pop. 14,774, with adjacent Midway), Baldwin co., central Ga., just S of Milledgeville. **2** Town (pop. 2,348), Worcester co., central Mass., on branch of Ware R. and 21 mi. WNW of Worcester, near Quabbin Reservoir; dairying. Settled 1737, inc. 1739. Includes villages of Gilbertville (pop. 1,039) and Wheelwright. **3** Village (pop. 297), Rock co., extreme SW Minn., near S.Dak. line, 8 mi. N of Luverne in grain and potato area. **4** Town (pop. 2,629), including Hardwick village (pop. 1,696), Caledonia co., N central Vt., 20 mi. NNE of Montpelier and on Lamoille R.; granite, wood and dairy products. Settled before 1800.

Hardwicke Bay, inlet of Spencer Gulf, South Australia, bet. Corny Point of Yorke Peninsula and S shore of Wardang Isl.; 33 mi. long, 20 mi. wide.

Hardy, county (□ 585; pop. 10,032), W.Va., in Eastern Panhandle; ⊙ Moorefield. Bounded E and S by Va.; drained by South Branch of the Potomac and by Cacapon R. Traversed by ridges (including North and Shenandoah mts.) and valleys of the Alleghenies. Includes Lost R. State Park and part of George Washington Natl. Forest. Agr. (livestock, dairy products, fruit). Small industries at Moorefield. Formed 1786.

Hardy. 1 Town (pop. 599), a ⊙ Sharp co., N Ark., 28 mi. W of Pocahontas and on Spring R.; fishing resort; timber. **2** Town (pop. 139), Humboldt co., N central Iowa, 23 mi. NNE of Fort Dodge, in agr. area. **3** Village (1940 pop. 854), Pike co., E Ky., in the Cumberlands near W.Va. line, 5 mi. SSE of Williamson, W.Va., in bituminous-coal-mining area. **4** Village (pop. 348), Nuckolls co., S Nebr., 7 mi. E of Superior, at Kansas line near Republican R.; dairy and poultry produce, livestock, grain. **5** Town (pop. 17), Kay co., N Okla., near Kansas line, 25 mi. NE of Ponca City, in agr. area.

Hardy Dam, Mich.: see MUSKEGON RIVER.

Hardy Peninsula, Chile: see HOSTE ISLAND.

Hardy River, Lower California, NW Mexico, rises from small L. Volcano (fed by overflow of the Colorado) in Imperial Valley near U.S. border, flows c.60 mi. SE to the Gulf of California opposite Montague Isl. Since 1909 the Hardy has formed, in almost its entire length, the lower course of Colorado R.

Hare Bay, inlet (20 mi. long, 10 mi. wide at entrance), NE N.F.: 51°17'N 55°50'W.

Harefield, England: see UXBRIDGE.

Hare Hill. 1 Hill (1,958 ft.), W N.F., at SW end of Grand L., 22 mi. SSW of Corner Brook. **2** Hill (995 ft.), S N.F., on W side of Burin Peninsula, near E side of Fortune Bay; highest point of Burin Peninsula.

Hareid or **Hareidland** (här'ādlän"), island (□ 67; pop. 5,431) in North Sea, More og Romsdal co., W Norway, one of the Sor Isls., SW of Alesund; 13 mi. long, 9 mi. wide; separated from mainland by narrow sound. Fishing and mfg. of fish products. Hareid village (pop. 744), on NE coast, makes wood products. Other villages: ULSTEINVIK and HJORUNGAVAG.

Hare Indian River, NW Mackenzie Dist., Northwest Territories, rises W of Great Bear L., flows 120 mi. W to Mackenzie R. at Fort Good Hope.

Hare Island or **Ile aux Lièvres** (ēl ō lyĕ'vrŭ), island (8 mi. long, 1 mi. wide), SE central Que., in the St. Lawrence, opposite Rivière du Loup. Just E are the Brandypot islets.

Harelbeke (hä'rŭlbākŭ), town (pop. 13,152), West Flanders prov., W Belgium, on Lys R. and 3 mi. NNE of Courtrai; textile industry; market center for tobacco-growing, cattle-raising area. Has 12th-cent. church. Town chartered 1153. Formerly spelled Harlebeke.

Haren (hä'rŭn), suburb 4 mi. NE of Brussels, Brabant prov., central Belgium; Portland cement; gasoline storage tanks. Airport.

Haren, village (pop. 391), in former Prussian prov. of Hanover, NW Germany, after 1945 in Lower Saxony, on the Ems (here joined by short Haren-Rütenbrock Canal) and 7 mi. NNW of Meppen; metalworking.

Haren, village (pop. 3,787), Groningen prov., N Netherlands, on the Hondsrug and 3 mi. SSE of Groningen; fruitgrowing, dairying.

Haren-Rütenbrock Canal (–rü'tŭnbrôk), NW Germany, connects Süd-Nord Canal (at Rütenbrock) with the Ems (at Haren). Length c.10 mi.

Hareskov (hä'rŭskou), town (pop. 1,147), Copenhagen amt, Zealand, Denmark, 11 mi. NW of Copenhagen.

Harewood, W.Va.: see BOOMER.

Harfleur (ärflûr'), town (pop. 5,052), Seine-Inférieure dept., N France, on Seine R. estuary and 4 mi. E of Le Havre; foundries; vinegar mfg. Important port during Middle Ages until rise of Le Havre. Its siege and capture (1415) by Henry V of England is described by Shakespeare. Damaged in Second World War. Shipping connection with Le Havre harbor via Tancarville Canal.

Harford (här'fŭrd), county (□ 448; pop. 51,782), NE Md.; ⊙ Bel Air. Bounded N by Pa. line, NE by the Susquehanna, SE and S by Chesapeake Bay. Piedmont agr. area (N) produces dairy products, vegetables, fruit, grain, poultry, and has stone quarries; coastal plain (S fringe) is occupied mostly by federal reservations (Aberdeen Proving Ground, Army Chemical Center, and Edgewood Arsenal). Commercial fisheries, shore resorts, some industries (especially vegetable canneries, clothing factories). Co. includes many large estates. Committee for Harford co. issued a declaration of independence from Britain (one of 1st in America) on March 22, 1775. Formed 1773.

Harg (här'yŭ), village (pop. 519), Sodermanland co., E Sweden, on short Nykoping R., just NW of Nykoping; cotton mills.

Hargaon, India: see SITAPUR, town, Sitapur dist.

Hargarten-aux-Mines (ärgärtĕn'-ō-mēn'), village (pop. 720), Moselle dept., NE France, 13 mi. WNW of Forbach; near-by rail junction of Hargarten-Falck is Saar border station.

Hargeisa (härgā'sä), town (pop. 15,000 to 20,000), ⊙ Br. Somaliland and of Hargeisa dist., W Br. Somaliland, in Ogo highland, on road and 90 mi. SW of Berbera; 9°31'N 44°3'E. Administrative center; residence of governor. Livestock raising. Airfield. Formerly only summer ⊙ of Br. Somaliland; became permanent ⊙ in March, 1941.

Hari, river, Afghanistan: see HARI RUD.

Haría (ärē'ä), village (pop. 2,347), Lanzarote, Canary Isls., 13 mi. N of Arrecife; cereals, grapes, fruit, vegetables. Flour milling, wine making, embroidery mfg. Its Atlantic port Arrieta (pop. 108) is 2 mi. E.

Hariana (hŭryä'nŭ), level area in S Punjab and S Patiala and East Punjab States Union, India; roughly bet. Ghaggar R. (N), sandy tracts of Thar Desert (W, S), and Jind and Rohtak (E). Once scene of flourishing Hindu civilization.

Hariana, town (pop. 6,417), Hoshiarpur dist., N central Punjab, India, 8 mi. NW of Hoshiarpur; wheat, sugar cane, corn, gram; hand-loom woolen weaving.

Harigaon (hä'rĭgoun), village (pop. 5,727), Ahmadnagar dist., E Bombay, India, 38 mi. N of Ahmadnagar; rail terminus; sugar milling.

Harihar (hŭrĭhŭr'), town (pop. 8,422), Chitaldrug dist., N Mysore, India, on Tungabhadra R. and 8 mi. WNW of Davangere, on Bombay border; road center; mfg. of cotton textiles, machine tools; known for fine handicrafts (leather footwear, woolen weaving, goldsmithing). Annual cattle fair. Large 13th-cent. Vishnuite-Sivaite temple contains substructure with inscriptions dating back to 7th cent. A.D.

Harij (hä'rĭj), village (pop. 4,540), Mehsana dist., N Bombay, India, 31 mi. WNW of Mehsana; rail spur terminus; local market for millet, cotton, salt, oilseeds.

Harim (hä'rĭm), town, Aleppo prov., NW Syria, on Turkish border, 38 mi. W of Aleppo; tobacco, cereals.

Harima (hä"rē'mä), former province in S Honshu, Japan; now part of Hyogo prefecture.

Harima Sea, Jap. *Harima-nada*, E section of Inland Sea, Japan, bet. Honshu (N) and NE coast of Shikoku (S); merges W with Hiuchi Sea; bounded E by Awaji-shima; connected with Philippine Sea by Naruto Strait and Kii Channel; c.50 mi. long, 40 mi. wide. Contains Shodo-shima. Takamatsu is on SW shore.

Häring (hâ'rĭng), village (pop. 1,793), Tyrol, W Austria, 6 mi. SSW of Kufstein; summer resort with mineral baths. Lignite mined near by.

Haringhata River, E Pakistan: see MADHUMATI RIVER.

Haringvliet (hä'rĭng-vlēt), SW Netherlands, N arm of Waal and Maas estuary, formed by branching of the HOLLANDSCHDIEP into the Volkerak and the Haringvliet, 12 mi. SW of Dordrecht; flows 21 mi. NW, past Hellevoetsluis, to North Sea; joined by Spui R. 14 mi. SW of Rotterdam. Forms SW boundary of Beijerland, Putten, and Voorne isls., NE boundary of Goeree and Overflakkee isls. Entire length navigable.

Haripad (hŭrĭpäd'), city (pop. 10,175), W Travancore, India, 30 mi. NNW of Quilon; coir rope and mats; cashew-nut processing.

Haripur (hŭrē'po͝or), town (pop. 9,322), Hazara dist., NE North-West Frontier Prov., W Pakistan, 18 mi. SW of Abbottabad; markets corn, wheat, barley, rapeseed; local trade in skins; handicraft cloth embroidering, shoe mfg.; apricot growing. Has small agr. farm. Sometimes called Haripur Hazara.

Hariq or **Al Hariq** (ăl hărēk'), town, S central Nejd, Saudi Arabia, 80 mi. SSW of Riyadh; 23°33'N 46°25'E. Grain, vegetables, fruit; stock raising.

Hari River (hä'rē), **Jambi River,** or **Djambi River** (both: jăm'bē), S central Sumatra, Indonesia, rises in Padang Highlands, flows SE, turning NE past Jambi, to Berhala Strait 55 mi. NE of Jambi; c.250 mi. long. Navigable for seagoing vessels below Jambi.

Hari Rud or **Heri Rud** (hŭ'rē ro͞od'), anc. *Arius*, river in Afghanistan, Iran, and Turkmen SSR (USSR), known as **Tedzhen River** (tĕjĕn') in lower course (Turkmen SSR); rises in the Koh-i-Baba, flows 700 mi. W, past Obeh and Herat, and N, past Zulfiqar and Serakhs (opposite Iranian Sarakhs), through the Kara-Kum desert to Tedzhen oasis, beyond which it disappears into the desert. Irrigates the richest agr. section of Afghan Herat prov., bet. Obeh and Ghurian, and the Turkmen Tedzhen oasis (dam above Tedzhen). Forms Iran-Afghanistan border bet. Islam Qala and Zulfiqar, and Iran-USSR line bet. Zulfiqar and Serakhs (Sarakhs). The lower course is sometimes spelled Tejen or Tejend.

Harjavalta (här'yäväl"tä), village (commune pop. 5,705), Turku-Pori co., SW Finland, on Kokemäki R. (rapids) and 17 mi. SE of Pori; copper-smelting center, serves Outokumpu mines. Large hydroelectric station. Site of sanitarium and mental hosp.

Harjedalen, province, Sweden: see JAMTLAND.

Harkany (hŏr'känyŭ), Hung. *Harkány,* town (pop. 914), Baranya co., S Hungary, at S foot of Villany Mts., 16 mi. S of Pecs; rail junction; hot sulphur springs.

Harkers Island (pop. 1,244), Carteret co., E N.C., in sheltered sound 4 mi. E of Beaufort; 5 mi. long, 1 mi. wide; bridged to mainland. Inhabited by fishermen.

Harkiko (härkē'kō), Ital. *Archico,* village, Massawa div., central Eritrea, fishing port on Red Sea, 8 mi. S of Massawa; cereals, sesame, vegetables.

Harkin, Mount (9,788 ft.), SE B.C., near Alta. border, in Rocky Mts., on SE edge of Kootenay Natl. Park, 30 mi. SW of Banff; 50°47'N 115°52'W.

Harksheide (härks'hī"dŭ), village (pop. 5,541), in Schleswig-Holstein, NW Germany, 12 mi. N of Hamburg city center; mfg. of chemicals.

Harlan (här'lŭn). **1** County (□ 469; pop. 71,751), SE Ky.; ⊙ Harlan. In the Cumberlands; bounded S and E by Va.; drained by Cumberland R. and its Poor and Clover forks; includes Kentenia State Forest, Big Black Mtn. (4,150 ft.; highest point in Ky.) and part of Pine Mtn. Rich bituminous- and cannel-coal mining area; leads Ky. counties in coal production. Hardwood timber; some farms (dairy products, poultry, livestock, corn, apples, Irish and sweet potatoes, tobacco). Labor conflicts bet. coal operators and miners in co. (nicknamed "Bloody Harlan") have been frequent and bitter; after 20 years of strife, mines were unionized in 1941. Formed 1819. **2** County (□ 575; pop. 7,189), S Nebr.; ⊙ Alma. Agr. region bounded S by Kansas; drained by Republican R., here impounded by Harlan Co. Dam (begun 1948; for flood control). Grain, livestock, dairy and poultry produce. Formed 1871.

Harlan. 1 City (pop. 3,915), ⊙ Shelby co., W Iowa, on West Nishnabotna R. (hydroelectric plant) and 37 mi. NE of Council Bluffs; corn cannery, rendering plant, cement works, machine shop (farm equipment). Settled 1858, inc. 1879. **2** City (pop. 4,786), ⊙ Harlan co., SE Ky., in the Cumberlands, on Clover Fork of Cumberland R. and 27 mi. NE of Middlesboro; coal-mining center in one of Ky.'s largest bituminous- and cannel-coal fields. Some lumbering, agr. (corn, potatoes) in region. City settled 1819 as Mt. Pleasant; grew as coal-shipping point after coming of railroad in 1911.

Harland (här'länt), town, central Lower Austria, near Traisen R., 3 mi. S of Sankt Pölten; textiles, thread.

Harlau (hûr'lŭoo), Rum. *Hârlău,* town (1948 pop. 4,172), Jassy prov., NE Rumania, in Moldavia, 24 mi. SE of Botosani; rail terminus in viticultural region; glass mfg., distilling, flour milling. Has 16th-cent. church, ruins of 17th-cent. palace.

Harlaw (här'lô, härlô'), locality in central Aberdeen, Scotland, 2 mi. NW of Inverurie; scene of battle (1411) in which earl of Mar defeated Highlanders under Donald, Lord of the Isles.

Harlebeke, Belgium: see HARELBEKE.

Harlech (här'lĭk, -lĕkh), town, NW Merioneth, Wales, on Cardigan Bay of Irish Sea, 5 mi. S of Portmadoc; seaside resort and agr. market. Has remains of Harlech Castle, built 1285 by Edward I, surrendered 1468 to Yorkists after stubborn defense, commemorated in Welsh battle song, *The March of the Men of Harlech.* Golf course is considered best in Wales. Harlech was anc. ⊙ Merioneth. Extending 3 mi. N from Harlech, up to 3 mi. wide, is triangular marsh area of Morfa Harlech.

Harlem, Netherlands: see HAARLEM.

Harlem (här'lŭm). **1** Village (pop. 1,411, with adjacent Hookers Point), Hendry co., S Fla. There is also a Harlem in Putnam co., N Fla., near Palatka. **2** Town (pop. 1,033), Columbia co., E Ga., 19 mi. WSW of Augusta; mfg. (brick, sewer pipe, clothing, wood products). **3** Town (pop. 1,107), Blaine co., N Mont., on Milk R. and 20 mi. E of Chinook; hq. and trading point for Fort Belknap Indian Reservation; grain, sugar beets, potatoes; rock quarries. Inc. 1910. **4** A residential and business district of N Manhattan borough of New York city, SE N.Y., bounded approximately by Central Park and 110th St. (S), East R. (E), Harlem R. (NE), 168th St. (N), and Amsterdam Ave. and Morningside Park (W). Largest Negro community (pop. more than 400,000) in U.S. grew up here after 1910; one of most congested districts in U.S., Harlem also has large colonies of Puerto Rican, Italian, and Latin American background. The Du. settlement of Nieuw Haarlem was est. here 1658 by Peter Stuyvesant; in the Revolution, Continental forces stopped the British advance up Manhattan in battle (Sept., 1776) of Harlem Heights. Area remained virtually rural until improvement in 19th cent. of transportation links with lower Manhattan. Public-housing projects (begun in 1930s) and other attempts to relieve unfavorable conditions have been made.

Harlem River, in New York city, SE N.Y., navigable tidal channel separating the N tip of Manhattan from the Bronx. Joins East R. at Hell Gate channel; 8 mi. long with short Spuyten Duyvil Creek (spī'tŭn dī'vŭl), now a ship canal, which joins W end of Harlem R. and the Hudson. Crossed by many bridges.

Harlesden, England: see WILLESDEN.

Harleston (härls'tŭn), town in parish of Redenhall with Harleston (pop. 1,645), S Norfolk, England, near Waveney R., 17 mi. S of Norwich; agr. market, with leather industry. Just ENE is agr. village of Redenhall, with 14th-cent. church.

Harle Syke, town in Burnley borough, E Lancashire, England; cotton milling.

Harleyville, agr. town (pop. 483), Dorchester co., SE central S.C., 20 mi. NW of Summerville.

Harlingen (här'lĭng-ŭn), town (pop. 10,865), Friesland prov., N Netherlands, on the Waddenzee, at W end of the Harlinger Trekvaart, and 16 mi. W of Leeuwarden; chief port for prov.; exports dairy products, potatoes, meat, garden produce; imports cotton, jute, coal. On site of town destroyed by the sea in 1134.

Harlingen (här'lĭnjŭn), city (pop. 23,229), Cameron co., extreme S Texas, 23 mi. NW of Brownsville; a barge port on channel (partly in Arroyo Colorado) to Gulf Intracoastal Waterway, and a trade, processing, shipping, mfg. center in rich irrigated citrus, truck, cotton area of lower Rio Grande valley; canneries, freezing and packing plants, cotton-processing plants, mfg. of canning and packing machinery, chairs. Founded c.1904 with coming of railroad.

Harlingerode (här"lĭng-ŭrō'dŭ), village (pop. 5,315), in Brunswick, NW Germany, after 1945 in Lower Saxony, at N foot of the upper Harz, 3 mi. NW of Bad Harzburg; woodworking, weaving.

Harlinger Trekvaart (här'lĭng-ŭr trĕk'värt), canal, Friesland prov., N Netherlands; extends 17 mi. E-W, bet. the Waddenzee at Harlingen and the WIJDE EE at Leeuwarden. Serves Franeker; carries dairy and agr. products.

Harlington, England: see HAYES AND HARLINGTON.

Harlow, residential town (1951 pop. 5,828), W Essex, England, near Stort R., 6 mi. S of Bishop's Stortford. Has Norman church. After Second World War it underwent great development as model residential town.

Harlowton (här'lōtŭn), city (pop. 1,733), ⊙ Wheatland co., central Mont., on Musselshell R. and 80 mi. NW of Billings; trade center for livestock area; railroad repair shops, stone quarries; flour, dairy products, grain. Inc. 1917.

Harlu, Karelo-Finnish SSR: see KHARLU.

Harman, village (pop. 146), Randolph co., E W.Va., 17 mi. E of Elkins.

Harmanec (här'mänyĕts), Hung. *Hermánd* (hĕr'mänd), village (pop. 845), central Slovakia, Czechoslovakia, on railroad and 7 mi. NW of Banska Bystrica; large paper mills.

Harmanli, Bulgaria: see KHARMANLII.

Harmarville, village (pop. c.900), Allegheny co., SW Pa., on the Allegheny opposite Oakmont and 10 mi. NE of downtown Pittsburgh; fuel and lubricant research plant.

Harmashatar, Mount (här'mŏsh-hŏtär), Hung. *Hármashatárhegy* (-hĕdyŭ), highest point (1,627 ft.) in N range of Buda Mts., N central Hungary. Residential dists. on E slopes; stalactite cave of Palvölgy near by.

Harmas Körös, Hungary: see KÖRÖS RIVER.

Harmelen (här'mŭlŭn), town (pop. 1,348), Utrecht prov., W central Netherlands, on the Old Rhine and 7 mi. W of Utrecht; machine shops; shipbuilding.

Harmignies (ärmēnyē'), town (pop. 1,015), Hainaut prov., SW Belgium, 5 mi. SE of Mons; cement mfg.

Harmon, county (□ 532; pop. 8,079), SW Okla.; ⊙ Hollis. Bounded S and W by Texas; drained by the Salt and Prairie Dog Town forks of Red R. Hilly agr. area (livestock, cotton, wheat, sweet potatoes). Mfg. at Hollis. Formed 1909.

Harmon. 1 Village (pop. 208), Lee co., N Ill., 9 mi. SSW of Dixon, in rich agr. area. **2** Section (pop. c.1,000) of Croton-on-Hudson, Westchester co., SE N.Y., on E bank of the Hudson, just N of Ossining; an important stop on N.Y. Central RR, at N end of its electrified section. Near by is Croton Point Park (recreation).

Harmondsworth, England: see YIEWSLEY AND WEST DRAYTON.

Harmon Field, N.F.: see STEPHENVILLE.

Harmony. 1 Agr. town (pop. 709), Somerset co., central Maine, 17 mi. NE of Skowhegan; wood products, yarn mills. **2** Village (pop. 1,022), Fillmore co., SE Minn., near Iowa line, 9 mi. SSE of Preston, in grain, livestock, and poultry area; dairy products. Near by is Niagara Cave, with 60-ft. waterfall 200 ft. below surface of earth. **3** Village (pop. 374), Iredell co., W central N.C., 14 mi. NNE of Statesville. **4** Borough (pop. 912), Butler co., W Pa., 12 mi. WSW of Butler. First settlement (1805) of Harmony Society.

Harnahalli, India: see HARANHALLI.

Harnai (hŭrnī'), village, Sibi dist., NE central Baluchistan, W Pakistan, in N Central Brahui Range, 38 mi. N of Sibi. Limestone, coal, gypsum deposits worked in hills (S).

Harnamganj, India: see KUNDA.

Harnes (ärn), town (pop. 11,634), Pas-de-Calais dept., N France, 4 mi. ENE of Lens; coal mines, coke ovens, limekilns, chemical plant.

Harnett (här'nĭt), county (□ 606; pop. 47,605), central N.C.; ⊙ Lillington. Forested sand-hills area; drained by Cape Fear R.; bounded SE by Little R. Farming (especially tobacco; cotton, corn); textile mfg., sawmilling. Formed 1855.

Harney, county (□ 10,132; pop. 6,113), SE central Oregon; ⊙ Burns. Livestock-grazing area bounded S by Nev. Lumber milling. Parts of Ochoco and Malheur natl. forests are in N, part of Great Sandy Desert in W. Steens Mtn. is in SE, Harney L. S of Burns. Formed 1889.

Harney, town (pop. 6), Harney co., E central Oregon, 11 mi. ENE of Burns.

Harney, Lake, E central Fla., on Volusia-Seminole co. line, 12 mi. ESE of Sanford; a shallow widening (c.4 mi. long, 2–3 mi. wide) of SAINT JOHNS RIVER.

Harney Lake, SE central Oregon, salt lake (□ c.60) just SW of Malheur L., 20 mi. S of Burns; c.10 mi. in diameter. Part of U.S. migratory bird refuge.

Harney Peak, SW S.Dak., 10 mi. NNE of Custer; highest point (7,242 ft.) in Black Hills and in S. Dak. Mt. Rushmore Natl. Memorial is near by.

Harnosand (hĕr"nŭsänd'), Swedish *Härnösand,* city (1950 pop. 15,263), ⊙ Vasternorrland co., NE Sweden, on Gulf of Bothnia, near mouth of Angerman R., 220 mi. N of Stockholm; 62°38'N 17°57'E. Port (ice-bound winter), shipping timber, pulp, cellulose, tar; timber yards, sawmills. Mfg. of plywood, wallboard, machinery, tobacco products. Seat of Lutheran bishop. Part of city is on Harno isl., Swedish *Härnön* (□ 15), just offshore (road bridge), with 18th-cent. town hall and large open-air mus. Founded in 14th cent.; chartered 1585. Sacked 1721 by Russians. First European city to be electrically lighted (1885). Sometimes spelled Hernosand, Swedish *Hernösand.*

Harö, Norway: see HAROY.

Haro (ä'rō), city (pop. 8,353), Logroño prov., N Spain, in Old Castile, near the Ebro, 22 mi. WNW of Logroño; chief wine-production center of La Rioja dist.; summer resort. Tanneries, cotton mills, vegetable canneries; mfg. of alcohol, liqueur, sandals, soap. Fruit, vegetables, cereals in area. Has Gothic church (16th cent.), 18th-cent. town hall, and many fine mansions of 17th–18th cent. Title of counts of Haro borne by lords of city since Middle Ages.

Harod, Well of, Palestine: see GILBOA.

Haroekoe, Indonesia: see HARUKU.

Harold, mining village (1940 pop. 694), Floyd co., E Ky., in Cumberland foothills, on Levisa Fork and 8 mi. WNW of Pikeville; bituminous coal.

Haroldswick, Scotland: see UNST.

Haromhuta (hä'rômhŏŏtŏ), Hung. *Háromhuta,* town (pop. 934), Zemplen co., NE Hungary, in Tokaj Mts., 10 mi. W of Satoraljaujhely; glass mfg.

Haro Strait (hâ'rō), channel of the Pacific, SW B.C. and NW Wash., at SE end of Vancouver Isl., joins straits of Georgia (N) and Juan de Fuca (S). Separates Vancouver and Saturna isls. (W) and San Juan and Stuart isls. (E). B.C.-Wash. boundary line runs through center of strait.

Haroué (ärŏŏā'), agr. village (pop. 261), Meurthe-et-Moselle dept., NE France, 15 mi. S of Nancy. Has 18th-cent. castle.

Harowabad, Iran: see KHALKHAL.

Haroy (här'ûü), Nor. *Harøy,* island (□ 5; pop. 1,083) in North Sea, More og Romsdal co., W Norway, one of the Nord Isls., 21 mi. W of Molde; 5 mi. long, 2 mi. wide. Formerly spelled Harö. At Steinshamn village (pop. 223) in N is a herring-meal factory.

Harpalpur (hŭrpäl'pŏŏr), village, NW Vindhya Pradesh, India, 17 mi. NNW of Nowgong; trades in wheat, cotton, sugar, millet; sugar and flour milling, hand-loom weaving.

Harpanahalli (hŭrpŭ'nŭhŭlē), town (pop. 11,716), Bellary dist., NW Madras, India, 40 mi. SW of Hospet; road center; peanut milling, hand-loom cotton and woolen weaving, cattle raising; silk growing.

Harpenden (här'pŭndŭn), residential urban district (1931 pop. 8,349; 1951 census 14,236), W Hertford, England, 5 mi. N of St. Albans. Site of Rothamsted Experimental Station (agr. research) and of St. George's coeducational school. Has late-Norman church.

Harper, town, ⊙ Maryland co., SE Liberia, port on Atlantic Ocean, on Cape Palmas, 255 mi. SE of Monrovia; trade center; copra, cassava, rice; fishing. Road to rubber plantation (N). Mission station. Airfield. Formerly called Cape Palmas.

Harper. 1 County (□ 801; pop. 10,263), S Kansas; ⊙ Anthony. Plains region, bordered S by Okla.; drained (NE) by Chikaskia R. Wheat, livestock. Formed 1873. **2** County (□ 1,034; pop. 5,977), NW Okla.; ⊙ Buffalo. Bounded N by Kansas; intersected by North Canadian and Cimarron rivers. Plains agr. area (livestock, wheat, barley, broom-corn). Oil and natural-gas wells. Formed 1907.

Harper. 1 Town (pop. 182), Keokuk co., SE Iowa, 8 mi. ENE of Sigourney; feed milling. **2** City (pop. 1,672), Harper co., S Kansas, 45 mi. SW of Wichita, in wheat area; flour milling. Settled 1877, inc. 1880.

Harpers Ferry. 1 Town (pop. 252), Allamakee co., extreme NE Iowa, on Mississippi R. and 32 mi. ESE of Decorah; dairy products, concrete blocks.

Sand and gravel pits near by. **2** Town (pop. 822), Jefferson co., W.Va., in Eastern Panhandle, 55 mi. NW of Washington, D.C., at meeting of W.Va., Va., and Md. and at confluence of Shenandoah R. with the Potomac, here cutting through the Blue Ridge. Scenic resort and residential town. Has Storer Col. (history mus.) A U.S. arsenal here (established 1796) was seized (1859) by John Brown in raid which led to his capture, trial, and execution. In Civil War, as key to the Shenandoah Valley, town was repeatedly abandoned and reoccupied by both sides; ultimately (in Gettysburg campaign) recovered and held by the Union for rest of war. Inc. 1763 on site of ferry established 1747.

Harpersville, town (pop. 348), Shelby co., central Ala., 24 mi. ESE of Birmingham.

Harpeth River, central Tenn., rises 10 mi. SW of Murfreesboro in Rutherford co., meanders 117 mi. generally NW, past Franklin, to Cumberland R. 5 mi. WNW of Ashland City.

Harp Island, Tuamotu Isls.: see HAO.

Harplinge (här'plĭng-ů), village (pop. 619), Halland co., SW Sweden, near the Kattegat, 6 mi. NW of Halmstad; grain, flax, sugar beets.

Harpster, village (pop. 236), Wyandot co., N central Ohio, 11 mi. NW of Marion.

Harpswell, resort town (pop. 1,644), Cumberland co., SW Maine, on peninsula (Harpswell Neck; W) and isls. (Orrs Isl., Bailey Isl., and Sebascodegan Isl., also called Great Isl. or East Harpswell Isl.; all bridge-linked), in Casco Bay, and 15 mi. NE of Portland. Includes Cundys Harbor, Orrs Island, and Harpswell Center villages, latter with church (1843) where Elijah Kellogg preached. Settled 1720, inc. 1758.

Harpswell Sound, SW Maine, arm of Casco Bay extending c.12 mi. bet. Harpswell Neck and Orrs and Sebascodegan isls.

Harput or **Kharput** (both: härpōōt'), village (pop. 2,095), Elazig prov., E central Turkey, 3 mi. NNE of Elazig, in the mts. near source of the Tigris; alt. c.4,200 ft. On an old trade route, it has been replaced by Elazig as trading center. Was known for its old Jacobite convent. Suffered heavily in Armenian massacre of 1895.

Harquahala Mountains (här"kwuhä'lů), in Yuma and Maricopa counties, W Ariz., E of Harcuvar Mts., WSW of Wickenburg; rise to 5,672 ft.

Harra or **Harrah** (här'rů), desert-type of Arabian Peninsula, consisting of scattered areas of corrugated and fissured lava beds overlying sandstone. It is most common bet. Khaibar and Taima oases in NW Arabia.

Harrachov (hä'räkhôf), village (pop. 1,553), N Bohemia, Czechoslovakia, at WNW foot of the Riesengebirge, 16 mi. E of Liberec, near Pol. border; noted glassworks; popular mtn. resort. Village of Novy Svet (nô'vĭ svĕt") and Novy Svet Pass are just NW.

Harrah (hă'rů). **1** Town (pop. 741), Oklahoma co., central Okla., 20 mi. E of Oklahoma City, and on North Canadian R., in agr. area; cotton ginning. **2** Town (pop. 297), Yakima co., S Wash., 15 mi. S of Yakima.

Harraiya, India: see HARAIYA.

Harran, Turkey: see HARAN.

Harrar, Ethiopia: see HARAR.

Harraseeket River (hărůsē'kĭt), SW Maine, inlet of Casco Bay near Freeport; c.4 mi. long.

Harrell (hă'rûl), town (pop. 342), Calhoun co., S Ark., 26 mi. E of Camden.

Harrell Store, town (pop. 147), Sampson co., S central S.C.

Harrellsville (hă'rûlzvĭl), town (pop. 167), Hertford co., NE N.C., 10 mi. E of Ahoskie; lumber.

Harricanaw River (hărĭkä'nô), W Que. and NE Ont., rises near Val d'Or, flows 250 mi. NW to James Bay of Hudson Bay, 50 mi. SW of Rupert House; crosses into Ont. near its mouth. Navigable for 50 mi.

Harrietsham (hă'rēůt-shům, hă'rĭsh-ům), town and parish (pop. 1,532), central Kent, England, 7 mi. ESE of Maidstone; agr. market, with tileworks. Has almshouses, built 1642, and church dating partly from 14th cent.

Harrietta, village (pop. 152), Wexford co., NW Mich., 15 mi. WNW of Cadillac, in farm area. Has state fish hatchery.

Harriman. 1 Village (pop. 676), Orange co., SE N.Y., 10 mi. WSW of Highland Falls. Harriman section of Palisades Interstate Park is just E. **2** or **Harriman Park,** village (pop. 1,078), Bucks co., SE Pa., on Delaware R., just above Bristol. **3** City (pop. 6,389), Roane co., E Tenn., near Tennessee R., 35 mi. W of Knoxville, in rolling hills; railroad, trade, and shipping center for fruitgrowing, timber, limestone area; lumber milling, mfg. of wood products, blankets, hosiery, agr. implements, paperboard. Watts Bar Reservoir is S. Platted 1889; inc. 1891.

Harriman Dam or **Davis Bridge Dam,** S Vt., power dam in Deerfield R., in Whitingham town. Earthfill construction; 200 ft. high, 1,250 ft. long; completed 1924. Impounds L. Whitingham (or Davis Bridge Reservoir), c.8 mi. long.

Harriman Park, Pa.: see HARRIMAN.

Harrington, former urban district (1931 pop. 4,128), W Cumberland, England, on Solway Firth and 5 mi. N of Whitehaven; steel production. Inc. 1934 in Workington.

Harrington. 1 City (pop. 2,241), Kent co., central Del., 16 mi. S of Dover; trading and shipping point in agr. area; feed and flour milling; makes shirts. Kent and Sussex Fairgrounds are here. Inc. 1869. **2** Town (pop. 853), Washington co., E Maine, on Pleasant Bay and 19 mi. SW of Machias; fishing, lumbering, resorts, canneries. **3** City (pop. 620), Lincoln co., E Wash., 13 mi. SSW of Davenport, in Columbia basin agr. region; wheat, cattle.

Harrington Harbour, village (pop. estimate 200), E Que., on largest of the Harrington Isls., a group of 12 islets in Gulf of St. Lawrence; 50°30'N 59°29'W; magnesite mining. Airfield.

Harrington Lake, Piscataquis co., central Maine, 40 mi. NE of Greenville, in wilderness recreational area; 4 mi. long. Joined by stream to Ripogenus L. to SW.

Harrington Park, borough (pop. 1,634), Bergen co., NE N.J., 11 mi. NE of Paterson. Inc. 1904.

Harrington Sound, landlocked lagoon (2¼ mi. long, 1½ mi. wide), E Bermuda Isl.; narrow, 200-ft. entrance in NW.

Harris, village (pop. 231), SE central Sask., 45 mi. SW of Saskatoon; flour milling, mixed farming.

Harris, village (pop. 1,265), E Montserrat, B.W.I., 4 mi. E of Plymouth; sea-island cotton, fruit.

Harris, S part of LEWIS WITH HARRIS isl., Outer Hebrides, Inverness, Scotland, sometimes referred to as Isle of Harris, though it is joined to the larger N part by 1-mi.-wide isthmus at Tarbert; 13 mi. long, 10 mi. wide. Has irregular coastline and mountainous interior, rising to 1,654 ft. in NW. Harris parish has pop. of 1,404. North Uist (S) is across the Sound of Harris (7 mi. wide), the only channel through the Outer Hebrides navigable for large vessels. On the sound is Renish Point (57°46'N 6°58'W). Harris is famous for its handwoven tweeds. Chief town is Tarbert, fishing port, with tweed weaving, on the isthmus; summer station for Norwegian whalers. On S coast, 12 mi. SW of Tarbert, is fishing village of Leverburgh, established 1918, adjoining fishing village of Obbe. Fishing village of Rodel has anc. church.

Harris. 1 County (□ 465; pop. 11,265), W Ga.; ⊙ Hamilton. Bounded W by Ala. line (formed here by Chattahoochee R.). Piedmont livestock, agr. (cotton, corn, grain, truck, fruit), and sawmilling area. Franklin D. Roosevelt State Park (NE). Langdale, Riverview, Bartletts Ferry, and Goat Rock dams create reservoirs on the Chattahoochee here. Formed 1827. **2** County (□ 1,747; pop. 806,701), S Texas; ⊙ HOUSTON, largest city in state, seaport, industrial center. On Gulf Coast plains and bounded SE by Galveston Bay; drained by San Jacinto R. and its tributaries. Forested in N; includes part of Sam Houston Natl. Forest. Large oil, natural gas production; also salt, sulphur, clay, cement (from oyster shell); a leading cattle-raising co.; dairying, poultry raising, agr. (especially rice, wheat, truck, feed). Bay resorts. Includes San Jacinto battlefield (state park). Formed 1836.

Harris. 1 Town (pop. 319), Osceola co., NW Iowa, 25 mi. NNW of Spencer, in livestock and grain area. **2** City (pop. 84), Anderson co., E Kansas, 20 mi. SSW of Ottawa; livestock, grain; dairying. **3** Village (pop. 569), Chisago co., E Minn., near St. Croix R., c.45 mi. N of St. Paul, in grain, potato, livestock area; dairy products. **4** Town (pop. 181), Sullivan co., N Mo., 14 mi. WNW of Milan.

Harris, Lake (c.11 mi. long, 6 mi. wide), Lake co., central Fla.; connected by canal with near-by L. Eustis, it forms part of lake system drained by Oklawaha R.

Harrisburg. 1 Town (pop. 1,498), ⊙ Poinsett co., NE Ark., 19 mi. S of Jonesboro, on Crowley's Ridge, in agr. area (cotton, rice, soybeans, livestock, dairy products); lumber and rice milling, cotton ginning. **2** City (pop. 10,999), ⊙ Saline co., SE Ill., 25 mi. ESE of West Frankfort; center of bituminous-coal-mining, agr., and timber area; mfg. (wood products, flour, brick). Shawnee Natl. Forest is S. Platted in 1850s; inc. 1861. Annexed Dorrisville in 1923. **3** Town (pop. 117), Boone co., central Mo., 15 mi. NNW of Columbia. **4** Village (pop. c.100), ⊙ Banner co., W Nebr., 20 mi. S of Scottsbluff; grain. **5** Village (pop. 344), on Franklin-Pickaway co. line, central Ohio, 13 mi. SW of Columbus. **6** City (pop. 862), Linn co., W Oregon, 18 mi. N of Eugene and on Willamette R.; lumber milling. **7** City (pop. 89,544), ⊙ Pa. and Dauphin co., S central Pa., 90 mi. WNW of Philadelphia and on Susquehanna R.; 40°15'N 76°53'W; alt. 374 ft. Important rail center, with coal and iron mines near by. Steel, clothing, lumber products, bricks, machinery, shoes, food products; printing; railroad shops. Settled by German sects and Scotch-Irish; became ⊙ Pa. 1812 and canal and railroad center in 19th cent. Buildings include the capitol (built 1906), state library, mus., and mental hosp. Laid out 1785, inc. as borough 1791, as city 1860. **8** Town (pop. 274), Lincoln co., SE S. Dak., 8 mi. S of Sioux Falls; panel silo factory is here.

Harrismith (hă'rĕsmĭth), town (pop. 10,513), SE Orange Free State, U. of So. Afr., near Natal border, on Wilge R. and 130 mi. SE of Vereeniging; alt. 5,321 ft., at foot of Platberg (7,462 ft.); cotton- and woolen-milling center; distributing point for E Orange Free State; agr. market. Resort. Named for Sir Harry Smith, a governor of Cape Colony. Near by are several caves with old Bushman paintings.

Harrison. 1 County (□ 479; pop. 17,858), S Ind.; ⊙ Corydon. Bounded E, S, and SW by Ohio R. (here forming Ky. line), and W by Blue R.; drained by Indian Creek and small Buck Creek. Agr. (grain, poultry); natural gas. Lumber milling; mfg. of furniture, wagons, glass, canned foods, dairy products. Stone quarries; timber. Formed 1808. **2** County (□ 693; pop. 19,560), W Iowa, on Nebr. line (W; formed here by Missouri R.); ⊙ Logan. Prairie agr. area (cattle, hogs, corn, wheat, fruit) drained by Boyer and Soldier rivers; bituminous-coal deposits. Formed 1851. **3** County (□ 308; pop. 13,736), N Ky.; ⊙ Cynthiana. Bounded NE by Licking R.; drained by South Fork of Licking R. and several creeks. Gently rolling upland agr. area, in Bluegrass region; burley tobacco, livestock, dairy products, poultry. Timber; limestone quarries. Some mfg. (especially whisky) at Cynthiana. Formed 1793. **4** County (□ 585; pop. 84,073), SE Miss.; ⊙ GULFPORT, port on Mississippi Sound (S). Biloxi and Wolf rivers drain co. Agr. (corn, pecans, truck), dairying, stock raising, lumbering; extensive sea-food industries. Includes part of De Soto Natl. Forest. BILOXI (seaport, resort) is in co. Formed 1841. **5** County (□ 720; pop. 14,107), NW Mo.; ⊙ Bethany. Borders Iowa on N; agr. (corn, wheat, oats), livestock. Formed 1845. **6** County (□ 411; pop. 19,054), E Ohio; ⊙ Cadiz. Drained by Stillwater and small Conotton creeks. Includes Tappan and Clendening reservoirs. Coal mining; agr. (cattle, sheep, grain, poultry; dairy products); mfg. at Cadiz and Scio; limestone quarries. Formed 1813. **7** County (□ 892; pop. 47,745), E Texas; ⊙ Marshall, commercial, industrial center. Bounded E by La. line, NE by Caddo L., SW by Sabine R.; drained by Little Cypress Bayou. Hilly wooded region (extensive lumbering); agr. (cotton, corn, forage crops, fruit, truck, peanuts), dairying, livestock (cattle, poultry, hogs, horses). Large clay-products industry; also oil, natural gas, lignite. Includes Caddo L. State Park (recreation). Formed 1839. **8** County (□ 418; pop. 85,296), N W.Va.; ⊙ CLARKSBURG. On Allegheny Plateau; drained by the West Fork (a headstream of the Monongahela) and its tributaries. Agr. (livestock, fruit, tobacco); natural-gas and oil wells, bituminous-coal mines; lumbering activities. Industries at Clarksburg. Formed 1784.

Harrison. 1 City (pop. 5,542), ⊙ Boone co., N Ark., c.60 mi. ENE of Fayettville, in the Ozarks. Commercial center for farm area (fruit, livestock, poultry). Mfg. (wood products, cheese, flour, clothing); die-casting plant, produce houses. Marble deposits. Platted c.1860, inc. 1876. Diamond Cave (stalactite and stalagmite formations) is near by. **2** Town (pop. 261), Washington co., E central Ga., 12 mi. SSE of Sandersville. **3** City (pop. 322), Kootenai co., N Idaho, 15 mi. NW of St. Maries and on E shore of Coeur d'Alene L.; agr. **4** Resort town (pop. 1,026), Cumberland co., SW Maine, 22 mi. W of Auburn, at N end of Long L.; mfg. (machinery, bldg. materials). Inc. 1805. **5** City (pop. 884), ⊙ Clare co., central Mich., 18 mi. N of Mt. Pleasant, in agr. area (poultry, grain, potatoes, beans; dairy products). Resort area (lakes; hunting, fishing). State park near by. Settled 1878, inc. as city 1891. **6** Village (pop. c.150), Madison co., SW Mont., 40 mi. SE of Butte and on branch of Jefferson R., just NE of Tobacco Root Mts., in ranching and mining region. **7** Village (pop. 492), ⊙ Sioux co., NW Nebr., 45 mi. WSW of Chadron, near Wyo. line, in ranching region; poultry products, grain, livestock, potatoes. Relics of prehistoric man found near by. **8** Town (pop. 13,490), Hudson co., NE N.J., industrial suburb across Passaic R. (bridged here) from Newark; mfg. (steel, elevators, pumps, radio equipment, gases, refrigerator equipment, ink, food products). Inc. 1869. **9** Residential village (1940 pop. 6,307) in Harrison town (1940 pop. 11,783), Westchester co., SE N.Y., bet. Mamaroneck (SW) and Rye (NE), near Long Island Sound; makes costume jewelry. **10** Village (pop. 1,943), Hamilton co., extreme SW Ohio, 19 mi. WNW of Cincinnati, and on Whitewater R., at Ind. line, contiguous to West Harrison, Ind.; makes footwear, farm implements, paperboard containers. Laid out 1813. **11** Urban township (pop. 15,116), Allegheny co., W central Pa., on Allegheny R. and 20 mi. NE of Pittsburgh; iron, steel. Includes NATRONA village.

Harrison, Cape, promontory on the Atlantic, SE Labrador; 54°46'N 58°26'W; site of air-navigation radio station, 130 mi. NE of Goose Bay air base.

Harrison Bay, N Alaska, shallow inlet of Beaufort Sea, bet. Cape Halkett (W) and Beechey Point (E), c.120 mi. ESE of Barrow; 70°40'N 151°15'W. Receives Colville R.

Harrisonburg. **1** Village (pop. 544), ⊙ Catahoula parish, E La., on Ouachita R. and 30 mi. NW of Natchez, Miss.; agr. (cotton, corn, sugar cane, grain, livestock, poultry). **2** City (pop. 10,810), in but independent of Rockingham co., NW Va., in central Shenandoah Valley, 23 mi. NNE of Staunton. Court house of Rockingham co. is here. Trade, shipping, industrial center in agr. area (poultry, fruit, livestock, dairy products); mfg. of textiles, shoes, furniture, clothing, poultry-raising equipment, wood products, plows, fertilizer, dairy products; flour milling; hatcheries. Marble and limestone quarrying, lumbering near by. Seat of Madison Col. and Eastern Mennonite Col. Hq. for George Washington Natl. Forest. Near-by Melrose Caverns (NE) and Massanutten Caverns (SE) attract visitors. Settled 1739.

Harrison Hot Springs, village (pop. estimate 500), S B.C., at S end of Harrison L., 12 mi. NE of Chilliwack; resort, with mineral springs.

Harrison Lake (□ 87), S B.C., 12 mi. NE of Chilliwack; 30 mi. long, 1–5 mi. wide. Contains Long Isl. (6 mi. long). Receives Lillooet R. (NW); drains S into Fraser R.

Harrison Mills, village (pop. estimate 200), S B.C., on Fraser R., at mouth of Harrison R. (outlet of Harrison L.), 5 mi. N of Chilliwack; lumbering, shingle milling.

Harrison Stickle, England: see LANGDALE PIKES.

Harrisonville, city (pop. 2,530), ⊙ Cass co., W Mo., near South Grand R., 32 mi. SSE of Kansas City; grain, cattle, poultry. Laid out 1837.

Harriston, town (pop. 1,305), S Ont., on Maitland R. and 40 mi. NW of Guelph; meat packing, dairying, lumbering, woodworking, stove mfg.

Harristown, agr. village (district pop. 347), E Co. Kildare, Ireland, 4 mi. S of Naas; cattle, horses; potatoes.

Harrisville. **1** City (pop. 485), ⊙ Alcona co., NE Mich., 30 mi. SSE of Alpena, on L. Huron; summer resort; nurseries; commercial fishing. State park near by. **2** Town (pop. 519), Cheshire co., SW N.H., in lake dist. 10 mi. E of Keene; woolen mills. **3** Village (pop. 868), Lewis co., N central N.Y., on West Branch of Oswegatchie R. and 33 mi. ENE of Watertown; paper milling. **4** Village (pop. 420), Harrison co., E Ohio, 8 mi. SE of Cadiz, in agr. and coal-mining area. **5** Borough (pop. 780), Butler co., W Pa., 4 mi. ESE of Grove City. **6** Village, Providence co., R.I.: see BURRILLVILLE. **7** Town (pop. 1,387), ⊙ Ritchie co., W W.Va., on North Fork of Hughes R. and 27 mi. E of Parkersburg, in oil-producing, livestock-raising, grain-growing region. Platted 1822.

Harrod, village (pop. 482), Allen co., W Ohio, 10 mi. ESE of Lima, in agr. area; wood products.

Harrodsburg (hă'rŭdzbûrg), city (pop. 5,262), ⊙ Mercer co., central Ky., near Salt R., 28 mi. SW of Lexington; tourist and health resort (mineral springs); trade center in Bluegrass agr. area (livestock, poultry, grain, burley tobacco); makes crushed rock, flour, ladies' coats. Holds annual (July) co. fair and foxhound show. PIONEER MEMORIAL STATE PARK here is on site of old Fort Harrod. City has many interesting early-19th-cent. bldgs. Near by are old Mud Meeting House (built c.1800) and Dix R. Dam. Harrodsburg is oldest settlement of Ky.; founded 1774 by James Harrod and others. George Rogers Clark was one of town's early leaders.

Harrodsburg Dam, Ky.: see DIX RIVER.

Harrogate (hă'rōgĭt), municipal borough (1931 pop. 39,770; 1951 census 50,454), West Riding, central Yorkshire, England, 13 mi. N of Leeds; health resort with over 80 mineral springs; mfg. of candy and chocolate; agr. market. Consists of Low Harrogate (W) and, c.250 ft. higher, High Harrogate (E). Has good climate (dry and bracing in uplands, mild in lower part). Medicinal properties of the springs discovered 1596. Resort formerly named Knaresborough Spa, after near-by town.

Harrogate (hă'rŭgăt), village, Claiborne co., NE Tenn., near Ky.-Va. line, 5 mi. S of Cumberland Gap. Seat of Lincoln Memorial Univ.

Harrold, town and parish (pop. 924), NW Bedford, England, on Ouse R. and 8 mi. NW of Bedford; leatherworks. Has 13th-14th-cent. church.

Harrold, town (pop. 263), Hughes co., central S. Dak., 22 mi. ENE of Pierre and on Medicine Knoll Creek; dairy products, livestock, poultry, grain.

Harrow, town (pop. 1,166), S Ont., near L. Erie, 17 mi. S of Windsor, in dairying, farming region.

Harrow or **Harrow-on-the-Hill,** residential urban district (1931 pop. 26,380; 1951 census 219,463), Middlesex, England, 11 mi. NW of London. Site of Harrow, famous public school, founded 1571. Its graduates include Byron, Galsworthy, Peel, Palmerston, and Churchill. St. Mary's church founded by Lanfranc in 11th cent., rebuilt in 14th cent. In 1934 and later, Harrow absorbed near-by areas, including Wealdstone.

Harrowsmith, village (pop. estimate 400), SE Ont., 15 mi. NW of Kingston; dairying, mixed farming.

Harrow Weald (wēld'), residential town, Middlesex, England, just N of Harrow-on-the-Hill. It was residence of W. S. Gilbert.

Hars, Mount (hărsh), Hung. *Hárshegy*, hill (1,502 ft.) in Buda Mts., N central Hungary; residential dist. of Hüvösvölgy and Lipotmezö Lunatic Asylum at foot.

Harsefeld (här'zŭfĕlt), village (pop. 3,830), in former Prussian prov. of Hanover, NW Germany, after 1945 in Lower Saxony, 10 mi. S of Stade; truck farming.

Harsens Island, SE Mich., in delta of St. Clair R. in L. St. Clair, opposite Walpole Isl., Ont.; c.5 mi. long, 3 mi. wide; summer resort, known for fishing. Sans Souci village is on E shore. Settled c.1779.

Harsin or **Hersin** (both: hĕrsēn'), town, Fifth Prov., in Kermanshah, W Iran, 30 mi. E of Kermanshah; grain, fruit, cotton, tobacco, dairy products; sheep raising. Tribal Lur pop.

Harsit River (här-shĕt'), Turkish *Harşit*, NE Turkey, rises in Gumusane Mts. 20 mi. W of Gumusane, flows 83 mi. NW to Black Sea near Tirebolu.

Harsova (hûr'shôvä), Rum. *Hârşova*, anc. *Carsium*, town (1948 pop. 3,762), Constanta prov., SE Rumania, in Dobruja, on Danube R. and 50 mi. NW of Constanta; small inland port; mfg. of tiles and bricks; stone and sand quarrying. Has notable remains of a Roman city and of a Turkish fortress.

Harspranget (här'sprông"ŭt), Swedish *Harsprånget*, village, Norrbotten co., N Sweden, on Lule R. and 65 mi. S of Kiruna, within Arctic Circle. Site of Sweden's highest waterfalls (246 ft.) and of major hydroelectric power station, completed 1950; power is supplied to mines at Kiruna, Gallivare, and Malmberget.

Harstad (här'stä), town (pop. 4,085), Troms co., N Norway, on E Hinnoy of the Vesteralen group, 30 mi. NW of Narvik; herring-fishing center, with shipyards, cold-storage plants, textile and lumber mills. Trade with Spitsbergen. Founded 1904. Near by is TRONDENES village.

Harsud (hŭrsōōd'), village, Nimar dist., W Madhya Pradesh, India, 31 mi. NE of Khandwa; cotton ginning; millet, wheat, oilseeds.

Harsum (här'zōōm), village (pop. 3,832), in former Prussian prov. of Hanover, NW Germany, after 1945 in Lower Saxony, 4 mi. N of Hildesheim; dairying, sawmilling.

Hart. **1** County (□ 257; pop. 14,495), NE Ga.; ⊙ Hartwell. Bounded E and N by S.C. line, formed here by Savannah and Tugaloo rivers. Piedmont agr. area (cotton, corn, hay, sweet potatoes). Formed 1853. **2** County (□ 425; pop. 15,321), central Ky.; ⊙ Munfordville. Bounded NE by Nolin R.; drained by Green R. Rolling agr. area (livestock, dairy products, poultry, burley tobacco, corn, wheat); some mfg., chiefly at Horse Cave. Resorts; includes part of MAMMOTH CAVE NATIONAL PARK; has other caves. Formed 1819.

Hart, city (pop. 2,172), ⊙ Oceana co., W Mich., 33 mi. NNW of Muskegon and on short Pentwater R., in fruitgrowing area; potatoes, beans; mfg. (canned goods, clothing, bowls); resort. Inc. as village 1885, as city 1947.

Harta (hŏr'tŏ), town (pop. 5,815), Pest-Pilis-Solt-Kiskun co., central Hungary, on the Danube and 34 mi. SW of Kecskemet; river port; barley, corn, cattle, poultry. Has penal colony.

Hartberg (härt'bĕrk), town (pop. 3,761), Styria, SE Austria, 28 mi. NE of Graz; market center; mfg. (agr. implements, leather goods); vineyards. Has 16th-cent. castle.

Hartburn, England: see STOCKTON-ON-TEES.

Hartebeest River (här'tŭbēst"), NW Cape Prov., U. of So. Afr., formed 7 mi. SE of Kenhardt by confluence of Zak R. and short Mottels R., flows 70 mi. NW, past Kenhardt, to Orange R. 3 mi. W of Kakamas.

Hartenstein (här'tŭn-shtīn), town (pop. 3,351), Saxony, E central Germany, in the Erzgebirge, near the Zwickauer Mulde, 9 mi. SE of Zwickau; textile milling and knitting; mfg. of machinery, aluminum products, shoes. Towered over by castle, rebuilt in 16th cent.

Hart Fell, Scotland: see MOFFAT HILLS.

Hartfield, town and parish (pop. 2,026), N Sussex, England, on Medway R. and 6 mi. ESE of East Grinstead; agr. market. Has 15th-cent. church.

Hartford, England: see CRAMLINGTON.

Hartford, county (□ 741; pop. 539,661), central and N Conn., on Mass. line, bisected by Connecticut R.; ⊙ Hartford, insurance center and state's largest city. Mfg. (airplanes, airplane engines and parts, machinery, hardware, tools, electrical equipment and appliances, brick, sports equipment, textiles, paper, clothing, cutlery, furniture, food products, carpets, silverware, rubber, leather, and wood products, soaps and cleansers, radios, chemicals, safety fuses, automobile parts, paint, metal products); agr. (tobacco, dairy products, poultry, truck, fruit, corn, potatoes, nursery products, seeds). Includes several state parks and forests. Drained by Farmington, Quinnipiac, Pequabuck, Hockanum, and Scantic rivers. Constituted 1666.

Hartford. **1** Town (pop. 1,655), Geneva co., SE Ala., 19 mi. SW of Dothan, bet. Choctawhatchee R. and Fla. line; pecan shelling, cotton ginning, lumber milling. Founded 1894. **2** City (pop. 865), Sebastian co., W Ark., 24 mi. S of Fort Smith, in coal-mining and diversified-agr. area. **3** City (pop. 177,397), coextensive with Hartford town, ⊙ Conn. and Hartford co., central Conn., on Connecticut R. and 34 mi. NNE of New Haven; 41°46'N 72°40'W. State's largest city; financial, industrial, commercial center; insurance business for which city is internationally famous began 1794. Mfg. (firearms, typewriters, airplane parts, tools, brushes, machinery, metal products, electrical equipment, and other products); tobacco packing. Port of entry. Trinity Col., Hartford Seminary Foundation, Univ. of Conn. schools of law and insurance, Hillyer Col., state trade school, art school, musical foundation, state institutions for the handicapped here. Settled as Newtown, 1635–36, on site of Dutch trading post (1633); town and city inc. 1784, consolidated 1896. Was site (1814) of Hartford Convention of New England Federalists during War of 1812. City manager-council govt. adopted 1947. One of strongest early Conn. colonies, Hartford was joint capital with New Haven until 1875. Considerable foreign shipping in 18th cent.; industrial development began in late 19th cent. Hartford *Courant* (founded 1764) is one of oldest U.S. newspapers. The Connecticut Wits flourished here in late-18th, early-19th cent. Henry Barnard, Harriet Beecher Stowe, Lydia Huntley Sigourney, Charles Dudley Warner, Mark Twain (whose home is now a library), and Horace Bushnell lived here; Noah Webster, John Fiske, and the elder J.P. Morgan b. here. Points of interest: Bushnell Park, Horace Bushnell Memorial (1930), old state house (1796; designed by Bulfinch), capitol (1872), state library and supreme court bldg. (1910; with Stuart's full-length portrait of Washington), and several libraries, museums, and parks. **4** Industrial village (pop. 1,909), Madison co., SW Ill., on the Mississippi and c.14 mi. NNE of downtown St. Louis, within St. Louis metropolitan area; oil refinery, large tannery. Inc. 1920. **5** Town (pop. 221), Warren co., S central Iowa, 15 mi. ESE of Des Moines; sorghum mill. **6** City (pop. 395), Lyon co., E central Kansas, on Neosho R. and 14 mi. SE of Emporia; grain, livestock. **7** City (pop. 1,564), ⊙ Ohio co., W Ky., on Rough R. and 25 mi. SSE of Owensboro, in coal, oil, timber, limestone, and agr. (corn, burley tobacco, hay) area. Founded c.1790. **8** Town (pop. 381), Oxford co., W Maine, 16 mi. SE of Rumford and on branch of Nezinscot R., in farming, recreational area; wood products. **9** Village (pop. 1,838), Van Buren co., SW Mich., 16 mi. NE of Benton Harbor and on Paw Paw R., in fruitgrowing area; nurseries. Ships fruit, truck. Mfg. of wreaths treated for permanence. Inc. 1877. **10** Village, Licking co., Ohio: see CROTON. **11** City (pop. 592), Minnehaha co., E S.Dak., 12 mi. WNW of Sioux Falls; livestock, grain, dairy products, poultry. **12** Town (pop. 5,827), Windsor co., E Vt., on the Connecticut, at mouth of White R., and 9 mi. E of Woodstock; textiles. Includes residential villages of Hartford and Wilder (pop. 1,097), industrial and transportation center WHITE RIVER JUNCTION, and Quechee (kwē'chē) village (woolen mills). Gateway to resort area (W). Large hydroelectric dam in the Connecticut at Wilder. Settled 1765. **13** or **Hartford City,** town (pop. 366), Mason co., W W.Va., on Ohio R. and 14 mi. NNE of Point Pleasant; saltworks. **14** City (pop. 4,549), Washington co., E Wis., on small Rubicon R. (tributary of Rock R.), near small Pike L. (resort), and 30 mi. NW of Milwaukee, in dairy and farm area; cheese, canned vegetables; mfg. of outboard motors, furniture, wood and metal products, leather and leather goods, automobile parts, chemicals, beverages. Settled c.1844, inc. 1883.

Hartford City. **1** City (pop. 7,253), ⊙ Blackford co., E Ind., 18 mi. N of Muncie, in rich agr. area (livestock; dairy products; soybeans, grain). Natural-gas and oil fields near by. Mfg. (glass, jute board, school supplies, hardware, caskets, doors, clothing, packed meat). Settled 1832, laid out 1839. **2** Town, Mason co., W.Va.: see HARTFORD.

Hartha (här'tä), town (pop. 8,522), Saxony, E central Germany, 7 mi. WSW of Döbeln; textile milling (wool, linen, cotton); mfg. of electric motors, furniture, buttons, shoes, cigars.

Harthau (här'tou), village (pop. 6,840), Saxony, E central Germany, 4 mi. S of Chemnitz; hosiery knitting, woolen milling, machinery mfg., metalworking.

Harth Forest (härt), Haut-Rhin dept., E France, extending c.15 mi. N–S near left bank of the Rhine, just E of Mulhouse. Traversed by sections of Rhone-Rhine and Huningue canals. Supplies Île-Napoléon paper mill (at W edge).

Hartington, town in parish of Hartington, Town Quarter (pop. 431), W Derby, England, 9 mi. SSE of Buxton; market center of lead-mining, limestone-quarrying, and dairying region, including surrounding parishes of Hartington, Middle Quarter (pop. 434), Hartington, Nether Quarter (pop. 438), and Hartington, Upper Quarter (pop. 2,074). The town has 14th-cent. church and 16th-cent. mansion.

Hartington, city (pop. 1,660), ⊙ Cedar co., NE Nebr., 45 mi. WNW of Sioux City, Iowa, near Missouri R.; grain. Inc. 1883.

Hart Island, N.Y.: see HARTS ISLAND.

Hartland, town (pop. 847), W N.B., on St. John R. (covered bridge) and 10 mi. N of Woodstock, near Maine border; agr. market in potato region; woodworking, mfg. of shoes, wire products, tiles, starch.

Hartland, town and parish (pop. 1,385), NW Devon, England, 13 mi. W of Bideford; agr. market. On the Atlantic, 2 mi. W, is fishing village of Hartland Quai (kē). Hartland Point is 3 mi. N.

Hartland. 1 Town (pop. 549), Hartford co., N Conn., in hilly region, on Mass. line and 21 mi. NW of Hartford; includes East Hartland village. Part of Barkhamsted Reservoir (on East Branch Farmington R.), state forests here. **2** Town (pop. 1,310), Somerset co., central Maine, on the Sebasticook and 7 mi. NNW of Pittsfield, in farming area; canning plant, tannery. Settled c.1800, inc. 1820. **3** Village (pop. c.200), Livingston co., SE Mich., 10 mi. NE of Howell, in farm area; handicrafts center. **4** Village (pop. 300), Freeborn co., S Minn., 13 mi. NNW of Albert Lea; dairy products. **5** Town (pop. 1,559), Windsor co., E Vt., on the Connecticut, just S of Hartford, in dairying area; wood products. Includes villages of North Hartland, at mouth of Ottauquechee R., and Hartland Four Corners. Settled 1763. **6** Village (pop. 1,190), Waukesha co., SE Wis., on Bark R. and 22 mi. W of Milwaukee, in dairying and farming area with resort lakes near by; dairy products, packing cases, steel products.

Hartland Point, high promontory, NW Devon, England, on the Atlantic, at entrance to Bristol Channel 14 mi. N of Bude; 51°2′N 4°31′W.

Hartlebury, town and parish (pop. 2,245), NW Worcester, England, 4 mi. S of Kidderminster; agr. market. Has castle begun by Bishop Cantelupe in early 12th cent.

Hartlepool (här′tülpōōl, härt′lē–), municipal borough (1931 pop. 20,537; 1951 census 17,217), E Durham, England, on North Sea and Hartlepool Bay, 9 mi. N of Middlesbrough; 54°42′N 1°12′W; seaport (with extensive docks), exporting coal and importing timber (pit props); shipbuilding, metalworking, producing iron, steel, machinery, boilers, electric generators, cement. A Saxon convent was founded here c.640. Has church of St. Hilda (1191) and remains of town wall and gate (13th cent.). In municipal borough (W) is town of Throston (pop. 8,797). Adjoining is WEST HARTLEPOOL.

Hartleton, borough (pop. 240), Union co., central Pa., 15 mi. WSW of Lewisburg.

Hartley, England: see SEATON DELAVAL.

Hartley, town (pop. 459), Salisbury prov., central Southern Rhodesia, in Mashonaland, on railroad and 65 mi. WSW of Salisbury; alt. 3,900 ft. Center of gold-mining area. Tobacco, cotton, peanuts, citrus fruit, dairy products.

Hartley, county (□ 1,489; pop. 1,913), extreme N Texas; ⊙ Channing. In high, grassy plains of the Panhandle, and bounded W by N.Mex. line; alt. 3,800–4,300 ft. Large-scale cattle-ranching area, growing some grain; natural-gas wells; glass sand, clay deposits. Includes Rita Blanca L. (recreational area). Formed 1876.

Hartley, town (pop. 1,611), O'Brien co., NW Iowa, 17 mi. W of Spencer; dairy, wood, and metal products. Inc. 1888.

Hartley Row, town in parish of Hartley Wintney (pop. 1,968), NE Hampshire, England, 7 mi. NW of Aldershot; agr. market.

Hartline, town (pop. 205), Grant co., E central Wash., 33 mi. NE of Ephrata, in wheat-growing region.

Hartly, town (pop. 139), Kent co., W Del., 10 mi. W of Dover, in agr. area.

Hartman. 1 Town (pop. 418), Johnson co., NW Ark., 8 mi. WSW of Clarksville, near Arkansas R. **2** Town (pop. 181), Prowers co., SE Colo., near Arkansas R. and Kansas line, 22 mi. E of Lamar.

Hartmanice (härt′mänyĭtsĕ), Ger. *Hartmanitz,* town (pop. 346), SW Bohemia, Czechoslovakia, 5 mi. SSW of Susice. Prasily (prä′shĭlĭ), Czech *Prášily,* summer resort, is 6 mi. SSW.

Hartmannsdorf (härt′mänsdôrf″), town (pop. 7,850), Saxony, E central Germany, 7 mi. NW of Chemnitz; mfg. of textiles (hosiery, gloves, underwear), machinery, electrical equipment.

Hartmannshof (–hōf″), village (pop. 1,203), Middle Franconia, N central Bavaria, Germany, 5.5 mi. ESE of Hersbruck; cement mfg., brewing. Hops, horse-radish. Large limestone quarry near by.

Hartmannswillerkopf (ärtmänzvĕlâr″kôf′) or **Vieil-Armand** (vyā-ärmä′), Ger. *Hartmannsweilerkopf* (härt′mäns-vī″lürkôpf), summit (3,136 ft.) of the SE Vosges, Haut-Rhin dept., E France, 4 mi. SSW of Guebwiller, commanding valleys of the Thur (S) and the Lauch (N). Scene (1915) of fierce struggles in First World War. Numerous war monuments, including natl. monument to 10,000 Fr. dead.

Hart Mountain (2,700 ft.), W Man., 27 mi. NNW of Swan River; highest point of Porcupine Mtn.

Hart Mountain, peak (8,020 ft.), S Oregon, rising from high plateau (c.7,000 ft.) in SE corner of Lake co., c.80 mi. SSW of Burns. Antelope refuge is here. Hart L. (6 mi. long, 2 mi. wide; half dry) is just W.

Hartney, town (pop. 509), SW Man., on Souris R. and 35 mi. SW of Brandon; grain elevators; stock.

Harton, England: see SOUTH SHIELDS.

Hartsburg. 1 Village (pop. 245), Logan co., central Ill., 38 mi. NW of Decatur, in agr. area (dairy products; livestock, grain). **2** Town (pop. 171), Boone co., central Mo., near Missouri R., 10 mi. NW of Jefferson City; grain, livestock.

Hartsdale, residential village (1940 pop. 2,664), Westchester co., SE N.Y., just SW of White Plains.

Hartsel, resort village (pop. c.50), Park co., central Colo., in Rocky Mts., 18 mi. SE of Fairplay; alt. 8,875 ft. Hot springs and Antero Reservoir near by.

Hartselle (härt′sĕl), city (pop. 3,429), Morgan co., N Ala., 12 mi. SSE of Decatur, in cotton, corn, and truck area; lumber milling, cotton ginning. Wm. B. Bankhead Natl. Forest is SW. Founded 1870, inc. 1875.

Hartshill, town and parish (pop. 2,542), N Warwick, England, 3 mi. NW of Nuneaton; coal mining, granite quarrying. Has remains of castle built 1125. Michael Drayton b. here.

Hartshorne (härts′hôrn), city (pop. 2,330), Pittsburg co., SE Okla., 13 mi. SE of McAlester and contiguous to Haileyville, in mining, lumbering, stock-raising, and agr. area (cotton, grain). Seat of Jones Acad., a U.S. school for Indians. Lumber and grain milling, cotton ginning. Rock quarries, natural-gas wells, coal mines. Settled c.1890.

Harts Island, SE N.Y., part of Bronx borough of New York city, in Long Island Sound, near City Isl. and Pelham Bay Park; c.1 mi. long. A naval prison and the city cemetery are here. Formerly site of city reformatory. Sometimes Hart Isl.

Harts River, U. of So. Afr.: see HARTZ RIVER.

Hartsville. 1 Town (pop. 340), Bartholomew co., S central Ind., on small Clifty Creek and 12 mi. ENE of Columbus, in agr. area. **2** Village, Berkshire co., Mass.: see NEW MARLBORO. **3** Town (pop. 5,658), Darlington co., NE S.C., 21 mi. NW of Florence; textiles, bricks, mattresses, furniture, paper, paper products, cottonseed oil. Seat of Coker Col. Experimental seed farm near by. **4** City (pop. 1,130), ⊙ Trousdale co., N Tenn., 38 mi. ENE of Nashville, in agr. area (tobacco, corn, wheat); woodworking. In Civil War, Federal garrison here was defeated (1862) by Gen. John H. Morgan. Settled in early 1800s; inc. 1913.

Har Tuv or **Hartuv** (härtōōv′), settlement (pop. 100), central Israel, in Judaean Hills, 13 mi. W of Jerusalem; cement works. Founded 1895; temporarily abandoned (1948) during Arab invasion. Sometimes spelled Hartov.

Hartville. 1 City (pop. 526), ⊙ Wright co., S central Mo., in the Ozarks, on Gasconade R. and 43 mi. E of Springfield; agr. **2** Industrial village (1940 pop. 1,019), Stark co., E central Ohio, 14 mi. SE of Akron; rubber goods, doors, ventilators, baskets; coal, limestone. **3** Town (pop. 229), Platte co., SE Wyo., on N.Platte R. and 22 mi. NE of Wheatland; alt. c.4,750 ft.; iron-ore mining near by.

Hartwell, city (pop. 2,964), ⊙ Hart co., NE Ga., 16 mi. NNW of Elberton, near S.C. line; mfg. (clothes, sheeting); ships cotton, corn. Named for Nancy Hart, Revolutionary heroine. Inc. 1856.

Hartwick, town (pop. 107), Poweshiek co., central Iowa, 8 mi. SSW of Belle Plaine, in agr. area.

Hartz River or **Harts River** (both: härts), SW Transvaal and NE Cape Prov., U. of So. Afr., rises in W Witwatersrand, NE of Lichtenburg, flows 270 mi. SW, past Schweizer Reneke and Taungs, to Vaal R. at Delport's Hope.

Hartzviller (ärtsvĕlâr′), Ger. *Harzweiler* (härts′vīlür), village (pop. 785), Moselle dept., NE France, 5 mi. SSE of Sarrebourg; crystal mfg.

Harue (hä″rōō′ā), town (pop. 11,099), Fukui prefecture, central Honshu, Japan, 5 mi. N of Fukui; rayon-textile center; sake.

Haruki, Japan: see KISHIWADA.

Haruku or **Haroekoe** (both: härōō′kōō), largest island (10 mi. long, 8 mi. wide; pop. 12,598) of Uliaser Isls., Indonesia, in Banda Sea, just E of Amboina and 4 mi. S of SW coast of Ceram across narrow Ceram Strait; 3°35′S 128°31′E. Generally low, rising in SW to 1,926 ft. Coconuts, cloves, sago. Also called Oma.

Harumukotan-kaikyo, Russian SFSR: see KURILE STRAIT.

Harumukotan-to, Russian SFSR: see KHARIMKOTAN ISLAND.

Harun, Jebel, or **Jabal Harun** (both: jĕ′bĕl härōōn′), mountain (4,383 ft.) of S central Jordan, W of Wadi Musa and overlooking ruins of Petra (N). It is the biblical Hor.

Harunabad, Iran: see SHAHABAD.

Harunabad (hä″rōōnäbäd′), town (pop. 4,888), Bahawalpur state, W Pakistan, 90 mi. ENE of Bahawalpur, on rail spur, wheat, millet, cotton; hand-loom weaving.

Harur (hŭrōōr′), town (pop. 5,211), Salem dist., S central Madras, India, 22 mi. ESE of Dharmapuri, in agr. area. Magnetite deposits near by.

Harut Rud (hä′rōōt rōōd′), river in W Afghanistan, rises in the Siah Koh (outlier of the Hindu Kush) 80 mi. SE of Herat, flows c.250 mi. SW, past Shindand and Anardarah, to the Hamun-i-Sabari, one of the lagoons of the Seistan depression on Iran line; intermittent flow in lower course. Also called Adraskan or Adraskand, particularly in upper course.

Harvard. 1 City (pop. 3,464), McHenry co., N Ill., near Wis. line, 26 mi. ENE of Rockford; railroad junction (with repair shops); trade center in dairying and resort area; mfg. of dairy products, clothing, hardware, bags. Inc. 1867. **2** Town (pop. 3,983), Worcester co., NE central Mass., 12 mi. ESE of Fitchburg. Has Harvard observatory. Settled 1704, inc. 1732. Includes Still River village, on Nashua R. In town is "Fruitlands," once scene of Bronson Alcott's cooperative community. **3** City (pop. 774), Clay co., S Nebr., 15 mi. E of Hastings; dairy and poultry produce, grain, livestock.

Harvard, Mount (14,399 ft.), central Colo., in Collegiate Range of Sawatch Mts., 23 mi. S of Leadville. Peak is 3d highest in Rocky Mts. of U.S.

Harvel, village (pop. 301), on Christian-Montgomery co. line, S central Ill., 30 mi. S of Springfield.

Harvestehude (härvĕ″stühōō′dü), residential district of Hamburg, NW Germany, on W shore of the Aussenalster, adjoining Eppendorf (N), Eimsbüttel (W), and Rotherbaum (S) dists.

Harvey, town (pop. 1,062), SW Western Australia, 80 mi. S of Perth; dairying and agr. center; butter. Harvey Weir and sawmills near by.

Harvey, village (pop. estimate c.200), SE N.B., near Shepody Bay, 10 mi. SW of Hopewell Cape, in mining region (albertite, oil shale, manganese).

Harvey, county (□ 540; pop. 21,698), S central Kansas; ⊙ Newton. Flat to gently rolling prairie, drained by Little Arkansas R. Wheat, livestock. Oil and natural-gas fields. Formed 1872.

Harvey. 1 Industrial city (pop. 20,683), Cook co., NE Ill., suburb 18 mi. S of Chicago; mfg. (Diesel engines, road machinery, trucks, railroad equipment, metal forgings and castings, stoves, auto parts, cartons). Thornton Jr. Col. is here. Inc. 1895. **2** Town (pop. 346), Marion co., S central Iowa, 10 mi. E of Knoxville, near Des Moines R.; brick and tile plant. Limestone quarries, sand and gravel pits near by. **3** Village (1940 pop. 3,615), Jefferson parish, SE La., on W bank (levee) of the Mississippi, opposite New Orleans; mfg. (machinery, boats, wood products, tin cans, chemicals, sugar and syrup, vegetable oils). Harvey Lock (425 ft. long) links the Mississippi to Gulf Intracoastal Waterway here. **4** Village (pop. c.200), Marquette co., NW Upper Peninsula, Mich., 4 mi. SE of Marquette; resort; fish hatchery. **5** City (pop. 2,337), Wells co., central N.Dak., on Sheyenne R. and 80 mi. NNE of Bismarck. Railway division point; dairy products, potatoes, wheat. Inc. 1906.

Harvey Bay, Australia: see TUMBY BAY.

Harvey Cedars, resort borough (pop. 106), Ocean co., E N.J., on Long Beach isl., S of Barnegat City, and 30 mi. NNE of Atlantic City. Artists' summer colony here.

Harvey Lake (□ 2.75; 3 mi. long, 1 mi. wide), SW N.B., 23 mi. SW of Fredericton.

Harveysburg, village (pop. 477), Warren co., SW Ohio, 20 mi. SSE of Dayton and on small Caesar Creek.

Harveyton, mining village (pop. 2,336, with adjacent Blue Diamond), Perry co., SE Ky., in Cumberland foothills, 5 mi. N of Hazard; bituminous coal.

Harveyville, city (pop. 236), Wabaunsee co., E central Kansas, 23 mi. SW of Topeka, in cattle, poultry, and grain region.

Harviell (här′vŭl), town (pop. 190), Butler co., SE Mo., in Ozark region, 8 mi. SW of Poplar Bluff.

Harwan (hŭr′vŭn), village, Anantnag dist., W central Kashmir, 7 mi. NE of Srinagar; headworks of water-supply system for Srinagar here. Buddhist ruins (some constructed in a peculiar pebble style) include stupa and extensive figured brick tiles; earliest ruins date from 4th cent. A.D.

Harwell (här′wŭl), village and parish (pop. 669), Berkshire, S England, 2 mi. W of Didcot; atomic research laboratory.

Harwich (hă′rĭj), municipal borough (1931 pop. 12,046; 1951 census 13,488), NE Essex, England, seaport and naval station on North Sea at estuary of the Stour and the Orwell, 70 mi. NE of London; 51°56′N 1°16′E. Port is fortified and is important destroyer and submarine station. Just W is Parkeston Quay, commercial port and terminal of passenger lines to Hook of Holland, Flushing, Antwerp, and Esbjerg, and of train ferry to Zeebrugge. There are several 16th–18th-cent. houses. Town sustained frequent air raids in Second World War, notably 1940–41. In municipal borough (S) is seaside resort of Dovercourt (pop. 7,855).

Harwich (här′wĭch), town (pop. 2,649), Barnstable co., SE Mass., on S coast of Cape Cod, 12 mi. E of Barnstable; summer resort; cranberries, truck. Once whaling and shipbuilding center. Settled c.1670, inc. 1694. Includes resort villages of Harwich Port (1940 pop. 522; yachting), North Harwich, East Harwich, South Harwich, and West Harwich. Pleasant L. (c.1.5 mi. long) is near.

Harwinton, town (pop. 1,858), Litchfield co., NW Conn., on Naugatuck R. and just SE of Torrington, in hilly region; agr. Settled 1730, inc. 1737.

Harwood, village (pop. estimate 200), S Ont., on Rice L., 13 mi. SE of Peterborough; fruit, dairying, mixed farming.

Harwood, England: see GREAT HARWOOD.

Harwood. 1 Town (pop. 141), Vernon co., W Mo., near Osage R., 14 mi. NE of Nevada. **2** Town (pop. 157), Gonzales co., S central Texas, 9 mi. E of Luling.

Harwood Heights, village (pop. 655), Cook co., NE Ill., NE suburb of Chicago.

Harworth, town and parish (pop. 6,092), N Nottingham, England, 8 mi. N of Worksop; coal mining. Has Norman church, rebuilt 19th cent., and 18th-cent. mansion containing notable Flemish paintings.

Harz (härts), mountain range in central Germany, bet. the Leine and the Elbe, extends c.60 mi. ESE from Innerste R., and occupies parts of Hanover and Saxony provs., Brunswick, and Anhalt. Rises to 3,747 ft. in the BROCKEN (legendary scene of the Walpurgis Nacht), in the Upper Harz (NW). It was formerly noted for numerous non-ferrous mineral deposits (especially silver); mining now is concentrated only in the RAMMELSBERG (2,085 ft.) and around CLAUSTHAL-ZELLERFELD; large copper-slate deposits in MANSFELD area. The Upper Harz, the higher part, has extensive moors and wastelands and a severe climate with heavy rainfall (64 inches annually on the Brocken). Main town in the Upper Harz is Goslar; Bad Harzburg, Bad Lauterberg, Braunlage, and Sankt Andreasberg (noted for its canary birds) are popular resorts. The Lower Harz (SE) is Devonian-slate plateau with mild climate; grain and cattle are raised. Main town in Lower Harz is Wernigerode; Blankenburg and Schierke are noted resorts. Bode and Wipper rivers rise here. The Harz was largely deforested in 1930s and '40s. Intensive uranium-ore prospecting began after Second World War. In anc. times the Harz seems to have been called Melicobus, a name which has come, in the last 2 centuries, to be applied, instead, to the MALCHEN, NNE of Bensheim.

Harzburg, Bad, Germany: see BAD HARZBURG.

Harzgerode (härts"gürō'dů), town (pop. 6,202), in former Anhalt State, central Germany, after 1945 in Saxony-Anhalt, in the Lower Harz, 10 mi. S of Quedlinburg; metal- and woodworking; climatic health resort. Has 16th-cent. palace. Silver and lead formerly mined here. Incorporates Alexisbad spa (NW), founded 1810.

Harzweiler, France: see HARTZVILLER.

Hasa (hă'sů) or **Al Ahsa** (ăl äsä'), province and E dependency (pop. 2,000,000) of Nejd, Saudi Arabia, on Persian Gulf; ⊙ Hofuf. Bounded N by Kuwait, Iraq, and their neutral zones, and S by Trucial Oman, it is bordered W by the sandy Dahana desert, and consists of the Summan plateau and the coastal lowland with salt marshes near the shore and steppe and desert inland. Richest agr. dists. are the oases of Hofuf and Qatif, where dates, wheat, barley, vegetables, and fruit are grown; large Bedouin pop. breeds sheep, camels, donkeys. Pearling is a secondary industry—at Jubail and Tarut Isl. Hasa is the region of Saudi Arabian oil production, with principal producing centers at Dhahran (in Dammam field), Abqaiq, Ain Dar, and Qatif. Other fields are Safaniya, Abu Hadriya, Fadhili, Ithmaniya, and Haradh. Refinery and loading terminal at Ras Tanura. Railroad (completed 1951) leads from Dammam deepwater port on Persian Gulf, past Hofuf and Haradh, toward Riyadh. In anc. times known as Bahrein, Hasa was nominally included (1819) in the Turkish vilayet of Basra, came under Wahabi control during 1821–33, and was occupied by Turkish forces in 1871. In 1913–14, the region was seized by Ibn Saud and attached to Nejd. Following the granting of an oil concession in 1933 to U.S. company, oil was discovered in 1936 and 1938. During Second World War began the rapid development of the region, which has made Saudi Arabia the 5th-largest oil producer in the world.

Hasa, town and oasis, Saudi Arabia: see HOFUF.

Hasakah, Al-, Syria: see HASEKE, EL.

Hasaki (hä"sä'kē) or **Hazaki** (hä"zä'kē), town (pop. 14,339), Ibaraki prefecture, central Honshu, Japan, on the Pacific, at mouth of Tone R., opposite Choshi; fishing center; rattan goods.

Hasanabad, India: see TAKI.

Hasan Abdal (hŭs'ŭn ăb'dŭl), town (pop. 8,089), Attock dist., NW Punjab, W Pakistan, 18 mi. ENE of Campbellpur; wheat. Various Moslem and Sikh legends about near-by tomb and spring. Also spelled Hassan Abdal.

Hasanah, Aden: see DATHINA.

Hasan Dag (häsän' dä), Turkish *Hasan Dağ*, peak (10,672 ft.), central Turkey, 29 mi. WNW of Nigde. Sometimes Buyukhasan, Turkish *Büyükhasan*.

Hasanganj (hŭs'ŭngŭnj), village, Unao dist., central Uttar Pradesh, India, on Sai R. and 18 mi. NNE of Unao; wheat, barley, rice, gram. Fruit orchards.

Hasani, Aden: see DATHINA.

Hasani, Greece: see ELLENIKON.

Hasankale, Turkey: see PASINLER.

Hasan Kiadeh (häsän' kēädě'), village, First Prov., in Gilan, N Iran, small Caspian port, 33 mi. NE of Resht, at mouth of the Sefid Rud.

Hasanparti or **Hassan Parthi** (both: hŭs'sŭnpŭr'tē), town (pop. 6,331), Warangal dist., E Hyderabad state, India, 6 mi. NW of Warangal; rice, oilseeds; silk weaving.

Hasanpur (hŭsŭn'po͝or), town (pop. 4,249), Moradabad dist., N central Uttar Pradesh, India, 31 mi. WSW of Moradabad; wheat, rice, pearl millet, mustard, sugar cane. Founded 1634.

Hasayan (hŭsīn'), town (pop. 2,187), Aligarh dist., W Uttar Pradesh, India, 13 mi. E of Hathras; wheat, barley, pearl millet, gram, corn. Also spelled Husain.

Hasbaya, Lebanon: see HASBEYA.

Hasbergen-Iprump (häs'bĕr"gŭn-ēpro͝omp'), village (commune pop. 7,918), in Oldenburg, NW Germany, after 1945 in Lower Saxony, 6 mi. W of Bremen, in peat region.

Hasbeya (häsbā'yů), Fr. *Hasbaya*, village (pop. 3,729), S Lebanon, at foot of Mt. Hermon, 22 mi. SE of Saida; alt. 2,500 ft.; sericulture, cotton, tobacco, cereals, almonds, olives, grapes. Iron deposits are found near by (NE). An old town, it was center of the Druses from 13th to 19th cent. One of the most important Druse shrines is the Khalwat el Bujad or Khalwat el Biyad, on a hill near by.

Hasbrouck Heights (hăz'bro͝ok), residential borough (pop. 9,181), Bergen co., NE N.J., 2 mi. S of Hackensack; mfg. (stationery, machine parts). Teterboro airport near by. Settled c.1685, inc. 1894.

Hascosay (hă'skōsā), island (2 mi. long, 1 mi. wide) of the Shetlands, Scotland, just off E coast of YELL.

Hase (hä'sā), town (pop. 5,007), Nara prefecture, S Honshu, Japan, 11 mi. SSW of Nara; rice, wheat, raw silk.

Haseke, El, or **Al-Hasakah** (both: ĕl hä'sĕků), Fr. *Hassetché*, town, ⊙ Jezire prov., NE Syria, on Khabur R. and 85 mi. NNE of Deir ez Zor; sheep raising.

Haselbach (hä'zůlbäkh), town (pop. 2,091), Thuringia, central Germany, on the Pleisse and 6 mi. N of Altenburg; lignite mining; glass mfg.

Haselberg, Russian SFSR: see KRASNOZNAMENSK.

Haselünne (hä'zůlü"ně), town (pop. 3,916), in former Prussian prov. of Hanover, NW Germany, after 1945 in Lower Saxony, on Haase R. and 8 mi. ESE of Meppen. Has 14th-cent. church.

Hasenkamp (häsĕnkämp'), village (pop. estimate 1,000), W Entre Ríos prov., Argentina, on railroad and 45 mi. NE of Paraná; grain, livestock, poultry.

Hasenpoth, Latvia: see AIZPUTE.

Hase River, Germany: see HAASE RIVER.

Hasharon, Israel: see RAMAT DAVID.

Hashihama (häshē'hämů), town (pop. 6,118), Ehime prefecture, N Shikoku, Japan, port on Hiuchi Sea, 3 mi. NW of Imabari; mfg. center (pottery, cotton textiles, soy sauce); shipbuilding, fishing. Exports pottery, agr. products.

Hashimoto (häshē'mōtō), town (pop. 9,319), Wakayama prefecture, S Honshu, Japan, on N central Kii Peninsula, 24 mi. SSE of Osaka; rail junction; commercial center for rice-growing, lumbering, stock-raising area.

Hashio (häshē'ō), town (pop. 4,731), Nara prefecture, S Honshu, Japan, 9 mi. SW of Nara; rice, watermelons, raw silk.

Hashir, Turkey: see PERVARI.

Hashtrud, Iran: see SARASKAND.

Hasiheisa or **El Hasiheisa** (ĕl häsē'häsů), town, Blue Nile prov., E central Anglo-Egyptian Sudan, in the Gezira, on left bank of Blue Nile (opposite Rufaa), on railroad, and 25 mi. NNW of Wad Medani; cotton, wheat, barley, corn, fruits, durra; livestock.

Hasikiya or **Hasikiyah** (häsĭkē'yů), uninhabited westernmost island (□ 1) of the Kuria Muria group, off SE Oman; rises to 501 ft.; 17°29'N 55°38'E. Guano was worked here in 1850s.

Hasilpur (hä'sĭlpo͝or), town (pop. 1,694), Bahawalpur State, W Pakistan, 55 mi. NE of Bahawalpur.

Hasiyah, Syria: see HISYA.

Haskeir or **Hyskier** (both: hůskēr'), rocky islet (pop. 3), Outer Hebrides, Inverness, Scotland, 8 mi. NW of North Uist, 12 mi. N of Heisker or Monach Isles; c.1 mi. long.

Haskell (hă'skŭl). **1** County (□ 579; pop. 2,606), SW Kansas; ⊙ Sublette. Flat to rolling prairie, with sand dunes in extreme N. Grain, livestock. Small natural-gas fields. Formed 1887. **2** County (□ 614; pop. 13,313), E Okla.; ⊙ Stigler. Bounded N by Canadian and Arkansas rivers. Agr. (cotton, corn, livestock, oats, barley); oil and natural-gas wells; coal mines; timber. Formed 1907. **3** County (□ 888; pop. 13,736), NW central Texas; ⊙ Haskell. Drained by Double Mtn. Fork of Brazos R. Agr. (cotton, grain sorghums, wheat, oats, barley, corn, legumes); dairying; livestock (beef cattle, horses, hogs, sheep). Oil, natural-gas wells. Formed 1858.

Haskell. 1 Town (pop. 209), Saline co., central Ark., 5 mi. SSW of Benton. **2** Village (pop. c.1,500) in Wanaque borough, Passaic co., NE N.J., on Wanaque R. and 10 mi. NW of Paterson; metal powder, calendars. **3** Town (pop. 1,676), Muskogee co., E Okla., 18 mi. WNW of Muskogee, near Arkansas R.; trade center in agr. area (cotton, corn, potatoes); cotton ginning, food canning; grain elevator, poultry hatchery; oil wells. Founded 1903. **4** City (pop. 3,836), ⊙ Haskell co., NW central Texas, c.50 mi. N of Abilene; trade, shipping center for cattle-ranching and agr. area (cotton, wheat); cotton gins, cottonseed oil mill, creamery. Settled 1882, inc. 1907.

Haskins, village (pop. 469), Wood co., NW Ohio, 6 mi. NNW of Bowling Green, near Maumee R., in agr. area.

Haskovo, Bulgaria: see KHASKOVO.

Haskoy or **Chaskoi** (häsků'ē), Turkish *Hasköy*, section (pop. 10,821) of Istanbul, Turkey; Jewish quarter.

Haslach (häs'läkh), town (pop. 2,490), N Upper Austria, on Grosse Mühl R. and 21 mi. NW of Linz, near Czechoslovak line; linen mfg.

Haslach, village (pop. 3,659), S Baden, Germany, in Black Forest, on the Kinzig and 14 mi. SSE of Offenburg; mfg. of chemicals, machinery; metal-working, lumber milling. Summer resort.

Hasland (hăz'lůnd), town and parish (pop. 3,339), NE Derby, England, just S of Chesterfield; steel milling.

Hasle (häs'lů), city (pop. 1,560), Bornholm amt, Denmark, on W shore of Bornholm isl.; brickworks, pottery, shipbuilding; granite quarry, fisheries.

Hasle bei Burgdorf (häs'lē bī bo͝org'dôrf), town (pop. 2,709), Bern canton, NW central Switzerland, on Emme R. and 3 mi. SSE of Burgdorf.

Hasleberg (häs'lůběrk"), commune (pop. 897), Bern canton, central Switzerland, N of Meiringen; Alpine tourist center.

Haslemere (hă'zůlmēr), residential urban district (1931 pop. 4,339; 1951 census 11,992), SW Surrey, England, 12 mi. SSW of Guildford; agr. market. Noted arts and crafts center, and scene of music festivals. Church contains grave of John Tyndall and a Burne-Jones window in memory of Tennyson, who lived near by. George Eliot lived at near-by Shottermill.

Hasletal or **Haslital** (both: häs'lĕtäl"), valley of upper Aar R., OBERHASLE dist., Bern canton, S central Switzerland, in Bernese Alps bet. Grimsel L. and L. of Brienz. Oberhasli hydroelectric works here. Chief town, Meiringen.

Haslett (hăz'lůt), village (1940 pop. 1,024, including near-by Lake Lansing village), Ingham co., S central Mich., 6 mi. E of Lansing, near L. Lansing (c.1½ mi. long, 1 mi. wide).

Haslev (hă'slĕv), town (pop. 5,020), Soro amt, Zealand, Denmark, 15 mi. SE of Soro; dairy plant, meat cannery, chemical plant; pottery, furniture, machinery.

Haslingden (hăz'–), municipal borough (1931 pop. 16,639; 1951 census 14,505), E central Lancashire, England, 4 mi. SSE of Accrington; cotton milling. Slate quarrying and coal mining near by. In the borough (S) is town of Helmshore, with cotton and woolen mills.

Haslital, Switzerland: see HASLETAL.

Hasparren (äspärĕn'), town (pop. 2,074), Basses-Pyrénées dept., SW France, 11 mi. SE of Bayonne; livestock market; footwear and chocolate mfg., dairying. Basque pop.

Haspe (häs'pů), SE industrial suburb (1925 pop. 25,688) of Hagen, W Germany, on the Ennepe; ironworks; mfg. of tools. Inc. 1929 into Hagen.

Hasper, Germany: see ENNEPETAL.

Haspres (äs'prů), town (pop. 2,776), Nord dept., N France, on the Selle and 9 mi. SW of Valenciennes; linen-mfg. center, in sugar-beet and hop-growing area.

Hasrun (häsro͞on'), Fr. *Hasroun*, village (pop. 2,237), N Lebanon, 15 mi. SE of Tripoli; alt. 4,100 ft.; summer resort; sericulture, cotton, cereals.

Hassa (häsä'), village (pop. 2,072), Hatay prov., S Turkey, 45 mi. NNE of Antioch; grain.

Hassan (hŭ'sŭn), district (□ 2,636; pop. 627,718), W Mysore, India; ⊙ Hassan. On Deccan Plateau; bordered W by Western Ghats (extensive coffee, tea, cardamom estates; timber, sandalwood); drained mainly by Hemavati R. Agr.: rice (terrace farming), sugar cane, millet, cotton. Coffee curing, rice milling, cotton ginning; chromite, asbestos, and kaolin working; handicrafts (biris, glass bangles, wickerwork); hand-loom weaving. Chief towns: Hassan, Hole Narsipur, Arsikere. Noted archaeological sites at Belur, Sravana Belgola.

Hassan, town (pop. 14,596), ⊙ Hassan dist., W central Mysore, India, 60 mi. NW of Mysore; road center; mfg. of agr. implements, domestic cutlery, firebricks, electric stoves, road tar. Annual cattle fair.

Hassan Abdal, W Pakistan: see HASAN ABDAL.

Hassan Parthi, India: see HASANPARTI.

Hassayampa River (hä"sēyäm'pů), W central Ariz., intermittent stream; rises S of Prescott, flows c.60 mi. S, past Wickenburg, to Gila R. W of Buckeye.

Hasse (hă'sē), village (pop. c.250), Comanche co., central Texas, near Leon R., 7 mi. NE of Comanche; rail point in agr., ranching area.

Hasselborg, Lake (hă'sůlbôrg) (4 mi. long), SE Alaska, central Admiralty Isl., 18 mi. NE of Angoon; 57°43'N 134°16'W; fishing, hunting.

Hasselby (hĕ'sůlbü"), Swedish *Hässelby*, residential town (pop. 2,686), Stockholm co., E Sweden, at E end of L. Malar, 10 mi. WNW of Stockholm; market gardening. Has 17th-cent. castle.

Hasselfelde (hä'sůlfĕl"dů), town (pop. 3,675), in former Brunswick exclave, central Germany, after 1945 in Saxony-Anhalt, in the lower Harz, 10 mi. SSE of Wernigerode; climatic health resort; wood-working, machinery mfg. In Middle Ages, silver and copper mined here.

Hassell (hă'zŭl), town (pop. 137), Martin co., E N.C., 14 mi. WNW of Williamston; lumber milling.

Hasselt (hä'sŭlt), town (pop. 29,369), ⊙ Limburg prov., NE Belgium, on Demer R. and 42 mi. ENE of Brussels, near Albert Canal; 50°56'N 5°20'E. Rail junction; liquor distilling; tobacco and gelatine mfg. Every 7 years town is scene of pilgrimage on Feast of the Assumption. Belgians defeated here (1831) by Dutch, in Belgian war of independence.

Hasselt, town (pop. 2,240), Overijssel prov., N central Netherlands, on the Zwartewater and 6 mi. N of Zwolle; dairying, hay pressing; chalk. Town chartered 1252.

Hassetché, Syria: see HASEKE, EL.

Hassfurt (häs'fŏŏrt"), town (pop. 5,882), Lower Franconia, N Bavaria, Germany, on the Main (canalized) and 20 mi. NW of Bamberg; rail junction; textile and leather mfg., printing, brewing, woodworking. Mineral (iron) springs. Has late-Gothic chapel and 15th-cent. town hall. Fluorspar mining in area.

Hassié, Syria: see HISYA.

Hasslarp (häs'lärp"), village (pop. 609), Malmohus co., S Sweden, 7 mi. NE of Halsingborg; sugar refining; grain, sugar beets, potatoes, stock.

Hasslau, Germany: see WILKAU-HASSLAU.

Hassleholm (hĕs"lŭhôlm'), Swedish *Hässleholm*, city (pop. 8,207), Kristianstad co., S Sweden, 17 mi. NW of Kristianstad; rail center; meat packing; mfg. of clothing, glassware, pharmaceuticals, machinery; cork processing. Chartered as town 1901; as city 1914.

Hasslingshausen (häs"lĭngs-hou'zŭn), village (pop. 5,309), in former Prussian prov. of Westphalia, W Germany, after 1945 in North Rhine-Westphalia, in the Ruhr, 3 mi. NW of Gevelsberg; grain.

Hassloch (häs'lôkh), town (pop. 11,243), Rhenish Palatinate, W Germany, 6 mi. E of Neustadt; wine; fruit (cherries, apricots, peaches), tobacco.

Hassum (hä'sŏŏm), village (pop. 825), in former Prussian Rhine Prov., W Germany, after 1945 in North Rhine-Westphalia, 4 mi. W of Goch; customs station near Dutch border.

Hasta, Italy: see ASTI, city.

Hastenbeck (häs'tŭnbĕk), village (pop. 1,000), in former Prussian prov. of Hanover, W Germany, after 1945 in Lower Saxony, 3 mi. SE of Hameln. Scene (1757) of Fr. victory over duke of Cumberland.

Hastière-Lavaux (ästyâr'-lävō'), village (pop. 950), Namur prov., S Belgium, on Meuse R. and 5 mi. SW of Dinant; tourist resort. Opposite, on right bank of river, is Hastière-par-delà (pop. 399) with old abbey church.

Hastings (hā'stĭngz), SE residential suburb and seaside resort of Bridgetown, SW Barbados, B.W.I.

Hastings, county (□ 2,323; pop. 63,322), SE Ont., on L. Ontario; ⊙ Belleville.

Hastings, village (pop. 754), SE Ont., on Trent R. and 18 mi. E of Peterborough; tanning, textile knitting, canoe building; grain elevators.

Hastings, county borough (1931 pop. 65,207; 1951 census 65,506), SE Sussex, England, on the Channel, 55 mi. SE of London; seaside resort and residential town, backed by cliffs, it has beaches, promenade, and gardens. It is one of the CINQUE PORTS. Overlooking the town are remains of castle dating from time of William the Conqueror. Has 11th- and 13th-cent. churches. In county borough (W) is resort and residential town of St. Leonards. The battle of Hastings (Oct. 14, 1066) was fought on hill on site of near-by town of BATTLE, 6 mi. inland.

Hastings, borough (pop. 14,623; metropolitan Hastings 20,330), E N.Isl., New Zealand, 12 mi. S of Napier; agr. center; fruit cannery, dehydration plant.

Hastings, town (1931 pop. 1,387), Sierra Leone colony, on Sierra Leone Peninsula, on railroad and 12 mi. SSE of Freetown; cassava, corn. Founded 1819.

Hastings. 1 Town (pop. 577), St. Johns co., NE Fla., near St. Johns R., 17 mi. SW of St. Augustine; potato-shipping center with agr. experiment station. **2** Town (pop. 308), Mills co., SW Iowa, on West Nishnabotna R. and 25 mi. SE of Council Bluffs, in agr. area. **3** City (pop. 6,096), ⊙ Barry co., SW Mich., 29 mi. SE of Grand Rapids and on Thornapple R., in agr. area; mfg. (auto parts, machinery, locks, furniture). Resort; several lakes near by. Indian mounds in vicinity. Settled c.1836; inc. as village 1855, as city 1871. **4** City (pop. 6,560), ⊙ Dakota co., SE Minn., on Mississippi R., at mouth of St. Croix R., and 20 mi. SE of St. Paul; trade and mfg. point in diversified-farming area; dairy products, flour, agr. and sports equipment. State hosp. for insane is here. Platted 1853, inc. 1857. **5** City (pop. 20,211), ⊙ Adams co., S Nebr., 23 mi. S of Grand Island and on West Fork of Big Blue R., near Platte R.; 40°35'N 98°23'W; alt. 1,932 ft. Trade, railroad, and mfg. center for extensive wheat region; automobile parts, farm equipment, brooms, bricks, air-conditioning apparatus; wheat, flour, corn products; grain. Episcopal cathedral, Hastings Col., and mus. here. State insane asylum near by. Founded 1872, inc. 1874. **6** Town (pop. 285), Jefferson co., S Okla., 21 mi. SSW of Duncan, in agr. area; cotton ginning. **7** Borough (pop. 1,846), Cambria co., SW central Pa., 25 mi. NNE of Johnstown; bottling works; bituminous coal; potatoes. Inc. 1894.

Hastings-on-Hudson, residential and industrial village (pop. 7,565), Westchester co., SE N.Y., on E bank of the Hudson, just N of Yonkers; mfg. (chemicals, copper wire, cables, asphalt blocks). Inc. 1879.

Hastings River, E New South Wales, Australia, rises in Great Dividing Range, flows 108 mi. S and E, past Wauchope, to the Pacific at Port Macquarie.

Hastveda (hĕst'vä"dä), Swedish *Hästveda*, village (pop. 468), Kristianstad co., S Sweden, 11 mi. NE of Hassleholm; rail junction; sawmilling, furniture.

Hasuda (hä"sŏŏ'dä) or **Hasuta** (-tä), town (pop. 8,634), Saitama prefecture, central Honshu, Japan, 6 mi. N of Omiya; rice, raw silk.

Hasuike (häsŏŏ'ēkä), town (pop. 4,675), Saga prefecture, W Kyushu, Japan, 3 mi. E of Saga; rice, wheat, raw silk.

Hasuta, Japan: see HASUDA.

Haswell, town (pop. 163), Kiowa co., E Colo., 20 mi. W of Eads; alt. 4,528 ft.

Hata (hä'tŭ), village, Gorakhpur dist., E Uttar Pradesh, India, 24 mi. E of Gorakhpur; rice, wheat, barley, oilseeds, sugar cane.

Hatay (hätī'), prov. (□ 2,205; 1950 pop. 296,277), S Turkey; ⊙ ANTIOCH. Borders W on Mediterranean, E and S on Syria. Amanos Mts. in W and N. Orontes R. in S. Iron deposits. ISKENDERUN (Alexandretta) is its port. Hatay prov. is the area of the sanjak of ALEXANDRETTA, which in 1920 was awarded to Syria and was returned in 1939 to Turkey.

Hatay Mountains, Turkey: see AMANOS MOUNTAINS.

Hatboro, borough (pop. 4,788), Montgomery co., SE Pa., 15 mi. NNE of Philadelphia; metal products, hosiery, cement blocks; agr. Hats for Continental army made here. Settled in early 18th cent., inc. 1871.

Hatch. 1 Village (pop. 1,064), Dona Ana co., SW N.Mex., on Rio Grande and 33 mi. NNW of Las Cruces, in irrigated agr. region. **2** Town (pop. 244), Garfield co., SW Utah, 15 mi. S of Panguitch.

Hatchet Bay, town (pop. 552), central Bahama Isls., on N Eleuthera Isl., 20 mi. NW of Governor's Harbour, 55 mi. ENE of Nassau; 25°20'N 76°28'W. Dairying, poultry farming.

Hatchie River (hă'chē), in Miss. and Tenn., rises in Union co., N Miss.; flows NNW into W Tenn., and WNW to Mississippi R. 30 mi. N of Memphis; c.175 mi. long. Receives Tuscambia R.

Hatchineha Lake (hă"chĭnē'ŭ), Polk co., central Fla., 11 mi. ESE of Haines City; c.7 mi. long, 2 mi. wide. Kissimmee R. connects it with L. Kissimmee (S) and with chain of lakes (including Tohopekaliga L.) to N.

Hatchville, Mass.: see FALMOUTH.

Hateg (hä'tsĕg), Rum. *Haţeg*, Ger. *Hötzing* (hû'tsĭng), Hung. *Hátszeg* (hät'sĕg), town (1948 pop. 3,210), Hunedoara prov., W central Rumania, in Transylvania, on railroad and 18 mi. S of Deva; livestock market; tanning, flour milling, vinegar making. Base for excursions into Retezat Mts. Still preserves colorful regional costumes.

Hatfield. 1 or **Bishop's Hatfield,** residential town (1951 pop. 9,258), central Hertford, England, near Lea R., 6 mi. E of St. Albans; aircraft works. The 13th-cent. church contains tombs of Salisbury family. Hatfield House, built 1610–11, is seat of marquess of Salisbury and contains noted paintings. There are remains of Hatfield Palace, built 1496 by Bishop of Ely; scene of imprisonment of Elizabeth just before her accession to throne. After 1946, developed as model residential town. **2** Town and parish (pop. 7,486), West Riding, S Yorkshire, England, 7 mi. NE of Doncaster; coal-mining center.

Hatfield. 1 Town (pop. 364), Polk co., W Ark., 10 mi. SW of Mena, near Okla. line; sawmilling. **2** Town (pop. 2,179), Hampshire co., W Mass., on Connecticut R. just above Northampton; wood products; barium-sulphate mine; tobacco. Settled 1661, set off from Hadley 1670. **3** Village (pop. 110), Pipestone co., SW Minn., near Rock R., 7 mi. ESE of Pipestone, in grain and potato area. **4** Borough (pop. 1,624), Montgomery co., SE Pa., 22 mi. N of Philadelphia; textiles, food products, stoves, paint. Settled 1860, inc. 1898.

Hatfield Peverel (pĕ'vŭrŭl), town and parish (pop. 1,892), central Essex, England, 6 mi. ENE of Chelmsford; agr. market. Has anc. priory church, restored in 19th cent.

Hatherleigh (hă'dhŭrlē), town and parish (pop. 1,130), W central Devon, England, 6 mi. NNW of Okehampton; agr. market; makes electrical appliances, agr. implements. Has 15th-cent. church.

Hathern (hă'dhŭrn), town and parish (pop. 1,225), N Leicester, England, 3 mi. NW of Loughborough; hosiery knitting, brick mfg. Has 14th-cent. church.

Hathersage (hă'dhŭrsĭj), town and parish (pop. 1,456), N Derby, England, 8 mi. SW of Sheffield; lead mining. Has 14th–15th-cent. church.

Hathigiripura, Ceylon: see KURUNEGALA.

Hathras (hä'trŭs), city (pop. 46,994), Aligarh dist., W Uttar Pradesh, India, 20 mi. S of Aligarh; road and trade center (wheat, barley, pearl millet, gram, cotton, corn, sugar cane); cotton milling, ginning, and baling, glass and cutlery mfg., oilseed milling. Strong Jat fort in early-19th cent. Saltpeter processing 5 mi. SE, at village of Lakhnau.

Hathwa, India: see SIWAN.

Hatia Island (hät'yŭ), E island of Ganges Delta, Noakhali dist., SE East Bengal, E Pakistan, in Bay of Bengal, 20 mi. S of Noakhali; 23 mi. long, 4–8 mi. wide; separated from Sandwip Isl. (E) by Hatia R. (an arm of Meghna R. delta mouth; c.23 mi. long) and from Dakhin Shahbazpur Isl. (W) by Shahbazpur R. Hatia village is in N central section. Steamer service with mainland. Subject to severe cyclones (over half of pop. destroyed in 1876). Large isl. just NW is also called Hatia.

Hatien (hä'tyĕn'), town, ⊙ Hatien prov. (□ 660; 1943 pop. 29,200), S Vietnam, in Cochin China, on Gulf of Siam and 155 mi. WSW of Saigon, on Cambodia line. Port of call for local shipping; exports pepper, dried and salt fish, straw bags, betel nuts, tortoise shells. Pop. largely Chinese. Linked with Chaudoc by Vinhte Canal. Limestone quarries. Former Khmer territory; passed 1798 to Annamese.

Hatiguanico River (ätēgwänē'kō) or **Gonzalo River** (gōnsä'lō), sluggish stream in W Cuba, rises near L. Tesoro, flows W through mangrove swamps to the Gulf of Matamanó.

Hatillo (ätē'yō), village, Duarte prov., central Dominican Republic, on Yuna R. and 23 mi. S of San Francisco de Macorís; iron and gold mining.

Hatillo, town (pop. 2,486), NW Puerto Rico, on the coast, on railroad and 7 mi. W of Arecibo; sugar-cane and coconut plantations.

Hatillo, El, Venezuela: see EL HATILLO.

Hatiman, Japan: see HACHIMAN, Shiga prefecture.

Hatinh (hä'tĭng'), town, ⊙ Hatinh prov. (□ 2,300; 1943 pop. 582,400), N central Vietnam, in Annam, on railroad and 25 mi. SE of Vinh, near South China Sea coast; trading center, fisheries. Head of road via Tanap to Thakhek (Laos) over Annamese Cordillera.

Hatinoe, Japan: see HACHINOHE.

Hatiozi, Japan: see HACHIOJI.

Hatirkul, India: see KONNAGAR.

Hatizyo-sima, Japan: see HACHIJO-JIMA.

Hatkalangda (hätkŭlŭng'dŭ) or **Hatkanagale** (hätkŭnŭg'ŭlä), town (pop. 3,323), Kolhapur dist., S Bombay, India, 13 mi. ENE of Kolhapur; sugar cane, tobacco. Sometimes spelled Hatkalangala.

Hatley, village (pop. 299), Marathon co., central Wis., 15 mi. ESE of Wausau, in dairying region.

Hato or **Hato Grotto** (hä'tō grô'tō), village and airfield, E central Curaçao, Du. West Indies, 5 mi. N of Willemstad.

Hato-Lia (hä'tōō-lēä'), town, Portuguese Timor, in central Timor, 21 mi. SW of Dili; cinnamon, coffee.

Hato Mayor (ä'tō mīōr'), town (1950 pop. 3,911), Seibo prov., E Dominican Republic, 22 mi. N of San Pedro de Macorís; agr. center (sugar cane, coffee, cacao, rice, fruit). First settled 1520.

Hato Rey (ä'tō rā'), N residential suburb of Río Piedras, N Puerto Rico, 5 mi. SE of San Juan; alcohol and rum distilling, dairying. Sanitariums; radio station.

Hatra, Iraq: see HADHR, AL.

Hatria, Italy: see ADRIA.

Hatsa (hät'sä'), village, Phongsaly prov., N Laos, port on the Nam Hou (head of navigation) 6 mi. ENE of Phongsaly.

Hatserim or **Hatzerim** (both: hätsĕrēm'), agr. settlement (pop. 100), S Israel, in the Negev, 5 mi. W of Beersheba; shoe mfg. Founded 1946.

Hatsor or **Hatsor-Barcai,** Israel: see BARCAI.

Hatsukaichi (hä'tsŏŏkī"chē), town and port (pop. 5,055), Hiroshima prefecture, SW Honshu, Japan, on Hiroshima Bay, 6 mi. SSW of Hiroshima; commercial center; toys, lumber, charcoal, sake. Exports mineral oil, sake, lumber.

Hatsu-shima, Japan: see ATAMI, Shizuoka prefecture.

Hatszeg, Rumania: see HATEG.

Hatta (hät'tŭ), village, Saugor dist., N Madhya Pradesh, India, on Sonar R. and 60 mi. ENE of Saugor; wheat, millet, oilseeds.

Hattem (hä'tŭm), town (pop. 5,378), Gelderland prov., N central Netherlands, on Ijssel R. and 3 mi. S of Zwolle, in residential area; enamelware mfg., knitting mills; quarrying. Gothic church, notable town gate.

Hatten (hä'tŭn) or **Kirchhatten** (kĭrkh'hä"tŭn), village (commune pop. 6,678), in Oldenburg, NW Germany, after 1945 in Lower Saxony, 12 mi. WSW of Delmenhorst; grain.

Hatteras (hă'tŭrŭs), resort village (1940 pop. 606), Dare co., E N.C., near SW end (Hatteras Inlet) of Hatteras Isl., W of Cape Hatteras; fishing.

Hatteras, Cape, E N.C., 65 mi. ESE of Belhaven; promontory on Hatteras Isl., narrow, curved barrier beach bet. the Atlantic and Pamlico Sound; 35°15'N 75°32'W. A point of danger to shipping because of frequent storms, it has long been known as the Graveyard of the Atlantic, and has been marked by lighthouses since 1798; the 2d and most famous lighthouse was in service from 1870 to 1936. Diamond Shoal Lightship, 17 mi. SE, marks treacherous shallows. A project to establish Cape Hatteras Natl. Seashore Recreational Area was authorized in 1937.

Hatteras Inlet, N.C., passage c.1 mi. wide, connecting Pamlico Sound with the Atlantic, at SW end of Hatteras Isl.

Hatteras Island, E N.C., name sometimes given to 40-mi. section of the Outer Banks extending S from New Inlet to Cape HATTERAS and thence SW to Hatteras Inlet, and lying bet. Pamlico Sound and the Atlantic. Site of fishing, resort villages (including Hatteras, Avon, Buxton), several coast guard stations.

Hatti, India: see HUTTI.

Hattiesburg, city (pop. 29,474), ⊙ Forrest co., SE Miss., c.85 mi. SE of Jackson and on Leaf R.; trade, rail, and industrial center for agr. and timber area; mfg. of naval stores, explosives, chemicals, pumps, cotton and silk goods, clothing; lumber milling. Mississippi Southern Col. and Mississippi Woman's Col. are here. Near-by Camp Shelby was active in Second World War. Settled in early 1880s.

Hattin, Horns of (hă'tĭn), mountain (1,069 ft.), Lower Galilee, NE Palestine, 5 mi. W of Tiberias. Scene (1187) of decisive defeat of Crusaders by Saladin.

Hattingen (hä'tĭng-ŭn), town (pop. 16,666), in former Prussian prov. of Westphalia, W Germany, after 1945 in North Rhine-Westphalia, on the Ruhr and 5 mi. S of Bochum city center; rail junction; steel mills. Coal and iron-ore mining. Was member of Hanseatic League.

Hatton, town (pop., including Dikoya, 5,391), Central Prov., Ceylon, on Hatton Plateau, 28 mi. S of Kandy; major tea-trade center of Ceylon. Administered jointly with Dikoya or Dickoya, 1.5 mi. S.

Hatton, town and parish (pop. 944), S Derby, England, on Dove R. and 9 mi. WSW of Derby; mfg. of electrical vehicles, bottles.

Hatton. 1 City (pop. 991), Traill co., E N.Dak., 30 mi. SW of Grand Forks; grain, livestock, dairy products. **2** Town (pop. 42), Adams co., SE Wash., 32 mi. SW of Ritzville, in Columbia basin agr. region.

Hattonchâtel (ätōshätĕl'), village (pop. 122), Meuse dept., NE France, on E slope of the Côtes de Meuse, 11 mi. NE of Saint-Mihiel; stone quarries.

Hatton Fields, village, Monterey co., W Calif., near Carmel.

Hatton Plateau, in Ceylon Hill Country, S central Ceylon, consists of parallel ridges (SE-NW) rising to crest line of 3–4,000 ft.; 23 mi. long, 18 mi. wide; average rainfall, 150 in. Main settlements: Hatton, Talawakele, Maskeliya.

Hattorf or **Hattorf am Harz** (hä'tôrf äm härts'), village (pop. 3,891), in former Prussian prov. of Hanover, W Germany, after 1945 in Lower Saxony, at S foot of the upper Harz, 5 mi. S of Osterode; woodworking.

Hatto-to, Pescadores: see PACHAO ISLAND.

Hattula (hät'tōōlä), village (commune pop. 6,603), Häme co., S Finland, in lake region, 6 mi. NNW of Hämeenlinna; grain, potatoes, livestock. Has church (1250), once R.C. shrine.

Hatuey (ätwā'), town (pop. 1,788), Camagüey prov., E Cuba, on railroad and 27 mi. ESE of Camagüey; sugar cane, cattle, lumber.

Hatutu (hä'tōō'tōō), uninhabited island, most northerly of Marquesas Isls., Fr. Oceania, S Pacific; 7°55'S 140°34'W; 4 mi. long, 1 mi. wide; rises to c.1,380 ft. Numerous ground doves unknown elsewhere in Pacific.

Hatvan (hŏt'vŏn), city (pop. 16,020), Heves co., N Hungary, on Zagyva R. and 30 mi. ENE of Budapest; rail center; textiles, chocolate, wine; sugar and alcohol refineries.

Hat Yai (hät'yī'), village (1937 pop. 5,834), Songkhla prov., S Thailand, in Malay Peninsula, 15 mi. SW of Songkhla; rail center on Singapore-Bangkok RR; junction for Malayan east-coast line and spur to Songkhla. Sometimes spelled Haad Yai and Had Yai.

Hatzerim, Israel: see HATSERIM.

Hatzic (hăt'sĭk), village (pop. estimate 500), SW B.C., on Fraser R. and 14 mi. W of Chilliwack; lumbering, dairying; fruit, vegetables.

Haubourdin (ōbōōrdē'), outer WSW suburb (pop. 10,014) of Lille, Nord dept., N France; textile milling (linen, cotton), mfg. (starch, chicory, cement, furniture, corsets), tanning.

Haubstadt (hôb'stŏt), town (pop. 894), Gibson co., SW Ind., 17 mi. N of Evansville, in grain-growing area.

Haucheun Island (hä'chŭn'), Mandarin *Hsia-ch'uan Shan* (shyä'chwän' shän'), in S.China Sea, part of Kwangtung prov., China, 70 mi. SW of Macau; 21°40'N 112°35'E; 10 mi. long, 1–5 mi. wide. Fisheries.

Haud (houd), arid plateau region in SE Ethiopia and Br. Somaliland, inhabited by nomadic Somali tribesmen grazing camels, sheep, and goats.

Haudainville (ōdēvēl'), village (pop. 535), Meuse dept., NE France, on the Meuse and Canal de l'Est, 3 mi. SSE of Verdun; limekilns, quarries.

Hauenstein (hou'ŭn-shtīn), village (pop. 3,004), Rhenish Palatinate, W Germany, in Hardt Mts., 11 mi. E of Pirmasens; potatoes, rye.

Hauenstein, mountain (2–3,000 ft.) in the Jura, N Switzerland, 2 mi. NNW of Olten; the Oberhauenstein (2–3,000 ft.) is 6 mi. W of Olten. Two railroad tunnels (one 5 mi. long, the other 1 mi. long) carry the Basel to Olten railway.

Hauge, Norway: see SOGNDAL, Rogaland co.

Haugen (hou'gŭn), village (pop. 246), Barron co., NW Wis., near small Bear L., 8 mi. N of Rice Lake; dairying.

Haugesund (hou'gŭsōōn), city (pop. 18,407), Rogaland co., SW Norway, port on North Sea, 35 mi. NNW of Stavanger; 59°25'N 5°19'E. Shipping center and home of large herring fleet; shipbuilding, mfg. of cast-iron products and canning metal; fish canneries; saltworks. Exports fresh, salted, canned, and frozen herring. Concrete causeway leads to Risoy (rēs'üü), Nor. *Risøy*, an isl. c.100 yards offshore, site of cold-storage plants and modern harbor facilities. Numerous Viking monuments near by, including grave of Harold I (with 56-ft. monument) at Haraldshaugen (1 mi. N).

Haughton (hô'tŭn), village (pop. 501), Bossier parish, NW La., 15 mi. E of Shreveport.

Haughton-le-Skerne, England: see DARLINGTON.

Haugsdorf (hougz'dôrf), village (pop. 1,606), N Lower Austria, on Pulkau R. and 23 mi. NNW of Stockerau, near Czechoslovak border; wine.

Hauhoi Wan, Hong Kong: see DEEP BAY.

Haukaban, Yemen: see SHIBAM.

Haukelifjell (houk'lĭfyĕl), mountains in SW Norway, extend from the valley Brattlandsdal and the glacier Breidfonn, in SE Hordaland co., E c.40 mi. to the Grungedal in Telemark co.; rises to 5,110 ft. in the Store Nup, 11 mi. ENE of Roldal. Traversed by highway; tourist area. Formerly spelled Haukelifjeld.

Haukipudas (hou'kĭpōō"däs), village (commune pop. 12,252), Oulu co., W Finland, near Gulf of Bothnia, 13 mi. NNW of Oulu; rail junction; lumber and pulp milling.

Haulbowline Island (hôlbō'lĭn) (1 mi. long), in Cork Harbour, SE Co. Cork, Ireland, just S of Cóbh; site of naval dockyard and repair installations.

Haunsheim (houns'hīm), village (pop. 894), Swabia, W Bavaria, Germany, 6 mi. WNW of Dillingen; chalk quarries.

Haunstetten (houn'shtĕ"tŭn), town (pop. 8,188), Swabia, W Bavaria, Germany, near the Lech, 4 mi. S of Augsburg; mfg. (textiles, precision instruments, toys).

Hauppauge (hō'pĕg", hō'pôg"), village (1940 pop. 804), Suffolk co., SE N.Y., on central Long Isl., 2 mi. SW of Smithtown Branch, in agr. area (potatoes, truck).

Haura, Haurah, or **Hawrah** (hou'rŭ), small sheikdom (pop. 300) of Eastern Aden Protectorate, on the Gulf of Aden, 110 mi. WSW of Mukalla; consists of Haura coastal village and environs. Protectorate treaty concluded in 1902.

Hauraki Gulf (hourä'kē), inlet of S Pacific, N N.Isl., New Zealand, extending into Firth of Thames (SE); 34 mi. E-W, 26 mi. N-S. Contains several islets; Great Barrier Isl. (N) forms breakwater. Auckland is on SW shore.

Hauraki Plains, county, New Zealand: see NGATEA.

Hauran (hourän') [Heb.,=hollow or cavernous land], district, SW Syria, E of the Jordan R. The name is derived from the numerous caverns in the mountainous NE, where rise the Jebel ed Druz. Hauran is largely a treeless area with rich lava soil. Most of the inhabitants are Druses, who migrated here from Lebanon in recent times. At least in part, Hauran belonged to biblical kingdom of Bashan, which the Israelites conquered. Later, part of Hauran was the Roman prov. Auranitis. There are many anc. towns (e.g., Busra, Der'a, Izra') and ruins, and inscriptions in Greek, Latin, and Arabic. In modern Syria, much of the area is included in the province (□ 1,726; 1946 pop. 118,801) of Hauran; ⊙ Der'a. Besides wheat, the major crop, the region grows corn, rice, lentils, apricots, pistachios, almonds, cotton, tobacco, beets.

Hauran, Wadi (wä'dē), largely dry stream, W Iraq, in Syrian Desert, extending c.200 mi. ENE from the Saudi Arabia line to the Euphrates bet. Haditha and Hit.

Haus (hous), village and canton (pop. 7,812), Hordaland co., SW Norway, at S tip of Osteroy, on Sor Fjord, 7 mi. NE of Bergen; agr., cattle raising. Lock factory near by.

Hausa (hou'sä), name referring to a group of former native states in W Africa and to its inhabitants of Negroid stock and Moslem religion. Region is now included in N Nigeria (Kano, Sokoto) and in adjacent territories of Fr. West Africa. The term is now strictly an ethnological one. Also spelled Haussa.

Hausach (hou'zäkh), town (pop. 2,381), S Baden, Germany, in Black Forest, on the Kinzig and 16 mi. SE of Offenburg; rail junction; mfg. of garments, metalworking, lumber milling. Summer resort.

Hauser (hô'zŭr) or **Hauser Lake,** town (pop. 70), Kootenai co., N Idaho, 12 mi. WNW of Coeur d'Alene. Small Hauser L. is N.

Hauser, Lake (hou'zŭr), W central Mont., in Lewis and Clark co., 10 mi. ENE of Helena; small widening of Missouri R.; recreation.

Haushabi or **Hawshabi** (hou'shäbē), tribal area (pop. 10,000) of Western Aden Protectorate, bet. Abdali and Amiri areas; ⊙ Museimir. Powerful tribe under feudal sultan's govt., controlling upper Wadi Tiban trade route to Yemen. Farming, stock raising. One of the original Nine Cantons; protectorate treaty concluded in 1895.

Hausham (hous'häm), village (pop. 6,662), Upper Bavaria, Germany, in Bavarian Alps, near the lake Schliersee, 14 mi. WSW of Rosenheim; lignite-mining center; textiles.

Hausien, Ethiopia: see HAUZEIN.

Hausruck Mountains (hous'rōōk), low range in SW central Upper Austria, bet. basins of the Inn and the Ager; extend c.15 mi. W from Haag, rising to 2,625 ft. in the Göbelsberg. Lignite mined at Thomasroith, Wolfsegg, and Ampflwang.

Haussa, W Africa: see HAUSA.

Haussonvillers (ōsōvēlâr'), village (pop. 393), Alger dept., N central Algeria, in Great Kabylia, on railroad and 12 mi. W of Tizi-Ouzou; tobacco and winegrowing.

Hauta, Hautah, or **Hawtah** (hou'tŭ). **1** Town and oasis (pop. 8,000), Wahidi sultanate of Balhaf, Eastern Aden Protectorate, 12 mi. NNE of Azzan. **2** Town, Quaiti state, Eastern Aden Protectorate: see QATN, AL.

Hauta, Hautah, or **Al-Hawtah** (ăl hou'tŭ), town (pop. 15,000), S central Nejd, Saudi Arabia, 80 mi. S of Riyadh, on the Tropic of Cancer; trading center; grain, vegetables, fruit; stock raising. Also called Hilla or Hillah.

Haut-Donnai, province, Vietnam: see DALAT.

Haute, Île (ēl ōt'), islet in the Bay of Fundy, off N N.S., in entrance of Minas Channel, 6 mi. SW of Cape Chignecto; 45°15'N 65°W.

Haute-Approuague, district, Fr. Guiana: see GRAND-PONT.

Haute Cime, Switzerland: see DENT DU MIDI.

Hautecombe, Abbey of, France: see BOURGET, LAC DU.

Haute-Deûle Canal (ōt-dûl'), in Nord dept., N France, connects the Scarpe (near Douai) with Lys R. (at Deûlémont), via lower course of Deûle R. Also called Deûle Canal.

Hautefort (ōtfôr'), village (pop. 330), Dordogne dept., SW France, 21 mi. ENE of Périgueux; rail junction.

Haute-Garonne (ōt-gärôn') [Fr.,=upper Garonne], department (□ 2,458; pop. 512,260), formed of parts of Languedoc and Gascony, S France; ⊙ Toulouse. Touches on Spain (S) in the central Pyrenees. Drained S-N by the Garonne and the Ariège, it extends across E part of Aquitaine Basin. Primarily agr., it has extensive wheat and corn fields, and grows wine, fruits, and vegetables. Horses, poultry, and cattle are raised. Important marble quarries. Industry, chiefly of the food-processing type, is centered at Toulouse, which also has chemical and machine-building plants. Electrometallurgy in Luchon Valley. Woolen mills at Saint-Gaudens and Montréjeau. Tourism and winter sports at Luchon, a popular spa.

Haute-Loire (ōt-lwär'), department (□ 1,931; pop. 228,076), in former Auvergne and Languedoc provinces, S central France; ⊙ Le Puy. Lies wholly within the Massif Central, bounded by the Montagnes de la Margeride (W) and the Monts du Vivarais (E). Central portion occupied by the Monts du VELAY, the basin of Le Puy and an arid granitic plateau topped by volcanic summits. Drained S-N by upper courses of Loire and Allier rivers. Rye, barley, wheat, oats, fruits and vegetables (especially lentils) grown around Le Puy and Brioude; sheep and cattle raised in uplands, chiefly near Mont Mézenc. Some coal and antimony mined near Brioude. Lacemaking (handmade in outlying villages and machine made in Le Puy) is the chief industry.

Hauteluce (ōtlüs'), village (pop. 105), Savoie dept., SE France, on the Doron de Beaufort and 11 mi. NE of Albertville, in the Beaufortin (Savoy Alps); alt. 4,765 ft. Resort; winter sports.

Haute-Mana, district, Fr. Guiana: see GRAND-PONT.

Haute-Marne (ōt-märn') department (□ 2,416; pop. 181,840), in Champagne, NE France; ⊙ Chaumont. S part occupied by Plateau of Langres. Drained S-N by Meuse, Marne, and Aube rivers; traversed S-N by Marne-Saône Canal. Poor agr. area with large forested tracts. Important metallurgical dist. in Saint-Dizier area (N). Artisan cutlery is made in Chaumont area, with centers at Nogent-en-Bassigny, Biesles, and Bologne; woodworking. Chief towns: Chaumont (glove mfg., tanning), Langres (old fortress), Saint-Dizier. Bourbonne-les-Bains is noted health resort.

Hauterive (ōt"rēv'), Ger. *Altenryf* (äl'tŭnrēf"), hamlet, Fribourg, canton, W Switzerland, on Sarine R. and 3 mi. SSW of Fribourg; hydroelectric plant. Former abbey with 12th-cent. church.

Hautes-Alpes (ōtzälp'), department (□ 2,178; pop. 84,932), in Dauphiné and part of N Provence, SE France; ⊙ Gap. Bounded by Italy (NE). Mountainous throughout, it contains Massif du Pelvoux (rising to 13,461 ft. at the Barre des Écrins), a section of the Cottian Alps (border range), and several minor ranges of Dauphiné Alps. Traversed NE-

SW by Durance R. valley, the only important artery of communication, with access to Italy via Montgenèvre Pass. Also drained by upper Drac R. (Champsaur valley), and minor tributaries of the Durance (Guisane, Guil, Buëch). Agr. insignificant. Mule and sheep raising. Dairying, cheese mfg. (in Queyras valley). Aluminum works at L'Argentière-la-Bessée, and chemical plant at La Roche-de-Rame powered by hydroelectricity. Lumber trade and woodworking, fruit shipping, distilling of lavender essence. Alpinism. Chief towns are Gap and Briançon (road and tourist center, former fortress). By Franco-Ital. treaty of 1947, dept. acquired 2 small areas (□ 24) near Montgenèvre Pass and Mont Thabor.

Haute-Sangha, Fr. Equatorial Africa: see BERBÉRATI.

Haute-Saône (ōt-sōn'), department (□ 2,075; pop. 202,573), in former Franche-Comté prov., E France; ⊙ Vesoul. Bounded by the Vosges (NE) and the Belfort Gap (E). Drained NE-SW by Saône and Ognon rivers. Dairying, potato and cherry growing, lumbering. Coal mined at Ronchamp. Chief industries: cotton milling, mfg. of hardware and textile machinery, lace mfg., woodworking, distilling. Principal towns are Vesoul (agr. market), Lure (textile center), Héricourt (metalworks), and Gray. Luxeuil-les-Bains is known for its mineral springs and Fougerolles for its kirsch.

Haute-Savoie (ōt-sävwä'), department (□ 1,775; pop. 270,468), in Savoy, SE France; ⊙ Annecy. Bounded by Switzerland (E), Italy (SE), L. Geneva (N), and Rhone R. (W). Occupied by limestone Savoy Alps and, in SE, by MONT BLANC massif, it contains highest peak of the Alps (15,781 ft.). Agr. (fruits, wine, cereals) and population concentrations in FAUCIGNY valley, in depression occupied by L. of Annecy, and in Fr. part of Geneva lowland. Cattle raising and intensive cheese mfg. in uplands. Arve, Giffre, Dranse, and Fier rivers, harnessed for hydroelectric power, activate aluminum (Thonon-les-Bains, Cran-Gevrier, Chedde) manganese, and electrochemical works. Other mfg.: watchmaking, paper milling, woodworking. Dept. has important tourist industry concentrated in Chamonix valley, at Saint-Gervais-les-Bains, and Mégève, along shores of L. of Annecy and L. Geneva. Évian-les-Bains and Thonon-les-Bains are popular spas. Dept. formed 1860 after Fr. annexation of Savoy.

Hautes Fagnes, Belgium: see HOHE VENN.

Hautes-Pyrénées (ōt-pērānā'), department (□ 1,751; pop. 201,954), in Gascony, SW France, bordering Spain; ⊙ Tarbes. S part lies in the central Pyrenees, accessible only through narrow valleys of the Gave de Pau, Neste, and upper Adour rivers. Region around and N of Tarbes is in Adour lowland adjoining the Lannemezan Plateau (E). Agr. (corn, wheat, wine, tobacco) limited to irrigated areas and mtn. valleys. Lumbering, grazing, slate and marble quarrying in the Pyrenees. Harnessed waterpower activates important electrometallurgical industry (Lannemezan, Hèches, Beyrède-Jumet). Dept. has popular spas (Bagnères-de-Bigorre, Barèges, Cauterets) and is a favorite mountain-climbing region. Chief towns are Tarbes (industrial and commercial center), Lourdes (famous pilgrimage place), and Bagnères-de-Bigorre (woolen textiles, electrical equipment). Many Sp. refugees have settled in dept.

Hautes-Rivières, Les (lā ōt-rēvyâr'), village (pop. 795), Ardennes dept., N France, on the Semoy, on Belg. border, 10 mi. NE of Mézières, in the Ardennes; custom house. Ironworks.

Haute-Vienne (ōt-vyĕn'), department (□ 2,145; pop. 336,313), W central France, occupying parts of Marche and Limousin; ⊙ Limoges. Crossed by W outliers of the Massif Central. Drained by Vienne R. Agr. limited to potatoes, buckwheat, rye, colza, and barley. Area noted for cattle, horses, sheep, and poultry. Here are the kaolin quarries which supply famous porcelain industry of Limoges and Sèvres. Dept. also has gold, antimony, and wolfram deposits. Harnessed waters of Vienne R. power paper mills and metalworks. Other industries: glove mfg., wool spinning. Chief towns are Limoges, Saint-Junien, Saint-Léonard-de-Noblat, and Saint-Yrieix-la-Perche.

Hauteville-Lompnès (ōtvēl'-lōpnĕs'), town (pop. 2,488), Ain dept., E France, in the S Jura, 15 mi. NNW of Belley; alt. 2,674 ft. Health resort; dairying; fine cutting-stone quarries near by. Sanatoriums.

Haute-Volta, Fr. West Africa: see UPPER VOLTA.

Haut-Koenigsbourg (ō-kĕnēgzbōōr'), Ger. *Hoh-Königsburg* (hō-kû'nĭksbōōrk), fortress in Bas-Rhin dept., E France, atop rocky height (c.2,500 ft.) of the E Vosges, overlooking Sélestat (5 mi. ENE). Built in 15th cent., it was restored (c.1900) by Emperor William II at public expense.

Haut-Mekong, province, Laos; see BAN HOUEI SAI.

Hautmont (ōmō'), town (pop. 14,127), Nord dept., N France, on the Sambre and 3 mi. SW of Maubeuge; metallurgical center (foundries, blast-furnaces, rolling mills, railroad engine works); chemical factories (sulphur, superphosphates, soap).

Haut-Mornag, Tunisia: see CRÉTÉVILLE.

Haut-Nyong (ō-nyông'), administrative region (□ 15,100; 1950 pop. 81,800), SE central and S Fr. Cameroons; ⊙ Abong-M'Bang. Adjoins Fr. Equatorial Africa on S. Drained by Dja and Nyong rivers. Located in tropical rain-forest zone, it has coffee plantations and wild-coffee fields.

Haut-Ogooué, Fr. Equatorial Africa: see FRANCEVILLE.

Hautrage (ōtrāzh'), town (pop. 3,412), Hainaut prov., SW Belgium, 9 mi. W of Mons; coal mining; ceramics.

Haut-Rhin (ō-rē'), department (□ 1,354; pop. 471,705), in Alsace, E France; ⊙ Colmar. Bounded by Germany (E), Switzerland (S), Belfort Gap (SW), and crest of the Vosges (W). Occupies S part of Alsatian lowland and contains highest summit of the Vosges (Ballon de Guebwiller). Drained by the Rhine (which forms Franco-German border), the Ill and its tributaries (Fecht, Lauch, Thur). Traversed by Rhone-Rhine Canal. Chief agr. crops: potatoes, vegetables (especially cabbage for sauerkraut), flax, hemp, cereals, tobacco, and fruits (cherries for kirsch distilling). Alsace wines grown on E slopes of Vosges at Guebwiller, Kaysersberg, Rouffach, Riquewihr (Riesling wines), Turckheim. Noted cheese made in Munster valley. Dept. has France's leading potash mines (N of Mulhouse), which supply numerous chemical plants. Chief industry is textile milling, with main centers at Mulhouse (cotton prints, sewing thread), Colmar, Guebwiller, Altkirch, Sainte-Marie-aux-Mines. Dept. also produces textile and printing machinery, electrical equipment (Saint-Louis), and paper (Île-Napoléon, Turckheim). Woodworking, tanning, alcohol distilling, vegetable processing. As part of Alsace-Lorraine, it was under Ger. administration, 1871–1918 and 1940–44.

Hauwara, Egypt: see HAWARA.

Hauzein (hou'zān), Ital. *Hausien*, town (pop. 2,471), Tigre prov., N Ethiopia, 20 mi. S of Adigrat; trade center (cereals, salt, honey, cotton goods).

Hauzenberg (hou'tsŭnbĕrk), village (pop. 5,906), Lower Bavaria, Germany, in Bohemian Forest, 10 mi. NE of Passau; makes apple wine; granite quarrying. Summer resort. Apples, cattle, hogs. Chartered c.1359.

Havana (hŭvă'nŭ), Sp. *La Habana* (lä ävä'nä), province (including Isle of Pines: □ 3,174; pop. 1,235,939), W Cuba; ⊙ Havana. Smallest, though most densely populated prov., bounded by Gulf of Mexico (N), Gulf of Batabanó (S); borders on Pinar del Río prov. (W) and Matanzas prov. (E). It is generally flat, with low hilly ranges in center, swamps in S. On N coast is sheltered Havana Harbor. Watered by numerous small rivers, among them the Almendares. Rich in minerals, especially copper, asphalt, petroleum (Bacuranao), marble (Isle of Pines). Thermal springs (Madruga, San Antonio de los Baños, Santa Fe). Fishing (sponge, lobster, tuna, etc.) on Gulf of Batabanó. Agr. products: sugar cane, tobacco, coffee, rice, cereals, vegetables, fruit. Also stock raising and dairying. Industries include sugar milling and refining, distilling, lumbering, tobacco processing, cigar making, tanning, centered at Guanabacoa, Regla, Marianao, and Havana city, the largest port of the West Indies.

Havana, Sp. *La Habana*, city (pop. 659,883), ⊙ Cuba and Havana prov., major port on sheltered Havana Bay on Gulf of Mexico, 100 mi. SSW of Key West (Fla.), and 1,120 mi. NNW of San Juan (Puerto Rico); 23°8'N 82°21'W. Largest city of the West Indies. It dominates Cuba's commercial, industrial, political, and social life. Through its fine, deep harbor (more than 2 sq. mi.) passes the bulk of the country's imports and about 1/5 of its exports (sugar cane, tobacco, tropical fruit). Its most famed industry is mfg. of cigars. It also has sugar refineries, rum and alcohol distilleries, breweries, meat-packing plants, textile mills, straw-hat factories, chemical factories, perfume plants, lumberyards. Havana owes much of its prosperity to its tourist trade, which reaches its peak during the winter. From here radiate international shipping lines and natl. and international airlines. The city's climate is humid, subtropical; mean annual temp. 76°F., average rainfall 43 inches. Hurricanes occur occasionally. It is a colorful metropolis, where old colonial atmosphere merges with the modern. The harbor's entrance is guarded (E) by old Morro Castle, built 1587–97, and Punta Castle (W). The old city (downtown, NW), now the chief business section, has remains of its wall (demolished 1863) and narrow cobblestone streets laid out in rectangular fashion. Has fine examples of Sp. architecture. Malecón thoroughfare is its principal artery. Adjoining are the spacious modern sections, distinguished by squares, boulevards, and parks. Among the noteworthy bldgs. and institutions are: Havana Univ., Natl. Library, Acad. of Science, Cathedral (built 1704 and containing, until 1898, supposed remains of Columbus), Bishop's Palace, Capitol, Presidential Palace, Centro Asturiano, Centro Gallego, Opera House, theater, bull ring, numerous churches and monuments. Havana is considered to have been founded 1519 by Diego de Velázquez, after an original settlement (1515) on S coast was moved (because of pirate attacks) to the present site. Since 1552 it has been ⊙, serving as a gateway to the New World. The city was frequently sacked. It was captured by the English in 1762 and held for a year. In 1898 the U.S. battleship *Maine* was blown up in Havana Harbor, an incident which led to the outbreak of the Spanish-American War and the ensuing blockade by the American fleet. The American occupation (1898–1902), though resented by the people, improved the sanitary conditions considerably. During the 1933 revolution against General Machado's dictatorship, the city was scene of street fighting. The Inter-American Conference of foreign ministers took place here in July, 1940. Immediately adjoining Havana are residential and industrial suburbs: Regla and Guanabacoa (E), Marianao (SW). The principal airport is Rancho Boyeros (S).

Havana. 1 Town (pop. 348), Yell co., W central Ark., 25 mi. WSW of Russellville; tourist resort near Magazine Mtn. **2** Town (pop. 1,634), Gadsden co., NW Fla., near Ga. line, 15 mi. NW of Tallahassee; canned foods (fruit, vegetables); feed, fertilizer. Settled 1904, inc. 1906. **3** City (pop. 4,379), ⊙ Mason co., central Ill., on Illinois R. (shipping), opposite mouth of Spoon R., and 32 mi. SW of Peoria; trade, shipping, and industrial center in agr. area; mfg. (farm machinery, cutlery, buckles, metal wheels, gasoline engines); commercial fisheries. Founded 1827, inc. 1853; important river port in early-19th cent. Site of Lincoln-Douglas debate is marked. Near by are resorts on lakes along Illinois R., Chautauqua Natl. Wildlife Refuge, and Dickson Mounds State Park. **4** City (pop. 215), Montgomery co., SE Kansas, 18 mi. WNW of Coffeyville, in livestock and grain area. Oil field here. **5** Village (pop. 267), Sargent co., SE N.Dak., 11 mi. S of Forman, at S.Dak. line.

Havannah, New Hebrides: see EFATE.

Havant (hă'vănt), former urban district (1931 pop. 4,350), SE Hampshire, England, on Langstone Harbour, 6 mi. NE of Portsmouth; agr. market. Just S, on Chichester Harbour, is village of Langston. In 1932 Havant, with Warblington and near-by areas, became part of Havant and Waterloo urban dist. (1951 census pop. 32,453).

Havasu Lake (hă'vŭsōō, hŭvă'sōō), on boundary bet. W Ariz. and SE Calif., reservoir (c.45 mi. long capacity 717,000 acre-ft.); formed in Colorado R by PARKER DAM.

Havdhem (hävd'hĕm"), village (pop. 481), Gotland co., SE Sweden, in S part of Gotland isl., 30 mi. S of Visby; grain, flax, potatoes, sugar beets.

Havelberg (hä'fŭlbĕrk), town (pop. 7,027), Brandenburg, E Germany, on the Havel near its mouth on the Elbe, and 18 mi. SE of Wittenberge; partly located on isl. in the Havel; shipbuilding; mfg. of chemicals, bricks. Has cathedral (1170), rebuilt in 15th cent.; late-Gothic church. Seat of bishopric 948–83 and 1150–1548. In Thirty Years War sacked (1627) by Danes.

Havelock (hăv'lŏk), village (pop. 1,113), SE Ont. 23 mi. ENE of Peterborough; dairying, lumbering mfg. of fishing tackle.

Havelock, village, N Swaziland, on Transvaal border, 25 mi. N of Mbabane; asbestos mining. Connected by aerial cableway with Barberton.

Havelock. 1 Town (pop. 307), Pocahontas co., N central Iowa, 35 mi. NW of Fort Dodge; livestock grain. **2** N suburb of Lincoln, Lancaster co., SE Nebr.; railroad repair shops. City annexed to Lincoln 1930.

Havel River (hä'fŭl), E Germany, rises in Mecklenburg lake region 6 mi. NW of Neustrelitz, flows generally S, past Zehdenick (N terminus of Voss Canal) and Oranienburg (junction of HOHENZOLLERN CANAL), whence it forms part of Berlin-Stettin Canal to Spandau dist. of Berlin; it continues W in lake-like expansion, past Potsdam (W terminus of Teltow Canal), through Schwielow L., to Plaue (here Plaue Canal links it with the Elbe); then meandering NNW, past Rathenow, it reaches the Elbe 6 mi. NW of Havelberg. Length, 215 mi. navigable for c.205 mi. At Berlin it receives the Spree, which links it with the Oder (E).

Havelte (hä'vŭltŭ), village (pop. 974), Drenthe prov., N central Netherlands, near the Smilder vaart, 6 mi. NNE of Meppel; meat packing, dairying, cattle raising.

Haven, city (pop. 720), Reno co., S central Kansas 13 mi. SE of Hutchinson, near Arkansas R., in wheat region; boilerworks. Oil and gas wells.

Havensville, city (pop. 208), Pottawatomie co., NE Kansas, 35 mi. NW of Topeka; cattle, grain.

Havercroft with Cold Hiendley, parish (pop. 2,038) West Riding, S Yorkshire, England. Includes coal mining towns of Havercroft, 6 mi. NNE of Barnsley and, just SE, South Hiendley.

Haverford (hă'vûrfŭrd), urban township (pop. 39,641), Delaware co., SE Pa., W residential suburb of Philadelphia; some mfg. (clay, concrete, and glass products). Includes villages of Llanerch (lă'nŭrk) (1940 pop. 2,512), Beechwood (1940 pop. 4,966), Manoa (mŭnō'ŭ), Preston (1940 pop. 2,825), Penfield, Brookline, South Ardmore, Oakmont, and part of Drexel Hill (partly in Upper Darby township). Haverford village, seat of Haverford Col., is in adjacent LOWER MERION.

Haverfordwest (hă'vûrfôrd-wĕst'), municipal borough (1931 pop. 6,121; 1951 census pop. 7,266) central Pembroke, Wales, 9 mi. NNW of Pembroke; agr. market; woolen mills. Has castle ruins (dating from c.1120) and 13th-cent. church. There are some remains of 12th-cent. Augustinian priory. A colony of Flemish weavers was established here 1107 by Henry I.

Haverhill (hā'vûrĭl), urban district (1931 pop. 3,828; 1951 census 4,096), SW Suffolk, England, 10 mi. ENE of Saffron Walden; agr. market; silk mills.

Haverhill. 1 City (pop. 47,280), Essex co., NE Mass., on Merrimack R. and 7 mi. NE of Lawrence; a leading shoe-mfg. center; manufacturers' supplies, leather, machinery, paper, electrical equipment, woolens, boxes. Whittier's birthplace (built 1688) is preserved. Bradford Jr. Col. here. Settled 1640, inc. as town 1645, as city 1869. **2** Town (pop. 3,357), Grafton co., W N.H., on the Connecticut and c.30 mi. above Lebanon; wood products. Includes WOODSVILLE village, Grafton County Farm at North Haverhill, and Pike village (bobbins, abrasives). Inc. 1763.

Haveri (hä'vārē), town (pop. 11,399), Dharwar dist., S Bombay, India, 50 mi. SSE of Dharwar; market center for cardamum, cotton, grain, chili; cotton ginning. Agr. school 4 mi. W, at Devihosur.

Haverodal, Sweden: see HALLSTAVIK-HAVERODAL.

Haverstraw (hă'vûrstrô"), village (pop. 5,818), Rockland co., SE N.Y., on W bank of the Hudson and 6 mi. NW of Ossining; mfg. (brick, cement, clothing, textiles); stone quarrying. Near by is Letchworth Village, a state institution for mental defectives. Inc. 1854.

Haviland (hă'vĭlŭnd). **1** City (pop. 606), Kiowa co., S Kansas, 20 mi. W of Pratt, in grain and livestock region. Seat of Friends Bible Col. **2** Village (pop. 235), Paulding co., NW Ohio, 10 mi. N of Van Wert; ceramics.

Havixbeck (hä'fĭksbĕk"), village (pop. 5,070), in former Prussian prov. of Westphalia, NW Germany, after 1945 in North Rhine-Westphalia, 9 mi. W of Münster; hog raising (ham). Has 14th-cent. church.

Havizeh, Iran: see HAWIZEH.

Havlickuv Brod (häv'lĕchkōōf brôt'), Czech *Havlíčkův Brod*, Ger. *Deutschbrod* (doich'brōt), town (pop. 11,792), E Bohemia, Czechoslovakia, on Sazava R. and 30 mi. NNE of Pardubice; rail center; potato and lumber trade; distilling; broadcloth mfg. Has 14th-cent. cathedral. Site of Zizka's victory (1422) over Emperor Sigismund. Until 1945, called Nemecky Brod, Czech *Německý Brod*.

Havoysund (häv'ûūsōōn), Nor. *Havøysund*, fishing village (pop. 456) in Masoy (Nor. *Måsøy*) canton (pop. 2,576), Finnmark co., N Norway, on fjord of Norwegian Sea, 30 mi. NE of Hammerfest.

Havré (ävrā'), town (pop. 4,805), Hainaut prov., SW Belgium, 5 mi. E of Mons; coal mining; mfg. of coal-tar chemicals; electric-power station. Has 16th-cent. church, Gothic castle. Ville-sur-Haine is just NNE.

Havre (hă'vûr), city (pop. 8,086), ⊙ Hill co., N Mont., on Milk R. and 105 mi. NE of Great Falls; livestock-shipping and railroad div. point with repair shops; gas wells; beverages, dairy products; potatoes, wheat. Jr. col., experimental farm run by Mont. State Col., fish hatchery here. Fresno Dam and Reservoir, parts of Milk R. irrigation project, are 13 mi. WNW, on Milk R. Near by are remains of Fort Assiniboine, established 1879. Founded 1887, inc. 1893.

Havre, Le (lù ä'vrù), city (1946 pop. 105,491; 1936 pop. 161,760), Seine-Inférieure dept., N France, on English Channel (at mouth of Seine R.) 110 mi. WNW of Paris and 45 mi. W of Rouen; 49°29'N 0°6'E. A leading commercial and transatlantic passenger seaport of France, with shipbuilding and repair yards, engine (diesel and steam) and boilerworks, and wire-drawing plants. Flour and sawmilling, cider distilling, brewing, mfg. of chemicals, dyes, hardware, work clothes. Active trade in imported coffee (roasted here), cotton, rum, pepper, hardwoods, and copper. Hides, leather goods, dyestuffs, and cotton cloth are exported. Harbor, protected by 2 long breakwaters, accommodates largest liners, and has extensive dock facilities (Bassin de L'Eure, Bassin Bellot, etc.). Bombed more than 170 times, 75% of Le Havre was leveled in Second World War. Reconstruction of port was begun immediately after its liberation in 1944; by 1949 Le Havre had become a leading petroleum port and had reached pre-war passenger traffic. Founded (1516) as Havre-de-Grâce by Francis I near Notre-Dame-de-Grâce chapel (only façade remains).

Havre Aubert (ōbâr') or **Amherst,** village (pop. 2,456), E Que., on E AMHERST ISLAND, one of the Magdalen Isls.; 47°15'N 61°50'W; fishing port. Airfield.

Havre aux Maisons, Que.: see HOUSE HARBOUR.

Havre Boucher (bōō-shā') or **Harbour au Bouche** (här'bùr ō bōōsh'), village (pop. estimate 300), E N.S., on George Bay, 22 mi. ENE of Antigonish; salmon fishing.

Havre de Grace (hă'vûr dù grăs', grās'), city (pop. 7,809), Harford co., NE Md., on Chesapeake Bay at mouth of the Susquehanna (bridged 1940) and 33 mi. NE of Baltimore; trade center for agr. area (truck, especially tomatoes; fruit, dairy products, poultry, corn), with granite quarries. Canneries; commercial fisheries. Resort center; sport fishing, yachting (annual July regatta), duck hunting (on near-by Susquehanna Flats). Near by are federal reservations (Aberdeen Proving Ground, Army Chemical Center, Perry Point veterans' hosp.), lighthouse (built 1827), beautiful estates. Settled 1658 as Susquehanna Lower Ferry; inc. as town 1785 and renamed; inc. as city 1879. Burned by the British in War of 1812.

Havre Saint Pierre (ä'vrù sẽ pyâr'), village (pop. estimate 1,000), E Que., on the St. Lawrence and 19 mi. ESE of Mingan; titanium-mining center; fish, fur, oil trading post.

Havrincourt (ävrēkōōr'), village (pop. 493), Pas-de-Calais dept., N France, 8 mi. SW of Cambrai; sugar-beet processing, brewing. Recaptured by British in 1917 in attack which preceded Hindenburg line break-through.

Havstenssund (häv"stān"sŭnd'), village (pop. 216), Goteborg och Bohus co., SW Sweden, on the Skagerrak, 12 mi. S of Stromstad; herring and lobster fishing.

Havza (hävzä'), village (pop. 3,539), Samsun prov., N Turkey, on railroad and 40 mi. SW of Samsun; cereals; hot springs.

Hawa (hä'wä) or **Mont Hawa** (mō hä'wä), village, Eastern Prov., NE Belgian Congo, 90 mi. NE of Irumu, near Uganda border; center of sericulture and apiculture; mfg. of fishing tackle.

Hawaii (hùwī'ē, hävä'ē, hùwä'yù), island (□ 4,021; pop. 67,683), T.H., largest of HAWAIIAN ISLANDS and southeasternmost; 19°30'N 155°30'W; ⊙ HILO, chief town. It comprises co. of Hawaii. Roughly triangular in shape, c.90 mi. long and c.75 mi. wide, Hawaii is geologically youngest of group and contains 3 mtn. masses: MAUNA LOA bearing KILAUEA (world's largest active volcano), MAUNA KEA, and HUALALAI. It has a generally rugged coast line, with a few good bathing beaches; climate ranges from tropical heat of S coastal areas to icy chill of mtn. summits; fern and bamboo forests, waterfalls, lava deserts (Kau and S KONA dists.), many valleys and gulches. Meat for the Territory is supplied chiefly by Parker Ranch (500,000 acres) in central area; N Kona dist. is the coffee belt; fertile KOHALA PENINSULA and the E coast are under sugar cultivation; S area has sisal production; Puna dist. has cattle, sisal. Railroad skirts scenic NE coast, and motor road goes around the isl. Deep-sea fishing off Kona coast; anc. city of refuge and Capt. Cook's monument in Kona. *Heiau* (anc. temples) scattered over isl. Parts of NE coast vulnerable to tidal waves. Formerly Owyhee.

Hawaiian Islands (hùwī'ùn), group of 20 isls. (□ 6,420; 1940 pop. 423,330; 1950 pop. 499,794), in N Pacific, c.2,400 mi. from San Francisco; officially known as Territory of Hawaii (and commonly called simply Hawaii), administered by governor appointed by U.S. President and confirmed by Congress; 18°55'–23°N 154°40'–162°W; ⊙ HONOLULU. Has 4 counties, HAWAII, HONOLULU, MAUI, KAUAI. The isls., surrounded by coral reefs, are volcanic, with soils formed by disintegrated lava rock and tufa (sulphur is only important mineral); they are mountainous, generally fertile, with mild climate (mean annual temp. 74.9°F.; annual rainfall varies among the isls. from 25 in. to 100 in.). There are 8 principal isls.: HAWAII (largest of group), OAHU (most important, seat of Honolulu and Univ. of Hawaii), MAUI, KAUAI, MOLOKAI (seat of KALAUPAPA leper settlement), LANAI, NIIHAU, and KAHOOLAWE. They contain some of the world's largest active and inactive volcanoes: on Hawaii, MAUNA KEA (13,825 ft.), MAUNA LOA (13,675 ft.); on Maui, HALEAKALA (10,032 ft.). Most important mtn. ranges are: on Oahu, WAIANAE RANGE (highest point 4,030 ft.) and KOOLAU RANGE (highest point 3,150 ft.); on Kauai, WAIALEALE (5,080 ft.). HAWAII NATL. PARK has luxuriant plant life and fern forests with what little remains of koa and sandalwood trees. Flora includes majagua, banyan, poinciana, fern, and algarroba plants, and mango, breadfruit, banana, coconut, ohia, and guava trees. The isls. have many species of birds and domestic animals, but no wild animals other than boars and goats. Sugar cane and pineapples are chief products; coffee is grown only in KONA dist. of Hawaii; other products are rice, sisal, cotton, meat. Most of trade is with U.S. Isls. are at junction of principal Pacific shipping routes, connected with Atlantic lines via Panama and Cape Horn; there is interisland steamship and airplane service, and steamship and airplane service to U.S., Orient, and Australia. Isls. were possibly visited by European navigators in 16th cent. When discovered 1778 by Captain Cook, isls. were under rule of 4 warring native kings. Group was united by Kamehameha I, king of Hawaii (enthroned 1790), who established dynasty lasting until 1873. Christianity was introduced in 1820 and became the national religion. Agitation for reforms (late 19th cent.) followed King Kalakaua's misrule; his successor, Queen Liliuokalani, was deposed in 1893 and provisional govt. established. A republic (1894) had Sanford B. Dole as president. Isls., annexed by U.S. in 1898, were constituted (1900) a Territory of U.S. under Dole as governor. Plebiscite (1940) showed Hawaiian people in favor of statehood. Mixed pop. composed roughly of Hawaiians and part-Hawaiians (15%), Japanese (32%), Caucasians (33%), Chinese, Filipinos, and other groups (20%). Education is free and compulsory, and literacy rate is high. The isls. constitute the most important Pacific outpost of U.S. defense (see PEARL HARBOR). For a time (Dec., 1941–March, 1943) in the Second World War isls. were under martial law. Isls. were called Sandwich Isls. by Capt. Cook.

Hawaii National Park comprises two areas (□ 275.7) on Hawaii and Maui isls., T.H. On Hawaii are KILAUEA (with fiery pit HALEMAUMAU) and MAUNA LOA (with volcano MOKUAWEOWEO); on Maui is HALEAKALA. Park established 1916 by act of Congress.

Hawal River, Nigeria: see GONGOLA RIVER.

Hawamdiya, El, or **Al-Hawamdiyah** (both: ĕl häwămdē'yù), village (pop. 15,504), Giza prov., Upper Egypt, on railroad and 6 mi. NW of Helwan; sugar-refining center.

Hawar, Qatar: see DUKHAN.

Hawara or **Hauwara** (hä'wärù), locality, Faiyum prov., Upper Egypt, SE of Faiyum; site of pyramid of Amenemhet III of XII dynasty.

Hawarden (hāwär'dùn), village (pop. 230), S central Sask., 50 mi. S of Saskatoon; grain elevators.

Hawarden (hā'wôrdùn), city (pop. 2,625), Sioux co., NW Iowa, on Big Sioux R. (forms S.Dak. line here) and 35 mi. N of Sioux City; rail junction; livestock shipping; feed milling. Sand and gravel pits near by. State park (N). Inc. 1887.

Hawarden (här'dùn), town and parish (pop. 9,230), Flint, Wales, 6 mi. W of Chester; coal mining; agr. market. Has ruins of 13th-cent. keep on grounds of Hawarden Castle, built 1752, home of Gladstone until his death. Gladstone established St. Deniol's Hostel and library for theological students. The 13th-cent. church has Burne-Jones window.

Hawarib, Aden: see HUWAIRIB.

Hawash, river, Ethiopia: see AWASH RIVER.

Hawata or **El Hawata** (ĕl häwä'tù), village, Kassala prov., NE Anglo-Egyptian Sudan, on right bank of Rahad R., on railroad and 65 mi. SW of Gedaref.

Hawatka, El, or **Al-Hawatkah** (both: ĕl häwăt'kù), village (pop. 10,962), Asyut prov., central Upper Egypt, on W bank of the Nile, on railroad, and 4 mi. SE of Manfalut; pottery making, wood and ivory carving; cereals, dates, sugar cane.

Hawdon, Lake (□ 53.5), SE South Australia, 165 mi. SSE of Adelaide, near Cape Jaffa; 16 mi. long, 5 mi. wide; shallow.

Hawea, Lake (hä'wēù) (□ 48), W central S.Isl., New Zealand, 100 mi. NW of Dunedin, near Southern Alps; 20 mi. long, 5 mi. wide.

Hawera (häwĕ'rù), borough (pop. 4,840), ⊙ Hawera co. (□ 191; pop. 5,608), W N.Isl., New Zealand, 40 mi. SSE of New Plymouth; cooperative dairy plant; sawmills.

Hawerib, Aden: see HUWAIRIB.

Hawes, town and parish (pop. 1,404), North Riding, NW Yorkshire, England, on Ure R. and 17 mi. N of Settle; resort, with knitting mills and dairy market.

Hawesville, city (pop. 925), ⊙ Hancock co., NW Ky., on the Ohio (ferry to Cannelton, Ind.) and 23 mi. ENE of Owensboro; shipping point for agr. area (burley tobacco, corn, wheat, truck). Coal mines, oil wells in region.

Hawes Water, lake in the Lake District, N Westmorland, England, 9 mi. S of Penrith; 3 mi. long, ½ mi. wide.

Hawi (hä'wē), village (pop. 956), N Hawaii, T.H., near Upolu Point.

Hawick (hô'ĭk), burgh (1931 pop. 17,059; 1951 census 16,718), W central Roxburgh, Scotland, in Teviotdale, on Teviot R. and 40 mi. SE of Edinburgh; woolen milling (tweed) and knitting center, with hosiery, textile-printing, and chemical works; agr. market. Features of town: Mote Hill, artificial mound 30 ft. high, old meeting place of Court of the Manor; Tower Hotel, former seat of Douglases of Drumlanrig and only house in Hawick not burned down by earl of Sussex in 1570; 18th-cent. Church of St. Mary, on site of church reputedly founded in 7th cent. by St. Cuthbert. At near-by Hornshole men of Hawick defeated (1514) English force; victory is commemorated annually by procession called the Riding of the Marches. Just N of Hawick is industrial suburb of Wilton. On Teviot R., 3 mi. SW of Hawick, are remains of 15th-cent. castle of Branxholm or Branksome (seat of barons of Buccleuch), destroyed in 1570 and scene of Scott's *The Lay of the Last Minstrel*. Present mansion dates from late 16th cent.

Hawizeh or **Havizeh** (both: hävēzĕ'), town, Sixth Prov., in Khuzistan, SW Iran, 40 mi. WNW of Ahwaz, in Arab tribal area, near Iraq line; grain, cotton, rice, dates.

Hawke, Cape, E New South Wales, Australia, in Pacific Ocean, near L. Wallis; 32°13'S 152°35'E. Rises to 777 ft.; lighthouse.

Hawke Bay, inlet of S Pacific, E N.Isl., New Zealand, bet. Mahia Peninsula (NE) and Cape Kidnappers (S); 50 mi. long, 35 mi. wide. Receives Wairoa R. Napier on SW shore, Wairoa on N.

Hawker, village (pop. 368), S South Australia, 90 mi. NNE of Port Pirie; wheat, wool.
Hawke's Bay, provincial district (□ 4,260; pop. 79,084), E N.Isl., New Zealand; chief town is Napier. Coastal plain, bounded W by Ruahine Range. Produces wool, frozen meat, timber. Area roughly divided into 2 land dists., Hawke's Bay and Gisborne.
Hawke's Bay, county, New Zealand: see NAPIER.
Hawkesbury, town (pop. 6,263), SE Ont., on Ottawa R. and 50 mi. W of Montreal; paper and lumber milling, woodworking, brick mfg. Paper mills have established "garden city" for their workers.
Hawkesbury, agr. village and parish (pop. 1,554), SW Gloucester, England, 14 mi. NE of Bristol. Has 14th-cent. church.
Hawkesbury Island (□ 159; 27 mi. long, 2–12 mi. wide), W B.C., in Douglas Channel (N arm of Hecate Strait), just N of Gribbell Isl.
Hawkesbury River, E New South Wales, Australia, rises in Great Dividing Range N of L. George, flows 293 mi. NE, past Goulburn, Penrith, and Windsor, to Broken Bay. Navigable 70 mi. below Windsor by small craft. Called Wollondilly R. bet. Goulburn and junction with Cox R., and Warragamba R. to junction with Nepean R.
Hawke's Harbour, settlement (pop. 14), on Hawke Isl. (5 mi. long, 5 mi. wide), just off SE Labrador; 53°1′N 55°50′W; whaling port.
Hawkeye, town (pop. 511), Fayette co., NE Iowa, 7 mi. WSW of West Union, in agr. area.
Hawkhurst, town and parish (pop. 3,075), S Kent, England, 17 mi. WSW of Ashford; agr. market. Has 15th-cent. church. Formerly important for its iron industry.
Hawk Inlet, village, SE Alaska, on NW shore of Admiralty Isl., 18 mi. SW of Juneau; fishing, fish processing, gold mining.
Hawkins, county (□ 494; pop. 30,494), NE Tenn.; ⊙ Rogersville. Bordered N by Va.; traversed by Clinch and Bays mts., ridges of the Appalachians; drained by Holston R. Includes part of Cherokee Reservoir. Hardwood timber; agr. (tobacco, corn, hay); livestock raising, dairying. Formed 1786.
Hawkins. 1 Village (pop. 493), Wood co., NE Texas, near Sabine R., 17 mi. N of Tyler, in oil area. Seat of Jarvis Christian Col. **2** Village (pop. 414), Rusk co., N Wis., 19 mi. ENE of Ladysmith; dairying, stock raising, farming; woodworking.
Hawkins Field, Miss.: see JACKSON.
Hawkins Peak (10,060 ft.), Alpine co., E Calif., in the Sierra Nevada, c.15 mi. S of L. Tahoe; flanks Ebbetts Pass on S.
Hawkinsville, city (pop. 3,342), ⊙ Pulaski co., S central Ga., on Ocmulgee R. and 39 mi. SSE of Macon; textile and lumber mills, peanut and pecan shelling plants. Inc. 1830.
Haw Knob, Tenn. and N.C.: see UNICOI MOUNTAINS.
Hawk Peak (10,600 ft.), SE Ariz., in Pinaleno Mts., near Mt. Graham, 13.5 mi. SW of Safford.
Hawk Point, town (pop. 254), Lincoln co., E Mo., near West Fork of Cuivre R., 8 mi. W of Troy.
Hawks Bill, peak (4,049 ft.) of the Blue Ridge, N Va., 12 mi. ENE of Shenandoah; highest point of Shenandoah Natl. Park.
Hawkshaw, England: see TOTTINGTON.
Hawkshead (hôks′hĕd), village and parish (pop. 535), N Lancashire, England, in the Lake District, 13 mi. NNE of Ulverston. Has 16th-cent. church with 13th-cent. tower, and grammar school which Wordsworth attended. Just S is lake of Esthwaite Water, 2 mi. long, ½ mi. wide.
Hawks Nest State Park, W.Va.: see GAULEY BRIDGE.
Hawkwell, agr. village and parish (pop. 1,744), SE Essex, England, 5 mi. NNW of Southend-on-Sea.
Hawley. 1 Town (pop. 244), Franklin co., NW Mass., 15 mi. W of Greenfield, in hilly area; apples. **2** Village (pop. 1,196), Clay co., W Minn., on Buffalo R. and 23 mi. E of Fargo, N.Dak.; trading and potato-shipping point in grain area; flour, dairy products. Settled c.1870. State game refuge near by. **3** Borough (pop. 1,602), Wayne co., NE Pa., 8 mi. SSE of Honesdale and on Lackawaxen R. Resort near L. Wallenpaupack. Textiles. Settled 1803, inc. 1884.
Haworth (hô′ûrth, hou′-, hô′wûrth), former urban district (1931 pop. 5,911), West Riding, W Yorkshire, England, 8 mi. NNW of Halifax; woolen and rayon milling, leather tanning. At the parsonage, now mus. and library, lived Patrick Brontë and his daughters. They are buried in Haworth church. Haworth inc. 1939 in Keighley.
Haworth. 1 (hā′wûrth, hô′-) Borough (pop. 1,612), Bergen co., NE N.J., 10 mi. ENE of Paterson. Inc. 1894. **2** (hā′wûrth) Town (pop. 254), McCurtain co., extreme SE Okla., 10 mi. ESE of Idabel.
Hawrah, Aden: see HAURA.
Haw River (hô), village (pop. 1,175), Alamance co., N central N.C., on Haw R. and 4 mi. E of Burlington; textile-milling center (cotton goods and yarn, hosiery). Settled 1747.
Haw River, N central N.C., rises NE of Kernersville, flows c.110 mi. E and SSE, joining Deep R. near Haywood to form Cape Fear R.
Hawshabi, Aden: see HAUSHABI.
Hawtah, Aden: see HAUTA.
Hawtah, Al-, Saudi Arabia: see HAUTA.
Hawthorn, municipality (pop. 40,467), S Victoria, Australia, 4 mi. E of Melbourne, in metropolitan area; commercial center for fruitgrowing region.
Hawthorn. 1 Town, Alachua co., Fla.: see HAWTHORNE. **2** Borough (pop. 666), Clarion co., W central Pa., on Redbank Creek and 14 mi. SSE of Clarion.
Hawthornden, Scotland: see BONNYRIGG AND LASSWADE.
Hawthorne. 1 City (pop. 16,316), Los Angeles co., S Calif., suburb 12 mi. SSW of downtown Los Angeles; industrial (aircraft, electrical equipment, building supplies), residential. Oil fields, truck farms near by. Seat of an aeronautical institute. **2** or **Hawthorn,** town (pop. 1,058), Alachua co., N Fla., 15 mi. ESE of Gainesville, in truck-farming area. **3** Town (pop. 1,861), ⊙ Mineral co., W Nev., near Walker L., c.95 mi. SE of Reno; alt. 4,375 ft. U.S. naval arsenal and ammunition depot; tourist center; gold, silver, tungsten. Inc. c.1940. Old mining town of Aurora is near. Wassuk Range W. **4** Residential borough (pop. 14,816), Passaic co., NE N.J., just NNE of Paterson; mfg. (chemicals, clothing, textiles, soap, machinery, metal products, glass, building blocks); rock quarries. Settled 1850, inc. 1898. **5** Village (1940 pop. 2,062), Westchester co., SE N.Y., 6 mi. N of White Plains, near Kensico Reservoir (E); mfg. (machinery, precision instruments and tools, aircraft and rifle parts).
Hawton, residential village and parish (pop. 849), E Nottingham, England, 2 mi. SSW of Newark; cement works. Has noted 14th-cent. church.
Haxtun (hăk′stŭn), town (pop. 1,006), Phillips co., NE Colo., near South Platte R., 17 mi. WNW of Holyoke; alt. 4,000 ft. Shipping point in irrigated grain and sugar-beet region.
Hay, municipality (pop. 2,963), S New South Wales, Australia, on Murrumbidgee R. and 265 mi. SE of Broken Hill; rail terminus; dairying and sheep center.
Hay, urban district (1931 pop. 1,509; 1951 census 1,452), E Brecknock, Wales, on Wye R. and 15 mi. NE of Brecknock; agr. market. Has Norman castle, rebuilt in 16th cent. Formerly a walled town.
Hay, Cape. 1 N extremity of Baffin Isl., E Franklin Dist., Northwest Territories, on Lancaster Sound; 73°53′N 79°49′W. **2** S extremity of Melville Isl., W Franklin Dist., Northwest Territories, on McClure Strait; 74°24′N 113°8′W. **3** NW extremity of Bylot Isl., E Franklin Dist., Northwest Territories, at E entrance of Lancaster Sound; 73°53′N 79°49′W.
Hay, Mount (8,870 ft.), on Alaska-B.C. border, St. Elias Mts., 75 mi. ESE of Yakutak; 59°15′N 137°36′W.
Hay, Shatt al, Iraq: see GHARRAF, SHATT AL.
Hayahoshi, Japan: see NENAKA.
Hayama (hä″yä′mä), town (pop. 15,495), Kanagawa prefecture, central Honshu, Japan, on NW Miura Peninsula, on NE shore of Sagami Bay, 5 mi. SW of Yokosuka; agr. (wheat, sweet potatoes, soybeans). Large estates here.
Hayame, Japan: see OMUTA.
Hayange (äyäzh′), Ger. *Hayingen* (hī′ĭng-ŭn), town (pop. 10,266), Moselle dept., NE France, 6 mi. WSW of Thionville; iron mines, steel mill. Mfg. of wooden railroad equipment. Large Polish pop.
Hayashi (hä″yä′shē), town (pop. 6,033), Tokushima prefecture, E central Shikoku, Japan, on Yoshino R. and 20 mi. W of Tokushima; raw-silk center; rice, wheat.
Hayashima (häyä′shĭmä), town (pop. 9,032), Okayama prefecture, SW Honshu, Japan, 6 mi. W of Okayama, in agr. area (rice, wheat, persimmons); floor mats, sake.
Hayashino (häyä′shĭnō), town (pop. 4,247), Okayama prefecture, SW Honshu, Japan, 10 mi. ESE of Tsuyama; rice, sake, persimmons, raw silk.
Hayatim, El, or **Al-Hayatim** (both: ĕl hăyă′tĭm), village (pop. 7,562), Gharbiya prov., Lower Egypt, 6 mi. SW of El Mahalla el Kubra; cotton.
Hayato (hä″yä′tō), town (pop. 19,465), Kagoshima prefecture, S Kyushu, Japan, 16 mi. NE of Kagoshima; tobacco-producing center; rice, raw silk; livestock. Has large Shinto shrine believed to occupy site of palace of Emperor Jimmu, 1st emperor of Japan.
Haybes (āb), village (pop. 1,652), Ardennes dept., N France, near Belg. border, in the Ardennes, 17 mi. N of Mézières, on entrenched Meuse R.; iron foundry. Slate quarries. Leveled in First World War. Also called Haybes-sur-Meuse.
Haycock, village (1939 pop. 81), W Alaska, SE Seward Peninsula, near Koyuk R., 18 mi. N of Koyuk; gold mining; trapping. School.
Haydarpasa (hīdär′pä-shä), Turkish *Haydarpaşa*, section of Istanbul, NW Turkey in Asia, part of Kadikoy, at entrance to the Bosporus on Sea of Marmara; terminus of Anatolian RR. Sometimes spelled Haidar Pasha.
Hayden. 1 Town (pop. 203), Blount co., N central Ala., 25 mi. N of Birmingham. **2** Village (pop. 1,494), Gila co., SE central Ariz., near junction of San Pedro and Gila rivers, 55 mi. NNE of Tucson; copper-smelting and reduction plants. **3** Town (pop. 767), Routt co., NW Colo., on Yampa R., W of Park Range, and 22 mi. W of Steamboat Springs; alt. 6,350 ft. Shipping point in sheep and cattle region. Routt Natl. Forest near by.
Hayden Lake. 1 In Kootenai co., NW Idaho, 4 mi. N of Coeur d'Alene, just W of Coeur d'Alene Mts.; 7 mi. long, 2 mi. wide. Used for irrigation. Resort village of Hayden Lake (pop. 39) is just W. **2** In Somerset co., central Maine, resort lake 4 mi. NW of Skowhegan; 3.5 mi. long.
Hayden Peak, Utah: see UINTA MOUNTAINS.
Haydenville, Mass.: see WILLIAMSBURG.
Haydock, urban district (1931 pop. 10,350; 1951 census 11,838), SW Lancashire, England, 3 mi. ENE of St. Helens; coal mining.
Haydon Bridge, town in parish of Haydon (pop. 2,050), S Northumberland, England, on South Tyne R. and 6 mi. W of Hexham; lead mining. Near by is 14th-cent. Langley Castle.
Haye, La, Netherlands: see HAGUE, THE.
Haye-Descartes, La (lä ā-dākärt′), village (pop. 1,477), Indre-et-Loire dept., W central France, on Creuse R. and 13 mi. NE of Châtellerault; poultry (mainly turkey) market. Has hydroelectric plant and paper factory. Birthplace of Descartes.
Haye-du-Puits, La (dü-pwē′), village (pop. 1,186), Manche dept., NW France, on Cotentin Peninsula, 18 mi. NNW of Coutances; rail junction; woodworking, dairying. Scene of heavy fighting (July, 1944) in Normandy campaign of Second World War, prior to Saint-Lô break-through.
Hayel, Saudi Arabia: see HAIL.
Haye-Pesnel, La (pĕnĕl′), agr. village (pop. 873), Manche dept., NW France, 8 mi. N of Avranches; cider distilling. Abbey of Lucerne (founded 1164) is 4 mi. W.
Hayes, residential town and parish (pop. 1,678), NW Kent, England, 2 mi. S of Bromley. William Pitt b. here. The church has Norman tower.
Hayes, town (pop. 1,400), Clarendon parish, S Jamaica, in irrigated Vere Plain (sugar cane), 4 mi. S of May Pen.
Hayes, county (□ 711; pop. 2,404), S Nebr.; ⊙ Hayes Center. Agr. area drained by Frenchman Creek and other branches of Republican R. Livestock, grain. Formed 1877.
Hayes, Fort, Ohio: see COLUMBUS.
Hayes, Mount (13,740 ft.), E Alaska, in Alaska Range, 90 mi. SSE of Fairbanks; 63°38′N 146°43′W.
Hayes and Harlington, residential and industrial urban district (1931 pop. 23,649; 1951 census 65,608), Middlesex, England, 13 mi. W of London; mfg. of radios, phonographs and phonograph records, aircraft, lubricating oil, food products. Has 13th-cent. church. William Pitt b. here. In urban dist. (S) is town of Harlington, with Norman church.
Hayes Center, village (pop. 361), ⊙ Hayes co., S Nebr., 30 mi. NW of McCook and on branch of Republican R.; dairy and poultry produce, livestock, grain.
Hayes Peninsula, NW Greenland, extends c.100 mi. into Baffin Bay and Smith Sound; 75°54′–79°10′N 64°–73°5′W; c.200 mi. wide, bet. Kane Basin (N) and Melville Bay (S). Deeply indented by Inglefield Bay and Wolstenholme Fjord. Thule and Etah settlements are on peninsula; Prudhoe Land and Inglefield Land forms its N part.
Hayes River, central and N Man., rises N of L. Winnipeg, flows 300 mi. NE, through several lakes, to Hudson Bay at York Factory.
Hayesville. 1 Town (pop. 137), Keokuk co., SE Iowa, 21 mi. E of Oskaloosa. Limestone quarries near by. **2** Town (pop. 356), ⊙ Clay co., W N.C., on Hiwassee R. and 80 mi. WSW of Asheville; resort; sawmilling. Chatuge Reservoir is just S. **3** Village (pop. 381), Ashland co., N central Ohio, 7 mi. SE of Ashland.
Hayfield, town and parish (pop. 2,593), NW Derby, England, 4 mi. S of Glossop, in The Peak; cotton milling, paper mfg. In parish (W) is textile-bleaching and -printing town of Birch Vale.
Hayfield, village (pop. 805), Dodge co., SE Minn., 20 mi. SW of Rochester in agr. area; dairy products.
Hayingen, France: see HAYANGE.
Hayingen (hī′ĭng-ŭn), town (pop. 673), S Württemberg, Germany, after 1945 in Württemberg-Hohenzollern, in Swabian Jura, 9 mi. S of Münsingen.
Hay Lake, Mich.: see NICOLET, LAKE.
Hay Lakes, village (pop. 199), central Alta., on small Little Hay L., 30 mi. SE of Edmonton; mixed farming, dairying.
Hayle (hāl), former urban district (1931 pop. 916), W Cornwall, England, on St. Ives Bay of the Atlantic and 7 mi. NE of Penzance; fishing port, seaside resort.
Haÿ-les-Roses, L' (lī-lā-rōz′), town (pop. 7,786), Seine dept., N central France, a residential S suburb of Paris, 5 mi. from Notre Dame Cathedral; rose gardens. Brickworks.
Hayling Island (4 mi. long, 1–4 mi. wide), just off SE coast of Hampshire, England, in the Channel at SE end of the Spithead, in Chichester Harbour; separated from mainland by narrow channel (bridged). Portsea Isl. is just W. Chief town, SOUTH HAYLING.
Haymana (hīmänä′), village (pop. 2,791), Ankara prov., central Turkey, 40 mi. SSW of Ankara; grain, fruit; mohair goats. Formerly Hamam or Sivrihamam.
Haymarket, town (pop. 213), Prince William co., N Va., 10 mi. NE of Warrenton, in agr. area.

Haymock Lake, Piscataquis co., N central Maine, 50 mi. NW of Millinocket, in wilderness recreational area; 2.5 mi. long, 1 mi. wide. Drains W into Eagle L.

Haymond, Ky.: see CROMONA.

Haynau, Poland: see CHOJNOW.

Haynes, village (pop. estimate 100), S central Alta., 18 mi. E of Red Deer; coal mining.

Haynes, village (pop. 145), Adams co., SW N.Dak., 8 mi. E of Hettinger, at S.Dak. line.

Haynesville. 1 Town (pop. 3,040), Claiborne parish, N La., 50 mi. NE of Shreveport, near Ark. line; oil and natural-gas wells, oil refineries; lumber milling; mfg. of solvents, chemicals; cotton ginning. Agr. (especially cotton). Inc. 1861. **2** Town (pop. 185), Aroostook co., E Maine, on the Mattawamkeag and 22 mi. SW of Houlton.

Hayneville (hān'vĭl), village (pop. c.2,000), ⊙ Lowndes co., S central Ala., 21 mi. SW of Montgomery.

Hayrabolu (hīrä'bôlōō), village (pop. 4,347), Tekirdag prov., Turkey in Europe, 26 mi. NW of Tekirdag, in rich grain-producing district; wheat, spelt, barley, rye, oats, canary-grass, corn; also flax, sugar beets. Sometimes spelled Airobol.

Hay River, village (district pop. 164), S Mackenzie Dist., Northwest Territories, on SW shore of Great Slave L., at mouth of Hay R., 70 mi. WSW of Fort Resolution; 60°51'N 118°44'W; fur-trading post; transshipment point for Yellowknife region, at N end of road from railhead at Grimshaw, Alta. Airfield, govt. radio and meteorological station; site of Anglican and R.C. mission and hosp. Fishing; oats and vegetables are grown. Trading post was established 1868.

Hay River, stream, W Canada, rises in NE corner of B.C., crosses into Alta., then turns NNE, crossing into Mackenzie Dist. of Northwest Territories, to Great Slave L. at Hay River village; 350 mi. long; 30 mi. from its mouth are the Alexandra Falls, c.150 ft. high.

Hay River, NW Wis., rises in Beaverdam L. (Barron co.), flows c.50 mi. S to Red Cedar R. 8 mi. N of Menomonie.

Hays, county (□ 670; pop. 17,840), S central Texas; ⊙ San Marcos. Crossed SW–NE by Balcones Escarpment, dividing prairies in SE from hilly N and W, part of Edwards Plateau; drained by San Marcos and Blanco rivers. Agr., livestock (especially in N); cotton, corn, wheat, grain sorghums, hay, flax; cattle, sheep, goats (wool, mohair marketed); also horses, mules, hogs; dairying. Limestone, clay. Tourist trade; springs, scenic hills, hunting, fishing attract visitors. Formed 1848.

Hays, city (pop. 8,625), ⊙ Ellis co., W central Kansas, on Big Creek and 90 mi. W of Salina; trade center for wheat- and oil-producing area; flour, ice cream. Oil wells near by. Fort Hays Kansas State Col. and agr. experiment station are here. Founded 1867 near Fort Hays (established 1865, abandoned 1889); inc. 1885. Trade stimulated by development (1936) of near-by oil fields.

Hays, Yemen: see HAIS.

Haysi (hā'sī), town (pop. 476), Dickenson co., SW Va., on Russell Fork and 26 mi. NE of Norton.

Hay Springs, village (pop. 1,091), Sheridan co., NW Nebr., 20 mi. SE of Chadron; dairy produce, livestock, grain, potatoes. Collection of prehistoric bones is here.

Haystack, Mount (4,918 ft.), Essex co., NE N.Y., a peak of the Adirondacks, just SE of Mt. Marcy and 14 mi. SSE of Lake Placid village.

Haystack Peak (12,101 ft.), highest point in Deep Creek Mts., Juab co., W Utah, near Nev. line.

Haysville, borough (pop. 177), Allegheny co., SW Pa., on Ohio R., opposite Coraopolis, and 10 mi. NW of Pittsburgh.

Hayti (hā'tī). **1** City (pop. 3,302), Pemiscot co., extreme SE Mo., near Mississippi R., 7 mi. NW of Caruthersville; processes cotton, lumber; ships stock, dairy products. **2** Town (pop. 413), ⊙ Hamlin co., E S.Dak., 18 mi. SSW of Watertown; dairy products, livestock, poultry, grain, potatoes.

Hayton, village and parish (pop. 1,112), NE Cumberland, England, 7 mi. ENE of Carlisle; cattle, sheep, oats. Has remains of Hayton Castle.

Hayward. 1 City (pop. 14,272), Alameda co., W Calif., 15 mi. SE of Oakland; E terminus of San Mateo Toll Bridge across San Francisco Bay. Poultry, rabbit, and pigeon center; flower, fruit, and vegetable growing; fruit canning; mfg. of poultry equipment, feed. Founded 1854, inc. 1876. **2** Village (pop. 241), Freeborn co., S Minn., near Iowa line, 6 mi. E of Albert Lea; dairy products. **3** Resort city (pop. 1,577), ⊙ Sawyer co., N Wis., on Namekagon R. and 55 mi. SE of Superior, in wooded lake region; dairy plants, boat yards. Camp Hayward (for migratory workers) was established here in 1934. Two state fish hatcheries and a govt. nursery are near by. Settled c.1881, inc. 1915.

Haywards Heath, former urban district (1931 pop. 5,391), central Sussex, England, 13 mi. N of Brighton; agr. market, with flour mills. Inc. 1934 in Cuckfield.

Haywood. 1 County (□ 543; pop. 37,631), W N.C.; ⊙ Waynesville. Partly (SE) in the Blue Ridge; bounded NW by Tenn. (Great Smoky Mts.); Balsam Mtn. is along W border; drained by Pigeon R.; partly in Great Smoky Mts. Natl. Park. Largely forested; farming (tobacco, apples, corn, dairy products), cattle raising, sawmilling. Resort area; mfg. at Canton and Waynesville. Formed 1808. **2** County (□ 519; pop. 26,212), W Tenn.; ⊙ Brownsville. Drained by Hatchie R. and South Fork of Forked Deer R. Agr. area (cotton, corn, livestock, truck); timber. Formed 1823.

Haywood, town (pop. 169), Chatham co., central N.C., 27 mi. WSW of Raleigh and on Haw R., near its confluence with Deep R. to form Cape Fear R.

Hazak, Turkey: see IDIL.

Hazaki, Japan: see HASAKI.

Hazar, Lake, Turkey: see GOLCUK, LAKE.

Hazara (hŭzä'rŭ), dist. (□ 3,000; 1951 pop. 846,-000), North-West Frontier Prov., Pakistan, at W end of Punjab Himalayas; ⊙ Abbottabad. Bounded by Indus R. (SW), Jhelum R. (SE). Mostly mountainous (forests have pine, fir, spruce); agr. in valleys (corn, wheat, barley, rice, rapeseed). Handicrafts (cloth, embroideries, woolen blankets), mule breeding. Pakistan Military Acad. at Kakul; Asokan rock edict near Mansahra. Annexed 1818 by Ranjit Singh. Dist. exercises political control over adjoining NW tribal area (pop. 192,000). Pop. 95% Moslem, 3% Hindu, 1% Sikh.

Hazarajat (hŭzä'rŭjät"), mountainous country of central Afghanistan, inhabited by the Hazaras, a Shiite Persian-speaking people of Mongolian descent; main town, Panjao. A little-developed region of high ranges and deep, narrow gorges, the Hazarajat is crossed by central Kabul-Bamian-Herat highway. Long independent, the Hazaras fell under Afghan rule in 1890s.

Hazard. 1 City (pop. 6,985), ⊙ Perry co., SE Ky., in Cumberland foothills, on North Fork Kentucky R. and 30 mi. W of Jenkins, W.Va. Trade, shipping, and industrial center for bituminous-coal-mining area; oil and gas wells, hardwood timber; oil refining, mfg. of stoves, ice cream, soft drinks; sawmilling. Surrounding mtn. regions, whose people retain old customs and speech, are sparsely settled and isolated. **2** Village (pop. 130), Sherman co., central Nebr., 14 mi. SSW of Loup City and on Mud Creek; recreation grounds near by.

Hazardville, Conn.: see ENFIELD.

Hazaribagh (hŭzä'rĭbäg), district (□ 7,016; pop. 1,751,339), central Bihar, India, in Chota Nagpur div.; ⊙ Hazaribagh. Foothills of Chota Nagpur Plateau in SW; drained by Damodar R. and tributaries of the Ganges. Major mica-mining area N (center at Kodarma); coal-mining area in SE (centers at Giridih and Bermo). Agr. (rice, rape and mustard, oilseeds, corn, sugar cane, barley, cotton); sal and mahua in forested areas.

Hazaribagh, town (pop. 24,918), ⊙ Hazaribagh dist., central Bihar, India, on Chota Nagpur Plateau, 60 mi. SSE of Gaya; road center; trades in rice, rape and mustard, oilseeds, corn, sugar cane, barley. Col.

Hazar Masjid Range or **Hezar Masjed Range** (both: hĕzär' mäsjĕd'), one of the Turkmen-Khurasan ranges, in NE Iran, a SE continuation of the Kopet Dagh; rises to 10,000 ft. N of Meshed.

Hazazon-Tamar, Palestine: see EN-GEDI.

Hazebrouck (äzbrōōk'), town (pop. 11,896), Nord dept., N France, 24 mi. WNW of Lille; rail junction and agr. trade center in dairying, flax- and potato-growing dist. Mfg. (cotton and linen cloth, lace curtains, jute bags, electric clocks, chicory). Damaged in both world wars.

Hazel. 1 Town (pop. 444), Calloway co., SW Ky., at Tenn. line, 40 mi. SSE of Paducah. **2** Town (pop. 161), Hamlin co., E S.Dak., 17 mi. SW of Watertown.

Hazel Crest, village (pop. 2,129), Cook co., NE Ill., S suburb of Chicago. Inc. 1911.

Hazel Green. 1 Town (pop. 264), Wolfe co., E central Ky., on Red R. and 45 mi. ESE of Winchester, in the Cumberlands. **2** Village (pop. 635), Grant co., extreme SW Wis., near Ill. line, 12 mi. E of Dubuque (Iowa), in livestock area; formerly an important lead-mining center.

Hazel Grove and Bramhall, urban district (1931 pop. 13,300; 1951 census 19,659), NE Cheshire, England. Includes cotton-milling towns of Hazel Grove (3 mi. SE of Stockport) and Bramhall (3 mi. S of Stockport). Coal mining near by. Has 15th-cent. mansion Bramhall Hall.

Hazelhurst, resort village, Oneida co., N Wis., 19 mi. NW of Rhinelander, in wooded lake region. Was formerly a lumbering town.

Hazel Park, city (pop. 17,770), Oakland co., SE Mich., a N residential suburb of Detroit. Inc. as city 1941.

Hazel Run, village (pop. 129), Yellow Medicine co., SW Minn., near Yellow Medicine R., 9 mi. WSW of Granite Falls; grain.

Hazelton, village (pop. estimate 500), W central B.C., on Skeena R., at mouth of Bulkley R., and 130 mi. NE of Prince Rupert; silver, lead, zinc, uranium mining; lumbering. New Hazelton (pop. estimate 200) is 4 mi. E.

Hazelton (hā'zŭltŭn). **1** Village (pop. 429), Jerome co., S Idaho, 15 mi. WNW of Burley; alt. 4,068 ft.; wheat, beans, potatoes. **2** Town, Gibson co., Ind.: see HAZLETON. **3** City (pop. 250), Barber co., S Kansas, 7 mi. NE of Kiowa, in cattle area. **4** Village (pop. 453), Emmons co., S N.Dak., 32 mi. SE of Bismarck.

Hazelton Peak, Wyo.: see BIGHORN MOUNTAINS.

Hazelwood. 1 Town (pop. 336), St. Louis co., E Mo. **2** Town (pop. 1,769), Haywood co., W N.C., just SSW of Waynesville, in mtn.-resort area; mfg. (furniture, textiles); tanning.

Hazen (hā'zŭn). **1** Town (pop. 1,270), Prairie co., E central Ark., 19 mi. N of Stuttgart; ships cotton, rice. **2** City (pop. 1,230), Mercer co., central N. Dak., 52 mi. NW of Bismarck and on Knife R.; lignite mines; wheat, corn.

Hazen, Lake (55 mi. long, 3–12 mi. wide), N Ellesmere Isl., NE Franklin Dist., Northwest Territories, at foot of United States Range, WNW of Lady Franklin Bay; 81°50'N 70°W.

Hazen Strait, W Franklin Dist., Northwest Territories, arm (60 mi. long, 50 mi. wide) of the Arctic Ocean, bet. South Borden Isl. and Melville Isl.; 76°N 110°W. Connects Prince Gustav Adolph Sea and Byam Martin Channel.

Hazerswoude (hä'zŭrsvou'dŭ), village (pop. 2,365), South Holland prov., W Netherlands, 6 mi. SE of Leiden; meat canning, pottery mfg.

Hazlehurst (hā'zŭlhûrst). **1** City (pop. 2,687), ⊙ Jeff Davis co., SE central Ga., c.45 mi. NNW of Waycross, near Altamaha R.; tobacco market; mfg. (clothes, boxes, wood chassis parts, naval stores). Settled late 1850s, inc. 1891. **2** City (pop. 3,397), ⊙ Copiah co., SW Miss., 32 mi. SSW of Jackson, in agr. and timber area; lumber, boxes; ships tomatoes, fruit. Founded 1857, inc. 1865.

Hazleton (hā'zŭltŭn). **1** or **Hazelton,** town (pop. 498), Gibson co., SW Ind., on White R. and 9 mi. N of Princeton; tomato cannery. **2** Town (pop. 550), Buchanan co., E Iowa, 5 mi. S of Oelwein; feed milling. Limestone quarries near by. **3** City (pop. 35,491), Luzerne co., E central Pa., 21 mi. SSW of Wilkes-Barre; alt. 1,700 ft. Mfg. (textiles, clothing, paper goods, radio and electrical equipment, shoes, machinery, metal products); railroad shops. Anthracite mines formerly important. Settled 1780, laid out 1836, inc. as borough 1856, as city 1892.

Hazo, Turkey: see KOZLUK.

Hazor (hāzôr'), anc. city, Upper Galilee, NE Palestine, SW of L. Hula, 6 mi. NE of Safad. In biblical history ⊙ King Jabin of Canaan. Site discovered 1928; excavations have yielded remains of acropolis dating from time of Solomon.

Hazor-Barcai, Israel: see BARCAI.

Hazorea (häzōrā'ä), settlement (pop. 450), NW Israel, at foot of Hills of Ephraim, at NW end of Plain of Jezreel, 13 mi. SSE of Haifa; mixed farming. Founded 1936.

Hazor'im, Israel: see SERGUNIA.

Hazrat Imam (hŭzrŭt' ĭmäm'), village, Kataghan prov., NE Afghanistan, 30 mi. N of Kunduz and on Panj R. (USSR line).

Hazro (hŭz'rō), town (pop. 11,186), Attock dist., NW Punjab, W Pakistan, 11 mi. NNE of Campbellpur; market center (wheat, millet, gram) for surrounding plain; small trade in tobacco and sugar; hand-loom weaving.

Hazu (hä'zōō), town (pop. 11,769), Aichi prefecture, central Honshu, Japan, on Atsumi Bay, 12 mi. S of Okazaki; flour milling, sake; fishing.

Hazzega (häz-zĕ'gä), Ital. *Azzega*, village, Asmara div., central Eritrea, on road and 9 mi. NE of Asmara; grain, fruit, vegetables; livestock. Tree nursery. Gold mining near by.

Heacham, town and parish (pop. 2,089), NW Norfolk, England, near The Wash, 2 mi. S of New Hunstanton; agr. market. John Rolfe b. here. The 14th-15th-cent. church contains an alabaster statue of Pocahontas.

Headford (hĕd'fŭrd), Gaelic *Lios na gCeann*, town (pop. 421), W central Co. Galway, Ireland, near NE shore of Lough Corrib, 14 mi. NNW of Galway; agr. market (sheep; potatoes, beets). Has Elizabethan castle.

Headington, England: see OXFORD.

Headland, town (pop. 2,091), Henry co., SE Ala., 9 mi. NNE of Dothan; peanut shelling; peanut and cottonseed products, fertilizer, lumber. State agr. experiment station here.

Headlands, village, Umtali prov., E Southern Rhodesia, in Mashonaland, on railroad and 18 mi. NNW of Rusape; alt. 5,147 ft. Tobacco, corn; livestock. Copper mining.

Headley, town and parish (pop. 1,973), E Hampshire, England, 9 mi. S of Aldershot; agr. market.

Head of Jeddore (jĕdôr'), village, S N.S., at head of Jeddore Bay, 30 mi. ENE of Halifax; fishing port; lumbering.

Head of the Harbor, village (pop. 334), Suffolk co., SE N.Y., on Stony Brook Harbor on N shore of Long Isl., 14 mi. E of Huntington, in summer-resort area.

Headrick (hĕ'drĭk), town (pop. 144), Jackson co., SW Okla., 11 mi. E of Altus, near North Fork of Red R., in cotton area.

Heads Nook, England: see WETHERAL.

Head Tide, Maine: see ALNA.

Heage (hēj), former urban district (1931 pop. 4,054), central Derby, England, 2 mi. NE of Belper. Inc. 1934 in Ripley.

Healdsburg (hēldz′bûrg), city (pop. 3,258), Sonoma co., W Calif., 13 mi. NW of Santa Rosa, and on Russian R., in resort region; fruit canning, drying, and shipping; wine making. Founded 1852, inc. 1874.

Healdton (hĕl′tŭn), town (pop. 2,578), Carter co., S Okla., 21 mi. W of Ardmore, in oil, agr., dairying, and stock-raising area; oil refining, cotton ginning; mfg. of cement blocks, mattresses, machine-shop products; oil wells.

Healesville, town (pop. 2,830), S central Victoria, Australia, on Yarra R. and 32 mi. ENE of Melbourne, in Great Dividing Range; rail terminus; mtn. resort.

Healey, town (pop. 1,690) in Whitworth urban dist., SE Lancashire, England, 3 mi. NNW of Rochdale, cotton milling. Site of Rochdale reservoir.

Healing Springs, resort village, Bath co., W Va., in the Alleghenies, 45 mi. WSW of Staunton; medicinal springs.

Healthshire Hills, low ridge in S Jamaica, adjoining Manatee Bay, 6 mi. WSW of Kingston. Its S portion, together with Manatee Bay shore line, was leased (1940) to U.S. for a naval base.

Healy, village (pop. 100), S central Alaska, near Mt. McKinley Natl. Park, 50 mi. S of Nenana, on Alaska RR; branch line to Healy R. coal field, 4 mi. E. Near by is Healy Fork (pop. 46).

Heanor (hē′nŭr, hā′–), urban district (1931 pop. 22,381; 1951 census 24,395), SE Derby, England, 8 mi. NE of Derby; coal mines, hosiery mills, ironworks, potteries. Has technical col. and church with 15th-cent. tower.

Heany Junction (hē′nē), village, Bulawayo prov., SW Southern Rhodesia, in Matabeleland, 15 mi. ENE of Bulawayo; alt. 4,462 ft. Rail junction (spur to West Nicholson); tobacco, corn, dairy products; livestock. Gold deposits.

Heap Bridge, England: see HEYWOOD.

Heapey, village and parish (pop. 504), central Lancashire, England, 2 mi. NE of Chorley; textile bleaching.

Heard (hûrd), county (□ 301; pop. 6,975), W Ga., on Ala. line; ⊙ Franklin. Piedmont area intersected by Chattahoochee R. Agr. (cotton, corn, hay, truck, fruit, livestock) and sawmilling. Formed 1830.

Heard Island, subantarctic islet (c.25 mi. long, 10 mi. wide) in S Indian Ocean, c.300 mi. SE of Kerguelen Isls.; 53°6′S 72°31′E. Volcanic isl., rising in Big Pen Peak to c.11,000 ft., is largely covered by snow and glaciers. Meteorological station. Discovered (1853) by U.S. Capt. John J. Heard. Formally annexed by Australia in Dec., 1947. Just N is Shag Isl.; the McDonald Isls. are W.

Hearne (hûrn), city (pop. 4,872), Robertson co., E central Texas, in the Brazos valley, c.50 mi. SSE of Waco; rail, highway junction; trade center for rich agr. area (cotton, alfalfa, truck, livestock); cotton processing, sand and gravel mining; railroad shops. Settled 1868, inc. 1871.

Hearst (hûrst), town (pop. 995), N central Ont., 60 mi. WNW of Kapuskasing; farming, lumbering.

Hearst Island, off Antarctica, in Weddell Sea off E coast of Palmer Peninsula; 69°30′S 62°W; 42 naut. mi. long, 12 naut. mi. wide; alt. 1,200 ft. Discovered 1928 by Sir Hubert Wilkins, who thought it was edge of Antarctic continent and named it Hearst Land. Rediscovered 1940 by U.S. expedition, which proved it was an isl.

Heart Island, Jefferson co., N N.Y., small island (.2 mi. long) of the Thousand Isls., in the St. Lawrence, just NW of Alexandria Bay. Boldt Castle here attracts tourists.

Heart River, rises in SW central N.Dak., flows NE and E, past Gladstone (here joined by Green R.), thence 180 mi. E to Missouri R. at Mandan. Being developed as part of Missouri Basin project.

Heart's Content, coast village (pop. 773), SE N.F., on NW coast of Avalon Peninsula, on inlet of Trinity Bay, 37 mi. NW of St. John's; 47°53′N 53°22′W; cod fishing and canning. Hydroelectric plant. Terminal of several transatlantic cables. Lumbering region.

Heartwell, village (pop. 125), Kearney co., S Nebr., 10 mi. NE of Minden, near Platte R.

Heath (hēth), town and parish (pop. 2,070), NE Derby, England, 5 mi. ESE of Chesterfield; coal mining.

Heath. 1 Town (pop. 305), Franklin co., NW Mass., 15 mi. E of North Adams; farming. **2** Village, Fergus co., Mont.: see LEWISTOWN.

Heath and Reach, agr. village and parish (pop. 1,022), SW Bedford, England, 2 mi. N of Leighton Buzzard.

Heath Charnock, parish (pop. 1,253), central Lancashire, England, 2 mi. SE of Chorley; cattle raising, dairying, potato and vegetable growing. Within the parish are a large hosp. and sanitarium, and Liverpool reservoir.

Heathcote (hēth′kōt), town (pop. 1,268), central Victoria, Australia, 65 mi. NNW of Melbourne, in sheep-raising, gold-mining area; magnesite.

Heathcote, New Zealand: see CHRISTCHURCH.

Heathfield, town and parish (pop. 3,659), E Sussex, England, 14 mi. N of Eastbourne; agr. market. Has 13th-cent. church. In Middle Ages Heathfield was important cannon-mfg. center.

Heath River, rises on Bolivia-Peru border at 13°47′S 69°W, flows c.100 mi. N along international line to Madre de Dios R. at Puerto Pardo and Puerto Heath. Named for American explorer who made an expedition along its course in 1880. Navigable for small launches.

Heath Row or **London Airport,** locality in Heston and Isleworth municipal borough, Middlesex, England, 15 mi. W of London; site of major airport.

Heath Springs, town (pop. 694), Lancaster co., N S.C., 9 mi. SE of Lancaster; sawmills.

Heathsville, village (pop. c.200), ⊙ Northumberland co., E Va., 65 mi. SE of Fredericksburg, in grain, truck, poultry region.

Heaton, England: see NEWCASTLE-UPON-TYNE.

Heaton Norris. 1 Suburb, Cheshire, England: see STOCKPORT. **2** S suburb of Manchester, SE Lancashire, England, on the Mersey; cotton milling. Adjacent is Heaton Mersey.

Heavener (hēv′nŭr), city (pop. 2,103), Le Flore co., SE Okla., 35 mi. SSW of Fort Smith (Ark.), just N of the Ouachita Mts., in pasture and farm area (cotton, corn, potatoes). Coal mines. Lumber mills, cotton gin. Ouachita Natl. Forest is just S. A state fish hatchery and an agr. experiment station are near by.

Hebardville, village (pop. 1,113), Ware co., SE Ga., just NW of Waycross. Also spelled Hebardsville.

Hebbal, India: see BANGALORE, city.

Hebbronville (hĕ′brŭnvĭl), village (pop. 4,302), ⊙ Jim Hogg co., extreme S Texas, c.55 mi. E of Laredo, in oil-producing region; cattle-shipping center; mfg. (cottonseed products, oil-field supplies).

Hebburn (hĕ′bûrn), urban district (1931 pop. 24,123; 1951 census 23,163), NE Durham, England, on Tyne R. estuary and 4 mi. E of Newcastle-upon-Tyne; shipbuilding, chemical, paint, electrical switchgear works. Coal is shipped.

Hebden Bridge or **Hebden Royd,** urban district (1931 pop. 6,312; 1951 census 10,233), West Riding, SW Yorkshire, England, on Calder R. and Rochdale Canal, 7 mi. W of Halifax; cotton milling, bleaching, and printing; has clothing mills, machine-tool works.

Heber (hē′bûr). **1** Village (1940 pop. 632), Imperial co., S Calif., 17 mi. N of Brawley, in IMPERIAL VALLEY. **2** City (pop. 2,936), ⊙ Wasatch co., N central Utah, 23 mi. NE of Provo, near Provo R., in mtn. region; alt. 5,595 ft.; trade center and cattle-shipping point; canned peas, cheese. Lead, silver, zinc mines in vicinity. City settled 1859 by Mormons. Hot-water pools of extinct geysers near by.

Heber Springs, town (pop. 2,109), ⊙ Cleburne co., N central Ark., c.55 mi. NNE of Little Rock; resort town in the Ozarks; medicinal springs. Agr., lumbering, stone quarrying in region. Laid out 1881.

Hébertville (ā″bâr′vĭl), village (pop. 1,025), central Que., 23 mi. W of Arvida; lumbering, dairying. Hébertville Station (pop. 950) is just E.

Hebet, Egypt: see BAHBIT EL HIGARA.

Hebgen Lake (hĕb′gŭn), SW Mont., in Gallatin co., at S end of Madison Range, just W of Yellowstone Natl. Park; artificial lake (15 mi. long, 6 mi. max. width) formed by Hebgen Dam in Madison R., which regulates water for hydroelectric plants.

Hebrides (hĕ′brĭdēz) or **Western Islands,** anc. *Hebudai, Hebudes, Ebudae,* and *Hebudae,* group (□ c.3,000) of c.500 isls. off W coast of Scotland, of which c.100 are inhabited. They are divided into the Inner Hebrides and the Outer Hebrides, separated by the straits of The Minch, the Little Minch, and the Sea of Hebrides. Inner Hebrides include SKYE, JURA, ISLAY, MULL, EIGG, COLL, IONA, STAFFA, COLONSAY, ORONSAY, RUM, TYREE, ULVA, and SCARBA; the Outer Hebrides, sometimes called Long Island, extend 130 mi. NNE-SSW bet. the Butt of Lewis (NNE) and Barra Head (SSW), and include LEWIS WITH HARRIS, NORTH UIST, BENBECULA, SOUTH UIST, BARRA, FLANNAN ISLES, and SAINT KILDA. Climate of the Hebrides is moist and little of soil is arable. Chief industries are fishing, cattle and sheep raising, and hand-weaving of tweeds (Harris tweeds). There is some whisky distilling and limestone and slate quarrying. Tourist trade is important. Administratively the isls. are divided bet. Ross and Cromarty, Inverness, and Argyll. Population has declined sharply in recent years, especially in the Inner Hebrides, many islanders emigrating to Canada. Gaelic, extensively spoken, is on the decline. In 8th cent. Celtic inhabitants of Hebrides came under Norwegian rule; in 1266 Alexander III of Scotland was ceded the isls. under treaty with Magnus VI. Local chieftains then held them in vassalage to the Scottish crown; by 1346 they were united under John Macdonald of Islay, "Lord of the Isles." In 1748 their incorporation with Scotland became final. The Hebrides were the Southern Isles of the Norwegians, Latin *Sodorenses,* a name surviving in title of bishop of Sodor and Man. In literature the Hebrides were made famous by the writings of Scott (*The Lord of the Isles*), Boswell, and William Black. There are numerous associations with Prince Charles Edward, the Young Pretender, who, aided by Flora Macdonald, hid on several of the isls. after failure of his 1745 uprising.

Hebrides, New: see NEW HEBRIDES.

Hebrides, Sea of the, or **Gulf of the Hebrides,** Scotland, arm of the Atlantic bet. the Inner Hebrides and the S Outer Hebrides, opening N on the Little Minch; c.30 mi. wide.

Hebron (hē′brŭn), village (pop. 166), NE Labrador, on N side of entrance of Hebron Fiord (30-mi.-long inlet of the Atlantic); 58°12′N 62°37′W; fishing port and seaplane anchorage.

Hebron, Arabic *El Khalil,* town (1946 pop. estimate 26,390) of Palestine, after 1948 in W Jordan, in Judaean Hills, 18 mi. SSW of Jerusalem; alt. 2,040 ft. It lies in flat valley (identified with biblical *Valley of Eshcol*), bet. hill ridges. Noted feature is the Haram, fortified structure enclosing Cave of Machpelah, traditional burial place of Sarah and Jacob. One of oldest towns in the world, Hebron figures in biblical history as *Kirjath-arba* or *Kiriath-arba,* and also as *Mamre.* Captured by Joshua, it was later David's ⊙. Captured from Edomites by Judas Maccabeus, it was subsequently burned by Romans. As St. Abraham it was seat of Crusaders' seigneurie and bishopric. There are remains of 12th-cent. Crusaders' cathedral.

Hebron. 1 Town (pop. 1,320), Tolland co., E central Conn., on Salmon R. and 18 mi. SE of Hartford, in agr. area. Includes Gilead and Amston villages and Amston L. (c.1 mi. long). Rev. Samuel Peters, Tory author of exaggerated account of Conn. "blue laws," lived here. Has 18th-cent. houses. Settled 1704, inc. 1708. **2** Village (pop. 696), McHenry co., NE Ill., near Wis. line, 11 mi. N of Woodstock, in dairying and resort area; makes dairy equipment, auto heaters. **3** Town (pop. 1,010), Porter co., NW Ind., 13 mi. SW of Valparaiso, in agr. area. **4** Agr. town (pop. 829), Oxford co., W Maine, 11 mi. NW of Auburn; orchard center. **5** Town (pop. 723), Wicomico co., SE Md., 6 mi. NW of Salisbury, in truck-farm and timber area; lumber mill, clothing factories. **6** City (pop. 2,000), ⊙ Thayer co., SE Nebr., 65 mi. SW of Lincoln and on Little Blue R.; dairy products, grain. Hebron Acad. here. City founded 1869. **7** Town (pop. 130), Grafton co., central N.H., on Newfound L. and 20 mi. NNW of Franklin, in agr., recreational area; summer camps, fishing, skiing. **8** City (pop. 1,412), Morton co., SW central N. Dak., 55 mi. W of Mandan. Brick and tile mfg. (clay deposits near by); dairy produce, livestock, poultry, wheat, corn, barley. State univ. mining experiment station is here. Inc. 1916. **9** Village (pop. 864), Licking co., central Ohio, 8 mi. SW of Newark; dairy products. Buckeye Lake Park (resort) is near by.

Hebron, Wales: see LLANGLYDWEN.

Hebros, nome, Greece: see HEVROS.

Hebros River, or **Hebrus River,** SE Europe: see MARITSA RIVER.

Hebudae, Hebudai, or **Hebudes,** Scotland: see HEBRIDES.

Heby (hā′bü″), village (pop. 1,106), Vastmanland co., central Sweden, 8 mi. E of Sala; rail junction; sawmills, brickworks.

Hecate Island, B.C.: see CALVERT ISLAND.

Hecate Strait (hĕ′kŭt) (160 mi. long, 40–80 mi. wide), W B.C., separates Queen Charlotte Isls. from mainland; joins Dixon Entrance (NNW) and Queen Charlotte Sound (SSE). Salmon and halibut fisheries.

Hecatompylus, Iran: see DAMGHAN.

Hecelchakán (āsĕlchäkän′), town (pop. 3,358), Campeche, SE Mexico, on NW Yucatan Peninsula, on railroad and 65 mi. SW of Mérida; agr. center (corn, sugar cane, henequen, tobacco, tropical fruit, livestock).

Heceta Beach (hŭsē′tŭ, hĕ′kŭtŭ), W Oregon, on the Pacific 22 mi. S of Waldport, just S of Heceta Head; state park.

Heceta Head (hĕ′kŭtŭ), W Oregon, coastal promontory c.20 mi. S of Waldport; lighthouse.

Hèches (ĕsh), village (pop. 390), Hautes-Pyrénées dept., SW France, on the Neste (hydroelectric plant) and 12 mi. ESE of Bagnères-de-Bigorre; electrometallurgy (lead and manganese ore smelting). Paper mill near by.

Hechingen (hĕ′khĭng-ŭn), town (pop. 6,119), Hohenzollern, S Germany, after 1945 in Württemberg-Hohenzollern, in Swabian Jura, 12 mi. SSW of Tübingen; rail junction; mfg. of office machines, knitwear; spinning, weaving. Has neoclassic castle and church. Site of research institute for biology and physics. Residence of dukes of Hohenzollern-Hechingen until 1849, when it passed to Prussia. Just N, towering above town, on top of Hohenzollern mtn. (2,805 ft.), is the castle of Hohenzollern (destroyed 1423; rebuilt in 1850s).

Hecho (ā′chō), town (pop. 875), Huesca prov., NE Spain, 16 mi. NW of Jaca, on S slopes of the Pyrenees; summer resort; cheese mfg.; flour mills. Because of its proximity to Fr. border, it was long a place of importance.

Hechtsheim (hĕkhts′hīm), village (pop. 4,247), Rhenish Hesse, W Germany, 3 mi. S of Mainz; wine.

Hecker, village (pop. 204), Monroe co., SW Ill., 22 mi. SSE of East St. Louis, in agr. area.

Hecklingen (hĕk′lĭng-ŭn), town (pop. 6,845), in former Anhalt state, central Germany, after 1945 in

Saxony-Anhalt, 3 mi. WSW of Stassfurt; potash mining; sugar refining, food canning; limestone- and brickworks.

Heckmondwike (hĕk'mŭndwīk), urban district (1931 pop. 8,991; 1951 census 8,648), West Riding, S central Yorkshire, England, 2 mi. WNW of Dewsbury; woolen milling, carpet weaving; also produces textile machinery, machine tools, shoes, asbestos, soap.

Heckscher State Park (hĕk'shûr), SE N.Y., recreational area (1,518 acres) on S Long Isl., on peninsula extending into Great South Bay SE of Islip. Bathing, picnicking, hiking, horseback riding.

Hecla (hĕ'klů), city (pop. 500), Brown co., N S.Dak., 33 mi. NNE of Aberdeen, near James R.; dairy produce, livestock, grain, potatoes.

Hecla, Cape (hĕ'klů), NE Ellesmere Isl., NE Franklin Dist., Northwest Territories, on Lincoln Sea of the Arctic Ocean; 82°54'N 64°40'W.

Hecla, Mount, peak (1,988 ft.) of South Uist, Outer Hebrides, Scotland.

Hecla and Griper Bay, inlet (85 mi. long, 25–60 mi. wide) of the Arctic Ocean, N Melville Isl., W Franklin Dist., Northwest Territories; 76°N 113°W.

Hector, village, SE B.C., near Alta. border, in Rocky Mts., in Yoho Natl. Park, 40 mi. NW of Banff; alt. 5,213 ft.; lumbering. Bet. this point and Field the Canadian Pacific RR passes through the SPIRAL TUNNELS.

Hector, village (pop. 1,196), Renville co., S central Minn., 14 mi. E of Olivia, in grain, potato, livestock area; dairy products, flour.

Hector, Mount (11,135 ft.), SW Alta., near B.C. border, in Rocky Mts., in Banff Natl. Park, 40 mi. NW of Banff; 51°39'N 116°16'W. At its foot is Hector L.

Hector Lake (4 mi. long, 1 mi. wide), SW Alta., near B.C. border, in Rocky Mts., in Banff Natl. Park, at foot of Mt. Hector, 45 mi. NW of Banff; alt. 5,704 ft. Drains SE into Bow R.

Heddal Lake (hĕd'däl), Telemark co., S Norway, extending 11 mi. S from Notodden (at mouth of Tinne R.). Sauer R., its outlet, flows S to Nor L. Steamboats ascend to Notodden from Skien. Also called Hitterdal.

Heddernheim (hĕ'dŭrnhīm), industrial suburb (pop., including settlement of Römerstadt, 7,233) of Frankfurt, W Germany, on the Nidda, 3.5 mi. N of city center; mfg. of aluminum and copper alloys.

Heddesheim (hĕ'dŭs-hīm), village (pop. 5,001), N Baden, Germany, after 1945 in Württemberg-Baden, 6 mi. ENE of Mannheim; tobacco, sugar beets, fruit.

Hédé (ādā'), agr. village (pop. 694), Ille-et-Vilaine dept., W France, 14 mi. NNW of Rennes. In near-by castle of Montmuran, Bertrand Du Guesclin was knighted in 1354.

Hedefors, Sweden: see LERUM.

Hedehusene (hā'dhůhōōsůnů), town (pop. 1,676), Copenhagen amt, Zealand, Denmark, 16 mi. W of Copenhagen; dairy products, cement, machinery.

Hedel (hā'důl), village (pop. 1,673), Gelderland prov., central Netherlands, on Bommelwaard isl., on Maas R. (bridge) and 4 mi. NNW of 's Hertogenbosch; shipbuilding, wooden-shoe mfg.; agr.

Hedemora (hā'dŭmōō"rä), city (pop. 4,564), Kopparberg co., central Sweden, on Dal R. and 25 mi. SE of Falun, in iron-mining region; iron works. Has 15th-cent. church, 18th-cent. town hall, mus. First mentioned as town 1414. Formerly scene of important annual trade fairs.

Hedemünden (hā"dümün'dŭn), village (pop. 1,745), in former Prussian prov. of Hanover, W Germany, after 1945 in Lower Saxony, on the Werra and 12 mi. SW of Göttingen; cement works.

Hedenstad (hā'dŭnstä), village in Övre Sandsvaer (Nor. *Øvre Sandsvaer*) canton (pop. 2,319), Buskerud co., SE Norway, in hilly region, 4 mi. S of Kongsberg; agr., lumbering; sawmilling. Silver mined in region. Skrim (skrĭm) mtn., 7 mi. S, rises 2,851 ft.

Hedensted (hā'dhŭnstĕdh), town (pop. 1,204), Vejle amt, E Jutland, Denmark, 7 mi. NE of Vejle; cement, margarine, tin products.

Hedervar (hā'dĕrvär), Hung. *Hédervár*, town (pop. 1,119), Györ-Moson co., NW Hungary, on Little SCHÜTT, isl. formed by the Danube, and 13 mi. NW of Györ; starch mfg., flour mills. Castle here.

He Devil Mountain, highest peak (9,387 ft.) in Seven Devils Mts., W Idaho, 35 mi. NW of McCall. Rises above Grand Canyon of the Snake R. (W).

Hedge End, town and parish (pop. 1,714), S Hampshire, England, 4 mi. E of Southampton; agr. market. Site of smallest church in England (First World War memorial).

Hedgesville, town (pop. 419), Berkeley co., NE W.Va., in Eastern Panhandle, 7 mi. NNW of Martinsburg.

Hedjaz, Saudi Arabia: see HEJAZ.

Hedjuff or **Hejaf** (hĕ'jŭf), E harbor section of Tawahi, on Aden peninsula and on Aden Bay; coaling piers, naval workshops.

Hedley, village (pop. estimate 600), S B.C., in Cascade Mts., on Similkameen R. and 26 mi. WSW of Penticton; alt. 4,500 ft.; gold and silver mining.

Hedley, town (pop. 588), Donley co., extreme N Texas, in the Panhandle, 15 mi. SE of Clarendon; shipping point for agr. area; cotton gins; clay products.

Hedmark (hĕd'märk), county [Nor. *fylke*] (□ 10,592; pop. 169,525), SE Norway, on Swedish border; ⊙ Hamar. Drained by Glomma R., which flows through the Osterdal, chief N-S valley, co. has undulating surface (S) with rich agr. land, and becomes rugged and mountainous (N), taking in E section of the Dovrefjell and Rondane mts. Pyrites mined at Folldal. Co. is densely forested; lumbering, mfg. of cardboard and cellulose, and woodworking are chief industries. Agr., stock raising. Hamar and Kongsvinger are the only cities.

Hedo, Cape (hā'dō), Jap. *Hedo-saki*, northernmost point of Okinawa, Okinawa Isls., in Ryukyu Isls., Japan, in E.China Sea; 26°52'N 128°16'E.

Hedon (hĕ'dŭn), municipal borough (1931 pop. 1,501; 1951 census 1,991), East Riding, SE Yorkshire, England, near Humber R. 6 mi. E of Hull; chemical center (industrial solvents). Has church begun 1180. Town was founded by the earls of Albermarle after Norman Conquest and became an important trade center, later displaced by the port of Hull.

Hedrick (hĕ'drĭk), town (pop. 733), Keokuk co., SE Iowa, 12 mi. NNE of Ottumwa; livestock, grain.

Hedrum (hĕd'rōōm), village and canton (pop. 6,515), Vestfold co., SE Norway, on Lagen R. and 5 mi. N of Larvik; market gardening, lumbering, tanning, stone cutting.

Heeg (hākh), village (pop. 1,214), Friesland prov., N Netherlands, on N shore of Fluessen L., 5 mi. SSW of Sneek; lake fishing.

Heemstede (hām'stādů), village (pop. 22,821), North Holland prov., W Netherlands, on the Ringvaart and 3 mi. S of Haarlem; flour milling, bulb growing.

Heer (hār), town (pop. 7,032), Limburg prov., SE Netherlands, 2 mi. E of Maastricht; chalk quarrying; ironworks; cement, candles.

Heer Arendskerke, 's, Netherlands: see 's HEER ARENDSKERKE.

Heerde (hār'dů), village (pop. 2,232), Gelderland prov., N central Netherlands, 12 mi. N of Apeldoorn; soap mfg.

Heerdt, Germany: see DÜSSELDORF.

Heerenberg, 's, Netherlands: see 's HEERENBERG.

Heerenveen (hā'rŭnvān), town (pop. 7,621), Friesland prov., N Netherlands, 12 mi. ESE of Sneek; mfg. of cement, agr. machinery and other metal products, bamboo products, oil and feed cakes, honey, edible fats, cigars; meat canning.

Heeren-Werve (hā'rŭn-vĕr'fů), village (pop. 5,997), in former Prussian prov. of Westphalia, W Germany, after 1945 in North Rhine-Westphalia, in the Ruhr, 3 mi. E of Kamen.

Heerhugowaard (hārhü'khōvärt), village (pop. 1,938), North Holland prov., NW Netherlands, 5 mi. NE of Alkmaar; cattle raising, dairying.

Heerlen (hār'lŭn), town (pop. 34,175; with suburbs 56,625), Limburg prov., SE Netherlands, 13 mi. ENE of Maastricht; rail junction; coal-mining center (site of Oranje–Nassau I coal mine, N); mfg. (briquettes, knitted textiles, iron, stoneware, cement, glassware, cigars), printing. Hq. of state mines administration; mining school. Has 13th-cent. parish church.

Heerlerheide (hār'lŭrhīdů), town (pop. 6,158), Limburg prov., SE Netherlands, 2.5 mi. NNW of Heerlen; coal mining.

Heerwegen, Poland: see POLKOWICE.

Heessen (hā'sŭn), village (pop. 10,887), in former Prussian prov. of Westphalia, NW Germany, after 1945 in North Rhine-Westphalia, on the Lippe and 2 mi. NE of Hamm; grain, cattle.

Heeze (hā'zů), village (pop. 2,650), North Brabant prov., SE Netherlands, 6 mi. SE of Eindhoven; wool spinning, ribbon weaving; agr., cattle raising.

Heflin, town (pop. 1,982), ⊙ Cleburne co., E Ala., near Tallapoosa R., 15 mi. E of Anniston; lumber milling, cotton ginning. Settled 1883, inc. 1892.

Heftsi Bah or **Heftziba** (both: hĕftsēbä'). **1** Settlement (pop. 400), NE Israel, at SE end of Plain of Jezreel, at N foot of Mt. Gilboa, 5 mi. WNW of Beisan; mixed farming, citriculture, stock raising. Marble quarry. Agr. school near by. Founded 1922. **2** Agr. settlement, W Israel, in Plain of Sharon, 2 mi. NW of Hadera. Both sometimes spelled Hefziba.

Hegenheim (äzhŭnĕm', Ger. hā'gŭnhīm), village (pop. 1,759), Haut-Rhin dept., E France, 3 mi. W of Basel; customs station on Swiss border opposite Allschwil; clock mfg.

Heggadadevankote or **Heggaddevankote** (hĕgŭdä'-vŭng-kōtĕ), town (pop. 1,474), Mysore dist., S Mysore, India, 25 mi. SW of Mysore; rice, millet, tobacco. Bamboo, sandalwood in near-by forests (tiger hunting).

Hegyalja (hĕ'dyĭyŏ), mountainous region in NE Hungary, embracing S slopes of a small spur of the Carpathians; extends 22 mi. bet. Szerencs and Sarospatak; alt. c.3,500 ft. Well-known Tokay wine produced here.

Hegyeshalom (hĕ'dyĕsh-hŏlôm), town (pop. 3,550), Györ-Moson co., NW Hungary, on Lajta R. and 24 mi. NW of Györ, on Austrian frontier; station on main Budapest-Vienna line; distillery, brickworks.

Heho (hā'hō), village, Yawnghwe state, Southern Shan State, Upper Burma, 15 mi. WSW of Taunggyi, on road and railroad to Thazi. Reached by railroad, 1921.

Hei, China: see HEI RIVER.

Heian-hokudo, Korea: see NORTH PYONGAN.

Heian-kyo, Japan: see KYOTO, city.

Heian-nando, Korea: see SOUTH PYONGAN.

Heiban (hābăn'), village, Kordofan prov., central Anglo-Egyptian Sudan, in Nuba Mts., on road and 50 mi. S of Delami; gum arabic, sesame, corn, durra; livestock.

Heichin, Formosa: see PINGCHEN.

Heidar, Jebel (jĕ'bĕl hādär') (3,435 ft.), Upper Galilee, N Israel, 8 mi. W of Safad.

Heide (hī'dů), town (pop. 22,094), in Schleswig-Holstein, NW Germany, 42 mi. E of Kiel; rail junction; center of oil-producing region; major market (grain, cattle, horses) of the Dithmarschen. Mfg. of machinery (wind turbines) and textiles; vegetable canning. Has late-Gothic church; also mus. First mentioned 1404. Was ⊙ peasant state of Dithmarschen from 1447 to 1559, when it burned down. Klaus Groth b. here.

Heidelberg (hī'dŭlbûrg), municipality (pop. 38,311), S Victoria, Australia, 7 mi. NNE of Melbourne; commercial center for agr. sheep-raising region.

Heidelberg (hī'dŭlbûrg, Ger. hī'dŭlbĕrk), city (1950 pop. 115,750), N Baden, Germany, after 1945 in Württemberg-Baden, on the canalized Neckar (dam and lock) and 11 mi. SE of Mannheim; 49°24'N 8°42'E. Celebrated chiefly for its university life and also for its castle, it is picturesquely situated at NW foot of the Königstuhl in a valley covered with orchards and vineyards. Also has mfg. of railroad cars, printing presses, precision instruments, tools, chains, fruit and vegetable preserves, cigars, fountain pens, furniture, pottery, textiles, soap. Printing. Cement and basalt works. First mentioned 1196, the city passed to counts palatine in 1225; served as residence of Electors Palatine until 1720. Was a center of Protestantism in 16th cent. Declined after ravages of Thirty Years War. City experienced rapid development after it came to Baden (1803). It was devastated by imperial troops under Tilly in 1622 and almost completely destroyed by the French in 1689 and 1693, so that most of the bldgs. are in baroque style, including the Church of Holy Ghost with tomb of Emperor Rupert. The red sandstone ruins of the large, mainly Renaissance castle (15th–17th cent.) tower above Heidelberg; in the castle cellar is the Heidelberg Tun, a gigantic wine cask with a capacity of about 49,000 gal. The Univ. of Heidelberg (Ruprecht-Karl-Universität) was founded 1386 by Elector Rupert I. Became a bulwark of the Reformation in 16th cent. After Napoleonic Wars it became the most famous university in Germany, its 19th-cent. student life of duels, songs, and romance being much publicized; the univ. has produced generations of scholars as well as dueling scars. Near MAUER, 6 mi. SE, was found (1907) the jawbone of the prehistoric man called Heidelberg man.

Heidelberg (hī'dŭlbûrg, Afrikaans hā'dŭlbĕrkh). **1** Town (pop. 3,172), SW Cape Prov., U. of So. Afr., at foot of the Langeberg range, on Duivenhoeks R. and 65 mi. W of Mossel Bay; agr. center (wool, grain, tobacco, aloes). **2** Town (pop. 7,138), S Transvaal, U. of So. Afr., on Biesbok Spruit R. and 30 mi. SE of Johannesburg; alt. 5,026 ft.; gold-mining center, leather mfg. Near by was hq. of Zulu chief Moselikatse. Heidelberg was ⊙ South African Republic during Transvaal revolt, 1880–81.

Heidelberg. 1 Village (pop. 61), Le Sueur co., S Minn., 38 mi. SSW of Minneapolis, in grain, livestock, poultry area. **2** Town (pop. 863), Jasper co., E central Miss., 16 mi. NNE of Laurel; oil refinery; lumber milling. Oil field near by. **3** Borough (pop. 2,250), Allegheny co., SW Pa., SW suburb of Pittsburgh.

Heidelsheim (hī'dŭls-hīm), town (pop. 3,004), N Baden, Germany, after 1945 in Württemberg-Baden, on the Saalbach and 2 mi. SE of Bruchsal; metalworking.

Heiden (hī'dŭn), town (pop. 2,904), Appenzell Ausser Rhoden half-canton, NE Switzerland, 7 mi. E of St. Gall; mountain health resort; silk and cotton textiles, embroideries.

Heidenau (hī'dŭnou), town (pop. 18,694), Saxony, E central Germany, in Saxonian Switzerland, on the Elbe and 8 mi. SE of Dresden, near Czechoslovak border; mfg. of printing presses, chemicals, rubber products, musical instruments, glass; paper milling, metalworking.

Heidenheim (hī'dŭnhīm). **1** Village (pop. 1,631), Middle Franconia, W Bavaria, Germany, 7 mi. S of Gunzenhausen; tanning, brewing. Former Benedictine abbey was founded 748 by St. Walburga and St. Winnebald, who both died here; the 12th-cent. Romanesque abbey church contains tomb of St. Winnebald and tombstone of St. Walburga; abbey secularized 1540. **2** City (pop. 34,694), N Württemberg, Germany, after 1945 in Württemberg-Baden, 20 mi. NNE of Ulm; 48°41'N 10°10'E, Industrial center; mfg. of machinery, turbines, armatures, tools, electrical goods, wine cloth, linen, calico, wool blankets, surgical dressings, furniture; paper, cigars, cigarettes. Has Renaissance castle, ruined fortress. Chartered in 15th cent.

Heidenreichstein (hī'dŭnrīkh'shtīn), town (pop. 3,421), NW Lower Austria, 9 mi. NE of Gmünd; rail terminus; linen.

Heidesheim or **Heidesheim am Rhein** (hī'dŭs-hīm äm rīn'), village (pop. 4,151), Rhenish Hesse, W Germany, near the Rhine, 6 mi. W of Mainz; mfg. of agr. machinery.

Heidmühle (hīt'mü"lŭ), village (commune pop. 15,912), in Oldenburg, NW Germany, after 1945 in Lower Saxony, in East Friesland, 7 mi. W of Wilhelmshaven, in peat region. Commune is called Oestringen (ûs'trĭng-ŭn).

Heidrick (hī'drĭk), village (1940 pop. 520), Knox co., SE Ky., 22 mi. NNW of Middlesboro, in the Cumberlands, near Cumberland R.

Heigun-shima (hāgo͞on'shĭmä), island (□ 7; pop. 3,848, including offshore islet), Yamaguchi prefecture, Japan, in Iyo Sea just off SW coast of Honshu, S of Yanai; 6 mi. long, 2 mi. wide. Mountainous, forested; rice, wheat, raw silk. Fishing.

Heiho (hā'hŭ'), former province (□ 45,900; 1940 pop. 149,987) of N Manchukuo, bet. right bank of Amur R. and Lesser Khingan watershed; ⊙ was Heiho (Aigun). Formed 1934 out of old Heilungkiang prov., it returned to the new Heilungkiang prov. (Manchuria) in 1946.

Heiho, town, Manchuria: see Aigun.

Hei Ho. 1 River, China and USSR: see Amur River. **2** River, Kansu prov., China: see Hei River.

Heihotun, Manchuria: see Aigun.

Heijo, Korea: see Pyongyang.

Heijthuijsen or **Heithuizen** (hī'toizŭn), village (pop. 1,619), Limburg prov., SE Netherlands, 7 mi. NW of Roermond; leather and wood products; agr. Also Heijthuizen, Heythuisen, and Heythuizen.

Heikei, Formosa: see Pingki.

Heikendorf (hī'kŭndôrf), village (commune pop., including Möltenort, 4,248), in Schleswig-Holstein, NW Germany, 5 mi. N of Kiel city center; seaside resort on Kiel Firth. Möltenort, just N, is site of U-boat memorial (built 1938) of First World War.

Heiko, Korea: see Pyonggang.

Heilbron (hĭl'brŏn), town (pop. 4,391), NE Orange Free State, U. of So. Afr., 40 mi. S of Vereeniging; alt. 5,150 ft.; agr. center (corn, cattle, sheep, horses, poultry, dairying); grain elevator, cold-storage plant. Site of Voortrekker Mus. (1934). Heilbron was ⊙ Orange Free State Republic, May 13–20, 1900. Near by Voortrekkers defeated (1836) force of native chief Mzilegasi.

Heilbronn (hīlbrôn'), city (1939 pop. 77,569; 1946 pop. 52,745; 1950 pop. 64,544), N Württemberg, Germany, after 1945 in Württemberg-Baden, port on canalized Neckar and 25 mi. N of Stuttgart; 49°8'N 9°13'E. Rail junction; industrial center; metal industry (steel and iron construction; cars, chassis, agr. machinery, tools, bells, electrotechnical equipment). Mfg. of chemicals (soda, industrial fats and oils, soap; vulcanizing), textiles (thread, canvas; weaving), sports goods (skis, tents, folding boats); food processing (sugar, preserves, vegetable oil, wine, spirits, beer). Other products: silverware, shoes, paper, glass, cigars. Tanning. Salt mining. New harbor (opened 1935) is head of small-steamer and Rhine-barge (1,200 tons) navigation on river trade route to Mannheim. Second World War destruction (about 80%) included inner city with 13th-cent. Kilian church and House of Teutonic Knights; 15th–16th-cent. city hall; 17th-cent. historical mus.; as well as E dists. Of anc. origin, Heilbronn became royal domain in 6th cent. Its favorable location on commercial routes and its active wine trade made for rapid development. Created free imperial city in 1281. Accepted Reformation after 1525. Declined after Thirty Years War. Recovery began in 2d half of 18th cent. and continued after city passed to Württemberg (1802) and rapidly became industrialized. Captured, after heavy fighting, by U.S. troops in April, 1945.

Heiligenbeil, Russian SFSR: see Mamonovo.

Heiligenberg (hī'lĭgŭnbĕrk"), village (pop. 876), S Baden, Germany, 7 mi. NE of Überlingen; woodworking. Late-16th-cent. Fürstenberg castle has noted carved ceiling.

Heiligenblut (–blo͞ot"), village (pop. 1,381), Carinthia, W central Austria, on Möll R. and 15 mi. N of Lienz, near the Grossglockner; tourist center (alt. 4,605 ft.). Starting point of the Grossglocknerstrasse over the Hohe Tauern. Gothic church (1483) is place of pilgrimage.

Heiligendamm, Germany: see Bad Doberan.

Heiligengrabe, Germany: see Pritzwalk.

Heiligenhafen (–hä'fŭn), town (pop. 8,623), in Schleswig-Holstein, NW Germany, port and seaside resort on the Baltic, 22 mi. NE of Eutin, opposite Fehmarn isl.; fishing fleet; mfg. (building materials, furniture, canned goods). Grain trade. Chartered 1305.

Heiligenhaus (–hous"), village (pop. 11,553), in former Prussian Rhine Prov., W Germany, after 1945 in North Rhine-Westphalia, 3 mi. W of Velbert; grain.

Heiligenkreuz (–kroits"), village (pop. 1,082), E Lower Austria, 6 mi. NNW of Baden, in the Wiener Wald. Has anc. abbey with 12th-cent. Romanesque church, large library; tombs of Babenberg family.

Heiligenroda (–rō'dŭ), village, Thuringia, central Germany, at SW foot of Thuringian Forest, 13 mi. SW of Eisenach; potash mining.

Heiligenstadt (–shtät"), E section of Döbling dist. of Vienna, Austria, 3 mi. N of city center. Was long residence of Beethoven.

Heiligenstadt, town (pop. 12,733), in former Prussian Saxony prov., central Germany, after 1945 in Thuringia, on the Leine and 18 mi. NW of Mühlhausen, 10 mi. E of Eichenberg; mfg. of tobacco products, paper, cardboard; metalworking, linen milling. Has several 14th-cent. churches; 18th-cent. castle. Was (1540–1802) ⊙ principality of Eichsfeld, property of the electors of Mainz.

Heiligenwald (–vält'), town (pop. 5,425), E central Saar, 3.5 mi. W of Neunkirchen; coal mining.

Heilsberg, Poland: see Lidzbark Warminski.

Heilsbronn (hīlsbrôn'), town (pop. 3,316), Middle Franconia, W Bavaria, Germany, 10 mi. ENE of Ansbach; tanning, brewing; rye, oats, wheat, hops. Former Cistercian abbey (1132–1555) has mid-12th-cent. church.

Heiltz-le-Maurupt (ĕlts-lŭ-mōrü'), agr. village (pop. 455), Marne dept., N France, 11 mi. ENE of Vitry-le-François.

Heilung Chiang, USSR and China: see Amur River.

Heilungkiang or **Hei-lung-chiang** (both: hā'lo͝ong'-jyäng'), province (□ 130,000; pop. 6,000,000) of N central Manchuria; ⊙ Tsitsihar. Bounded N by USSR along Amur R. (Chinese *Heilung Kiang*), W by Inner Mongolian Autonomous Region, S by Liaosi and Kirin, and SW by Sungkiang, it consists of the basins of the Amur (N) and Nonni (S) rivers, separated by the Lesser Khingan watershed. Agr. is concentrated in the valleys of Nonni R., Tao R., and Hulan R. (an affluent of the Sungari): soybeans, wheat, kaoliang, tobacco, and hemp are grown. The spurs of the Great Khingan Mts. (extreme N) have important timber reserves and constitute China's chief gold-mining area, with centers at Moho, Owpu, Huma, and Aigun. Some coal is mined at Kanho. Flour and soybean mills and distilleries provide the chief local industries. The chief centers, linked by good rail net, are Tsitsihar, Nunkiang, Aigun (on Amur R. opposite Blagoveshchensk), Pehan, Hailun, Suihwa (in Hulan R. agr. dist.), and Taonan (in Tao R. agr. dist.). Pop. is largely Chinese in agr. areas; there are Manchu minorities, Mongols (W and SW), and in the northernmost mtn. areas are Orochon, Solon, and Gold tribes. The name Heilungkiang was originally applied to the northernmost (□ 219,274; 1926 pop. 4,632,074; ⊙ Tsitsihar) of the original 3 Manchurian provs. N of the Sungari R., dissolved by Manchukuo regime in 1934. It was revived (1946) after Second World War as a Nationalist prov. (□ 99,522; pop. 2,860,037; ⊙ Pehan), then was reorganized along present lines in 1949.

Heilung Kiang, river, USSR and China: see Amur River.

Heilungkiang-cheng, Manchuria: see Aigun.

Heimaey, Iceland: see Vestmannaeyjar.

Heimiswil (hī'mĭsvēl), town (pop. 2,090), Bern canton, NW Switzerland, 13 mi. NE of Bern.

Heimsheim (hīms'hīm), town (pop. 1,108), N Württemberg, Germany, after 1945 in Württemberg-Baden, 9 mi. SE of Pforzheim; grain, cattle.

Heining (hī'nĭng), village (pop. 6,118), Lower Bavaria, Germany, on the Danube and 3 mi. W of Passau; grain, livestock. Gravel quarries in area.

Heinola (hā'nōlä), city (pop. 4,892), Mikkeli co., S Finland, on Saimaa lake system, 20 mi. NE of Lahti; rail terminus; plywood, bobbin, and spool mills; mfg. of wallboard and doors. Vacation and health resort. Site of teachers' seminary for women. Inc. 1839. It was ⊙ (1776–1843) of former co. of Kyminkartano.

Heinrichswalde, Russian SFSR: see Slavsk.

Heinsberg (hīns'bĕrk), town (pop. 2,152), in former Prussian Rhine Prov., W Germany, after 1945 in North Rhine-Westphalia, 7 mi. N of Geilenkirchen; basket mfg. Has 15th-cent. church.

Heinsch, Belgium: see Stockem.

Heinzenberg, Switzerland: see Domleschg.

Heirefos, Norway: see Herefoss.

Heirin, Formosa: see Pinglin.

Hei River, Chinese *Hei Ho* (hā'hŭ'), NW Kansu prov., China, rises in the Nan Shan as Kanchow R., flows over 300 mi. NW, past Changyeh, joining the Peita at Tingsin to form the Etsin Gol. Sometimes called Jo Shui, a name also applied to the Etsin Gol.

Heirnkut (hărn'ko͝ot) or **Fort Keary** (kâ'rē), village, S Naga Hills dist., Upper Burma, 27 mi. NNW of Homalin, in the Somra Tract.

Heis or **Hais** (hās), locality, NE Br. Somaliland, on Gulf of Aden, 35 mi. NW of Erigavo; water well.

Heis, Yemen: see Hais.

Heisaka (hā'säkä), town (pop. 13,322), Aichi prefecture, central Honshu, Japan, on Chita Bay, 22 mi. SSE of Nagoya; rice-growing, cotton-collection center. Fish hatcheries.

Heisdorf (hīs'dôrf), village (pop. 477), S central Luxembourg, 4 mi. N of Luxembourg city, near Alzette R.; lumber; rose growing.

Heise (hī'zē), town (pop. 87), Jefferson co., E Idaho, 20 mi. NE of Idaho Falls.

Heishan (hā'shän'), town, ⊙ Heishan co. (pop. 370,362), S central Liaosi prov., Manchuria, on railroad and 60 mi. NE of Chinchow; coal-mining center. Called Chenan until 1914.

Heisker (hĕ'skŭr) or **Monach Isles** (mŏ'nŭkh), group of small isls. (pop. 33) of the Outer Hebrides, Inverness, Scotland, separated from W coast of North Uist by 8-mi.-wide Sound of Monach, 12 mi. S of Haskeir or Hyskier isl. Westernmost isl., Shillay, is site of lighthouse (57°31'N 7°43'W).

Heissen (hī'sŭn), industrial suburb of Mülheim, W Germany, 3 mi. ENE of city center.

Heist (hīst), town (pop. 7,442), West Flanders prov., NW Belgium, on North Sea and 9 mi. N of Bruges; seaside resort. Formerly spelled Heyst. Resort of Duinbergen 2 mi. E.

Heist-op-den-Berg (–ōb-dăn-bĕrkh'), agr. village (pop. 10,922), Antwerp prov., N Belgium, near Grande Nèthe R., 8 mi. ESE of Lierre. Formerly spelled Heyst-op-den-Berg.

Heitaku, Korea: see Pyongtaek.

Heitersheim (hī'tŭrs-hīm), village (pop. 1,812), S Baden, Germany, 12 mi. SW of Freiburg; machinery mfg.; winegrowing. Has 16th-cent. castle.

Heithuizen, Netherlands: see Heijthuijsen.

Heito, Formosa: see Pingtung.

Heizyo, Korea: see Pyongyang.

Hejaf, Aden: see Hedjuff.

Hejaz or **Hedjaz** (hĕjăz', hē–), Arabic *Al-Hijaz* (ă hĭjăz'), viceroyalty (□ 150,000; pop. 1,500,000) of Saudi Arabia; ⊙ Mecca. Extending along Red Sea coast bet. Gulf of Aqaba and Asir, Hejaz consists of the barren Tihama coastal plain and a highland region (rises to 9,000 ft. in the Madian section) formed by the uptilting of W plateau edge of the Arabian shelf, which drops abruptly to the coastal plain. Vegetation is limited and agr. is possible only in a few inland wadies. Dates, millet, wheat, barley, and fruit are the chief crops in these favored spots; there is stock raising in the oases' drier margins. Pop. is concentrated in urban areas of Jidda (main port), Mecca, Taif (summer resort) and Medina—where pilgrim trade is the principal industry. Lesser Red Sea ports are Wejh, Yenbo, Rabigh, and Qunfidha. Following the fall (1258) of the Caliphate of Baghdad, Hejaz came under Egyptian control, followed in 1517 by Turkish control, although more or less nominal rule remained in the hands of the sherifs of Mecca of the Hashemite family. In early-19th cent., Hejaz was raided by the Wahabis, and peace was restored only in 1817 by Mohammed Ali, Turkish governor of Egypt. After 1845, Hejaz came again under direct Turkish control; and in order to improve communications, the Turks built the Hejaz railway (completed 1908; in disuse since First World War) from Damascus to Medina. Turkish control, however was challenged at this time by Husein ibn Ali, sherif of Mecca, who succeeded in expelling the Turks in 1916 during First World War and proclaimed him self king of Hejaz. Strained relations with Ibn Saud finally resulted in war, and in 1924–25 Hejaz fell to the ruler of Nejd. In 1926, Ibn Saud was declared king of Hejaz. Although the formal union of Hejaz and Nejd into Saudi Arabia was proclaimed in 1932, Hejaz continues to be administered provisionally under a 1926 constitution as a separate kingdom under a viceroy. It includes administratively the Kaf and Jauf areas of northern most Saudi Arabia.

Hejnice (hā'nyĭtsĕ), Ger. *Haindorf* (hīn'dôrf), village (pop. 1,689), N Bohemia, Czechoslovakia, at SW foot of Smrk peak of the Isergebirge, on railroad and 10 mi. NNE of Liberec. Health resort of Lazne Libwerda (läz'nyĕ lĭb'vĕrdä), Czech *Lázně Libwerda*, Ger. *Liebwerda* (lēb'vĕrdä), with carbonated springs, is just NNE.

Hejöcsaba (hĕ'yû-chŏbŏ), Hung. *Hejőcsaba*, town (pop. 5,036), Borsod-Gömör co., NE Hungary, just S of Miskolc; truck (apples, pears, lentils).

Hejrefos, Norway: see Herefoss.

Hekelgem (hā'kŭl-khĕm), agr. village (pop. 3,292), Brabant prov., central Belgium, 4 mi. SE of Alost. One mi. N is agr. village of Affligem (formerly spelled Afflighem), with ruins of 11th-cent. Benedictine abbey.

Hekido, Korea: see Pyoktong.

Hekimhan (hĕkĭmhän'), village (pop. 2,074), Malatya prov., E central Turkey, on railroad and 38 mi. NNW of Malatya; wheat, sugar beets.

Hekla (hĕk'lä), active volcano (4,747 ft.), S Iceland, 70 mi. E of Reykjavik; 64°N 19°40'W. Of its several craters the largest is c.400 ft. deep. Since 1104 over a score of eruptions have been recorded, the last in 1947. Major eruption in 1766 caused great loss of life.

Hekura-jima, Japan: see Wajima.

Hel, village and peninsula, Poland: see Hel Peninsula.

Hela, village, Poland: see Hel Peninsula.

Helagsfjallet, Swedish *Helagsfjället* (hä'läksfyĕ"lŭt), mountain (5,892 ft.), W Sweden, not far from the Norwegian border, and 70 mi. WSW of Ostersund; 62°55'N 12°28'E.

Helbra (hĕl'brä), town (pop. 10,218), in former Prussian Saxony prov., central Germany, after 1945 in Saxony-Anhalt, at E foot of the lower Harz, 3 mi. NW of Eisleben; copper-slate mining and smelting center.

Helchteren (hĕlkh'tůrůn), town (pop. 2,217), Limburg prov., NE Belgium, 9 mi. N of Hasselt; coal mining.

Heldburg (hĕlt'bo͝ork), town (pop. 1,581), Thuringia, central Germany, 11 mi. W of Coburg, in fruit-growing region; woodworking, toymaking. Has 16th-cent. church, and remains of medieval town walls; towered over by early-14th-cent. Heldburg castle.

Helden (hĕl'důn), village (pop. 1,033), Limburg prov., SE Netherlands, 8 mi. SW of Venlo; bricks, cigars, strawboard; agr.

Helder or **Den Helder** (důn hĕl'důr), town (pop. 28,729) and port, North Holland prov., NW Netherlands, on North Sea, at N end of NORTH HOLLAND CANAL and N tip of mainland, and 40 mi. N of Amsterdam. Separated by Marsdiep from Texel isl. (N); protected against tides by the Helderdijk (8-mi.-long granite dike). Main base of Netherlands navy at Willemsoord (newer; SE part of town) Navy Yard and Royal Naval Institute; fishing center. Naval battle (1673), when Dutch under De Ruyter and Tromp defeated English and Fr. fleets. In 1799, site of Br. and Rus. troop landing. Fortified (1811) by Napoleon.

Helderbergs, The, or **Helderberg Mountains** (hĕl'důrbûrg), E N.Y., N-facing limestone escarpment (c.1,700 ft. high) of the Catskills (part of Allegheny Plateau), along S side of Mohawk valley W of Albany.

Heldra (hĕl'drä), village (pop. 858), in former Prussian prov. of Hesse-Nassau, W Germany, after 1945 in Hesse, on the Werra and 7 mi. SE of Eschwege, opposite Treffurt; rail junction.

Heldrungen (hĕl'dro͝ong-ůn), town (pop. 3,830), in former Prussian Saxony prov., central Germany, after 1945 in Saxony-Anhalt, 13 mi. SSW of Sangerhausen; potash mining. Has old castle in which Thomas Münzer was imprisoned in 1525.

Helechal (ālächäl'), village (pop. 1,303), Badajoz prov., W Spain, 9 mi. ESE of Castuera, near Córdoba prov. border; olive-oil industry. Castle and sanctuary are NE.

Helechosa or **Helechosa de los Montes** (ālächō'sä dhā lōs mōn'tĕs), town (pop. 1,512), Badajoz prov., W Spain, near the upper Guadiana, 13 mi. NE of Herrera del Duque; olives, cereals, timber, livestock.

Helen or **Helen Mine,** village, central Ont., near Wawa L., 110 mi. NNW of Sault Ste. Marie; iron-mining center.

Helen, town (pop. 191), White co., NE Ga., 22 mi. WNW of Toccoa, near Chattahoochee R.; hosiery mfg., sawmilling. Summer resort.

Helen, Mount, Wyo.: see WIND RIVER RANGE.

Helena, Greece: see MAKRONESOS.

Helena. 1 (hĕ'lůnů) Town (pop. 421), Shelby co., central Ala., near Cahaba R., 15 mi. S of Birmingham. **2** (hĕ'lůnů) City (pop. 11,236), ⊙ Phillips co., E Ark., c.55 mi. SW of Memphis (Tenn.) and on Mississippi R.; rail center, hardwood market, and river port; ships lumber, cotton, farm products. Cotton processing, canning, woodworking; mfg. of hosiery, lard, veneers, fertilizer. In 1863 a Civil War battle, resulting in a Union victory, took place here. Inc. 1856. **3** (hĕlē'nů) Town (pop. 1,027), Telfair co., S central Ga., 32 mi. S of Dublin and on Little Ocmulgee R. adjacent to McRae (E); rail and processing center for timber and farm area (cotton, grain, corn), livestock, dairy products; mfg. (naval stores, lumber). **4** (hĕ'lůnů) City (pop. 17,581), ⊙ Mont. and Lewis and Clark co., SW central Mont., 50 mi. NNE of Butte, near Missouri R., in Prickly Pear valley, just E of Continental Divide; 46°35'N 112°2'W; alt. 4,160 ft. Trade center and resort in rich mining and agr. region; gold mines; concrete products, bricks and tiles, flour, grain, potatoes. Carroll Col., 2 cathedrals (Episcopal and R.C.) here. Other points of interest: capitol; Algeria Shrine Temple; Mt. Helena and Mt. Ascension; Fort Harrison, now used as veterans' hosp. Near by are Lakes Hauser and Sewall, small enlargements of Missouri R., and L. Helena. Founded in Last Chance Gulch 1864, when gold was discovered there; became territorial ⊙ 1874, state ⊙ 1894. Series of earthquakes, severest in 1935, caused extensive damage. **5** (hĕ'lůnů) Village (pop. 314), Sandusky co., N Ohio, 9 mi. W of Fremont, in agr. area. **6** (hĕlē'nů) Town (pop. 484), Alfalfa co., N Okla., 24 mi. WNW of Enid, in grain, livestock, and dairying area. **7** (hĕ'lůnů) Town (1940 pop. 497), Newberry co., NW central S.C., just W of Newberry.

Helena, Lake (hĕ'lůnů), W central Mont., in Lewis and Clark co., 7 mi. NNE of Helena; 3 mi. long, 2 mi. wide; fed by Missouri R. Used for recreation.

Helena Island (23 mi. long, 8 mi. wide), Parry Isls., N Franklin Dist., Northwest Territories, just off N Bathurst Isl.; 76°46'N 101°30'W.

Helena Island, Honduras: see SANTA ELENA ISLAND.

Helenaveen, Netherlands: see DE PEEL.

Helene, Greece: see MAKRONESOS.

Helen Mine, Ont.: see HELEN.

Helensburgh (hĕ'lĭnzbůrů), town (pop. 1,759), E New South Wales, Australia, 26 mi. S of Sydney; coal-mining center.

Helensburgh (hĕ'lĭnzbůrů), residential burgh (1931 pop. 8,893; 1951 census 8,760), SW Dumbarton, Scotland, on the Clyde at S end of Gare Loch, 8 mi. NW of Dumbarton; resort, port for Clyde and Gare Loch steamers. It was named after the wife of Sir James Colquhoun, who founded town in 1777.

Helen Shoal, China: see MACCLESFIELD BANK.

Helfta (hĕlf'tä), village (pop. 5,060), in former Prussian Saxony prov., central Germany, after 1945 in Saxony-Anhalt, at SE foot of the lower Harz, 3 mi. SE of Eisleben; copper-slate mining.

Helgeland (hĕl'gůlän), region in S part of Nordland co., N central Norway, consists of administrative dists. of North Helgeland (Nor. *Nord-Helgeland*) (□ 3,167; pop. 29,971) and South Helgeland (Nor. *Sør-Helgeland*) (□ 4,090; pop. 35,236). Extends N-S bet. Trondheim and Ran fjords; includes Borgefjell mts., Svartisen glacier, Vefsna valley, and off-coast isls. of Hestmanoy, Donna, and Torgoy. Fishing, fowl-egg and guano collecting; in Rana, N part of Helgeland, iron mining. Old Norse name *Hálogaland* covered area of entire present Nordland co.

Helgenaes, Denmark: see MOLS.

Helge River, Swedish *Helge å* (hĕl"gůō'), S Sweden, rises NE of Ljungby, flows c.200 mi. generally S, through L. Mockel, past Kristianstad, to Hano Bay of the Baltic at Ahus.

Helgoland (hĕl'gōlănd", Ger. hĕl'gōlänt"), rocky North Sea island (150 acres) of North Frisian group, NW Germany, c.40 mi. NW of Cuxhaven; formed of red sandstone; rises to c.155 ft. Was popular tourist resort before Second World War. Belonged to Holstein, 1402–1714; then was Danish possession until 1807, when Britain occupied isl. (formal cession 1814). Traded (1890) to Germany for Zanzibar. Ger. fortifications were razed after 1918. Refortified after 1935, isl. served as Ger. naval base in Second World War and sustained severe aerial bombings. After evacuation of pop. (mostly Frisian fishermen), British occupation authorities blew up fortifications and part of isl. (1947). Sometimes called Heligoland (hĕ'lĭgōlănd") in English.

Helice (hĕ'lĭsē), anc. city of Achaea, N Peloponnesus, Greece, near mouth of Selinous R., 20 mi. E of Patras. Sanctuary of Poseidon and seat of 1st Achaean League; destroyed (373 B.C.) by earthquake and replaced by Aigion. Modern village of Helike or Eliki (ĕlē'kē) (pop. 654) was formerly called Zevgolation.

Helicon (hĕ'lĭkŏn), Gr. *Helikon* or *Elikon* (both: ĕlĭkôn'), mountain group of Boeotia, E central Greece, bet. drained L. Copais and Gulf of Corinth. Rises to 5,736 ft., 10 mi. S of Levadia, in W section known as Palaiovouna; the E section, known as Zagora, rises to 5,009 ft. 11 mi. SE of Levadia. In Gr. legend, Helicon was the abode of the Muses. On Zagora's E slope is the Valley of the Muses, where an Ionic temple, theater, and statues were unearthed. Near by are the springs of Hippocrene and Aganippe. At E foot of the Zagora are THESPIAE and ASCRA.

Heliconia (ālēkōn'yä), town (pop. 1,706), Antioquia dept., NW central Colombia, on slopes of Cordillera Central, 12 mi. WSW of Medellín, in agr. region (coffee, sugar cane, yucca, bananas); alt. 4,724 ft. Salt and coal mines near by.

Heligoland, Germany: see HELGOLAND.

Helikon, Greece: see HELICON.

Héliopolis (ālyôpôlēs'), village (pop. 1,338), Constantine dept., NE Algeria, in the Constantine Mts., 2.5 mi. NNE of Guelma; winegrowing. Calamine and sulphur mining.

Heliopolis (hēlēŏ'půlĭs [Gr.,=city of the sun]. **1** Anc. city of Lower Egypt, in the Nile delta, c.6 mi. N of Cairo. Was noted as center of sun worship, and its god Ra or Re became (c.2600 B.C.) the state deity. Under the New Empire (c.1580–c.1090 B.C.), Heliopolis was seat of viceroy of N Egypt. The obelisks called Cleopatra's Needles (one of which is in London, one in N.Y.) were erected here. Its schools of philosophy and astronomy declined after founding of Alexandria in 332 B.C., but the city never wholly lost its importance until the Christian era. The Egyptian name was On, by which name it appears in the Bible; elsewhere in the Bible it is Beth-shemesh and Aven. Modern town of Matariya is partly on the site, marked by an obelisk. The modern Cairo suburb of Heliopolis is to the SE. **2** Residential suburb (pop. 165,132) of Cairo, Lower Egypt, c.5 mi. NE of Cairo city center; named for the anc. city whose site is NW. Has one of the 2 race tracks of Cairo, a civil airport, and 2 hospitals.

Heliopolis, Lebanon: see BAALBEK.

Helix (hē'lĭks), town (pop. 182), Umatilla co., NE Oregon, 15 mi. NNE of Pendleton.

Hell (hĕl), village (pop. 275) in Lanke canton, Nord-Trondelag co., central Norway, on Strinda Fjord (a bay in Trondheim Fjord), 16 mi. E of Trondheim; junction for Nordland RR and line to Storlien and Ostersund (Sweden).

Hella, El, Egypt: see HILLA, EL.

Hellada River, Greece: see SPERCHEIOS RIVER.

Hellam (hĕ'lům), borough (pop. 976), York co., S Pa., 7 mi. ENE of York. Post office name formerly Hallam.

Hell-Bourg (ĕl-bo͞or'), village (pop. 2,249), central Réunion isl., 11 mi. SW of Saint-André; alt. c.3,000 ft.; health resort in Salazie cirque; R.C. mission school, sanatorium.

Hellebaek (hĕ'lůbĕk), town (pop. 1,306), Frederiksborg amt, Zealand, Denmark, on the Oresund and 13 mi. NE of Hillerod; clothes mfg.

Hellemmes-Lille (hĕlĕm'-lēl'), E suburb (pop. 14,140) of Lille, Nord dept., N France; textiles (cotton and flax spinning, linen weaving); precision metalworks, breweries, brickworks.

Hellemo Fjord, Norway: see TYS FJORD.

Hellendoorn (hĕ'lůndōrn), village (pop. 2,448), Overijssel prov., E Netherlands, 9 mi. W of Almelo. Tuberculosis sanitarium.

Hellerau (hĕ'lůrou), residential village (pop. 5,861), Saxony, E central Germany, 5 mi. NNE of Dresden; market gardening; furniture mfg. Has noted arts and crafts school. Founded 1906.

Hellertown, borough (pop. 5,435), Northampton co., E Pa., just S of Bethlehem; electrical products, commercial gases; molding-sand quarry. Settled c.1740, inc. 1872.

Helles, Cape (hĕ'lůs), S tip of GALLIPOLI PENINSULA, Turkey in Asia, at mouth of Dardanelles.

Hellespont, Turkey: see DARDANELLES.

Hellesylt (hĕl'lůsült), village (pop. 237), in Sunnylven (formerly Sunelven or Sunnelven) canton (pop. 1,520), More og Romsdal co., W Norway, at head of Sunnylven Fjord, 35 mi. SE of Alesund; tourist center in Geiranger Fjord region.

Hellevoetsluis (hĕ'lůvo͞otslois'), town (pop. 872), South Holland prov., SW Netherlands, on S shore of Voorne isl. and 11 mi. SW of Vlaardingen, on the Haringvliet; agr. Former navy yard; embarkation point (1688) for William III on his expedition against James II of England. Ferry to Middelharnis, on Overflakkee isl.

Hell Gate, narrow channel of East R., SE N.Y., in New York city, N of Welfare Isl. and bet. Wards Isl. and Astoria, Queens. Spanned by Triborough highway bridge and by Hell Gate railroad bridge (1917), a connecting link for trains from the North to the South and West. Named Hellegat by Adriaen Block in 1614. It was long dangerous to ships because of rocks and strong currents.

Hell Gate River, Mont.: see CLARK FORK.

Hellier (hĕl'yůr), mining town (pop. 346), Pike co., E Ky., near Va. line, in the Cumberlands, 13 mi. SSE of Pikeville; bituminous coal mining, coke making.

Hellifield, agr. village and parish (pop. 1,026), West Riding, NW Yorkshire, England, near Ribble R. 9 mi. WNW of Skipton.

Hellín (ĕlyēn'), city (pop. 13,013), Albacete prov., SE central Spain, in Murcia, 35 mi. SSE of Albacete; industrial and trade center noted since Roman times for its important sulphur mines (14 mi. SSW, near confluence of Segura and Mundo rivers). Chemical works (resins, turpentine). Mfg. of footwear, tiles and pottery, wool blankets, felt hats, candy; esparto and hemp processing; rice-, flour-, and sawmilling; fruit canning. Gypsum and clay quarries. Two reservoirs and small hydroelectric plant on Mundo R. Airport.

Hellingly, town and parish (pop. 3,566), SE Sussex, England, on Cuckmere R. and 8 mi. N of Eastbourne; agr. market with flour mills. Has 12th-cent. church.

Hellior Holm, Scotland: see SHAPINSAY.

Hellisandur, Iceland: see SANDUR.

Hellocourt, France: see MOUSSEY.

Hell's Canyon, Idaho: see SNAKE RIVER.

Hell's Kitchen, SE N.Y., a district of Manhattan borough of New York city, along Hudson (North) R. waterfront approximately bet. 42d and 57th streets.

Hellville or **Hell-ville** (hĕlvēl'), main town (1948 pop. 4,046) and outlet of Nossi-Bé Isl., on its S coast, N Madagascar; 13°19'S 48°10'E. Ships sugar, vanilla, ilang-ilang, copra, black pepper, tropical fruit, coffee. Sugar milling; rice, manioc processing; mfg. of essential oils, soap, edible oils, rum, alcohol. Has seaplane base.

Hell-Ville, Réunion: see SALAZIE.

Hellyor Holm, Scotland: see SHAPINSAY.

Helmand River or **Hilmand River** (hĕl'můnd), anc. *Etymander* (ĕ"tĭmăn'důr), longest stream entirely in Afghanistan, 700 mi. long; rises 35 mi. W of Kabul on W slopes of Paghman Mts., flows generally SW, through heart of the mountainous Hazarajat, debouching at Girishk onto the S Afghan desert area, and enters the Seistan lake depression, which it fills during the spring flood. Receives the combined Arghandab-Tarnak-Arghastan rivers at Qala Bist. At Girishk, where river is crossed by Kandahar-Herat highway, a diversion dam (completed 1949) feeds Boghra Canal on W bank. Storage reservoir at Kajakai built to control the Helmand regime.

Helmarshausen (hĕl"märs-hou'zůn), town (pop. 1,919), in former Prussian prov. of Hesse-Nassau, W Germany, after 1945 in Hesse, on the Diemel and 10 mi. NNE of Hofgeismar; woodworking. Has ruined castle.

Helmbrechts (hĕlm'brĕkhts), town (pop. 8,051), Upper Franconia, NE Bavaria, Germany, in the Franconian Forest, 10 mi. SW of Hof; cloth and glass mfg., brewing. Chartered 1449. Limestone quarries in area.

Helmdange (hĕlmdăzh'), village (pop. 334), S central Luxembourg, on Alzette R. and 4 mi. N of Luxembourg city; tree and plant nurseries.

Helme River (hĕl'mů), central Germany, rises near S foot of the lower Harz 5 mi. SW of Bad Sachsa, flows c.55 mi. generally ESE, through the valley Goldene Aue, to the Unstrut 3 mi. SE of Artern.

Helmet Peak, Colo.: see LA PLATA MOUNTAINS.

Helmetta, borough (pop. 580), Middlesex co., E N.J., 8 mi. S of New Brunswick; snuff mfg. since early 19th cent.

Helminghausen (hĕl"mĭng-hou'zůn), village (pop. 352), in former Prussian prov. of Westphalia, W Germany, after 1945 in North Rhine-Westphalia, on the Diemel (dam and reservoir) and 7 mi. ESE of Brilon.

Helmington Row, town and parish (pop. 4,425), central Durham, England, 4 mi. NNW of Bishop Auckland; coal mining.

Helmond (hĕl'mônt), town (pop. 33,201), North Brabant prov., SE Netherlands, on Aa R. and the Zuid-Willemsvaart and 9 mi. ENE of Eindhoven; textile center (cotton, artificial silk, yarns, curtains, upholstering fabric), mfg. (cocoa, chocolate, cigars, strawboard, paper), woodworking. Has old castle, now used as town hall.

Helmsdale, town, SE Sutherland, Scotland, on Moray Firth, at mouth of Helmsdale R., 21 mi. NE of Dornoch; fishing port. Has ruins of anc. castle of dukes of Sutherland.

Helmsdale River, Sutherland, Scotland, formed by 2 short headstreams 7 mi. NNW of Kildonan, flows 20 mi. SE, past Kildonan, to Moray Firth at Helmsdale.

Helmshore, England: see HASLINGDEN.

Helmsley, (hĕlmz'lē, hĕmz'lē), village and parish (pop. 1,238), North Riding, NE Yorkshire, England, on Rye R. and 13 mi. NW of Malton; stone quarrying; agr. market. Has ruins of 12th-cent. castle, besieged by Fairfax 1644.

Helmstadt (hĕlm'shtät), village (pop. 1,591), Lower Franconia, NW Bavaria, Germany, 10 mi. WSW of Würzburg; vegetables.

Helmstedt (hĕlm'shtĕt), town (pop. 25,599), in Brunswick, NW Germany, after 1945 in Lower Saxony, 20 mi. E of Brunswick, 4 mi. NW of Marienborn (Saxony-Anhalt), in lignite- and potash-mining region; mfg. of machinery, household goods, chemicals, textiles, food products; fur processing, woodworking. Has Romanesque and Gothic churches; and the Juleum, Renaissance former univ. bldg. Founded in 9th cent.; chartered c.1300. Was member of Hanseatic League. Seat (1576–1809) of noted univ., a center of Protestant learning in 17th cent.; it was inc. (1810) into univ. of Göttingen. After 1945, major traffic check point bet. East and West Germany on route to Berlin. Formerly also spelled Helmstädt.

Helmville, village (pop. c.200), Powell co., W Mont., on branch of Blackfoot R. and 50 mi. WNW of Helena, in agr. and ranching region. Annual Labor Day rodeo.

Hel Peninsula, Pol. *Półwysep Hel* (pōō"wůvĭ'sĕp hĕl') or *Mierzeja Pucka* (myĕ-zhĕ'yä pōōts'kä), Ger. *Putziger Nehrung* (pōō'tsĭgůr nä'rōōng), Gdansk prov., N Poland, extends SE into Baltic Sea; separates Puck Bay (W) from the Baltic; 21 mi. long, up to 2 mi. wide. Hel, Ger. *Hela*, village on S tip of peninsula, is rail-spur terminus, fishing port, health resort; lighthouse. Jastarnia, village on middle of peninsula, is also a fishing port and health resort. In 17th cent., present peninsula was still a series of isls.; the peninsula was partially inundated in 1904 and 1914 by high seas. Pop. formerly largely Kashubs, with Germans only on SE tip, which had been yielded to Danzig in 1453; present pop. is Polish.

Helper, city (pop. 2,850), Carbon co., E central Utah, in canyon of Price R., 6 mi. NNW of Price; shipping center for coal-mining and agr. area (fruit, hay, sugar beets). Settled 1883, inc. 1907. Known as Pratts Siding until 1892. Scofield Dam, near by on Price R., is used for irrigation.

Helpfau-Uttendorf (hĕlp'fou-ōō'tůndôrf), town (pop. 2,672), W Upper Austria, 8 mi. SSE of Braunau; wheat, potatoes, cattle.

Helpston, village and parish (pop. 637) in the Soke of Peterborough, NE Northampton, England, 6 mi. NW of Peterborough; paper milling. Has church dating from 14th cent.

Helsby, town and parish (pop. 1,890), NW Cheshire, England, near Mersey R. 8 mi. NE of Chester; mfg. of electric cables, wood products.

Helsingborg, Sweden: see HALSINGBORG.

Helsinge (hĕl'sĭng-ů), town (pop. 1,646), Frederiksborg amt, Zealand, Denmark, 7 mi. NW of Hillerod.

Helsingfors, Finland: see HELSINKI.

Helsingor (hĕl'sĭng-ůr) or **Elsinore,** Dan. *Helsingør*, city (1950 pop. 21,010), port, Frederiksborg amt, Zealand, Denmark, on the Oresund, 14 mi. NE of Hillerod and 24 mi. N of Copenhagen; 56°2'N 12°37'E. Commercial and shipbuilding center; rubber mfg. Ferry to Halsingborg, Sweden. Site of Kronborg (built 1577–85; restored 1635–40), Elsinore castle of Shakespeare's *Hamlet*. City known in 13th cent.; prospered especially from 15th cent. to 1857 as port where Danish kings collected the Oresund ship dues.

Helsinki (hĕl'sĭngkē), Swedish *Helsingfors* (hĕl'sĭng-fôrz, Swed. hĕlsĭngfôrs', –fôsh'), city (pop. 359,813), ⊙ Finland and Uusimaa co., S Finland, Baltic port on Gulf of Finland, 250 mi. ENE of Stockholm, 180 mi. W of Leningrad; 60°10'N 24°58'E. Administrative, commercial, and intellectual center of Finland. Built on a peninsula, surrounded by isls., and protected by the isl. fortress of SUOMENLINNA, it is a rail center, is near an airport (at Malmi NNE), and has 3 sheltered harbors for passenger traffic, heavy freight, and local shipping; the port is icebound, Jan.-May. Exports include lumber, pulp, cellulose, plywood, paper. Industrial plants include shipyards, textile, hosiery, paper, and plywood mills, sugar refineries, distilleries; metal, machinery, and ceramics works; tobacco and coffee processing. Site of univ., founded (1640) at Turku, transferred (1828) to Helsinki; univ. observatory (1834); and technical col. (1877). Modern in character, predominantly built of light-colored native granite, Helsinki is called the "White City of the North." Features include railroad station, built (1919) by Saarinen, partly burned down (summer 1950); presidential residence, formerly Russian imperial palace; state council bldg., House of Representatives (1931), post office (1938), Natl. Theater (1902), Natl. Mus. (1910), opera house, conservatory, Russian Orthodox cathedral (1868), stadium (1938), and many modern residential and commercial bldgs. There are numerous modern statues. Mannerheim Way is city's chief street. Helsinki's social services are on notably high level. Mean temp. ranges from 22.4°F. (Feb.) to 62.2°F. (July); average annual rainfall is 27.5 in. Founded (1550) by Gustavus I of Sweden, Helsinki's growth dates from 1812, when ⊙ Finland was moved here from Turku by Alexander I of Russia. Though bombed several times during Russo-Finnish war of 1939–40 and in Second World War, Helsinki suffered only slight damage. Chosen as site of 1952 Olympic Games.

Helston (hĕl'stůn), municipal borough (1931 pop. 2,548; 1951 census 5,545), W Cornwall, England, on Cober R. and 10 mi. WSW of Falmouth; agr. market; tanning industry. Known for its Furry (or Flora) Dance, old flower and music festival (May 8th).

Heltau, Rumania: see CISNADIE.

Helvecia (ĕlvā'syä), village (pop. estimate 1,000), ⊙ Garay dept. (□ 1,555; 1947 pop. 12,501), E central Santa Fe prov., Argentina, on San Javier R. and 55 mi. NE of Santa Fe, in agr. area (livestock, grain).

Helvellyn (hĕlvĕ'lĭn), mountain (3,118 ft.) of the Cumbrians, England, on Cumberland and Westmorland border, 8 mi. SE of Keswick. Near summit is memorial to Charles Gough.

Helvetia, Latin name for SWITZERLAND.

Helvetia, village (1940 pop. 596), Clearfield co., W central Pa., 5 mi. S of Du Bois, in bituminous-coal region.

Helvick Head, cape, S Co. Waterford, Ireland, at entrance to Dungarvan Bay; 52°3'N 7°32'W.

Helvoirt or **Helvoort** (both: hĕl'vōrt), village (pop. 1,729), North Brabant prov., S Netherlands, 5 mi. SW of 's Hertogenbosch, in agr. and truck gardening area; fruitgrowing.

Helwan (hĕlwăn', hĕlwän') or **Hilwan** (hĭlwăn'), town (pop. 12,910; with suburbs, 24,661), Giza prov., Upper Egypt, 15 mi. SSE of Cairo city center 2 mi. E of the Nile; well-known health resort, with warm sulphur springs. Has meteorological observatory. Cement factory.

Helylä, Karelo-Finnish SSR: see KHYULYULYA.

Hematheia or **Imathia** (both: ēmăthē'ů), nome (□ 538; pop. 86,998), Macedonia, Greece; ⊙ Veroia. Situated on E slopes of the Vermion, it extends into Giannitsa lowland, drained by Aliakmon R. Agr.: wheat, vegetables, beans, wine. Textile milling at Veroia and Naousa. Formed after Second World War. Also spelled Ematheia.

Hemau (hā'mou), town (pop. 3,718), Upper Palatinate, central Bavaria, Germany, 14 mi. WNW of Regensburg; printing, woodworking, brewing.

Hemavati River (hămä'vŭtē), SW Mysore, India, rises in Western Ghats W of Mudigere, flows SSE past Sakleshpur, E past Hole Narsipur, and S to Krishnaraja Sagara (reservoir on Cauvery R.); c.130 mi. long. Feeds several irrigation channels.

Hemel Hempstead (hĕ'můl hĕm'stĭd), municipal borough (1931 pop. 15,119; 1951 census 23,523), SW Hertford, England, on Gade R. and 6 mi. W of St. Albans; straw-plaiting, paper milling, tanning, agr.-machinery mfg. Church (partly Norman) has leaded spire. In municipal borough (SW) is residential dist. of Boxmoor. Remains of Roman village found here.

Hemer (hā'můr), town (pop. 16,638), in former Prussian prov. of Westphalia, W Germany, after 1945 in North Rhine-Westphalia, 3 mi. E of Iserlohn; mfg. (machinery, wire, paper).

Hemet (hĕ'mĭt), city (pop. 3,386), Riverside co., S Calif., 27 mi. SE of Riverside, on W slope of Mt. San Jacinto; trading, processing center in agr. region (fruit, olives, walnuts). With near-by San Jacinto, holds annual Ramona Pageant, an adaptation of Helen Hunt Jackson's *Ramona*. Inc. 1910.

Hemfurth (hĕm'fōōrt"), village (pop. 588), in former Prussian prov. of Hesse-Nassau, W Germany, after 1945 in Hesse, on the Eder (dam) and 5 mi. NW of Bad Wildungen; hydroelectric plant.

Hemiksem (hä'mĭksům), town (pop. 9,321), Antwerp prov., N Belgium, on Scheldt R. and 5 mi. SW of Antwerp; mfg. (steel wire, nails, sulphuric acid, Portland cement, paving blocks). Formerly spelled Hemixem.

Hemingford (hĕ'mĭngfůrd), village (pop. 946), Box Butte co., NW Nebr., 18 mi. NW of Alliance; alt. 4,259 ft.; poultry products, grain, livestock, potatoes.

Hemingway, town (pop. 821), Williamsburg co., E S.C., 33 mi. SSE of Florence, in agr. area (tobacco, truck).

Hemis Gompa, Kashmir: see HIMIS GOMPA.

Hemixem, Belgium: see HEMIKSEM.

Hemlingby (hĕm'lĭngbü"), residential village (pop. 1,269), Gavleborg co., E Sweden, just SSE of Gavle.

Hemlock. 1 Village (1940 pop. 558), Saginaw co., E central Mich., 14 mi. W of Saginaw, in farm area. **2** Village (pop. 253), Perry co., central Ohio, 9 mi. SSE of New Lexington. **3** or **Eureka,** textile-mill village (pop. 1,990), Chester co., N S.C., just NE of Chester.

Hemlock Lake, Livingston co., W central N.Y., one of the Finger Lakes, 28 mi. S of Rochester, in agr. area; 7 mi. long. Supplies water to Rochester.

Hemmingford, village (pop. 429), S Que., 32 mi. S of Montreal, near N.Y. border; dairying, fruitgrowing, poultry raising.

Hemmingstedt (hĕ'mĭng-shtĕt), village (pop. 1,102), in Schleswig-Holstein, NW Germany, in the S Dithmarschen, 3 mi. S of Heide, in oil-producing region; refinery. Has monument (built 1900) commemorating defeat (1500) of Danes by peasants of the Dithmarschen.

Hemne, canton, Norway: see KYRKSAETERORA.

Hemnesberget (hĕm'näsbăr"gů), village (pop. 1,-225) in Hemnes canton (pop. 1,225), Nordland co., N central Norway, on Ran Fjord, 16 mi. WSW of Mo; port, with boat- and shipyards, lumber mills. Heavily damaged (1940) in Second World War.

Hemp, N.C.: see ROBBINS.

Hemphill (hĕmp'ĭl), county (□ 909; pop. 4,123), extreme N Texas; ⊙ Canadian. On high plains of the Panhandle, and bounded E by Okla. line; alt. 2,500–3,000 ft. Drained by Canadian and Washita rivers. Cattle-ranching region in N, producing also horses, mules, sheep, hogs, poultry; some agr. in S (wheat, grain sorghums, broomcorn, potatoes). Hunting, fishing in L. Marvin and Canadian R. regions. Formed 1876. Acquired parts of Ellis and Roger Mills counties, Okla., in relocation of 100th meridian (1930).

Hemphill, city (pop. 972), ⊙ Sabine co., E Texas, near La. line, c.50 mi. E of Lufkin; trade point in lumber, cotton, cattle area; lumber milling, cotton ginning. Inc. as city 1939.

Hempstead (hĕm'stĕd"), county (□ 735; pop. 25,080), SW Ark.; ⊙ Hope. Bounded SW by Red R. and N by Little Missouri R. Agr. area (cotton truck, fruit, livestock; dairy products); timber. Mfg. at Hope. Formed 1818.

Hempstead. 1 (hĕm'stĭd, –stĕd) Residential village (pop. 29,135), Nassau co., SE N.Y., on W Long Isl., 9 mi. E of Jamaica; some mfg. (clothing, textiles, radio equipment, wood and metal products lenses, machinery, aircraft and auto parts, truck bodies). Seat of Hofstra Col. Near by is Hempstead Lake State Park (903 acres) on shores of Hempstead Reservoir (c.1½ mi. long). Settled 1644, inc. 1853. **2** (hĕmp'stĕd") Town (pop. 1,395) ⊙ Waller co., S Texas, near Brazos R., c.50 mi. WNW of Houston, in agr., oil-producing, livestock area; ships truck, watermelons; recycling plant cotton gin. Near by is "Liendo," home of Elisabeth Ney. Founded 1835.

Hempstead Harbor (hĕm'stĭd, –stĕd), SE N.Y. inlet of Long Island Sound indenting N shore of W Long Isl., E of Manhasset Neck and c.5 mi. N of Hempstead; 4 mi. wide at entrance bet. Matinicock Point (E) and Prospect Point (W); 5 mi. long Roslyn is at its head; Glen Cove, Sea Cliff, Glenwood Landing, and Glen Head are on or near its shores.

Hemptinne-Saint-Benoit (hĕmptēn'-sē-bůnwä'), village, Kasai prov., S Belgian Congo, on right bank of Lulua R. and 95 mi. SE of Luebo, in fiber-growing area; noted R.C. missionary center with large seminary, Carmelite monastery, and mission schools. Also known as Bakonde.

Hems, Syria: see HOMS.

Hemsbach (hĕms'bäkh), village (pop. 3,969), N Baden, Germany, after 1945 in Württemberg-Baden, 3 mi. N of Weinheim; woodworking. Tobacco.

Hemse (hĕm'sů), town (pop. 612), Gotland co., SE Sweden, in S part of Gotland isl., 25 mi. S of Visby agr. center (grain, potatoes, flax, sugar beets). Has 13th-cent. church (rebuilt).

Hemsedal (hĕm'sůdäl), village and canton (pop. 1,478), Buskerud co., S Norway, in the Hemseda (tributary valley of the upper Hallingdal), 65 mi WSW of Lillehammer; agr., stock raising, lumbering. Surrounded by the Hemsedalsfjell.

Hemsedalsfjell (hĕm'sùdälsfyĕl"), mountain plateau (c.70 mi. long, 30 mi. wide) in Buskerud, Opland, and Sogn og Fjordane counties, S central Norway, bet. the upper Hallingdal and the Hallingskarv (S), Sogne Fjord (W), Jotunheim Mts. (N), and Valdres region (E); rises to 6,303 ft. in the Jokeleggja (Nor. *Jøkeleggja*) or Jokuleggi (Nor. *Jøkuleggi*).

Hemsworth, urban district (1931 pop. 13,002; 1951 census 13,654), West Riding, S Yorkshire, England, 7 mi. SE of Wakefield; coal mining. Has grammar school founded 1546 and hosp. founded 1555.

Hen (hān), village (pop. 509) in Adal (Nor. *Ådal*; sometimes spelled Aadal) canton (pop. 3,310), Buskerud co., SE Norway, on Begna R. and 4 mi. N of Honefoss, in agr. and lumbering region; rail junction; lumber and wood-pulp mills, hydro-electric plant.

Hen and Chickens, S Ont., group of islets at W end of L. Erie, 9 mi. W of Pelee Isl.

Henarejos (änärä'hōs), village (pop. 967), Cuenca prov., E central Spain, in the Serranía de Cuenca, 37 mi. ESE of Cuenca; cereals, grapes, saffron, honey, livestock. Flour milling; coal mining. Iron, gold, silver deposits.

Henares River (änä'rēs), New Castile, central Spain, rises NE of Sigüenza in Guadalajara prov., flows c.90 mi. SW, past Sigüenza, Guadalajara, and Alcalá de Henares, to Jarama R. (affluent of the Tagus) 9 mi. E of Madrid.

Henau (hĕ'nou), town (pop. 6,118), St. Gall canton, NE Switzerland, 12 mi. W of St. Gall.

Henbury, residential town and parish (pop. 2,823), SW Gloucester, England, 4 mi. NNW of Bristol.

Hencha, La (lä ĕnshä'), village, Sfax dist., E Tunisia, on railroad and 27 mi. N of Sfax; road junction; olive trees.

Henchir-Souatir (hĕnshēr'-swätēr'), village, Gafsa dist., W Tunisia, on railroad and 25 mi. WNW of Gafsa, in phosphate-mining area.

Hencida (hĕn'tsĭdŏ), town (pop. 2,676), Bihar co., E Hungary, on Berettyo R. and 8 mi. E of Berettyoujfalu; wheat, corn, cattle, poultry.

Hendaye (ãdī'), Sp. *Hendaya* (ĕndä'yä) town (pop. 5,306), Basses-Pyrénées dept., SW France, port on Bay of Biscay at the mouth of Bidassoa R. (Sp. border), opposite Fuenterrabia and 17 mi. SW of Bayonne; 43°22'N 1°47'W; international railroad station and customhouse; mfg. of small arms, liqueur, and berets; sardine canning, tanning, metal-working (zinc and lead). Hendaye-Plage (1 mi. N) is popular bathing resort with beach (2 mi. long), casino, and sanatoriums.

Hendek (hĕndĕk'), town (pop. 5,688), Kocaeli prov., NW Turkey, 18 mi. E of Adapazari; grain, tobacco.

Henderson, town (pop. 3,916), W central Buenos Aires prov., Argentina, 35 mi. SSE of Pehuajó; grain and livestock center; flour milling, dairying, liquor distilling.

Henderson. 1 County (□ 381; pop. 8,416), W Ill.; ⊙ Oquawka. Bounded W by the Mississippi; drained by Henderson Creek. Agr. (livestock, corn, wheat, oats, truck, poultry; dairy products); hardwood timber; limestone. Beaches, camp sites along the Mississippi. Formed 1841. **2** County (□ 440; pop. 30,715), W Ky.; ⊙ Henderson. Bounded N by the Ohio (Ind. line), E and SE by Green R.; drained by several creeks. Rolling plateau agr. area (tobacco, corn, wheat, livestock, fruit); bituminous-coal mines, oil wells; clay, sand, and gravel pits. Includes (in N) a part of Evansville (Ind.) metropolitan dist. Some mfg. at Henderson. Includes Diamond Isl., AUDUBON MEMORIAL STATE PARK, and several aquatic bird refuges; co. lies at crossing of 2 great inland migratory bird routes. Formed 1798. **3** County (□ 382; pop. 30,921), W N.C.; ⊙ Hendersonville. Partly in the Blue Ridge; bounded S by S.C.; drained by upper French Broad and Broad rivers; NW part in Pisgah Natl. Forest. Farming (vegetables, dairy products, poultry, apples, corn), textile mfg., saw-milling; chiefly a resort region. Formed 1838. **4** County (□ 515; pop. 17,173), W Tenn.; ⊙ Lexington. Drained by Big Sandy R. Agr. (cotton, corn, livestock, truck); lumbering. Includes Natchez Trace Forest State Park. Formed 1821. **5** County (□ 940; pop. 23,405), E Texas; ⊙ Athens. Bounded W by Trinity R., E by Neches R.; partly wooded (lumbering). Agr. (especially truck, fruit; also cotton, corn, grains, legumes), cattle, hogs, poultry. Oil, natural gas; lignite, clay, glass sand mined. Hunting; fishing in small lakes. Formed 1846.

Henderson. 1 Village (pop. 166), Knox co., NW central Ill., near Henderson Creek, 4 mi. N of Galesburg, in agr. and bituminous-coal area. **2** Town (pop. 208), Mills co., SW Iowa, near West Nishnabotna R., 25 mi. ESE of Council Bluffs, in grain and livestock region. **3** City (pop. 16,837), ⊙ Henderson co., W Ky., on left bank of the Ohio (bridges here and near by to Ind.) and 10 mi. S of Evansville, Ind., within its metropolitan dist. Important dark-tobacco shipping point and industrial center; mfg. of wood, wire, food, cotton, tobacco, and concrete products; furniture, clothing, industrial brushes, chemicals, processed oil, carbon black, plastics. U.S. ordnance works here. Has airport. Agr. in region (tobacco, corn, wheat, livestock, apples, peaches). John James Audubon lived here 1810–19; near by is AUDUBON MEMORIAL STATE PARK. City founded 1797 by Richard Henderson of the Transylvania Company; chartered 1893. **4** Town (pop. 106), Caroline co., E Md., near Del. line, 14 mi. WSW of Dover, Del.; vegetable canneries. **5** City (pop. 762), Sibley co., S Minn., on Minnesota R. and 45 mi. SW of Minneapolis, in grain, livestock, poultry area; dairy products. **6** Village (pop. 536), York co., SE central Nebr., 12 mi. SW of York. **7** Village (pop. 3,643), Clark co., SE Nev., 12 mi. SE of Las Vegas; trade center for agr. area. Mfg. of jet-engine and rocket fuels, chemicals; magnesium plant built here during Second World War was converted (1951) to titanium metal production. Hoover Dam and L. Mead are E. **8** City (pop. 10,996), ⊙ Vance co., N N.C., 40 mi. NNE of Raleigh; tobacco market; textile-mfg. center; cotton mills, jute-bagging plant, flour and lumber mills, fertilizer and truck assembly plants. Important tungsten mines near by. Settled 1814; inc. 1841; reinc. 1913. **9** City (pop. 2,532), ⊙ Chester co., SW Tenn., 16 mi. SE of Jackson, in timber and farm area; cotton ginning, grist milling. Seat of Freed-Hardeman Col. Chickasaw State Park, with Indian mounds, is near by. **10** City (pop. 6,833), ⊙ Rusk co., E Texas, 32 mi. ESE of Tyler; a principal commercial, processing center in rich East Texas oil field; petroleum refining, cotton processing, lumber milling, mfg. of oil-field equipment, clothing. Founded 1844, inc. 1877; early a lumbering town, then a cotton center, it became an oil city after oil discovery, 1930. **11** Town (pop. 483), Mason co., W W.Va., on the Ohio just SW of Point Pleasant.

Henderson Creek, W Ill., rises in branches near Galesburg, flows c.75 mi. W and SW, supplying water power near Oquawka, to the Mississippi 5 mi. above Burlington, Iowa.

Henderson Field, Solomon Isls.: see GUADALCANAL.

Henderson Harbor, resort village, Jefferson co., N N.Y., on Henderson Bay (an inlet of L. Ontario), 16 mi. SW of Watertown; fishing.

Henderson Island (7 naut. mi. wide), Antarctica, SE of Masson Isl., 4 mi. N of Queen Mary Coast; 66°22'S 97°5'E. Discovered 1912.

Henderson Island: see PITCAIRN ISLAND.

Henderson Lake, Essex co., NE N.Y., in the Adirondacks, c.60 mi. NNW of Glens Falls; c.1½ mi. long; resort. Drains S into Sanford L.

Henderson Mound, town (pop. 22), New Madrid co., extreme SE Mo., in Mississippi flood plain, 9 mi. NNE of New Madrid.

Hendersonville, city (pop. 6,103), ⊙ Henderson co., W N.C., 20 mi. SSE of Asheville, in the Blue Ridge; resort center; agr. trade; hosiery and rug mfg. Near by is Kanuga L. (kŭnōō'gŭ), an Episcopalian summer assembly center.

Hendijan, Iran: see HINDIJAN.

Hendley, village (pop. 130), Furnas co., S Nebr., 7 mi. W of Beaver City and on Beaver Creek.

Hendon, residential municipal borough (1931 pop. 115,682; 1951 census 155,835), Middlesex, England, 8 mi. NW of London. Site of Royal Air Force airfield, scene of annual air display. Has 14th–15th-cent. church. Hendon Hall was residence of Garrick. Municipal borough includes largely residential areas of: Edgware (NW), with aircraft, machine-tool, and light-metal works; Golders Green (SE); Mill Hill (NE), with R.C. missionary col.; Childs Hill (SE); Burn Oak (N).

Hendricks, county (□ 417; pop. 24,594), central Ind.; ⊙ Danville. Drained by Eel R., Mill Creek, and Whitelick R. Agr. (grain, livestock, fruit); canning, flour milling, processing of dairy products and lumber; timber. Formed 1823.

Hendricks. 1 Resort village (pop. 781), Lincoln co., SW Minn., on small lake, near S.Dak. line, and 9 mi. WNW of Ivanhoe, in grain and livestock area; dairy products. **2** Town (pop. 492), Tucker co., NE W.Va., on Black Fork of Cheat R. and 3 mi. SE of Parsons, in coal-mining and agr. area.

Hendrik-Capelle, Belgium: see HENRI-CHAPELLE.

Hendrik-Kapelle, Belgium: see HENRI-CHAPELLE.

Hendrix or **Kemp City,** town (pop. 152), Bryan co., S Okla., 15 mi. S of Durant, and on Red R.; cotton ginning. There is a town, Kemp, 3 mi. E.

Hendrum, village (pop. 352), Norman co., W Minn., on Red R. and 26 mi. N of Fargo, N.Dak.; dairy products.

Hendry, county (□ 1,187; pop. 6,051), S Fla.; ⊙ La Belle. Everglades sugar-cane, truck, and cattle area, crossed in NW corner by Caloosahatchee R.; touches L. Okeechobee (NE). Has Seminole Indian Reservation in SE. Formed 1923.

Henefer (hĕ'nùfùr), town (pop. 346), Summit co., N Utah, 29 mi. SE of Ogden and on Weber R.; alt. 5,337 ft.; agr., livestock.

Henegouwen, Belgium: see HAINAUT.

Henfield, town and parish (pop. 2,001), central Sussex, England, near Adur R., 9 mi. NW of Brighton; agr. market. Has 13th-cent. church.

Hengam, Iran: see HANGAM.

Hengchow. 1 City, Hunan prov., China: see HENGYANG. **2** Town, Kwangsi prov., China: see HENGHSIEN.

Hengchun or **Heng-ch'un** (hŭng'chŏŏn'), Jap. *Koshun* (kō'shōōn), town (1935 pop. 3,165), southernmost Formosa, 50 mi. SE of Pingtung; sugar milling; soybeans, peanuts. Limestone and oil deposits near by. Small port of TAPANLIEH is 3 mi. SSE.

Hengelo (hĕng'ùlō). **1** Town (pop. 1,697), Gelderland prov., E Netherlands, 8 mi. SE of Zutphen; sausages, wooden shoes; cattle and horse market. Also spelled Hengeloo. **2** Town (pop. 45,875), Overijssel prov., E Netherlands, on Twente Canal and 27 mi. E of Deventer; rail junction; textile and machinery center; motors, electrical instruments, salt, dairy products. Electric-power station. Sometimes spelled Hengeloo.

Hengersberg (hĕng'ùrsbĕrk), village (pop. 2,896), Lower Bavaria, Germany, at SW foot of the Bohemian Forest, near the Danube, 6 mi. SE of Deggendorf; wheat, vegetables, livestock. Has a mid-13th-cent. and a late-16th-cent. church.

Hengfeng (hŭng'fŭng'), town (pop. 3,982), ⊙ Hengfeng co. (pop. 57,620), NE Kiangsi prov., China, 24 mi. WSW of Shangjao and on railroad; pottery mfg.; coal mining. Until 1914, Hingan.

Henghsien (hŭng'shyĕn'), town, ⊙ Henghsien co. (pop. 295,575), S Kwangsi prov., China, 65 mi. ESE of Nanning and on left bank of Yü R.; rice, wheat, bamboo. Until 1912 called Hengchow.

Hengistbury Head, promontory of S Hampshire, England, on the Channel 2 mi. SE of Christchurch.

Hengoed (hĕng'goid), town (pop. 11,859) in Gelligaer urban dist., E Glamorgan, Wales, on Rhymney R.; coal mining.

Hengshan (hŭng'shän'). **1** Town, ⊙ Hengshan co. (pop. 446,092), E Hunan prov., China, on Siang R. and 26 mi. NNE of Hengyang; tea, rice, wheat, hemp. **Heng Shan** (2,953 ft.), one of the 5 sacred mts. of China, is 10 mi. W; pagodas on summit. **2** Town, ⊙ Hengshan co. (pop. 52,811), N Shensi prov., China, 40 mi. SW of Yülin, near Great Wall (Suiyuan line); agr. products. Saltworks near by. Until 1914, Hwaiyüan.

Hengshui (hŭng'shwā'), town, ⊙ Hengshui co. (pop. 154,760), S Hopeh prov., China, 35 mi. NW of Tehchow and on railroad; wheat, rice, millet, kaoliang.

Hengtowhotze or **Heng-t'ao-ho-tzu** (both: hŭng'-tou'hŭ'dzŭ), town, S Sungkiang prov., Manchuria, on Chinese Eastern RR and 33 mi. WNW of Mutankiang; lumbering center.

Hengyang (hŭng'yäng'), city (1946 pop. 181,424), central Hunan prov., China, port on left bank of Siang R. at mouth of Lei R., and 90 mi. SSW of Changsha; leading transportation center of Hunan prov., on Hankow-Canton RR, at junction of line to Kwangsi and Kweichow, and major road hub; airport. During Second World War, it was a U.S. air base, and was briefly captured (1944) by Japanese. Called Hengchow until 1912. It became an independent municipality in 1943, when the seat of Hengyang co. (1946 pop. 996,346) was moved to town of Situ, 12 mi. W, thereafter also called Hengyang.

Henik Lakes (hĕ'nĭk), S Keewatin Dist., Northwest Territories, group of 2 lakes S of Yathkyed L. South Henik L. (50 mi. long, 1–12 mi. wide) is at 61°30'N 97°35'W; just N is North Henik L. (18 mi. long, 10 mi. wide). Both drain E into Hudson Bay through Kaminak L.

Hénin-Liétard (ānē'-lyätär'), town (pop. 22,347), Pas-de-Calais dept., N France, 5 mi. E of Lens; coal-mining center; sugar refining, brewing.

Henjam, Iran: see HANGAM.

Henlawson, village (pop. 1,750), Logan co., SW W.Va., 4 mi. N of Logan, in coal-mining and agr. area.

Henley, town (pop. 64), Cole co., central Mo., on Osage R. and 18 mi. SSW of Jefferson City.

Henley and Grange, town (pop. 6,347), SE South Australia, on Gulf St. Vincent; consists of Henley, 5 mi. W of Adelaide, and Grange, 1.75 mi. N of Henley; bathing beaches.

Henley Harbour, village (pop. 50), SE Labrador, on inlet of the Atlantic, 20 mi. SW of Battle Harbour; 52°1'N 55°51'W; fishing port; lumbering.

Henley-in-Arden, town in parish of Wootton Wawen (pop. 2,264), W Warwick, England, on Alne R. and 8 mi. W of Warwick; produces cables and automobile electrical equipment. Has many old houses (including an inn dating from 1358), guild-hall (1448), and church dating from 15th cent. Just S is agr. village of Wootton Wawen with church dating from Saxon times.

Henley-on-Thames (tĕmz), residential municipal borough (1931 pop. 6,621; 1951 census 7,970), SE Oxfordshire, England, on the Thames and 7 mi. NNE of Reading, at foot of Chiltern Hills; chiefly known as scene of annual rowing regatta, instituted 1839. Has 14th-cent. church, grammar school founded 1605, and 5-arched stone bridge built 1786.

Henllan (hĕn'thlän). **1** Village and parish (pop. 182), SW Cardigan, Wales, on Teifi R. and 3 mi. E of Newcastle Emlyn; woolen milling. **2** Village, Denbigh, Wales: see DENBIGH.

Henlopen, Cape (hĕnlō'pŭn), Sussex co., SE Del., at S side of mouth of Delaware Bay, opposite Cape May, N.J.; 38°48'N 75°6'W. U.S. Fort Miles and naval radio station here; lightship offshore. Break-waters, both marked by lighthouses, protect harbor of refuge (Delaware Breakwater harbor) and Lewes harbor, both W of cape.

Henlow (-lō), town and parish (pop. 2,496), E Bedford, England, on Ivel R. and 4 mi. S of Biggleswade; agr. market. Has 15th-cent. church.

Henne, Germany: see MESCHEDE.

Henneberg (hĕ'nŭbĕrk), village (pop. 593), Thuringia, central Germany, 6 mi. SSW of Meiningen. Site of ruins of ancestral castle (destroyed 1525) of counts of Henneberg, who played important part in Thuringian history prior to 1353, when their property passed to house of Wettin.

Hennebont (ĕnbō'), town (pop. 5,058), Morbihan dept., W France, seaport at head of Blavet R. estuary and 5 mi. NNE of Lorient; foundries, forges; fish canning, woodworking, distilling. Suffered heavy damage in Second World War, including the massive 15th-cent. gate, 16th-cent. church, and many old houses.

Hennef (hĕ'nĕf), village (pop. 10,793), in former Prussian Rhine Prov., W Germany, after 1945 in North Rhine-Westphalia, on the Sieg and 3 mi. SE of Siegburg. Until 1934, called Geistingen.

Hennepin (hĕ'nŭpĭn), county (□ 565; pop. 676,579), E Minn.; ⊙ Minneapolis. Resort and industrial area bounded NE by Mississippi R., NW by Crow R., SE by Minnesota R. Industry and commerce at Minneapolis. L. Minnetonka in SW. Co. formed 1852.

Hennepin, village (pop. 312), ⊙ Putnam co., N central Ill., on Illinois R. (bridged) and 8 mi. SW of Spring Valley; grain elevator. Fishing in Senachwine and Sawmill lakes.

Hennersdorf, Czechoslovakia: see JINDRICHOV.

Hennersdorf or **Katholisch-Hennersdorf** (kätō'lĭsh-hĕ'nŭrsdôrf"), village, in Lower Silesia, after 1945 in Wroclaw prov., SW Poland, 12 mi. E of Görlitz. Here Frederick the Great defeated (Nov., 1745) Austrians and Saxons.

Hennessey (hĕ'nŭsē), city (pop. 1,264), Kingfisher co., central Okla., 21 mi. S of Enid, near the Turkey Creek, in grain and livestock area; cotton ginning, flour and feed milling, mfg. of auto trailers. Laid out 1889.

Hennigsdorf (hĕ'nĭkhs-dôrf), town (pop. 13,071), Brandenburg, E Germany, on the Havel and 12 mi. NW of Berlin; mfg. (steel products, locomotives, industrial ceramics).

Henniker (hĕ'nĭkŭr), town (pop. 1,675), Merrimack co., S central N.H., on the Contoocook and 15 mi. W of Concord; mfg. (paper, wood products, yarn); agr. (dairy products, poultry); lumber; summer resort. Seat of New England Col. Settled 1763–64, inc. 1768.

Henning. 1 Village (pop. 283), Vermilion co., E Ill., 12 mi. NNW of Danville, in agr. and bituminous-coal area. **2** Village (pop. 1,004), Otter Tail co., W Minn., 30 mi. E of Fergus Falls, near East Battle Lake in grain, livestock, poultry area; dairy products. Resort. **3** Town (pop. 493), Lauderdale co., W Tenn., 27 mi. SSW of Dyersburg, in cotton-growing area.

Henningsvaer (hĕn'nĭngsvăr), village (pop. 941) in Vagan canton, Nordland co., N Norway, on islet of same name in the Vesteralen group, just S of Austvagoy, 11 mi. SW of Svolvaer; fishing center; summer resort.

Hennock, agr. village and parish (pop. 1,046), S central Devon, England, 9 mi. SW of Exeter; granite quarrying. Has 15th-cent. church.

Hennstedt (hĕn'shtĕt), village (pop. 3,265), in Schleswig-Holstein, NW Germany, 7 mi. NE of Heide, in the N Dithmarschen; woodworking. Winter rye, potatoes.

Henri-Chapelle (ārē-shäpĕl'), Flemish *Hendrik-Kapelle* (formerly *Hendrik-Capelle*) (hĕn'drĭk-käpĕ'lŭ), village (pop. 1,538), Liége prov., E Belgium, 6 mi. NW of Eupen; agr., cattle raising, dairying. U.S. military cemetery (Second World War) here.

Henrichemont (ārēshmō'), village (pop. 1,453), Cher dept., central France, 16 mi. NNE of Bourges; tanneries, pottery works. Planned and founded by Sully in 1608.

Henrichenburg (hĕn'rĭkhŭnbŏŏrk"), village (pop. 2,429), in former Prussian prov. of Westphalia, W Germany, after 1945 in North Rhine-Westphalia, in the Ruhr, 5 mi. ESE of Recklinghausen; site of ship elevator joining Dortmund-Ems and Rhine-Herne canals (level difference: 45.9 ft.).

Henrico (hĕnrī'kō), county (□ 241; pop. 57,340), E central Va.; co. courthouse is at RICHMOND, in but independent of co. W part of co. is in piedmont, E part on coastal plain; bounded S by James R. (navigable to Richmond), N and NE by the Chickahominy. Truck, dairy and poultry farming; some tobacco growing, livestock raising (hogs, beef cattle, horses, mules). Civil War battlefields in co. are included in Richmond Natl. Battlefield Park. Formed 1634.

Henrietta. 1 City (pop. 462), Ray co., NW Mo., near Missouri R., 4 mi. SE of Richmond. **2** Textile village (pop. 3,494, with adjacent Caroleen and Avondale), Rutherford co., SW N.C., c.15 mi. W of Shelby. **3** Town (pop. 2,813), ⊙ Clay co., N Texas, 18 mi. ESE of Wichita Falls and on Little Wichita R.; shipping, processing center in cattle, cotton, oil area; mfg. of leather goods, tile, pottery, feed; cotton ginning, cottonseed-oil milling. Founded 1857, resettled 1873, inc. 1882.

Henrietta Island, Rus. *Ostrov Genriyetta,* northernmost of De Long Isls., in E.Siberian Sea, 355 mi. off N Yakut Autonomous SSR, Russian SFSR; 77°N 157°15'E. Arctic observation post.

Henrietta Maria, Cape, NE Ont., on Hudson Bay, on W side of entrance of James Bay; 55°9'N 82°20'W.

Henriette, village (pop. 57), Pine co., E Minn., 8 mi. WNW of Pine City, in grain, potato, livestock area.

Henrieville, town (pop. 114), Garfield co., S Utah, 30 mi. SE of Panguitch; alt. 6,000 ft.; agr.

Henry. 1 County (□ 565; pop. 18,674), SE Ala.; ⊙ Abbeville. Coastal plain bounded on E by Chattahoochee R. and Ga., drained (W) by Choctawhatchee R. Cotton, peanuts, corn; bauxite. Formed 1819. **2** County (□ 331; pop. 15,857), N central Ga.; ⊙ McDonough. Piedmont agr. (cotton, corn, grain, truck, fruit, pecans) and textile mfg. area. Formed 1821. **3** County (□ 826; pop. 46,492), NW Ill.; ⊙ Cambridge. Bounded NW by Rock R.; drained by Green and Edwards rivers; old Illinois and Mississippi Canal crosses co. Agr. (corn, oats, soybeans, wheat, truck, livestock, poultry; dairy products). Bituminous-coal mines. Mfg., including oil refining. Formed 1825. **4** County (□ 400; pop. 45,505), E Ind.; ⊙ New Castle. Agr. area (livestock, grain, truck, poultry). Mfg. (especially automobiles and auto equipment, canned goods, furniture, steel products, caskets, clothing) at New Castle and Knightstown. Drained by Big Blue R., Flatrock Creek, and small Fall Creek. Formed 1821. **5** County (□ 440; pop. 18,708), SE Iowa; ⊙ Mount Pleasant. Prairie agr. area (hogs, cattle, poultry, corn, oats, soybeans) drained by Skunk R.; limestone quarries. State parks. Formed 1836. **6** County (□ 289; pop. 11,394), N Ky.; ⊙ New Castle. Bounded E by Kentucky R.; drained by Little Kentucky R. and Floyds Fork. Gently rolling upland agr. area (burley tobacco, dairy products, livestock, corn, hay), in Bluegrass region. Zinc and lead mines here which produced during First World War were reopened at beginning of Second World War. Formed 1798. **7** County (□ 737; pop. 20,043), W central Mo.; ⊙ Clinton. Drained by South Grand R. Agr. (corn, wheat, oats, hay), livestock; coal. Formed 1834. **8** County (□ 416; pop. 22,423), NW Ohio; ⊙ Napoleon. Intersected by Maumee R. Diversified farming (corn, wheat, oats, sugar beets, truck); some mfg. at Napoleon. Formed 1824. **9** County (□ 599; pop. 23,828), NW Tenn.; ⊙ Paris. Bounded N by Ky., E by Kentucky Reservoir (Tennessee R.; here receives the Big Sandy); drained by East Fork Clarks R. and forks of the Obion. Agr. area (corn, cotton, tobacco, sweet potatoes, livestock); some mfg. at Paris. Timber; clay pits. Formed 1821. **10** County (□ 392; pop. 31,219), S Va.; co. courthouse is at Martinsville, in but independent of co. In S piedmont; bounded S by N.C.; drained by Smith and Mayo rivers. Agr. (especially tobacco; also hay, corn, poultry), dairying, livestock raising, beekeeping; lumbering. Mfg. of furniture and other wood products. Formed 1777.

Henry. 1 City (pop. 1,966), Marshall co., N central Ill., on Illinois R. (bridged here) and 28 mi. NNE of Peoria, in agr. area (corn, oats, wheat, livestock, poultry, fruit; dairy products); bituminous-coal mines; ships grain. Mfg. (bunting goods, rocker grates, cigars); nurseries; timber. Near by is Senachwine L. (waterfowl hunting, fishing). Founded in early 1840s; inc. 1854. **2** Village (pop. 171), Scotts Bluff co., extreme W Nebr., 20 mi. WNW of Scottsbluff and on N.Platte R. at Wyo. line. Near-by Horse Creek Treaty Monument commemorates large assembly (1851) of whites and Plains Indians to determine reservation boundaries. **3** Town (pop. 323), Codington co., E S.Dak., 18 mi. W of Watertown; pheasant hunting; potatoes, corn. **4** Town (pop. 200), Henry co., NW Tenn., 8 mi. SW of Paris.

Henry, Cape, SE Va., promontory at S side of entrance to Chesapeake Bay, opposite Cape Charles, 17 mi. E of Norfolk. Lighthouse, Cape Henry village, U.S. Fort Story, and Seashore State Park here. Cape Henry Memorial (part of Colonial Natl. Historical Park) marks 1st landing (1607) of Jamestown settlers.

Henry, Fort, fortification, SE Ont., on the St. Lawrence, near L. Ontario, at SW end of Rideau Canal, overlooking Kingston harbor. Built 1812, original fort was demolished 1832 and replaced by present structure. Later a mus., it was camp for prisoners of war in First and Second World Wars.

Henry, Fort, Tenn.: see FORT DONELSON NATIONAL MILITARY PARK.

Henry Clay, suburb (pop. 6,104) of Lexington, Fayette co., central Ky. There is also a hamlet called Henry Clay in Pike co., near Lookout.

Henryetta (hĕnrĕĕ'tŭ), city (pop. 7,987), Okmulgee co., E central Okla., 12 mi. S of Okmulgee, in diversified agr. area; glassmaking, oil refining, zinc smelting, cotton ginning. Coal mines; oil and natural-gas wells. Recreation park (with small L. Henryetta) is near by. Founded c.1900.

Henry Hudson Bridge, SE N.Y., over Spuyten Duyvil, connects N tip of Manhattan with the Bronx; a double-deck vehicular structure, it is 2,000 ft. long over all and 142 ft. above the water.

Henry Island, islet in Gulf of St. Lawrence, NE N.S., off W Cape Breton Isl., 5 mi. SW of Port Hood; 45°58'N 61°36'W.

Henry Kater, Cape, E Baffin Isl., E Franklin Dist., Northwest Territories, on Davis Strait, E extremity of Henry Kater Peninsula (55 mi. long, 7–23 mi. wide), forming N shore of Home Bay; 69°4'N 66°46'W.

Henry Mountains, in Garfield co., S Utah, W of Dirty Devil R., E of Escalante. Chief peaks: Mt. Hillers (10,650 ft.), Mt. Pennell (11,320 ft.), and Mt. ELLEN (11,485 ft.).

Henrys Fork, river, SE Idaho, rises in Henrys Lake (□ 8; 4 mi. long, 2 mi. wide; near Mont. line), flows c.110 mi. S and SW, past St. Anthony, to Snake R. 10 mi. SW of Rexburg. Island Park Dam (91 ft. high, 9,448 ft. long; completed 1938) is in upper course near Island Park. Used in irrigation of upper Snake R. valley; impounds Island Park L. (12 mi. long).

Henryville, village (pop. 429), S Que., 12 mi. SSE of St. Jean; dairying.

Hensall (hĕn'sôl), village (pop. 665), S Ont., 24 mi. SSE of Goderich; dairying, mixed farming.

Hensel (hĕn'sŭl), village (pop. 139), Pembina co., NE N.Dak., 8 mi. SSW of Cavalier. Formerly Canton.

Henshaw, Lake, Calif.: see SAN LUIS REY RIVER.

Hensies (ãsē'), town (pop. 3,167), Hainaut prov., SW Belgium, 12 mi. W of Mons, near Fr. border; coal mining.

Hensingham (hĕn'sĭng-ŭm), residential village and parish (pop. 2,116), W Cumberland, England, just SE of Whitehaven. Site of Whitehaven reservoir.

Hensley (hĕnz'lē), village (1940 pop. 574), Pulaski co., central Ark., 16 mi. SSE of Little Rock.

Hensley Field, Texas: see DALLAS, city.

Henstedt (hĕn'shtĕt), village (pop. 2,587), in Schleswig-Holstein, NW Germany, 16 mi. N of Hamburg; woodworking.

Henstridge, agr. village and parish (pop. 1,040), SE Somerset, England, 6 mi. ENE of Sherborne.

Hentey, Mongolia: see KENTEI.

Henty, town (pop. 836), S New South Wales, Australia, 120 mi. WSW of Canberra; rail junction; sheep, agr. center.

Henzada (hĕn'zŭdä'), Burmese *Hinthada* (hĕn"dhŭdä'), northernmost district (□ 2,807; 1941 pop. 693,271) of Irrawaddy div., Lower Burma; ⊙ Henzada. Bet. Arakan Yoma and Irrawaddy R. Protected by embankments along Irrawaddy R., it is an intensive rice-growing area. Forests at foot of Arakan Yoma. Pop. is 85% Burmese, 10% Karen.

Henzada, town (pop. 28,542), ⊙ Henzada dist., Lower Burma, on right bank of Irrawaddy R. opposite Tharrawaw (rail ferry) and 75 mi. NE of Bassein; river port and rail terminus of lines to Kyangin and Bassein; wood carving.

Hepburn, village (pop. 118), S central Victoria, Australia, 55 mi. NW of Melbourne, near Daylesford, on spur of Great Dividing Range; health resort with mineral springs.

Hepburn, village (pop. 317), central Sask., 28 mi. N of Saskatoon; mixed farming, dairying.

Hepburn, town (pop. 64), Page co., SW Iowa, near Nodaway R., 8 mi. N of Clarinda, in bituminous-coal-mining area.

Hephzibah (hĕp'zĭbŭ), town (pop. 525), Richmond co., E Ga., 12 mi. SSW of Augusta; clay mining.

Hepler, city (pop. 224), Crawford co., SE Kansas, 23 mi. NW of Pittsburg; agr., coal-mining.

Heppendorf (hĕ'pŭndôrf), village (pop. 5,092), in former Prussian Rhine Prov., W Germany, after 1945 in North Rhine-Westphalia, 14 mi. W of Cologne; sugar beets.

Heppenheim (hĕ'pŭnhīm), town (pop. 11,628), S Hesse, W Germany, in former Starkenburg prov., on the Bergstrasse, at W foot of the Odenwald, 3 mi. S of Bensheim; vineyards; fruit (peaches, apricots), almonds. Resort noted for its mild climate. The church of St. Peter, often called "the cathedral of the Bergstrasse," was rebuilt 1900–04. Town also has 13th-cent. castle, a former residence of archbishops of Mainz; 16th-cent., half-timbered town hall. Ruins of 12th-cent. castle Starkenburg on hill just NE. A royal villa, Heppenheim came to Lorsch abbey in 8th cent., passed to Mainz in 1232, and was chartered 1318. Sometimes called Heppenheim an der Bergstrasse.

Heppens, Germany: see RÜSTRINGEN.

Heppner, city (pop. 1,648), ⊙ Morrow co., N Oregon, on Willow Creek and c.45 mi. SW of Pendleton in wheat and livestock area; lumber milling, alcohol distilling. Founded 1873, inc. 1887.

Heptanesos, Greece: see IONIAN ISLANDS.

Heptarchy (hĕp'tärkē) [Gr.,=seven-kingdom], name applied to 7 kingdoms of Anglo-Saxon England: NORTHUMBRIA, EAST ANGLIA, MERCIA, ESSEX, SUSSEX, WESSEX, and KENT. Term probably 1st used in 16th cent. by writers who believed England was divided into just 7 kingdoms founded by Angles and Saxons. In fact political and geographical divisions of early England were more complex, and were fluid and shifting for centuries.

Hepworth, village (pop. 290), S Ont., 12 mi. NW of Owen Sound; dairying, mixed farming.
Hepworth, England: see NEW MILL.
Heraclea, Turkey, on the Aegean: see AYVALIK.
Heraclea Pontica, Turkey, on Black Sea: see EREGLI.
Heracleopolis (hŭră″klēō′pūlĭs, hē″rŭklē–), anc. city, N Egypt, near the Nile, SE of Faiyum. One of oldest of Egyptian cities, it was in existence before 3000 B.C. and was ⊙ (c.2445–c.2160) of the IX and X dynasties.
Heracleotica, Chersonesus: see SEVASTOPOL, Russian SFSR.
Heracleum, Crete: see CANDIA.
Heraclia, Greece: see HERAKLEIA.
Heradsvotn or **Heradhsvotn** (hyĕ′rädhsvŭ″tŭn), Icelandic *Héraðsvötn*, river, NW Iceland, rises in several headstreams on Hofsjokull, flows 70 mi. N to Skaga Fjord.
Herakleia or **Iraklia** (both: ērä′klēŭ), town (pop. 3,205), Serrai nome, Macedonia, Greece, 15 mi. NW of Serrai; cotton, barley, corn. Formerly called Tzoumagia (Tzoumayia, Jumaya, or Dzhumaya) or Kato (=lower) Tzoumagia, as opposed to Gorna (=upper) Dzhumaya, Bulgaria.
Herakleia or **Iraklia**, Aegean island (□ 7; pop. 227) in the Cyclades, Greece, S of Naxos isl.; 36°50′N 25°26′E; 5 mi. long, 2.5 mi. wide. Also spelled Heraclia.
Herakleion or **Iraklion** (both: ērä′klēōn), nome (□ 989; pop. 167,918), central Crete, bet. Mt. Dikte (E) and Mt. Ida (W); ⊙ Candia. The most fertile area of Crete; produces raisins, carobs, wheat, citrus fruits; olive oil; stock raising (sheep, goats, cows); fisheries. Main port, Candia, is on N shore.
Herakleion, city, Crete: see CANDIA.
Herakol Dag (hĕräkôl′ dä), Turkish *Herakol Dağ*, peak (9,655 ft.), SE Turkey in Van Mts., 10 mi. S of Perveri. Sometimes spelled Herekol.
Herald Harbor, summer resort, Anne Arundel co., central Md., on Severn R. 7 mi. NW of Annapolis.
Herald Island, Rus. *Ostrov Gerald* (□ 4), in W Chukchi Sea, in Khabarovsk Territory, Russian SFSR, 37 mi. E of Wrangel Isl.; 71°20′N 175°40′W. Rises to 650 ft. Discovered 1849 by Br. navigator Kellett.
Heras, Las. 1 Town, Comodoro Rivadavia military zone, Argentina: see COLONIA LAS HERAS. **2** Town, Mendoza prov., Argentina: see LAS HERAS.
Herastrau (hĕrŭ′strŭŏŏ), Rum. *Herăstrău*, N suburb (1948 pop. 5,902) of Bucharest, in Bucharest municipality, S Rumania, on left bank of Colentina R.
Herat or **Harat** (hŭrăt′), province (□ 50,000; pop. 1,150,000), NW Afghanistan; ⊙ Herat. Bounded W by Iran and N by Turkmen SSR (USSR), it is penetrated E by the wild outliers of the Hindu Kush (Band-i-Turkestan and Paropamisus Mts. in NE; Safed Koh and Siah Koh in SE) and forms desert lowland (*dasht*) along the W and N frontiers. It is drained by the rivers Murghab, Hari Rud, Harut Rud and Farah Rud, all of which disappear into the desert or into salt-lake depressions. Pop. and agr. is concentrated in a few oases producing grain (wheat, barley, millet, corn, rice), beans, oilseed, opium, cotton, fruit (peaches, pomegranates, melons), and wine. The Herat oasis along the Hari Rud is the largest, extending from Obeh to Ghurian, and containing 70% of pop.; other oases are Shindand (S) and Bala Murghab (N). Petroleum is produced at Tirpul; there are coal, silver-lead, iron, and rock-crystal deposits. Handicraft and a few minor industries are concentrated in Herat, the chief commercial center, handling trade with Iran (via Islam Qala) and USSR (via Torghondi and Maruchak). Pop. is ethnically diverse: Heratis (related to the Tadzhiks; NW) and Durani Afghans (SW) in oases, and seminomadic Persian-speaking peoples (Jamshidis, Firoz-Kohis, Taimanis, Hazaras) in mtn. and desert areas.
Herat or **Harat**, city (pop. 80–90,000), ⊙ Herat prov., NW Afghanistan, on right bank of the Hari Rud and 400 mi. W of Kabul; alt. 3,030 ft.; 34°22′N 62°9′E. Economic center of W Afghanistan; important highway crossing at heart of rich, densely populated, irrigated Hari Rud valley, 55–70 mi. from USSR and Iran borders. Large handicraft industry (silks, woolens, camel's-hair goods, rugs); auto repair shops, textile mill, cotton gins; flour, rice, and oilseed mills. Active karakul trade. Radio station. The present city (dating from 16th cent.) lies 3 mi. from the Hari Rud. It has mile-long walls on massive earthworks crossed by 5 gates. Divided into 4 quarters by main bazaar streets, meeting in domed central square known as Charsu. Dominated by citadel (N), the city contains 15th-cent. mosque Jama Masjid (NE), a lofty arched structure partly in ruins. Beyond the walls extends the new garden city with parks and orchards. The anc. *Alexandria Ariorum* of Alexander the Great, the city passed in A.D. 661 to the Arabs, under whose rule it became one of the leading centers of the Arab world, with pop. of 100,000. It suffered greatly in the Mongol conquest (1221), and was sacked again (1393) by Tamerlane. Subsequently it changed hands repeatedly bet. Persians and Afghans until the last Persian seizure (1856). The city was finally secured by the Afghans in 1861.
Herau, Iran: see KHALKHAL.
Hérault (ārō′), department (□ 2,403; pop. 461,100), in Languedoc, S France; ⊙ Montpellier. Traversed SW-NE by southernmost ranges of the Massif Central. Part of narrow coastal plain is occupied by lagoons of the Gulf of Lion. Drained by short streams (Orb, Hérault, Lez) which descend from the Cévennes. One of France's leading wine-growing depts., it also grows a variety of fruits (strawberries, apricots, almonds) and vegetables. The Mediterranean climate favors the olive and the mulberry tree. There are important bauxite mines at Villeveyrac and coal mines in Graissessac area; also many marble quarries and saltworks. Most major industries (distilling, mfg. of fertilizer, glass bottles, casks) are connected with viticulture. Some textile mills at Lodève and Bédarieux. Chief towns are Montpellier (commercial and cultural city), Béziers (wine-shipping center), and Sète (seaport).
Hérault River, Gard and Hérault depts., S France, rises at foot of Mont Aigoual, in the Cévennes, flows 100 mi. S, past Ganges and Pézenas, to the Gulf of Lion 3 mi. below Agde.
Herbault (ĕrbō′), village (pop. 622), Loir-et-Cher dept., N central France, 9 mi. W of Blois; small grains; sawmilling.
Herbede (hĕr′bŭdŭ), village (pop. 8,437), in former Prussian prov. of Westphalia, W Germany, after 1945 in North Rhine-Westphalia, on the Ruhr and 2 mi. SW of Witten; sandstone quarrying.
Herbert, town (pop. 824), S Sask., near Rush L., 27 mi. ENE of Swift Current; grain elevators, lumber and flour mills. Govt. experimental farm.
Herbert, Mount, New Guinea: see BISMARCK MOUNTAINS.
Herberton, town (pop. 900), NE Queensland, Australia, 40 mi. SSW of Cairns, on Atherton Tableland; mining center (tin, copper, silver, lead).
Herbertshöhe, Bismarck Archipelago: see KOKOPO.
Herbesthal (hĕr′bŭstäl), village, Liége prov., E Belgium, 8 mi. SW of Aachen; frontier station near Ger. border. Commune center of Lontzen (pop. 2,277) is 2 mi. NE.
Herbeumont (ĕrbûmō′), village (pop. 793), Luxembourg prov., SE Belgium, on Semois R. and 10 mi. SW of Neufchâteau, in the Ardennes; quarrying.
Herbiers, Les (lāzĕrbyā′), town (pop. 2,229), Vendée dept., W France, 14 mi. SSW of Cholet; hog market; mfg. of footwear and hosiery.
Herbignac (ĕrbēnyäk′), village (pop. 662), Loire-Inférieure dept., W France, 11 mi. NNW of Saint-Nazaire; dairying.
Herbillon (ĕrbēyō′), village (pop. 610), Constantine dept., NE Algeria, on the Mediterranean at foot of Edough range, 24 mi. WNW of Bône; fishing. Granite quarries.
Herb Lake, village, N central Man., on Wekusko L., 85 mi. E of Flin Flon; gold, lithium mines.
Herblay (ĕrblā′), town (pop. 4,823), Seine-et-Oise dept., N central France, an outer NW suburb of Paris, 13 mi. from Notre Dame Cathedral, on right bank of the Seine, opposite Saint-Germain forest.
Herbolzheim (hĕr′bôlts-hīm″), village (pop. 3,364), S Baden, Germany, at W foot of Black Forest, 9 mi. SW of Lahr; mfg. of machinery, textiles, tobacco; metal- and woodworking.
Herborn (hĕr′bôrn), town (pop. 8,326), in former Prussian prov. of Hesse-Nassau, W Germany, after 1945 in Hesse, in the Westerwald, on the Dill and 13 mi. NW of Wetzlar. Machinery mfg., metalworking. Has 13th-cent. castle, now housing noted Protestant theological seminary; and 16th-cent. town hall.
Herbrechtingen (hĕr′brĕkh″tĭng-ŭn), village (pop. 3,444), N Württemberg, Germany, after 1945 in Württemberg-Baden, 4 mi. S of Heidenheim; grain, cattle.
Hercegfalva (hĕr′tsĕkfŏlvŏ), market town (pop. 6,371), Fejer co., W central Hungary, 25 mi. SE of Szekesfehervar; wheat, corn, hemp; cattle, hogs.
Herceg Novi or **Khertseg Novi** (both: hĕr′tsĕk nô′vē), Ital. *Castelnuovo* (kästĕlnōō′vô), village (pop. 3,053), W Montenegro, Yugoslavia, port on Bay of Topla (NW inlet of Gulf of Kotor), on narrow-gauge railroad and 37 mi. W of Titograd, near Dalmatia (W) and Herzegovina (NW) borders. Tourist center (chiefly in summer) in forested hills (vineyards); noted for mild climate; sea bathing. Ruined Saracen and Sp. castles here. Savina, a medieval monastery, stands on shore E of town. Dates from 1382; in Dalmatia until 1921. Sometimes spelled Ercegnovi.
Hercegovina, Yugoslavia: see HERZEGOVINA.
Hercegszanto (hĕr′tsĕksäntō), Hung. *Hercegszántó*, town (pop. 3,493), Bacs-Bodrog co., S Hungary, 16 mi. S of Baja, on Yugoslav frontier.
Herchen (hĕr′khŭn), village (pop. 5,298), in former Prussian Rhine Prov., W Germany, after 1945 in North Rhine-Westphalia, on the Sieg and 13 mi. E of Siegburg.
Herchsheim (hĕrks′hīm), village (pop. 327), Lower Franconia, W Bavaria, Germany, 11 mi. S of Würzburg; grain, cattle.
Herculândia (ĕrkōōlän′dyŭ), city (pop. 1,419), W São Paulo, Brazil, on railroad and 30 mi. WNW of Marília, in region of pioneer settlements; coffee, cotton. Until 1944, called Herculânia.
Herculaneum (hûrkūlā′nēŭm), anc. city of Campania, S Italy, 5 mi. SE of Naples, at W foot of Vesuvius. Damaged by earthquake in A.D. 63; with Pompeii completely buried in A.D. 79. The site (now occupied by RESINA) was discovered in 1719; excavations, begun in 1735 and continued intermittently to the present time, have uncovered much of the city and yielded rich treasure in paintings, sculptures, and other antiquities.
Herculaneum, village (pop. 1,603), Jefferson co., E Mo., on Mississippi R. and 25 mi. S of St. Louis; lead smelters; marble quarries. Platted 1808.
Herculânia. 1 City, Mato Grosso, Brazil: see COXIM. **2** City, São Paulo, Brazil: see HERCULÂNDIA.
Hércules, Mexico: see CAYETANO RUBIO.
Hercules, residential and industrial town (pop. 41,857), S central Transvaal, U. of So. Afr., 3 mi. NNW of Pretoria; alt. 4,330 ft.
Hercules, town (pop. 343), Contra Costa co., W Calif., on San Pablo Bay, 12 mi. NE of Richmond; dynamite.
Hércules, Punta (pōōn′tä ĕr′kōōlĕs), cape in Chubut natl. territory, Argentina, on Atlantic coast; easternmost point of Valdés Peninsula; 42°37′S 65°36′W.
Herdecke (hĕr′dĕ″kŭ), town (pop. 12,409), in former Prussian prov. of Westphalia, W Germany, after 1945 in North Rhine-Westphalia, on the Ruhr, just N of Hagen; sandstone quarrying.
Herdorf (hĕr′dôrf), village (pop. 4,806), in former Prussian Rhine Prov., W Germany, after 1945 in Rhineland-Palatinate, 7 mi. SSW of Siegen.
Hered (hĕ′rād), Hung. *Heréd*, town (pop. 2,179), Nograd-Hont co., N Hungary, on branch of Zagyva R. and 29 mi. NE of Budapest; wheat, hemp, dairy.
Heredia (ārā′dyä), province (□ 1,100; 1950 pop. 51,760), N Costa Rica; ⊙ Heredia. Bounded N by San Juan R. (Nicaragua border), it lies largely in N lowlands drained by Sarapiquí R. Extends S across Barba volcano section of the Central Cordillera onto central plateau, where agr. and pop. are concentrated. Coffee, sugar cane, potatoes, grain, vegetables; dairying. Bananas and livestock are raised in sparsely settled Sarapiquí lowlands: Plateau section (served by railroads and Inter-American Highway) is site of principal centers. Heredia, Santo Domingo, San Isidro, and Barba.
Heredia, city (1950 pop. 11,967), ⊙ Heredia prov., central Costa Rica, on central plateau, on Inter-American Highway, on railroad and 6 mi. NNW of San José; alt. 3,822 ft.; 10°N 84°7′W. Commercial center in important coffee zone; mfg. of soap and matches, coffee processing; livestock trade. It has a Central Park, colonial churches (1797), and teachers col. One of oldest cities (founded 1571) on central plateau, it flourished during colonial times, but was later eclipsed by near-by San José.
Hereford or **Herefordshire** (hĕ′rŭfŭrd, –shĭr), county (□ 842.1; 1931 pop. 111,767; 1951 census 127,092), SW England; ⊙ Hereford. Bounded by Wales (W), Shropshire (N), Worcester (E), Gloucester (SE), and Monmouth (SW). Drained by Wye, Teme, Lugg, and Leadon rivers. Country is undulating, and on E border are Malvern Hills. Dairying (well-known Hereford cattle originate here); fruitgrowing (apples, pears); mfg. of cider and perry. Timber is plentiful. There are few industries. Besides Hereford, other towns are Ledbury, Leominster, and Ross. There are many traces of anc. occupation; Offa's Dyke crossed co.
Hereford, municipal borough (1931 pop. 24,163; 1951 census 32,490), ⊙ Herefordshire, England, in center of co., on the Wye and 120 mi. WNW of London; trade center for agr. area. The great cathedral (dating from 11th cent.) is one of the meeting places (with Gloucester and Worcester) of the Three Choirs. Has many 16th- and 17th-cent. bldgs., a grammar school founded 1384; remains of anc. castle and town walls; and a White Cross, commemorating end of Great Plague (1347). Nell Gwynn and David Garrick b. here. Mfg.: food processing, leather and leather products, agr. machinery, pharmaceuticals, tiles, wood products.
Hereford (hûr′fŭrd). **1** Village, Baltimore co., N Md., 20 mi. N of Baltimore. Site of cross-country racing courses for Grand Natl. Steeplechase and My Lady's Manor race, both held in April. **2** City (pop. 5,207), ⊙ Deaf Smith co., extreme N Texas, on the Llano Estacado on Tierra Blanca Creek, and c.45 mi. SW of Amarillo; shipping, processing center for wheat, cattle, and irrigated farm region, with flour mills, grain elevators, creamery, cannery, potato-handling plant. Buffalo L. (recreational center) is just E. City noted for residents' low rate of tooth decay, attributed to fluorine in the soil. Settled 1898, inc. 1906.
Hereford Inlet (hĕr′fŭrd), S N.J., passage (c.2 mi. wide) connecting the Atlantic and Intracoastal Waterway channel, bet. North Wildwood and S tip of Seven Mile Beach.
Herefordshire, England: see HEREFORD, county.
Herefordshire Beacon, England: see MALVERN HILLS.
Herefoss (hăr′ŭfôs), village and canton (pop. 582), Aust-Agder co., S Norway, on Herefoss L. (8-mi.-long widening of Tovdal R.), on railroad and 16 mi. WNW of Arendal. Has co. school. Formerly spelled Heirefos or Hejrefos.
Hereke (hĕrĕkĕ′), town (pop. 3,234), Kocaeli prov., NW Turkey, on railroad and 15 mi. W of Izmit; cotton and woolen goods.

Herekol Dag, Turkey: see HERAKOL DAG.
Herelen River, Mongolia: see KERULEN RIVER.
Herencia (ārĕn'syä), town (pop. 8,942), Ciudad Real prov., S central Spain, near Toledo prov. border, 40 mi. NE of Ciudad Real; agr. center on La Mancha plain (cereals, potatoes, grapes, olives, saffron). Olive-oil pressing, flour milling, cheese making, alcohol distilling; gypsum quarrying. Also exports wool.
Herencias, Las (läs ārĕn'syäs), village (pop. 1,332), Toledo prov., central Spain, on the Tagus and 7 mi. SW of Talavera de la Reina; grain, olives, grapes, cherries, melons, livestock.
Herend (hĕ'rĕnd), town (pop. 1,478), Veszprem co., NW central Hungary, on Sed R. and 8 mi. ENE of Veszprem; noted porcelain and faïence factories, founded 1837.
Herendeen Bay (hĕrŭndĕn'), village (1939 pop. 13), SW Alaska, on Alaska Peninsula, at head of Herendeen Bay, inlet (20 mi. long) of Bristol Bay of Bering Sea; 55°46'N 160°43'W; fishing. Surface coal veins in vicinity.
Hérens (ārā'), district (pop. 8,593), Valais canton, S Switzerland; extends W, E, and S of Val d'Hérens (valley watered by Borgne R.); includes commune of Ayent.
Herent (hā'rŭnt), town (pop. 8,421), Brabant prov., central Belgium, 2 mi. NNW of Louvain; ceramics. Just N is village of Wijchmaal (formerly spelled Wygmael); rice mills; food products.
Herentals (hā'rŭntäls), town (pop. 14,885), Antwerp prov., N Belgium, on Albert Canal and 18 mi. E of Antwerp; leather tanning, mfg. (shoes, leather products, electric bulbs), wool carding. Has 15th-cent. church, 16th-cent. town hall. Formerly spelled Herenthals.
Herenthout (hĕ'rŭnt-hout), town (pop. 5,092), Antwerp prov., NE Belgium, 15 mi. NE of Mechlin; agr. market (vegetables, potatoes).
Hereny (hĕ'rānyŭ), Hung. *Herény,* town (pop. 1,523), Vas co., W Hungary, 3 mi. NNW of Szombathely; flour mills.
Herfolge (hĕr'fŭlgŭ), Dan. *Herfølge,* town (pop. 1,023), Praesto amt, Zealand, Denmark, 21 mi. N of Praesto; pottery, cement.
Herford (hĕr'fôrt), city (1950 pop. 50,431), in former Prussian prov. of Westphalia, NW Germany, after 1945 in North Rhine-Westphalia, on the Werre and 9 mi. NE of Bielefeld; 52°7'N 8°40'E. Rail junction; mfg. of machinery, furniture, garments, cigars; food processing (sugar, chocolate). Has 11th–14th-cent. churches. Founded 823. Was member of Hanseatic League.
Hergiswil (hĕr'gĭsvēl"), resort town (pop. 2,437), Nidwalden half-canton, central Switzerland, on W shore of L. of Lucerne, at foot of the Pilatus, 4 mi. S of Lucerne; woodworking, glass.
Hergiswil bei Willisau (bīvĭ'lĭzou), town (pop. 2,-125), Lucerne canton, central Switzerland, on Enzwigger R. (affluent of Wigger R.) and 3 mi. SSW of Willisau; farming.
Herguijuela (ĕrgēhwä'lä), town (pop. 1,413), Cáceres prov., W Spain, 10 mi. SE of Trujillo; olive-oil processing; cereals, livestock.
Héricourt (ārēkōōr'), town (pop. 5,025), Haute-Saône dept., E France, in Belfort Gap, 7 mi. SW of Belfort; metalworking center; cotton milling. Scene of battle bet. Charles the Bold of Burgundy and the Swiss (1474) and of Franco-German engagement in 1871.
Hérimoncourt (ārēmōkōōr'), town (pop. 2,924), Doubs dept., E France, 6 mi. SE of Montbéliard; tool mfg., watchmaking.
Hérin (ārē'), residential town (pop. 3,549), Nord dept., N France, 3 mi. W of Valenciennes, in coal-mining dist.
Heringen (hā'rĭng-ŭn). **1** Village (pop. 4,459), in former Prussian prov. of Hesse-Nassau, W Germany, after 1945 in Hesse, on the Werra and 12 mi. E of Hersfeld; textiles. **2** or **Heringen an der Helme** (än dĕr hĕl'mŭ), town (pop. 3,185), in former Prussian Saxony prov., central Germany, after 1945 in Saxony-Anhalt, at S foot of the lower Harz, in Goldene Aue region, on the Helme and 6 mi. SE of Nordhausen; agr. market (grain, sugar beets, potatoes, livestock); flour milling.
Heringsdorf or **Seebad Heringsdorf** (zā'bät hā'rĭngsdôrf), village (pop. 2,616) in former Prussian Pomerania prov., E Germany, after 1945 in Mecklenburg, on NE shore of Usedom isl., 5 mi. NW of Swinemünde; popular seaside and health resort.
Herington, city (pop. 3,775), Dickinson co., central Kansas, 35 mi. ESE of Salina; shipping and trade center, with railroad repair shops, for livestock and grain area; cheese mfg. Monument to the missionary Juan de Padilla is here. Inc. 1887.
Hérinnes-lez-Pecq (ārĭn-lā-pĕk'), agr. village (pop. 1,563), Hainaut prov., SW Belgium, on Scheldt R. and 7 mi. N of Tournai.
Heri Rud, Afghanistan, Iran, and USSR: see HARI RUD.
Herisau (hā'rĭzou), town (1950 pop. 13,464), ⊙ Appenzell Ausser Rhoden half-canton, NE Switzerland, on Glatt R. (flows to Thur R.), 6 mi. SW of St. Gall; cotton textiles, embroideries, metal products; printing. Church (16th cent.). Health resorts, mtn. castles near by.
Hérisson (ārēsō'), village (pop. 611), Allier dept., central France, 13 mi. NNE of Montluçon; horse breeding. Has 15th-16th-cent. houses. Attracts painters.
Héristal, Belgium: see HERSTAL.
Herkimer (hûr'kŭmŭr), county (□ 1,442; pop. 61,407), central and N central N.Y.; ⊙ Herkimer. Long, narrow area, with N part extending into the Adirondacks, and S part in fertile Mohawk valley. Drained by Mohawk R., and by Unadilla, Black, and Moose rivers. Mfg., farming, and dairying in S. Many mtn. and lake resorts in N. Formed 1791.
Herkimer, industrial village (pop. 9,400), ⊙ Herkimer co., central N.Y., on Mohawk R. at mouth of West Canada Creek, and 13 mi. ESE of Utica; shipping, commercial, and trade center for surrounding Mohawk valley agr. and industrial area; mfg. (clothing, furniture, stone and paper products, footwear, machinery, hardware). Herkimer County Historical Society has important documents and exhibits here. Settled c.1725, inc. 1807.
Herkulesbad, Rumania: see BAILE-HERCULANE.
Herkulesfürdö, Rumania: see BAILE-HERCULANE.
Herlandsfoss (hăr'länsfôs), waterfall on small river on NW Osteroy, Hordaland co., SW Norway, 15 mi. NNE of Bergen; site of hydroelectric station serving Haus and Hosanger.
Herlany (hĕr'länĭ), Hung. *Rankfüred* (rŏngk'fürĕd), village, SE Slovakia, Czechoslovakia, in Presov Mts., 11 mi. NE of Kosice; health resort (alt. 1,312 ft.) with mineral springs and 130-ft. geyser.
Herlev (hĕr'lĕv), town (pop. 3,311), Copenhagen amt, Zealand, Denmark, 5 mi. W of Copenhagen.
Herlisheim, France: see HERRLISHEIM.
Herm (hûrm), island (320 acres; 1951 pop., including near-by Jethou isl., 49), one of Channel Isls., 2½ mi. E of Guernsey. Shell Beach, composed entirely of minute shells, is summer resort.
Hermagor (hĕr'mägôr), village (pop. 1,564), Carinthia, S Austria, near Gail R., 22 mi. W of Villach; leather goods, brewery.
Hermalle-sous-Argenteau (ĕrmäl'-sōōzärzhätō'), town (pop. 2,003), Liége prov., E Belgium, on Meuse R. and 7 mi. NE of Liége; coal mining. Has 12th-cent. castle, rebuilt in 17th cent., and church with tower built 1624.
Hermalle-sous-Huy (-sōō-wē'), village (pop. 1,-595), Liége prov., E central Belgium, 6 mi. ENE of Huy, near Meuse R.; chalk quarries, limekilns. Has 17th-cent. castle.
Herman. **1** Village (pop. 752), Grant co., W Minn., on small affluent of Mustinka R. and 15 mi. SW of Elbow Lake village, in grain, livestock, poultry area; dairy products. Numerous small lakes in vicinity. **2** Village (pop. 380), Washington co., E Nebr., 30 mi. NNW of Omaha, near Missouri R.; grain, livestock.
Hermann (hûr'mŭn), city (pop. 2,523), ⊙ Gasconade co., E central Mo., on Missouri R. and 41 mi. E of Jefferson City; mfg. (shoes, lumber products); flint, clay, diaspore mining. Inc. 1839.
Hermannsbad, Poland: see CIECHOCINEK.
Hermannsburg (hûr'mŭnzbŭrg), settlement, S central Northern Territory, Australia, 75 mi. WSW of Alice Springs, in Macdonnell Ranges. Ger. mission for aborigines; tourist center; sheep. Meteorite craters near by. Sometimes spelled Hermansburg.
Hermannsburg (hĕr'mänsbŏŏrk"), village (pop. 5,247), in former Prussian prov. of Hanover, NW Germany, after 1945 in Lower Saxony, 14 mi. N of Celle; mfg. of furniture, leather and wood products; bakery goods.
Hermannshöhle (hĕr'mäns-hû'lŭ), large stalactite cave, central Germany, in the lower Harz, S of Rübeland. Discovered 1866; fossil remains here.
Hermannstadt, Rumania: see SIBIU, city.
Hermanos, Los (lōs ĕrmä'nōs), small Caribbean island group and a federal dependency of Venezuela, E of Blanquilla isl., 50 mi. NW of Margarita Isl. Uninhabited; there are guano deposits.
Hermansburg, Australia: see HERMANNSBURG.
Hermansverk (hĕr'mänsvĕrk), village in Leikanger canton (pop. 2,601), Sogn og Fjordane co., W Norway, on N shore of Sogne Fjord, 10 mi. WSW of Sogndal; cans fruit, vegetables.
Hermansville, village (1940 pop. 874), Menominee co., SW Upper Peninsula, Mich., 24 mi. SE of Iron Mountain city and on Little Cedar R.; milling of hardwood flooring. Fox farm near by.
Hermanus (hûrmă'nŭs), town (pop. 4,490), SW Cape Prov., U. of So. Afr., on Walker Bay of the Atlantic, 55 mi. SE of Cape Town; fishing and seaside resort.
Hermanuv Mestec (hĕrzh'mänōōf myĕ'stĕts), Czech *Heřmanův Městec,* village (pop. 3,339), E Bohemia, Czechoslovakia, on railroad and 7 mi. SSE of Pardubice; shoe mfg.
Hermanville, village (pop. 255), Claiborne co., SW Miss., 8 mi. E of Port Gibson.
Hermel, Lebanon: see HERMIL.
Hermenault, L' (lĕrmnō'), village (pop. 478), Vendée dept., W France, 5 mi. NW of Fontenay-le-Comte; truck gardening.
Herment (ĕrmä'), village (pop. 326), Puy-de-Dôme dept., central France, in Auvergne Mts. 19 mi. NE of Ussel; cheese making.
Hermes (ârm), village (pop. 727), Oise dept., N France, on the Thérain and 9 mi. SE of Beauvais; brush and comb mfg., wood turning.
Hermeskeil (hĕr'mĕskīl"), village (pop. 3,344), in former Prussian Rhine Prov., W Germany, after 1945 in Rhineland-Palatinate, 16 mi. SE of Trier; rail junction on Saar border, opposite Nonnweiler.
Hermigua (ĕrmē'gwä), village (pop. 1,151), Gomera, Canary Isls., 7 mi. NW of San Sebastián; cereals, bananas, tomatoes, grapes, sugar cane, palm fibers; sheep. Flour milling, wine making.
Hermil (hĕr'mĭl) or **Hirmal** (hĭr'măl), Fr. *Hermel,* village (pop. 4,796), Bekaa prov., N Lebanon, near Syrian frontier, 60 mi. NE of Beirut; cereals, fruits. Also spelled Hirmil.
Herminie (hûr'mĭnē), village (pop. 2,072), Westmoreland co., SW Pa., 19 mi. SE of Pittsburgh.
Hermione or **Ermioni** (both: ĕrmēō'nē), town (pop. 2,868), Argolis and Corinthia nome, E Peloponnesus, Greece, port on Aegean Sea at SE end of Argolis Peninsula, 27 mi. ESE of Nauplia; iron pyrite deposits; stock raising (sheep, goats); fishing. Ruins include temple of Poseidon. Formerly called Kastri.
Hermiston, city (pop. 3,804), Umatilla co., N Oregon, 27 mi. NW of Pendleton, near Umatilla R., in poultry and truck-farming area of Columbia R. valley; dairy products, cattle medicines. Has branch agr. experiment station of Oregon State Col. Inc. 1910.
Hermitage, village (pop. 357), S N.F., on SE shore of Hermitage Bay, 80 mi. E of Burgeo; fishing; port with salmon canneries.
Hermitage. **1** Town (pop. 398), Bradley co., S Ark., 32 mi. ENE of El Dorado. **2** Town (pop. 204), ⊙ Hickory co., central Mo., in the Ozarks, on Pomme de Terre R. and 50 mi. N of Springfield.
Hermitage, home of Andrew Jackson, Davidson co., central Tenn., 12 mi. E of Nashville. The house, in a fine formal garden, was built 1819–31; a church on the grounds was built 1823. Jackson and his wife are buried in the plantation graveyard.
Hermitage Bay, inlet (30 mi. long, 10 mi. wide at entrance) of the Atlantic, S N.F.; 47°35'N 55°50'W. Many fishing settlements on its shores. N arm of Hermitage Bay is the Bay d'Espoir. Bay contains several isls.
Hermitage Castle, Scotland: see NEWCASTLETON.
Hermit Island, largest (13 mi. long, 5 mi. wide) of small group of 4 main islands and many rocks, in Tierra del Fuego, Chile, c.10 mi. NW of Cape Horn; Cape West is at 55°54'S 67°55'W.
Hermit Islands, small coral group (pop. c.30), Manus dist., Bismarck Archipelago, Territory of New Guinea, SW Pacific, 95 mi. WNW of Admiralty Isls.; c.5 isls. on reef 12 mi. long, 10 mi. wide; main isl. (Luf) is in lagoon; coconut plantations.
Hermleigh (hûrm'lē), town (pop. 671), Scurry co., NW central Texas, 10 mi. SE of Snyder; trade, shipping point for agr. and cattle-ranching area.
Hermon (hûr'mŭn). **1** Town (pop. 1,728), Penobscot co., S Maine, 7 mi. W of Bangor, in agr. area. Settled c.1790. **2** Village (pop. 547), St. Lawrence co., N N.Y., 20 mi. SE of Ogdensburg; cheese.
Hermon, Mount, Arabic *Jebel esh Sheikh* (jĕ'bĕl ĕsh-shākh') [mountain of the chief] or *Jebel eth Thelj* (ĕth-thĕlj') [snowy mountain], on Syria-Lebanon boundary, near Palestine line, 25 mi. WSW of Damascus; snow-capped massif rising to 9,232 ft., highest point in Anti-Lebanon mts. A sacred landmark in anc. Palestine, it is mentioned much in the Bible as Hermon, Sion, Senir, and Shenir. The Romans revered it, as did the Druses (a Druse shrine is near HASBEYA, in Lebanon). Anc. Caesarea Philippi was at its SW foot. The Arabic names for Mt. Hermon are also transliterated Jebel el Sheikh or Jabal al-Shaykh and Jebel el Thelj or Jabal al-Thalj.
Hermonthis, Egypt: see ARMANT.
Hermopolis, Greece: see HERMOUPOLIS.
Hermopolis Magna, Egypt: see ASHMUNEIN, EL.
Hermopolis Parva, Egypt: see DAMANHUR.
Hermosa (hûrmō'sŭ, Sp. ĕrmō'sä), town (1939 pop. 2,668; 1948 municipality pop. 8,437), Bataan prov., S Luzon, Philippines, at base of Bataan Peninsula, 36 mi. WNW of Manila; sugar cane, rice.
Hermosa, town (pop. 123), Custer co., SW S.Dak., 17 mi. S of Rapid City and on Battle Creek.
Hermosa Beach, resort and residential city (pop. 11,826), Los Angeles co., S Calif., 16 mi. SW of downtown Los Angeles, on Santa Monica Bay. Inc. 1907.
Hermosillo (ĕrmōsē'yō), city (pop. 18,601), ⊙ Sonora, NW Mexico, on Sonora R., on coastal plain of Gulf of California, on railroad and 220 mi. S of Tucson (Ariz.), 1,000 mi. NW of Mexico city; 29°4'N 110°58'W; alt. 778 ft. Situated in a generally hot, arid area. Commercial and shipping center for agr. area; produces tropical fruits (especially oranges), grain, corn, cotton. Outlet for the mtn. mining area (gold, copper, silver, molybdenum. It is a winter resort. Has foundries, shoe factory, brewery, food-processing plants, cold-storage plant. Industrial school, cathedral here. Guaymas, on Gulf of California, is its port.
Hermoso, Cerro (sĕ'rō ĕrmō'sō), Andean peak (15,-216 ft.), central Ecuador, 27 mi. ENE of Ambato; 1°10'S 78°14'W.
Hermoupolis or **Ermoupolis** (both: ĕrmōō'pôlĭs), also **Syros** or **Siros** (both: sē'rôs), city (1940 pop. 18,-925), ⊙ Cyclades nome, Greece, on E coast of Syros

isl., 75 mi. ESE of Athens; 37°26'N 24°56'E; major Aegean port, trading and commercial center. Shipbuilding; textile, glass, and leather industries. The old town, Ano [upper] Syros (1928 pop. 1,943), just N, dates from Venetian times. The new town (Hermoupolis) was founded (1820s) by refugees from Chios and Psara and developed rapidly as an Aegean transit port, eclipsed (late 19th cent.) by Piraeus. Sometimes spelled Hermopolis and Hermupolis.

Hermsdorf (hĕrms'dôrf), village (pop. 5,867), Thuringia, central Germany, 10 mi. W of Gera; china mfg., woodworking.

Hermsdorf, Poland: see SOBIECIN.

Hermupolis, Greece: see HERMOUPOLIS.

Hermus, town, Turkey: see GEDIZ.

Hermus River, Turkey: see GEDIZ RIVER.

Hernad River (hĕr'näd), Hung. *Hernád,* Slovak *Hornád* (hôr'nät), S Slovakia, Czechoslovakia, and NE Hungary, rises on N slope of the Low Tatra, 10 mi. SW of Poprad; flows E, past Spisska Nova Ves, and S, past Kosice, briefly along Czechoslovak-Hung. border, into Hungary, to Sajo R. SE of Miskolc. Length in Czechoslovakia, 105 mi.; total length, 165 mi.

Hernals (hĕrnäls'), outer NW district (□ 4; pop. 67,504) of Vienna, Austria.

Hernandarias (ĕrnändär'yäs), town (pop. estimate 1,500), W Entre Ríos prov., Argentina, port on Paraná R. and 70 mi. NE of Paraná. Limestone and gypsum works (deposits near by). Agr. (corn, wheat, livestock).

Hernandarias, town (dist. pop. 2,121), ⊙ Alto Paraná dept., E Paraguay, near upper Paraná R. (Brazil border), 190 mi. E of Asunción; 25°23'S 54°42'W. Maté, lumber, livestock. Formerly called Tacurupucú.

Hernández (ĕrnän'dĕs), town (pop. estimate 1,000), W Entre Ríos prov., Argentina, on railroad and 50 mi. SE of Paraná; flax, wheat, corn, livestock.

Hernando (ĕrnän'dō), town (pop. 4,753), central Córdoba prov., Argentina, 30 mi. W of Villa María; wheat, flax, corn, peanuts, sunflowers, fruit; flour milling.

Hernando (hûrnăn'dō), county (□ 488; pop. 6,693), W central Fla., bet. Withlacoochee R. (E) and Gulf of Mexico (W); ⊙ Brooksville. Lowland area with marshy coast and small scattered lakes. Agr. (poultry, cattle, hogs, corn, citrus fruit, peanuts); sawmilling; limestone quarrying. Formed 1843.

Hernando. 1 City (pop. 304), Citrus co., central Fla., 25 mi. SW of Ocala, on Tsala Apopka L.; fishing; phosphate quarrying. **2** Town (pop. 1,206), ⊙ De Soto co., extreme NW Miss., 22 mi. S of Memphis, Tenn; trade center for agr. region; sawmills, cotton gins. Arkabutla Reservoir is S. Inc. 1837.

Hernani (ĕrnä'nē), town (1939 pop. 968; 1948 municipality pop. 5,035), SE Samar isl., Philippines, on Philippine Sea, 60 mi. SE of Catbalogan; iron mining since 1934.

Hernani, town (pop. 2,356), Guipúzcoa prov., N Spain, on Urumea R. and 4 mi. S of San Sebastián; mfg. (paper, chemicals, cement, textiles). Lignite mines near by. Has Renaissance church. Played notable role in Carlist Wars (19th cent.).

Herndon. 1 City (pop. 321), Rawlins co., NW Kansas, on Beaver Creek and 16 mi. ENE of Atwood, near Nebr. line; grain, livestock. **2** Borough (pop. 677), Northumberland co., E central Pa., 11 mi. SSW of Sunbury and on Susquehanna R.; lumber, hosiery mfg. **3** Town (pop. 1,461), Fairfax co., N Va., 20 mi. WNW of Washington, D.C., in agr., dairying area. Inc. 1874; rechartered 1938.

Herne (hûrn), town and parish (pop. 2,269), NE Kent, England, near Thames estuary just S of Herne Bay; agr. market. Has 14th-cent. church where Nicholas Ridley later was a vicar.

Herne (hĕr'nū), city (1950 pop. 111,249), in former Prussian prov. of Westphalia, W Germany, after 1945 in North Rhine-Westphalia, in the Ruhr, port on Rhine-Herne Canal, adjoining (S) Bochum; coal-mining center; coke ovens, foundries; textile mfg. Has Renaissance castle with Gothic chapel. Chartered 1897.

Herne Bay (hûrn), urban district (1931 pop. 11,249; 1951 census 18,298), NE Kent, England, on Thames estuary, 7 mi. NNE of Canterbury; bathing resort, with pier and long esplanade.

Herne Hill (hûrn), residential district of Camberwell, London, England, S of the Thames, 4 mi. SSW of Charing Cross.

Herning (hĕr'nĭng), city (pop. 16,285), Ringkobing amt, W central Jutland, Denmark, 28 mi. E of Ringkobing; rail junction; machinery mfg., peat- and brickworks.

Hernosand, Sweden: see HARNOSAND.

Herod, town (pop. 126), Terrell co., SW Ga., 6 mi. S of Dawson.

Heroldsberg (hā'rôltsbĕrk"), village (pop. 3,513), Middle Franconia, N central Bavaria, Germany, 7 mi. NE of Nuremberg; woodworking, brewing. Hogs, horse-radish.

Heron Island, largest of Capricorn Isls., in Coral Sea, 40 mi. off Cape Capricorn on SE coast of Queensland, Australia; 5 mi. long, 2 mi. wide. Most southerly tourist resort within Great Barrier Reef; densely wooded; coral gardens.

Heron Lake, village (pop. 837), Jackson co., SW Minn., at N end of Heron L., 21 mi NW of Jackson, in grain, livestock, poultry area; dairy products.

Heron Lake (□ 13), Jackson co., SW Minn., 20 mi. NE of Worthington; 12 mi. long, 3 mi. wide. Has N outlet into Des Moines R. Abundance of game here.

Herowabad, Iran: see KHALKHAL.

Heroya (hăr'ûyä), Nor. *Herøya,* village (pop. 839) in Eidanger canton, Telemark co., S Norway, on Skien R., just SW of Porsgrunn; electrochemical works produce basic chemicals, magnesium, plastics.

Herpelje-Kozina (hĕr'pĕlyĕ-kô'zēnä), Ital. *Erpelle-Cosina* (ĕrpĕl'lĕ kôzē'nä), rail junction, SW Slovenia, Yugoslavia, 8 mi. ESE of Trieste. Until 1947, in Italy.

Herradura (ĕrädōō'rä), town (pop. estimate 700), ⊙ Laishi dept. (□ c.1,300; 1947 pop. 6,452), E Formosa natl. territory, Argentina, on Paraguay R. at mouth of the Río Salado, and 23 mi. SSW of Formosa. Agr. (corn, rice, cotton) and livestock center; lumbering.

Herradura, Cape, on the Pacific, in W Costa Rica, at entrance to Gulf of Nicoya; 9°38'N 84°41'W.

Herradura, La, Chile: see LA HERRADURA.

Herradura, La, Peru: see CHORILLOS.

Herradura, La, Salvador: see LA HERRADURA.

Herrang (hĕr'ĕng"), Swedish *Herräng,* village (pop. 600), Stockholm co., E Sweden, on Gulf of Bothnia, 40 mi. ENE of Uppsala; iron mines, smelters, and foundries. Mines, operated since 1584, are oldest in Sweden.

Herreid (hĕr'ĕd), city (pop. 633), Campbell co., N S.Dak., 80 mi. WNW of Aberdeen and on Spring Creek; grain, livestock, poultry.

Herrenalb (hĕ'rūnälp'), town (pop. 2,098), S Württemberg, Germany, after 1945 in Württemberg-Hohenzollern, in Black Forest, 14 mi. S of Karlsruhe; climatic health resort (alt. 1,204 ft.) with cold-water cures. Has ruins of anc. Cistercian abbey (destroyed 1642).

Herrenberg (hĕ'rūnbĕrk), town (pop. 5,605), N Württemberg, Germany, after 1945 in Württemberg-Baden, 10 mi. NW of Tübingen; rail junction: grain, cattle. Has 14th–15th-cent. church.

Herrenbreitungen, Germany: see BREITUNGEN.

Herrenleite Germany: see WEHLEN.

Herrera (ĕrā'rä), town (pop. estimate 500), ⊙ Avellaneda dept. (□ c.1,500; 1947 pop. 20,580), central Santiago del Estero prov., Argentina, near the Río Salado, on railroad, and 13 mi. W of Añatuya; agr. center (alfalfa, livestock).

Herrera, prov. (□ 568; 1950 pop. 49,960), S central Panama, on the Pacific; ⊙ Chitré. Occupies NE part of Azuero Peninsula and is bounded (N) by Santa María R. Important livestock region; agr. (corn, rice, beans, vegetables); gold mining in Los Pozos, Las Minas. Crossed by a branch of Inter-American Highway. Main centers are Chitré, Ocú, and Parita. Originally formed (1855) out of old Azuero prov.; was combined with Los Santos prov. (1864–1915, 1941–45).

Herrera, town (pop. 7,187), Seville prov., SW Spain, near Granada prov. border, 18 mi. ENE of Osuna; agr. center (olives, olive oil, cereals); liquor distilling, mfg. of plaster. Hydroelectric plant near by.

Herrera de Alcántara (dhā älkän'tärä), town (pop. 1,286), Cáceres prov., W Spain, near Tagus R. and Port. border, 15 mi. SSE of Castelo Branco (Portugal); cereals, livestock.

Herrera del Duque (dhĕl dōō'kā), town (pop. 4,429), Badajoz prov., W Spain, 75 mi. ENE of Mérida; agr. center (cereals, olives, grapes, cork, livestock); apiculture. Mineral springs.

Herrera de Pisuerga (dhā pēswĕr'gä), city (pop. 2,502), Palencia prov., N central Spain, near Pisuerga R., 43 mi. NNE of Palencia; tanning, flour- and sawmilling, mfg. of ceramics and burlap; ships cereals, potatoes, fruit.

Herreras, Los, Mexico: see LOS HERRERAS.

Herreruela de Oropesa (ĕrärwā'lä dhā ōrōpā'sä), village (pop. 1,031), Toledo prov., central Spain, 22 mi. W of Talavera de la Reina; cereals, grapes, sheep, hogs, cattle.

Herrick, village, NE Tasmania, 45 mi. NE of Launceston; rail terminus; sawmills.

Herrick. 1 Village (pop. 554), Shelby co., central Ill., 19 mi. NNE of Vandalia, in bituminous-coal and agr. area; hound-breeding kennels. **2** Town (pop. 169), Gregory co., S S.Dak., 7 mi. SE of Burke; small trading point for agr. area.

Herrieden (hĕ'rē"dŭn), town (pop. 1,851), Middle Franconia, W Bavaria, Germany, on the Altmühl and 5 mi. SW of Ansbach; potatoes, rye, oats, cattle, hogs.

Herrin, city (pop. 9,331), Williamson co., S Ill., c.55 mi. NNE of Cairo; trade center of bituminous-coal-mining area; agr. (corn, livestock; dairy products); lumber. Settled 1818, inc. 1900. Site of "Herrin Massacre" (1922), local clash in country-wide coal strike, which resulted in death of about 25 persons.

Herringen (hĕ'rĭng-ŭn), village (pop. 12,967), in former Prussian prov. of Westphalia, W Germany, after 1945 in North Rhine-Westphalia, in the Ruhr, near Lippe Lateral Canal, 3 mi. WSW of Hamm.

Herrings, village (pop. 192), Jefferson co., N N.Y., near Black R., 13 mi. E of Watertown; paper milling. Post office name formerly Herring.

Herrington Lake, Ky.: see DIX RIVER.

Herrliberg (hĕr'lēbĕrk"), town (pop. 2,002), Zurich canton, N Switzerland, on L. of Zurich and 7 mi. SSE of Zurich.

Herrlisheim (ĕrlēzĕm'), Ger. *Herlisheim* (hĕr'lĭshīm), town (pop 2,020), Bas-Rhin dept., E France, on the Zorn and 8 mi. SE of Haguenau, near Ger. border; hop growing.

Herrljunga (hĕr'yŭng"ä), village (pop. 1,909), Alvsborg co., SW Sweden, 20 mi. ENE of Alingsas; rail junction; woolen and lumber milling; mfg. of clothing, pianos.

Herrnburg (hĕrn'bŏŏrk), village (pop. 977), Mecklenburg, N Germany, 4 mi. ESE of Lübeck.

Herrnhut (hĕrn'hōōt'), town (pop. 2,024), Saxony, E central Germany, near the Neisse, in Upper Lusatia, 8 mi. NNW of Zittau; linen and woolen milling. Chief seat of the community of Moravian Brothers, founded 1722; has theological seminary.

Herrnsheim (hĕrns'hīm), village (pop. 451), Lower Franconia, W Bavaria, Germany, 17 mi. SE of Würzburg; grain, poultry.

Herrnstadt, Poland: see WASOSZ.

Herrsching (hĕr'shĭng), village (pop. 3,864), Upper Bavaria, Germany, on E shore of the Ammersee, 7.5 mi. W of Starnberg; textile mfg.; summer resort. S (1.5 mi.) is Andechs, with former Benedictine priory and 15th-cent. pilgrimage church.

Herrumblar, El (ĕl ĕrōōmblär'), town (pop. 927), Cuenca prov., E central Spain, 31 mi. NNE of Albacete; cereals, saffron, grapes, vetch, sheep, goats; lumbering.

Hers, river, France: see HERS RIVER.

Hersbruck (hĕrs'brŏŏk), town (pop. 8,323), Middle Franconia, N central Bavaria, Germany, on the Pegnitz and 7 mi. E of Lauf; mfg. of chemicals, precision instruments, metal products, textiles; woodworking, printing, brewing. Hops. Chartered c.1235. Sandstone quarries in area.

Herschel (hûr'shŭl), administrative district (□ 684; total pop. 48,394; native pop. 46,892), E Cape Prov., U. of So. Afr., on S Basutoland border, in Wittebergen mts., 30 mi. E of Aliwal North. Administered by local native-affairs council, established 1930, part of Ciskeian General Council. Cattle raising is chief occupation.

Herschel Island (11 mi. long, 2–7 mi. wide), N Yukon, in Beaufort Sea of the Arctic Ocean, on W side of entrance of Mackenzie Bay; 69°35'N 139°5'W. Herschel village, on E coast, has Royal Canadian Mounted Police post.

Herscher (hûr'shûr), village (pop. 515), Kankakee co., NE Ill., 13 mi. WSW of Kankakee, in agr. area.

Herseaux (ĕrsō'), Flemish *Herzeeuw* (hĕr'zāōō), town (pop. 7,088), West Flanders prov., W Belgium, 8 mi. S of Courtrai, near Fr. border; textiles.

Hersek, region, Yugoslavia: see HERZEGOVINA.

Herselt (hĕr'sŭlt), town (pop. 6,263), Antwerp prov., NE Belgium, 15 mi. NE of Louvain; agr. market (vegetables, potatoes).

Herserange (ârsûräzh'), E suburb (pop. 5,525) of Longwy, Meurthe-et-Moselle dept., NE France, near Luxembourg border, in iron-mining dist. of Longwy.

Hersey. 1 Town (pop. 116), Aroostook co., E Maine, 28 mi. WSW of Houlton. **2** Village (pop. 239), Osceola co., central Mich., 11 mi. N of Big Rapids and on Muskegon R., in lake and agr. area.

Hersfeld (hĕrs'fĕlt), city (pop. 19,625), in former Prussian prov. of Hesse-Nassau, W Germany, after 1945 in Hesse, on the Fulda and 32 mi. SSE of Kassel; 50°53'N 9°42'E. Rail junction; resort with mineral springs. Mfg.: textiles (jute, cloth, yarn, clothing), machinery, precision and optical instruments, plywood. Potash plants. Has ruins of large Romanesque abbey church, burned by French in 1761. Hersfeld developed around 8th-cent. Benedictine abbey, which was secularized and given to Hesse-Kassel in 1648.

Hersham, England: see WALTON AND WEYBRIDGE.

Hershey or **Central Hershey,** sugar-milling town (pop. 1,070), Havana prov., W Cuba, on railroad and 26 mi. E of Havana.

Hershey. 1 Village (pop. 573), Lincoln co., SW central Nebr., 12 mi. W of North Platte city and on S.Platte R.; sugar beets, livestock, grain. **2** Village (pop. 6,076, with adjacent Swatara Station), Dauphin co., S central Pa., 12 mi. E of Harrisburg. Owned by Hershey company; manufactures chocolate products. Dairying. Founded 1903.

Hersin, Iran: see HARSIN.

Hersin-Coupigny (ĕrsē'-kōōpēnyē'), town (pop. 5,989), Pas-de-Calais dept., N France, 6 mi. S of Béthune; coal mines; lime- and cementworks.

Hers River (âr), Ariège dept., S France, rises 3 mi. N of Ax-les-Thermes, flows 75 mi. NNW, past Bélesta and Mirepoix, to the Ariège above Cintegabelle. Pop. in Hers valley specializes in comb mfg. Formerly called Lhers.

Herstal (hĕrs'täl), Fr. *Héristal* (ārĕstäl'), town (pop. 27,092), Liége prov., E Belgium, on Meuse R. and Liége-Maastricht Canal, 3 mi. NE of Liége; firearms-mfg. center; motorcycles, electrical equipment (motors, transformers). Pepin of Héristal, 7th-cent. ruler of Frankish empire, b. here.

Herstelle (hĕr'shtĕ"lü), village (pop. 1,530), in former Prussian prov. of Westphalia, NW Germany, after 1945 in North Rhine-Westphalia, on left bank of the Weser and 2 mi. W of Karlshafen. Mentioned as early as 8th cent.

Herstmonceux, England: see HURSTMONCEUX.

Herta, Ukrainian SSR: see GERTSA.

Herten (hĕr'tün), town (pop. 35,704), in former Prussian prov. of Westphalia, W Germany, after 1945 in North Rhine-Westphalia, in the Ruhr, just W of Recklinghausen; mfg. of mining and agr. machinery, paper products; food processing (meat products, preserves). Coal mining. Has 16th-cent. castle. Chartered 1936.

Hertford or **Hertfordshire** (här'fůrd, härt'fůrd, -shĭr), county (□ 632.1; 1931 pop. 401,206; 1951 census 609,735), S England; ⊙ Hertford. Bounded by Buckingham (W), Bedford (NW), Cambridge (N), Essex (E), and Middlesex (S). Drained by Colne, Lea, Stort, and Gade rivers. Hilly, with pastures; dairying, fruitgrowing, truck gardening. There are various light industries, including making of motion pictures (Elstree). Urban areas are mostly residential; S part of co. is part of London suburban dist. Besides Hertford, other towns are St. Albans, dating from Roman times, Watford, Hemel Hempstead, Great Berkhampstead, Hitchin, and the garden cities of Welwyn Garden City and Letchworth. Shortened form for co. is Herts (härts).

Hertford, municipal borough (1931 pop. 11,378; 1951 census 13,890), ⊙ Hertfordshire, England, in E center of co., on the Lea and 20 mi. N of London; 51°48'N 0°5'W; agr. market, with flour mills, leatherworks, and electrical engineering industry. An important town in Saxon times; the Archbishop of Canterbury convened 1st natl. church council here in 673. Near by is a leading public school, Haileybury Col., founded 1805 by East Indian Company for training of its personnel, reestablished as public school (1862) by royal charter. Also near by are large orphanage and sanitarium. The castle, built c.905 and later rebuilt, was taken by French in 1216; one-time prison of John II of France and David, king of Scotland. It was royal castle until time of Charles I.

Hertford (hûrt'fůrd), county (□ 356; pop. 21,453), NE N.C.; ⊙ Winton. Bounded N by Va., E by Chowan R.; coastal plain (W) and tidewater (E); drained by Meherrin R. Agr. (peanuts, tobacco, cotton, corn); timber (pine, gum, oak). Formed 1759.

Hertford, town (pop. 2,096), ⊙ Perquimans co., NE N.C., 16 mi. SW of Elizabeth City and on Perquimans R.; sawmilling, fishing. Settled before 1700; inc. 1758.

Hertfordshire, England: see HERTFORD, county.

Hertogenbosch, 's, Netherlands: see 's HERTOGENBOSCH.

Herts, England: see HERTFORD, county.

Hertseliya, Israel: see HERZLIYA.

Hertzig, Belgium: see HACHY.

Herut or **Heruth** (both: hĕrōōt'), settlement (pop. 500), W Israel, in Plain of Sharon, 7 mi. NE of Herzliya; citriculture, mixed farming, flower growing. Founded 1930.

Herval, city, Brazil: see ERVAL.

Herval, Serra do, Brazil: see ERVAL, SERRA DO.

Hervás (ĕrväs'), town (pop. 4,097), Cáceres prov., W Spain, 10 mi. SW of Béjar; meat processing center (sausage, cured hams); mfg. of wool textiles, furniture, brandy; sawmilling; pepper shipping. Livestock, wine, fruit in area. Mineral springs.

Herve (ârv), town (pop. 3,761), Liége prov., E Belgium, 9 mi. E of Liége; market center for fruitgrowing, dairying region.

Hervey Bay, inlet of Pacific Ocean, SE Queensland, Australia, bet. Sandy Cape of Fraser Isl. (forming E shore) and Burnett Head; 50 mi. long, 35 mi. wide. Receives Burnett and Mary rivers.

Hervey Island: see MANUAE; COOK ISLANDS.

Herwen (hĕr'vůn), village (pop. 274), Gelderland prov., E Netherlands, 11 mi. SE of Arnhem; brick mfg.; agr.

Herxheim (hĕrks'hīm), village (pop. 5,695), Rhenish Palatinate, W Germany, 6 mi. SE of Landau; wine; also sugar beets, tobacco.

Héry (hārē'), village (pop. 1,006), Yonne dept., N central France, 8 mi. NNE of Auxerre; explosives mfg.

Herzberg (hĕrts'bĕrk). **1** or **Herzberg am Harz** (äm härts'), town (pop. 8,318), in former Prussian prov. of Hanover, W Germany, after 1945 in Lower Saxony, at S foot of the upper Harz, 6 mi. SE of Osterode; rail junction; mfg. (textiles, furniture, metal and wood products, paper). Has 16th-cent. castle. Was seat (1286–1596) of princes of Brunswick-Grubenhagen. **2** or **Herzberg an der Elster** (än dĕr ĕl'stůr), town (pop. 6,635), in former Prussian Saxony prov., central Germany, after 1945 in Saxony-Anhalt, on isl. formed by 2 arms of the Black Elster, 13 mi. NE of Torgau; metalworking, textile milling; mfg. of chemicals, furniture.

Herzebrock (hĕr'tsůbrôk), village (pop. 5,477), in former Prussian prov. of Westphalia, NW Germany, after 1945 in North Rhine-Westphalia, 6 mi. WSW of Gütersloh; hog raising.

Herzeeuw, Belgium: see HERSEAUX.

Herzegovina (hĕrtsůgōvē'nů), Serbo-Croatian *Hercegovina,* Turk. *Hersek* (hĕr'sĕk), S region (□ c.3,500; pop. c.315,000) of BOSNIA AND HERZEGOVINA, Yugoslavia, nearly coextensive with Mostar oblast; chief city, Mostar. Bounded E by Montenegro, N by Bosnia, W by Dalmatia, which separates it from the Adriatic except for narrow corridor extending to Neum on Neretva Channel. Generally mountainous; drained by Neretva R. Region originally called Hum; independent, except for brief intervals, after 10th cent.; passed (1284) under Serbian rule and (1325) to Bosnia. Resumed (1435) brief independence as a duchy (Herzegovina). Under Turkish rule (after 1483); it finally became part of Bosnia.

Herzliya or **Herzlia** (both: hĕrtslē'ä), settlement (1949 pop. 9,000), W Israel, in Plain of Sharon, near Mediterranean, on railroad and 8 mi. NE of Tel Aviv; health resort; agr. center in citrus-growing region; textile mills. Founded 1924. Sometimes spelled Hertseliya.

Herzogenaurach (hĕr'tsō"gůnou'räkh"), town (pop. 6,568), Upper Franconia, N Bavaria, Germany, 6 mi. WSW of Erlangen; mfg. of shoes, cloth, dyes; brewing. Has Gothic church.

Herzogenbuchsee (hĕr'tsōgůnbōōkh'zā), town (pop. 3,255), Bern canton, NW Switzerland, 8 mi. E of Solothurn; shoes, silk textiles, flour; tanning, metalworking, canning.

Herzogenburg (hĕrtsō'gůnbōōrk), town (pop. 4,671), central Lower Austria, on Traisen R. and 6 mi. NNE of Sankt Pölten; rail junction. Old abbey with large library.

Herzogenhorn, Germany: see BELCHEN.

Herzogenrath (hĕr'tsō"gůnrät'), village (pop. 8,193), in former Prussian Rhine Prov., W Germany, after 1945 in North Rhine-Westphalia, 6 mi. N of Aachen, opposite Kerkrade (Netherlands); rail junction; glassworks.

Hes, Yemen: see HAIS.

Hesarak, Iran: see HISARAK.

Hesban (hĕs'băn) or **Husban** (hōōs'băn), village, N central Jordan, 12 mi. SW of Amman; grain (wheat, barley), fruit. It was the biblical Heshbon.

Hesdin (ādē'), town (pop. 2,791), Pas-de-Calais dept., N France, on the Canche and 13 mi. ESE of Montreuil; road junction and market center; woodworking, tanning, hosiery mfg. Founded by Charles V in 1554; has 16th-cent. Gothic church and 17th-cent. town hall. Abbé Prévost b. here.

Heshbon, Jordan: see HESBAN.

Hesketh with Becconsall, parish (pop. 1,546), W Lancashire, England. Includes village of Hesketh Bank, near Ribble R. estuary 7 mi. WSW of Preston; dairy farming; wheat, barley, potatoes.

Hesket in the Forest, parish (pop. 1,822), central Cumberland, England. Includes cattle- and sheep-raising village of High Hesket, on Eden R. and 9 mi. NNW of Penrith, with 16th-cent. church and excavations which have yielded Viking arms. Just NNW is Low Hesket, on Eden R.

Hespeler (hĕ'spůlůr), town (pop. 3,058), S Ont., on Speed R. and 6 mi. N of Galt, in stock-raising region; woolen and flour mills; granite quarrying.

Hesperange (hĕspärăzh'), village (pop. 952), S Luxembourg, on Alzette R. and 3 mi. SSE of Luxembourg city; furniture mfg.; cherry growing.

Hesperia (hĕspēr'ēů), village (pop. 760), on Oceana-Newaygo co. line, W Mich., 26 mi. NNE of Muskegon and on White R., in resort and fruitgrowing area.

Hesperus (hĕ'spůrůs), village, La Plata co., SW Colo., on La Plata R. and 12 mi. W of Durango; seat of Fort Lewis Agr. and Mechanical Col.

Hesperus Peak (13,225 ft.), SW Colo., in La Plata Mts., 16 mi. NW of Durango.

Hess, Mount (12,030 ft.), E Alaska, in Alaska Range, 80 mi. S of Fairbanks; 63°37'N 147°6'W.

Hesse (hĕ'sē, hĕs), Ger. *Hessen* (hĕ'sůn), state (□ 8,153; 1946 pop. 3,995,678, including displaced persons 4,064,075; 1950 pop. 4,303,920), W Germany; ⊙ Wiesbaden. Formed 1945 through union of former Prussian prov. of HESSE-NASSAU (except MONTABAUR, which was ceded to Rhineland-Palatinate) and of former state of Hesse (see HESSE-DARMSTADT), except for left-bank RHENISH HESSE. Bounded by Württemberg-Baden (S), Rhineland-Palatinate (W), North Rhine-Westphalia (N), Thuringia (E), and Bavaria (E, SE). Consisting primarily of uplands, it includes the ODENWALD (SE), RHENISH SLATE MOUNTAINS (W, NW), and RHÖN MOUNTAINS (E). Drained by Rhine, Main, Lahn, Sieg (SW), Eder, Fulda, and Werra (NE) rivers. Heavily forested, except in Rhine plain (SW) and Frankfurt basin (center); cattle raised on numerous pastures; agr. (grain, potatoes) of secondary importance, only the BERGSTRASSE (fruit), the RHEINGAU (noted wine region), and region N of Hanau being really fertile. Mining: iron ore in valleys of the Lahn and the Dill, lignite in Kassel dist., potash around HERSFELD; fireclay quarries near GROSSALMERODE. Industries (metallurgy, machinery, chemicals) at FRANKFURT (Höchst), DARMSTADT, DILLENBURG, FULDA, GIESSEN, KASSEL, WETZLAR; HANAU is noted for its jewelry, OFFENBACH for leather goods. Frankfurt is commercial and financial center. The TAUNUS is frequented tourist region with numerous spas (WIESBADEN, BAD HOMBURG, BAD NAUHEIM, BAD SCHWALBACH, NIEDERSELTERS). Univ. at Frankfurt and MARBURG. Enfeoffed to dukes of Franconia and later to counts of Thuringia, Hesse emerged (1247) as landgraviate under a branch of house of Brabant. Territory was considerably enlarged (1479) through addition of county of Katzenellenbogen. At death (1567) of Landgrave Philip the Magnanimous, Hesse was divided among his 4 sons, the capitals being at Darmstadt, Kassel, Marburg and Rheinfels (see SANKT GOAR). Upon failure, shortly thereafter, of Marburg and Rheinfels lines, history of Hesse becomes that of Hesse-Darmstadt and HESSE-KASSEL. After capture (spring, 1945) of region by Americans, most of territory was constituted into state of Hesse (briefly known as Greater Hesse, Ger. *Gross-Hessen*) in U.S. occupation zone. New constitution ratified 1946. Joined (1949) the German Federal Republic (the West German state).

Hesse, Grand Duchy of, Germany: see HESSE-DARMSTADT.

Hesse-Cassel, Germany: see HESSE-KASSEL.

Hesse-Darmstadt (hĕ'sē-därm'shtät, -stăt, hĕs'-), Ger. *Hessen-Darmstadt* (hĕ'sůn-därm'shtät), former grand duchy of Germany. Formed 1567 at division of HESSE; ⊙ was DARMSTADT. Originally it comprised only small portion of territory inherited (1479) by Hessian landgraves. Was enlarged (1583, 1604) through addition of part of Hessen-Rheinfels (see SANKT GOAR) and Hessen-MARBURG. In 1622 the Homburg (see BAD HOMBURG) line branched off. Landgraves assumed (1806) grand ducal title; received considerable territory at Congress of Vienna. After HESSE-KASSEL was absorbed (1866) by Prussia, Hesse-Darmstadt (comprising provs. of RHENISH HESSE, STARKENBURG, and UPPER HESSE) became known simply as Hesse. Joined (1871) German Empire. Grand dukes (related through marriage with ruling houses of Great Britain and Russia) abdicated 1918. State of Hesse [Ger. *Volksstaat Hessen*] (□ 2,969; 1939 pop. 1,469,215) was constituted 1919. After capture by Americans (spring, 1945), the state, with exception of left-bank Rhenish Hesse, was inc. into new state of Hesse in U.S. occupation zone.

Hesse-Kassel or **Hesse-Cassel** (both: hĕ'sē-kä'sůl, hĕs'-), Ger. *Hessen-Kassel* or *Hessen-Cassel* (both: hĕ'sůn-kä'sůl), or **Electoral Hesse,** Ger. *Kurhessen* (kōōr"hĕ'sůn), former landgraviate of Germany. Formed 1567 at division of HESSE; ⊙ was KASSEL. Protestant landgraves subsequently increased their domain through acquisition of SCHMALKALDEN (1583) and part of Hessen-Rheinfels (see SANKT GOAR), part of Hessen-MARBURG (1604), Hersfeld and half of SCHAUMBURG (1648–49), and Fulda (1815). In 18th cent., rulers improved financial position by letting mercenaries for hire; many Hessians fought for British in American Revolution. Landgraves received (1803) electoral title; during 1807–13, Electoral Hesse formed part of kingdom of Westphalia. Congress of Vienna brought substantial territorial gains. Having sided with Austria in Austro-Prussian War (1866), Electoral Hesse was annexed to Prussia and became the administrative division [Ger. *Regierungsbezirk*] (□ 4-204; 1939 pop. 1,213,685) of Kassel in newly created prov. of HESSE-NASSAU. Was constituted briefly (1944–45) as separate Prussian prov. of Kurhessen (□ 3,552; pop. 971,887). After capture (spring, 1945) by Americans, it was inc. into new state of Hesse in U.S. occupation zone.

Hessel, resort village (pop. c.200), Mackinac co., SE Upper Peninsula, Mich., 17 mi. NE of St. Ignace, on L. Huron. A gateway to Les Cheneaux Isls. (just SE).

Hesselberg (hĕ'sůlbĕrk), highest elevation (2,260 ft.) of the Swabian Jura, Bavaria, Germany, 8 mi. E of Dinkelsbühl.

Hessen, Germany: see HESSE.

Hessen, Volksstaat, Germany: see HESSE-DARMSTADT.

Hesse-Nassau (hĕ'sē-nä'sô, hĕs'-), Ger. *Hessen-Nassau* (hĕ'sůn-nä'sou), former province (□ 6,505; 1939 pop. 2,675,111) of Prussia, W Germany, after 1945 included in HESSE (with exception of MONTABAUR); ⊙ was Kassel. Formed (1867–68) through union of HESSE-KASSEL, NASSAU, free city of FRANKFURT, Hesse-Homburg (see BAD HOMBURG)—all annexed to Prussia in 1866 as result of siding with Austria in Austro-Prussian War—and several other small territories. WALDECK was inc. in 1929. Prov. was divided 1944 into 2 separate provs., Nassau and Kurhessen (see HESSE-KASSEL).

Hessen-Cassel, Germany: see HESSE-KASSEL.

Hessen-Homburg, Germany: see BAD HOMBURG.

Hessen-Kassel, Germany: see HESSE-KASSEL.

Hessen-Marburg, Germany: see MARBURG.

Hessen-Nassau, Germany: see HESSE-NASSAU.

Hessen-Rheinfels, Germany: see SANKT GOAR.

Hessisch Lichtenau (hĕ'sĭsh lĭkh'tůnou), town (pop. 4,006), in former Prussian prov. of Hesse-Nassau, W Germany, after 1945 in Hesse, 12 mi. SE of Kassel; cotton weaving.

Hessisch Oldendorf (ôl'důndôrf), town (pop. 4,336), in former Prussian prov. of Hanover, W Germany, after 1945 in Lower Saxony, at S foot of Weser

Mts., near right bank of the Weser, 6 mi. NW of Hameln. Belonged to former Prussian prov. of Hesse-Nassau until 1932.

Hessle (hĕ'sŭl, hĕ'zŭl), residential former urban district (1931 pop. 6,429), East Riding, SE Yorkshire, England, on Humber R. and 4 mi. WSW of Hull. Has 13th-15th-cent. church. Inc. 1935 in Haltemprice.

Hesston, city (pop. 686), Harvey co., S central Kansas, 30 mi. NNW of Wichita, in wheat region. Has jr. col.

Hestan Island, islet in Solway Firth, just off S Kirkcudbright, Scotland, 7 mi. S of Dalbeattie; lighthouse (54°50'N 3°48'W).

Hester, town (pop. 31), Greer co., SW Okla., 6 mi. SSE of Mangum, near North Fork of Red R.

Hestmanoy (hĕst'män-ûü), Nor. *Hestmanøy* or *Hestmannen* [=horseman isl.], island (□ 4; pop. 182) in North Sea, on Arctic Circle, Nordland co., N central Norway, 40 mi. WNW of Mo; rises to 1,863 ft. in Hestman mtn., connected with folk legends.

Hesto (hĕ'stû), Dan. *Hestø*, Faeroese *Hestur*, island (□ 2; pop. 104) of the N Faeroe Isls., separated from SW Stromo by Hesto Fjord; highest point 1,401 ft. Fishing, sheep raising.

Heston and Isleworth (ī'zŭlwûrth), residential municipal borough (1931 pop. 75,460; 1951 census 106,636), Middlesex, England, W suburb of London. Includes town of Heston, 11 mi. W of London, with foundries, pharmaceutical works, and market gardens. Has 15th-cent. church. In municipal borough are towns of: Isleworth, with mfg. of paint, soap, vehicles, and flour; Hounslow (houns'lō), with foundries, formerly important coach stop on road to Southampton and Bath, and noted resort of highwaymen; and Osterley, site of 18th-cent. mansion of Osterley Park, belonging to earl of Jersey. Also in the borough is HEATH ROW, site of major airport.

Hestur, Faeroe Isls.: see HESTO.

Het Bildt or **Het Bilt,** Netherlands: see 'T BILDT.

Hetch Hetchy Valley, E central Calif., in Yosemite Natl. Park, on Tuolumne R.; reservoir here supplies water (via 156-mi. Hetch Hetchy Aqueduct) and power to San Francisco. O'Shaughnessy (or Hetch Hetchy) Dam (built 1923; 840 ft. long; enlarged to height of 430 ft. in 1938) turned the valley into a lake 7 mi. long.

Heteren (hā'tŭrŭn), village (pop. 834), Gelderland prov., central Netherlands, on Lower Rhine R. and 7 mi. WSW of Arnhem; brick mfg.; jam, syrups; fruit growing and canning; tree nurseries.

Hethersett, town and parish (pop. 1,241), central Norfolk, England, 5 mi. WSW of Norwich; agr. market, with farm-implement works. Has 14th-cent. church.

Hetland, town (pop. 123), Kingsbury co., E S.Dak., 16 mi. E of De Smet.

Het Loo, Netherlands: see APELDOORN.

Hetsugi (hätsōō'gē), town (pop. 6,972), Oita prefecture, NE Kyushu, Japan, 7 mi. SSE of Oita; agr. center (rice, wheat, barley); raw silk, lumber, charcoal.

Hettange-Grande (ĕtäzh'-gräd'), Ger. *Gross Hettingen* (grōs hĕ'tĭng-ŭn), town (pop. 3,290), Moselle dept., NE France, 4 mi. N of Thionville, in iron-mining dist. Also called Hettange-la-Grande.

Hettenleidelheim (hĕ'tŭnlī'dŭlhīm), village (pop. 2,405), Rhenish Palatinate, W Germany, in Hardt Mts., 13 mi. W of Frankenthal; clay pits.

Hettick, village (pop. 268), Macoupin co., SW Ill., 35 mi. SSW of Springfield, in agr. and bituminous-coal area.

Hettinger (hĕ'tĭnjŭr), county (□ 1,135; pop. 7,100), SW N.Dak.; ⊙ Mott. Agr. area drained by Cannonball R. Coal mines, farming, dairy products, wheat, poultry, grain. Formed 1883.

Hettinger, city (pop. 1,762), ⊙ Adams co., SW N.Dak., 110 mi. SW of Bismarck, near S.Dak. line; agr., dairying; bricks. Inc. 1916.

Hetton, urban district (1931 pop. 17,665; 1951 census 18,511), NE Durham, England. Includes coal-mining towns of: Hetton-le-Hole (pop. 5,478), 6 mi. NE of Durham, Hetton Downs (pop. 6,342), just N, and Easington Lane (pop. 5,845), just S.

Hettstedt (hĕt'shtĕt), town (pop. 10,118), in former Prussian Saxony prov., central Germany, after 1945 in Saxony-Anhalt, at E foot of the lower Harz, on the Wipper and 8 mi. SSE of Aschersleben; copper-slate mining and smelting center; copper and brass milling; mfg. of light metals and chemicals. Has remains of Gothic castle. Just E is scene of battle (1115) in which Emperor Henry V and Count Mansfeld were defeated by Saxons.

Het Zoute, Belgium: see KNOKKE.

Heubach (hoi'bäkh), town (pop. 3,677), Württemberg, Germany, after 1945 in Württemberg-Baden, 6 mi. ESE of Schwäbisch Gmünd; wine.

Heuchelheim (hoi'khŭlhīm), village (pop. 4,145), central Hesse, W Germany, in former Upper Hesse prov., 2 mi. W of Giessen; woodworking.

Heuchin (ûshē'), agr. village (pop. 515), Pas-de-Calais dept., N France, 7 mi. NNW of Saint-Pol.

Heukelum or **Heukelom** (both: hû'kŭlŭm), village (pop. 765), South Holland prov., W Netherlands, 5 mi. NE of Gorinchem; mfg. (bricks, cement); cattle raising.

Heukuppe, Austria: see RAXALPE.

Heule (hû'lŭ, Fr. ûl), town (pop. 8,219), West Flanders prov., W Belgium, 2 mi. NW of Courtrai; textile industry; agr. market. Has 16th-cent. church.

Heungshan, China: see CHUNGSHAN, Kwangtung prov.

Heusay, Belgium: see BEYNE-HEUSAY.

Heuscheuer Mountains (hoi'shoi"ŭr), Ger. *Heuscheuer Gebirge* (gŭbĭr'gŭ), Pol. *Góry Stołowe* (gōō'rĭ stôwô'wĕ), range of the Sudetes in Lower Silesia (after 1945, SW Poland), near Czechoslovak border, W of Glatz (Klodzko); extend c.10 mi. NW-SE; highest point (3,018 ft.) is 7 mi. NW of Polanica Zdroj. Separated from Reichenstein Mts. (S) by the Glatzer Neisse. NW slope extends toward Teplice, Czechoslovakia.

Heusden (hûz'dŭn). **1** Agr. village (pop. 5,049), East Flanders prov., NW Belgium, on Scheldt R. and 4 mi. SE of Ghent. Cistercian monastery (1247–1578). **2** Village (pop. 7,517), Limburg prov., NE Belgium, 8 mi. NNW of Hasselt; agr., cattle raising.

Heusden, town (pop. 1,751), North Brabant prov., S central Netherlands, on Bergsche Maas R. and 7 mi. WNW of 's Hertogenbosch; shipbuilding; basket weaving.

Heusenstamm (hoi'zŭn-shtäm), village (pop. 4,215), S Hesse, W Germany, in former Starkenburg prov., 3 mi. SSE of Offenbach; tanning.

Heusweiler (hois'vī"lŭr), town (pop. 5,262); S central Saar, 8 mi. NNW of Saarbrücken; coal mining.

Heusy (ûzē'), town (pop. 3,700), Liége prov., E Belgium, S residential suburb of Verviers; wool spinning, weaving.

Heuvelton (hū'vŭltŭn), village (pop. 712), St. Lawrence co., N N.Y., on Oswegatchie R. and 6 mi. SE of Ogdensburg; cheese, feed, wood products.

Hève, La (lä ĕv'), cape on English Channel, in Seine-Inférieure dept., N France, 3 mi. NW of Le Havre, at mouth of Seine R. estuary; 49°30'N 0°4'E. Rises c.350 ft. above beach of SAINTE-ADRESSE. Its 2 lighthouses were damaged 1939–45.

Hevenk, Turkey: see BOZOVA.

Hever (hā'vŭr), agr. village (pop. 2,496), Brabant prov., central Belgium, 11 mi. NW of Louvain.

Heverlee (hā'vŭrlā), Fr. *Héverlé* (āvŭrlā'), residential town (pop. 11,832), Brabant prov., central Belgium, on Dyle R., S suburb of Louvain. Anc. castle, once residence of chamberlains of Brabant, now owned by Univ. of Louvain. Premonstratensian abbey was founded c.1130; most extant bldgs. date from 15th–17th cent.

Heves (hĕ'vĕsh), county (□ 1,492; pop. 334,411), N Hungary; ⊙ Eger. Includes Matra Mts. (N) and part of the Alföld (SE); drained by Tarna, Zagyva, Eger rivers. Agr. (grain, watermelons, vineyards, tobacco, caraway seed), livestock region (cattle, pigs, sheep, poultry). N part heavily forested. Industry at Eger and Gyöngyös.

Heves, town (pop. 10,605), Heves co., N Hungary, 18 mi. ENE of Jaszbereny; watermelons, vineyards, hemp and hemp products, lumber. Lignite deposits near by.

Hevizszentandras (hā'vĭs-sĕntŏndräsh), Hung. *Hévizszentandrás*, town (pop. 871), Zala co., W Hungary, 17 mi. ESE of Zalaegerszeg; rye, wine. On near-by small lake, fed by hot springs, is Hevizfürdö, Hung. *Hévizfürdő*, a health resort.

Hevne, Norway: see KYRKSAETERORA.

Hevros or **Evros** (both: ĕv'rôs), nome (□ 1,635; pop. 154,945), W Thrace, Greece; ⊙ Alexandroupolis. Bordered N by Bulgaria, E by Turkey in Europe (along Maritsa R.), S by Aegean Sea, W by Macedonia. Orestias lowland (NE), drained by Arda and Maritsa rivers, is chief agr. area (silk, tobacco, wheat, cotton, dried fruit). Fisheries and salt pans along coast, W of Maritsa R. delta. Includes Aegean isl. of SAMOTHRACE. Main towns are Alexandroupolis (port), Didymoteikhon, and Souphlion. Served by Salonika-Adrianople RR. Sometimes spelled Hebros.

Hevros River, SE Europe: see MARITSA RIVER.

Hewell Island (hū'ŭl), Knox co., S Maine, in Penobscot Bay, 4.5 mi. SSE of South Thomaston; 1 mi. long.

Hewitt, village (pop. 312), Todd co., W central Minn., 27 mi. NNW of Long Prairie; dairy products.

Hewlett (hū'lĭt), residential village (1940 pop. 3,485), Nassau co., SE N.Y., near S shore of W Long Isl., 6 mi. SE of Jamaica; makes cosmetics.

Hewlett Bay Park, residential village (pop. 466), Nassau co., SE N.Y., on S shore of W Long Isl., on small Hewlett Bay, just S of Valley Stream.

Hewlett Harbor, residential village (pop. 411), Nassau co., SE N.Y., on S shore of W Long Isl., just S of Lynbrook.

Hewlett Neck, residential village (pop. 369), Nassau co., SE N.Y., on S shore of W Long Isl., just S of Valley Stream.

Hewlett Point, N.Y.: see MANHASSET BAY.

Heworth, England: see GATESHEAD.

Hexham (hĕk'sŭm), urban district (1931 pop. 8,888; 1951 census 9,715), S Northumberland, England, on the Tyne and 19 mi. W of Newcastle-upon-Tyne; agr. market, with agr.-machinery works. Remains of a monastery founded 674 by St. Wilfrid are now part of 13th-cent. abbey. Has 15th-cent. Moot Hall and 14th-cent. prison. Battle of Hexham (1464), in which Edward IV defeated the Lancastrians, was fought 2 mi. SE.

Hex River Mountains, SW Cape Prov., U. of So. Afr., extend 30 mi. ENE from upper Breede R. valley near Worcester; rise to 7,386 ft. on Matroosberg, 20 mi. E of Ceres.

Heybeli Island (hābĕlē') (pop. 4,213), one of Princes Isls., in Sea of Marmara, NW Turkey, 12 mi. SE of Istanbul, of which it is part, included in Adalar dist.; 1 mi. long. Formerly Khalki or Copper Isl.

Heybridge, town and parish (pop. 2,061), E central Essex, England, on Blackwater R. opposite Maldon; iron foundries. Has Norman church.

Heyburn (hā'bŭrn), village (pop. 539), Minidoka co., S Idaho, 5 mi. SW of Rupert and on Snake R.; alt. 4,342 ft.; ships grain, livestock.

Heyburn, Lake, E Okla., reservoir c.11 mi. long, impounded by dam in small Polecat Creek, c.11 mi. WSW of Sapulpa.

Heydebreck, Poland: see KEDZIERZYN.

Heydekrug, Lithuania: see SILUTE.

Heyrieux (ārēû'), village (pop. 1,086), Isère dept., SE France, 14 mi. SE of Lyons; footwear mfg.

Heys, Yemen: see HAIS.

Heysham, England: see MORECAMBE AND HEYSHAM.

Heyst, Belgium: see HEIST.

Heyst-op-den-Berg, Belgium: see HEIST-OP-DEN-BERG.

Heytesbury (hāts'bŭrē), agr. village and parish (pop. 454), W Wiltshire, England, on Wylye R. and 4 mi. ESE of Warminster. Has 13th-15th-cent. church.

Heythuisen, Netherlands: see HEIJTHUIJSEN.

Heywood, town (pop. 961), SW Victoria, Australia, 185 mi. WSW of Melbourne; rail junction; cattle center; cheese.

Heywood (hā'–), municipal borough (1931 pop. 25,968; 1951 census 25,193), SE Lancashire, England, 8 mi. N of Manchester; cotton milling, mfg. of metal products, leather. Has 17th-cent. mansion. In municipal borough is paper-milling village (pop. 2,969) of Heap Bridge.

Heyworth (hā'wûrth), village (pop. 1,072), McLean co., central Ill., 10 mi. S of Bloomington; trade center in agr. area (corn, grain, soybeans, livestock).

Hezar Masjed Range, Iran: see HAZAR MASJID RANGE.

Hialeah (hīŭlē'ŭ), residential city (pop. 19,676), Dade co., S Fla., just NW of Miami and part of Greater Miami. Seat of famed Hialeah Park race track. Mfg. (preserves, candy, dairy and wood products). Settled 1921, inc. 1925.

Hiangcheng or **Hsiang-ch'eng** (both: shyäng'-chŭng'), town, ⊙ Hiangcheng co. (pop. 228,761), NW central Honan prov., China, 35 mi. NW of Yencheng; tobacco center; wheat, rice, beans, kaoliang.

Hiaty, Paraguay: see HYATY.

Hiawassee (hīŭwŏ'sē), resort town (pop. 375), ⊙ Towns co., NE Ga., near N.C. line 34 mi. NW of Toccoa, on Chatuge Reservoir.

Hiawatha (hīŭwä'thŭ). **1** City (pop. 3,294), ⊙ Brown co., NE Kansas, 37 mi. W of St. Joseph, Mo.; trade center for stock-raising and agr. area (grain, apples); dairying. Davis Memorial, with 11 statues of John Davis and wife, is in cemetery. Founded 1857, inc. 1859. **2** Town (pop. 1,421), Carbon and Emery counties, E central Utah, 15 mi. SW of Price.

Hibaiyo (ēbī'yō), town (1939 pop. 9,744) in Guihulñgan municipality, Negros Oriental prov., E Negros isl., Philippines, on Tañon Strait, 32 mi. ENE of Binalbagan; agr. center (corn, coconuts, sugar cane).

Hibar, Saudi Arabia: see TURAIF.

Hibbing, village (pop. 16,276), St. Louis co., NE Minn., in Mesabi iron range and c.60 mi. NW of Duluth; resort in lake and forest region; iron mining; dairy products, beverages, foundry products. Settled as lumbering point. Platted and inc. 1893. Moved to present site after 1917 to make way for operation of large open-pit iron mine. Village has well-equipped high school, junior col., and large auditorium.

Hibernia: see IRELAND.

Hibernia (hībûr'nēŭ), village, Morris co., N N.J., 5 mi. NNE of Dover. Until c.1912 was thriving iron-mining town; Hibernia Furnace here furnished munitions in Revolution.

Hibi, Japan: see TAMANO.

Hibiki Sea (hēbē'kē), Jap. *Hibiki-nada*, S arm of Sea of Japan, bet. SW coast of Honshu (E) and small isls. (W) which form E boundary of Tsushima Strait; connected with Suo Sea (SE) by Shimonoseki Strait; merges with Genkai Sea (SW). Wakamatsu on SE shore.

Hicacos Peninsula (ēkä'kōs), narrow spit (11 mi. long NE-SW), Matanzas prov., NW Cuba, 20 mi. ENE of Matanzas, flanking NW Cárdenas Bay, and terminating in Hicacos Cape. Has saltworks. Near its base is the Varadero beach resort.

Hichuloma (hēchōolō'mä), village, La Paz dept., W Bolivia, on SE slopes of Cordillera de La Paz 19 mi. NE of La Paz, on La Paz–Chulumani road; terminus of La Paz–Yungas RR.

Hickam Field, U.S. army air base, S Oahu, T.H., 12 mi. NW of Honolulu, near Pearl Harbor. Completed 1935, it was bombed (Dec. 7, 1941) by the Japanese.

Hickman. 1 County (□ 248; pop. 7,778), SW Ky.; ⊙ Clinton. Bounded W by the Mississippi (Mo. line); drained by Obion Creek and Bayou de Chien. Gently rolling agr. area (livestock, grain, dark tobacco, cotton, fruit). Includes Columbus Belmont Battlefield State Park. Formed 1821. **2** County (□ 613; pop. 13,353), central Tenn.; ⊙ Centerville. Drained by Duck R. and tributaries. Livestock raising, dairying, general agr.; phosphate mining; lumbering. Some mfg. at Centerville. Formed 1807.

Hickman. 1 Town (pop. 2,037), ⊙ Fulton co., extreme SW Ky., on bluffs above left bank of the Mississippi and 36 mi. WSW of Mayfield. Trade and shipping center for agr. area (cotton, corn, hay), with timber; mfg. of food products, veneer, concrete products; lumber mills, cotton gins. Flood wall (1934) protects city. Reelfoot L. is 8 mi. SW. Settled 1819; inc. 1834. **2** Village (pop. 279), Lancaster co., SE Nebr., 12 mi. S of Lincoln; dairy and poultry produce, grain, livestock.

Hickman, Mount (9,700 ft.), NW B.C., near Alaska border, in Coast Mts., 70 mi. NE of Wrangell; 57°16′N 131°7′W.

Hickory, county (□ 410; pop. 5,387), central Mo.; ⊙ Hermitage. In the Ozarks; drained by Pomme de Terre and Little Niangua rivers. Agr. (corn, wheat, oats, hay), livestock. Formed 1845.

Hickory. 1 or **Hickory Grove,** town (pop. 185), Graves co., SW Ky., on Mayfield Creek and 5 mi. N of Mayfield; clay pits. **2** Town (pop. 614), Newton co., E central Miss., 19 mi. W of Meridian. **3** City (pop. 14,755), Catawba co., W central N.C., 45 mi. NW of Charlotte, in the piedmont. Hosiery and furniture mfg. center with abundant hydroelectric power from near-by dams (form Hickory L., Lookout Shoals L.) in Catawba R.; mfg. of textiles, cordage, wagons, boxes, springs, foundry products. Seat of Lenoir-Rhyne Col. (Lutheran; coeducational; 1891). Founded 1874; inc. 1884; annexed Highland and West Hickory in 1931. **4** Town (pop. 112), Murray co., S Okla., 17 mi. SSW of Ada, in agr. area.

Hickory Flat, village (pop. 345), Benton co., N Miss., 13 mi. NW of New Albany, in Holly Springs Natl. Forest; sawmills.

Hickory Grove. 1 Town, Graves co., Ky.: see HICKORY. **2** Town (pop. 275), York co., N S.C., 10 mi. W of York.

Hickory Lake, N.C.: see CATAWBA RIVER.

Hickory Ridge, town (pop. 345), Cross co., E Ark., 27 mi. NW of Wynne.

Hickox, town (pop. 139), Brantley co., SE Ga., 22 mi. E of Waycross.

Hicksville. 1 Residential village (1940 pop. 6,835), Nassau co., SE N.Y., on W Long Isl., 6 mi. ENE of Mineola, in potato- and cabbage-growing area; mfg. (cement products, clothing, fertilizer, glass products, machinery, truck bodies, knit goods); nurseries. Founded 1648. **2** Village (pop. 2,629), Defiance co., NW Ohio, near Ind. line, 20 mi. W of Defiance; shipping and processing center in farming and dairying area; mfg. (wood products, food products, cigars). Founded 1836.

Hico (hī′kō), city (pop. 1,212), Hamilton co., central Texas, on Bosque R. and c.60 mi. NW of Waco, in agr. area; ships poultry; grain milling, dairying.

Hicpochee, Lake, Fla.: see CALOOSAHATCHEE RIVER.

Hida (hē′dä), former province in central Honshu, Japan; now part of Gifu prefecture.

Hida or **Hita** (hē′tä), city (1940 pop. 36,293; 1947 pop. 46,234), Oita prefecture, N central Kyushu, Japan, on Chikugo R. and 38 mi. WNW of Oita, on forested plateau (alt. 2,000 ft.); rice, lumber; fishing (with cormorants). Large gold mine near by.

Hida (hē′dä), Hung. *Hidalmás* (hĕ′dŏlmäsh), village (pop. 1,956), Cluj prov., W central Rumania, 24 mi. NNW of Cluj; agr. center; coal mining. In Hungary, 1940–45.

Hidaka (hēdä′kä) or **Hitaka** (hētä′kä), town (pop. 8,713), Hyogo prefecture, S Honshu, Japan, 31 mi. ESE of Tottori, in agr. area (rice, wheat, fruit, flowers, poultry); home industries (leather goods, straw products, cutlery, soy sauce). Fishing.

Hidalgo (ēdäl′gō), state (□ 8,058; 1940 pop. 771,818; 1950 pop. 840,760), central Mexico, N of Mexico state; ⊙ Pachuca. Extremely mountainous; crossed by the Sierra Madre Oriental; consists mainly of central plateau with high valleys (center and S), sloping toward NW. NE tip is Gulf lowland. Drained by Moctezuma and Tula rivers. Temperate climate in uplands, cold in high sierras, tropical in NE. Apart from arid SE plains around Pachuca and Apam, where maguey—Hidalgo's main agr. product—is grown on large scale, it is a fertile, well-irrigated region. Produces corn, wheat, barley, tobacco, cotton, sugar cane, fruit, vegetables; provides good pastures. The torrid NE lowlands are given to cultivation of rice, sugar cane, coffee, and tropical fruit; they are rich in fine woods such as mahogany, cedar, rosewood, ebony. The sierras produce timber. Hidalgo has been known since early colonial days for its large silver deposits; also has gold, lead, copper, mercury, manganese, antimony, iron, sulphur, and zinc mines; main mining centers are Pachuca, Zimapán, Huichapan, Mineral del Monte. Metallurgical industry is concentrated at Pachuca; flour and textile mills, tanneries, distilleries at Pachuca, Tulancingo, Tepeji del Río. The area was site of several anc. Indian cultures, including the Toltec, whose capital was at Tula. Region was conquered by the Spanish in 1530, and formed N part of Mexico state until 1869.

Hidalgo. 1 Town (pop. 513), Coahuila, N Mexico, on the Rio Grande (Texas border) and 75 mi. SE of Piedras Negras; cattle grazing. **2** or **Ciudad Hidalgo** (syōōdädh′), city (pop. 7,594), Michoacán, central Mexico, on central plateau surrounded by peaks, on railroad and 35 mi. E of Morelia; agr. center (grain, sugar cane, beans, fruit, livestock); tanning, lumbering, flour milling, soapmaking; forest products (resins, turpentine, etc.). It is the old Tarascan town Taximaroa. **3** Town (pop. 1,783), Nuevo León, N Mexico, on railroad, on Salinas R. and 23 mi. NW of Monterrey; grain, livestock. Formerly San Nicolás. **4** Town (pop. 1,194), Tamaulipas, N Mexico, at E foot of Sierra Madre Oriental, near Nuevo León border, 40 mi. NNW of Ciudad Victoria; sugar cane, beans, livestock.

Hidalgo (hĭdăl′gō). **1** County (□ 3,447; pop. 5,095), extreme SW N.Mex.; ⊙ Lordsburg. Livestock and agr. region; watered N by Gila R.; bounded by Ariz. (W) and Mexico (S, SE). Mining (copper, silver, gold, lead) near Lordsburg. Includes part of Coronado Natl. Forest and ranges of Continental Divide in S. Formed 1919. **2** County (□ 1,541; pop. 160,446), extreme S Texas; ⊙ Edinburg. S part is in rich irrigated valley of the Rio Grande (Mex. border), producing large part of Texas citrus crop, huge truck crops, cotton; N part has ranches (beef and dairy cattle, goats, sheep). Packing, canning industries are important; oil, natural-gas production and refining, clay mining, brick and tile mfg. Winter-resort area. Formed 1852.

Hidalgo. 1 (hī′dŭlgō) Village (pop. 167), Jasper co., SE Ill., 21 mi. E of Effingham, in agr. area. **2** (hĭdăl′gō) Village (1940 pop. 645), Hidalgo co., extreme S Texas, port of entry on the Rio Grande (bridged) opposite Reynosa, Mexico, and c.7 mi. S of McAllen, in irrigated agr. area (citrus, truck, cotton).

Hidalgo, Salina de, Argentina: see SALINA GRANDE.

Hidalgo, Villa, Mexico: see VILLA HIDALGO.

Hidalgo del Parral (– dĕl päräl′) or **Parral,** city (pop. 24,231), Chihuahua, N Mexico, in E outliers of Sierra Madre Occidental, 120 mi. SSE of Chihuahua; alt. 6,397 ft. One of largest Mex. mining towns (notably silver; and lead, gold, zinc). Agr. center (cereals, cattle); flour milling. Area has been known since early Sp. conquest for its mineral riches. A Franciscan mission was established here in 1714. Villa was assassinated in the town.

Hidalgotitlán (ēdälgōtētlän′), town (pop. 1,131), Veracruz, SE Mexico, on Isthmus of Tehuantepec, on Coatzacoalcos R. and 17 mi. SSW of Minatitlán; fruit, livestock.

Hidalmas, Rumania: see HIDA.

Hidas (hĭ′dŏsh), town (pop. 2,375), Baranya co., S Hungary, 12 mi. SW of Szekszard; enamelware.

Hidasnemeti (hĭ′dŏsh-nāmĕtē), Hung. *Hidasnémeti,* town (pop. 804), Abauj co., NE Hungary, on Hernad R. and 33 mi. NE of Miskolc, near Czechoslovak line; rail junction.

Hidayatpur, India: see GURGAON, town.

Hiddekil, river, Mesopotamia: see TIGRIS RIVER.

Hidden Inlet, fishing village (1939 pop. 13), extreme SE Alaska, on Pearse Canal, 60 mi. SE of Ketchikan; 54°59′N 130°21′W.

Hiddenite, village (pop. c.300), Alexander co., W central N.C., 6 mi. ESE of Taylorsville. Here the gem hiddenite was discovered (c.1879) and mined for a time.

Hidden Peak, Kashmir: see GASHERBRUM I.

Hidden Reservoir, Calif.: see FRESNO RIVER.

Hidden River Cave, Ky.: see HORSE CAVE, town.

Hiddensee (hĭ′dŭnzā″) or **Hiddensoe** (hĭ′dŭnzō″), Baltic island (□ 7; pop. 1,434), N Germany, just W of Rügen isl., 2 mi. off Mecklenburg coast; 11 mi. long, 1–2 mi. wide. Low and level, rising toward N, with even coast line (W) and slightly indented E coast. Frequented as seaside resort; fishing is chief occupation. Main village, Kloster; near by are remains of 13th-cent. Cistercian monastery. Viking gold utensils have been found here. Site of ornithological station and of biological research station of Greifswald univ. Isl. was separated (1308) from Rügen isl. by major storm wave.

Hidden Valley, Colo.: see ROCKY MOUNTAIN NATIONAL PARK.

Hidra (hē′drä), Nor. *Hidra* or *Hitterøy,* island (□ 8; pop. 901) in North Sea, Vest-Agder co., S Norway, at mouth of a fjord near Flekkefjord. Fishing, shipping; kieselguhr quarrying. Stone Age findings made near by. Fortified during Danish-English war (1807–14). Sometimes spelled Hitra. Formerly Hitterö.

Hiechechin Bay, China: see KITCHIOH BAY.

Hieflau (hēf′lou), village (pop. 1,766), Styria, central Austria, on the Enns and 8 mi. NW of Eisenerz; rail junction; ironworks, hydroelectric station.

Hiendelaencina (yĕn″däläĕn-thē′nä), town (pop. 439), Guadalajara prov., central Spain, 33 mi. NNE of Guadalajara; grain growing; sheep raising. Has abandoned silver mines.

Hienghene (yĕn′gĕn′), village (dist. pop. 1,849), New Caledonia, on E coast, 145 mi. NW of Nouméa; agr. products, livestock.

Hiephoa (hyĕp′hwä′), village, Cholon prov., S Vietnam, 25 mi. NW of Saigon; sugar-growing center; sugar mill, distillery.

Hierapetra or **Ierapetra** (both: yĕrä′pĭtrŭ), town (pop. 4,949), Lasethi nome, E Crete, port on S coast, 17 mi. S of Hagios Nikolaos. Trades in carobs, raisins; olive oil.

Hierapolis (hīūră′pŭlĭs) [Gr.,=holy city], anc. city of Phrygia, W Asia Minor, on a tributary of the Maeander just N of Laodicea, c.120 mi. ESE of Smyrna, Turkey. Anciently devoted to worship of Greek goddess Leto, it became an early seat of Christianity. Noted for its extensive Roman ruins.

Hierissos or **Ierissos** (both: yĕrĭsôs′), town (pop. 2,768), Chalcidice nome, Macedonia, Greece, port on Gulf of Hierissos (Acanthus) of Aegean Sea, 23 mi. E of Polygyros; olive oil, wine; timber. Near by was anc. Acanthus.

Hieroconpolis, Egypt: see KOM EL AHMAR, EL.

Hierro (yĕ′rō) or **Ferro** (fĕ′rō), smallest and westernmost island (□ 107; pop. 8,849) of the Canary Isls., 40 mi. SW of Gomera and 40 mi. S of Palma, in Santa Cruz de Tenerife prov., Spain; 27°45′N 18°W. Chief town and port, Valverde. Isl. is 18 mi. long NE-SW. Has an abrupt coast line and rises in volcanic interior to 4,330 ft. (Alto de Mal Paso). Large tracts are wooded. Because of scarcity of water, there are only a few fertile valleys, yielding cereals, grapes, potatoes, tomatoes, figs, almonds. Also exports wine and cheese. Sheep, cattle, and goats are raised. Its iron deposits are not exploited. Hierro was anciently thought to be the end of the world, and the longitude of Hierro's westernmost point, Cape Orchilla, was 1st used by Mercator, noted 16th-cent. geographer, as the prime meridian and a convenient dividing line bet. the Eastern and Western hemispheres. Confirmed 1634 as the zero meridian by a geographical congress in Paris, it remained in use until the adoption (1884) of the Greenwich meridian. The Hierro meridian was originally defined as 20°W of Paris (i.e., 17°40′W of Greenwich), but the actual longitude of Cape Orchilla is 18°20′W of Greenwich.

Hiersac (yĕrsäk′), village (pop. 536), Charente dept., W France, 7 mi. W of Angoulême; winegrowing, horse raising.

Hiers-Brouage (yâr-brōōäzh′), village (pop. 486), Charente-Maritime dept., W France, near Bay of Biscay, 8 mi. SW of Rochefort; saltworks. Nearby Brouage, a former fortress and port, now almost abandoned, preserves ramparts built (1630–40) by Richelieu and old arsenal. Champlain b. here.

Hietzing (hĭt′sĭng), outer WSW district (□ 6; pop. 48,345) of Vienna, Austria. Has palace and park of SCHÖNBRUNN; Lainz zoological garden.

Higashi-ichiki (hēgä′shē-ē′chĭkē), town (pop. 20,616), Kagoshima prefecture, S Kyushu, Japan, on NW Satsuma Peninsula, 13 mi. WNW of Kagoshima; commercial center in livestock, rice-growing area; raw silk.

Higashi-iwase, Japan: see TOYAMA, city.

Higashi-kamiura (–kämŭ′rä), town (pop. 6,594), Oita prefecture, E Kyushu, Japan, on Hoyo Strait, 23 mi. SE of Oita; fishing center.

Higashi-kata, Ryukyu Isls.: see KONIYA.

Higashi-kushira (–kōō′shĭrä), town (pop. 11,845), Kagoshima prefecture, S Kyushu, Japan, on E Osumi Peninsula, 29 mi. ESE of Kagoshima, just SE of Kushira; commercial center in agr. area (rice, wheat); raw silk, lumber.

Higashi-maizuru, Japan: see MAIZURU.

Higashi-mizuhashi, Japan: see MIZUHASHI.

Higashi-murayama (–mōōrä′yämŭ), town (pop. 17,099), Greater Tokyo, central Honshu, Japan, 6 mi. NE of Tachikawa; agr. (sweet potatoes, rice, wheat); raw silk.

Higashi-naibuchi, Russian SFSR: see UGLEZAVODSK.

Higashine (hēgä′shĭnä), town (pop. 15,487), Yamagata prefecture, N Honshu, Japan, 14 mi. NNE of Yamagata, in agr. area (rice, wheat, tobacco); silk cocoons.

Higashi-nogami (hēgä′shĭ-nōgä′mē), town (pop. 6,967), Wakayama prefecture, S Honshu, Japan, on W Kii Peninsula, 8 mi. SE of Wakayama, in agr. area (rice, citrus fruit); raw silk, lumber.

Higashi-nomi-shima, Japan: see NOMI-SHIMA.

Higashi-tsuge, Japan: see TSUGE.

Higashi-uji (hēgä′shē-ōō′jē), town (pop. 10,776), Kyoto prefecture, S Honshu, Japan, 8 mi. SSE of Kyoto, just E of Uji, in rice-growing area; mulberry fields. Until early 1940s, called Uji.

Higashi-yoshitomi (hēgä′shĭyō′shĭtō″mē), town (pop. 7,555), Fukuoka prefecture, N Kyushu, Japan, 25 mi. SSE of Moji; rice. Sometimes called Yoshitomi.

Higaturu (hēgätōōrōō′), town, Territory of Papua, SE New Guinea, 30 mi. ENE of Kokoda, in rice-growing area. Govt. station.

Higaza or **Hijazah** (hĭgä′zŭ, –jă′–), village (pop. 18,294), Qena prov., Upper Egypt, 7 mi. SE of Qus; pottery making, sugar refining; cereals, dates.

Higbee, city (pop. 674), Randolph co., N central Mo., 9 mi. SSW of Moberly; agr.

Higden, town (pop. 115), Cleburne co., N central Ark., 11 mi. WNW of Heber Springs, in the Ozarks.

Higganum, Conn.: see HADDAM.

Higgins, city (pop. 675), Lipscomb co., extreme N Texas, in the Panhandle, c.40 mi. SW of Woodward, Okla.; trade, shipping point in wheat and cattle region.

Higgins Bay, resort village, Hamilton co., E central N.Y., in the Adirondacks, on Piseco L., c.40 mi. NE of Utica.

Higgins Lake, N central Mich., 5 mi. W of Roscommon; c.7 mi. long, 4 mi. wide. State park on S shore; resorts; fishing. Joined to Houghton L. (S) by small passage.

Higginson, town (pop. 131), White co., central Ark., 4 mi. SSE of Searcy.

Higginsport, village (pop. 385), Brown co., SW Ohio, on the Ohio and 6 mi. SSW of Georgetown.

Higginsville, city (pop. 3,428), Lafayette co., W central Mo., near Missouri R., 12 mi. SE of Lexington; agr., especially corn; mfg. (flour, shoes, brick, tile); coal. Laid out 1869.

Higgston, town (pop. 155), Montgomery co., E central Ga., 3 mi. W of Vidalia.

Higham, Derby, England: see SHIRLAND AND HIGHAM.

Higham Ferrers (hī'ŭm fĕ'rŭrz), municipal borough (1931 pop. 2,930; 1951 census 3,679), E Northampton, England, on Nene R. and 4 mi. E of Wellingborough; leather and shoe mfg. Has 13th-14th-cent. church.

High and Low Bishopside, England: see PATELEY BRIDGE.

High Atlas, Fr. Morocco: see ATLAS MOUNTAINS.

Highbank, township (pop. 263), E central S.Isl., New Zealand, 45 mi. W of Christchurch and on S shore of Rakaia R.; agr. center. Hydroelectric plant.

High Bentham, England: see BENTHAM.

High Blantyre, Scotland: see BLANTYRE.

Highbridge, England: see BURNHAM-ON-SEA.

High Bridge. 1 Village, Jessamine co., central Ky., on Kentucky R. (here flowing through deep gorge), at Dix R. mouth, and 20 mi. SW of Lexington, in Bluegrass region; limestone quarrying. DIX RIVER Dam and High Bridge State Park (named for a 317-ft.-high rail bridge across Kentucky R.) are near by. **2** Borough (pop. 1,854), Hunterdon co., W N.J., on South Branch of Raritan R. and 15 mi. E of Phillipsburg; metal products; poultry, truck. State park near by. Settled before 1750, inc. 1898.

Highbridge, SE N.Y., a residential section of SW Bronx borough of New York city.

High Commission Territories, South Africa: see BECHUANALAND PROTECTORATE; BASUTOLAND; SWAZILAND.

High Crompton, England: see CROMPTON.

High Crosby, England: see CROSBY-ON-EDEN.

Higher Bebington, England: see BEBINGTON.

Higher Walton, town in Walton-le-Dale urban dist., W central Lancashire, England, 3 mi. SE of Preston; cotton milling.

High Falls, village, Ulster co., SE N.Y., on Rondout Creek and 10 mi. SW of Kingston, in resort and agr. area.

Highfield, village (pop. 5,410, with adjacent Lyndora), Butler co., W Pa., just W of Butler.

Highgate, village (pop. 311), S Ont., 20 mi. ENE of Chatham; dairying, mixed farming, lumbering.

Highgate (hī'gĭt), suburb of London, residential district in Hornsey municipal borough, E Middlesex, England, 5 mi. NNW of Charing Cross. Reputedly named for 14th-cent. toll gate at entrance to a bishop's estate when district was forest and hunting ground. Highgate was residence of Coleridge, Bacon, and George Eliot. Whittington Stone, at foot of Highgate Hill, is connected with legend of Dick Whittington. Highgate Cemetery has graves of George Eliot, Faraday, Karl Marx.

Highgate, town (pop. 2,400), St. Mary parish, N Jamaica, in uplands, on railroad and 23 mi. NNW of Kingston; fruitgrowing, stock grazing.

Highgate (hī'gāt″), town (pop. 1,681), Franklin co., NW Vt., on L. Champlain, at Que. line, at mouth of Missisquoi R., and 8 mi. N of St. Albans; metal products; lime, lumber. Port of entry. Highgate Springs is resort village.

High Harrogate, England: see HARROGATE.

High Hesket, England: see HESKET IN THE FOREST.

High Hill, town (pop. 224), Montgomery co., E central Mo., 9 mi. SE of Montgomery City.

High Island, village (pop. c.500), Galveston co., S Texas, 32 mi. NE of Galveston, bet. Gulf coast (S) and Gulf Intracoastal Waterway; oil-field center, on salt dome in marshland.

High Island, island, Mich.: see BEAVER ISLANDS.

Highland. 1 County (□ 554; pop. 28,188), SW Ohio; ⊙ Hillsboro. Drained by East Fork of Little Miami R. and by Paint Creek, and small White Oak and Rattlesnake creeks. Agr. (livestock, grain, tobacco, poultry; dairy products); mfg. at Hillsboro and Greenfield; limestone quarries. Formed 1805. **2** County (□ 416; pop. 4,069), NW Va.; ⊙ Monterey. In the Alleghenies; bounded (W, N) by W.Va.; drained by Jackson and Cowpasture rivers and South Branch of the Potomac. Livestock-raising area; lumbering, lumber milling; some agr. (grain, potatoes); maple sugar. Formed 1847.

Highland. 1 Village (1940 pop. 2,411), San Bernardino co., S Calif., 5 mi. E of San Bernardino; citrus fruit. **2** City (pop. 4,283), Madison co., SW Ill., 27 mi. ENE of East St. Louis, in dairying and agr. area (corn, wheat, poultry, livestock); mfg. (pipe organs, road machinery, trucks, shoes, paint, beverages, feed, shoe polish). Founded 1831 by Swiss; inc. 1863. **3** Town (pop. 5,878), Lake co., extreme NW Ind., 7 mi. SW of Gary, near Ill. line; truck farming. Settled 1850, inc. 1910. **4** City (pop. 717), Doniphan co., extreme NE Kansas, 22 mi. NNW of Atchison, in agr. region (apples, grain, livestock, poultry). Seat of Highland Jr. Col. **5** Plantation (pop. 56), Somerset co., central Maine, 8 mi. N of Bingham. **6** Village (pop. 3,035), Ulster co., SE N.Y., on W bank of the Hudson (here crossed by Mid-Hudson Bridge), opposite Poughkeepsie; summer resort; mfg. (wine, clothing). **7** Former town, Catawba co., N.C.: see HICKORY. **8** Village (pop. 280), Highland co., SW Ohio, 10 mi. N of Hillsboro and on small Rattlesnake Creek. **9** Village (pop. 1,030), Allegheny co., SW Pa. **10** Village (pop. 1,920, with adjacent West Clarkston), Asotin co., extreme SE Wash. There are also communities called Highland in Spokane and Clark counties. **11** Village (pop. 785), Iowa co., SW Wis., 14 mi. NW of Dodgeville; makes cheese, beer; timber.

Highland Beach. 1 Town (pop. 52), Palm Beach co., SE Fla. **2** Town (pop. 5), Anne Arundel co., central Md., 3 mi. SE of Annapolis, on Chesapeake Bay in shore-resort area.

Highland Falls, summer-resort village (pop. 3,930), Orange co., SE N.Y., on W bank of the Hudson and 10 mi. S of Newburgh, just S of West Point, in poultry, dairying, and fruitgrowing area. Seat of Ladycliff Col. Settled 1800, inc. 1906.

Highland Heights. 1 City (pop. 1,569), Campbell co., N Ky., near the Ohio, 8 mi. S of downtown Cincinnati. **2** Village (pop. 762), Cuyahoga co., N Ohio, an E suburb of Cleveland.

Highland Lake. 1 Village, Cumberland co., Maine: see WESTBROOK. **2** Resort village, Sullivan co., SE N.Y., on small Highland L., 13 mi. SW of Monticello.

Highland Lake. 1 Litchfield co., NW Conn., lake in Winchester town, adjacent to Winsted; 2 mi. long; resorts. **2** In Cheshire and Sullivan counties, SW N.H., narrow resort lake (6 mi. long) near Stoddard, 16 mi. NNE of Keene.

Highland Mills, village (1940 pop. 764), Orange co., SE N.Y., 8 mi. W of Highland Falls; mfg. of cord and twine.

Highland Park. 1 N residential section of LOS ANGELES city, Los Angeles co., S Calif., near Pasadena. Founded 1887; annexed 1895 by Los Angeles. **2** Village (pop. 1,933, with adjacent Belmont), Pinellas co., W Fla. There is also a Highland Park in Polk co., central Fla., near Lake Wales. **3** Village (pop. 52), Polk co., central Fla., just S of Lake Wales. **4** City (pop. 16,808), Lake co., NE Ill., beautiful suburb N of Chicago, on L. Michigan. Settled 1834; named Highland Park in 1854; inc. 1867. Ravinia Park is a summer music center. U.S. Fort Sheridan is near by. **5** Village (pop. 1,058, with College Park), Saline co., S Ill. **6** Village (pop. 1,665, with adjacent Splane Place), Ouachita parish, N La. **7** City (pop. 46,393), Wayne co., SE Mich., surrounded by Detroit, c.6 mi. NW of downtown Detroit. Mfg. (automobiles, trucks, steel tubing, marine and industrial engines, air-conditioning and heating equipment, auto parts). Seat of Lawrence Inst. of Technology and a jr. col. Laid out 1818; inc. as village 1889, as city 1918. Grew after 1909, when Ford plant (later moved to Dearborn) was built here. **8** Residential borough (pop. 9,721), Middlesex co., E N.J., on Raritan R. opposite New Brunswick. Settled on site of 17th-cent. Indian village, inc. 1905. **9** Town (pop. 476), Tulsa co., NE Okla., a suburb of Tulsa. **10** Village, Delaware co., Pa.: see UPPER DARBY. **11** Village (pop. 1,212), Mifflin co., central Pa., near Lewistown. **12** Village (pop. 4,846, with adjacent Litz Manor), Sullivan co., NE Tenn., suburb just E of Kingsport. **13** Town (pop. 11,405), Dallas co., N Texas, residential suburb N of Dallas. Settled 1907, inc. 1913.

Highland Peak (10,955 ft.), Alpine co., E Calif., in the Sierra Nevada, c.30 mi. SSE of L. Tahoe.

Highlands, county (□ 1,041; pop. 13,636), S central Fla., bounded E by Kissimmee R.; ⊙ Sebring. Rolling terrain with many lakes, notably L. Istokpoga; SE corner of co. in Everglades. Citrus-fruit and cattle area; also truck and poultry farming. Formed 1921.

Highlands. 1 Resort borough (pop. 2,959), Monmouth co., E N.J., bet. Navesink R. and Sandy Hook Bay, 5 mi. NE of Red Bank; seafood, truck. On near-by Navesink Highlands is 1 of most powerful lighthouses in U.S. First U.S. Navy wireless station (1903) near by. Inc. 1900. **2** Town (pop. 515), Macon co., W N.C., 13 mi. SE of Franklin, near Ga. line; mtn. resort. **3** Village (pop. 2,723), Harris co., S Texas, 18 mi. E of Houston and on San Jacinto R., in agr. area; canneries.

Highlands Forge Lake, N.Y.: see WILLSBORO.

Highlands of Navesink, N.J.: see NAVESINK HIGHLANDS.

Highland Springs, residential village (pop. 3,171), Henrico co., E central Va., just E of Richmond.

Highlandville, town (pop. 46), Christian co., SW Mo., in the Ozarks, near James R., 20 mi. S of Springfield.

Highley, town and parish (pop. 2,095), SE Shropshire, England, on Severn R. and 7 mi. NW of Kidderminster; coal mining.

Highmore, city (pop. 1,158), ⊙ Hyde co., central S.Dak., 45 mi. ENE of Pierre; trading center for farming region; dairy products, livestock, grain. State experiment farm near by.

Highmount, resort village, Ulster co., SE N.Y., in the Catskills NW of Kingston and near Belle Ayr Mtn. (skiing).

High Ongar, England: see ONGAR.

High Peak, England: see PEAK, THE.

High Peak, highest peak (6,683 ft.) in Zambales prov., central Luzon, Philippines, c.30 mi. W of Tarlac.

High Plains, Texas and N.Mex.: see LLANO ESTACADO.

High Point, city (pop. 39,973), Guilford co., N central N.C., 14 mi. SW of Greensboro, in the piedmont. A leading U.S. furniture mfg. center; also noted for its hosiery mills; mfg. of textiles, clothing, veneer, plywood, crates, paperboard boxes, excelsior, mirrors, paint, varnish, auto bodies, metal goods. Exhibits for buyers held in large Southern Furniture Exposition Bldg. Seat of High Point Col. (Methodist; 1920). A farm trade center until beginning of furniture industry in 1888. Laid out 1853; inc. 1859.

High Point. 1 Summit (1,801 ft.) of Kittatinny Mtn. ridge, extreme NW N.J.; highest point in state, with view of 3 states. Has war memorial tower (225 ft. high). Surrounding region included in High Point State Park (c.10,900 acres), year-round forest recreational area. **2** Summit (3,075 ft.) in the Catskills, Ulster co., SE N.Y., 15 mi. W of Kingston.

High Prairie, village (pop. 643), W Alta., 65 mi. SE of Peace River and 15 mi. W of Lesser Slave L.; lumbering, mixed farming, wheat.

High River, town (pop. 1,674), S Alta., at foot of Rocky Mts., 35 mi. SSE of Calgary; coal mining; grain, dairying. In oil-producing region.

High Rock Lake (c.15 mi. long), central N.C., E of Salisbury; formed by power dam in Yadkin (Pee Dee) R., 15 mi. S of Lexington.

High Shoals, town (1940 pop. 217), Oconee, Walton, and Morgan counties, NE central Ga., 12 mi. SW of Athens and on Apalachee R.

Highshoals or **High Shoals,** village (1940 pop. 812), Gaston co., S N.C., 9 mi. N of Gastonia; textile mfg.

High Sierras, Calif.: see SIERRA NEVADA.

Highspire, residential borough (pop. 2,799), Dauphin co., S Pa., 6 mi. SE of Harrisburg and on Susquehanna R. Settled 1775, laid out 1814, inc. 1867.

Highsplint, mining village (pop. 1,506), Harlan co., SE Ky., in the Cumberlands, on Clover Fork of Cumberland R. and 10 mi. ENE of Harlan; bituminous coal.

High Springs, city (pop. 2,088), Alachua co., N Fla., near Santa Fe R., 21 mi. NW of Gainesville; agr. trade and shipping point; railroad shops. Quarries (phosphate, flint) near by. Founded c.1885.

High Tatra, mountains, Czechoslovakia and Poland: see TATRA MOUNTAINS.

Hightown, England: see SPENBOROUGH.

Hightstown, borough (pop. 3,712), Mercer co., central N.J., near Millstone R., 12 mi. ENE of Trenton; farm trade center (truck, grain, nursery products); mfg. (rugs, lace). Peddie School for boys here. Near by (4 mi. SE) is former Jersey Homesteads, now ROOSEVELT borough. Hightstown settled 1721, inc. 1853.

High Veld, U. of So. Afr.: see NORTHERN KARROO.

High Willhays, England: see DARTMOOR.

Highwood, city (pop. 3,813), Lake co., NE Ill., N suburb of Chicago, on L. Michigan, 12 mi. NNW of Evanston. Inc. 1888.

Highwoods, town (pop. 40), Marion co., central Ind., NW suburb of Indianapolis.

Highworth, town and parish (pop. 2,144), NE Wiltshire, England, 6 mi. NE of Swindon; agr. market in dairying region. Has 15th-cent. church.

High Wycombe or **Wycombe** (wĭ'kŭm), officially **Chepping Wycombe,** sometimes **Chipping Wycombe,** municipal borough (1931 pop. 27,988; 1951 census 40,692), S Buckingham, England, on the Wye and 13 mi. SSE of Aylesbury, 28 mi. WNW of London; lumber and furniture center, producing also shoes, agr. machinery, electrical instruments, paper. Has 13th-cent. church and Knights Templars Hosp. The Guildhall dates from 18th cent. Roman remains found here. Town is associated with Disraeli, who fought several elections here. In municipal borough are towns of Wycombe Marsh (SE), with paper mills, and West Wycombe (NW; pop. 3,304).

Higo (hē'gō), former province in W Kyushu, Japan; now part of Kumamoto prefecture.

Higüei, Dominican Republic: see HIGÜEY.
Higuer, Cape (ēgĕr′), Fr. *Figuier* (fēgyā′), headland on Bay of Biscay, Guipúzcoa prov., N Spain, near Fr. border, 2 mi. N of Fuenterrabía; 43°25′N 1°47′W. Lighthouse.
Higuera, La, Chile: see LA HIGUERA.
Higuera de Arjona (ēgā′rä dhā ärhō′nä), town (pop. 3,552), Jaén prov., S Spain, 18 mi. NW of Jaén; agr. trade (olive oil, cereals, vegetables).
Higuera de Calatrava (kälätrā′vä), town (pop. 1,567), Jaén prov., S Spain, 21 mi. WNW of Jaén; olive oil, cereals.
Higuera de las Dueñas (läs dwā′nyäs), town (pop. 832), Ávila prov., central Spain, on SE slopes of Sierra de Gredos, 21 mi. NE of Talavera de la Reina; cereals, fruit, stock.
Higuera de la Serena (lä särā′nä), town (pop. 2,720), Badajoz prov., W Spain, in La Serena region, 11 mi. SW of Castuera; cereals, chick-peas, olives, grapes, tubers, livestock.
Higuera de la Sierra (syĕ′rä), town (pop. 2,094), Huelva prov., SW Spain, 7 mi. SE of Aracena; lumbering and agr. (cereals, olives, fruit, acorns, chestnuts, cork, chick-peas); charcoal burning. Antimony and silver-bearing lead deposits. Its railroad station is 4½ mi. NE. Sometimes called Higuera junto a Aracena.
Higuera de Llerena (lyārā′nä), town (pop. 1,100), Badajoz prov., W Spain, 11 mi. N of Llerena; cereals, chick-peas, livestock.
Higuera de Vargas (vär′gäs), town (pop. 4,122), Badajoz prov., W Spain, 30 mi. S of Badajoz; agr. center (flour, olive oil; timber, charcoal, acorns, cork, livestock).
Higuera la Real (lä rääl′), town (pop. 5,524), Badajoz prov., W Spain, in the Sierra Morena, near Huelva prov. border, 13 mi. SSE of Jerez de los Caballeros; flour-milling center in agr. region (cereals, olives, livestock).
Higueras (ēgā′räs), town (pop. 1,010), Nuevo León, N Mexico, 27 mi. NE of Monterrey; grain, cactus fibers, stock.
Higueritas (ēgārē′täs), village (1930 pop. 230), Coquimbo prov., N central Chile, 14 mi. N of Ovalle; rail junction in copper-mining area; fruitgrowing.
Higuerote (ēgārō′tā), town (pop. 1,730), Miranda state, N Venezuela, port on the Caribbean, and 55 mi. E of Caracas. Linked by railroad with Río Chico and El Guapo. Port in cacao-growing region; exports hides, coffee, fruit.
Higueruela (ēgārwā′lä), town (pop. 2,198), Albacete prov., SE central Spain, 23 mi. E of Albacete; wine, saffron, cereals.
Higüey or **Higüei** (ēgwā′), town (1950 pop. 5,208), La Altagracia prov., SE Dominican Republic, 23 mi. ESE of Seibo, in agr. region (cacao, corn, rice, cattle); dairy products. Known for its shrine of the Virgin, with magnificent altar, attracting many pilgrims from the isl. Town was founded 1502 by Juan Ponce de León.
Higuito River, Honduras: see JICATUYO RIVER.
Hihya (hĭ′hyä), town (pop. 11,130), Sharqiya prov., Lower Egypt, on the Bahr Muweis and 8 mi. NE of Zagazig; cotton.
Hiisijärvi (hē′sĭyăr″vē), village in Ristijärvi commune (pop. 3,684), Oulu co., E central Finland, 30 mi. ENE of Kajaani; iron deposits.
Hiitola, Karelo-Finnish SSR: see KHIITOLA.
Hiiumaa or **Khiuma** (hē′ōōmä), Ger. *Dagden* (däk′dûn), Rus. *Dago* (dä′gû), Swedish *Dagö* (dä′gû), second-largest island (□ 373) of Estonia, in Baltic Sea, N of Saare isl. (separated by Soela Sound), 14 mi. off mainland; 37 mi. long, 28 mi. wide. Level terrain; poor sandy soils on limestone base. Some agr., stock raising (cattle, sheep); fisheries. Cotton-textile mfg. at Kardla, its main town and port. It was ruled after 1200 by Livonian Knights; isl. passed 1561 to Sweden; occupied 1710 by Russia.
Híjar (ē′här), town (pop. 3,280), Teruel prov., E Spain, 18 mi. WNW of Alcañiz; olive-oil processing, mfg. of candy and chocolate. Fruit, wheat, sheep in area. Irrigation reservoir near by. Coal mines.
Hijaz, Al-, Saudi Arabia: see HEJAZ.
Hijazah, Egypt: see HIGAZA.
Hiji (hē′jē), town (pop. 5,251), Oita prefecture, NE Kyushu, Japan, on SW Kunisaki Peninsula, 10 mi. NNW of Oita, on N shore of Beppu Bay; rice-growing center; sake.
Hijili, India: see KHARAGPUR.
Hijiri, Mount (hējē′rē) Jap. *Hijiri-dake* (9,936 ft.), central Honshu, Japan, on Shizuoka-Nagano prefecture border, 30 mi. SW of Kofu.
Hijo (ē′hō), town (1939 pop. 5,608), center of Tagum (tä′gōōm) municipality (1948 pop. 29,678), Davao prov., S central Mindanao, Philippines, at head of Davao Gulf, 26 mi. NE of Davao; abacá, coconuts.
Hijuelas (ēhwā′läs), town (pop. 1,963), Valparaiso prov., central Chile, on Aconcagua R. and 33 mi. NE of Valparaiso; agr. center (wine, hemp, fruit, grain, cattle).
Hikari (hēkä′rē), city (1940 pop. 21,786; 1947 pop. 36,050), Yamaguchi prefecture, SW Honshu, Japan, port on Suo Sea, just SE of Kudamatsu; agr. center; exports rice, raw silk, fish. Formed in early 1940s by combining adjacent towns of Hikari and Murozumi.
Hikawa (hēkä′wä), town (pop. 7,276), Greater Tokyo, central Honshu, Japan, 17 mi. NW of Hachioji; lumbering; raw silk.
Hike-shima, Japan: see SHIMONOSEKI.
Hiketa (hēkä′tä), town (pop. 7,286), Kagawa prefecture, NE Shikoku, Japan, on Harima Sea, 14 mi. NW of Tokushima; fishing port; canned fish, soy sauce, sake.
Hiki (hē′kē), town (pop. 5,580), Wakayama prefecture, S Honshu, Japan, on Philippine Sea, on S Kii Peninsula, 12 mi. SSE of Tanabe, in agr. area (rice, citrus fruit); raw silk, poultry.
Hikimoto (hēkē′mōtō), town (pop. 4,574), Mie prefecture, S Honshu, Japan, on E Kii Peninsula, on Kumano Sea, 38 mi. SW of Uji-yamada; fishing, agr., livestock raising.
Hikkaduwa (hĭk′kŭdōōvŭ), village (pop., including near-by villages, 3,500), Southern Prov., Ceylon, on SW coast, 10 mi. NNW of Galle; trades in vegetables, graphite, rubber, rice, tea, cinnamon, coral lime.
Hikone (hēkō′nä), city (1940 pop. 36,143; 1947 pop. 46,049), Shiga prefecture, S Honshu, Japan, on E shore of L. Biwa, 38 mi. WNW of Nagoya; textile center (cotton, silk, linen); pottery, cement, metalwork.
Hiko-shima, Japan: see SHIMONOSEKI.
Hikueru (hēkōōĕ′rōō), atoll (pop. 169), central Tuamotu Isls., Fr. Oceania, S Pacific; 17°36′S 142°40′W; pearl shell. Formerly Melville Isl.
Hikuma, Japan: see SHIZUOKA, city.
Hikurangi (hēkōōrăng′gē), town (pop. 1,030), N N.Isl., New Zealand, 90 mi. NNW of Auckland; coal mines; manganese, mercury.
Hilbersdorf (hĭl′bûrsdôrf). **1** Village (pop. 2,321), Saxony, E central Germany, at N foot of the Erzgebirge, on the Freiberger Mulde and 3 mi. E of Freiberg; mining (lead, tin, zinc, nickel). Inc. mining locality of Muldenhütten. **2** NNE industrial suburb of Chemnitz, Saxony, E central Germany.
Hilbert, village (pop. 648), Calumet co., E Wis., 14 mi. SE of Appleton; produces cheese, canned vegetables.
Hilbringen (hĕl′brĭng-ûn), town (pop. 1,413), NW Saar, on Saar R., just W of Merzig; iron smelting.
Hilchenbach (hĭl′khûnbäkh), town (pop. 3,812), in former Prussian prov. of Westphalia, W Germany, after 1945 in North Rhine-Westphalia, 9 mi. NE of Siegen; forestry.
Hilda, town (pop. 304), Barnwell co., W S.C., 27 mi. SW of Orangeburg.
Hildasay (hĭl′dúsā), island (1 mi. long) of the Shetlands, Scotland, off SW coast of Mainland isl., in the Deeps, 3 mi. W of Scalloway.
Hildburghausen (hĭlt′bōōrk-hou′zûn), town (pop. 7,870), Thuringia, central Germany, on the Werra and 15 mi. NW of Coburg; printing, wood- and metalworking, basket weaving. Has town hall, rebuilt 1572; former ducal palace (17th cent.), now mus.; 18th-cent. church. Insane asylum. Chartered 1324, town was ⊙ duchy of Saxe-Hildburghausen (1683–1826), then passed to Saxe-Meiningen. Bibliographic Inst., founded here 1828, was moved to Leipzig in 1874.
Hildebran, town (pop. 529), Burke co., W central N.C., 4 mi. WSW of Hickory; hosiery mfg.
Hilden (hĭl′dûn), town (pop. 24,345), in former Prussian Rhine Prov., W Germany, after 1945 in North Rhine-Westphalia, 7 mi. SE of Düsseldorf (linked by tramway); rail junction; Solingen steelworks; mfg. of machinery, bicycles, abrasives, artificial silk, textiles, umbrellas, varnish; dyeing, tanning. Has 12th-cent. late-Romanesque church. Chartered 1861.
Hilden, town (pop. 522), S Co. Antrim, Northern Ireland, on Lagan R. just NE of Lisburn; mfg. of twine, fish nets.
Hildenborough, town and parish (pop. 2,078), W Kent, England, 2 mi. NW of Tonbridge; agr. market; cricket-ball works.
Hildesheim (hĭl′dûs-hīm), city (1939 pop. 72,101; 1946 pop. 58,973; 1950 pop. 71,821), in former Prussian prov. of Hanover, NW Germany, after 1945 in Lower Saxony, on the Innerste and 17 mi. SE of Hanover; connected by short canal with Weser-Elbe Canal (10 mi. N); 52°9′N 9°58′E. Rail junction; foundries; mfg. of metal structural forms, machinery (agr., dairying), furnaces, chemicals, pharmaceuticals, cosmetics, dyes, rubber goods, textiles, shoes, washing machines, radios, furniture, organs, paper products. Food processing (dried vegetables, canned goods, meat and flour products, sugar), brewing, tanning, sawmilling. Hildesheim, frequently called the "North German Nuremberg," suffered severe destruction (about 50%) during Second World War. Heavily damaged were: Romanesque cathedral (founded 842), with Gothic additions; all of the noted Romanesque-Gothic churches; several museums (including contents). Gothic old town hall was gutted. Almost all of the numerous late-Gothic and Renaissance timbered houses were completely destroyed. Only noteworthy bldg. to escape damage was Romanesque church in W suburb of Moritzberg. Bishopric, founded 815, was cultural center of N Germany in 11th cent. Bishops were princes of the empire (13th cent.–1803). Town, chartered 1249, was member of Hanseatic League. Accepted Reformation in 1542; bishopric remained R.C. Passed to Prussia in 1803, to Hanover in 1815.
Hildreth, village (pop. 374), Franklin co., S Nebr., 40 mi. SW of Hastings; dairying, poultry, grain, livestock.
Hilgard, Mount, peak (11,527 ft.) in Fish Lake Plateau, S central Utah, 30 mi. ESE of Richfield.
Hilham (hĭ′lûm), town (pop. 177), Overton co., N Tenn., 7 mi. WNW of Livingston.
Hili, India: see HILLI.
Hilibandar, India: see HILLI.
Hill. 1 County (□ 2,944; pop. 14,285), N Mont.; ⊙ Havre. Agr. area bordering on Sask. and Alta.; drained by Milk R. Grain, livestock. Rocky Boy's Indian Reservation in SE. Formed 1912. **2** County (□ 1,028; pop. 31,282), N central Texas; ⊙ Hillsboro. Rich blackland prairies; bounded W by Brazos R. Agr. (especially cotton; also corn, grains, clover seed, hay, legumes, fruit, truck); livestock (cattle, poultry, hogs, sheep, horses); dairying; wool shipped. Mfg., processing at Hillsboro. In W is Whitney Dam (begun 1946) in Brazos R. Formed 1853.
Hill, town (pop. 310), Merrimack co., S central N.H., 5 mi. NNW of Franklin. Flood-control dam on Pemigewasset R. caused village to be moved to new site and rebuilt as model town, 1940–41. Original town settled 1768.
Hill 60, low ridge just SE of Ypres, West Flanders prov., W Belgium. In First World War, scene of heavy fighting (especially in 1915) in battles of Ypres.
Hill 70, height bet. Lens and Loos, Pas-de-Calais dept., N France, attacked with heavy losses by British in 1915 in battle of Loos, and carried by them (1917) in battle of Lens.
Hill 112, Calvados dept., NW France, 6 mi. SW of Caen, bet. Odon (W) and Orne (E) rivers. Scene of heavy fighting in battle for Caen (July, 1944), in Normandy campaign, Second World War. Monument.
Hill 204, Aisne dept., N France, 2 mi. W of Château-Thierry. Site of Aisne-Marne American Memorial commemorating successful Franco-American defense (June, 1918) of road to Paris.
Hill 304, France: see CUMIÈRES-LE-MORT-HOMME.
Hill 609 or **Djebel Tahent** (jĕ′bĕl tähĕnt′), height in N Tunisia, 13 mi. SW of Mateur, hotly contested in last phase of Tunisian campaign, and finally captured by Americans May 1, 1943.
Hilla or **Hillah** (hĭl′lù, hĭl′lù), province (□ 2,041; pop. 261,903), central Iraq, on the Euphrates; ⊙ Hilla. Dates, wheat, barley, corn, sesame. The Euphrates divides at Al Musaiyib into 2 branches, the Shatt Hilla and the Shatt Hindiya, which later rejoin. Basra-Baghdad RR parallels river. In the prov. are ruins of some of the greatest cities of antiquity: BABYLON, KISH, BORSIPPA.
Hilla or **Hillah**, town (pop. 51,361), ⊙ Hilla prov., central Iraq, on the Shatt Hilla (branch of the Euphrates), on railroad, and 60 mi. S of Baghdad; dates. Almost wholly built (c.1100) of bricks from the ruins of BABYLON, just NNE.
Hilla or **Hillah**, Saudi Arabia: see HAUTA.
Hilla, El, or **Al-Hillah** (both: ĕl), village (pop. 5,811), Qena prov., Upper Egypt, on E bank of the Nile opposite Isna; pottery making; cereals, sugar cane, dates. Sometimes spelled El Hella. It is on site of anc. Contra Latopolis.
Hilla, Shatt, or **Shatt Hillah** (shăt), river, central Iraq, an arm (c.120 mi. long) of the Euphrates, branching off the Euphrates below Al Musaiyib and flowing SE past Hilla, Diwaniya, and Rumaitha, to Samawa, where it unites with the Shatt Hindiya branch to reform the Euphrates. Irrigates Hilla and Diwaniya provs. Construction of the HINDIYA barrage has made it a canal.
Hillaby, Mount (hĭ′lùbē), hill (1,104 ft.), highest in Barbados, B.W.I., 7 mi. NNE of Bridgetown.
Hill Air Force Base, Utah: see OGDEN.
Hillburn, village (pop. 1,212), Rockland co., SE N.Y., in the Ramapos, at N.J. line, just W of Suffern, in resort area; mfg. of railroad equipment. Inc. 1893.
Hill City. 1 City (pop. 1,432), ⊙ Graham co., NW Kansas, on South Fork Solomon R. and 45 mi. NW of Hays; wheat. Laid out 1880, inc. 1888. **2** Resort village (pop. 501), Aitkin co., N central Minn., on small lake, 32 mi. N of Aitkin, in grain, potato, livestock region; dairy products. **3** Town (pop. 361), Pennington co., W S.Dak., 20 mi. SW of Rapid City, in Black Hills; alt. 4,976 ft. Agr.; gold, tungsten mines; timber. Near-by artificial lake used for recreation.
Hillcrest. 1 Residential village (1940 pop. 1,245), Broome co., S N.Y., suburb of Binghamton. **2** Village (pop. 2,826), Wichita co., N Texas.
Hillcrest Heights, town (pop. 91), Polk co., central Fla., 6 mi. SSE of Lake Wales, near Crooked L.
Hillebyn (hĭl′lùbün″), residential village (pop. 847), Gavleborg co., E Sweden, 4 mi. NNE of Gavle. Includes Varva (vär′vä) village.
Hillegersberg (hĭl′ĭ-khûrzbĕrkh′), residential town, South Holland prov., W Netherlands, 3 mi. N of Rotterdam; vegetable growing.
Hillegom (hĭl′ù-khôm), town (pop. 10,832), South Holland prov., W Netherlands, 7 mi. SSW of Haarlem and on the Ringvaart; important flower-

bulb-growing center; mfg. (cement, wood products); cattle raising.

Hill End, town (pop. 347), E central New South Wales, Australia, 120 mi. NW of Sydney; gold-mining center.

Hiller, village (pop. 1,326), Fayette co., SW Pa.

Hillerod (hĭ'lûrûdh), Dan. *Hillerød,* city (1950 pop. 10,023; 15,667, with Frederiksborg castle parish), ⊙ Frederiksborg amt, NE Zealand, Denmark, 20 mi. NNW of Copenhagen; 55°56'N 12°18'E. Mfg. (agr. machinery), brickworks, slaughterhouses, meat canneries; rail junction. On 3 isls. in small Frederiksborg L. is Frederiksborg, castle erected 1602–20 on site of earlier castle.

Hillers, Mount, Utah: see HENRY MOUNTAINS.

Hillersluis, Netherlands: see ROTTERDAM.

Hillesoy, Norway: see KVALOY, Troms co.

Hillestad, Norway: see BOTNE.

Hilli (hĭl'lē), town (pop. 6,952), West Dinajpur dist., N West Bengal, India, on Jamuna R. (tributary of the Atrai) and 60 mi. ENE of English Bazar; major rice-milling center; rice, jute, sugar cane, rape and mustard. Also called Hilibandar; also spelled Hili.

Hilliard. 1 Town (pop. 607), Nassau co., extreme NE Fla., 28 mi. NW of Jacksonville. **2** Village (pop. 610), Franklin co., central Ohio, 10 mi. WNW of Columbus, in agr. area.

Hillingdon, England: see UXBRIDGE.

Hill Island, SE Ont., on Ont.-N.Y. border, in the St. Lawrence, in Thousand Isls., 25 mi. ENE of Kingston; connected with Wellesley Isl., N.Y., and with Ont. mainland by Thousand Islands International Bridge.

Hillman. 1 Village (pop. 442), Montmorency co., N Mich., 22 mi. W of Alpena and on Thunder Bay R. **2** Village (pop. 85), Morrison co., central Minn., 24 mi. E of Little Falls; dairy products. Inc. 1938.

Hill Military Reservation, Va.: see FREDERICKSBURG.

Hillmorton, England: see RUGBY.

Hill of Beath, village and hill (705 ft.), SW Fifeshire, Scotland, 4 mi. ENE of Dunfermline; coal mining.

Hillrose, town (pop. 190), Morgan co., NE Colo., on South Platte R. and 16 mi. ENE of Fort Morgan; alt. 4,900 ft.

Hills. 1 Town (pop. 248), Johnson co., E Iowa, 7 mi. S of Iowa City, near Iowa R. **2** Village (pop. 520), Rock co., extreme SW Minn., on small tributary of Rock R., near Iowa line, and 19 mi. W of Sioux Falls, S.Dak., in grain, potato, livestock area; dairy products, cattle feed.

Hills and Dales, village (pop. 125), Stark co., E central Ohio, 4 mi. NW of Canton.

Hillsboro or **Hillsborough,** county (□ 890; pop. 156,987), S N.H., on Mass. line; ⊙ Manchester and Nashua. Mfg. center of N.H., one of leading industrial counties of U.S.; shoes, textiles, wood products, paper, tools, and machinery. Granite quarrying, lumbering, resorts, agr. (dairy products, poultry, stock). Water power furnished by Contoocook, Piscataquog, Souhegan, Merrimack, and Nashua rivers. Formed 1769.

Hillsboro. 1 Town (pop. 257), Lawrence co., NW Ala., near Wheeler Reservoir (in Tennessee R.), 12 mi. WNW of Decatur. **2** City (pop. 4,141), ⊙ Montgomery co., S central Ill., 8 mi. E of Litchfield, in agr. and bituminous-coal-mining area; corn, wheat, hay, livestock, poultry; mfg. of paper boxes, glass jars; zinc smelters. Inc. 1855. **3** Town (pop. 526), Fountain co., W Ind., 15 mi. WNW of Crawfordsville, in agr. and bituminous-coal area; feed, clay products. **4** Town (pop. 253), Henry co., SE Iowa, 12 mi. SW of Mount Pleasant; limestone quarries. **5** City (pop. 2,150), Marion co., central Kansas, 45 mi. N of Wichita, near Cottonwood R., in agr. area (winter wheat, corn, poultry, livestock); flour milling, bookbinding. Oil wells near by. Seat of Tabor Col. Founded 1879, inc. 1884. **6** Town (pop. 141), Fleming co., NE Ky., 36 mi. ESE of Cynthiana, in agr. area. **7** Town (pop. 179), Caroline co., E Md., on Tuckahoe Creek and 12 mi. NE of Easton. **8** Town (pop. 390), ⊙ Jefferson co., E Mo., near Mississippi R., 35 mi. SW of St. Louis; agr. **9** or **Hillsborough,** town (pop. 2,179; village pop. 1,670), Hillsboro co., S N.H., on the Contoocook (water power) and 19 mi. WSW of Concord. Textiles, clothing mills, lumber, dairy products, poultry, livestock. Franklin Pierce mansion, restored 1925, was built 1804 by president's father. Settled 1741, inc. 1772. **10** Village (pop. c.300), Sierra co., SW N.Mex., in SE foothills of Black Range, near Rio Grande, 24 mi. SW of Truth or Consequences; alt. 5,236 ft.; livestock. Once a busy silver-mining point with pop. (1886) of 5,000. Gila Natl. Forest just W. **11** Town (pop. 1,329), ⊙ Orange co., N central N.C., 11 mi. NW of Durham; mfg. of textiles, furniture, wood products. An early ⊙ prov. of N.C.; in 1768, scene of disturbances by the Regulators. Thomas Hart Benton b. here. Settled before 1700; platted 1754. **12** City (pop. 1,331), ⊙ Traill co., E N.Dak., 39 mi. N of Fargo and on Goose R.; grain, livestock, dairy products, potatoes. Platted 1880, inc. 1881. **13** City (pop. 5,126), ⊙ Highland co., SW Ohio, 34 mi. WSW of Chillicothe; trade center for stock-raising, farming, and limestone-quarrying area; mfg. (trousers, agr. machinery, foundry products). In 1873, Women's Temperance Crusade was founded here. Several mound builders' forts are near by. Platted 1807. **14** City (pop. 5,142), ⊙ Washington co., NW Oregon, on Tualatin R. and 14 mi. W of Portland; trade and shipping point; food processing (quick-frozen fruits and vegetables), canning, dairying; lumber, bricks and tiles. Settled c.1845, inc. 1876. **15** City (pop. 8,363), ⊙ Hill co., N central Texas, 32 mi. N of Waco; trade, shipping center for rich blackland agr. area (cotton; also livestock, dairying). Cotton, cottonseed, dairy-products processing, textile milling, mfg. of clothing, feed, concrete blocks, heaters. Seat of a jr. col. and a childrens' home. Inc. 1853. **16** Town (pop. 129), Loudoun co., N Va., 10 mi. NW of Leesburg. **17** Village (pop. 241), Pocahontas co., E W.Va., 9 mi. SW of Marlinton. Droop Mtn. Battlefield State Park is just SW. **18** City (pop. 1,341), Vernon co., SW Wis., on tributary of Baraboo R. and 45 mi. ESE of La Crosse, in timber and farm area; dairy products, flour, lumber. Settled 1854; inc. as village in 1885, as city in 1939.

Hillsboro Bay, Fla.: see TAMPA BAY.

Hillsboro Beach, village (pop. 84), Broward co., S Fla., near Pompano. Also spelled Hillsborough Beach.

Hillsboro River, central and W Fla., rises N of Lakeland, flows c.55 mi. NW and then SW to Hillsboro Bay (an arm of Tampa Bay), at Tampa.

Hillsborough, village (pop. estimate c.700), SE N.B., on Petitcodiac R. estuary and 13 mi. SE of Moncton; ships oil shale, albertite, manganese, coal, gypsum. Settled 1765.

Hillsborough, town (pop. 272), W Carriacou, Grenadines, B.W.I., 35 mi. NE of St. George's, Grenada; 12°28'N 61°27'W. Has fine harbor. Cotton, limes.

Hillsborough (hĭlz'bûrû), town (pop. 1,199), N Co. Down, Northern Ireland, 11 mi. SW of Belfast; linen milling; agr. market (flax). Hillsborough Castle is official residence of governor of Northern Ireland. Fort dates from 17th cent. and church was built 1774.

Hillsborough, county (□ 1,040; pop. 249,894), W Fla., on Gulf coast and bounded S and partly W by Tampa Bay; ⊙ Tampa. Rolling and level terrain with many small lakes; drained by Hillsboro R. Agr. (citrus fruit; truck, especially tomatoes and strawberries; peanuts; corn), dairying, poultry raising, fishing. Mfg. (food, tobacco, and wood products). Some quarrying (phosphate, sand, shells). Formed 1834.

Hillsborough, residential town (pop. 3,552), San Mateo co., W Calif., c.15 mi. S of San Francisco, near San Mateo. Inc. 1910.

Hillsborough Bay, inlet (10 mi. long, 10 mi. wide at entrance) of Northumberland Strait, S central P.E.I. Receives Hillsborough R. at its head at Charlottetown. St. Peters Isl. is in entrance of bay.

Hillsborough Beach, Fla.: see HILLSBORO BEACH.

Hillsborough River, central P.E.I., rises 18 mi. ENE of Charlottetown, flows 30 mi. W and SW, past Charlottetown, to Hillsborough Bay at Charlottetown.

Hillsborough River, narrow lagoon (c.18 mi. long) in Volusia co., NE Fla., sheltered from the Atlantic by barrier beach; extends S from Ponce de Leon Inlet (at S end of Halifax R. lagoon) to N end of Mosquito Lagoon. Followed by Intracoastal Waterway.

Hillsburgh, village (pop. estimate 500), S Ont., 18 mi. NNE of Guelph; dairying, mixed farming.

Hillsdale, village (pop. estimate 400), S Ont., 17 mi. W of Orillia; dairying, mixed farming.

Hillsdale, county (□ 601; pop. 31,916), S Mich.; ⊙ Hillsdale. Bounded S by Ohio line; drained by headstreams of the Kalamazoo and by St. Joseph R. Agr. (grain, fruit, soybeans, livestock, poultry; dairy products). Mfg. at Hillsdale, Jonesville, and Reading. Many small lakes. Organized 1835.

Hillsdale. 1 City (1940 pop. 142), Miami co., E Kansas, 30 mi. SSW of Kansas City, Kansas; cattle raising, farming. **2** City (pop. 7,297), ⊙ Hillsdale co., S Mich., 25 mi. SSW of Jackson and on St. Joseph R. Trade and mfg. center (auto and airplane parts, tools, food products, clothing, brooms). Seat of Hillsdale Col., with 60-acre Slayton Arboretum. Indian mounds near by. Settled 1834; inc. as village 1847, as city 1869. **3** Town (pop. 2,902), St. Louis co., E Mo., just NW of St. Louis. **4** Borough (pop. 4,127), Bergen co., NE N.J., 8 mi. N of Hackensack; concrete products; fruit, truck. Inc. 1923. **5** Village, Columbia co., SE N.Y., near Mass. line, 8 mi. W of Great Barrington, Mass. Skiing at near-by Catamount Mtn. in the Berkshires. **6** Town (pop. 104), Garfield co., N Okla., 13 mi. NW of Enid, in agr. area.

Hillsgrove, village (pop. c.1,000) in Warwick city, Kent co., E central R.I., 7 mi. SSW of Providence, near Pawtuxet R.; mfg. (heaters, iron castings, beverages). R.I. state airport here.

Hillside, residential town (pop. 3,645), SW Southern Rhodesia, 3 mi. SSE of Bulawayo. Has govt. preparatory school.

Hillside. 1 Village (pop. 2,131), Cook co., NE Ill., W suburb of Chicago, 10 mi. E of Wheaton. Inc. 1905. **2** Village (1940 pop. 1,605), Prince Georges co., central Md., ESE suburb of Washington. **3** Township (pop. 21,007), Union co., NE N.J., SW suburb of Newark; mfg. (machinery, metal products; rubber, asbestos, cork, and paper goods; hydrogen, pharmaceuticals, plastics; silica, quartz, concrete and stone products); dairy products. Inc. 1913.

Hillside Gardens, village (pop. 1,012, with adjacent Riverside), Jackson co., S Mich.

Hill States, India: see PUNJAB HILL STATES.

Hill Station, Sierra Leone: see FREETOWN.

Hillston, town (pop. 829), S central New South Wales, Australia, on Lachlan R. and 260 mi. ESE of Broken Hill; sheep and agr. center.

Hillsview, town (pop. 68), McPherson co., N S.Dak., 55 mi. WNW of Aberdeen.

Hillsville, town (pop. 764), ⊙ Carroll co., SW Va., in the Blue Ridge, 12 mi. NE of Galax; agr. (grain, cabbage); timber.

Hillswick, village on NW coast of Mainland isl., Shetlands, Scotland, on N shore of St. Magnus Bay, 25 mi. NNW of Lerwick; fishing port and tourist resort. Near by are the Drongs, a series of interesting rock formations.

Hill Tippera, state, India: see TRIPURA.

Hilltonia, town (pop. 318), Screven co., E Ga., 10 mi. NNW of Sylvania.

Hilltop, village (pop. 2,459, with near-by Scarbro and Glen Jean), Fayette co., S central W.Va., 11 mi. N of Beckley, in coal region.

Hilltown, agr. village (district pop. 842), S Co. Down, Northern Ireland, on Bann R. and 8 mi. ENE of Newry; flax, oats; sheep raising. Angling resort.

Hillview, village (pop. 419), Greene co., W Ill., near Illinois R., 24 mi. SW of Jacksonville, in agr. and bituminous-coal area.

Hillview Reservoir (90 acres), Westchester co., SE N.Y., in Yonkers; part of New York city water-supply system; completed 1915. Terminus of Catskill and Delaware aqueducts, and head of tunnel system delivering water to boroughs of New York city.

Hilmand River, Afghanistan: see HELMAND RIVER.

Hilo (hē'lō), city (pop. 27,198), ⊙ Hawaii co., E Hawaii, T.H., on Hilo Bay; port of entry. Seat of airport, Lyman Mus. with collection of Hawaiiana, beach park on Coconut Isl. in bay, Rainbow Falls in outskirts of city. Severely damaged in recent years by tidal waves. Has fruit canneries, rice mill, iron works; exports agr. produce (sugar, coffee, rice, fruits).

Hilo Bay, crescent-shaped indention, only anchorage on E coast, Hawaii, T.H.; exposed to NE trade wind, vulnerable to tidal waves. Coconut Isl., in the bay, has beach park.

Hilongos (hēlông'gōs, ē–), town (1939 pop. 3,195; 1948 municipality pop. 27,310), W Leyte, Philippines, on Canigao Channel; agr. center (rice, coconuts, corn).

Hilpoltstein (hĭl'pôlt-shtīn″), town (pop. 3,029), Middle Franconia, central Bavaria, Germany, 18 mi. SSE of Nuremberg; mfg. of metal products, toys, chemicals; printing, lumber milling, brewing. Has ruins of castle and medieval fortifications.

Hilsbach (hĭls'bäkh), town (pop. 1,837), N Baden, Germany, after 1945 in Württemberg-Baden, 13 mi. ENE of Bruchsal; sandstone quarries.

Hilschbach, Saar: see RIEGELSBERG.

Hilton. 1 Village, Perry co., Ky.: see HILTONIAN. **2** Village (pop. 1,036), Monroe co., W N.Y., 13 mi. NW of Rochester; canning, flour milling; agr. (fruit, wheat, truck).

Hiltonbeach or **Hilton Beach,** village (pop. 182), S central Ont., on St. Joseph Isl., on St. Joseph Channel of L. Huron, 28 mi. SE of Sault Ste. Marie; lumbering.

Hiltonhead, village, S.C.: see HILTON HEAD ISLAND.

Hilton Head Island, S S.C., one of Sea Isls., SW of Port Royal Sound, 17 mi. ENE of Savannah, Ga.; c.12 mi. long, 1–5 mi. wide. Hiltonhead village (pop. 985) on W shore.

Hiltonian or **Hilton,** village (1940 pop. 548), Perry co., SE Ky., in Cumberland foothills, 3 mi. N of Hazard, in bituminous-coal-mining area.

Hilton Park, suburb (pop. 14,960, with adjacent Newsome Park) of Newport News, Warwick co., SE Va.

Hilton Village or **Hilton,** residential suburban village (pop. 4,486), Warwick co., SE Va., on the James just N of Newport News. Has Mariners' Mus. (1930). Near by was fought (June 10, 1861) the battle of Big Bethel, one of 1st battles of Civil War, in which a Union attack was repulsed.

Hiltrup (hĭl'trŏŏp), village (pop. 6,341), in former Prussian prov. of Westphalia, NW Germany, afters 1945 in North Rhine-Westphalia, 3 mi. S of Münster; dairying.

Hilvan (hĭlvän'), village (pop. 1,316), Urfa prov., S Turkey, 32 mi. NNE of Urfa; wheat, barley, sesame, lentils. Also called Karacurun.

Hilvarenbeek (hĭl'värûnbāk), town (pop. 2,930), North Brabant prov., S Netherlands, 6 mi. SSE of Tilburg; shoe mfg.

Hilversum (hĭl'vûrsûm), city (pop. 85,051), North Holland prov., W central Netherlands, 16 mi. SE of Amsterdam; rail junction; residential town; health resort, with several sanatoria; radio-broadcasting center. Mfg. (electrical machinery, radios, carpets, dyes, furniture, cigars); diamond polishing. Noted for modern architecture.

Hilwan, Egypt: see HELWAN.

Hima (hī'mŭ), village (1940 pop. 649), Clay co., SE Ky., in Cumberland foothills, 35 mi. N of Middlesboro, in coal, timber, and agr. area.

Himachal Pradesh (hĭmä'chŭl prŭdäsh'), chief commissioner's state (□ 10,600; 1951 census pop. 989,437), NW India; ⊙ SIMLA. Lies in W Himalayas; consists of 2 sections separated by Kangra dist. of Punjab; larger S area bordered E by Tibet, S by Uttar Pradesh, and W by Punjab, detached E section of Patiala and East Punjab States Union, and Bilaspur; N area bordered N and W by Kashmir. Lofty mtn. ranges and narrow river valleys characterize most of state. Drained N by Chenab R., S by Sutlej and Beas rivers. Extensive coniferous forests (deodar, pine) provide chief source of income; potatoes, fruit (apples, peaches), nuts, rock salt (mined in Mandi dist.), ginger, and turmeric are other export products. Wheat, rice, corn grown in lower valleys; sheep and goat raising; hand-loom woolen weaving, wood carving. Large hydroelectric plant at Jogindarnagar. Principal towns are Chamba, Mandi, and Nahan; several picturesque hill resorts situated around Punjab town of Simla. State was formed 1948 by merger of former PUNJAB princely states of Chamba, Mandi, and Suket, and former Punjab Hill states of Bashahr, Sirmur, Jubbal, Keonthal, Baghal, Bhajji, Kumharsain, Tharoch, Balsan, Mailog, Baghat, Dhami, Kuthar, Sangri, Mangal, Kunihar, Bija, and Darkoti. Now divided into 4 dists.: Chamba, Mahasu, Mandi, Sirmur. Pop. 96% Hindu, 3% Moslem.

Himalayas (hĭmä'lŭyŭz, hĭmŭlā'ŭz) or **The Himalaya** [Sanskrit,=abode of snow], anc. *Imaus*, great mountain system bet. the high plateau of central Asia and the alluvial plains of the Indian subcontinent, enclosed within arms of Indus (N and W) and Brahmaputra (N and E) rivers and containing some of the highest peaks in the world. From the Indus bend the Himalayas extend c.1,500 mi. ESE in a broad curve, through NW Pakistan, Kashmir, N India, S Tibet, Nepal, Sikkim, and Bhutan, to the Brahmaputra bend; 100–150 mi. wide. Geographically divided into 4 sections: PUNJAB HIMALAYAS, bet. Indus and Sutlej rivers; KUMAUN HIMALAYAS, bet. Sutlej and Kali (Sarda) rivers; NEPAL HIMALAYAS, bet. Kali and Tista rivers; and ASSAM HIMALAYAS, bet. Tista and Brahmaputra rivers. The Himalayas are sometimes considered to be structurally related to the Hindu Kush and Baluchistan ranges in the W and to the mts. of Sikang (China) and W Burma in the E. On the NW the upper Indus separates the system from Karakoram, Ladakh, and Kailas ranges, and on the N and NE the upper Brahmaputra separates it from Kailas and Nyenchen Tanglha ranges (S limits of the Trans-Himalayas). The Himalayan ranges may be grouped into 3 longitudinal zones, descending from N to S: Great Himalayas, or main range, with a crest-line of c.20,000 ft., perpetually snow-clad and including such famous peaks as Mt. EVEREST (29,002 ft.; world's highest point), KANCHENJUNGA (28,146 ft.), Makalu (27,790 ft.), Dhaulagiri (26,810 ft.), NANGA PARBAT (26,660 ft.), NANDA DEVI (25,645 ft.), and Namcha Barwa (25,445 ft.); Lesser Himalayas, with an alt. of 7–15,000 ft., running parallel to and sometimes merging with main range and enclosing noted Vale of KASHMIR and NEPAL VALLEY; and the Outer Himalayas (2–5,000 ft.), consisting mainly of SIWALIK RANGE. The E Himalayas are structurally simpler than the W section, where the main range throws off lateral spurs—ZASKAR RANGE and PIR PANJAL RANGE. All of major rivers rising in the Himalayas flow S; the Jhelum, Chenab, Ravi, and Beas drain into the Indus to Arabian Sea, while Jumna, Ganges, Sarda, Gogra, Gandak, Kosi, Tista, and Subansiri rivers flow into Bay of Bengal via the Ganges Delta. The snow line varies bet. 15,000 and 19,000 ft. (E-W), and glaciers descend to 11–15,000 ft. The Himalayas, which form a barrier to the cold air currents of central Asia from the N and to the moisture-laden winds from the S, may be divided into E and W climatic regions. The E region (Assam and Nepal Himalayas), characterized by heavy monsoon rainfall (90–120 in.), rises abruptly from swampy, undulating ground of the Terai and Duars (S) through successive belts of dense subtropical (Outer Himalayas), live oak (5–9,000 ft.), and coniferous (9–12,000 ft.) forests to alpine zone (12–16,000 ft.; rhododendrons, grass tufts) and perpetual snow line. Sal timber in monsoon forests and tea gardens on lower slopes are important. The W region, comparatively drier (rainfall 20–70 in., decreasing E-W), rises more gradually from the plains and passes through belts of scattered scrub and bamboo, temperate forests (5–12,000 ft.; oak, pine, deodar), and alpine wastes (12–17,000 ft.) to the snow line. Grain, corn, potatoes, fruit, and spices are grown in places throughout the lower Himalayan valleys. Mtn. goats and sheep graze in upland pastures, and yaks are used as pack animals; elephants, tigers, leopards, and rhinoceroses are common at base of E Himalayas. Most accessible mineral deposits are found in the W, where small amounts of iron ore, slate, rock salt, graphite, gold, and sapphires are worked. The Himalayan rivers, with their perennial flow, offer much scope for hydroelectric power and irrigation development. Besides the Jogindarnagar works (Himachal Pradesh, India), other projects include those on the Sutlej (at Bhakra), KOSI RIVER, and Sarda R. The towering ranges present an almost insuperable barrier to travel, even by air, and the small trade existing bet. India and Tibet is an arduous undertaking. Railroads reach only to the S foothills, whence the main routes follow mere footpaths across primitive bridges, ropeways, and high mtn. passes. In Kashmir, roads from Srinagar to Gilgit and Leh run via Burzil Pass (13,775 ft.) and Zoji La respectively; Gartok (W Tibet) is reached from India through Shipki Pass (c.15,400 ft.) from Simla and via Anta Dhura and Lipu La passes from Tanakpur; Jelep La (c.14,390 ft.) and Natu La passes lie on main India-Tibet trade route bet. Kalimpong and Gyangtse through Chumbi Valley. Himalayan hill resorts (bet. 6,000 and 8,000 ft.) of SIMLA, NAINI TAL, Mussoorie, and DARJEELING are popular summer retreats from the heat of the Indian plains; SRINAGAR, in the Vale of Kashmir, is famous for its picturesque setting. Other important towns include Jammu (Kashmir), Dehra (Uttar Pradesh, India), the Nepalese cities of Katmandu, Patan, and Bhadgaon, Gangtok (⊙ Sikkim), and Punakha (⊙ Bhutan). The hill people are mostly of Mongolian stock, although in the W Kashmiris predominate. Geologically the Himalayas were formed during the Tertiary era by a powerful compression of the central Asian upland against the Indian peninsula—which has left the S slopes generally steeper than those on the N. In this mtn.-building era the great Alpine and Andean uplifts also occurred. The Great and Lesser Himalayan ranges are composed of crystalline rocks with igneous intrusions, deeply eroded and flanked by thick, unfossiliferous sediments, while the outer ranges consist entirely of late Tertiary sediments, highly fossiliferous. The great mtn. wall, which gives rise to some of the most sacred rivers of India and which is associated with many legends in Hindu mythology, bulks large in the Indian imagination. On isolated slopes are the retreats of rishis (holy sages), gurus, and Tibetan monks. Most of the lofty peaks have been attempted by mtn. climbers in recent years, but the highest still remain unconquered; ANNAPURNA (26,502 ft.) was (1950) highest scaled. The region is subject to severe earthquakes, considerable damage being caused by landslides and floods, especially in 1897 and 1950.

Himamaylan (hēmämī'län, ēmä–), town (1939 pop. 3,389; 1948 municipality pop. 33,984), Negros Occidental prov., W Negros isl., Philippines, on Panay Gulf, 7 mi. S of Binalbagan; agr. center (rice, coconuts).

Himarë (hēmä'rŭ) or **Himara** (hēmä'rä), Ital. *Chimara*, anc. *Chimaera*, town (1945 pop. 2,150), S Albania, 27 mi. SE of Valona, near Ionian Sea coast (its ports are SPILË and Port PALERMO); citrus-growing center; oranges, lemons.

Himatnagar (hĭmŭt'nŭgŭr), town (pop. 6,426), ⊙ Sabar Kantha dist., N Bombay, India, 45 mi. NNE of Ahmadabad; market center for grain, oilseeds, cloth fabrics; cotton ginning, hand-loom weaving, oilseed milling, mfg. of matches, pottery, glass. Sandstone quarries near by. Was ⊙ former Western India state of Idar. Sometimes spelled Himmatnagar; formerly called Ahmadnagar.

Himayat Sagar, India: see HYDERABAD, city.

Himberg (hĭm'bĕrk), town (pop. 2,732), after 1938 in Schwechat dist. of Vienna, Austria, 9 mi. SSE of city center; vineyards.

Himedo (hēmā'dō), largest village (pop. 6,562) of Kami-shima, Amakusa Isls., Japan, in Kumamoto prefecture, on E coast of isl.; fishing.

Himeji (hēmā'jē), city (1940 pop. 104,259; 1947 pop. 197,299), Hyogo prefecture, S Honshu, Japan, 32 mi. WNW of Kobe. Rail and industrial center; cotton-textile mills, chemical plants, engineering works; leather goods, woodworking. Site of 10th-cent. Buddhist temple. Remains of 14th-cent. castle near by. Bombed (1945) in Second World War. Since c.1947, includes former city of SHIKAMA (S) and several neighboring towns.

Himera (hĭ'mŭrŭ), ancient Greek colony on N coast of Sicily, near mouth of the Himera Septentrionalis (Grande R.). Founded by Zancleans (Messinians) in 648 B.C.; attained great power and, aided by Syracusans, defeated Carthaginians in 480 B.C. Carthage razed the town in 409 B.C.; inhabitants fled to their outpost at Thermae Himerenses, 7 mi. W. Ruins include Doric temple and tombs.

Himera Meridionalis, Sicily: see SALSO RIVER.

Himera Septentrionalis, Sicily: see GRANDE RIVER.

Himi (hē'mē). **1** Town, Ehime prefecture, Japan: see SAIJO. **2** Town (pop. 22,764), Toyama prefecture, central Honshu, Japan, at base of Noto Peninsula, fishing port on SW shore of Toyama Bay; fish processing. Summer resort.

Himis Gompa (hē'mēs gôm'pä), noted Buddhist monastery, Ladakh dist., E central Kashmir, in Zaskar Range, near the Indus, 20 mi. SSE of Leh. Founded 17th cent. Large annual (June) festival with devil dance. Also spelled Hemis Gompa.

Himlerville or **Beauty,** town (pop. 577), Martin co., E Ky., in Cumberland foothills, near Tug Fork, 27 mi. N of Pikeville.

Himmelberg (hĭ'mŭlbĕrk), town (pop. 2,434), Carinthia, S Austria, 15 mi. NW of Klagenfurt; lumber and paper mills; summer resort.

Himmelbjaerget (hĭ'mŭlbyĕr-khŭt), group of hills, E Jutland, Denmark, rising to 531 ft. Largely wooded, with several lakes (largest, JUL LAKE) traversed by Guden R.

Himmelpforten (hĭ'mŭlpfôr'tŭn), village (pop. 2,137), in former Prussian prov. of Hanover, NW Germany, after 1945 in Lower Saxony, 7 mi. W of Stade; flour milling; cattle.

Himmelriiki, Finland: see PALLAS MOUNTAINS.

Himmelsthür (hĭ'mŭlstür'), village (pop. 2,482), in former Prussian prov. of Hanover, NW Germany, after 1945 in Lower Saxony, 3 mi. WNW of Hildesheim; apparel.

Himmerland (hĭ'mŭrlăn), sometimes called **Himmersyssel** (–sü"sŭl), hilly region, N Jutland, Denmark, along the Kattegat and bet. Lim Fjord and Mariager Fjord; highest point, 374 ft. Unfertile; largely moor and forest area.

Himminghausen (hĭ"mĭng-hou'zŭn), village (pop. 531), in former Prussian prov. of Westphalia, NW Germany, after 1945 in North Rhine-Westphalia, 5 mi. N of Bad Driburg; rail junction.

Himoga-an, Philippines: see HIMUGAAN.

Himugaan (hēmōōgä-än', ēmōō–), town (1939 pop. 5,391) in Sagay municipality, Negros Occidental prov., N Negros isl., Philippines, on Visayan Sea, 35 mi. NE of Bacolod; agr. center (rice, sugar cane). Also spelled Himoga-an.

Hinagu (hēnä'gōō), town (pop. 8,171), Kumamoto prefecture, W Kyushu, Japan, on Yatsushiro Bay, 27 mi. SSW of Kumamoto; hot-springs resort in agr. area.

Hinase (hēnä'sä) or **Hinashi** (–shē), town (pop. 8,077), Okayama prefecture, SW Honshu, Japan, on Harima Sea, 18 mi. ENE of Okayama; fishing center. Rice, wheat, persimmons, sake.

Hinatuan (hēnätōō'än, ēnä'twän), town (1939 pop. 2,660; 1948 municipality pop. 12,395), Surigao prov., Philippines, on NE coast of Mindanao. Sawmill near by.

Hin Boun, Nam, Laos: see PAK HIN BOUN.

Hinche (ēsh), town (1950 census pop. 4,511), Artibonite dept., E central Haiti, on fertile plain, 45 mi. NE of Port-au-Prince; cotton, fruit, cattle. Airfield.

Hinchinbrook, Cape (hĭn'chĭnbrŏŏk), S Alaska, S tip of Hinchinbrook Isl.; 60°16'N 146°37'W.

Hinchinbrooke, England: see HUNTINGDON.

Hinchinbrook Entrance, S Alaska, bet. Hinchinbrook Isl. (E) and Montague Isl. (W), joins Gulf of Alaska and Prince William Sound.

Hinchinbrook Island (22 mi. long, 4–13 mi. wide), S Alaska, in Gulf of Alaska, at mouth of Prince William Sound, 20 mi. SW of Cordova; 60°23'N 146°25'W; rises to 2,815 ft. Nuchek village is in W.

Hinchinbrook Island (hĭn'chĭnbrŏŏk) (□ 152; pop. 9,223), in Coral Sea just off E coast of Queensland, Australia, within Great Barrier Reef, N of Lucinda Point; 20 mi. long, 9 mi. wide; mountainous, rising to 3,650 ft. Cape Sandwich, its N point (18°14'S 146°19'E), forms S side of entrance to Rockingham Bay. Timber, agr. products.

Hinckley, urban district (1931 pop. 16,030; 1951 census 39,088), SW Leicester, England, 11 mi. NE of Coventry; hosiery and shoe center; textile printing; mfg. of electrical appliances and pharmaceuticals. Has notable 13th-cent. church.

Hinckley. 1 Village (pop. 774), De Kalb co., N Ill., 16 mi. W of Aurora, in rich agr. area; brick, tile, cement blocks. **2** Village (pop. 902), Pine co., E Minn., on small affluent of Kettle R. and 14 mi. N of Pine City, in grain, livestock, poultry area; dairy products. **3** Town (pop. 589), Millard co., W Utah, 5 mi. SW of Delta; alt. 4,600 ft.; agr., livestock.

Hinckley Reservoir, N.Y.: see WEST CANADA CREEK.

Hindaun (hĭndoun'), town (pop. 13,804), E Rajasthan, India, 75 mi. ESE of Jaipur; markets cotton, wheat, barley, millet, oilseeds. Sandstone quarried near by. Cotton ginning at rail station, 1 mi. N.

Hindelang (hĭn'dŭläng), village (pop. 5,039), Swabia, SW Bavaria, Germany, in Allgäu Alps, 4 mi. E of Sonthofen; brewing, dairying, tanning; summer and winter resort (alt. 2,706 ft.).

Hindeloopen (hĭn'dŭlōpŭn), town (pop. 924), and port, Friesland prov., N Netherlands, on the IJsselmeer, 13 mi. WSW of Sneek; furniture mfg.; fishing; summer resort. Has 17th-cent. church and town hall. Once famous for making painted furniture.

Hindenburg (hĭn'dŭnbûrg, Ger. hĭn'dŭnbŏŏrk) or **Zabrze** (zäb'zhĕ), industrial city (1939 pop. 126,220; 1946 census pop. 104,184; 1950 pop. estimate 132,900) in Upper Silesia, after 1945 in Katowice prov., S Poland, 11 mi. WNW of Katowice, 100 mi. SE of Breslau (Wroclaw); 50°18'N 18°47'E. Important rail junction; coal-mining and steel-milling center; mfg. of machinery, chemicals, glass. Gas works supply Upper Silesian industrial dist. by pipe-line system. Founded 13th cent., Zabrze passed 1742 to Prussia; renamed Hindenburg in 1915; returned to Poland in 1945, and its old name restored. In 1927, many adjacent communes were incorporated into the city. Until 1939, Ger. frontier station on Pol. border, opposite Chorzow. Considerably damaged in Second World War.

Hindenburgdamm (hĭn'dŭnbo͝ork"däm'), dike (8 mi. long), on North Sea coast of Schleswig-Holstein, NW Germany, carrying railroad bet. Sylt isl. and mainland; 26 ft. high, c.160 ft. wide. Built 1923–27.

Hinderwell, former urban district (1931 pop. 2,146), North Riding, NE Yorkshire, England, near North Sea, 8 mi. WNW of Whitby; agr. market. Just NNW, on a small creek flowing into the North Sea, is resort and fishing village of Staithes. James Cook b. here.

Hindhead, England: see FRENSHAM.

Hindian, Iran: see HINDIJAN.

Hindijan or **Hendijan** (both: hĕndējän'), town (1942 pop. estimate 2,000), Sixth Prov., in Khuzistan, SW Iran, 85 mi. E of Abadan, and on Zuhreh R. (here called Hindijan R.) just above its mouth on Persian Gulf; stock raising; grain, cotton. Also called Hindian.

Hindiya or **Hindiyah** (hĭndē'yŭ), town, Hilla prov., central Iraq, on the Shatt Hindiya (branch of the Euphrates), and 12 mi. WNW of Hilla; dates, corn, millet. Here is a floating bridge. The Hindiya barrage is 10 mi. NNE at the bifurcation of the Hilla and Hindiya branches of the Euphrates. Built in 1911 and repaired in 1917 mainly to feed the Hilla branch which had dried out, the barrage feeds numerous irrigation canals. Also called Tuwairij, Tuwairiq, Tuwayriq, or Tuwayrij.

Hindiya, Shatt, or **Shatt Hindiyah** (shät), river, central Iraq, an arm (c.130 mi. long) of the Euphrates, branching off the Euphrates below Al Musaiyib (S of which is the Hindiya barrage), and flows past Al Kufa to Samawa, where it joins the Shatt Hilla branch to reform the Euphrates.

Hindley (hĭnd'lē), urban district (1931 pop. 21,632; 1951 census 19,414), S Lancashire, England, 3 mi. SE of Wigan; cotton milling. Has 17th-cent. church, rebuilt in 18th cent.

Hindman (hīn'mŭn), town (pop. 521), ⊙ Knott co., E Ky., in Cumberland foothills, 13 mi. ENE of Hazard, in coal-mining and agr. area. Seat of Hindman Settlement School (founded 1902; 1st of its type in Ky.). At near-by Pippapass is Caney Jr. Col. and Community Center.

Hindmarsh (hīnd'märsh), NW suburb (pop. 14,537) of Adelaide, SE South Australia, on N shore of Torrens R.; flour mill.

Hindmarsh, Lake, salt lake (□ 47), W central Victoria, Australia, 200 mi. NW of Melbourne; 12 mi. long, 5 mi. wide; frequently dry. Jeparit village near S shore.

Hindol (hĭn'dōl), village, Dhenkanal dist., E central Orissa, India, 45 mi. WNW of Cuttack; exports timber. Was ⊙ former princely state of Hindol (□ 291; pop. 58,505) in Orissa States; state inc. 1949 into newly-created Dhenkanal dist.

Hindoli (hĭndō'lē), village, SE Rajasthan, India, 13 mi. NW of Bundi; millet, gram.

Hindostan, India: see HINDUSTAN.

Hindoy, Norway: see HINNOY.

Hinds (hīndz), county (□ 877; pop. 142,164), W Miss.; ⊙ JACKSON (⊙ Miss.) and Raymond. Bounded E by Pearl R., NW and partly W by Big Black R. Agr. (cotton, corn, truck), cattle and poultry raising. Timber; natural gas. Formed 1821.

Hindsboro (hīndz'bŭrō), village (pop. 377), Douglas co., E central Ill., 18 mi. NE of Mattoon, in agr. area.

Hind's Hill (2,158 ft.), W central N.F., 45 mi. E of Corner Brook, overlooking Hind's L.

Hind's Lake (□ 14), W central N.F., 40 mi. E of Corner Brook, at foot of Hind's Hill; 7 mi. long, 3 mi. wide.

Hindubagh (hĭn'do͞obäg), village, Zhob dist., NE Baluchistan, W Pakistan, on Zhob R. and 60 mi. NE of Quetta; market center for wheat, rice, felts. Chromite mined in hills (S); asbestos deposits in Toba-Kakar Range (N).

Hindu Kush (hĭn'do͞o ko͞osh'), Pashto *Hindu Koh* (kō'), one of the main mountain systems in central Asia, situated largely in NE Afghanistan; extends from the Pamir mountain knot at W termination (37°N 74°E) of the Karakoram southwestward for 400 mi. to 35°N 68°E in central Afghanistan near the Bamian valley. The E section, on Afghanistan-Pakistan (Chitral state) line, rivals the Karakoram in the height of its peaks and the extent of its glaciers; here rises the Tirich Mir (25,263 ft.), the system's culminating peak. In W section, the Hindu Kush fans out in several outliers, covering most of central Afghanistan. These are the Koh-i-Baba, Band-i-Turkestan, Paropamisus Mts., Safed Koh, Siah Koh, and the jumbled ranges of the Hazarajat. In Afghanistan, the Hindu Kush forms the natural divide bet. Badakhshan, Kataghan, and Afghan Turkestan (N), and Nuristan and the Kabul and Jalalabad valleys (S). It is crossed by the Baroghil, Dorah, and Khawak passes; near W end the Shikari Pass (a gorge) is used by Kabul–Mazar-i-Sharif highway. Alexander the Great and Tamerlane crossed the Hindu Kush at Khawak Pass. The system is generally treeless, except in wooded Nuristan.

Hindupur (hĭn'do͞opo͝or), city (pop. 19,049), Anantapur dist., W Madras, India, near Penner R., 60 mi. S of Anantapur; road junction; trade center; cloth goods, jaggery; peanut milling, hand-loom woolen weaving; silk growing. Corundum mines near by. Notable 16th-cent. Sivaite temple 8 mi. E, at village of Lepakshi.

Hindur, India: see NALAGARH.

Hindustan (hĭn"do͞ostăn') [Persian,=Hindu land], a vague term, usually applied to the Ganges Plain of N India, bet. the Himalayas (N) and Deccan Plateau (S). Name derived from the river Indus (Sanskrit *Sindhu*) and used by anc. Persians to designate the land just E of the Indus. Used variably throughout Indian history—generally in contradistinction to the Deccan of peninsular India—it gradually came to mean the whole of N India from Punjab to Assam. Hindustan has also been applied to the whole Indian subcontinent; to the smaller region of the Ganges Plain where Hindi is largely spoken; and, after creation of Pakistan in 1947, to the republic of India. Also spelled Hindostan.

Hi-Nella (hī"-nĕ'lŭ), borough (pop. 237), Camden co., SW N.J., 8 mi. SE of Camden.

Hines, town (pop. 918), Harney co., E central Oregon, just S of Burns; lumber mills; alt. 4,155 ft.

Hinesburg, town (pop. 1,120), Chittenden co., NW Vt., 12 mi. SSE of Burlington; lumber. Settled just after Revolution.

Hines Creek, village (pop. estimate 200), W Alta., near Peace R., 50 mi. W of Peace River town; lumbering, mixed farming, wheat.

Hinesville, town (pop. 1,217), ⊙ Liberty co., SE Ga., 33 mi. WSW of Savannah, in farm area. U.S. Camp Stewart near by.

Hingan, province, Manchuria: see HSINGAN.

Hingan or **Hsing-an** (both: shĭng'an'). **1** Town Kiangsi prov., China: see HENGFENG. **2** Town, ⊙ Hingan co. (pop. 152,366), NE Kwangsi prov., China, on railroad and 30 mi. NE of Kweilin; paper-milling center; tung-oil processing; timber, bamboo, beans, wheat, sweet potatoes. **3** Town, Shensi prov., China: see ANKANG.

Hinganghat (hĭng'gŭngät), town (pop. 28,040), Wardha dist., central Madhya Pradesh, India, on tributary of Wardha R. and 45 mi. SSW of Nagpur; major cotton-textile center in important Indian cotton tract; millet, wheat, oilseeds, rice; turmeric growing.

Hingcheng or **Hsing-ch'eng** (both: shĭng'chŭng'), town, ⊙ Hingcheng co. (pop. 235,385), SW Liaosi prov., Manchuria, 40 mi. SW of Chinchow and on railroad, near Gulf of Liaotung; gold deposits, coal and manganese mines; brick and tiles, bean cakes, hog bristles, felt products. Until 1914 called Ningyüan.

Hingene (hĭn'hĕnŭ), town (pop. 4,647), Antwerp prov., N Belgium, 11 mi. SW of Antwerp; market gardening, dairying. Has 12th-cent. castle.

Hinghai or **Hsing-hai** (both: shĭng'hī'), town, ⊙ Hinghai co. (pop. 40,000), E Tsinghai prov., China, 120 mi. SW of Sining and on highway to Jyekundo; cattle raising; agr. products. Until 1939 called Tahopa.

Hingham, town and parish (pop. 1,322), central Norfolk, England, 13 mi. WSW of Norwich; agr. market. Has 14th-cent. church.

Hingham (hĭng'ŭm). **1** Town (pop. 10,665), Plymouth co., E Mass., on Hingham Bay (arm of Boston Bay), 12 mi. SE of Boston; summer resort. Ships built here during Second World War. Settled c.1633, inc. 1635. Includes villages of South Hingham (1940 pop. 545) and Hingham Center. **2** Town (pop. 214), Hill co., N Mont., 35 mi. W of Havre; storage and shipping point for livestock, grain.

Hingho or **Hsing-ho** (both: shĭng'hŭ'), town (pop. 9,189), ⊙ Hingho co. (pop. 102,972), easternmost Suiyuan prov., China, 55 mi. W of Kalgan, near Great Wall (Chahar line); wheat, millet, beans. Graphite found near by. Was in N Shansi until 1914, and in Chahar, 1914–28.

Hinghsien or **Hsing-hsien** (both: shĭng'shyĕn'), town, ⊙ Hinghsien co. (pop. 80,371), NW Shansi prov., China, 70 mi. N of Lishih, near Yellow R.; wheat, ramie, timber. Coal mining near by.

Hinghwa or **Hsing-hua** (both: shĭng'hwä'). **1** Town, Fukien prov., China: see PUTIEN. **2** Town (pop. 55,245), ⊙ Hinghwa co. (pop. 172,478), N Kiangsu prov., China, 40 mi. NE of Yangchow, in rice region; wheat, beans, corn, cotton.

Hinghwa Bay or **Hsing-hua Bay,** inlet of Formosa Strait, in Fukien prov., China, 40 mi. S of Foochow; 20 mi. wide, 15 mi. long. On its shore, near Putien (formerly Hinghwa), the Hinghwa dialect (intermediary bet. N and S Fukienese) is spoken.

Hingi or **Hsing-i** (both: shĭng'yē'), town (pop. 12,201), ⊙ Hingi co. (pop. 189,568), SW Kweichow prov., China, 145 mi. SW of Kweiyang; alt. 4,265 ft.; major commercial center; cotton-textile and pottery mfg., embroidered-goods making. Timber, wheat, millet, tobacco. Mercury mined near by. The name Hingi was applied until 1913 to ANLUNG, 30 mi. E. Present site was formerly known as Hwangtsaopa.

Hingjen or **Hsing-jen** (both: shĭng'rŭn'), town (pop. 10,931), ⊙ Hingjen co. (pop. 99,615), SW Kweichow prov., China, 65 mi. SW of Anshun; alt. 4,513 ft.; cotton textiles, embroidered goods; rice, millet. Mercury and coal deposits near by. Until 1914 called Sincheng.

Hingking, Manchuria: see SINPIN.

Hingkwo or **Hsing-kuo** (both: shĭng'gwô'). **1** Town, Hupeh prov., China: see YANGSIN. **2** Town (pop. 14,235), ⊙ Hingkwo co. (pop. 196,761), S Kiangsi prov., China, 38 mi. NNE of Kanchow; cotton weaving. Tungsten, bismuth, and iron mines.

Hinglé, Le, France: see DINAN.

Hinglung or **Hsing-lung** (both: shĭng'lŏng'), town, ⊙ Hinglung co. (pop. 21,393), S Jehol prov., China, 70 mi. NE of Peking, in mtn. region; gold mining. Until 1949 in Hopeh.

Hinglungchen, Manchuria: see MINGSHUI.

Hingning or **Hsing-ning** (both: shĭng'nĭng). **1** Town, Hunan prov., China: see TZEHING. **2** Town (pop. 21,167), ⊙ Hingning co. (pop. 451,770), E Kwangtung prov., China, on Mei R. and 27 mi. WSW of Meihsien; coal-mining center; cotton milling; rice, potatoes, tea.

Hingoli (hĭngō'lē), town (pop. 14,601), Parbhani dist., N Hyderabad state, India, 40 mi. NNW of Nander; rail spur terminus; cotton-trade center in agr. area (millet, wheat); cotton ginning. Experimental cattle farm. Temple at Aundah, 14 mi. SSW, is noted example of medieval Hindu architecture.

Hingol River (hĭng-gōl'), longest river (c.350 mi.) in Baluchistan, W Pakistan; rises on W slope of Central Brahui Range, c.15 mi. SSW of Kalat town, flows S, through barren hill ranges, cutting through E end of Makran Coast Range (gorge used by Alexander the Great in 325 B.C.), to Arabian Sea 55 mi. E of Ormara. In middle course, called Nal. Main tributary, Mashkai R. (right).

Hingping or **Hsing-ping** (both: shĭng'bĭng'), town (pop. 7,620), ⊙ Hingping co. (pop. 153,809), S central Shensi prov., China, 30 mi. W of Sian and on Lunghai RR; cotton weaving; rice, wheat, beans, ramie.

Hingshan or **Hsing-shan** (both: shĭng'shän'). **1** Town (pop. 14,755), ⊙ Hingshan co. (pop. 90,486), W Hupeh prov., China, 15 mi. NNE of Tzekwei; timber center; millet, wheat. Iron deposits near by. Sometimes spelled Singshan. **2** City, N Sungkiang prov., Manchuria, China, 40 mi. N of Kiamusze; rail terminus, and major coal-mining center. Mines extend along rail spur to Haoli or Haolikang, 20 mi. S.

Hingwen or **Hsing-wen** (both: shĭng'wŭn'), town (pop. 8,915), ⊙ Hingwen co. (pop. 81,846), SW Szechwan prov., China, 40 mi. SW of Luhsien; paper milling; rice, millet, wheat, sweet potatoes. Sometimes spelled Singwen.

Hingyeh or **Hsing-yeh** (both: shĭng'yĕ'), town, ⊙ Hingyeh co. (pop. 125,689), SE Kwangsi prov., China, 17 mi. NW of Watlam, near Kwangtung line; rice, millet, tea, indigo.

Hinigaran (hēnēgä'rän, ēnē–), town (1939 pop. 6,306; 1948 municipality pop. 29,017), Negros Occidental prov., W Negros isl., Philippines, on Guimaras Strait, 5 mi. N of Binalbagan; agr. center (rice, sugar cane).

Hinis (hŭnŭs'), Turkish *Hınıs,* village (pop. 2,511), Erzurum prov., E Turkey, 45 mi. SE of Erzurum; naphtha, grain.

Hinlopen Strait (hĭn'lōpŭn), Nor. *Hinlopenstredet,* passage (100 mi. long, 7–30 mi. wide) of Arctic Ocean, extending NW–SE bet. West Spitsbergen (W) and Northeast Land (E) of Spitsbergen group. Receives extensive glaciers on both shores. Contains several isls. (SE), including Wilhelmoya (vĭl'hĕlm-ûyä), Nor. *Wilhelmøya* (□ 39), 79°4'N 20°25'E, which rises to 1,821 ft.

Hinna, Ethiopia: see IMI.

Hinnoy (hĭn'ûü), Nor. *Hinnøy,* island (□ 849; pop. 23,965) in North Sea, in Nordland and Troms counties, N Norway, largest of the VESTERALEN group and of Norway, separated from mainland by narrow strait. Isl. is 55 mi. long (N-S), up to 30 mi. wide; rises to 4,153 ft. in Moysalen peak (SW). Fishing is chief occupation; some agr. Main village: Harstad (N). Sometimes spelled Hindoy, Nor. *Hindøy.*

Hino (hē'nō). **1** Town (pop. 16,967), Greater Tokyo, central Honshu, Japan, just S of Tachikawa; rice, wheat, raw silk. **2** Town (pop. 7,954), Shiga prefecture, S Honshu, Japan, 40 mi. WSW of Nagoya; agr. center (rice, wheat, tea, market produce); sawmilling.

Hinojal (ēnōhäl'), village (pop. 2,357), Cáceres prov., W Spain, 17 mi. NNE of Cáceres; livestock, cereals.

Hinojales (ēnōhä'lĕs), town (pop. 1,145), Huelva prov., SW Spain, in the Sierra Morena, 8 mi. N of Aracena; olives, cereals, honey, cork, timber.

Hinojedo (ēnōhā'dhō), village (pop. 917), Santander prov., N Spain, 12 mi. E of Santander; zinc and lead processing, sulphuric-acid mfg.

Hinojos (ēnō'hōs), town (pop. 2,583), Huelva prov., SW Spain, 22 mi. WSW of Seville; vegetables, fruit, timber; viticulture and apiculture. Olive-oil extracting, flour- and sawmilling. Limestone quarries and kilns.

Hinojosa de Duero (ēnōhō'sä dhā dhwā'rō), town (pop. 1,849), Salamanca prov., W Spain, 31 mi. NNW of Ciudad Rodrigo; cheese and meat processing, flour milling; livestock, olive oil, fruit, wine. Dominated by hill with ruins of anc. castle. Topaz quarries near by.

Hinojosa del Duque (dhĕl dōō'kä), town (pop. 13,393), Córdoba prov., S Spain, in the Sierra Morena, 50 mi. NW of Córdoba; agr. trade center. Olive-oil processing, sawmilling, tanning; ships wool. Cereals, wine, lumber, livestock in area. Lead deposits near by.

Hinojosa del Valle (vä'lyä), town (pop. 1,255), Badajoz prov., W Spain, 18 mi. SE of Almendralejo; cereals, acorns, livestock.

Hinojosa de San Vicente (dhā sän' vēsĕn'tā), town (pop. 1,172), Toledo prov., central Spain, 10 mi. NE of Talavera de la Reina; olives, grapes, potatoes, cherries, onions, figs; sericulture.

Hinojosas or **Hinojosas de Calatrava** (ēnōhō'säs dhā käläträ'vä), town (pop. 2,402), Ciudad Real prov., S central Spain, 27 mi. SSW of Ciudad Real; grain, olives, livestock; lead mining.

Hinojosos, Los (lōs ēnōhō'sōs), town (pop. 2,195), Cuenca prov., E central Spain, 50 mi. SW of Cuenca; olives, cereals, grapes, livestock.

Hinomi Point (hēnō'mē), Jap. *Hinomi-saki*, promontory in Shimane prefecture, SW Honshu, Japan, in Sea of Japan, just NW of Taisha; 35°26'N 132°38'E; lighthouse.

Hinsdale, county (□ 1,057; pop. 263), SW central Colo.; ⊙ Lake City. Tourist and agr. area, drained by headwaters of Rio Grande. Livestock. Includes parts of San Juan Mts. and San Juan, Gunnison, Rio Grande, and Uncompahgre natl. forests. Formed 1874.

Hinsdale. 1 Residential village (pop. 8,676), on Cook-Du Page co. line, NE Ill., W suburb of Chicago, just W of La Grange, in dairying and fruitgrowing area; nurseries. Inc. 1873. **2** Town (pop. 1,560), Berkshire co., W Mass., in the Berkshires, 7 mi. E of Pittsfield; resort; dairying. Settled 1763, inc. 1804. **3** Town (pop. 1,950), including Hinsdale village (pop. 1,247), Cheshire co., extreme SW N.H., on the Connecticut below Brattleboro, Vt., at mouth of Ashuelot R.; water power runs its mills (paper, metal products). Settled c.1742, inc. 1753.

Hinterpommern, region, Europe: see POMERANIA.

Hinterrhein River (hĭn'tûrīn"), a headstream of the Rhine, E Switzerland, rises in Adula group of Lepontine Alps, flows E, through Rheinwald valley, thence N, past Thusis, joining the Vorderrhein W of Chur to form the Rhine. Length, 35 mi.

Hinterrugg, Switzerland: see CHURFIRSTEN.

Hinton, England: see SHARPNESS.

Hinton. 1 Town (pop. 345), Plymouth co., NW Iowa, 10 mi. NNE of Sioux City; livestock, grain. **2** Town (pop. 1,025), Caddo co., W central Okla., 22 mi. W of El Reno, in agr. area (cotton, wheat, corn); cotton ginning, flour milling; grain elevators. **3** City (pop. 5,780), ⊙ Summers co., SE W.Va., on New R., near Greenbrier R. mouth, and 18 mi. SE of Beckley; railroad shops; shipping point for agr. area (fruit, tobacco, livestock); processes lumber, dairy products, beverages. Bluestone Dam is just S. Settled 1831; inc. 1880.

Hintonburg, suburb of Ottawa, SE Ont.

Hinunangan (hēnōōnäng'gän, ēnōō–), town (1939 pop. 1,972; 1948 municipality pop. 17,556), SE Leyte, Philippines, on small inlet of Surigao Strait; agr. center (corn, hemp).

Hinwil (hĭn'vēl), town (pop. 3,040), Zurich canton, N Switzerland, 15 mi. ESE of Zurich; cotton and silk textiles, clothing; metalworking.

Hinzir Dagi (hŭnzŭr' dä'ŭ), Turkish *Hınzır Dağı*, peak (9,022 ft.), central Turkey, in Tecer Mts., 45 mi. ENE of Kayseri.

Hiogo, Japan: see KOBE.

Hipólito (ēpō'lētō), village (pop. 1,136), Coahuila, N Mexico, in outliers of Sierra Madre Oriental, on railroad and 33 mi. NW of Saltillo; alt. 4,042 ft. Corn, beans, alfalfa, istle fibers, cattle. Cooperative settlement.

Hippenus, Palestine: see ASHDOD.

Hipperholme (–hōm), former urban district (1931 pop. 5,383), West Riding, S Yorkshire, England, 2 mi. E of Halifax; woolen milling, leather tanning; electric-cable works. Inc. 1937 in Brighouse.

Hippo, Algeria: see BÔNE.

Hippone, Algeria: see BÔNE.

Hippo Regius, Algeria: see BÔNE.

Hippos (hĭ'pŏs), anc. city of Palestine, just E of Sea of Galilee; one of the Decapolis.

Hippo Zarytus, Tunisia: see BIZERTE.

Hirado (hērä'dō), chief town (pop. 16,397) on Hirado-shima, Nagasaki prefecture, Japan, port on NE coast of isl., opposite NW tip of Hizen Peninsula, Kyushu; known for porcelain ware. Exports timber, fish, porcelain ware. Opened in 16th cent. to foreign trade. In early 17th cent., Du. and English factories were built here.

Hirado-shima (–shĭmä), island (□ 66; pop. 40,834, including offshore islets), Nagasaki prefecture, Japan, in E.China Sea, just off NW coast of Hizen Peninsula, Kyushu; 20 mi. long, 5 mi. wide; hilly, with rugged coast; fertile, forested. Sweet potatoes, timber, fish. Chief town is Hirado, porcelain-ware center.

Hirael, Wales: see BANGOR.

Hirafuku (hērä'fōōkōō), town (pop. 1,844), Hyogo prefecture, S Honshu, Japan, 24 mi. NW of Himeji, in agr. area; processed tea, cutlery, soy sauce; woodworking.

Hirai (hērī'), town (pop. 8,839), Kagawa prefecture, NE Shikoku, Japan, 7 mi. SE of Takamatsu; commercial center in truck-gardening area; grain.

Hiraiso (hērī'sō), town (pop. 10,533), Ibaraki prefecture, central Honshu, Japan, on the Pacific, 8 mi. E of Mito; fishing port; summer resort.

Hirakata (hērä'kätŏŏ). **1** Town (pop. 3,321), Ibaraki prefecture, central Honshu, Japan, on the Pacific, 19 mi. NNE of Hitachi; fishing port. **2** Town (pop. 41,041), Osaka prefecture, S Honshu, Japan, 14 mi. NE of Osaka; lumbering and agr. center; poultry. Includes (since early 1940s) former town of Tonoyama. **3** Town (pop. 4,177), Saitama prefecture, central Honshu, Japan, 5 mi. NW of Omiya; raw silk, rice, wheat, soy sauce.

Hirakud, India: see SAMBALPUR, town, Orissa.

Hiram (hī'rŭm). **1** Town (pop. 299), Paulding co., NW Ga., 23 mi. WNW of Atlanta, in agr. area. **2** Town (pop. 804), Oxford co., W Maine, on Saco R. and 33 mi. NW of Portland; wood products. **3** Village (pop. 986), Portage co., NE Ohio, 23 mi. NE of Akron; seat of Hiram Col.

Hirao (hērä'ō), town (pop. 5,725), Yamaguchi prefecture, SW Honshu, Japan, 17 mi. SE of Tokuyama; rice, wheat, raw silk.

Hiraoka (hērä'ôkä), town (pop. 12,838), Osaka prefecture, S Honshu, Japan, just E of Fuse; commercial center in agr. area (rice, wheat); wire factory, flour mill; poultry.

Hirapur, India: see BURNPUR.

Hirara (hērä'rä), city (1950 pop. 28,504) on Miyako-jima of Sakishima Isls., in the Ryukyus, port on W coast of isl., in East China Sea; agr. center (sugar cane, sweet potatoes). Exports raw sugar, livestock. Also called Taira.

Hirasawa (hērä'säwŏŏ), town (pop. 6,079), Akita prefecture, N Honshu, Japan, on Sea of Japan, 8 mi. SW of Honjo; oil refining; agr., fishing.

Hirata (hērä'tä), town (pop. 9,439), Shimane prefecture, SW Honshu, Japan, 14 mi. W of Matsue across L. Shinji; commercial center in agr., livestock area; silk-textile mills, canneries, sake breweries; soy sauce, raw silk.

Hiratsuka (hērä'tsōōkä), city (1940 pop. 43,148; 1947 pop. 45,507), Kanagawa prefecture, central Honshu, Japan, on N shore of Sagami Bay, 19 mi. WSW of Yokohama; mfg. (silk textiles, soy sauce); beach resort. Fishery.

Hirekerur (hĭrā'kärōōr), village (pop. 4,195), Dharwar dist., S Bombay, India, 75 mi. SSE of Dharwar; chili, rice, sugar cane, betel leaf.

Hire Vadvatti (hē'rā vŭd'vŭt-tē), town (pop. 3,265), Dharwar dist., S Bombay, India, 55 mi. ESE of Dharwar; local market for cotton, peanuts, wheat, millet. Sometimes spelled Hirewadwadi.

Hirgis Nuur, Mongolia: see KIRGIS NOR.

Hiri (hē'rē), volcanic island (2 mi. in diameter; pop. 1,156), N Moluccas, Indonesia, in Molucca Sea, just N of Ternate; 0°53'N 127°19'E; mountainous, rising to 2,067 ft. Fishing.

Hiriyur (hĭrĭyōōr'), town (pop. 3,417), Chitaldrug dist., NE Mysore, India, on Vedavati (Hagari) R. and 24 mi. SE of Chitaldrug; road center; coconuts, rice, sugar cane; cotton ginning.

Hirm (hĭrm), Hung. *Félszerfalva* (fāl'sĕrfŏlvŏ), village (pop. 909), Burgenland, E Austria, 5 mi. SSW of Eisenstadt; sugar refining.

Hirmal, Lebanon: see HERMIL.

Hirmil, Lebanon: see HERMIL.

Hirna (hĭr'nä), village (pop. 1,000), Harar prov., E central Ethiopia, in Chercher highlands, 20 mi. ENE of Asba Tafari; coffee-collecting center.

Hiro, Japan: see HIROHATA.

Hirochi, Russian SFSR: see PRAVDA.

Hirod, India: see FRENCH ROCKS.

Hirohata (hērō'hätŏŏ), town (1945 pop. estimate 15,165), Hyogo prefecture, S Honshu, Japan, on Harima Sea, 4 mi. SW of Himeji; commercial center in agr. area (rice, wheat, tobacco, fruit, truck, poultry). Home industries (woodworking, floor mats, bamboo ware). Fishing. Formed in early 1940s by combining former villages of Hiro (1940 pop. 8,285) and Yawata (1940 pop. 3,606). Since c.1947, part of Himeji.

Hiromi (hērō'mē), town (pop. 5,385), Gifu prefecture, central Honshu, Japan, 7 mi. NW of Tajimi; rice, wheat; spinning.

Hirono (hērō'nō), town (pop. 6,175), Fukushima prefecture, central Honshu, Japan, on the Pacific, 13 mi. NNE of Taira; rice, silk cocoons, charcoal.

Hiroo (hērō'), town (pop. 9,064), S Hokkaido, Japan, fishing port on the Pacific, 45 mi. S of Obihiro; agr., lumbering; fish canning.

Hirosaki (hērō'säkē), city (1940 pop. 51,498; 1947 pop. 63,669), Aomori prefecture, N Honshu, Japan, 21 mi. SW of Aomori; mfg. (textiles, lacquer ware), woodworking, soybean processing, sake brewing. Has 17th-cent. Buddhist temple and remains of feudal castle.

Hirose (hērō'sā). **1** Town (pop. 4,929), Shimane prefecture, SW Honshu, Japan, 10 mi. SE of Matsue; home industries (incense sticks, brilliantine, sake). **2** Town (pop. 6,604), Yamaguchi prefecture, SW Honshu, Japan, 17 mi. NE of Tokuyama, in agr. and forested area; rice, raw silk, charcoal.

Hiroshima (hĭ"rōshē'mŭ, Jap. hē"rō'shĭmä), prefecture [Jap. *ken*] (□ 3,258; 1940 pop. 1,869,540; 1947 pop. 2,011,498), SW Honshu, Japan; ⊙ HIROSHIMA. Bounded S by Hiroshima Bay and Hiuchi Sea (central section of Inland Sea). Prefecture includes offshore isls. of NOMI-SHIMA, KURAHASHI-JIMA, ITSUKU-SHIMA, KAMI-KAMAKARI-JIMA, OSAKI-KAMI-SHIMA, IKUCHI-JIMA, INNO-SHIMA, MUKAI-SHIMA, OSAKI-SHIMO-SHIMA, SAKI-SHIMA, TA-JIMA, and several smaller islets. Generally mountainous, with fertile valleys. Small streams drain agr. and livestock-raising areas. Hot springs at Shobara in interior. Rice and wheat are grown extensively; some tobacco fields in S. Raw silk is produced everywhere. Mfg. of writing brushes, fountain pens, insecticide (made from chrysanthemums), dyes, floor mats, textiles, soy sauce. Exports sake, fountain pens, lumber, charcoal, textiles. Principal centers: Hiroshima, KURE (naval base), ONOMICHI, FUKUYAMA, MIHARA.

Hiroshima, city (1940 pop. 343,968; 1947 pop. 224,100), ⊙ Hiroshima prefecture, SW Honshu, Japan, on Hiroshima Bay, 180 mi. W of Osaka; 34°23'N 132°28'E. On delta of Ota R., whose 7 mouths divide city into 6 isls. connected by 81 bridges. Mfg. center; textile mills, rubber-goods factories, canneries, sake breweries; produces machinery, paper umbrellas; citrus fruit, persimmons, oysters, processed seaweed. Exports canned goods, rayon, machinery, sake. Sentei Park is known for its landscape gardens. The sacred isl. of Itsukushima is near by. Hiroshima founded 1594 as castle city. Hq. of military operations in Sino-Japanese War (1894–95) and Russo-Japanese War (1904–05). In Second World War, it was the target (Aug. 6, 1945) of 1st atomic bomb ever dropped on a populated area. Some 150,000 people were killed or wounded; 75% of bldgs. were destroyed or severely damaged. Sometimes spelled Hirosima.

Hiroshima Bay, Jap. *Hiroshima-wan*, inlet of Inland Sea, SW Honshu, Japan; Kurahashi-jima forms E side of entrance; 20 mi. N-S, 15 mi. E-W. Contains Nomi-shima, Itsuku-shima, and many smaller isls. Hiroshima is at head of bay, Kure is on E shore.

Hirotani (hē"rō'tänē), town (pop. 5,721), Hyogo prefecture, S Honshu, Japan, 11 mi. SSW of Toyooka, in agr. area (rice, wheat, flowers, poultry); home industries (woodworking, cutlery, straw products).

Hirsau (hĭr'zou), village (pop. 1,441), S Württemberg, Germany, after 1945 in Württemberg-Hohenzollern, in Black Forest, on the Nagold and 1.5 mi. N of Calw; health resort. Has ruins of noted Benedictine monastery (destroyed 1692).

Hirschaid (hĭr'shīt), village (pop. 2,405), Upper Franconia, N Bavaria, Germany, on Ludwig Canal, near Regnitz R., and 7 mi. SE of Bamberg; hydroelectric station; lumber and paper milling.

Hirschau (hĭr'shou), town (pop. 4,190), Upper Palatinate, N central Bavaria, Germany, 8 mi. NNE of Amberg; textile and porcelain mfg., brewing; carp hatcheries. Has late-Gothic church and mid-16th-cent. town hall. Jerome of Prague was captured here (1415) after his escape from Council of Constance.

Hirschberg (hĭrsh'bĕrk). **1** Town (pop. 3,357), Thuringia, central Germany, on the Thuringian Saale and 8 mi. NW of Hof; textile and paper milling, tanning, wood- and metalworking; mfg. of machinery, glass. Has 17th-cent. former palace of princes of Reuss. **2** Town (pop. 1,425), in former Prussian prov. of Westphalia, W Germany, after 1945 in North Rhine-Westphalia, 6 mi. N of Meschede; forestry.

Hirschberg or **Jelenia Gora** (yĕlĕn'yä gōō'rä), Pol. *Jelenia Góra*, city (1939 pop. 35,296; 1946 pop. 39,050) in Lower Silesia, after 1945 in Wroclaw prov., SW Poland, at N foot of the Riesengebirge, on Bobrawa R. and 60 mi. WSW of Breslau (Wroclaw); 50°54'N 15°44'E. Rail junction; textile (linen, woolen, rayon) and paper milling, mfg. of machinery, optical lenses, glass, castings, chemicals, pharmaceuticals, tiles; wood-pulp processing; tourist center. Has one of 6 Churches of Grace allowed Silesian Protestants (1707) under Treaty of Altranstädt. First mentioned c.1280; chartered 1312. Passed to Bohemia after 1368. In Thirty Years War, captured by Swedes; burned (1634) by imperial forces; passed 1741 to Prussia. Linen-milling center in 18th cent.

Hirschfelde (hĭrsh'fĕl"dŭ), town (pop. 3,897), Saxony, E Germany, near Czechoslovak border, in Upper Lusatia, on the Lusatian Neisse and 5 mi. NNE of Zittau; lignite mining; cotton and linen milling; synthetic-oil and calcium-nitrogen plants.

Hirschhorn or **Hirschhorn am Neckar** (hĭrsh'hôrn" äm nĕ'kär), town (pop. 3,065), S Hesse, W Germany, in former Starkenburg prov., at S foot of the Odenwald, on the Neckar and 10 mi. ENE of Heidelberg; woodworking. Has 13th-cent. castle.

Hirsilä (hĭr'sĭlä), village in Orivesi commune (pop. 8,481), Häme co., SW Finland, 25 mi. NE of Tampere; shoe mfg.

Hirsingue (ērsĕg'), Ger. *Hirsingen* (hĕr'sĭng-ŭn), village (pop. 1,300), Haut-Rhin dept., E France, on upper Ill R. and 3 mi. S of Altkirch; cotton spinning, cap mfg.

Hirson (ērsō'), town (pop. 10,208), Aisne dept., N France, on the Oise and 32 mi. NE of Laon; rail and metallurgical center (steel-casting mill, iron foundries, forges); glassworks. Wool spinning in area.

Hirst, England: see Ashington.
Hirta, Scotland: see Saint Kilda.
Hirtshals (hĭrts'häls), fishing village (pop. 2,133), Hjorring amt, N Jutland, Denmark, on the Skagerrak and 9 mi. N of Hjorring; rail terminus. Cable to Arendal, Norway.
Hirtzenberg (hĭrt'sŭnbĕrkh), mountain (1,525 ft.) of the Ardennes, Luxembourg prov., SE Belgium, 2 mi. SW of Arlon.
Hiruma (hērōō'mä), town (pop. 6,496), Tokushima prefecture, NE Shikoku, Japan, on Yoshino R. and 40 mi. W of Tokushima; tobacco-producing center; rice, wheat, raw silk.
Hisaga-shima (hēsägä'shĭmä) or **Hisaka-shima** (hēsäkä'–), island (□ 15; pop. 3,869) of isl. group Gotoretto, Nagasaki prefecture, Japan, in E.China Sea, 50 mi. W of Kyushu; 5.5 mi. long, 4 mi. wide. Large bay indents N coast; hilly. Fishing; cattle raising. Sometimes called Hisaka.
Hisai (hēsī'), town (pop. 14,975), Mie prefecture, S Honshu, Japan, 4 mi. SW of Tsu; livestock and agr. (rice, wheat) center; raw silk, lumber.
Hisaka or **Hisaka-shima,** Japan: see Hisaga-shima.
Hisanohama (hē'sänōhämŭ), town (pop. 6,211), Fukushima prefecture, central Honshu, Japan, on the Pacific, 8 mi. NE of Taira; agr., fishing.
Hisarak or **Hesarak** (both: hĕsäräk'), village, Second Prov., in Teheran, N central Iran, 30 mi. WNW of Teheran, just off highway to Kazvin; has noted medical institute; serum production.
Hisaronu, Gulf of, Turkey: see Syme, Gulf of.
Hiseville (hīz'vĭl, hĭs'vĭl), town (1940 pop. 196), Barren co., S Ky., 10 mi. NE of Glasgow.
Hishikari (hĕshē'kärē), town (pop. 12,214), Kagoshima prefecture, S Kyushu, Japan, 30 mi. N of Kagoshima; livestock and agr. (rice, wheat) center; lumber. Alkaline hot springs near by.
Hisnumansur, Turkey: see Adiyaman.
Hisoy (hēs'ûü), Nor. *Hisøy,* island (□ 3.5; pop. 2,148) in the Skagerrak, Aust-Agder co., S Norway, 1 mi. off coast S of Arendal; pilot station, formerly fortified; fishing, sailing, light mfg., some shipbuilding. Stone Age findings made here.
Hispalis, Spain: see Seville, city.
Hispania (hĭspā'nēŭ, –nyŭ), Lat. name for Iberian Peninsula including present-day Spain and Portugal.
Hispanic America: see Spanish America.
Hispaniola (hĭ"spănēō'lŭ), Sp. *Española* (ĕspänyō'lä), island (□ c.30,000), West Indies, 2d largest of the Greater Antilles, bet. Cuba and Puerto Rico, separated from the former by c.55-mi.-wide Windward Passage, from the latter by 75-mi.-wide Mona Passage; approximately bet. 17°35'–20°N and 68°20'–74°30'W. Its W third is occupied by Haiti, the rest by the Dominican Republic. Has an equable, tropical climate of little seasonal change, relieved by NE trade winds; average annual temp. 77°F. in the lowlands. Predominantly mountainous, it is traversed W-E by several wooded ranges, such as Cordillera Central, which has the highest peak in the West Indies (see Monte Tina and Pico Trujillo). These enclose deep, fertile plains, where the bulk of the mainly rural pop. is concentrated: the Cibao, La Vega Real, Seibo, and San Juan plains in Dominican Republic; Cul-de-Sac, Artibonite, and Central plains in Haiti. Largest river is the Artibonite (Artibonito), flowing mostly through Haitian territory. Main crops: sugar cane, coffee, cotton, cacao, tobacco, bananas, rice. The extensive forests yield fine timber (mahogany, lignum vitae, cedar, etc.). Its mineral resources have so far been little exploited. Originally called Quisqueya and Haiti by native Arawak Indians, it was named by Columbus La Isla Española when he made his 1st landing here, near Cape Saint Nicolas (NW Haiti), on Dec. 6, 1492. The Indian pop. soon almost entirely vanished, and Negro slaves were introduced beginning in early 16th cent. For political and cultural history, see the articles on the respective countries. The isl. has been variously called; during 19th cent. both Haiti and Santo Domingo were frequently used interchangeably, though towards late 19th cent. Haiti prevailed as designation for the entire isl.; in modern usage the tendency has been to revert to Hispaniola.
Hissar (hĭs-sär'), district (□ 5,439; pop. 1,034,601), S Punjab, India; ⊙ Hissar. On NE edge of Thar Desert; bordered N and SE by Patiala and East Punjab States Union (in which it has an enclave), S by Rajasthan. Irrigated by branches of Sirhind and Western Jumna canals; agr. (millet, gram, cotton, oilseeds); hand-loom weaving, cattle breeding. Chief towns: Bhiwani, Hissar, Hansi, Sirsa. Several outbreaks occurred here during Sepoy Rebellion of 1857. Original dist. (□ 5,213; pop. 1,006,709) enlarged (1948) by inc. of former Punjab state of Loharu.
Hissar, town (pop. 28,618), ⊙ Hissar dist., S Punjab, India, on branch of Western Jumna Canal and 150 mi. S of Jullundur; rail junction; trade center for cotton, cattle, grain, oilseeds; cotton ginning, hand-loom weaving. Veterinary col. Large cattle farm (□ c.60) extends N and W. Town built 1356 by Firuz Shah III, king of Delhi.
Hissar, Tadzhik SSR: see Gissar.
Hissarlik, Turkey: see Troy.
Hissmofors, Sweden: see Krokom.

Histiaia or **Istiaia** (both: ēstēä'yŭ), Lat. *Histiaea* (hĭstē'ŭ), town (pop. 5,358), NW Euboea, Greece, 43 mi. NW of Chalcis; wheat, wines, olive oil, citrus fruit, livestock. Also spelled Istiea; formerly Xerochori or Xirokhori.
Histon, town and parish (pop. 1,722), central Cambridge, England, 3 mi. N of Cambridge; agr. market with canning industry (fruit, jam, vegetables). Has 14th-15th-cent. church.
Histria, Rumania: see Istria.
Hisua (hĭs'wŭ), town (pop. 7,608), Gaya dist., central Bihar, India, 26 mi. E of Gaya; rice, gram, wheat, barley; pottery mfg. Hindu cave sculpture and inscriptions 9 mi. NNW, at Rajpind Cave.
Hiswa or **Hiswah** (hĭs'wŭ), Arab village (1946 pop. 708) of Aden Colony, on mainland, 4 mi. SW of Sheikh Othman, on Aden Bay at mouth of the Wadi Kebir (arm of the Wadi Tiban); irrigated agr.
Hisya (hĭs'yŭ) or **Hasiyah** (hä'sĭyŭ), Fr. *Hassié,* town, Homs prov., W Syria, 22 mi. S of Homs; cereals.
Hit (hĭt), village, Dulaim prov., central Iraq, on the Euphrates and 32 mi. WNW of Ramadi; dates, sesame, millet, corn. Site of anc. Mesopotamian city of *Is* (ĭs), whose bitumen wells were utilized in the construction of the walls of Babylon.
Hita, Japan: see Hida.
Hita (ē'tä), town (pop. 559), Guadalajara prov., central Spain, 15 mi. NNE of Guadalajara; cereals, olives, vegetables.
Hitachi (hētä'chē), former province in central Honshu, Japan; now Ibaraki prefecture.
Hitachi, city (1940 pop. 82,885; 1947 pop. 50,159), Ibaraki prefecture, central Honshu, Japan, on the Pacific, 19 mi. NE of Mito; mining center (gold, silver, copper); smelting.
Hitaka, Japan: see Hidaka.
Hitchcock, county (□ 722; pop. 5,867), S Nebr.; ⊙ Trenton. Agr. area bounded S by Kansas; drained by Republican R. Grain, livestock, dairy and poultry produce. Formed 1873.
Hitchcock. 1 Town (pop. 166), Blaine co., W central Okla., 9 mi. NNE of Watonga, in cotton-producing area. **2** Town (pop. 227), Beadle co., E central S.Dak., 20 mi. NNW of Huron. **3** Village (pop. 1,105), Galveston co., S Texas, 15 mi. WNW of Galveston.
Hitchin, urban district (1931 pop. 14,383; 1951 census 19,959), N Hertford, England, 14 mi. NW of Hertford; mfg.: leather, pharmaceuticals, agr. machinery, boilers; lavender distilling, straw-plaiting; agr. market. Has 12th-15th-cent. parish church; old almshouse, once part of 14th-cent. Gilbertine priory. George Chapman b. here.
Hitchins, village (1940 pop. 983), Carter co., NE Ky., 21 mi. SW of Ashland, in agr. and clay-producing area; makes firebrick.
Hitchita (hĭ'chĭtô), town (pop. 141), McIntosh co., E Okla., 14 mi. ESE of Okmulgee, in agr. area; cotton ginning.
Hither Pomerania, region, Europe: see Pomerania.
Hiti, Tuamotu Islands: see Raevski Islands.
Hito, El (ĕl ē'tō), town (pop. 827), Cuenca prov., E central Spain, 35 mi. WSW of Cuenca; grain- and winegrowing; stock raising.
Hitoichi (hētō'ĕchē), town (pop. 3,610), Akita prefecture, N Honshu, Japan, 6 mi. N of Showa, on Hachiro-gata lagoon; rice growing.
Hitokappu Bay, Russian SFSR: see Kasatka.
Hitoyoshi (hētō'yōshē), city (1940 pop. 32,890; 1947 pop. 43,824), Kumamoto prefecture, W central Kyushu, Japan, on Kuma R. and 40 mi. S of Kumamoto; rail junction; major lumber center; alcoholic beverages, tea. Hot-springs resort.
Hitra (hĭt'rä). **1** Island (□ 218; pop. 3,103) in North Sea, Sor-Trondelag co., central Norway, separated from mainland by Trondheim Channel, 37 mi. W of Trondheim; 29 mi. long, 12 mi. wide. Animal husbandry, herring fishing, boatbuilding; whaling station. Fur farming. Deposits of iron ore and galena, not mined since late 19th cent. Formerly called Hitteren. **2** Island, Vest-Agder co., Norway: see Hidra.
Hitterdal (hĭ'tŭrdŏl), village (pop. 262), Clay co., W Minn., 26 mi. ENE of Fargo, N.Dak.; dairy products.
Hitterdal Lake, Norway: see Heddal Lake.
Hitteren, Norway: see Hitra, Sor-Trondelag co.
Hitteroy, Norway: see Hidra.
Hitzacker (hĭts'ä"kŭr), town (pop. 3,799), in former Prussian prov. of Hanover, NW Germany, after 1945 in Lower Saxony, on left bank of the Elbe and 26 mi. ESE of Lüneburg; metal- and woodworking. Mineral baths.
Hitzendorf (hĭt'sŭndôrf), village (pop. 2,081), Styria, SE Austria, 6 mi. WSW of Graz; corn, cattle.
Hiu, New Hebrides: see Torres Islands.
Hiuchi Sea (hū'chē), Jap. *Hiuchi-nada,* or **Bingo Sea,** central section of Inland Sea, Japan, bet. S coast of Honshu and N coast of Shikoku; merges E with Harima Sea, W with Iyo Sea; c.60 mi. E-W, c.35 mi. N-S. Contains many isls.; largest is Omishima. Imabari is on SW shore.
Hiunghsien or **Hsiung-hsien** (both: shyŏŏng'shyĕn'), town, ⊙ Hiunghsien co. (pop. 108,965), central Hopeh prov., China, 35 mi. ENE of Paoting, near small Siting L.; wheat, rice, millet, kaoliang.

Hiva Oa (hē'vä ō'ä) or **Hivaoa,** volcanic island (pop. 847), 2d largest but most important of Marquesas Islands, Fr. Oceania, S Pacific; 9°46'S 139°W. Seat of Atuona, ⊙ Marquesas Isls. Circumference c.60 mi.; central mtn. range rises to 4,130 ft.; large fertile plateau. Good harbor (Bay of Traitors), protected by ridges 3,000 ft. high, is on S coast. Exports copra. Formerly Dominica.
Hiw or **Hu** (hōō), anc. *Diospolis Parva,* village (pop. 13,120), Qena prov., Upper Egypt, 3 mi. SE of Nag Hammadi; cereals, sugar cane, dates.
Hiwada (hēwä'dä), town (pop. 7,231), Fukushima prefecture, N central Honshu, Japan, 4 mi. N of Koriyama; rice, soybeans, tobacco.
Hiwaki (hēwä'kē), town (pop. 14,013), Kagoshima prefecture, SW Kyushu, Japan, 20 mi. NW of Kagoshima; commercial center in rice-growing area; raw silk.
Hiwasa (hēwä'sä), town (pop. 5,810), Tokushima prefecture, E Shikoku, Japan, on Philippine Sea, 23 mi. S of Tokushima; fishing and agr. center; rice, wheat, raw silk.
Hiwassee River (hīwŏ'sē), in Ga., N.C., and Tenn., rises in the Blue Ridge in Towns co., N Ga.; flows N into SW corner of N.C., past Hayesville, and NW, past Murphy, into SE Tenn., to Tennessee R. (Chickamauga Reservoir) 31 mi. NE of Chattanooga; 132 mi. long. In N.C., Apalachia, Hiwassee, and Chatuge dams are major TVA units. Hiwassee Dam (307 ft. high, 1,287 ft. long; completed 1940) is 10 mi. WNW of Murphy; concrete, straight gravity, overflow construction; used for hydroelectric power and flood control. Impounds Hiwassee Reservoir (□ c.10; 22 mi. long, capacity 438,000 acre-ft.) in Cherokee co., N.C.
Hixton, village (pop. 315), Jackson co., W central Wis., on Trempealeau R. and 38 mi. SE of Eau Claire, in dairying region.
Hiyama (hēyä'mä), town (pop. 2,823), Akita prefecture, N Honshu, Japan, 5 mi. SE of Noshiro; rice, bamboo ware.
Hizan (hĭzän'), village (pop. 563), Bitlis prov., SE Turkey, 25 mi. SE of Bitlis; wheat, millet, barley. Formerly Karasufla or Karasusufla.
Hizen (hē'zän), former province in NW Kyushu, Japan; now Nagasaki and Saga prefectures.
Hizen Peninsula, NW Kyushu, Japan, in E.China Sea; branches into 3 sprawling peninsulas: Sonogi Peninsula (SW), Nomo Peninsula (S), Shimabara Peninsula (SE). Indented by Omura Bay (W), Tachibana Bay (S), Ariakeno-umi and Shimabara Bay (E); joined to Kyushu mainland by neck c.30 mi. wide; major portion of peninsula is c.50 mi. long. Contains Nagasaki prefecture and part of Saga prefecture. Nagasaki city in S, Sasebo in W, Karatsu in N. Formerly site of Hizen prov.
Hizume (hēzōō'mā), town (pop. 3,161), Iwate prefecture, N Honshu, Japan, on Kitakami R. and 10 mi. S of Morioka; rice.
Hjallerup (yä'lŭrōōp), town (pop. 1,058), Hjorring amt, N Jutland, Denmark, 21 mi. SSE of Hjorring.
Hjalmar, Lake, Swedish *Hjälmaren* (yĕl'märŭn) (□ 190), S central Sweden, extends E from Orebro; 40 mi. long (E-W), 2–12 mi. wide; max. depth 59 ft. Drains E into L. Malar by Eskilstuna R. (20 mi. long); connects N by Hjalmar Canal (8 mi. long) with Arboga R., 3 mi. E of Arboga. Formerly spelled L. Hjelmar, Swedish *Hjelmaren.*
Hjarno (yärn'ŭ), Dan. *Hjarnø,* low island (□ 1.2; pop. 180), Denmark, at mouth of Horsens Fjord, off E Jutland; farming.
Hjartdal, Norway: see Sauland.
Hjelmar, Lake, Sweden: see Hjalmar, Lake.
Hjo (yōō), city (pop. 3,121), Skaraborg co., S Sweden, on W shore of L. Vatter, 45 mi. N of Jonkoping; health and tourist resort; lake port. Metalworking. Chartered in 16th cent.
Hjoringsnes, Norway: see Hjorungavag.
Hjorring (yŭ'rĭng), Dan. *Hjørring,* Denmark's most northerly amt (□ 1,102; pop. 169,688), N Jutland, N of Lim Fjord; ⊙ Hjorring. Includes isls. Laeso and Hirsholm in the Kattegat, Gjol in Lim Fjord. Drained by Rye and Uggerby rivers. Hilly in E and SE; soil rather poor. Agr., dairy farming. The chief cities are Frederikshavn, Bronderslev, Hjorring.
Hjorring, Dan. *Hjørring,* city (1950 pop. 14,093), ⊙ Hjorring amt, N Jutland, Denmark, 90 mi. N of Aarhus; 57°28'N 9°59'E. Textile mills, meat-packing plants, iron foundries, machine shops; rail junction. City dates from 12th cent.
Hjorundfjord, canton, Norway: see Oye.
Hjorund Fjord, inlet, Norway: see Stor Fjord.
Hjorungavag (yŭ'rōōng-ävôg"), Nor. *Hjørungavåg,* village in Hareid canton, More og Romsdal co., W Norway, on E shore of Hareid isl., 9 mi. SSW of Alesund; fishing and sealing; shipyards. Scene of naval battle in 986 bet. viking kings. Sometimes called Hjoringsnes.
Hjosen Fjord, Norway: see Josen Fjord.
Hjulsbro (yüls'brōō"), village (pop. 543), Ostergotland co., SE Sweden, on Stang R. and 4 mi. SE of Linkoping; ironworks.
Hkamti Long (käm'tē lông'), former group of 8 Shan states (□ 296; pop. 5,349) of Myitkyina dist., Upper Burma, in Putao region, after 1947 inc. into Kachin State.
Hladir, Norway: see Lade.

Hlaingbwe (hŭlĭng'bwĕ"), village, Thaton dist., Lower Burma, in Tenasserim, on Hlaingbwe R. (headstream of Gyaing R.) and 45 mi. NNE of Moulmein; rice, teak forests (govt. reserves).
Hlaing River, Burma: see MYITMAKA RIVER.
Hlatikulu (hlätēkōō'lōō), village, ⊙ Southern Dist., S Swaziland, 50 mi. SSE of Mbabane.
Hlegu (hŭlĕ'gōō), village, Insein dist., Lower Burma, 22 mi. NNE of Rangoon; road center.
Hliboka, Ukrainian SSR; see GLYBOKA.
Hlinik nad Vahom, Czechoslovakia: see BYTCA.
Hlinsko (hlĭn'skô), town (pop. 5,189), E Bohemia, Czechoslovakia, on Chrudimka R., on railroad and 20 mi. SSE of Pardubice, in sugar-beet and potato dist.; fur-processing center; also has cotton and jute mills. Bathing place of Hamry (hăm'rĭ) is 2 mi. SSE.
Hlohovec (hlô'hôvĕts), Hung. *Galgóc* (gŏl'gōts), town (pop. 8,723), W Slovakia, Czechoslovakia, on Vah R. and 15 mi. NW of Nitra, in agr. area (wheat, sugar beets, barley); rail junction; distilling, woodworking. Formerly also known as Frastak, Slovak *Fraštak*, Ger. *Freistadl.* Former fortress of Leopoldov, Ger. *Leopoldstadt*, Hung. *Lipótvár*, now converted into state penitentiary, is just NW, across the Vah.
Hlotse, Basutoland: see LERIBE.
Hlubocepy (hlōō'bôchĕ"pĭ), Czech *Hlubočepy*, SSW suburb (pop. 4,364) of Prague, Czechoslovakia, on left bank of Vltava R., 4 mi. from city center; large cement works, lime kilns.
Hluboczek Wielki, Ukrainian SSR: see VELIKI GLUBOCHEK.
Hluboka nad Vltavou (hlōō'bôkä näd' vŭl"tävō), Czech *Hluboká nad Vltavou*, Ger. *Frauenberg* (frou'ŭnbĕrk), town (pop. 2,537), S Bohemia, Czechoslovakia, on Vltava R., on railroad and 6 mi. NNW of Budweis. Famous for 19th-cent. castle, built in Tudor style and containing collections of paintings, tapestry, furniture, and arms; park and game preserve adjoin castle. Carp breeding and fishing in near-by fish ponds; noted Bezdrev pond (□ 2) is 2 mi. W.
Hlucin (hlōō'chēn), Czech *Hlučín*, Ger. *Hultschin*, town (pop. 5,064), NE Silesia, Czechoslovakia, on railroad and 6 mi. NW of Ostrava; agr. center (sugar beets, oats). Anthracite mining in vicinity.
Hluhluwe Game Reserve, U. of So. Afr.: see ZULULAND.
Hnifsdalur (hŭnēfs'dä"lür), Icelandic *Hnífsdalur*, fishing village (pop. 290), Isafjardar co., NW Iceland, on Vestfjarda Peninsula, on Isafjardardjup, 3 mi. N of Isafjordur.
Hnusta (hŭnōō'shtä), Slovak *Hnúšta*, Hung. *Nyustya* (nyōō'styŏ), town (pop. 1,682), S central Slovakia, Czechoslovakia, in Slovak Ore Mts., on railroad and 38 mi. ESE of Banska Bystrica; iron mining.
Ho (hō), town (pop. 5,818), S Br. Togoland, administered as part of Eastern Prov., Gold Coast colony, 45 mi. NE of Akuse; road junction; cacao, palm oil and kernels, cotton.
Hoabinh (hwä'bĭng'), town, ⊙ Hoabinh prov. (□ 1,800; 1943 pop. 84,400), N Vietnam, in Tonkin, on Black R. and 35 mi. SW of Hanoi, in forested region; gums and resin. Prehistoric caves.
Hoang Ho, China: see YELLOW RIVER.
Hoback River, W Wyo., rises in NW Sublette co., flows c.30 mi. NW, through picturesque Hoback Canyon, past N Wyoming Range, to Snake R. 10 mi. S of Jackson.
Hobara (hōbä'rä), town (pop. 7,448), Fukushima prefecture, N Honshu, Japan, 7 mi. NE of Fukushima; rice, raw silk.
Hobart (hō'bärt hō'bûrt), city (pop. 56,640; metropolitan Hobart 76,534), ⊙ Tasmania, Australia, on W shore of Derwent R. estuary; 42°51'S 147°20'E. Chief port of state; rail terminus; zinc refinery, cement works, woolen mills, meat-packing plants, fruit canneries, flour mills. Mt. Wellington (4,166 ft.) is W, behind city. Floating bridge (built 1941) links Hobart with E Derwent shore; its floating portion is 3,168 ft. long. Seat of Univ. of Tasmania, Tasmanian Mus. (1861), art gall., Anglican and R.C. cathedrals, Parliament House. Founded 1804. Mild, equable climate.
Hobart. 1 (hō'bärt, hō'bûrt) City (pop. 10,244), Lake co., extreme NW Ind., 7 mi. SE of Gary; mfg. (clay products, packed meat); clay pits; grain, dairy products, livestock. L. George (recreation) is near by. Settled c.1849, inc. 1921. **2** (hō'bärt, hō'bûrt) Village (pop. 618), Delaware co., S N.Y., in the Catskills, on West Branch of Delaware R. and 20 mi. ESE of Oneonta, in resort area; feed, and lumber milling. **3** (hō'bûrt) City (pop. 5,380), Kiowa co., SW Okla., c.65 mi. W of Chickasha; trade center for rich agr. area (cotton, grain, alfalfa, sorghums, poultry; dairy products); cotton gins and compress, cold-storage plants, creameries, cottonseed and feed mills. Oil field near by. Seat of Kiowa Co. Jr. Col. Inc. 1901.
Hoba West, South-West Africa: see GROOTFONTEIN.
Hobbs, city (pop. 13,875), Lea co., SE N.Mex., on Llano Estacado, near Texas line, 95 mi. SE of Roswell. Trade center in livestock, grain area; oil-well supplies, oil refineries. Air Force base near. Founded 1907. Grew rapidly after discovery of oil and gas (1927) in vicinity. Railroad arrived 1930.
Hobbs Coast, Antarctica, along coast of Marie Byrd Land, extends NE from Emory Land Bay to W edge of Getz Shelf Ice; 75°45'S 135°–140°30'W. Discovered 1940 by U.S. expedition.
Hobdo, Mongolia: see KOBDO.
Hoberg (hō'bûrg), town (pop. 90), Lawrence co., SW Mo., in the Ozarks, on Spring R. and 4 mi. SW of Mt. Vernon.
Hobe Sound (hōb), resort village (1940 pop. 554), Martin co., SE Fla., 30 mi. SSE of Fort Pierce, near Jupiter Isl.
Hobgood (hŏb'gōōd), town (pop. 603), Halifax co., NE N.C., 12 mi. NE of Tarboro; lumber milling.
Hobkirk, agr. village and parish (pop. 524), central Roxburgh, Scotland, 6 mi. ESE of Hawick.
Hobkirks Hill, S.C.: see CAMDEN.
Hobo (ō'bō), town (pop. 1,681), Huila dept., S central Colombia, in upper Magdalena valley, 27 mi. SSW of Neiva; rice, cacao, coffee, livestock.
Hoboken (hō'bōkŭn), town (pop. 31,941), Antwerp prov., N Belgium, on Scheldt R., 4 mi. SW of Antwerp; shipbuilding center; copper, tin, and silver refining; wool combing.
Hoboken. 1 (hō"bō'kĭn) City (pop. 492), Brantley co., SE Ga., 13 mi. E of Waycross. **2** (hō'bōkŭn, hō'bŭkŭn) City (pop. 50,676), Hudson co., NE N.J., on Hudson R. opposite lower Manhattan (ferry, tunnel, subway connections), just N of Jersey City. Port of entry, commercial and industrial center, with marine and railway terminals; shipbuilding, mfg. (food products, electrical equipment, furniture, excavating and hoisting machinery, clothing, chemicals, drafting and scientific instruments). Seat of Stevens Inst. of Technology. Dutch trade and farming began here c.1630. Area deeded by Indians to Stuyvesant 1658, sold 1711 to N.Y. merchant from whose Tory descendants it was confiscated in Revolution, purchased by John Stevens 1784, town laid out 1804, inc. as city 1855. Brewery built here 1642. Stevens operated here 1st steam ferry (1811) and 1st locomotive to pull train on track (1824). Industrialization and growth of transportation came in mid-19th cent. The John Jacob Astor home (1828) was gathering-place for noted authors of early 19th cent.; the *Talisman* edited here by Bryant, Sands, and Verplanck.
Hobro (hō'brō), city (pop. 7,699), Randers amt, E Jutland, Denmark, at head of Mariager Fjord, 36 mi. NNW of Aarhus; meat cannery, brewery, iron foundry.
Höbsögöl, Mongolia: see KHUBSUGUL.
Hobson, New Zealand: see DARGAVILLE.
Hobson, town (pop. 205), Judith Basin co., central Mont., on Judith R. and 21 mi. W of Lewistown; trading point in wheat region; flour, livestock, poultry products.
Hobson City, residential town (pop. 672), Calhoun co., E Ala., just SW of Anniston.
Hobson Lake (20 mi. long, 1–2 mi. wide), E B.C., in Cariboo Mts., in Wells Gray Provincial Park, 120 mi. N of Kamloops; alt. 2,735 ft. Drains S into North Thompson R. through Clearwater L.
Hobson's Bay, S Victoria, Australia, N arm of Port Phillip Bay; 12 mi. long, 7 mi. wide; receives Yarra R. Port Melbourne on N shore, Williamstown on SW shore.
Hocabá (ōkäbä'), town (pop. 1,774), Yucatan, SE Mexico, 26 mi. ESE of Mérida; rail junction; henequen growing.
Hochalmspitze (hōkh'älm'shpĭtsŭ), peak (11,007 ft.) of the Hohe Tauern, S Austria, SE of the Ankogel, in NW Carinthia.
Hochang (hŭ'jäng'), town (pop. 11,380), ⊙ Hochang co. (pop. 130,334), westernmost Kweichow prov., China, 30 mi. NE of Weining; papermaking, wool-textile weaving; grain. Iron mines, lead deposits near by.
Hochburg-Ach (hōkh'bōōrk-äkh'), town (pop. 2,427), W Upper Austria, on the Inn, opposite Burghausen, Germany, and 12 mi. SW of Braunau; wheat, potatoes.
Hochdorf (hōkh'dôrf), town (pop. 3,510), Lucerne canton, central Switzerland, 8 mi. N of Lucerne; cement, chemicals, milk, fats, beer, flour.
Hochelaga (hō"shŭlä'gŭ), former co. of S Que., inc. in MONTREAL ISLAND.
Hochelaga, district of MONTREAL, Que., and name of former Indian village on site of which city is built.
Hochemmerich, Germany: see RHEINHAUSEN.
Hocheng (hŭ'jŭng'). **1** Town, ⊙ Hocheng co. (pop. 50,247), SE Kansu prov., China, 50 mi. SSW of Lanchow; gold mines, saltworks. **2** Town, Sinkiang prov., China: see HORGOS.
Höchenschwand (hû'khŭn-shvänt'), village (pop. 516), S Baden, Germany, in Black Forest, 8 mi. NNW of Waldshut; climatic health resort (alt. 3,307 ft.).
Höcherberg, Saar: see MITTELBEXBACH.
Hochfeiler (hōkh'fīlŭr), Ital. *Gran Pilastro*, highest peak (11,555 ft.) of Zillertal Alps, on Austro-Ital. border and 12 mi. E of Brenner Pass.
Hochfeld (hōkh'fĕlt), SW industrial district of DUISBURG, Germany, on right bank of the Rhine; deep-water port.
Hochfelden (ōkfĕldĕn', Ger. hōkh'fĕldŭn), town (pop. 2,565), Bas-Rhin dept., E France, on the Zorn and Marne-Rhine Canal, and 15 mi. NW of Strasbourg; agr. trade center; metalworks, brewery.
Hochfilzen (hōkh'fĭltsŭn), village (pop. 659), Tyrol, W Austria, 11 mi. E of Kitzbühel, in Kitzbühel Alps. Just E is Griessen Pass (alt. 3,123 ft.) with railroad and highway into Salzburg.
Hochgolling (hōkh'gôlĭng), highest peak (9,393 ft.) of the NIEDERE TAUERN, central Austria, on Styria-Salzburg border.
Hoch Hagi, Czechoslovakia: see VYSNE HAGY.
Hochheim or **Hochheim am Main** (hōkh'hīm äm mīn'), town (pop. 5,786), in former Prussian prov. of Hesse-Nassau, W Germany, after 1945 in Hesse, on right bank of the canalized Main and 16 mi. WSW of Frankfurt; noted for its sparkling Hochheimer ("hock") wine.
Ho-chiang, China: see HOKIANG.
Ho-chien, China: see HOKIEN.
Hochih or **Ho-ch'ih** (both: hŭ'chŭ'), town, ⊙ Hochih co. (pop. 98,173), NW Kwangsi prov., China, 95 mi. WNW of Liuchow, near railroad; tin- and mercury-mining center; tung-oil and tobacco processing, cotton-textile mfg.; rice, millet, indigo.
Ho-ching. 1 Town, Shansi prov., China: see HOTSIN. **2** Town, Sinkiang prov., China: see HOTSING.
Ho-ch'iu, China: see HWOKIU.
Hochkirch (hōkh'kĭrkh"), village (pop. 963), Saxony, E central Germany, in Upper Lusatia, 7 mi. ESE of Bautzen. Scene (Oct., 1758) of defeat of Prussians under Frederick the Great by Austrians commanded by Daun and Loudon.
Hochkönig (hōkh'kûnĭkh), highest peak (9,639 ft.) of ÜBERGOSSENE ALM in Salzburg Alps, W central Austria; copper deposits near Mitterberg village at SE foot.
Hochlantsch (hōkh'läntsh), peak (5,650 ft.) of Fischbach Alps, in Styria, SE central Austria, 8 mi. ESE of Bruck an der Mur; has interesting limestone formations (gorges, caves).
Hochneukirch (hōkh'noi'kĭrkh"), village (pop. 5,408), in former Prussian Rhine Prov., W Germany, after 1945 in North Rhine-Westphalia, 5 mi. S of Rheydt; rail junction.
Hochobir (hōkh"ō'bēr) Slovenian *Ojsterc*, peak (7,026 ft.) of the Obir (mtn. in the Karawanken), S Austria, 12 mi. SE of Klagenfurt, bet. the Drau and Yugoslav border.
Hochow. 1 Town, Anhwei prov., China: see HOHSIEN. **2** Town, Kansu prov., China: see LINSIA. **3** Town, Szechwan prov., China: see HOCHWAN.
Hochschwab (hōkh'shväp), peak (7,474 ft.) in Styria, central Austria, highest of Hochschwab Alps, 15 mi. NNW of Bruck an der Mur. Its springs supply drinking water for Vienna.
Hochspeyer (hōkh'shpī"ŭr), village (pop. 3,086), Rhenish Palatinate, W Germany, 5 mi. E of Kaiserslautern; grain, potatoes.
Höchst (hûkhst). **1** Industrial suburb (pop. 18,641, including incorporated dists., 51,452) of FRANKFURT, Hesse, W Germany, on right bank of the canalized Main and 6 mi. W of city center; a seat of Ger. chemical industry (especially dyes). Tilly here defeated Christian of Brunswick in 1622. **2** or **Höchst im Odenwald** (ĭm ō'dŭnvält), village (pop. 3,437), S Hesse, W Germany, in former Starkenburg prov., in the Odenwald, on the Mümling, 8 mi. N of Michelstadt; woodworking.
Hochstadt, Czechoslovakia: see VYSOKE NAD JIZEROU.
Höchstädt or **Höchstädt an der Donau** (hûkh'shtĕt än dĕr dō'nou), town (pop. 227), Swabia, W Bavaria, Germany, on the Danube and 4 mi. NE of Dillingen; mfg. of chemicals. Has several Gothic churches; late-16th-cent. castle with watchtower dating from 1292. Founded by the Hohenstaufen, it was chartered c.1280. Two battles of War of the Spanish Succession took place near by, in 1703 and 1704 (see BLENHEIM).
Höchstadt or **Höchstadt an der Aisch** (hûkh'shtät än dĕr ĭsh'), town (pop. 3,291), Upper Franconia, N Bavaria, Germany, on the Aisch and 12 mi. NW of Erlangen; mfg. of chemicals, leather and metal products; brewing; hops. Has early 15th-cent. church; and a chapel (1513).
Hochstetter Foreland (hŏk'stĕtŭr, hōkh'stĕtŭr), Dan. *Hochstetters Forland*, peninsula (75 mi. long, 20–55 mi. wide), NE Greenland, on Greenland Sea; 75°35'N 20°50'W. Generally ice-free, mountainous surface rises to over 4,000 ft. At SE tip, near 75°8'N 19°37'W, is meteorological station and hunting outpost, until 1941 operated by Norway, then dismantled; rebuilt after 1945.
Höchst im Odenwald, Germany: see HÖCHST.
Hochstuhl (hōkh'shtōōl), Slovenian *Stol*, highest peak (7,342 ft.) of the Karawanken, on Austro-Yugoslav border, SSW of Klagenfurt, Austria.
Hochtaunus, Germany: see TAUNUS.
Hochtor, peak, Austria: see ENNSTAL ALPS.
Ho-ch'ü, China: see HOKÜ.
Ho-ch'uan, China: see HOCHWAN.
Hochvogel (hōkh'fōgŭl), peak (8,507 ft.) in Allgäu Alps on Austro-Ger. border, 8 mi. E of Obersdorf.
Hochwan or **Ho-ch'uan** (both: hŭ'chwän'), town (pop. 40,086), ⊙ Hochwan co. (pop. 712,340), S central Szechwan prov., China, on Kialing R., at

mouth of Fow R., and 35 mi. NW of Chungking city; tung-oil trading center; paper milling, match mfg. Agr.: rice, millet, wheat, rapeseed, oranges, medicinal herbs. Sulphur and iron mines near by. Until 1913 called Hochow.

Hochwang (hōkh'väng), peak (8,317 ft.) in the Alps, E Switzerland, 5 mi. ENE of Chur.

Hockanum, village, Conn.: see EAST HARTFORD.

Hockanum River (hŏ'kŭnŭm), central Conn., rises in Shenipsit L., flows c.25 mi. SW, past Rockville, Talcottville, and Manchester (water power), to the Connecticut at East Hartford.

Hockenheim (hô'kŭnhīm), town (pop. 11,198), N Baden, Germany, after 1945 in Württemberg-Baden, on the Kraichbach and 5 mi. E of Speyer, in tobacco area; mfg. of cigars, cigarettes, clothing; woodworking.

Hocking, county (□ 421; pop. 19,520), S central Ohio; ⊙ Logan. Intersected by Hocking R. and small Rush, Salt, and Monday creeks. Agr. (livestock; dairy products; grain); mfg. at Logan; coal mining; clay, sand, and gravel pits. Formed 1805.

Hocking, village (pop. 1,004, with adjacent The Plains), Athens co., SE Ohio, on Hocking R., just N of Athens.

Hocking River, SE Ohio, rises in Fairfield co., flows c.100 mi. SW, past Lancaster, Logan, Nelsonville, and Athens, to the Ohio 22 mi. SW of Marietta.

Hockley, town and parish (pop. 2,017), SE Essex, England, 5 mi. NNW of Southend-on-Sea; agr. market. Has Norman church.

Hockley, county (□ 903; pop. 20,407), NW Texas; ⊙ Levelland. Rich agr. region, with extensive irrigated areas; cotton, grain sorghums, corn, wheat, potatoes, truck, fruit; dairying, livestock (beef cattle, hogs, poultry; some sheep, horses, mules). Large oil production. Formed 1876.

Hocmon (houk'mōn'), town, Giadinh prov., S Vietnam, 10 mi. NW of Saigon; rice center.

Hoctún (ōktōōn'), town (pop. 1,868), Yucatan, SE Mexico, 28 mi. ESE of Mérida; henequen, sugar cane, corn.

Hodaka, Mount, Japan: see HOTAKA, MOUNT.

Hodal (hō'dŭl), town (pop. 8,661), Gurgaon dist., SE Punjab, India, 45 mi. SSE of Gurgaon; wheat, millet, cotton, sugar cane; cotton ginning.

Hoddesdon (hŏdz'dŭn), residential urban district (1931 pop. 6,811; 1951 census 13,728), E Hertford, England, 4 mi. SE of Hertford; mfg.: electrical equipment, clothing, pharmaceuticals. Roman remains excavated. Near by is Rye House, scene of plot (1683) to assassinate Charles II and his brother.

Hoddom, Scotland: see ECCLEFECHAN.

Hodeida, Hodeidah, Hudaida, or **Al-Hudaydah** (ăl hōdā'dŭ), city (pop. 26,000), ⊙ Hodeida prov. (pop. 720,000), W Yemen, port on Red Sea, 160 mi. N of the strait Bab el Mandeb, 90 mi. SW of Sana (linked by motor road); 14°47'N 42°46'E. Chief port of Yemen, Hodeida is also hq. of foreign consular and steamship offices. Exports coffee, hides and skins, and has a small weaving, dyeing, and tanning industry. A semicircular wall separates the old inner town from scattered suburbs amid palm groves and gardens. The city's prominence dates from mid-19th cent., when it was occupied (1849) by the Turks and developed as Yemen's chief port, supplanting the old Mocha. After First World War, it was briefly held (1919) by the British, and then (until 1921) by Asir. In 1934, it was briefly captured in Ibn Saud's raid.

Hodgdon (hŏj'dŭn), town (pop. 1,162), Aroostook co., E Maine, 5 mi. S of Houlton, in agr., lumbering area. Inc. 1832.

Hodge, paper-milling village (pop. 1,386), Jackson parish, N central La., on Dugdemona R. and 40 mi. WSW of Monroe, in agr. area; cannery.

Hodgeman, county (□ 860; pop. 3,310), SW central Kansas; ⊙ Jetmore. Rolling prairie region, watered by Pawnee R. Grain, livestock. Formed 1879.

Hodgenville (hŏj'ĭnvĭl), town (pop. 1,695), ⊙ Larue co., central Ky., on Nolin R. and 45 mi. S of Louisville, in agr. (burley tobacco, corn, livestock), limestone-quarries, gas-wells, and timber area; mfg. of concrete blocks; feed, flour, and lumber mills. Gateway to ABRAHAM LINCOLN NATIONAL HISTORICAL PARK (S). Settled c.1789.

Hodges. 1 Town (pop. 220), Franklin co., NW Ala., 30 mi. SSW of Tuscumbia. **2** Town (pop. 275), Greenwood co., W S.C., 8 mi. NW of Greenwood.

Hodges Hill (1,868 ft.), central N.F., 14 mi. NW of Grand Falls.

Hodgeville, village (pop. 224), S Sask., on Wiwa Creek and 40 mi. ESE of Swift Current; grain elevators, dairying.

Hodgkins, village (pop. 536), Cook co., NE Ill., W suburb of Chicago.

Hodmezövasarhely (hōd'mĕzûvä"shärhĕē), Hung. *Hódmezővásárhely*, city (1941 pop. 61,776), in but independent of Csongrad co., S Hungary, near the Tisza, 15 mi. NE of Szeged; rail center. Mfg. (agr. implements, pottery), sawmills, flour mills, distilleries, brickworks. Agr. school. Grain, cattle raised near by. In the administrative reorganization of 1950 it lost its large rural suburban area.

Hodna (hŏd'nŭ, Fr. ôdnä'), interior drainage basin in Constantine dept., NE Algeria, at N edge of the Sahara, forming a break in the Saharan Atlas (Oulad-Naïl Mts., SW; Aurès massif, E), and separated from the Tell (N) by the Hodna Mts. The bottom of the arid depression (alt. 1,280 ft.) is occupied by the Chott el Hodna, a playa lake of varying size (c.50 mi. long, 10 mi. wide). Only settlements, near basin's edges, are Bou Saâda (SW) and M'Sila (N).

Hodna Mountains, range of the Tell Atlas, in NE Algeria, extending c.80 mi. ESE from Aumale, and bounding the Hodna depression on N. Rise to 6,000 ft. Oak and cedar forests. Phosphate mines on N slope at Tocqueville.

Hodonin (hô'dônyĕn), Czech *Hodonín*, Ger. *Göding* (gû'dĭng), town (pop. 13,103), S Moravia, Czechoslovakia, on Morava R. and 34 mi. SE of Brno; rail junction; main agr. center of Moravian Slovakia; tobacco processing, sugar refining; large brickkilns and brickyards. Near-by petroleum deposits have been exploited commercially since 1933. Has noted ethnographic mus. Thomas G. Masaryk b. here.

Hodsag, Yugoslavia: see ODZACI.

Hodslavice, Czechoslovakia: see NOVY JICIN.

Hodsock, town and parish (pop. 4,307), N Nottingham, England, 4 mi. NNE of Worksop; coal mining.

Hodur (hōdōōr'), Ital. *Oddur*, town (pop. 2,500), in the Upper Juba, Ital. Somaliland, 170 mi. NW of Mogadishu, on plateau (alt. 1,500 ft.) bet. Webi Shebeli and Juba rivers; 4°8'N 43°54'E. Road junction. Trade in hides, ivory, myrrh, frankincense, gum arabic; wood carving. Fort, airfield.

Hoedic or **Hoëdic** (ôĕdĕk'), island (pop. 185), in Bay of Biscay, off Brittany coast (Morbihan dept.), W France, 12 mi. SE of tip of Quiberon Peninsula; 2 mi. long, ½ mi. wide. Isl. is a remnant of coastline which once joined Quiberon Peninsula to Pointe du Croisic. Fisheries.

Hoedjes Bay, U. of So. Afr.: see SALDANHA.

Hoegaarden (hōō'gärdŭn), Fr. *Hougarde* (ōōgärd'), town (pop. 4,513), Brabant prov., central Belgium, 3 mi. SW of Tirlemont; sugar refining.

Hoehne (hō'nē), village, Las Animas co., S Colo., on Purgatoire R. and 10 mi. NE of Trinidad, in irrigated agr. region (sugar beets, alfalfa, beans); alt. c.5,710 ft.

Hoei, Belgium: see HUY.

Hoeilaart (hōō'ēlärt), town (pop. 6,349), Brabant prov., central Belgium, 8 mi. SE of Brussels; market center for grape-growing area. Formerly spelled Hoeylaert.

Hoeksche Waard, Netherlands: see BEIJERLAND.

Hoek van Holland, Netherlands: see HOOK OF HOLLAND.

Hoendiep (hōōn'dēp), canal, Friesland and Groningen provs., N Netherlands; extends 16 mi. E-W, bet. Groningen and the KOLONELSDIEP at Stroobos (10 mi. ESE of Dokkum); 7 ft. deep. Navigable by ships to 250 tons. Joined by Van Starkenborgh Canal at Noordhornerga (WNW of Groningen).

Hoenheim (ôĕnĕm'), Ger. *Hönheim* (hûn'hīm), outer N suburb (pop. 3,397), of Strasbourg, Bas-Rhin dept., E France, on Marne-Rhine Canal; brick- and tileworks. Furniture mfg., enameling.

Hoensbroek (hōōnz'brōōk), town (pop. 8,825; commune pop. 16,042), Limburg prov., SE Netherlands, 3 mi. WNW of Heerlen; iron industry. Near by are open-pit lignite workings.

Hoerhkwosze, China: see HORGOS.

Hoeryong (hû'rĕŭng'), Jap. *Kainei*, town (1944 pop. 24,330), N.Hamgyong prov., N Korea, on Tumen R. (Manchuria line) and 32 mi. NW of Najin; commercial center in agr. area. Coal near by.

Hoeselt (hōō'sŭlt), town (pop. 4,250), Limburg prov., NE Belgium, 5 mi. N of Tongres; agr. market (fruit, potatoes, tobacco).

Hoeylaert, Belgium: see HOEILAART.

Hoey's Bridge (hō'ēz), village, Rift Valley prov., W Kenya, on railroad and 35 mi. NNW of Eldoret; pyrethrum, sisal, coffee, corn.

Hof, Czechoslovakia: see DVORCE.

Hof (hōf), city (1950 pop. 60,867), Upper Franconia, NE Bavaria, Germany, on the Saxonian Saale and 70 mi. NE of Nuremberg, 8 mi. S of Gutenfürst; 50°19'N 11°55'E. Communications center near Czechoslovak line, with airport and customs station; textile center (cotton, wool, synthetic wool, thread, felt, rugs). Metal industry (iron foundries; heavy machinery, precision instruments); breweries, glassworks, lumber and paper mills, tanneries. Has mid-16th-cent. city hall; the 2 old churches (mid-11th cent. and early-13th cent.) were renovated after disastrous fire of 1823. Hof was founded in 13th cent. by dukes of Meran, and was chartered bet. 1288 and 1319. Passed to Hohenzollern line in 14th cent. Seriously devastated by religious wars and Seven Years War. Became part of Bavaria in 1810. In 19th cent., industrialization of textile craft brought tremendous expansion and increase of pop. Repeatedly bombed in Second World War; captured by U.S. troops in spring, 1945. After 1945, traffic check point bet. East and West Germany.

Hof, Norway: see EIDSFOSS.

Hofei (hŭ'fā'), city (1934 pop. estimate 70,000), ⊙ North Anhwei, China, NW of Chao L., 90 mi. W of Nanking, and on railroad; 117°16'E 31°53'N. Administrative center, in rice-growing region; cotton and silk weaving; wheat, sweet potatoes, tobacco, lacquer. Projected junction for rail line to Sinyang (Honan). Li Hung-chang, Chinese statesman (1823–1901), was b. here. Until 1912 called Lüchow, Hofei became an independent municipality in 1947. Was ⊙ Anhwei in late 1940s.

Hofeng (hŭ'fŭng'). **1** Town (pop. 9,507), ⊙ Hofeng co. (pop. 80,893), SW Hupeh prov., China, near Hunan line, 35 mi. SE of Enshih; rice, wheat, beans, cotton. Also written Haofeng. **2** Town, Sinkiang prov., China: see HOSHUTOLOGOI.

Hoffman. 1 Village (pop. 575), Grant co., W Minn., 14 mi. SE of Elbow Lake village, in agr. area (grain, fruit, livestock, poultry); dairy products. **2** Town (pop. 398), Richmond co., S N.C., 13 mi. NE of Rockingham. **3** Town (pop. 302), Okmulgee co., E central Okla., 6 mi. ENE of Henryetta, in agr. area; cotton ginning.

Hoffman Island, SE N.Y., artificial island (c.10 acres) in Lower New York Bay, just off E Staten Isl.; part of Richmond borough of New York city. Created 1872, it was formerly a quarantine station; now site of maritime training school.

Hoffman Mountain (3,715 ft.), Essex co., NE N.Y., in the Adirondacks, 15 mi. SSE of Mt. Marcy and just NW of Schroon Lake village.

Hofgastein, Austria: see BAD HOFGASTEIN.

Hofgeismar (hōf"gīs'mär), town (pop. 7,711), in former Prussian prov. of Hesse-Nassau, W Germany, after 1945 in Hesse, 13 mi. NNW of Kassel; mfg. of machinery, precision instruments, chemicals; woodworking. Has Gothic church.

Hofheim (hōf'hīm). **1** or **Hofheim in Unterfranken** (ĭn ōōn'tŭrfrăng"kŭn), village (pop. 1,889), Lower Franconia, N Bavaria, Germany, 14 mi. NE of Schweinfurt; machine shop; woodworking, lumber and flour milling. **2** Town (pop. 9,226), in former Prussian prov. of Hesse-Nassau, W Germany, after 1945 in Hesse, at S foot of the Taunus, 10 mi. W of Frankfurt; wine. Was Roman fort. **3** Village (pop. 3,629), Rhenish Hesse, W Germany, after 1945 in Hesse, near the Rhine, 2.5 mi. NE of Worms; rail junction; grain.

Hofkirchen (hōf'kĭr"khŭn), village (pop. 913), Lower Bavaria, Germany, on the Danube and 17 mi. ENE of Passau; wheat, barley, horses, cattle. Chartered 1387.

Hofmeyr (hôf'mī"ŭr), town (pop. 1,449), SE Cape Prov., U. of So. Afr., 70 mi. WNW of Queenstown; rail terminus; sheep, grain, feed crops. Salt pans in region.

Hofn or **Hofn i Hornafirdi** (hû'pŭn ē hôrd'näfĭr"dhē), Icelandic *Höfn í Hornafirði*, fishing village (pop. 400), Austur-Skaftafell co., SE Iceland, on Horna Fjord; 64°15'N 15°11'W.

Hofors (hōō"fôrs', –fôsh'), village (pop. 6,887), Gavleborg co., E Sweden, 17 mi. WSW of Sandviken; large iron- and steelworks, sawmills.

Hofsjokull (hôfs'yû"kütŭl), Icelandic *Hofsjökull*, extensive glacier, central Iceland, rises to 5,581 ft. at 64°46'N 18°43'W.

Hofstade (hōf'städŭ), town (pop. 4,475), East Flanders prov., N central Belgium, on Dender R. and 2 mi. N of Alost; artificial silk, matches.

Hofu, Japan: see BOFU.

Hofuf or **Hufuf** (both: hōōfōōf'), city (pop. 100,000), ⊙ Hasa, E Saudi Arabia, on railroad and 70 mi. SW of Dhahran, 180 mi. ENE of Riyadh; 25°23'N 49°34'E. Commercial center in rich Hasa oasis, largest in Hasa prov., producing dates, wheat, barley, fruit. Textile weaving; copper- and brasswork; mfg. of swords and daggers. Pop. is 75% Sunni, 25% Shiah. Hofuf is linked by road with its Persian Gulf port Oqair. Oil field of Ithmaniya is SW. Mubarraz is a major N oasis-suburb. Hofuf, originally called Hasa, was hq. of Karmathian terrorist movement (10th cent.).

Hoganas (hû'gänĕs", hû"gänĕs'), Swedish *Höganäs*, city (pop. 6,699), Malmohus co., SW Sweden, on W coast of Kullen peninsula, on the Kattegat, at N end of the Oresund, 12 mi. NNW of Halsingborg; coal-mining center, with iron, brick, pottery, and furniture works.

Hogansburg, village (pop. c.250), Franklin co., N N.Y., on St. Regis R. near its mouth on the St. Lawrence, and 11 mi. ENE of Massena. Near by is St. Regis Indian Reservation (partly in Canada).

Hogansville, city (pop. 3,769), Troup co., W Ga., 11 mi. NE of La Grange; cotton market with textile mills, cannery. Inc. 1870.

Hogatza River (hōgăt'sŭ), W central Alaska, rises in S foothills of Brooks Range near 66°55'N 153°50'W, flows 130 mi. SSW to Koyukuk R. at 66°N 155°23'W.

Hogback Mountain. 1 Peak in Mont.: see SNOWCREST MOUNTAINS. **2** Peak (3,226 ft.) in the Blue Ridge, NW S.C., 6 mi. W of Landrum, near N.C. line.

Hog Bay, Australia: see PENNESHAW.

Hogbo, Sweden: see SKOGSBO.

Hogen, Formosa: see FENGYÜAN.

Hogfors, Finland: see KARKKILA.

Hogfors (hûg"fôrs', –fôsh'), Swedish *Högfors*, village (pop. 259), Vastmanland co., central Sweden, in Bergslag region, 7 mi. E of Fagersta, in iron-mining region; ironworks, foundries (established in 17th cent.).

Hoggar Mountains, Algeria: see AHAGGAR MOUNTAINS.

Hog Harbour, New Hebrides: see ESPIRITU SANTO.
Hog Head, Cape, SW Co. Kerry, Ireland, on E side of entrance of Ballinskelligs Bay, 4 mi. SE of Ballinskelligs; 51°47'N 10°14'W.
Hoghton (hô'tůn, hō'–), village and parish (pop. 978), central Lancashire, England, on Darwen R. and 5 mi. W of Blackburn; cotton milling. Has ruins of 16th-cent. Hoghton Tower.
Hog Island, narrow islet (4 mi. long), N central Bahama Isls., just off NE New Providence Isl., and protecting Nassau harbor. Has a popular beach.
Hog Island (□ 22), Essequibo co., N Br. Guiana, in Essequibo R. estuary, SSW of Wakenaam and Leguan isls., 25 mi. W of Georgetown; rice growing.
Hog Island, islet in the Shannon, SW Co. Clare, Ireland, just S of Kilrush.
Hog Island. 1 In SW Maine, at mouth of Fore R., in Casco Bay; site of Fort Gorges, abandoned harbor defense completed 1865. **2** In Mich.: see BEAVER ISLANDS. **3** In SE Pa., along W shore of Delaware R., in S Philadelphia; separated from mainland by creek. In First World War, important govt. shipyard here; now an industrial and shipping area and site of municipal airport. **4** In E Va., barrier island bet. the Atlantic and Hog Island Bay (9 mi. long N-S, 6 mi. wide), 18 mi. NE of Cape Charles city; 6 mi. long; lighthouse. Great Machipongo Inlet (mă-chĭpŏng'gō), at S end, links bay and ocean; Little Machipongo Inlet is at N end.
Hog Islands, Sp. *Cayos Cochinos* or *Islas Cochinos* (kī'lōs, ē'släs kōchē'nōs), archipelago (□ 725 acres) in Bay Islands dept., N Honduras, in Caribbean Sea, c.8 mi. off N Honduras coast, 22 mi. ENE of La Ceiba. Consist of 2 larger isls. (Big Hog Isl., Little Hog Isl.) and 13 islets. Coconuts.
Hog Islands, group in the Atlantic, SW Co. Kerry, Ireland, near mouth of Kenmare R., W of Lamb's Head. Main isls. are Scariff and Deenish.
Hogla (hōglä'), settlement (pop. 220), W Israel, in Plain of Sharon, 4 mi. S of Hadera; mixed farming. Founded 1933.
Hogland, Russian SFSR: see SURSAARI.
Hogolu, Caroline Isls.: see TRUK.
Hogoro (hōgō'rō), village, Central Prov., central Tanganyika, 35 mi. NNE of Gulwe on new rail spur from Msagali (10 mi. NW of Gulwe), in area designated for peanut-growing scheme.
Hog Point, easternmost point of Borneo, in Sulu Sea, at tip of wide NE peninsula; 5°19'N 119°16'E.
Hog Point, Indonesian *Tanjung Tua* (tänjŏŏng' tōōä'), Du. *Varkenshoek* (vär'kůns-hōōk''), promontory on Sunda Strait, at E side of entrance to Lampung Bay, at S tip of Sumatra, Indonesia; 5°54'S 105°43'E.
Hogsby (hûks'bü''), Swedish *Högsby*, village (pop. 1,250), Kalmar co., SE Sweden, on Em R. and 17 mi. WSW of Oskarshamn; woodworking; bricks.
Hogs Fjord (hûks), Nor. *Høgsfjord*, or **Hole Fjord** (hû'lů), Nor. *Hølefjord*, SE arm of Bokn Fjord, Rogaland co., SW Norway, extends c.17 mi. to Dirdal in Ryfylke region; herring fisheries. Name Hogsfjord is sometimes applied to HOLE village on W shore.
Hogsjo (hûg'shû''), Swedish *Högsjö*, village (pop. 578), Sodermanland co., E Sweden, 19 mi. W of Katrineholm; woolen mills.
Hogsty Reef (hŏg'stī''), central Bahama Isls., 40 mi. NW of Great Inagua Isl., 310 mi. SE of Nassau; 21°40'N 73°50'W. The reef is c.6 mi. long (W-E), 3 mi. wide. Off it are 2 small cays. Called Les Etoiles on early Fr. charts.
Hogue, La, France: see SAINT-VAAST-LA-HOUGUE.
Högyesz (hû'dyās), Hung. *Hőgyész*, town (pop. 3,541), Tolna co., SW central Hungary, 16 mi. NW of Szekszard; vineyards.
Hogyoshin, Korea: see PANGOJIN.
Hoh, Turkey: see SIVRICE.
Hohe Acht (hō'ů äkht'), highest peak (2,447 ft.) of the Eifel, W Germany, 2 mi. E of Adenau.
Hohe Eule (oi'lů), Pol. *Góra Sowia* (gōō'rä sô'vyä), highest peak (3,327 ft.) of the Eulengebirge, in Silesia, after 1945 in SW Poland, 11 mi. S of Schweidnitz (Swidnica).
Hohegeiss (hō'ůgīs'), village (pop. 1,864), in Brunswick, NW Germany, after 1945 in Lower Saxony, in the upper Harz, 5 mi. SE of Braunlage, 2 mi. W of Benneckenstein (E Germany); climatic health resort and winter-sports center (alt. 2,105 ft.); woodworking.
Hohenau (hō'ůnou), town (pop. 3,852), NW Lower Austria, near Czechoslovak border, 35 mi. NNE of Vienna; oil and sugar refineries.
Hohenau (ōěnou'), town (dist. pop. 6,569), Itapúa dept., SE Paraguay, 20 mi. NE of Encarnación; agr. center (oranges, maté, wine, livestock); sawmilling. A Ger. colony founded 1898, it stretches SE to the Paraná. Sometimes Colonia Hohenau.
Hohenberg (hō'ůnběrk), town (pop. 2,136), S Lower Austria, on Traisen R. and 20 mi. S of Sankt Pölten; machinery mfg.
Hohenberg or **Hohenberg an der Eger** (än děr ā'gůr), village (pop. 1,412), Upper Franconia, NE Bavaria, Germany, on the Eger and 6 mi. SE of Selb, on Czechoslovak border; porcelain mfg., lumber and flour milling.
Hohenbruck, Czechoslovakia: see TREBECHOVICE POD OREBEM.
Hoheneck (hō'ůněk''), NE suburb of LUDWIGSBURG, Germany, on the Neckar; resort with hot mineral springs.
Hohenelbe, Czechoslovakia: see VRCHLABI.
Hohenems (hō'ůn-ěms), town (pop. 6,791), Vorarlberg, W Austria, 4 mi. SSW of Dornbirn; textiles, chemicals; mineral springs. Castle, ruins of fortress on near-by mtn.
Hohenfriedeberg (hōůnfrēt'běrk) or **Dobromierz** (dôbrôm'yězh), commune (pop. 7,421) in Lower Silesia, after 1945 in Wroclaw prov., SW Poland, 9 mi. NNW of Waldenburg (Walbrzych). Here Prussians under Frederick the Great defeated (1745) Austrians and Saxons in Second Silesian War. Sometimes Hohenfriedberg. After 1945, briefly called Wysoka Gora, Pol. *Wysoka Góra*.
Hohenfurth, Czechoslovakia: see VYSSI BROD.
Hohenheim (hō'ůnhīm''), S suburb of Stuttgart, Germany, 5 mi. S of city center; site of noted agr. col., housed in 18th-cent. castle; large botanical garden.
Hohenkirchen (hō''ůnkĭr'khůn), village (commune pop. 6,118), in Oldenburg, NW Germany, after 1945 in Lower Saxony, in East Friesland, near North Sea, 6 mi. N of Jever, in peat region. Commune is called Wangerland (väng'ůrlänt).
Hohenleuben (–loi'bůn), town (pop. 2,250), Thuringia, central Germany, 8 mi. NW of Greiz; cotton and woolen milling. Near by are ruins of Reichenfels castle.
Hohenlimburg (–lĭm'bōōrk), town (pop. 21,346), in former Prussian prov. of Westphalia, W Germany, after 1945 in North Rhine-Westphalia, on the Lenne and 4 mi. E of Hagen; steel and wire mills, limestone- and glassworks; textile mfg. Noted castle Hohenlimburg, built c.1230, towers above town. Until 1879, called Limburg.
Hohenlinden (–lĭn'důn), village (pop. 1,619), Upper Bavaria, Germany, 20 mi. E of Munich; known for the decisive victory of Moreau over the Austrians on Dec. 3, 1800.
Hohenmauth, Czechoslovakia: see VYSOKE MYTO.
Hohenmölsen (–mûl'zůn), town (pop. 5,513), in former Prussian Saxony prov., central Germany, after 1945 in Saxony-Anhalt, 7 mi. ESE of Weissenfels; lignite mining; brick mfg. Scene (1080) of battle in which King (later Emperor) Henry IV was defeated by the rival King Rudolf of Swabia, who was killed in battle.
Hohen Neuendorf (noi'ůndôrf), village (pop. 9,353), Brandenburg, E Germany, 12 mi. NW of Berlin; optical- and radio-equipment mfg.
Hohe Nock, Austria: see SENGSENGEBIRGE.
Hohenrain (–rīn''), town (pop. 2,061), Lucerne canton, central Switzerland, 9 mi. N of Lucerne; agr.
Hohensaaten (–zä'tůn), village (pop. 1,186), Brandenburg, E Germany, 14 mi. ENE of Eberswalde, and on Oder R., which here branches into the East Oder (or Reglitz) and the West Oder. HOHENZOLLERN CANAL connects here with the Oder in flight of 4 locks and continues to Stettin as part of BERLIN-STETTIN CANAL, utilizing the canalized West Oder.
Hohensalza, Poland: see INOWROCLAW.
Hohensalzburg, Russian SFSR: see LUNINO, Kaliningrad oblast.
Hohenschwangau, Germany: see SCHWANGAU.
Hohenstadt, Czechoslovakia: see ZABREH.
Hohenstaufen (–shtou'fůn), historic peak (2,244 ft.) in the Swabian Jura, Germany, 4 mi. NE of Göppingen. Has ruins of ancestral Hohenstaufen castle, destroyed 1525.
Hohenstein, Poland: see OLSZTYNEK.
Hohenstein-Ernstthal (–shtīn-ěrns'täl), town (pop. 17,729), Saxony, E central Germany, 10 mi. W of Chemnitz, in coal-mining region; textile center (cotton, wool, silk, carpets); mfg. of machinery.
Hohen Tauern (hō'ůn tou'ůrn), Alpine crest (8,081 ft.) in Hohe Tauern range of Eastern Alps, on Salzburg-Carinthia line, S Austria, just N of Mallnitz. Pierced by Tauern RR tunnel.
Hohentengen (–těng'ůn), village (pop. 683), S Baden, Germany, at S foot of Black Forest, on the Rhine (Swiss border; bridge) and 11 mi. ESE of Waldshut; strawberries.
Hohentwiel (hō''ůntvēl'), phonolite peak (2,260 ft.), a Württemberg exclave in S Baden, Germany, just W of Singen. On summit are ruins of anc. fortress, seat (10th cent.) of dukes of Swabia; sold to Württemberg in 16th cent; razed by French in 1800; mentioned in Scheffel's novel *Ekkehard*.
Hohenwald (hō'ůnwôld), town (pop. 1,703), ⊙ Lewis co., central Tenn., 60 mi. SW of Nashville, in forest and farm region; lumber milling; shoes, canned vegetables. Meriwether Lewis Natl. Monument is SE.
Hohenwart (hō''ůnvärt'), village (pop. 1,461), Upper Bavaria, Germany, on Paar R. and 12 mi. S of Ingolstadt; cattle, sheep, rye, oats.
Hohenwartetalsperre (hō''ůnvär'tůtäl'shpě''rů), irrigation dam and reservoir, Thuringia, central Germany, on the Thuringian Saale and 5 mi. SE of Saalfeld; hydroelectric power station.
Hohenwarthe (–tů), village (pop. 1,112), in former Prussian Saxony prov., central Germany, after 1945 in Saxony-Anhalt, on the Elbe, at SW end of Ihle Canal (ship elevator), here connected with the Weser-Elbe Canal by aqueduct across the Elbe.
Hohenwestedt (–vā'shtět), village (pop. 5,321), in Schleswig-Holstein, NW Germany, 13 mi. W of Neumünster; weaving, woodworking. Agr. school.
Hohenzieritz (hō''ůntsē'rĭts), village (pop. 476), Mecklenburg, N Germany, 6 mi. NNE of Neustrelitz. Queen Louise of Prussia died (1810) in hunting lodge here.
Hohenzollern (hō''ůntsō'lůrn), former Prussian province (□ 441, including several exclaves; 1946 pop. 75,951; 1950 pop. 85,863), S Germany; ⊙ was Sigmaringen. After 1945 part of Württemberg-Hohenzollern. A narrow, knee-shaped strip in the Swabian Jura, it is bounded by S Baden (S) and S Württemberg. Drained by Danube and Neckar rivers. Grain and cattle in mtn. valleys. Main industry, concentrated at and around Hechingen, is knitwear mfg. Hohenzollern, equivalent to the former Prussian administrative division [Ger. *Regierungsbezirk*] Sigmaringen, was formed 1849, when the principalities of Hohenzollern-Hechingen and Hohenzollern-Sigmaringen were deeded by their respective rulers to Prussia. Joined 1945 to S Württemberg to form Ger. state of Württemberg-Hohenzollern.
Hohenzollern, mountain, Germany: see HECHINGEN.
Hohenzollern Canal, E Germany, extends 40 mi. E from the Havel at Oranienburg to the Oder at Hohensaaten (4 locks); ship elevator at Niederfinow. Navigable for barges up to 600 tons. Supersedes FINOW CANAL. Forms part of BERLIN-STETTIN CANAL.
Hoher Bogen (hō'ůr bō'gůn), Czech *Osek* (ô'sěk), peak (3,517 ft.) of Bohemian Forest, in Bavaria, near Ger.-Czech border, 5 mi. NNE of Kötzting.
Hoher Böhmerwald, Czechoslovakia and Germany: see BOHEMIAN FOREST.
Hoher Göll, Austria and Germany: see HAGENGEBIRGE.
Hohe Rhön (hō'ů rûn'), main range (SE) of the Rhön Mts., W central Germany; rises to 3,117 ft. in the Wasserkuppe. Gersfeld is the most frequented resort; mineral springs at Brückenau (SW foot).
Hoher Kasten (hō'ůr käs'tůn), peak (5,899 ft.) in the Alps, NE Switzerland, 5 mi. SE of Appenzell.
Hoher Lindkogel, Austria: see WIENER WALD.
Hohe Rone (hō'ů rō'nů), mountain (4,044 ft.) in the Alps, N central Switzerland, 8 mi. E of Zug.
Hoher Taunus, Germany: see TAUNUS.
Hohe Tatra, mountains, Czechoslovakia and Poland: see TATRA MOUNTAINS.
Hohe Tauern (hō'ů tou'ůrn), S Austria, range of Eastern Alps, mainly along East Tyrol-Carinthia-Salzburg line; extends from Katschberg Pass c.70 mi. W to Zillertal Alps at Ital. border, rising to 12,460 ft. in the Grossglockner. Includes some of Austria's highest peaks: GROSSVENEDIGER, SONNBLICK, DREIHERRNSPITZE, ANKOGEL, HOCHALMSPITZE. The Grossglocknerstrasse, highway from Heiligenblut to Bruck, passes E of the Grossglockner, reaching 8,215 ft. at Hochtor Tunnel; a branch road leads to base of Pasterze glacier. Tauern RR (built 1901–08), bet. Spittal an der Drau and Schwarzach, traverses range (N-S) via 5-mi.-long Tauern Tunnel (alt. 3,890 ft.); highest station at Mallnitz. The Zillertal Alps are sometimes considered W outliers.
Hohe Venn (hō'ů fěn'), Fr. *Hautes Fanges* (ōt fāzh'), northernmost and highest section of the ARDENNES, E Belgium, on German line, bordered by the Amblève (S,W), the Rur (E), and the Vesdre (N); rises to 2,283 ft. in the Botrange, highest peak in Belgium. Desolate, sparsely populated region; extensive moors. Treaty of Versailles awarded E (German) half to Belgium.
Hoh-Königsburg, France: see HAUT-KOENIGSBOURG.
Hohndorf (hōn'dôrf), village (pop. 7,117), Saxony, E central Germany, 8 mi. E of Zwickau; coal mining; rayon mfg.
Hohneck (ōněk', Ger. hō'něk), summit (4,465 ft.) of the central Vosges, E France, on Vosges-Haut-Rhin dept. border, 6 mi. W of Munster, overlooking Col de la Schlucht (N). Road to summit.
Hohnstein (hōn'shtīn), town (pop. 1,451), Saxony, E central Germany, in Saxonian Switzerland, 8 mi. E of Pirna; woodworking.
Hohoe (hōhō'ā), town, S Br. Togoland, administered as part of Eastern Prov., Gold Coast colony, 38 mi. N of Ho; cacao, cotton, cassava, corn.
Hohohoto, China: see KWEISUI.
Hohokus or **Ho-Ho-Kus** (both: hōhō'kůs), borough (pop. 2,254), Bergen co., NE N.J., on small Hohokus R., just N of Ridgewood; textile bleaching. Has 2 notable 18th-cent. houses. Inc. 1908.
Höhr-Grenzhausen (hûr'-grěnts'hou''zůn), town (pop. 6,192), in former Prussian prov. of Hesse-Nassau, W Germany, after 1945 in Rhineland-Palatinate, 6 mi. NE of Coblenz; pottery works.
Hoh River (hō), NW Wash., formed in Olympic Natl. Park by N and S forks (each c.20 mi. long) rising N and S of Mt. Olympus; flows c.30 mi. SW from junction to Pacific Ocean at Hoh Indian Reservation.
Höhscheid (hû'shīt), S suburb (1925 pop. 15,854) of Solingen, W Germany. Inc. 1929 into Solingen.
Ho-hsi, China: see HOSI.
Hohsien (hŭ'shyěn'). **1** Town, ⊙ Hohsien co. (pop. 352,731), E Anhwei prov., China, near Kiangsu line, 35 mi. SW of Nanking, and on Yangtze R.;

rice, wheat, cotton, rapeseed. Until 1912, Hochow. **2** Town, ⊙ Hohsien co. (pop. 247,531), E Kwangsi prov., China, 60 mi. N of Wuchow, near Kwangtung line; rice, sweet potatoes, peanuts, timber. Tin mining, coal and tungsten deposits near by. **3** Town, Shansi prov., China: see HWOHSIEN.

Hohultslatt (hō″hŭltslĕt′), Swedish *Hohultslätt*, village (pop. 802), Kronoberg co., S Sweden, 15 mi. N of Nybro; woodworking, furniture mfg.

Hohwald, Le (lü ōväld′), Ger. *Hohwald* (hō′vält), village (pop. 579), Bas-Rhin dept., E France, in the E Vosges, 12 mi. NNW of Sélestat; resort in densely wooded area (valley of small Andlau R.).

Hoianger, Norway: see HOYANGER.

Hoifung (hoi′fōōng′), Mandarin *Haifeng* (hī′fŭng), town (pop. 24,023), ⊙ Hoifung co. (pop. 356,360), SE Kwangtung prov., China, 60 mi. E of Waiyeung; fisheries and saltworks on Honghai Bay (SW); rice, wheat. Tin mining. Also spelled Haifung.

Hoihong (hoi′hông′), Mandarin *Hai-k'ang* (hī′käng′), town (pop. 16,644), ⊙ Hoihong co. (pop. 220,935), SW Kwangtung prov., China, 25 mi. SW of Chankiang; economic center of Luichow Peninsula; fisheries, saltworks. Sugar cane, potatoes, peanuts, bamboo. Until 1912 called Luichow. Sometimes spelled Hoikong.

Hoihow (hoi′hou′), Mandarin *Hai-k'ou* (hī′kō′), town (pop. 60,000), N Hainan, Kwangtung prov., China, port on Hoihow Bay of Hainan Strait, at mouth of Nantu R., 3 mi. N of Kiungshan; commercial center of N Hainan; exports hemp, matting, medicinal herbs, poultry and livestock, sugar, eggs, and betel nuts. Tanning, food canning, glassworking, cotton milling. Supplanted (1876) old treaty port of Kiungshan as deep-water anchorage. Boat connection with Hoion on Luichow Peninsula across strait.

Hoikin (hoi′gĕn′), Mandarin *K'ai-chien* (kī′jyĕn′), town (pop. 5,497), ⊙ Hoikin co. (pop. 74,124), W Kwangtung prov., China, 25 mi. NE of Wuchow; rice, wheat, beans, sugar cane. Gold mining near by. Sometimes spelled Kaikien.

Hoikong, China: see HOIHONG.

Hoima (hōē′mä), town, Western Prov., Uganda, 30 mi. SW of Masindi; agr. trade center (cotton, tobacco, coffee, bananas, corn). Hq. Bunyoro dist., inhabited by the Nyoro tribe.

Hoion (hoi′ŏn′, hoing′ŏn′), Mandarin *Haian* (hī′än), village, SW Kwangtung prov., China, port on Hainan Strait, at S tip of Luichow Peninsula, 45 mi. S of Hoihong. Boat connection with Hoihow on Hainan isl. across strait. Sometimes spelled Hoihang or Haihan.

Hoiping (hoi′pĭng′), Mandarin *K'ai-p'ing* (kī′pĭng′), town (pop. 4,764), ⊙ Hoiping co. (pop. 436,866), S Kwangtung prov., China, 21 mi. NW of Toishan; rice, wheat, cotton, sugar. Gold mining near by.

Hoisington (hoi′zĭngtŭn), city (pop. 4,012), Barton co., central Kansas, 11 mi. N of Great Bend, in wheat, livestock, and poultry area; dairying; railroad maintenance. Inc. 1886.

Hoixuan (hoi′sōōn′), town, Thanhhoa prov., N central Vietnam, 65 mi. SW of Hanoi.

Hoja Ancha (ō′hä än′chä), village, Guanacaste prov., NW Costa Rica, on Nicoya Peninsula, 6 mi. SSE of Nicoya; livestock; rice, corn, beans, coffee.

Hoje Moen, Denmark: see MOEN.

Hojer (hû′yûr), Dan. *Højer*, Ger. *Hoyer*, town (pop. 1,345) and port, Tonder amt, SW Jutland, Denmark, on North Sea and 7 mi. WNW of Tonder. Fisheries; serves as port for Tonder. Belonged to Germany before 1920 plebiscite.

Hojo (hō′jō′). **1** Town (pop. 8,632), Ehime prefecture, N Shikoku, Japan, on Iyo Sea, 9 mi. N of Matsuyama; fishing port; agr. center (rice, wheat). **2** Town (pop. 8,350), Hyogo prefecture, S Honshu, Japan, 11 mi. NE of Himeji; rail terminus; agr. center (rice, wheat, tobacco, flowers, poultry); woodworking; bamboo ware, floor mats, tiles. **3** Town (pop. 5,876), Ibaraki prefecture, central Honshu, Japan, 9 mi. NW of Tsuchiura; rice growing, lumbering, cotton milling.

Hojo, Korea: see POSONG.

Hojung (hŭ′rōōng′), town, W central Hupeh prov., China, 35 mi. NW of Shasi; commercial center; exports silk.

Hojvendsyssel, Denmark: see VENDSYSSEL.

Hokah (hō′kû), village (pop. 643), Houston co., extreme SE Minn., near Mississippi R., 8 mi. WSW of La Crosse, Wis., in grain, potato, and livestock area; dairy products.

Hoke (hōk), county (□ 414; pop. 15,756), S central N.C.; ⊙ Raeford. Forested sand-hills; farming (cotton, tobacco, grain, corn, peaches), sawmilling. Formed 1911.

Hokendauqua (hŏkûndô′kwû), village (1940 pop. 1,336), Lehigh co., E Pa., on Lehigh R., opposite North Catasauqua, and 4 mi. N of Allentown.

Hokes Bluff, town (pop. 1,158), Etowah co., NE Ala., 8 mi. E of Gadsden. Inc. since 1940.

Hoki (hō′kē), former province in SW Honshu, Japan; now part of Tottori prefecture.

Hokiang or **Ho-chiang** (both: hŭ′jyäng′), former province (□ 52,280; pop. 6,949,405) of NE Manchuria, China, on Sungari R.; ⊙ was Kiamusze. Formed 1946 out of Manchukuo's Sankiang prov., it was inc. 1949 into the enlarged Sungkiang prov.

Hokiang or **Ho-chiang,** town (pop. 20,190), ⊙ Hokiang co. (pop. 415,241), S Szechwan prov., China, on right bank of Yangtze R., at mouth of the small Ho Kiang, and 24 mi. ESE of Luhsien; match mfg.; hog bristles, rice, wheat, sugar cane, indigo.

Hokianga, county, New Zealand: see RAWENE.

Hokianga Harbour (hōkēăng′gû), N N.Isl., New Zealand, 120 mi. NW of Auckland, on Tasman Sea; outlet for kauri gum. Small settlement (Omapere) at entrance; Rawene on S shore.

Hokien or **Ho-chien** (both: hŭ′jyĕn′), town, ⊙ Hokien co. (pop. 379,600), central Hopeh prov., China, 45 mi. SE of Paoting; straw plait, soap, pottery, paper; pears, jujubes, melons. Formerly an important city, it declined when by-passed by railroad.

Hoking or **Hao-ch'ing** (both: hou′chĭng′), town, ⊙ Hoking co. (pop. 83,586), NW Yunnan prov., China, near Yangtze R., 60 mi. N of Tali; alt. 6,831 ft.; iron and lead-zinc mining; smelters; chemical industry.

Hokitika (hō″kĭtē′kû), borough (pop. 2,742) and port, ⊙ Westland co. (□ 4,410; pop. 4,294), on W coast of S.Isl., New Zealand, at mouth of Hokitika R., 75 mi. SSW of Westport; gold mines, sawmills. Summer resort at near-by L. Kanieri.

Hokiu, China: see HWOKIU.

Hokkaido (hōkī′dō), island (□ c.29,600; including offshore isls.: □ 30,077; 1940 pop. 3,272,718; 1947 pop. 3,852,821), northernmost and 2d largest of 4 main isls. of Japan; ⊙ SAPPORO. Isl. is bet. Sea of Japan (W) and the Pacific (E), just N of Honshu across Tsugaru Strait, just S of Sakhalin across La Pérouse Strait; 41°24′–45°31′N 139°50′–145°45′E; 260 mi. N-S, 280 mi. E-W, with irregularly shaped SW peninsula. Largely mountainous, with active and inactive volcanic cones principally in central area. Its E mtn. mass (continuation of Kurile Isls. volcanic chain) rises to 7,513 ft. at Asahi-dake. Many hot springs in SW part. Ishikari R. (largest river of isl.) drains extensive fertile plain in W central area. Climate differs from that of other home isls. of Japan; its winters are much longer and more severe, partly because of Okhotsk Current, which chills its shores. Mean annual temp. 41°F.; annual rainfall 40 in.; has 6-month cover of snow 10–20 in. deep. Heavy fog (June–July) on E coast; monsoon winds on W coast, which is frequently icebound in winter. Isl. is densely forested, and until 1890s the interior was virtually inaccessible. Among the many varieties of trees are beech, oak, elm, maple, fir, and spruce. Fauna includes grizzly bears, deer, wolves, foxes, wild ducks, and quail. Heavy concentration of pop. in W and SW areas. Hokkaido is only isl. in Japan proper inhabited by the aboriginal Ainus (pop. c.15,000). Although large areas are unfit for agr. there are farm products, including soybeans, potatoes, and sugar beets. Conditions for rice growing are unfavorable, but some rice is grown. Sawmilling, stock raising, and dairying are important industries. One of major fishing centers of world, isl. produces cod, herring, and sardines. Yubari (or Ishikari) coal field is one of Japan's main producers of coal. Sulphur, iron, and some gold are mined. Small oil fields in N, W, and SW. Principal centers: Sapporo, HAKODATE (chief port), OTARU, MURORAN, ASAHIGAWA, KUSHIRO, OBIHIRO, ABASHIRI. Japanese 1st settled in 16th cent. on SW peninsula, which became domain of Matsumae family during Tokugawa period. Then called Yezo (also spelled Yesso, Yedzo, and Ezo), isl. was renamed Hokkaido following restoration (1868) of imperial power and establishment of colonial office to encourage settlement. Hokkaido ceased being a mere territory and became (1885) a *cho* (administrative unit roughly similar to prefecture or *ken*). Govt. of Hokkaido includes small offshore isls. of OKUSHIRI-SHIMA, REBUN-JIMA, and RISHIRI-SHIMA; until 1945 it included the Kuriles, which became Rus. territory under terms of Yalta agreement. Sometimes called Hokushu.

Hokkiang, China: see FUTSING.

Hokko, Formosa: see PEIKANG.

Hoko, Korea: see POHANG.

Hoko-retto, Formosa: see PESCADORES.

Hokota (hōkō′tä), town (pop. 6,384), Ibaraki prefecture, central Honshu, Japan, 15 mi. SSE of Mito, on N shore of lagoon Kita-ura; rice, wheat, charcoal.

Hoko-to, Pescadores: see PENGHU ISLAND.

Hokow or **Ho-k'ou** (both: hŭ′kō′). **1** Town, NE Kiangsi prov., China, 20 mi. SW of Shangjao and on Kwangsin R.; paper mfg. **2** Town, Sikang prov., China: see YAKIANG. **3** Town, Suiyuan prov., China: see TOKOTO. **4** Town, SE Yunnan prov., China, on Red River (Vietnam border), opposite Laokay, 65 mi. SE of Mengtsz, and on Kunming-Hanoi RR; commercial center. Opened to foreign trade in 1896.

Hokshan (Cantonese hôk′sän′), Mandarin *Haoshan* (hou′shän′), town (pop. 39,915), ⊙ Hokshan co. (pop. 206,751), S Kwangtung prov., China, 18 mi. WNW of Sunwui; tea.

Hokü or **Ho-ch'ü** (both: hŭ′jü′), town, ⊙ Hokü co. (pop. 112,130), northwesternmost Shansi prov., China, at the Great Wall, 65 mi. NW of Ningwu and on Yellow R., at Shensi-Suiyuan line; wheat, kaoliang, millet.

Hokubu-shoto, Ryukyu Isls.: see AMAMI-GUNTO.

Hokumon, Formosa: see PEIMEN.

Hokusei, Korea: see PUKCHONG.

Hokushu, Japan: see HOKKAIDO.

Hokuto, Formosa: see PEITOW.

Hol (hōl). **1** Village and canton (pop. 3,533), Buskerud co., S Norway, at E foot of Hallingskarv mts., in the Hallingdal, on railroad and 70 mi. NW of Honefoss; agr., stock raising, lumbering, fishing, hunting. **2** Canton, Nordland co., Norway: see STAMSUND.

Hölak, Czechoslovakia: see TRENCIANSKA TEPLA.

Holalkere (hō′lŭlkĕrĕ), town (pop. 4,146), Chitaldrug dist., N central Mysore, India, 20 mi. SW of Chitaldrug; agr. market (millet, oilseeds, cotton); cotton ginning, hand-loom weaving. Manganese mines 5 mi. NE.

Holan (hŭ′län′), town, ⊙ Holan co. (pop. 66,650), SE Ningsia prov., China, on railroad and 20 mi. NNE of Yinchwan, near Yellow R., at E foot of Alashan (Holan) Mts.; cattle raising; grain, licorice. Until 1942 called Siehkangpao.

Holandsfjorden (hō′länsfyōrdûn), village in Meloy canton, Nordland co., N Norway, on small Holands Fjord, at foot of Svartisen glacier, 30 mi. NW of Mo; tourist center. Graphite mine.

Holan Mountains, China: see ALASHAN MOUNTAINS.

Holar or **Holar i Hjaltadal** (hō′lär ē hyäl′tädäl″), Icelandic *Hólar í Hjaltadal*, locality, Eyjafjardar co., N Iceland, on the Eyjafjardara and 20 mi. SSW of Akureyri. See (1106–1801) of bishopric; educational center in early Middle Ages. Printing press with movable type established here 1530; Holar subsequently became publishing center.

Holbaek (hôl′bĕk), amt (□ 676; pop. 126,162), NW Zealand, Denmark, on the Kattegat (N) and the Great Belt (W); ⊙ Holbaek. Includes Samso, Sejero, and Nekselo isls. Large marshes. Dairy farming, peat; briquettes.

Holbaek, city (1950 pop. 14,417), ⊙ Holbaek amt, N Zealand, Denmark, port on Holbaek Fjord and 35 mi. W of Copenhagen; 55°43′N 11°43′E. Rail junction; mfg. (machinery, paper, hardware), fishing, shipbuilding. Dates from 13th cent.

Holbaek Fjord, Denmark: see ISE FJORD.

Holbeach (hŏl′–), former urban district (1931 pop. 6,112), Parts of Holland, SE Lincoln, England, 7 mi. E of Spalding; agr. market in bulb- and fruit-growing region. A market town chartered in 1252; has 14th-cent. Gothic church.

Holbeck (hŏl′bĕk), town (pop. 32,565) in Leeds county borough, West Riding, S central Yorkshire, England, just S of Leeds; textile printing, metal casting, mfg. of textile machinery, soap, flour.

Holberg Inlet (hōl′bûrg), SW B.C., N arm of Quatsino Sound, N Vancouver Isl., in lumbering, fishing area; 21 mi. long, 1 mi. wide. Holberg village is at W end.

Holborn (hō′bûrn), metropolitan borough (1931 pop. 38,860; 1951 census 24,806) of London, England, N of the Thames, 1 mi. N of Charing Cross. Business and residential area, it includes district of BLOOMSBURY, with Univ. of London, British Mus., Gray's and Lincoln's inns (Inns of Court), Royal Col. of Surgeons, and diamond-trade center of Hatton Gardens. Many bldgs. destroyed or damaged in Second World War air raids.

Holborn Head, Scotland: see SCRABSTER.

Holbrook (hŏl′brōōk), village (pop. 973), S New South Wales, Australia, 105 mi. WSW of Canberra; tin-mining center.

Holbrook (hōl′brōōk). **1** Town (pop. 2,336), ⊙ Navajo co., E central Ariz., on Little Colorado R. and c.90 mi. ESE of Flagstaff; trade and tourist center in agr. area (livestock and poultry raising, dairying); helium field near by. Petrified Forest Natl. Monument is 15 mi. E; Hopi and Navajo Indian reservations are N. Settled in 1870s, inc. 1917. **2** Town (pop. 4,004), Norfolk co., E Mass., 5 mi. N of Brockton; mfg. (disinfectants, insecticides, shoes, rubber soles); dairying. Settled 1710, inc. 1872. **3** Village (pop. 398), Furnas co., S Nebr., 33 mi. ENE of McCook and on Republican R.; grain, livestock, dairy and poultry produce.

Holcomb (hŏl′kûm). **1** Village (pop. 229), Grenada co., NW central Miss., 20 mi. NNE of Greenwood. **2** Agr. town (pop. 505), Dunklin co., extreme SE Mo., near St. Francis R., 12 mi. N of Kennett. **3** Village (pop. 313), Ontario co., W central N.Y., 20 mi. SE of Rochester, in fruit- and truck-growing area; canned foods, wood products.

Holcombe (hō′kûm), town in Ramsbottom urban dist., SE Lancashire, England, 4 mi. NNW of Bury; cotton milling.

Holcombe Rogus (hō′kûm rō′gûs), agr. village and parish (pop. 478), E Devon, England, 8 mi. NE of Tiverton. Has 15th-cent. church and a Tudor mansion.

Holden, village (pop. 382), central Alta., 30 mi. NE of Camrose; dairying, mixed farming.

Holden. 1 Agr. town (pop. 754), Penobscot co., S Maine, just SE of Brewer. National Grange of Patrons of Husbandry founded here 1867. **2** Agr. town (pop. 5,975), Worcester co., central Mass., 7 mi. NNW of Worcester. Settled 1723, inc. 1741,

Includes village of Jefferson. **3** City (pop. 1,765), Johnson co., W central Mo., 14 mi. W of Warrensburg; grain, livestock; coal. Laid out 1857. **4** Town (pop. 476), Millard co., W central Utah, 10 mi. NNE of Fillmore; alt. 5,115 ft.; agr., livestock. **5** Coal-mining village (pop. 2,229, with near-by Beebe), Logan co., SW W.Va., 5 mi. WSW of Logan.

Holdenville, city (pop. 6,192), ⊙ Hughes co., central Okla., 8 mi. SE of Wewoka; trade center for oil and agr. area (cotton, corn, watermelons); cotton ginning, meat packing; grain elevators; oil wells and refineries. L. Holdenville (c.3 mi. long; fishing) and site of old Fort Holmes are near by. Laid out 1895, inc. 1898.

Holderness (hŏl'–), low, fertile peninsula in SE Yorkshire, England, bet. North Sea and Humber R. estuary. Its S extremity is Spurn Head, a narrow, 4-mi. promontory at mouth of Humber R. opposite Grimsby, with 2 lighthouses and a near-by lightship.

Holderness, resort town (pop. 731), Grafton co., central N.H., on Squam L. and Pemigewasset R. and just W of Plymouth.

Holdfast, village (pop. 243), S central Sask., near Last Mountain L., 50 mi. NW of Regina; wheat.

Holdingford, village (pop. 458), Stearns co., central Minn., near Mississippi R., 18 mi. NW of St. Cloud, in grain, livestock, poultry area; dairy products, flour.

Holdrege (hŏl'drĭj), city (pop. 4,381), ⊙ Phelps co., S Nebr., 50 mi. WSW of Hastings; flour; livestock, grain, dairy produce. Orphans' home here. Settled 1883, inc. 1884.

Hold with Hope, Cape, wide headland, E Greenland, on Greenland Sea; 73°22'–73°53'N 20°20'W. First sighted and named (1607) by Hudson. Forms N side of entrance to Franz Josef Fjord.

Hole (hû'lů), Nor. *Høle,* village (pop. 252; canton pop. 1,072), Rogaland co., SW Norway, on Hogs Fjord, 10 mi. SE of Stavanger; quarrying of kieselguhr and other insulation materials. Sometimes called Hogsfjord, Nor. *Høgsfjord.*

Hole (hōō'lů), village (pop. 1,613), Kopparberg co., central Sweden, on West Dal R. and 60 mi. W of Falun; tanning, stock raising. Includes Idback (ĕd'bĕk"), Swedish *Idbäck,* village.

Hole Fjord, Norway: see HOGS FJORD.

Hole in the Wall, Bahama Isls.: see GREAT ABACO ISLAND.

Hole Narsipur (hō'lā nŭr'sĭpōōr), town (pop. 9,303), Hassan dist., W central Mysore, India, on Hemavati R. and 17 mi. SSE of Hassan; grain, rice; handicraft wickerwork. Chromite and asbestos workings near by. Also written Hole-Narsipur or Holenarsipur.

Holesov (hô'lĕshôf), Czech *Holešov,* Ger. *Holleschau* (hô'lůshou), town (pop. 6,599), E central Moravia, Czechoslovakia, on railroad and 8 mi. NNW of Gottwaldov; agr. center (sugar beets, wheat, barley, oats).

Holesovice-Bubny (hô'lĕshô"vĭtsĕ-bōōb'nĭ), Czech *Holešovice-Bubny,* NNE district (pop. 61,922) of Prague, Czechoslovakia, on left bank of Vltava R., 2 mi. from city center; main river port, with dockyards, machine shops, and electrical works.

Holetown, town (pop. 470), W Barbados, B.W.I., 6 mi. N of Bridgetown, surrounded by sugar plantations. Has an old fort. Site where English made their 1st landing, in 1605, is commemorated by a column. Formerly called Jamestown.

Holetta, Ethiopia: see OLETTA.

Holgate (hŏl'gāt), village (pop. 1,092), Henry co., NW Ohio, 10 mi. S of Napoleon, in dairying, poultry-raising, and grain-producing dist.

Holguera (ōlgā'rä), village (pop. 1,091), Cáceres prov., W Spain, 17 mi. SW of Plasencia; cereals, olive oil, pepper, tobacco.

Holguín (ōlgēn'), city (pop. 35,865), Oriente prov., E Cuba, on Central Highway, on railroad, and 19 mi. SSW of its port Gibara, 65 mi. NNW of Santiago de Cuba; communication and trading center for agr. region (sugar cane, tobacco, coffee, corn, fruit, cattle); apiculture, poultry raising. Has airfield. Industries include sawmilling, tanning, quarrying; mfg. of furniture, tiles, peanut oil. Gold and manganese deposits near by. A well-built city, with La Periquera (city hall), theater, Spanish Colonial Bldg., several churches, fine parks, and with noted La Cruz Hill in outskirts, whose top is reached by long flight of steps. Holguín was an insurgent center during Ten Years War (1868–78) and 1895–98 revolution.

Holic (hô'lĭch), Slovak *Holíč,* Hung. *Holics* (hô'lĭch), village (pop. 5,353), W Slovakia, Czechoslovakia, 13 mi. ENE of Breclav; rail junction; ceramics mfg.

Holice (hô'lĭtsĕ), Ger. *Holitz* (hō'lĭts), town (pop. 5,695), E Bohemia, Czechoslovakia, on railroad and 11 mi. ENE of Pardubice, in sugar-beet and potato region; sugar milling, distilling, mfg. of hand-worked footwear.

Holikachuk (hōlĭ'kůchŭk), Indian village (pop. 98), W Alaska, on Innoko R. and 50 mi. N of Holy Cross; salmon fishing; fur-trading post. Formerly spelled Holocachaket or Hologachaket.

Holin, Mongolia: see KARAKORUM.

Holinkoerh (hŭ'lĭn'kŭr'), Mongolian *Horinkar* (hōrĭngkär'), town (pop. 5,839), ⊙ Holinkoerh co. (pop. 71,737), E Suiyuan prov., China, 33 mi. S of Kweisui; cattle raising; millet, rice, licorice.

Holitna River (hōlĭt'nů), W Alaska, rises near 60°25'N 158°20'W, flows 170 mi. N to Kuskokwim R. at Sleetmute.

Holitz, Czechoslovakia: see HOLICE.

Holker, England: see LOWER HOLKER.

Holkham Bay, England: see WELLS.

Holla, Norway: see ULEFOSS.

Hollabrunn (hôl'äbrōōn), town (pop. 6,431), N Lower Austria, 13 mi. NNW of Stockerau; corn, cattle, vineyards.

Hollam's Bird Island, islet, W South-West Africa, in the Atlantic; 24°38'S 14°31'E. Guano.

Holland (hô'lůnd), popular name for the present-day NETHERLANDS, stemming from the former county (of the Holy Roman Empire) which became the chief member of the United Provs. of the Netherlands. Since 1840 it has formed 2 provs., NORTH HOLLAND and SOUTH HOLLAND, in the W Netherlands. Created early 10th cent., it originally controlled also Zeeland and medieval Friesland. Its count, William II, was elected (1247) German king. It led in the struggle (16th–17th cent.) for Dutch independence and its history became virtually identical with that of the Netherlands.

Holland, village (pop. estimate 350), S Man., 50 mi. ESE of Brandon; lumbering, grain elevators.

Holland, village (pop. 2,649), Singapore isl., 4 mi. NW of Singapore; rubber. Pop. is Chinese.

Holland. 1 Town (pop. 501), Dubois co., SW Ind., 36 mi. NE of Evansville, in agr. area. **2** Town (pop. 221), Grundy co., central Iowa, 25 mi. WSW of Waterloo, in agr. area. **3** Agr. town (pop. 377), Hampden co., S Mass., on headstream of Quinebaug R. and 22 mi. E of Springfield. **4** City (pop. 15,858), Ottawa co., SW Mich., 24 mi. SW of Grand Rapids and on Black R., near Black L., in tulip-producing, orchard, and farm area (celery, sugar beets, livestock, poultry; dairy products). Mfg. (furnaces, airplane motors, machinery, air-conditioning equipment, metal and rubber products, furniture, glass, chemicals, drugs, shoes, canned goods). Ships tulip bulbs, chicks. Tulip growing is an important industry, and an annual four-day festival is held by the town's Du. descendants. Seat of Hope Col. and Western Theological Seminary. Its Netherlands Mus. contains historical relics. State park near by. Settled by Dutch in 1847; inc. as city 1867. **5** Village (pop. 263), Pipestone co., SW Minn., on fork of Rock R. and 9 mi. NE of Pipestone, in agr. area. **6** Agr. town (pop. 409), Pemiscot co., extreme SE Mo., in Mississippi flood plain, 15 mi. SW of Caruthersville. **7** Residential village (1940 pop. 642), Erie co., W N.Y., on small Cazenovia Creek and 25 mi. SE of Buffalo; wood containers, machinery; dairy products, poultry. **8** Village (pop. 714), Lucas co., NW Ohio, 9 mi. WSW of Toledo. **9** Town (pop. 674), Bell co., central Texas, 22 mi. W of Temple, near Little R.; trade point in cotton, grain, truck, dairying area. **10** Town (pop. 406), Orleans co., N Vt., on Que. line, 10 mi. E of Newport. **11** Town (pop. 289), Nansemond co., SE Va., 12 mi. WSW of Suffolk; peanuts, lumber.

Holland, Parts of, SE administrative division of LINCOLNSHIRE, England.

Hollandale (hŏ'lůndāl"). **1** Village (pop. 360), Freeborn co., S Minn., 12 mi. NE of Albert Lea, in grain, livestock, poultry area. Inc. 1934. **2** Town (pop. 2,346), Washington co., W Miss., 20 mi. SSE of Greenville, and on small Deer Creek, in agr. and timber area; cotton ginning, lumber milling. **3** Village (pop. 281), Iowa co., S Wis., 11 mi. SE of Dodgeville, in agr. area.

Holland Bay, small inlet of the Caribbean on E Jamaica coast, on Jamaica Channel, and 38 mi. E of Kingston. Receives Plantain Garden R. Adjoining is village of Holland.

Hollandia (hŭlăn'dēů), town (dist. pop. 6,228), ⊙ Netherlands New Guinea, port on Humboldt Bay, at foot of Cyclops Mts. and near border of Australian Territory of New Guinea; 2°32'S 140°43'E; trade center. In Second World War Hollandia was major Jap. air base. Taken April, 1944, by U.S. forces, it became (Sept., 1944) hq. of Gen. Douglas MacArthur.

Holland Patent, village (pop. 400), Oneida co., central N.Y., 10 mi. N of Utica.

Hollandschdiep or **Hollandsch Diep** (hô"länts-dēp'), W Netherlands, outlet of Maas R.; formed by junction of New Merwede R. and Bergsche Maas R. 6 mi. SSE of Dordrecht; flows 15 mi. W, past Lage-Zwaluwe, Moerdijk, Willemsdorp, and Willemstad, dividing into the Volkerak (which continues as the Krammer) and the Haringvliet 12 mi. SW of Dordrecht. Forms S boundary of Beijerland isl. Entire length navigable.

Hollandsche Ijssel River or **Hollandsche Ijsel River** (hô'läntsů ī'sůl), W Netherlands, branches from Lek R. near Vreeswijk; flows 48 mi. NNW, past Ijsselstein, and WSW, past Montfoort, Gouda, Nieuwerkerk, and Krimpen aan den Ijssel, to New Maas R. just E of Rotterdam. Joined by branch of Merwede Canal 2 mi. E of Ijsselstein. Navigable from Lek R. to Gouda by ships to 200 tons with draught to 5 ft., from Gouda to New Maas R. by ships to 1,000 tons with draught to 10 ft. Sometimes spelled Hollandsche Yssel; sometimes called simply Ijssel (not to be confused with larger stream in central Netherlands called IJSSEL RIVER).

Hollandsche Yssel River, Netherlands: see HOLLANDSCHE IJSSEL RIVER.

Holland Tunnel, SE N.Y., vehicular tunnel (2 tubes) under the Hudson R. bet. Manhattan borough of New York city and Jersey City, N.J. Completed 1927, it is 9,250 ft. long.

Hollansburg, village (pop. 295), Darke co., W Ohio, 11 mi. SW of Greenville, at Ind. line; cheese, canned tomatoes.

Hollenbek (hô'lůnbāk), village (pop. 571), in Schleswig-Holstein, NW Germany, 6 mi. SE of Mölln, 5 mi. NW of Zarrentin.

Hollenberg, city (pop. 97), Washington co., NE Kansas, on Little Blue R., near Nebr. line, and 12 mi. NNE of Washington; grain, cattle. Inc. 1937.

Höllengebirge (hû'lůn-gůbĭr'gů), mountain range in the Salzkammergut, in S Upper Austria, bet. Attersee and L. Traun; rises to 6,107 ft. in the Höllenkogel; bleak rough slopes.

Hollenstein or **Hollenstein an der Ybbs** (hôl'ůnshtīn, än dĕr ĭps'), town (pop. 2,073), SW Lower Austria, on Ybbs R. and 11 mi. S of Waidhofen; cutlery.

Höllental (hû'lůntäl), SE Lower Austria, valley of Schwarza R. bet. the Raxalpe and the Schneeberg; beautiful scenery. Reichenau is its trade center.

Holleschau, Czechoslovakia: see HOLESOV.

Holley, village (pop. 1,551), Orleans co., W N.Y., on the Barge Canal and 22 mi. WNW of Rochester; canning; mfg. of cider, vinegar, feed. Agr. (truck, fruit, grain, potatoes). Inc. 1867.

Hollfeld (hôl'fĕlt), town (pop. 1,860), Upper Franconia, N Bavaria, Germany, on the Wiesent and 13 mi. W of Bayreuth; flour and lumber milling. Has late-18th-cent. church.

Holliday. 1 Town (pop. 196), Monroe co., NE central Mo., 17 mi. ENE of Moberly. **2** Town (pop. 1,007), Archer co., N Texas, 12 mi. SSW of Wichita Falls; trade point in oil-producing and irrigated farm area. L. Wichita is just E.

Hollidaysburg, borough (pop. 6,483), ⊙ Blair co., S central Pa., 6 mi. S of Altoona; railroad shops; metal products, explosives. Portage RR carried canal boats over Allegheny Mts. to Johnstown in mid-19th cent. Settled 1768, laid out 1820.

Hollidays Cove, former city, Brooke and Hancock counties, NW W. Va.; it was absorbed 1947 by WEIRTON.

Hollinger Mines, Ont.: see PORCUPINE.

Hollingworth, former urban district (1931 pop. 2,299), NE Cheshire, England, 3 mi. ESE of Stalybridge; rayon milling. Site of Manchester reservoir. Inc. 1936 in Longdendale.

Hollins, village, Roanoke co., SW Va., 5 mi. NNE of Roanoke. Hollins Col. for Women (1842) here.

Hollins Green, England: see RIXTON WITH GLAZEBROOK.

Hollinwood, SW suburb of Oldham, SE Lancashire, England; cotton milling, mfg. of radio receivers, electrical equipment, pharmaceuticals, machinery.

Hollis (hŏ'lĭs). **1** Town (pop. 1,214), York co., SW Maine, 15 mi. W of Portland and on the Saco; wood products. Inc. 1798. **2** Rural town (pop. 1,196), Hillsboro co., S N.H., on Mass. line, just W of Nashua. **3** A residential section of E central Queens borough of New York city, SE N.Y.; some mfg. (wood products, thermometers). **4** City (pop. 3,089), ⊙ Harmon co., SW Okla., 33 mi. W of Altus, near Texas line, in livestock, cotton, and wheat area; cotton ginning; mfg. of furniture, cottonseed and dairy products. Natural-gas wells near by. Inc. as town 1905, as city 1929.

Hollister (hŏ'lĭstůr). **1** City (pop. 4,903), ⊙ San Benito co., W Calif., 40 mi. SE of San Jose, in San Benito valley; canneries, creameries; meat-, fruit-, and vegetable-packing plants; vegetable and flower-seed growing. Has a jr. col. Holds annual rodeo. Settled 1868, inc. 1874. **2** Village (pop. 80), Twin Falls co., S Idaho, 15 mi. SW of Twin Falls; alt. 4,500 ft. **3** Resort city (pop. 542), Taney co., S Mo., in the Ozarks, on L. Taneycomo (formed by White R.), just S of Branson. **4** Town (pop. 172), Tillman co., SW Okla., 9 mi. ESE of Frederick, in cotton and grain area.

Holliston, town (pop. 3,753), including Holliston village (pop. 1,908), Middlesex co., E central Mass., 22 mi. SW of Boston; shoes. Settled c.1659, inc. 1724.

Hollognes-aux-Pierres (ôlô"nyů-ō-pyâr'), town (pop. 5,657), Liége prov., E Belgium, 5 mi. W of Liége; zinc and lead processing.

Holloman Air Force Base, N.Mex.: see ALAMOGORDO.

Holloway. 1 Village (pop. 264), Swift co., SW Minn., near Pomme de Terre R., 16 mi. WSW of Benson, in grain and potato area. **2** Village (pop. 654), Belmont co., E Ohio, 11 mi. SW of Cadiz, in coal-mining area.

Hollowayville, village (pop. 89), Bureau co., N Ill., 8 mi. E of Princeton, in agr. and bituminous-coal area.

Hollow Rock, town (pop. 397), Carroll co., NW Tenn., 9 mi. ENE of Huntingdon, in cotton, livestock area.

Hollum (hô'lŭm), village (pop. 878), Friesland prov., N Netherlands, on Ameland isl. and 6 mi. W of Nes; dairying; resort.

Holly. 1 Town (pop. 1,236), Prowers co., SE Colo., on Arkansas R., near Kansas line, and 24 mi. E of Lamar in grain region; alfalfa meal, dairy, poultry, truck products. **2** Village (pop. 2,663), Oakland co., SE Mich., 20 mi. NW of Pontiac and on Shiawassee R., in an area of many lakes; mfg. (auto parts, pianos). Settled 1836, inc. 1865.

Hollyford, Gaelic *Cluain Mhurchaidh*, village, W Co. Tipperary, Ireland, 12 mi. NW of Cashel; copper mining.

Holly Grove, town (pop. 761), Monroe co., E central Ark., 21 mi. ENE of Stuttgart, in agr. area.

Holly Hill. 1 Town (pop. 3,232), Volusia co., NE Fla., suburb of Daytona Beach, in an area noted for its flowers; coquina quarries. **2** Town (pop. 1,116), Orangeburg co., S central S.C., 27 mi. ESE of Orangeburg, in truck, livestock, cotton area; fertilizer, lumber, lime, ice. Santee-Cooper hydroelectric and navigation development is E. Inc. 1887.

Hollymount, Gaelic *Maolda*, town (pop. 155), S Co. Mayo, Ireland, on Robe R. and 5 mi. NE of Ballinrobe; agr. market (cattle; potatoes).

Holly Pond, town (pop. 182), Cullman co., N Ala., 13 mi. E of Cullman, near Mulberry Fork.

Hollyridge or **Holly Ridge,** town (pop. 1,082), Onslow co., E N.C., near the coast 29 mi. NE of Wilmington. Inc. after 1940.

Holly River State Park (c.7,300 acres), central W.Va., in the Alleghenies, 21 mi. S of Buckhannon, along a fork of small Holly R. (right tributary of the Elk). Wooded recreational area (set aside 1938); facilities for fishing, swimming, other sports.

Holly Shelter Swamp (□ c.100), SE N.C., NE of Wilmington, and bordering Northeast Cape Fear R. on E; includes Holly Shelter Game Refuge (c.30,000 acres), E of Burgaw. Angola Swamp is N.

Holly Springs. 1 Town (pop. 386), Cherokee co., NW Ga., 4 mi. S of Canton. **2** City (pop. 3,276), ⊙ Marshall co., N Miss., c.40 mi. SE of Memphis, Tenn.; trade and market center for cotton-growing and dairying region; mfg. of stoneware, brick; cotton gins; clay deposits. Rust Col., Mississippi Industrial Col., and an agr. experiment station are here. Has many fine ante-bellum homes. Inc. 1837. In Civil War, town was captured (1862) by Confederates, thus delaying Grant's advance against Vicksburg. **3** Town (pop. 406), Wake co., central N.C., 14 mi. SW of Raleigh.

Hollywood. 1 Town (pop. 477), Jackson co., NE Ala., near Tennessee R., 35 mi. E of Huntsville. **2** Section (pop. c.185,000) of Los ANGELES city, S Calif., lying to NW of downtown dist. and adjoining Beverly Hills (W); center of the world's motion-picture industry. Hollywood's 1st moving picture (1911), filmed by Nestor Company, was followed by an influx of other companies, and the city's 1910 pop. of 4,000 soon multiplied. Although most of the major studios are now in near-by dists. (e.g., Culver City, Burbank, Los Angeles proper), Hollywood is still the industry's focal point. It is also a Western radio and television broadcasting center. Has extensive shopping and business dists. (including exotically designed theaters), and residential sections extending far up slopes (locally the Hollywood Hills) of Santa Monica Mts. (N). Seat of Immaculate Heart Col. Points of interest include Hollywood Bowl, seating 20,000 for outdoor concerts, operas, ballets; Griffith Park (c. 3,800 acres of foothills and canyons, with motor roads, hiking trails, playgrounds, picnic grounds), which includes Griffith Observatory and Planetarium, the Greek Theater (seats 4,000), and a zoo; Barnsdall Park, site of California Art Club (art and craft exhibits). Founded in late 1880s; inc. 1903; consolidated with Los Angeles in 1910. **3** City (pop. 14,351), Broward co., S Fla., 17 mi. N of Miami, on Atlantic coast; tourist resort; vegetable canning, citrus-fruit packing; limestone quarrying. Has military acad. Founded 1921, inc. 1925; began and developed as a resort city. **4** Village, St. Marys co., S Md., 5 mi. NE of Leonardtown, near Patuxent R. Resorts near by (Sandgates, Clarks Wharf; swimming, fishing, duck hunting, boating). Near by are "Sotterley" (built 1730; restored) and Resurrection Manor, one of oldest manorial grants (1650) in Md. **5** Town (pop. 79), Dunklin co., extreme SE Mo., near St. Francis R., 15 mi. SSW of Kennett. **6** Town (pop. 246), Charleston co., SE S.C., 17 mi. W of Charleston.

Hollywood Beach, Md.: see CHESAPEAKE CITY.

Hollywood-by-the-Sea, village (pop. 1,000, with adjacent Silver Strand Beach), Ventura co., S Calif.

Hollywood Park, Calif.: see INGLEWOOD.

Holman Island (hōl'mŭn), trading post, W Victoria Isl., SW Franklin Dist., Northwest Territories, on Amundsen Gulf at entrance of Prince Albert Sound; 70°44'N 117°45'W; radio station; site of R.C. mission.

Holmavik (hōl'mävēk"), Icelandic *Hólmavík*, fishing village (pop. 411), ⊙ Strandа co., NW Iceland, on Vestfjarda Peninsula, 45 mi. SE of Isafjordur, on Steingrim Fjord, 15-mi.-long W arm of Huna Bay.

Holmberg (ōm'bĕrk), village (pop. estimate 1,000), SW Córdoba prov., Argentina, 5 mi. SW of Río Cuarto; grain, flax, livestock.

Holmdel (hōlm'dĕl), village in Holmdel township (pop. 1,380), Monmouth co., E N.J., 6 mi. W of Red Bank, in farm area.

Holme Cultram, England: see SILLOTH.

Holmen (hōl'mŭn), village (pop. 584), La Crosse co., W Wis., 10 mi. N of La Crosse, in farm and dairy region; sawmill, cannery.

Holmenkollen (hôl'mŭnkôl"lŭn), suburb (pop. 260) of Oslo, SE Norway, in hilly region, 8 mi. NW of city center, on electric railroad; popular ski resort; scene of annual ski-jump competition. Until 1948, in Akershus co.

Holmes, England: see ROTHERHAM.

Holmes (hōmz). **1** County (□ 483; pop. 13,988), NW Fla., on Ala. line (N) and bounded E by Holmes Creek; ⊙ Bonifay. Rolling agr. area (corn, peanuts, cotton, vegetables, livestock) drained by Choctawhatchee R.; has forest industries (lumber, naval stores). Formed 1848. **2** County (□ 764; pop. 33,301), central Miss.; ⊙ Lexington. Bounded E by Big Black R.; also drained by Yazoo R. Agr. (cotton, corn); timber; clay deposits. Formed 1833. **3** County (□ 424; pop. 18,760), central Ohio; ⊙ Millersburg. Intersected by Killbuck Creek and Walhonding R. Agr. (livestock; dairy products; grain); mfg. at Millersburg; coal mines, sandstone quarries, gravel pits. Formed 1825.

Holmes Beach, town (pop. 137), Manatee co., SW Fla.

Holmes Chapel (hōmz), village in Church Hulme parish (pop. 1,143), central Cheshire, England, on Dane R. and 8 mi. ESE of Northwich; flour milling. Site of agr. and horticultural col. affiliated with Manchester Univ. Has 14th-cent. church.

Holmes Creek, NW Fla., rises in Geneva co., SE Ala., flows SW, into Fla., to Choctawhatchee R. 21 mi. SE of De Funiak Springs; c.60 mi. long; navigable below Vernon.

Holmestrand (hôl'mŭsträn), city (pop. 2,195), Vestfold co., SE Norway, on W shore of Oslo Fjord, on railroad and 35 mi. SSW of Oslo; aluminum mfg.; dairy plant; tourist resort.

Holmesville, village (pop. 392), Holmes co., central Ohio, 33 mi. ESE of Mansfield and on Killbuck Creek.

Holmfield, village (pop. estimate 200), SW Man., on Whitemud R. and 9 mi. ESE of Killarney; grain, stock.

Holmfirth (hōm'–), urban district (1931 pop. 10,407; 1951 census 19,073), West Riding, SW Yorkshire, England, 5 mi. S of Huddersfield; woolen mills, chemical works. Near by are stone quarries. In urban dist. are woolen-milling suburbs of Cartworth (S), Wooldale (NE), and Netherthong (NNW).

Holm of Huip, Scotland: see STRONSAY.

Holm of Papa, Scotland: see PAPA WESTRAY.

Holmsbu (hôlms'bōō), town (pop. 416), Buskerud co., SE Norway, on E side of Drammen Fjord near its mouth on Oslo Fjord, 14 mi. SE of Drammen; fruitgrowing, fishing. Dates from Middle Ages. Chief town of Hurum peninsula (15 mi. long, 4–8 mi. wide), which is bet. Drammen Fjord (W) and Oslo Fjord (E). Hurum canton (pop. 6,160) is lumbering and market-gardening region; industries include mfg. of cellulose, explosives.

Holmslands Klit, Denmark: see RINGKOBING FJORD.

Holmsund (hôlm'sŭnd"), village (pop. 3,733), Vasterbotten co., N Sweden, on Gulf of Bothnia, at mouth of Ume R., 10 mi. SSE of Umea, of which it is outport; lumber milling, woodworking.

Holne (hōn), agr. village and parish (pop. 301), S Devon, England, on Dart R. and 8 mi. NW of Totnes. Has medieval stone bridge and 15th-cent. church. Charles Kingsley b. here.

Holoby, Ukrainian SSR: see GOLOBY.

Holocachaket, Alaska: see HOLIKACHUK.

Hologachaket, Alaska: see HOLIKACHUK.

Holon (hōlōn'), residential settlement (1949 pop. 13,000), W Israel, in Plain of Sharon, near Mediterranean, just SE of Jaffa, 3 mi. S of Tel Aviv; industrial center; textile milling, metalworking; mfg. of silverware, leather goods, food products. Has textile school. Founded 1933.

Holopaw (hō'lĭpô"), village (1940 pop. 1,196), Osceola co., central Fla., 34 mi. SE of Orlando; lumber milling.

Holoubkov (hô'lōpkôf), village (pop. 746), SW Bohemia, Czechoslovakia, on railroad and 14 mi. ENE of Pilsen; machine-tool mfg.

Holowno, Ukrainian SSR: see GOLOVNO.

Holroyd, W suburb (pop. 24,129) of Sydney, E New South Wales, Australia; mfg. (textiles, pottery, flour).

Holsenoy (hôl'sŭn-ûü), Nor. *Holsenøy* or *Holsnøy*, island (□ 34; pop. 2,571) in North Sea, Hordaland co., SW Norway, 9 mi. NNW of Bergen; 13 mi. long, 5 mi. wide; covered with moors and lakes.

Hols Fjord, Norway: see TYRI FJORD.

Holstebro (hôl'stŭbrō"), city (pop. 13,212), Ringkobing amt, W Jutland, Denmark, on Stor R. and 23 mi. NE of Ringkobing; rail junction; brewery, meat cannery, dairy plant, machine shops; hydroelectric plant.

Holstebro River, Denmark: see STOR RIVER.

Holsted (hâl'stĕdh), town (pop. 1,106), Ribe amt, S central Jutland, Denmark, 18 mi. ENE of Esbjerg.

Holstein (hōl'stīn, Ger. hôl'shtīn), region in NW Germany, S of Eider R., forming S part of SCHLESWIG-HOLSTEIN. Created (1111) county of Holy Roman Empire and given to Schauenburg (see SCHAUMBURG-LIPPE) family. In 1386, Danish duchy of SCHLESWIG became hereditary fief of counts of Holstein, after whose extinction (1459) both Holstein and Schleswig passed in personal union to Denmark. Annexed (1864–66) by Prussia, Holstein and Schleswig were constituted as Prussian prov. of Schleswig-Holstein.

Holstein (hōl'stēn). **1** Town (pop. 1,336), Ida co., W Iowa, 18 mi. S of Cherokee, in livestock and grain area. Settled 1882. **2** Village (pop. 187), Adams co., S Nebr., 15 mi. SW of Hastings and on branch of Little Blue R.

Holsteiner Schweiz, Germany: see PLÖN.

Holsteinsborg (hôl'stänsbôr"), Eskimo *Sisimiut*, town (pop. 763), ⊙ Holsteinsborg dist. (pop. 1,471), SW Greenland, on Davis Strait, at mouth of Amerdiok Fjord (15 mi. long); 66°55'N 53°43'W. Fishing port, with fish and shrimp cannery; meteorological and radio station. Founded 1760. Sometimes spelled Holstensborg or Holstenborg.

Holston Mountains (hōl'stŭn), in NE Tenn. and SW Va., ridge (2,500–4,000 ft.) of the Appalachians bet. South Fork Holston R. (N) and Iron Mts. (SE); from Elizabethton, Tenn., extend c.30 mi. NE to Damascus, Va.; highest point (c.4,300 ft.) is 7 mi. NE of Elizabethton. Included in Cherokee and Jefferson natl. forests. Sometimes considered a range of Unaka Mts.

Holston River, NE Tenn., just W of Kingsport formed by junction of North and South forks; flows c.115 mi. SW, through Great Appalachian Valley, joining French Broad R. 4½ mi. above Knoxville to form Tennessee R. North Fork (c.120 mi. long) rises in N Smyth co., SW Va., flows SW, through Washington and Scott counties, into NE Tenn. South Fork (c.110 mi. long) rises in S Smyth co., Va., flows SW into Tenn., then NE to join North Fork; receives Middle Fork (c.60 mi. long) in S Washington co., Va. In Tenn. are 2 TVA dams: CHEROKEE DAM on the Holston, and, on South Fork, South Holston Dam (c.285 ft. high, 1,600 ft. long; for flood control, hydroelectric power), designed to impound reservoir extending c.25 mi. upstream and covering □ 12.5.

Holsworthy (hōlz'wûr-dhē, hŏl'zûrē), urban district (1931 pop. 1,403; 1951 census 1,550), W Devon, England, 9 mi. E of Bude; agr. market and hunting center. Scene of St. Peter's Fair, annual horse festival. Has 13th-cent. church.

Holt, Argentina: see IBICUY.

Holt. 1 Town and parish (pop. 1,940), N Norfolk, England, 11 mi. ENE of Fakenham; agr. market. Has 16th-cent. school and 14th-cent. church. **2** Agr. village and parish (pop. 1,030), W Wiltshire, England, 3 mi. ENE of Bradford-on-Avon; leather mfg. Has 15th-cent. church.

Holt, Norway: see NES, village, Aust-Agder co.

Holt. 1 County (□ 456; pop. 9,833), NW Mo.; ⊙ Oregon. Bet. Missouri (W and S) and Nodaway (E) rivers; drained by Tarkio R. Agr. (corn, wheat, oats, apples), stock raising. Formed 1841. **2** County (□ 2,408; pop. 14,859), N Nebr.; ⊙ O'Neill. Agr. region bounded N by Niobrara R.; drained by Elkhorn R. Grain, livestock, dairy and poultry produce. Formed 1876.

Holt. 1 Village (pop. 2,453, with adjacent Fox), Tuscaloosa co., W Ala., on Black Warrior R. and 5 mi. NE of Tuscaloosa; iron and coal products, chemicals, paper. **2** Town (1940 pop. 303), Okaloosa co., NW Fla., near Blackwater R., 35 mi. NE of Pensacola, in agr. area. **3** or **Holt Mine,** mining village, Muhlenberg co., W Ky., 5 mi. NE of Greenville; bituminous coal. There are also hamlets called Holt in Lawrence and Breckenridge counties. **4** Village (1940 pop. 1,818), Ingham co., S central Mich., 7 mi. SSE of Lansing, in agr. area (livestock, poultry, grain; dairy products); meat packing. **5** Village (pop. 172), Marshall co., NW Minn., 12 mi. N of Thief River Falls, in agr. area; dairy products. **6** Town (pop. 270), Clay and Clinton counties, W Mo., on Fishing R. and 28 mi. NE of Kansas City.

Holt, town and parish (pop. 1,103), E Denbigh, Wales, on the Dee (14th-cent. bridge) and 5 mi. ENE of Wrexham; agr. market. Has 15th-cent. church.

Holtaalen, Norway: see HALTDALEN.

Holte (hôl'tŭ), town (pop. 7,311), Copenhagen amt, Denmark, 8 mi. N of Copenhagen; truck produce. Includes communities of Sollerod, Overod, and Dronninggaard.

Holtemme River (hôl'tĕ"mŭ), central Germany, rises in the upper Harz at foot of the Brocken, flows 28 mi. ENE, past Wernigerode and Halberstadt, to the Bode 2 mi. NE of Gröningen.

Holten (hôl'tŭn), village (pop. 1,547), Overijssel prov., E Netherlands, 10 mi. E of Deventer; dairying, milk-powder mfg., cattle raising.

Holtenau (hôl'tŭnou), district (since 1922) of Kiel, NW Germany, 3.5 mi. N of city center, on W bank of Kiel Firth, at E end of Kiel Canal (locks; bridge). Airport with seaplane base.

Holt Mine, Ky.: see HOLT.

Holton (hōl'tùn), city (pop. 2,705), ⊙ Jackson co., NE Kansas, 29 mi. N of Topeka, in livestock and grain region; dairy products. Laid out 1857 by Free Staters; inc. 1870. Potawatomi Indian Reservation is near by.

Holtville (hōlt'vĭl), city (pop. 2,472), Imperial co., S Calif., 10 mi. E of El Centro, in IMPERIAL VALLEY; ships truck. Inc. 1908.

Holtz Bay, Alaska: see ATTU ISLAND.

Holualoa (hō'lōō-älō'ä), village (pop. 475), W Hawaii, T.H., near Kailua Bay, in the Kona dist.; produces coffee.

Holung (hŭ'lōōng'), town, ⊙ Holung co. (pop. 137,608), E Kirin prov., Manchuria, 20 mi. S of Yenki, near Tumen R. (Korea line); gold and chromite mining; lumbering. Formerly called Talatze.

Holwerd (hōl'vûrt), village (pop. 1,651), Friesland prov., N Netherlands, near the Waddenzee, 12 mi. NNE of Leeuwarden; wheat, flax, potatoes. Ferry to Ameland isl. on near-by coast.

Holy Cross, village (pop. 158), W Alaska, on Yukon R. at mouth of Innoko R. and 120 mi. NE of Bethel; 62°12'N 159°47'W; fur trading. Jesuit mission and school. Established 1887.

Holycross, Gaelic *Mainistir na Croise Naomhtha,* agr. village (district pop. c.1,000), central Co. Tipperary, Ireland, on Suir R. and 4 mi. SW of Thurles; beets, potatoes. Site of ruins of abbey founded 1182 by Donal O'Brien.

Holy Cross. 1 Locality, St. Joseph co., Ind.: see SOUTH BEND. **2** Town (pop. 139), Dubuque co., E Iowa, 17 mi. WNW of Dubuque; limestone quarry.

Holy Cross, Mount of the, peak (13,986 ft.) in Sawatch Mts., W central Colo., 18 mi. NW of Leadville. Near its summit, snow-filled crevices c.50 ft. wide form a huge cross more than 1,000 ft. long, with 750-ft. arms. Formerly (1929–50) Holy Cross Natl. Monument; site now administered by U.S. Forest Service.

Holyhead (hŏ'lēhĕd), Welsh *Caer Gybi* (kĭr gŭ'bē), urban district (1931 pop. 10,700; 1951 census 10,569), at N end of HOLY ISLAND or Holyhead Isl., W Anglesey, Wales, on Irish Sea, 19 mi. NW of Caernarvon; 53°19'N 4°38'W; chief port on mail and passenger route to Dublin, with direct rail connection with mainland of Wales and England. Has 7,860-ft.-long breakwater and 15th-cent. church. Rocky promontory of North Stack, 2 mi. WNW, has coves and sea inlets; 3 mi. W is promontory of South Stack, site of lighthouse (53°18'N 4°42'W).

Holyhead Island, Wales: see HOLY ISLAND.

Holy Island (hō'lē) or **Lindisfarne** (lĭn'dĭsfärn), island (3 mi. long, 1 mi. wide) in North Sea just off E coast of Northumberland, England, SE of Berwick-on-Tweed, and connected with mainland at low tide. On W coast is agr. village and parish (pop. 287) of Holy Island. Church and monastery, founded 635 by St. Aidan, were 1st establishment of Celtic Christianity in England. St. Cuthbert was bishop of Lindisfarne. In 793 settlement was burned by Danes and subsequently rebuilt; in 883 the bishopric was moved to the mainland. In 1093 a Benedictine priory was founded here; there are remains of its church and of a 16th-cent. castle. The *Lindisfarne Gospels* or *Book of Durham,* an illuminated Latin MS written here before 700, is now in British Mus. in London.

Holy Island or **Iniscaltra** (ĭ"nĭskäl'trù), islet in Lough Derg, Ireland, 4 mi. E of Scariff, Co. Clare. Site of 10th-cent. round tower and of remains of several churches and monastic bldgs. established in 7th cent., destroyed by the Danes, and rebuilt by Brian Boru.

Holy Island (pop. 19), Buteshire, Scotland, in Firth of Clyde just off E coast of Arran, sheltering harbor of Lamlash.

Holy Island or **Holyhead Island** (hŏ'lē–), Anglesey, Wales, in Irish Sea, just off W coast of Anglesey isl., linked by rail and road bridges; 7 mi. long, 4 mi. wide. Chief town, HOLYHEAD.

Holy Loch, Scotland: see KILMUN.

Holyoke (hōl'yōk). **1** Town (pop. 1,558), ⊙ Phillips co., NE Colo., on Frenchman Creek, near Nebr. line, and 45 mi. E of Sterling; livestock, grain, dairy and poultry products. Inc. 1888. **2** City (pop. 54,661), Hampden co., S Mass., on Connecticut R. (water power) and 7 mi. N of Springfield; mfg. (paper and paper products, textiles, machinery, steel products, electrical supplies). Has a jr. col. Settled 1745, set off from West Springfield 1850, inc. as city 1873. Includes part of Mt. Tom State Park.

Holyoke, Mount, Mass.: see HOLYOKE RANGE.

Holyoke Range, W central Mass., E–W range just N of South Hadley; c.8 mi. long; rises to 1,106 ft. in Mt. Norwottock (nôrwŏ'tŭk). Mt. Holyoke (878 ft.), at W end, has road to summit hotel.

Holyrood, Scotland: see EDINBURGH.

Holyrood, city (pop. 748), Ellsworth co., central Kansas, 23 mi. NE of Great Bend; shipping point in wheat region; flour. Oil wells near by.

Holywell, England: see EARSDON.

Holywell (hŏ'lē–), urban district (1931 pop. 3,424; 1951 census 8,196), Flint, Wales, near the Dee, 4 mi. WNW of Flint; woolen milling, paper mfg., livestock market. Has Gothic chapel built by Margaret, mother of Henry VII, on site of St. Winifred's Well, which, according to legend, sprang up on site of beheading of St. Winifred. It is Roman Catholic place of pilgrimage, and one of "Seven Wonders of Wales." On the Dee, 2 mi. NE, is small port of Greenfield.

Holywood (hŏ'lēwŏŏd), urban district (1937 pop. 5,078; 1951 census 6,316), NE Co. Down, Northern Ireland, on SE coast of Belfast Lough, 6 mi. NE of Belfast; port and seaside resort. The monastery founded here in 7th cent. by St. Laserian was succeeded in early 13th cent. by Franciscan establishment, burned 1572, of which there are some remains. In urban dist. is seaside resort of Marino.

Holzen (hôl'tsùn), village (pop. 1,197), in former Prussian prov. of Hanover, W Germany, after 1945 in Lower Saxony, 12 mi. NE of Holzminden; asphalt quarries. Until 1941 in Brunswick.

Holzgerlingen (hôlts'gĕr'lĭng-ùn), village (pop. 3,382), N Württemberg, Germany, after 1945 in Württemberg-Baden, 3 mi. S of Böblingen; cattle.

Holzhausen (hôlts'hou"zùn), village (pop. 6,742), Saxony, E central Germany, 4 mi. ESE of Leipzig city center; mfg. (precision instruments, construction machinery).

Holzheim (hôlts'hīm), village (pop. 5,082), in former Prussian Rhine Prov., W Germany, after 1945 in North Rhine-Westphalia, 2.5 mi. SSW of Neuss.

Holzkirchen (hôlts'kĭr"khùn), village (pop. 4,299), Upper Bavaria, 10 mi. NE of Bad Tölz; rail junction; brewing, metal- and woodworking.

Holzminden (hôlts'mün"dùn), town (pop. 19,906), in former Pruss an prov. of Hanover, NW Germany, after 1945 in Lower Saxony, port on right bank of the Weser and 34 mi. N of Kassel; rail junction; mfg. of plywood, furniture, essential oils, wood alcohol, machinery, building materials, glass, wax paper; leather- and metalworking. Silver-fox farm. Has architectural institute (founded 1831). Chartered c.1200. Plundered and completely burned (1640) by imperial troops. Until 1941 in Brunswick.

Holzweissig (hôlts"vī'sĭkh), village (pop. 8,000), in former Prussian Saxony prov., central Germany, after 1945 in Saxony-Anhalt, just S of Bitterfeld; lignite mining.

Holzwickede (hôltsvĭ'kùdù), town (pop. 8,332), in former Prussian prov. of Westphalia, W Germany, after 1945 in North Rhine-Westphalia, in the Ruhr, 3 mi. W of Unna; rail junction; coal mining.

Homa (hō'mä), village, Nyanza prov., W Kenya, on Kavirondo Gulf of L. Victoria, 36 mi. SW of Kisumu; apatite deposits. Also Homa Bay.

Homalin (hō'mùlĭn"), village, Upper Chindwin dist., Upper Burma, on left bank of Chindwin R. (head of navigation) and 120 mi. NNE of Kalewa; tea plantations; jungle-covered area.

Homathko River (hōmăth'kō), SW B.C., rises in Coast Mts. near 51°50'N 124°45'W, flows 80 mi. generally S to head of Bute Inlet.

Hombeek (hōm'bāk), agr. village (pop. 3,123), Antwerp prov., N central Belgium, 2 mi. WSW of Mechlin.

Homberg (hŏm'bûrg, Ger. hôm'bĕrk). **1** Town (pop. 6,164), in former Prussian prov. of Hesse-Nassau, W Germany, after 1945 in Hesse, 19 mi. SSW of Kassel; lumber. In 1526, at a synod held in the Gothic church, the introduction of the Reformation into Hesse was decided. **2** Town (pop. 2,305), central Hesse, W Germany, in former Upper Hesse prov., on the Ohm and 17 mi. NE of Giessen; lumber milling. **3** Town (pop. 27,117), in former Prussian Rhine Prov., W Germany, after 1945 in North Rhine-Westphalia, in the Ruhr, port on left bank of the Rhine, nearly opposite Duisburg; 51°27'N 6°42'E. Coal-mining center; iron foundries; mfg. of machinery, synthetic oil, dyes, lithopone, textiles. Coal harbor.

Hombetsu (hōmbā'tsōō), town (pop. 13,615), S central Hokkaido, Japan, 25 mi. NE of Obihiro; flour milling, stock raising, hemp clothmaking. Sometimes called Pombetsu.

Hombori (hōmbōrē'), village, E central Fr. Sudan, Fr. West Africa, in hilly region (Hombori mts.), 120 mi. WSW of Gao; rice, millet; livestock.

Hombourg (ōbōōr'), Flemish *Homburg* (hôm'bûrkh), agr. village (pop. 1,552), Liége prov., E Belgium, 8 mi. NNW of Eupen.

Hombourg, Saar: see HOMBURG.

Hombourg-Haut (ōbōōr'-ō'), Ger. *Oberhomburg* (ō'bùrhôm'bōōrk), town (pop. 2,438), Moselle dept., NE France, 4 mi. NE of Saint-Avold, in coal-mining dist. Boilerworks; mfg. of auto springs.

Hombrechtikon (hômbrĕkh'tĭkôn), town (pop. 2,627), Zurich canton, N Switzerland, 13 mi. SE of Zurich; metalworking, silk textiles.

Hombre Muerto, Salar de (sälär' dā ōm'brā mwĕr'tō), salt desert (□ 241) in Puna de Atacama, N Catamarca prov., Argentina, extends c.20 mi. N–S and E–W on Salta prov. border. Contains borax and sodium chloride. Sierra del Hombre Muerto, 80 mi. SE, is a 40-mi. subandean range rising to 16,500 ft.

Hombre Pintado, Venezuela: see EL MENE.

Homburg, Belgium: see HOMBOURG.

Homburg (hŏm'bûrg, Ger. hôm'bōōrk). **1** or **Homburg am Main** (äm mīn'), village (pop. 966), Lower Franconia, NW Bavaria, Germany, on the Main (canalized) and 13 mi. W of Würzburg; wine-growing ("Kalmut" wine). Chartered 1332. Just N is grotto where St. Burchard died. Ruins of anc. castle Homburg are ½ mi. NE of GÖSSENHEIM. **2** or **Bad Homburg,** town, Hesse, Germany: see BAD HOMBURG.

Homburg, Fr. *Hombourg* (õbōōr'), city (pop. 19,490), SE Saar, frontier station near Ger. border, near Blies R., 18 mi. ENE of Saarbrücken, 5 mi. NNW of Zweibrücken; rail junction; steel industry; metal- and woodworking, brewing; mfg. of machinery, ceramics, glass, electrical equipment. Power station. Seat of Saar Univ., founded 1948. Homburg dist. formed part (1815–1919) of Bavarian Palatinate. Near by are remains of several anc. castles.

Home Bay, E Baffin Isl., E Franklin Dist., Northwest Territories, inlet (40 mi. long, 50 mi. wide at mouth) of Davis Strait; 68°40'N 67°30'W. Bounded N by Henry Kater Peninsula.

Homebush, municipality (pop. 3,501), E New South Wales, Australia, 7 mi. W of Sydney, in metropolitan area; govt.-owned abattoirs; mfg. (radios, phonograph records). Included 1947 in STRATHFIELD.

Home Corner, village (pop. 3,950), Grant co., NE central Ind., suburb of Marion.

Homécourt (ômākōōr'), town (pop. 6,702), Meurthe-et-Moselle dept., NE France, in Briey iron basin on Orne R. and 3 mi. SE of Briey; iron mines, blast furnaces, and steel mills for naval construction. Phosphate extraction near by. Has metallurgical school.

Homecroft, town (pop. 659), Marion co., central Ind.

Homedale, village (pop. 1,411), Owyhee co., SW Idaho, on Snake R. and 15 mi. W of Caldwell, near Oregon line, in Idaho section of Owyhee irrigation project; grain, potatoes, sugar beets, sheep.

Home Hill, town (pop. 2,198), E Queensland, Australia, on Burdekin R. and 50 mi. SE of Townsville; sugar center.

Homei (hŭ'mā'), Jap. *Wabi* (wä'bē), town (1935 pop. 5,755), W central Formosa, 4 mi. NW of Changwa and on railroad; sugar refining, hatmaking.

Home Island, Singapore colony: see COCOS ISLANDS.

Homel, Belorussian SSR: see GOMEL, city.

Homeland, town (pop. 276), Charlton co., SE Ga., 2 mi. NNW of Folkston.

Homer, village (pop. 434), S Alaska, on Kachemak Bay, SW Kenai Peninsula, 75 mi. WSW of Seward; 59°36'N 151°25'W. Connected by highway with Seward and Cook Inlet towns, it is trading center for rich farming region (c.500,000 acres). Fishing, fish processing, coal mining; copper and gold deposits near by. Center of proposed farm expansion on Kenai Peninsula.

Homer. 1 Town (pop. 340), ⊙ Banks co., NE Ga., 18 mi. E of Gainesville, in agr. area; lumber. **2** Village (pop. 1,030), Champaign co., E Ill., 16 mi. ESE of Champaign, in agr. area; corn, wheat, soybeans, livestock, poultry, dairy products. **3** Town (pop. 4,749), ⊙ Claiborne parish, N La., 45 mi. NE of Shreveport; trade center in oil, timber, and cotton area; cotton ginning, lumber milling; mfg. of bricks, dairy products, beverages. Settled 1830, inc. 1850. **4** Village (pop. 1,301), Calhoun co., S Mich., 22 mi. SW of Jackson and on a branch of Kalamazoo R., in area producing wheat, corn, and hay; mfg. (flour, dry-milk products). Settled 1832, inc. 1871. **5** Village (pop. 345), Dakota co., NE Nebr., 12 mi. S of Sioux City, Iowa, near Missouri R.; farm trading center. Site of 18th-cent. Omaha Indian village near by. **6** Village (pop. 3,244), Cortland co., central N.Y., in the Tioughnioga valley, just N of Cortland; farm trade center, with mfg. of clothing, soap, canned foods, feed, sporting goods; sand and gravel pits. Settled 1791, inc. 1835.

Homer City, borough (pop. 2,372), Indiana co., SW central Pa., 5 mi. S of Indiana; bituminous coal; metal products; agr. Inc. 1872.

Homerville, city (pop. 1,787), ⊙ Clinch co., S Ga., 25 mi. WSW of Waycross, near Okefenokee Swamp; pulpwood, naval stores. Founded on the railroad 1859, inc. as town 1869, as city 1931.

Homestead. 1 City (pop. 4,573), Dade co., S Fla., 28 mi. SW of Miami; truck-produce packing and shipping center. Has agr. experiment station. Royal Palm State Park, a wildlife sanctuary, is near by; Everglades Natl. Park is W. **2** Village, Iowa co., Iowa; see AMANA. **3** SW suburb (pop. 3,688) of Omaha, Douglas co., E Nebr., on Missouri R. **4** Industrial borough (pop. 10,046), Allegheny co., SW Pa., on Monongahela R. opposite SE Pittsburgh; iron and steel works. Most of huge works for which borough was noted are now included in adjacent MUNHALL borough. Famous Homestead strike, one of bitterest U.S. labor disputes, broke out here in 1892 and lasted nearly 5 months. Inc. 1880.

Homestead National Monument of America, Nebr.: see BEATRICE.

Homeville, village (pop. 2,353), Erie co., N Ohio.

Homewood. 1 City (pop. 12,866), Jefferson co., N central Ala., SE suburb of Birmingham; woodworking. Inc. 1921 as Edgewood, renamed 1926. **2** Residential village (pop. 5,887), Cook co., NE Ill., S suburb of Chicago, in agr. area; mfg. (neckwear, lumber). Washington Park Race Track is near by. Glenwood Manual Training School for boys is here. Platted as Hartford in 1852; inc. 1893. **3** Suburb of Annapolis, Anne Arundel co., central Md. **4** Borough (pop. 316), Beaver co., W Pa., 3 mi. N of Beaver Falls and on Beaver R.

Homildon, England: see HUMBLEDON.

Hominabad, India: see HOMNABAD.

Hominy, city (pop. 2,702), Osage co., N Okla., 29 mi. NW of Tulsa, in agr. and oil-producing area; mfg. of oil-field equipment, cottonseed products, feed; cotton ginning. Established as an Indian subagency in 1874; laid out 1905, inc. 1908.

Homme-d'Armes, L', France: see SAVASSE.

Hommelvik (hôm'mülvĕk), village (pop. 2,106) in Malvik canton (pop. 4,391), Sor-Trondelag co., central Norway, on S shore of Trondheim Fjord, on railroad and 12 mi. E of Trondheim; iron casting, woodworking. Exports lumber.

Homnabad (hōm'näbäd), town (pop. 8,894), Atraf-i-Balda dist., W central Hyderabad state, India, in enclave within Bidar dist., 23 mi. WSW of Bidar; millet, cotton, rice. Road junction is 2 mi. W. Sometimes spelled Hominabad.

Homocea (hômô'chä), village (pop. 2,253), Putna prov., E Rumania, 20 mi. NNW of Tecuci.

Homochitto River (hōmüchĭ'tů, -tē), SW Miss., rises in Copiah co., flows c.90 mi. SW and W, past Bude, entering the Mississippi through several channels in Wilkinson co.

Homoíne (ōmōōē'nĭ), village, Sul do Save prov., SE Mozambique, on road and 15 mi. W of Inhambane; coffee, cotton, mafura.

Homokbalvanyos, Yugoslavia: see BAVANISTE.

Homonhon Island (hōmōnhōn') (□ 40; 1939 pop. 1,825), Samar prov., Philippines, bet. Leyte Gulf and Philippine Sea, 14 mi. S of narrow SE peninsula of Samar isl.; 12 mi. long, 4 mi. wide. Deeply indented in E by Casogoran Bay. Hilly, rising to 1,120 ft. Rice growing. Chromite deposits.

Homonna, Czechoslovakia: see HUMENNE.

Homorod (hōmôrŏd'), Hung. *Homoród* (hô'môrōd), village (pop. 1,503), Sibiu prov., central Rumania, on railroad and 25 mi. SE of Sighisoara; lumbering center; stud farm. Has noted 15th-cent. fortified church.

Homosassa (hō"müsă'sů), fishing village (pop. c.300), Citrus co., central Fla., c.60 mi. NNE of Tampa, on Gulf coast. The Homosassa Isls., a group of many small mangrove isls., are just offshore. Homosassa Springs, a resort, is 2 mi. ENE.

Homs (hôms), town (pop. 2,553), Tripolitania, Libya, port on Mediterranean Sea, 65 mi. ESE of Tripoli; highway junction. Commercial and tourist center; esparto grass processing, olive-oil pressing. Formerly called Lebda. Near by are extensive Roman ruins (harbor, forum, temples, baths, theater) of Leptis Magna, an important Phoenician port and later a Roman colony. Septimius Severus b. here. Archaeological mus. Town bombed (1942) in Second World War.

Homs (hôms) or **Hums** (hōōms), province (□ 16,400; 1946 pop. 224,523), central Syria; ⊙ HOMS. Extends from NE tip of Lebanon E and SE to borders of Iraq and Jordan. Mainly desert. In W is an area irrigated by the Orontes and L. Homs; millet, wheat, corn, cotton are grown. Crossed E-W by the Kirkuk (Iraq)-Tripoli (Lebanon) oil pipe line, which passes through PALMYRA. Rail line N to Hama and Aleppo, and S to Baalbek, Beirut, and Damascus. Important ruins, especially of the Roman period, are at Homs, Palmyra, and Er Rastan. Also spelled Hems and Hims.

Homs or **Hums,** Lat. *Emesa* (ĕ'mĕsä), city (pop. c.100,000), ⊙ Homs prov., W Syria, on the Orontes 7 mi. below L. Homs, and 85 mi. NNE of Damascus, in a fertile plain; alt. 1,600 ft. Communications center on the Damascus-Aleppo road and railroad; commercial center in well-irrigated area (sericulture; cereals, fruit); silk weaving, jewelry mfg. At Emesa, in anc. times, was a great temple to the sun-god, whence came Heliogabalus, the priest who became Roman emperor in A.D. 218. Aurelian here defeated (272) Zenobia of Palmyra. The Arabs took Emesa in 7th cent. It later passed to the Turks, in whose hands it remained—except for the short period after 1832 when Ibrahim Pasha of Egypt defeated the Turks and took the city—until the creation of modern Syria after First World War. There are almost no remains of its past. Sometimes spelled Hems and Hims.

Homs, Lake, irrigation reservoir (□ 23) on the Orontes (dammed), Homs prov., W Syria, 7 mi. SW of Homs, near Lebanese border; 9 mi. long, c.2 mi. wide. Qattine is on NE shore. Sometimes called L. Qattine.

Homún (ōmōōn'), town (pop. 1,783), Yucatan, SE Mexico, 27 mi. SE of Mérida; henequen, sugar cane, corn.

Hon, Tripolitania: see HUN.

Honaker (hŏ'nĭkůr), town (pop. 847), Russell co., SW Va., in the Alleghenies, near Clinch R., 40 mi. SW of Bluefield.

Honam (hô'näm'), Mandarin *Honan* (hŭ'nän'), S suburb of Canton, Kwangtung prov., China, on right bank of Canton R., opposite Canton proper (linked by bridge); commercial and industrial center; produces cement, matting. Has shipyards, warehouses, stock exchange.

Honan (hō'năn', Chinese hŭ'nän') [Chinese,=S of the (Yellow) river], province (□ 55,000; pop. 25,000,000) of N central China; ⊙ Kaifeng. Bounded N by Pingyuan and Shansi along Yellow R., W by Shensi, S by Hupeh (in part along Tungpeh Mts.), and E by Anhwei. Honan lies at the contact zone of China's W central mtn. belt, the NW loess highlands, and the N China plain. Largely mountainous (alt. 7,800 ft.) in W, where the Sung and Funiu Mts. are the last outliers of the Kunlun system, Honan slopes gradually E to Hwai R. valley of N Anhwei. There the predominantly loess soils of the NW merge with the fertile river alluvium. Only the sheltered SW agr. valleys of Tan, Pai, and Tang rivers (with center at Nanyang), oriented toward Yangtze R. basin, have a generally mild climate, permitting the production of rice, silk, cotton. The remainder of the prov., exposed to cold N winds and winter dust storms, has typically N agr. production of wheat, millet, fruit, beans, and some cotton. Here the chief agr. areas are Lo R. valley and the E plain of Hwai R. basin. Peanuts, sesame, and *tihwang* (medicinal plant) are also grown. Coal and iron are exploited on a small scale near Lushan. The chief urban centers are, in addition to the old cities of Kaifeng and Loyang, the SW agr. center of Nanyang, the E commercial center of Chowkiakow, and the railroad towns of Sinyang (S), Yencheng (center), and especially Chengchow (N). Here cross 2 of China's major railroad lines, the E-W Lunghai RR and the N-S Peking-Hankow RR. Pop. is homogeneously Chinese, speaking N Mandarin dialect. The prov. is the earliest region of Chinese settlement; Loyang and Kaifeng were among China's earliest capitals. The name Honan was 1st used in the Tang dynasty (618–906). During Second World War, the prov. was partly occupied by the Japanese, mainly along the railroad lines. Passed 1948–49 to the Chinese Communists. The section N of Yellow R. was separated (1949) from Honan to form the new prov. of Pingyuan.

Honan. 1 City, Honan prov., China: see LOYANG. **2** Suburb, Kwangtung prov., China: see HONAM.

Honavar (hō'nävŭr), town (pop. 8,939), Kanara dist., S Bombay, India, port on Arabian Sea, at mouth of Sharavati R., 42 mi. SE of Karwar; agr. market (rice, coconuts, spices); fish-supplying center (mackerel, sardines, catfish, seerfish); sandalwood and ivory carving, fruit canning, mfg. of coir products; exports matchwood. Handicraft school. Casuarina plantations near by. Fortified 1505 by Portuguese; seized 1783 from Hyder Ali by British.

Honaz Dag (hônäz' dä), Turkish *Honaz Dağ*, peak (8,435 ft.), SW Turkey, 12 mi. SE of Denizli.

Honchong (hôn'choung'), town, Hatien prov., S Vietnam, on Gulf of Siam, 17 mi. SE of Hatien; fishing center; pepper plantations.

Honctö, Rumania: see GURAHONT.

Honda (ōn'dä), city (pop. 12,424), Tolima dept., W central Colombia, port on Magdalena R. (Cundinamarca dept. border), on Ibagué–La Dorada highway, and 60 mi. NW of Bogotá. It grew as an important river-rail transshipping point bet. lower and upper Magdalena R., obstructed here by the Honda Falls; its commerce was supplemented by the building (1884) of the railroad from Puerto Salgar, on the Magdalena opposite La Dorada, directly to Bogotá and Girardot. Trading and processing center in agr. region (tobacco, cacao, bananas, rice, corn, yucca, sugar cane, livestock); ships coffee, cacao, hides, gold and silver; flour milling, brewing, soapmaking. Airport. Thermal springs and petroleum deposits near by. An old colonial town, founded c.1565. It was severely damaged by 1805 earthquake.

Honda, Ensenada, Puerto Rico: see ENSENADA HONDA.

Honda Bay (ōn'dä), on Caribbean N coast of Guajira peninsula, N Colombia, SW of Point Gallinas; 12°20'N 71°45'W; c.6 mi. wide. Saltworks.

Honda Bay, sheltered inlet, NW Cuba, just N of town of Bahía Honda, 50 mi. WSW of Havana. Seaplane anchorage.

Hondagua, Philippines: see LOPEZ.

Honddu River (hôn'dhē), Brecknock, Wales, rises on Mynydd Eppynt, flows 10 mi. SE to the Usk at Brecknock.

Hondo (hōn'dō), town (pop. 16,805), on Shimo-jima of Amakusa Isls., Japan, in Kumamoto prefecture, on E coast of isl., 20 mi. NE of Ushibuka; mfg. center; dolls, camellia oil, porcelain ware, raw silk.

Hondo, island, Japan: see HONSHU.

Hondo (hŏn'dō), city (pop. 4,188), ⊙ Medina co., SW Texas, W of San Antonio in ranching and irrigated farm area (cattle, sheep, goats, grain). Medina L. (müdē'nů) (irrigation, recreation) is 17 mi. NE. Inc. after 1940.

Hondo, Río (rē'ō ōn'dō), short stream on Tucumán–Santiago del Estero prov. border, NW Argentina; formed by union of the Río Chico and Marapa R., flows c.5 mi. to the Salí (upper course of the Río Dulce) at Río Hondo town. The name Río Hondo is sometimes applied to the Santiago del Estero section of the Río DULCE.

Hondo, Río, or **Hondo River,** river in Yucatan Peninsula, on Mexico–Br. Honduras border, rises as Río Azul NE of Uaxactún (Guatemala), flows c.130 mi. NE, along international border, to Chetumal Bay (Caribbean Sea) at Chetumal. Used for logging.

Hondón de las Nieves (ōndōn' dhā läs nyā'vĕs), town (pop. 1,117), Alicante prov., E Spain, 9 mi. NW of Elche; footwear mfg., olive-oil processing.

Hondores, Peru: see ONDORES.

Hondschoote (ōskōt', Flemish hōnt'skhōtů), frontier town (pop. 2,002), Nord dept., N France, near Belg. border, 10 mi. SE of Dunkirk; agr. market; flax processing, brewing.

Hondsrug (hōnz'rûkh), plateau in Drenthe and Groningen provs., N central Netherlands; extends 30 mi. NNW-SSE, bet. Emmen and Groningen; highest alt. 100 ft.

Honduras (hŏndōō'rŭs, -dyōō'-), republic (□ 59,160; 1945 pop. 1,200,542; 1950 pop. 1,533,625), Central America; ⊙ TEGUCIGALPA. With a c.350-mi. coast line in N along the Caribbean, it extends c.175 mi. southward to the Gulf of FONSECA on the Pacific Ocean. Borders W on Guatemala, SW on Salvador, E and NE on Nicaragua, with which it disputes N section of the MOSQUITO COAST bet. Patuca and Coco rivers (the *de facto* boundary follows COLÓN MOUNTAINS). The Bay Isls. in Bay of Honduras belong to it. Honduras is situated approximately bet. 13°–16°N and 83°15'–89°15'W. It is almost entirely mountainous, except for the narrow coastal strips, the lower river valleys, and the undeveloped Mosquito Coast, which is still inhabited by Indian tribes. It is crossed by the main cordillera of Central America, which rises to c.7,000 ft. in the more elevated S section, sending off spurs that enclose fertile interior valleys and plateaus, among them 40-mi.-long COMAYAGUA valley. Several block ranges are in the N. There are no active volcanoes, but rich volcanic soil abounds. Along the rift valley which cuts across N-S from the ULÚA RIVER and L. YOJOA basin to the Pacific, is an intercoastal highway (POTRERILLOS to SAN LORENZO). The country is well drained. Principal rivers emptying into the Caribbean are the navigable (c.125 mi. upstream) Ulúa R. (with Comayagua-Humuya tributary), AGUÁN RIVER, and PATUCA RIVER. The CHOLUTECA RIVER flows to the Pacific. The climate is hot and humid in tropical coastal lowlands, where rainfall is heavy, especially in N; and more healthful in the interior uplands. Rainy season May–Dec. Tegucigalpa (alt. 3,070 ft.) has an equable spring climate all year round. Honduras is rich in mineral resources. Gold and silver, worked since colonial days and still making up 20–25% of all exports, are extracted chiefly from the rich Rosario mine at SAN JUANCITO near the capital in vicinity of YUSCARÁN (El Paraíso dept.), and, since 1940s, at EL MOCHITO mine W of L. Yojoa. The country ranks 3d (after Mexico and Peru) among silver-producing nations of Latin America. Antimony is mined near SANTA ROSA (Copán dept.). Exploited minerals include copper, iron, zinc, coal, and petroleum. The luxuriant lowlands yield important revenue in forest products, especially mahogany, pine, naval stores, vanilla, rubber, and sarsaparilla. The leading export, however, is bananas (34% in 1948–49), though the acreage has recently been greatly reduced because of plant disease. Bananas are grown on large U.S.-owned plantations on the Caribbean coast, and shipped through the ports of TRUJILLO, LA CEIBA, TELA, and PUERTO CORTÉS. The latter also loads coffee. Among minor crops grown for foreign trade—generally on small holdings—are: coffee raised on slopes at 1,500–4,000 ft.; coconuts, mainly from Bay Isls.; tobacco (W Honduras); citronella and lemon grass; abacá (Manilla hemp) and henequen. Beef, hides, and reptile skins are also exported. Principal trade is with U.S., which also provides most of the imports; trade also with Salvador. Though the pop. is overwhelmingly agrarian, only a small fraction of the land is cultivated. Corn, rice, wheat, beans, sugar cane, cotton, fruit (near La Esperanza) are grown for home consumption. There is cigar mfg. and a few industries for domestic use, such as mfg. of matches, cigarettes, textiles, clothing, shoes; food processing, distilling, brewing, brick making. Commerce and industry are centered at SAN PEDRO SULA, Puerto Cortés, and Tegucigalpa. Other interior cities are Santa Rosa (center of tobacco industry), Comayagua (⊙ until 1880), DANLI, JUTICALPA, COPÁN (noted for its Maya ruins with hieroglyphics and remarkable calendar). The Inter-American Highway, near the Pacific coast, passes through CHOLUTECA in the S. Only Pacific port is AMAPALA on Tigre Isl. ROATÁN is the port of entry for Bay Isls. Beach resorts at CEDEÑO (S) and Tela (N). Inadequate transportation has impeded development. Railroads (total mileage, c.650 mi.) are confined to N coast serving the plantations. Both San Pedro Sula and Tegucigalpa are, however, served by natl. and international airlines. The capital is also seat of country's only univ. Half the mestizo pop. (87% of the total) is illiterate. Negroes from Jamaica were introduced to work the banana plantations in N, where English is now widely spoken. Majority of the people are R.C. The coast of Honduras was visited (1502) by Columbus on his 4th voyage. In early colonial days the region became part of captaincy general of Guatemala, which included most of Central America. Gained (1821) independence from Spain. Was briefly included in Iturbide's Mexican Empire, and 1823–38 a member of Central American Federation, of which the Honduran patriot Francisco Morazán was president (1830–38). Thereafter bloody wars were fought to control Honduras. The Bay Isls. were transferred (1859) from Great Britain, who had long controlled the Mosquito Coast. William Walker attempted a "liberation" in 1860. In 1933 the boundary with Guatemala was finally fixed. For further information see separate articles on towns, cities, physical features, and the following 17 depts.: ATLÁNTIDA, BAY ISLANDS, COLÓN, COMAYAGUA, COPÁN, CORTÉS, CHOLUTECA, EL PARAÍSO, FRANCISCO MORAZÁN, INTIBUCÁ, LA PAZ, LEMPIRA, OCTEPEQUE, OLANCHO. SANTA BÁRBARA, VALLE, YORO.

Honduras, British: see BRITISH HONDURAS.

Honduras, Cape, or **Punta Castilla** (pōōn'tä kästē'yä), northernmost point of Honduras mainland, on Caribbean Sea, 7 mi. NNW of Trujillo; 16°1'N 86°2'W. Site of Puerto Castilla.

Honduras, Gulf of, or **Bay of Honduras,** wide inlet of Caribbean Sea on coasts of Honduras, Guatemala, and Br. Honduras; mostly bet. 16° and 18°N, 86° and 88°W. Includes Bay of Amatique. Receives Motagua R. It contains the cays of Br. Honduras (N) and the Bay Isls. of Honduras (E).

Honea Path (hŭ'nēū păth", hŭ'nē), town (pop. 2,840 Anderson and Abbeville counties, NW S.C., 16 mi. ESE of Anderson; cotton and synthetic textiles, clothing, cottonseed oil.

Honecohe (hôn'koi'), village, Khanhhoa prov., S central Vietnam, minor port on Bengoi Bay of South China Sea, 22 mi. N of Nhatrang; salines. Serves Ninhhoa (8 mi. SW). Also spelled Honkhoi.

Honefoss (hû'nûfôs), Nor. *Hønefoss*, city (pop. 3,554), Buskerud co., SE Norway, center of Ringerike region, on Begna R. at mouth of short Rand R., and 25 mi. NW of Oslo; rail center; paper milling, woodworking, brewing, food packing; mfg. of truck and bus bodies. Falls in center of town power hydroelectric plant.

Honeoye (hŭ'nēoi"), resort village, Ontario co., W central N.Y., at N end of Honeoye L., 27 mi. S of Rochester.

Honeoye Creek, N.Y.: see HONEOYE LAKE.

Honeoye Falls, resort village (pop. 1,460), Monroe co., W N.Y., on Honeoye Creek and 15 mi. S of Rochester; mfg. (butter and other dairy products, textiles, electrical machinery, truck bodies); agr. (grain, potatoes). Inc. 1838. Honeoye village is 12 mi. S, on Honeoye L.

Honeoye Lake, Ontario co., W central N.Y., one of the Finger Lakes, W of Canandaigua L. and 25 mi. S of Rochester; 4 mi. long, up to ¾ mi. wide; resorts. Drained by Honeoye Creek, which flows c.35 mi. NW and W, past Honeoye Falls, to Genesee R. 5 mi. N of Avon.

Honesdale (hōnz'dāl), borough (pop. 5,662), ⊙ Wayne co., NE Pa., 24 mi. ENE of Scranton and on Lackawaxen R.; shoes, textiles. First trial run of a locomotive in U.S. made here (1829). Settled 1803, inc. 1831. Was W terminus of Delaware and Hudson Canal.

Honey (ōnā'), town (pop. 811), Puebla, central Mexico, in Sierra Madre Oriental, on Hidalgo border, 12 mi. WNW of Huauchinango; rail terminus; iron mining.

Honeybrook, borough (pop. 864), Chester co., SE Pa., 22 mi. E of Lancaster; candy; rock quarries.

Honey Grove, city (pop. 2,340), Fannin co., NE Texas, 21 mi. WSW of Paris; shipping, processing center for dairy, cotton, poultry, truck area; machine-shop products, cement blocks. Near by is large game and reforestation preserve. Inc. 1872.

Honey Island, village (1940 pop. 610), Hardin co., E Texas, 30 mi. NW of Beaumont, in agr. area.

Honey Island Swamp, La.: see PEARL RIVER.

Honey Lake (c.12 mi. wide; intermittently dry bed), Lassen co., NE Calif., at E base of the Sierra Nevada, near Nev. line; alt. 3,949 ft. Receives Susan R. Its valley has irrigated agr.

Honey Springs, town (1940 pop. 342), Dallas co., N Texas, S suburb of Dallas.

Honeyville, town (pop. 599), Box Elder co., N Utah, 10 mi. NNW of Brigham; alt. 5,269 ft.; agr.

Honfleur (õflûr'), town (pop. 7,783), Calvados dept., NW France, seaport on S shore of Seine R. estuary on English Channel, 7 mi. SE of Le Havre; processes imported coal and hardwoods; exports cider, dairy produce, fruits (chiefly to England). Boatbuilding. Has 15th-cent. wooden church, mus. of ethnography and Norman art, and a picturesque small harbor (begun 1668 by order of Louis XIV). Important center of navigation and exploration in 16th and 17th cent.

Hong (hûng), Dan. *Høng*, town (pop. 1,458), Holbaek amt, W Zealand, Denmark, 22 mi. SW of Holbaek; machinery mfg.

Honga, village, Md.: see HOOPER ISLANDS.

Hongal, India: see BAILHONGAL.

Honga River (hŏng'gù), E Md., wide arm of Chesapeake Bay, bet. Hooper Isls. (W) and the Eastern Shore (E), in Dorchester co.; c.15 mi. long.

Hongay (hôn'gī'), town, Quangyen prov., N Vietnam, in Tonkin, on Along Bay at entrance to Port Courbet (inlet), 80 mi. E of Hanoi. Extensive open-cast anthracite mines, coal distributing and exporting center; coke-, briquette- and coal-treating plant. Fisheries. Sometimes called Port Courbet.

Höngen (hûng'ùn), village (pop. 9,393), in former Prussian Rhine Prov., W Germany, after 1945 in North Rhine-Westphalia, 8 mi. NE of Aachen; coal mining.

Honghai Bay (hông'hī'), Mandarin *Hunghai* (hŏŏng'-hī'), shallow inlet of S.China Sea, in Kwangtung prov., China, 10 mi. SW of Hoifung; 25 mi. wide, 10 mi. long. Exposed to winds. Port of Swabue on E shore.

Hongkew (hŏng'kyōō', hông–), NE industrial section of Shanghai, China, on Whangpoo R., in former U.S. concession of International Settlement.

Hong Kong (hŏng'kŏng', hông'kông'), Chinese Mandarin *Hsiang-chiang* (shyäng'jyäng') or *Hsiang kang* (shyäng' gäng'), British crown colony (□ 391; 1931 pop. 849,751; 1949 pop. estimate 1,850,000; almost entirely Chinese) in S China, adjoining Kwangtung prov., 40 mi. E of Macao, across Canton (Pearl) R. estuary, 90 mi. SE of Canton (linked by railroad); ⊙ Hong Kong (Victoria). Situated bet. 22°9'–22°35'N and 113°50'–114°30'E, the colony of Hong Kong consists of a British-owned section (Hong Kong isl. and the KOWLOON peninsula), and a leased section known as the NEW TERRITORIES. Hong Kong isl. (□ 32; 1949 pop. estimate 950,000) is an irregular, indented isl., 11 mi. long, 2–5 mi. wide, rising in broken, abrupt peaks to 1,823 ft. in Mt. Victoria. It is separated (N) from Kowloon peninsula of Chinese mainland by 1-mi.-wide strait constituting spacious Hong Kong harbor, one of the best deepwater anchorages in the world. The subtropical climate of Hong Kong is governed by the monsoons: the cool, dry, NE monsoon (Oct.–April), and the hot, humid, SW monsoon (May–Sept.) that is occasionally accompanied by typhoons. Mean annual rainfall is 85 inches, ¾ of which fall during the summer. Unlike the intensive agr. of the New Territories, there is little land suitable for tillage on Hong Kong isl. Granite is quarried, there is some fishing along the coast, and a ranch and dairy farm supplies the isl. pop. On N shore of Hong Kong isl., on strait (ferry service) separating it from Kowloon, is the city of Victoria (1949 pop. estimate 880,000), commonly known as Hong Kong, the urban center and administrative seat of the colony. Extending over 5 mi. along the harbor, Victoria presents a picturesque appearance as it stretches from reclaimed shoreland up the hillsides of Victoria Peak. The seat of the Univ. of Hong Kong (1912), the city has cotton mills, machinery plants, and a naval dockyard. It is, however, primarily an administrative and management center (hq. of numerous large banks and corporations). With its great natural harbor, Hong Kong is the principal deepwater port and distributing center for S China, with the overseas docks situated on the Kowloon side. Its all-important transit trade with China consists of coal, cotton and cotton goods, iron and steel, sent to the mainland; and hides, nuts, oils, sugar, silk, tea, tin, and tungsten, shipped from the mainland. Local trade is carried on by river steamers and junks within the Canton R. delta. In addition to its premier shipping position, Hong Kong is a leading international air hub (airport at Kaitak) on trunk routes from Britain and the U.S. to the Far East. The colony is administered by an appointed governor with the aid of executive and legislative councils. Formerly a desolate isl. inhabited by fishermen, Hong Kong was occupied in 1841 by the British for the purpose of creating a trade center free from Chinese control. The cession was confirmed in 1842 by the Treaty of Nanking. The Kowloon peninsula and adjacent isls. were added in 1860 to the crown colony; and in 1898 the New Territories were leased to Britain for 99 years. Hong Kong's phenomenal development began in 1851 with the discovery of gold in Australia and the ensuing Chinese emigration. Such factors as the opening of China to foreign trade and the building of the Suez Canal also contributed to Hong Kong's growing prosperity. The outbreak of the Sino-Japanese War brought 500,000 refugees from China. Hong Kong itself was captured in 1941 after a brief campaign and remained under Jap. rule until 1945. After the war, it failed to regain fully its former importance in trade, although the advent (1949) of Chinese Communist control on the mainland, which caused another great pop. influx, made Hong Kong the main clearing house bet. China and the West.

Hongo (hōng-gō'). **1** Town (pop. 2,395), Aichi prefecture, central Honshu, Japan, 31 mi. ENE of Okazaki; lumbering. **2** Town (pop. 3,911), Fukushima prefecture, N central Honshu, Japan, 3 mi. SW of Wakamatsu; rice, silk cocoons, pottery. **3** Town (pop. 4,066), Hiroshima prefecture, SW Honshu, Japan, 30 mi. E of Hiroshima; sake, soy sauce, rice, charcoal, persimmons.

Hongsong (hông'sŭng'), Jap. *Kojo*, town (1949 pop. 17,314), S. Chungchong prov., S Korea, 40 mi. N of Kunsan; rice, soybeans, cotton, tobacco; lumber.

Hongu (hōng-gōō'), resort village (pop. 1,045), Wakayama prefecture, S Honshu, Japan, on S Kii Peninsula, on Kumano R. and 15 mi. NW of Shingu; citrus fruit, raw silk; lumber.

Hongwon (hông'wŭn'), Jap. *Kogen*, town (1944 pop. 25,663), S.Hamgyong prov., N Korea, on E.Korea Bay, 22 mi. NE of Hungnam; fishing center; chemicals.

Hönheim, France: see HOENHEIM.

Honiara (hōnēä'rä), coast town, NW Guadalcanal, Solomon Isls., SW Pacific; ⊙ Br. protectorate.

Honister Crag, mountain (1,750 ft.), SW Cumberland, England, 8 mi. SW of Keswick. Slate.

Honiton (hŭ'nĭtŭn, hŏ'–), municipal borough (1931 pop. 3,008; 1951 census 4,614), E Devon, England, on Otter R. and 15 mi. ENE of Exeter; agr. market in farming and dairying region; well-known lace-mfg. center. The 14th-cent. St. Margaret's almshouse was formerly a leper hosp. Parish church founded 1482.

Honjo (hōnjō'). **1** Town (pop. 18,251), Akita prefecture, N Honshu, Japan, on Sea of Japan, 23 mi. SSW of Akita; collection center for lumber, rice; sake brewing. **2** Town (pop. 12,190), Miyazaki prefecture, E Kyushu, Japan, 7 mi. NW of Miyazaki; agr. center (rice, wheat, sweet potatoes); livestock. **3** Town (pop. 23,011), Saitama prefecture, central Honshu, Japan, 12 mi. SE of Maebashi, in agr. area (rice, wheat); raw-silk center.

Honkhoi, Vietnam: see HONECOHE.

Honley, former urban district (1931 pop. 4,611), West Riding, SW Yorkshire, England, 3 mi. S of Huddersfield; woolen and silk milling; textile-machinery works. Inc. 1938 in Holmfirth.

Honmura, Japan: see NII-JIMA.

Honnali (hŏnä'lē), town (pop. 4,645), Shimoga dist., NW Mysore, India, on Tungabhadra R. and 21 mi. N of Shimoga; rice milling; handicraft wickerwork. Granite quarrying near by.

Honnedaga Lake (hŏnùdä'gù, –dō'gù), Herkimer co., N central N.Y., in the Adirondacks, 35 mi. NE of Utica; c.4 mi. long; fishing.

Honnef (hô'nĕf), town (pop. 13,610), in former Prussian Rhine Prov., W Germany, after 1945 in North Rhine-Westphalia, on right bank of the Rhine (landing) and 9 mi. SE of Bonn; resort with alkaline salt spring. Has late-Gothic church.

Hönningen (hû'nĭng-ùn), village (pop. 4,287), in former Prussian Rhine Prov., W Germany, after 1945 in Rhineland-Palatinate, on right bank of the Rhine and 9 mi. NW of Neuwied; carbonic-acid processing.

Honningsvag (hôn'nĭngsvôg), Nor. *Honningsvåg*, village (pop. 1,124) in Kjelvik canton (pop. 3,528), on SE Mageroy, Finnmark co., N Norway, on Porsang Fjord of Barents Sea, 55 mi. ENE of Hammerfest; fishing center.

Honno (hōn-nō'), town (pop. 5,337), Chiba prefecture, central Honshu, Japan, on central Chiba Peninsula, 4 mi. N of Mobara; rice, raw silk, poultry.

Hono (hûn'û"), Swedish *Hönö*, fishing village (pop. 2,425), Goteborg och Bohus co., SW Sweden, on isl. (□ 2) of Hono in the Kattegat, 10 mi. W of Goteborg.

Honokaa (hō'nōkä'), village (pop. 1,022), NE Hawaii, T.H., 35 mi. NW of Hilo, on elevated coast; sugar mill; macadamia nuts.

Honokahua (hō'nōkähōō'ä), village (pop. 477), N Maui, T.H.; taro, cattle.

Honolulu (hŏ'nŭlōō'lŭ, hō'nō–, –lōō), city (pop. 248,034), ⊙ Territory of Hawaii, on SE shore of OAHU; 21°18'N 157°51'W. With Palmyra, it constitutes Honolulu co. (□ 603; pop. 347,529), and is chief port of HAWAIIAN ISLANDS, with steamship and airplane service to U.S., Orient, Australasia; port of entry. It is in a narrow plain between the sea and Koolau Range; Nuuanu Pali connects city with windward part of the isl. Seat of Univ. of Hawaii (1907), Bishop Mus. (1889), Acad. of Arts (1926), Punahou Acad. (1841), Lunalilo Home for Aged, Queen's Hosp., and Kamehameha Schools. Largest parks are Moana and Kapiolani. PUNCHBOWL is heavily populated. A beach and Fort De Russy are at Waikiki. Iolani Palace is Territorial capitol, with statue of Kamehameha I near by. Chief industrial establishments: sugar refineries, pineapple canneries, ironworks; chief exports: sugar, fruits, coffee. Tourist trade is important.

Honomu (hŏ'nùmōō'), coast village (pop. 600), E Hawaii, T.H., 10 mi. N of Hilo; grows sugar cane.

Honor, village (pop. 269), Benzie co., NW Mich., 22 mi. SW of Traverse City, near Platte L.

Honquan (hŭn'kwän), town, Thudaumot prov., S Vietnam, on Saigon-Locninh RR and 60 mi. N of Saigon, near Cambodia line: sawmilling center; rubber and citronella plantations.

Honrubia (ōnrōō'vyä), town (pop. 2,012), Cuenca prov., E central Spain, 32 mi. SSW of Cuenca; saffron- and grain-growing center.

Honsater (hûns'ĕ'tûr), Swedish *Hönsäter*, village (pop. 778), Skaraborg co., S Sweden, on E shore of L. Vaner, 14 mi. WSW of Mariestad; grain.

Honshu (hŏn′shōō, Jap. hō′shōō), largest and principal island (□ c.88,000; including offshore isls.: □ 88,745; 1940 pop. 55,993,219; 1947 pop. 58,769,968) of Japan, bet. Sea of Japan (W) and the Pacific (E); separated from Hokkaido (N) by Tsugaru Strait, from Kyushu (SW) by Shimonoseki Strait, and from Shikoku (S) by Inland Sea; 33°57′–41°33′N 130°56′–140°35′E. Long, curved, and narrow; c.800 mi. long, c.30–150 mi. wide; broadest in central portion. Structurally, Honshu is divided into 2 regions by the Fossa Magna, a great depressed zone cutting across central Honshu from the Pacific to Sea of Japan. Along this zone runs a volcanic chain, rising to 12,389 ft. at Fujiyama (highest peak of Japan). Just W of the Fossa Magna is a group of peaks (c.10,000 ft. high) sometimes called Japanese Alps. Highest of the many active volcanoes is Mt. Asama. Hot springs occur in all parts of the isl.; most important in central area. Most of the rivers are short and swift, feeding numerous small hydroelectric plants. Only a very few of the larger rivers are navigable, and none (including the Shinano, largest on isl.) has a drainage basin of any size. L. Biwa, a fresh-water lake in S, is largest in Japan. There are several lagoons; largest is on E coast. Because of predominantly mountainous terrain, there is a limited amount of arable land. The few lowland regions, mostly in coastal areas, are densely populated. Major centers are all located in lowlands: TOKYO (⊙ Japan) and YOKOHAMA (principal port for foreign trade) are on KWANTO plain, the largest in Japan; OSAKA, KYOTO, and KOBE are in lowlands comprising the Kinki dist.; and NAGOYA, NIIGATA, and SENDAI (only large city in N) are also located on plains. Mean annual temp. ranges from 48°F. in N to 59°F. in S. There is great regional diversity in climatic conditions. N Honshu (sometimes called the Tohoku or Ou dist.) represents a transitional zone bet. cold Hokkaido and temperate and subtropical areas further S. Partly influenced by Okhotsk Current chilling its shores, the winter temperatures in N are frequently below freezing and there is a snow cover throughout the winter months. Central Honshu has a temperate climate, with warm Japan Current bringing mild winters to E coastal areas; in the Tokyo area temp. range is 37°–75°F. In contrast to the foggy and cool W coast, the Pacific side is warm and sunny. Summer months are particularly hot and uncomfortable in landlocked region around the Inland Sea. Mean annual rainfall is 44 in. in N, 66 in. in SW, with particularly heavy rainfall (80–100 in.) on W coast bordering Sea of Japan. Wet monsoon season (*baiu*) occurs in summer; typhoons striking Honshu in Sept. and Oct. bring torrential rains which often cause serious floods. Humidity is generally high in all parts of isl. Earthquakes occur frequently, especially in the Fujiyama section and in regions bordering on Sea of Japan and W section of Inland Sea. Isl. has a wealth of valuable forests: in S and SW are camphor trees, oaks, and black pines (*Pinus thunbergii*); on rest of isl. are cedars, hemlocks, beeches (almost extinct), horse chestnuts, cypresses, firs, and Korean pines (*Pinus koraiensis*). Characteristic flowers are wisteria, camellias, cherry and plum blossoms, azaleas, peonies, chrysanthemums, and lotus. The rich fauna is closely related to that of the Asian continent. Animals include antelope, deer, wild boars, bears, foxes, badgers, squirrels, and monkeys; among the birds are pheasants, herons, hawks, and crows (the most common). The cold Okhotsk and warm Japan currents washing both shores of the isl. provide the habitat for diverse species of fish; off E coast, around Chiba Peninsula, is a mingling of subarctic and subtropical fish. Commercially important fish are bonitos, cod, tuna, sardines, and herring. Pop., primarily engaged in agriculture, is thickly clustered along fertile coastal areas. N Honshu is sparsely settled because of difficult climate and relatively infertile soil. Rice is principal crop in all parts of isl. Other important grains are wheat, rye, barley, oats, and millet. Cotton, sweet potatoes, and citrus fruit are grown only in S and SW, and tea primarily in Shizuoka prefecture in central area. Mulberry trees are grown mostly in the interior where irrigation is not possible; raw silk is produced everywhere except in N. In central and S Honshu, there is a variety of agr. products including peppermint, soybeans, tobacco, giant radishes (*daikon*), and fruit (persimmons, pears, grapes, peaches); AOMORI prefecture in N is principal apple-growing region. Honshu's mineral resources are varied but largely inadequate for industrial needs of the isl. The Joban field N of Tokyo is principal producer of coal, mostly bituminous and of poor quality; there are minor fields in extreme SW. Oil fields are in N, paralleling W coast; some iron is mined also in N. There are small scattered mines producing copper, lead, zinc, and silver. Shipbuilding, metallurgical, chemical, and textile industries are important. There are 3 great industrial areas: Osaka-Kobe region (the Kinki dist.); Tokyo-Yokohama belt on Kwanto plain, and Nagoya. Chief handicraft center is Kyoto. Principal ports are Yokohama, Osaka, Kobe, SHIMONOSEKI (opposite Moji on Kyushu, and guarding W entrance to Inland Sea), and Aomori (in extreme N); only important port on the Sea of Japan is Niigata. Honshu is divided into 34 prefectures; most important are TOKYO, OSAKA, KYOTO, YAMAGUCHI, NARA, AICHI, MIYAGI, NIIGATA, and HIROSHIMA. Sometimes spelled Honshiu and Honsyu; formerly sometimes called Hondo.

Hont, Netherlands: see WESTERN SCHELDT.

Hontalbilla (ōntälvē′lyä), town (pop. 1,134), Segovia prov., central Spain, 28 mi. N of Segovia; cereals, grapes, chicory, resins.

Hontanaya (ōntänī′ä), town (pop. 1,125), Cuenca prov., E central Spain, 45 mi. ESE of Aranjuez; cereals, olives, anise, vegetables, timber, livestock; apiculture. Limestone quarrying.

Honto, Russian SFSR: see NEVELSK.

Hontoria del Pinar (ōntō′ryä dhĕl pēnär′), town (pop. 1,049), Burgos prov., N Spain, on Burgos-Soria RR, on highway, and 37 mi. W of Soria; cereals, vegetables, livestock, timber, naval stores. Flour milling, sawmilling. Iron and coal deposits.

Hoo (hōō), town and parish (pop. 2,120), N Kent, England, on Medway R. and 4 mi. NNE of Chatham; agr. market, with brickworks. Just S, in Medway R., is extensive salt marsh.

Hood, county (□ 426; pop. 5,287), N central Texas; ⊙ Granbury. Drained by Brazos R. Agr. (mainly peanuts; also corn, grains, hay, fruit, truck, pecans); livestock (cattle, goats, sheep, hogs); dairying; wool, mohair marketed. Formed 1866.

Hood, Fort, Texas: see KILLEEN.

Hood, Mount (11,245 ft.), N Oregon, highest point in state, in Cascade Range 45 mi. ESE of Portland. Snow-capped volcanic cone (last activity in mid-19th cent.) with large glaciers. Mt. Hood Recreational Area here. Skiing facilities. Ascended by aerial tramway c.3 mi. long.

Hood Bay, SE Alaska, inlet (13 mi. long, 5 mi. wide at mouth) of Chatham Strait, on W coast of Admiralty Isl., just S of Angoon. Hood Bay or Killisnoo fishing village (pop. 31) is on N shore.

Hood Canal, W Wash., narrow, curved W arm of PUGET SOUND, extending from entrance on Admiralty Inlet c.75 mi. along E side of Olympic Peninsula.

Hood Island, Galápagos: see ESPAÑOLA ISLAND.

Hood River, county (□ 529; pop. 12,740), N Oregon; ⊙ Hood River. Mt. HOOD (highest point in state) is in Cascade Range here. Columbia R. forms N boundary. Agr., particularly fruit growing in irrigated Hood R. valley; also wheat, truck; dairying, lumbering. Formed 1908.

Hood River, city (pop. 3,701), ⊙ Hood River co., N Oregon, on Columbia R. (here forming Wash. line) at mouth of Hood R. and c.55 mi. ENE of Portland. Trade, packing, shipping center for irrigated orchards (pears, apples, cherries), truck and dairy farms of Hood R. valley, stretching to base of Mt. Hood, 25 mi. S, whose glaciers feed the river. Has agr. experiment station of Oregon State Col. Settled 1854, inc. 1895. Annual music festival.

Hoofddorp-Haarlemmermeer, Netherlands: see HAARLEMMERMEER.

Hooge (hō′gů), North Sea island (□ 2.6; pop. 204) of North Frisian group, NW Germany, in Hallig Isls., 14 mi. off Schleswig-Holstein coast; grazing.

Hoogeveen (hō′khůvān), town (pop. 9,059), Drenthe prov., NE central Netherlands, 12 mi. E of Meppel; egg market; mfg. (aluminumware, concrete, wooden shoes), food canning, vegetable and rose growing, cattle raising, dairying, peat production. A fen colony dating from 17th cent.

Hoogezand (hō′khůzänt), town (pop. 3,040), Groningen prov., N Netherlands, on the Winschoter Diep and 9 mi. ESE of Groningen; mfg. (machinery, potato flour, strawboard, auto and cycle tires), dairying.

Hooghly (hōō′glē), district (□ 1,209; pop. 1,416,013), S central West Bengal, India; ⊙ Chinsura. Bounded E by Hooghly R.; drained by Damodar and Rupnarayan rivers. Swampy alluvial tract, rising in NW; rice, jute, potatoes, pulse, sugar cane. Highly industrialized section in area W of Hooghly R.; jute milling (center at Champdani), rice and cotton milling; chemical and glass mfg., jute pressing at Konnagar. Hooghly Col. at Chinsura; large annual mela near Serampore. Satgaon for 1500 years was mercantile ⊙ lower Bengal. Oldest Moslem bldgs. in Bengal near Hooghly. Former Eur. settlements include Hooghly (Portuguese), Serampore (Danish), Chinsura (Dutch), and Chandernagore (French). Also spelled Hugli.

Hooghly, town (pop., including CHINSURA, 49,081), Hooghly dist., S central West Bengal, India, on Hooghly R. and 18 mi. N of Calcutta city center, in heavy industrial area; rice milling. Has Moslem imambara with 277-ft.-long façade. Founded 1537 by Portuguese following decline of Satgaon; scene (1632) of Port. slaughter by Shah Jehan. First English factory founded 1651; abandoned 1690 for Calcutta. Sacked 1742 by Mahrattas. Also spelled Hugli. Rubber-goods mfg. 2 mi. N, at Sahaganj. Tomb and mosque ruins (oldest Moslem bldgs. in Bengal) 5 mi. N, at Tribeni.

Hooghly River, an arm of the Ganges, West Bengal, India, formed by junction of BHAGIRATHI RIVER and Jalangi R. at Nabadwip, where the Bhagirathi becomes known as the Hooghly; flows c.160 mi. S, through heavily industrialized area, past Hooghly, Naihati, Bhatpara, Chandernagore, Barrackpore, Serampore, Bally, Howrah, Calcutta, Garden Reach, Budge-Budge, Diamond Harbour, and Sagar Isl., to Bay of Bengal, forming estuary mouth 3–20 mi. wide. W boundary of Ganges Delta. Navigable by large ocean liners to Calcutta, although difficult to navigate because of sandbars and a strong tidal bore; difference in depth bet. wet and dry seasons, 20′11″. Spanned by pontoon bridge bet. Howrah and Calcutta, by Willingdon Bridge bet. Bally and Baranagar. Also spelled Hugli. Main tributaries: Damodar, Rupnarayan, and Kasai rivers. Lighthouse on Sagar Isl., another 13 mi. ENE of Contai.

Hoogkarspel (hōkh-kär′spůl), village (pop. 1,886), North Holland prov., NW Netherlands, 7 mi. NE of Hoorn; dairy farming.

Hoogkerk-Vierverlaten, Netherlands: see VIERVERLATEN.

Hooglede (hōkh′lādů), agr. village (pop. 4,477), West Flanders prov., W Belgium, 3 mi. NW of Roulers. Scene of Austrian defeat (1794) by French.

Hoogstraeten, Belgium: see HOOGSTRATEN.

Hoogstraten (hōkh′strätůn), agr. village (pop. 3,926), Antwerp prov., N Belgium, near Netherlands border, 20 mi. NE of Antwerp. Has 16th-cent. Gothic, 17th-cent. baroque churches. Formerly spelled Hoogstraeten.

Hook, town in parish of Hook with Warsash (pop. 1,310), NE Hampshire, England, 6 mi. E of Basingstoke; agr. market, with farm-implement works. Has late-Norman church.

Hooker, county (□ 722; pop. 1,061), central Nebr.; ⊙ Mullen. Agr. area drained by Middle Loup and Dismal rivers. Livestock, grain. Formed 1889.

Hooker, city (pop. 1,842), Texas co., extreme NW Okla., on high plains of the Panhandle, 20 mi. NE of Guymon; shipping and trading point in wheat-growing area; natural gas. Inc. 1907.

Hooker, Mount, Wyo.: see WIND RIVER RANGE.

Hooker Island, in S Franz Josef Land, Russian SFSR, in Arctic Ocean; 20 mi. long, 15 mi. wide; rises to 1,483 ft.; 80°15′N 53°E. Govt. observation station on Tikhaya Bay of NW coast. Discovered 1880 by Br. explorer Leigh Smith.

Hookers Point, village (pop. 1,411, with adjacent Harlem), Hendry co., S Fla. There is also a Hookers Point in Hillsborough co., W Fla., near Tampa.

Hookerton (hōō′kûrtůn), town (pop. 253), Greene co., E central N.C., 11 mi. N of Kinston, in agr. area.

Hook Head or **Hook Point,** cape, SW Co. Wexford, Ireland, at entrance to Waterford Harbour, 12 mi. SE of Waterford; lighthouse (52°7′N 6°56′W).

Hook Mountain Park, N.Y.: see NYACK.

Hook Norton, agr. village and parish (pop. 1,153), W Oxfordshire, England, 8 mi. SW of Banbury. Church dates from Norman times.

Hook of Holland, Du. *Hoek van Holland* (hōōk′ fän hô′länt), town (pop. 2,536) and port, South Holland prov., SW Netherlands, at North Sea end of the New Waterway, 10 mi. SW of The Hague; terminus of cross-channel boats from Harwich (England); port for Westland agr. area. Exports fruit, vegetables, eggs, herrings; pottery mfg., meat-packing plant.

Hook Point, Ireland: see HOOK HEAD.

Hooks, town (pop. 2,319), Bowie co., NE Texas, 15 mi. W of Texarkana, in agr. area. Inc. after 1940.

Hooksett (hōōk′sĭt), town (pop. 2,792), Merrimack co., S N.H., at falls of the Merrimack, bet. Concord and Manchester. Seat of Mt. St. Mary Col. Inc. 1822.

Hooksiel (hōk′zēl), fishing village (commune pop. 5,592), in Oldenburg, NW Germany, after 1945 in Lower Saxony, in East Friesland, on North Sea, 8 mi. NNW of Wilhelmshaven. Commune is called Minsen (mĭn′zůn) after a village 6 mi. NNW.

Hookstown, borough (pop. 247), Beaver co., W Pa., 5 mi. ESE of East Liverpool, Ohio.

Hoole (hōōl), residential urban district (1931 pop. 5,889; 1951 census 9,054), W Cheshire, England, 2 mi. NE of Chester; agr. market for dairying and cheese-mfg. region.

Hoolehua (hō′ōlāhōō′ä), village (pop. 974), W central Molokai, T.H.; pineapples.

Hoonah (hōō′nů), village (pop. 558), SE Alaska, on N shore of Chichagof Isl., on Icy Strait 40 mi. WSW of Juneau; fishing, fish processing, lumbering, fur farming. School. Harbor is called Port Frederick.

Hoopa (hōō′pů), village (pop. c.150), Humboldt co., NW Calif., on a tributary of Klamath R. and 30 mi. NE of Eureka; hq. Hoopa Indian Reservation.

Hooper. 1 Town (pop. 103), Alamosa co., S Colo., in San Luis Valley, 20 mi. N of Alamosa; alt. 7,500 ft. **2** Village (pop. 859), Dodge co., E Nebr., 12 mi. N of Fremont and on Elkhorn R.; cement products; grain, livestock, poultry and dairy produce. **3** Village, Broome co., N.Y.: see ENDWELL.

Hooper Bald, N.C.: see UNICOI MOUNTAINS.

Hooper Bay, Eskimo village (pop. 295), W Alaska, on Hooper Bay (15 mi. long) of Bering Sea, 4 mi. ESE of Point Dall; 61°33′N 165°48′W. R.C. mission, school.

Hooper Islands, E Md., 3 low marshy islands extending c.12 mi. N–S in Chesapeake Bay, N of Hooper Strait; separated from mainland by Honga R.; bridged to mainland (N). Bridges connect N and middle isls. Fisheries (fish, crabs, oysters); seafood packing houses, vegetable canneries. Excellent sport fishing, duck and goose hunting. Villages are Honga (hŏng'gŭ) and Fishing Creek (1940 pop. 544; ships seafood), on N isl.; Hoopersville (seafood shipping) on middle isl. Lower isl. is uninhabited hunting grounds.

Hooper Strait, E Md., narrow channel of Chesapeake Bay, bet. Bloodsworth Isl. (S) and Dorchester co. shore and Hooper Isls. (N).

Hoopersville, Md.: see HOOPER ISLANDS.

Hoopeston (hōōp'stŭn), city (pop. 5,992), Vermilion co., E Ill., 23 mi. N of Danville; canning center (corn, beans); mfg. of canning machinery, castings; agr. (vegetables, livestock, poultry; dairy products). Platted 1871, inc. 1877.

Hoople, village (pop. 447), Walsh co., NE N.Dak., 13 mi. NW of Grafton and on branch of Park R.; ships potatoes.

Hooppole (hōōp'pōl″), village (pop. 195), Henry co., NW Ill., 30 mi. E of Moline, in agr. and bituminous-coal area.

Hoor (hû'ûr″), Swedish *Höör,* town (pop. 1,963), Malmohus co., S Sweden, 20 mi. NE of Lund; agr. market (grain, potatoes, stock).

Hoorn (hōrn), city (pop. 13,711), North Holland prov., NW Netherlands, on the Ijsselmeer and 13 mi. E of Alkmaar; rail junction; center of vegetable and dairy-farming area. Founded 1311, it was medieval ⊙ West Friesland. Was port for Amsterdam until construction of North Sea Canal. Birthplace of Willem Schouten (1580–1625), 1st to circumnavigate Cape Horn, which he named after his birthplace. Abel Janszoon Tasman also b. here.

Hoorn, Cape, Chile: see HORN, CAPE.

Hoorn Islands, Fr. *Îles Horn,* island group (pop. 2,005), WALLIS AND FUTUNA ISLANDS protectorate, SW Pacific, 120 mi. SW of Wallis Islands; 14°15'S 178°5'W; comprises 2 volcanic isls. (FUTUNA and uninhabited ALOFI) and some coral islets. Also called Futuna Isls.

Hoosac Range (hōō'sŭk), in SW Vt. and NW Mass., S continuation of GREEN MOUNTAINS of Vt.; N–S range lying mainly E of Hoosic R., in N Berkshire co., Mass.; rises to c.3,000 ft. Sometimes considered part of BERKSHIRE HILLS region. E of North Adams, range is pierced E–W by Hoosac Tunnel.

Hoosac Tunnel, village in FLORIDA town, Berkshire co., NW Mass., 6 mi. E of North Adams, at E end of Hoosac Tunnel (c.25,000 ft. long; completed 1873), which carries railroad under Hoosac Range.

Hoosick Falls (hōō'sĭk, –zĭk), industrial village (pop. 4,297), Rensselaer co., E N.Y., on Hoosic R. (water power from falls), near Vt. line, and 27 mi. NE of Albany, in dairying area; mfg. (knitwear, electrical equipment, machinery, paper products). Bennington Battlefield Park is NE. Small lakes (resorts) are near by. Inc. 1827.

Hoosic River, in Mass. and N.Y., rises in Hoosac Range in NW Mass., flows c.70 mi. N, NW, and W, past Adams, North Adams, and Williamstown, Mass., across SW corner of Vt., and past Hoosick Falls, N.Y. (water power), to the Hudson c.14 mi. above Troy.

Hoosier Pass (hōō'zhûr) (11,541 ft.), central Colo., in Rocky Mts., bet. Park and Summit counties. Crossed by highway. Mt. Lincoln is near by.

Hoover Dam, in Black Canyon, on Colorado R., at Nev.-Ariz. line, and 25 mi. SE of Las Vegas, Nev. Authorized 1928, begun 1931, dedicated 1935, completed 1936. Called Hoover Dam (1930), changed to Boulder Dam (1933), renamed Hoover Dam (1947). It is 727 ft. high, 1,282 ft. long; constructed by Bureau of Reclamation. Dam is key unit of projects on Colorado R. Is used for flood control, irrigation (see IMPERIAL VALLEY), and hydroelectric power (supplied to Los Angeles and areas in Ariz. and Nev.). L. MEAD is formed by the dam. BOULDER CITY, Nev., was built to house workers on the project. A recreational area surrounds project.

Hooversville, borough (pop. 1,240), Somerset co., SW Pa., on Stony Creek and 10 mi. S of Johnstown. Inc. 1896.

Hop (hōp), village in Fana canton, Hordaland co., SW Norway, 4 mi. S of Bergen; knitting mill.

Hopa (hôpä'), village (pop. 3,508), Coruh prov., NE Turkey, port on Black Sea, 27 mi. NW of Artvin, 20 mi. SSW of Batum, USSR; manganese, lead.

Hopatcong (hōpăt'kŏn, –kŏng), borough (pop. 1,173), Sussex co., N N.J., 10 mi. SE of Newton and on **Lake Hopatcong** (c.7 mi. long), in hilly region NW of Dover; largest lake entirely in N.J. Resorts include Landing, Mt. Arlington, Lake Hopatcong.

Hop Bottom, borough (pop. 375), Susquehanna co., NE Pa., 11 mi. SSE of Montrose; summer resort.

Hope, village (pop. 56), S Alaska, on N shore of Kenai Peninsula, on Turnagain Arm, 23 mi. SSE of Anchorage, on highway from Seward; gold mining. Scene (1896) of gold rush.

Hope, village (pop. 515), SW B.C., on Fraser R., at mouth of Coquihalla R., and 27 mi. NE of Chilliwack, in mining (gold, silver) and lumbering region.

Hope, agr. village and parish (pop. 730), N Derby, England, just E of Castleton, in The Peak; cementworks. Has 14th-cent. church and remains of 10th-cent. Saxon cross. Near by, site of excavation of a Roman settlement.

Hope or **Hope Gardens,** agr. station, St. Andrew parish, SE Jamaica, on Hope R. and 3 mi. NE of Kingston; comprises Jamaica School of Agr., research laboratories, and botanical gardens. Also a tourist site. Was once part of large Hope sugar estate, which prospered in 18th cent. Bought by govt. in 1913.

Hope. 1 City (pop. 8,605), ⊙ Hempstead co., SW Ark., 30 mi. ENE of Texarkana; commercial and shipping center for farm products, especially watermelons. Cotton processing; mfg. of wood products, baskets, bricks, insecticides. State univ. agr. experiment station is near by. Settled 1874, inc. 1875. **2** Village (pop. 111), Bonner co., N Idaho, on E shore of Pend Oreille L., 14 mi. E of Sandpoint. **3** Town (pop. 1,215), Bartholomew co., S central Ind., 39 mi. SSE of Indianapolis, in agr. area (truck, grain); lumber milling. **4** City (pop. 480), Dickinson co., central Kansas, 28 mi. ESE of Salina, in grain, livestock, and poultry area; dairy products. **5** Town (pop. 504), Knox co., S Maine, 10 mi. NNW of Rockland, in agr., resort region; wood products, canned foods. **6** Village (pop. c.300) in Hope township (pop. 681), Warren co., NW N.J., on small Beaver Brook, near Jenny Jump Mtn. and 8 mi. NW of Hackettstown; hosiery, canned fruits and vegetables, dairy products. Has 18th-cent. buildings, including stone mill built 1768 by Moravian settlers. **7** Town (pop. 186), Eddy co., SE N.Mex., on branch of Pecos R. and 40 mi. NW of Carlsbad; corn, cotton, alfalfa. **8** City (pop. 470), Steele co., E N.Dak., 14 mi. SSE of Finley; dairy products, grain, potatoes. **9** Village, Providence co., R.I.: see SCITUATE.

Hope, town and parish (pop. 4,128), Flint, Wales, on Alyn R. and 8 mi. SW of Flint; coal mining. Just SSW is town of Caergwrle (kĭrgōōr'lā), with colliery equipment works.

Hope, Mount, R.I.: see BRISTOL, town.

Hope, Point, headland, NW Alaska, on Chukchi Sea; 68°20'N 166°45'W. Site of Point Hope village.

Hope Bay, town (pop. 1,240), Portland parish, NE Jamaica, on the coast, on railroad and 7 mi. W of Port Antonio, in fruitgrowing region (bananas, coconuts, cacao).

Hopedale, village (pop. 167), E Labrador, on the Atlantic; 55°28'N 60°12'W; fishing port and seaplane anchorage.

Hopedale. 1 Village (pop. 574), Tazewell co., central Ill., 14 mi. SE of Pekin, in agr. and bituminous-coal area. **2** Town (pop. 3,479), including Hopedale village (pop. 2,797), Worcester co., S Mass., 17 mi. SE of Worcester; textiles. Once a Christian communistic community (1841–c.1857); later developed as textile "company town." Settled 1660, inc. 1886. **3** Village (pop. 888), Harrison co., E Ohio, 6 mi. NE of Cadiz, in coal-mining area.

Hopefield, town (pop. 1,512), SW Cape Prov., U. of So. Afr., near Great Berg R., 35 mi. NW of Malmesbury; grain-growing center.

Hope Fountain, village, Bulawayo prov., SW Southern Rhodesia, in Matabeleland, 10 mi. SSE of Bulawayo; tobacco, corn, dairy products.

Hope Gardens, Jamaica: see HOPE.

Hopeh or **Hopei** (hō'pā', Chinese hŭ'bā') [Chinese, =N of the (Yellow) river], northernmost province (□ 50,000; pop. 27,000,000) of China proper; ⊙ Paoting. Situated on Gulf of Chihli of Yellow Sea, Hopeh is bounded N along the Great Wall by the Manchurian provs. of Liaosi and Jehol, NW by Chahar (in part also along the Great Wall), W by Shansi, S by Pingyuan (which separates it from the Yellow R.), and SE by Shantung. Hopeh lies entirely on the alluvial, level N China plain, bounded W and NW by the Shansi and Inner Mongolian plateaus. Its unimportant streams (Lwan, Pai, Yungting, and Huto rivers) are connected N to S by the Grand Canal. The continental climate is marked by hot summers, with monsoon rains in July and Aug., and cold winters, in which rivers freeze about mid-Nov. Dust storms frequently blow (March–June) from the deserts (NW) before the rains come. Agr., limited to one crop a year, is widely diversified: winter wheat, barley, and beans are sown in the winter; kaoliang and millet, in the spring; and corn, soybeans, sweet potatoes, peanuts, and sesame, in the summer. Hopeh ranks 2d in China's coal production (2d only to Liaotung), with the leading mines in the Kailan dist. (Tangshan, Kaiping, Lwanhsien), and at Lincheng, Tsingsing, and Mentowkow. Gold is mined along Jehol line (N) and iron near Tangshan. The leading cities are: Peking, the political and cultural center of China; Tientsin, N China's main port and industrial center; Chinwangtao, port for the Kailan coal mines; Shanhaikwan, a traditional gateway to Manchuria; and the modern rail center of Shihkiachwang. Hopeh is well supplied with rail lines; river navigation is negligible. Pop. is homogeneously Chinese, speaking N Mandarin dialect. One of the earliest regions of Chinese settlement, the prov. was originally called Chi, for the early name of Peking. It was 1st protected (300 B.C.) by a Great Wall against inroads from the N. The name Hopeh was 1st used in the Tang dynasty (A.D. 618–906). In 1421, when the Mings transferred their capital from Nanking to Peking, the prov. was named Chihli [Chinese, =directly ruled] or Pechili. The previous name was restored in 1928, when the natl. capital returned to Nanking. During Sino-Japanese War, Hopeh was held (1937–45) by the Japanese, who had begun in 1933 to exert pressure upon the prov. from Manchuria. Communist control became complete in 1949.

Hopelawn, N.J.: see WOODBRIDGE.

Hopelchén (ōpĕlchĕn'), town (pop. 1,089), Campeche, SE Mexico, on Yucatan Peninsula, 45 mi. E of Campeche; timber, sugar, chicle, fruit, henequen.

Hopeless Reach, Australia: see SHARK BAY.

Hopeman, fishing village, N Moray, Scotland, on Moray Firth, 2 mi. ENE of Burghead.

Hope Mills, town (pop. 1,077), Cumberland co., S central N.C., 7 mi. SSW of Fayetteville; mfg. of cotton yarn.

Hopen (hō'pŭn), island (□ 23) of the Norwegian possession Svalbard, in Barents Sea of Arctic Ocean, SE of Spitsbergen group; 76°35'N 25°30'E. Isl. is 20 mi. long (SW-NE), 1 mi. wide; rises to 1,198 ft. Site of meteorological radio station. Pop. in winter 1948–49 was 4.

Hope River, St. Andrew parish, SE Jamaica, flows c.15 mi. S, entering the Caribbean 5 mi. ESE of Kingston. Used for water supply of Kingston and suburbs.

Hopes Advance, Cape, N Que., on Hudson Strait, on W side of entrance of Ungava Bay; 61°2'N 69°30'W.

Hopetoun, small port, S Western Australia, on Indian Ocean and 230 mi. SSW of Kalgoorlie; head of railroad to Ravensthorpe; wheat. Exports gold.

Hope Town, town (pop. 214), N Bahama Isls., on cay just off E central Great Abaco Isl., 115 mi. NNE of Nassau; 26°32'N 76°58'W. Fishing and trading. Lighthouse.

Hopetown, town (pop. 2,342), E central Cape Prov., U. of So. Afr., on Orange R. (bridge) and 75 mi. SW of Kimberley; diamond mining, stock raising, dairying. Salt pans in region. Airfield. First diamonds in South Africa discovered here 1867.

Hope Valley, village (1940 pop. 907) in Hopkinton town, Washington co., SW R.I., on Wood R. (bridged here) and 11 mi. NNE of Westerly, in agr. area; mfg. (cotton fabrics, woolens, fish line, wood products). Prudence Crandall b. here.

Hopeville, town (1940 pop. 92), Clarke co., S Iowa, 13 mi. WSW of Osceola.

Hopewell, village (pop. estimate 350), NE N.S., 8 mi. SSW of New Glasgow; dairying, farming.

Hopewell, town (pop. 1,570), Hanover parish, NW Jamaica, on coast, 6 mi. W of Montego Bay; rice, bananas, yams.

Hopewell. 1 Borough (pop. 1,869), Mercer co., W N.J., 11 mi. N of Trenton, in agr. region (poultry, truck, dairy products); mfg. (metal products, jewelry, canned goods). Has Baptist Church (1748); monument (1865) to John Hart, who lived here; historical mus. Home for juvenile delinquents, here, is former Lindbergh estate deeded (1941) to state. Settled before 1700, inc. 1891. **2** Borough (pop. 360), Bedford co., S Pa., 15 mi. NE of Bedford and on Raystown Branch of Juniata R. **3** City (pop. 10,219), in but independent of Prince George co., E Va., on James R., at Appomattox R. mouth, and 7 mi. NE of Petersburg. Founded 1913 as munitions center; now produces rayon, chemicals, cans, paper. City Point (freight-steamer wharves), settled 1613, was annexed 1923; Grant had his base of operations here, 1864–65. Inc. 1916. **4** Residential and industrial suburb (pop. 1,159), Marion co., N W.Va., just E of Fairmont; glass mfg.

Hopewell Cape, village (district pop. 1,122), ⊙ Albert co., SE N.B., at head of Shepody Bay, at mouth of Petitcodiac R., and 19 mi. SE of Moncton; lumbering.

Hopewell Village National Historic Site (848 acres; established 1938), SE Pa., just SE of Birdsboro. Iron-making village of 18th and 19th cent., active from c.1770 to 1883; includes parts of old cold-blast iron furnace and associated structures, Bird manor house (1744), and other old buildings (some restored).

Hopin (hō'pĭn), village, Myitkyina dist., Kachin State, Upper Burma, on railroad and 65 mi. SW of Myitkyina.

Hoping or **Ho-p'ing** (hŭ'pĭng', hō'–, Cantonese wô'-pĭng'), town (pop. 4,341), ⊙ Hoping co. (pop. 161,216), NE Kwangtung prov., China, at S foot of Kiulien Mts., 30 mi. ENE of Linping, near Kiangsi prov. border; rice, beans. Tungsten mining near by.

Hôpital, L' (lōpētäl'), Ger. *Spittel* (shpĭ'tŭl), town (pop. 5,060), Moselle dept., NE France, on Saar border, 8 mi. WSW of Forbach, at N edge of Forest of Saint-Avold; coal mines.

Hôpitaux-Neufs, Les (lāz ōpētō-nûf'), village (pop. 202), Doubs dept., E France, near Swiss border, 9 mi. S of Pontarlier, in the E Jura; alt. 3,248 ft. Winter-sports resort. Sawmilling.

Hopkins. 1 County (□ 555; pop. 38,815), W Ky.; ⊙ Madisonville. Bounded E by Pond R., W by

Tradewater R. Rolling agr. area (livestock, grain, burley tobacco, dairy products, poultry, fruit); important bituminous-coal mines; oil wells, hardwood timber; some mfg. Includes Dawson Springs State Park and part of Pennyrile State Forest. Formed 1806. **2** County (□ 793; pop. 23,490), NE Texas; ⊙ Sulphur Springs. Bounded N by South Fork of Sulphur R.; drained by White Oak Bayou. Prairies in W; hilly in E. Dairying (a leading Texas co.); agr. (cotton, corn, peanuts, grains, sweet potatoes, fruit, truck); poultry, hogs, sheep, cattle; lumbering. Oil wells; clay mining. Mfg., farm-products processing at Sulphur Springs. Formed 1846.

Hopkins. 1 Village (pop. 531), Allegan co., SW Mich., 8 mi. NNE of Allegan, in farm area. **2** Village (pop. 7,595), SW suburb of Minneapolis, Hennepin co., E Minn., in truck-farming area; berries, vegetables, ice cream. Makes agr. equipment. Co. fair takes place here. Settled c.1850. **3** City (pop. 825), Nodaway co., NW Mo., near One Hundred and Two R., 14 mi. N of Maryville; grain, livestock.

Hopkins Landing, village, SW B.C., on Thornbrough Channel of Howe Sound, 20 mi. NW of Vancouver; lumber-shipping port.

Hopkins River, S Victoria, Australia, rises in Great Dividing Range SW of Ararat, flows 135 mi. S, past Allansford, to Indian Ocean just E of Warrnambool.

Hopkinsville, city (pop. 12,526), ⊙ Christian co., SW Ky., 60 mi. W of Bowling Green, in tobacco region. Important dark-tobacco and livestock market; mfg. of clothing; wood, cement, and limestone products, dairy products, packed meat, soft drinks, fertilizer, snuff; flour and feed mills; airport. Coal mines, gas wells, hardwood timber, and stone quarries are near by. Seat of Bethel Woman's Col. and Western State Hosp. At Fairview (E) is Jefferson Davis Memorial Park. U.S. Fort Campbell (formerly Camp Campbell) and Campbell Air Force Base are 17 mi. S. Inc. 1804.

Hopkinton. 1 Town (pop. 731), Delaware co., E Iowa, on Maquoketa R. and 31 mi. WSW of Dubuque; lumber and feed mills, creamery. **2** Rural town (pop. 3,486), including Hopkinton village (pop. 1,829), Middlesex co., E central Mass., 26 mi. WSW of Boston; cotton thread. Settled c.1715, inc. 1744. **3** Town (pop. 1,831), Merrimack co., S N.H., just W of Concord; agr., machinery, wood products. Legislature met here occasionally, 1798–1807. Congregational church (1789) has Revere bell; Long Memorial Library has N.H. Antiquarian Society collection. Settled 1736, inc. 1765. Contoocook village (kŭntōō'kŭk), on Contoocook R., is business center of town. **4** Town (pop. 3,676), Washington co., SW R.I., 30 mi. SSW of Providence, in agr. area; mfg. (textiles, yarn, twine, wood products). Includes villages of ASHAWAY, Canonchet, HOPE VALLEY, Hopkinton, and ROCKVILLE, and part of POTTER HILL village. Set off from Westerly and inc. 1757.

Hopland, village (pop. c.600), Mendocino co., NW Calif., in Russian R. valley, 13 mi. S of Ukiah; hops.

Hopong (hō'pông), central state (myosaship) (□ 212; pop. 11,617), Southern Shan State, Upper Burma; ⊙ Hopong, village on Thazi-Kengtung road, 10 mi. E of Taunggyi, at head of road (S) to Loikaw.

Hoppenhof, Latvia: see APE.

Hoppo (hăp'pō'), Mandarin *Ho-p'u* (hŭ'pōō'), town (pop. 67,173), ⊙ Hoppo co. (pop. 609,146), SW Kwangtung prov., China, port in Lim R. delta on Gulf of Tonkin, 85 mi. WNW of Chankiang; pearl-fishing center; sugar cane, rice, vegetable oil. Iron mining near by. Opened to foreign trade in 1877; later superseded by Pakhoi. Until 1912 called Limchow or Lienchow.

Hoppo, Formosa: see PEIPU.

Hop River, village, Conn.: see COLUMBIA.

Hop River, E central Conn., small stream formed by several branches near Andover, flows c.15 mi. SE and E to Willimantic R. just NW of Willimantic. Site of Andover Dam (for flood control) is 8 mi. W of Willimantic.

Hopton, England: see MIRFIELD.

Ho-p'u, China: see HOPPO.

Hopwood, village (pop. 1,099), Fayette co., SW Pa., 2 mi. SE of Uniontown; coal, coke. Founded 1791.

Hoquiam (hō'kwĭm, hō'kwēŭm), city (pop. 11,123), Grays Harbor co., W Wash., on Grays Harbor adjoining Aberdeen, at mouth of Hoquiam R.; cellulose, lumber, fish, agr., dairy products. Indian Agency hq. for local reservations. Settled 1859, inc. 1890.

Hor, Jordan: see HARUN, JEBEL.

Hora Abyata (hō'rä ä'byätä), saline lake (□ c.90), S central Ethiopia, in Great Rift Valley, bet. lakes Zwai and Shala, and parallel to L. Langana (2 mi. E), 90 mi. S of Addis Ababa; 7°40'N 38°35'E; alt. 5,161 ft.; 12 mi. long, 11 mi. wide. Receives (N) outlet of L. Zwai. During flood periods receives waters of L. Langana and overflows (SW) into L. Shala.

Horace. 1 City (pop. 258), Greeley co., W Kansas, just W of Tribune, in agr. and cattle area. **2** Village (pop. 190), Cass co., E N.Dak., 10 mi. SW of Fargo.

Horahora (hô'rŭhô"rŭ), village (pop. 368), N central N.Isl., New Zealand, 20 mi. SE of Hamilton and on Waikato R.; hydroelectric plant.

Horaidha, Aden: see HUREIDHA.

Hor al Hammar, Iraq: see HAMMAR, HOR AL.

Horana (hō'rŭnŭ), town (pop. 3,654), Western Prov., Ceylon, 20 mi. SSE of Colombo; extensive rubber, rice, coconut-palm, cinnamon, and jack-tree plantations; vegetables. Anc. Buddhist monastery and temple near by.

Horaschdowitz, Czechoslovakia: see HORAZDOVICE.

Hora Svateho Sebestiana (hô'rä svä'tĕhô shĕ'bĕs-tyĕä"nä), Czech *Hora Svatého Šebestiána,* Ger. *Sebastianberg* (zäbä'styänbĕrk"), village (pop. 242), NW Bohemia, Czechoslovakia, in the Erzgebirge, on railroad and 17 mi. W of Most; peat extraction.

Hora Svate Kateriny (svä'tä kä'tĕrzhĭnĭ), Czech *Hora Svaté Kateřiny,* Ger. *Katharinaberg* (kätärē'-näbĕrk), village (pop. 373), NW Bohemia, Czechoslovakia, in the Erzgebirge, 10 mi. NW of Most, near Ger. border; old mining settlement.

Horatio, town (pop. 776), Sevier co., SW Ark., 7 mi. S of De Queen, near Little R.; distribution, shipping point for farm area (fruit, vegetables).

Horazdovice (hô'räzhdô"vĭtsĕ), Czech *Horažďovice,* Ger. *Horaschdowitz,* town (pop. 2,747), S Bohemia, Czechoslovakia, on Otava R., on railroad and 10 mi. NW of Strakonice; mfg. of knitgoods (hosiery, gloves). Pearl oysters bred in river.

Horb or **Horb am Neckar** (hôrp' äm nĕ'kär), town (pop. 2,920), S Württemberg, Germany, after 1945 in Württemberg-Hohenzollern, in Black Forest, on the Neckar and 12.5 mi. E of Freudenstadt; rail junction; textile mfg. Has Gothic church.

Horbourg (ôrbōōr'), Ger. *Horburg* (hôr'bōōrk), village (pop. 1,022), Haut-Rhin dept., E France, on the Ill and 2 mi. E of Colmar; biscuit mfg., vegetable (especially asparagus) shipping and preserving. Damaged in Second World War.

Horbury, urban district (1931 pop. 7,791; 1951 census 7,966), West Riding, S central Yorkshire, England, on Calder R. and 3 mi. SW of Wakefield; woolen milling and printing, coal mining, mfg. of leather goods.

Horby (hûr'bü"), Swedish *Hörby,* town (pop. 2,789), Malmohus co., S Sweden, near Ring L., 20 mi. ENE of Lund; agr. market (grain, potatoes, stock); light industries. Site of radio station.

Horcajada, La (lä ôrkähä'dhä), town (pop. 1,802), Ávila prov., central Spain, 40 mi. WSW of Ávila; cereals, vegetables, livestock; flour milling.

Horcajo de las Torres (ôrkä'hō dhä läs tō'rĕs), town (pop. 1,265), Ávila prov., central Spain, 30 mi. E of Salamanca; wheat, rye, barley, carobs, grapes, livestock; flour milling.

Horcajo de los Montes (dhä lōs mōn'tĕs), town (pop. 1,335), Ciudad Real prov., S central Spain, 45 mi. NW of Ciudad Real; cereals, cork, honey, livestock; apiculture. Lumbering, olive-oil extracting. Lead and silver mining.

Horcajo de Santiago (säntyä'gō), town (pop. 3,068), Cuenca prov., E central Spain, 34 mi. ESE of Aranjuez; agr. center (grapes, saffron, cereals, anise, olives, cumin, livestock). Alcohol distilling, tartaric-acid mfg., flour milling, cheese making. Hydroelectric plant.

Horcasitas or **San Miguel de Horcasitas** (sän mēgĕl' dā ôrkäsē'täs), town (pop. 715), Sonora, NW Mexico, on San Miguel R. and 33 mi. NE of Hermosillo; corn, wheat, beans, fruit, livestock.

Horche (ôr'chā), town (pop. 1,714), Guadalajara prov., central Spain, 7 mi. SE of Guadalajara; wheat, olives, livestock. Flour milling, olive-oil pressing; mfg. of soft drinks, soap, plaster.

Horconcitos (ôrkōnsē'tōs), village (pop. 875), Chiriquí prov., W Panama, near the Pacific, 20 mi. ESE of David; leatherworking center; livestock.

Horcones Valley (ōrkō'nĕs), NW Mendoza prov., Argentina, at S part of Aconcagua massif, near Chile border, along Horcones R., a headstream of Mendoza R.

Hordaland (hôr'dälän"), county [Nor. *fylke*] (□ 6,126; pop. 188,389), SW Norway; ⊙ BERGEN. Regionally it comprises 3 main areas: South Hordaland (Nor. *Sunnhordland,* formerly *Søndhordland*), which includes the area around mouth of Hardanger Fjord, as well as the isls. Bomlo, Stord, and Tysnesoy; and North Hordaland (Nor. *Nordhordland*), N of Bergen, comprising the coast and the isls. Askoy, Holsenoy, Radoy, and Fedje; and HARDANGER, around the inner Hardanger Fjord. Bedrock is cut by large igneous outcrops and Silurian formations running, like the Hardangerfjell, NE to SW. Mild climate, with very heavy precipitation. Agr. (rye, oats, potatoes; fruitgrowing). Industries at Bergen, ODDA, and in villages along the fjord. Active fishing (herring) along coast. Good road net in N part of co.; railroad Bergen-Oslo. Until 1918, co. (then called *amt*) was named Sondre Bergenhus or Sondre Bergenhuus.

Hörde (hûr'dŭ), industrial suburb (1925 pop. 34,694) of Dortmund, W Germany, adjoining (S) city center; steel plants. Coal mining. Inc. 1929 into Dortmund.

Hordio (hôrdē'ō), town (pop. 1,120), in the Mijirtein, N Ital. Somaliland, 100 mi. SSE of Alula, on Indian Ocean, on a bay enclosed by Hafun peninsula; extensive saltworks.

Hordle, agr. village and parish (pop. 1,642), SW Hampshire, England, 3 mi. W of Lymington. Extensive deposits of marine-fossil shells have been found here.

Hordnaes, Norway: see HORNNES.

Hords Creek Reservoir, central Texas, a unit of Colorado R. flood-control project, on Hords Creek (a tributary of Pecan Bayou) in Coleman co., W of Coleman; construction begun 1947. Planned capacity, c.49,000 acre-ft.; dam 91 ft. high, c.6,200 ft. long.

Hördt (hûrt'), village (pop. 2,033), Rhenish Palatinate, W Germany, near the Rhine, 10 mi. ESE of Landau; grain, tobacco, sugar beets.

Hordville, village (pop. 116), Hamilton co., SE central Nebr., 25 mi. NE of Grand Island and on Platte R.

Horeb, Mount (hō'rĕb), mountain mentioned in the Bible, perhaps Mt. SINAI.

Horezu (hôrăz'), village (pop. 1,257), Valcea prov., S central Rumania, in Walachia, 16 mi. WNW of Ramnicu-Valcea; shoe mfg., flour milling, lumbering. Sometimes spelled Hurezu. The 17th-cent. Horezu monastery, founded by Constantine Brancovan, and often visited by Carmen Sylva, is 2 mi. N. Near by are 15th-cent. Bistrita monastery, restored in 19th cent., and 17th-cent. church of former Arnota monastery.

Horfield, N industrial district (pop. 27,973), of Bristol, SW Gloucester, England.

Horgen (hôr'gŭn), town (1950 pop. 10,049), Zurich canton, N Switzerland, on L. of Zurich and 9 mi. SSE of Zurich; metalworking, textiles.

Horgheim (hôrg'hām), village in Grytten canton, More og Romsdal co., W Norway, on Rauma R., on railroad and 9 mi. SSE of Andalsnes; tourist center in the valley Romsdal.

Horgos (hôr'gōs'), Chinese *Hocheng* (hŭ'jŭng'), town, ⊙ Horgos co. (pop. 26,394), NW Sinkiang prov., China, 20 mi. E of Panfilov (USSR), 30 mi. WNW of Suiting; major highway crossing on Soviet border; livestock, wheat; carpets. Sometimes spelled Hoerhkwosze or Ho-erh-kuo-ssu.

Horgos or **Khorgosh** (both: hôr'gôsh), Serbo-Croatian *Horgoš,* village (pop. 7,615), Vojvodina, N Serbia, Yugoslavia, near Tisa R., 14 mi. E of Subotica, in the Backa, near Hung. border; rail junction.

Hori, Formosa: see PULI.

Horice (hôr'zhĭtsĕ), Czech *Hořice,* Ger. *Horschitz* (hôr'shĭts), town (pop. 6,794), NE Bohemia, Czechoslovakia, on railroad and 9 mi. SW of Dvur Kralove, in sugar-beet and potato region; mfg. (machinery, textiles); biscuits; fruit trade. Has large sculptors' and stone-cutters' school (sandstone quarries near by).

Horice na Sumave (nä' shōōmä"vyĕ), Czech *Hořice na Šumavě,* Ger. *Höritz* (hû'rĭts), village (pop. 468), S Bohemia, Czechoslovakia, in Bohemian Forest, on railroad and 7 mi. SW of Cesky Krumlov; summer resort noted for annual Passion Play performances.

Horicon (hŏ'rēkŏn). **1** Village, Warren co., N.Y.: see BRANT LAKE. **2** City (pop. 2,664), Dodge co., S central Wis., on Rock R. and 10 mi. E of Beaver Dam, in farm (dairy, livestock, poultry, grain) area; makes farm machinery, iron and steel products, canned foods, cheese. Inc. 1897.

Horigome, Japan: see SANO, Tochigi prefecture.

Horin, Formosa: see FENGLIN.

Horinkar, China: see HOLINKOERH.

Horinouchi (hōrēnō'chē). **1** Town (pop. 12,550), Niigata prefecture, central Honshu, Japan, 15 mi. SSE of Nagaoka; rice, silk cocoons; textiles. **2** Town (pop. 5,838), Shizuoka prefecture, central Honshu, Japan, 7 mi. SW of Shimada; rice, tea, livestock.

Höritz, Czechoslovakia: see HORICE NA SUMAVE.

Hork River, Sweden: see ARBOGA RIVER.

Horley, residential town and parish (pop. 7,749), SE Surrey, England, on Mole R. and 5 mi. SSE of Reigate; agr. market. Has 15th-cent. church and old inn.

Horme, L' (lôrm), town (pop. 3,198), Loire dept., SE central France, in the Jarez, on Gier R. and 8 mi. ENE of Saint-Étienne; coal mining, steel milling (naval armament), mfg. of precision tools.

Hormigas de Afuera Islands (ôrmē'gäs dā äfwā'rä), 2 small isls. 40 mi. off coast of W central Peru, W of Lima; 55°58'S 77°47'W; guano deposits.

Hormigueros (ôrmēgā'rōs), town (pop. 1,773), W Puerto Rico, 4 mi. S of Mayagüez, in sugar-growing region. Famed for its shrine of Our Lady of Montserrate. Mfg. of cigars. Eureka sugar mill is 1½ mi. SE on railroad.

Hormoz, Iran: see HORMUZ.

Hormuz (hôr'mŭz) or **Ormuz** (ôr'mŭz), Persian *Hormoz* (hōrmōz'), Persian Gulf island of SE Iran, in Strait of Hormuz, 10 mi. SE of Bandar Abbas; 5 mi. long, 3½ mi. wide. Ferrous-oxide (red ocher) and rock-salt mining. Hormuz village is on N shore. The name Hormuz (anc. *Harmozia*) referred originally to a mainland port, 20 mi. E of isl. at mouth of Minab R., visited 325 B.C. by Nearchus, admiral of Alexander the Great. The mainland Hormuz flourished under Arab rule (8th cent.) and was visited (13th cent.) by Marco Polo. In 14th cent. the center of trade was transferred to Hormuz isl., which had supremacy over Persian Gulf trade during next 2 centuries, having supplanted Qish. Hormuz isl. next fell to the Portuguese (1507–14), who were ousted in turn by combined Persian-English forces in 1622. Abbas the Great then returned the seat of trade to the mainland, founding BANDAR ABBAS.

Hormuz, Strait of, or **Strait of Ormuz,** channel connecting the Persian Gulf with the Gulf of Oman of Arabian Sea, and separating Iran and Arabia; 40–60 mi. wide. Of great strategic importance, it contains the isls. of Qishm, Hormuz, and Hangam.

Horn (hôrn), town (pop. 4,230), N Lower Austria, 17 mi. N of Krems; corn, vineyards. Has Gothic church.

Horn, town (pop. 4,389), in former Lippe, NW Germany, after 1945 in North Rhine-Westphalia, on N slope of Teutoburg Forest, 5 mi. SSE of Detmold; woodworking.

Horn, village (pop. 2,296), Limburg prov., SE Netherlands, 2.5 mi. WNW of Roermond; cattle raising, agr. Has 15th-cent. Horn Castle.

Horn, Cape, Sp. *Cabo de Hornos,* steep, rocky headland (alt. 1,391 ft.), the southernmost point of South America, on small Horn Isl. (5 mi. long), in Tierra del Fuego, Magallanes prov., Chile; 55°59'S 67°16'W. Discovered 1616 by the Du. navigator Schouten and named for Hoorn, Netherlands. FALSE CAPE HORN is 35 mi. NW.

Horn, the, Australia: see BUFFALO, MOUNT.

Hornachos (ôrnä'chōs), town (pop. 6,847), Badajoz prov., W Spain, in Sierra de Hornachos, 20 mi. ESE of Almendralejo; spa and agr. center (cereals, oranges, cork, olives, livestock).

Hornachos, Sierra de (syĕ'rä dhä), low W spur of the Sierra Morena, Badajoz prov., W Spain; extends c.25 mi. NW; rises to 1,870 ft.

Hornachuelos (ôrnäch-wä'lōs), town (pop. 4,031), Córdoba prov., S Spain, 27 mi. W of Córdoba; olive-oil processing. Agr. trade (cereals, cork, livestock); lumber.

Hornad River, Czechoslovakia and Hungary: see HERNAD RIVER.

Hornavan (hŏorn'ä"vän), lake (□ 97), an expansion (50 mi. long, 1–2 mi. wide) of Skellefte R., Lapland, N Sweden, 100 mi. W of Boden. Connects SE with L. Uddjaur.

Hornbach (hôrn'bäkh), town (pop. 1,153), Rhenish Palatinate, W Germany, on small Hornbach R. and 4 mi. S of Zweibrücken, on French border; grain. Has ruins of former Benedictine abbey, founded in 8th cent.

Hornbaek (hôrn'bĕk), town (pop. 1,405), Frederiksborg amt, Zealand, Denmark, on the Oresund and 12 mi. NNE of Hillerod; fisheries.

Hornbeak, town (pop. 309), Obion co., NW Tenn., 17 mi. SW of Union City.

Hornbeck, town (pop. 524), Vernon parish, W La., 56 mi. W of Alexandria, near Texas line; agr.; mfg. of wood products.

Hornberg (hôrn'bĕrk), village (pop. 3,103), S Baden, Germany, in Black Forest, 22 mi. SE of Offenburg; mfg. of ceramics, cotton, machinery, paper; metal- and woodworking, lumber milling. Climatic health resort (alt. 1,180 ft.).

Hornbostel (hôrn'bôs"tùl), village (pop. 1,012), in former Prussian prov. of Hanover, NW Germany, after 1945 in Lower Saxony, near the Aller, 10 mi. WNW of Celle, in oil dist.

Hornburg (hôrn'bŏŏrk), town (pop. 3,491), in Brunswick, NW Germany, after 1945 Lower Saxony, 9 mi. SSE of Wolfenbüttel; mfg. of chemicals; metal- and woodworking. Has many 16th-cent., half-timbered houses. Until 1941 in former Prussian Saxony prov.

Hornby Island (□ 11), SW B.C., in Strait of Georgia off Vancouver Isl., just E of Denman Isl. and 16 mi. SE of Courtenay; 6 mi. long, 4 mi. wide; fishing, lumbering.

Horncastle, urban district (1931 pop. 3,496; 1951 census 3,809), Parts of Lindsey, central Lincolnshire, England, on Bain R. and 18 mi. E of Lincoln; leather and agr.-machinery works; agr. market in fruitgrowing area. Scene of noted horse fair, described in George Borrow's *Romany Rye.* Has 13th-cent. church and remains of wall of the Roman station *Banovallum.*

Hornchurch, residential urban district (1931 pop. 28,417; 1951 census 104,128), SW Essex, England, 2 mi. ESE of Romford; machinery industry. Has 15th-cent. church.

Horndal (hôrn'däl"), village (pop. 1,643), Kopparberg co., central Sweden, on L. Ross, Swedish *Rossen* (rô'sùn), (3 mi. long), 12 mi. NE of Avesta, in iron-mining region; ironworks, sawmills.

Horneburg (hôr'nùbŏŏrk), village (pop. 3,334), in former Prussian prov. of Hanover, NW Germany, after 1945 in Lower Saxony, 7 mi. SSE of Stade; paper- and sawmilling.

Hornefors (hûr"nùfôrs', –fôsh'), Swedish *Hörnefors,* village (pop. 1,569), Vasterbotten co., N Sweden, on Gulf of Bothnia, 19 mi. SW of Umea; pulp mills, sulphite works. Has old church. Scene (1809) of battle bet. Swedes and Russians.

Hornelen, Norway: see BREMANGER.

Hornell (hôrnĕl'), city (pop. 15,049), Steuben co., S N.Y., on Canisteo R. and c.45 mi. WNW of Elmira; mfg. of textiles, clothing, furniture, wood and metal products; railroad shops. Agr. (truck, potatoes, wheat, fruit; dairy products). Settled 1789; inc. as village in 1852, as city in 1888. Grew mainly after coming of Erie RR (1850).

Hornepayne, village (pop. estimate 1,000), N central Ont., 200 mi. N of Sault Ste. Marie; alt. 1,074 ft.; gold mining, lumbering.

Hornersville, town (pop. 875), Dunklin co., extreme SE Mo., in Mississippi flood plain, 14 mi. S of Kennett.

Horne Srnie (hôr'nyā sŭr'nyĕ), Slovak *Horné Srnie,* Hung. *Felsőszernye* (fĕl'sûsĕrnyĕ), village (pop. 1,580), W Slovakia, Czechoslovakia, on railroad and 8 mi. NNE of Trencin; large cementworks.

Horn Head, promontory, N Co. Donegal, Ireland, 3 mi. N of Dunfanaghy; 53°14'N 7°59'W.

Horni Becva River, Czechoslovakia: see BECVA RIVER.

Horni Benesov (hôr'nyē bĕnĕshôf), Czech *Horní Benešov,* Ger. *Bennisch* (bĕ'nĭsh), village (pop. 1,530), central Silesia, Czechoslovakia, 30 mi. NNE of Olomouc; rail terminus in iron-mining area.

Horni Blatna (blät'nä), Czech *Horní Blatná,* Ger. *Platten* or *Bergstadt Platten* (bĕrk'shtät plä'tùn), town (pop. 766), W Bohemia, Czechoslovakia, in the Erzgebirge, on railroad and 5 mi. NNE of Nejdek, near Ger. border; iron mining. Sometimes called Blatna Horni.

Horni Briza (bûrzhē'zä), Czech *Horní Bříza,* village (pop. 1,694), W Bohemia, Czechoslovakia, on railroad and 7 mi. NNW of Pilsen; kaolin and fire-clay quarrying.

Hornick, town (pop. 310), Woodbury co., W Iowa, on West Fork Little Sioux R. and 25 mi. SE of Sioux City, in agr. area.

Horni Dvoriste (dvôr'zhĭshtyĕ), Czech *Horní Dvořiště,* village (pop. 747), S Bohemia, Czechoslovakia, 26 mi. S of Budweis; customs station on Austrian border.

Horni Litvinov, Czechoslovakia: see LITVINOV.

Hornillo, El (ĕl ôrnē'lyō), town (pop. 791), Ávila prov., central Spain, in the Sierra de Gredos, 35 mi. SW of Ávila; olives, grapes, beans, apricots, walnuts, livestock. Lumbering; flour milling, olive-oil pressing.

Hornindal Lake (hôr'nĭndäl), Nor. *Hornindalsvatn,* lake (□ 20; 16 mi. long) in Sogn og Fjordane co., W Norway, 50 mi. ENE of Floro; deepest lake (1,600 ft. deep) in Europe. Drains into Nord Fjord at Nordfjordeid. Hornindal village is on NE shore.

Horni Plana (hôr'nyē plä'nä), Czech *Horní Planá,* Ger. *Oberplan* (ō'bûrplän), town (pop. 805), S Bohemia, Czechoslovakia, in Bohemian Forest, near Austrian border, on Vltava R., on railroad and 25 mi. SW of Budweis; graphite mining; glass making; lumbering.

Horni Poustevna, Czechoslovakia: see DOLNI POUSTEVNA.

Hornisgrinde (hôr'nĭsgrĭn"dù), mountain (3,819 ft.) in the Black Forest, S Germany, 10 mi. S of Baden-Baden.

Horn Island (□ 19), in Torres Strait 20 mi. N (across Endeavour Strait) of Cape York Peninsula, N Queensland, Australia, near Prince of Wales Isl. Circular, 15 mi. in circumference; rises to 376 ft. Wooded, sandy; uninhabited.

Horn Island, Chile: see HORN, CAPE.

Horn Island (c.14 mi. long), SE Miss., one of isl. chain in the Gulf of Mexico, partly sheltering Mississippi Sound (N), 10 mi. S of Pascagoula; lighthouse (30°14'N 88°29'W). To E is deepwater channel (Horn Island Pass) leading from the Gulf to Pascagoula Bay.

Horni Slavkov (hôr'nyē släf'kôf), Czech *Horní Slavkov,* Ger. *Schlaggenwald* (shlä'gùnvält), village (pop. 1,493), W Bohemia, Czechoslovakia, on railroad and 20 mi. ENE of Cheb; porcelain mfg.

Hornitos (hôrnē'tùs), town (pop. 126), Mariposa co., central Calif., 18 mi. NE of Merced. Has bldgs. dating from gold rush days.

Hornnes (hôrn'nās), village and canton (pop. 1,400), Aust-Agder co., S Norway, on Otra R. and 30 mi. N of Kristiansand. Formerly spelled Hordnaes.

Hornopiren Volcano (ōrnōpē'rĕn), Andean peak (5,480 ft.) in Llanquihue prov., S central Chile, 40 mi. SE of Puerto Montt.

Hornos, Cabo de, Chile: see HORN, CAPE.

Hornos Islands (ôr'nōs), group of small rocky islets in the Río de la Plata, Colonia dept., SW Uruguay, 4 mi. NW of Colonia city, 25 mi. NE of Buenos Aires.

Hornoy (ôrnwä'), village (pop. 706), Somme dept., N France, 18 mi. WSW of Amiens; brick mfg.; livestock.

Horn Peak, Colo.: see SANGRE DE CRISTO MOUNTAINS.

Hornsberg (hôrns'bĕr"yù), village (pop. 4,015), Jamtland co., N central Sweden, on Froso isl. in Stor L., just W of Ostersund (bridge); tourist resort; dairying.

Hornsby, town (pop. 8,286), E New South Wales, 13 mi. NW of Sydney; coal-mining center; pottery, watches.

Hornsby, town (pop. 280), Hardeman co., SW Tenn., 30 mi. S of Jackson, in farm area; lumber.

Hornsea (hôrn'sē), urban district (1931 pop. 4,450; 1951 census 5,324), East Riding, SE Yorkshire, England, on North Sea 14 mi. NE of Hull; seaside resort. Has 14th-15th-cent. church, rebuilt by Sir Gilbert Scott. Just inland from the town is the lake Hornsea Mere.

Hornsey (hôrn'zē), residential municipal borough (1931 pop. 95,523; 1951 census 98,134), Middlesex, England, N suburb of London. In municipal borough are residential dists. of: HIGHGATE (W; pop. 13,479); Finsbury Park (SE; pop. 3,414); Muswell Hill (N; pop. 16,145); and Crouch End (S; pop. 7,279).

Hornslet (hôrns'lĕt), town (pop. 1,401), Randers amt, E Jutland, Denmark, 14 mi. SE of Randers; furniture, woodworking.

Hornstein (hôrn'shtīn), Hung. *Szarvkő* (sôrf'kû), village (pop. 2,466), Burgenland, E Austria, on W slope of Leitha Mts. and 4 mi. NW of Eisenstadt; sugar beets, vineyards.

Hornsundtind (hôrn'sŏŏntĭn"), mountain (4,692 ft.), S West Spitsbergen, Spitsbergen group, near S shore of Horn Sound (Nor. *Hornsund;* 15-mi.-long inlet of Arctic Ocean), 90 mi. S of Longyear City; 76°55'N 16°10'E. First climbed (1897) by Sir Martin Conway.

Hornu (ôrnü'), town (pop. 11,229), Hainaut prov., SW Belgium, 6 mi. WSW of Mons; coal mining.

Hörnum, Germany: see RANTUM-HÖRNUM.

Horobetsu (hōrōbā'tsōō), village (pop. 18,581), SW Hokkaido, Japan, 12 mi. NNE of Muroran, in mtn. area; principal hot-spring resort of isl. (hot springs area is called Noboribetsu). Hot Spring Research Inst. of Hokkaido Imperial Univ. here. Near by is extinct volcano Io-zan, where large quantities of sulphur have been mined since 1874.

Horochow, Ukrainian SSR: see GOROKHOV.

Horodenka, Ukrainian SSR: see GORODENKA.

Horodyszcze, Belorussian SSR: see GORODISHCHE, Baranovichi and Pinsk oblasts.

Horodziej, Belorussian SSR: see GORODEYA.

Horonai, Japan: see MIKASA.

Horonai-kawa, Russian SFSR: see PORONAI RIVER.

Hororata (hô'rŏŏrä'tù), township (pop. 251), ⊙ Selwyn co. (□ 954; pop. 1,466), E central S.Isl., New Zealand, 35 mi. W of Christchurch; agr.

Horoshiri-dake, Japan: see POROSHIRI-DAKE.

Horovice (hôr'zhôvĭtsĕ), Czech *Hořovice,* Ger. *Horschowitz* (hôr'shōvĭts), town (pop. 4,533), W central Bohemia, Czechoslovakia, on railroad and 29 mi. SW of Prague, in potato- and barley-growing dist.; iron foundries; mfg. of metal and wooden furniture, enamelware.

Horowhenua, New Zealand: see LEVIN.

Horps, Le (lù ôr'), village (pop. 238), Mayenne dept., W France, 10 mi. NE of Mayenne; horse raising.

Horqueta (ôrkā'tä), town (dist. pop. 14,171), Concepción dept., central Paraguay, 25 mi. E of Concepción (connected by rail line); cattle-raising and lumbering center; tanneries.

Horqueta, Cerro (sĕ'rō), peak (7,441 ft.) in continental divide of W Panama, 29 mi. N of David. Just W is Horqueta Pass, on road from David (in Pacific lowland) to Chiriquí Lagoon of the Caribbean.

Horra, La (lä ō'rä), town (pop. 1,383), Burgos prov., N Spain, 11 mi. WNW of Aranda de Duero; grain- and winegrowing.

Horrem (hô'rùm), village (pop. 5,303), in former Prussian Rhine Prov., W Germany, after 1945 in North Rhine-Westphalia, on the Erft and 10 mi. W of Cologne; rail junction.

Horry (ŏ'rē"), county (□ 1,152; pop. 59,820), E S.C.; ⊙ Conway. Bounded W by Little Pee Dee R., SE by the Atlantic, NE by N.C.; drained by Waccamaw R. Intracoastal Waterway canal passes near coast. Summer resort area; includes Myrtle Beach (state park here). Lumbering, agr. (especially tobacco; also melons, strawberries, truck, cotton, corn). Hunting and fishing attract tourists. Formed 1785 as Kingston, renamed 1801.

Hörsching (hûr'shĭng), town (pop. 3,982), central Upper Austria, 7 mi. SW of Linz; rye, potatoes.

Horschitz, Czechoslovakia: see HORICE.

Horschowitz, Czechoslovakia: see HOROVICE.

Horse Cave, town (pop. 1,545), Hart co., central Ky., 32 mi. ENE of Bowling Green. Tourist resort for Ky. limestone cave region and an E gateway to MAMMOTH CAVE NATIONAL PARK; agr. (livestock, dairy products, poultry, burley tobacco, corn, wheat); mfg. of cheese, processed tobacco, concrete products; flour and lumber mills. Hidden River Cave, with an underground river containing blind fish, is here.

Horse Creek, in SE Wyo. and W Nebr., rises in Laramie Mts. near Laramie, Wyo.; flows 136 mi. E, N, and E, past La Grange, to N.Platte R. near Morrill, Nebr., just E of Nebr. line. Dammed 6 mi. N of La Grange.

Horsefly Lake (28 mi. long, 1–2 mi. wide), S central B.C., in Cariboo Mts., 120 mi. SE of Prince George, S of Quesnel L. Drained W into Fraser R. by Quesnel R.

Horsehead Lake, Kidder co., central N.Dak., 50 mi. ENE of Bismarck; 6 mi. long.

Horseheads, village (pop. 3,606), Chemung co., S N.Y., 5 mi. N of Elmira; mfg. (brick, optical goods, metal and wood products, feed); sand, gravel pits. Agr. (dairy products; poultry, apples). Settled 1789, inc. 1837.

Horse Island, Scotland: see ARDROSSAN.

Horse Islands, N.F.: see SAINT BARBE ISLANDS.

Horseley Heath, England: see TIPTON.

Horse Mesa Dam (mā'sù), S central Ariz., on Salt R. and c.40 mi. ENE of Phoenix. Unit in Salt R. irrigation project; concrete arch dam (300 ft. high, 803 ft. long), completed 1927. Used for irrigation and power. Forms reservoir (17 mi. long) with capacity of 245,100 acre-ft.

Horseneck Beach, Mass.: see WESTPORT.

Horsens (hôr'sùns), city (1950 pop. 35,898), Skanderborg amt, E Jutland, Denmark, port on Horsens Fjord and 24 mi. SSW of Aarhus. Commercial, shipping, industrial center; rail junction; hydroelectric plant. Textile mills; mfg. (machinery, rubber, tobacco products), meat and dairy packing, fishing.

Horsens Fjord (c.13 mi. long), E Jutland, Denmark; inlet of the Kattegat. At mouth are Hjarno and Alro isls.; Horsens city at head.

Horse Shoe Bend, town (pop. 401), Boise co., W Idaho, 21 mi. N of Boise.

Horseshoe Lake, Alexander co., extreme S Ill., c.12 mi. NW of Cairo; c.7 mi. long. State game preserve; fishing.

Horseshoe Mountain, peak (13,902 ft.) in Rocky Mts., bet. Park and Lake counties, central Colo.

Horsforth (hôrs'fûrth), urban district (1931 pop. 11,776; 1951 census 14,105), West Riding, central Yorkshire, England, on Aire R. and 5 mi. NW of Leeds; woolen milling and printing, leather tanning; soapworks.

Horsham (hôr'shùm), municipality (pop. 6,388), W central Victoria, Australia, on Wimmera R. and 170 mi. WNW of Melbourne; rail and commercial center for wheat-raising area; flour mills. Longerenong Agr. Col. near by.

Horsham, urban district (1931 pop. 13,580; 1951 census 16,682), N Sussex, England, 18 mi. NNW of Brighton; agr. market, with mfg. of shoes, agr. machinery, chemicals, pharmaceuticals. Has 13th-cent. church. The Causeway, an old cobbled street, has several 16th–17th-cent. houses. Christ's Hosp., a public school, was moved to Horsham from London in 1902. Field Place, birthplace of Shelley, is in near-by Warnham parish.

Horsham, village (pop. 2,174), Montgomery co., SE Pa., 12 mi. NE of Norristown.

Horsham Saint Faith (hôr'shùm sùnt), agr. village in parish of Horsham St. Faith with Newton St. Faith (pop. 870), central Norfolk, England, 4 mi. N of Norwich; site of U.S. bomber station in Second World War. There are remains of 12th-cent. priory; church dates from 15th cent. Just N is agr. village of Newton St. Faith.

Horsovsky Tyn (hôr'sôfskē tĭn"), Czech *Horsovský Tyn*, Ger. *Bischofteinitz* (bĭ"shôftī'nĭts), town (pop. 2,393), SW Bohemia, Czechoslovakia, on Radbuza R., on railroad and 24 mi. SW of Pilsen, in woolen- and linen-spinning dist.; lumbering, glass mfg. (mirrors at Stankov). Zinc and strontium mining near by.

Horst (hôrst), village (pop. 4,906), in Schleswig-Holstein, NW Germany, 4 mi. NNW of Elmshorn; knitwear; food processing.

Horst, town (pop. 2,953), Limburg prov., E Netherlands, 8 mi. NW of Venlo; mfg. (lace, cigars, fur products), peat digging, poultry breeding.

Horstead, agr. village in parish of Horstead with Stanninghall (pop. 677), E central Norfolk, England, on Bure R. and 7 mi. NNE of Norwich; flour milling. Has 14th-cent. church, formerly a place of pilgrimage. Just S is agr. village of Stanninghall.

Hörstein (hûr'shtīn), village (pop. 1,917), Lower Franconia, NW Bavaria, Germany, 6 mi. NNW of Aschaffenburg; wine.

Horstmar (hôrst'mär), town (pop. 2,782), in former Prussian prov. of Westphalia, NW Germany, after 1945 in North Rhine-Westphalia, 5 mi. SSW of Burgsteinfurt; dairying.

Horst Wessel Stadt, Germany: see FRIEDRICHSHAIN.

Horta (ôr'tù), district (□ 295; pop. 52,731) of the Azores, covering FAIAL ISLAND, PICO ISLAND, FLORES ISLAND, CORVO ISLAND; ⊙ Horta (on Faial).

Horta, city (pop. 8,184), ⊙ Horta dist., central Azores, on SE shore of FAIAL ISLAND, facing Pico Isl. (5 mi. E) across Faial Channel, 75 mi. WSW of Angra do Heroísmo; 38°32'N 28°37'W. Has excellent harbor, with refueling and ship-repair yards; also junction of numerous submarine cables. Important seaplane base for trans-Atlantic flights. Has powerful naval radio transmitter. Exports cattle, dairy produce, salted fish, wine, oranges. Whaling industry yields sperm oil. Damaged by 1926 earthquake. Became an Allied naval and air base in Second World War.

Horta or **Horta de San Juan** (ôr'tä dhä sän' hwän'), town (pop. 1,739), Tarragona prov., NE Spain, 9 mi. SW of Gandesa; olive-oil processing, brandy distilling, flour milling; wheat, wine, almonds and other nuts.

Hortaleza (ôrtälā'thä), town (pop. 1,005), Madrid prov., central Spain, 4 mi. NNE of Madrid; cereals, grapes.

Horten (hôr'tùn), city (pop. 10,964), Vestfold co., SE Norway, port on W shore of Oslo Fjord, 35 mi. S of Oslo; 59°30'N 10°29'E. Terminus of rail spur. Together with Karljohansvern (kärl"yō'hänsvĕrn), just N, it forms Norway's chief naval base. Fortifications, shipyards; mfg. of naval munitions, aircraft assembling, brewing. Has naval col., officers' school and technical col., observatory, naval mus.

Hortensias, Chile: see LAS HORTENSIAS.

Hortobagy (hôr'tôbädyù), Hung. *Hortobágy*, section (□ 104) of the ALFÖLD, E Hungary, belonging to Debrecen. Characteristics of the *puszta* (pasturelands of the Alföld) are preserved here for tourist trade; large herds of cattle. In July or August a fata morgana is frequently visible. New irrigation development.

Hortobagy River, Hung. *Hortobágy*, E Hungary, rises 15 mi. WNW of Hajduböszörmeny; flows 70 mi. SE, draining the Hortobagy; joins Berettyo Canal 9 mi. E of Kisujszallas to form another, shorter, Berettyo R.

Horton, agr. village and parish (pop. 1,156), S Buckingham, England, 3 mi. E of Windsor. Residence of Milton for 6 years; his mother is buried here.

Horton. 1 City (pop. 2,354), Brown co., NE Kansas, c.40 mi. NNE of Topeka; trading point, with railroad repair shops, in grain, livestock, and fruit area; dairy products. Has agency hq. for Potawatomi Indian Reservation (SW). Small Mission L., just NE, is source of city's water supply Founded 1886, inc. 1887. **2** Village, Jackson co., S Mich., 9 mi. SW of Jackson, in farm and lake-resort area. **3** Resort village, Delaware co., S N.Y., in the Catskills, on Beaver Kill and c.50 mi. W of Kingston.

Hortonia, Lake, W Vt., in Sudbury town, 15 mi. NW of Rutland; c.2 mi. long; resort.

Horton Kirby, town and parish (pop. 2,086), NW Kent, England, on Darent R. and 4 mi. SSE of Dartford; paper milling. Has 13th-cent. church.

Horton Plains, tableland (alt. 7,000 ft.) in S Ceylon Hill Country, S central Ceylon; rise to 7,857 ft. in Kirigalpotta, to 7,741 ft. in Totapola peaks.

Horton River, N Mackenzie Dist., Northwest Territories, rises N of Great Bear L., flows c.275 mi. generally NW to Franklin Bay, arm of Amundsen Gulf.

Hortonville, village (pop. 1,081), Outagamie co., E Wis., 11 mi. NW of Appleton, in dairying and fruitgrowing area; canning.

Horvik (hûr"vēk'), Swedish *Hörvik*, fishing village (pop. 549), Blekinge co., S Sweden, on E shore of Listerland peninsula, on the Baltic, 6 mi. E of Solvesborg.

Horw (hôrf), town (pop. 3,553), Lucerne canton, central Switzerland, near L. of Lucerne, 2 mi. S of Lucerne; chemicals, cement; woodworking.

Horwich (hŏ'rĭj, –ĭch), urban district (1931 pop. 15,680; 1951 census 15,552), central Lancashire, England, 5 mi. WNW of Bolton; cotton milling, locomotive building, paper mfg. Site of Liverpool reservoir.

Horyniec (hôrĭn'yĕts), Rus. *Gorynets* (gôrē'nyĕts), village, Rzeszow prov., SE Poland, 12 mi. ENE of Lubaczow; health resort (sulphur springs); sawmilling.

Horyn River, European USSR: see GORYN RIVER.

Horyu (hōrū'), town (pop. 6,578), Ishikawa prefecture, central Honshu, Japan, on N Noto Peninsula, 15 mi. E of Wajima; rice, raw silk.

Horyuji (hōrū'jē), village (1940 pop. 2,663), Nara prefecture, S Honshu, Japan, 5 mi. SW of Nara; rice, wheat, raw silk. Site of Horyu-ji, oldest Buddhist temple in Japan, built in 7th cent., with grave of Jimmu, 1st emperor of Japan.

Hosadurga, India: see HOSDURGA.

Hosanagara (hō'sŭnŭgŭrŭ), town (pop. 1,372), Shimoga dist., NW Mysore, India, on Sharavati R. and 35 mi. W of Shimoga; rice, betel palms and vines; cinnamon-oil extracting, handicraft wickerwork. Called Kallurkotte until 1893, when it succeeded Nagar (7 mi. S) as a subdivisional administrative hq. of dist. Also spelled Hosanagar.

Hosanger (hō'sängùr), village and canton (pop. 2,722), Hordaland co., SW Norway, on NW shore of Osteroy, on Oster Fjord, 14 mi. NNE of Bergen; agr., cattle raising, fishing; lumber mills. Disused copper and nickel mines.

Hosanna, Ethiopia: see HOSSEINA.

Hoschton (hōōsh'tùn), agr. town (pop. 378), Jackson co., NE central Ga., 22 mi. WNW of Athens.

Hosdurga (hōs'dōōrgŭ), town (pop. 3,922), Chitaldrug dist., N central Mysore, India, 30 mi. SSW of Chitaldrug; coconuts, oilseeds; coir products (rope, sacks); hand-loom cotton and woolen weaving, handicraft cap making. Cattle grazing in NW hills (manganese deposits). Hosdurga Road, rail station, is 10 mi. WNW. Also spelled Hosadurga.

Hose, agr. village and parish (pop. 421), NE Leicester, England, 6 mi. N of Melton Mowbray; cheese. Has 15th-cent. church.

Hoseason Island (hōzā'ùsùn), Antarctica, off NW coast of Palmer Peninsula, in the South Pacific; 63°45'S 61°40'W; 7 naut. mi. long, 3 naut. mi. wide; rises to 1,900 ft.

Hosford, village (1940 pop. 654), Liberty co., NW Fla., 31 mi. W of Tallahassee; lumber milling.

Hosh or **El Hosh** (ĕl hōsh'), village, Blue Nile prov., E central Anglo-Egyptian Sudan, in the Gezira, near railroad and 20 mi. S of Wad Medani; cotton, wheat, barley, corn, fruits; livestock.

Hoshan, town, China: see HWOSHAN.

Ho Shan, mountains, China: see TAIYO MOUNTAINS.

Hoshang, China: see DURBULDJIN.

Hoshangabad (hōshŭng-gäbäd'), district (□ 5,858; pop. 837,942), NW Madhya Pradesh, India, on Deccan Plateau; ⊙ Hoshangabad. Bordered N by Narbada R. and Bhopal; mainly in level, fertile wheat tract of Narbada valley, with densely forested spurs of Satpura Range (S) and outliers of Vindhya Range (NW). Wheat, millet, cotton, oilseeds (chiefly sesame) in alluvial valley; mahua, date palms, mangoes; betel farms. Teak, sal, salai, bamboo, and khair on S hills; lac growing. Coal deposits S of Gadarwara; marble quarries near Narsinghpur. Flour, oilseed, and dal milling, cotton ginning, sawmilling, cutch processing; sandstone quarrying; cattle raising. Harda and Hoshangabad are agr. trade centers. Pachmarhi (climatic health resort) is summer hq. of Madhya Pradesh govt. Dist. enlarged in early 1930s by merger of former dist. of NARSINGHPUR (E) and in 1948 by inc. of former Central India state of MAKRAI. Pop. 80% Hindu, 17% tribal (mainly Gond), 3% Moslem.

Hoshangabad, town (pop. 13,290), ⊙ Hoshangabad dist., NW Madhya Pradesh, India, on Narbada R. and 140 mi. NW of Nagpur; agr. trade center (wheat, cotton, millet, oilseeds); roofing tiles (red sandstone quarries near by), brassware, bamboo canes. Rail junction of Itarsi is 10 mi. SSE.

Hoshe, China: see USHAKTAL.

Hoshiarpur (hōsh'yärpŏŏr), district (□ 2,195; pop. 1,170,323), N central Punjab, India; ⊙ Hoshiarpur. Largely in Bist Jullundur Doab, bet. Sutlej R. (SE) and Beas R. (NW); bordered E by foothills of E Punjab Himalayas, parallel to (and W of) which runs W Siwalik Range; seasonal torrents flow SW. Agr. (wheat, gram, corn, sugar cane, cotton); hand-loom weaving. Chief towns: Hoshiarpur, Tanda-Urmar, Dasuya.

Hoshiarpur, town (pop. 35,345), ⊙ Hoshiarpur dist., N central Punjab, India, 24 mi. NE of Jullundur; rail spur terminus; trades in wheat, gram, maize, mangoes, sugar; mfg. of shellac, rosin, turpentine, aerated water; beeswax refining, hand-loom silk weaving, oilseed pressing; handicrafts (ivory and brass inlay work, fibre products, leather goods). Has col.

Hoshih, China: see USHAKTAL.

Hoshihtolokai, China: see HOSHUTOLOGOI.

Hoshui (hŭ'shwā'), town, ⊙ Hoshui co. (pop. 26,115), SE Kansu prov., China, 55 mi. NE of Kingchwan; grain.

Hoshun (hŭ'shōōn'), town, ⊙ Hoshun co. (pop. 71,731), E Shansi prov., China, 30 mi. S of Pingting; wheat, beans, kaoliang. Coal mining.

Hoshutologoi (hōshōōtōlōgoi'), Chinese *Hofeng* (hŭ'fŭng'), town, ⊙ Hoshutologoi co. (pop. 12,156), N Sinkiang prov., China, 140 mi. E of Chuguchak and on highway; coal-mining center; cattle raising; agr. products. Sometimes spelled Hoshihtolokai.

Hosi or **Ho-hsi** (both: hŭ'shē'), town, ⊙ Hosi co. (pop. 54,993), SE central Yunnan prov., China, 60 mi. S of Kunming, on small lake; rice, wheat, millet, beans. Manganese mines near by.

Hoskins, village (pop. 171), Wayne co., NE Nebr., 16 mi. SW of Wayne and on branch of Elkhorn R.

Hoskote (hōs'kōtĕ), town (pop. 6,226), Bangalore dist., E Mysore, India, 15 mi. NE of Bangalore; rice milling, tobacco curing; handicrafts (silk cloth, lacquerware, coir mats).

Hosmer (hŏz'mùr), city (pop. 533), Edmunds co., N S.Dak., 23 mi. WNW of Ipswich; trading point for agr. area.

Hosoda (hōsō'dä), town (pop. 7,842), Miyazaki prefecture, SE Kyushu, Japan, 25 mi. SSW of Miyazaki; rice, livestock; lumber.

Hososhima, Japan: see TOMISHIMA.

Hospers (hŏ'spùrz), town (pop. 604), Sioux co., NW Iowa, 9 mi. SSW of Sheldon; livestock, grain.

Hospet (hōs'pĕt), city (pop. 26,023), Bellary dist., NW Madras, India, 37 mi. WNW of Bellary; rail junction; agr. trade center; rice milling, jaggery. Famous ruins of anc. city of Vijayanagar 6 mi. NW, at HAMPI. Dam and power plant under construction on the Tungabhadra, 4 mi. W, at Mallapuram (or Malapuram) village; part of irrigation and hydroelectric project. Rail spur to Gunda Road, rail junction 7 mi. S, with spurs to Swamihalli (manganese ore) and Kotturu.

Hospital (ōspētäl'), village (1930 pop. 240), Santiago prov., central Chile, on railroad and 30 mi. S of Santiago; resort in agr. area.

Hospital, Gaelic *Óspidéal Ghleann Áine*, town (pop. 635), E Co. Limerick, Ireland, 12 mi. W of Tipperary; agr. market (dairying, cattle raising; grain, potatoes).

Hospital, Cuchilla del (kōōchē'yä dhĕl ōspētäl'), hill range, Rivera dept., NE Uruguay, branches off from the Cuchilla de Santa Ana NE of Yaguarí, extends 20 mi. SSW, forming watershed bet. the Arroyo Yaguarí (NE) and the Río Negro (SW).

Hospital de Órbigo (dhā ôr'vēgō), town (pop. 1,109), Leon prov., NW Spain, 9 mi. E of Astorga; beans, potatoes, sugar beets, tobacco.

Hospitalet (ōspētälĕt'), outer industrial suburb (pop. 25,515) of Barcelona, Barcelona prov., NE Spain, in Catalonia, 4 mi. WSW of city center, on Llobregat coastal plain. Steel mills; mfg. also includes chemicals (fertilizers, lubricants, dyes, insecticides), electrical equipment, auto accessories, cement, rayon and other textiles, brandy. Truck farming.

Hospitalet-du-Larzac, L' (lōpĕtälā'-dü-lärzäk'), village (pop. 250), Aveyron dept., S France, on the Causse du Larzac, 10 mi. SE of Millau; cheese making.

Hospitalet-près-l'Andorre, L' (–prĕ-lädôr'), village (pop. 119), Ariège dept., S France, near Andorra and Sp. border, on the Ariège and 27 mi. SSE of Foix; alt. 4,711 ft. Customhouse on trans-Pyrenean RR. Electrochemical and metallurgical plant. Winter sports.

Hossegor, France: see CAPBRETON.

Hosseina (hōsā'nä), Ital. *Hosanna,* town, Arusi prov., S central Ethiopia, 70 mi. E of Jimma. Trade center (coffee, beeswax, hides).

Hosston, village, Caddo parish, extreme NW La., near Red R., 25 mi. N of Shreveport; oil refining.

Hosszuaszo, Rumania: see VALEA-LUNGA.

Hosszufalu, Rumania: see SATULUNG.

Hosszuheteny (hôs'sōōhĕtänyü), Hung. *Hosszúhetény,* town (pop. 3,212), Baranya co., S Hungary, in Mecsek Mts., 8 mi. NE of Pecs; beer.

Hosszumező, Rumania: see CAMPULUNG-PE-TISA.

Hosszupalyi (hôs'sōōpälyĭ), Hung. *Hosszúpályi,* town (pop. 5,094), Bihar co., E Hungary, 10 mi. SE of Debrecen; hemp, tobacco, hogs.

Hosszuperesztег (hôs'sōōpĕ"rĕstĕg), Hung. *Hosszúpereszteg,* town (pop. 1,995), Vas co., W Hungary, 21 mi. SE of Szombathely; wheat, potatoes, honey.

Hostalrich (ōstälrēch'), town (pop. 1,026), Gerona prov., NE Spain, 19 mi. SSW of Gerona; cork, lumber, fruit.

Hostau, Czechoslovakia: see HOSTOUN.

Hoste Island (ōs'tā), Tierra del Fuego, Chile, one of the larger isls. (c.90 mi. long) of the archipelago, just W of Navarino Isl.; 54°55'–55°44'S 68°–70°W. It has several irregular, large peninsulas, notably Hardy Peninsula, which extends SE, terminating in FALSE CAPE HORN.

Hostinne (hô'styĭnä), Czech *Hostinné,* Ger. *Arnau* (är'nou), town (pop. 4,671), NE Bohemia, Czechoslovakia, on Elbe R., on railroad and 34 mi. SE of Liberec; large paper mills; silk textiles. Dam across Elbe R., c.2 mi. downstream. Health resort of Fort (fôrsht), Czech *Fořt,* Ger. *Forst* (fôrsht), is 6 mi. NNW.

Hostivar (hô'styĭvärsh), Czech *Hostivař,* SE mfg. suburb (pop. 6,244) of Prague, Czechoslovakia, 5 mi. from city center; aluminum alloys, electrical products; foundries.

Hostos (ō'stōs), village (1950 pop. 631), Duarte prov., E central Dominican Republic, in fertile La Vega Real valley, on railroad and 33 mi. E of La Vega; cacao, rice. Until 1928, La Ceiba.

Hostotipaquillo (ōstōtēpäkē'yō), town (pop. 2,014), Jalisco, W Mexico, 55 mi. NW of Guadalajara; alt. 4,235 ft.; silver, gold, lead, copper mining.

Hostoun (hô'stōnyü), Czech *Hostouň,* Ger. *Hostau* (hô'stou), village (pop. 630), SW Bohemia, Czechoslovakia, on railroad and 30 mi. SW of Pilsen, in lumbering region.

Hostun (ōstü'), village (pop. 137), Drome dept., SE France, 17 mi. NE of Valence; kaolin quarries.

Hostyn, mountain, Czechoslovakia: see BYSTRICE POD HOSTYNEM.

Hosur (hō'sōōr), town (pop. 6,457), Salem dist., W Madras, India, near SE border of Mysore, 23 mi. SE of Bangalore; rail spur terminus; mfg. of tiles, sandalwood oil; silk growing. Livestock research center; remount depot. C. Rajagopalachari, 1st Indian governor-general of India, b. in near-by village.

Hoszcza, Ukrainian SSR: see GOSHCHA.

Hota (hō'tä), town (pop. 7,571), Chiba prefecture, central Honshu, Japan, on W Chiba Peninsula, on Uraga Strait, 12 mi. N of Tateyama; beach resort; agr., fishing.

Hotaka (hōtä'kä), town (pop. 7,848), Nagano prefecture, central Honshu, Japan, 9 mi. NW of Matsumoto; rice, raw silk.

Hotaka, Mount, Jap. *Hotaka-dake,* peak (10,527 ft.), central Honshu, Japan, on Gifu-Nagano prefecture border, 20 mi. WNW of Matsumoto; highest peak in Chubu-sangaku Natl. Park. Sometimes called Hodaka.

Hotavila, Ariz.: see HOTEVILA.

Hotchkiss, town (pop. 715), Delta co., W Colo., on branch of Gunnison R., just W of West Elk Mts., and 20 mi. ENE of Delta, in fruit-growing region; alt. 5,369 ft.

Hotei, Formosa: see PUTAI.

Hotei (hōtā'), town (pop. 10,650), Aichi prefecture, central Honshu, Japan, 12 mi. N of Nagoya; agr. center (rice, herbs); raw silk, textiles.

Hötensleben (hû'tünslā"bün), village (pop. 5,570), in former Prussian Saxony prov., central Germany, after 1945 in Saxony-Anhalt, 8 mi. S of Helmstedt; lignite mining; sugar refining.

Hotevila or **Hotevilla** (hō'tüvĭ"lü), Hopi Indian pueblo, NE Ariz., atop a mesa c.65 mi. N of Winslow, in Hopi Indian Reservation; alt. c.5,900 ft. Founded 1906 by dissenting residents of Oraibi. Sometimes Hotavila.

Hotham, Cape (hŏ'thüm, hŭ'dhüm), NW Northern Territory, Australia, bet. Clarence Strait and Van Diemen Gulf of Timor Sea; 12°3'S 131°18'E.

Hotham, Mount (6,100 ft.), E central Victoria, Australia, in Australian Alps, 130 mi. ENE of Melbourne; winter sports (May-Sept.).

Hotham Inlet (hŏ'tüm), NW Alaska, arm (50 mi. long, 5–20 mi. wide) of Kotzebue Sound; extends SE from Kotzebue, forms E side of Baldwin Peninsula. Receives Kobuk R. At head of inlet is Selawik L.

Hotien, China: see KHOTAN.

Hoti Mardan, W Pakistan: see MARDAN, town.

Hotin, Ukrainian SSR: see KHOTIN.

Hotseh or **Ho-tse** (hŭ'dzŭ'), town, ⊙ Hotseh co. (pop. 434,763), S Pingyuan prov., China, 90 mi. E of Sinsiang; trade center; cotton weaving; wheat, kaoliang, millet. Called Tsaochow until 1913. Until 1949 in Shantung prov.

Hotsin or **Ho-ching** (both: hŭ'jĭng'), town, ⊙ Hotsin co. (pop. 98,214), SW Shansi prov., China, 55 mi. NNE of Yüngtsi, and on Fen R. just above its confluence with Yellow R.; persimmons, wheat, kaoliang, millet.

Hotsing or **Ho-ching** (both: hŭ'jĭng'), town, ⊙ Hotsing co. (pop. 9,842), central Sinkiang prov., China, 20 mi. NNW of Kara Shahr; cattle, agr. products. Saltworks, coal mines near by.

Hot Spring, county (□ 621; pop. 22,181), central Ark.; ⊙ Malvern. Drained by Ouachita R. and small Caddo R. Agr. (cotton, corn, sweet potatoes, livestock). Mfg. at Malvern. Barite and rutile mining; bentonite, sand, gravel deposits; timber. Remmel Dam forms L. Catherine here. Co. has state park. Formed 1829.

Hot Springs, village (pop. 29), central Alaska, near Tanana R., 40 mi. ESE of Tanana; supply point for placer gold-mining and farming region; health resort for Fairbanks area.

Hot Springs, county (□ 2,022; pop. 5,250), N central Wyo.; ⊙ Thermopolis. Mining and agr. region; drained by Bighorn R. Coal, oil; livestock, grain, sugar beets. Part of Absaroka Range in W. Formed 1911.

Hot Springs. **1** City (pop. 29,307), ⊙ Garland co., central Ark., c.45 mi. WSW of Little Rock and on Ouachita R., in Ouachita Mts. Health and pleasure resort, and commercial center for wide area. Adjoining is Hot Springs Natl. Park (1,019.1 acres; established 1921), famous year-round spa with 47 mineral hot springs, numerous bathhouses, and Army-Navy hosp. (established 1882; present structure completed 1933). Springs, long used by Indians for medicinal purposes, were probably visited (c.1541) by DeSoto; area set aside as govt. reservation 1832. Near by are lakes Catherine and Hamilton (formed by dams in Ouachita R.) and Ouachita Natl. Forest. City settled 1807, inc. 1851. **2** Town (pop. 733), Sanders co., NW Mont., 60 mi. NNW of Missoula; resort; farming equipment, lumber mill; dairy products. Mineral waters used for medicinal purposes. **3** Town, Sierra co., N.Mex.: see TRUTH OR CONSEQUENCES. **4** Town (pop. 721), Madison co., W N.C., 25 mi. NW of Asheville and on French Broad R., near Tenn. line; mtn. resort; lumber milling. **5** City (pop. 5,030), ⊙ Fall River co., SW S.Dak., 45 mi. SSW of Rapid City, just S of Black Hills, and on Fall R. Health resort; sulphur hot springs; dairy products, timber, sandstone, alfalfa seed. Several sanitariums and hosps. are here; near by are Fossil Cycad Natl. Monument, Harney Natl. Forest, Wind Cave Natl. Park, Jewel Cave Natl. Monument, and Custer State Park. First settled 1879, inc. 1882. **6** Health-resort village (1940 pop. 611), Bath co., W Va., in the Alleghenies, 40 mi. WSW of Staunton; medicinal springs.

Hot Springs District (□ c.1,000), N central and central N.Isl., New Zealand, extends S from area near Bay of Plenty to volcanic region around L. TAUPO. Mineral springs, geysers, active and inactive volcanoes. ROTORUA is chief health resort. Sometimes called Thermal Springs Dist.

Hot Springs National Park, Ark.: see HOT SPRINGS, city.

Hot Sulphur Springs, town (pop. 263), ⊙ Grand co., N Colo., on Colorado R., in W foothills of Front Range, and 65 mi. WNW of Denver; alt. 7,655 ft. Resort; hq. of Arapaho Natl. Forest and Williams Fork game preserve. Mineral springs here.

Hottah Lake (□ 377), W central Mackenzie Dist., Northwest Territories, 60 mi. S of Port Radium; 65°5'N 118°30'W; 40 mi. long, 1–20 mi. wide. Drained N into Great Bear L. by Camsell R. (50 mi. long).

Hotte, Massif de la (mäsēf' dü lä ôt'), range in SW Haiti, stretches through Tiburon Peninsula for c.130 mi. to Jacmel; rises to over 7,500 ft.

Hottentots Holland Mountains (hŏ'tüntŏts"), SW Cape Prov., U. of So. Afr., extend c.20 mi. in a semicircle NE and then NW from E side of False Bay; rise to 5,217 ft. on Sneeuwkop, 8 mi. ENE of Somerset West. Crossed by railroad and road on Sir Lowry Pass (1,530 ft.), 6 mi. SE of Somerset West. In early days of Cape Colony range represented E limit of Dutch rule.

Hotzenplotz, Czechoslovakia: see OSOBLAHA.

Hötzing, Rumania: see HATEG.

Hou-, for Chinese names beginning thus and not found here: see under How-.

Hou, Nam (näm'hōō'), river in N Laos, rises on Chinese frontier N of Muong Hou Neua, flows c.280 mi. S in valley (rice fields) and deep gorge to Mekong R. 10 mi. N of Luang Prabang; navigable up to Hatsa (port of Phongsaly).

Houaïlou (wäēlōō'), village (dist. pop. 2,351), New Caledonia, on E coast, 85 mi. NW of Nouméa; agr. products, livestock.

Houaphan, Laos: see SAMNEUA.

Houat (wä), island (pop. 331), in Bay of Biscay off Brittany coast (Morbihan dept.), W France, 7 mi. SE of tip of Quiberon Peninsula; 2.5 mi. long, 1 mi. wide. Port of Houat (on N shore) difficult of access. Fishing.

Houches, Les (lā ōōsh'), Alpine village (pop. 171), Haute-Savoie dept., SE France, resort at SW end of Chamonix valley, 4 mi. SW of Chamonix; alt. 3,304 ft. Winter sports. Aerial tramway to Bellevue height (5,945 ft.; hotel).

Houdain (ōōdē'), industrial town (pop. 1,869), Pas-de-Calais dept., N France, 7 mi. SW of Béthune, in coal-mining dist.

Houdan (ōōdā'), town (pop. 1,952), Seine-et-Oise dept., N central France, 14 mi. NW of Rambouillet; poultry-raising center. Has picturesque 15th-16th-cent. wooden houses and 12th-cent. keep.

Houdeng-Aimeries (ōōdā-āmrē'), town (pop. 7,863), contiguous with **Houdeng-Goegnies** (–gŭnyē') (pop. 9,165), Hainaut prov., S Belgium, 10 mi. E of Mons; mfg. (glass, ceramics, cement).

Houeillès (wĕyĕs'), village (pop. 576), Lot-et-Garonne dept., SW France, in the Landes, 16 mi. WNW of Nérac; lumber trade, poultry.

Houffalize (ōōfälēz'), town (pop. 1,079), Luxembourg prov., SE Belgium, on headstream of Ourthe R. and 9 mi. NNE of Bastogne, in the Ardennes; tourist resort; cattle and pig market. In Second World War suffered much destruction in Battle of the Bulge (1944–45).

Hougarde, Belgium: see HOEGAARDEN.

Houghton (hou'tün), NE suburb of Johannesburg, S Transvaal, U. of So. Afr.

Houghton (hō'tün), county (□ 1,030; pop. 39,771), NW Upper Peninsula, Mich.; ⊙ Houghton. Includes S part of Keweenaw Peninsula, extending into L. Superior; partly bounded SE by Keweenaw Bay; drained by Ontonagon and Sturgeon rivers. Intersected NE by KEWEENAW WATERWAY. Copper-mining region, traversed by Copper Range. Some mfg. at Hancock and Houghton. Stock raising, agr. (potatoes, truck, fruit, hay), dairying, commercial fishing, lumbering. Resorts. A state park, fish hatchery, and several lakes are in co. Organized 1846.

Houghton. **1** Village (pop. 3,829), ⊙ Houghton co., NW Upper Peninsula, Mich., opposite Hancock, on Keweenaw Waterway (port facilities). Shipping, distribution, and industrial center for Keweenaw Peninsula. Mfg. (explosives, wood products), copper mining and refining, commercial fishing, farming. Seat of Mich. Col. of Mining and Technology; has mainland hq. of Isle Royale Natl. Park. Settled 1851, inc. 1867. **2** Village (pop. c.500), Allegany co., W N.Y., on Genesee R. and 22 mi. S of Warsaw; makes fish traps. Agr. (dairy products; fruit, grain). Seat of Houghton Col. (1923). **3** Town (pop. 1,005), King co., W Wash., on E shore of L. Washington, just S of Kirkland.

Houghton, Port (hō'tün, hū'tün), SE Alaska, arm (20 mi. long) of Stephens Passage, 75 mi. SE of Juneau; 57°19'N 133°27'W.

Houghton Lake (hō'tün), Roscommon co., N central Mich., c.20 mi. WNW of West Branch; largest lake of state (c.16 mi. long, 7 mi. wide). Source of Muskegon R. Houghton Lake, resort village, is on SW shore. Year-round fishing; winter sports, hunting. State park; waterfowl feeding grounds.

Houghton-le-Spring (hō'tün-lü-, hou'–), urban district (1931 pop. 10,616; 1951 census 30,676), NE Durham, England, 6 mi. SW of Sunderland; coal mining. Has 13th-cent. church containing tomb of Bernard Gilpin (d.1583), founder of local grammar school. In urban dist. (N) is town of Philadelphia, with coal mines, metal and concrete works.

Houghton Regis (hō'tün rē'jĭs), town and parish (pop. 2,459), S Bedford, England, just N of Dunstable; limestone quarries, cement works. Has 14th-cent. church. In parish (WSW) is quarrying village of Sewell.

Hougue, La, France: see SAINT-VAAST-LA-HOUGUE.

Houilles (ōōē'), town (pop. 20,559), Seine-et-Oise dept., N central France, an outer NW suburb of Paris, 9 mi. from Notre Dame Cathedral, near right bank of the Seine; mfg. (pharmaceuticals, varnishes, biscuits, underwear).

Houlgate (ōōlgät'), village (pop. 1,660), Calvados dept., NW France, fashionable bathing resort on English Channel just E of mouth of Dives R., 15 mi. NE of Caen.

Houlka (hŭl'kü), town (pop. 545), Chickasaw co., NE central Miss., 24 mi. SW of Tupelo.

Houlme, Le (lü ōōlm'), town (pop. 2,941), Seine-Inférieure dept., N France, 5 mi. NNW of Rouen; linoleum mfg.

Houlton (hōl'tün), town (pop. 8,377), including Houlton village (pop. 6,029), ⊙ Aroostook co., E Maine, on Meduxnekeag R. and 100 mi. NNE of Bangor, near N.B. line. Trade, rail, shipping center or large potato-growing area; commercial center or tourist region (hunting, fishing, canoeing); port of entry. Mfg. (machine parts, tools, bldg. materials). Seat of Ricker Col. U.S. air base built near by in 1941.

ouma (hō'mŭ), city (pop. 11,505), ⊙ Terrebonne parish, SE La., at head of navigation on Bayou Terrebonne, c.45 mi. SW of New Orleans; port on Gulf Intracoastal Waterway; canning and shipping center for sea food, vegetables. Agr. (sugar cane, corn, potatoes, truck); sugar milling; lumber, furs. Oil wells. Founded 1834, inc. 1848.

oumeiré, Syria: see HAMRA, EL.

oumt-Souk (hōōmt'-sōōk') or **Djerba** (jûr'bŭ), town, ⊙ Djerba dist., SE Tunisia, on N shore of DJERBA isl., 40 mi. E of Gabès; chief trade center for isl.'s lush agr. (olives, figs, pomegranates, pears, grapes, dates); sponge fishing. Handicraft industries (colorful silk and woolen cloth, jewelry). Airfield. Ruins of a Spanish fort.

ound, town and parish (pop. 4,110), S Hampshire, England, near Hamble R. estuary, 5 mi. ESE of Southampton; agr. market. Has 13th-cent. church.

oundé (hōōn'dā), town (pop. c.1,200), W Upper Volta, Fr. West Africa, on road to Ouagadougou and 65 mi. ENE of Bobo-Dioulasso; peanuts, shea nuts, subsistence crops; livestock. Manganese deposits near by.

ounslow, England: see HESTON AND ISLEWORTH.

ouplines (ōōplēn'), NE suburb (pop. 4,484) of Armentières, Nord dept., N France, on the Lys (Belg. border); linen-weaving center; truck.

ourn, Loch (lŏkh hōōrn), inlet of W Inverness, Scotland, extends 14 mi. inland from Sound of Sleat.

ourtin or **Hourtins** (ōōrtē'), village (pop. 783), Gironde dept., SW France, 33 mi. NW of Bordeaux; sawmilling, fishing. Bathing resort on Hourtin L. (10 mi. long, 2.5 mi. wide), separated from Bay of Biscay by a dune belt 2 mi. wide.

ousatonic, village, Mass.: see GREAT BARRINGTON.

ousatonic River (hōōsŭtŏ'nĭk), in Mass. and Conn., rises in the Berkshires in NW Mass., flows c.130 mi. generally S, past Pittsfield, Lee, and Great Barrington, Mass., and New Milford, Derby (receives Naugatuck R. here), and Shelton, Conn., to Long Isl. Sound at Milford. Power dam near Monroe, Conn., forms L. Zoar (6 mi. long). Navigable to Shelton and Derby (power dam here).

ousay, Scotland: see OUT SKERRIES.

ouse Harbour or **Havre aux Maisons** (ä'vr ō năzō'), village (pop. 1,559), E Que., on Alright Isl., one of the Magdalen Isls.; 47°24'N 61°49'W; fishing port.

ouse Island, SW Maine, small isl. off South Portland; one of 1st settlements in Casco Bay area; fortified since 17th cent. Fort Scammel built 1808; rebuilt 1862; now abandoned.

Houstka, Czechoslovakia: see STARA BOLESLAV.

Houston (hōō'stŭn), agr. village in Houston and Killellan parish (pop. 2,591), N Renfrew, Scotland, 6 mi. W of Renfrew.

Houston. 1 (hū'stŭn) County (□ 578; pop. 46,522), extreme SE Ala.; ⊙ Dothan. Bounded E by Chattahoochee R. and Ga., S by Fla. Rich agr. region (peanuts, cotton, corn, potatoes, melons; hogs, beef cattle). Formed 1903. **2** (hou'stŭn) County (□ 379; pop. 20,964), central Ga.; ⊙ Perry. Bounded E by Ocmulgee R. Coastal plain agr. (cotton, corn, melons, truck, peanuts, pecans, peaches, livestock) and timber area. Formed 1821. **3** (hū'stŭn) County (□ 565; pop. 14,435), extreme SE Minn.; ⊙ Caledonia. Agr. area drained by Root R.; bounded E by Mississippi R. and Wis., S by Iowa. Livestock, dairy products, grain, potatoes. Formed 1854. **4** (hū'stŭn) County (□ 207; pop. 5,318), NW Tenn.; ⊙ Erin. Bounded W by Kentucky Reservoir (Tennessee R.). Livestock raising, dairying, agr. (corn, tobacco, sweet potatoes). Formed 1871. **5** (hū'stŭn) County (□ 1,232; pop. 22,825), E Texas; ⊙ Crockett. Bounded W by Trinity R., E by Neches R.; includes part of Davy Crockett Natl. Forest. Rolling wooded area (much lumbering); agr. (cotton, corn, pecans, grains, fruit, truck), cattle, hogs, poultry; dairying. Some oil, natural gas. Lumber milling, oil refining, mfg., produce processing. Formed 1837.

Houston. 1 (hū'stŭn) Town (pop. 291), Perry co., central Ark., 15 mi. WSW of Conway, near Arkansas R. **2** (hou'stŭn) Town (pop. 332), Kent co., central Del., 16 mi. S of Dover; canning. **3** (hū'stŭn) Village (pop. 973), Houston co., extreme SE Minn., on Root R. and 17 mi. W of La Crosse, Wis., in grain, livestock, and poultry area; dairy products, flour, cattle feed. **4** (hū'stŭn) Town (pop. 1,664), a ⊙ Chickasaw co., NE central Miss., 30 mi. SSW of Tupelo, in agr. (cotton, corn), dairying, and timber area; mfg. of clothing. Near by are Indian mounds and Geology Hill. Inc. 1837. **5** (hū'stŭn) City (pop. 1,277), ⊙ Texas co., S central Mo., in the Ozarks, 32 mi. SW of Salem; dairying, recreational center; lumber and stave factory. **6** (hū'stŭn, hou'stŭn) Borough (pop. 1,957), Washington co., SW Pa., 5 mi. N of Washington. Laid out 1871, inc. 1901. **7** (hū'stŭn) City (1940 pop. 384,514; 1950 pop. 596,163), ⊙ Harris co., S Texas, on Gulf coastal plain c.20 mi. NW of Galveston Bay, c.145 mi. ESE of Austin; 29°45'N 95°21'W; max. alt. 74 ft. Largest city and mfg. center of Texas, and one of greatest U.S. cargo ports, on artificial port connected by deepwater Houston Ship Channel (50 mi. long) to Gulf of Mexico. Port of entry. Exports petroleum, cotton and cottonseed products, sulphur, grain, chemicals, lumber, rice, mfgd. goods; imports coffee, jute, newsprint, bananas, sugar, lumber. Rail (6 lines), highway focus; cotton, livestock market. Huge oil-refining industry is supplied by local fields and by pipelines. One of nation's chemical-mfg. centers (sulphuric acid and other sulphur derivatives, phosphates and acids, chlorine, glycerine, caustic soda, isopropyl and ethyl alcohol; also plastics, fungicides, insecticides), based on Gulf Coast natural resources (petroleum, natural gas, sulphur, salt). Here and in industrial suburbs (Pasadena, Deer Park, others) are shipyards, cottonseed, rice, and flour mills, cotton compresses, meat-packing plants, textile mills, railroad shops, and plants producing paper, cement (from Galveston Bay oyster shell), synthetic rubber, lumber, firearms, steel, metal products (iron, tin, aluminum), oil-field equipment (especially steel pipe), furniture, food products. Seat of Rice Inst., Univ. of Houston, Univ. of Texas school of dentistry, South Texas Colleges, Texas State Univ. for Negroes. Texas Medical Center has Baylor Univ. medical school, many hosps. Has mus. of fine arts, zoological gardens, mus. of natural history, and several parks (notably Hermann Park). Battlefield of SAN JACINTO is c.15 mi. E. Near by is U.S. Ellington Air Force Base, active military airfield in both world wars. Settlement in area begun 1823 at near-by Harrisburg (now part of Houston); Houston, founded 1836 as a rival town, served (1837–39) as ⊙ Texas Republic; grew as railroad shipping center but expanded enormously after dredging of Ship Channel (1912–14) and development of Gulf Coast oil fields. Shipbuilding, other war industries of Second World War caused further growth. In 1948, absorbed adjoining Galena Park, Bellaire, West University Place, Southside Place, and South Houston.

Houston, Fort Sam, Texas: see SAN ANTONIO.

Houstonia (hŭstō'nēŭ), town (pop. 309), Pettis co., central Mo., 15 mi. NNW of Sedalia.

Houston Ship Channel (hū'stŭn), S Texas, dredged deepwater channel c.50 mi. long, connecting port of Houston with the Gulf of Mexico via Buffalo Bayou, San Jacinto R., and Galveston Bay. Vehicular tunnels under channel at Pasadena (just E of Houston) and under San Jacinto R. section, bet. Baytown and La Porte. Development began 1912; channel has since been deepened and widened to accommodate large vessels.

Hout Bay (hout), Afrikaans *Houtbaai* (–bī'), town (pop. 1,904), SW Cape Prov., U. of So. Afr., on Hout Bay (3 mi. long, 8 mi. wide) of the Atlantic, 10 mi. SSW of Cape Town; rock-lobster fishing center; fruit. Near-by fort, dating from Dutch days, is now natl. monument.

Houth, Yemen: see HUTH.

Houthalen (hou'tälŭn), town (pop. 7,185), Limburg prov., NE Belgium, 7 mi. N of Hasselt; coal mining. Formerly spelled Houthaelen.

Houtman Abrolhos (hout'mŭn ŭbrŏl'yōōsh), small archipelago in Indian Ocean, 35 mi. off W coast of Western Australia; 28°18'–29°21'S 113°36'–114°11'E. Extends 50 mi. N–S. Comprises 3 coral groups: WALLABI ISLANDS (N), EASTER ISLANDS (central), PELSART ISLANDS (S). Low, sandy; mangrove forests. Tourist resorts. Sometimes called Houtman Rocks and, popularly, Abrolhos Isls.

Hou-tsang, Tibet: see TSANG.

Houtskar (hōt'shâr"), Swedish *Houtskär*, Finnish *Houtskari* (hōt'skä"rē), island (7 mi. long, 1–3 mi. wide), Turku-Pori co., SW Finland, in strait bet. the Baltic and Gulf of Bothnia, 35 mi. WSW of Turku. On N coast is Houtskar fishing village (commune pop. 1,389). Pop. is entirely Swedish-speaking.

Houtzdale (houts'dāl), borough (pop. 1,306), Clearfield co., central Pa., 22 mi. N of Altoona; bituminous coal, clay; creamery. Laid out 1870, inc. 1872.

Hova (hōō'vä"), village (pop. 756), Skaraborg co., S Sweden, 18 mi. NE of Mariestad; grain, stock.

Hovden, Norway: see BO.

Hove (hōv), municipal borough (1931 pop. 54,993; 1951 census 69,435), S Sussex, England, on the Channel just W of Brighton; seaside resort and residential dist., with some mfg. (leather, shoes, pharmaceuticals). Has art gall., mus., and 13th-cent. church. There is also large Druid stone.

Hovedoy (hō'vŭd-ûü), Nor. *Hovedøy*, islet in Oslo Fjord, just S of Oslo city center, opposite Akershus fortress; seaside resort. Has remains of Cistercian abbey, founded 1147 by English monks and destroyed 1532.

Hövel, Germany: see BOCKUM-HÖVEL.

Hövelhof (hû'fŭlhōf"), village (pop. 5,283), in former Prussian prov. of Westphalia, NW Germany, after 1945 in North Rhine-Westphalia, 8 mi. NW of Paderborn; pumpernickel.

Hoven (hō'vŭn), town (pop. 552), Potter co., N central S.Dak., 18 mi. NNE of Gettysburg; dairy products, livestock, grain.

Hovenaset (hōō'vŭnĕ"sŭt), Swedish *Hovenäset*, village (pop. 467), Goteborg och Bohus co., SW Sweden, on the Skagerrak, 7 mi. NW of Lysekil; seaside resort; stone quarrying.

Hovenweep National Monument (hō'vŭnwēp) (299.34 acres; established 1923), SW Colo. and SE Utah, c.65 mi. WNW of Durango, Colo. Pre-Columbian Indian ruins, abandoned c.600 years ago, include cliff dwellings, pueblos, and multiple-chamber towers. Best preserved is Hovenweep Castle.

Hovik (hû'vĭk, –vēk), Nor. *Høvik*, village (pop. 5,637) in Baerum canton, Akershus co., SE Norway, at head of Oslo Fjord, on railroad and 6 mi. WSW of Oslo city center; metalworking, glass mfg.; seaside resort.

Hovin (hō'vĭn), village and canton (pop. 730), Telemark co., S Norway, on E shore of Tinn L., 50 mi. NNW of Skien; lumbering; small copper mine.

Hovmantorp (hōv'mäntôrp"), village (pop. 1,115), Kronoberg co., S Sweden, on N side of L. Rottne, Swedish *Rottnen* (rôt'nŭn) (7 mi. long, 1–4 mi. wide), 14 mi. ESE of Vaxjo; metal and glassworks.

Howard, village (pop. 1,042), Queensland, Australia, 150 mi. N of Brisbane, near Hervey Bay; coal mines.

Howard. 1 County (□ 600; pop. 13,342), SW Ark.; ⊙ Nashville. Drained by Saline and Little Missouri rivers. Agr. (fruit, cotton, alfalfa, vegetables, corn). Cotton ginning, sawmilling; mfg. of wood and cement products. Timber; cinnabar mines. Formed 1873. **2** County (□ 293; pop. 54,498), central Ind.; ⊙ KOKOMO. Rich agr. area (livestock, corn, grain, poultry, soybeans, truck); diversified mfg. Drained by Wildcat Creek. Formed 1844. **3** County (□ 471; pop. 13,105), NE Iowa, on Minn. line (N); ⊙ Cresco. Rolling prairie agr. area (hogs, cattle, poultry, corn, oats) drained by Upper Iowa, Wapsipinicon, and Turkey rivers. Limestone quarries, sand and gravel pits. Formed 1851. **4** County (□ 251; pop. 23,119), central Md.; ⊙ Ellicott City. Bounded NE by Patapsco R., W and SW by Patuxent R. Mostly rolling piedmont, with SE part in coastal plain. Agr. produce (dairy products, poultry, truck, apples, some grain) marketed in metropolitan dist. of Baltimore (E). Includes part of Patapsco State Park. Formed 1851. **5** County (□ 469; pop. 11,857), central Mo.; ⊙ Fayette. On Missouri R.; agr. (corn, wheat, oats, apples), cattle, poultry. Formed 1816. **6** County (□ 566; pop. 7,226), E central Nebr.; ⊙ St. Paul. Agr. region drained by N.Loup and Middle Loup rivers. Grain, livestock, dairy and poultry produce. Formed 1871. **7** County (□ 912; pop. 26,722), NW Texas; ⊙ Big Spring. Rolling plains, drained by tributaries of Colorado R.; alt. 2,400–2,800 ft. Livestock (beef cattle, horses, mules, sheep, hogs, poultry); agr. in E (cotton, grain sorghums, some truck, fruit); dairying. Oil, natural-gas fields; oil refining, processing of clay and farm products. Includes a state park. Formed 1876.

Howard. 1 City (pop. 1,149), ⊙ Elk co., SE Kansas, on headstream of Elk R. and 55 mi. ESE of Wichita; trade center for livestock region; mfg. of livestock remedies. Oil and gas wells near by. Founded 1870, inc. 1877. **2** Borough (pop. 754), Centre co., central Pa., 9 mi. NE of Bellefonte and on Bald Eagle Creek. **3** City (pop. 1,251), ⊙ Miner co., SE central S.Dak., 50 mi. NW of Sioux Falls; trading center for agr. area; grain, dairy produce, cattle, poultry. Platted 1881.

Howard Beach, SE N.Y., a section of S Queens borough of New York city, on N shore of Jamaica Bay; resort.

Howard City. 1 Village (pop. 791), Montcalm co., central Mich., 32 mi. NNE of Grand Rapids and on short Tamarack R., in agr. and lake-resort area (grain, potatoes, beans, poultry, livestock; dairy products); oil and gas wells. **2** Village, Howard co., Nebr.: see BOELUS.

Howard Field, military reservation, Balboa dist., S Panama Canal Zone, at SE foot of Cerro Galera, 5 mi. SW of Panama city. Fort Kobbe adjoins E.

Howard Lake, resort village (pop. 931), Wright co., S central Minn., on small lake and c.40 mi. W of Minneapolis, in diversified-farming area; dairy products.

Howard Mountain, Colo.: see NEVER SUMMER MOUNTAINS.

Howden (hou'dŭn), town and parish (pop. 2,154), East Riding, SE Yorkshire, England, near Ouse R., 3 mi. N of Goole; agr. market. Has church dating mainly from 14th cent.

Howdon, England: see WALLSEND.

Howe (hou). **1** Town (pop. 486), Le Flore co., E Okla., 32 mi. SSW of Fort Smith (Ark.), in agr. area. **2** Town (pop. 572), Grayson co., N Texas, 9 mi. S of Sherman, in agr. area.

Howe, Cape, southeasternmost point of Australia, on boundary bet. New South Wales and Victoria; forms S end of entrance to Disaster Bay of Tasman Sea; 37°31'S 149°58'E.

Howe Caverns, N.Y.: see HOWES CAVE.

Howe Island (□ 12), SE Ont., one of the Thousand Isls., in the St. Lawrence, near its outlet from L. Ontario, 8 mi. E of Kingston; 8 mi. long, 3 mi. wide. Separated from mainland by narrow Bateau Channel.

Howell, county (□ 920; pop. 22,725), S Mo.; ⊙ West Plains. In the Ozarks; drained by Eleven Point R. Livestock and agr. region (corn, hay); pine timber; stone quarries. Part of Mark Twain Natl. Forest here. Formed 1857.

Howell. 1 Town (pop. 169), Echols co., S Ga., 13 mi. E of Valdosta, near Alapaha R. **2** City (pop. 4,353), ⊙ Livingston co., SE Mich., 33 mi. ESE of Lansing, on small Thompson L., in agr. and dairying area; mfg. (electric motors, chemicals, metal products, fishing tackle). Summer resort. Settled 1834; inc. as village 1863, as city 1915. **3** Town (pop. 176), Box Elder co., NW Utah, 30 mi. W of Logan.

Howells, village (pop. 784), Colfax co., E Nebr., 20 mi. N of Schuyler and on branch of Elkhorn R.; grain.

Howe of the Mearns (mârnz), fertile lowland area in S Kincardine, Scotland, centered on Laurencekirk, extending E to North Sea coast. The Mearns is anc. name of Kincardine co.

Howerla, Ukrainian SSR: see GOVERLA.

Howes Cave (houz), village, Schoharie co., E central N.Y., 32 mi. W of Albany; cement mfg. Tourist trade attracted by Howe Caverns, among largest in NE U.S., with underground stream and lake. Near by are Secret Caverns.

Howe Sound, inlet (26 mi. long, 1–10 mi. wide) of Strait of Georgia, SW B.C., 10 mi. NW of Vancouver. Receives Squamish R. at head; contains Gambier, Bowen, Anvil, and Keats isls. Fishing and lumbering area; copper mining at Brittania Beach on E shore.

Howey-in-the-Hills, town (pop. 188), Lake co., central Fla., 10 mi. SE of Leesburg, on L. Harris; citrus-fruit packing and canning.

Howick (hou'ĭk), village (pop. 484), SW Que., near Châteauguay R., 15 mi. ESE of Valleyfield; dairying.

Howick, town (pop. 1,885), central Natal, U. of So. Afr., on Umgeni R. and 12 mi. NW of Pietermaritzburg; rubber and lumbering industry; resort. Just E are noted falls (364 ft. high) of Umgeni R.; hydroelectric power.

Howkan Island, Alaska: see LONG ISLAND.

Howland (hou'lŭnd), town (pop. 1,441), Penobscot co., central Maine, 30 mi. N of Bangor and on Penobscot R., at mouth of the Piscataquis; plywood, paper mills. Inc. 1826.

Howland Island (hou'–) (□ 1), central Pacific, near equator, c.1,620 mi. SW of Honolulu, T.H.; 0°48'N 176°38'W. Discovered 1842 by American traders; claimed 1857 by U.S. Worked for guano by American and later by British guano companies, Howland became in the 1930s important as air base for Honolulu-Australia route. American colonists arrived from Hawaii 1935; isl. placed under Dept. of Interior 1936. Landing field completed 1937.

Howli or **Houli** (both: hō'lē'), Jap. *Kori* (kō'rē), town (1935 pop. 1,691), W central Formosa, 4 mi. N of Fengyüan and on railroad; sugar milling, hat mfg.; rice, tobacco, fruit.

Howlung or **Houlung** (both: hō'lŏŏng'), Jap. *Koryu* (kō'ryōō), town (1935 pop. 5,105), NW Formosa, minor port on W coast, on railroad and 17 mi. SW of Sinchu; rice, sweet potatoes, peanuts, watermelons; fish products (mullet, sardines).

Howpi or **Houpi** (both: hō'bē'), Jap. *Koheki* (kō'-hākē), town, W central Formosa, on railroad and 9 mi. SSW of Kiayi; rail junction for Kwantzeling resort.

Howrah (hou'rä), district (□ 561; pop. 1,490,304), S West Bengal, India; ⊙ Howrah. Bounded E by Hooghly, W by Rupnarayan rivers; drained by the Damodar. Alluvial soil (swamps towards W); rice, jute, pulse, potatoes, coconuts, betel nuts. Heavy industrial area centered around Howrah; iron- and steel-rolling works, cotton and jute milling, glass mfg.; railroad workshops at Liluah. Engineering Col., Royal Botanical Gardens at Sibpur.

Howrah, city (□ 10.18; pop., including suburbs, 379,292), ⊙ Howrah dist., S West Bengal, India, on Hooghly R. (pontoon bridge; opened 1874) opposite Calcutta. Rail and road junction; trade and industrial center; jute pressing and milling, cotton, rice, flour, and dal milling, sawmilling, cotton ginning and baling, mfg. of chemicals, glass, hosiery, cigarettes, batteries, rice mills, rope; general engineering works. Main N suburbs include SALKHIA, LILUAH, and GHUSURI. Sibpur (including Shalimar area; S) is S industrial suburb, with jute pressing, mfg. of paint, soap, perfume, toys, and brushes, and railroad workshop. Engineering Col., noted Royal Botanical Gardens (270 acres; founded 1786), with famous 163-year-old banyan tree, here.

Howrah Salkia, India: see SALKIA.

Howson Peak (hou'sŭn) (9,000 ft.), W central B.C., in Coast Mts., 30 mi. SW of Smithers; 54°25'N 127°45'W.

Howtao or **Hou-t'ao** (hō'tou'), agr. district of W Suiyuan prov., China, on N bank of Yellow R. bend, W of Paotow; chief town is Wuyüan. Long colonized by Chinese, the oasis has an elaborate irrigation system, permitting intensive agr.

Howth (houdh, hōdh), Gaelic *Beann Eadair*, suburb (pop. c.5,000) of Dublin, E Co. Dublin, Ireland, on the Irish Sea, 9 mi. ENE of Dublin, on a peninsula at foot of Hill of Howth; 53°23'N 6°4'W; fishing port and seaside resort. Has anc. castle and 16th-cent. Col. of Howth. Until 1830, when superseded by Dún Laoghaire (Kingstown), Howth was terminal of Dublin mail steamers from England. Part of Dublin since 1940.

Howth, Hill of, hill on a peninsula (5 mi. long, 2 mi. wide) in the Irish Sea, E Co. Dublin, Ireland, forming N shore of Dublin Bay; rises to 560 ft. At E extremity is Lion's Head promontory, with fishing village of Baily or Bailey; site of lighthouse (53°21'N 6°3'W), built 1814.

Howu Island, China: see LINCOLN ISLAND.

Hoxie (hŏk'sē). **1** Town (pop. 1,855), Lawrence co., NE Ark., 20 mi. NW of Jonesboro, bet. Black and Cache rivers; rail junction, in farm area. **2** City (pop. 1,157), ⊙ Sheridan co., NW Kansas, 30 mi. E of Colby; shipping and trading point in grain and livestock region.

Hoxsie, R.I.: see WARWICK.

Höxter (hûk'stûr), town (pop. 13,029), in former Prussian prov. of Westphalia, NW Germany, after 1945 in North Rhine-Westphalia, on left bank of the Weser and 26 mi. E of Paderborn; mfg. of chemicals. Cement works. Has 13th-cent. church, 14th-cent. town hall. Was member of Hanseatic League. Just E are baroque bldgs. of noted former Benedictine abbey of Corvey or Korvey (founded 822; secularized 1803), with Romanesque church. Hoffmann von Fallersleben buried here.

Hoxton, district of Shoreditch, London, England, N of the Thames, 2.5 mi. NE of Charing Cross; furniture-mfg. center. Mary Lamb was patient in private asylum here.

Hoy, island (□ 61.6, including GRAEMSAY, FLOTTA, and FARA isls.; pop. 955), 2d-largest of the Orkneys, Scotland, 9 mi. N of mainland of Caithness across Pentland Firth, and 2 mi. S of Pomona isl. across Hoy Sound; 13 mi. long, 6 mi. wide. Hilly, rising to 1,564 ft. on Ward Hill (NE); coastline has high cliffs, rising to over 1,000 ft. on W coast. Long Hope, 4-mi.-long inlet on SE coast, forms good natural harbor (it is former naval anchorage). On NW coast is the Old Man of Hoy, conspicuous detached sandstone pinnacle, 450 ft. high. Linksness (NE) is chief port. Near by is Dwarfie Stone, a great sandstone block from which a cave is hollowed; it is object of Scandinavian folk tales. At W extremity of isl. is promontory of Rora Head, 58°52'N 3°24'W. Hoy forms W boundary of SCAPA FLOW anchorage.

Hoya (hō'yä), town (pop. 4,359), in former Prussian prov. of Hanover, NW Germany, after 1945 in Lower Saxony, on the Weser and 8 mi. SSW of Verden; cattle.

Hoya (hō'yä), town (pop. 11,930), Greater Tokyo, central Honshu, Japan, just W of Tokyo; agr. (rice, wheat, radishes, sweet potatoes); raw silk.

Hoya-Gonzalo (oi'ä-gōnthä'lō), town (pop. 1,438), Albacete prov., SE central Spain, 17 mi. ESE of Albacete; livestock, wine, saffron, cereals.

Hoyales de Roa (oiä'lĕs dhä rō'ä), town (pop. 949), Burgos prov., N Spain, 9 mi. W of Aranda de Duero; cereals, truck, grapes.

Hoyang (hŭ'yäng'), town, ⊙ Hoyang co. (pop. 145,728), E Shensi prov., China, 95 mi. NE of Sian, near Yellow R.; cotton weaving; rice, wheat.

Hoyanger (hû'üängûr), Nor. *Hoyanger*, village (pop. 2,690) in Kyrkjebo (Nor. *Kyrkjebø*) canton (pop. 4,854), Sogn og Fjordane co., W Norway, landing on N shore of Sogne Fjord, 65 mi. NNE of Bergen; large hydroelectric works; aluminum-smelting center. Tourist center. Formerly spelled Hoianger, Nor. *Høianger*. At Vadheim (pop. 328), 8 mi. W, mining of salt, potassium chlorate, metallic sodium.

Hoyer, Denmark: see HOJER.

Hoyerswerda (hoi″ûrsvĕr'dä), town (pop. 7,274), in former Prussian Lower Silesia prov., E central Germany, after 1945 in Saxony, in Upper Lusatia, on the Black Elster and 25 mi. S of Cottbus, in lignite-mining region; railroad repair shops; glass-, brickworks.

Hoylake, town in Hoylake and West Kirby urban dist. (1931 pop. 16,631; 1951 census 30,920), on Wirral peninsula, NW Cheshire, England, on Irish Sea at mouth of the Dee, 7 mi. W of Birkenhead; seaside resort with golf links. Has church of 14th–15th cent.

Hoyland, Norway: see GANDDAL.

Hoyland Nether, urban district (1931 pop. 15,214; 1951 census 15,707), West Riding, S Yorkshire, England, 8 mi. N of Sheffield; coal-mining center. In urban dist. (E) is coal-mining village of St. Helens.

Hoyland Swaine, former urban district (1931 pop. 792), West Riding, S Yorkshire, England, 5 mi. W of Barnsley; coal mining. Inc. 1938 in Penistone.

Hoyleton (hoil'tŭn), village (pop. 462), Washington co., SW Ill., 9 mi. SW of Centralia, in agr. and bituminous-coal area.

Hoym (hoim), town (pop. 4,567), in former Anhalt state, central Germany, after 1945 in Saxony-Anhalt, at N foot of the lower Harz, 7 mi. E of Quedlinburg, in lignite-mining region. Has 13th-cent. palace.

Hoyocasero (oiōkäsä'rō), town (pop. 982), Ávila prov., central Spain, in fertile Alberche valley, at N foot of the Sierra de Gredos, 21 mi. SW of Ávila; cereals, vegetables, forage. Lumbering; flour milling, woolen milling.

Hoyo de Manzanares (oi'ō dhä män-thänä'rĕs), town (pop. 600), Madrid prov., central Spain, in hills of the Sierra de Guadarrama, 18 mi. NW of Madrid; summer resort, dairying.

Hoyo de Pinares, El (ĕl, pēnä'rĕs), town (pop. 2,720), Ávila prov., central Spain, 18 mi. SE of Ávila. Surrounding pine forests (timber, pine cones) are its mainstay; also raises grapes, cereals, fruit, livestock. Olive-oil pressing, flour milling, dairying; ceramics mfg.

Hoyos (oi'ōs), town (pop. 1,703), Cáceres prov., W Spain, 50 mi. NNW of Cáceres; olive-oil processing; stock raising; citrus and other fruit.

Hoyo Strait (hō'yō), Jap. *Hoyo-kaikyo*, Japan, bet. Kyushu (W) and Shikoku (E); connects Iyo Sea (SW section of Inland Sea) with Philippine Sea; c.60 mi. long, c.35 mi. wide. Beppu Bay is largest inlet. Sometimes called Bungo Strait.

Hoyran, Lake, Turkey: see EGRIDIR, LAKE.

Hoyt, city (pop. 246), Jackson co., NE Kansas, 1[illegible] mi. N of Topeka, in livestock and grain region.

Hoytville, village (pop. 340), Wood co., NW Ohio, 14 mi. SSW of Bowling Green and on Middle Branch of Portage R.

Hoyün (hō'yün'), Mandarin *Hoyüan* (hŭ'yüän'), town (pop. 13,356), ⊙ Hoyün co. (pop. 202,893), [illegible] central Kwangtung prov., China, on East R. and 50 mi. NNE of Waiyeung; rice, sugar, vegetable oil. Tungsten and tin mining near by.

Hozan, Formosa: see FENGSHAN.

Hozan, Korea: see PUNGSAN.

Hozat (hôzät'), village (pop. 1,595), Tunceli prov., E central Turkey, 30 mi. N of Elazig; grain. Formerly Dersim.

Hpimaw (pē'mô), village, Myitkyina dist., Kachin State, Upper Burma, 20 mi. ENE of Htawgaw, on Chinese Yunnan prov. border.

Hpungan Pass (pŏŏng-gän') (alt. 10,000 ft.), on Burma-India border, 30 mi. WNW of Putao; 27°30'N 96°55'E. Difficult route, rarely used by natives.

Hrabusice (hrä'bŏŏshĭtsĕ), Slovak *Hrabušice*, Hung. *Káposztafalva* (kä'pôstôfŏl″vŏ), village (pop. 1,538), NE Slovakia, Czechoslovakia, on Hornad R., on railroad and 7 mi. SE of Poprad; woodworking industry.

Hradcany (hrä'chänĭ), Czech *Hradčany*, E dist. (pop. 7,209) of Prague, Czechoslovakia, on left bank of Vltava R., on Hradcany hill. Site of famous Hradcany castle, revered in Czech history. The castle, of legendary foundation (probably 9th cent.), became the residence of various dynasties; surrounding fortified walls are mostly of 12th cent. neglected during Reformation and greatly damaged by fire in 1541; later restored, becoming under Rudolph II (16th cent.) an outstanding center of science and art. Second Defenestration of Prague took place from castle windows in 1618, precipitating Thirty Years War. Twice occupied by Prussia under Maria Theresa; temporary asylum for Charles X in 1832. Residence of Czech president since 1918, except for 1939–45 period of Ger. occupation. Present form dates mostly from end of 18th cent. Notable features are: St. Vitus Cathedral (926–1929), originally a rotunda erected by St. Wenceslaus (St. Wenceslaus and St. John of Nepomuk are buried here); St. George Basilica (925); royal palace, with 15th-cent. Vladislav Hall, 16th-cent. Spanish Hall, 12th-cent. Black Tower.

Hradec, Silesia, Czechoslovakia: see OPAVA.

Hradec Kralove (hrä'dĕts krä'lôvä), Czech *Hradec Králové*, Ger. *Königgrätz* (kû'nĭkhgräts), city (pop. 19,242; metropolitan area pop. 51,480), ⊙ Hradec prov. (□ 1,636; pop. 552,780), NE Bohemia, Czechoslovakia, on Elbe R., at Orlice R. mouth, and 62 mi. ENE of Prague; 50°13'N 15°49'E. Important rail communications center; mfg. (industrial machinery, pianos, musical wind instruments, furniture, photographic equipment, soap, beer, textiles), fur dressing; center of tanning industry of E Bohemia. Intensive growing of cabbages, sugar beets, fruit in vicinity. Airport. R.C. bishop's see. Noted for 14th-cent. early Gothic cathedral and 17th-cent. baroque church. Institute for glass industry, medical school, leather-trade school, mus. Originally a 14th-cent. fortress, its growth as modern community began with razing of fortifications in 1884. Memorable battle of SADOVA or Königgrätz (1866) fought near by.

Hradec u Opavy, Czechoslovakia: see OPAVA.

Hradek, Czechoslovakia: see MIROSOV.

Hradek nad Nisou (hrä'dĕk näd' nyĭ″sō), Czech *Hrádek nad Nisou*, Ger. *Grottau* (grô'tou), village (pop. 2,642) N Bohemia, Czechoslovakia, on Lusatian Neisse R., on railroad and 11 mi. NW of Liberec, near Ger.-Polish border across from Zittau; oats, potatoes; lignite mining.

Hranice (hrä'nyĭtsĕ), Ger. *Mährisch-Weisskirchen* (mâ'rĭsh-vīs'kĭrkhŭn), town (pop. 11,225), E Bohemia, Czechoslovakia, on right bank of Becva R. and 21 mi. ESE of Olomouc; rail junction; mfg. of machinery (notably motors, pumps). Military acad. Health resort of Teplice nad Becvou, with mineral baths, is just S.

Hranovnica (hrä'nôvnyĭtsä), Hung. *Szepesvéghely* (sĕ'pĕzhvāk″hā), village (pop. 1,482), N Slovakia, Czechoslovakia, 5 mi. S of Poprad; woodworking (notably construction materials).

Hrastnik (hräst'nĭk), Ger. *Hrastnig* (hräst'nĭk), village (pop. 5,767), central Slovenia, Yugoslavia, near Sava R., 29 mi. ENE of Ljubljana; mfg. of hollow glass, paints, varnishes, superphosphates, sulphuric acid. Brown-coal mines at near-by hamlets of Dol and Ojstro.

Hrensko (hûrzhĕn'skô), Czech *Hřensko*, village (pop. 366), N Bohemia, Czechoslovakia, on right bank of the Elbe (Ger. border), opposite Schöna, and 6 mi. N of Decin; popular excursion center.

Hrisey (hûrēs'ā"), Icelandic *Hrísey*, fishing village (pop. 316), Eyjafjardar co., N Iceland, on Hrisey isl. (30 mi. long) in Eyja Fjord, 20 mi. NNW of Akureyri.

Hronov (hrô'nôf), Ger. *Hronow*, village (pop. 3,989), NE Bohemia, Czechoslovakia, in the Sudetes, on railroad and 16 mi. ENE of Dvur Kralove; textile mfg. (notably linen). Has 14th-cent. church. Chalybeate springs.

Hron River (hrôn), Ger. *Gran* (grän), Hung. *Garam* (gŏ'rŏm), S Slovakia, Czechoslovakia, rises on SE slope of Kralova Hola, flows W, bet. the Low Tatra and Slovak Ore Mts., past Banska Bystrica, and S, past Zvolen, to the Danube opposite Esztergom, Hungary; c.170 mi. long.

Hrotovice (hrô'tôvĭtsĕ), Ger. *Hrottowitz*, town (pop. 1,415), S Moravia, Czechoslovakia, 26 mi. WSW of Brno; barley, oats.

Hrubieszow (hûrōōbyĕ'shōōf), Pol. *Hrubieszów*, Rus. *Grubeshov* or *Grubeshov'* (grōōbā'shŭf), town (pop. 12,984), Lublin prov., E Poland, on railroad and 28 mi. E of Zamosc, near Bug R. (Ukrainian SSR border); mfg. of candy, soap; chicory drying, flour milling; brickworks. Before Second World War, pop. 50% Jewish.

Hruschau, Czechoslovakia: see HRUSOV.

Hrusica (hrōō'shĭtsä), Slovenian *Hrušica*, mountain in Dinaric Alps, SW Slovenia, Yugoslavia; culminates in Nanos peak (over 4,000 ft.), Ital. *Monte Re*, 15 mi. NE of Trieste.

Hrusov (hrōō'shôf), Czech *Hrušov*, Ger. *Hruschau* (hrōō'shou), town (pop. 7,892), NE Silesia, Czechoslovakia, on right bank of Ostravice R., at its influx into the Oder, on railroad and just N of Ostrava; mfg. of chemicals (notably soda and drugs) and earthenware. Part of industrial complex of Greater OSTRAVA.

Hrusovany (hrōō'shôvänĭ), Czech *Hrušovany*, Ger. *Grusbach* (grōōs'bäkh), village (pop. 2,250), S Moravia, Czechoslovakia, 27 mi. SSW of Brno; agr. center (barley, oats); sugar refining.

Hrvatska, Yugoslavia: see CROATIA.

Hsahtung (shätōōng', Burmese shä'doun), S state (myosaship) (□ 471; pop. 11,965) of Southern Shan State, Upper Burma, on the Nam Pawn; ⊙ Hsihseng.

Hsamonghkam (shämōng'käm'), W state (myosaship) (□ 479; pop. 25,091), Southern Shan State, Upper Burma; ⊙ Hsamonghkam, village on Thazi-Shwenyaung RR and 20 mi. WSW of Taunggyi.

Hsawnghsup (shông'shōōp'), Burmese *Thaungdut* (thoun-dōōt'), former Shan state (□ 567; pop. 7,239), Upper Chindwin dist., Upper Burma; ⊙ Thaungdut. In Manipur hills, bet. Manipur (India) border and Chindwin R.; teak, wood-oil trees. Shan (Thai) pop. influenced by near-by Nagas and Manipuris.

Hsenwi (shĕnwē'), village, ⊙ North Hsenwi state, Northern Shan State, Upper Burma, on Burma Road and 29 mi. NE of Lashio; head of road (E) to Kunlong. Ruins of old capital near by.

Hsenwi, North, and South Hsenwi, states, Burma: see NORTH HSENWI; SOUTH HSENWI.

Hsi-, for Chinese names beginning thus and not found here: see under SI-.

Hsi, lake, China: see WEST LAKE.

Hsi, river, China: see WEST RIVER.

Hsia-, for Chinese names beginning thus and not found here: see under SIA-.

Hsia-chiang, China: see SIAKIANG.

Hsia-ching, China: see SIATSING.

Hsia-i, China: see SIAYI.

Hsia-kuan, China: see SIAKWAN.

Hsia-men, China: see AMOY.

Hsiang-, for Chinese names beginning thus and not found here: see under SIANG-.

Hsiang-ch'eng, China: see HIANGCHENG.

Hsiang Chiang, China: see SIANG RIVER.

Hsiang-hsiang, China: see SIANGSIANG.

Hsiang-shan, China: see CHUNGSHAN, Kwangtung prov.

Hsiao-, for Chinese names beginning thus and not found here: see under SIAO-.

Hsiao-i, China: see SIAOYI.

Hsi Chiang, China: see WEST RIVER.

Hsi-ch'uan, China: see SICHWAN.

Hsieh-ka-erh, Tibet: see SHEKAR.

Hsien-, for Chinese names beginning thus and not found here: see under SIEN-.

Hsien-chü, China: see SIENKÜ.

Hsi-feng, China: see SIHFENG.

Hsihseng (shē'shăng), village, ⊙ Hsahtung state, Southern Shan State, Upper Burma, 45 mi. SSE of Taunggyi, on road to Loikaw.

Hsi-hsia, China: see TANGUT.

Hsi-hsiang, China: see SISIANG.

Hsi Hu, China: see WEST LAKE.

Hsi-hua, China: see SIHWA.

Hsi-nan, China: see SAINAM.

Hsin-ch'ang, China: see SUNCHONG.

Hsincheng, Manchuria: see FUYÜ, Kirin prov.

Hsin-chiang, province, China: see SINKIANG, province.

Hsin-chiang, town, China: see SINKIANG, town.

Hsin-chiang, Formosa: see SINKANG.

Hsin-chien, China: see SINKIEN.

Hsin-ching, China: see SINTSING.

Hsin-chi-pu-k'o, Tibet: see SENGE.

Hsin-chuang, China: see SINCHWANG.

Hsin-chuang, Formosa: see SINCHWANG.

Hsin-feng, China: see SUNFUNG.

Hsing-, for Chinese names beginning thus and not found here: see under HING-.

Hsingan or **Hingan** (both: shĭng'än'), former province (□ 160,670; 1940 pop. 2,095,292) of W Manchukuo; ⊙ was Hailar. Formed 1932 out of Inner Mongolian section of Manchuria, it was divided in 1934 into North Hsingan, East Hsingan, South Hsingan, and West Hsingan provs. North Hsingan and East Hsingan provs. were joined in 1946 to form the new prov. (NW Manchuria) of Hsingan or Hingan (□ 107,605; 1946 pop. 322,173; ⊙ was Hailar), which was in turn inc. 1949 into the Inner Mongolian Autonomous Region. In 1946, South Hsingan became part of Liaopeh prov. and West Hsingan part of Jehol prov.; both later were inc. (1949) into Inner Mongolian Autonomous Region.

Hsingan, Mongolian league, China: see KHINGAN.

Hsing-hai, China: see HINGHAI.

Hsing-hua, town, China: see HINGHWA.

Hsing-hua Bay, China: see HINGHWA BAY.

Hsing-k'ai Hu, Manchuria and USSR: see KHANKA, LAKE.

Hsing-kuo, China: see HINGKWO.

Hsin-ho, China: see DUSHAMBA.

Hsin-hsiang, China: see SINSIANG.

Hsin-hsing, China: see SUNHING.

Hsin-hua, China: see SINHWA.

Hsin-hua, Formosa: see SINHWA.

Hsin-hui, China: see SUNWUI.

Hsin-i, China: see SUNYI.

Hsinking, Manchuria: see CHANGCHUN.

Hsipaw (sēbô'), SW state (sawbwaship) (□ 4,591; pop. 148,731), Northern Shan State, Upper Burma; ⊙ Hsipaw. Central plain along Myitnge R., with hills (6,000 ft.) NW and SE. Rice, cotton, ginger. Coal deposits. Served by Mandalay-Lashio RR.

Hsipaw, town (pop. 4,849), ⊙ Hsipaw state, Northern Shan State, Upper Burma, on Myitnge R. and Mandalay-Lashio RR, and 35 mi. SW of Lashio; road S to Loilem. Trading center; tea and tung plantations; brine wells.

Hsiu-, for Chinese names beginning thus and not found here: see under SIU-.

Hsiu-jen, China: see SOUYEN.

Hsiung-, for Chinese names beginning thus and not found here: see under SIUNG-.

Hsiu Shui, China: see SIU RIVER.

Hsü-, for Chinese names beginning thus and not found here: see under SÜ-.

Hsüan, for Chinese names beginning thus and not found here: see under SÜAN-.

Hsüan-hua, China: see SÜANHWA.

Hsüchang or **Hsü-ch'ang** (shü'chäng'), town, ⊙ Hsüchang co. (pop. 286,517), N central Honan prov., China, on Peking-Hankow RR and 60 mi. SW of Kaifeng; tobacco center; exports hides, wheat, beans, melons. Until 1913 called Hsüchow.

Hsüeh-, for Chinese names beginning thus and not found here: see under SÜEH-.

Hsü-i, China: see CHUYI.

Hsün-, for Chinese names beginning thus and not found here: see under SÜN-.

Hsün Chiang, China: see SÜN RIVER.

Hsün-i, China: see SÜNYI.

Htawgaw (tô'-gô), village, Myitkyina dist., Kachin State, Upper Burma, near Nmai R., 70 mi. NE of Myitkyina.

Htugyi (tōō'jē"), village, Henzada dist., Lower Burma, on railroad and 25 mi. NW of Henzada.

Hua-, for Chinese names beginning thus and not found here: see under HWA-.

Huaca, La, Peru: see LA HUACA.

Huacachi (wäkä'chē), town (pop. 1,228), Ancash dept., W central Peru, on E slopes of Cordillera Blanca, 40 mi. ENE of Huarás; barley, potatoes; sheep raising.

Huacachina (wäkächē'nä), village (pop. 18), Ica dept., SW Peru, 3 mi. WSW of Ica; resort; thermal baths.

Huacaibamba (wäkī bäm'bä), town (pop. 510), Huánuco dept., central Peru, on W slopes of Cordillera Central, on Marañón R. and 34 mi. SE of Huacrachuco; sugar cane, corn.

Huacana, La, Mexico: see LA HUACANA.

Huacaraje (wäkärä'hä), village (pop. c.1,000), Beni dept., NE Bolivia, on Huacaraje R. (branch of the Itonamas) and 29 mi. SE of Magdalena, in the llanos; cotton, rice.

Huacaya (wäkī'ä), town, Chuquisaca dept., SE Bolivia, on Huacaya R. (left affluent of the Pilcomayo) and 37 mi. NNW of Villa Montes; corn, sugar cane, fruit.

Huachacalla (wächäkä'yä), town (pop. c.3,000), Oruro dept., W Bolivia, near confluence of Turco and Lauca rivers, in the Altiplano, 95 mi. SW of Oruro; alt. 12,231 ft.; alpaca, potatoes.

Huachi or **San Miguel de Huachi** (sän' mēgĕl' dā wä'chē), village, La Paz dept., W Bolivia, at confluence of Santa Elena and Bopi rivers (here forming Beni R.), 50 mi. NNE of Chulumani; coffee, cacao, coca, quina. Site of mission.

Huachipato, Chile: see SAN VICENTE, Concepción prov.

Huacho (wä'chō), city (pop. 13,320), ⊙ Chancay prov. (□ 2,651; pop. 103,220), Lima dept., W central Peru, Pacific port on Huacho Bay (2 mi. wide, 1 mi. long), on Pan American Highway and 75 mi. NW of Lima (connected by railroad). Cotton ginning, cotton-seed milling; mfg. of oil, soap, candles; rice milling. Shipping point for products of surrounding region (cotton, sugar cane); fisheries. Salt is mined near by. Huacho port (pop. 545) is an adjoining settlement (tramway connection).

Huachón (wächōn'), town (pop. 1,330), Pasco dept., central Peru, in Cordillera Oriental, on a branch of La Oroya–Cerro de Pasco RR and 21 mi. E of Cerro de Pasco; grain, potatoes.

Huachuca Mountains (wŭchōō'kŭ), in Cochise co., SE Ariz., S of Fort Huachuca near Mex. line; MILLER PEAK (9,445 ft.) is highest point. **Huachuca Peak** (8,406 ft.), also in range, is 4 mi. S of Fort Huachuca. Range lies in section of Coronado Natl. Forest.

Huaco (wä'kō), town (pop. estimate 500), N central San Juan prov., Argentina, 18 mi. NE of Jachal; cereal, wine, livestock. Warm sulphur springs.

Huacrachuco (wäkrächōō'kō), town (pop. 778), ⊙ Marañón prov. (□ 2,142; enumerated pop. 21,882, plus estimated 6,000 Indians), Huánuco dept., central Peru, on W slopes of Cordillera Central of the Andes, 105 mi. NW of Huánuco; 8°38'S 76°53'W; alt. 11,975 ft. Agr. products (barley, potatoes); sheep raising.

Huafo Island, Chile: see GUAFO ISLAND.

Huagaruancha, Cerro (sĕ'rō wägärwän'chä), Andean peak (18,858 ft.), Pasco dept., central Peru, in Cordillera Oriental, 25 mi. ENE of Cerro de Pasco.

Hua Hin (hōō'ŭ hĭn'), village (1937 pop. 5,150), Prachuabkhirikhan prov., S Thailand, on Gulf of Siam, on railroad and 85 mi. SSW of Bangkok. Largest seaside resort of Thailand; site of royal residence.

Huahine (hōō'ähē'nä), volcanic island (□ 28; pop. 2,464), Leeward group, SOCIETY ISLANDS, Fr. Oceania, S Pacific, 25 mi. E of Raiatea. Consists of 2 isls. divided by isthmus; circumference 20 mi. Fertile and mountainous; Mt. Turi (2,230 ft.) highest peak. Exports copra. Chief town, Fare.

Hua-hsien, China: see FAHSIEN.

Huahua River or **Wawa River** (both: wä'wä), NE Nicaragua, rises in E outlier of Cordillera Isabella c.15 mi. NE of Bonanza, flows c.100 mi. ESE, through hardwood and banana dist., to Caribbean Sea 11 mi. SSW of Puerto Cabezas, here forming Carata Lagoon. Navigable in part.

Huahuaxtla (wäwä'slä), town (pop. 1,607), Puebla, central Mexico, in foothills of Sierra Madre Oriental, 20 mi. E of Zacatlán; corn, sugar cane, fruit.

Huaicho, Bolivia: see PUERTO ACOSTA.

Huai-hua, China: see HWAIHWA.

Huai-jou, China: see HWAIJU.

Huailas, province, Peru: see CARÁS.

Huailas, city, Peru: see HUAYLAS.

Huaillabamba (wīyäbäm'bä), town (pop. 1,241), Cuzco dept., S central Peru, on Urubamba R. and 5 mi. SE of Urubamba; cereals, potatoes. Sometimes Huayllabamba.

Huaillati (wīyä'tē), town (pop. 811), Apurímac dept., S central Peru, in Andean valley, 15 mi. S of Cotabambas; grain, livestock.

Huaillay or **Huayllay** (wīyī'), town (pop. 593), Pasco dept., central Peru, in Cordillera Occidental of the Andes, 24 mi. SSW of Cerro de Pasco; alt. c.14,000 ft. Road junction near SW branch of Cerro de Pasco–La Oroya RR. The Bosque de Rocas [Sp.,= rock forest], an unusually eroded rock formation, is near by.

Huainacotas (wīnäkō'täs), town (pop. 1,114), Arequipa prov., S Peru, in high Andean valley of Cordillera Occidental, 8 mi. NE of Cotahuasi; cereals, potatoes, stock; silver and gold mining.

Huaina Potosí, Bolivia: see HUAYNA POTOSÍ.

Huaina Putina, **Huaynaputina** (both: wī"näpōōtē'nä), or **Omate** (ōmä'tä), dormant Andean volcano (over 13,000 ft.), Moquegua dept., S Peru, SE of Nevado de Pichu Pichu and 45 mi. SE of Arequipa. Sp. colonial chronicles record evident eruptions, 1582–1783, the most severe in 1667. Town of Omate is at S foot.

Huaitará (wītärä'), city (pop. 718), Huancavelica dept., S central Peru, on Huaitará R. (left affluent of the Pisco) and 23 mi. S of Castrovirreyna; alt. 9,613 ft. Wheat, corn, barley, livestock. Also spelled Huaytará. Was ⊙ Castrovirreyna prov., 1919–42.

Huaitiquina Pass (wītēkē'nä) (14,025 ft.), in the Andes, on Argentina-Chile border; 23°44'S 67°13'W.

Huai Yot (hōō'ī yôt'), village (1937 pop. 2,737), Trang prov., S Thailand, on Malay Peninsula, 20 mi. N of Trang and on railroad. Highway to west-coast port of Krabi. Sometimes spelled Huey Yot.

Huajicori (wähēkō'rē), town (pop. 550), Nayarit, W Mexico, on Acaponeta R. and 12 mi. N of Acaponeta; corn, sugar cane, beans, cattle; silver and gold mining.

Huajuápan or **Huajuápan de León** (wawhä'pän dā lāōn'), city (pop. 4,275), Oaxaca, S Mexico, in Sierra Madre del Sur, on Inter-American Highway and 45 mi. NW of Nochixtlán; alt. 5,085 ft. Agr. center (cereals, coffee, sugar cane, fruit). Oil deposits near by. Airfield.

Hualahuises (wäläwē'sĕs), town (pop. 1,950), Nuevo León, N Mexico, in foothills of Sierra Madre Oriental, 8 mi. WNW of Linares; grain, livestock.

Hualaihué (wälīwā'), village (1930 pop. 50), Llanquihue prov., S central Chile, on a headland in Gulf of Ancud, 40 mi. SSE of Puerto Montt; dairying, lumbering. Sometimes Gualaihué.

Hualalai (hōō'älälä'ē), mountain (8,275 ft.), near W coast, Hawaii, T.H.

Hualañé (wälänyā'), village (pop. 1,010), Curicó prov., central Chile, on Mataquito R. and 32 mi. W of Curicó; rail terminus; agr. center (grain, beans, wine, livestock).

Hualgayoc (wälgīōk'), city (pop. 1,277), ⊙ Hualgayoc prov. (□ 2,140; pop. 102,482), Cajamarca dept., NW Peru, in Cordillera Occidental, 28 mi. NNW of Cajamarca, on road from Pacasmayo (Libertad dept.); alt. 11,548 ft. Silver-mining center; agr. products (corn, barley, potatoes).

Hualla (wä'yä), town (pop. 2,525), Ayacucho dept., S central Peru, on E slopes of Cordillera Occidental, 47 mi. SSE of Ayacucho; grain, livestock.

Huallaga, province, Peru: see SAPOSOA.

Huallaga River (wäyä'gä), central and N Peru, rises in the Andes S of Cerro de Pasco (Pasco dept.) in Cordillera Occidental, flows N, past Huánuco and Tingo María (Huánuco dept.), then NE, past Picota, Shapaja, Chasuta, and Yurimaguas (San Martín and Loreto depts.), entering the Amazon basin to join Marañón R. at 5°10'S 75°33'W. Estimated length, 700 mi. Navigable for small craft up to Tingo María (385 mi.), for large vessels to Lagunas (30 mi.).

Huallanca (wäyäng'kä). **1** Village (pop. 299), Ancash dept., W central Peru, on Santa R. and 5 mi. NE of Huaylas; rail terminus; corn, wheat. At steep gorge of Santa R. (Canyón de Perote) near by is a large govt. hydroelectric project. **2** City (pop. 1,490), Huánuco dept., central Peru, in the Andes, 12 mi. SW of La Unión; grain, potatoes, alfalfa; sheep raising. Silver mining near by.

Huallay Grande (wäyī' grän'dä), town (pop. 1,638), Huancavelica dept., S central Peru, in Cordillera Occidental, 3 mi. NNE of Lircay; grain, alfalfa, cattle, sheep.

Hualpai Mountains (wäl'pī), range in Mohave co., W Ariz.; extends c.50 mi. S from point near Kingman. Hualpai Peak (8,266 ft.), 12 mi. SE of Kingman, is highest point. NE extension (sometimes known as Peacock Mts.) rises to 6,268 ft. in Peacock Peak, 17 mi. ENE of Kingman.

Hualqui (wäl'kē), town (pop. 2,127), Concepción prov., S central Chile, on railroad, on Bío-Bío R. and 13 mi. SE of Concepción; agr. center (cereals, lentils, beans, potatoes, livestock); flour milling. Sometimes Gualqui.

Huamachuco (wämächōō'kō), city (pop. 2,450), ⊙ Huamachuco prov. (□ 1,247; pop. 49,385), Libertad dept., NW Peru, in Cordillera Occidental of the Andes, 70 mi. ENE of Trujillo; alt. 10,859 ft. Agr. products (wheat, corn, potatoes).

Huamalíes, Peru: see LLATA.

Huamanga, Peru: see AYACUCHO.

Huamanguilla (wämäng-gē'yä), town (pop. 1,351), Ayacucho dept., S central Peru, in the Andes, 12 mi. N of Ayacucho; sugar cane, coffee, coca; vineyards.

Huamantanga (wämäntäng'gä), town (pop. 1,372), Lima dept., W central Peru, in Cordillera Occidental, 5 mi. WNW of Canta; grain, potatoes, livestock.

Huamantla (wämän'tlä), officially Huamantla de Juárez, city (pop. 7,287), Tlaxcala, central Mexico, at NE foot of Malinche volcano, on railroad and 25 mi. NE of Puebla; alt. 8,225 ft. Agr. center (corn, wheat, barley, alfalfa, beans, maguey, livestock); flour milling, pulque distilling. Many churches. Airfield.

Huambo, Angola: see NOVA LISBOA.

Huamuxtitlán (wämōōstētlän'), city (pop. 1,786), Guerrero, SW Mexico, in Sierra Madre del Sur, 50 mi. ENE of Chilapa; alt. 3,691 ft.; cereals, sugar cane, fruit.

Huan-, for Chinese names beginning thus and not found here: see under HWAN-; WAN-.

Huanacache or **Guanacache** (both: wänäkä'chā), swamp and lake district of Argentina, on borders of San Juan, Mendoza, and San Luis provs., formed by San Juan, Mendoza, and Bermejo rivers; extends c.90 mi. SE and S. It is drained by the Desaguadero, part of the Río SALADO. Popular fishing area.

Huañamarca, Lake, Bolivia: see UINAMARCA, LAKE.

Huanay, Bolivia: see GUANAY.

Huancabamba (wäng-käbäm'bä). **1** Town, Pasco dept., central Peru, on E slopes of Cordillera Oriental, 6 mi. NW of Oxapampa; coffee, cacao, fruit. **2** City (pop. 2,580), ⊙ Huancabamba prov. (□ 2,532; pop. 51,613), Piura dept., NW Peru, in Cordillera Occidental of the Andes, on Huancabamba R. and 80 mi. E of Piura, near Peru-Ecuador boundary; alt. 6,420 ft. Trade in tobacco, coffee, cacao, hides; cattle raising.

Huancabamba River, NW Peru, rises in Cordillera Occidental 15 mi. N of Huancabamba (Piura dept.), flows 120 mi. S and NE, past Huancabamba, to Marañón R. 9 mi. SE of Jaén (Cajamarca dept.). Also called Chamaya R. in lower course.

Huancané (wäng-känā'), town (pop. c.1,150), Oruro dept., W Bolivia, in the Altiplano, 55 mi. SSE of Oruro, on Oruro-Uyuni RR; alt. 12,185 ft.; corn, potatoes, quinoa.

Huancané, town (pop. 2,595), ⊙ Huancané prov. (□ 3,855; pop. 111,927), Puno dept., SE Peru, on the Altiplano, near N shore of L. Titicaca, 48 mi. NNE of Puno; alt. 12,631 ft. Trade center; potatoes, barley, quinoa, livestock.

Huancapi (wäng-kä'pē), town (pop. 2,415), ⊙ Víctor Fajardo prov. (□ 1,385; pop. 39,177), Ayacucho dept., S central Peru, on E slopes of Cordillera Occidental, 40 mi. SSE of Ayacucho; alt. 10,607 ft. Grain, alfalfa, livestock.

Huancapón (wäng-käpōn'), town (pop. 978), Lima dept., W central Peru, in Cordillera Occidental, 17 mi. SW of Cajatambo; grain; cattle raising.

Huancarama (wäng-kärä'mä), town (pop. 1,500), Apurímac dept., S central Peru, in Andean spur, 13 mi. W of Abancay; gold and coal mining; potatoes, grain, stock.

Huanca Sancos (wäng'kä säng'kōs), city (pop. 1,893), Ayacucho dept., S central Peru, in Cordillera Occidental, 45 mi. SSW of Ayacucho; stock-raising center (cattle, sheep, llamas, vicuñas, alpacas); grain, alfalfa.

Huancavelica (wäng-kävälē'kä), department (□ 8,300; pop. 265,557), S central Peru; ⊙ Huancavelica. Mainly mountainous, drained by Mantaro R., which separates Cordillera Central from Cordillera Occidental. Wheat, barley, corn, alfalfa; cattle and sheep raising in mts.; sugar cane, mostly used for distilling, in valleys of Cordillera Central. Mining and smelting (silver, lead, mercury) in area of Castrovirreyna, Huancavelica, and Lircay. Main centers: Huancavelica, Acobamba, Pampas. Dept. is served by Huancayo-Huancavelica RR.

Huancavelica, city (pop. 8,139), ⊙ Huancavelica dept. and Huancavelica prov. (□ 1,936; pop. 63,571), S central Peru, on Huancavelica R. (right affluent of the Mantaro) and 50 mi. SSE of Huancayo, 140 mi. ESE of Lima (connected by railroad); 12°46'S 75°2'W; alt. 12,401 ft. Mining and smelting center (mercury, silver, lead); flour milling; exports wool. Flourished in colonial period following opening (16th cent.) of mercury mines. It declined in 19th cent., but resumed its mining activity after construction (1926) of railroad from Huancayo. The Potochi thermal springs are in NE outskirts.

Huancayo (wäng-kī'ō), city (pop. 28,680), ⊙ Junín dept. and Huancayo prov. (□ 1,388; enumerated pop. 132,632, plus estimated 5,000 Indians), central Peru, on Mantaro R. and 120 mi. E of Lima, 45 mi. SE of La Oroya (connected by rail and highway); 12°4'S 75°12'W; alt. 10,731 ft. One of the most important agr. centers of Peru, shipping especially wheat. Has brewery, flour mills, dairies; mfg. of textiles, furniture, soap, silver articles; tanning; processing of ceramics, lime, and gypsum; lumber milling; trade in agr. products (wheat, corn, alfalfa). Tourist resort, known for its colonial architecture. An Amer. magnetic observatory is 12 mi. S. City was an old Inca center, situated on one of imperial highways (later used by Pizarro in his conquest of Peru). In 1931, dept. ⊙ was moved here from Cerro de Pasco.

Huanchaca (wänchä'kä), town, Potosí dept., SW Bolivia, on W slopes of Cordillera de Chichas and 15 mi. NE of Uyuni, on rail branch; alt. 14,895 ft. With near-by PULACAYO, it is main silver-mining center of Bolivia.

Huanchaco (wäng-chä'kō), town (pop. 520), Libertad dept., NW Peru, Pacific port, on railroad and 7 mi. WNW of Trujillo; fisheries.

Huan Chiang, China: see WAN RIVER.

Huandacareo (wändäkärā'ō), town (pop. 3,445), Michoacán, central Mexico, on NW shore of L. Cuitzeo, 22 mi. NW of Morelia; agr. center (cereals, fruit, stock).

Huando (wän'dō), town (pop. 1,224), Huancavelica dept., S central Peru, in Cordillera Occidental, on Huancayo-Huancavelica RR and 15 mi. NNE of Huancavelica; grain, corn, alfalfa, livestock.

Huang-, for Chinese names beginning thus and not found here: see under HWANG-.

Huang-ch'iao, China: see HWANGKIAO.

Huang-ch'uan, China: see HWANGCHWAN.

Huang-hua, China: see HWANGHWA.

Huang-kang, China: see UNGKUNG.

Huang-pu, China: see WHAMPOA.

Huanguelén (wäng-gälĕn'), town (pop. 3,002), W central Buenos Aires prov., Argentina, 28 mi. E of Guaminí; rail junction in grain-growing area.

Huanímaro (wänē'märō), town (pop. 2,311), Guanajuato, central Mexico, on central plateau, 22 mi. SSW of Irapuato; alt. 5,840 ft.; cereals, alfalfa, beans, sugar cane, fruit.

Huaniqueo (wänēkā'ō), officially Huaniqueo de Morales, town (pop. 2,003), Michoacán, central Mexico, 30 mi. NW of Morelia; cereals, fruit, livestock.

Hunoquite (wänōkē'tä), town (pop. 700), Cuzco dept., S Peru, 33 mi. SSW of Cuzco; grain.

Huanta (wän'tä), city (pop. 4,874), ⊙ Huanta prov. (□ 2,373; enumerated pop. 55,985, plus estimated 10,000 Indians), Ayacucho dept., S central Peru, in the Andes, 15 mi. NNW of Ayacucho (connected by highway); alt. 10,552 ft. Sugar cane, coca, coffee, grain. Gold, silver, lead, copper mining near by.

Huantajaya, Chile: see GUANTAJAYA.

Huantán (wäntän'), town (pop. 1,098), Lima dept., W central Peru, in Cordillera Occidental, 6 mi. E of Yauyos; potatoes, grain, livestock.

Huantar (wäntär'), town (pop. 1,123), Ancash dept., W central Peru, on E slopes of Cordillera Blanca, 22 mi. ENE of Huarás; barley, potatoes.

Huantraicó, Sierra de (syĕ'rä dā wäntrīkō'), subandean range in N Neuquén natl. territory, Argentina, 25 mi. E of Chos Malal; c.20 mi. long; rises to c.6,000 ft. Has coal deposits.

Huánuco (wä'nōōkō), department (□ 15,431; enumerated pop. 251,833, plus estimated 25,000 Indians), central Peru; ⊙ Huánuco. Bordered by middle Huallaga R. (NE), upper Marañón R. (NW), and Cordillera Blanca of the Andes (SW). Crossed N-S by Cordillera Central (W of Huallaga R.) and E by Cordillera Oriental. Corn, barley, potatoes; sheep and cattle raising in mts.; coca, cacao, and coffee in subtropical valleys on slopes of mtn. ranges. Rubber exploitation; lumbering in E tropical regions toward Pachitea R. Oil is found at Agua Caliente on the Pachitea. Dept. is served by highway from Cerro de Pasco (SW) to Pucallpa (NE). Main centers: Huánuco, Acomayo, Margos.

Huánuco, city (pop. 12,877), ⊙ Huánuco dept. and Huánuco prov. (□ 3,868; pop. 72,856), central Peru, on E slopes of Cordillera Central, on Huallaga R., on highway, and 50 mi. N of Cerro de Pasco, 155 mi. NNE of Lima; 9°55'S 76°12'W; alt. 6,273 ft. Local trade center. Factories produce brandy, timber, agr. products (coca, sugar cane, cotton, coffee, cacao, fruit). Tourist resort. Airport. Cotton ginning and sugar milling near by. Bishopric. Has Superior Court of Justice, govt. bldg., public school, colonial style churches. Founded by the Spaniards in 1539, it became an important center in colonial times, declining afterward.

Huanuni (wänōō'nē), town (pop. c.8,600), ⊙ Pantaleón Dalence prov., Oruro dept., W Bolivia, on W slope of Cordillera de Azanaques and 28 mi. SSE of Oruro, on Machacamarca-Uncía RR; alt. 12,871 ft. Major tin-mining center.

Huanusco (wänōō'skō), town (pop. 733), Zacatecas, N central Mexico, 22 mi. ESE of Tlaltenango.

Huanzo, Cordillera de (kôrdīyä'rä dā wän'sō), section of Cordillera Occidental of the Andes, S Peru, on Ayacucho-Apurímac dept. border, extends c.100 mi. from Cotahuasi W to Puquio; rises to c.20,000 ft.

Huapango, Lake (wäpäng'gō), artificial lake in Mexico state, central Mexico, 30 mi. ENE of El Oro; c.12 mi. long.

Huapi Mountains or **Wapi Mountains** (both wä'pē), S central Nicaragua, E spur of main continental divide; extend from area of Camoapa c.100 mi. E toward Pearl Lagoon; rise to c.4,000 ft. Form watershed bet. Río Grande (N) and Escondido R. (S).

Huaquechula (wäkächōō'lä), town (pop. 1,433), Puebla, central Mexico, 12 mi. SW of Atlixco; cereals, sugar cane, vegetables, livestock.

Huaqui, Bolivia: see GUAQUI.

Huaquirca (wäkēr'kä), town (pop. 786), Apurímac dept., S central Peru, on affluent of Pachachaca R. and 2½ mi. N of Antabamba; grain, stock.

Huara (wä'rä), town (pop. 1,794), Tarapacá prov., N Chile, on railroad and 30 mi. NE of Iquique; nitrate mining and refining. Flourished c.1900.

Huaral (wäräl'), town (pop. 5,012), Lima dept., W central Peru, on coastal plain, 35 mi. NNW of Lima; rail junction on Chancay-Palpa RR and line from Lima, in cotton-growing area; cotton ginning, mfg. of soap.

Huarás or **Huaraz** (both: wäräs'), city (pop. 12,099), ⊙ Ancash dept. and Huarás prov. (□ 1,628; pop. 74,748), W central Peru, in the Callejón de Huaylas, on Santa R., on road, and 50 mi. ESE of Casma, 175 mi. NNW of Lima; 9°32'S 77°32'W; alt. 9,931 ft. Predominantly Indian. It is a commercial center for an agr. region (wheat, corn, potatoes) and mining area (silver, lead, copper, coal). Also weaving of native textiles, brewing, mfg. of candy. Hot springs in vicinity. Bishopric. Has archaeological mus. Tourist resort. Huascarán, highest peak in Peru, is 30 mi. N. Huarás suffered severely in earthquake of 1941.

Huari (wä'rē), town (pop. c.1,900), Oruro dept., W Bolivia, in the Altiplano, 75 mi. SSE of Oruro, on Oruro-Uyuni RR; alt. 12,165 ft.; brewery. Annual fair of cattle and agr. products.

Huari, city (pop. 2,106), ⊙ Huari prov. (□ 2,096; pop. 98,294), Ancash dept., W central Peru, on E slopes of Cordillera Blanca of the Andes, 24 mi. ENE of Huarás; alt. 3,158 ft. Agr. products (barley, corn, potatoes). Lead, silver mined near by.

Huariaca (wäryä'kä), town (pop. 1,593), Pasco dept., central Peru, on Huallaga R. and 17 mi. NNE of Cerro de Pasco; wheat, barley. Lead and silver mining near by.
Huarina (wärē'nä), village (pop. c.11,700), La Paz dept., W Bolivia, on L. Titicaca and 36 mi. NW of La Paz; alt. 12,549 ft.; potatoes, sheep. Here Gonzalo Pizarro defeated (1547) rebelling Diego Centeno.
Huarmaca (wärmä'kä), town (pop. 428), Piura dept., NW Peru, on W slopes of Cordillera Occidental, 23 mi. SSW of Huancabamba; corn, wheat, potatoes.
Huarmey, province, Peru: see CASMA.
Huarmey (wärmā'), town (pop. 1,333), Ancash dept., W central Peru, on coastal plain, near mouth of small Huarmey R., on Pan-American Highway and 40 mi. SSE of Casma; corn, fruit. Its port, Puerto Huarmey, on the Pacific, is 3 mi. SW.
Huarochirí, province, Peru: see MATUCANA.
Huarochirí (wärōchērē'), city (pop. 1,865), Lima dept., W central Peru, on Mala R., just opposite San Lorenzo de Quinti, and 55 mi. ESE of Lima; wheat, corn.
Huarocondo (wärōkōn'dō), town (pop. 2,755), Cuzco dept., S central Peru, in the Andes, on railroad and 22 mi. WNW of Cuzco; grain growing; marble and gypsum quarries.
Huarón (wärōn'), village (pop. 1,361), Pasco dept., central Peru, in Cordillera Occidental of the Andes, 24 mi. SSW of Cerro de Pasco, near SW branch of La Oroya–Cerro de Pasco RR.; alt. c.15,000 ft. Mining center (copper, silver, gold); smelter.
Huarte (wär'tā), town (pop. 1,049), Navarre prov., N Spain, 3 mi. NE of Pamplona; flour milling, meat packing; cereals, fruit.
Huásabas (wä'säbäs), town (pop. 803), Sonora, NW Mexico, on Bavispe R. and 115 mi. NE of Hermosillo; livestock, wheat.
Huasca (wä'skä), officially Huasca de Ocampo, town (pop. 1,269), Hidalgo, central Mexico, 12 mi. NE of Pachuca; corn, maguey, beans, livestock.
Huascarán (wäskärän'), extinct Andean volcano (22,205 ft.) in Ancash dept., W central Peru, in Cordillera Blanca, 9 mi. ENE of Yungay; 9°7'S 77°37'W. Highest elevation in Peru, and one of the highest in the Andes, it is in a massif containing other impressive snow-capped peaks.
Huasco, department, Chile: see VALLENAR.
Huasco (wäs'kō), town (pop. 1,537), Atacama prov., N central Chile, Pacific port near mouth (2 mi. SW) of Huasco R., 30 mi. WNW of Vallenar, 95 mi. SW of Copiapó; 28°28'S. Rail terminus; trading and mfg. center. Ships copper, cobalt, nickel, other ores; also exports noted Huasco wines, currants, goatskins. Copper smelters, wineries. Agr.: corn, alfalfa, clover. Deposits of high-grade iron ores near by (so far little exploited). Airport. Formerly also spelled Guasco. Heavily damaged in 1922 earthquake.
Huasco Bajo (bä'hō), village (1930 pop. 565), Atacama prov., N central Chile, on Huasco R., on railroad and 3 mi. E of Huasco, in agr. area (alfalfa, corn, wine, cattle, goats).
Huasco River or **Guasco River**, Atacama prov., N Chile, formed 20 mi. SE of Vallenar by confluence at NW foot of Sierra de Tatul of 2 headstreams, flows c.60 mi. WNW, past Vallenar and Huasco Bajo, to the Pacific 2 mi. NE of Huasco; c.140 mi. long, with longest tributary. Irrigates agr. area where alfalfa, corn, oranges, and wine are grown, cattle and goats are raised. Rich mining area.
Huaspán or **Waspán** (wäspän'), village, Cabo Gracias a Dios territory, Zelaya dept., NE Nicaragua, on Coco R. and 70 mi. WSW of Cabo Gracias a Dios; hardwood lumbering.
Huaspuc River or **Waspuc River** (both: wäspōōk'), N Nicaragua, rises as Pis Pis R. in Bonanza gold-mining area (hydroelectric station), flows 70 mi. N, past Morabila (gold mining), to Coco R. at Huaspuc. Sometimes spelled Waspook.
Huasteca, La (lä wästä'kä), Gulf lowlands in NE Mexico, comprise central and lower Pánuco R. basin of Veracruz and Tamaulipas; rise near slopes of Sierra Madre Oriental in Hidalgo and San Luis Potosí. Fertile region with abundant rain, tropical in the plains. Excellent pastures for stock raising; produces on large scale sugar cane, cereals, fruit. Center of Mexico's petroleum industry.
Huata, Bolivia: see SANTIAGO DE HUATA.
Huatabampo (wätäbäm'pō), city (pop. 5,643), Sonora, NW Mexico, on the Gulf of California, near Mayo R. mouth (irrigation area), 110 mi. SE of Guaymas; agr. center (chick-peas, cereals, fruit).
Huata Peninsula, Bolivia: see ACHACACHI PENINSULA.
Hua-ti, China: see FATI.
Huatlatlauca (wätlätlou'kä), town (pop. 1,124), Puebla, central Mexico, near Atoyac R., 27 mi. SSE of Puebla; corn, sugar cane, fruit, livestock.
Huatusco (wätōō'skō), officially Huatusco de Chicuellar, city (pop. 6,539), Veracruz, E Mexico, in Sierra Madre Oriental, 50 mi. W of Veracruz; agr. center (bananas, corn, coffee, sugar cane).
Huauchinango (wouchēnäng'gō), city (pop. 5,779), Puebla, central Mexico, in SE Sierra Madre Oriental, on railroad and 45 mi. E of Pachuca; alt. 4,888 ft. Processing and agr. center (corn, coffee, sugar cane, tobacco, vegetables, fruit); floriculture; tanning, lumbering, shoe mfg. Necaxa dam and hydroelectric plant are near by.
Huauco, Peru: see SUCRE.
Huaura (wou'rä), town (pop. 1,161), Lima dept., W central Peru, on coastal plain, on Huaura R. and 2 mi. NNE of Huacho (connected by railroad and tramway). Center of important cotton and sugar-cane area; cotton ginning, sugar milling.
Huaura River, Lima dept., W central Peru, rises in Cordillera Occidental of the Andes 17 mi. W of Yanahuanca, flows 90 mi. SW and W, past Sayán and Huaura, to the Pacific. Irrigation works are 1 mi. WNW of Huacho in lower course.
Huautla (wou'tlä). **1** Town (pop. 2,307), Hidalgo, central Mexico, in Sierra Madre Oriental foothills, 12 mi. SE of Huejutla; agr. center (corn, rice, sugar cane, tobacco, fruit, livestock). **2** Officially Huautla de Jiménez, town (pop. 3,314), Oaxaca, S Mexico, in Sierra Madre del Sur, 40 mi. SE of Tehuacán; alt. 5,623 ft. Agr. center (cereals, sugar cane, fruit, tobacco).
Huayacocotla (wīäkōkō'tlä), town (pop. 1,040), Veracruz, E Mexico, in Sierra Madre Oriental, 35 mi. SW of Chicontepec; cereals, sugar cane, coffee.
Huaycho, Bolivia: see PUERTO ACOSTA.
Huayday (wīdī'), village (pop. 185), Libertad dept., NW Peru, in Cordillera Occidental, 20 mi. NNW of Otusco; anthracite deposits.
Huaylas, province, Peru: see CARÁS.
Huaylas or **Huailas** (both: wī'läs), town (pop. 1,246), Ancash dept., W central Peru, in the Callejón de Huaylas, 13 mi. NNW of Carás; wheat, corn.
Huaylas, Callejón de (käyĕhōn' dā), valley of upper SANTA RIVER in Cordillera Occidental of the Andes, Ancash dept., W central Peru, bet. Cordillera Negra (W) and Cordillera Blanca (E). Extends 100 mi. SSE from area of Huallanca to area of Chiquián. Silver, lead, and copper mines at Recuay, Carhuás, and Carás. Agr.: wheat, corn, fruit, potatoes. Main centers: Huarás, Yungay, Huaylas.
Huayllabamba, Peru: see HUAILLABAMBA.
Huayllay, Peru: see HUAILLAY.
Huayna Potosí (wī'nä pōtōsē'), peak (20,328 ft.) in Cordillera de La Paz, W Bolivia, 17 mi. NNW of La Paz; site of tin mines. Formerly also Huaina Potosí.
Huaynaputina, Peru: see HUAINA PUTINA.
Huayopota (wīōpō'tä), town (pop. 606), Cuzco dept., S central Peru, on affluent of Urubamba R. and 11 mi. SSE of Quillabamba. Sugar, coffee, cacao; liquor distilling, sugar milling.
Huazalingo (wäsäling'gō), town (pop. 470), Hidalgo, central Mexico, 14 mi. SW of Huejutla; corn, rice, sugar cane, tobacco, livestock.
Hubalta (hŭbôl'tŭ), village (pop. estimate 350), S Alta., near Bow R., E suburb of Calgary.
Hubbard, county (□ 932; pop. 11,085), NW central Minn.; ⊙ Park Rapids. Agr. area watered in S by small lakes. Dairy products, potatoes; peat deposits. Includes state forests in N and SE. Co. formed 1883.
Hubbard. **1** Town (pop. 836), Hardin co., central Iowa, 27 mi. NW of Marshalltown; feed, concrete blocks, dairy products. **2** Village (pop. 145), Dakota co., NE Nebr., 13 mi. SW of Sioux City, Iowa, near Missouri R. **3** Industrial village (pop. 4,560), Trumbull co., NE Ohio, 5 mi. NE of Youngstown, near Pa. line; mfg. of steel specialties and other metal products; has greenhouses. Settled 1803, inc. 1869. **4** City (pop. 493), Marion co., NW Oregon, 25 mi. SSW of Portland; berries. **5** City (pop. 1,768), Hill co., central Texas, 29 mi. NE of Waco; trade, shipping center in cotton-growing area; has mineral wells.
Hubbard, Mount (14,950 ft.), on Yukon-Alaska border in St. Elias Mts., 140 mi. W of Whitehorse, 60 mi. NNE of Yakutat; 60°19'N 139°4'W.
Hubbard Glacier (50 mi. long), SE Alaska, on Disenchantment Bay at head of Yakutat Bay; 60°2'N 139°25'W; part of St. Elias Mts. glacier system.
Hubbard Lake, NE Mich., 15 mi. SSW of Alpena; c.7 mi. long, 3 mi. wide; fishing. Source of a branch of Thunder Bay R. Hubbard Lake, resort village, is near N end.
Hubbardston. **1** Agr. town (pop. 1,134), Worcester co., N central Mass., 18 mi. NNW of Worcester, near Wachusett Mtn. Settled 1737, inc. 1767. **2** Village (pop. 335), on Ionia-Clinton co. line, S central Mich., 14 mi. NE of Ionia and on Fish Creek, in farm area.
Hubbardton, town (pop. 332), Rutland co., W Vt., 12 mi. NW of Rutland, at N end of L. Bomoseen. Scene, July 7, 1777, of Br. victory over Seth Warner.
Hubbell. **1** Village (pop. 1,690), Houghton co., NW Upper Peninsula, Mich., 7 mi. NE of Houghton, on Torch L. (connected by deepwater channel to Keweenaw Waterway), in copper-mining area; copper refining. **2** Village (pop. 199), Thayer co., SE Nebr., 12 mi. SSE of Hebron, at Kansas line, and on branch of Little Blue R.
Hubertusburg (hōōbĕr'tōōsbōōrk"), hunting lodge, Saxony, E central Germany, 10 mi. ENE of Grimma, 24 mi. E of Leipzig. Peace treaty bet. Prussia, Saxony, and Austria, at conclusion of Seven Years War, was signed here in Feb., 1763. Built 1721–33 for electors of Saxony, it is now insane asylum.
Hubli (hōōb'lē), city (pop., including suburban area, 98,751), Dharwar dist., S Bombay, India, 12 mi. SE of Dharwar; rail (workshops) and road junction; important cotton market; cotton ginning and milling, handicraft cloth weaving, mfg. of chemicals, biri; rice milling; copper, brass, and iron goods. Arts, engineering, commercial cols. Held 14th–16th cent. by Vijayanagar kings.
Hubsugul, Mongolia: see KHUBSUGUL.
Hucal, Argentina: see BERNASCONI.
Hucclecote, town and parish (pop. 1,272), N central Gloucester, England, 3 mi. E of Gloucester; aircraft works.
Huchow, China: see WUHING.
Huchu (hōō'jōō'), town, ⊙ Huchu co. (pop. 112,683), NE Tsinghai prov., China, 20 mi. NE of Sining, on Kansu border; cattle raising; agr. products. Until 1931 called Weiyüanpu.
Huckarde (hōō'kär"dù), district (since 1914) of Dortmund, W Germany, on Dortmund-Ems Canal and 2 mi. NW of city center; extensive port facilities.
Hückelhoven (hü'kùlhō"fùn), agr. village (pop. 13,992), in former Prussian Rhine Prov., W Germany, after 1945 in North Rhine-Westphalia, near the Rur, 20 mi. NNE of Aachen. Enlarged 1935 through incorporation of Hilfarth, Ratheim, and part of Klein Gladbach.
Hückeswagen (hü'kùsvä"gùn), town (pop. 12,421), in former Prussian Rhine Prov., W Germany, after 1945 in North Rhine-Westphalia, 5 mi. E of Wermelskirchen; mfg. of cloth. Bever dam and reservoir 1.5 mi. E.
Hucknall or **Hucknall Torkard** (hŭk'nùl tôr'kùrd), urban district (1931 pop. 17,338; 1951 census 23,213), W Nottingham, England, 6 mi. NNW of Nottingham; coal mines, hosiery mills. Has 14th-cent. church, with tomb of Byron.
Hucknall-under-Huthwaite, England: see HUTHWAITE.
Hucqueliers (ükùlyā'), agr. village (pop. 616), Pas-de-Calais dept., N France, 10 mi. NE of Montreuil.
Hudaida, Yemen: see HODEIDA.
Hudaydah, Al-, Yemen: see HODEIDA.
Huddersfield, (hŭ'dùrz–), county borough (1931 pop. 113,475; 1951 census 129,021), West Riding, SW Yorkshire, England, on Colne R. and 15 mi. SW of Leeds; 53°39'N 2°47'W; important woolen-, cotton-, and silk-milling center; mfg. of machinery, chemical and aniline dyes, clothing. The proximity of coal and good transportation facilities by river, canal, and rail contributed to its development. Has church (c.1100) rebuilt 1836; Cloth Hall, built 1766; and Tolson Memorial Mus. In county borough are textile-milling suburbs of Marsh (pop. 7,582), Moldgreen (pop. 11,479), Paddock (pop. 8,601), Birkby (pop. 7,680), Lindley (pop. 7,565), Longwood (pop. 6,290), Lockwood (pop. 7,660), Dalton, Bradley and Deighton (pop. 6,244), and Almondbury (äl'mùndbùrē, ā'mùnd–, ô'mùnd–) (pop. 8,435).
Huddinge (hŭ'dĭng-ù), village (pop. 1,154), Stockholm co., E Sweden, 7 mi. SW of Stockholm city center; hosiery knitting, concrete mfg.
Hude (hōō'dù), village (commune pop. 10,275), in Oldenburg, NW Germany, after 1945 in Lower Saxony, 8 mi. NW of Delmenhorst; rail junction. Has ruined 13th-cent. monastery.
Hudiksvall (hü'dĭksväl'), city (pop. 7,829), Gavleborg co., E Sweden, on Hudiksvall Fjord, Swedish *Hudiksvallsfjärden*, 15-mi.-long inlet of Gulf of Bothnia, 45 mi. S of Sundsvall; seaport, timber-shipping center; rail junction. Metalworking, sawmilling; mfg. of chemicals. Has archaeological mus. Chartered as city in 16th cent. Near by are several winter-sports resorts.
Hudin (hōōdēn'), locality, SE Br. Somaliland, on road and 50 mi. N of Las Anod; water well.
Hudlice (hōōd'lĭtsĕ), Ger. *Hudlitz* (hōōd'lĭts), village (pop. 1,436), central Bohemia, Czechoslovakia, 5 mi. W of Beroun; iron mining. Historian Josef Jungmann b. here.
Hudson. **1** Village (pop. estimate 700), NW Ont., on inlet of L. Seul, 12 mi. W of Sioux Lookout, in gold-mining, dairying, grain-growing region. **2** Village (pop. 731), S Que., on L. of the Two Mountains, 8 mi. E of Rigaud; dairying, potato growing; resort.
Hudson, county (□ 45; pop. 647,437), NE N.J., bounded by Passaic R. and Newark Bay (W), and Hudson R. and Upper New York Bay (E); ⊙ JERSEY CITY, a commercial and transportation center of New York metropolitan area. Heavily industrialized, with varied mfg., oil refining, shipbuilding, rail and ocean shipping. Drained by Hackensack R. Formed 1840.
Hudson. **1** Town (pop. 365), Weld co., N Colo., near South Platte R., 30 mi. NE of Denver; alt. 5,000 ft. **2** Town (pop. 339), McLean co., central Ill., 8 mi. N of Bloomington, in rich agr. area. L. Bloomington is near by. **3** Town (pop. 420), Steuben co., NE Ind., 32 mi. N of Fort Wayne; potatoes, onions. **4** Town (pop. 613), Black Hawk co., E central Iowa, 8 mi. SW of Waterloo, in agr. area. **5** City (pop. 194), Stafford co., S central Kansas, 40 mi. W of Hutchinson, near Rattlesnake Creek, in wheat area. **6** Agr. town (pop. 455), Penobscot co., S central Maine, just NW of Old

Town. **7** Town (pop. 8,211), Middlesex co., E central Mass., on Assabet R. and 14 mi. NE of Worcester; shoes, textiles, machine tools, plastics, rubber clothing. Settled 1699, inc. 1866. **8** City (pop. 2,773), Lenawee co., SE Mich., on Tiffin R. and 16 mi. WSW of Adrian; shipping point for rich farm area; mfg. (fruit sprayers, car washers, harnesses, food products). Indian mounds near by. Settled 1834; inc. as village 1853, as city 1893. **9** Town (pop. 4,183), including Hudson village (pop. 2,382), Hillsboro co., S N.H., on the Merrimack opposite Nashua; agr. Inc. 1722 as Nottingham, named Hudson 1830. **10** City (pop. 11,629), ⊙ Columbia co., SE N.Y., on E bank of the Hudson and 28 mi. S of Albany, in diversified-farming area; mfg. (matches, cement, food and leather products, knit goods, furniture); limestone quarrying. Rip Van Winkle Bridge (3 mi. SW) crosses the Hudson to Catskill. A state training school for girls is here. Settled 1662, inc. 1785. Was whaling and sealing port until early-19th cent. **11** Town (pop. 922), Caldwell co., W central N.C., 5 mi. SE of Lenoir; cotton mills. **12** Village (pop. 1,538), Summit co., NE Ohio, 11 mi. NE of Akron; photographic equipment, sheet metal, fireworks, gaskets, textiles. Western Reserve Acad. (1826) is here. Settled 1799, inc. 1837. **13** Town (pop. 500), Lincoln co., SE S.Dak., 14 mi. SSE of Canton and on Big Sioux R.; trading center for rich corn-producing area; dairy produce, livestock, poultry. **14** City (pop. 3,435), ⊙ St. Croix co., W Wis., on St. Croix R. and 15 mi. E of St. Paul (Minn.), in dairying and grain-growing area; railroad workshops; mfg. of dairy products, furniture, refrigerators. A near-by park has Indian mounds. Inc. 1856. **15** Town (pop. 293), Fremont co., W central Wyo., on Popo Agie R. and 9 mi. NE of Lander; alt. 5,094 ft. Trading and cattle-shipping point in fruit and vegetable region; coal mines. Near by is state school for mental defectives.

Hudson Bay, large inland sea (□ c.475,000), E central Canada, bounded by Ont. (S), Man. (SW), Keewatin Dist. (W) and Franklin Dist. (N) of the Northwest Territories, and Ungava Peninsula, Que. (E); 52°–62°50′N 76°–95°W. It is 850 mi. long, 650 mi. wide, including JAMES BAY, its SE arm. Average depth is 70 fathoms; maximum depth of 141 fathoms has been chartered in center of bay. It is connected with the Atlantic by Hudson Strait (NE) and with the Arctic Ocean by Foxe Channel (N); its N entrance is sheltered by Southampton, Coats, and Mansel isls. Bay contains isls. of Akimiski, Coats, Mansel, and Charlton, and the isl. groups Belcher, Ottawa, Sleeper, and Twin isls., all near the rocky E shore. Receives Churchill, Nelson, Severn, Albany, Ekwan, Attawapiskat, Abitibi, Moose, Harricanaw, Nottaway, and Great Whale rivers; combined drainage basin of rivers flowing into bay is 1,379,160 sq. mi. There are important cod and salmon fisheries; whaling was formerly carried on. Churchill is chief port on bay; trading posts include Chesterfield Inlet, Eskimo Point, York Factory, Fort Severn, Fort Albany, Moosonee, Moose Factory, Rupert House, Old Factory River, and Port Harrison. Coral Harbour, on S Southampton Isl., is air base. Bay is navigable from mid-July to Oct. Discovered 1610 by Henry Hudson, bay was explored by Sir Thomas Button (1612), William Baffin (1615), Jens Munck (1619), Luke Foxe, and Thomas James (1631). Radisson reached it overland (1662) and Groseilliers built 1st trading post (1668) at mouth of Rupert R. Bet. 1682 and 1713 French made repeated attempts to establish themselves here and at times were in complete control of the bay; Treaty of Utrecht (1713) assigned all Fr. posts to England. Hudson's Bay Co. was chartered 1760 and held exclusive trading rights in bay's watershed area until territory was acquired by Canada in 1869, when bay's designation became that of an inland sea of the Dominion. Hudson Bay railroad to Churchill was completed from The Pas, 1929; grain shipments to Europe began 1931. Another railroad reached Moosonee from North Bay, 1932.

Hudson Bay Junction, village (pop. 793), E Sask., 80 mi. SW of The Pas; railroad junction for The Pas–Flin Flon mining region; lumbering, clay quarrying, mixed farming.

Hudson Falls, village (pop. 7,236), ⊙ Washington co., E N.Y., on E bank of the Hudson and 3 mi. E of Glens Falls, in diversified-farming area; lumber and paper milling; mfg. of clothing, machinery, wood and cement products. Limestone quarrying. Settled 1761, inc. 1810.

Hudson Heights, village (pop. 715), S Que., on L. of the Two Mountains, 7 mi. E of Rigaud; dairying, potato growing.

Hudson Island, Gilbert Isls.: see NANUMANGA.

Hudson River, in N.Y. and N.J., rises as Opalescent R. in tiny L. Tear of the Clouds near Mt. Marcy in the Adirondacks, receives several small headstreams, flows S to Corinth, E to Hudson Falls, then generally S, forming N.Y.–N.J. line for c.17 mi. near its mouth, to Upper New York Bay at New York city, where its lowest section, an important part of the harbor, is called North R.; c.315 mi. long; drains □ 13,370. A drowned river valley for its lower 150 mi., the Hudson also has a deep submarine canyon extending for 200 mi. seaward from its mouth. Tidal to Albany, head of channel for ocean-going vessels; Troy is at head of 12-ft. channel. One of the world's important commercial waterways, the Hudson is linked to the Great Lakes, L. Champlain, and the St. Lawrence by N.Y. State Barge Canal system, including canalized Mohawk R., chief tributary of the Hudson, which enters at Cohoes. Falls in the upper Hudson furnish water power. The section (2–3 mi. wide) bet. Westchester and Rockland counties, N.Y., is known as TAPPAN ZEE. Scenic Catskill Mts. descend to W bank in Greene and Ulster counties, N.Y.; the rugged Hudson highlands (part of Appalachian system) lie along both banks S of Newburgh; the PALISADES (Palisades Interstate Park here) extend along W bank in S N.Y. and N N.J. U.S. Military Acad. at West Point and the Roosevelt home at Hyde Park overlook the river. At New York city (max. width of river here, 4,400 ft.), the Holland and Lincoln tunnels, a railroad tunnel, subways, ferries, and the GEORGE WASHINGTON BRIDGE are links with N.J. Other N.Y. cities on the Hudson are Cohoes, Troy, Albany, Hudson, Kingston, Poughkeepsie, Newburgh, Peekskill, Yonkers; in N.J. are Weehawken, Hoboken, and Jersey City. First explored by Henry Hudson in 1609, and long of strategic importance to the Indians, the Hudson was an important highway for the first settlers, and scene of many historic Revolutionary events. Its valley near Tarrytown was scene of Irving's *Legend of Sleepy Hollow*. First bridged below Albany in 1889; Bear Mtn. Bridge near Peekskill (1924) was 1st highway crossing below Albany. Also crossed by Rip Van Winkle Bridge at Catskill and Mid-Hudson Bridge at Poughkeepsie.

Hudson Strait, N Que. and SE Franklin Dist., Northwest Territories, arm (450 mi. long, 40–150 mi. wide) of the Atlantic, extending from N extremity of Labrador to Hudson Bay at NW extremity of Ungava Peninsula, opposite Southampton Isl.; 60°30′–64°N 64°30′–78°W. Ungava Bay, N Que., is S arm. At E entrance of strait are Killinek and Resolution isls.; at W entrance are Salisbury and Nottingham isls. Foxe Channel connects strait with Foxe Basin and thence with other arms of the Arctic Ocean. Trading posts on strait include Lake Harbour on Baffin Isl. and Sugluk on Ungava Peninsula. Ice-free from mid-July until Oct., strait is navigable with ice breakers during greater part of the year. Reputedly entered by Sebastian Cabot, 1498, E end of Hudson Strait was explored by Sir Martin Frobisher, 1576–78, and by John Davis, 1585–87; in 1610 Henry Hudson 1st navigated its full length. It later became main route of Hudson's Bay Co. vessels and, since 1931, of grain ships from Churchill.

Hudsonville, village (pop. 1,101), Ottawa co., SW Mich., 11 mi. SW of Grand Rapids, in orchard, dairy, and farm area; mfg. of baskets. Inc. 1926.

Hudspeth (hŭd'spĕth), county (□ 4,533; pop. 4,298), extreme W Texas; ⊙ Sierra Blanca. Bounded N by N.Mex. line, S by the Rio Grande (Mex. border); 3d largest co. in state. High plateau region (alt. c.3,500 ft.) with mts. (up to c.7,500 ft.) surrounding a central bolson with intermittent drainage into large playas (saltworks; figured in Salt War, 1877) in NE. Part of Sierra Diablo is in E, Eagle Peak in SE, Quitman Mts. in S, Sierra Blanca mtn. in S center, Finlay Mts. in W center, Hueco Mts. in NW, scattered mts. in N. Irrigated agr. (water from Elephant Butte Reservoir, N.Mex.) in Rio Grande valley (cotton, alfalfa); cattle, sheep; minerals (chiefly copper). Formed 1917.

Hue or **Hué** (hwā), city (1936 pop. 40,000), ⊙ central Vietnam and Thuathien prov. (□ 1,800; 1943 pop. 407,000), on Hanoi-Saigon RR, 5 mi. from South China Sea coast, on short Hue R. (head of navigation); 16°29′N 107°34′E. Former capital of Annam; commercial center; rice- and sawmilling; mfg. of silk and cotton textiles, lime, cement. Airport. Hue consists of the Annamese citadel on left bank, European quarter on right bank, and commercial sections (N) along the lower Hue R. The walled Annamese city (built in early 19th cent. in imitation of Chinese capitals) consists concentrically of the Capital City (administrative offices) and the Royal City or palace grounds (royal palaces, temples). It is linked by rail and road bridges with the European right-bank section. On Hue's SW outskirts, on the left bank, are a 17th-cent. Buddhist shrine and a temple dedicated to Confucius. The noted Temple of Heaven, foremost Annamese religious edifice, is just S of the European quarter, and, upstream, scattered along the right bank, are the royal tombs of Annam's rulers since 1802. First mentioned c.200 B.C. when it was seat of Chinese military command, it passed A.D. c.200 to the Chams, was captured repeatedly by the Chinese, and was annexed by Annam in 1312. After 1635, Hue was the seat of the Annamese Nguyen line, which controlled S Annam and modern Cochin China. It became (1802) ⊙ united empire of Annam, was captured (1883) by the French and remained ⊙ Fr. protectorate of Annam until 1945–46, when it was heavily damaged in civil troubles.

Huechucuicui Point (wāchōōkwē'kwē), Pacific cape at NW tip of Chiloé Isl., S Chile, 11 mi. NW of Ancud; 41°47′S 74°2′W.

Huechulafquén, Lake (wāchōōläfkĕn') (□ 32; alt. 3,180 ft.), in the Andes, SW Neuquén natl. territory, Argentina, S of Lanín Volcano, and extending c.20 mi. E from Chile border; drained by an affluent of Collón Curá R. Also spelled Huechulaufquén and Huechulauquén.

Huechupín (wāchōōpēn'), village (1930 pop. 597), Ñuble prov., S central Chile, 14 mi. WSW of Chillán, in agr. area (grain, wine, potatoes, vegetables, livestock).

Hueco Mountains (wā'kō), extreme W Texas and S N.Mex., N–S range c.55 mi. long, NE of El Paso; rise to 6,767 ft. in Cerro Alto Peak (sĕ'rō äl'tō), Texas. At Hueco Tanks (c.25 mi. ENE of El Paso) are caves, natural rock reservoirs, and pictographs left by tribes whose stronghold this was; camp grounds here. Diablo Bolson is E.

Huecú, El, Argentina: see EL HUECÚ.

Huedin (hwädēn'), Hung. *Bánffy-Hunyad* (bäm'fē-hōō'nyŏt), town (1948 pop. 5,134), Cluj prov., W central Rumania, in Transylvania, on Rapid Körös R. and 28 mi. WNW of Cluj; rail junction and trading center, notably for lumber; flour milling, mfg. of hats. Has 16th-cent. church. Most of inhabitants are Magyars. In Hungary, 1940–45.

Huehuetán (wāwātän'), town (pop. 2,423), Chiapas, S Mexico, in Pacific lowland, on railroad and 10 mi. SE of Huixtla; coffee, sugar cane, fruit, livestock.

Huehuetenango (wāwātānäng'gō), department (□ 2,857; 1950 pop. 205,110), W Guatemala; ⊙ Huehuetenango. On Mex. border; drained by headstreams of Grijalva system (W) and Lacantún R. (N and E); contains highest (W) sec. of Cuchumatanes Mts. Wheat, corn, beans, sheep raising on slopes; coffee, sugar cane, tropical fruit in lower part. Local industries: textile weaving, pottery making. Lead mining near Chiantla and San Miguel Acatán. Main commercial center, Huehuetenango.

Huehuetenango, city (1950 pop. 5,740), ⊙ Huehuetenango dept., W Guatemala, near headstreams of Chiapas R., 80 mi. NW of Guatemala; 15°18′N 91°28′W; alt. 6,200 ft. Commercial center of NW highlands and Cuchumatanes Mts.; flour milling, tanning, wool processing and milling. Trades in pottery, leather, and textiles. Founded in 17th cent. after downfall of old Indian capital of Zaculeu, 1 mi. W.

Huehuetla (wāwā'tlä). **1** Town (pop. 1,594), Hidalgo, central Mexico, in E foothills of Sierra Madre Oriental, 50 mi. NE of Pachuca; corn, sugar cane, coffee, fruit, beans, livestock. **2** Town (pop. 1,141), Puebla, central Mexico, in SE foothills of Sierra Madre Oriental, 28 mi. ESE of Huauchinango; sugar cane, coffee, tobacco, fruit.

Huehuetlán (wāwĕtlän'). **1** Officially Huehuetlán el Chico, town (pop. 2,453), Puebla, central Mexico, 21 mi. SW of Matamoros; alt. 3,245 ft.; agr. center (corn, rice, sugar cane, fruit, livestock). **2** Officially Santo Domingo Huehuetlán, town (pop. 2,023), Puebla, central Mexico, 21 mi. S of Puebla; cereals, sugar cane, fruit, livestock.

Huehuetlán el Chico, Mexico: see HUEHUETLÁN.

Huehuetoca (wāwātō'kä), town (pop. 437), Mexico state, central Mexico, on railroad and 28 mi. N of Mexico city; alt. 7,411 ft.; corn, maguey, stock.

Huejotitán (wāhōtētän'), town (pop. 417), Chihuahua, N Mexico, 30 mi. WNW of Hidalgo del Parral; corn, cotton, beans, sugar cane, tobacco.

Huejotzingo (wāhōtsĭng'gō), city (pop. 4,904), Puebla, central Mexico, on central plateau, 15 mi. NW of Puebla; alt. 7,480 ft. Rail terminus; fruitgrowing center (apples, pears, plums, figs, nuts); cider mfg.; handwoven serapes. Has 17th-cent. church and a monastery of San Francisco.

Huejúcar (wāhōō'kär), town (pop. 1,972), Jalisco, N central Mexico, on Zacatecas border, 19 mi. NNW of Colotlán; alt. 6,338 ft.; cereals, vegetables, stock.

Huejuquilla el Alto (wāhōōkē'yä ĕl äl'tō), town (pop. 1,751), Jalisco, W Mexico, near Zacatecas border, 50 mi. NW of Colotlán; alt. 5,577 ft.; cereals, alfalfa, beans, stock.

Huejutla (wāhōō'tlä), city (pop. 4,322), Hidalgo, central Mexico, in E foothills of Sierra Madre Oriental, near Veracruz border, 75 mi. NNE of Pachuca; agr. center (corn, rice, sugar cane, tobacco, coffee, fruit, cattle); cigars. Oil deposits near by.

Huelgoat (wĕlgôä'), village (pop. 1,690), Finistère dept., W France, 30 mi. NE of Quimper; candy making. Summer resort.

Huellelhue (wāyĕl'wā), village (pop. 1,562), Valdivia prov., S central Chile, on Calle-Calle R., on railroad, and 7 mi. ENE of Valdivia, in lumbering and agr. area (cereals, potatoes, peas, apples, livestock). Also spelled Hueyelhue.

Huelma (wĕl'mä), town (pop. 5,432), Jaén prov., S Spain, in mountainous dist., 20 mi. SE of Jaén; mfg. of esparto rope, soap; olive-oil and cheese processing, flour milling. Stock raising, lumbering. Trades in wool. Iron and lead deposits.

Huelmó (wĕlmō'), village (1930 pop. 403), Llanquihue prov., S central Chile, on Reloncaví Sound, and 13 mi. SSW of Puerto Montt, in agr. area (wheat, flax, potatoes, livestock); dairying. Small isl. of Huelmó is just off the coast.

Huelva (wĕl′vä), province (□ 3,894; pop. 366,526), SW Spain, in Andalusia; ⊙ Huelva. Borders S on the Atlantic, bounded W by Portugal along Guadiana and Chanza rivers; Badajoz prov. is N, Seville prov. E. Watered by the Río Tinto and Odiel R., which join S of Huelva city to form a navigable estuary. Has 2 principal regions: mountainous area (N) is formed by wooded spurs of the Sierra Morena, chiefly Sierra de Aracena; in S are fertile, low plains (called La Campiña) adjoined SE by the marshy, scantily populated, alluvial Las Marismas along the lower Guadalquivir. Climate is temperate to subtropical, cooler in the sierras. Huelva ranks among the leading mining areas in Spain and was renowned as such since Phoenician days; the Ríotinto dist. is its most productive area. Copper is chief mineral; also iron, copper-iron pyrite, argentiferous lead, manganese, antimony, sulphur, graphite, coal, peat, limestone, jasper, marble. Agr. products include wheat, corn, barley, olives and olive oil, acorns, chestnuts, cork, chick-peas, almonds, peaches, oranges, figs (dried). Noted for its wines (La Palma, Niebla, Bollullos par del Condado), and brandies. Considerable stock raising is carried on, mainly of hogs. Next to mining, the Atlantic fisheries of tuna and sardines, based at Ayamonte, Isla-Cristina, and Huelva (with salting and canning plants), are a major source of prov.'s income. The hilly ranges yield a variety of timber (oak, walnut, poplar, beech, pine). Huelva city, its trading and processing center, is an important ore-shipping port, linked by narrow-gauge railroad with the interior mines (Ríotinto, Zalamea la Real, Nerva, Tharsis).

Huelva, city (pop. 50,837), ⊙ Huelva prov., SW Spain, major Andalusian ore-shipping port near the Atlantic, on peninsula formed by Odiel and Tinto rivers (which join 3 mi. S), 50 mi. W of Seville, 280 mi. SW of Madrid; 37°16′N 6°58′W. From the city radiate railroad lines to Seville, Mérida, the Port. border, and to the chief interior mining towns, such as Ríotinto, whose important output of minerals (copper, iron and copper pyrites, silver-bearing lead ore, manganese, sulphur) it exports, thus making it one of Spain's busiest ports. It also ships cork and fish (mainly tunny from Isla-Cristina), and has large fisheries of its own. Among its industrial works are fish canneries, flour mills, wineries, shipyards; mfg. of chemicals, fertilizers, insecticides, furniture, food products, olive oil. The city is a fertile region where olives, grapes, and fruit thrive. Few historic bldgs. are left of the anc. city, once a Phoenician trading center and a Roman colony. A Roman aqueduct, recently repaired, supplies the city with water. There are a customhouse, modern harbor installations, a natl. institute, bull ring, and fine beaches. Across the Río Tinto, 3 mi. SE, is La Rábida monastery, where Columbus worked out his plans. He sailed on his 1st voyage from Palos, 3½ mi. SE of Huelva. A huge statue (1892) of Columbus is just S of La Rábida.

Huéneja (wā′nāhä), town (pop. 2,568), Granada prov., S Spain, 13 mi. SE of Guadix; olive-oil processing; stock raising, lumbering; cereals, vegetables, sugar beets. Mineral springs. Rich iron mines near by.

Hueneme, Calif.: see PORT HUENEME.

Huépac (wā′päk), town (pop. 654), Sonora, NW Mexico, on Sonora R. (irrigation) and 75 mi. NE of Hermosillo; livestock, wheat, corn, vegetables, sugar cane; silver, gold, lead, zinc mining.

Huequén (wākĕn′), village (pop. 1,042), Malleco prov., S central Chile, 3 mi. SE of Angol, in fruit-growing area (apples).

Huércal de Almería (wĕr′käl dhā älmärē′ä), N suburb (pop. 2,592) of Almería, Almería prov., S Spain; flour milling, grape shipping. Mineral springs. Lead, zinc, and magnesite mines near by.

Huércal-Overa (–ōvä′rä), town (pop. 4,180), Almería prov., S Spain, near Almanzora R., 48 mi. NE of Almería; olive-oil processing, flour milling, mfg. of sandals and tiles; ships oranges, dried figs, esparto. Livestock market. Gypsum quarries.

Huércanos (wĕr′känōs), town (pop. 1,089), Logroño prov., N Spain, 12 mi. WSW of Logroño; cereals, potatoes, sugar beets, wine.

Huerfano (wâr′fŭnō), county (□ 1,578; pop. 10,549), S Colo.; ⊙ Walsenburg. Coal-mining and livestock grazing area, bounded W by Sangre de Cristo Mts.; drained by Cucharas and Huerfano rivers. Part of San Isabel Natl. Forest and Wet Mts. in N. Formed 1861.

Huerfano River, S Colo., rises in several branches in Sierra Blanca, flows 99 mi. E and NE to Arkansas R. E of Pueblo.

Huerta, La, Argentina: see LA HUERTA.

Huerta, Sierra de la (syĕ′rä dā lä wĕr′tä), pampean range in E San Juan prov., Argentina, 60 mi. NE of San Juan; extends c.50 mi. N–S; rises to c.8,000 ft. Has gold mines, and silver, lead, arsenic, and sulphur deposits.

Huerta del Rey (wĕr′tä dhĕl rā′), town (pop. 1,468), Burgos prov., N Spain, 40 mi. SE of Burgos; cereals, vegetables, resins, livestock. Lumbering; flour milling; plaster and tile mfg.

Huerta de Valdecarábanos (dhā väl″dā kärä′vänōs), town (pop. 2,393), Toledo prov., central Spain, 12 mi. S of Aranjuez; cereals, hemp, saffron, grapes, sugar beets, livestock.

Huerta Grande (wĕr′tä grän′dā), town (pop. 2,314), NW Córdoba prov., Argentina, 30 mi. NW of Córdoba; tourist resort in N Córdoba hills; lime and marble quarries; stock raising.

Huertas (wĕr′täs), village (pop. 103), Nuevo León, N Mexico, on railroad and 13 mi. SE of Monte-morelos; spas.

Huertgen, Germany: see HÜRTGEN.

Huerva River (wĕr′vä), in Teruel and Saragossa provs., NE Spain, rises at NE edge of the central plateau 10 mi. NW of Montalbán, flows 90 mi. generally N to the Ebro at Saragossa. Irrigation reservoirs. Olive groves.

Huesa (wā′sä), town (pop. 2,308), Jaén prov., S Spain, 40 mi. E of Jaén; olive-oil processing, flour milling; cereals, esparto, lumber. Gypsum quarries. Mineral springs near by.

Huesca (wĕ′skä), province (□ 6,054; pop. 231,647), NE Spain, in Aragon; ⊙ Huesca. Bounded N by crest of the central Pyrenees (Fr. border), which here rise to 11,168 ft. in the Pico de Aneto (highest in Pyrenees) and slope S toward the Ebro plain. In N are anc. dists. of Sobrarbe and Ribagorza. Sp. prov. 2d in hydroelectric power. Watered by Cinca and Gállego rivers, which feed network of irrigation canals. Lead, manganese, bauxite deposits. Essentially agr.: wine, olive oil, livestock, cereals, sugar beets. Chief towns: Huesca, Barbastro, Jaca.

Huesca, anc. *Osca,* city (pop. 16,943), ⊙ Huesca prov., NE Spain, in Aragon, 40 mi. NE of Saragossa, at foot of central Pyrenees; 42°8′N 0°25′W; agr. center (wine, livestock, cereals, fruit), with some industry (cement, linen, candy and chocolate, flour products). Episcopal see. Has Gothic cathedral (15th-16th cent.), Romanesque church (12th cent.) with cloisters, anc. town hall, and remains of old walls. Palace of former univ. (founded 1354, abolished 19th cent.), with historic 12th-cent. vaulted hall, is now seat of provincial institute. In Roman times, Quintus Sertorius here founded (77 B.C.) a school. It was an important town under the Moors; and after Peter I of Aragon liberated it (1096), it was residence of kings of Aragon until 1118.

Huéscar (wĕ′skär), city (pop. 5,453), Granada prov., S Spain, 26 mi. NE of Baza; agr. trade center. Olive pressing, flour milling, wood turning, chocolate mfg. Wine, cereals, esparto, truck produce; stock raising, lumbering. Has 16th-cent. church.

Huetamo (wātä′mō), officially Huetamo de Núñez, town (pop. 4,794), Michoacán, central Mexico, in Río de las Balsas valley, 75 mi. SSE of Morelia; agr. center (sugar, coffee, fruit, cereals); tanning.

Huete (wā′tā), city (pop. 2,695), Cuenca prov., E central Spain, on railroad to Madrid and 30 mi. W of Cuenca; agr. center in irrigated region (saffron, grapes, honey, cereals, livestock). Mfg. of flour, chocolate, jute bags. Flourished in Middle Ages.

Huétor-Santillán (wā′tōr-säntēlyän′), town (pop. 1,440), Granada prov., S Spain, 6 mi. NE of Granada; olive oil, cereals, truck produce. Sand pits, and silver-bearing lead mines near by.

Huétor-Tájar (–tä′här), town (pop. 3,668), Granada prov., S Spain, near Genil R., 6 mi. ENE of Loja; olive-oil processing, flour milling. Cereals, sugar beets, fruit, lumber.

Huétor-Vega (–vā′gä), SE suburb (pop. 1,952) of Granada, Granada prov., S Spain; olive oil, sugar beets, truck produce, cereals.

Huetter (hŭ′tŭr), village (pop. 84), Kootenai co., N Idaho.

Huévar (wā′vär), town (pop. 1,694), Seville prov., SW Spain, 15 mi. W of Seville (linked by rail); olives, cereals, grapes, livestock.

Huevos Island (wā′vōs) (253 acres; alt. 680 ft.), off NW Trinidad, B.W.I., in the Dragon's Mouth, bet. Chacachacare isl. (W) and Monos Isl. (E). Bathing resort.

Huexoculco (wāhōkōōl′kō), officially Santa María Huexoculco, town (pop. 1,816), Mexico state, central Mexico, 24 mi. SE of Mexico city; cereals, fruit, stock.

Huexotla (wāhō′tlä), town (pop. 720), Mexico state, central Mexico, 4 mi. SSW of Texcoco; site of many archaeological remains (temples, pyramids, etc.).

Huey (hū′ē), village (pop. 175), Clinton co., SW Ill., 9 mi. WNW of Centralia, in agr., bituminous-coal, and oil-producing area.

Hueyapan (wäā′pän). **1** Town (pop. 2,408), Morelos, central Mexico, 16 mi. W of Atlixco; corn, sugar cane, fruit. **2** Town (pop. 1,298), Puebla, central Mexico, in Sierra Madre Oriental, on railroad and 6 mi. SE of Tulancingo; cereals, sugar cane, vegetables. **3** Officially Hueyapan de Ocampo, town (pop. 1,616), Veracruz, SE Mexico, in Gulf lowland, 17 mi. NW of Acayucan; sugar cane, fruit.

Hueycantenango (wākäntänäng′gō), town (pop. 1,921), Guerrero, SW Mexico, in Sierra Madre del Sur, 26 mi. E of Chilpancingo; cereals, sugar cane, fruit, stock.

Hueyelhue, Chile: see HUELLELHUE.

Hueyotlipan (wäōtlē′pän). **1** Officially San Felipe Hueyotlipan, town (pop. 1,386), Puebla, central Mexico, 2 mi. N of Puebla; rail terminus; fruit-growing center (apples, pears, figs, nuts). **2** Officially Santo Tomas Hueyotlipan, town (pop. 1,528), Puebla, central Mexico, 25 mi. ESE of Puebla; cereals, vegetables. **3** Officially San Ildefonso Hueyotlipan, town (pop. 1,444), Tlaxcala, central Mexico, 13 mi. NW of Tlaxcala; maguey, corn, wheat, beans, livestock.

Hueypoxtla (wāpōs′tlä), town (pop. 1,253), Mexico state, central Mexico, 33 mi. N of Mexico city; grain, maguey, stock.

Hueytamalco (wātämäl′kō), town (pop. 780), Puebla, E Mexico, in foothills of Sierra Madre Oriental, 10 mi. NE of Teziutlán; sugar cane, fruit.

Hueytepec, Sierra de (syĕ′rä dā wātāpĕk′), range in Chiapas, S Mexico, a N spur of Sierra Madre, E of Tuxtla; extends c.60 mi. NW-SE, forming E watershed of upper Grijalva R. Rises, in Cerro Zontehuitz, to 9,376 ft.; the Cerro Hueytepec rises to 8,946 ft. It is a fertile and forested area. San Cristóbal de las Casas is its center.

Hueytlalpan (wätläl′pän), town (pop. 1,808), Puebla, central Mexico, in foothills of Sierra Madre Oriental, 25 mi. SE of Huauchinango; coffee, tobacco, sugar cane, fruit.

Huey Yot, Thailand: see HUAI YOT.

Huez (wĕz′), village (pop. 455), Isère dept., SE France, in Grandes-Rousses range of the Dauphiné Alps, overlooking Oisans valley, 3 mi. NNE of Le Bourg-d'Oisans; cheese mfg. L'Alpe d'Huez (1 mi. NNE; alt. 5,725 ft.) noted for winter sports.

Huffman, village (pop. 1,141), Jefferson co., N central Ala., 11 mi. NE of Birmingham.

Hüfingen (hü′fĭng-ŭn), village (pop. 2,277), S Baden, Germany, in Black Forest, on the Breg and 9 mi. S of Villingen; rail junction; metal- and wood-working, lumbering. Remains of Roman bath.

Hufuf, Saudi Arabia: see HOFUF.

Hughenden (hū′ŭndŭn), town (pop. 1,745), central Queensland, Australia, on Flinders R. and 190 mi. WSW of Townsville; rail junction; fruit and livestock center.

Hughenden, village (pop. 168), E Alta., near small Hughenden L., 23 mi. S of Wainwright; grain elevators, lumbering, mixed farming.

Hughenden (hū′ŭndŭn), residential parish (pop. 3,238), S Buckingham, England, just N of High Wycombe. Parish includes Hughenden Manor, seat of Disraeli, who is buried here.

Hughes, Indian village (pop. 49), central Alaska; on Koyukuk R. and 80 mi. NW of Tanana; 66°3′N 154°13′W; fur-trading post; trapping; gold mining near by. Airfield.

Hughes, town (pop. estimate 2,000), S Santa Fe prov., Argentina, 70 mi. SW of Rosario; agr. center (corn, flax, wheat, livestock, poultry).

Hughes (hūz). **1** County (□ 810; pop. 20,644), central Okla.; ⊙ Holdenville. Intersected by Canadian and North Canadian rivers; includes L. Holdenville. Agr. (cotton, corn, peanuts, watermelons, cattle, hogs, poultry). Some mfg. at Holdenville and Wetumka. Oil and natural-gas wells; oil refining, gasoline mfg. Formed 1907. **2** County (□ 762; pop. 8,111), central S.Dak.; ⊙ Pierre. Agr. region bounded S by Missouri R. and watered by intermittent streams; Crow Creek Indian Reservation in SE. Dairy products, livestock, wheat, corn, barley. Formed 1873.

Hughes, town (pop. 1,686), St. Francis co., E Ark., 27 mi. WSW of Memphis (Tenn.), and on the Mississippi, in agr. area (cotton, alfalfa, soybeans); cotton ginning, alfalfa and lumber milling. Hunting, fishing. Founded 1913.

Hughes, Port, inlet of Spencer Gulf, South Australia, on W Yorke Peninsula; 10 mi. long, 3 mi. wide. Moonta town near E shore.

Hughes River, W W.Va., formed in W Ritchie co. by junction of North Fork (c.50 mi. long; flows generally SW) and South Fork (c.40 mi. long; flows generally W); flows 18 mi. W to Little Kanawha R. 5 mi. N of Elizabeth.

Hughes Springs, town (pop. 1,445), Cass co., NE Texas, 35 mi. NNW of Marshall; resort, with mineral springs; lumber milling; nursery.

Hugheston, village (pop. 1,796, with adjacent London), Kanawha co., W W.Va., on Kanawha R. and c.18 mi. SE of Charleston.

Hughestown, borough (pop. 1,888), Luzerne co., NE central Pa., 8 mi. NE of Wilkes-Barre. Inc. 1879.

Hughesville. 1 Village (pop. c.350), Charles co., S Md., 28 mi. SSE of Washington; tobacco market and farm trade center. **2** Borough (pop. 2,095), Lycoming co., N central Pa., on Muncy Creek and 17 mi. E of Williamsport; furniture. Laid out 1816, inc. 1852.

Hughson (hū′sŭn), village (pop. 1,816), Stanislaus co., central Calif., in San Joaquin Valley, 7 mi. SE of Modesto; dairying, irrigated farming and fruitgrowing.

Hughsonville (hū′sŭnvĭl), resort village, Dutchess co., SE N.Y., near the Hudson, 13 mi. S of Poughkeepsie.

Hugh Town, village, ⊙ SCILLY ISLANDS, England, on SW side of SAINT MARY'S; fishing center, tourist resort. Star Castle (1593) is now hotel.

Hugli, India: see HOOGHLY.

Hugo (hū′gō). **1** Town (pop. 943), ⊙ Lincoln co., E Colo., on Big Sandy Creek and 90 mi. SE of Denver; alt. 4,970 ft. Livestock, grain, dairy products. **2** Village (pop. 440), Washington co., E Minn., 16 mi. NNE of St. Paul, in lake region; grain, potatoes, livestock. **3** City (pop. 5,984), ⊙ Choctaw co., SE Okla., c.50 mi. E of Durant, near Red R.; railroad and trade center for agr. area (cotton, grain, peanuts). Cotton ginning, peanut processing; creosoting works; lumber, flour, feed milling; mfg. of mattresses, soap, insecticides, bus bodies, dairy products; railroad shops. Inc. 1908.

Hugo Reservoir, Okla.: see KIAMICHI RIVER.

Hugoton (hū'gōtŭn), city (pop. 2,781), ⊙ Stevens co., SW Kansas, 22 mi. WNW of Liberal; shipping point in Great Plains wheat area; center of a major natural-gas field, with pipelines to NE U.S. Founded 1885, inc. 1910.

Huguenot Park (hū'gŭnŏt), SE N.Y., a section of Richmond borough of New York city, on S Staten Isl.

Huhí (ōōē'), town (pop. 1,793), Yucatan, SE Mexico, 33 mi. SE of Mérida; henequen, sugar cane, corn.

Hühnerstock (hü'nŭrshtôk"), peak (10,864 ft.) in Bernese Alps, S central Switzerland, 10 mi. S of Meiringen.

Huhsien (hōō'shyĕn'), town (pop. 5,443), ⊙ Huhsien co. (pop. 127,656), S central Shensi prov., China, 25 mi. WSW of Sian; cotton, rice, wheat, beans.

Hui-, for Chinese names beginning thus and not found here: see under HWEI-.

Huichapan (wēchä'pän), city (pop. 1,927), Hidalgo, central Mexico, on central plateau, 60 mi. WNW of Pachuca; alt. 6,896 ft. Silver, gold, lead, copper mining; winegrowing. Thermal springs near by.

Hui-chi, China: see WAITSAP.

Huichon (hōō'ē'chŭn'), Jap. *Kisen,* town (1944 pop. 14,619), N.Pyongan prov., N Korea, on Chongchon R. and 85 mi. NNE of Pyongyang, in stock-raising and agr. area (rice, soy beans, cotton). Produces textiles (silk, hemp), vegetable oil, woodwork, paper.

Hui-chuan, China: see HWEICHWAN.

Huicungo (wēkōōng'gō), town (pop. 544), San Martín dept., N central Peru, on affluent of Huallaga R. and 28 mi. S of Saposoa; coca, tobacco, yucca.

Huigra (wē'grä), village, Chimborazo prov., S central Ecuador, on Guayaquil-Quito RR, on Chanchán R. and 10 mi. WSW of Alausí; alt. c.4,000 ft. Trading post; cereals, potatoes, sheep.

Huíla (wē'lŭ), province (□ 85,741; pop. 473,041), SW Angola; ⊙ Sá da Bandeira. Bounded W by the Atlantic, S by South-West Africa. From arid, narrow coastal strip rises escarpment of Serra da Chela, beyond which extends central Angola's plateau. Drained by Cunene R., which forms part of Angola's S border in lower course. Fertile upland areas around Sá da Bandeira are linked to Mossâmedes (prov.'s best port) by rail. In 1946 the prov. was administratively subdivided into 3 dists.: Huíla (⊙ Sá da Bandeira), Mossâmedes (⊙ Mossâmedes), and Cunene (⊙ Roçadas).

Huíla, town, Huíla prov., SW Angola, on road and 10 mi. SSE of Sá da Bandeira; meat processing, sawmilling. Agr. school.

Huila (wē'lä), department (□ 7,992; 1938 pop. 216,676; 1950 estimate 239,840), S central Colombia; ⊙ Neiva. Consists of the Magdalena valley flanked by Cordillera Central and Cordillera Oriental. Climate is tropical in Magdalena valley, cooler in uplands. Mineral resources include silver and gold (Aipe, La Plata, Campoalegre), alum (Agrado), asphalt (Garzón). Main agr. crops: rice, cacao, tobacco, cotton, coffee, pita and fique fibers. Considerable stock raising (cattle, horses, mules). Neiva, its only important city, does mfg. of panama hats, fiber products, cotton goods. The region is rich in archaeological and paleontological remains. The noted Guácharos Caves are S of Pitalito.

Huila, Nevado del (nāvä'dō dĕl), snow-capped Andean volcanic peak (18,865 ft.), S central Colombia, on Huila-Tolima-Cauca dept. border, highest in Cordillera Central, 50 mi. SE of Cali; 3°N 76°W. Second only to Pico Cristóbal Colón in Colombia.

Hui-lai, China: see HWEILAI.

Huiliches, Argentina: see JUNÍN DE LOS ANDES.

Huillapima (wīyäpē'mä), village (pop. estimate 500), SE Catamarca prov., Argentina, on La Rioja–Catamarca RR and 22 mi. SW of Catamarca; dairying and grain-milling center.

Huimanguillo (wēmäng-gē'yō), city (pop. 2,491), Tabasco, SE Mexico, on Grijalva R. (Chiapas border) and 33 mi. WSW of Villahermosa; agr. center (bananas, tobacco, mangoes, rice, coffee, beans). Airfield.

Huimilpan (wēmēl'pän), town (pop. 1,115), Querétaro, central Mexico, 15 mi. SSE of Querétaro; alt. 7,575 ft.; grain, sugar cane, alfalfa, vegetables, stock.

Huinca Renancó (wĭng'kä rānäng-kō'), town (pop. 4,497), S Córdoba prov., Argentina, 120 mi. S of Río Cuarto; rail junction, connected with Bahía Blanca and San Rafael (Mendoza prov.); agr. center (cereals, flax, alfalfa, livestock).

Huisne River (wēn), Sarthe dept., W France, rises 6 mi. SW of Mortagne (Orne dept.), flows 80 mi. generally SW, past Nogent-le-Rotrou and La Ferté-Bernard, to the Sarthe 1 mi. SW of Le Mans. Not navigable.

Huistán (wēstän'), town (pop. 556), Chiapas, S Mexico, in Sierra de Hueytepec, 11 mi. E of San Cristóbal de las Casas; wheat, fruit.

Huitepec (wētäpĕk'), town (pop. 1,514), Hidalgo, central Mexico, 22 mi. WSW of Huejutla; corn, rice, sugar cane, tobacco, fruit.

Huitiupan (wētū'pän), town (pop. 373), Chiapas, S Mexico, in N outliers of Sierra Madre, 8 mi. NE of Simojovel; corn, fruit.

Huitzilac (wētsēläk'), town (pop. 797), Morelos, central Mexico, 8 mi. N of Cuernavaca; wheat, fruit, livestock.

Huitzilan (wētsē'län), town, (pop. 2,358), Puebla, central Mexico, in foothills of Sierra Madre Oriental, 17 mi. E of Zacatlán; corn, tobacco, sugar cane, fruit.

Huitziltepec (wētsēltāpĕk'). **1** Town (pop. 1,504), Guerrero, SW Mexico, on N slopes of Sierra Madre del Sur, 14 mi. N of Chilpancingo; cereals, sugar cane, fruit, forest products (resins, vanilla). **2** Officially Santa Clara Huitziltepec, town (pop. 840), Puebla, central Mexico, on railroad and 29 mi. SE of Puebla; cereals, vegetables.

Huitzitzilingo (wētsētsēlĭng'gō), town (pop. 1,717), Hidalgo, central Mexico, 16 mi. W of Huejutla; corn, rice, tobacco, sugar cane, fruit.

Huitzizilapan or **San Lorenzo Huitzizilapan** (sän lōrĕn'sō wētsēsēlä'pän), town (pop. 2,063), Mexico state, central Mexico, 22 mi. W of Mexico city; cereals, stock.

Huitzuco (wētsōō'kō), officially Huitzuco de los Figueroa, town (pop. 3,946), Guerrero, SW Mexico, in N outliers of Sierra Madre del Sur, 13 mi. E of Iguala; mercury mining; cereals, sugar cane, fruit, timber.

Huixcolotla (wēskōlō'tlä), officially San Salvador Huixcolotla, town (pop. 2,364), Puebla, central Mexico, 30 mi. ESE of Puebla; cereals, maguey, fruit. Sometimes Huizcolotla.

Huixquilucan (wēskēlōō'kän), officially Huixquilucan de Degollado, town (pop. 1,660), Mexico state, central Mexico, 14 mi. WSW of Mexico city; cereals, stock.

Huixtla (wēs'tlä), city (pop. 6,828), Chiapas, S Mexico, in Pacific lowland, on railroad and 23 mi. NW of Tapachula. Trading, processing, and agr. center (coffee, sugar cane, cacao, cotton, fruit, livestock); mfg. (furniture, shoes).

Hui-yang, China: see WAIYEUNG.

Hui-yüan, China: see HWEIYÜAN.

Huizcolotla, Mexico: see HUIXCOLOTLA.

Huizen (hoi'zŭn), village (pop. 11,395), North Holland prov., W central Netherlands, on the IJsselmeer and 6 mi. NNE of Hilversum; fishing. Has important radio transmitter.

Hukae-sima, Japan: see FUKAE-SHIMA.

Hukawng Valley (hōō'koun), circular basin (□ 2,000) of Kach n State, Upper Burma, drained by headwaters of Chindwin R.; main village, Maingkwan. Surrounded by mts. (Kumon Range; E), it connects S with Mogaung valley. Agr.: rice, tobacco, cotton, opium. Amber mines on S edge. Pop. is largely Kachin. Scene of heavy fighting during Second World War, when the Ledo Road was laid through the valley.

Hukeri (hōōkā'rē), town (pop. 7,703), Belgaum dist., S Bombay, India, 28 mi. NNE of Belgaum; tobacco, millet, peanuts, chili, sugar cane. Moslem ruins (16th cent.) near by.

Hukow or **Hu-k'ou** (both: hōō'kō') [Chinese,=lake mouth], town (pop. 5,227), ⊙ Hukow co. (pop. 94,269), northernmost Kiangsi prov., China, 20 mi. E of Kiukiang, and on right bank of Yangtze R. (Anhwei line), at N end of 30-mi.-long Hukow Canal linking Poyang L. and the Yangtze; river navigation hub and transshipment point.

Hukow or **Hu-k'ou** (both: hōō'kō'), Jap. *Koko* (kō'kō), village (1935 pop. 2,654), NW Formosa, on railroad and 7 mi. NE of Sinchu, in oil field; rice, sweet potatoes, vegetables, oranges, livestock.

Hu-kuan, China: see HUKWAN.

Hu-kuang, China: see HUKWANG.

Hukue, Japan: see FUKUE, Aichi prefecture.

Hukui, Japan: see FUKUI, city.

Hukuntsi (hōōkōōn'tsē) or **Gukunsi** (gōō–), village (pop. c.1,450), N Kgalagadi dist., SW Bechuanaland Protectorate, in Kalahari Desert, 280 mi. WNW of Mafeking; 24°3'S 21°32'E; important road junction.

Hukuoka, Japan: see FUKUOKA, city, Fukuoka prefecture.

Hukvaldy, Czechoslovakia: see SKLENOV.

Hukwan or **Hu-kuan** (both: hōō'gwän'), town, ⊙ Hukwan co. (pop. 121,118), SE Shansi prov., China, 8 mi. SE of Changchih; coal mining; chestnuts, medicinal herbs.

Hukwang or **Hu-kuang** (both: hōō'gwäng'), ancient province of S central China, centered at Tungting L. Divided in 1660s into Hupeh (N) and Hunan (S) provs.

Hula (hōō'lä), town (pop. 2,000), Sidamo-Borana prov., S Ethiopia, on road and 22 mi. SSE of Yirga-Alam; 6°20'N 38°39'E; alt. c.9,200 ft. Commercial center (coffee, hides, livestock). Coptic churches. Formerly Agheressalam.

Hula, Lake (hōō'lä), **Lake Huleh, Lake Hule** (hōō'lä), or **Waters of Merom** (mē'rŭm), Hebrew *Yam Samkho* or *Yam Hulata,* Arabic *Bahr el Huleh* or *Bahr al-Hulah,* expansion (□5.5) of headwaters of the Jordan, NE Israel, near Syrian border, 9 mi. NE of Safad; alt. 230 ft; 3 mi. long, 1–3 mi. wide. The Jordan proper is formed here, leaves lake at S end. On W shore are settlements of Hulata and Yesud ha Ma'ala; fisheries are important. Swamp region on N shore partly drained (1930s). In 1951 further drainage of the area by Israel precipitated an armed clash with Syria.

Hulah Dam, Okla.: see CANEY RIVER.

Hulan (hōō'län'), town (pop. 46,000), ⊙ Hulan co. (pop. 326,657), W Sungkiang prov., Manchuria, on railroad and 16 mi. N of Harbin, and on Hulan R. near its mouth on the Sungari; agr. center; flour and soybean milling, sugar refining, match mfg., tanning.

Hulan River, Chinese *Hulan Ho* (hōō'län' hŭ'), N central Manchuria, rises in S outlier of the Lesser Khingan Mts., flows c.250 mi. SW and S, through densely populated agr. dist. (sugar beets, wheat, soybeans), to Sungari R. below Hulan. Navigable in lower course; frozen Nov.-April.

Hulata (hōōlätä'), settlement (pop. 330), Upper Galilee, NE Israel, on SW shore of L. Hula, 9 mi. NE of Safad; fishing, mixed farming, mat weaving, waterfowl breeding. Founded 1936.

Hulda (hōōldä'), settlement (pop. 400), W Israel, on W slope of Judaean Hills, 6 mi. SE of Rehovot; grain, fruit, olives; dairying, poultry, sheep raising, beekeeping. Founded 1909. Scene (1948) of heavy fighting during Arab invasion.

Hule, Lake, Israel: see HULA, LAKE.

Huletts Landing (hū'lĭts), resort village, Washington co., E N.Y., on L. George, 8 mi. NW of Whitehall.

Hulikal Drug, hill, India: see COONOOR.

Hulin (hōō'lĭn'), town, ⊙ Hulin co. (pop. 45,000), E Sungkiang prov., Manchuria, river port on Ussuri R. (USSR border), opposite Iman and 220 mi. ENE of Mutankiang; rail terminus; agr. center (beans, kaoliang); fisheries.

Hulin (hōō'lēn), Czech *Hulín,* village (pop. 4,046), W central Moravia, Czechoslovakia, 21 mi. SSE of Olomouc; agr. center (wheat, sugar beets).

Hulin Rocks, Northern Ireland: see MAIDENS, THE.

Hull, county (□ 139; pop. 41,434), SW Que., on Ont. border, on Ottawa R.; ⊙ Hull.

Hull, city (pop. 32,947), ⊙ Hull co., SW Que., on Ottawa R., at mouth of Gatineau R. opposite Ottawa, on Ont. border; paper and lumbering center, with iron and steel foundries, mfg. of matches, cement, jute bags, furniture, mattresses; mica processing. Hydroelectric station.

Hull, officially **Kingston-upon-Hull,** county borough (1931 pop. 313,544; 1951 census 299,068), East Riding, SE Yorkshire, England, 50 mi. E of Leeds and on N shore of the Humber at mouth of the Hull, 20 mi. from North Sea; 53°45'N 0°20'W; major port for Yorkshire, with fine rail and water connections. Chief imports: iron ore, wool, hides, timber; exports: textiles, salt, machinery. Industries include shipbuilding, coal mining, leather tanning, chemical making, oil distilling, metalworking, paper milling, textile milling. It is also an important fishing port. Has two 14th-cent. churches, Trinity House (1369; an institution for sailors), a grammar school founded 1486 and attended by Wilberforce (b. here), Wilberforce Mus., Municipal Mus., Royal Institution, an art gall., University Col. Town was founded in late 13th cent. by Edward I and construction of the extensive docks was begun c.1775. In Second World War (particularly in 1941) city sustained damage from air raids. N industrial section of city is called Sculcoates.

Hull. 1 Town (pop. 153), Madison co., NE Ga., 6 mi. NE of Athens. **2** Village (pop. 489), Pike co., W Ill., near the Mississippi, 17 mi. SSE of Quincy, in agr. area. **3** Town (pop. 1,127), Sioux co., NW Iowa, 27 mi. N of Le Mars; livestock, grain. Inc. 1888. **4** Town (pop. 3,379), Plymouth co., E Mass., on narrow Nantasket Peninsula in Massachusetts Bay and 10 mi. ESE of Boston; summer resort. Settled 1624, inc. 1644. Resort villages include Allerton, Kenberma (1940 pop. 567), NANTASKET BEACH. **5** Village (1940 pop. 668), Liberty co., E Texas, 32 mi. W of Beaumont, in oil, timber, farm area.

Hullet, Norway: see KONGSVOLL.

Hull Island, atoll (□ 1.5; pop. 530), Phoenix Isls., S Pacific, 110 mi. SW of Canton Isl.; 4°30'S 172°11'W; on reef 4.5 mi. long, 2.5 mi. wide. Discovered 1840 by Americans, included 1937 in Br. colony of Gilbert and Ellice Isls. Site of anc. Polynesian shrine. Best potential seaplane base in group; surveyed 1939 by New Zealand and U.S. Also called Orona.

Hull Island, Tubuai Isls.: see MARIA ISLAND.

Hull Mountain (6,954 ft.), Lake co., NW Calif., 34 mi. N of Lakeport, in the Coast Ranges.

Hull River, SE Yorkshire, England, rises near Great Driffield, flows 23 mi. S to Humber R. at Hull.

Hulme (hŭm), SW suburb of Manchester, SE Lancashire, England, included in borough; metalworking, soap mfg., flour milling.

Hulmeville (hŭm'vĭl), borough (pop. 860), Bucks co., SE Pa., 4 mi. NW of Bristol.

Hulpe, La (lä ülp'), Flemish *Terhulpen* (tĕrhŭl'pŭn), town (pop. 4,271), Brabant prov., central Belgium, 9 mi. SE of Brussels; paper mfg.

Hüls (hüls), town (pop. 10,500), in former Prussian Rhine Prov., W Germany, after 1945 in North Rhine-Westphalia, 3 mi. NW of Krefeld; mfg. (synthetic rubber, textiles, machinery, glassware).

Hulst (hŭlst), town (pop. 4,547), Zeeland prov., SW Netherlands, on Flanders mainland, 11 mi. ESE of Terneuzen, near Belg. border; market center; mfg. of cigars, tobacco; knitting mills. Site of 15th-cent. church.

Hultschin, Czechoslovakia: see HLUCIN.

Hultsfred (hŭlts'frād"), town (pop. 2,562), Kalmar co., SE Sweden, 30 mi. NW of Oskarshamn; rail junction; sawmilling, metalworking.

Hulun, Manchuria: see HAILAR.

Hulunbuir, Manchuria: see BARGA.

Hulun Nor (hōōlōōn' nōr') or **Dalai Nor** (dälī'), largest lake of Manchuria, in NW Inner Mongolian Autonomous Region, 100 mi. W of Hailar; 35 mi. long, 10 mi. wide (in 1946), 3–5 ft. deep. Of fluctuating level, it is the flood reservoir of the Argun R., with which it is connected by a channel (N). Receives Kerulen R. (SW) and Orchun R. (E; outlet of Bor Nor.)

Hulusiau, Indonesia: see SIAU.

Hulutao (hōō'lōō'dou'), town, SW Liaosi prov., Manchuria, port on Gulf of Liaotung, on rail spur and 27 mi. S of Chinchow; ships coal from Pehpiao mines and lead-zinc concentrates; has lead smelter and chemical plant. Founded in 1908, it rivals the older shallow port of Yingkow as a result of its more favorable harbor site.

Hulutun, Formosa: see FENGYÜAN.

Hum or **Khum** (hōōm), village, S Herzegovina, Yugoslavia, 7 mi. NNE of Dubrovnik, near Croatia border; rail junction.

Huma (hōō'mä'), town, ⊙ Huma co. (pop. 8,209), N Heilungkiang prov., Manchuria, 110 mi. NNW of Aigun and on right bank of Amur R. (USSR border); gold-mining center. Until 1914, Kuchan. Gold mining near Chinshanchen, 13 mi. NNW.

Humacao (ōōmäkou'), town (pop. 10,851), E Puerto Rico, 28 mi. SE of San Juan, near the coast, on railroad, linked with its port Playa de Humacao or Punta Santiago (5 mi. ENE), in broad sugar- and tobacco-growing valley; 18°9'N 65°49'W. Trading, sugar-milling and -refining center; mfg. of textiles, needlework, and cigars; extracting of castor oil. Seat of senatorial dist. Port of entry.

Humahuaca (ōōmäwä'kä), town (1947 census pop. 2,076), ⊙ Humahuaca dept. (□ 1,525; 1947 pop. 11,456), N central Jujuy prov., Argentina, in the Quebrada de Humahuaca Valley (upper Río Grande de Jujuy valley), on railroad and 70 mi. N of Jujuy. Health resort; mining, lumbering, agr. center. Zinc, silver, copper deposits. Potatoes, alfalfa, corn, wheat, fruit, livestock.

Humahuaca, Quebrada de, Argentina: see GRANDE DE JUJUY, RÍO.

Humai, Peru: see HUMAY.

Humaitá (ōōmĭtä'), village (pop. c.1,600), Pando dept., N Bolivia, on Orton R. and 24 mi. WNW of Riberalta; rubber. Also spelled Humaytá.

Humaitá (ōōmĭtä'). **1** Town, Acre territory, Brazil: see PÔRTO VALTER. **2** City (pop. 759), S Amazonas, Brazil, steamer and hydroplane landing on left bank of Madeira R., and 100 mi. NE of Pôrto Velho; rubber, Brazil nuts, cacao, hides. Formerly also spelled Humaytá.

Humaitá, town (dist. pop. 4,212), Ñeembucú dept., S Paraguay, on Paraguay R. (Argentina border) above its confluence with the Paraná, and 19 mi. SW of Pilar; minor port and agr. center (cotton, corn, sugar cane, oranges, cattle). Here are ruins of fort and of the church of San Carlos, bombarded 1867 by allied fleet in War of the Triple Alliance and now revered as natl. shrine.

Humanes (ōōmä'nĕs), officially Humanes de Mohernando, town (pop. 1,085), Guadalajara prov., central Spain, near Henares R., 14 mi. N of Guadalajara; cereals, olives, grapes, sheep, goats. Flour milling, meat-products mfg.

Humansdorp (hü'mänsdôrp"), town (pop. 2,174), S Cape Prov., U. of So. Afr., near St. Francis Bay of the Indian Ocean, 50 mi. W of Port Elizabeth; agr. center (stock, wheat, fruit, vegetables).

Humansville, city (pop. 803), Polk co., SW central Mo., in the Ozarks, bet. Sac R. and Pomme de Terre R., 15 mi. NNW of Bolivar; grain products.

Humarock, Mass.: see MARSHFIELD.

Humay (ōōmī'), town (pop. 358), Ica dept., SW Peru, on Pisco R. and 22 mi. E of Pisco; cotton, grapes, vegetables. Also Humai.

Humaya (ōōmī'ä), village (pop. 1,740), Lima dept., W central Peru, on Huaura R., on Huaura-Sayán RR and 13 mi. ENE of Huaura; cotton-growing center.

Humayrah, Al-, Syria: see HAMRA, EL.

Humaytá, Bolivia: see HUMAITÁ.

Humaytá, Brazil: see HUMAITÁ, Amazonas.

Humbe (hōōm'bā), town, Huíla prov., S Angola, near Cunene R., on road and 150 mi. SE of Sá da Bandeira; cattle raising, dairying.

Humbeek (hûm'bāk), agr. village (pop. 2,454), Brabant prov., central Belgium, 8 mi. N of Brussels. Has 17th-cent. castle.

Humbermouth (hŭm'bûrmŭth, –mouth), village (pop. 1,914), W N.F., on Humber R. estuary, on railroad, and 3 mi. E of Corner Brook; lumbering center, agr. market (dairying, cattle raising; potatoes, vegetables).

Humber River, central and W N.F., issues from Alder L., 10 mi. SW of head of White Bay at 49° 29'N 57°6'W, flows SW, through Deer L., past Corner Brook, to the Bay of Islands 12 mi. WNW of Corner Brook; 75 mi. long. Valley is noted for fertility.

Humber River, anc. *Abus,* navigable estuary of Trent and Ouse rivers on E coast of England bet. Yorkshire and Lincolnshire, opening on North Sea at Spurn Head; 40 mi. long, 1–8 mi. wide. Principal ports: Hull, Grimsby.

Humberstone (hŭm'bûrstŭn, –stōn), village (pop. 2,963), S Ont., on L. Erie, at S end of Welland Ship Canal, opposite Port Colborne. Humberstone Lock, on the canal, is one of world's largest lift locks.

Humberstone, residential town and parish (pop. 3,267), central Leicester, England, just E of Leicester; shoe industry.

Humberto I (ōōmbĕr'tō prēmā'rō), town (pop. estimate 1,500), central Santa Fe prov., Argentina, 65 mi. NW of Santa Fe; agr. center (alfalfa, flax, wheat); dairying, tanning. The livestock includes nutria.

Humberto de Campos (ōōmbĕr'tōō dĭ kăm'pōōs), city (pop. 824), N Maranhão, Brazil, 55 mi. ESE of São Luís; saltworks; manioc meal, corn. Formerly called Miritiba.

Humbird, village (pop. c.400), Clark co., central Wis., 36 mi. SE of Eau Claire, in dairying and farming area (corn, hay, strawberries); makes cheese, canned foods.

Humble (hŭm'bŭl, ŭm'–), city (pop. 1,388), Harris co., S Texas, 17 mi. N of Houston, in oil field; lumber milling. Founded 1888, inc. 1933. Had oil boom, 1904.

Humbledon (hŭm'bŭldŭn) or **Homildon** (hŏ'mĭldŭn), parish (pop. 132), N Northumberland, England, just NW of Wooler, SE of Flodden. In the plain before **Humbledon Hill** Sir Henry Percy (Hotspur) and others won their notable victory over the Scots in 1402.

Humboldt (hŭm'bōlt), town (pop. 1,798), central Sask., 65 mi. E of Saskatoon; grain elevators, railroad yards, cold-storage plant, oil refinery, dairies. Resort with medicinal springs. Small lakes near by.

Humboldt. 1 County (□ 3,573; pop. 69,241), NW Calif., on Pacific coast; ⊙ Eureka. Cape Mendocino is westernmost point of Calif. Mainly in Coast Ranges; part of Klamath Mts. is in E and NE. Drained by Klamath, Trinity, Mad, Eel, and Mattole rivers. Includes large Hoopa Indian Reservation and part of Trinity Natl. Forest (E). Co. has 400,000 acres of redwoods (*Sequoia sempervirens*), about ½ of world's total stand; in state parks (notably Humboldt State Redwood Park and Prairie Creek State Park along Redwood Highway) are preserved c.21,000 acres of the finest groves. World's tallest tree (364 ft.) is near Dyerville. Logging (redwood, Douglas fir, cedar, spruce), lumber milling; dairying, sheep raising (for Merino wool), farming (truck, apples, berries, nuts; seed growing), poultry raising. Noted recreational area (fishing, camping, hiking, bathing). Ocean fisheries. Some quarrying and mining (sand, gravel, clay, gold); natural-gas wells. Formed 1853. **2** County (□ 435; pop. 13,117), N central Iowa; ⊙ Dakota City. Prairie agr. area (hogs, cattle, corn, oats, soybeans) drained by Des Moines and East Des Moines rivers. Bituminous-coal deposits, limestone quarries. Formed 1857. **3** County (□ 9,702; pop. 4,838), NW Nev.; ⊙ Winnemucca. Ranching and mining area watered by Quinn, Little Humboldt, and Humboldt rivers and bordering on Oregon. Livestock; silver, copper, gold. Santa Rosa Range is in NE, in part of Toiyabe Natl. Forest. Summit Lake Indian Reservation is in W, Black Rock Desert in SW. Formed 1861.

Humboldt. 1 Village (pop. 295), Coles co., E central Ill., 9 mi. N of Mattoon, in rich agr. area. **2** City (pop. 3,219), Humboldt co., N central Iowa, on Des Moines R., near mouth of the East Des Moines, and 15 mi. N of Fort Dodge; concrete and wood products, beverages. Limestone quarries, sand pits near by. Settled 1863, inc. 1869. **3** City (pop. 2,308), Allen co., SE Kansas, on Neosho R. and 9 mi. N of Chanute; oil-shipping point in oil and grain region; mfg. of bricks, tiles, cement products. Laid out 1857; inc. as village 1866, as city 1870. **4** Village (pop. 143), Kittson co., extreme NW Minn., near Red R. and Man. line, 12 mi. NW of Hallock. **5** City (pop. 1,404), Richardson co., extreme SE Nebr., 19 mi. WNW of Falls City and on N.Fork of Nemaha R.; flour, feed; grain. Settled c.1856. **6** Town (pop. 450), Minnehaha co., E S.Dak., 20 mi. WNW of Sioux Falls; chemicals; grain, hogs, dairy produce. **7** City (pop. 7,426), Gibson co., NW Tenn., 15 mi. NNW of Jackson; rail junction; trade and shipping center for agr. area (cotton, corn, fruit, vegetables); mfg. of shoes, shipping cartons, fertilizers, cotton yarn; marble and granite works.

Humboldt Bay, inlet (7 mi. N–S, 5 mi. E–W) of the Pacific, N New Guinea; Hollandia on W shore. In Second World War U.S. troops landed here April, 1944.

Humboldt Bay, sheltered Pacific inlet (c.14 mi. long, c.1–5 mi. wide), Humboldt co., NW Calif. Eureka is on S shore, Arcata on N shore.

Humboldt Current: see PERU CURRENT.

Humboldt Glacier, NW Greenland; 79°30'N 64°W. The largest known glacier, it discharges into Kane Basin along 60-mi.-long front. Discovered (1853–55) by E. K. Kane.

Humboldt Mountains, range of the Nan Shan system, N Tsinghai prov., China, rising to c.20,000 ft. Named for 19th-cent. German explorer.

Humboldt Peak (14,044 ft.), S Colo., in Sangre de Cristo Mts., Custer co.

Humboldt Peak, Venezuela: see CORONA, LA.

Humboldt Range, NW Nev., in Pershing co., extending generally N–S along E bank of Humboldt R. Rises to 9,835 ft. in Star Peak, at N end. Humboldt Sink is just SW.

Humboldt River, N Nev., formed by confluence of E and N forks in Elko co., flows W past Elko, then SW past Winnemucca and Lovelock, to Humboldt Sink near Humboldt Range; c.300 mi. long. Rye Patch Dam (75 ft. high, 914 ft. long; completed 1936), 21 mi. NNE of Lovelock, forms Humboldt Reservoir (c.20 mi. long; capacity 179,000 acre-ft.) and is main unit in Humboldt irrigation project. Agr. (alfalfa, barley, oats, wheat), stock raising, dairying. River (named by Frémont) was important 19th-cent. route for emigrants from Salt Lake City to central Calif.

Humboldt Salt Marsh, W Nev., in Churchill co., NE of Fallon; 15 mi. long, 6 mi. wide. Fed by intermittent affluents from Clan Alpine Mts. (E).

Humboldt Sink (11 mi. long, max. width 4 mi.), W Nev., N of Carson Sink, c.30 mi. N of Fallon; intermittently dry lake bed fed at times by Humboldt R. Also known as Humboldt L.

Hume (hūm). **1** Village (pop. 448), Edgar co., E Ill., 15 mi. NNW of Paris, in agr. area; ships grain. **2** Town (pop. 474), Bates co., W Mo., 12 mi. W of Rich Hill; agr.; coal.

Hume Dam, Australia: see HUME RESERVOIR.

Humen, town, China: see TAIPING, Kwangtung prov.

Hu Men, river mouth, China: see BOCA TIGRIS.

Humenne (hōō'mĕnyā), Slovak *Humenné,* Hung. *Homonna* (hô'môn-nŏ), town (6,020), E Slovakia, Czechoslovakia, on Laborec R. and 31 mi. ESE of Presov; rail junction; agr. center; sugar mills.

Hume Reservoir (hūm), largest reservoir (□ 70) of Australia, on Murray R., near Albury, on boundary bet. New South Wales and Victoria; extends into both states; semicircular, c.45 mi. long, 3 mi. wide; used for irrigation. Hume Dam (1937), on W side of reservoir, is 1,042 ft. long, 200 ft. high.

Humeston (hū'mŭstŭn), town (pop. 750), Wayne co., S Iowa, 15 mi. SW of Chariton; livestock, grain.

Humewood, S residential suburb of Port Elizabeth, S Cape Prov., U. of So. Afr.; site of Driftsands airport. Resort.

Humilladero (ōōmēlyā-dhä'rō), town (pop. 1,098), Málaga prov., S Spain, 10 mi. NW of Antequera; olive-oil industry; cereals.

Humlebaek (hōōm'lûbĕk), town (pop. 744) and port, Frederiksborg amt, Zealand, Denmark, on the Oresund and 9 mi. ENE of Hillerod; fisheries, brickworks.

Hummelo (hŭ'mŭlō), agr. village (pop. 255), Gelderland prov., E Netherlands, 4 mi. NW of Doetinchem.

Hummelstadt, Poland: see LEWIN.

Hummelstown, borough (pop. 3,789), Dauphin co., S central Pa., 8 mi. E of Harrisburg and on Swatara Creek; clothing mfg., lumber; limestone; agr. Founded c.1740, laid out 1762, inc. 1874.

Humnoke (hŭm'nōk), town (pop. 263), Lonoke co., central Ark., 12 mi. WNW of Stuttgart.

Humocaro Alto (ōōmōkä'rō äl'tō), town (pop. 1,224), Lara state, NW Venezuela, in N Andean spur, 55 mi. SW of Barquisimeto; alt. 3,589 ft.; coffee, cacao, sugar cane, cereals, stock.

Humocaro Bajo (bä'hō), town (pop. 1,193), Lara state, NW Venezuela, in N Andean spur, 50 mi. SW of Barquisimeto; alt. 3,668 ft.; coffee, sugar cane, cereals, fruit, stock.

Humorului, Rumania: see GURA-HUMORULUI.

Humos, Cape (ōō'mōs), Pacific headland in Maule prov., S central Chile, 6 mi. SW of Constitución; 35°23'S 72°31'W.

Humos Island, Chile: see CHONOS ARCHIPELAGO.

Humpata (hōōmpä'tä), town (pop. 490), Huíla prov., SW Angola, 10 mi. SW of Sá da Bandeira; alt. 6,150 ft. Dairying, wool clipping, skin curing. Settled 1876 by Boers from Transvaal. Majority of Boer pop. resettled in South-West Africa 1928–29. Formerly called São Januaria.

Humphrey. 1 Town (pop. 629), Jefferson and Arkansas counties, central Ark., 21 mi. NE of Pine Bluff, in agr. (cotton) area. **2** Village (pop. 593), Christian co., central Ill., 18 mi. SSE of Springfield, in agr. and bituminous-coal-mining area. **3** Village (pop. 761), Platte co., E Nebr., 19 mi. NNW of Columbus and on branch of Elkhorn R.; flour; grain.

Humphrey Island: see MANIHIKI.

Humphrey Point, NE Alaska, near Yukon border, cape on Beaufort Sea, W of Mackenzie Bay; 69° 58'N 142°31'W. Eskimo settlement and trading post (1939 pop. 24) here.

Humphreys. 1 County (□ 410; pop. 23,115), W Miss.; ⊙ Belzoni. Bounded partly W by Sunflower R.; also drained by Yazoo R. and tributaries. Agr. (cotton, corn); lumbering. Formed 1918. 2 County (□ 555; pop. 11,030), central Tenn.; ⊙ Waverly. Bounded W by Tennessee R.; drained by Duck and Buffalo rivers. Includes part of Kentucky Reservoir. Timber, livestock raising, dairying, agr. (corn, peanuts). Formed 1809.

Humphreys, town (pop. 185), Sullivan co., N Mo., 12 mi. SW of Milan.

Humphreys, Fort, Va.: see BELVOIR, FORT.

Humphreys, Mount (13,972 ft.), E Calif., in the Sierra Nevada, on Fresno-Inyo co. line, 17 mi. WSW of Bishop.

Humphreys Peak (12,655 ft.), N Ariz., 10 mi. N of Flagstaff, on rim of eroded volcano (SAN FRANCISCO PEAKS); highest point in state.

Humpolec (hŏŏm'pôlĕts), Ger. *Gumpolds* (gŏŏm'pôlts), town (pop. 5,083), SE Bohemia, Czechoslovakia, 11 mi. SW of Havlickuv Brod, in barley, rye, and timber region; rail terminus; mfg. of woolen textiles. Has 13th-cent. St. Nicholas church and 13th-cent. synagogue.

Humptulips River (hŭmtōō'lŭps, –lŭpsh), SW Wash., formed N of Hoquiam by W and E forks (each c.30 mi. long) rising in Olympic Natl. Park; flows c.20 mi. SW to Grays Harbor.

Hums, Syria: see HOMS.

Humshaugh (hŭmz'hăf), agr. village and parish (pop. 394), S central Northumberland, England, on North Tyne R. and 5 mi. NNW of Hexham; limestone quarrying.

Humurgan, Turkey: see SURMENE.

Humuya (ōōmōō'yä), town (pop. 238), Comayagua dept., W central Honduras, on Comayagua R. (here called Humaya R.) and 14 mi. SSW of Comayagua; grain, sugar cane.

Humuya River, Honduras: see COMAYAGUA RIVER.

Hun, China: see YUNGTING RIVER.

Hun (hŏŏn) or **Hon** (hōn), oasis (1950 pop. 3,500), SE Tripolitania, Libya, near Fezzan border, 150 mi. SSW of Sirte, in an oasis; road junction. Trade center (dates, figs, barley, livestock, hides). Under Italian administration (c.1911–43), was capital of S military territory (Libyan Sahara).

Huna (hōō'nä'), Mongolian league in N Inner Mongolian Autonomous Region, Manchuria; formed 1949 through union of BARGA and BUTEHA (Nonni R.) leagues, on W and E slopes, respectively, of the Great Khingan Mts. Huna is derived from the "hu" of Hulunbuir (Barga) and "na," from the Daur name for Nonni R.

Hunabasi, Japan: see FUNABASHI.

Huna Bay (hōō'nŭ), Icelandic *Húnaflói* (hōō'näflō"ē), inlet (65 mi. long, 2–40 mi. wide) of Greenland Sea, NW Iceland; 65°45'N 20°55'W; forms E side of Vestfjarda Peninsula. Fishing ports on bay are Holmavik, Blonduos, Skagastrond.

Hunakawaminato, Japan: see FUNAKAWAMINATO.

Hunan (hōō'nän') [Chinese,=S of the lake], province (□ 80,000; pop. 28,000,000) of S central China, S of Tungting L.; ⊙ Changsha. Bordered N by Hupeh (in part along Yangtze R.), W by Szechwan and Kweichow, S by Kwangsi and Kwangtung, and E by Kiangsi, Hunan is hilly in S and W and becomes (NE) an alluvial lowland in Tungting basin. The uplands, consisting largely of red sandstone, intersected by limestone and granite, include the Nan Ling (S; crossed by Cheling Pass), the Süehfeng and Wuling mts. (W), and the Heng Shan, one of China's 5 sacred mts. The Siang R. valley, which forms the main N–S corridor, and the lesser Tzu and Yüan rivers drain through Tungting L. into the Yangtze. The climate is of the temperate continental type, with warm summers and cool winters. Rice is the outstanding summer crop (yielding 2 crops), particularly in the "rice bowl" of Tungting L. Wheat, beans, rapeseed, and barley are grown in winter. Hunan is one of China's chief tea producers, and exports ramie, cotton, tobacco, oranges, and tea oil. Timber (pine, oak, cedar, camphor) is floated down the Yüan and Tzu rivers from the SW hills. The prov. abounds in mineral resources. Bituminous coal of good coking grade is found in Siangtan-Pingsiang area and anthracite farther S. Foremost among China's minerals are the lead-zinc of Shuikowshan (near Changning), the antimony of Sikwangshan (near Sinhwa), and the tin and tungsten of Sianghwaling (near Linwu), all of which are smelted at Changsha. An extension of the Kweichow mercury field is exploited near Fenghwang. Among handicraft industries, the embroidery, linen, porcelain, and paper are important. The leading urban centers are, in addition to Changsha, the provincial communications hub of Hengyang, the NW trade center of Changteh, and Yoyang (at outlet of Tungting L.). Hunan is served by Hankow-Canton RR, which follows Siang–Lei R. valley, and has branches from Hengyang to Kwangsi, and from Chuchow to Kiangsi and toward Kweichow. Pop., concentrated in the Siang and lower Yüan valleys, is overwhelmingly Chinese and speaks the Hunanese variety of Mandarin. In the Changteh region, the SW Mandarin dialect is spoken; and there are aboriginal Miao and Yao groups in W and S hills. Under Chinese rule since 3d cent. B.C., the region, traditionally called Siang for its main river, was part of the Chu kingdom of the Five Dynasties (907–960). Its present name, 1st used (12th cent.) under the Sung dynasty, was revived in 1660s by the Manchus when the anc. prov. of Hukwang was divided into Hupeh and Hunan. During Second World War, Hunan was sporadically invaded by the Japanese, who finally obtained control (1944–45) of main transportation lines. It passed to Communist rule in 1949.

Hunavatn (hōō'nävä"tŭn), Icelandic *Húnavatn*, county [Icelandic *sýsla*] (pop. 3,500), NW Iceland; ⊙ Blonduos. On S and E shores of Huna Bay. Marshy on coast; hilly inland, with fertile valleys. Sheep and horse raising, fishing. Thingeyrar is anc. judicial and literary center.

Hunchun or **Hun-ch'un** (hŏŏn'chŏŏn'), town, ⊙ Hunchun co. (pop. 116,938), E Kirin prov., Manchuria, 45 mi. E of Yenki, near USSR and Korea borders; gold deposits; lumbering; match mfg. An old commercial center opened to foreign trade in 1905, it was, however, by-passed by railroad and it subsequently declined. A Russo-Chinese border treaty was signed here, 1886.

Hundested (hōō'nŭstĕdh), village (pop., with adjacent village of Lynaes, 2,521), Frederiksborg amt, Zealand, Denmark, at mouth of Ise Fjord, 17 mi. WNW of Hillerod; fisheries, cannery.

Hundholmen, Norway: see KJOPSVIK.

Hundred, town (pop. 587), Wetzel co., NW W.Va., 26 mi. W of Morgantown, in oil, natural-gas, and agr. area.

Hundred and Two River, Iowa and Mo.: see ONE HUNDRED AND TWO RIVER.

Hundsfoss, Norway: see HUNSFOSS.

Hunedoara (hōōnädwä'rä), Ger. *Eisenmarkt* (ī'zŭnmärkt), Hung. *Vajdahunyad* (voi'dŏhōō"nyŏt), town (1948 pop. 7,018), Hunedoara prov., W central Rumania, in Transylvania, in E foothills of the Poiana-Rusca, 8 mi. S of Deva; rail terminus; center of a metallurgical dist. (blast furnaces, iron foundries, engineering works). Noted for its historic Hunyadi Castle built in 15th cent. on site of 13th-cent. fortress, and 15th-cent. Uniate church. Iron mining at near-by Teliuc (tĕlyōōk') and Ghelar (gälär'), to S and SW.

Hünfeld (hün'fĕlt), town (pop. 3,905), in former Prussian prov. of Hesse-Nassau, W Germany, after 1945 in Hesse, 9 mi. NNE of Fulda; rail junction; textile mfg.

Hungary (hŭng'gŭrē), Hung. *Magyarország* (mŏ'dyŏrō"säg) [Magyar land], since 1949 officially **Hungarian People's Republic,** Hung. *Magyar Népköztársaság*, country (□ 35,902; 1941 pop. 9,316,613) of SE central Europe; ⊙ Budapest. Bounded N by Czechoslovakia, in part along Danube and Ipel (Ipoly) rivers, NE by the Transcarpathian oblast of the Soviet Ukraine, E by Rumania, S by Yugoslavia, in part along Drava and Mur rivers, and W by Austria, Hungary lies largely in the middle Danubian (Hungarian or Pannonian) basin, ringed W by the Alps, and N and E by the Carpathians. The Danube bisects the country along its N–S course, separating the ALFÖLD or Great Hungarian Plain (E) from the DUNANTUL or Transdanubia (W). The fertile Alföld, which is bisected in turn by the Tisza R., extends beyond the Hung. borders into Rumania, Yugoslavia, and the Ukraine. It is a level, sedimentary basin covered by a layer of loess and by once-drifting sand dunes that have largely been anchored by vegetation and now produce rye, potatoes, and fruit. The hilly Dunantul contains elongated L. BALATON, Hungary's leading resort area. S of the lake are low hills rising to 2,237 ft. in the Mecsek Mts. N of L. Balaton are old, peneplained hill ranges oriented SW–NE: the Bakony, Vertes, Gerecse, and Buda mts. This line of hills is continued beyond the Danube elbow in the Börzsöny, Cserhat, Matra (with Hungary's highest peak, Mt. Kekes, 3,330 ft.), Bükk, and Tokaj-Eperjes mts. In the extreme NW is a small mtn.-ringed replica of the Alföld, the Little Alföld, which extends across the Danube into Czechoslovakia. Situated bet. 46° and 48°N, Hungary has a moderate continental climate. The Dunantul is more exposed to Atlantic maritime influences, and the Alföld has rather dry, hot summers and variable winters. The spring and autumn seasons are generally short. Winds blow predominantly from the NW, rainfall is 25–30 in. yearly, most of it falling in early summer. The Danube is a major international waterway, navigable in its entire Hung. section. It receives, in Hungary, the Leitha, Raab, and the combined Sio-Sarviz rivers (right) and the Ipel (left). The Tisza, of more irregular regime, receives the Sajo (with the Hernad) and the Zagyva rivers (right) and the Somes (Szamos) Körös, and Mures (Maros) rivers (left). Despite the continental climate and occasionally poor soils, agr. plays a leading role in the Hung. economy; 60% of the total area is under cultivation, of which in turn 60% is under grains; pastures cover 18% of the country, notably in the remaining *puszta* areas of the Bugac Steppe (S of Kecskemet) and the Hortobagy (W of Debrecen). Forests (12% of total area) are mainly in Bakony and Matra mts. Considerable sections are under garden crops (melons) and vineyards (Tokay wine is famous). Extensive irrigation and flood control in the Alföld have increased the agr. yield since 19th cent.; since the Second World War even the Hortobagy *puszta* is being irrigated for rice production. Of the dominant grain production, wheat and corn lead in sown acreage and are grown mainly in the Alföld and the S Dunantul. Secondary grains are rye (on the fixed dunes of the Nyirseg and the Kiskunsag), barley (in the Little Alföld and on the Matra and Bükk slopes), and oats (for fodder). Potatoes are widely grown. Sugar beets, flax, hemp, tobacco, and paprika are the chief industrial crops. Fruit is cultivated near Kecskemet and Nagykörös. Hungary is a country of intensive livestock raising; beef cattle, hogs, horses, and sheep constitute the principal stock. Poultry, notably fattened geese, are raised on grain. Agr. production is the basis for the important food-processing industry: flour milling (mainly at Budapest), sugar refining (Hatvan, Szerencs, Sarvar), starch and alcohol processing, fruit and vegetable canning, and meat packing. Next to the food industry are the mfg. of shoes and other leather goods, woodworking (handicraft industry at Nagyteteny), paper mfg., and cotton milling. Although minerals play a secondary role in the Hung. economy, they have given rise, in conjunction with imported coke and iron ore, to machinery, chemical, and metallurgical industries. Lignite, one of the leading mineral resources, is mined in the Vertes Mts. (Tatabanya), the Gerecse Mts. (Dorog, Tokod), and in Bakony Mts. (Varpalota); coal and lignite in Ozd and Salgotarjan areas, and anthracite in Mecsek Mts. (Pecs, Komlo). Petroleum is drilled at Lispe (Lispeszentadorjan) and natural gas at Lovaszi near Mur R. (Yugoslav border). While very little iron ore is produced, manganese, and particularly bauxite (18–20% of world reserves), are mined in Vertes and Bakony mts. Heavy industry is centered at Budapest (including Csepel and Pestszentlörinc), Miskolc-Diosgyör, Györ, Ozd, Salgotarjan, and Pecs. Development of heavy industry also begun after Second World War at Dunapentele. Other industrial centers, engaged mainly in food processing and textile milling, are Szeged, Debrecen, Hodmezövasarhely, Bekescsaba, Mako, Szolnok, and Kecskemet. Hungary has a well-developed rail net, radiating from Budapest, though lacking transverse lines. It is crossed by the Orient Express. River navigation on the Danube and the Tisza is aided by a navigable canal (begun after Second World War) bet. Dunaharaszti on the Danube and Ujkecske on the Tisza. Trade moves by the Danube and the railroads and is now primarily with the USSR and E European countries, rather than with Germany and Austria, as it was before the Second World War. Agr. products constitute half the exports, the principal items being corn, dressed poultry, beans, cattle, tomato products, sugar, and oilseeds, in addition to cotton fabrics. The share of industry in the export trade increased after the Second World War, while industrial raw materials accounted for the major imports. Hungary's once heterogeneous pop. has become quite homogeneous since the First World War as the result of the separation of non-Hungarian territories. Since the Second World War, during which Hungary briefly regained some lost areas, the pop. is 97% Magyar, with Germans, Slovaks, Yugoslavs, and Rumanians the main minorities. Budapest contains 17% of the total pop. The rest lives chiefly in middle-sized "towns," really rural agglomerations or garden cities covering very large areas. The largest of these garden cities (Szeged, Debrecen, Kecskemet, Hodmezovasarhely, Bekescsaba) lost their rural suburbs in the 1950 reorganization. Only a small proportion of the rural pop. lives in isolated farmsteads. Pop. is 65% R.C. and 20% Calvinist (Reformed Church). In Roman times, cis-Danubian Hungary constituted parts of Pannonia (conquered A.D. 10). In the course of the great migrations, the area was settled for brief periods by the Huns, the Ostrogoths, and the Avars. In the late 9th cent., the Magyars, a Ugric tribe, settled in the middle Danubian basin, founding their 1st dynasty under the semilegendary Arpad. Early Magyar expansion toward the West was halted by King Otto I at the battle of Lechfeld (955). Under St. Stephen (1001–38) the Christianization of the Magyars was completed and natl. consolidation begun. Petchenegs and Cumans from S Russia raided Transylvania in 11th cent., but they and other elements (Slavic, German, and Latin) were absorbed into the existing Hung. feudal system. After c.1100, Croatia was in personal union with Hungary, which later (until 14th cent.) also dominated Bosnia. Andrew II granted (1222) to the nobles the Golden Bull (the "Magna Carta of Hungary"). After the country had been briefly occupied (1241) by the Mongols, it fell into anarchy. The Arpad line died out (1301) and the magnates (powerful nobles) elected (1308) Charles I, the 1st of the Angevin line. Under his son, Louis I, Hungary reached its greatest territorial expansion when it was joined (1370) with Poland in a personal union, resumed briefly (1440–44) under Ladislaus III of Poland. John Hunyadi, voivode of Transylvania, halted (middle 15th cent.) the threatening

Turks and the Hung. Renaissance took place under his son, King Matthias Corvinus (1458–90). However, renewed division made Hungary an easy Turkish prey at the battle of Mohacs (1526), which ended the powerful, independent Hungary of the Middle Ages. In the long wars that followed, Hungary fell into 3 parts: the western, under Austrian control after 1526; the central plains, under complete Turkish domination after 1541; and Transylvania, under Turkish suzerainty. Following the liberation (1686) of Budapest by the Hapsburgs, Austria gained most of Hungary by the Peace of Karlowitz (1699), control over Transylvania being confirmed in 1711, and the Banat by the Treaty of Passarowitz (1718). The Peace of Belgrade (1739) confirmed the Hapsburgs in their control of Hungary, which remained an Austrian crownland until the Hungarian revolution of 1848. The struggle for independence, led by Kossuth, who proclaimed (1849) a short-lived independent republic, was suppressed by Austria with Russian aid and was followed by ruthless reprisals. However, Austria was obliged to compromise with Magyar natl. aspirations in the *Ausgleich* of 1867, which set up the Austro-Hungarian dual monarchy, with the 2 countries nearly equal partners. The collapse of the dual monarchy at the close of the First World War led to the establishment (1918) of a republic under Michael Karolyi, followed (1919) by the short rule of the Communist Bela Kun. Following Rumanian intervention, the reins passed to Admiral Horthy, leader of counter-revolutionary forces, who, in 1920, became regent of a kingdom without a king, but identified with the crown of St. Stephen. By the Treaty of Trianon (1920), Hungary lost nearly 70% of its territory, including Slovakia, Ruthenia, Transylvania, the Banat, Burgenland, Croatia-Slavonia, and Fiume. The frustration of Magyar revisionist sentiment by the Little Entente and France drove Hungary into friendship with Italy and ultimately (1941) into alliance with Nazi Germany in the Second World War. Bet. 1938 and 1944, Hungary temporarily regained the S fringes of Slovakia, Ruthenia, N Transylvania, the Backa, SE Baranya, and Yugoslav areas along the Mur R. Hungary was occupied (1944–45) by the Soviet Army; a provisional govt. established in 1944 at Debrecen signed an armistice in 1945. The peace treaty of 1947 restored the country to the area within the Trianon boundaries, but provided for the cession of the Rusovce (Oroszvar) bridgehead (□ 33) opposite Bratislava, to Czechoslovakia. In 1946 a republic had been proclaimed and the new coalition regime instituted long-needed land reforms. However, in early 1948, the Communist minority by a coup d'état gained full control and proclaimed (1949) a people's republic fully aligned with the Soviet bloc. Since late 1949 industry has been entirely nationalized and the collectivization of agr. progressed through 1950 and 1951. After the Second World War, Hungary was divided administratively into 25 counties (Hung. *megye* or *vármegye*): ABAUJ, BACS-BODROG, BARANYA, BEKES, BIHAR, BORSOD-GÖMÖR, CSANAD, CSONGRAD, FEJER, GYÖR-MOSON, HAJDU, HEVES, JASZ-NAGYKUN-SZOLNOK, KOMAROM-ESZTERGOM, NOGRAD-HONT, PEST-PILIS-SOLT-KISKUN, SOMOGY, SOPRON, SZABOLCS, SZATMAR-BEREG, TOLNA, VAS, VESZPREM, ZALA, and ZEMPLEN. In 1950, the counties were reorganized. The 19 new divisions and their capitals are Bacs-Kiskun (⊙ Kecskemet), Baranya (⊙ Pecs), Bekes (⊙ Bekescsaba), Borsod-Abauj-Zemplen (⊙ Miskolc), Csongrad (⊙ Hodmezövasarhely), Fejer (⊙ Szekesfehervar), Györ-Sopron (⊙ Györ), Hajdu-B har (⊙ Debrecen), Heves (⊙ Eger), Komarom (⊙ Tatabanya), Nograd (⊙ Salgotarjan), Pest (⊙ Budapest, greatly enlarged 1949 through inc. of suburbs), Somogy (⊙ Kaposvar), Szabolcs-Szatmar (⊙ Nyiregyhaza), Szolnok (⊙ Szolnok), Tolna (⊙ Szekszard), Vas (⊙ Szombathely), Veszprem (⊙ Veszprem), and Zala (⊙ Zalaegerszeg). The Hung. counties referred to throughout this book are those in existence up to the 1950 reorganization.

Hungcheng or **Hung-ch'eng** (hŏŏng'chŭng'), village, SE Ningsia prov., China, 12 mi. SE of Yinchwan, across Yellow R., at the Great Wall (Suiyuan line); handles Yinchwan's river trade.

Hung-chiang, China: see HUNGKIANG.

Hung-ch'iao, China: see HUNGJAO.

Hungen (hŏŏng'ŭn), town (pop. 2,923), central Hesse, W Germany, in former Upper Hesse prov., 12 mi. SE of Giessen; lumber milling. Has 15th–16th-cent. castle.

Hungerburg, Estonia: see NARVA-JOESUU.

Hungerford, town and parish (pop. 2,870), SW Berkshire, England, on Kennet R. and 9 mi. W of Newbury; agr. market. Has 14th-cent. church. In town hall is drinking horn given to town by John of Gaunt.

Hunghai Bay, China: see HONGHAI BAY.

Hung Ho, China: see RED RIVER.

Hunghoa (hŏŏng'hwä'), town, Phutho prov., N Vietnam, on Red R. and 37 mi. WNW of Hanoi. Former Annamese citadel.

Hungjao (hŏŏng'jou'), Mandarin *Hung-ch'iao* (-chyou'), village, Kiangsu prov., China, 11 mi. W of Shanghai; one of Shanghai's military airports.

Hungkiang or **Hung-chiang** (both: hŏŏng'jyäng'), town, W Hunan prov., China, port on upper Yüan R. and 8 mi. SE of Kienyang; distributing center of SW Hunan; exports tung oil, hides, bamboo.

Hungkiatun, Manchuria: see CHINSI.

Hungnam (hŏŏng'näm'), Jap. *Konan* (kō'nä), city (1944 pop. 143,600), S.Hamgyong prov., N Korea, at mouth of Tongsongchon R. SE of Hamhung; industrial center (gold refinery; aluminum, chemical, and nitrogen-fertilizer plants); fisheries. Coal mined near by. Was small fishing village until late 1920s. Heavily bombed in Korean war (1950).

Hungry, village (pop. 52), SW central Alaska, near middle Kuskokwim R.

Hungry Hill, mountain (2,251 ft.), SW Co. Cork, Ireland, highest point of Caha Mts., 6 mi. ENE of Castletown Bere.

Hungry Horse, village (pop. 1,335, with adjacent Government Village), Flathead co., NW Mont., on South Fork Flathead R. near site of Hungry Horse Dam, and 18 mi. NE of Kalispell.

Hungry Horse Dam, NW Mont., in narrow canyon of South Fork Flathead R., S of Glacier Natl. Park and 26 mi. NE of Kalispell. A major unit in development program for Columbia R. basin, dam was authorized 1944 by Congress, built by Bureau of Reclamation; 564 ft. high, 2,115 ft. long; of concrete, arch-gravity construction; for hydroelectric power, irrigation, and flood control. At max. capacity, its reservoir will extend c.35 mi. upstream.

Hungshankiao, China: see LINSEN.

Hungshui, China: see KINGTAI; MINLO.

Hungshuipao, China: see KINGTAI.

Hungshui River, Chinese *Hungshui Ho* (hŏŏng'-shwā' hŭ'), main left headstream of West R., S China; 900 mi. long; rises in Kweichow-Yunnan border region in 2 branches (Peipan and Nanpan rivers) which join at Kweichow-Kwangsi line, traverses Kwangsi in deep sandstone gorges, obstructed by rapids, past Tsinkong (head of junk navigation), and joins YÜ RIVER at Kweihsien to form WEST RIVER (here called Sün R.). The Hungshui is sometimes known as the Pak [Chinese *Pak Ho*] below mouth of Liu R. (its chief left affluent).

Hungtow Island (hŏŏng'tō'), Chinese *Hung-t'ou Hsü* (shü) or *Lan Hsü* (län), Jap. *Koto-sho* (kō'tō-shō'), island off SE Formosa, 45 mi. E of Cape Olwanpi; 22°3'N 121°33'E; 8 mi. long, 1.5-4 mi. wide. Formerly called Botel Tobago. The Little Hungtow Isl. is 3 mi. S.

Hungtung (hŏŏng'dŏŏng'), town, ⊙ Hungtung co. (pop. 112,300), S Shansi prov., China, on Fen R., on railroad and 15 mi. NNE of Linfen; cotton weaving; wheat, corn, millet.

Hungtze Lake, Chinese *Hung-tze Hu* (hŏŏng'dzŭ' hōō), on Kiangsu-Anhwei border, China; occupies irregular basin 5–30 mi. wide (E–W), 65 mi. long. Receives Hwai R.; connected with Kaoyu L. and with Grand Canal. Navigable; abounds in fish.

Hungund (hōōn'gŏŏnd), town (pop. 6,748), Bijapur dist., S Bombay, India, 60 mi. SSE of Bijapur; cotton, peanuts, millet, wheat; cotton ginning.

Hungya (hŏŏng'yä'), town (pop. 16,916), ⊙ Hungya co. (pop. 195,527), W Szechwan prov., China, 30 mi. NW of Loshan, on Sikang line; paper milling, Chinese-wax processing; rice, wheat, millet. Copper and iron deposits near by.

Hungyen (hŏŏng'yĕn'), town, (1936 pop. 4,000), ⊙ Hungyen prov. (□ 350; 1943 pop. 533,300), N Vietnam, in Tonkin, near Red R., 30 mi. SE of Hanoi. Timber center; woodcarving. Important European trading center in 17th cent. Declined following changes in river course.

Hun Ho, China: see YUNGTING RIVER.

Huningue (ünĕg'), Ger. *Hüningen* (hü'nĭng-ŭn), town (pop. 2,946), Haut-Rhin dept., E France, on left bank of the Rhine (at junction of S branch of Rhone-Rhine Canal), 3 mi. N of Basel; customs and transshipment station on Ger. and near Swiss border; mfg. (plastics, chemicals, silk fabrics, baby carriages, water-repellent cartons). Near by is a fish hatchery. Purchased and fortified by Louis XIV; besieged by Austrians in 1815, and captured by Germans in 1871.

Huni Valley (hōō'nē), town, Western Prov., SW Gold Coast colony, 13 mi. NNE of Tarkwa; rail junction in gold-mining region; cacao, cassava, corn. Copper, platinum, nickel deposits.

Hunkers, borough (pop. 404), Westmoreland co., SW central Pa., 8 mi. SSW of Greensburg.

Hunn, Norway: see FREDRIKSTAD.

Hunnebostrand (hŭ"nŭbōō"stränd'), village (pop. 1,585), Goteborg och Bohus co., SW Sweden, on Skagerrak, 12 mi. NNW of Lysekil; seaside resort; stone quarries. Near by is 4th-cent. burial mound.

Hunnewell (hŭ'nēwĕl"). **1** City (pop. 103), Sumner co., S Kansas, at Okla. line, 16 mi. S of Wellington, in wheat area. **2** City (pop. 293), Shelby co., NE Mo., near Salt R., 7 mi. W of Monroe City; dairying.

Hunnur (hōōn'nŏŏr), town (pop. 3,905), Bijapur dist., S Bombay, India, 2 mi. W of Jamkhandi; cotton, millet, peanuts.

Hun River: China: see YUNGTING RIVER.

Hünsdorf (hüns'dôrf), town (pop. 195), S central Luxembourg, on Alzette R. and 6 mi. N of Luxembourg city; mfg. of mining and blast-furnace equipment, metal casting and stamping.

Hunsfoss or **Hundsfoss** (both: hōōns'fôs), waterfall (46 ft.) on Otra R., Vest-Agder co., S Norway, 8 mi. N of Kristiansand; hydroelectric plant powers paper factory.

Hunslet Carr and Middleton, industrial town (pop. 19,916) in Leeds county borough, West Riding, S central Yorkshire, England, just S of Leeds; coal mines, iron and steel foundries and rolling mills; produces locomotives, engines, machine tools, textile machinery, leather, paper, aniline dyes.

Hunsrück (hōōns'rük"), mountain region, W Germany, bet. Rhine (E), Mosel (N), Saar (W), and Nahe (S) rivers; rises to 2,677 ft. in the Erbeskopf. Densely forested; wine grown on N and S rim. Main town: Simmern. Geologically it is considered part of Rhenish Slate Mts.

Hunstanton, England: see NEW HUNSTANTON.

Hunsur (hōōn'sōōr), town (pop. 7,919), Mysore dist., SW Mysore, India, on Lakshmantirtha R. and 25 mi. W of Mysore; road center; depot for timber from mts. of Coorg state (W); processing of coffee, tobacco, spices (pepper, cardamom). Cattle farm breeds well-known Mysore bullocks, sheep.

Hunsworth, England: see SPENBOROUGH.

Hunt, county (□ 910; pop. 42,731), NE Texas; ⊙ Greenville. Rich blackland prairie in W and NW; timbered in E; drained by Sabine R. and South Fork of Sulphur R. Agr. (especially cotton; also corn, clover, grains, pecans, fruit, truck); dairying; poultry, cattle, hogs, sheep. Some oil production. Mfg., processing at Greenville and Commerce. Formed 1846.

Hunt, Mount (9,000 ft.), SE Yukon, near Northwest Territories border, in Mackenzie Mts.; 61°28'N 129°14'W.

Hunter. 1 Town (pop. 286), Woodruff co., E central Ark., 20 mi. W of Forrest City. **2** City (pop. 236), Mitchell co., N central Kansas, 50 mi. NW of Salina; grain, livestock. **3** Town (pop. 134), Carter co., S Mo., in the Ozarks, near Current R., 27 mi. WNW of Poplar Bluff. **4** Resort village (pop. 526), Greene co., SE N.Y., in the Catskills, on Schoharie Creek and 17 mi. W of Catskill; mfg. of clothing. **5** Village (pop. 417), Cass co., E N.Dak., 30 mi. NW of Fargo and on branch of Elm R.; dairy products, livestock, grain, potatoes. **6** Town (pop. 279), Garfield co., N Okla., 16 mi. NE of Enid, in grain and livestock area.

Hunter, Mount (14,960 ft.), S central Alaska, in Alaska Range, in Mt. McKinley Natl. Park, 130 mi. NNW of Anchorage; 62°57'N 151°5'W.

Hunter, Port, or **Newcastle Harbour,** estuary of Hunter R. opening into the Pacific, E New South Wales, Australia; 2d largest harbor of state; semicircular, 3 mi. long, 2 mi. wide. Coal-loading port of Newcastle is on S shore, near entrance. Small peninsula (site of Stockton) forms N side of entrance.

Hunter Air Force Base, Ga.: see SAVANNAH.

Hunterdon, county (□ 435; pop. 42,736), W N.J., bounded W by Delaware R.; ⊙ Flemington. Agr. area (poultry, truck, grain, fruit, dairy products, livestock); mfg. (iron and steel products, paper, machinery, clothing, porcelain and rubber goods). Includes Voorhees State Park. Drained by the Musconetcong R. and by South Branch of Raritan R. Musconetcong Mtn. is in W. Co. formed 1714.

Hunter Island (□ 129), SW B.C., in NE part of Queen Charlotte Sound, 6 mi. S of Bella Bella; 51°55'N 128°5'W; 21 mi. long, 3–10 mi. wide. Rises to 2,950 ft.

Hunter Island, tract of land in NW Ont., extending N from Minn. border, 100 mi. W of Fort William; 50 mi. long, 30 mi. wide. Region of small lakes and streams, flowing into Rainy R.

Hunter Island, Marshall Isls.: see KILI.

Hunter Islands, island group in Bass Strait, 3 mi. off NW coast of Tasmania; comprise Hunter Isl., Three Hummock Isl., and several small islets; mountainous. Hunter Isl. (□ 33; 14 mi. long, 4 mi. wide) is largest; formerly called Barren Isl.

Hunte River (hōōn'tŭ), NW Germany, rises in the Wiehen Mts. 4 mi. N of Melle, flows c.120 mi. generally N, past Wildeshausen and Oldenburg city, to the Weser at Elsfleth. Canalized lower course forms part of Ems-Hunte Canal, which connects Ems and Weser rivers.

Hunter Liggett Military Reservation, Calif.: see JOLON.

Hunter Mountain (4,025 ft.), Greene co., SE N.Y., in the Catskills, 19 mi. W of Catskill.

Hunter River, E New South Wales, Australia, rises in Liverpool Range, flows 287 mi. SW, past Muswellbrook and Denman, and SE, past Singleton, Maitland, Morpeth, and Raymond Terrace, to Pacific Ocean at Port Hunter (site of Newcastle). Navigable by steamer for 23 mi. below Morpeth. Coal mines in river valley; frequent floods. Goulburn R., main tributary.

Hunter's Hill, municipality (pop. 11,497), E New South Wales, Australia, on N shore of Parramatta R. and 4 mi. NW of Sydney, in metropolitan area; shipyards. Linked by bridge with Drummoyne, on S shore of river.

Hunter's Island, N.Y.: see PELHAM BAY PARK.

Hunter's Quay, resort on Firth of Clyde, in DUNOON burgh, E Argyll, Scotland.

Hunters River, village (pop. estimate 400), central P.E.I., on Hunter R. and 15 mi. WNW of Charlottetown; mixed farming, dairying; potatoes.

Hunter's Road, township (pop. 43), Gwelo prov., central Southern Rhodesia, in Matabeleland, on railroad and 20 mi. N of Gwelo; alt. 4,218 ft. Gold mining.

Huntersville, textile town (pop. 916), Mecklenburg co., S N.C., 12 mi. N of Charlotte; cotton milling.

Huntingburg, industrial city (pop. 4,056), Dubois co., SW Ind., c.40 mi. NE of Evansville, in agr. area (grain, poultry, strawberries; dairy products); mfg. (pottery, brick, electronic equipment, furniture and wood products, packed meat); poultry hatcheries; clay pits; rose greenhouses.

Huntingdon, county (□ 361; pop. 12,394), S Que., on Ont. and N.Y. borders, on the St. Lawrence; ⊙ Huntingdon.

Huntingdon. 1 Village (pop. estimate 200), SW B.C., on Wash. border, 10 mi. S of Mission; dairying; stock, fruit, hops. **2** Town (pop. 1,952), ⊙ Huntingdon co., S Que., on Châteauguay R. and 40 mi. SW of Montreal, near N.Y. border; woolen milling, lumbering, dairying.

Huntingdon or **Huntingdonshire** (-shĭr), county (□ 365.6; 1931 pop. 56,206; 1951 census 69,273), S central England; ⊙ Huntingdon. Bounded by Northampton (W and N), Cambridge (E), and Bedford (SW). Drained by Ouse R. and Nene R. Undulating farming and grazing land. NE part is in The Fens. Besides Huntingdon, other towns are Old Fletton (bricks), St. Ives, and St. Neots. Chief industries are brewing and malting, mfg. of agr. machinery, fruit and vegetable canning, paper making. Shortened form is Hunts.

Huntingdon, municipal borough (1931 pop. 4,106; 1951 census 5,282), ⊙ Huntingdonshire, England, in center of co., on Ouse R. and 60 mi. N of London, on the anc. Ermine Street; 52°20′N 0°11′E; jam, fruit, and vegetable canneries, agr.-machinery works, brickworks, breweries. Oliver Cromwell, b. here, attended the grammar school where Samuel Pepys later also studied. Just W is large estate of Hinchinbrooke, bought from the Cromwells by earl of Sandwich.

Huntingdon, county (□ 895; pop. 40,872), S central Pa.; ⊙ Huntingdon. Hilly region, drained by Juniata R. Tussey Mtn. lies along W and part of N border, Tuscarora Mtn. along SE border. Clay, bituminous coal, glass sand; mfg. (bricks, paper, metal products, textiles). Formed 1787.

Huntingdon. 1 Industrial borough (pop. 7,330), ⊙ Huntingdon co., S central Pa., 21 mi. E of Altoona and on Juniata R.; mfg. (paper, boilers, radiators, silk products); bituminous coal, glass sand; timber. Juniata Col. here. Settled c.1755, laid out 1767, inc. 1796. Lincoln Caverns are W. **2** Town (pop. 2,043), ⊙ Carroll co., NW Tenn., 34 mi. NE of Jackson; shipping point for cotton, grain, sweet potatoes, tomatoes; lumber and grain milling. Settled and inc. 1821.

Huntingdonshire, England: see HUNTINGDON, county.

Hunting Island, Beaufort co., S S.C., one of Sea Isls., just E of St. Helena Isl., to which it is connected by highway bridge; c.5 mi. long. State park (c.5,000 acres), resort colony, and wildlife sanctuary here.

Huntington, county (□ 390; pop. 31,400), NE central Ind.; ⊙ Huntington. Agr. area (grain, truck, poultry, livestock, and soybeans; dairy products). Diversified mfg. at Huntington. Limestone quarrying; timber. Drained by Wabash, Salamonie, and Little rivers, and by small Longlois Creek. Formed 1832.

Huntington. 1 Town (pop. 744), Sebastian co., W Ark., 22 mi. SSE of Fort Smith, in agr. area. **2** City (pop. 15,079), ⊙ Huntington co., NE central Ind., on Little R. near its mouth on the Wabash, and 24 mi. SW of Fort Wayne; farm trade center. Mfg. of rubber goods, furniture, cranes, asbestos, radios, phonographs, machinery, automobile parts, furnaces, paint, disinfectants, food products; printing. Limestone quarrying. Seat of Huntington Col. **3** Town (pop. 1,257), Hampshire co., SW Mass., in the Berkshires, 10 mi. NW of Westfield and on Westfield R. (dammed here to form Knightville Reservoir); textiles. Settled 1769, inc. 1775. **4** or **Huntington Village,** village (pop. 9,324), Suffolk co., SE N.Y., on N shore of W Long Isl., at head of Huntington Harbor, 14 mi. NE of Mineola, in suburban residential and resort region; part of Huntington town (1940 pop. 31,768). Mfg.: coats, luggage, machinery, cement blocks, aircraft parts, auto bodies, boats. Walt Whitman's birthplace is near by. **5** Town (pop. 733), Baker co., E Oregon, 25 mi. N of Vale and on Burnt R., near its confluence with the Snake; alt. 2,113 ft. Stockyards. **6** City (pop. 1,039), Angelina co., E Texas, 10 mi. ESE of Lufkin, near Angelina R., in pine, cotton, cattle area; lumber and grain milling, cotton ginning. Inc. 1938. **7** City (pop. 1,029), Emery co., central Utah, 20 mi. SSW of Price; alt. 5,900 ft.; agr. Settled 1878, inc. 1891. **8** Town (pop. 601), Chittenden co., NW Vt., on small Huntington R. (water power) and 17 mi. SE of Burlington; lumber, dairy products. Includes part of Camels Hump State Forest. **9** City (pop. 86,353), ⊙ Cabell co., in Cabell and Wayne counties, W W.Va., on the Ohio and 190 mi. SW of Pittsburgh; 38°25′N 82°25′W; alt. c.550 ft. Largest city in state; commercial (wholesale and market) and mfg. center for bituminous-coal, oil, natural-gas, and farm (especially tobacco, fruit) region; important railroad city (huge repair shops); river port (ships coal). Industries include reduction and fabrication of nickel alloys (especially monel metal), mfg. of railroad equipment, steel rails, glass, furniture, footwear, ceramics, chemicals (dyes), electrical goods, textiles, wood products, flour and other foods, tobacco products. Seat of Marshall Col. State institutions here include industrial school for girls, hosp. for the insane, children's home. Along river here is 11-mi. flood wall. City founded 1871 as W terminus of Chesapeake & Ohio RR.

Huntington Bay, village (pop. 585), Suffolk co., SE N.Y., on N shore of Long Isl., on inlet of Huntington Bay, just NE of Huntington, in summer-resort area. Site of capture of Nathan Hale by the British is marked.

Huntington Bay, SE N.Y., an arm of Long Island Sound indenting N shore of Long Isl. N of Huntington, which is at head of Huntington Harbor (c.2 mi. long), bay's S arm; c.4½ mi. wide at entrance bet. Lloyd Point (W) and Eatons Neck Point (E); 3½ mi. long. Northport Bay and Centerport Harbor connect with Huntington Bay on SE, Lloyd Harbor adjoins on W. Resort area.

Huntington Beach, city (pop. 5,237), Orange co., S Calif., 13 mi. SE of Long Beach, on coast; oil and natural-gas fields (discovered 1920); oil refineries. Inc. 1909.

Huntington Harbor, N.Y.: see HUNTINGTON BAY, inlet.

Huntington Lake, Fresno co., E central Calif., in the Sierra Nevada, 45 mi. NE of Fresno; 6 mi. long; summer, winter resort. Impounded in a tributary of the San Joaquin by Huntington Lake No. 1 Dam (165 ft. high, 1,310 ft. long; for power; completed 1917). Receives water through tunnel from Florence L. (12 mi. E).

Huntington Park, residential city (pop. 29,450), Los Angeles co., S Calif., suburb 5 mi. S of downtown Los Angeles, in industrial area; iron and steel products, oil-field equipment, food products. Oil and gas wells, oil refineries near by. Inc. 1906.

Huntington Station, village (pop. 9,924), Suffolk co., SE N.Y., on N shore of W Long Isl., just S of Huntington, in truck-farm and summer-resort area; mfg. (clothing, aircraft and marine instruments, auto bodies, sheet-metal and wood products); sand, gravel.

Huntington Village, N.Y.: see HUNTINGTON, village.

Huntington Woods, city (pop. 4,949), Oakland co., SE Mich., residential suburb N of Detroit. Inc. as village 1926, as city 1932.

Hunting Valley, village (pop. 477), on Cuyahoga-Geauga co. line, N Ohio, an E suburb of Cleveland.

Huntland, town (pop. 285), Franklin co., S Tenn., near Ala. line, 55 mi. W of Chattanooga.

Huntleigh (hŭnt′lē), town (pop. 180), St. Louis co., E Mo., W of St. Louis.

Huntley. 1 Village (pop. 830), McHenry co., NE Ill., 11 mi. NW of Elgin, in dairying area. Summer resorts near by. **2** Village (pop. c.150), Yellowstone co., S Mont., on Yellowstone R. and 12 mi. NE of Billings. Huntley Dam and administrative center for Huntley irrigation project here. **3** Village (pop. 98), Harlan co., S Nebr., 9 mi. NNE of Alma and on branch of Republican R.

Huntly, borough (pop. 2,870), N N.Isl., New Zealand, on Waikato R. and 55 mi. S of Auckland; rail junction; coal mines. School of mines.

Huntly, burgh (1931 pop. 3,779; 1951 census 4,197), NW Aberdeen, Scotland, on Deveron R. and 33 mi. NW of Aberdeen; agr. market, with woolen and hosiery milling, bacon and ham curing, mfg. of agr. machinery and oleomargarine; summer and angling resort. The 14th-cent. Huntly Castle (formerly Strathbogie Castle) was seat of earls of Huntly. George Macdonald b. here.

Hunt River, S central R.I., rises NE of Exeter, flows SE, then NE, bet. East Greenwich and North Kingstown towns, to Narragansett Bay SE of East Greenwich village; c.8 mi. long. Called Potowomut R. in lower course, where it is S boundary of Potowomut Peninsula.

Hunts, England: see HUNTINGDON, county.

Huntsdale, town (pop. 50), Boone co., central Mo., on Missouri R. and 8 mi. W of Columbia.

Hunts Peak (12,446 ft.), S central Colo., in N tip of Sangre de Cristo Mts., bet. Fremont and Saguache counties.

Huntspill, agr. village and parish (pop. 1,448), N central Somerset, England, near Parrett R. estuary, 2 mi. S of Burnham-on-Sea. Has 15th-cent. church.

Hunt's Point, SE N.Y., a residential and industrial section of S Bronx borough of New York city, at confluence of Bronx and East rivers.

Huntsville, town (pop. 2,800), SE central Ont., bet. small L. Vernon (W) and Fairy L. (E), 25 mi. N of Bracebridge; tanning, woodworking, diatomite processing; resort.

Huntsville. 1 City (pop. 16,437), ⊙ Madison co., N Ala., 85 mi. N of Birmingham, bet. Tennessee R. and Tenn. line; textile center; mfg. (work clothes and cotton fabrics, shoes, farm implements; metal, wood, and rubber products; cottonseed oil, beverages). U.S. arsenal here. Has fine ante-bellum homes. Settled 1807, inc. 1811. Site of constitutional convention (1819), and briefly state ⊙. Near by are Ala. Agr. and Mechanical Inst. (at Normal), Oakwood Col. (in suburban Oakwood) and a state park. **2** Town (pop. 1,010), ⊙ Madison co., NW Ark., 24 mi. E of Fayetteville, in the Ozarks; lumber, flour, canned foods. **3** City (pop. 1,520), ⊙ Randolph co., N central Mo., 5 mi. W of Moberly; grain, coal. Founded c.1830. **4** Village (pop. 408), Logan co., W central Ohio, 6 mi. NNW of Bellefontaine, in agr. area. **5** Village (pop. c.2,000), ⊙ Scott co., N Tenn., 45 mi. NW of Knoxville; lumbering. **6** City (pop. 9,820), ⊙ Walker co., E central Texas, c.65 mi. N of Houston; a trade, shipping, processing center; lumber milling, cotton ginning, dairying. Seat of the state penitentiary and a state teachers col. Restored home of Sam Houston and a memorial mus. are here. A state park and a state fish hatchery are near by. Inc. 1845. **7** Town (pop. 494), Weber co., N Utah, on Pine View Reservoir (in Ogden R.) and 12 mi. E of Ogden in irrigated agr. area; alt. 4,920 ft. Wasatch Range near by.

Huntsville Park, Ala.: see MERRIMACK.

Hunucmá (hōōnōōkmä′), town (pop. 4,655), Yucatan, SE Mexico, 16 mi. W of Mérida; rail junction; henequen-growing center.

Hunyani River (hōōnyä′nē), in N Southern Rhodesia and W Mozambique, rises 5 mi. W of Marandellas, flows 260 mi. W and N, past Sinoia, to the Zambezi in Mozambique. Prince Edward Dam on its upper course, 10 mi. S of Salisbury, supplies that city with water. Receives Angwa R. (left).

Hunyüan (hōōn′yüän′), town, ⊙ Hunyüan co. (pop. 176,872), SW Chahar prov., China, 35 mi. SE of Tatung; ramie weaving; wheat, millet, kaoliang, potatoes. Until 1949 in N Shansi.

Hunza (hōōn′zä), feudatory state (□ 3,900; pop. 15,341) in Gilgit Agency, NW Kashmir; ⊙ BALTIT. Bounded N by Afghanistan, S by Nagar state and Hunza R.; the Hindu Kush lies along N border; N end of Karakoram mtn. system in center. Misgar village, in E, is on important trade route leading, via Kilik Pass, into China. In 1869, state recognized suzerainty of maharaja of Jammu and Kashmir; in 1888, combined with Nagar state and ejected Kashmir troops from Chalt (recaptured same year). Kashmir troops removed (1906) from Hunza and Nagar after disturbances following re-establishment (1889) of Gilgit Agency. Held after 1948 by Pakistan. Prevailing mother tongue, Burushaski.

Hunza, village, Kashmir: see BALTIT.

Hunza River, N Kashmir, rises in N Karakoram mtn. system, in headstreams joining 10 mi. E of Misgar; flows S, W past Baltit and Nagar, along Hunza-Nagar state border, and S to Gilgit R. just E of Gilgit; c.120 mi. long.

Huo-, for Chinese names beginning thus and not found here: see under Hwo-.

Huo-chia, China: see HWOKIA.

Huo-ch'iu, China: see HWOKIU.

Huongkhe (hwŭng′khā′), town, Hatinh prov., N central Annam, on railroad and 15 mi. WSW of Hatinh; betel nuts, rubber, tangerines; forestry. Coal and iron deposits near by.

Huon Gulf (hū′ŭn), NE New Guinea, bounded by Huon Peninsula (N) and coast of Morobe dist. (S); 80 mi. wide, 65 mi. deep. Lae and Salamaua are its harbors.

Huon Islands, uninhabited coral group (160 acres), SW Pacific, 170 mi. NW of New Caledonia, of which it is a dependency; 18°1′S 162°55′E; comprise 3 isls.

Huon Peninsula, NE New Guinea, bet. Astrolabe Bay and Huon Gulf; 60 mi. wide; Finschhafen in E, Lae in S. Occupied 1942 by Japanese, taken 1943 by Allies.

Huon River, S Tasmania, rises in mts. 50 mi. W of Hobart, flows 105 mi. E, past Huonville and Franklin, to D'Entrecasteaux Channel, forming estuary 2.5 mi. wide. Cygnet is at head of N inlet of estuary. Coal mined along banks.

Huonville (hū′ŭnvĭl), town (pop. 884), SE Tasmania, 17 mi. SW of Hobart and on Huon R.; fruit canneries.

Huounta or **Wounta** (both: wōn′tä), village, Zelaya dept., E Nicaragua, minor Caribbean port, at mouth of Cucalaya R., 15 mi. N of Prinzapolka; coconuts, hardwood.

Hupeh or **Hupei** (both: hōō′pā′, Chinese hōō′bā′) [Chinese,=north of the lake], province (□ 70,000; pop. 25,000,000) of central China, N of Tungting L.; ⊙ Wuchang. Bounded N by Honan, W by Shensi and Szechwan, S by Hunan (in part along Yangtze R.) and Kiangsi (along Mufow Mts.), and E by Anhwei, the prov. of Hupeh lies largely on the alluvial, lake-studded, central Yangtze plain. In the W rise sandstone mts. forming part of the E rim of the Red Basin of Szechwan. Through these uplands, in picturesque gorges, flow the rivers Yangtze and Han, the principal streams of the prov., which have their confluence in the great

Wuhan conurbation. Hupeh has a moderate continental climate, with cool winters, and hot, wet summers favorable to agr. Rice and cotton are the leading summer crops; wheat, barley, and beans are raised during the winter. There is important tea production on N slopes of Mufow Mts. (Kiangsi border), and prov. also exports ramie and tung oil. Mushrooms are collected in W hills. Outside of Manchuria, it has China's chief iron mines, near Tayeh, whose ore is smelted at Hanyang with Pingsiang coking coal. There are minor coal, gypsum, and salt deposits. Hupeh's economic activity (mfg., trade) is centered at the Wuhan tri-city area, comprising Hankow, Hanyang, and Wuchang. Other important centers are the Yangtze ports of Shasi and Ichang and the Han ports of Fancheng and Kwanghwa (Laohokow). Hupeh owes its economic importance to its favorable location at the junction of the Yangtze and the N–S Peking-Hankow-Canton RR. Pop. is entirely Chinese and speaks the SW Mandarin dialect. Originally joined with Hunan in the anc. prov. of Hukwang, Hupeh was separated in 1660s. During Second World War, Hupeh was partly occupied by Japanese, mainly in Hankow area. It passed in 1949 to Chinese Communist control.

Hupei, China: see HUPEH.

Hur, Turkey: see MUTKI.

Huraidha, Aden: see HUREIDHA.

Hur al-Hammar, Iraq: see HAMMAR, HOR AL.

Huraydah, Aden: see HUREIDHA.

Hurayn, Egypt: see HUREIN.

Hurbanovo (hŏŏr'bänôvô), town (pop. 3,578), S Slovakia, Czechoslovakia, on railroad and 8 mi. NNE of Komarno; agr. center (wheat, corn, tobacco). Has meteorological observatory. Until 1948, called Stara Dala, Czech *Stará Ďala,* Hung. *Ógyalla.*

Hurdland, agr. town (pop. 268), Knox co., NE Mo., near Salt R., 7 mi. W of Edina.

Hurdsfield, village (pop. 223), Wells co., central N.Dak., 20 mi. SW of Fessenden.

Hureidha, Horaidha, Huraidha, or **Huraydah** (all: hŏŏrā'dhŭ), town (pop. 2,000), Quaiti state, Eastern Aden Protectorate, 35 mi. SW of Shibam; chief town of the Wadi 'Amd; place of religious teaching; mosques. Airfield.

Hurein or **Hurayn** (both: hōō'rān), village (pop. 7,561), Gharbiya prov., Lower Egypt, 6 mi. S of El Santa; cotton. Sometimes Hurin.

Hurezu, Rumania: see HOREZU.

Hurghada (hŏŏr'gădŭ), Arabic *El Ghardaqa* or *Al-Ghardaqah* (both: ĕl gär'däkŭ), town (pop. 2,727), ⊙ Red Sea Frontier Prov., E Egypt, on Red Sea at entrance to Gulf of Suez, 100 mi. NE of Qena. Important producer of crude oil, which is refined at Suez. In vicinity are molybdenite deposits.

Huriel (ürēĕl'), village (pop. 787), Allier dept., central France, 7 mi. WNW of Montluçon; brick and tile mfg., dairying.

Hurin, Egypt: see HUREIN.

Hurka River, Manchuria: see MUTAN RIVER.

Hurley, town and parish (pop. 1,252), E Berkshire, England, on the Thames and 4 mi. WNW of Maidenhead; agr. market. Has Norman church and remains of Norman monastery.

Hurley. 1 Village (pop. 2,079), Grant co., SW N.Mex., in foothills of Pinos Altos Mts., 10 mi. SE of Silver City; alt. 5,748 ft. Copper-ore mill and steam plant here; mill processes ore from open-pit copper mines at near-by Santa Rita. Agr. and livestock in vicinity. Gila Natl. Forest is N. **2** Village in Hurley town (1940 pop. 1,530), Ulster co., SE N.Y., just W of Kingston, in summer-resort and agr. area. **3** City (pop. 474), Turner co., SE S. Dak., 8 mi. S of Parker. **4** City (pop. 3,034), ⊙ Iron co., N Wis., on Montreal R., opposite Ironwood (Mich.), in Gogebic Range; iron-mining center (ironworks, machine shops). Founded 1885, it was a boom town (mining, lumbering) until c.1910. Inc. 1918.

Hurleyville (hûr'lĭvĭl), resort village (1940 pop. 661), Sullivan co., SE N.Y., 6 mi. N of Monticello.

Hurlford, town in Riccarton parish, N Ayrshire, Scotland, on Irvine R. and 2 mi. ESE of Kilmarnock; hosiery mills, ironworks, fire-clay works.

Hurlingham, town (pop. 11,396) in Greater Buenos Aires, Argentina, 15 mi. WNW of Buenos Aires; residential and fashionable sport center; also produces tires and rubber articles, soap powder, typewriter utensils.

Hurlock (hûr'lŏk"), town (pop. 944), Dorchester co., E Md., on Delmarva Peninsula, 13 mi. ENE of Cambridge; shipping, packing point for truck-farm area; makes tin cans, clothing.

Hurn, agr. village and parish (pop. 864), SW Hampshire, England, 5 mi. NE of Bournemouth; major airport.

Huron (hyŏŏ'rŭn), county (□ 1,245; pop. 43,742), S Ont., on L. Huron; ⊙ Goderich.

Huron. 1 County (□ 822; pop. 33,149), E Mich., at tip of the Thumb; ⊙ Bad Axe. Bounded E and N by L. Huron, W by Saginaw Bay; drained by headwaters of the Cass and by small Pigeon and Willow rivers. Farm area (beans, sugar beets, grain, chicory, livestock; dairy products). Commercial fishing, farm-products processing. Lake resorts; small game hunting. Organized 1859. **2** County (□ 497; pop. 39,353), N Ohio; ⊙ Norwalk. Drained by Huron and Vermilion rivers. Agr. area (fruit, grain, truck, livestock, dairy products); mfg. at Bellevue, Norwalk, New London; gravel pits. Formed 1815.

Huron. 1 City (pop. 128), Atchison co., extreme NE Kansas, 13 mi. WNW of Atchison, in corn belt. **2** Village (pop. 2,515), Erie co., N Ohio, on harbor on L. Erie, at mouth of Huron R., 10 mi. ESE of Sandusky; fishing; coal and iron-ore transshipping; tourist resort. Makes cement blocks, boats, sauerkraut, pickles. Settled c.1805. **3** City (pop. 12,788), ⊙ Beadle co., E central S.Dak., 110 mi. E of Pierre and on James R.; 44°22'N 98°15'W. Trade and shipping center for large agr. area; meat products, beverages, feed, lumber; dairy products, poultry, grain. Has state fair, weather bureau station, and Huron Col. Airport near by. Platted 1879, inc. 1883.

Huron, Lake, U.S. and Canada, 2d largest of the GREAT LAKES; covering □ 23,010 (of which □ 13,675 are in Canada), it is 206 mi. long, 183 mi. wide, including Georgian Bay arm, and lies c.580 ft. above sea level; max. depth is 750 ft. Bounded N and E by Ont. (Canada), W by Mich. Receives waters of L. Superior (NW) via St. Marys R. (whose rapids are by-passed by SAULT SAINTE MARIE CANALS), and of L. Michigan (W) via Straits of Mackinac; empties into L. Erie (S) through St. Clair R., St. Clair L., and Detroit R. GEORGIAN BAY indents Ont. coast, SAGINAW BAY is in Mich., and NORTH CHANNEL lies bet. Manitoulin Isls. (N) and Ont. shore. Mackinac Isl. is in Mich. portion. Carries heavy commerce, chiefly iron ore, grain, coal, and limestone, and has valuable fisheries. Chief ports in Mich. are Bay City, Alpena, Cheboygan; in Ont., Goderich, Collingwood, and Midland. Subject to violent storms, lake is generally icebound from mid-December to early April. It was probably the 1st of the Great Lakes to be visited by white men; Étienne Brulé is believed to have visited Georgian Bay c.1612 or earlier, and in 1615 Champlain traversed part of lake.

Huron Bay, Mich., narrow inlet of L. Superior indenting N shore of Upper Peninsula, c.20 mi. SE of Houghton and just E of Keweenaw Bay, from which it is separated by narrow peninsula (c.18 mi. long) terminating in Point Abbaye (ă'bā).

Huron Mountains (c.1,500–c.1,800 ft.), granitic range in NW Marquette co., Upper Peninsula, Mich., extending c.20 mi. NW-SE near S shore of L. Superior. Wilderness recreational region (hunting, fishing), with lakes (INDEPENDENCE, Ives, Mountain, others).

Huron River. 1 In SE Mich., rises in small lakes in Oakland and Livingston counties, flows SW and S to Dexter, then SE, past Ann Arbor, Ypsilanti, and Belleville, to L. Erie just SE of Rockwood; c.97 mi. long. Utilized for power. **2** In N Ohio, formed by East and West branches in S Erie co., flows c.11 mi. N to L. Erie at Huron. East Branch rises in Huron co., flows c.32 mi. N. West Branch rises near Shiloh, flows c.38 mi. N, past Monroeville, to union with East Branch.

Hurricane. 1 Town (pop. 1,271), Washington co., SW Utah, near Virgin R., 17 mi. ENE of St. George, in fruit area. Settled 1906. **2** Trading village (pop. 1,463), Putnam co., W W.Va., 22 mi. W of Charleston, in tobacco-growing, coal-mining area. Inc. 1888.

Hurricane Creek, Ark.: see BAUXITE.

Hurricane Island, Knox co., S Maine, in Penobscot Bay, 3 mi. WSW of Vinalhaven village, Vinalhaven Isl.; ¾ mi. long.

Hurricane Mountain (3,687 ft.), Essex co., NE N.Y., in the Adirondacks, 12 mi. NE of Mt. Marcy and 13 mi. ESE of Lake Placid village.

Hurst, town in Ashton-under-Lyne borough, SE Lancashire, England; cotton milling.

Hurst, city (pop. 858), Williamson co., S Ill., 7 mi. WNW of Herrin, in bituminous-coal-mining and agr. area.

Hurstmonceux or **Herstmonceux** (both: hûrstmŭnsōō'), agr. village and parish (pop. 1,532), SE Sussex, England, near the Channel, 8 mi. N of Eastbourne. Site of 1446 castle, restored 1907. After Second World War it was decided (1946) to move govt. meteorological station and time clocks to the castle grounds from Greenwich, the move to be completed by 1953. Greenwich, however, continues to be the point from which longitude is reckoned.

Hurstpierpoint (hûrst"pēr'point), town and parish (pop. 3,064), central Sussex, England, 7 mi. N of Hove; agr. market; flour mills. Site of Hurstpierpoint Col., a public school.

Hurstville, municipality (pop. 33,939), E New South Wales, Australia, 9 mi. SSW of Sydney, in metropolitan area; industrial center; brass foundries; mfg. (pottery, shoes, bicycles, furniture).

Hurstville, town (pop. 83), Jackson co., E Iowa, 2 mi. N of Maquoketa; hybrid seed corn.

Hurstwood, England: see WORSTHORNE WITH HURSTWOOD.

Hürtgen (hürt'gŭn), village (pop. 458), in former Prussian Rhine Prov., W Germany, after 1945 in North Rhine-Westphalia, 8 mi. SW of Düren. Near-by Hürtgen Forest was scene of heavy fighting in Nov., 1944. Sometimes spelled Huertgen.

Hürth (hürt), town (pop. 31,248), in former Prussian Rhine Prov., W Germany, after 1945 in North Rhine-Westphalia, 5 mi. SW of Cologne; lignite-mining center; mfg. of machinery, chemicals, textiles; woodworking. Potteries. Lignite-fed power plant. Truck farming (fruit, vegetables).

Hurtsboro, town (pop. 920), Russell co., E Ala., 28 mi. SW of Phenix City; lumber.

Hurum, Norway: see HOLMSBU.

Hurup (hōō'rōōp), town (pop. 1,730), Thisted amt, N Jutland, Denmark, 17 mi. SW of Thisted; lime and chalk kilns.

Husain, India: see HASAYAN.

Husain Sagar, India: see HYDERABAD, city.

Husan, Korea: see PUSAN.

Husavik (hōō'sävēk"), Icelandic *Húsavík,* town (pop. 1,236), ⊙ Thingeyjar co., N Iceland, on Skjalfandi Bay, 30 mi. NE of Akureyri; fishing port. Sulphur formerly shipped from here.

Husban, Jordan: see HESBAN.

Huseyinabat, Turkey: see ALACA.

Hushu (hōō'shōō'), town, SW Kiangsu prov., China, 22 mi. SE of Nanking; commercial center.

Hushukwan, China: see SOOCHOW.

Husi (hōōsh), Rum. *Huşi,* town (1948 pop. 16,605), Barlad prov., E Rumania, in Moldavia, c.190 mi. NNE of Bucharest, 40 mi. SE of Jassy; rail terminus and commercial center noted for its wine; also mfg. of candles, soap, dyes, bricks, knitwear; flour milling, tanning. Extensive vineyards in vicinity. Founded in 15th cent. Has 15th-cent. cathedral built by Stephen the Great, valuable library. Orthodox bishopric. Treaty of Prut (Pruth) was signed here (1711) bet. Russia and Turkey. Occupied by USSR troops (1944).

Husiatyn, Ukrainian SSR: see GUSYATIN.

Husinec, Czechoslovakia: see PRACHATICE.

Huskvarna (hüs'kvär"nä), city (1950 pop. 12,645), Jonkoping co., S Sweden, at S end of L. Vatter, 5 mi. E of Jonkoping; firearms, sewing machines, foundry products, dyes, brushes. Trade center in Middle Ages. Chartered 1911. Sometimes spelled Husqvarna.

Husn, El, or **Al-Husn** (both: ĕl-hōō'sŭn), village (pop. c.4,500), N Jordan, 6 mi. SSE of Irbid; road junction near oil pipe line; grain, vineyards, olives. Also spelled Husun.

Husn al 'Abr (hōō'sŭn ăl ä'bŭr), desert outpost of Quaiti state, Eastern Aden Protectorate, 90 mi. WSW of Shibam, and on caravan route to Yemen; 16°5'N 47°15'E. Airfield; radio station. Hq. of Sei'ar tribal country. Also called Al 'Abr.

Husnumansur, Turkey: see ADIYAMAN.

Husovice, Czechoslovakia: see BRNO.

Husqvarna, Sweden: see HUSKVARNA.

Hussar (hōōzär'), village (pop. 130), S Alta., 30 mi. S of Drumheller; wheat.

Hussein-Dey (üsĕ'-dā'), town (pop. 26,657), Alger dept., N central Algeria, industrial SE suburb of Algiers, on Algiers Bay; metalworks (founding and stamping, boilermaking; structural shapes, agr. machinery), sawmills (barrels, crates); wool washing, mfg. of corks, electrical equipment, paint, varnish, lubricating oil, rubber goods, flour products. Here Charles V (in 1541) and O'Reilly (in 1775) made their unsuccessful landings on Algerian coast. Named after Algiers' last dey.

Hussigny-Godbrange (üsēnyē'-gōbrāzh'), commune (pop. 2,671), Meurthe-et-Moselle dept., NE France, on Luxembourg border, opposite Differdange, and 5 mi. ESE of Longwy; blast furnaces, foundries; pharmaceuticals. Iron mines.

Hustad (hōō'stä), village and canton (pop. 2,299), More og Romsdal co., W Norway, on an inlet of North Sea, 22 mi. SW of Kristiansund; fisheries, cod-liver-oil refineries. At Vikan, 2 mi. WSW, is a chemical plant. Sea along the coast is here called Hustadvika.

Huste, Ukrainian SSR: see KHUST.

Hüsten, Germany: see NEHEIM-HÜSTEN.

Hustisford (hŭ'stĭsfôrd"), village (pop. 622), Dodge co., S central Wis., 14 mi. SE of Beaver Dam and on Rock R., here dammed to form Sinissippi L. (sĭ"nŭsĭ'pē) (c.3 mi. long); dairy products, canned vegetables.

Hustler, village (pop. 194), Juneau co., central Wis., c.50 mi. E of La Crosse, in farming area.

Hustonville (hū'stŭnvĭl"), town (pop. 435), Lincoln co., central Ky., 13 mi. S of Danville, in agr. area.

Hustopece (hōō'stôpĕchĕ), Czech *Hustopeče,* Ger. *Auspitz* (ous'pĭts), town (pop. 2,495), S Moravia, Czechoslovakia, on railroad and 18 mi. SSE of Brno; barley, wheat growing; exports fruit and vegetables. T. G. Masaryk was schoolboy here. Dolni Vestonice (dôl'nyĕ vyĕ'stônyĭtsĕ), Czech *Dolní Věstonice,* site of important prehistoric finds, is 5 mi. SW.

Husum (hōō'zōōm), town (pop. 23,551), in Schleswig-Holstein, NW Germany, on small Husumer Au R. near its mouth (harbor) on North Sea, and 20 mi. W of Schleswig, in North Friesland; rail junction; airfield (N); horse-breeding center, noted for its cattle markets; deep-sea fishing. Food processing (sugar, canned fish), spinning, weaving; mfg. of chemicals, machinery, watches umbrellas, garments; woodworking, brewing, distilling. Has 16th-cent. castle, 19th-cent. church and town hall.

Husum is most important town on Schleswig-Holstein's W coast. Flourished 14th-17th cent. Chartered c.1600. Theodor Storm b. here.

Husum (hü'sŭm"), village (pop. 1,848), Vasternorrland co., NE Sweden, on Gulf of Bothnia, 14 mi. E of Ornskoldsvik; pulp mills.

Husun, Jordan: see Husn, El.

Huszt, Ukrainian SSR: see Khust.

Hutagawa, Japan: see Futagawa.

Hutan Melintang or **Utan Melintang** (hōōtän' mŭlĭn"täng'), town (pop. 1,518), SW Perak, Malaya, minor fishing port on lower Bernam R. (Selangor line), 11 mi. SW of Telok Anson; coconuts.

Hutchins, town (pop. 743), Dallas co., N Texas, just SSE of Dallas.

Hutchinson. 1 County (□ 814; pop. 11,423), SE S.Dak.; ⊙ Olivet. Agr. and cattle-raising area drained by James R. Dairy products, poultry, corn, wheat, barley, oats. Formed 1862. **2** County (□ 884; pop. 31,580), extreme N Texas; ⊙ Stinnett. On high treeless plains of the Panhandle, here broken by gorge of Canadian R.; alt. 3,000–3,500 ft. Much of co. underlaid by huge Panhandle natural-gas and oil field; here is one of world's largest natural-gas pumping stations, and large carbon-black and oil-refining industries; mfg. of petroleum products, synthetic rubber, printer's ink; some agr. (grain, sorghums); livestock (beef and dairy cattle, hogs, sheep, horses, mules, poultry). Formed 1876.

Hutchinson. 1 City (pop. 33,575), ⊙ Reno co., S central Kansas, on left bank of Arkansas R., near mouth of Cow Creek, and 40 mi. NW of Wichita; trade, industrial, and shipping center. Processes salt from salt beds largely within city limits; refines oil from near-by wells. There are flour mills, meat-packing plants, and railroad repair shops. Also mfg. of fiber and dairy products, airplane parts, agr. equipment, oil-well supplies. Has jr. col. and state reformatory. State fair takes place here annually in Sept. Laid out 1871, inc. 1872. Grew after discovery of salt (1887) and development of oil fields. City and environs much damaged by floods in 1929 and 1941. **2** City (pop. 4,690), McLeod co., S central Minn., on South Fork Crow R. and c.55 mi. W of Minneapolis; mfg. point (paint, concrete products) in grain, livestock, and truck-farming area; dairy products, beverages. Founded 1855, inc. 1881. Part of settlement burned in Sioux uprising of 1862.

Hutchinson River, small stream in SE N.Y., rises in S Westchester co., flows generally S through the Bronx to Eastchester Bay in Pelham Bay Park. Paralleled by landscaped highway.

Hutch Mountain, peak (8,650 ft.) in high plateau (c.7,000 ft.), Coconino co., central Ariz., c.30 mi. SE of Flagstaff.

Huth (hōōth), town (pop. 2,000), ⊙ Huth prov. (pop. 160,000), N central Yemen, on central plateau, 45 mi. SE of Sada. Sometimes spelled Houth.

Huthwaite or **Hucknall-under-Huthwaite** (hŭk'nŭl, hōōth'wāt), former urban district (1931 pop. 5,092), W Nottingham, England, 2 mi. W of Sutton-in-Ashfield; coal mines, hosiery and shoe mills. Inc. 1935 in Sutton-in-Ashfield.

Huto, town, China: see Hutow.

Huto River, Chinese *Huto Ho* (hōō'dô' hŭ'), in Shansi and Hopeh provs., China, rises on N slope of Wutai Mts. near Hopeh-Shansi-Chahar line, flows over 400 mi. S and E, into Shansi, past Taihsien and Tingsiang, and into Hopeh, past Chengting and Sienhsien, to area of Tientsin, where it joins Pai R. Called Tzeya R. in lower course.

Hutow or **Huto** (both: hōō'dô'), town, N central Kiangsu prov., China, 45 mi. ESE of Hwaiyin; commercial center.

Hutsonville, village (pop. 647), Crawford co., SE Ill., on the Wabash (bridged here) and 26 mi. SSW of Terre Haute (Ind.), in agr. area (wheat, corn, livestock, hay, alfalfa); flour mill.

Hutt, New Zealand: see Wellington, city.

Hüttenberg (hü'tŭnbĕrk), town (pop. 2,216), Carinthia, S Austria, 16 mi. SSW of Judenburg; summer resort. Iron mines near by have been worked since anc. times.

Huttenheim (ütŭnĕm'), Ger. *Hüttenheim* (hü'tŭnhīm), village (pop. 1,629), Bas-Rhin dept., E France, on the Ill and 9 mi. NE of Sélestat; cotton milling.

Hüttenrode (hü"tŭnrō'dŭ), village (pop. 2,029), in former Brunswick exclave, central Germany, after 1945 in Saxony-Anhalt, in the lower Harz, 3 mi. SW of Blankenburg; iron mining and smelting; lime processing.

Hutti (hōōt'tē) or **Hatti** (hŭt'tē), village, Raichur dist., SW Hyderabad state, India, 45 mi. W of Raichur; gold mines, abandoned in 1920 and reopened in 1949.

Huttig (hŭ'tĭg), lumber town (pop. 1,038), Union co., S Ark., 30 mi. ESE of El Dorado, near La. line; pine and hardwood timber; woodworking. Inc. 1904.

Hutto (hŭ'tō), town (pop. 529), Williamson co., central Texas, 22 mi. NNE of Austin; rail point in cotton, grain, truck area.

Hutton. 1 Residential town and parish (pop. 2,142), SW Essex, England, 2 mi. NE of Brentwood. **2** Residential village and parish (pop. 1,129), W Lancashire, England, 3 mi. SW of Preston; truck gardening.

Huttonsville, town (pop. 227), Randolph co., E W.Va., 16 mi. SSW of Elkins.

Hüttschlag (hüt'shläk), village (pop. 659), Salzburg, W central Austria, on N slope of the Hohe Tauern, 16 mi. S of Bischofshofen. Pyrite deposits near by.

Huttwil (hōōt'vēl), town (pop. 4,364), Bern canton, NW central Switzerland, on Langeten R. and 22 mi. NE of Bern; shoes, knit goods, pastry; tanning, canning, woodworking.

Hutubi (hōōtōōbē'), Chinese *Changhwa* or *Ch'ang-hua* (both: chäng'hwä'), town, ⊙ Hutubi co. (pop. 22,466), central Sinkiang prov., China, 40 mi. WNW of Urumchi, and on highway N of the Tien Shan; cattle raising; wheat, rice, fruit. Coal and gold mines. Sometimes spelled Hutupi.

Hutupi, China: see Hutubi.

Huvadu Atoll, Maldive Isls.: see Suvadiva Atoll.

Huvek, Turkey: see Bozova.

Hüvösvölgy, Hungary: see Hars, Mount.

Huvvinahadagalli, India: see Hadagalli.

Huwairib or **Huwayrib** (hōōwī'rĭb), village, ⊙ Atifi sheikdom, Subeihi tribal area, Western Aden Protectorate, 65 mi. W of Aden, and on the small Wadi Timnan 10 mi. from its mouth on Gulf of Aden. Also spelled Hawarib and Hawerib.

Huwei (hōō'wā'), Jap. *Kobi* (kō'bē), town (1935 pop. 9,813), W central Formosa, 15 mi. N of Kiayi; sugar-milling center; rice, sweet potatoes, peanuts. Sometimes spelled Fuwei.

Huxley, village (pop. estimate 100), S central Alta., 70 mi. NE of Calgary; coal mining.

Huxley, town (pop. 422), Story co., central Iowa, 20 mi. N of Des Moines; livestock, grain.

Huxley, Mount (12,560 ft.), SE Alaska, in St. Elias Mts., 20 mi. N of Icy Bay; 60°20'N 141°10'W.

Huy (wē), Flemish *Hoei* (hwē), town (pop. 13,179), Liége prov., E central Belgium, on Meuse R. and 18 mi. SW of Liége; industrial center (leather tanning, mfg. of steel products, paper); horse and cattle market. Has church of Notre Dame (completed in 16th cent.), 14th-cent. fountain, and remains of medieval abbey, founded by Peter the Hermit on his return from 1st Crusade. Town captured several times by French in 17th cent.

Huyamampa (ōōyämäm'pä), village (pop. estimate 500), W central Santiago del Estero prov., Argentina, on railroad and 25 mi. N of Santiago del Estero, in corn and livestock area; lumbering. Salt deposits near by.

Huyo, Korea: see Puyo.

Hüyten, Mongolia: see Tabun Bogdo.

Huyton with Roby (hī'tŭn, rō'bē), urban district (1931 pop. 5,199; 1951 census 55,783), SW Lancashire, England. Includes residential and granite-quarrying town of Huyton, 6 mi. E of Liverpool, having 15th-cent. church with 14th-cent. arches and a font of Saxon or Norman origin. Just E is residential town of Roby.

Huzurabad (hōōzōōr'äbäd), town (pop. 8,161), Karimnagar dist., E Hyderabad state, India, 23 mi. SE of Karimnagar; cotton ginning, rice milling.

Huzurnagar (hōōzōōr'nŭgŭr), village (pop. 2,253), Nalgonda dist., SE Hyderabad state, India, 42 mi. SE of Nalgonda; rice milling, cotton ginning, castor-oil extraction.

Hval Fjord, Iceland: see Faxa Bay.

Hval Islands (väl), Nor. *Hvaler* [=whale islands], group of 22 islands coextensive with Hvaler canton (□ 33; pop. 3,473), SE Norway, in the Skagerrak, near Swedish boundary line, along E shore of mouth of Oslo Fjord. Largest isl. is Kjerkoy (Nor. *Kjerkøy*) (□ 11.5; pop. 1,367), 10 mi. S of Fredrikstad, Norway, and 8 mi. NW of Stromstad, Sweden. Fishing, fish canning, stone quarrying are chief occupations; seaside resorts.

Hvalpsund, Denmark: see Skive Fjord.

Hval Sund, Greenland: see Whale Sound.

Hvannadalshnjukur (hwä'nädäls"hŭnyōō"kür) or **Hvannadalshnukur** (–hŭnōō"kür), Icelandic *Hvannadalshnjúkur* or *Hvannadalshnúkur*, highest peak (6,952 ft.) of Iceland, in SE part of isl., near the coast, at S edge of Vatnajokull glacier region; 64°1'N 16°40'W. Oraefajokull (û'rīväyû"kütŭl), Icelandic *Öræfajökull*, glacier, surrounds peak.

Hvar (khvär), Ital. *Lesina* (lĕzē'nä), village, S Croatia, Yugoslavia, port on W coast of Hvar Isl., 22 mi. S of Split; resort. R.C. bishopric. Once a leading center of Croatian culture; called "museum of architecture and art." Has 12th-cent. cathedral, arsenal (built 1300), Renaissance loggia (1515–17), 16th-cent. Sp. and Venetian forts, Franciscan church and monastery.

Hvar Island, anc. *Pharos*, Ital. *Lesina* (lĕzē'nä), Dalmatian island (□ 120) in Adriatic Sea, S Croatia, Yugoslavia, S of Split; 40 mi. long E–W; rises to 2,053 ft. Marble deposits; growing of chrysanthemums. Chief villages: Hvar, Starigrad, Jelsa. Was site of anc. prosperous Gr. colony on N coast. Hvar Channel, Serbo-Croatian *Hvarski Kanal*, separates it from Brac Isl. (N).

Hven, island, Sweden: see Ven.

Hveragerdi (hwĕ'rägĕr"dhē), Icelandic *Hveragerði*, town (pop. 485), Arne co., SW Iceland, 25 mi. ESE of Reykjavik; noted for its fruit, vegetables, and flowers, grown in hothouses. Near by are several natural hot springs. Also spelled Hveragerdhi.

Hvidtland, Russian SFSR: see Belaya Zemlya.

Hvita (hwēt'ou"), Icelandic *Hvítá*. **1** River, SW Iceland, rises in the Hvitarvatn, a lake at S edge of Langjokull, flows 80 mi. SW to confluence with Sog R. 10 mi. NE of Eyrarbakki, forming Olfusa R. Receives several streams from Hofsjokull. On upper course is Gullfoss, large waterfall. **2** River, W Iceland, rises on Eiriksjokull, flows 50 mi. WSW to Borgar Fjord, arm of Faxa Bay. Noted for its salmon.

Hvitarvatn (hwēt'ourvä"tŭn), Icelandic *Hvítárvatn*, lake (□ 13.5), W Iceland, at SE edge of Langjokull, 70 mi. ENE of Reykjavik; 7 mi. long, 1–2 mi. wide. Drained S by Hvita R.

Hvitsten (vēt'stän), town (pop. 76), Akershus co., SE Norway, on E shore of Oslo Fjord narrows, 4 mi. SSE of Drobak; mfg. of chemicals, paint, lacquer. Surrounded by Vestby canton (pop. 3,711). Also spelled Hvitstein.

Hvittingfoss (vĭt'tĭngfôs), village (pop. 578) in Ytre Sandsvaer canton (pop. 3,188), Buskerud co., SE Norway, on Lagen R. (falls) and 20 mi. SSW of Drammen; paper- and sawmilling. Power station supplies Tonsberg. Sometimes spelled Vittingfoss.

Hwaan or **Hua-an** (hwä'än'), town (pop. 1,243), ⊙ Hwaan co. (pop. 51,745), S Fukien prov., China, 50 mi. NNW of Lungki and on Kiulung R.; rice, sugar cane, sweet potatoes. Coal, iron, silver, lead, and molybdenum deposits near by. Until 1928 called Hwafeng.

Hwachow, China: see Hwahsien, Shensi prov.

Hwachwan or **Hua-ch'uan** (both: hwä'chwän'), town, ⊙ Hwachwan co. (pop. 180,000), N Sungkiang prov., Manchuria, 25 mi. NE of Kiamusze and on right bank of Sungari R.; barley, rye, soybeans, buckwheat, kaoliang, hemp. Formerly called Yüehlaichen.

Hwafeng, China: see Hwaan.

Hwahsien or **Hua-hsien** (hwä'shyĕn'). **1** Town, ⊙ Hwahsien co. (pop. 610,559), W central Pingyuan prov., China, on main road and 40 mi. NE of Sinsiang, near railroad (Taokow station); rice, ramie, wheat, beans. Until 1949 in Honan prov. **2** Town (pop. 4,115), ⊙ Hwahsien co. (pop. 134,548), E Shensi prov., China, in Wei R. valley, 50 mi. ENE of Sian, and on Lunghai RR; cotton weaving; indigo, fruit, ramie. Until 1913, called Hwachow.

Hwai, China: see Hwai River.

Hwaian or **Huai-an** (both: hwī'än'). **1** Town, ⊙ Hwaian co. (pop. 131,789), central Chahar prov., China, on road and 30 mi. SW of Kalgan; grain, grapes. Until 1928 in Chihli (Hopeh). The name Hwaian was formerly applied to a town 6 mi. NE. **2** Town (pop. 35,443), ⊙ Hwaian co. (pop. 267,533), N Kiangsu prov., China, 8 mi. SE of Hwaiyin and on Grand Canal; agr. center (rice, wheat, corn, kaoliang, beans). Saltworks. An old city, dating from 12th cent., it was founded on old arm of Yellow R. Visited by Marco Polo, who called it Coigangui. It flourished until 1852, when Yellow R. changed its course.

Hwai Ho, China: see Hwai River.

Hwaihwa or **Huai-hua** (both: hwī'hwä'), town, ⊙ Hwaihwa co. (pop. 116,298), W Hunan prov., China, 32 mi. ENE of Chihkiang; antimony and iron mining.

Hwaijen or **Huai-jen** (both: hwī'rŭn'). **1** Town, ⊙ Hwaijen co. (pop. 79,230), SW Chahar prov., China, 20 mi. SSW of Tatung and on railroad; rice, millet, beans, timber. Until 1949 in N Shansi. **2** Town, Liaotung prov., Manchuria, China: see Hwanjen.

Hwaiju or **Huai-jou** (both: hwī'rō'). **1** Town, ⊙ Hwaiju co. (pop. 60,712), N Hopeh prov., China, 30 mi. NNE of Peking and on railroad; grapes, pears, peaches, grain. **2** Town, Sikang prov.: see Chanhwa.

Hwaiking, China: see Tsinyang.

Hwailai or **Huai-lai** (both: hwī'lī'), town, ⊙ Hwailai co. (pop. 163,336), E Chahar prov., China, near Great Wall (Hopeh line), 50 mi. SE of Kalgan, and on railroad; grain, fruit, timber, sesame oil. Until 1928 in Chihli (Hopeh) prov.

Hwailu or **Huai-lu** (both: hwī'lōō'), town, ⊙ Hwailu co. (pop. 294,543), SW Hopeh prov., China, 10 mi. WNW of Shihkiachwang, near railroad; rice, wheat, beans. Known for its stoneware. Also written Hwolu.

Hwaining, China: see Anking.

Hwai River, Chinese *Hwai Ho* or *Huai Ho* (both: hwī' hŭ'), E central China, rises in Tungpeh Mts. on Honan-Hupeh border, flows 600 mi. ENE, past old Sihsien (Honan prov.), Showhsien, Pengpu, and Wuho (Anhwei prov.), into Hungtze L. Among its numerous tributaries are Ying, Kwo, and Kwei rivers (left), and Pi R. (right). Known as the "river without a mouth," the Hwai spills over in flood beyond Hungtze L. into the canals of the alluvial N Kiangsu lowland and to the Yellow Sea. Its lower course below Chengyangkwan was used (1938–46) by the diverted Yellow R. Construction of a permanent channel linking Hungtze L. and the Yellow Sea is projected. The river is navigable below Sinyang, situated on a right headstream.

Hwaite or **Huai-te** (both: hwī'dŭ'), town, ⊙ Hwaite co. (pop. 389,867), W Kirin prov., Manchuria, 28 mi. W of Changchun, near Liaosi line; kaoliang, beans, millet. Formerly called Pakiachen.

Hwaiyang or **Huai-yang** (both: hwī'yäng'), town, ⊙ Hwaiyang co. (pop. 156,560), E Honan prov., China, 85 mi. SSE of Kaifeng; mfg. (fans, bamboo articles, cotton textiles); sesame, watermelons, wheat, beans. Until 1913 called Chenchow. Commercial center of CHOWKIAKOW is 15 mi. SW, on Sha R.

Hwaiyang Mountains, China: see TAPIEH MOUNTAINS.

Hwaiyin or **Huai-yin** (both: hwī'yĭn'), town (1935 pop. 80,615; 1948 pop. 47,295), N Kiangsu prov., China, 100 mi. N of Chinkiang, and on Grand Canal, E of Hungtze L.; agr. center (wheat, beans, corn, kaoliang, rapeseed). Until 1914 called Tsingkiangpu. Was ⊙ Hwaiyin co. (1948 pop. 369,123) until 1949, when city became an independent municipality.

Hwaiyüan or **Huai-yüan** (both: hwī'yüän'). **1** Town, ⊙ Hwaiyüan co. (pop. 530,128), N Anhwei prov., China, on Hwai R. at mouth of Kwo R., and 10 mi. WNW of Pengpu; rice, wheat, cotton, beans, tobacco. Coal mining at the Shunkeng Shan, 30 mi. SW. **2** Town, Kwangsi prov., China: see SANKIANG. **3** Town, Shensi prov., China: see HENGSHAN.

Hwajung or **Hua-jung** (both: hwä'rŏŏng'), town, ⊙ Hwajung co. (pop. 291,427), NE Hunan prov., China, on N shore of Tungting L., 32 mi. WNW of Yoyang, on Hupeh line; rice, wheat, cotton.

Hwalien, Hua-lien, or **Hua-lien-kang** (hwä'lyĕn'-gäng'), Jap. *Karen* or *Karenko* (kä'rānkō), town (1935 pop. 15,464), E central Formosa, port on E coast, 50 mi. S of Ilan; N terminus of E coast railroad; industrial center; nonferrous-metals refining (aluminum, nickel, cobalt), chemical mfg. (nitrogen fixation, ammonia). Linked (since 1931) by coastal highway with Suao and N Formosa. City developed after 1878. Its shallow anchorage was replaced (1930s) by modern harbor at Milun (Jap. *Beiron*), 2 mi. N.

Hwalung or **Hua-lung** (both: hwä'lŏŏng'), town, ⊙ Hwalung co. (pop. 58,978), E Tsinghai prov., China, 45 mi. NE of Sining; trades in wool, furs, felt, vegetable oil. Until 1912 named Payenyungko; also formerly called Payung (1912–1928) and Payen (1928–31).

Hwa Mountains, Chinese *Hwa Shan* or *Hua Shan* (both: hwä' shän'), S Shensi prov., China, near Honan line; rise to 7,218 ft. in the sacred mtn. Hwa Shan (Buddhist shrine), 10 mi. S of Hwayin.

Hwan-, for Chinese names beginning thus and not found here: see under WAN-.

Hwan, province, China: see ANHWEI.

Hwang, river, China: see YELLOW RIVER.

Hwangan or **Huang-an** (both: hwäng'än'), town (pop. 30,888), ⊙ Hwangan co. (pop. 326,171), E Hupeh prov., China, near Honan line, 60 mi. NNE of Hankow; rice, wheat, peanuts, cotton. Asbestos deposits near by.

Hwangchow, China: see HWANGKANG.

Hwangchung or **Huang-chung** (both: hwäng'jŏŏng'), town, ⊙ Hwangchung co. (pop. 220,884), NE Tsinghai prov., China, 12 mi. SW of Sining; wool textiles; tanning, vegetable-oil processing; gypsum quarrying. Site of KUMBUM lamasery. Until 1928 in Kansu prov.

Hwangchwan or **Huang-ch'uan** (both: hwäng'-chwän'), town, ⊙ Hwangchwan co. (pop. 217,391), SE Honan prov., China, 55 mi. E of Sinyang; rice center; cotton weaving; hides, bamboo articles. Copper deposits near by. Formerly Kwangchow.

Hwanghae (hwäng'hă'), Korean *Hwanghae-do*, Jap. *Kokai-do*, province [Jap. and Korean *do*] (□ 6,463; 1944 pop. 2,013,166), central Korea, N of 38°N, bounded W by Korea Bay and S by Yellow Sea; ⊙ HAEJU. Includes PAENGNYONG ISLAND and numerous islets. Terrain is relatively low, with fertile plains producing soybeans, wheat, fruit, rice, and tobacco. Gold, iron, coal are mined. Numerous fisheries. Haeju, KYOMIPO, and SARIWON are principal centers. The small area S of 38°N was briefly included (1945-50) in Kyonggi prov.

Hwang Hai: see YELLOW SEA.

Hwang Ho, China: see YELLOW RIVER.

Hwanghsien or **Huang-hsien** (both: hwäng'shyĕn'). **1** Town, ⊙ Hwanghsien co. (pop. 116,535), W Hunan prov., China, on Yüan R. and 32 mi. WSW of Chihkiang, on Kweichow line; rice, wheat, cotton. Mercury mining. **2** Town (1922 pop. estimate 80,000), ⊙ Hwanghsien co. (pop. 463,366), NE Shantung prov., China, on road and 12 mi. E of Lungkow, near N coast; silk weaving, noodle making; pears, grain.

Hwanghwa or **Huang-hua** (both: hwäng'hwä'), town, ⊙ Hwanghwa co., E Hopeh prov., China, 50 mi. SSE of Tientsin, near Gulf of Chihli; salt-extracting center. Originally called Hantsun, later (1937–49) Sinhai.

Hwangju (hwäng'jōō'), Jap. *Koshu*, town (1944 pop. 16,993), Hwanghae prov., central Korea, N of 38°N, 24 mi. S of Pyongyang; iron mining.

Hwangkang or **Huang-kang** (both: hwäng'gäng'), town (pop. 53,448), ⊙ Hwangkang co. (pop. 826,791), E Hupeh prov., China, on left bank of Yangtze R., opposite Ocheng, and 35 mi. ESE of Wuchang; tobacco processing, cotton-textiles mfg. The name Hwangkang was applied 1929–32 to Twanfeng, 13 mi. N. Present Hwangkang was called Hwangchow until 1912.

Hwangkiao or **Huang-ch'iao** (both: hwäng'chyou'), town, N Kiangsu prov., China, 25 mi. SE of Taichow; commercial center.

Hwangkutun, Manchuria: see LUNGHWA.

Hwangling or **Huang-ling** (both: hwäng'lĭng'), town, ⊙ Hwangling co. (pop. 25,479), N central Shensi prov., China, 70 mi. S of Yenan, in mtn. region; wheat, beans, millet. Until 1944 called Chungpu. Site of tomb of Hwang-ti (2697–2597 B.C.), legendary founder of Chinese Empire.

Hwanglung or **Huang-lung** (both: hwäng'lŏŏng'), town, ⊙ Hwanglung co. (pop. 59,124), central Shensi prov., China, 85 mi. SSE of Yenan; wheat, millet, beans. Until 1941 called Shihpu.

Hwangmei or **Huang-mei** (both: hwäng'mā'), town (pop. 21,349), ⊙ Hwangmei co. (pop. 323,254), SE Hupeh prov., China, near Anhwei line, 100 mi. ESE of Hankow; ramie, rice, wheat, cotton. Has noted monastery.

Hwang Mountains, Chinese *Hwang Shan* or *Huang Shan* (hwäng' shän'), S Anhwei prov., China, rise to 8,694 ft. 30 mi. NNW of Tunki.

Hwangpei or **Huang-p'ei** (both: hwäng'pā'), town (pop. 41,084), ⊙ Hwangpei co. (pop. 540,115), E Hupeh prov., China, on rail spur and 25 mi. NNE of Hankow; rice, wheat, cotton, peanuts, tobacco. Also written Hwangpo.

Hwangping or **Huang-p'ing** (both: hwäng'pĭng'), town (pop. 3,868), ⊙ Hwangping co. (pop. 116,512), E Kweichow prov., China, 80 mi. ENE of Kweiyang and on main road to Hunan; cotton weaving, tobacco processing, embroidery making; wheat, millet, beans. Gypsum quarrying near by.

Hwangpo, China: see HWANGPEI.

Hwangpoo River, China: see WHANGPOO RIVER.

Hwangpu River, China: see WHANGPOO RIVER.

Hwang Shan, China: see HWANG MOUNTAINS.

Hwangshihkang (hwäng'shŭ'gäng') or **Huang-shih-chiang** (–jyäng'), town, SE Hupeh prov., China, port on right bank of Yangtze R. and 13 mi. NE of Tayeh; cement and lime works. At Shihhweiyao (just SE), connected by rail with Tiehshan iron mine of Tayeh, iron ore is transferred to Yangtze R. vessels.

Hwang Shui, China: see SINING RIVER.

Hwangtsun, China: see TAHING.

Hwangyen or **Huang-yen** (both: hwäng'yĕn'), town (pop. 21,475), ⊙ Hwangyen co. (pop. 519,648), SE Chekiang prov., China, 15 mi. SSE of Linhai, near Taichow Bay of E.China Sea; orange-growing center; rice, wheat, cotton, tobacco.

Hwangyüan or **Huang-yüan** (both: hwäng'yüän'), town, ⊙ Hwangyüan co. (pop. 29,526), NE Tsinghai prov., China, on Sining R. and 33 mi. WNW of Sining, and on route to Tibet and Jyekundo; major commercial center for Tibetan trade, handling wool, salt, wheat, sugar, tea, cotton cloth. Until 1912 called Tangar, Tenkar, or Donkyr. Before 1928 in Kansu prov.

Hwaning or **Hua-ning** (both: hwä'nĭng'), town (pop. 3,944), ⊙ Hwaning co. (pop. 84,498), SE central Yunnan prov., China, 60 mi. SSE of Kunming, near railroad; rice, millet, beans, sugar cane, cotton. Lead deposits near by. Until 1913 called Ningchow; later, briefly, Ninghsien; and, 1914–31, Lihsien.

Hwanjen or **Huan-jen** (both: hwän'rŭn'), town, ⊙ Hwanjen co. (pop. 127,231), SE Liaotung prov., Manchuria, 40 mi. SW of Tunghwa; road center. Until 1914 called Hwaijen.

Hwan Mountains, Chinese *Hwan Shan* or *Huan Shan* (hwän' shän'), low hill range in N central Anhwei prov., China, forming divide bet. Hwai and Yangtze R. systems.

Hwannan, China: see ANHWEI.

Hwanpeh or **Hwanpei,** China: see ANHWEI.

Hwan Shan, China: see HWAN MOUNTAINS.

Hwantai or **Huan-t'ai** (both: hwän'tī'), town, ⊙ Hwantai co. (pop. 279,071), central Shantung prov., China, 12 mi. NNE of Chowtsun; silk weaving; rice, beans, kaoliang. Until 1914, Sincheng.

Hwaping or **Hua-p'ing** (both: hwä'pĭng'). **1** Town, ⊙ Hwaping co. (pop. 22,425), SE Kansu prov., China, 60 mi. NE of Tienshui; millet, beans. **2** Town, ⊙ Hwaping co. (pop. 32,113), N Yunnan prov., China, 60 mi. ENE of Likiang, in mtn. region, near Sikang line; timber, rice, millet, beans. Old town of Hwaping is 25 mi. SSE.

Hwa Shan, China: see HWA MOUNTAINS.

Hwashulintze, Manchuria: see HWATIEN.

Hwate or **Hua-te** (both: hwä'dŭ'), town, ⊙ Hwate co., N Chahar prov., China, 85 mi. NNW of Kalgan, near Inner Mongolian line; cattle raising; grain.

Hwatien or **Hua-tien** (both: hwä'dyĕn'), town, ⊙ Hwatien co. (pop. 175,032), S central Kirin prov., Manchuria, 60 mi. S of Kirin, on Sungari reservoir; gold and coal mining; lead deposits; grain, beans, hemp, tobacco. Formerly called Hwashulintze.

Hwating or **Hua-t'ing** (both: hwä'tĭng'), town, ⊙ Hwating co. (pop. 43,920), SE Kansu prov., China, 20 mi. SW of Pingliang; cotton textiles; wheat, beans, kaoliang. Coal mines near by.

Hwayin or **Hua-yin** (both: hwäng'yĭn'), town, ⊙ Hwayin co. (pop. 108,416), E Shensi prov., China, in Wei R. valley, near Yellow R. bend, at foot of the Hwa Shan, 70 mi. ENE of Sian, and on Lunghai RR; resort center; mfg. (straw shoes, cotton textiles); rice, wheat, beans. The Hwa Shan is ascended from here.

Hwayüan or **Hua-yüan** (both: hwä'yüän'), town, E Hupeh prov., China, 50 mi. NW of Hankow and on Peking-Hankow RR; commercial center.

Hwei, China: see HWEI RIVER.

Hweian or **Hui-an** (both: hwā'än'), town (pop. 12,040), ⊙ Hweian co. (pop. 376,994), SE Fukien prov., China, 35 mi. SSW of Putien, on E.China Sea coast; sweet potatoes, rice, wheat, peanuts.

Hweichang or **Hui-ch'ang** (both: hwā'chäng'), town (pop. 10,812), ⊙ Hweichang co. (pop. 115,782), S Kiangsi prov., China, 56 mi. ESE of Kanchow and on Kung R. (right headstream of Kan R.); rice, peanuts, beans; mfg. of porcelain. Tungsten and bismuth mines.

Hweichow. 1 Town, Anhwei prov., China: see SIHSIEN. **2** Town, Kwangtung prov., China: see WAIYEUNG.

Hweichwan or **Hui-chuan** (both: hwā'jwän'), town, ⊙ Hweichwan co. (pop. 70,954), SE Kansu prov., China, 70 mi. S of Lanchow; wheat, millet, beans. Until 1944 called Kwanpao.

Hwei Ho, China: see HWEI RIVER.

Hweihsien or **Hui-hsien** (both: hwā'shyĕn'). **1** Town, ⊙ Hweihsien co. (pop. 133,974), SE Kansu prov., China, 50 mi. SSE of Tienshui; rice, wheat, millet. **2** Town, ⊙ Hweihsien co. (pop. 96,258), SW Pingyuan prov., China, 10 mi. N of Sinsiang; cotton weaving, tobacco processing; wheat, kaoliang. Until 1949 in Honan prov.

Hweilai or **Hui-lai** (both: hwā'lī'), town (pop. 18,239), ⊙ Hweilai co. (pop. 266,335), SE Kwangtung prov., China, near coast, 32 mi. SW of Swatow; tin-mining center; rice, wheat, peanuts, pineapples.

Hweili or **Hui-li** (both: hwā'lē'), town, ⊙ Hweili co. (pop. 217,800), SE Sinkang prov., China, near Yangtze R. (Yunnan line), 85 mi. S of Sichang, and on highway; trading center, exporting cotton goods, tobacco, paper. Rice, wheat, cotton, ramie. Lead-zinc deposits. Until 1938 in Szechwan.

Hweimin or **Hui-min** (both: hwā'mĭn'), town, ⊙ Hweimin co. (pop. 298,473), NW Shantung prov., China, on road and 60 mi. NNE of Tsinan; commercial center of NW Shantung; cotton and silk weaving; kaoliang, wheat, millet, beans. Until 1913 called Wuting.

Hweinan or **Hui-nan** (both: hwā'nän'), town, ⊙ Hweinan co. (pop. 97,399), NE Liaotung prov., Manchuria, 65 mi. NNE of Tunghwa, on Sungari reservoir; wheat, soybeans.

Hweining or **Hui-ning** (both: hwā'nĭng'), town, ⊙ Hweining co. (pop. 96,383), SE Kansu prov., China, 75 mi. ESE of Lanchow; licorice-producing center; wheat, beans, millet, ramie. Coal mines near by.

Hweinung or **Hui-nung** (both: hwā'nŏŏng'), town (pop. 8,476), ⊙ Hweinung co. (pop. 65,144), SE Ningsia prov., China, near Yellow R. (Suiyuan line), 50 mi. NNE of Yinchwan; wheat, millet, beans. Until 1942 called Paofeng.

Hweipeh, Manchuria: see HAILUNG.

Hwei River, Chinese *Hwei Ho* or *Hui Ho* (both: hwā' hŭ'), N Anhwei prov., China, rises on Honan line N of Pohsien, flows 150 mi. SE to Hwai R. near Wuho.

Hweishui or **Hui-shui** (both: hwā'shwā'), town (pop. 9,633), ⊙ Hweishui co. (pop. 141,572), S Kweichow prov., China, 30 mi. S of Kweiyang; cotton textiles; tobacco processing; embroideries. Rice, wheat, beans. Until 1940s called Tingfan.

Hweitseh or **Hui-tse** (both: hwā'dzŭ'), town (pop. 15,213), ⊙ Hweitseh co. (pop. 178,208), NE Yunnan prov., China, 100 mi. NE of Kunming; alt. 7,251 ft.; major mining center for nonferrous metals (copper, lead, zinc); smelting, chemical industries; tung-oil processing, cotton milling. Hot springs near by. Until 1929 called Tungchwan.

Hweitung or **Hui-t'ung** (both: hwā'tŏŏng'). **1** Town, ⊙ Hweitung co. (pop. 184,689), SW Hunan prov., China, near Kweichow line, 30 mi. S of Chihkiang; rice, wheat, cotton. Gold mining near by. **2** Town, Hainan, Kwangtung prov., China: see KIUNGTUNG.

Hweiyüan or **Hui-yüan** (both: hwā'yüän'), town, NW Sinkiang prov., China, in Ili dist., 23 mi. WSW of Kuldja, near Ili R.; 44°N 80°54'E. The so-called new Kuldja, town was founded c.1760 by the Chinese and was destroyed in 1860s during a Moslem rebellion. Sometimes called Ili.

Hwohsien or **Huo-hsien** (both: hwô'shyĕn'), town, ⊙ Hwohsien co. (pop. 62,311), S Shansi prov., China, on Fen R., on railroad and 35 mi. N of Linfen, at W foot of Taiyo (Hwo) Mts.; wheat, cotton, corn. Also written Hohsien.

Hwokia or **Huo-chia** (both: hwŭ'jyä'), town, ⊙ Hwokia co. (pop. 188,725), SW Pingyuan prov., China, on Wei R. and 10 mi. WSW of Sinsiang, on railroad; agr. center. Until 1949 in Honan prov.

Hwokiu or **Huo-ch'iu** (both: hwô'chyō'), town, ⊙ Hwokiu co. (pop. 500,516), N Anhwei prov., China, near Honan line, 70 mi. NW of Hofei, in lake area; rice, wheat, hemp, beans, corn; winegrowing. Also spelled Hokiu (or Ho-ch'iu).

Hwolu, China: see HWAILU.

Hwo Mountains, China: see TAIYO MOUNTAINS.

Hwoshan or **Huo-shan** (both: hwô'shän'), town, ⊙ Hwoshan co. (pop. 139,880), N Anhwei prov., China, on Pi R. and 65 mi. WSW of Hofei, at foot of the peak Hwo Shan, in Tapieh Mts.; tea-growing center; rice, hemp, tung oil, lacquer; vegetable-tallow processing (soap, candles). Also written Hoshan.

Hwo Shan, mountains, China: see TAIYO MOUNTAINS.

Hwoshao Island (hwô'shou'), Chinese *Huo-shao Tao* (dou), Jap. *Kasho-to* (kä'shō-tō'), volcanic island (□ 11; 1935 pop. 2,274) off SE Formosa, 20 mi. SE of Taitung; sweet potatoes, rice, peanuts, livestock; fisheries. Main village is Nanliao (Jap. *Nanryo*) (1935 pop. 943).

Hyannis (hīă'nĭs). **1** Village (pop. 4,235) in BARNSTABLE town, Barnstable co., SE Mass., on S shore of Cape Cod, 3 mi. SSE of Barnstable; summer resort and Cape business center, at terminus of rail spur; cranberries, truck, fishing. Has state teachers col. and Mass. Maritime Acad. Hyannis Port is SW, on Nantucket Sound. **2** Village (pop. 432), ⊙ Grant co., W central Nebr., 60 mi. E of Alliance; resort; livestock, grain, poultry produce, potatoes. Recreation grounds near by.

Hyattsville (hī'ŭtsvĭl), town (pop. 12,308), Prince Georges co., central Md., residential suburb just NE of Washington, at head of Anacostia R. Inc. 1880.

Hyattville, village (pop. c.100), Big Horn co., N Wyo., on branch of Bighorn R., just W of Bighorn Mts., and 24 mi. ESE of Basin, in bean-growing area; alt. c.4,450 ft.

Hyaty or **Hiaty** (yätē'), town (dist. pop. 5,706), Guairá dept., S Paraguay, on railroad and 4 mi. NW of Villarrica; sugar cane, cotton, oranges.

Hybla or **Hybla Major,** Sicily: see PATERNÒ.

Hybo (hü'bōō"), village (pop. 624), Gavleborg co., E Sweden, near Ljusna R., 4 mi. SE of Ljusdal; linen milling, woodworking.

Hydaburg (hī'dùbûrg), town (pop. 341), SE Alaska, on W coast of Prince of Wales Isl., 23 mi. SE of Craig; fishing, fish processing, lumbering; Haida Indian settlement.

Hydaspes, river, Kashmir and W Pakistan: see JHELUM RIVER.

Hyde, municipal borough (1931 pop. 32,075; 1951 census 31,498), NE Cheshire, England, 7 mi. ESE of Manchester; cotton mills, machine works, iron foundries; mfg. of soap, starch, chemicals, rubber and ebonite products. In the borough (S) is leather-mfg. suburb of Gee Cross.

Hyde. 1 County (□ 634; pop. 6,479), E N.C.; ⊙ Swanquarter. Forested and swampy tidewater area; bounded S by Pamlico Sound; crossed by Alligator-Pungo R. Canal; includes Ocracoke Isl. and Mattamuskeet L. Fishing, farming (hogs, poultry, soybeans, cotton), sawmilling. Formed 1705. **2** County (□ 869; pop. 2,811), central S. Dak.; ⊙ Highmore. Agr. area drained by intermittent streams; Missouri R. and Crow Creek Indian Reservation in SW corner. Dairy products, livestock, grain. Formed 1873.

Hyden (hī'dùn), town (pop. 647), ⊙ Leslie co., SE Ky., in Cumberland foothills, on Middle Fork Kentucky R. and 12 mi. WSW of Hazard. Seat of Frontier Nursing Service Hosp. (built 1928), which serves a primitive mtn. region.

Hyde Park, village (pop. 841), Demerara co., N Br. Guiana, landing on right bank of Demerara R. and 23 mi. SSW of Georgetown, in agr. region (sugar cane, rice, fruit); 6°30'N 58°16'W. Just SE a U.S. army base (with Atkinson airfield) was established 1940.

Hyde Park, public park (364 acres) in Westminster, London, England, N of the Thames, 2 mi. W of Charing Cross, bounded by Park Lane (E), Knightsbridge (S), Kensington Gardens (W), and Bayswater Road (N). At NE corner is Marble Arch (triumphal arch formerly at entrance to Buckingham Palace, erected by George IV), the meeting place of soap-box orators. Features of park are Rotten Row, famous bridle path, and the Serpentine, artificial lake constructed from the Westbourne rivulet for Queen Caroline in 1733. Park originally belonged to the manor of Hyde, property of Westminster Abbey; under Henry VIII the park was laid out and used as hunting ground; races held here in time of Charles II. In 1712 the duke of Hamilton and Lord Mohun fought fatal duel here. In 1851 1st great international exhibition was held here.

Hyde Park. 1 Section of BOSTON, Mass. **2** Village (pop. 1,059) in Hyde Park town (1940 pop. 4,056), Dutchess co., SE N.Y., on E bank of the Hudson and 5 mi. N of Poughkeepsie, in diversified-farming area. The Franklin D. Roosevelt Natl. Historic Site (33.23 acres; established 1944) is here, including bldg. that was birthplace and home of Franklin D. Roosevelt and garden in which he is buried. Franklin D. Roosevelt Library (opened 1941) contains historical material relating to Roosevelt's career from 1910 to 1945. Vanderbilt Mansion Natl. Historic Site (211.7 acres) was established in 1940 for preservation of a sumptuous American residence of period 1880–1900. **3** Borough (pop. 758), Westmoreland co., SW central Pa., on Kiskiminetas R. just E of Leechburg. **4** Town (pop. 644), Cache co., N Utah, 8 mi. N of Logan; alt. 4,449 ft. **5** Town (pop. 1,291), including Hyde Park village (pop. 440), ⊙ Lamoille co., N central Vt., 23 mi. N of Montpelier; lumber; asbestos; metal products. Settled 1787. North Hyde Park village is a woodworking center.

Hyder (hī'dùr), village (pop. 31), SE Alaska, on B.C. border, at head of Portland Canal, 2 mi. S of Stewart, B.C.; supply point; port of entry; small-scale mining (gold, silver, lead, tungsten).

Hyderabad or **Haidarabad** (both: hī'dùrùbăd", -bäd"), constituent state (□ 82,313; 1941 pop. 16,338,534; 1951 census pop. 18,652,964), S central India, on DECCAN PLATEAU; ⊙ Hyderabad. Bordered W and NW by Bombay, N and NE by Madhya Pradesh; SE and S by Madras. From Ajanta Hills in NW, and Penganga and Wardha rivers on N border, terrain slopes generally SE in undulating plains to Kistna R. and its right affluent, the Tungabhadra, on S border. Godavari R. crosses state from W to E in N portion, partly forming E border. Over-all climate is tropical savanna, with annual rainfall averaging 25 in.; temp. ranges from a minimum of 65°F. in Jan. to a maximum of 111°F. in May. NW area of state, marked off by the Manjra, right tributary of Godavari R., is characterized by fertile black soil producing cotton, wheat, millet, and oilseeds (chiefly peanuts). The less fertile red-soil plains covering rest of the state, assisted by numerous irrigation works (reservoirs and canals) on Manjra and Musi rivers, grow rice, millet, tobacco, sugar cane, and oilseeds (peanuts, castor beans, sesame). Small, widely-dispersed forest tracts produce teak, ebony, bamboo, and gum arabic. Cattle raising (draft animals, sheep, goats) and poultry farming is widespread. Coal mined at Kottagudem and Rajura; iron ore worked at Yellandlapad (graphite, mica, and marble quarrying); abandoned gold mines at Hutti reopened 1949. Hyderabad has several cotton-milling centers, notably Aurangabad, Gulbarga, Hyderabad, and Warangal. Other industries include rice, oilseed, paper, and silk milling, vegetable, tobacco, and sugar processing, tanning, mfg. of cement, glass, matches, chemical fertilizer, cotton, and woolen. Hand-loom weaving, dyeing, bidri, and pottery are among the more important handicrafts. Principal cities are Hyderabad, Warangal, Gulbarga, Aurangabad, Jalna, Nander, Raichur, Nizamabad, Latur, Parbhani, Bidar, and Bodhan. Major rail lines, with junctions at Kazipet, Hyderabad, and Wadi, traverse state, connecting it with ports of Bombay and Madras and with New Delhi. Airports at Hyderabad and Warangal. State's pop. comprises Hindus (82%), Moslems (12%), aboriginal tribes (4%; mostly Gonds and Bhils), and Christians (1%). Main languages, Marathi and Telugu (W and E of Manjra R. respectively). Literacy is low (9%). The famous caves of AJANTA (c.200 B.C. to A.D. c.600) and rock-cut temples of ELLORA (c.3d-13th cent. A.D.) testify to spread of Buddhism, Brahmanism, and Jainism over the region during Andhra and Gupta empires and the indigenous dynasties which succeeded them. In 14th cent., Delhi sultans invaded the area and, in 16th cent., their viceroys of the South seceded and founded independent Deccan sultanates. These were annexed to Mogul empire by Aurangzeb in 1687; a Mogul viceroy became effectively independent of Delhi's control in 1724 and established dynastic seat of Nizams of Hyderabad in Hyderabad city. After alternately joining forces with the French and English against the Mysore sultans (Hyder Ali and Tippoo Sahib) and the Mahrattas, the Nizams finally came under Br. protection in 1800 and state's approximate present boundaries were established, the Nizams retaining titular authority over Berar, in present Madhya Pradesh. Hyderabad was largest in area and by far the most populous of the princely states of India. Following Br. withdrawal from India in Aug., 1947, Hyderabad and India agreed to defer final decision on state's accession to India for a year. But in Sept., 1948, after the Nizam's failure to check widespread plundering in Hyderabad and border areas of Madras by militant bands of fanatic Hyderabad Moslems, the Indian army entered Hyderabad in a 5-day police action, and the state was placed under a temporary military govt., which was ended following Hyderabad's formal accession to the republic of India as a constituent state in Jan., 1950. Exclaves were exchanged with Bombay and Madras. State comprises 17 dists.: Adilabad, Atraf-i-Balda, Aurangabad, Baghat, Bidar, Bir, Gulbarga, Karimnagar, Mahbubnagar, Medak, Nalgonda, Nander, Nizamabad, Osmanabad, Parbhani, Raichur, Warangal. Hyderabad was formerly called Nizam's Dominions.

Hyderabad, city (including SECUNDERABAD and suburban areas, □ 79; pop. 739,159), ⊙ Hyderabad state and Atraf-i-Balda and Baghat dists., India, on Deccan Plateau, on Musi R. and 380 mi. ESE of Bombay; 17°23'N 78°29'E. Road and rail junction; airports; commercial and industrial center; cotton milling, silk weaving, gunmaking, mfg. of bricks, tiles, glassware, cigarettes, paper, buttons, flour products; locomotive and railway-car works (in E area, known as Lalaguda or Lalguda), pharmaceutical works, tanneries. Has Osmania Univ. (founded 1918; uses Urdu language as medium of instruction), Nizam's Col., and a large industrial research laboratory. On left (N) bank of the Musi are industrial and commercial sections of Begampett or Begumpet (airport) and Sultan's Bazaar, the residential section of Jubilee Hill, the Residency (built 1803; until 1947 seat of state's Br. resident), and public gardens surrounding a notable archaeological mus. On right bank of river is original walled city (founded 1589), containing several mosques and palaces and the Char Minar, built 1591, a building with 4 arches through which the old city's main streets pass. First Nizam established Hyderabad as seat of his dominions in 1724. Main road to cantonment area of Secunderabad (N) leads along E bank of Husain Sagar (reservoir). Large experimental farm is near Himayat Sagar (reservoir; SW). Noted fort GOLCONDA is 5 mi. W of city. Often called Hyderabad Deccan to distinguish it from city of same name in Sind, Pakistan. Sometimes spelled Haidarabad.

Hyderabad, district (□ 4,476; pop. 758,748), S central Sind, W Pakistan; ⊙ Hyderabad. Bounded W by Indus R., S by Rann of Cutch. Flat alluvial plain, irrigated by Fuleli Canal and S branches of Rohri Canal; rice, millet, cotton, wheat. Cotton ginning, handicrafts (cloth, blankets, saddles, pottery, metalware), embroidering, fruitgrowing (mangoes, dates, plaintains, peaches, mulberries); camel breeding; fishing (chiefly shad) in the Indus. Natural salt deposits (S); some fuller's earth mined. City of Hyderabad is a trade center; was ⊙ Sind until 1843, when near-by Br. victories resulted in annexation of prov. to Br. India. Sometimes spelled Haidarabad.

Hyderabad, city (pop., including cantonment area, 134,693), ⊙ Sind and Hyderabad dist., W Pakistan, near left bank of Indus R., 90 mi. NE of Karachi; rail and road junction; important trade center; airport. Cotton ginning and milling, rice and oilseed milling, tanning, mfg. of agr. machinery, aerated water; handicrafts (embroideries, silk fabrics, lacquer ware, jewelry), cement and metalworks, motion picture studios. Markets millet, rice, wheat, cotton, and fruit (mangoes, dates, pomegranates, peaches). Medical school, commercial and agr. cols. Was old ⊙ Sind until its surrender to British in 1843, when Sir Charles Napier defeated emirs of Sind in near-by battles of Miani and Dabo, and again became ⊙ after 1950, replacing Karachi. Sometimes spelled Haidarabad.

Hyderabad Deccan, India: see HYDERABAD, state and city, India.

Hydernagar, India: see NAGAR, Mysore.

Hydetown, borough (pop. 530), Crawford co., NW Pa., on Oil Creek and 3 mi. NW of Titusville.

Hydeville, Vt.: see CASTLETON.

Hydra or **Idhra** (hī'drù, Gr. ēdh'rù), Lat. *Hydrea* (hīdrē'ù), island (□ 20; pop. 3,739) in Aegean Sea off E Peloponnesus, Greece, part of Attica nome, 4 mi. off Argolis Peninsula; 13 mi. long, 2 mi. wide. Largely barren rock, with most of its pop. in town of Hydra, port on N shore. Fishing (notably for sponges), trading. Town flourished as a trade and commercial center under Turkish rule (in 1821 pop. was 26,000), and its seafaring people played an important role in Gr. war of independence. Also spelled Idra and Ydra.

Hydraotes, river, India and Pakistan: see RAVI RIVER.

Hydrea, Greece: see HYDRA.

Hydro (hī'drō), town (pop. 714), Caddo co., W central Okla., 34 mi. W of El Reno, in agr. area (cotton, grain).

Hyères (yâr'), town (pop. 15,020), Var dept., SE France, near the Rade d'Hyères (a bay of the Mediterranean), 10 mi. E of Toulon, at SW foot of Monts des Maures; noted winter resort at W end of Fr. Riviera, with mild climate (average temp. 60°F.) and subtropical vegetation. Mfg. (olive oil, essences, baskets, aluminum household articles, woodworking machinery). Ships local fruits (strawberries), flowers (violets), and vegetables, and salt worked at Salins-d'Hyères (4 mi. E; fishing port). Has picturesque old town, ruined castle, and statue of Massillon (b. here). La Plage d'Hyères (3 mi. SSE) is a popular beach resort, damaged during Allied landings (Aug., 1944) in Second World War.

Hyères, Iles d' (ēl dyâr'), island group in the Mediterranean just off S coast of France at Hyères, administratively in Var dept. Chief isls. are, E–W, LEVANT, PORT-CROS, and PORQUEROLLES. They protect the **Rade d'Hyères,** a sheltered bay (10 mi. wide, 6 mi. deep), extending from Giens Peninsula (SW) to Cap Bénat (E).

Hyesanjin (hyä'sän'jĭn'), Jap. *Kaizanchin* (kī'zän'-chĭn), town, S Hamgyong prov., NE Korea, 110 mi. NNE of Hamhung and on Yalu R. (Manchuria line), opposite Changpai; rail terminus. Reached 1950 by U.S. troops in Korean war.

Hyle Fjord, Norway: see SAND FJORD.

Hylestad, Norway: see NOMELAND.

Hylike, Lake, or **Lake Iliki** (both: ēlĭkē'), Lat. *Hylice* (hī'lĭsē) (□ 8.5), in Boeotia nome, E central Greece, on lower Cephisus R., N of Thebes; 6 mi. long, 3 mi. wide. Formerly called Likeri.

Hylla, Norway: see Rora.

Hyltebruk (hül″tůbrük'), village (pop. 1,822), Jonkoping co., S Sweden, on Nissa R. and 30 mi. WSW of Varnamo; paper mills, sulphite works.

Hylton, England: see Castletown.

Hymera (hīmā'rů), town (pop. 1,069), Sullivan co., SW Ind., 21 mi. SSE of Terre Haute, in agr. area; bituminous-coal mining. Shakamak State Park is near by. Platted 1870.

Hymettus (hīmĕ'tůs), Gr. *Hymettos* or *Imittos* (both: ēmētôs'), mountain range in Attica nome, E central Greece, extends from just E of Athens 10 mi. S to coast of Saronic Gulf; rises to 3,367 ft. 5 mi. E of Athens. Known for its honey; site of white-marble quarries.

Hyndman (hīnd'můn), borough (pop. 1,322), Bedford co., S Pa., on Wills Creek and 22 mi. SW of Bedford; lumber milling. Laid out 1840, inc. 1877. Severely damaged by fire, 1949.

Hyndman, Mount, or **Hyndman Peak,** highest (12,078 ft.) of Pioneer Mts., central Idaho, 11 mi. ENE of Sun Valley.

Hynes (hīnz), unincorporated town, Los Angeles co., S Calif., 12 mi. SSE of downtown Los Angeles; alfalfa-hay market, dairying center; clay products, furniture. Fruit, poultry farms.

Hynes Bay, Texas: see San Antonio Bay.

Hyogo (hyō'gō), prefecture [Jap. *ken*] (□ 3,213; 1940 pop. 3,221,232; 1947 pop. 3,057,444), S Honshu, Japan; ⊙ Kobe, a major port of Japan. Bounded N by Sea of Japan, S by Harima Sea and Osaka Bay; includes Awaji-shima. Generally mountainous terrain, drained by small streams. Hot springs in coastal area of Inland Sea. Extensive truck gardening and poultry raising; fishing. Chief agr. products: rice, wheat, tobacco, tea. Saltmaking on S coast. Home industries (cutlery, woodworking, leather goods, straw products, raw silk). Produces machinery, textiles, pottery, dyes, chemicals, matches. Silver, copper, and gold mined at Ikuno. Industrial centers: Kobe, Himeji, Amagasaki, Akashi. Other centers: Shikama, Itami, O-o.

Hyogo, port, Japan: see Kobe.

Hyonnae (hyŭn'nä'), Jap. *Kennai*, town (1944 pop. 16,198), Kangwon prov., central Korea, N of 38°N, 55 mi. NNE of Seoul, in agr. area (potatoes, grain).

Hypanis, Russia: see Bug River (Southern Bug).

Hypate or **Ipati** (both: ēpä'tē), village (pop. 2,166), Phthiotis nome, E central Greece, 10 mi. W of Lamia. Health resort; sulphur springs. Also spelled Ypati.

Hyphasis, river, India: see Beas River.

Hyrcania (hûrkā'nēů), province of anc. Persian Empire, on SE shore of Caspian Sea, corresponding to modern Gurgan prov. and E part of Mazanderan prov. of Iran.

Hyrum (hī'rům), city (pop. 1,704), Cache co., N Utah, on Little Bear R., 7 mi. S of Logan, and near Wasatch Range; alt. 4,706 ft.; dairy products, canned vegetables. Settled 1860. Hyrum Dam, just SW, impounds water for irrigation of surrounding region.

Hyrum Dam, Utah: see Little Bear River.

Hysham (hī'shům), town (pop. 410), ⊙ Treasure co., S central Mont., near Yellowstone R., 70 mi. NE of Billings; shipping point for livestock, sugar beets, grain.

Hyskier, Scotland: Haskeir

Hythe (hīth), village (pop. 288), W Alta., near B.C. border, on Beaverlodge R. and 32 mi. WNW of Grande Prairie; lumbering, mixed farming.

Hythe (hīdh). **1** Suburb, Hampshire, England: see Dibden. **2** Municipal borough (1931 pop. 8,398; 1951 census 9,218), SE Kent, England, on the Channel, 5 mi. W of Folkestone; seaside resort and agr. market, with breweries. It was one of the Cinque Ports; the harbor is now silted up. Has 13th-cent. church. Near by is Saltwood Castle, former property of archbishops of Canterbury and reputed scene of plot to murder Thomas à Becket. The 23-mi.-long Royal Military Canal, terminating at Hythe, is now used for boating. W 3 mi. is village and parish of Lympne (lĭm) (pop. 598), the Roman *Portus Lemanis;* here are an important airfield and cross-Channel flight-control station, and Studfall Castle, once residence of archbishops of Canterbury. **3** Suburb, Surrey, England: see Egham.

Hyttefoss (hüt'tůfôs), waterfall (171 ft.) on Nid R., in Sor-Trondelag co., central Norway, just W of Selbu L., 13 mi. S of Trondheim; hydroelectric plant. Also spelled Hyttfoss.

Hyuga (hū'gä), former province in E Kyushu, Japan; now Miyazaki prefecture.

Hyuga Sea (hū'gä), Jap. *Hyuga-nada*, N arm of Philippine Sea, forms wide bight in E Kyushu, Japan, bet. Cape Sen (N) and Point Tozaki (S); c.75 mi. wide.

Hyvinkää (hü'vĭn-kä″), Swedish *Hyvinge* (hü'vĭng-ů), town (pop. 10,536), Uusimaa co., S Finland, 30 mi. N of Helsinki; rail junction; woolen-milling center; granite quarries. Vacation and winter-sports resort; site of sanitarium.

I

I, China: see I Mountains; I River.

Iacanga (yäkăng'gů), city (pop. 1,910), central São Paulo, Brazil, near Tietê R., 30 mi. N of Bauru; coffee processing, pottery mfg.; cattle raising.

Iacobeni (yäkōbăn'), village (pop. 1,165), Suceava prov., N Rumania, on Bistrita R., on railroad and 7 mi. NNW of Vatra-Dornei; health resort (alt. 2,789 ft.) in the E Carpathians. Also manganese-mining center; limestone quarrying; mfg. of agr. tools. Established by Ger. colonists.

Iaco River (yä'kōō), Acre territory, westernmost Brazil, rises in Peru near 11°S 71°40'W, flows c.250 mi. NE to the Purus below Sena Madureira (head of navigation).

Iaeger (yā'gůr), mining town (pop. 1,271), McDowell co., S W.Va., on Tug Fork and 13 miles W of Welch, in semibituminous-coal field; lumber milling.

Ialomita, province, Rumania: see Calarasi.

Ialomita River (yä'lômētsä), Rum. *Ialomița*, S central and S Rumania, rises in Bucegi Mts. 5 mi. NW of Sinaia, flows S past Pucioasa and Targoviste, and E past Slobozia, to the lower Danube 3 mi. W of Harsova; 200 mi. long. Receives Prahova R. (left). Upper valley is noted for its stalactite caverns, formerly site of anc. hermitage.

Ialpug or **Ialpuh,** lagoon, Ukrainian SSR: see Yalpug Lagoon.

Ialysus, Greece: see Trianta.

Ian (yē'än'), town, ⊙ Ian co. (pop. 180,489), W central Heilungkiang prov., Manchuria, 70 mi. E of Tsitsihar; soybeans, rye, millet, corn. Called Lungchüanchen until 1929.

Ianca (yäng'kä), village (pop. 2,986), Galati prov., SE Rumania, on railroad and 24 mi. SW of Braila; agr. center.

Ianstown, Scotland: see Buckie.

Iara (yä'rä), Hung. *Alsójara* (ŏl'shōyŏrŏ), village (pop. 1,634), Cluj prov., NW central Rumania, 12 mi. W of Turda.

Iasi, Rumania: see Jassy.

Iasmos (yäs'môs), village (pop. 3,671), Rhodope nome, W Thrace, Greece, on railroad and 10 mi. W of Komotine; tobacco, wheat, vegetables.

Iatrinoli, Italy: see Taurianova.

Iatt, Lake (ī'ůt), Grant parish, central La., 3 mi. NE of Colfax; c.7 mi. long. Entered N by short Iatt Creek; drains S through outlet to Red R.

Iauaretê or **Iuaretê** (you-ärĭtā'), town (pop. 520), NW Amazonas, Brazil, post on Colombia border, on Uaupés R. at mouth of Papury R., and 150 mi. WNW of Uaupés. Formerly spelled Jauaretê or Yauaretê.

Iavello, Ethiopia: see Yavello.

Iba (ē'bä), town (1939 pop. 3,078; 1948 municipality pop. 9,741), ⊙ Zambales prov., central Luzon, Philippines, near W coast, 45 mi. WSW of Tarlac; trade center for rice-growing area. Mineral pigments.

Ibadan (ē″bädän', ēbä'dän), city (pop. 387,133), ⊙ Western Provinces, SW Nigeria, in Oyo prov., on railroad and 70 mi. NNE of Lagos; alt. 651 ft.; 7°23'N 3°53'E. Largest city of Nigeria. Commercial center in agr. area (cacao, cotton, yams, corn); cacao industry, processing of palm oil and kernels, cotton weaving, cigarette mfg. Most populous city of Yoruba tribe. Has Univ. Col. (established 1947), teachers colleges, hosp., town hall of Roman design. Site of Moor plantation; hq. of Nigerian Agr. Dept. Airfield.

Ibagué (ēbägā'), city (pop. 27,448), ⊙ Tolima dept., W central Colombia, on E slopes of Cordillera Central, 80 mi. WSW of Bogotá (connected by rail and highway); 4°26'N 75°14'E; alt. c.4,200 ft. Major commercial link bet. Magdalena and Cauca valleys, the latter reached by Pan-American Highway over cordillera to Armenia (Antioquia dept.). Trade and shipping center for gold-mining and processing industries in agr. region (principally coffee; but also rice, sugar cane, corn, potatoes, bananas, yucca, silk, livestock). Coffee, sugar, and flour mills; brewery; mfg. of chocolate, soap, tobacco products. Airport. Coal, silver, and sulphur deposits near by. Old colonial city founded 1550. It has a conservatory and San Simón Col.

Ibahernando (ēväĕrnän'dō), village (pop. 2,773), Cáceres prov., W Spain, 10 mi. SSW of Trujillo; cereals, olive oil, wine, livestock.

Ibaiti (ēbītē'), city (pop. 906), NE Paraná, Brazil, on rail spur and 10 mi. WSW of Tomazina; coffee and rice processing; coal deposits. Until 1944, called Barra Bonita.

Ibajay (ēbähī'), town (1939 pop. 2,214; 1948 municipality pop. 24,086), Capiz prov., NW Panay isl., Philippines, on Sibuyan Sea, 45 mi. WNW of Capiz; agr. center (tobacco, rice).

Ibañeta, Puerto de, Spain: see Roncesvalles.

Ibáñez, Chile: see Puerto Ibáñez.

Ibar (ē'bůr), peak (8,747 ft.) in E Rila Mts., W Bulgaria, 12 mi. SE of Samokov.

Ibara (ēbä'rä) or **Ihara** (ēhä'rä), town (pop. 13,340), Okayama prefecture, SW Honshu, Japan, 9 mi. NE of Fukuyama; distribution center for agr. area; textiles, sake, soy sauce, dried mushrooms.

Ibaraki (ēbä'räkē), prefecture [Jap. *ken*] (□ 2,352; 1940 pop. 1,620,000; 1947 pop. 2,013,735), central Honshu, Japan; ⊙ Mito. Bounded E by the Pacific, S by Tone R.; generally mountainous and forested. Fertile valleys produce rice, tobacco, wheat; lumbering, raw-silk production. Many resorts and fishing ports on coast. Part of Joban coal field is in N border area; gold, silver, and copper are mined in Hitachi region. Textile mfg., woodworking. Principal centers: Mito, Hitachi, Tsuchiura.

Ibaraki, town (pop. 14,243), Osaka prefecture, S Honshu, Japan, 13 mi. NNE of Osaka; distribution center for agr., poultry-raising area; largely residential.

Ibarlucea (ēbärlōōsā'ä), town (pop. estimate 1,000), S Santa Fe prov., Argentina, 10 mi. NW of Rosario; agr. (corn, flax, wheat, livestock).

Ibarra (ēbä'rä), city (1950 pop. 14,221), ⊙ Imbabura prov., N Ecuador, on Pan-American Highway, on railroad and 50 mi. NE of Quito, in a high Andean valley, near Ecuadorian lake dist., surrounded by the peaks Cotacachi (W) and Imbabura (SW); 0°21'N 78°7'W; alt. 7,300 ft. Trading center in fertile agr. region (coffee, sugar cane, cotton, cereals, potatoes, fruit, stock); mfg. of native woolen goods, cotton products, fine silverwork, wood carvings, *aguardiente*, furniture, Panama hats; saltworks. The bishopric has notable shrine. An old Indian town, it was largely destroyed by 1868 earthquake.

Ibarreta (ēbärā'tä), town (pop. estimate 2,000), central Formosa natl. territory, Argentina, on railroad and 125 mi. NW of Formosa; agr. center (corn, cotton, livestock).

Ibar River (ē'bär), S central Yugoslavia, rises in Mokra Planina c.10 mi. ESE of Berane, flows E, past Rozaj and Kosovska Mitrovica, and N, past Raska, to Western Morava R. just below Rankovicevo town; c.150 mi. long. Navigable for c.130 mi. Receives Sitnica R. (right). Kopaonik mtn. range lies E of its middle course; paralleled by railroad below Kosovska Mitrovica.

Ibars de Urgel (ēvärs' dhā ōōrhĕl'), village (pop. 1,494), Lérida prov., NE Spain, on Urgel Canal and 19 mi. ENE of Lérida, in well-irrigated agr. area (cereals, olive oil, wine, almonds).

Ibatuba, Brazil: see Soledade de Minas.

Ibb (ĭb), town (pop. 7,000), ⊙ Ibb prov. (po[illegible] 410,000), S Yemen, on plateau, 95 mi. S of San[illegible] and on main route to Taiz; alt. 6,700 ft. Tradi[illegible] center; tanning, mfg. of saddles and harnesse[illegible] stock raising. Situated on mtn. ridge, it is a walle[illegible] town of lofty stone-built houses, entered by castle-like gate.

Ibbenbüren (ĭ'bůnbü″růn), town (pop. 12,541), in former Prussian prov. of Westphalia, NW Germany, after 1945 in North Rhine-Westphalia, at N foot of Teutoburg Forest, 11 mi. E of Rheine; rail junction; mfg. of textiles (linen, cotton), machinery, leather goods. Summer resort. Coal mined in vicinity.

Ibdes (ēv'dhĕs), town (pop. 1,722), Saragossa prov., NE Spain, 14 mi. SW of Calatayud; cereals, fruit.

Ibefun (ēbāfā'), town, Ijebu prov., Western Provinces, SW Nigeria, 12 mi. SW of Ijebu Ode; cacao industry; cotton weaving, indigo dyeing; palm oil and kernels. Sometimes spelled Ibefon.

Ibembo (ēbĕm'bō), village, Eastern Prov., N Belgian Congo, on Itimbiri R., 50 mi. W of Buta; steamboat landing and trading center; rice, cotton. Has hosp. for Europeans. Across Itimbiri is the R.C. mission of Tongerloo-Saint-Norbert (tõzhârlōō'-sē-nôrbâr') with native teachers' school and small seminary.

Ibenthann, Germany: see Maxhütte.

Iberá, Esteros del (ĕstä'rōs dĕl ēbärá'), region of swamps and lakes in Corrientes prov., Argentina, extending c.150 mi. NE-SW bet. Paraná R. and Uruguay R. Includes the lakes Iberá, Luna, and Itatí. Subtropical forests cover most of the area.

Iberá, Lake (□ 140), in the Esteros del Iberá (swamps), N central Corrientes prov., Argentina, 70 mi. NE of Mercedes; c.20 mi. long.

Iberia (ībē'rēů), in anc. geography, a country bet. the Greater Caucasus and Armenia, corresponding approximately to modern E Georgia.

Iberia, parish (□ 588; pop. 40,059), S La.; ⊙ New Iberia. On Gulf coast; bounded SW by Vermilion Bay, E by Grand L. (widening of Atchafalaya R.); intersected by Bayou Teche. Includes Avery, Jefferson, and Weeks isls. (salt domes). Oil and gas wells, huge salt mines, sulphur mines; fisheries. Rich agr. area (sugar cane, rice, cotton, corn, oats, pecans, sweet potatoes; dairy products). Processing of farm products and some other mfg. at New Iberia. Hunting, fur trapping. Parish is crossed by Gulf Intracoastal Waterway. Formed 1850.

Iberia, town (pop. 595), Miller co., central Mo., 13 mi. NW of Dixon; agr. Has a jr. col.

Iberian Gates, USSR: see DARYAL GORGE.

Iberian Mountains, Spain: see IBÉRICA, CORDILLERA.

Iberian Peninsula, SW Europe, comprises SPAIN and PORTUGAL. The Pyrenees, which form entire length of its land boundary (NE), are an effective barrier to communication with other parts of continental Europe. In S, at Gibraltar, peninsula is separated from Africa by the narrow Strait of Gibraltar. Peninsula's E coast is washed by the Mediterranean; its W and N coasts border on the Atlantic. Cape Roca (in Portugal) is westernmost point of continental Europe, and Cape St. Vincent (also in Portugal) is its southwesternmost headland. Peninsula takes its name from an anc. people whom the Greeks named Iberians probably after the Ebro.

Ibérica, Cordillera (kôrdhēlyä'rä ēvä'rēkä), or **Iberian Mountains** (ībĭr'ēŭn), mountain system on E edge of the great central plateau (Meseta) of Spain, extends in a wide arc (c.250 mi. long) from Sierra de la DEMANDA southward to the Júcar R. basin, roughly separating Old and New Castile from Aragon and Valencia. Rises in Sierra del MONCAYO to c.7,590 ft. Among other subranges are Sierra CEBOLLERA and Serranía de CUENCA. Sometimes called Sistema Ibérico.

Iberus, river, Spain: see EBRO RIVER.

Iberville (ē'bûrvĭl, Fr. ēbârvēl'), county (□ 198; pop. 10,273), S Que., near N.Y. border, on Richelieu R.; ⊙ Iberville.

Iberville, town (pop. 3,454), ⊙ Iberville co., S Que., on Richelieu R. and 22 mi. SE of Montreal; mfg. of chemicals, pottery; iron founding, woodworking; market in dairying region. Site of American mother-house of the Marist Brothers.

Iberville (ī'bûrvĭl), parish (□ 611; pop. 26,750), SE central La.; ⊙ Plaquemine. Bounded W by Atchafalaya R.; intersected by Mississippi R. Agr. (sugar cane, corn, hay, rice, fruit, vegetables); sugar refineries, cotton and moss gins, lumber mills. Oil and gas fields; fisheries; timber. Drained by Grand R. Locks connect a branch (Plaquemine–Morgan City waterway) of Gulf Intracoastal Waterway with the Mississippi here. Includes migratory bird refuge. Formed 1805.

Ibex (ī'bĕks), peak (8,263 ft.) in SW Palni Hills, SW Madras, India, 10 mi. NW of Periyakulam.

Ibha, Saudi Arabia: see ABHA.

Ibi (ē'bē), town (pop. 5,370), Gifu prefecture, central Honshu, Japan, 11 mi. WNW of Gifu, in rice-growing area. Has agr. and forestry schools.

Ibi (ēbē'), town (pop. 4,990), Benue prov., Northern Provinces, E central Nigeria, port on Benue R. and 25 mi. N of Wukari; salt mining; cassava, durra, yams. Br. commercial station in 19th cent.

Ibi (ē'vē), town (pop. 3,314), Alicante prov., E Spain, 8 mi. SW of Alcoy; ice-cream and biscuit factories; toy mfg., olive-oil processing. Wine.

Ibiá (ēbyä'), city (pop. 4,029), W Minas Gerais, Brazil, in the Serra da Canastra, 90 mi. ENE of Uberaba; rail junction; cotton, coffee, cattle, dairy products. Spa of Araxá is 25 mi. WSW.

Ibiapaba, Serra, Brazil: see GRANDE, SERRA.

Ibiapina (ēbyŭpē'nŭ), city (pop. 1,122), NW Ceará, Brazil, in the Serra Grande, 40 mi. SW of Sobral, on Piauí border; distilling. Ships coffee, tobacco, lumber.

Ibiapinópolis, Brazil: see SOLEDADE, Paraíba.

Ibibobo (ēbēbō'bō), village (pop. c.350), Tarija dept., SE Bolivia, in the Chaco, on Pilcomayo R. and 38 mi. SE of Villa Montes. Sometimes spelled Ivi Bobo.

Ibicuí River (ēbēkwē'), SW Rio Grande do Sul, Brazil, rises N of Santa Maria, flows c.300 mi. W to Uruguay R. (Argentina border) 30 mi. NE of Uruguaiana. Navigable. Old spelling, Ibicuhy.

Ibicuy (ēbēkwē'), town (pop. estimate 1,000), SE Entre Ríos prov., Argentina, port on Paraná Ibicuy R. and 45 mi. S of Gualeguay; rail terminus (Holt station); stock-raising center; ships cereals.

Ibi Gamin, mountain, India: see KAMET.

Ibipetuba (ēbēpĭtōō'bŭ), city (pop. 1,456), W Bahia, Brazil, on the Rio Prêto (navigable) and 80 mi. W of Barra; hides, sugar, manioc. Formerly called Santa Rita do Rio Prêto, then Rio Prêto until 1944.

Iboporã (ēbēpōō'rã'), city (pop. 1,219), N Paraná, Brazil, on railroad and 7 mi. ENE of Londrina, in pioneer coffee zone; sawmilling, brick mfg.

Ibirá (ēbērä'), city (pop. 2,613), N São Paulo, Brazil, 20 mi. SSE of São José do Rio Prêto; resort with mineral springs (established 1928); pottery mfg., corn milling.

Ibiraci (ēbērŭsē'), city (pop. 2,007), SW Minas Gerais, Brazil, near São Paulo border, 40 mi. NW of Passos; coffee, sugar, livestock. Formerly spelled Ibiracy.

Ibiraçu (ēbērŭsōō'), city (pop. 695), central Espírito Santo, on railroad and 35 mi. N of Vitória; coffee, bananas, manioc. Until 1944, called Pau Gigante.

Ibirama (ēbērä'mŭ), city (pop. 997), E central Santa Catarina, Brazil, in Itajaí Açu R. valley, 30 mi. WSW of Blumenau. Agr. colony settled in 19th cent. by Germans and Slavs. Until 1944, called Hamônia (old spelling, Hammonia).

Ibirarema (ēbērŭrā'mŭ), city (pop. 840), W São Paulo, Brazil, on railroad and 13 mi. NW of Ourinhos; rice, corn, coffee, poultry. Until 1944, Pau d' Alho.

Ibi River, Japan: see KISO RIVER.

Ibitinga (ēbētēng'gŭ), city (pop. 5,203), central São Paulo, Brazil, near Tietê R., on railroad and 75 mi. WSW of Ribeirão Prêto; agr.-processing center (manioc flour, sausages, soft drinks); cotton, coffee, and rice processing. Oil-shale deposits.

Ibiúna (ēbyōō'nŭ), city (pop. 1,099), SE São Paulo, Brazil, 40 mi. W of São Paulo, near Sorocaba R. reservoir; grain, citrus fruit. Until 1944, called Una.

Ibiza, Balearic Isls.: see IVIZA.

Iblei, Monti (mōn'tē ēblā'), mountain range, SE Sicily; extends 25 mi. NW from Cassibile R. to Caltagirone; rises to 3,231 ft. in Monte Lauro.

Ibo (ē'bō), town (1950 commune pop. 2,613), Niassa prov., N Mozambique, on Ibo Isl. (□ 17) in Mozambique Channel just off mainland, 45 mi. N of Pôrto Amélia; 12°20'S 40°38'E. Oil-seed processing. Ships copra, ivory, wax, cashew nuts, ebony. Founded 17th cent. Became a slave-trading center. Has 3 old forts.

Iboti, Brazil: see NEVES PAULISTA.

Ibra (ĭ'brŭ, ĭbrä'), chief town (pop. 4,000) of Sharqiya dist. of interior Oman, 65 mi. S of Muscat, across Eastern Hajar hill country; date groves.

Ibrahimiya, El, or **Al-Ibrahimiyah** (both: ĕl ĭbrähĭmē'yŭ), town (pop. 7,370; with suburbs, 11,919), Sharqiya prov., Lower Egypt, 10 mi. NNE of Zagazig; cotton, cereals.

Ibrahimiya Canal, Upper Egypt, runs parallel (W) to the Nile, extending c.200 mi. from Asyut to Giza prov.; navigable in some parts. The Bahr Yusuf branches off it at Dairut. Beni Suef is on it. With its numerous tributaries, it is an important irrigation canal.

Ibrahimpatan or **Ibrahim Patan** (ĭbrä'hēm pŭtŭn'), town (pop. 5,702), Baghat dist., S central Hyderabad state, India, 17 mi. SE of Hyderabad; rice, oilseeds.

Ibrany (ĭ'brănyŭ), Hung. *Ibrány*, town (pop. 7,043), Szabolcs co., NE Hungary, 12 mi. N of Nyiregyhaza; wheat, potatoes, cattle, hogs.

Ibresi (ēbryĭsē'), town (1948 pop. over 2,000), central Chuvash Autonomous SSR, Russian SFSR, on railroad and 35 mi. NNE of Alatyr; woodworking. Oil-shale deposits near by.

Ibri or **'Ibri** (ĭbrē'), chief town (pop. 5,000) of Dhahira dist. of interior Oman, at foot of Western Hajar hill country, 140 mi. WSW of Muscat; fruitgrowing center; dates, limes, mangoes, pomegranates. Large mosque.

Ibros (ē'vrōs), town (pop. 4,098), Jaén prov., S Spain, 9 mi. ESE of Linares; soap, essential-oil mfg., olive-oil processing; wine and cereals.

Ibshawai or **Ibshaway** (ĭb'shăwī), village (pop. 7,351), Faiyum prov., Upper Egypt, on railroad and 10 mi. WNW of Faiyum; cotton, cereals, sugar, fruits.

Ibstock, town and parish (pop. 5,365), NW Leicester, England, 12 mi. WNW of Leicester; coal mining. Has 14th-cent. church.

Ibura, Brazil: see RECIFE.

Iburg (ē'bōōrk), village (pop. 2,780), in former Prussian prov. of Hanover, NW Germany, after 1945 in Lower Saxony, on S slope of Teutoburg Forest, 8 mi. S of Osnabrück; summer resort. Has castle (rebuilt in 17th cent.), once residence of bishops of Osnabrück.

Iburi Bay, Japan: see UCHIURA BAY.

Ibusuki (ēbōō'sōōkē), town (pop. 28,908), Kagoshima prefecture, S Kyushu, Japan, on SE Satsuma Peninsula, 23 mi. SSE of Kagoshima; hot-springs resort; agr. center (tobacco, rice, melons); kaolin. Agr. and forestry schools.

Ibyar (ĭb'yär), village (pop. 13,984), Gharbiya prov., Lower Egypt, 3 mi. ENE of Kafr el Zaiyat; cotton, cereals, rice, fruits.

Ica (ē'kä), department (□ 9,799; pop. 144,547), SW Peru, bet. the Pacific and Cordillera Occidental of the Andes; ⊙ Ica. Includes Chincha and Viejas isls. Situated chiefly on coastal plain, it is irrigated by the Chincha, Pisco, Ica, and Río Grande. Peru's 2d largest cotton-producing center, important also for viticulture and fruitgrowing. Alcohol distilling; produces Pisco brandy. Fishing at Pisco and San Andrés; fish canning at San Andrés. Gold placers near Nazca; iron deposits at Marcona; thermal baths at Huacachina. Railroad runs bet. Ica and Pisco port.

Ica, city (pop. 21,437), ⊙ Ica dept. and Ica prov. (in 1940: □ 6,198; pop. 76,024), SW Peru, on Ica R. and 160 mi. SE of Lima (connected by highway); 14°4'S 75°42'W. Commercial and industrial center in major irrigated cotton and wine region. Cotton ginning, cottonseed-oil milling, mfg. (soap, candles), textile milling, tanning, distilling. Railroad to its port Pisco. Founded 1563 by the Spaniards, it has been twice destroyed by earthquake. In 1941 Nazca prov. (pop. 12,083) was formed from part of Ica prov.

Icacos, Punta, Nicaragua: see CORINTO.

Icacos Point (ēkä'kōs), SW Trinidad, B.W.I., W section of the SW peninsula, on the Serpent's Mouth, and 10 mi. off Venezuela coast, terminating in Icacos Point headland at 10°2'N 61°55'W.

Içana (ēsä'nŭ), town (pop. 38), NW Amazonas, Brazil, on right bank of the Rio Negro just below influx of Içana R., and 40 mi. NNW of Uaupés. Until 1944, called São Felipe or São Felippe.

Icaño (ēkä'nyō), town (pop. estimate 500), SE Catamarca prov., Argentina, 31 mi. SE of Catamarca; educational center of La Paz dept.

Icaria or **Ikaria** (īkâ'rēŭ, Gr. ēkŭrē'ŭ), Greek Aegean island (□ 99; pop. 11,614), SW of Samos isl., in Samos nome; 37°35'N 26°20'E; 25 mi. long (NE–SW), 6 mi. wide; rises to 3,389 ft. (SW). Lumbering (charcoal production); figs, wine, fruit, grain; charcoal. Sulphur radioactive springs. Main town is Hagios Kyrikos, on E shore. Formerly called Nicaria or Nikaria, and, under Turkish rule (until 1913), Akhigria. In Gr. mythology. Icarus fell into the sea here after his flight. The Aegean Sea off the coast of Asia Minor was known as Icarian Sea in antiquity.

Icarian Sea, Greece: see AEGEAN SEA.

Içá River, Brazil: see PUTUMAYO RIVER.

Ica River (ē'kä), Ica dept., SW Peru, rises in Cordillera Occidental SSW of Huaitará, flows 100 mi. S, past Ica, to the Pacific NW of San Nicolás. Irrigates agr. region (cotton, grapes).

Icatu (ēkŭtōō'), city (pop. 359), N Maranhão, Brazil, on Monim R. near its mouth on São José Bay of the Atlantic, and 23 mi. ESE of São Luís; alcohol distilling; corn, manioc, sugar growing.

Icaturama, Brazil: see SANTA ROSA DE VITERBO.

Ice Bay, Nor. *Isfjorden* (ēs"fyôr'dŭn), inlet (35 naut. mi. long, 30 naut. mi. wide) of Indian Ocean, in Antarctica, bet. Enderby Land (E) and Queen Maud Land (W), in 67°45'S 50°E. Discovered 1930 by Hjalmar Riiser-Larsen, Norwegian explorer.

Icel (ĭchĕl'), Turkish *Içel*, province (□ 6,061; 1950 pop. 317,853), S Turkey; ⊙ MERSIN. On the Mediterranean, bordered NW by Taurus Mts., drained by lower course of Goksu R. Zinc, chromium, copper, iron, lignite; cotton, sesame, grain, oranges; camels. In it is the anc. city of Tarsus. Formerly called Mersin.

Iceland (īs'lŭnd), Icelandic *Ísland* (ēs'länt"), republic and island (□ 39,700; 1949 pop. 141,042), westernmost state of Europe, in the North Atlantic just S of the Arctic Circle, c.500 mi. NW of Scotland, c.600 mi. W of Norway, and c.175 mi. SE of Greenland; 63°24'–66°32'N 13°28'–24°32'W; ⊙ REYKJAVIK. It is 300 mi. long (E–W), up to 190 mi. wide. Surface consists of uninhabited central plateau averaging 2,000–2,500 ft. high. On S and W sides of the plateau are extensive glacier regions, notably the VATNAJOKULL (S), which rises to 6,952 ft. on Hvannadalshnjukur, highest peak of Iceland. Other high glaciated elevations are Hofsjokull (5,581 ft.), Eiriksjokull (5,495 ft.), and Eyjafjallajokull (5,466 ft.). There are over 100 volcanoes, many still active; Hekla (4,747 ft.) has had over a score of eruptions since 1104 (the latest was in 1947). There are numerous hot springs, many of which are exploited for heating purposes; noted is the Geysir or Great Geysir. Coast line is rugged and deeply indented by numerous fjords and bays, especially on W and N coasts. Large Vestfjarda Peninsula extends NW into Denmark Strait; it is rugged and mountainous, partly glaciated. Country is drained by many glacier streams; largest are Jokulsa a Fjollum, Thjorsa, Hvita, and Fnjoska rivers. Noted waterfalls are Dettifoss, Gullfoss, and Ljosafoss (major power station). Large parts of country are covered with lava fields, among them the vast Odadahraun (N), on slope of Askja volcano. Among large lakes are Myvatn, Thingvallavatn, and Thorisvatn. The few small isls. off coasts include VESTMANNAEYJAR (SW) and Grimsey (N, within Arctic Circle). Timber is virtually absent, but extensive grazing lands support sheep, and there are also goats, cattle, and horses. Feed crops, potatoes, vegetables are grown; also some fruit in hothouses. Fishing is chief occupation; cod and herring constitute greatest part of catch and main export. Several factories process, freeze, and can fish. There are cod-liver-oil refineries. Only about ¼ of Iceland is habitable, and all the towns and larger villages are on W, N, and E coasts; S coast is very sparsely populated. Cities are Reykjavik, Akureyri, Hafnarfjordur, Vestmannaeyjar, Siglufjordur, Isafjordur, Akranes, Neskaupstadur, Saudarkrokur, Olafsfjordur, and Seydisfjordur. These cities are independent of Iceland's 18 counties (Icelandic *sýslur*). Climate is generally mild and humid and the S coast, washed by the North Atlantic Drift, is ice-free. At Reykjavik average annual temp. ranges from 30°F. (Jan.) to 52°F. (July); mean annual rainfall 34 inches. Some ports on N coast are blocked by ice floes in late winter and early spring. Iceland may have been the anc. THULE. Before 9th cent. A.D. it was visited by Irish monks, who abandoned it on arrival (c.850–870) of Norse settlers; 874 is generally accepted as date of 1st permanent settlement. The Althing (a general assembly) was established (930) at Thingvellir; Christianity introduced 1000. In mid-13th cent. Iceland entered into union with Norway; passed (1380) to Denmark. Most of pop. was wiped out (1402–04) by the plague. In mid-16th cent. Lutheranism was forcibly introduced; Catholic bishopric of Skalholt abolished 1550. In 17th and 18th cent. country suffered from great devastation caused by volcanic eruptions, notably that of 1783; at about the same time British, Spanish, Algerian, and Turkish privateers raided its ports and ruined its trade. The Althing, abolished 1798, was reestablished in 1843. Restrictions on foreign trade were lifted, 1854. Denmark granted (1874) home rule to Iceland, which became (1918) a sovereign state, in personal union with Denmark, whose king was also king of Iceland. With German occupation (1940) of Denmark a regent was appointed in Iceland; at the same time the British sent a force to defend the isl.; U.S. forces replaced (1941) the British and established military and air bases, of which Keflavik (Meeks Field) was the most important. After referendum (1944) the union with Denmark was ended and the republic proclaimed, June 17. Iceland joined the United Nations in 1946.

Icemorelee (ĭs'môr″lē), town (1940 pop. 527), Union co., S N.C., just NW of Monroe.

Ice Mountain, W.Va.: see ROMNEY.

Ichalkaranji (ĭchŭlkŭr'ŭnjē), town (pop. 18,573), Kolhapur dist., S Bombay, India, 16 mi. E of Kolhapur; trade center for millet, sugar cane, tobacco, cotton, wheat; cotton milling, hand-loom weaving (noted for its saris); engineering workshop. Annual fair.

Ichamati River, E Pakistan: see JAMUNA RIVER.

Ichang. 1 (yē'jäng') Town, ⊙ Ichang co. (pop. 192,779), S Hunan prov., China, near Kwangtung line, on Hankow-Canton RR and 55 mi. NW of Kükong; rice, wheat, beans, corn. Coal, tin, tungsten, and arsenic found near by. **2** or **I-ch'ang** (ē'chäng', yē'chäng'), town (pop. 80,979), ⊙ Ichang co. (pop. 368,123), SW central Hupeh prov., China, port on left bank of Yangtze R., at E end of the Yangtze gorges, and 65 mi. WNW of Kiangling; terminus of navigation for ocean-going steamers from Shanghai, and transshipment point for river steamers to Chungking; airport. Rice, tea, beans, cotton. Iron and coal deposits near by. Opened to foreign trade in 1876.

Ichapur (ĭch'äpōōr). **1** Town, Madras, India: see ICHCHAPURAM. **2** Village, 24-Parganas dist., SE West Bengal, India, on Hooghly R. and 15.5 mi. N of Calcutta city center; ordnance factory and depot. Sometimes called Ichapur-Nawabganj.

Ichawaynochaway Creek (ĭ″chŭwänŏ'chŭwä), SW Ga., rises NE of Cuthbert, flows c.65 mi. SSE, past Morgan, to Flint R. 13 mi. SW of Newton.

Ichchapuram (ĭ'chŭpōōrŭm), town (pop. 11,159), Vizagapatam dist., NE Madras, India, 110 mi. NE of Vizianagaram; saltworks (large salt pans on Bay of Bengal; E). Moslem pilgrimage center. Sometimes called Ichapur.

Ichendorf, Germany: see QUADRATH-ICHENDORF.

Icheng. 1 or **I-ch'eng** (yē'chŭng'), town (pop. 15,230), ⊙ Icheng co. (pop. 152,657), N central Hupeh prov., China, 22 mi. SSE of Siangyang and on right bank of Han R.; peas, wheat, sesame. Called Tzechung, 1944–49. **2** (yē'jŭng') Town (1935 pop. 56,632), ⊙ Icheng co. (1946 pop. 243,340), N Kiangsu prov., China, 17 mi. SW of Yangchow and on Yangtze R.; rice, wheat, beans.

I-ch'eng, Shansi prov., China: see YICHENG.

Ichenhausen (ĭ″khŭnhou'zŭn), town (pop. 3,705), Swabia, W Bavaria, Germany, on the Günz and 7 mi. S of Günzburg; textile mfg., woodworking. Chartered 1406.

Ichenheim (ĭ'khŭnhĭm), village (pop. 1,950), S Baden, Germany, 7 mi. WSW of Offenburg; tobacco industry.

Ichhawar (ĭchä'vŭr), town (pop. 3,997), W Bhopal state, India, 29 mi. SW of Bhopal; agr. (gram, wheat).

Ichiba (ēchē'bä), town (pop. 6,890), Tokushima prefecture, E Shikoku, Japan, 15 mi. W of Tokushima; rice, wheat.

Ichibusa-yama (ēchē'bōōsä-yä″mä), second highest peak (5,650 ft.) of Kyushu, Japan, in center of isl., 38 mi. WSW of Nobeoka; highest peak of Miyazaki prefecture.

Ichihazama, Japan: see ICHINOHAZAMA.

Ichijo (ēchē'jō), town (pop. 7,533), Tokushima prefecture, E Shikoku, Japan, 10 mi. WNW of Tokushima; rice-growing center. Until 1923, called Shichijo.

Ichikawa (ēchē'käwŭ), city (1940 pop. 58,060; 1947 pop. 74,522), Chiba prefecture, central Honshu, Japan, adjacent to Funabashi (E), 10 mi. E of Tokyo; mfg. (woolen goods, sake), metalworking. Sometimes spelled Itikawa.

Ichikawa-daimon (ēchē'käwä-dī″mō), town (pop. 8,831), Yamanashi prefecture, central Honshu, Japan, 8 mi. SSE of Kofu; paper milling, rice growing.

Ichiki (ēchē'kē) or **Ichiku** (ēchē'kōō), town (pop. 10,803), Kagoshima prefecture, S Kyushu, Japan, on NW Satsuma Peninsula, 17 mi. WNW of Kagoshima; rice-producing center; sake, charcoal. Has teachers col., feudal castle. Until 1932, called Nishi-ichiki.

Ichilo, province, Bolivia: see BUENA VISTA, Santa Cruz dept.

Ichilo River (ēchē'lō), on Cochabamba–Santa Cruz dept. border, central Bolivia; rises at NE end of Cordillera de Cochabamba NNW of Comarapa; flows 170 mi. N, mostly through tropical lowlands, joining the Chaparé 80 mi. S of Trinidad to form MAMORÉ RIVER. Navigable for 110 mi. above mouth. Receives the Chimoré (left).

Ichinohazama (ēchĭnōhä'zämŭ) or **Ichihazama** (ēchĭhä'zämä), town (pop. 7,524), Miyagi prefecture, N Honshu, Japan, 12 mi. N of Furukawa; wheat, silk cocoons.

Ichinohe (ēchĭnō'ā), town (pop. 5,129), Iwate prefecture, N Honshu, Japan, 23 mi. SSW of Hachinohe; rice, silk cocoons, poultry.

Ichinomiya (ēchĭnō'mēä). **1** City (1940 pop. 70,792; 1947 pop. 62,460), Aichi prefecture, central Honshu, Japan, 13 mi. NNW of Nagoya; textile center; woolen fabrics, dyes, clothing. Bombed (1945) in Second World War. Sometimes spelled Itinomiya. **2** Town (pop. 7,013), Chiba prefecture, central Honshu, Japan, on E Chiba Peninsula, 21 mi. SE of Chiba; rice, wheat, raw silk, poultry.

Ichinomoto (ēchĭnō'mōtō), town (pop. 6,734), Nara prefecture, S Honshu, Japan, 4 mi. S of Nara; rice, wheat, raw silk. Agr. school.

Ichinoseki (ēchĭnō'sākē), town (pop. 14,431), Iwate prefecture, N Honshu, Japan, 36 mi. NNW of Ishinomaki; mfg. (textiles, chemicals), sake brewing. Sometimes spelled Itinoseki.

Ichinskaya Sopka (ēchēn'skĭŭ sôp'kŭ), extinct volcano (11,834 ft.) in central range of Kamchatka Peninsula, Russian SFSR, 185 mi. NNW of Petropavlovsk.

Ichise, Japan: see URAYASU, Tottori prefecture.

Ichki or **Ichki-Grammatikovo,** Russian SFSR: see SOVETSKI, Crimea.

Ichnya (ēch'nyŭ), town (1926 pop. 11,983), SE Chernigov oblast, Ukrainian SSR, 24 mi. SE of Nezhin; distilling, flour milling; leather products.

Ichoa River, Bolivia: see ISIBORO RIVER.

Ichoca (ēchō'kä), town (pop. c.4,200), La Paz dept., W Bolivia, at SE end of Cordillera de Tres Cruces, 18 mi. S of Inquisivi; alt. 11,811 ft.; grain, potatoes, *oca*.

Ichon (ē'chŭn'), Jap. *Risen*, town (1949 pop. 14,500), Kyonggi prov., central Korea, S of 38°N, 32 mi. SE of Seoul; soybeans, tobacco, hemp, cotton.

Ichow. 1 Town, Hopeh prov., China: see YIHSIEN. **2** Town, Liaosi prov., Manchuria, China: see IHSIEN. **3** Town, Shantung prov., China: see LINI.

Ichtegem (ĭkh'tŭ-khŭm), town (pop. 5,317), West Flanders prov., NW Belgium, 13 mi. SW of Bruges; agr. market (grain, stock). Partly-Romanesque church. Center of pottery industry in Middle Ages.

Ichtiman, Bulgaria: see IKHTIMAN.

I-ch'uan, China: see ICHWAN.

Ichun or **I-ch'un** (yē'chōōn'), town (pop. 19,455), ⊙ Ichun co. (pop. 262,694), W Kiangsi prov., China, 110 mi. SW of Nanchang and on Yüan R.; mfg. (ramie cloth, tea oil, bamboo paper). Coal and gold mines. Until 1912, Yüanchow.

Ichün (yē'jün'), town, ⊙ Ichün co. (pop. 40,278), central Shensi prov., China, 80 mi. N of Sian, in mtn. region; wheat, millet, beans.

Ichuña (ēchōō'nyä), town (pop. 167), Moquegua dept., S Peru, in Cordillera Occidental, on affluent of Tambo R. and 60 mi. NE of Moquegua; grain, stock.

Ichwan or **I-ch'uan** (both: yē'chwän'). **1** Town, ⊙ Ichwan co. (pop. 232,261), NW Honan prov., China, 13 mi. SW of Loyang; wheat, millet, beans. Until 1933 called Nantitien. **2** Town, ⊙ Ichwan co. (pop. 33,446), E Shensi prov., China, 50 mi. SE of Yenan; millet, wheat, beans. Oil deposits near by.

Ickenham, England: see UXBRIDGE.

Icklesham (ĭ'kŭl-shŭm), agr. village and parish (pop. 1,583), E Sussex, England, 6 mi. NE of Hastings. Has Norman church.

Icknield Street (ĭk'nēld), Saxon name for anc. road in Britain, used by Romans, crossing Berkshire hills and Chilterns.

Icla (ē'klä), town (pop. c.3,420), Chuquisaca dept., S central Bolivia, 14 mi. SE of Tarabuco; corn, vegetables, fruit.

Icó (ēkô'), city (pop. 3,044), SW Ceará, Brazil, near Jaguaribe R., 32 mi. E of Iguatu; irrigated agr. (cotton, sugar); cattle raising.

Icod (ēkōdh'), city (pop. 4,010), Tenerife, Canary Isls., near Atlantic coast, served by adjoining port of Puerto de San Marcos or Calela de San Marcos (pop. 106), 30 mi. WSW of Santa Cruz de Tenerife. Agr. center (bananas, tomatoes, grapes, potatoes, cattle). Flour milling, mfg. of embroidery and chocolate. Also a resort with benign climate. Has a tree over 3,000 years old.

Icolmkill, Scotland: see IONA.

Iconha (ēkō'nyŭ), city (pop. 671), S Espírito Santo, Brazil, 22 mi. NE of Cachoeiro de Itapemirim; coffee; monazitic-sand quarries.

Iconium, Turkey: see KONYA, city.

Iconoclast Mountain (10,630 ft.), SE B.C., in Selkirk Mts., on E edge of Hamber Provincial Park, 35 mi. NE of Revelstoke; 51°27'N 117°45'W.

Icononzo (ēkōnōn'sō), town (pop. 1,516), Tolima dept., W central Colombia, on W slopes of Cordillera Oriental, 40 mi. SW of Bogotá; alt. 4,338 ft. Coffeegrowing center; sugar cane, corn, bananas, yucca, vegetables, cattle. A notable natural bridge, with hieroglyphic inscriptions, is near by.

Icoraci (ēkōōrŭsē'), town (pop. 8,082), E Pará, Brazil, landing on right bank of Pará R. (Amazon delta) and 10 mi. N of Belém; terminus of branch railroad. Resort. Until 1944, Pinheiro.

Icoya (ēkoi'ä), village (pop. c.2,500), Cochabamba dept., W central Bolivia, in Cordillera de Cochabamba, 45 mi. W of Cochabamba; barley, potatoes. Tungsten deposits at Kami are just NW.

Icpic, Alaska: see IKPEK.

Icy Bay (12 mi. long, 8 mi. wide), SE Alaska, at head of the Panhandle, on Gulf of Alaska, 70 mi. WNW of Yakutat; 59°55'N 141°33'W; receives Guyot and Malaspina glaciers.

Icy Cape. 1 In S Alaska, on Gulf of Alaska at W entrance to Icy Bay, 75 mi. WNW of Yakutat; 59°55'N 141°38'W. **2** In NW Alaska, on Chukchi Sea, at W edge of naval oil reserve; 70°20'N 161°50'W. Akeonik settlement here.

Icy Strait, SE Alaska, bet. Chichagof Isl. and the mainland, extends 40 mi. NW from Chatham Strait (58°7'N 135°W) to Glacier Bay (58°22'N 136°W) and Cross Sound.

Ida, Japan: see TAGAWA.

Ida, county (□ 431; pop. 10,697), W Iowa; ⊙ Ida Grove. Prairie agr. area (cattle, hogs, poultry, corn, oats, barley) drained by Maple and Soldier rivers; sand and gravel pits (N), bituminous-coal deposits (S). Formed 1851.

Ida, village (1940 pop. 500), Monroe co., extreme SE Mich., 9 mi. W of Monroe, in farm area.

Ida, Lake, Douglas co., W Minn., just S of L. Miltona, 5 mi. N of Alexandria; 5 mi. long, 2 mi. wide. Fishing resorts.

Ida, Mount, Asia Minor: see IDA MOUNTAINS.

Ida, Mount (10,472 ft.), E B.C., in Rocky Mts., 100 mi. E of Prince George; 54°3'N 120°20'W.

Ida, Mount (ī'dŭ), Gr. *Ide* or *Idhi* (both: ē'dhē), highest peak (8,058 ft.) of Crete, near its center, 23 mi. SW of Candia. A grotto on its slope is commonly identified with the cave where Zeus was raised, according to a Cretan myth. Also called Psiloriti.

Idabel (ī'dŭbĕl), city (pop. 4,671), ⊙ McCurtain co., extreme SE Okla., c.40 mi. E of Hugo, in farming and lumbering region; saw- and gristmills, cotton gins, ironworks; mfg. of concrete blocks. Inc. 1906.

Ida Grove, city (pop. 2,202), ⊙ Ida co., W Iowa, on Maple R. and c.50 mi. ESE of Sioux City, in livestock and grain area. Settled 1856, inc. 1887.

Idah (ēdä'), town (pop. 4,824), Kabba prov., Northern Provinces, S central Nigeria, on Niger R. and 50 mi. S of Lokoja; agr. trade center; shea-nut processing, cotton weaving; palm oil and kernels, durra, corn, plantains, yams. Limestone deposits. A Br. commercial station in 19th cent.

Idaho (ī'dŭhō), state (land □ 82,808; with inland waters □ 83,557; 1950 pop. 588,637; 1940 pop. 524,873), NW U.S., bordered W by Oregon and Wash., N by British Columbia, E by Mont. and Wyo., S by Utah and Nev.; 12th in area, 43d in pop.; admitted 1890 as 43d state; ⊙ Boise. The southern, rectangular part (310 mi. E–W, 175 mi. N–S) of Idaho stands on the 42d parallel and has a long panhandle extending N to the 49th parallel (Canadian border), where it is only 45 mi. wide; the over-all length of the state is 480 mi. The "Gem State" is almost wholly mountainous, with the main ranges of the Rockies running NNW–SSE along the Mont. line. In the S, however, is the wide valley of the SNAKE RIVER which enters from Wyo., traverses the S part of the state in a sweeping arc, and forms part of the W boundary, where it has cut the deepest gorge (4,000–7,500 ft.) in the U.S.; the Snake R. Plain lies in the Columbia Plateau region. In the N are the S Selkirk Mts.—separating Priest L. and PEND OREILLE LAKE—the COEUR D'ALENE MOUNTAINS, and Coeur d'Alene L. The Clearwater Mts. (8–9,000 ft.) and the Salmon River Mts. (8–10,000 ft.), large mtn. masses, almost uninhabited, in the center of the state form a barrier bet. the N and S parts of Idaho. In the W, overlooking the Snake R. canyon, are the Seven Devils Mts., while along the Mont. boundary is the BITTERROOT RANGE, rising to peaks of 9–10,000 ft. Bordering the Snake R. Plain on the N are the Sawtooth Mts., Pioneer Mts., Lost R. Range (with Borah Peak, 12,655 ft., highest point in Idaho), and Lemhi Range; SE of the Snake valley are outliers of the Teton and Wasatch ranges. The Snake R. Plain (c.350 mi. long, 30–50 mi. wide) is a region of lava beds, strange volcanic formations (such as those in CRATERS OF THE MOON NATIONAL MONUMENT), sand dunes, and irrigated farm land; it merges in the S and SW with the desert-like Great Basin sections of Utah and Nev. The chief affluents in Idaho of the Columbia-Snake river system are the Salmon, Payette, St. Joe, and Pend Oreille. The climate of Idaho is mainly of the dry continental type, with cold winters and hot summers; annual rainfall is 8–20 in., and the winter snowfall in the mts. is 40–100 in. Boise has a mean temp. of 74°F. in July and 29°F. in Jan. Agr. is confined to the Snake R. Plain and the Palouse R. basin (NW), which comprises the E edge of the INLAND EMPIRE.

The crop season varies (E–W) from 120 to 200 days. There are over 40,000 farms in Idaho with an average acreage of 300. The principal crops are wheat, potatoes, alfalfa, dry beans, sugar beets, hay, apples, barley, prunes, and oats. Irrigation is important; the major projects include the AMERICAN FALLS DAM, MINIDOKA DAM, and the Arrowrock and Anderson Ranch dams. Dry farming is also practiced, especially in the Palouse basin where wheat is extensively grown. Potatoes are an Idaho specialty and are cultivated chiefly in the upper Snake valley. Fruit orchards are found in the mtn. valleys N of Boise, near Twin Falls, and at other places along the Snake. There is some dairying, and in the drier areas cattle and sheep are raised; the state is a leading producer of cheese, butter, and wool. Idaho's valuable timber resources include western white pine, yellow pine, Douglas fir, lodgepole pine, white fir, and Engelmann spruce, much of which is inaccessible. Public lands comprise 64% of the state's area, some 21,000,000 acres lying in 19 natl. forests. Most of the lumber mills are in the N half of the panhandle and in the mtn. valleys N of Boise. Idaho is rich in minerals and ranks high in the production of lead, silver, zinc, copper, and gold, with many deposits still undeveloped. The main mining dist. is Shoshone co. (lead, silver) in the Coeur d'Alene Mts. near KELLOGG (smelters) and Wallace. Other minerals include extensive phosphate rock deposits (SE), building stone, clay, antimony, manganese, cobalt (at Forney), mercury, and tungsten. Beet-sugar refining, flour milling, vegetable and fruit canning, and meat packing are the main industries in the Snake valley towns of BOISE (largest in Idaho), POCATELLO, IDAHO FALLS, NAMPA, TWIN FALLS, and CALDWELL, and in the N the processing of lumber and agr. products is centered in LEWISTON, COEUR D'ALENE, and Moscow. At Arco an atomic energy processing plant was begun in 1949. Idaho's natural setting has given it a wealth of scenic attractions and resort areas, chief among which are Craters of the Moon Natl. Monument, SUN VALLEY on the W slope of the Pioneer Mts., the beautiful N lakes of Pend Oreille, Coeur d'Alene, and Priest, the vast mtn. areas with their hunting, fishing, and skiing, the SHOSHONE FALLS on the Snake, and the many natl. forests and state parks; a small section of Yellowstone Natl. Park is in E Idaho. The Univ. of Idaho (at Moscow) and Idaho State Col. (at Pocatello) are the leading educational institutions. The 1st white exploration of the region was by Lewis and Clark (1805), who descended the Clearwater and lower Snake rivers on their way to the Pacific. They were followed by Br. and American fur traders, and a few trading posts were established, including Fort Hall (1834). The area was part of the Oregon country and the famous Oregon Trail followed most of the Snake R. valley. The whole of Idaho came under American jurisdiction in 1846; it was partly in Washington territory, partly in Oregon territory 1853–59; entirely in Washington territory 1859–63. Organized as a separate territory in 1863, it included Mont. (until 1864) and most of Wyo. (until 1868); Boise became the capital in 1864. The 1st permanent settlement was founded (1860) by the Mormons at Franklin (SE), and thousands of other settlers arrived with the discovery of gold at Orofino in the same year and at several other places soon afterwards. In the next few years towns grew up, sheep and cattle ranching and irrigated agr. were begun, and several Indian wars were fought. The late 19th cent. saw the booms brought about by the discovery of rich silver and lead mines and the coming of the railroads. The physical and economic differences bet. N and S Idaho, accentuated by the central mtn. barrier and the poor N–S communications, have produced a strong intrastate sectionalism. The panhandle, with its predominantly mining and lumbering economy, is oriented toward Wash. and Mont.; Boise is the regional center of the SW part of the state; and the large Mormon pop. in the SE has close contacts with Salt Lake City, Utah. Moreover, N Idaho is in the Pacific Time Zone while S Idaho is in the Mtn. Time Zone. However, all attempts to change the state's boundaries along geographical lines have failed. For further information see articles on the cities, towns, and physical features, and the 44 counties: ADA, ADAMS, BANNOCK, BEAR LAKE, BENEWAH, BINGHAM, BLAINE, BOISE, BONNER, BONNEVILLE, BOUNDARY, BUTTE, CAMAS, CANYON, CARIBOU, CASSIA, CLARK, CLEARWATER, CUSTER, ELMORE, FRANKLIN, FREMONT, GEM, GOODING, IDAHO, JEFFERSON, JEROME, KOOTENAI, LATAH, LEMHI, LEWIS, LINCOLN, MADISON, MINIDOKA, NEZ PERCE, ONEIDA, OWYHEE, PAYETTE, POWER, SHOSHONE, TETON, TWIN FALLS, VALLEY, WASHINGTON.

Idaho, county (□ 8,515; pop. 11,423), central Idaho; ⊙ Grangeville. Agr. and mining area bounded E by Bitterroot Range and Mont., W by Grand Canyon of the Snake R. and Oregon; drained by Clearwater and Salmon rivers. Wheat, livestock; copper, gold, silver, lead. Includes Nezperce Natl. Forest and part of Salmon R. primitive area. Seven Devils Mts. are in W, Salmon River Mts. in SE, and Clearwater Mts. in NE. Formed 1861.

Idaho City, village (pop. 246), ⊙ Boise co., SW Idaho, on small affluent of Boise R. and 24 mi. NE of Boise, in mtn. area; alt. 4,200 ft.; lumber milling, placer mining for gold. Important gold-mining center in 1860s (estimated pop. 30,000).

Idaho Falls, city (pop. 19,218), ⊙ Bonneville co., SE Idaho, on left bank of Snake R. and 45 mi. NNE of Pocatello; alt. 4,709 ft. Shipping center for irrigated agr. area (sugar beets, potatoes, wheat, seed peas, alfalfa, livestock); food processing (beet sugar, flour, dairy products, beverages), metalworking, lumbering. Silver, lead, gold mines near by. U.S. atomic-reactor testing station is 30 mi. W, on Snake R. Plain. Has large, municipally owned hydroelectric plant. The Latter-Day Saints Temple was opened 1945. Early settlement here (established in 1860s) was 1st known as Taylor's Bridge, after 1872 as Eagle Rock. Chartered as city 1890–91 and named Idaho Falls.

Idaho Springs, city (pop. 1,769), Clear Creek co., N central Colo., on Clear Creek, in Front Range, and 26 mi. W of Denver; alt. 7,500 ft. Trade center, resort with hot mineral springs. Gold, silver, lead, and copper mines in vicinity. Newhouse, or Argo, Tunnel extends from point on Clear Creek c.4 mi. N to Central City; used to drain mines and transport ore. Near by are site of 1st important gold strike (1859) in Colo. and Edgar mine, operated by Colo. School of Mines for instruction of students. Settled 1859–60, inc. 1885.

Idahue (ēdä'wā), town (pop. 1,312), O'Higgins prov., central Chile, on Cachapoal R. and 25 mi. SW of Rancagua; agr. center (wheat, alfalfa, potatoes, beans, fruit, livestock); flour milling, dairying.

Idako, Japan: see ITAKO.

Idalium (īdā'lēŭm), anc. city in S central Cyprus near site of present-day village of DHALI or Dali, 15 mi. NW of Larnaca. It had a temple devoted to Aphrodite of Apollo. An inscription found here in 19th cent. gave key to Cypriote language. Idalium is believed to have been center of a kingdom which in 6th or 7th cent. B.C. became part of Citium.

Idalou (īdŭlōō'), town (pop. 1,014), Lubbock co., NW Texas, on the Llano Estacado, 11 mi. NE of Lubbock.

Ida Mountains or **Mount Ida** (ī'dŭ), Turkish *Kaz Dağı* (käz' däŭ"), range in NW Turkey just NW of Edremit (Adramyttium), S of Kucuk Menderes (Scamander) R.; the site of anc. Troy was NW, on the Aegean. From its highest peak (5,797 ft.), Mt. Gargarus, Turkish *Kaz Dağı*, is a fine view of the Sea of Marmara and the Aegean. The mountain was dedicated in anc. times to the worship of Cybele, who was therefore sometimes called Idae Mater.

Idanha (īdă'nŭ), town (pop. 442), Marion co., NW Oregon, on North Santiam R. and c.50 mi. ESE of Salem.

Idanha-a-Nova (ēdä'nyä-nô'vŭ), town (pop. 5,069), Castelo Branco dist., central Portugal, 16 mi. ENE of Castelo Branco; agr. trade center (wheat, corn, beans, olives, wine, livestock). Has remains of medieval fortifications.

Idanre (ēdän'rē), town, Ondo prov., Western Provinces, S Nigeria, 18 mi. E of Ondo; cacao, palm oil and kernels, timber, rubber, cotton.

Idappadi or **Edappadi** (both: ĕd'ŭp-pŭdē), town (pop. 18,046), Salem dist., S central Madras, India, on branch of Cauvery R. and 24 mi. WSW of Salem; trade center in tobacco area; castor- and peanut-oil extraction. Limestone, saltpeter, and mica workings near by.

Idar (ĭd'ŭr), former princely state (□ 1,668; pop. 307,798) in Rajputana States, India; ⊙ was Himatnagar. Rulers were Rajputs. In Western India States agency from 1924 to early 1940s, when transferred to Rajputana States; since 1949, inc. into Sabar Kantha and Mehsana dists. of Bombay.

Idar, town (pop. 6,550), Sabar Kantha dist., N Bombay, India, 17 mi. N of Himatnagar; market center for grain, oilseeds, sugar cane; pottery and wooden-toy mfg.; distillery.

Idar-Oberstein (ē'där-ō'bŭr-shtīn), town (pop. 22,754), in former Prussian Rhine Prov., W Germany, after 1945 in Rhineland-Palatinate, 30 mi. E of Trier; 49°43'N 7°19'E. A center of Ger. precious- and semiprecious-stone polishing industry; jewelry mfg., metalworking. Has 2 ruined castles. Research institute for precious stones. Town formed 1933 through incorporation of Idar, Oberstein (both chartered 1865), Algenrodt, and Tiefenstein. In BIRKENSTEIN principality of Oldenburg until 1937.

Idawgaw, Nigeria: see IDOGO.

Idback, Sweden: see HOLE.

Idd, canton, Norway: see KORNSJO.

Idde Fjord, Norway: see HALDEN.

Iddo (ē'dō), town (pop. 640) in Lagos township, Nigeria colony, on Iddo Isl. (1 mi. long, ½ mi. wide) in Lagos Lagoon, bet. Lagos Isl. (connected by Carter Bridge) and mainland; rail terminus; linked with Ebute Metta (on mainland) by rail and road causeway. Sawmilling.

Ide, Mount, Crete: see IDA, MOUNT.

Ideal, town (pop. 318), Macon co., central Ga., 9 mi. NW of Oglethorpe, in farm area; clothes mfg.

Idel or **Idel'** (ēdyĕl'), town (1939 pop. over 500), E Karelo-Finnish SSR, on Murmansk RR and 28 mi. SSW of Belomorsk; sawmilling.

Ideles (ēdlĕs'), oasis, Saharan Oases territory, S Algeria, on N slope of Ahaggar Mts., 80 mi. N of Tamanrasset; 23°49'N 5°58'E.

Idenburg, Mount, Netherlands New Guinea: see NASSAU RANGE.

Idenburg River (ī'dŭnbûrg), chief tributary of Mamberamo R., W New Guinea, in Du. section of isl., rises in NE slopes of Orange Range, flows c.230 mi. generally NW to junction (c.160 mi. WSW of Hollandia, in marshy area) with Rouffaer R. to form the Mamberamo. Sometimes called Taritalu.

Idensalmi, Finland: see IISALMI.

Ider, river, Mongolia: see IDER RIVER.

Ider River (ē'dĕr), Mongolian *Iderin Gol* or *Ideriin Gol* (ē'dĕrēn gōl'), right headstream of Selenga R., in NW Mongolian People's Republic; rises in the Khangai Mts. 50 mi. ENE of Uliassutai, flows 281 mi. ENE, joining the river Muren to form the Selenga 35 mi. SE of Muren town. Sometimes spelled Eder.

Idfa (ĭd'fă), village (pop. 9,941), Girga prov., central Upper Egypt, 4 mi. NW of Sohag; cotton, cereals, dates, sugar. Sometimes Edfa.

Idfina or **Edfina** (ĭdfē'nă), village (pop. 4,816), Beheira prov., Lower Egypt, on Rosetta branch of the Nile and 9 mi. SE of Rosetta; cotton, rice, cereals.

Idfu (ĭd'fōō) or **Edfu** (ĕd'fōō), anc. *Apollonopolis Magna*, town (pop. 18,404), Aswan prov., S Egypt, on W bank of Nile R., on railroad, and 60 mi. N of Aswan; trading center (grain, cotton, dates). Site of the famous temple of Horus (built 237 B.C.–57 B.C.), begun by Ptolemy III, and one of the finest extant examples of Egyptian temple architecture.

Idhi, Mount, Crete: see IDA, MOUNT.

Idhomeni, Greece: see EIDOMENE.

Idhra, Greece: see HYDRA.

Idice River (ē'dēchĕ), N central Italy, rises in Etruscan Apennines 6 mi. NNW of Firenzuola, flows 45 mi. N and E to Reno R. 2 mi. S of Argenta. Receives Savena R. (left). Canalized in lower course; used for irrigation.

Idil (ĭdĭl'), Turkish *Idil*, village (pop. 1,344), Mardin prov., SE Turkey, 65 mi. E of Mardin; cereals, lentils. Also called Hazak.

Idiofa (ēdyō'fä), village, Leopoldville prov., SW Belgian Congo, 50 mi. ENE of Kikwit; native trade (palm products, fibers). Jesuit mission.

Idisat, El, Egypt: see ARMANT.

Iditarod (īdĭ'tŭräd), village (1939 pop. 1), W Alaska, on Iditarod R. and 9 mi. NNW of Flat; placer gold mining. Scene (1908) of gold rush.

Iditarod River, W Alaska, rises N of Russian Mission, near 61°47'N 159°W, flows 150 mi. in an arc NE, N, and finally W, to Innoko R. at 63°2'N 158°45'W. Placer gold mining in valley.

Idjil, Fr. West Africa: see FORT GOURAUD.

Idjwi Island (ēj'wē) (□ c.96), E Belgian Congo, in L. Kivu; 25 mi. long, 5–8 mi. wide. Mountainous; forests (N), banana groves (S). Sometimes called Kwidjwi.

Idkerberget (ĭt'kûrbĕr"yŭt), village (pop. 660), Kopparberg co., central Sweden, in Bergslag region, 10 mi. SW of Borlange; iron mining.

Idku (ĭd'kōō) or **Edku** (ĕd'kōō), town (pop. 27,321; with suburbs, 30,136), Beheira prov., Lower Egypt, on N shore of L. Idku, 26 mi. ENE of Alexandria; rice milling, silk weaving, fisheries.

Idku, Lake, or **Lake Edku**, salt lake (□ 57, not including marshes), Lower Egypt, 14 mi. E of Alexandria; 15 mi. long, 3 mi. wide; fisheries. Separated from Abukir Bay (N) by narrow sandbank and connected with the bay by short canal El Ma'adiya, said to be old Canopic branch of the Nile.

Idle, England: see BRADFORD.

Idlewild Airport, N.Y.: see NEW YORK INTERNATIONAL AIRPORT.

Idlewilde, village (pop. 1,387, with near-by Parrish Court), Alleghany co., W Va., near Covington.

Idlib (ĭd'lĭb), town, Aleppo prov., NW Syria, 36 mi. SSW of Aleppo; cotton, olives, cereals, tobacco.

Idmiston, agr. village and parish (pop. 1,140), SE Wiltshire, England, 6 mi. NE of Salisbury. Has 14th-15th-cent. church.

Idogo or **Idawgaw** (ēdō'gō), Abeokuta prov., Western Provinces, SW Nigeria, 8 mi. WSW of Ilaro; rail spur terminus; cotton weaving, indigo dyeing; cacao, palm oil and kernels. Phosphate deposits.

Idomeni, Greece: see EIDOMENE.

Idra, Greece: see HYDRA.

Idrija (ē'drēä), Ital. *Idria* (ē'drēä), village (pop. 5,148), W Slovenia, Yugoslavia, 23 mi. W of Ljubljana; major mercury-mining center; lace making. Until 1947, in Italy.

Idrinskoye (ēdrēn'skŭyŭ), village (1926 pop. 2,990), SW Krasnoyarsk Territory, Russian SFSR, 45 mi. NNE of Minusinsk; dairy farming.

Idris Dag (ĭdrĭs' dä), Turkish *Idris Dağ*, peak (6,512 ft.), central Turkey, 24 mi. ENE of Ankara.

Idritsa (ē'drētsŭ), town (1948 pop. over 10,000), SW Velikiye Luki oblast, Russian SFSR, 60 mi. W of Velikiye Luki; rail junction; metalworking, hemp retting.

Idro (ē'drô), commune (pop. 1,128), Brescia prov., Lombardy, N Italy, on S shore of Lago d'Idro, 19 mi. NNE of Brescia. Contains Crone (commune seat; pop. 635) and several other villages. Brick, lime, wood, charcoal industries.

Idro, Lago d' (lä'gō dē'drō), or **Eridio** (ĕrē'dyō), lake (□ 4.2) in Brescia prov., Lombardy, N Italy, bet. lakes Garda (E) and Iseo (W), 18 mi. NE of Brescia; 6 mi. long, up to 1¼ mi. wide, alt. 1,207 ft., max. depth 400 ft. Traversed by Chiese R. Used for irrigation and hydroelectric power.

Idstedt (ĭt'shtĕt), village (pop. 769), in Schleswig-Holstein, NW Germany, 5 mi. N of Schleswig, in the Angeln. Scene (1850) of decisive victory of Danes over Schleswig-Holsteiners.

Idstein (ĭt'shtīn), town (pop. 5,771), in former Prussian prov. of Hesse-Nassau, W Germany, after 1945 in Hesse, in the Taunus, 9 mi. NNE of Wiesbaden; leather mfg. Has 15th-cent. castle.

Idua Oron, Nigeria: see ORON.

Idumania, England: see BLACKWATER RIVER.

Idumea, Palestine: see EDOM.

Idutywa (ĭdōō'tĭwù), village (pop. 737), E Cape Prov., U. of So. Afr., 45 mi. SW of Umtata; center of Idutywa Reserve (□ 448; pop. 37,381; native pop. 36,851) of Transkei dist. of the Transkeian Territories; stock, dairying, grain.

'Idwa, El, Egypt: see EDWA, EL.

Idyllwild, Calif.: see SAN JACINTO MOUNTAINS.

Idylside, village (pop. 1,172), Will co., NE Ill.

Idzhevan (ējĭvän'), town (1926 pop. 2,261), NE Armenian SSR, 20 mi. SW of Akstafa (Azerbaijan); lumber milling, rug mfg. Lithographic-stone quarries near by. Formerly Karavansarai.

Idzu, Japan: see IZU.

Idzuhara, Japan: see IZUHARA.

Idzumi, Japan: see IZUMI, province.

Idzumo, Japan: see IZUMO, province.

Ie-jima (ē-ä'jĭmä), volcanic island (□ 9; 1950 pop. 6,530) of Okinawa Isls., in the Ryukyus, in East China Sea, just off W coast of Okinawa; 5.5 mi. long, 2.5 mi. wide; surrounded by coral reef. Produces raw sugar. Airfield. Part of battle of Okinawa fought here in Second World War. Ernie Pyle's grave is here.

Ieki (ē-ä'kē), town (pop. 3,789), Mie prefecture, S Honshu, Japan, 13 mi. SW of Tsu; rice, raw silk, lumber.

Ielsi (yĕl'sē), town (pop. 3,340), Campobasso prov., Abruzzi e Molise, S central Italy, 8 mi. ESE of Campobasso. Formerly also Jelsi.

Iepê (yĭpā'), city (pop. 1,061), W São Paulo, Brazil, near Paranapanema R., 45 mi. SE of Presidente Prudente; coffee, cotton, grain.

Ieper, Belgium: see YPRES.

Ierapetra, Crete: see HIERAPETRA.

Ierhkoszetang, China: see IRKESHTAM, USSR.

Ierissos, Greece: see HIERISSOS.

Iernut (yĕr'nōōts), Rum. *Iernuț*, Hung. *Radnót* (rŏd'nōt), village (pop. 2,458), Mures prov., central Rumania, on Mures R., on railroad and 27 mi. NE of Blaj; agr. center; flour milling, reed weaving.

Ierseke, Netherlands: see YERSEKE.

Ierzu (yĕr'tsōō), village (pop. 3,963), Nuoro prov., E central Sardinia, 45 mi. NE of Cagliari; wine, fruit; lignite deposits. Has grotto, nuraghi. Formerly spelled Jerzu.

Iesi (yā'zē), anc. *Aesis*, town (pop. 18,008), Ancona prov., The Marches, central Italy, near Esino R., 15 mi. SW of Ancona. Silk, woolen, and paper mills, foundry; mfg. of agr. machinery, furniture, macaroni, soap, matches, liquor. Bishopric. Has cathedral, early Renaissance palace, remains of 14th-cent. town walls. Emperor Frederick II b. here. Formerly also Jesi.

Iesolo (yā'sôlô), village (pop. 1,171), Venezia prov., Veneto, N Italy, on N shore of Lagoon of Venice, 16 mi. NE of Venice; sea bathing resort. Has ruined Romanesque church (11th cent.). Called Cavazuccherina until c. 1930.

Iet (yĕt), village, in the Upper Juba, on Ethiopia–Ital. Somaliland border, 70 mi. ENE of Dolo, in durra-growing region; water hole. Also spelled Yet.

If (ēf), rocky islet off S coast of France, 2 mi. SW of harbor of Marseilles, Bouches-du-Rhône dept. Chateau d'If, a castle built here 1524 by Francis I, was long used as state prison and has been made famous by Alexandre Dumas's *The Count of Monte Cristo.*

Ifach, rock, Spain: see CALPE.

Ifag (ēfäg'), town, Begemdir prov., NW Ethiopia, near E shore of L. Tana, on road and 45 mi. SSE of Gondar, in agr. (cereals, grapes) and cattle-raising region; road junction; coffee market.

Ifakara (ēfäkä'rä), town, Eastern Prov., Tanganyika, on road and 90 mi. SSW of Kilosa, in Kilombero (kĕlōmbĕ'rō) Valley (c.70 mi. long); cotton center; livestock.

Ifalik (ē'fälĕk), atoll (□ c.1; pop. 214), Yap dist., W Caroline Isls., W Pacific, 40 mi. SE of Woleai; 2 mi. long, 1.6 mi. wide; 5 wooded islets on reef.

Ifanadiana (ēfänädyä'nù), town, Fianarantsoa prov., E Madagascar, on highway and 40 mi. NE of Fianarantsoa; trading center; coffee plantations. Gold and iron mined near by.

Ife (ē'fā), town (pop. 24,170), Oyo prov., Western Provinces, SW Nigeria, 45 mi. ENE of Ibadan; gold-mining center; cotton weaving, cacao industry, processing of palm oil and kernels. Seat of the Oni, spiritual leader of Yoruba tribe.

Ifeng (yē'fŭng'), town (pop. 9,923), ⊙ Ifeng co. (pop. 88,031), NW Kiangsi prov., China, 70 mi. WSW of Nanchang; rice, wheat; ramie weaving. Until 1914 called Sinchang.

Iffezheim (ĭ'fŭts-hīm), village (pop. 2,225), S Baden, Germany, 3.5 mi. SW of Rastatt; lumber milling.

Iffley, England: see OXFORD.

Ifield (ī'fēld), town and parish (pop. 4,680), N Sussex, England, 6 mi. NE of Horsham; agr. market. Has 13th-cent. church.

Ifigguig, Djebel (jĕ'bĕl ēfēg-gēg'), southwesternmost high peak (11,663 ft.) of the High Atlas, SW Fr. Morocco, overlooking the Sous lowland (S), 20 mi. N of Taroudant; 30°46'N 8°53'W.

Ifni (ĭf'nē, ēf'nē), territory (□ c.675; pop. 45,852), a Spanish enclave on SW coast of Fr. Morocco, politically part of Sp. West Africa; ⊙ Sidi Ifni. Shaped like a rectangle, 35 mi. long, 15 mi. wide. Reached by southwesternmost spurs of the Anti-Atlas range at edge of Sahara Desert. Arid climate permits only scattered subsistence agr. (barley) and nomadic stock raising (sheep, goats, camels, horses). Some irrigated patches grow alfalfa, corn, tomatoes. Argan trees yield olive-like oil. Territory is inhabited by the Ait Ba Amarán, a Berber tribe. Its only town, **Sidi Ifni** (pop. 905; urban dist. pop. 7,651, including 1,500 Europeans), is ⊙ SPANISH WEST AFRICA. Handicraft industries (furniture, carpets, jewelry); grain milling, oil pressing. Airfield; lighthouse (29°23'N 10°11'W). Territory was awarded to Spain in 1860. Effective Sp. occupation dates from 1934.

Ifo (ē'fō), town, Abeokuta prov., Western Provinces, SW Nigeria, 12 mi. ESE of Ilaro; rail and road junction; cotton weaving, indigo dyeing; cacao, palm oil and kernels, cotton, yams, corn, cassava, plantains. Phosphate deposits.

Iforas, Adrar des (ädrär' dāzēfôrä'), highland of the Sahara, along Fr. Sudan–Algeria border, c.300 mi. NE of Timbuktu. A SW extension of the Ahaggar massif; rises over 2,000 ft.

Ifrane (ēfrän'), city (pop. 4,281), Meknès region, N central Fr. Morocco, on N spur of the Middle Atlas, 35 mi. SE of Meknès; alt. 4,400 ft. A leading summer resort and one of sultan's summer residences, situated amidst natl. forest (□ 77) of cedars and oaks. Hotels, casino, summer colonies. Airfield.

Ifugao, Philippines: see MOUNTAIN PROVINCE.

Iga (ē'gä), former province in S Honshu, Japan; now part of Mie prefecture.

Igal (ĭ'gŏl), town (pop. 2,375), Somogy co., SW Hungary, 14 mi. NNE of Kaposvar; wine.

Igaliko (ĭgä'lĭkō), settlement (pop. 137), Julianehaab dist., SW Greenland, at head of Igaliko Fjord, 25 mi. NE of Julianehaab; 60°58'N 45°24'W; sheep raising. Meteorological and radio station. The old Norse *Gardar*, it was seat (c.10th cent.) of the *Gardar Thing*, parliament of Norse Eastern Settlement; after 1126 it was see of Greenland bishopric. Region 1st settled (c.985) by Eric the Red.

Igaliko Fjord, inlet (35 mi. long, 1–3 mi. wide) of the Atlantic, SW Greenland. Near mouth is Julianehaab.

Igalula (ēgälōō'lä), village, Western Prov., W central Tanganyika, on railroad and 20 mi. SE of Tabora; beeswax; livestock.

Iganga (ēgäng'gä), town, Eastern Prov., SE Uganda, 22 mi. NE of Jinja; cotton, tobacco, coffee, bananas, corn. Missionary-teaching center.

Igaraçu (ēgùrùsōō'), city (pop. 2,013), E Pernambuco, NE Brazil, on inlet of the Atlantic, and 15 mi. NNW of Recife; sugar, coconuts. One of oldest Port. settlements (16th cent.) in Brazil, with several 16th-cent. churches, and convent of São Francisco noted for its Dutch tiles and sculpture. Formerly spelled Iguarassú.

Igara-Paraná River (ēgä'rä-päränä'), Amazonas commissary, SE Colombia, rises near 74°W near Caquetá R., flows c.250 mi. SE, through densely forested tropical lowlands, to Putumayo R. (Peru border).

Igarapava (ēgùrùpä'vù), city (pop. 4,710), NE São Paulo, Brazil, near the Rio Grande, on railroad and 22 mi. SSE of Uberaba (Minas Gerais); sugar milling, distilling (rum, alcohol), cotton and rice processing.

Igarapé Açu (ēgùrùpĕ' äsōō'), city (pop. 2,005), E Pará, Brazil, on Belém-Bragança RR and 65 mi. NE of Belém; Brazil nuts, rubber, cacao, corn.

Igarapé Miri (mērē'), city (pop. 771), E Pará, Brazil, 50 mi. SW of Belém.

Igarka (ēgär'kŭ), largest Siberian city (1939 pop. estimate c.20,000) N of Arctic Circle, in N Krasnoyarsk Territory, Russian SFSR, on Yenisei R. and 140 mi. S of Dudinka; lumber port; sawmilling center; graphite processing. Founded 1928.

Igatimí or **Ygatimí** (ēgätēmē'), town (dist. pop. 1,962), Caaguazú dept., S central Paraguay, 160 mi. NE of Asunción; maté, lumber.

Igatpuri (ĭgŭt'pōōrē), town (pop. 8,173), Nasik dist., central Bombay, India, in Western Ghats, on railroad (workshops) and 27 mi. SW of Nasik; health resort (sanitarium); millet, wheat, gur.

Igbaja (ēb-bä'jä), town (pop. 6,142), Ilorin prov., Northern Provinces, SW central Nigeria, 22 mi. ESE of Ilorin; shea-nut processing, cotton weaving; cassava, yams, corn; cattle, skins.

Igbaras (ēgbä'räs), town (1939 pop. 3,853; 1948 municipality pop. 15,968), Iloilo prov., S Panay isl., Philippines, 20 mi. W of Iloilo; rice-growing center.

Igdir (ēdĭr'), Turkish *Iğdır*, town (pop. 8,644), Kars prov., NE Turkey, bet. Mt. Ararat and Aras R., 70 mi. SE of Kars, 7 mi. from USSR border; cotton gin.

Igdlorssuit (ĭglôkhsh'wĭt), fishing and hunting settlement (pop. 161), Umanak dist., W Greenland, on E Ubekendt Isl., on Igdlorssuit Sound, 50 mi. NW of Umanak; 71°14'N 53°32'W. Radio station.

Igea (ēhā'ä), town (pop. 1,540), Logroño prov., N Spain, 16 mi. S of Calahorra; olive-oil processing; wine, fruit, vegetables, honey.

Igel (ē'gùl), village (pop. 688), in former Prussian Rhine Prov., W Germany, after 1945 in Rhineland-Palatinate, on the Mosel and 5 mi. SW of Trier, near Luxembourg line. The sandstone Igel obelisk (75 ft. high) is one of the most remarkable Roman remains N of the Alps.

Igelsta (ē'gùlstä"), village (pop. 608), Stockholm co., E Sweden, on Galo Fjord, just E of Sodertalje; sawmills.

Iggesund (ĭ'gùsünd"), village (pop. 2,943), Gavleborg co., E Sweden, on small inlet of Gulf of Bothnia, 5 mi. S of Hudiksvall; iron, steel, and sulphite works.

Igharghar, Oued (wĕd' ēgärgär'), wadi in Saharan Oases territory, central Algeria, rises on N slope of the Ahaggar Mts., flows c.800 mi. N (entirely underground) to the Oued Rhir oases near Touggourt. Some of its waters reach the Chott Merouane (arm of the Chott Melrhir).

Ighil M'Goun, Fr. Morocco: see M'GOUN, DJEBEL.

Ightham (ī'tùm), village and parish (pop. 1,589), W central Kent, England, 10 mi. W of Maidstone; stone quarrying. Has 14th-cent. moated house and Norman church. Pre-Roman earthworks near by. Just ENE is village of Borough Green; leatherworks.

Igilgili, Algeria: see DJIDJELLI.

Igis (ē'gĭs), town (pop. 2,424), Grisons canton, E Switzerland, near the Rhine, 6 mi. N of Chur; includes Landquart Dorf, hamlet.

Igiugig (ĭg'yùgĭg), village (1939 pop. 21), S Alaska, on Kvichak R., at SW end of Iliamna L., 40 mi. SW of Newhalen; fishing; supply point for sportsmen; trapping.

Iglas (ĭglăs'), village, Aligarh dist., W Uttar Pradesh, India, 11 mi. NNW of Hathras; wheat, barley, millet, gram.

Iglau, Czechoslovakia: see JIHLAVA.

Iglawa River, Czechoslovakia: see JIHLAVA RIVER.

Iglesia, department, Argentina: see RODEO.

Iglesia (ēglā'syä), town (pop. estimate 1,000), central San Juan prov., Argentina, in irrigated valley, 36 mi. WSW of Jachal; alt. 6,500 ft.; alfalfa, wheat, wine, livestock; flour milling.

Iglesias (ēglā'zyäs), town (pop. 13,860), Cagliari prov., SW Sardinia, 31 mi. WNW of Cagliari; center of SW mining dist. (Iglesiente). Lead-zinc-silver mines at near-by MONTEPONI, San Giovanni, Nebida, Masua, Malacalzetta, San Benedetto; lignite and iron; wine, olive oil, furniture; gasworks, foundry, tanneries. Bishopric. Has cathedral (built 1285–88), castle (built 1325; now a factory), 16th-cent. church of San Francesco, mining school with mineralogical mus.

Iglesuela, La (lä ēgläswā'lä), town (pop. 1,238), Toledo prov., central Spain, 18 mi. NNE of Talavera de la Reina; cereals, grapes, olives, acorns, livestock. Lumber; flour milling, olive-oil pressing.

Igli (ēglē'), Saharan outpost and oasis, Aïn-Sefra territory, W Algeria, on the Oued Saoura, 75 mi. S of Colomb-Béchar, at NW edge of the Great Western Erg; 30°28'N 2°17'W.

Iglino (ē'glĭnŭ), village (1948 pop. over 2,000), E Bashkir Autonomous SSR, Russian SFSR, on railroad and 19 mi. NE of Ufa; dairying, truck.

Iglo, Czechoslovakia: see SPISSKA NOVA VES.

Igloo, village (1939 pop. 114), NW Alaska, on Seward Peninsula, 45 mi. N of Nome; fox-farming center; supply point for gold prospectors. Also called Marys Igloo.

Igloo, S.Dak.: see EDGEMONT.

Igloolik Island (ĭglōō'lĭk) (10 mi. long, 1–7 mi. wide), SE Franklin Dist., Northwest Territories, in Foxe Basin, just off NE Melville Peninsula; 69°24'N 81°49'W. Formerly site of trading post, radio station, and R.C. mission.

Igls (ē'gùls), village, Tyrol, W Austria, at foot of the Patscherkofel (cable car), 2 mi. S of Innsbruck; summer resort; winter sports.

Ignace (ĭg'nùs), village (pop. estimate 300), W Ont., on Agimak L. (5 mi. long), 50 mi. SSE of Sioux Lookout, in gold-mining, lumbering region.

Ignacio (ĭgnä'shō), town (pop. 526), La Plata co., SW Colo., on Los Pinos R., in foothills of San Juan Mts., and 17 mi. SE of Durango; alt. 6,432 ft. Hq. of Colsolidated Ute Indian Reservation; livestock, grain, dairy and poultry products. U.S. school and hosp. for Indians here.

Ignacio Allende or **Villa Ignacio Allende** (vē'yä ēgnä'syō äyĕn'dā), town (pop. 2,201), Durango, N Mexico, on railroad and 50 mi. NE of Durango; grain, cotton, vegetables, stock.

Ignacio de la Llave (ēgnä'syō dā lä yä'vā), town (pop. 1,841), Veracruz, SE Mexico, in Sotavento lowlands, 15 mi. WSW of Alvarado; fruit, livestock. Formerly San Cristóbal de la Llave.

Ignacio Uchoa, Brazil: see UCHÔA.

Ignaluk, Alaska: see LITTLE DIOMEDE ISLAND.

Ignatovka (ĕgnä'tŭfkŭ), town (1939 pop. over 2,000), central Ulyanovsk oblast, Russian SFSR, 40 mi. SW of Ulyanovsk; woolen milling, distilling.

Ignatovo, Russian SFSR: see BOLSHOYE IGNATOVO.

Igneada (ĕnĕ'ädä"), Turkish *İğneada*, village (pop. 713), Kirklareli prov., Turkey in Europe, on Black Sea 7 mi. from Bulgarian line, 40 mi. ENE of Kirklareli. Just E, across a small inlet, is Cape Igneada (sometimes spelled Iniada; anc. *Thynias*); 41°52'N 28°3'E.

Igniarfik (ĭngnyäkh'fĭk), fishing settlement (pop. 71), Egedesminde dist., W Greenland, on Davis Strait, 40 mi. SSW of Egedesminde; 68°9'N 53°10'W.

Ignusi, Greece: see OINOUSA.

Igodovo (ē'gŭdŭvŭ), village (1926 pop. 258), SW central Kostroma oblast, Russian SFSR, 25 mi. S of Galich; flax.

Igoumenitsa, Greece: see EGOUMENITSA.

Igra (ēgrä'), village (1948 pop. over 500), central Udmurt Autonomous SSR, Russian SFSR, 48 mi. N of Izhevsk, near railroad; rye, oats. Quartz sand deposits near by (N, S).

Igreja Nova (ĕgrā'zhŭ nô'vŭ), city (pop. 2,400), E Alagoas, NE Brazil, near left bank of lower São Francisco R., 12 mi. NNW of Penedo; sugar, rice, livestock. Formerly Triumpho.

Iguaçu or **Iguassú** (ēgwŏosōō'), former federal territory (□ 25,427; 1944 pop. estimate 104,700), S Brazil, on Paraguay and Argentina border. Created as a frontier defense zone in 1943, it was dissolved in 1946, and area was reincorporated into Paraná and Santa Catarina. Seat of govt. was at Iguaçu (now called Laranjeiras do Sul).

Iguaçu. **1** Town, Bahia, Brazil: see ITAETÊ. **2** City, Paraná, Brazil: see LARANJEIRAS DO SUL.

Iguaçu, river and falls, Brazil and Argentina: see IGUASSÚ.

Iguak, Alaska: see OHOGAMIUT.

Iguala (ēgwä'lä), city (pop. 12,756), Guerrero, SW Mexico, on affluent of the Río de las Balsas and 80 mi. SSW of Mexico city, on railroad. Important mining (silver, gold, copper, lead), lumbering, and agr. center (cereals, coffee, sugar cane, tobacco, fruit); tanning, vegetable-oil extracting, alcohol distilling, coffee processing, cigar making, silversmithing; mfg. of sweets, soap, jewelry. Airfield. The famous Plan of Iguala, outlining certain principles of Mexican independence, was proclaimed here 1821 by Agustín de Iturbide with the acquiescence of guerrilla leader Vicente Guerrero; the plan was later abandoned when Iturbide made himself emperor.

Igualada (ēgwälä'dhä), city (pop. 15,311), Barcelona prov., NE Spain, in Catalonia, 30 mi. WNW of Barcelona; leading center of the leather and cotton industries; mfg. of glue, brandy, alcohol, cement, shoes; lumbering; agr. trade (wine, olive oil, cereals, fruit). Gypsum quarries in vicinity. Terminus of branch railway from Martorell.

Igualapa (ēgwälä'pä), town (pop. 1,406), Guerrero, SW Mexico, in Pacific lowland, 8 mi. WNW of Ometepec; fruit, sugar cane, livestock.

Igualeja (ēgwälā'hä), town (pop. 1,529), Málaga prov., S Spain, 7 mi. S of Ronda; grapes, fruit, truck produce, corn, chestnuts, timber. Marble and graphite quarrying, iron mining.

Iguape (ēgwä'pĭ), city (pop. 3,531), S São Paulo, Brazil, 95 mi. SW of Santos; fishing port on the Ribeira de Iguape near its mouth on a tidal inlet protected from the open Atlantic by a long, narrow isl. Fish processing, rice milling, lumbering, caustic-soda mfg. Large apatite deposits discovered in area (1947). Center of lowland region settled largely by Japanese immigrants.

Iguarassú, Brazil: see IGARAÇU.

Iguaratinga, Brazil: see SÃO FRANCISCO DO MARANHÃO.

Iguassú Falls or **Iguaçu Falls** (both: ēgwŏosōō'), Sp. *Iguazú* [Guarani,=big waters], cataract on Iguassú R. (Brazil-Argentina border) 14 mi. above its influx into the Paraná; 25°41'S 54°27'W. Over its irregular, 2.5-mi.-long crest line, hundreds of falls, separated from each other by rocky, tree-covered isls., drop c.210 ft. into a narrow gorge. Of the 2 main sections, the receding horseshoe belongs to Brazil. The falls, higher and wider than Niagara, have enormous, as yet undeveloped, hydroelectric power potential, and present one of South America's great natural spectacles. Accessible by air and river (Paraná R. navigation), they attract tourists from both countries, which have established natl. parks (Argentina in 1928, Brazil in 1939) on either side, in a wild, subtropical setting. Fine hotels have been recently built. Though explored in colonial days and named Santa María Falls, they were 1st mapped in 1892.

Iguassú River or **Iguaçu River**, Sp. *Iguazú*, in Paraná, SE Brazil, rises in the Serra do Mar just E of Curitiba, flows W in a meandering course to the Paraná at Argentina-Brazil-Paraguay border 3 mi. below Foz do Iguaçu (Brazil). In last 75 mi. of course it forms Brazil-Argentina border; the famous IGUASSÚ FALLS are 14 mi. above its mouth. Navigable only bet. Pôrto Amazonas and União da Vitória in Brazil. Receives the Rio Negro (left). Length estimated up to 820 mi.

Iguatama (ēgwŏotä'mŭ), city (pop. 1,157), SW central Minas Gerais, Brazil, on railroad and 50 mi. W of Divinópolis. Diamond washings in headwaters of São Francisco R. (W). Until 1944, Pôrto Real.

Iguatemi River (ēgwŏotĭmē'), southernmost Mato Grosso, Brazil, rises in the Serra de Amambaí near Paraguay border, flows 120 mi. ESE to the Paraná (right bank) 20 mi. above Guaíra Falls. Used for maté shipments from Ponta Porã area to Paraguay and Argentina. Formerly spelled Iguatemy.

Iguatu (ēgwŏotōō'), city (pop. 7,249), S Ceará, Brazil, on Fortaleza-Crato RR and 190 mi. SSW of Fortaleza; trade center of irrigated agr. region shipping cotton, tobacco, carnauba, manioc, cattle. Airfield. Called Telha until 1874. Magnesite mining. Dam at Orós (28 mi. ENE) impounds waters of Jaguaribe R. for irrigation and flood control.

Iguatzio, Mexico: see IHUATZIO.

Iguazú, village and department, Argentina: see PUERTO IGUAZÚ.

Iguazú, river and falls, Brazil and Argentina: see IGUASSÚ.

Igueña, Spain: see TREMOR.

Iguidi, Erg, Algeria: see ERG.

Igumale (ĭgōōmä'lĕ), town (pop. 4,021), Benue prov., Northern Provinces, S central Nigeria, on railroad and 33 mi. SSW of Oturkpo; shea nuts, cassava, durra, yams. Sometimes spelled Ogumali.

Igumen, Belorussian SSR: see CHERVEN.

Igushik (ĭgōō'shĭk, ĭ–), village (1939 pop. 16), SW Alaska, on W shore of Nushagak Bay, at mouth of small Igushik R., 30 mi. SW of Dillingham; salmon fishing and canning.

Iguvium, Italy: see GUBBIO.

Ihara, Japan: see IBARA.

Ihden (ĭ'dĕn) or **Ihdin** (ĭ'dĭn), Fr. *Ehdène*, village, N Lebanon, 12 mi. SE of Tripoli; alt. 8,000 ft.; summer resort; sericulture, cotton, cereals, fruit.

Iheya-shoto (ēhā'yä-shōtō'), volcanic island group (□17; 1950 pop. 9,539) of Okinawa Isls., in the Ryukyus, in the Philippine Sea, 18 mi. NW of Okinawa. Comprises Iheya-ushiro-jima (largest; 8 mi. long, 1.5 mi. wide), Ijina-shima (also called Iheya-mae-shima), and several smaller islets. Hilly; surrounded by coral reef. Produces sugar cane, sweet potatoes, rice.

Ihing or **I-hsing** (both: ē'shĭng', yē'–), town (pop. 93,463), ⊙ Ihing co. (pop. 630,655), S Kiangsu prov., China, near Chekiang line, 45 mi. W of Soochow, across Tai L.; agr. center (rice, tea, wheat, beans); pottery mfg. Kaolin quarries near by.

Ihle Canal (ē'lŭ), central Germany, extends c.20 mi. NE from the Elbe at Hohenwarthe (junction with Weser-Elbe Canal) to Plaue Canal 5 mi. W of Genthin. Navigable for 1,000-ton vessels.

Ihlen (ĭ'lŭn), village (pop. 135), Pipestone co., SW Minn., near S.Dak. line, 7 mi. SSW of Pipestone, in grain and potato area. State park here.

Ihlienworth (ē'lyŭnvôrt"), village (pop. 3,036), in former Prussian prov. of Hanover, NW Germany, after 1945 in Lower Saxony, 12 mi. SE of Cuxhaven; food processing.

Ihna River, Poland: see INA RIVER.

Ihnasya el Madina or **Ihnasiyat al-Madinah** (both: ĭnä'sĭyŭ ĕl mădē'nŭ), village (pop. 10,708), Beni Suef prov., Upper Egypt, 9 mi. W of Beni Suef; cotton, cereals, sugar cane.

I Ho, China: see I RIVER.

Iholdy (ēôldē'), village (pop. 183), Basses-Pyrénées dept., SW France, 20 mi. SE of Bayonne; corn, livestock.

Ihosy (ēhōō'sē, yōōsh), town, Fianarantsoa prov., SE Madagascar, on highway and 90 mi. SW of Fianarantsoa; cattle market. Garnets and mica are mined near by. Has military airfield, hosp. for natives, R.C. and Protestant missions.

Ihrhove (ēr'hō"fŭ), village (pop. 1,753), in former Prussian prov. of Hanover, NW Germany, after 1945 in Lower Saxony, 4 mi. S of Leer; rail junction; sawmilling.

Ihringen (ē'rĭng-ŭn), village (pop. 3,335), S Baden, Germany, at S foot of the Kaiserstuhl, 10 mi. WNW of Freiburg; noted for its wine.

Ihsien (ē'shyĕn', yē'–). **1** Town, ⊙ Ihsien co. (pop. 56,761), S Anhwei prov., China, 20 mi. WNW of Tunki; tea, tung oil, lacquer. **2** Town, Hopeh prov., China: see YIHSIEN. **3** Town (1938 pop. 30,275), ⊙ Ihsien co. (1946 pop. 330,216), Liaosi prov., Manchuria, 29 mi. N of Chinchow; rail junction; coal-mining center; bricks and tiles. Grain, cotton, hides, skins. Called Ichow until 1913. **4** Town, Shantung prov., China: see YIHSIEN.

I-hsing, China: see IHING.

Ihtiman, Bulgaria: see IKHTIMAN.

I-huang, China: see IHWANG.

Ihuatzio (ēwät'syō), town (pop. 1,206), Michoacán, central Mexico, on E shore of L. Pátzcuaro, 25 mi. WSW of Morelia; native handicrafts. Old Indian town with subterranean passages and other archaeological remains. Sometimes spelled Iguatzio.

Ihwang or **I-huang** (both: yē'hwäng'), town (pop. 7,985), ⊙ Ihwang co. (pop. 78,398), E central Kiangsi prov., China, 25 mi. S of Fuchow; rice; ramie weaving, straw-paper making. Coal mining, lime quarrying. Also Yihwang.

Ii (ē), Swedish *Ijo* (ē'ō), village (commune pop. 5,465), Oulu co., W Finland, on Gulf of Bothnia at mouth of Ii R. (rail and road bridges), 20 mi. N of Oulu; timber-shipping port.

Iida (ē'dä). **1** Town (pop. 3,174), Ishikawa prefecture, central Honshu, Japan, on NE Noto Peninsula, on Sea of Japan, 32 mi. NE of Nanao; rice, raw silk. Fishing. **2** City (1940 pop. 28,494; 1947 pop. 30,295), Nagano prefecture, central Honshu, Japan, on Tenryu R. and 60 mi. ENE of Nagoya; mfg. (sake, twine), woodworking; raw silk. Includes (since 1937) former town of Kami-iida.

Iidakawa, Japan: see SHOWA, Akita prefecture.

Iino (ē'nō). **1** Town (pop. 3,255), Fukushima prefecture, N central Honshu, Japan, 8 mi. SSE of Fukushima; raw silk. **2** Town (pop. 19,735), Miyazaki prefecture, S central Kyushu, Japan, 34 mi. WNW of Miyazaki; horse-breeding and agr. (rice, wheat) center; sawmills.

Iinokawa (ē'nōkäwŭ) or **Iinogawa** (–gäwŭ), town (pop. 7,395), Miyagi prefecture, N Honshu, Japan, 6 mi. N of Ishinomaki; rice, silk cocoons, tea.

Iioka (ē'ôkä), town (pop. 9,161), Chiba prefecture, central Honshu, Japan, at NE base of Chiba Peninsula, 6 mi. WSW of Choshi; summer resort; fishing center.

Ii River, Finnish *Iijoki* (ē'yō"kē), Swedish *Ijo älv*, N central Finland, rises in lake region near 66°N 28°E, flows 150 mi. in winding course generally SW, past Pudasjärvi, to Gulf of Bothnia at Ii. Timber-floating route.

Iisalmi (ē'säl"mē), Swedish *Idensalmi* (ē'dŭnsäl"mē), city (pop. 4,424), Kuopio co., S central Finland, in lake region, 50 mi. NNW of Kuopio; rail junction; lumber and flour mills; light industry. Near-by lakes yield iron by dredging.

Iittala (ēt'tälä), village in Kalvola (käl'vōlä) commune (pop. 4,866), Häme co., S Finland, in lake region, 12 mi. NW of Hämeenlinna; glassworks.

Iitti (ēt'tē), Swedish *Iittis* (ē'tĭs), village (commune pop. 10,750), Kymi co., SE Finland, in lake region, 25 mi. E of Lahti; lumbering. Until 1949 in Uusimaa co.

Iiyama (ē'yämä), town (pop. 10,299), Nagano prefecture, central Honshu, Japan, 17 mi. NE of Nagano; commercial center for rice-growing area.

Iizaka (ē'zäkä), town (pop. 8,277), Fukushima prefecture, N Honshu, Japan, 5 mi. NNW of Fukushima; coal mining.

Iizuka (ē'zōōkä), city (1940 pop. 46,685; 1947 pop. 47,321), Fukuoka prefecture, N Kyushu, Japan, 17 mi. E of Fukuoka; rail and commercial center for coal-mining area.

Ij or **Y** (both: ī), Du. *IJ*, inlet of the Ijsselmeer, North Holland prov., NW Netherlands, on which Amsterdam is located. Receives Amstel R. at Amsterdam; connected with North Sea by North Sea Canal, with Lek R. and Waal R. by Merwede Canal.

Ijebu (ējäbōō'), province (□ 2,456; pop. 305,898), Western Provinces, SW Nigeria; ⊙ Ijebu-Ode. Mainly in rain-forest zone, with some fresh-water and mangrove-swamp forests (S). Main products: cacao, palm oil and kernels, rubber, kola nuts. Food crops: rice, corn, yams, cassava, plantains. Hardwood lumbering. Pop. is largely Yoruba. Main centers: Ijebu-Ode, Shagamu.

Ijebu Igbo (ēb-bōō'), town, Ijebu prov., Western Provinces, SW Nigeria, 12 mi. NNE of Ijebu-Ode; road center; cacao, hardwood, rubber, palm oil and kernels.

Ijebu-Ode (–ōdā'), town (pop. 27,909), ⊙ Ijebu prov., Western Provinces, SW Nigeria, 40 mi. S of Ibadan; 6°49'N 3°55'E. Agr. and trade center; cacao industry; hardwood, rubber, palm oil and kernels. Has hosp.

Ijerseke, Netherlands: see YERSEKE.

Ijil, Fr. West Africa: see FORT GOURAUD.

Ijina-shima, Japan: see IHEYA-SHOTO.

Ijlst (īlst), Du. *IJlst*, town (pop. 1,357), Friesland prov., N Netherlands, 2 mi. SW of Sneek; machinery, tools, drainage pumps, toys, skates. Sometimes spelled Ylst.

Ijmuiden (ī'moi"dŭn), Du. *IJmuiden*, town (pop. 22,121) and port, North Holland prov., W Netherlands, on North Sea and 14 mi. WNW of Amsterdam, at W end of NORTH SEA CANAL; fishing center; ice and cement mfg. Steel plant and paper mills at VELSEN, 2 mi. E; Velsen commune includes Ijmuiden. Ger. torpedo-boat base in Second World War. Sometimes spelled Ymuiden.

Ijo, village, Finland: see II.

Ijo älv, Finland: see II RIVER.

Ijofin (ējō'fĕn), town, Abeokuta prov., Western Provinces, SW Nigeria, on Dahomey frontier, 16 mi. WSW of Ado; cotton weaving, indigo dyeing; cacao, palm oil and kernels. Phosphate deposits.

Ijselmeer, Netherlands: see IJSSELMEER.

Ijsel River, Netherlands: see IJSSEL RIVER.

Ijselstein, Netherlands: see IJSSELSTEIN.

Ijsselmeer or **Ijselmeer** (both: ī'sŭlmār), Du. *IJsselmeer* or *IJselmeer*, shallow fresh-water lake in N and central Netherlands; formed from the old Zuider Zee by building of Ijsselmeer Dam [Du. *Afsluitdijk*], which extends 19 mi. from Den Over (North Holland prov.) to a point 1½ mi. SW of Zurich (Friesland prov). Dam, completed 1932, has navigation locks and drainage sluices at both ends and carries a roadway. The Ijsselmeer borders provs. of North Holland, Utrecht, Gelderland, Overijssel, and Friesland. Receives Vecht R. near Muiden, Ijssel R. NW of Kampen, and the Zwartewater W of Zwartsluis. Considerable areas of the sea have been reclaimed, including WIERINGERMEER POLDER, BEEMSTER POLDER, and NORTH EAST POLDER. Further reclamations are planned. Main towns on lake: Amsterdam (on Ij or Y inlet), Harderwijk, Stavoren, Medemblik, Enkhuizen, and Hoorn. Prior to building of Ijsselmeer Dam, the sea here was an important fishing ground. Of the isls. of the old Zuider Zee, only Marken remains as an isl., the former isls. of Wieringen, Urk, and Schokland having been incorporated into the reclaimed land areas. Sometimes spelled Ysselmeer.

Ijsselmonde (–mōndů), Du. *IJsselmonde*, island (15 mi. long, 5 mi. wide), South Holland prov., SW Netherlands, surrounded by Noord R. (E), Old Maas R. (S and SW), and New Maas R. (N). Strawberries and vegetables are grown; also dairying. The town of Ijsselmonde (pop. 8,156) is on the New Maas, 3 mi. E of Rotterdam. Besides Ijsselmonde, other towns are Bardendrecht, Pernis, Ridderkerk. Sometimes spelled Ysselmonde.

Ijssel River or **Ijsel River,** Du. *IJssel*, E and central Netherlands, branches from the Lower Rhine 2.5 mi. SE of Arnhem, flows 72 mi. N, past Doesburg, Zutphen, and Deventer, to the Ijsselmeer 4 mi. WNW of Kampen. Joined by Old Ijssel R. at Doesburg, by Twente Canal 2 mi. NNW of Zutphen, by Overijssel Canal at Deventer; connected with the Zwartewater at Zwolle. Sometimes spelled Yssel or Ysel. Not to be confused with shorter river in W Netherlands called HOLLANDSCHE IJSSEL RIVER.

Ijsselstein (–stīn), Du. *IJsselstein*, town (pop. 4,348), Utrecht prov., W central Netherlands, on Hollandsche Ijssel R. and 6 mi. SSW of Utrecht; bricks, woodworking, furniture; agr., cattle raising, dairying. Sometimes spelled Ysselstein or Ijselstein.

Ijuí (ēzhwē'), city (pop. 5,523), NW Rio Grande do Sul, Brazil, on railroad and 26 mi. NW of Cruz Alta; center of agr. colony; cattle and hog raising; processing of meat, grain, and maté. Mineral springs near by. Formerly spelled Ijuhy.

Ijuin ējōō'ēn), town (pop. 15,837), Kagoshima prefecture, S Kyushu, Japan, on N Satsuma Peninsula, 10 mi. WNW of Kagoshima; rail junction. Known for Satsuma porcelain ware. Inhabited by descendants of colony of potters brought from Korea in 16th cent. Sometimes spelled Izyuin.

Ijuí River, N Rio Grande do Sul, Brazil, rises in the Serra Geral, flows 225 mi. W to Uruguay R. E of Concepción de la Sierra (Argentina). Not navigable. Formerly spelled Ijuhy.

Ijzendijke (ī'zůndī"ků), Du. *IJzendijke*, town (pop. 1,494), Zeeland prov., SW Netherlands, on Flanders mainland and 9 mi. W of Terneuzen, near Belg. border; mfg. (Venetian blinds, wooden shoes), dairy products. First known in 10th cent.; trade center in Middle Ages. Sometimes Yzendyke.

Ikaalinen (ī'kälĭ"nĕn), Swedish *Ikalis* (ē'kälĭs), town (pop. 456), Turku-Pori co., SW Finland, in lake region, 30 mi. NW of Tampere; health resort.

Ikaho (ēkä'hō), town (pop. 3,846), Gumma prefecture, central Honshu, Japan, 11 mi. NW of Maebashi; hot springs.

Ikali (ēkä'lē), village, Equator Prov., NW Belgian Congo, on Luilaka R. and 130 mi. SSE of Boende; terminus of steam navigation in palm-growing region.

Ikalis, Finland: see IKAALINEN.

Ikamiut (ĭkäm'yōōt), fishing settlement (pop. 95), Christianshaab dist., W Greenland, on inlet of Disko Bay, 25 mi. ESE of Egedesminde; 68°38'N 51°50'W.

Ikang (ēkäng'), town, Calabar prov., Eastern Provinces, SE Nigeria, on inlet of Bight of Biafra (Br. Cameroons frontier), 20 mi. SE of Calabar; minor port of entry; fishing industry; coconuts, plantains, bananas.

Ikara (ē'kärä), town (pop. 3,002), Zaria prov., Northern Provinces, N central Nigeria, 35 mi. ENE of Zaria; agr. trade center (cotton, peanuts, locust beans). Surrounding dist. freed of tsetse flies in connection with pop. resettlement scheme. Sometimes spelled Ikare.

Ikaria, Greece: see ICARIA.

Ikaruga (ēkä'rōōgä), town (pop. 3,697), Hyogo prefecture, S Honshu, Japan, 7 mi. W of Himeji; rice.

Ikast (ē'käst), town (pop. 3,059), Ringkobing amt, central Jutland, Denmark, 35 mi. E of Ringkobing; textiles. chemicals.

Ikatan (ēkätän'), village (pop. 25), on SE Unimak Isl., SW Alaska; 54°45'N 163°19'W.

Ikatek or **Ikateq** (both: ī'kätĕk), meteorological station and landing field, SE Greenland, on inlet of Denmark Strait, 35 mi. NE of Angmagssalik; 65°56'N 36°33'W.

Ikazaki (ēkä'zäkē), agr. town (pop. 3,974), Ehime prefecture, W Shikoku, Japan, 22 mi. SSW of Matsuyama, in mtn. area.

Ikeda (ēkä'dä). **1** Town (pop. 15,349), S central Hokkaido, Japan, on Tokachi R. and 12 mi. E of Obihiro; rail junction; agr. (rice, soybeans), livestock; lumbering; hemp weaving. **2** Town (pop. 6,716), on Shodo-shima, Kagawa prefecture, Japan, on S coast of isl.; agr. center (tobacco, wheat, rice, sweet potatoes); soy sauce, noodles. **3** City (pop. 42,733), Osaka prefecture, S Honshu, Japan, 13 mi. NNW of Osaka; charcoal-collection center. **4** Town (pop. 5,314), Nagano prefecture, central Honshu, Japan, 14 mi. NNW of Matsumoto; rice, wheat, raw silk. **5** Town (pop. 9,298), Tokushima prefecture, NE central Shikoku, Japan, on Yoshino R. and 42 mi. W of Tokushima; agr. center (rice, wheat, tobacco).

Ikegawa (ēkä'gäwä), town (pop. 8,897), Kochi prefecture, central Shikoku, Japan, 22 mi. WNW of Kochi; commercial center in agr. area (soybeans, tea, sugar beets, wheat).

Ikei or **Ikey** (ēkyā'), village (1939 pop. over 500), S Irkutsk oblast, Russian SFSR, 30 mi. SW of Tulun, in agr. area.

Ikeja (ēkäd'yä), town, Nigeria colony, on railroad and 9 mi. NNW of Lagos. Site of Lagos airport.

Ikela (ēkĕ'lä), Equator Prov., central Belgian Congo, on Tshuapa R. and 175 mi. ESE of Boende; steamboat landing and trading center in palm-growing region; rubber plantations in vicinity.

Ikelemba River (ēkĕlĕm'bä), W Belgian Congo, rises 25 mi. SW of Befale, flows c.200 mi. NW and SW, past Balangala and Bombimba, to Congo R. opposite Coquilhatville. Navigable for steamboats for 85 mi. below Bombimba, for barges below Balangala.

Ikerasak (ĭkĕ'räsäk), fishing and hunting settlement (pop. 112), Umanak dist., W Greenland, on small Ikerasak Isl. in Qarajaq Ice Fjord, 20 mi. SE of Imanak; 70°30'N 51°19'W. Radio station.

Ikere (ē'kārä), town, Ondo prov., Western Provinces, S Nigeria, 16 mi. N of Akure; cacao industry; palm oil and kernels, rubber, timber.

Ikervar (ĭ'kĕrvär), Hung. *Ikervár*, town (pop. 2,275), Vas co., W Hungary, on Raba R. and 13 mi. E of Szombathely; honey, wheat.

Ikeshinden (ēkā'shēndän), town (pop. 7,513), Shizuoka prefecture, central Honshu, Japan, 13 mi. SSW of Shimada; rice, wheat, tea.

Ikey, Russian SFSR: see IKEI.

Ikh Chao, China: see ORDOS DESERT.

Ikhe Aral Nor, Mongolia: see KHARA USU.

Ikhe Bogdo or **Yihe Bogdo** (both: ē'khä bŏg'dō), highest peak (over 13,000 ft.) of Gobi section of Altai Mts., in E Mongolian People's Republic, 250 mi. SE of Uliassutai; 45°N 100°24'E. Also called Barun Bogdo or Baruun Bogdo.

Ikhtiman (ĭkhtēmän'), city (pop. 6,516), Sofia dist., W central Bulgaria, at S foot of Ikhtiman Sredna Gora, on right tributary of Topolnitsa R. and 30 mi. SE of Sofia; agr. center in Ikhtiman Basin (□ 45; average alt. 3,000 ft.; hardy grain, potatoes, flax, livestock); shoe mfg. Asbestos quarried near by. Sometimes spelled Ichtiman or Ihtiman.

Ikhtiman Sredna Gora, Bulgaria: see SREDNA GORA.

Iki, Japan: see IKI-SHIMA.

Ikire (ēkyĭ'rē), town (pop. 20,920), Oyo prov., Western Provinces, SW Nigeria, 20 mi. E of Ibadan; road center; cotton weaving; cacao, palm oil and kernels, cotton. Sawmilling near by.

Ikirun (ēkĭ'rōōn), town (pop. 23,874), Oyo prov., Western Provinces, SW Nigeria, on railroad and 65 mi. NE of Ibadan; cotton weaving, shea-nut processing, cacao industry.

Iki-shima (ēkē'shĭmä), island (□53; pop. 50,637, including offshore islets), Nagasaki prefecture, Japan, in Tsushima Strait, 13 mi. N of NW coast of Kyushu; 8.5 mi. long, 5 mi. wide; hilly, fertile; agr. Chief town, Mushozu. Site of ruins of 16th-cent. castle built by Hideyoshi. Sometimes called Iki.

Ikitsuki-shima (ēkē'tsōōkē"shĭmä), island (□6; pop. 9,993), Nagasaki prefecture, Japan, in E. China Sea, just NW of Hirado-shima, 8 mi. W of Hizen Peninsula, Kyushu; 6 mi. long, 2 mi. wide; hilly. Rice, sweet potatoes, fish. Chief town, Ikitsuki, is on E coast.

Ikiz Tepe (ĭkĭz' tĕpĕ"), Turkish *İkiz Tepe*, peak (5,580 ft.), Amanos Mts., S Turkey, 16 mi. WNW of Antioch, 4 mi. from Mediterranean coast.

I-k'o-chao, China: see ORDOS DESERT.

Ikole (ē'kôlä), town, Ondo prov., Western Provinces, S Nigeria, 40 mi. N of Owo; cacao industry; palm oil and kernels, kola nuts.

Ikom (ēkôm'), town (pop. 1,787), Ogoja prov., Eastern Provinces, SE Nigeria, port on Cross R. (head of high-water navigation) and 28 mi. ESE of Obubra; trade center; hardwood and rubber; palm oil and kernels, cacao, kola nuts.

Ikoma (ēkō'mä), town (pop. 9,903), Nara prefecture, S Honshu, Japan, 7 mi. W of Nara; rail junction; mtn. resort. Buddhist temple on near-by Mt. Ikoma (2,120 ft.).

Ikon-Khalk (ēkôn"-khälk'), village (1939 pop. over 500), N Cherkess Autonomous Oblast, Stavropol Territory, Russian SFSR, on Little Zelenchuk R. and 8 mi. WNW of Cherkessk; grain, livestock.

Ikonnikovo, Russian SFSR: see GORKOVSKOYE.

Ikopa River (ēkōō'pů), central and NW Madagascar, main tributary of the Betsiboka, rises 25 mi. SSE of Tananarive, flows 250 mi. NNW to Betsiboka R. just above Maevatanana. Mantasoa reservoir (completed 1939), the largest of Madagascar, is at its source; used for irrigation (notably of Betsimitatra rice fields) and fishing. Several barrages regulate the Ikopa near Tananarive. Valley has gold placers.

Ikornnes (ē'kôrn-näs), village in Sykkylven canton, More og Romsdal co., W Norway, on a S inlet of Stor Fjord, 14 mi. ESE of Alesund; mfg. of springs and mattresses. Formerly spelled Ekornnes.

Ikorodu (ēkōrōdōō'), town (pop. 13,598), Nigeria colony, 15 mi. NNE of Lagos (across lagoon); port and market; cacao, palm oil and kernels, rice.

Ikot Ekpene (ēkôt' ĕp-pĕ'nĕ), town (pop. 805), Calabar prov., Eastern Provinces, SE Nigeria, on headstream of Kwa Ibo R. and 25 mi. E of Aba; road center; toy making; raffia industry; palm oil and kernels, kola nuts. Has hosp.

Ikoyi (ēkô'yē), residential town (pop. 3,953) in Lagos township, Nigeria colony, on E end of Lagos Isl. Has R.C. mission, hosp.

Ikpek or **Icpic** (ēk'pĭk), village (pop. 26), W Alaska, near Nome.

Ikramovo, Uzbek SSR: see DZHUMA.

Ik River (ēk), in E European Russian SFSR, rises in W foothills of the S Urals 10 mi. S of Belebei, flows S, W, NNW, past Oktyabrski (Bashkir Autonomous SSR) and Muslyumovo, and WNW to Kama R. 9 mi. E of Bondyuzhski; 326 mi. long. Receives Usen (right) and Menzelya (left) rivers.

Ikryanoye (ēkryä'nŭyů), village (1926 pop. 2,296), E Astrakhan oblast, Russian SFSR, on Bakhtemir arm of Volga R. delta mouth and 22 mi. SSW of Astrakhan; caviar; fisheries; fruit, cotton.

Iksha (ēk'shŭ), town (1939 pop. over 500), N central Moscow oblast, Russian SFSR, on Moscow Canal, 12 mi. S of Dmitrov; metalworks (wire, nails).

Ikskile or **Ikshkile** (ēk'shkēlā), Lettish *Ikšķile*, Ger. *Uexküll*, village, central Latvia, in Vidzeme, on right bank of the Western Dvina and 17 mi. SE of Riga; summer resort.

I-ku-ch'i Hu, Tibet: see NGANGTSE TSO.

Ikuchi-jima (ēkōō'chē-jĭmä), island (□ 12; pop. 16,713), Hiroshima prefecture, Japan, in Hiuchi Sea (central section of Inland Sea), 6 mi. S of Mihara on SW Honshu, bet. Omi-shima (W) and Inno-shima (E); 5.5 mi. long, 3 mi. wide; mountainous. Fishing, raw-silk production. Setoda is chief town.

Ikuji (ēkōō'jē), town (pop. 6,677), Toyama prefecture, central Honshu, Japan, on E shore of Toyama Bay, at delta mouth of Kurobe R., 18 mi. NE of Toyama; fishing center; sake, soy sauce. Mineral springs.

Ikuno (ēkōō'nä), town (pop. 8,948), Hyogo prefecture, S Honshu, Japan, 3 mi. NNE of Himeji; mining center (silver, copper, gold).

Ikura (ēkōō'rä), town (pop. 5,697), Kumamoto prefecture, W Kyushu, Japan, port on Shimabara Bay, 10 mi. NW of Kumamoto; exports rice.

Ikushumbetsu, Japan: see MIKASA.

Ikva River (ēk'vŭ), Pol. *Ikwa* (ēk'vä), W Ukrainian SSR, rises S of Brody in Volyn-Podolian Upland, flows E, N past Dubno, and WNW to Styr R. S of Lutsk; 100 mi. long.

Ila (ī'lů), town (pop. 225), Madison co., NE Ga., 15 mi. NNE of Athens, in farm area.

Ilabaya, Bolivia: see GUACHALLA.

Ilabaya (ēläbī'ä), town (pop. 119), Tacna dept., S Peru, in Andean foothills, on affluent of Locumba R. and 32 mi. ESE of Moquegua; grapes, fruit, stock; wine and liquor distilling. Silver deposits near by.

Ilacaon Point (ēläkä'ōn, –koun'), northernmost point of Negros isl., Philippines, in Guimaras Strait, near its entrance; 11°N 123°11'E.

Ilagan (ēlä'gän), town (1939 pop. 5,850; 1948 municipality pop. 35,384), ⊙ Isabela prov., N Luzon, Philippines, on Cagayan R. and 100 mi. NE of Baguio; agr. center (rice, corn).

Ilaiyankudi, India: see ILAYANGUDI.

Ilaló, Cerro (sĕ'rō ēlälō'), Andean peak (10,433 ft.) in Pichincha prov., N central Ecuador, 7 mi. E of Quito. At its foot is the spa Tingo.

Ilam or **'Ilam** (ēläm'), town (pop. 6,626), Fifth Prov., W Iran, 60 mi. SW of Kermanshah; main town of the Pusht Kuh; sheep raising; grain. Sometimes spelled Elam, Eilam, or Eylam.

Ilam (ĭläm'), town, E Nepal, 33 mi. WSW of Darjeeling; alt. 4,125 ft. Nepalese military post; road leads to Darjeeling.

Ilama (ēlä'mä), town (pop. 916), Santa Bárbara dept., W Honduras, on Ulúa R. and 10 mi. NNE of Santa Barbara; commercial center; palm-hat mfg., mat weaving, ropemaking; coffee, sugar cane.

Ilamatlán (ēlämätlän'), town (pop. 896), Veracruz, E Mexico, in Sierra Madre Oriental, on Puebla border, 22 mi. SW of Chicontepec; corn, sugar cane, coffee.

Ilan (yē'län'), Jap. *Giran* (gē'rän), town (1940 pop. 36,371), N Formosa, near E coast, 25 mi. SE of Taipei, and on railroad; commercial center in agr. area (rice, sugar cane, ramie, citrus fruit); rice and sugar milling; mfg. of gold and silver foil; sawmilling, fish processing.

Ilan (yē'län'), town (pop. 30,000), ⊙ Ilan co. (pop. 250,000), NW Sungkiang prov., Manchuria, on right bank of Sungari R., at mouth of Mutan R., and 50 mi. SW of Kiamusze; agr. and lumbering center; flour and soybean milling, fur processing. Gold mining; oil-shale deposits. One of oldest towns of Manchuria, dating from 12th cent.; it was the economic center of the lower Sungari valley until supplanted in Manchukuo by Kiamusze. A former treaty port, it was previously called Sansing.

Ilaniya or **Ilanya** (ēlänē'ä), settlement (pop. 260), Lower Galilee, N Israel, 7 mi. ENE of Nazareth; mixed farming. Founded 1902. Also called Sejera (sĕjĕrä').

Ilanski or **Ilanskiy** (ēlän'skē), city (1939 pop. over 10,000), SE Krasnoyarsk Territory, Russian SFSR, 11 mi. E of Kansk and on Trans-Siberian RR; metalworking; railroad shops.

Ilanz (ēlänts'), Romansh *Glion*, town (pop. 1,494), Grisons canton, E central Switzerland, on the Vorderrhein and 18 mi. WSW of Chur.

Ilaro (ēlä'rō), town (pop. 6,175), Abeokuta prov., Western Provinces, SW Nigeria, on rail spur and 30 mi. SW of Abeokuta; major cacao-producing center; cotton weaving, indigo dyeing; palm oil and kernels. Phosphate deposits.

Ilava (ĭ'lyävä), Slovak *Il'ava*, Hung. *Illava* (ĭl'lŏvŏ), town (pop. 2,043), W Slovakia, Czechoslovakia, on Vah R., on railroad and 12 mi. NE of Trencin; old trading center; furniture mfg. Has large penitentiary.

Ilave (ēlä'vä), town (pop. 1,843), Puno dept., SE Peru, on W shore of L. Titicaca, at mouth of small Ilave R., 30 mi. ESE of Puno (connected by road); alt. 13,097 ft. Grain, quinoa, potatoes, livestock.

Ilawa (ēwä'vä), Pol. *Iława*, Ger. *Deutsch Eylau* (doich' ī'lou), town (1939 pop. 13,922; 1946 pop. 2,220) in East Prussia, after 1945 in Olsztyn prov., NE Poland, at S end of L. Jeziorak, 40 mi. SE of Marienburg (Malbork); rail junction; grain and cattle market. Until 1939, Ger. frontier station near Pol. border. Its Ger. pop. left after Second World War.

Ilayangudi (ĭlŭyäng'gŏŏdē) or **Ilaiyankudi** (-kŏŏdē), town (pop. 12,291; ¾ Moslem), Ramnad dist., S Madras, India, 39 mi. SE of Madura; betel farms.

Ilbono (ēlbô'nô), village (pop. 2,007), Nuoro prov., E Sardinia, 31 mi. SSE of Nuoro.

Ilchester (ĭl'chĭstûr), agr. village and parish (pop. 485), S Somerset, England, on Yeo R. and 5 mi. NW of Yeovil. Has 13th-cent. church. Roger Bacon b. here. Site of important Roman station.

Ilchester (ĭl'chĕ"stûr, ĭl'chĭstûr), village (pop. c.300), Howard co., central Md., on Patapsco R. and 9 mi. WSW of downtown Baltimore. Near by is boxboard mill (at Thistle).

Ileanda (ēlyän'dä), Hung. *Nagyilonda* (nŏ'dyē"-lôndŏ), village (pop. 1,338), Cluj prov., N Rumania, near Somes R., on railroad and 18 mi. NW of Dej; agr. center. Sulphurous springs near by. In Hungary, 1940–45.

Île aux Noix (ēl ō nwä'), islet in Richelieu R., S Que., 30 mi. SE of Montreal. Fort Île-aux-Noix was built here by the French (1759) after Br. capture of Ticonderoga and Crown Point; Br. advance on Montreal was considerably held up here. Fort was rebuilt (1775) by General Montgomery's American forces and became base of operations against Quebec. British built Fort Lennox here (1812), garrisoned until 1869.

Ilebo, Belgian Congo: see PORT-FRANCQUI.

Île-Bouchard, L' (lēl-bōōshär'), village (pop. 1,222), Indre-et-Loire dept., W central France, on Vienne R. and 9 mi. ESE of Chinon; winegrowing, livestock raising. Has 4 old churches.

Île-de-France (ēl-dù-fräs'), region and former province, N central France, at center of Paris Basin; ⊙ Paris. Including parts of Beauce and Brie districts and of the Vexin, Île-de-France is now largely comprised in Seine, Seine-et-Marne, Seine-et-Oise, Oise, and Aisne depts. Drained by the Seine, which receives its chief tributary, the Marne, just above Paris. Has large forests (notably those of Fontainebleau, Compiègne, and Rambouillet), and fertile agr. regions which supply metropolitan area with cereals, vegetables, fruits, dairy produce. The Paris area, though lacking raw materials, is most industrialized region of France, with large metallurgical industry (automobiles, aircraft, bicycles, machinery) and highly diversified luxury and consumer industries. Important or historical cities are Paris, Beauvais, Compiègne, Fontainebleau, Laon, Meaux, Melun, Nemours, Saint-Cloud, Saint-Germain-en-Laye, Senlis, Soissons, Versailles, and numerous Parisian suburbs in Seine and Seine-et-Oise depts. Île-de-France was the cradle of French monarchy. Though the name dates only from 15th cent., region was comprised in duchy of France or Francia as early as 10th cent. When Hugh Capet, duke of France and count of Paris, became king in 987, his domains became the nucleus of the evergrowing crownland, which by 1483 comprised major part of present France. At that time Île-de-France, with the addition of various fiefs to the crown, was made a province subject to *Parlement* of Paris. Broken up into present depts. in 1790.

Île de France, island in Indian Ocean: see MAURITIUS.

Île du –, in French names: see under following part of the name; e.g., for Île du Diable, see DIABLE, ÎLE DU.

Île d'Yeu, France: see YEU, ÎLE D'.

Île Jésus (ēl zhāzü'), county (□ 93; pop. 21,631), S Que., coextensive with JESUS ISLAND; ⊙ Ste. Rose. Formerly called Laval.

Ilek (ēlyĕk'), village (1926 pop. 5,428), S Chkalov oblast, Russian SFSR, on right bank of Ural R. (landing), at mouth of Ilek R., and 70 mi. WSW of Chkalov; metalworking; grain and livestock trade. Before First World War, called Iletski Gorodok.

Ilek River, NW Kazakh SSR and S Chkalov oblast, Russian SFSR; rises in Mugodzhar Hills NE of Kandagach (Kazalch SSR), flows N, past Alga and Aktyubinsk, and generally WNW to Ural R. at Ilek; 330 mi. long. Nonnavigable.

Île Maligne (ēl mùlēn'), town (pop. 455), central Que., on Île d'Alma, on Saguenay R. and 2 mi. NE of St. Joseph d'Alma; aluminum mill; hydroelectric plant.

Île-Napoléon, France: see ILLZACH.

Ilerda, Spain: see LÉRIDA, city.

Île-Rousse, L' (lēl-rōōs'), town (pop. 2,018), NW Corsica, port on the Mediterranean, 10 mi. NE of Calvi, with shipping service to Nice, Toulon, Marseilles; tourist resort; mfg. (cheese, olive oil, cigars), lobster fishing. Just N is Pietra peninsula (formerly an isl.) with lighthouse. Founded 1758 by Paoli as rival to Genoese stronghold of Calvi.

Île Royale, former French name of CAPE BRETON ISLAND, N.S.

Île-Saint-Denis, L' (lēl-sē-dùnē'), town (pop. 3,058), Seine dept., N central France, a N suburb of Paris, 6 mi. from Notre Dame Cathedral, on isl. (3 mi. long) in Seine R., opposite Saint-Denis; metal and chemical works; mfg. of perfumes, ties.

Île Saint Jean, official name for PRINCE EDWARD ISLAND during French regime in Canada.

Îles du –, in French names: see under following part of the name; e.g., for Îles du Salut, see SALUT, ÎLES DU.

Ilesha (ēlä'shä), town (pop. 21,892), Oyo prov., Western Provinces, SW Nigeria, 60 mi. ENE of Ibadan; gold-mining center; cotton weaving; cacao, palm oil and kernels.

Îles Laval (ēl läväl'), town (pop. 358), SW Que., at SW end of Jesus Isl., on L. of the Two Mountains, 15 mi. W of Montreal; resort.

Ilet, town, Russian SFSR: see KRASNOGORSKI.

Ilet River or **Ilet' River** (ēlyĕt'yù), Mari Autonomous SSR, Russian SFSR, rises 7 mi. E of Paranga, flows 120 mi. generally SW, past Krasnogorski, to the Volga 3 mi. WNW of Volzhsk; logging.

Iletsk, Russian SFSR: see SOL-ILETSK.

Iletskaya Zashchita, Russian SFSR: see SOL-ILETSK.

Iletski Gorodok, Russian SFSR: see ILEK, village.

Ilfeld (ĭl'fĕlt), village (pop. 2,506), in former Prussian Saxony prov., central Germany, after 1945 in Thuringia, at S foot of the lower Harz, 6 mi. N of Nordhausen; climatic health resort. Site of former Premonstratensian monastery (founded 1196), converted into school in 1546.

Ilford (ĭl'–), residential municipal borough (1931 pop. 131,061; 1951 census 184,707), SW Essex, England, 11 mi. ENE of London; mfg. of photographic materials, paper, telephone and telegraph equipment, dies, tools, light metals, and tiles.

Ilfracombe (ĭlfrùkōōm'), urban district (1931 pop. 9,175; 1951 census 9,218), N Devon, England, at mouth of Bristol Channel, 10 mi. NNW of Barnstaple; seaside resort, fishing port, and agr. market. Has Norman manor, 14th-cent. church, and 16th-cent. lighthouse (51°12'N 4°8'W). Noted for mild climate.

Ilgaz (ŭlgäz'), village (pop. 1,588), Cankiri prov., N central Turkey, on Devrez R. and 22 mi. N of Cankiri; grain, potatoes, vetch, mohair goats. Formerly Kochisarbala.

Ilgaz Mountains, N Turkey, extend 100 mi. WSW of Boyabat, bet. the Arac and Goksu (N) and Devrez and Kizil Irmak (S); rise to 8,415 ft. in Ilgaz Dag. Towns of Kargi and Tosya on S slope.

Ilgin (ŭlgŭn'), Turkish *Ilgın*, village (pop. 4,240), Konya prov., W central Turkey, near S end of L. Cavuscu, on railroad and 40 mi. NW of Konya; wheat.

Ilhabela (ēlyùbĕ'lù), city (pop. 805), SE São Paulo, Brazil, port on NW coast of SÃO SEBASTIÃO ISLAND, 60 mi. ENE of Santos; fishing; coffee trade. Until 1944, Formosa; originally, Villa Bella.

Ilha dos Pombos (ē'lyù dōōs pōm'bōōs), island in Paraíba R., on Rio de Janeiro-Minas Gerais state line, Brazil, 5 mi. NNE of Carmo; site of hydroelectric station supplying Rio de Janeiro city; built 1920–23.

Ilha Grande Bay (ē'lyù grän'dĭ), on SE coast of Brazil, in Rio de Janeiro state, 70 mi. W of Rio; 30 mi. wide, 15 mi. long; heavily indented by spurs of the Serra do Mar reaching the coast. On it are towns of Angra dos Reis and Parati. Athwart SE entrance lies Ilha Grande, a mountainous isl. (alt. 3,200 ft.) c.15 mi. long.

Ílhavo (ē'lyùvō), town (pop. 6,031), Aveiro dist., N central Portugal, near Aveiro lagoon (inlet of the Atlantic), 3 mi. SSW of Aveiro; equips high-sea fishing fleets; saltworks. Marine mus.

Ilhéus (ēlyĕ'ōōs), city (1950 pop. 23,006), SE Bahia, Brazil, on the Atlantic at mouth of Cachoeira R., and 130 mi. SSW of Salvador; 14°48'S 39°2'W. Important cacao-shipping port exporting over half of Brazil's crop; also ships coffee, sugar, tobacco, lumber, piassava. Terminus of railroad tapping cacao-growing hinterland. Has airport on Bahia-Rio de Janeiro route. Settled in 16th cent. as head of a hereditary captaincy; inc. into Bahia in 18th cent. Formerly spelled Ilhéos. Old name, São Jorge dos Ilhéos.

Ili (ē'lē', yē'lē'), district of W Sinkiang prov., China, in the W Dzungaria, on USSR border; main town, Kuldja. Situated in region of upper reaches of Ili R. and enclosed by the Tien Shan (S) and the Borokhoro Range (N), it is oriented W toward the lower Ili R. valley in the Kazakh SSR. Its chief centers are Kuldja, Hweiyüan, and Suiting, all of which once had the name Ili. The dist. was the scene of a Moslem rebellion (1860s) and was occupied by Russia (1871–81). It was part of the temporary East Turkestan Republic (1944–50).

Ili, river, China and USSR: see ILI RIVER.

Ili (ēlyē'), town (1939 pop. over 10,000), S Alma-Ata oblast, Kazakh SSR, on Turksib RR, on Ili R. and 40 mi. N of Alma-Ata; shipyards; lumber milling, sugar and meat processing. Formerly called Ilisk, Iliisk, or Iliysk.

Ilia, Greece: see ELIS, nome.

Ilia (ē'lyä), Hung. *Marosillye* (mŏ'rôshĕl-lyĕ), village (pop. 1,031), Hunedoara prov., W central Rumania, on Mures R., on railroad and 12 mi. WNW of Deva; gold production. Former fortress against the Turks.

Iliamna (ĭlēăm'nù), village (pop. 43), S Alaska, on N shore of Iliamna L., 120 mi. W of Homer; 59°45'N 153°53'W. Gold mining, trapping; supply point for sport fishermen on Iliamna L. Airbase. Newhalen village (pop. 48) is 3 mi. WSW; Old Iliamna village is 35 mi. E.

Iliamna Lake (75 mi. long, 10–25 mi. wide), S Alaska, at base of Alaska Peninsula, W of Cook Inlet; 59°41'N 154°19'W. Alaska's largest lake, game-fishing center noted for rainbow trout. On shores are Iliamna and Newhalen villages. Drains W into Bristol Bay through Kvichak R.

Iliamna Volcano (10,085 ft.), active volcano, S Alaska, W of Cook Inlet, 150 mi. SW of Anchorage; 60°2'N 153°6'W.

Iliang (yē'lyäng'). **1** Town (pop. 9,913), ⊙ Iliang co. (pop. 95,973), E Yunnan prov., China, 30 mi. ESE of Kunming and on railroad; alt. 5,052 ft.; coal-mining center; chemical industry; iron smelting, tung-oil processing. Rice, wheat, millet, tea. **2** Town, Yunnan prov., China: see YILIANG.

Iliatenco (ēlyätĕng'kō), town (pop. 1,708), Guerrero, SW Mexico, in Sierra Madre del Sur, 60 mi. SE of Chilapa; cereals, fruit, livestock.

Ilic (ĭlĭch'), Turkish *Iliç*, village (pop. 1,413), Erzincan prov., E central Turkey, on Euphrates R., on railroad, and 55 mi. WSW of Erzincan; grain.

Ilich or **Il'ich** (ēlyēch'), town (1939 pop. over 10,000), S South Kazakhstan oblast, Kazakh SSR, on spur of Trans-Caspian RR and 50 mi. SW of Tashkent; cotton-ginning center in Golodnaya Step irrigation area. Near by are state cotton farms of Pakhta-Aral (12,000 acres) and Imeni 30 Oktyabrya (19,000 acres), among largest of USSR.

Ilicha, Port, Azerbaijan SSR: see PORT ILICHA.

Ilich Bay or **Il'ich Bay**, inlet of Caspian Sea, Azerbaijan SSR, on S shore of Apsheron Peninsula, 4 mi. SSW of Baku; oil fields.

Ilici, Spain: see ELCHE.

Ilidza or **Ilidzha** (ē'lĭjä), Serbo-Croatian *Ilidža*, village, S Bosnia, Yugoslavia, on railroad and 7 mi. W of Sarajevo; health resort; sulphur springs and baths. Known since Roman period; popular under Turkish rule.

Iliff (ī'lĭf), town (pop. 235), Logan co., NE Colo., on South Platte R., near Nebr. line, and 11 mi. NE of Sterling, in sugar-beet region.

Iligan (ēlē'gän), village (1939 pop. 2,580; 1948 municipality pop. 25,725), Lanao prov., W central Mindanao, Philippines, on Iligan Bay, 30 mi. SW of Cagayan; rice, corn.

Iligan Bay, inlet (30 mi. long, 30 mi. wide) of Mindanao Sea, Philippines, in N central Mindanao. On it are Kolambugan, Oroquieta, and Ozamiz (Misamis). PANGUIL BAY is inlet's SW arm.

Ilihuli Shan, Manchuria: see ILKURI MOUNTAINS.

Iliki, Lake, Greece: see HYLIKE, LAKE.

Ilim Range (ēlyēm'), central Irkutsk oblast, Russian SFSR, forms divide bet. upper Lena and Ilim rivers; highest point 3,300 ft. Angara-Ilim iron-ore basin is NW.

Ilim River, Irkutsk oblast, Russian SFSR, rises in Ilim Range, flows 225 mi. N, past Ilimsk and Nizhne-Ilimsk, through Angara-Ilim iron-ore basin to Angara R. 100 mi. N of Zayarsk. Navigable for 125 mi. below Ilimsk.

Ilimsk (ēlyēmsk'), village (1939 pop. over 500), central Irkutsk oblast, Russian SFSR, on Ilim R. and 200 mi. NE of Tulun, in Angara-Ilim iron-ore basin.

Ilin, China: see YILIN.

Ilin Island (ēlēn') (□ 30; 11 mi. long, 4 mi. wide; 1939 pop. 1,376), Mindoro prov., Philippines, in Mindoro Strait, just off S coast of Mindoro isl. 4 mi. S of San Jose; hilly, rises to 666 ft.; rice.

Iliniza, Cerro (sĕ'rō ēlēnē'sä), Andean peak (17,405 ft.) in Cotopaxi prov., central Ecuador, 18 mi. W of Cotopaxi volcano; 0°40'S 78°42'W.

Ilino or **Il'ino** (ēlyē'nù), village (1926 pop. 776), S Velikiye Luki oblast, Russian SFSR, near Western Dvina R., 37 mi. S of Toropets; dairying; flax retting.

Ilinskaya or **Il'inskaya** (ēlyēn'skīù), village (1926

pop. 13,634), E Krasnodar Territory, Russian SFSR, 20 mi. NNE of Kropotkin; flour mill, metalworks; wheat, sunflowers, castor beans.

Ilinski or **Il'inskiy** (-skē). **1** Town, Karelo-Finnish SSR: see OLONETS. **2** Town (1940 pop. 2,841), on W coast of S Sakhalin, Russian SFSR, 17 mi. NNE of Tomari, at narrowest section of isl.; N terminus (1948) of W coast railroad; herring-fishing center. Under Jap. rule (1905–45), called Kushunnai.

Ilinsko-Podomskoye or **Il'insko-Podomskoye** (ēlyēn'skŭ-pŭdôm'skŭyŭ), village (1939 pop. under 500), S Archangel oblast, Russian SFSR, on left affluent of Vychegda R. and 45 mi. ESE of Kotlas; flax processing, dairying. Formerly called Ilinskoye.

Ilinskoye or **Il'inskoye** (-skŭyŭ). **1** Village, Archangel oblast, Russian SFSR: see ILINSKO-PODOMSKOYE. **2** Village (1926 pop. 2,142), central Molotov oblast, Russian SFSR, on right tributary of Kama R. and 19 mi. SW of Chermoz; flax and food processing; grain, livestock. **3** Village (1926 pop. 206), E central Yaroslavl oblast, Russian SFSR, 15 mi. N of Rostov; potatoes, chicory.

Ilinskoye-Khovanskoye or **Il'inskoye-Khovanskoye** (-khŭvän'skŭyŭ), village (1926 pop. 1,439), W Ivanovo oblast, Russian SFSR, 45 mi. W of Ivanovo; potatoes, wheat.

Ilinsko-Zaborskoye or **Il'insko-Zaborskoye** (ēlyēn'skŭ-zŭbôr'skŭyŭ), village (1926 pop. 558), NW Gorki oblast, Russian SFSR, 32 mi. N of Semenov; flax.

Ilintsy or **Il'intsy** (ēlyēn'tsē), town (1926 pop. 11,552), E Vinnitsa oblast, Ukrainian SSR, 33 mi. ESE of Vinnitsa; sugar refining.

Iliodhromia or **Iliodromia**, Greece: see HALONNESOS.

Ilion: see TROY.

Ilion (ĭ'lēŭn), industrial village (pop. 9,363), Herkimer co., central N.Y., on Mohawk R. and the Barge Canal, and 11 mi. SE of Utica, in dairying and truck-farming area; mfg. (firearms, ammunition, typewriters, furniture, cutlery, clothing); summer resort. Inc. 1852.

Ilipa (ĭl'ĭpŭ), anc. town of Spain, near modern Seville, where Scipio Africanus Major defeated Hasdrubal (206 B.C.). The overthrow of Carthaginian power in Spain paved the way for the defeat of Hannibal at Zama (202 B.C.).

Ili River (ē'lē, yē'lē'), in China and USSR, formed by junction 65 mi. E of Kuldja in Sinkiang prov., China, of 2 branches—the Kunges, 140 mi. long, rising in E Tien Shan, China; and the Tekes, 270 mi. long, rising in central Tien Shan, Kazakh SSR. It flows 590 mi. W, past Kuldja, bet. the Dzungarian Ala-Tau and the Trans-Ili Ala-Tau, into Kazakh SSR and, passing Ili, turns NW through desert area and into SW end of L. Balkhash through a delta. Important for irrigation; navigable in middle course to Bakanas. Receives Chilik and Kaskelen rivers.

Ilirska Bistrica, Yugoslavia: see BISTRICA, SW Slovenia.

Ilisesti (ēlēshĕsht'), Rum. *Ilișești*, village (pop. 2,739), Suceava prov., N Rumania, 10 mi. WSW of Suceava; leather tanning.

Ilissos River, Greece: see EILISSOS RIVER.

Ilium: see TROY.

Iliyantsi (ĭlē'äntsē), agr. village (pop. 1,120), Sofia dist., W Bulgaria, 4 mi. N of Sofia; rail junction.

Ilja, Belorussian SSR: see ILYA.

Ilkal (ĭl'kŭl), town (pop. 17,660), Bijapur dist., S Bombay, India, 65 mi. SE of Bijapur; market center for cotton, peanuts, millet, wheat; handicraft cloth weaving and dyeing.

Ilkeston (ĭl'kĭstŭn), municipal borough (1931 pop. 32,813; 1951 census 33,674), E Derby, England, on Erewash R. and 8 mi. ENE of Derby; coal and iron mining; mfg. of rayon, silk, hosiery, lace, earthenware. Mineral springs. Has church built in late 12th cent. EASTWOOD is 3 mi. NNE, in Nottingham.

Ilkeston Junction, E suburb of Ilkeston, W Nottingham, England, on Erewash R.; leather- and metalworking.

Ilkhuri Mountains, Manchuria: see ILKURI MOUNTAINS.

Ilkley, anc. *Olicana*, urban district (1931 pop. 9,736; 1951 census 17,265), West Riding, W central Yorkshire, England, on Wharfe R. and 10 mi. NNW of Bradford; resort with mineral springs. Has remains of Roman fort. The churchyard contains 3 sculptured Saxon crosses.

Ilkuri Mountains or **Ilkhuri Mountains** (ēlkhōō̆rē'), Chinese *Ilihuli Shan* (yē'lē'hōō'lē' shän'), NE spur of the Great Khingan Mts., NW Manchuria, continued SE by Lesser Khingan Mts.; rise to 6,050 ft. Sometimes called Ilkhuri Alin.

Ill, river, France: see ILL RIVER.

Illahun (ĭl-lă'hōōn), **El Lahun**, or **Al-Lahun** (both: ĕl lă'hōōn), village (pop. 5,430), Faiyum prov., Upper Egypt, on the Bahr Yusuf, on railroad, and 11 mi. SE of Faiyum; cotton, cereals, sugar cane, fruits. Site of the pyramid built (c.1900 B.C.) by Sesostris II.

Illampu (ēyämpōō'), W Bolivia, highest mountain in the Eastern Cordillera of the Andes, in N part (Cordillera de La Paz) of range, c.5 mi. SE of Sorata. Consists of 2 peaks, Illampu (21,275 ft.) and Ancohuma (äng-kō-ōō'mä) (21,490 ft.). Sometimes called Mt. Sorata (sōrä'tä).

Illana (ēlyä'nä), town (pop. 2,074), Guadalajara prov., central Spain, 45 mi. ESE of Madrid; cereals, olives, grapes, livestock; olive-oil pressing.

Illana Bay (ēyä'nä, ēlyä'nä), inlet of Moro Gulf in SW coast of Mindanao, Philippines; 50 mi. wide at mouth, 40 mi. long. Pagadian is on NW shore, Cotabato on SE shore. Bongo Isl. is in it.

Illapel (ēyäpĕl'), town (pop. 6,085), ⊙ Illapel dept. (□ 3,994; pop. 52,709), Coquimbo prov., N central Chile, on Illapel R. (affluent of the Choapa), on railroad and 120 mi. S of La Serena; agr. center, with mild climate; grain, fruit, cattle. In colonial times noted for its gold deposits.

Illarionovo (ēlŭrēô'nŭvŭ), town (1939 pop. over 500), central Dnepropetrovsk oblast, Ukrainian SSR, 10 mi. ESE of Dnepropetrovsk, across Dnieper R.

Illasi (ēl-lä'zē), village (pop. 1,369), Verona prov., Veneto, N Italy, 9 mi. ENE of Verona, in fruit-growing region; wine.

Illaunamid or **Illaunimmul**, rocky islet in the Atlantic, W Co. Galway, Ireland, 10 mi. SW of Clifden; 2 lighthouses (53°24'N 10°14'W).

Illava, Czechoslovakia: see ILAVA.

Illawarra District (ĭ"lŭwă'rŭ), New South Wales, Australia, on E coast, extends 50 mi. S from Helensburgh to Nowra and lower Shoalhaven R.; contains Illawarra L. Known for coastal scenery; many seaside resorts. Produces dairy foods, coal. Wollongong (coal-mining center), chief town.

Illawarra Lake, lagoon (□ 13), E New South Wales, Australia, on coast, near Wollongong, in Illawarra Dist., 45 mi. S of Sydney; 4 mi. long, 3 mi. wide.

Illawarra North, municipality (pop. 1,810), E New South Wales, Australia, on the Pacific, 40 mi. SW of Sydney, in coal-mining area.

Ille or **Ille-sur-la-Têt** (ēl-sür-lä-tĕt'), town (pop. 3,711), Pyrénées-Orientales dept., S France, on the Têt and 14 mi. W of Perpignan; noted orchards and olive groves. Fruit preserving and shipping.

Illecillewaet River (ĭ"lŭsĭ'lŭwĭt, -wĕt, -wăt), SE B.C., rises in Illecillewaet Glacier in Selkirk Mts., Glacier Natl. Park, flows c.50 mi. W to Columbia R. at Revelstoke.

Ille-et-Vilaine (ēl-ā-vēlĕn'), department (□ 2,700; pop. 578,246), in Brittany, W France, on English Channel; ⊙ Rennes. Mostly flat. Drained by the Vilaine, Ille, Rance, and Couesnon rivers. A leading cider-making region, with extensive apple and pear orchards. Other crops: wheat, barley, oats, potatoes, tobacco, hemp. One of France's chief dairy-farming and beekeeping areas. Some iron deposits (in S); granite quarries. Principal industries are tanning and brush mfg. at Rennes, shoe mfg. at Fougères, vegetable canning, and oyster fishing (Cancale). Coastal tourist resorts are Dinard, Saint-Malo (chief port), and Saint-Servan.

Ille-Rance Canal (ēl-räs'), Côtes-du-Nord and Ille-et-Vilaine depts., W France, connects Dinan (on the Rance) with Rennes (on the Vilaine at the mouth of the Ille); c.40 mi. long. Takes imported British coal inland from Saint-Malo.

Ille River (ēl), Ille-et-Vilaine dept., W France, rises in Boulet L. 5 mi. SE of Combourg, flows 28 mi. S, joining the Vilaine at Rennes. Its channel used by Ille-Rance Canal, which connects Dinan and Rennes.

Iller River (ĭ'lŭr), Germany, rises in Allgäu Alps near Austrian border, flows 91 mi. N, past Kempten, to the Danube at Neu-Ulm. In middle and upper course it forms boundary between Bavaria and Württemberg-Hohenzollern.

Illertissen (ĭ"lŭrtĭ'sŭn), village (pop. 4,637), Swabia, SW Bavaria, Germany, near the Iller, 13 mi. SSE of Ulm; mfg. of chemicals, textiles, ceramics; metal- and woodworking, tanning. Has Renaissance castle. Chartered 1430.

Illesca, Cerro (sĕ'rō ēyĕs'kä), small hilly range on Pacific coast of Piura dept., NW Peru, extends c.20 mi. S from Aguja Point; rises to 1,696 ft. At its S foot are the now-abandoned Reventazón sulphur mines.

Illescas (ēlyĕ'skäs), town (pop. 2,168), Toledo prov., central Spain, on railroad and 21 mi. SSW of Madrid; wheat, carobs, olives, potatoes, cattle, hogs. Olive-oil pressing, sawmilling, plaster and soap mfg. Has Caridad church and hospital. Francis I of France lived here.

Illescas (ēyĕ'skäs), village, Florida dept., SE central Uruguay, in the Cuchilla Grande Principal, on railroad and road, and 13 mi. SW of José Batlle y Ordóñez, on Lavalleja dept. line; agr. settlement; wheat, corn, oats, cattle.

Ille-sur-la-Têt, France: see ILLE.

Illiberis, Spain: see GRANADA, city.

Illiers (ēlyā'), town (pop. 2,226), Eure-et-Loir dept., NW central France, on the Loir and 15 mi. SW of Chartres; agr. market in horse-raising area; dairying.

Illilouette Fall, Calif.: see YOSEMITE NATIONAL PARK.

Illimani (ēyēmä'nē), Andean peak (21,185 ft.) in Cordillera de La Paz, W Bolivia, 25 mi. SE of La Paz. Tungsten deposits at SE foot.

Illimo (ēyē'mō), town (pop. 2,018), Lambayeque dept., NW Peru, on coastal plain, on Leche R. and 15 mi. N of Lambayeque, on Pan American Highway; rice, corn, wheat, fruits; apiculture.

Illingen (ĭ'lĭng-ŭn), town (pop. 4,955), central Saar, 6 mi. WNW of Neunkirchen, in coal-mining region.

Illinois (ĭlŭnoi'), state (land □ 55,947; with inland waters, but without □ 1,526 of L. Michigan, □ 56,400; 1950 pop. 8,712,176; 1940 pop. 7,897,241), central U.S., in the Middle West, bordered N by Wis., W by Iowa and Mo., S by Ky., E by Ind.; 23d in area, 4th in pop.; admitted 1818 as 21st state; ⊙ Springfield. Extends 385 mi. N–S, 215 mi. E–W. It is bounded largely by natural features, including the Mississippi R. for its entire W border, L. Michigan (NE), Wabash R. along S part of E border, and Ohio R. (S). The "Prairie State" lies in the vast interior plains region and consists of fairly level prairie land, sloping gently southward from 1,241 ft. near Wis. line to 279 ft. at confluence of Mississippi and Ohio rivers near Cairo. Variations in topography are largely determined by glacial deposits left by the Pleistocene ice sheets, which covered all of Ill. except the extreme NW (part of Wisconsin Driftless Area) and the far S. Across S Ill. runs an E extension (rising to c.1,000 ft.) of the Ozark Mts. The state is drained by the ILLINOIS RIVER and the Rock, Sangamon, Kaskaskia, Big Muddy, Little Wabash, and Embarrass rivers. The larger river courses are flanked by picturesque limestone bluffs. Climate is predominantly continental, with subtropical conditions prevailing in extreme S region (known locally as Egypt). Extremes in temp. are common, especially in the N; annual rainfall averages 30–35 in. over most of the state, increasing to c.45 in. in the S. Chicago has mean temp. of 25°F. in Jan., 73°F. in July, and 33 in. of annual rainfall. Growing season varies from 150 days along N border to 200 days at S tip. Natural vegetation consisted of prairie grassland and, in S, oak-hickory forest. Ill. is an important agr. state, ranking high in the production of corn and hogs (2d only to Iowa), oats (3d), hay, winter wheat, soybeans (1st; more than ⅓ of U.S. output), cattle, poultry, and dairy products. Vast stretches of level terrain are conducive to mechanized farming. About ⅔ of the total crop acreage (20,500,000) is in corn, raised chiefly in N half of state, where the oat crop is also concentrated. The wheat areas are W central and SW, while hay and soybeans are grown throughout. Other crops include rye, barley, potatoes, buckwheat, and fruit (apples, peaches; in S and W); cotton is grown on the river-bottom lands of the 3 southernmost counties. Truck farms are localized near the large cities. Cash-grain farming centers in the E central sector, but the bulk of Ill.'s agr. forms the basis of a flourishing livestock industry, including (1950) 3,159,000 head of cattle (raised throughout, but especially numerous in N and NW), 6,285,000 hogs (chiefly W and NW in corn belts), 180,000 horses, and 585,000 sheep. The N border counties lie in a major dairying area, producing large quantities of cheese, milk, margarine, and ice cream. Beef cattle are also important, and CHICAGO, with its huge stockyards and meat-packing plants, is the world's largest livestock market. Poultry farming is carried on mainly in the SW. Total commercial forest land amounts to some 3,300,000 acres; chief timber species are oak, hickory, maple, elm, ash, beech, cottonwood, and basswood; natl. forest reserves (S) comprise 812,654 acres. Bituminous coal is the chief mineral product, in which it ranks 3d in U.S. output; the Eastern Interior Coal Field underlies more than half the state, with the main mining centers in Franklin, Williamson, Marion, Perry, Sangamon, Fulton, and Vermilion counties. The coal is of medium grade, adequate for most industrial uses but not for the NE lakeside steel industry, which is supplied largely by the Appalachian fields. Petroleum is obtained in the S half of the state, mainly bet. Kaskaskia and Wabash rivers; refineries at Roxana, Wood River, East St. Louis, and Hartford in the St. Louis conurbation and at Lockport, Lemont, Centralia, Lawrenceville, and Robinson. Other minerals are fluorspar (over 50% of U.S. output; mostly from Hardin co.), natural gas and gasoline, tripoli, peat, lead, zinc, sand and gravel, and limestone. Ill. is a leading mfg. state, making a wide variety of products, including agr. machinery, packed meat, steel, furniture, electrical machinery, petroleum and machine-shop products, food, corn products, railway equipment, cement, footwear, confectioneries, distilled liquors, home appliances and luxury goods, and clothing; commercial printing and publishing are important. Over 70% of the mfg., as well as over 50% of the state's pop., is centered in Cook co., where Chicago, the metropolis of the Midwest and the nation's 2d largest city, is situated. The city has profited by its strategic location at the S tip of L. Michigan to become the world's largest rail hub and a major road and air center and inland port (bulk of shipments handled at CALUMET HARBOR); besides its pre-eminence as a livestock and grain market, it also is the center of a heavy industrial concentration, including its suburbs Cicero and Chicago Heights and the Calumet region (part of its huge metropolitan area) which extends SE into Ind. Other mfg. centers are East Saint Louis and surrounding industrial towns (e.g., Alton, Belleville, Granite City) of St. Louis metropolitan dist., Peoria, Rockford, Rock Island and Moline (farm equipment), Springfield, Joliet, Decatur, Aurora, Elgin (watches), Quincy, Waukegan, Champaign, and Galesburg. The Argonne Natl. Laboratory (atomic research) is near Lemont. Ill.'s industrial development has been favored by the state's central location, its easy access to raw materials, abundant labor supply, and large local and Western markets. The state is served by dense road and rail networks and by the c.325-mi.-long ILLINOIS WATERWAY, which links L. Michigan at Chicago with the Mississippi above St. Louis. Leading educational institutions are Univ. of Ill. (at Urbana), Northwestern Univ. (at Evanston), Bradley Univ. (at Peoria), and Univ. of Chicago, De Paul Univ., Loyola Univ., Roosevelt Col., and Ill. Inst. of Technology (all at Chicago). Numerous earthen mounds throughout the state attest to the early Mound Builders' culture which existed in the Mississippi basin. The Kaskaskia, Sac, and Fox were the principal Indian tribes in Ill. at the time of the 1st white exploration, notably by Father Marquette and Jolliet, who traveled up the Illinois R. in 1673, and by La Salle, who built Fort Crève Coeur, near present Peoria, in 1680. Missionary settlements were made at CAHOKIA (1699) and KASKASKIA (1703) on the Mississippi, and in 1720s Ill. became part of French prov. of Louisiana. Ceded to the British in 1763, the area was the scene of several skirmishes during the Revolution, when George Rogers Clark led the colonial forces in this section. Under the Ordinance of 1787 Ill. was included in the NORTHWEST TERRITORY; part of Indiana Territory 1800; with Wis., made a separate territory 1809. Recurrent trouble with the British and Indians culminated in the War of 1812, marked by the massacre of the garrison of Fort Dearborn (later Chicago), which had been founded 1803 on the portage bet. L. Michigan and the upper Illinois R. Statehood was achieved (1818) in a period of rapid pop. growth, the majority of settlers (mostly farmers) coming from the South, although later on, in the internal improvements era, most settlers were from the Northeast. The Black Hawk War (1832) with the Sac and Fox resulted in the expulsion of the last remaining Indians from Ill., and soon after 1844, when their leaders Joseph and Hyrum Smith were murdered, the Mormons were forced to leave NAUVOO and migrate to Utah. Development of the land proceeded apace with the arrival of more immigrants (including Europeans), the building of railroads, and the opening of the prairies to farming and coal mining. The slavery question, dramatized by the famous Lincoln-Douglas debates in 1858, divided the state into Northern and Southern factions and led to the formation (1856) of the state Republican party at Bloomington. In 1860, however, Lincoln, who had lived at Springfield since 1837, was elected president and in the ensuing Civil War Ill. rallied to the Union cause. The latter half of the 19th cent. was a period of great industrial (machine shops, stockyards) and agr. (mechanized corn and wheat farming) expansion. However, farmer discontent with exorbitant railroad rates and high price of manufactured goods gave rise to the powerful Granger movement, while organized labor grew in strength and industrial strikes became numerous. Chicago, where the violent Haymarket riot (1886) and Pullman strike (1894) took place, was the center of a strong trade union movement and was later the birthplace of the Socialist Party (1901; headed by Eugene Debs), Industrial Workers of the World (1905), and Communist Party (1919). In the early 20th cent. labor conditions improved and Ill. was a leader in progressive social legislation. State politics have since responded to conflicting farmer, labor, and management forces, as well as to strong isolationist sentiment. For further information see articles on cities, towns, geographic features, and the 102 counties: ADAMS, ALEXANDER, BOND, BOONE, BROWN, BUREAU, CALHOUN, CARROLL, CASS, CHAMPAIGN, CHRISTIAN, CLARK, CLAY, CLINTON, COLES, COOK, CRAWFORD, CUMBERLAND, DE KALB, DE WITT, DOUGLAS, DU PAGE, EDGAR, EDWARDS, EFFINGHAM, FAYETTE, FORD, FRANKLIN, FULTON, GALLATIN, GREENE, GRUNDY, HAMILTON, HANCOCK, HARDIN, HENDERSON, HENRY, IROQUOIS, JACKSON, JASPER, JEFFERSON, JERSEY, JO DAVIESS, JOHNSON, KANE, KANKAKEE, KENDALL, KNOX, LAKE, LA SALLE, LAWRENCE, LEE, LIVINGSTON, LOGAN, MCDONOUGH, MCHENRY, MCLEAN, MACON, MACOUPIN, MADISON, MARION, MARSHALL, MASON, MASSAC, MENARD, MERCER, MONROE, MONTGOMERY, MORGAN, MOULTRIE, OGLE, PEORIA, PERRY, PIATT, PIKE, POPE, PULASKI, PUTNAM, RANDOLPH, RICHLAND, ROCK ISLAND, ST. CLAIR, SALINE, SANGAMON, SCHUYLER, SCOTT, SHELBY, STARK, STEPHENSON, TAZEWELL, UNION, VERMILION, WABASH, WARREN, WASHINGTON, WAYNE, WHITE, WHITESIDE, WILL, WILLIAMSON, WINNEBAGO, WOODFORD.

Illinois and Michigan Canal, Ill.: see ILLINOIS WATERWAY.

Illinois and Mississippi Canal, NW Ill., abandoned waterway (75 mi. long) bet. the Mississippi at Rock Island and Illinois R. near Bureau. Opened 1907; soon abandoned because of rail competition.

Illinois River. 1 In Ark. and Okla., rises in the Ozarks in Benton co., NW Ark., flows W and SW into Okla., past Watts (dam impounds small L. Francis here), to Arkansas R. just S of Gore; 145 mi. long. In lower course c.7 mi. NW of Vian is site of dam (160 ft. high) impounding Tenkiller Ferry Reservoir (capacity 630,000 acre-ft.) for flood control, hydroelectric power. **2** In Ill., formed 45 mi. SW of Chicago by confluence of Des Plaines and Kankakee rivers, flows W, past Morris, Ottawa, La Salle, Peru, and Spring Valley to Depue, where it makes a great bend to SW and flows past Peoria (principal city and port on river), Pekin, Havana, and Beardstown, thence S to the Mississippi at Grafton; 273 mi. long. State's principal internal waterway and a link in shipping route bet. the Great Lakes and the Gulf of Mexico, it is part of ILLINOIS WATERWAY system. Principal cargoes carried (chiefly by barges) are coal, grain, petroleum. Marseilles Canal around rapids at Marseilles and several locks and dams aid navigation. Right-bank tributaries include the Fox, Spoon, and La Moine rivers; left tributaries are the Vermilion, the Mackinaw, and the Sangamon. Illinois-Kankakee system (420 mi. long, to farthest headstream) drains □ 27,900. In wide flood plain of its lower 200 mi., the Illinois has formed many bayou lakes (e.g., Senachwine L., Meredosia L.) which afford waterfowl hunting. Widened section (c.15 mi. long) above Peoria is called L. Peoria.

Illinois Waterway, commercial and pleasure-craft route (c.325 mi. long) in Ill., extending from L. Michigan at Chicago to the mouth of Illinois R. on the Mississippi at Grafton, 38 mi. above St. Louis, Mo.; toll-free; operated by U.S. Army Corps of Engineers. From L. Michigan, it follows CHICAGO RIVER and its South Branch and the SANITARY AND SHIP CANAL to DES PLAINES RIVER (locks) at Lockport, thence the Des Plaines and the ILLINOIS RIVER to the Mississippi, thus forming part of Great Lakes-to-Gulf Waterway, connecting Great Lakes with Gulf of Mexico. In Chicago area, the CALUMET SAG CHANNEL, and Grand Calumet, Little Calumet, and CALUMET rivers link main waterway with L. Calumet, South Chicago Harbor, and Indiana Harbor (bet. East Chicago and Gary, Ind.) Principal cargoes carried on waterway are coal, building materials, petroleum, grain, steel products, sulphur, limestone; most of shipping is by barge. Old Illinois and Michigan Canal (96 mi. long; completed 1848, unused since 1900), part of which is paralleled by present waterway, was former shipping link bet. Chicago R. and Illinois R. at La Salle. Recreational areas (Illinois and Michigan Canal Parkway) have been developed along it.

Illiopolis, (ĭlēō'pùlĭs), village (pop. 833), Sangamon co., central Ill., 15 mi. W of Decatur, in agr. and bituminous-coal area; ships grain.

Illkirch-Graffenstaden (ēlkĭrsh'-gräfĕnstädĕn', Ger. ĭl'kĭrkh-grä'fùn-shtädùn), town (pop. 7,656), Bas-Rhin dept., E France, on the Ill, on Rhone-Rhine Canal, and 5 mi. SSW of Strasbourg; industrial center; metalworks (locomotives, machine tools, woodworking machinery) and glassworks; aluminum smelting, rubber and wax mfg. Poultry and vegetable shipping. Capitulation of Strasbourg signed here 1681.

Illmitz (ĭl'mĭts), village (pop. 2,210), Burgenland, E Austria, 11 mi. NE of Sopron, Hungary, across Neusiedler L.; vineyards.

Illmo (ĭl'mō), city (pop. 1,247), Scott co., SE Mo., near Mississippi R., 6 mi. S of Cape Girardeau; agr.; clothing factories. Inc. 1906.

Illnau (ĭl'nou), town (pop. 3,925), Zurich canton, N Switzerland, on Kempt R. (affluent of Töss R.) and 9 mi. E of Zurich; metalworking; cotton textiles, flour.

Illogan (ĭlō'gùn, ĭlŭ'–), town and parish (pop. 8,008), W Cornwall, England, 2 mi. NW of Redruth; tin and copper mining.

Íllora (ē'lyōrä), town (pop. 4,498), Granada prov., S Spain, 17 mi. NW of Granada; olive-oil processing, brandy distilling, flour milling. Cereals, sugar beets, wine, fruit; lumbering.

Ill River, W Austria, rises in glacier of Piz Buin of Silvretta Group, flows c.45 mi. NW, through MONTAFON valley, past Bludenz and Feldkirch, to the Rhine 5 mi. W of Feldkirch. Hydroelectric works in upper course.

Ill River (ēl), Haut-Rhin and Bas-Rhin depts., E France, rises on N slopes of the Jura, S of Ferrette (near Swiss border), flows 127 mi. NNE in a course almost parallel to the Rhine, draining Alsatian lowland, past Mulhouse, Sélestat, Erstein, and Strasbourg, to the Rhine below La Wanzenau. Navigable in Strasbourg area. Receives Thur, Fecht, and Bruche rivers (left), all rising in the Vosges.

Illueca (ēlūā'kä), town (pop. 1,993), Saragossa prov., NE Spain, 13 mi. N of Calatayud; woolen mills, shoe factory; olive oil, wine, pears.

Illuxt, Latvia: see ILUKSTE.

Illyria (ĭlĭ'rēù), anc. region of vague limits on N and E shores of the Adriatic, occupied in prehistoric times by a group of Indo-European speaking tribes. Among the Illyrian peoples were the tribes later called the Dalmatians and the Pannonians; therefore sometimes Illyria is taken in the widest sense to include the whole area occupied by the Pannonians, and thus to reach from Epirus N to the Danube. More usually today Illyria is used to mean only the Adriatic coast N of central Albania and W of the Dinaric Alps. The Romans undertook to conquer the Illyrians in the 3d cent. B.C. An Illyrian kingdom had been set up with the capital at Scodra (modern Scutari, Albania), and trouble over Illyrian piracy led the Romans to conduct 2 victorious Illyrian wars (229–228, 219 B.C.). After the Dalmatians had split from this kingdom, the Romans conquered its king, Genthius, and established (168–167 B.C.) one of the earliest of Roman colonies as Illyricum (ĭlĭ'rĭkùm). The colony was enlarged by the total conquest of Dalmatia in several wars. Illyricum was expanded by conquests (12–11 B.C.) of the Pannonians. At the time of the stubborn revolt of the Illyrians (A.D. 6–9) the territory was split into the provs. of Dalmatia and Pannonia, but the term *Illyricum* was still used. It was later given to one of the great prefectures of the late Roman Empire. Illyricum then included much of the region N of the Adriatic as well as a large part of the Balkan Peninsula. When Napoleon revived (1809) the name for the Illyrian Provs. of his empire he included much of the region N of the Adriatic and what is today E Yugoslavia. Roughly the same region was included in the administrative dist. of Austria called (1816–49) the Illyrian kingdom.

Illzach (ēlzäk', Ger. ĭlt'säkh), N suburb (pop. 1,710) of Mulhouse, Haut-Rhin dept., E France, on the Ill; textile bleaching, mfg. (brushes, chemicals, fertilizer). Large paper mill at Île-Napoléon (2 mi. E), near junction of Rhone-Rhine and Huningue canals.

Ilmen, Lake, or **Lake Il'men'** (ĭl'mùn, Rus. ēl'-mĭnyù) (□ 425-850), in Novgorod oblast, Russian SFSR, just S of Novgorod; 26 mi. long (E-W), 21 mi. wide, 32 ft. deep. Its 52 inlets include Msta, Pola, Lovat, and Shelon rivers; empties (N) through Volkhov R. into L. Ladoga. Near NE shore, Siversov and Vishera canals connect Msta and Volkhov rivers, by-passing the lake as part of Vyshnevolotsk canal system. Shipbuilding, fishing, lumbering, agr. along its shores. Novgorod lies near N, Staraya Russa near S shore. In 9th–12th cent., lake was part of important waterway connecting Baltic and Black seas.

Ilmenau (ĭl'mùnou), town (pop. 18,603), Thuringia, central Germany, in Thuringian Forest, on Ilm R. and 20 mi. SSW of Erfurt, in fluorspar-mining region; china- and glass-mfg. center; also mfg. of optical and precision instruments, electric lamps, leather, machinery; woodworking. Climatic health resort. Has Gothic church, rebuilt 1609; palace (17th cent.); 18th-cent. town hall. First mentioned in 10th cent., it was silver- and copper-mining center in 17th and early-18th cent. Frequented by Goethe, whose cottage on Kickelhahn (kĭ'kùlhän") mtn. (2,825 ft.), 2 mi. SW, was rebuilt in 1874 after fire.

Ilmenau. 1 Town, S Krakow prov., Poland: see JORDANOW. **2** Town, SE Krakow prov., Poland: see LIMANOWA.

Ilmenau River, NW Germany, formed below Uelzen, flows c.60 mi. N and NW, past Lüneburg (head of navigation), to the Elbe 2 mi. N of Winsen.

Ilminster, urban district (1931 pop. 2,232; 1951 census 2,610), S Somerset, England, on Isle R. (short tributary of Parrett R.) and 10 mi. SE of Taunton; agr. market; mfg. (lace, cement). Has 15th-cent. church and 16th-cent. grammar school.

Ilm River (ĭlm), central Germany, rises in Thuringian Forest SW of Ilmenau, flows 75 mi. NE, past Ilmenau and Weimar, to the Thuringian Saale 7 mi. WSW of Naumburg.

Ilnitskaya or **Il'nitskaya** (ēl'nyĭtskīŭ), Czech *Ilnica* (ĭl'nyĭtsä), Hung. *Ilonca* (ĭ'lôngkŏ), village (1941 pop. 5,607), central Transcarpathian Oblast, Ukrainian SSR, on railroad and 15 mi. NW of Khust; lignite mining.

Ilo (ē'lō), town (pop. 1,043), Moquegua dept., S Peru, Pacific port at mouth of Moquegua R. (irrigation), 37 mi. SW of Moquegua (linked by rail); 17°37'S 71°19'W. With a well-protected harbor, Ilo is shipping center for fertile irrigation area (olives, wine, figs, cotton). Fishing, fruit canning, and olive-oil extracting. Airfield. Its rail station, Pacocha, is 1½ mi. S.

Ilobasco (ēlōbä'skō), city (pop. 3,632), Cabañas dept., N central Salvador, 25 mi. ENE of San Salvador; major pottery center; clays quarried near by. Agr., livestock raising.

Ilobu (ēlô'bōō), town, Oyo prov., Western Provinces, SW Nigeria, 7 mi. NW of Oshogbo; cotton weaving; cacao, palm oil and kernels, cotton, yams, corn, cassava, plantains.

Ilocos Norte (ēlō'kōs nôr'tā), province (□ 1,308; 1948 pop. 251,455), NW Luzon, Philippines, bounded W and N by S.China Sea; ⊙ LAOAG, chief port. Largely mountainous, with fertile coastal strip; drained by many small streams. Rice is grown extensively. There are chrome-ore deposits and manganese mines.

Ilocos Sur (sōōr'), province (□ 1,037; 1948 pop. 276,278), N Luzon, Philippines, bounded W by S.China Sea; ⊙ VIGAN. Generally level, except in

E part. Rice is grown in coastal areas. One of chief centers of weaving industry.

Ilog (ē'lōg), town (1939 pop. 3,244; 1948 municipality pop. 21,645), Negros Occidental prov., W Negros isl., Philippines, near Panay Gulf, 13 mi. SSW of Binalbagan; agr. center (rice, sugar cane).

Iloilo (ē"lōē'lō), province (□ 2,048; 1948 pop. 816,382), E Panay isl., Philippines, bounded E by Visayan Sea and Guimaras Strait, SE by Panay Gulf; ⊙ Iloilo. Includes GUIMARAS ISLAND. Mountainous, with fertile valleys. Agr. (rice, sugar cane, coconuts), horse breeding.

Iloilo, city (1939 pop. 62,954; 1948 metropolitan area pop. 110,122), ⊙ Iloilo prov., SE Panay isl., Philippines, port on Iloilo Strait (1½–4 mi. wide), opposite Guimaras Isl., 290 mi. SSE of Manila; 10°42'N 122°34'E. Terminus of railroad from Capiz. Chief commercial center of the isl., exporting sugar, rice, hemp. Produces *jusi* and piña cloth, guano, and phosphate rock. The Central Philippine Col. of Jaro is here.

Iloilo Strait, Philippines: see GUIMARAS STRAIT.

Ilok (ē'lôk), Hung. *Újlak* (ōō'ēlŏk), village, NE Croatia, Yugoslavia, on the Danube and 28 mi. E of Vinkovci, in winegrowing region. Has castle noted for its wine cellars.

Ilonca, Ukrainian SSR: see ILNITSKAYA.

Ilonga, Tanganyika: see KILOSA.

Ilopango (ēlōpäng'gō), town (pop. 1,068), San Salvador dept., S central Salvador, on railroad and Inter-American Highway, 5 mi. E of San Salvador, near W shore of L. Ilopango; pleasure resort; agr. (tobacco, sugar cane). Site of San Salvador airport (commercial and military).

Ilopango, Lake (□ 30), on San Salvador–La Paz–Cuscatlán dept. border, S central Salvador, 6 mi. E of San Salvador; 8 mi. long, 5 mi. wide; alt. 1,450 ft. Occupies old volcanic crater; sulphurous water. Popular tourist resort, with center at Asino, small port on W shore, near Ilopango town. Ilopango volcano (150 ft. high, 500 ft. across) appeared 1880 in center of lake. Outlet (E) drains into Jiboa R.

Ilorin (ēlô'rĕn), province (□ 17,719; pop. 453,347), Northern Provinces, W Nigeria; ⊙ Ilorin. Bounded W by Dahomey, E by Niger R.; largely savanna pasture land, with some deciduous forest (SE). Gold mining (N) near Kaiama and Bussa. Agr. (shea nuts, cotton, yams, corn, durra); cattle raising. Pop. largely Yoruba (S, near Ilorin). Main centers: Ilorin, Jebba, Offa. E section of former Borgu kingdom forms a div. (⊙ KAIAMA) of prov.

Ilorin, city (pop. 47,412), ⊙ Ilorin prov., Northern Provinces, W Nigeria, on railroad and 160 mi. NNE of Lagos; 8°45'N 4°32'E. Major agr. trade center (palm oil, rubber). Mfg. (baskets, pottery); shea-nut processing, cotton weaving; yams, corn, durra; cattle, skins. Has hosp. Airfield. One of the most populous cities of Yoruba tribe in Northern Provinces of Nigeria; surrounded by a mud wall.

Ilosva, Ukrainian SSR: see IRSHAVA.

Ilovaisk or **Ilovaysk** (ēlŭvīsk'), city (1939 pop. over 10,000), central Stalino oblast, Ukrainian SSR, in the Donbas, 13 mi. SE of Makeyevka; rail junction; metalworks.

Ilova River (ē'lôvä), N Croatia, Yugoslavia, in Slavonia; rises in Bilo Gora 5 mi. S of Virovitica, flows c.50 mi. SW to Lonja R. 5 mi. S of Kutina.

Ilovatka (ēlŭvät'kŭ), village (1939 pop. over 2,000), NE Stalingrad oblast, Russian SFSR, on left bank of Volga R. and 36 mi. NE of Kamyshin; metalworks; wheat, fruit.

Ilovlinskaya (ē'lŭvlyĭnskīŭ), village (1926 pop. 2,067), central Stalingrad oblast, Russian SFSR, on Ilovlya R., near its confluence with the Don, and 45 mi. NW of Stalingrad; rail junction; dairying center. S terminus of Volga lateral railroad (built during Second World War).

Ilovlya River (ē'lŭvlyŭ), in S European Russian SFSR, rises W of Zolotoye (Saratov oblast), flows c.150 mi. SSW, past Solodcha, to Don R. below Ilovlinskaya.

Ilov-vrakh or **Il'ov-Vrakh** (ē'lôf-vräkh'), peak (5,915 ft.) in Males Mts., on Yugoslav-Bulgarian line, 17 mi. SSW of Gorna Dzhumaya, Bulgaria. Also called Dzhama or Dzhema.

Ilpela Pass (ēlpā'lä) (1,520 ft.), in the Andes, on Argentina-Chile border, W of L. Lacar; 40°10'S 71°50'W.

Ilpyrski or **Il'pyrskiy** (ēl'pĭrskē), town (1949 pop. over 500), NE Koryak Natl. Okrug, Kamchatka oblast, Khabarovsk Territory, Russian SFSR, on Bering Sea, 150 mi. NE of Palana, on Cape Ilpyr; 59°50'N 164°10'E. Fish cannery.

Ilsenburg (ĭl'zŭnbŏŏrk), town (pop. 6,713), in former Prussian Saxony prov., central Germany, after 1945 in Saxony-Anhalt, at N foot of the upper Harz, 5 mi. WNW of Wernigerode; mfg. of electric vehicles; steel milling (foundry established 1540), copper smelting and refining. Climatic health resort. First Ger. country boarding school founded here in 1898. Town grew around castle 1st mentinoed in 10th cent. and converted 1003 into Benedictine monastery. Of the monastery, the Romanesque church and bldgs. (converted 1609 into palace) are extant.

Ilshofen (ĭls'hō"fŭn), town (pop. 983), N Württemberg, Germany, after 1945 in Württemberg-Baden, 9 mi. NE of Schwäbisch Hall; grain, cattle.

Ilsington (ĭl'zĭngtŭn), agr. village and parish (pop. 1,135), central Devon, England, 6 mi. NW of Newton Abbot, at E end of Dartmoor. Has 14th-cent. church, old thatched cottages.

Ilski or **Il'skiy** (ēl'skē), town (1926 pop. 9,476), W Krasnodar Territory, Russian SFSR, on railroad and 21 mi. SW of Krasnodar; oil wells.

Ilubabor or **Ilubbabor** (ēlōō'bäbōr), province (□ 19,000), SW Ethiopia; ⊙ Gore. Situated bet. Baro and Akobo rivers, borders on Anglo-Egyptian Sudan. Consists (W–E) of lowland, plateau (1,500 –3,000 ft.), and mtn. region (6,000–8,000 ft.). Largely forested with grasslands in W. Lowland is seasonally swampy and infested by malaria and tsetse fly; drained by Gila R. Agr. (durra, corn, rice, beans, cotton, tobacco), stock raising, fishing. Chief products are coffee, largely gathered from wild plants, beeswax, and hides. Gold deposits along Akobo and Baro rivers. Trade centers, Gore and Burei. Annexed 1887 by Ethiopia.

Ilukste (ē'lōōkstā), Lettish *Ilūkste*, Ger. *Illuxt*, city (pop. 1,300), SE Latvia, in Zemgale, 11 mi. NW of Daugavpils, near left bank of the Western Dvina; agr. market (rye, fodder); wool processing, flour milling.

Ilumán (ēlōōmän'), village, Imbabura prov., N Ecuador, in the Andes, 9 mi. WSW of Ibarra, in agr. region (cereals, fruit, coffee, stock); weaving of Indian shawls and other woolen goods.

Ilung (yē'lōōng'), town (pop. 18,465), ⊙ Ilung co. (pop. 319,686), N Szechwan prov., China, 25 mi. E of Langchung; sugar cane, sweet potatoes, cotton, beans.

Iluro, France: see OLORON-SAINTE-MARIE.

Ilva, Italy: see ELBA.

Ilversgehofen (ĭl'fūrsgŭhō"fŭn), industrial N suburb of Erfurt, Thuringia, central Germany.

Ilvesheim (ĭl'fŭs-hīm), village (pop. 3,989), N Baden, Germany, after 1945 in Württemberg-Baden, on the canalized Neckar and 4 mi. E of Mannheim; tobacco.

Ilwaco (ĭlwŏ'kō), town (pop. 628), Pacific co., SW Wash., at mouth of the Columbia, 12 mi. NW of Astoria, Oregon; salmon, oysters, tuna, cranberries.

Ilya or **Il'ya** (ēlyä'), Pol. *Ilja*, village (1939 pop. over 500), E Molodechno oblast, Belorussian SSR, on Ilya R. (left tributary of Viliya R.) and 19 mi. NE of Molodechno; rye, oats, flax.

Ilyaly or **Il'yaly** (ēlyä'lē), town (1932 pop. estimate 1,500), NE Tashauz oblast, Turkmen SSR, on Khiva oasis, 17 mi. W of Tashauz; cotton.

Ilyas Dag (ĭlyäs' dä), Turkish *Ilyas Dağ*, peak (1,991 ft.), on Marmara Isl., NW Turkey, in Sea of Marmara.

Ilych River (ēlych'), in Komi Autonomous SSR, Russian SFSR, rises in the N Urals at 63°15'N, flows c.200 mi. S and W to Pechora R. at Ust-Ilych, 20 mi. SE of Troitsko-Pechorsk. Forms N border of Pechora-Ilych game reserve.

Ilza (ē'ōō-zhä), Pol. *Iłża*, Rus. *Ilzha* (ēl'zhä), town (pop. 3,813), Kielce prov., E central Poland, 17 mi. SSE of Radom; flour milling, tanning, brewing; stone quarrying. Castle ruins near by.

Ilz River (ĭlts), Bavaria, Germany, rises in the Bohemian Forest near Czechoslovak border, flows 36 mi. S to the Danube at Passau.

Ima (ē'mä), town (pop. 7,886), Niigata prefecture, central Honshu, Japan, 7 mi. NE of Nagaoka; rice, raw silk.

Imabari (ēmä'bärē), city and port (1940 pop. 55,557; 1947 pop. 52,026), Ehime prefecture, N Shikoku, Japan, on Hiuchi Sea, 21 mi. NE of Matsuyama; mfg. center; cotton-textile mills, woodworking factories. Fishery. Exports copper, fodder, oil cakes. Formerly sometimes called Imaharu and Imabaru.

Imabuku (ēmä'bōōkōō) or **Imafuku** (ēmä'fōōkōō), town (pop. 7,237), Nagasaki prefecture, NW Kyushu, Japan, on N coast of Hizen Peninsula, 13 mi. N of Sasebo; coal-mining center.

Imad or **'Imad** (ĭmäd'), village (1946 pop. 155), Aden Colony, 5 mi. NE of Sheikh Othman, at W limit of Fadhli sultanate.

Imaharu, Japan: see IMABARI.

Imai (ēmī'), town (pop. 4,796), Nara prefecture, S Honshu, Japan, on N Kii Peninsula, 12 mi. SSW of Nara; rice.

Imaichi (ēmī'chē). **1** Town, Shimane prefecture, Japan: see IZUMO, city. **2** Town (pop. 17,746), Tochigi prefecture, central Honshu, Japan, 16 mi. NW of Utsunomiya; hot-springs resort. Sometimes spelled Imaiti.

Imaise (ēmī'sä), town (pop. 10,133), Aichi prefecture, central Honshu, Japan, just W of Ichinomiya; woolen mills.

Imaiti, Japan: see IMAICHI, Tochigi prefecture.

Imaklit Island, SFSR: see RATMANOV ISLAND.

Imam-Nezer or **Imam-Nazar** (ēmäm"-nyĭzyĕr', –nŭzär'), village, SE Chardzhou oblast, Turkmen SSR, on Afghan frontier, 39 mi. S of Kerki; customs station; trade with Andkhui.

Iman (ēmän'), city (1939 pop. over 10,000), W Maritime Territory, Russian SFSR, on Ussuri R. (opposite Hulin, Manchuria), at mouth of Iman R., on Trans-Siberian RR and 125 mi. NNE of Voroshilov; sawmilling center; flour mills. Iron deposits near by.

Imandra, Lake (ē'mŭndrŭ) (□ 300), in SW central Murmansk oblast, Russian SFSR; 50 mi. long, 15 mi. wide, 220 ft. deep. Of glacial origin; consists of 3 deeply indented sections connected by narrow passages; contains 90 isls. Receives 26 rivers; empties through the Niva (S) into Kandalaksha Bay of White Sea. Railroad passes along E shore; Monchegorsk lies on NW shore.

Iman River (ēmän'), W Maritime Territory, Russian SFSR, rises in S Sikhote-Alin Range, flows 220 mi. N and W to Ussuri R. at Iman. Gold along its upper course. Lumber floating.

Imao (ēmä'ō), town (pop. 6,822), Gifu prefecture, central Honshu, Japan, 13 mi. SW of Gifu; rice, raw silk.

Imari (ēmä'rē), town (pop. 21,677), Saga prefecture, NW Kyushu, Japan, on N Hizen Peninsula, 12 mi. NE of Sasebo, at head of inlet of E.China Sea; rail junction; porcelain, silk, cotton, paper. Coal mines in vicinity.

Imaruí (ēmŭrwē'), city (pop. 1,250), SE Santa Catarina, Brazil, on inlet of the Atlantic, 10 mi. N of Laguna; sugar cane, coffee, lumber. Formerly spelled Imaruhy.

Imataca, Brazo (brä'sō ēmätä'kä), southernmost major arm of Orinoco R. delta, Delta Amacuro territory, NE Venezuela; branches off from the main arm, the Río Grande, flows c.60 mi. E to the Atlantic in the Boca Grande (or Boca de Navíos) at Curiapo.

Imataca, Sierra (syĕ'rä), low mountain range in E Venezuela, in Delta Amacuro territory and Bolívar state; outlier of Guiana Highlands S of lower Orinoco R. and N of Upata; c.90 mi. long W–E; rises to c.2,700 ft. Rich iron deposits. El Pao is a mining center.

Imathia, Greece: see HEMATHEIA.

Imatong Mountains (ēmä'tông), on Uganda–Anglo-Egyptian Sudan border, SE of Juba; rise to 10,456 ft. in Mt. Kinyeti.

Imatra (ĭ'mäträ), town (pop. 27,794), Kymi co., SE Finland, near USSR border, on Vuoksi R. (descends 60 ft. in rapids several thousand feet long) and 20 mi. ENE of Lappeenranta; major hydroelectric station, serving Helsinki and most of S Finland; iron, steel, and copper works. Tourist resort. Inc. 1948.

Imazu (ēmä'zōō). **1** Town (pop. 5,540), Hiroshima prefecture, SW Honshu, Japan, on inlet of Hiuchi Sea, 3 mi. NE of Onomichi; rice-growing center; raw silk, soy sauce, floor mats. **2** Town (pop. 6,636), Oita prefecture, N Kyushu, Japan, on Suo Sea, 34 mi. SE of Yawata; rice, wheat. **3** Town (pop. 5,907), Shiga prefecture, S Honshu, Japan, on NW shore of L. Biwa, 15 mi. NW of Hikone, in rice-growing area; rail terminus.

Imbabura (ēmbäbōō'rä), prov. (□ 2,136; 1950 pop. 139,785), N Ecuador, in the Andes, just N of the equator; ⊙ Ibarra. A mountainous region including many volcanic peaks (Imbabura, Cotacachi, Yanaurcu) and several picturesque crater lakes (San Pablo, Cuicocha), because of which it is often called the Lake District of Ecuador. The climate is semitropical to temperate in the settled, fertile valleys. Among mineral resources are manganese, iron, and salt; but stock raising (cattle, sheep, llamas) and agr. predominate. Main crops are cereals, potatoes, sugar cane, cotton, coffee, fruit. The towns of Ibarra, Otavalo, Cotacachi, and Atuntaqui have leather, textile, and food industries. The large Indian pop. weaves native cotton and woolen goods. The 1868 earthquake damaged the prov. severely.

Imbabura, Cerro (sĕ'rō), extinct Andean volcano (15,026 ft.), Imbabura prov., N Ecuador, 7 mi. SW of Ibarra.

Imbe (ēm'bā), town (pop. 5,382), Okayama prefecture, SW Honshu, Japan, 14 mi. ENE of Okayama, in agr. area (rice, wheat); pottery making.

Imbert (ēmbĕrt'), town (1950 pop. 1,706), Puerto Plata prov., N Dominican Republic, on railroad and 10 mi. W of Puerto Plata; agr. center (cacao, coffee, sugar). Sugar mill near by. Until 1925, called Bajabonico.

Imbetiba, Brazil: see MACAÉ.

Imbituba (ēmbētōō'bŭ), town (pop. 3,408), SE Santa Catarina, Brazil, port on the Atlantic, 45 mi. S of Florianópolis; rail terminus. Ships coal mined in Tubarão region to Rio de Janeiro steel mill at Volta Redonda. Harbor improvements recently completed.

Imbituva (–vŭ), city (pop. 1,657), S central Paraná, Brazil, on road and 28 mi. WSW of Ponta Grossa; woodworking, linen milling; maté, tobacco, grain, cattle. Formerly Santo Antônio de Imbituva.

Imbler, city (pop. 149), Union co., NE Oregon, 12 mi. NE of La Grande and on Grande Ronde R.; ships grain.

Imboden (ĭm'bō"dŭn), town (pop. 447), Lawrence co., NE Ark., 36 mi. NW of Jonesboro and on Spring R.; cotton, lumber.

Imbros (ĭm'brŭs, –ŏs), Turkish *İmroz* (ĭmrôz'), largest Turkish island (□ 108; pop. 6,359), in Aegean Sea 10 mi. off coast of Gallipoli Peninsula, in Canakkale prov., European Turkey, near entrance to the Dardanelles; 19 mi. long, 8 mi. wide; rises to 1,959 ft. Largely of volcanic stone and unproductive except for some grain and beans. Imroz

village (pop. 2,004) is in E part. Occupied by Greece in First World War, when it was also an Allied base during Gallipoli campaign; returned to Turkey 1923 by Treaty of Lausanne.
Imbuial, Brazil: see BOCAIÚVA DO SUL.
Imen (yē'mŭn'), town (pop. 2,836), ⊙ Imen co. (pop. 46,208), central Yunnan prov., China, 45 mi. SW of Kunming; alt. 5,229 ft.; iron smelting; rice, wheat, millet, beans. Copper, iron mines near by.
Imera Meridionale, Sicily: see SALSO RIVER.
Imera Settentrionale, Sicily: see GRANDE RIVER.
Imeretia or **Imeritia** (ĭmûrĭ'shû), Rus. *Imeretiya*, hilly region of W central Georgian SSR; drained by upper Rion R. Vineyards, sericulture, grain, livestock. Main towns: Kutaisi (mfg.), Chiatura (manganese mines), Tkibuli (coal mines). Passed (1804) to Russia.
Imeretian Range, Georgian SSR: see ADZHAR-IMERETIAN RANGE.
Imerigsoq, Greenland: see KRONPRINSEN ISLANDS.
Imerina (ēmĕrē'nŭ) or **Emyrna** (ĕmĕr'nŭ), Fr. *Imérina* or *Emyrne*, mountainous region in heart of Madagascar, embracing 12 hills and centered on Tananarive; rises to 4,835 ft. Once forested, it is now chiefly agr., with rice, pulse, and corn as main crops. Horse breeding, cattle raising. Has primarily a historic significance as cradle of Malagasy kings of Hova tribe. Formerly noted as center of slave traffic. First European explorers penetrated here in 1770. Fell to France 1895. For more details see MADAGASCAR.
Im Fout Dam, Fr. Morocco: see OUM ER RBIA.
Imi (ē'mē) or **Hinna** (hĭ'nä), village (pop. 300), Harar prov., SE Ethiopia, on the Webi Shebeli (here called Wabi) and 110 mi. SE of Ginir; cattle, camels; dum nuts, cereals.
Imienpo or **I-mien-p'o** (yē'myĕn'pô') town, SW Sungkiang prov., Manchuria, on Chinese Eastern RR and 85 mi. SE of Harbin; trade center; flour and soybean mills.
Imini, Fr. Morocco: see OUARZAZATE.
Imi n'Tanout (ēmēn'tänōōt'), village, Marrakesh region, SW Fr. Morocco, near SW extremity of the High Atlas, 60 mi. SW of Marrakesh; argan and chestnut trees.
Imishly (ēmĭshlē'), town (1948 pop. over 2,000), S Azerbaijan SSR, on left bank of Aras R., on railroad and 25 mi. WSW of Sabirabad; cotton-ginning center in cotton dist.; developed in late 1930s.
Imittos, Greece: see HYMETTUS.
Imjar (ēmjär'), landing, SE shore of Gozo, Maltese Isls., 3½ mi. ESE of Victoria. Ferry to Marfa Peninsula on Malta. Just SW is 18th-cent. Fort Chambray.
Imlay City, village (pop. 1,654), Lapeer co., E Mich., 11 mi. ESE of Lapeer, in area producing celery, onions, and potatoes; mfg. of foundry products. Indian mounds near by. Inc. 1873.
Immendingen (ĭ'mŭndĭng"ŭn), village (pop. 1,508), S Baden, Germany, in Black Forest, on the Danube (which here diminishes in volume through seepage), and 5 mi. SW of Tuttlingen; rail junction; metalworking; summer resort (alt. 2,160 ft.).
Immenhausen (ĭ"mŭnhou'zŭn), town (pop. 3,680), in former Prussian prov. of Hesse-Nassau, W Germany, after 1945 in Hesse, 7 mi. N of Kassel; pharmaceuticals. Has 15th-cent. church.
Immenreuth (ĭ"mŭnroit'), village (pop. 1,054), Upper Palatinate, NE Bavaria, Germany, 14 mi. ESE of Bayreuth; mfg. of glass beads and costume jewelry.
Immensee (ĭ'mŭnzā"), village, Schwyz canton, N central Switzerland, just E of Küssnacht, on L. of Zug, at N foot of the Rigi.
Immenstadt (ĭ'mŭn-shtät), town (pop. 8,281), Swabia, SW Bavaria, Germany, in Allgäu Alps, 12 mi. SSW of Kempten; rail junction; mfg. of agr. machinery, musical instruments, textiles, twine, brushes, whips; dairying (butter, milk, cheese), brewing, printing, woodworking. Summer and winter resort (alt. 2,300 ft.). Has early-17th-cent. castle and mid-17th-cent. town hall. Chartered c.1360. Small picturesque Alp L. is 1 mi. NW.
Immingham, town and parish (pop. 2,423), Parts of Lindsey, N Lincolnshire, England, on Humber R. and 7 mi. NW of Grimsby; paint works. Has church dating from 13th cent. In parish (NE) on Humber R. is port of Immingham Docks, a satellite of the port of Grimsby; and (N) on Humber R. is small port of South Killingholme Haven, where the Pilgrim Fathers embarked for Holland (1608).
Immokalee (ĭmŏ'kŭlē), village (1940 pop. 875), Collier co., S Fla., 32 mi. ESE of Fort Myers; truck farming.
Immola (ĭm'mōlä), village in Ruokolahti commune (pop. 8,227), Kymi co., SE Finland, near USSR border, at E end of L. Saimaa, near mouth of Vuoksi R., 25 mi. ENE of Lappeenranta; cellulose milling.
Imogene (ĭ'mŭjēn"), town (pop. 274), Fremont co., SW Iowa, 8 mi. NNW of Shenandoah; livestock, grain.
Imola (ē'mōlä), anc. *Forum Cornelii*, town (pop. 20,800), Bologna prov., Emilia-Romagna, N central Italy, on Santerno R. and 20 mi. SE of Bologna, on the Aemilian Way. Rail junction; mfg. (agr. machinery, bicycles, packing boxes, cement, pottery, shoes, wine, alcohol); foundries. Bishopric. Has cathedral (1187–1271; remodeled 18th cent.), citadel (1332; reinforced 1472–73), 16th-cent. town hall, several fine Renaissance palaces. Became a free commune in 11th cent.; later ruled by various tyrants; passed to Pope Julius II in early 16th cent. Damaged in Second World War by air and artillery bombing.
Imón (ēmōn'), town (pop. 392), Guadalajara prov., central Spain, 8 mi. NW of Sigüenza; saltworking center; lumbering, grain growing, sheep raising.
Imo River (ē'mō), S Nigeria, in forest belt, rises W of Okigwi, flows 150 mi. S, through rich oil-palm region, to Gulf of Guinea below Opobo. Also called Opobo R. in lower course.
Imotski (ē'môtskē), village (pop. 2,199), S Croatia, Yugoslavia, 38 mi. E of Split, near Bosnia-Herzegovina border, in Dalmatia; local trade center; bricks, tobacco. Roman ruins near by. In Middle Ages, called Emotha or Imotha, later Imoschi or Imoski. Passed 1718 from Turkish rule to Venetian Dalmatia.
I Mountains, Chinese *I Shan* (yē'shän'), central Shantung prov., China, E of the Tai Mts.; rise to 3,248 ft. 30 mi. N of Ishui.
Imperatriz (ēmpĭrŭtrēz'), city (pop. 1,178), W Maranhão, Brazil, on Tocantins R. (Goiás border) and 125 mi. N of Carolina; ships manioc meal, babassu and copaiba oil, cotton. Airport.
Imperia (ēmpä'rēä), province (□ 457; pop. 158,470), Liguria, NW Italy; ⊙ Imperia. Comprises W RIVIERA DI PONENTE, enclosed by Ligurian Alps; drained by Roya and Taggia rivers. Mtn. terrain, rising to 7,218 ft. in Mt. Saccarello (N), covers 82% of area. Bordered W by Fr. dept. of Alpes-Maritimes. A leading prov. of Liguria for olive oil, flowers, and wood; economy based on agr. (olives, grapes, flowers, citrus fruit, peaches) and tourist trade (San Remo, Bordighera) of the Riviera and alpine foothills bordering it. Industry limited to Imperia. From1860 to 1923, called Porto Maurizio.
Imperia, town (pop. 20,916), ⊙ Imperia prov., Liguria, NW Italy, port on Gulf of Genoa, 60 mi. SW of Genoa, in olive- and grape-growing region; 43°53'N 8°1'E. Consists of Imperia Ponente (formerly Porto Maurizio; pop. 9,668) and adjacent Imperia Levante (formerly Oneglia; pop. 11,248), united 1923 to form Imperia. Imperia Ponente is a winter resort with olive-oil refineries; has cathedral, 14th-cent. sanctuary. From 1860 to 1923, capital of Porto Maurizio prov. (now Imperia prov.). Imperia Levante is 2d to Savona as chief industrial and commercial center of Riviera di Ponente; iron- and steelworks; macaroni flour, canned fruits and vegetables, glass, soap, cement. Noted for its olive oil. In Second World War, port and industrial areas damaged.
Imperial, village (pop. 393), S central Sask., 70 mi. NNW of Regina; wheat, stock.
Imperial, Chile: see NUEVA IMPERIAL.
Imperial (ēmpärēäl'), town (pop. 3,296), Lima dept., W central Peru, on irrigated coastal plain, on Lima-Cañete highway, and 5 mi. ENE of Cañete; road junction; sugar plantations in surrounding area.
Imperial, county (□ 4,284; pop. 62,975), S Calif.; ⊙ El Centro. Bounded S by Mexico border, E by Colorado R. (Ariz. line). In Colorado Desert; desert ranges (low Superstition Mts., W; Chocolate Mts., E), enclose IMPERIAL VALLEY, winter-garden agr. region irrigated by ALL-AMERICAN CANAL; drainage channels (New and Alamo rivers) carry waste water to SALTON SEA (NW). Part of PALO VERDE VALLEY in NE. Yuma Indian Reservation is in SE; Anza Desert State Park in W. Ships huge quantities of lettuce, melons, vegetables; also important are livestock, dairy products, alfalfa, flax, grain, citrus fruit. Quarrying and mining (gypsum, gold, sand, gravel); mud volcanoes produce carbon dioxide gas for refrigeration. Chief communities are Brawley, Calexico, Calipatria, El Centro. Formed 1866; irrigation development was begun in 1900.
Imperial. **1** City (pop. 1,759), Imperial co., S Calif., 10 mi. S of Brawley; oldest community in IMPERIAL VALLEY. Hq. of Imperial Irrigation Dist. and seat of co. fair. Stockyards; rice mill; packs, ships truck. Founded 1902, inc. 1904. **2** Village (pop. 1,563), ⊙ Chase co., S Nebr., 55 mi. WNW of McCook in Great Plains region; grain, livestock, poultry produce, potatoes. Settled c.1885. **3** Village (pop. 1,895), Allegheny co., W Pa., 17 mi. W of downtown Pittsburgh. **4** Village (pop. c.175), Pecos co., extreme W Texas, 29 mi. NNE of Fort Stockton; trading point in irrigated area of Pecos valley.
Imperial Beach, resort village (pop. c.300), San Diego co., S Calif., on the coast, 9 mi. S of downtown San Diego.
Imperial Canal (ēmpärēäl'), Navarre and Saragossa, NE Spain, starts from the Ebro below Tudela, runs 60 mi. SE along right bank of river, which it reenters 12 mi. SE of Saragossa. Begun by Emperor Charles V (16th cent.) for navigation, it is now used for irrigation.
Imperial Canal, Calif. and Lower California: see IMPERIAL VALLEY.
Imperial Dam, in Colorado R. (forming Ariz.-Calif. line), 15 mi. NE of Yuma, Ariz., near mouth of Gila R.; weir-type dam (3,475 ft. long, including diversion structures and dike; 31 ft. high) completed 1938 by Bureau of Reclamation; used to divert water into ALL-AMERICAN CANAL. Laguna Dam (completed 1909) is 4 mi. S; used for tailwater control in connection with Imperial Dam.
Imperial River (ēmpärēäl'), Cautín prov., S central Chile, formed by union of Cautín R. and the lesser Quepe R. 3 mi. SE of Nueva Imperial, flows c.35 mi. W, past Nueva Imperial, Carahue, and Puerto Saavedra, to the Pacific. Navigable c.20 mi. for small craft. The Imperial is sometimes considered to include the Cautín; total length c.135 mi.
Imperial Valley, in S Calif., and N Lower California, Mexico; below-sea-level region of COLORADO DESERT, occupies basin (Salton Sink) S of Salton Sea; bounded W by desert ranges, E by sand hills and Chocolate Mts. Little rainfall; 300-day growing season; subject to extreme temperatures (to 115° F.) and wide daily temp. ranges. Once covered by Gulf of California, it was cut off from gulf by growing delta of Colorado R.; its rich soils were 1st irrigated c.1900, but disastrous floods of the Colorado (see SALTON SEA) hindered development until completion of control works (1907). Irrigation, supplied to c.1,000,000 acres by old Imperial (or Alamo) Canal, which passes through Mexico, and by new ALL-AMERICAN CANAL from the Colorado, produces huge crops of truck, fruit, grain, cotton, dates, alfalfa; dairying is extensive. Cities (settled since 1900) in IMPERIAL co., Calif., are Brawley, Calexico, Calipatria, El Centro, Holtville, Imperial, Niland, Westmorland. Mexicali (Mexico) is center of important Mex. cotton dist. Valley recovered rapidly from earthquakes which caused much damage in 1940.
Imperoyal (ĭm"pŭroi'ŭl), locality (pop. estimate 1,200), S N.S., on Halifax Harbour, near its mouth on the Atlantic, 6 mi. SE of Halifax; petroleum-refining center.
Impfondo (ēmpfōndō'), town, ⊙ Likouala region (□ 23,940; 1950 pop. 22,500), N Middle Congo territory, Fr. Equatorial Africa, on right bank of Ubangi R. and 440 mi. NNE of Brazzaville; steamboat landing and native market for palm products, kola nuts, copal; cacao plantations. Meteorological station. Formerly also called Desbordesville.
Imphal (ĭm'pŭl), city (pop. 99,716), ⊙ Manipur, NE India, on Imphal (Manipur) R. and 140 mi. ESE of Shillong; road and trade center (rice, mustard, sugar cane, tobacco, fruit). Linked with Burma via Tamu and Tiddim routes. Figured in Jap. invasion of India in 1944.
Imphal River, India: see MANIPUR RIVER.
Imphy (ēfē'), industrial village (pop. 1,533), Nièvre dept., central France, on right bank of Loire R. and 6 mi. SE of Nevers; steel mills.
Impilakhti (ēm'pēlŭkhtyē), Finnish *Impilahti* (ĭm'-pĭlätē), town (1947 pop. over 500), SW Karelo-Finnish SSR, on L. Ladoga, on railroad and 14 mi. ESE of Sortavala.
Impington, agr. village and parish (pop. 1,429), S Cambridge, England, 3 mi. N of Cambridge. Has 14th–15th-cent. church. It is associated with Samuel Pepys.
Imp Mountain, N.H.: see CARTER-MORIAH RANGE.
Impruneta (ēmprōōnā'tä), town (pop. 2,324), Firenze prov., Tuscany, central Italy, 6 mi. S of Florence; mfg. (chemicals, pottery). Has basilica of Santa Maria dell'Impruneta (rebuilt 15th cent.; heavy war damage repaired). Partly destroyed by bombing (1944) in Second World War.
Imroz, Turkey: see IMBROS.
Imrun, Turkey: see PUTURGE.
Imst, resort town (pop. 4,025), Tyrol, W Austria, on the Inn and 31 mi. W of Innsbruck; cotton mills; lumberyards.
Imtandzha (ēmtŭnjä'), village, N Yakut Autonomous SSR, Russian SFSR, near upper Bytantai R. (tributary of the Yana), in Verkhoyansk Range, 155 mi. SW of Verkhoyansk; tin (extensive), lead, zinc deposits.
Imuris (ēmōō'rēs), town (pop. 934), Sonora, NW Mexico, on Magdalena R. (irrigation), on railroad and 40 mi. S of Nogales; wheat, corn, cotton, alfalfa, sugar cane.
Imus (ē'mōōs), town (1939 pop. 2,875; 1948 municipality pop. 23,685), Cavite prov., S Luzon, Philippines, 12 mi. SSW of Manila, near Bacoor Bay; agr. center (rice, fruit, coconuts).
'Imwas, Jordan: see EMMAUS.
In, Russian SFSR: see SMIDOVICH, Khabarovsk Territory.
Ina (ē'nä), town (pop. 23,249), Nagano prefecture, central Honshu, Japan, on Tenryu R. and 27 mi. S of Matsumoto; raw silk. Agr. school.
Ina (ī'nŭ), town (pop. 432), Jefferson co., S Ill., 12 mi. S of Mount Vernon; agr.; feed milling.
Inaba (ēnä'bä), former province in SW Honshu, Japan; now part of Tottori prefecture.
Inabe (ēnä'bā), town (pop. 7,719), Mie prefecture, S Honshu, Japan, 8 mi. WNW of Kuwana; rice, wheat, poultry, raw silk. Formed in early 1940s by combining former villages of Kasada, Oizumihara, and Oizumi.
Inabu (ēnä'bōō), town (pop. 5,919), Aichi prefecture, central Honshu, Japan, 23 mi. E of Seto; saw-

milling, tea processing; charcoal, raw silk. Villages of Inahashi and Busetsu were combined in late 1930s to form town of Inatake, which was renamed Inabu in early 1940s.

Inaccessible Island, uninhabited rocky islet (2 mi. long, ¾ mi. wide) in S Atlantic, 12 mi. SW of Tristan da Cunha, with which it is a dependency (since 1938) of St. Helena; 37°17'S 12°40'W.

Inaccessible Islands, westernmost of South Orkney Isls., in the South Atlantic, 23 naut. mi. W of Coronation Isl.; 60°35'S 46°43'W. Steep pinnacle rocks of 400–700 ft. elev. Discovered 1821.

Inachos River or **Inakhos River** (both: ē'nŭkhôs), in E Peloponnesus, Greece, rises in Artemision Mts., flows 15 mi. SSE to Gulf of Argolis 4 mi. W of Nauplia.

Inagua (ĭnä'gwŭ), islands and district (□ 560; pop. 890), southernmost isls. of the Bahamas, consisting of GREAT INAGUA ISLAND (also called Inagua Isl.; S) and Little Inagua Isl. (NE), situated SW of the Caicos Isls. and 55 mi. NE of Cape Maisí (E Cuba), 350 mi. SE of Nassau. Only Great Inagua Isl. is inhabited, with chief settlement at Matthew Town. Salt panning is main activity.

Inahashi, Japan: see INABU.

Inajaroba, Brazil: see SANTA LUZIA DO ITANHI.

Inakhos River, Greece: see INACHOS RIVER.

Inambari (ēnämbä'rē) or **Boca del Punkire** (bō'kä dĕl pōōng-kē'rä), village (pop. 62), Madre de Dios dept., SE Peru, landing at junction of Inambari and Madre de Dios rivers, 38 mi. W of Puerto Maldonado, in rubber region.

Inambari River, SE Peru, rises in several branches in the Nudo de Apolobamba of the Andes near Sandia, flows 210 mi. NW and NE, past Santo Domingo and Puerto Leguía, to Madre de Dios R. at Inambari.

Inami (ēnä'mē). **1** Town (pop. 7,820), Toyama prefecture, central Honshu, Japan, 18 mi. E of Kanazawa; silk textiles. **2** Town (pop. 4,006), Wakayama prefecture, S Honshu, Japan, on Philippine Sea, on SW coast of Kii Peninsula, 11 mi. NW of Tanabe; fishing; rice, citrus fruit, raw silk.

Inangahua, New Zealand: see REEFTON.

Inaniwa (ēnä'nĭwä), town (pop. 3,227), Akita prefecture, N Honshu, Japan, 6 mi. SE of Yuzawa; rice, tobacco.

Inaouene, Oued (wĕd' ēnäwĕn'), stream in N Fr. Morocco, rises on S slope of Rif Mts. N of Taza, flows c.75 mi. W to the Sebou 13 mi. N of Fez.

Iñapari (ēnyäpä'rē), town (pop. 138), ⊙ Tahuamanu prov. (□ 5,169; enumerated pop. 1,404, plus estimated 6,000 Indians), Madre de Dios dept., SE Peru, landing on Acre R., at Brazil-Bolivia border, opposite Bolpebra (Bolivia), and 55 mi. W of Cobija (Bolivia), in rubber region; 19°57'S 69°33' W. Sometimes called Tacna.

Inarajan (ĭnŭrä'jŭn), town (pop. 814) and municipality (pop. 1,494), S Guam, on coast; rice paddies, livestock.

Inari (ĭ'närē), Swedish *Enare* (ā'närŭ), village (commune pop. 4,568), Lapi co., N Finland, at SW end of L. Inari, 90 mi. SW of Kirkenes; Lapp trading center; fishing. On branch of Arctic Highway (Rovaniemi-Pechenga). After Second World War, Lapps evacuated from Pechenga region resettled here.

Inari, Lake, Finnish *Inarijärvi* (ĭ'näreyăr"vē), Swedish *Enare* (□ 535), Lapland, N Finland, bet. USSR and Norwegian borders, 45 mi. SW of Kirkenes; 69°N 28°E. It is 50 mi. long (ENE-WSW), 1–25 mi. wide. Receives Ivalo R. (SW); drained E by Pats R. Contains over 3,000 islets. Shores are steep, rocky, and wooded; good fishing attracts many tourists. Inari village on W shore.

Ina River (ē'nä), Ger. *Ihna* (ē'nä), in Pomerania, after 1945 in NW Poland, rises 13 mi. N of Recz, flows S past Recz, WNW, NNW past Stargard and Goleniow, and W to N end of Damm L. opposite Police; length, 70 mi.

Inariyama (ēnä'rē'yämŭ), town (pop. 4,818), Nagano prefecture, central Honshu, Japan, 9 mi. SW of Nagano; rice, raw silk.

Inatake, Japan: see INABU.

Inatomi, Japan: see TATSUNO, Nagano prefecture.

Inatori (ēnä'tōrē), town (pop. 7,586), Shizuoka prefecture, central Honshu, Japan, on E Izu Peninsula, on Sagami Sea, 25 mi. SSE of Numazu; fishing port. Orange orchards.

Inawashiro (ēnäwä'shĭrō), town (pop. 6,568), Fukushima prefecture, N Honshu, Japan, 11 mi. ENE of Wakamatsu, near L. Inawashiro; rice, raw silk.

Inawashiro, Lake, Jap. *Inawashiro-ko* (□ 40), N Honshu, Japan, 4 mi. E of Wakamatsu; roughly circular, 7 mi. in diameter.

'Inaybah, Egypt: see 'INEIBA.

'Inaza or **'Inazah** (ĭ'năzŭ), village, S Jordan, on Hejaz RR and 20 mi. NNE of Ma'an; grain, camels, goats. Sometimes spelled 'Uneiza and 'Aneiza.

Inazawa (ēnä'zäwŭ), town (pop. 22,283), Aichi prefecture, central Honshu, Japan, 10 mi. NW of Nagoya; textile mills.

Inca (ĕng'kä), city (pop. 10,799), Majorca, Balearic Isls., 17 mi. NE of Palma (linked by rail and highway); industrial and agr. center for fertile inland region (grapes, almonds, capers, sheep). Sawmilling, tanning, alcohol distilling, wine making, vegetable canning; mfg. of shoes, lace, cotton and hemp goods, wood pulp, cardboard, starch, soap, jewelry, oxygen. Cement-gravel quarries. Venerable city with magnificent Santa María la Mayor church (begun in 13th cent.).

Inca, Lake (ĕng'kä), in the Andes, Aconcagua prov., central Chile, just N of Portillo, near Argentina border; 3 mi. long. Tourists.

Inca, Paso del (pä'sō dĕl) (15,520 ft.), pass in the Andes, on Argentina-Chile border, on road bet. San Juan (Argentina) and Tránsito (Chile); 28°40'S 69°48'W.

Inca de Oro (ĕng'kä dā ō'rō), town (pop. 2,324), Atacama prov., N Chile, on railroad and 45 mi. NNE of Copiapó; copper and gold mining.

Incahuasi, Cerro (sĕ'rō ĕng-käwä'sē), Andean volcano (21,720 ft.) on Argentina-Chile border, 90 mi. SW of Antofagasta (Argentina); 27°2'S.

Ince, Cape (ĭnjĕ'), Turkish *İnce*, on Black Sea, N Turkey, 12 mi. WNW of Sinop; northernmost point of Anatolia; 42°6'N 34°58'E. Sometimes spelled Inje and Indje.

Ince-in-Makerfield, urban district (1931 pop. 21,761; 1951 census 20,414), S Lancashire, England, just SSE of Wigan; cotton milling, coal mining. In urban dist. is coal-mining town of Bryn (brĭn).

Incesu (ĭnjĕsōō'), Turkish *İncesu*, village (pop. 4,663), Kayseri prov., central Turkey, on railroad and 19 mi. WSW of Kayseri; wheat, rye, barley.

Inch, agr. village and parish (pop. 3,966, including part of Stranraer burgh), W Wigtown, Scotland, just SSE of Stranraer.

Inchagoill (ĭn"chŭgoil'), island (108 acres) in Lough Corrib, NW Co. Galway, Ireland, 4 mi. SW of Cong; site of 2 anc. church ruins.

Inchard, Loch, Scotland: see KINLOCHBERVIE.

Inchbrayock, Scotland: see MONTROSE.

Inchcape Rock, Scotland: see BELL ROCK.

Inchcolm (ĭnch'kŭm) [Gaelic,=island of Columba], island in Firth of Forth, off coast of S Fifeshire, Scotland, 2 mi. S of Aberdour. Has noted ruins of abbey of St. Columba, founded 1123 by Alexander I; near church is an older oratory. As "St. Colme's Inch" isl. figures in *Macbeth*. Just SE, in Firth of Forth, is lighthouse (56°1'N 3°17'W).

Inchenhofen (ĭn"khŭnhō'fŭn), village (pop. 1,064), Upper Bavaria, Germany, 21 mi. SE of Donauwörth; brickworks; brewing. Has mid-15th-cent. pilgrimage church. Chartered 1400.

Inches, village in Douglas parish, S Lanark, Scotland; coal mining.

Inchgarvie (ĭnch"gär'vē), islet in the Firth of Forth, West Lothian, Scotland, just NNW of Queensferry. It is a support of the Forth Bridge. Has fort, built c.1490, restored 1779.

Inchicore (ĭn"chĭkôr'), Gaelic *Inse Chaoir*, W suburb of Dublin, Co. Dublin, Ireland; railroad shops, paper mills.

Inchinnan (ĭn-shĭ'nŭn), town and parish (pop. 1,288), NE Renfrew, Scotland, on White Cart Water at mouth of Black Cart Water (bridge), just WNW of Renfrew; automobile tire mfg. Near bridge is "Argyll Stone," marking site of arrest of earl of Argyll in 1685.

Inch Island (4 mi. long, 3 mi. wide) in SE part of Lough Swilly, E Co. Donegal, Ireland, 7 mi. NW of Londonderry.

Inchkeith (ĭnch-kēth'), fortified island (1 mi. long) in Firth of Forth, off S coast of Fifeshire, Scotland, 3 mi. SE of Kinghorn. A monastery was established here c.700. In 1547, after battle of Pinkie, the English fortified isl.; from 1549 until 1567 it was garrisoned by the French. At N end (56°2'N 3°8'W) is lighthouse (1803).

Inchmahome, Scotland: see MENTEITH, LAKE OF.

Inchmarnock (ĭnch-mär'nŭk), island (pop. 14), Buteshire, Scotland, in the Sound of Bute just off W coast of Bute isl.; 2½ mi. long, 1 mi. wide.

Inchnadamph, Scotland: see ASSYNT.

Inchon, Korea: see CHEMULPO.

Incio (ēn'thyō), village (pop. 163), Lugo prov., NW Spain, 12 mi. NE of Monforte, in iron-mining area.

Incirli, Turkey: see KARASU.

Incomati River, Mozambique: see KOMATI RIVER.

Inconfidencia, Brazil: see CORAÇÃO DE JESUS.

Incoronata, island, Yugoslavia: see KORNAT ISLAND.

Indaal, Loch, Scotland: see ISLAY.

Indaial (ēndĭäl'), city (pop. 1,151), NE Santa Catarina, Brazil, on Itajaí Açu R., on railroad and 10 mi. W of Blumenau; agr. colony. Formerly spelled Indayal.

Indaiatuba (ēndī"ŭtōō'bŭ), city (pop. 2,641), SE central São Paulo, Brazil, on railroad and 16 mi. SW of Campinas; woodworking; sugar, cotton, coffee.

Indaki, Afghanistan: see CHIHAL SATUN.

Indal River, Swedish *Indalsälven* (ĭn'däls-ĕl"vŭn), N central Sweden, rises in Norwegian border mts. S of Storlien, flows in winding course generally E, over the TANNFORSEN, through Stor L., to KRANGEDE (falls; power station); thence flows SE, over several smaller falls, past Hammarstrand, Ragunda, and Bispgarden, to Gulf of Bothnia 10 mi. NE of Sundsvall. Length, 220 mi. Important logging route.

Indan, Philippines: see VINZONS.

Indang (ĕndäng'), town (1939 pop. 3,131; 1948 municipality pop. 15,989), Cavite prov., S Luzon, Philippines, 29 mi. SSW of Manila; agr. center (rice, fruit, coconuts).

Indanza (ĕndän'sä), village, Santiago-Zamora prov., SE Ecuador, on E slopes of the Andes, 40 mi. SE of Cuenca; stock, fruit, timber.

Indaparapeo (ĕndäpäräpā'ō), town (pop. 2,757), Michoacán, central Mexico, 15 mi. NE of Morelia; cereals, vegetables, fruit, livestock.

Indapur (ĭndä'pŏŏr), town (pop., including suburban area, 6,919), Poona dist., central Bombay, India, 80 mi. SE of Poona; road junction; market center (sugar cane, millet); handicraft cloth weaving.

Indargarh (ĭn'dŭrgŭr), village, E Rajasthan, India, 45 mi. NNE of Kotah; wheat, barley; handicraft pottery and lacquered woodwork.

Indaw (ĭn'dô). **1** Village, Katha dist., Upper Burma, on railroad and 12 mi. W of Katha. **2** Village, Upper Chindwin dist., Upper Burma, 25 mi. E of Mawlaik; oil field (opened 1918).

Indawgyi Lake (ĭndôjē'), largest lake (□ 80) in Burma, in Myitkyina dist., Kachin State, 65 mi. WSW of Myitkyina. Surrounded by thickly wooded hills; theme of many Burmese legends.

Indé (ĕndā'), town (pop. 1,482), Durango, N Mexico, 60 mi. NNE of Santiago Papasquiaro; alt. 6,102 ft.; silver, gold, lead, copper mining.

Indefatigable Island, Galápagos: see CHAVES ISLAND.

Independence, county (□ 755; pop. 23,488), NE central Ark.; ⊙ BATESVILLE. Bounded E by Black R.; drained by White R.; part of Ozarks in W. Agr. (cotton, corn, truck, fruit, hay, livestock). Mfg. at Batesville. Manganese and bauxite mines, black marble and limestone quarries; timber. Founded 1820.

Independence. **1** Village (1940 pop. 569), ⊙ Inyo co., E Calif., in Owens Valley, 35 mi. S of Bishop; mining (gold, salt, lead, mercury); stock raising, farming. Winter-sports center. Mt. Whitney is S. Large fish hatchery and old Fort Independence are near by. Railroad station is Kearsarge (5 mi. E). **2** City (pop. 4,865), ⊙ Buchanan co., E Iowa, on Wapsipinicon R. and 23 mi. E of Waterloo; canned corn, dressed poultry, feed, dairy and metal products. Limestone quarries, sand and gravel pits near by. A state hosp. for the insane (1873) is here. Founded 1847, inc. 1864. **3** City (pop. 11,335), ⊙ Montgomery co., SE Kansas, on Verdigris R. and 14 mi. NNW of Coffeyville; processing center for oil and grain region; mfg. (oil-well bombs, cement, wood products, bricks and tiles). Oil and gas wells in vicinity. Has jr. col. Near by is site of Rebel Creek Battle, where small detachment of Confederate officers was wiped out (1863) by band of Osage Indians. Founded 1869, inc. 1870. **4** Town (pop. 285), a ⊙ Kenton co., N Ky., 9 mi. S of Covington. **5** Town (pop. 1,606), Tangipahoa parish, SE La., 40 mi. ENE of Baton Rouge; strawberries, truck; canneries; box and crate mfg. Inc. 1903. **6** Village (1940 pop. 159), Tate co., NW Miss., c.30 mi. SSE of Memphis (Tenn.), near Arkabutla Reservoir. **7** City (pop. 36,963), ⊙ Jackson co., W Mo., 12 mi. E of Kansas City. Mfg. (farm machinery, furnaces, stoves, cement, tile, flour); agr. (potatoes, corn, wheat). Hq. of Reorganized Church of Jesus Christ of Latter Day Saints. Home of President Harry S. Truman. Was starting point for mid-19th-cent. westbound expeditions. Settled 1825, inc. 1849. **8** Village (pop. 3,105), Cuyahoga co., N Ohio, a S suburb of Cleveland; makes pottery, heating apparatus. A state park (boating, fishing, swimming) is here. **9** City (pop. 1,987), Polk co., NW Oregon, on Willamette R. and 10 mi. SW of Salem; hop-raising center. Inc. 1874. **10** Town (pop. 486), ⊙ Grayson co., SW Va., in the Blue Ridge, 13 mi. WSW of Galax, near N.C. line; hosiery mfg. **11** City (pop. 1,088), Trempealeau co., W Wis., on Trempealeau R. and 31 mi. S of Eau Claire, in dairy and farm area (tobacco, grain); grain milling; dairy products. Settled 1856; inc. as village in 1876, as city in 1942.

Independence, Fort, Mass.: see CASTLE ISLAND.

Independence, Lake, Marquette co., NW Upper Peninsula, Mich., 22 mi. NW of Marquette, bet. Huron Mts. (W and SW) and L. Superior; c.2 mi. long, 1½ mi. wide.

Independence, Mount, W Vt., hill in Orwell town, near L. Champlain, opposite Ticonderoga, N.Y.; site of Revolutionary defenses.

Independence Fjord, inlet (80 mi. long, 8–15 mi. wide) of Greenland Sea, NE Greenland; 81°40'–82°16'N 21°50'–33°50'W. Extends W to edge of inland icecap, where it receives large Academy Glacier. Forms SE boundary of Peary Land.

Independence Island, Line Isls.: see MALDEN ISLAND.

Independence Mountains, NE Nev., in Elko co., N of Humboldt R., NW of Elko. Rises to more than 9,000 ft. in Lone Mtn., at N end.

Independence Pass, Colo.: see SAWATCH MOUNTAINS.

Independencia, dept., Argentina: see PATQUIA.

Independencia, town, Argentina: see VILLA INDEPENDENCIA.

Independencia (ĕndāpĕndĕn'syä), town (pop. c.5,200), ⊙ Ayopaya prov., Cochabamba dept., W central Bolivia, in N outliers of Cordillera de Cochabamba, 50 mi. WNW of Cochabamba; alt. 9,081 ft.; corn, wheat, potatoes.

Independência (ēndĭpēndān'syŏŏ). **1** City (pop. 608), W Ceará, Brazil, 28 mi. SE of Crateús; cheese mfg.; cotton, carnauba, skins. **2** City, Paraíba, Brazil: see GUARABIRA. **3** Town, Rio Grande do Norte, Brazil: see PENDÊNCIA.

Independencia (ēndāpāndān'syä), province (1950 pop. 20,892), SW Dominican Republic, bet. L. Enriquillo and Haiti border; ⊙ Jimaní. Formed 1949 out of W Bahoruco prov.

Independencia, town (dist. pop. 4,304), Guairá dept., S Paraguay, 10 mi. E of Villarrica; viticultural center; also cotton, corn, peanuts, tobacco, livestock; lumbering. German colony.

Independencia, Uruguay: see FRAY BENTOS.

Independencia, town (pop. 2,122), Táchira state, W Venezuela, in Andean spur, 5 mi. W of San Cristóbal; alt. 4,180 ft.; coffee, grain, cattle.

Independencia, La, Mexico: see LA INDEPENDENCIA.

Independencia Bay, inlet of the Pacific, Ica dept., SW Peru, 25 mi. S of Pisco; 17 mi. wide, 5 mi. long. Guano deposits on small isls., including Viejas Isl.

Independenta (ēndĕpĕndān'tsä), Rum. *Independența,* village (pop. 4,615), Galati prov., E Rumania, on railroad and 14 mi. W of Galati.

Independent Oman: see OMAN.

Inderagiri River, Indonesia: see INDRAGIRI RIVER.

Inderborski or **Inderborskiy** (ēndyĭrbôr'skē), town (1939 pop. over 2,000), N Guryev oblast, Kazakh SSR, on Ural R., near Inder L., and 95 mi. N of Guryev; borax-extracting center.

Inder Lake, Kazakh SSR: see INDERBORSKI.

Inderoy, Norway: see STRAUMEN.

Indetu (ĭn'dĕtōō), village (pop. 300), Arusi prov., S central Ethiopia, near the upper Webi Shebeli (here called Wabi), 65 mi. NW of Ginir.

Index, town (pop. 211), Snohomish co., NW Wash., 32 mi. ESE of Everett and on Skykomish R., in Cascade Range. Gold, silver, copper, antimony deposits; granite quarries.

Indherred, Norway: see INNHERAD.

Indi (ĭn'dē), village (pop. 5,497), Bijapur dist., S Bombay, India, 29 mi. NE of Bijapur; millet, peanuts, cotton, wheat.

India, officially also known by the anc. name *Bharat,* republic (□ 1,138,814; 1951 pop. 356,891,624; in 1941, pop. of the area now constituting the republic was 314,830,190; all figures without Kashmir and without nontabulated Assam tribal areas) and member (but not a dominion) of the Br. Commonwealth of Nations; ⊙ NEW DELHI. About ⅓ the size of the U.S., India is the world's 2d most populous nation (after China). Welded to the S central rim of Asia by the Himalayas, the country stretches S from 33°N (at S border of Kashmir) and at the Tropic of Cancer thrusts in a triangular-shaped peninsula (1,300 mi. wide at its base) into the Indian Ocean bet. the Bay of Bengal (E) and the Arabian Sea (W), its coast line totaling c.3,500 mi. Cape Comorin (8°5'N) is its S tip. India borders NE on Burma (along a series of mtn. ranges); N (along the Himalayas) on Tibet, Bhutan and Sikkim (Indian protectorates), Nepal, and Kashmir (object, after 1947, of conflicting Indian and Pakistani claims); and NW on West Pakistan. In NE, forming an enclave bet. the states of West Bengal and Assam, is East Pakistan. Ceylon lies just off SE coast across Palk Strait and Gulf of Mannar. The Andaman and Nicobar Isls. in Bay of Bengal and Laccadive Isls. in Arabian Sea belong to India. Vestiges of pre-British trading empires in India are the small coastal enclaves of Karikal, Mahé, Pondicherry, and Yanam, belonging to France, and Goa, Damão, and Diu, which make up Portuguese India. The majestic HIMALAYAS (which in India rise to 25,645 ft. in Nanda Devi and to 25,447 ft. in Kamet), the world's most formidable mtn. barrier, limit travel to a few lofty passes, notably the Jelep La and Natu La on the main India-Tibet trade route through Chumbi Valley NE of Darjeeling. In the N reaches of this mtn. system rise the 3 great rivers of the Indian subcontinent—the Indus, Ganges, and Brahmaputra. The alluvial plain of the Ganges lies bet. the Himalayas and the dissected plateaus of the central Indian upland. To the NW, beyond the Aravalli Range in Rajasthan, is the THAR DESERT, merging with the swampy Rann of Cutch to the S. In peninsular India, the DECCAN PLATEAU, scarped by the Eastern and Western GHATS, is buttressed on the N by Satpura and Vindhya ranges, which are drained by the Narbada and the Tapti, the country's main W-flowing rivers; to the NE lie the broken hill ranges of the CHOTA NAGPUR PLATEAU, N of the Chhattisgarh Plain, which comprises the upper basin of the E-flowing Mahanadi R. The main rivers of peninsular India, the Godavari, Kistna, and Cauvery, break through the Eastern Ghats and form broad deltas on the wide E coast. The much narrower W coast, consisting of MALABAR COAST (S), KONKAN (center), and fertile GUJARAT plain (N), curves round the Gulf of Cambay in the N onto KATHIAWAR peninsula. India's climate is essentially tropical, with diurnal and annual ranges of temperature more marked in the central and N regions than in the S. Seasons are determined by a system of monsoon winds. In 4 months (June–Sept.) the SW monsoon brings most of the country's rainfall, shedding 100–200 in. on W slopes of the Western Ghats and decreasing as it advances NE across the peninsula. Becoming resaturated during its passage over the Bay of Bengal, it releases over 100 in. in places in Bengal and Assam (world's heaviest precipitation —c.450 in. a year—is recorded at Cherrapunji). The extreme variability of these rains causes droughts and floods that threaten some part of India with famine almost once a decade. This hot monsoon season (mean temp. averages 80°–90°F. all over India) is followed by a cooler, dry period (Oct.–Feb.; c.60°–70°F. in N India and c.75°–80°F. in S peninsula). In May a max. of almost 100°F. is reached in Madras and c.110°F. in Delhi; scorching winds blow in the Ganges Plain. About 70% of the pop. of India engage in agr. Rice is extensively grown in Ganges valley and the wetter coasts; wheat and sugar cane in upper Ganges Plain and in Punjab; cotton in NW Deccan Plateau and in Punjab; oilseeds (peanuts, linseed, castor beans, rape, sesame) and tobacco in Deccan Plateau dists. and N Madras. Millet (a major food staple), corn, barley, and gram grow in widespread areas. India is a leading producer of tea (mainly in Assam hills) and jute (in West Bengal). There are plantations of coffee, tea, rubber, and spices (pepper, cardamom) in the Anaimalai and Cardamom hills (S section of Western Ghats). Thick coconut groves on Malabar Coast yield coir and copra; here also grows most of the country's cashew-nut crop. Bananas are found chiefly in E coast deltaic tracts; many regional varieties of mango exist. Although India ranks high as a world producer of food crops, the output is far from sufficient for the enormous pop. Fragmentation of holdings, absentee landlordism, peasant indebtedness (to the parasitic moneylenders), outmoded methods of crop production, and social prejudice against certain improvements are characteristic of contemporary Indian agr. Irrigation works on the Cauvery, Kistna, and Periyar rivers in the peninsula and extensive canal systems fed by the Ganges, Jumna, and Sutlej rivers in the N have brought large areas under cultivation. Since Pakistan has ½ the subcontinent's rice and wheat lands and ⅔ of the jute acreage, to compensate for this loss India has inaugurated vast reclamation projects (also furnishing hydroelectric power) on Godavari, Kistna, Mahanadi, Tungabhadra, Damodar, Kosi, and Sutlej rivers. India's c.150,000,000 head of cattle are used primarily as draft animals, but their working efficiency is impaired by the great number of old or diseased stock, a condition perpetuated by the Hindu religious ban on cow killing and the lack of eugenic breeding. Trading in hides and skins is carried on, and sheep raising supports a domestic woolen industry and a small export trade in wool. Coastal fisheries and, to a lesser extent, inland fisheries and pearling grounds (in Gulf of Mannar) are locally important. India's forested area (over □ 80,000) includes deodar, oak, and pine (in the Himalayas); sal, an important timber species (mainly in lower Himalayas and E central India); teak, blackwood, and ebony (in Western Ghats); sandalwood (especially in Mysore forests); and bamboo (extensively grown; utilized in paper mfg.). Lac (notably in Chota Nagpur), tanning materials, honey, and silkworms (chiefly SW Madras) are other forest produce. Casuarinas are numerous along E coast, a major area for jaggery- and fiber-yielding palmyra and areca palms. Among the wide variety of wildlife are leopards and panthers, tigers (now mainly confined to S Himalayan slopes, E Rajasthan jungles, S fringes of Ganges Delta), elephants (Assam hills, S Mysore), rhinoceroses, and cheetahs (on N Deccan Plateau, where they are trained to hunt antelope). Aside from mica, manganese, ilmenite, and monazite, in which the country ranks high, India's mineral resources, though large, have not been fully exploited. The Chota Nagpur Plateau region of S Bihar, SW West Bengal, and N Orissa is the most important mining area, producing most of India's coal (notably Jharia and Raniganj coal fields), iron (hematite), mica (India produces c.60% of world output), and copper. Lesser amounts of coal are worked in SE Hyderabad, S Madhya Pradesh, and along SE Madras coast (lignite); iron in Mysore; and mica in N Madras and central Rajasthan. India exports most of its manganese, mined in Madhya Pradesh, Madras, Bombay, and Mysore. Ilmenite and the strategic mineral monazite are found in Travancore's beach sands. There are workings of magnesite (in Chalk Hills of Madras), gold (in Kolar Gold Fields in Mysore), and of bauxite, chromite, steatite, gypsum, building stone, salt, fire clay, asbestos, corundum, and fuller's earth. India is deficient in petroleum (only fields are in Assam), lead, and sulphur, and produces no tin or zinc. Industries are predominantly devoted to agr. processing and mfg. of light consumers' goods. Cotton textiles are by far the most important industry, centering in Bombay, Ahmadabad, Coimbatore, Sholapur, and Nagpur. Other manufactures include woolen (Cawnpore) and silk (Benares, Mysore) textiles, leather goods (Cawnpore, Madras), jute products (West Bengal; output seriously diminished when partition left Calcutta's mills dependent on E Pakistan's raw jute), steel (largest works at Jamshedpur in Chota Nagpur), refined sugar (main centers in Uttar Pradesh), paper, cement, glass, cigarettes, bricks and tiles, paint, and matches. India's motion-picture industry, which centers in Bombay, is 2d only to that of the U.S. Industrial development during and since Second World War includes factories for airplane mfg. (at Bangalore), automobile assembling, agr. machinery, machine tools, chemicals, aluminum products (in Bihar and Travancore), power alcohol, rayon; also telephones, radios, plywood, plastics. Because of the relatively small amount of industrial fuel many industries are powered by hydroelectricity; chief works are in Kolaba dist. (Bombay), at Mettur (Madras), near Sivasamudram isl. (Mysore), and at Jogindarnagar (Himachal Pradesh); schemes are projected in the Damodar Valley and at Bhakra (Bilaspur). Of India's many noted handicrafts (or cottage industries), cotton weaving is the most prevalent; others include woolen carpets, silks and brocades, brass and ivory ware, pottery, coir matting. The principal ports (CALCUTTA, MADRAS, and Vizagapatam on E coast, BOMBAY and COCHIN on W coast) handle the bulk of India's exports (jute goods, tea, cotton cloth, hides and skins, manganese, mica, shellac, coir and copra, tobacco, spices) and imports (machinery, cotton, metals, grain, piece goods, chemicals). Chief inland cities are HYDERABAD, AHMADABAD, DELHI, CAWNPORE (Kanpur), AMRITSAR, LUCKNOW, HOWRAH, NAGPUR, AGRA, BENARES (Banaras), ALLAHABAD, POONA, BANGALORE, and MADURA. India has c.34,000 mi. of railway track (chiefly broad gauge). Roads are mostly unmetaled and unusable in the rainy season. From the international air centers of Calcutta, Bombay, and Delhi, domestic air routes radiate to all major Indian cities. Inland water transport is relatively unimportant. Leading educational institutions include univs. of Calcutta, Bombay, and Madras, Benares Hindu Univ., Aligarh Muslim Univ., Visva-Bharati (at Santiniketan), Indian School of Mines and Applied Geology (at Dhanbad), Patna Univ., East Punjab Univ. (at Solan), and Andhra Univ. (at Waltair). Most popular of the country's resorts are the hot-weather retreats of SIMLA, Mussoorie, Naini Tal, Almora, and DARJEELING in the Himalayas and Matheran, Mahabaleshwar, Ootacamund, and Kodaikanal in the Western Ghats. Benares, Allahabad, Hardwar, Dwarka, Conjeevaram, Kumbakonam, Muttra (Mathura), Puri, and Nasik are major Hindu pilgrimage centers; Amritsar is the holy city of the Sikhs; and Satrunjaya hill near Palitana is sacred to the Jains. Visited by Indians of all sects are SEVAGRAM, last home of Mahatma Gandhi, and Rajghat, in Delhi, where his body was cremated. Outstanding archaeological landmarks are the cave temples of Ajanta, Ellora, Karli, and Elephanta, the Buddhist remains at Sarnath, Sanchi, and Buddh Gaya, and the noted temple sites at Belur, Madura, Tanjore, Abu (Jain), Bhubaneswar, Konarak, Mahabalipuram, and Khajraho. India is far from being linguistically homogeneous. English is in official usage, although the Indian constitution of 1950 provided for the gradual introduction (within 15 years) of Hindi, the vernacular of the upper Ganges Plain and, to a certain extent, a lingua franca throughout India. Other major languages are Bengali, Bihari, Telugu (spoken in Andhra), Marathi (Maharashtra), Tamil (Tamilnad), Rajasthani, Punjabi, Kanarese (Kanara), Oriya (Orissa), Gujarati (Gujarat), Malayalam (Travancore-Cochin), and Assamese, all of which are subdivided into several local dialects. The historical discussion which follows is that of the Indian subcontinent. Earliest known civilization was that of the Indus valley, most notably revealed in the remains (4000–2000 B.C.) at MOHENJO-DARO in Sind and at Harappa in the Punjab. The Vedic Aryans are generally believed to have entered India c.1500 B.C. via the passes of the NW. Establishing their original homeland, *Aryavarta,* in the plains of Punjab and the upper Ganges, they moved eastward down the Ganges valley and then southward over the peninsula, developing over a period of c.2,000 years a Brahamanic civilization. Important kingdoms were MAGADHA (⊙ Pataliputra, modern Patna), Kosala (⊙ Ajodhya), and Avanti (⊙ Ujjain). The name of a semi-legendary dynasty—Bharat—survives as the alternate name of the new Indian republic. In this period the caste system was developed, establishing separate social groups based on hereditary occupations, and the basic treatises of Hindu philosophical speculation, culminating in the Upanishads, were formulated. Buddhism and Jainism arose in Bihar c.6th cent. B.C. The anc. Persian prov. of Gandhara along the middle Indus valley was reached in 326 B.C. by Alexander the Great, who penetrated as far as Beas R. The great Mauryan emperor Asoka (c.273–232 B.C.) expanded his domain from its nucleus in Bihar to include most of India except the S tip of the peninsula, where the Chera, Chola, and Pandya kings flourished. About this time Buddhism, which Asoka adopted as the state religion, spread over E Asia and Hindu culture was 1st carried to the Malay Archipelago by the colonizing S Indian dynasties (Tamils). In 4th and 5th cent. A.D., N India experienced the "golden age" of the Guptas, when Hindu art and literature reached a high level. After several invasions by White Huns (5th cent.), a strong kingdom (⊙ Kanauj) was established by Harsha in the 1st half of 7th cent., when the noted Chinese pilgrim Hsüan-tsang visited India. Medieval dynasties in peninsular India included the Chalukyas and Cholas, while in Bengal the Pal and Sen kings held sway (8th–13th cent.), and in Assam the Ahoms were powerful. The period bet. 700 and 1200 saw the rise of several Rajput tribes, who later valiantly resisted the Moguls in their hill forts in Rajputana. Islam was 1st brought to India by Arabs, who, along with sea merchants from Alexandria and Rome, were early traders with India and permanently settled in Sind in A.D. 712. Moslem invasions from the NW began with the plundering raids (1001–1025) of Mahmud of Ghazni. The Turko-Afghan Delhi sultans, who reached the region of present Delhi state after subduing Punjab in 1193, conquered most of N India to Bengal from 12th to early 13th cent. and in 14th cent. expanded over the Deccan Plateau, where they were succeeded by several separate rebel kings—the Deccan sultans (e.g., at Bijapur, Ahmadnagar, Golconda), who combined to defeat the Hindu Vijayanagar kings of KANARA in 1565. The Mogul empire, founded by Baber after battle of PANIPAT (1526), was consolidated (1556–76) by Akbar and reached its greatest territorial extent under Aurangzeb (1658–1707). The Moguls were the 1st rulers since Asoka's time to give all India a semblance of unified administration. Akbar was noted for his organizing genius, religious tolerance, and patronage of learning, while under Jahangir and Shah Jehan Mogul architecture reached its peak with such bldgs. as the Taj Mahal and Moti Masjid (Pearl Mosque) at Agra, Red Fort at Delhi, and Jami Masjid at Fatehpur Sikri. With the rise of the Mahratta power, centered in the Western Ghats under Sivaji, and the militant Sikh nation in Punjab, the Mogul empire disintegrated during 18th cent. into virtually independent chieftainships, such as Hyderabad. Meanwhile, in 16th and 17th cents., the Portuguese, Dutch, Danes, French, and English had established small trading settlements on E and W coasts and along Hooghly R. in Bengal. Taking advantage of native princely rivalries, the British and French struggled for commercial supremacy, and, after victories at PLASSEY (1757) and BUXAR (1764) which ended Moslem control in Bengal, forces of the Br. East India Co. under Robert Clive triumphed over the French in the CARNATIC. In 1774 Warren Hastings became the Company's 1st governor-general. By 1819 the British were firmly entrenched, having concluded successful military campaigns against Hyder Ali and Tippoo Sahib of Mysore (1769–99), the Mahrattas (1775–1819), and the Gurkhas of Nepal (1814–16). Subsequent conquests included Assam (1826), Sind (1843), prompted by the debacle of the 1st Afghan War (1839–42), Punjab (1849) after 2 short Sikh wars, and Oudh (1856); other areas were brought within the British sphere by a system of treaty alliances with native princes. Major developments in administration and social reform in 1st half of 19th cent. were the creation of a govt. bureaucracy (with Indians holding only subordinate positions), the establishment of higher education on the English model (univs. of Calcutta, Bombay, and Madras founded 1857), and the suppression of infanticide, suttee, slavery, and thuggee. The impact of an alien culture, regret for past glories, and Br. territorial encroachments formed the background for the bloody Sepoy Rebellion of 1857. The mutiny, confined to the upper Ganges Plain, was rigorously suppressed after a year. In 1858 an act of parliament transferred the Company's authority to the Br. crown (Victoria was proclaimed Empress of India in 1877) and provided for India's govt. by a viceroy in India and a secretary of state for India in the Br. cabinet. In 2d half of 19th cent. extensive railroad and irrigation canal building took place and commercial agr. (cotton, wheat, jute) became dominant. India supplied raw materials for Br. industries and at the same time was made a market for their finished products. These events seriously undermined the old rural structure, which was based on the self-sufficient village economy of subsistence agr. and handicraft mfg. Further imperial expansion brought Kashmir (1885), Burma (1886), and Baluchistan (1891) within the Indian Empire. In 1885 the Indian Natl. Congress was formed and declared its long-range goal to be the attainment of self-government within the Br. Empire by constitutional means. The partition of Bengal (1905) by Viceroy Curzon, without regard for its cultural homogeneity, gave rise to violent agitation. The reforms of 1909 provided for a separate Moslem electorate, as requested by the Moslem League (formed 1906), and gave disproportionate representation to Europeans and wealthy Indian landlords. During the First World War both Congress and the League, influenced by official statements promising constitutional reform, backed the govt. war effort, and Indian troops served in the Middle East and France. The Government of India Act of 1919, however, fell far short of nationalist hopes and in the same year public opinion was incensed by the notorious Amritsar massacre. In the 1920s, under the leadership of Mahatma Gandhi, the nationalist movement spread rapidly to all parts of India. Although Hindus and Moslems both demanded independence (*swaraj*) from the British, many Moslems were afraid lest their rights be ignored by the Hindu majority in an independent India, and accordingly the Moslem League, under Mohammed Ali Jinnah, held back from a united front with the Congress. Three conferences held in London in 1930–32 led to the Government of India Act of 1935, which provided for an enlarged franchise and autonomous provincial govts.; Burma was separated from India at this time. Elections were held in 1937 and the new govts. took office, but the provision made in the constitution for an eventual federation of Br. India and the Indian States was not implemented. The INDIAN EMPIRE therefore consisted of the provs. of BRITISH INDIA, comprising 55% of total area and 76% of total pop., and the INDIAN (or Native) STATES; in 1941—□ 1,581,410; including nontabulated Assam tribal areas, □ 1,609,598; pop. 388,997,955. On the outbreak of the Second World War, the viceroy's arbitrary declaration that India was a belligerent exasperated Indian opinion. With the failure of the 1942 Cripps mission to arrive at a satisfactory solution for the transfer of power to Indian hands, the Congress, led by Jawaharlal Nehru, issued its "Quit India" resolution, authorizing Gandhi to launch a nonviolent resistance campaign; the British immediately outlawed the Congress party and imprisoned all its leaders. In the meantime the Moslem League had increased its demands and in 1940 officially endorsed the PAKISTAN or Moslem autonomy idea, strongly opposed by Congress. At the war's end the Congress leaders were released. Anti-British feeling ran high during the trial (1946) of officers of the "Indian Natl. Army," which had fought with the Japanese to win India from the British. However, the Br. (Labour) govt. in the same year offered complete independence to India and the new viceroy, Lord Mountbatten, finally persuaded Congress to accept, reluctantly, the partition of the country into 2 dominions, India and Pakistan, which took effect Aug. 15, 1947. At the London Conference of 1949 India accepted membership in the Br. Commonwealth as an equal partner and independent nation. The division of Punjab and Bengal bet. Pakistan and India resulted in serious communal riots and the mass migration of millions of people to and from the new dominions. At this time a vast administrative reorganization was begun. By Jan. 26, 1950, when India became a sovereign republic, all acceding princely states had been brought within the constitutional framework, some being inc. into adjacent provs. (e.g., Deccan States into Bombay, Orissa States into Orissa, Cooch Behar into West Bengal), others merging to form unions (e.g., Rajputana States into Rajasthan, Western India States into Saurashtra, W Central India states into Madhya Bharat), and a few retaining their territorial identity (e.g., Hyderabad, Mysore, Cutch); also numerous small detached enclaves were absorbed by surrounding units. The new India's foreign policy was dominated in the early years by friction with Pakistan, especially over the KASHMIR dispute. India now comprises the following 27 constituent states: ASSAM, BIHAR, BOMBAY, HYDERABAD, MADHYA BHARAT, MADHYA PRADESH (former Central Provs. and Berar), MADRAS, MYSORE, ORISSA, PATIALA AND EAST PUNJAB STATES UNION (PEPSU), PUNJAB, RAJASTHAN, SAURASHTRA, TRAVANCORE-COCHIN, UTTAR PRADESH (formerly United Provs.), West BENGAL, and (administered by central govt. through chief commissioners) AJMER, ANDAMAN AND NICOBAR ISLANDS, BHOPAL, BILASPUR, COORG, CUTCH, DELHI, HIMACHAL PRADESH, MANIPUR, TRIPURA, and VINDHYA PRADESH; the protectorate of SIKKIM is included in the India census figures. For further information see those articles.

India, Yugoslavia: see INDJIJA.

India, La, Nicaragua: see LA INDIA.

Indiahoma (ĭn″dēŭhō′mŭ), town (pop. 319), Comanche co., SW Okla., 20 mi. W of Lawton, S of the Wichita Mts.; trade center for agr. area; cotton ginning.

Indiana, state (land □ 36,205; with inland waters, but without □ 228 of L. Michigan, □ 36,291; 1950 pop. 3,934,224; 1940 pop. 3,427,796), E central U.S., in the Middle West; bordered N by Mich., W by Ill., S by Ky., E by Ohio; 37th in area, 12th in pop.; admitted 1816 as 19th state; ⊙ Indianapolis. The "Hoosier State," measuring 260 mi. N–S, 150 mi. E–W at its widest points, is one of the prairie states. It is bounded NW by L. Michigan, S by the Ohio R., and SW by the Wabash R., which, with its major tributaries (White R., Tippecanoe R.), drains most of the state. The major portion of Ind. is fairly level, sometimes rolling prairie land with an average elev. of c.700 ft. (state's highest point, 1,240 ft., is near E border). Surface features (especially in N) are largely determined by continental glaciation, and till plains, glacial lakes (NE), and terminal moraines are characteristic. In the NW, around L. Michigan, are sand dunes. The only unglaciated section, in the S, is a comparatively rugged region of rounded hills and steep valleys, of predominantly limestone formation with sinkholes and caves. The state has a humid continental climate with relatively hot summers and cold winters; rainfall, well distributed throughout the year, varies from 35–40 in. in N to 40–45 in. in S. South Bend (N) has mean temp. of 35°F. in Jan., 80°F. in July, and 40 in. of rain. The picturesque valley of the Ohio is subject to occasional floods. The growing season averages 160 (NE) to 180 (SW) days a year. Native vegetation consisted of oak-hickory forest with small areas of chestnut oak—yellow poplar (S) and prairie grass (W). Over 85% of the state's total area is classified as farm and range land, just over half of which is in crops. Corn is by far the major crop and is grown (for feed and cash) extensively throughout the N half of the state. Winter wheat is raised largely in the S third, oats center and N, hay mostly NE, soybeans in the N, and tobacco in the S. Truck farming is important and the muck soil region in the N produces large amounts of cabbages, onions, potatoes, celery, melons, and peppermint and spearmint (Ind. processes ⅔ of U.S. output of these mint oils). The state ranks 2d to Calif. in the production of tomatoes for canning (canneries center around Elwood). There are grape, apple, and peach orchards (mostly S). Livestock includes (1950) 1,760,000 cattle, 4,611,000 hogs, and 454,000 sheep. Dairying is concentrated near urban centers, especially in the far N; hogs are numerous in the N half of the state (part of Corn Belt). Poultry is raised on most farms. Total commercial forest area comprises 3,358,000 acres; chief timber species are oak, maple, beech, walnut, ash, basswood, elm, chestnut; natl. forest reserves total 784,650 acres. The state's most valuable mineral is bituminous coal, mined largely in Vigo, Knox, Pike, and Warrick counties, which lie in the Eastern Interior Coal field in SW and central W Ind. Coal is suitable for most domestic industries but not for the NW lakeside iron and steel plants, which obtain coking coal from the Appalachian fields. Almost all of the limestone used for building purposes in the U.S. comes from S central and S Ind., where Bloomington and Bedford are major quarrying centers. Principal petroleum fields are in central E part of the state and in Posey co. (SW); some natural gas is produced; large oil refineries are at Whiting and East Chicago. Clay (around Brazil), sand and gravel, and sandstone are also worked. Ind. has a wide variety of industries, the most important being the steel works of GARY, HAMMOND and EAST CHICAGO, in the heavily industrialized CALUMET region, strategically located at the S end of L. Michigan, midway bet. L. Superior iron mines and Appalachian coal fields. Other industries include mfg. of motor vehicles and parts, agr. and electrical machinery; food processing, meat packing; metal works, railroad and machine shops; mfg. of chemicals, cement, furniture, glass products, electrical appliances, soap, and clothing. INDIANAPOLIS, the state's largest city, FORT WAYNE, SOUTH BEND, and EVANSVILLE are important commercial and mfg. centers, while Terre Haute, Muncie, Anderson, Kokomo, Richmond, Elkhart, Logansport, and New Albany also have diversified manufactures. Ind.'s proximity to raw materials and the large Midwestern markets and its good transportation facilities (Indianapolis is a major rail and road hub) have contributed to its industrial development. Michigan City, on L. Michigan, is a popular summer resort, and the large Wyandotte and Marengo caves (S) are also tourist attractions. Ind. figures prominently in American literature and is the native state of James Whitcomb Riley, Theodore Dreiser, Booth Tarkington, George Ade, and William Vaughan Moody. Leading educational institutions are Ind. Univ. (at Bloomington), Purdue Univ. (at Lafayette), Univ. of Notre Dame (at Notre Dame, N suburb of South Bend), Butler Univ. (at Indianapolis), and De Pauw Univ. (at Greencastle). Several of the river valleys have remains of the anc. Mound Builders' culture. The Ind. region was 1st explored (1679) by the French fur trader La Salle, who found the Miami Indians the dominant tribe at the time. Other French trappers followed and a trading post was established at VINCENNES in 1702, the 1st permanent settlement in Ind. British influence among the Indians increased throughout the 18th cent. and by the Treaty of Paris (1763) France surrendered her western territory to England. In order to create some administrative order, the area was annexed to the prov. of Quebec in 1774, but the campaigns of George Rogers Clark, climaxed by the capture of Vincennes (1779), during the Revolution, were largely responsible for England's ceding the area to the U.S. in 1783. By the Ordinance of 1787 Ind. became part of the NORTHWEST TERRITORY. Indian depredations were temporarily halted by the battle of Fallen Timbers (in Ohio) in 1794, and in 1800 Indiana Territory was created, comprising present states of Ind., Ill., Wis., Mich., and part of Minn. Indian resistance to white encroachment culminated in the Battle of Tippecanoe (1811), at which Gov. William Henry Harrison defeated a confederacy under Tecumseh and the Prophet. The War of 1812 finally removed the British and Indian threat to the Northwest. Ind. became a state (1816), with its present boundaries, during a period of rapid settlement; internal improvements, such as roads and canals, further developed the area, as corn, wheat, and fruit were widely grown by the Hoosier farmers. With the coming of the railroads, mining and mfg. had their beginnings. During the Civil War, Ind.—a Northern state—suffered a Confederate raid in 1863. As the growth of industries upset the old agrarian structure, and farmers sought relief from high prices and railroad rates, land monopolies, and indebtedness, the Granger movement and Greenback and Populist parties dominated Ind. politics bet. 1875 and 1900. Eugene Debs, a native Indianian, figured prominently in the nascent labor movement at turn of the century. Important industrial plants (oil refineries, steel mills) were constructed in the Calumet region in the early years of the 20th cent. Although the farmers' problems remain, Ind.'s economy has been bolstered by manufactures, which during the Second World War almost tripled in value. For further information see articles on cities, towns, geographical features, and the 92 counties: Adams, Allen Bartholomew, Benton, Blackford, Boone, Brown, Carroll, Cass, Clark, Clay, Clinton, Crawford, Daviess, Dearborn, Decatur, De Kalb, Delaware, Dubois, Elkhart, Fayette, Floyd, Fountain, Franklin, Fulton, Gibson, Grant, Greene, Hamilton, Hancock, Harrison, Hendricks, Henry, Howard, Huntington, Jackson, Jasper, Jay, Jefferson, Jennings, Johnson, Knox, Kosciusko, Lagrange, Lake, La Porte, Lawrence, Madison, Marion, Marshall, Martin, Miami, Monroe, Montgomery, Morgan, Newton, Noble, Ohio, Orange, Owen, Parke, Perry, Pike, Porter, Posey, Pulaski, Putnam, Randolph, Ripley, Rush, Saint Joseph, Scott, Shelby, Spencer, Starke, Steuben, Sullivan, Switzerland, Tippecanoe, Tipton, Union, Vanderburgh, Vermillion, Vigo, Wabash, Warren, Warrick, Washington, Wayne, Wells, White, Whitley.

Indiana, county (□ 831; pop. 77,106), W central Pa.; ⊙ Indiana. Coal-mining, mfg., agr. region; bounded S by Conemaugh R.; drained by other tributaries of Allegheny R. Bituminous coal, coke, natural gas, limestone; mfg. (clay and glass products, rubber tires, metal products, food products); agr. (grain, potatoes, clover, poultry, livestock, dairy products). Formed 1803.

Indiana, borough (pop. 11,743), ⊙ Indiana co., W central Pa., 45 mi. ENE of Pittsburgh; bituminous coal; mfg. (rubber tires, food products, clay products, furniture). State teachers col. here. Settled c.1772, laid out 1805, inc. 1816.

Indiana Harbor, Ind.: see East Chicago.

Indianapolis (ĭn″dēŭnă′pŭlĭs), city (pop. 427,173), largest city and ⊙ Ind. and Marion co., central Ind., on West Fork of White R. and c.175 mi. SE of Chicago; 39°45′N 86°10′W; alt. c.750 ft. An important Middle West railroad and highway focus; port of entry; largest U.S. city not on navigable waterway. State's banking, commercial, and agr. market center (grain, livestock). Large stockyard, railroad shops, flour and hosiery mills; printing and publishing; mfg. of pharmaceuticals, automobile bodies and parts, machinery, metal products, hardware, construction materials, paint, food products, clothing. Seat of Butler Univ., units of Indiana Univ., John Herron Art Inst., Indiana Central Col., Marian Col., a Carmelite monastery, a music conservatory; has a symphony orchestra. Here are a correctional school for girls and a women's prison. Points of interest: the capitol (1888); state library, with historical collections; World War Memorial Plaza; natl. hq. of American Legion (in a war memorial bldg.); home of James Whitcomb Riley; motor speedway (near by; scene of annual auto races); state fairgrounds; a state fish hatchery. U.S. Fort Benjamin Harrison (established 1903), with an air force base, is near by. Settled 1819, laid out 1821, inc. 1847. Became ⊙ Ind. in 1825. Lincoln's body lay in state here in 1865.

Indian Arm, SW B.C., N arm (13 mi. long, 1 mi. wide) of Burrard Inlet, 8 mi. NE of Vancouver. Receives small Indian R. at head. On both shores mts. rise to 3–5,000 ft.

Indian Creek, town (pop. 44), Dade Co., S Fla., near Miami Beach. Sometimes called Indian Creek Village.

Indian Creek, S Ind., rises in SW Clark co., flows c.60 mi. SW to the Ohio 11 mi. SW of Corydon.

Indian Desert, India: see Thar Desert.

Indian Empire or **India**, those parts of the Indian subcontinent which were formerly directly or indirectly under British rule or protection; comprised British India, with 55% of total area and 76% of total pop., and Indian (or Native) States; ⊙ was New Delhi, seat of the viceroy or governor-general. Until 1937 included Burma and Aden. In 1941: □ 1,581,410; including nontabulated Assam tribal areas, □ 1,609,598; pop. 388,997,955. In accordance with Indian Independence Act of 1947, Indian Empire was partitioned into self-governing dominions of India and Pakistan.

Indian Head, town (pop. 1,354), S Sask., 40 mi. E of Regina; grain elevators, flour mills; site of Dominion experimental and forestry farm.

Indian Head, town (pop. 491), Charles co., S Md., on the Potomac c.28 mi. below Washington; has naval ordnance proving ground (1892), ordnance, disposal school, and powder plant.

Indian Hill, village (pop. 2,090), Hamilton co., extreme SW Ohio, suburb c.10 mi. NE of downtown Cincinnati. Inc. 1941.

Indian Hills, town (pop. 291), Jefferson co., N Ky., a suburb of Louisville.

Indian House Lake (□ 125), NE Que., on George R.; 56°N 64°30′W; 35 mi. long, 2 mi. wide. On E shore hills rise to c.1,800 ft. On lake is air base.

Indian Island, Knox co., S Maine, small lighthouse isl. off harbor of Rockport.

Indian Islands, N.F.: see East Indian Island; West Indian Island.

Indian Lake, resort village, Hamilton co., NE central N.Y., in the Adirondacks, near N end of Indian L. (□ c.7; c.7 mi. long), c.45 mi. NW of Glens Falls; lumber.

Indian Lake. 1 In Upper Peninsula, Mich.: see Indian River, stream. **2** In N.J.: see Denville. **3** In Logan co., W central Ohio, 9 mi. NW of Bellefontaine; c.4 mi. in diameter. State park; fishing, duck hunting. Source of Great Miami R.

Indian Lorette, Que.: see Loretteville.

Indian Oaks, village (1940 pop. 681), Tarrant co., N Texas, NE suburb of Fort Worth.

Indian Ocean, anc. *Oceanus Indicus*, smallest (□ 28,350,000) of the 3 great oceans of the world, bounded by Asia (N), Australia (E), Antarctica (S), and Africa (W). It is separated from the Pacific Ocean by the Sunda Isls., through which the chief passages are the Strait of Malacca, Sunda Strait, and the Timor Sea. On S coast of Australia, the Indian and Pacific oceans communicate via Bass Strait, with 147°E as the conventional dividing line S of Tasmania. Links with the Atlantic are via the Suez Canal and also S of Cape of Good Hope across 20°E. Mean depth of the Indian Ocean is 13,000 ft.; greatest depth, 24,440 ft. in Java Trench off S Java. The Indian Ocean forms 2 major indentations—Arabian Sea and Bay of Bengal (with Andaman Sea)—in S coast of Asia. Principal isls. are Madagascar, Comoro Isls., Réunion, Mauritius, and Seychelles, off Africa; Ceylon, Laccadives, Maldives, Chagos Archipelago, Andaman, Nicobar, Christmas, and Cocos Isls., off Asia. In S Indian Ocean are Amsterdam, St. Paul, Kerguelen, and Crozet isls. of France; Heard Isl. of Australia; and Marion and Prince Edward isls. of U. of So. Afr. A notable feature of Indian Ocean submarine topography is a series of curved parallel ridges trending N–S in the W section. Situated largely S of the equator, the Indian Ocean has a counterclockwise circulation consisting of the West Australian, Equatorial, and Mozambique currents. N of the equator, the currents are greatly influenced by the monsoon: they vary with the SW summer monsoon and the NE winter monsoon, the former bringing warm, moist marine air from the Indian Ocean to S Asia. Long navigated by Arab, Indian, and Chinese traders, the Indian Ocean was penetrated (1498) by Vasco da Gama en route to India. Following the opening (1869) of the Suez Canal, the N Indian Ocean became the direct shipping lane bet. Europe and the Far East. The greatest modern ports are Aden, Bombay, Colombo, Calcutta, and Rangoon in Asia; Perth in Australia; and Mombasa, Lourenço Marques, and Durban in Africa.

Indianola (ĭn″dēŭnō′lŭ). **1** Village (pop. 392), Vermilion co., E Ill., 14 mi. SSW of Danville, in agr. and bituminous-coal area. **2** City (pop. 5,145), ⊙ Warren co., S central Iowa, 16 mi. S of Des Moines; mfg. (metal products, brooms, feed). Seat of Simpson Col. (coeducational; 1860). State park near by. Inc. 1863. **3** City (pop. 4,369), ⊙ Sunflower co., W Miss., 24 mi. E of Greenville, near Sunflower R., in rich agr. area (cotton, corn, alfalfa); cottonseed products; cotton compress. Settled in mid-19th cent.; inc. 1886. **4** City (pop. 738), Red Willow co., S Nebr., 10 mi. E of McCook and on Republican R.; grain, livestock, dairy and poultry produce. **5** Town (pop. 314), Pittsburg co., SE Okla., 16 mi. N of McAlester, and on Canadian R.; cotton ginning. **6** Vanished port, Calhoun co., S Texas, on Matagorda Bay, c.11 mi. SE of Port Lavaca. Founded 1844, it was once most active port in state and port of entry for many immigrants; destroyed by hurricanes of 1875 and 1886.

Indian Orchard, Mass.: see Springfield.

Indian Pass. 1 In Essex co., NE N.Y., gorge (c.1,300 ft. deep, c.1 mi. long) in the Adirondacks, bet. Wallface Mtn. (W) and Mt. MacIntyre (E), c.6 mi. WNW of Mt. Marcy; hiking trails. **2** In Wyo.: see Wind River Range.

Indian Peak (9,817 ft.), SE B.C., near Alta. border, in Rocky Mts., near SE side of Kootenay Natl. Park, 20 mi. SSW of Banff; 50°55′N 115°45′W.

Indian Pond, Somerset co., W central Maine, 12 mi. NW of Greenville; 5 mi. long. Receives 2 Moosehead L. outlets, which then flow S as Kennebec R.

Indian River, village (pop. 48), E Alaska, on Copper R. and 120 mi. NE of Valdez, on Tok Cut-off.

Indian River, county (□ 511; pop. 11,872), central Fla., on the Atlantic (E); ⊙ Vero Beach. Coastal lowland bordered by barrier beach enclosing Indian R. lagoon; interior is a marshy peat area containing L. Wilmington. Co. forms part of Indian River dist. noted for its citrus fruit (especially oranges); also a truck and tourist region; sugar cane grown around Fellsmere. Formed 1925.

Indian River, village (pop. c.500), Cheboygan co., N Mich., 18 mi. SSW of Cheboygan, on SE shore of Burt L., in resort and forest area.

Indian River. 1 In Sussex co., SE Del., formed by small streams just W of Millsboro (dam here); flows 6 mi. E to Indian River Bay. **2** In E Fla., one of longest (c.120 mi.) and straightest lagoons of state, sheltered from the Atlantic by barrier beach (broken by several inlets), and connected with Mosquito Lagoon (N) and Banana R. lagoon (E) by passages. Parallels E coast from a point near Volusia-Brevard co. line (N) to St. Lucie Inlet (S); average width 2 mi., max. width 5½ mi. (near Merritt Isl.). Followed by Intracoastal Waterway, and connected (at S end) with Okeechobee Waterway. Along its shores are many resorts (Titusville, Cocoa, Melbourne, Vero Beach, Fort Pierce). Indian River dist., including Indian River, Brevard, and St. Lucie counties, is noted for its citrus fruit. **3** In S Upper Peninsula, Mich., rises in SE Alger co., flows SE to Indian L. (c.6 mi. long, 4 mi. wide) just NW of Manistique, then short distance E to Manistique R.; c.40 mi. long. Sometimes called Big Indian R. Two state parks are on lake shore. **4** In N N.Y., rises in N Lewis co., flows NW to Antwerp, and SW, past Philadelphia, then generally N, past Theresa, to S end of Black L. in St. Lawrence co.; c.80 mi. long. At Natural Bridge, river has cut a limestone bridge and caverns.

Indian River Bay, SE Del., lagoon (c.6 mi. long, 2 mi. wide) at mouth of Indian R., just S of Rehoboth Bay, to which it is joined by channels. Barrier beach, cut by dredged inlet, protects bay from the Atlantic.

Indian Rocks Beach South Shore, town (pop. 198), Pinellas co., W Fla., 14 mi. NW of St. Petersburg.

Indian Springs, hamlet, Clark co., S Nev., c.40 mi. NW of Las Vegas. Hq. for Air Force bombing and gunnery range (□ c.5,000; to NW), which includes Atomic Energy Commission installations and Frenchman Flat, desert basin which was site (Jan., 1951) of experimental atomic explosions.

Indian States or **Native States**, the semi-independent states of the former Br. Indian Empire, ruled by Indian princes in treaty relation with Br. Govt. at New Delhi; name used in contradistinction to the provs. of British India. The 560 odd states varied in area from a few acres to the 82,313 sq. mi. of Hyderabad. Most of larger states held direct relations with governor-general through respective Residents, but the vast majority were grouped into agencies (e.g., Central India, Deccan States, Eastern States, Gujarat States, Punjab States, Rajputana States, Western India States), administered by Residents or Political Agents. Principal states included Hyderabad, Kashmir, Mysore, Travancore, Gwalior, Baroda, Jodhpur, Jaipur, Udaipur, Indore, Navanagar, Kalat, and Manipur. In 1941: total □ 715,964; pop. 93,189,233. In 1947–49 all states, except Kashmir, were incorporated into India or Pakistan.

Indian Stream, Coos co., N N.H., rises near Que. line, flows c.25 mi. S to the Connecticut below Pittsburg.

Indian Stream Republic, short-lived independent territory at headwaters of Connecticut R., over which neither U.S. nor Canadian jurisdiction was established. Set up 1832 by local inhabitants; annexed 1835 by N.H.; awarded to U.S. by Webster-Ashburton Treaty of 1842.

Indian Territory, in U.S.: see Oklahoma.

Indian Tibet, Kashmir: see Ladakh.

Indiantown Gap Military Reservation, Pa.: see Annville.

Indian Trail, town (pop. 308), Union co., S N.C., 14 mi. SE of Charlotte.

Indian Village, town (pop. 57), St. Joseph co., N Ind.

Indiaroba (ēndyŏŏrô′bŭ), city (pop. 554), S Sergipe, NE Brazil, on Bahia border, 16 mi. S of Estância; sugar. Until 1944, called Espírito Santo.

Indiga (ēndyēgä′), village (1939 pop. over 500), W Nenets Natl. Okrug, Archangel oblast, Russian SFSR, port on Barents Sea, 110 mi. W of Naryan-Mar; fish cannery.

Indigirka River (ĭn″dĭgēr′kŭ, Rus. ēndyĭgēr′kŭ), NE Yakut Autonomous SSR, Russian SFSR, NE Siberia, rises on Oimyakon Plateau SE of Oimyakon; flows 1,113 mi. N, cutting through Cherski Range and through tundra zone, past Khonu (head of navigation), Druzhina, and Chokurdakh, to E. Siberian Sea, forming large delta mouth. Main tributaries, Selennyakh (left) and Moma (right) rivers. Ice-free June–Sept.

Indija, Yugoslavia: see INDJIJA.

Indin Lake (25 mi. long, 1–8 mi. wide), S central Mackenzie Dist., Northwest Territories, 120 mi. NNW of Yellowknife; 64°15′N 115°15′W; drains S into Great Slave L. by Snare R. Gold deposits discovered here 1945.

Indio (ĭn′dēō), city (pop. 5,300), Riverside co., S Calif., in Coachella Valley, 60 mi. ESE of Redlands; trade center for irrigated agr. region (dates, citrus fruit, cotton, alfalfa). Desert resort. Joshua Tree Natl. Monument is NE. Founded 1876 on railroad; inc. 1930.

Indirab, Afghanistan: see BANU.

Indispensable Strait, Solomon Isls., SW Pacific, separates Malaita (E) and isls. of Guadalcanal and Santa Isabel (W); 40 mi. wide.

Indje, Cape, Turkey: see INCE, CAPE.

Indjija or **Indyiya** (both: ĕn′dyēyä), Serbo-Croatian *Inđija,* Hung. *India* (ĭn′dēō), village (pop. 7,588), Vojvodina, N Serbia, Yugoslavia, 25 mi. NW of Belgrade, in the Srem; rail junction.

Indochina or **French Indochina** (ĭn′dōchī″nü), Fr. *Indochine française,* group (□ 272,200; pop. 27,-000,000) of 3 states (VIETNAM, LAOS, CAMBODIA) associated with France within the French Union, in SE Asia, on E coast of Indochinese Peninsula (which it shares with Burma, Thailand, and Malaya) on South China Sea. Prior to European intervention (16th cent.), the cultures of Indochina, formed by currents of influence coming from China and India, resulted in growth and decline of Khmer empire in Cambodia, the rise and fall of Champa, and the steady expansion of ANNAM. In 19th-cent. race for colonial empire, Indochina fell to France. COCHIN CHINA (annexed 1863–67 by France as a colony) and the protectorates of Cambodia, Annam, and TONKIN were combined (1887) into the Union of Indochina (⊙ Saigon; after 1902, Hanoi), joined (1893–1904) by Laos and (1898) by the Fr.-leased territory of Kwangchowan (see CHANKIANG). Japanese intervention (1940) in Indochina became a major issue (1941) bet. Japan and U.S. and precipitated the diplomatic exchanges cut short by Jap. attack on Pearl Harbor. Fr. plans (during Second World War) for a federation of Indochina within the French Union, although accepted by Cambodia and Laos, failed as a result of Annamese nationalist revolt leading to the formation of Vietnam. Amid French-Vietminh warfare (after 1946), protracted negotiations regarding the juridical status of Indochina resulted in agreements finally ratified in early 1950. According to these, the 3 constituent Indochinese states of Vietnam, Laos, and Cambodia, although provided with certain common Fr. advisory services, are individually associated with France within the French Union and recognized by the U.S.

Indonesia (ĭndōnē′zhŭ), republic (less Western New Guinea: □ 575,893; 1930 pop. c.60,250,000; 1950 pop. estimate 80,000,000), Malay Archipelago, SE Asia; ⊙ JAKARTA. Consists of large isl. group of volcanic origin, extending c.3,000 mi. E–W in Indian and Pacific oceans bet. W coast of Malay Peninsula and Australasia, crossed by the Equator. Comprises the Sunda Isls. (JAVA, SUMATRA, BORNEO, and CELEBES), the LESSER SUNDA ISLANDS (including BALI, FLORES, and part of TIMOR), the MOLUCCAS (including AMBOINA, CERAM, and HALMAHERA), RIOUW ARCHIPELAGO, and a vast number of small isls. The most important, in terms of density of population and cultural development, are Java, Bali, and Sumatra. Among and around the isls. are the Java, Flores, Timor, Arafura, Banda, Ceram, Molucca, and Celebes seas, and Macassar and Malacca straits. All larger isls. are crossed by central volcanic mtn. ranges; highest peaks are Mt. Kinabalu (13,455 ft.), North Borneo; Mt. Kerinchi (12,487 ft.), Sumatra; Mt. Mahameru (12,060 ft.), Java; and Mt. Rantemario (11,286 ft.), Celebes. Small KRAKATOA ISLAND, in Sunda Strait bet. Java and Sumatra, is noted for its still-active volcano. Mtn. slopes of all isls. are heavily wooded; where cleared, they support extensive plantations of tobacco, rubber, tea, coffee, sugar (cultivated largely on Java), cinchona. Rice and tapioca, grown in fertile coastal plains, are principal food crops. Other products are black and white pepper, nutmeg, mace, rattan, kapok, damar, palm oil, palm kernels, copra. The forests also produce teak, ebony, sandalwood, camphor, and other fine woods. Fishing is major occupation in the smaller isls. Indonesia has vast mineral wealth; important quantities of tin are mined on isls. of BANGKA and BILLITON. There are major oil fields in Sumatra, especially in PALEMBANG region; also in Java (Surabaya region), and in Celebes (Tarakan, Balikpapan, and Banjermasin are centers). There are major coal mines in the Ombilin region (W Sumatra) and in E Borneo. Manganese, nickel, silver, gold, platinum, phosphate, sulphur, and diamonds are among other minerals worked. Principal industries process native raw materials; there are tin and petroleum refineries, oil presses, rubber, sugar, rice, tapioca, and lumber mills; tea- and tobacco-curing works, and plants mfg. etheric oils and forest extracts. Other industries include cotton milling and printing (especially batik), shoe mfg., metal- and woodworking. Larger rivers are harnessed for irrigation and power purposes. Large fleet of steamers and schooners serves interisland transportation. Java is traversed by 2 E–W railroads, connected by ferry with SE Sumatra, where a rail line leads to Palembang. Another railroad system exists in NW Sumatra. Air transportation is rapidly developing, and Jakarta is a stop on all Europe-Australia airlines. Principal cities of Indonesia are Jakarta (formerly Batavia) and its port of Tanjungpriok, Surabaya, Semarang, Bandung, Solo (Surakarta), Jogjakarta, Bogor, and Cheribon on Java; Palembang, Medan, and Padang on Sumatra; Macassar, Banjermasin, and Manado on Celebes; Pontianak, Balikpapan, and Tarakan on Borneo; and Denpasar and Singaraja on Bali. In E Indonesia Amboina and Ternate are important towns. Climate is tropical and humid, but becomes more temperate in hill and mtn. regions. Indonesian animal life roughly forms connecting link bet. fauna of Asia and that of Australia; great variety of large mammals and reptiles inhabit interior of larger isls., and richly colored birds abound. Ethnologically Indonesia is divided bet. Malayan and Papuan groups, with many inhabitants of central Indonesia representing a transition bet. these types. Each group has numerous subdivisions; Malayans range from highly cultured and civilized Javanese and Balinese to such primitive, seminomadic groups as the Dyaks of the interior of Borneo. Several great migrations many centuries ago from Asia and the Pacific have created a very complex ethnic structure. Moslems form great majority of pop., followed by Animists; Hindus and Christians form relatively small groups. Chinese are most numerous of the nonindigenous pop.; the so-called Coast Malays, who live in coastal regions of larger isls., are of mixed stock, Chinese, Malayan, Indian, and Arab. Indonesian language is a variant of Malay. Early in Christian era, Indonesia came under influence of Indian civilization through gradual influx of Indian traders and Buddhist and Hindu monks; great native empires that began to emerge were closely bound up with Hinduism and Buddhism. By 7th cent., Sumatra had become 1st important political center of the archipelago; in 14th cent. it was succeeded by Java which for 2 centuries was nucleus of a vast empire dominating almost all Indonesia. In early 13th cent. infiltration of Islam had begun with arrival of Arab traders, and by end of 16th cent. it had replaced Buddhism and Hinduism as dominant religion. Under Islamic control, Indonesia soon degenerated into many small and weak states, which fell easy prey to European imperialism. In 1511 the Portuguese captured strategic commercial center of Malacca on Malay Peninsula, and from there established trading posts in Indonesia. Dutch followed in 1596, and the English in 1600. In early 17th cent. rivalry became intense with appearance on the scene of the Dutch East India Company and the English East India Company. Dutch soon ousted Portuguese, who only retained E part of Timor, but only after a series of Anglo-Dutch conflicts (1610–23) did the Dutch emerge as dominant power in Indonesia. Dutch East India Company expanded its control over entire region in 17th and 18th cent.; taken over (1798) by Dutch govt., its holdings became known as Netherlands East Indies or Dutch East Indies. Dutch rule was briefly broken (1811–15) during Napoleonic Wars when isls. were occupied by British under Sir Thomas Raffles. Dutch exploited riches of archipelago and built up the colony during 19th and early 20th cent. Indonesian movement for independence began at outset of 20th cent., but remained weak and ineffective until outbreak of Second World War; it was active, especially in Java and parts of Sumatra, during the occupation (beginning in early 1942) of the region by the Japanese. At the close of the Second World War, Indonesian nationalists proclaimed (Aug., 1945) the independent "Republic of Indonesia" (⊙ Jogjakarta), claiming jurisdiction over Java, Madura, and Sumatra. Thus began a 5-year period of political adjustment, sometimes accompanied by violence, before a united country of Indonesia emerged in the fall of 1950. As a countermove to the 1945 establishment of an Indonesia republic, the Dutch sponsored a number of rival autonomous states among the other parts of the archipelago. After a period of hostilities and negotiations, the Dutch and Indonesians signed (March, 1947) the Cheribon (or Linggajati) Agreement. This agreement recognized the *de facto* authority of the Republic over Java, Madura, and Sumatra. However, there were differences over the interpretation of the agreement and in July, 1947, hostilities were resumed, briefly interrupted (Jan., 1948) by the Renville truce. A new Dutch attack (Dec., 1948) led to the occupation of Jogjakarta and most of the territory of the Republic, which could engage, now, only in guerrilla warfare. Through U.N. intervention, negotiations were resumed at a conference (late 1949) at the Hague, and on Dec. 28th Indonesia became a sovereign country, the "United States of Indonesia"; this was a confederation consisting of what remained of the "Republic of Indonesia" and 15 Dutch-supported states which had been established in the rest of the archipelago. The status of Netherlands (or Western) New Guinea remained undecided. The federation as such was short-lived, however, and by Aug., 1950, all components of it became part of a unified country called, finally, the Republic of Indonesia; it was admitted in Sept., 1950, to the United Nations. The country was administratively divided into 10 new provs.: North Sumatra, Central Sumatra, South Sumatra; West Java, Central Java, East Java; Borneo; Celebes; the Lesser Sundas; and the Moluccas. The Republic remained linked to the Netherlands only through a loose union under the Dutch crown. The question of Netherlands New Guinea continued to be a source of dispute bet. the Netherlands and Indonesia in 1951. The Javanese name Nusantara is sometimes applied to the archipelago.

Indonesian Borneo: see BORNEO.

Indor, Israel: see EN-DOR.

Indore (ĭndôr′), former princely state (□ 9,934; pop. 1,513,966) of Central India agency; ⊙ was Indore. Consisted of several detached areas, mainly on Malwa plateau and in Narbada R. valley. Founded by Mahratta leader, Malhar Rao Holkar, in early-18th cent.; greatly expanded by Jaswant Rao Holkar, until checked by British in early-19th cent. In 1948, merged with Madhya Bharat.

Indore, city (pop. 203,695), summer ⊙ Madhya Bharat (winter ⊙ at Lashkar) and ⊙ Indore dist., India, 420 mi. SSW of New Delhi, on S Malwa plateau; 22°43′N 75°52′E. Road junction, airport; major cotton-milling center; trades in grain (wheat, millet), cotton, textiles, oilseeds, opium; cotton ginning, flour and oilseed milling, mfg. of hosiery, blankets, chemicals, tents, furniture, sports goods, bobbins, brushes; engineering and metalworks, dairy farms. Has cols., medical col., Inst. of Plant Industry, and several fine palaces. Cenotaphs of Holkar family in W outskirts. Founded early-18th cent.; became ⊙ princely state of Indore in 1818. Was hq. of former Central India agency.

Indragiri River (ĭndrŭgĭ′rē), **Kuantan River,** or **Koeantan River** (both: kwäntän′), central Sumatra, Indonesia, rises in Padang Highlands near Bukittinggi, flows generally E past Rengat, thence through marshy area to Berhala Strait 45 mi. ENE of Rengat; 250 mi. long. Also spelled Inderagiri.

Indramayu, Indramaju, or **Indramajoe** (all: ĭndrŭmī′-ōō), town (pop. 21,190), W Java, Indonesia, near the N coast, 30 mi. NW of Cheribon, near Indramayu Point; rice-production center. Formerly an important trade center, then called Dermayo.

Indramayu Point, promontory on Java Sea, NW Java, Indonesia, near town of Indramayu; 6°15′S 108°19′E.

Indraprastha, India: see DELHI, state.

Indrapura or **Indrapoera** (both: ĭndrŭpōō′rŭ). **1** Village (dist. pop. 21,582), NE Sumatra, Indonesia, 50 mi. ESE of Medan, in area producing rubber and palm oil. Airfield. **2** Village (dist. pop. 16,385), central Sumatra, Indonesia, near Indian Ocean, 90 mi. SSE of Padang; 2°4′S 100°55′E; tea, pepper. The Dutch gained foothold here in 1668; area was under Br. rule (1685–93). Formerly ⊙ sultanate of Indrapura (abolished 1792).

Indrapura Peak, Indonesia: see KERINCHI, MOUNT.

Indravati River (ĭndrä′vŭtē), SW Orissa and SE Madhya Pradesh, India, rises in Eastern Ghats c.25 mi. SSW of Bhawanipatna (Orissa), flows 315 mi. SSW, W, and SSW, past Jagdalpur, to Godavari R. at Hyderabad border.

Indre (ĕ′drü), department (□ 2,666; pop. 252,075), central France, formed by parts of Berry, Orléanais, Marche, and Touraine provinces; ⊙ Châteauroux. Gently sloping region at S margin of Paris Basin. Drained by Indre and Creuse rivers, which flank the marshy Brenne dist. (W). Dept. produces wheat, oats, vegetables (mainly artichokes and beans), and some wine; cattle and sheep raising. Although chiefly agr., it has textile, iron, leather, and parchment manufactures and handicraft industries. Chief towns: Châteauroux, Issoudun, Argenton, Le Blanc.

Indre, W suburban commune (pop. 4,477) of Nantes, Loire-Inférieure dept., W France. It includes La Basse-Indre (blast furnaces, forges, tinplate works) on right bank of Loire R. and 6 mi. W of Nantes, and Indret isl. (in Loire R. opposite La Basse-Indre), with important naval machine shops and arsenal.

Indre Arna (ĭn′rŭ är′nä), village in Haus canton, Hordaland co., SW Norway, on an inlet of Sor Fjord, on railroad and 5 mi. E of Bergen; furniture.

Indre-et-Loire (ĕ′drü-ā-lwär′), department (□2,378; pop. 349,685), in Touraine, W central France; ⊙ Tours. Traversed by the flood plain of the Loire and drained by its large tributaries, the Cher, Indre, and Vienne; a region of fertile valleys and poor interfluvial uplands; produces wine, vegetables, small grains, and flowers; center of tanning industry. Chief towns: Tours, a railroad hub and regional commercial center; and Chinon, known for its wines. The dept. contains several of the famous Loire valley châteaux (Chinon, Chenonceaux, Amboise, Azay-le-Rideau).

Indre River, Indre and Indre-et-Loire depts., central France, rises in foothills of Massif Central 5 mi. NW of Boussac, flows 165 mi. NW, past La Châtre, Châteauroux, Châtillon-sur-Indre, Loches, and Azay-le-Rideau, to the Loire 25 mi. below Tours.

Indret, France: see INDRE.

Indur, Israel: see EN-DOR.

Indura (ĕndōō′rŭ), town (1931 pop. 2,650), W Grodno oblast, Belorussian SSR, 15 mi. S of Grodno, near Pol. border; distilling, brewing.

Indus River (ĭn′dŭs), Sanskrit *Sindhu,* longest (c.1,900 mi.) of Himalayan rivers, running NW, through W Tibet and central Kashmir, and generally SSW through W Pakistan into Arabian Sea SE of Karachi. Rises in Kailas Range (at alt. c.17,000 ft.) near Senge (or Senge Khambab) village in SW Tibet, c.50 mi. NNE of Manasarowar L.; flows N and W for 195 mi. as the Senge Khambab, then NW, into Kashmir, cutting through Ladakh Range, past Leh and Skardu (alt. 8,900 ft.), twisting through deep gorges and picturesque valleys; SE of Gilgit it bends sharply S, skirting NW end of Punjab Himalayas, into North-West Frontier Prov. (W Pakistan). At Attock (alt. 1,100 ft.) it passes through narrow gorge; lower down, at Kalabagh, it debouches onto Punjab plains, continuing S in a broad, braided channel (¼–2 mi. wide), through Pakistan Punjab and Sind, past Sukkur and Hyderabad, emptying into Arabian Sea SE of Karachi by many mouths; its delta (□ 3,000) is a level, muddy area with little cultivation. The Indus is fed by great glaciers of Karakoram and Hindu Kush mtn. ranges and receives drainage of such noted peaks as K², Nanga Parbat, Tirich Mir, Sikaram, and Takht-i-Sulaiman. Receives Shyok R. near Skardu, Kabul R. at Attock, Kurram R. W of Mianwali, and, ESE of Rajanpur, the Panjnad, which brings to it the combined waters of the 5 rivers of the Punjab (Sutlej, Beas, Ravi, Chenab, and Jhelum). Total catchment basin, □ 380,000. Volume of water is extremely variable and serious floods have occurred, chiefly in Pakistan Punjab, where the river has been known to extend 10–25 mi. in width. The Indus is navigable only for small river craft, and is little used for transportation. In N Sind is 1-mi.-long SUKKUR BARRAGE, headworks of one of largest canal-irrigation systems in the world; farther upstream, in Mianwali dist. (Pakistan Punjab), an irrigation and hydroelectric project is under construction with headworks just below Kalabagh. Agr. is chief activity throughout the valley; wheat, corn, rice, millet are general crops, while in lower course dates, mangoes, and other fruit are also grown; camels, sheep, cattle raised in Sind and Punjab; mahseer (N) and Indian shad (S) abound in the river. Situated bet. mts. of NW frontier and arid plains on E, the Indus has been a significant landmark in Indian history. Along its banks flourished the highly-developed Indus Valley Civilization (bet. 4,000–2,000 B.C.), relics of which have been excavated at MOHENJO-DARO in Sind. It was crossed (325 B.C.) by Alexander the Great, and later by many other invaders of N India. Until British inc. Baluchistan and North-West Frontier Prov. into the Indian Empire in latter half of 19th cent., the Indus was often considered the frontier of NW India.

Industrial City Gardens, town (1940 pop. 734), Chatham co., E Ga., 5 mi. NW of Savannah.

Industrialny or **Industrial′nyy** (ĕndōōstrēăl′nē), shipbuilding suburb (1940 pop. over 500) of Petropavlovsk, Kamchatka oblast, Khabarovsk Territory, Russian SFSR.

Industriya, Russian SFSR: see APATITY.

Industry. 1 Village (pop. 496), McDonough co., W Ill., 9 mi. SSE of Macomb; agr. (grain, livestock); bituminous-coal mines. **2** Town (pop. 315), Franklin co., W central Maine, 7 mi. NE of Farmington.

Indwe (ĭnd′wē), town (pop. 2,366), E Cape Prov., U. of So. Afr., in Stormberg range, 40 mi. NE of Queenstown; agr. center (dairying, grain). Former coal-mining center; mines were opened 1859, closed down 1918, except for shafts now worked to cover local needs.

Indyiya, Yugoslavia: see INDJIJA.

Inebolu (ĭnĕ′bôlōō), Turkish *İnebolu,* village (pop. 4,302), Kastamonu prov., N Turkey, port on Black Sea, 40 mi. N of Kastamonu; shipbuilding, mercury reserve; hemp, wheat, corn. Sometimes spelled Ineboli.

Inegol (ĭnĕgûl′), Turkish *İnegöl,* town (pop. 15,165), Bursa prov., NW Turkey, 25 mi. ESE of Bursa; wheat, barley, corn; copper near by.

'Ineiba or **'Inaybah** (both: ĭnā′bŭ), village (pop. 2,014), Aswan prov., S Egypt, on W bank of Nile R. and 60 mi. NE of Wadi Halfa; cereals, dates. Also spelled Eneiba.

Ineli, Greece: see PALEOMYLOS.

Ineu (ĕnā′ōō), Hung. *Borosjenő* (bô′rôsh-yĕnû), (pop. 7,043), Arad prov., W Rumania, on White Körös R. and 30 mi. NE of Arad; rail junction; mfg. of furniture; wine production.

Inevi, Turkey: see CIHANBEYLI.

Inez (ī′nĕz), town (pop. 622), ⊙ Martin co., E Ky., in Cumberland foothills, 28 mi. N of Pikeville, in coal, oil, and agr. area.

Inezgane (ēnĕzgän′), town (pop. 4,674), Agadir frontier region, SW Fr. Morocco, on right bank of the Oued Sous, 7 mi. SE of Agadir; trade center (olives, almonds, truck). Airfield 3 mi. NW.

Infanta (ĭnfăn′tŭ, Sp. ēnfän′tä), town (1939 pop. 2,103; 1948 municipality pop. 19,006), Quezon prov., central Luzon, Philippines, near Polillo Strait, 45 mi. ENE of Manila; fishing and agr. center (coconuts, rice).

Infantas, Colombia: see BARRANCABERMEJA.

Infantes or **Villanueva de Infantes** (vēlyänwā′vä dhä ēnfän′tĕs), city (pop. 9,859), Ciudad Real prov., S central Spain, in New Castile, 50 mi. ESE of Ciudad Real; agr. center (olives, cereals, grapes, livestock); olive-oil pressing, flour milling, cheese processing; mfg. of woolen goods, firearms, plaster. Had greater importance as center of anc. Campo de Montiel. The writer Francisco de Quevedo is buried here.

Inferior, Laguna (lägōō′nä ēnfĕryōr′), lagoon in Oaxaca, S Mexico, on Isthmus of Tehuantepec, 18 mi. SE of Juchitán; connected through narrow channels with Laguna Superior and Gulf of Tehuantepec.

Infesta, Portugal: see SÃO MAMEDE DE INFESTA.

Infiesto (ēmfyĕ′stō), town (pop. 1,774), Oviedo prov., NW Spain, 24 mi. E of Oviedo; agr. center shipping almonds, nuts, apples. Vegetable canning, cider distilling; stock raising. Has fish hatchery. Mineral springs near by.

Infreschi, Punta degli (pōōn′tä dĕlyēnfrā′skē), promontory, S Italy, 4 mi. SE of Camerota, at NW end of Gulf of Policastro; 40°N 15°25′E.

Ingá (ēng-gä′). **1** City (pop. 3,218), E Paraíba, NE Brazil, on railroad and 18 mi. E of Campina Grande; cotton, sugar, coffee, tobacco, wool. **2** City, Paraná, Brazil: see ANDIRÁ.

Ingabu (ĭn′gŭbōō), village, Henzada dist., Lower Burma, on railroad and 16 mi. NW of Henzada.

Ingalls (ĭng′gŭlz). **1** Town (pop. 666), Madison co., E central Ind., on small Lick Creek and 24 mi. NE of Indianapolis, in agr. area. **2** City (pop. 173), Gray co., SW Kansas, on Arkansas R. and 6 mi. WNW of Cimarron; grain, cattle.

Ingalls, Mount (ĭng′gŭlz, –gôlz″) (8,377 ft.), Plumas co., NE Calif., in the Sierra Nevada, 17 mi. E of Quincy; copper mine on its slopes.

Ingalls Park (ĭng′gŭlz), village (pop. 6,840), Will co., NE Ill.

Inganda, Belgian Congo: see BOENDE.

Ingatestone and Fryerning, agr. parish (pop. 2,352), S central Essex, England. Includes market town of Ingatestone, 6 mi. SW of Chelmsford, with church dating from c.1000 and 16th-cent. Ingatestone Hall; and, just W, agr. village of Fryerning.

Ingavi, province, Bolivia: see VIACHA.

Ingavi (ēng-gä′vē), village, Pando dept., N Bolivia, on Orton R. and 50 mi. W of Riberalta; rubber.

Ingavi, military post (Fortín Ingavi), Boquerón dept., N Paraguay, in the Chaco, on road from Ravelo (Bolivia), and 145 mi. N of Mariscal Estigarribia. Area was awarded to Paraguay by the Chaco Peace Conference (signed 1938).

Ingelfingen (ĭng′ŭlfĭng″ŭn), town (pop. 1,812), N Württemberg, Germany, after 1945 in Württemberg-Baden, on the Kocher and 14 mi. SSW of Mergentheim; wine.

Ingelheim or **Ingelheim am Rhein** (ĭng′ŭlhīm äm rīn′), town (pop. 11,899), Rhenish Hesse, W Germany, on left bank of the Rhine and 10 mi. W of Mainz; mfg. (agr. machinery, chemicals); noted red wine. Market center for wine, fruit, and vegetable region. Has 13th-cent. church. Formed 1939 through unification of Nieder-Ingelheim, Ober-Ingelheim, and Frei-Weinheim.

Ingelmunster (ĭng′ŭlmŭnstŭr), town (pop. 9,107), West Flanders prov., W Belgium, 7 mi. N of Courtrai; textiles, carpets.

Ingenbohl (ĭng′ŭnbōl″), town (pop. 3,958), Schwyz canton, central Switzerland, near L. of Lucerne, 2 mi. SW of Schwyz; cementworks. Its resort of BRUNNEN is on lake.

Ingende (ĭng-gĕn′dā), village, Equator Prov., W Belgian Congo, on Ruki R. at confluence of Momboyo and Busira rivers, and 40 mi. ESE of Coquilhatville; trading and agr. center (palm products, bananas, manioc), steamboat landing.

Ingeniero Balloffet (ēnhĕnyā′rō bälōfā′), town (pop. estimate 500), SE central Mendoza prov., Argentina, near Atuel R. (irrigation), on railroad and 36 mi. SE of San Rafael; agr. center (wine, fruit, potatoes); wine making, dried-fruit processing, alcohol distilling, sawmilling.

Ingeniero Boasi, Argentina: see SARMIENTO, Santa Fe prov.

Ingeniero Giagnoni (hēänyō′nē), town (pop. estimate 700), N Mendoza prov., Argentina, on railroad and 30 mi. SE of Mendoza; agr. center; wine making, dried-fruit processing.

Ingeniero Huergo or **Ingeniero Luis A. Huergo** (lwēs′ ä′ wĕr′gō), village (pop. estimate 1,500), N Río Negro natl. territory, Argentina, in Río Negro valley (irrigation area), on railroad and 17 mi. E of Fuerte General Roca; agr. center (alfalfa, fruit, wine, potatoes); wine making, lumbering.

Ingeniero Jacobacci (häkōbä′chē), town (1947 pop. 2,311), S Río Negro natl. territory, Argentina, on railroad and 45 mi. W of Maquinchao; stock raising (cattle, goats). Diatomite deposits.

Ingeniero Luiggi (lōōē′zhē), town (pop. estimate 2,500), NE La Pampa natl. territory, Argentina, 45 mi. WNW of General Pico; rail terminus; grain and livestock center; flour milling, dairying.

Ingeniero Luis A. Huergo, Argentina: see INGENIERO HUERGO.

Ingeniero Montero Hoyos (mōntā′rō oi′ōs) or **Puerto Pailas** (pwĕr′tō pī′läs), village (pop. c.1,300), Santa Cruz dept., central Bolivia, on Río Grande and 35 mi. E of Santa Cruz; sugar cane, corn.

Ingeniero White or **Puerto Ingeniero White** (pwĕr′tō, wīt′), S suburb (pop. estimate 10,000) and main port of Bahía Blanca, SW Buenos Aires prov., Argentina, 350 mi. SW of Buenos Aires, 14 mi. inland. Modern harbor facilities (oil tanks, cranes, grain elevators); rail terminus.

Ingenio (ēnhā′nyō), village (pop. 4,331), Grand Canary, Canary Isls., 13 mi. S of Las Palmas; grain-growing and flour-milling center.

Ingenio San Antonio, Nicaragua: see SAN ANTONIO.

Ingermanland (ĭng′gŭrmŭnlănd) or **Ingria** (ĭng′grēŭ), Rus. *Ingriya,* ancient district of Russia, bet. lakes Peipus and Ladoga; now in Leningrad oblast, Russian SFSR. Originally under Novgorod, dist. was long disputed by Swedes and Russians; finally annexed to Russia under Peter the Great by Treaty of Nystad (1721).

Ingerois, Finland: see INKEROINEN.

Ingersheim (ĕzhĕrzĕm′, Ger. ĭng′ŭrs-hīm), town (pop. 2,289), Haut-Rhin dept., E France, on the Fecht and 3 mi. WNW of Colmar, in winegrowing area; hosiery and carton mfg.

Ingersoll, town (pop. 5,782), S Ont., on Thames R. and 18 mi. ENE of London; mfg. of furniture, hardware, tools; flour and lumber milling, dairying, milk canning.

Ingersoll (ĭng′gŭrsôl), town (pop. 78), Alfalfa co., N Okla., 3 mi. NW of Cherokee, in grain-growing area.

Ingham (ĭng′ŭm), town (pop. 3,036), E Queensland, Australia, 55 mi. NW of Townsville; sugar-producing center; connected with Lucinda Point (its port) by electric railroad.

Ingham, county (□ 559; pop. 172,941), S central Mich.; ⊙ Mason. LANSING (⊙ Mich.) is in co. Drained by Grand and Red Cedar rivers, and small Sycamore Creek. Agr. (livestock, poultry, fruit, grain, sugar beets, corn, hay, beans, truck, dairy products). Mfg. at LANSING. Clay, coal deposits. Formed 1838.

Inghok, China: see YUNGTAI.

Ingichka (ēn-gēch′kŭ), town (1945 pop. over 500), W Samarkand oblast, Uzbek SSR, c.15 mi. S of Aktash; mining.

Ingierstrand Bad (ĭng′ērsträn bäd′), village in Oppegard canton, Akershus co., SE Norway, on E shore of Bunde Fjord (SE arm of Oslo Fjord), 7 mi. S of Oslo; seaside resort. Amundsen's residence is now mus.

Inginiyagala (ĭng″gĭnĭyŭgä′lŭ), village, Uva Prov., E Ceylon, on the Gal Oya and 37 mi. ENE of Badulla. Projected dam (3,600 ft. long, 122 ft. high) will form lake (□ 30); irrigation project (□ 188) to be largely under sugar cane.

Ingleburn (ĭng′gŭlbŭrn), municipality (pop. 3,270), E New South Wales, Australia, 18 mi. SW of Sydney, in metropolitan area; coal-mining center.

Inglefield Gulf, inlet (60 mi. long, 10–20 mi. wide), of N Baffin Bay, NW Greenland; 77°27′N 68°W. Extends to edge of inland icecap; receives several glaciers. At mouth Northumberland Isl. (20 mi. long, 7 mi. wide), Herbert Isl. (19 mi. long, 2–6 mi. wide), and HAKLUYT ISLAND divide approaches to gulf into Murchison (N) and Whale (S) sounds.

Inglefield Land, ice-free region, NW Greenland, on Smith Sound and Kane Basin, bet. Humboldt Glacier (N) and Prudhoe Land (S), in N part of Hayes Peninsula; 78°45′N 69°W.

Ingleside, village (pop. 1,424), San Patricio co., S Texas, 12 mi. ENE of Corpus Christi, across Corpus Christi Bay; oil refining.

Inglestat, Alaska: see KOYUK.

Ingleton (ĭng′gŭl–), village and parish (pop. 2,227), West Riding, W Yorkshire, England, 15 mi. ENE of Lancaster; granite quarries.

Inglewood. 1 Village (pop. 800), SE Queensland, Australia, 135 mi. WSW of Brisbane; rail junction in wheat-raising area; cyanide works. **2** Municipality (pop. 925), N central Victoria, Australia, 105 mi. NW of Melbourne, near Loddon R.; rail junction in gold-mining area; eucalyptus oil.

Inglewood, borough (pop. 1,295), ⊙ Inglewood co. (□ 187; pop. 3,053), W N.Isl., New Zealand, at base of Mt. Egmont, 11 mi. SE of New Plymouth; dairy plants.

Inglewood, residential and industrial city (pop. 46,185), Los Angeles co., S Calif., suburb c.10 mi. SW of downtown Los Angeles; mfg. of aircraft, machinery, metal products, pottery; oil refining. Has Hollywood Park race track. Los Angeles International Airport near by. Laid out 1887, inc. 1908.

Inglis Island, Australia: see ENGLISH COMPANY'S ISLANDS.

Ingoda River (ēn-gŭdä′), S central Chita oblast, Russian SFSR, rises near Sokhondo peak in Borshchovochny Range, flows 500 mi. generally NE, past Ulety, Chita, and Karymskoye, joining Onon R. t[o] form Shilka R. 15 mi. above Shilka. Navigable below Chita. Trans-Siberian RR runs along its lower course.

Ingolstadt (ĭng'gôl-shtät), city (1950 pop. 40,270), Upper Bavaria, Germany, on the Danube and 43 mi. N of Munich; 48°46'N 11°25'E. Road and trade center; mfg. of textile machinery; textile (cotton, wool, silk) and fur industries; woodworking, brewing. Has remains of 14th-cent. fortifications; also Church of Our Blessed Lady (1425–1500), and baroque church. First mentioned 725, Ingolstadt was chartered 1250. Ducal residence from 13th to 15th cent. Site of Bavarian univ. (founded 1472; transferred to LANDSHUT in 1800), where Petrus Apianus and Johann Eck taught. City was captured by U.S. troops in spring, 1945. Second World War destruction (30%) included baroque Augustinian church; Gothic New Castle was damaged. Eck buried here.

Ingomar (ĭng'gŭmär). **1** Village (1940 pop. 262), Union co., N Miss., 6 mi. SSW of New Albany, in agr. and dairying area. **2** Village (pop. c.300), Rosebud co., SE central Mont., 40 mi. NW of Forsyth, in sheep region; wool.

Ingonish (ĭng-gŭnĭsh'), village (pop. estimate 400), NE N.S., on NE coast of Cape Breton Isl., 40 mi. NNW of Sydney; fishing port, tourist resort. Extending W is Cape Breton Highland Natl. Park.

Ingram (ĭng'grŭm). **1** Borough (pop. 4,236), Allegheny co., SW Pa., W suburb of Pittsburgh. Inc. 1902. **2** Village (pop. c.450), Kerr co., SW Texas, on Guadalupe R. and c.60 mi. NW of San Antonio; trading point in ranching area(sheep, goats). State fish hatchery. **3** Village (pop. 146), Rusk co., N Wis., 14 mi. ENE of Ladysmith, in dairying and stock-raising area.

Ingrandes (ēgrãd'), village (pop. 809), Maine-et-Loire dept., W France, on the Loire and 19 mi. WSW of Angers; winegrowing, dairying; coal deposits near by. Damaged in Second World War.

Ingria, Russia: see INGERMANLAND.

Ingrid Christensen Coast (ĭng'grĭd krĭ'stĭnsĭn), Antarctica, on Indian Ocean, extends from Mt. Caroline Mikkelsen at head of Sandefjord Bay (74°E) to 81°E. Discovered 1935 by Klarius Mikkelsen, Norwegian explorer.

Ingrow, England: see KEIGHLEY.

Ingulets (ēn-gōōlyĕts'), town (1939 pop. over 500), SW Dnepropetrovsk oblast, Ukrainian SSR, on right bank of Ingulets R. and 14 mi. SSW of Krivoi Rog; iron mining. Village of Ingulets (1926 pop. 2,230) is across Ingulets R., 2 mi. NE.

Ingulets River, S Ukrainian SSR, rises N of Kirovograd in Volyn-Podolian Upland, flows 335 mi. generally S, past Aleksandriya (Kirovograd oblast), through Krivoi Rog iron region, past Kalininskoye (head of navigation) to Dnieper R. above Kherson; steep banks in middle course. Navigable for 68 mi. above mouth.

Ingul River (ēn-gōōl'), S Ukrainian SSR, rises NW of Kirovograd in Volyn-Podolian Upland, flows 215 mi. S, past Kirovograd, to Southern Bug R. at Nikolayev; granite and limestone formations along course. Navigable for 20 mi. above mouth.

Ingur River (ēn-gōōr'), NW Georgian SSR, rises in the Greater Caucasus, at S foot of peak Dykh-Tau; flows 125 mi. W and SW, through Svanetia, to Black Sea at Anaklia. Forms border of Abkhaz Autonomous SSR in lower course. Powers Zugdidi paper mill.

Ingurtosu (ēng-gōōrtô'sōō), village (pop. 373), Cagliari prov., SW Sardinia, 14 mi. N of Iglesias; lead-zinc-silver mine.

Ingush, in Rus. names: see CHECHEN-INGUSH.

Ingwavuma (ĭng"wŭvōō'mŭ), town (pop. 139), NE Natal, U. of So. Afr., in Zululand, on Swaziland border, 75 mi. E of Piet Retief.

Ingwiller (ēgvēlâr'), Ger. *Ingweiler* (ĭng'vīlŭr), town (pop. 2,432), Bas-Rhin dept., E France, on the Moder and 11 mi. NNE of Saverne; brewing, mfg. (kitchen ranges, stoves, furniture, thermometers). Castle of Lichtenberg is 4 mi. N on a height of the Vosges.

Inha (ĭn'hä), village in Ähtäri commune (pop. 8,392), Vaasa co., W Finland, in lake region, 55 mi. WNW of Jyväskylä; steel and lumber mills.

Inhaca Island (ēnyä'kä), off S coast of Mozambique, guarding entrance to Delagoa Bay, 20 mi. E of Lourenço Marques; c.5 mi. long.

Inhambane (ēnyămbä'nă), town (pop. 5,134), ⊙ Sul do Save prov., SE Mozambique, port on Mozambique Channel of Indian Ocean, 230 mi. NE of Lourenço Marques; 23°51'S 35°24'E. Exports sugar, cotton, timber, peanuts, rubber, mafura, corn, copra, cashew nuts. Mfg. (soap, brick, pottery). Sugar mills at near-by Mutamba and Maxixe. Linked by rail with Inharrime (50 mi. SSW). Airport. Harbor is on deep, sheltered bay. An old Arab settlement, it was visited 1498 by Vasco da Gama. Also ⊙ Inhambane dist. (□ 25,579; 1950 pop. 570,044).

Inhambupe (ēnyămbōō'pĭ), city (pop. 2,585), NE Bahia, Brazil, 25 mi. N of Alagoinhas; tobacco, coffee, oranges.

Inhaminga (ēnyämĭng'gŭ), village, Manica and Sofala prov., central Mozambique, on railroad and 100 mi. N of Beira; hardwood lumbering, pottery mfg.; cotton.

Inhandava (ēnyăndä'vŭ), town (pop. 1,677), E central Rio Grande do Sul, Brazil, on Taquari R. and 4 mi. SSE of Estrêla; rye, oats, manioc. Until 1944, called Bom Retiro.

Inhangapi (ēnyăng-gŭpē'), city (pop. 98), E Pará, Brazil, 40 mi. E of Belém.

Inharrime (ēnyärē'mă), village, Sul do Save prov., SE Mozambique, 50 mi. SSW of Inhambane (linked by rail); cotton, coffee, manioc, mafura. R.C. mission here.

Inhomirim (ē"nyōōmērēn'), town (pop. 3,441), central Rio de Janeiro state, Brazil, 19 mi. N of Rio; rail junction; oranges.

Inhuçu or **Inhussu** (ēnyōōsōō'), city (pop. 1,247), NW Ceará, Brazil, in the Serra Grande, near Camocim-Crateús RR, 40 mi. SSW of Sobral; cattle, coffee, cotton. Founded in 18th cent. Until 1944, called Campo Grande.

Inhumas (ēnyōō'mŭs), city (pop. 2,004), S central Goiás, central Brazil, 20 mi. NW of Goiânia.

Inhussu, Brazil: see INHUÇU.

Iniada, Cape, Turkey: see IGNEDA.

Iniesta (ēnyĕ'stä), town (pop. 4,008), Cuenca prov., E central Spain, 32 mi. N of Albacete; agr. center (saffron, cereals, grapes, sheep); lumbering; liquor distilling.

Ining (yē'nĭng'). **1** Town, Kiangsi prov., China: see SIUSHUI. **2** Town, ⊙ Ining co. (pop. 47,132), NE Kwangsi prov., China, 12 mi. WNW of Kweilin; rice, wheat, beans, sugar cane, cotton, ramie. **3** Town, Sinkiang prov., China: see KULDJA.

Inini (ēnēnē'), territory (□ c.30,300; pop. 5,024), S Fr. Guiana, bordering S on Brazil (Tumuc-Humac Mts.). Vast, densely forested hinterland, separated from the Atlantic by narrow coastal strip, Fr. Guiana proper. Includes low outliers of the Guiana Highlands and is intersected by many streams which, in spite of their rapids, are navigable for small craft. Little exploited and unexplored, the region yields some rosewood, fine cabinet wood, balata, and alluvial gold (Saint-Élie). The chief outposts are Grand-Pont, Maripa, Maripasoula, and P.I. Set up 1930 as a separate unit, it was reunited in 1946 as a dependency of Fr. Guiana. Largely inhabited by Indian and Negro tribes.

Inini River, S Fr. Guiana, rises at S foot of Chaîne Granitique, flows c.100 mi. W, through tropical forests, to Maroni R. at 3°40'N 54°2'W. Interrupted by rapids. Gold placers near source.

Inírida River (ēnē'rēdä), Vaupés commissary, SE Colombia, flows c.450 mi. E in meandering course, forming side channels, oxbows, and isls., through wild rain forests to Guaviare R. just before latter joins Orinoco R. Cataracts make it unnavigable.

Iniscaltra, Ireland: see HOLY ISLAND.

Inishark, Ireland: see INISHSHARK.

Inishbofin (ĭ"nĭshbŏ'fĭn). **1** Island (295 acres; 1 mi. long) off NW Co. Donegal, Ireland, 5 mi. ENE of Bloody Foreland. **2** Island (2,374 acres; 3½ mi. long, 2 mi. wide; rises to 292 ft.) in the Atlantic, 4 mi. NNW of NW coast of Co. Galway, Ireland. Surrounded by several small rocky islets, largest of which is Inishshark.

Inishcrone, Ireland: see INNISCRONE.

Inisheer or **Inishere** (both: ĭ"nĭ-shēr'), Gaelic *Inis Thiar*, rocky island (1,148 acres; 2 mi. long, 2 mi. wide; rises to 202 ft.) of the ARAN ISLANDS, in Galway Bay off SW Co. Galway, Ireland, 24 mi. SW of Galway. Has prehistoric fort, remains of church of St. Kevin, and medieval stronghold of the O'Briens. On S coast of isl. is lighthouse (53°3'N 9°31'W).

Inishglora (ĭ"nĭsh-glô'rŭ), island (60 acres; 1 mi. long) just off Mullet Peninsula, NW Co. Mayo, Ireland, 3 mi. W of Binghamstown; site of remains of church built by St. Brendan.

Inishkeen, Ireland: see INNISKEEN.

Inishmaan (ĭ"nĭshmän'), Gaelic *Inis Mheadhóin*, rocky island (2,252 acres; 3 mi. long, 2 mi. wide; rises to 275 ft.) of the ARAN ISLANDS, Ireland, in Galway Bay off SW Co. Galway, 25 mi. WSW of Galway. Has prehistoric fort (Dun Chonchobair) and remains of anc. oratory.

Inishmore (ĭ"nĭshmôr'). **1** or **Deer Island** (462 acres; 2 mi. long) in Fergus R. estuary, S Co. Clare, Ireland, 7 mi. S of Ennis. **2** also called **Aran-na-naomh** or **Aranmore** (ă"rŭnmôr'), rocky island (□ 12; 9 mi. long, 2½ mi. wide; rises to 403 ft.), largest of the ARAN ISLANDS, SW Co. Galway, Ireland, in Galway Bay, 27 mi. WSW of Galway. Towns on isl. are Kilronan, Killeany, Onagh. Fishing is carried on. There are numerous remains of 6th-cent. churches and monastic establishments, and several prehistoric forts. Arkyn Castle held out against Cromwell for a year after capture of Galway. After fall of Galway in 1691 isl. was garrisoned for several years by William III's troops.

Inishmulclohy, Ireland: see CONEY ISLAND.

Inishmurray (ĭ"nĭshmŭr'ē), island (209 acres; 1 mi. long) at entrance to Donegal Bay, N Co. Sligo, Ireland, 14 mi. NW of Sligo. Contains large number of antiquities, including pagan stone fort (converted into monastery in 6th cent. by St. Molaise) and 3 anc. oratories.

Inishowen Head (ĭ"nĭsh-ō'ĭn), promontory, NE Co. Donegal, Ireland, on W side of entrance to Lough Foyle, 6 mi. NE of Moville; lighthouse (55°13'N 6°56'W).

Inishshark or **Inishark** (both: ĭ"nĭ-shärk'), island (615 acres; 1½ mi. long) off NW Co. Galway, Ireland, just W of Inishbofin isl.

Inishturk (ĭ"nĭshtûrk'), island (136 acres; 2½ mi. long, rises to 629 ft.) off NW Co. Galway, Ireland, 15 mi. NNW of Clifden. Has remains of church built by St. Columba.

Inistioge, Gaelic *Inis Tēog*, town (pop. 292), E Co. Kilkenny, Ireland, on the Nore (bridged) and 9 mi. NW of New Ross; agr. market (cattle; barley, potatoes). Has remains of Austin priory (1210).

Initao (ēnētou'), town (1939 pop. 2,717; 1948 municipality pop. 36,534), Misamis Oriental prov., N Mindanao, Philippines, 23 mi. W of Cagayan; agr. center (corn, coconuts). Chromite deposits.

Inje, Cape, Turkey: see INCE, CAPE.

Inke (ĭng'kĕ), town (pop. 2,731), Somogy co., SW Hungary, on branch of Zala R. and 11 mi. E of Nagykanizsa.

Inkerman (ĭng'kŭrmŭn, Rus. ēn-kyĭrmän'), E suburb of Sevastopol, S Crimea, Russian SFSR, at head of Sevastopol Bay, at mouth of Chernaya R., on railroad and 3 mi. E of Sevastopol; residential area; truck produce. Limestone quarries. Cave dwellings (dating from 3d-4th cent. A.D.), cut into limestone rock, and ruins of 14th-cent. Gothic fortress near by. Site of Rus. defeat (Nov., 1854) by Franco-English forces in Crimean War.

Inkermann (ēngkĕrmän'), village (pop. 3,331), Oran dept., N Algeria, near the Chéliff, on railroad and 25 mi. NE of Relizane; trade center in irrigated valley growing cotton and citrus fruit. Grain and cattle market.

Inkeroinen (ĭng'kĕroi"nĕn), Swedish *Ingerois* (ĭng'-ŭrois), village in Anjala commune (pop. 5,004), Kymi co., SE Finland, on Kymi R. and 16 mi. N of Kotka; rail junction; lumber, pulp, and paper mills.

Inkisi (ĭngkē'sē), village, Leopoldville prov., W Belgian Congo, on Inkisi R., on railroad, and 140 mi. ENE of Boma; trading center; sugar cane, coffee, native foodstuffs.

Inkisi River, W Belgian Congo, rises in NW Angola, flows generally NNW, past Lemfu, Inkisi, and Kisantu to Congo R. 40 mi. SW of Leopoldville. Has 2 hydroelectric power stations at Sanga.

Inkom (ĭng'kŭm), town (pop. 434), Bannock co., SE Idaho, 12 mi. SE of Pocatello.

Inks Lake, Texas: see ROY INKS DAM.

Inkster. **1** Village (pop. 16,728), Wayne co., SE Mich., residential suburb 14 mi. WSW of downtown Detroit; truck and poultry farming; mfg. of flower pots. Has modern psychopathic hosp. Settled 1825, inc. 1927. **2** City (pop. 304), Grand Forks co., E N.Dak., 32 mi. NW of Grand Forks.

Inkur (ēn-kōōr'), town (1942 pop. over 500), SW Buryat-Mongol Autonomous SSR, Russian SFSR, on Dzhida R. just S of Gorodok.

Inland Empire, in NW U.S., name given to vast region of Columbia R. basin in E Wash., N Oregon E of the Cascades, and N Idaho, and sometimes including NW Mont.; Spokane (Wash.) is chief center. Dry farming (wheat) and livestock grazing have long predominated, but large-scale irrigation is contemplated through the COLUMBIA RIVER project, so as to increase the variety of the region's agr. produce. Mining and lumbering are important in Idaho and Mont. portions.

Inland Passage, B.C. and Alaska: see INSIDE PASSAGE.

Inland Sea, Jap. *Seto-naikai* (□ 3,668), arm of Philippine Sea, bet. Honshu (N) and Shikoku and Kyushu (S); connected with Philippine Sea by Hoyo Strait (W) and Kii Channel (E); c.240 mi. long, c.540 mi. wide. Sections of it are variously called SUO SEA (W), IYO SEA (SW), HIUCHI SEA (central), HARIMA SEA (E). OSAKA BAY is an E arm. Many fishing ports. AWAJI-SHIMA is largest of many isls. dotting the sea. Inland Sea Natl. Park (□ 706), established in 1934, covers area bet. Shodo-shima (E) and Tomo (W) in Hiroshima prefecture; includes pine-clad shores of Kagawa, Okayama, and Hiroshima prefectures. Sea formerly sometimes called Seto-chi-umi.

Inland Waterway, U.S.: see INTRACOASTAL WATERWAY.

Inle Lake (ĭn'lā'), in Yawnghwe state, Southern Shan State, Upper Burma, on Shan Plateau, SW of Taunggyi; 12 mi. long, 4 mi. wide; alt. c.3,000 ft. Source of Nam Pilu, it is fed by small streams N and W and is bordered by floating isls. (cultivated) of decayed vegetable matter. Fisheries; rice area.

Inlet, resort village, Hamilton co., NE central N.Y., in the Adirondacks, bet. 2 lakes of Fulton Chain of Lakes, c.50 mi. NNE of Utica.

Inman. **1** City (pop. 615), McPherson co., S central Kansas, 15 mi. NE of Hutchinson, in wheat region; flour milling. Oil wells near by. **2** Village (pop. 237), Holt co., N Nebr., 8 mi. SE of O'Neill and on Elkhorn R. **3** Town (pop. 1,514), Spartanburg co., NW S.C., 12 mi. NW of Spartanburg; mfg. (textiles, bricks, concrete blocks, beverages); ships peaches, apples, cotton. **4** Village (pop. 1,165, with near-by Linden and Laurel), Wise co., SW Va., 3 mi. N of Big Stone Gap.

Inman Mills, village (pop. 1,776), Spartanburg co., NW S.C., NW of Spartanburg and near Inman; textile mills.

Inn, river: see INN RIVER.
Innai (ĕn-nī'), town (pop. 4,883), Akita prefecture, N Honshu, Japan, 9 mi. SSW of Yuzawa; silver mining.
Innamincka (ĭ'nŭmĭng'kŭ), settlement, NE South Australia, on Barcoo R. and 390 mi. NNE of Port Pirie, near Queensland border; cattle.
Inner Hebrides, Scotland: see HEBRIDES.
Innerleithen (ĭnŭrlē'dhŭn), burgh (1931 pop. 2,359; 1951 census 2,361), E Peebles, Scotland, on the Tweed and 5 mi. ESE of Peebles; health resort, with woolen (tweed) milling and hosiery knitting. Reputed site of Scott's *St. Ronan's Well*.
Inner Mongolia, China: see MONGOLIA.
Inner Sound, strait (5–8 mi. wide) bet. mainland of W Ross and Cromarty, Scotland, and Raasay isl., linking The Minch (N) and Loch Alsh (S).
Innerste River (ĭ'nŭrstŭ), NW Germany, rises in the upper Harz near Clausthal-Zellerfeld, flows c.50 mi. N and NW, past Hildesheim, to the Leine 1 mi. NW of Sarstedt.
Innertkirchen (ĭ'nŭrtkĭr'khŭn), village (pop. 1,362), Bern canton, S central Switzerland, on Aar R. and 2 mi. SE of Meiringen, in valley among peaks of Bernese Alps; alt. 2,086 ft. Has hydroelectric plant. Also known as Hof.
Innherad (ĭn'hărād), region around inner Trondheim Fjord, Nord-Trondelag co., central Norway. Steinkjer and Levanger are its centers. Formerly spelled Indherred.
Innichen, Italy: see SAN CANDIDO.
Inniscrone (ĭ"nĭskrōn') or **Inishcrone** (ĭ"nĭshkrōn'), Gaelic *Inis Easgrach Abhann*, town (pop. 484), NW Co. Sligo, Ireland, on Killala Bay, 5 mi. E of Killala; fishing port.
Innisfail (ĭ'nĭsfāl"), town (pop. 2,621), NE Queensland, Australia, 45 mi. SSE of Cairns, on coast; sugar-producing center; sugar mill. Mean annual rainfall 144 in.
Innisfail (ĭ'nĭsfāl), town (pop. 1,272), S central Alta., near Red Deer R., 18 mi. SSW of Red Deer; grain elevators, dairying, ranching. Coal and sandstone are worked near by.
Innisfallen (ĭ"nĭsfô'lŭn), islet in Lough Leane, one of the Lakes of Killarney, Ireland, 3 mi. SW of Killarney; site of ruins of 6th-cent. abbey founded by St. Finian. Isl. is the "sweet Innisfallen" of Moore's poem.
Innisfree, village (pop. 258), E Alta., 28 mi. W of Vermilion; dairying, grain, stock.
Innisfree, small island in Lough Gill, NE Co. Sligo, Ireland. Celebrated in Yeats's poem.
Innishannon (ĭ'nĭ-shă'nŭn), Gaelic *Inis Eoghanain*, town (pop. 196), S Co. Cork, Ireland, on Bandon R. and 12 mi. SW of Cork; agr. market (potatoes, oats; dairying).
Inniskeen (ĭ"nĭskēn') or **Inishkeen** (ĭ"nĭsh–), Gaelic *Inis Caoin Deagha*, agr. village (district pop. 926), SE Co. Monaghan, Ireland, on Fane R. and 7 mi. W of Dundalk; flax, oats, potatoes. Has anc. round tower.
Innokentyevka or **Innokent'yevka** (ēnŭkĕn'tyĭfkŭ), village (1939 pop. over 500), SE Amur oblast, Russian SFSR, on Amur R. (landing), opposite Wuyün, on spur of Trans-Siberian RR and 120 mi. ESE of Blagoveshchensk, in agr. area (grain, soybeans). Cossack village, founded 1858.
Innokentyevski or **Innokent'yevskiy** (ēnŭkĕn'tyĭfskē), town (1939 pop. over 2,000), SE Khabarovsk Territory, Russian SFSR, port on Sea of Japan, 20 mi. S of Sovetskaya Gavan; fish canning.
Innoko River (ĭnō'kō), W Alaska, rises near 63°N 156°30'W, flows first N, then in a winding course generally SW, to Yukon R. opposite Holy Cross; c.450 mi. long. Receives Iditarod R.
Inno-shima (ĕn'nō'shĭmä), island (□ 14; pop. 38,439, including offshore islets), Hiroshima prefecture, Japan, in Hiuchi Sea (central section of Inland Sea), 3 mi. S of Onomichi on SW Honshu, bet. Mukai-shima (N) and Ikuchi-jima (SW); 5 mi. long, 3 mi. wide. Mountainous, fertile; rice, sweet potatoes, citrus fruit. Habu is chief town.
Inn River, anc. *Aenus*, in central Europe, rises in Grisons canton, Switzerland, 2 mi. NW of resort hamlet of Maloja, flows NE through ENGADINE valley, past Saint Moritz, enters Tyrol (Austria) at Finstermünz Pass, continues past Innsbruck and Solbad Hall (head of navigation) to Kufstein (near Ger. border). Flows N, past Rosenheim (Bavaria), then generally E to the Danube at Passau. Forms Austro-Ger. border in lower course. Length, 317 mi. Receives the Salzach (right). Agr. in middle and lower valley. Numerous hydroelectric plants (Innsbruck, Jenbach, Mühldorf).
Innsbruck (ĭnz'brŏŏk, Ger. ĭns'–), city (1951 pop. 94,599), ⊙ Tyrol, W Austria, on the Inn (several bridges), at mouth of the Sill, and 60 mi. S of Munich, Germany; beautifully situated in Eastern Alps; alt. 1,883 ft. Includes old and new town, several suburbs (Hötting, Mühlau, Wilten, Pradl). Rail and market center; hydroelectric plant; mfg. (textiles, processed food), glass painting, mosaic works. Points of interest: Hofkirche, 16th-cent. Franciscan church with monument of Maximilian I; Fürstenburg, 15th-cent. castle with the Goldene Dachl, a balcony with gilded copper roof; univ. (founded 1677); column of St. Anne (1706); Ferdinandeum and other museums; botanical garden with collection of alpine plants. Summer and winter resort; excellent view of surrounding mts. from the adjoining Isel (S). Became hq. of Fr. occupation zone in 1945.
Innuit, Mount (4,554 ft.), E Labrador, at head of Nachvak Fiord; 59°2'N 64°9'W.
Innvik, Norway: see OLDE LAKE.
Ino (ē'nō), town (pop. 10,363), Kochi prefecture, S Shikoku, Japan, on Niyodo R. and 6 mi. W of Kochi; connected with Kochi by electric railway; major paper-milling center.
Inola (ĭnō'lŭ), town (pop. 294), Rogers co., NE Okla., 25 mi. E of Tulsa, in stock-raising and agr. area.
Inongo (ēnông'gō), town (1946 pop. c.2,100), ⊙ Lake Leopold II dist. (□ 56,763; 1948 pop. c.337,000), Leopoldville prov., W Belgian Congo, on E Shore of L. Leopold II, 270 mi. NE of Leopoldville; trading center in region noted for palm products; steamboat landing. Has R.C. mission, native teachers and trade schools, hosp. for Europeans. Airport.
Inonu (ēnŭnü'), Turkish *İnönü*, town (pop. 4,151), Bilecik prov., NW Turkey, on railroad and 20 mi. WNW of Eskisehir. Scene of Turkish victory over the Greeks after First World War; Gen. Ismet Pasha, who commanded the Turks and later took his name from the town, succeeded (1938) Ataturk as president of Turkey.
Inowroclaw (ēnôvrôts'wäf), Pol. *Inowrocław*, Ger. *Hohensalza* (hōŭnzäl'tsä), city (pop. 35,808), Bydgoszcz prov., central Poland, 21 mi. SW of Torun, near Notec R. Rail junction; trade center; a leading city in the Kujawy; health resort, with salt-water springs, hot, salt, and mud baths; many hospitals. Mfg. of machinery, pumps, bricks, glass; brass working, beet-sugar milling, brewing. Rock salt (c.500 ft. underground) and gypsum (for art uses) worked in vicinity. Passed 1772 to Prussia; reverted 1919 to Poland. Here, in 1909, a church collapsed when the dissolution of underground salt created an underground cave. During Second World War the town suffered relatively little damage.
Inoz, Turkey: see ENOS.
Inquisivi (ĭng-kēsē'vē), town (pop. c.3,100), ⊙ Inquisivi prov., La Paz dept., W Bolivia, on E slopes of Cordillera de Tres Cruces and 70 mi. ESE of La Paz; alt. 9,711 ft.; grain, potatoes; *oca*, orchards; distilling industry.
Inrim, Bismarck Archipelago: see LORENGAU.
Inrin, Formosa: see YÜANLIN.
Inriville (ēnrēvēl'), town (pop. 2,139), E Córdoba prov., Argentina, on the Río Tercero and 20 mi. SW of Marcos Juárez; mfg. of agr. implements; agr. center (corn, wheat, flax, alfalfa, oats); horticulture; cattle raising.
Ins (ĭns), Fr. *Anet* (ănā'), town (pop. 2,054), Bern canton, W Switzerland, 16 mi. WNW of Bern.
In-Salah (ĕn'-sälä'), oasis (pop. 4,429), Saharan Oases territory, central Algeria, chief of the Tidikelt oases, 230 mi. S of El-Goléa; 27°12'N 2°29'E. Important caravan station and junction of desert automobile tracks; exports dates. Handicraft industries (carpets, leather goods). Airport at Aoulef, 90 mi. WSW.
Insar (ēnsär'), village (1926 pop. 4,617), S Mordvinian Autonomous SSR, Russian SFSR, on Issa R. (right branch of Moksha R.) and 26 mi. WSW of Ruzayevka; bast-fiber processing, metalworking; hemp, legumes.
Insar River, Mordvinian Autonomous SSR, Russian SFSR, rises just SE of Kadoshkino, flows ENE, past Ruzayevka, and N, past Saransk, Romodanovo, and Lada, to Alatyr R. just NE of Kemlya; length, c.80 mi.
Insch (ĭnch), town and parish (pop. 1,249), central Aberdeen, Scotland, 10 mi. WNW of Inverurie; agr. market. Near by is Leslie Castle (1661).
Inscription Point, E New South Wales, Australia, on S shore of Botany Bay; 30°S 151°13'E. Site of monument in honor of Capt. Cook's landing (1770) and establishment of Br. claim.
Insein (ĭn'sān"), district (□ 1,903; 1941 pop. 387,345), Pegu div., Lower Burma, bet. Irrawaddy R. and on S spurs of Pegu Yoma; ⊙ Insein. Part of the Irrawaddy delta, it is drained by Myitmaka R. Rice fields and fisheries in plains; teak forests on Pegu Yoma. Served by Rangoon-Mandalay RR.
Insein, town (pop. 20,487), ⊙ Insein dist., Lower Burma, port on Myitmaka R. (here called Hlaing R.) and Rangoon-Mandalay RR, 5 mi. N of Rangoon. Woolen mills, railroad shops.
Inselsberg (ĭn'zŭlsbĕrk), second-highest peak (3,005 ft.) of the Thuringian Forest, central Germany, 13 mi. SW of Gotha.
Insh, agr. village, E Inverness, Scotland, near the Spey, 5 mi. E of Kingussie, on Loch Insh (1 mi. long).
Inside Passage, natural, protected waterway, c.950 mi. long, off the coast of British Columbia and SE Alaska. It threads through the ALEXANDER ARCHIPELAGO. From Seattle, Wash., to Skagway, Alaska, or via Cross Sound to the Gulf of Alaska, the route uses channels and straits bet. isls. and the mainland which afford protection from the storms of the Pacific. Snow-capped mts., forests, waterfalls, glaciers, and the many deep, narrow channels give it great scenic beauty. It was known to Spanish, Russian, English, and American explorers, many of whom gave names to the isls. and waterways. It is the route generally used by steamers bet. the U.S. and Alaska. Also called Inland Passage.
Insiza, township (pop. 52), Bulawayo prov., SW central Southern Rhodesia, in Matabeleland, on railroad and 45 mi. NE of Bulawayo; alt. 4,640 ft. Tobacco, corn; livestock. Insiza dist. has gold, asbestos, copper mines.
Insjon (ĭn'shŭn"), Swedish *Insjön*, village (pop. 1,600), Kopparberg co., central Sweden, on East Dal R. and 17 mi. NW of Borlange; woodworking, copper mining.
Inskaya (ēn'skĭŭ), railway junction on Turksib RR, just S of Novosibirsk, Novosibirsk oblast, Russian SFSR; freight yards; sawmilling; metalworks.
Insko (ē'nyŭskō), Pol. *Ińsko*, Ger. *Nörenberg* (nû'rŭnbĕrk), town (1939 pop. 3,012; 1946 pop. 296) in Pomerania, after 1945 in Szczecin prov., NW Poland, on small lake, 40 mi. E of Stettin.
Insoemanai, Indonesia: see WAKDE ISLANDS.
Insoemoar, Netherlands New Guinea: see WAKDE ISLANDS.
Inspiration, company-owned town (1940 pop. 711), Gila co., SE central Ariz., in Pinal Mts., just N of Miami; copper-processing.
Insterburg, Russian SFSR: see CHERNYAKHOVSK.
Inster River (ĭn'stŭr), former East Prussia, right headstream of Pregel R., in Kaliningrad oblast, Russian SFSR, rises NE of Dobrovolsk, flows 45 mi. W and SW, joining the Angerapp at Chernyakhovsk to form Pregel R.
Instinción (ēnstēnthyōn'), town (pop. 1,209), Almería prov., S Spain, at foot of the Sierra de Gádor, 15 mi. NW of Almería; ships grapes; produces olive oil, cereals. Iron mines near by.
Institute, W.Va.: see CHARLESTON.
Insu (ĕn'sōō), town, Western Prov., SW central Gold Coast colony, on railroad and 19 mi. NNE of Tarkwa; gold-mining; cacao, cassava, corn.
Insull, mining village, Harlan co., SE Ky., in the Cumberlands, 16 mi. NE of Middlesboro; bituminous coal.
Insumanai, Netherlands New Guinea: see WAKDE ISLANDS.
Insumar, Netherlands New Guinea: see WAKDE ISLANDS.
Insuta, Gold Coast: see NSUTA.
Inta (ĕn'tŭ), town (1944 pop. over 500), NE Komi Autonomous SSR, Russian SFSR, on Inta R. (right affluent of the Kos-Yu), on N.Pechora RR and 150 mi. SW of Vorkuta; coal-mining center in Pechora basin. Developed during Second World War.
Intan, Malaya: see KLIAN INTAN.
Intendente Alvear (ēntĕndĕn'tā älvāär'), town (1947 pop. 2,734), ⊙ Chapaleufú dept. (pop. 8,251), NE La Pampa prov., Argentina, 33 mi. NNE of General Pico; agr. center (wheat, corn, barley, alfalfa, livestock); dairy industry.
Inter-American Highway, section, 3,349 mi. long, of the PAN AMERICAN HIGHWAY system from NUEVO LAREDO, Mexico, to Panama city, Panama. Much of the highway had been built by the countries concerned prior to Dec., 1941, but wartime necessity led the U.S. Congress to appropriate $20,000,000 to assist completion; subsequent aid was granted, but later work was done by each nation on its own. In 1950 there remained uncompleted sections in Chiapas (Mexico), Guatemala, Costa Rica, and W Panama; some other sections are passable only in the dry season.
Interamna Nahars, Italy: see TERNI, city.
Intercourse, village (1940 pop. 518), Lancaster co., SE Pa., 10 mi. E of Lancaster, in rich agr. area.
Interior, town (pop. 126), Jackson co., SW central S.Dak., 25 mi. WSW of Kadoka, just E of Badlands Natl. Monument; center of tourist trade.
Interior and Labuan (läbōōän'), residency (□ 8,042; 1931 pop. 88,887), Br. North Borneo; ⊙ BEAUFORT. Until 1946, when LABUAN isl. was included, it was called simply Interior residency.
Interlachen (ĭn'tŭrlä"kŭn), town (pop. 297), Putnam co., N Fla., 15 mi. W of Palatka.
Interlaken (ĭn'tŭrlä'kŭn), town (pop. 4,059), Bern canton, central Switzerland, on Aar R. and on the Bödeli (lowland), bet. lakes of Thun and Brienz, 26 mi. SE of Bern; largest resort (mainly summer) in Bernese Alps; alt. 1,860 ft. Mfg. (woolen textiles); printing. From the Höheweg, its main street, magnificent view of the Jungfrau. Old monastery bldg. (1130), castle (1750).
Interlaken, village, central Tasmania, 50 mi. N of Hobart, bet. L. Sorell and L. Crescent; sheep.
Interlaken. 1 (ĭn'tŭrlä"kŭn) Village, Berkshire co., Mass.: see STOCKBRIDGE. **2** (ĭn'tŭrlä"kŭn) Borough (pop. 833), Monmouth co., E N.J., near coast, just N of Asbury Park. **3** (ĭn'tŭrlä"kŭn) Village (pop. 770), Seneca co., W central N.Y., in Finger Lakes region, near Cayuga L., 17 mi. NW of Ithaca; canned foods, lumber, railroad ties; agr. (fruit, wheat).
Interlochen (ĭn'tŭrlŏ"kŭn), resort village, Grand Traverse co., NW Mich., near Duck and Green lakes, 10 mi. SSW of Traverse City, in fruitgrowing area. Site of Natl. Music Camp, which presents summer concerts. State park near by.

Intermediate Lake, Mich.: see CENTRAL LAKE, village.

International Falls, city (pop. 6,269), ⊙ Koochiching co., N Minn., on Rainy R. near its mouth in Rainy L., opposite Fort Frances, Ont., and c.140 mi. NW of Duluth. Lumber and summer-excursion center in dairying and truck-farming area; port of entry; dairy products, insulation material. Large paper mill and sawmill here. Growth followed construction of paper mill (1904) at falls in Rainy R. Toll bridge across river connects city with Fort Frances.

Interstate Park (730 acres), mainly in Polk co., Wis., with 150 acres in Chisago co., Minn.; comprises villages of St. Croix Falls and Taylors Falls, on St. Croix R. Its central feature is the scenic gorge called the Dalles of the St. Croix, with rock walls c.200 ft. high; there are curious rock formations and potholes.

Intervale, N.H.: see CONWAY.

Inthanon Peak (ĭn'tŭnôn') or **Angka Peak** (äng'kä), highest peak (8,452 ft.) of Thailand, 35 mi. WSW of Chiangmai, in spur of Thanon Tong Chai Range; 18°35'N 98°30'E.

Intibucá (ēntēbōōkä'), department (□ 1,057; 1950 pop. 65,299), SW Honduras, on Salvador border; ⊙ La Esperanza. Astride continental divide (Sierra de Opalaca), sloping into valleys of Río Grande de Otoro (N) and Lempa R. (S). Mainly agr. (corn, beans, rice, tobacco, coffee); cattle, hogs. Mat-, basket-, and ropemaking are local industries. Main centers, La Esperanza and adjoining Intibucá. Formed 1883.

Intibucá, town (pop. 2,235), Intibucá dept., SW Honduras, in Sierra de Opalaca, adjoining (N) LA ESPERANZA; alt. 6,529 ft.; mat weaving, basketmaking. Pop. largely Indian.

Intorsatura-Buzaului (ēntôrsŭtōō'rä-bōōzŭ'ōōlōōē) or **Intorsura-Buzaului** (ēntôrsōō'rä), Rum. *Intorsătura-Buzăului* or *Intorsura-Buzăului*, Hung. *Bodzaforduló* (bôd'zōfôrdōōlō), village (pop. 2,012), Stalin prov., central Rumania, on Buzau R. and 22 mi. E of Stalin (Brasov); rail terminus, agr. center.

Intorsura-Buzaului, Rumania: see INTORSATURA-BUZAULUI.

Intotto (ĭntō'tō), Ital. *Entotto*, village, Shoa prov., central Ethiopia, on road and 3 mi. N of Addis Ababa. Has ruins of palace and churches. Was capital of Ethiopia (c.1880–89) until replaced by Addis Ababa.

Intra (ēn'trä), town (pop. 9,011), Novara prov., Piedmont, N Italy, port on W shore of Lago Maggiore, 18 mi. SE of Domodossola; commercial center; textiles (cotton, silk), machinery (textile, quarry), glass, hats, sausage. Small mus.

Intracoastal Waterway, U.S., toll-free route for commercial and pleasure craft extending for c.3,100 mi. along the Atlantic and Gulf of Mexico coasts from Boston, Mass., to mouth of the Rio Grande at Brownsville, Texas. Federally maintained, it follows bays, sounds, and rivers, many of which have been deepened by dredging, land-cut canals, and occasional reaches in the Atlantic and the Gulf; minimum depth for most of its length is 12 ft., although there are sections 7 and 9 ft. deep. Its sections and connecting waterways include CAPE COD CANAL; Delaware R. as far upstream as Trenton, N.J.; CHESAPEAKE AND DELAWARE CANAL, connecting Delaware R. with Chesapeake Bay; Dismal Swamp Canal and Albemarle and Chesapeake Canal, connecting S part (Hampton Roads) of Chesapeake Bay with Albemarle Sound; OKEECHOBEE WATERWAY across the Fla. peninsula, which connects the E coast section of waterway (extending as far S as Key West) with the beginning at Fort Myers of the Gulf Intracoastal Waterway, continuing W to the Rio Grande. The Gulf section, much of it following landcut canals, is particularly important commercially, carrying heavy traffic in petroleum, chemicals, sulphur, sugar, pulpwood, iron and steel, building materials, salt, agr. products, seafood, and manufactured goods. It crosses the Mississippi delta near New Orleans, and is connected with the Mississippi by locks, giving Waterway traffic access to the river's great basin and the Great Lakes region. Principal ports are Boston, New York, Trenton, Baltimore, Norfolk (and other Hampton Roads points), Wilmington and Beaufort, N.C.; Charleston, Savannah, Jacksonville, Miami, Key West, Pensacola, Mobile, Gulfport, Biloxi, New Orleans, Morgan City, Lake Charles, Orange, Port Arthur, Beaumont (these last 3 on SABINE-NECHES WATERWAY), Houston (on Houston Ship Channel), Galveston, Texas City, Freeport, Corpus Christi, and Brownsville. Further improvements authorized include deepening and widening of several sections and construction across Fla. of a channel bet. Palatka (at head of present branch of Atlantic section extending up St. Johns R.) and Withlacoochee Bay, on the Gulf coast. Waterway was formerly sometimes known as Inland Waterway; its Gulf portion was formerly the Intracoastal Canal.

Introbio (ēntrō'byō), village (pop. 778), Como prov., Lombardy, N Italy, 9 mi. NNE of Lecco; hardware mfg.

Introdacqua (ēntrôdä'kwä), town (pop. 2,552), Aquila prov., Abruzzi e Molise, S central Italy, 3 mi. SW of Sulmona; woolen mills.

Inubo, Cape (ēnōōbō'), Jap. *Inubo-saki*, Chiba prefecture, central Honshu, Japan, near Choshi, at NE tip of base of Chiba Peninsula, in the Pacific; 35°42'N 140°52'E; important lighthouse. Formerly sometimes called Inuboye.

Inubushi, Japan: see SANO, Tochigi prefecture.

Inui (ēnōō'ē), town (pop. 4,020), Shizuoka prefecture, central Honshu, Japan, 20 mi. NNE of Hamamatsu; lumbering.

Inukai (ēnōō'kī), town (pop. 3,804), Oita prefecture, NE Kyushu, Japan, 12 mi. S of Oita; lumber, rice.

Inútil, Bahía, Chile: see USELESS BAY.

Inuyama (ēnōō'yämŭ), town (pop. 19,548), Aichi prefecture, central Honshu, Japan, on Kiso R. and 16 mi. N of Nagoya; rice-growing center; pottery, sake, *konnyaku* (paste made from devil's-tongue). Fishing (with cormorants). Has feudal castle.

Inver, Loch, Scotland: see LOCHINVER.

Inverallochy (ĭn"vŭră'lŏkh-ē), fishing village in Rathen parish, NE Aberdeen, Scotland, on North Sea, 3 mi. ESE of Fraserburgh. Near by is Inverallochy Castle, anc. stronghold of the Comyns. Just W of Inverallochy is fishing village of Cairnbulg, with another castle (restored) of the Comyns.

Inveraray (ĭn"vŭrâr'ē), burgh (1931 pop. 455; 1951 census 503), ⊙ Argyllshire, Scotland, in center of co., on Loch Fyne, 45 mi. NW of Glasgow. The 18th-cent. Inveraray Castle, designed by Robert Adam, is seat of duke of Argyll.

Inverbervie (–bûr'vē) or **Bervie,** burgh (1931 pop. 1,032; 1951 census 885), SE Kincardine, Scotland, on North Sea at mouth of Bervie Water, 9 mi. SSW of Stonehaven; fishing port, agr. market. Just S are ruins of 16th-cent. Hallgreen Castle.

Invercargill (–kär'gĭl), city (pop. 23,470; metropolitan Invercargill 27,583), ⊙ Southland co. (□ 3,736; pop. 23,805), S S.Isl., New Zealand, on inlet of Foveaux Strait; 46°20'S 168°20'E. Agr. center; flour, timber, brick. Its port is near-by Bluff.

Inverell (ĭn"vûrĕl'), municipality (pop. 6,530), NE New South Wales, Australia, on Macintyre R. and 220 mi. NNW of Newcastle; rail terminus; mining center (silver-lead, tin, diamonds); dairy foods, fruit, tobacco.

Inveresk (ĭn"vûrĕsk'), town and parish (pop. 20,700, including Musselburgh burgh), NE Midlothian, Scotland, on Esk R. just S of Musselburgh; agr. market. Site of battle of Pinkie (1547) in which duke of Somerset defeated the Scots.

Invergarry (ĭn"vûrgă'rē), agr. village, central Inverness, Scotland, in GLENGARRY near Loch Oich, 7 mi. SW of Fort Augustus. Has ruins of anc. Invergarry Castle, burned 1745 by duke of Cumberland, seat of the Macdonnells of Glengarry, whose last chief was reputedly the prototype of Fergus MacIvor in Scott's *Waverley*.

Invergordon (–gôr'dŭn), burgh (1931 pop. 1,417; 1951 census 1,514), E Ross and Cromarty, Scotland, on Cromarty Firth, 15 mi. N of Inverness; 57°43'N 4°8'W; important naval base. Scene of naval mutiny in 1931.

Invergowrie (–gou'rē), village in Longforgan parish, SE Perthshire, Scotland, on the Firth of Tay, 3 mi. W of Dundee; paper milling. Has remains of 15th-cent. church.

Inver Grove, village (pop. 667), Dakota co., E Minn., on Mississippi R. just S of St. Paul, in grain, potato, stock area.

Inverkeilor (–kē'lûr), agr. village and parish (pop. 1,206), E Angus, Scotland, on Lunan Water near the coast, and 6 mi. N of Arbroath.

Inverkeithing (–kē'thĭng), burgh (1931 pop. 3,185; 1951 census 3,703), SW Fifeshire, Scotland, near the Firth of Forth, 4 mi. SE of Dunfermline; paper-milling center; stone quarries near by. On the Firth of Forth is port, with shipyards. Has 14th-cent. Hospitium of Grey Friars and 16th-cent. market cross. Town was residence of David I; in 1651 Cromwell defeated supporters of Charles II at battle of Inverkeithing. On the Firth of Forth, 2 mi. S, is market town of North Queensferry, N terminal of the Forth Bridge (see QUEENSFERRY). Just NW is ROSYTH.

Inverkip (ĭn"vûrkĭp'), agr. village and parish (pop. 11,180, including part of burghs of Greenock and Gourock), NW Renfrew, Scotland, on Firth of Clyde, 6 mi. WSW of Greenock. Just N is Ardgowan (ärdgou'ŭn), with whisky distillery.

Inverloch, village (pop. 491), S Victoria, Australia, 70 mi. SSE of Melbourne, near Wonthaggi, on small inlet of Bass Strait; seaside resort.

Inverlochy, Scotland: see FORT WILLIAM.

Invermay, village (pop. 226), SE Sask., near small Saline and Stonewall lakes, 33 mi. WNW of Canora; mixed farming.

Invermere, resort village (pop. estimate 450), SE B.C., on slope of Rocky Mts., on Windermere L., 50 mi. SSW of Banff; alt. 2,624 ft. Site of Dominion agr. experiment station.

Inverness (ĭn"vûrnĕs', ĭn'vûrnĕs"), county (□ 1,409; pop. 20,573), NE N.S., in E part of Cape Breton Isl., on Gulf of St. Lawrence; ⊙ Port Hood.

Inverness. 1 Town (pop. 2,975), E N.S., on W coast of Cape Breton Isl., on Northumberland Strait, 55 mi. W of Sydney; coal mining; coal-shipping port. **2** Village (pop. 212), ⊙ Megantic co., S Que., 16 mi. NW of Thetford Mines; copper, magnesite mining; dairying; cattle, pig raising; lumbering.

Inverness or **Inverness-shire** (ĭn"vûrnĕs', –shĭr), largest county (□ 4,211.1; 1931 pop. 82,108; 1951 census 84,924) of Scotland; ⊙ Inverness. Bounded by Perthshire and Argyll (S), the Atlantic (W), Ross and Cromarty (N), Nairn and Moray (NE), and Banff and Aberdeen (E). Drained by the Spey, Findhorn, Beauly, Spean, Nairn, and Garry rivers. Co. includes several isls. of the Inner and Outer Hebrides (S part of Lewis with Harris, North and South Uist, Skye, Scalpay, Eigg, Barra, Rum, Raasay, and others). A part of the Highlands, its surface is very mountainous, with the Grampian and Cairngorm mts.; Ben Nevis (4,406 ft.) is highest peak in Great Britain, and there are many peaks over 3,500 ft. Inverness is crossed by the Caledonian Canal, following geological fault of the great Glen of Scotland, extending from Moray Firth to the Atlantic, through lochs Ness, Oich, Lochy, and Linnhe. Other lakes are lochs Ericht, Arkaig, Laggan, Garry; on W coast are numerous sea lochs. Sheep grazing and fishing are important; industries are slate and granite quarrying, aluminum processing (Inverlochy and Foyers), and woolen milling (the Hebrides are noted for their tweeds). Hydroelectric power resources are being developed (Lochaber scheme). Other towns are Fort Augustus, Fort William, and Kingussie. Co. has many associations with 1715 Jacobite rising and subsequent flight of Prince Charles Edward with Flora Macdonald to the Hebrides. There are numerous tourist resorts.

Inverness, burgh (1931 pop. 22,583; 1951 census 28,115), ⊙ Inverness-shire, Scotland, in N part of co., on narrows bet. Beauly Firth and Moray Firth, at mouth of Ness R. and near NE end of Caledonian Canal; 57°29'N 4°14'W. "Capital of the Highlands," it is a commercial center and seaport, with shipbuilding yards, iron foundries, woolen mills, tanneries, whisky distilleries, railroad shops. It is scene of annual Highland Gathering (Sept.). Notable bldgs. include 18th-cent. High Church, Dunbar's Hosp. (1688, now residential bldgs.), modern Episcopal Cathedral, and Highland Mus. Present castle (1835) contains county offices and is on site of Macbeth's Castle, which was razed in revenge for Duncan's murder, and was succeeded by castle built by Malcolm Canmore or David I and destroyed by Robert the Bruce in 1307. Inverness was a center of Highland warfare. In 1652 Cromwell built a fort here, razed after the Restoration. A later structure was destroyed in 1745 uprising. Town is noted for purity of English spoken here.

Inverness (ĭn'vûrnĕs"). **1** Town (pop. 1,471), ⊙ Citrus co., central Fla., c.60 mi. NNE of Tampa, on Tsala Apopka L.; agr. trade center; vegetable packing; fishing; phosphate quarrying. **2** Village (pop. 1,110), Cook co., NE Ill. **3** Town (pop. 1,010), Sunflower co., W Miss., 8 mi. SSE of Indianola, in rich cotton-growing area.

Inverness-shire, Scotland: see INVERNESS, county.

Inversnaid (ĭn"vûr-snād'), resort village, NW Stirling, Scotland, on NE shore of Loch Lomond. Site of fort dating from 1713. Just N is Rob Roy's Cave, where Robert Bruce hid after 1306 battle of Dalry.

Inveruno (ēnvĕrōō'nō), village (pop. 4,324), Milano prov., Lombardy, N Italy, 17 mi. WNW of Milan; foundry, cotton mill.

Inverurie (ĭn"vûrōōr'ē), burgh (1931 pop. 4,524; 1951 census 5,054), central Aberdeen, Scotland, on Urie R. just above its mouth on Don R., and 14 mi. NW of Aberdeen; agr. market, with paper and oatmeal milling, agr. machinery mfg.

Investigator Islands, in Great Australian Bight, 4 mi. off W coast of Eyre Peninsula, South Australia; 40-mi. chain comprising FLINDERS ISLAND, Pearson and Waldegrave isls. Sandy, hilly.

Investigator Strait, channel of Indian Ocean, forms SW entrance to Gulf St. Vincent, SE South Australia, bet. S coast of Yorke Peninsula and N coast of Kangaroo Isl.; merges with Backstairs Passage (E); 60 mi. long, 35 mi. wide.

Invisible Peak, Idaho: see LOST RIVER RANGE.

Inwood, village (pop. estimate 400), S Ont., 10 mi. ESE of Petrolia; dairying, mixed farming.

Inwood. 1 Town (pop. 644), Lyon co., NW Iowa, 38 mi. NNW of Le Mars, in livestock and grain area. **2** Residential village (1940 pop. 8,022), Nassau co., SE N.Y., on W Long Isl., near E shore of Jamaica Bay, 9 mi. SW of Hempstead; mfg. (clothing, dishcloths, wood and plastic products). **3** A residential district of NW Manhattan borough of New York city, SE N.Y., along the Hudson and Harlem rivers. Contains Inwood Hill Park and Fort Tryon Park, site of the Cloisters, noted mus. of medieval art.

Inyanga (ēnyäng'gä), township (pop. 348), Umtali prov., E Southern Rhodesia, in Mashonaland, in Inyanga Mts., 45 mi. NE of Rusape (linked by road); alt. 5,514 ft. Fruitgrowing center (pears, apples, citrus fruit); livestock raising. Police post. Rhodes Inyanga Estate, a tourist resort with hotel, is 6 mi. S, at road junction. There are some old ruins near by (NW).

Inyanga Mountains, NE Southern Rhodesia, N of Umtali; extend c.50 mi. N–S along Mozambique border; rise to 8,517 ft. at Mt. Inyangani, highest point of Southern Rhodesia.

Inyan Kara Creek (ĭn'yŭn kâ'rŭ), NE Wyo., rises in Black Hills near Inyan Kara Mtn., flows W and NW 43 mi. to Belle Fourche R. 16 mi. NE of Moorcroft.

Inyan Kara Mountain (6,374 ft.), peak in Black Hills, NE Wyo., 14 mi. S of Sundance.

Inyantue (ēnyäntōō'ä) village, Bulawayo prov., W Southern Rhodesia, in Matabeleland, on railroad and 17 mi. SE of Wankie, in Wankie coal area; coal mining.

Inya River (ĕn'yŭ), in Kemerovo and Novosibirsk oblasts, Russian SFSR, rises in central Kuznetsk Basin, flows 331 mi. generally WNW, past Leninsk-Kuznetski, Promyshlennaya, and Toguchin, to Ob R. just above Novosibirsk.

Inyati (ēnyä'tē), township (pop. 164), Bulawayo prov., SW central Southern Rhodesia, in Matabeleland, 36 mi. NNE of Bulawayo; tobacco, corn, peanuts; livestock. Gold deposits. Hq. of native commissioner for Bubi dist.; police post. Seat of London Missionary Society.

Inyazura (ēnyäzōō'rä), township (pop. 517), Umtali prov., E Southern Rhodesia, in Mashonaland, on railroad and 12 mi. SSE of Rusape; alt. 3,994 ft. Tobacco, corn; livestock.

Inyo (ĭn'yō), county (□ 10,091; pop. 11,658), E Calif.; ⊙ Independence. Crest of Sierra Nevada (High Sierras) along W boundary; contains Mt. WHITNEY (14,495 ft.), highest peak in U.S., and 9 other peaks over 14,000 ft. In E, intersected by Nev. line, is DEATH VALLEY NATIONAL MONUMENT, which has lowest point (280 ft. below sea level) in Western Hemisphere. Bet. the Sierra Nevada and Panamint Range (W wall of Death Valley) are arid basins (notably OWENS VALLEY), Inyo Mts., and other ranges. E of Death Valley is Amargosa Range. Owens R. supplies water to Los Angeles Aqueduct; Amargosa R., Furnace Creek vanish in Death Valley. Includes Fort Independence and Paiute Indian reservations. Partly in Inyo Natl. Forest. Mining of lead, tungsten, talc (in all of which co. is a leading Calif. producer), molybdenum, zinc, silver; extraction of borates, potash, salt, and soda. Some irrigated farming (in Owens Valley), stock raising, dairying. Camping, hunting, fishing, and winter sports in mts.; winter resorts in Death Valley. Formed 1866.

Inyokern (ĭn"yōkûrn'), village, Kern co., S central Calif., in Mojave Desert, 45 mi. NNE of Mojave. U.S. naval ordnance test station, airfield are near by, on China L.

Inyo Mountains (ĭn'yō), E Calif., range along E side of Owens Valley, extending 70 mi. SSE from S end of White Mts., SE of Bishop, to point just SE of Owens L. Rise to 11,127 ft. at Waucoba Mtn. (wôkō'bŭ), 18 mi. SE of Big Pine. Crossed by Westgard Pass (alt. 7,276 ft.) just NE of Big Pine.

Inywa (ĭn'yŭwä), village, Katha dist., Upper Burma, on left bank of Irrawaddy R. and 20 mi. S of Katha, at mouth of Shweli R.

Inzá (ēnsä'), town (pop. 458), Cauca dept., SW Colombia, in Cordillera Central, 40 mi. ENE of Popayán; alt. 5,755 ft. Archaeological ruins found here c.1935.

Inza (ēn'zŭ), city (1944 pop. over 10,000), W Ulyanovsk oblast, Russian SFSR, near Inza R. (right tributary of Sura R.; 64 mi. long), 85 mi. WSW of Ulyanovsk; rail junction; wood-cracking center; mfg. (tripoli bricks, liquor), basket making. Tripoli quarries near by. Became city in 1946.

Inzago (ēnzä'gô), village (pop. 4,137), Milano prov., Lombardy, N Italy, near Adda R., 15 mi. ENE of Milan; silk mill.

Inzer (ēn'zyĭr), town (1939 pop. over 2,000), E Bashkir Autonomous SSR, Russian SFSR, in the S Urals, on Inzer R. and 40 mi. NW of Beloretsk, on rail spur; mining center in Komarovo-Zigazinski iron dist. Until 1946, Inzerski Zavod.

Inzer River, Bashkir Autonomous SSR, Russian SFSR, rises in the S Urals WNW of Tirlyanski, flows SSW, NNW, past Inzer, and W to Sim R. just above its mouth; 185 mi. long.

Inzersdorf (ĭnt'sûrsdôrf), town (pop. 5,754), after 1938 in Liesing dist. of Vienna, Austria, 4 mi. S of city center; machine mfg.

Inzhavino (ēnzhä'vēnŭ), village (1926 pop. 2,793), E Tambov Oblast, Russian SFSR, on Vorona R. and 24 mi. SSW of Kirsanov; rail terminus; sunflower-oil press, metalworks.

Ioannina (yôä'nēnŭ), nome (□ 1,947; pop. 161,637), Epirus, Greece; ⊙ Ioannina. Bounded NW by Albania, E by the Pindus, and S by Tzoumerka massif, it is drained by Aoos (N) and Arachthus (S) rivers and contains L. Ioannina. Major stock-raising region, known for its cheese, milk, and skin exports. Served by major highway bet. Albania and Greece.

Ioannina, city (1951 pop. 32,268), ⊙ Epirus and Ioannina nome, Greece, on L. Ioannina, 200 mi. NW of Athens; commercial center; silk milling, brocade mfg.; agr. trade (corn, wheat, wine, fruit). Airport. Seat of Greek metropolitan. Has remains of lofty Iron Castle and Byzantine churches. Founded in Byzantine times, it was taken 1081 by the Normans, became (1204) ⊙ independent despotat of Epirus, later succeeded by Arta. Under Turkish rule (after 1430), it became famous as residence of Ali Pasha, the "Lion of Janina" (Ioannina). Passed to Greece in 1913. Severely damaged in Second World War. Formerly variously spelled Janina (jä'nēnŭ), Jannina, Yanina (yä'nēnŭ), Yannina.

Ioannina, Lake, anc. *Pambotis*, lake (□ 8.5), in Ioannina nome, S Epirus, Greece; 5 mi. long, 3 mi. wide. Ioannina stands on W shore. Important fisheries.

Ioco (īō'kō), town (pop. estimate 1,000), SW B.C., at W end of Burrard Inlet of the Strait of Georgia, 10 mi. ENE of Vancouver, opposite Port Moody; oil refinery.

Iokanga or **Iokan'ga** (ēŭkän'yŭgŭ), village, NE Murmansk oblast, Russian SFSR, on Barents Sea, on Kola Peninsula, just SE of Gremikha, 180 mi. ESE of Murmansk; fish cannery. Pop. largely Lapp (Saami).

Iokhannes, Russian SFSR: see SOVETSKI, Leningrad oblast.

Iola (īō'lŭ). **1** Village (pop. 213), Clay co., S central Ill., 22 mi. NE of Salem, in agr., oil, and natural-gas area. **2** City (pop. 7,094), ⊙ Allen co., SE Kansas, on Neosho R. and 35 mi. W of Fort Scott; trade center for grain and livestock region; dairying; mfg. of cement, bricks, clothing, candy. Co. fair and Southeastern Kansas Exposition take place here annually in Aug. Has jr. col. Founded 1859, inc. 1870. **3** Village (pop. 867), Waupaca co., central Wis., 22 mi. E of Stevens Point, in agr. area (dairy products; potatoes, poultry).

Iolcus, Greece: see VOLOS.

Iolotan or **Iolotan'** (ēŭ"lŭtän'yŭ), city (1932 pop. estimate 3,160), central Mary oblast, Turkmen SSR, on Murgab R., on railroad and 35 mi. SE of Mary; cotton-ginning center. Irrigation dam.

Ioma (īō'mŭ), town, Northern Div., Territory of Papua, SE New Guinea, 90 mi. NE of Port Moresby; rubber, coconuts.

Iona (īō'nŭ) or **Icomkill** (ī"kōmkĭl') [*Iona* miswritten for Irish *Ioua*=island; *Icomkill*, Irish,=island of Columcille], island (pop. 141) of the Inner Hebrides, Argyll, Scotland, off SW coast of Mull, from which it is separated by the 1-mi.-wide Sound of Iona. It is 3½ mi. long and 1½ mi. wide. Surface is hilly, rising to 332 ft.; there are shell beaches. Isl. is famous as early center of Celtic Christianity; in 563 St. Columba (or St. Columcille), with 12 companions, landed here from Ireland, founding a monastery, which was burned by Danes in 9th cent., and rebuilt by Queen Margaret in 1072. From here St. Columba began conversion of Scotland. In 1203 a Benedictine monastery and nunnery (remains) were established here. In N part of isl. is the Cathedral, formerly Church of St. Mary, dating from late 12th or early 13th cent. There are remains of several anc. crosses. A cemetery near 12th-cent. chapel of St. Oran contains sculptured tombstones and is reputed burial place not only of many Scottish kings and chieftains, but also of several Irish, Norwegian, and French sovereigns. Chief industries are farming, fishing, marble quarrying; tourist trade is important. Plan to restore anc. buildings of Iona was halted by Second World War, but was resumed in 1947.

Iona. 1 Village (pop. 502), Bonneville co., SE Idaho, near Snake R., 5 mi. ENE of Idaho Falls, in irrigated region; alt. 4,788 ft. **2** Village (pop. 355), Murray co., SW Minn., 5 mi. SSW of Slayton, in grain area.

Ionava, Lithuania: see JONAVA.

Ione. 1 (īō'nē) Village (pop. 1,071), Amador co., central Calif., 33 mi. SE of Sacramento; clay products. Seat of state industrial school for boys. **2** (īōn') City (pop. 262), Morrow co., N Oregon, 16 mi. NW of Heppner. **3** (īōn') Town (pop. 714), Pend Oreille co., NE Wash., 25 mi. NE of Colville and on Clark Fork R.; lumber.

Ionia (īō'nēŭ), anc. region of Asia Minor, occupying a narrow coastal strip of W Anatolia (now Turkey) and adjacent Aegean isls. (most of which now belong to Greece). Settled, presumably before 1000 B.C., by Greek settlers, the region became one of the most important of anc. times and a great center of Athenian art, literature, and philosophy. There came to be 12 important cities—Miletus, Myus, Priene, Samos, Ephesus, Colophon, Sebedus, Teos, Erythrae, Chios, Clazomenae, and Phocaea—linked in a loose religious league centering on the temple of Poseidon at Mycale. Smyrna, an Aeolian foundation, later joined the league. The cities sent traders and colonists into the Mediterranean as far as Spain and to the Black Sea shores. Invaded by Cimmerians (7th cent. B.C.) and, later, by Lydians, they came under Persian rule (6th cent. B.C.) under Cyrus the Great and thenceforth their fate hinged on the Persian-Greek wars. Alexander the Great of Macedon took them, and they continued important through the Roman and Byzantine empires. With the Turkish conquest, the cities and their culture were destroyed.

Ionia, county (□ 575; pop. 38,158), S central Mich.; ⊙ Ionia. Intersected by Grand R., and drained by Flat, Lookingglass, and Maple rivers. Livestock, dairy products, poultry, grain, corn, beans, peas, potatoes, fruit. Mfg. at Ionia, Belding, and Portland. Lake resorts. Organized 1837.

Ionia. 1 Town (pop. 301), Chickasaw co., NE Iowa, 12 mi. ESE of Charles City, in livestock and grain area. **2** City (pop. 6,412), ⊙ Ionia co., S central Mich., 30 mi. E of Grand Rapids and on Grand R., in agr. area (grain, fruit, livestock); mfg. (furniture, auto parts, pottery, tile, food products); ships beans. Has a state reformatory and a state hosp. for the criminally insane. Settled 1833; inc. as village 1865, as city 1873. **3** Town (pop. 120), Benton co., central Mo., 15 mi. S of Sedalia.

Ionian Islands (īō'nēŭn), Gr. *Ionioi Nesoi* or *Ionioi Nisoi*, island group in Ionian Sea, off W coast of Greece, constituting essentially the nomes of CORFU, LEUKAS, CEPHALONIA, and ZANTE, named for the 4 largest isls. The lesser isls. are ITHACA and PAXOS. Cythera, off S coast of Peloponnesus, was (until 1864) politically part of the Ionian Isls. Largely mountainous, the isls. reach their highest point at Mt. Ainos (5,315 ft.) on Cephalonia. The climate is warm, with c.50 in. annual rainfall. Currants (S), wine, olive oil, fruit are the leading products. The isls. had no unified history until they passed (14th–15th cent.) to Venice, which held them until the dissolution of the Venetian republic by the Treaty of Campo Formio (1797). The isls. went to France, but were seized (1799) by a Russo-Turkish fleet and constituted (1800–07) into a republic under Rus. occupation and Ottoman protection. In 1807, by the Treaty of Tilsit, Russia restored the islands to France. The Treaty of Paris (1815) established a British protectorate (□ 1,041) over the Ionian Islands, which were at last ceded to Greece in 1864. During their separate political existence, they were often called Heptanesos [Gr.,=7 islands], for the 7 largest isls.

Ionian Sea, section of Mediterranean Sea, bet. Greece (E) and Sicily and the foot of the Italian peninsula (W); connected by Strait of Otranto with Adriatic Sea and with Tyrrhenian Sea by Strait of Messina. Its principal ports are Patras, Corfu, Taranto (naval base), Catania, Syracuse. Ionian Isls. are off Greek coast. The Ionian Sea forms the gulfs of Patras, Corinth, Arta, Taranto, and Squillace.

Ionio (yô'nyô), province (□ 940; pop. 321,888), Apulia, S Italy; ⊙ Taranto. On Gulf of Taranto; narrow coastal plain, bordered by Apennine foothills. Agr. (olives, grapes, figs, cereals, tobacco); livestock raising. Fishing and mfg. at Taranto. Formed 1923 from Lecce prov.; until c.1937 called Taranto, a name restored once more in 1951.

Ionishkis, Lithuania: see JONISKIS.

Iora River (ēō'rŭ), in Georgian and Azerbaijan SSRs, rises on S slope of Mt. Barbalo in the E Greater Caucasus, flows S past Tianeti, and SE through dry steppe in lower course, to Mingechaur Reservoir on Kura R.; 180 mi. long. Irrigates Samgora steppe, E of Tiflis. Sometimes spelled Iori.

Ios (ē'ôs) or **Nios** (nē'ôs), Aegean island (□ 43; 1940 pop. 2,041) in the Cyclades, Greece, SSW of Naxos isl.; 36°42'N 25°25'E; 12 mi. long, 5 mi. wide; rises to 2,410 ft. Produces olive oil, wine, cotton, barley. Main town, Ios (1928 pop. 1,472), is on NW shore. One legend says it is the burial place of Homer.

Iosco (īŏs'kō), county (□ 547; pop. 10,906), NE Mich.; ⊙ Tawas City, Port on Tawas Bay. Bounded E by L. Huron; drained by Au Sable and Au Gres rivers and small Tawas R. Agr. area (livestock, grain, potatoes, corn, onions); dairy products. Commercial fishing, lumber milling, woodworking; cement plants. Resorts; hunting, fishing. Includes part of Huron Natl. Forest, also Tawas and Van Ettan lakes. Organized 1857.

Ioshkar-Ola or **Yoshkar-Ola** (yŭshkär"-ŭlä'), city (1939 pop. 27,052), ⊙ Mari Autonomous SSR, Russian SFSR, on Lesser Kokshaga R. and 400 mi. ENE of Moscow, on rail spur from Zelenodolsk; 56°38'N 47°55'E. Agr.-processing center (grain, flax, meat, sunflower oil); mfg. (movie projectors, furniture, bricks, vitamins), sawmilling. Has forestry and teachers colleges. Founded 1578 as Muscovite stronghold of Tsarev-Gorod na Kokshage; later renamed Tsarevokokshaisk; called (1918–29) Krasnokokshaisk.

Iota (īō'tŭ), village (pop. 1,162), Acadia parish, S La., 11 mi. NW of Crowley, in rice-growing area; rice, lumber, and feed mills; cotton gins. Inc. 1902.

Iotry, Lake (yōō'trē) (□ 45), Tuléar prov., SW Madagascar, 15 mi. SE of Morombe; 10 mi. long, 7 mi. wide.

Iowa (ī'ŭwŭ), state (land □ 55,986; with inland waters □ 56,280; 1950 pop. 2,621,073; 1940 pop. 2,538,268), U.S., in the Midwest, bordered by Minn. (N), Mo. (S), Wis. and Ill. (E), S.Dak. and Neb. (W); 24th in area, 22d in pop.; admitted 1846 as 29th state; ⊙ Des Moines. Iowa is rectangular in shape, c.300 mi. E-W, 200 mi. N-S. The "Hawkeye State," situated bet. the Mississippi (E) and the Missouri and Big Sioux (W), is largely a gently rolling plain underlain by nearly horizontal strata (limestone, dolomite, sandstone, shale); glaciation (except in the NE driftless area) leveled hills and filled valleys. Glacial till, often 100 ft. deep, covers the N and central part of the state, and loess the remainder. The most rugged areas are the hilly NE part (called Little Switzerland by Iowans) and the steep bluffs rising c.100–300 ft. above the Mississippi and Missouri. In general, the surface slopes gradually from Osceola co. (NW), where Ocheyedan Mound rises to an alt. of 1,675 ft. (highest in the state), to Lee co. (SE), where the alt. drops to 480 ft. Accordingly, the eastern ⅔ of the state drains SE into the Mississippi through the Des Moines, Skunk, Iowa, Cedar, Wapsipinicon, and Turkey rivers; and the western ⅓ drains SW and S into the Missouri through the Nishnabotna, Boyer, Little Sioux, Floyd, Nodaway, Little Platte, Thompson, and Chariton rivers. On the Mississippi at Keokuk is a large hydroelectric plant. There are groups of small glacial lakes (Spirit, Clear, Storm, Okoboji) in the N (especially in Dickinson co.). Many marshes and other wet lands in the poorly drained areas have been reclaimed for agr., so that Iowa has long been a national leader in the use of drainage tile. Originally most (c.85%) of the state was tall grass prairie with hardwood forests in the more humid E and along rivers. Of the original forest area c.50% (2,500,000 acres) remains, chiefly mixed hardwoods, birch, and pine. Iowa has a wet continental climate characterized by cold winters (with heavy snowfalls) and hot summers (with thundershowers). Typical temperature range is from −25°F. to 100°F. Rainfall ranges from 26–36 inches (NW to SE) and averages 32 inches. Because of its rich prairie soils, large level areas (ideally suitable for mechanized agr.), adequate growing season (140–170 days from NW to SE), and favorable rainfall regime (wet spring for plant growth, less wet summer for ripening), Iowa is the richest farm state in the U.S. and the symbol of the Corn Belt. Almost all (c.95%) of the state is in farms, c.65% in crops and 30% in pastures. Modern farming methods and soil conservation practices (sheet and gully erosion are serious problems) are typical. Iowa leads the nation in corn and oats (c.20% of U.S. crop), hogs, poultry, eggs, and in Western and native cattle fattened here for market. Other important farm products are hay, soybeans (c.15% of U.S. crop), barley, wheat, flaxseed, rye, potatoes, fruit, truck crops, sheep, turkeys. Corn is grown chiefly in the W and in wide belt across S central part of state, oats in the N and N central parts, soybeans in the E central part, hay in the NE, wheat in SW, and barley, rye, and flaxseed in NW. Most of the grain (corn, oats) is fed to livestock; the E and W lead in meat production; only the N and N central parts of the state are cash grain areas. The NE is the chief dairying region and the S is a pasture area. Although most of the pop. is engaged in farming, mfg. and mining are also important and widespread. The principal industry is the processing of farm products—meat, poultry, and egg packing; mfg. of dairy products; food canning; grain milling (corn syrup, oil, and starch; flour, feed, breakfast cereals). Other manufactures include machinery (agr. and industrial), washing machines, foundry products, furnaces, railroad equipment, auto accessories, fountain pens, buttons, calendars, cosmetics, cement, brick and tile. Iowa has extensive deposits of bituminous coal (mined chiefly bet. Des Moines and the Mo. line) in the center, S, and SW, and the state is a leading U.S. gypsum producer (mined around Fort Dodge). Limestone, dolomite, shale, clay, sand and gravel are quarried throughout much of the state and around Dubuque are lead and zinc deposits. The state has an even distribution of population, with most of the people living on farms and in small towns. Important cities include Des Moines (the largest), Sioux City, Davenport, Cedar Rapids, Waterloo, Dubuque, Council Bluffs, Ottumwa, Mason City, Clinton, Burlington, Fort Dodge, Marshalltown, Muscatine, Iowa City, Keokuk, Fort Madison, and Ames. The Mississippi and Missouri carry a large volume of barge traffic. Iowa is a leading state educationally. Literacy is almost universal, and there are many institutions of higher learning, including the State Univ. of Iowa (Iowa City), Iowa State Col. of Agriculture and Mechanic Arts (Ames), Drake Univ. (Des Moines), Grinnell Col. (Grinnell), Coe Col. (Cedar Rapids), and Cornell Col. (Mt. Vernon). Iowa was visited by Marquette and Jolliet in 1673 as they traveled down the Mississippi, and later by La Salle. They were followed by other Frenchmen, fur traders who crossed the land and paddled up most of the rivers. Late in 18th cent. Julien Dubuque opened lead mines near the present city of Dubuque. Iowa became part of the U.S. by the Louisiana Purchase in 1803. After an influx of settlers, who displaced the Indians, Iowa was organized as a territory in 1838. A system of public schools was established in 1839 and soon colleges were founded. Iowans built a rural civilization like that of New England, from which many of them came. Later immigrants included Germans, Czechs, Dutch, and Scandinavians. With the coming of railroads (by 1869 state had been spanned), Iowa became especially prosperous. In the Civil War, Iowa, a land of small independent farmers, sided with the Union. During the hard times of the late 19th cent. the Granger Movement and Greenback and Populist parties flourished. Generally, however, agr. prosperity grew, furthered by considerable crop and livestock research and energetic farm organizations. In recent years more industry has been attracted into the state and a well-balanced economy achieved. For further information see also the articles on the cities, towns, physical features, and the 99 counties: ADAIR, ADAMS, ALLAMAKEE, APPANOOSE, AUDUBON, BENTON, BLACK HAWK, BOONE, BREMER, BUCHANAN, BUENA VISTA, BUTLER, CALHOUN, CARROLL, CASS, CEDAR, CERRO GORDO, CHEROKEE, CHICKASAW, CLARKE, CLAY, CLAYTON, CLINTON, CRAWFORD, DALLAS, DAVIS, DECATUR, DELAWARE, DES MOINES, DICKINSON, DUBUQUE, EMMET, FAYETTE, FLOYD, FRANKLIN, FREMONT, GREENE, GRUNDY, GUTHRIE, HAMILTON, HANCOCK, HARDIN, HARRISON, HENRY, HOWARD, HUMBOLDT, IDA, IOWA, JACKSON, JASPER, JEFFERSON, JOHNSON, JONES, KEOKUK, KOSSUTH, LEE, LINN, LOUISA, LUCAS, LYON, MADISON, MAHASKA, MARION, MARSHALL, MILLS, MITCHELL, MONONA, MONROE, MONTGOMERY, MUSCATINE, O'BRIEN, OSCEOLA, PAGE, PALO ALTO, PLYMOUTH, POCAHONTAS, POLK, POTTAWATTAMIE, POWESHIEK, RINGGOLD, SAC, SCOTT, SHELBY, SIOUX, STORY, TAMA, TAYLOR, UNION, VAN BUREN, WAPELLO, WARREN, WASHINGTON, WAYNE, WEBSTER, WINNEBAGO, WINNESHIEK, WOODBURY, WORTH, WRIGHT.

Iowa. **1** County (□ 584; pop. 15,835), E central Iowa; ⊙ Marengo. Rolling prairie agr. area (cattle, hogs, poultry, corn, oats) drained by Iowa R. and by forks of English R. Formed 1843. **2** County (□ 761; pop. 19,610), S Wis.; ⊙ Dodgeville. Bordered N by Wisconsin R.; also drained by Pecatonica and Blue rivers. Dairying and stock-raising area, with dairy-products processing as chief industry. Lead and zinc deposits. Includes Tower Hill State Park. Formed 1829.

Iowa, village (pop. 1,125), Calcasieu parish, SW La., 11 mi. E of Lake Charles.

Iowa City, city (pop. 27,212), ⊙ Johnson co., E Iowa, on both banks of Iowa R. and 23 mi. SSE of Cedar Rapids; mfg. (calendars, yearbooks, dairy and wood products, feed, beverages, concrete). Limestone quarries near by. Municipal airport. Seat of State Univ. of Iowa (established 1847; opened 1855) with a fine general hosp. Library of state historical society, and U.S. veterans' hosp. here. Near by are the state sanatorium for the tubercular and the villages of the AMANA Society. Town was founded 1839 as capital of Iowa Territory, and inc. 1853. Seat of govt. was moved to Des Moines in 1857 and the old stone capitol (begun 1840) was given to the univ. With arrival of railroad (1855), city became an important outfitting center for westward trails. Growth further stimulated by opening of univ.

Iowa Falls, city (pop. 4,900), Hardin co., central Iowa, on Iowa R. (dammed here for power) and 38 mi. NNW of Marshalltown; rail junction; agr.-processing center (packed poultry and eggs, dairy products, feed, tankage); concrete blocks. Limestone quarries near by. Has Ellsworth Jr. Col. (coeducational) and mus. of pioneer relics. Annual state Baptist convention held here. Settled 1853, inc. 1889.

Iowa Park, town (pop. 2,110), Wichita co., N Texas, 11 mi. W of Wichita Falls, in oil, agr. area (cotton, cattle, wheat); mfg. of oil-field supplies. Texas-Okla. Fair, Southwestern Oil Exposition held here. Seat of agr. experiment station.

Iowa River, central and SE Iowa, rises in East and West branches in Hancock co., N Iowa, flows generally SE from their junction near Belmond, past Iowa Falls (where it forms a gorge with rapids), Marshalltown, and Iowa City, to the Mississippi 20 mi. S of Muscatine; 329 mi. long, from head of longest headstream.

Io-zan, Japan: see HOROBETSU.

Ipala (ēpä'lä), town (1950 pop. 2,003), Chiquimula dept., E Guatemala, at NE foot of the volcano Ipala (5,480 ft.), 14 mi. SSW of Chiquimula; road center; corn, wheat, livestock.

Ipameri (ēpümĭrē'), city (pop. 7,192), SE Goiás, central Brazil, on railroad and 100 mi. SE of Goiânia; cattle-shipping center; meat processing, rice hulling. Rock crystals and rutile exploited in area. Airfield. Formerly spelled Ipamery.

Ipamu, Belgian Congo: see MANGAI.

Ipanema (ēpünä'mü). **1** City (pop. 1,965), E Minas Gerais, Brazil, 35 mi. NNE of Manhuassu; agr. trade. Formerly called José Pedro. **2** Village, São Paulo, Brazil: see SOROCABA.

Ipati, Greece: see HYPATE.

Ipatovo (ēpä'tüvŭ), village (1926 pop. 9,877), N Stavropol Territory, Russian SFSR, on railroad, on Kalaus R. and 60 mi. NE of Stavropol; flour milling, dairying; metalworks. Until 1930s, Vinodelnoye.

Ipauçu (ēpousōō'), city (pop. 2,344), SW central São Paulo, Brazil, on railroad and 16 mi. E of Ourinhos; coffee processing, distilling, pottery mfg. Formerly spelled Ipaussú.

Ipava (īpā'vü), village (pop. 667), Fulton co., W central Ill., 20 mi. SW of Canton, in agr. and bituminous-coal area; ships grain.

Ipeh or **Ipei** (both: yē'bā'), town, ⊙ Ipeh co. (pop. 45,611), N Kwangsi prov., China, 50 mi. NNW of Ishan, near Kweichow line; rice, wheat, beans. Until 1914 called Anhwa.

Ipek, Yugoslavia: see PEC.

Ipel River (ĭ'pĕl), Slovak *Ipel'*, Ger. *Eipel* (ī'pül), Hung. *Ipoly* (ĭ'poi), in S Slovakia, Czechoslovakia, rises on S slope of Slovak Ore Mts., 25 mi. ENE of Zvolen; flows c.50 mi. S, then generally SW, forming Czechoslovak-Hung. border, to the Danube E of Esztergom; total length c.150 mi.

Iphofen (ĭp'hō"fün), town (pop. 2,328), Middle Franconia, W Bavaria, Germany, 16 mi. ESE of Würzburg; gypsum, flour, and lumber milling; wine-growing. Has Gothic church. Sand and limestone quarries in area.

Ipiales (ēpyä'läs), town (pop. 8,343), Nariño dept., SW Colombia, in the Andes, on Carchi R. and 35 mi. SW of Pasto, on Ecuador border opposite Tulcán (linked by bridge and highway); alt. 7,516 ft. Customs station, and trading and textile-milling center in agr. region (corn, wheat, sugar cane, coffee, cacao, cotton, fruit, stock). Airport. In hills near by is the shrine of Nuestra Señora de las Lajas.

Ipiaú (ēpyäōō'), city (pop. 3,806), Bahia, Brazil, on the Rio de Contas and 23 mi. SE of Jiquié; ships cacao and coffee. Until 1944, called Rio Novo.

Ipin (ē'pĭn', yē'pĭn'), town (pop. 80,439), ⊙ Ipin co. (pop. 799,940), SW Szechwan prov., China, near Yunnan border, on Yangtze R., at mouth of Min R., and 135 mi. SW of Chungking city; commercial port and head of navigation on Yangtze R.; trade in tung oil and medicinal herbs; match mfg.; rice, wheat, sugar cane, sweet potatoes. Until 1913 called Süchow and Suifu.

Iping (ī'pĭng), village and parish (pop. 432), W Sussex, England, on Rother R. and 3 mi. WNW of Midhurst; paper milling.

Ipiranga (ēpērăng'gü). **1** City (pop. 992), S central Paraná, Brazil, 26 mi. WNW of Ponta Grossa; coffee and lard processing; maté, rice, corn, grapes. Coal deposits. Formerly spelled Ypiranga. **2** Town, E Rio Grande do Sul, Brazil, 5 mi. NNW of Gravataí, 15 mi. NE of Porte Alegre; oil refinery.

Ipiros, Greece: see EPIRUS.

Ipixuna (ēpēshōō'nü), city (pop. 732), N central Maranhão, Brazil, on Mearim R. and 125 mi. S of São Luís; cotton, manioc, sugar. Until 1944, called São Luís Gonzaga.

Ipoh (ēpō'), largest town (pop. 80,894) of Perak, W Malaya, 110 mi. NNW of Kuala Lumpur, on railroad and on Kinta R.; leading tin-mining center of Malaya and transportation hub of Kinta Valley; Br. resident; marble quarry and rubber plantations near by. Pop. is 70% Chinese, 18% Indian. Succeeded Taiping as greatest tin center of Malaya.

Ipojuca (ēpōōzhōō'kü), city (pop. 1,451), E Pernambuco, NE Brazil, near the Atlantic, 27 mi. SSW of Recife; sugar, coconuts. Clay deposits.

Ipoly River, Czechoslovakia and Hungary: see IPEL RIVER.

Ipolysag, Czechoslovakia: see SAHY.

Iporanga (ēpōōrăng'gü), city (pop. 453), S São Paulo, Brazil, on Ribeira R. and 75 mi. SSW of Itapetininga; lead, silver, vanadium, gold, copper deposits. Formerly spelled Yporanga.

Ippesheim (ĭ'püs-hīm), village (pop. 745), Middle Franconia, W Bavaria, Germany, 10 mi. SSE of Kitzingen; vineyards. Has 17th-cent. church with Romanesque tower.

Ippy (ēpē'), village, central Ubangi-Shari, Fr. Equatorial Africa, 45 mi. NE of Bambari; cotton center; diamond mining in vicinity. R.C. and Protestant missions.

Iprump, Germany: see HASBERGEN-IPRUMP.

Ipsala (ĭpsälä'), Turkish *Ipsala*, anc. *Cypsela*, village (pop. 2,931), Adrianople prov., Turkey in Europe, near Maritsa R. (Greek frontier), 50 mi. SSW of Adrianople; wheat, rice, rye, sugar beets.

Ipsambul, Egypt: see ABU SIMBEL.

Ipsara, Greece: see PSARA.

Ipsheim (ĭps'hīm), village (pop. 1,200), Middle Franconia, W Bavaria, Germany, 4 mi. NE of Windsheim; grain, hops, sheep.

Ipsus (ĭp'süs), anc. town of central Phrygia, W central Asia Minor, whose site is NW of present-day Afyonkarahisar, Turkey. Antigonus I was here defeated and slain by his rivals Seleucus and Lysimachus in 301 B.C.

Ipswich (ĭp'swĭch), city (pop. 26,218), SE Queensland, Australia, on Bremer R. and 20 mi. WSW of Brisbane; principal coal-mining center of state; woolen mills.

Ipswich, county borough (1931 pop. 87,502; 1951 census 104,788), ⊙ Suffolk, England, in SE of co., at head of Orwell R. estuary, 70 mi. NE of London; 52°3'N 1°10'E. Port and industrial center; railroad workshops, mfg. (leather, shoes, agr. machinery, nonferrous metals, electrical equipment, feed cakes, sugar). Has many old bldgs., including 1567 Sparrowe's House, 1477 grammar school, and several 15th-cent. churches. Natural History Mus. is here. Wolsey's Gate is relic of col. founded by Cardinal Wolsey, b. here. Ipswich is of anc. origin; it was the Saxon Gyppeswyk (after upper course of Orwell R., which is called Gipping R.). Was residence of Gainsborough.

Ipswich, town (pop. 1,170), St. Elizabeth parish, W Jamaica, on Kingston–Montego Bay RR and 21 mi. SSE of Montego Bay, in agr. region (corn, vegetables, livestock).

Ipswich. 1 Town (pop. 6,895), including Ipswich village (pop. 4,952), Essex co., NE Mass., on Ipswich R. (here crossed by bridge built 1764) and 11 mi. NNE of Salem; summer resort; hosiery, stone monuments; truck; shellfishery. Settled 1633 in area called Agawam; inc. 1634. 2 City (pop. 1,058), ⊙ Edmunds co., N S.Dak., 25 mi. W of Aberdeen, in farming and cattle-raising region.

Ipswich Bay, E Mass., bight (c.6 mi. wide) of the Atlantic, E of Ipswich; sheltered on S and E by Cape Ann.

Ipswich River, NE Mass., rises in NE Middlesex co., flows c.35 mi. generally NE, past Ipswich, to S end of Plum Island Sound (arm of Ipswich Bay), N of Cape Ann.

Ipu (ēpōō'), city (pop. 4,874), W Ceará, Brazil, on E slope of Serra Grande, 50 mi. SSW of Sobral, and on Camocim-Crateús RR; cotton, sugar, tobacco, skins. Gold, nitrate, iron deposits near by.

Ipueiras (ēpwā'rŭs), city (pop. 1,399), W Ceará, Brazil, on Camocim-Crateús RR and 60 mi. SSW of Sobral; cotton, sugar, tobacco.

Ipun Island, Chile: see CHONOS ARCHIPELAGO.

Iput River or **Iput' River** (ēpōōt'yŭ), W European USSR, rises E of Klimovichi (Belorussian SSR) in Smolensk-Moscow Upland, flows 295 mi. E, S, and WSW in wide bend, past Surazh (Bryansk oblast) and Dobrush, to Sozh R. at Gomel. Navigable for 20 mi., to Dobrush.

Iqlid or **Eqlid** (both: ĕklēd'), town, Seventh Prov., in Fars, S central Iran, 90 mi. N of Shiraz.

Iqlit (ĭk'lēt), village (pop. 6,839), Aswan prov., S Egypt, 30 mi. N of Aswan; cereals, dates.

Iquique (ēkē'kā), city (1940 pop. 38,094, 1949 estimate 35,985), ⊙ Tarapacá prov. and Iquique dept. (□ 10,883; 1940 pop. 77,304), N Chile, port on the Pacific, 900 mi. N of Santiago, 250 mi. NNE of Antofagasta, at edge of Atacama Desert; 20°12'S 70°9'W. Rail terminus; trading and mfg. center. Ships nitrates, iodine, salt. Petroleum refinery, sugar refinery, cement factory, fish-canning plants. Airport. It is linked by rail with rich nitrate fields for which it serves as outlet. With a moderate but almost totally dry climate, it depends for its water supply on the oasis of Pica, 55 mi. SE. On its N coast are considerable guano deposits. In the S it is adjoined by Cavancha, a beach resort on Cavancha Peninsula. Iquique harbor is protected by Serrano Isl. City was founded in 16th cent. in connection with the discovery of the rich Guantajaya silver mines. Taken (1879) from Peru in the War of the Pacific, it was ceded to Chile by Ancón treaty (1883). In 1868 and 1877 it was partially destroyed by earthquakes.

Iquitos (ēkē'tōs), city (pop. 34,231), ⊙ Loreto dept. and Maynas prov. (in 1940: □ 52,409; enumerated pop. 103,331, plus estimated 60,000 Indians), NE Peru, port on left bank of the upper Amazon and 900 mi. W of Manaus (Brazil), 640 mi. NNE of Lima, at Nanay R. mouth, c.2,300 mi. upstream from the Atlantic, from which it can be reached by ocean-going vessels drawing 14 ft.; 3°45'S 72°15'W. Has tropical, humid climate. The farthest inland port of major size in the world, it trades in rubber, balata, chicle, medicinal plants, tagua nuts, timber, cotton, rice, coffee, tobacco, hides. Industries include sawmilling, cotton ginning, liquor distilling, soapmaking, mfg. of straw hats. Airport. Its port facilities comprise repair yards and drydock. It prospered during the rubber boom of the early 20th cent. Founded 1863 as Peruvian settlement at site of a fishing village which dates back to 16th cent. Maynas prov., of which Iquitos is ⊙, was called Bajo Amazonas until 1943, when part of the prov. was taken to form new provs. At Nanay R. mouth near by (SW) are lumber mills (mahogany, cedar), considered to be the largest in Latin America. Adjoining S is a small naval base. Although there is launch service some distance up Marañón and Ucayali rivers, the Andes are so formidable a barrier to transport that Iquitos has been oriented toward the Atlantic rather than the Pacific.

Ira, town (pop. 141), Rutland co., W central Vt., 6 mi. SW of Rutland; lumber, dairy products.

Iraan (ī'rŭ-ăn", īrăn'), village (pop. 1,196), Pecos co., extreme W Texas, on Pecos R. and c.55 mi. E of Fort Stockton; oil-field trading point; agr. (livestock, grain).

Irabu-shima (ērăbōō'shĭmä), volcanic island (□ 15; 1950 pop. 11,431, including adjacent Shimoji-shima) of Sakishima Isls., in the Ryukyus, bet. East China Sea (W) and Philippine Sea (E), 3.5 mi. W of Miyako-jima; 5 mi. long, 3 mi. wide. Generally low, fertile (sugar cane). Fishing. Just off its W coast is Shimoji-shima (3 mi. long, 1.5 mi. wide). Coral reef encircles both isls.

Iracoubo (ērăkōōbō'), town (commune pop. 1,109), N Fr. Guiana, near the coast, 70 mi. WNW of Cayenne; coffee, sugar cane, corn, fruit.

Iraí (ēräē'), city (pop. 1,439), N Rio Grande do Sul, Brazil, on Uruguay R. (Santa Catarina border) and 70 mi. WNW of Erechim; mineral springs. Semiprecious stones near by. Old spelling, Irahy.

Irak: see IRAQ.

Iraklia, Greece: see HERAKLEIA.

Iraklion, nome, Crete: see HERAKLEION.

Iraklion, city, Crete: see CANDIA.

Irala (ērä'lä), town (dist. pop. 1,174), Alto Paraná dept., SE Paraguay, near upper Paraná R. (Argentina border), 115 mi. ESE of Villarrica; maté, lumber.

Iramba Plateau (ērăm'bä), central Tanganyika, c.100 mi. N of Manyoni. Gold deposits.

Irámuco (ērä'mōōkō), town (pop. 7,028), Guanajuato, central Mexico, near E shore of L. Cuitzeo, 11 mi. WSW of Acámbaro; grain, sugar cane, fruit, vegetables, stock.

Iran (ĭrăn', ērän', īrăn'), independent kingdom (□ 630,000; 1940 pop. 16,549,837; 1949 pop. estimate 18,387,000) of SW Asia, universally known in English as **Persia** (pûr'zhŭ, –shŭ) before 1935, and still commonly called by that name; ⊙ Teheran (Tehran). Bounded S by Gulf of Oman and the Persian Gulf of the Arabian Sea, W by Iraq and Turkey, N by the Azerbaijan and Armenian SSRs, the Caspian Sea, and the Turkmen SSR of USSR, and E by Afghanistan and Pakistan, Iran constitutes a land bridge bet. S Asia and the approaches to Europe and Africa. Topographically, it consists of a vast central plateau (4,000 ft. high), ringed by great mtn. arcs sweeping around the plateau's N (Elburz system) and W and S (Zagros system) margins. These folded mtn. barriers, rising to 18,600 ft. in Mt. Demavend of the Elburz system, separate the plateau from narrow coastal lowlands along the Caspian (N) and Persian Gulf (S) shores. The country's climate corresponds to the distinct Iranian type, marked by extreme continentality, very low rainfall and high winds, which intensify the temperature extremes. These extremes occur as the plateau is alternately exposed to the influences of the dry, hot monsoonal summer from NW India and the Siberian winter anticyclone sweeping in from the NE. The mtn. barriers restrict maritime influences to the coastal lowlands, creating the special humid subtropical regime in the Caspian lowland and the hot, oppressive Persian Gulf summer climate. Rainfall of 40 inches annually occurs only in NW Iran and on the Caspian shore. Arid plateau conditions, with less than 5 inches of rainfall in SE, have caused the formation of the great interior salt deserts, the Dasht-i-Kavir (NW) and the Dasht-i-Lut (SE). Because of the aridity, there are few perennial streams. The Caspian receives the Aras, Sefid Rud, Gurgan, and Atrek rivers; the Persian Gulf, the Karun R. Zaindeh R. is the principal stream of the interior drainage plateau. Of the many salt lakes and marshes, L. Urmia (NW) is the largest. Pop. is densest (over 60 per sq. mi.) in the high-rainfall areas and in the few isolated, irrigated agr. sites. The majority (60%) of pop. belong to the Iranian language group. They include the Shiite Persians (the dominant element), the tribal Sunni Kurds of Kurdistan, the Caspian coastal splinter groups (Talishi, Gilaki, Mazanderani), and the Baluch tribes of Iranian Baluchistan (SE). Turkic elements (35% of total pop.) predominate along country's N margins and include the Turks of Azerbaijan and Khamseh (NW) and the Turkmen of Khurasan (NE). The remainder is made up of various small groups, such as the Jews, the Gregorian Armenians, the Nestorian Syriac-speaking Assyrians, Yezidis and R.C. Chaldeans of Azerbaijan, and the Zoroastrians (Parsis or Ghebers) centered at Yezd. Iran's tribal pop. (2–3 million) includes, in addition to the Kurds and Baluchis, the Turkic Qashqai tribes and the Lur tribes, the latter consisting of the Little Lurs (Faili) and the Great Lurs (Bakhtiari, Mamassani, Kuhgalu). There is an Arab minority in Khuzistan (notably in the Dasht-i-Mishan). About 80% of the people of Iran are dependent on agr. in an area suffering from great disadvantages in terrain and climate. Only 10% of the land is cultivated (of which ⅓ is under irrigation) and 15% is available for grazing, while the rest is mountainous or forest-covered or barren desert. Another 20–30% could be cultivated if irrigation were expanded. Primitive shifting cultivation methods are the rule in the few fertile patches, irrigated by *qanats* (underground channels), wells, or rudimentary canals. Only the Caspian subtropical littoral and parts of Azerbaijan have favorable growing conditions, resulting in an exportable surplus and in the concentration in these regions of the chief commercial crops. Wheat and barley are the principal food crops, covering ⅔ of the land under cultivation. Millet and corn are of minor importance; rice grows on the Caspian coast and where irrigation water is abundant (Khuzistan, Shiraz). Cotton is the leading cash crop and is associated with sericulture in the Caspian provs., where tea (at Lahijan), tobacco, and citrus fruit are also grown. The Iranian sugar supply stems chiefly from beets (refineries at Karaj, Kahrizak, and Veramin near Teheran, Marvdasht near Shiraz, Shahabad, Miyanduab, Arak, and Meshed) and some cane cultivation on the Caspian and in Khuzistan. Fruit and nuts form an important element in the Iranian diet; these are figs, peaches, melons, pomegranates, while raisins, dried apricots, almonds, and pistachio nuts are also exported. Olives grow in the Rudbar-Manjil area of the Elburz and dates along the Persian Gulf. The arid plateau sections produce vegetable dyes (indigo, henna, madder, saffron) and gums (gum arabic, asafetida, and tragacanth). The cultivation of the opium poppy is restricted by the govt. Stock raising, chiefly under tribal nomadic conditions of transhumance in the Zagros ranges, plays a major role in the economy. Sheep (50%) and goats (25%) constitute the largest herds, with lesser numbers of horned cattle, mules, horses, and camels. Forestry is profitable only on the Caspian slopes of the Elburz; and there are fisheries in the Caspian (sturgeon, caviar), under joint Soviet-Iranian operation, and in the Persian Gulf (sardines). Iran's otherwise indifferent mineral resources are eclipsed by the petroleum deposits, in Khuzistan in the foothills of the Zagros, whose exploitation has put the country in 4th place among the world's oil producers. The production centers—Masjid-i-Sulaiman, Haft Kel, Gach Saran, Agha Jari, White Oil Springs, and Lali—are linked by pipe line with the great refinery of Abadan or with the loading port of Bandar Mashur. A smaller field, Naft-i-Shah, on the Iraq border is linked by pipe line with the Kermanshah refinery. An oil concession, 1st granted in 1901 to W. K. D'Arcy, an Englishman, passed later to the Anglo-Iranian Oil Company, whose 1933 accord was ended in 1951 by nationalization of the Iranian oil industry. Among Iran's other minerals are coal (mined at Shimshak, Abiak, Zirab), copper and lead (near Anarak, Abbasabad), iron oxide (Hormuz isl.), turquoise (near Nishapur), and sulphur and salt. Iran's industry was restricted to handicrafts and small-scale plants until a program of industrialization was started in 1930s by Riza Shah, who developed a modern food-processing (flour, rice, sugar, alcohol) and light-mfg. industry. Cotton goods are produced by the modern plants of Shahi and Behshahr and the older centers of Isfahan, Kazvin, Kerman, Meshed, and Yezd, many of which also have a wool-weaving industry. Silk textiles are made at Chalus, and jute is milled at Resht. Other modern plants (mainly in Teheran area) make metal goods, armaments, cement, glass, matches, paper, soap, and leather goods. Rugs are among Iran's best-known exports and continue to be woven on a handicraft basis in such centers as Kerman, Kashan, Isfahan, and Hamadan. Gold- and silverwork, mosaics, embroidery, and wood carving are also carried on by time-honored handicraft methods. Iran's main urban centers are Teheran, Tabriz, Isfahan, Meshed, Shiraz, Resht, Hamadan, Kermanshah, Ardebil, Yezd, and Kerman. These cities are linked by an inadequate transportation system of a few year-round roads and the Trans-Iranian RR and its branches. This rail system (begun in 1927) links Teheran with Tabriz, with the Persian Gulf ports of Khurramshahr and Bandar Shahpur, with Yezd and Meshed, and with the Caspian port of Bandar Shah. Tabriz is also connected by rail with Julfa on USSR border, and the W Pakistan railroad from Quetta penetrates to Zahidan in SE Iran, both lines dating from First World War. The lower Karun R. is the only navigable waterway, and there are airfields in all principal cities. Iran's ports on the Persian Gulf include, in addition to the modern rail termini, the older and once-flourishing harbors of Bushire and Bandar Abbas, which have only road connections with the interior. On the Caspian, the railhead of Bandar Shah is rivaled by the ports of Pahlevi and Naushahr. Nearly all of the country's foreign trade is sea-borne and the bulk passes through the port of Khurramshahr. Iran exports, aside from petroleum (its chief source of wealth), rugs, dried fruit, medicinal plants and seeds, gums, and wool. Its imports are sugar and tea; cotton, silk, and woolen goods; metal products and machinery, automobiles, and pharmaceuticals. Iran has several Shiite pilgrimage centers, notably Meshed, Qum, and Rai (near Teheran); and several modern Caspian seaside resorts (Babulsar, Ramsar). The earliest political organization in the territory of modern Iran was the state of ELAM in modern Khuzistan, which flourished after 1200 B.C. and was conquered by the Assyrians in 645 B.C. By that time, the anc. Persians, a nomadic tribe that presumably had filtered S from the Caucasus onto the Iranian plateau, was established in Fars (the anc. Persis) under rulers that claimed descent from one Achaemenes (Hakhamanesh). The Persians were associated with MEDIA in the overthrow of Assyria in late-7th cent. B.C., but soon emerged under Cyrus II (the Great) as the dominant power; and, having captured the Median capital of Ecbatana in 550 B.C., supplanted the great Median empire. In an amazingly short time, Cyrus extended his rule NW to Asia Minor, where he defeated Croesus, the Lydian king, and thus established the greatness of the Achaemenian Persian Empire. Under Darius I (the Great; ruled 521–485 B.C.), the empire reached its greatest territorial extent: E to NW India and Afghanistan, NW to Danube, and W to Egypt. Its capitals were Persepolis, Susa, and Ecbatana. However, in Greece the Achaemenids became embroiled in the fruitless Persian Wars and were defeated at Marathon (490 B.C.) under Darius and again at Salamis (480 B.C.) under Xerxes I. Through the late-5th and early 4th-cent. B.C., internecine struggles weakened the Achaemenian empire, and with the rise of Alexander the Great, the end came. Alexander crossed the Hellespont in 334, defeated the Persians in a series of battles (Granicus, Issus, Gaugamela), and by 328 had the entire empire under its control. Upon Alexander's death, his empire was torn apart by the quarrels of his Hellenistic successors, the Diadochi; and Persia fell (after 312) to Seleucus I and his successors, the Seleucids. The NE prov. (BACTRIA, PARTHIA), however, broke away from the Seleucids in c.250 B.C. and established independent and expanding states. Under Arsaces I and his successors (the Arsacids), the Parthians extended their rule W to the Euphrates and advanced in their victorious struggles against Rome through the 1st cent. B.C. They were overthrown and their capital, Ctesiphon, captured in A.D. c.226 by the Sassanids, a native Persian dynasty founded by Ardashir (Artaxerxes) I and named for his ancestor Sassan. The Sassanids, who rejected Hellenism and revived the Achaemenian era with its Zoroastrian religion, were finally defeated in 642 at Nehavend by the rising Arab caliphate state. Under Arab rule, Persia was converted to Islam, although some of its native religions (Zoroastrianism, Manichaeism) still survived. Persia began to flourish in the scientific and literary spheres during this period and many of the notable figures under the caliphate were Persian-born: Avicenna and Rhazes in medicine, Firdausi and Omar Khayyam in poetry and mathematics, Al-Gazel (Ghazali) in theology, Tabari in history are best known. After early control by the Omayyad caliphs, the Shiite faction, which had flourished in Persia after the schism, aided the Abbasids in obtaining control of the caliphate in 750. Under the Abbasids, the center of gravity of the caliphate moved eastward toward Persia with the establishment of the capital of Baghdad. But, following the dynasty's prime (786–809) under Harun al-Rashid, a slow process of disintegration began with the rise of several independent dynasties on Persian soil during 9th cent. These were in quick succession the Tahirids (820–872) of Khurasan, the Saffarids (867–908) of Seistan, and the Samanids (892–999) of Bukhara. Under the Samanids, Persian scholarship flourished, but the dynasty fell to the rising power of Ghazni, which maintained its control over Persia until the coming of the Seljuk Turks. These horsemen from the Turkmen steppes ruled the country (1037–1194) under nominal caliphate sovereignty and reached their zenith under Malikshah (1072–92) and his illustrious Persian vizier Nizam al-Mulk. The Seljuk realm disintegrated in 12th cent., and Persia passed to the Turkish Khwarizm (Khorezm) shahs, whose territory reached its greatest extent under Muhammad (1200–20). Now Jenghiz Khan was approaching and his Mongols spread destruction as they swept (1221) through N Persia. His grandson Hulagu captured Baghdad in 1258 and thus effectively ended the long rule of the Abbasid caliphate. Hulagu founded the Mongol kingdom of the Ilkhans with his seat at Maragheh. The Ilkhan realm was divided (c.1330) into minor dynasties, all of which fell (1380s) before the renewed Mongol sweep under Tamerlane. After his death (1405), his successors (the Timurids), notably Shah Rukh (until 1447), ruled Persia through 15th cent., until internecine strife encouraged the rise of a new native Persian dynasty, the Safavids (1499–1736). Founded at Tabriz by Ismail (died 1524), who made Shiism the state religion, this dynasty reached its peak under Abbas I (the Great; 1587–1628). Abbas reorganized the army, defeated the Ottoman Turks, and, with English aid, expelled the Portuguese from Hormuz; he founded the port Bandar Abbas. His creation of a strong state with capital at Isfahan and with its boundaries nearly those of Sassanian times, and the secularization of the royal power marked the national rebirth of Persia. The fall of the Safavids was brought about (1722) by the raids of the Ghilzai Afghans, but Persian power rose anew under Nadir Shah, an Afshar tribesman from Khurasan, who expelled the Afghans (1729–30). His greatest adventure was the invasion of India (1731), from which he brought back fabulous wealth, including the Koh-i-noor diamond and the Peacock Throne of the Moguls. Nadir Shah, assassinated in 1747, was followed by the brief Zand dynasty (1750–79) of Fars, under Karim Khan, a humane ruler who moved his capital to Shiraz. After his death, the rival Kajar (Qajar) tribe, led by Agha Mohammed Khan, seized power and founded (1794) a dynasty (⊙ Teheran) that was to last until 1925. During the Kajar rule, Persia gradually lost ground under the increasing pressure of the European nations. Fath Ali (1797–1834) ceded the Caucasian territories beyond the Aras R. to Russia by the treaties of Gulistan (1813) and Turkmanchai (1828); and under Nasr-ed-Din (1848–96), Persia was forced to accept (1857) the British-aided independence of Afghanistan and to evacuate Herat. Nasr-ed-Din, however, was the 1st to shake the country loose from its inertia, was interested in modernization, and favored British influence. Under his successor, Muzaffar-ed-Din (1896–1906), Russia's influence reached its peak; and by the Anglo-Russian agreement of 1907, spheres of influence were created in Persia. These lasted until after the First World War, during which the country underwent actual occupation by the 2 powers. A constitutional govt. had been granted (1906) by the Shah after a revolutionary outbreak; but in 1921, Riza (Reza) Khan, an army officer, effected a coup d'état and established a military dictatorship. He was subsequently (1925) elected shah, which thus created the new Pahlevi dynasty. Riza Shah, ruling the country with an iron hand, introduced sorely needed reforms, reorganized the army, and made a definite effort to industrialize the country. During the Second World War, however, Britain and the USSR charged Iran with pro-Axis activity, occupied the country, and forced the abdication (1941) of Riza Shah in favor of his son, Mohammed Riza Shah. Foreign troops were withdrawn in 1946 after a short-lived, Soviet-supported autonomous movement in Azerbaijan had been suppressed under U.N. direction. Following the abortive Seven-Year Plan (1949) for the development of the country, Iran once more asserted itself economically, in forcing (1951) the nationalization of the British-owned oil industry. A constitutional monarchy, Iran has a bicameral legislature: the upper house (senate) was convened for the 1st time in 1949 and is composed of 60 members, 30 appointed by the shah and 30 elected by the people; the lower house (Majlis) consists of elected representatives. Executive power is vested in a cabinet whose premier is appointed by the shah subject to parliamentary approval. As part of Riza Shah's reforms, Iran was divided (1928) into 26 provs., later (1934) increased to 32. In 1938, the country was divided into 10 provs., known as *ustan* or *ostan*. These provs., officially identified by numbers, but also known by the name of the largest component former prov., are: First Prov. or GILAN (⊙ Resht), Second Prov. or TEHERAN (⊙ Teheran), Third Prov. or E AZERBAIJAN (⊙ Tabriz), Fourth Prov. or W Azerbaijan (⊙ Rizaiyeh), Fifth Prov. or KERMANSHAH (⊙ Kermanshah), Sixth Prov. or KHUZISTAN (⊙ Ahwaz), Seventh Prov. or FARS (⊙ Shiraz), Eighth Prov. or KERMAN (⊙ Kerman), Ninth Prov. or KHURASAN (⊙ Meshed), and Tenth Prov. or ISFAHAN (⊙ Isfahan).

Iraniel (ĭrŭnyĕl'), town (pop. 8,709), S Travancore, India, 30 mi. SE of Trivandrum; coir rope and mats, copra, palmyra jaggery. Monazite workings near by. Formerly spelled Eraniel. Also called Neyyur.

Iran Mountains (ĭrăn'), range in N central Borneo, on border bet. Sarawak (W) and Indonesian Borneo (E), c.170 mi. S of Brunei town; extends c.50 mi. N-S; rises to c.8,000 ft.

Iranshahr (ērănshä'hûr), town (1942 pop. 2,245), Eighth Prov., in Baluchistan, SE Iran, 15 mi. E of old fortress of Bampur, which it has largely superseded as an agr. center; dates, corn, barley, cotton. Sometimes called Fahraj, it is commonly identified with anc. *Pura*, the ⊙ Gedrosia, where Alexander the Great passed in 325 B.C. on his return from India. The modern town dates from 1892.

Irapa (ērä'pä), town (pop. 3,309), Sucre state, NE Venezuela, port on S coast of Paria Peninsula, on Gulf of Paria, 45 mi. E of Carúpano, in goat-grazing region.

Irapiranga, Brazil: see ITAPORANGA D'AJUDA.

Irapuã (ērŭpwä'), city (pop. 1,033), N central São Paulo, Brazil, 17 mi. NW of Novo Horizonte; rice, coffee, sugar.

Irapuato (ērăpwä'tō), city (pop. 32,377), Guanajuato, central Mexico, on central plateau, 35 mi. SE of León; alt. 5,656 ft. Rail junction; mining (silver, gold), mfg., and agr. center (cereals, alfalfa, sugar cane, tobacco, fruit, vegetables, livestock); tanneries, flour mills, iron foundries; mfg. of matches, shoes, clothing, toys, cigars, wine, liquor, glycerin. Mineral springs near by. Has radio stations, airfield. Founded 1547. Site of many battles during colonial and revolutionary wars.

Iraq or **Irak** (both: ĭrăk', ērăk'), kingdom (□ 168,040; 1947 pop. 4,799,500), SW Asia; ⊙ BAGHDAD. Approximately coextensive with the historic region of MESOPOTAMIA, it occupies the structural depression bet. the plateaus of Iran (E) and Arabia (W), extending from short, c.55-mi.-long frontage at head of the Persian Gulf c.600 mi. NW (maximum width c.400 mi.) to the Armenian highlands of KURDISTAN, where it borders on Turkey. Along mountainous NE and E frontier (Zagros Mts.) lies Iran. With Syria and Jordan (W) and Saudi Arabia (SW) it shares the great Syrian Desert. S of it are Kuwait and a neutral territory of rhomboid shape. Iraq is roughly bet. 29°5'–37°20'N and 38°45'–48°30'E. Three physiographic regions may be distinguished: the NE highlands (rising above 10,000 ft.), the rugged and sparsely wooded home of the Kurds, with some good pastures and fertile peneplains (e.g., Sulaimaniya); the vast Syrian Desert, contiguous with the Arabian Desert and inhabited by some nomadic and seminomadic tribes who raise on its fringes famed Arabian horses, sheep, camels, and other livestock; and the all-important lowland bet. the mts. and the desert watered by the EUPHRATES RIVER and TIGRIS RIVER, the lifeblood of the country since time immemorial. In and astride the fork of these streams lie all the major cities and most of the productive areas. The N section of the riparian plain (Al Jazira) corresponds to anc. ASSYRIA, which had its historic capital at NINEVEH near modern MOSUL. It is a monotonous, rolling plain, interspersed by a few low ridges. Cultivated tracts are along the Euphrates and Tigris and the latter's tributaries, the Great Zab R. and Little Zab R. The region is important for its enormous, largely British-controlled oil reserves. Though the deposits—mentioned in the Old Testament as "fiery furnaces"—were known to the ancients, petroleum production was started only in the 1920s, when oil soon became the country's leading export and source of revenue. Principal oilfields are centered around Mosul (Qaiyara and Ain Zalah fields), KIRKUK (Baba Gurgur field), and KHANAQIN (Naft Khaneh field). Refineries are at the Khanaqin suburb of Alwand and the Kirkuk suburb of BABA GURGUR. Petroleum is conveyed by pipe lines from Kirkuk to HADITHA (which has also an oil refinery) on the Euphrates; near by, the pipe lines branch off, 2 lines leading to Tripoli (Lebanon) and 2 to Haifa (Israel). A new line to Baniyas (Syria) was begun after 1950. Some oil is also railed S to BASRA and shipped from there. Lower Iraq from the vicinity of Baghdad to the Persian Gulf roughly corresponds to anc. BABYLONIA, whose anc. metropolis was BABYLON near present-day HILLA on Shatt Hilla branch of the Euphrates. (CHALDAEA, originally the southernmost portion of the Euphrates-Tigris valley, is sometimes extended to include all of Babylonia.) This immensely fertile region, in the glacial age still a part of the Persian Gulf, consists of alluvial matter, which is thrusting into the sea at the rate of c.1½ mi. a century. It is a delta country of extensive marshes, large lakes (e.g., Hor al HAMMAR, Hor SANNIYA), old arms and branches of the rivers (e.g., Shatt HILLA, Shatt HINDIYA, Shatt al GHARRAF), and innundation canals. The 2 rivers unite at Al QURNA to form the 120-mi.-long SHATT AL ARAB, which flows SE past Basra (with adjoining MA'QIL, head of ocean-going navigation) to the sea at FAO. Since there is very little rainfall (less than 10 in.), agr. depends entirely on irrigation. Iraq has excessively hot summers, while its winters are quite cool, considering the latitude. In Baghdad the temp. rises in Aug. frequently to 115°F., while the Jan. mean is barely 40°F. The Kurdish uplands have a rigorous mtn. climate with snowfall. Rains occur almost entirely during the winter (Nov.-April). Rainfall increases towards N and is highest in the mts. In the mtn. region are now grown tobacco and fruit of the temperate and subtropical climes. The plains of upper Iraq receive enough rain to permit dry farming, mainly of barley and wheat as winter crops. Though irrigation is still below the level reached by the anc. civilizations of Mesopotamia, large projects have been inaugurated, foremost the Hindiya barrage on lower Euphrates, Kut barrage on lower Tigris, and the barrage on DIYALA RIVER (Tigris affluent) which waters entire prov. of Diyala. Here rice has become the leading subsistence crop, followed by corn, millet, sorghum, sesame, vegetables. All commercial crops are topped by dates, of which Iraq furnishes about ¾ of the world trade, and which in export value is exceeded only by petroleum. Continuous groves of date palms line the Shatt al Arab, but reach as far N as 'ANA on the upper Euphrates. Date palms provide the native population with food, liquor (arrack), mattings, building material, textile fibers, and rope. Other agr. products include opium, hemp, lentils, and licorice. Some high-quality cotton is planted with good results. Wool and skins constitute a considerable export. Sheep are mainly raised in the N, beef cattle and buffaloes in the lowland. Kurdistan yields mohair. There are some salt, low-grade coal, sulphur, limestone, marble, and gypsum deposits; rich copper veins were discovered in NE bet. Penjwin and 'Amadiya. Except for the oil refineries, there are no industries of any importance, though tobacco mfg., arrack distilling, cotton ginning, and brick making are fairly widespread. Mosul (once famous for its "muslin" cottons) and KADHIMAIN have spinning mills; tanneries at Baghdad; licorice processing at KUT. Communication has long relied on river navigation. The lower Shatt al Arab is a fine deep-draft channel, and the Tigris can be ascended by shallow-draft steamers upstream to Baghdad, and beyond Baghdad to Mosul by smaller boats in the high-water season, but the sluggish, sand-choked Euphrates (with Shatt al Gharraf) is of little use. Rafts are used above Mosul for downstream traffic. Of Iraq's 1,555 mi. of railroad track, about ⅓ is standard gauge. A meter-gauge line links Mosul with Baghdad and Basra, where it branches off to Iran. Beyond Mosul a rail line was built (1940) to Tel Kotchek, thus completing the BAGHDAD RAILWAY, finally linking Iraq with Turkey and the European rail net. ERBIL in N Iraq is terminus of railroad from Baghdad via Kirkuk.

There are airports at Baghdad, Basra, Rutba, and Habbaniya. By far the leading city of the country is Baghdad, famed through the Arabian Nights as seat of Harun-al-Rashid. Basra in the S is the principal port and center of date trade, while Mosul serves as market center of the N. Among other trading towns, not so far mentioned, are Nasiriya, Samawa, Ramadi, Diwaniya, Mandali, and Ba'qba. Karbala, Najaf, Samarra, and Kadhimain are religious sites. The kingdom has no university, but there are several professional schools. The present pop. is predominantly of Arabic stock and Moslem religion (Sunnite and Shiite sects). There are Kurdish (c.15%) and Turkish minorities in the N; Iranians live near international line in the E. The once large Jewish pop. in the cities has largely emigrated to Israel. A few Assyrians survive. Scattered religious groups include c.120,000 Christian Arabs (Orthodox, Catholic, Protestant, and others), besides Mandaeans, Yazidis, Bahais, etc. Arabic, the official language, is spoken by the majority of the people. Anc. Mesopotamia has seen the passing of many races and empires. Though opinion is still divided as to the origin of civilization, in this region certainly flourished some of the world's oldest and most remarkable cultures. Ur of Chaldaea has been called the globe's oldest city. The legendary Garden of Eden was most likely located in Babylonia. Now ruined sites of Babylon, Kish, Ashur, Calah, Nineveh, Larsa, Eridu, Lagash, Nippur, Ctesiphon, etc. recall the countries of the Bible, the anc. Sumer, Hittite, Babylonian, Assyrian, Persian, and Arab realms. Here, at Gaugamela near Erbil, Alexander the Great triumphed (331 B.C.) over the Persians. Fabulous Baghdad rose to become for centuries the center of the Arab world. Iraq is a veritable treasure house of antiquities, and recent archaeological excavations have greatly expanded our knowledge of the dawn of history. Decline set in with wanton Mongol invasion in 1298. Despite fierce resistance, Mesopotamia fell to the Ottoman Turks in the 16th cent., and passed under immediate Turkish suzerainty in 19th cent., when it came to constitute the 3 Turkish provs. (*vilayets*) of Basra, Baghdad, and Mosul. During the First World War nationalists from this area joined with Arabs in other parts of the Ottoman Empire in support of the Allies, and the military occupation by the British (in the Mesopotamia campaign, begun 1915) was welcomed. A 1920 revolt was put down by the British. Late that year the Treaty of Sèvres established Iraq as a mandate of the League of Nations under Br. administration, and in 1921 the country became a kingdom headed by Feisal I. In 1930 a treaty with Britain provided for termination of the mandate, and Iraq was admitted to the League of Nations. Domestic politics remained turbulent, wavering bet. pro-British and anti-British factions. After the fall of France in Second World War a pro-Axis coup d'état (1941) led to Br. intervention. In Jan., 1943, Iraq declared war on the Axis powers and soon afterwards adhered to the declaration of the United Nations. A forceful member of the Arab League, Iraq joined in 1948 in the unsuccessful war against the newly formed state of Israel. For further information see separate articles on cities, towns, physical features, historic regions and sites, and the following 14 provs. (*liwas*); 'Amara, Baghdad, Basra, Diwaniya, Diyala, Dulaim, Erbil, Hilla, Karbala, Kirkuk, Kut, Mosul, Muntafiq, Sulaimaniya. The North Desert prov. (□ 36,558) and the South Desert prov. (□ 29,228) are outside these administrative units.

'Iraq, Iraq-i-Ajam, or 'Iraq-i-'Ajam (ĕräk'ē-äjäm'), former province of W central Iran, on central Iranian plateau, corresponding to anc. Media. Iraq-i-Ajam, meaning Persian Iraq, was 1st used under the Seljuk Turks to differentiate region from the Arabian Iraq. Its chief cities were Isfahan, Hamadan, Qum, and Sultanabad (modern Arak). After 1928, the name became restricted to its central section around Sultanabad, and the spelling was changed to Arak. It was also spelled Irak and Araq.

Irará (ērŭrä'), city (pop. 1,524), E Bahia, Brazil, 25 mi. WNW of Alagoinhas; tobacco, coffee, oranges, cotton.

Irasburg (ī'rŭzbûrg), town (pop. 711), Orleans co., N Vt., 10 mi. SSW of Newport and on Black R.; lumbering, dairying. Settled 1798 on Ira Allen's 1781 grant.

Irati (ērŭtē'), city (pop. 4,780), S Paraná, Brazil, on railroad and 50 mi. SW of Ponta Grossa; sawmilling center; maté processing, grain milling. Formerly Iraty.

Irawadi, Burma: see Irrawaddy.

Irazú (ērăsōō'), highest volcano (11,260 ft.) in the Cordillera Central, central Costa Rica, 8 mi. NE of Cartago (linked by road); 9°59'N 83°50'W. Ascended by tourists, it offers views of Atlantic and Pacific coasts.

Irbeiskoye or Irbeyskoye (ērbyā'skŭyŭ), village (1939 pop. over 2,000), SE Krasnoyarsk Territory, Russian SFSR, 40 mi. S of Kansk and on Kan R, in agr. area.

Irbe Strait (ēr'bā), joins Baltic Sea and Gulf of Riga, separating Cape Kolka (Latvia; S) from Saare isl. (Estonia; N); 17 mi. wide. Receives small Irbe R. of Kurzeme, Latvia, on S shore.

Irbid (ĭr'bĭd), town (pop. c.7,000), N Jordan, 40 mi. N of Amman; alt. 1,920 ft.; road and agr. center; grain (wheat, barley), olives.

Irbit (ērbēt'), city (1939 pop. estimate 23,500), SE central Sverdlovsk oblast, Russian SFSR, on Nitsa R. (landing), at mouth of Irbit R. (right tributary), on railroad and 105 mi. NE of Sverdlovsk. Mfg. center (motorcycles, peat-extracting machinery, diatomite chemicals, bricks); flour milling, distilling, tanning, meat preserving, dairying. Has old churches. Founded 1643 as Irbitskaya Sloboda; chartered 1776. Developed as timber-, livestock-, and grain-trading center. Prior to 1930s, site of noted annual fair.

Irbitskiye Vershiny, Russian SFSR: see Altynai.

Irbitski Zavod, Russian SFSR: see Krasnogvardeiski, Sverdlovsk oblast.

Irboska, Russian SFSR: see Novo-Izborsk.

Irchester (ûr'–), town and parish (pop. 2,503), E Northampton, England, 2 mi. SE of Wellingborough; leather and shoe mfg. Has church dating from 13th cent. Site of Saxon and Roman camps. Just NW, on Nene R., is ironstone-quarrying town of Little Irchester.

Irebu (ērĕ'bōō), village, Equator Prov., W Belgian Congo, on left bank of Congo R. opposite the influx of the Ubangi, at mouth of Irebu channel (outlet of L. Tumba), and 65 mi. SSW of Coquilhatville; training center for native troops; steamboat landing. Has R.C. mission.

Iredell (ī'r'dŭl), county (□ 591; pop. 56,303), W central N.C.; ⊙ Statesville. In piedmont area; bounded SW by Catawba R.; drained by tributaries of Yadkin R. Farming (tobacco, cotton, corn, wheat, hay, poultry, dairy products), mfg. of textiles and furniture, sawmilling. Formed 1788.

Iredell (īrŭdĕl'), city (pop. 394), Bosque co., central Texas, on Bosque R. and c.50 mi. NW of Waco, in farm area.

Ireg, Yugoslavia: see Irig.

Iregszemcse (ĭ'rĕksĕm-chĕ), town (pop. 4,484), Tolna co., W central Hungary, 29 mi. NE of Kaposvar; agr., cattle.

Ireland, Gaelic *Eire* (â'rŭ) [to it are related the poetic *Erin* and, perhaps, the Latin *Hibernia*], island (□ 32,375; land area □ 31,839; 1951 census pop. 4,329,587), 2d largest of the British Isles. In the Atlantic, it is separated from Great Britain (E) by the North Channel, Irish Sea, and St. George's Channel. Politically divided into Northern Ireland (NE), a part of the United Kingdom of Great Britain and Northern Ireland, and the republic of Ireland (□ 27,137; land □ 26,601; 1946 pop. 2,953,452; 1951 pop. 2,958,878; ⊙ Dublin). Isl. consists of a central lowland, enclosed (S, W, and N) by mts. Principal physical regions are: Mountainous moorland (SE) of the Wicklow Mts., rising to 3,039 ft. on Lugnaquillia; this region extends N to vicinity of Dublin and is drained by Slaney, Ouoca, Barrow, and Liffey rivers. To its S lie the fertile Wexford uplands, rising to 2,610 ft. on Mt. Leinster in Blackstairs Mts. S Ireland (Cork and Waterford) is region of rolling hills, with parallel E-W valleys; drained by Blackwater, Lee, Bandon, and Suir rivers; has fertile soil; important dairying and pig-raising industry. SW Ireland (Kerry) forms mountainous peninsula, with Carrantuohill mtn. rising to 3,414 ft. in the Macgillycuddy's Reeks range. Here is picturesque Killarney lake dist. SW coast is deeply indented by Dunmanus, Bantry, Dingle, and Tralee bays and Kenmare R.; Valentia isl., just offshore, is terminus of transatlantic cables. Co. Kerry peninsula borders N on long Shannon R. estuary (major hydroelectric plant near Limerick), which forms S shore of hilly upland peninsula of Co. Clare (W). Surface rises to 1,745 ft. near Lough Derg, large expansion of the Shannon. N shore of Co. Clare peninsula is deeply indented by Galway Bay, with Aran Isls.; N of Galway Bay is hilly peninsula formed by cos. Galway, Mayo, and Sligo. Rocky coast indented by Clew and Blacksod bays. Large lakes here include loughs Corrib, Mask, and Conn. Region drained by Clare, Suck, and Moy rivers. Coastal region of Co. Donegal (NW) is rocky and hilly, rises to over 2,000 ft., and is indented by Donegal Bay, Lough Swilly, and Lough Foyle. Aran and Tory are offshore isls. In NE part of Ireland is political territory of Northern Ireland, consisting of plateau, c.500 ft. high, bordered by higher hills; in SE part of region, near border of Irish republic, Mourne Mts. rise to 2,796 ft. on Slieve Donard. Center of region slopes down to Lough Neagh, largest lake in the British Isles. Northern Ireland is drained by Lagan, Bann, Blackwater, Mourne, Foyle, and Main rivers. Coast is deeply indented by Lough Foyle (N), Belfast Lough (E), and Strangford Lough (SE). Central and E part of Ireland consists of lowland region, partly boggy (includes extensive Bog of Allen), drained into Irish Sea by Boyne, Blackwater, and Liffey rivers, and into Atlantic by the Shannon and its tributaries. Dublin is its economic center. Damp pastures predominate; cattle raising, horse breeding are important. While Northern Ireland has commercially-worked bauxite deposits in Co. Antrim, republic of Ireland has few mineral resources. A little coal is mined in S central Ireland; iron, copper, barites, and lead are also worked on small scale. Gypsum, marble, limestone, flagstone, and slate are quarried in quantity. Peat supplies are ample. Irish industry is of minor economic importance; textile milling (linen, wool, cotton), shoe mfg., brewing (Dublin is important center), distilling, biscuit baking are leading mfg. industries. Agr. is Ireland's principal occupation; leading crops are potatoes, oats, wheat, barley, rye, turnips, and vegetables. Stock raising (cattle, pigs, sheep, poultry) and dairying are important; large quantities of bacon, meat, eggs, butter are exported, especially to Great Britain. Fishing. The Shannon is chief inland waterway of Ireland and affords, together with Grand and Royal canals, E-W connection across center of the country. Railroads connect principal towns. Shannon Airport at Rineanna, near Limerick, is one of major European transatlantic airports. Air services connect Dublin with Great Britain and the Continent. Among mail-steamer routes bet. Ireland and Great Britain are Dún Laoghaire–Holyhead, Dublin–Liverpool, and Rosslare–Fishguard. Principal Irish cities are Dublin, Cork, Limerick, Dún Laoghaire, Waterford, Galway, Dundalk, Drogheda, Sligo, Wexford, Tralee, Kilkenny, Bray, Clonmel. Cóbh (formerly Queenstown) is Ireland's chief transatlantic port. Climate is maritime in character; SE part of country has warm summers and mild winters, while remainder has cool summers and mild winters. On W coast annual rainfall ranges from 40 to 80 inches, in E Ireland it ranges from 30 to 40 inches. Vast majority of pop. is Roman Catholic; this is a cardinal factor, as religion has been intimately connected with Irish politics since 16th cent. Gaelic is spoken by c.25% of country's pop.; its spread is encouraged by govt. Several centuries before Christian era Ireland was conquered by Celtic tribes, who established their own culture. Anglo-Saxon invasion of Britain had little influence on Ireland; though they occupied Britain for 400 years, the Romans never came to Ireland. Isl. was invaded by 4 successive peoples; from the last of them, the Milesians, modern Irish are reputedly descended. Until 8th cent. A.D., when Norse raids began, Irish culture flourished. Country was ruled by petty provincial kings, who served the Ard-Ri high king of all Ireland, at Tara. A period of great achievement in literature, music, and sculpture was punctuated by clan warfare. Gaelic influence was extended to Scotland. Although earlier missionaries had visited Ireland, greatest contribution to introduction of Christianity was made in 5th cent. by St. Patrick. The Book of Kells is outstanding example of cultural and artistic achievement of early Christian era; among noted scholars and missionaries of the time were St. Columba, St. Columban, and St. Bridget, who founded great monastery at Kildare. At end of 8th cent. coastal regions of Ireland were settled by Norsemen, who founded Dublin, Waterford, and Limerick; Norse power was broken (1014) at Clontarf by Brian Boru, high king of Ireland. Civil strife broke out once more. In 12th cent. overlordship of Ireland was granted to Henry II of England by Pope Adrian IV; English conquest was begun (1169) by Richard Strongbow (Richard de Clare), earl of Pembroke. In 1171 Henry went to Ireland to establish his overlordship. Invasion opened Anglo-Irish struggle that has continued essentially to present time. Early days of English rule were chaotic; clan struggles continued and land was seized, giving rise to landlord-tenant problem that was to continue for many centuries. Only Henry VIII brought all Ireland under English control and introduced English system of land tenure. Parliament (1541) at Dublin contained Irish chiefs as well as English nobles, but legislative power for Ireland had already been vested (1495) in English Parliament under Poyning's Law, in force until 1782. With introduction of the Reformation in England Anglo-Irish differences were intensified by religious conflict. In time of Elizabeth 3 major Irish rebellions were ruthlessly crushed; Protestant Scotch settlers were planted in Ulster and took root there, thus paving way to 20th-cent. conflict bet. Ireland and Northern Ireland. Another rebellion began (1641) at time of the English Commonwealth; lasting for 10 years, it cost 600,000 lives and was brutally crushed by Cromwell. Irish economic and agr. development was virtually halted by restrictive laws. An independent but ineffective Parliament met in 1782. Peasants' condition remained deplorable and a further unsuccessful rising took place (1798), led by Wolfe Tone. As a result Pitt united (1800) Ireland with Great Britain in the United Kingdom of Great Britain and Ireland, Irish being represented in British Parliament. Irish Catholic disabilities were removed (1829) under Catholic Emancipation Act; further discontent was removed by disestablishment (1869) of Church of Ireland. Serious economic problems arose from absentee landlordism and a growing pop.; potato blight in the 1840s and resulting famine reduced pop. from c.8,500,000 to c.6,500,000 by 1854—1,000,000 having died of starvation an c.1,500,000 having emigrated, mostly to the United States. In 1870 Home Rule movement to end the union had gained momentum under leadership of Parnell; nationalism was stimulated further by a revival of Gaelic literature in late-19th cent. Constitutional Home Rule movement was supplemented and later superseded by Sinn Fein movement, aiming at complete Irish independence. Easter Rebellion (1916) was crushed, but led to guerrilla warfare, which British tried to suppress with auxiliaries called the Black and Tans, who terrorized (1920) the country. In 1921 British prime minister Lloyd George began negotiations with Sinn Fein leader De Valera. The 6 northern Protestant counties had accepted (1920) dominion status under 4th Home Rule Bill, and in 1921 Irish Free State was established in remainder of country. Sovereign country of Ireland was established when new constitution became effective, Dec., 1937; the new state of Ireland or Eire was to be associated with the British Commonwealth of Nations in external affairs only. Special agreement with Great Britain ended trade war bet. the countries and returned British-held ports, including Cóbh, and Lough Swilly to Irish control. During Second World War Ireland remained neutral; as Irish industry came to virtual standstill, large numbers of Irish workers sought employment in Great Britain and Northern Ireland. In April, 1949, republic of Ireland was established, which formally claims jurisdiction over Northern Ireland. Legislative power is vested in bi-cameral parliament, consisting of First Chamber (*Dáil Éireann*) and Second Chamber (*Seanad Éireann*). Executive power is vested in prime minister; president signs and promulgates laws. Administratively Ireland is divided into 26 counties: Carlow, Cavan, Clare, Cork, Donegal, Dublin, Galway, Kerry, Kildare, Kilkenny, Leitrim, Laoighis (Leix), Limerick, Longford, Louth, Mayo, Meath, Monaghan, Offaly, Roscommon, Sligo, Tipperary, Waterford, Westmeath, Wexford, and Wicklow. Cavan, Donegal, and Monaghan are in Ulster.

eland Island (1½ mi. long, ¼ mi. wide), northwesternmost part of Bermuda, at entrance to Great Sound, W of Hamilton. A narrow channel cuts it in two. Has Br. naval base.

eland's Eye, islet in the Irish Sea just N of Howth, E Co. Dublin, Ireland. Has remains of anc. chapel, built on site of 7th-cent. church of St. Nessan.

eland's Eye Island (□ 2; pop. 132), SE N.F., on NW side of Trinity Bay, 35 mi. NNW of Carbonear; 48°13′N 53°30′W. Fishing.

emel or **Iremel'** (ērŭmyĕ′lyŭ), peak (5,197 ft.) in S Urals, Russian SFSR, SW of Zlatoust; 54°30′N. The Belaya and Ai rivers rise here.

ene, town (pop. 374), Turner, Clay, and Yankton counties, SE S.Dak., 20 mi. NE of Yankton; livestock, poultry, corn, barley, oats.

eng River, Brazil and Br. Guiana: see Maú River.

eton, town (pop. 573), Sioux co., NW Iowa, 32 mi. N of Sioux City, in livestock and grain area.

galem, Ethiopia: see Yirga-Alam.

Ganim or **Ir Gannim,** Israel: see Qiryat Nahum.

giz (ērgēs′), village (1939 pop. over 500), SE Aktyubinsk oblast, Kazakh SSR, on Irgiz R. and 90 mi. NE of Chelkar, on dry steppe; dairying. Founded 1847 in Rus. conquest of Kazakhstan.

giz River. 1 In E Aktyubinsk oblast, Kazakh SSR, rises in SE foothills of the S Urals c.70 mi. SE of Orsk, flows S, through salt steppe, past Karabutak, and SE, past Irgiz, to lake Chelkar-Tengiz; 300 mi. long. **2** Name of 2 left affluents of lower Volga R., in Kuibyshev and Saratov oblasts, SE European Russian SFSR. **Greater Irgiz River,** Rus. *Bolshoi Irgiz*, rises in the Obshchi Syrt 50 mi. SSW of Buzuluk, flows 355 mi. generally WSW, past Pugachev and Sulak, to the Volga opposite Volsk. Navigable at high water in lower course. **Lesser Irgiz River,** Rus. *Maly Irgiz*, flows intermittently WSW, parallel to and N of the Greater Irgiz, past Ivantayevka (Saratov oblast) to an arm of the Volga near Alekseyevka; 110 mi. long.

herm (ēgârm′), village, Agadir frontier region, SW Fr. Morocco, in the Anti-Atlas, 36 mi. SE of Taroudant; alt. 5,665 ft.

hir, Fr. Morocco: see Ouarzazate.

i (ē′rē′), Jap. *Riri*, city (1949 pop. 46,674), N.Cholla prov., S Korea, 13 mi. ESE of Kunsan, in agr. area (rice, soybeans, hemp, cotton); rail center; rice refining, sake brewing.

ian: see New Guinea.

idere, Bulgaria: see Ardino.

ig (ē′rĭk), Hung. *Ireg* (ĭr′ĕg), village, Vojvodina, N Serbia, Yugoslavia, 11 mi. S of Novi Sad, at S foot of Fruska Gora, in the Srem.

iga (ērē′gä), town (1939 pop. 5,126; 1948 municipality pop. 42,049), Camarines Sur prov., SE Luzon, Philippines, on railroad and 29 mi. NW of Legaspi; agr. center (rice, abacá, corn).

igny (ērēnyē′), village (pop. 910), Rhône dept., E central France, on right bank of the Rhone and 6 mi. S of Lyons; meat processing, fiber mfg., strawberry shipping.

igoyen, Argentina: see Bernardo de Irigoyen, Santa Fe prov.

iha, Syria: see Eriha.

Iriklinski or **Iriklinskiy** (ērĭklyēn′skē), town (1946 pop. over 500), NE Chkalov oblast, Russian SFSR, in SE foothills of S Urals, on Ural R. and 30 mi. N of Orsk, in gold-mining region.

Irimbo (ērēm′bō), town (pop. 847), Michoacán, central Mexico, 6 mi. E of Hidalgo; rail junction; corn, stock.

Iringa (ērĭng′gä), town (pop. c.5,500), Southern Highlands prov., S central Tanganyika, 110 mi. S of Dodoma; agr. trade center; tobacco (flue cured), tea, wheat, cattle, sheep, goats. Govt. African primary school. Airfield. Limestone deposits.

Irinjalakuda (ĭrĭnjä′lŭko͝odŭ), city (pop. 17,330), W Cochin, India, 25 mi. N of Ernakulam; coir products (rope, mats); betel-nut curing, rice milling. Also spelled Irinjalakkuda.

Iriomote-jima (ērē′ōmōtä-jĭ′mä), volcanic island (□ 144; 1950 pop. 9,908, including offshore islets) of Sakishima Isls., in the Ryukyus, bet. East China Sea (W) and Philippine Sea (E), 10 mi. W of Ishigaki-shima; 18 mi. long, 9 mi. wide. Mountainous, rising to c.1,670 ft. Coal mining.

Irion (ĕr′ēŭn), county (□ 1,073; pop. 1,590), W Texas; ⊙ Mertzon. Broken prairie, drained by Middle Concho R. and spring-fed small streams; alt. c.2,000–2,500 ft. Ranching region (sheep, goats, some cattle), ships wool and mohair; some agr. (grain sorghums, alfalfa, cotton, hogs, poultry). Formed 1889.

Iriona (ēryō′nä), town (pop. 66), Colón dept., N Honduras, ⊙ Iriona dist. (□ c.15,000; pop. 11,003), in Mosquitia, port on Caribbean Sea, on railroad and 55 mi. E of Trujillo; transit center bet. Trujillo and Mosquitia region of E Honduras; coconuts, livestock.

Iriondo, department, Argentina: see Cañada de Gómez.

Iriondo, village, Argentina: see Tapso.

Iripau, Society Isls.: see Tahaa.

Iriri, Fr. Morocco: see Ouarzazate.

Iri River, Greece: see Eurotas River.

Irish Free State: see Ireland.

Irish Sea, arm of the Atlantic, separating Ireland from England, Scotland, Wales; 130 mi. long, 130 mi. wide; □ 40,000; mean depth 200 ft. Joins the Atlantic by North Channel (N) and St. George's Channel (S). In it are isls. of Man, Anglesey, and Holyhead. Chief ports on Irish Sea are Dublin and Dundalk (Ireland); Barrow-in-Furness, Heysham, Fleetwood, Liverpool, and Birkenhead (England); and Holyhead (Wales).

Irishtown, village (pop. 358), NW Tasmania, 110 mi. WNW of Launceston; sheep.

Iris River, Turkey: see Yesil Irmak.

Iriston (ērĭstôn′), village (1926 pop. 3,193), central North Ossetian Autonomous SSR, Russian SFSR, on railroad (Beslan station), on Terek R. and 13 mi. NNW of Dzaudzhikau; corn, wheat, hemp; essential oils. Until 1941, Tulatovo.

Irituia (ērētō͞o′yŭ), city (pop. 399), E Pará, Brazil, 90 mi. SE of Belém; Brazil nuts, rubber.

I River, Chinese *I Ho* (yē′hŭ′), S central Shantung prov., China, rises in the I Mts., flows over 150 mi. S, past Ishui and Lini, to Grand Canal on Kiangsu line, 40 mi. E of Süchow. Sometimes spelled Yi R.

Irka, Aden: see Irqa.

Irkeshtam (ĭrkĕshtäm′), village, Osh oblast, Kirghiz SSR, on USSR-China border, on major trade route bet. Kashgar and Osh, and 85 mi. SE of Osh. **Irkestan** or **Ierhkoszetang,** in Sinkiang prov., China, is village opposite, across the international line.

Irkleyev (ērklyä′ŭf), village (1926 pop. 1,928), SW Poltava oblast, Ukrainian SSR, 16 mi. SE of Zolotonosha; metalworks.

Irkut River (ērko͞ot′), in SW Buryat-Mongol Autonomous SSR and SE Irkutsk oblast, Russian SFSR, rises in Eastern Sayan Mts., flows 270 mi. W, past Kyren, to Angara R. at Irkutsk.

Irkutsk (ĭrko͞otsk′), oblast (□ 301,900; 1939 pop. 1,286,696) in S Siberian Russian SFSR; ⊙ Irkutsk. Bounded SE by L. Baikal, SW by Eastern Sayan Mts.; extends N into Central Siberian Plateau along upper Lower Tunguska R., NE to Patom Plateau. Drained by upper Lena and Angara rivers. Pop. includes Russians, Buryat-Mongols (in Ust-Orda Natl. Okrug), and Evenki (N and NE). Forests (mainly coniferous) cover 70–80% of region. Steppe and wooded steppe along Trans-Siberian RR (S) contain major industrial centers of Irkutsk. Coal (Cheremkhovo), salt (Usolye); other mineral deposits include iron in Angara-Ilim area, gold (Bodaibo), mica (Mama, Slyudyanka), and asbestos. Main exports: lumber, gold, furs. Projected harnessing of Angara R. water power aims to transform region into a major industrial area (electrometallurgy, chemicals). Agr. shows shift from rye to spring wheat production; potatoes, vegetables, dairying, poultry raising. Formed 1937 out of E.Siberian Territory.

Irkutsk, city (1926 pop. 108,129; 1939 pop. 243,380), ⊙ Irkutsk oblast, Russian SFSR, on Angara R. at mouth of Irkut R., on Trans-Siberian RR and 2,600 mi. ESE of Moscow, 35 mi. W of L. Baikal; 52°17′N 104°20′E. Major transportation and industrial center of E Siberia; river port; terminus of highways to Mongolia and upper Lena R. Shipping point for freight to Yakut Autonomous SSR and gold-mining areas. Aircraft and auto assembly; mfg. (gold-mining equipment, building materials); sawmilling (wood-pulp production), mica processing, leather and textile mfg. Long a Siberian cultural center; has univ. (1918), agr., medical, and teachers colleges, mineralogical and metallurgical schools; seat of a branch of USSR Acad. of Sciences. Has historical, regional, and art museums, and several theaters. City proper, with most cultural institutions, is located on right Angara bank opposite Irkut R. mouth. Across Angara R. (permanent bridge built in 1930s) is industrial Sverdlov suburb, site of rail station. Further north, across Irkut R., are industrial suburbs of Lenino (inc. 1930 into Irkutsk; railroad shops) and Zhilkino (meat, flour, soap, livestock feed). Founded 1652 on isl. in Irkut R.; transferred 1669 to present site. Became city in 1683; developed as administrative and commercial center; until c.1900, 2d-largest city (after Tomsk) of Siberia. Industrialization followed construction (1898) of Trans-Siberian RR and development of Cheremkhovo (or Irkutsk) coal basin.

Irlam (ûr′lŭm), urban district (1931 pop. 12,901; 1951 census 15,063), S Lancashire, England, on Manchester Ship Canal and 7 mi. WSW of Manchester; steel production; mfg. of soap. Includes (SW) town of Cadishead (kă′dĭs-hĕd, kĕ′–), on Manchester Ship Canal; benzol refining, tar distilling, paper milling.

Irlbach (ĭrl′bäkh), village (pop. 1,300), Lower Bavaria, Germany, on the Danube and 9 mi. ESE of Straubing; brewing. Has 19th-cent. castle.

Irma, village (pop. 345), E Alta., near Sask. border, 17 mi. WNW of Wainwright; oil drilling, dairying; grain, mixed farming.

Irmak (ĭrmäk′), rail junction, Ankara prov., central Turkey, 30 mi. E of Ankara.

Irmãos, Serra dos, Brazil: see Dois Irmãos, Serra dos.

Irminger Sea, part of North Atlantic Ocean, off SE Greenland, linked by Denmark Strait with Greenland Sea of Arctic Ocean. The Irminger Current, a branch of the North Atlantic Current, flows N and W, past S coast of Iceland, and joins the East Greenland Current issuing from Denmark Strait.

Irminio River (ērmē′nyô), SE Sicily, rises on Monte Lauro, flows 28 mi. SSW, past Ragusa, to Mediterranean Sea 6 mi. E of Cape Scaramia. Sometimes called Ragusa R.

Irmino (ĕr′mēnŭ), city (1939 pop. over 10,000), W Voroshilovgrad oblast, Ukrainian SSR, in the Donbas, 3 mi. NW of Kadiyevka; coal-mining center; chemical works. Formerly Irminski Rudnik. The Stakhanovite movement to increase production started here, 1935.

Irmo (ûr′mō), town (pop. 281), Lexington co., central S.C., 9 mi. WNW of Columbia, near L. Murray.

Iro, river, Mongolia: see Iro River.

Iro, Cape (ē′rō), Jap. *Iro-zaki*, Shizuoka prefecture, central Honshu, Japan, in Philippine Sea; southernmost point of Izu Peninsula; 34°36′N 138°51′E; lighthouse.

Irois, Cape (ērwä′), westernmost headland of Tiburon Peninsula, Haiti, 5 mi. SSW of Anse-d'Hainault; 18°26′N 74°28′W.

Iron. 1 County (□ 1,197; pop. 17,692), SW Upper Peninsula, Mich.; ⊙ Crystal Falls. Bounded S by Wis. line; drained by Brule, Michigamme, Paint, and Iron rivers. Part of Ottawa Natl. Forest in W. Includes part of Menominee iron range (mining). Lumbering. Agr. (livestock, poultry, potatoes, truck, grain, fruit; dairy products). Some mfg. at Crystal Falls. Many small lakes (resorts) and streams. Univ. of Mich. forestry school's summer camp is here. Formed and organized 1885. **2** County (□ 554; pop. 9,458), SE central Mo.; ⊙ Ironton. Partly in St. Francois Mts.; includes Taum Sauk Mtn. (1,772 ft.), highest point in state. Agr., mining (manganese, lead, iron, granite); oak, pine timber; resorts. Includes parts of Clark Natl. Forest. Formed 1857. **3** County (□ 3,300; pop. 9,642), SW Utah; ⊙ Parowan. Mtn. and plateau region bordering on Nev. Agr. near Parowan; iron mining in Iron Mts. (S). Cedar Breaks Natl. Monument and part of Dixie Natl. Forest in Markagunt Plateau (SE). Kolob Terrace S of Cedar City; desert area in N. Formed 1850. **4** County (□ 748; pop. 8,714), N Wis.; ⊙ Hurley. Bounded partly N by L. Superior and Montreal R. (here forming Mich. border); drained by tributaries of Bad R. and by Montreal. R. Gogebic Range (valuable source of iron ore) extends across co. S half of Iron co. is largely wooded, with many lakes, and forms a large resort area. Iron mining is principal industry. Formed 1893.

Iron or **Iron Junction,** village (pop. 128), St. Louis co., NE Minn., just S of Mesabi iron range, 8 mi. SSW of Virginia, in grain and potato area. Iron mines near by.

Iron, Lough (lŏkh), lake (2½ mi. long, ½ mi. wide), NW Co. Westmeath, Ireland, 7 mi. NW of Mullingar.

Iron Acton, agr. village and parish (pop. 1,084), SW Gloucester, England, 9 mi. NE of Bristol. Has 14th-cent. church.

Iron Belt, village (pop. c.500), Iron co., N Wis., 6 mi. WSW of Hurley; iron mining.

Ironbridge, England: see WENLOCK.

Iron City, town (pop. 293), Seminole co., extreme SW Ga., 16 mi. WNW of Bainbridge, in farm area.

Irondale. 1 City (pop. 1,876), Jefferson co., N central Ala., just E of Birmingham; iron castings, lumber. **2** Town (1940 pop. 71), Adams co., N central Colo., near South Platte R., just NE of Denver; alt. 5,115 ft. **3** Town (pop. 443), Washington co., E central Mo., in Ozarks, on Big R. and 9 mi. W of Flat River. **4** Village (pop. 775), Jefferson co., E Ohio, 15 mi. NNW of Steubenville, near the Ohio; clay products, lumber.

Irondequoit (ûrŏn'dĭkwoit", –kwŏt"), town (1940 pop. 23,376), Monroe co., W N.Y., on L. Ontario and Irondequoit Bay, just N of downtown Rochester and partly enclosed by the city. Settled 1791, organized 1839.

Irondequoit Bay, Monroe co., W N.Y., inlet of L. Ontario just NE of Rochester; c.4 mi. long, ½–1 mi. wide. Receives small Irondequoit Creek from S.

Iron Gate or **Iron Gates,** Rum. *Porțile de Fier* (pôr'tsēlĕ dă fyâr'), Serbo-Croatian *Đerdap* (dyĕr'-däp), Ger. *Eisenernes Tor* (ī'zûrnĕs tôr'), gorge (c.2 mi. long; 16-ft. fall) of the Danube on Rum.-Yugoslav border, 3 mi. below Varciorova, bet. Orsova and Turnu-Severin (W Rumania). Here the river narrows to break through bet. S end of the Carpathians and N outliers of the Balkans. Navigation obstacles here were removed by construction (1896) of Sip Canal, with regulation works chiefly on Yugoslav side.

Iron Gate, town (pop. 725), Alleghany co., W Va., on Jackson R. just E of Clifton Forge; tannery.

Iron Junction, Minn.: see IRON.

Iron Knob, village (pop. 628), S South Australia, in Middleback Range, NE Eyre Peninsula, 155 mi. NE of Port Lincoln; head of railroad to Whyalla. Iron mines.

Iron Mine Hill, village, Gwelo prov., central Southern Rhodesia, in Matabeleland, on railroad, and 33 mi. ENE of Gwelo; alt. 4,752 ft. Iron mining.

Iron Monarch, Australia: see MIDDLEBACK RANGE.

Iron Mountain, city (pop. 9,679), ⊙ Dickinson co., SW Upper Peninsula, Mich., c.50 mi. W of Escanaba, near Wis. line. Distribution point for Menominee iron range. Mfg. (wood auto parts, chemicals, dairy products). Veterans' hosp. near by. Livestock, fruit, truck, and hay are produced; timber. Resort (winter sports). Settled 1879, inc. 1889.

Iron Mountain (325 ft.), Polk co., central Fla., near Lake Wales. Site of the Singing Tower (with a carillon of 71 bells) and of a bird sanctuary and park established by Edward W. Bok and opened in 1929.

Iron Mountains. 1 In NE Tenn. and SW Va., ridge (2,500–4,500 ft.) of the Appalachians bet. Holston (SW) and Stone (E) mts.; from Doe R. near Elizabethton, Tenn., extend c.80 mi. NE to New R. SE of Wytheville, Va. A spur in Va., just NE of Tenn.-N.C. line, includes Mt. ROGERS (5,720 ft.) and White Top Mtn. (5,520 ft.). Included in Cherokee and Jefferson natl. forests. Sometimes considered a range of Unaka Mts. **2** In Iron and Washington counties, SW Utah; rise to 7,828 ft. in Iron Mtn., 17 mi. W of Cedar City. Iron is mined.

Iron Ridge, village (pop. 341), Dodge co., S central Wis., near Rock R., 15 mi. ESE of Beaver Dam, in dairying region.

Iron River. 1 City (pop. 4,048), Iron co., SW Upper Peninsula, Mich., 33 mi. NW of Iron Mountain city and on Iron R., in iron-mining and lumbering region; agr. (livestock, poultry, truck, potatoes; dairy products). Lake resort. Ottawa Natl. Forest is near by. Settled by iron-ore prospectors c.1881; inc. as village 1885, as city 1926. **2** Village (1940 pop. 748), Bayfield co., extreme N Wis., 25 mi. W of Ashland, in lake-resort region; lumbering, dairying, farming.

Iron River, SW Upper Peninsula, Mich., rises in small lakes in SW Iron co., flows c.25 mi. SE, past Stambaugh, to Brule R. 5 mi. SE of Caspian.

Iron Station, town (pop. 232), Lincoln co., S N.C., 6 mi. SE of Lincolnton.

Ironton. 1 Town (pop. 6), Ouray co., SW Colo., near Ouray. **2** Village (pop. 828), Crow Wing co., central Minn., on Cuyuna iron range, 14 mi. NE of Brainerd, in lake and forest area; grain, potatoes. Iron mines near by. State forests in vicinity. **3** City (pop. 1,148), ⊙ Iron co., SE central Mo., in St. Francois Mts., 18 mi. S of Flat River; tourist, farm trade; iron, lead mines. Civil War battle of Pilot Knob, fought near by on Sept. 27, 1864, resulted in reverse for Confederates under Sterling Price. Clark Natl. Forest near by; Taum Sauk Mtn., highest point in Mo., W. Founded 1857. **4** City (pop. 16,333), ⊙ Lawrence co., S Ohio, on the Ohio (bridged) and 4 mi. NNW of Ashland, Ky.; river port and railroad center, in coal, limestone, and fruit area. Mfg.: fabricated iron and steel, cement, brick, tile, electrical goods, stoves, machinery, auto parts. Laid out 1848, inc. 1851. **5** Village (pop. 176), Sauk co., S central Wis., on Baraboo R. and 21 mi. WNW of Baraboo, in dairy and livestock region.

Ironville, England: see ALFRETON.

Ironwood, city (pop. 11,466), Gogebic co., W Upper Peninsula, Mich., on Montreal R., opposite Hurley, Wis. Trade center for Gogebic Range iron-mining region; lumbering, dairy and truck farming. Has jr. col. Some of the world's deepest mines are here. Hq. for Ottawa Natl. Forest here. Founded 1885, inc. 1889.

Iroquois (ĭ'rŭkwoi), village (pop. 956), SE Ont., on the St. Lawrence and 15 mi. NE of Prescott; linen and lumber milling, furniture mfg., dairying.

Iroquois, county (□ 1,222; pop. 32,348), E Ill., on Ind. line (E); ⊙ Watseka. Agr. (corn, oats, wheat, soybeans, livestock, poultry). Mfg. (dairy products, canned foods, clothing, monuments, soft drinks, batteries). Drained by Iroquois R. and small Sugar Creek. Formed 1833.

Iroquois. 1 Village (pop. 232), Iroquois co., E Ill., on Iroquois R. (bridged here) and 25 mi. SSE of Kankakee, in agr. area. **2** City (pop. 413), Kingsbury and Beadle counties, E central S.Dak., 15 mi. W of De Smet; livestock, dairy products, poultry, grain. Near by is artificial lake.

Iroquois Falls, town (pop. 1,302), E central Ont., on Abitibi R. and 27 mi. SE of Cochrane; pulp, paper, and sulphite milling center. Near by are waterfalls and hydroelectric station.

Iroquois River, in NW Ind. and NE Ill., rises in Jasper co., NW Ind., flows WSW to Watseka, Ill., then generally N to Kankakee R. c.4 mi. above Kankakee; c.85 mi. long.

Iro River (ē'rō), Mongolian *Yöröö Gol* (yû'rû gōl'), N Mongolian People's Republic, rises in Kentei Mts. 50 mi. NE of Ulan Bator, flows 200 mi. NW to Orkhon R. 25 mi. S of Sukhe Bator. Freezes Nov.–April; subject to great floods following rains. Used for timber floating. Has gold mines, sawmill, and Russian agr. settlements along its course.

Irosin (ērōsēn'), town (1939 pop. 5,610; 1948 municipality pop. 19,317), Sorsogon prov., extreme SE Luzon, Philippines, 19 mi. S of Sorsogon; agr. center (abacá, coconuts, rice).

Irpen or **Irpen'** (ērpyĕn'yŭ), town (1926 pop. 2,513), N central Kiev oblast, Ukrainian SSR, on railroad and 13 mi. NW of Kiev; sawmilling, tanning.

Irqa, 'Irqa, or **'Arqa** (all: ĭrkä'), small sheikdom (pop. 500) of Eastern Aden Protectorate, on Gulf of Aden, 130 mi. WSW of Mukalla; consists of Irqa village and environs. Protectorate treaty concluded in 1902. Sometimes spelled Irka.

Irrawaddy (ĭr"ŭwŏ'dē), Burmese *Iyawadi* (ā'yäwŭ-dē), administrative division (□ 13,578; 1941 pop. 2,659,126) of Lower Burma; ⊙ Bassein. Comprises nearly the entire Irrawaddy R. delta and, in NW, the S foothills of Arakan Yoma. Divided into dists. of Bassein, Henzada, Maubin, Myaungmya, Pyapon. Major rice-growing region (annual rainfall, 100 in.); important fisheries. Served by Irrawaddy delta steamers and Bassein-Henzada-Kyangin RR. Dense pop. (200 per sq. mi.) is 75% Burmese, 20% Karen, 5% Indian. Formerly part of prov. of Pegu, annexed 1852 by British and inc. 1862 into Br. (Lower) Burma. Also spelled Irawadi.

Irrawaddy River, main stream and economic lifeline of Burma and one of great rivers of SE Asia, traversing the entire length of Burma from N to S and forming a vast delta on the Andaman Sea, one of the world's leading rice-producing areas. It rises in northernmost Kachin State in 2 headstreams, the Mali and Nmai rivers, which enclose The Triangle and join at 25°45'N, 25 mi. N of Myitkyina. The combined stream flows S through defiles strewn with rapids, past Myitkyina, Bhamo (head of navigation), Mandalay, Pakokku, and bet. the Pegu Yoma and Arakan Yoma, past Yenangyaung, Thayetmyo, and Prome. The delta begins 180 mi. from the sea, N of Henzada bet. Bassein R. (westernmost and principal arm flowing past Bassein) and the Irrawaddy proper, here linked by Twante Canal with Rangoon; the delta arms empty into the Andaman Sea over 150-mi. front of tidal forests. Receives Mogaung, Mu, Chindwin (chief affluent), and Mon rivers on right; Taping, Shweli, and Myitnge rivers on left. Year-round steamer navigation to Bhamo (872 river mi. from Rangoon); shallow-draught launches during low-water season (Oct.–Feb.) negotiate the rapids to Myitkyina, 90 mi. above Bhamo. Petroleum barges (from Chauk, Yenangyaung, and Minbu oil fields) and teak rafts constitute most of the traffic. Total length: 1,000 mi.; including Nmai headstream, 1,300 mi. Headwaters are claimed by China. Also spelled Irawadi.

Irricana (ĭ"rŭkä'nŭ), village (pop. 150), S central Alta., near Rosebud R., 28 mi. NE of Calgary; rail junction in irrigated area.

Irrsee, Austria: see MONDSEE.

Irsa (ĭr'shŏ), town (pop. 7,393), Pest-Pilis-Solt-Kiskun co., central Hungary, 10 mi. NW of Cegled; distilleries; grain, cattle, fruit (apples, pears, cherries).

Irsava, Ukrainian SSR: see IRSHAVA.

Irsha (ēr'shŭ), town (1939 pop. over 500), SE Krasnoyarsk Territory, Russian SFSR, 40 mi. SW of Kansk; lignite mines.

Irshava (ērshä'vŭ), Czech *Iršava* (ĭr'shävä), Hung. *Ilosva* (ĭ'lôshvŏ), village (1941 pop. 3,863), S central Transcarpathian Oblast, Ukrainian SSR, on railroad and 17 mi. SE of Mukachevo; iron mining.

Irsina (ērsē'nä), town (pop. 8,149), Matera prov., Basilicata, S Italy, near Bradano R., 20 mi. WNW of Matera, in cereal- and grape-growing region. Has cathedral and mus. of antiquities.

Irthington, village and parish (pop. 646), N Cumberland, England, 7 mi. NE of Carlisle; cattle, sheep, oats. Has church of Norman origin and remains of Hadrian's Wall.

Irthlingborough (ăr'tŭlbŭrŭ), urban district (1931 pop. 4,715; 1951 census 5,015), E Northampton, England, on Nene R. (crossed by 14th-cent. bridge) and 4 mi. ENE of Wellingborough; leather tanning and shoe mfg.; ironstone quarrying and iron smelting. Has 13th-cent. church.

Irtysh River (ĭrtĭsh'), chief tributary of the Ob, in Kazakh SSR and W Siberian Russian SFSR; 1,844 mi. long. Rises in Sinkiang prov., China, on W slope of the Mongolian Altai Mts.; flows W as the Black Irtysh until it enters L. Zaisan (Kazakh SSR), which it leaves as the Irtysh proper; then going N and NW, it breaks through side ranges of Altai Mts., past Ust-Kamenogorsk (hydroelectric dam near by) and Semipalatinsk, through W Kulunda Steppe, past Pavlodar, into Russian SFSR, past Omsk and Tobolsk, to Ob R. at Khanty-Mansisk. Chief affluents: Narym, Bukhtarma, Om, and Tara (all right), Osha, Ishim, Vagai, Tobol, and Konda (all left) rivers. Middle course drains excellent agr. areas of W Siberia. Navigation begins at Semipalatinsk for steamers (for smaller craft at L. Zaisan) during April–Nov., and at Tobolsk during May–Nov. Until Russia's appearance on the Irtysh (at Tara, 1594), its banks were occupied successively by Mongols, Kalmyks, and Chinese. Rus. conquest of basin was completed in 1860s.

Irtyshskoye (ērtĭsh'skŭyŭ), village (1926 pop. 3,170), N Pavlodar oblast, Kazakh SSR, on Irtysh R. and 95 mi. NNW of Pavlodar; wheat.

Irumagawa (ērōōmä'gäwŭ), town (pop. 12,447), Saitama prefecture, central Honshu, Japan, 6 mi. SW of Kawagoe, in agr. area (rice, wheat); textiles.

Irumu (ērōō'mōō), town, ⊙ Kibali-Ituri dist. (□ 40,763; 1948 pop. c.860,000), Eastern Prov. NE Belgian Congo, on Shari R. near its confluence with Ituri R. and 315 mi. ENE of Stanleyville commercial center in region of white settlement Large hospitals for Europeans and natives. Airport Has decreased in importance since development o Bunia and of mining centers in the Kilo-Moto gol fields.

Irún (ērōōn'), frontier city (pop. 7,790), Guipúzcoa prov., N Spain, in the Basque Provs., on left ban of Bidassoa R. (Fr. border) and 10 mi. E of Sa Sebastián; customs station; commercial and indus trial center. Rolling-stock mfg.; cementworks; als makes matches, electrical equipment, liqueurs Has Renaissance church and 17th-cent. town hall Iron and lead mines near by. Strongly defended b Loyalists in Sp. civil war of 1936–39, it was burne before its surrender to the Nationalists in 1936.

Irupana (ērōōpä'nä), city (pop. c.3,300), La Pa dept., W Bolivia, in the Yungas, c.5 mi. SE o Chulumani, on road; alt. 6,059 ft.; in subtropica agr. area (coffee, cacao, quina).

Irurita (ērōōrē'tä), village (pop. 1,666), Navarr prov., N Spain, in the W Pyrenees, 22 mi. NNE o Pamplona; flour milling, chocolate mfg.; lumbe milling.

Iruya (ērōō'yä), village (pop. estimate 350) ⊙ Iruya dept. (□ 1,360; 1947 pop. 4,578), N Salt prov., Argentina, 60 mi. NW of Orán, in stock raising area.

Irvine (ĕr'vĭn), town (pop. 261), SE Alta., nea Sask. border, 19 mi. ESE of Medicine Hat; grai elevators. Coal and gas deposits near by.

Irvine (ûr'vĭn), burgh (1931 pop. 12,032; 1951 cen sus 14,741), N Ayrshire, Scotland, on Irvine R near its mouth on Firth of Clyde, 22 mi. SW o Glasgow; 55°37'N 4°41'W; port (shipping coal an chemicals) and mfg. center, with chemical work ironworks, sawmills, shipbuilding yards, glas works. Port was enlarged 1873 and later.

Irvine (ûr'vĭn), city (pop. 3,259), ⊙ Estill co., central Ky., on Kentucky R. and 38 mi. SE o Lexington, in truck-farming area; clothing mfg railroad shops, oil refineries, sawmills. Oil well timber near by. Cumberland Natl. Forest is just E

Irvine River (ûr'vĭn), Ayrshire, Scotland, rises o Lanark border 3 mi. NE of Darvel, flows 29 mi. W past Darvel, Newmilns and Greenholm, Galstor Kilmarnock, Dreghorn, and Irvine, to Firth o Clyde just WSW of Irvine.

Irvines Landing, village (pop. estimate 500), SW B.C., on Malaspina Strait of Strait of Georgia, a mouth of Jervis Inlet, 30 mi. N of Nanaimo; lum ber-shipping port.

Irvinestown (ûr'vĭnztoun), town (pop. 974), N C Fermanagh, Northern Ireland, 9 mi. N of Ennis killen; agr. market (potatoes, cattle).

Irving. 1 Village (pop. 539), Montgomery co., central Ill., 14 mi. E of Litchfield, in agr. a bituminous-coal area. **2** City (pop. 279), Marsha co., NE Kansas, on Big Blue R. and 2? mi. N o Manhattan; grain. **3** Town (pop. 2,621), Dalla co., N Texas, an outer WNW suburb of Dalla cotton ginning, mfg. (kitchen equipment, bldg. ma terials, beverages).

Irvington. **1** Village (1940 pop. 894), Alameda co., W Calif., 25 mi. SE of Oakland, in orchard and vineyard region; wine making, stove mfg. **2** Village (pop. 379), Washington co., SW Ill., 7 mi. S of Centralia, in fruitgrowing area. **3** Town (pop. 831), Breckinridge co., NW Ky., 40 mi. SW of Louisville; trade center in agr. (burley tobacco, corn, wheat, hay), limestone-quarries, and timber area. **4** Industrial town (pop. 59,201), Essex co., NE N.J., W suburb of Newark; metal and rubber products, leather, clothing, toys, hardware, tools, paper, pigments. Settled 1692 as Camptown, renamed 1852 for Washington Irving. Inc. as village 1874, as town 1898. **5** Residential village (pop. 3,657), Westchester co., SE N.Y., on E bank of the Hudson, bet. Dobbs Ferry (S) and Tarrytown; mfg. (textiles, metal, and quartz products, machinery, boats, religious articles); hothouse flowers, vegetables. Here at "Nevis," once estate of Alexander Hamilton's son, are a Columbia Univ. arboretum, a children's mus., and a cyclotron (supported by Columbia Univ. and the U.S. navy) begun 1947. Home for cardiac children here. Settled c.1655, inc. 1872. Originally called Dearman; renamed (1854) for Washington Irving, who bought the estate "Sunnyside" (extant) here in 1835. **6** Resort and fishing village (1940 pop. 673), Lancaster co., E Va., on the Rappahannock (ferry) near Chesapeake Bay, and 45 mi. N of Newport News; packs and cans seafood. Near by is Christ Church (1732).

Irvona (ûrvō'nù), borough (pop. 915), Clearfield co., W central Pa., 20 mi. NNW of Altoona.

Irwell River (ûr'wĕl), SE Lancashire, England, rises just N of Bacup, flows 40 mi. S, past Bacup, Bury, Radcliffe, and Manchester, to Mersey R. at Irlam. Receives Roch R. 2 mi. S of Bury.

Irwin, county (□ 372; pop. 11,973), S central Ga.; ⊙ Ocilla. Coastal plain agr. (cotton, corn, tobacco, peanuts, peaches, livestock) and timber area drained by Alapaha and Satilla rivers. Jefferson Davis Memorial State Park (W). Formed 1818.

Irwin. **1** Town (pop. 147), Bonneville co., SE Idaho, on Snake R. and c.40 mi. E of Idaho Falls. **2** Village (pop. 85), Kankakee co., NE Ill., 7 mi. SW of Kankakee, in agr. area. **3** Town (pop. 381), Shelby co., W Iowa, on West Nishnabotna R. and 11 mi. NE of Harlan. **4** Borough (pop. 4,228), Westmoreland co., SW Pa., 16 mi. SE of Pittsburgh; coal, limestone; foundry products, electrical equipment. W terminus of 1st section of Pennsylvania Turnpike. Laid out 1853, inc. 1864.

Irwin Canal, irrigation channel in Mandya dist., S Mysore, India; from dam on Cauvery R. at Krishnarajasagara extends 28 mi. NE to 9,000-ft.-long underground tunnel, from which subsidiary canals (total length, 180 mi.) branch out, irrigating over 120,000 acres.

Irwinton, town (pop. 700), ⊙ Wilkinson co., central Ga., 27 mi. E of Macon, in agr. (cotton, corn, truck, potatoes) and kaolin area.

Irymple (ĭrĭm'pùl), town (pop. 1,718), NW Victoria, Australia, near Mildura, 205 mi. ENE of Adelaide, in fruitgrowing area; dried fruit.

Is, Iraq; see HIT.

Is (ēs), town (1939 pop. over 2,000), W Sverdlovsk oblast, Russian SFSR, in the central Urals, on Is R. (left tributary of Tura R.) and 60 mi. NNW of Nizhni Tagil; rail junction on spur from Vyya; center of gold-mining region. Developed in 1930s; called Sverdlovski Priisk until 1933.

Isa (ē'sä), town (pop. 5,292), Yamaguchi prefecture, SW Honshu, Japan, 15 mi. W of Yamaguchi; rice, charcoal, lumber; paper milling, marble quarrying.

Isa (ē'sä), town (pop. 15,677), Sokoto prov., Northern Provinces, NW Nigeria, 45 mi. NNW of Kaura Namoda; cotton, millet; cattle, skins.

Isaac Arriaga (ēsäk' äryä'gä), town (pop. 1,886), Michoacán, central Mexico, 10 mi. N of Puruándiro; cereals, livestock. Formerly Santa Ana.

Isaac Lake (28 mi. long, 1–2 mi. wide), E B.C., in Cariboo Mts., 70 mi. ENE of Quesnel; alt. 3,200 ft. Drains SE through Lanezi L. and Cariboo R. into Quesnel R.

Isaacs Harbour, village (pop. estimate 400), E N.S., on Isaacs Harbour R., near its mouth on the Atlantic, 17 mi. SSW of Guysborough; lobster, haddock fishing. In gold-mining region.

Isabel. **1** City (pop. 205), Barber co., S Kansas, 14 mi. SE of Pratt, in cattle and wheat region. **2** Town (pop. 511), Dewey co., N central S.Dak., 17 mi. W of Timber Lake; lignite mines near by; dairy produce, poultry, livestock, grain.

Isabela or **La Isabela** (ĭzùbĕ'lù, Sp. lä ēsäbä'lä), ruined town in Puerto Plata prov., N Dominican Republic, on the coast, 25 mi. WNW of Puerto Plata. Founded 1493 by Columbus, it is reputedly 1st town settled by the Spanish on American soil.

Isabela, province (□ 4,069; 1948 pop. 264,495), N Luzon, Philippines, bounded E by Philippine Sea; ⊙ ILAGAN. Fertile central region is drained by Cagayan R. and its tributary, Magat R. Part of Sierra Madre is on E coast. Corn and tobacco are grown.

Isabela. **1** Town (1939 pop. 5,285; 1948 municipality pop. 33,743), Negros Occidental prov., W Negros isl., Philippines, 9 mi. E of Binalbagan; agr. center (rice, sugar cane); sugar milling. **2** Town (1939 pop. 1,000), a chief town of Basilan Isl., Zamboanga prov., Philippines, on Basilan Strait opposite Zamboanga; small port, shipping lumber. Fishing, agr. (coconuts, corn, rice).

Isabela, town (pop. 6,895), NW Puerto Rico, near the Atlantic, on railroad and 9 mi. NE of Aguadilla; agr. center in fertile irrigated region (sugar cane, tobacco, cotton, coffee, vegetables, tropical fruit). Site of experimental station and agr. col. of the Univ. of Puerto Rico. The Isabela hydroelectric plant is c.3 mi. SSE. Isabela Segunda is on N Vieques Isl.

Isabela, Cape, headland on N coast of Dominican Republic, 23 mi. WNW of Puerto Plata; 19°58'N 71°W. The ruined town of ISABELA, reputedly the 1st town settled by Spanish in America, is near by.

Isabela, La, Cuba: see ISABELA DE SAGUA.

Isabela, La, village (pop. 199), Guadalajara prov., central Spain, 3 mi. SSE of Sacedón, 28 mi. ESE of Guadalajara; thermal springs.

Isabela de Sagua (dā sä'gwä) or **La Isabela,** town (pop. 3,470), Las Villas prov., central Cuba, port for Sagua la Grande, on Nicholas Channel, 37 mi. N of Santa Clara. Rail terminus; sugar-shipping and fishing (sharks, oysters, crabs) center. Also a seaside resort. Seaplane anchorage.

Isabela Island or **Albemarle Island** (□ 2,249; 1950 pop. 308), largest of the Galápagos Isls., Ecuador, in the Pacific, 90 mi. W of Puerto Baquerizo (San Cristóbal Isl.), on the equator, bet. 0°10'N–1°5'S and 90°48'W–91°35'W. A volcanic, L-shaped isl. (c.80 mi. long), it has many craters, the highest (SW) rising to 4,698 ft. Sparsely settled, its main products are potatoes, cattle, wild hogs, reptile hides, fish (tuna, lobster, corvina). VILLAMIL, on S coast, is its main port and site of penal colony.

Isabela Segunda (sāgōōn'dä), **Isabela II,** or **Vieques** (vyā'kĕs), town (pop. 3,085), on N shore of Vieques Isl., off E Puerto Rico, 50 mi. ESE of San Juan; 18°9'N 65°26'W. Main town and landing of the isl., in sugar-growing and stock-raising region. U.S. naval base.

Isabel II Canal (ēsävĕl' sāgōōn'dä) or **Lozoya Canal** (lōthoi'ä), Madrid prov., central Spain, begins near confluence of Lozoya and Jarama rivers (reservoirs) E of Patones, and flows c.40 mi. S to Madrid, which it supplies with water. Begun 1902.

Isabelia, Cordillera (kôrdēyā'rä ēsäbä'lyä), N central Nicaragua, E spur of main continental divide; extends from area bet. Condega and San Rafael del Norte 150 mi. generally ENE to Bonanza mining dist.; forms watershed bet. Coco R. (N) and Río Grande (S); rises to over 6,500 ft. in Saslaya peak. Sometimes called Yeluca Mts.

Isabella (ĭzùbĕ'lù), county (□ 572; pop. 28,964), central Mich.; ⊙ Mt. Pleasant. Drained by Chippewa and Pine rivers. Stock and poultry raising, dairying, agr. (sugar beets, beans, grain, corn, hay, potatoes). Mfg. at Mt. Pleasant. Oil wells, refineries. Organized 1859.

Isabella, village (1940 pop. 810), Polk co., SE Tenn., near Ga.-N.C.-Tenn. border, 50 mi. E of Chattanooga; copper mining and smelting.

Isabella, Cape, SE Ellesmere Isl., NE Franklin Dist., Northwest Territories, on Smith Sound; 78°21'N 75°W. Named (1818) by John Ross after one of his expedition vessels.

Isabella Dam, Calif.: see KERN RIVER.

Isabella River, rises in small lake in Lake co., NE Minn., flows 30 mi. W, through Superior Natl. Forest, to Bald Eagle L. SE of Ely. Drains L. Isabella (3 mi. long, 2 mi. wide).

Isaccea (ēsäk'chä), Lat. *Noviodunum,* town (1948 pop. 4,653), Galati prov., SE Rumania, in Dobruja, on Danube R. and 17 mi. WNW of Tulcea; inland port trading in fish, lumber, grain. Extensive vineyards and marble quarries in vicinity (S). Has 16th-cent. mosque.

Isachsen, Cape, NW extremity of Ellef Ringnes Isl., N Franklin Dist., Northwest Territories, on the Arctic Ocean; 79°25'N 105°30'W.

Isachsen Peninsula, formerly Isachsen Island, Canada: see ELLEF RINGNES ISLAND.

Isady, Russian SFSR: see SEMIBRATOVO.

Isafjardar or **Isafjardhar** (ē'säfyär"dhär), Icelandic *Ísafjarðar,* county [Icelandic *sýsla*] (pop. 3,884), NW Iceland; ⊙ Isafjordur, a city in but independent of the co. Covers central and W part of Vestfjarda Peninsula. Rocky coast line. Fishing. Main towns and villages are Bolungarvik, Flateyri, and Sudureyri.

Isafjardardjup or **Isafjardhardjup** (ē'säfyär'dhärdyōōp"), Icelandic *Ísafjarðardjúp,* inlet (50 mi. long, 1–12 mi. wide) of Denmark Strait, NW Iceland, on NW coast of Vestfjarda Peninsula; 66°5'N 22°45'W. Extends numerous arms (S). On a S arm, near its mouth, is Isafjordur city.

Isafjordur or **Isafjordhur** (ē'säfyûr"dhûr), Icelandic *Ísafjörður,* city (pop. 2,857), ⊙ and in but independent of Isafjardar co., NW Iceland, on Vestfjarda Peninsula, on S arm of Isafjardardjup, 140 mi. NNW of Reykjavik; 66°4'N 23°9'W; fishing and commercial center.

Isagarh (ĭs'ăgûr), village, E Madhya Bharat, India, 38 mi. ENE of Guna; millet, wheat, gram.

Isahaya (ēsä'häyû), city (1940 pop. 44,418; 1947 pop. 64,183), Nagasaki prefecture, W Kyushu, Japan, on S central Hizen Peninsula, 12 mi. NE of Nagasaki; rail junction; rice, raw silk.

Isaka (ēsä'kä), village, Western Prov., N central Tanganyika, on railroad and 75 mi. N of Tabora; peanuts, millet. Gold and limestone deposits.

Isa Khel (ĭs'ŭ kāl), town (pop. 7,931), Mianwali dist., NW Punjab, W Pakistan, 15 mi. WNW of Mianwali; local market for wheat, gram, cattle. Also written Isakhel.

Isakly (ēsäk'lē), village (1939 pop. over 2,000), NE Kuibyshev oblast, Russian SFSR, on Sok R. and 21 mi. NNE of Sergiyevsk; dairying; wheat, sunflowers, legumes.

Isakogorka (ēsä"kŭgôr'kŭ), S suburb (1926 pop. 2,384) of Archangel, Archangel oblast, Russian SFSR, on railroad and 7 mi. S of city center; rail junction of branch to Molotovsk.

Isaku, Japan: see IZAKU.

Isandhlwana (ēsändlwä'nù), agr. village, Zululand, central Natal, U. of So. Afr., near Buffalo R., 30 mi. ESE of Dundee; mission station. During Zulu War (1879) British force was annihilated here by Cetewayo's troops. Louis Napoleon, son of Napoleon III, serving with British, was killed 20 mi. NNE.

Isangi (ēsäng'gē), village, Eastern Prov., central Belgian Congo, on left bank of Congo R. at mouth of Lomami R. and 70 mi. WNW of Stanleyville; steamboat landing and transshipment point. R.C. mission. Former Arab post, it still preserves picturesque ruins of old mosque. Local Negro tribe, the Topoke, is noted for its inordinate tattooing.

Isangila (ēsäng-gē'lä), village, Leopoldville prov., W Belgian Congo, on right bank of Congo R. and 45 mi. NE of Boma. Though this section of Congo R. is part of the noted Livingstone Falls, the river is navigable bet. here and Manyanga. British explorer Capt. J. K. Tuckey reached Isangila from W in 1876.

Isanlu Makatu (ēshän'lōō mäkä'tōō), town, Kabba prov., Northern Provinces, W central Nigeria, 38 mi. NW of Kabba; tin-mining center; columbite and tantalite also mined; shea-nut processing.

Isanti (ī'säntē), county (□ 442; pop. 12,123), E Minn.; ⊙ Cambridge. Agr. area drained by Rum R. Dairy products, grain, livestock, poultry; peat. Co. formed 1849.

Isanti, village (pop. 422), Isanti co., E Minn., on Rum R. and 36 mi. N of Minneapolis; dairy products.

Isarco River (ēzär'kô), Ger. *Eisack,* N Italy, rises in the Alps 1 mi. W of Brenner Pass, flows 55 mi. generally S, past Bressanone and Bolzano, to Adige R. 4 mi. SW of Bolzano.

Isarog, Mount (ēsärōg'), extinct volcano (6,482 ft.), Camarines Sur prov., SE Luzon, Philippines, 10 mi. E of Naga. Numerous streams rise here. Sulphur mining.

Isar River (ē'zär), Bavaria, Germany, rises in the Karwendelgebirge 6 mi. NE of Innsbruck, flows generally NNE, through Scharnitz Pass gorge (Austro-German border), past Bad Tölz, Munich, Freising, and Landshut, to the Danube 2.5 mi. SSE of Deggendorf. Length 163 mi. Receives the Loisach, the Würm, and the Amper (right). Regulated bet. Lenggries and Wolfratshausen. Large hydroelectric plants below Munich.

Isaszeg (ĭ'shŏsĕg), town (pop. 6,495), Pest-Pilis-Solt-Kiskun co., N central Hungary, on Rakos R. and 15 mi. E of Budapest; distilleries. Hungarian victory here (1849) over Austrian forces.

Isauria (īsô'rēù), anc. district of S central Asia Minor, on borders of Pisidia and Cilicia. It was a wild region inhabited by marauding bands, partially checked by the Romans in 1st cent. B.C. but not completely subdued until arrival of the Seljuk Turks.

Isawa (ēsä'wä), town (pop. 5,845), Yamanashi prefecture, central Honshu, Japan, 4 mi. E of Kofu; rice, raw silk. Sericulture school.

Isayevo-Dedovo, Russian SFSR: see OKTYABRSKOYE, Chkalov oblast.

Isbarta, Turkey: see ISPARTA, town.

Isbergues (ēzbârg'), town (pop. 3,994), Pas-de-Calais dept., N France, on Aire–La Bassée Canal and 11 mi. NW of Béthune; blast furnaces, forges.

Isca, England: see CAERLEON.

Isca Damnoniorum, England: see EXETER.

Íscar (ē'skär), town (pop. 2,998), Valladolid prov., N central Spain, 22 mi. SE of Valladolid; flour- and sawmills; grain, chicory, sheep.

Iscayachi (ēskäyä'chē), town (pop. c.1,500), Tarija dept., S Bolivia, 20 mi. W of Tarija; road center; vineyards, fruit, grain.

Ischia (ē'skyä), rocky island (□ 18; pop. 30,418), Napoli prov., S Italy, near NW entrance to Bay of Naples, 18 mi. WSW of Naples; in 8-mi.-wide channel separating it from Cape Miseno lies Procida isl. Ischia is 5 mi. long, 4 mi. wide; rises to 2,589 ft. in Monte Epomeo (center). Health resort, noted for its warm mineral springs and scenery. Inhabited since anc. times; repeatedly abandoned because of its volcanic eruptions (last occurred in 1302). Agr. (grapes, olives, citrus fruit, cereals); fishing. Exports wine. Ischia (pop. 2,858), principal town, is on NE coast; bishopric. First built by Greeks in 5th cent. B.C. on an islet (site of imposing 15th-cent. castle), now connected with town by a stone causeway. Other towns include Casamicciola, Forio, and Lacco Ameno.

Ischia di Castro (dē kä'strô), village (pop. 2,899), Viterbo prov., Latium, central Italy, 20 mi. WNW of Viterbo.

Ischilín, department, Argentina: see DEÁN FUNES.

Ischilín, Sierra de (syĕ'rä dā ēschēlēn'), pampean mountain range of Sierra de Córdoba, NW Córdoba prov., Argentina; extends c.12 mi. S from Deán Funes; rises to c.3,000 ft.

Ischitella (ēskētĕl'lä), town (pop. 5,187), Foggia prov., Apulia, S Italy, on Gargano promontory, 15 mi. W of Vieste, in sheep-raising and agr. (olives, grapes) region.

Ischl, Austria: see BAD ISCHL.

Ischua (ĭ'shōōū, ĭ'shōōä''), village (pop. c.200), Cattaraugus co., W N.Y., on Ischua Creek and 12 mi. N of Olean.

Ischua Creek, W N.Y., rises W of Machias, flows c.30 mi. S to Allegheny R. at Olean; below influx of small Oil Creek it is called Olean Creek.

Iscia Baidoa, Ital. Somaliland: see ISHA BAIDOA.

Ise (ē'sā), former province in S Honshu, Japan; now part of Mie prefecture.

Ise Bay, Jap. *Ise-wan*, inlet of Philippine Sea, central Honshu, Japan; bounded E by Chita Peninsula; 15 mi. long, 5–10 mi. wide. Has 2 arms: CHITA BAY (NE) and ATSUMI BAY (E). Nagoya is at head of bay, Tsu and Uji-yamada on W shore. Formerly sometimes called Owari Bay.

Ise Fjord (ē'sù fyôr'') (20 mi. long), N Zealand, Denmark. Branches into Roskilde Fjord (25 mi. long) on E side, Nykobing Bay, Lamme Fjord, and Holbaek Fjord on W side. Oro isl. (□ 6; pop. 782) is 11 mi. S of mouth.

Iseghem, Belgium: see IZEGEM.

Isehara (ēsā'härù), town (pop. 7,669), Kanagawa prefecture, central Honshu, Japan, 6 mi. NNW of Hiratsuka; rice, tobacco.

Isel or **Iselberg** (ē'zùlbĕrk), hill (2,460 ft.) just S of Innsbruck, Tyrol, W Austria, with excellent view. Site of battle (1809) bet. Austrians and French. Also called Berg Isel.

Iselle (ēzĕl'lĕ), village (pop. 137), Novara prov., Piedmont, N Italy, 2 mi. W of Swiss border, near S entrance to Simplon Tunnel, 8 mi. NW of Domodossola; customs station.

Isel River (ē'zùl), S Austria, rises in the Grossvenediger of the Hohe Tauern, flows 30 mi. SE, through East Tyrol, to the Drau at Lienz.

Isen (ē'zùn), village (pop. 1,631), Upper Bavaria, Germany, on the Isen and 10 mi. SE of Erding; mfg. of textiles, bricks, tiles; metalworking. Has late-12th-cent. church. Chartered 1434.

Isen, Korea: see KWANGCHON.

Isen River (ē'zùn), Bavaria, Germany, rises 4 mi. S of Isen, flows 40 mi. E to the Inn, 1.5 mi. N of Altötting.

Iseo (ēzā'ô), town (pop. 2,881), Brescia prov., Lombardy, N Italy, port on SE shore of Lago d'Iseo, 12 mi. NW of Brescia. Resort; silk and flax mills, dyeworks, tannery, lime kilns, pottery factory; fishing; peat digging.

Iseo, Lago d' (lä'gô dēzā'ô), or **Sebino** (sĕbē'nô), anc. *Lacus Sebinus*, lake (□ 23.5) in Lombardy, N Italy, in Brescia (E) and Bergamo (W) provs., 18 mi. E of Bergamo; 15.5 mi. long, up to 3 mi. wide, alt. 610 ft., max. depth 820 ft. Fishing; fish hatcheries. Used for irrigation. In center of lake is Monte Isole or Montisola, largest fresh-water isl. (□ 5; pop. 1,582) in Italy; c.2 mi. long, 1 mi. wide; rises to 1,965 ft. Lake traversed by Oglio R. On its picturesque banks are Iseo, Pisogne, and Lovere. Small steamers ply bet. them.

Iseran, Col de l' (kôl dù lēzùrä'), Alpine pass (9,085 ft.), Savoie dept., SE France, bet. Graian Alps (E) and Massif de la Vanoise (W), connects upper Isère R. valley (Tarentaise; N) with Arc R. valley (Maurienne; S). Scenic road (one of highest in Europe) bet. Bourg-Saint-Maurice (20 mi. NW) and Lanslebourg (12 mi. SE) completed 1937.

Isère (ēzâr'), department (□ 3,180; pop. 574,019), in Dauphiné, SE France; ⊙ Grenoble. Extending E from the Rhone (below Lyons), it includes the Pre-Alpine massifs of Grande Chartreuse and Vercors and part of Massif du Pelvoux (rising to 13,461 ft.). Dept. is bisected by Isère R., which, bet. Chambéry trough and Grenoble, flows in fertile Grésivaudan valley. Agr. (tobacco, corn, potatoes, wheat, wine; chestnuts, peaches) in Alpine basins and in Rhone valley just SE of Lyons. Most mineral deposits too remote from railroads for economic exploitation. Anthracite mined N of La Mure, iron near Allevard. Extensive hydroelectric developments in gorges of the Romanche (Chambon Dam; power plants in Livet-et-Gavet commune), and of the Drac (Sautet Dam; power plants near La Mure, at Avignonet, Pont-de-Claix) activate electrometallurgical (aluminum, steel, electrical equipment) and electrochemical works at Grenoble, Villard-Bonnot, Allevard, Pont-de-Claix, Livet. Dept. also produces kid gloves (at Grenoble), woolens (at Vienne), and has numerous paper mills and cementworks. It exports Grande Chartreuse liqueur. Chief towns are Grenoble and Vienne. The Grésivaudan valley is densely populated.

Isère River, SE France, an important stream of Fr. Alps, rises in Graian Alps near Ital. border above Val-d'Isère, flows generally W through Savoy Alps in deep TARENTAISE valley, turns SW near Albertville, traversing the COMBE DE SAVOIE, and, bet. Montmélian and Grenoble, the fertile GRÉSIVAUDAN glacial trough. Below Grenoble it veers NW at foot of the Grande Chartreuse, winds around Vercors massif (S), and continues SW, past Romans-sur-Isère, to the Rhone 4 mi. above Valence. Length: 180 mi. Receives the Arly (right), Arc, Drac, and Bourne rivers (left). Upper valley has numerous hydroelectric plants which power chemical and metallurgical works.

Isergebirge (ē'zùrgùbĭr''gù), Czech *Jizerské Hory* (yĭ'zùrskä hō'rĭ), Pol. *Góry Izerskie* (gōō'rĭ ēzĕr'-skyĕ), mountain range of the Sudetes, in N Bohemia, Czechoslovakia, and Lower Silesia (after 1945, SW Poland); extend c.20 mi. bet. Chrastava, Czechoslovakia (W), and headwaters of Kwisa (Queis) R. (E); rise to 3,681 ft. in Smrk, to c.3,675 ft. in Jizera peaks. Novy Svet Pass is at S foot.

Ise River (īz), Northampton, England, rises just N of Naseby, flows 20 mi. E and S, past Kettering, to Nene R. at Wellingborough.

Iserlohn (ē''zùrlōn'), city (1950 pop. 46,104), in former Prussian prov. of Westphalia, W Germany, after 1945 in North Rhine-Westphalia, 14 mi. SE of Dortmund; wire mills; mfg. of springs, needles, bronze goods, chemicals. Active trade. Has 11th- and 14th-cent. churches.

Isernia (ēzĕr'nyä), town (pop. 7,826), Campobasso prov., Abruzzi e Molise, S central Italy, 23 mi. W of Campobasso; macaroni factories, woolen mills, foundry; lace mfg. Bishopric. Badly damaged (1943) in Second World War.

Iser River, Czechoslovakia: see JIZERA RIVER.

Isesaki, Japan: see ISEZAKI, Gumma prefecture.

Iset River or **Iset' River** (ēsyĕt'yù), in SW Siberian Russian SFSR, rises in the central Urals c.10 mi. NE of Bilimbai, flows SE, forming dammed Iset L. (□ 8; Sredne-Uralsk on E shore), Verkhne-Iset pond (W of Sverdlovsk city center) and Nizhne-Iset pond (S of Sverdlovsk city center), past Sverdlovsk and Aramil, and generally ESE, past Kamensk-Uralski, Kataisk, Dalmatovo, and Shadrinsk, to Tobol R. 4 mi. S of Yalutorovsk; length, c.325 mi. Lumber floating. Part of projected Kama-Irtysh waterway. Dammed at Sverdlovsk for industrial water supply. Receives Techa and Miass rivers.

Isetskoye (ēsyĕt'skŭyù), village (1926 pop. 848), SW Tyumen oblast, Russian SFSR, on Iset R. and 40 mi. SW of Yalutorovsk, in agr. area (grain, livestock).

Iseum, Egypt: see BAHBIT EL HIGARA.

Iseyin (ēsā'ē), town (pop. 36,805), Oyo prov., Western Provinces, SW Nigeria, 25 mi. WNW of Oyo; cotton-weaving center; metalworking; cacao, palm oil and kernels.

Isezaki (ēsā'zäkē). **1** or **Isesaki** (ēsā'säkē), city (1940 pop. 40,004; 1947 pop. 46,046), Gumma prefecture, central Honshu, Japan, 8 mi. SE of Maebashi; silk-textile center. **2** Town, Tottori prefecture, Japan: see URAYASU.

Isfahan (ĭs'fùhän'', -hăn'') or **Esfahan** (ĕsfähän'), former province (□ 50,000; pop. 1,105,956) of central Iran; ⊙ Isfahan. Bounded N by Kashan and Gulpaigan, W by Luristan and Khuzistan, S by Fars, and E by Yezd, it is situated in E margins of the Zagros ranges and extends onto the central plateau. Agr. is concentrated along Zaindeh R.; grain, tobacco, cotton, opium. Stock raising in Bakhtiari tribal country (W). Highways radiate from Isfahan to other important centers (Nejafabad, Shahriza, Ardistan). Isfahan prov. was joined (1938) with Yezd prov. to form Iran's Tenth Province (□ 100,000; pop. 1,431,762).

Isfahan or **Esfahan**, anc. *Aspadana* (ăs''pùdä'nù), city (1940 pop. 204,598), ⊙ Tenth Prov., W central Iran, 210 mi. S of Teheran and on Zaindeh R.; alt. 5,200 ft.; 32°40'N 51°40'E. Iran's 3d-largest city and chief city of former Isfahan prov., situated on E edge of the Zagros ranges in basin watered by Zaindeh R.; center of rich agr. region and outlet for animal products of Bakhtiari country (SW), major textile-milling center; cotton, silk, and woolen goods; carpets, brocade, metalwork, foodstuffs and dried fruit. Highway hub, linked with Teheran, Arak, Shiraz, and Yezd. Airport. The city's heart is the Maidan-i-Shah (royal square), a vast enclosure surrounded by bazaars (N); the Lutfullah mosque with blue-tiled dome (E); the great 17th-cent. Masjid-i-Shah (royal mosque; S), one of the outstanding examples of Persian architecture, and the Ali Kapu gate (W), leading to the former royal gardens. These gardens contain numerous courts and pavilions, of which the Chihil Satun (40 pillars) is noted as the former throne hall. The Shah Hussain madrasah (1710) was originally a school for dervishes. The broad esplanade, Chehar Bagh, leads to the arcaded bridge (one of 3 across the Zaindeh), which links Isfahan proper with the right-bank suburb of Julfa or Jolfa. Julfa was founded in 1603, settled by Armenian artisans from Julfa in Azerbaijan, and is seat of Armenian bishopric. Situated on line of march of Alexander the Great, Isfahan 1st achieved prominence as provincial capital under the Baghdad caliphs and in 11th cent. as temporary capital of Seljuk realm. It fell in 1387 to Tamerlane, who is said to have erected a great skull tower following massacre of local pop. It was under the Safavid dynasty, however, that Isfahan reached the zenith of its development. The residence was transferred here (1590) from Kazvin by Abbas the Great, who built many of the sumptuous edifices of the city. In 17th cent., Isfahan's pop. was more than 500,000. Its decline began in 1722 with its sacking by the Ghilzai Afghans, and it did not regain its former glory after its recapture (1729) by Nadir Shah. It was formerly spelled Ispahan.

Isfana (ēsfùnä'), village (1939 pop. over 500), W Osh oblast, Kirghiz SSR, on N slope of Turkestan Range, 30 mi. S of Leninabad; wheat.

Isfara (ēsfùrä'), town (1948 pop. over 10,000), E Leninabad oblast, Tadzhik SSR, on railroad and 15 mi. SE of Kanibadam, in oil-producing area; fruit-canning (apricots), tobacco industry; cotton. Ozocerite quarries near by.

Isfarain or **Esfarayen** (both: ĕsfärīn'), agr. district of Khurasan, Ninth Prov., NE Iran, 30 mi. SSE of Bujnurd, across the Ala Dagh; irrigated agr. (grain, fruit). Main village is Mianabad.

Isfendiyar Mountains, Turkey: see KURE MOUNTAINS.

Is Fjord (ēs), Nor. *Isfjorden*, inlet (70 mi. long, 8–20 mi. wide) of Arctic Ocean, W West Spitsbergen, Spitsbergen group; 78°5'–78°27'N 13°35'–17°20'E. On S shore of mouth is Cape Linné; on Advent Bay, on S shore of fjord, are Grumant City and Longyear City, coal-mining settlements. Extends several arms: Gront Fjord, Nor. *Grønfjorden* (Barentsburg settlement on E shore), extends 10 mi. S; Sassen Fjord and Tempel Fjord extend 20 mi. E; Bille Fjord extends 18 mi. NE; and Dickson Fjord extends 30 mi. N. Several extensive glaciers drain into the fjord, which is open to shipping, July–Sept. On Tempel and Bille fjords are gypsum and anhydrite deposits, not worked now.

Isha Baidoa (ē'shä bī'dwä), Ital. *Iscia Baidoa*, town (pop. 10,000), in the Upper Juba, S central Ital. Somaliland, 135 mi. WNW of Mogadishu, on Hodur plateau; 3°7'N 43°38'E. Road junction, agr. trade center (cereals, livestock). Has fort.

Ishan (yē'shän'), town, ⊙ Ishan co. (pop. 288,264), N Kwangsi prov., China, 45 mi. WNW of Liuchow and on railroad; cotton textiles; rice, millet, tea, beans, peanuts. Until 1913 called Kingyüan.

I Shan, mountains, China: see I MOUNTAINS.

Ishawooa Pass, Wyo.: see ABSAROKA RANGE.

Isherim (ēshùrēm'), peak (4,367 ft.) in the Urals, Russian SFSR, at junction of N and central Urals; 61°N. The Vishera and Lozva rivers rise near by.

Isheyevka (ēshyā'ùfkŭ), town (1939 pop. over 2,000), N Ulyanovsk oblast, Russian SFSR, on Sviyaga R. and 9 mi. NNW of Ulyanovsk; woolen milling.

Ishibashi (ēshē'bäshē), town (pop. 6,946), Tochigi prefecture, central Honshu, Japan, 9 mi. S of Utsunomiya; agr. (gourds, rice).

Ishibe (ēshē'bā), town (pop. 4,217), Shiga prefecture, S Honshu, Japan, 17 mi. E of Kyoto; rice.

Ishidoriya, Japan: see ISHITORIYA.

Ishigaki (ēshē'gäkē), city (1950 pop. 19,868), on Ishigaki-shima of Sakishima Isls., in the Ryukyus, on S coast of isl.; agr. center (rice, sugar cane, sweet potatoes); sake, dried tuna.

Ishigaki-shima (ēshē'gäkē''shĭmä), largest island (□ 83; 1950 pop. 27,907) of Sakishima Isls., in the Ryukyus, bet. East China Sea (W) and Philippine Sea (E), 230 mi. WSW of Okinawa; 24°24'N 124°12'E; 11 mi. long (with long peninsula in N), 8.5 mi. wide. Mountainous, rising to 1,670 ft. Produces pottery, sake, raw silk, dried tuna. Agr. products include sweet potatoes, sugar cane, rice. Formerly called Pachungsan. Chief town, Ishigaki.

Ishige (ēshē'gā), town (pop. 7,177), Ibaraki prefecture, central Honshu, Japan, 13 mi. WNW of Tsuchiura; rice, silk cocoons.

Ishih (yē'shû'), town, ⊙ Ishih co. (pop. 77,937), SW Shansi prov., China, 35 mi. NE of Yüngtsi; corn, beans, wheat.

Ishii (ēshē'), town (pop. 6,588), Tokushima prefecture, E Shikoku, Japan, 6 mi. W of Tokushima; livestock-raising, rice-growing center.

Ishiji (ēshē'jē), town (pop. 3,692), Niigata prefecture, central Honshu, Japan, on Sea of Japan, 11 mi. NE of Kashiwazaki; agr., fishing, oil drilling.

Ishikari (ēshkä'rē), town (pop. 8,745), SW Hokkaido, Japan, fishing port on Ishikari Bay, at mouth of Ishikari R., 13 mi. N of Sapporo; agr. (rice, wheat). Oil field (opened 1887) near by.

Ishikari, coal field, Japan: see YUBARI.

Ishikari Bay, Jap. *Ishikari-wan*, inlet of Sea of Japan, in W Hokkaido, Japan; 50 mi. long, 30 mi. wide. Otaru is on S shore. Also called Otaru Bay; formerly sometimes Strogonov Bay.

Ishikari River, Jap. *Ishikari-gawa*, second largest river of Japan, in W Hokkaido; rises on Asahi-dake 30 mi. E of Asahigawa, flows W, past Asahigawa and Fukagawa, SSW, past Sunagawa and Ebetsu, and WNW to Ishikari Bay at Ishikari; 227 mi. long. Drains mtn. area and Yubari coal field.

Ishikawa (ēshkä'wä), prefecture [Jap. *ken*] (□ 1,619; 1940 pop. 757,676; 1947 pop. 927,743), central Honshu, Japan; ⊙ KANAZAWA. Bounded W and N by Sea of Japan, E by Toyama Bay; NANAO is principal port. Roughly half of prefecture is on

Noto Peninsula (N). Extensive coastal area is generally flat and fertile, interior is mountainous and forested. Hot springs on SW coast and on Noto Peninsula. Rice growing, lumbering, raw-silk production. Mfg. (textiles, porcelain, lacquer ware). Principal centers: Kanazawa, Nanao, KOMATSU.

Ishikawa. **1** Town (pop. 8,157), Aomori prefecture, N Honshu, Japan, 5 mi. SE of Hirosaki; rice, lumber. **2** Town (pop. 8,532), Fukushima prefecture, central Honshu, Japan, 17 mi. SSE of Koriyama; mining (tourmaline, rock crystal).

Ishikawa, city (1950 pop. 17,795), on central Okinawa, in the Ryukyus, 18 mi. NNE of Naha, on E coast; fishing port.

Ishim (ēshēm'), city (1936 pop. estimate 34,500), SE Tyumen oblast, Russian SFSR, on Ishim R., on Trans-Siberian RR and 160 mi. SE of Tyumen; center of agr. area; meat packing, flour milling, distilling. Founded 1670; chartered 1782.

Ishimbai or **Ishimbay** (ēshēmbī'), city (1939 pop. over 10,000), W central Bashkir Autonomous SSR, Russian SFSR, on W slope of the S Urals, on Belaya R. and 90 mi. S of Ufa, on rail spur from Sterlitamak; major petroleum center (cracking plant; pipe line to Chernikovsk); sawmilling. Developed in 1930s; became city in 1940.

Ishimori (ē'shĭmōrē) or **Ishinomori** (ē'shĭnō'mōrē), town (pop. 7,227), Miyagi prefecture, N Honshu, Japan, 5 mi. SE of Wakayanagi; rice, wheat, silk cocoons.

Ishim River, in N Kazakh SSR and Tyumen oblast, Russian SFSR, largest left tributary of Irtysh R.; rises N of Karaganda, flows W, past Akmolinsk and Atbasar, and N, past Petropavlovsk, into Russian SFSR, past Ishim, through Ishim Steppe (flour mills), to Irtysh R. at Ust-Ishim, 110 mi. ESE of Tobolsk; 1,123 mi. long. Navigable below Vikulovo. Receives Nura (intermittently) and Koluton rivers.

Ishim Steppe, black-earth area of W.Siberian Plain, Russian SFSR, bet. lower Irtysh and Tobol rivers; drained by lower Ishim R. Rich agr. area (wheat, dairy farming).

Ishinden, Japan: see ISSHINDEN.

Ishinomaki (ēshē'nōmäkē), city (1940 pop. 36,442; 1947 pop. 46,745), Miyagi prefecture, N Honshu, Japan, port on Ishinomaki Bay, at mouth of Kitakami R., 25 mi. ENE of Sendai; fish canneries, building-stone quarries. Exports fish. Sometimes spelled Isinomaki.

Ishinomaki Bay, Jap. *Ishinomaki-wan,* inlet of Pacific Ocean, in Miyagi prefecture, N Honshu, Japan; sheltered E by Ojika Peninsula; 25 mi. E-W, 10 mi. N-S. Contains, near Matsushima, hundreds of pine-clad islets. Ishinomaki is on N, Sendai on W shore. Also called Sendai Bay.

Ishinomori, Japan: see ISHIMORI.

Ishioka (ēshē'ōkä), town (pop. 25,969), Ibaraki prefecture, central Honshu, Japan, 8 mi. NE of Tsuchiura; textiles, soy sauce, sake; sawmilling.

Ishitoriya (ēshĭtō'rēä) or **Ishidoriya** (–dō'rēä), town (pop. 6,371), Iwate prefecture, N Honshu, Japan, on Kitakami R. and 14 mi. S of Morioka; rice, sake.

Ishitsuka, Japan: see ISHIZUKA.

Ishizuchi, Mount (ēshē'zōōchē), Jap. *Ishizuchi-yama,* highest peak (6,497 ft.) of Shikoku, Japan, in Ehime prefecture, 11 mi. SSW of Saijo. Site of Shinto temple. Cherry and fir trees on slopes. Sometimes spelled Isizuti.

Ishizuka (ēshē'zōōkä) or **Ishitsuka** (ēshē'tsōōkä), town (pop. 5,844), Ibaraki prefecture, central Honshu, Japan, 8 mi. NW of Mito; sawmilling, weaving.

Ishkashim (ēshkŭshēm'), village (1948 pop. over 2,000), SW Gorno-Badakhshan Autonomous Oblast, Tadzhik SSR, in the Pamir, on Panj R. (Afghanistan border) and 55 mi. S of Khorog; horses.

Ishkuman (ĭsh'kōōmŭn), feudatory state (□ 1,600; pop. 4,282) in Gilgit Agency, NW Kashmir; ⊙ Ishkuman. In trans-Indus extension of N Punjab Himalayas; traversed (N–S) by Ishkuman R. (left tributary of Gilgit R.). Held after 1948 by Pakistan.

Ishkuman, village, ⊙ Ishkuman state, Gilgit Agency, NW Kashmir, 55 mi. NW of Gilgit.

Ishlei-Pokrovskoye or **Ishley-Pokrovskoye** (ēshlyā"-pŭkrôf'skŭyŭ), village (1939 pop. over 500), N Chuvash Autonomous SSR, Russian SFSR, 10 mi. SE of Cheboksary; wheat, rye, oats.

Ishmant (ĭsh'mănt) or **Ashmant** (ăsh'–), village (pop. 6,517), Beni Suef prov., Upper Egypt, on Ibrahimiya Canal, on railroad and 15 mi. NNE of Beni Suef; cotton, cereals, sugar cane.

Ishm River (ē'shŭm) or **Ishmi River** (ēsh'mē), Albanian coastal stream, formed by 3 parallel mtn. torrents rising in area of Tirana, flows c.25 mi. NW to Drin Gulf of the Adriatic 12 mi. S of Lesh.

Ishpeming (ĭsh'pŭmĭng), city (pop. 8,962), Marquette co., NW Upper Peninsula, Mich., 14 mi. SW of Marquette, in Marquette Iron range; dynamite mfg.; marble quarrying, lumbering. Livestock, poultry, and truck are raised. Ski tournaments held here since 1888. Inc. as village 1871, as city 1873.

Ishpeming Point, Mich.: see ISLE ROYALE NATIONAL PARK.

Ishpushta (ĭshpōōsh'tŭ), village, Kataghan prov., NE Afghanistan, on N slopes of the Hindu Kush, 37 mi. SW of Doshi, near Surkhab R.; site of one of Afghanistan's leading coal mines.

Ishtib, Yugoslavia: see STIP.

Ishtykhan (ĕshtĭkhän'), village (1939 pop. over 500), W Samarkand oblast, Uzbek SSR, c.20 mi. E of Katta-Kurgan, bet. Zeravshan R. arms; cotton.

Ishuatán (ēswätän'), town (pop. 501), Chiapas, S Mexico, 38 mi. NNE of Tuxtla; corn, fruit.

Ishui (yē'shwā), town, ⊙ Ishui co. (pop. 630,000), S central Shantung prov., China, on I River and 50 mi. NNE of Lini; cotton weaving; sericulture; wheat, millet.

Ishurdi (ĭshōōr'dē), village, Pabna dist., W East Bengal, E Pakistan, 14 mi. NW of Pabna; rail junction (workshops); rice milling, tobacco processing; rice, jute, rape and mustard, tobacco.

Isiboro River (ēsēbō'rō), Cochabamba dept., central Bolivia, rises in Serranía de Mosetenes NNE of Cochabamba, flows 130 mi. NE, through tropical lowlands, to the Secure c.20 mi. W of Limoquije. Receives Ichoa R. (left). Navigable for 110 mi.

Isigny (ēzēnyē'). **1** or **Isigny-sur-Mer** (–sür-mâr'), town (pop. 2,053), Calvados dept., NW France, port at confluence of Vire and Aure rivers, near English Channel, 14 mi. N of Saint-Lô; dairying center; cider distilling, meat canning. American troops landed at near-by Utah Beach (NW) and Omaha Beach (NE) on June 6, 1944, in Second World War. **2** or **Isigny-le-Buat** (–lü-bwä'), village (pop. 27), Manche dept., NW France, 10 mi. SE of Avranches.

Isili (ē'zēlē), village (pop. 2,570), Nuoro prov., S central Sardinia, 36 mi. N of Cagliari; domestic weaving (carpets, blankets), lead working; lignite deposits. Site of agr. penal colony; nuraghi.

Isil-Kul or **Isil'-Kul'** (ēsēl"-kōōl'), city (1939 pop. over 10,000) SW Omsk oblast, Russian SFSR, on Trans-Siberian RR and 85 mi. W of Omsk; metalworks.

Isin or **Issin** (ī'sĭn), anc. city, ⊙ Semitic kingdom of N Babylonia; its site is in SE central Iraq, in Diwaniya prov., 20 mi. ESE of Diwaniya, 18 mi. S of site of Nippur and 80 mi. NW of site of Ur, across the Euphrates. Established c.3000 B.C., it at one time controlled Nippur and Ur. Excavations.

Isinglass River, SE N.H., rises in W Strafford co., flows c.15 mi. E to the Cocheco below Rochester.

Isinomaki, Japan: see ISHINOMAKI.

Isiolo (ēsēō'lō), town (pop. c.500), ⊙ Northern Frontier Prov., central Kenya, N of Mt. Kenya, 120 mi. NNE of Nairobi; 0°25'N 37°37'E; agr. and trade center; coffee, sisal, wheat, corn; livestock. Quarantine camp. Airfield.

Isipattana, India: see SARNATH.

Isiro, Belgian Congo: see PAULIS.

Isis River, England: see THAMES RIVER.

Isizuti, Mount, Japan: see ISHIZUCHI, MOUNT.

Iskander (ēskŭndyĕr'), town (1939 pop. over 2,000), SE South Kazakhstan oblast, Kazakh SSR, on Chirchik R. and 25 mi. NE of Tashkent (linked by railroad); cotton, fruit.

Iskanderun, Turkey: see ISKENDERUN.

Iskar River or **Isker River** (ē'skŭr), anc. *Oescus,* NW Bulgaria, formed 4 mi. S of Samokov by confluence of 3 headstreams (Beli Iskar, Cherni Iskar, Levi Iskar) rising in N Rila Mts.; flows N, past Samokov, through Sofia Basin and W Balkan Mts., and NE to the Danube at Boril; 250 mi. long. In W Balkan Mts. it forms a 40-mi.-long gorge N of Kurilo, used by railroad and highway. Receives Malki Iskar and Panega rivers (right). Stock raising in valley N of W Balkan Mts.

Iskelib, Turkey: see ISKILIP.

Iskenderun (ĭskĕn'dĕrōōn), Turkish *İskenderun,* formerly **Alexandretta** (ă"lĭgzăndrĕ'tŭ), Fr. *Alexandrette,* town (1950 pop. 22,946), HATAY prov., S Turkey, port, rail terminus at head of Gulf of Iskenderun (inlet—45 mi. long, 28 mi. wide—at NE extremity of the Mediterranean), 27 mi. N of Antioch; 36°35'N 36°15'E. It was long the port for Aleppo and the outlet for N Syria, especially, in modern times, from 1920 to 1937, when it was part of Syria (see ALEXANDRETTA, SANJAK OF). Sometimes spelled Iskanderun and Iskenderon.

Isker, USSR: see SIBIR.

Isker River, Bulgaria: see ISKAR RIVER.

Iskilip (ĭskĭlĭp'), Turkish *Iskilip,* town (1950 pop. 10,683), Corum prov., N central Turkey, near the Kizil Irmak, 28 mi. NW of Corum; wheat, mohair goats. Formerly Iskelib.

Iski-Naukat (ēskē"-nŭōōkät'), village (1932 pop. estimate 5,000), N Osh oblast, Kirghiz SSR, 19 mi. SW of Osh; wheat, tobacco.

Iskininski or **Iskininskiy** (ēskē'nyĭnskē), oil town (1948 pop. over 2,000), N Guryev oblast, Kazakh SSR, on rail spur and 40 mi. E of Guryev, in Emba oil fields.

Iskitim (ēskĭtyēm'), city (1939 pop. over 10,000), E Novosibirsk oblast, Russian SFSR, on Turksib RR and 30 mi. SSE of Novosibirsk; cement-milling center. Developed after 1935.

Iskrets (ē'skrĕts), village (pop. 2,908), Sofia dist., W Bulgaria, in W Balkan Mts., on Iskrets R. (left tributary of Iskar R.) and 20 mi. N of Sofia; grain, sheep. Tuberculosis sanatorium near by.

Isla, river: see ISLA RIVER.

Isla, Cabo de la (kä'bō dā lä ēs'lä), headland on Caribbean coast of Margarita Isl. (NE), Nueva Esparta state, NE Venezuela, 10 mi. N of La Asunción; 11°11'N 63°58'W.

Isla, La, Mexico: see LA ISLA.

Isla Cabellos (ē'slä käbĕ'yōs) or **Cabellos,** town (pop. 1,200), Artigas dept., NW Uruguay, 55 mi. WSW of Artigas, 35 mi. SSE of Bella Unión; rail and road center; cereals, cattle, sheep.

Isla-Cristina (–krēstē'nä), city (pop. 9,756), Huelva prov., SW Spain, in Andalusia, on peninsula at the Guadiana estuary, 4 mi. ESE of Ayamonte, 21 mi. W of Huelva; fishing (tuna, sardines) and canning center. Mfg. of fertilizers; saltworks. Sometimes written Isla Cristina.

Isla de León, Cádiz prov., Spain: see LEÓN ISLAND; SAN FERNANDO.

Isla de Maipo (dā mī'pō), town (pop. 2,254), Santiago prov., central Chile, surrounded by arms of Maipo R., 25 mi. SW of Santiago; resort and agr. center (wheat, alfalfa, fruit, livestock).

Isla de Pinos, Cuba: see PINES, ISLE OF.

Isla Grande (grän'dā), U.S. air and naval base in NE Puerto Rico, just S of San Juan, across San Antonio Channel and W of Santurce. International airport. Its S section with dry dock is called Miraflores, adjacent to which are large metalworks.

Islahiye (ĭslä'hĭyĕ), Turkish *Islahiye* or *İslâhiye,* village (pop. 4,313), Gaziantep prov., S Turkey, on railroad and 40 mi. W of Gaziantep; wheat, barley, rice, lentils.

Islamabad, Kashmir: see ANANTNAG, town.

Islamabad, E Pakistan: see CHITTAGONG, city.

Isla Mala, Uruguay: see MAYO, 25 DE.

Isla Mayor (ē'slä mīôr'), sprawling village (pop. 1,664) and island, Seville prov., SW Spain, formed by right arm of the lower Guadalquivir 13 mi. SSW of Seville. Isl. is c.25 mi. long N–S, up to 9 mi. wide; largely marshland, used for stock raising.

Islamnagar (ĭslăm'nŭgŭr), town (pop. 7,307), Budaun dist., N central Uttar Pradesh, India, 31 mi. NW of Budaun; trades in wheat, pearl millet, mustard, sugar cane.

Islamorada, Fla.: see FLORIDA KEYS.

Islampur. **1** Village, Bihar, India: see FATWA. **2** Town, Bombay, India: see URUN ISLAMPUR.

Islampur, E Pakistan: see JAMALPUR.

Islam Qala or **Eslam Qala** (ĭslăm' kŭ'lŭ), frontier post, Herat prov., NW Afghanistan, on Iranian border, 65 mi. WNW of Herat, near the Hari Rud. Formerly called Kafir Qala; also spelled Islam Kala or Eslam Kala.

Islam-Terek, Russian SFSR: see KIROVSKOYE, Crimea.

Isla Mujeres (ēs'lä mōōhä'rĕs), town (pop. 557), Quintana Roo, SE Mexico, on small Mujeres Isl. (□ 1.3), 5 mi. off NE Yucatan Peninsula, 190 mi. E of Mérida; saltworks; fishing. Formerly belonging to great Maya federation, isl. has many archaeological remains.

Island, Icelandic name for ICELAND.

Island, county (□ 206; pop. 11,079), NW Wash.; ⊙ Coupeville. Group of several isls. (WHIDBEY ISLAND and CAMANO ISLAND are largest) in Puget Sound, NW of Everett. Dairy products, grain, poultry; fishing and summer resorts. Formed 1853.

Island, town (pop. 566), McLean co., W Ky., 20 mi. ENE of Madisonville, in agr., timber, and coal area.

Island Beach, borough (pop. 13) and beach, Ocean co., E N.J., on lower 8 mi. of peninsula bet. Barnegat Bay and the Atlantic, S of Seaside Park and N of Barnegat Inlet. Beach noted for plant and bird life. Borough set off from Berkeley township and inc. 1933.

Island City, town (pop. 138), Union co., NE Oregon, on Grande Ronde R. and 4 mi. E of La Grande; alt. 2,743 ft.

Island Falls. **1** Village (pop. estimate 100), NE Ont., on Abitibi R. (66-ft. falls) and 40 mi. NNW of Cochrane; hydroelectric-power center, supplying Cochrane mining region. **2** Village, E Sask., on Churchill R. (falls) and 55 mi. NNW of Flin Flon; hydroelectric-power center, supplying Flin Flon and Sherridon mining region.

Island Falls, town (pop. 1,237), Aroostook co., E central Maine, 22 mi. SW of Houlton and on Mattawamkeag L.; trade center for agr., lumbering, recreation (hunting, fishing) area. Settled 1843, inc. 1872.

Island Heights, resort borough (pop. 795), Ocean co., E N.J., on Toms R., near Barnegat Bay, just E of Toms River village; summer camps.

Island Lake (□ 550), E Man., on Ont. border; 55 mi. long, 20 mi. wide; drains into Hudson Bay.

Island Number 10, Tenn.: see NEW MADRID, city, Mo.

Island Park. **1** Resort village, Fremont co., E Idaho, 35 mi. NE of St. Anthony. Island Park Dam in Henrys Fork is near by. **2** Village (pop. 1,357), Hennepin co., E Minn., on small island in L. Minnetonka and 20 mi. W of Minneapolis. **3** Village (pop. 2,031), Nassau co., SE N.Y., on isl. off S shore of W Long Isl., 7 mi. S of Hempstead, in shore-resort area. Connected by causeways to Long Beach (S) and to Long Isl. Inc. 1926. **4** Village (pop. 1,322, with near-by The Hummocks),

Newport co., SE R.I., on Rhode Isl., 2 mi. E of Portsmouth.

Island Park Dam, Idaho: see HENRYS FORK.

Island Pond, village, Vt.: see BRIGHTON.

Island Pond, lake, N.H.: see HAMPSTEAD.

Islands, Bay of, inlet (20 mi. long, 10 mi. wide at entrance) of the Gulf of St. Lawrence, W N.F., 20 mi. N of Corner Brook; 49°10'N 58°15'W. Contains Tweed, Pearl, Woods, Guernsey, and Governors isls. E shore is deeply indented by 3 arms; S arm receives Humber R. estuary. On shore are several fishing settlements.

Islands, Bay of, inlet of S Pacific, extreme N N.Isl., New Zealand; 5 mi. wide; Russell is on S shore. Deep-sea fishing. Visited 1835 by Darwin. Formerly visited by whalers.

Island View, village (pop. 18), Koochiching co., N Minn., on Rainy L., 9 mi. E of International Falls.

Isla Pucú (ē'slä pōōkōō'), town (dist. pop. 6,028), La Cordillera dept., S central Paraguay, 45 mi. E of Asunción, in agr. area (fruit, tobacco, livestock).

Isla River (ī'lů). **1** In Angus and Perthshire, Scotland, rises 10 mi. SSE of Braemar, flows 46 mi. S and SW, past Coupar-Angus, to the Tay 4 mi. WSW of Coupar-Angus. **2** In Banffshire and Aberdeen, Scotland, rises 3 mi. SE of Dufftown, flows 18 mi. NE, past Dufftown and Keith, to Deveron R. just N of Rothie-may.

Islas de la Bahía, Honduras: see BAY ISLANDS.

Isla Umbú (ē'slä ōōmbōō'), town (dist. pop. 3,146), Ñeembucú dept., S Paraguay, 13 mi. SE of Pilar; stock-raising center; tanneries.

Isla Verde (vĕr'dä), town (pop. 2,877), SE Córdoba prov., Argentina, 45 mi. SSW of Marcos Juárez; corn, wheat, flax, alfalfa, cattle; flour milling, dairying.

Isla Verde, bathing resort, NE Puerto Rico, 5½ mi. E of San Juan. Surrounded by coconut groves.

Islay, province, Peru: see MOLLENDO.

Islay (ī'lā, ī'lů), island (□ 233.7, including Oversay; pop. 4,970), Inner Hebrides, most southerly of the Hebrides, Argyll, Scotland, separated from Jura (NE) by 1-mi.-wide Sound of Islay, and 14 mi. W of the Kintyre peninsula. Isl. is 25 mi. long, up to 19 mi. wide, and rises to 1,544 ft. It is deeply indented by Loch Indaal, on S coast, 12 mi. long and 8 mi. wide at mouth, and by Loch Gruinart (lŏkh grĭn'yûrt) (N), 5 mi. long and 2 mi. wide at mouth. Chief town, PORT ELLEN; other towns are Port Askaig (NE), Bowmore (center), Port Charlotte (W, on Loch Indaal), Bridgend (center), and Portnahaven (SW). Rudh'a'Mhail is the N promontory (55°55'N 6°9'W). On the Mull of Oa, the S headland (55°35'N 6°19'W), is a tower in memory of American soldiers and sailors drowned when transport *Tuscania* was torpedoed in 1918. Islay has been scene of several major shipwrecks. Main industries are fishing, stock raising, dairying, farming, whisky distilling, marble and slate quarrying. There is an airfield near Port Ellen. Isl. is former seat of the Lords of the Isles (the Macdonalds and Campbells).

Isle, river, France: see ISLE RIVER.

Isle, resort village (pop. 674), Mille Lacs co., E Minn., on SE shore of Mille Lacs L. and 40 mi. N of Princeton, in grain, livestock, and poultry area; dairy products. Granite quarries near by.

Isle-Adam, L' (lēl-ädä'), town (pop. 4,016), Seine-et-Oise dept., N central France, on left bank of braided Oise R. and 7 mi. NE of Pontoise; fashionable resort (river beach); mfg. of gardening implements. Its Renaissance church damaged in Second World War. Villiers de l'Isle-Adam b. here.

Isle au Haut (ēl" ō hō'), town (pop. 82), Knox co., S Maine, on Isle au Haut (□ c.9) and adjacent isls., 25 mi. ESE of Rockland in Isle au Haut Bay. Part of the isl. is in Acadia Natl. Park.

Isle-en-Dodon, L' (-ā-dôdō'), village (pop. 1,557), Haute-Garonne dept., S France, on Save R. and 20 mi. NNE of Saint-Gaudens; fruitgrowing, poultry raising.

Isleham (īz'lům), agr. village and parish (pop. 1,487), E Cambridge, England, 7 mi. N of Newmarket; limestone quarrying. Has 11th-cent. chapel and 14th-cent. church.

Isle-Jourdain, L' (lēl-zhōōrdē'). **1** Village (pop. 1,910), Gers dept., SW France, on the Save and 18 mi. W of Toulouse; agr. market in fruitgrowing valley. **2** Village (pop. 1,043), Vienne dept., W central France, on Vienne R. and 14 mi. N of Confolens; flour milling. Hydroelectric plant.

Isle La Motte (īl" lů mŏt'), island and town, Grand Isle co., NW Vt., in L. Champlain, 14 mi. W of St. Albans; 6 mi. long, 2 mi. wide; bridged to Alburg. Isle La Motte town (pop. 295), chartered 1779, was site of Fr. Fort St. Anne (c.1665), 1st white settlement in Vt., abandoned long before permanent settlement began c.1788. Marble (including black variety), fruit.

Isle of Ely, Isle of Man, Isle of Pines, etc.: for places beginning thus, see under main part of name; e.g., see ELY, ISLE OF, and MAN, ISLE OF, etc.

Isle of Hope, resort town (1940 pop. 526), Chatham co., E Ga., 6 mi. SSE of Savannah, near the Atlantic.

Isle of Palms, beach resort, Charleston co., SE S.C., on Isle of Palms isl. (5.5 mi. long), 8 mi. E of Charleston. Bridged to Sullivans Isl. (SW). Intracoastal Waterway passes to W.

Isle of Springs, S Maine, in Sheepscot R. just W of Boothbay Harbor town; c.½ mi. in diameter. Formerly Sweet Isl.

Isle of Whithorn, Scotland: see WHITHORN.

Isle of Wight, county (□ 321; pop. 14,906), SE Va.; ⊙ Isle of Wight. In tidewater region; bounded W by Blackwater R., NE by the James (bridged here). Sandy soils produce peanuts, corn, truck, cotton; co. is known for Smithfield hams from peanut-fed hogs. Some lumbering, lumber milling. Old bldgs. include one of oldest churches in America, at Benn's Church. Formed 1634.

Isle of Wight, village (pop. c.100), ⊙ Isle of Wight co., SE Va., 23 mi. W of Portsmouth.

Isle River (ēl), Dordogne and Gironde depts., SW France, rises in Monts du Limousin, flows 145 mi. WSW through a fertile valley, past Périgueux, Mussidan, and Guîtres, to the Dordogne at Libourne. Receives the Auvézère (left) and the Dronne (right). Navigable in lower half of its course.

Isle Royale National Park (īl' roi'ůl) (□ 209.1; established 1940), N Mich., wilderness area on Isle Royale and more than 200 surrounding islets, in L. Superior near Ont. line, NW of Keweenaw Peninsula. Isle Royale (c.45 mi. long, 9 mi. wide), largest in L. Superior, extends SW-NE; its irregular coast line provides excellent harbors. Wooded, hilly terrain (highest alt. 1,307 ft., at Ishpeming Point in central ridge) shelters moose, beavers, coyotes, minks, muskrats. Of its numerous small lakes, largest is Siskiwit L. (7 mi. long, 1.5 mi. wide), in S. Fishing, boating; camp sites at principal harbors, including Rock Harbor (NE), Washington Harbor (SW), and Siskiwit Bay (sĭ'skĭwĭt) (large inlet in S shore). Isl. has boat connections with Keweenaw Peninsula and with points in Minn. (Duluth, Grand Marais, Grand Portage) and Ont. (Fort William). Govt. lighthouses are maintained on offshore isls.; park hq. (during summer) on small Mott Isl. (NE); mainland hq. at Houghton, on Keweenaw Peninsula. Isl. was worked for copper in prehistoric times; visited early in 17th cent. by Etienne Brulé. Became part of U.S. in 1783, under Treaty of Paris. Intermittent copper mining in 19th cent.; now supports small-scale lumbering, trapping and commercial fishing.

Isle Saint George, Ohio: see BASS ISLANDS.

Islesboro or **Islesborough,** island and town (pop. 529), Waldo co., S Maine, in Penobscot Bay SE of Belfast; c.11.5 mi. long, .5–1.5 mi. wide. Includes resort villages of Darkharbor, Pripet, North Islesboro.

Isles Dernieres (ēl" dârnyâr'), S La., uninhabited island chain (c.18½ mi. long), 38 mi. S of Houma, bet. Caillou Bay and L. Pelto (N) and Gulf of Mexico (S); once a continuous barrier beach. Fashionable mid-19th-cent. resorts here were destroyed by hurricane (1856) which took many lives.

Islesford, Maine: see CRANBERRY ISLES.

Isles of Shoals, Maine and N.H., islands 10 mi. SE of Portsmouth, N.H. Appledore, Cedar, Duck, and Smuttynose (or Haley's) isls. are in Maine; Lunging, White (lighthouse), and Star isls. are in N.H. Resorts on Appledore and Star isls.

Isle-sur-la-Sorgue, L' (lēl-sür-lä-sôrg'), town (pop. 3,464), Vaucluse dept., SE France, on the Sorgue and 12 mi. E of Avignon; road and rail junction; wool-blanket and rug-mfg. center. Trade in potatoes, early fruits, vegetables, and wines. Also makes plastics, glues. Alcohol distilling. Has beautifully decorated 14th–17th-cent. church.

Isle-sur-le-Doubs, L' (-lů-dōō'), town (pop. 2,494), Doubs dept., E France, on Doubs R. and Rhone-Rhine Canal, and 11 mi. SW of Montbéliard; metalworking, furniture and crate mfg., fruit preserving.

Isle-sur-Serein, L' (-sürě'), village (pop. 505), Yonne dept., N central France, on Serein R. and 8 mi. NE of Avallon; cementworks.

Isleta (ēslā'tä), peninsula (c.3 mi. long, 2 mi. wide), NE Grand Canary, Canary Isls., 3 mi. N of Las Palmas. On its isthmus is Puerto de la Luz.

Isleta (īslě'tů), pueblo (□ 320.8), Bernalillo co., central N.Mex. Isleta village (1948 pop. 1,462) is on W bank of the Rio Grande and 13 mi. S of Albuquerque; alt. 4,898 ft. Principal fiesta Aug. 28, St. Augustine's day. Older village on this site discovered (c.1540) by Spaniards and abandoned during Pueblo revolt of 1680.

Isleton (īl'tůn), city (pop. 1,597), Sacramento co., central Calif., 28 mi. S of Sacramento, and on Sacramento R., in its delta; asparagus-canning and -packing center; also packs fruit, other truck. Founded 1874, inc. 1923.

Islettes, Les (lāzēlět'), village (pop. 635), Meuse dept., NE France, in defile of the Argonne, 5 mi. ENE of Sainte-Menehould; furniture, bottles.

Isle Verte (ēl vârt'), village (pop. estimate 1,000), S Que., on the St. Lawrence and 16 mi. NE of Rivière du Loup; dairying, lumbering, peat-moss mfg. Opposite is Île VERTE.

Isleworth, England: see HESTON AND ISLEWORTH.

Islington (ĭz'lĭngtůn), W suburb (pop. estimate 3,000) of Toronto, S Ont.

Islington (ĭz'–), metropolitan borough (1931 pop. 321,795; 1951 census 235,645) of London, England, N of the Thames, 2.5 mi. NNE of Charing Cross. Industrial and workers' residential dist., it is site of King's Cross (one of principal rail stations for N England and Scotland), Royal Agr. Hall (1861), several hospitals, and Pentonville and Holloway prisons. Among Islington residents were Charles and Mary Lamb, John Spencer, Francis Bacon, and Oliver Goldsmith.

Islington, Mass.: see WESTWOOD.

Islip (ī'slĭp), residential village (pop. 5,254), Suffolk co., SE N.Y., on S shore of Long Isl., on Great South Bay, just E of Bay Shore, in resort and duck-farming area; mfg. (canvas products, clothing, radios, machinery, aircraft parts); fisheries; flower growing. Heckscher State Park (recreation facilities) is near by.

Islip Terrace, residential village (pop. 1,579), Suffolk co., SE N.Y., on central Long Isl., 2 mi. NE of Islip, in diversified-farming area; mfg. of sweaters and knit goods.

Isluga Volcano (ēslōō'gä), Andean peak (18,145 ft.), N Chile, near Bolivia border; 19°10'S.

Isly (ēslē'), short stream of NE Fr. Morocco, just W of Oujda, near Algerian border. Here, in 1844, Fr. general Bugeaud defeated Abd-el-Kader and a Moroccan army in a decisive battle.

Ismail, Ukrainian SSR: see IZMAIL, city.

Ismailia, Ismailiya, or **Isma'iliyah** (ĭz"mālē'ä, ĭs"–, ēs"–, –mä–; ĭz"māē'lyů, ĭs"–), town (pop. 53,594; with suburbs, 68,338), in the Canal Governorate, NE Egypt, at mid-point of Suez Canal, on L. Timsah, and 45 mi. NNW of Suez. It is on Ismailia Canal and has rail connections with Cairo, Suez, and Port Said. Has hosp., coast-guard station, customs hq. Mfg. of confectioneries, electric-light bulbs. Founded 1863 by Ferdinand de Lesseps as base for construction of the canal.

Ismailia Canal, navigable fresh-water canal, E Egypt, extending c.80 mi. in Wadi Tumilat from Cairo to Ismailia and L. Timsah on the Suez Canal. At Nifisha, just W of Ismailia, it branches off S and at Ismailia it continues N as the El 'Abbasiya Canal. It was constructed (c.1860) to supply the villages on the projected Suez Canal with drinking water. Used chiefly for irrigation.

Ismailly (ēsmē'lē), village (1932 pop. estimate 2,470), E central Azerbaijan SSR, on S slope of the Greater Caucasus, 55 mi. ENE of Yevlakh; wheat, livestock; lumbering.

Ismaros (ē'smůrôs), hill range in W Thrace, Greece, on Aegean Sea, rises to 2,224 ft. 17 mi. SE of Komotine.

Ismay (ĭz'mā), town (pop. 182), Custer co., E Mont., on O'Fallon Creek and 50 mi. E of Miles City.

Ismeli, Russian SFSR: see OKTYABRSKOYE, Chuvash oblast.

Ismid, Turkey: see IZMIT.

Isna (ĭs'nů) or **Esna** (ĕs'nů) anc. *Latopolis*, town (pop. 20,085; with suburbs, 25,775), Qena prov., Upper Egypt, on W bank of the Nile, on railroad, and 85 mi. NNW of Aswan, 29 mi. S of Luxor; pottery making, wool spinning and weaving. Site of ruins of the old temple of Khnum, built in Ptolemaic period. Sometimes spelled Esneh.

Isnello (ēzněl'lō), village (pop. 3,381), Palermo prov., N Sicily, in Madonie Mts., 7 mi. S of Cefalù.

Isnik, Turkey: see IZNIK.

Isnotú (ēsnōtōō'), town (pop. 899), Trujillo state, W Venezuela, in Andean spur, 7 mi. WNW of Valera; coffee, grain, sugar.

Isny (ĭs'nē, ĭs'nů), town (pop. 4,962), S Württemberg, Germany, after 1945 in Württemberg-Hohenzollern, in the Allgäu, 13 mi. W of Kempten; textile mfg., woodworking. Summer resort and winter-sports center. Has 13th- and 17th-cent. churches. Was free imperial city.

Isobe (ēsō'bā), town (pop. 5,873), Gumma prefecture, central Honshu, Japan, 3 mi. SW of Annaka; rice. Hot springs.

Isohama (ēsō'hämů), town (pop. 15,618), Ibaraki prefecture, central Honshu, Japan, on the Pacific, 7 mi. SE of Mito; fishing port; summer resort.

Isohara (ēsō'härů), town (pop. 13,141), Ibaraki prefecture, central Honshu, Japan, 14 mi. NNE of Hitachi; mining of anthracite coal, cotton-textile mfg., sawmilling.

Isoka (ēsō'kä), township (pop. 75), Northern Prov., NE Northern Rhodesia, 110 mi. E of Kasama; road junction; corn, wheat; livestock.

Isokyrö (ī'sōkü"rů), Swedish *Storkyro* (stōōr'kü"rō), village (commune pop. 7,948), Vaasa co., W Finland, 20 mi. ESE of Vaasa, in lumbering, grain-growing region. Has 14th-cent. church. Just S is locality of Napue (nä'pōōě), scene (1714) of Russian victory over Finns.

Isola (ē'zōlä), village (pop. 87), Brescia prov., Lombardy, N Italy, in Val Camonica, on small branch of Oglio R. and 9 mi. SE of Edolo. Has one of major Ital. hydroelectric plants.

Isola, Slovenian *Izola* (ē'zōlä), town (pop. 6,777), S Free Territory of Trieste, fishing port on Gulf of Trieste, 9 mi. SW of Trieste, on little isl. linked to mainland; fish and vegetable canning, dairying, wine making, boatbuilding, distilling, brick mfg. Has 15th-cent. cathedral. Placed 1947 under Yugoslav administration.

Isola (ĭsō'lů), town (pop. 450), Humphreys co., W Miss., 8 mi. NW of Belzoni, in rich cotton area.

Isola della Scala (ē'zôlä dĕl'lä skä'lä), town (pop. 2,821), Verona prov., N Italy, on Tartaro R. and 11 mi. S of Verona; rail junction; mfg. (tower clocks, scales).

Isola del Liri (dĕl lē'rē), town (pop. 3,076), Frosinone prov., Latium, S central Italy, 12 mi. ENE of Frosinone, on isl. in Liri R., which here forms several waterfalls utilized for industrial power. A major paper mfg. center; foundries, felt and woolen mills, cementworks, macaroni factories, cellulose plant.

Isola di Capo Rizzuto (dē kä'pô rētsōō'tô), village (pop. 3,905), Catanzaro prov., Calabria, S Italy, bet. capes Rizzuto and Colonne, 9 mi. S of Crotone; olive oil, wine.

Isola Dovarese (dôvärā'zē), village (pop. 1,834), Cremona prov., Lombardy, N Italy, on Oglio R. and 15 mi. ENE of Cremona.

Isola Vicentina (vēchĕntē'nä), village (pop. 1,488), Vicenza prov., Veneto, N Italy, 7 mi. NW of Vicenza; alcohol distillery.

Isole, Monte, Italy: see ISEO, LAGO D'.

Isonzo River (ēzôn'tsô), anc. *Sontius,* Slovenian *Soča* (sô'chä), NW Yugoslavia and NE Italy, rises in Slovenia on NW slope of Triaglav, flows 84 mi. generally S, past Bovec, Kobarid, Tolmin, and Kanal (Yugoslavia), and Gorizia (Italy) to Gulf of Trieste (Adriatic Sea) 12 mi. NW of Trieste. Scene (1915–17) of Austro-Ital. battles.

Isorella (ēzôrĕl'lä), village (pop. 1,852), Brescia prov., Lombardy, N Italy, 17 mi. SSE of Brescia.

Iso Saimaa, Finland: see SAIMAA.

Ispahan, Iran: see ISFAHAN, city.

Isparta (ĭspär'tä), Turkish *Isparta* or *İsparta,* prov. (□ 3,209; 1950 pop. 186,152), W central Turkey; ⊙ Isparta. Bordered NE by Sultan Mts.; drained by Kopru and Aksu rivers. In it is L. Egridir. Products include rose petals, attar of roses, carpets, hides, sulphur, grain.

Isparta, Turkish *Isparta* or *İsparta,* town (1950 pop. 18,394), ⊙ Isparta prov., W central Turkey, rail terminus 105 mi. W of Konya; cotton spinning, carpet weaving; attar of roses; wheat, barley, beans, onions, tobacco. Sometimes called Sparta or Isbarta. Formerly Hamitabat.

Isperikh (ēspĕrēkh'), village (pop. 3,564), Ruse dist., NE Bulgaria, 20 mi. NE of Razgrad; market center; grain, sunflowers. Until 1934, Kemanlar.

Ispica (ē'spēkä), town (pop. 11,095), Ragusa prov., SE Sicily, 10 mi. SE of Modica; wine. Called Spaccaforno until 1935. Cava d'Ispica is near MODICA.

Ispir (ĭspĭr'), Turkish *İspir,* village (pop. 2,206), Erzurum prov., NE Turkey, on Coruh R. and 40 mi. NNW of Erzurum, in mountainous area; alt. c.6,500 ft.; barley, potatoes.

Ispiriz Dag (ĭspĭrĭz' dä), Turkish *İspiriz Dağ,* peak (11,604 ft.), E Turkey, 40 mi. SE of Van.

Ispravnaya (ēsprăv'nīŭ), village (1926 pop. 7,857), central Cherkess Autonomous Oblast, Stavropol Territory, Russian SFSR, on Great Zelenchuk R. and 25 mi. SW of Cherkessk; orchards, grain; livestock.

Israel (ĭz'rēůl, –rāĕl, –růĕl), republic (□ 8,050; 1951 pop. estimate 1,414,500), W Asia, on Mediterranean; ⊙ JERUSALEM. Bordering on Gulf of Aqaba of Red Sea, it is bounded SW by Sinai Peninsula of Egypt, E by Jordan (with which it has 330-mi.-long border), NE by Syria, N by Lebanon. In the SW is the Egyptian-held Gaza strip of Palestine. Sandy, even coast line on Mediterranean (W) is 120 mi. long. Narrow fertile lowland (comprising plains of Zevulun, Sharon, and Judaea) along the sea rises (E) to highlands of Galilee and Judaea (S spur of Lebanon and Anti-Lebanon ranges) and attains c.2,500 ft. in Jerusalem region. Terrain then drops steeply to Jordan valley, which is generally below sea level, and its expansions of L. Hula, the Sea of Galilee, and the Dead Sea (surface 1,292 ft. below sea level). S Israel, consisting of the arid NEGEV region, which extends S to Elath on Gulf of Aqaba, is being irrigated and settled on large scale. Central highlands of N Israel are cut by Plain of Jezreel (Esdraelon) bet. Mt. Carmel (NW) and Jordan valley near Beisan (SE). Highest elevation is Jebel Jarmaq (3,963 ft.) in Upper Galilee; other notable elevations include mts. Carmel, Tabor, and Gilboa. Besides the all-important Jordan, there are intermittent streams, among them the Kishon and the Yarkon. Extensive swamps in plains of Sharon and Jezreel and in L. Hula region have been reclaimed since 1919. There are 4 main climatic zones: coastal plain has dry subtropical climate, with abundant winter rains; central highlands are cool and dry in summer, cold and rainy in winter; Jordan valley is hot and dry in summer and has mild winter climate (Tiberias is a popular resort in this zone); the Negev is hot and dry in summer, cold and dry in winter. There are abrupt diurnal temperature changes, except in coastal plain. Until recent times citrus fruit (oranges, grapefruit), grown in irrigated sandy soil along coast, constituted chief Israeli crop and largest export item, followed by wines and olive products. A more balanced agr. was achieved after Second World War by increase of area devoted to wheat and barley (which thrive in Galilee), vegetables, deciduous fruit, and bananas. Dairying, poultry raising, and fishing (in Mediterranean and L. Hula) are of increasing importance, and there is an extensive afforestation program. Israel's mineral wealth, apart from salt pans at Atlit on the Mediterranean, is concentrated in Dead Sea; major chemical plant at its S end extracts potash and numerous other basic chemicals. Important industries are fruit canning and processing, metalworking, textile milling, oil refining, diamond polishing; mfg. of clothing, shoes, food products (notably chocolate, candy, and olive oil), chemicals, pharmaceuticals, dyes, soap, cement, radios, electrical equipment, plastics, wood and tobacco products, artificial teeth; handicrafts, automobile assembly. Because of the rapid increase in pop., the construction industry is of primary importance and employs large number of workers. Chief cities and towns are TEL AVIV (including Jaffa), HAIFA, Jerusalem (the section called the Old City is in Arab hands), Lydda, Ramat Gan, Bnei Braq, Natanya, Petah Tiqva, Ramle, Acre, Tiberias, Safad, Nazareth, and Beersheba. Prevalent types of rural settlement are the *moshav ovdim* (cooperative smallholders' settlement on privately-owned land), the *kibbutz* and *kvutsa* (communal settlements, usually affiliated with a political party), and the *moshav shitufi* (communal settlement, with division of profits among the members). There are numerous cooperative enterprises, and the trade union organization (*Histadrut*) also owns diverse industrial enterprises, especially in the construction industry. Agr. marketing is almost entirely on a cooperative basis. Chief means of transportation is the dense road network; a N–S railroad serves entire coastal plain, with spur to Jerusalem and direct connections to Syria and Turkey and to Egypt. Narrow-gauge line connects Haifa with Jordan valley. Lydda is one of world's main airline hubs; there are also airfields at Haifa and Tel Aviv. Chief seaport is Haifa; open roadsteads at Tel Aviv and Jaffa. Branch of oil pipe line from Kirkuk (Iraq) to Haifa was closed in 1948. Univ. at Jerusalem; technical col. at Haifa. Israel is a parliamentary democracy, with executive power vested in a cabinet, headed by prime minister, and the president; legislative branch is a unicameral parliament (*Knesset*). The Jews' long struggle for an independent state in Palestine came to a head after the Second World War, and, with the intervention of the U.N., the new state was set up. With the end of British mandate over PALESTINE (see that article for history of the region prior to this event), independent state of Israel was proclaimed (May 14, 1948) in Tel Aviv, power being vested in provisional state council and in provisional govt. The U.S. accorded immediate *de facto* recognition; the USSR accorded (May 17, 1948) *de jure* recognition. Provisional govt. offices were established at Hakyria, suburb of Tel Aviv. First parliamentary elections held Jan., 1949; 1st session took place (Feb. 14, 1949) at Jerusalem. On Feb. 16, 1949, Dr. Chaim Weizmann was elected president of Israel. The election of a govt. brought recognition by Great Britain and *de jure* recognition by U.S. Almost entire Arab pop. had already evacuated the region allocated (Nov. 29, 1947) by the U.N. to the proposed Jewish state. With the declaration of Israel's independence, the neighboring Arab countries invaded Israel. Israeli forces of the *Haganah* (defense army) gradually pushed the Arab forces out of Israel and also occupied the N frontier region of Galilee not previously allocated to Israel. In Jerusalem, however, Jordan's forces held the Old City and gained control of main road from W at Latrun, besieging the New City held by the Jews. The siege of the New City was later relieved. An armistice was called (June 11, 1948) by U.N. Special Commission on Palestine (UNSCOP), but hostilities were renewed (July 9, 1948) and Israeli forces captured additional territory and opened up communication with the isolated Negev. A new armistice was signed (July 18, 1948) at Rhodes under UNSCOP auspices. On Sept. 17, Count Folke Bernadotte, chief U.N. mediator, was assassinated by Jewish terrorists. Israeli authorities outlawed the secret groups. Jordan annexed the part of Palestine neither assigned to nor taken by Israel. Israel became a member of the U.N. in May, 1949. Jerusalem was declared ⊙ Israel, Dec. 14, 1949. Jewish immigrants, who had been flocking to Israel even before its independence, increased enormously in volume in 1948. By the end of Nov., 1950, 500,000 immigrants had entered the country, chiefly from displaced-persons camps in Germany and detention camps in Cyprus, Eastern Europe, Yemen, North Africa, and Iraq. This large influx, coupled with the need for vast investment in housing and production facilities, placed a heavy strain on the economy of the country.

Israel River (ĭz'rēůl), Coos co., N N.H., rises in Presidential Range, flows c.25 mi. NW to the Connecticut near Lancaster.

Issa (ē'sů), village (1926 pop. 4,712), N Penza oblast, Russian SFSR, on Issa R. (right branch of Moksha R.) and 12 mi. SSW of Ruzayevka, in hemp area; hemp processing; legumes, orchards.

Issa, island, Yugoslavia: see VIS ISLAND.

Issano or **Issano Landing** (ĭsä'nō), village (pop. 353), Essequibo co., central Br. Guiana, communication point on Mazaruni R. and 70 mi. SW of Bartica (connected by road).

Issaquah (ĭ'sůkwä), town (pop. 955), King co., W central Wash., 15 mi. ESE of Seattle; lumber, dairy products, poultry.

Issaquena (ĭsůkwē'nů), county (□ 415; pop. 4,966), W Miss.; ⊙ Mayersville. Drained by winding bayous; the Mississippi (here the La. line) forms co.'s W boundary, the Yazoo partly its S and E boundaries. Agr. (cotton, corn, oats); timber. Includes part of Delta Natl. Forest. Has oxbow lakes along the Mississippi. Formed 1844.

Issel, river, Germany and Netherlands: see OLD IJSSEL RIVER.

Isselburg (ĭ'sůlbōōrk), town (pop. 2,443), in former Prussian Rhine Prov., W Germany, after 1945 in North Rhine-Westphalia, 6 mi. W of Bocholt, near Dutch border; tobacco.

Issele Uku (ē'shĕlā ōō'kōō), town, Benin prov., Western Provinces, S Nigeria, 20 mi. WNW of Asaba; road center; palm oil and kernels, kola nuts, yams, cassava, corn, plantains. Lignite deposits.

Isser, Oued (wĕd' ēsâr'), stream of Alger dept., N central Algeria, rises in the Tell Atlas S of Berrouaghia, flows 87 mi. NE, past Palestro and Bordj-Ménaïel, to the Mediterranean 35 mi. ENE of Algiers.

Isserville (ēsârvēl'), village (pop. 1,307), Alger dept., N central Algeria, near the Oued Isser, 21 mi. W of Tizi-Ouzou; wine, olives, tobacco. Essential oils shipped from Les Issers railroad station, 1 mi. N.

Isshiki (ēs'shĭkē), town (pop. 21,476), Aichi prefecture, central Honshu, Japan, on Chita Bay and 25 mi. SSE of Nagoya; spinning mills; acetylene-gas plant. Fishing.

Isshinden or **Ishinden** (ēshēn'dăn), town (pop. 5,981), Mie prefecture, S Honshu, Japan, just N of Tsu; agr. center (rice, wheat, market produce); rayon textiles, sake, soy sauce. Has 15th-cent. temple.

Issia (ē'syä), village (pop. c.800), W central Ivory Coast, Fr. West Africa, 30 mi. SSW of Daloa; coffee, cacao, palm kernels.

Issigeac (ēsēzhäk'), village (pop. 563), Dordogne dept., SW France, 10 mi. SE of Bergerac; flour milling; prune, wine, tobacco growing.

Issin, Iraq: see ISIN.

Issoire (ēswär'), town (pop. 6,218), Puy-de-Dôme dept., central France, near the Allier, 18 mi. SSE of Clermont-Ferrand; agr. trade center; mfg. (toys, furniture, paints); linen weaving and embroidering. Has 12th-cent. Romanesque church.

Issoudun (ēsōōdŭ'), anc. *Uxellodunum,* town (pop. 11,189), Indre dept., central France, on Théols R. and 18 mi. NE of Châteauroux; morocco-leather-mfg. center with tanneries, foundries, fertilizer and parchment factories; mfg. (heating equipment, paint brushes, labels). Surrounded by truck gardens, vineyards. Medieval stronghold fought over by Richard Coeur de Lion and Philip Augustus.

Is-sur-Tille (ēsūr-tēl'), town (pop. 2,479), Côte-d'Or dept., E central France, 14 mi. N of Dijon; lumber market.

Issus (ĭ'sůs), anc. town of SE Asia Minor, in Cilicia, near head of the Mediterranean gulf now called Gulf of Iskenderun; its site was 5 mi. NW of modern Dortyol, Turkey. Scene of several important battles, among them the victory of Alexander the Great in 333 B.C. over Darius III of Persia. In A.D. 194 Septimus Severus here defeated Pescennius Niger for the throne of Roman Empire.

Issyk (ēsĭk'), village (1948 pop. over 500), S Alma-Ata oblast, Kazakh SSR, 20 mi. E of Alma-Ata; irrigated agr. (wheat, tobacco, fruit, truck produce).

Issyk-Ata (–ŭtä'), village, S Frunze oblast, Kirghiz SSR, on N slope of Kirghiz Range, 20 mi. S of Kant; health resort (alt. 5,990 ft.).

Issyk-Kul or **Issyk-Kul'** (–kōōl') [Kirghiz,=hot lake], oblast (□ 16,300, including lake area; 1946 pop. estimate 175,000), E Kirghiz SSR; ⊙ Przhevalsk. Includes highest mts. (E) of Kirghiz SSR (Khan-Tengri, Pobeda Peak). A lake, the Issyk-Kul, in N, has wheat and opium cultivation along shores. Sheep and horses raised in mtn. valleys. Coal mining at Dzhargalan. Fisheries at Rybachye. Tourist area; many health resorts (Koisara, Dzhety-Oguz). Shipping on lake; railroad runs W from Rybachye to Frunze and Lugovoi. Pop.: Kirghiz, Russians. Formed 1939.

Issyk-Kul or **Issyk-Kul',** second-largest (□ 2,395; exceeded only by L. Titicaca) mountain lake of the world, in Issyk-Kul oblast, Kirghiz SSR, in Tien Shan mtn. system, bet. the Kungei Ala-Tau (N) and Terskei Ala-Tau (S); 105 mi. long, 35 mi. wide, alt. 5,193 ft., max. depth 2,303 ft. Slightly saline (.5%); ice-free in winter; shipping route Rybachye-Pristan Przheval'sk. Tourist area; health resorts along shores. Receives many streams, including Tyup R. (E); intermittent link with Chu R. (W).

Issy-les-Moulineaux (ēsē'-lā-mōōlēnō'), town (pop. 39,818), Seine dept., N central France, just SSW of Paris, 4 mi. from Notre Dame Cathedral, port on left bank of the Seine, opposite Boulogne-Billancourt, and just W of Vanves; automobile and aircraft plants; mfg. (electrical equipment, munitions, hosiery, chocolate), woodworking. Natl. tobacco factory. Its airport (just N) forms part of city of Paris.

Issy-l'Évêque (–lāvĕk'), village (pop. 490), Saône-et-Loire dept., E central France, 23 mi. SW of Autun; cattle.

Istahbanat or **Estahbanat** (both: ĕstäbänät'), town, Seventh Prov., in Fars, S Iran, 15 mi. WSW of Niriz; grain, opium, cotton, figs, saffron. Coal and lead deposits near by. Also known as Savanat.

Istakhr, Iran: see PERSEPOLIS.

Istalif (ĭstä'lĭf), town (pop. 10,000), Kabul prov., E Afghanistan, 22 mi. NNW of Kabul, in picturesque site on slopes of Paghman Mts.; handicrafts; weaving; graphite mining. Summer resort. Stormed (1842) by British in 1st Afghan War.

Istalloskö, Mount (ĭsh'täl-lōsh-kû), Hung. *Istállós-kő,* highest point (3,145 ft.) of Bükk Mts., NE Hungary. Istalloskö Cave, on N slope, contains remains from Stone Age.

Istán (ĕstän'), town (pop. 1,551), Málaga prov., S Spain, in coastal spur of the Cordillera Penibética, 30 mi. WSW of Málaga; cork, corn, carob beans, oranges, figs, almonds, esparto, resins.

Istanbul (ĭstănbōōl'), Turkish *İstanbul* (ĭstäm'bōōl"), province (□ 2,081; 1950 pop. 1,179,666), NW Turkey, on both sides of the Bosporus; ⊙ Istanbul. Bordered on N by Black Sea, on S by Sea of Marmara and Samanli Mts. Commercial and industrial concentration on both sides of Bosporus. Some cereals grown; deposits of cement, coal, lignite, copper; salt-water fishing.

Istanbul, Turkish *İstanbul,* largest city (1950 pop. 1,000,022) of Turkey, ⊙ Istanbul prov., NW Turkey, on both sides of the Bosporus at its entrance on the Sea of Marmara; 41°5'N 28°55'E. Its name was officially changed from Constantinople (kŏn"stăntĭnō'pŭl) to Istanbul in 1930; the history of Constantinople is given below. Modern Istanbul, a major seaport at one of the strategic sites of the world, is the rail, mfg., commercial, and financial center of Turkey, although the ⊙ was moved to Ankara in 1923. It handles 60% of Turkey's imports and much of its exports, has shipbuilding yards, and produces textiles, pottery, leather products, tobacco, liqueurs, cement, glass, flour, canned goods, soap, and other products. The European part of Istanbul is terminus of the Orient Express, and at Haydarpasa station, on the Asiatic side, begins the Baghdad Railway. The part of Istanbul corresponding to historic Constantinople is situated entirely on the European side. It rises on both sides of the Golden Horn, an inlet of the Bosporus, on one of the finest sites of the world, and, like Rome, is built on seven hills. Several miles of its anc. moated and turreted walls are still standing. Outside the walls and N of the Golden Horn are the commercial quarter of Galata, originally a Genoese settlement; the quarter of Pera, which under the sultans was reserved for foreigners; and Chaskoi or Haskoy, the Jewish quarter. The Golden Horn is crossed by a famous bridge, leading into the historic quarter of Stambul, the anc. core of the city. The quarter of Phanar, formerly reserved for the Greeks, is in NW part of city, near former site of palace of Blachernae of the Byzantine emperors. The 11 administrative districts of Istanbul do not correspond to these 4 historic quarters; the largest among them are Beyoglu, Fatih, and Eminonu on the European side, and Kadikoy and Scutari or Uskudar on the Asiatic side. Istanbul has a univ. (at Beyazit), founded 1453 as a theological school and completely secularized in 1933; School of Economics (1883); Robert Col. (at Bebek; 1863); American Col. for Girls (at Arnavutkoy; 1871); Technical Univ. (1773, reorganized 1944). Also see of patriarch of Greek Orthodox Church, of a Latin-rite patriarch of Catholic Church, and of patriarch of Armenian Church. The great Byzantine monument is the Hagia Sophia, originally a church, after 1453 a mosque, now a mus., one of the world's noblest works of architecture. Recent excavations on site of the former Byzantine palaces have brought to light many fine works of art, but Istanbul as a whole has few monuments of the Byzantine past besides the walls, Hagia Sophia, and some isolated ruins. City was destroyed (1509) by earthquake; rebuilt by Sultan Bajazet II. Turkish culture reached its height in 16th cent. and it is from that period that date most of its magnificent mosques, notably those of Bajazet II, Suleiman I, and Ahmed I. They all reflect the influence of Hagia Sophia and give the skyline of Istanbul its character—a succession of perfectly proportioned domes broken by minarets. In the gardens by the Bosporus stand the buildings of the Seraglio, the former palace of the sultans, now a mus. In 19th cent. the sultans shifted their residence to the Dolma Bagtche palace and the Tildiz Kiosk, N of Pera on the Bosporus. The environs of Istanbul, particularly the villas, gardens, and castles along the Bosporus, are famed for their beauty. Always a cosmopolitan city, Istanbul has preserved much of its international and polyglot character, and Greeks, Armenians, and Jews continue to form a large part of the pop. Constantinople was founded (A.D. 330) at anc. Byzantium as the new ⊙ of the Roman Empire by Constantine I, after whom it was named. The largest and most splendid European city of the Middle Ages, Constantinople shared the glories and vicissitudes of the Byzantine Empire which, in the end, was reduced to the city and its environs. Though besieged innumerable times by various peoples, it was taken only three times: in 1204, by the crusaders in the Fourth Crusade; in 1261, by Michael VIII; and in 1453 by Sultan Mohammed II. Constantinople was surrounded by a triple wall of fortifications, begun (5th cent.) by Theodosius II. An earlier inner wall was erected by Constantine I. The city on the Bosporus presented the aspect of an impregnable fortress enclosing a sea of magnificent palaces and gilded domes and towers. At its greatest period, in the 10th cent., it had about 1,000,000 inhabitants, representing nearly every race in the world. Scores of churches, public edifices, and monuments lined the broad arcaded avenues and squares. Probably no city in Europe ever possessed as many artistic and literary treasures as Constantinople before it was sacked in 1204 and in 1453. Virtually depopulated when it fell (1453) to the Turks, the city soon flourished again under the sultans (whose court was called the Sublime Porte) as the ⊙ Ottoman Empire and as one of the great political and commercial centers of Europe. After the First World War it was occupied (1918–23) by the Allies.

Istanos, Turkey: see KORKUTELI.

Ister, anc. name for DANUBE RIVER.

Isthmia (ĭsth'mēŭ, Gr. ĕsthmē'ŭ), village (pop. 1,177), Argolis and Corinthia nome, NE Peloponnesus, Greece, port at SE end of Corinth Canal, 4 mi. ESE of Corinth. Near by took place the Isthmian games of Corinth.

Istiaia, Greece: see HISTIAIA.

Istib, Yugoslavia: see STIP.

Istiea, Greece: see HISTIAIA.

Istisu (ĕstyĭsōō'), village, SW Azerbaijan SSR, on Karabakh Upland of the Lesser Caucasus, in the Kurdistan, on Terter R. and 11 mi. SSW of Kelbadzhar; health resort.

Istmina (ĕstmē'nä), town (pop. 1,601), Chocó dept., W Colombia, landing on San Juan R. and 38 mi. S of Quibdó; gold and platinum mining. Founded 1784. The rich Andagoya placers are 4 mi. S.

Istok (ē'stôk), village, SW Serbia, Yugoslavia, 20 mi. WSW of Mitrovica, in the Metohija, at S foot of Mokra Planina.

Istokpoga, Lake (ĭstŭpō'gŭ), Highlands co., S central Fla., 25 mi. NW of L. Okeechobee; c.10 mi. long, 5 mi. wide; connected by channel (N) with lakes Weohyakapka and Kissimmee; has short outlet (dredged) at E end to Kissimmee R.

Istoro Nal (ĭstō'rō näl'), mountain (24,271 ft.) in the Hindu Kush, Chitral state, N North-West Frontier Prov., W Pakistan, N of Tirich Mir.

Istra (ē'strŭ), city (1926 pop. 4,296), central Moscow oblast, Russian SFSR, on Istra R. and 30 mi. WNW of Moscow; clothing mfg., silk milling. Until c.1930, called Voskresensk. Near by is famous Novo-Iyerusalimski [Rus.,=new Jerusalem] monastery, built (17th cent.) after model of Holy Sepulchre; has regional mus. Chartered 1781. During Second World War, briefly held (1941) by Germans in Moscow campaign.

Istra, Yugoslavia: see ISTRIA.

Istranca Mountains (ĭsträn'jä), Turkish *İstranca,* Bulgarian *Strandzha* (strän'jŭ), coastal range along Black Sea coast of Bulgaria and Turkey, extending c.85 mi. SE across the international line; rise to c.3,400 ft. Heavily wooded. Also spelled Istranja.

Istra River (ē'strŭ), Moscow oblast, Russian SFSR, rises in Klin-Dmitrov Ridge NW of Solnechnogorsk, flows c.50 mi. SE, past Istra, to Moskva R. 6 mi. SSE of Pavlovskaya Sloboda; reservoir and hydroelectric station in upper course.

Istres (ēs'trŭ), town (pop. 3,325), Bouches-du-Rhône dept., SE France, near W shore of Étang de Berre, 24 mi. NW of Marseilles; chemical works based on near-by saltworks. Naval flying school.

Istria (ĭ'strēŭ, Rum. ē'stryä), village (pop. 2,300), Constanta prov., SE Rumania, in Dobruja, on W shore of L. Sinoe, 27 mi. N of Constanta; noted as site of the ruins of anc. city of Histria, lying just SE, the object of extensive excavations. Histria was founded by Milesians in 7th cent. B.C. as a trading colony, then passed successively under Macedonian (339 B.C.) and Roman (72 B.C.) domination; destroyed by the Goths (A.D. 238), it was rebuilt by Constantine the Great, and destroyed again by the Barbarians.

Istria or **Istrian Peninsula** (ĭ'strēŭ, –ŭn), Serbo-Croatian *Istra* (ē'strä), Ger. *Istrien* (ĭ'strēŭn), peninsula (□ c.1,500–2,000) projecting into N Adriatic Sea, mostly in Yugoslavia; bounded (N) by the KARST. Free Territory of TRIESTE is on NW shore. Consists of 3 regions (so named for the prevailing soils): mountainous, karstlike White Istria (N), which culminates in UCKA peak; Yellow Istria (center); and Red Istria (S). Pop., which comprised (1945) Croats (55%), Italians (24%), and Slovenes (18%), engaged largely in agr. (olives, fruit, cereals, wine), mule raising, and fishing (sardines, tuna). Deposits of coal (at RASA), salt, and bauxite. Chief towns: PULA, OPATIJA. Originally inhabited by an Illyrian race, it passed (c.177 B.C.) to Rome. After decline of Rome, it was invaded by Ostrogoths, Avars, and Slavs, but remained under nominal Byzantine rule until 752. Held by various overlords until NE Istria passed (1374) to the Hapsburgs and SW Istria (1420) to Venice. During Napoleonic era, entire peninsula passed successively to Austria (1797), Italy (1805), and Illyrian Provs. (1809). Finally granted to Austria in 1815, it was made (1816) part of kingdom of Illyria and (1849) a prov. (□ 1,914; 1910 pop. 403,566) of Küstenland. Istria was ceded to Italy in 1919 and became Pola (after 1937, Istria) prov. (□ 1,436; pop. 294,492) within Venezia Giulia. In 1947, most of Istria passed to Yugoslavia, where it was divided along ethnic lines bet. Croatia and Slovenia, while a NW section formed the Free Territory of Trieste.

Istrouma (ĭstrōō'mŭ), village (1940 pop. 3,679), East Baton Rouge parish, SE central La., just NE of Baton Rouge.

Isuru (ēsōō'rōō), village, Eastern Prov., NE Belgian Congo, 11 mi. W of Kilo-Mines; gold mining and processing. Sometimes spelled Issuru.

Isurugi (ēsōō'rōōgē), town (pop. 10,112), Toyama prefecture, central Honshu, Japan, 14 mi. NE of Kanazawa; commercial center for rice-growing area; silk textiles.

Isvoron, Greece: see STRATONIKE.

Iswaripur (ĭs'vŭrēpŏŏr"), village, Khulna dist., SW East Bengal, E Pakistan, in the Sundarbans, 45 mi. SW of Khulna; road terminus; rice, jute, oilseeds. Was ⊙ 16th-cent. independent Moslem kingdom until defeated 1576 by Akbar's Hindu general.

Isyangulovo (ēsyŭn-gōō'lŭvŭ), village (1948 pop. over 2,000), S Bashkir Autonomous SSR, Russian SFSR, on Greater Ik R. and 70 mi. NE of Chkalov; wheat, rye, oats, livestock.

Iszkaszentgyörgy (ĭs'kŏsĕnd-dyûr"dyû), mining town (pop. 1,342), Fejer co., N central Hungary, on SE slope of Bakony Mts., 6 mi. NW of Szekesfehervar; bauxite mine.

Ita, Japan: see TAGAWA.

Itá (ētä'), town (dist. pop. 18,517), Central dept., S Paraguay, 26 mi. SE of Asunción; processing and agr. center (cotton, sugar cane, tobacco, fruit); vegetable-oil mfg., liquor distilling, tanning. Founded 1536.

Itabaiana (ētŭbīä'nŭ). **1** City (pop. 7,972), E Paraíba, NE Brazil, on right bank of Paraíba R. and 35 mi. SW of João Pessoa; road and rail junction (spur to Campina Grande) and important trade center (cotton, livestock, leather, cereals). Called Tabaiana, 1944–48. Formerly spelled Itabayanna. **2** City (pop. 4,422), central Sergipe, NE Brazil, on W slope of Serra Itabaiana, 30 mi. NW of Aracaju; agr. trade center (cotton, manioc, cereals, livestock). Has model farms.

Itabaiana, Serra (sĕ'rŭ), hill range in E Sergipe, NE Brazil, forming escarpment above coastal lowland c.25 mi. NW of Aracaju. Rises to 2,800 ft. Dense forest cover.

Itabaianinha (ētŭbīŭnē'nyŭ), city (pop. 1,778), S Sergipe, NE Brazil, on railroad and 22 mi. W of Estância; sugar, cotton, livestock.

Itabapoana (ētŭbŭpōä'nŭ), town (pop. 1,941), NE Rio de Janeiro state, Brazil, on the Atlantic at mouth of Itabapoana R. (Espírito Santo border), and 36 mi. NNE of Campos; sugar cane, fish.

Itabapoana River, E Brazil, rises at S foot of the Pico da Bandeira, flows c.100 mi. SE, through sugar-growing valley forming Espírito Santo–Rio de Janeiro border, to the Atlantic at Itabapoana.

Itabashi, Formosa: see PANKIAO.

Itabayanna, Brazil: see ITABAIANA, Paraíba.

Itaberá (ētŭbĭrä'), city (pop. 1,160), S São Paulo, Brazil, 19 mi. NW of Itapeva; coffee, cotton, tobacco, grain.

Itaberaba (ētŭbĭrä'bŭ), city (pop. 2,700), E central Bahia, Brazil, on rail spur, and 100 mi. W of Cachoeira; tobacco, coffee, manioc, livestock. Asbestos deposits.

Itaberaí (ētŭbĭräē'), city (pop. 1,488), S central Goiás, central Brazil, 50 mi. NW of Goiânia; distilling, cattle shipping. Emeralds and beryls found in area. Formerly spelled Itaberahy.

Itabira (ētŭbē'rŭ), city (pop. 4,685), E central Minas Gerais, Brazil, in an offshoot of the Serra do Espinhaço, 50 mi. NE of Belo Horizonte; leading iron-mining center of Brazil. Surrounding city are Cauê peak (4,281 ft.), an iron mtn. containing over 100,000,000 tons of ore (67% pure hematite), now actively worked; and Conceição peak with similar deposits. Crushed ore is shipped 300 mi. by narrow-gauge railroad through Rio Doce valley to recently modernized port of Vitória (Espírito Santo). Semiprecious stones and graphite also found in area. Originally called Itabira or Itabira de Matto Dentro, it was renamed Presidente Vargas 1944, but became Itabira again 1948.

Itabirito (ētŭbērē'tōō), city (pop. 4,918), S central Minas Gerais, Brazil, on railroad and 25 mi. SSE of Belo Horizonte; iron-mining center, 2d only to Itabira, working high-grade hematite ore of cone-shaped Itabirito peak. Pig-iron plant. Ore is shipped by rail to Rio de Janeiro.

Itaboraí (ētŏobŏŏrăē'), city (pop. 1,032), S central Rio de Janeiro state, Brazil, on railroad and 19 mi. NE of Niterói; alcohol distilling; poultry, sugar, fruit. Formerly spelled Itaborahy.

Itabuna (ētŏobōō'nŭ), city (1950 pop. 26,312), SE Bahia, Brazil, head of navigation on Cachoeira R. 20 mi. W of Ilhéus (linked by rail); cacao-growing and -processing center; also ships livestock, rice, wine.

Itacaré (ētŭkŭrĕ'), city (pop. 1,649), E Bahia, Brazil, on the Atlantic at mouth of the Rio de Contas, 35 mi. N of Ilhéus; ships cacao, piassava, manioc. Formerly called Barra do Rio de Contas.

Itacê (ētŭsā'), town (pop. 206), central Goiás, central Brazil, 90 mi. NNE of Goiás city; abandoned gold mine. Until 1944, called Pilar.

Itacoatiara (ētŭkwŭtyä'rŭ), city (pop. 4,741), E Amazonas, Brazil, steamer and hydroplane landing on left bank of the Amazon below influx of the Madeira, and 110 mi. E of Manaus; ships rubber, Brazil nuts, cacao, guarana, hardwood, fish, and copaiba. Tinted petroglyphs found here. Old name, Serpa.

Itacolomi, Pico de (pē'kŏŏ dĭ ētŭkŏŏlŏŏmē'), mountain (5,896 ft.) in offshoot of the Serra do Espinhaço, SE central Minas Gerais, Brazil, just SW of Ouro Prêto.

Itacurubí de la Cordillera (ētäkŏŏrŏŏbē' dā lä kôrdĭyä'rä), town (dist. pop. 9,202), La Cordillera dept., S central Paraguay, in Cordillera de los Altos, 55 mi. ESE of Asunción. Resort and agr. center (fruit, maté, tobacco, cattle); tanning, tile making.

Itacurubí del Rosario (dĕl rōsär'yō), town (dist. pop. 9,454), San Pedro dept., central Paraguay, 75 mi. NE of Asunción; lumbering, agr. (oranges, maté, livestock); tanneries, distilleries, sawmills.

Itacurussá (ētŭkŏŏrŏŏsä'), town (pop. 958), SW Rio de Janeiro state, Brazil, on Sepetiba Bay of the Atlantic, on railroad and 40 mi. W of Rio; its small port is to be rebuilt for export of iron ore from Minas Gerais.

Itaetê (ētītā'), town (pop. 469), central Bahia, Brazil, W terminus of railroad from Salvador, and 26 mi. SE of Andaraí; diamond shipping. Until 1944, called Iguaçu (formerly spelled Iguassú).

Itaguá (ētägwä'), town (dist. pop. 12,358), Central dept., S Paraguay, 23 mi. ESE of Asunción, in agr. area (fruit, tobacco, cotton, rice). Known for its fine lace. Tanneries. Notable 19th-cent. church. Sometimes spelled Itauguá.

Itaguaçu (ētŭgwŭsōō'), city (pop. 791), central Espírito Santo, Brazil, 45 mi. NW of Vitória; coffee, corn. Old spelling, Itaguassú.

Itaguaí (ētŭgwäē'), city (pop. 872), SW Rio de Janeiro state, Brazil, on railroad and 32 mi. W of Rio. At near-by site called Kilometro 47, on Rio–São Paulo highway, is Rural Univ. (founded 1943; operated by federal govt.).

Itaguatins (ētŭgwŭtēns'), city (pop. 960), northernmost Goiás, N central Brazil, on left bank of Tocantins R. (rapids) and 15 mi. S of Imperatriz (Maranhão); babassu nuts, mangabeira rubber. Until 1944, called Santo Antônio da Cachoeira.

Itagüí (ētägwē'), town (pop. 1,455), Antioquia dept., NW central Colombia, in Cordillera Central, on Porce R., on railroad and 6 mi. SSW of Medellín; alt. 5,331 ft. Resort in agr. region (sugar cane, coffee, corn, yucca, bananas); textile milling.

Itahana (ētä'hänŭ), town (pop. 2,695), Gumma prefecture, central Honshu, Japan, 4 mi. W of Takasaki; rice, wheat.

Itaí (ētäē'), city (pop. 1,232), S São Paulo, Brazil, 25 mi. SSW of Avaré; tanning, lumber shipping. Formerly Itahy.

Itá-Ibaté (ētä'-ēbätā'), village (pop. estimate 1,000), N Corrientes prov., Argentina, river port on Paraná R. (Paraguay border) and 95 mi. E of Corrientes; rice, citrus fruit, livestock.

Itaiópolis (ētīô'pŏŏlēs), city (pop. 722), N Santa Catarina, Brazil, 28 mi. S of Mafra. Agr. colony (grain, livestock, timber) founded 1891 by English and Slav settlers. Formerly spelled Itayopolis.

Itaipava (ētīpä'vŭ), town (pop. 1,122), central Rio de Janeiro state, Brazil, in the Serra do Mar, on railroad and 10 mi. N of Petrópolis; dairy produce, poultry, vegetables, fruit, flowers. Sanatorium.

Itaipu (ētīpōō'), town, S Rio de Janeiro state, Brazil, on the Atlantic, 7 mi. SE of Niterói; bathing resort.

Itaituba (ētītōō'bŭ), city (pop. 381), W Pará, Brazil, head of navigation on left bank of Tapajós R. and 140 mi. SSW of Santarém; bituminous schist deposits.

Itajaí (ētŭzhäē'), city (1950 pop. 20,017), NE Santa Catarina, Brazil, Atlantic port at mouth of Itajaí Açu R., and 50 mi. N of Florianópolis; port for Blumenau (25 mi. W; river navigation) and its fertile agr. hinterland settled by German immigrants in mid-19th cent. Exports timber (cedar and rosewood, mahogany), dairy products, sugar, rice, meat. Textile mills. Iron, molybdenum deposits in area. Airfield. Formerly spelled Itajahy.

Itajaí Açu River (äsōō'), E Santa Catarina, Brazil, rises in several headstreams in the Serra do Mar, flows c.125 mi. E, through fertile, thickly settled lowland, past Rio do Sul and Blumenau (head of navigation), to the Atlantic at Itajaí.

Itajobi (ētŭzhŏŏbē'), city (pop. 2,166), N central São Paulo, Brazil, 13 mi. SSW of Catanduva; cotton ginning, wine making; cotton, coffee, cattle.

Itajubá (ētŭzhŏŏbä'), city (1950 pop. 21,255), SW Minas Gerais, Brazil, on slope of Serra da Mantiqueira, near São Paulo border, 110 mi. NE of São Paulo city; ships coffee, sugar, tobacco, lard; mfg. (textiles, matches, hats). Has electrotechnical institute (founded 1913).

Itaka (ētä'kŭ), town (1939 pop. over 500), central Chita oblast, Russian SFSR, 20 mi. N of Ksenyevka; gold mining.

Itakhola (ĭtä'kōlŭ), village, Sylhet dist., E East Bengal, E Pakistan, 60 mi. SSW of Sylhet; rice, tea, oilseeds; umbrella mfg. Tea processing near by.

Itako (ētä'kō) or **Idako** (–dä'kō), town (pop. 7,035), Ibaraki prefecture, central Honshu, Japan, 22 mi. NW of Choshi, on canal connecting (S) lagoon Kasumi-ga-ura with Kita-ura. Summer resort; rice growing, fishing, mfg. (textiles, sake).

Itala (ētä'lä), town (pop. 500), in the Benadir, S Ital. Somaliland, fishing port on Indian Ocean, 80 mi. NE of Mogadishu, in durra-growing region. Also El Athale.

Italaque (ētälä'kā), town (pop. c.10,900), La Paz dept., W Bolivia, in Cordillera Real, 15 mi. NE of Puerto Acosta; *oca*, barley, potatoes.

Italian Mountain, peak (13,350 ft.) in Rocky Mts., Gunnison co., W central Colo.

Italian Riviera, Italy: see RIVIERA.

Italian Somaliland (sōmä'lēlănd) or **Somalia** (sōmä'-lēŭ), Ital. trust territory (□ c.194,000; 1947 pop. estimate 970,000), E Africa, on Gulf of Aden and Indian Ocean; ⊙ Mogadishu. Consists of a coastal strip (90–250 mi. wide) extending from the "horn" of E Africa SW to Kenya border, bounded W by Ethiopia and Br. Somaliland. Its rather straight coast line (paralleled by sand dunes in S) has no natural harbors; on it are capes Guardafui (at tip of "horn") and Hafun (Africa's easternmost point). Mountainous in N (outliers of Br. Somaliland's Ogo highland and Haud plateau); elsewhere, a broad, arid lowland sloping gently from Ethiopia's Ogaden plateau toward Indian Ocean. Its dry, tropical climate has 2 short rainy periods (March–April; Oct.–Nov.), with little rainfall (less than 20 in.). Commercial agr. limited to lower valleys of territory's 2 perennial streams, Webi Shebeli and Juba rivers. Irrigated plantation crops (cotton, sugar, tobacco, castor beans, bananas, peanuts) grown at Villabruzzi, Genale, Afgoi, and Alessandra. Native subsistence agr. includes durra, corn, barley, millet, sesame, and beans. Nomadic stock raising (camels, sheep, goats) is chief occupation. Gums and resins are collected in N coastal area, which supplies ½ of world's frankincense. Skins and hides (antelope, leopard) are also exported. Tunny fisheries; mother-of-pearl. Saltworks at Hordio and on Hafun peninsula. The following regions are usually distinguished: Mijirtein (N), Mudugh (center), Benadir (S coastal strip), and Upper Juba (SW). Chief coastal towns are Mogadishu and Kismayu (main ports), Brava, Merca, Obbia, Hafun, Bender Kassim. Bardera, Isha Baidoa, and Lugh Ferrandi are main inland centers. Roads (c.7,000 mi.) radiate from Mogadishu to N coast, Ethiopia, and Kenya. Lower Webi Shebeli and Juba rivers navigable for dhows. Native pop. is largely Somali (Moslem), with some Bantu tribes in SW; c.25,000 Arabs in coastal towns. Less than 4,000 Italians remained in 1948. Italy 1st asserted its authority here in 1889. It enlarged its zone of influence by leasing (1892) and subsequently purchasing (1905) several coastal stations from the Sultan of Zanzibar. JUBALAND was acquired from Kenya in 1925, and incorporated into colony in 1926. After Italo-Ethiopian War, Ital. Somaliland was combined with Ethiopia's Ogaden region into a "government" of newly formed Ital. East Africa. Conquered by British (1941) during Second World War, it remained under their military administration until 1950, when, pursuant to a United Nations decision, Italy assumed control of its former colony until 1959, the provisional date for its independence.

Italica, Sp. *Itálica* (ētä'lēkä), ruined Roman town, Seville prov., SW Spain, just NW of Santiponce, 5 mi. NW of Seville. Founded c.205 B.C. by Scipio Africanus for retired soldiers. Noted as birthplace of Emperor Hadrian, and probably of Trajan and Theodosius. Has remains of amphitheater.

Italy, Latin and Ital. *Italia* (ētä'lyä), republic (□ 116,224; 1936 census pop. 42,918,726; 1948 pop. estimate 46,110,000), S Europe; ⊙ ROME. Extends bet. 36°39'–47°5'N and 6°33'–18°31'E. A closely knit geographical unit before it became a modern nation, the country is tied to the continent along the borders of France (NW) and Switzerland and Austria (N) by Europe's greatest divide, the Alps, from which Italy thrusts c.600 mi. SE as a narrow, boot-shaped peninsula (up to 200 mi. wide) into the Mediterranean Sea, bet. the Adriatic Sea (E) and the Tyrrhenian Sea (W). Only in its frontier with Yugoslavia (NE), in the low, tumbled Julian Alps of Istria, does the boundary lack clear definition; and it is here, therefore, where disputes led to the creation (1947) of Free Territory of Trieste under U.N. supervision. Off the SW tip of Italy, across the Strait of Messina, is the triangular isl. of SICILY (□ 9,831). Its other major isl., SARDINIA (□ 9,196), lies c.240 mi. W of Naples, just S of Fr. isl. of Corsica. Several smaller isls. fringe the W coast, such as ELBA (□ 86), renowned as Napoleon's place of exile; enchanting CAPRI and ISCHIA off Naples; and volcanic LIPARI ISLANDS, with active STROMBOLI and VULCANO islets. PANTELLERIA and LAMPEDUSA (Pelagian isls.), former island strongholds bet. Sicily and North African coast of Tunisia, are scattered over the sealane that connects the E and W Mediterranean basins. The Ionian Sea (SE), linked with the Adriatic by Strait of Otranto, washes the S peninsula and W Greece. The Ligurian Sea (NW) separates the Italian Riviera from Corsica. Sovereign enclaves within Italy are the old republic of SAN MARINO near Rimini and VATICAN CITY (set up 1929) in Rome. Highest peak entirely on Italian soil is the Gran Paradiso (13,323 ft.) in Graian Alps (Val d'Aosta) near the Mont Blanc massif, which belongs largely to France. The Monte Rosa, on the border in the Pennine Alps, belongs mostly to Switzerland. On the S slopes of the Rhaetian Alps is the beautiful lake dist. (the lakes MAGGIORE, LUGANO, COMO, and GARDA). Though a powerful barrier, the Alps are crossed by international highways and railroads, notably at the passes Mont Cenis (tunnel), Fréjus, and Little St. Bernard from France; at Great St. Bernard, Simplon (tunnel), St. Gotthard (tunnel), Bernina, and Maloja from Switzerland; and at the Brenner Pass from Austria. The backbone of Italy is the APENNINES, a large deforested range which branches off the Ligurian Alps (spur of Maritime Alps) at Ligurian coast and traverses the entire length of the peninsula, continuing on into Sicily. It splits into several plateaus and subranges which encircle small inland basins and coastal lowlands; in N are the Apuane Alps (with Carrara marble quarries), part of Etruscan Apennines which center near Florence; the desolate Abruzzi E of Rome rises in the GRAN SASSO D'ITALIA to Monte Corno (9,560 ft.). Characteristic of the Apennines are their volcanic features, exemplified in lava fields, frequent earthquakes, *sofiones*, and famed active craters such as VESUVIUS (3,891 ft.) towering over Naples, Mt. ETNA (10,705 ft.) above Messina, and the Lipari Isls. Despite its long maritime frontage (c.2,500 mi.), Italy has comparatively few good harbors. Apart from the navigable Po and the Adige, there are only minor rivers paralleling each other on both sides of the peninsula. Among the most important of these are the Arno of Tuscany, and the Tiber, near whose mouth lies Rome. Piave and Isonzo rivers (NE) are known chiefly for military reasons. In general, Italy enjoys a Mediterranean climate, with hot, dry summers and mild, humid winters. The peninsula's more arid E coast lies in rainshadow of the Apennines. While rainfall generally decreases towards S, temperatures increase. Sicily is subtropical (e.g., TAORMINA is a winter resort). The RIVIERA coast E and W of Genoa (with resorts of BORDIGHERA, SAN REMO, RAPALLO, etc.) and the lake dist. of Lombardy are famed for their fine climate and setting. The hot, dry *sirocco* from the Sahara frequently sweeps over the South. Malaria, long a curse of the country, still ravages the S marshy lowlands but is on the wane in the PONTINE MARSHES (now largely drained) and the Po valley. The latter, colder in winter than the S Alpine slopes, is Italy's only region with a continental type of climate, showing marked seasonal changes. Here, in an area constituting c.15% of entire country (drainage basin □ 28,945), with c.40% of its pop., centers Italy's economic life. This fertile, alluvial land, the one major plain of the country, extends S and E of the Alpine crescent to the N Apennines. The valley yields the bulk of the country's wheat, corn, oats, rye, potatoes, barley, hemp, meat, and dairy products; and virtually all the rice, silk, and sugar beets. The lower slopes are used for fruitgrowing and grazing. The Alps provide the hydroelectric power necessary to supply large-scale industries, since Italy is poor in all mineral resources, and especially lacks coal (though there are some deposits in Tuscany and Sardinia). Natural gas and oil deposits are developed in Pavia and Piacenza provs. Hub and 2d city of the nation is MILAN, economically unsurpassed even by Rome. It has been the industrial (textiles, chemicals, publishing, machinery) center and banking hq. since early Middle Ages. A number of industrial towns surround it. Italy's leading industry, textile milling, is carried on also at TURIN (which also makes automobiles, electrical equipment, etc.), ALESSANDRIA, COMO, BERGAMO, BIELLA, and BRESCIA; food processing is dominant at PAVIA, LODI, CREMONA, and MANTOVA; ASTI is renowned for its sparkling wines; AOSTA has electrometallurgical industries. Mfg. becomes less important towards E coast of Po valley, where historic VERONA, VICENZA, and PADUA, within productive agr. region, lie on Milan-Venice RR. A string of trading and mfg. towns on another railroad from Milan follows N Apennine piedmont: PIACENCA, PARMA, REGGIO NELL'EMILIA, MODENA, and, principally, BOLOGNA, an industrial and communications center, celebrated for its anc. univ. (faculty of law). Ravenna, a silted-up port now c.12 mi. inland from the Adriatic coast, is known for its Byzantine art treasures. The major Mediterranean port of Genoa, on Ligurian coast, today surpasses in trade its former rival, Venice, the picturesque island city on the opposite coast amidst the Adriatic lagoons. Venice is still noted for its glassware. Another Adriatic port, Ancona, lies on NE bulge of peninsula. S of the Po, the peninsula proper is made up of an intricate pattern of verdant slopes, arid mts., and interior and coastal depressions. Much of the area has suffered from erosion, large landholding, overpopulation, malaria, and warfare. There are a few productive stretches, principally in the Arno basin of Tuscany from Florence to Livorno, and in the Campania around Naples. Main crops are wheat, alfalfa, citrus, olives, tomatoes, and wine. The Pontine Marshes S of Rome, reclaimed in 1930s, now support a number of agr. towns (Littoria, Nettuno, Anzio). Sheep and goats are grazed widely. Cheese is exported. Tuscany is the only section, apart from Sardinia, with fairly substantial mineral resources (iron, lignite, magnesite, zinc, mercury, building stone), but industries are few. Several hydroelectric plants have been built. Central Italy contains the great cultural and historic centers of Florence, Pisa, Siena, Perugia, Assisi, Urbino, and Rome itself, "the Eternal City" and a treasure-house of Western Civilization. Civitavecchia serves as port of Rome. The treasures of those towns and the numerous spas and resorts (e.g., Viareggio, Fiuggi, Alban Hills) attract tourists from all nations. Spezia in Tuscany is a naval base and has, like Genoa in N and Palermo on Sicily, major shipyards. S Italy is, together with Sardinia, Italy's most backward region. Only Naples, the lively port on a beautiful Mediterranean bay, is a great urban center. Near by are the picturesque towns of Salerno, Sorrento, and Amalfi; the ruins of excavated Pompeii and Herculaneum; and the vacation paradise of Capri. A belt of olive trees stretches bet. Bari and Brindisi, the Adriatic ports of S Italy. The port of Taranto (naval base) lies on a gulf inside the heel of Italy. Port of Reggio di Calabria, on tip of the toe, faces Strait of Messina. Overpopulated Sicily, breadbasket of the anc. world, does not fare much better than the S peninsula. The rugged hills of the interior are unsuitable for settlements, and most of the people live in or around the few large cities along coast: Palermo, Messina, Catania, Syracuse, Agrigento. Wheat is grown widely; citrus (especially lemons) in irrigated areas; sheep grazing in hills. The isl. yields large amount of sulphur; also asphalt and rock salt. Italy's chief mining region is in Sardinia (zinc, lead, silver, lignite, manganese, iron, antimony, molybdenum, copper, barite, kaolin, anthracite, talc, salt), which, however, are insufficient for country's needs. The isl. of Elba has iron deposits furnishing about 90% of the iron from the inadequate Italian resources. To keep its industry going and supply a rapidly increasing pop., Italy has to import coal, metals, all kinds of raw materials (textile fibers, timber, wood pulp, paper, rubber), machinery, fertilizers, wheat, and foodstuff. Principal exports are subtropical fruit, winter vegetables, and consumer goods such as textiles, hats, automobiles, wine, cheese, etc. The unfavorable trade balance is somewhat eased by the large tourist trade and the savings sent by Italians from abroad. Although always in the front rank of European culture, Italy nevertheless still has a high percentage of illiterates (up to 50% in S). To its high intellectual tradition testify 27 universities, among them Bari, Bologna, Florence, Milan, Padua, Palermo, Pisa, Rome, Turin, Venice. There are small minorities in the N: German-speaking (0.5%) in Trentino-Alto Adige (Italian Tyrol); French-speaking (0.2%) in Val d'Aosta of W Alps; Yugoslavs (1%) live in Friuli-Venezia-Giulia. An overwhelming majority of all the Italians are R.C. Ethnologically the Italians are of as varied a stock as any European nation. Among early inhabitants were probably Ligurians and Ibezians, who succumbed to invading Etruscans from Asia Minor. The Etruscans established a great culture in central Italy. Their advance was checked in S by Samnites. The Latins, along coast of Latium, and Sabines were ancestors of the Romans. The history of Italy from 5th cent. B.C. to 5th cent. A.D. is largely that of the rise and fall of Rome. All of Italy was thoroughly latinized. In 5th cent. it was invaded by successive waves of Barbarian tribes from N (Visigoths, Ostrogoths, Lombards, Huns, etc.). Normans and Saracens gained foothold in S during Middle Ages. The peninsula became a pawn of foreign empires, chiefly German, French, and Spanish, disintegrated into sometimes powerful city states (Venice, Genoa, etc.), republics (e.g., Florence, Siena, Lucca), duchies (Ferrara, Modena, Milan, Savoy), and kingdoms (Sardinia, Naples). After Congress of Vienna (1814–15) only 3 major powers were left, the Kingdom of the Two Sicilies in S, the Papal States in center, and Sardinia with Piedmont and Savoy (NW). Lombardy and Venetia belonged to Austria. Though the concept of a united Italy had been kindled in the Renaissance (Machiavelli, Cesare Borgia, Rienzi), Italy as a modern state emerged through efforts of the Risorgimento movement, of which the liberal Mazzini was the 1st great leader; he proclaimed (1849) short-lived republic at Rome. Unification gained momentum after Peace of Zurich (1859), when Victor Emmanuel II, assisted by Cavour and Garibaldi, obtained Lombardy from Austria. Tuscany (with Lucca), Modena, Parma, and Romagna (with Bologna) were joined (1860) to Kingdom of Sardinia by plebiscite, followed soon by Naples and Sicily, and by the Papal States of Marches and Umbria. In 1861 Victor Emmanuel became king of Italy. Defeat (1866) of Austria won Venetia. Remainder of Papal States were seized (1870). Italy concluded (1882) Triple Alliance with Germany and Austria and embarked upon industrial and colonial expansion. Italy acquired Eritrea and part of Somaliland, but was checked (1896) by Ethiopians at Aduwa. War with Turkey (1911–12) yielded Libya. Overpopulation led in early 20th cent. to mass emigration to North and South America. Italy sided (1915) in First World War with the Allies and obtained at Paris Peace Conference S Tyrol, Trieste, Istria, part of Carniola, several Dalmatian isls., and the Dodecanese (which had been kept by Greeks, though ceded 1913 by the Turks to Italy). Fiume was taken (1921) by D'Annunzio. The Fascist dictatorship was inaugurated (1922) by Mussolini's March on Rome. Lateran Treaty (1929) with Pope established sovereign Vatican City. Conquest of Ethiopia in 1935–36 and ineffective sanctions imposed by League of Nations (from which it withdrew in 1937) drew Italy closer to Germany and Japan, with whom it formed the "Axis." Thus committed to aggression, Italy embarked upon the dictatorial road to natl. disaster. It intervened in the Spanish Civil War (1936–39) on behalf of the Insurgents, occupied (1939) Albania, and, after a brief neutrality, entered (1940) the Second World War on Germany's side, declaring war on collapsing France and embattled Great Britain. The same year attacks were launched on Greece and Egypt. Joined (1941) Germany and Japan in war against Russia and U.S. In 1943, when all African colonies were lost, and Sicily had been invaded by the Allies, Mussolini fell. He was replaced by Gen. Badoglio, who declared war on Germany. German resistance turned all Italy into a battlefield. Unpopular Victor Emmanuel III abdicated (1944) in favor of his son Humbert II. Germans signed (1945) their surrender at Caserta. A referendum (1946) established the republic by small margin. In the peace treaty (1947) Italy renounced claims to her colonial possessions, lost most of Venezia-Giulia (the remainder is now Friuli-Venezia-Giulia) to Yugoslavia, and small border strips—including Tenda (Fr. Tende) and Briga (Fr. Brigue)—to France. Trieste was set up as a Free Territory. Concession of Tientsin (obtained 1902) was returned to China and the islet of Saseno (occupied 1914) to Albania. Italian Somaliland became (1950) an Italian trusteeship under U.N., to expire in 1959. In 1950 the U.N. decided Eritrea was to be given its freedom in a federation with Ethiopia, to become effective 1952. Libya (consisting of Tripolitania, Cyrenaica, and Fezzan) was to have its independence in 1952. After the war, Italy's economy largely recovered, aided by U.S. under European Recovery Program, but the political scene remained unsettled and the country was still faced by 2 major problems—overpopulation and wasteful large estates. The new democratic constitution provides for a chamber of deputies, a senate, and a president elected for 7 years by the 2 houses. Certain privileges of autonomy were granted to Sicily, Sardinia, Trentino-Alto Adige, Val d'Aosta, and Friuli-Venezia-Giulia. Italy joined (1949) the North Atlantic Treaty. For further information, see articles on cities, towns, physical features, and the 91 provs. included in the following 19 regions: Abruzzi e Molise, Basicata (Lucania), Calabria, Campania, Emilia-Romagna, Friuli-Venezia-Giulia, Latium, Liguria, Lombardy, Marches, Piedmont, Puglia, Sicily, Sardinia, Trentino-Alto Adige, Tuscany, Umbria, Val d'Aosta, Veneto.

Italy, town (pop. 1,185), Ellis co., N central Texas, c.40 mi. S of Dallas; trade, shipping point in rich blackland agr. area (cotton, corn, grain).

Itamaracá Island (ētŏŏmŭrŏŏkä'), in the Atlantic, off coast of Pernambuco, NE Brazil, 20 mi. N of Recife; c.9 mi. long, 4 mi. wide; separated from mainland by narrow channel. Just S is city of Igaraçu.

Itamarandiba (ētŏŏmŭrăndē'bŭ), city (pop. 1,860), NE central Minas Gerais, Brazil, in the Serra da Penha, 60 mi. NE of Diamantina; tourmalines found here; also has iron and kaolin deposits.

Itamaraty, Brazil: see Pedro Segundo.

Itambacuri (ētămbŏŏkŏŏrē'), city (pop. 2,308), NE Minas Gerais, Brazil, 20 mi. SW of Teófilo Otoni; coffee, lard, alcohol; mica mines. Formerly spelled Itambacury.

Itambé (ētămbĕ'). **1** City (pop. 2,203), S Bahia, Brazil, on the Rio Pardo and 30 mi. SSE of Vitória da Conquista; livestock, cotton, coffee. **2** City, Pernambuco, Brazil: see També.

Itambé, Pico do (pē'kŏŏ dŏŏ), peak (6,155 ft.) in central Minas Gerais, Brazil, 20 mi. SE of Diamantina, in E outlier of the Serra do Espinhaço. Jequitinhonha R. rises here. Large iron deposits.

Itami (ētä'mē), city (1940 pop. 33,579; 1947 pop. 53,296), Hyogo prefecture, S Honshu, Japan, just N of Amagasaki and Nishinomiya; sake-producing center. Resort area. Airfield.

Itamorotinga, Brazil: see Serra Branca.

Itanhaém (ētŭnyäē'), city (pop. 928), SE São Paulo, Brazil, unsheltered port on the Atlantic, on railroad and 35 mi. SW of Santos; fishing. Church and convent bldgs. date from 1534. Sometimes spelled Itanhaen.

Itanhandu (ētŭnyăndŏŏ'), city (pop. 2,660), S Minas Gerais, Brazil, in the Serra da Mantiqueira, on railroad and 20 mi. N of Cruzeiro (São Paulo); tobacco-growing center.

Itanoishi, Japan: see Banzai.

Itany River (ētänē'), Du. *Litani* (lē'tänē), in the Guianas, rises in Tumuc-Humac Mts. near Brazil line, flows c.100 mi. through tropical forests along S border of Fr. and Du. Guiana to Maroni R. (of which it is also considered the upper course) at 3°18'N 54°5'W.

Itaocara (ētoukä'rŭ), city (pop. 1,225), NE Rio de Janeiro state, Brazil, on Paraíba R. above influx of Pomba R., and 50 mi. W of Campos; coffee, sugar.

Itapagé (ētŭpŭzhĕ'), city (pop. 1,745), N Ceará, Brazil, in Uruburetama hills, 75 mi. W of Fortaleza; cotton, coffee, sugar. Until 1944, called São Francisco.

Itaparica (ētŭpŭrē'kŭ). **1** City (pop. 2,125), E Bahia, Brazil, fishing port at N tip of Itaparica Isl., 12 mi. NW of Salvador; oil and natural-gas wells. Ships whale oil, salt, coconuts, fruit. Its fort (built 1711) was attacked in 1823 by Port. fleet. **2** City, Pernambuco, Brazil: see Petrolândia.

Itaparica Island, in Todos os Santos Bay of the Atlantic, E Bahia, Brazil, 10 mi. W of Salvador; 18 mi. long, 5 mi. wide. Itaparica city is at N tip. Petroleum recently discovered here. Saltworks.

Itapé (ētäpā'), town (dist. pop. 5,820), Guairá dept., S Paraguay, 12 mi. SW of Villarrica; alcohol- and liquor-distilling center in agr. area (sugar cane, tobacco, maté, cattle). Founded 1680. Sometimes spelled Ytapé.

Itapecerica (ētŭpĭsĭrē'kŭ). **1** City (pop. 4,219), S central Minas Gerais, Brazil, 25 mi. SW of Divinópolis; rail-spur terminus; agr. trade (coffee, fruit, dairy products, sugar). Graphite deposits. **2** City, São Paulo, Brazil: see Itapecerica da Serra.

Itapecerica da Serra (dä sĕ'rŭ), city (pop. 693), SE São Paulo, Brazil, 20 mi. SW of São Paulo; timber; kaolin quarries; mica, gold deposits. Until 1944, Itapecerica.

Itapecuru Mirim (ētŭpĭkŏŏrŏŏ' mērēn'), city (pop. 1,825), N Maranhão, Brazil, on lower Itapecuru R., on São Luís–Teresina RR and 60 mi. S of São Luís; sugar, cotton, babassu nuts, rubber, tobacco. Road to Brejo.

Itapecuru River, Maranhão, NE Brazil, rises in the Serra do Itapecuru, flows NE, past Colinas, to Caxias (head of navigation), then NW, past Codó, Coroatá, and Itapecuru Mirim, to São José Bay of the Atlantic just below Rosário. Length, c.400 mi. Its valley, Brazil's leading babassu-nut-growing area, has diversified agr. (cotton, sugar, tobacco) and dense pop. Below Caxias it is followed by São Luís–Teresina RR.

Itapema (ētŭpä'mŭ), town (pop. 1,428), E Santa Catarina, Brazil, on the Atlantic, and 15 mi. S of Itajaí; sugar, rice, bananas; fishing.

Itapemirim (ētŭpĭmērēn'), city (pop. 2,721), S Espírito Santo, Brazil, on the Atlantic, near mouth of Itapemirim R., 23 mi. ESE of Cachoeiro de Itapemirim (rail link); sugar, coffee, rice, bananas.

Itapemirim River, S Espírito Santo, Brazil, rises near Alegre, flows 50 mi. ESE, past Cachoeiro de Itapemirim, to the Atlantic just N of Itapemirim. Not navigable.

Itaperuna (ētŭpĭrŏŏ'nŭ), city (pop. 6,697), NE Rio de Janeiro state, Brazil, on Muriaé R., on railroad and 55 mi. NW of Campos; coffee- and rice-processing center; dairying, alcohol distilling, cotton ginning, mfg. of chemicals.

Itapetininga (ētŭpĭtēnēng'gŭ), city (pop. 12,786), S central São Paulo, Brazil, on railroad and 90 mi. W of São Paulo, in fertile cotton-growing valley. Agr.-trade and -processing center; cheese factories, cottonseed-oil mills. Trade in cattle (for São Paulo slaughterhouses), cotton, grain. Founded at end of 18th cent. Has fine old church.

Itapeva (ētŭpā'vŭ), city (pop. 4,545), S São Paulo, Brazil, on railroad and 60 mi. SW of Itapetininga; livestock center; cotton processing. Copper and marble deposits. Airfield. Until mid-1930s, called Faxina.

Itapicuru River (ē"tŭpēkŏŏrŏŏ'), NE Bahia, Brazil, rises near Jacobina, flows c.250 mi. generally ESE, past Queimadas and Cipó, to the Atlantic below Conde.

Itapipoca (ētŭpēpō'kŭ), city (pop. 2,627), N Ceará, Brazil, terminus of railroad from Fortaleza (75 mi. ESE) projected to reach Sobral (55 mi. WSW); cotton-growing center on N slope of Uruburetama hills; coffee, carnauba wax.

Itapira (ētŏŏpē'rŏŏ). **1** City, Bahia, Brazil: see UBAITABA. **2** City (pop. 7,872), E São Paulo, Brazil, near Minas Gerais border, on railroad and 35 mi. NNE of Campinas; mfg. of shoes, hats, chairs, tile, bricks, sugar, alcohol; coffee processing. Limestone, marble deposits near by.

Itapiranga (ētŏŏpērăng'gŏŏ), city (pop. 176), E Amazonas, Brazil, on left bank of the Amazon and 40 mi. NE of Itacoatiara.

Itapoama (ētŏŏpōä'mŏŏ), city (pop. 1,232), S Espírito Santo, Brazil, 12 mi. E of Cachoeiro de Itapemirim; coffee, manioc, bananas. Until 1944, called Rio Novo.

Itápolis (ētä'pŏŏlēs), city (pop. 4,893), central São Paulo, Brazil, 40 mi. WNW of Araraquara; rail-spur terminus; pottery mfg.; coffee, cotton, rice, and corn processing; distilling.

Itaporanga (ētŏŏpŏŏrăng'gŏŏ). **1** City (pop. 2,312), W Paraíba, NE Brazil, 40 mi. SE of Cajàzeiras; cotton, rice, sugar, goat cheese. Called Misericórdia until 1939; Itaporanga, 1939–43; and again Misericórdia, 1944–48. **2** City (pop. 960), S São Paulo, Brazil, near Paraná border, 55 mi. SSW of Avaré; cotton, corn, beans, manioc, coffee.

Itaporanga d'Ajuda (dăzhōō'dŏŏ), city (pop. 1,980), E Sergipe, NE Brazil, on lower Vasa Barris R., on railroad and 18 mi. SW of Aracaju; ships sugar, cattle; sugar milling. Until 1944, called Itaporanga; and Irapiranga, 1944–48.

Itapúa (ētäpōō'ä), department (□ 6,380; pop. 104,706), SE Paraguay; ⊙ Encarnación. Forested lowlands bounded S and E by upper Paraná R. (Argentina border) and Tebicuary R. (NW). Has subtropical, humid climate. Some copper deposits. A rich lumbering and agr. area producing maté, cotton, corn, rice, tobacco, sugar cane, wine, cattle. Sawmilling and processing industries concentrated at Encarnación, Carmen del Paraná, Hohenau, Coronel Bogado, San Pedro del Paraná. Area was colonized by 18th-cent. Jesuit missions. In recent years, Ger., Russian, and Czech colonies were founded.

Itapucumi (ētäpōōkōō'mē), village, Concepción dept., N central Paraguay, on Paraguay R. and 60 mi. NW of Concepción; marble and lime quarrying; limekilns, small cement plant.

Itapuí (ētŏŏpwē'), city (pop. 3,036), central São Paulo, Brazil, on Tietê R., on railroad and 9 mi. WNW of Jaú; cotton, coffee, and rice processing. Formerly Bica de Pedra.

Itaquara (ētŏŏkwä'rŏŏ), city (pop. 1,773), E Bahia, Brazil, on railroad and 75 mi. SW of Nazaré; coffee, fruit, manioc.

Itaquari (ētŏŏkwŏŏrē'), town (pop. 2,670), central Espírito Santo, Brazil, on inlet of Espírito Santo Bay, opposite Vitória; metalworks.

Itaqui (ētŏŏkē'), city (pop. 7,121), W Rio Grande do Sul, Brazil, on Uruguay R. (Argentina border) at influx of Aguapey R., opposite Alvear (Argentina), on railroad and 55 mi. NE of Uruguaiana. Exports oranges and bergamots (for essential oils) to Argentina; slaughterhouses; horse raising, flax growing. Airfield. Formerly spelled Itaquy.

Itararé (ētŏŏrŏŏrě'), city (pop. 5,033), S São Paulo, Brazil, near Paraná border, on railroad to Jaguariaíva, and 90 mi. N of Curitiba; livestock center; grain, cotton, fruit; lumbering.

Itararé River, S Brazil, left tributary of Paranapanema R., forms São Paulo–Paraná border throughout its N-S course of 120 mi.

Itaretama (ētŏŏrĭtä'mŏŏ), city (pop. 1,596), central Rio Grande do Norte, NE Brazil, 70 mi. W of Natal; rail junction (spur to Pedro Avelino); livestock, cheese, carnauba wax. Gypsum and marble quarries. Until 1944, called Lajes (formerly spelled Lages).

Itarsi (ĭtär'sē), town (pop. 14,269), Hoshangabad dist., NW Madhya Pradesh, India, in fertile Narbada valley, 10 mi. SSE of Hoshangabad; rail junction (workshops); trade center; cattle market. Products of dense teak, sal, and khair forests (S) include lac and cutch.

Itasca (ītă'skŭ), county (□ 2,663; pop. 33,321), N Minn.; ⊙ Grand Rapids. Agr., resort, and mining area on Mississippi R.; numerous lakes, including Bowstring L., in W, and Pokegama L., near Grand Rapids. Dairy products, potatoes; peat deposits. Iron is mined in Mesabi iron range, in SE Parts of Greater Leech Lake Indian Reservation, Chippewa Natl. Forest, and Winnibigoshish L. in W; state forest in N. Formed 1849.

Itasca. 1 (ītă'skŭ) Village (pop. 1,274), Du Page co., NE Ill., WNW of Chicago and 15 mi. ESE of Elgin, in dairying area. **2** (ĭtă'skŭ) City (pop. 1,718), Hill co., N central Texas, c.40 mi. SSE of Fort Worth; trade center in cotton, grain area; cotton textile mfg. Settled 1882, inc. as city 1910.

Itasca, Lake (ītă'skŭ), small, shallow lake in Clearwater co., NW central Minn., on Mississippi R. and 23 mi. SW of Bemidji; 3.5 mi. long, max. width 1.5 mi. Discovered 1832 by Henry Schoolcraft and considered to be source of Mississippi R.; included in state park 1891. Later geographers consider the source to be small creeks above the lake.

Itasy, Lake (ētä'sē) (□ c.35, including adjoining swamps), central Madagascar, 28 mi. WSW of Tananarive; c.10 mi. long, 10 mi. wide; 19°5'S 46°48'E. Drains into Tsiribihina R. Center of fishing and agr. activities (peanuts, tobacco, corn, pulse, aleurites, patchouli).

Itat (ētät'), village (1926 pop. 2,750), NE Kemerovo oblast, Russian SFSR, on Trans-Siberian RR and 50 mi. E of Mariinsk, in agr. area.

Itata, department, Chile: see QUIRIHUE.

Itata River (ētä'tä), S central Chile, in Concepción and Ñuble provs., rises in Andes foothills W of Yungay, flows 110 mi. NW, through the irrigated central valley, to the Pacific 16 mi. NNE of Tomé. It is joined by its main tributary, the Ñuble, 20 mi. W of Chillán. The Itata-Ñuble is c.150 mi. long. A swift, torrential stream, it is navigable only a short distance for small craft.

Itatí (ētätē'), village (pop. estimate 2,000), ⊙ Itatí dept. (□ c.300; pop. 5,257), NW Corrientes prov., Argentina, port on Paraná R. (Paraguay border) and 40 mi. ENE of Corrientes, in agr. area (corn, rice, cotton, oranges); stock raising, fishing; tanning. Has old church of Our Lady of Itatí. Founded 1516.

Itatí, Lake (12 mi. long, 4 mi. wide), W central Corrientes prov., Argentina, at SW end of Esteros del Iberá, 30 mi. N of Mercedes. The Corrientes R. flows through part of it.

Itatiaia (ētŏŏtyī'ŏŏ), agr. town (pop. 1,288), W Rio de Janeiro state, Brazil, on Paraíba R., on railroad and 25 mi. W of Barra Mansa, near São Paulo border; cattle. Bauxite deposits. Starting point for Itatiaia Natl. Park (N). Until 1943, called Campo Belo.

Itatiaia, mountain (9,145 ft.) in the Serra da Mantiqueira, SE Brazil, on Minas Gerais–Rio de Janeiro border, 30 mi. WNW of Barra Mansa. Surrounding it is a natl. park (□ 46), established 1937. Peak also called Agulhas Negras [Port.,=black needles].

Itatiba (ētŏŏtē'bŏŏ), city (pop. 5,145), E São Paulo, Brazil, 16 mi. SE of Campinas; rail-spur terminus in coffee zone; textile milling, distilling.

Itatinga (ētŏŏtēng'gŏŏ), city (pop. 1,388), S central São Paulo, Brazil, 20 mi. E of Avaré; rail-spur terminus; butter processing, flour milling, tanning.

Itatupã (ētŏŏtōōpă'), town (pop. 322), NE Pará, Brazil, on N coast of Gurupá Isl. in Amazon delta, 40 mi. SSW of Macapá. Until 1943, Sacramento.

Itaú (ētäōō'), town (pop. c.500), Tarija dept., S Bolivia, on Itaú R. (branch of Tarija R.) and 23 mi. NNW of Yacuiba; tobacco, cotton.

Itaú, Sierra del (syĕ'rä dĕl), subandean mountain range in NE Salta prov., Argentina, and parallel to Bolivia-Argentina border, NW of Tartagal; extends c.45 mi. NNE–SSW; rises to c.3,500 ft.

Itaú de Minas, Brazil: see PASSOS.

Itauguá, Paraguay: see ITAGUÁ.

Itaúna (ētäōō'nŭ), city (pop. 5,035), S central Minas Gerais, Brazil, on railroad and 40 mi. WSW of Belo Horizonte; ships coffee, sugar cane, cattle; textile milling.

Itaverá (ētŏŏvĭrä'), city (pop. 589), SW Rio de Janeiro state, Brazil, in the Serra do Mar, on railroad and 25 mi. SW of Barra do Piraí; pyrite mining. Reservoir and hydroelectric plant (E). Until 1943, called Rio Claro.

Itawah, India: see ETAWAH.

Itawamba (ĭtŭwäm'bŭ), county (□ 541; pop. 17,216), NE Miss., borders E on Ala.; ⊙ Fulton. Drained by East Fork of Tombigbee R. Agr. (cotton, corn, sorghum); lumbering. Formed 1836.

Itayanagi (ētä'yänägē), town (pop. 8,616), Aomori prefecture, N Honshu, Japan, 6 mi. N of Hirosaki; rice, apples.

Itayopolis, Brazil: see ITAIÓPOLIS.

Itbayat Island (ētbä'yät), largest island (□ 33; 1948 pop. 1,954) of Batan Isls., Batanes prov., N Philippines, in Luzon Strait, 200 mi. N of Luzon; 20°46'N 121°50'E; 11 mi. long, 4 mi. wide, generally flat. Corn, rice.

Itchen River, Hampshire, England, rises just E of New Alresford, flows 25 mi. W and SW, past New Alresford and Winchester, to Southampton Water at Southampton. Navigable below Winchester.

Itea (ētā'ŭ), town (pop. 2,532), Phocis nome, W central Greece, port on Bay of Crisa (or Itea) of Gulf of Corinth, 7 mi. S of Amphissa; wheat; olive oil; wine; fisheries.

Itebej, Itebei, or Itebey (all: ē'tĕbā), Hung. *Ittebe* (ĭt'tĕbĕ), village (pop. 5,195), Vojvodina, NE Serbia, Yugoslavia, near Rum. border, on Begej Canal and 20 mi. NE of Zrenjanin, in the Banat. Pop. is largely Serbian. Until 1947, called Srpski Itebej, Hung. *Felsőittebe*. Novi Itebej, Hung. *Alsóittebe*, smaller village, with Magyar pop., is just SW.

Iténez, Bolivia: see MAGDALENA.

Iténez River, Bolivia: see GUAPORÉ RIVER.

Ithaca (ĭ'thĭkŭ), Gr. *Ithake* or *Ithaki* (both: ĭthä'kē), island (□ 37.2; pop. 7,083) of Ionian group, Greece, off NE Cephalonia (separated by 2–3-mi.-wide Thaka Strait), in Leukas nome; main town, Ithaca (38°23'N 20°42'E). Nearly bisected by Gulf of Molo, it consists of two mountainous sections rising to 2,645 ft. (N); 14 mi. long, 3 mi. wide. Agr.: currants, wine, olive oil. Fisheries. Commonly identified with home of Homer's Odysseus (Ulysses), although some archaeologists (including W. Dörpfeld) have connected anc. Ithaca with modern Leukas. Since the Middle Ages it has shared the history of Cephalonia. Cyclopean walls and other remains have been found. Sometimes called Thiaki.

Ithaca, Gr. *Ithake* or *Ithaki*, town (pop. 3,120), on E shore of Ithaca isl., Greece, on well-sheltered inlet of Gulf of Molo (Ionian Sea); trade in currants, olives, wine; fisheries. Dates from 16th cent. Also called Vathy or Vathi.

Ithaca. 1 Village (pop. 2,377), ⊙ Gratiot co., central Mich., 34 mi. WSW of Saginaw, in agr. area (livestock; poultry, beans, sugar beets; dairy products); mfg. (chemicals, flour, feed). Inc. 1869. **2** Village (pop. 140), Saunders co., E Nebr., 30 mi. W of Omaha and on branch of Platte R. **3** City (pop. 29,257), ⊙ Tompkins co., W central N.Y., in Finger Lakes region, at S end of Cayuga L., 45 mi. SSW of Syracuse; mfg. (firearms, business machines, salt, fertilizers, cement; clay and wood products; clothing, electric clocks). Agr. (dairy products; grain, poultry). Seat of Cornell Univ. and Ithaca Col. Renwick Bird Sanctuary adjoining Stewart Park, and a state tuberculosis hosp. are here. Taughannock Falls State Park is near by. Settled c.1790, inc. 1888. **4** Village (pop. 146), Darke co., W Ohio, 12 mi. SSE of Greenville, in agr. area.

Ithmaniya or **Ithmaniyah** (ĭthmănē'yŭ), oil field in Hasa, Saudi Arabia, 17 mi. SW of Hofuf; discovered 1950.

Ithome, Mount, or **Mount Ithomi** (both: ē-thō'mē) (2,617 ft.), in SW Peloponnesus, Greece, 14 mi. NW of Kalamata. Ruins of anc. MESSENE on W slopes; ruined monastery on summit.

Itigi (ētē'gē), town, Central Prov., central Tanganyika, on railroad and 25 mi. W of Manyoni; cotton, peanuts, gum arabic, beeswax, livestock.

Itikawa, Japan: see ICHIKAWA.

Itil (ē'tēl), former town in Volga delta, SE European USSR, on site of modern ASTRAKHAN. Was ⊙ Khazar state (8th–10th cent.).

Itil, river, Russian SFSR: see VOLGA RIVER.

Itimadpur (ĭtĭmäd'pŏŏr), town (pop. 5,383), Agra dist., W Uttar Pradesh, India, 12 mi. ENE of Agra; pearl millet, gram, wheat, barley. Founded 16th cent. Also spelled Itmadpur.

Itimbiri River (ētĭmbē'rē), right tributary of Congo R., N Belgian Congo. Rises as Rubi R. 3 mi. W of Niapu, flows c.165 mi. W, past Buta, to Ekwangatana, where it becomes the Itimbiri and flows c.180 mi. SW, past Aketi and Ibembo, to Congo R. 25 mi. SE of Bumba; total length c.350 mi. Navigable for 160 mi. below Aketi. It is an important freight waterway, carrying agr. produce of Uele region, notably cotton and rice.

Itinga (ētēng'gŭ), city (pop. 1,100), NE Minas Gerais, Brazil, on left bank of Jequitinhonha R. and 20 mi. NE of Araçuaí; rice, manioc.

Itinomiya, Japan: see ICHINOMIYA, Aichi prefecture.

Itinoseki, Japan: see ICHINOSEKI.

Itiquira River (ētēkē'rŭ), S central Mato Grosso, Brazil, a subtributary of São Lourenço R., rises near Alto Araguaia, flows 150 mi. W to the Pequiri, which in turn enters the São Lourenço. Diamond washings near headwaters.

Itirapina (ētērŏŏpē'nŭ), city (pop. 3,791), E central São Paulo, Brazil, 17 mi. SSE of São Carlos; rail junction; coffee, cotton, grain, cattle.

Itivdlek or **Itivdleq** (both: ĭtĭv'lĕk), fishing settlement (pop. 82), Holsteinsborg dist., SW Greenland, on islet in Davis Strait, at mouth of Itivdleq Fjord (30 mi. long), 25 mi. SSE of Holsteinsborg; 66°34'N 53°29'W.

Itkillik River (ĭtkĭ'lĭk), N Alaska, rises in N Brooks Range near 68°10'N 150°W, flows c.180 mi. N to Colville R. near its mouth at 70°3'N 151°2'W.

Itlidim (ĭtlē'dĭm), village (pop. 8,821), Asyut prov., central Upper Egypt, on W bank of the Nile, on Ibrahimiya Canal, on railroad, and 15 mi. SSE o Minya; cereals, dates, sugar cane.

Itmadpur, India: see ITIMADPUR.

Itmida or **Itmidah** (ĭtmē'dŭ), village (pop. 11,143), Daqahliya prov., Lower Egypt, 6 mi. NE of Mit Ghamr; cotton, cereals.

Ito (ētō'), town (pop. 34,643), Shizuoka prefecture, central Honshu, Japan, on E Izu Peninsula, on Sagami Sea, 16 mi. SE of Numazu, in agr. area (rice, tea, oranges, camellia oil). Health resort with numerous hot springs.

Itoda (ētō'dä), town (pop. 14,196), Fukuoka prefecture, N Kyushu, Japan, 14 mi. S of Yawata; coal mining center.

Itogon (ētō'gōn), town (1939 pop. 4,293; 1948 municipality pop. 16,970), Benguet sub-prov., Mountain Prov., N Luzon, Philippines, 6 mi. ESE of Baguio; gold mining.

Itoigawa (ētō'ēgäwŭ) or **Itoikawa** (–käwŭ), town (pop. 12,179), Niigata prefecture, central Honshu, Japan, on Toyama Bay, 22 mi. WSW of Takada, in rice-growing area; sake, soy sauce; fishing.

Itoman (ētō'mä), town (1950 pop. 14,837), on Okinawa of Okinawa Islands, in the Ryukyus, 5 mi. S of Naha; fishing port; ironworks (agr. implements).

Itonamas, Lake (ētōnä'mäs), Beni dept., NE Bolivia, 50 mi. SSE of Magdalena; 10 mi. long, c.5 mi. wide. Inlet: SAN MIGUEL RIVER. Outlet: Itonamas R. Also called L. San Luis and L. Carmen.

Itonamas River, Beni dept., NE Bolivia, rises in L. Itonamas 50 mi. SSE of Magdalena, flows c.120 mi. NNW, past Magdalena, to Guaporé R. on Brazil border, 4 mi. SE of Forte Príncipe da Beira

(Brazil). Receives Machupo R. (left). Navigable for c.70 mi. below Magdalena.

Iton River (ētō'), Eure dept., NW France, rises 6 mi. N of Mortagne, flows c.70 mi. generally NE, past Breteuil and Évreux, to the Eure above Louviers. It flows partially underground above Évreux, and feeds Paris water supply.

Itozaki, Japan: see MIHARA, city.

Ítrabo (ē'trävō), town (pop. 1,845), Granada prov., S Spain, 8 mi. WNW of Motril; olive-oil processing; raisins, almonds, wine.

Itri (ē'trē), town (pop. 6,219), Latina prov., Latium, S central Italy, 6 mi. NNW of Gaeta; cork industry. Damaged in Second World War.

Itsa (ĭt'sä) or **Etsa** (ĕt'sä), village (pop. 4,779), Faiyum prov., Upper Egypt, on railroad and 5 mi. SW of Faiyum; cotton, cereals, sugar cane, fruits.

Itsukaichi (ētsōōkĭ'chē). **1** Town (pop. 7,315), Greater Tokyo, central Honshu, Japan, 8 mi. NW of Hachioji; textiles; lumbering. **2** Town (pop. 9,600), Hiroshima prefecture, SW Honshu, Japan, on Hiroshima Bay, just W of Hiroshima; commercial center for rice-growing, stock-raising area; fishery.

Itsuku-shima (ētsōōkōō'shĭmä), sacred island (□12; pop. 5,197), Hiroshima prefecture, Japan, in Hiroshima Bay opposite Kuba, 6 mi. SW of Hiroshima; 6 mi. long, 2.5 mi. wide. Site of anc. Shinto shrine and 9th-cent. Buddhist temple. A huge camphor-wood *torii* built in 1875 lies c.530 ft. from the shore. A pagoda, 5 stories high, was built in 1407; Senjo-kaku (Hall of a Thousand Mats) was built by Hideyoshi in 16th cent. Many cherry trees. Tame deer on grounds of shrine. Also called Miya-jima; sometimes spelled Ituku-sima.

Itta Bena (ĭ"tŭ bē'nŭ), town (pop. 1,725), Leflore co., W central Miss., 9 mi. W of Greenwood, in cotton-growing area.

Ittebe, Yugoslavia: see ITEBEJ.

Ittiri (ēt'tērē), town (pop. 7,971), Sassari prov., NW Sardinia, 9 mi. S of Sassari. Has 2 medieval churches, monastery ruins. Numerous nuraghi near by.

Itu (ētōō'), city (pop. 13,729), S São Paulo, Brazil, on railroad and 45 mi. NW of São Paulo; industrial center (cotton textiles, chemicals, flour products, alcohol); metalworking, agr. processing (rice, corn, cotton, oranges). Slate quarries. Hydroelectric plant on Tietê R. (just N). Founded 1657. Has two 17th-cent. churches, an 18th-cent. convent, and a historical mus. Formerly spelled Ytú.

Itu (yē'dōō'), **1** Town (pop. 12,147), ⊙ Itu co. (pop. 250,949), SW Hupeh prov., China, 45 mi. WNW of Kiangling, and on Yangtze R. at mouth of Ching R.; medicinal herbs, rice, wheat, beans, cotton. Coal and iron deposits near by. **2** Town, Shantung prov., China: see YITU.

Itu (ē'chōō), town, Calabar prov., Eastern Provinces, SE Nigeria, on Cross R. (head of year-round navigation) and 30 mi. NW of Calabar; road center; palm oil and kernels, kola nuts. Has leper settlement.

Itu Aba Island (ē'tōō ä'bä), Chinese *Taiping* or *T'ai-p'ing* (both: tī'pĭng'), Chinese dependency in Tizard Bank, S.China Sea, c.600 mi. SE of Hainan; 10°23'N 114°21'E; ½ mi. wide, ¾ mi. long. Guano; fisheries. Has lighthouse, military post, meteorological and radio station. Occupied by France (1933–39), by Japan (1940–45); passed to China after Second World War.

Ituaçu or **Ituassú** (ētwŭsōō'), city (pop. 1,354), S central Bahia, Brazil, on railroad and 70 mi. S of Andaraí; diamonds, gold, and semiprecious stones (aquamarines, amethysts) found in area.

Ituango (ētwäng'gō), town (pop. 2,854), Antioquia dept., NW central Colombia, in Cauca valley, 55 mi. NNW of Medellín; alt. 4,921 ft.; corn, beans, coffee, cattle, hogs. Gold deposits near by.

Ituassú, Brazil: see ITUAÇU.

Ituberá (ētōōbĭrä'), city (pop. 2,065), E Bahia, Brazil, 45 mi. SSW of Nazaré; vegetable-oil processing, coffee, and lumber shipping. Until 1944, called Santarém.

Ituiutaba (ētōōyōōtä'bŭ), city (pop. 4,002), westernmost Minas Gerais, Brazil, in the Triângulo Mineiro, 70 mi. W of Uberlândia; cattle raising, sugar growing. Formerly spelled Ituyutaba.

Ituku-sima, Japan: see ITSUKU-SHIMA.

Itula (ētōō'lä), village, Kivu prov., E Belgian Congo, on Elila R. and 95 mi. SW of Costermansville; communications point; palm products.

Itumbiara (ētōōmbyä'rŭ), city (pop. 2,128), S Goiás, central Brazil, on right bank of Paranaíba R. (Minas Gerais border) and 70 mi. NW of Uberlândia; cattle raising. Extensive nitrate deposits. Until 1944 called Santa Rita or Santa Rita do Paranaíba.

Itun (yē'dōōn'), town, ⊙ Itun co. (pop. 11,622), W Sikang prov., China, on highway and 40 mi. SE of Paan, in mtn. region; wheat, beans, millet. Until 1913 called Taso.

Ituna (ĭtū'nŭ), agr. village (pop. 422), SE Sask., in the Beaver Hills, 45 mi. W of Yorkton.

Itung or **I-t'ung** (yē'tōōng'), town, ⊙ Itung co. (pop. 381,025), SW Kirin prov., Manchuria, 40 mi. S of Changchun, near Liaotung and Liaosi lines; beans, millet, corn, rice, wheat, tobacco, hemp.

Ituni, village, Berbice co., N central Br. Guiana, on small affluent of the Berbice, on railroad and 30 mi. S of Mackenzie.

Itupeva, Brazil: see JUNDIAÍ, São Paulo.

Itupiranga (ētōōpĕrăng'gŭ), city (pop. 517), E Pará, Brazil, on left bank of Tocantins R. and 5 mi. NW of Marabá. Railroad around rapids of Tocantins R. under construction here.

Iturbe (ētōōr'bā), town (dist. pop. 6,946), Guairá dept., S Paraguay, on branch of Tebicuary R., on railroad and 20 mi. S of Villarrica; agr. center (fruit, wine, sugar cane, livestock); alcohol and liquor distilling, wine making, sugar refining.

Iturbide (ētōōrbē'dā). **1** City, Guanajuato, Mexico: see ALVARO OBREGÓN. **2** Town (pop. 480), Nuevo León, N Mexico, in Sierra Madre Oriental, 23 mi. WSW of Linares; alt. 4,900 ft.; grain, livestock. **3** Town, San Luis Potosí, Mexico: see VILLA HIDALGO.

Ituri River, Belgian Congo: see ARUWIMI RIVER.

Iturralde, Bolivia: see SAN BUENAVENTURA.

Iturup Island (ētōōrōōp'), Jap. *Etorofu-to* (ătō'rō'-fōō-tō'), largest (□ 2,587) and most important of Kurile Isls., Russian SFSR, in S section of main chain; separated from Urup Isl. (N) by Friz Strait, from Kunashir Isl. (S) by Yekaterina Strait; 44°55'N 147°40'E; 126 mi. long, 28 mi. wide. Largely mountainous; rises to 5,207 ft. Hunting (bears, red foxes, rabbits) for fur; fishing, whaling, lumbering (pine forests), and sulphur mining are chief economic activities. Main centers: Kurilsk, Kuibyshevo, Kasatka (chief port; on Hitokappu Bay). First visited (1643) and named Staten Isl. by Du. navigator De Vries. Reached by Russians in 1760s; occupied (1800) by Japan.

Ituverava (ētōō"vĭrä'vŭ), city (pop. 4,836), NE São Paulo, Brazil, on railroad and 60 mi. N of Ribeirão Prêto; livestock center.

Ituyutaba, Brazil: see ITUIUTABA.

Ituzaingó (ētōōsĭng-gō'). **1** Town (pop. estimate 9,000) in Greater Buenos Aires, Argentina, 17 mi. WSW of Buenos Aires; agr. and industrial center (paper, cardboard; sawmills). Alfalfa, grain, livestock; plant nurseries. **2** Town (pop. 2,232), ⊙ Ituzaingó dept. (□ c.3,200; pop. 14,318), N Corrientes prov., Argentina, port on Paraná R. (Paraguay border) 10 mi. S of Apipé Rapids, and 50 mi. WSW of Posadas; farming center (oranges, maté, tobacco, cotton, livestock).

Ituzaingó, village, San José dept., S Uruguay, on railroad and 3 mi. NW of Santa Lucía, in agr. region (cereals, livestock). Founded 1875. Mental hosp. near by.

Itwari, India: see NAGPUR, city.

Ityai el Barud or **Ityay al-Barud** (both: ĭt'yĭl bä'-rōōd), village (pop. 6,726), Beheira prov., Lower Egypt, railway junction 17 mi. SE of Damanhur. Cotton, rice, cereals. Important freight yard. Sometimes Teh el Barud. The ruins of anc. Naucratis are 4 mi. W.

Itzalco, Salvador: see IZALCO, city.

Itzapa or **San Andrés Itzapa** (sän' ändrĕs' ētsä'pä), town (1950 pop. 3,981), Chimaltenango dept., S central Guatemala, 2.5 mi. SSW of Chimaltenango; alt. 5,971 ft.; corn, wheat, beans.

Itzehoe (ĭ'tsühō), town (pop. 34,182), in Schleswig-Holstein, NW Germany, harbor on the Stör, and 32 mi. NW of Hamburg; main town of Steinburg dist.; mfg. of cement, machinery, pumps, chemicals, textiles, nets, wallpaper; sugar refining, woodworking. Former Cistercian nunnery now houses Protestant sisterhood. Founded c.800. Chartered 1238.

Itzer (ētzâr'), village, Meknès region, central Fr. Morocco, in upper Moulouya valley, on S slope of the Middle Atlas, 22 mi. NW of Midelt; market. Oak forests.

Itzimná (ētsēmnä'), town (pop. 2,221), Yucatan, SE Mexico, 2 mi. N of Mérida; henequen.

Itz River (ĭts), Germany, rises N of Bavarian-Thuringian border, flows 40 mi. S, past Coburg, to the Main 2 mi. S of Rattelsdorf. Receives the Rodach (right).

Itztacoyotla (ētstäkoiō'tlä), town (pop. 1,012), Hidalgo, central Mexico, in Sierra Madre Oriental, 50 mi. N of Pachuca; corn, wheat, sugar cane, stock raising.

Iuaretê, Brazil: see IAUARETÊ.

Iubdo, Ethiopia: see YUBDO.

Iuka. **1** (ī'ūkŭ) Village (pop. 450), Marion co., S Ill., 19 mi. ENE of Centralia, in agr., oil, and bituminous-coal area. **2** (iū'kŭ) City (pop. 129), Pratt co., S Kansas, 6 mi. N of Pratt, in wheat area. **3** (iū'kŭ) Town (pop. 1,527), ⊙ Tishomingo co., extreme NE Miss., 22 mi. ESE of Corinth, near Woodall Mtn. and near Pickwick Landing Reservoir in Tennessee R.; mfg. of brick, tile, crossties; lumber milling. Limestone, sandstone, clay deposits; mineral spring. Inc. 1857. A Civil War battle was fought here in 1862. Fine ante-bellum houses survive.

Iulis, Greece: see KEA.

Iúna (yōō'nŭ), city (pop. 818), SW Espírito Santo, Brazil at foot of the Pico da Bandeira, 45 mi. NW of Cachoeiro de Itapemirim; coffee, bananas; sawmill. Until 1944, called Rio Pardo.

Iuripick, Caroline Isls.: see EAURIPIK.

Iva (ī'vŭ), town (pop. 1,164), Anderson co., NW S.C., 14 mi. S of Anderson, in agr. area; textile mill. Founded c.1885.

Ivahy River, Brazil: see IVAÍ RIVER.

Ivailovgrad or **Ivaylovgrad** (ēvī'lôvgrät), city (pop. 2,419), Khaskovo dist., SE Bulgaria, on E slope of Rhodope Mts., near Arda R. and Greek border, 40 mi. SE of Khaskovo; sericulture center in agr. area; exports tobacco, cotton, silk, sesame-oil, sweet potatoes, almonds. Lead and copper deposits near by (W). Until 1934, Orta-koi.

Ivaí River (ēväē'), central and NW Paraná, Brazil, rises in the Serra de Esperança E of Guarapuava, flows c.400 mi. NW to the Paraná 80 mi. above Guaíra Falls. Navigable in lower course. Formerly spelled Ivahy.

Ivalo (ī'välō), village in Inari commune (pop. 4,568), Lapi co., N Finland, on Ivalo R., Finnish *Ivalojoki* (–yō"kē) (120 mi. long), near its mouth on S shore of L. Inari, 95 mi. SW of Kirkenes; junction on Arctic Highway (Rovaniemi-Pechenga); gold mine.

Ivancice (ī'vänchĭtsĕ), Czech *Ivančice*, Ger. *Eibenschitz* (ī'bŭnshĭts), town (pop. 4,595), S Moravia, Czechoslovakia, on Jihlava R., on railroad and 12 mi. SW of Brno; agr. center, noted for vegetables (notably horse-radishes) and fruit.

Ivanec (ē'vänĕts), village (pop. 2,949), N Croatia, Yugoslavia, on railroad and 12 mi. WSW of Varazdin, at N foot of the Ivanscica; local trade center; lignite mine.

Ivanestii-Noui, Ukrainian SSR: see NOVAYA IVANOVKA.

Ivan-Franko (ēvän"-frän'kŭ), town (1931 pop. 2,597), central Lvov oblast, Ukrainian SSR, 12 mi. WNW of Lvov; sawmilling, lumbering. Fisheries along small lake (just N). Until 1941, called Yanov, Pol. *Janów*.

Ivangorod, Poland: see DEBLIN.

Ivangorod (ēvän'gŭrŭt), town (1947 pop. over 2,000), W Leningrad oblast, Russian SFSR, on Narva R. (Estonian border) opposite Narva; site of Ivangorod castle fortress (built 1492 under Ivan III). Until 1945, in Estonia as part of Narva city.

Ivangrad (ē'vängrät"), town (pop. 3,894), E Montenegro, Yugoslavia, on Lim R. and 40 mi. NE of Titograd; road junction; trade center (cattle, corn). Dates from 1862. Called Berane until 1948. Monastery of Djurdjevi Stupovi near by.

Ivanhoe, village (pop. 351), W central New South Wales, Australia, 180 mi. ESE of Broken Hill; sheep center.

Ivanhoe. **1** Village (pop. 1,172), Tulare co., central Calif., 5 mi. NE of Visalia. **2** Village (pop. 682), ⊙ Lincoln co., SW Minn., near S.Dak. line, 23 mi. W of Marshall, in grain, livestock, and poultry area; dairy products. **3** Village (1940 pop. 1,023), Wythe co., SW Va., near New R., 10 mi. SSE of Wytheville; makes industrial gases.

Ivanic Grad (ē'vänich grät'), Serbo-Croatian *Ivanić Grad*, village, N Croatia, Yugoslavia, on Lonja R., on railroad and 22 mi. ESE of Zagreb, in Slavonia; center of winegrowing region. Fortress in Turkish wars.

Ivanichi (ēvä'nyĕchē), Pol. *Iwanicze* (ēvänyē'chē), village (1939 pop. over 500), SW Volyn oblast, Ukrainian SSR, near Pol. border (Bug R.), 13 mi. S of Vladimir-Volynski; rail junction; wheat, barley, livestock.

Ivanishchi (ēvä'nyĕshchē), town (1926 pop. 1,078), S central Vladimir oblast, Russian SFSR, 25 mi. S of Vladimir; glassworks. Called Ukrepleniye Kommunizma (early 1920s–1942).

Ivanitsa (ēvä'nyētsŭ), agr. town (1926 pop. 4,685), SE Chernigov oblast, Ukrainian SSR, 16 mi. NE of Priluki; metalworks.

Ivanjica or **Ivanyitsa** (both: ē'vänyĭtsä), village (pop. 1,467), W Serbia, Yugoslavia, on Western Morava R. and 25 mi. SW of Rankovichevo town; hydroelectric plant. Antimony mine (Lisanski Rudnik) and smelter 4 mi. NE.

Ivanjska, Ivanska, or **Ivan'ska** (all: ē'vänskä), village (pop. 5,750), NW Bosnia, Yugoslavia, 11 mi. NNW of Banja Luka.

Ivanka or **Ivanka pri Dunaji** (ĭ'vän-kä prĭ' dōō"-näyĭ), Slovak *Ivánka*, Hung. *Pozsonyivánka* (pô'-zhōnyĭvängkō), village (pop. 3,073), SW Slovakia, Czechoslovakia, on railroad and 7 mi. NE of Bratislava; airport.

Ivankov (ēvän'kŭf), agr. town (1926 pop. 2,886), N Kiev oblast, Ukrainian SSR, on Teterev R. (head of navigation) and 45 mi. NW of Kiev; flax, potatoes.

Ivankovo or **Ivan'kovo** (ēvä'nyŭkŭvŭ). **1** Town (1939 pop. over 2,000), SE Kalinin oblast, Russian SFSR, 12 mi. SW of Kimry and on right bank of Volga R., at E end of Volga Reservoir and at efflux of Moscow Canal; site of dam and hydroelectric station (completed 1937); rail spur terminus (Bolshaya Volga station). **2** Village (1939 pop. under 500), NE Tula oblast, Russian SFSR, 11 mi. SW of Kashira; wheat.

Ivankovski or **Ivan'kovskiy** (ēvänkôf'skē), town (1949 pop. over 500), SW Ivanovo oblast, Russian SFSR, near Gavrilov-Posad.

Ivan Mountains (ē'vän), in Dinaric Alps, Yugoslavia, on Bosnia–Herzegovina line; highest point (5,720 ft.) is 8 mi. N of Konjic. Sarajevo-Konjic RR passes through 3,172-ft.-high Ivan Saddle, which lies 8 mi. NNE of Konjic.

Ivanopol or **Ivanopol'** (ēvŭnô'pŭl), town (1926 pop. 7,147), S Zhitomir oblast, Ukrainian SSR, 16 mi. W of Berdichev; sugar refining. Until 1946, Yanushpol.

Ivanovka (ēvä'nŭfkŭ). **1** Village (1939 pop. over 2,000), N Frunze oblast, Kirghiz SSR, in Chu valley, on railroad and 28 mi. E of Frunze; sugar beets. **2** Village (1926 pop. 2,964), SE Amur oblast, Russian SFSR, 20 mi. ENE of Blagoveshchensk, in agr. area (grain, soybeans). **3** Village (1948 pop. over 2,000), NW Chkalov oblast, Russian SFSR, 60 mi. ENE of Buzuluk; wheat, sunflowers, livestock. **4** Village (1926 pop. 2,057), SW Maritime Territory, Russian SFSR, 30 mi. ENE of Voroshilov, on road, in agr. area (grain, soybeans, sugar beets, rice). **5** Village (1926 pop. 2,457), E Kherson oblast, Ukrainian SSR, 40 mi. WSW of Melitopol; flour, dairy products; metalworks. **6** Village (1926 pop. 2,286), S Odessa oblast, Ukrainian SSR, 35 mi. NNW of Odessa; cotton, wheat. Until 1945, Yanovka. **7** Town (1926 pop. 4,590), SW Voroshilovgrad oblast, Ukrainian SSR, in the Donbas, 7 mi. N of Krasny Luch; machine mfg. Formerly also called Malaya Ivanovka.

Ivanovo (ēvä'nŭvŭ), oblast (□ 9,500; 1946 pop. estimate 1,500,000) in central European Russian SFSR; ⊙ Ivanovo. On level plain bet. Volga and Klyazma rivers; drained by Nerl, Uvod, and Teza rivers (left affluents of the Klyazma); mixed forest zone; marshes (SE). Mineral resources include peat (W of Ivanovo and in SE; peat-power station at Komsomolsk), phosphorites near Kineshma, quartz sands. Principal textile-producing region of USSR; cotton-milling centers at Ivanovo, Kokhma, Shuya, Teikovo, Rodniki, Furmanov, and Vichuga; linen milling (Privolzhsk, Puchezh); also production of chemicals (acids, alkalis, dyes), flax fibers, starch. Handicraft industries (homespun goods, embroidery, weaving shuttles, carved wooden articles). Sawmilling along Volga R. (Kineshma, Novaya Slobodka). Textile and peat-working machine mfg. (Ivanovo). Agr. supplies industrial centers with vegetables, potatoes, dairy products; chicory and tobacco (W), wheat, flax, fodder crops (E). Chiefly railroad and highway transportation. Formed 1929 out of Ivanovo-Voznesensk govt. (formed 1918) and govts. of Vladimir, Kostroma, and Yaroslavl; originally called Ivanovo Industrial Oblast.

Ivanovo. 1 Town (1937 pop. 3,070), SW Pinsk oblast, Belorussian SSR, 25 mi. W of Pinsk; flour milling, sawmilling; stone quarrying. Until 1945, Yanov, Pol. *Janów* or *Janów Poleski*. **2** City (1926 pop. 111,443; 1939 pop. 285,069), ⊙ Ivanovo oblast, Russian SFSR, on Uvod R. and 155 mi. NE of Moscow; 57°N 40°55'E. Major cotton-milling center (full production cycle); mfg. (textile and peat-working machines, print dresses), flax-processing mills, food processing. Textile, chemical, medical, agr., and teachers colleges, microbiological institute. Site of one of largest theaters of USSR. Ivanovo dates from 1328; became commercial center in 17th cent.; 1st textile mill in 1751. Combined (1871) with left-bank town of Voznesensk (dating from early 19th cent.) to form Ivanovo-Voznesensk. Scene of early strike movements (1883, 1885, 1905); temporary ⊙ (1918) of revolutionary govt. Renamed Ivanovo, 1932. Was ⊙ Ivanovo-Voznesensk govt. (1918–29).

Ivanovo-Alekseyevka (–ŭlyĭksyā'ŭfkŭ), village, N Talas oblast, Kirghiz SSR, 2 mi. from Talas; wheat, horses.

Ivanovo-Voznesensk, Russian SFSR: see IVANOVO, city, Ivanovo oblast.

Ivanovskoye. 1 Village, Leningrad oblast, Russian SFSR: see KINGISEPP. **2** Village, Moscow oblast, Russian SFSR: see SMYCHKA.

Ivanscica (ē'vänshchĭtsä), Serbo-Croatian *Ivanščica*, mountain (3,480 ft.), N Croatia, Yugoslavia, 13 mi. SW of Varazdin.

Ivanska, Yugoslavia: see IVANJSKA.

Ivanteyevka (ēvŭntyā'ŭfskē). **1** City (1939 pop. over 10,000), E central Moscow oblast, Russian SFSR, on Ucha R. and 4 mi. SE of Pushkino; woolen- and cotton-milling center; knitwear. Called Ivanteyevski after 1928, until it became city in 1938. **2** Village (1926 pop. 2,850), NE Saratov oblast, Russian SFSR, on Lesser Irgiz R., on railroad and 22 mi. NNE of Pugachev; wheat, cattle.

Ivanyitsa, Yugoslavia: see IVANJICA.

Ivashchenkovo, Russian SFSR: see CHAPAYEVSK.

Ivato, Madagascar: see TANANARIVE.

Ivatsevichi (ēvŭtsyĕ'vēchē), Pol. *Iwacewicze* (ēvätsĕvē'chĕ), town (1931 pop. 2,000), NE Brest oblast, Belorussian SSR, 8 mi. ESE of Kossovo; distilling, flour milling, sawmilling.

Ivaylovgrad, Bulgaria: see IVAILOVGRAD.

Ivdel or **Ivdel'** (ēvdyĕl'), city (1948 pop. over 10,000), N Sverdlovsk oblast, Russian SFSR, in SE foothills of the N Urals, on Ivdel R. (right tributary of Lozva R.) and 75 mi. N of Serov, on railroad; sawmilling center; mfg. of motorcycles; manganese and magnetite mining. Became city in 1943.

Ivel River (ī'vŭl), Hertford and Bedford, England, rises just N of Baldock, flows 30 mi. N, past Biggleswade, to the Ouse 3 mi. N of Sandy. Navigable below Biggleswade.

Ivenets (ēvyĭnyĕts'), Pol. *Iwieniec* (ēvyĕ'nyĕts), town (1931 pop. 2,230), NE Baranovichi oblast, Belorussian SSR, 29 mi. N of Stolbtsy, in woodland; concrete-block mfg., tanning, flour milling.

Iver (ī'vŭr), residential town and parish (pop. 4,919), SE Buckingham, England, 2 mi. SW of Uxbridge; makes cables and tile. Has Saxon church with 13th-15th-cent. additions.

Ivesdale, village (pop. 407), on Champaign-Piatt co. line, E central Ill., 15 mi. SW of Champaign, in agr. area.

Ivesti (ēvĕsht'), Rum. *Iveşti*, agr. village (pop. 2,353), Putna prov., E Rumania, on Barlad R., on railroad and 14 mi. SSE of Tecuci.

Ivey, town (pop. 46), Wilkinson co., central Ga., 11 mi. SSW of Milledgeville.

Ivi, Cape (ēvē'), headland of Oran dept., NW Algeria, on the Mediterranean, at E end of Gulf of Arzew, 14 mi. NNE of Mostaganem; 36°7'N 0°14'E; lighthouse.

Ivi Bobo, Bolivia: see IBIBOBO.

Ivigtut (ĭvĭkh'to͝ot), settlement (pop. 141), Frederikshaab dist., SW Greenland, on Arsuk Fjord (20-mi.-long inlet of the Atlantic), 70 mi. SE of Frederikshaab; 61°12'N 48°10'W; site of world's largest cryolite mine. Radio station. In Second World War site of U.S. military base.

Ivindo River (ēvēndō'), in S Fr. Cameroons and N Gabon, Fr. Equatorial Africa, rises on Cameroons-Gabon border 20 mi. ENE of Minvoul, flows c.225 mi. S and SW, past Makokou, to Ogooué R. 15 mi. E of Booué. Its middle course is navigable intermittently for c.200 mi.; rapids in lower course. Sometimes called Livindo R.

Ivinghoe, town and parish (pop. 763), E Buckingham, England, 8 mi. E of Aylesbury; agr. market.

Ivinhema River (ēvēnyā'mù), S Mato Grosso, Brazil, rises in the Serra de Amambaí in several headstreams (Dourados, Brilhante, Vacoaria rivers), flows SE to the Paraná near 22°45'S 53°40'W. Length, including the Rio Brilhante, c.220 mi. Used for barge shipments of maté from Ponta Porã region to Paraguay and Argentina. Formerly spelled Ivinheima.

Ivins (ī'vĭnz), town (pop. 95), Washington co., SW Utah, near Shebit Indian Reservation, 5 mi. NW of St. George.

Iviza, Sp. *Ibiza* (both: ēvē'thä), anc. *Ebusus*, smallest island (including adjacent islets: □ 221; pop. 33,961) of the 3 principal Balearic Isls., in the W Mediterranean, 55 mi. SW of Majorca, 90 mi. ESE of Valencia; chief town and port, Iviza. Roughly 25 mi. long NE–SW, 12 mi. wide. Surrounded by tiny islets. Low ridge rises in the Atalayasa to 1,558 ft. Towards S shore are extensive saltworks, representing, together with fisheries, principal source of income. Has a generally dry and hot climate. Undulated surface is well wooded. There are also lead deposits. Chief crops include cereals, figs, almonds, carobs, grapes, olives, potatoes. Hog raising. Has some minor processing industries. Among leading towns, apart from Iviza, are the small port San Antonio Abad and Santa Eulalia del Río. Picturesque isl. attracts tourists and artists. Arouses great interest for its Roman and Phoenician remains (necropolises). Occupied early during Sp. civil war (1936–39) by Nationalists, it was, together with adjacent Formentera, temporarily held by the Loyalists. Iviza and Formentera were anciently called *Pityusae*, derived from Greek word for pine trees.

Iviza, Sp. *Ibiza*, chief city (pop. 9,644) of Iviza isl., Balearic Isls., port on SE coast, 80 mi. SW of Palma (Majorca), 105 mi. ESE of Valencia; 38°55'N 1°25'E. Ships chiefly salt, wool, fruit. Region produces carobs, almonds, figs, grapes, potatoes; hogs. Liquor distilling, wine making (vermouth), sawmilling, printing, fish curing; mfg. of cloth, lace, soap, ice. Lobster fisheries. The picturesque city is a favorite tourist site. Whitewashed houses are grouped around old castle which once protected city against pirate attacks. Has fine collegiate church (former cathedral) and renowned archaeological mus., best of its kind in Spain for Phoenician and Carthaginian remains. In vicinity are several remarkable Phoenician necropolises.

Ivnya (ēv'nyŭ), village (1926 pop. 1,959), SW Kursk oblast, Russian SFSR, 12 mi. SW of Oboyan; sugar refinery.

Ivohibe (ēvōōhē'bā), village, Fianarantsoa prov., SE central Madagascar, 70 mi. SSE of Fianarantsoa; trading outpost; rice, manioc, cattle. R.C. and Protestant missions; hosp. for natives.

Ivo Lake, Swedish *Ivösjön* (ē'vû-shûn") (16 mi. long, 7–10 mi. wide), S Sweden, extends NW from Bromolla. Drains SE into the Baltic. Contains Ivo, Swedish *Ivön*, island (□ 4.9; pop. 330).

Ivolginsk (ē'vŭlgĕnsk), village (1939 pop. over 500), SE Buryat-Mongol Autonomous SSR, Russian SFSR, 20 mi. SW of Ulan-Ude; truck produce, wheat, livestock.

Ivoloina (ēvōōlōōē'nŭ), village, Tamatave prov., E Madagascar, near coast, on the Canal des Pangalanes, and NNW of Tamatave; site of oldest (1898) agr. station in Madagascar, specializing in tropical cultures (coffee, cacao, sugar cane, clove, vanilla, essential oils, rice; papayas, bananas). Experimental distilleries.

Ivondro River (ēvōōn'drōō), E Madagascar, rises 50 mi. NNE of Moramanga, flows 100 mi. in a wide curve NE and E, cutting through Canal des Pangalanes to the Indian Ocean 5 mi. S of Tamatave. Used for water power.

Ivor (ī'vŭr), town (pop. 377), Southampton co., SE Va., near Blackwater R., 34 mi. SE of Petersburg; makes staves.

Ivory Coast, Fr. *Côte d'Ivoire* (kōt'dēvwär'), French overseas territory (□ c.127,800; pop. c.2,031,000), S Fr. West Africa, on Gulf of Guinea of the Atlantic; ⊙ Abidjan. Borders N on Upper Volta and Fr. Sudan, NW on Fr. Guinea, W on Liberia (Cavally R.), E on Gold Coast. Fringed by a string of coastal lagoons. Rises gently from low alluvial belt to well-wooded interior tableland. Several large rivers (impeded by rapids) flow N–S, such as Sassandra, Bandama, and Camoé rivers. Has a typically equatorial climate with heavy rainfall. There are 2 rainy and 2 dry seasons. The very fertile soil yields, principally, cacao; this is surpassed in export volume, however, by hardwood (mahogany) from interior rain forests. Other important products are dried and fresh bananas, palm kernels, palm oil, shea-nut butter, peanuts, pineapples, coffee, cotton, rubber, kola nuts, sesame, sisal, kapok, vanilla, orange essences. Subsistence crops: millet, corn, rice, manioc, yams. Some stock raising (goats, sheep, cattle). Coastal fishing for native consumption. A few minor industries: lumbering, extraction of vegetable oils, fiber ginning. Gold placers are worked along rivers and in Bouaké dist. Big game abounds. Most of the trade passes through Abidjan, served by auxiliary ports of Grand-Bassam and Port-Bouet. The latter is the terminus of railroad to interior, now extended beyond Bobo-Dioulasso, Upper Volta. Intercolonial routes join the region with other territories in Fr. West Africa. Fr. occupation of the coast was accomplished by 1884. In 1889 Captain Binger reached the Niger from here. The French set up (1891) protectorate which soon became a colony and was incorporated into Fr. West Africa in 1904. Grand-Bassam was ⊙ until 1900, followed by Bingerville, which was replaced (1935) by Abidjan. The Ivory Coast now is represented by 2 deputies in Fr. National Assembly.

Ivory Coast, the coastal region of W Africa along the Gulf of Guinea bet. the Gold Coast and the Grain Coast (Liberia); 3°–7°30'W. Back of it is the French territory to which it gave its name.

Ivoryton, Conn.: see ESSEX.

Ivot (ē'vŭt), town (1926 pop. 3,696), NE Bryansk oblast, Russian SFSR, 7 mi. NW of Dyatkovo; glassworks.

Ivrea (ēvrā'ä), anc. *Eporedia*, town (pop. 8,737), Torino prov., Piedmont, NW Italy, on Dora Baltea R. and 29 mi. NNE of Turin; mfg. center; cotton and rayon textiles, typewriters, adding machines, macaroni. Bishopric. Has cathedral (969–1002; frequently rebuilt), seminary (1715–63), and picturesque castle of Conte Verde (1358; now a prison). Originally a Salassi town; captured by Romans in 100 B.C. In Middle Ages became seat of marquisate, whose lord, Berengar II, crowned himself king of Italy in 950. Passed to house of Savoy in 14th cent.

Ivrindi (ĭvrĭndĭ'), Turkish *İvrindi*, village (pop. 1,932), Balikesir prov., NW Turkey, 22 mi. WSW of Balikesir; cereals.

Ivry-la-Bataille (ēvrē'-lä-bätī'), village (pop. 1,279), Eure dept., NW France, on left bank of Eure R. and 17 mi. SE of Évreux; mfg. of wooden musical instruments and of plastics (especially combs). Here Henry IV won a stirring victory (1590) over Catholic League.

Ivry-sur-Seine (–sür-sĕn'), city (pop. 40,377), Seine dept., N central France, just SSE of Paris, 3 mi. from Notre Dame Cathedral, port on left bank of Seine R. below influx of the Marne; forges, foundries; mfg. (refractory products, chemicals, varnish, Portland cement, electric bulbs, ball-bearings, cider, chocolate). Insane asylum.

Ivy or **Ivy Depot,** village, Albemarle co., central Va., 7 mi. W of Charlottesville. Meriwether Lewis b. here, 1774.

Ivybridge, former urban district (1931 pop. 1,609), S Devon, England, 10 mi. E of Plymouth; agr. market; paper mfg. Has old bridge.

Ivye or **Iv'ye** (ē'vyĭ), Pol. *Iwje* (ē'vyĕ), town (1931 pop. 2,730), SW Molodechno oblast, Belorussian SSR, 19 mi. ENE of Lida; rail spur terminus; tanning, flour milling, alcohol distilling, mfg. of sweets.

Ivyland, borough (pop. 358), Bucks co., SE Pa., 16 mi. NNE of Philadelphia.

Ivywild, village (pop. 2,849), El Paso co., E central Colo., just W of Colorado Springs.

Iwabune (ēwä'bōōnä) or **Iwafune** (ēwä'fōōnä), town (pop. 5,289), Niigata prefecture, central Honshu, Japan, on Sea of Japan, 3 mi. SW of Murakami; fishing port.

Iwacewicze, Belorussian SSR: see IVATSEVICHI.

Iwade (ēwä'dā), town (pop. 4,574), Wakayama prefecture, S Honshu, Japan, on W Kii Peninsula, 9 mi. E of Wakayama, in rice-growing area; cotton textiles, raw silk. Agr. school.

Iwadeyama (ēwädä'yämŏŏ), town (pop. 9,075), Miyagi prefecture, N Honshu, Japan, 7 mi. N of Furukawa; rice, raw silk, bamboo ware.

Iwafune, Japan: see IWABUNE.

Iwagasaki (ēwägä'sä'kē), town (pop. 5,351), Miyagi prefecture, N Honshu, Japan, 9 mi. NW of Wakayanagi; horse breeding, rice, raw silk.

Iwagawa, Japan: see IWAKAWA.

Iwai (ēwī'). **1** Town (pop. 6,475), Ibaraki prefecture, central Honshu, Japan, 15 mi. SE of Koga, on small lake; agr. (rice, tobacco), lumbering. **2** Town (pop. 2,469), Tottori prefecture, S Honshu, Japan, 8 mi. ENE of Tottori; hot-springs resort; rice, raw silk.

Iwai-shima, Japan: see NAGA-SHIMA, Yamaguchi prefecture.

Iwaizumi (ēwī'zōōmē), town (pop. 6,115), Iwate prefecture, N Honshu, Japan, 16 mi. NW of Miyako; lumbering, poultry raising; sandstone quarrying.

Iwakawa (ēwä'käwŏŏ) or **Iwagawa** (ēwä'gäwŏŏ), town (pop. 11,062), Kagoshima prefecture, S Kyushu, Japan, on N Osumi Peninsula, 26 mi. E of Kagoshima; rice-producing center.

Iwaki (ēwä'kē), former province in N Honshu, Japan; now part of Miyagi and Fukushima prefectures.

Iwakuni (ēwä'kōōnē), city (1940 pop. 51,045; 1947 pop. 57,661), Yamaguchi prefecture, SW Honshu, Japan, on Nishiki R. and 22 mi. SW of Hiroshima, across Hiroshima Bay. Rail junction; mfg. center (textiles, flour, soy sauce). Site of feudal castle. Known for Kintai Bridge (1673) with series of 5 arches totaling length of 750 ft. Includes (since 1940) former town of Marifu just E of city.

Iwakura (ēwä'kōōrä), town (pop. 13,327), Aichi prefecture, central Honshu, Japan, 9 mi. NNW of Nagoya; agr. center (rice, wheat), poultry; raw silk; textiles.

Iwama (ēwä'mä), town (pop. 10,052), Ibaraki prefecture, central Honshu, Japan, 7 mi. N of Ishioka; rice, silk cocoons.

Iwamatsu (ēwä'mätsōō), town (pop. 5,478), Ehime prefecture, W Shikoku, Japan, 7 mi. SSW of Uwajima; rice, wheat, raw silk.

Iwami (ēwä'mē), former province in SW Honshu, Japan; now part of Shimane prefecture.

Iwami, town, Japan: see MASUDA, Shimane prefecture.

Iwami-gotsu, Japan: see GOTSU.

Iwamizawa (ēwämē'zäwŏŏ), city (1940 pop. 33,519; 1947 pop. 42,978), W central Hokkaido, Japan, 24 mi. ENE of Sapporo; agr. center (rice, wheat, hemp); mfg. (gunpowder, soy sauce). Has agr. school.

Iwamura (ēwä'mōōrä), town (pop. 5,134), Gifu prefecture, central Honshu, Japan, 18 mi. E of Tajimi; rice, lumber.

Iwamurata (ēwämōō'rätŏŏ) or **Iwamurada** (–dŏŏ), town (pop. 10,240), Nagano prefecture, central Honshu, Japan, 15 mi. ESE of Ueda; rice, wheat, raw silk.

Iwanai (ēwänī'), town (pop. 21,281), SW Hokkaido, Japan, port on Sea of Japan, 29 mi. WSW of Otaru; fishing center; vegetable canning. Exports coal, cod-liver oil.

Iwanicze, Ukrainian SSR: see IVANICHI.

Iwanuma (ēwä'nōōmä), town (pop. 10,971), Miyagi prefecture, N Honshu, Japan, on Abukuma R. and 10 mi. S of Sendai; commercial center for agr., horse-breeding area.

Iwasaki (ēwä'sä'kē), town (pop. 2,871), Akita prefecture, N Honshu, Japan, 3 mi. NNE of Yuzawa; rice growing.

Iwase (ēwä'sä), town (pop. 11,336), Ibaraki prefecture, central Honshu, Japan, 20 mi. W of Mito, in agr. area; clay-slate quarrying.

Iwashiro (ēwä'shīrō), former province in N Honshu, Japan; now part of Fukushima prefecture.

Iwata (ēwä'tä), town (pop. 34,185), Shizuoka prefecture, central Honshu, Japan, 7 mi. E of Hamamatsu, in forested area; paper milling, stock raising. Formed in early 1940s by combining former towns of Nakaizumi (1940 pop. 13,302) and Mitsuke (1940 pop. 10,268).

Iwataki (ēwä'täkē), town (pop. 5,872), Kyoto prefecture, S Honshu, Japan, on inlet of Wakasa Bay, 3 mi. NW of Miyazu, in rice-growing area; silk textiles, raw silk.

Iwate (ēwä'tā), prefecture (Jap. *ken*) (□ 5,882; 1940 pop. 1,095,793; 1947 pop. 1,262,743), N Honshu, Japan; ⊙ MORIOKA. Bounded E by the Pacific; mountainous terrain, drained by Kitakami R. Chief port, KAMAISHI. Major stock-raising area. Extensive lumbering, fishing, raw-silk culture, agr. (soybeans, rice, potatoes, tobacco). Iron, gold, silver, and copper mines. Mfg. (silk textiles, lacquer ware, chemicals), sake brewing. Principal centers: Morioka, Kamaishi, MIYAKO.

Iwatsu (ēwä'tsōō) or **Iwazu** (–zōō), town (pop. 12,465), Aichi prefecture, central Honshu, Japan, 19 mi. SE of Nagoya; agr. center (rice, wheat); raw silk.

Iwatsuki (ēwä'tsōōkē), town (pop. 12,610), Saitama prefecture, central Honshu, Japan, 5 mi. NE of Omiya; mfg. (dolls, textiles).

Iwaya (ēwä'yä), town (pop. 9,677), on Awaji-shima, Hyogo prefecture, Japan, 10 mi. SW of Kobe across Osaka Bay; fishing center; rice, wheat, fruit, market produce, flowers; pottery making.

Iwayado (ēwä″yädō'), town (pop. 9,345), Iwate prefecture, N Honshu, Japan, 4 mi. NNE of Mizusawa; rice, silk cocoons. Has sericulture school.

Iwazu, Japan: see IWATSU.

Iwieniec, Belorussian SSR: see IVENETS.

Iwje, Belorussian SSR: see IVYE.

Iwo (ē'wō), town (pop. 57,191), Oyo prov., Western Provinces, SW Nigeria, near railroad (Iwo station is 5 mi. S), 25 mi. NE of Ibadan; road center; indigo dyeing, cotton weaving; cacao, palm oil and kernels.

Iwo Jima (ē'wō jē'mŏŏ, Jap. ēwō' jĭmä), volcanic island (□ c.8), most important and largest of Volcano Isls., W Pacific, c.145 naut. mi. S of Chichi-jima, Bonin Isls.; 24°47′N 141°20′E. Extinct volcano, Mt. Suribachi (sŏŏr″ēbä'chē, Jap. sōōrē'-bä'chē) in S, rises to 546 ft. Formerly (under the Japanese) it had important sulphur mines. In Second World War, the heavily fortified isl. was site of Jap. air base. The U.S. marines' flag-raising (Feb., 1945) on Mt. Suribachi was high point in battle to secure S part of isl. The costly battle of Iwo Jima ended March, 1945, and isl. was occupied by U.S.; radio beacon was placed on Kangaku, an offshore islet. Also Io-jima; formerly Sulphur Isl.

Iwu (yē'wōō'). **1** Town (pop. 12,716), ⊙ Iwu co. (pop. 328,173), central Chekiang prov., China, 28 mi. NE of Kinhwa and on railroad; rice, ham, tung oil. Manganese, silver, coal mining near by. **2** Town (pop. 3,280), easternmost Sinkiang prov., China, 50 mi. NE of Hami; cattle; gold and copper mines.

Iwuy (ēvwē'), town (pop. 3,229), Nord dept., N France, on the Escaut and 6 mi. NE of Cambrai; mfg. (furniture, handkerchiefs, sugar).

Ixcamilpa (ēskämēl'pä), town (pop. 980), Puebla, central Mexico, 40 mi. SSW of Matamoros; corn, sugar cane, stock.

Ixcapuzalco (–pōōsäl'kō), town (pop. 572), Guerrero, SW Mexico, on S slope of central plateau, 21 mi. WSW of Taxco; cereals, sugar cane, fruit.

Ixcaquixtla (–kē'slä), officially San Juan Ixcaquixtla, town (pop. 2,716), Puebla, central Mexico, on central plateau, 50 mi. SE of Puebla; corn, sugar cane, fruit, livestock. Pre-Columbian ruins near by.

Ixcateopan (–täōpän'), town (pop. 1,324), Guerrero, SW Mexico, on S slope of central plateau, 17 mi. WSW of Taxco; cereals, sugar cane, fruit, timber.

Ixcatepec (–täpĕk'), town (pop. 856), Veracruz, E Mexico, in Sierra Madre Oriental foothills, 40 mi. NW of Tuxpan; cereals, sugar cane, coffee, fruit.

Ixchiguán (ēks-chēgwän'), town (1950 pop. 657), San Marcos dept., SW Guatemala, in the Sierra Madre, 16 mi. NNW of San Marcos; alt. 10,325 ft. Corn, wheat, fodder grasses; livestock.

Ixelles (ēksĕl'), Flemish *Elsene* (ĕl'sŭnŭ), SE suburb (pop. 92,211) of Brussels, Brabant prov., central Belgium; mfg. (metals, chemicals, textiles, wood products, foodstuffs), printing. Has 17th- and 18th-cent. bldgs. of former Cistercian monastery, now housing military cartographic inst. and higher inst. of decorative arts.

Ixhuacán (ēswäkän'), officially Ixhuacán de los Reyes, town (pop. 1,270), Veracruz, E Mexico, in Sierra Madre Oriental, 17 mi. SW of Jalapa; corn, fruit.

Ixhuatán or **Santa María Ixhuatán** (sän'tä märē'ä ēkswätän'), town (pop. 2,285), Santa Rosa dept., S Guatemala, in Pacific piedmont, 6 mi. SE of Cuilapa; alt. 4,035 ft.; coffee, sugar cane; livestock.

Ixhuatlán (ēswätlän'). **1** or **Ixhuatlán-Córdoba** (–kôr'dōbä), town (pop. 1,770), Veracruz, E Mexico, in Sierra Madre Oriental, 12 mi. N of Córdoba; coffee, corn, fruit. **2** or **Ixhuatlán de Madero** (dā mädä'rō), town (pop. 1,025), Veracruz, E Mexico, in Sierra Madre Oriental foothills, 40 mi. SE of Tuxpan; corn, sugar cane, fruit. **3** Town, Veracruz, Mexico, near Minatitlán: see CHAPOPOTLA.

Ixhuatlancillo (ēswätlänsē'yō), town (pop. 2,900), Veracruz, E Mexico, in Sierra Madre Oriental, 4 mi. NW of Orizaba; coffee, sugar cane, tobacco, fruit.

Ixiamas (ēsēä'mäs), town (pop. c.2,100), La Paz dept., NW Bolivia, 60 mi. NNW of San Buenaventura; cacao, sugar cane, tobacco.

Ixil (ē-shēl'), town (pop. 790), Yucatan, SE Mexico, 16 mi. NE of Mérida; henequen.

Iximché, Guatemala: see TECPÁN.

Ixitlán (ēhētlän'), officially San Miguel Ixitlán, town (pop. 736), Puebla, central Mexico, 24 mi. SE of Acatlán; corn, sugar cane, stock.

Ixmatlahuacán (ēsmätläwäkän'), town (pop. 557), Veracruz, SE Mexico, in Sotavento lowlands, 6 mi. NNW of Cosamaloapan; sugar cane, bananas.

Ixmiquilpan (ēsmēkēl'pän), city (pop. 1,543), Hidalgo, central Mexico, on Tula R., on Inter-American Highway and 40 mi. NW of Pachuca; alt. 5,734 ft. Cereals, maguey, livestock; native textiles. Anc. Indian capital.

Ixopo (ēksō'pō), town (pop. 1,503), S Natal, U. of So. Afr., on small Ixopo R. and 40 mi. SW of Pietermaritzburg; rail junction; stock, fruit.

Ixtacalco (ēstäkäl'kō), town (pop. 5,245), Federal Dist., central Mexico, on railroad and 3 mi. SSE of Mexico city; mfg. and agr. (cereals, livestock); chemical plants, tanneries. Connected by canal with "floating gardens" of Xochimilco.

Ixtacamaxtitlán (ēstäkämästētlän'), town (pop. 563), Puebla, central Mexico, 27 mi. SSE of Zacatlán; corn, maguey. Silver, gold, copper deposits near.

Ixtacihuatl, Ixtaccihuatl, or **Iztaccihuatl** (all: ēs″-täsē'wätŏŏl) [Aztec,=white woman], dormant volcano (17,342 ft.), central Mexico, on Puebla-Mexico state border, N of the Popocatepetl, 35 mi. SE of Mexico city; 19°11′N 98°38′W. A twin volcano of irregular shape, and snow-capped, it is also popularly known as the Sleeping Woman. Last eruption, 1868.

Ixtacomitán (ēstäkōmētän'), town (pop. 1,031), Chiapas, S Mexico, 45 mi. N of Tuxtla; rice, fruit.

Ixtacuixtla or **San Felipe Ixtacuixtla** (sän fālē'pä ēstäkwē'slä), town (pop. 1,530), Tlaxcala, central Mexico, 9 mi. W of Tlaxcala; maguey-growing center. Thermal springs near by.

Ixtaczoquitlán (ēstäksōkētlän'), town (pop. 871), Veracruz, E Mexico, in Sierra Madre Oriental, on railroad and 3 mi. NE of Orizaba; coffee, sugar cane, fruit.

Ixtahuacán. 1 or **San Ildefonso Ixtahuacán** (sän' ēldäfōn'sō ēkstäwäkän'), town (pop. 1,082), Huehuetenango dept., W Guatemala, near Cuilco R., 21 mi. WNW of Huehuetenango; alt. 5,600 ft.; coffee, sugar cane, fruit, vegetables. **2** Town, Sololá dept., Guatemala: see SANTA CATARINA.

Ixtapa (ēstä'pä). **1** Town (pop. 822), Chiapas, S Mexico, in N spur of Sierra Madre, 13 mi. E of Tuxtla; alt. 3,664 ft.; cereals, fruit, livestock. **2** Officially San José Ixtapa, town (pop. 1,506), Puebla, central Mexico, 19 mi. S of Serdán; grain, vegetables.

Ixtapalapa (ēstäpälä'pä), town (pop. 9,238), Federal Dist., central Mexico, 6 mi. SE of Mexico city; agr. suburb (cereals, fruit, livestock). Situated at foot of Cerro de la Estrella (8,071 ft.), on top of which Aztecs lit fires at beginning of 52-year cycles.

Ixtapaluca (ēstäpälōō'kä), town (pop. 1,660), Mexico state, central Mexico, 19 mi. SE of Mexico city; cereals, maguey, stock.

Ixtapan (ēstäpän'), town (pop. 1,716), Mexico state, central Mexico, 45 mi. SW of Toluca; sugar cane, coffee, fruit.

Ixtapan de la Sal (dā lä säl'), town (pop. 1,541), Mexico state, central Mexico, 32 mi. S of Toluca; sugar cane, coffee, cereals, fruit. Thermal springs.

Ixtapan del Oro (dĕl ō'rō), town (pop. 785), Mexico state, central Mexico, 40 mi. W of Toluca; grain, fruit, stock.

Ixtapangajoya (ēstäpäng-gähoi'ä), town (pop. 121), Chiapas, S Mexico, in Gulf lowland, 37 mi. S of Villahermosa; fruit.

Ixtapa Point (ēstäpä), cape on Pacific coast of Guerrero, SW Mexico, 23 mi. SW of La Unión; 17°38′N 101°40′W.

Ixtenco (ēstĕng'kō), officially San Juan Ixtenco, town (pop. 4,356), Tlaxcala, central Mexico, at E foot of Malinche volcano, 25 mi. NE of Puebla; agr. center (corn, wheat, barley, alfalfa, beans, stock).

Ixtepec (ēstä'pĕk). **1** Officially Ciudad Ixtepec, city (pop. 7,069), Oaxaca, S Mexico, in Pacific lowland of Isthmus of Tehuantepec, 18 mi. NE of Tehuantepec. Rail terminus; lumbering, processing, and agr. center (rice, sugar cane, coffee, tobacco, fruit, vegetables); sawmilling, coffee processing, sugar refining. An airfield was maintained here by U.S. forces during Second World War. Formerly sometimes San Jerónimo Ixtepec. **2** Town (pop. 2,013), Puebla, central Mexico, in E foothills of Sierra Madre Oriental, 25 mi. SE of Huauchinango; sugar cane, coffee, tobacco, fruit.

Ixtlahuaca (ēsläwä'kä), officially Ixtlahuaca de Rayón, town (pop. 1,094), Mexico state, central Mexico, on Lerma R. and 40 mi. WNW of Mexico city; cereals, fruit, stock. Silver deposits near by.

Ixtlahuacán (ēsläwäkän'), town (pop. 1,127), Colima, W Mexico, on coastal plain, 16 mi. S of Colima; rice, corn, sugar cane, coffee, tobacco, fruit.

Ixtlahuacán de los Membrillos (dā lōs mämbrē'yōs), town (pop. 1,881), Jalisco, central Mexico, near L. Chapala, on railroad and 25 mi. SSE of Guadalajara; wheat-growing center.

Ixtlahuacán del Río (dĕl rē'ō), town (pop. 1,599), Jalisco, central Mexico, on affluent of Santiago R. and 14 mi. NE of Guadalajara; grain, sugar cane, fruit, stock.

Ixtlán (ēslän'). **1** Town (pop. 4,017), Michoacán, central Mexico, on central plateau, 26 mi. SW of La Piedad; agr. center (cereals, fruit, vegetables, livestock). Geysers and springs with radioactive properties are near by. **2** or **Ixtlán de Juárez** (dā whä'rĕs), town (pop. 1,075), Oaxaca, S Mexico, surrounded by spurs of Sierra Madre del Sur, 25 mi. NE of Oaxaca; alt. 6,187 ft.; silver, gold, lead, copper, zinc mining. **3** or **Ixtlán del Río** (dĕl rē'ō), town (pop. 4,720), Nayarit, W Mexico, amid W outliers of Sierra Madre Occidental, on railroad and 50 mi. SE of Tepic; mining (silver, gold, lead) and agr. center (corn, beans, sugar cane, bananas); sugar refineries, tanneries.

Iya (ē'yä), town (pop. 3,648), Shimane prefecture, SW Honshu, Japan, on SW shore of lagoon Nakano-no-umi, 5 mi. SE of Matsue; rice, sake; fishing.

Iyang (yē'yäng'). **1** Town, ⊙ Iyang co. (pop. 114,700), NW Honan prov., China, in Sung Mts., 40 mi. SSW of Loyang; rice, wheat, beans. Tin mines near by. **2** Town, Honan prov., China: see YIYANG. **3** Town, Hunan prov., China: see YI-YANG. **4** Town (pop. 9,285), ⊙ Iyang co. (pop. 95,516), NE Kiangsi prov., China, 35 mi. WSW of Shangjao and on Kwangsin R., on railroad; coal mining.

Iya River (ēyä'), SW Irkutsk oblast, Russian SFSR, rises in Eastern Sayan Mts., flows 370 mi. NE, past Tulun, to Oka R. (tributary of Angara R.) 35 mi. SSE of Bratsk.

Iyo (ē'yō), former province in W Shikoku, Japan; now Ehime prefecture.

Iyo-nada, Japan: see IYO SEA.

Iyo-nagahama, Japan: see NAGAHAMA, Ehime prefecture.

Iyo-ozu, Japan: see OZU, Ehime prefecture.

Iyo-saijo, Japan: see SAIJO, Ehime prefecture.

Iyo-sakurai, Japan: see SAKURAI, Ehime prefecture.

Iyo Sea (ē'yō), Jap. *Iyo-nada,* SW section of Inland Sea, Japan, bet. SW coast of Honshu and NW coast of Shikoku; merges with Hoyo Strait (S), Suo Sea (W), and Hiuchi Sea (E). Its largest inlet is Hiroshima Bay. Contains numerous isls.; O-shima (in Yamaguchi prefecture) is largest.

Izabal (ēsäbäl'), department (□ 3,489; 1950 pop. 55,635), E Guatemala; ⊙ (since 1920) Puerto Barrios. On Gulf of Honduras of Caribbean Sea (forming Bay of Amatique). Includes L. Izabal and its outlet, Río Dulce, separated from lower Motagua R. valley by the Sierra del Mico. Hot, humid climate. Agr.: bananas (centered at Bananera), abacá, corn, beans, coconuts. Lumbering in tropical forests. Railroad serves Motagua R. valley. Main centers: Puerto Barrios (chief port and rail terminus), Lívingston (port and ⊙ until 1920).

Izabal, village (pop. 87), Izabal dept., E Guatemala, port on S shore of L. Izabal, 40 mi. WSW of Puerto Barrios; grain, bananas, coconuts. Once a thriving port on water route bet. sea and highlands; declined after building of Guatemala–Puerto Barrios RR. Subjected to pirate raids in 17th cent.

Izabal, Lake, largest in Guatemala, in Izabal dept., 20 mi. SW of Bay of Amatique (inlet of Caribbean Sea), into which it drains via Río DULCE; 30 mi. long, 15 mi. wide, 69 ft. deep; alt. 26 ft. Receives Polochic R. (W). In Sp. colonial times, scene of active trading bet. highlands and sea. Formerly called Golfo Dulce.

Izaku (ēzä'kōō) or **Isaku** (ēsä'-), town (pop. 19,955), Kagoshima prefecture, SW Kyushu, Japan, on W Satsuma Peninsula, 13 mi. WSW of Kagoshima; agr. center (rice, wheat); silk, tiles.

Izalco (ēsäl'kō), city (pop. 8,319), Sonsonate dept., W Salvador, at SW foot of volcano Izalco, 5 mi. NE of Sonsonate; pottery and basket making; grain, fruit, sugar cane, livestock. Limestone quarries. City formed 1869 out of adjacent ladino town of Dolores and Indian settlement of Asunción. Sometimes spelled Itzalco.

Izalco, active volcano (6,184 ft.) in Sonsonate dept., W Salvador, 9 mi. NE of Sonsonate. Izalco city at SW foot. Of recent formation, it 1st appeared in 1770. Known as "Lighthouse of the Pacific" because of its continuous activity.

Izamal (ēsämäl'), town (pop. 5,305), Yucatan, SE Mexico, 39 mi. E of Mérida; rail terminus; agr. center (henequen, sugar cane, corn). Site of anc. Maya town (believed to be older than Chichén Itzá), an aboriginal Mecca. Many religious remains, pyramids, mausoleum, etc. The present-day monastery and cathedral were erected 1553 on site of Maya temples.

Izard (ĭ'zûrd), county (□ 574; pop. 9,953), N Ark.; ⊙ Melbourne. Bounded SW by White R.; drained by Strawberry R. Agr. (livestock, poultry, cotton, grain, hay; dairy products); lumber milling, cotton ginning; glass sand, gravel pits. Formed 1825.

Izatnagar, India: see BAREILLY, city.

Izberbash (ēzbyĭrbäsh'), city (1949 pop. over 2,000), E Dagestan Autonomous SSR, Russian SFSR, on Caspian coastal railroad and 36 mi. SSE of Makhachkala; petroleum center; metalworks. Developed mainly after Second World War.

Izberdei, Russian SFSR: see PETROVKA, Tambov oblast.

Izdeshkovo (ēzdyĕsh'kŭvŭ), town (1948 pop. over 2,000), central Smolensk oblast, Russian SFSR, 25 mi. W of Vyazma; limestone works; peat working, flax retting.

Izeaux (ēzō'), village (pop. 1,289), Isère dept., SE France, 18 mi. NW of Grenoble; shoe mfg.

Izeda (ēzä'dŭ), village (pop. 1,216), Bragança dist., N Portugal, 17 mi. S of Bragança; wheat, rye, almonds.

Izegem (ĭ'zŭ-khŭm), town (pop. 16,787), West Flanders prov., W central Belgium, 5 mi. ESE of Roulers; cotton-milling center. Formerly spelled Iseghem.

Izeh (ēzĕ'), town (pop. 2,010), Sixth Prov., SW Iran, 80 mi. NE of Ahwaz, on mtn. plain near upper Karun R.; center of Bakhtiari region; sheep raising; rugmaking. Situated on site of Sassanian city of Izeh (ruins, inscriptions), it was later known as Malamir before regaining the anc. name.

Izel (ēzĕl'), village (pop. 1,642), Luxembourg prov., SE Belgium, on Semois R. and 21 mi. W of Arlon, in the Ardennes; lumbering, agr.

Izena-shima, Ryukyu Isls.: see IHEYA-SHOTO.

Izera, peak, Czechoslovakia: see JIZERA.

Izernore (ēzĕrnôr'), village (pop. 277), Ain dept., E France, in the Jura, 5 mi. NW of Nantua; woodworking. Roman ruins.

Izerskie, Góry, Poland and Czechoslovakia: see ISERGEBIRGE.

Izhevsk (ē'zhĭfsk), city (1939 pop. 175,740), ⊙ Udmurt Autonomous SSR, Russian SFSR, on Izh R. (here forming small lake) and 600 mi. ENE of Moscow; 56°51'N 53°13'E. Rail junction; metallurgical center; mfg. (lathes, agr. machinery, motorcycles, musical instruments, shotguns, building materials), woodworking, sawmilling, brewing. Medical and teachers colleges. Has regional mus., old cathedral, and several monuments. Founded 1760; assaulted by peasant rebels under Yemelyan Pugachev in 1774. Developed in early 1800s as shotgun mfg. center; became city in 1917. Formerly Izhevski Zavod.

Izhevskoye (–skŭyŭ), village (1926 pop. 6,540), central Ryazan oblast, Russian SFSR, in Oka R. valley, 40 mi. E of Ryazan; truck produce, wheat.

Izh Island, Yugoslavia: see IZ ISLAND.

Izhma (ēzh'mŭ). **1** Town (1948 pop. over 500), central Komi Autonomous SSR, Russian SFSR, on upper Izhma R. (head of navigation), on N.Pechora RR and 5 mi. NE of Ukhta, in oil fields. **2** Village (1948 pop. over 2,000), N central Komi Autonomous SSR, Russian SFSR, on Izhma R. (landing) and 100 mi. N of Ukhta; agr.; reindeer raising. Center of Zyryan resistance (19th cent.) against Rus. domination.

Izhma River, in Komi Autonomous SSR, Russian SFSR, rises in S Timan Ridge, flows 320 mi. N, through forested region, past Krutaya, Izhma town, and Izhma village, to Pechora R. at Ust-Izhma, 20 mi. ESE of Ust-Tsilma. Navigable for 190 mi. below Ukhta (oil fields).

Izhmorskoye (ēzhmôr'skŭyŭ,–mŭrskoi'ŭ), village (1926 pop. 905), N Kemerovo oblast, Russian SFSR, on Trans-Siberian RR and 25 mi. ENE of Anzhero-Sudzhensk, in agr. area.

Izhora River (ēzhô'rŭ), Leningrad oblast, Russian SFSR, rises W of Gatchina, flows 50 mi. E and N, past Kolpino (shipyards), to Neva R. at Ust-Izhora.

Izh River (ēsh), in E European Russian SFSR, rises E of Yakshur-Bodya, flows 132 mi. generally S, past Izhevsk, to Kama R. E of Bondyuzhski. Lumber floating.

Izieux (ēzyû'), town (pop. 8,126), Loire dept., SE central France, in the Jarez, on Gier R. and 6 mi. ENE of Saint-Étienne; mfg. of rayon, braids and laces, textile machinery; metal plating.

Iz Island (ēsh), Serbo-Croatian *Iž,* Ital. *Eso* (ē'zō), Dalmatian island in Adriatic Sea, W Croatia, Yugoslavia; 7 mi. long, 1 mi. wide. Chief village, Iz Veliki, Serbo-Croatian *Iž Veliki,* Ital. *Eso Grande,* is 7 mi. WSW of Zadar. Sometimes spelled Izh.

Izki or **Azki** (both: ĭzkē'), town (pop. 4,000), Oman Proper, 70 mi. SW of Muscat, at S foot of the Jabal Akhdar; strategic center controlling Wadi Sama'il route from coast to interior. Sometimes spelled Ziki and Zikki.

Izmail (ēzmēl'), oblast (□ 4,800; 1947 pop. estimate 700,000), SW Ukrainian SSR, on Black Sea, in S Bessarabia; ⊙ Izmail. Bounded by Kiliya arm (Rum. border) of Danube R. delta (S), Moldavian SSR (N), Dniester Liman (NE); mainly steppe lowland whose intermittent rivers (e.g., Kogalnik R.) drain into characteristic lagoons (limans) of Danube delta and Black Sea coast. Agr. (corn, wheat, barley, mustard); vineyards, orchards. Sheep, horse, and cattle raising. Industry (flour milling, tanning, weaving) is centered in Izmail, Kiliya, and Belgorod-Dnestrovski. Important sturgeon fisheries (black caviar) along coast. Pop. largely Ukrainian, Russian, Bulgarian. Formed 1940 (confirmed 1947) out of Rum. depts. of Ismail and Cetatea-Alba of S Bessarabia; occupied (1941–44) by Rum. troops.

Izmail, Rum. *Ismail* (ēsmēl'), city (1941 pop. 17,569), ⊙ Izmail oblast, Ukrainian SSR, in Bessarabia, port on Kiliya arm (Rum. border) of Danube R. delta, 120 mi. SW of Odessa, 40 mi. E of Galatz; 45°21'N 28°50'E. Rail terminus; commercial center in winegrowing dist.; flour milling, tanning, mfg. of vegetable oils, soap, bricks; lumber mill. Naval flotilla base (repair yards). Has ruins of Turkish citadel. First mentioned in 16th cent.; became, under Turkish rule, a strong fortress; captured by Russians in 1770 and again, under Suvarov, in 1790, after costly assault. Passed (1812) to Russia; returned (1856–78) to Moldavia; passed (1918–40; 1941–44) to Rumania, where it was ⊙ Ismail dept. (□ 1,626; 1930 pop. 225,509). Its cession to USSR, effected 1940, was confirmed 1947.

Izmailovo or **Izmaylovo** (ēzmī'lŭvŭ). **1** W suburb of Moscow, Russian SFSR, within Moscow city limits. Was 17th-cent. summer residence of Russian tsars; has 17th-cent. cathedral and castle towers. **2** Town (1926 pop. 2,744), central Ulyanovsk oblast, Russian SFSR, 7 mi. NE of Barysh; woolens; sawmilling. Sometimes called Izmailovka.

Izmalkovo (ēzmäl'kŭvŭ), village (1939 pop. 2,259), E central Orel oblast, Russian SFSR, 21 mi. WNW of Yelets; potatoes.

Izmir, Turkey: see SMYRNA.

Izmit, province, Turkey: see KOCAELI.

Izmit (ĭzmĭt'), Turk. *İzmit,* city (1950 pop. 35,564), ⊙ Kocaeli prov., NW Turkey in Asia, port at head of Gulf of Izmit on Sea of Marmara, 55 mi. ESE of Istanbul, on railroad; 40°47'N 29°53'E. Center of rich tobacco dist.; mfg. of paper and pulp products, beer, cement, chemicals. Naval base. Izmit is on site of anc. Nicomedia, founded 264 B.C. by Nicomedes I on site of the Megaran city of Astacus (destroyed by Lysimachus). Nicomedia was ⊙ of Bithynia and later seat of Diocletian and Constantine the Great. Hannibal died here. There are only scanty ruins. Sometimes spelled Ismid.

Izmit, Gulf of, Turkish *İzmit,* long narrow inlet at E end of Sea of Marmara, NW Turkey, 15 mi. SE of Istanbul; 45 mi. long. Town of Izmit at E end, Golcuk on S shore.

Iznájar (ēthnä'här), town (pop. 2,187), Córdoba prov., S Spain, on Genil R. and 15 mi. SE of Lucena; olive-oil processing, flour milling. Gypsum quarries near by.

Iznalloz (ēthnälyōth'), town (pop. 3,480), Granada prov., S Spain, 16 mi. NNE of Granada; brandy distilling, flour milling. Olive oil, sugar beets, cereals, vegetables, livestock; lumber.

Iznate (ēthnä'tā), town (pop. 685), Málaga prov., S Spain, 14 mi. ENE of Málaga; grapes, raisins, olives and olive oil, cereals.

Iznatoraf (ēthnätōräf'), town (pop. 3,923), Jaén prov., S Spain, 4 mi. NE of Villacarrillo; olive-oil processing; cereals, vegetables. Gypsum quarries. Has remains of anc. walls.

Iznik or **Isnik** (both: ĭznĭk'), Turkish *İznik,* anc. *Nicaea* (nīsē'ŭ), also *Nice* (nīs), village (pop. 2,958), Bursa prov., NW Turkey, at E end of L. Iznik, 25 mi. SSW of Izmit, 38 mi. ENE of Bursa, in a grain area. Known for its tiles since Middle Ages. An anc. town of Bithynia, Nicaea flourished under the Romans and was scene (A.D. 325) of the 1st ecumenical council called by Constantine the Great. City was captured 1078 by Seljuk Turks, 1097 by Crusaders, 1330 by Ottoman Turks. There are ruins.

Iznik, Lake, or **Lake Isnik,** Turkish *İznik,* anc. *Ascanius,* lake (□ 80), NW Turkey, 23 mi. NE of Bursa; 20 mi. long, 7 mi. wide; alt. 260 ft.

Iznoski (ēznôs'kē), village (1926 pop. 464), N Kaluga oblast, Russian SFSR, 45 mi. NW of Kaluga; peat works.

Izoard, Col d' (kôl dēzōär'), pass (alt. 7,726 ft.) of the Cottian Alps, in Hautes-Alpes dept., SE France, on Briançon-Guillestre road (*route des Alpes*), 7 mi. SE of Briançon. Just E is the Pic de Rochebrune.

Izobilnoye or **Izobil'noye** (ēzŭbēl'nŭyŭ), village (1939 pop. over 2,000), NW Stavropol Territory, Russian SFSR, on railroad and 25 mi. NNW of Stavropol, in wheat and sunflower area; flour milling. Until middle 1930s, called Izobilno-Tishchenskoye. A smaller village (1939 pop. over 500), 5 mi. S, was formerly called Izobilnoye; since 1930s, Staro [old]-Izobilnoye.

Izola, Free Territory of Trieste: see ISOLA.

Izoplit (ēzŭplyēt'), town (1946 pop. over 500), SE Kalinin oblast, Russian SFSR, near Volga R., c.20 mi. SE of Kalinin; mfg. of insulating materials.

Izozog, Bañados de (bänyä'dōs dā ēsōsōk'), marshy area in Santa Cruz dept., SE Bolivia, at N edge of the Chaco, 80 mi. NE of Charagua; 80 mi. long, c.30 mi. wide. Receives the Parapetí; has several outlets, one of which flows to L. CONCEPCIÓN (N). Also called Bañados del Parapetí.

Izra' (ĭzrä') or **Azra'** (äzrä'), Fr. *Ezraa* or *Ezra,* anc. *Zoroa,* town, Hauran prov., SW Syria, on railroad and 19 mi. NNE of Der'a; cereals, wheat. Has ruins dating from Roman era.

Izsak (ĭ'zhäk), Hung. *Izsák,* town (pop. 7,988), Pest-Pilis-Solt-Kiskun co., central Hungary, 17 mi. SW of Kecskemet; grain, tobacco, cherries, apricots; cattle.

Iztaccihuatl, Mexico: see IXTACIHUATL.

Iztapa (ēstä'pä), town (1950 pop. 427), Escuintla dept., S Guatemala, on the Pacific, at mouth of Michatoya R., and 7 mi. E of San José; tropical resort. Sometimes called Puerto de Iztapa.

Iztochno Shivachevo, Bulgaria: see GOLYAMO SHIVACHEVO.

Izu (ē'zōō) or **Idzu** (ē'dzōō), former province in central Honshu, Japan; now part of Shizuoka prefecture.

Izúcar de Matamoros, Mexico: see MATAMOROS.

Izuhara (ēzōō'härŭ), town (pop. 10,105), on SE coast of Tsushima, Nagasaki prefecture, Japan, on Tsushima Strait; chief town of isl.; fishing. Site of ruins of castle built in 16th cent. by Hideyoshi. Sometimes spelled Idzuhara.

Izu Islands, Japan: see IZU-SHICHITO.

Izumi or **Idzumi** (both: ēzōō'mē), former province in S Honshu, Japan; now part of Osaka prefecture.

Izumi. 1 Town (pop. 9,318), Gifu prefecture, central Honshu, Japan, 4 mi. ENE of Tajimi; rice, wheat, raw silk. **2** Town (pop. 21,791), Kagoshima prefecture, W Kyushu, Japan, 35 mi. NNW of Kagoshima; commercial center for agr. area (tobacco, rice, soybeans, sweet potatoes). Business col. Airfield bombed (1945) in Second World War.

3 Town (pop. 16,179), Osaka prefecture, S Honshu, Japan, just E of Izumi-otsu; rice-producing center.
Izumikawa (ēzōōmē'kāwŭ), town (pop. 8,763), Ehime prefecture, N Shikoku, Japan, just S of Niihama; agr. center (rice, wheat); livestock; raw silk. Copper mines near by.
Izumi-otsu (ēzōō'mē'ō'tsōō), city (1940 pop. 27,800; 1947 pop. 30,652), Osaka prefecture, S Honshu, Japan, on Osaka Bay, 13 mi. SW of Osaka; commercial center in rice-growing area; home industries (cotton and woolen textiles, straw products). Fishery. Until early 1940s, called Otsu.
Izumo or **Idzumo** (both: ēzōō'mō), former province in SW Honshu, Japan; now part of Shimane prefecture.
Izumo, city (pop. 43,855), Shimane prefecture, SW Honshu, Japan, 18 mi. WSW of Matsue; commercial center in agr. area; textile mills. Has agr. school. Formed in early 1940s by combining town of Imaichi with surrounding villages. Sometimes called Izumo-imaichi.
Izumozaki (ēzōō'mō'zäkē), town (pop. 7,675), Niigata prefecture, central Honshu, Japan, on Sea of Japan, 11 mi. NW of Nagaoka; fishing, oil drilling.
Izumrud (ēzŏŏmrōōt') [Rus.,=emerald], town (1939 pop. over 2,000), S Sverdlovsk oblast, Russian SFSR, on left tributary of Pyshma R. and 6 mi. NW of Asbest; noted emerald-mining center.
Izu-nagaoka (ē'zōō-nägä'ôkä), town (pop. 6,761), Shizuoka prefecture, central Honshu, Japan, on NW Izu Peninsula, 7 mi. SE of Numazu; rice, raw silk. Hot springs.
Izu-no-shichito, Japan: see IZU-SHICHITO.
Izu Peninsula (ē'zōō), Jap. *Izu-hanto,* Shizuoka prefecture, central Honshu, Japan, bet. Suruga Bay (W) and Sagami Bay (E); 40 mi. long, 10–20 mi. wide; mountainous. Known for hot springs, seaside resorts. Atami is chief town.
Izushi (ēzōō'shē), town (pop. 5,851), Hyogo prefecture, S Honshu, Japan, 6 mi. SSE of Toyooka; pottery, textiles.
Izu-shichito (ē'zōō-shĭchĭtō), island group (□ 116; 1940 pop. 31,967; 1947 pop. 38,683), Greater Tokyo, Japan, bet. Philippine Sea (W) and the Pacific (E), S of Sagami and Tokyo bays, off central Honshu; 30°29'-34°44'N 139°24'-140°19'E. Comprises chain of volcanic isls. extending c.300 mi. N-S. Includes O-SHIMA (largest isl.), TO-SHIMA, NII-JIMA, KOZU-SHIMA, MIYAKE-JIMA, MIKURA-JIMA, HACHIJO-JIMA, KO-JIMA, AOGA-SHIMA, TORI-SHIMA. BAYONNAISE ROCKS, SMITH ISLAND, and LOT'S WIFE are uninhabited rocks. Isls. are generally mountainous; many have active volcanoes; best-known, Mt. Mihara on O-shima. Japan Current flows N along W side of isls. Mean annual temp. 64°F.; mean annual rainfall 135 in. Abundant bird life, poisonous snakes, fruit bats, rats. Extensive mulberry fields on larger isls.; stock raising, dairying, fishing, farming. Important products: silk textiles, camellia oil. Isl. group is in administrative sphere of Greater Tokyo. In feudal times, used as a place of exile for political prisoners. The island group is sometimes called Izu-shoto, and sometimes Anglicized as Izu Isls. Formerly Izu-no-shichito.
Izvarino (ēzvä'rĭnŭ), town (1926 pop. 1,768), SE Voroshilovgrad oblast, Ukrainian SSR, in the Donbas, 5 mi. E of Krasnodon; coal mines. Formerly Izvarinski Rudnik.
Izvestiya Tsik Islands (ēzvyĕs'tyēŭ tsĭk'), in Kara Sea of Arctic Ocean, 100 mi. off NW Taimyr Peninsula, in Krasnoyarsk Territory, Russian SFSR; 75°50'N 82°30'E.
Izvestkovy or **Izvestkovyy** (ēzvyĭstkô'vē), town (1948 pop. over 500), NW Jewish Autonomous Oblast, Russian SFSR, on Trans-Siberian RR and 125 mi. W of Birobidzhan; junction for railroad to coal fields of the Bureya Range, in Khabarovsk Territory; limestone works.
Izvestnyaki, Russian SFSR: see NOVO-TROITSK.
Izvornik, Yugoslavia: see ZVORNIK.
Izyaslav (ēzyŭsläf'), city (1926 pop. 11,707), N Kamenets-Podolski oblast, Ukrainian SSR, on Goryn R. and 11 mi. WSW of Shepetovka; metal and food industries. Formerly called Zaslavl, then (in 1920s) Izyaslavl, and, until c.1935, Zaslav. Dates from 14th cent.
Izylbash, Russian SFSR: see MOLOTOVO, Omsk oblast.
Izyuin, Japan: see IJUIN.
Izyum (ēzyōōm'), city (1932 pop. estimate 13,690), E Kharkov oblast, Ukrainian SSR, on the Northern Donets and 70 mi. SE of Kharkov; metalworking center; railroad shops; ceramic industry; sawmilling. Founded in late 17th cent. as fortress against Tatars. Phosphorite and lignite deposits near by.
Izzan, Aden: see AZZAN.

J

Ja'alan, Oman: see JA'LAN.
Jääski, Russian SFSR: see LESOGORSKI.
Jabal [Arabic,=mountain], for Arabic names beginning thus: see under following part of the name.
Jabalah, Syria: see JEBLE.
Jabalí, El, Nicaragua: see SANTO DOMINGO.
Jabalí Island (häbälē'), off Atlantic coast, SW Buenos Aires prov., Argentina, S of San Blas Bay, 45 mi. ENE of Carmen de Patagones; 8 mi. long, 3 mi. wide.
Jabalón River, Spain: see JAVALÓN RIVER.
Jabalpur, India: see JUBBULPORE.
Jabalquinto (hävälkēn'tō), town (pop. 3,098), Jaén prov., S Spain, near confluence of Guadalimar and Guadalquivir rivers, 7 mi. SW of Linares; olive oil, cereals.
Jabal-us-Siraj (jŭ'bŭl-ōōs-sĭräj'), industrial town (pop. over 2,000), Kabul prov., E Afghanistan, 40 mi. N of Kabul, and on Salang R. (short left tributary of Ghorband R.), at foot of the Hindu Kush; modern cotton mill; hydroelectric station. Iron deposits near by.
Jabarhera (jŭbŭrhā'rŭ), town (pop. 2,261), Saharanpur dist., N Uttar Pradesh, India, 16 mi. SE of Saharanpur; wheat, rice, rape and mustard, gram, corn. Also spelled Jhabrera.
Jabbeke (yä'bākŭ), agr. village (pop. 2,611), West Flanders prov., NW Belgium, 6 mi. WSW of Bruges.
Jabbok River, Jordan: see ZERQA', WADI.
Jabiri (jä'bērē), town (pop. 3,795), N Br. Cameroons, administered as part of Bornu prov. of Nigeria, near Fr. Cameroons border, 50 mi. S of Kikwa; peanuts, millet, cotton; cattle, skins.
Jablanica or **Yablanitsa** (both: yä'blänĭtsä), village, N Herzegovina, Yugoslavia, on the Neretva, on railroad and 14 mi. SSE of Prozor; climatic resort; tourist center for excursions into near-by mts. Hydroelectric plant, large dam and reservoir.
Jablanica or **Yablanitsa,** mountain (7,403 ft.) in the Pindus system, on Yugoslav-Albania border, bet. the Black Drin and the Shkumbi, 10 mi. NW of Struga.
Jablonec or **Jablonec nad Nisou** (yä'blônĕts näd' nyĭsō), Ger. *Gablonz* (gä'blônts), city (pop. 23,112; pop. of urban area 44,000), N Bohemia, Czechoslovakia, in the Sudetes, on Lusatian Neisse R., on railroad and 6 mi. SE of Liberec. The cradle of Bohemian glass industry, it now makes all types of glass articles, from tableware to ornaments. Especially known for artificial jewelry (Jablonec goods) made of glass, metal, and (lately) plastic, developed after Napoleonic Wars. Imitation beads, pearls, and bangles are exported to Africa and India. Woolen and cotton textiles, paper mills also important. Has Gothic and 17th-cent. churches, Moorish-style synagogue, mus. with collections of Bohemian cut glass.
Jablonica Pass, Ukraine: see YABLONITSA PASS.
Jablonkow, Czechoslovakia: see JABLUNKOV.
Jablonne v Podjestedi (yä'blônä fpôd'yĕshtyĕdē), Czech *Jablonné v Podještědí,* Ger. *Deutsch Gabel* (doich' gä"bŭl), town (pop. 1,944), N Bohemia, Czechoslovakia, 32 mi. ENE of Prague; rail junction; summer resort; mfg. (brushes, brooms), basketwork. Formerly known as Nemecke Jablonne, Czech *Německé Jablonné.*
Jablonow, Ukrainian SSR: see YABLONOV.
Jablunkov (yä'blōōn-kôf, Ger. *Jablunkau,* Pol. *Jabłonków* (yäbwôn'kōōf), town (pop. 4,702), SE Silesia, Czechoslovakia, in the Beskids, on Olse R., on railroad and 23 mi. SE of Ostrava, near Pol. border; mfg. of metal goods. Jablunkov Pass (alt. 1,807 ft.), with railroad tunnel, is 4 mi. S.
Jabneel, Palestine: see JAMNIA.
Jabneh, Israel: see JAMNIA.
Jaboatão (zhŭbōōtou'ō). **1** City (1950 pop. 34,788), Pernambuco, NE Brazil, on railroad, 11 mi. WSW of Recife; cotton, sugar, tobacco, rice. Here were fought 2 battles in Dutch Wars (17th cent.). **2** City, Sergipe, Brazil: see JAPOATÃ.
Jabón (häbōn'), town (pop. 596), Lara state, NW Venezuela, in Segovia Highlands, 35 mi. SW of Carora; corn, goats.
Jaboticabal (zhŭbōōtē"kŭbäl'), city (pop. 11,592), N central São Paulo, Brazil, 33 mi. WSW of Ribeirão Prêto; rail junction. Mfg. of agr. machinery, pottery, macaroni; sugar refining, alcohol distilling, cotton ginning. Trades in livestock, coffee, fruit. Has agr. school with airfield.
Jabrin (jäbrēn'), town and oasis in S Hasa, Saudi Arabia, 150 mi. S of Hofuf, near Tropic of Cancer.
Jabugo (hävōō'gō), town (pop. 1,842), Huelva prov., SW Spain, in the Sierra Morena, 10 mi. W of Aracena; acorns, chestnuts, walnuts, olives, fruit, hogs; mfg. of meat products; sawmilling.
Jabuka Island (yä'bōōkä), Ital. *Pomo* (pô'mô), Dalmatian island (□ 1) in Adriatic Sea, S Croatia, Yugoslavia, c.55 mi. SW of Split.
Jabukovac or **Yabukovats** (both: yä'bōōkôvāts), village, E Serbia, Yugoslavia, 11 mi. NNW of Negotin.
Jabwot (jäb'wōt), coral island (pop. 94), Ralik Chain, Kwajalein dist., Marshall Isls., W central Pacific, 10 mi. N of Ailinglapalap; 7°44'N 168°59'E; c.10 mi. in circumference; phosphorite deposit.
Jaca (hä'kä), city (pop. 7,633), Huesca prov., NE Spain, in Aragon, near Fr. border, on S slopes of the central Pyrenees, on Aragon R. and 30 mi. NNW of Huesca; communications and processing center, strategically placed in the Aragon valley, through which passes the trans-Pyrenean RR to Saragossa. Trades in livestock, cereals, fruit. Mfg. of cement, candy, chocolate; flour milling; lumbering. City is a bishopric and seat of a summer univ. Among its outstanding bldgs. are a cathedral (built 11th-15th cent., restored in 19th) with Byzantine, Romanesque, and Gothic features; and a plateresque town hall (1554). On a N hill towers the magnificent citadel, begun 1593 by Philip II. The medieval town walls have Roman remains. Hermitage of the Virgin of the Grotto is near by. Of Iberian origin, Jaca was held by the Moors from 8th to early 11th cent. During the reconquest it was ⊙ Aragon until Huesca was taken (1096). During the Peninsular War, Jaca was occupied (1809–14) by the French.
Jacala (häkä'lä), town (pop. 1,325), Hidalgo, central Mexico, in Sierra Madre Oriental, on Inter-American Highway and 70 mi. NNW of Pachuca; alt. 4,567 ft.; corn, wheat, beans, potatoes, fruit, livestock.
Jacaleapa (häkälää'pä), town (pop. 1,220), El Paraíso dept., S Honduras, 5 mi. WSW of Danlí; tobacco, corn, beans.
Jacaltenango (häkältänäng'gō), town (1950 pop. 3,298), Huehuetenango dept., W Guatemala, on W slopes of Cuchumatanes Mts., 30 mi. NW of Huehuetenango; alt. 5,700 ft. Mfg. (palm-leaf hats, textiles); crude sugar production; stock raising.
Jacareí (zhŭkŭrĭ-ē'), city (pop. 11,797), E São Paulo, Brazil, on Paraíba R., on railroad and 45 mi. ENE of São Paulo. Textile milling; mfg. of pottery, tile, flour products; dairying, distilling. Old spelling, Jacarehy.
Jacarèzinho (zhŭkŭrĕ"zē'nyōō), city (pop. 5,135), NE Paraná, Brazil, on railroad and 75 mi. E of Londrina; furniture mfg., coffee and rice processing; cotton, tobacco, grain, cattle.
Jachal (hächäl'), town (1947 pop. 3,957), ⊙ Jachal dept. (□ c.8,500; pop. 16,857), central San Juan prov., Argentina, on Jachal or Zanjón R. and 90 mi. N of San Juan; farming center (alfalfa, wheat, corn, wine, olives, livestock). Lime deposits; sawmills. Irrigation dam and coal mines near by.
Jachal River, Argentina: see ZANJÓN RIVER.
Jachymov (yä'khĭmôf), Czech *Jáchymov,* Ger. *Joachimsthal* or *Sankt Joachimsthal* (zängkt yōä'khēmstäl), town (pop. 6,806), W Bohemia, Czechoslovakia, in the Erzgebirge, 10 mi. N of Carlsbad, near Ger. border. Rail terminus; a leading European pitchblende-mining center, with production of uranium and radium; lead, silver, nickel, cobalt, and bismuth mining; woodworking, lace making. Noted health resort, with thermal radioactive springs (81°F.) and baths. Has 16th-cent. church, 2 town halls, castle. Main silver-mining center of Holy Roman Empire. Ger. word *Thaler,* from which *dollar* is derived, is an abbreviation of Joachimsthaler, a coin 1st struck here in 16th cent.
Jacinto Aráuz (häsēn'tō ärous'), town (pop. estimate 1,500), SE La Pampa natl. territory, Argentina, on railroad and 85 mi. SE of General Acha; wheat and livestock center.
Jacinto City (jusĭn'tō), town (pop. 6,856), Harris co., S Texas, just E of Houston. Inc. since 1940.
Jaci-Paraná (zhŭsē'-pŭrŭnä'), town (pop. 240), W Guaporé territory, W Brazil, on Madeira-Mamoré RR and 50 mi. SW of Pôrto Velho; rubber. Until 1944, called Generoso Ponce.
Jack, county (□ 944; pop. 7,755), N Texas; ⊙ Jacksboro. Drained by West Fork of Trinity R.; includes part of L. Bridgeport. Livestock (cattle, sheep, goats, poultry); wool, mohair marketed. Oil wells; agr. (grain, cotton, corn, peanuts, pecans, fruit, truck); timber. Formed 1856.
Jackfish, village (pop. estimate 250), central Ont., on Jackfish Bay of L. Superior, 14 mi. E of Schreiber; gold mining.
Jackfish Bay, Lake co., NE Minn., near Ont. line, 10 mi. NE of Ely in resort area, in Superior Natl. Forest; 7 mi. long, 1 mi. wide. Also known as Jackfish L.
Jackfish Lake (10 mi. long, 6 mi. wide), W Sask., 17 mi. N of North Battleford. Drains S into North Saskatchewan R. Just E is Murray L. (6 mi. long, 3 mi. wide).
Jackman, plantation (pop. 964), Somerset co., W Maine, 25 mi. W of Moosehead L., 15 mi. E of Que. line, 33 mi. NW of Greenville; port of entry; center of wilderness hunting, fishing, camping region; lumbering.
Jacksboro. 1 Coal-mining village (1940 pop. 577), ⊙ Campbell co., NE Tenn., 28 mi. NW of Knoxville. **2** City (pop. 2,951), ⊙ Jack co., N Texas,

50 mi. SSE of Wichita Falls; trade, shipping center in ranching, oil, timber area; oil refining, flour and lumber milling; sheep, cattle, mohair. Settled around Fort Richardson (founded 1867; extant); inc. 1899.

Jacks Mountain, NE-SW ridge (c.2,000 ft.), central Pa., runs c.70 mi. NE from central part of Huntingdon co. to N part of Snyder co.; Juniata R. crosses at Mount Union; sandstone, ganister, silica.

Jackson. **1** County (□ 1,124; pop. 38,998), NE Ala.; ⊙ Scottsboro. Agr. region bordering on Ga. and Tenn., drained by Tennessee and Paint Rock rivers and Guntersville Reservoir. Cotton, corn, timber; deposits of coal and limestone. Formed 1819. **2** County (□ 637; pop. 25,912), NE Ark.; ⊙ Newport. Drained by Black, White, and Cache rivers, and by small Village Creek. Agr. (cotton, rice, corn, pecans, livestock). Mfg. at Newport. Sand and gravel pits. Formed 1829. **3** County (□ 1,623; pop. 1,976), N Colo.; ⊙ Walden. Agr. area, bordering on Wyo.; drained by headwaters of North Platte R. Livestock, lumber. Includes parts of Routt and Arapaho natl. forests. Part of Park Range in W and Medicine Bow Mts. in E. Formed 1909. **4** County (□ 942; pop. 34,645), NW Fla., on Ala. (N) and Ga. (E; Chattahoochee R.) lines; ⊙ Marianna. Rolling agr. area (peanuts, corn, cotton, vegetables, hogs) with many small lakes; drained by Chipola R. Some mfg. (food products; lumber, naval stores), and limestone quarrying. Formed 1822. **5** County (□ 337; pop. 18,997), NE central Ga.; ⊙ Jefferson. Piedmont area drained by Oconee R. Agr. (cotton, corn, hay, sweet potatoes, apples, peaches, poultry) and textile mfg. Formed 1796. **6** County (□ 603; pop. 38,124), SW Ill.; ⊙ Murphysboro. Bounded SW by Mississippi R.; drained by Big Muddy and Little Muddy rivers and Beaucoup Creek. S section lies in Ill. Ozarks. Agr. area (corn, wheat, livestock, truck, fruit; dairy products), with some mfg. (clothing, railroad equipment, beverages, flour, silica and iron products). Bituminous-coal mining. Includes part of Shawnee Natl. Forest and Giant City State Park. Formed 1816. **7** County (□ 520; pop. 28,237), S Ind.; ⊙ Brownstown. Bounded S by Muscatatuck R.; drained by East Fork of White R. and tributaries of the Muscatatuck. Agr. area (grain, livestock, truck, poultry), with diversified mfg., timber. Formed 1815. **8** County (□ 644; pop. 18,622), E Iowa, on Ill. line (E; formed here by Mississippi R.); ⊙ Maquoketa. Prairie agr. area (hogs, cattle, poultry, corn, oats, alfalfa) drained by Maquoketa and North Fork Maquoketa rivers; limestone quarries. Has state parks. Formed 1837. **9** County (□ 656; pop. 11,098), NE Kansas; ⊙ Holton. Rolling prairie, watered by headstreams of Delaware R. Livestock, grain. Potawatomi Indian Reservation is W of Mayetta. Formed 1857. **10** County (□ 337; pop. 13,101), SE central Ky.; ⊙ McKee. In Cumberland foothills; drained by headstreams of Rockcastle R. and by several creeks. Includes part of Cumberland Natl. Forest. Mtn. agr. area (livestock, fruit, tobacco, hay, corn); coal mines, timber. Formed 1858. **11** Parish (□ 583; pop. 15,434), N central La.; ⊙ Jonesboro. Agr. area (cotton, corn, hay, peanuts, sweet and white potatoes, poultry; dairy products); timber. Sawmills, cotton gins. Drained by Dugdemona R. and Bayou Castor. Formed 1845. **12** County (□ 705; pop. 107,925), S Mich.; ⊙ Jackson. Drained by Grand and Raisin rivers and headstreams of the Kalamazoo. Agr. (grain, corn, hay, fruit, livestock, poultry; dairy products). Mfg. at Jackson. Contains many small lakes (fishing, bathing). Organized 1832. **13** County (□ 698; pop. 16,306), SW Minn.; ⊙ Jackson. Agr. area bordering Iowa and watered by Des Moines R. and headwaters of Little Sioux R. Corn, oats, barley, livestock, potatoes. Includes part of Coteau des Prairies. Heron L. is in NW. Formed 1857. **14** County (□ 744; pop. 31,401), extreme SE Miss.; ⊙ Pascagoula. Borders E on Ala., S on Mississippi Sound. Drained by Pascagoula and Escatawpa rivers. Agr. (cotton, corn, pecans, livestock), dairying; fisheries; lumbering. Includes part of De Soto Natl. Forest. Formed 1812. **15** County (□ 603; pop. 541,035), W Mo.; ⊙ Independence. Bounded N by Missouri R.; Kansas R. enters the Missouri at NW corner. Agr. (wheat, corn, oats, dairy products); mfg. and livestock industries centered at Kansas City. Formed 1826. **16** County (□ 499; pop. 19,261), W N.C.; ⊙ Sylva. Partly in the Blue Ridge; bounded S by S.C.; Balsam Mtn. in E, Cowee Mts. in W; drained by Tuckasegee R. Included in Nantahala Natl. Forest. Glenville Reservoir in S. Farming (livestock, apples, clover, potatoes, corn), lumbering, mica and talc mining; resort region. Formed 1851. **17** County (□ 420; pop. 27,767), S Ohio; ⊙ Jackson. Drained by Little Scioto R. and small Symmes and Little Raccoon creeks. Includes Buckeye Furnace and Leo Petroglyph state parks, and Canter's Cave. Agr. area (livestock, grain, fruit, dairy products); mfg. at Jackson, Oak Hill, Wellston; coal mining. Formed 1816. **18** County (□ 780; pop. 20,082), SW Okla.; ⊙ Altus. Bounded S by Texas; drained by Red R. and its North, Salt, and Prairie Dog Town forks. Agr. (cotton, wheat, alfalfa). Irrigation from ALTUS DAM. Mfg. at Altus. Oil, natural-gas wells. Formed 1907. **19** County (□ 2,817; pop. 58,510), SW Oregon; ⊙ Medford. Mtn. area bordering on Calif. and crossed by Rogue R. Poultry, fruit, nuts, truck. Includes parts of Siskiyou Mts. and Rogue River Natl. Forest. Formed 1852. **20** County (□ 809; pop. 1,768), SW central S.Dak.; ⊙ Kadoka. Agr. area watered by intermittent streams; bounded on S by White River. Livestock, grain. Part of Badlands Natl. Monument in SW. Formed 1883 and later absorbed into other counties; reconstituted 1914. **21** County (□ 327; pop. 12,348), N central Tenn.; ⊙ Gainesboro. Crossed by Cumberland R. Agr. (tobacco, livestock, corn); oil wells; timber. Formed 1801. **22** County (□ 854; pop. 12,916), S Texas; ⊙ Edna. On Gulf coastal plain; touches on Lavaca and Matagorda bays in S. Drained by Lavaca and Navidad rivers. Oil, natural-gas wells; cattle ranching; agr. (cotton, corn, grains, flax, fruit, vegetables); dairying, livestock raising (hogs, poultry). Formed as municipality 1835, as county 1836. **23** County (□ 463; pop. 15,299), W W.Va.; ⊙ Ripley. Bounded NW by Ohio R. (Ohio line); drained by small creeks. Natural-gas and oil wells; some coal; agr. (livestock, dairy products, fruit, tobacco). Small industries at Ripley, Ravenswood. Formed 1831. **24** County (□ 1,000; pop. 16,073), W central Wis.; ⊙ Black River Falls. Intersected by Black, Buffalo, and Trempealeau rivers. Dairying area; also general farming (potatoes, canning crops), stock raising. Some mfg. Formed 1853.

Jackson. **1** Town (pop. 3,072), Clarke co., SW Ala., on Tombigbee R. (railroad bridge) and 60 mi. N of Mobile; lumber, hosiery. Artesian mineral wells and Salt Springs State Park near by. Inc. 1816. **2** City (pop. 1,879), ⊙ Amador co., central Calif., 40 mi. ESE of Sacramento and on short Jackson Creek; trade and mining center in Mother Lode country. Gold mines, marble quarries, clay pits, farms, vineyards near by. Argonaut and Kennedy quartz mines, operating since early 1850s, are more than 1 mi. deep. Founded during gold rush; made co. seat in 1851; inc. 1905. **3** City (pop. 2,053), ⊙ Butts co., central Ga., c.40 mi. SE of Atlanta; cotton milling, vegetable canning; mfg. of clothing, boxes, toys. State park and Lloyd Shoals Reservoir near by. Inc. 1826. **4** City (pop. 1,978), ⊙ Breathitt co., E central Ky., in the Cumberlands, on North Fork Kentucky R. and 24 mi. NNW of Hazard; trade center for coal-mining, lumbering, and agr. (livestock, corn, poultry, fruit, truck, potatoes, tobacco) area; makes staves, soft drinks. Seat of Lees Jr. Col. (1864; Presbyterian; coeducational). Forestry experiment station of Univ. of Ky. is just SE, at Quicksand. **5** Town (pop. 6,772), East Feliciana parish, SE central La., 27 mi. N of Baton Rouge, in agr. area. Has state mental hosp. **6** Town (pop. 258), Waldo co., S Maine, 14 mi. NNW of Belfast; agr., lumbering. **7** City (pop. 51,088), ⊙ Jackson co., S Mich., c.70 mi. W of Detroit and on Grand R. Industrial, rail, and commercial center, in agr. area; mfg. (auto and airplane parts, tools, wheels, metal products, radios, furniture, paper, wood products, clothing, drugs, medicines, food products); railroad shops. Has jr. col. Near by is a state prison. A tablet marks the site of the founding in Jackson of the Republican party (July 6, 1854). Settled 1829; inc. as village 1843, as city 1857. **8** City (pop. 3,313), ⊙ Jackson co., SW Minn., on Des Moines R., near Iowa line, and 27 mi. W of Fairmont; trade and shipping point in grain, livestock, and poultry area; dairy, wood products. Settled before 1857, scene of Sioux uprising 1862, inc. 1881. **9** City (pop. 98,271), ⊙ Mississippi and a ⊙ Hinds co., W Miss., on Pearl R. and 195 mi. S of Memphis, Tenn.; 32°17′N 90°12′W; alt. c.300 ft. State's largest city, and its railroad, shipping, and industrial center. Industries produce lumber, wood products, furniture, clothing, cottonseed oil, fluorescent lamps, vehicle-body parts, steel and iron castings, packed meat, filtering compound; railroad shops are important; a natural-gas field is just S. Seat of Millsaps Col. (Methodist; coeducational; opened 1892), Belhaven Col. (Presbyterian; for women; 1894), Jackson Col. (Negro; state supported; coeducational; 1877), and of several state institutions for the physically and mentally handicapped. U.S. military air base (Hawkins Field) and Tougaloo Col. are near by. Points of interest: the old capitol (1839), the new capitol (1903), governor's mansion 1(1842), art gall., state mus. and library, state fairgrounds, and a notable Confederate monument. Laid out as state capital in 1821, on site of a trading post; legislature 1st met here in 1822; town was inc. in 1833. In Civil War, town was a center of military activity in Vicksburg campaign; Sherman virtually destroyed it in 1863. Jackson grew rapidly in 20th cent. (pop. has tripled since 1920); the opening of near-by natural-gas fields in 1930s stimulated its industrial growth. **10** City (pop. 3,707), ⊙ Cape Girardeau co., SE Mo., near Mississippi R., 10 mi. NW of Cape Girardeau; shoes, bricks; grain, lumber, dairy products. Founded c.1815. **11** Village (pop. 200), Dakota co., NE Nebr., 8 mi. W of Sioux City, Iowa, near Missouri R. and S.Dak. line. **12** Resort town (pop. 344), Carroll co., E N.H., on Ellis R. and 12 mi. NNW of Conway; winter sports center. Partly in White Mtn. Natl. Forest. **13** Town (pop. 843), ⊙ Northampton co., NE N.C., 14 mi. SE of Roanoke Rapids; agr. trade center; sawmills. **14** City (pop. 6,504), ⊙ Jackson co., S Ohio, 28 mi. NE of Portsmouth; steel mills, foundries; also produces cigars, clay products, lumber. Coal mines; gas wells; clay, sand, gravel, and silica pits. Buckeye Furnace and Leo Petroglyph state parks, and Canter's Cave are near by. Founded 1817. **15** Village (pop. c.1,000), Aiken co., W S.C., near Savannah R., 18 mi. SSW of Aiken. Grew with establishment near by (1951) of Savannah R. Plant of Atomic Energy Commission. **16** City (pop. 30,207), ⊙ Madison co., W Tenn., on South Fork of Forked Deer R. and 75 mi. NE of Memphis. Rail junction (repair shops); industrial and shipping center for timber, agr. (corn, potatoes, strawberries, tomatoes) area; mfg. of wood products, furniture, cotton, cottonseed products, paper boxes, beverages, steel products; meat packing, sawmilling. Seat of Lane Col., Union Univ., Lambuth Col. Points of interest include West Tenn. fairgrounds, grave of "Casey" Jones. Prehistoric mounds, state forest nursery, West Tenn. Agr. Experiment Station are near by. Settled 1819; inc. as town 1823, as city 1845. **17** Village (pop. 361), Washington co., E Wis., 23 mi. NNW of Milwaukee, in dairying and farming area; cannery. **18** Town (pop. 1,244), ⊙ Teton co., NW Wyo., on branch of Snake R., just S of Grand Teton Natl. Park, and 65 mi. E of Idaho Falls, Idaho; alt. c.6,200 ft. Resort and trading point in JACKSON HOLE; agr., livestock. Hq. of Teton Natl. Forest. Rodeo takes place annually. Hunting and dude ranches in vicinity.

Jackson, Fort. **1** Fort in La.: see TRIUMPH. **2** Fort in S.C.: see COLUMBIA.

Jackson, Lake, Prince William co., N Va., impounded by hydroelectric dam in Occoquan Creek, 4 mi. SE of Manassas; c.2 mi. long; resort.

Jackson, Mount. **1** Peak in Mont.: see LEWIS RANGE. **2** Peak in N.H.: see PRESIDENTIAL RANGE.

Jackson, Port, or **Sydney Harbour** (□ c.22), inlet of Pacific Ocean, E New South Wales, Australia; best harbor on E coast of Australia; 1.5 mi. wide at mouth, 12 mi. long; broken into many coves. Parramatta R. is W arm. Site of naval base. Contains COCKATOO ISLAND with large shipyards. SYDNEY, on S shore, is connected with N suburbs by Sydney Harbour Bridge (1932) with arch span of 1,650 ft. Principal suburbs on N shore are Manly and Mosman, on S shore Vaucluse, Woollahra, and Paddington. In Second World War, port was Allied naval base.

Jacksonburgh or **Jacksonburg**, village (pop. 114), Butler co., extreme SW Ohio, 7 mi. W of Middletown.

Jackson Center. **1** Village (pop. 698), Shelby co., W Ohio, 12 mi. NE of Sidney; food and dairy products, clothing, lumber. **2** Borough (pop. 266), Mercer co., W Pa., 6 mi. NE of Mercer.

Jackson Gulch Dam, Colo.: see MANCOS RIVER.

Jackson Harbor, Wis.: see WASHINGTON ISLAND.

Jackson Heights, SE N.Y., a residential section of NW Queens borough of New York city.

Jackson Hole, fertile valley (6–8 mi. wide, 48 mi. long; alt. 6–7,000 ft.), in Teton co., NW Wyo.; extends N from Jackson bet. Teton Range and Continental Divide; drained by Jackson L. and headwaters of Snake R. Jackson Hole Natl. Monument, established 1943, was abolished 1950 and its area added mostly to Grand Teton Natl. Park; the rest was added to Teton Natl. Forest and Jackson Hole Wildlife Park (established 1948; stocked with elk, deer, bison, antelope,and moose).

Jackson Junction, town (pop. 107), Winneshiek co., NE Iowa, 18 mi. SW of Decorah; limestone quarries.

Jackson Lake. **1** Reservoir in Ga.: see LLOYD SHOALS RESERVOIR. **2** Lake in NW Wyo., in Jackson Hole, in Grand Teton Natl. Park; 2d largest lake in Wyo. (□ 40; 18 mi. long, average width 4 mi.); alt. c.6,750 ft. Fed and drained by Snake R. Jackson L. Dam (finished 1911; 70 ft. high, 4,920 ft. long) is in SE corner of lake at Moran; part of Minidoka irrigation project.

Jackson Mountains, NW Nev., in Humboldt co., E of Black Rock Desert, rising to 8,800 ft. in King Lear peak.

Jackson Peak, Wyo.: see WIND RIVER RANGE.

Jacksonport. **1** Town (1940 pop. 215), Jackson co., NE Ark., 3 mi. NW of Newport and on White R. **2** Fishing village,, Door co., NE Wis., on Door Peninsula, on L. Michigan, 13 mi. NE of Sturgeon Bay. Formerly a lumber port.

Jackson River, W Va., rises in the Alleghenies in W Highland co., flows SSW, past Covington, and ENE, past Clifton Forge, joining Cowpasture R. SE of Iron Gate to form James R.; c.75 mi. long. Site of Gathright Dam (găth′rīt), for flood control and power, is 12 mi. N of Covington; site of auxiliary dam (Falling Spring Dam) is 6 mi. N of Covington.

Jackson's Bay, village (pop. 51), New Zealand, southernmost settlement on W coast of S.Isl., 150 mi. SW of Hokitika, on SW shore of Jackson's Bay (13 mi. wide); tourist center.

Jackson Springs, town (pop. 246), Moore co., central N.C., 13 mi. WNW of Southern Pines.

Jacksonville. 1 City (pop. 4,751), Calhoun co., E Ala., 12 mi. NNE of Anniston, in cotton and dairying area; cotton fabrics, yarn, lumber. State teachers col. here. Fort McClellan near by. **2** City (pop. 2,474), Pulaski co., central Ark., 13 mi. NE of Little Rock, in farm area (corn, cotton, truck, fruit, livestock; dairy products). Mfg. (lumber, furniture, concrete vaults, metal cabinets, electric motors, chemicals). Inc. as city 1941. **3** City (pop. 204,517), ⊙ Duval co., NE Fla., 2d largest city in state, with a deepwater port on St. Johns R. (bridged here) near its mouth on the Atlantic; one of chief Southern commercial centers on Atlantic coast, with extensive rail, air, and highway connections; port of entry; popular year-round tourist resort; site of large naval air training station (established 1940). City has many wood and metal-processing industries, producing lumber, furniture, boxes, millwork, creosoted woods, naval stores, paper, and iron and steel products (machinery, pipes, castings); also manufactures cigars, concrete blocks, glassware, fertilizers, feeds, and meat products. Boatbuilding, fishing, and citrus-fruit canning and packing are carried on. Exports include lumber, naval stores, fruit, crushed oyster shells, and machinery. The Spanish built Fort St. Nicholas on site in 1740. Lewis Hogan settled here in 1816. In 1822 the city was laid out and named for Andrew Jackson, and was inc. in 1832; it annexed South Jacksonville in 1932. City's growth was halted by the Seminole War, and by the Civil War, during which city was occupied several times by Union troops, and the greater part of it destroyed. The construction of a good harbor and railroads in late-19th cent. stimulated development. Large section of city destroyed by fire in 1901; rebuilding followed. Places of interest: public library, municipal docks and yards, Hemming Park with Confederate monument, war-memorial fountain, and Oriental Gardens. **4** City (pop. 20,387), ⊙ Morgan co., W central Ill., 31 mi. W of Springfield; rail and trade center in agr. area (corn, grain; dairy products; livestock); meat packing; mfg. of clothing, steel products, shoes, wire novelties, cigars. Seat of Illinois Col., MacMurray Col., state schools for deaf and blind, state hosp. for the insane. One of state's oldest cities; laid out 1825, inc. 1840. Was a station of the Underground Railroad. Lincoln was well known here; Stephen A. Douglas and William Jennings Bryan were residents. **5** Town (pop. 177), Randolph co., N central Mo., 11 mi. N of Moberly. **6** Resort town (pop. 3,960), ⊙ Onslow co., E N.C., on New R. and 36 mi. S of Kinston; fishing, sawmilling. U.S. Camp Lejeune (Marine base) is 10 mi. SE. **7** Village (pop. 657), Athens co., SE Ohio, 9 mi. N of Athens, and on small Sunday Creek, in coal-mining area. **8** City (pop. 1,193), Jackson co., SW Oregon, 5 mi. WSW of Medford. **9** Borough (pop. 204), Indiana co., SW central Pa., 9 mi. SW of Indiana. **10** City (pop. 8,607), Cherokee co., E Texas, 27 mi. S of Tyler; tomato-shipping center, in rich truck-farming region; canneries, lumber mills, mfg. of bus bodies, clothing, beverages; nurseries. Has 2 jr. colleges. A state park is N. Founded near by 1847; moved to present site 1872. **11** Village, Windham co., Vt.: see WHITINGHAM.

Jacksonville Beach, city (pop. 6,430), Duval co., NE Fla., 17 mi. ESE of Jacksonville, on the Atlantic; resort with concrete industry. Inc. 1907.

Jacktown, town, Sinoe co., SE Liberia, on Sinoe R. and 14 mi. NNE of Greenville; citrus fruit, palm oil and kernels, cacao, coffee.

Jack Wade, village (1939 pop. 21), E Alaska, near Yukon border, 65 mi. W of Dawson; gold placers.

Jacmel (zhäkmĕl'), coast town (1950 census pop. 8,545), Ouest dept., S Haiti, port on the Caribbean, at base of Tiburon Peninsula, 24 mi. SW of Port-au-Prince; commercial center, shipping bananas, coffee, and other products of fertile region (cottonseed, cacao, orange peel, beeswax, honey, precious timber, dyewood). Vessels anchor offshore. Airfield. Manganese deposits near by.

Jaco (yä'kōō), uninhabited island (□ 5) off E tip of Timor, belonging to Portuguese Timor, in Timor Sea; 8°26'S 127°20'E. Also spelled Yako, and called Nusa Besi.

Jacobabad (jā'kŭbäbäd"), town (pop. 21,588), ⊙ Upper Sind Frontier dist., N Sind, W Pakistan, 255 mi. NNE of Karachi; rail junction; trade center (grain, ghee, leather goods); markets millet, rice, wheat; rice milling, handicrafts (carpets, saddlery, palm mats). Founded 1847 by Gen. John Jacob; frontier post before Br. occupation of Quetta. Noted for intense summer heat (known to reach 127°F. in June).

Jacobi Island, Alaska: see YAKOBI ISLAND.

Jacobina (zhŏŏkōōbē'nŭ), city (pop. 4,389), NE central Bahia, Brazil, near head of Itapicuru R., on railroad and 55 mi. SSW of Senhor do Bonfim; old gold-mining and -washing center. Manganese mines in Serra da Jacobina (NW). Aquamarines and amethysts found in area. City ships cattle and caroa fibers.

Jacob Riis Park (rēs), SE N.Y., a municipal park of New York city, on Rockaway Peninsula in S Queens borough; ocean bathing; recreational facilities. Marine Parkway bridge across Rockaway Inlet is here.

Jacobshagen, Poland: see DOBRZANY.

Jacobs Pillow, Mass.: see LEE.

Jacobus (jŭkō'bŭs), borough (pop. 706), York co., S Pa., 6 mi. SSE of York.

Jacomino (häkōmē'nō), town (pop. 6,121), Havana prov., W Cuba, 3 mi. SE of Havana; trading, dairying, lumbering center; mfg. of tiles.

Jacona (häkō'nä), town (pop. 5,750), Michoacán, central Mexico, on central plateau, 2 mi. SSW of Zamora; agr. center (cereals, sugar cane, fruit, stock).

Jacque Peak (jăk) (13,205 ft.), in Rocky Mts., Summit co., NW central Colo. Also known as Eagle River Peak.

Jacques Cartier (zhäk kärtyā'), former co. of SW Que., inc. in MONTREAL ISLAND co.

Jacques Cartier, Mount, or **Tabletop,** peak (4,160 ft.), E Que., on N side of Gaspé Peninsula, 70 mi. W of Gaspé; 48°59'N 65°57'W; highest peak of Shickshock Mts., in Gaspesian Provincial Park.

Jacuhy, city, Brazil: see SOBRADINHO.

Jacuhy River, Brazil: see JACUÍ RIVER.

Jacuí, city, Brazil: see SOBRADINHO.

Jacuí River (zhŏŏkwē'), central Rio Grande do Sul, Brazil, rises in the Serra Geral NE of Cruz Alta, flows 280 mi. S and E, past Cachoeira do Sul and Rio Pardo, through São Jerônimo coal basin, to Pôrto Alegre, where it is joined by 3 short streams (Caí, Sinos, Gravataí) to form the Guaíba, a shallow, widening estuary at N end of the Lagoa dos Patos. Navigable for river steamers beyond Cachoeira do Sul; used for coal shipments to seaports. Receives the Taquari (left). Its valley, settled by German immigrants after 1824, is a rich agr. dist. Rice is grown in flood plain. Formerly spelled Jacuhy.

Jacumba (hŏŏkŭm'bŭ), resort village (pop. c.500), San Diego co., S Calif., at Mexico border, c.55 mi. ESE of San Diego; hot springs. Carrizo Gorge is near by.

Jacupiranga (zhŏŏkōōpērăng'gŭ), city (pop. 823), S São Paulo, Brazil, in the Ribeira de Iguape valley, 27 mi. W of Iguape; apatite mined here for Santo André superphosphate plant.

Jacura (häkōō'rä), town (pop. 505), Falcón state, NW Venezuela, 40 mi. NW of Tucacas; corn, yucca, fruit.

Jacutinga (zhŏŏkōōtēng'gŭ), city (pop. 3,358), SW Minas Gerais, Brazil, near São Paulo border, on railroad and 35 mi. S of Poços de Caldas; coffee-growing center. Mica deposits.

Jadacaquiva (hädäkäkē'vä), town (pop. 699), Falcón state, NW Venezuela, on Paraguaná Peninsula, 13 mi. WSW of Pueblo Nuevo; goat grazing.

Jadar or **Yadar** (both: yä'där), county (pop. 59,818), W Serbia, Yugoslavia; ⊙ LOZNICA. Drained by Jadar R. (right affluent of the Drina).

Jadar River or **Yadar River,** E Bosnia, Yugoslavia, rises at W foot of Krk mtn., flows c.40 mi. NW and N to Drinjaca R. 7 mi. S of Zvornik. Another Jadar R., in W Serbia, is a right affluent of Drina R.

Jade (yä'dŭ), village (commune pop. 7,422), in Oldenburg, NW Germany, after 1945 in Lower Saxony, 6 mi. SE of Varel, in peat region.

Jade Bay (yä'dŭ), Ger. *Jadebusen* (yä"dŭbōō'zŭn), North Sea inlet in Oldenburg, NW Germany; 10 mi. long, 10 mi. wide. Formed by floods (1218, 1511). Receives small Jade R. Wilhelmshaven is near its mouth (W).

Jadidah, Al-, Egypt: see GIDIDA, EL.

Jadita, Lebanon: see JEDITA.

Jadotville (zhädōvēl'), city (1948 pop. 34,570), ⊙ Lualaba dist. (□ 46,796; 1948 pop. c.278,000), Katanga prov., SE Belgian Congo, 65 mi. NW of Elisabethville; leading center of copper and cobalt industry in Belgian Congo; railroad junction with large workshops. Processes copper, zinc, and cadmium ores; has major chemical works (sulphuric acid, hydrogen chloride, sodium chlorate, caustic soda, glycerin, reagents for copper industry, disinfectants). Industries are concentrated in the 2 suburbs of Panda (just SSW) and Shituru (8 mi. ESE). There are Benedictine and Methodist missions; hospitals and schools for Europeans and natives, including a junior college. Geological mus. Food-staple farms and tobacco plantations near by.

Jadraque (hädhrä'kā), town (pop. 1,553), Guadalajara prov., central Spain, on Henares R., on railroad and 24 mi. NNE of Guadalajara, in horticultural region; also cereals, grapes, fruit, livestock. Gypsum quarrying; plaster mfg. Has ruins of old castle.

Jadra River, Swedish *Jädraån* (yĕd'räōn"), E Sweden, rises SW of Bollnas, flows 50 mi. generally SE to Stor L. at Sandviken.

Jaederen, Norway: see JAEREN.

Jaegerspris (yā'yŭrsprēs), town (pop. 1,106), Frederiksborg amt, Zealand, Denmark, 13 mi. SW of Hillerod; orchards.

Jaegervasstind, Norway: see LYNGEN FJORD.

Ja-ela (jŭä'lŭ), town (pop. 3,082), Western Prov., Ceylon, 10 mi. NNE of Colombo; mat weaving; coconuts, rice, cinnamon. Also written Jaela.

Jaén (häān'), city (pop. 555), ⊙ Jaén prov. (□ 3,920; enumerated pop. 24,666, plus estimated 30,000 Indians), Cajamarca dept., NW Peru, in Cordillera Occidental, 100 mi. N of Cajamarca; 5°21'S 78°28'W; alt. 2,428 ft. Agr. products (wheat, cacao, coffee, sugar cane, tobacco); cattle raising.

Jaen, town (1939 pop. 2,211; 1948 municipality pop. 14,516), Nueva Ecija prov., Philippines, on Pampanga R. and 11 mi. SSW of Cabanatuan; agr. center (rice, corn).

Jaén, province (□ 5,209; pop. 753,308), S Spain, in NE Andalusia; ⊙ Jaén. Bounded N by the Sierra Morena; crossed by several mtn. ranges; includes plain in central and NW section. Drained by Guadalquivir R. and its tributaries and by the Segura, which rises here. Climate almost temperate (though hot in summer), with sufficient rainfall. Has some dams and hydroelectric-power plants. Lead mines in the Sierra Morena (Linares, La Carolina, Santa Elena dists.) among richest in Europe; also some iron and copper. Lead widely exported. Gypsum, limestone, and marble quarries; some saltworks; mineral springs. Stock raising (including fine breeds of horses); lumbering in mtn. areas. Besides mining, agr. is chief resource; Jaén is 1st prov. in Spain for olive-oil production (⅓ of total). Broad Guadalquivir valley has hills covered with olive groves, vineyards, and fruit orchards, and fertile plains yielding large crops of cereals. Produces also esparto, vegetables, some potatoes, and tobacco. Except for mining and metalworking (Linares, La Carolina), industries are mostly derived from agr.: olive oil and esparto processing, brandy and liqueur distilling, flour- and sawmilling, tanning. Makes also soap, pottery, footwear, furniture, some chemicals. Chief cities: Jaén, Linares, Úbeda, Andújar, Baeza.

Jaén, city (pop. 48,003), ⊙ Jaén prov., S Spain, in Andalusia, picturesquely situated in hilly dist., 185 mi. S of Madrid, 40 mi. N of Granada; 37°46'N 3°47'W. Agr. trade center (olive oil); chemical works (iron oxide, fertilizers, essential oils), brandy and liqueur distilleries, brewery, tannery. Other mfg.: colored tiles, hemp rope, furniture, hats, flour products, chocolate. Limestone and gypsum quarries near by. Episcopal see since 13th cent. Has narrow, irregular streets, and remains of Moorish walls and citadel. Imposing Renaissance cathedral (16th-18th cent.), flanked by tall towers, on site of anc. mosque. Also notable are 17th-cent. town hall, episcopal palace, seminary, and some fine mansions. Founded by Romans; conquered by Moors (8th cent.), under whom it was (11th cent.) ⊙ small principality; liberated 1246 by Ferdinand III of Castile. King Ferdinand IV died (1312) here. Briefly held (1808) by French. In last civil war, city remained in Loyalist hands till March, 1939.

Jaeren (yăr'ŭn), lowland region in Rogaland co., SW Norway, extending from Egersund c.25 mi. N along North Sea and c.10 mi. inland. Unlike the rest of Norwegian coast, it is unprotected by offshore isls. Partly covered with lakes, woods, and moors, it has good soil and is Norway's best agr. area. Exports food and dairy products via Sandnes and Stavanger. Formerly spelled Jaederen.

Jafarabad (jä"fŭräbäd'), town (pop. 6,319), S Saurashtra, India, port on Gulf of Cambay, on Kathiawar peninsula, 75 mi. SE of Junagarh; trades in timber, ghee, oilseeds; fishing (chiefly Bombay duck) off coast. Lighthouse (SE). Founded c.1575. Was ⊙ former princely state of Jafarabad (□ 53; pop. 13,837) of Western India States agency; state merged 1948 with Saurashtra. Also Jafrabad.

Ja'fariyah, Al-, Egypt: see GA'FARIYA, EL.

Jaffa (jă'fŭ, yä'fä), anc. *Joppa* or *Japho*, town (1946 pop. estimate 101,580), W Israel, in Plain of Sharon, on Mediterranean, just S of TEL AVIV, into which it was inc. in 1950. Largely evacuated (1948) by Arab pop. New industries include mfg. of radio receivers. Has Casa Nova Hospice (1654) and several mosques and Christian churches. Port, formerly citrus-export center, is now of little importance. Mentioned in anc. Egyptian records, and in Old Testament in connection with Jonah; in New Testament connected with story of Peter. Disputed by Maccabees and Syrians, and subject to repeated foreign conquests, Jaffa was destroyed (A.D. 68) by Vespasian. Early Christian episcopal see; during Crusades twice captured (1191) by Richard Coeur de Lion. Destroyed (1345) by Mohammedans. Later became chief port for pilgrims to Jerusalem. Captured (1799) by Napoleon, by British (1917), and by Israelis (1948).

Jaffa, village (pop. 4,872, with near-by Schoolfield), Pittsylvania co., S Va., 2 mi. WSW of Danville.

Jaffa, Cape (jă'fŭ), SE South Australia, in Indian Ocean, at SW end of Lacepede Bay; 36°57'S 139°40'E.

Jaffna (jăf'nŭ), town (pop. 62,922), ⊙ Northern Prov. and Jaffna dist. (□ 1,265; pop. 424,634), Ceylon, on SW Jaffna Peninsula, on Jaffna Lagoon, 190 mi. N of Colombo. Road and trade (grain, tobacco, coconut, chili, mangoes, pan, yams) center; small port (trades with India and Burma); chank, bêche-de-mer, and turtle fishing. Several colleges; meteorological observatory. Well-preserved Du. fort (built 1680) contains oldest Du. church (1706) in

Ceylon. Major saltern of Jaffna Peninsula 2 mi. E, at Chiviyateru. Town captured by Portuguese in 1617; last Port. stronghold in Ceylon when taken (1658) by Dutch; occupied by English in 1795. Original *Dalada* [=tooth of Buddha], believed brought to Jaffna from Kandy for protection, taken from here by Portuguese, and destroyed at Goa in 1560. Also called Jaffnapatam.

Jaffna Lagoon, bet. Jaffna Peninsula (N) and Ceylon proper (S); c.50 mi. long, 10 mi. wide; separated from Palk Strait (NW) by Mandaitivu, Velanai, and Karaitivu isls. Chank and bêche-de-mer fishing. Large govt. saltern near Elephant Pass. Jaffna and Chavakachcheri are on N shore.

Jaffna Peninsula, northernmost part of Ceylon; separated from India by Palk Strait, from Ceylon proper by Jaffna Lagoon; c.55 mi. long, up to 15 mi. wide. Composed of extensive Miocene limestone beds with intensively-cultivated red (tobacco main cash crop) and grey (rice, chili, yams, pan) soils; extensive coconut- and palmyra-palm plantations. Except for Colombo area, the most thickly populated (Jaffna Tamils form 90% of pop.) section of Ceylon. Main towns: Jaffna, Kankesanturai, Chavakachcheri, Point Pedro. Rail and road connection with Ceylon via Elephant Pass. Karaitivu, Velanai, Mandaitivu, Punkudutivu, and Delft isls. lie off SW shore. Annual rainfall, 25–50 in.

Jaffrey, town (pop. 2,911), Cheshire co., SW N.H., on the Contoocook and 15 mi. SE of Keene; includes Jaffrey village (resort), EAST JAFFREY, and Mt. MONADNOCK. Mfg. (boxes, wood products, nails, matches). Winter sports. Settled c.1758, inc. 1773.

Jafr, El, or Al-Jafr (both: ĕl-jä'fûr), village, E Jordan, in desert area 25 mi. ENE of Ma'an; police post; sheep, goat raising.

Jafura or **Jafurah** (jăfōō'rü), sandy desert, N outlier of the Rub' al Khali, Saudi Arabia, W of Qatar peninsula.

Jagadalpur, India: see JAGDALPUR.

Jagadhri (jŭgä'drē), town (pop. 16,422), Ambala dist., E Punjab, India, 34 mi. SE of Ambala; trade center for grain, cotton, timber, borax, sugar cane; paper milling, cotton ginning, chemical mfg., handicraft cloth weaving and dyeing; copper, brass utensils. Village of Sugh, 4 mi. SE, has ruins of 7th-cent. Buddhist and Brahman seat of learning.

Jagadishpur, India: see JAGDISPUR.

Jagalur (jō'gŭlōōr), town (pop. 2,888), Chitaldrug dist., N Mysore, India, 20 mi. N of Chitaldrug; cattle grazing in near-by scrub forests.

Jagannath, India: see PURI, town.

Jagannathapuram, India: see COCANADA.

Jagannathganj, E Pakistan: see JAMALPUR.

Jagdalak (jŭg'dŭlŭk) or **Jigdalik** (jĭg'dŭlĭk), village, Eastern Prov., Afghanistan, 40 mi. W of Jalalabad and on highway to Kabul; ruby mining. Silk mill.

Jagdalpur (jŭg'dŭlpŏŏr), town (pop. 11,304), ⊙ Bastar dist., SE Madhya Pradesh, India, on Indravati R. and 155 mi. S of Raipur; rice, millet, oilseeds. Surrounded by dense forests (sal, bamboo, myrobalan). Was ⊙ former princely state of Bastar, one of Chhattisgarh States; state ⊙ moved here from Bastar village, 11 mi. NW, in 18th cent. Sometimes spelled Jagadalpur; sometimes called Bastar.

Jagdispur or **Jagdishpur** (both: jŭgdēs'pŏŏr), town (pop. 10,658), Shahabad dist., W Bihar, India, on Son Canals branch and 16 mi. WSW of Arrah; sugar-processing center; rice, gram, wheat, oilseeds, barley, corn.

Jägerndorf, Czechoslovakia: see KRNOV.

Jagersfontein (yä'khŭrsfôntān"), town (pop. 1,905), SW Orange Free State, U. of So. Afr., 70 mi. SW of Bloemfontein; alt. 4,618 ft.; diamond-mining center; gold deposits near by. Airfield. First diamond discovered here 1878; mines closed 1932; reopened 1949.

Jagersfontein Road, U. of So. Afr.: see TROMPSBURG.

Jaggayyapeta (jŭgī'yŭpĕtŭ), town (pop. 10,037), Kistna dist., NE Madras, India, on left tributary of Kistna R. and 40 mi. NW of Bezwada; cotton ginning, hand-loom silk weaving; rice, peanuts. Has Buddhist stupa. Bamboo, myrobalan in near-by forests. Also spelled Jaggayapet or Jaggiahpet.

Jaghatai or **Jaghatay** (jägätī'), village, Ninth Prov., in Khurasan, NE Iran, 45 mi. NW of Sabzawar, at N foot of short Jaghatai range; grain, silk. Copper deposits near by.

Jaghatu River, Iran: see ZARINEH RIVER.

Jaghbub, Cyrenaica: see JARABUB.

Jagnair (jŭgnīr'), town (pop. 3,648), Agra dist., W Uttar Pradesh, India, 33 mi. SW of Agra; pearl millet, gram, wheat, barley, oilseeds. Also spelled Jagner.

Jagner, India: see JAGNAIR.

Jagniatkow, Poland: see AGNETENDORF.

Jagodina, Yugoslavia: see SVETOZAREVO.

Jagraon (jŭg'roun), town (pop. 26,704), Ludhiana dist., central Punjab, India, 24 mi. WSW of Ludhiana; trades in wheat, gram, sugar cane, horses; hand-loom woolen weaving, cotton ginning, ivory carving; metalware.

Jagstfeld, Germany: see BAD FRIEDRICHSHALL.

Jagsthausen (yäkst"hou'zün), village (pop. 961), N Württemberg, Germany, after 1945 in Württemberg-Baden, on the Jagst and 16 mi. NE of Heilbronn; wine. Has castle, supposedly birthplace of Götz von Berlichingen. Small collection of local relics includes iron hand of the hero.

Jagst River (yäkst), S Germany, rises 8 mi. E of Ellwangen, meanders generally N and W, past Crailsheim, to the canalized Neckar at Bad Friedrichshall. Length, over 100 mi.

Jagtial (jŭg'tyŭl), town (pop. 16,294), Karimnagar dist., NE central Hyderabad state, India, 29 mi. NNW of Karimnagar; millet, rice, oilseeds, cotton. Near-by forests supply bamboo pulp to Sirpur paper mill.

Jaguaquara (zhŏŏgŏŏkwä'rŏŏ), city (pop. 2,980), E Bahia, Brazil, on railroad and 20 mi. NNE of Jiquiê; coffee, tobacco, livestock.

Jaguarão (zhŏŏgwŭrā'ō), city (pop. 10,660), S Rio Grande do Sul, Brazil, on Jaguarão R. (Uruguay border; international bridge), opposite Río Branco, on railroad and 75 mi. SW of Pelotas; stock-raising and -shipping center; trades in cereals, wool, wine. Airfield; custom station.

Jaguarão River, Sp. *Yaguarón*, rises in Brazil in S Rio Grande do Sul E of Bagé, flows 135 mi. SE to Mirim L., forming (through most of its course) Brazil-Uruguay border. Crossed by international road and railroad bridge bet. Jaguarão (Brazil) and Río Branco (Uruguay).

Jaguarari (zhŏŏgwŭrŭrē'), city (pop. 1,561), N Bahia, Brazil, on railroad to Juàzeiro and 13 mi. N of Senhor do Bonfim; sugar cane, cotton, tobacco; rose-quartz and kaolin deposits. Formerly spelled Jaguarary.

Jaguari (zhŏŏgwŭrē'). **1** City (pop. 3,226), W central Rio Grande do Sul, Brazil, on railroad and 55 mi. WNW of Santa Maria; cattle raising. Formerly spelled Jaguary. **2** Town, São Paulo, Brazil: see JAGUARIÚNA.

Jaguariaíva (zhŏŏgwŭrē"äē'vŭ), city (pop. 3,516), E Paraná, Brazil, 85 mi. NNW of Curitiba; rail junction; important meat-packing center (hogs); mfg. of dairy products, paper, tannin; corn and rice milling. Airfield. Old spelling, Jaguariahyva.

Jaguaribe (zhŏŏgwŭrē'bĭ), city (pop. 1,404), E Ceará, Brazil, on Jaguaribe R. and 60 mi. NE of Iguatu; cotton, sugar, cattle. Formerly called Jaguaribe Mirim.

Jaguaribe River, Ceará, NE Brazil, rises on E slope of Serra Grande near 6°S 41°W, flows E, past Jucás and Iguatu, then NE, past Limoeiro do Norte, to the Atlantic 12 mi. below Aracati (head of navigation). Length, c.350 mi. Irregular volume. Several irrigation dams projected or under construction, notably at Orós and Cariús. Cotton grown in valley.

Jaguaripe (–pĭ), city (pop. 1,149), E Bahia, Brazil, on inlet of the Atlantic, 8 mi. SE of Nazaré; ceramics; ships lumber, piassava, sea shells.

Jaguariúna (zhŏŏgwŭryōō'nŭ), town (pop. 1,210), E São Paulo, Brazil, 15 mi. N of Campinas; rail junction; coffee. Until 1944, called Jaguari.

Jaguaruana (zhŏŏgwŭrwä'nŭ), city (pop. 2,163), NE Ceará, Brazil, on left bank of lower Jaguaribe R. and 20 mi. S of Aracati; cotton, carnauba wax. Until 1944, called União.

Jaguaruna (zhŏŏgwŭrōō'nŭ), city (pop. 1,130), SE Santa Catarina, Brazil, near the Atlantic, on railroad and 18 mi. SW of Laguna; lumbering.

Jaguary, Brazil: see JAGUARI, Rio Grande do Sul.

Jagüel, Sierra de (syĕ'rä dā hägwĕl'), subandean mountain range in NW La Rioja prov., Argentina, N of Vinchina; extends c.30 mi. SSW from Catamarca prov. border; rises to c.10,000 ft. Sometimes called Sierra de Vinchina.

Jagüey Grande (hägwā'grän'dā), town (pop. 4,374), Matanzas prov., W Cuba, on railroad and 45 mi. SE of Matanzas; agr. center (sugar cane, honey, poultry, cattle); lumbering and charcoal burning. The Australia sugar central is 2 mi. S.

Jaguito, El, Panama: see EL JAGUITO.

Jahanabad (jŭhä'näbäd). **1** Town (pop. 10,842), Gaya dist., W central Bihar, India, on Ganges Plain, on tributary of the Ganges and 30 mi. N of Gaya; road junction; trades in rice, gram, oilseeds, wheat, barley. Saltpeter processing near by. **2** Town, West Bengal, India: see ARAMBAGH.

Jahangirabad (jŭhäng-gē'räbäd), town (pop. 12,922), Bulandshahr dist., W Uttar Pradesh, India, 14 mi. E of Bulandshahr; hand-loom weaving; trades in wheat, oilseeds, barley, jowar, sugar cane. Founded 16th cent.

Jahazpur (jŭhäz'pŏŏr), town (pop. 4,253), S central Rajasthan, India, 12 mi. SSW of Deoli; millet, wheat, oilseeds.

Jahnsdorf (yäns'dôrf), village (pop. 4,377), Saxony, E central Germany, at N foot of the Erzgebirge, 7 mi. SSW of Chemnitz; hosiery knitting.

Jahorina or **Yakhorina** (both: yä'khôrēnä), mountain in Dinaric Alps, SE Bosnia, Yugoslavia; extends c.10 mi. NW-SE. Highest point (6,284 ft.) is 12 mi. SSE of Sarajevo.

Jahra or **Al-Jahrah** (ăljärä'), village (pop. 1,000), Kuwait, 20 mi. W of Kuwait town; irrigated agr. center; wheat, barley, lucerne, dates, melons.

Jahrom, Iran: see JAHRUM.

Jahrum or **Jahrom** (both: järōm'), town (1940 pop. 23,390), Seventh Prov., in Fars, S Iran, 100 mi. SE of Shiraz; dates, tobacco, grain, opium, cotton.

Jahú, Brazil: see JAÚ.

Jahuel (häwĕl'), village (1930 pop. 311), Aconcagua prov., central Chile, mtn. resort in Andean foothills, 10 mi. NE of San Felipe; alt. 3,900 ft. Has noted thermal springs and mineral waters. Sometimes Baños de Jahuel or Termas de Jahuel.

Jahwarian, W Pakistan: see JHAWARIAN.

Jaicós (zhīkôs'), city (pop. 1,163), E central Piauí, Brazil, 65 mi. SE of Oeiras; carnauba wax, maniçoba rubber, hides. Airfield.

Jaihun River, Central Asia: see AMU DARYA.

Jailolo, town and island, Indonesia: see HALMAHERA.

Jailolo Passage or **Djailolo Passage** (both: jīlō'lō), channel (c.100 mi. wide) connecting Ceram Sea with the Pacific, bet. Halmahera (W) and Raja Ampat Isls. (E); contains numerous islets.

Jaime Prats (hī'mā präts'), village (pop. estimate 500), SE central Mendoza prov., Argentina, near Atuel R. (irrigation), 36 mi. SE of San Rafael. Rail terminus; agr. center (wine, alfalfa, grain, livestock; apiculture); mfg. of tomato extracts. Formerly Atuel Sud.

Jainad, Thailand: see CHAINAT.

Jainagar, India: see JAYNAGAR, Bihar.

Jainpur, India: see JIANPUR.

Jainti, India: see RAJABHAT KHAWA.

Jaintia Hills (jīnt'yŭ), range, W Assam, India, forming part of W Assam Range, bet. Brahmaputra valley (N) and Shillong Plateau (S) which separates them from Khasi Hills; c.130 mi. long E-W; rise to c.4,430 ft.

Jaipur (jī'pŏŏr), former princely state (□ 15,610; pop. 3,040,876) in Rajputana States, India; ⊙ was Jaipur. Established in 12th cent. by Kachwaha Rajputs who made their ⊙ at Amber (country also known as Amber). Recognized Mogul supremacy in 16th and 17th cent. Jaipur city became ⊙ in 1728. Suffered Mahratta invasions in late-18th and early-19th cent.; treaty of alliance concluded with British in 1818. In 1949, joined union of Rajasthan. Sometimes spelled Jeypore.

Jaipur, city (pop. 175,810), ⊙ Rajasthan and Jaipur dist., India, 145 mi. SW of New Delhi. Rail and road junction; airport; important commercial center; trades in grain, wool, cotton, building stone, metal, cloth fabrics, salt; mfg. of carpets, blankets, shoes, drugs, aerated water, pottery, glass, sports equipment; cotton ginning, hand-loom weaving, distilling; engineering and metalworks. Its handicrafts are famous, especially jewelry, enamel and metalwork, printed cloths, marble inlays, and ivory products. Has large banking business. Overlooked by forested hills (N, E), city proper is enclosed by wall with 7 gateways; has wide, regularly laid out streets. Contains maharaja's palace, Univ. of Rajputana (founded 1947) with affiliated arts and technical cols., astronomical observatory, School of Art (handicraft industries), and elaborate Hawa Mahal (Hall of the Winds). Many bldgs. painted a rose-pink. Village of Sanganer, 7 mi. S, has some fine temples. Jaipur was founded in 1728, replacing Amber (5 mi. N) as ⊙ Jaipur state. Sometimes spelled Jeypore.

Jaipurhat (jī'pŏŏrhät), village, Bogra dist., N central East Bengal, E Pakistan, 30 mi. NW of Bogra; rice milling; rice, jute, rape and mustard. Also spelled Joypurhat; also written Jaipur Hat.

Jaipur Residency, India: see RAJPUTANA STATES.

Jais (jīs), town (pop. 8,754), Rae Bareli dist., central Uttar Pradesh, India, 20 mi. W of Rae Bareli; trades in rice, wheat, barley, oilseeds, cotton cloth. Jama Masjid built from remains of Hindu temple.

Jaisalmer (jī'sŭlmär), former princely state (□ 15,980; pop. 93,246) in Rajputana States, India; ⊙ was Jaisalmer. Established in 12th cent. by a Rajput clan; raided in late-13th cent. by Ala-ud-din, king of Delhi; made treaty with British in 1818. In 1949, joined union of Rajasthan.

Jaisalmer, town (pop. 7,340), ⊙ Jaisalmer dist., W Rajasthan, India, on Thar Desert, 200 mi. W of Jaipur; caravan center; trades in wool, hides, camels, sheep, salt, fuller's earth; handicrafts (blankets, saddlery). A walled town, founded in 1156; noted for its bldgs. of yellowish-brown stone and for several Jain temples. Was ⊙ former Rajputana state of Jaisalmer.

Jai Samand, lake, India: see DHEBAR LAKE.

Jaitaran (jītä'rŭn), town (pop. 4,543), central Rajasthan, India, 55 mi. E of Jodhpur; millet.

Jaito or **Jaitu** (jī'tōō), town (pop. 11,435), W Patiala and East Punjab States Union, India, 10 mi. SSE of Kot Kapura; agr. market center (gram, wheat, millet, cotton); hand-loom weaving, oilseed milling. Annual cattle fair.

Jaivergi, India: see JEVARGI.

Jajarkot (jä'jŭrkōt), village, W central Nepal, 22 mi. N of Sallyana. Nepalese military post; castle ruins. Absorbed by Gurkhas in late-18th cent. Also spelled Jajekot.

Jajarm or **Jajorm** (jäjōrm'), town, Ninth Prov., in Khurasan, NE Iran, on road and 60 mi. SW of Bujnurd; grain, gums.

Jajce, Yaitse, or **Yaytse** (all: yī'tsĕ), town (pop. 5,177), W central Bosnia, Yugoslavia, on Vrbas R., on railroad and 30 mi. S of Banja Luka. Hydroelectric plant at c.100-ft.-high waterfall at mouth of Pliva R. (tributary of the Vrbas); electrochemical (calcium carbide, ferrosilicon, caustic soda) and electrometallurgical (ferromanganese, spiegeleisen) industries; lumber works. Ruined 13th-cent. castle (captured by the Turks in 1528) and Franciscan church with tomb of last Bosnian king here; seat of Bosnian kings in early-15th cent. Site of 2d session (1943) of provisional parliament which drafted post-war constitution of Yugoslavia.

Jajja Abbasian (jŭj'jŭ ŭb-bŭs'yŭn), town (pop. 473), Bahawalpur state, W Pakistan, 9 mi. NW of Khanpur, on rail spur.

Jajó (hähō'), town (pop. 791), Trujillo state, W Venezuela, in Andean spur, 17 mi. S of Valera; alt. 5,892 ft.; wheat, corn, potatoes.

Jajome Alto (hähō'mā äl'tō), resort, E central Puerto Rico, in Cordillera Central, 6 mi. NNW of Guayama; governor's summer residence. SE is a replica of the Grotto of Our Lady of Lourdes.

Jajorm, Iran: see JAJARM.

Jajpur (jäj'pōōr), town (pop. 11,188), Cuttack dist., E Orissa, India, on Baitarani R. and 38 mi. NE of Cuttack; Hindu pilgrimage center (annual festival fair); rice growing. Col. Was ⊙ Orissa (A.D. c.500–950) under Hindu dynasty.

Jaj Rud (jäj' rōōd'), river of N Iran, rises in Elburz mts. 25 mi. NNE of Teheran, flows c.80 mi. S, past Latiyan (projected dam), and through Veramin plain, to Namak L. salt flats.

Jak (yäk), Hung. *Ják*, town (pop. 2,533), Vas co., W Hungary, 7 mi. SSW of Szombathely; distilleries, sawmills. Has Romanesque church.

Jakarta or **Djakarta** (jŭkär'tŭ, jäkär'tä), formerly **Batavia** (bŭtā'vēŭ, –vyŭ), city (pop. 533,015), ⊙ INDONESIA, NW Java, on Jakarta Bay (inlet of Java Sea) at mouth of Chiliwong R., 580 mi. SSE of Singapore; 6°10'S 106°50'E. Commercial and industrial center, with its port at near-by TANJUNGPRIOK. The city is divided into 2 sections: the old town (with Javanese, Chinese, and Arab quarters), and a modern residential garden suburb. City is intersected by canals crossed by drawbridges; railroads link Jakarta with Surabaya and other centers. Kemayoran (Kemajoran) airport is 6 mi. SE. There are railroad shops, iron foundries, tanneries, sawmills, textile mills, printing and chemical plants, soap and leather-goods factories, auto-assembly plant. Univ. of Indonesia is here; archaeological and ethnological museums and several late-17th-cent. churches. Has magnetic-meteorological observatory at 6°11'0"S 106°49'50"E. Jan Pieterszoon Coen founded (1619) fort of Batavia adjacent to Indonesian town of Jakarta which was destroyed 1620; rebuilt, the town was called Batavia. Town was hq. of Br. rule (1811–16). In Second World War, it was briefly (in Jan., 1942) hq. of Allied Far East Command. After the war, during Du.-Indonesian strife, it was hq. of U.N. conciliation commission. Cheribon (or Linggajati) Agreement was signed here March, 1947.

Jakatala, India: see WELLINGTON.

Jakhal (jä'kŭl), village, Hissar dist., S Punjab, India, 45 mi. NNE of Hissar; rail junction.

Jakhau (jŭkou'), town (pop. 3,460), SW Cutch, India, near Arabian Sea, 60 mi. W of Bhuj; market center for wheat, fish, barley.

Jakin (jā'kĭn), town (pop. 264), Early co., SW Ga., 7 mi. WNW of Donalsonville, near the Chattahoochee R.

Jakkampatti, India: see ANDIPATTI.

Jakkur, India: see BANGALORE, city.

Jakobsberg (yä'kôpsbĕr"yŭ), residential village (pop. 1,338), Stockholm co., E Sweden, 11 mi. NW of Stockholm city center.

Jakobshavn (yä'kôps-houn"), Eskimo *Ilulissat*, town (pop. 593), ⊙ Jakobshavn dist. (pop. 896), W Greenland, in Disko Bay, at mouth of Jakobshavn Ice Fjord; 69°13'N 51°4'W; fishing port and hunting base; meteorological and radio station, hosp. Founded 1741.

Jakobshavn Ice Fjord, Dan. *Jacobshavns Isfjord*, inlet (25 mi. long, 3–6 mi. wide) of Disko Bay, W Greenland; 69°10'N 50°35'W. At its head it receives large Jakobshavn Glacier, Dan. *Jakobshavns Isbrae*.

Jakobstad (yä'kôpstäd"), Finnish *Pietarsaari* (pē'ĕtärsä"rē), city (pop. 7,836), Vaasa co., W Finland, on Gulf of Bothnia, 50 mi. NE of Vaasa; seaport, shipping tobacco and wood products; rail terminus. Tobacco-processing center, with lumber, pulp, cellulose, and lace mills, machine shops, chicory works. Radio station. Pop. is predominantly Swedish-speaking. Has 13th-cent. church. City founded 1652. Finnish natl. poet, Runeberg, b. here.

Jakobstadt, Latvia: see JEKABPILS.

Jakupica or **Yakupitsa** (both: yä'kōōpētsä), mountain, N Macedonia, Yugoslavia; highest peak (8,331 ft.), Solunska Glava or Mokra, is 20 mi. SSW of Skoplje. Also spelled Jakubica or Yakubitsa.

Jal (jăl), village (pop. 2,047), Lea co., extreme SE N.Mex., on Llano Estacado, near Texas line, 40 mi. S of Hobbs; oil-field supplies. Settled c.1916, inc. 1928. Boomed with discovery of oil (1927) in vicinity.

Jala (hä'lä), town (pop. 2,727), Nayarit, W Mexico, at E foot of Ceboruco volcano, 45 mi. SE of Tepic; corn, beans, sugar cane, fruit, cattle.

Jalacingo (häläsĭng'gō), city (pop. 2,357), Veracruz, E Mexico, in Sierra Madre Oriental, 33 mi. NW of Jalapa; agr. center (corn, sugar cane, coffee, tobacco, fruit).

Jalahalli, India: see BANGALORE, city.

Jalakandapuram (jä'lŭnkŭndŭpōōrŭm") or **Jalakantapuram** (–tŭ–), town (pop. 6,576), Salem dist., S central Madras, India, 20 mi. WNW of Salem; castor beans, peanuts, millet; cotton weaving. Sometimes spelled Jalakandpuram.

Jalalabad (jŭlä'läbäd", jŭlä'lŭbăd"), town (pop. over 20,000), ⊙ Eastern Prov., Afghanistan, 75 mi. E of Kabul and on Kabul R. just above mouth of Kunar R.; alt. 1,950 ft.; 34°26'N 70°27'E. Center of large irrigated plain producing dried fruit, almonds, citrus fruit, grain, and handicraft articles (semiprecious stones, silk goods). Major transit-trade center, handling 50% of Afghanistan's exports and imports, on Kabul-Peshawar route via Khyber Pass. Old walled town contains former royal winter residence (1892) in subtropical garden; it also has large bazaars (E), handicraft shops and modern factories (rice, flour, paper, sugar) in NE, and residential section (NW). Garden suburbs extend outside of walled town. Founded 1570 by the Mogul Akbar, Jalalabad passed to the Afghans in 1834. Defended by British troops in 1841–42 during 1st Afghan War, town was again occupied (1879–80) in 2d Afghan War, when the British built Fort Sale (1 mi. E of city), still used by Afghan troops. Sometimes spelled Jelalabad.

Jalalabad (jŭlä'läbäd). **1** Town (pop. 7,134), Ferozepore dist., W Punjab, India, 31 mi. SW of Ferozepore; wheat, millet, cotton; hand-loom weaving, cattle breeding. **2** Town (pop. 5,947), Muzaffarnagar dist., N Uttar Pradesh, India, 18 mi. NW of Muzaffarnagar; wheat, gram, sugar cane, oilseeds. Ruins of 18th-cent. Afghan fort (S). **3** Town (pop. 7,217), Shahjahanpur dist., central Uttar Pradesh, India, 18 mi. SW of Shahjahanpur; wheat, rice, gram, oilseeds, sugar cane. Founded 13th cent.

Jalali (jŭlä'lē), town (pop. 8,378), Aligarh dist., W Uttar Pradesh, India, 11 mi. E of Aligarh; wheat, barley, gram, corn, pearl millet. Extensive imambarahs.

Jalalpur (jŭläl'pōōr). **1** Village (pop. 5,666), Surat dist., N Bombay, India, on Purna R. and 18 mi. S of Surat; market center for timber, rice, fruit; millet, sugar cane, plantains; salt drying. Also spelled Jalalpore. **2** Town (pop. 2,247), Fyzabad dist., E central Uttar Pradesh, India, on Tons R. and 15 mi. SE of Fyzabad; rice, wheat, gram, sugar cane. Has 18th-cent. imambarah.

Jalalpur, village, Jhelum dist., N Punjab, W Pakistan, near Jhelum R., 25 mi. SW of Jhelum. Identified by some as site from which Alexander the Great crossed the Jhelum to defeat Porus in battle of Hydaspes (326 B.C.), afterwards erecting town of *Bucephala*, in memory of his famous horse. Others place site near town of Jhelum. Also called Jalalpur Kiknan.

Jalalpur Jattan (jŭt'tŭn), town (pop. 16,663), Gujrat dist., NE Punjab, W Pakistan, 8 mi. NE of Gujrat; local market center; wheat, millet, rice; hand-loom weaving, mfg. of tongas, confectioneries. Also called Jalalpur.

Jalalpur Pirwala (pĕr'välŭ), town (pop. 6,269), Multan dist., S Punjab, W Pakistan, 50 mi. SSW of Multan; wheat, millet, oilseeds. Annual festival fair. Sometimes called Jalalpur.

Ja'lan or **Ja'alan** (both: jä'lăn), sandy desert district of E Oman, on landward side of Eastern Hajar hill country and extending to Arabian Sea S of Ras al Hadd.

Jalan Bahru (jŭlän' bä'rōō), village (pop. 740), NW Perak, Malaya, 23 mi. NW of Taiping, in Krian rice dist.

Jalance (hälän'thā), town (pop. 2,315), Valencia prov., E Spain, 22 mi. S of Requena; flour milling, fruit canning, olive-oil processing; esparto.

Jalandhar, India: see JULLUNDUR, district.

Jalangi River (jŭlŭng'gē), E West Bengal, India, a main distributary of Ganges Delta, leaves Padma R. 14 mi. SSE of Rajshahi, flows generally S past Krishnagar, and W, joining Bhagirathi R. at Nabadwip to form Hooghly R.; c.120 mi. long. Main distributary, Jamuna R. (left).

Jalán River (hälän'), E central Honduras, rises NW of Guaimaca, flows SE, past Guaimaca, E, and NE to Guayape R. in Olancho Valley, 4 mi. SE of Juticalpa; length, c.100 mi. Gold placers along upper course.

Jalapa (hälä'pä), department (□ 797; 1950 pop. 74,574), E central Guatemala; ⊙ Jalapa. In E highlands, on continental divide; drained by affluents of Motagua R. (N) and Ostúa R. (inlet of L. Güija; S); includes volcanoes Alzatate and Jumay. Agr. and livestock-raising region; corn, wheat, beans, tobacco, rice; dairying (cheese production); lumbering. Chromite mining (N of Jalapa). Main centers: Jalapa, Jilotepeque.

Jalapa, city (1950 pop. 6,605), ⊙ Jalapa dept., E central Guatemala, in highlands, 36 mi. E of Guatemala; 14°38'N 89°59'W; alt. 4,530 ft. Commercial and road center in agr. and livestock area; corn, beans, wheat, cattle, hogs; dairying. Chromite mines (N).

Jalapa. **1** Town (pop. 1,010), Tabasco, SE Mexico, on affluent of Grijalva R. and 20 mi. SSE of Villahermosa; rice, coffee, beans, fruit. **2** Officially Jalapa Enríquez, city (pop. 39,530), ⊙ Veracruz, E Mexico, at E foot of the Cofre de Perote, in Sierra Madre Oriental, 55 mi. NW of Veracruz, 150 mi. E of Mexico city, on a railroad to the coast; alt. 4,465 ft.; 19°31'N 96°55'W. Rail junction. Health resort. Processing center for rich coffee- and tobacco-growing area producing also sugar cane, citrus fruit, bananas, pineapples. Coffee processing, flour milling, sugar refining, food canning, tanning; mfg. of cotton goods, soap, chocolate, cigars, ceramics. Once important producer of jalap drug. Situated in a beautiful tropical region, with a cool climate. Has cathedral, convent of San Francisco, old churches, govt. palace, state univ.

Jalapa, town (1950 pop. 550), Nueva Segovia dept., NW Nicaragua, at E foot of Sierra de Jalapa, 32 mi. NE of Ocotal; tobacco center; sugar cane, coffee, rice, corn.

Jalapa, Sierra de, Nicaragua and Honduras: see DIPILTO, SIERRA DE.

Jalapahar (jälä'pŭhär), town (pop. 905), Darjeeling dist., N West Bengal, India; S suburb of Darjeeling; highest point, c.7,870 ft. Former Br. cantonment.

Jalapilla, Mexico: see ORIZABA.

Jalaput (jŭlä'pōōt), village, Koraput dist., SW Orissa, India, on Machkund R. and 28 mi. S of Jeypore, near Madras border; site of projected dam and hydroelectric plant.

Jalarpet, India: see TIRUPPATTUR, North Arcot dist.

Jalatlaco (hälätlä'kō), town (pop. 3,199), Mexico state, central Mexico, 25 mi. SW of Mexico city; agr. center (cereals, vegetables, stock); dairying.

Jalaun (jä'loun), district (□ c.1,590; pop. c.482,384), S Uttar Pradesh, India; ⊙ Orai. Bounded NE by the Jumna; irrigated by distributaries of Betwa Canal. Agr. (gram, wheat, mustard, jowar, linseed, pearl millet, sesame); babul plantations near KALPI. Main towns: Kalpi, Kunch, Orai. S area of dist. was formerly part of Br. Bundelkhand. Dist. enlarged 1950 by inc. of several former petty states.

Jalaun, town (pop. 10,375), Jalaun dist., S Uttar Pradesh, India, 12 mi. NW of Orai; trades in gram, wheat, oilseeds, jowar, pearl millet. Was ⊙ 18th-cent. Mahratta state.

Jalca, La, Peru: see LA JALCA.

Jalcomulco (hälkōmōōl'kō), town (pop. 1,112), Veracruz, E Mexico, in Sierra Madre Oriental, 17 mi. SE of Jalapa; corn, coffee, fruit.

Jaldak (jŭl'dŭk), town (pop. over 2,000), Kandahar prov., SE Afghanistan, on Tarnak R. and 60 mi. NE of Kandahar, on highway to Kabul.

Jaldessa (jäldĕ'sä), Ital. *Gildessa*, village (pop. 500), Harar prov., E central Ethiopia, 19 mi. ENE of Diredawa.

Jaldhaka River (jŭlä'kŭ), in N India and E Pakistan, rises in W Assam Himalayas in SE Sikkim, India, 15 mi. E of Gangtok; flows S and SSE, past Matabhanga (West Bengal) and Kurigram (East Bengal) to the Brahmaputra 10 mi. SSE of Kurigram; total length, c.145 mi. Receives Dharla R. (arm of the Torsa) 18 mi. S of Cooch Behar; below this confluence also known as Dharla.

Jalesar (jŭlā'sŭr), town (pop. 12,743), Etah dist., W Uttar Pradesh, India, 22 mi. WSW of Etah; hand-loom cotton weaving, saltpeter processing, mfg. of glass bangles; wheat, pearl millet, barley, corn, oilseeds, cotton. Ruins of 15th-cent. fort.

Jaleswar (jŭlā'svŭr), village, Balasore dist., NE Orissa, India, on Subarnarekha R. and 28 mi. NE of Balasore; rice milling, hand-loom weaving.

Jaleswar, town, SE Nepal, in the Terai, near India border, 35 mi. NNW of Darbhanga (India); trades in rice, corn, wheat, barley, oilseeds, jute.

Jalgaon (jäl'goun). **1** Town (pop. 48,596), ⊙ East Khandesh dist., NE Bombay, India, near Girna R., 225 mi. NE of Bombay; cotton market; trades in millet, linseed, sesame, wheat; cotton ginning and milling, oilseed milling, handicraft cloth weaving, mfg. of ice, buttons. Has col. **2** Town (pop. 10,599), Buldana dist., W Madhya Pradesh, India, 38 mi. NW of Akola; millet, wheat; cotton ginning, oilseed milling.

Jalhay (zhälā'), village (pop. 1,429), Liége prov., E Belgium, 5 mi. ESE of Verviers; agr., lumbering.

Jaligny (zhälēnyē'), village (pop. 333), Allier dept., central France, in Sologne Bourbonnaise, on the Besbre and 9 mi. N of Lapalisse; flour milling, woodworking.

Jalingo (jälĭng'gō), town (pop. 1,803), Adamawa prov., Northern Provinces, E Nigeria, 85 mi. WSW of Yola; cassava, durra, yams; cattle, skins.

Jalisco (hälē'skō), state (□ 31,152; 1940 pop. 1,418,310; 1950 pop. 1,744,700), W and central Mexico; ⊙ GUADALAJARA. Bordering W on the Pacific, it is surrounded by Nayarit (Ameca R.), Zacatecas, and Aguascalientes (N), Guanajuato (E), Colima and Michoacán (S). It has a narrow coastal plain but is otherwise mountainous; traversed NW–SE by the Sierra Madre Occidental, locally sometimes known as Sierra de Nayarit or Sierra de Jalisco. State comprises largely the W part of central plateau (c.6,000 ft.), flanked SW by volcanic peaks, including the Nevado de Colima and Volcán de Colima. Jalisco is intersected by

Santiago R. (lower course of Lerma R.), which issues from L. Chapala; it contains numerous smaller lakes such as the Magdalena and Sayula. Climate varies greatly: hot and humid on the coast, subtropical to temperate on the plateau, cool in the sierras. Uplands are rich in silver, gold, lead, copper, and zinc, mined at Ahualulco, Guachinango, Etzatlán, Hostotipaquillo; mercury near Guzmán. There is a rich and varied agr.: mainly corn, wheat, beans, chick-peas on the plateau; citrus fruit, cotton, sugar cane, sweet potatoes, tobacco in the warmer sections; bananas and forest products (rubber, palm oil, timber) in the tropical W. Stock raising in elevated regions. Rural industries: lumbering, mining, flour milling, cotton ginning, sugar refining, native handicrafts (pottery), tequila distilling. Guadalajara is a major mfg. center. L. Chapala, largest in Mexico, is a noted tourist dist. The region, long a stronghold of Indian resistance, was conquered (1529) by Nuño de Guzmán and later included in Nueva Galicia. It played an important part in the independence movement. Temporarily occupied by the French invaders, it was liberated 1866. Nayarit formed a part of the state until 1884.

Jalisco, town (pop. 2,105), Nayarit, W Mexico, near Pacific coast, 4 mi. SSW of Tepic; alt. 3,340 ft. Agr. center (corn, beans, sugar cane, coffee, bananas, cattle). Has federal school. Old Aztec town.

Jallieu (zhälyû'), town (pop. 4,398), Isère dept., SE France, adjoining BOURGOIN (S), on the Bourbre and 25 mi. SE of Lyons; textile printing, silk milling, carton mfg.

Jallo (jŭl'lō), village, Lahore dist., E Punjab, W Pakistan, 9 mi. E of Lahore; mfg. of footwear, rosin, turpentine. Dairy farm (S).

Jalna (jäl'nŭ), town (pop., including NE suburb of Kadirabad, 38,096), Aurangabad dist., NW Hyderabad state, India, 37 mi. E of Aurangabad; road junction; agr. trade center (chiefly cotton, millet, wheat, peanuts); cotton and oilseed milling, biri mfg. Kadirabad suburb is sometimes spelled Qadirabad or Khadirabad.

Jalo, Cyrenaica: see GIALO.

Jalón (hälōn'), town (pop. 1,978), Alicante prov., E Spain, 26 mi. ENE of Alcoy; olive-oil processing; raisins, wine, almonds.

Jalón River, in Soria and Saragossa provs., NE central Spain, rises at NE edge of the central plateau 6 mi. S of Medinaceli, flows 145 mi. generally NE, past Calatayud, to the Ebro 2 mi. W of Alagón. Used for irrigation and hydroelectric power. Olive groves and vineyards along its course.

Jalor (jä'lōr), town (pop. 7,967), ⊙ Jalor dist., SW central Rajasthan, India, 70 mi. SSW of Jodhpur; local market for cotton, millet, oilseeds, wheat; handicrafts (cloth fabrics, saddlery, metal vessels). Noted hill fort (S) dates from c.11th cent.; a medieval Rajput stronghold. Sometimes spelled Jhalore.

Jalostotitlán (hälōstōtētlän'), town (pop. 6,467), Jalisco, central Mexico, on interior plateau, 65 mi. NE of Guadalajara; alt. 5,500 ft.; agr. center (corn, wheat, beans, chick-peas, stock).

Jalovec (yä'lôvěts), Ital. *Glalluz* (glāl-lōōts'), peak (8,671 ft.) in Julian Alps, NW Slovenia, Yugoslavia, 8 mi. WNW of Triglav peak. On Yugoslav-Ital. border until 1947.

Jalpa (häl'pä), town (pop. 3,085), Zacatecas, N central Mexico, on Juchipila R. and 27 mi. SE of Tlaltenango; alt. 5,900 ft.; agr. center (grain, beans, sugar cane, stock).

Jalpa de Méndez (dā měn'děs), town (pop. 2,906), Tabasco, SE Mexico, on arm of Grijalva R. and 17 mi. NW of Villahermosa; corn, rice, beans, tobacco, fruit, stock.

Jalpaiguri (jŭlpī'gōōrē), district (□ c.2,600; pop. c.1,150,000), N West Bengal, India; ⊙ Jalpaiguri. Bounded N by Bhutan, E by Assam, S by Cooch Behar dist. and East Bengal (E Pakistan), W by Bihar; drained by upper Atrai, Tista, Jaldhaka, and Torsa rivers. Alluvial soil; rice, tea, tobacco (major tea- and tobacco-growing dist. of West Bengal), rape and mustard, jute, sugar cane, potatoes, tamarind. Spurs of W Assam Himalayan foothills in NE; extensive sal, sissoo, and khair tracts. WESTERN DUARS in E; sal, sissoo, and bamboo tracts. Minerals include coal deposits near Bagrakot, copper-ore deposits (Buxa Duar, Matiali); limestone quarries near Bhutan border. Rice milling, sawmilling, tea processing; rail workshops at Domohani. Noted for wild game (elephants, tigers, rhinoceroses, buffaloes). Part of anc. Kamarupa and Buddhist Pal kingdom. Ruins of city of Bhitargarh (built c.9th cent. A.D.) in S. Under 16th-cent. Koch kingdom (absorbed 1639 into Mogul empire); passed to English in 1765. Original dist. (□ 3,050; pop. 1,089,513) was reduced 1947 by transfer of SW portion into Dinajpur dist. of East Bengal, following creation of Pakistan. Pop. 50% Hindu, 23% Moslem, 25% tribal (including Mech, Mangar, Kami, Newar).

Jalpaiguri, town (pop. 27,766), ⊙ Jalpaiguri dist., N West Bengal, India, on Tista R. and 50 mi. SE of Darjeeling; trade center (rice, tea, rape and mustard, tobacco, jute, potatoes, tamarind); jute pressing, sawmilling, match mfg. Has col. Railroad workshops 4 mi. NNE, across river, at Domohani. Early-17th-cent. Sivaite temple 9 mi. E, at Jalpes.

Jalpan (häl'pän). **1** Town (pop. 511), Puebla, central Mexico, 22 mi. NNE of Huauchinango; sugar cane, coffee, fruit. **2** City (pop. 1,317), Querétaro, central Mexico, in a valley of Sierra Madre, 75 mi. NE of Querétaro; alt. 2,539 ft.; grain, sugar cane, bananas, dates, pineapples, pomegranates, limes, sweet potatoes, coffee, maguey.

Jalpatagua (hälpätä'gwä), town (1950 pop. 1,185), Jutiapa dept., SE Guatemala, in highlands, 13 mi. SW of Jutiapa; corn, beans, livestock.

Jalpes, India: see JALPAIGURI, town.

Jaltenango (hältěnäng'gō), town (pop. 1,301), Chiapas, S Mexico, in Sierra Madre, 30 mi. SSW of Venustiano Carranza; cereals, sugar cane, fruit, stock. Called Angel Albino Corzo until 1934.

Jaltenco (hältěng'kō), officially San Andrés Jaltenco, town (pop. 1,464), Mexico state, central Mexico, 23 mi. N of Mexico city; cereals, fruit, stock.

Jaltepeque Lagoon (hältāpā'kā), Sp. *Estero Grande de Jaltepeque*, salt-marsh inlet of Pacific Ocean, in La Paz dept., S Salvador, 25 mi. SE of San Salvador; 15 mi. long, c.1 mi. wide. Salt extraction. Port of La Concordia at W end.

Jáltipan (häl'tēpän), town (pop. 4,547), Veracruz, SE Mexico, on Isthmus of Tehuantepec, 12 mi. W of Minatitlán; agr. center (rice, fruit, coffee, livestock).

Jaltocán (hältōkän'), town (pop. 2,519), Hidalgo, N Mexico, in foothills of Sierra Madre Oriental, 8 mi. W of Huejutla; rice, corn, sugar cane, tobacco, coffee, fruit.

Jaluit (jä'lōōĭt), atoll (□ 4; pop. 862), Ralik Chain, Majuro dist., Marshall Isls., W central Pacific, 200 mi. SE of Kwajalein; 6°3'N 169°34'E; 30 mi. long, 12 mi. wide; 84 islets, of which Jaluit isl. (former ⊙ Marshall Isls.) is most important. Produces copra. In Second World War, Jaluit (southernmost Jap. air base of Ralik Chain) taken 1944 by U.S. forces.

Jama (zhämä'), anc. *Zama*, village, Maktar dist., N central Tunisia, 18 mi. N of Maktar. Near by, Hannibal was defeated (202 B.C.) by Scipio Africanus Major in one of history's decisive battles, ending the strength of Carthage.

Jamaari (jŭ'märē), town (pop. 5,327), Bauchi prov., Northern Provinces, N Nigeria, 20 mi. W of Azare; agr. trade center; cotton, peanuts. durra, cattle, skins. Sometimes spelled Jamaare.

Jamaica (jŭmā'kŭ), island (□ 4,411; 1943 pop. 1,237,063; 1947 estimate 1,297,900) and Br. colony in the West Indies; the colony (□ 4,705; 1943 pop. 1,249,871; 1947 estimate 1,316,554) includes Jamaica isl. and its dependencies (CAYMAN ISLANDS, TURKS AND CAICOS ISLANDS, and the uninhabited Pedro and Morant Cays); ⊙ KINGSTON. The leading possession of the Br. West Indies and 3d largest isl. of the Greater Antilles, Jamaica is c.90 mi. S of Cuba, separated E from Haiti (Hispaniola isl.) by 120-mi.-wide Jamaica Channel; c.500 mi. SSE of Miami, Fla.; and c.600 mi. NNE of Colón, Panama. Roughly elliptical, isl. is about 140 mi. long (W–E), up to 50 mi. wide, bet. 17°43'–18°32'N and 76°11'–78°21'W. Has varied climate, equable and tropical along coast, cool and healthful in the mts. Mean annual temp. of Kingston, 78.7°F. Rainy seasons occur May-June and Sept.-Nov., with average rainfall about 77 inches. Occasionally visited by hurricanes; disastrous earthquakes in 1692 and 1907. The isl. is indented by many fine bays; apart from a few alluvial plains, mostly along S and W coast, it is predominantly mountainous, formed by igneous rocks, overlaid by limestone formations, with extensive plateaus, subterranean basins, and caverns. Main range, running W–E, and adjoined by parallel subranges, terminates towards E in picturesque wooded Blue Mts., with Blue Mountain Peak (7,520 ft.), highest in the isl. Of the many rivers, only the largest, Black R. (44 mi. long), is partly navigable; others are Minho, Cobre, White, Plantain Garden rivers, and the Rio Grande. Mineral deposits are thus far of little economic importance, though there are extensive bauxite and gypsum deposits; also gold, iron, manganese, copper, cobalt, lead, zinc, ocher, and building materials. Salt panning is the principal industry of the Turks and Caicos Isls. Mineral springs at Milk River (Clarendon parish) and Bath (St. Thomas parish). Jamaica's main sources of income are its tourist trade and intensive agr. Sugar has been the leading crop since colonial days, but great strides have been made in diversification. The isl. is now one of the world's principal suppliers of bananas, and has a virtual monopoly on annatto and pimento. Other important products are: coffee, cacao, coconuts, tobacco, citrus fruit, ginger, sisal; these are exported, as are processed goods (copra, rum, fruit juices, beeswax, honey, hides, tortoise shells, cigars, essential oils, dyewood extracts). The forests yield cedar, mahogany, logwood, greenheart, broadleaf, rosewood, juniper, etc. Fisheries on coast. The isl. has about 20 sugar factories, a large condensed-milk factory at Bog Walk, and various processing plants in the main towns. There is otherwise little industrialization. Kingston, largest city and commercial hub of Jamaica, has one of the finest harbors in the West Indies. Other ports are Montego Bay (NW), Port Antonio (NE), Falmouth (N), Savanna-la-Mar (SW), Port Royal (S, on Palisadoes peninsula), and Morant Bay (SE). Spanish Town, 2d largest city, is the chief communications center, linked by railroad with Kingston, Port Antonio, and Montego Bay. Jamaica was discovered May 3, 1494, by Columbus, who called it St. Jago, but the native Indian name Xaymaca [= well watered] prevailed. A 1st Sp. settlement was made (1509) at present-day St. Ann's Bay under direction of Diego Columbus. Harsh Sp. rule soon led to the extinction of the aboriginal inhabitants, and Negroes were introduced in increasing numbers. After 2 unsuccessful attacks (1596 and 1643), the British captured the isl. (1655) under Admiral Penn and Gen. Venables, sent by Cromwell against Hispaniola. In Treaty of Madrid (1670), Spain finally ceded it to England. Buccaneers, who made their hq. at Port Royal, brought great wealth; but that city was almost entirely engulfed in 1692 earthquake. Since then Spanish Town and Kingston have become more prominent. During 18th cent. the colony suffered from hurricanes and earthquakes; slave revolts led to a war with the maroons, who achieved quasi-independence in the interior. Slave trade was stopped in 1807, and slavery abolished in 1833. Another uprising was suppressed in 1865. Poverty, mainly an outcome of overpopulation, continues. The establishment of Jamaica Welfare (1937) introduced important social and cultural developments. The 1944 hurricane caused great economic loss. A new constitution was promulgated in 1945, granting increasing self-government. Several bases on S shore were leased to the U.S. in 1940. Administratively Jamaica is divided into 15 parishes; of these Kingston, St. Andrew, and Port Royal are amalgamated for local govt. purposes. The 3 counties, Surrey (E), Middlesex (center), and Cornwall (W), created in 1758, no longer have political significance. Of the pop. only about 1% is white, an estimated 78% is Negro, 17.5% colored; the remainder are East Indian, Chinese, Syrian, and others. English is spoken throughout the island.

Jamaica (hämī'kä), town (pop. 2,524), Oriente prov., E Cuba, on railroad and 5 mi. NE of Guantánamo; agr. center (cacao, coffee, fruit, sugar cane). The sugar central Romelie is 3 mi. SE.

Jamaica (jŭmā'kŭ). **1** Town (pop. 303), Guthrie co., W central Iowa, 11 mi. W of Perry, in agr. area. **2** A commercial, industrial, and administrative center (with a co. courthouse) in central Queens borough of New York city, SE N.Y.; chief transfer station of Long Isl. RR and a subway terminus and highway hub. Diversified mfg.; extensive residential sections. Points of interest include King Mansion (c.1750) and edifice (1813) of First Presbyterian Church, organized 1662. Main bldg. of Queens Borough Public Library, and Jamaica Race Track are here. Settled in mid-17th cent., it was 1st ⊙ Queens co. **3** Town (pop. 597), Windham co., SE Vt., on West R. and 20 mi. NNW of Brattleboro, in hunting, fishing region; lumber, sports equipment. Partly in Green Mtn. Natl. Forest.

Jamaica Bay, SE N.Y., shallow inlet (□ c.18.5) of the Atlantic indenting S shore of W Long Isl., in Brooklyn and Queens boroughs; sheltered on S by Rockaway Peninsula, and connecting SW with ocean via Rockaway Inlet (bridged). Part of Port of New York. Marshy isls. support Cross Bay Parkway, spanning bay N-S. Floyd Bennett Field is on SW shore; N.Y. International Airport at Idlewild is on NE shore near Jamaica.

Jamaica Channel, in the Caribbean, separating Jamaica (W) from Hispaniola isl. (E) and forming SW continuation of Windward Passage; 120 mi. wide bet. 74°30'–76°1'W. In the channel are Navassa Isl. (N) and Morant Cays (at its S entrance).

Jamaica Plain, Mass.: see BOSTON.

Jamaica Square, N.Y.: see SOUTH FLORAL PARK.

Jamaliyah, Al-, Egypt: see GAMALIYA, EL.

Jamalpur (jŭmäl'pōōr), town (pop. 39,401), Monghyr dist., NE central Bihar, India, 6 mi. S of Monghyr; rail junction; major railway workshops; locomotive mfg., iron and steel foundries. Slate quarries 7 mi. SW, at Dharahra.

Jamalpur, town (pop. 29,139), Mymensingh dist., NE East Bengal, E Pakistan, on the old Brahmaputra and 31 mi. WNW of Mymensingh; rail junction (Singjhani station), with spur to Jagannathganj (16 mi. SW); trade center (rice, jute, oilseeds, sugar cane, tobacco). Jute-pressing center 15 mi. SW, at Sarishabari; metalware mfg. 14 mi. NW, at Islampur.

Jamapa (hämä'pä), town (pop. 636), Veracruz, E Mexico, in Gulf lowland, 13 mi. SW of Veracruz; fruit.

Jamay (hämī'), town (pop. 5,892), Jalisco, central Mexico, on E shore of L. Chapala, 50 mi. SE of Guadalajara; agr. center (wheat, corn, oranges, beans, alfalfa, stock).

Jambeiro (zhāmbā'rŏŏ), city (pop. 638), E São Paulo, Brazil, 17 mi. E of Jacareí.
Jambeli Channel (hämbā'lē), on coast of Guayas prov., SW Ecuador, separates Puná Isl. from the coast and links Gulf of Guayaquil with Guayas R. estuary; c.50 mi. long, 7–20 mi. wide.
Jamberoo (jăm"bŭrōō'), municipality (pop. 921), E New South Wales, Australia, near coast, 55 mi. SSW of Sydney; coal mining.
Jambes (zhāb), town (pop. 9,707), Namur prov., S central Belgium, near Sambre R., just SE of Namur; machine mfg.; jam.
Jambi or **Djambi** (both: jäm'bē), town (pop. 22,071), SE Sumatra, Indonesia, port on Hari R. and 125 mi. NW of Palembang; 1°35'S 103°37'E; trade center for area producing rubber, timber, rattan, oil, and lignite. Port is accessible to ocean-going vessels. Chief exports: rubber, oil.
Jambi River, Indonesia: see Hari River.
Jambol, Bulgaria: see Yambol.
Jambughoda (jŭmbŏŏgō'dŭ), village, Panch Mahals dist., N Bombay, India, 29 mi. SSE of Godhra; agr. market (oilseeds, cotton, grain); rice husking. Was ⊙ former princely state of Jambughoda, in Gujarat States, Bombay; state inc. 1949 into Panch Mahals dist.
Jambukeswaram, India: see Srirangam, city.
Jambusar (jŭm'bōōsŭr), town (pop. 14,207), Broach dist., N Bombay, India, 27 mi. NNW of Broach; rail junction; markets millet, wheat, cotton; tanning, cotton ginning, calico printing; handicrafts (toys, ivory armlets).
Jamda, India: see Girna River.
Jamdena, Indonesia: see Tanimbar Islands.
James, former co., E Tenn.: see Hamilton, co.
James, Lake, N.C.: see Catawba River.
Jamesabad (jāmz'äbäd"), village, Thar Parkar dist., S Sind, W Pakistan, on Jamrao Canal and 31 mi. WSW of Umarkot; local market (cotton, millet, wheat, rice); handicraft cloth and carpet weaving, cotton ginning.
James Bay, S arm (275 mi. long, 135 mi. wide) of Hudson Bay, bet. NE Ont. and NW Que.; 51°10'–56°6'N 78°31'–82°45'W. It is very shallow and receives Eastmain, Rupert, Nemiscau, Nottaway, Harricanaw, Moose, Albany, Attawapiskat, and Ekwan rivers. Bay contains Akimiski, Bear, Charlton, Twin, and several other isls. Fort Albany, Moosonee, Moose Factory, Rupert House, Eastmain, and Fort George are chief Hudson's Bay Co. posts on or near the bay. Discovered (1610) by Henry Hudson, it is named after Capt. Thomas James, who explored it, 1631.
Jamesburg, borough (pop. 2,307), Middlesex co., E N.J., 10 mi. S of New Brunswick. Inc. 1887.
James City, county (□ 150; pop. 6,317), SE Va.; co. courthouse is at Williamsburg, in but independent of co., which was colonial ⊙ of Va. Co. also includes Jamestown Island, site of 1st permanent English settlement in America; both places included in Colonial Natl. Historical Park. In tidewater region, along S shore (James R.) of peninsula bounded N by York R.; co. bounded W by the Chickahominy. Agr. (truck, tobacco, corn, potatoes, fruit), dairying, livestock raising; some timber. Extensive fishing, oystering. Formed 1634.
James Craik or **James Craig** (both: zhā'mĕs krāk'), town (pop. 2,267), central Córdoba prov., Argentina, 70 mi. SE of Córdoba; rail junction and agr. center (alfalfa, wheat, corn, flax, livestock; dairy products).
James Creek, Pa.: see Marklesburg.
James Island, village (pop. estimate 500), SW B.C., on James Isl. (2 mi. long, 1 mi. wide), in Haro Strait, off SE Vancouver Isl., 14 mi. N of Victoria; fishing, lumbering.
James Island, Chile: see Chonos Archipelago.
James Island, Galápagos: see Santiago Island.
James Island, Charleston co., SE S.C., one of Sea isls., on SW side of Charleston Harbor; 9 mi. long. Bridged to mainland (N), Johns Isl. (W), and Folly Isl. (SE). U.S. quarantine station.
Jameson (jā'mĭsŭn), town (pop. 185), Daviess co., NW Mo., on Grand R. and 27 mi. NW of Chillicothe.
Jameson Point, Knox co., S Maine, forms N side of Rockland harbor; has breakwater, lighthouse.
James Peak (13,260 ft.), N central Colo., in Front Range, c.35 mi. WNW of Denver. Moffat Tunnel passes through part of mtn.
Jamesport. 1 City (pop. 720), Daviess co., NW Mo., near Grand R., 18 mi. NW of Chillicothe. **2** Village (1940 pop. 510), Suffolk co., SE N.Y., on NE Long Isl., near Great Peconic Bay, 4 mi. ENE of Riverhead, in summer-resort area; duck raising; fishing.
James River. 1 In S central Mo., rises in the Ozarks 17 mi. E of Springfield, flows c.80 mi. SW to White R. S of Galena. **2** In N.Dak. and S.Dak., rises in central N.Dak., flows SSE, past Jamestown and across S.Dak., past Huron and Mitchell, to Missouri R. at Yankton; 710 mi. long, not navigable. Often called Dakota R. **3** In Va., formed in N Botetourt co. by junction of Jackson and Cowpasture rivers; flows SE past Buchanan, NE, crossing the Blue Ridge NW of Lynchburg, again SE past Lynchburg, NE, and generally SE past Richmond (at fall line; head of tidewater, c.100 mi. above mouth), to Hampton Roads at Newport News; 340 mi. long. Drops in scenic Balcony Falls in its gorge through the Blue Ridge and again in 3-mi. series of rapids (84-ft. drop; waterpower) above Richmond; lower course is estuary up to 5-mi. wide near mouth. Appomattox and Chickahominy rivers are chief tributaries. Navigable to Richmond for deep drafts; chief cargoes are coal, petroleum, agr. produce, lumber, fertilizers, merchandise. Spanned by 4½-mi.-long bridge just above Newport News. River's lower course, rich in historical associations, was region of 1st permanent English settlement in New World; Jamestown Island, 1st settled in 1607, and other historic towns and plantations are here. In Civil War, river was avenue of Union attempts (during which Dutch Gap Canal below city was constructed) to take Richmond. Old James R. and Kanawha Canal (abandoned in 1880s) formerly paralleled river from Richmond W to Buchanan, whence a road continued to the Kanawha in W.Va.
James Ross Island, Antarctica: see Ross Island.
James Ross Strait, arm (110 mi. long, 30–40 mi. wide) of the Arctic Ocean, S Franklin Dist., Northwest Territories, bet. King William Isl. (SW) and Boothia Peninsula (NE); 70°N 96°W. Connects N with sea area leading to McClintock Channel and Franklin Strait.
Jamestown, town (pop. 1,386), S South Australia, 34 mi. E of Port Pirie; wheat; wool, sheep, dairy products; wine, timber.
Jamestown, Barbados, B.W.I.: see Holetown.
Jamestown, town (pop. 1,547), port and ⊙ Saint Helena, in S Atlantic, on James Bay, on isl.'s NW shore. Ships flax fibers (phormium tenax) and some lily bulbs. Once a busy coaling station on East India route, it lost its importance after opening of Suez Canal. Still supplies water to vessels. Adjoining are barracks and batteries. Plantation House (governor's residence) and the cathedral of St. Paul's are c.2 mi. S in the uplands.
Jamestown, town in Bonhill parish, S Dumbarton, Scotland, on Leven R. just N of Bonhill; textile printing and bleaching.
Jamestown, town (pop. 1,312), E Cape Prov., U. of So. Afr., 30 mi. SSE of Aliwal North, in foothills of Drakensberg range; sheep, wool, grain.
Jamestown. 1 Town (pop. 84), Independence co., NE central Ark., 6 mi. SW of Batesville. **2** Village (1940 pop. 698), Tuolumne co., central Calif., c.45 mi. E of Stockton; gold-mining center in Mother Lode country; received its nickname "Jimtown" in gold rush. Table Mountain is near by. **3** Town (pop. 118), Boulder co., N Colo., in foothills of Front Range, 8 mi. NW of Boulder; alt. c.7,000 ft. Supply point in gold-mining region. Rocky Mtn. Natl. Park near by. **4** Town (pop. 718), Boone co., central Ind., 17 mi. SE of Crawfordsville, in agr. area; lumber, flour. **5** City (pop. 494), Cloud co., N Kansas, 11 mi. W of Concordia, in wheat region. **6** Town (pop. 1,064), ⊙ Russell co., S Ky., in Cumberland foothills, 27 mi. WSW of Somerset; makes wood products, woolens; flour milling. Wolf Creek Dam in Cumberland R. is SW. **7** Town (pop. 245), Moniteau co., central Mo., near Missouri R., 11 mi. NNE of California. **8** City (pop. 43,354), Chautauqua co., extreme W N.Y., at SE end of Chautauqua L., 27 mi. S of Dunkirk; furniture-mfg. center, also producing textiles, toys, tools, and washing, milking, and voting machines. Ships dairy products. Founded c.1806; inc. as village in 1827, as city in 1886. Predominantly Swedish in pop. since coming of skilled Swedish workers in c.1850; noted for cooperative community services. **9** Village (pop. 748), Guilford co., N central N.C., 5 mi. NE of High Point; mfg. of cotton yarn, paperboard containers. **10** City (pop. 10,697), ⊙ Stutsman co., SE central N.Dak., 100 mi. E of Bismarck and on James R. Railroad junction, shipping center for wheat and livestock; flour mills, grain elevators, stockyards; dairy products, poultry, flax. Seat of Jamestown Col. and state insane asylum. Settled 1872, inc. 1896. **11** Village (pop. 1,345), Greene co., S central Ohio, 10 mi. ESE of Xenia, and on small Caesar Creek, in livestock and grain area; food canning, furniture mfg. Settled 1806, laid out 1815. **12** Borough (pop. 931), Mercer co., NW Pa., 22 mi. SW of Meadville and on Shenango R.; paint mfg.; dairy products, grain, potatoes; railroad shops. **13** Resort town (pop. 2,068), including Jamestown village (pop. 1,757), Newport co., S R.I., coextensive with Conanicut Isl. (kŭnă'nĭkŭt) (c.9 mi. long, 1–2 mi. wide), in Narragansett Bay W of Newport; farming. Bridge (1940) connects with North Kingstown (W). Beavertail Light, at S tip of isl., was established before 1750. Several pre-Revolutionary bldgs. remain. Inc. 1678. **14** Town (pop. 2,115), ⊙ Fentress co., N Tenn., 65 mi. NW of Knoxville, in hilly coal and timber area; lumbering. Alvin C. York Agr. Inst. and Pickett State Park near by. Settled 1827; inc. 1837.
Jamestown Bay district, SE Alaska, on W shore of Baranof Isl., 4 mi. E of Sitka; 57°3'N 135°17'W; fishing.
Jamestown Island (1,559.5 acres), SE Va., in James R. (bridge, ferry connections), 35 mi. NW of Norfolk; isl., then a peninsula, was site of 1st permanent English settlement (May 13, 1607) in America. Colonists, though ably led by John Smith and befriended at first by the Indians, experienced great hardships; during severe winter of 1609–10 (the "starving time"), only arrival of Lord De la Warr, with supplies and more colonists, saved settlement from abandonment. Introduction of tobacco culture (c.1612) by John Rolfe gave colony an economic foothold; town grew, becoming seat of govt. of Va. in 1619, when House of Burgesses (1st representative legislative assembly in New World) met here. Burned during Bacon's Rebellion (1676) and later rebuilt, Jamestown suffered permanent decline after 1699, when Williamsburg (6 mi. NE) became capital. Only relics of early settlement are church tower (c.1639), on site of 1st Anglican church in America, the old cemetery, and utensils and bldg. foundations excavated by Natl. Park Service. All but 22 acres (Jamestown Natl. Historical Site, administered by Association for the Preservation of Virginia Antiquities) now included in Colonial National Historical Park.
Jamesville. 1 Village (1940 pop. 933), Onondaga co., central N.Y., 5 mi. SE of Syracuse; chemicals, cement. **2** Town (pop. 529), Martin co., NE N.C., on Roanoke R. and 9 mi. SE of Williamston.
Jamikunta (jŭmĭkōōn'tŭ), town (pop. 5,162), Karimnagar dist., E Hyderabad state, India, 23 mi. ESE of Karimnagar; rice milling. Sometimes spelled Jumekoonta, Jammikunta.
Jamilena (hämēlä'nä), town (pop. 3,260), Jaén prov., S Spain, 7 mi. WSW of Jaén; olive oil, cereals, livestock. Mineral springs.
Jamiltepec (hämēltāpĕk'), town (pop. 2,141), Oaxaca, S Mexico, in Pacific coast lowland, 90 mi. SW of Oaxaca; cereals, sugar cane, coffee, cotton, fruit, vegetables, timber. Airfield.
Jam Jodhpur (jŭm' jōd'pōōr), town (pop. 7,248), W central Saurashtra, India, 39 mi. S of Jamnagar; markets millet, cotton, oilseeds, gram; cotton ginning, flour and oilseed milling, hand-loom weaving.
Jam jo Tando, W Pakistan: see Tando Jam.
Jamkhandi (jŭm'kŭndē), town (pop. 15,940), Bijapur dist., S Bombay, India, 35 mi. SW of Bijapur; local trade center for cotton and silk fabrics, wheat, millet; cotton ginning, hand-loom weaving. Was ⊙ former princely state of Jamkhandi (□ 522; pop. 126,272) in Deccan States, Bombay; state inc. 1949 into dists. of Dharwar, Bijapur, Belgaum, Sholapur, Satara North, and Ahmadnagar.
Jammalamadugu (jŭ'mŭlŭmŭ"dōōgōō), town (pop. 9,653), Cuddapah dist., central Madras, India, on Penner R. and 38 mi. NW of Cuddapah; peanut milling; rice, cotton, turmeric; handicraft lacquerware. Extensive limestone quarrying near by.
Jammikunta, India: see Jamikunta.
Jammu (jŭm'ōō), province (□ 12,378; pop. 1,981,-433), SW Kashmir state; ⊙ Jammu. Comprises dists. of Jammu, Kathua, Udhampur, Riasi, and Mirpur and dependencies (*jagirs*) of Punch and Chineni. Area was old kingdom of Dogra Rajputs, who maintained semi-independence during Mogul occupation (1586–1750) of Kashmir Valley. Came under Sikh control in 1819, and in 1820 Gulab Singh, a Dogra, was made Raja of Jammu for distinguished service in Ranjit Singh's army. Gulab Singh conquered Ladakh (1830s) and in 1846 was acknowledged (by British) ruler of most of present Kashmir state; died in 1857. Prov. continued under rule of Dogra maharajas of Jammu and Kashmir until after 1948, when, following Indian-Pakistani hostilities in Kashmir, dists. of Jammu, Kathua, Udhampur, Riasi (renamed Rajaori), the new Doda dist., and dependencies of Chineni and part of Punch remained under Indian administration; Mirpur and most of Punch lay in Pakistan-held territory. Formerly Jummoo.
Jammu, district (□ 1,147; pop. 431,362), Jammu prov., SW Kashmir; ⊙ Jammu. Bounded S by W Pakistan; drained by Chenab R.; foothills of Siwalik Range in N. Agr. (wheat, rice, bajra, corn, barley, oilseeds, sugar cane, cotton, spices). Main centers: Jammu, Akhnur, Samba, Nawanshahr. Pop. 60% Hindu, 39% Moslem. Prevailing mother tongue, Dogri. Formerly spelled Jummoo.
Jammu, city (pop., including cantonment area, 58,847), ⊙ Jammu prov. and dist., Kashmir, on left tributary of Chenab R. and 95 mi. S of Srinagar. Winter ⊙ Kashmir; rail spur terminus; mfg. of silk, drugs, rubber goods, pottery; rice and oilseed milling; tannery, indianite factory; trades in grain, sugar cane, cotton. Col., Drug Research Laboratory. Palace, built 1775. Was ⊙ early Dogra Rajputs, defeated early-19th cent. by Sikhs. Sometimes called Jammu Tawi. Formerly spelled Jummoo.
Jammu and Kashmir, Asia: see Kashmir, state.
Jamnagar (jäm'nŭgŭr) or **Navanagar** (nŭvä'nŭgŭr), city (pop. 71,588), ⊙ Halar dist., W Saurashtra, India, on Kathiawar peninsula, 45 mi. WNW of Rajkot. Commercial center; rail junction (workshops); airport; agr. market (oilseeds, cotton, millet, garden vegetables); cotton, oilseed, and flour milling, tanning, mfg. of chemicals, matches, paint, soap, tiles, pottery; metalworks (wire, tin products, pipes, nut crackers, brassware), sawmills. Handicrafts include cloth weaving, em-

broidering, dyeing, cosmetic and bangle making. Has noted solarium. Port, on Gulf of Cutch, is 4 mi. NW, at Bedi. City founded 1540 by Jadeja Rajputs; was ⊙ former princely state of Navanagar.

Jamner (jäm′när), town (pop. 9,025), East Khandesh dist., NE Bombay, India, 19 mi. SE of Jalgaon; rail terminus; market center for cotton, peanuts, millet; cotton ginning.

Jamnia (jăm′nēŭ), biblical *Jabneel* (jăb′nēĕl, jăb′-nēl) and *Jabneh* (jăb′nŭ, –nē) [Heb.,=God causes to build], town, W Israel, in Judaean Plain. The modern settlement (pop. 350), called Yavne (yäv′-nā), 18 mi. S of Haifa, was founded 1941 near site of the anc. city; mixed farming, citriculture. The biblical city, an important center of Philistia, was sacked by Judas Maccebeus and later rebuilt. In the years just before the destruction (A.D. 70) of Second Temple it became a Jewish cultural center. Vespasian spared it at request of Johanan ben Zaccai, who moved here after fall of Jerusalem and made it center of Judaism. For some time it was seat of the Sanhedrin. As Ybelin it was fortified by Crusaders. In 1948 the town was scene of battle bet. Jews and Arabs.

Jamnitz, Czechoslovakia: see JEMNICE.

Jamnotri (jŭmnō′trē), noted Hindu shrine, Tehri dist., N Uttar Pradesh, India, in W Kumaun Himalayas, 45 mi. N of Tehri; small wooden temple. Hot springs (194.7°F.) near by.

Jamoigne (zhämwän′yŭ), village (pop. 1,173), Luxembourg prov., SE Belgium, in the Ardennes, on Semois R. and 19 mi. W of Arlon; agr. Has 16th-cent. church.

Jampur (jäm′po͝or), town (pop. 11,862), Dera Ghazi Khan dist., SW Punjab, W Pakistan, 28 mi. S of Dera Ghazi Khan; local market (wheat, millet, dates, indigo); hand-loom weaving, lacquered woodwork.

Jamrao Canal (jäm′rou), irrigation canal, E Sind, W Pakistan; from Eastern Nara Canal (17 mi. NE of Mohattanagar) runs 125 mi. S, past Jamesabad, to point c.15 mi. SW of Nabisar Road. Has several branches. Opened 1899.

Jamrud (jŭmro͞od′), fort at E mouth of Khyber Pass, Khyber agency, W North-West Frontier Prov., W Pakistan, 10 mi. W of Peshawar; military post; toll station. Built 1836 by Sikhs.

Jämsänkoski (yăm′săn-kōs″kē), village (commune pop. 4,510), Häme co., S central Finland, in Päijänne lake region, 30 mi. SW of Jyväskylä; pulp, cellulose, and paper mills.

Jamsar (jŭm′sŭr), village, N Rajasthan, India, 17 mi. NNE of Bikaner. Near-by gypsum deposits worked.

Jamshedpur (jŭmshäd′po͝or), city (□ c.22; pop. 148,711), Singhbhum dist., SE Bihar, India, on Subarnarekha R. and 140 mi. WNW of Calcutta. Major industrial center; principal iron- and steel-works of India (opened 1907), with tinplate, cable, and steel-wire plants; mfg. of agr. implements, enameled ironware, locomotive engine parts; oil and flour milling. Natl. Metallurgical Laboratory. City formerly called Sakchi. Rail station just S, at Tatanagar.

Jamtland (yĕmt′länd), Swedish *Jämtland*, county [Swedish *län*] (□ 19,966; 1950 pop. 144,137), NW Sweden; ⊙ Ostersund. On Norwegian border, its N part comprises Jamtland province [Swedish *landskap*] (□ 14,543; pop. 126,747); its S part comprises Harjedalen, Swedish *Härjedalen* (hĕr′yüdä″-lŭn), prov. (□ 4,961; pop. 14,390). Surface is hilly, becoming mountainous near Norwegian border, where it rises to 5,892 ft. on Helagsfjall. Of its many lakes, Stor L. is largest. Drained by Ljusna, Indal, and several other rivers. Dairying, lumbering, and quarrying (limestone, marble, talc) are chief occupations. There are numerous health and winter-sports resorts. Ostersund is only city; Sveg and Stromsund are towns. Formerly spelled Jemtland.

Jamui (jŭmo͞o′ē), town (pop. 10,682), Monghyr dist., central Bihar, India, on tributary of the Ganges and 32 mi. SSW of Monghyr; road and trade (rice, corn, gram, wheat, barley) center. Mica mines 15 mi. SE, near Nawadih.

Jamuna River (jŭ′mo͞onŭ). **1** In E Pakistan, main channel of lower BRAHMAPUTRA RIVER; leaves the Brahmaputra proper (old Brahmaputra) N of Bahadurabad Ghat, flows 100 mi. S to Padma (Ganges) R. N of Goalundo. **2** In Indian and Pakistan Bengal, left tributary of the Atrai, rises 30 mi. WNW of Rangpur, flows c.100 mi. S, past Phulbari, Hilli, and Naogaon, to Atrai R. 28 mi. NE of Rajshahi. **3** In Indian and Pakistan Bengal, a main distributary of Ganges Delta, leaves Jalangi R. 19 mi. SSE of Rajshahi, flows 225 mi. S, past Chuadanga, Bangaon, Basirhat, Taki, Debhata, and Kaliganj, through the Sundarbans (here partly forming India–E Pakistan border), to Bay of Bengal, forming estuary mouth. In upper course, above Basirhat, called Ichamati; in parts of lower course, also called Kalindi and Raimangal. Navigable throughout course. **4** In N India: see JUMNA RIVER.

Jamundá River (zhŭmo͞ondä′), N Brazil, rises in the Guiana Highlands, flows c.400 mi. SE, forming Amazonas-Pará border, to the Amazon (left bank) at Faro. Also spelled Nhamundá.

Jamundí (hämo͞ondē′), town (pop. 1,718), Valle del Cauca dept., W Colombia, in Cauca valley, on railroad and 12 mi. SSW of Cali; sugar cane, tobacco, coffee, cacao, bananas, corn, rice, yucca, stock.

Jamursba, Tandjung, Netherlands New Guinea: see GOOD HOPE, CAPE OF.

Jana, La (lä hä′nä), town (pop. 1,732), Castellón de la Plana prov., E Spain, 10 mi. WNW of Vinaroz; olive-oil processing; cereals, wine.

Janakkala (yä′näk-kälä), village (commune pop. 11,357), Häme co., S Finland, in lake region, 8 mi. SE of Hämeenlinna; grain, potatoes, livestock; lumbering.

Janamuato (hänämwä′tō), village (pop. 1,890), Michoacán, central Mexico, 3 mi. NW of Puruándiro; cereals, livestock.

Janaúba (zhünäo͞o′bŭ), city, N Minas Gerais, Brazil, 60 mi. NE of Montes Claros; terminus (1948) of railroad from Corinto, to be continued to Bahia via Monte Azul.

Jand (jŭnd), town (pop. 6,134), Attock dist., NW Punjab, W Pakistan, 30 mi. SW of Campbellpur; rail junction; hand-loom weaving; wood products.

Janda, Laguna de (lägo͞o′nä dhä hän′dä), shallow lake (8 mi. long, up to 3 mi. wide), Cádiz prov., SW Spain, near Atlantic coast, 30 mi. SE of Cádiz. Through it flows Barbate R. Here, and not on the Guadalete R., was most likely fought the decisive "battle of Guadalete" in which the last Visigothic king, Roderick, was defeated (July 19, 711) by the Moors under Tarik.

Jandakot, town (pop. 231), SW Western Australia, SE suburb of Fremantle; wool scouring.

Jandaq (jändäk′), village, Tenth Prov., in Yezd, central Iran, 145 mi. N of Yezd, in the desert Dasht-i-Kavir; barley, gums; camel breeding.

Jandiala Guru (jŭndyä′lŭ go͞o′ro͞o), town (pop. 11,520), Amritsar dist., W Punjab, India, 10 mi. ESE of Amritsar; local trade in wheat, cotton, gram, rice, oilseeds; hand-loom weaving (cotton, woolen); copper- and brassware. Sometimes called Jandiala.

Jandía Peninsula (händē′ä), SW extremity of Fuerteventura, Canary Isls., 30 mi. SW of Puerto de Cabras; ends in **Jandía Point,** 28°3′N 14°30′W. Rises to highest point (2,648 ft.) of isl.

Jane Franklin, Cape, NW King William Isl., S Franklin Dist., Northwest Territories, on Victoria Strait; 69°36′N 98°20′W. Remains of camp, graves, and other relics of Franklin expedition, 1847–48, were found here by McClintock (1859) and Hall (1861–65).

Jane Lew, town (pop. 491), Lewis co., central W. Va., 12 mi. S of Clarksburg.

Janesville. 1 Town (pop. 445), on Black Hawk-Bremer co. line, E central Iowa, on Cedar R. and 12 mi. NNW of Waterloo; feed milling. Limestone quarries, sand and gravel pits near by. **2** Village (pop. 1,287), Waseca co., S Minn., just S of L. Elysian, 10 mi. WNW of Waseca, in grain, livestock, poultry area; dairy products, flour, cattle feed. Platted 1855, deserted in Sioux outbreak of 1862, inc. 1870. **3** City (pop. 24,899), ⊙ Rock co., S Wis., on Rock R. and 32 mi. SSE of Madison; commercial and industrial center in tobacco-growing and dairying area; mfg. (automobiles, fountain pens, textiles); tobacco warehouses. Has a mus. and a state school for the blind. Ella Wheeler Wilcox was born near by. Settled 1835, inc. 1853.

Jangaon (jŭn′goun), town (pop. 7,036), Nalgonda dist., E central Hyderabad state, India, 24 mi. NE of Bhongir; rice and castor-bean milling.

Jangipur (jŭng′gĭpo͝or), town (pop. 16,903), Murshidabad dist., central West Bengal, India, on the Bhagirathi and 28 mi. NNW of Berhampore; cotton weaving; rice, gram, oilseeds, jute, barley. Reputedly founded by Jahangir. Silk-trade center in 18th cent. Extensive silk growing near by.

Jangshahi, W Pakistan: see JUNGSHAHI.

Janicho, Mexico: see JANITZIO.

Jánico (hä′nēkō), officially Santo Tomás de Jánico, town (1950 pop. 759), Santiago prov., N central Dominican Republic, 11 mi. SW of Santiago, in agr. region (tobacco, cacao, coffee).

Janik, Turkey: see SAMSUN, province.

Janikow, Poland: see JANKAU.

Janina, Greece: see IOANNINA.

Jäniskoski, Russian SFSR: see PATS RIVER.

Janitza, Greece: see GIANNITSA.

Janitzio (hänēt′syō), island (c.1 mi. long; pop. 771), in L. Pátzcuaro, Michoacán, central Mexico, 7 mi. NNW of Pátzcuaro; native fishing village. Sometimes Janicho.

Janiuay (hänēwī′), town (1939 pop. 3,845; 1948 municipality pop. 44,348), Iloilo prov., S central Panay isl., Philippines, 17 mi. NNW of Iloilo; agr. center (rice, sugar cane); sugar milling.

Janja or **Yanya** (both: yänyä), village (pop. 5,538), NE Bosnia, Yugoslavia, near Drina R. (Serbia border), 6 mi. S of Bijeljina.

Janjevo or **Yanyevo** (both: yä′nyĕvô), village, S Serbia, Yugoslavia, 8 mi. SSE of Pristina, in the Kosovo; handicraft (jewelry).

Janjgir (jänj′gēr), village, Bilaspur dist., E central Madhya Pradesh, India, 28 mi. ESE of Bilaspur; rice and oilseed milling, shellac mfg. Includes adjoining railway settlement of Naila.

Janjira (jŭnjē′rŭ), former princely state (□ 326; pop. 103,557) in Deccan States, Bombay, India; ⊙ was Murud. Inc. 1949 into Kolaba dist.

Jankampet, India: see BODHAN.

Jankau, Czechoslovakia: see JANKOV.

Jankau (yäng′kou) or **Janikow** (yänē′ko͞of), Pol. *Janików*, village in Lower Silesia, after 1945 in Wroclaw prov., SW Poland, 13 mi. SE of Breslau (Wroclaw). In Thirty Years War, scene (Feb., 1645) of decisive victory of Swedes under Torstensson over imperial forces under Emperor Ferdinand and Hatzfeld. After 1937, called Grünaue; sometimes called Jankowitz.

Jankov (yän′kôf), Ger. *Jankau* or *Jankow*, village (pop. 565), S Bohemia, Czechoslovakia, 4 mi. ENE of Votice. Bavarian and Imperialist armies defeated here (1645) by Swedish commander Torstensson, during Thirty Years War.

Jankovac, Hungary: see JANOSHALMA.

Jankowitz, Poland: see JANKAU.

Jan Mayen (yän′ mī′ŭn), island (□ 144; pop. 8), Norwegian possession in Arctic Ocean, E of Greenland and NE of Iceland, c.640 mi. W of Tromso, Norway; 70°58′–71°10′N 7°56′–8°21′W. Isl. is 39 mi. long (SW–NE), 9 mi. wide; rises to 8,347 ft. in the Beerenberg (NE), extinct volcano. Site (since 1921) of observatory of Norwegian Meteorological Inst. and of radio station. Visited by whalers, sealers, and fox hunters. Discovered 1607 by Henry Hudson; shortly afterwards Dutch captain Jan Mayen established whaling base here. During 1st International Polar Year (1882–83), isl. was site of Austrian meteorological station. Placed under Norwegian sovereignty in 1929; during Second World War, site of U.S. meteorological station. Gulf Stream and cold East Greenland Current meet near by; fog and stormy weather prevail on isl. In winter, surrounded by drift ice. Temp. ranges bet. −25°F. (Dec.) and 50°F. (July).

Jannina, Greece: see IOANNINA.

Janos (hä′nōs), town (pop. 909), Chihuahua, N Mexico, on affluent of Casas Grandes R. and 90 mi. SE of Douglas, Ariz.; alt. 4,453 ft.; cotton, cereals, cattle.

Janos, Mount (yä′nôsh), Hung. *Jánoshegy*, highest point (1,738 ft.) in S range of Buda Mts., N central Hungary; residential dists. on E slope.

Janoshalma (yä′nôsh-hŏl″mŏ), Hung. *Jánoshalma*, Serbo-Croatian *Jankovac*, town (pop. 15,933), Bacs-Bodrog co., S Hungary, 12 mi. SW of Kiskunhalas; distilleries, flour mills, brickworks.

Janoshaza (yä′nôsh-häzŏ), Hung. *Jánosháza*, town (pop. 4,227), Vas co., W Hungary, 26 mi. SE of Szombathely; potatoes, honey.

Janoshida (yä′nôsh-hĭdŏ), Hung. *Jánoshida*, town (pop. 4,487), Jasz-Nagykun-Szolnok co., E central Hungary, on Zagyva R. and 11 mi. SE of Jaszbereny; barley, wheat, cattle, hogs.

Janov, Lithuania: see JONAVA.

Janow (yä′no͞of), Pol. *Janów*, Rus. *Yanov* (yä′nŭf). **1** or **Janow Lubelski** (lo͞obĕl′skē), Pol. *Janów Lubelski*, Rus. *Yanov Lyubelski* or *Lyubel′ski* (both: lyo͞obĕl′skē), town (pop. 3,793), Lublin prov., E Poland, 17 mi. SSE of Krasnik; stone quarrying; sawmilling, tanning, brewing. **2** or **Janow Podlaski** (pôdlä′skē), Pol. *Janów Podlaski*, Rus. *Yanov Podlyaski* (pôdlyä′skē), town (pop. 2,450), Lublin prov., E Poland, 12 mi. NNE of Biala Podlaska, near Bug R. (Belorussian SSR border). Rail spur terminus; flour milling, tanning, tile mfg. (clay pit); horse-breeding station. Sometimes called Janow nad Bugiem.

Janow or **Janow Poleski** (yä′nôf pôlĕs′kē). **1** Town, Pinsk oblast, Belorussian SSR: see IVANOVO. **2** Town, Lvov oblast, Ukrainian SSR: see IVAN-FRANKO. **3** Town, Ternopol oblast, Ukrainian SSR: see YANOV, town.

Janowiec or **Janowiec Wielkopolski** (yänô′vyĕts vyĕlkôpôl′skē), Ger. *Janowitz* (yä′nōvĭts), town (1946 pop. 2,809), Poznan prov., W central Poland, on Welna R. and 34 mi. NE of Poznan; rail junction; mfg. of cement, bricks; tanning, flour milling.

Janpur (jŭn′po͝or), town (pop. 958), Bahawalpur state, W Pakistan, 60 mi. SW of Bahawalpur; dates.

Jansath (jän′sŭt), town (pop. 7,541), Muzaffarnagar dist., N Uttar Pradesh, India, 14 mi. SE of Muzaffarnagar; wheat, gram, sugar cane, oilseeds. Home of Jansath Sayids, chief power in Delhi empire in early-18th cent. Hydroelectric station 3 mi. NNW, near village of Chitaura.

Jansen, village (pop. 244), Jefferson co., SE Nebr., 5 mi. NE of Fairbury.

Jansenville, town (pop. 1,980), SE Cape Prov., U. of So. Afr., on Sundays R. and 50 mi. S of Graaff Reinet; stock, grain, feed crops, fruit.

Janske Lazne (yän′skā läz′nyĕ), Czech *Janské Lázně*, Ger. *Johannisbad* (yōhä′nĭsbät), village (pop. 725), NE Bohemia, Czechoslovakia, in the Riesengebirge, on railroad and 33 mi. ESE of Liberec; health resort (alt. 2,020 ft.) with thermal (82°F.) and chalybeate springs, especially equipped since 1935 for cure of poliomyelitis. Also noted as winter-sports center, with excellent skiing facilities on slopes of *Cerna Hora* (chĕr′nä hô′rä), Ger. *Schwarzenberg*; cable railway leads to top.

Jan Smuts Airport, U. of So. Afr.: see KEMPTON PARK.

Jantetelco (häntätĕl'kō), town (pop. 1,021), Morelos, central Mexico, 13 mi. SE of Cuautla; rice, sugar cane, fruit.

Jan Tiel (yän tēl'), village, S Curaçao, Du. West Indies, beach resort on coastal lagoon, and 3 mi. ESE of Willemstad.

Jantra Khani, Nepal: see OKHALDHUNGA.

Jantra River, Bulgaria: see YANTRA RIVER.

Januária (zhŭnwä'rēŭ), city (pop. 5,747), N Minas Gerais, Brazil, river port on São Francisco and 90 mi. NNW of Montes Claros (connected by new road); ships cotton, sugar cane, resins. Zinc deposits. Has hosp. Airfield. First settled in late 17th cent.

Janville (zhāvēl'), village (pop. 1,187), Eure-et-Loir dept., N central France, in the Beauce, 20 mi. N of Orléans; wheat, oats, merino sheep.

Janvrin Island (3 mi. long, 2 mi. wide), in the Atlantic, E N.S., off S Cape Breton Isl., just E of Madame Isl., at entrance of the Strait of Canso; 45°32'N 61°10'W.

Janwada (jŭnvä'dŭ), village (pop. 2,536), Bidar dist., W central Hyderabad state, India, 8 mi. NW of Bidar; cotton, rice, sugar cane.

Janzé (zhāzā'), town (pop. 2,203), Ille-et-Vilaine dept., W France, 13 mi. SE of Rennes; market center (poultry, cheese, cider).

Janzur, Egypt: see GANZUR.

Jaochow, China: see POYANG.

Jaoho (rou'hŭ'), town, ⊙ Jaoho co. (pop. 25,000), NE Sungkiang prov., Manchuria, 125 mi. SSW of Khabarovsk, and on left bank of Ussuri R. (USSR line), opposite Bikin; cattle raising; beans, kaoliang. The name Jaoho was formerly applied to a town 30 mi. N, on Ussuri R. Present Jaoho was then called Twanshantze.

Jaoping or **Jao-p'ing** (both: rou'pĭng'), town (pop. 17,184), ⊙ Jaoping co. (pop. 354,810), E Kwangtung prov., China, 40 mi. NNE of Swatow; rice, wheat, sugar cane. Kaolin quarrying near by.

Jaora (jou'rŭ), town (pop. 25,501), W Madhya Bharat, India, 22 mi. NNE of Ratlam; trades in corn, millet, cotton, sugar cane, opium; sugar milling, cotton ginning, hand-loom weaving. Was ⊙ former princely state of Jaora (□ 601; pop. 116,953) of Central India agency; state established early-19th cent. by Pathan chieftain, since 1948 merged with Madhya Bharat.

Jaoyang (rou'yäng'), town, ⊙ Jaoyang co. (pop. 192,741), S central Hopeh prov., China, 45 mi. SSE of Paoting, near Huto R.; wheat, beans, kaoliang, peanuts.

Japan (jăpăn', jŭ-), Jap. *Nippon* (nĭ'pŏn, Jap. nēpôn') or *Nihon* (nēhôn'), empire, occupying crescent-shaped archipelago off the Pacific E coast of Asia; ⊙ TOKYO. Post-Second World War Japan (□ 140,680.9; 1947 pop. 78,627,000; 1950 pop. 83,199,637), largely reduced in territory, but swollen in population through repatriation of many Japanese from overseas, is comprised of, apart from numerous offshore isls., the 4 principal home isls., N–S: HOKKAIDO, HONSHU (by far the largest, with c.60% of the area and almost 75% of the people), SHIKOKU, and KYUSHU (see separate articles on these isls. for detailed geographic and economic information). Before the Second World War, the Japanese Empire was at its height and included: the S part (called Karafuto) of SAKHALIN; KURILE ISLANDS; RYUKYU ISLANDS; FORMOSA and the PESCADORES; KOREA; KWANTUNG leased territory in S Manchuria (with Dairen and Port Arthur); VOLCANO ISLANDS; BONIN ISLANDS; MARCUS ISLAND; and the former German isl. groups held as mandates from the League of Nations—the CAROLINE ISLANDS with the PALAU ISLANDS, the MARSHALL ISLANDS, and the MARIANAS ISLANDS (except Guam)—all the islands now constituting a U.N. trust territory administered by the U.S. This empire then constituted □ 262,939, 1940 pop. 105,226,101; pre-war Japan proper (which included the Ryukyus and the Kuriles as well as the 4 home isls.) had □ 147,707, 1940 pop. 73,114,308. Japan also controlled the puppet state of Manchukuo. During the 1st successful years of the Second World War it held in addition vast territories in China, the Philippines, Malaya, the Malay Archipelago, Hongkong, Hainan, Indochina, Thailand, and Burma. Japan proper forms a c.1,000-mi.-long arc (maximal width, c.200 mi.), separated in N by narrow La Pérouse Strait from Russian-held Sakhalin and in SW by c.130-mi.-wide Korea and Tsushima straits from Korea. The nearest point of China is c.500 mi. SW across the East China Sea. Japan's concave W shore is washed by the Sea of Japan. SE Honshu is separated from Shikoku by the all-important Inland Sea, dotted by many islets. Bet. Honshu and Kyushu, Shimonoseki Strait is crossed by railroad tunnel. Corresponding in latitude roughly to the U.S. East Coast from Maine to Florida, the Japanese archipelago is situated approximately bet. 31°–45°N and 128°30'–146°E. Physiographically it is a long volcanic mtn. chain lifted above the ocean. Its landscape is of unusual charm and variety, with shapely, snow-capped mts., terraced hillsides, small verdant plains, carefully planned gardens, and gushing streams and waterfalls. A part of the Tertiary ranges that border the Pacific, it lies within one of the globe's most active and disaster-ridden earthquake zones. In the center of Honshu, rising to 12,389 ft., is the now dominant (since 1707) FUJIYAMA, Japan's highest peak and most famous landmark. The mountainous surface has narrow valleys, a rocky coast line, and scattered alluvial fans. The many short, swift rivers have a high hydroelectric potential. Only major fresh-water lake is L. BIWA in S Honshu, near Kyoto. On the narrow coastal lowlands all the economic life of the country is carried on. Here are situated the large cities and practically all the arable land (c.16% of the total area). Japan's people (with one of the world's highest birthrates) crowd these plains. Pop. density, about 500 persons per sq. mi. for the country as a whole, is about 3,100 per sq. mi. in the settled areas. The people draw extensively on the vast interior mtn. forests (covering more than half of the archipelago) and the upland water-power resources. The enormously rich fishing grounds provide, in a country with little stock raising, a major food item (bonito, cod, sardine, mackerel, herring, tuna, shark, etc.) and account for ½ to ⅔ of the world's catch. The agr. land is occupied by small farms, on the average barely exceeding 2 acres. (Large estates were split up after the Second World War.) The soil is intensively cultivated. Irrigated rice fields, furnishing the chief food crop, make up more than ½ the acreage. Also widely raised are barley, wheat, rye, oats, millet, potatoes, sweet potatoes, soybeans, peas, beans, radishes (the oversized *daikons*), and a great variety of fruit (peaches, pears, grapes, apples, persimmons, tangerines). The celebrated cherry trees, cultivated for their blossoms, are a familiar sight. By painstaking methods Japan is able to grow about 80% of its vegetal food requirements. The most important cash crop is mulberry trees for the raising of silkworms; silk is a chief export item, furnishing in normal times the great bulk of world supply. Other agr. yields include tea, tobacco, flax, hemp, cotton, pyrethrum, camphor. Hokkaido in the N is the principal dairying region. There the climate is characterized by long, cold winters with 6 months of snow cover. Similar conditions prevail in N Honshu. The E coast of the main isl. is tempered by the warm Japan Current, while the W coast along Japan Sea is chilled by the cold Okhotsk Current. Maritime and continental influences combine, and climatic variations are considerable. S Honshu, Shikoku, and Kyushu are subtropical, well suited for the growing of citrus fruit. In Tokyo (at 35°41'N; annual mean temp. 57°F.) winters are somewhat cooler and summers more humid than in New York. Annual mean temp. ranges bet. 41°F. in Hokkaido to c.60°F. in Kyushu. Rainfall reaches 125 inches in S and along parts of the W coast. Typhoons occasionally harass the isls. in Sept. and Oct. Mineral resources are few; only copper, gold, and sulphur deposits suffice for home needs. Gold, sulphur, mercury, and zinc are shipped in small amounts. There are scattered low-grade coal mines (e.g., CHIKUHO in Kyushu, JOBAN N of Tokyo, YUBARI on Hakodate, etc.), but coking coal and anthracite have to be imported. Other minerals include silver, lead, asbestos, salt. The few iron pyrite mines are insufficient for Japan's highly advanced siderurgical industry, which has to import c.80% of its ore. There is a small output in petroleum, principally in NW Honshu. Despite these drawbacks, the Japanese were able to build up a formidable industrial economy. Largest industry is in textiles, which turn out, apart from silk, large quantities of cotton, woolen, and rayon goods—principal articles for foreign trade. Among other major industries are mfg. of chemicals, machinery, and appliances, lumber and wooden articles. Though there are few consumer goods—from the finest precision instruments, drugs, porcelain, and artificial pearls to automobiles—that the country does not produce, its output has suffered through war-time bombing and post-war trade restrictions. Among the leading industrial centers are Tokyo—one of the globe's largest cities; OSAKA, with textile and metal plants; NAGOYA, also a textile center; KYOTO, the old imperial city, hq. of traditional arts and crafts. Heavy industries are mainly concentrated on Kyushu in the cities of YAWATA, WAKAMATSU, FUKUOKA, NAGASAKI, and KOKURA. The principal ports are YOKOHAMA, KOBE, OSAKA, KURE, SHIMONESEKI, NIIGATA, and AOMORI on Honshu; MOJI on Kyushu; HAKODATE and MURORAN on Hokkaido. Japan is served by a good railnet (c.17,000 mi.). Paved automobile roads are relatively scarce. Before the Second World War Japan owned the 3d largest merchant marine, including a modern whaling fleet. Education, partly modeled after the U.S., is compulsory. There are many institutions of univ. rank, among them the universities of Tokyo, Kyoto, Osaka, and Nagoya, Tohoku univ. in Sendai, Kyushu univ. in Fukuoka, and Hokkaido univ. in SAPPORO. Religious affiliations are largely divided (though sometimes held simultaneously) bet. Buddhism and Shintoism. Roman Catholics (chiefly in Nagasaki) and Protestants maintain small communities. Today a rather homogeneous nation, the Japanese are, however, of varied racial origin, believed to be of S and N Mongoloid, Indonesian, and some Malayo-Polynesian stock. The only ethnic minority is the aboriginal, hirsute Ainus—somewhat resembling the Veddas of India—who were most likely absorbed by the Japanese in their gradual penetration of the N archipelago, and of whom only about 20,000 survive in Hokkaido. Japan's early history is lost in legend. The divine origin of the Empire—supposedly founded in 660 B.C. by Jimmu Tenno, the alleged forbear of the present dynasty—was held as official dogma until 1945. Knowledge about the early period is scant, apart from some records dating back to c.400 B.C. The country came early into contact with Korea, and possibly through Korea with the great civilization of China. During 6th cent. A.D. Buddhism was introduced, and Chinese art, written language, literature, philosophy, and political principles were to leave a permanent imprint. At that time an attempt was made to set up a centralized govt. with Nara as ⊙; Kyoto soon succeeded it. Occupation of the main isl. was not completed before the 10th cent. Powerful families and Buddhist priesthood contributed to the decline of imperial rule, while provincial gentry built up their own strength, and a feudal system developed. Civil warfare was almost continuous in 12th cent. Upon the victory of Yoritomo of the Minamoto family temporal power fell to a regime of so-called *shoguns*, whose successive families instituted a rule of military dictatorships (1192–1867), while the imperial court remained in seclusion. In 1274 and again in 1281 Japan was invaded by the Mongols under Kublai Khan, who failed to subdue it. Until arrival of Europeans in 16th cent., extensive commerce was carried on with the Asiatic mainland. First European contact was made (1542) by Portuguese sailors, but the earlier voyages (13th cent.) of Marco Polo to E Asia brought some knowledge about Japan, which as Zipangu was to haunt Columbus. Christianity was introduced by St. Francis Xavier, who reached Japan in 1549. During this epoch the Japanese gained a foothold in S Hokkaido. By the beginning of the 17th cent. most seafaring European nations were admitted, but before long there was a revulsion against Christianity, and only the Dutch were allowed to trade; they were confined to a trading post at Nagasaki. In the late-16th cent. 3 great warriors, Nobunaga, Hideyoshi, and Ieyasu established military control. Hideyoshi's invasions of Korea in 1592 and 1596 failed. Ieyasu set himself up as *shogun* at Yedo (the present Tokyo) and inaugurated the efficient but repressive feudal govts. of the Tokugawa. The Tokugawa system introduced a rigid social hierarchy, headed by the *Samurai* overlords, who subscribed to the *Bushido* code of honor. Oppressions of the peasants led to sporadic uprisings. Yet production and trade expanded, flourishing cities grew up, and a rising merchant class acquired great economic power. For more than 2 centuries Japan remained virtually isolated, and no Japanese was permitted to leave the isls. A rapid transformation of the country's entire structure was precipitated by the mission of Commodore Perry, who in 1854 (he 1st entered Tokyo Bay outside Uraga in 1853) forced the opening of trade with the West. In 1867 the *shogun* was compelled to resign and by the Meiji Restoration (dated from 1868) supreme power was transferred to the imperial line. Thus was initiated a total revolution of the Japanese political, economic, and cultural structure unparalleled in history. The nation embraced the technological civilization of the Occident, and with it some of the more dubious imperialistic practices. Within a short time Japan became a modern capitalistic state and a great naval and military power. Feudalism was abolished in 1871. In 1889 a constitution was granted, modeled on that of Prussia. Industrial development was actively fostered by the state working in close cooperation with the great merchant houses, the *zaibatsu* family trusts. Nationalistic feelings ran high. The pseudo-historic researches of eager scholars did their bit to redress old myths of racial superiority and imperial glory. By 1899 Japan disclaimed the extraterritorial rights of foreign nations, but not until 1911 was full tariff autonomy gained. Japan embarked on the road to conquest. The First Sino-Japanese War (1894–95) led to acquisition of Formosa and Pescadores, as well as the Liaotung Peninsula, which, however, the great powers forced her to relinquish. An alliance with Great Britain in 1902 increased Japanese prestige, which was further enhanced by the victorious conclusion of the Russo-Japanese War (1904–05), in which the Japanese won one of the decisive naval battles of modern times near Tsushima isl. The Treaty of Portsmouth ending the war recognized Japan as a world power. The lease of Kwantung (S Liaotung Peninsula) granted a foothold in Manchuria. It annexed (1910) Korea outright, but the "Twenty-One Demands" on China's sovereignty were rejected through intervention of other nations. During the First World War the Japanese secured the German interests in SHANTUNG (later restored to China) and received the German-owned isls. in the Pacific as mandates. In 1918 Japan took the lead in the Allied military expedition into Siberia until 1922. Trade and industry, though interrupted by 1923 earthquake, continued to expand. But nationalistic army elements clamored for more spectacular ventures. In 1931 the Kwantung army provoked an incident at Mukden and promptly overran all of Manchuria, which was detached from China and set up as the puppet state of Manchukuo. Military extremists—among the most notorious of whom was the Black Dragon Society—instigated the assassination of Prime Minister Inukai in 1932 and attempted a coup d'état in 1936. In July, 1937, after an incident at Peiping (Marco Polo Bridge), Japanese troops invaded the N provs. of China and established a puppet govt. at Nanking. Since Japan adhered to the Anti-Comintern Pact, relations with Russia worsened, leading (1938–39) to armed clashes on the Manchurian border. Japan drifted into the Fascist camp and became (1940), after outbreak of the Second World War, a full-fledged partner of the Axis powers. In 1940 Japan sent troops into French Indochina and announced its design for a "Greater East Asia Co-Prosperity Sphere." In April, 1941, neutrality treaty with Russia was concluded. In Oct., 1941, the militarists achieved complete control, when Gen. Hideki Tojo assumed the premiership. While special Japanese envoys conferred in Washington, Japan opened on Dec. 7, 1941, hostilities against the U.S. and Great Britain by striking at Pearl Harbor, Singapore, the Philippines, and other Pacific possessions. Spectacular initial successes brought Japan to the doors of India, but by the end of 1942 the tide had begun to turn. Isl. by isl. the Allies fought their way toward Japan and by the time atomic bombs were dropped on HIROSHIMA and Nagasaki Japan had already been badly bombed. Formal surrender was made on the U.S. battleship *Missouri* in Tokyo Harbor Sept. 2, 1945. Allied terms had been laid down at the previous Potsdam Conference. The empire was to be reduced to the home isls., it was to be demilitarized, industries were to be geared to peacetime needs, and responsible govt. was to be instituted. Until these conditions were fulfilled, Japan was to be under Allied military occupation, which began immediately to function under Gen. Douglas MacArthur as Supreme Commander of the Allied Powers; Lieut. Gen. Matthew B. Ridgway replaced him in 1951. A Far Eastern Commission, representing 11 Allied nations, was to supervise general policy. In 1946 Japan adopted a new democratic constitution (put into effect in 1947), and parliamentary rule began to function. The emperor publicy disclaimed divine attributes, recognizing the sovereignty of the people. The new constitution lowered the voting age from 25 to 20 and gave franchise to women. Steps were undertaken to curtail the *zaibatsu* family trusts. In 1949 the Allied military govt. turned over many of the responsibilities to local authorities. Japan is administratively divided into 45 prefectures called, variously, *fu*, *ken*, and *to*, from N–S: AOMORI, IWATE, MIYAGI, AKITA, YAMAGATA, FUKUSHIMA, IBARAKI, TOCHIGI, GUMMA, SAITAMA, CHIBA, TOKYO, KANAGAWA, NIIGATA, TOYAMA, ISHIKAWA, FUKUI, YAMANASHI, NAGANO, GIFU, SHIZUOKA, AICHI, MIE, SHIGA, KYOTO, OSAKA, HYOGO, NARA, WAKAYAMA, TOTTORI, SHIMANE, OKAYAMA, HIROSHIMA, YAMAGUCHI, TOKUSHIMA, KAGAWA, EHIME, KOCHI, FUKUOKA, SAGA, NAGASAKI, KUMAMOTO, OITA, MIYAZAKI, KAGOSHIMA. The isl. of Hokkaido forms an administrative unit (Jap. *cho*) of its own, somewhat similar in status to the other prefectures.

Japan, Sea of, arm of Pacific Ocean, bet. Asian mainland and Japan; 1,000 mi. long, 500 mi. wide. Bounded W by Maritime Territory of Russian SFSR and by Korea, E by Jap. isls. of Honshu and Hokkaido and by Sakhalin. It is linked with E.China Sea by Korea Strait, with Japan's Inland Sea by Shimonoseki Strait, with the open Pacific by Tsugaru Strait, and with Sea of Okhotsk by La Pérouse Strait and Tatar Strait. While these straits are quite shallow (up to 500 ft.), the sea itself reaches depths of nearly 13,000 ft. It is traversed by a warm current (Tsushima branch of Japan Current) moving N along the Japanese coast and a cold flow (branch of Okhotsk Current) S along the Asian shore. The latter brings floating ice as far S as the Wonsan-Otaru line. The Sea of Japan receives no major streams except for the Suifun and Tuman rivers; it contains the Korean Ullung Isl. and the Jap. isl. group of Oki-gunto. Main ports are Sovetskaya Gavan and Vladivostok in USSR; Najin, Chongjin, Hungnam, and Wonsan in Korea; Otaru, Niigata, Tsuruga, and Maizuru in Japan.

Japan Current, Jap. *Kuroshio* [=black stream], warm ocean current originating in Philippine Sea; enters East China Sea and flows N along E shores of Formosa and S Ryukyu Isls. to about 26°N, where it forks, with main stream moving N along E shores of Kyushu, Shikoku, and Honshu, then turning E past Aleutian Isls. and S along North American coast. Offshoot of the stream, known as Tsushima Current, enters Sea of Japan through Korea Strait and flows N along W shores of Kyushu and Honshu. Main stream meets Okhotsk Current in the Pacific at about 38°N; its W offshoot meets a branch of Okhotsk Current at about 40°N. Japan Current warms shores of S Japan.

Japanese Alps, a name sometimes given to the volcanic ranges extending N-S through central and widest portion of Honshu, Japan. Highest peak, Mt. Hotaka (10,527 ft.).

Japanese Alps National Park: see CHUBU-SANGAKU NATIONAL PARK.

Japan Trench, submarine depression in North Pacific Ocean, extending in a concave curve from Bonin Isls. along E coast of N Honshu and Hokkaido to the Kuriles. The TUSCARORA DEEP (27,929 ft.; N) was long considered the greatest ocean depth in the world. However, the depth of 30,954 ft. was sounded in 1926 at 30°49'N 142°18'E by the Japanese ship *Manshu*, and the Ramapo Deep (1st thought to be 34,626 ft., later corrected to 34,038 ft.) was sounded during Second World War at 30°43'N 142°28'E by the *U.S.S. Ramapo*. The deepest part of the ocean is in the MINDANAO TRENCH.

Japara or **Djapara** (jäpä'rä), town (pop. 8,356), central Java, Indonesia, on Java Sea, 30 mi. NE of Semarang; trade center for agr. and forested area (sugar, rice, kapok, teak, cassava). Has mosque dating from 16th–17th cent., when town was seat of important Moslem sultanate. It was supplanted (early 19th cent.) by near-by Kudus. Sometimes spelled Djepara.

Japaratuba (zhŏopŏorŏotōō'bŏo), city (pop. 2,457), NE Sergipe, NE Brazil, on railroad and 23 mi. N of Aracaju; ships sugar, alcohol, fruit.

Japen Islands or **Jappen Islands** (yä'pŏon), group (□ 10,907; pop. 28,684), Netherlands New Guinea, in Geelvink Bay; 1°45'S 136°10'E; consists of 3 isls. Largest isl., Japen (c.100 mi. long, c.15 mi. wide), is hilly, with central mountainous area rising to 4,718 ft.; chief settlement is Serui or Seroei (both: sŏorōō'ē'). Other isls. of group are Mios Num or Mios Noem (both: myōs' nōōm'), 16 mi. long, 3 mi. wide, and 10 mi. NW of Japen; and Kurudu or Koeroedoe (both: kōōrōō'dōō), 7 mi. long, and 5 mi. SE of Japen. Agr., fishing. Also spelled Yapen and Yappen.

Japho, Palestine: see JAFFA.

Japla, India: see DALTONGANJ.

Japoatã (zhŏopōōtã'), city (pop. 2,424), NE Sergipe, NE Brazil, 14 mi. S of Propriá; sugar, rice, cotton. Kaolin quarries. Until 1944, spelled Jaboatão.

Japonski Island (jŏopŏn'skē), islet (1939 pop. 39), SE Alaska, in Alexander Archipelago, in Sitka Sound, just W of Sitka; 57°3'N 135°22'W. Site of U.S. naval base in Second World War; installations now occupied by school. Russians had magnetic observatory here.

Jappen Islands, Netherlands New Guinea: see JAPEN ISLANDS.

Japurá River (zhŏopōōrä'), W Amazonas, Brazil, called CAQUETÁ RIVER along its upper course in Colombia. From junction of Caquetá and Apaporis rivers at Brazil-Colombia line, it flows c.400 mi. ESE to the Amazon above Tefé. Total length (with Caquetá R.) probably c.1,150 mi., although estimates range up to 1,700 mi. Navigable in Brazil. In its lower course it is linked to the Amazon by a network of channels forming lakes seasonally. Sometimes spelled Yapurá and Yupurá.

Jaqué (häkā'), village (pop. 358), Darién prov., E Panama, on Pacific Ocean, and 60 mi. S of La Palma; stock raising, lumbering.

Jar (yär), village (pop. 2,839) in Baerum canton, Akershus co., SE Norway, on railroad and 5 mi. W of Oslo city center.

Jara, Cerrito (sĕrē'tō hä'rä), hill on Bolivia-Paraguay border, 65 mi. SW of Puerto Suárez (Bolivia), in the Chaco; 19°48'S 58°23'W. Boundary marker established (1938) in Chaco Peace Conference.

Jara, La (lä hä'rä), high region in W central Spain, cutting across Cáceres and Toledo prov. border along left bank of the Tagus. The Montes de Toledo range is S. Picturesque wooded upland. Raises grain and livestock.

Jara, Villa, Mexico: see VILLA JARA.

Jarabacoa (häräbäkō'ä), town (1950 pop. 2,596), La Vega prov., central Dominican Republic, in the Cordillera Central, on Yaque del Norte and 10 mi. SW of La Vega; resort in fruitgrowing valley. Has fine mtn. climate. Just E are Jimenoa falls, a tourist site and hydroelectric project. Nickel deposit near by.

Jarabub (järäbōōb'), Arabic *Jaghbub*, Ital. *Giarabub*, village (pop. c.250), E Cyrenaica, Libya, near Egyptian border, 140 mi. S of Bardia, in an oasis at N edge of Libyan Desert; date growing. Has small meteorological observatory; 29°45'N 24°31'E. Holy city of the Senusi, with sanctuary containing tomb of founder of sect. Awarded to Italian Libya by Italo-Egyptian treaty of 1925.

Jarabulus, Syria: see JERABLUS.

Jaraco (hä'rä'kō), village (pop. 2,548), Valencia prov., E Spain, near the Mediterranean, 7 mi. NNW of Gandía; rice, oranges, vegetables.

Jarácuaro (härä'kwärō), small island and town (pop. 875), Michoacán, central Mexico, in L. Pátzcuaro, 6 mi. NW of Pátzcuaro; fruitgrowing, fishing.

Jaradu, Egypt: see GARADU.

Jarafuel (häräfwĕl'), town (pop. 2,437), Valencia prov., E Spain, 25 mi. S of Requena; mfg. of walking canes; olive-oil processing, flour milling; lumbering. Saffron, wax, honey.

Jaraguá (zhŏorŏogwä'). **1** Harbor district, Alagoas, Brazil: see MACEIÓ. **2** City (pop. 1,477), S central Goiás, central Brazil, on the Rio das Almas (headstream of Tocantins R.) and 60 mi. N of Goiânia; tobacco, livestock, rare skins; tanning. Gold placers (abandoned). **3** City, Santa Catarina, Brazil: see JARAGUÁ DO SUL.

Jaraguá do Sul (dōō sōōl'), city (pop. 2,537), NE Santa Catarina, Brazil, on railroad and 18 mi. SW of Joinvile; has textile mill. Until 1944, Jaraguá.

Jarahueca (häräwä'kä), village (pop. 352), Las Villas, central Cuba, on railroad and 23 mi. SE of Caibarién, in agr. region (sugar cane, cattle). Has deposits of light oil.

Jaraicejo (härī-thā'hō), town (pop. 2,419), Cáceres prov., W Spain, 16 mi. NNE of Trujillo; flour milling; stock raising; cereals, cork. Has plateresque parochial church.

Jarai Plateau, Vietnam: see KONTUM PLATEAU.

Jaraíz (häräēth'), town (pop. 5,761), Cáceres prov., W Spain, 18 mi. E of Plasencia; pepper- and paprika-shipping center; mfg. of soap, baskets, candy; food processing, olive pressing, sawmilling; figs, fruit, wine, tobacco.

Jaral or **Jaral del Progreso** (häräl' dā prōgrā'sō), city (pop. 5,325), Guanajuato, central Mexico, on central plateau, 20 mi. SW of Celaya, just E of Valle de Santiago. Rail terminus; agr. center (rice, corn, alfalfa, sugar cane, vegetables, fruit, stock).

Jaral, El, Honduras: see EL JARAL.

Jarales (hărä'lĕs), village (pop. 1,199), Valencia co., W central N.Mex., on Rio Grande and 33 mi. S of Albuquerque; trading point in irrigated region; grain, livestock, fruit. Manzano Range and part of Cibola Natl. Forest E.

Jarama River (härä'mä), New Castile, central Spain, rises in the Somosierra range near Segovia prov. border, flows c.100 mi. S, almost entirely through Madrid prov., to the Tagus 2 mi. W of Aranjuez. Its lower course is accompanied by a canal. Widely used for irrigation of central plateau (Meseta). Receives Lozoya, Manzanares, Henares, and Tajuña rivers. At its lower course the Nationalist advance was held (Feb., 1937) during Sp. civil war.

Jaramillo (härämē'yō), village (pop. estimate 500), SE Comodoro Rivadavia military zone, Argentina, on railroad, near Deseado R. (irrigation area), 70 mi. NW of Puerto Deseado; fruitgrowing and sheep-raising center. Petrified forest near by.

Jarandilla (härändē'lyä), town (pop. 3,030), Cáceres prov., W Spain, 24 mi. ENE of Plasencia; agr. trade center (livestock, cereals, wine, flax, honey); ships pepper; footwear mfg., meat processing, olive pressing, flour- and sawmilling. Has medieval castle, the residence (1556–57) of Emperor Charles V before he moved to Yuste.

Jaranwala (jŭrän'välŭ), town (pop. 9,833), Lyallpur dist., E Punjab, W Pakistan, 20 mi. ESE of Lyallpur; rail junction; market center (grain, oilseeds, cotton); oilseed, flour, and rice milling, cotton ginning; engineering and metalworks.

Jarash, Jordan: see JERASH.

Jarbo (yĕr'bō"), Swedish *Järbo*, village (pop. 1,275), Gavleborg co., E Sweden, on Jadra R. and 9 mi. NW of Sandviken; woolen milling.

Jarboesville, Md.: see LEXINGTON PARK.

Jarbridge, village (pop. c.300), Elko co., NE Nev., 29 mi. E of Mountain City, near Idaho line; gold.

Jardim (zhärdēn'), city (pop. 2,218), southernmost Ceará, Brazil, in the Serra do Araripe, near Pernambuco border, 27 mi. SSE of Crato; sugar, cotton, cattle. Gypsum quarries; copper deposits.

Jardim de Piranhas (dĭ pērä'nyŏos), city (pop. 688), S Rio Grande do Norte, NE Brazil, near Paraíba border, 21 mi. W of Caicó; livestock.

Jardim do Seridó (dōō sĭrĕdô'), city (pop. 869), S Rio Grande do Norte, NE Brazil, on Borborema Plateau, 24 mi. SE of Caicó; mining of rare minerals (beryl, tantalite, columbite).

Jardín (härdēn'), town (pop. 2,453), Antioquia dept., NW central Colombia, in Cordillera Occidental, 50 mi. SSW of Medellín; alt. 5,928 ft. Coffeegrowing; corn, beans, sugar cane, yucca fibers; textile milling. Founded 1872.

Jardine (järdēn'), village (pop. c.300), Park co., S Mont., near Yellowstone R., just W of Absaroka Range, c.40 mi. S of Livingston; alt. c.7,000 ft.; arsenic mines and reduction works. Yellowstone Natl. Park just S.

Jardines Bank (härdē'nĕs), shoal off S Cuba, extending c.70 mi. E from Isle of Pines, bounded N by Zapata Peninsula and fringed by numerous keys E of Los Canarreos archipelago; includes the keys Cantiles, Rosario, and Largo. The E section is called Jardinillos Bank.

Jardines de la Reina (dā lä rā'nä), archipelago of coral reefs (c.85 mi. long NW–SE) off Caribbean coast of E Cuba, 70 mi. SW of Camagüey. More than 400 keys, consisting of Cayos de las DOCE LEGUAS (NW) and Laberinto de las Doce Leguas (SE), separated by the Canal de Caballones; bounded by the Gran Banco de Buena Esperanza (NE), sometimes considered to be a part of the Jardines de la Reina.

Jardines del Rey, Cuba: see CAMAGÜEY ARCHIPELAGO.

Jardinillos Bank (härdēnē'yōs), shoal (c.25 mi. long) off S Cuba, 45 mi. SW of Cienfuegos, an E continuation of the Jardines Bank.

Jardinópolis (zhärdēnô'pōōlēs), city (pop. 3,660), NE São Paulo, Brazil, on railroad and 11 mi. NNE of Ribeirão Prêto, in coffee zone; pottery; hats.

Jardón, Argentina: see RANCÚL.

Jaremcze, Ukrainian SSR: see YAREMCHA.

Jarez (zhärā'), region in Loire dept., E central France, extending NE from Saint-Étienne bet. the Monts du Lyonnais (N) and the Mont Pilat (S) along the valley of the Gier. Includes E section of Saint-Étienne coal field and industrial dist. Densely populated, it contains mfg. centers of Izieux, Saint-Chamond, L'Horme, La Grand-Croix, Lorette, Rive-de-Gier. Formerly spelled Jarrez or Jarret.

Jargeau (zhär-zhō'), village (pop. 1,327), Loiret dept., N central France, on left bank of the Loire and 11 mi. ESE of Orléans; metalworking. Here Joan of Arc was wounded in a battle (1429) in which English were defeated.

Jaria Jhanjail, E Pakistan: see SHAMGANJ.

Jari River (zhùrē'), N Brazil, rises on S slope of the Serra de Tumucumaque, flows c.350 mi. SE, forming Pará State–Amapá territory border, to the Amazon delta opposite Gurupá Isl. Navigable in lower course. Formerly spelled Jary.

Ja River, Cameroons: see N'GOKO RIVER.

Jarkent, Kazakh SSR: see PANFILOV.

Jarlsberg og Larvik, Norway: see VESTFOLD.

Jarmaq, Jebel (jĕ'bĕl jär'mäk), or **Jebel Jermaq** (jĕr'–), highest peak (3,963 ft.) of Upper Galilee, N Israel, 5 mi. WNW of Safad; 33°N 35°24'E.

Jarmen (yär'mùn), town (pop. 5,408), in former Prussian Pomerania prov., N Germany, after 1945 in Mecklenburg, on the Peene and 13 mi. SSW of Greifswald; rail junction; agr. market (grain, sugar beets, stock).

Jarna (yĕr'nä"), Swedish *Järna*, village (pop. 813), Stockholm co., E Sweden, 7 mi. SSW of Sodertalje; rail junction; luggage mfg.

Jarnac (zhärnäk'), town (pop. 3,624), Charente dept., W France, on Charente R. and 7 mi. E of Cognac; brandy-distilling center; flour milling, printing. Here, in 1569, the Catholics under the duke of Anjou (later King Henry III) defeated the Huguenots, whose leader, Louis I de Condé, was killed.

Jarnages (zhärnazh'), village (pop. 432), Creuse dept., central France, 10 mi. E of Guéret; livestock raising.

Jarnforsen (yĕrn'fôr"sùn, –fô"shùn), Swedish *Järnforsen*, village (pop. 572), Kalmar co., SE Sweden, on Em R. and 19 mi. E of Vetlanda; sawmilling, furniture mfg.

Jarny (zhärnē'), town (pop. 6,989), Meurthe-et-Moselle dept., NE France, in Briey iron basin, 13 mi. WNW of Metz; rail junction; mfg. of metal bldg. materials; breweries; explosives mfg. Iron mine at Droitaumont (1 mi. S).

Jaro (hä'rō), town (1939 pop. 4,198; 1948 municipality pop. 19,650), N central Leyte, Philippines, 15 mi. WSW of Tacloban, in mountainous area; agr. center (rice, coconuts).

Jarocin (yärô'chĭn), Ger. *Jarotschin* (yärô'chĭn), town (1946 pop. 11,818), Poznan prov., W Poland, 38 mi. SSE of Poznan; rail junction; mfg. (cement goods, bricks, agr. machinery and tools, furniture, roofing materials, beet sugar, flour, leather). Castle ruins.

Jaromer (yä'rômyĕrsh), Czech *Jaroměř*, town (pop. 7,281), NE Bohemia, Czechoslovakia, on Elbe R. and 7 mi. SE of Dvur Kralove; processes hides, furs, jute; mfg. of driving belts, industrial leather goods, textile machinery. Has old belfry, noted church. A stronghold of Hussites in 1421; later (1634–45) occupied by Swedes. Rail junction of JOSEFOV is 2 mi. downstream. Health resort of Velichovsky (vĕ'lĭkhôfskĭ) is 3 mi. W.

Jaronú or **Central Jaronú** (sĕnträl' hārōnōō'), modern sugar-mill village (pop. 925), Camagüey prov., E Cuba, on railroad and 29 mi. N of Camagüey.

Jaroslavice (yä'rôslävĭtsĕ), Ger. *Joslowitz* (yô'slôvĭts), village (pop. 1,337), S Moravia, Czechoslovakia, 10 mi. SW of Znojmo, near Austrian border; vineyards; barley, oats.

Jaroslaw (yärô'swäf), Pol. *Jarosław*, Ger. *Jaroslau* (yä'rôslou), Rus. *Yaroslav* (yŭrùsläf'), town (pop. 19,376), Rzeszow prov., SE Poland, on San R., on railroad and 16 mi. N of Przemysl; flour milling, mfg. of metal- and cement ware, lumbering; brickworks. Included (1382) in Poland; passed (1772) to Austria; returned to Poland in 1919.

Jarotschin, Poland: see JAROCIN.

Jarpas (yĕrp'ōs"), Swedish *Järpås*, village (pop. 405), Skaraborg co., SW Sweden, 10 mi. SW of Lidkoping; metalworking.

Jarpen (yĕr'pùn), Swedish *Järpen*, village (pop. 1,117), Jamtland co., NW Sweden, on upper Indal R. at mouth of small Jarp R. (Swedish *Järpström*), 35 mi. WNW of Ostersund; cellulose mills; hydroelectric station.

Jarque (här'kā), town (pop. 1,215), Saragossa prov., NE Spain, 14 mi. NNW of Calatayud; flour milling; olive oil, potatoes, sugar beets, fruit.

Jarratt, town (pop. 574), Greensville and Sussex counties, S Va., near Nottoway R., 28 mi. S of Petersburg; rail junction; makes insulating board.

Jarrie (zhärē'), village (pop. 1,109), Isère dept., SE France, on height overlooking Romanche R., 6 mi. SSE of Grenoble; electrochemical works (sodium, chlorine, ammonia), plaster factory.

Jarrie, La (lä), village (pop. 524), Charente-Maritime dept., W France, 7 mi. ESE of La Rochelle; flour milling, truck gardening, distilling.

Jarrow (jă'rō), municipal borough (1931 pop. 32,018; 1951 census 28,541), NE Durham, England, on Tyne R. estuary and 5 mi. E of Newcastle-upon-Tyne; shipbuilding; foundries; machinery, chemical, paper, electrical-equipment works. Has basilica founded 685 by Benedict Biscop and now incorporated in St. Paul's church. Near by is site of Saxon monastery where the Venerable Bede worked bet. 682 and 735, when he died here. The shipyards, established 1851 by Sir Charles Palmer, were closed down in 1920s, resulting in widespread unemployment and "hunger marches" on London in the early 1930s. In the Second World War the yards were reopened.

Jaruco (härōō'kō), town (pop. 4,648), Havana prov., W Cuba, on small Jaruco R. and 23 mi. ESE of Havana; rail junction and agr. center (sugar cane, fruit, vegetables). Copper deposits near by. Adjoining (W) are the Escaleras de Jaruco, a picturesque hilly range.

Jarva-Jaani, Yarva-Yani, or **Yyarva-Yani,** Est. *Järva-Jaani* (all: yăr'vä-yä'nē), agr. town (pop. 830), N central Estonia, 16 mi. NE of Paide.

Jarvakandi, Yarvakandi, or **Yyarvakandi,** Est. *Järvakandi* (all: yăr'väkändē), town (commune pop. 2,002), W central Estonia, on rail spur and 16 mi. S of Rapla; glassworking center.

Jarved (yĕr'vād"), Swedish *Järved*, village (pop. 900), Vasternorrland co., NE Sweden, on small inlet of Gulf of Bothnia, just SE of Ornskoldsvik; shoe mfg. Includes Alne (äl'nù) village.

Järvenpää (yăr'vĕnpă"), Swedish *Träskända* (trā'shĕn"dä), village in Tuulusa commune (pop. 16,079), Uusimaa co., S Finland, on 5-mi.-long Tuusula L., 20 mi. NNE of Helsinki; lumber mills, rubber works. Site of agr. col. and of domestic-science teachers' school. Near by, on lake, are houses of many authors and artists; here is "Ainola," since 1904 residence of Sibelius.

Jarville-la-Malgrange (zhärvēl'-lä-mälgrāzh'), SSE suburb (pop. 4,782) of Nancy, Meurthe-et-Moselle dept., NE France, on Meurthe R. and Marne-Rhine Canal; steel mills, foundries, railroad shops, mfg. of furniture, wallpaper.

Jarvis, village (pop. 591), S Ont., 11 mi. E of Simcoe; grist milling, dairying; bees, poultry.

Jarvis Island, isolated Pacific island (□ 1), Line Isls., near equator, 1,100 mi. E of Howland; 0°22'S 160°3'W. Claimed 1857 by U.S. and worked for its guano; annexed 1889 by Great Britain. American colonists brought from Hawaii 1935, Jarvis placed under Dept. of Interior 1936. It is on direct Hawaii-N.Z. route.

Jarvis Sound, S N.J., inlet (1½ mi. long, ¾ mi. wide) just N of Cape May Harbor, to which it is joined by Intracoastal Waterway channel, which enters from Richardson Sound (N).

Jarvso (yĕrfs'ū"), Swedish *Järvsö*, village (pop. 800), Gavleborg co., E central Sweden, on Ljusna R. and 7 mi. SSE of Ljusdal; tourist resort.

Jaryczow Nowy, Ukraine: see NOVY YARYCHEV.

Jary River, Brazil: see JARI RIVER.

Jasa Tomic or **Yasha Tomich** (both: yä'shä tô'mĭch), Serbo-Croatian *Jaša Tomić*, Hung. *Módos* (mō'dôsh), village, Vojvodina, NE Serbia, Yugoslavia, on Tamis R., on railroad and 23 mi. E of Zrenjanin, on Rum. border, in the Banat.

Jasdan (jŭs'dŭn), town (pop. 7,276), central Saurashtra, India, 32 mi. SE of Rajkot; market center (millet, cotton, ghee); oilseed milling, match mfg., hand-loom weaving. Rail spur terminus just E. Was ⊙ former Western Kathiawar state of Jasdan (□ 296; pop. 37,679) of Western India States agency; state merged 1948 with Saurashtra.

Jasenovac (yäsĕ'nôväts), village, N Croatia, Yugoslavia, on Sava R., opposite Una R. mouth, and 30 mi. SE of Sisak, in Slavonia; trade center in plum-growing region; poultry raising. In Second World War, site of a concentration camp.

Jashpur (jŭsh'pōōr), former princely state (□ 1,955; pop. 223,612) of Chhattisgarh States, India; ⊙ was Jashpurnagar. Since 1948, inc. into Raigarh dist. of Madhya Pradesh.

Jashpurnagar (jŭsh'pōōrnŭgŭr"), village, Raigarh dist., E Madhya Pradesh, India, 85 mi. NNE of Raigarh; rice, oilseeds. Lac grown in near-by sal forests. Was ⊙ former princely state of Jashpur, one of Chhattisgarh States.

Jasien (yä'shĕnyù), Pol. *Jasień*, Ger. *Gassen* (gä'sùn), town (1939 pop. 3,186; 1946 pop. 1,180) in Brandenburg, after 1945 in Zielona Gora prov., W Poland, 16 mi. E of Forst; rail junction; agr. market (grain, potatoes, livestock). After 1945, briefly called Goclaw, Pol. *Gocław*.

Jasikan (jäsēkän'), town, S Br. Togoland, administered as part of Eastern Prov., Gold Coast colony, 17 mi. N of Hohoe; cacao market. Also spelled Gjasikan.

Jasin (jŭsĭn'), town (pop. 2,152), Settlement of Malacca, SW Malaya, 15 mi. NE of Malacca; rice, rubber.

Jasina, Ukrainian SSR: see YASINYA.

Jasiolda River, Belorussian SSR: see YASELDA RIVER.

Jask (jäsk), town (1940 pop. 4,938), Eighth Prov., in Makran, SE Iran, port on Gulf of Oman, 145 mi. SE of Bandar Abbas; airport, wireless station, customs and police station. Fishing.

Jaslo (yä'swô), Pol. *Jasło*, town (pop. 3,563), Rzeszow prov., SE Poland, on Wisloka R. and 31 mi. SW of Rzeszow. Rail junction; center of region producing petroleum and natural gas (gas pipe line to Ostrowiec, Radom, Sandomierz); flour milling, lumbering, tanning, mfg. of cement ware, food processing. Explosives factory planned here before Second World War. Manganese ore in vicinity. During Second World War, under Ger. rule called Jessel.

Jasmergarh (jŭsmär'gŭr), village, Kathua dist., SW Kashmir, 17 mi. WNW of Kathua; wheat, rice, corn, bajra. Sometimes spelled Jasmirgarh.

Jasmund Lake, Germany: see RÜGEN.

Jasna Gora, Poland: see CZESTOCHOWA.

Jaso (jŭsō'), village, central Vindhya Pradesh, India, 25 mi. SE of Panna; agr. (millet, wheat, gram). Was ⊙ former petty state of Jaso (□ 72; pop. 8,727) of Central India agency; since 1948, state merged with Vindhya Pradesh.

Jasonville (jā'sùnvĭl), city (pop. 2,937), Greene co., SW Ind., 24 mi. SSE of Terre Haute, in agr. area (grain, fruit); makes cold-storage lockers, rubber goods; timber; bituminous-coal mines. State park near by.

Jasov (yä'sôf), Hung. *Jászó* (yä'sō), village (pop. 1,372), S Slovakia, Czechoslovakia, on Bodva R., on railroad and 13 mi. WSW of Kosice. Noted for 18th-cent. monastery with large library, art collections, and botanical gardens. Has castle ruins, stalactite caverns. Numerous prehistoric remains near by.

Jasper, town (pop. estimate 1,000), W Alta., near B.C. border, in Rocky Mts., on Athabaska R. and 200 mi. WSW of Edmonton; alt. 3,470 ft.; tourist center in Jasper Natl. Park. Overlooked by peaks over 10,000 ft. high.

Jasper. 1 County (□ 373; pop. 7,473), central Ga.; ⊙ Monticello. Bounded W by Ocmulgee R. (forms Lloyd Shoals Reservoir here); drained by Little R. Piedmont agr. (cotton, corn, truck, livestock) and timber area. Formed 1807. **2** County (□ 495; pop. 12,266), SE central Ill.; ⊙ Newton. Agr. (livestock, poultry, redtop seed, corn, wheat; dairy products). Some mfg. (wood products, brooms, beverages). Drained by Embarrass R. Formed 1831. **3** County (□ 562; pop. 17,031), NW Ind.; ⊙ Rensselaer. Bounded N by Kankakee R.; drained by Iroquois R. Farming, stock raising; some flour and lumber milling, dairying. Formed 1835. **4** County (□ 736; pop. 32,305), central Iowa; ⊙ Newton. Prairie agr. area (hogs, cattle, poultry, corn, oats, wheat), drained by Skunk and North Skunk rivers, and with bituminous-coal deposits mined in SW. Formed 1846. **5** County (□ 683; pop. 18,912), E central Miss.; ⊙ Paulding and Bay Springs. Drained by Tallahala Creek and short Tallahoma Creek, and by affluents of Leaf R. Agr. (corn, cotton); lumbering. Oil fields. Includes part of Bienville Natl. Forest. Formed 1833. **6** County (□ 642; pop. 79,106), SW Mo.; ⊙ Carthage. In Ozark region; drained by Spring R. Agr. (grain, poultry, strawberries), dairying; mfg. (notably at JOPLIN); lead, zinc mines; marble, limestone quarries; oak timber. Formed 1841. **7** County (□ 578; pop. 10,995), extreme S S.C.; ⊙ Ridgeland. Bounded W by Savannah, NE by Coosawhatchie, SE by Broad rivers. Agr. area (corn, potatoes, tomatoes), livestock; timber. Formed 1912. **8** County (□ 969; pop. 20,049), E Texas; ⊙ Jasper. Bounded W by Neches R. Heavily wooded; lumbering chief industry. Includes part of Angelina Natl. Forest. Diversified agr.; livestock raising, dairying. Clay, fuller's earth mining. Formed 1836.

Jasper. 1 City (pop. 8,589), ⊙ Walker co., NW central Ala., 35 mi. NW of Birmingham, in cotton, corn, and truck area; lumber and lumber products, cotton, building materials. Coal mines near by. Settled 1815. **2** Town (pop. 407), ⊙ Newton co., NW Ark., 15 mi. SSW of Harrison, in the Ozarks; lead and zinc mining; lumber milling. **3** City (pop. 2,327), ⊙ Hamilton co., N Fla., near Ga. line, 15 mi. N of Live Oak; trade and processing center, in tobacco and timber region. Settled c.1825. **4** Town (pop. 1,380), ⊙ Pickens co., N Ga., c.50 mi. N of Atlanta; textile and lumber mills. Inc. 1857. **5** City (pop. 5,215), ⊙ Dubois co., SW Ind., on Patoka R. and 45 mi. NE of Evansville, in agr. area (grain, strawberries); mfg. (desks, canned goods, wood products, gloves); bituminous-coal mines; timber. Settled 1830. **6** Village (pop. 840), Pipestone and Rock counties, SW Minn., near S.Dak. line, 11 mi. SSW of Pipestone, in agr. area (grain, livestock, poultry, potatoes); dairy products. Silica quarries near by. **7** City (pop. 776), Jasper co., SW Mo., near branch of Spring R., 11 mi. N of Carthage; dairying; grain products. **8**

Village (pop. 1,198), ⊙ Marion co., SE Tenn., near Ala. and Ga. lines, 18 mi. W of Chattanooga, in fertile Sequatchie R. valley (dairying, tobacco and cotton growing); makes hosiery, pottery. **9** City (pop. 4,403), ⊙ Jasper co., E Texas, c.60 mi. NNE of Beaumont in pine-woods area; lumber milling, wood-products mfg.; ships cattle, agr. produce; canneries. Fish hatchery near by. Settled 1824; inc. 1926.

Jasper Lake (8 mi. long, 1 mi. wide), expansion of Athabaska R., W Alta., in Rocky Mts., in Jasper Natl. Park, 13 mi. N of Jasper. N end of lake was last site of Jasper House, Hudson's Bay Co. trading post, moved here 1801 from Brûlé L., abandoned 1875.

Jasper National Park (□ 4,200), W Alta., on B.C. border, in Rocky Mts., 170 mi. WSW of Edmonton; 130 mi. long, 45 mi. wide. Noted for its spectacular alpine scenery. Within park are some of the highest peaks of Canadian Rockies (Mts. Chown, Edith Cavell, Fryatt, Chaba, Alberta, Dais, Columbia, Kitchener, Athabaska, Poboktan, Balinhard; Sunwapta Peak, Simon Peak, and The Twins) and part of the large Columbia Icefield. Athabaska R. rises in S part of park. Lakes include Maligne and Jasper. Jasper is chief tourist resort. Yellowhead Pass (W) is important route into B.C. Big game abounds. Park was established 1907. Borders S on Banff Natl. Park and W on Hamber Provincial Park, B.C.

Jaspur (jŭs'pŏŏr), town (pop. 18,250), Naini Tal dist., N Uttar Pradesh, India, 9 mi. NW of Kashipur; hand-loom cotton weaving; trades in rice, wheat, mustard, sugar cane, timber.

Jasrana (jŭsrä'nŭ), town (pop. 2,084), Mainpuri dist., W Uttar Pradesh, India, 22 mi. W of Mainpuri; wheat, gram, pearl millet; barley, jowar.

Jassans-Riottier (zhäsā'-rēōtyā'), village (pop. 893), Ain dept., E France, on left bank of the Saône and 2 mi. E of Villefranche; sawmilling, mfg. of fertilizer and work clothing.

Jasso, Mexico: see TULA, Hidalgo.

Jassy or **Iasi** (both: yä'sē, Rum. yäsh), Rum. *Iaşi*, city (1948 pop. 94,075), ⊙ Jassy prov., NE Rumania, in Moldavia, c.200 mi. NNE of Bucharest in a region of vineyards near Prut R.; 47°10'N 27°37'E. Historical, cultural, and commercial center; important rail junction; specializes in production of textiles (notably cotton, silk, wool, rugs, knitwear); mfg. of furniture, metal articles, soap, candles, cosmetics, pharmaceuticals. Food and tobacco processing, tanning, printing. Jassy is well known for its educational institutions: univ. (founded 1860), academies of music, art, and drama. Its 17th-cent. Trei Ierarhi [=three hierarchs] church is an outstanding memento of Moldavian architecture. Also notable are 15th-cent. St. Nicholas church with exterior frescoes, several 17th-cent. churches, natl. theater, botanical gardens, and museums. First mentioned in 1408, Jassy became an Orthodox bishopric in 15th cent. and succeeded (1565) Suceava as ⊙ Moldavia. Was repeatedly burned and sacked by Turks, Tatars, and Russians. Treaty of Jassy (1792) put end to Russo-Turkish War of 1787–92. During 19th cent. city developed into a cultural center of first importance. In First World War it was temporarily ⊙ Rumania. Russian troops occupied it in 1944. Until 1941 it had large Jewish pop., which was massacred, on German instigation, in one of worst pogroms in history.

Jastrebarsko (yä'strĕbärskô), village (pop, 1,558), N Croatia, Yugoslavia, on railroad and 16 mi. SW of Zagreb; trade center in winegrowing region; fishery. Castle. Formerly called Jaska.

Jastrowie (yästrô'vyĕ), Ger. *Jastrow* (yä'strō), town (1939 pop. 5,891; 1946 pop. 2,891) in Pomerania, after 1945 in Koszalin prov., NW Poland, 20 mi. N of Schneidermühl (Pila); agr. market (grain, sugar beets, potatoes, livestock); woolen milling. Until 1938, in former Prussian prov. of Grenzmark Posen–Westpreussen.

Jaswantnagar (jŭs'vŭntnŭgŭr), town (pop. 6,942), Etawah dist., W Uttar Pradesh, India, 10 mi. NW of Etawah; road center; mfg. of ornamental brassware; trades in pearl millet, wheat, barley, oilseeds, yarn, cattle.

Jaszalsoszentgyörgy (yä'sŏl-shōsĕnd-dyûr"dyû), Hung. *Jászalsószentgyörgy*, town (pop. 5,340), Jasz-Nagykun-Szolnok co., E central Hungary, on Zagyva R. and 3 mi. W of Jaszladany; corn, wheat, hogs, sheep.

Jaszapati (yä'sŏpätĭ), Hung. *Jászapáti*, town (pop. 12,150), Jasz-Nagykun-Szolnok co., E central Hungary, 10 mi. E of Jaszbereny; wheat, corn, vineyards; horses, hogs.

Jaszarokszallas (yä'särôksäl-läsh), Hung. *Jászárokszállás*, town (pop. 14,310), Jasz-Nagykun-Szolnok co., N central Hungary, on short Gyöngyös R. and 10 mi. SSE of Gyöngyös; wheat, corn, vineyards.

Jaszbereny (yäs'bĕrānyû), Hung. *Jászberény*, city (pop. 31,070), Jasz-Nagykun-Szolnok co., central Hungary, on Zagyva R. and 19 mi. S of Gyöngyös; market center for agr. (wheat, corn), livestock region; tobacco-shipping center. Agr. school, mus. of folk art here.

Jaszdozsa (yäs'dō-zhŏ), Hung. *Jászdózsa*, town (pop. 4,509), Jasz-Nagykun-Szolnok co., E central Hungary, on Tarna R. and 6 mi. SSE of Jaszarokszallas; corn, potatoes, horses.

Jaszfelsöszentgyörgy (yäs'fĕl-shûsĕnd-dyûr"dyû), Hung. *Jászfelsőszentgyörgy*, town (pop. 2,770), Jasz-Nagykun-Szolnok co., central Hungary, on Zagyva R. and 6 mi. W of Jaszbereny; vineyards.

Jaszfenyszaru (yäs'fānyûsŏrŏŏ), Hung. *Jászfényszaru*, town (pop. 8,017), Jasz-Nagykun-Szolnok co., central Hungary, on Zagyva R. and 7 mi. S of Hatvan; wheat, corn, hogs; vineyards.

Jaszjakohalma (yäs'yäkōhōlmŏ), Hung. *Jászjákóhalma*, town (pop. 4,386), Jasz-Nagykun-Szolnok co., central Hungary, on Tarna R. and 4 mi. E of Jaszbereny; corn, melons, hogs.

Jaszkarajenö (yäs'kŏrŏyĕnû), Hung. *Jászkarajenő*, town (pop. 7,003), Pest-Pilis-Solt-Kiskun co., central Hungary, 10 mi. SSW of Szolnok; flour mills; wheat, barley, paprika; horses.

Jaszkiser (yäs'kĭshär), Hung. *Jászkisér*, town (pop. 7,258), Jasz-Nagykun-Szolnok co., central Hungary, 5 mi. SE of Jaszapati; tobacco-shipping center.

Jaszladany (yäs'lŏdänyû), Hung. *Jászladány*, town (pop. 10,098), Jasz-Nagykun-Szolnok co., central Hungary, 13 mi. N of Szolnok; wheat, paprika, cattle, hogs.

Jasz-Nagykun-Szolnok (yäs'-nŏ'dyûkŏŏn-sôl'nôk), Hung. *Jász-Nagykun-Szolnok*, county (□ 2,096; pop. 439,959), E central Hungary; ⊙ Szolnok. Level region in the Alföld, drained by Tisza and Zagyva rivers. Agr. (wheat, barley, corn), wine; honey, tobacco, sugar beets also raised; livestock (cattle, hogs, horses, sheep), poultry in SE; some fruit (apples, pears) in N. Regulation of Tisza R. in 19th cent. and recent govt. swamp-draining projects have greatly increased arable areas. Industry at Szolnok (soap- and candleworks, distillery), Jaszbereny, Karcag (flour mill, brickworks), and Mezötur (flour mills).

Jaszo, Czechoslovakia: see JASOV.

Jaszszentandras (yäs'sĕntŏndräsh), Hung. *Jászszentandrás*, town (pop. 5,199), Jasz-Nagykun-Szolnok co., E central Hungary, 5 mi. W of Heves; vineyards.

Jasztelek (yäs'tĕlĕk), Hung. *Jásztelek*, town (pop. 2,745), Jasz-Nagykun-Szolnok co., E central Hungary, on Zagyva R. and 5 mi. ESE of Jaszbereny; wheat, potatoes, cattle, vineyards.

Jataí (zhŭtäē'), city (pop. 2,438), SW Goiás, central Brazil, 50 mi. W of Rio Verde; coffee, grapes, livestock. Formerly spelled Jatahy.

Jataté River (hätätä'), in Chiapas, S Mexico, rises in Sierra de Hueytepec S of Ocosingo, flows c.150 mi. SE, to join Lacantún R. (Usumacinta system) near Guatemala border.

Jath (jŭt), town (pop. 7,556), Satara South dist., S Bombay, India, 45 mi. ENE of Sangli; local market for millet, cotton, wheat, rice. Was ⊙ former princely state of Jath (□ 972; pop. 107,036) in Deccan States, Bombay; state inc. 1949 into Satara South, Sholapur, and Belgaum dists., Bombay.

Jati (jä'tē), village, Tatta dist., SW Sind, W Pakistan, 85 mi. ESE of Karachi; market center for salt, millet, rice. Also called Mughalbhin.

Jatibonico (hätēbōnē'kō), town (pop. 3,486), Camagüey prov., E Cuba, on Río Jatibonico del Sur, on Central Highway, on railroad and 27 mi. W of Ciego de Ávila, in agr. region (sugar cane, tobacco, livestock). Mfg. of pottery and cigars. The sugar central of Jatibonico is just SE.

Jatibonico del Norte, Río (rē'ō, dĕl nôr'tā), central Cuba, rises in the Sierra de Jatibonico 8 mi. SSE of Caibarién, flows c.40 mi. along Las Villas–Camagüey prov. border to N coast. Has irregular course, obstructed by cataracts, and flowing partly through subterranean trench (2½ mi. long). The Jatibonico del Sur flows S c.60 mi. along prov. border.

Jatinã (zhŭtēnä'), city (pop. 1,038), W central Pernambuco, NE Brazil, on left bank of São Francisco R. (Bahia border) and 60 mi. SW of Serra Talhada; cotton, cereals. Until 1944, called Belém.

Játiva or **Játiba** (both: hä'tēvä), anc. *Saetabis*, city (pop. 17,496), Valencia prov., E Spain, 35 mi. SSW of Valencia. Industrial and agr. trade center on fertile plain (oranges, rice) at foot of hill crowned by 15th-cent. castle and fortifications (formerly a state prison). Rice milling and shipping, brandy and liqueur distilling, tanning; cementworks. Other mfg.: paper, bicycles, knit goods, linen, burlap, felt hats, leather goods, and toys. Has remains of anc. walls and Moorish bldgs., and Gothic collegiate church (15th cent.; restored), silk exchange, and several convents and fine mansions. Noted under Romans for its linen. Moors founded here 1st paper factory in Europe. Was temporary residence (14th cent.) of Borja or Borgia family. Took active part in War of the Comunidades (1520–21) against royalists and opposed (1707) Philip V in War of Spanish Succession. Pope Alexander VI and the painter Ribera were b. here. At near-by Canals, Pope Calixtus III was b.

Jatiwangi or **Djatiwangi** (both: jätēwäng'ē), town (pop. 11,022), W Java, Indonesia, 30 mi. W of Cheribon; trade center for agr. area (rice and sugar); sugar and textile mills.

Jatobá (zhŭtŏŏbä'). **1** City (pop. 1,283), W Paraíba, NE Brazil, 12 mi. SSE of Cajàzeiras; cotton, sugar, tobacco. Formerly called São José de Piranhas. **2** City, Pernambuco, Brazil: see PETROLÂNDIA.

Jatta Ismail Khel (jŭt'tŭ ĭsmīl' khāl'), village, Kohat dist., E North-West Frontier Prov., W Pakistan, 18 mi. SSW of Kohat. Rock salt quarried (S) and largely exported to Kohat and other towns of prov. Gypsum deposits (S). Sometimes called Jatta.

Jaú (zhä-ŏŏ'), city (pop. 18,201), central São Paulo, Brazil, near Tietê R., 100 mi. WNW of Campinas; agr.-processing center at E edge of coffee zone. Mfg. of agr. machinery, furniture; manioc and cottonseed-oil processing, brewing, distilling. Trades in coffee, sugar, potatoes, rice, livestock. Has noteworthy church and town hall. Airfield. Formerly spelled Jahú.

Jau, Oman: see BARAIMI.

Jauareté, Brazil: see IAUARETÊ.

Jauer, Poland: see JAWOR.

Jauernig, Czechoslovakia: see JAVORNIK.

Jauf, Al Jauf, or **Al-Jawf** (ăl jouf'), town and oasis, N Hejaz, northernmost Saudi Arabia, at N edge of the Nafud, 250 mi. E of Ma'an, at head of the Wadi Sirhan; 29°58'N 39°34'E. Agr. center; dates, wheat, barley, millet, corn, alfalfa, vegetables, fruit. Handicrafts (weaving, leatherworking). A major caravan center bet. Syrian Desert and central Arabian Peninsula, it forms a long, narrow belt of gardens and palm groves, dominated (SE) by a stone castle. Also called Jauf al Amir (or Jauf el Amr), the oasis was formerly considered part of Jebel Shammar.

Jauf or **Jawf,** large oasis in Yemen hinterland, at edge of the desert Rub' al Khali; 16°10'N 44°50'E. Here are the ruins of Ma'in, ⊙ Minaean kingdom (c.1200–650 B.C.), which was succeeded by the Sabaean kingdom of MARIB.

Jaugada (jou'gŭdŭ), ruined fort in Ganjam dist., SE Orissa, India, on Rushikulya R. and 14 mi. NNE of Berhampur; contains Asokan rock edicts.

Jauja (hou'hä), city (pop. 8,276), ⊙ Jauja prov. (□ 4,200; enumerated pop. 110,790, plus estimated 5,000 Indians), Junín dept., central Peru, on railroad, on Mantaro R. and 25 mi. NW of Huancayo; 11°47'S 75°30'W; alt. 11,187 ft. Flour milling, lumbering; agr. products (wheat, potatoes); cattle and sheep raising. Health resort.

Jaumave (houmä'vä), town (pop. 1,839), Tamaulipas, NE Mexico, in E outliers of Sierra Madre Occidental, 28 mi. SW of Ciudad Victoria; henequen, cereals, stock.

Jaungulbene, Latvia: see GULBENE.

Jaunjelgava or **Yaunyelgava** (youn'yĕl"gävä), Ger. *Friedrichstadt*, city (pop. 2,153), S central Latvia, in Zemgale, on left bank of the Western Dvina and 45 mi. SE of Riga; leather mfg., sawmilling. Has castle, botanic garden.

Jaunlatgale, Russian SFSR: see PYTALOVO.

Jaun Pass (youn) (4,957 ft.) in Bernese Alps, W central Switzerland, N of Zweisimmen; joins Bern and Fribourg cantons.

Jaunpur (joun'pŏŏr), district (□ 1,555; pop. 1,387,439), SE Uttar Pradesh, India; ⊙ Jaunpur. On Ganges Plain; drained by Gumti R. Agr. (barley, rice, corn, wheat, sugar cane, gram, mustard, millets); mango, nahua, sissoo, and babul groves. Main towns: Jaunpur, Machhlishahr, Shahganj.

Jaunpur, town (pop. 44,833), ⊙ Jaunpur dist., SE Uttar Pradesh, India, on the Gumti and 35 mi. NW of Benares; road center; perfume mfg.; trades in grains, sugar cane, oilseeds. Fort, built 1360 by Firoz Shah Tughlak, who founded town, with mosque built from ruined temples. Other mosques include Jami Masjid (completed c.1478) and Atala Masjid (built 1408 on site of Hindu temple). Was ⊙ strong independent Moslem kingdom, 1397–1478; conquered 1559 by Akbar. Buddhist monasteries formerly stood by river. Passed to British in 1775.

Jáuregui (hou'rāgē), town (pop. estimate 1,800), Buenos Aires prov., Argentina, 4 mi. SW of Luján; livestock center; linen mill.

Jauru River (zhourŏŏ'), W central Mato Grosso, Brazil, rises in the Serra dos Parecis, flows c.170 mi. SSE to the Paraguay below Cáceres. Diamonds, sapphires, and rubies found in stream.

Java (jä'vŭ), Indonesian *Djawa*, island (□ 48,842; pop. 39,755,902, including offshore isls.), Greater Sundas, INDONESIA, bet. Java Sea (N) and Indian Ocean (S), 20 mi. SE of Sumatra across Sunda Strait, just W of Bali across Bali Strait, c.220 mi. S of Borneo across Java Sea; 6°5'–8°52'S 105°18'–114°36'E. Only the 4th largest isl. of Indonesia, but the most important culturally, politically, and economically. The long, narrow isl. (650 mi. long, 40–130 mi. wide) has E–W volcanic mtn. range (with several active volcanoes) traversing its length and rising to 12,060 ft. in Mt. Mahameru. In W part is extensive highland region; wide fertile plain along irregular N coast. Rivers are mostly short and torrential, largest being the Solo and Brantas (important for irrigation). Warm and humid in coastal regions; cool and dry in interior highlands. Annual mean temp. ranges from 60° to 80°F. Heavy rainfall during period of W monsoon (Nov.–March); dry the rest of the year. Luxuriant tropical vegetation and dense forests of casuarina, teak, sago palms, banyans. Wild animals include tigers, rhinoceroses, apes, panthers. In highlands in Preanger region are grown rubber, tea, coffee, tobacco, and cinchona; mtn. slopes have terraced rice fields. Sugar cane and kapok are grown in E part of isl. Other crops: peanuts, cassava. Producing most of world's supply of quinine, Java also exports rubber, sugar, teak. There are oil fields and sulphur, gold, and phosphate mines. Industries: textile milling, tanning, metal-working; mfg. of drugs, chemicals, glass, tiles. Java is known for silver craft and batik work. Surplus inhabitants are moved to near-by isls., but Java remains one of most densely populated areas of world. Here, near TRINIL, were found (1891–92) fossilized remains of Java man (*Pithecanthropus erectus*). Malayan inhabitants include the Javanese in central and E Java, the Sudanese in W, and Madurese in E. Numerous Chinese and Arabs live in coastal areas. Java has been predominantly Moslem since 15th cent., but Buddhism and Hinduism have left greatest effect on artistic life of the Javanese. Best known of Buddhistic remains is monumental shrine BOROBUDUR. Largest city is JAKARTA (formerly Batavia), ⊙ Indonesia, with its port at TANJUNGPRIOK. Main trade centers: JOGJAKARTA, SOLO (Surakarta), SEMARANG, BOGOR, BANDUNG, CHERIBON, PEKALONGAN, SUKABUMI, MALANG, KEDIRI. Colonization of central and E Java was begun in 7th cent. by Hindus. In 11th and 12th cent. Hindu-Javanese kingdom of East Java included Bali, Madura, and parts of Sumatra and Malay Peninsula. The Hindu-Javanese state of Majapahit (founded 1293) flourished in 14th cent.; it was succeeded in 16th cent. by Moslem state of Mataram. Following the Portuguese, the Dutch came 1596 and established ⊙ at Batavia in 1619. Java was occupied (1811–16) by the British under Raffles. In Second World War, Java was left open to Jap. invasion by the disastrous Allied defeat in battle of Java Sea (Feb., 1942). At end of war, roughly half (central and W sections) came under control of the original Republic of Indonesia. The Du.-sponsored autonomous states of East Java and West Java (formed 1948) became part of Indonesia in 1950, and the isl. (with Madura) was divided into 3 provinces.

Java (jă'vŭ), city (pop. 433), Walworth co., N S.Dak., 8 mi. E of Selby; trading point for cattle-raising region; dairy products, livestock, poultry, grain.

Javadi Hills (jŭvä'dē), E outlying group of S Eastern Ghats (separated by upper Palar R. valley), E central Madras, India; c.60 mi. long, up to c.35 mi. wide; rise to over 1,000 ft. Chief products: sandalwood, tanbark, nux vomica, hemp narcotics, tamarind, beeswax. Cheyyar R. rises on central plateau. Historic rock fortresses at Karnaticgarh peak (SE; 3,180 ft.) and Kailasagarh peak (NE; c.2,740 ft.).

Java Head or **Gede Point,** westernmost point of Java, Indonesia, in Indian Ocean, opposite Prinsen isl.; 6°46'S 105°12'E.

Javalón River or **Jabalón River** (both: hävälōn'), Ciudad Real prov., S central Spain, in New Castile, rises near Albacete prov. border SE of Montiel, flows c.100 mi. W and NW, past Valdepeñas, to the Guadiana 11 mi. SW of Ciudad Real.

Javari River (zhŭvŭrē'), Sp. *Yavarí* (yävärē'), on Brazil-Peru border, rises near 7°S 74°W, flows c.600 mi. NE, bet. Loreto dept. (Peru) and Amazonas (Brazil), to the Amazon near Benjamin Constant. Navigable. Old Braz. spelling, Javary.

Java Sea (jä'vŭ), part of the Pacific, bet. Borneo (N) and Java (S), connected with S.China Sea by Karimata Strait, with Celebes Sea by Macassar Strait, and with Indian Ocean by Sunda Strait; c.600 mi. E–W, c.200 mi. N–S. In Second World War scene of disastrous Allied naval defeat (Feb. 27–March 1, 1942) which exposed Java to Jap. invasion.

Java Trench, submarine depression in Indian Ocean, off S coast of Java. Here the greatest depth (24,440 ft.) of the Indian Ocean was obtained (1925–28) at 10°21'S 110°6'E, E of Christmas Isl.

Jávea (hä'väā), seaport (pop. 4,275), Alicante prov., E Spain, in picturesque site on the Mediterranean, 22 mi. SE of Gandía; exports raisins, wine, citrus from fertile hinterland. Olive-oil processing, straw-hat mfg. Has remains of anc. walls and medieval castle. Stalactite caves near by.

Javie, La (lä zhävē'), village (pop. 230), Basses-Alpes dept., SE France, on the Bléone and 8 mi. NE of Digne, in Provence Alps; alt. 2,260 ft. Fruitgrowing.

Javier Island (hävēr'), just off coast of Aysén prov., S Chile, on inner Gulf of Peñas; 47°5'S 74°20'W; 14 mi. long, 1–7 mi. wide.

Javor, Germany: see GREAT ARBER.

Javorice (yä'vôrĭtsĕ), second-highest mountain (2,738 ft.) in Bohemian-Moravian Heights, SW Moravia, Czechoslovakia, 16 mi. SW of Jihlava; granite quarries at SE foot.

Javorina (yä'vôrĭnä), village (pop. 407), N Slovakia, Czechoslovakia, on NE slope of the High Tatra, 16 mi. NNW of Poprad, near Pol. border; part of commune of Vysoke Tatry; alt. 3,280 ft.; woodworking. Noted natural park and game reserve to SE. Javorina, together with surrounding area, was inc. into Poland after Munich Pact (1938); returned to Slovakia after partition (1939) of Poland.

Javor Mountains or **Yavor Mountains** (both: yävôr'), in Dinaric Alps, E Bosnia, Yugoslavia; extend c.15 mi. NW–SE; highest peak (5,041 ft.) is 4 mi. ESE of Han Pijesak.

Javornik (yä'vôrnyĕk), Czech *Javorník*, Ger. *Jauernig* (you'ŭrnĭkh), village (pop. 1,678), NW Silesia, Czechoslovakia, 14 mi. NW of Jesenik, near Pol. border, in textile-mfg. and oat-growing area; rail terminus. Has old castle.

Javornik, Slovak *Javorník*, highest mountain (3,512 ft.) of the Javorniky, NW Slovakia, Czechoslovakia, 35 mi. SE of Ostrava.

Javornik or **Yavornik** (both: yä'vôrnĭk), mountain (3,483 ft.) in Dinaric Alps, E Bosnia, Yugoslavia, 7 mi. NNE of Kladanj; Drinjaca R. flows along S and E foot.

Javorniky (yä'vôrnyēkĭ), Slovak *Javorníky*, Hung. *Fehér Karpatok* (fĕ'hâr kŏr'pŏtôk), mountain range, NW Slovakia, Czechoslovakia; extends c.40 mi. NE–SW, bet. Cadca (N) and Lysa Pass (S); rises to 3,512 ft. in Javornik mtn.

Jawad (jä'vŭd), town (pop. 7,214), W Madhya Bharat, India, 9 mi. N of Nimach; market center for cotton, millet, wheat, gram; oilseed milling, cotton ginning; handicrafts (cloth, bracelets).

Jawar (jä'vŭr), town (pop. 2,055), W Bhopal state, India, 60 mi. WSW of Bhopal; agr. (wheat, gram, cotton, millet); hand-loom weaving.

Jawf, Yemen: see JAUF.

Jawf, Al-, Saudi Arabia: see JAUF.

Jawhar (jŭv'är), village, Thana dist., W Bombay, India, 50 mi. NNE of Thana, on outlier of Western Ghats; agr. market (millet, pulse). Teak in near-by forests. Was ⊙ former princely state of Jawhar (□ 308; pop. 65,126) in Gujarat States, Bombay; state inc. 1949 into Thana dist.

Jawor (yä'vôr), Ger. *Jauer* (you'ŭr), town (1939 pop. 13,817; 1946 pop. 9,690) in Lower Silesia, after 1945 in Wroclaw prov., SW Poland, 11 mi. S of Liegnitz (Legnica); linen milling, metalworking, mfg. of leather goods, chemicals, soap, stoves; granite quarrying. Has late-Gothic church. In 14th cent., ⊙ principality under branch of Pol. Piast dynasty.

Jaworow, Ukrainian SSR: see YAVOROV.

Jaworzno (yävôzh'nô), town (pop. 17,506), Krakow prov., S Poland, 12 mi. E of Katowice; coal mining; mfg. of chemicals, wood products, flour. Abandoned galena mine.

Jaxartes River, Central Asia: see SYR DARYA, river.

Jay, county (□ 386; pop. 23,157), E Ind., bounded E by Ohio line; ⊙ Portland. Agr. area (livestock, grain, poultry, soybeans, truck). Mfg. especially of stone, clay, and glass products; vehicle parts, dairy and food products; lumber milling. Natural-gas and oil wells; timber. Drained by Salamonie R. Formed 1835.

Jay. 1 Town (pop. 547), Santa Rosa co., NW Fla., 38 mi. N of Pensacola, near Ala. line. **2** Town (pop. 3,102), Franklin co., W central Maine, on the Androscoggin just above Livermore Falls. Village (pop. 1,135) of Chisholm (chĭ'zŭm) has pulp and paper mills; North Jay has granite quarries. Inc. 1795. **3** Resort village, Essex co., NE N.Y., in the Adirondacks, on East Branch of Ausable R. and 26 mi. SSW of Plattsburg. **4** Town (pop. 697), ⊙ Delaware co., NE Okla., near Ark. line, 25 mi. SE of Vinita; trade center for agr. area (fruit, berries, livestock); limestone quarries; timber. **5** Town (pop. 243), Orleans co., N Vt., on Que. line, 11 mi. W of Newport. Jay Peak is SW.

Jay, Fort, N.Y.: see GOVERNORS ISLAND.

Jayabhum, Thailand: see CHAIYAPHUM.

Jayanca (hīăng'kä), town (pop. 3,413), Lambayeque dept., NW Peru, on coastal plain, on Pan-American Highway and 22 mi. NNE of Lambayeque, in irrigated Leche R. valley (rice, corn, fruit); rice milling; apiaries, vineyards.

Jayankondacholapuram (jŭyŭng"kōndŭchō'lŭpōōrŭm or **Jayamkondacholapuram** (jŭyŭm"–), town (pop. 10,831), Trichinopoly dist., S Madras, India, 50 mi. NE of Trichinopoly; cotton weaving; brass vessels. Near-by village of Gangaikondapuram is site of large 11th-cent. Dravidian temple. Formerly spelled Jeyamkondacholapuram.

Jayaque (hīä'kā), city (pop. 3,191), La Libertad dept., SW Salvador, in coastal range, 8 mi. W of Nueva San Salvador; coffee-growing center; coffee processing, light mfg. Gypsum and marble deposits near by.

Jayena (hīā'nä), town (pop. 1,584), Granada prov., S Spain, 20 mi. SW of Granada; olive oil, cereals; lumber. Completely destroyed in 1884 by earthquake; was soon rebuilt.

Jayhun River, Central Asia: see AMU DARYA.

Jaykaynagar, India: see ASANSOL.

Jaynagar (jī'nŭgŭr). **1** Town (pop. 4,337), Darbhanga dist., N Bihar, India, 33 mi. NNE of Darbhanga, near Nepal border; rail terminus; rice, corn, sugar cane, barley, oilseeds. Also spelled Jainagar. **2** Town (pop. 14,218), 24-Parganas dist., SE West Bengal, India, on rail spur and 28 mi. SSE of Calcutta city center; rice, jute, pulse. Also spelled Joynagar. Rail spur terminus 8 mi. SW, at Lakshmikantapur.

Jay Peak (3,861 ft.), in Green Mts., N Vt., near Que. line, 15 mi. W of Newport; N terminus of Long Trail.

Jayton, town (pop. 635), Kent co., NW Texas, 40 mi. NNE of Snyder; trading, shipping point for cattle and agr. region; cotton gins, cottonseed-oil mill.

Jayuri, Cerro (sĕ'rō hīōō'rē), Andean peak (18,543 ft.), Apurímac dept., S central Peru, 6 mi. NNW of Abancay.

Jayuya (hīōō'yä), town (pop. 2,303), central Puerto Rico, in Caribbean Natl. Forest, 14 mi. N of Ponce, in sugar- and coffeegrowing region; alt. 2,420 ft.; sugar milling, sawmilling, mfg. of cigars. Starting point for ascent of Tres Picachos peak, 3 mi. E.

Jazira, Al, or **Al Jazirah** (äl jäzē'rŭ), the region of Mesopotamia bet. the Tigris and the Euphrates in NE Syria and NW Iraq, NW of Baghdad. Sometimes El Jezireh or El Jezire.

Jazirah, province, Syria: see JEZIRE.

Jazirat Shandawil, Egypt: see GEZIRET SHANDAWIL.

Jaz Murian (jäz' mōōrēän'), salt-lake depression in SE Iran, 200 mi. SE of Kerman; receives Bampur (E) and Halil (W) rivers.

Jazygia (jūzĭ'jŭ), Hung. *Jászság* (yäs'-shäg), region in NE central Hungary, E of Budapest, on right bank of Tisza R.; chief town, Jaszbereny. Its name is related to the Jazyges, a tribe of Sarmatian origin, thought to have settled here in early Middle Ages.

Jazzin, Lebanon: see JEZZIN.

Jbail, Lebanon: see BYBLOS.

Jdeide, Lebanon: see JUDEIDE.

Jeandelaincourt (zhădlĕkōōr'), village (pop. 298) Meurthe-et-Moselle dept., NE France, 11 mi. N o Nancy; tileworks.

Jeanerette (jĕnŭrĕt'), town (pop. 4,692), Iberi parish, S La., on navigable Bayou Teche and 1 mi. SE of New Iberia; market center for oil an agr. area (sugar cane, cotton, rice, peppers, pecans) Sugar milling; mfg. of machine-shop products, agr machinery, boats, wood products, mattresses. A U.S. experimental livestock farm is near by.

Jeannette (jŭnĕt'), city (pop. 16,172), Westmore land co., SW Pa., 21 mi. ESE of Pittsburgh; mfg (glass, rubber, and metal products, beverages, ce ment); coal, shale. Laid out 1888, inc. as boroug 1889, as city 1937.

Jeannette, Mount (11,700 ft.), SW Yukon, nea Alaska border, in St. Elias Mts., 200 mi. W o Whitehorse; 60°31'N 140°57'W.

Jeannette Island, Rus. *Ostrov Zhannetta,* eastern most of De Long Isls., in E.Siberian Sea, 345 mi. o N Yakut Autonomous SSR, Russian SFSR; 76 35'N 158°30'E.

Jean-Rabel (zhă-räbĕl'), town (1950 census pop 1,205), Nord-Ouest dept., NW Haiti, near NW tip of Hispaniola isl., 23 mi. WSW of Port-de-Paix agr. center (sugar cane, bananas, fruit). Its port Bord-de-Mer-Jean-Rabel, is 4 mi. NNW.

Jeantown, Scotland: see LOCHCARRON.

Jebail, Lebanon: see BYBLOS.

Jebba (jĕ'bä), town (pop. 768), Ilorin prov., Northern Provinces, W Nigeria, on Niger R. (head o navigation), on railroad, and 50 mi. NNE of Ilorin agr. trade center; shea-nut processing, cotto weaving; cassava, yams, durra. Bridge across Niger R. is one of main crossing points along its lowe course. Was ⊙ N Nigeria (1898–1902) before it transfer to Zungeru.

Jebeil, Lebanon: see BYBLOS.

Jebel [Arabic=mountain], for names beginning thu and not found here: see under following part of th name.

Jebel, Bahr el, Anglo-Egyptian Sudan: see BAHR E JEBEL.

Jebel Aulia or **Jebel Auliya** (jĕ'bĕl ou'lĭyŭ), villag (pop. 3,573), Khartoum prov., central Anglo Egyptian Sudan, on White Nile and 25 mi. S o Khartoum, near the hill Jebel Aulia. The Whit Nile storage dam (completed here 1937) consists o 2-mi.-long embankment (W) and 1-mi.-long ma sonry dam (E) with lock and sluices. Backing u of river during flood season (July–Oct.) is felt 38 mi. upstream. Sluices are opened Feb.–May.

Jebel-Bereket, Turkey: see OSMANIYE.

Jebel ed Druz, Jebel el Druz, Jabal al-Duruz (all jĕ'bĕl ĕd-drōōz'), or **Jebel Druze** [Arabic,=mtn. o the Druses], province (□ 2,584, 1946 pop. 88,787) extreme S Syria, at E edge of the HAURAN, border ing S on Jordan; ⊙ Es SUWEIDA. Plateau and mtn area rising to 5,900 ft. in the Jebel ed Druz or Jebe Druze (sometimes Jebel Druse), a few miles E o Es Suweida. Some wheat, corn, and millet grow There are extensive remains of Roman cities a Shahba and Kanawat. This area, home of th Druses, was given a kind of autonomous status after First World War, in French-mandated Syria The Druses revolted against the French in 192 but agreed (1942) to incorporation into the repub lic of Syria.

Jebelein or **El Jebelein** (ĕl jĕbĕlän'), town, Blue Nil prov., E central Anglo-Egyptian Sudan, on righ bank of the White Nile, on road, and 40 mi. SSE o Kosti; cotton, sesame, corn, durra, gum arabic livestock.

Jebel et Tur or **Jebel et Tor,** Palestine: see GERIZIM MOUNT.

Jeberos (hävä'rōs), town (pop. 981), Loreto dept., N central Peru, in Amazon basin, 45 mi. N of Yurimaguas; banana and tobacco growing. Founded 1640; was once ⊙ dept. Sometimes Jeveros.

Jeble or **Jabalah** (both: jĕ'blū), Fr. *Djéblé*, town, Latakia prov., NW Syria, on the Mediterranean Sea, 14 mi. SE of Latakia; sericulture, cotton, tobacco, cereals. Site of a once flourishing Phoenician town, also important in Byzantine times; extensive ruins remain.

Jebus, Palestine: see JERUSALEM.

Jech Doab, W Pakistan: see CHAJ DOAB.

Jechica Island, Chile: see CHONOS ARCHIPELAGO.

Jechnitz, Czechoslovakia: see JESENICE.

Jedburgh (jĕd'bürü), burgh (1931 pop. 3,058; 1951 census 4,083), ⊙ Roxburghshire, Scotland, in E part of co., on Jed Water and 40 mi. SE of Edinburgh; woolen milling, leather tanning, artificial-silk mfg. There are remains of Augustinian abbey founded 1118 by David I. A castle (no remains) was given to England under Treaty of Falaise (1174) as security for ransom for William I; it was Scottish royal residence until pulled down in 1409. Town was much affected by border warfare and was noted for "Jeddart (or Jethart) Justice" (hanging first, trial afterward). Sir David Brewster and Mary Somerville b. here. The poet James Thomson and Samuel Rutherford (b. near by) were educated in Jedburgh. Town's noted residents included Mary Queen of Scots, Prince Charles Edward, Wordsworth, and Burns.

Jedda or **Jeddah**, Saudi Arabia: see JIDDA.

Jeddo, borough (pop. 262), Luzerne co., E central Pa., 5 mi. NE of Hazleton.

Jeddore Harbour (jĕdôr'), inlet (7 mi. long, 3 mi. wide) of the Atlantic, S N.S., 30 mi. ENE of Halifax; 44°45'N 63°1'W. At head of bay is Head of Jeddore.

Jedeideh, Lebanon: see JUDEIDE.

Jedita or **Jadita** (both: jĕdē'tä), Fr. *Djedita*, town (pop. 1,796), Bekaa prov., central Lebanon, 18 mi. E of Beirut; grapes, cereals, fruit. Summer resort.

Jedrzejow (yĕjĕ'yŏof), Pol. *Jędrzejów*, town (pop. 10,998), Kielce prov., S central Poland, 21 mi. SSW of Kielce. Rail junction, mfg. of bricks, metalware; brewing, flour milling, sawmilling, tanning; gypsum mining. In Rus. Poland, 1815–1919, called Andreyev. Before Second World War, pop. 40% Jewish.

Jedwabne (yĕdväb'nĕ), town (pop. 1,670), Bialystok prov., NE Poland, 12 mi. NE of Lomza.

Jed Water, river, Roxburgh, Scotland, rises in Cheviot Hills, flows 21 mi. N, past Jedburgh, to Teviot R.

Jefara, Tripolitania: see GEFARA.

Jeff, mining village (1940 pop. 769), Perry co., SE Ky., in Cumberland foothills, on North Fork Kentucky R. and 4 mi. SE of Hazard; bituminous coal.

Jeff Davis. 1 County (□ 331; pop. 9,299), SE central Ga.; ⊙ Hazlehurst. Bounded NW by Ocmulgee R., N by Altamaha R.; drained by Little Satilla R. Coastal plain agr. (tobacco, corn, truck, sugar cane, peanuts, pecans, livestock) and forestry (lumber, naval stores) area; textile mfg. at Hazlehurst. Formed 1905. **2** County (□ 2,258; pop. 2,090), extreme W Texas; ⊙ Fort Davis. High plateau (c.4,500–8,382 ft.), extending to the Rio Grande in W; rises to scenic Davis Mts. (with state park; tourist area), including Mt. Livermore (8,382 ft.; 2d highest peak in state) and Mt. Locke, with observatory. Part of Sierra Vieja is in W. Cattle-ranching area; also sheep, goats, horses; fruit (chiefly apples). Formed 1887.

Jeffers, village (pop. 516), Cottonwood co., SW Minn., 14 mi. NNW of Windom, in grain and livestock area; dairy products.

Jefferson. 1 County (□ 1,117; pop. 558,928), N central Ala.; ⊙ Birmingham. Industrial area crossed by Locust Fork. Coal and iron mining, limestone quarrying. Iron and steel products are made at Birmingham, Bessemer, Fairfield, Tarrant, and Leeds. Formed 1819. **2** County (□ 890; pop. 76,075), central Ark.; ⊙ PINE BLUFF. Intersected by Arkansas R.; drained by small Plum Bayou. Agr. (cotton, hay, grain, rice, livestock); timber. Mfg. at Pine Bluff. Has state park. Formed 1829. **3** County (□ 786; pop. 55,687), central Colo.; ⊙ Golden. Coal-mining and irrigated agr. region, bounded E by South Platte R.; drained by Clear Creek. Sugar beets, beans, livestock. Fur farms. Includes parts of Arapaho, Pike, and Roosevelt natl. forests, and part of Front Range in W. Formed 1861. **4** County (□ 598; pop. 10,413), NW Fla.; ⊙ Monticello. Bounded by Ga. line (N), Gulf of Mexico (S), and Aucilla R. (E). Lowland area, partly swampy, with rolling terrain and L. Miccosukee in N. Agr. (corn, peanuts, cotton, vegetables, tung nuts, hogs, cattle) and some forestry (lumber, naval stores). Formed 1827. **5** County (□ 532; pop. 18,855), E Ga.; ⊙ Louisville. Coastal plain agr. (cotton, corn, peanuts) and sawmilling area drained by Ogeechee R. Formed 1796. **6** County (□ 1,089; pop. 10,495), E Idaho; ⊙ Rigby. Livestock-raising and irrigated agr. area in Snake River Plain. Clover, legumes, sugar beets, potatoes, orchards. Formed 1913. **7** County (□ 574; pop. 35,892), S Ill.; ⊙ Mount Vernon. Agr. (livestock, fruit, poultry, clover seed, corn, wheat). Mfg. (railroad cars, clothing, shoes, stoves, feed, food products). Bituminous-coal mining. Drained by Big Muddy R. Formed 1819. **8** County (□ 366; pop. 21,613), SE Ind.; ⊙ Madison. Bounded partly S by Ohio R. (here forming Ky. line); drained by Big Creek. Agr. (tobacco, grain, livestock); diversified mfg., oil refining; timber. Contains Clifty Falls State Park. Formed 1810. **9** County (□ 436; pop. 15,696), SE Iowa; ⊙ Fairfield. Prairie agr. area (hogs, cattle, poultry, corn, soybeans, hay) drained by Skunk R.; coal mines, limestone quarries. Formed 1839. **10** County (□ 549; pop. 11,084), NE Kansas; ⊙ Oskaloosa. Hilly area, crossed by Delaware R.; bounded S by Kansas R. Corn, stock, and poultry raising; dairying. Formed 1855. **11** County (□ 375; pop. 484,615), N Ky.; ⊙ LOUISVILLE, state's largest city and a metropolis of the South. Bounded W by Ohio R. (Ind. line), drained by Floyds Fork and several creeks. Industry in Louisville metropolitan area, where a large part of state's mfg. products is produced. Agr. (especially potatoes, onions; also burley tobacco, livestock, grain, fruit); minerals (phosphate, fluorspar, stone, clay, sand, gravel). Formed in 1780 from old Kentucky co., Va., becoming one of 3 counties of Ky. dist. of Va. **12** Parish (□ 409; pop. 103,873), extreme SE La.; ⊙ Gretna. Situated in the delta of the Mississippi, which intersects parish; bounded S by Gulf of Mexico, N by L. Pontchartrain. Important industrial parish, adjoining (in N) New Orleans. Fisheries; dairying, truck farming; oil and natural-gas wells. Traversed by Gulf Intracoastal Waterway. Formed 1825. **13** County (□ 520; pop. 11,306), SW Miss.; ⊙ Fayette. Bounded W by the Mississippi, here the La. line. Includes part of Homochitto Natl. Forest. Agr. (cotton, corn); lumbering. Formed 1802. **14** County (□ 667; pop. 38,007), E Mo.; ⊙ Hillsboro. On Mississippi R. (E) and Meramec R. (NE); drained by Big R. Agr. (corn, wheat, barley, livestock); shoe factories, textile and grain mills; silica, barite mines. Formed 1818. **15** County (□ 1,651; pop. 4,014), SW central Mont.; ⊙ Boulder. Agr. and mining region drained by Boulder R.; bounded S by Jefferson R., W by Continental Divide. Livestock; gold, silver, lead, zinc. Part of Deerlodge Natl. Forest in W, part of Helena Natl. Forest in NE. Formed 1865. **16** County (□ 577; pop. 13,623), SE Nebr.; ⊙ Fairbury. Agr. region bounded S by Kansas; drained by Little Blue R. Grain, livestock, dairy and poultry produce. Formed 1871. **17** County (□ 1,293; pop. 85,521), N N.Y.; ⊙ Watertown. Bounded W by L. Ontario and NW by St. Lawrence R.; resorts and state parks on L. Ontario and in the Thousand Isls. region of the St. Lawrence. Drained by Black and Indian rivers (water power). Dairying and iron-producing area, with mfg., especially at Watertown and Carthage. Fisheries; limestone, talc deposits. Formed 1805. **18** County (□ 411; pop. 96,495), E Ohio; ⊙ STEUBENVILLE. Bounded E by Ohio R., here forming W.Va. line; drained by small Yellow and Cross creeks. Coal mining; mfg. at Steubenville; agr. (truck, fruit, livestock; dairy products); ceramics plants. Formed 1797. **19** County (□ 755; pop. 11,122), S Okla.; ⊙ Waurika. Bounded S by Red R., here forming Texas line; and drained by Beaver and Mud creeks. Stock-raising, agr. (cotton, grain, corn, poultry; dairy products). Mfg. at Waurika. Oil and natural-gas wells. Formed 1907. **20** County (□ 1,794; pop. 5,536), central Oregon; ⊙ Madras. Mt. Jefferson is in Cascade Range on W boundary. Part of Warm Springs Indian Reservation in NW. Drained by Deschutes R. Livestock grazing; quicksilver mining. Formed 1914. **21** County (□ 652; pop. 49,147), W central Pa.; ⊙ Brookville. Agr. and mfg. area; bounded N by Clarion R.; drained by other tributaries of Allegheny R. Bituminous coal; mfg. (clay products, glass, butter, gloves, caskets); meat packing; buckwheat; clay, glass sand mining. Formed 1804. **22** County (□ 318; pop. 19,667), E Tenn.; ⊙ Dandridge. In Great Appalachian Valley; traversed by Bays Mtn.; bounded NW by Holston R.; drained by French Broad R. Includes parts of Cherokee and Douglas reservoirs. Livestock raising, dairying, agr. (tobacco, fruit, corn, hay). Zinc mines, limestone quarries. Formed 1792. **23** County (□ 945; pop. 195,083), SE Texas; ⊙ BEAUMONT. On Gulf coastal plain; bounded E by Sabine L. (here forming La. line) and Neches R., S by Gulf of Mexico; crossed by Gulf Intracoastal Waterway. Sabine-Neches Waterway gives access from Gulf to deep-water ports of Beaumont and Port Arthur, important oil-shipping, oil refining, and industrial centers. Oil, natural-gas fields. Cattle raising, dairying, agr. (rice, wheat, fruit, truck). Fishing, duck hunting. Formed 1836. **24** County (□ 1,812; pop. 11,618), W Wash.; ⊙ Port Townsend. Bounded W by Pacific Ocean, E and N by Hood Canal and Puget Sound; peaks of Olympic Mts. in interior. Includes Hoh Indian Reservation and parts of Quinault Indian Reservation and Olympic Natl. Park. Lumber, wood pulp, fish, livestock, dairy products. Formed 1852. **25** County (□ 211; pop. 17,184), northeasternmost of W.Va., at tip of Eastern Panhandle; ⊙ Charles Town. In S part of Great Appalachian Valley; Blue Ridge is along SE border. Bounded NE by Potomac R. (Md. line), SE and SW by Va.; drained by Shenandoah R., which joins the Potomac at HARPERS FERRY, and by short Opequon Creek. Scenic resort region. Agr. (livestock, especially horses; dairying, fruit); limestone and dolomite quarrying. Industry at Ranson, Charles Town. Formed 1801. **26** County (□ 564; pop. 43,069), S Wis.; ⊙ Jefferson. Drained by Rock, Bark, and Crawfish rivers. Dairying (chief industry), stock raising, farming (corn, oats). Some mfg. Has lake resorts. Formed 1836.

Jefferson. 1 Village (pop. c.50), Park co., central Colo., on headstream of Tarryall Creek, in Rocky Mts., and 50 mi. SW of Denver; alt. 9,500 ft. Shipping point for livestock and timber. **2** City (pop. 2,040), ⊙ Jackson co., NE central Ga., 15 mi. NW of Athens; mfg. (textiles, plastics). Dr. Crawford W. Long performed an operation here in 1842 using ether as an anesthetic. Inc. 1806. **3** City (pop. 4,326), ⊙ Greene co., central Iowa, on Raccoon R. and c.50 mi. NW of Des Moines; rail junction; agr. trade center; dairy products, feed, tankage. Sand and gravel pits near by. Settled c.1854, inc. 1871. **4** Town (pop. 1,215), Lincoln co., S Maine, on Damariscotta L. and 24 mi. NE of Bath. **5** Village, Worcester co., Mass.: see HOLDEN. **6** Resort town (pop. 728), Coos co., N N.H., in White Mts., on Israel R. and 10 mi. SW of Berlin. Includes Riverton village. **7** Resort town (pop. 359), ⊙ Ashe co., NW N.C., 25 mi. NW of North Wilkesboro, in the Blue Ridge and Yadkin Natl. Forest. **8** Village (pop. 1,844), ⊙ Ashtabula co., extreme NE Ohio, 9 mi. S of Ashtabula, in livestock and dairying area; produces light bulbs, baskets, lumber; stone working. Founded c.1804. **9** Town (pop. 179), Grant co., N Okla., 8 mi. SSW of Medford, in agr. area. **10** City (pop. 636), Marion co., W Oregon, 8 mi. NNE of Albany and on Santiam R.; feed. **11** Borough (pop. 575), Greene co., SW Pa., 7 mi. ENE of Waynesburg. **12** Borough (pop. 449), York co., S Pa., 12 mi. SSW of York. **13** Town (pop. 556), Chesterfield co., N S.C., 60 mi. NNE of Columbia; fertilizer. **14** Town (pop. 466), Union co., SE S.Dak., 10 mi. SE of Elk Point, near Big Sioux R. **15** City (pop. 3,164), ⊙ Marion co., E Texas, on Cypress Bayou and 14 mi. N of Marshall; a trade, shipping, processing center for oil, cotton, truck, lumbering area; gasoline plant; lumber milling; mfg. of syrup, cottonseed oil, soap, canned foods, brooms, furniture. Caddo L. (hunting, fishing) is just E. Grew as a river port and lumbering center in area settled in 1830s; reached pop. of c.30,000 in 1875, later declined. **16** Industrial city (pop. 3,625), ⊙ Jefferson co., S Wis., at confluence of Crawfish and Rock rivers, 30 mi. ESE of Madison, in dairying and farming region; mfg. (furniture, shoes, woolen goods, wood products, sausage, evaporated milk). Settled c.1836, inc. 1878.

Jefferson, Fort, Fla.: see FORT JEFFERSON NATIONAL MONUMENT.

Jefferson, Mount. 1 Peak in Nev.: see TOQUEMA RANGE. **2** Peak in N.H.: see PRESIDENTIAL RANGE. **3** Peak (10,495 ft.) in NW central Oregon, in Cascade Range, 65 mi. ESE of Salem. Mount Jefferson Primitive Area here.

Jefferson Barracks, Mo., a military base, is near SAINT LOUIS.

Jefferson City. 1 City (pop. 25,099), ⊙ Missouri and ⊙ Cole co., on right bank of Missouri R. and 110 mi. W of St. Louis. Trade and industrial center of farming region. Railroad shops, river traffic; mfg. (grain, wood, and dairy products, shoes, clothing, bricks, printing); zinc, lead, clay mines in vicinity. Lincoln Univ., jr. col., state penitentiary here; boys' reformatory near by. Laid out 1822, inc. 1825. **2** Village (pop. c.80), Jefferson co., SW central Mont., on Prickly Pear Creek and 15 mi. S of Helena; gold and silver mines near by. **3** Town (pop. 3,633), Jefferson co., E Tenn., near Cherokee Dam (Holston R.), 26 mi. ENE of Knoxville; mfg. of springs, canned foods. Seat of Carson-Newman Col. Zinc mines near by. Settled c.1810; inc. 1900.

Jefferson Davis. 1 Parish (□ 658; pop. 26,298), SW La.; ⊙ Jennings. Bounded E and SE by Bayou Nezpique and Mermentau R. Oil, natural gas, lumber. Agr. (rice, cotton, corn, sweet potatoes). Rice milling, cotton ginning, metalworking, oil refining. Includes L. Arthur (fishing, camping). Formed 1910. **2** County (□ 414; pop. 15,500), S central Miss.; ⊙ Prentiss. Drained by tributaries of Leaf and Pearl rivers. Agr. (cotton, corn); lumbering. Formed 1906.

Jefferson Island, one of the Five Isls., in Iberia parish, S La., a salt dome rising from prairies just E of L. Peigneur, 9 mi. W of New Iberia. Large rock-salt mine (producing since 1921); oil wells; sulphur deposits.

Jefferson River, SW Mont., rises in Gravelly Range, near Yellowstone Natl. Park (here known as Red Rock R.); flows W, through Upper and Lower Red Rock lakes, thence N, past Dillon (here it becomes Beaverhead R.); joined by Big Hole and Ruby rivers at Twin Bridges; continues N and E as Jefferson R. to point just NE of Three Forks, where it joins Madison and Gallatin rivers to form the Missouri. Length, 207 mi.

Jefferson Springs, resort village, Rutherford co., central Tenn., on Stones R. and 24 mi. SE of Nashville.

Jeffersontown, town (pop. 1,246), Jefferson co., N Ky., 12 mi. ESE of Louisville; residential community within Louisville metropolitan dist.; some agr. (potatoes, corn, apples, peaches); nurseries.

Jeffersonville. 1 City (pop. 787), ⊙ Twiggs co., central Ga., 19 mi. ESE of Macon; market center for pecan, farm, and timber region; sawmilling. **2** Village (pop. 326), Wayne co., SE Ill., 29 mi. ENE of Mount Vernon, in agr. area. **3** City (pop. 14,685), ⊙ Clark co., SE Ind., on the Ohio (bridged here), E of New Albany and opposite Louisville (Ky.), of whose metropolitan area it is a part; river port, with shipyards, railroad-car works; mfg. of foundry and wood products, machinery, canned goods, animal oils, soap, clothing. Seat of U.S. army quartermaster depot and a state prison. Settled 1802. Inundated by flood in 1937. **4** Village (pop. 450), Sullivan co., SE N.Y., 10 mi. W of Liberty, in resort area; produces lumber, machinery. **5** Village (pop. 865), Fayette co., S central Ohio, 10 mi. NW of Washington Court House, in stock-raising and farming area. **6** Village (pop. 2,452), Montgomery co., SE Pa., just NW of Norristown, near Schuylkill R. **7** Village, Lamoille co., Vt.: see CAMBRIDGE.

Jeffs, village (pop. 2,211, with near-by Messick), York co., SE Va., near Chesapeake Bay, 7 mi. N of Hampton.

Jefren (jĕ'frĕn), town (pop. 7,740), W Tripolitania, Libya, on the plateau Gebel Nefusa, 30 mi. WSW of Garian; alt. 2,230 ft.; road junction; olive oil, barracans, carpets, terra-cotta ware. Has power station.

Jega (jä'gä), town (pop. 9,007), Sokoto prov., Northern Provinces, NW Nigeria, on Zamfára R. and 70 mi. SW of Sokoto; agr. trade center (cotton, millet, rice, cattle, skins).

Jegervasstind, Norway: see LYNGEN FJORD.

Jegindo (yā'yĭndû"), Dan. *Jegindø*, island (□ 3.1; pop. 754) in W Lim Fjord, NW Jutland, Denmark, 1 mi. S of Mors isl.; highest point, 43 ft.; flat and fertile.

Jegun (zhügŭ'), village (pop. 489), Gers dept., SW France, 10 mi. NW of Auch; brandy distilling.

Jehlam River, Kashmir and W Pakistan: see JHELUM RIVER.

Jehol (jŭhōl'), Chinese *Jeho* (rŭ'hŭ'), province (□ 40,000; pop. 5,000,000) of SW Manchuria; ⊙ Chengteh (formerly Jehol). Bounded S by Hopeh along the Great Wall, W by Chahar, N by Inner Mongolian Autonomous Region along upper Liao R., and E by the Liaosi corridor separating it from the Gulf of Chihli, Jehol slopes SE from the Mongolian plateau. It has a rugged, rocky topography, extending in a wedge bet. the N China and Manchuria plains. The prov. is drained by the Lwan (SW) and Liao (N) rivers; its continental climate is typical of N China. Insufficient rainfall restricts agr. to the cultivation of wheat, barley, kaoliang, corn, and beans. The original forest areas have been largely cut over and remain only in isolated sections, such as the old Weichang hunting grounds. Pehpiao, near E border, is one of Manchuria's leading coal-mining centers; gold, iron, and oil shale are also found. S Jehol is served by railroad (through Chengteh, Pingchüan, and Chaoyang), with branch line to Chihfeng. Trade is primarily in Mongolian products, such as wool, skins, and hides. Jehol was originally inhabited by the Mongolian leagues of Josoto (S) and Jooda (N). Chinese penetration, originally along Lwan R. valley (SE), dates from the Ming dynasty. The Weichang area was later set aside as an imperial hunting ground by the Manchus, who also built a summer capital at Chengteh. During 19th cent., Chinese colonization penetrated the entire Josoto league, and in 1914 Jehol was separated from Chihli (Hopeh) prov. and set up as a special administrative dist., raised to full prov. status in 1928. In Manchukuo (after 1933), the Jooda league (N of Liao R.) was created (1934) West Hsingan prov., while the Fusin-Pehpiao-Chaoyang area passed to Chinchow prov. In 1946, Jehol was reconstituted briefly within its original limits; then present Jehol was formed in 1949, when the Jooda league passed to the Inner Mongolian Autonomous Region.

Jehol, city, Manchuria: see CHENGTEH.

Jeida, Israel: see RAMAT YISHAI.

Jeinemeni, Cerro (sĕ'rō hānĕmā'nē), Andean peak (8,530 ft.) in Aysén prov., S Chile, bet. L. Buenos Aires and L. Cochrane, 110 mi. SSE of Puerto Aysén.

Jeiseyville (jē'sēvĭl), village (pop. 199), Christian co., central Ill., on South Fork of Sangamon R. and 20 mi. SSE of Springfield, in agr. and bituminous-coal area.

Jejuí-guazú (hāwhē'-gwäsōō'), river in central Paraguay, rises on W slopes of Cordillera de Mbaracayú near Brazil line, flows c.150 mi. W to Paraguay R. 13 mi. SW of San Pedro.

Jejuri (jä'jōōrē), town (pop. 2,929), Poona dist., central Bombay, India, 25 mi. SE of Poona; Hindu pilgrimage center.

Jekabpils or **Yekabpils** (yā'kāpēls), Lettish *Jēkabpils*, Ger. *Jakobstadt* (yä'kôp-shtät), city (pop. 5,826), S central Latvia, in Zemgale, on left bank of the Western Dvina, opposite Krustpils, and 75 mi. ESE of Riga; mfg. (musical instruments, leather goods, potato flour, beer, liquors); dairying, lime works. Important trading center in 15th cent. Formerly also called Jekabmiests.

Jekyll Island, one of the Sea Isls., in Glynn co., SE Ga., off the coast, 5 mi. SE of Brunswick; c.7 mi. long, 1–2 mi. wide. Covered by virgin forests. Made a state park in 1947, it was formerly a winter-resort colony of large estates.

Jelalabad, Afghanistan: see JALALABAD.

Jelapang (jŭlä"päng'), village (pop. 1,327), central Perak, Malaya, 3 mi. NW of Ipoh; tin mining.

Jelawat (jŭlä'wät), village (pop. 518), N Kelantan, Malaya, 12 mi. SE of Kota Bharu; rice, coconuts.

Jelebu (jŭlĕ'bōō), district (□ 528; pop. 19,285) in N Negri Sembilan, Malaya; main town, Kuala Klawang. One of the original Negri Sembilan states.

Jelec, Czechoslovakia: see USTEK.

Jelenia Gora, Poland: see HIRSCHBERG.

Jelep La (jĕ'lĕp lä'), pass (alt. c.14,390 ft.) in SW Assam Himalayas, on Tibet-India border, 16 mi. ENE of Gangtok (India); road leads from Sikkim into Chumbi Valley, Tibet; main India-Tibet trade route.

Jelgava or **Yelgava** (yĕl'gävä), Ger. *Mitau* (mē'tou), Rus. (until 1917) *Mitava* (mētä'vä), city (pop. 34,099), W central Latvia, chief city of Zemgale, on Lielupe R. and 25 mi. SW of Riga; 56°39'N 23°43'E. Major rail hub, textile and sugar-refining center, in fertile agr. area (grain, flax, sugar beets); mfg. (linen goods, oilcloth, rope, woolens, leather goods, bricks, tiles), agr. processing (sugar, flour, dairy products, tobacco, beer), sawmilling. Agr. fairs. Has 18th-cent. palace by Rastrelli (residence of former dukes of Courland), historical mus., 16th-cent. Trinity Church, 18th-cent. town hall. Founded 1266 by Teutonic Knights, it became (1561) ⊙ Courland, with which it passed to Russia in 1795. Before First World War Jelgava had c.47,000 inhabitants (c.50% Germans, and c.25% Jews); before its occupation (1915–18) by the German army its population was evacuated to inner Russia. In 1919, during struggle for Latvian independence, Jelgava was occupied in turn by the Soviets, by German free corps, and by the Latvians. In independent Latvia (1920–40), Jelgava was ⊙ Zemgale. Little of the original pop. remained after its occupation (1941) by the Germans and its reconquest (1944) by the Red Army in the Second World War.

Jelks, Ark.: see PATTERSON.

Jellico (jĕ'lĭkō), city (pop. 1,556), Campbell co., NE Tenn., at Ky. line, 45 mi. NNW of Knoxville, in foothills of the Cumberlands. Coal-mining center; mfg. of brass bearings, lumbering. U.S. mine rescue station, with first-aid school for miners, here. Settled 1795.

Jellicocreek (jĕ'lŭkōkrēk') or **Jellico,** village (1940 pop. 667), Whitley co., SE Ky., in the Cumberlands, 6 mi. SW of Williamsburg, in coal-mining area.

Jellicoe (jĕ'lĭkō), village (pop. estimate 350), N central Ont., near L. Nipigon, 110 mi. NE of Port Arthur; alt. 1,087 ft.; gold mining.

Jelling (yĕ'lĭng), town (pop. 1,086), Vejle amt, E Jutland, Denmark, 5 mi. NW of Vejle; cement.

Jellison, Cape, Hancock co., S Maine, peninsula on W shore of Penobscot Bay and 8 mi. NE of Belfast. Fort Point has lighthouse.

Jeloy, Norway: see MOSS.

Jelsa (yĕl'sä), Ital. *Gelsa* (jĕl'sä), village, S Croatia, Yugoslavia, port on N coast of Hvar Isl., 13 mi. E of Hvar, in Dalmatia; resort; center of winegrowing region.

Jelsava (yĕl'shävä), Slovak *Jelšava*, Hung. *Jólsva* (yōlz'vŏ), village (pop. 2,456), S central Slovakia, Czechoslovakia, on railroad and 47 mi. WSW of Kosice; iron mining. Magnesite mining in vicinity. Has noted 19th-cent. Empire-style castle. Chyzne or Chyzne Vode iron mines are 3 mi. NW.

Jelsi, Italy: see IELSI.

Jemaa (jĕmä'), town (pop. 1,014), Plateau Prov., Northern Provinces, central Nigeria, 10 mi. SSE of Kafanchan; tin-mining center.

Jemaja, Indonesia: see ANAMBAS ISLANDS.

Jemaluang (jŭmä"lōōäng'), town (pop. 1,276), NE Johore, Malaya, 10 mi. S of Mersing; road junction; tin mining. Sometimes Bandar Jemaluang.

Jemappe (zhümäp'), town (pop. 3,743), Namur prov., S central Belgium, on Sambre R. and 10 mi. W of Namur; glass mfg. In near-by grotto are prehistoric relics.

Jemappes (zhümäp'), town (pop. 12,812), Hainaut prov., SW Belgium, on Condé-Mons Canal and 3 mi. W of Mons; coal-shipping center; coal mining; glass blowing, soda mfg. Site of 1st battle of Fr. Revolutionary War, when French under Dumouriez decisively defeated Austrians (1792).

Jember or **Djember** (both: jĕmbĕr'), town (pop. 20,222), E Java, Indonesia, 95 mi. SE of Surabaya, at foot of Mt. Argapura; trade center for agr. area (sugar, tobacco, corn, peanuts); lumber mills, machine shops.

Jemelle (zhümĕl'), town (pop. 2,105), Namur prov., SE central Belgium, 6 mi. SW of Marche; railroad shops; stone quarrying.

Jementah (jŭmĕn"tä'), village (pop. 950), NW Johore, Malaya, 10 mi. SW of Segamat, near Negri Sembilan line; rubber.

Jemeppe or **Jemeppe-sur-Meuse** (zhümĕp'-sür-mûz'), town (pop. 14,083), Liége prov., E Belgium, on Meuse R. and 4 mi. WSW of Liége; mfg. (soda, machinery).

Jemes, N.Mex.: see JEMEZ PUEBLO.

Jemez Creek (hā'mĕs), N central N.Mex., rises in several branches near Redondo Peak, flows S, past Jemez Springs village, and SE to Rio Grande 5 mi. N of Bernalillo; c.60 mi. long.

Jemez Mountains, N.Mex.: see VALLE GRANDE MOUNTAINS.

Jemez Pueblo or **Jemez,** pueblo (□ 68.6), Sandoval co., NW central N.Mex. Jemez village (1948 pop. 892) is on Jemez Creek and 24 mi. NW of Bernalillo; alt. 5,585 ft. Sometimes Jemes. Chief activities are weaving and basket making. Fiesta Nov. 12 honors St. Didacus. Near by are Valle Grande Mts. and Jemez State Monument, with ruins of Mission of San José de Jémez (1617). Village settled c.1700.

Jemez Springs, village (pop. c.500), Sandoval co., N central N.Mex., on Jemez Creek, in Valle Grande Mts., and 50 mi. N of Albuquerque; alt. 6,195 ft.; farm trading point. Jemez Pueblo Indian village is 10 mi. S.

Jemison (jĭ'mŭsŭn, jĕ'mŭsŭn), town (pop. 847), Chilton co., central Ala., 11 mi. NW of Clanton; lumber.

Jemmapes (zhümäp'), town (pop. 4,536), Constantine dept., NE Algeria, 15 mi. SE of Philippeville; winegrowing center; olives, cork, cereals. Mercury mined at Ras-el-Ma (6 mi. SW).

Jemnice (yĕm'nyĭtsĕ), Ger. *Jamnitz* (yäm'nĭts), town (pop. 3,034), S Moravia, Czechoslovakia, 26 mi. S of Jihlava; rail terminus; oats; coffee processing. Has forest rangers' school.

Jemo (jĕ'mō), uninhabited coral island, Ratak Chain, Marshall Isls., W central Pacific, 20 mi. NE of Likiep; 5 mi. long.

Jemseg (jĕm'sĕg), village (pop. estimate c.100), S N.B., on short Jemseg stream (connecting Grand L. with St. John R.) and 40 mi. N of St. John.

Jemtland, county and province, Sweden: see JAMTLAND.

Jena (yā'nä), city (pop. 82,722), Thuringia, central Germany, on the Thuringian Salle and 25 mi. E of Erfurt; 50°56'N 29°15'E. Univ. city and industrial center, with metal- and woodworking, publishing, mfg. of machinery and chemicals, and the famed optical and precision instruments of the Zeiss works (the Zeiss factories, bombed during Second World War, were partly removed after 1945 by the Russian occupation authorities). The univ. (founded 1558) reached its academic zenith in late 18th cent., when Schiller, Fichte, Hegel, Schelling, and Schlegel taught here; its bldgs. (completed 1908) were damaged in Second World War. Jena has 14th-cent. town hall; 15th-16th-cent. church; Schiller's residence, where he wrote *Wallenstein;* botanical gardens with inspector's lodge, where Goethe wrote *Herrmann und Dorothea;* several museums. Site of planetarium; seismographic institute. Chartered 1230, the town passed to house of Wettin in 15th cent. Carl Zeiss founded the optical works here in 1846. On E bank of river is the suburb WENIGENJENA, with many cultural associations. On NW outskirts of city is site of battle of Jena (Oct. 14, 1806), where Napoleon decisively defeated the Prussian forces. In the Second World War, Jena and its suburbs were captured by American forces in April, 1945.

Jena (jē'nŭ), town (pop. 1,438), ⊙ La Salle parish, central La., 34 mi. NE of Alexandria; sugar cane, cotton, rice; sawmills, cotton gins, ironworks. Oil fields near by. Inc. 1927.

Jenbach (yĕn'băkh), town (pop. 4,527), Tyrol, W Austria, on Inn R. and 13 mi. ENE of Innsbruck; rail junction. Large hydroelectric plant; ironworks; mfg. (agr. machinery, tools); lumberyards. Summer resort; cogwheel railroad to the Achensee, whose water supplies hydroelectric plant.

Jen-chin-li, Tibet: see RINCHENLING.

Jen-ch'iu, China: see JENKIU.

Jenera (jĕ'nĭrŭ), village (pop. 316), Hancock co., NW Ohio, 11 mi. SSW of Findlay.

Jenhsien (rŭn'shyĕn'), town, ⊙ Jenhsien co. (pop. 107,825), SW Hopeh prov., China, 10 mi. ENE of Singtai; wheat, kaoliang, millet, beans.

Jen-hua, China: see YANFA.

Jenhwai or **Jen-huai** (both: rŭn'hwī'), town (pop. 2,148), ⊙ Jenhwai co. (pop. 247,172), N Kweichow prov., China, 35 mi. W of Tsunyi, near Szechwan line; wine center; papermaking, lacquer and tung-oil processing; timber, millet, wheat, beans. Coal mines near by.

Jenin (jĕnēn'), town (1946 pop. estimate 4,310) in Palestine, after 1948 in W Jordan, near S edge of Plain of Jezreel, on railroad and 30 mi. SE of Haifa. Identified as *En-gannim* of the Old Testament.

Jenkinjones, village (pop. 1,859), McDowell co., S W.Va., at Va. line, 10 mi. W of Bluefield, in bituminous-coal region.

Jenkins, county (□ 351; pop. 10,264), E Ga.; ⊙ Millen. Coastal plain agr. (cotton, corn, truck, livestock) and timber area intersected by Ogeechee R. Formed 1905.

Jenkins. 1 Mining town (pop. 6,921), Letcher co., SE Ky., in the Cumberlands, at Va. line, 70 mi. ENE of Middlesboro. Center of important bituminous-coal region; stone quarrying. POUND GAP is just SE. 2 Village (pop. 170), Crow Wing co., central Minn., 21 mi. NNW of Brainerd, in region of lakes and woods; grain. 3 Town (pop. 39), Barry co., SW Mo., in the Ozarks, 17 mi. SE of Monett.

Jenkinsburg, town (pop. 166), Butts co., central Ga., 4 mi. WNW of Jackson.

Jenkintown, residential borough (pop. 5,130), Montgomery co., SE Pa., 10 mi. N of Philadelphia; metal products, paper. Seat of Beaver Col. Settled 1750, inc. 1874.

Jenkiu or **Jen-ch'iu** (both: rŭn'chyō'), town, ⊙ Jenkiu co. (pop. 265,264), central Hopeh prov., China, 35 mi. ESE of Paoting; rice, wheat, corn.

Jenks, town (pop. 1,037), Tulsa co., NE Okla., 10 mi. S of Tulsa, and on Arkansas R.; coal mining.

Jenné, Fr. West Africa: see DJENNÉ.

Jenner, resort village, Sonoma co., W Calif., at mouth of Russian R. on the Pacific, 22 mi. W of Santa Rosa. Also called Jenner-by-the-sea. State park near by.

Jennersdorf (yĕ'nûrsdôrf), village (pop. 1,816), Burgenland, E Austria, near the Raab, 33 mi. ESE of Graz; orchards (cherries, peaches), vineyards.

Jennertown or **Jennerstown,** borough (pop. 376), Somerset co., SW Pa., 12 mi. SW of Johnstown.

Jennings, county (□ 377; pop. 15,250), SE Ind.; ⊙ Vernon. Bituminous-coal and agr. area (livestock, grain, tobacco). Mfg. at North Vernon. Timber; limestone quarries. Drained by small Vernon, Graham, and Sand creeks. Formed 1816.

Jennings. 1 Town (pop. 549), Hamilton co., N Fla., near Ga. line, 23 mi. NNW of Live Oak; lumbering. 2 City (pop. 330), Decatur co., NW Kansas, on Prairie Dog Creek and 23 mi. SW of Norton; agr., stock raising. 3 City (pop. 9,663), ⊙ Jefferson Davis parish, SW La., 33 mi. E of Lake Charles city; trade center for agr. area (corn, rice, potatoes, cotton, trunk); flower growing (Easter lilies). Rice milling, cotton ginning; mfg. of machinery, beverages, metal and machine-shop products, petroleum products. Fishing, timber, oil field near by. Settled 1884. 4 Town (pop. 15,282), St. Louis co., E Mo., near Mississippi R., just N of St. Louis. 5 Town (pop. 338), Pawnee co., N Okla., 17 mi. SE of Pawnee, in agr. area.

Jenny Jump Mountain (c.1,100 ft.), ridge of Appalachians in NW N.J., NW of Belvidere. State park here.

Jenny Lind Island or **Lind Island** (17 mi. long, 10 mi. wide), S Franklin Dist., Northwest Territories, in Queen Maud Gulf, at SW end of Victoria Strait, off SE Victoria Isl.; 68°52'N 101°30'W.

Jenolan Caves, Australia: see OBERON.

Jensen, village, Uintah co., NE Utah, on Green R. and 12 mi. SE of Vernal; hq. for Dinosaur Natl. Monument (N). Oil refinery.

Jenshow or **Jen-shou** (both: rŭn'shō'), town (pop. 36,091), ⊙ Jenshow co. (pop. 968,981), W Szechwan prov., China, 45 mi. S of Chengtu; rice, sweet potatoes, sugar cane, wheat, millet. Kaolin quarrying, oil deposits, saltworks near by.

Jens Munk Island (45 mi. long, 17 mi. wide), SE Franklin Dist., Northwest Territories, at head of Foxe Basin, off NW Baffin Isl.; 69°42'N 79°40'W.

Jeparit, village (pop. 740), W central Victoria, Australia, on Wimmera R. and 205 mi. WNW of Melbourne, near S shore of L. Hindmarsh; rail junction; sheep, wheat.

Jepelacio (hāpäläs'yō), town (pop. 745), San Martín dept., N central Peru, in E outliers of the Andes, 5 mi. SSE of Moyobamba; sugar cane, rice, corn.

Jeppe (jĕ'pē), E suburb of Johannesburg, S Transvaal, U. of So. Afr.

Jequetepeque (hākätāpā'kā), town (pop. 809), Libertad dept., NW Peru, on coastal plain, near mouth of Jequetepeque R., 7 mi. NW of San Pedro, in irrigated agr. area (rice, alfalfa).

Jequetepeque River, NW Peru, rises in Cordillera Occidental of the Andes 15 mi. SE of Cajamarca, flows 100 mi. W across Cajamarca and Libertad depts., past Chilete, to the Pacific 2 mi. W of Jequetepeque. Feeds numerous irrigation channels in lower course.

Jequié, Brazil: see JIQUIÉ.

Jequitinhonha (zhĭkētēnyō'nyŭ), city (pop. 3,612), NE Minas Gerais, Brazil, on navigable Jequitinhonha R. and 90 mi. NNE of Teófilo Otoni; rock crystals and semiprecious stones found here.

Jequitinhonha River, E Brazil, rises in the Serra do Espinhaço S of Diamantina (Minas Gerais), flows over 500 mi. NE, emptying into the Atlantic in a common delta with the Rio Pardo just N of Belmonte (Bahia). Receives the Araçuaí (right). Navigable bet. Araçuaí (city) and Bahia border (Salto Grande falls), and again near mouth. Diamond washings in headwaters; rock crystals and semiprecious stones found in valley. Lower course also called Rio Grande do Belmonte.

Jerablus or **Jarabulus** (both: jĕrä'blo͞os), Fr. *Djérablous*, town, Aleppo prov., NW Syria, on W bank of the Euphrates, at Turkish border, and 65 mi. NE of Aleppo; cereals. Across the border in Turkey is site of anc. CARCHEMISH.

Jérada, Fr. Morocco: see DJÉRADA.

Jerai, Gunong, Malaya: see KEDAH PEAK.

Jerantut (jŭrän"to͞ot'), village (pop. 770), central Pahang, Malaya, 28 mi. SE of Kuala Lipis; junction of highway and E coast railroad; rice, rubber.

Jerash or **Jarash** (both: jĕ'räsh), town (pop. c.2,500), N Jordan, 22 mi. N of Amman; road junction, tourist resort; wheat, vineyards. It is on site of the anc. Gerasa (jĕ'rŭsŭ), a city of the Decapolis, and there are extensive ruins of its great Roman period. Sometimes spelled Gerash.

Jerauld (jĕ'rŭld), county (□ 528; pop. 4,476), SE central S.Dak.; ⊙ Wessington Springs. Agr. area watered by intermittent streams. Dairy produce, livestock, poultry, grain. Formed 1883.

Jerba, Tunisia: see DJERBA.

Jerécuaro (hārā'kwärō), town (pop. 2,464), Guanajuato, central Mexico, on affluent of Lerma R. and 33 mi. S of Querétaro, on railroad; alt. 6,227 ft. Grain, sugar cane, alfalfa, fruit, vegetables.

Jerejak, Pulan (po͞olän'jŭrĕ"jäk'), island in S Penang Channel, NW Malaya, off E coast of Penang; 2 mi. long, 1 mi. wide. Has quarantine station and leper hospital of Penang harbor.

Jérémie (zhārāmē'), town (1950 census pop. 11,138), Sud dept., SW Haiti, port on NW coast of Tiburon Peninsula, on Gulf of Gonaïves, 120 mi. W of Port-au-Prince; 18°39'N 74°8'W. Ships produce of fertile region (cacao, coffee, sugar cane, bananas, mangoes, logwood, hides). Fishing; mfg. of soap. Airfield.

Jeremoabo (zhĭrĭmōä'bo͝o), city (pop. 1,966), NE Bahia, Brazil, on Vasa Barris R. and 105 mi. NW of Aracaju (Sergipe); nitrate deposits. Formerly spelled Geremoabo.

Jerer River (jĕrĕr') or **Tug Jerer** (to͝og jĕrĕr'), Ital. *Gerrer*, in Harar prov., SE Ethiopia, rises in mts. at edge of Great Rift Valley, 20 mi. NW of Jijiga, flows intermittently c.180 mi. SE, past Jijiga and Dagahbur, through the Ogaden to Fafan R. 20 mi. S of Sassabaneh.

Jeresa (hārā'sä), village (pop. 1,958), Valencia prov., E Spain, 4 mi. NW of Gandía; rice, oranges, wine, vegetables.

Jeres del Marquesado (hā'rĕs dhĕl märkāsä'dhō), town (pop. 2,672), Granada prov., S Spain, 8 mi. SSW of Guadix; cereals, chestnuts; livestock. Copper deposits.

Jerez (hārĕs'), town (1950 pop. 1,432), Jutiapa dept., SE Guatemala, in highlands, at SW foot of Chingo volcano, near Salvador line, 16 mi. SE of Jutiapa; corn, beans, livestock.

Jerez, Mexico: see GARCÍA, Zacatecas.

Jerez or **Jerez de la Frontera** (hĕrĕth' dhā lä frōntā'rä), second largest city (pop. 65,166) of Cádiz prov., SW Spain, in Andalusia, near the Atlantic, 14 mi. NE of Cádiz. Hq. of large wine industry, whose sherry (named for the town) has gained world-wide fame. Also produces cognac; and bottles, barrels, cement; and is an active trading center for fertile agr. region (grapes, cereals, olives, vegetables, oranges, livestock; cork, timber). The rich and handsome city, surrounded by vineyards, has notable religious bldgs., such as 15th-cent. Santiago church, Gothic church of San Miguel (begun 1462), ruins of San Francisco convent. The alcazar is a memento of the Moorish period. A special feature are the extensive *bodegas* (wineries). Jerez was captured by the Moors in 711 and, after several attempts, finally retaken in 1264 by Alfonso X of Castile. The Cartuja, former charterhouse, built in elaborate baroque, is 3 mi. E; it is a natl. monument. Jerez probably originated from the Phoenician *Xera*. Formerly spelled Xerez or Xeres.

Jerez de los Caballeros (dhā lōs kävälyā'rōs), city (pop. 12,486), Badajoz prov., W Spain, in Estremadura, in outliers of the Sierra Morena, near Port. border, 40 mi. ESE of Badajoz. Processing, lumbering, and agr. center (cereals, olives, grapes, livestock; cork). Olive-oil pressing, liquor distilling, meat packing, sawmilling, wood turning, tanning; copper, tungsten, and iron mining. Its chief industry is mfg. of bottle corks. Founded in 1229, it was formerly known as Jerez de Badajoz, but later was named Jerez de los Caballeros for the Knights Templars, to whom the city had been given. Balboa was b. here.

Jergucat (yĕrgo͞otsät') or **Jergucati** (yĕrgo͞otsä'tē), village (1930 pop. 657), S Albania, near Gr. line, 12 mi. SE of Argyrokastron; road junction. Also spelled Gjorgucat (Gjorgucati) and Jorgucat (Jorgucati).

Jérica (hā'rēkä), town (pop. 2,013), Castellón de la Plana prov., E Spain, 30 mi. WSW of Castellón de la Plana; burlap mfg.; olive oil, wine, fruit. Remains of medieval walls and castle.

Jericho (jĕ'rĭkō), village (pop. 302), central Queensland, Australia, 280 mi. W of Rockhampton; rail junction; sheep.

Jericho (jĕ'rĭkō), Arabic *Eriha*, village of Palestine, after 1948 in W Jordan, in Jordan valley, near N end of Dead Sea, at E foot of Judaean Hills, 14 mi. ENE of Jerusalem; 820 ft. below sea level. Captured by Joshua from Canaanites; later repeatedly destroyed and rebuilt, it figures in a number of biblical stories. Among its later captors was Herod the Great, who made it winter residence. Just W of modern village, excavations (1950) have yielded remains of Hellenic fortress (2d cent. B.C.) and of the Jericho of Herod. Just NE is locality of Tell es Sultan, scene (1907–35) of excavations yielding remains of wall believed to be that of the 1st Jericho.

Jericho (jĕ'rĭkō, jĕ'rēkō). 1 Village (1940 pop. 551), Nassau co., SE N.Y., on W Long Isl., just N of Hicksville, in suburban residential and agr. area. 2 Wool-shipping point, Juab co., central Utah, 20 mi. WNW of Nephi, on railroad; sheep-shearing center for wide region. 3 Town (pop. 1,135), including Jericho village (1940 pop. 254), Chittenden co., NW Vt., 10 mi. E of Burlington. Settled in late 18th cent. 4 Suburb (pop. 4,687, with near-by Lloyd Place and Pleasant Hill) of Suffolk, Nansemond co., SE Va.

Jericho Bay, Hancock co., S Maine, bounded W, S, and E by Deer Isl., Isle au Haut, and Swans Isl.; opens NE into Blue Hill Bay.

Jerichow (yā'rĭ-khō), town (pop. 3,680), in former Prussian Saxony prov., central Germany, after 1945 in Saxony-Anhalt, near the Elbe, 10 mi. SE of Stendal; agr. market (sugar beets, grain, potatoes, livestock); limestone quarrying. Has noted 12th-cent. church of former Premonstratensian monastery (founded 1144; dissolved 1552).

Jericó (hārēkō'), town (pop. 4,922), Antioquia dept., NW central Colombia, on E slopes of Cordillera Occidental, near Cauca R., 35 mi. SSW of Medellín; alt. 6,453 ft. In fertile agr. region (coffee, corn, potatoes, tobacco, sugar cane, beans, bananas, vegetables, stock). Mfg. of textile goods.

Jerico Springs (jĕ'rĭkō), city (pop. 235), Cedar co., W Mo., in Ozark region, 24 mi. SE of Nevada.

Jerilderie (jŭrĭl'dŭrē), village (pop. 803), S New South Wales, Australia, 190 mi. W of Canberra; wheat, sheep.

Jerim (jĕrēm'), Chinese *Che-li-mu* (jŭ'lē'mo͞o), Mongolian league in SE Inner Mongolian Autonomous Region, Manchuria, in upper Liao R. valley; main town, Tungliao. Formerly part of South Hsingan prov. in Manchukuo, it was inc. 1946 into Liaopeh prov. and 1949 into Inner Mongolian Autonomous Region. Sometimes spelled Cherim.

Jerimoth Hill (jûrĭ'mŭth) (812 ft.), highest point in R.I., in Foster town, near Conn. line c.20 mi. W of Providence.

Jermaq, Jebel, Israel: see JARMAQ, JEBEL.

Jerma River or **Yerma River** (both: yĕr'mä), in W Bulgaria and SE Yugoslavia, rises in Krajiste highland, SW of Trin (Bulgaria); flows c.45 mi. NE and N, past Trin, to Nisava R. 8 mi. SE of Pirot (Yugoslavia).

Jermyn (jûr'mĭn), borough (pop. 2,535), Lackawanna co., NE Pa., 10 mi. NE of Scranton and on Lackawanna R.; anthracite; casket factory; agr. Inc. 1870.

Jerome (jŭrōm'), county (□ 593; pop. 12,080), S Idaho; ⊙ Jerome. Livestock-raising and irrigated agr. area bounded S by Snake R. and in Snake River Plain. Potatoes, apples, sugar beets, alfalfa, dairy products. Formed 1919.

Jerome. 1 Town (pop. 1,233), Yavapai co., central Ariz., in Black Hills, 25 mi. NE of Prescott; alt. 5,435 ft.; copper mining; pyrite deposits. Grew in 1880s after discovery of copper in '70s; inc. 1899. 2 Town (pop. 82), Drew co., SE Ark., 9 mi. S of Dermott, near Bayou Bartholomew. 3 City (pop. 4,523), ⊙ Jerome co., S Idaho, near Snake R., 12 mi. NNW of Twin Falls, in irrigated agr. area (grain, truck, fruit, poultry); dairy products, flour. Laid out 1907, inc. 1909. 4 Village (pop. 689), Sangamon co., central Ill., just SW of Springfield, in agr. and bituminous-coal area.

Jerome Park, SE N.Y., a residential section of central Bronx borough of New York city. A division of Hunter Col. is here. Van Cortlandt and Bronx parks are adjacent.

Jeromesville, village (pop. 513), Ashland co., N central Ohio, 8 mi. SE of Ashland and on Jerome Fork of Mohican R. Formerly Jeromeville.

Jerry City, village (pop. 360), Wood co., NW Ohio, 8 mi. SSE of Bowling Green, in agr. area.

Jersey (jûr'zē), anc. *Caesarea*, island (□ 44.9; 1945 census pop. 44,382; 1951 census 57,296), largest and southernmost of Channel Isls., 15 mi. W of Normandy coast of France, and 18 mi. SE of Guernsey; ⊙ St. Helier. It is 11 mi. long, 5 mi. wide. Its mild climate (plants requiring subtropical conditions grow without protection), moderate rainfall (30–35 in.), and beautiful scenery have contributed to its development as a vacation resort. It cultivates and exports early vegetables (especially potatoes and tomatoes); also dairying, cattle raising (Jersey cattle), granite quarrying. Inhabitants are mostly of Norman descent. English, French, and local dialects are spoken. Occupied (1940–45) by Germany in Second World War.

Jersey, county (□ 374; pop. 15,264), W Ill.; ⊙ Jerseyville. Bounded S by the Mississippi and W by Illinois R.; drained by Macoupin Creek. Agr. (apples, corn, wheat, livestock). Mfg. (shoes, leather, concrete products, flour, cigars, beverages, lumber). Bituminous-coal mining. Resorts on Illinois R. Includes Pere Marquette State Park. Formed 1839.

Jersey, town (pop. 182), Walton co., N central Ga., 7 mi. SW of Monroe.

Jersey City, city (pop. 299,017), ⊙ Hudson co., NE N.J., on peninsula bet. Hackensack R. (W) and Hudson R. (E), opposite lower Manhattan, with which it is connected by ferry, Holland Tunnel (vehicular), and subway; 2d largest city in state; part of Port of N.Y., it is a port of entry, commercial and industrial center, important rail and ocean shipping terminal. Produces packed meat, ink, chemicals, cans, machine-shop and foundry products, petroleum products, steel and metal products, soap, pencils and other graphite goods, cosmetics, cigarettes, footwear, elevators, paint, food products, coke, clocks, clothing. St. Peter's Col., John Marshall Col., state teachers col., and a jr. col. here; has fine public library (1889) and modern medical center. Area acquired by Michiel Pauw (1630) as patroonship of Pavonia; early Dutch trading posts established in this area at Paulus Hook, Communipaw, and Horsimus (1st permanent N.J. settlement). Near-by Bergen was stockaded village dating from before 1620; had 1st municipal govt. in N.J. (1661), 1st church (1660), and 1st school (1662). British rule began 1664; fort at Paulus Hook captured in Revolution by "Light-Horse Harry" Lee, 1779. Town of Jersey, including Bergen, inc. 1804; Hudson City and Greenville added to form present Jersey City, renamed 1836. Coming of railroads and old Morris Canal in 1830s stimulated industrial growth. City adopted commission govt., 1913. In Aug., 1916, Ger. sabotage caused devastating explosion of munitions plant at Black Tom (or Black Tom Isl.) on the waterfront. Points of interest: Fraser's statue of Lincoln (1929) in Lincoln Park; war memorial designed by Martigny.

Jersey Homesteads, N.J.: see ROOSEVELT.

Jersey Shore, borough (pop. 5,595), Lycoming co., N central Pa., 7 mi. WSW of Williamsport and on West Branch of Susquehanna R.; agr.; metal products; railroad shops. Settled 1785, inc. 1826.

Jerseyville, city (pop. 5,792), ⊙ Jersey co., W Ill., 17 mi. NNW of Alton; trade and shipping center in agr. area (apples, corn, wheat, livestock). Mfg.: shoes, leather, concrete products, machinery, flour, cigars, beverages. Platted 1834, inc. 1855.

Jerte (hĕr'tā), town (pop. 1,931), Cáceres prov., W Spain, 23 mi. NE of Plasencia; olive-oil processing; fruit, wine, honey.

Jerteh (jûr"tĕ'), village (pop. 686), N Trengganu, Malaya, 7 mi. SW of Kuala Besut; road junction.

Jerumenha (zhĭrōōmā'nyů), city (pop. 459), W central Piauí, Brazil, on Gurgueia R. and 40 mi. SW of Floriano, in cattle region; carnauba wax, hides. Formerly spelled Jeromenha.

Jerusalem (jůrōō'sůlům), Hebrew *Yerushalayim*, Arabic *El Quds esh Sherif* or *El Kuds*, anc. *Hierosolyma*, city (1946 pop. estimate 164,440), central Palestine, on rocky ridge in Judaean Hills, 35 mi. SE of Tel Aviv; 31°47'N 35°13'E; alt. 2,439 ft. Railroad terminus. Since 1948 the New City (1950 pop. estimate 110,000) has been held by Israel, who made it their ⊙, and the Old City, Arab-held, has been inc. into Jordan. Jerusalem is the holy city of Judaism and Christianity, and site of numerous Moslem shrines; in Jewish and Christian literature often called Zion, it is associated with the Messiah. Almost all holy sites of the 3 faiths are concentrated in the Old City (E), enclosed by wall built (1542) by Suleiman I, with 8 gates, including Jaffa, New, Damascus, Herod's, and Zion gates. Overlooked by Mt. Zion (SW), site of King David's tomb, Old City contains Moslem quarter (E) with the walled Haram esh-Sherif, which contains 7th-cent. Dome of the Rock and mosques of Omar and Aksa; incorporates only remaining wall of Temple of Solomon, which, as the Wailing Wall, is principal holy place of Judaism. Christian quarter (NW) is site of Church of the Holy Sepulcher and of the Via Dolorosa. Armenian quarter is in SW part of Old City; Jewish quarter (S), with Hurva synagogue, was largely destroyed (1948). SE of Old City is the City of David, anc. *Ophel*, scene of important excavations. It is bounded by valleys of the Kidron (SE) and of Hinnom (S), which meet at pool of Siloam. Opposite are Garden of Gethsemane and Mt. of Olives. Also under Arab control are all approaches to Mt. Scopus (NNE), site of bldgs. of Hebrew Univ. (now housed in Terra Sancta Col. in Israeli suburb of Rehavia) and of Hadassah Medical Center. In the New City (W) are 14th-cent. Citadel, on site of Herod's fortress, bldgs. of Israeli parliament, supreme court, Jewish agency; also Palestine Archaeological Mus., many churches, monasteries, and synagogues; railroad station. New City is Jerusalem's economic center; chief industries are printing, handicrafts, metalworking; mfg. of food products, pharmaceuticals, leather and glass products, cigarettes. Radio-assembly and shoe-mfg. plants under construction. Jerusalem is at least as old as 15th cent. B.C. In the Bible it is first mentioned (except for possible allusion as Salem in Genesis) as Jebus; the Jebusite fortress of Zion was captured (1048 B.C.) by David, who made it his ⊙ and brought the Ark here. Under Solomon, the great Temple was built. Among city's subsequent captors was (333 B.C.) Alexander the Great. Antiochus Epiphanes razed (168 B.C.) Jerusalem and massacred inhabitants; Jerusalem was then captured by Maccabeans, succeeded by the Herods. Herod the Great rebuilt the Temple and beautified city. Titus totally destroyed (A.D. 70) Jerusalem, on whose site Hadrian established (A.D. 130) new city of *Aelia Capitolina*. A Christian shrine under Constantine, whose mother Helena established (3d cent.) Church of the Holy Sepulcher, city was sacked (615) by Persians and fell (637) to Moslems, and it became their chief shrine after Mecca. Captured (1099) by Crusaders, who erected the Latin Kingdom of Jerusalem; fell (1187) to Saladin. In First World War entered (1917) by British under Allenby; subsequently became ⊙ British mandated territory of Palestine. Damaged (1927) by earthquake, it was scene (1936–39) of repeated Moslem riots. After the partition of Palestine, and with British withdrawal, fighting broke out (May 14, 1948) bet. Jews and Arabs; Old City surrendered to Arabs May 28, 1948, while Israel controlled the New City. Jerusalem was proclaimed ⊙ Israel on Dec. 14, 1949. Suburbs include Talpioth (SSE), Katamon (SSW), Qiryat Shmuel (SW), and Rehavia (W); among New City's noted sections are the Russian Compound and Mea Shearim.

Jerusalem, village (pop. 175), Monroe co., E Ohio, 11 mi. SSE of Barnesville, in agr. area.

Jerusalem Mills, Md.: see KINGSVILLE.

Jervaulx (jûr'vō, jär'–), village, North Riding, N Yorkshire, England, on Ure R. and 10 mi. S of Richmond. Near by are remains of Jervaulx Abbey, a Cistercian abbey founded 1156 and dismantled 1537. The last abbot was executed after taking part in the Pilgrimage of Grace (1536).

Jervis, Cape (jär'vĭs), SE South Australia, at E side of entrance to Gulf St. Vincent; 35°38'S 138°6'E.

Jervis Bay (jär'vĭs), inlet of Pacific Ocean, E New South Wales, Australia, bet. Point Perpendicular (NE) and Governor Head; 3 mi. wide at mouth; 10 mi. long, 6 mi. wide. Sheltered by Bowen Isl. and 2 small peninsulas forming N and S shores. Harbor and portion (□ 28) of S peninsula transferred (1915) to the Commonwealth by New South Wales for port to be connected by rail with Canberra (85 mi. inland, in Australian Capital Territory). Royal Australian Naval Col., at Captain's Point on S shore, removed (1930) to Flinders naval base, Victoria. Summer resorts on W and S shores.

Jervis Inlet (jär'vĭs), SW B.C., NE arm (51 mi. long, 1–8 mi. wide) of Malaspina Strait of Strait of Georgia; mouth opposite Texada Isl., head near 50°13'N 123°58'W. At mouth is Nelson Isl. (12 mi. long, 5 mi. wide).

Jervois (jûr'vĭs), village (pop. 385), SE South Australia, 55 mi. ESE of Adelaide and on Murray R., near Tailem Bend; dairy products, livestock.

Jerxheim (yĕrkh'hīm), village (pop. 2,394), in Brunswick, NW Germany, after 1945 in Lower Saxony, 11 mi. SW of Helmstedt, 14 mi. WNW of Oschersleben; rail junction; woodworking.

Jerzu, Sardinia: see IERZU.

Jeschken, peak, Czechoslovakia: see JESTED.

Jesenice (yĕ'sĕnyĭtsĕ), Ger. *Jechnitz* (yĕkh'nĭts), town (pop. 1,125), W Bohemia, Czechoslovakia, on railroad and 25 mi. N of Pilsen.

Jesenice or **Jesenice na Gorenjskem** (yĕ'sĕnētsĕ nä gôr'ĕnskĕm), Ger. *Assling* (ä'slĭng), village (pop. 13,458), NW Slovenia, Yugoslavia, on the Sava Dolinka and 35 mi. NNW of Ljubljana, near Austrian border, at S foot of the Karawanken. Rail junction, with lines to Ljubljana, Trieste, Villach (Austria), and Tarvisio (Italy); industrial center (iron-and steelworks here and in vicinity). Skiing, mtn. climbing.

Jesenik (yĕ'sĕnyĕk), Czech *Jeseník*, Ger. *Freiwaldau* (frī'väldou), town (pop. 5,873), NW Silesia, Czechoslovakia, on railroad and 45 mi. N of Olomouc; textile (chiefly linen) and furniture mfg.; granite quarrying. Noted health and winter-sports resort (alt. 1,387 ft.) in Jeseniky mts., with main spa facilities at Jesenik Lazne (yĕ'sĕnyĕk läz'nā), Czech *Jeseník Lázně*, just NW. Has 15th-cent. castle, 18th-cent. town hall, several sanatoriums, 4-mi. bobsled run. Known for its healthful waters since 13th cent. Until 1946, called Fryvaldov; Jesenik Lazne was called Gräfenberk or Gräfenberg. Chain works of *Česka Ves* (chĕ'skä vĕs") are 2 mi. NNE.

Jeseniky (yĕ'sĕnĕkĭ), Czech *Jeseníky*, Ger. *Altvater Gebirge* (ält'fä"tůr gůbĭr'gů), mountain range of the Sudetes, W Silesia and NW Moravia, Czechoslovakia; from Czechoslovak-Pol. border NE of Stare Mesto extend c.50 mi. SE to Moravian Gate; lie bet. Kralicky Sneznik mtn. group (W) and Oder Mts. (SE). Rise to 4,888 ft. in Praded mtn. Extensive forests and pastures; great power resources; scattered iron and graphite deposits on Moravian slopes; marble quarries and numerous mineral springs in N. Noted for health resorts (Jesenik Lasne, Karlova Studanka) and textile industries.

Jesenske (yĕ'sĕnskā), Slovak *Jesenské*, town (pop. 1,567), S Slovakia, Czechoslovakia, 50 mi. SE of Banska Bystrica, in tobacco-growing area; rail junction. Until 1949, called Feldince, Hung. *Feled.*

Jesi, Italy: see IESI.

Jesmond, England: see NEWCASTLE-UPON-TYNE.

Jessamine (jĕ'sůmĭn), county (□ 177; pop. 12,458), central Ky.; ⊙ Nicholasville. Bounded SW and SE by Kentucky R. Gently rolling upland agr. area in Bluegrass region; dairy products, livestock, poultry, burley tobacco, corn, wheat, truck. Limestone quarries. Includes part of High Bridge State Park. Formed 1798.

Jessel, Poland: see JASLO.

Jesselton, town (1951 pop. 11,266, with environs), ⊙ Br. North Borneo and West Coast residency, chief port of colony on small inlet of S.China Sea, 1,000 mi. ENE of Singapore; 5°59'N 116°4'E. Rail and trade center for agr. and stock-raising area; exports rubber. Has rice mills, fisheries. Trade is largely controlled by the Chinese. Founded 1899. Severely damaged in Second World War. Became ⊙ colony in June, 1947, supplanting Sandakan.

Jessen (yĕ'sůn), town (pop. 5,043), in former Prussian Saxony prov., central Germany, after 1945 in Saxony-Anhalt, on the Black Elster and 14 mi. ESE of Wittenberg; metalworking, flour milling; mfg. of furniture, bricks.

Jessnitz (yĕs'nĭts), town (pop. 11,534), in former Anhalt state, central Germany, after 1945 in Saxony-Anhalt, near the Mulde, 5 mi. N of Bitterfeld; paper milling, woodworking.

Jessore (jůsôr'), district (□ c.2,600; 1951 pop. 1,708,000), East Bengal, E Pakistan, in Ganges Delta; ⊙ Jessore. Bounded W by West Bengal, E by Madhumati R.; drained by river arms of Ganges Delta. Alluvial plain (rice, jute, linseed, tobacco, sugar cane, wheat); bamboo, moringa, and tamarind groves, areca and date palms in dispersed forest area. Extensive marshes, in S and SE, largely responsible for high malarial mortality. Jessore is main industrial center; sugar-candy mfg. at Jhenida. Part of 16th-cent. independent Moslem kingdom until defeated 1576 by Akbar's Hindu general. Original dist. (□ 2,925; 1941 pop. 1,828,216) was in former Br. Bengal prov., India, until inc. 1947 into new prov. of East Bengal, following creation of Pakistan; SW portion inc. into Twenty-four Parganas dist., West Bengal, India. Formerly called Yasohara.

Jessore, town (1941 pop. 18,410), ⊙ Jessore dist., SW East Bengal, E Pakistan, on river arm of Ganges Delta and 85 mi. SW of Dacca; road and trade center (rice, jute, linseed, tobacco, sugar cane, tamarind); celluloid and plastic mfg., rice and oilseed milling. Formerly called Yasohara and Kasba.

Jessup, Lake, Seminole co., E central Fla., 13 mi. NE of Orlando; c.10 mi. long, 1–3 mi. wide; N end connected with St. Johns R.

Jessups or **Jessup,** village, Howard co., central Md., 14 mi. SW of downtown Baltimore. Seat of state reformatory for women.

Jested (yĕsh'tyĕt), Czech *Ještěd*, Ger. *Jeschken* (yĕsh'kůn), highest peak (3,314 ft.) of Lusatian Mts., N Bohemia, Czechoslovakia, 3 mi. SW of Liberec. Noted winter-sports resort; cable railway to summit. Amethyst and agate deposits, stone quarries.

Jestetten (yā'shtĕ"tůn), village (pop. 1,453), S Baden, Germany, near the Rhine (bridge), 4 mi. SE of Schaffhausen, near Swiss border; strawberries.

Jesup (jĕ'sůp). **1** Town (pop. 4,605), ⊙ Wayne co., SE Ga., c.55 mi. SW of Savannah, near Altamaha R.; trade and processing center for agr. and timber area; mfg. (clothes, furniture, lumber, naval stores). Inc. 1870. **2** Town (pop. 1,158), Buchanan co., E Iowa, 14 mi. E of Waterloo; butter mfg.

Jesup, Fort, La.: see MANY.

Jesús (hāsōōs'), village (pop. 1,763), Iviza, Balearic Isls., 1 mi. NNE of Iviza; cereals, fruit, livestock.

Jesús, town (dist. pop. including TRINIDAD, 16,777), Itapúa dept., SE Paraguay, 22 mi. NNE of Encarnación; maté center; viticulture. Former Jesuit mission, founded 1685. Just NE, at Tabarangué (täbäräng-gā'), is fine Jesuit church begun 1767.

Jesús. 1 Resort (pop. 19), Arequipa dept., S Peru, SE suburb of Arequipa; thermal springs. **2** City (pop. 1,401), Cajamarca dept., NW Peru, in Cordillera Occidental, 10 mi. SE of Cajamarca; hot springs. The Inca thermal baths, Sp. *Baños del Inca*, are just N.

Jesús Carranza (kärän'sä), town, (pop. 1,407), Veracruz, SE Mexico, on navigable affluent of Coatzacoalcos R., on Isthmus of Tehuantepec, and 50 mi. SW of Minatitlán. Rail junction. Tropical fruit, livestock. Formerly Santa Lucrecia.

Jesús del Río, Colombia: see ZAMBRANO.

Jesús de Machaca (dā mächä'kä), town (pop. c.7,700), La Paz dept., W Bolivia, in the Altiplano, 11 mi. SSE of Guaqui; potatoes, barley, sheep.

Jesús de Otoro (dā ōtō'rō), town (pop. 1,379), Intibucá dept., W central Honduras, 20 mi. NE of La Esperanza, near Río Grande de Otoro; palm-hat mfg.; livestock.

Jesus Island or **Île Jésus** (ēl zhāzü'), island (□ 93; pop. 21,631), S Que., bet. Mille Îles R. (NW) and R. des Prairies (SE), just N of Montreal Isl.; 23 mi. long, 6 mi. wide. Chief centers on isl. are Laval des Rapides, Ste Dorothée, and L'Abord à Plouffe. Market gardening and dairying center. Isl. is coextensive with Île Jésus co.

Jesús María (hāsōōs' märē'ä), town (pop. 6,194), ⊙ Colón dept. (□ c.1,500; pop. 43,538), N central Córdoba prov., Argentina, 30 mi. N of Córdoba. Resort and farming center; (corn, wheat, flax, potatoes, livestock); toolmaking, sawmilling, flour milling. Formerly a Jesuit mission, founded 1618. Has 18th-cent. church.

›sús María, town (pop. 572), Santander dept., N entral Colombia, 20 mi. N of Chiquinquirá, in a mall valley of Cordillera Oriental.

›sús María. 1 Town (pop. 1,534), Aguascalientes, N central Mexico, on San Pedro R. and 6 mi. NW of Aguascalientes; cereals, fruit, vegetables, to-›acco, livestock. 2 Town (pop. 1,196), Jalisco, entral Mexico, 15 mi. E of Atotonilco el Alto; ;rain, beans, livestock.

›swantpur, India: see BANGALORE, city.

›t, town (pop. 371), Alfalfa co., N Okla., 25 mi. NW of Enid, in agr. area (wheat, livestock, poul-ry). Great Salt Plains Dam is 5 mi. NE.

›tafe (hätä'fä), town (1939 pop. 2,030; 1948 mu-icipality pop. 15,804), N Bohol isl., Philippines, 0 mi. NNE of Tagbilaran; agr. center (rice, corn, oconuts).

talsar (jä'tŭlsŭr), village, S central Saurashtra, ndia, 2 mi. SW of Jetpur; rail junction.

thou (zhütōō'), island (44 acres; 1951 pop., in-luding isl. of Herm, 49), one of Channel Isls., 3 ni. E of Guernsey.

tmore, city (pop. 988), ⊙ Hodgeman co., SW cen-ral Kansas, on small affluent of Pawnee R. and 24 ni. NNE of Dodge City; grain, livestock. State ark near by.

tpur (jät'pŏŏr), town (pop. 28,406), S central aurashtra, India, on Bhadar R. and 40 mi. SSW of Rajkot; agr. market center (millet, oilseeds, wheat, otton); handicraft cloth weaving. Was ⊙ former Western Kathiawar state of Jetpur (□ 120; pop. 5,145) of Western India States agency; state nerged 1948 with Saurashtra.

tte (zhĕt), residential town (pop. 29,396), Brabant rov., central Belgium, NW suburb of Brussels; esort.

umont (zhūmō'), town (pop. 6,008), Nord dept., I France, on Belg. border opposite Erquelinnes, mi. ENE of Maubeuge, on the Sambre; custom tation; has important electrical industry, marble nd granite quarries. Produces machine tools and one-polishing equipment.

vany, Czechoslovakia: see KOSTELEC NAD CERNY-I LESY.

vargi (jä'vŭrgē) or Jivargi (jĭvŭr'gē), village (pop. ,128), Gulbarga dist., W Hyderabad state, India, 2 mi. S of Gulbarga; millet, rice. Sheep raising ear by. Sometimes spelled Jaivergi.

ver (yä'vŭr), town (pop. 10,342), in Oldenburg, NW Germany, after 1945 in Lower Saxony, in East Friesland, 10 mi. WNW of Wilhelmshaven; main own of Friesland dist.; rail junction; woolen mill-g, brewing, meat processing. Horse and cattle narkets. Has 17th-cent. town hall.

veros, Peru: see JEBEROS.

vicko (yĕ'vĭchkô), Czech *Jevíčko*, town (pop. ,575), W Moravia, Czechoslovakia, on railroad nd 24 mi. W of Olomouc; health resort with sana-orium for tubercular patients.

war (jä'vŭr), town (pop. 8,592), Bulandshahr ist., W Uttar Pradesh, India, 20 mi. WSW of Khurja; hand-loom cotton weaving; wheat, oil-eeds, barley, cotton, jowar, corn.

we, Estonia: see JOHVI.

wel Cave National Monument (1,274.56 acres; stablished 1908), SW S.Dak., 13 mi. W of Custer, n high plateau (5,200–5,800 ft.). Series of small ubterranean chambers fretted with jewellike cal-ite crystals.

well, county (□ 915; pop. 9,698), N Kansas; ⊙ Mankato. Rolling plain area, bordering N on Nebr. Grain, livestock. Formed 1870.

well. 1 Town (pop. 973), Hamilton co., central owa, 19 mi. N of Ames, in livestock and grain rea. Platted 1880. 2 City (pop. 593), Jewell co., I Kansas, 9 mi. SSE of Mankato, in grain and vestock area.

wett (jōō'ĭt). 1 Village (pop. 253), Cumberland o., SE central Ill., 20 mi. SSE of Mattoon, in agr. rea. 2 Resort village, Greene co., SE N.Y., in the Catskills, 23 mi. E of Catskill. 3 Village (pop. ,019), Harrison co., E Ohio, 6 mi. N of Cadiz and n small Conotton Creek; coal mining; sawmilling. aid out 1851, inc. 1886. 4 Town (pop. 598), Leon o., E central Texas, c.60 mi. ESE of Waco; trade oint in farm area.

wett City, Conn.: see GRISWOLD.

wish Autonomous Oblast, popularly called Biro-idzhan (bērūbējän'), administrative division □ 13,800; 1939 pop. 108,419; 1946 pop. estimate 50,000) of S Khabarovsk Territory, Russian SFSR, in the Soviet Far East; ⊙ Birobidzhan. ies bet. Amur R. (Manchuria border; S) and Bureya Range (N); drained by Bira and Bidzhan ivers (left affluents of Amur R.). Agr. (wheat, oats, oybeans, truck produce) in S and SE sections, umbering and gold mining in N, iron and tin min-ng W in Little Khingan Range. Larger settle-nents are on Trans-Siberian RR (N); produce tex-iles, leather, clothing goods. Percentage of Jewish op. estimated variously bet. 25% and more than 0%. Formed 1934 for Jewish agr. colonization.

yamkondacholapuram, India: see JAYANKONDA-HOLAPURAM.

ypore (jä'pōr, jī'pŏŏr). 1 Town (pop. 12,504), Koraput dist., SW Orissa, India, 240 mi. SW of Cuttack; trades in rice, hides, forest produce (sal, eak, bamboo, lac); rice milling, tanning; tile-works, distillery (arrack). Has col. 2 City, Raja-sthan, India: see JAIPUR, city.

Jezerce (yĕzĕr'tsä), peak (8,464 ft.) in North Albanian Alps, on Albanian-Yugoslav border, 10 mi. SSW of Gusinje.

Jezerska Cesma or **Yezerska Chesma** (both: yĕ'-zĕrskä chĕs'mä), Serbo-Croatian *Jezerska Česma*, peak (8,541 ft.) in Sar Mts., Yugoslavia, on Serbia-Macedonia border, 10 mi. NNE of Tetovo; chromium mining.

Jezerski Vrh, Yugoslavia and Austria: see SEEBERG PASS.

Jeziorak, Lake (yĕ-zhô'räk) or **Jezierzyce, Lake** (yĕ-zhĕ-zhĭ'tsĕ), Ger. *Geserich* (gā'zūrĭkh) (□ 12), in East Prussia, after 1945 in N Poland, N of Ilawa; 18 mi. long N-S, 1–5 mi. wide; drains SW into the Vistula.

Jeziorany (yĕ"zhôrä'nĭ), Ger. *Seeburg* (zā'bŏŏrk), town (1939 pop. 3,022; 1946 pop. 1,248) in East Prussia, after 1945 in Olsztyn prov., NE Poland, in Masurian Lakes region, 17 mi. NNE of Allenstein (Olsztyn); grain and cattle market.

Jeziory, Belorussian SSR: see OZERY, Grodno oblast.

Jezire, Jezira, or **Jazirah** (all: jĕzē'rū) [Arabic, = island], Fr. *Djézireh* or *Djéziret*, province (□ 8,331; 1946 pop. 151,173), NE Syria, in the Syrian Desert, bordering N on Turkey and E on Iraq; ⊙ El Haseke. The desert is here somewhat irrigated by Khabur R., an affluent of the Euphrates. Grows cotton, rice, corn, millet. Sheep raising. Rich oil deposits, largely unexploited.

Jezireh, El, Mesopotamia: see JAZIRA, AL.

Jezreel (jĕz'rēĕl) or **Yizre'el** (yĭzrĕ-ĕl'), agr. settlement, N Israel, in SE part of Plain of Jezreel, at NW foot of Mt. Gilboa, 4 mi. SE of Afula. Modern Jewish settlement founded 1948 on site of village of Zir'in, abandoned by Arab pop. Jezreel figures in biblical history. Important road junction in Roman times; during Crusades called Le Petit Gerin.

Jezreel, Plain of, or **Plain of Esdraelon** (ĕs'drūē'lŭn), Hebrew *'Emeq Jezreel*, plain (□ c.200), N Israel, extending c.25 mi. NW–SE bet. Jordan valley near Beisan and SE foot of Mt. Carmel, SE of Haifa; separates Lower Galilee (N) from Samaria (S); drained by Kishon R. Here are numerous agr. settlements; Afula is economic center of region. In biblical history noted as site of battlefield of MEGIDDO.

Jezupol, Ukrainian SSR: see ZHOVTEN, Stanislav oblast.

Jezzin or **Jazzin** (both: jĕz-zēn'), Fr. *Djezzine*, town (pop. 4,348), S Lebanon, 12 mi. E of Saida; summer resort; sericulture, cereals, oranges. Has waterfall 130 ft. high. Sometimes spelled Jezzeen.

Jhabrera, India: see JABARHERA.

Jhabua (jäb'wŭ), village, ⊙ Jhabua dist., SW Madhya Bharat, India, 40 mi. SW of Ratlam; local market (corn, millet, timber); cotton ginning. Was ⊙ former princely state of Jhabua (□ 1,265; pop. 178,327) of Central India agency; a Rajput state, founded 16th cent., since 1948 merged with Madhya Bharat.

Jhagadia (jō'gŭdyŭ), town (pop. 4,209), Broach dist., N Bombay, India, 11 mi. E of Broach; rail junction; trades in cotton, tobacco, millet, timber.

Jhajjar (jŭj'jŭr), town (pop. 13,919), Rohtak dist., SE Punjab, India, 20 mi. SSE of Rohtak; trade center for grain, salt, cloth fabrics; millet, gram, cotton; hand-loom weaving, embroidering, dyeing, pottery mfg.

Jhalakati (jälŭkä'tē), town (pop. 9,184), Bakarganj dist., S East Bengal, E Pakistan, on Bishkhali R. (distributary of Arial Khan R.) and 12 mi. WSW of Barisal; trade center (rice, oilseeds, jute, sugar cane, sundari timber, betel nuts); rice and oilseed milling.

Jhalawan (jŭlŭvän'), largest division (□ 20,483; pop. 52,272) of Kalat state, E Baluchistan, W Pakistan. Bordered E by Kirthar Range; hilly region, watered by Hingol, Porali, and Hab rivers. Agr. (wheat, millet, rice, barley, pomegranates, apricots, mulberries); livestock raising; hand-loom carpet weaving, palm-mat and bag making. Chief villages: Khuzdar, Nal. Pop. 99% Moslem.

Jhalawar (jä'lŭvär), former princely state (□ 824; pop. 122,299) in Rajputana States, India; ⊙ was Brijnagar. Created 1838 from original Kotah state. In 1948, merged with union of Rajasthan.

Jhalawar, district, SE Rajasthan, India; ⊙ Brijnagar.

Jhalida or **Jhalda** (both: jŭl'dŭ), town (pop. 7,182), Manbhum dist., SE Bihar, India, 25 mi. W of Purulia; rice, corn, oilseeds, bajra, sugar cane; lac growing, mfg. (cutlery, shellac, firearms).

Jhalod (jä'lōd), town (pop. 6,750), Panch Mahals dist., N Bombay, India, 40 mi. NE of Godhra; market center for corn, rice, wheat, cotton cloth; pottery, lac bracelets. Flagstone quarried near by.

Jhalore, India: see JALOR.

Jhalrapatan (jälrŭpä'tŭn), town (pop. 6,059), SE Rajasthan, India, 4 mi. S of Brijnagar; trades in wheat, cotton, oilseeds, millet, cattle; hand-loom weaving, oilseed pressing, pottery making. Sometimes called Patan.

Jhalrapatan Chhaoni, India: see BRIJNAGAR.

Jhalu (jä'lōō), town (pop. 6,953), Bijnor dist., N Uttar Pradesh, India, 6 mi. ESE of Bijnor; rice, wheat, gram, sugar cane.

Jhang (jŭng), district (□3,415; 1951 pop. 875,000), central Punjab, W Pakistan; ⊙ Jhang-Maghiana. Bounded S by Ravi R.; includes parts of Rechna Doab (E), Chaj Doab (N), and Sind-Sagar Doab (W); drained by Chenab and Jhelum rivers. Wheat, cotton, millet grown in large alluvial areas; hand-loom weaving; cattle breeding. Chief towns: Jhang-Maghiana, Chiniot. Formerly included present Lyallpur dist.

Jhang-Maghiana (jŭng' mŭgyä'nŭ), city (1941 pop. 50,051), ⊙ Jhang dist., central Punjab, W Pakistan, 120 mi. WSW of Lahore; trades in grain, wool, and cloth fabrics; cotton ginning, hand-loom weaving, mfg. of pottery, locks, leather goods, metalware. Has col. Formerly 2 towns, joined to form a municipality.

Jhansi (jän'sē), district (□ c.3,670; pop. c.784,700), S Uttar Pradesh, India; ⊙ Jhansi. Drained by Betwa R.; irrigated by Betwa Canal; foothills of Vindhya Range in S. Agr.: jowar, oilseeds, wheat, gram, barley, rice, corn. Main centers: Jhansi, Lalitpur, Mau, Barwa Sagar. Archaeological landmarks include remains at Deogark and near Mahonri and Lalitpur. Formerly part of Br. Bundelkhand. Ruled by Chandel and Bundela Rajput dynasties until conquered (18th cent.) by Mahrattas. Last Mahratta raja died without issue in 1853 and the state was escheated to Great Britain and made a dist.; his widow, Rani of Jhansi, entered into coalition with other native rulers and became an important military leader during Sepoy Rebellion of 1857. Original dist. (□ 3,606; 1941 pop. 773,002) enlarged 1950 by inc. of several former petty states.

Jhansi, city (pop., including rail settlement and cantonment, 103,254), ⊙ Jhansi dist., S Uttar Pradesh, India, 130 mi. SW of Cawnpore; rail junction (workshops); road and trade (grain, oilseeds, cotton) center; iron- and steel-rolling mill; rubber-goods and brassware mfg. Soil survey laboratory. Main part of city (N), surrounded by a wall, developed around a fort built 1613 by Bundela Rajputs and strengthened by Mahrattas in 1742. Founded 1613. Site of massacre of British men, women, and children during Sepoy Rebellion of 1857. Acquired by British in 1886. Hydroelectric plant for Betwa power project 18 mi. S, at Dukwan village.

Jharia or **Jherria** (both: jär'ryŭ), town (pop. 18,037), Manbhum dist., SE Bihar, India, near Damodar R., 28 mi. N of Purulia; coal-mining center in Jharia coal field.

Jharsuguda (jär'sōōgōōdŭ), town (pop. 8,032), Sambalpur dist., NW Orissa, India, 27 mi. N of Sambalpur; rail junction (workshops); trades in rice, timber, oilseeds, hides; biri mfg. Sometimes called Jharsugra. Mfg. of paper, pencils, nibs, penholders near by, at Brajrajnagar village.

Jhawarian (jŭvär'yän), town (pop. 6,016), Shahpur dist., central Punjab, W Pakistan, 18 mi. N of Sargodha; wheat, cotton, millet; cotton ginning. Sometimes spelled Jahwarian.

Jhelum (jä'lōōm), district (□ 2,774; pop. 629,658), N Punjab, W Pakistan; ⊙ Jhelum. Bounded E and S by Jhelum R.; crossed S by E Salt Range. Plateau (N, center) and riverbank area produce wheat, millet, oilseeds. Petroleum wells at Balkassar and Joya Mair; extensive coal and rock salt deposits (works at Khewra and Dandot) in Salt Range. Trade centers: Jhelum, Pind Dadan Khan.

Jhelum, town (pop., including SW cantonment area, 33,191), ⊙ Jhelum dist., N Punjab, W Pakistan, on Jhelum R., on railroad (workshops) and 95 mi. NNW of Lahore. Trade center; timber depot (logs floated down river from N forests collected here); wheat, millet; sawmills; boat building, pottery mfg. Pakistan Military Col. Considered by some to be near point of Jhelum R. (*Hydaspes*) crossing by Alexander the Great in 326 B.C.; others locate site at Jalalpur.

Jhelum Canal, Lower, irrigation channel in N Punjab, W Pakistan; from left bank of Jhelum R. (headworks near Rasul, Gujrat dist.) runs 39 mi. SW. Here it divides into 2 main branches, with N branch flowing c.110 mi. S, S branch flowing c.85 mi. S; numerous distributaries. Irrigates extensive areas of Gujrat, Shahpur, and Jhang dists. in Chaj Doab. Opened 1901.

Jhelum Canal, Upper, irrigation channel mainly in Gujrat dist., N Punjab, W Pakistan; from left bank of Jhelum R. (headworks at Mangla in SW Kashmir) runs 85 mi. S and SE to CHENAB RIVER 5 mi. W of Wazirabad. Used chiefly as feeder for Lower Chenab Canal. Opened 1915.

Jhelum River, anc. *Hydaspes*, in Kashmir and W Pakistan, westernmost of 5 rivers of the Punjab. Rises in a spring near town of Vernag, at foot of Banihal Pass on N slope of Pir Panjal Range. Flows NW through Vale of Kashmir, past Anantnag and Srinagar, through Wular L., thence W past Baramula, cutting through N extension of Pir Panjal Range, past Muzaffarabad (here receives Kishanganga R. from NE), thence almost due S along borders of Kashmir (E) and North-West Frontier Prov. and Pakistan Punjab (W), SW past Jhelum town, across Punjab plains and again S to

Chenab R. 10 mi. SW of Jhang-Maghiana; total length, c.480 mi. Near Mangla are headworks of Upper Jhelum Canal, while at Rasul Lower Jhelum Canal takes off. River crossed in 326 B.C. by Alexander the Great, who defeated Porus here; site located near Jalalpur by some, near Jhelum town by others. Known as the Veth in Kashmir; sometimes spelled Jehlam.

Jhenida (jā'nĭdŭ), village, Jessore dist., W East Bengal, E Pakistan, on distributary of the Madhumati and 26 mi. N of Jessore; trades in rice, jute, linseed, sugar cane, pepper; sugar-candy mfg.

Jherria, India: see JHARIA.

Jhind, India: see JIND.

Jhinjhak (jĭn'jŭk), town (pop. 2,387), Cawnpore dist., S Uttar Pradesh, India, on Lower Ganges Canal and 38 mi. WNW of Cawnpore; gram, wheat, jowar, barley, mustard.

Jhinjhana (jĭnjä'nŭ), town (pop. 5,562), Muzaffarnagar dist., N Uttar Pradesh, India, 29 mi. W of Muzaffarnagar; wheat, gram, sugar cane, oilseeds. Has tomb of Moslem saint (built 1495), 17th-cent. mosque.

Jhinkpani, India: see CHAIBASA.

Jhuldabhaj, India: see BARAUNI.

Jhumra, W Pakistan: see CHAK JHUMRA.

Jhunjhunu (jōōn'jōōnōō), town (pop. 16,874), ⊙ Jhunjhunu dist., NE Rajasthan, India, 90 mi. NNW of Jaipur; local trade center (wool, cattle, hides, grain).

Jhusi (jōō'sē), town (pop. 2,962), Allahabad dist., SE Uttar Pradesh, India, at Jumna R. mouth, 4 mi. E of Allahabad city center; sugar processing. Gold coins dating from Gupta empire found here, also copperplate of a Pratihara Rajput king dated A.D. 1027. Area identified with *Pratisthan* or *Kesi* of the Puranic histories, when it was ⊙ 1st king of the Lunar dynasty.

Jiaganj, India: see AZIMGANJ.

Jianpur (jē'ŭnpŏŏr), village, Azamgarh dist., E Uttar Pradesh, India, 11 mi. NE of Azamgarh; rice, barley, wheat, sugar cane. Also called Sagri and Jainpur.

Jibacoa (hēbäkō'ä), town (pop. 1,026), Havana prov., W Cuba, on railroad and 30 mi. E of Havana, in sugar-growing region.

Jibhalanta, Mongolia: see ULIASSUTAI.

Jibiya (jĭ'bĭyä), town (pop. 4,787), Katsina prov., Northern Provinces, N Nigeria, on upper Kebbi R. and 28 mi. WNW of Katsina, on Fr. West African border; peanuts, cotton; cattle, skins. Also spelled Jibia.

Jibla or **Jiblah** (jĭ'blŭ), town (pop. 3,000), Ibb prov., S Yemen, 3 mi. SW of Ibb.

Jiblea or **Jiblea-Veche** (zhē'blyä-vā'kā), agr. village (pop. 1,214), Valcea prov., S central Rumania, on Olt R., on railroad and 15 mi. WNW of Curtea-de-Arges.

Jibliya or **Jibliyah,** Kuria Muria Isls.: see QIBLIYA.

Jiboa River (hēbō'ä), S Salvador, rises near San Rafael, flows c.45 mi. SSW, through La Paz dept., to the Pacific 17 mi. ESE of La Libertad. Receives waters of L. Ilopango (right).

Jibon (zhē'bôn), Hung. *Zsibó* (zhē'bō), village (pop. 3,518), Cluj prov., NW Rumania, near Somes R., 10 mi. NE of Zalau; rail junction; coal mining, mfg. of alcohol. In Hungary, 1940–45.

Jibuti, Fr. Somaliland: see DJIBOUTI.

Jicaral (hēkäräl'), village, Puntarenas prov., W Costa Rica, small Pacific port on Gulf of Nicoya, on Nicoya Peninsula, and 20 mi. W of Puntarenas; lumbering.

Jicaral, El, Nicaragua: see EL JICARAL.

Jicarilla Mountains (hĭkûrē'ŭ), S central N.Mex., N range of Sacramento Mts., in Lincoln co.; lies in part of Lincoln Natl. Forest. Prominent peak, Jicarilla Mtn. (c.8,200 ft.). Gold is mined.

Jícaro, Guatemala: see EL JÍCARO.

Jícaro, El, Nicaragua: see EL JÍCARO.

Jícaro Galán (hē'kärō gälän'), village (pop. 140), Valle dept., S Honduras, 3 mi. ESE of Nacaome; major road center, on Inter-American Highway and road to Tegucigalpa.

Jícaro River, NW Nicaragua, rises in Sierra de Dipilto near Jalapa, flows c.50 mi. S and SE, past El Jícaro and San Albino gold mines (hydroelectric station), to Coco R. below Quilalí.

Jicatuyo River (hēkätōō'yō), W Honduras, rises as Alash R. in Andean divide S of San Marcos (Ocotepeque dept.), flows N, past Cucuyagua (here called Higuito R.), and generally E, to Ulúa R. 3 mi. NNW of Santa Bárbara; length, c.100 mi.

Jicin (yĭ'chēn), Czech *Jičín*, Ger. *Gitschin* (gĭ'chĭn), town (pop. 10,651), N Bohemia, Czechoslovakia, 26 mi. SSE of Liberec; rail junction; mfg. of machinery, motors, pianos. Has 17th-cent. castle built by Wallenstein, remains of medieval fortifications (notably Walditz gate). Emperor Francis of Austria held conference here (1813) with Prussian and Russian representatives, before battle of Leipzig. Picturesque formations of sandstone rocks (Prachov rocks), part of so-called BOHEMIAN PARADISE, are 3–6 mi. NW.

Jico (hē'kō), town (pop. 5,804), Veracruz, E Mexico, at SE foot of Cofre de Perote, 10 mi. SSW of Jalapa; alt. 4,314 ft.; rail terminus; orangegrowing.

Jidda, Jedda, Jiddah, or **Jeddah** (all: jĭ'dŭ, jĕ'dŭ), city (pop. 60,000), central Hejaz, Saudi Arabia, major Red Sea port 40 mi. W of Mecca (linked by road); 21°29'N 39°11'E. Principal harbor of Hejaz and port of entry on pilgrimage route to Mecca, handling 90% of pilgrim trade; airport (N). Local mfg. (rugs, mats, pottery, clothing, religious articles), dhow building; fishing and pearling. A cosmopolitan center with mixed Arabian, Persian, Indian, and Negro pop. Jidda is walled and is built largely of coral rock, with its W section standing on land reclaimed from Red Sea. City's residential section (N) is seat of foreign diplomatic missions to Saudi Arabia; there is a large bazaar (S). Reputed tomb of Eve, beyond N gate, was demolished in 1927 by the Wahabis. Jidda's commercial prosperity dates from Turkish rule of Hejaz, when it developed as a pilgrimage center. It fell to Husein ibn Ali of Mecca in 1916 and to Ibn Saud in 1925. Sometimes spelled Judda or Juddah.

Jigat, India: see DWARKA.

Jigdalik, Afghanistan: see JAGDALAK.

Jigjiga, Ethiopia: see JIJIGA.

Jigni (jĭg'nē), village, Hamirpur dist., S Uttar Pradesh, India, on Dhasan R. and 45 mi. NW of Mahoba. Was ⊙ former petty state of Jigni (□ 22; pop. 4,745) of Central India agency; in 1948, state merged with Vindhya Pradesh, in 1950, inc. into Hamirpur dist. of Uttar Pradesh.

Jiguaní (hēgwänē'), town (pop. 4,715), Oriente prov., E Cuba, on Central Highway, on railroad and 13 mi. E of Bayamo; dairying center. Also produces sugar cane, fruit, coffee, cacao. Granite quarrying. In its picturesque surroundings are ruins of a colonial castle and the Pepú caves.

Jigüero, Point (hēgwā'rō), on NW coast of Puerto Rico, 9 mi. SW of Aguadilla; 18°22'N 67°16'W.

Jigüey Bay (hēgwā'), shallow inlet of Old Bahama Channel, off Camagüey prov., E Cuba, bet. Cayo Romano and Cuba, 30 mi. E of Morón; c.30 mi. long NW-SE, 6 mi. wide. Receives Caunao R. and small Jigüey R.

Jihchao (rŭ'jou'), town, ⊙ Jihchao co. (pop. 497,523), SE Shantung prov., China, 60 mi. SW of Tsingtao, near Yellow Sea; pongee and cotton weaving.

Jih-k'o-tse, Tibet: see SHIGATSE.

Jihlava (yĭkh'lävä), Ger. *Iglau* (ĭ'glou), city (pop. 23,413), ⊙ Jihlava prov. (□ 2,568; pop. 422,533), W Moravia, Czechoslovakia, in Bohemian-Moravian Heights, on Jihlava R. and 48 mi. WNW of Brno; 49°24'N 15°35'E. Rail junction; noted for woolen textile and leather (footwear, gloves) industries; mfg. (furniture, pianos, automobile bodies, saws, files), tobacco processing, tanning. Former silver-mining center. Retains parts of its old fortifications, 13th- and 16th-cent. Gothic churches, 16th-cent. town hall, old city gate. Has a radio station. Famous in Czechoslovakian history as site of signing of the "Compactata"—the Magna Carta of the Hussite church—in 1436. Cejle-Kostelec, 4 mi. SW, is known for its smoked meats and preserves.

Jihlava River, Ger. *Iglawa* (ĭ'glävä), SW Moravia, Czechoslovakia, rises in Bohemian-Moravian Heights 3 mi. NE of Pocatky, flows NNE, E, past Jihlava, and SE, past Trebic and Ivancice, to Svratka R. 19 mi. S of Brno; 57 mi. long.

Jihun River, Turkey: see CEYHAN RIVER.

Jihyüeh Lake (rŭ'yüĕ'), Chinese *Jih-yüeh T'an* (tän) [Sun-Moon Lake], Jap. *Jitsugetsu Tan* (jētsōō'gĕtsōō tän'), mountain lake (□ 2) in central range of Formosa, 24 mi. SE of Taichung; 15 ft. deep; alt. 2,400 ft. A scenic water-body, it consists of 2 sections, Sun L. (NE) and Moon L. (SW). It feeds Formosa's largest hydroelectric plant (completed 1934). Formerly called L. Candidius, for a Dutch missionary.

Jijelli, Algeria: see DJIDJELLI.

Jijiga (jĭ'jĕgä), Ital. *Giggiga*, town (pop. 11,000), Harar prov., E central Ethiopia, on plateau, on Jerer R. and 45 mi. E of Harar; 9°20'N 42°45'E. Commercial center (coffee, hides, wax) at junction of roads to Addis Ababa, Berbera (Br. Somaliland), and Mogadishu (Ital. Somaliland). Airfield. Occupied by Italians (1936) in Italo-Ethiopian War and by British (1941) in Second World War. Sometimes written Jigjiga.

Jijona (hēhō'nä), city (pop. 5,076), Alicante prov., E Spain, 15 mi. N of Alicante; candy- and conserve-mfg. center, shipping nougats and raisins. Olive-oil processing, flour- and sawmilling. Sheep raising; honey, cereals, vegetables in area. Has remains of Moorish castle.

Jilava (zhē'lävä), village (pop. 2,546), Bucharest prov., S Rumania, 7 mi. S of Bucharest; rubber processing; dairying.

Jilawiyah, Al-, Egypt: see GILAWIA, EL.

Jilemnice (yĭ'lĕmnyĭtsĕ), Ger. *Starkenbach* (shtär'kŭnbäkh), town (pop. 3,362), NE Bohemia, Czechoslovakia, in foothills of the Riesengebirge, 23 mi. SE of Liberec. Rail junction; summer and winter resort noted for skiing facilities; mfg. of textiles (notably linen), skis, sleighs; paper mills. Has old castle, mus.

Jiloca River or **Giloca River** (both: hēlō'kä), in Teruel and Saragossa provs., NE Spain, rises in the Montes Universales N of Teruel, flows c.80 mi. NNW to the Jalón at Calatayud.

Jilolo, Indonesia: see HALMAHERA.

Jilotepec (hēlōtāpĕk'). **1** Officially Jilotepec de Abasolo, city (pop. 1,359), Mexico state, central Mexico, 40 mi. NW of Mexico city; cereals, fruit, livestock. Airfield. **2** Town (pop. 1,129), Veracruz, E Mexico, in Sierra Madre Oriental, 6 mi. N of Jalapa; corn, coffee, fruit.

Jilotepeque or **San Luis Jilotepeque** (sän lwēs' hēlōtāpā'kā), town (1950 pop. 4,098), Jalapa dept., E central Guatemala, in highlands, 15 mi. E of Jalapa; corn, beans.

Jilotlán de los Dolores (hēlōtlän' dā lōs dōlō'rĕs), town (pop. 901), Jalisco, central Mexico, 45 mi. E of Colima; sugar cane, corn, fruit.

Jilotzingo (hēlōtsĭng'gō), officially Santa Ana Jilotzingo, town (pop. 2,595), Mexico state, central Mexico, 17 mi. WNW of Mexico city; cereals, livestock.

Jilove (yē'lôvā), Czech *Jílové*, Ger. *Eule* (oi'lĕ), town (pop. 2,256), S central Bohemia, Czechoslovakia, on railroad and 13 mi. SSE of Prague; excursion center. Former gold-mining settlement. *Velké Popovice* (vĕl'kā pô'pôvĭtsĕ) breweries are 6 mi. NE.

Jimaní (hēmänē'), town (1935 pop. 423; 1950 pop. 487), Bâhoruco prov., SW Dominican Republic, bet. L. Enriquillo and Haiti border, 30 mi. W of Neiba; coffee, fruit, timber. Became (1949) ⊙ newly formed Independencia prov.

Jimasa (jēmäsä'), Chinese *Fuyüan* (fōō'yüän'), town, ⊙ Jimasa co. (pop. 21,526), E central Sinkiang prov., China, 70 mi. E of Urumchi and on branch of Silk Road.

Jimbolia (zhēmbô'lyä), Hung. *Zsombolya* (zhôm'bôlyŏ), Ger. *Hatzfeld* (häts'fĕlt), village (pop. 10,781), Timisoara prov., W Rumania, 25 mi. W of Timisoara; rail junction and frontier station on Yugoslav border; mfg. of clay products, felt hats, combs, buttons, flour.

Jimena (hēmä'nä), town (pop. 3,392), Jaén prov., S Spain, 18 mi. ENE of Jaén; olive-oil processing, flour milling, soap mfg.; cereals, fruit. Stone quarries.

Jimena de la Frontera (dhä lä frōntā'rä), city (pop. 4,979), Cádiz prov., SW Spain, 21 mi. N of Algeciras; agr. center (cereals, vegetables, fruit, tubers, livestock); cork, timber; apiculture; mfg. of shoes; limekilns. At site of old Iberian settlement; has Moorish castle.

Jiménez, Argentina: see GRAMILLA.

Jiménez, canton, Costa Rica: see JUAN VIÑAS.

Jiménez (hēmā'nĕs), village (dist. pop. 3,318), Limón prov., E Costa Rica, 3 mi. E of Guápiles, on railroad; rubber, bananas, corn, livestock.

Jiménez. 1 City (pop. 5,175), Chihuahua, N Mexico, on plateau E of Sierra Madre Occidental, on Florido R. and 125 mi. SE of Chihuahua; alt. 5,530 ft. Rail junction; mining center (fluorspar, mercury); silver, gold, lead, copper deposits; cotton ginning. The region near by is known for large number of meteorites, some of them discovered by the Spaniards in 16th and 17th cent., and now exhibited in School of Mines in Mexico city. **2** Town (pop. 622), Coahuila, N Mexico, near the Rio Grande (Texas border), 27 mi. NW of Piedras Negras; wheat, bran, cattle; istle fibers, candelilla wax. **3** or **Santander Jiménez** (säntändĕr'), town (pop. 1,639), Tamaulipas, NE Mexico, 55 mi. NE of Ciudad Victoria; cereals, sugar cane, beans, livestock.

Jimenez, town (1939 pop. 4,404; 1948 municipality pop. 25,352), Misamis Occidental prov., W Mindanao, Philippines, port on Panguil Bay, 11 mi. SSE of Oroquieta; agr. center (corn, coconuts); ships copra.

Jiménez, Villa, Mexico: see VILLA JIMÉNEZ.

Jiménez del Teul (dĕl tĕōōl'), town (pop. 288), Zacatecas, N central Mexico, near Durango border, 35 mi. NW of Valparaíso; maguey, corn, livestock raising.

Jimenoa (hēmänô'ä), falls and hydroelectric project, La Vega prov., central Dominican Republic, on affluent of the Yaque del Norte, just E of Jarabacoa, 10 mi. SW of La Vega.

Jimera de Libar (hēmā'rä dhä lēvär'), town (pop. 1,034), Málaga prov., S Spain, on Guadiaro R., on railroad and 9 mi. SW of Ronda; acorns, almonds, grapes, olives, wheat, vegetables; flour milling. Has mineral springs.

Jim Hogg, county (□ 1,139; pop. 5,389), extreme S Texas; ⊙ Hebbronville. Petroleum-producing ranching co.; mainly cattle; also horses, mules, goats; some agr. (peanuts, cotton, corn), dairying. Formed 1913.

Jimma (jĭ'mä), Ital. *Gimma*, town (pop. 15,000), ⊙ Kaffa prov., SW Ethiopia, on an affluent of Gojab R. and 150 mi. SW of Addis Ababa; 7°39'N 36°50'E; road junction; alt. c.5,740 ft. Situated in fertile, mountainous region, but town is hot and malarial. Commerical and mfg. center; coffee, cereals, hides, wax, salt; milling (flour, lumber), tanning, cotton weaving, metal working. Has leprosarium. Airfield. Occupied by Italians (1936) in Italo-Ethiopian War and by British (1941) in Second World War. Jiran, on a hill 4 mi. ENE, is a sultan's seat.

Jimokuji (jēmō'kōōjē), town (pop. 9,939), Aichi prefecture, central Honshu, Japan, just NW of Nagoya; rice, wheat, radishes, raw silk.

Jimramov (yĭm'rämôf), village (pop. 1,050), W Moravia, Czechoslovakia, in Bohemian-Moravian Heights, 35 mi. NNW of Brno; excursion center; shoe-making industry.

Jimsah, Egypt: see GEMSA.

Jim Wells, county (□ 846; pop. 27,991), S Texas; ⊙ Alice. Bounded NE by Nueces R. and small Agua Dulce and San Diego creeks. Large oil, natural-gas production; agr. (partly irrigated): grain sorghums, cotton, corn, flax, peanuts, citrus, other fruit; dairying, livestock (cattle, sheep, goats, hogs); beekeeping. Sulphur mining. Formed 1911.

Jin, Tell, or **Tall Jin** (both: tĕl'jēn'), Fr. *Tell Djin,* town, Aleppo prov., NW Syria, on railroad and 26 mi. SSW of Aleppo; cotton, cereals.

Jinayfah, Egypt: see GINEIFA.

Jind (jēnd), former princely state (□ 1,299; pop. 361,812) of Punjab States, India; ⊙ was Sangrur; comprised several detached areas. Formed 1763 by Sikhs on breakup of Mogul empire. Since 1948, merged with Patiala and East Punjab States Union. Sometimes spelled Jhind.

Jind, town (pop. 14,909), S central Patiala and East Punjab States Union, India, 70 mi. S of Patiala; rail junction; local trade in millet, gram, wheat; cotton ginning. Sometimes spelled Jhind.

Jindrichov (yĭn'dŭrzhĭkhôf), Czech *Jindřichov,* Ger. *Hennersdorf* (hĕ'nŭrzdôrf), village (pop. 1,268), N Silesia, Czechoslovakia, on railroad and 14 mi. NNW of Krnov; oats.

Jindrichuv Hradec (yĭn'dŭrzhĭkhōof hrä'dĕts), Czech *Jindřichův Hradec,* Ger. *Neuhaus* (noi'hous), town (pop. 9,099), S Bohemia, Czechoslovakia, in foothills of Bohemian-Moravian Heights, 26 mi. NE of Budweis; rail junction; mfg. of linen and cotton goods, ceramics, mother-of-pearl buttons, glass. Pond fishing in vicinity. Noted for castle mus. (Gothic to Renaissance), 13th-cent. Hunger Tower, 15th-cent. Gothic church.

Jinguji (jēng-gōō'jē), town (pop. 5,790), Akita prefecture, N Honshu, Japan, 4 mi. NW of Omagari; agr., sake brewing.

Jinja (jĭn'jŭ, jēn'jä), town (pop. 8,410), ⊙ Eastern Prov. (□ 15,233, including 3,535 sq. mi. of lakes; pop. 1,514,428), SE Uganda, port on N shore of L. Victoria at efflux of the Victoria Nile (here forming Ripon Falls), 45 mi. ENE of Kampala, on railroad; alt. 3,753 ft. Agr. and commercial center; processing of soybeans and tobacco (cigarettes), cotton and sugar milling; fisheries. Army cantonment, R.C. mission (N). At Owen Falls (1.5 downstream) construction of dam (for Nile water storage) and major hydroelectric station was begun in 1949.

Jinotega (hēnōtä'gä), department (□ 5,870; 1950 pop. 47,103), N Nicaragua, on Honduras border; ⊙ Jinotega. Colón Mts. in NW, Cordillera Isabelia in S; drained by Coco and Bocay rivers. Agr. concentrated in SW part, site of main populated centers. Coffee (Yalí), sugar cane (La Concordia), wheat (San Rafael del Norte), potatoes, grain, fodder crops. Lumber in undeveloped NE area is floated down Coco and Bocay rivers. Flour milling at Jinotega. Main centers linked by road with Matagalpa.

Jinotega, city (1950 pop. 4,687), ⊙ Jinotega dept., W central Nicaragua, 70 mi. NNE of Managua; commercial center; coffee processing, flour milling, tanning, mfg. (hats, mats).

Jinotepe (hēnōtä'pä), city (1950 pop. 7,128), ⊙ Carazo dept., SW Nicaragua, on railroad, on Inter-American Highway and 22 mi. SSE of Managua; 11°55'N 86°12'W. Agr.-processing and commercial center in coffee area; rice, sugar cane, sesame, livestock. Limestone, saltworks, lumber trade. Became city in 1883, ⊙ dept. in 1891.

Jinsen, Korea: see CHEMULPO.

Jintotolo Channel (hēntōtō'lō), Philippines, bet. Masbate isl. (N) and Panay (S), connecting Visayan Sea with Sibuyan Sea; 20 mi. wide.

Jintsu River (jēn'tsōō), Jap. *Jintsu-gawa,* central Honshu, Japan, rises in mts. W of Mt. Hotaka, flows 78 mi. WNW, past Toyama, to Toyama Bay (inlet of Sea of Japan). Hydroelectric plants on upper course. Sometimes spelled Zintu.

Jintur (jĭntōōr'), town (pop. 7,384), Parbhani dist., NW Hyderabad state, India, 24 mi. NNW of Parbhani; cotton, millet, wheat. Cotton ginning near by.

Jipijapa (hēpēhä'pä), city (1950 pop. 7,605), Manabí prov., W Ecuador, in Pacific lowlands, on highway, and 80 mi. NW of Guayaquil. Noted for mfg. of Panama hats (jipijapa hats), it is also a trading center for rich agr. region (coffee, cacao, rice, tagua nuts); rice milling. Mfg. also of hammocks, baskets. Sulphur baths in vicinity.

Jiquié (zhĕkyĕ'), city (1950 pop. 21,322), E Bahia, Brazil, on left bank of the Rio de Contas, on Rio de Janeiro–Bahia highway, and 125 mi. SW of Salvador; W terminus of railroad from São Roque do Paraguaçu and Nazaré. Asbestos-mining center; also ships tobacco, cacao, sugar, coffee, livestock. Iron deposits near by. Formerly spelled Jequié.

Jiquilisco (hēkēlē'skō), city (pop. 6,414), Usulután dept., SE Salvador, on railroad and 9 mi. W of Usulután; commercial center at road junction for Puerto El Triunfo; grain, livestock raising.

Jiquilisco Bay, lagoonlike inlet of Pacific Ocean, in Usulután dept., SE Salvador, S of Usulután; 25 mi. long, 1–2 mi. wide. Fisheries; salt extraction. Puerto El Triunfo on N shore.

Jiquilpan (hēkēl'pän). **1** Town (pop. 1,113), Jalisco, W Mexico, 13 mi. SW of Sayula; grain, beans, sugar cane, fruit. **2** Officially Jiquilpan de Juárez, city (pop. 7,560), Michoacán, central Mexico, on central plateau, 60 mi. SE of Guadalajara; agr. center (cereals, sugar cane, tobacco, beans, fruit, livestock); flour milling.

Jiquipilas (hēkēpē'läs), town (pop. 1,870), Chiapas, S Mexico, on N slopes of Sierra Madre, 36 mi. E of Tuxtla; corn, beans, sugar cane, fruit.

Jiquipilco (hēkēpēl'kō), officially San Juan Jiquipilco, town (pop. 5,241), Mexico state, central Mexico, 32 mi. WNW of Mexico city; agr. center (cereals, fruit, stock).

Jiquitaia, Brazil: see PRADO.

Jiran, Ethiopia: see JIMMA.

Jirays, Egypt: see GIREIS.

Jirgalanta, Mongolia: see KOBDO, city.

Jirikov (yĭr'zhēkôf), Czech *Jiříkov,* Ger. *Georgswalde* (gāôrks'väldŭ), town (pop. 3,850), N Bohemia, Czechoslovakia, 32 mi. NE of Usti nad Labem, on Ger. border opposite Ebersbach and Neugersdorf; rail junction; piano mfg.

Jiring, Annam: see DJIRING.

Jirja, Egypt: see GIRGA.

Jirkov (yĭr'kôf), Ger. *Görkau* (gûr'kou), village (pop. 4,247), NW Bohemia, Czechoslovakia, on railroad and 8 mi. WSW of Most; coal mining; textiles. Medicinal bitter waters exported from Zajecice (zä'yĕchĭtsĕ), Czech *Zaječice,* just SE.

Jiroft, Iran: see SABZAWARAN.

Jish, Israel: see GISCHALA.

Jisr el Majami' or **Jisr al-Majami'** (both: jĭ'sûr ĕl-măjă'mē), frontier post in N Jordan, 17 mi. WNW of Irbid, with rail and road bridge over Jordan R., below mouth of Yarmuk R. Hydroelectric station is just N at Naharayim.

Jisr esh Sheikh Hussein, Jordan: see JISR SHEIKH HUSSEIN.

Jisr esh Shughur, Jisr el Shughur, or **Jisr al-Shughur** (all: jĭs'rĕsh-shōōgōōr'), Fr. *Djisr el Choghour,* town, Aleppo prov., NW Syria, near Turkish border, 55 mi. WSW of Aleppo; surrounded by marshes; cereals, tobacco.

Jisr Sheikh Hussein or **Jisr Shaykh Husayn** (both: jĭ'sûr shākh' hōōsān'), frontier post in N Jordan, 17 mi. WSW of Irbid, with road bridge over Jordan R. Also called Jisr esh Sheikh Hussein.

Jissa, Jissah, or **Bandar Jissah** (bändär' jĭs'sŭ), inlet of Gulf of Oman, in Oman, 5 mi. SE of Muscat; good natural harbor sheltered by rocky islet.

Jitotol (hētōtōl'), town (pop. 684), Chiapas, S Mexico, in N spur of Sierra Madre del Sur, 27 mi. NE of Tuxtla; alt. 5,082 ft.; cereals, tobacco, fruit.

Jitra (jĕ'trä), village (pop. 1,175), N Kedah, Malaya, 11 mi. NNE of Alor Star; rubber, rice plantations.

Jitsugetsu Tan, Formosa: see JIHYÜEH LAKE.

Jitsu-to, Ryukyu Isls.: see TOKARA-GUNTO.

Jitto, Ryukyu Isls.: see TOKARA-GUNTO.

Jiu River (zhē'ōō) or **Jiul** (zhē'ōōl), Ger. *Schyl* (shül), SW and S Rumania, in Transylvania and Oltenia, formed by 2 headstreams just S of Petrosani, cuts a deep gorge (Surduc or Vulcan pass) through the Transylvanian Alps, thence flows S to the Danube 28 mi. W of Corabia; 135 mi. long. Upper Jiu R. valley is the leading coal-mining region of Rumania.

Jiutepec (hūtāpĕk'), town (pop. 870), Morelos, central Mexico, 5 mi. SE of Cuernavaca; sugar cane, rice, fruit, stock.

Jivargi, India: see JEVARGI.

Jiwani, Cape (jēwä'nē, jēvä'nē), SW Baluchistan, W Pakistan, on E Gwatar Bay of Arabian Sea, near Iran line; 25°10'N 61°47'E. Seaplane base.

Jiza, El, or **Al-Jizah** (both: ĕl jē'zŭ), village (pop. c.500), N central Jordan, on Hejaz RR and 18 mi. S of Amman; road junction, airfield.

Jizah, Al-, Egypt: see GIZA.

Jizan, Saudi Arabia: see QIZAN.

Jizay, Egypt: see GIZAI.

Jizera (yĭ'zĕrä), Ger. *Sichhübel* (zĭkh'hü"bŭl), Pol. *Izera* (ēzĕ'rä), second-highest peak (c.3,675 ft.) of the Isergebirge, in N Bohemia, Czechoslovakia, 10 mi. NE of Liberec.

Jizera River, Ger. *Iser* (ē'zûr), N Bohemia, Czechoslovakia, rises in the Isergebirge, at S foot of Smrk mtn., on Pol. border; flows SSE, along border for c.8 mi., and generally SSW, past Turnov and Mlada Boleslav, to Elbe R. at Tousen; 100 mi. long.

Jizerske Hory, Czechoslovakia: see ISERGEBIRGE.

Jizodo (jēzō'dō'), town (pop. 5,168), Niigata prefecture, central Honshu, Japan, 6 mi. W of Sanjo; rice collection.

J. K. Nagar, India: see ASANSOL.

Joaçaba (zhōŭsä'bŭ), city (pop. 2,087), W Santa Catarina, Brazil, on Peixe R., on railroad and 70 mi. SSW of União da Vitória (Paraná); livestock center (cattle, horses); meat preserving, fruit and maté shipping. Originally called Limeira; then Cruzeiro do Sul, c.1928–38; and Cruzeiro, 1939–43.

Joachimsthal, Czechoslovakia: see JACHYMOV.

Joachimsthal (yō'äkhĭmstäl", yōä'khĭmstäl"), town (pop. 4,105), Brandenburg, E Germany, near Grimnitz and Werbellin lakes, 10 mi. NNW of Eberswalde; market gardening, dairying; forestry; mfg. of tiles, mirrors, glass. Noted boys' school (Joachimsthalsches Gymnasium) founded here in 1607, moved to Berlin in 1650, finally moved in 1912 to Templin. W of the town extends the Schorfheide, former royal hunting ground. Town founded 1604 by Elector Joachim Frederick.

Joal (zhwäl), village, W Senegal, Fr. West Africa, on the Atlantic, 55 mi. SE of Dakar; fishing and oyster-breeding center. R.C. mission.

Joannes, Brazil: see MARAJÓ.

Joannès (zhôänĕs'), village, W Que., 15 mi. E of Rouyn; gold mining.

Joanópolis (zhwŭnô'pōōlĕs), city (pop. 1,029), E São Paulo, Brazil, near Minas Gerais border, 50 mi. NNE of São Paulo; dairying.

João Alfredo (zhwä'ō älfrä'dōō), city (pop. 1,672), E Pernambuco, NE Brazil, on Capiberibe R. and 10 mi. WSW of Limoeiro; cotton.

João Belo, Vila de, Mozambique: see VILA DE JOÃO BELO.

João Coelho (kwä'lyōō), city (pop. 2,194), E Pará, Brazil, on Belém-Bragança RR and 25 mi. NE of Belém; cacao, Brazil nuts, cereals. Until 1944, Santa Isabel.

João Monlevade, Brazil: see MONLEVADE.

João Pessoa (pĕsō'ŭ). **1** City, Amazonas, Brazil: see EIRUNEPÉ. **2** City, Espírito Santo, Brazil: see MIMOSO DO SUL. **3** City (1950 pop. 90,853), ⊙ Paraíba, NE Brazil, on right bank of Paraíba R. 11 mi. above its mouth on the Atlantic, and 65 mi. N of Recife. Through its port Cabedelo (11 mi. NNE), it exports cotton, sugar, and agave fibers, and also rare minerals mined in Borborema Plateau; small ships reach city proper. Expanding industries include portland-cement plant, and factories producing cigars, footwear, and soft drinks. From a height the residential and administrative dist. overlooks the low-lying commercial part of the city. Connected by rail and road with port of Cabedelo, and with Natal (N), Recife (S), and inland city of Campo Grande. Airport. City has many fine palm-lined squares and parks, a state normal school, several colonial churches, and the outstanding 17th-cent. baroque convent of São Francisco. Tambaú (4 mi. NE on the Atlantic) is city's finest beach. Founded 1585, it was 1st called Philippéa, then Frederikstad under Dutch occupation (17th cent.). Known as Parahyba (sometimes spelled Parahiba) from 19th cent. until 1930, when it received its present name in memory of a patriot killed in the Vargas revolution. **4** City, Piauí, Brazil: see PÔRTO.

João Pinheiro (pēnyä'rōō), city (pop. 1,053), W Minas Gerais, Brazil, 55 mi. SE of Paracatu; cattle.

João Ribeiro (rēbä'rōō), city (pop. 1,966), S central Minas Gerais, Brazil, 18 mi. W of Conselheiro Lafaiete; manganese and iron (mined in area) and local limestone shipped to Volta Redonda (Rio de Janeiro) steel mill. Until 1940, called Entre Rios.

Joaquim Távora (zhwŭkē' tä'vōōrŭ), city (pop. 1,640), NE Paraná, Brazil, on railroad and 23 mi. S of Jacarèzinho; sawmilling; rice, corn, coffee, cotton.

Joaquin (wäkēn'), town (pop. 579), Shelby co., E Texas, near the Sabine, 45 mi. SSE of Marshall, in truck-farming, lumbering area.

Joaquín Suárez, Uruguay: see SUÁREZ.

Joaquín V. González (hwäkēn' vä' gōnsä'lĕs), town (1947 pop. 4,020), SE Salta prov., Argentina, on Pasaje or Juramento R., on railroad and 85 mi. ESE of Salta; agr. center (rice, corn, alfalfa, cotton, livestock); sawmills. Formerly Kilómetro 1082.

Joazeiro. 1 City, Bahia, Brazil: see JUÀZEIRO. **2** City, Ceará, Brazil: see JUÀZEIRO DO NORTE.

Job (jōb), village (1940 pop. 184), Randolph co., E W.Va., 15 mi. ESE of Elkins.

Jobabo (hōbä'bō), town (pop. 2,664), Oriente prov., E Cuba, near Jobabo R., 22 mi. WSW of Victoria de las Tunas; sugar-milling center.

Jobabo River, E Cuba, along Oriente-Camagüey prov. border; flows c.45 mi. S to the swamps at head of the Gulf of Guacanayabo.

Joban (jō'bä), major coal field of Japan, in Ibaraki and Fukushima prefectures, central Honshu, on the Pacific, c.120 mi. NNE of Tokyo; 50 mi. N-S, 2–12 mi. E-W. Provides fuel for industrial Tokyo-Yokohama area.

Jobares, river, India: see JUMNA RIVER.

Jobat (jō'bŭt), former princely state (□ 131; pop. 20,945) of Central India agency, lying in W Vindhya Range. Since 1948, merged with Madhya Bharat.

Jobos (hō'bōs), village (pop. 653), S Puerto Rico, on railroad and 3 mi. SW of Guayama; sugar growing. Port of entry. Puerto Jobos, a sugar-loading port, is 1½ mi. W.

Jobourg, Nez de (nā dŭ zhôbōōr'), headland of Cotentin Peninsula, Manche dept., NW France, on Race of Alderney of English Channel, 11 mi. ESE of Alderney; 49°41'N 1°57'W.

Jobson, Argentina: see VERA.

Jocassee (jōkă'sē), summer resort, Oconee co., NW S.C., in Blue Ridge, 33 mi. WNW of Greenville.

Jochmus Lake, Australia: see GALILEE, LAKE.

Jockgrimm (yôk'grĭm"), village (pop. 2,401), Rhenish Palatinate, W Germany, near the Rhine, 8 mi. NW of Karlsruhe; grain, tobacco.

Jockis, Finland: see JOKIOINEN.

Jocoaitique (hōkwītē'kä), town (pop. 652), Morazán dept., NE Salvador, near Honduras border, 17 mi. N of San Francisco; henequen center; cordage mfg.

Jocoro (hōkō'rō), city (pop. 1,563), Morazán dept., E Salvador, on branch of Inter-American Highway and 13 mi. NE of San Miguel, in gold- and silver-mining dist.; grain, sugar cane, indigo.

Jocotán (hōkōtän'), town (1950 pop. 1,088), Chiquimula dept., E Guatemala, on branch of Chiquimula R. and 11 mi. E of Chiquimula; corn, beans, livestock.

Jocotenango (hōkōtänäng'gō), town (1950 pop. 1,129), Sacatepéquez dept., S central Guatemala, 2 mi. NW of Antigua; alt. 5,052 ft.; coffee. Founded 1542.

Jocotepec (hōkōtāpěk'), town (pop. 4,950), Jalisco, W Mexico, near W shore of L. Chapala, 27 mi. SSW of Guadalajara; beans, grain, fruit, livestock.

Jocotitlán (hōkōtētlän'), town (pop. 2,720), Mexico state, central Mexico, 40 mi. NW of Mexico city; cereals, stock.

Jódar (hō'dhär), city (pop. 11,808), Jaén prov., S Spain, 12 mi. S of Úbeda; olive-oil and esparto processing; mfg. of felt hats, baskets, soap; brandy distilling, flour milling. Agr. trade (cereals, wine, esparto, livestock). Marble and gypsum quarries.

Jo Daviess (dā'vĭs), county (□ 614; pop. 21,459), extreme NW Ill., bounded N by Wis. line and W by the Mississippi (here forming Iowa line); ⊙ Galena. Drained by Apple, Plum, and Galena rivers. Agr. (livestock, poultry, corn, oats, barley, alfalfa). Lead and zinc mines; timber. Mfg.: dairy products, beverages, gloves and mittens, metal products, stoves, mining machinery, lubricating oil, thermometers, flour, feed, wool cloth. Includes hilly area near Wis. line; Charles Mound (1,241 ft.), highest point in Ill., is here. Contains Apple River Canyon State Park and portion of Upper Mississippi River Natl. Wildlife Refuge. Formed 1827.

Jodhpur (jŏd'pŭr, jōd'pŏŏr) or **Marwar** (mär'vär), former princely state (□ 36,120; pop. 2,555,904) in Rajputana States, India; ⊙ was Jodhpur. Established in early-13th cent. by Rathor Rajputs. Invaded 16th-17th cent. by Moguls, late-18th cent. by Mahrattas. Sought Br. protection by alliance in 1818. In 1949, joined union of Rajasthan.

Jodhpur, city (pop. 126,842), ⊙ Jodhpur dist., W central Rajasthan, India, on Thar Desert, 180 mi. WSW of Jaipur. Rail junction (workshops); airport; trade center (cotton, wool, cattle, salt, hides, building stone); markets millet, oilseeds, wheat; mfg. of cotton textiles, metal tools (blades, shovels), polo sticks and balls, ice, pharmaceutical products; engineering workshops. Handicrafts include ivory goods, glass bangles, cutlery, dyed cloth, and lacquer work. Sandstone quarried 2 mi. NW. At suburban village of Mahamandir (NE) is ink factory; has richly decorated temple. City contains walled N area with hill fort, several handsome palaces, technical and arts colleges, and mus.; water supply tanks are W. Founded in 1459, it soon replaced Mandor (4 mi. N) as ⊙ Rajput state of Jodhpur. Jodhpur breeches named after city, where they 1st became popular.

Jodiya (jōd'yŭ), town (pop. 8,956), NW Saurashtra, India, near Gulf of Cutch, 21 mi. NE of Jamnagar; from wharf (2 mi. NW) exports cotton, wool, and oilseeds; handicraft cloth weaving, oilseed pressing, cotton ginning.

Jodoigne (zhôdwän'yû), Flemish *Geldenaken* (gĕl'dŭnäkŭn), town (pop. 4,136), Brabant prov., central Belgium, 6 mi. SSW of Tirlemont; agr. market.

Joeirana (zhwärä'nŭ), city, NW Espírito Santo, Brazil, claimed as **Ataléia** by Minas Gerais, near São Mateus R. (N branch), 35 mi. SE of Teófilo Otoni (Minas Gerais), in disputed Serra dos Aimorés region.

Joensuu (yô'ĕnsōō), city (pop. 7,584), Kuopio co., E Finland, on lake of the Saimaa system, 70 mi. ESE of Kuopio; rail junction; timber-shipping port, with large lumber and plywood mills. Trade center of N Karelia. Radio station. Has town hall (1913) by Saarinen, with N Karelia mus. Inc. 1848.

Joerg Plateau (yûrg), highland area back of Orville Escarpment, Antarctica; 76°S 67°W. Discovered 1948 by U.S. expedition led by Finn Ronne.

Joeuf (zhûf), town (pop. 9,271), Meurthe-et-Moselle dept., NE France, in Briey iron basin, on Orne R. and 4 mi. SE of Briey, adjoining Homécourt; forges. Iron mined near by.

Joffre, Mount (jŏ'fŭr) (11,316 ft.), SE B.C., on Alta. border, in Rocky Mts., 50 mi. SSE of Banff; 50°31'N 115°14'W.

Joffreville (zhôfrûvēl'), village, Majunga prov., N Madagascar, at foot of Mt. Ambre, 20 mi. S of Diégo-Suarez; climatic resort (alt. c.3,900 ft.); cinchona plantations. Formerly called Camp d'Ambre.

Jofra, Tripolitania: see GIOFRA.

Jog (jōg), settlement (pop. 6,183), Shimoga dist., NW Mysore, India, on Sharavati R., near rail terminus at Talguppa (6 mi. E), and 55 mi. WNW of Shimoga. Headworks of Mahatma Gandhi Hydroelectric Works near by; consist of storage dam on the Sharavati and hydroelectric plant, in operation since 1948. Project in no way impairs beauty of famous Gersoppa Falls (1.5 mi. W; downstream). The system, with substations at Shimoga and other towns of W Mysore, is intended to aid industrial expansion in this mountainous area and to merge its power with that of SIVASAMUDRAM and SHIMSHA FALLS, in SE part of state.

Jogbani (jōg'bŭnē), village, Purnea dist., NE Bihar, India, on Nepal border, 45 mi. NNW of Purnea; rail terminus.

Joge (jō'gā), town (pop. 4,253), Hiroshima prefecture, SW Honshu, Japan, 20 mi. NNW of Onomichi; livestock; sawmilling.

Jogeshvari (jōgāsh'vŭrē), village, Bombay Suburban dist., W Bombay, India, on Salsette Isl., 14 mi. N of Bombay city center; mfg. (matches, chemicals, rubber goods); rice growing. Has col. Has large Brahmanic cave temple of late-7th cent. Sometimes spelled Jogeshwari or Jogeswar.

Jogeva or **Yygeva,** Est. *Jõgeva* (all: yû'gĕvä), Ger. *Laisholm,* city (pop. 1,144), E Estonia, on railroad and 28 mi. NNW of Tartu; agr. market (flax); clay quarry, sawmill.

Joggins (jŏ'gĭnz), town (pop. 1,109), N N.S., on Chignecto Bay, 16 mi. SW of Amherst; coal mining.

Jogindarnagar (jō'gĭndŭrnŭgŭr''), town (pop. 2,749), N central Himachal Pradesh, India, 20 mi. NNW of Mandi, in S Punjab Himalayas; rail terminus. Hydroelectric plant (in operation since 1932) supplied by dam (3 mi. NNE) across Uhl R.; powers industries in large cities of Indian Punjab.

Jogipet (jō'gĭpāt), town (pop. 5,233), Medak dist., central Hyderabad state, India, near Manjra R., 40 mi. NNW of Hyderabad; rice, sugar cane.

Jogjakarta or **Djokjakarta** (both: jōgyŭkär'tŭ, jōgjŭ–, native jōk''yäkär'tä), town (pop. 136,646), S Java, Indonesia, 170 mi. WSW of Surabaya, at foot of Mt. Merapi; 7°48'S 110°22'E; cultural and trade center for agr. area (rice, rubber, copra, sugar). In center of town is vast walled palace (1760) of sultan of Jogjakarta. Town is known for drama and dance festivals. Has highly developed handicraft industry (batik, copper and silver craft). There are railroad workshops, textile mills, tanneries. Town was heavily damaged by 1867 eruption of Mt. Merapi. After Second World War, Jogjakarta was ⊙ original Republic of INDONESIA; occupied (Dec., 1948–July, 1949) by Du. troops. Also spelled Jokyakarta and Jokjakarta.

Johana (jō'hänä), town (pop. 5,047), Toyama prefecture, central Honshu, Japan, 15 mi. ESE of Kanazawa; rail terminus; lacquer ware, silk textiles. Radioactive mineral springs.

Johanna Island, Comoro Isls.: see ANJOUAN ISLAND.

Johannedal (yōōhä'nŭdäl''), village (pop. 888), Vasternorrland co., E Sweden, on small inlet of Gulf of Bothnia, 5 mi. NE of Sundsvall, opposite Alno isl.; sawmilling.

Johannes, RSFSR: see SOVETSKI, Leningrad oblast.

Johannesburg (jōhă'nĭsbûrg, Afrikaans yōhä'nŭsbûrkh''), city (pop. 606,016; including suburbs 765,457), S Transvaal, U. of So. Afr., on WITWATERSRAND, 800 mi. NE of Cape Town, 300 mi. NW of Durban, 30 mi. SSW of Pretoria; 26°11'S 28°3'E; alt. 5,740 ft. Largest city and commercial center of the U. of So. Afr. Rail, commercial, and industrial center of the Witwatersrand gold fields, city is surrounded by important gold mines. Site of Univ. of the Witwatersrand (1922), originally founded as So. Afr. School of Mines in Kimberley, transferred here 1904; Witwatersrand Technical Col.; Union Observatory (26°10'55''S 28°4'30''E; alt. 5,925 ft.), established 1903, with photographic telescope of Leiden Univ., Netherlands; and Yale-Columbia Southern Station observatory (26°11'14''S 28°1'45''E; alt. 5,712 ft.), established 1925. Notable features include stock exchange, So. Afr. Railways hq., municipal art gallery, Geological Mus. (1895), Africana Mus. (1935), So. Afr. Inst. of Medical Research, Public Library (1935), Anglican cathedral (1928), R.C. pro-cathedral, and many modern office and residential bldgs. Main shopping center is Eloff St. and other streets in immediate vicinity of new railroad station. Among industries are metal- and woodworking, textile milling, mfg. of machinery, chemicals, drugs, furniture, leather, clothing, food products. Mean temp. ranges from 49.5°F (July) to 68.5°F (Jan.); average annual rainfall 32.6 in. Airports serving city are Palmietfontein (international), 13 mi. SE; Rand Airport (domestic), 8 mi. ESE; Vaaldam (seaplanes), 50 mi. SSE; new Jan Smuts international airport at Kempton Park, 13 mi. ESE. Chief suburbs within municipality (□ 84) are Mayfair, Fordsburg (W), Melville (NW), Rosebank (N), Houghton, Norwood (NE), Jeppe, Malvern (E), City Deep (SE), Rosettenville, Ophirton (S), Orlando (SW). Founded 1886 as gold-mining settlement, city grew rapidly with development of mining industry. In recent times city has been scene of frequent native labor disturbances.

Johannesburg (jōhă'nĭsbûrg), mining camp (pop. c.100), Kern co., S central Calif., in Rand Mts. (silver, tungsten, gold mines), near Randsburg.

Johanngeorgenstadt (yōhän'gäôr'gŭn-shtät), town (pop. 6,559), Saxony, E central Germany, in the Erzgebirge, 11 mi. S of Aue; frontier station on Czechoslovak border, opposite Potucky, in uranium-mining region, with concentrating plant; mfg. of kid gloves and musical instruments; metal- and woodworking, paper milling. Winter-sports center. Founded 1654 as silver-mining settlement by Bohemian Protestants.

Johannisbad, Czechoslovakia: see JANSKE LAZNE.

Johannisberg (yōhä'nĭsbĕrk), village (pop. 2,122), in former Prussian prov. of Hesse-Nassau, W Germany, after 1945 in Hesse, in the Rheingau, near the Rhine, 12 mi. WSW of Wiesbaden. Noted vineyards of near-by Johannisberg castle yield one of finest Ger. wines. The castle, built 1757–59, was given (1816) as imperial fief to Metternich.

Johannisburg, Poland: see PISZ.

Johannisthal (yōhä'nĭstäl), section of Treptow dist., SE Berlin, Germany, 7 mi. SE of city center; 52°23'N 13°32'E. Airport. Mfg. of electrical equipment; moving-picture studios. After 1945 in Soviet sector.

Johen (jō'hān), town (pop. 4,418), Ehime prefecture, SW Shikoku, Japan, 18 mi. S of Uwajima; rice. Sometimes spelled Zyohen.

Johi (jō'hē), village, Dadu dist., W Sind, W Pakistan, 10 mi. W of Dadu; market center (wheat, millet, rice, wool, mangoes); handicraft carpet weaving.

Jöhlingen (yû'lĭng-ŭn), village (pop. 3,221), N Baden, Germany, after 1945 in Württemberg-Baden, 8 mi. ENE of Karlsruhe; fruit.

John Day, resort city (pop. 1,597), Grant co., NE central Oregon, on John Day R., just N of Canyon City, and near Strawberry Mts.; dairying. Hq. of near-by Malheur Natl. Forest. Chromite deposits near.

John Day River, N Oregon, rises in several branches in Strawberry Mts., NE Oregon, flows 281 mi. W and N to Columbia R. 28 mi. ENE of The Dalles; not navigable. Used for irrigation.

John Martin Dam, SE Colo., on Arkansas R. and 15 mi. E of Las Animas. Concrete and earthfill dam completed 1948; length is 2.6 mi. (including earth abutments, dikes, and concrete spillway); 153 ft. high; used for flood control and irrigation. Forms John Martin Reservoir (□ 27.5; 14 mi. long, 2 mi. wide; known, until 1940, as Caddoa Reservoir).

John Muir Trail (mūr), Calif., mountain footpath c.200 mi. long, follows crest of the Sierra Nevada from Yosemite Natl. Park (N) to Mt. Whitney in Sequoia Natl. Park (S).

John o'Groat's House (grōts), locality, NE Caithness, Scotland, on the Pentland Firth, 14 mi. N of Wick, near Duncansbay Head. It is often erroneously named as northernmost point of isl. of Britain; the phrase "from Land's End to John o'Groat's" is commonly used to denote greatest land distance in Britain (876 mi.). The house, of which there are no remains, was, according to legend, built in octagonal shape by a Dutchman, John de Groot or John o'Groat, who settled in Scotland in 16th cent.

Johns, Ala.: see NORTH JOHNS.

Johnsburg, village (pop. c.300), Warren co., E N.Y., in the Adirondacks, 26 mi. NW of Glen Falls; resort; lumbering.

Johnshaven (jŏnz'hāvŭn), fishing port in Benholm parish, SE Kincardine, Scotland, on North Sea, 6 mi. ESE of Laurencekirk.

Johns Island, Charleston co., S S.C., one of Sea Isls., c.5 mi. WSW of Charleston; c.11 mi. long, 5–10 mi. wide. Separated from mainland (NE) and James Isl. (E) by Stono R. (bridged), by narrow channels from Wadmalaw Isl. (W) and Kiawah Isl. (S). Truck farming area.

Johnson. 1 County (□ 676; pop. 16,138), NW Ark.; ⊙ Clarksville. Bounded S by Arkansas R.; drained by small Mulberry R. and Piney Creek. Agr. area livestock, poultry, cotton, fruit. Natural-gas wells, coal mines; timber. Part of Ozark Natl. Forest is in N. Formed 1833. **2** County (□ 313; pop. 9,893), E central Ga.; ⊙ Wrightsville. Bounded W by Oconee R.; drained by Ohoopee R. Coastal plain agr. area (cotton, corn, potatoes truck, fruit). Formed 1858. **3** County (□ 345; pop. 8,729), S Ill., in Ill. Ozarks; ⊙ Vienna. Agr. area (fruit, corn, wheat; dairy products; livestock). Lumbering; wood products. Drained by Cache R.; includes part of Shawnee Natl. Forest. Formed 1812. **4** County (□ 315; pop. 26,183), central Ind.; ⊙ Franklin. Drained by West Fork of White R. and tributaries of its East Fork. Agr. (wheat, corn, livestock, vegetables; dairy products); mfg. at Franklin, Greenwood, Edinburg. Formed 1815. **5** County (□ 620; pop. 45,756), E Iowa; ⊙ Iowa City. Prairie agr. area (corn, hogs, cattle, poultry) drained by Iowa R.; limestone quarries. Includes Lake Macbride State Park. Formed 1839. **6** County (□ 476; pop. 62,783), E Kansas; ⊙ Olathe. Rolling plain area with low hills; bounded N by Kansas R., E by Mo. Stock raising, corn growing, dairying. Scattered oil and gas fields. Residential and suburban area in N, near Kansas City, Kansas. Formed 1855. **7** County (□ 264; pop. 23,846), E Ky.; ⊙ Paintsville. Drained by Levisa Fork; Dewey Dam in S. Mtn. agr. area in foothills of the Cumberlands; livestock, poultry, corn, soybeans, Irish potatoes, apples, lespedeza, tobacco. Coal mines, oil wells. Formed 1843. **8** County (□ 826, pop. 20,716), W central Mo; ⊙ Warrensburg. Drained by Blackwater R. Agr. (corn, wheat, oats, hay), livestock; coal mines, stone quarries, clay pits. Formed 1834. **9** County (□ 377; pop. 7,251), SE Nebr.; ⊙ Tecumseh. Agr. area drained by branches of Nemaha R. Feed, livestock, fruit, grain, dairy and poultry produce.

Formed 1856. **10** County (□ 299; pop. 12,278), extreme NE Tenn.; ⊙ Mountain City. Bounded N by Va., E and SE by N.C.; Stone Mts. lie along N.C. line; traversed by Iron Mts.; drained by Watauga R. Includes parts of Watauga Reservoir and Cherokee Natl. Forest. Lumbering, agr. (tobacco, truck, fruit), livestock. Formed 1836. **11** County (□ 740; pop. 31,390), N central Texas; ⊙ Cleburne, shipping, processing center. Bounded SW by Brazos R.; drained by tributaries of the Brazos (in W) and the Trinity (in E). Rich agr. area: cotton, corn, oats, other grains, peanuts, pecans, fruit, truck; extensive dairying; poultry, cattle, hogs, sheep; wool marketed. Clay, limestone, gravel. Mfg., processing at Cleburne. Includes state park (recreation). Formed 1854. **12** County (□ 4,175; pop. 4,707), N central Wyo.; ⊙ Buffalo. Agr. and coal-mining region; watered by Powder R. Grain, livestock, sugar beets. Part of Bighorn Natl. Forest and Bighorn Mts. in NW. Formed 1875.

Johnson. 1 City (pop. 994), ⊙ Stanton co., SW Kansas, 50 mi. SW of Garden City, in wheat area. **2** Village (pop. 54), Big Stone co., W Minn., 20 mi. NNE of Ortonville; grain. **3** Village (pop. 262), Nemaha co., SE Nebr., 8 mi. W of Auburn, in agr. region. **4** Town (pop. 1,527), including Johnson village (pop. 900), Lamoille co., N central Vt., on Lamoille R. and 10 mi. NE of Mt. Mansfield; lumber, talc; textiles, clothing, machinery. State normal school here. Settled 1784.

Johnsonburg. 1 Village (pop. c.150), Warren co., NW N.J., 9 mi. SW of Newton, in hilly region; summer engineering camp of Stevens Institute here. **2** Borough (pop. 4,567), Elk co., N central Pa., 32 mi. S of Bradford and on Clarion R.; paper, wood pulp, metal products, chemicals; agr. Settled 1810, laid out 1888.

Johnson City. 1 Industrial village (pop. 19,249), Broome co., S N.Y., on the Susquehanna, bet. Endicott (5 mi. W) and Binghamton (just E), with which 2 towns it comprises the Triple Cities; large shoe industry (Endicott-Johnson Shoe Company). Also produces machinery, shoe-mfg. supplies and equipment, cameras, felt, confectionery. Inc. 1892. **2** City (pop. 27,864), Washington co., NE Tenn., 90 mi. ENE of Knoxville, in Great Appalachian Valley. Rail junction; trade and shipping point for surrounding mountainous area of timber, farms, limestone quarries; an important burley tobacco market; mfg. of wood products (especially hardwood flooring), bricks, textiles, pig iron; foundry and limestone products, dairy products; flour and sawmilling. Seat of East Tenn. State Col. and U.S. soldiers' home. Near by are Milligan Col. and Haynes-Tipton house (c.1770). Settled before 1800; inc. 1869. **3** Village (pop. 648), ⊙ Blanco co., S central Texas, c.40 mi. W of Austin and on Pedernales R.; trade point in livestock, agr. area; cotton gin.

Johnson Creek, village (pop. 575), Jefferson co., S Wis., on small Johnson Creek and 5 mi. N of Jefferson, in dairying region; ships dairy products, eggs.

Johnson Island, Chile: see CHONOS ARCHIPELAGO.

Johnsonville, town, Montserrado co., W Liberia, 10 mi. ENE of Monrovia, on road; palm oil and kernels, rubber, coffee.

Johnsonville. 1 Village (pop. 105), Wayne co., SE Ill., 24 mi. NE of Mount Vernon, in agr. area; oil wells. **2** Town (pop. 616), Florence co., E S.C., 30 mi. SSE of Florence, near Lynches R.; lumber.

Johnston. 1 County (□ 795; pop. 65,906), central N.C.; ⊙ Smithfield. On coastal plain; drained by Neuse R. and its tributary. Agr. (especially tobacco; cotton, corn); timber (pine, gum). Cotton and lumber milling, tobacco processing. Formed 1746. **2** County (□ 657; pop. 10,608), S Okla.; ⊙ Tishomingo. Bounded by L. Texoma and Washita R.; drained by Blue R. Stock raising, agr. (cotton, corn, alfalfa). Sand and gravel pits; timber. Formed 1907.

Johnston. 1 or **Johnston Station,** village (1940 pop. 527), Polk co., central Iowa, near Des Moines R., 7 mi. NW of Des Moines. U.S. Camp Dodge near by was active in Second World War. **2** Town (pop. 12,725), Providence co., N central R.I., just W of Providence; agr., mfg. (textiles, paper boxes, yarns, hosiery, toys). Thornton village (1940 pop. 2,018) is administrative center. Set off from Providence and inc. 1759. **3** Town (pop. 1,426), Edgefield co., W S.C., 10 mi. ENE of Edgefield; textile milling, canning, sawmilling, cotton ginning.

Johnston City (jŏn'sŭn), city (pop. 4,479), Williamson co., S Ill., 5 mi. S of West Frankfort, in bituminous-coal-mining and agr. area (corn, wheat, hay; dairy products). Inc. 1905.

Johnstone (jŏnz'tŭn), burgh (1931 pop. 12,841; 1951 census 15,661), central Renfrew, Scotland, on Black Cart Water and 10 mi. W of Glasgow; steel, cotton, and flax milling, iron and brass founding, mfg. of machinery, machine tools, and thread.

Johnstone Lake (□ 123), S Sask., 22 mi. SW of Moose Jaw; 20 mi. long, 12 mi. wide.

Johnstone Strait, SW B.C., joins Queen Charlotte Strait with Strait of Georgia, via Discovery Passage, separating Vancouver Isl. from mainland; 70 mi. long, 2–3 mi. wide. Mainland shore deeply indented. Alert Bay is at W entrance.

Johnston Island (pop. 69), in N Pacific, c.715 mi. SW of Honolulu, T.H.; 16°45'N 169°30'W; c.3,000 ft. long, 600 ft. wide. Discovered 1807 by British, claimed 1858 by U.S. A bird reservation for years, it was commissioned a naval air station 1941.

Johnstons Station or **Johnston Station,** village (1940 pop. 121), on Lincoln-Pike co. line, SW Miss., on the Bogue Chitto and 7 mi. N of McComb.

Johnston Station, Iowa: see JOHNSTON.

Johnstown. 1 Gaelic *Baile Sheagháin*, agr. village (district pop. 176), E Co. Kildare, Ireland, on the Grand Canal and 2 mi. NE of Naas; cattle, horses; potatoes. **2** Gaelic *Cúirt an Phúca*, town (pop. 296), NW Co. Kilkenny, Ireland, 13 mi. WNW of Kilkenny; agr. market (cattle; barley, potatoes).

Johnstown. 1 Town (pop. 897), Weld co., N Colo., near South Platte R., 40 mi. N of Denver, in grain and sugar-beet region; alt. 4,820 ft. Beet sugar, evaporated milk. **2** Town (pop. 24), Bates co., W Mo., 14 mi. E of Butler. **3** Village (pop. 109), Brown co., N Nebr., 10 mi. W of Ainsworth. **4** Industrial city (pop. 10,923), ⊙ Fulton co., E central N.Y., near Mohawk R., 10 mi. WNW of Amsterdam; mfg. center for knitted and leather gloves and mittens, leather apparel and footwear; also makes glove lasts, cotton fleece, textiles, glue, gelatin, wood and paper products, machinery, sporting goods. Johnson Hall (1762) and other 18th-cent. bldgs. remain. Last battle of the Revolution in N.Y. fought near by, Oct. 25, 1781. Elizabeth Cady Stanton was b. here. Founded 1762; inc. as city in 1895. **5** Village (pop. 1,220), Licking co., central Ohio, 16 mi. WNW of Newark, and on Raccoon Creek, in diversified-farming area; rubber products, flour, feed. **6** Industrial city (pop. 63,232), Cambria co., SW central Pa., 55 mi. ESE of Pittsburgh at confluence of Conemaugh R. and Stony Creek, in a beautiful mtn. region. Iron and steel, bituminous coal, clay products, machinery, machine tools, clothing, packed meat, chemicals, beverages, furniture. First domestic steel rails produced here 1867. Flooded 1889 with great loss of life. Settled 1794, laid out 1800.

Johoji (jō'-hō'jē), town (pop. 8,408), Iwate prefecture, N Honshu, Japan, 33 mi. N of Morioka; rice, soybeans, potatoes; makes lacquer ware. Sometimes spelled Zyohozi.

Johol (jôhôl'), town (pop. 664), S Negri Sembilan, Malaya, 23 mi. ESE of Seremban; rice, rubber. Chief town of Johol, one of the original Negri Sembilan states.

Johore (jŭhôr', jōhōr'), southernmost state (□ 7,321; pop. 738,251; with transients, 741,791) of Malaya, bet. South China Sea and Strait of Malacca; ⊙ Johore Bharu. Bounded NW by Malacca and Negri Sembilan and N by Pahang, it is separated from Singapore isl. (S) by narrow Johore Strait. Generally flat and jungle-covered, it rises in isolated peaks to over 3,000 ft. (highest is Mt. Ophir, 4,187 ft.) and is drained by Muar, Endau, and Johore rivers. Agr.: rubber, coconuts, oil palm, pineapples (canning at Skudai, Kota Tinggi). Iron mining at Endau and Yong Peng; bauxite deposits. Bisected by main Malayan rail line, it also has a sparse road net serving the isolated cultivated areas. Chief centers, besides Johore Bharu, are Bandar Maharani (or Muar), Bandar Penggaram (or Batu Pahat), and Kluang. Pop. is 48% Chinese, 42% Malay. Johore fell (15th cent.) under rule of sultans of Malacca. Following fall of Malacca to Portuguese (1511), the fugitive sultan of Malacca founded the kingdom of Johore-Riouw which declined (18th cent.) when seat of power moved from Johore (⊙ Kota Tinggi) to Riouw. The Johore governors of the sultan became increasingly independent and were recognized as such by the British in the cession of Singapore (1819, 1824). Formal Br. treaty relations with Johore were established (1885) and a Br. protectorate accepted 1914. Ruled by a sultan, Johore was one of the unfederated Malay States until it joined the Federation of Malaya after the Second World War.

Johore Bharu or **Johore Bahru** (bä'rōō), town (pop. 38,826), ⊙ Johore, Malaya, 14 mi. NNW of Singapore, on Johore Strait opposite Singapore isl., at road and rail causeway; 1°27'N 104°46'E. Trade center for rubber, pineapples, palm oil; canning, oil milling. Has sultan's palace, large mosque, tree-lined avenues and gardens. Pop. is 40% Chinese, 36% Malay, 13% Indian.

Johore River, Johore, S Malaya, formed 15 mi. NW of Kota Tinggi, flows 40 mi. SE, past Kota Tinggi, to Singapore Strait forming wide estuary in low mangrove coast.

Johore Strait or **Tebrau Strait,** Malay *Selat Tebrau* (sŭlät' tĕbrou'), arm of Singapore Strait bet. Singapore isl. and Johore at S tip of Malay Peninsula; 30 mi. long, ¾–3 mi. wide; crossed in center by rail and road causeway (3,442 ft. long; completed 1924) linking Johore Bharu and Woodlands on Singapore isl. E of causeway is deep-water access channel to Br. base on N side of Singapore isl.

Jöhstadt (yû'shtät), town (pop. 2,497), Saxony, E central Germany, in the Erzgebirge, 6 mi. SE of Annaberg; frontier station on Czechoslovak border, opposite Vejprty; cotton and rayon milling and knitting. Founded 1517 as silver-mining settlement.

Johvi or **Yykhvi,** Est. *Jõhvi* (all: yûkh'vē), Ger. *Jewe*, city (pop. 2,043), NE Estonia, on railroad and 27 mi. W of Narva, in oil-shale mining area; brewery.

Joice, town (pop. 244), Worth co., N Iowa, 19 mi. NW of Mason City; livestock-shipping point.

Joigny (zhwänyē'), town (pop. 5,511), Yonne dept., N central France, on the Yonne and 15 mi. NNW of Auxerre; winegrowing center; woodworking, fruit and snail preserving, cider distilling. Has two 16th-cent. churches.

Joiner, town (pop. 596), Mississippi co., NE Ark., 27 mi. NNW of Memphis (Tenn.), near the Mississippi.

Joinerville, village (1940 pop. 633), Rusk co., E Texas, 5 mi. W of Henderson, in East Texas oil field.

Joinvile (zhoinvē'lĭ), city (1950 pop. 21,102), NE Santa Catarina, Brazil, on an Atlantic inlet, opposite São Francisco isl., on railroad and 90 mi. NNW of Florianópolis. State's chief industrial center, with textile mills, breweries, distilleries; maté processing, furniture mfg., shipbuilding. Ships rice, sugar, tapioca, corn, tobacco, arrowroot, and dairy products via seaport of São Francisco do Sul (12 mi. NE). Airfield. Iron deposits in area. Founded c.1850 by German immigrants as center of agr. colony (sometimes called Doña Francisca). Formerly spelled Joinville.

Joinville, Algeria: see BLIDA.

Joinville, Brazil: see JOINVILE.

Joinville (zhwēvēl'), town (pop. 3,162), Haute-Marne dept., NE France, on Marne R. and Marne-Saône Canal, 16 mi. SE of Saint-Dizier; metal foundries, paper and flour mills, shoe factory. Has ruined castle of seneschals of Champagne (most famous was Jean de Joinville). Here treaty allying Spain with the League was signed in 1584.

Joinville Island (join'vĭl, zhwēvēl'), Antarctica, off NE tip of Palmer Peninsula; 63°15'S 55°50'W; 41 naut. mi. long, 20 naut. mi. wide. Discovered 1838 by Dumont d'Urville, Fr. navigator.

Joinville-le-Pont (zhwēvēl'-lù-pō'), residential town (pop. 13,319), Seine dept., N central France, a SE suburb of Paris, 6 mi. from Notre Dame Cathedral, at neck of Marne R. meander and at SE edge of Bois de Vincennes, with large movie studios; woodworking, mfg. (perfumes, morocco leather, false pearls, seltzer water).

Jojima (jō'jĭmä), town (pop. 7,089), Fukuoka prefecture, NW Kyushu, Japan, 7 mi. E of Saga; rice-producing center. Site of feudal castle.

Jojutla (hōhōō'tlä), city (pop. 4,451), Morelos, central Mexico, on S slope of central plateau, on railroad and 22 mi. S of Cuernavaca; alt. 2,936 ft. Agr. center (rice, sugar cane, melons, tropical fruit, livestock). L. Tequesquitengo, popular fishing and hunting resort, is 4 mi. N.

Jokela (yō'kĕlä), village in Hyvinkää rural commune (pop. 5,006), Uusimaa co., S Finland, 25 mi. N of Helsinki; match mfg.

Jokeleggja, Norway: see HEMSEDALSFJELL.

Jokioinen (yō'kē-oi"nĕn), Swedish *Jockis* or *Jokkis* (both: yô'kĭs), village (commune pop. 5,956), Häme co., SW Finland, 35 mi. WSW of Hameenlinna; metalworking. Site of experimental farm and plant nursery.

Jokjakarta, Indonesia: see JOGJAKARTA.

Jokkis, Finland: see JOKIOINEN.

Jokkmokk (yôk'môk"), village (pop. 1,437), Norrbotten co., N Sweden, within Arctic Circle, on headstream of Lule R. and 70 mi. NW of Boden; road and trade center.

Jokneam (jŏk'nēăm), **Yokne'am,** or **Yokneam** (all: yōknā-äm'), settlement (pop. 700), NW Israel, in Plain of Jezreel, near SE foot of Mt. Carmel, 13 mi. SSE of Haifa; mixed farming. Modern village founded 1935. Of biblical origin. In immediate vicinity is site of anc. locality of *Caymont*, 12th–13th-cent. ⊙ Crusaders' Seigneurie of Caymont. Remains of castle.

Jokuleggi, Norway: see HEMSEDALSFJELL.

Jokulsa (yû'külsou"), Icelandic *Jökulsá*. **1** or **Jokulsa a Bru** (ou brōō'), Icelandic *Jökulsá á Brú*, river, E Iceland, rises at E edge of Vatnajokull, flows 100 mi. NE to Atlantic 30 mi. NNW of Seydisfjordur. **2** or **Jokulsa a Fjollum** (ou fyût'-lŭm), Icelandic *Jökulsá á Fjöllum*, river, E Iceland, rises at N edge of Vatnajokull glacier region, flows 130 mi. N to Axar Fjord of Greenland Sea. Its several waterfalls include the Dettifoss, 30 mi. above mouth.

Jokyakarta, Indonesia: see JOGJAKARTA.

Jolalpan (hōläl'pän), town (pop. 1,598), Puebla, central Mexico, 30 mi. SW of Matamoros; corn, rice, fruit, sugar, stock.

Jolburi, Thailand: see CHONBURI.

Jolfa, Iran: see JULFA.

Joliba River, West Africa: see NIGER RIVER.

Joliet. 1 (jō'lēĕt") City (pop. 51,601), ⊙ Will co., NE Ill., on Des Plaines R. section of Illinois Waterway, and c.30 mi. SW of Chicago; important rail (with repair shops) and industrial center, near bituminous-coal mines and limestone quarries. Mfg.: wallpaper, chemicals, steel products, dairy products, furnaces, clothing, petroleum products, farm machinery; household, bakery, and packaging equipment; roofing materials, jewelry, soap, barrels, beverages, cartons. Sand and gravel pits. The state penitentiary, a jr. col., the Col. of St. Francis, Pilcher Park Arboretum, and a large excavated Indian mound are here. Settled 1831, laid out 1834, inc. 1837; known as Juliet for many years. **2** (jōlēĕt') Town (pop. 410), Carbon co., S Mont., on Red Lodge Creek and 30 mi. SW of Billings; shipping point in irrigated region.

Joliette (zhôlyĕt'), county (□ 2,506; pop. 31,713), S Que., on the St. Lawrence; ⊙ Joliette.

Joliette, city (pop. 12,749), ⊙ Joliette co., S Que., on L'Assomption R. and 35 mi. NNE of Montreal; steel and paper milling, mica mining, limestone quarrying, textile milling, knitting, dyeing, tobacco processing; mfg. of hosiery, biscuits; tree nurseries. Seat of R.C. bishop; site of seminary.

Jolley, town (pop. 195), Calhoun co., central Iowa, 27 mi. W of Fort Dodge, in agr. area.

Jolo, village (1940 pop. 1,303), McDowell co., S W.Va., near Dry Fork, 14 mi. SW of Welch, in bituminous-coal region.

Jolo Island (hō'lō, hōlō') or **Sulu Island** (sōō'lōō), chief island (□ 345; 1948 pop. c.116,000) of SULU ARCHIPELAGO, Sulu prov., Philippines, bet. Sulu Sea and Celebes Sea, 80 mi. SW of Zamboanga; 37 mi. long (E-W), 12 mi. max. width, narrowing to 3-mi. isthmus in E center; 6°N 121°E. Mountainous (rising to 2,664 ft.), but fertile (rice, coconuts, cassava, fruit); heavily wooded. Many Moros live here. With offshore isls. (e.g., Pata, Cabucan, Capual) and islets, it forms the Jolo Group. On NW coast of Jolo is town of Jolo (1939 pop. 6,272; 1948 municipality pop. 18,282), ⊙ Sulu prov., port of entry, and long the trading center of the archipelago; ships large quantities of mother-of-pearl, and also pearls, hemp, fruit. A walled city, it was long capital of Sulu chieftains (Mohammedan since 14th cent.).

Jolon (hŭlōn'), hamlet, Monterey co., W Calif., in valley of Coast Ranges, 35 mi. NW of Paso Robles. Near by are Hunter Liggett Military Reservation and restored Mission San Antonio de Padua (founded 1771).

Jolstra Lake (yûl'strä), Nor. *Jølstravatn*, formerly *Jølstervand*, lake (□ 15) in Sogn og Fjordane co., W Norway, at W foot of the glacier Jostedalsbre, 40 mi. E of Floro; c.20 mi. long; tourist attraction.

Jolsva, Czechoslovakia: see JELSAVA.

Joly (zhôlē'), village, S Que., 30 mi. SW of Quebec; garnet mining.

Joly, Mont (mō), summit (8,300 ft.) of Savoy Alps, 5 mi. S of Saint-Gervais-les-Bains. View of Mont Blanc (8 mi. E).

Jomala (yō'mälä), village (commune pop. 3,524), Aland co., SW Finland, in central part of Aland isl., 5 mi. N of Mariehamn; grain.

Jomalig Island (hōmä'lĭg) (□ 20), one of the Polillo Isls., Quezon prov., Philippines, in Philippine Sea, just SE of Patnanongan Isl., 19 mi. E of Polillo Isl.; 14°42'N 122°22'E; 9 mi. long, 3 mi. wide. Fishing.

Jomanes, river, India: see JUMNA RIVER.

Jo-Mary Lakes, central Maine, 10 mi. SW of Millinocket; chain of 3 lakes (Upper, Middle, and Lower), each c.3 mi. long, joined to Pemadumcook L. to N.

Jombang or **Djombang** (both: jōmbäng'), town (pop. 20,380), E Java, Indonesia, on Brantas R. and 40 mi. WSW of Surabaya; trade center for agr. area (rice, corn, cassava, peanuts).

Jomolhari, mountain, Bhutan and Tibet: see CHOMO LHARI.

Jomsburg, Poland: see WOLIN, town.

Jomulco (hōmōōl'kō), town (pop. 1,436), Nayarit, W Mexico, at E foot of Ceboruco volcano, 45 mi. SE of Tepic; corn, beans, sugar cane, fruit, cattle.

Jona (yō'nä), town (pop. 3,252), St. Gall canton, N Switzerland, near Rapperswil; cotton textiles, woodworking.

Jonacatepec (hōnäkätäpĕk'), city (pop. 2,152), Morelos, central Mexico, 32 mi. ESE of Cuernavaca; agr. center (rice, coffee, sugar cane, limes and other fruit). Airfield.

Jonai, Formosa: see TAIPEI.

Jonava, Ionava, or **Yonava** (yō'nävä), Ger. *Janow*, Rus. *Janov*, city (pop. 5,465), central Lithuania, on Viliya R. and 20 mi. NE of Kaunas; furniture mfg. center; chemicals, matches, shoes, felt, cement, rope; sawmilling. In Rus. Kovno govt. until 1920.

Joncs, Plaine des (plĕ' dā zhō'), low, swampy region of S Vietnam, just N of Mekong delta and W of Saigon; periodically flooded, traversed by the West Vaico R. Sparsely populated.

Jones. 1 County (□ 402; pop. 7,538), central Ga.; ⊙ Clinton. Bounded SW by Ocmulgee R. Intersected by fall line. Agr. (peaches, cotton, corn, pimientos, truck, livestock) and sawmilling area. Part of Chattahoochee Natl. Forest. in W. Formed 1807. **2** County (□ 585; pop. 19,401), E Iowa; ⊙ Anamosa. Prairie agr. area (cattle, hogs, poultry, corn, oats, wheat) drained by Wapsipinicon and Maquoketa rivers. Limestone quarries, sand and gravel pits. Has state park. Formed 1837. **3** County (□ 706; pop. 57,235), SE Miss.; ⊙ LAUREL and Ellisville. Drained by Leaf R. and Tallahala Creek. Includes part of Chickasawhay Natl. Forest. Agr. (cotton, corn, sweet potatoes, poultry); lumbering, lumber milling; naval stores. Formed 1826. **4** County (□ 467; pop. 11,004), E N.C.; ⊙ Trenton. Forested and swampy tidewater area; drained by Trent R. Includes part of Croatan Natl. Forest (SE) and Whiteoak Swamp (S). Farming (especially tobacco; corn, cotton), timber (pine, gum); sawmilling. Formed 1778. **5** County (□ 973; pop. 2,281), S central S.Dak.; ⊙Murdo. Agr. area drained by Bad R. and numerous creeks; bounded S by White R. Livestock, poultry, grain. Formed 1916. **6** County (□ 959; pop. 22,147), W central Texas; ⊙ Anson. Rolling plains, drained by Clear Fork of Brazos R. Rich agr. co. (cotton, corn, grain sorghums, some fruit, truck); livestock (cattle, hogs, sheep, goats). Oil wells; gypsum, clay deposits. Formed 1858.

Jones, town (pop. 476), Oklahoma co., central Okla., 15 mi. ENE of Oklahoma City, and on North Canadian R., in oil-producing and agr. area; cotton ginning.

Jones Beach State Park (2,413 acres), SE N.Y., on barrier isl. off SE shore (causeway connections) of Long Isl., 5 mi. S of Wantagh. Noted outing resort; ocean and bay beaches, boardwalk; facilities for boating, fishing, games, dancing, and concerts; has marine stadium for water spectacles. Developed after 1929.

Jonesboro. 1 City (pop. 16,310), a ⊙ Craighead co., NE Ark., c.60 mi. NW of Memphis (Tenn.), on Crowley's Ridge; distribution center for farm area (cotton, corn, rice, fruit, livestock, poultry). Seat of Ark. State Col. Mfg. of wood products, flour, shoes, hosiery, brick; cotton ginning and compressing, rice and feed milling. Founded 1859, inc. 1883. **2** City (pop. 1,741), ⊙ Clayton co., N central Ga., 17 mi. S of Atlanta, in agr. area; mfg. (textile, wood, and cement products). Historical mus. near by on site of Civil War battle of Jonesboro in Sherman's Atlanta campaign (1864). Settled 1823, inc. 1859. **3** City (pop. 1,607), ⊙ Union co., S Ill., 30 mi. N of Cairo, in Ill. Ozarks; agr. (fruit, wheat, corn, truck); limestone quarries. Laid out 1816, inc. 1857. A Lincoln-Douglas debate was held here in 1858. **4** Town (pop. 1,973), Grant co., E central Ind., on Mississinewa R. and 6 mi. S of Marion; farm trading center in agr. area; mfg. (feed, electric wire and cable). Platted 1837. **5** Town (pop. 3,097), ⊙ Jackson parish, N central La., 40 mi. WSW of Monroe, in agr. area (cotton, corn, potatoes, truck; dairy products; poultry); cotton gins, lumber mills; mfg. of wood products. **6** or **Jonesborough,** agr. town (pop. 459), Washington co., E Maine, at mouth of Chandler R., 7 mi. SW of Machias. **7** Former town, Lee co., N.C.: see SANFORD. **8** Town (pop. 1,126), ⊙ Washington co., NE Tenn., 6 mi. WSW of Johnson City. Laid out 1779; oldest town in Tenn.; was 1st ⊙ State of Franklin. Andrew Jackson admitted to law practice here in 1788. Among many old bldgs. is an inn built c.1798.

Jonesburg, town (pop. 433), Montgomery co., E central Mo., 13 mi. SE of Montgomery City.

Jones Mill or **Jones Mills,** industrial village (pop. 1,069), Hot Spring co., central Ark., near Remmel Dam and L. Catherine, 7 mi. NW of Malvern; aluminum plant.

Jones Pass (12,453 ft.), N central Colo., in Front Range, bet. Grand and Clear Creek counties. Beneath pass is Jones Pass, or Williams Fork, Tunnel (c.3 mi. long; finished 1939), unit in Denver sewage-disposal system.

Jonesport, town (pop. 1,727), Washington co., E Maine, on peninsula W of Wohoa Bay and 15 mi. SW of Machias; summer resort, fishing center. Port of entry. Settled 1763–4; inc. 1832; included Beals until 1925.

Jones Sound, NE Franklin Dist., Northwest Territories, arm (250 mi. long, 15–60 mi. wide) of Baffin Bay, bet. Ellesmere Isl. (N) and Devon Isl. (S); 76°N 85°W. At Baffin Bay end is Cobourg Isl. Discovered (1616) by William Baffin.

Jonestown. 1 Town (pop. 741), Coahoma co., NW Miss., 10 mi. NE of Clarksdale, in agr. area. **2** Borough (pop. 853), Lebanon co., SE central Pa., 6 mi. NW of Lebanon and on Swatara Creek.

Jonesville, village (pop. 98), S Alaska, in Matanuska Valley, on rail spur and 16 mi. NE of Matanuska village; coal mining.

Jonesville. 1 Town (pop. 225), Bartholomew co., S central Ind., 10 mi. S of Columbus, in agr. area. **2** Town (pop. 1,954), Catahoula parish, E La., on Ouachita R. (Black R.), at influx of Tensas and Little rivers, and 24 mi. W of Natchez (Miss.), in agr. area (corn, cotton, potatoes); lumbering; cooperage; fisheries; cotton and moss ginning. Built on site of anc. Indian village. Inc. 1904. **3** Village (pop. 1,594), Hillsdale co., S Mich., 4 mi. NNW of Hillsdale and on St. Joseph R., in diversified agr. area; mfg. (store fixtures, paint brushes, toys, cigars, food products). Settled 1828, inc. 1855. **4** Town (pop. 1,768), Yadkin co., N N.C., on Yadkin R. opposite Elkin, in tobacco area. **5** Town (pop. 1,345), Union co., N S.C., 14 mi. ESE of Spartanburg; textile mills. Settled 1808, inc. 1876. **6** Town (pop. 597), ⊙ Lee co., extreme SW Va., near Powell R., 17 mi. SE of Harlan, Ky.

Jongka or **Jongkha** (both: jông'kä), Chinese *Jung-ha* (rŏŏng'hä'), town [Tibetan *dzong*], S Tibet, in N Nepal Himalayas, on Trisuli R. near its source and 90 mi. N of Katmandu (Nepal); 28°58'N 85°12'E. Sometimes spelled Dzongka.

Jonglei (jông-lā'), village, Upper Nile prov., S central Anglo-Egyptian Sudan, on right bank of the Bahr el Jebel (white Nile) and 50 mi. NNW of Bor. Bet. here and Malakal (200 mi. N) a canal to by-pass the Sudd marshes is planned.

Jong River (jông), S Sierra Leone, formed 10 mi. W of Yele by union of Teye and Pampana rivers; flows c.100 mi. S past Mano, to Sherbro R. (inlet of the Atlantic) opposite Bonthe. Navigable in lower course. Sometimes called Teye River.

Jongsong La, pass, India and Nepal: see SINGALILA RANGE.

Joniskis, Ionishkis, or **Yonishkis** (yō'nēshkēs), Lith. *Joniškis*, Ger. *Janischken*, Rus. *Yanishki*, city (pop. 5,132), N Lithuania, 24 mi. NNE of Siauliai, near Latvian border; mfg. (shoes, furniture), flour milling, dairying, flax processing. Dates from 15th cent. In Rus. Kovno govt. until 1920.

Jonkoping (yûn'chû"pĭng), Swedish *Jönköping*, county [Swed. *län*] (□ 4,449; 1950 pop. 271,905), S Sweden; ⊙ Jonkoping. Extends S from L. Vatter; forms N part of SMALAND prov. Marshy, undulating surface is studded with many lakes; drained by Em, Laga, and Nissa rivers. Rye and oats are grown, cattle are raised. Industries include mfg. of matches (centered on Jonkoping city), paper and textile milling, wood- and metalworking, furniture mfg. Cities are Jonkoping, Nassjo (railroad center), Huskvarna, Varnamo, Vetlanda, Eksjo, Tranas, and Granna.

Jonkoping, Swed. *Jönköping*, city (1950 pop. 44,685), ⊙ Jonkoping co., S Sweden, at S end of L. Vatter, 80 mi. E of Goteborg; 57°47'N 14°9'E. Rail junction; center (since 1844) of Swedish match-mfg. industry, with some of the world's largest match factories. Paper and textile mills, machinery and shoe factories. Served by Gota Canal steamers. Has several 14th- and 17th-cent. churches, 17th-cent. courthouse and town hall. Chartered 1284, the city was built on piles over a marsh. Destroyed (1612) by its citizens to prevent sacking by Danes; rebuilt by Gustavus Adolphus. A. V. Rydberg b. here. Just S are small Munk L., Swedish *Munksjön*, and Rock L., Swedish *Rocksjön*.

Jonotla (hōnō'tlä), town (pop. 1,375), Puebla, central Mexico, 28 mi. E of Huauchinango; sugar, coffee, tobacco, fruit.

Jonquière (zhōkyâr'), town (pop. 13,769), S central Que., on Sable R. (tributary of Saguenay R.) and 9 mi. WSW of Chicoutimi; railroad workshops; pulp milling.

Jonquières (zhōkyâr'), village (pop. 807), Vaucluse dept., SE France, 5 mi. ESE of Orange; fruit and vegetable preserving, olive-oil mfg.

Jonsered (yôn'sûrĕd"), village (pop. 2,033), Goteborg och Bohus co., SW Sweden, on Save R. and 7 mi. ENE of Goteborg; cotton and linen milling, metal- and woodworking.

Jonte River (zhōt), Lozère and Aveyron depts., S France, rises at Mont Aigoual E of Meyrueis, flows 25 mi. W bet. Causse Méjan (N) and Causse Noir (S) to the Tarn at Peyreleau.

Jonuta (hōnōō'tä), town (pop. 1,053), Tabasco, SE Mexico, on Usumacinta R., near Campeche border, and 45 mi. SE of Alvaro Obregón; rice, beans, tobacco, fruit.

Jonzac (zhōzäk'), town (pop. 2,570), Charente-Maritime dept., W France, on the Seugne and 18 mi. SSW of Cognac; brandy distilling, biscuit mfg. Stone quarries near by.

Jooda or **Jouda** (both: jōdä'), Chinese *Chao-wu-ta* (jou'wōō'dä'), Mongolian league in S Inner Mongolian Autonomous Region, Manchuria, N of upper Liao R.; main centers are Kailu, Tapanshang, Linsi, Kingpeng, and Lupeh. Originally part of N Jehol, it was constituted in 1934 as West Hsingan prov. of Manchukuo; it reverted in 1946 to Jehol, and passed in 1949 to Inner Mongolian Autonomous Region. Sometimes spelled Chao Uda.

Jopala (hōpä'lä), town (pop. 1,150), Puebla, central Mexico, 24 mi. E of Huauchinango; sugar, coffee, fruit.

Joplin (jŏp'lĭn), city (pop. 38,711), Jasper and Newton counties, SW Mo., at edge of the Ozarks, near Spring R., 140 mi. S of Kansas City; alt. 1,039 ft. Railroad center; agr. shipping and industrial city; stockyards, meat-packing houses, mineral-processing plants; mfg. (leather goods, metal products, sewer pipe, explosives, lumber, food products); important zinc and lead mines, limestone quarries. Jr. col. Settled c.1840, inc. 1873.

Joppa, Palestine: see JAFFA.

Joppa (jŏ'pŭ). **1** Village (pop. 513), Massac co., extreme S Ill., on Ohio R. and 23 mi. NNE of Cairo. Steam power plant here for Atomic Energy Commission plant near Paducah, Ky. **2** Hamlet, Harford co., NE Md., near Little Gunpowder Falls (stream), 17 mi. NE of Baltimore. Near by is site of Joppa Town, ⊙ old Baltimore co. (1712–68), which was a major American tobacco market until c.1750.

Joquicingo (hōkēsĭng'gō), officially Joquicingo de León Guzmán, town (pop. 1,684), Mexico state, central Mexico, 21 mi. SE of Toluca; sugar cane, cereals, stock.

Jora (jō'rŭ), town (pop. 4,970), NE Madhya Bharat, India, 24 mi. WNW of Lashkar; gram, millet, wheat. Also called Jora Alapur; sometimes Joura.

Jorat (zhôrä'), chain of heights in W Switzerland, bet. Bernese Alps and the Jura; forms watershed bet. lakes of Neuchâtel and Geneva. Rises to c.3,000 ft. in Mt. Jorat; Lausanne is on its S slopes.

Joravarnagar, India: see WADHWAN, town.

Jordan, Arabic *Al Urduniyah* (ăl ŏŏrdŏŏnē'yä), formerly *Trans-Jordan* or *Transjordania,* now officially named the **Hashemite Kingdom of the Jordan,** kingdom (□ c.37,000), SW Asia, bordering N (partly along Yarmuk R.) on Syria, NE on Iraq, E and S on Saudi Arabia, W on Israel; ⊙ AMMAN. Before the incorporation (1950) of E central sections of PALESTINE its pop. was estimated at 450,000, but this has swelled since then to more than 1,000,000, of which a great many are refugees from the area of the new state of Israel. Jordan extends roughly bet. 29°15'–33°25'N and 35°–39°E. Boundaries with Saudi Arabia and, particularly, Israel are still disputed. The country lies now astride the JORDAN RIVER, thus including most of the highlands of SAMARIA (chief town, NABLUS) and JUDAEA (chief town, HEBRON), with the Old Town section of JERUSALEM and with BETHLEHEM. What was Trans-Jordan occupies the biblical lands of GILEAD, EDOM, MOAB, and AMMON. Most distinctive physical feature is the deep Jordan valley —frequently called El GHOR—which together with the saline DEAD SEA and the Wadi 'Araba forms one continuous depression to the Gulf of Aqaba of the Red Sea, where Jordan owns a short, c.15-mi.-long maritime strip. This depression, part of the GREAT RIFT VALLEY of Africa and the Near East, is 1,292 ft. below sea level at the surface of the Dead Sea. Both sides are lined by steep cliffs. E of the Jordan R. the mts. descend more gently to merge with the SYRIAN DESERT. The Samarian and Judaean hills rise above 3,000 ft. (Mt. Ebal, 3,084 ft.), while S of MA'AN near Gulf of Aqaba elevation attains 5,686 ft. Most of the uplands consist of barren, calcareous rock in advanced stage of soil erosion. Some pine forests are in N center, particularly on slopes of the Jebel 'Ajlun. Virtually all land E of the so-called Hejaz RR (from Damascus, past Amman, to Ma'an, beyond which it is in disrepair) is desert. Among the few oases is that of Azraq in N, which has salt and gypsum deposits near by. Jordan adjoins in NW the fertile Plain of Jezreel (Esdraelon). The climate, influenced by the Mediterranean, has dry, hot summers; winters are mild and cool with occasional torrential rains. In the Jordan valley bananas and subtropical fruit (citrus) thrive. There is little irrigation, and the area supports only a small, largely seminomadic population. Barely 5% of the land is under cultivation, but agr. and grazing are the chief occupations; in it are engaged 85% of the people. Methods employed remain antiquated. Among the chief crops are wheat, barley, lentils, kersenneh, corn, millet, beans, peas, sesame. Olives and grapes are grown with good results in the N. Stock raised includes goats, sheep, cattle, donkeys, camels. Fishing in Gulf of Aqaba. In normal times, principal exports include live animals, skins and hides, wool, vegetables, raisins, fruit, cereals. However, in recent years imports exceeded exports almost 10 fold. Of the diverse mineral resources, phosphates, potash (from Dead Sea), kaolin, silica, and ocher play a certain part in foreign trade. Oil deposits have been reported in the S. There are also copper and iron ores. Besides some mining, cloth weaving, lumbering, and native handicrafts, there is processing of agr. and livestock products. Nablus makes olive oil and soap. Jordan has few large towns. These are, apart from those already mentioned, IRBID, a flourishing road and agr. center; SALT, on road to Jerusalem across strategic Allenby Bridge; JERASH, a resort with vineyards; KALLIA, on Dead Sea, with potash works (damaged during Arab-Jewish hostilities); JERICHO, near N end of Dead Sea, visited in winter; JENIN, at S edge of the Plain of Jezreel; TAFILA, with manganese deposits. Both Amman and MAFRAQ have airfields, where British units are stationed. The pipe line crossing N Jordan from Kirkuk (Iraq) to Haifa (Israel) was closed in 1948. The country has c.360 mi. of all-weather roads. The Jordan people are predominantly of Arab stock and Moslem (Sunnite) religion. Apart from various religious groups in and around Jerusalem, there are about 40,000 Christian Arabs, and a small Circassian minority settled by the Turks in the 1880s. The majority speak Arabic, the official language. Modern Jordan occupies a land saturated with religious and historic associations. Next to Jerusalem, Bethlehem is one of the most sacred sites in Christendom. Amman, KERAK, and JERASH have extensive ruins of many epochs. PETRA, a city hewn out of rock, is not the least remarkable of them all. Remains of Graeco-Roman culture abound. The area of Jordan (for early history see also PALESTINE) corresponds approximately to the lordships of Montreal and Krak in the Latin Kingdom. It fell to the Ottoman Empire in the 16th cent. and remained under Turkish rule until the end of the First World War. In 1920 Jordan was part of the short-lived Kingdom of Syria under Feisal I, but it was quickly subjugated by the British. Originally part of the Br. mandate of Palestine, Trans-Jordan (i.e., "land beyond the Jordan") was established (1923) as a semi-independent emirate under Abdullah ibn Hussein, though still under suzerainty of the British. In S, the Ma'an dist. (with Aqaba) was annexed in 1925. Trans-Jordan supported the Allies during the Second World War, and in 1946 the mandate was terminated and a kingdom proclaimed. A treaty in 1948 set forth the relations bet. the United Kingdom and the Kingdom of Trans-Jordan. While fully independent, Trans-Jordan was to receive an annual subsidy for its British-trained Arab Legion (comprising c.14,000 officers and men) and Britain continued to maintain garrisons at the principal airports. Trans-Jordan was not admitted to the United Nations, though it became a member of the Arab League, whose opposition against Zionist aims it endorsed. In 1948, upon withdrawal of the British from Palestine, it dispatched its Arab Legion against Jewish forces. While Arab troops were unsuccessful in occupying the newly-proclaimed state of Israel, Trans-Jordan troops did hold most of the part of E central Palestine which the United Nations had designated Arab territory. Late in 1949 Jordan concluded a truce with Israel, and formally annexed the occupied portion of Palestine. The name Jordan was generally adopted in 1949, though the official change (to Hashemite Kingdom of the Jordan) had already been made upon establishment of the kingdom in 1946. Jordan is a constitutional monarchy, administratively divided into districts and the large E desert tracts; E of the Jordan R. are 'Ajlun, Amman, Belqa, Karak, Ma'an; W of the Jordan are Ramallah, Nablus, and Hebron.

Jordan, Philippines: see GUIMARAS ISLAND.

Jordan. 1 City (pop. 1,494), Scott co., S Minn., near Minnesota R., 28 mi. SW of Minneapolis; trading point in grain, livestock, poultry area; dairy products, beverages, cattle feed. Sand and gravel pits near by. Platted 1854, inc. as village 1872, as city 1891. **2** Village (1940 pop. 677), ⊙ Garfield co., E central Mont., 80 mi. NW of Miles City; trading point in irrigated ranching region; grain, livestock. **3** Village (pop. 1,295), Onondaga co., central N.Y., 17 mi. W of Syracuse, in farming, dairying, poultry-raising area; mfg. of furniture. Inc. 1835.

Jordan Dam, central Ala., on Coosa R., 17 mi. NNE of Montgomery. Privately built power dam (125 ft. high, 2,066 ft. long) completed 1929; forms small reservoir (□ 7.7). Hydroelectric plant.

Jordânia (zhôrdä'nyů), city (pop. 1,818), NE Minas Gerais, Brazil, on Bahia border, 80 mi. W of Canavieiras (Bahia); agr. settlement. Until 1944, called Palestina.

Jordania, S.C.: see LONSDALE.

Jordanne River (zhôrdän'), Cantal dept., S central France, rises on S slopes of Puy Mary in Massif du Cantal, flows 22 mi. SW into the Cère 2 mi. below Aurillac.

Jordanow (yôrdä'nŏŏf), Pol. *Jordanów,* town (pop. 2,638), Krakow prov., S Poland, on Skawa R. and 29 mi. S of Cracow; flour milling, sawmilling, tanning; stone quarrying. During Second World War, under Ger. rule, called Ilmenau (ĭl'mŭnou).

Jordan River, B.C.: see RIVER JORDAN.

Jordan River, the great river of Palestine, rising in several headstreams in Anti-Lebanon mts. of Syria and Lebanon, and flowing over 200 mi. S to the Dead Sea. The Jordan proper is formed in L. Hula (alt. 230 ft.), whence it flows S through the Sea of Galilee and through the great depression called The Ghor to the Dead Sea (1,292 ft. below sea level); all lie in the GREAT RIFT VALLEY. Its upper course is precipitous, its middle and lower course sluggish. Chief tributary is the Yarmuk (left). The Jordan formerly marked E border of British mandate in Palestine, except in extreme N. After the partition of Palestine (May, 1948), much territory W of it was occupied by Jordan and annexed April, 1950, so that the S half of the river is in Jordan and N half makes part of Israel-Jordan and Israel-Syria borders. Allenby Bridge (Jerusalem-Amman road) is chief crossing. Several fords mentioned in Old Testament; in New Testament scene of baptism of Jesus. Hydroelectric power plant at Naharayim; further water-power and irrigation development projected.

Jordan River, rises in Utah L., N central Utah, flows 60 mi. N, past Salt Lake City, to Great Salt L. near Bountiful. Crossed by numerous bridges in Salt Lake City and used for irrigation. Agr., mining, smelting, and mfg. in valley.

Jordans, England: see CHALFONT SAINT GILES.

Jordan Valley, town (pop. 236), Malheur co., SE Oregon, near Idaho line, 50 mi. SW of Nampa, Idaho, and on Jordan R.; alt. 4,389 ft.; sheep.

Jordão, Brazil: see FOZ DO JORDÃO.

Jorge Island, Chile: see CHONOS ARCHIPELAGO.

Jorge Montt Island (hōr'hā mōnt'), off coast of S Chile, 90 mi. WNW of Puerto Natales, just NE of Nelson Strait; 51°20'S; 28 mi. long, 25 mi. wide. Uninhabited.

Jorgucat or **Jorgucati,** Albania: see JERGUCAT.

Jorhat (jōr'hät), town (pop. 11,664), ⊙ Sibsagar dist., E central Assam, India, in Brahmaputra valley, on tributary of the Brahmaputra and 165 mi. NE of Shillong; rail junction, with spur to Kokilamukh (steamer service), 8 mi. NW; road and trade center (tea, rice, rape and mustard, sugar cane, jute); makes Assamese jewelry. Assam Agr. Col. here. Was ⊙ Ahom (Shan) kingdom in late-18th cent.

Jorm, Afghanistan: see JURM.

Jorn (yûrn), Swedish *Jörn,* village (pop. 983), Vasterbotten co., N Sweden, 35 mi. NW of Skelleftea; rail junction; sawmills.

Jornada del Muerto (hôrnä'dů děl mwâr'tō), arid region of desert and lava beds in S N.Mex.; extends N–S along Rio Grande, just W of San Andres Mts., in Socorro, Sierra, and Dona Ana counties. Once crossed by El Camino Real (early trade route); area was much feared by travelers because of robbers and danger of death by thirst. Now crossed by railroad and highways; irrigated in places.

Joroinen (yō'roiněn), Swedish *Jorois* (yô'rois), village (commune pop. 8,346), Mikkeli co., SE Finland, on lake of Saimaa system, 40 mi. NW of Savonlinna; agr. center (grain, potatoes, stock; dairying).

Jorpeland (yûr'půlän), Nor. *Jørpeland,* village (pop. 1,837) in Strand canton (pop. 4,408), Rogaland co., SW Norway, on SE shore of Bokn Fjord, 12 mi. ENE of Stavanger; industrial center producing steel and steel products. At village of Fiska (fĭsk'ô), Nor. *Fiskå,* 7 mi. N, mfg. of iron alloys and insulation materials.

Jorullo (hōrōō'yō), volcano (4,330 ft.) in Michoacán, central Mexico, on SW slope of central plateau, 33 mi. SE of Uruapan. It was created in 1759, when it erupted violently, destroying what had been a rich agr. area. Has numerous craters and fumaroles; inactive since 1860.

Jos (jôs), town (pop. 11,854), ⊙ Plateau Prov., Northern Provinces, central Nigeria, on Bauchi Plateau, on railroad and 140 mi. SSE of Kano; alt. 4,010 ft.; 9°56'N 8°54'E. Major tin-mining center; butter factory; cassava, millet, durra. Airfield.

Josanicka Banja or **Yoshanichka Banya** (both: yô'shänĭchkä bän'yä), Serbo-Croatian *Jošanička Banja,* village, S central Serbia, Yugoslavia, on railroad 23 mi. S of Rankovicevo; health resort.

José Batlle y Ordóñez (hōsā' bät'yä ē ōrdō'nyěs) or **Batlle y Ordóñez,** town (pop. 7,000), Lavalleja dept., SE central Uruguay, in the Cuchilla Grande Principal, on railroad (Nico Pérez station) and 45 mi. WSW of Treinta y Tres, on Florida dept. line. Local trade center; rail and road junction; airport. Agr. products (wheat, corn, oats); cattle, sheep. Until 1907 called Nico Pérez, a name still applied to the town section extending W into Florida dept.

José Bonifácio (zhōōzĕ' bōnēfä'syōō). **1** City, Rio Grande do Sul, Brazil: see ERECHIM. **2** City (pop. 1,900), N São Paulo, Brazil, 25 mi. SW of São José do Rio Prêto; coffee, cotton, rice, and macaroni processing; sawmilling.

José Cardel (hōsā' kärděl') or **Antigua Veracruz** (äntē'gwä väräkrōōs'), town (pop. 2,041), Veracruz, E Mexico, in Gulf lowland, on railroad and 15 mi. NW of Veracruz; coffee, fruit, livestock. Cortés landed here in April, 1519.

José C. Paz (sā' päs'), town (pop. 3,707), Buenos Aires prov., Argentina, 2.5 mi. NW of San Miguel; mfg.: ceramics, dairy products, canned foods; flower growing.

José de Alencar, Brazil: see ALENCAR.

José de Freitas (zhōōzĕ' dĭ frā'tůs), city (pop. 1,576), N Piauí, Brazil, 28 mi. NNE of Teresina; carnauba wax, maniçoba rubber. Until 1939, called Livramento.

José de la Isla, Mexico: see SAN JOSÉ DE LA ISLA.

José de San Martín (hōsā' dā sän märtēn'), village (pop. estimate 600), ⊙ Tehuelches dept., SW Chubut natl. territory, Argentina, 85 mi. SE of Esquel. Resort, sheep-raising center; brewery. Formerly Colonia San Martín.

José Enrique Rodó, Uruguay: see RODÓ.

Josefina, Argentina: see COLONIA JOSEFINA.

Josefov (yô'sěfôf). **1** Ger. *Josefstadt* (yō'zěfshtät), town (pop. 3,660), NE Bohemia, Czechoslovakia, on Elbe R. and 8 mi. SSE of Dvur Kralove; rail junction; lumbering trade; mfg. of clothing, underwear, embroidery. A fortress until 1890, it still preserves much of its fortifications. Town of JAROMER is 1 mi. NNW. **2** NNW district (pop. 2,829) of Prague, central Bohemia, Czechoslovakia, on right bank of Vltava R. Site of former ghetto almost entirely demolished at end of 19th cent.; still retains remarkable 14th-cent. synagogue, 18th-cent. Jewish town hall, and famous Jewish cemetery used from 1439 to 1787.

Josefstadt (yō'zěfshtät), district (□ .4; pop. 42,178) of Vienna, Austria, just W of city center.

Josefstadt, Czechoslovakia: see JOSEFOV, town.

José Ignacio, Lake (hōsā' ēgnä'syō), fresh-water coastal lagoon (6 mi. long, 2½ mi. wide), Maldonado dept., S Uruguay, 13 mi. ENE of Maldonado.

José Ignacio Point, headland, Maldonado dept., S Uruguay, 19 mi. E of Maldonado city; 34°51'S 54°37'W.

José Ingenieros (ēnhěnyā'rōs), town (pop. estimate 2,000) in W Greater Buenos Aires, Argentina; residential and industrial center; shoes, blinds; metalworks; dairy products.

José Néstor Lencinas, Argentina: see Las Catitas.

Josen Fjord (yû'sûn), Nor. *Jøsenfjord,* NE branch of Bokn Fjord, Rogaland co., SW Norway, extends from Ombo 16 mi. ENE. Sometimes spelled Hjosen.

Joseni (zhôsän'), Hung. *Gyergyóalfalu* (dyĕr'dyōōlfŏlōō), village (pop. 7,022), Mures prov., E central Rumania, near Mures R., 15 mi. W of Gheorgheni; mineral springs. In Hungary, 1940–45.

Jose Pañganiban (hōsā' pä"nyûgänēbän'), town (1939 pop. 5,761; 1948 municipality pop. 8,485), Camarines Norte prov., SE Luzon, Philippines, port on small inlet of Philippine Sea, 105 mi. NW of Legaspi; 14°17'N 122°41'E. Trade center for mining area (iron, gold); sawmilling. Exports iron ore. Formerly Mambulao (mämbōō'lou).

José Pedro Varela (pā'drō värā'lä), town (pop. 2,700), Lavalleja dept., SE Uruguay, on railroad (Corrales station) and highway, and c.16 mi. SW of Treinta y Tres. Road junction; commercial, distributing center; wheat, corn, cattle, sheep.

Joseph. 1 City (pop. 666), Wallowa co., NE Oregon, 6 mi. SE of Enterprise; alt. 4,191 ft.; lumber milling. Wallowa L. just S. **2** Town (pop. 208), Sevier co., SW central Utah, 10 mi. SW of Richfield and on Sevier R.; alt. 5,435 ft.; agr.

Joseph, Lake (12 mi. long, 4 mi. wide), S Ont., in Muskoka lake region, 16 mi. SE of Parry Sound.

Joseph Bonaparte Gulf, arm of Timor Sea, N Australia, bet. Cape Londonderry (W) and Point Blaze (E); 225 mi. E–W, 100 mi. N–S; divides into Cambridge Gulf (W; site of Wyndham) and Queen's Channel (E).

Joseph Henry, Cape, NE Ellesmere Isl., NE Franklin Dist., Northwest Territories, on Lincoln Sea of the Arctic Ocean, NE extremity of Fielden Peninsula; 82°49'N 63°35'W.

Josephine, county (□ 1,625; pop. 26,542), SW Oregon; ⊙ Grants Pass. Mtn. area bordering on Calif. and crossed (in N) by Rogue R. Fruit, poultry; lumber, gold. Includes part of Siskiyou Natl. Forest, in Siskiyou Mts. Oregon Caves Natl. Monument in SE. Formed 1856.

Josephinenhütte, Poland: see Szklarska Poreba.

José Trujillo Valdez (hōsā' trōōhē'yō väldēs'), town (1950 pop. 2,020), Bahoruco prov., SW Dominican Republic, near L. Enriquillo, 5 mi. W of Neiba; coffee, cereals, fruit, timber. Sometimes Trujillo Valdez.

Joshimath (jō'shēmŭt), village, Garhwal dist., N Uttar Pradesh, India, at confluence of headstreams of the Alaknanda, 55 mi. NE of Pauri. Winter hq. of chief priest of Badrinath.

Joshin, Korea: see Songjin.

Joshua (jŏsh'wä), village (1940 pop. 525), Johnson co., N central Texas, 20 mi. S of Fort Worth in dairy, cotton, truck area.

Joshua Tree National Monument (jŏ'shōōû, jŏ'shûwû) (□ 1,086.2; established 1936), S Calif. 70 mi. E of San Bernardino. Colorful desert area including several stands of rare, rapidly diminishing Joshua Tree (*Yucca brevifolia;* 10–38 ft. high, with clusters of large white blossoms) and other desert flora. Monument hq. just N, at Twentynine Palms. Prehistoric artifacts have been found in Pinto Basin (E).

Jo Shui, China: see Etsin Gol; Hei River.

Joslowitz, Czechoslovakia: see Jaroslavice.

Josoto or **Josotu** (jōsōtōō'), Chinese *Cho-so-t'u* (jō'sō'tōō'), Mongolian league in S Jehol prov., Manchuria, S of upper Liao R. Extensively colonized by Chinese.

Jos Plateau, Nigeria: see Bauchi Plateau.

Jossefors (yû"sûfôrs',–fôsh'), Swedish *Jössefors,* village, Varmland co., W Sweden, on By R. (falls), at N end of Glaf Fjord, 4 mi. WNW of Arvika; paper mill, sulphite works, hydroelectric plant.

Josselin (zhôsûlĕ'), town (pop. 2,011), Morbihan dept., W France, on Oust R. (Brest-Nantes Canal) and 7 mi. W of Ploërmel; tanning, woodworking. Has fine 15th-cent. castle.

Jossund, canton, Norway: see Lysoysundet.

Jostedalsbre (yô'stûdälsbrā"), glacier in Sogn og Fjordane co., W Norway, 100 mi. NE of Bergen, bet. Nord and Sogne fjords, W of Jotunheim Mts. Largest ice field (□ 340) on European mainland, it is 60 mi. long, 15 mi. wide. Rises to 6,700 ft. Sends off numerous glaciers into near-by valleys. Village of Jostedal is at its E foot, 25 mi. N of Sogndal.

Jost Van Dyke (yōst" văn dīk', jōst"), islet (pop. 238, including adjoining Little Jost Van Dyke), Br. Virgin Isls., 4 mi. W of Tortola; 18°27'N 64°45'W. Rugged, mountainous, rising to 1,070 ft. Dr. William Thornton, a designer of the Washington capitol, b. here. Little Jost Van Dyke isl. is just E.

Josvafö (yōsh'vŏfû), Hung. *Jósvafő,* town (pop. 607), Abauj co., NE Hungary, 29 mi. NNW of Miskolc; entrance to Josvafö Cave, one of Baradla Caves.

Jotiba's Hill, India: see Panhala.

Jotsoma (jōtsō'mŭ), village, Naga Hills dist., E Assam, India, in Naga Hills, 3 mi. W of Kohima; rice, cotton, oranges. Former stronghold of Naga tribes.

Jotunheim Mountains (yō'tŏŏnhām), Nor. *Jotunheimen* [=giant's home], range in Opland and Sogn og Fjordane counties, S central Norway, extend c.70 mi. bet. head of Sogne Fjord (WSW) and the upper Gudbrandsdal (ENE). Highest range in Scandinavia, it rises to 8,097 ft. in the peak Galdhopiggen (gäl'hûp"pĭgûn), Nor. *Galdhøppigen,* 80 mi. NW of Lillehammer, at 61°38'N 8°18'E. Other peaks are the Glittertind (glĭt'tûrtĭn) (8,048 ft.); Skagastolstind (skä'gästûlstĭn"), Nor. *Skagastølstindane* (7,887 ft.); and Knutsholtind (kûnōōts'hôltĭn) (7,680 ft.). On S slope of range are Steinbusjo, Bygdin, and Vinsteren lakes. On lower slopes are extensive summer-grazing areas. Region is setting of numerous sagas and legends, and of Ibsen's *Peer Gynt.* Sometimes called Jotunfjell. SW section of range near head of Sogne Fjord is called Sognefjell.

Jouarre (zhwär'), village (pop. 927), Seine-et-Marne dept., N central France, 2 mi. S of La Ferté-sous-Jouarre; millstone mfg. Former seat of Benedictine convent. Behind 15th-cent. church is crypt containing 7th–13th-cent. sarcophagi.

Joub el Jarrah, Syria: see Jubb el Jarra.

Joubert, Point (zhōōbâr'), on coast of Fr. Guiana, at mouth of Sinnamary R., 50 mi. NW of Cayenne; 5°23'N 52°57'W.

Jouda, Manchuria: see Jooda.

Joudreville (zhōōdrûvēl'), town (pop. 2,051), Meurthe-et-Moselle dept., NE France, 8 mi. WNW of Briey; iron mines.

Joué-lès-Tours (zhwā-lā-tōōr'), town (pop. 2,717), Indre-et-Loire dept., W central France, 2 mi. SW of Tours; food-processing center; vineyards.

Jouet-sur-l'Aubois (zhwā-sür-lōbwä'), village (pop. 1,046), Cher dept., central France, on Aubois R. and Berry Canal, and 9 mi. WNW of Nevers; cement mfg. and shipping.

Jougne (zhōō'nyû), resort (pop. 234), Doubs dept., E France, on Swiss border, opposite Vallorbe, 10 mi. S of Pontarlier; alt. 3,280 ft. Customhouse. Winter sports.

Jounié, Lebanon: see Juniye.

Joura, India: see Jora.

Jourdanton (jûr'dûntûn), city (pop. 1,481), ⊙ Atascosa co., SW Texas, 35 mi. S of San Antonio, near Atascosa R.; rail, trade center in agr. area (peanuts, corn, cotton); cotton ginning.

Joure (you'rû), town (pop. 4,353), Friesland prov., N Netherlands, 8 mi. SE of Sneek; gold- and silverware mfg., furniture; tree nursery.

Jourimain, Cape (jōōr'ĭmăn,–mûn, Fr. zhōōrēmē'), promontory on Northumberland Strait, SE N.B., 32 mi. ENE of Sackville; 46°10'N 63°49'W.

Joutseno (yōt'sĕnō), village (commune pop. 9,527), Kymi co., SE Finland, near USSR border, near S shore of L. Saimaa, 12 mi. ENE of Lappeenranta; lumber and cellulose mills.

Joux, Fort de, France: see Cluse-et-Mijoux, La.

Joux, Lac de (läk dû zhōō'), lake (6 mi. long, max. depth 112 ft., alt. 3,296 ft.), Vaud canton, W Switzerland, in the Jura. Small Lac Brenet is N, just beyond embankment. Orbe R. enters Lac de Joux from S and leaves Lac Brenet in N. **Vallée de Joux** extends W of lake and river to Fr. border.

Jouy-sur-Morin (zhwē-sür-môrē'), village (pop. 661), Seine-et-Marne dept., N central France, on the Grand-Morin and 9 mi. ESE of Coulommiers; paper milling.

Jovellanos (hōvĕyä'nōs), town (pop. 7,036), Matanzas prov., W Cuba, on Central Highway and 29 mi. ESE of Matanzas. Rail junction and commercial center in sugar-growing region. Has foundries, machine shops, tobacco factories. The Soledad and San Vicente sugar centrals are near by (E).

Jovero, Dominican Republic: see Miches.

Jovet, Mont (mō zhôvā'), peak (8,409 ft.) of Savoy Alps, Savoie dept., SE France, bet. Isère R. (N) and Doron de Bozel R. (S), overlooking Moutiers (6 mi. W). Hostel near summit.

Joveymand, Iran: see Gonabad.

Jovita (hōvē'tä), town (pop. estimate 2,000), S Córdoba prov., Argentina, 100 mi. SSE of Río Cuarto; cereals, flax, sunflowers, cattle; dairying.

Jowai (jō'vī), village, Khasi and Jaintia Hills dist., W central Assam, India, in Khasi Hills, 22 mi. ESE of Shillong; rice, sesame, cotton.

Joy, village (pop. 505), Mercer co., NW Ill., 26 mi. SW of Rock Island, in agr. and bituminous-coal area.

Joya, La, Bolivia: see La Joya.

Joyabaj (hô-yäbäkh'), town (1950 pop. 1,260), Quiché dept., W central Guatemala, on S slope of Sierra de Chuacús, 23 mi. E of Quiché; alt. 4,200 ft.; corn, beans, livestock.

Joya Mair, W Pakistan: see Balkassar.

Joyce's Country, mountainous district of NW Co. Galway, Ireland, extending bet. Killary Harbour (W) and Lough Mask (E). Noted for picturesque scenery. Named for a Welsh family that came here in 12th cent.

Joyeuse (zhwäyûz'), village (pop. 1,084), Ardèche dept., S France, at foot of the Cévennes, 12 mi. SW of Aubenas; clothing, tanning extracts.

Joynagar, India: see Jaynagar, West Bengal.

Joyo, Korea: see Yangyang.

Joypurhat, E Pakistan: see Jaipurhat.

Jozan, Korea: see Songsan.

Jozankei, Japan: see Sapporo.

Jozsa (yō'zhŏ), Hung. *Józsa,* town (pop. 4,018), Hajdu co., E Hungary, 6 mi. NW of Debrecen; grain, cattle, hogs.

J. P. Koch Fjord (kŏk), inlet (70 mi. long, 2–10 mi. wide) of Lincoln Sea of Arctic Ocean, Peary Land region, N Greenland; 82°35'N 42°30'W. Receives large glacier. It is the W part of what was long thought to be Peary Channel.

Juab (jōō'ăb), county (□ 3,412; pop. 5,981), W Utah; ⊙ Nephi. Mining and agr. area watered in SE by Sevier R. Gypsum, quartz (for electronic equipment), rock salt, silver; beef cattle, alfalfa. Part of Goshute Indian Reservation is in NW on Nev. line. Co. formed 1852.

Juanacatlán (hwänäkätlän'), town (pop. 2,587), Jalisco, central Mexico, on Santiago (Lerma) R. and 16 mi. SE of Guadalajara; wheat, vegetables, stock. Hydroelectric plant. The famous falls here are 2d only to Niagara on North American continent; of immense horseshoe formation, they are 524 ft. wide, 70 ft. high.

Juana Díaz (hwä'nä dē'äs), town (pop. 4,743), S central Puerto Rico, 8 mi. ENE of Ponce; rail terminus in sugar-growing region; mfg. of cigars. Gypsum, marble, manganese deposits near by. U.S. military reservation and airfield is c.3 mi. S.

Juan Aldama (hwän äldä'mä), town (pop. 5,506), Zacatecas, N central Mexico, on interior plateau, near Durango border, 32 mi. NW of Nieves; alt. 6,637 ft. Silver mining; agr. (maguey, corn, livestock). Formerly San Juan de Mezquital.

Juan B. Arruabarrena (bā' ärwäbärä'nä), town (pop. estimate 2,000), NE Entre Ríos prov., Argentina, 75 mi. NNW of Concordia; rail junction (San Jaime station) and agr. center (flax, corn, livestock, poultry); corn milling. Formerly called Frontera.

Juan B. Molina (mōlē'nä), town (pop. estimate 1,000), SE Santa Fe prov., Argentina, 38 mi. S of Rosario; agr. center (corn, flax, livestock).

Juan de Acosta (dā äkōs'tä), town (pop. 1,841), Atlántico dept., N Colombia, in Caribbean lowlands, 20 mi. SW of Barranquilla; cotton growing; corn, yucca, stock.

Juan de Fuca Strait (wän" dû fū'kû) (c.100 mi. long, 11–17 mi. wide), SW B.C. and NW Wash., bet. Vancouver Isl. (N) and Wash. mainland (S), leading from the Pacific to Haro Strait and Strait of Georgia. Victoria is at NE end of strait; on SE shore is Port Angeles. Reputedly discovered 1592 by Juan de Fuca (a Greek sailor in the service of Spain), it was rediscovered (1787) by Capt. Charles Barkley and explored (1792) by Capt. George Vancouver.

Juan de Mena (hwän' dā mā'nä), town (dist. pop. 4,469), La Cordillera dept., S central Paraguay, 60 mi. ENE of Asunción; fruit, livestock. Formerly called San Rafael.

Juan de Nova Island (nō'vä), small island, dependency of Madagascar, in Mozambique Channel of Indian Ocean, 90 mi. off W coast; 17°5'S 42°18'E. Guano deposits. Also known as Saint-Christophe.

Juan Díaz (dē'äs), village (pop. 821), Panama prov., central Panama, in Pacific lowland, on Inter-American Highway and 7 mi. NE of Panama city; coconuts; stock raising, lumbering.

Juan Fernández Islands (fĕrnän'dēs) (pop. 434), Chilean group in the South Pacific, c.400 mi. W of Valparaiso, Chile; 33°36'–33°48'S 78°45'–80°47'W. Consist of 2 main isls., a small islet, and scattered rocks. The 2 larger isls. (c.100 mi. apart, E-W) are Más a Tierra (E; □ 36; c.13 mi. long) and Más Afuera (□ 33; c.6 mi. long); small Santa Clara Isl. (c.5 mi. in circumference) is just off SW tip of Más a Tierra. Volcanic in origin, rugged (El Yunque, on Más a Tierra, rises to 3,000 ft.; Más Afuera Isl. rises to 5,415 ft.), and heavily wooded, the isls. have a moderate, pleasant climate. Chief occupation is fishing for giant lobsters, which are shipped to Santiago and Buenos Aires. Discovered by the navigator Juan Fernández before 1572, possibly in 1563, they won fame when Defoe wrote *Robinson Crusoe,* generally acknowledged to have been inspired by the sojourn (1704–08) on Más a Tierra of Alexander Selkirk. In First World War, Cumberland Bay on NE Más a Tierra was site of naval battle (1915) when Ger. cruiser *Dresden* was sunk by a Br. squadron; Salinas Point, next to small village San Juan Bautista on N coast, has a lighthouse. The archipelago is under administration of Valparaiso prov.

Juan Gallegos Island (gäyā'gōs) (c.4 mi. long, 1½ mi. wide), in Gatun L., Panama Canal Zone, 9 mi. SSE of Colón. Covered by jungle, rises to 410 ft. On it is Monte Lirio railroad station of transisthmian railroad.

Juan Godoy (hwän' gōdoi'), village (1930 pop. 45), Atacama prov., N central Chile, 32 mi. S of Copiapó; rail terminus in copper- and silver-mining area.

Juan Griego or **Juangriego** (grēā'gō), town (pop. 3,104), port on Margarita Isl. in the Caribbean, Nueva Esparta state, NE Venezuela, 7 mi. NW of La Asunción; fishing (pearls, sardines, mackerel, tuna, herring).

Juan Gualberto Gômez, Cuba: see Sabanilla.

Juan Guerra (gĕ'rä), town (pop. 1,190), San Martín dept., N central Peru, landing on affluent of Mayo R. and 8 mi. S of Tarapoto, in agr. region (tobacco, coffee, cotton, sugar cane).

Juan Gulf (zhwã'), on the Mediterranean, off Alpes-Maritimes dept., SE France, on Fr. Riviera, bet. Cap de la Croisette (W) and Cap d'Antibes (E); 4 mi. wide, 2 mi. deep. Good fleet anchorage sheltered by Îles de Lérins (S). On it are resorts of Juan-les-Pins and Golfe-Juan. Formerly spelled Jouan.

Juanjuí (hwän-hwē'), city (pop. 2,254), ⊙ Mariscal Cáceres prov. (□ 8,186; enumerated pop. 9,457, plus estimated 2,000 Indians), San Martín dept., N central Peru, landing on Huallaga R. and 80 mi. SSE of Moyobamba, on road; coca, bananas, yucca.

Juankoski (yo͞o'än-kōs"kē), Swedish *Strömsdal* (strûms'däl"), village (commune pop. 2,495), Kuopio co., S central Finland, in Saimaa lake region, 20 mi. NE of Kuopio; pulp and board mills.

Juan Lacaze or **Juan L. Lacaze** (hwän' ĕ'lĕ läkä'sä), town (pop. 7,000), Colonia dept., SW Uruguay, on N bank of the Río de la Plata and 23 mi. E of Colonia. The dept.'s leading port, visited by ocean-going vessels; exports cereals, cattle, and building material to Buenos Aires (55 mi. W). Textile and paper mills. Quarries near by (NW). Officially called Sauce until 1909; its port is still sometimes referred to as Puerto Sauce or Puerto del Sauce.

Juan-les-Pins (zhwã'-lā-pē'), town (pop. 2,764), Alpes-Maritimes dept., SE France, 1 mi. SSW of Antibes, on sheltered Juan Gulf; noted summer resort on Fr. Riviera.

Juan Mata Ortíz (hwän mä'tä ōrtēs') or **Mata Ortíz**, town (pop. 1,104), Chihuahua, N Mexico, near Casas Grandes R., on railroad and 140 mi. SW of Ciudad Juárez; cotton, cereals, livestock. Formerly Pearson.

Juan Ortíz, town (pop. estimate 1,500), SE Santa Fe prov., Argentina, near Paraná R., 10 mi. NNW of Rosario; agr. center (flax, corn, wheat, alfalfa, livestock); paper and chemical industries.

Juan Soldado, Cerro de (sĕ'rō dā hwän' sōldä'dō), pre-Andean mountain (3,900 ft.), Coquimbo prov., N central Chile, near Pacific coast, N of La Serena; limestone and high-grade iron-ore deposits. Cement plant near by.

Juan Stuven Island (sto͞o'vĕn), off coast of Aysén prov., S Chile, just S of Guayaneco Isls.; 48°S 75°W; c.20 mi. long. Uninhabited.

Juan Vicente (vēsĕn'tā), beach resort, Oriente prov., E Cuba, on Nipe Bay (Atlantic), 2 mi. NW of Mayarí, 50 mi. N of Santiago de Cuba.

Juan Viñas (vē'nyäs), town (1950 pop. 407), ⊙ Jiménez canton, Cartago prov., Costa Rica, in Reventazón R. valley, near railroad, on branch of Inter-American Highway and 12 mi. ENE of Cartago. Sugar-cane center; sugar mill; coffee, stock.

Juan W. Gez (hĕs'), village (pop. estimate 500), N central San Luis prov., Argentina, at S foot of Sierra de San Luis, on railroad and 20 mi. ESE of San Luis; alt. 3,100 ft.; resort in wheat and livestock area. Formerly La Cumbre.

Juárez (hwä'rĕs), town (pop. 7,687), ⊙ Juárez dist. (□ 2,083; pop. 17,591), S central Buenos Aires prov., Argentina, 44 mi. SW of Tandil; agr. center (oats, wheat, flax, sheep, cattle).

Juárez. 1 Town (pop. 164), Chiapas, S Mexico, in Gulf lowland, 27 mi. SW of Villahermosa; cacao, rice. **2** City, Chihuahua, Mexico: see CIUDAD JUÁREZ. **3** Town (pop. 1,024), Coahuila, N Mexico, near Don Martín dam, in irrigated low plain, 26 mi. SE of Sabinas; cereals, fruit, istle fibers, cattle. **4** Town (pop. 761), Hidalgo, central Mexico, 50 mi. NNW of Pachuca; corn, wheat, beans, fruit, livestock. **5** Town (pop. 1,041), Nuevo León, N Mexico, 13 mi. E of Monterrey; chick-peas, grain, livestock.

Juárez, Sierra (syĕ'rä), range in N Lower California, NW Mexico, extends c.90 mi. SE from U.S. border, W of Laguna Salada; rises to 6,675 ft. Gold placers.

Juárez, Villa, Mexico: see VILLA JUÁREZ.

Juárez Celman, Argentina: see LA CARLOTA.

Juaso (jwä'sō), town (pop. 1,862), Ashanti, S central Gold Coast, on railroad and 40 mi. ESE of Kumasi; gold mining; cacao, cassava, corn.

Juayúa (hwäyo͞o'ä), city (pop. 3,619), Sonsonate dept., W Salvador, on Río Grande and 8 mi. N of Sonsonate; coffee-growing center; coffee processing.

Juàzeiro (zhwo͝ozā'ro͞o), city (1950 pop. 42,703), N Bahia, Brazil, on right bank of São Francisco R., opposite Petrolina (Pernambuco), 280 mi. N of Salvador; 9°25'S 40°31'W. Downstream end of river navigation from Pirapora (Minas Gerais), and terminus of railroad from Salvador; important center for shipping of caroa fibers. Railroad bridge to Petrolina built 1951. Rock crystals found in area. Has 18th-cent. church. Formerly spelled Joazeiro.

Juàzeiro do Norte (do͞o nôr'tĭ), city (pop. 23,490), S Ceará, Brazil, on Fortaleza-Crato RR and 6 mi. E of Crato; center of fertile agr. area growing sugar, cotton, cereals; sugar distilling, cotton ginning. Large recent pop. increase. Until 1944, called Juàzeiro; previously spelled Joazeiro.

Juba (jo͞o'bä), town (pop. 8,500), ⊙ Equatoria prov., S Anglo-Egyptian Sudan, on left bank of the Bahr el Jebel (White Nile) and 750 mi. S of Khartoum; 4°52'N 31°37'E. Southern gateway into Sudan, head of navigation from Khartoum on the White Nile, and transfer point for road service from Nimule (on Uganda border); administrative and commercial center. Mission station. Airfield.

Jubail or **Jubayl** (jo͝obāl'), town in Hasa, E Saudi Arabia, port on Persian Gulf, 55 mi. NNW of Dhahran; trading center; pearling. Was major Hasa port in 1920s and 1930s until development of oil industry. Also called Jubail al Bahri.

Jubaland (jo͞o'bülănd) or **Trans-Juba**, Ital. *Oltre Giuba* (ōl'trä jo͞o'bä), region of Ital. Somaliland bet. Juba R. (E) and Kenya (W), with narrow frontage on Indian Ocean (S). Formerly a part of Kenya, it was ceded (1925) to Italy, and formed a separate territory (⊙ Kismayu) until its incorporation (1926) into Ital. Somaliland.

Jub al-Jarrah, Syria: see JUBB EL JARRA.

Juban Bey, Syria: see CHOBAN BEY.

Juba River (jo͞o'bä), Ital. *Giuba*, Somali *Ganana*, in S Ital. Somaliland, formed at Dolo (Ethiopia) by confluence of GANALE DORYA and Dawa rivers, meanders c.545 mi. S, past Lugh Ferrandi, Bardera, and Giumbo, to Indian Ocean 10 mi. NE of Kismayu. Navigable for dhows to Bardera. Has 2 flood seasons (April–June, Sept.–Nov.) and variable width (260–1,150 ft.). Its valley, together with that of the Webi Shebeli, is the chief agr. region of Ital. Somaliland. Principal crops: corn, durra, sesame, rice. Formed border bet. Kenya and Ital. Somaliland until 1925, when JUBALAND was transferred to Ital. rule.

Jubayl, Lebanon: see BYBLOS.

Jubayl, Saudi Arabia: see JUBAIL.

Jubbal (jo͝ob'bŭl), former princely state (including dependencies, □ 297; pop. 29,802) of Punjab Hill States, India, SE of Simla; ⊙ was Deorha. Since 1948, merged with Himachal Pradesh.

Jubb el Jarra or **Jub al-Jarrah** (both: jo͝ob' ĕl jär-rä'), Fr. *Joub el Jarrah*, town, Homs prov., W Syria, 36 mi. ENE of Homs; cereals.

Jubbulpore (jŭb'ŭlpôr), Hindi *Jabalpur* (jŭbŭl'po͝or), district (□ 3,919; pop. 910,603), N Madhya Pradesh, India; ⊙ Jubbulpore. Bordered N and E by Vindhya Pradesh; S escarpment of central Vindhya Range in NW, spurs of Satpura Range in SE; drained by Narbada R. and its tributaries (S) and by tributaries of the Son (N). Wheat, gram, rice, millet, oilseeds in alluvial river valleys; tamarind, mahua, mangoes. Bamboo, sal, ebony, sunn hemp in forested hills (lac growing). Flour, rice, and dal milling, sawmilling, shellac mfg. Katni and Jubbulpore are rail junctions and industrial centers (ordnance, cement) near extensive bauxite, limestone, steatite, clay, and ocher workings. A rock edict of Asoka, 22 mi. N of Sihora, proves extension of his empire over N part of prov. in 3d cent. B.C. Dist. abounds in other Buddhist remains and in Hindu and Jain temple ruins (many dating from 5th cent. A.D.). Pop. 72% Hindu, 19% tribal (mainly Gond), 7% Moslem, 1% Christian.

Jubbulpore, Hindi *Jabalpur*, city (pop. including cantonment, 178,339), ⊙ Jubbulpore dist., N Madhya Pradesh, India, near Narbada R., 150 mi. NNE of Nagpur; rail and road junction; industrial center in agr. area (wheat, gram, rice, millet, oilseeds); ammunition depot; ordnance-mfg. center (gun carriages); major cement-, iron-, ceramics-, and glassworks; flour and dal milling, sawmilling, mfg. of textiles, telephone parts, furniture; lapidary industry. Has col., industrial school. Experimental farm (silk raising; dairy products). Limestone, bauxite, clay, and steatite workings near by.

Jubeil, Lebanon: see BYBLOS.

Jübek (yü'bĕk), village (pop. 1,617), in Schleswig-Holstein, NW Germany, 7 mi. NW of Schleswig; rail junction; sawmilling.

Jubilee Lake (6 mi. long, 4 mi. wide), SE N.F., 30 mi. N of Fortune Bay; 48°3'N 55°10'W.

Jublains (zhüblē'), village (pop. 278), Mayenne dept., W France, 6 mi. SE of Mayenne. Has remains of 3d-cent. Roman camp, enclosed by a double wall.

Jubones River (ho͞obō'nĕs), S Ecuador, rises in the Andes S of Cuenca, flows c.100 mi. W, past Pasaje, to the Jambeli Channel on the Pacific, 7 mi. NNE of Machala.

Jubrique (ho͞ovrē'kā), town (pop. 1,656), Málaga prov., S Spain, 12 mi. S of Ronda; grapes, chestnuts, olives; liquor distilling, sawmilling.

Juby, Cape (jo͞o'bē), or **Cape Yubi** (yo͞o'bē), headland on coast of NW Africa, in Sp. West Africa, opposite Canary Isls., 150 mi. E of Las Palmas; 27°57'N 12°55'W. On it is town of Villa Bens (formerly Tarfaia or Tarfaya).

Júcaro (ho͞o'kärō), village (pop. 868), Camagüey prov., E Cuba, landing on the Caribbean, 16 mi. SSW of Ciego de Ávila (linked by rail). Ships timber.

Júcar River (ho͞o'kär), E Spain, in Cuenca, Albacete, and Valencia provs.; rises on W slopes of the Montes Universales, flows S, past Cuenca, turning E near La Roda, to the Mediterranean at Cullera; 310 mi. long. In lower course it feeds several irrigation canals.

Jucás (zho͞okäs'), city (pop. 825), S Ceará, Brazil, on upper Jaguaribe R. and 22 mi. SW of Iguatu; coffee, cotton, tobacco. Magnesite deposits. Irrigation dam and reservoir under construction at Cariús, just SE. Until 1944, called São Mateus (formerly spelled São Matheus).

Jüchen (yü'khŭn), village (pop. 5,151), in former Prussian Rhine Prov., W Germany, after 1945 in North Rhine-Westphalia, 5 mi. SSE of Rheydt.

Jucheng or **Ju-ch'eng** (both: ro͞o'chŭng'), town, ⊙ Jucheng co. (pop. 140,235), SE Hunan prov., China, near Kwangtung-Kiangsi line, 55 mi. NNE of Kükong; rice, wheat, cotton, hemp. Tungsten, tin, bismuth, and zinc found near by. Until 1913, Kweiyang.

Juchipila (ho͞ochēpē'lä), city (pop. 2,821), Zacatecas, N central Mexico, on Juchipila R. and 32 mi. SSE of Tlaltenango; alt. 4,429 ft.; agr. center (grain, sugar cane, tobacco, fruit, stock).

Juchipila River, in Zacatecas, N central Mexico, rises on interior plateau N of Villanueva, flows S c.120 mi., past Villanueva, Jalpa, and Juchipila, to Santiago (Lerma) R. 28 mi. NNW of Guadalajara.

Juchique de Ferrer (ho͞ochē'kā dā fĕrĕr'), town (pop. 529), Veracruz, E Mexico, 27 mi. NE of Jalapa; corn, coffee.

Juchitán (ho͞ochētän'), officially Juchitán de Zaragoza, city (pop. 14,550), Oaxaca, S Mexico, in S lowland of Isthmus of Tehuantepec, on railroad, on Inter-American Highway bet. Mexico city and Guatemala, and 15 mi. ENE of Tehuantepec. Trading, processing, and agr. center (rice, sugar cane, coffee, tropical fruit, vegetables, livestock); sugar refining, saltmaking; mfg. of soap, palm-fiber cloth. Airfield. Colorful market. An old Indian city, it rivals Tehuantepec as cultural center of Zapotec Indians.

Juchitepec (ho͞ochētäpĕk'), officially Juchitepec de Mariano Riva Palacio, town (pop. 3,682), Mexico state, central Mexico, 29 mi. SSE of Mexico city; agr. center (cereals, vegetables, stock).

Juchitlán (ho͞ochētlän'), town (pop. 2,354), Jalisco, W Mexico, 31 mi. S of Ameca; alt. 4,058 ft.; agr. center (grain, sugar cane, flax, fruit, tobacco).

Juchow, China: see LINJU.

Jucuapa (ho͞okwä'pä), city (pop. 6,711), Usulutan dept., E Salvador, near Inter-American Highway, 12 mi. NNE of Usulután, at NE foot of volcano Jucuapa (alt. 5,540 ft.); coffee, grain, livestock.

Jucuarán (ho͞okwärän'), town (pop. 1,404), Usulután dept., SE Salvador, 13 mi. SE of Usulután, at W end of Jucuarán coastal range (rising to 3,113 ft.); grain; lumbering; collecting of medicinal plants.

Jucurutu (zho͞oko͞oro͞oto͞o'), city (pop. 807), central Rio Grande do Norte, NE Brazil, on Piranhas R. and 35 mi. S of Açu; cotton. Formerly called São Miguel de Jucurutu.

Jud (jŭd), village (pop. 175), La Moure co., SE central N.Dak., 12 mi. NW of Edgeley.

Juda, village, Green co., S Wis., 7 mi. E of Monroe, in livestock, dairy, and grain region.

Judaea or **Judea** (jo͞odē'ŭ), Greco-Roman name for S Palestine, the area now occupied by SW Israel and W Jordan. The southernmost of the Roman divisions of Palestine, it was cut off from the Mediterranean by a strip of Samaria. It bordered E on the Jordan and the Dead Sea, and its N boundary with Samaria ran WSW from the Jordan E of Mt. Ebal; its S boundary ran ESE-WNW from Engedi nearly to Ashdod. Idumaea was to S. It is a hilly region sloping steeply toward Dead Sea and gently toward Judaean Plain and Mediterranean. Rises to 3,340 ft. 3 mi. N of Hebron. Jerusalem is chief city; in densely populated and agr. Judaean Plain are Lydda, Ramle, Rishon le Zion, and Rehovot. Rugged E part of region is known as Wilderness of Judaea.

Judda or **Juddah**, Saudi Arabia: see JIDDA.

Judea, Palestine: see JUDAEA.

Judeide, Jdeide, or **Judaydah** (all: jo͝odā'dŭ, jŭdā'dŭ), Fr. *Djedeide* or *Jedeideh*, village, central Lebanon, near Mediterranean Sea, 5 mi. E of Beirut; sericulture, cotton, tobacco, cereals, lemons.

Judenburg (yo͞o'dŭnbo͝ork), city (pop. 10,285), Styria, S central Austria, on Mur R. and 37 mi. WNW of Graz; steel- and ironworks; scythes; summer resort. Once important Roman road center; has 9th-cent. church, 15th-cent. bell tower. Stalactite cave, ruins of Liechtenstein castle near by.

Judendorf-Strassengel (yo͞o'dŭndôrf-shträs'ĕngŭl), town (pop. 2,362), Styria, SE Austria, 7 mi. NW of Graz; grain, cattle.

Judge and Clerk: see MACQUARIE ISLAND.

Judge Daly Promontory (dā'lē), NE Ellesmere Isl., NE Franklin Dist., Northwest Territories, peninsula (100 mi. long, 10–48 mi. wide), on Kennedy Channel; 81°N 67°W. Terminates NE at Cape Baird. Rises to c.6,000 ft. near base of peninsula.

Judith, Point, R.I.: see POINT JUDITH.

Judith Basin, county (□ 1,880; pop. 3,200), central Mont.; ⊙ Stanford. Agr. region drained by branches of Judith R. Grain, livestock. Part of Lewis and Clark Natl. Forest and Little Belt Mts. in SW. Formed 1920.

Judith Gap, city (pop. 175), Wheatland co., central Mont., 17 mi. N of Harlowton.

Judith River, central Mont., rises in Little Belt Mts., flows 124 mi. NE, past Utica and Hobson, to Missouri R. 18 mi. NW of Winifred.

Judson. 1 Town (pop. 96), Parke co., W Ind., 28 mi. NNE of Terre Haute, in agr. and bituminous-coal area. **2** Village (pop. 11,008, with near-by Brandon), Greenville co., NW S.C., a suburb of Greenville.

Judsonia (jŭdsō'nēŭ), town (pop. 1,122), White co., central Ark., c.50 mi. NE of Little Rock and on Little Red R., in strawberry-producing area; ships strawberries, strawberry plants. Cotton ginning, box mfg.

Juelsminde (yo͞ol'smĭnü), town (pop. 1,036), Vejle amt, E Jutland, Denmark, on the Little Belt, and 19 mi. E of Vejle; cement, paint; fish canning.

Jue Shan (jü' shän'), Mandarin *Ch'ü Shan* (chü'), island of Chusan Archipelago, in E.China Sea, Chekiang prov., China; 30°28'N 122°20'E; 9 mi. long, 3 mi. wide.

Juggernaut, India: see Puri, TOWN.

Jugohama, Japan: see OKACHI.

Jugon (zhügõ'), village (pop. 443), Côtes-du-Nord dept., W France, on lake formed by Arguenon R., 13 mi. WSW of Dinan; tanning, fishing.

Jugoslavia: see YUGOSLAVIA.

Jugsalai, India: see TATANAGAR.

Juhaynah, Egypt: see GILHEINA.

Juhi (jo͞o'hē), suburban town (pop. 54,092) in Cawnpore municipality, Cawnpore dist., S Uttar Pradesh, India, 2.5 mi. SW of Cawnpore city center; oilseed milling, soap mfg. Also called Juhi Bari.

Juhu (jo͞o'ho͞o), town (pop. 3,393), Bombay Suburban dist., W Bombay, India, on Salsette Isl., 12 mi. N of Bombay city center; popular bathing resort on Arabian Sea; fishing.

Juian (rwā'än'), town (pop. 36,042), ⊙ Juian co. (pop. 538,810), SE Chekiang prov., China, 15 mi. S of Wenchow, on E.China Sea; fishing port; saltworks; rice, wheat, tea, indigo.

Juichang or **Jui-ch'ang** (rwā'chäng'), town (pop. 4,957), ⊙ Juichang co. (pop. 115,380), N Kiangsi prov., China, 18 mi. WSW of Kiukiang; rice, cotton, tea, tobacco; exports hemp, indigo. Iron and anthracite mines. Also spelled Shuichang.

Juicheng or **Jui-ch'eng** (rwā'chŭng'), town, ⊙ Juicheng co. (pop. 66,239), SW Shansi prov., China, 25 mi. ESE of Yüngtsi, near Yellow R. (Honan line); mfg. (bamboo articles, cotton textiles); wheat. Until 1912 called Kiangchow.

Jui-chin, China: see JUIKIN.

Juichow, China: see KAOAN.

Juifang (rwā'fäng'), Jap. *Zuiho* (zo͞o'ēhō), town, N Formosa, on railroad and 5 mi. ESE of Keelung; gold-mining center; also silver and copper mining.

Juigalpa (hwēgäl'pä), city (1950 pop. 3,245), ⊙ Chontales dept., S Nicaragua, 65 mi. E of Managua (linked by road); agr. center (sugar cane, coffee, grain), livestock; beverage mfg., coffee processing, tanning.

Juigné-sur-Sarthe (zhwēnyā'-sür-särt'), village (pop. 264), Sarthe dept., W France, 3 mi. NE of Sablé-sur-Sarthe; anthracite mine.

Juikin or **Jui-chin** (both: rwā'jĭn'), town (pop. 21,769), ⊙ Juikin co. (pop. 184,631), S Kiangsi prov., China, 68 mi. E of Kanchow and on Kung R. (right headstream of Kan R.); ramie, rice, tea, tobacco, sugar cane. Gold and anthracite mines. Also spelled Shuikin. Was hq. (1927–34) of Chinese Communists.

Juili (rwā'lē'), district (pop. 13,660) of westernmost Yunnan prov., China, on Shweli R. (Burma border). Its administrative seats of LASA (winter and spring) and MENGMAO (summer and fall) are also known as Juili.

Juili River, China: see SHWELI RIVER.

Juillac (zhwēyäk'), village (pop. 826), Corrèze dept., S central France, in Brive Basin, 15 mi. NW of Brive-La-Gaillarde; chestnut trade; vegetable canning, furniture mfg.

Juimand, Iran: see GONABAD.

Juist (yüst), North Sea island (□ 6.5; pop. 1,625) of East Frisian group, Germany, off Ems R. estuary, 7 mi. NW of Norddeich (steamer connection); 9 mi. long (E-W), c.½ mi. wide (N-S). Nordseebad Juist (center) is resort.

Juiz de Fora (zhwēs' dĭ fô'rü), city (1950 pop. 86,819), southern Minas Gerais, Brazil, in a valley of the Serra da Mantiqueira, on Paraibuna R. and 80 mi. N of Rio de Janeiro; 21°46'S 43°38'W; alt. 2,170 ft. Rail junction; leading industrial center of Minas Gerais and its 2d largest city, on Belo Horizonte–Rio de Janeiro highway; sometimes called "The Manchester of Brazil," it is 1st in production of knitted goods. Other industries are sugar refining, metal- and woodworking, brewing, tire mfg. Ships tobacco products, coffee, cereals, vegetable oil, medicinal plants. Has schools of engineering (founded 1914), law, pharmacy, and dentistry; and noted mus. Temperate climate. Old name, Parahybuna.

Jujo, Korea: see YUSONG.

Jujurieux (zhüzhürēû'), village (pop. 1,124), Ain dept., E France, at foot of the SW Jura, 12 mi. SW of Nantua; silk weaving, cement mfg.

Jujuy (ho͞o-ho͞o'ē), province (□ 22,962; pop. 166,700), NW Argentina; ⊙ Jujuy. In the Andes and the *puna* region, bordering Chile and Bolivia. Drained by the Río Grande de Jujuy and San Francisco R. Its lower mtn. ranges are covered with forests. Climate varies according to alt., but the fertile inhabited valleys have humid, semitropical climate. Among its rich mineral resources are lead (Aguilar, Humahuaca, Mina Pirquitas), iron (Sierra de Zapla), tin (Cerro Galán, Rinconada dept.), copper (Purmamarca), kaolin, sodium and borax salts (Salar de Caurchari, Salinas Grandes). Agr. mainly in irrigated valleys: sugar cane, corn, alfalfa, fruit, potatoes, grapes, cotton, tobacco, livestock (cattle, sheep); donkeys and llamas also raised in higher altitudes. Fisheries in main rivers. Rural industries: mining, lumbering, spinning, dairying, cotton ginning. Mfg. concentrated at Jujuy, La Esperanza, San Pedro, Ledesma, La Mendieta, Palpalá. Major resorts, noted for mild winters, are Reyes, Humahuaca, and Jujuy. Prov. was founded 1834, when it was separated from Salta. When Los Andes territory was dissolved (1943), Susques dept. (SW) was inc. into Jujuy prov.

Jujuy, city (pop. 30,764), ⊙ Jujuy prov. and Jujuy dept. (□ 960; 1947 pop. 42,016), NW Argentina, on S bank of the Río Grande de Jujuy, on railroad, and 800 mi. NW of Buenos Aires, 45 mi. NNE of Salta; 24°12'S 65°17'W; alt. 4,215 ft. Resort, agr., trade, mining, and lumbering center. Mfg.: lead foundry, flour- and sawmills, dairy industry. Trade in timber, minerals, and agr. products (grain, fruit, livestock). Asphalt and lead deposits near by. Hydroelectric station on the river. Fisheries. Has administrative bldgs., govt. house, cathedral, 17th-cent. chapel, natl. col., historical mus., seismographic station. An old colonial city, founded 1593 near an Indian village.

Jujuy River, Argentina: see GRANDE DE JUJUY, Río.

Jukao (ro͞o'gou'), town (1935 pop. 183,268), ⊙ Jukao co. (1946 pop. 1,541,192), N Kiangsu prov., China, 65 mi. E of Yangchow; agr. center (wheat, rice, rapeseed, corn, cotton).

Jukkasjarvi, Sweden: see KIRUNA.

Julamerk, Turkey: see HAKARI, town.

Julesburg (jo͞olz'bûrg), town (pop. 1,951), ⊙ Sedgwick co., extreme NE Colo., on South Platte R., near Nebr. line, and 55 mi. NE of Sterling; trade center and railroad div. point in sugar-beet region; flour. Fish hatchery here. Founded 1881, inc. 1886.

Julfa or **Jolfa** (both: jōlfä'). **1** Town, Third Prov., in Azerbaijan, NW Iran, 65 mi. NNW of Tabriz, and on Aras R. (USSR border), adjoining Dzhulfa; road center and terminus of railroad from Tabriz. Pop. largely Armenian. Sometimes spelled Djulfa. **2** Suburb of ISFAHAN, Tenth Prov., Iran.

Juli (ho͞o'lē), town (pop. 2,630), ⊙ Chucuito prov. (□ 4,826; pop. 127,815), Puno dept., SE Peru, on SW shore of L. Titicaca, near mouth of small Juli R., 40 mi. SE of Puno (connected by steamer service and road); alt. 12,697 ft. Potatoes, quinoa, barley, livestock (sheep, llamas, alpacas, vicuñas).

Juliaca (ho͞olyä'kä), city (pop. 7,002), ⊙ San Román prov. (□ 11,228; pop. 31,663), Puno dept., SE Peru, on the Altiplano, 24 mi. NNW of Puno; alt. 12,730 ft. Rail junction of lines from Arequipa and Cuzco; commercial center. Native woolen textiles; wool, hides; barley, potatoes, livestock.

Juliaetta (jo͞o"lyŭĕ'tŭ), village (pop. 365), Latah co., W Idaho, 18 mi. SE of Moscow and on Potlatch R.; grain, potatoes, beans, livestock.

Julia Molina or **Villa Julia Molina** (vē'yä ho͞ol'yä mōlē'nä), town (1950 pop. 5,249), Samaná prov., N Dominican Republic, on the coast, 29 mi. E of San Francisco de Macorís, in rice- and cacao-growing region.

Julian, village (pop. 123), Nemaha co., SE Nebr., 8 mi. N of Auburn, near Missouri R.

Juliana Canal (Du. yülēä'nä), Limburg prov., SE Netherlands; extends 21 mi.N-S, lateral to non-navigable section of Maas R. bet. Maasbracht (5.5 mi. SW of Roermond) and Borgharen (1.5 mi. N of Maastricht). Navigable by ships up to 2,000 tons; chiefly carries coal.

Julian Alps (jo͞o'lyŭn), Slovenian *Juliske Alpe*, Ital. *Alpi Giulie*, Ger. *Julische Alpen*, division of Eastern Alps, NW Yugoslavia and NE Italy; extend SE from Carnic Alps at Tarvisio to Ljubljana area. Bounded N by Karawanken range, NW by Fella R. and Camporosso Pass, E by upper Sava R. Divided by Predil Pass into 2 subgroups. Constitute part of watershed bet. Adriatic Sea and Black Sea. Highest peak, Triglav (c.9,395 ft.). Others are Jôf del Montasio, Skrlatica, Mt. Mangart, Jalovec, Mt. Canin, and Krn. High intermontane valleys include the Planica, Trenta, Vrata, Kot, and Krma. Tourist resorts on Bled and Bohinj lakes. Rich flora; numerous chamois.

Julianehaab (yo͞olyä'nühôp"), town (pop. 936), ⊙ Julianehaab dist. and colony (pop. 4,186), SW Greenland, on Igaliko Fjord, near its mouth on the Atlantic; 60°43'N 46°1'W. Seaport and trade center of S Greenland, in most populous part of isl. Has hosp., radio station. Meat and wool packing, seal hunting; fish canning near by. In cattle-sheep-, goat-raising region. Founded 1775. Near by was site of *Brattahlid*, 1st Norse settlement in Greenland, founded (985) by Eric the Red.

Jülich (yü'lĭkh), town (1939 pop. 11,587; 1946 pop. 6,831), in former Prussian Rhine Prov., W Germany, after 1945 in North Rhine-Westphalia, on the Rur and 15 mi. NE of Aachen; rail junction; leatherworking, paper milling, sugar refining. Duchy of Jülich, of which it was ⊙, was created (1356) from counties of Jülich and Berg. Passed 1524 to dukes of Cleves, and after 1666 to a branch of house of Wittelsbach; and to Prussia in 1815. Town practically obliterated by air attacks and artillery shelling (Nov., 1944–Feb., 1945).

Juliénas (zhülyānä'), village (pop. 218), Rhône dept., E central France, 8 mi. SW of Mâcon; noted wines.

Julier, Piz, Switzerland: see PIZ JULIER.

Julier Pass (zhülyā') (7,507 ft.), in Rhaetian Alps, SE Switzerland, 5 mi. WSW of St. Moritz; connects Upper Engadine and Oberhalbstein valleys. Used since antiquity, it is crossed by modern Julier Road (built 1820–40), from Chur to Silvaplana.

Julimes (ho͞olē'mĕs), town (pop. 1,093), Chihuahua, N Mexico, on Conchos R. (irrigation) and 40 mi. ESE of Chihuahua; alt. 3,838 ft.; grain, beans, cattle. Sulphur thermal springs.

Julin, Poland: see WOLIN, town.

Julio, 9 de, department, Argentina: see SIERRA COLORADA.

Julio, 9 de, city, Argentina: see NUEVE DE JULIO.

Julio, 18 de, Uruguay: see DIEZ Y OCHO DE JULIO.

Juliobona, France: see LILLEBONNE.

Juliobriga, Portugal: see BRAGANÇA.

Júlio de Castilhos (zho͞o'lyo͝o dĭ kŭstē'lyo͝os), city (pop. 2,649), central Rio Grande do Sul, Brazil, in the Serra Geral, on railroad and 30 mi. N of Santa Maria; cattle slaughtering and by-products processing; rice, tobacco.

Juliomagus, France: see ANGERS.

Jul Lake (yo͞ol), Dan. *Julsø*, largest (5 mi. long, 1 mi. wide) of the Himmelbjaerget lakes, E Jutland, Denmark, c.20 mi. W of Aarhus; surrounded by forests.

Jullouville, France: see BOUILLON.

Jullundur (jŭlŭn'dŭr), district (□ 1,334; pop. 1,127,190), central Punjab, India; ⊙ Jullundur. Bounded S by Sutlej R., W by Patiala and East Punjab States Union. Agr. (wheat, corn, gram, cotton, sugar cane); carpentry, hand-loom weaving. Chief towns: Jullundur, Kartarpur, Phillaur, Nakodar. Formerly also spelled Jalandhar.

Jullundur, city (pop., including cantonment area, 135,283), ⊙ Jullundur dist., India, 215 mi. NNW of New Delhi, 75 mi. ESE of Lahore. Rail and road junction; trade center; agr. market (wheat, sugar cane, gram, cotton); mfg. of silk fabrics, celluloid toys, cigarettes, nuts, bolts, agr. implements, hosiery, flour; hand-loom weaving, dyeing, tanning, oilseed pressing. Noted handicraft carpentry, especially lacquered woodwork, ivory inlays, and carriages. Col., engineering institute, Western Univ. Agr. farm just S. Was ⊙ Rajput kingdom when visited (7th cent. A.D.) by Hsüan-Tsang; taken by Ranjit Singh in 1811.

Jumaima, Saudi Arabia: see RAFHA.

Jumaisa, Iraq: see SUWAIRA.

Jumaitepeque (ho͞omītāpā'kā), extinct volcano (5,938 ft.), Santa Rosa dept., S Guatemala, 5 mi. NNE of Cuilapa. On N slope is Jumaitepeque village (pop. 2,208). Sometimes spelled Jumaytepeque.

Jumay (ho͞omī'), extinct volcano (7,218 ft.), Jalapa dept., E central Guatemala, 3 mi. N of Jalapa.

Jumaya, Greece: see HERAKLEIA.

Jumaytepeque, Guatemala: see JUMAITEPEQUE.

Jumbilla (ho͞ombē'yä), town (pop. 674), ⊙ Bongará prov. (in 1940: □ 8,683; enumerated pop. 7,598, plus estimated 20,000 Indians), Amazonas dept., N Peru, on E Andean slopes, 25 mi. NNE of Chachapoyas; sugar cane, cotton, coca, fruit.

Jumbo Mountain (11,217 ft.), SE B.C., in Selkirk Mts., 70 mi. NNE of Nelson; 50°24'N 116°34'W.

Jumbor, Thailand: see CHUMPHON.

Jumeaux (zhümō'), village (pop. 986), Puy-de-Dôme dept., central France, on the Allier and 9 mi. SSE of Issoire; mfg. of cigarette paper.

Jumekoonta, India: see JAMIKUNTA.

Jumento Cays, Bahama Isls.: see RAGGED ISLAND AND CAYS.

Jumet (zhümā'), town (pop. 28,764), Hainaut prov., S central Belgium, 3 mi. N of Charleroi; glass-mfg. center (window glass, bottles, mirrors); coal mine.

Jumièges (zhümyĕzh'), village (pop. 1,044), Seine-Inférieure dept., N France, in Seine R. and 13 mi. W of Rouen. Has ruins of well-known Benedictine abbey (founded 7th cent.) with 11th-cent. abbatial church.

Jumilhac-le-Grand (zhümēläk'-lü-grã'), village (pop. 533), Dordogne dept., SW France, on Isle R. and 19 mi. ESE of Nontron; flour milling, fruit and early-vegetable shipping.

Jumilla (ho͞omē'lyä), city (pop. 15,426), Murcia prov., SE Spain, 16 mi. N of Cieza; wine-producing center. Brandy and alcohol distilling, esparto processing, flour- and sawmilling, olive pressing; mfg. of footwear, knit goods, furniture, baskets, candy, sausage. Ships saffron, almonds, and olives. Limestone and gypsum quarries, saltworks near by. Has 15th-cent. church, medieval castle.

Jumiltepec (ho͞omĕltāpĕk'), town (pop. 1,204), Morelos, central Mexico, 30 mi. E of Cuernavaca; corn, sugar cane, fruit, stock.

Jumla (jo͝om'lŭ), town, W Nepal, on left tributary of Karnali (Gogra) R. and 20 mi. NW of Katmandu; corn, millet, vegetables, fruit. Important Nepalese military post.

Jummoo, Kashmir: see JAMMU.

Jumna Canal, Eastern (jo͝om'nŭ), important irrigation system in Uttar Pradesh, India; from left bank of Jumna R. (headworks at Tajewala, Punjab) runs 130 mi. S, parallel to river's left bank, to point just E of Delhi. Irrigates Saharanput, Muzaffarnagar, and Meerut dists. in rich agr. area. Opened 1830.

Jumna Canal, Western, important irrigation system in Punjab and in Patiala and East Punjab States Union, India. From headworks on Jumna R. at Tajewala (Ambala dist.) it parallels right bank of river for 52 mi. SW, whence a right branch flows c.150 mi. WSW to Sirsa (Hissar dist.). Main canal again divides, 31 mi. SSW, into 2 branches: W branch flows c.120 mi. WSW, past Hansi and Hissar, to NE of Bhadra (Rajasthan); E branch flows c.75 mi. SSE to New Delhi. System has numerous distributaries. Original channel (to Hissar) built in mid-14th cent.; repaired by Akbar in 1568. Other branches constructed in 1870s.

Jumna River, N India, rises in W Kumaun Himalayas near Jamnotri, flows generally SW through Kumaun Himalayas and Siwalik Range (here forming SE border of Himachal Pradesh), S along Indian Punjab-Uttar Pradesh border, past Delhi, Brindaban, and Muttra, and SE past Agra, Etawah, Kalpi, Hamirpur, and Mau to the Ganges at Allahabad, forming one of most sacred confluences in India; length, c.860 mi. W boundary of Ganges-Jumna Doab. Chief tributaries: Chambal, Sind, Betwa, and Ken rivers, all flowing from S. Feeds Eastern and Western Jumna Canals and AGRA CANAL; drains total area of □ c.118,000. The *Jomanes* of Pliny, *Diamouna* of Ptolemy, *Jobares* of Arrian. Also spelled Jamuna and Yamuna.

Jumneta, Poland: see WOLIN, town.

Jumonji (jōō'mōnjē), town (pop. 5,456), Akita prefecture, N Honshu, Japan, 6 mi. SSW of Yokote; agr. (rice, fruit), stock raising.

Jump River, N central Wis., formed by 2 forks rising in Price co., flows c.70 mi. SW, through wooded region, to Chippewa R. 13 mi. S of Ladysmith.

Junacas (hōōnä'käs), town (pop. c.2,400), Tarija dept., S Bolivia, on road and 18 mi. NE of Tarija; vineyards; fruit, grain, livestock.

Junagarh (jōōnä'gŭr) or **Junagadh** (–gŭd), former princely state (□ 3,337; pop. 670,719) of Western India States agency, on S Kathiawar peninsula, India; ⊙ was Junagarh. In 1947, despite predominantly Hindu pop., Moslem ruler acceded to Pakistan; however, India took over administration of state; since 1949 merged with Saurashtra.

Junagarh or **Junagadh,** city (pop. 58,111), ⊙ Sorath dist., S Saurashtra, India, 55 mi. SSW of Rajkot, near Girnar hill; rail junction; agr. market (cotton, millet, oilseeds, sugar cane); local trade in ghee, salt, timber, building stone; mfg. of pharmaceutical products, hats, brass- and copperware; hand-loom weaving, embroidering, oilseed pressing. Has col., mus., technical school, and several fine tombs of former rulers. On E side is Uparkot, the walled citadel of old Hindu kings. Some rock-cut Buddhist caves date from 3d cent. B.C. A Rajput stronghold until captured in 15th cent. by Moslems. Was ⊙ former Western India state of Junagarh.

Junan (rōō'nän'), town, ⊙ Junan co. (pop. 611,482), SE central Honan prov., China, 45 mi. SSE of Yencheng; millet, beans. Until 1913, Juning.

Juncal (hōōng-käl'), town (pop. estimate 1,000), S Santa Fe prov., Argentina, 55 mi. SSW of Rosario, in grain and livestock area.

Juncal, Cerro (sĕ'rō), Andean peak (19,880 ft.) on Argentina-Chile border, N of Nevado del Plomo massif; 33°6'S.

Juncal, Lake (hōōng-käl') (□ 50), E Río Negro natl. territory, Argentina, 4 mi. S of Viedma, along the lower course of the Río Negro; 24 mi. long, 2–4 mi. wide.

Juncos (hōōng'kōs), town (pop. 8,285), E Puerto Rico, 21 mi. SE of San Juan; sugar- and tobacco-growing center; alcohol distilling. Large sugar mill 1 mi. N.

Juncosa (hōōng-kō'sä), village (pop. 1,011), Lérida prov., NE Spain, 19 mi. SSE of Lérida; sheep raising; olive oil, wine, almonds.

Junction. 1 Village (pop. 239), Gallatin co., SE Ill., 17 mi. E of Harrisburg, in agr. area. **2** City (pop. 2,471), ⊙ Kimble co., W central Texas, on Edwards Plateau, c.100 mi. NW of San Antonio, at junction of North Llano and South Llano rivers to form Llano R.; important market and shipping center for wool, mohair, livestock; tile mfg.; also agr. (cotton, grain) in area. Scenery, hunting, fishing attract visitors. Settled 1876, inc. 1928. **3** Town (pop. 285), ⊙ Piute co., S Utah, 22 mi. E of Beaver and on Piute Reservoir (impounds water of Sevier R. for irrigation); alt. 6,250 ft. Agr. and cattle area.

Junction City. 1 Town (pop. 259), Talbot co., W Ga., 32 mi. ENE of Columbus; furniture mfg. **2** Village (pop. 353), Marion co., S Ill., 3 mi. N of Centralia, in agr., oil, and bituminous-coal area. **3** City (pop. 13,462), ⊙ Geary co., E central Kansas, at confluence of Smoky Hill and Republican rivers (here forming Kansas R.) c.60 mi. W of Topeka; trade and shipping center, with railroad repair shops, for grain and livestock area; flour milling, dairying. Limestone quarries near by. Founded 1858, inc. 1859. Grew as supply point for Fort Riley (4 mi. NE; active military post, established 1852 for protection of travelers on Santa Fe Trail). Marshall Air Force Base is near fort. **4** Town (pop. 988), Boyle co., central Ky., 4 mi. S of Danville, in outer Bluegrass region; makes tobacco baskets. **5** Town (pop. 1,527; in Ark., 1,013; in La., 514), in Claiborne and Union parishes, N La., and in Union co., S Ark., 14 mi. S of El Dorado, Ark.; lumber milling; truck, dairy products, poultry, watermelons. **6** Village (pop. 805), Perry co., central Ohio, 5 mi. W of New Lexington; pottery, lumber; coal mining. **7** City (pop. 1,475), Lane co., W Oregon, 12 mi. NNW of Eugene, near Willamette R.; shipping point for seeds and canned goods; lumber milling, canning, dairying. Inc. 1872. **8** Village (pop. 330), Portage co., central Wis., 14 mi. NNE of Wisconsin Rapids; railroad junction; makes cheese.

Jundiaí (zhōōndyäē'). **1** City, Paraná, Brazil: see CINZAS. **2** City (1950 pop. 39,560), SE São Paulo, Brazil, 28 mi. NNW of São Paulo; rail center (end of line to Santos); cotton textile mills, foundries, match and pottery factories. Agr. trade (grapes, wine, grain, coffee). Tungsten ore mined at near-by Itupeva. Founded 1655. Formerly spelled Jundiahy.

Jundiaí River, Rio Grande do Norte, NE Brazil, flows 50 mi. E to the Potengi just above Natal. Navigable below Macaíba. Intermittent-flowing stream. Formerly spelled Jundiahy.

Juneau (jōō'nō), city (pop. 5,956), ⊙ Alaska, in SE part of territory, near Yukon border, on Gastineau Channel, just across from Douglas Isl. (suspension bridge to Douglas), at foot of Mt. Juneau (3,590 ft.) and Mt. Robert (3,600 ft.); 58°18'N 134°24'W. Sea and fishing port, ice-free the year round, with salmon canneries, lumber mills; supply center for gold-mining, fur-farming region; port of entry. Has many territorial and Federal offices; Alaska Historical Library. Airport; seaplane base. Mean temp. ranges from 27.8°F (Jan.) to 56.7°F (July); mean annual rainfall 83.72 inches. Founded 1880 after gold strike near by, later declined in importance; ⊙ moved here 1900 from Sitka; govt. offices were not transferred until 1906.

Juneau, county (□ 795; pop. 18,930), central Wis.; ⊙ Mauston. Predominantly agr. area (dairy products, livestock, potatoes, canning crops). Processing of dairy products is principal industry. Bounded E by Wisconsin R.; drained by Yellow, Lemonweir, and Baraboo rivers. Dells of the Wisconsin in SE. Includes Necedah Natl. Wildlife Refuge, Rocky Arbor State Park. Formed 1856.

Juneau, city (pop. 1,444), ⊙ Dodge co., S central Wis., 7 mi. SE of Beaver Dam, in dairying region; produces hemp, boilers, cheese, canned vegetables. Inc. 1887.

Juneda (hōōnā'dhä), town (pop. 3,165), Lérida prov., NE Spain, 12 mi. ESE of Lérida; soap mfg., olive-oil and wine processing; agr. trade (cereals, sugar beets, tobacco).

Junee (jōō'nē'), municipality (pop. 4,010), S New South Wales, Australia, 95 mi. WNW of Canberra; rail junction; sheep, agr. center.

June Lake, Mono co., E Calif., resort lake in the Sierra Nevada, S of Mono L. and c.50 mi. NW of Bishop; c.1½ mi. long; trout fishing.

Jung-, for Chinese names beginning thus and not found here: see under YUNG-.

Jung, river, China: see JUNG RIVER.

Junga (jōōng'gŭ), village, central Himachal Pradesh, India, 6 mi. SSE of Simla; local market for corn, rice, timber. Was ⊙ former Punjab Hill state of Keonthal.

Jungapeo (hōōng-gäpā'ō), town (pop. 1,890), Michoacán, central Mexico, 20 mi. S of Hidalgo; cereals, fruit, livestock.

Jungaria, China: see DZUNGARIA.

Jungbunzlau, Czechoslovakia: see MLADA BOLESLAV.

Jungchang or **Jung-ch'ang** (rōōng'chäng'), town (pop. 29,567), ⊙ Jungchang co. (pop. 349,577), S Szechwan prov., China, on railroad and 65 mi. WSW of Chungking city; ramie-producing center; exports hog bristles; grows rice, sugar cane, wheat, rapeseed, kaoliang. Coal mines near by.

Jungcheng or **Jung-ch'eng** (rōōng'chŭng'). **1** Town, ⊙ Jungcheng co. (pop. 88,882), central Hopeh prov., China, 25 mi. NE of Paoting; winegrowing center; wheat, kaoliang, chestnuts. **2** Town, ⊙ Jungcheng co. (pop. 277,985), easternmost Shantung prov., China, 25 mi. ESE of Weihai on Yellow Sea; fisheries, saltworks.

Jung-chiang, China: see JUNGKIANG.

Jung-ching, China: see JUNGKING.

Jungfrau (yōōng'frou) [Ger.,=the virgin], peak (13,653 ft.) in Bernese Alps, S central Switzerland, 11 mi. SSE of Interlaken, on border of Bern and Valais cantons. First ascended in 1811. Jungfrau Firn extends to SE. The Jungfraujoch, pass bet. the Jungfrau and the Mönch, is highest point (11,412 ft.; also given as 11,342 ft.) in Europe reached by rail; noted for fine views and sports; Alpine research station here. The Sphinx, rocky peak (11,733 ft.) above the Jungfraujoch, has a meteorological station.

Jung-ha, Tibet: see JONGKA.

Jungho, China: see YUNGHO, Shansi prov.

Junghsien (rōōng'shyĕn'). **1** or **Yunghsien** (yōōng'–), town, ⊙ Junghsien co. (pop. 185,000), N Kwangsi prov., China, 50 mi. N of Liuchow and on Liu R.; cotton-textiles mfg., papermaking, tung-oil processing; rice, peanuts, beans, sweet potatoes. **2** Town, Kwangsi prov., China: see JUNGYÜN. **3** Town (pop. 13,625), ⊙ Junghsien co. (pop. 523,307), SW Szechwan prov., China, 38 mi. E of Loshan; match mfg.; rice, sweet potatoes, millet, kaoliang, wheat. Coal mining and kaolin quarrying, also saltworks near by.

Jungkiang or **Jung-chiang** (both: rōōng'jyäng'), town (pop. 8,176), ⊙ Jungkiang co. (pop. 81,721), SE Kweichow prov., China, 135 mi. SE of Kweiyang; lumbering center; cotton textiles, embroideries; rice, wheat, tobacco. Antimony deposits near by. Until 1913 called Kuchow.

Jungking or **Jung-ching** (rōōng'jĭng'), town, ⊙ Jungking co. (pop. 67,765), E Sikang prov., China, near Szechwan line, 50 mi. ESE of Kangting, on highway; tea, medicinal herbs, rice, corn, kaoliang. Lead-zinc mines. Until 1938 in Szechwan.

Junglinster (yōōng-lĭn'stŭr), village (pop. 826), E Luxembourg, 9 mi. NE of Luxembourg city; sawmills; fruitgrowing (plums).

Jung River (rōōng) or **Yung River** (yōōng), Mandarin *Yung Kiang* or *Yung Chiang* (both: jyäng'), SE Kwangsi prov., China, rises near Kwangtung line, flows c.100 mi. NNE, past Paklow (head of navigation) and Jungyün, to Sün section of West R. at Tengyün. In connection with portage linking it to upper reaches of Lim R. near Watlam, it forms Kwangsi-Kwangtung trade route.

Jungshahi (jōōngshä'hē), village, Tatta dist., SW Sind, W Pakistan, 45 mi. E of Karachi; rice, millet; mfg. of pottery, clays, paint pigments, glass. Sometimes spelled Jangshahi.

Jungwoschitz, Czechoslovakia: see MLADA VOZICE.

Jungyang (rōōng'yäng'), town, ⊙ Jungyang co. (pop. 110,029), N Honan prov., China, 20 mi. W of Chengchow and on Lunghai RR; cotton weaving; wheat, millet, timber, indigo.

Jungyün (Cantonese yōōng'yün'), Mandarin *Junghsien* (rōōng'shyĕn'), town, ⊙ Jungyün co. (pop. 304,815), SE Kwangsi prov., China, 60 mi. SW of Wuchow, in pine and bamboo woods; rice, millet, wheat.

Juniata (jōōnēă'tŭ), county (□ 387; pop. 15,243), central Pa.; ⊙ Mifflintown. Agr. area, drained by Juniata R. Blacklog Mtn. lies along SW, Shade Mtn. along NW border; Tuscarora Mtn. forms SE border. Dairying, fruitgrowing; mfg. (shirts, textiles), grist mills, sawmills; ganister deposits. Formed 1831.

Juniata, village (pop. 365), Adams co., S Nebr., 5 mi. W of Hastings and on branch of Little Blue R.

Juniata River, scenic stream, central Pa., formed 6 mi. NW of Huntingdon by junction of Little Juniata R. (c.30 mi. long) and Frankstown Branch (c.15 mi. long); flows 95 mi. generally E, past Huntingdon, Mount Union, and Lewistown, to Susquehanna R. just above Duncannon; breaks through Jacks Mtn. at Mount Union and through Tuscarora Mtn. at Millerstown. Raystown Branch rises in Allegheny Mts. in E Somerset co., winds E. past Bedford, and NNE to Juniata R. just below Huntingdon; 105 mi. long.

Junikabura, Japan: see TSUCHIZAWA.

Junín, department, Argentina: see SANTA ROSA, San Luis prov.

Junín (hōōnēn'). **1** City (pop. 36,667), ⊙ Junín dist. (□ 870; pop. 53,257), N Buenos Aires prov., Argentina, on the Río Salado and 150 mi. W of Buenos Aires, in agr. area (grain, fruit, livestock). Rail junction (workshops) and commercial center; mfg. of metal goods, ceramics, furniture; brewing. Has technical and natl. col., conservatory. **2** Town (pop. estimate 1,000), ⊙ Junín dept. (□ 130; pop. 17,434), N Mendoza prov., Argentina, in Mendoza R. valley (irrigation area), 27 mi. SE of Mendoza, in wine and fruit area; apiculture; wine making, dried-fruit processing, sawmilling.

Junín, village (pop. 4), Tarapacá prov., N Chile, port on the Pacific, 4 mi. SSE of Pisagua; rail terminus, formerly shipping nitrate; almost abandoned in 1930s.

Junín, department (□ 11,166; enumerated pop. 363,212, plus estimated 20,000 Indians), central Peru; ⊙ Huancayo (since 1931). Bordered by Ene and Tambo rivers (E), Cordillera Oriental (NE), and Cordillera Occidental (W). Includes L. Junín; drained by Mantaro and Perené rivers. Cordillera Central crosses dept. NW–SE. Important mining region, with centers at La Oroya (metallurgy), Morococha (copper), and Cercapuquio (cadmium). Hydroelectric plants at La Oroya and Pachach[illegible] fed by water reservoirs on Yauli and Mantaro rivers. Agr. (wheat, barley, potatoes); cattle and sheep raising in mts.; subtropical products (coffee, cacao, sugar cane) on E slopes of the Andes; rubber and lumbering in E tropical lowlands toward the Perené. Thermal baths at Llocllapampa and Yauli. Served by trans-Andean railroad from Lima. Main centers: Huancayo, La Oroya, Juaja, Tarma. Until 1931, dept. ⊙ was Cerro de Pasco. Pasco prov. separated (1944) from Junín to form Pasco dept.

Junín, town (pop. 3,058), ⊙ Junín prov. (pop. 18,372; created 1944), Junín dept., central Peru, in Cordillera Central of the Andes, just SE of L. Junín, on railroad and 90 mi. NW of Huancayo, 37 mi. SSE of Cerro de Pasco; alt. c.14,000 ft. Agr. products: potatoes, grain, livestock. Here Bolívar defeated the Spaniards in 1824.

Junín, Lake (14 mi. long, 6 mi. wide), Junín dept., central Peru, in Cordillera Central of the Andes, 8 mi. NNW of Junín; alt. 13,560 ft. Outlet; Mantaro R.

Junín de los Andes (dä lōs än′dĕs), village (pop. estimate 1,000), ⊙ Huiliches dept. (1947 pop. 5,509), SW Neuquén natl. territory, Argentina, in Argentinian lake dist., 90 mi. SW of Zapala. Resort; sheep, cattle raising, silver-fox farming.

Juning, China: see JUNAN.

Junio, 4 de, district, Argentina: see LANÚS.

Junio, 4 de, town, Argentina: see CUATRO DE JUNIO.

Junior, town (pop. 729), Barbour co., E W.Va., on Tygart R. and 5 mi. NW of Elkins, in agr. and coal-mining area.

Junipero Serra Peak, Calif.: see SANTA LUCIA RANGE.

Junisho (jo͞o′nĕshō), town (pop. 5,559), Akita prefecture, N Honshu, Japan, 7 mi. SE of Odate; rice, silk cocoons; mining (gold, silver, copper, lead). Hot springs near by.

Juniville (zhünēvēl′), village (pop. 689), Ardennes dept., N France, 8 mi. S of Rethel; stock raising.

Juniye or **Juniyah** (both: jo͞onē′yù), Fr. *Djouni, Jounié,* or *Jounieh,* village, central Lebanon, near the Mediterranean, overlooking a little bay, 9 mi. NE of Beirut; sericulture, cotton, cereals, oranges.

Junk, Liberia: see MARSHALL.

Junkceylon, Thailand: see PHUKET.

Junken, Cape (jŭng′kŭn), S Alaska, on S Kenai Peninsula, 30 mi. ESE of Seward; 59°55′N 148°39′W.

Junnar (jo͞on′nŭr), town (pop. 9,951), Poona dist., central Bombay, India, in Western Ghats, 50 mi. N of Poona; market center for millet, wheat, rice. Anc. Buddhist center (c.1st–3d cent. A.D.). Near-by hill fort of Shivner was birthplace (1627) of Sivaji; later a Mahratta stronghold.

Juno, W.Va.: see CARETTA.

Junonis Promontorium, Spain: see TRAFALGAR, CAPE.

Junqueiro (zho͞ongkā′ro͞o), city (pop. 856), E Alagoas, NE Brazil, 26 mi. N of Penedo; sugar, hides.

Junquera, La (lä ho͞ong-kā′rä), town (pop. 794), Gerona prov., NE Spain, 11 mi. NNW of Figueras; customs station near Fr. border on road to Perthus pass. Lumbering; cork, cereal, and wine processing.

Junsen, Korea: see SUNCHON.

Junta, La, Limón, Costa Rica: see LA JUNTA.

Juntas, Las, Costa Rica: see LAS JUNTAS.

Junten, Korea: see SUNCHON.

Juntura (jŭntŭr′ù, –työr′ù), town (pop. 107), Malheur co., E Oregon, 45 mi. WSW of Vale, on Malheur R. at mouth of North Fork.

Junturas, Las, Argentina: see LAS JUNTURAS.

Junun (jo͞o″no͞on′), village (pop. 465), W central Kedah, Malaya, on railroad and 16 mi. SSE of Alor Star; rice.

Juodkrante or **Yuodkrante** (yo͞oôdkrän′tä), Lith. *Juodkrantė,* Ger. *Schwarzort* (shvärts′ôrt), climatic and seaside resort (1941 pop. 346), W Lithuania, on lagoon side of Courland Spit, 11 mi. S of Memel; fisheries; amber diggings. In Memel Territory, 1920–39.

Juoksengi (yo͞o′ôksĕng″ē), village (pop. 762), Norrbotten co., N Sweden, on Torne R. (Finnish border) and 50 mi. N of Haparanda; livestock.

Jupiá (zho͞opyä′), village, SE Mato Grosso, Brazil, on right bank of Paraná R. (São Paulo border). River is here spanned by 3,330-ft. steel bridge of São Paulo–Corumbá RR.

Jupille (zhüpēl′), town (pop. 8,261), Liége prov., E Belgium, on Meuse R. and 3 mi. E of Liége; coal mining; metal industry. Favorite residence of Pepin of Héristal, who died here, and of Charlemagne.

Jupilles (zhüpē), village (pop. 220), Sarthe dept., W France, 17 mi. SE of Le Mans; mfg. of wooden shoes.

Jupiter. 1 Town (pop. 313), Palm Beach co., SE Fla., 16 mi. N of West Palm Beach, on Atlantic coast, near S end of Jupiter Isl. **2** Town (pop. 136), Buncombe co., W N.C., 11 mi. NNW of Asheville.

Jupiter Island, Martin co., SE Fla., barrier beach on the Atlantic, separated from mainland by narrow channel; 15 mi. long. At N end is St. Lucie Inlet, [illegible]t S end Jupiter Inlet. Lighthouse (26°55′N [illegible]0°5′E) at S tip.

[illegible]queri, Brazil: see MAIRIPORÃ.

[illegible]iá (zho͞okyä′), town (pop. 459), S São Paulo, [illegible] head of navigation on Juquiá R. and 25 mi. [illegible] Iguape; terminus of railroad from Santos, [illegible]ing Japanese settlements in Registro-Iguape [illegible]

[illegible]a River, S São Paulo, Brazil, rises in the Serra do Mar 35 mi. W of Santos, flows 100 mi. SW, past Juquiá (head of navigation), joining Ribeira R. above Registro to form Ribeira de Iguape R.

Juquila (ho͞okē′lä), officially Santa Catarina Juquila, town (pop. 1,405), Oaxaca, S Mexico, in Sierra Madre del Sur, 70 mi. SW of Oaxaca; cereals, sugar, coffee, fruit, vegetables, stock.

Jura (jo͞or′ù, Fr. zhürä′, Ger. yo͞o′rä), department (□ 1,952; pop. 216,386), E France, in old Franche-Comté prov.; ⊙ Lons-le-Saunier. Bounded by Switzerland (SE), and traversed S–NE by the Jura. W part occupied by the REVERMONT and BRESSE regions. Drained by the Ain and Brenne (S), Loue and Doubs (N) rivers, all rising in the Jura and flowing into Rhone basin. Cereals, rapeseed, poultry in the Bresse, wines in the Revermont and along W slopes of the Jura. Cattle raising, mfg. of Gruyère and blue cheese important throughout dept., with centers at Morez and Lons-le-Saunier. Extensive lumbering in mts. (fir trees) and in wooded tracts E of Dôle. Marble quarries at Saint-Amour, Balanod, and Molinges; saltworks at Salins-les-Bains and near Lons-le-Saunier. Mfg., chiefly of the artisan type, includes clockmaking, diamond and gem cutting, wood turning, and the working of plastics, ivory, and horn. Chief towns are Lons-le-Saunier (cheese and wine trade), Dôle (metallurgical and chemical industries), Saint-Claude (brier pipes, plastic articles, carved and inlaid ornaments), and Morez (optical and clockmaking center).

Jura or **Jura Mountains,** mountain range along Franco-Swiss border, occupying parts of French Franche-Comté (Ain, Jura, Doubs depts.) and of Swiss cantons of Vaud, Neuchâtel, Bern, Solothurn, and Basel. Extends in an arc in parallel folded ridges (rising above 5,500 ft.) for c.160 mi. from Rhone R. gorge (S) to the Rhine near Basel (NE). It is up to 40 mi. wide, cut by several transverse gorges locally known as "cluses." Geologically, the Jura belongs to the Alpine system. Its predominating fossiliferous limestone formations have given the Jurassic period its name. Highest peaks: Crêt de la Neige (5,652 ft.), Mont Reculet (5,643 ft.), both in Fr. part of S Jura, Mont Tendre (5,520 ft.) and Dôle (5,513 ft.), both in Switzerland. Chief passes: Col de la Faucille (4,340 ft.) and the "cluse" of Pontarlier. The steep E slopes overlook Swiss lakes of Geneva, Neuchâtel, and Biel, and Aar R. valley. The Doubs, Loue, and Ain rivers, which rise here, drain longitudinal valleys on Fr. side. On NW and W the Jura is bounded by the Belfort Gap, Doubs and Saône river valleys. Pastoral and forest industries predominate. Because of difficult transverse communications, large cities (Basel, Mulhouse, Belfort, Besançon, Geneva, Neuchâtel, Biel) are found along base in marginal lowlands. In smaller towns, skilled mtn. population produces watches (particularly in Le Locle, La Chaux-de-Fonds, Granges), carved wood products and plastics (Saint-Claude). Cheese is exported. Wooded slopes, picturesque valleys, Karst-like limestone formations, numerous waterfalls, attract tourists to widely scattered small resorts. The Swabian and Franconian Jura in SW Germany (bet. Neckar, Danube, and Main rivers), though geologically a continuation of the Jura beyond the Rhine graben, is considered a geographically separate upland region.

Jura (jo͞or′ù), island (□ 146.5, including Fladda, Lunga, Scarba, and Skervuile isls.; pop. 364) of the Inner Hebrides, Argyll, Scotland, separated from N part of Kintyre peninsula (E) by 4-mi.-wide Sound of Jura, from Islay (SW) by 1-mi.-wide Sound of Islay, and from Scarba (N) by strait of CORRYVRECKAN. Isl. is 28 mi. long, 8 mi. wide. Traversed by a central range of hills rising to 2,571 ft. in the PAPS OF JURA (SW). W coast is deeply indented by Loch Tarbert. Chief villages: Ardlussa (NE) and Craighouse (SE). Fishing, stock raising (sheep, cattle, goats), and crofting are main occupations. Red deer are numerous. There are traces of anc. entrenchments.

Juraciszki, Belorussian SSR: see YURATISHKI.

Juradó (ho͞orädō′), town (pop. 263), Chocó dept., NW Colombia, minor port on the Pacific near Panama border, 20 mi. NNW of Cape Marzo; coconuts, vegetable ivory, oranges.

Juramento River, Argentina: see SALADO, Río.

Jurançon (zhüräsō′), SW suburb (pop. 3,838) of Pau, Basses-Pyrénées dept., SW France; metalworking, tanning, meat processing, mfg. of furniture, shoes, cheese. Extensive high-quality vineyards in area. Sanatoriums.

Jurba, Al (ăl jo͞or′bù), town, ⊙ Maflahi sheikdom of Upper Yafa, Western Aden Protectorate, 6 mi. SW of Mahjaba.

Jurbarkas or **Yurbarkas** (yo͞orbär′käs), Ger. *Jurburg* or *Georgenburg,* city (pop. 5,221), SW Lithuania, on right bank of Neman R. and 45 mi. WNW of Kaunas; mfg. of shoes, furniture; sawmilling, oilseed pressing, brewing. Dates from 14th cent., when Teutonic Knights built Georgenburg castle; passed (16th cent.) to Lithuania; in Rus. Kovno govt. until 1920.

Jurbise (zhürbēz′), Flemish *Jurbeke* (yür′bĕkù), village (pop. 1,261), Hainaut prov., SW Belgium, on Dender R. and 6 mi. NNW of Mons; agr.; pottery mfg.

Jurburg, Lithuania: see JURBARKAS.

Jurema (zho͞orā′mù), city (pop. 1,673), E central Pernambuco, NE Brazil, 28 mi. NE of Garanhuns; coffee, sugar, corn.

Jurf al-Darawish, Jordan: see JURUF EL DARAWISH.

Jurf ed Darawish, Jordan: see JURUF EL DARAWISH.

Jurilovca (zho͞orēlôv′kä), village (pop. 3,991), Galati prov., SE Rumania, on L. Razelm, 12 mi. SE of Babadag; fishing port, center for production of black caviar.

Juripiranga (zho͞orēpērăng′gù), town (pop. 2,136), E Paraíba, NE Brazil, on Pernambuco border, 30 mi. SW of João Pessoa; cotton, pineapples. Until 1944, called Serrinha.

Jurisdicciones, Cerro Las (sĕ′rō läs ho͞orēsdēksyō′näs), Andean peak (12,631 ft.) of Cordillera Oriental, on Norte de Santander–Magdalena dept. border, N Colombia, 45 mi. W of Cúcuta.

Jurm or **Jorm** (jo͞orm), town (pop. over 2,000), Afghan Badakhshan, NE Afghanistan, on left tributary of Kokcha R. and 22 mi. SE of Faizabad.

Jurques (zhürk), village (pop. 193), Calvados dept., NW France, 14 mi. NNE of Vire; iron mining.

Jur River (jo͞or), SW Anglo-Egyptian Sudan, rises on Nile-Congo watershed S of Wau, flows over 350 mi. N and E, past Wau and Gogrial, joining Tonj R. in L. AMBADI to form the Bahr el Ghazal. Navigable (July–Oct.) below Wau.

Juruá River (zho͞orwä′), Amazonas, Brazil, rises in Peru just S of Brazil border, flows c.1,200 mi. NE in meandering course across Acre territory, past Cruzeiro do Sul (head of navigation) and Eirunepé, to the Amazon (right bank) below Fonte Boa. Traverses rubber-growing region.

Juruena River (zho͞orwā′nù), left headstream of the Tapajós, in N Mato Grosso, Brazil, rises in the Serra dos Parecis near 14°30′S 59°0′W, flows 500 mi. N, forming Mato Grosso–Amazonas border for c.120 mi. before its confluence with São Manuel R. at Pará-Amazonas-Mato Grosso frontier, where joint streams form TAPAJÓS RIVER. Chief tributary, Arinos R. (right). Not navigable.

Juruf el Darawish, Juruf ed Darawish, or **Juruf al-Darawish** (all: jo͞oro͞of′ ĕd-därä′wēsh), village, S central Jordan, on Hejaz RR and 18 mi. SE of Tafila; camel raising. Manganese deposits near by. Also spelled Jurf ed Darawish or Jurf al-Darawish.

Juruti (zho͞oro͞otē′), city (pop. 508), westernmost Pará, Brazil, on right bank of the Amazon, near Amazonas line, and 40 mi. WSW of Óbidos; rubber, Brazil nuts, jute.

Jusepín (ho͞osäpēn′), town (pop. 1,449), Monagas state, NE Venezuela, 22 mi. W of Maturín; oil wells, linked by pipe line with Caripito.

Jushan (ro͞o′shän′), town, ⊙ Jushan co., E Shantung prov., China, 20 mi. NE of Haiyang, near Yellow Sea.

Jushqan, Iran: see MEIMEH.

Juslibol (ho͞oslēvōl′), N suburb (pop. 4,446) of Saragossa, Saragossa prov., NE Spain.

Jussey (zhüsā′), village (pop. 1,935), Haute-Saône dept., E France, near the Saône, 19 mi. NW of Vesoul; dairying, sawmilling; hand embroidery.

Justice, village (pop. 854), Cook co., NE Ill., W suburb of Chicago.

Justin, town (pop. 496), Denton co., N Texas, 13 mi. SW of Denton.

Justiniano Posse (ho͞ostēnyä′nō pō′sā), town (pop. 2,653), E Córdoba prov., Argentina, 45 mi. SE of Villa María; wheat, flax, corn, livestock; dairying.

Justo Daract (ho͞os′tō därăkt′), town (1947 pop. 4,737), E San Luis prov., Argentina, on railroad, on the Río Quinto and 22 mi. SE of Mercedes; agr. center (alfalfa, corn, wheat, livestock); lumbering.

Justoy (yo͞ost′ûü), Nor. *Justøy,* island (□ 3; pop. 316) in the Skagerrak, Aust-Agder co., S Norway, 3 mi. S of Lillesand.

Jutaí River (zho͞otäē′), W Amazonas, Brazil, rises near 6°S 70°W, flows NE to the Amazon (right bank). Navigable in lower course. Estimated length, up to 800 mi. Formerly spelled Jutahy.

Jüterbog (yü′tùrbōk), town (pop. 15,137), Brandenburg, E Germany, 20 mi. ENE of Wittenberg; rail junction; mfg. of paper products and stationery, furniture; food canning. Has 12th- and 15th-cent. churches, several 15th-cent. town gates. Chartered 1174; was property of archbishops of Magdeburg; passed to Saxony in 1648. Went to Prussia in 1815. Formerly military center with extensive training grounds.

Jutfaas, Netherlands: see JUTPHAAS.

Jutiapa (ho͞otyä′pä), department (□ 1,243; 1950 pop. 136,213), SE Guatemala, on Pacific Ocean and Salvador border; ⊙ Jutiapa. In SE highlands, sloping S to Pacific coastal plain; drained by the Río de la Paz (which forms its SE border); includes volcanoes Suchitán and Moyuta. Chingo volcano and L. Güija are on Salvador border. Mainly agr. (corn, beans, fodder grasses, rice); extensive livestock raising (hogs, cattle). Coffee and sugar cane grown on lower slopes. Main centers are Jutiapa and Ascención Mita, served by Inter-American Highway.

Jutiapa, city (1950 pop. 5,141), ⊙ Jutiapa dept., SE Guatemala, near Inter-American Highway, 45 mi. ESE of Guatemala, in highlands; 14°17′N 89°53′W; alt. 2,926 ft. Commercial center in dairying region; corn, beans, livestock.

Juticalpa (ho͞otēkäl′pä), city (pop. 3,372), ⊙ Olancho dept., central Honduras, in Olancho Valley, on Juticalpa R. (left affluent of Guayape R.) and 75 mi. NE of Tegucigalpa (linked by road); 14°38′N 86°15′W; alt. 1,476 ft. Commercial center in livestock area; dairying; coffee, tobacco, rice. Has govt. buildings, col. Airfield (W). Founded c.1260; became city in 1835. Flourished in 19th cent. through trade with Caribbean ports and placer mining in near-by Guayape R.

Jutland (jŭt′lŭnd), Dan. *Jylland* (yül′lăn), also known as Cimbric Peninsula, anc. *Chersonesus*

Cimbrica [=Cimbric Chersonese], peninsula of N Europe comprising continental Denmark and Germany N of Eider R. Bounded by the Skagerrak and North Sea (N and W), by the Kattegat and the Little Belt (E). Danish peninsula proper (less its N tip, which—cut off by LIM FJORD—constitutes isls. of Thy and Vendsyssel) has □ 9,186, pop. 1,491,850; with Thy and Vendsyssel it has □ 10,990, pop. 1,753,189; all Danish Jutland, with its small satellite isls., has □ 11,411, pop. 1,826,056. S part of peninsula, called South Jutland, Dan. *Sønderjylland*, coincides with former Danish duchy of SCHLESWIG. Swept by North Sea winds, the sand dunes and shallow inlets of W Jutland afford few harbors (Esbjerg is only good port); land is sparsely vegetated. Pop. is mostly on E seaboard, which is fertile (agr., dairying, livestock raising) and has a number of ports, including Aarhus, Aalborg, Frederikshavn. Jutland has many lakes, of which the Himmelbjaerget group is most important. Guden R. is largest stream. On May 31, 1916, was fought c.60 mi. W of Jutland the battle of Jutland, only major engagement bet. Ger. and Br. fleets in First World War. Known in Germany as the battle of the Skagerrak, it resulted in loss to the Germans of 11 ships and c.2,500 dead, to the British of 14 ships and c.6,000 dead. Although the battle could be called a tactical German success, they gained no advantage from it and the German fleet remained bottled up in harbor for the rest of the war.

Jutogh (jōōtōg'), town (pop. 634), central Himachal Pradesh, India, cantonment 3 mi. W of Simla.

Jutphaas (yût'fäs), town (pop. 1,260), Utrecht prov., central Netherlands, on Merwede Canal and 4 mi. SSW of Utrecht; soap mfg.; truck gardening. Sometimes spelled Jutfaas.

Jutrosin (yōōtrô'shĕn), Ger. *Jutroschin* (yōōtrô'shĭn), town (1946 pop. 1,389), Poznan prov., W Poland, 11 mi. WSW of Krotoszyn; mfg. of cement goods, flour milling, sawmilling.

Juupajoki, Finland: see KORKEAKOSKI.

Juvavum, Austria: see SALZBURG, city.

Juventino Rosas (hōōvĕntē'nō rō'säs), city (pop. 6,831), Guanajuato, central Mexico, on central plateau, 30 mi. SSE of Guanajuato; alt. 5,643 ft. Agr. center (wheat, corn, alfalfa, beans, sugar cane, cotton, fruit, stock). Santa Cruz or Santa Cruz de Galeana until 1938.

Juvigny (zhüvēnyē'). **1** Village (pop. 224), Aisne dept., N France, 5 mi. N of Soissons. Captured (1918) by Americans cooperating with French in surprise tank attack. **2** or **Juvigny-le-Tertre** (–lü-tĕr'trü), village (pop. 350), Manche dept., NW France, in Normandy Hills, 16 mi. E of Avranches; horse raising. Damaged in Second World War.

Juvigny-sous-Andaine (–sōōzädĕn'), village (pop. 235), Orne dept., NW France, 7 mi. ESE of Domfront; sawmilling.

Juvisy-sur-Orge (zhüvēzē'-sür-ôrzh'), town (pop. 7,787), Seine-et-Oise dept., N central France, on left bank of the Seine and 11 mi. S of Paris; mfg. (machine tools, bottle caps, malt, chicory, cement pipes). Freight yards. Observatory.

Juwaimisa, Iraq: see SUWAIRA.

Juxtlahuaca (hōōsläwä'kä), town (pop. 2,117), Oaxaca, S Mexico, in Sierra Madre del Sur, 22 mi. W of Tlaxiaco; alt. 5,413 ft.; cereals, sugar, coffee, fruit, stock.

Juymand, Iran: see GONABAD.

Ju-yüan, China: see YÜYÜAN.

Júzcar (hōōth'kär), town (pop. 520), Málaga prov., S Spain, 7 mi. S of Ronda; olives, grapes, cereals, oranges, nuts; flour milling, liquor distilling.

Juzennecourt (zhüzĕnkōōr'), agr. village (pop. 232), Haute-Marne dept., NE France, on Blaise R. and 9 mi. NW of Chaumont.

Juzna Morava River, Yugoslavia: see SOUTHERN MORAVA RIVER.

Juzni Brod, Yugoslavia: see BROD, Macedonia.

Jyderup (yü'dhürōōp), town (pop. 1,560), Holbaek amt, Zealand, Denmark, 12 mi. WSW of Holbaek; explosives, briquettes.

Jyekundo (jüĕkōōndō'), Chinese *Yüshu* (yü'shōō'), town, ⊙ Jyekundo co. (pop. 67,000), S Tsinghai prov., China, on trade route to Chamdo, near Sikang line and Yangtze R., 380 mi. SW of Sining; major trading center, handling Tibetan products, tea, grain, and wool.

Jylland, Denmark: see JUTLAND.

Jyväskylä (yü'văskü"lă), city (pop. 28,682), Vaasa co., S central Finland, on small lake near N end of L. Päijänne, 80 mi. NE of Tampere; rail junction; pulp-, paper-, and plywood-milling center; mfg. of matches, margarine, machinery. Airfield. Site of pedagogical col. Univ. summer extension courses held here. City founded 1837. First secondary school with Finnish as language of instruction was founded here in 1858. Black granite is quarried near by.

K

K2 or **Mount Godwin Austen**, second-highest peak (28,250 ft.) in the world and highest peak in main range of Karakoram mtn. system, N Kashmir, at 35°53'N 76°31'E. Notable climbing expeditions made by duke of Abruzzi in 1909 and by Americans in 1938 (led by Dr. Charles Houston) and 1939 (led by Fritz Wiessner; 4 perished). Highest point reached up to 1950 was 27,500 ft., climbed in 1939. All 3 expeditions used SE (Abruzzi) ridge.

K5, peak, China: see MUZTAGH.

Kaaden, Czechoslovakia: see KADAN.

Ka'aiti, Aden: see QUAITI.

Kaakamo River, Finnish *Kaakamojoki* (kä'kämō-yō"kē), NW Finland, rises N of Tornio, flows 40 mi. generally S to Gulf of Bothnia 4 mi. SW of Kemi. Boundary (from 1374) bet. bishoprics of Uppsala and Turku; later, until 1809, border bet. Sweden and Finland.

Kaa-Khem, Russian SFSR: see YENISEI RIVER.

Kaakhka (kääkh-kä'), town (1926 pop. 2,072), SE Ashkhabad oblast, Turkmen SSR, on Trans-Caspian RR and 75 mi. SE of Ashkhabad, in orchard area. Called Ginsburg, c.1920–27.

Kaala, Mount (kä-ä'lä), W Oahu, T.H., highest point (4,030 ft.) of Waianae Range and of the isl.

Kaala-Gomen (–gō'mĕn), village (pop. 1,211), W New Caledonia, 170 mi. NW of Nouméa; agr. produce, stock; meat cannery at near-by Ouaco.

Kaapland, U. of So. Afr.: see CAPE OF GOOD HOPE PROVINCE.

Kaap Plateau (käp), region in N part of the Northern Karroo, N Cape Prov., U. of So. Afr., in Griqualand West, bet. Orange R. (S), Asbestos Mts. (W), Kalahari Desert (N), and Hartz and Vaal rivers (E and SE); 3,700–5,000 ft. high.

Kaapstad, U. of So. Afr.: see CAPE TOWN.

Kaaterskill Clove (kä'túrzkĭl, –skĭl, kô'–), SE N.Y., in the Catskills, scenic gorge of small Kaaterskill Creek, extends c.5 mi. bet. Haines Falls village (W; noted waterfall here) and Palenville (E). Traversed by highway.

Kaatsheuvel (käts'hûvúl), village (pop. 6,521), North Brabant prov., S Netherlands, 7 mi. NNW of Tilburg; leather tanning, shoe mfg.

Kab, El, or **Al-Kab** (both: ĕl käb'), village (1937 pop. 334), Aswan prov., S Egypt, 12 mi. NNW of Idfu. Site of ruins of anc. Nekheb or Nikhab, Gr. *Eileithyaspolis*, anc. ⊙ of Upper Egypt.

Kaba (kŏ'bŏ), town (pop. 7,103), Hajdu co., E Hungary, 22 mi. SW of Debrecen; rail center; flour mills; wheat, corn, paprika; cattle.

Kabadian, Tadzhik SSR: see MIKOYANABAD.

Kabaena (käbī'nä), island (□ 338; pop. 9,040), Indonesia, off SE coast of Celebes, at E side of entrance to Gulf of Bone; 5°15'S 121°55'E; 30 mi. long, 20 mi. wide. Partly mountainous, rising to c.5,400 ft. in center of isl. Buffalo raising, agr. (sago, coconuts).

Kabakovsk, Russian SFSR: see SEROV.

Kabaktan (kŭbŭktän'), town (1939 pop. over 500), S Yakut Autonomous SSR, Russian SFSR, in Stanovoi Range, near upper Aldan R., 170 mi. SW of Aldan; gold mining.

Kabala (käbä'lä), town (pop. 3,064), Northern Prov., N Sierra Leone, on road and 60 mi. NNE of Makeni; trade center; peanuts, rice, hides and skins. Has Church of England mission, school. Hq. Koinadugu dist.

Kabale (käbä'lā), town (pop. c.5,000), SW Uganda, in mtn. and lake region, 65 mi. SW of Mbara; alt. c.6,000 ft. Agr. trade center; coffee, corn, millet; cattle, sheep, goats. Tourist center for surrounding mts. and L. Bunyoni (bōōnyō'nē) (SW). Hq. Kigezi dist., inhabited by Bantu-speaking Chiga tribe. Gold, tin, tungsten deposits. Kikungiri, 2 mi. S, is R.C. mission center.

Kabalo (käbä'lō), town, Katanga prov., E Belgian Congo, on Lualaba R., on railroad, and 160 mi. W of Albertville; transshipment point for produce of middle Lualaba region and for imports from E Africa. African staples (manioc, yams, sweet potatoes) are grown on a large scale in vicinity. Has R.C. and Protestant missions. Airport.

Kabambare (käbämbä'rā), village, Kivu prov., central Belgian Congo, 70 mi. ESE of Kasongo; tin mining, cotton growing, cotton ginning; also tantalite mining.

Kabankalan (käbängkä'län), town (1939 pop. 4,656; 1948 municipality pop. 47,817), Negros Occidental prov., W Negros isl., Philippines, 15 mi. S of Binalbagan; sugar mill, distillery; gypsum mine.

Kabansk (kŭbänsk'), village (1926 pop. 2,233), S Buryat-Mongol Autonomous SSR, Russian SFSR, on Selenga R., near Trans-Siberian RR (Timlyui station), and 45 mi. WNW of Ulan-Ude; dairy plant, fish canneries. Oil and natural gas deposits.

Kabara, Fiji: see KAMBARA.

Kabara (käbärä'), village, central Fr. Sudan, Fr. West Africa, port for Timbuktu (just N) on left bank of the Niger. Meteorological station.

Kabardian Autonomous Soviet Socialist Republic (kŭbär'dēŭn), Rus. *Kabardinskaya Avtonomnaya SSR*, autonomous republic (□ 4,550; 1946 pop. estimate 300,000) in S European Russian SFSR; ⊙ Nalchik. On N slopes of the central Greater Caucasus; extends from peaks in Caucasus crest (S; Elbrus, Koshtan-Tau, Dykh-Tau, Shkhara), through Caucasus front ranges broken by deep river gorges, to level Kabardian plain, its chief economic dist.; includes basin of Terek R. (N) and its affluents (Malka and Baksan rivers). Corn (processed at Dokshukino), wheat, sunflowers, common and ambary hemp, fruit, garden crops. Poultry in lowlands, livestock raising (dairying) in mtn. meadows. Industry, largely based on agr., produces flour, vegetable oil, alcohol, starch, jams, and canned goods. Molybdenum mining at Tyrny-Auz; hydroelectric station near Baksan. Lumbering on Caucasus slopes. Pop. largely (60%) Kabardian (a Circassian group; 164,106 in 1939), Russian, and Ukrainian. Main centers: Nalchik, Prokhladny. Since 1825 under Russian rule; briefly (1921) in Mountain Autonomous SSR, then separated as Kabardian Autonomous Oblast; renamed Kabardino-Balkar Autonomous Oblast with inc. (1922) of Balkar-inhabited mtn. dist.; became autonomous SSR in 1936. The Balkars, a Moslem, Turkic-speaking mtn. people, were resettled in 1944, presumably because they collaborated with the Germans, and the region became the Kabardian Autonomous SSR; a Balkar dist. along upper Baksan R. passed to Georgian SSR. Sometimes called Kabardinian Autonomous SSR.

Kabardino-Balkar Autonomous Oblast, Russian SFSR: see KABARDIAN AUTONOMOUS SOVIET SOCIALIST REPUBLIC.

Kabare (käbä'rā), village, Kivu prov., E Belgian Congo, 7 mi. WSW of Costermansville; alt. 6,232 ft. Center of an area of European agr. colonization (notably coffee plantations). Has large R.C. mission.

Kabarnet, town, Rift Valley prov., W Kenya, on road and 35 mi. E of Eldoret; coffee, wheat, corn, wattle growing.

Kabasalan (käbäsälän'), town (1939 pop. 3,437; 1948 municipality pop. 19,037), Zamboanga prov., W Mindanao, Philippines, near head of Sibuguey Bay, 45 mi. W of Pagadian; coconuts, corn, rice.

Kabaw Valley (kŭbô'), longitudinal lowland in Upper Burma, on Manipur (India) border, bet. Manipur and Chin hills (W) and Chindwin R.; 100 mi. long, it is sometimes defined as including additional 60-mi. section of Myittha valley (S). Valley is used by major Burma-India trade route via Kalemyo, Tamu, and Imphal.

Kabba (kä'bä'), province (□ 10,953; pop. 463,531), Northern Provinces, SW central Nigeria; ⊙ Lokoja. Savanna (N), deciduous forests (S); drained by Niger and Benue rivers. Tin and columbite mining at Egbe; coal, lignite, and limestone deposits (SE); iron deposits (Lokoja). Mainly agr.: shea nuts, cotton, palm oil and kernels around Niger-Benue river confluence; cassava, durra, yams; sackmaking. Chief centers: Lokoja, Kabba, Okene.

Kabba, town (pop. 9,221), Kabba prov., Northern Provinces, S central Nigeria, 45 mi. W of Lokoja; agr. trade center; shea-nut processing, cotton weaving, sackmaking; cassava, corn, durra.

Kabbani River (kŭ'bŭnē), in W Madras and S Mysore, India, rises in the Wynaad in Western Ghats, W of Gudalur; flows N and generally ENE past Sargur and Nanjangud to Cauvery R. at Tirumakudal Narsipur; c.120 mi. long.

Kabe (kä'bā), town (pop. 8,249), Hiroshima prefecture, SW Honshu, Japan, 9 mi. NNE of Hiroshima; commercial center for agr. area (rice, wheat); sake, soy sauce, ironware.

Kabel Station (kä'bŭl stätēōn'), village, Surinam dist., N central Du. Guiana, on Surinam R., on Paramaribo-Dam RR serving near-by gold fields, and 65 mi. S of Paramaribo. Bauxite deposits in vicinity.

Kabelvag (kä'bŭlvôg), Nor. *Kabelvåg*, village (pop. 1,333) in Vagan (Nor. *Vågan*) canton (pop. 5,527), Nordland co., N Norway, on S Austvagoy of Lofoten Isls., on Vest Fjord, 4 mi. SW of Svolvaer; cod-fishing center; summer resort. Church built 1120. Formerly called Kapelvagar.

Kaberamaido (käbĕrämī'dō), village, Northern Prov., E central Uganda, 30 mi. W of Soroti, near L. Kyoga; cotton, peanuts, sesame.

Kabete (käbĕ'tā), village, Central Prov., S central Kenya, on railroad and 7 mi. W of Nairobi; coffee center; sisal, wheat, corn; dairying. Veterinary research station (bacteriological inst.) and experimental farm. Radio broadcasting station.

Kabetogama, Lake (kăbŭtō'gŭmŭ), largely in St. Louis co., NE Minn., just S of Rainy L., 16 mi. ESE of International Falls; □ 31; 20 mi. long, max. width 5 mi. Famous scenic lake with numerous fishing resorts, several peninsulas, and many small isls. within state forest. E outlet is Namakan L., on Ont. line.

Kabgaye (käbgā'), village, central Ruanda-Urundi, in Ruanda, 23 mi. WSW of Kigali; alt. 6,100 ft. R.C. missionary center with 2 seminaries, trade and teachers' schools for natives. Has noted mus. of native life. Residence of vicar apostolic of Ruanda.

Kabilcoz, Turkey: see SASUN.

Kabin, Turkey: see BESIRI.

Kabinakagami Lake (kă"bĭnŭkă'gŭmē) (16 mi. long, 10 mi. wide), central Ont., 150 mi. W of Timmins; drains N into Kenogami R.

Kabinburi (kŭbĭn'bōōrē'), village (1937 pop. 4,189), Prachinburi prov., S Thailand, on Bang Pakong R. (high-water head of navigation), on Bangkok-Pnompenh RR, and 80 mi. ENE of Bangkok; rice; gold. Local name, Kabin. Also spelled Krabin and Krabinburi.

Kabinda, district and town, Angola: see CABINDA.

Kabinda (käbĕn'dä), village, ⊙ Kabinda dist. (□ 33,654; 1948 pop. c.685,000), Kasai prov., SE Belgian Congo, 110 mi. SE of Lusambo; trading and cotton center, road communications hub; cotton ginning. Has hosp. for Europeans, R.C. mission, several trade schools and school for mulattoes.

Kabir Kuh (kăbĕr' kōō'), mountain range in SW Iran, in the Pusht Kuh (Zagros system), on right bank of upper Karkheh R.; rises to 9,000 ft. at 33°20'N 46°40'E.

Kabo (kŭbō'), village, Shwebo dist., Upper Burma, on Mu R. and 27 mi. NNW of Shwebo; site of major irrigation headworks feeding Shwebo and Yeu canals.

Kaboeroeang, Indonesia: see KABURUANG.

Kabol, Yugoslavia: see KOVILJ.

Kabolela (käbōlĕ'lä), village, Katanga prov., SE Belgian Congo, 15 mi. NW of Jadotville; copper mining and concentrating; also cobalt mining.

Kabongo (kābông'gō), village, Katanga prov., SE Belgian Congo, 95 mi. NNE of Kamina; cotton ginning. R.C. and Protestant missions.

Kaboudia, Ras (räs' käbōōdyä'), cape on the Mediterranean coast of E Tunisia, 40 mi. NNE of Sfax; 35°13'N 11°10'E. Also spelled Ras Kapoudia.

Kabru (kä'brōō), peak (24,002 ft.) in Singalila Range, on undefined Nepal-Sikkim (India) border, 40 mi. NNW of Darjeeling, at 27°36'N 88°7'E. Ascent in 1883 claimed by W. W. Graham.

Kabul (kä'bŏŏl, kŭbōōl'), province (□ 40,000; pop. 2,500,000), E central Afghanistan; ⊙ Kabul. Occupied almost entirely by the mountainous Hazarajat, where the Hari Rud, Helmand, and Kabul rivers rise, the prov. extends SE to the Pakistan line near the Gumal R., and includes the rich economic areas (E) of Kabul city and the Samt-i-Shimali, where irrigated agr., industry, and pop. are concentrated. In addition to Kabul, main centers are Ghazni (on Kabul-Kandahar road), Charikar (metal industry), and Jabal-us-Siraj (cotton mill). Panjao is the main town of the Hazarajat. Pop. is Ghilzai Afghan in Ghazni area (S), Hazara in the Hazarajat (W), and Tadzhik in the developed Kabul area (E).

Kabul, city (pop. 300,000), ⊙ Afghanistan and Kabul prov., on Kabul R. above mouth of Logar R., and 140 mi. WNW of Peshawar (Pakistan; linked by highway through Khyber Pass); alt. 5,895 ft.; 34°30'N 69°13'E. The political, economic, and cultural center of Afghanistan, Kabul is wedged in a triangular valley, overlooked S by the Sherdarwaza Hill (7,254 ft.) and W by Asmai Hill (6,893 ft.). The narrow gorge bet. these 2 hills, known as the Guzargah Pass or Deh Mozang Pass, is crossed by Kabul R. and constitutes the W access route to the city. The old right-bank section with its narrow, crooked streets contains the extensive bazaars (the Chahar Chatta; destroyed by British in 1842; restored 1850) and, on the river bank, the public gardens with the tomb of Timur Shah. The modern left-bank garden city (development began in late-19th cent.) includes the Arg or royal palace, as well as administrative and business bldgs. The old royal residence in the Bala Hissar fort (SE) is now a military col. In N outskirts are the airport, the new fort (on site of 19th-cent. British Sherpur cantonment), and the radio station. In NW outskirts is Bagh-i-Bala, residence of Habibullah (ruled 1901–19) and residential suburb. Flanking the highway from Peshawar (E) are the parade grounds and the royal cemetery. Industries are concentrated (W) in the so-called Mashin-Khana, a govt. complex including a mint and also an ordnance works producing arms, boots, saddles, textiles, soap, and wood products. Kabul also has auto repair shops, food-processing and -canning factories, cotton and wool-weaving mills, and a cement plant. Beyond the Guzargah Pass extends the CHAHARDEH plain, a W extension of Kabul, containing beautiful gardens (Baber's tomb) and the suburb of DAR-UL-FANUN, with Kabul univ. The city proper is the seat of Habibia, Istiqlal, and Nijat colleges. Identified with the *Orthospana* or *Cabura* of Alexander the Great, Kabul 1st gained prominence in 16th cent., when Baber made it (1504) capital of the Mogul Empire; the capital was transferred to Delhi area after 1526. The city remained under Mogul rule until its capture (1738) by Nadir Shah and succeeded Kandahar as ⊙ Afghanistan under Timur Shah (ruled 1773–93). Kabul was the scene of massacres (1842, 1879) of British garrisons during 1st and 2d Afghan Wars.

Kabul River, anc. *Cophus,* in E Afghanistan and W Pakistan, rises in Paghman Mts. at foot of Unai Pass 45 mi. W of Kabul, flows 320 mi. E, past Kabul, Jalalabad, and Nowshera, to the Indus just N of Attock. Receives Panjshir, Kunar, and Swat rivers (left), Logar R. (right). Irrigates Jalalabad valley in Afghanistan and Peshawar dist. in Pakistan (headworks at Warsak). Alexander the Great invaded India (327 B.C.) via the Kabul R. valley, which is used since 1945 by new Peshawar-Jalalabad-Kabul highway.

Kaburuang or **Kaboeroeang** (käbōōrwäng'), island (□ 36; pop. 3,072), Talaud Isls., Indonesia, 10 mi. S of Karakelong; 3°47'N 126°48'E; 10 mi. long, 5 mi. wide; hilly, forested. Timber, copra, sago, nutmeg; fishing.

Kabushia or **Kabushiya** (kŭbōō'shĭyŭ), town Northern Prov., Anglo-Egyptian Sudan, on right bank of the Nile, on railroad and 25 mi. NE of Shendi; cotton, wheat, barley, corn, fruit, durra; livestock. Near by (N) is site of anc. city of MEROË.

Kabutarahang (käbōō"tärähäng'), town, Fifth Prov., in Hamadan, W Iran, 32 mi. NNE of Hamadan; grain, opium, fruit; sheep raising.

Kabylia (kŭbĭl'yŭ), Fr. *Kabylie* (käbēlē'), mountainous coastal region of Algeria, in NE Alger and N Constantine depts., extending from the Mitidja lowland near Algiers (W) to Philippeville area (E), and reaching up to 30 mi. inland. It is geographically divided by the Sahel-Soummam valley into 2 sections, Great Kabylia (W) and Little Kabylia (E). The former has the more rugged terrain, including the DJURDJURA range, and has its main center at Tizi-Ouzou. It is densely populated, grows olives on mtn. slopes, wheat, tobacco, wine, and figs in sheltered valleys. Cork is exploited in coastal strip bet. Dellys and Bougie (Kabylia's chief port). Little Kabylia, longitudinally traversed by the BABOR range, is Algeria's ranking cork-producing region. Its main port is Djidjelli, but there are few inland towns. Scattered mineral deposits (only a few economically exploited) yield iron, lead, zinc, copper. The Mediterranean shore of Kabylia is followed (with interruptions) by a scenic highway. Peopled by fiercely independent Berbers, Kabylia offered desperate resistance to Fr. occupation. Even after Abd-el-Kader's surrender, the Kabylians fought Fr. expeditions throughout the 1850s, and were not pacified until the failure of the 1871 insurrection.

Kacanik or **Kachanik** (both: kä'chänĭk), Serbo-Croatian *Kačanik,* village (pop. 5,489), S Serbia, Yugoslavia, on Lepenac R., on railroad and 18 mi. NNW of Skoplje, near Macedonia border, in the Kosovo. Kacanik defile, Serbo-Croatian *Kačanička Klisura,* bet. Sar Mts. and Crna Gora, extends from Kacanik SSE along Lepenac R. into Macedonia.

Kacergine or **Kachergine** (kächĕrgēnā'), Lith. *Kačerginė,* town, S central Lithuania, on left bank of the Neman and 7 mi. W of Kaunas; summer resort.

Kacha, Nigeria: see KATCHA.

Kacha (kŭchä'), town (1939 pop. over 500), SW Crimea, Russian SFSR, on Black Sea coast, N of Kacha R. mouth, 12 mi. N of Sevastopol; fisheries; fish processing.

Kachannagar, India: see BURDWAN, city.

Kachanovo (kŭchä'nŭvŭ), Latvian *Kačanava* (kächä'nävä), village (1945 pop. over 500), SW Pskov oblast, Russian SFSR, 32 mi. SW of Pskov; flax, grain. In Rus. Pskov govt. until 1920; in Latvian Latgale prov. until 1945.

Kachar, India: see CACHAR.

Kacha River, S Crimea, Russian SFSR, rises in Crimean Mts. WSW of Alushta, flows c.40 mi. W to Black Sea 7 mi. N of Sevastopol.

Kachchhiahana, India: see SAUSAR.

Kachek (gä'jĕk'), Mandarin *Chia-chi* (jyä'jē'), town (pop. 5,500), E Hainan, Kwangtung prov., China, on Wanchüan R. and 50 mi. S of Kiungshan; commercial center; exports poultry, livestock, rattan cane, fruit; cotton milling.

Kacheliba (kächĕlē'bä), town, Rift Valley prov., W Kenya, on right bank of Turkwell R. near Uganda border, on road, and 32 mi. N of Kitale; sisal, coffee, wheat, corn.

Kachemak Bay (kă'chŭmăk"), S Alaska, arm (40 mi. long, 20 mi. wide) of Cook Inlet, SW Kenai Peninsula; 59°34'N 51°31'W. Seldovia village, S; Homer village, N.

Kachergine, Lithuania: see KACERGINE.

Kach Gandava, W Pakistan: see KACHHI.

Kachh, India: see CUTCH, state.

Kachhi (kŭch'ē), NE division (□ 5,330; pop. 86,112) of Kalat state, E Baluchistan, W Pakistan. A dry, low-lying plain (extends into S Sibi dist.), bounded W, N, and NE by Central Brahui Range; watered by seasonal mtn. streams, including Nari and Bolan rivers. Agr. (millet, wheat, rice, cotton); handicrafts (cloth, carpets, embroideries, leather goods, palm mats). Sulphur and gypsum deposits in NW section. Noted for its camels and horses. Chief villages: Lahri, Bhag, Gandava. Pop. 92% Moslem. Sometimes spelled Cutchi; formerly called Kach (Cutch) Gandava.

Kachhwa (kŭch'vŭ), town (pop. 4,330), Mirzapur dist., SE Uttar Pradesh, India, near the Ganges, 10 mi. ENE of Mirzapur; rice, barley, gram, wheat, oilseeds.

Kachia (kä'chä), town (pop. 891), Zaria prov., Northern Provinces, central Nigeria; 60 mi. SE of Kaduna; cotton, peanuts, ginger. Tin mining.

Kachikawa, Japan: see KASUGAI.

Kachin State (kŭchĭn'), constituent unit (□ 33,871; 1941 pop. 427,625) of Union of Burma, in northernmost Upper Burma, on China and Assam borders; ⊙ Myitkyina. Located in the N mtn. region known as the Kachin hill tracts, it includes the central Kumon Range and The Triangle, and is drained by headstreams (Mali and Nmai rivers) of the Irrawaddy and the upper basin of the Chindwin (Hukawng Valley). Contains Indawgyi L., largest in Burma. Subsistence agr. (rice, vegetables, tobacco, cotton, opium); sugar cane near Myitkyina (mill at Sahmaw). Jade mining (at Lonkin, Tawmaw), amber (on S edge of Hukawng Valley). Main centers, Myitkyina, Bhamo, Mogaung, Maingkwan, Sadon, and Putao, are served by railroad from Mandalay, Irrawaddy R. navigation, and Ledo (Stilwell) Road (built during Second World War). Pop. is 30% Thai, 25% Burmese, and 20% Kachin. The Kachins (or Jinghpaws), a Mongoloid race of the Tibeto-Burman group, migrated (8th cent.) from E Tibet by way of Nmai and Mali headstreams of the Irrawaddy. Nearly half their total number (175,000) lives in N Shan State. The Kachin State was formed out of Bhamo and Myitkyina states by virtue of 1947 constitution. The N section of Kachin State is claimed by China.

Kachiry (kŭchērē'), village (1939 pop. over 500), N Pavlodar oblast, Kazakh SSR, on Irtysh R. and 65 mi. NNW of Pavlodar, in agr. area (wheat).

Kachreti (kŭchryĕ'tyē), village (1939 pop. over 500), E Georgian SSR, 45 mi. E of Tiflis; rail junction for Mirzaani oil fields.

Kachuga (kŭchōō'gŭ), town (1939 pop. over 10,000), SE Irkutsk oblast, Russian SFSR, port on Lena R. (high-water head of navigation) and 135 mi. NNE of Irkutsk (linked by highway); transit center on Irkutsk–upper Lena R. route, in agr. and livestock area; shipbuilding, sawmilling, woodworking. Also known as Kachug.

Kacina, Czechoslovakia: see SEDLEC.

Kackar Dag (kächkär' dä), Turkish *Kaçkar Dağ,* highest peak (12,917 ft.) of Rize Mts., NE Turkey, 38 mi. ESE of Rize.

Kaczawa River, Poland: see KATZBACH, river.

Kada (kä'dä) or **Kata** (kä'tä), town (pop. 6,170), Wakayama prefecture, S Honshu, Japan, on strait bet. Osaka Bay and Kii Channel, 7 mi. NW of Wakayama; rail terminus; fishing center; rice, citrus fruit; cotton flannel. Summer resort.

Kada-boaz Pass, Bulgaria-Yugoslavia: see BELOGRADCHIK PASS.

Kadaiyam, India: see KADAYAM.

Kadaiyanallur, India: see KADAYANALLUR.

Kadamdzhai, Kirghiz SSR: see FRUNZE, town, Osh oblast.

Kadan (kä'dänyŭ), Czech *Kadaň,* Ger. *Kaaden* (kä'dŭn), town (pop. 5,062), NW Bohemia, Czechoslovakia, on Ohre R., on railroad and 8 mi. SW of Chomutov. Has 15th-cent. town hall. Franciscan monastery with late-Gothic church just outside of town.

Kadarbana (kŭdŭr'bŭnŭ) or **Katerban** (kŭtär'bŭn), town, S Nepal, in the Terai, near India border, 25 mi. ENE of Motihari (India); rice, wheat, barley, corn, jute.

Kadarkut (kŏ'dŏrkōōt), Hung. *Kadarkút,* town (pop. 3,232), Somogy co., SW Hungary, 12 mi. SW of Kaposvar; wheat, corn.

Kadayam or **Kadaiyam** (kŭdŭyŭm'), town (pop. 3,545), Tinnevelly dist., S Madras, India, 22 mi. WNW of Tinnevelly; silk growing.

Kadayanallur (kŭdä"yŭnŭl-lōōr'), town (pop. 29,652), Tinnevelly dist., S Madras, India, 9 mi. NNE of Tenkasi; major cotton-weaving center. Formerly spelled Kadaiyanallur.

Kade (kä'dā), town, Eastern Prov., central Gold Coast colony, 14 mi. NE of Oda; rail terminus; diamond-mining center.

Kadéï River (kädā'), main headstream of Sanga R. in E Fr. Cameroons and W Ubangi-Shari (Fr. Equatorial Africa), rises on Fr. Cameroons–Fr. Equatorial Africa border 15 mi. NW of Baboua, flows in Fr. Cameroons S past Batouri, and turns E and SE, crossing into Fr. Equatorial Africa, joining another headstream at Nola to form the Sanga; c.250 mi. long.

Kadesh (kā'dĕsh), anc. city of W Syria, on the Orontes, near Homs; a capital of the Hittites, who were here defeated c.1300 B.C. by Ramses II.

Kadhimain, Al (äl kä'dhĭmĭn), or **Al-Kazimayn** (kä'zĭ-), town, Baghdad prov., central Iraq, on Tigris R., on railroad, and 5 mi. NW of Baghdad; dates, sesame, fruit; textile mill. Has notable mosques.

Kadi (kŭd'ē), town (pop. 17,165), Mehsana dist., N Bombay, India, 20 mi. SSW of Mehsana; trades in millet, cotton, cloth fabrics; cotton ginning and milling, handicraft cloth weaving, calico printing, oilseed milling; copper and brass products.

Kadiak, Alaska: see Kodiak.

Kadiam, India: see Dowlaiswaram.

Kadijica or **Kadiyitsa** (both: kä'dēyĭtsä), Bulg. *Ogreyak* (ô'grĕyäk), highest peak (6,337 ft.) of Males Mts., on Yugoslav-Bulgarian line, 8 mi. NE of Berovo, Yugoslavia.

Kadikoy (kädĭkû'ē), Turkish *Kadıköy*, city (pop. 66,540), Istanbul prov., NW Turkey in Asia, at S entrance of the Bosporus on the Sea of Marmara opposite Istanbul, of which it forms a part; rail terminus and commercial center. On site of anc. Chalcedon.

Kadima, Israel: see Qadima.

Kadina (kŭdī'nŭ), town (pop. 1,744), S South Australia, on W Yorke Peninsula, 55 mi. SSW of Port Pirie, near Wallaroo; rail junction; wheat, wool, sheep. Salt, gypsum, limestone, some copper.

Kadinhani (kädŭn'hänŭ"), Turkish *Kadınhanı*, village (pop. 4,338), Konya prov., W central Turkey, 29 mi. NNW of Konya; wheat. Formerly Saideli or Saiteli.

Kadipur (kä'dēpŏŏr), village, Sultanpur dist., E central Uttar Pradesh, India, 20 mi. ESE of Sultanpur; rice, wheat, gram, barley, oilseeds.

Kadirabad, India: see Jalna.

Kadiri (kŭ'dĭrē), town (pop. 11,885), Anantapur dist., W Madras, India, 55 mi. SE of Anantapur; road center; grain trade; jaggery. Hq. of regional malaria control. Sheep grazing in near-by forested hills (bamboo, satinwood).

Kadiri, Indonesia: see Kediri.

Kadirli (kädĭrlĭ'), village (pop. 3,345), Seyhan prov., S Turkey, 50 mi. NE of Adana; grain. Formerly Karszulkadriye.

Kadiyevka (kä'dyĕûfkŭ), city (1926 pop. 17,224; 1939 pop. 68,360), SW Voroshilovgrad oblast, Ukrainian SSR, in the Donbas, 30 mi. W of Voroshilovgrad; coal-mining center; chemical and metallurgical works. Called Sergo (1937–43). Its satellite towns include Irmino, Almaznaya, Bryanski, Golubovka, Krivorozhye.

Kadiyitsa, peak, Bulgaria: see Kadijica.

Kadjebi (käjĕ'bē), town, S Br. Togoland, administered as part of Eastern Prov., Gold Coast colony, near Fr. Togoland border, 27 mi. N of Hohoe; cacao market.

Kadmat Island, India: see Cardamum Island.

Kadmous, Syria: see Qadmus, El.

Kadnikov (käd'nyĭkŭf), city (1926 pop. 2,319), central Vologda oblast, Russian SFSR, 24 mi. NNE of Vologda, in flax, potato, dairy-farming region. Place of exile under tsars. Chartered 1780.

Kado (kä'dō), town (pop. 7,191), Akita prefecture, N Honshu, Japan, on Sea of Japan, 12 mi. SSE of Noshiro; rice, raw silk; fishing, lumbering.

Kadogawa (kädō'gäwŭ), town (pop. 14,862), Miyazaki prefecture, E Kyushu, Japan, on Hyuga Sea, 7 mi. S of Nobeoka; agr. and fishing center; rice, wheat, barley, millet.

Kadoka (kŭdō'kŭ), town (pop. 584), ⊙ Jackson co., SW central S.Dak., 70 mi. SW of Pierre and 25 mi. E of Badlands Natl. Monument; tourist center; agr., livestock.

Kadom (kä'dŭm), village (1926 pop. 8,370), E Ryazan oblast, Russian SFSR, on Moksha R. and 27 mi. NE of Sasovo; boatbuilding, woodworking.

Kadoshkino (kä'dŭshkēnŭ), town (1939 pop. over 500), S Mordvinian Autonomous SSR, Russian SFSR, on railroad, 20 mi. W of Ruzayevka; hemp.

Kadugannawa (kŭdŏŏgŭnä'vŭ), town (pop. 1,317), Central Prov., Ceylon, on Kandy Plateau, 8 mi. WSW of Kandy; tea, rice, vegetables. Anc. Buddhist temples near by.

Kadugli (kä'dŏŏglē), village, Kordofan prov., central Anglo-Egyptian Sudan, in Nuba Mts., on road and 70 mi. S of Dilling; gum arabic; livestock.

Kadui or **Kaduy** (kŭdŏŏ'ē), town (1948 pop. over 2,000), SW Vologda oblast, Russian SFSR, on Suda R. and 27 mi. W of Cherepovets; food processing, veneering.

Kaduna (kä'dŏŏnä', kädŏŏ'nä), town (pop. 10,628), ⊙ Northern Provinces, N central Nigeria, in Zaria prov., on Kaduna R. and 130 mi. SW of Kano; 10°31'N 7°25'E. Rail junction; agr. center (cotton, ginger, durra). Has teachers col., general hosp., technical inst. Airfield.

Kaduna River, central Nigeria, rises on Bauchi Plateau SW of Jos, flows c.325 mi. NW and SW, past Kaduna and Zungeru, to Niger R. at Mureji. Navigable (July-Oct.) below Zungeru for barges.

Kadur (kŭdŏŏr'), district (□ 2,775; pop. 358,290), W Mysore, India; ⊙ Chikmagalur. On Deccan Plateau; bordered W by Western Ghats, rising to over 6,000 ft. on crest. Baba Budan Range, highest ridge (to over 6,000 ft.) in Mysore, in central area; noted coffee plantations; important iron mines supply iron- and steelworks at Bhadravati. Drained mainly by Tunga and Bhadra rivers (headstreams of the Tungabhadra). Extensive coffee, cardamom, tea, and pepper estates in W foothills (bamboo, sandalwood); rice (terrace farming), sugar cane, millet, cotton, coconuts. Coffee and tea processing, hand-loom weaving; handicrafts (biris, wickerwork). Chief towns: Chikmagalur, Tarikere, Birur.

Kadur, town (pop. 4,484), Kadur dist., W central Mysore, India, 20 mi. NE of Chikmagalur; tobacco, cotton, millet; handicraft biri making.

Kaduy, Russian SFSR: see Kadui.

Kady or **Kadyy** (kŭdē'), village (1948 pop. over 2,000), S Kostroma oblast, Russian SFSR, 45 mi. NE of Kineshma; flax.

Kadzharan (kŭjŭrän'), town (1947 pop. over 500), S Armenian SSR, in Zangezur Range (alt. 8,000 ft.), 15 mi. WSW of Kafan (rail spur terminus); molybdenum- and copper-mining center; concentrating plant. Developed after Second World War.

Kadzhisai or **Kadzhisay** (kŭjĕsī'), town (1947 pop. over 500), SW Issyk-Kul oblast, Kirghiz SSR, near S shore of Issyk-Kul (lake), on small stream Kadzhi-Sai and 70 mi. WSW of Przhevalsk; coal mining (begun in late 1940s).

Kadzusa, Japan: see Kazusa, province.

Kaechon (kä'chŭn'), Jap. *Kaisen*, town (1944 pop. 18,381), S.Pyongan prov., N Korea, 40 mi. NNE of Pyongyang, in mining area (coal, iron); graphite works.

Kaédi (käē'dē), town (pop. c.5,000), S Mauritania, Fr. West Africa, on right bank of Senegal R. at mouth of Gorgol R., and 195 mi. E of Saint-Louis. Produces gum, hides, skins, butter for export, subsistence crops (millet, potatoes); livestock.

Kaélé (käē'lā), village, Nord-Cameroun region, N Fr. Cameroons, 45 mi. SE of Maroua, near Fr. Equatorial Africa border; native trade center; stock raising.

Kaena Point (kä-ā'nä), W tip of Oahu, T.H.

Kaeo (kī'ō), township (pop. 317), ⊙ Whangaroa co. (□ 240; pop. 2,428), N N.Isl., New Zealand, 130 mi. NNW of Auckland; center of fruitgrowing area.

Kaersorssuak or **Qaersorssuaq** (both: kĭkhsôkh'-shwäk), island (10 mi. long, 3–5 mi. wide), W Greenland, in Baffin Bay, 4 mi. SE of Upernavik; 72°42'N 55°55'W. Rises to 3,467 ft. Site of noted bird cliffs. Discovered (1587) by Davis, who named W extremity Sanderson's Hope. Also spelled Kaersorsuak.

Kaersut or **Qaersut** (both: kĭkh'sŏŏt), fishing and hunting settlement (pop. 106), Umanak dist., W Greenland, on N shore of Nugssuak peninsula, on Umanak Fjord, 13 mi. WNW of Umanak; 70°44'N 52°39'W. Radio station.

Kaesong (kă'sŭng'), Jap. *Kaijo* or *Kaizyo* (both: kī'jō'), city (1949 pop. 88,708), Kyonggi prov., central Korea, S of 38°N, 36 mi. NW of Seoul; commercial center for ginseng-growing area. Known for fine porcelain ware. An anc. cultural center, Kaesong was ⊙ (10th–14th cent.) of Korea, preceding Seoul. Here are anc. tombs of Korean kings. Sometimes called Songdo; also spelled Kaisong. Here were held (beginning July, 1951) the 1st truce conferences in the Korean War.

Kaf or **Qaf** (käf), town and oasis in Hejaz, northernmost Saudi Arabia, in the Wadi Sirhan, 170 mi. NW of Jauf, near Jordan line; 31°25'N 37°22'E.

Kafa, prov., Ethiopia: see Kaffa.

Kafan (kŭfän'), city (1932 pop. estimate 4,060), SE Armenian SSR, on rail spur and 55 mi. E of Nakhichevan; copper-mining center; smelting works. Shipping point for Kadzharan molybdenum mines.

Kafanchan (käfäshä'), town (pop. 1,977), Plateau Prov., Northern Provinces, central Nigeria, 45 mi. SW of Jos; rail junction; tin-mining center.

Kafer Bouhoum, Syria: see Kafr Behum.

Kaffa or **Kafa** (kä'fä), Ital. *Caffa*, province (□ 19,000), SW Ethiopia; ⊙ Jimma. Extends W of Omo R. and borders on Anglo-Egyptian Sudan. Consists largely of fertile, forested mountainous region (5,000–11,000 ft. high), including the Enarea dist., with lowland in S near L. Rudolf. Drained by Gojab, Gibbe, and Kibish rivers. Chief products: coffee, cereals, hides, beeswax. Coffee is native to region, and wild coffee accounts for most of crop. Trade centers: Jimma, Bonga, Jiran, Maji, Wota. Iron mining at Omo. Crossed by road in N. Formerly a kingdom, it was Christianized in 16th cent., rivaled Ethiopia (18th-early 19th cent.), and was incorporated into it in 1897. Has Hamite pop., considerably reduced by slave trade which persisted until recently.

Kaffa, Russian SFSR: see Feodosiya.

Kaffraria (kŭfrâ'rēŭ), region in E Cape Prov., U. of So. Afr., bet. Great Fish R. (S) and Basutoland and Natal borders (N), bounded by the Indian Ocean (E). Consists of the Transkeian Territories and British Kaffraria, formerly a prov. (founded 1847, ⊙ Kingwilliamstown), extending N to Great Kei R. Members of German legion who had fought in Crimean War were settled here 1858. Annexed to Cape Colony 1865.

Kaffrine (käfrēn'), town (pop. c.1,600), W Senegal, Fr. West Africa, on Saloum R., on Dakar-Niger RR, and 35 mi. E of Kaolack; peanut growing.

Kafirevs, Cape, Greece: see Kaphereus, Cape.

Kafirevs Channel, Greece: see Kaphereus Channel.

Kafiristan, Afghanistan: see Nuristan.

Kafirnigan River (kŭfĕrnyēgän'), Stalinabad oblast, Tadzhik SSR, rises in several branches in E Gissar Range, flows WSW, past Ramit and Ordzhonikidzeabad, and S, past Mikoyanabad and Shaartuz, to the Amu Darya; 220 mi. long. Rich cotton areas along middle and lower course. Receives (right) Dyushambinka R., on which is Stalinabad. Joined to the Surkhan Darya by Gissar Canal, at Gissar.

Kafir Qala, Afghanistan: see Islam Qala.

Kafr Behum (kă'fûr bĕhōōm'), **Kifrabhum** (kĭ'-frăbhōōm'), or **Kafr Buhum** (bōōhōōm'), Fr. *Kafer Bouhoum*, town, Hama prov., W Syria, on railroad and 5 mi. SSW of Hama; cotton, cereals.

Kafr Biheida or **Kafr Bihaydah** (both: kă'fûr bĭhā'-dŭ), village (pop. 6,495), Daqahliya prov., Lower Egypt, 5 mi. NNE of Mit Ghamr; cotton, cereals.

Kafr Buhum, Syria: see Kafr Behum.

Kafr Bulin (bōō'lēn), village (pop. 7,015), Beheira prov., Lower Egypt, 3 mi. SE of Kom Hamada; cotton. Has canal regulator.

Kafr Dawud or **Kafr Da'ud** (dă'-ōōd), village (pop. 6,569), Beheira prov., W Lower Egypt, on Rosetta branch of the Nile and 22 mi. SSE of Kom Hamada; cotton.

Kafr el Battikh or **Kafr al-Battikh** (both: kă'frĕl băt'tĕk), village (pop. 15,303), Gharbiya prov., Lower Egypt, on railroad, near mouth of Damietta branch of the Nile, 5 mi. W of Damietta; cotton, fruits.

Kafr el Dawar, Kafr ed Dawar, or **Kafr al-Dawwar** (all: kă'frĕd-dou'wär), village (pop. 10,946; with suburbs, 13,507), Beheira prov., Lower Egypt, 15 mi. ESE of Alexandria; cotton ginning, cigarette mfg.; cotton, rice, cereals. Also spelled Kafr el Dauwar.

Kafr el Sheikh, Kafr esh Sheikh, or **Kafr al-Shaykh** (all: kă'frĕsh shākh'), town (pop. 15,508), Gharbiya prov., Lower Egypt, on railroad and 22 mi. NNW of Tanta; cotton ginning, cigarette mfg.; cotton, cereals, rice, fruits.

Kafr el Zaiyat, Kafr ez Zaiyat, or **Kafr al-Zayyat** (all: kă'frĕz-zī'yăt), agr. and industrial town (pop. 21,600), Gharbiya prov., Lower Egypt, on Rosetta branch of the Nile, on Cairo-Alexandria RR, and 11 mi. WNW of Tanta; cotton ginning, wool spinning, cigarette mfg., important chemical industry (cottonseed oil, soap, phosphates, fatty acids). Agr.: cotton, cereals, rice, fruits.

Kafr Kila el Bab or **Kafr Kila al-Bab** (both: kă'fûr kĭlăl'-băb'), village (pop. 8,831), Gharbiya prov., Lower Egypt, 11 mi. SE of Tanta; cotton.

Kafr Saqr (să'kûr), village (pop. 4,197), Sharqiya prov., Lower Egypt, on the Bahr Muweis, on railroad and 16 mi. NNE of Zagazig; cotton. Sometimes spelled Kafr Sakr.

Kafr Shibin (shĭbēn'), village (pop. 8,311), Qalyubiya prov., Lower Egypt, 18 mi. N of Cairo; cotton, flax, cereals, fruits.

Kafr Shukr (shōō'kûr), village (pop. 7,146), Daqahliya prov., Lower Egypt, on Damietta branch of the Nile and 11 mi. S of Mit Ghamr; cotton, cereals.

Kafubu (käfōō'bōō), village, Katanga prov., SE Belgian Congo, on railroad and 8 mi. SE of Elisabethville; agr. center; large citrus-fruit plantations, vineyards, and cattle-raising farms. Has R.C. mission, small seminary, and school of agr.

Kafue (käfōō'ā), township (pop. 349), Central Prov., Northern Rhodesia, on left bank of Kafue R., on railroad and 25 mi. S of Lusaka; tobacco, wheat, corn; livestock; fishing. Junction of road to Salisbury, Southern Rhodesia.

Kafue River, central Northern Rhodesia, rises on Belgian Congo border W of Elisabethville, flows in winding course SE, past Nchanga and Nkana mines in copper belt, then SW, and E past Namwala and Kafue, to Zambezi R. opposite (NNW of) Chirundu, Southern Rhodesia; length, c.600 mi. Drains Lukanga Swamp, W of Broken Hill, in middle course. Flows through **Kafue Gorge** near its confluence with the Zambezi, 50 mi. SE of Lusaka; potential hydroelectric site.

Kafulafuta (käfōōläfōō'tä), township (pop. 6), Western Prov., N central Northern Rhodesia, near Belgian Congo border, on railroad and 19 mi. SSE of Ndola. Kafulafuta Mission is 28 mi. W, on Kafulafuta R. (left affluent of Kafue R.).

Kafu River (kä'fōō), W Uganda, rises in marshes W of L. Kyoga, flows c.150 mi. WSW to S end of L. Albert. Called Nkusi R. in lower course.

Kagachi (kä"gä'chē), town (pop. 4,175), Oita prefecture, NE Kyushu, Japan, 30 mi. N of Oita, on Suo Sea; lumber, rice.

Kagal (kä'gŭl), town (pop. 8,031), Kolhapur dist., S Bombay, India, 10 mi. SE of Kolhapur; market center for rice, sugar cane, tobacco, mangoes; handicraft cloth weaving.

Kagalaska Island (kăgŭlă'skŭ) (9 mi. long, 7 mi. wide), Andreanof Isls., Aleutian Isls., SW Alaska, just E of Adak.

Kagalnik or **Kagal'nik** (kŭgăl'nyĭk). **1** Village (1926 pop. 8,819), SW Rostov oblast, Russian SFSR, on Taganrog Gulf of Sea of Azov, at mouths of Kagalnik R. and S arm of Don R. delta, 5 mi. SW of Azov; fisheries. **2** Village, S Rostov oblast, Russian SFSR: see Kagalnitskaya.

Kagalnik River or **Kagal'nik River**, S Rostov oblast, Russian SFSR, rises N of Mechetinskaya, flows c.70 mi. WNW, past Kagalnitskaya and Samarskoye, to Sea of Azov, here joining S arm of Don R. delta mouth at Kagalnik.

Kagalnitskaya or **Kagal'nitskaya** (kŭgăl'nyĭtskīŭ), village (1926 pop. 5,904), S Rostov oblast, Russian SFSR, on Kagalnik R., on railroad and 33 mi. SE of Rostov; flour milling, metalworking; wheat, sunflowers, castor beans. Formerly also Kagalnik.

Kagami (kä″gä′mē), town (pop. 10,863), Kumamoto prefecture, W Kyushu, Japan, on Yatsushiro Bay, 16 mi. S of Kumamoto; rice-producing center; raw silk. Agr. school.

Kagan (kŭgän′), city (1932 pop. estimate 14,300), S Bukhara oblast, Uzbek SSR, on Trans-Caspian RR (junction for Termez and Stalinabad) and 8 mi. SE of Bukhara; rail center (repair shops); tobacco and wine processing, cotton ginning, cottonseed-oil extraction. Developed in late-19th cent. around BUKHARA station; residence of Rus. political agent to khan of Bukhara. Until c.1935, called Novaya Bukhara [Rus.,=new Bukhara].

Kaganovich (kŭgŭnô′vĭch), district of Greater Baku, Azerbaijan SSR, on S Apsheron Peninsula, E of Baku; oil fields. Main centers: Zykh, Imeni L. M. Kaganovicha.

Kaganovich. **1** Village (1939 pop. over 2,000), NW Frunze oblast, Kirghiz SSR, in Chu valley, near railroad (Novotroitski station), 15 mi. W of Frunze; machine repair shops; sugar beets (refinery at adjoining Krasno-Oktyabrski). Until 1937, Novo-Troitskoye. **2** Rail station, Amur oblast, Russian SFSR: see YEKATERINOSLAVKA. **3** City (1939 pop. over 10,000), S Moscow oblast, Russian SFSR, on Oka R. and 3 mi. E of Kashira; electric-power center; site of Kashira power plant (based on Moscow Basin lignite), which supplies Moscow with electricity. Formerly Ternovski; called Ternovsk (1932–c.1935). **4** Town (1939 pop. over 10,000), E Tula oblast, Russian SFSR, near railroad (Tovarkovo station), 7 mi. SSE of Bogoroditsk; lignite-mining center in Moscow Basin; flour and sugar milling.

Kaganovicha, Imeni (ē′mĭnyĕ kŭgŭnô′vĭchŭ), town (1948 pop. over 2,000), central Chita oblast, Russian SFSR, on Trans-Siberian RR and 150 mi. ENE of Chita; junction for railroad to Bukachacha coal mines.

Kaganovicha, Imeni L. M. **1** Town (1939 pop. over 500) in Kaganovich dist. of Greater Baku, Azerbaijan SSR, on S Apsheron Peninsula, 7 mi. E of Baku, in Kara-Chukhur oil field (developed 1932); truck produce; vineyards. **2** City, Voroshilovgrad oblast, Ukrainian SSR: see POPASNAYA.

Kaganovichabad (kŭgŭnô″vĭchŭbät′), village (1939 pop. over 2,000), S Stalinabad oblast, Tadzhik SSR, in Vakhsh valley, 18 mi. SSW of Kurgan-Tyube (linked by narrow-gauge railroad); long-staple cotton, truck produce; metalworks. Developed in 1930s.

Kaganovichesk (kŭgŭnô″vēchĕsk′), town (1948 pop. over 2,000), E Chardzhou oblast, Turkmen SSR, 5 mi. SSE of Chardzhou; cotton, orchards; metalworks. Site of anc. Amul, later known as Chardzhui. Following rise of new city of Chardzhui (see CHARDZHOU), it was called Stary Chardzhui [Rus., =old Chardzhui] until 1937.

Kaganovichi Pervye or **Kaganovichi Pervyye** (kŭgŭnô′vēchē pyĕr′vēŭ) [Rus.,=Kaganovichi No. 1], agr. town (1926 pop. 3,158), NW Kiev oblast, Ukrainian SSR, on Uzh R. (head of navigation) 75 mi. NW of Kiev; hemp. Until c.1935, called Khabno or Khabnoye, and later (until c.1940), Kaganovich.

Kagarko (kägär′kō), town (pop. 1,487), Zaria prov., Northern Provinces, central Nigeria; 70 mi. SSE of Kaduna; tin, columbite, wolfram mining. Sometimes spelled Kagerko.

Kagarlyk (kŭgŭrlĭk′), town (1926 pop. 8,060), central Kiev oblast, Ukrainian SSR, 40 mi. SSE of Kiev; sugar-refining center; flour mill, metalworks.

Kagato (kä″gä′tō), town (pop. 2,289), Okayama prefecture, SW Honshu, Japan, 12 mi. ENE of Okayama, in agr. area (rice, wheat, pears, peppermint); raw silk.

Kagawa (kä″gä′wä), prefecture [Jap. *ken*] (□ 718; 1940 pop. 730,394; 1947 pop. 917,673), NE Shikoku, Japan; ⊙ TAKAMATSU, its chief port. Bounded NW by Hiuchi Sea (central section of Inland Sea), NE by Harima Sea (E section of Inland Sea). Includes offshore isl. of SHODO-SHIMA. Generally mountainous and forested terrain. Agr. (tobacco, rice, sweet potatoes, oranges, apples). Mfg. (cotton textiles, paper, pottery, dolls), woodworking. Large production of salt in coastal towns; many fishing ports. Chief centers (all on N coast): Takamatsu, MARUGAME, SAKAIDE.

Kagawong (kă′gŭwŏng), village (pop. estimate 200), S central Ont., on N Manitoulin Isl., on North Channel of L. Huron, 17 mi. WSW of Little Current; fishing, lumbering.

Kagayan, Philippines: see CAGAYAN SULU ISLAND.

Kage (kō′gŭ), Swedish *Kåge*, village (pop. 1,340), Vasterbotten co., N Sweden, on small inlet of Gulf of Bothnia, 5 mi. N of Skelleftea; cattle; dairying.

Kagera National Park (käge′rä, –gā′–) (□ 780; established 1934), NE Ruanda-Urundi, in Ruanda, along Kagera R. (Tanganyika territory border). Mostly a barren and semi-arid terrain, especially known for great herds of antelopes and zebras and other animals. Gabiro is administrative center.

Kagera River or **Alexandra Nile,** in E central Africa, formed along Ruanda-Urundi–Tanganyika border (near 2°30′S 30°45′E) by junction of the Ruvuvu and the Nyawarongo, flows N along border through marshy, lake-studded region, then turns E, forming section of Uganda-Tanganyika boundary, to W shore of L. Victoria 25 mi. N of Bukoba. Length, c.250 mi. Lower course navigable. Used for hydroelectric power. As the chief tributary of L. Victoria, the Kagera is usually considered the headstream of the Victoria Nile; its furthest branch, the Luvironza, is taken as the remotest source of the Nile. The Kagera was 1st explored by Oskar Baumann 1892–93.

Kagerko, Nigeria: see KAGARKO.

Kagerod (kō′gŭrûd″), Swedish *Kågeröd,* village (pop. 746), Malmohus co., S Sweden, 16 mi. ESE of Halsingborg; grain, cattle.

Kagi, Formosa: see KIAYI.

Kagizman (käŭzmän′), Turkish *Kağızman,* town (pop. 6,634), Kars prov., NE Turkey, on Aras R. and 32 mi. S of Kars; arsenic, some gold.

Kagmari, E Pakistan: see TANGAIL.

Kagna River (kŭg′nŭ), in SW Hyderabad state, India, rises in 2 forks joining near Dharur (Atraf-i-Balda dist.), flows 70 mi. WSW, past Tandur, to Bhima R. 7 mi. S of Shahabad.

Kagoro (kä′gōrō), town, Zaria prov., Northern Provinces, central Nigeria, on railroad and 5 mi. E of Kafanchan; tin-mining center.

Kagoshima (kä″gō′shĭmä), prefecture [Jap. *ken*] (□ 3,515; 1940 pop. 1,589,467; 1947 pop. 1,746,305), S Kyushu, Japan; ⊙ Kagoshima, its chief port. Mainland portion bounded W by E.China Sea, S by Kagoshima Bay, Osumi Strait, and Ariake Bay; prefecture includes TANEGA-SHIMA, YAKU-SHIMA, NAGA-SHIMA and SHISHI-JIMA of AMAKUSA ISLANDS, and KOSHIKI-RETTO. Satsuma and Osumi peninsulas comprise major part of prefecture. Mountainous; hot springs in Kirishima Natl. Park. No large streams. Gold and silver mines in S, iron and copper in W. Subtropical vegetation, with gum, camphor, and lichee trees. Principal agr. products are sweet potatoes, tobacco, soybeans; livestock breeding; sawmilling. Outlying isls. produce sugar cane, sweet potatoes, fish. Kagoshima is chief mfg. center.

Kagoshima, city and port (1940 pop. 190,257; 1947 pop. 170,416), ⊙ Kagoshima prefecture, S Kyushu, Japan, on E Satsuma Peninsula, on W shore of Kagoshima Bay, opposite Sakura-jima, 600 mi. WSW of Tokyo; 31°35′N 130°33′E. Principal port of S Kyushu; cultural and mfg. center; silk and cotton clothing, tinware. Known for Satsuma porcelain ware. Navy yard. Exports logs, lumber, wood products. Seat of Nishi-honganji, a great Buddhist temple; historical mus. Birthplace of Takamori Saigo, Toshimichi Okubo, Heihachiro Togo, Prince Iwao Oyama. St. Francis Xavier landed here 1549. In feudal times, city was seat of lords of Satsuma. Bombed 1863 by British. Center of Satsuma Rebellion (1877), which resulted in destruction of city. Damaged 1914 by eruption of volcano on near-by Sakura-jima. Bombed 1945 in Second World War. Sometimes spelled Kagosima.

Kagoshima Bay, Jap. *Kagoshima-wan,* inlet of E. China Sea, S Kyushu, Japan, in Kagoshima prefecture, bet. Satsuma Peninsula (W) and Osumi Peninsula (E); c.45 mi. long, 13 mi. wide. Sakura-jima (NW projection of Osumi Peninsula) is opposite Kagoshima on W shore of bay.

Kagul (kŭgōōl′), Rum. *Cahul* (kähōōl′), city (1930 pop. 11,370; 1941 pop. 7,375), S Moldavian SSR, in Bessarabia, on Prut R. (Rum. border) and 30 mi. NNE of Galati; flour milling, wine making. Passed (1812) to Russia; returned briefly (1856–78) to Moldavia. While in Rumania (1918–40, 1941–44), it was ⊙ Cahul dept. (□ 1,715; 1941 pop. 203,260).

Kagul Lagoon, Rum. *Cahul,* SW Izmail oblast, Ukrainian SSR, near Danube R., SE of Reni; 15 mi. long, 6 mi. wide (in S). Receives minor Kagul R. (N).

Kaguyak (kăgū′yăk). **1** Fishing village, S Alaska, S Kodiak Isl., 80 mi. SW of Kodiak; 56°52′N 153°46′W. **2** Fishing village, S Alaska, on Shelikof Strait, NE Alaska Peninsula, in Katmai Natl. Monument, 80 mi. NW of Kodiak. Formerly spelled Kayuyak or Kayayak.

Kahama (kähä′mä), town, Western Prov., NW central Tanganyika, on road and 80 mi. N of Tabora; peanuts, millet, corn; cattle, sheep, goats.

Kahawa (kähä′wä), town (pop. c.1,500), S central Kenya, on railroad and 10 mi. NNE of Nairobi; coffee center; sisal, wheat, corn.

Kahawatta or **Kahawatte** (kŭhŭvŭt′tŭ), town (pop. 717), Sabaragamuwa Prov., SW central Ceylon, 15 mi. ESE of Ratnapura; rubber, tea, rice, vegetables.

Kahe (kä′hā), locality, Northern Prov., Tanganyika, at S foot of Kilimanjaro, 12 mi. SE of Moshi. Junction of rail lines from Tanga and Mombasa (Kenya).

Kahemba (kähĕm′bä), village, Leopoldville prov., SW Belgian Congo, 140 mi. S of Kikwit, near Angola border; customs station, native trade center; copal.

Kahili (kähē′lē), peak (3,016 ft.), Kauai, T.H.

Kahl or **Kahl am Main** (käl′ äm mīn′), village (pop. 4,146), Lower Franconia, NW Bavaria, Germany, on small Kahl R. near its junction with the Main (canalized), and 9 mi. NW of Aschaffenburg; mfg. of metal and wood products.

Kahla (kä′lä), town (pop. 9,342), Thuringia, central Germany, on the Thuringian Saale and 9 mi. S of Jena; glass- and china-mfg. center. Towered over by 12th-cent. Leuchtenburg castle. Has 15th-cent church and remains of medieval town walls.

Kahl am Main, Germany: see KAHL.

Kahle Asten (kä′lŭ äs′tŭn), highest peak (2,759 ft.) of the Rothaargebirge, W Germany, 2 mi. W o Winterberg. Lenne R. rises here.

Kahlenberg, Austria: see WIENER WALD.

Kahlotus (kălō′tŭs), town (pop. 151), Franklin co. SE Wash., 35 mi. NE of Pasco, in Columbia basir agr. region.

Kahlur, India: see BILASPUR, state.

Kahmard, Afghanistan: see KAMARD.

Kahoka (kŭhō′kŭ), city (pop. 1,847), ⊙ Clark co. extreme NE Mo., near Des Moines R., 48 mi. ENE of Kirksville; grain; cheese mfg. Laid out 1851.

Kahoolawe (kähōōlä′vä, –wä, kähō′lä′–), island (□ 45), SW of Maui, T.H., from which it is separated by Alalakeiki Channel; 9 mi. long, 6 mi. wide Highest point 1,444 ft.; volcanic rocks, but no craters. Has poor soil, used for some cattle grazing Formerly a prison isl.; now leased to a private citizen. Sometimes written Kahulaui.

Kahrizak (kärēzäk′), village, Second Prov., in Teheran, N Iran, 10 mi. S of Teheran and on road to Qum; grain, cotton, sugar beets, truck produce sugar refinery.

Kahror or **Kahror Pakka** (kä′rōr pŭk′kŭ), town (pop. 11,348), Multan dist., S Punjab, W Pakistan 45 mi. SE of Multan; trades in wheat, cloth fabrics wool; cotton ginning, handicraft cloth printing.

Kahta (kyätä′), Turkish *Kâhta,* village (pop. 1,391) Malatya prov., E central Turkey, 45 mi. SSE of Malatya; barley, wheat, chick-peas, lentils, tobacco. Also Koluk.

Kahuku (kähōō′kōō), village (pop. 1,605), Oahu T.H., on NE coast; sugar industry. It is near **Kahuku Point,** the N tip of Oahu; 21°42′N 157°59′W.

Kahulaui, T.H.: see KAHOOLAWE.

Kahului (kä′hōōlōō′ē), village (pop. 6,306), N Maui T.H., on **Kahului Harbor,** principal Maui port for sugar export. Port of entry.

Kahusi Range (kähōō′sē), group of extinct volcanoes in E Belgian Congo, extending c.60 mi. parallel to W shore of L. Kivu; rises to 10,738 ft.; bamboo forests. First explored and mapped 1930–32.

Kai (kī), former province in central Honshu, Japan; now part of Yamanashi prefecture.

Kaiafa, Lake, Greece: see ZACHARO.

Kaiama (kāyä′mä), town (pop. 1,392), Ilorin prov., Northern Provinces, W Nigeria, 60 mi. NW of Jebba; gold-mining center; shea-nut processing, cotton weaving; cassava, millet, durra; cattle, skins. Hq Borgu div. (□ 10,908; pop. 40,145), the E section of former Borgu kingdom.

Kaiapha, Lake, Greece: see ZACHARO.

Kaiapoi (kī′ūpoi), borough (pop. 1,723), E S.Isl., New Zealand, 10 mi. N of Christchurch, at mouth of Waimakariri R.; wool, frozen meat, fish.

Kaibab Plateau (kī′băb, –băb), high tableland (7,500–9,300 ft.) largely in Coconino co., N Ariz., extends N from Grand Canyon, past Marble Gorge, into S Utah. Includes part of Kaibab Natl. Forest.

Kaibara (kībä′rä), town (pop. 6,745), Hyogo prefecture, S Honshu, Japan, 12 mi. SSW of Fukuchiyama; agr. center (chestnuts, mushrooms, rice, wheat, poultry). Raw silk.

Kaiba-to, Russian SFSR: see MONERON ISLAND.

Kaibitsy, Russian SFSR: see BOLSHIYE KAIBITSY.

K'ai-chiang, China: see KAIKIANG.

K'ai-chien, China: see HOIKIN.

Kaichow. **1** Town, Kweichow prov., China: see KAIYANG. **2** Town, Pingyuan prov., China: see PUYANG.

Kaidaichi (kīdī′chē) or **Kaitaichi** (kītī′chē), town (pop. 5,961), Hiroshima prefecture, SW Honshu, Japan, 5 mi. E of Hiroshima; rail junction; rice, wheat, raw silk; fishery.

Kaidanovo, Belorussian SSR: see DZERZHINSK, Minsk oblast.

Kaieiewaho Channel, T.H.: see KAUAI CHANNEL.

Kaien Island (kān) (6 mi. long, 4 mi. wide), W B.C., in Chatham Sound, off Tsimpsean Peninsula, near mouth of Skeena R. On NW coast is Prince Rupert city. Isl. is linked with mainland (S) by railroad and road bridges.

Kaieteur Falls (kī′ūtōōr″, kī″ūtōōr′), central Br. Guiana, on Potaro R., in outliers of the Guiana Highlands, and 100 mi. SW of Bartica; 5°10′N 59°28′W. A majestic landmark, the falls—c.350 ft. wide and several times as high as Niagara—drop 741 ft. from a sandstone tableland into a wide basin, where it drops another 71 ft. A notable tourist site, it can be reached by plane from Georgetown or by road from Bartica. The falls were discovered 1870 by Barrington Brown of the Geological Survey. The surrounding region has been proclaimed Kaieteur Natl. Park. There are other impressive waterfalls in the vicinity.

Kaifeng or **K'ai-feng** (kī′fŭng′), city (1936 pop. 303,422), ⊙ Honan prov., E central China, near Yellow R., on Lunghai RR, and c.370 mi. SSW of Peking; 34°48′N 114°21′E. Trading center; silk weaving, flour milling; peanuts, wheat, millet, melons, fruit. Soda and salt worked near by. Situated near CHAOKOW, where Yellow R. broke through its dike (1938) on its SE course, Kaifeng has been menaced by Yellow R. floods throughout its history. The old walled city (2.5 mi. by 3 mi.) includes Honan univ. (in former Examination Hall), military barracks (in former Sung palace), and the Sun Yat-sen Park, with lake. A modern S commercial suburb adjoins the railroad station. An anc. city, it was an imperial residence in the Five Dynasties (907–960) and the Northern Sung dynasty (960–1127). It was site of an early Jewish colony, with record of a 12th-cent. synagogue. Became ⊙ Honan in the Mongol dynasty (1280–1368) and remained the economic and transportation center of the prov. until supplanted (early 20th cent.) by rail hub of Chengchow. During Sino-Japanese War, it was held (1938–45) by Japanese. Fell 1948 to the Communists. It became an independent municipality in 1949.

Kaihsien or **K'ai-hsien** (kī'shyĕn'), town (pop. 21,351), ⊙ Kaihsien co. (pop. 606,586), E Szechwan prov., China, 25 mi. N of Wanhsien; rice, sweet potatoes, sugar cane, millet, rapeseed, medicinal herbs. Gypsum quarrying, coal and sulphur deposits, saltworks near by.

Kaihwa or **K'ai-hua** (both: kī'hwä'). **1** Town (pop. 5,858), ⊙ Kaihwa co. (pop. 114,617), SW Chekiang prov., China, near Kiangsi-Anhwei line, 32 mi. WNW of Chühsien; rice, wheat, bamboo shoots, tung oil. **2** Town, Yunnan prov., China: see Wenshan.

Kaihwachen, Manchuria: see Chanyü.

Kaihyo-to, Russian SFSR: see Tyuleni Island.

Kai Islands or **Kei Islands** (both: kī), group (□ 555; pop. 50,648), S Moluccas, Indonesia, in Banda Sea, 170 mi. SE of Ceram; 5°37'S 132°44'E; includes Nuhu Chut (largest), Nuhu Rowa, and the small groups, Tayandu Isls. and Kur Isls. Chief products: timber, trepang, copra, sago. Colonized by the Dutch after 1645. Also called Key Isls. and Ewab Isls.

Kaijo, Korea: see Kaesong.

Kaikalur (kī'kŭlōōr), village, Kistna dist., NE Madras, India, in Kistna R. delta, 13 mi. SSE of Ellore; rice, peanuts, tobacco.

Kaikiang or **K'ai-chiang** (both: kī'jyäng'), town (pop. 20,803), ⊙ Kaikiang co. (pop. 213,295), E Szechwan prov., China, 27 mi. ESE of Tahsien; paper milling, match mfg.; produces rice, millet, sweet potatoes, wheat, medicinal herbs. Until 1914 called Sinning.

Kaikien, China: see Hoikin.

Kaiko, Formosa: see Haikow.

Kaikoura (kīkōōr'ŭ), township (pop. 1,119), ⊙ Kaikoura co. (□ 929; pop. 3,424), E S.Isl., New Zealand, 65 mi. SSW of Blenheim, on small peninsula; dairying, fishing.

Kaikoura Ranges, E S.Isl., New Zealand, consist of 2 chains (Inland Kaikouras and Seaward Kaikouras) extending 25 mi. parallel with E coast, flanking lower course of Clarence R.; highest peak is Tapuaenuku (9,465 ft.); forested slopes.

Kailahun (kīlähōōn'), town (pop. 2,611), South-Eastern Prov., E Sierra Leone, near Moa R. (Fr. Guinea border), 85 mi. ENE of Bo and 15 mi. NE of railhead at Pendembu; road and trade center; palm oil and kernels, cacao, rice, coffee. Has hosp.

Kailali (kĭlä'lē), town, SW Nepal, in the Terai, on small Kateni R. and 16 mi. NE of Palia (India), 2 mi. NE of rail spur terminus at Chandan Chauki (India); rice, jute, oilseeds, sabai grass, vegetables.

Kailan (kī'län'), **Kailwan,** or **K'ai-luan** (both: kī'lwän'), coal-mining district in NE Hopeh prov., China, extending along Peking-Mukden RR, from Kaiping to Lwanhsien (Lanhsien), for which it is named. Includes coal-mining centers of Tangshan, Kaiping, and Lwanhsien.

Kailar, Greece: see Ptolemais.

Kailas (kīläs'), Tibetan *Kang* (or *Gang*) *Rimpoche* (käng' rĭm'pōchĕ, gäng'), peak (22,028 ft.) in Kailas Range, SW Tibet, N of Manasarowar L., 75 mi. SE of Gartok, at 31°5'N 81°20'E. Hindu pilgrimage center, encircled by path much used by pilgrims. Famous in Sanskrit literature as the paradise of Siva and Parvati.

Kailasagarh, peak, India: see Javadi Hills.

Kailashahar (kī'läshŭhŭr), village, Tripura, NE India, on tributary of the Kusiyara and 48 mi. NE of Agartala; trades in rice, cotton, tea, mustard, jute. Also spelled Kailasahar.

Kailas-Karakoram Range (kīläs'-kă'rŭkō"rŭm), S lateral range of Karakoram mtn. system, N Kashmir; from Hunza R. bend extends c.200 mi. SE to main bend of Shyok R.; parallels main range. Consists of 4 groups (NW–SE): Rakaposhi, Haramosh, Masherbrum, and Saltoro ranges. Masherbrum (25,660 ft.) is highest peak; average alt., c.18–19,700 ft. Chang Chenmo and Pangong ranges are SE extensions.

Kailas Range (kīläs'), mountain range of the SW Trans-Himalayas, SW Tibet; from upper Indus R. it extends c.360 mi. ESE, from c.80°E to c.85°E; c.20 mi. wide. Highest peaks are Kailas (22,028 ft.) in W and Lombo Kangra (23,165 ft.) in E. Gives rise to Indus R. (near village of Senge) and to headstreams of the Brahmaputra.

Kailiu, Cape (kä'ēlē'ōō), on NW coast, Kauai, T.H.

Kailo (kī'lō), village, Kivu prov., E Belgian Congo, 135 mi. NNW of Kasongo; center of tin-mining area; tin concentrating; also wolfram mining.

Kailu or **K'ai-lu** (kī'lōō'), town, ⊙ Kailu co. (pop. 31,667), S Inner Mongolian Autonomous Region, Manchuria, 50 mi. W of Tungliao, in Jooda league. Founded 1908; in Jehol until 1949.

Kailua (kä'ēlōō'ŭ), village (pop. 326), E Oahu, T.H., 13 mi. NE of Honolulu, on Kailua Bay.

Kailua Bay. 1 W Hawaii, T.H., chief landing in Kona dist. for cattle shipment. The 1st missionaries in Hawaii landed here in 1820. **2** E Oahu, T.H., near Mokapu Point.

K'ai-luan, China: see Kailan.

Kailwan, China: see Kailan.

Kaimakchalan, mountain range, Greece and Yugoslavia: see Kajmakcalan.

Kaimakli Beuyuk (kīmä'klē bäyōōk'), NE suburb (pop. 3,683), of Nicosia, N central Cyprus; wheat, barley, vetches; sheep, goats. Kaimakli Kutchuk adjoins W.

Kaimakli Kutchuk (kōōchōōk') or **Omorphita** (ômôr'fētä), N suburb (pop. 2,252) of Nicosia, N central Cyprus; citrus fruit, wheat; sheep, goats. Kaimakli Beuyuk adjoins E.

Kaimanawa Mountains (kīmă'nŭwŭ), central N.Isl., New Zealand, extend 40 mi. S from SE shore of L. Taupo; rise to 5,558 ft.; hot springs on W slopes.

Kaimes, Scotland: see Muirkirk.

Kaimganj (kīm'gŭnj), town (pop. 9,466), Farrukhabad dist., central Uttar Pradesh, India, 18 mi. NW of Farrukhabad; wheat, gram, corn, tobacco. Founded 1713 by 1st nawab of Farrukhabad.

Kaimpur, W Pakistan: see Qaimpur.

Kaimur Hills (kī'mōōr), NE branch of Vindhya Range, central India; from S Jubbulpore dist. in Madhya Pradesh extend c.300 mi. ENE, across Vindhya Pradesh and Mirzapur dist. of Uttar Pradesh, to just E of Sasaram (Shahabad dist., Bihar); c.10–35 mi. wide; up to c.2,000 ft. high. Drained largely by Son R.

Kain (kē), village (pop. 4,692), Hainaut prov., SW Belgium, 2 mi. N of Tournai, near Scheldt R.; liquor distilling; agr. Site of former Cistercian nunnery.

Kain, Iran: see Qain.

Kainan (kīnä'), city (1940 pop. 29,091; 1947 pop. 33,692), Wakayama prefecture, S Honshu, Japan, on inlet of Kii Channel, on W coast of Kii Peninsula, just SE of Wakayama; rail junction; home industries (lacquer ware, umbrellas). Fishing. Harbor for sailboats and other small craft.

Kainan, Korea: see Haenam.

Kainar or **Kaynar** (kīnär'), village (1939 pop. over 500), NW Semipalatinsk oblast, Kazakh SSR, 165 mi. WSW of Semipalatinsk; cattle.

Kainardzha or **Kaynardzha** (kīnär'jä), Rum. *Cainargeana-Mica*, village (pop. 2,296), Ruse dist., NE Bulgaria, in S Dobruja, 15 mi. SE of Silistra; grain, sheep. A peace treaty was concluded here (1774), by which Turkey ceded to Russia the Crimea and S Ukraine. Called Kuchuk Kainarji or Kutchuk Kainarji under Turkey. In Rumania 1913–40.

Kainary or **Kaynary** (kīnä'rē), Rum. *Căinari*, village (1941 pop. 2,043), SE Moldavian SSR, on Botna R., on railroad and 22 mi. SW of Bendery; rail junction; corn, wheat, stock; carpet weaving.

Kainda, Kirghiz SSR: see Molotovsk, Frunze oblast.

Kaindorf (kīn'dôrf), village (pop. 2,051), Styria, SE Austria, 19 mi. S of Graz; grain, cattle.

Kainei, Korea: see Hoeryong.

Kainsk, Russian SFSR: see Kuibyshev, city, Novosibirsk oblast.

Kaintira, India: see Athmallik, village.

Kai o Kalohi (kī'ōkälō'hē), channel bet. Lanai and Molokai isls., T.H., 7 naut. mi. wide.

Kaipara Harbour (kī'pŭrŭ), N N.Isl., New Zealand, 25 mi. NNW of Auckland; 40 mi. long, 5 mi. wide; connected with Tasman Sea by passage 5 mi. wide. Receives Wairoa R. Several small villages surround harbor. Outlet for dairy products, timber.

Kaiparowits Plateau (kŭpă'rŭwĭts) (c.7–8,000 ft.), S Utah; sparsely settled tableland W of Colorado R., bet. Escalante and Paria rivers; sheep and cattle grazing.

Kaiping or **K'ai-p'ing** (kī'pĭng'). **1** Town, NE Hopeh prov., China, on railroad and 5 mi. NE of Tangshan; major coal-mining center of Kailan dist. Spur leads to Makiakow mine, 3 mi. N. **2** Town, Kwangtung prov., China: see Hoiping.

Kaipong Islands (gī'pông'), Mandarin *Chia-p'eng* (jyä'pŭng'), group in S.China Sea, Kwangtung prov., China, off Canton R. estuary, extending 10 mi. SW–NE at 21°50'N 114°W. Largest isl. (NE) is Pak Tsim (päk'jēm'), Mandarin *Pei Chien*, 3 mi. long.

Kaira (kī'rŭ), district, N Bombay, India; ⊙ Kaira. Bounded S and E by Mahi R., SW by Sabarmati R., N by Sabar Kantha dist. Agr. (millet, rice, tobacco, cotton, oilseeds); hand-loom weaving, cloth printing; metal products. Cotton mills at Nadiad, Petlad, Cambay. Other important towns: Kapadvanj, Anand, Borsad. Under Rajput dynasties (8th–13th cent.). Original dist. (□ 1,617; 1941 pop. 914,957) enlarged by inc. (1949) of several former Gujarat states, including Cambay and Balasinor, and parts of former Baroda state. Pop. 86% Hindu, 9% Moslem, 3% Christian.

Kaira, town (pop. 7,311), ⊙ Kaira dist., N Bombay, India, 19 mi. SSE of Ahmadabad; market center for rice, millet, cloth fabrics; cotton and rice milling, cotton-cloth printing, match mfg. Very old site (c.5th cent. B.C.).

Kairana (kīrä'nŭ), town (pop. 22,644), Muzaffarnagar dist., N Uttar Pradesh, India, 30 mi. WSW of Muzaffarnagar; sugar processing, ornamental-curtain mfg.; trades in wheat, gram, sugar cane, oilseeds.

Kairanga, New Zealand: see Palmerston North.

Kairiru (kīrērōō'), volcanic island, Sepik dist., Territory of New Guinea, SW Pacific, just off NE coast of New Guinea; c.9 mi. long; rises to 3,350 ft.; coconut plantation.

Kairouan or **Kairwan** (kärwän', Fr. kĕrwã'), Arabic *Qairwan*, city (pop. 32,299), ⊙ Kairouan dist. (□ 2,690; pop. 181,127), E central Tunisia, on rail spur 32 mi. SW of Sousse and 80 mi. S of Tunis, in a semi-arid lowland; 35°40'N 10°6'E. A holy city of the Moslems (pilgrimages), it also attracts non-Moslem tourists. Its magnificent mosques are open to visitors of other faiths. The town walls, gateways, water reservoirs, and markets are also noteworthy. Kairouan is well-known for its carpets and leather goods. Trade in cereals, olives, sheep, wool, and skins. Airfield. Founded A.D. 671 by the Arab conqueror Sidi Okba (for whom the Great Mosque is named). Capital of Aglabite dynasty during 9th cent.

Kairuku, Papua: see Yule Island.

Kaisarganj (kī'sŭrgŭnj), village, Bahraich dist., N Uttar Pradesh, India, 22 mi. S of Bahraich; rice, wheat, corn, gram.

Kaisargarh, peak, W Pakistan: see Takht-i-Sulaiman.

Kaisaria, Turkey: see Kayseri.

Kaisariane or **Kaisariani** (both: käsärēänē'), ESE suburb (pop. 20,151) of Athens, Greece, 2 mi. from city center.

Kaisatskoye or **Kaysatskoye** (kīsät'skŭyŭ), village (1939 pop. over 2,000), NE Stalingrad oblast, Russian SFSR, on railroad (Kaisatskaya station) and 40 mi. N of Elton; wheat, cattle, sheep.

Kaisen, Korea: see Kaechon.

Kaiseraugst, Switzerland: see Augst.

Kaiseregg (kī'zŭrĕk), peak (7,181 ft.) in Bernese Alps, W central Switzerland, 7 mi. NNW of Zweisimmen.

Kaisergebirge (kī'zŭrgŭbĭr'gŭ), W mountain group of Salzburg Alps, Tyrol, W Austria, E of Kufstein; rises to 7,688 ft. in the Ellmauer Haltspitze.

Kaiserin-Augusta River, New Guinea: see Sepik River.

Kaiseroda (kī"zŭrō'dä), village (pop. 240), Thuringia, central Germany, on the Werra and 13 mi. SSW of Eisenach; potash mining.

Kaiser Peak (kī'zŭr) (10,300 ft.), E central Calif., in the Sierra Nevada, 50 mi. NE of Fresno.

Kaiserslautern (kī"zŭrslou'tŭrn), city (1939 pop. 70,713; 1946 pop. 55,932; 1950 pop. 62,395), Rhenish Palatinate, W Germany, on the Lauter and 30 mi. W of Ludwigshafen; 49°27'N 7°47'E. Rail transshipment point; industrial center; metalworking. Textile (wool, worsted) and tobacco (cigars, cigarettes, pipe tobacco) industries; mfg. of furniture, beer. Has early-14th-cent. church; mid-19th-cent. Fruchthalle. Second World War destruction (c.60%) included late-13th-cent. church. Kaiserslautern was 1st mentioned c.800. Emperor Frederick Barbarossa built castle here c.1150. Chartered 1276. Seat (1849) of provisional govt. of Rhenish Palatinate. Captured by U.S. troops in March, 1945.

Kaiserstuhl (kī'zŭr-shtōōl), volcanic massif on right bank of the Rhine, S Baden, Germany, 8 mi. NW of Freiburg; rises to 1,734 ft. in the Totenkopf (to'tŭn-kôpf). One of Germany's warmest regions. Noted for wine and fruit.

Kaiserswerth (kī"zŭrsvârt'), district (since 1929) of Düsseldorf, W Germany, on right bank of the Rhine (landing) and 6 mi. N of city center. Has early-Romanesque church. Site of noted school for deaconesses, founded 1836.

Kaiser Wilhelm Canal, Germany: see Kiel Canal.

Kaiser Wilhelm II Land, Antarctica: see Wilhelm II Coast.

Kaiser-Wilhelmsland: see New Guinea, Territory of.

Kaishantun or **K'ai-shan-t'un** (kī'shän'tōōn'), town, SE Kirin prov., Manchuria, on railroad and 20 mi. SE of Yenki, on Tumen R. (Korea line); wood-pulp mill; rayon mfg.

Kaisheim (kīs'hīm), village (pop. 1,864), Swabia, W Bavaria, Germany, 3 mi. NNE of Donauwörth; textile mfg. Former Cistercian monastery (founded c.1135), with late-Gothic church, was converted into prison in 1816.

Kaishow (gī'shō) or **Chieh-shou** (jyĕ'shō'), town, N Kiangsu prov., China, on E shore of Kaoyu L., 15 mi. N of Kaoyu, and on Grand Canal; commercial center.

Kaishu, Korea: see Haeju.

Kaisiadorys, Kaishyadoris, or **Kayshyadoris** (kīsh'-yädōrēs'), Lith. *Kaišiadorys*, Rus. *Koshedary*, city (1925 pop. 1,540), S central Lithuania, 20 mi. E of Kaunas; rail junction; mfg. (shoes, lubricating oils, bone meal, bricks, flour). Has mus. In Rus. Vilna govt. until 1920.

Kaisong, Korea: see Kaesong.

Kaisyu, Korea: see HAEJU.

Kaitaia (kītī'ů), borough (pop. 1,209), ⊙ Mangonui co. (□ 960; pop. 7,576), N N.Isl., New Zealand, 145 mi. NW of Auckland; dairying center.

Kaitaichi, Japan: see KAIDAICHI.

Kaitak, Hong Kong: see KOWLOON.

Kaitangata (kītăng'gŭtů), borough (pop. 1,351), SE S.Isl., New Zealand, on Clutha R. and 45 mi. SW of Dunedin; coal mines.

Kaithal (kī'tŭl), town (pop. 22,325), Karnal dist., E Punjab, India, 35 mi. WNW of Karnal; market center for wheat, millet, cotton, rice; cotton ginning, saltpeter refining; metalwork, pottery, lacquered woodwork. Large bathing tank.

Kaitieke, New Zealand: see RAURIMU.

Kaitung or **K'ai-t'ung** (kī'tŏŏng'), town, ⊙ Kaitung co. (pop. 88,619), SW Heilungkiang prov., Manchuria, 40 mi. SSE of Taonan, and on railroad, near Kirin line; kaoliang, millet, sheepskins.

Kaiwi Channel (kä-ē'wē), bet. Molokai and Oahu isls., T.H., 23 naut. mi. wide.

Kaiya, China: see KERIYA.

Kaiyang or **K'ai-yang** (kī'yäng'), town (pop. 3,588), ⊙ Kaiyang co. (pop. 137,570), central Kweichow prov., China, 35 mi. NNE of Kweiyang; lacquer processing; wheat, millet. Iron, bauxite, and mercury deposits, and saltworks near by. Until 1914 called Kaichow, and 1914–30, Tzekiang.

Kaiyüan or **K'ai-yüan** (kī'yüăn'). **1** Town (1938 pop. 34,380), ⊙ Kaiyüan co. (1946 pop. 396,150), NE Liaosi prov., Manchuria, 40 mi. SSW of Szeping and on railroad; one of chief soybean centers in Manchuria; soybean oil and cake; rice and flour mills. Consists of old walled Chinese city (N), dating from 13th cent.; and the new rail town of Sunkiatai. **2** Town (pop. 5,996), ⊙ Kaiyüan co. (pop. 82,854), SE Yunnan prov., China, on railroad and 95 mi. SE of Kunming, on highway leading E to Kweichow; alt. 3,445 ft.; center of antimony-mining dist.; cotton-textile mfg., rice milling. Wheat, millet, beans, fruit. Until 1931, Ami.

Kaizanchin, Korea: see HYESANJIN.

Kaizuka (kīzōō'kä), city (1940 pop. 42,797; 1947 pop. 47,129), Osaka prefecture, S Honshu, Japan, adjacent to Kishiwada (NE), 17 mi. SW of Osaka; mfg. (textiles, dyes, celluloid, flour).

Kaizyo, Korea: see KAESONG.

Kajaani (kä'yänē), Swedish *Kajana* (kī'änä"), city (pop. 10,077), Oulu co., central Finland, port on tributary of Oulu R. (falls), just above its mouth on L. Oulu, 90 mi. SE of Oulu; lumber center, with lumber, cellulose, paper, and flour mills. Site of power station, teachers' seminary, dist. hosp. Has mus., ruins of 17th-cent. castle. Founded 1651; sacked (1712) by Russians. For some time residence of Lönnrot, compiler of the *Kalevala*.

Kajakai or **Kajkai** (kŭjŭkī'), village, Kandahar prov., S central Afghanistan, 45 mi. NE of Girishk and on Helmand R.; storage dam built here c.1950 regulates the Helmand's seasonal level changes.

Kajang (käjäng'), town (pop. 7,543), SE Selangor, Malaya, on railroad and 12 mi. SSE of Kuala Lumpur, on Langat R.; rubber-growing center; rice, cattle, hogs.

Kajan River (kŭjän'), E Borneo, Indonesia, rises in Iran Mts. on boundary bet. Sarawak and Indonesian Borneo, flows E through mountainous area, turns generally ENE past Tanjungselor to Celebes Sea, 25 mi. E of Tanjungselor; c.250 mi. long. Sometimes spelled Kayan; also called Bulungan.

Kajiado (käjēä'dō), village, Masai dist., S Kenya, on railroad (at road crossing) and 35 mi. ENE of Magadi; stock raising; coffee, wheat, peanuts, corn. Marble quarrying near by.

Kajikazawa (käjēkä'zäwů), town (pop. 6,095), Yamanashi prefecture, central Honshu, Japan, 11 mi. SW of Kofu; umbrellas.

Kajiki (kä"jē'kē), town (pop. 19,527), Kagoshima prefecture, S Kyushu, Japan, 13 mi. NE of Kagoshima, on N shore of Kagoshima Bay; livestock and agr. (rice) center.

Kajkai, Afghanistan: see KAJAKAI.

Kajmakcalan, Kaimakchalan, or **Kaymakchalan** (kīmäkchä'län), Serbo-Croatian *Kajmakčalan*, Gr. *Voras* (vô'rùs), peak in Nidze massif on Yugoslav-Greek border, E of Pelagonija valley; rises to 8,280 ft. 15 mi. NW of Edessa (Greece). The name Kajmakcalan is sometimes applied to the entire Nidze massif.

Kajora, India: see RANIGANJ.

Kaka (kä'ků), village, Upper Nile prov., S central Anglo-Egyptian Sudan, on left bank of the White Nile, on road and 80 mi. NNE of Malakal. Shilluk tribes in area.

Kakabeka Falls, village (pop. estimate 450), W Ont., on Kaministikwia R. (130-ft. falls) and 17 mi. W of Fort William; hydroelectric-power center; dairying, grain growing.

Kakagi Lake (20 mi. long, 6 mi. wide), W Ont., 3 mi. E of head of Whitefish Bay (L. of the Woods), 40 mi. SE of Kenora.

Kakamega (käkämĕ'gä), town (pop. c.5,000), W Kenya, on road and 28 mi. N of Kisumu; 0°17'N 34°37'E. Center of gold field (extending S to Tanganyika border), discovered 1930. Also pyrite mining. Asbestos-cement sheet mfg. Airfield. Kavirondo tribal reserve.

Kakamoeka (käkämwĕkä'), village, SW Middle Congo territory, Fr. Equatorial Africa, on Kouilou R. and 50 mi. NNE of Pointe-Noire; terminus of navigation; gold mining, plantations.

Kakanda (käkän'dä), village, Katanga prov., SE Belgian Congo, 28 mi. NW of Jadotville; copper mining.

Kakanj, Kakan, or **Kakan'** (all: kä'känyů), village, central Bosnia, Yugoslavia, on Bosna R., on railroad and 10 mi. ESE of Zenica, in Sarajevo coal area; brown-coal mine.

Kaka River (kä'kä), La Paz dept., W Bolivia; formed by confluence of Mapiri and Coroico rivers at Puerto Ballivián; flows 40 mi. N to Beni R. at Puerto Pando. Sometimes called Mapiri R.

Kakata (kä'kätä), town, Central Prov., W Liberia, 35 mi. NE of Monrovia, on road; palm oil and kernels, cassava, rice, poultry. Site of Booker T. Washington inst. (agr. and technical school); mission station.

Kakaur (kŭkour'), town (pop. 3,041), Bulandshahr dist., W Uttar Pradesh, India, 12 mi. SW of Bulandshahr; wheat, oilseeds, cotton, barley, corn, jowar. Also spelled Kakor and Kakore.

Kake (kāk), village (pop. 376), SE Alaska, on N shore of Kupreanof Isl., 40 mi. WNW of Petersburg; fishing, fish processing, lumbering. School.

Kake (kä'kā), town (pop. 5,820), Hiroshima prefecture, SW Honshu, Japan, 17 mi. NNW of Hiroshima; commercial center for agr. and livestock area; rice, raw silk, lumber; textiles.

Kakeda (kä"kā'dä), town (pop. 4,328), Fukushima prefecture, N Honshu, Japan, 7 mi. ENE of Fukushima; agr., raw silk.

Kakegawa (käkā'gäwů), town (pop. 16,955), Shizuoka prefecture, central Honshu, Japan, 25 mi. SW of Shizuoka; agr. center (rice, tea); raw silk, textiles.

Kaketsuka (käkā'tsŏŏkä) or **Kakezuka** (–zōō–), town (pop. 7,062), Shizuoka prefecture, central Honshu, Japan, on Philippine Sea, at mouth of Tenryu R., 5 mi. SE of Hamamatsu; rice, raw silk.

Kakhetia (kůkē'shů), Rus. *Kakhetiya* (kŭkhĕ'tyēŭ), major wine-producing region of E Georgian SSR, drained by upper Alazan R. Chief towns: Telavi, Signakhi, Gurdzhaani. Wine-making centers: Tsinandali, Napareuli.

Kakhetian Range, S spur of the E Greater Caucasus, in E Georgian SSR; extends in arc from Mt. Barbalo c.75 mi. S and SE to area of Gurdzhaani; forms watershed bet. Iora and Alazan rivers; rises to 6,530 ft. Vineyards on Alazan R. slopes.

Kakhi (kŭkhē'), village (1948 pop. over 2,000), N Azerbaijan SSR, on S slope of the Greater Caucasus, on road and 22 mi. NW of Nukha; rice, tobacco, sericulture; lumbering.

Kakhib (kŭkhēp'), village (1932 pop. estimate 1,300), central Dagestan Autonomous SSR, Russian SFSR, 8 mi. SW of Khunzakh, near the Avar Koisu; grain, sheep. Pop. largely Avar.

Kakhonak (kăk'hōnăk), village (pop. 60), SW Alaska, on S shore of Iliamna L., at base of Alaska Peninsula; 59°26'N 154°54'W.

Kakhovka (kŭkhôf'kŭ), city (1939 pop. over 10,000), central Kherson oblast, Ukrainian SSR, on Dnieper R. (landing), opposite Berislav, and 40 mi. ENE of Kherson; tractor plant; cotton ginning, flour milling.

Kaki Bukit (kä'kē bōō'kĭt), village (pop. 1,273), Perlis, NW Malaya, near Thailand border, 13 mi. N of Kangar, on slopes of the Gunong China; tin mining.

Kakinada, India: see COCANADA.

Kakino (käkē'nō), town (pop. 5,220), Mie prefecture, S Honshu, Japan, 17 mi. W of Uji-yamada; lumber, charcoal, rice, tea.

Kakinoura-shima (käkēnō'rä'shĭmä), island (□ 2; pop. 19,226), Nagasaki prefecture, Japan, in E. China Sea, just off NW coast of Sonogi Peninsula, Kyushu; 2.5 mi. long, 1 mi. wide; sandstone.

Kakioka (kä"kē'ōkä), town (pop. 5,170), Ibaraki prefecture, central Honshu, Japan, 11 mi. N of Tsuchiura; rice, wheat.

Kakira (käkē'rä), village, Eastern Prov., SE Uganda, 8 mi. NE of Jinja; sugar mill.

Kakisaki (käkē'sä'kē) or **Kakizaki** (–zä'kē), town (pop. 9,455), Niigata prefecture, central Honshu, Japan, 14 mi. NE of Takada; rice, silk cocoons.

Käkisalmi, Russian SFSR: see PRIOZERSK.

Kakitumba (käkētŏŏm'bä), village, NE Ruanda-Urundi, in Ruanda, on Kagera R., on Uganda and Tanganyika borders, and 65 mi. NE of Kigali; customs station; coffee growing.

Kakizaki, Japan: see KAKISAKI.

Kakkapalliya (kŭk"kŭpŭl'lĭyŭ), village (pop. 832), North Western Prov., Ceylon, 3.5 mi. SSE of Chilaw; paper mfg.; rice, coconut palms.

Kakogawa (käkō'gäwů), town (pop. 24,610), Hyogo prefecture, S Honshu, Japan, 9 mi. ESE of Himeji; commercial and mfg. center; woolen and leather goods, cutlery.

Kakontwe (käkōnt'wä), village, Katanga prov., SE Belgian Congo, 8 mi. W of Jadotville. Copper mining, flour milling (manioc, wheat, corn), palm-oil milling, limestone quarrying; explosives mfg.

Kakopetria (käkôpē'trēä), summer resort (pop. 1,003), Nicosia dist., W central Cyprus, in Olympus Mts., 28 mi. WSW of Nicosia. Chromite ore is mined and concentrated near by.

Kakor, India: see KAKAUR.

Kakori (kä'kōrē), town (pop. 8,073), Lucknow dist., central Uttar Pradesh, India, 8 mi. W of Lucknow city center; wheat, rice, gram, millet, oilseeds. Has 16th-17th-cent. dargahs.

Kakoulima (käkōōlē'mä), village, W Fr. Guinea, Fr. West Africa, on railroad and 25 mi. NE of Conakry; bananas, palm kernels. The Kakoulima mtn. (3,688 ft.) and resort area adjoins E.

Kakrala (kŭkră'lů), town (pop. 8,603), Budaun dist., central Uttar Pradesh, India, 11 mi. SSE of Budaun; wheat, pearl millet, mustard, barley, gram. Serai.

Kaktovik (käk'tōvĭk), village (pop. 44), E central Alaska, near Fairbanks.

Kakuda (kä"kōō'dä), town (pop. 11,973), Miyagi prefecture, N Honshu, Japan, on Abukuma R. and 20 mi. SSW of Sendai; rice, wheat, raw silk.

Kakudate (käkōō'dä'tä) or **Kakunodate** (käkōō'nōdä"tä), town (pop. 8,458), Akita prefecture, N Honshu, Japan, 25 mi. ESE of Akita; sake, silk cocoons, livestock, rice.

Kakul (kä'kōōl), village, Hazara dist., NE North-West Frontier Prov., W Pakistan, 3 mi. NE of Abbottabad; site of Pakistan Military Acad. (opened Jan., 1948).

Kakumabetsu, Russian SFSR: see SHELEKHOVO.

Kakumagawa (käkōōmä'gäwů), town (pop. 4,387), Akita prefecture, N Honshu, Japan, 7 mi. NW of Yokote; rice, sake, peat.

Kakunodate, Japan: see KAKUDATE.

Kakuzan, Korea: see KWAKSAN.

Kal (käl), Hung. *Kál*, agr. town (pop. 4,749), Heves co., N Hungary, on Tarna R. and 9 mi. N of Heves.

Kala, for Afghan names beginning thus: see under QALA.

Kala, Azerbaijan SSR: see KALININA, IMENI.

Kalaa, for Arabic names beginning thus and not found here: see under QAL'A.

Kalaa-Djerda (kälä-ä'-jĕrdä'), village, Le Kef dist., W Tunisia, on railroad and 35 mi. NNW of Kasserine; important phosphate mines.

Kalaa-Kebira (–kĕbērä'), town (pop. 14,282), Sousse dist., E Tunisia, in the coastal strip (*Sahel*), 6 mi. NW of Sousse; olive groves, olive and flour mills.

Kalaa-Srira (–srērä'), village, Sousse dist., E Tunisia, 5 mi. W of Sousse; junction of Tunis-Gabès and Sousse-Tozeur rail lines. Silo. Olives, vegetables, sheep.

Kalaat, for Arabic names beginning thus and not found here: see under QAL'AT.

Kalaat-es-Senam (kälä-ät'-ĕs-sĕnäm'), village, Le Kef dist., W Tunisia, near Algerian border, on rail spur and 35 mi. SSW of Le Kef; phosphate mines. Zinc and lead mining on slope of Djebel bou Jaber (on frontier, 5 mi. SW; rail terminus).

Kalabagh (kä'läbäg), town (pop. 8,714), Mianwali dist., NW Punjab, W Pakistan, on Indus R. and 26 mi. N of Mianwali; wheat; hand-loom weaving; metal products. Rock salt quarried in near-by hills; coal mines, alum deposits. Mari Indus is 1 mi. S, across river; small rail depot for coal and salt. Headworks of Thal canal irrigation project 4 mi. S.

Kalabahi, Indonesia: see ALOR.

Kalabak, Bulgaria-Greece: see RADOMIR.

Kalabaka, Greece: see KALAMBAKA.

Kalabaki, Greece: see KALAMBAKI.

Kalabi, Belgian Congo: see KANUNKA.

Kalabo (kälä'bō), township (pop. 174), Barotse prov., W Northern Rhodesia, 40 mi. NW of Mongu; cattle, sheep, goats; corn, millet. Airfield.

Kalabsha or **Kalabshah** (kăläb'shů), village (1937 pop. 956), Aswan prov., S Egypt, on W bank of the Nile and 40 mi. S of Aswan. Site of Roman temple built during reign of Augustus on site of earlier sanctuary built by Thutmose III (c.1450 B.C.).

Kalach (kŭlăch'). **1** or **Kalach on Don**, Rus. *Kalach-na-Donu*, town (1948 pop. over 10,000), S central Stalingrad oblast, Russian SFSR, on left bank of Don R., 45 mi. W of Stalingrad, at W terminus of the Volga-Don Canal; metalworks. Encirclement of Ger. Stalingrad besiegers was completed (Nov., 1942) near by. **2** City (1948 pop. over 10,000), E Voronezh oblast, Russian SFSR, 33 mi. SE of Buturlinovka; rail terminus; meat-packing center; flour milling. Became city in 1945.

Kalachinsk (kŭlä'chĭnsk), town (1926 pop. 4,243), SE Omsk oblast, Russian SFSR, on Trans-Siberian RR and 45 mi. E of Omsk; metalworks.

Kaladan River (kůlůdăn', –dŭn'), main stream of N Arakan coast, Lower Burma, formed in Chin Hills on India border at 22°47'N by junction of Boinu and Tyao rivers, flows 200 mi. through Indian Lushai Hills and Burmese Arakan Hill Tracts, past Paletwa (head of navigation) and Kyauktaw, to Bay of Bengal at Akyab, where it is linked by tidal creeks with Mayu and Lemro rivers. Navigable for 96 mi.

Kaladgi (kŭlăd'gē), village, Bijapur dist., S Bombay, India, on Ghatprabha R. and 13 mi. W of Bagalkot; peanuts, cotton. Sandstone, slate, and flagstone quarried near by.

Ka Lae (kä lī'), point, S extremity of Hawaii, T.H.; 18°54'N 155°41'W.

Kalagarh (kä'lăgŭr), village, Garhwal dist., N Uttar Pradesh, India, on Ramganga R. and 22 mi. SE of Kotdwara, at foot of Siwalik Range. Just N, 340-ft.-high irrigation and power dam is planned.

Kalahandi (kälä'hŭndē), district (□ 4,388; pop. 794,440), SW Orissa, India; ⊙ Bhawanipatna. Bordered W by Madhya Pradesh; crossed (N–S) by several ranges of Eastern Ghats. Rice is chief crop; forests yield sal and bamboo. Created 1949 by merger of former princely state of Kalahandi (□ 3,559; pop. 597,940) of Chhattisgarh States and S subdivision (□ 829; pop. 196,500) of original Sambalpur dist.

Kalahari Desert (kä"lŭhä'rē), arid plateau region (3,500–4,000 ft.) in S Africa, in Bechuanaland Protectorate and British Bechuanaland, bet. Orange R. (S) and Zambezi R. (N); South-West Africa is on W. Near S border of Bechuanaland Protectorate are extensive sand-dune areas; further N numerous dry lake-beds occur and water is believed to be available below the surface. Bushman grass and Tsama melons grow in parts of region; Hottentots and Bushmen live here. In SW part of region is the Kalahari Natl. Park.

Kalahari National Park (□ 3,729), NW Bechuanaland dist., N Cape Prov., U. of So. Afr., c.250 mi. N of Upington, in the panhandle bet. Bechuanaland Protectorate (E and N) and South-West Africa (W). Reserve contains gemsbok, springbok, wildebeest, hartebeest, elands, kudus, ostriches, steenbok, duiker, lions, leopards, hyenas, jackals.

Kalahasti (kä'lŭhŭstē), town (pop. 14,704), Chittoor dist., E central Madras, India, 55 mi. NE of Chittoor; rice and oilseed milling; ceramics, metalworks; noted handicrafts include cotton fabrics and glass bangles. Annual temple fair.

Kalaheo (kä'lähä'ō), village (pop. 973), S Kauai, T.H.; pineapple plantations.

Kalah Shergat, Iraq: see SHARQAT.

Kalai-Khumb (kŭlī"-khōomp'), village (1926 pop. 230), S Garm oblast, Tadzhik SSR, in the Pamir, on Panj R. (Afghanistan border) and 45 mi. SE of Garm; gold placers; sheep, goats.

Kalai-Lyabiob, Tadzhik SSR: see TADZHIKABAD.

Kalai-Mirzabai, Tadzhik SSR: see KALININABAD.

Kala-i-Mor (–mōr), town (1948 pop. over 500) S Mary oblast, Turkmen SSR, 30 mi. NE of Kushka, on railroad to Mary and on Kushka R.; karakul state farm.

Kalai-Vamar, Tadzhik SSR: see RUSHAN.

Kalaiya (kŭlī'yŭ), town, S Nepal, in the Terai, 8 mi. ENE of Birganj; rice, wheat, barley, mustard, millet.

Kalajoki (kä'läyō"kē), village (commune pop. 7,123), Oulu co., W Finland, on Gulf of Bothnia at mouth of Kala R., 40 mi. NE of Kokkola; granite quarries; seaside resort.

Kalakan (kŭlŭkän'), town (1939 pop. over 500), NW Chita oblast, Russian SFSR, on Vitim R. and 250 mi. NE of Chita; agr., lumbering. Was ⊙ former Vitim-Olekma Natl. Okrug.

Kalakh, Iraq: see CALAH.

Kalakh, Tell, Syria: see TELKALAKH.

Kalakhiri Range or **Kalakiri Range** (käläkē'rē), on Thailand-Malaya border, on Malay Peninsula, forming S continuation of Sithammarat Range; rises to 5,035 ft. Crossed by Malaya-Thailand highway bet. Kroh and Betong.

Kalam or **Kallam** (both: kŭl'lŭm), town (pop. 5,396), Osmanabad dist., W Hyderabad state, India, on Manjra R. and 28 mi. N of Osmanabad; millet, wheat, rice; cotton ginning.

Kalama (kŭlă'mŭ), town (pop. 1,121), Cowlitz co., SW Wash., 10 mi. S of Kelso and on Columbia R., near mouth of Kalama R.; river and rail shipping point. Timber, strawberries, fish, truck. State fish hatchery here. Founded 1870, ⊙ Cowlitz co. until 1932.

Kalamai, Greece: see KALAMATA.

Kalama River (kŭlă'mŭ), SW Wash., rises SW of Mt. St. Helens, flows c.45 mi. SW to Columbia R. below Kalama; salmon hatchery near mouth.

Kalamas River, Greece: see THYAMIS RIVER.

Kalamat (kä'lämät), Ital. *Chelamet* (kĕlämĕt'), village, Keren div., N Eritrea, 25 mi. NE of Keren, in agr. (cereals, fruit, vegetables) and livestock region; road junction.

Kalamata (kälŭmä'tŭ), Gr. *Kalamai* (kŭlä'mā), city (1951 pop. 38,363), ⊙ Messenia, SW Peloponnesus, Greece, port on Gulf of Messenia, 85 mi. SSE of Patras; major commercial and industrial center. Fisheries; silk spinning, flour milling, mfg. of cigarettes, liquors. Coaling station with repair docks. Connected by rail with Patras and Argos. Exports local agr. products (figs, citrus fruits, olives, olive oil, cotton, silk), imports timber, textiles, manufactured goods. Developed after 1204 under Fr. Crusaders who established feudal state, built castle (NE); later ruled by Venetians and (1459–1821) by Turks. Destroyed 1825 in Gr. war of independence.

Kalamata, Gulf of, Greece: see MESSENIA, GULF OF.

Kalamazoo (kă"lŭmŭzōō'), county (□ 567; pop. 126,707), SW Mich.; ⊙ KALAMAZOO. Drained by Kalamazoo R. and short Portage R. Livestock, dairy products, fruit, grain, corn, celery, peppermint. Mfg. at Kalamazoo. Numerous small lakes. Organized 1830.

Kalamazoo, city (pop. 57,704), ⊙ Kalamazoo co., SW Mich., c.55 mi. NE of South Bend (Ind.) and on Kalamazoo R. (water power). Industrial center, especially important for paper making; also mfg. of stoves, furnaces, pharmaceuticals, fishing tackle, auto parts, metal products, air-conditioning equipment, electrical goods, essential oils, foodstuffs, clothing; oil refining. Rail and commercial center of rich celery-growing area, also producing fruit, pansy plants, peppermint. Has Kalamazoo Col., a state teachers col., Nazareth Acad., an art institute and a natural-history mus. A state hosp. for the mentally ill is here. Settled 1829; inc. as village 1838, as city 1884.

Kalamazoo River, S and SW Mich., formed by junction of North and South branches at Albion, flows NW, past Marshall, Battle Creek, Kalamazoo, Otsego, and Allegan, to L. Michigan at Saugatuck; c.138 mi. long. Power development.

Kalamb (kŭl'ŭmb), village (pop., including factory area of Walchandnagar, 8,403), Poona dist., central Bombay, India, on Nira R. and 16 mi. SE of Baramati; agr. market (sugar cane, peanuts, millet); sugar and oilseed milling, dairy farming, soap mfg.

Kalambaka or **Kalabaka** (both: kälŭbä'kŭ), town (pop. 3,690), Trikkala nome, Thessaly, Greece, 14 mi. NW of Trikkala, on Peneus R. where it enters Thessalian plain; narrow-gauge rail terminus; trade in corn, wheat, vegetables, cheese. The anc. Aeginium, it was known as Stagous in Byzantine times and received present name under Turkish rule. Meteora monasteries are just N. Also spelled Kalampaka.

Kalambaki or **Kalabaki** (both: kälŭbä'kē), town (pop. 2,873), Drama nome, Macedonia, Greece, 8 mi. S of Drama; tobacco, barley; wine; olive oil.

Kalambo Falls (kaläm'bō), on short Kalambo R., at Northern Rhodesia–Tanganyika border, near SE shore of L. Tanganyika, 20 mi. NW of Abercorn. Falls, featured by single 704-ft. drop, descend 3,000 ft. in 6-mi. course through a volcanic gorge from plateau to L. Tanganyika.

Kalambur, India: see KOLAMBUR.

Kalamnuri (kŭlŭmnōō'rē), town (pop. 6,222), Parbhani dist., N Hyderabad state, India, 36 mi. N of Nander; cotton, millet, wheat.

Kalamos (kä'lŭmôs), Ital. *Calamo* (kä'lämō), island (□ 7.3; pop. 1,044) in Ionian Sea, Greece, in Acarnania nome, 1.5 mi. off central Greek mainland (E); 38°37'N 20°55'E; 7 mi. long, 1–3 mi. wide, rises to 2,445 ft. Chief town, Kalamos, is on NE shore. Fisheries.

Kalampaka, Greece: see KALAMBAKA.

Kalamunda (kă'lŭmŭn'dŭ), residential town (pop. 1,343), SW Western Australia, 11 mi. ESE of Perth and on W slopes of Darling Range; orchards.

Kalan (kälän'), village (pop. 762), Tunceli prov., E central Turkey, 25 mi. S of Erzincan; grain. Formerly Mameki.

Kalanaur (kŭlä'nour), village, Gurdaspur dist., NW Punjab, India, 14 mi. W of Gurdaspur. Akbar proclaimed emperor here, in 1556.

Kalanchak (kŭlŭnchäk'), village (1926 pop. 7,868), S Kherson oblast, Ukrainian SSR, near Perekop Isthmus, 40 mi. SE of Kherson, on railroad; dairy farming; metalworking.

Kalangadoo, village (pop. 329), SE South Australia, 220 mi. SSE of Adelaide, and on Naracoorte–Mt. Gambier RR; dairy products, livestock.

Kalang River (käläng'), arm of the Brahmaputra, in central Assam, India; leaves river 8 mi. E of Silghat, flows 100 mi. SW, through rice, jute, tea, and rape and mustard area, past Samaguri, Nowgong, and Raha, returning to the Brahmaputra 15 mi. NE of Gaunati. Left tributaries drain Nowgong dist.

Kalaniya, Ceylon: see KELANIYA.

Kalao (kŭlou'), coral island (pop. 1,074), Indonesia, in Flores Sea, 70 mi. N of Flores, near Bonerate; 7°18'S 120°57'E; 18 mi. long, 4 mi. wide; fishing.

Kalaotowa or **Kalaotoa** (both: kŭloutō'ŭ), coral island (6 mi. long, 6 mi. wide; pop. 1,646), Indonesia, in Flores Sea, 75 mi. N of Flores; 7°23'S 121°48'E; fishing.

Kala Oya (kä'lŭ ō'yŭ), river, NW Ceylon, rises in NW extension of Ceylon Hill Country, SW of Dambulla; flows 97 mi. N and WNW to Dutch Bay NNE of Kalpitiya, entering it in 2 streams.

Kalarash (kŭlŭräsh'), Rum. *Călăraşi* (kŭlŭräsh'), city (1930 pop. 10,818; 1941 pop. 6,514), central Moldavian SSR, on Byk R., on railroad and 30 mi. NW of Kishinev, in fruit- and winegrowing dist.; wine making, oilseed milling, fruit processing.

Kala River, Finnish *Kalajoki* (kä'läyō"kē), W Finland, rises in lake region E of Kokkola, flows 80 mi. NW, past Haapajärvi and Ylivieska, to Gulf of Bothnia at Kalajoki. Logging route.

Kalarne (chĕ'lärnŭ), Swedish *Kälarne*, village (pop. 594), Jamtland co., N central Sweden, on small An L., Swedish *Ansjö* (än'shû"), 40 mi. WSW of Solleftea; dairying.

Kalashnikovo (kŭläsh'nyĭkŭvŭ), town (1939 pop. 1,842), central Kalinin oblast, Russian SFSR, 38 mi. NW of Kalinin; glassworks; power station.

Kalasin (kä'lŭsĭn'), town (1947 pop. 6,940), ⊙ Kalasin prov. (□ 2,028; 1947 pop. 307,793), E Thailand, on Korat Plateau, on Phao R. and 20 mi. N of Mahasarakham; rice, tobacco; buffalo and horse raising. Sometimes spelled Kalasindhu. Formed in 1940s out of Mahasarakham prov.

Kalat, Kalat-i-Nadiri, or **Kalat-e-Naderi** (kälät' ĕnädĕrē'), village, Ninth Prov., in Khurasan, NE Iran, 50 mi. NNE of Meshed, near USSR border; wheat; sheep raising, sheepskins. Near by is natural fortress called Kalat-i-Nadiri used as treasure cache by Nadir Shah.

Kalat (kŭlät'), princely state (□ 30,799; 1951 pop. 283,000), E Baluchistan, W Pakistan; administrative hq. at Mastung; residence of khan at Kalat. Bounded E by Sind, W by Kharan and Makran. Comprises 3 divisions: SARAWAN, JHALAWAN, KACHHI. A mountainous area, crossed by Central Brahui and Pab ranges; Kachhi plain in NE. Annual rainfall averages 5–10 in., with rivers seasonal; agr. (wheat, barley, millet, fruit) is difficult. Livestock raising; handicrafts (cloth, felt goods, palm mats). Established in 17th cent.; made treaty 1876 with British by which the khan was recognized as leader of confederacy of princely states (Kalat, Las Bela, Kharan, Makran). Acceded 1948 to Pakistan. Sometimes spelled Khelat.

Kalat, town (1941 pop. 2,463), Kalat state, Baluchistan, W Pakistan, in Sarawan div., 85 mi. SSW of Quetta; trades in wheat, millet, wool, salt, tobacco; handicrafts (carpets, embroideries, palm mats, leather goods). Residence of khan of Kalat. Sometimes spelled Khelat.

Kalata or **Kalatinski Zavod,** Russian SFSR: see KIROVGRAD.

Kalat-i-Ghilzai (kŭlät'-ĭ-gĭlzī'), town (pop. 7,000), Kandahar prov., SE Afghanistan, on Tarnak R. and 80 mi. NE of Kandahar, on highway to Kabul; alt. 5,543 ft.; road junction in oasis; irrigated agr. Fort was occupied in 1842 and 1879–80 by British garrison.

Kalau, Germany: see CALAU.

Kalaupapa (kälä'ōōpä'pä), leper settlement constituting KALAWAO co., Molokai, T.H.; on small N peninsula (Makanalua), shut off by rock wall 1,600 ft. high. Established 1860, now a modern govt. leprosarium. The Belgian martyr Father Damien worked and died here.

Kalaus River (kŭlŭōōs'), Stavropol Territory, Russian SFSR, rises 10 mi. NE of Kursavka, flows N, past Petrovskoye (rail bridge) and Ipatovo, and E, disappearing N of Arzgir into marshes of Manych Depression; 245 mi. long. Floods in spring; dries up during summer in upper and lower portions.

Kalavad (kä'lavŭd), town (pop. 5,546), W central Saurashtra, India, 26 mi. SE of Jamnagar; millet, oilseeds, cotton. Sometimes spelled Kalawad.

Kalavasos (kälävăsôs'), village (pop., including adjacent Drapia and Parsada, 1,243), Larnaca dist., S Cyprus, 22 mi. WSW of Larnaca. Has pyrite mines. Ore is shipped by rail to Vasilikos R. estuary near Zyyi, where it is crushed and shipped. Mfg. of plaster board. Sometimes Kalavassos

Kalavryta or **Kalavrita** (both: kŭlä'vrĭtŭ), anc. *Cynaetha* (sĭnē'thŭ), town (pop. 2,712), Achaea nome, N Peloponnesus, Greece, on rail spur, on Vouraikos R. and 24 mi. SE of Patras; summer resort; wine, livestock (sheep, goats). Ruined feudal castle. At monastery of Hagia Laura or Ayia Lavra (founded 961), just SW, Greeks 1st rallied (1821) in Gr. war of independence. In vaulted cave, 5 mi. NE, is monastery of Megaspelaion or Megaspilaion, said to date from 4th cent. and famed for successful defense (1827) against Turks.

Kalaw (kŭlô'), town (pop. 3,621), Hsamonghkam state, Southern Shan State, S Upper Burma, 35 mi. WSW of Taunggyi, on road and railroad to Thazi; hill resort. Gold deposits near by. Reached by railroad, 1915.

Kalawao (kä'läwou'), called a co. (□ 14; pop. 335), officially a dist. of Maui co., on Makanalua Peninsula, N Molokai, T.H.; consists only of KALAUPAPA leper settlement. Controlled by Territorial Bd. of Hosps. and Settlements; has no local govt., but is represented in Territorial legislature.

Kalawewa (kŭlŭvā'vŭ), village, North Central Prov., Ceylon, 25 mi. SSE of Anuradhapura; extensive rice plantations; coconut palms, vegetable gardens. Land development project (□ 15). Kala Wewa irrigation tank is just E; 6 mi. long, 3 mi. wide.

Kalawsk, Poland: see WEGLINIEC.

Kalba or **Kalbah** (kăl'bŭ), sheikdom (□ 25; pop. 2,000) in Trucial Oman, on Gulf of Oman, forming an enclave in Fujaira sheikdom; agr. (dates, tobacco, wheat). Consists of town of Kalba (airfield) and environs. Long a dependency of Sharja; joined trucial league in 1937.

Kalba Range (kŭlbä'), W branch of Altai Mts., in E Kazakh SSR; extends c.150 mi. NW from Irtysh R. (in East Kazakhstan oblast) to Turksib RR; rises to 5,250 ft.; extensive gold, tin, and tungsten deposits. Formerly called Kolba Range.

Kalbe or **Kalbe an der Milde** (käl'bŭ än dĕr mĭl'dŭ), town (pop. 2,571), in former Prussian Saxony prov., central Germany, after 1945 in Saxony-Anhalt, on small Milde R. and 9 mi. N of Gardelegen; hops, grain, potatoes, livestock. Has remains of old castle. Also spelled Calbe.

Kaldenkirchen (käl"dŭn-kĭr'khŭn), town (pop. 5,753), in former Prussian Rhine Prov., W Germany, after 1945 in North Rhine-Westphalia, 15 mi. W of Krefeld; customs station and rail junction on Dutch border.

Kaldi Dag (käldĭ' dä), Turkish *Kaldi Dağ*, highest peak (12,251 ft.) of the Ala Dag, S Turkey, 30 mi. SE of Nigde.

Kaldzhir River, Kazakh SSR: see MARKA-KUL.

Kalé (kälā'), village, SW Fr. Sudan, Fr. West Africa, on the Senegal, on Dakar-Niger RR, and 70 mi. SE of Kayes; peanuts, livestock.

Kale, Turkey: see KARLIOVA.

Kalecik (kälĕjĭk'), village (pop. 4,109), Ankara prov., central Turkey, on railroad and 32 mi. ENE of Ankara; wheat, barley; mohair goats.

Kaledupa or **Kaledoepa** (both: kälĕdōō'pŏŏ), island (□ 30; pop. 10,343), Tukangbesi Isls., Indonesia, bet. Flores and Molucca seas, just SE of Wangi-wangi; 5°41'S 123°39'E; 12 mi. long, 3 mi. wide; generally low. Fishing, agr. (coconuts, sago).

Kalehe (kälā'hā), village, Kivu prov., E Belgian Congo, on W shore of L. Kivu, 30 mi. N of Costermansville; center of European agr. settlement; boat landing. Coffee and palm plantations; palm-oil milling.

Kalemba, Belgian Congo: see KAMPENE.

Kalemyo (kŏŏlā'myō), village, Upper Chindwin dist., Upper Burma, on Myittha R. and 15 mi. W of Kalewa, on road to Chin Hills, in Kabaw Valley.

Kale Sultaniye, Turkey: see CANAKKALE, town.

Kaleva (kă'lŏŏvŏŏ, kŏŏlē'vŏŏ), village (pop. 346), Manistee co., NW Mich., 18 mi. NE of Manistee.

Kalewa (kŏŏlā'wä"), village, Upper Chindwin dist., Upper Burma, on right bank of Chindwin R. (landing) at mouth of Myittha R., 140 mi. NW of Mandalay; head of roads to Manipur (India) via Tiddim and Tamu; coal deposits near by.

Kalga (kŭlgä'), village (1948 pop. over 2,000), SE Chita oblast, Russian SFSR, 110 mi. ENE of Borzya, in agr. area; metalworks.

Kalgan (kälgän'), Chinese *Changkiakow* or *Chang-chia-k'ou* (both: jäng'jyä'kō'), city (1941 pop. 86,084; 1947 pop. 151,234), ⊙ Chahar prov., China, on railroad and 95 mi. NW of Peking, at gate in the Great Wall; leading commercial and communications center of Inner Mongolia; exports hides, sheep, horses. Transit trade in tea, sugar, flour, cloth. Handicraft industry (copper- and ironware, leather goods, rugs). Situated on affluent of Yang R., in pass of Yin Mts., Kalgan consists of right-bank Chinese town and left-bank Mongol commercial section and railroad settlement. The "gate" to Mongolia, city is linked by highways with Ulan Bator and Tolun. Developed as a military and trade center under the Manchu dynasty, Kalgan handled most of China's tea trade with Russia. It was reached 1909 by railroad from Peking. Separated 1928 from Chihli (Hopeh) to become ⊙ Chahar. During Sino-Japanese War, it was held (1937–45) by the Japanese and became ⊙ South Chahar autonomous govt. Passed to Communist control in 1948. As ⊙ Wanchüan co. (1914–47), Kalgan was also called Wanchüan (wän'chüän') until 1947, when it became an independent municipality, and when the co. seat was moved to a town 10 mi. W, thereafter called Wanchüan.

Kalghatgi (kŭl'gŭtgē), village (pop. 4,285), Dharwar dist., S Bombay, India, 19 mi. S of Dharwar; rice, millet, cotton; rice milling.

Kalgin Island (kăl'gĭn) (13 mi. long, 2–4 mi. wide), S Alaska, in Cook Inlet, 90 mi. SW of Anchorage; 60°26'N 151°57'W.

Kalgoorlie and Boulder (kălgŏŏr'lē), municipality (pop. 22,380), S central Western Australia, 340 mi. ENE of Perth; 30°45'S 121°33'E. Principal mining town of state; center of E.Coolgardie Goldfield. Adjacent towns of Kalgoorlie and Boulder (sometimes called Boulder City) combined in 1947. On Trans-Australian RR; junction of rail lines to Esperance and Laverton; airport. Gold mines near by began operating 1893. Water supply from Mundaring Weir in Darling Range.

Kalhat or **Qalhat** (kälhăt'), town, E Oman, on Gulf of Oman, 80 mi. SE of Muscat, at foot of Eastern Hajar hill country. Was major port in 15th and 16th cent. prior to rise of Muscat under Portuguese.

Kaliakra, Cape (kälēäk'rä), Rum. *Caliacra*, on Black Sea, in NE Bulgaria, 30 mi. NE of Stalin; 43°21'N 28°28'E. Medieval ruins and lighthouse are on 200-ft. cliffs. The coastal waters, abounding in porpoises, have been made a natl. park.

Kalibo (kälē'bō), town (1939 pop. 4,313; 1948 municipality pop. 17,842), Capiz prov., N Panay isl., Philippines, on small inlet of Sibuyan Sea, 28 mi. WNW of Capiz; agr. center (tobacco, rice).

Kalida (kŭlī'dŭ), village (pop. 533), Putnam co., NW Ohio, 17 mi. NNW of Lima; livestock, poultry, grain.

Kali Gandaki River (kälē gŭn'dŭkē), central Nepal, rises in N Nepal Himalayas c.30 mi. NNE of Muktinath, near undefined Nepal-Tibet border; flows SSW past Baglung and Kusma, and E past Riri Bazar, joining Trisuli R. 55 mi. W of Katmandu to form GANDAK RIVER; total length, c.200 mi. Also called Krishna Gandaki.

Kaliganj (kä'lēgŭnj). **1** Village, Dacca dist., E East Bengal, E Pakistan, on tributary of Dhaleswari R. and 16 mi. NE of Dacca; rice, jute, oilseeds; sugar milling. **2** Village, Khulna dist., SW East Bengal, E Pakistan, in the Sundarbans, on Jamuna R. and 40 mi. SW of Khulna. Trades in rice, jute, oilseeds; mfg. of pottery, cutlery, horn implements.

Kalikata, India: see CALCUTTA.

Kalima-Kingombe (kälē'mä-kĭng-gōm'bā), village (1948 pop. 2,291), Kivu prov., E Belgian Congo, near Ulindi R., 125 mi. N of Kasongo; center of tin-mining area employing c.11,000 workers; tin concentrating, also tantalite mining. Has hospitals for Europeans and natives; 2 hydroelectric plants near by. Kamisuku (kämēsōō'kōō) tin mines are 7 mi. NE.

Kalimantan: see BORNEO.

Kali Mas River (kä'lēmäs'), principal stream in Brantas delta, E Java, Indonesia, branches from the Brantas 8 mi. W of Mojokerto, flows 40 mi. NE, past Surabaya, to Madura Strait 3 mi. N of Surabaya. Sometimes called Mas R.

Kalimnos, Greece: see KALYMNOS.

Kalimpong (kä'lĭmpōng), town (pop. 11,958), Darjeeling dist., N West Bengal, India, on Tista R. and 13 mi. E of Darjeeling, in extreme SW Assam Himalayan foothills. Terminus of main trade route to Tibet; trade center for Tibetan goods; handicraft cotton-weaving center; soda-drink mfg. Residence of Bhutanese political officer. Cinchona plantation 6 mi. NE. Rail station 4 mi. SW, at Gielkhola.

Kalin (kälŭn'), Turkish *Kalın*, village (pop. 830), Sivas prov., N central Turkey, 15 mi. WSW of Sivas; rail junction.

Kalina, Belgian Congo: see LEOPOLDVILLE, city.

Kali Nadi (kä'lē nŭdē'), river, W Uttar Pradesh, India, rises c.20 mi. N of Meerut, flows c.250 mi. S and SE through Ganges-Jumna Doab to the Ganges SSE of Farrukhabad.

Kalindi River, India: see JAMUNA RIVER.

Kalinga, Philippines: see MOUNTAIN PROVINCE.

Kalingapatam, India: see CHICACOLE.

Kalinin (kŭlĭ'nĭn, kŭlē'nĭn, Rus. kŭlyē'nyĭn), oblast (□ 25,500; 1946 pop. estimate 2,250,000) in W central European Russian SFSR; ⊙ Kalinin. In Valdai Hills watershed area; drained by upper Msta, upper Mologa, Tvertsa, and Volga rivers; typical moraine region (W), marshy lowland (E). W section abounds in lakes (L. Seliger, L. Peno, L. Volgo). Sandy and clayey soils restrict agr. use (flax, potatoes, vegetables, dairy farming); extensive grazing lands; forests (pine, fir, oak) in NE. Chief mineral resources: peat (power plants), quartz (glassworks), limestone. Textile industry, with cotton milling along Moscow-Leningrad RR (Kalinin, Vyshni Volochek, Novo-Zavidovski), linen milling (Rzhev, Bezhetsk). Lignite mining near Selizharovo. Machine mfg. (railroad rolling stock, textile and peat-working machines) at Kalinin, leather and shoe industries (Kimry, Ostashkov), sawmilling (along rail lines), paper milling (Kuvshinovo), glassworking, porcelain mfg. Handicrafts around Kimry (footwear) and Ostashkov (net making). Filling of Volga Reservoir (hydroelectric plant at Ivankovo) and construction of Moscow Canal furthered economic development of region. Formed 1935 out of Moscow oblast.

Kalinin, city (1926 pop. 108,413; 1939 pop. 216,131), ⊙ Kalinin oblast, Russian SFSR, on Volga R., at mouth of the Tvertsa, and 100 mi. NW of Moscow; 56°52'N 35°55'E. Transportation and industrial center at junction of Volga R., Moscow-Leningrad RR, and several main highways; railway-car works, machine mfg. (textile and peat-working equipment), cotton, clothing, and knitting mills; mfg. (silicate bricks, photo-engraving equipment, rubber goods, plastics, rayon). Shipyards. Teachers col. Has 17th-cent. cathedral (tombs of princes of Tver) and regional mus. in 14th-cent. castle. In SW suburb of Zheltikovo is 14th-cent. monastery (place of exile of Aleksei Petrovich). The city, founded as Tver, dates from 1135; became (1240) ⊙ Tver principality, a rival of Moscow, to which it fell (1486). Developed into important trading center (18th cent.) on Vyshnevolotsk Canal system. Destroyed by fire (end of 18th cent.) and rebuilt with wide squares and avenues. River trade declined after construction of Moscow-Leningrad RR, which marked start of city's industrialization. Was ⊙ Tver govt. until 1929; city called Tver until 1933. During Second World War, held briefly (1941) by Germans and severely damaged.

Kalinina, Imeni (ē'mĭnyē kŭlyē'nyĭnŭ), town (1939 pop. over 2,000) in Azizbekov dist. of Greater Baku, Azerbaijan SSR, on E Apsheron Peninsula, 18 mi. ENE of Baku, in Kala oil field (developed in 1930s).

Kalinina, Imeni M. I., town (1939 pop. over 500), NW Gorki oblast, Russian SFSR, 25 mi. WNW of Vetluga; paper-milling center (cardboard articles). Before 1938, called Kartonnaya Fabrika.

Kalininabad (kŭlyē"nyĭnŭbät'), village, central Leninabad oblast, Tadzhik SSR, on N slope of Turkestan Range, 15 mi. SE of Ura-Tyube; wheat, horses. Until c.1935, Kalai-Mirzabai.

Kalinin Bay (kă'lĭnĭn, kŭlē'–), district (pop. 11), SE Alaska, on N shore of Kruzof Isl., on Salisbury Sound, 25 mi. NW of Sitka; fishing.

Kalinindorf, Ukrainian SSR: see KALININSKOYE, Kherson oblast.

Kaliningrad (kŭlĭ'nĭngrăd, –lē'–, Rus. kŭlyē"nyĭn-grät'), detached oblast (□ 6,100; 1950 pop. estimate 900,000) of W European Russian SFSR, on Baltic Sea; ⊙ Kaliningrad. Formed after Second World War out of N portion of former East Prussia; bounded by Lithuania (N, E) and Poland (S). Its Baltic shore consists of Courland and Vistula lagoons, separated by Samland peninsula. Largely a humid lowland with moderate continental climate; drained by Pregel and Neman rivers. Agr. (potatoes, sugar beets, rye, barley, dairy cattle, hogs), lumbering (paper and pulp milling), fishing, amber extracting (Yantarny). Noted seaside resorts (Svetlogorsk, Zelenogradsk). Main industrial centers: Kaliningrad (Königsberg), Chernyakhovsk (Insterburg), Sovetsk (Tilsit), Gusev (Gumbinnen). Dense rail and road net. Originally part of East Prussia, area was assigned (1945) to the USSR by Potsdam Conference. First constituted by Russians as a special Königsberg okrug; became an oblast in April, 1946; renamed Kaliningrad in July, 1946.

Kaliningrad. 1 Formerly **Königsberg** (kŭ'nĭkhsbĕrk), city (1939 pop. 372,164), ⊙ Kaliningrad oblast, Russian SFSR, icefree Baltic seaport on Pregel R., near its mouth in Vistula Lagoon, and 340 mi. NE of Berlin, 680 mi. W of Moscow; 54°43'N 20°30'E. Major industrial and commercial center, connected by 20-mi. deep-water channel with its outer port and naval base Baltisk; mfg. of freight cars, paper-milling equipment, cranes, amber articles; shipbuilding, paper and pulp milling, food processing (meat, flour, dairy goods, lard, margarine, yeast). Trade in grain, pulses (mainly lentils), lumber, and flax. Teachers col. Originally founded (1255) as a fortress of Teutonic Knights and named Königsberg, allegedly for King Ottocar II of Bohemia; consisted at first of 3 separate towns of Altstadt (chartered 1286), Löbnicht (1300), and Kneiphof (1327). Joined Hanseatic League (1340). After loss of Marienburg (1457) to Poland, became seat of grand masters of Teutonic Knights and (1525–1618) residence of dukes of Prussia. Was the Prussian coronation city; here Elector Frederick III of Brandenburg crowned himself (1701) first king (Frederick I) of Prussia; William I was crowned here, 1861. After 18th cent., ⊙ East Prussia. Occupied (1758–62) by Russians during Seven Years War; fortified after 1843; again an objective of the Russians during First World War. During Second World War, its capture (April, 1945) by Soviet troops following 2-month siege left the old city in ruins, including its 14th-cent. cathedral with adjoining tomb of Kant (b. here 1724), old quadrangular castle of Teutonic Knights and dukes of Prussia, and oldest (1544) Prussian univ. Along with N part of East Prussia, it passed (1945) to USSR. The new Soviet city (renamed Kaliningrad in 1946) was laid out after 1945 in former residential NW suburbs. **2** City (1939 pop. over 10,000), central Moscow oblast, Russian SFSR, on railroad (Podlipki station) and 1.5 mi. NE of Mytishchi; textiles. Originally called Podlipki; later (1928–38), Kalininski.

Kalinino (kŭlyē'nyĭnŭ). **1** Village (1939 pop. over 2,000), NW Armenian SSR, on Lori Steppe, 33 mi. NE of Leninakan; livestock, grain, potatoes. Until 1930s, Vorontsovka. **2** Village (1939 pop. over 500), SE Amur oblast, Russian SFSR, on Amur R. (landing) and 130 mi. ESE of Blagoveshchensk, in agr. area (grain, soybeans). **3** Village (1939 pop. over 500), central Chuvash Autonomous SSR, Russian SFSR, on Greater Tsivil R. and 18 mi. ENE of Shumerlya; grain. Until 1939, Norusovo.

Kalininsk (kŭlyē'nyĭnsk). **1** City, Karelo-Finnish SSR: see PETROZAVODSK. **2** Town (1939 pop. over 500), NE Tashauz oblast, Turkmen SSR, on Khiva oasis, 25 mi. NW of Tashauz; cotton. Until 1936, Porsy. Formerly also called Kalinin. **3** City (1939 pop. over 10,000), central Stalino oblast, Ukrainian SSR, in the Donbas, 3 mi. NE of Gorlovka; coal-mining center. Until c.1935, Bairak.

Kalininski, Russian SFSR: see KALININGRAD, Moscow oblast.

Kalininskoye (–skŭyŭ). **1** Village (1939 pop. over 2,000), W Frunze oblast, Kirghiz SSR, in Chu valley, on railroad (Karabalty station) and 37 mi. W of Frunze; sugar beets (refinery at adjoining Karabalty); essential oils. Until 1937, called Karabalty. **2** Village (1939 pop. over 2,000), W Kherson oblast, Ukrainian SSR, on Ingulets R. (head of navigation) and 36 mi. NNE of Kherson; flour mill, metalworks. Village was a Jewish settlement called Seidemenukha; renamed Kalinindorf c. 1928, and became Kalininskoye 1944.

Kalinjar (kä'lĭnjŭr), village, Banda dist., S Uttar Pradesh, India, 33 mi. SSE of Banda; Sivaite pilgrimage site. Famous anc. fort and city which figured in the Mahabharata. Was civil ⊙ Chandel Rajputs after its transfer (c.1182) from Mahoba. Noted Afghan, Sher Shah, killed here in 1545. Stormed by Akbar's troops in 1569; occupied by British in 1812. Has extensive cave inscriptions, 12th-cent. ruins. Also called Tarahti.

Kalinjara (–jŭrŭ), village, S Rajasthan, India, 16 mi. SSW of Banswara; corn, rice; hand-loom weaving. Ruined Jain temple.

alinkovichi (kŭlyĕn'kuvēchē), city (1926 pop. ;,152), central Polesye oblast, Belorussian SSR, 6 ni. NNE of Mozyr; rail junction; sawmilling, wood listilling, clothing mfg.

alino (kŭlyē'nŭ), town (1943 pop. over 500), E Molotov oblast, Russian SFSR, 8 mi. WSW (under urisdiction) of Chusovoi; rail junction; peat.

alinovik (kä'lĕnôvĭk), village, SE Bosnia, Yugolavia, 23 mi. S of Sarajevo. Near-by Treskavica ntn. rises NNW, Lelija mtn. S.

alinovka (kŭlyē'nufkŭ). **1** Village (1939 pop. ,049), N central Kaliningrad oblast, Russian SFSR, 11 mi. N of Insterburg, on narrow-gauge ailroad. Until 1945, in East Prussia where it was alled Aulowönen or Gross Aulowönen (grōs" u'lōvû"nŭn) and, later (1938–45), Aulenbach ou'lŭnbäkh). **2** Town (1926 pop. 2,418), N Vinitsa oblast, Ukrainian SSR, 15 mi. N of Vinnitsa; ail junction; metalworks, sugar refinery.

alinovo (kŭlyē'nuvŭ). **1** Town (1944 pop. over 00), W central Sverdlovsk oblast, Russian SFSR, ear Tavatui L., 23 mi. S of Nevyansk; precioustone mining. **2** Town (1926 pop. 5,210), W Voroshilovgrad oblast, Ukrainian SSR, in the Donbas, mi. SE of Popasnaya; coal mines.

aliparhi, India: see Raniganj.

ali River, India and Nepal: see Sarda River.

aliro (kälē'rō), town, Eastern Prov., SE Uganda, n railroad and 35 mi. NE of Jinja; cotton, tobacco, offee, bananas, corn.

alisch, Poland: see Kalisz.

ali Sindh River (kä'lē sĭnd), W central India, rises n Vindhya Range c.30 mi. ESE of Indore, flows .220 mi. N, past Sonkach and Sarangpur, to Chambal R. 12 mi. SE of Kakheri. Sometimes spelled Kali Sind.

alisizo (kälēsē'zō), town, Buganda prov., S Uganla, 15 mi. SSW of Masaka; cotton, coffee, bananas, orn, millet.

alispell (kă'lĭspĕl", –pĕl'), city (pop. 9,737), ⊙ Flathead co., NW Mont., c.100 mi. NNW of Missoula and on Flathead R., near Flathead L. nd Glacier Natl. Park; tourist and trade center or rich agr. region; silver, lead mines; lumber mill; lour, cereals, peas, grain, fruit. Radio station ere. Inc. 1892.

alisz (kä'lēsh), Ger. *Kalisch* (kä'lĭsh), Rus. *Kalish* (kä'lēsh), city (pop. 48,092), Poznan prov., W central Poland, on Prosna R. and 60 mi. W of Lodz; ail junction; industrial center; mfg. of embroideries, laces, metal products, foodstuffs; tanning, flour milling, sawmilling. Lignite deposits in vicinity. Has modern central section, park, several bridges. One of oldest Pol. towns, 1st mentioned in 2d cent. A.D. by Ptolemy; it lay on anc. Roman route at a convenient crossing of the Prosna, whose 2 small tributaries provided the town's defenses. Town moved to a river isl. in 13th cent.; was then 2d-largest town (after Poznan) in the Wielkopolska, with a flourishing weaving industry; its church was founded c.1220. Passed 1793 to Prussia, 1815 to Rus. Poland; after 1903, following building of a railroad, became an important point near Ger. frontier; was ⊙ of Kalish govt. In treaty signed here (1813), Prussia and Russia formed an alliance against Napoleon I.

Kalisz Pomorski (pômôr'skē), Ger. *Kallies* (kä'lēs), town (1939 pop. 4,016; 1946 pop. 1,175) in Pomerania, after 1945 in Koszalin prov., NW Poland, in lake region, 40 mi. ESE of Stargard; paper mfg.

Kalitva River (kŭlyĕt'vŭ), Rostov oblast, Russian SFSR, rises E of Chertkovo, flows c.130 mi. S, through steppe, past Krivorozhye and Litvinovka, to Northern Donets R. at Belaya Kalitva.

Kaliua (kälēōō'ä), village, Western Prov., W Tanganyika, 70 mi. W of Tabora. Rail junction (spur to Mpanda mining area). Also spelled Kaliuwa.

Kaliub, Egypt: see Qalyub.

Kalivia, Greece: see Kalyvia.

Kaliwungu or **Kaliwoengoe** (both: kälēwŏŏng'ōō), town (pop. 17,357), N central Java, Indonesia, near Java Sea, 10 mi. W of Semarang; trade center in agr. area (sugar, rice, peanuts, tobacco, coffee, kapok).

Kalix (kä'lĭks), village (pop. 1,708), Norrbotten co., N Sweden, on small inlet of Gulf of Bothnia at mouth of Kalix R., 30 mi. W of Haparanda; sawmills. Has 15th-cent. church. Limestone and quartz deposits near by.

Kalix River, Swedish *Kalix älv* (ĕlv'), Lapland, N Sweden, rises near Norwegian border WNW of Kiruna, flows 270 mi. in wide arc SE and S, past Overkalix, to Gulf of Bothnia at Kalix. Important logging route.

Kalk (kälk), industrial suburb of Cologne, W Germany, adjoining (E) Deutz; rail junction; iron foundries; mfg. of machinery, tools, chemicals.

Kalka (käl'kŭ), town (pop. 9,766), Ambala dist., E Punjab, India, on railroad (workshops) and 33 mi. NNE of Ambala, in small enclave in Patiala and East Punjab States Union; trades in spices, wheat, maize, bamboo; mfg. of aerated water, snuff, millstones. Limestone quarried just E. Acquired 1843 by British from Patiala state as depot for Simla.

Kalkali Ghat, India: see Patharkandi.

Kalkandelen, Yugoslavia: see Tetovo.

Kalkar (käl'kär), town (pop. 2,287), in former Prussian Rhine Prov., W Germany, after 1945 in North Rhine-Westphalia, 7 mi. SE of Cleves. Has 15th-cent. church and town hall. Gen. Seydlitz b. here. Until 1936, spelled Calcar.

Kalkara (kälkä'rä), town (pop. 2,068), E Malta, on inlet of Grand Harbour, c.1 mi. E of Valletta; fishing, boat repairing. Heavily damaged during Second World War. Its 19th-cent. parish church and Villa Bighi, which housed naval hosp., were completely destroyed. Severely damaged also was the adjoining baroque Fort Risacoli (1670) at E entrance of Grand Harbour opposite Fort St. Elmo. Sometimes spelled Calcara.

Kalkaska (kălkă'skŭ), county (□ 564; pop. 4,597), NW central Mich.; ⊙ Kalkaska. Drained by Manistee and Boardman rivers. Stock raising, dairying, agr. (potatoes, grain, fruit); logging. Many lakes (fishing), resorts. Includes a state forest and a state game refuge. Organized 1871.

Kalkaska, village (pop. 1,250), ⊙ Kalkaska co., NW central Mich., 22 mi. ESE of Traverse City and on Boardman R.; supply center for farm and lake area; flour milling. Inc. 1887.

Kalken (käl'kŭn), town (pop. 4,807), East Flanders prov., NW Belgium, on Scheldt R. and 9 mi. E of Ghent; agr. market. Gothic church. Formerly spelled Calcken.

Kalkfontein, South-West Africa: see Karasburg.

Kalkuda (kŭl'kŏŏdŭ), village (pop., including nearby villages, 671), Eastern Prov., Ceylon, on E coast, 18 mi. NNW of Batticaloa; extensive coconut-palm plantations.

Kalla, Lake, Finnish *Kallavesi* (käl'lävĕ"sē) (30 mi. long, 1–10 mi. wide), S central Finland. On W shore is Kuopio. Dotted with numerous isls. Forms part of Saimaa lake system, through which it drains into L. Ladoga.

Kalladi or **Kallady** (kŭl'lŭdē), village (pop. 725), Eastern Prov., Ceylon, on long lagoon near E coast, 1 mi. E of Batticaloa; coconut-palm plantations; paper mill.

Kallai, India: see Calicut.

Kallakurchi or **Kallakurichi** (both: kŭl"lŭkŏŏr'ĭchē), town (pop. 9,124), South Arcot dist., SE central Madras, India, 55 mi. W of Cuddalore; rice, millet; cotton and woolen weaving. Trades in timber and gum arabic from Kalrayan Hills (W; magnetite deposits). Formerly also spelled Kallakkurichchi.

Kallam, India: see Kalam.

Kallands (kă'lŭndz), village, central Alaska, on Yukon R. and 30 mi. W of Tanana; supply point for placer gold-mining dist.

Kallang (kä"läng'), NE section of Singapore city, Singapore isl., at mouth of small Kallang R.; site of Singapore civil airport and seaplane base.

Kallaste (kä'lästä), city (pop. 1,605), E Estonia, on L. Peipus, 25 mi. NE of Tartu; agr. market; flax, oats. Pop. largely Russian.

Kallayi, India: see Calicut.

Kalle (kä'lŭ), village (pop. 5,113), in former Prussian prov. of Westphalia, W Germany, after 1945 in North Rhine-Westphalia, 3 mi. E of Meschede; forestry.

Kallfallet (chĕl'fä"lŭt), Swedish *Källfallet*, village (pop. 397), Vastmanland co., central Sweden, in Bergslag region, 15 mi. SW of Fagersta; iron and copper mining.

Kallham (käl'häm), town (pop. 2,576), central Upper Austria, 17 mi. WNW of Wels; potatoes, rye, hogs.

Kallia (kăl-lē'ŭ), settlement of Palestine, after 1948 in W Jordan, at N end of Dead Sea, near mouth of the Jordan, 16 mi. E of Jerusalem; 1,292 ft. below sea level. Entirely destroyed (1948) when region was invaded by Jordan forces, it had been site of important potash-extracting and refining plant. Just SW was site of popular health resort.

Kallidaikurichi or **Kulladakurichi** (kŭl"lĭdī'kŏŏrĭchē), town (pop. 16,031), Tinnevelly dist., S Madras, India, on Tambraparni R. opposite Ambasamudram and 15 mi. WSW of Tinnevelly; cotton-weaving center; sesame-oil extraction. Also spelled Kallidaikurichchi.

Kallidromon or **Kallidhromon** (both: kŭlĭ'dhrômôn), mountain massif in Phthictis nome, central Greece, rises to 4,589 ft. 12 mi. SSE of Lamia. Also called Koukos.

Kallies, Poland: see Kalisz Pomorski.

Kallifiton, Greece: see Kalliphyton.

Kallinge (kä'lĭng-ŭ), village (pop. 3,606), Blekinge co., S Sweden, 12 mi. NW of Karlskrona; iron- and steelworks.

Kallipeuke or **Kallipevki** (both: kälĭpĕf'kē), village (pop. 1,559), Larissa nome, NE Thessaly, Greece, on slope of the Lower Olympus, 16 mi. ENE of Elasson; chromite mining. Formerly Nezeros.

Kalliphyton or **Kallifiton** (both: kŭlē'fĭtôn), town (pop. 3,186), Drama nome, Macedonia, Greece, 4 mi. ENE of Drama; tobacco, barley; olive oil. Formerly called Ravika; sometimes Kallifytos.

Kallipolis, Turkey: see Gallipoli.

Kallithea (kälĭthä'ŭ), SW suburb (1951 pop. 46,848) of Athens, Greece, 2.5 mi. from city center; cotton textile mfg.

Kallmorberget, Sweden: see Karrgruvan.

Kallmünz (käl'münts), village (pop. 2,438), Upper Palatinate, E central Bavaria, Germany, on the Nab, opposite mouth of Vils R., and 12 mi. NNW of Regensburg; grain, cattle.

Kallo (kälō'), town (pop. 2,457), East Flanders prov., N Belgium, on Scheldt R. and 7 mi. WNW of Antwerp; beet-sugar refining. Has two 16th-cent. forts. Here Duke of Parma threw a 2,400-ft. bridge across the Scheldt during 1583 siege of Antwerp. Formerly spelled Calloo or Kalloo.

Kallo (käl'lō), Hung. *Kálló*, town (pop. 2,444), Nograd-Hont co., N Hungary, 25 mi. NE of Budapest; potatoes, cattle.

Kallo-Knipplan (chĕl'û"-kŭnĭp'plän"), Swedish *Källö-Knipplan*, fishing village (pop. 557), Goteborg och Bohus co., SW Sweden, on islet (123 acres) of same name in the Skagerrak, 12 mi. WNW of Goteborg.

Kallone, Gulf of, or **Gulf of Kalloni** (both: kälônē'), inlet of Aegean Sea in S Lesbos isl., Greece; 13 mi. long, to 5 mi. wide. Kallone (pop. 2,472) is near N shore.

Kallosemjen (käl'lō-shĕmyān), Hung. *Kállósemjén*, town (pop. 4,636), Szabolcs co., NE Hungary, 12 mi. SE of Nyiregyhaza; agr. market for wheat, tobacco, cattle.

Kallsoy, Faeroe Isls.: see Kalso.

Kallurkot or **Kalur Kot** (kŭlŏŏr' kōt'), town (pop. 4,001), Mianwali dist., W Punjab, W Pakistan, 33 mi. SSW of Mianwali; wheat, millet, dates.

Kallurkotte, India: see Hosanagara.

Kallviken, Sweden: see Framby.

Kalmak Kure (kälmäk' kŏŏrā'), Chinese *Chaosu* (jou'sōō'), town, ⊙ Kalmak Kure co. (pop. 28,746), W Sinkiang prov., China, near Tekes R., in the Tien Shan, near USSR border, 60 mi. SSW of Kuldja; livestock, agr. products.

Kalmalo (käl'mäl'ō), town (pop. 4,888), Sokoto prov., Northern Provinces, NW Nigeria, on Fr. West Africa border opposite Birni-N'Konni, 45 mi. N of Sokoto; tobacco, millet, rice; cattle, skins. Sometimes spelled Kalmaloo.

Kalmanka (kŭlmän'kŭ), village (1939 pop. over 2,000), central Altai Territory, Russian SFSR, on Ob R. and 40 mi. S of Barnaul, near Turksib RR; metalworks.

Kalmar (käl'mär), county [Swedish *län*] (□ 4,484; 1950 pop. 236,762), SE Sweden, on the Baltic; ⊙ Kalmar. Includes Oland isl.; mainland section of co. includes E part of Smaland prov. Surface is undulating, generally wooded. Marshy in W; coastal region has fertile soil with large meadow areas. Sheep raising and dairying. Chief industries are woodworking, mfg. of matches, furniture, glass, metal products. Cities are Kalmar, Vastervik, Oskarshamn, Nybro, Vimmerby, and Borgholm. Sometimes spelled Calmar.

Kalmar, city (1950 pop. 27,049), ⊙ Kalmar co., SE Sweden, port on the Baltic, opposite Oland isl. across Kalmar Sound (car ferry to Farjestaden, on Oland isl.), 190 mi. SSW of Stockholm; 56°40'N 16°22'E. Commercial center of SE Sweden, with shipyards, paper mills, food-canning plants; mfg. of matches, tiles, chocolate, margarine. Airport. City, partly built on small isl. in Kalmar Sound, has 17th-cent. cathedral. Its great medieval castle (12th cent.) withstood 24 sieges bet. 1307 and 1611, was rebuilt (16th cent.) on small peninsula in S part of city; now houses archaeological and ethnological mus. Of commercial importance since 9th cent.; scene (1397) of Kalmar Union under which crowns of Denmark, Norway, and Sweden were united. Sometimes spelled Calmar.

Kalmar Sound, strait (85 mi. long, 4–14 mi. wide) of the Baltic, bet. SE Sweden and Oland isl. Chief ports on strait are Kalmar, Oskarshamn (mainland), Borgholm, and Farjestaden (Oland isl.).

Kalmeshwar (kŭlmāsh'vŭr), town (pop. 5,620), Nagpur dist., central Madhya Pradesh, India, 12 mi. WNW of Nagpur; cotton ginning; millet, wheat, oilseeds.

Kalmis, Belgium: see Calamine, La.

Kalmit, Germany: see Hardt Mountains.

Kalmius River or **Kal'mius River** (käl'mēōōs), Stalino oblast, Ukrainian SSR, rises in Donets Ridge S of Artemovsk, flows 110 mi. S, past Stalino, to Sea of Azov at Zhdanov.

Kalmthout (kälmt'hout), town (pop. 8,836), Antwerp prov., N Belgium, near Netherlands border, 12 mi. NNE of Antwerp; market gardening, in marshy region. Sometimes spelled Kalmpthout.

Kalmuck, in Rus. names: see Kalmyk.

Kalmunai (kŭl'mōōnī), town (pop. 3,161), Eastern Prov., Ceylon, on E coast, 24 mi. SSE of Batticaloa; resort.

Kalmyk Autonomous Soviet Socialist Republic (kăl'mĭk), former administrative division (□ 28,650; 1939 pop. 220,723) of SE European Russian SFSR; ⊙ Elista. Pop. was largely Kalmyk (Mongol nomads of Lamaist Buddhist religion; immigrated from Asia in early 18th cent.). Formed 1920 as autonomous oblast; gained status of autonomous SSR in 1935. Was part of Lower Volga Territory (1928–34) and in Stalingrad Territory (1934–36). Divided among adjacent divisions upon its dissolution in 1943, following collaboration of local pop. with Germans. Newly formed Astrakhan oblast received major portion, including its capital (renamed Stepnoi). SW panhandle of Manych Depression passed to Stavropol Territory (S) and Rostov oblast (N); Stalingrad oblast gained NW section. Also spelled Kalmuck.

Kalmykovo (kŭlmĭ'kŭvŭ, kŭlmĭkô'vŭ), village (1926 pop. 1,329), S West Kazakhstan oblast, Kazakh SSR, on Ural R. and 150 mi. S of Uralsk; millet; cattle.
Kalmytski Bazar, Russian SFSR: see PRIVOLZHSKI, Astrakhan oblast.
Kalna (käl'nŭ), town (pop. 12,562), Burdwan dist., central West Bengal, India, on the Bhagirathi and 32 mi. E of Burdwan; rice milling, cotton weaving; trades in rice, potatoes, wheat, sugar cane, gram. Site of 109 Siva lingam temples (built 1809), Moslem fort ruins.
Kalnibolotskaya (kŭlnyēbŭlôt'skīŭ), village (1926 pop. 10,997), NE Krasnodar Territory, Russian SFSR, on Yeya R. and 17 mi. ENE of Tikhoretsk; flour mill, metalworks; wheat, sunflowers, castor beans.
Kalnik (käl'nĭk), mountain (2,109 ft.), N Croatia, Yugoslavia, in Slavonia, 13 mi. SSE of Varazdin, in lignite area.
Kalni River, E Pakistan: see SURMA RIVER.
Kalo Bay, Denmark: see MOLS.
Kalocsa (kŏ'lô-chŏ), city (pop. 12,341), Pest-Pilis-Solt-Kiskun co., S central Hungary, near the Danube, 23 mi. N of Baja; rail terminal, river port, market center. Agr. experiment station; breweries, brickworks, flour mills. Created bishopric by St. Stephen; became seat of an archbishop in 12th cent. Has archiepiscopal palace (18th cent.), library, R.C. acad., observatory. Beautiful embroidery produced in vicinity. Grain, potatoes, cattle, horses.
Kalofer (kälô'fĕr), city (pop. 4,291), Plovdiv dist., central Bulgaria, on S spur of Kalofer Mts., at Krastets Pass, on Tundzha R. and 8 mi. E of Karlovo; summer resort; horticulture, wine making. Once a Turkish cloth-weaving town; declined following Bulg. uprising (1877), when it was burned by Turks. Khristo Botev b. here.
Kalofer Mountains, central Bulgaria, highest section of Balkan Mts., extend c.20 mi. bet. Troyan Mts. (W) and Shipka Mts. (E); rise to 7,793 ft. at Botev Peak. Its S spur is crossed by Krastets Pass.
Kalogrea, Cape, or **Cape Kalogria,** Greece. **1** In Macedonia: see KANASTRAION, CAPE. **2** In Peloponnesus: see PAPAS, CAPE.
Kalol (kä'lōl). **1** Town (pop. 17,879), Mehsana dist., N Bombay, India, 25 mi. SSE of Mehsana; rail junction; market center; trades in millet, pulse, wheat, oilseeds; cotton milling, handicraft cloth weaving, thread and bobbin mfg., bone crushing. **2** Town (pop. 6,879), Panch Mahals dist., N Bombay, India, 15 mi. SW of Godhra; local market for timber, millet, wheat.
Kaloleni (kälōlĕ'nē), village, Coast prov., SE Kenya, 27 mi. N of Mombasa; mission; sugar cane, fruits.
Kalomo (kälō'mō), township (pop. 194), Southern Prov., Northern Rhodesia, on railroad and 70 mi. NE of Livingstone; farming and ranching center; tobacco, corn, wheat, truck; cattle, sheep, goats. Was ⊙ Barotseland–North-Western Rhodesia until formation (1911) of Northern Rhodesia.
Kalona (kŭlō'nŭ), town (pop. 947), Washington co., SE Iowa, near English R., 15 mi. SW of Iowa City; feed, processed turkeys, dairy and metal products.
Kalopanayiotis (kälōpänäyō'tēs), summer resort (pop. 1,099), Nicosia dist., W central Cyprus, in Olympus Mts., 33 mi. WSW of Nicosia; alt. 2,350 ft. Fruitgrowing center (grapes, peaches, pears, olives). Known for its sulphur springs.
Kaloshino (kŭlô'shēnŭ), NE suburb of Moscow, Russian SFSR, just N of Izmailovo. Inc. into city c.1940.
Kalotina (kälō'tēnä), village (pop. 1,354), Sofia dist., W Bulgaria, near Yugoslav border, on Nisava R. and 30 mi. NW of Sofia; rye, potatoes. Has 16th-cent. church. Once a Roman settlement, Calotina, on road from Pannonia to Byzantium. Berende (pop. 387), across the Nisava, has 14th-cent. church.
Kalovo (kä'lôvô), village (pop. 3,799), Ruse dist., NE Bulgaria, 10 mi. NNE of Razgrad; wheat, rye, sunflowers.
Kaloyanovo (kälôyä'nôvô), village (pop. 3,410), Plovdiv dist., W central Bulgaria, 14 mi. N of Plovdiv; rye, potatoes, livestock. Formerly Seldzhikovo.
Kaloz (kä'lôz), Hung. *Káloz,* town (pop. 4,590), Fejer co., W central Hungary, near Sarviz R., on Malom Canal and 17 mi. SSE of Szekesfehervar; wheat, rye, cattle, poultry.
Kalpentyn, Ceylon: see KALPITIYA, village.
Kalpi (kăl'pē), town (pop. 11,530), Jalaun dist., S Uttar Pradesh, India, on the Jumna (bridged) and 21 mi. ENE of Orai; trades in gram, wheat, oilseeds, jowar, cotton, ghee. Has 15th-cent. Afghan ruins. Captured by Afghans in 1196; became an important fortress of Moslem power; taken by Mogul emperor, Humayun, in 1527; stormed by Afghans under Sher Shah in 1540. Hq. of Mahrattas in Bundelkhand during 18th cent. Scene (1477) of great battle bet. Jaunpur kingdom and Delhi sultan. Formerly an important cotton center of East India Co. Near by is site of important Br. victory (1858) over native leaders, including Rani of Jhansi, during Sepoy Rebellion.
Kalpitiya (kŭl'pĭtĭyŭ), fishing village (pop. 1,584), North Western Prov., Ceylon, on Kalpitiya Peninsula, on Dutch Bay, 15 mi. NNW of Puttalam; coconut palms. Ruins of Du. fort (built 1646). Ceylonese Christian pilgrimage center at St. Anna's Church, 10 mi. SSW. Formerly called Kalpentyn. **Kalpitiya Peninsula,** in SE Gulf of Mannar, extends 27 mi. N–S, parallel to mainland; forms W shore of Dutch Bay and Puttalam Lagoon.
Kalrayan Hills (kŭlrä'yŭn), outlier of S Eastern Ghats, S central Madras, India, NE of Salem; c.25 mi. long, c.20 mi. wide; rise to over 4,000 ft. in SW plateau (magnetite deposits); timber, gum arabic, tanbark. Gadilam R. rises in E foothills.
Kalsdorf (käls'dôrf), town (pop. 2,936), Styria, SE Austria, near Mur R., 7 mi. S of Graz; ironworks.
Kalshing, Czechoslovakia: see CHVALSINY.
Kalsi (käl'sē), village, Dehra Dun dist., N Uttar Pradesh, India, near the Jumna, 19 mi. NNW of Dehra. Large quartz boulder near by bears edicts of Asokan.
Kalsia (kŭls'yŭ), former princely state (□ 188; pop. 67,393) of Punjab Hill States, India; ⊙ was Chhachhrauli. Consisted of several detached areas in Ambala and Ferozepore dists. Since 1948, merged with Patiala and East Punjab States Union.
Kalsia, town, India: see CHHACHHRAULI.
Kalskag (kăl'skăg), Eskimo village (pop. 136), W Alaska, on lower Kuskokwim R. and 70 mi. NE of Bethel; 61°32'N 160°22'W; supply point for trappers.
Kalso (käl'sû), Dan. *Kalsø,* Faeroese *Kallsoy,* island (□ 12; pop. 338) of the NE Faeroe Isls.; c.10 mi. long, 1½ mi. wide. Mountainous terrain; highest point is Naestinde (2,591 ft.), near N tip. Fishing, sheep raising.
Kalsubai Peak (kŭlsōō'bī) (5,400 ft.), in Western Ghats, Nasik dist., N central Bombay, India, 27 mi. SSW of Nasik.
Kaltag (kăl'tăg), village (pop. 119), W Alaska, on Yukon R. and 200 mi. E of Nome; 64°19'N 158°44'W; trapping, logging.
Kaltasa (kŭltŭsä'), village (1939 pop. over 500), NW Bashkir Autonomous SSR, Russian SFSR, 25 mi. S of Yanaul; wheat, rye, oats, livestock.
Kaltbrunn (kält'brŏŏn), town (pop. 2,246), St. Gall canton, NE Switzerland, 4 mi. E of L. of Zurich; silk textiles.
Kaltenbrunn (käl"tŭnbrŏŏn'), village (pop. 1,100), Upper Palatinate, NE Bavaria, Germany, 10 mi. WSW of Weiden; hops, hogs.
Kaltendorf, Germany: see OEBISFELDE.
Kaltenkirchen (käl"tŭn-kĭr'khŭn), village (pop. 4,483), in Schleswig-Holstein, NW Germany, 19 mi. N of Hamburg; metalworking, sawmilling, food processing.
Kaltenleutgeben (kältŭnloit'gābŭn), town (pop. 1,906), after 1938 in Liesing dist. of Vienna, Austria, 10 mi. SW of city center; rail terminus; baths.
Kaltennordheim (käl"tŭn-nôrt'hīm), town (pop. 2,251), Thuringia, central Germany, in the Hohe Rhön, 12 mi. WNW of Meiningen; woodworking, furniture mfg., wool weaving.
Kalterherberg (käl"tŭrhĕr'bĕrk), village (pop. 1,906), in former Prussian Rhine Prov., W Germany, after 1945 in North Rhine-Westphalia, on Belgian frontier (customs station), 17 mi. S of Stolberg.
Kaltern, Italy: see CALDARO.
Kaltimo (käl'tĭmō), village in Eno commune (pop. 10,443), Kuopio co., SE Finland, on Pieli R. and 18 mi. NE of Joensuu; pulp and board mills, quartz quarries.
Kaluga (kŭlōō'gŭ), oblast (□ 11,600; 1946 pop. estimate 1,050,000) in W central European Russian SFSR; ⊙ Kaluga. In Ugra-Oka river basin, bet. Smolensk-Moscow Upland (N) and Central Russian Upland (S); in mixed forest zone; sandy soils. Basic crops, coarse grain, wheat and potatoes (NE), hemp (S); fodder crops, fruit, vegetables. Dairy cattle, hogs raised. Main mineral resources: peat, quartz, phosphorites. Rural industries based on lumber (paper milling at Kondrovo, woodworking), agr. (fruit canning, dairying, flour milling, distilling), and minerals (peat, glass, porcelain, and phosphate-fertilizer industries). Textile milling at Borovsk (woolens) and Balabanovo (cotton); machinery is made at Kaluga and Lyudinovo. Formed 1944 out of Tula and other oblasts.
Kaluga, city (1939 pop. 89,484), ⊙ Kaluga oblast, Russian SFSR, on high left bank of Oka R. and 90 mi. SW of Moscow; 54°31'N 36°15'E. Machine-building center; mfg. (railroad hand cars, steam generators, iron and steel products, electrical, telephone, and telegraph equipment, weights, measuring instruments); woodworking (matches), food processing, glass and leather industries. Hydroelectric project. Teachers col., regional mus., palace of Marina Mniszek (residence of 2d false Dmitri, who was murdered here, 1610). Dates from 14th cent. Chartered 1389, when it passed to Moscow; developed into trading center which flourished until early 19th cent. Was ⊙ Kaluga govt. until 1929. During Second World War, briefly held (1941) by Germans in drive on Moscow.
Kalu Ganga (kä'lōō gŭng'gŭ), river, SW Ceylon, rises in S Ceylon Hill Country, in several headstreams joining near Ratnapura; flows W past Ratnapura and SW to Indian Ocean at Kalutara; 70 mi. long.
Kalugerovo (kälōō'gĕrôvô), village (pop. 3,041), Plovdiv dist., W central Bulgaria, on Topolnitsa R. and 11 mi. NW of Pazardzhik; vineyards, rice, truck produce. Formerly Gelvere.
Kalugumalai (kŭl"ŏŏgōōmŭlī'), town (pop. 6,232), Tinnevelly dist., S Madras, India, 30 mi. N of Tinnevelly; seasonal cattle-trade center during temple pilgrimage festivals. Has rock-carved Jain figures.
Kalukhali (kälŏŏkä'lē), village, Faridpur dist., S central East Bengal, E Pakistan, near Padma R., 24 mi. NW of Faridpur; rail junction, with spurs to Faridpur and to Bhatiapara Ghat, 39 mi. SSE.
Kalule-Sud (kälōōlā'-süd'), village, Katanga prov., SE Belgian Congo, on railroad and 75 mi. NW of Jadotville, in cattle-raising region.
Kalundborg (kä'lŏŏnbôr), city (pop. 7,875) and port, Holbaek amt, NW Zealand, Denmark, on Kalundborg Fjord and 58 mi. W of Copenhagen. Meat canning, fertilizer and machinery mfg., tanning, shipbuilding, fishing. Has 12th-cent. church.
Kalundborg Fjord (8 mi. long), W Zealand, Denmark, bet. Rosnaes (N) and Asnaes (S) peninsulas; fisheries.
Kalundu, Belgian Congo: see UVIRA.
Kalupara Ghat (kŭlōōpä'rŭ gät), village, Puri dist., E Orissa, India, 27 mi. WNW of Puri, near Chilka L.; trades in rice, fish; ice mfg.
Kalur Kot, W Pakistan: see KALLURKOT.
Kalush (kä'lŏŏsh), Pol. *Kałusz* (kä'wŏŏsh), city (1931 pop. 12,131), NW Stanislav oblast, Ukrainian SSR, on left tributary of Lomnitsa R. and 17 mi. WNW of Stanislav; mining center (salt and potash deposits); petroleum and natural-gas extracting; cement mfg., iron casting, agr. processing (cereals, hides, fruit, hops), sawmilling. Passed from Poland to Austria (1772); reverted to Poland (1919); ceded to USSR in 1945.
Kaluszyn (käwōō'shĭn), Pol. *Kałuszyn,* Rus. *Kalushin* (kälōō'shĭn), town (pop. 2,554), Warszawa prov., E central Poland, 34 mi. E of Warsaw; mfg. of shingles, tanning, brewing, flour milling.
Kalutara (kŭl'ŏŏtŭrŭ) [Singhalese,=black port] town (pop. 18,801), ⊙ Kalutara dist. (□ 624; pop., including estate pop., 458,198), Western Prov., Ceylon, on SW coast, at mouth of the Kalu Ganga (1,200-ft. bridge), 24 mi. SSE of Colombo; fishing and trade (tea, rubber, coconuts, rice, mangosteens, cinnamon, graphite) center; basket and mat weaving; govt. arrack distillery. Du. fort ruins. Large arrack distilleries in dist.
Kaluzhskoye (kŭlōō'shskŭyŭ), village (1939 pop. 611), N central Kaliningrad oblast, Russian SFSR, on railroad and 12 mi. NNE of Chernyakhovsk. Until 1945, in East Prussia and called Grünheide (grün'hīdŭ).
Kalvakurti, India: see KALWAKURTI.
Kalvan (kŭl'vän), village, Nasik dist., central Bombay, India, on Girna R. and 38 mi. NNE of Nasik; gur, millet, rice. Sometimes spelled Kalwan.
Kalvarija or **Kalvariya** (kälvä'rēä), Pol. *Kalwaria,* city (pop. 5,433), SW Lithuania, on upper Sheshupe R. and 10 mi. SSE of Marijampole, near Pol. border; agr. market; mfg. of shoes, furniture; sawmilling, oilseed pressing, flour milling. Dates from 13th cent. (castle ruins); passed 1795 to Prussia, 1815 to Rus. Poland; in Suvalki govt. until 1920.
Kalvo Bay, Denmark: see MOLS.
Kalvola, Finland: see IITTALA.
Kalvsund (kälv"sünd'), fishing village (pop. 145), Goteborg och Bohus co., SW Sweden, on Bjorkon (byûrk'ŭn"), Swedish *Björkön,* islet in the Skagerrak, 10 mi. WNW of Goteborg.
Kalwakurti or **Kalvakurti** (both: kŭlvŭkŏŏr'tē), town (pop. 5,170), Mahbubnagar dist., S Hyderabad state, India, 33 mi. E of Mahbubnagar; millet, rice, castor beans, peanuts. Also Kalvakurthi.
Kalwan, India: see KALVAN.
Kalwaria, Lithuania: see KALVARIJA.
Kalwaria or **Kalwaria Zebrzydowska** (kälvär'yä zĕb"zhĭdôf'skä), town (pop. 1,816), Krakow prov., S Poland, 18 mi. SW of Cracow; rail junction; furniture mfg. Pilgrimage center; monastery.
Kalya or **Kal'ya** (kŭlyä'), town (1947 pop. over 500), N Sverdlovsk oblast, Russian SFSR, 36 mi. N of Karpinsk; bauxite-mining center, supplying Krasnoturinsk aluminum works; gold placers.
Kalyan (kŭl'yän), town (pop. 31,356), Thana dist., W Bombay, India, on Ulhas R. and 26 mi. NE of Bombay, in the Konkan; rail junction (workshops), road center; trade in rice, cloth fabrics, tobacco, fish; rice, cotton, and oilseed milling, bone crushing, mfg. of ice, leather goods, bricks, tiles. Rayon mill. Substation for power lines of Andhra R. valley hydroelectric scheme; steam-electric plant is 1 mi. SW, at Chole.
Kalyandrug (kŭlyän'drōōg), town (pop. 5,984), Anantapur dist., W Madras, India, 34 mi. WSW of Anantapur; oilseed milling, hand-loom woolen weaving. Corundum mining near by.
Kalyani (kŭl'yŭnē), town (pop. 12,542), Gulbarga dist., W Hyderabad state, India, in enclave within Bidar dist., 38 mi. N of Gulbarga; millet, rice.
Kalyazin (kŭlyä'zĭn), city (1939 pop. over 10,000), SE Kalinin oblast, Russian SFSR, on Volga R. and 40 mi. NNE of Kimri; rail junction; shoe, felt-boot, and clothing mfg.; handicrafts; sawmills. Site of strongly fortified Makaryev monastery (15th cent.), now a mus. Rus. fabulist Krylov b. near by. Chartered 1775.

Kalymnos or **Kalimnos** (both: kä'lēmnôs), Ital. *Calino* (kälē'nô), Lat. *Calymna* (kŭlĭm'nŭ), Aegean island (□ 41; pop. 11,864) in the Dodecanese, Greece, off Turkish Bodrum peninsula; 37°N 27'E; 12 mi. long, 6 mi. wide, rises to 2,228 ft. Produces olive oil, beans, figs, almonds, citrus fruits. Major sponge-fishing center. Main town, Kalymnos (pop. 8,505), is on SE shore.

Kalyubiya, Egypt: see Qalyubiya.

Kalyvia or **Kalivia** (both: kŭlē'vēŭ). **1** Town (pop. 2,859), Attica nome, E central Greece, on railroad and 15 mi. SE of Athens; wheat, vegetables, straw; wine. **2** Town, Attica nome, Greece, WNW of Athens: see Aspropyrgos.

Kam, China: see Kham.

Kama (kä'mä), village, Kivu prov., E Belgian Congo, on Elila R. and 70 mi. NNE of Kasongo; gold-mining center; rice processing.

Kama (kä'mä), village, Thayetmyo dist., Upper Burma, on Irrawaddy R. and 20 mi. SSE of Thayetmyo.

Kama, river, Russian SFSR: see Kama River.

Kamabai (kämäbī'), village (pop. 700), Northern Prov., N central Sierra Leone, 20 mi. NNE of Makeni; palm oil and kernels, cacao, coffee. Has Wesleyan medical mission and school.

Kamachumu (kämächoo'moo), village, Lake Prov., NW Tanganyika, 22 mi. SSW of Bukoba, near SW shore of L. Victoria; coffee, tobacco, corn, livestock.

Kamae (kämä'ā), town (pop. 5,346), Oita prefecture, E Kyushu, Japan, 36 mi. SSE of Oita, on Hyuga Sea; fishing center.

Kamai, Belgian Congo: see Luisa.

Kamaing (kŭmīng'), village, Myitkyina dist., Kachin State, Upper Burma, on Mogaung R. and 40 mi. W of Myitkyina. In Second World War, scene of fighting.

Kamaishi (kämī'shē), city (1940 pop. 42,167; 1947 pop. 28,907), Iwate prefecture, N Honshu, Japan, port on the Pacific, 50 mi. SE of Morioka; iron-mining center (smelting); fish processing. Exports marine products, pig iron. Sometimes spelled Kamaisi.

Kamakhya, India: see Gauhati.

Kamakou, Mount (kä'mäkō'), E Molokai, T.H., highest peak (4,958 ft.) on isl.

Kamakura (kämä'koorä), city (1940 pop. 40,151; 1947 pop. 55,168), Kanagawa prefecture, central Honshu, Japan, at base of Miura Peninsula, on NE shore of Sagami Bay, just NW of Yokosuka; religious center; meat-processing plants; largely residential. Known for its *daibutsu* [Jap.,=great Buddha], a 42-ft. bronze figure of Buddha cast in 1252. A 30-ft. statue of Kannon (Goddess of Mercy) and tomb of Yoritomo also here. Natl. Art Mus. has art objects of Kamakura and Ashikaga periods. Hq. of Yoritomo and his descendants (1192–1333); under Ashikaga shogunate (1333–1573) it was govt. hq. of Eastern Japan. Severely damaged in earthquake of 1923.

Kamakwi (kämä'kwē), town (pop. 1,490), Northern Prov., NW Sierra Leone, on road and 65 mi. NNE of Port Loko; center of trade with Fr. Guinea. Has hosp. Also called Makwi.

Kamalapuram (kä'mŭläpoorŭm). **1** Village, Anantapur dist., Madras, India: see Hampi. **2** Town (pop. 5,937), Cuddapah dist., N central Madras, India, near Penner R., 13 mi. NW of Cuddapah; cotton, rice, melons. Limestone quarrying near by.

Kamalganj (kŭm'ŭlgŭnj), town (pop. 3,149), Farrukhabad dist., central Uttar Pradesh, India, on tributary of the Ganges and 9 mi. SSE of Farrukhabad; wheat, gram, jowar, corn, potatoes, tobacco.

Kamalia (kŭmäl'yŭ), town (pop. 14,295), Lyallpur dist., E central Punjab, W Pakistan, 55 mi. SSW of Lyallpur; market center (wheat, millet, cotton, ghee, wool); cotton ginning, handicraft cloth weaving and printing.

Kamamaung (kŭmä"moung'), village, Salween dist., Lower Burma, 60 mi. N of Moulmein, on Salween R. (head of navigation) at mouth of Yunzalin R.

Kaman (kä'mŭn), town (pop. 9,204), E Rajasthan, India, 33 mi. NNW of Bharatpur; millet, gram, wheat; hand-loom weaving. A place of Hindu pilgrimage.

Kaman (kämän'), village (pop. 3,988), Kirsehir prov., central Turkey, 28 mi. NW of Kirsehir; grain, linseed, mohair goats.

Kamaniola (kämänyō'lä), village, Kivu prov., E Belgian Congo, on Ruzizi R. and 20 mi. SSE of Costermansville; terminus of railroad from Uvira (Kalundu); cotton growing, cotton ginning.

Kamaran Islands (kămărăn'), dependency (□ 22; pop. 2,200) of Aden Colony, in Red Sea, off Yemen coast, 200 mi. N of the strait Bab el Mandeb; includes main Kamaran Isl. (10 mi. long, 5 mi. wide) off Salif and near-by smaller isls. Kamaran Isl. has airfield, post and telegraph office, as well as quarantine station for pilgrims traveling to Mecca. Formerly a Turkish possession, the Kamaran group was occupied in 1915 by the British. Its status having been left indeterminate by the Treaty of Lausanne (1923), the group is directed by a civil administrator under the governor of Aden.

Kamard or **Kahmard** (kŭmŭrd'), village, Kabul prov., E Afghanistan, at N foot of the Hindu Kush, 105 mi. NW of Kabul, and on Kamard R. (left tributary of the Surkhab); 35°20'N 67°38'E. Sulphur deposits in valley, chiefly at Dasht-i-Safed (15 mi. E).

Kamareddi or **Kamaredi** (both: kämärā'dē), town (pop. 5,282), Nizamabad dist., central Hyderabad state, India, 30 mi. SE of Nizamabad; rice, oilseeds; distillery. Formerly called Kamareddipet.

Kamarhati (kämärhä'tē), town (pop. 42,545), 24-Parganas dist., SE West Bengal, India, on Hooghly R. and 7 mi. N of Calcutta city center; jute and cotton milling, mfg. of rubber goods, cement, pottery, paint; tannery.

Kama River (kä'mŭ, kŭ'–), chief left tributary of the Volga, E European Russian SFSR; 1,262 mi. long. Rises in low outliers of the central Urals just N of Kuliga (Udmurt Autonomous SSR), flows N past Loino (head of shallow-draught navigation for near-by Rudnichny phosphorite field), and turning E and S past Borovsk (port of Solikamsk), Berezniki, and Molotov (hydroelectric dam site), and SW past Sarapul and Chistopol to the Volga at Kamskoye Ustye [=Kama mouth]. Receives Vishera, Chusovaya, and Belaya rivers (left), Vyatka R. (right). Navigable for 6–6½ months, the Kama carries lumber, paper, ferrous metals (downstream), petroleum, salt, and cement (upstream). Regular river-steamer traffic is planned to be extended above Molotov to Solikamsk with completion of Molotov dam.

Kamarkhali Ghat, E Pakistan: see Madhukhali.

Kamarlu or **Kamarlyu,** Armenian SSR: see Artashat.

Kamas (kă'mŭs), town (pop. 721), Summit co., N central Utah, on diversion canal and 12 mi. E of Park City; alt. 6,473 ft.

Kamashi (kŭmŭshē'), village (1939 pop. over 500), central Kashka-Darya oblast, Uzbek SSR, on railroad and 35 mi. E of Karshi; wheat.

Kamatanda (kämätän'dä), village, Katanga prov., SE Belgian Congo, 10 mi. E of Jadotville; rail junction, copper-mining center.

Kamatapur (kŭmä'täpoor), ruined city, Cooch Behar dist., NE West Bengal, India, near the Jaldhaka, 12 mi. SSW of Cooch Behar. Founded early-15th cent. as ⊙ Khen kingdom; abandoned late-15th cent. after overthrow of Khens by Afghans. Also called Rajpat. Figured prominently on early maps of India as Comotay.

Kamay (kă'mā), village (pop. c.700), Wichita co., N Texas, 18 mi. WSW of Wichita Falls, near Wichita R.; oil-field center. Formerly Kemp City.

Kamayut (kŭmä"yoot'), NW suburb (pop. 7,256) of Rangoon, Lower Burma, on railroad and 6 mi. from central Rangoon; mfg. of tobacco products, rubber shoes.

Kambaengbejr, Thailand: see Kamphaengphet.

Kambam, town, India: see Cumbum, Madura dist.

Kambam Valley (kŭm'bŭm), along E slopes of S Western Ghats, SW Madras, India, bet. Palni Hills (N) and Varushanad and Andipatti hills (SE); drained by upper Vaigai R. and its left affluent, the Suruli; irrigated by Periyar Lake project. Mainly agr. (rice, grain, tobacco); date and coconut palms. Chief products of near-by hills: tea, coffee, cardamom, timber. Main towns: Bodinayakkanur, Cumbum. Sometimes spelled Cumbum.

Kambar (kŭm'bŭr), town (pop. 11,681), Larkana dist., NW Sind, W Pakistan, 12 mi. WNW of Larkana; market center for local produce (rice, millet, wheat); trades in mangoes, dates, fresh-water fish; handicraft cloth weaving, rice milling.

Kambara (kämbä'rä), limestone island (□ 12; pop. 513), Lau group, Fiji, SW Pacific; 18°57'S 178°57'W; 4.5 mi. long, 3 mi. wide; rises to 470 ft.; copra. Sometimes spelled Kabara.

Kambara (kämbä'rä), town (pop. 17,065), Shizuoka prefecture, central Honshu, Japan, on N shore of Suruga Bay, at mouth of Fuji R., 10 mi. NE of Shizuoka; citrus-fruit center.

Kambarka (kŭmbär'kŭ), city (1926 pop. 6,256), SE Udmurt Autonomous SSR, Russian SFSR, near Kama R., on railroad and 20 mi. SE of Sarapul; mfg. center (wagons, carts). Founded 1767; became city in 1945. Formerly Kambarski Zavod.

Kambaye, Belgian Congo: see Kanda-Kanda.

Kambe. 1 Town, Mie prefecture, Japan: see Suzuka. **2** Village, Nara prefecture, Japan: see Ouda.

Kambia (kämbē'ä), town (pop. 2,664), Northern Prov., NW Sierra Leone, near Fr. Guinea border, on Great Scarcies R. (head of navigation) and 25 mi. NNW of Port Loko; palm oil and kernels, piassava, rice. Hq. Kambia dist.

Kambing, Portuguese Timor: see Atauro.

Kambo-ho, Korea: see Kwanmo, Mount.

Kambove (kämbō'vā), village, Katanga prov., SE Belgian Congo, 10 mi. NW of Jadotville; copper-mining center; rail terminus; cobalt and platinum-palladium are also mined. Has Protestant mission. Copper deposits of Kambove were exploited by Swahilis of E African coast before the arrival of white African explorers.

Kamburg, Germany: see Camburg.

Kamchatka (kămchăt'kŭ, Rus. kŭmchät'kŭ), oblast (□ 490,425; pop. c.150,000) in NE Khabarovsk Territory, Siberian Russian SFSR, on Bering Sea; ⊙ Petropavlovsk. Includes Kamchatka Peninsula, Komandorski Islands, Koryak National Okrug, Chukchi National Okrug. Fishing (chief industry), fur trapping, lumbering; some agr. along Kamchatka R.; fish canning along coast. Formed 1932 within former Far Eastern Territory; placed 1938 in Khabarovsk Territory.

Kamchatka Gulf, inlet of the Pacific, on E coast of Kamchatka Peninsula, Russian SFSR, bet. Kronotski Cape (S) and Ust-Kamchatsk (N), where it receives Kamchatka R., 85 mi. wide.

Kamchatka Peninsula, large peninsula (□ 104,200) of NE Siberia; part of Kamchatka oblast, Khabarovsk Territory, Russian SFSR; separates Sea of Okhotsk (W) from Bering Sea and Pacific Ocean (E). Extends from 51° to 61°N lat.; 750 mi. long, up to 300 mi. wide; terminates S in Cape Lopatka, beyond which lie Kurile Isls. Linked to mainland (N) by 63-mi.-wide isthmus. Central valley (drained by Kamchatka R.) is enclosed by 2 parallel longitudinal volcanic ranges. Central (or E) range rises to 11,834 ft. in Ichinskaya Sopka; W range rises to 15,666 ft. in Klyuchevskaya Sopka, the highest of 13 active (of 38) volcanoes. Hot springs are abundant. Peat marshes along W coast; forests on lower mtn. slopes. Climate is severe; rain averages over 32 in. yearly on E coast. Fishing and crabbing are chief industries, mainly off W coast, with canneries along the littoral (near Ust-Bolsheretsk and Sobolevo). Hunting, lumbering, reindeer raising; petroleum and coal deposits. Agr. along Kamchatka R. Pop. chiefly Russian, with some Kamchadales and Koryaks (N). Main center, Petropavlovsk. Discovered 1697 by Rus. explorer Atlasov; Rus. conquest completed 1732.

Kamchatka River, Kamchatka Peninsula, Russian SFSR, rises in S central mtn. range of the peninsula, flows N, through a wide, densely populated agr. valley, past Milkovo (head of shallow-draught navigation) and Sredne-Kamchatsk, and E, past Nizhne-Kamchatsk, to Kamchatka Gulf of the Pacific at Ust-Kamchatsk; 335 mi. long.

Kamchiya River (käm'chēä), E Bulgaria, formed at Rakla by confluence of Golyama Kamchiya and Luda Kamchiya rivers; flows 23 mi. E, through Longosa alluvial flood plain (□ c.65; oak and elm forests), past Rakovets, to the Black Sea 13 mi. S of Stalin. Navigable 4–5 mi. in lower course. Also called Ticha R.

Kamdoli (kŭmdō'lē), town (pop. 3,010), Dharwar dist., S Bombay, India, 24 mi. SE of Dharwar; local cotton market.

Kamechlié, Syria: see Qamishliye, El.

Kameda (kämä'dä). **1** Town (pop. 4,389), Akita prefecture, N Honshu, Japan, 8 mi. NNE of Honjo; rice, silk cocoons. **2** Town (pop. 18,694), Niigata prefecture, central Honshu, Japan, 5 mi. SE of Niigata, in rice-growing area; textile center (silk, cotton flannel).

Kamehameha, Fort (kämä'ŭmä'ŭ), at Pearl Harbor, S Oahu, T.H.; hq. of coast defenses of Oahu; established 1909.

Kamembe (kämĕm'bā), village, W Ruanda-Urundi, in Ruanda, on S shore of L. Kivu, near Belgian Congo border, 85 mi. SW of Kigali; municipal airport for Costermansville (Belgian Congo); customs.

Kamen (kä'mŭn), town (pop. 14,808), in former Prussian prov. of Westphalia, W Germany, after 1945 in North Rhine-Westphalia, in the Ruhr, 4 mi. N of Unna; foundries. Coal mining.

Kamen or **Kamen-on-Ob** (kä'mĭnyŭ, ōb), Rus. *Kamen'-na-Obi* (–nŭ-ô'bē), city (1926 pop. 22,982), NW Altai Territory, Russian SFSR, port on Ob R. and 105 mi. WNW of Barnaul, in agr. area; power plant, iron foundry, brickworks.

Kamenets (kä'mĭnyĭts), Pol. *Kamieniec* or *Kamieniec Litewski* (kämyĕ'nyĕts lyĭtĕf'skē), town (1931 pop. 3,001), W Brest oblast, Belorussian SSR, on Lesna R. and 20 mi. NNE of Brest; flour milling, tanning, mfg. (bricks, tiles). Has ruins of old tower. Founded in 13th cent.

Kamenets-Podolski or **Kamenets-Podol'skiy** (–pŭdôl'skē), oblast (□ 8,000; 1946 pop. estimate 1,800,000), W Ukrainian SSR; ⊙ Proskurov. In Volyn-Podolian Upland; bounded S by Dniester R., W by Zbruch R.; wooded steppe region. Chiefly agr. (except extreme N), with sugar beets, wheat, fruit orchards, tobacco, corn; dairy farming. Phosphorite and peat deposits. Industry includes sugar refining, fruit canning, dairying (S), lumbering, paper milling, ceramics (N). Chief centers: Proskurov, Kamenets-Podolski, Shepetovka. Formed 1937.

Kamenets-Podolski or **Kamenets-Podol'skiy,** city (1926 pop. 32,051), S Kamenets-Podolski oblast, Ukrainian SSR, in Podolia, on Smotrich R. (left affluent of the Dniester) and 55 mi. SSW of Proskurov; rail terminus; road center; machine shops, lumber and clothing mills, meat packing, fruit canning. Teachers col. Has remains of 14th-cent. castle. Former ⊙ Podolia; after 1434 under Poles; annexed 1793 to Russia. Pop. 40% Jewish until Second World War, when city was held (1941–43) by Germans. Called Kamenets-Podolsk until 1944.

Kamenica, Kamenitsa, Kamenica Valjevska, or **Kamenitsa Valyevska** (all: kä'mĕnĭtsä, vä'lyĕfskä), village (pop. 2,631), W Serbia, Yugoslavia, 9 mi. WNW of Valjevo.

Kamenice nad Lipou (kä'mĕnyĭtsĕ nad' lĭpō), Ger. *Kamnitz an der Linde* (käm'nĭts än dĕr lĭn'dŭ), town (pop. 2,533), S Bohemia, Czechoslovakia, in

Bohemian-Moravian Heights, on railroad and 11 mi. NNE of Jindrichuv Hradec; barley, oats; textiles.

Kamenicky Senov (kä'mĕnĭtsē shĕ'nôf), Czech *Kamenický Šenov*, Ger. *Steinschönau* (shtīn'shû-nou), town (pop. 3,445), N Bohemia, Czechoslovakia, on railroad and 22 mi. NE of Usti nad Labem; glass mfg. and refining; a center of Bohemian cut-glass industry, dating from 17th cent.

Kamenitsa (kämĕnē'tsä), village (pop. 4,274), Plovdiv dist., SW Bulgaria, on Chepino R. and 20 mi. SW of Pazardzhik; health resort with thermal springs; sawmilling; flax, vegetables, fruit.

Kamenka (kä'myĭn-kŭ). **1** Village, NW West Kazakhstan oblast, Kazakh SSR, on railroad (Shipovo station) and 45 mi. W of Uralsk; cattle, horses. **2** Town (1926 pop. 7,022), NE Moldavian SSR, on Dniester R. and 70 mi. N of Kishinev; grape-cure resort; wines, flour. **3** Town (1948 pop. over 2,000), N Archangel oblast, Russian SFSR, 12 mi. NNW of Mezen, across Mezen R.; sawmilling. Formerly called Okulovski. **4** Town (1939 pop. over 500), NE Ivanovo oblast, Russian SFSR, on Volga R. and 14 mi. NNW of Vichuga; cotton mill. **5** Town (1926 pop. 5,229), central Penza oblast, Russian SFSR, on railroad (Belinskaya station) and 40 mi. W of Penza; flour-milling center in grain and sugar-beet area; mfg. of farm implements. Also known as Kamenka Belinskaya or Belinskaya Kamenka. **6** Village (1926 pop. 2,035), SE central Tambov oblast, Russian SFSR, 45 mi. SSE of Tambov; wheat, sunflowers, essential-oil plants. **7** Town (1948 pop. over 2,000), S central Voronezh oblast, Russian SFSR, on railroad (Yevdakovo station) and 18 mi. SE of Ostrogozhsk; dairy plant. **8** Suburb, Dnepropetrovsk oblast, Ukrainian SSR: see FRUNZENSKI. **9** Town (1926 pop. 2,444), N Kirovograd oblast, Ukrainian SSR, 16 mi. SE of Smela; sugar refining, distilling, lumber milling. Called (1930–44) Kamenka-Shevchenkovskaya. **10** or **Kamenka-Dneprovskaya** (–dŭnyĭprôf'skĭŭ), town (1926 pop. 9,466), W Zaporozhe oblast, Ukrainian SSR, on arm of Dnieper R., opposite Nikopol; flour milling. Originally called Malaya Znamenka; later also Kamenka-na-Dnepre [Rus.,=Kamenka on the Dnieper].

Kamenka Belinskaya, Russian SFSR: see KAMENKA, Penza oblast.

Kamenka-Bugskaya (kä'myĭn-kŭ-bōōk'skĭŭ), city (1931 pop. 7,935), central Lvov oblast, Ukrainian SSR, on Bug R. and 20 mi. NE of Lvov; agr. processing (grain, potatoes, hops), tanning, soap mfg., sawmilling. Has ruins of old monastery. Under Austrian rule (1772–1918); reverted to Poland (1919); ceded to USSR in 1945. Until 1940, called Kamenka-Strumilovskaya, Pol. *Kamionka Strumilowa.*

Kamenka-Dneprovskaya, Ukrainian SSR: see KAMENKA, Zaporozhe oblast.

Kamen-Kashirski or **Kamen'-Kashirskiy** (kä'mĭn-yŭ-kŭshĭr'skē), Pol. *Kamień Koszyrski* (kä'myĕn-yŭ kôshĭr'skē), city (1931 pop. 2,150), N Volyn oblast, Ukrainian SSR, in Pripet Marshes, on right tributary of Pripet R. and 30 mi. NNE of Kovel; rail terminus; flour milling, distilling, brick mfg. A Pol. frontier stronghold on Lith. border in 14th cent.; passed to Russia (1795); reverted to Poland (1921); ceded to USSR in 1945.

Kamenka-Strumilovskaya, Ukrainian SSR: see KAMENKA-BUGSKAYA.

Kamennogorsk (kämyĭnŭgôrsk'), city (1945 commune pop. 7,964), NW Leningrad oblast, Russian SFSR, on Vuoksi R. and 20 mi. NE of Vyborg; sugar-milling center. Called Antrea while in Finland (until 1940) and, until 1948, in USSR.

Kamenno-Millerovo (kä"myĭnŭ-mē'lyĭrŭvŭ), town (1939 pop. over 500), S Voroshilovgrad oblast, Ukrainian SSR, in the Donbas, 10 mi. WNW of Rovenki; coal mines.

Kamennomostskaya (–môst'skĭŭ), town (1939 pop. over 500), S central Krasnodar Territory, Russian SFSR, on Belaya R. and 20 mi. S of Maikop (linked by rail); gypsum quarries.

Kamenny Brod or **Kamennyy Brod** (kä'myĭnē brôt"), town (1939 pop. over 500), W Zhitomir oblast, Ukrainian SSR, 18 mi. SE of Novograd-Volynski; ceramic industry.

Kameno (kä'mĕnô), village (pop. 3,894), Burgas dist., E Bulgaria, on railroad and 10 mi. WNW of Burgas, in sugar-beet area; sugar refinery. Formerly called Kayalii.

Kamenolomni (kä"myĭnŭlôm'nyē), town (1939 pop. over 2,000), SW Rostov oblast, Russian SFSR, just S of Shakhty; machine mfg.; stone quarries.

Kamen-Rybolov or **Kamen'-Rybolov** (kä"mĭnyŭ-rĭbŭlôf'), village (1926 pop. 680), SW Maritime Territory, Russian SFSR, on L. Khanka and 65 mi. N of Voroshilov, on branch of Trans-Siberian RR, in rice-growing area; grain, soybeans. Former river-road transfer point on Khabarovsk-Vladivostok route.

Kamensk (kä'myĭnsk). **1** or **Kamenski Zavod,** ironworks, Russian SFSR: see KAMENSK-URALSKI. **2** or **Kamensk-Shakhtinski** or **Kamensk-Shakhtinskiy** (–shäkh'tyĭnskē), city (1936 pop. estimate 25,400), W Rostov oblast, Russian SFSR, on right bank of Northern Donets R. (landing) and 75 mi. NNE of Rostov. Industrial center in E Donets Basin; locomotive and car repair shops, chemical plant (potash, nitrogen fixation); lumber milling, distilling. Coal mining at Gundorovka (W). Originally a Cossack village; became city in 1927. During Second World War, held (1942–43) by Germans.

Kamenski or **Kamenskiy** (kä'myĭnskē), town (1926 pop. 5,645), S Saratov oblast, Russian SFSR, 13 mi. SW of Krasnoarmeisk; mfg. of agr. implements, flour milling. Until 1941 (in German Volga Autonomous SSR), Grimm.

Kamenskoye (–skŭyŭ). **1** Village (1926 pop. 216), NW Koryak Natl. Okrug, Kamchatka oblast, Khabarovsk Territory, Russian SFSR, port on Penzhina Bay of Sea of Akhotsk, at mouth of Penzhina R., 290 mi. N of Palana, in lignite area. Trading post; fisheries; reindeer raising. **2** City, Dnepropetrovsk oblast, Ukrainian SSR: see DNEPRODZERZHINSK.

Kamensk-Shakhtinski, Russian SFSR: see KAMENSK, Rostov oblast.

Kamensk-Uralski or **Kamensk-Ural'skiy** (kä"-myĭnsk-ōōräl'skē), city (1926 pop. 5,367; 1939 pop. 50,897), S Sverdlovsk oblast, Russian SFSR, in E foothills of the central Urals, on Iset R. and 55 mi. SE of Sverdlovsk. Rail junction (Sinarskaya station); a major bauxite-mining and aluminum-refining center; ferrous metallurgy (largely pig iron), based on local hematite deposits; mfg. (machine tools, pipes, building materials), woodworking, food processing. Founded 1682 as ironworks called Kamenski Zavod (later Kamensk); renamed Kamensk-Uralski (c.1930); became city in 1935. Largely developed after construction (1935–37) of pipe foundry and aluminum plant.

Kamenz (kä'mĕnts), town (pop. 13,862), Saxony, E Central Germany, in Upper Lusatia, on the Black Elster and 25 mi. NE of Dresden; woolen and linen milling; mfg. of glass, china, machinery, musical instruments. Kaolin quarrying. Lessing b. here. Town destroyed by fire in 1842. Marienstern Cistercian convent, founded 1264, is 6 mi. ESE.

Kamenz, Poland: see KAMIENIEC.

Kameoka (kämā'ôkä), town (pop. 9,652), Kyoto prefecture, S Honshu, Japan, 10 mi. W of Kyoto; commercial center in rice-growing area; sake, dried mushrooms; woodworking. Agr. school.

Kamerun: see CAMEROONS.

Kamesaki, Japan: see HANDA, Aichi prefecture.

Kameshkir Russki, Russian SFSR: see RUSSKI KAMESHKIR.

Kameshkovo (kä'myĭshkŭvŭ), town (1926 pop. 3,992), N Vladimir oblast, Russian SFSR, 13 mi. W of Kovrov, near railroad (Derbenevo station); cotton-milling center. Textile school. In early 1920s, also called Imeni Sverdlova.

Kameshli, Syria: see QAMISHLIYE, EL.

Kamesnica, peak, Yugoslavia: see DINARA.

Kamet (kŭ'māt, kŭmät'), mountain (25,447 ft.) in SE Zaskar Range, in Garhwal dist., N Uttar Pradesh, India, near Tibet (border undefined), 14 mi. NE of Badrinath. First scaled (1931) by English group including noted Himalayan climbers Frank S. Smythe and Eric Shipton; for 5 years highest mtn. climbed by man. A Sherpa porter was 1st to set foot on summit. Sometimes called Ibi Gamin.

Kametsu (kämā'tsōō), largest town (1950 pop. 12,438) on Tokuno-shima of isl. group Amami-gunto, in Ryukyu Isls., on SE coast of isl.; agr. center (sugar cane, sweet potatoes).

Kameyama (kämā'yämŭ), town (pop. 16,195), Mie prefecture, S Honshu, Japan, 7 mi. WSW of Suzuka; rail junction; agr. center (rice, wheat, tea, poultry); cotton textiles.

Kami, Bolivia: see ICOYA.

Kami (kä'mē), town (pop. 4,469), Okayama prefecture, SW Honshu, Japan, just S of Tsuyama, in rice-growing area; wheat, charcoal, raw silk.

Kamiah (kă'mēī), village (pop. 812), Lewis co., W Idaho, 10 mi. E of Nezperce and on South Fork of Clearwater R.

Kamibun (kämē'bōōn), town (pop. 3,695), Ehime prefecture, N Shikoku, Japan, 2 mi. ENE of Mishima; rice.

Kamidaki (kämē'dä'kē), town (pop. 3,997), Toyama prefecture, central Honshu, Japan, 7 mi. SE of Toyama; rice growing.

Kamien or **Kamien Pomorski** (kä'myĕnyŭ pômôr'-skē), Pol. *Kamień Pomorski.* **1** Ger. *Kamin* (kämēn'), town (pop. 1,275), Bydgoszcz prov., NW Poland, on railroad and 35 mi. NW of Bydgoszcz, flour milling. **2** Ger. *Cammin* (kämēn'), town (1939 pop. 6,055; 1946 pop. 1,576) in Pomerania, after 1945 in Szczecin prov., NW Poland, on Kamien Lagoon (E arm of Oder R. estuary mouth), opposite Wolin isl., and 40 mi. NNE of Stettin. Seaport; fish and cattle market; health resort with mineral springs; woodworking. Bishopric, moved here (1175) from Wolin, again moved in 1574 to Köslin (Koszalin). Town passed 1679 to Brandenburg. In Second World War, c.50% destroyed. Seat (1933–45) of Protestant bishopric.

Kamieniec (kämyĕn'yĕts), Ger. *Kamenz* (kä'mĕnts), town (1939 pop. 2,510; 1946 pop. 2,137) in Lower Silesia, after 1945 in Wroclaw prov., SW Poland, on the Glatzer Neisse and 6 mi. SE of Zabkowice; in nickel-mining, grain-growing region; rail junction. Has 14th-cent. church of former monastery (1210). Chartered after 1945 and briefly called Kamienice.

Kamieniec, Belorussian SSR: see KAMENETS.

Kamien Koszyrski, Ukrainian SSR: see KAMEN-KASHIRSKIY.

Kamien Lagoon (kä'myĕn), Pol. *Zalew Kamieński* (zä'lĕf kämyĕ'nyŭskē), Ger. *Camminer Boden* (kämē'nŭr bō'dŭn), expansion (□ 3.5) of Dievenow R. (E arm of Oder R. estuary mouth), in Pomerania, after 1945 in NW Poland, bet. Wolin isl. (W) and mainland (E); drains N into the Baltic. Kamien Pomorski (Cammin) is on E shore. Also called Plycizna Kamienska, Pol. *Płycizna Kamieńska.*

Kamienna Gora (kämyĕ'nä gōō'rä), Pol. *Kamienna Góra,* Ger. *Landeshut* (län'dŭs-hōōt), town (1939 pop. 13,688; 1946 pop. 12,754) in Lower Silesia, after 1945 in Wroclaw prov., SW Poland, at E foot of the Riesengebirge, on Bobrawa R. and 11 mi. W of Waldenburg (Walbrzych); coal mining; cotton and linen milling, metalworking, mfg. of machinery, shoes, leather goods. Has one of 6 Churches of Grace (1709–30) allowed Silesian Protestants under Treaty of Altranstädt (1707). In 1745, Prussians defeated Austrians here; in Seven Years War, scene (1760) of Austrian victory over Prussians.

Kamienna River, E central Poland, rises 12 mi. SSW of Szydlowiec, flows c.80 mi. generally E, past Skarzysko-Kamienna, Wierzbnik, and Ostrowiec, to Vistula R. 24 mi. SSW of Pulawy.

Kamienna-Skarzysko, Poland: see SKARZYSKO-KAMIENNA.

Kamienski, Zalew, Poland: see KAMIEN LAGOON.

Kami-Furano (kä'mē-fōō'ränō), village (pop. 12,587), central Hokkaido, Japan, 22 mi. S of Asahigawa; hot-springs resort; agr. (rice, potatoes).

Kamigori (kämē'gō'rē), town (pop. 6,964), Hyogo prefecture, S Honshu, Japan, 22 mi. WNW of Himeji, in agr. area (rice, wheat, market produce, flowers).

Kami-hasami (kä'mēhä"sämē), town (pop. 10,463), Nagasaki prefecture, NW Kyushu, Japan, on NW Hizen Peninsula, 10 mi. E of Sasebo; rice; pottery. Some gold mined near by.

Kamiichi (kämē'chē). **1** Town (pop. 3,287), Nara prefecture, S Honshu, Japan, on N central Kii Peninsula, 20 mi. S of Nara; raw silk, rice, wheat. **2** Town (pop. 10,195), Toyama prefecture, central Honshu, Japan, 8 mi. E of Toyama; rice-growing center; silk textiles. Prefectural agr. school.

Kami-iida, Japan: see IIDA, Nagano prefecture.

Kamiiso (kämē'ēsō), town (pop. 17,579), SW Hokkaido, Japan, on inlet of Tsugaru Strait, 6 mi. NW of Hakodate; cement making; lumbering, fishing.

Kami-kamakari-jima (kämē'-kämä'kä'rē-jĭmä) or **Kami-kamagari-jima,** island (□ 9; pop. c.10,000), Hiroshima prefecture, Japan, in Hiuchi Sea (central section of Inland Sea) just SE of Kure (on SW Honshu); 5 mi. long, 2 mi. wide. Mountainous, fertile (rice, sweet potatoes). Fishery.

Kami-koma (kämē'-kō'mä), town (pop. 3,847), Kyoto prefecture, S Honshu, Japan, 19 mi. S of Kyoto; rice, wheat, fruit.

Kami-koshiki-shima (kä'mē-kōshĭkē'shĭmä), island (□ 21; pop. 10,833 including offshore islets) of isl. group Koshiki-retto, Kagoshima prefecture, Japan, in E.China Sea 14 mi. off SW coast of Kyushu; 9 mi. long, 4 mi. wide; irregular coastline; mountainous. Produces rice, wheat. Fishing.

Kamiluk Lake (kă'mĭlŭk) or **Kamilukuak Lake** (kămĭlŭ'kwăk) (30 mi. long, 20 mi. wide), SW Keewatin Dist., Northwest Territories, on Mackenzie Dist. border; drains into Dubawnt L. (S); 62°25'N 101°40'W. On S shore is trading post.

Kami-mizo, Japan: see SAGAMIHARA.

Kamin, Poland: see KAMIEN, Bydgoszcz prov.

Kamina (kämē'nä), village (1948 pop. 2,209), ⊙ Upper Lomami dist. (□ 63,993; 1948 pop. c.405,000), Katanga prov., SE Belgian Congo, on railroad and 260 mi. NW of Elisabethville; road junction; agr. trade center. Has R.C. mission. Airfield.

Kaminada (kämē'nädä), town (pop. 6,817), Ehime prefecture, W Shikoku, Japan, on Iyo Sea, 13 mi. SW of Matsuyama; commercial center in agr. area producing oranges.

Kaminak Lake (kă'mĭnăk) (40 mi. long, 1–22 mi. wide), SW Keewatin Dist., Northwest Territories, 60 mi. W of Tavani; 62°12'N 95°W. Drains E into Hudson Bay.

Kaministikwia River (kŭmĭ"nĭstĭ'kwēŭ), W Ont., issues from Dog L., flows S to Kakabeka Falls (hydroelectric station), thence E to Thunder Bay of L. Superior at Fort William; 60 mi. long.

Kaminokae (kämē'nōkä'ā), town (pop. 5,027), Kochi prefecture, S Shikoku, Japan, on Tosa Bay, 26 mi. SW of Kochi; major fishing center.

Kaminokawa (kämēnō'käwŭ), town (pop. 8,172), Tochigi prefecture, central Honshu, Japan, 9 mi. S of Utsunomiya; rice, tobacco, wheat.

Kaminoyama (kämēnō'yämŭ), town (pop. 16,586), Yamagata prefecture, N Honshu, Japan, 7 mi. SSW of Yamagata; agr. center (rice, grapes, persimmons). Known for hot springs since 15th cent.

Kaminski or **Kaminskiy** (kŭmēn'skē), town (1947 pop. over 500), N Ivanovo oblast, Russian SFSR, 11 mi. WNW of Rodniki; cotton milling. Until 1947, Gorki-Pavlovy.

Kaminuriak Lake (kămĭnyŏŏ'rēăk) (□ 360), Keewatin Dist., Northwest Territories, near 63°N 95°45'W.

Kamionka Strumilowa, Ukrainian SSR: see KAMENKA-BUGSKAYA.

Kamishak Bay (kă'mĭshăk), (45 mi. wide at mouth, 20 mi. long), S Alaska, on W side of mouth of Cook Inlet, W of Seldovia; 59°18'N 153°30'W. Contains Augustine Isl.

Kami-shikuka, Russian SFSR: see LEONIDOVO.

Kami-shima (kämē'shĭmä), island (□ 89; pop. 59,760 including offshore islets) of Amakusa Isls., in E.China Sea, Japan, in Kumamoto prefecture, off W coast of Kyushu; nearly connected with Shimo-jima (W); 12 mi. E–W, 10 mi. N–S. Mountainous, fertile (rice); fishing. Largest village, Himedo.

Kamisuku, Belgian Congo: see KALIMA-KINGOMBE.

Kami-suwa, Japan: see SUWA, city.

Kamiteru, Japan: see NAGAHAMA, Shiga prefecture.

Kamituga (kämētŏŏ'gä), village, Kivu prov., E Belgian Congo, 65 mi. SW of Costermansville; center of gold-mining operations employing c.7,000, workers; gold processing. Hydroelectric plant.

Kamiyashiro, Japan: see UJI-YAMADA.

Kamkeut (kämkût'), town, Cammon prov., central Laos, in Annamese Cordillera, 65 mi. WSW of Vinh (linked by road).

Kamkong, China: see TSINGMAI.

Kamlin or **El Kamlin** (ĕl kămlēn'), town, Blue Nile prov., E central Anglo-Egyptian Sudan, in the Gezira, on left bank of Blue Nile, near railroad, 60 mi. SE of Khartoum; cotton, wheat, barley, corn, fruits, durra; livestock.

Kamloops (kăm'lōōps), city (pop. 5,959), S B.C., on Thompson R., at confluence of North and South Thompson rivers, near Kamloops L., 160 mi. NE of Vancouver; alt. 1,160 ft.; rail junction and chief divisional point in B.C. of Canadian Pacific and Canadian National RRs; fruitgrowing, dairying, stock-raising center; distributing point for agr. and mining (coal, gypsum, metals) region; lumbering. Has large Hudson's Bay Co. store. Founded 1812 as Fort Thompson, fur-trading post of the North West Co.; later renamed Fort Kamloops. A village which grew here during the Cariboo gold rush was reached 1885 by Canadian Pacific RR.

Kamloops Lake (20 mi. long, 20 mi. wide), S B.C., expansion of Thompson R., 6 mi. W of Kamloops.

Kammersee, Austria: see ATTERSEE, lake.

Kamnik (käm'nĭk), Ger *Stein* (shtīn), village (pop. 4,950), N Slovenia, Yugoslavia, 13 mi. NNE of Ljubljana, at S foot of Savinja Alps. Terminus of railroad to Ljubljana; light metallurgy; mfg. of gunpowder. Tourist center. Castle ruins and church with fine frescoes near by. Until 1918, in Carniola.

Kamnik Mountains, Yugoslavia: see SAVINJA ALPS.

Kamnitz an der Linde, Czechoslovakia: see KAMENICE NAD LIPOU.

Kamo (kä'mō). **1** or **Gamo** (gä'mō), town (pop. 16,216), Kagoshima prefecture, S Kyushu, Japan, 13 mi. N of Kagoshima; tobacco-producing, mining center (gold, silver). **2** Town (pop. 27,588), Niigata prefecture, central Honshu, Japan, 18 mi. S of Niigata; textile center; sugar refining. **3** Town (pop. 8,438), Okayama prefecture, SW Honshu, Japan, 8 mi. NNE of Tsuyama, in agr. area (rice, wheat). Produces charcoal, *konnyaku* (paste made from devil's tongue). **4** Town (pop. 7,919), Shimane prefecture, SW Honshu, Japan, 12 mi. SW of Matsue; commercial center in rice-growing area. **5** Town, Tokushima prefecture, Japan: see TOKUSHIMA, city. **6** Town (pop. 7,096), Yamagata prefecture, N Honshu, Japan; fishing port on Sea of Japan, 5 mi. WNW of Tsuruoka; summer resort.

Kamo (kä'mō), township (pop. 556), NW N.Isl., New Zealand, 85 mi. NNW of Auckland; coal mines, mineral springs.

Kamogata (kämō'gätŭ), town (pop. 10,507), Okayama prefecture, SW Honshu, Japan, 20 mi. WSW of Okayama; agr. (rice, wheat, pears, peppermint).

Kamogawa (kämō'gäwŭ), town (pop. 9,182), Chiba prefecture, central Honshu, Japan, on SE coast of Chiba Peninsula, 17 mi. NE of Tateyama; fishing, agr. (rice, wheat).

Kamojima (kämō'jĭmä), town (pop. 7,647), Tokushima prefecture, E Shikoku, Japan, 11 mi. W of Tokushima; mfg. (dolls, textiles).

Kamoke (kä'mōkā), town (pop. 11,602), Gujranwala dist., E Punjab, W Pakistan, 12 mi. S of Gujranwala; market center (rice, wheat, millet); rice milling. Sometimes spelled Kamonki.

Kamola (kämō'lä), village, Katanga prov., SE Belgian Congo, c.35 mi. SW of Manono; tin mining; power plant.

Kamon (kä'môn), Hung. *Kámon*, town (pop. 2,480), Vas co., W Hungary, just N of Szombathely; wheat, potatoes, fruit.

Kamona, Japan: see TOKUSHIMA, city.

Kamo River, Japan: see YODO RIVER.

Kamoto, Belgian Congo: see KOLWEZI.

Kamouraska (kămŏŏră'skŭ), county (□ 1,038; pop. 25,535), SE Que., on Maine border, on the St. Lawrence; ⊙ St. Pascal.

Kamouraska, village (pop. 571), SE Que., on the St. Lawrence and 15 mi. ESE of La Malbaie; dairying: resort.

Kamp, Netherlands: see CAMPERDOWN.

Kampa, Tibet: see KHAMBA.

Kampala (kämpä'lä), town (pop. 22,094), ⊙ Buganda prov., S Uganda, 19 mi. NNE of Entebbe, near N shore of L. Victoria; 0°19'N 32°34'E; alt. 3,811 ft. Chief commercial center of Uganda. Terminus of rail line from Mombasa; agr. and livestock market; exports cotton, coffee, sugar cane; processes tobacco (cigarettes), hides, skins. Town lies amid several hills. Main govt., residential, and business area is N of rail station. Old Kampala (W) is site of old fort (govt. hq. until 1905; now a mus.). In N outskirts are Makerere (site of col. founded 1938, technical and other schools) and Mulago (govt. hosp. and medical school). Mengo (SW) is hq. of native govt. of Buganda.

Kampar (käm"pär'), town (pop. 17,499), S central Perak, Malaya, at foot of central Malayan range, on railroad and 20 mi. SSE of Ipoh; a tin-mining center of Kinta Valley.

Kampar River, central Sumatra, Indonesia, rises in Padang Highlands in mts. E of Mt. Ophir, flows c.200 mi. generally E through marshy area to Strait of Malacca near Mendol isl.

Kampen (käm'pŭn), town (pop. 22,088), Overijssel prov., N central Netherlands, on Ijssel R., near the Ijsselmeer, and 8 mi. WNW of Zwolle; dairy products, soap, cigars, tobacco, enamelware, magnesite; shipbuilding. Has 14th-cent. town hall, 14th-cent. church, several other 14th- and 15th-cent. buildings, theological col. Trading center and member of Hanseatic League in 15th cent.

Kampene (kämpĕ'nā), village, Kivu prov., E Belgian Congo, 55 mi. N of Kasongo; center of gold-mining area employing c.3,000 workers; rice processing. Tin and wolfram are also mined in vicinity (E and S). Gold mines of Kalemba (kälĕm'bä) are 25 mi. N, those of Kisulu (kēsŏŏ'lōō) 15 mi. NNW.

Kampengpet, Thailand: see KAMPHAENGPHET.

Kamperduin, Netherlands: see CAMPERDOWN.

Kampeska (kămpĕ'skŭ), village and township (pop. 300), Codington co., E S.Dak., 10 mi. W of Watertown. Just N is L. Kampeska (4 mi. long, 3 mi. wide), used for recreation.

Kamphaengphet (käm'păng'pāt'), town (1947 pop. 4,143), ⊙ Kamphaengphet prov. (□ 3,436; 1947 pop. 65,742), central Thailand, on Ping R. and 200 mi. NNW of Bangkok; anc. walled town, in rice-growing region; teak lumbering. Sometimes spelled Kampengpet and Kambaengbejr.

Kampil (kŭm'pĭl), village, Farrukhabad dist., central Uttar Pradesh, India, near Kaimganj. Was ⊙ anc. Panchala kingdom (figured in the Mahabharata). Jain temple, ruins of fort built by 13th-cent. Afghan leader. Extensive Hindu ruins near by.

Kampi-ya-Moto (käm'pē-yä-mō'tō), village, Rift Valley prov., W Kenya, on railroad and 15 mi. N of Nakuru; coffee, wheat, corn. Also called Kampiya.

Kampli (kŭm'plē), town (pop. 7,903), Bellary dist., NW Madras, India, on Tungabhadra R. and 28 mi. NW of Bellary; rice milling; bamboo coracles; coconut palms, plantain.

Kamp-Lintfort (kämp'-lĭnt'fôrt), town (pop. 24,315), in former Prussian Rhine Prov., W Germany, after 1945 in North Rhine-Westphalia, in the Ruhr, 6 mi. NW of Moers; coal mining; mfg. (textiles, clothing, leather goods). Has former Cistercian abbey Kamp (founded 1123; destroyed 16th cent.; rebuilt 1700–14). Town formed 1934 through incorporation of Kamp, Lintfort, and 4 neighboring villages.

Kamponde (kämpōn'dā), village, Kasai prov., S Belgian Congo, on railroad and 100 mi. WSW of Kabinda; center of native schooling, including noted agr. school and junior college. R.C. missions.

Kampong (kämpŏŏng') [Malay, =village]. For Malaya names beginning thus and not found here, see under following part of the name.

Kampong Dew (dĕv'), village (pop. 244), NW Perak, Malaya, c.10 mi. NW of Taiping, in Krian rice dist.

Kampong Koh (kō'), village (pop. 2,152), W Perak, Malaya, 5 mi. ESE of Lumut; rubber.

Kampong Loyang (lō"yäng'), fishing village (pop. 461), E Singapore isl., on Johore Strait, 2 mi. WSW of Changi.

Kampong Raja (rä'jä), village (pop. 1,630), N Trengganu, Malaya, 2 mi. S of Kuala Besut; rice plantations.

Kampong Sungei Tengah (sōōng-ā' tĕng'ä), village (pop. 1,383), NE Singapore isl., 8 mi. NE of Singapore; rubber. Pop. is Chinese.

Kampot (käm'pôt'), town (1936 pop. 5,530), ⊙ Kampot prov. (□ 6,500; 1948 pop. 253,092), SW Cambodia, shallow port on Gulf of Siam, 80 mi. SSW of Pnompenh, at foot of Elephant Range; center of Cambodian pepper culture; rice, sugar palms, tobacco. Limestone and phosphate extraction. In 19th cent. the chief port of Cambodia, it has been partly replaced by the deep-water ports of Ream and Kep.

Kamp River (kämp), N Lower Austria, rises near NW border of Lower Austria, flows 68 mi. E and S, past Zwettl Stadt, to the Danube 10 mi. E of Krems.

Kampsville, resort village (pop. 437), Calhoun co., W Ill., on Illinois R. (ferry) and 37 mi. NW of Alton. Bartholomew Beach here is summer resort.

Kamptee (käm'tē), town (pop., including cantonment, 26,930), Nagpur dist., central Madhya Pradesh, India, on Kanhan R. and 8 mi. NE of Nagpur; trade center (mainly cotton); cotton ginning, tea processing; cement works, tanneries. Sandstone and marble quarries near by. Formerly spelled Kamthi.

Kampti (kämp'tē), village (pop. c.900), SW Upper Volta, Fr. West Africa, near Ivory Coast border and 80 mi. SE of Bobo-Dioulasso; peanuts, shea nuts, sesame; cattle, sheep, goats. R.C. mission.

Kamrar (kăm'rär), town (pop. 261), Hamilton co., central Iowa, 7 mi. SE of Webster City, in agr. area.

Kamrej (käm'rāj), town (pop. 1,755), Surat dist., N Bombay, India, on Tapti R. and 10 mi. NE of Surat; cotton, millet.

Kamrup (käm'rōōp), district (□ 3,844; pop. 1,264,-200), W Assam, India; ⊙ Gauhati. Mainly in Brahmaputra valley; spurs of Jaintia Hills (S); swamp lakes (center SE); bounded N by Bhutan, W by Manas R.; traversed by Brahmaputra R. and drained by its tributaries. Mainly alluvial soil; rice, mustard, jute, cotton, tea; lac growing, sal timbering, silk growing in dispersed forest area; cotton ginning and baling, flour, rice, and oilseed milling, mfg. of silk cloth, soap. Gauhati Univ. and Earle Law Col. at Gauhati, Vishnuite col. (founded 15th cent.) at Barpeta. Pilgrimage centers at Kamakhya (Sivaite temple) and Hajo (Vishnuite temple). Gauhati was ⊙ anc. Hindu kingdom of Kamarupa (from which present dist. derives its name) and of late-18th-cent. Ahom (Shan) kingdom. Pop. 55% Hindu, 29% Moslem, 15% Animist tribes.

Kamsack (kăm'săk), town (pop. 1,754), SE Sask., on Assiniboine R. at mouth of Whitesand R., and 35 mi. NE of Yorkton; distributing center; grain elevators; lumbering, dairying, stock raising; natural-gas production.

Kamsar, Iran: see QAMSAR.

Kamsdorf (käms'dôrf), two adjoining villages (Grosskamsdorf, pop. 1,298; Kleinkamsdorf, pop. 1,392), in former Prussian Saxony prov. exclave, central Germany, after 1945 in Thuringia, 4 mi. E of Saalfeld; iron-mining center supplying Maxhütte steelworks at Unterwellenborn-Röblitz.

Kamskoye Ustye or **Kamskoye Ust'ye** (käm'skŭyŭ ōō'styĭ), town (1926 pop. 2,530), SW Tatar Autonomous SSR, Russian SFSR, port on right bank of the Volga, opposite mouth of Kama R., and 40 mi. S of Kazan; freight-transfer point; alabaster and gypsum quarrying; building-material mfg.; fisheries; apples. Until c.1928, Bogorodsk.

Kamta Rajaula (käm'tŭ rŭjou'lŭ), former petty state (□ 13; pop. 1,411) of Central India agency, SW of Karwi, one of the CHAUBE JAGIRS. Since 1948, merged with Vindhya Pradesh.

Kamthi, India: see KAMPTEE.

Kamudi (kŭm'ŏŏdē) or **Kamuti** (kŭm'ŏŏtē), town (pop. 10,735), Ramnad dist., S Madras, India, 39 mi. SSE of Madura, in cotton area; cotton weaving, bell-metal wares.

Kamuela, T.H.: see WAIMEA.

Kamuli (kämōō'lē), town, Eastern Prov., SE central Uganda, 35 mi. NNW of Jinja, near railroad; cotton, tobacco, coffee, bananas, corn. Mission.

Kamunting (kämōōn"tĭng'), village (pop. 1,723), NW Perak, Malaya, on railroad and 2 mi. NNW of Taiping; tin mining.

Kamuti, India: see KAMUDI.

Kamvali, Belgian Congo: see LUISHIA.

Kamvounia (kämvōō'nēŭ), Lat. *Cambunia* (kămbū'nēŭ), mountain massif on Macedonia-Thessaly line, Greece, forming divide bet. Aliakmon and upper Titaresios rivers; rises to 4,849 ft. in the Amarvik, 20 mi. SE of Kozane.

Kamysh-Burun, Russian SFSR: see KERCH, city.

Kamyshevakha (kŭmĭshĭvä'khŭ). **1** Town (1939 pop. over 500), W Voroshilovgrad oblast, Ukrainian SSR, in the Donbas, on railroad, 5 mi. N of Popasnaya. **2** Village (1926 pop. 3,018), N Zaporozhe oblast, Ukrainian SSR, on Konka R. and 15 mi. SE of Zaporozhe; truck produce.

Kamyshevatskaya (kŭmĭshĕvät'skīŭ), village (1926 pop. 9,542), NW Krasnodar Territory, Russian SFSR, on Sea of Azov, 25 mi. SW of Yeisk; wheat, sunflowers, cotton, dairying, fisheries.

Kamyshin (kŭmĭ'shĭn), city (1926 pop. 18,477; 1936 pop. estimate 29,800), NE Stalingrad oblast, Russian SFSR, port on right bank of the Volga (opposite Nikolayevski), at mouth of small Kamyshinka R., and 100 mi. NNE of Stalingrad, in melon-growing area. Rail terminus; agr. center; canned goods (fruit, meat), bakery products, alcohol, flour; mfg. (lacquers, glassware). Trades in melons, grain, timber. Rail-river transfer point. Has agr. experimental station (melon culture). Founded (1668) by Moscow as a fortress to protect the Volga route; scene of unsuccessful attempt (1697) to build a Volga-Don canal via Kamyshinka and Ilovlya rivers. Chartered 1780; called Dmitriyevsk until named Kamyshin in 1784. Volga dam project here.

Kamyshla (kŭmĭsh'lŭ), village (1926 pop. 3,109), NE Kuibyshev oblast, Russian SFSR, on Sok R. and 45 mi. ENE of Sergiyevsk; wheat, sunflowers.

Kamyshlov (kŭmĭshlôf', -mĭsh'lŭf), city (1936 pop. estimate 20,000), S Sverdlovsk oblast, Russian SFSR, on Pyshma R., on Trans-Siberian RR and

75 mi. E of Sverdlovsk; rail repair shops; tanning, flour milling, mfg. of building materials, metalworking; tripoli quarrying. Has old churches. Founded 1666 as fortress of Kamyshevskaya Sloboda; chartered 1771.

Kamysh-Zarya (kŭmĭsh'-zŭryä'), town (1939 pop. over 500), E Zaporozhe oblast, Ukrainian SSR, 38 mi. N of Osipenko; rail junction (Tsarekonstantinovka station).

Kamyzyak (kŭmĭzyäk'), village (1926 pop. 3,145), E Astrakhan oblast, Russian SFSR, on Kamyzyak arm (40 mi. long) of Volga R. delta mouth and 15 mi. S of Astrakhan; fisheries; fruit, cotton.

Kan, province, China: see KIANGSI.

Kan, river, China: see KAN RIVER.

Kan (kän), village, Second Prov., in Teheran, N Iran, 10 mi. NW of Teheran; grain, fruit (pomegranates, figs). Formerly called Kand.

Kanab (kunăb'), resort city (pop. 1,287), ⊙ Kane co., S Utah, on Kanab Creek and 55 mi. S of Panguitch, near Ariz. line; alt. 4,973 ft. Trade center for ranching and agr. area (alfalfa, livestock); lumbering. Settled 1864. Zion Natl. Park is NW; Grand Canyon Natl. Park is S.

Kanab Creek, rises in Kane co., S Utah, flows 90 mi. S, past Kanab, Utah, and through canyon in Kanab Plateau, N Ariz., to Colorado R. at E end of Grand Canyon Natl. Monument. Artifacts of cliff dwellers have been found on its banks.

Kanabec (kunā'bĭk), county (□ 525; pop. 9,192), E Minn.; ⊙ Mora. Agr. area drained by Snake R. Dairy products, livestock, poultry, grain. Formed 1858.

Kanab Plateau (kunăb'), tableland (c.6,000 ft.) in Mohave co., NW Ariz., extends N from Colorado R. and is W of Kaibab Plateau. Crossed (N-S) by Kanab Creek. Includes part of Colorado Natl. Monument in S.

Kanacea, Fiji: see KANATHEA.

Kanada (kä"nä'dä), town (pop. 8,247), Fukuoka prefecture, N Kyushu, Japan, 12 mi. S of Yawata; coal-mining center.

Kanadukattan or **Kanadukathan** (kä"nädŏŏkä'tŭn), village (pop. 10,287), Ramnad dist., S Madras, India, 7 mi. N of Karaikudi; residential and financial center of Chetty merchant community. Trade in foreign luxury goods.

Kanaga, Lake, Ill.: see EFFINGHAM, city.

Kanaga Island (kună'gu) (30 mi. long, 4-8 mi. wide), Andreanof Isls., Aleutian Isls., SW Alaska, 10 mi. W of Adak Isl.; 51°47'N 177°15'W; rises to 4,416 ft. on Kanaga Volcano (N). Fox farming.

Kanagawa (känä'gäwŭ), prefecture [Jap. *ken*] (□ 908; 1940 pop. 2,188,974; 1947 pop. 2,218,120), central Honshu, Japan; ⊙YOKOHAMA, a major port. Bounded S by Sagami Bay, E by Uraga Strait and Tokyo Bay. Urban belt in E merges with Tokyo (N). Agr. (rice, tobacco, potatoes, tea, soybeans, oranges), fishing, raw-silk production; mfg. (textiles, sake, pharmaceutical products). Heavy industry at Yokohama and KAWASAKI. Other centers: YOKOSUKA (site of naval base), KAMAKURA (religious center), ODAWARA, HIRATSUKA, FUJISAWA.

Kanagawa. 1 Town, Kanagawa prefecture, Japan: see YOKOHAMA. **2** Town (pop. 2,662), Okayama prefecture, SW Honshu, Japan, 9 mi. N of Okayama; rice, wheat, raw silk.

Kanagi (kä"nä'gē) or **Kanaki** (-kē), town (pop. 7,463), Aomori prefecture, N Honshu, Japan, 16 mi. WNW of Aomori; commercial center for agr. area.

Kanai, China: see YINGKIANG.

Kanakanak (kună'kunăk), village (pop. 88), S Alaska, on W shore of Nushagak Bay, 6 mi. SW of Dillingham; fishing and fish processing. School, hosp., radio station.

Kanaker (kŭnŭkyĕr'), N suburb (1932 pop. estimate 2,770) of Erivan, Armenian SSR, on railroad, in orchard area on Zanga R.; building-stone quarrying, metalworking. Site of hydroelectric station (Kanakerges), with reservoir.

Kanaki, Japan: see KANAGI.

Kanal (känäl'), Ital. *Canale* (känä'lĕ), village (1936 pop. 493), W Slovenia, Yugoslavia, on Isonzo R., on railroad and 10 mi. N of Gorizia. Until 1947, in Italy.

Kananga, Belgian Congo: see LULUABOURG.

Kananur, India: see CANNANORE, city.

Kanara (kŭ'nŭrŭ), Kanarese *Karnatak*, region (□ c.60,000) of S Deccan Plateau, India, named for its Kanarese-speaking people. Mainly in Mysore, it extends W over Kanara dist. (Bombay) and N through Bellary dist. (Madras) into SW Hyderabad. Was center of 16th-cent. Vijayanagar kings (⊙ was Hampi), who were forced onto plains SE of the plateau after their defeat (1565) by Deccan sultans at battle of Talikota. Kanara became an important prov. of the Mahrattas under Sivaji in 1670s. In 18th cent., the English restricted the term CARNATIC to the plains area.

Kanara, district (□ 3,961; pop. 441,157), S Bombay, India, on W edge of Deccan Plateau; ⊙ Karwar. Crossed N-S by Western Ghats, with narrow coastal strip on Arabian Sea (W); bounded NW by Goa, SE by Mysore; drained by several mtn. streams and S by Sharavati R. (Gersoppa Falls on Mysore border). Rice milling, betel and pepper farming. Coastal area has fishing centers (mackerel, sardines, catfish); ports at Karwar, Honavar, and Kumta; coconut plantations (coir processing), saltworks. Teak, bamboo, and blackwood in N forests (timber depot at Dandeli). Manganese ore deposits. Honavar and other ports fortified by Portuguese in 17th cent. Formed part of Kanara dist. of Madras presidency until 1864, when dist. was divided into Kanara dist. of Bombay presidency and SOUTH KANARA dist. of Madras presidency. Pop. 88% Hindu, 8% Moslem, 4% Christian. Also called North Kanara; formerly spelled Canara.

Kanarak, India: see KONARAK.

Kanarraville (kună'rŭvĭl), town (pop. 263), Iron co., SW Utah, near Zion Natl. Monument, 10 mi. SW of Cedar City; alt. 5,750 ft.; ranching.

Kanasashi (känä'sä'shē), town (pop. 1,940), Shizuoka prefecture, central Honshu, Japan, 2 mi. ENE of Kega; rice, tea.

Kanash (kŭnäsh'), city (1936 pop. estimate 14,100), E Chuvash Autonomous SSR, Russian SFSR, 43 mi. SSE of Cheboksary; rail junction; metalworking, poultry and meat preserving. Sack- and mat-making near by.

Kanasín (känäsēn'), town (pop. 2,420), Yucatan, SE Mexico, on railroad and 5 mi. SE of Mérida; henequen.

Kanastraion, Cape (känustrā'ôn), Lat. *Canastraeum* (kănustrē'ŭm), SE extremity of Kassandra prong of Chalcidice peninsula, Greek Macedonia, on Aegean Sea; 39°54'N 23°44'E. Formerly called Kalogrea (Kalogria) and Paliouri (Paliuri).

Kanatak (kună'tŭk), village (1939 pop. 134), S Alaska, NE Alaska Peninsula, at SW end of Shelikof Strait, 140 mi. W of Kodiak; fishing and trapping. Scene of oil boom in 1900s.

Kanatha, Syria: see KANAWAT.

Kanathea (känädhā'ä) or **Kanacea,** limestone island (□ 5; pop. 122), Lau group, Fiji, SW Pacific; 2 mi. long; copra.

Kanaud, India: see MOHINDARGARH.

Kanauj or **Kannauj** (kŭnouj'), town (pop. 21,994), Farrukhabad dist., central Uttar Pradesh, India, near the Ganges, 31 mi. SE of Farrukhabad; noted for its mfg. of perfume. Has 15th-cent. mosques and tombs. A very anc. city (called *Kanogiza* by Ptolemy), it was important during Gupta empire (320 B.C.-A.D. c.480) and again as the ⊙ and brilliant cultural center of Harsha's empire (early 7th cent.), when it was visited by Hsüan-tsang. Underwent a period of decline under successive Indian principalities after Harsha's death; sacked by Mahmud of Ghazni in 1019; was ⊙ Rajput (Rathor) kingdom from 1019 to 1194, when it was defeated by Afghans; town declined rapidly thereafter. During 18th cent., under nawabs of Oudh and Farrukhabad and, at times, Mahrattas. Humayun was defeated (1540) near by, by Sher Shah.

Kanaung (kän'-oun'), village, Henzada dist., Lower Burma, on right bank of Irrawaddy R. and 37 mi. NNW of Henzada.

Kanaura (känä'ŏŏrä), town (pop. 8,090), Okayama prefecture, SW Honshu, Japan, on Hiuchi Sea, 7 mi. E of Fukuyama, in agr. area (rice, wheat, peppermint, poultry); raw silk.

Kanavino, Russian SFSR: see GORKI, city, Gorki oblast.

Kanawat or **El Qanawat** (ĕl kănăwăt'), town, Jebel ed Druz, S Syria, just NE of Es Suweida in the mts.; alt. 4,000 ft. Extensive remains of anc. Roman city of Kanatha, a member of the Decapolis.

Kanawha (kunô'wŭ), county (□ 908; pop. 239,629), W W.Va.; ⊙ CHARLESTON, the state ⊙. On Allegheny Plateau; bounded W by Coal R.; drained by Kanawha, Elk, and Pocataliço rivers. Includes state forest and small Booker T. Washington State Park. Bituminous-coal region; natural-gas and oil wells. Industry at Charleston, South Charleston, Dunbar. Agr. (corn, dairy products, livestock, poultry, tobacco); nurseries. Formed 1788.

Kanawha, town (pop. 747), Hancock co., N Iowa, 35 mi. WSW of Mason City, in agr. area.

Kanawha Plateau, W.Va. and Ohio: see ALLEGHENY PLATEAU.

Kanawha River, SW W.Va., with its headstreams the principal river system of state, formed at Gauley Bridge by confluence of New and Gauley rivers; flows 97 mi. NW, past Charleston, to Ohio R. at Point Pleasant. Has dams (hydroelectric plants) and navigation locks; flood-control works on tributaries. Its valley, with rich coal and natural-gas fields and enormous reserves of salt brine, is one of world's great chemical-mfg. regions; Charleston is its industrial center.

Kanaya (kä"nä'yä), town (pop. 12,808), Shizuoka prefecture, central Honshu, Japan, 18 mi. SW of Shizuoka; tea, raw silk.

Kanayama, Formosa: see KINSHAN.

Kanayama (kä"nä'yämŭ). **1** Town (pop. 3,404), Gifu prefecture, central Honshu, Japan, 23 mi. N of Tajimi; sawmilling. **2** or **Kaneyama** (kä"nā'yämä), town (pop. 2,366), Miyagi prefecture, N Honshu, Japan, 5 mi. SSE of Kakuda; copper mining.

Kanazawa (kä"nä'zäwŭ). **1** City (1940 pop. 186,297; 1947 pop. 231,441), ⊙ Ishikawa prefecture, central Honshu, Japan, on Sea of Japan, 100 mi. NNW of Nagoya and on small Ono R. Mfg. center (silk textiles, porcelain, weaving machinery, lacquer ware), metalworking. Has medical col. Kenroku Park (22 acres) is known for its landscape gardens laid out in 17th cent. Seat (16th-19th cent.) of Maeda clan. Originally called Yamazaki. Includes (since 1935) former town of Ono. **2** Town, Kanagawa prefecture, Japan: see YOKOHAMA.

Kanazu (kä"nä'zōō), town (pop. 5,225), Fukui prefecture, central Honshu, Japan, 10 mi. N of Fukui; rice, wheat; weaving.

Kanbalu (kän'bulōō), village, Shwebo dist., Upper Burma, on railroad and 45 mi. NNW of Shwebo.

Kanbauk (känbouk'), village, Tavoy dist., Lower Burma, in Tenasserim, minor port on inlet of Andaman Sea, on road and 40 mi. NNW of Tavoy.

Kanbe (kämbĕ'), town (pop. 6,575), Insein dist., Lower Burma, 10 mi. WSW of Rangoon.

Kanbo, Mount, Korea: see KWANMO, MOUNT.

Kanchanaburi or **Kanburi** (kän'chänäbŏŏrē, kän'-bŏŏrē'), town (1947 pop. 7,342), ⊙ Kanchanaburi prov. (□ 7,518; 1947 pop. 140,198), S Thailand, on Mae Klong R. at mouth of Khwae Noi R., on railroad and 70 mi. WNW of Bangkok; paper mfg.; tobacco and kapok plantations. Ruby and sapphire mining at Bo Phloi (N); lead mining near by. A walled town, it was built (18th cent.) as military base against Burmese armies.

Kanchanpur, Nepal: see BILAURI.

Kanchenjunga (kŭn'chŭnjŭng"-gŭ), Tibetan *Gangchhendzönga* (gängchĕn'dzŭng'gä), Nepali *Kumbhkaran Lungur* (kŏŏmb'kŭrŭn lŏŏng-gōōr'), third-highest mountain in the world, in Singalila Range of E Nepal Himalayas, on undefined Nepal-Sikkim (India) border, 105 mi. NW of Darjeeling, at 27°42'N 88°9'E. Consists of 5 peaks; highest is 28,146 ft. First climbing attempts made in 1904 by a Br. party, in 1905 by a Swiss party. Other attempts include the arduous 1929 Bavarian expedition (led by Paul Bauer), 1930 Dyhrenfurth expedition, and 1931 Bavarian expedition (also led by Bauer), which attained highest point (26,220 ft.) reached up to 1950. Usual route is NNE ridge via the NE spur. Zemu Glacier, on E slope, descends into Sikkim state. Formerly spelled Kinchinjunga.

Kanchi, India: see CONJEEVERAM.

Kan Chiang, China: see KAN RIVER.

Kanchipuram, India: see CONJEEVERAM.

Kanchow or **Kan-chou** (both: gän'jō'). **1** Town, Kansu prov., China: see CHANGYEH. **2** City (1948 pop. 58,582), ⊙, but independent of, Kanhsien co. (1948 pop. 314,475), SW Kiangsi prov., China, 200 mi. SSW of Nanchang, and on Kan R. at junction of Kung and Tsang rivers; major commercial center in rice and ramie area. Tungsten, tin, bismuth, and gold mines near by. Became U.S. air base in Second World War, and was briefly captured (1945) by Japanese from Kwangtung. Called Kanhsien from 1911 until it became (1949) an independent municipality.

Kanchrapara (känchräpä'rŭ), town (pop. 24,015), 24-Parganas dist., SE West Bengal, India, near the Hooghly, 26 mi. NNE of Calcutta city center; large railroad workshops; jute milling.

Kanchriech (kän'shrĕch), town, Preyveng prov., S Cambodia, 45 mi. ENE of Pnompenh; corn, rice.

Kanchu or **Kanchuh** (both: gän'jōō'), village, S Kwangtung prov., China, on West R. branch of Canton R. delta and 23 mi. SW of Canton; former port of call.

Kanchüan or **Kan-ch'üan** (gän'chüän'), town, ⊙ Kanchüan co. (pop. 7,444), N Shensi prov., China, 25 mi. SSW of Yenan; wheat, beans. Petroleum, coal, and salt found near by.

Kanchumiao, Manchuria: see GANJUR.

Kanczuga (känyŭchōō'gä), Pol. *Kańczuga,* town (pop. 1,955), Rzeszow prov., SE Poland, 19 mi. ESE of Rzeszow; brewing, cement mfg.

Kand, Iran: see KAN.

Kand, peak, W Pakistan: see TOBA-KAKAR RANGE.

Kanda (kän'dä), town (pop. 11,482), Fukuoka prefecture, N Kyushu, Japan, 12 mi. ESE of Yawata, on Suo Sea; rice-producing center. Has feudal castle.

Kandagach (kŭndŭgäch'), town (1948 pop. over 2,000), N central Aktyubinsk oblast, Kazakh SSR, on Trans-Caspian RR, on Ilek R. and 100 mi. S of Aktyubinsk, in phosphorite area; junction for railroads to Guryev (SW) and Orsk (N).

Kandaghat (kŭndŭgät'), village, ⊙ Kohistan dist., E Patiala and East Punjab States Union, India, in outer W Kumaun Himalayas, on railroad and 10 mi. SSW of Simla.

Kandahar or **Qandahar** (kŭndŭhär', kăn'dŭhär), province (□ 50,000; pop. 1,050,000), SE Afghanistan; ⊙ Kandahar. Bounded S and SE by Baluchistan (Pakistan), it consists of N mtn. section in outliers of the Hindu Kush, and S Registan desert section on Baluchistan border. Pop. and agr. economy are concentrated at foot of mts., in oases watered by Helmand, Arghandab, Tarnak, and Arghastan rivers. These oases, including Girishk (irrigation dam), Kandahar, and Kalat-i-Ghilzai, are linked by Kabul-Kandahar-Herat highway. Trade with Pakistan passes through Spinbaldak. Agr. products: wheat, rice, cotton, fruit. Mining of gold and semiprecious stones (handicrafts). Pop. is nearly entirely Afghan: Durani in W, Ghilzai in NE. Baluch nomads in S desert.

Kandahar or **Qandahar,** city (pop. 60,000), ⊙ Kandahar prov., S Afghanistan, 285 mi. SW of Kabul, on level plain bet. Tarnak and Arghandab rivers;

31°27'N 65°43'E. Leading commercial center of S Afghanistan, at junction of auto routes from Kabul, Herat, and Chaman (Pakistani rail terminus), in populous irrigated oasis (wheat, rice, cotton, sugar cane, sesame, fruit); textile factories (cotton and wool weaving); food processing (fruit canning and drying); power plants. The old city, oblong in shape, is surrounded by a well-preserved, 27-ft.-high wall and a wide ditch, separating it from the new garden suburbs. It contains the citadel (N); the tomb of Ahmed Shah Durani, founder (1747) of modern Afghanistan, with prominent gilded dome (W); regional mus. and library. Active trade in dried fruit, tobacco, karakul. Probably founded or rebuilt by Alexander the Great as *Alexandria Arachosiorum*, the city was destroyed by Jenghiz Khan (1222) and by Tamerlane (15th cent.). It belonged to the Moguls (16th cent.), then the Persians (17th cent.), and became 1st capital of modern Afghanistan under the Ghilzai (1709) and again under the Durani (1747). It was occupied by the British in the 1st (1839–42) and 2d (1878–81) Afghan Wars. Ruins of old Kandahar, destroyed 1738 by Nahir Shah, are 3 mi. W.

Kandahar (kŭndŭhär'), town (pop. 5,950), Nander dist., N Hyderabad state, India, 21 mi. SSW of Nander; millet, cotton, wheat. Also spelled Khandhar and Qandhar.

Kanda-Kanda (kän'dä-kän'dä), village, Kasai prov., S Belgian Congo, on left bank of Luilu R., a headstream of the Sankuru, near railroad, and 80 mi. SW of Kabinda; trading center in cotton and native-staples growing area; cottonseed-oil milling. Cattle farms at Kambaye (kämbä'yä), 15 mi. ENE. Thielen-Saint-Jacques R.C. mission is 7 mi. S.

Kandal, province, Cambodia: see PNOMPENH.

Kandalaksha (kŭndŭläk'shŭ), Finnish *Kannanlahti* (kän'nänlätē), city (1939 pop. over 10,000), SW Murmansk oblast, Russian SFSR, port at head of Kandalaksha Bay of White Sea, at mouth of Niva R., on Murmansk RR and 125 mi. S of Murmansk. Aluminum and superphosphate works (based on Kirovsk apatite and nephelite deposits); sawmilling, wood- and metalworking, fish canning. Granite quarries. Hydroelectric station at Nivski (N). Settlement at present site was known to Vikings. In Karelian Autonomous SSR (1920–38).

Kandalaksha Bay, Rus. *Kandalakshskaya Guba*, northwesternmost and deepest section of White Sea, in N European USSR, bet. Kola Peninsula (NE) and Karelia (SW); 130 mi. long, 60 mi. wide at mouth, 1,115 ft. deep; SW coast is deeply indented and strewn with isls. Port of Kandalaksha lies at head of inlet.

Kandalasskiye Kopi (kŭndŭlä'skēŭ kô'pē), village, central Yakut Autonomous SSR, Russian SFSR, on Lena R. and 25 mi. N of Yakutsk; lignite mines.

Kandangan (kändäng'än) or **Kendangan** (kĕn–), town (pop. 9,774), SE Borneo, Indonesia, 60 mi. NE of Banjermasin; trade center for rubber-growing region.

Kandanghaur or **Kandanghaoer** (both: kändäng'-our), town (pop. 11,623), NW Java, Indonesia, near Java Sea, 40 mi. WNW of Cheribon; rice-growing center.

Kandanur (kŭndŭnŏŏr'), town (pop. 6,899), Ramnad dist., S Madras, India, 5 mi. NE of Karaikudi; residence of Chetty merchant community.

Kandava (kän'dävä), Ger. *Kandau*, city (pop. 1,718), NW Latvia, in Kurzeme, 16 mi. SSE of Talsi; grain, fodder, potatoes. Castle ruins.

Kandavu or **Kadavu** (both: kändä'vōō), volcanic island (□ 157; pop. 6,548), most southwesterly of Fiji isls., SW Pacific, 50 mi. S of Viti Levu across Kandavu Passage; 35 mi. long. Central mtn. range, with fertile slopes, rises (SW) to Mt. Washington (2,750 ft.). Isthmus connects SW and NE parts of isl. Many good harbors (best: Ngaloa Harbor, near S end of isthmus). Produces copra, fruits.

Kandel (kän'dŭl), town (pop. 4,391), Rhenish Palatinate, W Germany, 9 mi. SSE of Landau; cigar mfg., woodworking.

Kandel, mountain (4,071 ft.) in the Black Forest, S Germany, 7 mi. NE of Freiburg. Tourist center of Waldkirch is at NW foot.

Kandela or **Kandhila** (both: kŭndhē'lŭ), village (pop. 2,150), Arcadia nome, E Peloponnesus, Greece, 16 mi. N of Tripolis; wheat, tobacco, livestock (sheep, goats). Sometimes spelled Kandila.

Kandelion or **Kandhilion** (both: kŭndhē'lēôn), mountain in NW Euboea, Greece, extends 10 mi. along W coast SE of Limne; rises to 3,919 ft. 17 mi. NW of Chalcis. Also called Kandili.

Kandergrund (kän'dŭrgrōōnt"), village (pop. 823), Bern canton, SW central Switzerland, on Kander R. and 13 mi. SW of Interlaken; hydroelectric plant; matches.

Kandern (kän'dŭrn), village (pop. 2,082), S Baden, Germany, on SW slope of Black Forest, 7 mi. N of Lörrach; mfg. of pottery, paper, machinery; metal- and woodworking, lumber milling. Summer resort (alt. 1,155 ft.).

Kander River (kän'dŭr), S central Switzerland, rises near the Blümlisalp in Bernese Alps, flows 27 mi. N, past Frutigen, to L. of Thun 3 mi. S of Thun. Kandergrund and Spiez hydroelectric plants are on it.

Kandersteg (kän'dŭrshtāk"), village (pop. 835), Bern canton, SW central Switzerland, in Bernese Alps, at N end of Lötschberg Tunnel, on Kander R. and 16 mi. SSW of Interlaken; resort (alt. 3,860 ft.). Has 16th-cent. church.

Kandhila, Greece: see KANDELA.

Kandhilion, Greece: see KANDELION.

Kandhkot (kŭnd'kōt), village, Upper Sind Frontier dist., N Sind, W Pakistan, 45 mi. E of Jacobabad; local market for millet, rice, wheat, fruit; embroidering, rice milling.

Kandhla (kän'dlŭ), town (pop. 13,594), Muzaffarnagar dist., N Uttar Pradesh, India, on Eastern Jumna Canal and 28 mi. WSW of Muzaffarnagar; cotton-cloth mfg.; trades in wheat, gram, sugar cane, oilseeds.

Kandi (kän'dē), town (pop. c.5,900), N Dahomey, Fr. West Africa, on motor road and 325 mi. N of Porto-Novo; 11°8'N 2°56'W. Agr. center (cotton, kapok, shea nuts, peanuts, corn, millet). Cotton, kapok ginning. Airfield; customhouse; garrison.

Kandi, town (pop. 16,652), Murshidabad dist., central West Bengal, India, 17 mi. WSW of Berhampore; metalware mfg.; rice, gram, oilseeds, jute.

Kandil Dag (kändĭl' dä), Turkish *Kandil Dağ*, peak (12,841 ft.), E Turkey, 16 mi. SE of Karakose.

Kandili, Greece: see KANDELION.

Kandira (kändŭrä'), Turkish *Kandıra*, village (pop. 6,238), Kocaeli prov., NW Turkey, 23 mi. NE of Izmit, near Black Sea; oats, wheat, hemp.

Kandiyohi (kăn"dēyō'hē), county (□ 824; pop. 28,644), SW central Minn.; ⊙ Willmar. Agr. area watered by several lakes. Corn, oats, barley, livestock, dairy products, poultry. Formed 1858.

Kandiyohi, village (pop. 293), Kandiyohi co., S central Minn., 6 mi. E of Willmar; dairy products.

Kandiyohi Lake, Kandiyohi co., S central Minn., 9 mi. SSE of Willmar; 3.5 mi. long, 2 mi. wide.

Kandla (kŭnd'lŭ), village, S Cutch, India, 12 mi. SE of Anjar; port (opened early 1930s) on Gulf of Cutch; rail terminus; trades in grain, cloth fabrics, timber; saltworks.

Kandos, town (pop. 1,757), E New South Wales, Australia, 105 mi. W of Newcastle; agr. and sheep center; Portland cement.

Kandrian (kän'drēän), village on S coast of New Britain, Territory of New Guinea, 50 mi. W of Gasmata, which it replaced (1949) as local govt. station; seaplane landing.

Kandry (kŭndrē'), village (1939 pop. over 500), W Bashkir Autonomous SSR, Russian SFSR, on railroad and 75 mi. WSW of Ufa; wheat, rye, oats.

Kandrzin, Poland: see KEDZIERZYN.

Kandukur (kŭndōōkōōr'), town (pop. 10,396), Nellore dist., E Madras, India, 55 mi. N of Nellore; cattle breeding (annual fair); millet, cotton. Saltworks E, on Coromandel Coast of Bay of Bengal.

Kandy (kăn'dē), Singhalese *Maha Nuwara* [=great city], city (□ 11; pop., including PERADENIYA, 50,767), ⊙ Central Prov. and Kandy dist. (□ 911; pop., including estate pop., 707,319), Ceylon, on Kandy Plateau, on the Mahaweli Ganga and 60 mi. NE of Colombo; alt. 1,602 ft. Road junction; trade center (tea, rubber, cacao, vegetables, rice, cardamom). Main part of city overlooks scenic artificial lake; near its N shore is famous *Dalada Maligawa* [=temple of the tooth] containing what is supposed to be Buddha's tooth (original, brought to Ceylon in 4th cent. A.D., believed taken by Portuguese from Jaffna and destroyed at Goa in 1560). Has palace of kings of Kandy, art mus., oriental library, meteorological observatory. Residence of governor-general of Ceylon. Became last ⊙ independent kings of Ceylon in 1592; it remained Ceylon's ⊙ through domination of isl. by Portuguese and Dutch until 1815, when the English exiled the last king to India. During Second World War, hq. (1944–45) of South East Asia Command. Annual religious festival, during which noted devil dances are held. Limestone quarries, brick- and tileworks in Kandy dist. Formerly spelled Candy.

Kandy Plateau (average alt., 1,500–3,000 ft.), in W Ceylon Hill Country, S central Ceylon; c.25 mi. long N–S, up to 10 mi. wide; drained by upper Mahaweli Ganga. Chief centers: Kandy, Gampola.

Kane. 1 County (□ 516; pop. 150,388), NE Ill.; ⊙ Geneva. Agr. area (dairy products; livestock, grain), with industrial centers along Fox R. producing varied manufactures. Limestone quarries. Drained by Fox R. and small Mill Creek. Formed 1836. **2** County (□ 4,105; pop. 2,299), S Utah; ⊙Kanab. Grazing and agr. area bordering on Ariz., bounded on E and SE by Colorado R., and drained, in W half, by Paria and Virgin rivers. Kaiparowits Plateau is in E, part of Bryce Canyon Natl. Park and Paunsaugunt Plateau in NW. Formed 1864.

Kane. 1 Village (pop. 485), Greene co., W Ill., 22 mi. NNW of Alton, in agr. area. **2** Borough (pop. 5,706), McKean co., N Pa., 22 mi. SSW of Bradford. Oil wells and refineries; mfg. (toys, wood products, clothing, leather products, glass); health resort; agr. Natural gas near by. Laid out 1860. **3** Village, Big Horn co., N Wyo., on Bighorn R., at mouth of Shoshone R., near Mont. line, and 9 mi. E of Lovell; lumber-shipping point.

Kane Basin, in the Arctic, bet. Ellesmere Isl. (Canada) and NW Greenland (E); expansion (110 mi. long, 50–120 mi. wide) of sea passage bet. the Lincoln Sea of the Arctic Ocean and the Atlantic; 79°N 70°W. Opens N on Kennedy Channel, S on Smith Sound to Baffin Bay. Receives the great Humboldt Glacier in E.

Kanegasaki (känägä'sä'kē), town (pop. 10,010), Iwate prefecture, N Honshu, Japan, on Kitakami R. and 13 mi. S of Hanamaki; commercial center for agr. area (rice, wheat); poultry; sawmilling.

Kaneko (känä'kō), town (pop. 4,026), Gumma prefecture, central Honshu, Japan, 4 mi. W of Maebashi; raw silk, rice.

Kanem (kä'nĕm, känĕm'), former state of N central Africa, roughly coextensive with present Kanem administrative region (□ 56,000; 1950 pop. 117,-900), W Chad territory, Fr. Equatorial Africa, adjacent to Fr. Cameroons; ⊙ Moussoro; old ⊙ was Mao. Located bet. NE shores of L. Chad and SE fringes of the Sahara, it is a semi-desert country. Its Moslem pop. is of Negroid-Hamitic stock. Sedentary *Kanembous* practice agr. (sesame, millet, some hard wheat, vegetables, dates), natron extracting, fishing. Nomadic Tedas and Dazas tend oxen, horses, sheep, camels. A powerful Negro kingdom (11th–15th cent.) stretching from Sudan to Egypt, Kanem later became vassal successively to Bornu, Baguirmi, and Wadai sultanates. Occupied by France 1903, pacified by 1912.

Kanen, China: see KUMYAN.

Kaneohe (kä'nāō'hā), village (pop. 3,208), E Oahu, T.H., on Kaneohe Bay; coral gardens.

Kaneohe Bay, on E shore of Oahu, T.H.; protected by coral reefs, dotted with isls. Naval air station here attacked by Japanese on day of Pearl Harbor raid, Dec. 7, 1941.

Kanev (kä'nyĭf), city (1926 pop. 8,085), E Kiev oblast, Ukrainian SSR, port on Dnieper R. and 65 mi. SE of Kiev; metalworks. Grave of Shevchenko is 4 mi. away, on the hill Chernaya Gora.

Kanevskaya (–skīŭ), village (1926 pop. 17,241), NW Krasnodar Territory, Russian SFSR, 75 mi. N of Krasnodar; flour mill, metalworks; dairying; wheat, sunflowers, cotton, southern hemp.

Kaneyama (känä'yämŭ). **1** Town (pop. 1,988), Gifu prefecture, central Honshu, Japan, 8 mi. NNW of Tajimi; sawmilling. **2** Town, Miyagi prefecture, Japan: see KANAYAMA. **3** Town (pop. 9,947), Yamagata prefecture, N Honshu, Japan, 8 mi. NNE of Shinjo; rice, raw silk, lumber.

Kanezawa (känä'zäwŭ), town (pop. 7,818), Akita prefecture, N Honshu, Japan, 4 mi. N of Yokote; rice, silk cocoons.

Kang or **K'ang,** China: see KHAM.

Kanga (käng'gä), village, Eastern Prov., NE Belgian Congo, 15 mi. NW of Kilo-Mines; gold mining.

Kangahun (käng-gähōōn'), village (pop. 760), South-Western Prov., SW Sierra Leone, on railroad and 12 mi. ESE of Moyamba; palm oil and kernels, piassava, rice.

Kangal (kängäl'), village (pop. 2,107), Sivas prov., central Turkey, 40 mi. SSE of Sivas; wheat, barley.

Kangamiut or **Kangâmiut** (kängä'myōōt), fishing settlement (pop. 316), Sukkertoppen dist., SW Greenland, at S tip of small Kangamiut Isl. in Davis Strait, 30 mi. NNW of Sukkertoppen; 65°49'N 53°20'W. Radio station. Original site of Sukkertoppen settlement, founded here 1761.

Kangan (käng-gän'), town (1940 pop. 3,514), Seventh Prov., S Iran, on Persian Gulf, 110 mi. SE of Bushire; grain, dates. Airfield.

Kangar (käng"är'), town (pop. 3,970), ⊙ Perlis, NW Malaya, port on Perlis R., 7 mi. from coast and 70 mi. N of George Town, in rice-growing area; administrative hq. of Perlis (raja's residence at Arau).

Kangaroo Island (□ 1,680), in Indian Ocean, 27 mi. S of Yorke Peninsula, South Australia; 90 mi. long, 33 mi. wide. Forms S shore of Investigator Strait. Structurally part of Mt. Lofty Ranges on mainland. Nepean Bay (E) is best of several harbors. E peninsula forms S shore of Backstairs Passage. Large reservation (Flinders Chase; at W end) for native flora and fauna. Feldspar, tourmaline. Produces barley, sheep, wool, salt, gypsum, eucalyptus oil. Summer resorts. Chief town is Kingscote.

Kangaroo Lake, Wis.: see BAILEYS HARBOR.

Kangas (käng'äs), village in Ylivieska commune (pop. 9,332), Oulu co., W Finland, 40 mi. SSE of Raahe; lumber and paper mills.

Kangâtsiak or **Kangâtsiaq** (both: kängät'syäk), fishing settlement (pop. 190), Egedesminde dist., W Greenland, on small isl. in Davis Strait, 30 mi. SW of Egedesminde; 68°18'N 53°27'W.

Kangavar (kängävär'), town (1940 pop. 15,588), Fifth Prov., in Kermanshah, W Iran, 50 mi. ENE of Kermanshah and on road to Hamadan; grain, tobacco, cotton; sheep raising.

Kangayam, India: see TIRUPPUR.

Kangaz (kŭn-gäs'), Rum. *Congaz* (kôn-gäz'), village (1941 pop. 5,911), S Moldavian SSR, on Yalpug R. and 22 mi. NE of Kagul; barley, corn; sheep raising.

Kangdong (käng'dông'), Jap. *Koto*, township (1944 pop. 12,848), S.Pyongan prov., N Korea, 20 mi. NE of Pyongyang, in coal-mining area.

Kangean Islands (käng"ēän'), small group (□ 258; pop. 40,743), Indonesia, in Java Sea, 75 mi. N of Bali; 6°57'S 115°42'E; comprises 3 isls. surrounded by c.60 islets. Largest isl. is Kangean (□ 188), 25 mi. long, 12 mi. wide, generally low, rising in NE to

1,192 ft. Chief products: coconuts, teak, salt, fish, cattle. Chief town is Arjasa or Ardjasa. The other large isls. (SE of Kangean) are Paliat (pä″lēät′; 9 mi. long, 3 mi. wide) and Sepanjang or Sepandjang (sŭpänjäng′; 10 mi. long, 5 mi. wide).

Kangek or **Kangeq** (both: kä′ngĕk), fishing settlement (pop. 143), Godthaab dist., SW Greenland, on islet in the Atlantic, at S end of Davis Strait, at mouth of Godthaab Fjord, 10 mi. WSW of Godthaab; 64°6′N 52°2′W. Radio station.

Kangerdluarssuk (kängĕrlwäkh′shŏŏk), fishing settlement, Sukkertoppen dist., SW Greenland, on Davis Strait, at mouth of Sondre Isorfoq Fjord, 13 mi. ESE of Sukkertoppen. Eudialyte deposits found here.

Kangerdlugssuak or **Kangerdlugssuaq** (both: kängĕrlŏŏkh′shwäk), inlet (45 mi. long, 3–9 mi. wide) of Denmark Strait, SE Greenland; 68°20′N 32°15′ W. Extends NW bet. sheer mts. (rising steeply to over 8,500 ft.) to edge of inland icecap, where it receives several large glaciers, including Kangerdlugssuak Glacier. At mouth, near 68°10′N 31°20′W, is meteorological and radio station.

Kanggye (käng′gyā′), Jap. *Kokai*, town (1944 pop. 30,013), N.Pyongan prov., N Korea, 95 NW of Hungnam; collection center for agr. products, textiles. Graphite mined near by.

Kanggyong (käng′gyŭng′), Jap. *Kokei*, town (1946 pop. 20,327), S.Chungchong prov., S Korea, on Kum R. and 20 mi. NE of Kunsan; commercial center for textile-making area; fish processing; rice.

Kanghoa, Korea: see KANGHWA ISLAND.

Kanghsien or **K'ang-hsien** (käng′shyĕn′), town, ⊙ Kanghsien co. (pop. 104,175), SE Kansu prov., China, 50 mi. E of Wutu; wheat, kaoliang, beans. Gold deposits near by. Until 1928 called Paimawan.

Kanghwa Island (käng′whä′), Korean *Kanghwa-to*, Jap. *Koka-to* (□ 163; 1946 pop. 98,414, including near-by islets), Kyonggi prov., Korea, in Yellow Sea, 30 mi. NW of Seoul, at mouth of Han R., nearly connected with W coast of mainland; roughly rectangular, 16 mi. long, 9 mi. wide. Hilly, fertile. Agr. (rice, wheat, soybeans, millet, cotton), fishing. Formerly a fortress, the isl. was stormed by the French in 1866 and by the Americans in 1871. Chief town is Kanghwa (1946 pop. 13,027) near E coast. Sometimes spelled Kangwha and Kanghoa.

Kangjin (käng′jĕn′), Jap. *Koshin*, town (1949 pop. 19,433), S.Cholla prov., S Korea, 23 mi. SE of Mokpo; agr. (rice, barley, soybeans, cotton); textiles, metalwork.

Kangley (kăng′lē), village (pop. 296), La Salle co., N Ill., on Vermilion R., just NW of Streator.

Kanglo or **K'ang-lo** (both: käng′lô′), town, ⊙ Kanglo co. (pop. 63,987), SE Kansu prov., China, 55 mi. S of Lanchow; rice, beans, kaoliang. Until 1930 called Sintsi.

Kang-ma, Tibet: see KHAMBA.

K'ang-ma, Tibet: see KANGMAR.

Kangmar or **Khangmar** (khäng′mär), Chinese *K'ang-ma* (käng′mä′), village, S Tibet, on the Nyang Chu, on main India-Lhasa trade route and 26 mi. SSE of Gyangtse; alt. 13,900 ft. Wheat, barley, vegetables. Hot spring just N.

Kangnung (käng′nŏŏng′), Jap. *Koryo*, town (1949 pop. 30,278), Kangwon prov., central Korea, S of 38°N, near E coast, 65 mi. E of Chunchon; agr. center (rice, persimmons, hemp).

Kango (käng-gō′), village, NW Gabon, Fr. Equatorial Africa, on right shore of Gabon estuary, 50 mi. ESE of Libreville; agr. center, with coffee, cacao, and experimental rubber plantations; manioc, groundnuts, corn also grown on large scale. Some gold mining. Center for treatment of trypanosomiasis.

Kangpao or **K'ang-pao** (käng′bou′), town, ⊙ Kangpao co. (pop. 69,546), N Chahar prov., China, 70 mi. N of Kalgan, at Inner Mongolia border; cattle.

Kangping or **K'ang-p'ing** (käng′pĭng′), town, ⊙ Kangping co. (pop. 172,823), central Liaosi prov., Manchuria, 60 mi. SW of Szeping; kaoliang, beans, rye, cotton. Former Mongol area, colonized after 1880 by Chinese.

Kangra (käng′grŭ), district (□ 9,979; pop. 899,377), NE Punjab, India; ⊙ Dharmsala. Bordered N by Kashmir and Himachal Pradesh, S by Himachal Pradesh, E by Tibet (frontier undefined); crossed by Punjab Himalayas (in NE section peaks rise to over 20,000 ft.). Chenab, Ravi, and Beas rivers rise in dist. E section comprises subdivisions of KULU, LAHUL, SPITI, and SARAJ. Main crops are wheat, corn, rice, barley, tea, gram, and spices; fruit grown in Kulu valley. Hand-loom woolen and cotton weaving, basket making. Forests of deodar, pine, oak, bamboo. Chief villages: Palampur, Kulu, Nagar, Nurpur. For centuries area was dominated by Rajput princes, who long resisted Moslem penetrations. Largely annexed by Ranjit Singh in 1828, after he had overcome the Gurkhas.

Kangra, village, Kangra dist., N Punjab, India, on railroad and 9 mi. SSW of Dharmsala; local trade center for wheat, rice, tea, corn, wool; handicrafts (enamel work, printed cloths). Annual Hindu festival fair. For many centuries a Rajput stronghold, known as Nagarkot; plundered by Mahmud of Ghazni in 1009; later garrisoned by Moguls. Destroyed by earthquake in 1905.

Kangri, peak, Bhutan and Tibet: see KULA KANGRI.

Kangri, Turkey: see CANKIRI.

Kang Rimpoche, Tibet: see KAILAS, peak.

Kangshan (gäng′shän′), Jap. *Okayama* (ōkä′yämä), town (1935 pop. 4,383), S Formosa, 10 mi. N of Kaohiung and on railroad; agr. center (sugar cane, rice, bananas); has large airfield and airplane repair and assembly plant.

Kangso (käng′sŭ′), Jap. *Kosei*, township (1944 pop. 12,264), S.Pyongan prov., N Korea, 15 mi. WSW of Pyongyang; coal mining.

Kangting or **K'ang-ting** (käng′dĭng′), town, Sikang prov. and Kangting co. (pop. 36,760), SW China, on highway and 275 mi. W of Chungking, near Szechwan line; alt. 8,500 ft.; 30°3′N 102°2′E. Commercial center, trading in musk, furs, wool, medicinal herbs, yak tails; tea processing, cotton and silk weaving. Gold mines near by. Until 1913 called Tatsienlu, Tibetan *Tarchendo*. Was ⊙ Sikang prov. until 1950, when it became ⊙ Tibetan Autonomous Dist.

Kangto (kängtō′), peak (23,260 ft.) in main range of central Assam Himalayas, on undefined Tibet-Assam (India) border; 27°50′N 92°30′E.

Kangu (käng′gōō), village, Leopoldville prov., W Belgian Congo, on railroad and 40 mi. NNW of Boma; palm-oil milling, coffee and rubber plantations. Also a mission center, with several trade schools, and seat of vicar apostolic of Boma.

Kangurt (kŭn-gōōrt′), village (1939 pop. over 500), W Kulyab oblast, Tadzhik SSR, 28 mi. NW of Kulyab; wheat.

Kangwha Island, Korea: see KANGHWA ISLAND.

Kangwon (käng′wŭn′), Korean *Kangwon-do*, Jap. *Kogen-do*, province [Korean and Jap. *do*] (□ 10,141; 1944 pop. 1,856,707), central Korea, bounded E by Sea of Japan; ⊙ CHUNCHON. Largely mountainous and forested terrain, drained by Han R. Scenic Diamond Mts. are near E coast. A major silk-producing area, the prov. also has an important fishing industry. Scattered gold and tungsten mines; SAMCHOK is major coal-mining center. Potatoes are chief crop; rice, wheat, millet, hemp also grown. The prov. is divided into 2 roughly equal parts by the 38th parallel.

Kanhan River (kŭnhän′), in central Madhya Pradesh, India, rises in central Satpura Range E of Betul, flows 120 mi. E and SE, past Khapa and Kamptee, to Wainganga R. 7 mi. SW of Bhandara. Receives Pench R.

Kanheri, India: see BORIVLI.

Kanho (gän′hŭ′), village, W central Heilungkiang prov., Manchuria, on Inner Mongolian line, 55 mi. NW of Nunkiang; coal mining.

Kanhsien, China: see KANCHOW, Kiangsi prov.

Kani (kŭnē′), village, Lower Chindwin dist., Upper Burma, on right bank of Chindwin R. and 30 mi. NW of Monywa.

Kani (kä′nē), village (pop. c.2,700), central Ivory Coast, Fr. West Africa, 37 mi. N of Séguéla; coffee, palm kernels, cotton, rice.

Kaniama (känyä′mä), village, Katanga prov., SE Belgian Congo, on railroad and 95 mi. NW of Kamina; cotton ginning.

Kaniapiskau, Lake (kănyŭpĭ′skō″) (□ 375), N central Que., on Hudson Bay–St. Lawrence watershed; 54°10′N 69°50′W; alt. 1,850 ft.; 20 mi. long, 12 mi. wide; drained by Kaniapiskau R.

Kaniapiskau River, N Que., issues from L. Kaniapiskau, on Hudson Bay–St. Lawrence watershed, flows 450 mi. generally NNW to confluence with Larch R. 50 mi. SW of Fort Chimo, forming Koksoak R., which flows NW to Ungava Bay.

Kanibadam (kŭnyēbŭdäm′), city (1932 pop. estimate 16,450), E Leninabad oblast, Tadzhik SSR, on Great Fergana Canal, on railroad and 40 mi. E of Leninabad; fruit- and vegetable-canning center; mfg. of cotton gins, cottonseed-oil milling.

Kanie (känē′ā), town (pop. 15,035), Aichi prefecture, central Honshu, Japan, 7 mi. W of Nagoya; rice-growing center; textiles.

Kanieri (kănĕr′ē), township (pop. 269), W S.Isl., New Zealand, 3 mi. SE of Hokitika; gold-mining center.

Kanigiri (kŭ′nĭgĭrē), town (pop. 6,376), Nellore dist., E Madras, India, 75 mi. NNW of Nellore; mfg. of spinning instruments, scissors, razors; millet, cotton. Granite quarries near by.

Kaniguram (kŭnĭgŭrŭm′), village, South Waziristan agency, SW North-West Frontier Prov., W Pakistan, 20 mi. NE of Wana, in N Sulaiman Range; trades in hides and corn.

Kanin, Italy and Yugoslavia: see CANIN, MOUNT.

Kanin (kä′nyĭn), town (1942 pop. over 500), E central Komi Autonomous SSR, Russian SFSR, on right bank of Pechora R., on N.Pechora RR just E of Kozhva, 150 mi. NE of Ukhta. Placed (1949) under jurisdiction of Pechora city, 20 mi. N. Called Kanin Nos until 1942.

Kanina (känē′nä), town (pop. 1,500), ⊙ Hajr prov., Quaiti state, Eastern Aden Protectorate, in the Wadi Hajr.

Kanin Nos (nôs″), NW cape of Kanin Peninsula, in Barents Sea, in Nenets Natl. Okrug, Archangel oblast, Russian SFSR; 68°27′N 43°10′E; lighthouse.

Kanin Peninsula, in Nenets Natl. Okrug, Archangel oblast, Russian SFSR; projects N into Barents Sea bet. White Sea (W) and Chesha Bay (E); terminates NW in cape Kanin Nos; low tundra (S), hilly (N); fishing, fur trapping, reindeer raising. Shoina is on W coast.

Kanisah, Jabal al-, Lebanon: see KENISA, JEBEL EL.

Kanita (känē′tä), town (pop. 6,640), Aomori prefecture, N Honshu, Japan, on W Aomori Bay, 16 mi. NNW of Aomori; agr., fishing, sawmilling.

Kaniva, village (pop. 910), W Victoria, Australia, 230 mi. WNW of Melbourne; wheat, oats, barley.

Kanjamalai (kŭn′jŭmŭlī″), hill (3,236 ft.), SW outlier of Shevaroy Hills, S central Madras, India, WSW of Salem; c.5 mi. long, c.2 mi. wide; extensive magnetite, magnesite, and chromite mining. Chalk Hills (NNE) are a major source of India's magnesite.

Kanjiza, Kanyizha, Stara Kanjiza, or **Stara Kanyizha** (all: stä′rä, kä′nyĭzhä), Serbo-Croatian *Stara Kanjiža*, Hung. *Magyarkanizsa* (mŏ′dyŏrkŏ″nĭzhŏ), village (pop. 12,404), Vojvodina, N Serbia, Yugoslavia, on Tisa R., on railroad and 18 mi. E of Subotica, near Hung. border; mineral baths. Novi Knezevac (formerly Nova Kanjiza), village, is E, across the Tisa.

Kanju, Korea: see HAMJONG.

Kankakee (kăngkŭkē′), county (□ 680; pop. 73,524), NE Ill., on Ind. line (E); ⊙ Kankakee. Agr. (corn, oats, soybeans, wheat, livestock, poultry). Limestone deposits. Mfg.: farm machinery, wood products, brick, tile, clothing, stoves, paint, fiber drums, hosiery, dairy and food products, textiles. Drained by Kankakee and Iroquois rivers. Formed 1853.

Kankakee, city (pop. 25,856), ⊙ Kankakee co., NE Ill., on Kankakee R. (bridged here) and 50 mi. SSW of Chicago; industrial and shipping center in agr. area (corn, oats, soybeans, livestock, poultry; dairy products); mfg. (brick, tile, clothing, furniture, stoves, paint, farm machinery, fiber drums, hosiery); limestone quarries; flower growing. Seat of Olivet Nazarene Col., and a state hosp. for insane. Sculptures by George Grey Barnard, who went to school here, are in high school. Inc. 1855.

Kankakee River, in Ind. and Ill., rises near South Bend, N Ind., flows SW to a point near Kankakee, thence NW, joining Des Plaines R. SW of Joliet to form Illinois R.; c.135 mi. long.

Kankan (kän-kän′, kăkā′), town (pop. c.15,650), E central Fr. Guinea, Fr. West Africa, on Milo R. (Niger affluent), and 175 mi. SW of Bamako; road junction in interior highlands, terminus of railroad from Conakry; 10°20′N 9°15′W. Trading, stock-raising, and agr. center; rice, corn, yam, potatoes, rubber; cattle, sheep. Brickmaking. Has R.C. and Protestant missions. Airfield. Bordo agr. school is near by. Gold placers in dist.

Kankanhalli (käng′känhŭlē), town (pop. 6,338), Bangalore dist., SE Mysore, India, on tributary of Cauvery R. and 30 mi. SSW of Bangalore; trades in bamboo, sandalwood from near-by hills; sawmilling, cattle grazing.

Kankari, Turkey: see CANKIRI, town.

Kanke, India: see RANCHI, city.

Kanker (käng′kār), town (pop. 5,173), Baster dist., E central Madhya Pradesh, India, on small affluent of Mahanadi R. and 30 mi. S of Dhamtari; rice, millet, oilseeds. Sal, bamboo, myrobalan in dense forest area (S). Was ⊙ former princely state of Kanker (□ 1,413; pop. 149,471), one of the Chhattisgarh States, since 1948 inc. into Bastar dist.

Kankesanturai (kŭngkāsŭn′tōōrī), town (pop. 1,909), Northern Prov., Ceylon, on N Jaffna Peninsula, on Palk Strait, 10 mi. NNE of Jaffna; rail terminus; seaport (trades in grain, sugar); cement mfg.; lighthouse. Extensive tobacco cultivation 5 mi. S, near Chunnakam, a betel-leaf market; also spelled Chunakam.

Kan Kiang, China: see KAN RIVER.

Kanko, city, Korea: see HAMHUNG.

Kan-ko, river, Korea: see HAN RIVER.

Kankroli (käng′krōlē), village, S central Rajasthan, India, on S shore of Raj Samand, 35 mi. NNE of Udaipur; place of Hindu pilgrimage; Vishnuite temple.

Kanku (gän′gōō′), town, ⊙ Kanku co. (pop. 157,536), SE Kansu prov., China, 30 mi. NNW of Tienshui; tobacco center; wool textiles, hides, grain, timber, licorice. Until 1928 called Fukiang.

Kankyo-hokudo, Korea: see NORTH HAMGYONG.

Kankyo-nando, Korea: see SOUTH HAMGYONG.

Kannabe (kän-nä′bā), town (pop. 6,761), Hiroshima prefecture, SW Honshu, Japan, 3 mi. N of Fukuyama; commercial center in agr. area (rice, wheat); raw silk.

Kannad (kŭn′nŭd), town (pop. 5,490), Aurangabad dist., NW Hyderabad state, India, 29 mi. NNW of Aurangabad; cotton, millet, oilseeds. Sheep raising in near-by hills.

Kannambadi, India: see KRISHNARAJASAGARA.

Kannan (gän′nän′), town, ⊙ Kannan co. (pop. 106,038), W Heilungkiang prov., Manchuria, 50 mi. NNW of Tsitsihar, at Inner Mongolian line; wheat, soybeans, corn, millet, kaoliang. Called Kantsingtze until 1926.

Kannanlahti, Russian SFSR: see KANDALAKSHA.

Kannapolis (kŭnă′pŭlĭs), mill village (pop. 28,448), Cabarrus and Rowan counties, central N.C., 22 mi. NNE of Charlotte; a company-owned textile-mfg. and-finishing center (sheets, towels, blankets). Founded 1906 around mills established 1877.

Kannauj, India: see KANAUJ.

Kanniyai, Ceylon: see TRINCOMALEE.

Kanniyakumari, India: see COMORIN, CAPE.

Kannod (kŭn-nōd′), town (pop. 5,095), S Madhya Bharat, India, 55 mi. ESE of Indore; market center for wheat, cotton, corn, timber; cotton ginning.

Kannonji (kän″nōn′jē) or **Kanonji** (kä″nōn′jē), town (pop. 23,801), Kagawa prefecture, N Shikoku, Japan, port on Hiuchi Sea, 14 mi. SW of Marugame; mfg. and fishing center; spinning mills, woodworking factories; dolls, sake, raw silk, rice jelly. Exports cotton thread, wheat, sugar, tiles, sake.

Kannoura (känō′rä), fishing town (pop. 4,076), Kochi prefecture, SE Shikoku, Japan, on Philippine Sea, 44 mi. E of Kochi.

Kano (kä′nō), town (pop. 6,736), Yamaguchi prefecture, SW Honshu, Japan, 12 mi. N of Tokuyama; lumbering center; charcoal, tea, dried mushrooms.

Kano (kä′nō), province (□ 16,625; pop. 2,374,253), Northern Provinces, N Nigeria; ⊙ Kano. Bounded N by Fr. West Africa. Savanna (S), scrub vegetation (N). Mainly agr. (cotton, peanuts, millet); cattle raising. Cotton weaving, metal-, brass-, and leatherworking. Tin mining at Tudun Wada and Ruruwei (S) and near Gwaram (SE). Chief centers: Kano, Hadejia, Gumel. Pop. largely Hausa and Fulah. Includes Kano emirate, the successor of an original Hausa state, conquered (c.1800) by the Fulah; came (1903) under Br. rule.

Kano, city (pop. 89,162), ⊙ Kano prov., Northern Provinces, N Nigeria, on railroad and 700 mi. NE of Lagos; alt. 1,570 ft.; 12°N 8°30′E. Major commercial and mfg. center of N Nigeria; peanut products, cotton and leather goods, soap, biltong, metalware; livestock market. Trade in agr. products (cotton, peanuts, poultry, hides and skins). Surrounded by 11-mi. wall (40 ft. thick at base; 30–50 ft. high). City is of Moorish design; has large mosque, modern hosp., school for Mohammedan law. International airport. Built on site of older 9th-cent. city, present Kano dates from 16th cent., when it was the main seat of the Hausas. Flourished in 19th cent. under Fulah rule as a caravan and trade emporium. Captured 1903 by the British.

Kanogiza, India: see KANAUJ.

Kanonji, Japan see KANNONJI.

Kanopolis (kănō′pūlĭs), city (pop. 743), Ellsworth co., central Kansas, on Smoky Hill R. and 4 mi. ESE of Ellsworth, in wheat and livestock area; salt mining. Kanapolis Reservoir (□ 21.7; 25.6 mi. long) is formed by Kanopolis Dam, 12 mi. SE on Smoky Hill R. Kanopolis Dam, completed in 1948 by U.S. Army Engineers, is a flood-control dam of Missouri R. Basin project; consists of concrete spillway and earth-fill dikes and abutments; 131 ft. high, total length 15,810 ft.

Kanorado (kănūrā′dō), city (pop. 285), Sherman co., NW Kansas, 17 mi. W of Goodland, at Colo. line; shipping point in agr. area.

Kanosh (kŭnŏsh′), town (pop. 476), Millard co., W Utah, 15 mi. SSW of Fillmore; alt. 5,125 ft.; grain, alfalfa.

Kanowit (känōwĕt′), town (pop. 1,430), central Sarawak, on Rajang R. and 26 mi. SE of Sibu.

Kanowna (kŭnou′nŭ), village, S central Western Australia, 11 mi. NNE of Kalgoorlie; gold mining.

Kanoya (känō′yä), city (1940 pop. 46,841; 1947 pop. 62,497), Kagoshima prefecture, S Kyushu, Japan, on central Osumi Peninsula, 22 mi. SE of Kagoshima across Kagoshima Bay; commercial center in agr. area (rice, wheat); raw silk. Airfield bombed (1945) in Second World War.

Kanpetlet (kän′pĕt′lĕt″), village, ⊙ S.Chin Hills dist., Upper Burma, 70 mi. WSW of Pakokku.

Kanpur, India: see CAWNPORE.

Kanra-san, Korea: see HALLA, MOUNT.

Kan River, Chinese *Kan Chiang* or *Kan Kiang* (both: gän′ jyäng′), chief river of Kiangsi prov., China, rises in the Nan Ling in 2 branches (Tsang and Kung rivers) joining at Kanchow, flows N through wide central valley of Kiangsi prov., past Wanan, Kian, Changshu (rail bridge), and Nanchang, to Poyang L., forming vast delta with Fu R. (E). Navigable for junks below Kanchow and for steamers up to Nanchang. Total length, including Kung headstream, 540 mi. Receives Yüan R. (left).

Kan River (kän), S Krasnoyarsk Territory, Russian SFSR, rises in Eastern Sayan Mts., flows N, past Irbeiskoye and Kansk, and W to Yenisei R. 50 mi. NE of Krasnoyarsk; 318 mi. long.

Kansai, Formosa: see KWANSI.

Kansai or **Kansay** (kŭnsī′), town (1948 pop. over 10,000), N Leninabad oblast, Tadzhik SSR, on S slope of Kurama Range, 17 mi. NNE of Leninabad; lead-zinc mine and works.

Kansas (kăn′zŭs), state (land □ 82,113; with inland waters □ 82,276; 1950 pop. 1,905,299; 1940 pop. 1,801,028), central U.S., bordered S by Okla., E by Mo., N by Nebr., W by Colo.; 13th in area, 31st in pop.; admitted 1861 as 34th state; ⊙ Topeka. Comprising the geographic center (Smith co., 2 mi. NW of Lebanon) of continental U.S., the "Sunflower State" (or "Jayhawker State") lies midway bet. the Mississippi R. and the Rocky Mts. in the vast GREAT PLAINS and interior lowlands regions. Except in the NE, where the Missouri R. forms the boundary, the state is rectangular in shape, measuring 410 mi. E-W and 208 mi. N–S. Lacking in prominent features, the land descends gradually from 4,135 ft. on the W border to c.750 ft. in the SE. Its entire drainage falls into the Missouri-Mississippi system via the KANSAS RIVER, formed by junction of Republican R. and SMOKY HILL RIVER (with tributary Solomon and Saline rivers), and the ARKANSAS RIVER, with its tributary Cimarron (SW) and Neosho (SE) rivers. Kansas may be divided into 3 physiographic sections, though boundaries are vague and the middle section is actually a transition zone bet. the other two. In the W are the high plains, a gently rolling, mostly treeless expanse, which descends on the E over an irregular escarpment to the low plains region, marked by badland erosion, steep slopes, and isolated buttes. In E Kansas the prairie land is characterized by broad valleys of deep, fertile soil and low hill ridges, such as the FLINT HILLS. Subsections of these main divisions are found in the NE corner, which consists of an undulating plain of glacial till and loess deposits, and in the SW, S of the Arkansas R., where an E–W belt of sand hills and eroded cliffs occurs. Its remoteness from mtn. ranges and any sizable body of water influences the state's continental type of climate. Rainfall varies from 10–20 in. in the extreme W to c.40 in. in the SE. Temperatures are often extreme in winter and summer, and the open plains are subject to dust and hail storms and tornadoes. These wind-eroded surfaces do not absorb water easily and are exposed to serious floods during heavy rains. Topeka has mean temp. of 29° F. in Jan., 80°F. in July, and 32 in. of annual rainfall; Dodge City has mean temp. of 31°F. in Jan., 79°F. in July, and 19 in. of rain. Original vegetation was predominantly short buffalo grass in the W and tall prairie grass in the E, with forests comprising a negligible area. Most E river valleys have stretches of oak-hickory woodland, while black walnut, box elder, and cottonwood are other species found in the state. Kansas is primarily an agr. and stock-raising state, with over 48,500,000 acres—or c.92% of its total land area—in farm and range land. Wheat is the great field crop, the state producing the highest percentage (c.20%) of hard winter wheat in the U.S. Because of vast stretches of level terrain in the central and W parts, its farming is highly commercialized and mechanized (almost all of the crop is harvested by combines). Kansas ranks 1st in milling flour from wheat, the chief mills being at Wichita, SALINA, TOPEKA, NEWTON, HUTCHINSON, and Kansas City. Corn and oats, in NE and E, are also major crops, while grain sorghums, barley, oilseeds, hay, potatoes, and rye are raised in smaller amounts, mainly in the E. Broomcorn is grown in the extreme SW counties, sugar beets in irrigated dists. along Arkansas R., and apples in the Missouri valley (NE). Cattle total c.3,500,000 head and are distributed throughout the state. Beef cattle production is a major industry, centering at KANSAS CITY (2d only to Chicago in stockyards and meat-packing plants) and WICHITA, the state's largest cities. Dairying and poultry farming are important in the E half of the state. Hogs (c.1,200,000), are raised in the corn belt, especially in NE. Petroleum ranks 1st in value of the mineral resources in Kansas; chief oil fields are in the central and SE parts, with refineries at CHANUTE, COFFEYVILLE, EL DORADO, MCPHERSON, and Wichita. Natural gas (helium plant at Dexter), coal (mainly SE and E around PITTSBURG and Pleasanton), zinc and lead (extreme SE corner), rock salt (center), building stone, volcanic ash, and sand and gravel are also produced. Manufactures include cement, agr. implements, airplanes (Wichita and Kansas City), food and dairy products, metal goods, and lumber products. Besides industrial centers mentioned above, other trading and mfg. towns are LEAVENWORTH, EMPORIA, ATCHISON (railroad shops), ARKANSAS CITY, Lawrence, Independence, Ottawa, and Dodge City. Principal educational institutions consist of Univ. of Kansas (at Lawrence and Kansas City), Kansas State Col. of Agr. and Applied Science (at Manhattan), Municipal Univ. of Wichita, and Washburn Municipal Univ. of Topeka. A large federal prison is at Fort Leavenworth. At the time of Coronado's search for QUIVIRA in 1541, the Kansas plains were inhabited by the Wichita, Pawnee, Osage, and Kansa Indians, for the last of whom the state is named. Another Spaniard, de Oñate, probably explored S Kansas in 1601, and in the late 17th and early 18th cent. the French entered the region. Ceded to Spain in 1762 and returned to France in 1800, the area was transferred to the U.S. by the Louisiana Purchase of 1803. Further exploration was undertaken by Lewis and Clark (1804), Zebulon Pike (1806), and Stephen Long (1819). Although the wind-swept plains at first deterred settlers, development of the area proceeded along with the opening of the Santa Fe Trail (1825), the establishment of Fort Leavenworth (1827) and trading and missionary posts, the explorations of Frémont and Kit Carson (1842–48), and the great westward migrations of the mid-19th cent. By the Kansas-Nebraska Act of 1854 Kansas was organized as a separate territory with the right to decide the slavery issue on the basis of "popular soverignty," a provision which repealed the Missouri Compromise of 1820. Immigration was accelerated as both pro- and anti-slavery forces sought control of the territory. For several years "bleeding Kansas" experienced virtual civil war and was the scene of John Brown's 1st battles against slavery; but by 1859 the numerically superior Free Staters had triumphed and statehood soon followed (1861). In the *post-bellum* period development was furthered by the extension of the railroads, the liquidation of hostile Indian tribes, the availability of land under the Homestead Law (1862), and the great cattle boom of the '70s and '80s, when the cowboy and cow town—such as ABILENE on the Chisholm Trail from Texas—were characteristic of the pioneer life on the Kansas plains. The introduction of Turkey red wheat in 1874 and the beginning of large-scale commercial agr. were important events. Oil and natural gas were discovered c.1890. However, there were periodic droughts and depressions, and the farmers' reaction to the hard times found political expression in the Granger movement and the Populist party, which rose to power in Kansas in the 1890s. But as conditions improved the average Kansan came to typify the conservative Republicanism of the Midwest, and his strong bent for moral reform was evidenced by the widespread support for prohibition—dramatized by saloon-smashing Carry Nation in the '90s—which was legally enforced from 1881 to 1949. Since the state's prosperity depends largely on its farms, efforts have been made to alleviate the hardships due to natural causes; there are reclamation and conservation projects, such as Kanopolis Dam on the Smoky Hill R. For further information see articles on the cities, towns, and physical features, and the 105 counties: ALLEN, ANDERSON, ATCHISON, BARBER, BARTON, BOURBON, BROWN, BUTLER, CHASE, CHAUTAUQUA, CHEROKEE, CHEYENNE, CLARK, CLAY, CLOUD, COFFEY, COMANCHE, COWLEY, CRAWFORD, DECATUR, DICKINSON, DONIPHAN, DOUGLAS, EDWARDS, ELK, ELLIS, ELLSWORTH, FINNEY, FORD, FRANKLIN, GEARY, GOVE, GRAHAM, GRANT, GRAY, GREELEY, GREENWOOD, HAMILTON, HARPER, HARVEY, HASKELL, HODGEMAN, JACKSON, JEFFERSON, JEWELL, JOHNSON, KEARNY, KINGMAN, KIOWA, LABETTE, LANE, LEAVENWORTH, LINCOLN, LINN, LOGAN, LYON, MCPHERSON, MARION, MARSHALL, MEADE, MIAMI, MITCHELL, MONTGOMERY, MORRIS, MORTON, NEMAHA, NEOSHO, NESS, NORTON, OSAGE, OSBORNE, OTTAWA, PAWNEE, PHILLIPS, POTTAWATOMIE, PRATT, RAWLINS, RENO, REPUBLIC, RICE, RILEY, ROOKS, RUSH, RUSSELL, SALINE, SCOTT, SEDGWICK, SEWARD, SHAWNEE, SHERIDAN, SHERMAN, SMITH, STAFFORD, STANTON, STEVENS, SUMNER, THOMAS, TREGO, WABAUNSEE, WALLACE, WASHINGTON, WICHITA, WILSON, WOODSON, WYANDOTTE.

Kansas, village (pop. 835), Edgar co., E Ill., 13 mi. WSW of Paris; dairy products, livestock.

Kansas City. 1 City (pop. 129,553), ⊙ Wyandotte co., NE Kansas, largely on right bank of Missouri R., at mouth of Kansas R., and contiguous with Kansas City, Mo.; 39°7′N 94°38′W; alt. 773 ft. Second-largest city in state. With Kansas City, Mo., it forms commercial, industrial, transportation, and cultural center for extensive wheat-growing and stock-raising area on central plains. City is 2d-largest livestock market in U.S., with stockyards and meat-packing plants. Chief industries: food processing (flour, dairy products, canned goods), oil refining; grain storage; mfg. of structural-steel products, soap, cement, airplanes and airplane parts, fiber boxes, bricks and tiles; railroad maintenance. Oil and gas wells and limestone deposits are near by. Site of city was visited (1804) by Lewis and Clark. Settled (1843) by Wyandot Indians, who sold their claim (1855) to white settlers. The white settlement, known as Wyandotte, was inc. 1859. After completion of railroad (1866), trade increased and stockyards were built. Old Kansas City (platted 1868, inc. 1872) and several other towns established in vicinity were later annexed by Wyandotte, and the consolidated communities became known (1886) as Kansas City. Argentine (metalworking suburb) became part of city by petition (1909); Rosedale, on S bank of Kansas R., was included in 1922. Arrival of freed Negroes ("Exodusters") and European immigrants in late 1800s was additional factor in growth. State school for blind, 2 theological seminaries (R.C. and Baptist), conservatory of music, school of medicine of Univ. of Kansas, and an Air Force base are here. Industrial districts were damaged by great flood of July, 1951. **2** City (pop. 456,622), on Clay-Jackson co. line, W Mo., on S bank of Missouri R., at mouth of Kansas R., 235 mi. WNW of St. Louis; 39°6′N 94°37′W; almost in geographical center of U.S.; alt. 944 ft. Second-largest city in Mo. and one of leading cities in central U.S. for industry, agr. products, transportation. One of most important hay-market and seed-distribution centers of world. Port of entry. Meat packing, flour milling; poultry and grain market. Offices of major livestock industry located here, while packing plants and most stockyards are in adjoining Kansas City, Kansas. Situated near mid-continent oil fields; coal, lead, zinc mines; limestone quarries. Mfg. of farm machinery, automobiles, refrigerators, furniture, electrical equipment; metal, lumber and food products, bakery goods, cosmetics, chemicals, medicines, dental supplies, paints, soap, clothing. Printing. Oil refining at suburb (E) of Sugar Creek. Important railroad (12 trunk lines) and airline focus; has railroad yards. Annual American Royal livestock show. Univ. of Kansas City, Rockhurst Col., Col. of St. Teresa, Col. of Osteopathy and Surgery, Natl. Col. for Christian workers, 2 yr. colleges, William Rockhill Nelson Gall. of Art, art institute, conservatory of music; Philharmonic Orchestra. Hq. Unity School of Christianity. Area was on route of the Santa Fe and Oregon trails; several historic posts such as Westport, settled in 1820s, were starting points for many western expeditions. Inc. 1853. Extensively damaged by great flood of July, 1951.

Kansas River, NE Kansas, formed by confluence of Smoky Hill and Republican rivers at Junction City, flows c.170 mi. E, past Manhattan (near which it receives Big Blue R.), Topeka, and Lawrence, to Missouri R. bet. Kansas City in Kansas and Kansas City in Mo.; not extensively navigable. Drainage area (□ 61,300), includes N Kansas and parts of S Nebr. and E Colo. Hydroelectric plants in basin. Agr. (wheat, corn, hay, oats, potatoes) and stock raising are leading activities in river area. Sometimes known as Kaw River.

Kansen, Korea: see HANCHON.

Kansenia (kănsĕn'yä), village, Katanga prov., SE Belgian Congo, on railroad and 65 mi. NW of Jadotville; agr. and cattle-raising center. Also a climatic resort. Benedictine mission.

Kansera, El, dam, Fr. Morocco: see BETH, OUED.

Kanshirei, Formosa: see KWANTZELING.

Kansk (kănsk), city (1939 pop. over 10,000), SE Krasnoyarsk Territory, Russian SFSR, on Kan R., on Trans-Siberian RR and 110 mi. E of Krasnoyarsk. Industrial center in lignite-mining area; cotton and sawmills, iron foundry, leather works, distillery, dairy plant. Lignite mines. Founded 1628; tsarist exile settlement.

Kansongwe, Belgian Congo: see LUISHIA.

Kansu (kăn'sōō', gän'sōō'), province (□ 150,000; pop. 7,000,000) of NW China; ⊙ Lanchow. Bounded SE by Shensi and Szechwan, the prov. extends NW to Sinkiang, forming a Chinese wedge bet. Tibetan Tsinghai (S) and Mongolian Ningsia (N) provs. Loess hills (SE) are drained by the upper Yellow R., which receives Sining R. (left) and Tao R. (right), upper Wei R., and upper reaches of the Kialing. In the NW, descending from the Nan Shan to the Mongolian tableland, are Hei and Peita rivers, which combine to form the Etsin Gol. The continental climate is conditioned by the nearness of the Gobi desert, with only 15–20 inches of rainfall (largely in July and Aug.). Agr., important only in the SE loess hills, produces wheat, millet, kaoliang, vegetables, and fruit. Opium, cotton, and tobacco are the only cash crops. Camels, cattle, and sheep (wool exports) are raised chiefly in NW. Except for petroleum at Yümen (leading Chinese producer) and coal at Shantan and Yungchang, mineral resources are little exploited. The leading centers are Lanchow, Tienshui, Pingliang, and, in the NW corridor along the Silk Road leading to Sinkiang, Wuwei, Changyeh, and Kiuchüan. It is to this great road, protected formerly by the Great Wall (of which sections remain), that Kansu owes its importance as a transit region. Pop. is almost entirely Chinese, speaking N Mandarin dialect, with Salar (Turkic) language isl. SW of Lanchow, on Tsinghai line. There are also small Tibetan and Mongolian minorities. The traditional name of prov. is Lung. The name Kansu, 1st used by the Yüan (Mongol) dynasty, is a combination of Kanchow (present Changyeh) and Suchow (present Kiuchüan). Kansu prov. originally included modern Sinkiang. Following the organization of Sinkiang, it was joined 1882 to Shensi, then became a separate prov. in 1911. The Sining and Ningsia city areas formed part of Kansu until 1928. Prov. was devastated and depopulated during Moslem revolt (1861–78), by catastrophic earthquake (1920), and by famines, notably in 1929–30. It remained in Chinese hands during Sino-Japanese War, and passed 1949–50 to Chinese Communist control.

Kant (känt) [Kirghiz,=sugar], town (1939 pop. over 2,000), N Frunze oblast, Kirghiz SSR, in Chu valley, on railroad and 13 mi. E of Frunze; beet-sugar refining center. Founded 1932.

Kantagi (kŭntŭgē'), town (1948 pop. over 2,000), central South Kazakhstan oblast, Kazakh SSR, in the Kara-Tau, 25 mi. NE of Turkestan; lead and zinc mines.

Kantalai (kŭn'tŭlī), village, Eastern Prov., Ceylon, 20 mi. SW of Trincomalee; rice and coconut-palm plantations, vegetable gardens. Just W is Kantalai Tank (4.5 mi. long, 2 mi. wide; built A.D. c.275 by King Maha Sena), a large irrigation lake.

Kantanagar (kăn'tŭnŭgŭr), village, Dinajpur dist., NW East Bengal, E Pakistan, on tributary of the Mahananda and 12 mi. N of Dinajpur; rice, jute, sugar cane. Annual fair. Noted 18th-cent. Vishnuite temple.

Kantang (kän'täng'), village (1937 pop. 3,931), Trang prov., S Thailand, on W coast of Malay Peninsula, at mouth of Trang R., 15 mi. SSW of Trang; small port on Strait of Malacca; rail terminus of line from Cha Mai; rice, rubber, pepper.

Kantara (käntä'rä), summer resort in Kyrenia Mts. of NE Cyprus, 20 mi. N of Famagusta. Has a noted castle.

Kantara, El- (ĕl-kătärä'), village, Constantine dept., NE Algeria, guarding a defile through the Aurès massif, 25 mi. N of Biskra. The El-Kantara defile was used by Romans (remains of bridge) and by caravans to Touggourt, and is now used by Batna-Biskra road and railroad.

Kantara, El, Egypt: see QANTARA, EL.

Kantara, El- village, SE Tunisia, on SE shore of Djerba isl. (ferry to mainland), 13 mi. SSE of Houmt-Souk; dates, olives, apples, pears.

Kantarawadi or **Kantarawaddy** (kăn'tŭräwädē'), former Karenni state (□ 3,161; pop. 30,677) of Upper Burma; ⊙ was Loikaw. Hilly jungle (teak). Wet paddy. Pop.: Red Karens, Burmese, Shans. Included former states of Nammekon and Naungpale. Since 1947, part of the Karenni State.

Kantchari (känchä'rē), village, SE Upper Volta, Fr. West Africa, on road and 70 mi. SSW of Niamey; peanuts, shea nuts, beeswax; cattle, sheep, goats. Airfield.

Kantemirovka (kŭntyĭmĕr'ŭfkŭ), village (1926 pop. 11,316), S Voronezh oblast, Russian SFSR, 38 mi. SSE of Rossosh; flour milling, metalworking, woodworking.

Kanth (känt), town (pop. 9,011), Moradabad dist., N central Uttar Pradesh, India, near Ramganga R., 17 mi. NNW of Moradabad; sugar refining, hand-loom cotton weaving; wheat, rice, pearl millet, sugar cane.

Kanth, Poland: see KATY.

Kanthal, India: see PARTABGARH, former princely state.

Kanthan (kän"tän'), village (pop. 580), central Perak, Malaya, just N of Chemor, on railroad and 10 mi. NNE of Ipoh; rubber.

Kanthi, India: see CONTAI.

Kantilo (kŭn'tĭlō), village, Puri dist., E Orissa, India, on Mahanadi R. and 55 mi. NW of Puri; local market for sal timber, rice; handicraft brassware.

Kantipura, Nepal: see KATMANDU.

Kantishna (kăntĭsh'nŭ), district, S central Alaska, N of Mt. McKinley Natl. Park, 100 mi. SW of Nenana; gold mining. Rich mineral region, with lead, zinc, copper, gold, silver, antimony deposits.

Kantishna River, S tributary of Tanana R., central Alaska, rises on N slope of Mt. McKinley, flows 200 mi. NE, past Toklat, to Tanana R. at 64°45'N 149°58'W. Upper course called McKinley R. Receives Toklat R.

Kanto, Japan: see KWANTO.

Kanto, town, Korea: see WANDO.

Kan-to, island, Korea: see WAN ISLAND.

Kanto, Manchuria: see KWANTUNG.

Kantorjanosi (kän'tôryänô-shē), Hung. *Kántorjánosi*, town (pop. 3,318), Szatmar-Bereg co., NE Hungary, 20 mi. E of Nyiregyhaza; potatoes, grain, hemp, tobacco, livestock.

Kantorp, Sweden: see SKOLDINGE.

Kantse or **Kan-tzu** (both: gän'dzŭ'), town, ⊙ Kantse co. (pop. 10,063), N Sikang prov., China, on Yalung R., on highway and 160 mi. NW of Kangting; alt. 10,780 ft.; trade center of NE Sikang; wheat, rice. Silver-lead found near by. Site of major lamasery (making art articles, sculpture).

Kantsingtze, Manchuria: see KANNAN.

Kantsu, Japan: see KOZU-SHIMA.

Kantunil (kăntōōnēl'), town (pop. 1,350), Yucatan, SE Mexico, 9 mi. S of Izamal; henequen, sugar cane, corn.

Kantunil-Kin (–kēn'), town (pop. 577), Quintana Roo, SE Mexico, on E Yucatan Peninsula, near Yucatan border, 45 mi. ESE of Tizimín; chicle, henequen, fruit. Archaeological remains near by.

Kanturk (kăntûrk'), Gaelic *Ceann Tuirc*, town (pop. 1,577), NW Co. Cork, Ireland, 12 mi. WNW of Mallow; agr. market (dairying; potatoes, oats). Has uncompleted Elizabethan castle, now property of National Trust.

Kantyshevo, Russian SFSR: see NARTOVSKOYE.

Kan-tzu, China: see KANTSE.

Kanuga Lake, N.C.: see HENDERSONVILLE.

Kanukov, Russian SFSR: see PRIVOLZHSKI, Astrakhan oblast.

Kanuku Mountains (kŭnōō'kōō), S Br. Guiana, spur of the Guiana Highlands, extending c.80 mi. E from Brazil border just N of 3°N. A sandstone plateau (rising to c.2,500 ft.), mostly covered by savanna grassland, where cattle of the Rupununi valley are raised. Deposits of uranium ore.

Kanuma (kä"nōō'mä), town (pop. 32,037), Tochigi prefecture, central Honshu, Japan, 8 mi. W of Utsunomiya; mfg. (hemp goods, incense), woodworking, charcoal making.

Kanunka (känōōng'kä), village, Katanga prov., SE Belgian Congo, on railroad and 15 mi. NNW of Jadotville; iron mining. Near-by Kalabi (kälä'bē), 5 mi. NE, has copper mines.

Kanuparti (känōōpŭr'tē), village, Guntur dist., NE Madras, India, on Buckingham Canal and 12 mi. NE of Ongole; salt refining.

Kanwa, India: see KHANUA.

Kanyankaw (känyäng'kô), **Kanyankwa** (–kwä), or **Kayiankor,** town, Western Prov., SW Gold Coast colony, 22 mi. NW of Takoradi; gold-mining center; cacao, palm oil and kernels.

Kanye (kä'nyä), town (pop. 22,922), ⊙ Ngwaketse dist., SE Bechuanaland Protectorate, 60 mi. NNW of Mafeking; asbestos mines; hq. of Bangwaketse tribe. Airfield; hosp. Road junction. Irrigation dam near by.

Kanyizha, Yugoslavia: see KANJIZA.

Kanyü (gän'yü'), town, ⊙ Kanyü co. (pop. 462,767), S Shantung prov., China, 20 mi. N of Sinhai, near Yellow Sea; agr. center (wheat, beans, kaoliang, cotton). Saltworks near by. Its port Tsingkow, just SE, has been superseded by Lienyün. Until 1949 in Kiangsu.

Kanyutkwin (kŭnyōōt"kwĭn'), village, Toungoo dist., Lower Burma, on Rangoon-Mandalay RR and 40 mi. S of Toungoo.

Kanzaki (känzä'kē), town (pop. 7,781), Saga prefecture, NW Kyushu, Japan, 6 mi. NE of Saga; commercial center for agr. area; sake, noodles.

Kao (kä'ô), uninhabited island, W of Haabai group, central Tonga, S Pacific; volcanic; rises to 3,380 ft.

Kaoan (gou'ăn'), town (pop. 4,585), ⊙ Kaoan co. (pop. 244,565), NW Kiangsi prov., China, 34 mi. WSW of Nanchang and on Kin R.; rice, cotton, ramie, peanut and sesame oil. Anthracite mines; lime quarrying. Until 1912 called Juichow.

Kaocheng. 1 or **K'ao-ch'eng** (kou'chŭng'), town, ⊙ Kaocheng co. (pop. 175,610), NE Honan prov., China, near Yellow R., on Pingyuan border, 35 mi. ENE of Kaifeng. **2** or **Kao-ch'eng** (gou'chŭng'), town, ⊙ Kaocheng co. (pop. 242,059), SW Hopeh prov., China, 20 mi. E of Shihkiachwang and on railroad; cotton, wheat, millet.

Kao-ch'iao, China: see KAOKIAO.

Kao-ch'ing, China: see KAOTSING.

Kaochow, China: see MOWMING.

Kaohiung, Kaosiung, or **Kaohsiung** (gou'shyōōng'), Jap. *Takao* (tä'kou), city (1940 pop. 152,365; 1950 pop. 275,563), S Formosa, on W coast, 28 mi. S of Tainan; 22°38'N 120°18'E. Leading port of S Formosa; rail and highway terminus; exports sugar, rice, pineapples, bananas. A major industrial center, it produces aluminum, cement, superphosphate fertilizer; has iron foundry, oil refinery, shipyards; and processes fish and agr. products (sugar, alcohol, rice, fruit). City consists of old Chinese fishing section of Kihow (Ch'i-hou) at tip of peninsula (W) and modern quarter adjoining the harbor (E), which is situated on a sheltered lagoon. Developed originally as a commercial port after 1858, Kaohiung became an industrial center under Jap. rule (1895–1945). Until 1920, called Takow (Jap. *Taku*). The name Kaohiung is also applied officially to FENGSHAN, 5 mi. E.

Kaohsien (gou'shyĕn'), town (pop. 11,651), ⊙ Kaohsien co. (pop. 176,053), SW Szechwan prov., China, 25 mi. S of Ipin; rice, sweet potatoes, wheat, medicinal plants.

Kaohsiung, Formosa: see KAOHIUNG.

Kao-i, China: see KAOYI.

Kaokiao or **Kao-ch'iao** (both: gou'chyou'), town, S Kiangsu prov., China, 10 mi. E of Chinkiang, on isl. in Yangtze R.; commercial center.

Kaokoveld Mountains (kou"kōfĕlt'), range in NW South-West Africa, extends c.450 mi. SE from Angola border along E edge of Namib Desert, parallel to the Atlantic; rises to 8,550 ft. on Brandberg, 100 mi. N of Swakopmund. On E side of range are several native reserves.

Kaolack (kou'läk), town (pop. c.32,550), W Senegal, Fr. West Africa, inland port on right bank of Saloum R. and 95 mi. ESE of Dakar; rail terminus and peanut-trading center; stock raising; vegetable-oil extracting. Airfield, military camp, radio station, customhouse, R.C. mission. The port is accessible to ships drawing up to 12 ft., while larger vessels dock at Foundiougne, 26 mi. W.

Kaolan, China: see LANCHOW.

Kaolikung Mountains (gou'lē'gōōng'), SE outlier of Tibetan highlands, on China-Burma border, extend over 200 mi. N–S bet. Salween R. and Nmai headstream of the Irrawaddy. Rise to 13,000 ft.

Kaoling (gou'lĭng'), town (pop. 5,509), ⊙ Kaoling co. (pop. 51,061), S central Shensi prov., China, 22 mi. NE of Sian, near junction of King and Wei rivers; rice, wheat, corn, cotton.

Kaomi (gou'mē'), town, ⊙ Kaomi co. (pop. 498,442), E Shantung prov., China, 40 mi. NW of Tsingtao and on railroad to Tsinan; millet and wheat center; straw plait; peanuts, kaoliang.

Kaoming, China: see KOMING.

Kaonde-Lunda (koun'dā-lōōn'dä), former province of NW Northern Rhodesia. Chief towns: Balovale, Kasempa, Solwezi, Mwinilunga. Absorbed 1946 by Western Prov.

Kaoping or **Kao-p'ing** (gou'pĭng'), town, ⊙ Kaoping co. (pop. 244,583), SE Shansi prov., China, 30 mi. S of Changchih; silk weaving; sericulture; millet, kaoliang, rice, wheat. Iron mines near by.
Kaoshun (gou'shŏŏn'), town, ⊙ Kaoshun co. (pop. 252,039), S Kiangsu prov., China, on Anhwei line, 50 mi. S of Nanking; rice, wheat, rapeseed, beans. Coal deposits near by.
Kaosiung, Formosa: see KAOHIUNG.
Kaotai or **Kao-t'ai** (both: gou'tī'), ⊙ Kaotai co. (pop. 60,416), NW Kansu prov., China, on left bank of Hei R. and 45 mi. NW of Changyeh, near the Great Wall; alt. 4,658 ft. Oil, coal, gold deposits near by.
Kaotang or **Kao-t'ang** (gou'täng'), town, ⊙ Kaotang co. (pop. 192,171), northeasternmost Pingyuan prov., China, near Shantung-Hopeh line, 45 mi. WNW of Tsinan; cotton center; peanut-oil processing; wheat, millet, potatoes, beans. Until 1949 in Shantung prov.
Kaotsing or **Kao-ch'ing** (both: gou'chĭng'), town, ⊙ Kaotsing co. (pop. 131,282), NW Shantung prov., China, on Yellow R. and 50 mi. NE of Tsinan; peanuts, melons, poultry, hides. Co. was formed in 1949 through union of Kaoyüan (town, 20 mi. SE) and Tsingcheng (town, 5 mi. SSE).
Kaoukab, Syria: see KAUKAB.
Kaoyang (gou'yäng'), town, ⊙ Kaoyang co. (pop. 154,092), central Hopeh prov., China, 20 mi. SE of Paoting; cotton center; rice, wheat, beans.
Kaoyao, China: see KOYIU.
Kaoyi or **Kao-i** (both: gou'yē'), town, ⊙ Kaoyi co. (pop. 64,458), SW Hopeh prov., China, 35 mi. S of Shihkiachwang and on Peking-Hankow RR; cotton, wheat, pears.
Kaoyu (gou'yōō'), town (1935 pop. 62,731), ⊙ Kaoyu co. (1946 pop. 670,808), N Kiangsu prov., China, 25 mi. N of Yangchow, on E shore of Kaoyu L. and on Grand Canal; rice center; wheat; fisheries.
Kaoyüan, China: see KAOTSING.
Kaoyu Lake, Chinese *Kaoyu Hu* (gou'yōō' hōō'), on Kiangsu-Anhwei border, China, W of Grand Canal; occupies irregular basin 7–15 mi. wide (E–W), 25 mi. long (N–S). Through canal and small lakes, it is connected with Hungtze L. (NW) and with Yangtze R. (S) near Yangchow.
Kapaa (kŭpä'), coast town (pop. 3,177), E Kauai, T.H.; cooperative pineapple plantation, cannery.
Kapaau-Halaula (kä'pä-ou' hä'lä-ōō'lä), village (pop. 1,307), N Hawaii, T.H., on Kohala Peninsula; sugar cane cultivated. Kamehameha I b. near by; his statue stands in village. Formerly called Kapaau.
Kapadvanj (kŭp'ŭdvŭnj), town (pop. 20,075), Kaira dist., N Bombay, India, 31 mi. E of Ahmadabad; rail terminus; trade center (rice, millet, corn); cotton ginning, handicraft cloth weaving, oilseed milling, mfg. of glass bangles, soap, leather jars for ghee. Agate, onyx found in bed of small stream (N). Sometimes spelled Kapadwanj.
Kapal or **Kopal** (kŭpäl'), village (1939 pop. over 2,000), E Taldy-Kurgan oblast, Kazakh SSR, in the Dzungarian Ala-Tau, 35 mi. E of Taldy-Kurgan; irrigated agr. (wheat); sheep. Founded 1847 as Rus. military post. Near by (NE) are warm springs and resort of Arasan-Kapal or Arasan-Kopal.
Kapalaoa (kä'pŭlä-ō'ŭ), peak (3,436 ft.), central Kauai, T.H.
Kapanga (käpäng'gä), village, Katanga prov., S Belgian Congo, on Lulua R. and 165 mi. WNW of Kamina; cotton ginning. R.C. and Protestant missions.
Kapapa (käpä'pŭ), island, Oahu, T.H., off E coast, in Kaneohe Bay; Territorial bird reservation.
Kapar (kä"pär'), village (pop. 1,035), W Selangor, Malaya, 9 mi. NW of Klang; coconuts.
Kapasi, India: see KAPSI.
Kapasin or **Kapasan** (both: kŭpä'sŭn), town (pop. 6,085), S Rajasthan, India, 20 mi. W of Chitor; agr. (millet, cotton, wheat); cotton ginning.
Kapela, Velika, and **Kapela, Mala,** mountain ranges, Yugoslavia: see VELIKA KAPELA.
Kapelle (käpĕ'lŭ). **1** Town, North Brabant prov., Netherlands: see 's GREVELDUIN-CAPELLE. **2** Agr. village (pop. 1,917), Zeeland prov., SW Netherlands, on South Beveland isl. and 3 mi. ESE of Goes; vegetable canning. Village of Biezelinge (pop. 1,004) is 1 mi. SW.
Kapelle aan den Ijssel, Netherlands: see CAPELLE AAN DEN IJSSEL.
Kapellen (käpĕ'lŭn), Fr. *Capellen-lez-Anvers* (käpĕl-lā-ävâr'), residential town (pop. 9,788), Antwerp prov., N Belgium, 7 mi. N of Antwerp.
Kapelle-op-den-Bos (käpĕ'lŭ-ōb-dŭn-bōs'), Fr. *Capelle-au-Bois* (käpĕl-ō-bwä'), town (pop. 3,380), Brabant prov., central Belgium, near Willebroek Canal, 12 mi. N of Brussels; mfg. (drainage pipes). Formerly spelled Kapelle-op-den-Bosch.
Kapelvagar, Norway: see KABELVAG.
Kapenguria (käpĕng-gōōrē'ä), town, Rift Valley prov., W Kenya, near Uganda boundary, on road and 18 mi. NNE of Kitale; sisal, coffee, tea, wheat, corn. Asbestos deposits. Suk tribe inhabits area.
Kapeshticë (käpĕshtē'tsŭ) or **Kapeshtica** (–tsä), village (1930 pop. 605), SE Albania, on Gr. border, 11 mi. E of Koritsa; customs station on Koritsa-Kastoria road.
Kapfenberg (käp'fŭnbĕrk), city (pop. 21,552), Styria, SE central Austria, on Mürz R. and 3 mi. NNE of Bruck; iron- and steelworks, lumberyards.
Kaphereus, Cape, or **Cape Kafirevs** (both: käfīrĕfs'), Lat. *Caphereus* (kŭfēr'ūs), SE extremity of Euboea, Greece, on Aegean Sea at NE entrance of Kaphereus Channel; 38°9'N 24°36'E. Formerly called Cape d'Oro or Cape Doro.
Kaphereus Channel or **Kafirevs Channel,** in Aegean Sea, Greece, separates Euboea (NW) from Andros (SE); 8 mi. wide. Formerly called Doro Channel or Channel d'Oro.
Kapi Dag (käpŭ' dä), Turkish *Kapı Dağ*, peak (8,035 ft.), W central Turkey, 2 mi. SE of Uluborlu.
Kapidagi Peninsula (käpŭ'däŭ"), Turkish *Kapıdağı*, anc. *Cyzicus* (sĭ'zĭkŭs), NW Turkey, extends into Sea of Marmara 70 mi. SW of Istanbul, bet. gulfs of Erdek (W) and Bandirma (E); 19 mi. wide, 8 mi. long; rises to 2,640 ft. Sometimes spelled Kapu Dagh. Town of Erdek on SW shore. In anc. times the notable city of CYZICUS was at its base.
Kapilavastu, Nepal: see PADERIA.
Kapilmuni (kŭpĭl'mōōnē), village, Khulna dist., SW East Bengal, E Pakistan, on river arm of Ganges Delta and 18 mi. WSW of Khulna; rice, jute, oilseeds. Large annual fair.
Kapingamarangi (käpĭng'ŭmŭräng'ē), atoll (pop. 511), southernmost of Caroline Isls., Ponape dist., W Pacific; 1°4'N 154°46'E; 6.5 mi. long, 4.5 mi. wide; rises to 12 ft.; 31 coral islets on reef. Polynesian natives. In Second World War, it was 1st of Carolines to be bombed by U.S.
Kapiri Mposhi (käpē'rĕmpō'shē), township (pop. 184), Central Prov., Northern Rhodesia, on railroad and 40 mi. NNE of Broken Hill; junction of road to Abercorn; tobacco, wheat, corn; cattle, sheep, goats.
Kapisa, Afghanistan: see BAGRAM.
Kapisigdlik (käpĭsĭg'lĭk), fishing settlement (pop. 143), Godthaab dist., SW Greenland, on Godthaab Fjord, near its head, 50 mi. ENE of Godthaab; near 64°35'N 50°10'W.
Kapit (kŭpĭt'), town (pop. 1,398), S Sarawak, in W Borneo, on Rajang R. and 80 mi. ESE of Sibu; lumbering, agr. (rice, sago), fishing.
Kapiti Island (käpē'tē), uninhabited island in Cook Strait, New Zealand, 30 mi. NNE of Wellington; 10 mi. long, 2 mi. wide; game reservation. Sometimes called Entry Isl.
Kaplan (kă'plŭn), town (pop. 4,562), Vermilion parish, S La., 60 mi. ESE of Lake Charles city, in rice-growing area; rice milling. Inc. 1902.
Kaplice (käp'lĭtsĕ), Ger. *Kaplitz*, town (pop. 1,588), S Bohemia, Czechoslovakia, on Malse R., on railroad and 9 mi. SW of Cesky Krumlov; pottery mfg., tanning.
Kapnikbanya, Rumania: see CAPNIC.
Kapoeas Mountains, Borneo: see KAPUAS MOUNTAINS.
Kapoeas River, Borneo: see KAPUAS RIVER.
Kapolna (kä'pôlnŏ), Hung. *Kápolna*, town (pop. 1,767), Heves co., N Hungary, on Tarna R. and 12 mi. SW of Eger; tobacco. Hungarians defeated here (1849) by Austrians.
Kapolnokmonostor, Rumania: see COPALNIC-MONASTUR.
Kapong (käpông'), village (1937 pop. 1,027), Phangnga prov., S Thailand, in Malay Peninsula, 16 mi. NNW of Phangnga; tin mining.
Kapos River (kŏ'pôsh), SW and central Hungary, rises 10 mi. W of Kaposvar, flows c.65 mi. E, past Kaposvar and Dombovar, and N to SIO RIVER 6 mi. W of Simontornya; flow regulated (as Kapos Canal) bet. Dombovar and Sio R.
Kaposvar (kŏ'pôsh-vär), Hung. *Kaposvár*, city (pop. 32,985), ⊙ but independent of Somogy co., SW Hungary, on Kapos R. and 29 mi. NW of Pecs; rail center; sugar and alcohol refining, mfg. (machinery, soap, candles); brewery, flour mill, brickworks; agr. (wine, onions, tobacco) near by.
Kapoudia, Ras, Tunisia: see KABOUDIA, RAS.
Kapoutzedes or **Kapoutzidhes,** Greece: see PYLAIA.
Kappa, village (pop. 125), Woodford co., central Ill., on Mackinaw R. and 32 mi. E of Peoria, in agr. and coal area.
Kappanzan, Formosa: see KIAOPANSHAN.
Kappel am Albis (käpĕl' äm äl'bĭs), also known as **Cappel** (käpĕl'), village (pop. 635), Zurich canton, N Switzerland, 10 mi. S of Zurich. Here Zwingli fell in battle in 1531.
Kappeln (kä'pŭln), town (pop. 4,841), in Schleswig-Holstein, NW Germany, on the Schlei near its mouth on the Baltic, 18 mi. NE of Schleswig, in the Angeln; fishing and excursion port; food processing (smoked herring, canned milk), metal- and woodworking. Trade (grain, wood). Has baroque church. First mentioned 1357.
Kappelrodeck (kä'pŭlrō'dĕk), village (pop. 3,022), S Baden, Germany, on W slope of Black Forest, 11 mi. NE of Offenburg; noted for its red wine. Lumber and paper milling, woodworking. Has 11th-cent. castle, renovated in 19th cent.
Kappelshamn (kä'pŭls-hä"mŭn), village (pop. 224), Gotland co., SE Sweden, on N coast of Gotland isl., 25 mi. NE of Visby; grain, potatoes, sugar beets, flax. Has remains of prehistoric fortifications.
Kappl (kä'pŭl), village (pop. 1,752), Tyrol, W Austria, in Rhaetian Alps, on Trisanna R. and 10 mi. WSW of Landeck; main town of the Paznauntal; cattle.
Kapraina, Greece: see CHAIRONEIA.
Kaprijke (kä'prĭkŭ), agr. village (pop. 3,150), East Flanders prov., NW Belgium, 3 mi. NE of Eekloo. Formerly spelled Caprycke.
Kapronca, Yugoslavia: see KOPRIVNICA.
Kaprun (kä'prōōn), village (pop. 4,836), Salzburg, W central Austria, on right affluent of the Salzach, 23 mi. SW of Bischofshofen; large hydroelectric works, generated by the Kessel Falls (kĕ'sŭl) (c.200 ft. high). Main installations are at Limberg Dam; other reservoirs are upstream at Moserboden.
Kapsabet (käpsäbĕt'), town (pop. c.800), Rift Valley prov., W Kenya, 30 mi. NE of Kisumu; coffee, tea, wheat, corn. Gold fields just W. Hq. of dist. inhabited by Nandi tribe.
Kapsali, Greece: see KYTHERA.
Kapsi (käp'sē), town (pop. 2,694), Kolhapur dist., S Bombay, India, 25 mi. S of Kolhapur; tobacco, chili, sugar cane. Also spelled Kapshi or Kapasi.
Kapuas Mountains or **Kapoeas Mountains** (both: kŭpōōäs'), central Borneo, on boundary bet. SE Sarawak and Indonesian Borneo, c.50 mi. SE of Sibu; extends c.120 mi. generally E–W; highest peak is 5,797 ft.
Kapuas River or **Kapoeas River,** Borneo, rises in Kapuas Mts. in central part of isl., on boundary bet. Sarawak and Indonesian Borneo, flows 710 mi. WSW in winding course, past Sintang, through marshy delta to S.China Sea 20 mi. SW of Pontianak. Navigable c.560 mi. by small craft. N stream in Kapuas delta flows past Pontianak to S.China Sea 10 mi. WNW of Pontianak.
Kapu Dagh, Turkey: see KAPIDAGI PENINSULA.
Kapunda (kŭpŭn'dŭ), town (pop. 1,236), SE South Australia, 45 mi. NNE of Adelaide; livestock; marble, flagstones. Formerly important copper-mining center.
Kapurthala (kŭpōōr'tŭlŭ), town (pop. 26,067), ⊙ Kapurthala dist., N Patiala and East Punjab States Union, India, 12 mi. WNW of Jullundur; trades in wheat, gram, sugar cane, tobacco; mfg. of pharmaceutical products, chemicals, paints, varnish. Has col. Fruitgrowing near by. Was ⊙ former princely state of Kapurthala (□ 645; pop. 378,380) of Punjab States, India, in Bist Jullundur Doab, mainly along E bank of Beas R. Since 1948, state merged with Patiala and East Punjab States Union.
Kapuskasing (kă"pŭskā'sĭng, –zĭng), town (pop. 3,431), central Ont., on Kapuskasing R. and 80 mi. NW of Timmins; paper milling (newsprint); farming center. Airfield. Agr. experiments were begun here 1913. Site of large prisoner-of-war camp during First World War.
Kapuskasing River, N Ont., rises near 48°N 83°5'W, flows 160 mi. NE, past Kapuskasing, to Mattagami R. at 49°50'N 82°W.
Kapustin Yar (kŭpōō'styĭn yär"), village (1926 pop. 13,013), NE Astrakhan oblast, Russian SFSR, near Akhtuba R., on railroad and 60 mi. ESE of Stalingrad; fruit, truck.
Kaputh, Germany: see CAPUTH.
Kapuvar (kŏ'pōōvär), Hung. *Kapuvár*, town (pop. 10,173), Sopron co., W Hungary, 21 mi. ESE of Sopron; agr. market center (wheat, corn); distilleries, flour mills.
Kara (kŭr'ŭ), town (pop. 4,445), Allahabad dist., SE Uttar Pradesh, India, on the Ganges and 34 mi. WNW of Allahabad; gram, wheat, barley, pearl millet, oilseeds.
Kara (kä'rŭ), village, E Nenets Natl. Okrug, Archangel oblast, Russian SFSR, port on Kara Bay (W inlet of Baidarata Bay), near mouth of Kara R., 120 mi. N of Vorkuta; govt. observation station.
Kara, El, Egypt: see QARA, EL.
Kara Agach, Bulgaria: see LEVSKI, city.
Kara-Amid, Turkey: see DIYARBAKIR, city.
Kara-Aul (kŭrä"-ŭōōl'), village, W Semipalatinsk oblast, Kazakh SSR, 115 mi. SSW of Semipalatinsk; cattle.
Karababa Dag (kä"räbäbä' dä), Turkish *Karababa Dağ*, peak (7,693 ft.), central Turkey, 15 mi. SE of Akdagmadeni, overlooking the Kizil Irmak.
Karabagh, Azerbaijan SSR: see NAGORNO-KARABAKH AUTONOMOUS OBLAST.
Kara-bair, Bulgaria: see BURGAS, city.
Karabakh, Azerbaijan SSR: see NAGORNO-KARABAKH AUTONOMOUS OBLAST.
Karabakh Range (kŭrŭbäkh'), branch of the Lesser Caucasus, in SW Azerbaijan SSR; extends from Armenian SSR c.70 mi. SE to Aras R.; rises to 11,000 ft. Forms W border of Nagorno-Karabakh Autonomous Oblast. **Karabakh Steppe** lies at its E foot. **Karabakh Upland** is a plateau bet. Karabakh and Zangezur ranges.
Kara Balkan Mountains, Bulgaria: see CHERNATITSA MOUNTAINS.
Karabalty (kŭrä"bŭltē'), town (1939 pop. over 2,000), W Frunze oblast, Kirghiz SSR, in Chu valley, just S of KALININSKOYE (called Karabalty until 1937) and 37 mi. W of Frunze; beet-sugar refinery. Until 1937, Imeni Mikoyana.
Karabanovo (kŭrŭbä'nŭvŭ), city (1926 pop. 11,240), NW Vladimir oblast, Russian SFSR, 5 mi. S of Aleksandrov; cotton-milling center. Became city in 1938.

Karabash (kŭrŭbäsh′), city (1926 pop. 3,187; 1936 pop. estimate 28,500), N central Chelyabinsk oblast, Russian SFSR, on NE slope of the S Urals, 20 mi. SW of Kyshtym, on rail spur; major copper-mining and -smelting center, based on extensive deposits exploited since 1830; pyrite mining. First copper works established 1834; largely developed in 1920s; became city in 1933. Formerly called Karabashski Zavod.

Kara Bay, Russian SFSR: see KARA, village.

Karabekaul (kŭrä″byĕkŭōōl′), town (1939 pop. over 500), central Chardzhou oblast, Turkmen SSR, on the Amu Darya and 50 mi. SE of Chardzhou; cotton, vineyards.

Kara-Bogaz-Gol (kŭrä″-bŭgäs″-gôl′), town (1932 pop. estimate 4,000), NW Ashkhabad oblast, Turkmen SSR, port on Caspian Sea, at entrance to gulf Kara-Bogaz-Gol, 70 mi. N of Krasnovodsk; center of Glauber's-salt-extracting industry.

Kara-Bogaz-Gol, shallow gulf on E shore of Caspian Sea, in Ashkhabad oblast, Turkmen SSR; 100 mi. long, 60–90 mi. wide. Separated from Caspian Sea by 70-mi.-long sandspit broken by narrow strait at Kara-Bogaz-Gol town; acts as natural evaporating basin, with intensive depositing of mirabilite (Glauber's salt). Chief extraction centers: Sartas, Chagala, Kizyl-Kup, Kara-Bogaz-Gol.

Karabudakhkent (kŭrä″bōōdŭkhkyĕnt′), village (1926 pop. 3,220), E Dagestan Autonomous SSR, Russian SFSR, on Caspian Sea coastal plain, 18 mi. SSE of Makhachkala; wheat, cotton (irrigation).

Karabuk (käräbük′), Turkish *Karabük*, town (pop. 10,682), Zonguldak prov., N Turkey, on Yenice R., on railroad, and 6 mi. SW of Safranbolu; iron and steel mills, blast furnaces, chemical works. A new industrial town developed after 1940.

Karabulak (kŭrä″bōōläk′), town (1939 pop. over 2,000), central Taldy-Kurgan oblast, Kazakh SSR, on the Kara-Tal and 8 mi. SE of Taldy-Kurgan; beet-sugar refinery.

Karabunar (kärä′bōōnär′). **1** Village, Burgas dist., Bulgaria: see SREDETS. **2** Village (pop. 3,300), Plovdiv dist., W central Bulgaria, 9 mi. NW of Pazardzhik; winegrowing center; rice, hemp, truck produce.

Karaburun (kä″räbōōrōōn′) or **Karaburuni** (–rōō′nē), peninsula of SW Albania, at Strait of Otranto, on W side of Bay of Valona; 10 mi. long, 3 mi. wide. Forms NW extremity of ACROCERAUNIA (for which it is sometimes named) and terminates in Cape LINGUETTA; rises to 2,753 ft.

Karaburun, village (pop. 762), Smyrna prov., W Turkey, port on Gulf of Smyrna, 40 mi. WNW of Smyrna; mercury; tobacco, olives, raisins. Formerly Ahirli. It lies near the tip of the **Karaburun Peninsula** (60 mi. long, 15 mi. wide), which extends into Aegean Sea bet. Gulf of Smyrna and Chios isl.; rises to 3,976 ft. Town of Cesme on W shore, Urla near its base.

Karaburun Steppe (kŭrä″bōōrōōn′), in W Armenian SSR, on SW slope of Mt. Aragats; traversed by Leninakan–Erivan RR. Site of irrigation project (50-mi.-long canal system from Akhuryan S to Oktemberyan area).

Karabutak (–bōōtäk′), village (1939 pop. over 500), NE Aktyubinsk oblast, Kazakh SSR, on Irgiz R. and 125 mi. E of Aktyubinsk; millet; sawmilling.

Karaca, village, Turkey: see SIRAN.

Karacabey (kä″räjäbā′), town (pop. 11,104), Bursa prov., NW Turkey, on Simav R. and 22 mi. ESE of Bandirma; agr. center (wheat, barley, oats, rye, corn, beans, onions); iron near by. Formerly Mihalic or Mikhalitch.

Karacadag (käräjä′dä), Turkish *Karacadağ*, village (pop. 198), Kirklareli prov., European Turkey, at Bulgarian line 28 mi. NE of Kirklareli.

Karaca Dag, Turkish *Karaca Dağ*. **1** Peak (5,655 ft.), central Turkey, 27 mi. SE of Haymana. **2** Peak (6,430 ft.), S central Turkey, 12 mi. ENE of Karapinar.

Karacali Dag (käräjälē′ dä), Turkish *Karacali Dağ*, peak (6,296 ft.), SE Turkey, 26 mi. SW of Diyarbakir, bet. the Tigris and the Euphrates.

Karacasu (käräjäsōō′), village (pop. 4,692), Aydin prov., W Turkey, 26 mi. W of Denizli; figs, barley, cotton.

Karachai Autonomous Oblast or **Karachay Autonomous Oblast** (kŭrŭchī′), former administrative division (□ 3,800; 1939 pop. 149,925) of S European Russian SFSR; ⊙ Mikoyan-Shakhar. Pop. was largely Karachai (a Turkic ethnic group, 75,737 in 1939). Under Russian rule since 1828, it was (after 1921) in Mountain Autonomous SSR; later became part of Karachai-Cherkess Autonomous Oblast (formed 1922); Karachai unit was separated (1926) to become an autonomous oblast. Upon its dissolution (1944), after collaboration of local pop. with Germans, its major (S) portion became part of Georgian SSR, including the capital (renamed KLUKHORI) and TEBERDA resort; Stavropol Territory obtained N section, including ORDZHONIKIDZEVSKI coal mine; W mtn. section passed to Cherkess Autonomous Oblast.

Karachala (kŭrä″chŭlä′), town (1939 pop. over 500), E Azerbaijan SSR, on SE Shirvan Steppe, on lower Kura R. and 7 mi. S of Ali-Bairamly; cotton-ginning center for cotton dist. developed in late 1930s.

Karachev (kŭrŭchôf′, –rä′chĭf), city (1926 pop. 13,065), NE Bryansk oblast, Russian SFSR, 25 mi. ESE of Bryansk; major hemp-milling center; wood-working plant, sawmill, oil press, distillery. One of principal hemp-shipping points of USSR. Dates from 1146.

Karachi, former district, Sind, W Pakistan: see TATTA.

Karachi (kŭrä′chē), city (□ 72; 1941 pop. 359,492, including cantonment areas 386,655; 1951 pop. 1,005,000), ⊙ Pakistan, in the new Karachi administrative area (formerly part of Sind), on Arabian Sea just NW of Indus R. delta, 550 mi. NW of Bombay, 660 mi. WSW of New Delhi; 24°52′N 67°5′E. Pakistan's chief seaport and shipping point for agr. produce of extensive irrigated areas in Sind and Punjab; rail terminus; international airport. Serves as seaport entry for Afghanistan. Mean temp. ranges from 90°F. in June to 57°F. in Jan.; annual rainfall, 8 in. Exports wheat, cotton, oilseeds, gram, barley, hides, bone fertilizer, salt, and wool; imports textiles, machinery, metals (iron, steel), petroleum, coal, hardware, and sugar. Main industries are agr. processing (flour, cotton, rice, oilseeds), fish curing, woolen milling, salt panning, kerosene canning, mfg. of chemicals, cement, tiles, matches, leather goods, glass, bicycle parts, ice; also metal and engineering works, sawmills, railroad workshops. Handicrafts (pottery, carpets, cloth fabrics, metalware). Harbor (SW) is protected by breakwaters, including Manora headland (lighthouse; cantonment) at entrance (S); opposite Manora is Kiamari section (wharves, oil installations), formerly an isl. but now connected to Karachi by 2-mi.-long mole. To N is city proper, with its crowded markets, public bldgs., commercial offices, and parks. Seat of Univ. of Sind (founded 1947 as affiliating and examining body). To NE are airfields, dairy farms, and military arsenal. An 18th-cent. coastal fort, Karachi was acquired (1843) by British from emirs of Sind and made seat of Sind govt.; after 1950 Hyderabad once more became ⊙ Sind. With extensive harbor development and construction of railroad into hinterland, it progressed rapidly as a port and commercial center for NW India; now occupies important position on intercontinental air routes. Became ⊙ Pakistan in 1947 and experienced enormous pop. growth. In 1948, Karachi administrative area (□ 812; 1951 pop. 1,118,000) was created to include Karachi city and the surrounding area; thus it is separated from Karachi dist. and is under direct administration of central govt.

Karachi (kŭrŭchē′), health resort (1939 pop. over 500), W Novosibirsk oblast, Russian SFSR, on Trans-Siberian RR and 40 mi. E of Tatarsk; dairying. It is on **Lake Karachi** (2 mi. long, 1 mi. wide), known for its mud baths.

Kara-Chukhur, Azerbaijan SSR: see KAGANOVICHA, IMENI L. M., town.

Karacurun, Turkey: see HILVAN.

Karad (kŏ′räd), Hung. *Karád*, town (pop. 3,817), Somogy co., SW Hungary, 23 mi. N of Kaposvar; wine.

Karad (kŭr′äd), town (pop. 17,996), Satara North dist., central Bombay, India, on Kistna R. and 31 mi. SSE of Satara; road junction; trade center (millet, wheat, peanuts); cotton and silk milling, handicraft cloth weaving and dyeing, mfg. of agr. implements, cots, soap.

Kara Dag (kärä′ dä), Turkish *Kara Dağ*. **1** Peak (7,451 ft.), S central Turkey, 16 mi. NNW of Karaman. **2** Peak (11,910 ft.), SE Turkey, 7 mi. N of Hakari. **3** Peak (9,940 ft.), N central Turkey, 15 mi. W of Erzincan.

Karadag (kŭrŭdäk′), town (1945 pop. over 500) in Molotov dist. of Greater Baku, Azerbaijan SSR, 16 mi. SW of Baku; oil fields (developed 1937).

Kara Dagh, Iran: see QARA DAGH.

Kara-Darya or **Kara-Dar'ya** (kŭrä″-dŭryä′), village (1926 pop. 5,573), W Samarkand oblast, Uzbek SSR, on the Ak Darya (S arm of Zeravshan R.) and 9 mi. N of Katta-Kurgan; cotton. Until c.1935, Paishambe or Peishambe.

Kara Darya or **Kara Dar'ya.** **1** A headstream of the Syr Darya in Kirghiz and Uzbek SSRs; rises in several branches in Fergana Range, on China border; flows c.170 mi. NW, past Uzgen, into Fergana Valley and E Uzbek SSR, joining Naryn R. near Balykchi to form the Syr Darya. Lower course used for irrigation. **2** River, Uzbek SSR: see ZERAVSHAN RIVER.

Karadeniz Bogazi, Turkey: see BOSPORUS.

Karadzica or **Karadzhitsa** (both: kärä′jĭtsä), Serbo-Croatian *Karadžica*, mountain, N Macedonia, Yugoslavia; highest peak (8,111 ft.) is 17 mi. SSW of Skoplje.

Karafoca, Turkey: see FOCA.

Karafuto, Russian SFSR: see SAKHALIN.

Karaga (kŭrŭgä′), village, central Koryak Natl. Okrug, Kamchatka oblast, Khabarovsk Territory, Russian SFSR, on NE coast of Kamchatka Peninsula, 100 mi. E of Palana, in reindeer-raising area; fisheries.

Karagai or **Karagay** (kŭrŭgī′), village (1926 pop. 1,030), W Molotov oblast, Russian SFSR, on right tributary of Kama R. and 30 mi. WNW of Krasnokamsk; food processing; rye, oats, flax, livestock.

Karaganda (kŭ″rŭgŭndä′), oblast (□ 156,700; pop. c.500,000), central Kazakh SSR; ⊙ Karaganda. Extends from L. Balkhash (SE) nearly to Aral Sea (W); includes, in N, Kazakh Hills and dry steppe, in S, Bet-Pak-Dala desert area; drained by Nura R. and the Sary-Su. Most extensive mining region of Kazakh SSR: Karaganda coal basin, Kounradski and Dzhezkazgan copper mines, iron (Atasuski), manganese (Dzhezdinski), tungsten (Akchatau), molybdenum, corundum, and lead-zinc deposits. Large copper-smelting industry; iron and steel metallurgy (Temir-Tau). Agr. (millet, wheat) near Karaganda; livestock raising (sheep, camels, cattle). Trans-Kazakhstan RR runs N–S, with branches to Baikonur (W) and Balkhash (SE). Pop.: Kazakhs, Russians. Formed 1932.

Karaganda, city (1926 pop. 116; 1939 pop. 165,937; 1947 pop. estimate 220,000), ⊙ Karaganda oblast, Kazakh SSR, in Kazakh Hills, near Nura R., on railroad and 490 mi. NNW of Alma-Ata; 49°45′N 73°10′E. Center of Karaganda coal basin (one of largest in USSR; developed after 1928; coking coal); mfg. of mining equipment; sawmilling; brick- and cementworks. Teachers col. New coal center of Saran or Saran' is 12 mi. WSW. Large metallurgical plant and power works at near-by Temir-Tau (NW). Founded 1928, Karaganda began large-scale production in 1930; reached 1931 by railroad; made a city in 1934.

Karagash (kŭrŭgäsh′), village (1926 pop. 3,282), SE Moldavian SSR, on left bank of Dniester R. and 5 mi. SSE of Tiraspol; hq. of Karagash irrigation system (vegetable growing).

Karaginski Island or **Karaginskiy Island** (kŭrŭgĕn′skē) (□ 775), in SW Bering Sea, in Koryak Natl. Okrug, Kamchatka oblast, Khabarovsk Territory, Russian SFSR; separated by 29-mi.-wide Litke Strait from NE Kamchatka Peninsula; 69 mi. long, up to 25 mi. wide; rises to 3,140 ft. Fish-canning center on W coast; fur farms.

Karagiye Sink, Kazakh SSR: see BATYR DEPRESSION.

Karagwe (kärä′gwā), former native kingdom in E Africa, just W of L. Victoria. It is now part of Tanganyika. Its lake port is Bukoba. The Karagwe tin mines (at Murongo, Kikagati) are 80 mi. W of lake along Kagera R. (Uganda–Tanganyika–Ruanda-Urundi border).

Karahisar or **Karahissar,** Turkey. **1** City, Afyonkarahisar prov., W central Turkey: see AFYONKARAHISAR, city. **2** Town, Giresun prov., N Turkey: see SEBINKARAHISAR.

Karaidel or **Karaidel'** (kŭrīdyĕl′), village (1932 pop. estimate 790), N Bashkir Autonomous SSR, Russian SFSR, on Ufa R. (landing) and 65 mi. SSW of Krasnoufimsk; distilling, lumbering. Also written Kara-Idel. Karaidelski, town (1944 pop. over 500), is 5 mi. E; glassworks.

Karaikudi or **Karaikkudi** (both: kŭrī′kōōdē), city (pop. 28,908), Ramnad dist., S Madras, India, 45 mi. ENE of Madura; residential and financial center of Chetty merchant community; trades in foreign luxury goods. Electro-chemical research institute (opened 1949).

Kara Irtis River, China and USSR: see BLACK IRTYSH RIVER.

Karaisali (kärīsälŭ′), Turkish *Karaisalı*, village (pop. 1,051), Seyhan prov., S Turkey, 24 mi. NW of Adana; wheat, barley, vetch, sesame, cotton. Formerly Ceceli.

Kara Isen (kärä′ ēsĕn′), village (pop. 3,697), Pleven dist., N Bulgaria, 16 mi. S of Svishtov; wheat, corn, livestock.

Karaitivu (kŭrītē′vōō). **1** Island (pop. 11,784) in Northern Prov., Ceylon, bet. Jaffna Lagoon (E) and Palk Strait (W); joined by causeway (N) to Jaffna Peninsula, by ferry to Velanai isl. (S). Extensive rice, coconut, and palmyra-palm plantations. Lighthouse on NW shore. Hospital for infectious diseases at fort off SW coast. **2** Two islands, North Western Prov., Ceylon; see KARATIVU.

Karaj (käräj′), town (1940 pop. estimate 15,000), Second Prov., in Teheran, N Iran on road and railroad to Kazvin and 25 mi. WNW of Teheran, on Karaj R. (tributary of Shur R.); industrial center; beet-sugar refinery, chemical factory (superphosphate, insecticide). Site of agr. col. Steel mill is planned here, as well as irrigation and hydroelectric project on Karaj R. Linked by Elburz mtn. highway with Caspian Sea at Chalus.

Karajgaon, India: see KARASGAON.

Karak (kä′räk), village (pop. 342), W Pahang, Malaya, 12 mi. SE of Bentong; tin mining, rubber.

Karak, Al-, Jordan: see KERAK.

Kara-Kala (kŭrä″-kŭlä′), town (1948 pop. over 2,000), SW Ashkhabad oblast, Turkmen SSR, near Iran border, 35 mi. S of Kizyl-Arvat and on Sumbar R. (right affluent of the Atrek); subtropical agr. (guayule, date palms, figs).

Karakalli, Turkey: see OZALP.

Kara-Kalpak Autonomous Soviet Socialist Republic (kŭrä″-kŭlpäk′, kä′rŭ-kŭlpäk′) (□ 61,600; 1946 pop. estimate 600,000), NW Uzbek SSR; ⊙ Nukus. Includes parts of the deserts Ust-Urt and Kyzyl-Kum, and the Amu Darya delta on Aral Sea. Extensive cotton cultivation along the Amu Darya and in its delta; alfalfa crop rotation. Fisheries in

Aral Sea. Cotton ginning. Railroad from Chardzhou to Khodzheili and Kungrad. Formerly Kara-Kalpak Autonomous Oblast (created 1925) and part of Kazak Autonomous SSR, in 1932 it became Kara-Kalpak Autonomous SSR within Russian SFSR; joined Uzbek SSR in 1936. Turtkul and Chimbai were former capitals. Tamdy-Bulak dist. ceded (1943) to Bukhara oblast. Also called Kara-Kalpakistan.

Karakas (kŭrŭkäs'), village (1939 pop. under 500), E East Kazakhstan oblast, Kazakh SSR, 80 mi. NW of Zaisan, on L. Zaisan, at efflux of Irtysh R.; fish processing.

Kara Kash or **Qara Qash** (kärä' käsh'), Chinese *Moyü* (mô'yü') [black jade], town, ⊙ Kara Kash co. (pop. 135,380), SW Sinkiang prov., China, 20 mi. NW of Khotan, and on Kara Kash R. (tributary of Khotan R.); jade-mining center; cotton textiles. Sericulture; cattle raising; fruit.

Karakelong (käräkĕlông'), largest island (□ c.380; pop. 12,921) of Talaud Isls., Indonesia, 190 mi. NE of Celebes; 4°17'N 126°49'E; 48 mi. long, 12 mi. wide. Rises to 2,264 ft. Timber, copra, sago, nutmeg; fishing. On W coast is Beo, chief town and port of group.

Karakhoto (kä"räkhō'tō), Mongolian *Hara Hoto* (hărä' hōtō'), Chinese *Heicheng* or *Hei-ch'eng* (hā'chŭng') [black city], ruined town in Ningsia section of Inner Mongolia, China, in Etsin Gol valley; 41°45'N 101°24'E. A trade center after c.1000 in the Tangut kingdom, it was reported (13th cent.) by Marco Polo as Etzina, and was destroyed in 14th cent. The remains were discovered (1909) by Russian explorer Kozlov.

Karakilisa, Armenian SSR: see SISIAN.

Karakilisse, Turkey: see KARAKOSE.

Kara-Kirghiz Autonomous Oblast, USSR: see KIRGHIZIA.

Kara-Kishlak (kŭrä"-kēshläk'), village (1939 pop. over 500), E Samarkand oblast, Uzbek SSR, c.20 mi. SE of Gallya-Aral; cotton, grain, livestock.

Karaklis. 1 City, N Armenian SSR: see KIROVAKAN. **2** Village, S Armenian SSR: see SISIAN.

Karakocan (kärä'kôchän"), Turkish *Karakoçan*, village (pop. 546), Elazig prov., E central Turkey, 47 mi. ENE of Elazig; grain, legumes, fruit. Formerly Tepe or Tepekoy.

Karakol, Kirghiz SSR: see PRZHEVALSK.

Karakoram or **Karakorum** (kă"rŭkō'rŭm, kä"–) [Turkic,=black gravel], mountain system in N Kashmir; from 74°E, near Afghanistan border, extends c.300 mi. SE to main bend of Shyok R. Consists of 4 ranges: main range (also called Great Karakoram and sometimes Muztagh-Karakoram), AGHIL-KARAKORAM RANGE (N lateral range), KAILAS-KARAKORAM RANGE (S lateral range), and LADAKH RANGE (trans-Shyok lateral range). The main Karakoram has some of the highest peaks of the world, including K^2 or Mt. Godwin Austen (28,250 ft.), Gasherbrum I (26,470 ft.), and Broad Peak (26,400 ft.), and the giant glaciers Siachen, Biafo, and Baltoro. Main pass, Karakoram Pass. Range separated from Kunlun mts. (N) by Yarkand R., from Punjab Himalayas (S) by the Indus.

Karakoram Pass (alt. 18,290 ft.), in Aghil-Karakoram Range, NE Kashmir, 95 mi. N of Leh; important pass on main Kashmir-China trade route.

Karakoro River (käräkō'rō), W Fr. West Africa, rises in S Mauritania, near Kiffa, flows c.180 mi. S, most of its course along Mauritania–Fr. Sudan border, to Senegal R. 45 mi. WNW of Kayes.

Karakorum (kă"rŭkō'rŭm,kä"–), Chinese *Holin* (hŭ'lĭn'), ruins of old Mongol capital, on Orkhon R., near modern Erdeni Dzu (or Erdeni Dzuu), in North Khangai aimak, central Mongolian People's Republic, 200 mi. WSW of Ulan Bator; 47°13'N 102°46'E. Residences of Turkic tribes (Huns, Avars, Uigurs) existed intermittently in this area during the 1st millenium of the Christian era and reached their greatest prominence during 7th–9th cent. Karakorum itself was established (c.1220) as residence of Jenghiz Khan; it remained as Mongol hq. until latter was transferred (1267) to Peking under Kublai Khan. It was visited by papal missions under Plano Carpini (1245–47) and William of Rubruk (1253–55). Karakorum later was abandoned; but on its site appeared in 1586 the monastery of Erdeni Dzu. The ruins of the anc. Mongol city were discovered in 1889 by Russian explorer N. M. Yadrintsev, who also uncovered the ORKHON RIVER inscriptions.

Karakose (kärä'kûsĕ), Turk. *Karaköse*, town (1950 pop. 10,013), ⊙ Agri prov., E Turkey, on Murat R. and 95 mi. E of Erzurum. Formerly Karakilisse.

Karakubstroi, Ukrainian SSR: see KOMSOMOLSKOYE, Stalino oblast.

Karakul or **Karakul'** (kŭrä"kōōl'), village (1926 pop. 837), SW Bukhara oblast, Uzbek SSR, on Trans-Caspian RR, on Zeravshan R. and 35 mi. SW of Bukhara; cotton-ginning center.

Kara-Kul or **Kara-Kul'**, mountain lake (□ 140) in the Pamir, NE Gorno-Badakhshan Autonomous Oblast, Tadzhik SSR, near China-USSR border, just W of Osh-Khorog highway, 135 mi. NE of Khorog; 775 ft. deep; alt. 12,980 ft.

Kara-Kuldzha or **Kara-Kul'dzha** (kŭrä"-kōōl'jŭ), village (1939 pop. over 500), NE Osh oblast, Kirghiz SSR, 17 mi. SE of Uzgen; cotton.

Karakulino (kŭrŭkōōlyē'nŭ), village (1939 pop. over 2,000), SE Udmurt Autonomous SSR, Russian SFSR, on right bank of Kama R. (landing) and 60 mi. SSE of Izhevsk; food processing.

Karakulskoye or **Karakul'skoye** (kŭrŭkōōl'skŭyŭ), village (1926 pop. 1,710), E Chelyabinsk oblast, Russian SFSR, on Ui R. and 32 mi. E of Troitsk; wheat, rye, oats, livestock. Formerly Karakulski.

Kara Kum or **Qara Qum** (kärä' kōōm'), Chinese *Weili* (wā'lē'), town and oasis (pop. 10,022), central Sinkiang prov., China, 25 mi. SSE of Kurla and on highway; sericulture; carpet mfg.; livestock. Gold mines near by.

Kara-Kum (kŭrä"-kōōm'), extensive desert in Turkmen SSR; bounded N by the Ust-Urt plateau and the Amu Darya, S by the Kopet-Dagh; 600 mi. long, 200–250 mi. wide. Traversed by Trans-Caspian RR (SE); includes Tedzhen and Murgab oases. Sulphur mining at Serny Zavod and Darvaza; extensive semi-nomadic raising of goats, camels, and karakul sheep. In 1951 was begun the Turkmen Canal to cross the Kara-Kum from Takhia-Tash on the Amu Darya to Krasnovodsk on the Caspian Sea. The desert ARAL KARA-KUM lies NE of Aral Sea.

Kara-Kum Canal, waterway project to link the Amu Darya with Murgab and Tedzhen oases, Turkmen SSR. Construction begun 1948, later abandoned.

Karakuni-dake, Japan: see KIRISHIMA-YAMA.

Karakuyu (kärä'kōōyōō"), village (pop. 409), Afyonkarahisar prov., W central Turkey, 2 mi. E of Dinar; rail junction.

Karalis, Turkey: see BEYSEHIR, LAKE.

Karaman (kärämän'), anc. *Laranda*, town (1950 pop. 13,605), Konya prov., S central Turkey, on railroad and 65 mi. SE of Konya, at N foot of Taurus Mts., on edge of great central plain of Asia Minor; alt. 3,409 ft.; wheat, barley. Has old castle, mosques. Sometimes spelled Caraman; formerly called Darende. An early stronghold of the Isaurians, it was destroyed by its people when besieged by Perdiccas in 4th cent. B.C. In Middle Ages it was ⊙ independent kingdom of Karamania (kärŭmā'nēŭ), which succumbed to the Ottoman Turks in 15th cent. The term Karamania has at various times meant: the area of Konya prov.; a larger area N of Taurus Mts. and including regions to W of Konya; and an area including the Taurus Mts. down to the coast.

Karamanovo (kärämä'nôvô), village (pop. 3,518), Pleven dist., N Bulgaria, 11 mi. ESE of Svishtov; grain, vineyards, stock.

Kara-Mazar (kŭrä"-mŭzär'), village, NE Leninabad oblast, Tadzhik SSR, on S slope of Kurama Range, 30 mi. NE of Leninabad; lead-zinc-silver mining center.

Karambakudi (kŭrŭm'bŭkōōdē), town (pop. 4,015), Trichinopoly dist., S Madras, India, 23 mi. ENE of Pudukkottai; rice, peanuts, millet. Also spelled Karambakkudi or Karambakudy.

Karamea Bight (kärŭmē'ŭ), inlet of Tasman Sea, NW S.Isl., New Zealand, N of Westport; 65 mi. long, 15 mi. wide. Receives Buller R.; Cape Foulwind at S end.

Karamoja, district, Uganda: see MOROTO.

Karamursel (kärä' mürsĕl"), Turkish *Karamürsel*, village (pop. 2,762), Kocaeli prov., NW Turkey, on Gulf of Izmit, 17 mi. WSW of Izmit; grain.

Karamyshevo (kŭrūmĭ'shĭvŭ), village (1939 pop. over 500), central Pskov oblast, Russian SFSR, 17 mi. ESE of Pskov; flax, dairy products.

Karan or **Karan'** (kŭrän'yŭ), town (1939 pop. over 500), S Stalino oblast, Ukrainian SSR, 12 mi. SE of Volnovakha.

Karand, Iran: see KARIND.

Karanfil Dag (kärämfĭl' dä), Turkish *Karanfil Dağ*, peak (10,154 ft.), S Turkey, in the Ala Dag, 32 mi. E of Ulukisla.

Karangan (kŭräng"än'), village, S Kedah, Malaya, 22 mi. E of George Town; tin and tungsten mining.

Karanja (kä'rŭnjŭ), town (pop. 18,126), Akola dist., W Madhya Pradesh, India, 36 mi. ESE of Akola; cotton ginning, oilseed milling.

Karanji (kŭr'ŭnjē), village (pop. 2,065), Ahmadnagar dist., E Bombay, India, 15 mi. E of Ahmadnagar; cotton, millet; cotton ginning, handicraft cloth weaving.

Karansebes, Rumania: see CARANSEBES.

Karantaba (käräntä'bä), village (pop. 49), MacCarthy Isl. div., E central Gambia, on right bank of Gambia R. (wharf) and 14 mi. ENE of Georgetown; peanuts, beeswax, hides and skins. A Br. trading post dating from c.1780. Formerly called Pisania.

Karany (kä'rānē), Czech *Kárany*, village, N central Bohemia, Czechoslovakia, on Elbe R. and 16 mi. ENE of Prague, opposite Celakovice; supplies Prague with water.

Kara Orman or **Karaorman** (both: kä'räôr"män), mountain (5,084 ft.) in the Pindus system, W Macedonia, Yugoslavia, E of the Black Drin, 7 mi. NNE of Struga.

Karapcha, Bulgaria: see MALOMIR.

Karapchu (kŭräp'chōō), Rum. *Carapciu* (käräp'-chōō), village (1941 pop. 1,507), SW Chernovtsy oblast, Ukrainian SSR, in N Bukovina, on Sereth R. and 7 mi. SE of Storozhinets; rail junction; lignite mining.

Karapinar (kärä'pŭnär"), Turkish *Karapınar*, town (pop. 6,168), Konya prov., SW central Turkey, 60 mi. ESE of Konya; salt, figs, cereals. Formerly Sultaniye.

Kara River (kä'rŭ), N European Russian SFSR, rises in the N Urals, flows 130 mi. N to Kara Bay of Baidarata Bay; forms border bet. Nenets Natl. Okrug (European USSR) and Yamal-Nenets Natl. Okrug (Asiatic USSR). Receives Silova R. (left).

Karasburg (kä'räsbûrkh), formerly **Kalkfontein** (kälk"fôntān'), town, S South-West Africa, 110 mi. SSE of Keetmanshoop, 160 mi. WNW of Upington; distributing center for S part of country, in Karakul-sheep-raising region.

Kara Sea (kä'rŭ), Rus. *Karskoye More*, section of Arctic Ocean off Russian SFSR; bounded S by coast of W Siberia, W by Novaya Zemlya, N by line joining capes Kohlsaat and Molotov at 82°N lat., E by Severnaya Zemlya. Receives Ob, Yenisei, Pyasina, and Taimyra rivers. Generally not over 650 ft. deep; navigable only during ice-free Aug.–Sept. River mouths abound in fish. Main ports: Novy Port, Dickson Harbor.

Karasgaon (kŭr'ŭsgoun), town (pop. 7,129), Amraoti dist., W Madhya Pradesh, India, 8 mi. NE of Ellichpur; millet, wheat; cotton ginning. Sometimes spelled Karajgaon.

Kara Shahr or **Qara Shahr** (kärä' shä'hûr), Chinese *Yenki* or *Yen-ch'i* (both: yĕn'chē'), town and oasis (pop. 19,899), central Sinkiang prov., China, W of lake Bagrach Kol, 130 mi. SSW of Urumchi; 42°4'N 86°19'E. Road junction on highway S of the Tien Shan; horse-raising center; mfg. (saddles, carpets); sericulture.

Karash River, Rumania and Yugoslavia: see CARAS RIVER.

Karasjok (kä'räshōk), Lapp village (pop. 356; canton pop. 1,581), Finnmark co., N Norway, near Finnish border, on Karasjok R. (tributary of Tana R.) and 96 mi. SE of Hammerfest. Airfield; tuberculosis sanitarium. First settled by Finns; church established 1807.

Karas Mountains, South-West Africa: see GROSSE KARRAS MOUNTAINS.

Karasouli, Greece: see POLYKASTRON.

Karas River, Rumania and Yugoslavia: see CARAS RIVER.

Kara Strait, USSR: see KARSKIYE VOROTA.

Kara-Su, rivers, Bulgaria and Greece: see STRUMA RIVER; MESTA RIVER.

Karasu (kä"rä'sōō), town (pop. 6,042), Mie prefecture, S Honshu, Japan, on W shore of Izu Bay, 5 mi. SSE of Tsu; rice, wheat, poultry; raw silk.

Karasu (käräsōō'), village (pop. 2,906), Kocaeli prov., NW Turkey, port on Black Sea at mouth of Sakarya R., 26 mi. NNE of Adapazari; grain, potatoes. Formerly Incirli.

Kara Su or **Karasu**, name sometimes given to the W headstream of the EUPHRATES which combines with the MURAT RIVER in E central Turkey. Several minor streams of Turkey are also called Kara Su.

Karasu (kŭrŭsōō'). **1** Village, NE Kustanai oblast, Kazakh SSR, 80 mi. SSE of Kustanai; cattle. **2** Town (1939 pop. over 2,000), NE Osh oblast, Kirghiz SSR, in Fergana Valley, 12 mi. NNE of Osh, at junction (Karasu-Uzbekski station) of railroads to Osh, Kok-Yangak, and Andizhan; cotton-ginning center. **3** Village, Uzbek SSR: see VOROSHILOVO.

Kara-Su, lake, Kazakh SSR: see KARASUK LAKES.

Kara-Su, river, Russian SFSR: see KARASUK RIVER.

Karasubazar, Russian SFSR: see BELOGORSK.

Karasufla, Turkey: see HIZAN.

Karasuk (kŭrŭsōōk'), town (1926 pop. 2,682), SW Novosibirsk oblast, Russian SFSR, on railroad, on Karasuk R. and 55 mi. NNW of Slavgorod; dairying, meat packing.

Karasuk Lakes, group of salt lakes on NW Kulunda Steppe, on border of Altai Territory, Russian SFSR, and Pavlodar oblast, Kazakh SSR. Karasuk L. or Kara-Su (□ 2), in Pavlodar oblast, Kazakh SSR, is largest of the group and is 60 mi. NW of Slavgorod.

Karasuk River, Novosibirsk oblast, Russian SFSR, rises on E Baraba Steppe, flows 220 mi. SW, past Kochki, Krasnozerskoye, and Karasuk, to one of Karasuk Lakes. Also known in lower course as Kara-Su.

Karasu Mountains (käräsōō'), E central Turkey, extend 70 mi. E from Tercan, bet. Euphrates R. (N) and Tuzla R. (S); rise to 10,335 ft. in Saksak Dag.

Karasuyama (kärä'sōōyämŭ), town (pop. 11,337), Tochigi prefecture, central Honshu, Japan, 16 mi. ENE of Utsunomiya; commercial center for agr. area (rice, wheat, tobacco).

Karata, Ethiopia: see KORATA.

Karata (kŭrŭtä'), village (1939 pop. over 500), W Dagestan Autonomous SSR, Russian SFSR, in the E Greater Caucasus, on right branch of the Andi Koisu and 8 mi. SE of Botlikh; woolen milling; grain, sheep raising. Dist. inhabited by Akhvakh, one of mtn. tribes of Dagestan.

Kara-Tag (kŭrä"-täk'), village (1926 pop. 2,217), NW Stalinabad oblast, Tadzhik SSR, on S slope of

Gissar Range, 22 mi. W of Stalinabad, in wheat area. Coal and phosphorite deposits.

Kara-Tal (-täl'), river in Taldy-Kurgan oblast, Kazakh SSR, rises in the Dzungarian Ala-Tau, flows 220 mi. NNW, past Taldy-Kurgan, through Sary-Ishik-Otrau (desert), to S L. Balkhash. Upper course irrigates sugar-beet and rice area; salt lakes and fisheries near mouth.

Karatas, Cape (kärätäsh'), Turkish *Karataş*, on SE Mediterranean coast of Asia Minor, Turkey, at W entrance to Gulf of Iskenderun; 36°33'N 35°19'E.

Kara-Tau (kŭrä"-tou'). **1** W branch of Tien Shan mountain system, S Kazakh SSR, extends 210 mi. NW from Turksib RR parallel to the Syr Darya; metamorphic schists; rises to 6,035 ft. Cotton grown on irrigated slopes. Large lead-zinc mines at Kantagi and Achisai; extensive phosphorite deposits at Chulak-Tau; **2** Range on Mangyshlak Peninsula, Guryev oblast, Kazakh SSR; rises to 1,742 ft.; coal and manganese deposits.

Karategin Range (kŭrŭtyĭgēn'), NE Stalinabad oblast, Tadzhik SSR, along Vakhsh R., to area of Faizabad; rises to c.12,000 ft. The Karategin country was a division of former Bukhara Khanate.

Kara Tepe, Afghanistan: see TORGHONDI.

Karatina (kärätē'nä), town, Central Prov., S central Kenya, on railroad and 12 mi. ESE of Nyeri; dried vegetables; livestock.

Karativu (kŭrŭtē'vōō), 2 low-lying islands off W coast of Ceylon, separated from mainland by Portugal Bay; larger isl. (N; 8 mi. long, 1 mi. wide) has fishing camps; smaller isl. (S) is 2 mi. long. Also spelled Karaitivu; also written Kara Tivu.

Karaton (kŭrŭtôn'), oil town (1945 pop. over 500), W Guryev oblast, Kazakh SSR, near Caspian Sea, 31 mi. SSW of Koschagyl, in Emba oil field.

Karatoya River (kŭrŭtō'yŭ), Indian and Pakistan Bengal, formed 12 mi. WSW of Rangpur by junction of headstreams; flows c.150 mi. SSE, past Bogra, Sherpur, and Ulapara, to Atrai R. 3 mi. NNW of Bera. Another Karatoya R. is upper course of the Atrai.

Karatsu (kä"rä'tsōō), city and port (1940 pop. 31,342; 1947 pop. 49,668), Saga prefecture, NW Kyushu, Japan, on N Hizen Peninsula, 24 mi. NNE of Sasebo, on Genkai Sea; coal-loading port. Known for pottery. Summer resort. Site of castle built in 16th cent. by Hideyoshi during his invasion of Korea.

Kara-Turgai River, Kazakh SSR: see TURGAI RIVER.

Karatuzskoye (kŭrŭtōō'skŭyŭ), village (1926 pop. 3,811), S Krasnoyarsk Territory, Russian SFSR, 45 mi. E of Minusinsk, in hemp-growing area; dairy farming.

Kara-Tyube (kŭrä"-tyōōbyĕ'). **1** Village (1948 pop. over 10,000), E West Kazakhstan oblast, Kazakh SSR, 135 mi. SE of Uralsk; cattle. **2** Village, NE Osh oblast, Kirghiz SSR, on railroad and 35 mi. E of Uzgen, in Uzgen coal basin.

Karaul (kŭrŭōōl'), village, W Taimyr Natl. Okrug, Krasnoyarsk Territory, Russian SFSR, N of Arctic Circle, on Yenisei R. and 80 mi. NW of Dudinka; fisheries.

Karauli (kŭrou'lē), city (pop. 19,177), E Rajasthan, India, 80 mi. ESE of Jaipur; agr. market (millet, gram, wheat, cotton); hand-loom weaving (carpets), biri mfg. Founded mid-14th cent. Was ⊙ former princely state of Karauli (□ 1,227; pop. 152,413) in Rajputana States, India; in 1949, state joined union of Rajasthan.

Kara-Unkurt, Kirghiz SSR: see KUM-BEL.

Kara-Uzyak (kŭrä"-ōōzyäk') village (1939 pop. over 500), central Kara-Kalpak Autonomous SSR, Uzbek SSR, in the Amu Darya delta, 60 mi. NNW of Nukus; cotton.

Karavan (kŭrŭvän'). **1** Village (1948 pop. over 2,000), W Dzhalal-Abad oblast, Kirghiz SSR, in SE foothills of Chatkal Range, 70 mi. NW of Dzhalal-Abad; wheat. **2** Village (1939 pop. over 500), NE Osh oblast, Kirghiz SSR, 5 mi. E of Kizyl-Kiya; wheat.

Karavansarai, Armenian SSR: see IDZHEVAN.

Karavas (käräväs'), town (pop. 2,156), Kyrenia dist., N Cyprus, 15 mi. NW of Nicosia; citrus fruit, almonds, carobs, olive oil; goats, sheep.

Karavassara, Greece: see AMPHILOCHIA.

Karavasta Lagoon, Albania: see KRAVASTA LAGOON.

Karavostasi (kärävôstä'sē) or **Xeros** (ksĕrôs'), village (pop. 1,759), Nicosia dist., NW Cyprus, minor port on Morphou Bay, 30 mi. W of Nicosia, in agr. region (citrus fruit, almonds, olive oil; sheep, goats). Fishing. Ships pyrites from near-by Mavrovouni and Skouriotissa mines (Evrykhou Valley). Just W are ruins of anc. city of Soli.

Karawa (kärä'wä), village, Equator Prov., NW Belgian Congo, 100 mi. NW of Lisala; cotton ginning. Protestant mission.

Karawanken (käräväng'kŭn), Slovenian *Karavanke*, Ital. *Caravanche*, range of Eastern Alps along Yugoslav-Austrian border; extend c.50 mi. E from Tarvisio, forming continuation of Carnic Alps. A limestone formation (except for schist outcrop in W), becoming steeper in E. Highest peak, Hochstuhl (7,342 ft.). Crossed by Wurzen, Loibl, and Seeberg passes. Railroad connecting Villach (Austria) with Jesenice (Yugoslavia) passes through Karawanken Tunnel (5 mi. long, just over 2,000 ft. high). Excellent view of Carinthian lakes and of Klagenfurt (N). Pop. largely Slovenian.

Karayazi (kärä'yăzŭ"), Turkish *Karayazı*, village (pop. 251), Erzurum prov., NE Turkey, 33 mi. ESE of Erzurum; grain. Formerly Cullu and Bayrakdar.

Karayazy, village, Georgian SSR: see GARDABANI.

Karayazy Steppe (kŭrŭyä'zē), in E Georgian and W Azerbaijan SSRs, bet. Iora and Kura rivers, SE of Tiflis; dry salt steppe, partially irrigated for wheat and cotton growing; average alt., 1,000 ft.; winter pastures.

Karb, Poland: see BOBREK.

Karbala (kär'bŭlŭ, -bälä) or **Kerbela** (kûr'bŭlŭ), province (□ 2,275; pop. 276,670), W central Iraq, extending from the Euphrates valley WSW into the Syrian Desert (the desert area, which extends to the Saudi Arabia line, is not included in the prov. area); ⊙ Karbala. Served by Basra-Baghdad RR. In the E there is date cultivation. In the prov. are several sacred Moslem shrines, at Karbala, NAJAF, and KUFA.

Karbala or **Kerbela**, city (pop. 122,719), ⊙ Karbala prov., central Iraq, at the edge of the Syrian Desert, 10 mi. from the Euphrates, on railroad, and 55 mi. SSW of Baghdad; 32°7'N 44°2'E. An important Moslem pilgrimage city, and a tourist and trade (dates, religious objects, hides, wool) center. Here was killed (A.D. 680) the Moslem saint Husein (also spelled Hosain, Husain, Hussain, etc.), grandson of Mohammed, and his tomb ranks with that of Ali at Najaf as one of the greatest shrines of pilgrims of the Shiite sect. The tomb, with a gilded dome and 3 minarets, was destroyed 1801 by Wahabis, but it was quickly restored by contributions from Persians and other Shiites. Persian pilgrims to Mecca usually begin their journey at Karbala, often bringing the bones of their dead for burial here.

Karbitz, Czechoslovakia: see CHABAROVICE.

Karcag (kŏr'tsŏg), city (pop. 25,551), Jasz-Nagykun-Szolnok co., E central Hungary, 35 mi. ENE of Szolnok; rail junction; flour mill, brickworks; wheat, corn, melons, cattle, hogs. Agr. school. Formerly spelled Karczag.

Karcal Dag (kärchäl' dä), Turkish *Karçal Dağ*, peak (10,990 ft.), NE Turkey, 18 mi. NNE of Artvin.

Karchana (kŭr'chŭnŭ), village, Allahabad dist., SE Uttar Pradesh, India, 13 mi. SSE of Allahabad; gram, rice, barley, wheat, sugar cane.

Karcsa (kŏr'chŏ), town (pop. 2,435), Zemplen co., NE Hungary, 25 mi. N of Nyiregyhaza; grain, potatoes, cattle, hogs.

Karczag, Hungary: see KARCAG.

Kardam (kärdäm'), village (pop. 3,048), Kolaravgrad dist., NE Bulgaria, on Cherni Lom R. and 2 mi. NE of Popovo; poultry, oil-bearing plants, truck. Formerly Khaidar.

Kardamyla or **Kardhamila** (both: kärdhä'mĭlŭ), town (pop. 4,676), N Chios isl., Greece, 11 mi. N of Chios city; olive oil, wine, wheat, barley.

Kardaun, Italy: see CARDANO.

Kardeljevo (kär'dĕlyĕvô), town, S Croatia, Yugoslavia, Adriatic port at Neretva R. mouth, 10 mi. W of Metkovic, in Dalmatia. Deep-water port (exports timber); supplanted the older Metkovic after Second World War; terminus of railroad from Sarajevo. Until 1949 called Ploce (plô'chĕ), Serbo-Croatian *Ploče*.

Kardhamila, Greece: see KARDAMYLA.

Karditsa or **Kardhitsa** (both: kärdhē'tsŭ), nome (□ 936; pop. 130,960), SW Thessaly, Greece; ⊙ Karditsa. Bounded W by Pindus system and N Peneus R., it includes S portion of Trikkala lowland. Agr.: corn, wheat, vegetables; livestock raising. Industry centered at Karditsa, served by narrow-gauge railroad from Volos.

Karditsa or **Kardhitsa**, city (pop. 14,024), ⊙ Karditsa nome, SW Thessaly, Greece, on narrow-gauge railroad and 15 mi. SE of Trikkala; trading center for corn, vegetables, tobacco, cotton, dairy products, livestock. Developed during Turkish rule (after 15th cent.) Also Karditza and Carditsa.

Kardiva Channel, seaway in Indian Ocean, along c.4°50'N; runs bet. central Maldive Isls.

Kardla or **Kyardla**, Est. *Kärdla* (all: kărd'lä), Ger. *Kertel*, city (pop. 1,454), Baltic port on N shore of Hiiumaa isl., Estonia, 30 mi. W of Haapsalu; agr. market (barley, potatoes); mfg. of woolens.

Kardymovo (kŭrdĭ'mŭvŭ), village (1939 pop. over 500), central Smolensk oblast, Russian SFSR, 15 mi. ENE of Smolensk; dairying center.

Kardzhali, Bulgaria: see KIRDZHALI.

Kareima (kŭrā'mŭ), village, Northern Prov., Anglo-Egyptian Sudan near 4th Nile Cataract, 5 mi. N of Merowe; 18°33'N 31°51'E. Terminus of rail spur from Abu Hamed and transfer point for steamers to Kerma (above 3d cataract). Tourist base for near-by Napata ruins, Kuru and Nuri pyramid fields. Airfield. Also spelled Karima.

Kareli (kŭrā'lē), town (pop. 2,992), Hoshangabad dist., NW Madhya Pradesh, India, 8 mi. W of Narsinghpur; dal milling, sawmilling; wheat, oilseeds. Sometimes called Kareliganj.

Kareli (kŭrĕ'lyē), village (1939 pop. over 2,000), central Georgian SSR, on railroad and 12 mi. W of Gori; agr., orchards.

Karelia (kŭrē'lyŭ) or **Karelo-Finnish Soviet Socialist Republic** (kŭrē'lō), constituent republic (□ 68,900; 1947 pop. estimate 600,000) of NW European USSR; ⊙ Petrozavodsk. Extends 350 mi. from Kola Peninsula (N) to lakes Onega and Ladoga (S), bet. Finland (W) and the White Sea (E). Prolonged glaciation has left its imprint on the granitic terrain covered by thousands of lakes (15% of total area; Vygozero, Segozero, Topozero) and coniferous forests (⅔ of area). Short rivers (rapids) furnish water power. Subarctic humid continental climate with mean temp. of 14°-18°F. (Jan.) and 61°-64°F. (July); yearly precipitation (over 20 in.) results in marshiness due to reduced evaporation. Pop. consists of related Karelians and Finns (23%), and, in E, Russians (63%). Administratively, Karelia is divided directly into *raions* (*rayons*) and independent cities. Lumbering and paper and pulp milling are the leading industries, with principal centers at Belomorsk and Kem (sawmilling), Segezha, Kondopoga, Pitkyaranta, Kharlu, Lyaskelya, and Suoyarvi (paper and pulp). Industry is powered by hydroelectric stations (largest at Sunski); supplied with machinery by Petrozavodsk. Related industries produce plywood, veneers, furniture, prefabricated housing, and river barges. Building stone (marble, quartzite, red granite, porphyry) and mica are quarried. Bog iron ore (mined since 17th cent.) and also magnetite (Gimoly), titaniferous iron ore (Pudozhgora) and lead-zinc ores (Pitkyaranta) supply the metallurgical industry. Agr. plays secondary role and is devoted to dairy farming (butter, cheese) and cultivation of fodder crops, potatoes, vegetables, rye, oats, and barley. Fisheries (whitefish, oysters) abound in lakes, rivers, and the White Sea. Main industrial centers (Petrozavodsk, Sortavala, Medvezhyegorsk, Kondopoga, and Belomorsk) are linked by White Sea-Baltic Canal (built 1933) and Murmansk RR (built 1916). Timber and lumber products, paper, building stone, and mica are exported. The Karelians, first located in 9th cent. N of L. Ladoga, came (c.12th cent.) under Rus. rule and were temporarily dominated (1617-1721) by Swedes. Constituted originally (1920) as Karelian Workers' Commune, the area became (1923) Karelian Autonomous SSR. Following Soviet-Finnish war of 1939-40, the autonomous republic absorbed nearly the entire territory ceded by Finland, except for S Karelian Isthmus bet. Leningrad and Vuoksi R. (which passed to Russian SFSR); raised (1940) to status of union republic (Karelo-Finnish SSR). After Second World War, when over half its area was held (1941-44) by Germans and Finns, the N Karelian Isthmus (including Vyborg, Primorsk, and Priozersk) also passed (1944) to Russian SFSR.

Karelian Autonomous Soviet Socialist Republic, USSR: see KARELIA.

Karelian Isthmus (-lyŭn), lake-studded glacial land bridge in Leningrad oblast, Russian SFSR, bet. Gulf of Finland and L. Ladoga; 90 mi. long, 25-70 mi. wide. Chief cities: Leningrad (S), Vyborg (NW), Priozersk (NE). Entire isthmus came under USSR control after Finland was forced to cede N section in 1940. Scene of fighting in Russo-Finnish war (1939-40) and Second World War (1941-44).

Karelian National Okrug, former autonomous unit (□ 2,300; pop. c.150,000) in Kalinin oblast, Russian SFSR; ⊙ Likhoslavl; existed 1937-39.

Karelo-Finnish Soviet Socialist Republic, USSR: see KARELIA.

Karema (kärĕ'mä), town, Western Prov., SW Tanganyika, 50 mi. SW of Mpanda; fishing; rice, corn, beeswax. Mission. Chromite and gold deposits near by.

Karen, Formosa: see HWALIEN.

Karene, district, Sierra Leone: see BATKANU.

Karenko, Formosa: see HWALIEN.

Karenni State (kŭrĕn'nē; Burmese kŭyĭn'nē), constituent unit (□ 4,506; 1941 pop. 70,493) of Union of Burma, in SE Upper Burma, on Thailand line; ⊙ Loikaw. Bounded N by Shan State and traversed N-S by Salween R., it coincides roughly with the Karenni hills, a S extension of Shan Plateau, rising to over 8,000 ft. Agr.: hill rice, corn, millet, lac; vast teak forests. Tungsten and tin mines at Mawchi. Served by road from Toungoo. Pop. is 70% Karen, 20% Shan (Thai). The Karens, a people of Thai-Chinese origin, numbered 1,400,000 (1931) in all Burma, only 4% of which (known as Red Karens) lived in the Karenni State. The great majority are found in Tenasserim and the Irrawaddy delta. Originally Animists, they have been converted to Buddhism and, in part, to Christianity (chiefly as Baptists). A pact concluded (1875) bet. Britain and Burma recognized the independence of Karenni, which consisted originally of 5, later of 3, states (Kantarawadi, Bawlake, Kyebogyi). It was not considered part of Br. Burma, but stood in treaty relationship to the Crown. According to the 1947 Burma Constitution, the 3 Karenni states form a constituent unit of the Union of Burma known as the Karenni State.

Karera (kŭrā'rŭ). **1** Town (pop. 4,002), NE Madhya Bharat, India, 31 mi. E of Shivpuri; agr. (millet, gram, wheat, corn). **2** Village, Rajasthan, India: see BHUPALSAGAR.

Karf, Poland: see BOBREK.

Karfreit, Yugoslavia: see CAPORETTO.
Kargali (kŭrgŭlyē′), village (1948 pop. over 2,000), central Tatar Autonomous SSR, Russian SFSR, 15 mi. SE of Chistopol; wheat, livestock. Lignite deposits near by. Sometimes spelled Kargaly.
Kargalinskaya (kŭrgŭlyĕn′skīŭ), village (1926 pop. 2,201), E Grozny oblast, Russian SFSR, on railroad, on Terek R. and 13 mi. SW of Kizlyar, in cotton dist.; wine making.
Kargaly, Russian SFSR: see KARGALI.
Kargapolye or **Kargapol'ye** (kŭrgŭpô′lyĭ), village (1948 pop. over 2,000), N Kurgan oblast, Russian SFSR, on Miass R. and 30 mi. ESE of Shadrinsk; metalworks; flour mill, dairy plant.
Kargasok (kŭrgŭsôk′), village (1939 pop. over 500), central Tomsk oblast, Russian SFSR, on Ob R., near mouth of Vasyugan R., and 25 mi. WNW of Narym, in agr. area; river port; airfield.
Kargat (kŭrgät′), village (1939 pop. over 10,000), central Novosibirsk oblast, Russian SFSR, on Kargat R., on Trans-Siberian RR and 100 mi. W of Novosibirsk; processing of grain, meat, and dairy.
Kargat River, Novosibirsk oblast, Russian SFSR, rises on NE Baraba Steppe, flows 180 mi. SW, past Kargat and Zdvinsk, to SE L. Chany.
Karghalik or **Qarghaliq** (kärgälĭk′), Chinese *Yeh-cheng* or *Yeh-ch'eng* (yĕ′chŭng′), town and oasis (pop. 37,190), SW Sinkiang prov., China, 35 mi. SSE of Yarkand, at edge of Taklamakan Desert; 37°54′N 77°26′E. Trade route leads S across Karakoram Pass to Leh (Kashmir); sericulture; carpets. Copper, salt found near by.
Kargi (kärgŭ′), Turkish *Kargı*, village (pop. 2,283), Kastamonu prov., N Turkey, on the Kizil Irmak and 40 mi. ENE of Kastamonu; cereals.
Kargil (kŭr′gĭl), village, ⊙ Kargil tahsil (□ 7,392; pop. 52,853), Ladakh dist., central Kashmir, in Deosai Mts., on Suru R. and 80 mi. NE of Srinagar; pulse, wheat, corn. Fort. Scene of fighting (1948) during India-Pakistan struggle for control. Buddhist cave monastery is 15 mi. SE, at Shergol (sometimes spelled Shargol).
Kargi Road, India: see KOTA.
Kargopol or **Kargopol'** (kär′gŭpŭl), city (1926 pop. 3,449), SW Archangel oblast, Russian SFSR, on Onega R., at its outlet from L. Lacha, and 60 mi. NW of Konosha; agr. center (flour, dairy products); fisheries. Chartered 1380; formerly a salt-trading center on Vologda-Onega route.
Kargowa (kärgô′vä), Ger. *Unruhstadt* (ŏŏn′rōō-shtät″), town (1939 pop. 1,713; 1946 pop. 1,403) in Brandenburg, after 1945 in Zielona Gora prov., W Poland, 18 mi. NE of Grünberg (Zielona Gora); candy mfg., flour milling. Chartered 1661. Briefly occupied, 1918–19, by Poles. In Second World War, c.45% destroyed.
Karguiri (kärgē′rē), village, S Niger territory, Fr. West Africa, on Nigeria border and 75 mi. SE of Zinder. Customhouse.
Karhal (kŭr′hŭl), town (pop. 5,811), Mainpuri dist., W Uttar Pradesh, India, 16 mi. SSW of Mainpuri; wheat, gram, pearl millet, corn, barley.
Karhula (kär′hŏŏlä), village in Kymi commune (pop. 25,193), Kymi co., SE Finland, near USSR border, on Gulf of Finland, 2 mi. N of Kotka; rail terminus; glassworks, steel, pulp, paper, and board mills, machine shops.
Kari, Formosa: see KIALI.
Karia ba Mohammed (käryä′ bä mōhäm-mĕd′), village, Fez region, N Fr. Morocco, near the Sebou, 25 mi. NW of Fez; agr. (wheat, barley, vegetables); horse raising.
Karia de Arkeman (kär′yä dā ärkā′män), village (pop. 505), Kert territory, E Sp. Morocco, on a lagoon of the Mediterranean (Mar Chica), 15 mi. SE of Melilla; fishing.
Kariai, Greece: see KARYAI.
Kariatein, Syria: see QARYATEIN, EL.
Kariba Gorge (kärē′bä), defile on Zambezi R., at Northern Rhodesia–Southern Rhodesia border, 50 mi. SSE of Lusaka, near mouth of Sanyati R.; dam, hydroelectric plant, steel-mfg. center, and irrigation scheme planned here.
Karibib (kärĭbĭb′), town (pop. 835), W South-West Africa, 90 mi. NW of Windhoek; tin, lithium mining; marble quarries (now closed). Otjimbingwe reserve of Hottentot, Damara, and Herero tribes is 35 mi. SE.
Karihaara (kä′rĭhä″rä), NW suburb of Kemi, Lapi co., NW Finland, on islet in Gulf of Bothnia, at mouth of Kemi R.; lumber and pulp mills.
Karikal (kä′rĭkäl), settlement (after 1947, officially "free city"; □ 52; pop. 70,541) of Fr. India, within Tanjore dist., S Madras, India, on Coromandel Coast of Bay of Bengal, in Cauvery R. delta, 150 mi. S of Madras; divided into 6 communes. Largely agr. (rice, plantain, millet, tobacco, sugar cane, coconuts). Acquired by French in 1739; Fr. authority finally established in 1817. Formerly spelled Carical.
Karikal, town (commune pop. 23,008), ⊙ Karikal settlement, Fr. India, port on Coromandel Coast of Bay of Bengal, 70 mi. S of Pondicherry, at mouth of Cauvery R. delta arm; terminus of rail spur from Peralam; exports rice, oilseeds.
Karikawa (kärē′käwŭ), town (pop. 5,918), Yamagata prefecture, N Honshu, Japan, 9 mi. ENE of Tsuruoka; rice, silk cocoons.
Karima, Anglo-Egyptian Sudan: see KAREIMA.
Karimata Islands (kärēmä′tŭ), Indonesia, in Karimata Strait, off SW coast of Borneo; 1°36′S 108°53′E; comprises 2 large isls.: Karimata (10 mi. long, 7 mi. wide) and Serutu or Seroetoe (8 mi. long, 2 mi. wide) surrounded by c.60 islets. Fishing. Chief port of group is Padang on SE coast of Karimata isl.
Karimata Strait, channel (c.125 mi. wide) connecting Java Sea (S) with S.China Sea (N), bet. Billiton (W) and SW Borneo (E). Karimata Isls. here.
Karimganj (kŭrēm′gŭnj), town (pop. 7,813), Cachar dist., S Assam, India, in Surma Valley, on Kusiyara R. and 28 mi. W of Silchar; trades in rice, tea, mustard; tea processing. Rice research station. Until 1947, in Sylhet dist.
Karimnagar (kŭrēm′nŭgŭr), district (□ 5,722; pop. 1,355,415), E Hyderabad state, India, on Deccan Plateau; ⊙ Karimnagar. Bounded N by Godavari R.; mainly lowland, drained by tributaries of the Godavari. Largely sandy red soil; millet, rice, oilseeds (chiefly peanuts, sesame), cotton. Bamboo (used in paper mfg.), teak, ebony in forests (E, W). Rice and oilseed milling, cotton ginning, poultry farming. Main towns: Karimnagar (noted silver filigree), Jagtial. Became part of Hyderabad during state's formation in 18th cent. Pop. 90% Hindu, 5% Moslem, 1% Christian.
Karimnagar, town (pop. 17,437), ⊙ Karimnagar dist., E central Hyderabad state, India, 85 mi. NNE of Hyderabad; road center in agr. area (millet, rice, oilseeds, cotton); noted silver filigree.
Karimun Islands or **Karimoen Islands** (both: kärēmōōn′), small group of Riouw Archipelago, Indonesia, in S.China Sea at entrance to Strait of Malacca, bet. Singapore and Sumatra. Largest of several isls. is Kundur or Koendoer (18 mi. long, 10 mi. wide); site of Ungar or Oengar, chief port of group. N of Kundur is Karimun Besar or Great Karimun (12 mi. long, 5 mi. wide). Chief products of group are sago, coconuts, pepper, gambier, firewood; some tin is mined. Fishing industry is important.
Karimunjawa Islands or **Karimoendjawa Islands** (both: kärēmōōnjä′vŭ), group (□ 19; pop. 1,231), Indonesia, in Java Sea, 80 mi. N of Semarang, Java; 5°48′S 110°20′E. Comprise c.25 isls., largest being Karimunjawa (4 mi. in diameter, rising to 1,660 ft.) and Kemujan or Kemoedjan (4 mi. long). Many of smaller isls. are barren and uninhabited. Coconut growing and fishing on larger isls.
Karin (kärēn′), town, NE Br. Somaliland, minor port on Gulf of Aden, in lowland, 60 mi. ENE of Berbera; gums, resins; fisheries.
Karind, Karand, or **Kerend** (all: kĕrĕnd′), town (1942 pop. estimate 15,000), Fifth Prov., in Kermanshah, W Iran, 50 mi. W of Kermanshah, and on road to Iraq line at Qasr-i-Shirin; grain, fruit, dairy products; sheep raising. Metalwork (hand-made rifles and knives).
Karingon (chĕ′rĭng-ŭn″), Swedish *Käringön*, fishing village (pop. 332), Goteborg och Bohus co., SW Sweden, on isl. (575 acres) of same name in the Skagerrak, 12 mi. SSW of Lysekil; seaside resort.
Karintorf (kŭrĭntôrf′), town (1948 pop. over 2,000), central Kirov oblast, Russian SFSR, 27 mi. E of Kirov; peat works.
Karis (kä′rĭs), Finnish *Karjaa* (kär′yä), town (pop. 3,809), Uusimaa co., S Finland, near Gulf of Finland, 40 mi. W of Helsinki; rail center, in lumbering and dairying region.
Karisimbi, Mount (kärēsēm′bē), extinct volcano and highest peak (c.14,780 ft.) of the Virunga range, E central Africa, on Belgian Congo and Ruanda-Urundi border, 18 mi. NE of Goma; part of the SE section of Albert Natl. Park set aside for preservation of outstanding flora (hagenias, giant lobelias, senecios, heather-trees) and of the gorilla species. Occasionally covered with snow, its summit is believed by natives to be the place of sojourn of pure souls.
Karistos, Greece: see KARYSTOS.
Karitaina, Greece: see KARYTAINA.
Kariwano (kärē′wänō), town (pop. 4,202), Akita prefecture, N Honshu, Japan, 8 mi. NW of Omagari; rice, silk cocoons.
Kariya (kä″rē′yä). **1** Town (pop. 29,353), Aichi prefecture, central Honshu, Japan, 13 mi. SSE of Nagoya; textiles, pottery. **2** Town (pop. 7,013) on Awaji-shima, Hyogo prefecture, Japan, on Osaka Bay, 14 mi. NNE of Sumoto, in agr. area (rice, wheat, market produce, flowers).
Karjaa, Finland: see KARIS
Karjat (kŭr′jŭt). **1** Village (pop. 6,376), Ahmadnagar dist., E Bombay, India, 40 mi. SE of Ahmadnagar; agr. market (millet, gur). **2** Village (pop. 2,245), Kolaba dist., W Bombay, India, 32 mi. E of Bombay; timber depot (teak, blackwood); rice.
Karkabat (kärkäbät′), Ital. *Carcabat*, village (pop. 650), Agordat div., W Eritrea, on Barka R. and 60 mi. NW of Agordat, in irrigated cotton-growing region. Alluvial gold deposits near by.
Karkal or **Karkala** (kär′kälŭ), town (pop. 9,012), South Kanara dist., W Madras, India, 26 mi. NNE of Mangalore; rice milling, mfg. of potstone culinary vessels (steatite quarries near by). Has monolithic Jain statue. Other noted Jain archaeological remains 10 mi. S, at village of Mudbidri.
Karkamb (kŭr′kŭmb), town (pop. 6,473), Sholapur dist., E central Bombay, India, 42 mi. WNW of Sholapur; market center; cotton dyeing, handicraft cloth weaving, betel farming.
Karkamis, Turkey: see CARCHEMISH.
Karkar (kär′kär), volcanic island (□ 140; pop. c.9,000), Madang dist., Territory of New Guinea, SW Pacific, 9 mi. NE of New Guinea; 15 mi. long; rises to 4,900 ft.; active volcano; coconuts, cacao. Formerly Dampier Isl.
Karkaralinsk (kär″kŭrŭlyĕnsk′), city (1948 pop. over 500), E Karaganda oblast, Kazakh SSR, 105 mi. ESE of Karaganda; road center in Kazakh Hills; cattle; meat packing. Lead-silver deposits. Formerly called Karkaraly. Founded 1824 in Rus. conquest of Kazakhstan.
Karkeln, Russian SFSR: see MYSOVKA.
Karkheh River or **Kerkheh River** (both: kärkhĕ′), anc. *Choaspes* (kōăs′pēz), in Khuzistan, SW Iran, formed by 2 headstreams rising in W Zagros mts. and joining 70 mi. NW of Dizful, flows 200 mi. SSE, disappearing into Tigris marshes on Iraq border. Length, including longest headstream, 350 mi.
Karkinit Gulf (kŭrkĭnyēt′), shallow N inlet of Black Sea in USSR, bet. Ukrainian mainland (N) and Crimea (S); 15-50 mi. wide, 65 mi. long. Separated by Perekop Isthmus (E) from Sivash lagoon. Main ports: Skadovsk, Khorly (N), Chernomorskoye (S).
Karkkila (kärk′kĭlä), Swedish *Högfors* (hŭgfôrs′, –fôsh), town (pop. 4,466), Uusimaa co., S Finland, 35 mi. NW of Helsinki; rail terminus; metal-working.
Karkloof Falls, on Umgeni R., central Natal, U. of So. Afr., N of Pietermaritzburg; drops 350 ft. in a series of cascades.
Karkonosze, Poland and Czechoslovakia: see RIESENGEBIRGE.
Karksi, Estonia: see NUIA.
Karkuk, Iraq: see KIRKUK, city.
Karkur (kärkōōr′), settlement (pop. 1,000), W Israel, in Plain of Sharon, 5 mi. NE of Hadera; starch and glucose mfg.; citriculture. Founded 1913.
Karla Lake, Greece: see VOIVEIS, LAKE.
Karl Alexander Island, in N Franz Josef Land, Russian SFSR, in Arctic Ocean; 22 mi. long, 10 mi. wide; 81°30′N 57°30′E.
Karla Libknekhta, Nikolayev oblast, Ukrainian SSR: see SHIROKOLANOVKA.
Karla Libknekhta, Imeni (ē′mĭnyē kär′lŭ lyēp′-knyĭkhtŭ). **1** N iron mining suburb (1939 pop. over 10,000) of Krivoi Rog, Dnepropetrovsk oblast, Ukrainian SSR, 4 mi. NNE of city center, at Shmakovo station, on right bank of Saksagan R. Until c.1926, called Shmakovski Rudnik. **2** Town (1926 pop. 1,491), NE Stalino oblast, Ukrainian SSR, in the Donbas, 7 mi. NNE of Artemovsk; salt mines.
Karla Marksa, Imeni (ē′mĭnyē kär′lŭ mär′ksŭ). **1** E suburb (1926 pop. 2,692) of Dnepropetrovsk, Dnepropetrovsk oblast, Ukrainian SSR, on left bank of Dnieper R., 6 mi. ENE of city center. Called Rybalskaya until 1920s. **2** Town (1926 pop. 4,511), E Stalino oblast, Ukrainian SSR, in the Donbas, 4 mi. NW of Yenakiyevo; coal mines. Until c.1926, Sofiyevski Rudnik.
Karli (kär′lē), village (pop. 634), Poona dist., central Bombay, India, 32 mi. NW of Poona. In near-by hills are noted Buddhist cave temples (c.1st cent. A.D.). Main cave is one of largest in India (124 ft. long, 45 ft. wide, 46 ft. high); noted for its rows of well-preserved pillars and fine sculptures. Also spelled Karla or Karle.
Karlikova, Greece: see MIKROPOLIS.
Karlin (kär′lēn), Czech *Karlín*, industrial ENE suburb of Prague, Czechoslovakia; gasworks.
Karlingen, France: see CARLING.
Karlino (kärlē′nô) or **Korlino** (kôrlē′nô), Ger. *Körlin* or *Körlin an der Persante* (kŭr′lĭn än dĕr pĕrzän′tŭ), town (1939 pop. 3,421; 1946 pop. 2,115) in Pomerania, after 1945 in Koszalin prov., NW Poland, on Prosnica (Persante) R. and 16 mi. SW of Köslin (Koszalin); mfg. of machinery, bricks; sawmilling, flour milling. Has late-Gothic church.
Karliova (kärlŭ′ôvä″), Turkish *Karlıova*, village (pop. 508), Bingol prov., E central Turkey, 40 mi. NE of Bingol; grain. Formerly Kale.
Karljohansvern, Norway: see HORTEN.
Karl Libknekht (kärl lyĕp′knyĭkht), town (1948 pop. over 2,000), W central Kursk oblast, Russian SFSR, near Seim R., 30 mi. W of Kursk; sugar refinery. Until 1930, Penski Sakharni Zavod.
Karlo, Finland: see HAILUOTO.
Karlobag (kär′lôbäk), Ital. *Carlopago* (kärlôpä′gô), village, W Croatia, Yugoslavia, on Velebit Channel of Adriatic Sea, at W foot of Velebit Mts., 29 mi. N of Zadar; small lumber-exporting seaport; resort.
Karloca, Yugoslavia: see KARLOVCI.
Karlova, Yugoslavia: see MILOSEVO.
Karlovac (kär′lôväts). **1** Ger. *Karlstadt* (kärl′shtät), Hung. *Károlyváros* (kä′roivä″rôsh), city (pop. 23,885), ⊙ Karlovac oblast (formed 1949), N Croatia, Yugoslavia, near confluence of Kupa and Korana rivers, 30 mi. SW of Zagreb, in the Pokupje. Industrial and trade center; mfg. of

textiles, leather goods, chemicals; lumber, iron, and machine works. Founded 1579; former fortress on Turkish frontier. Hydroelectric plant and summer resort near by, on Korana R. **2** Village, Serbia, Yugoslavia: see Rankovicevo, Vojvodina, Serbia.

Karlova Studanka, Czechoslovakia: see Vrbno.

Karlovci, Karlovtsi, Sremski Karlovci, or **Sremski Karlovtsi** (all: srĕm'skē, kär'lôftsē), Hung. *Karlóca* (kŏr'lōtsŏ), Ger. *Karlowitz* (kär'lŭvĭts), village (pop. 5,670), Vojvodina, N Serbia, Yugoslavia, on the Danube, on railroad and 6 mi. SE of Novi Sad, in the Srem, at NE foot of Fruska Gora. Seat of Serbian patriarch (1690; 1713–1918), when it was a political and cultural center of Serbia. By treaty signed here (1699), Turkey ceded to Austria all of Hungary (except the Banat), Transylvania, and Croatia-Slavonia, to Venice the Peloponnesus and Dalmatia, and returned Podolia to Poland.

Karlovka (kär'lŭfkŭ), town (1926 pop. 6,083), E Poltava oblast, Ukrainian SSR, 27 mi. ESE of Poltava; sugar refinery, machine works, distillery.

Karlovo (kär'lôvô), city (pop. 8,862), Plovdiv dist., central Bulgaria, at S foot of Troyan Mts., 34 mi. N of Plovdiv; rail junction; summer resort; major rose-oil extracting center in Karlovo Basin; textile mfg., wine making. Technical school. Has old clock tower and mosque. Under Turkish rule, 15th–19th cent. Health resort Banya (pop. 1,590), 5 mi. S, has thermal springs.

Karlovo Basin, valley (□ 110; average alt. 1,150 ft.) in central Bulgaria, bet. Troyan Mts. (N) and Sredna Gora (S); drained by Strema R. Noted rose-growing region; vineyards, cotton, tobacco, nuts, mint, medicinal herbs. Main center, Karlovo.

Karlovy Vary, Czechoslovakia: see Carlsbad.

Karlowitz, Czechoslovakia: see Velke Karlovice.

Karlowitz, Yugoslavia: see Karlovci.

Karlsbad, Czechoslovakia: see Carlsbad.

Karlsbad, Latvia: see Rigas Jurmala.

Karlsborg (kärlsbôr'yŭ). **1** Village (pop. 3,952), Skaraborg co., S central Sweden, on NW shore of L. Vatter, 18 mi. W of Motala; E terminus of central section of Gota Canal. Garrison town; metalworking. Has old fortress. Sometimes spelled Carlsborg. **2** Village (pop. 919), Norrbotten co., N Sweden, on small inlet of Gulf of Bothnia, near mouth of Kalix R., 25 mi. W of Haparanda; lumber and pulp milling, woodworking.

Karlsbrunn, Czechoslovakia: see Vrbno.

Karlsburg, Rumania: see Alba-Iulia.

Karlshafen (kärls"hä'fŭn), town (pop. 3,687), in former Prussian prov. of Hesse-Nassau, W Germany, after 1945 in Hesse, on the Weser (landing), at mouth of Diemel R., and 22 mi. N of Kassel; tobacco mfg.; saline baths. Founded 1699 and settled by Huguenots. Also spelled Carlshafen.

Karlshamn (kärls-hä'mŭn, kärls'hä"–), city (1950 pop. 10,691), Blekinge co., S Sweden, on the Baltic, 25 mi. W of Karlskrona; seaport and commercial center; rail junction. Metalworking, sugar refining; mfg. of oilcake, margarine, fruit wine. Ships stone quarried near by. Has church (1702) and ruins of old castle. Inc. 1664, later fortified, it became fishing center. Napoleon's continental blockade gave new impetus to its trade. Sometimes spelled Carlshamn.

Karlshorst (kärls'hôrst"), residential section of Lichtenberg dist., E Berlin, Germany, 7 mi. E of city center. Scene (May 8, 1945) of ratification of Ger. surrender at end of Second World War. After 1945 in Soviet sector, and site of Soviet army and administrative hq. for East Germany.

Karlskoga (–kōō"gä), city (1950 pop. 31,303), Orebro co., S central Sweden, at N end of L. Mockel, 25 mi. W of Orebro; steel mills, foundries, chemical works, sawmills. Inc. 1940 as city. Its E section is suburb of Bofors, with noted armament works.

Karlskrona (kärlskrōō'nä), city (1950 pop. 30,997), ⊙ Blekinge co., S Sweden, on mainland and on small isls. (rail and road bridges) in the Baltic, 100 mi. ENE of Malmo; 56°9'N 15°35'E. Chief Swedish naval base (since 1680), with shore fortifications and extensive docks, cut out of granite. Air base. Shipbuilding, metalworking, brewing, sawmilling; mfg. of naval supplies, clothing. Granite is quarried and shipped. Has 17th-cent. church and 18th-cent. town hall. Sometimes spelled Carlscrona.

Karlsruhe (kärls'rōō"ŭ, kärls"rōō'ŭ), city (1950 pop. 198,014), former ⊙ Baden, Germany, after 1945 administrative center of North Baden (a div. of Württemberg-Baden), 4 mi. E of the Rhine (bridge), 32 mi. S of Mannheim; 49°1'N 8°23'E. Important industrial and rail and road center (near Alsace border), with inland harbor and airport (NW outskirts). Large railroad repair shops; noted metal (machinery, gas and electric stoves, steam engines, bicycles, sewing machines, tools) and chemical (perfumes, soap) industries. Food processing, brewing, paper milling, printing. Pottery works. Active river trade (coal, food); harbor (c.3 mi. from center of city), built 1898–1920, connected with the Rhine by c.1-mi.-long canal. City is laid out in fan shape, with streets converging upon 18th-cent. castle with large park in back. Founded 1715 by a margrave of Baden-Durlach near his hunting lodge. Developed in 19th cent. in neoclassic style; all noteworthy bldgs., including the castle, were destroyed or heavily damaged in Second World War. Site of oldest Ger. institute of technology (founded 1825), where Hertz discovered radio waves. Painter Thoma was director (1899–1919) of noted art gall. Karl Benz b. in W suburb of Mühlburg. Seat of Protestant bishop. Sometimes spelled Carlsruhe.

Karlsruhe (kärlz'rōō), village (pop. 282), McHenry co., central N.Dak., 32 mi. ESE of Minot.

Karlstad (kärl'städ"), city (1950 pop. 35,651), ⊙ Varmland co., SW central Sweden, on Tingvalla isl. and on N shore of L. Vaner, at mouth of Klara R., 160 mi. W of Stockholm; 59°23'N 13°31'E. Port, with important lumber, pulp, and textile mills, shipyards; mfg. of chemicals, leather goods, fishing gear, clothing, matches. Seat of Lutheran bishop. Has cathedral (1723–30) and county mus. There are noted mineral springs. Originally called Tingvalla, known as trade center since Middle Ages. Chartered 1584, when it was renamed Karlstad. Treaty of Karlstad (1905) ended union bet. Norway and Sweden. Sometimes spelled Carlstad.

Karlstad (kärl'stăd"), village (pop. 804), Kittson co., NW Minn., 37 mi. NNW of Thief River Falls, in grain and dairy area.

Karlstadt (kärl'shtät), town (pop. 4,989), Lower Franconia, NW Bavaria, Germany, on the Main (canalized) and 13 mi. NW of Würzburg; mfg. of cement, lime, paper, pottery; brewing. Barley, hops. Surrounded by walls; has Gothic church and 15th-cent. town hall. Carlstadt (Andreas Bodenstein), Protestant reformer, b. here. On opposite side of Main are ruins of castle Karlsburg, founded by Charles Martel and destroyed in Peasants War.

Karlstadt, Yugoslavia: see Karlovac, Croatia.

Karlstejn (kärl'shtān), Czech *Karlštejn* or *Karlův Tyn* (kär'lōōf tĭn"), village, W central Bohemia, Czechoslovakia, on Berounka R., on railroad and 15 mi. SW of Prague. Famous for 14th-cent. castle (now a mus.), former seat of Charles IV and depository, until 1414, of crown jewels of Holy Roman Empire. Popular summer resort of Budnany (bŏŏd'nyänĭ), Czech *Budňany*, is just S, on Berounka R.

Karluck, Alaska: see Karluk.

Karluk (kär'lŭk), village (pop. 41), S Alaska, W Kodiak Isl., on Shelikof Strait, 80 mi. WSW of Kodiak; salmon fishing (cannery at Uyak Bay.) Near by is salmon hatchery. Sometimes spelled Karluck.

Karluv Tyn, Czechoslovakia: see Karlstejn.

Karlyuk (kŭrlyōōk'), town (1939 pop. over 500), SE Chardzhou oblast, Turkmen SSR, on S spur of the Baisun-Tau, 65 mi. ESE of Kerki; cotton, wheat.

Karma, Anglo-Egyptian Sudan: see Kerma.

Karma (kär'mŭ), town (pop. 2,918), Allahabad dist., SE Uttar Pradesh, India, 10 mi. S of Allahabad; gram, rice, barley, wheat, oilseeds, sugar cane.

Karma, Ras, Socotra: see Qadhub.

Karmakchi (kŭrmŭkchē'), village (1926 pop. 2,280), central Kzyl-Orda oblast, Kazakh SSR, on the Syr Darya, near Trans-Caspian RR (Dzhusaly station), and 85 mi. NW of Kzyl-Orda; rice.

Karmala (kŭrmä'lŭ), town (pop. 7,310), Sholapur dist., E central Bombay, India, 70 mi. NW of Sholapur; market center for millet, oilseeds, cattle; handicraft cloth weaving, dal milling, cotton ginning.

Karmanovo (kŭrmä'nŭvŭ), village (1939 pop. over 500), NE Smolensk oblast, Russian SFSR, 20 mi. NNW of Gzhatsk; flax.

Karmaskaly (kŭrmŭskä'lē), village (1926 pop. 3,001), central Bashkir Autonomous SSR, Russian SFSR, 27 mi. SSE of Ufa; distilling; wheat, truck, livestock.

Karmir Bazar, Azerbaijan SSR: see Krasny Bazar.

Karmoy (kärm'ûü), Nor. *Karmøy*, island (□ 68; pop. 16,541) in North Sea at mouth of Bokn Fjord, Rogaland co., SW Norway, separated from mainland by narrow sound; 18 mi. long (N–S), 6 mi. wide. Harbors at Kopervik, Skudeneshavn, Akrahamn, Avaldsnes, Torvastad. Copper mining at Visnes. Fishing (herring, mackerel, lobster). Sometimes spelled Karmö.

Karnack (kär'năk), village, Harrison co., NE Texas, 14 mi. NE of Marshall; Caddo L. State Park (hunting, fishing, boating) is just NE.

Karnak (kär'năk), **El Karnak,** or **Al-Karnak** (both: ĕl), village (pop. 10,865), Qena prov., Upper Egypt, on E bank of the Nile and 1 mi. NE of Luxor, 450 mi. S of Cairo. Consists of New Karnak (pop. 3,700) and Old Karnak (pop. 7,165). Occupies part of site of anc. Thebes; it has the famous temple of Amon (Ammon) or temple of Karnak, with the "Great Hall of Columns" in front of it and with avenues of sphinxes on either side. Temple was founded by the 1st monarchs of the XII dynasty, and from the Middle Empire to the Ptolemaic period most of the Pharoahs added to the shrine. The ruins of Karnak, of which the temple of Amon is the most important, are considered among the most beautiful in the world.

Karnak (kär'năk), village (pop. 792), Pulaski co., extreme S Ill., 23 mi. NNE of Cairo; logging, lumber milling.

Karnal (kŭrnäl'), district (□ 3,126; pop. 994,575), E Punjab, India; ⊙ Karnal. Bounded E by Jumna R.; has several enclaves in Patiala and East Punjab States Union (NW); irrigated by Western Jumna Canal system. Agr. (wheat, gram, millet, maize, rice, cotton); hand-loom weaving. Chief towns: Panipat (famous battleground), Karnal, Kaithal, Shahabad. Area has many anc. sites connected with legends of Mahabharata (see Kurukshetra).

Karnal, town (pop. 37,444), ⊙ Karnal dist., E Punjab, India, 140 mi. SE of Jullundur, just E of Western Jumna Canal; trade center for grain, salt, metal, corn, cotton; vegetable-oil and saltpeter refining, agr. machinery mfg., button making, hand-loom weaving, liquor and perfume distilling; dairy farm, metalworks. Scene of Nadir Shah's victory (1739) over Mogul emperor, Muhammad Shah.

Karnali River, Tibet and Nepal: see Gogra River.

Karnaphuli River (kŭr'nŭpōōlē), in Assam (India) and East Bengal (E Pakistan), rises in W Lushai Hills, flows S, past Barkal, and SW, past Rangamati and Chittagong, to Bay of Bengal 8 mi. SSW of Chittagong; 146 mi. long. Navigable by steamer to Rangamati. Hydroelectric project.

Karnaprayag, India: see Chamoli.

Karnatak, India: see Kanara, region.

Karnatic, India: see Carnatic.

Karnaticgarh, peak, India: see Javadi Hills.

Karnaukhovka (kŭrnŭōō'khŭfkŭ), town (1926 pop. 3,735), central Dnepropetrovsk oblast, Ukrainian SSR, 5 mi. E of Dneprodzerzhinsk.

Karnes (kärnz), county (□ 758; pop. 17,139), S Texas; ⊙ Karnes City. Drained by San Antonio R. Agr.: corn, grain sorghums, flax (a leading U.S. flax co.); also cotton, peanuts, fruit, truck; livestock (cattle, horses, sheep, turkeys). Oil, natural-gas wells, clay, fuller's earth deposits. Formed 1854.

Karnes City, town (pop. 2,588), ⊙ Karnes co., S Texas, c.50 mi. SE of San Antonio, near San Antonio R.; trade, shipping center in cotton, corn, flax, truck, livestock area; cotton gins, hatcheries. Settled 1885, inc. 1914.

Karnische Alpen, Austria and Italy: see Carnic Alps.

Karnobat (kärnôbät'), city (pop. 10,225), Burgas dist., E Bulgaria, 26 mi. WNW of Burgas; rail junction; sheep-raising center, cattle market. Has ruins of Turkish fortress.

Karns City, borough (pop. 508), Butler co., W Pa., 12 mi. NE of Butler; oil refinery.

Kärnten, Austria: see Carinthia.

Karo La (kä'rō lä'), pass (alt. c.15,000 ft.) in E Himalayas, S Tibet, on main India-Lhasa trade route and 15 mi. WSW of Nagartse. In 1904, scene of battle bet. Tibetans and British expedition under Younghusband.

Karolyvaros, Yugoslavia: see Karlovac, Croatia.

Karonga (kärông'gä), town (pop. 205), Northern Prov., Nyasaland, port near N tip of L. Nyasa, 140 mi. NNE of Mzimba; 9°54'S 33°55'E. Fishing; rice, cotton. Landing field. Arab slave-trading center in 1880s, '90s. Attacked by Germans, 1914.

Karoola (kŭrōō'lŭ), village (pop. 133), N Tasmania, 12 mi. N of Launceston; oil shale.

Karoonda (kărōōn'dŭ), village (pop. 341), SE South Australia, 75 mi. ESE of Adelaide; rail junction; agr. center; wheat.

Karor (kŭrōr'), town (pop. 4,696), Muzaffargarh dist., SW Punjab, W Pakistan, 80 mi. NNW of Muzaffargarh; wheat, dates. Sometimes called Karor Lal Isa.

Karora (kärō'rä), Ital. *Carora*, village, on Eritrea-Anglo-Egyptian Sudan border, near Red Sea, on Asmara–Port Sudan road, and 70 mi. SE of Tokar; frontier and police posts; livestock market.

Karos (kä'rôs) or **Keros** (kĕ'rôs), Aegean island (□ 6; pop. 10) in the Cyclades, Greece, SE of Naxos isl.; 36°52'N 25°40'E; 4 mi. long, 1.5 mi. wide; fisheries.

Karpacz (kär'päch), Ger. *Krummhübel* (krŏŏm'-hü"bŭl), commune (1939 pop. 2,209; 1946 pop. 10,543) in Lower Silesia, after 1945 in Wroclaw prov., SW Poland, near Czechoslovak border, in the Riesengebirge, at N foot of the Schneekoppe, on small river (irrigation dam) and 9 mi. S of Hirschberg (Jelenia Gora); popular health and winter-sports resort. Large orphanage here. Until early 19th cent., noted for its trade in medicinal herbs.

Karpas Peninsula (kärpäs'), NE promontory of Cyprus, juts c.50 mi. into the Mediterranean, narrowing from a c.10-mi.-wide base to Cape Andreas. It is traversed by outliers of the Kyrenia or Karpas Mts. Sometimes spelled Carpas or Karpass.

Karpatalja, Ukraine see Transcarpathian Oblast.

Karpathos (kär'pŭthôs), Ital. *Scarpanto* (skärpän'-tō), Lat. *Carpathus* (kär'pŭthŭs), third largest island (□ 111; pop. 7,396) in the Dodecanese, Greece, in Aegean Sea, SW of Rhodes (separated by 30-mi.-wide Karpathos Strait; shipping route); bet. 35°25'N and 35°50'N, at 27°10'E. It is 30 mi. long, 2–6 mi. wide; rises to 3,986 ft. Barley, wheat, olive oil, grapes, chick-peas, potatoes; stock raising (sheep, goats); fishing; gypsum deposits. Airport. Main town, Pegadia or Pigadhia (pop. 1,002), is on SE shore.

Karpatska Ukraina, Ukrainian SSR: see TRANSCARPATHIAN OBLAST.
Karpenesion or **Karpenision** (both: kärpĕnē'sēôn), town (pop. 3,796), ⊙ Eurytania nome, central Greece, 35 mi. W of Lamia (linked by road); alt. 3,280 ft., highest nome capital of Greece; livestock center; dairy products (cheese, milk). Seat of bishop. Marco Bozzaris fell here (1823) in battle against the Turks. Also spelled Karpenission.
Kärpf (kĕrpf), peak (9,178 ft.) in Glarus Alps, E central Switzerland, 4 mi. E of Linthal.
Karpilovka (kŭrpē'lŭfkŭ), village (1939 pop. over 500), S Bobruisk oblast, Belorussian SSR, 37 mi. SSW of Bobruisk; food products.
Karpinsk (kŭrpēnsk'), city (1939 pop. over 10,000), W Sverdlovsk oblast, Russian SFSR, in NE foothills of the central Urals, on railroad (Bogoslovsk station) and 23 mi. WNW of Serov; bituminous-coal-mining center. Known as Bogoslovsk or Bogoslovski Zavod prior to First World War; called Ugolny c.1935–41; became city in 1941 and renamed Karpinsk for Rus. geologist Alexander Karpinski. Aluminum refinery 5 mi. E at Krasnoturinsk.
Karpogory (kŭrpŭgô'rē), village (1926 pop. 684), S Archangel oblast, Russian SFSR, on Pinega R. and 120 mi. ESE of Archangel; lumbering.
Karpushikha (kŭrpōōshē'khŭ), town (1939 pop. over 500), SW central Sverdlovsk oblast, Russian SFSR, 8 mi. NW (under jurisdiction) of Kirovgrad, on rail spur; copper- and zinc-mining center, supplying Kirovgrad refinery.
Karradi (kär-rä'dē), village, Muntafiq prov., SE Iraq, on the Shatt al Gharraf and 50 mi. N of Nasiriya; grain, dates.
Karrats Fjord (kä'räts fyōr'), inlet (70 mi. long, 3–17 mi. wide) of Baffin Bay, W Greenland; 71° 30'N 53°W. Separated from Umanak Fjord (S) by Ubekendt and Upernivik isls. Receives large glacier at its head. Mts. rise steeply to over 7,000 ft. on both shores. Extends 40-mi. arm (N), called Uvkusigsat Fjord.
Karrgruvan (chĕr'grü"vän), Swedish *Kärrgruvan*, village (pop. 1,520), Vastmanland co., central Sweden, in Bergslag region, 7 mi. NE of Fagersta; iron mining, metalworking. Vacation resort. Includes Spannarhyttan (spĕ'närhü'tän), Swedish *Spännarhyttan*, and Kallmorberget (käl'môrbĕr"-yüt), mining villages.
Karroo, plateau area of U. of So. Afr.: see SOUTHERN KARROO; GREAT KARROO; NORTHERN KARROO.
Kars (kärs), prov. (□ 7,107; 1950 pop. 409,138), NE Turkey, on USSR line; ⊙ Kars. The Aras and Arpa Chai rivers form part of border with Armenian SSR; on S are Aras Mts.; in SE is Mt. Ararat, near Iranian line. Arsenic and some gold at Kagizman; also lignite. Mountainous and heavily forested. Stock raising and agr. The region was taken from the Turks by the Russians many times in 19th cent.; last returned to Turkey by treaty in 1921.
Kars, anc. *Chorsa*, town (1950 pop. 20,524), ⊙ Kars prov., Turkey, on Kars R., on railroad, 110 mi. ENE of Erzurum, 40 mi. SW of Leninakan (USSR), in a mountainous region; alt. 5,750 ft.; 40°42'N 43°5'E. Market for butter, cheese, hides, cattle, sheep; wheat, barley, potatoes. An old fortified town of Armenia, with a 16th-cent. fortress, it was taken from the Turks by the Russians in 1828, 1855, and finally annexed in 1878. Returned to Turkey 1921 by terms of a treaty with USSR.
Karsakpai or **Karsakpay** (kŭrsŭkpī'), town (1932 pop. estimate 15,000), W Karaganda oblast, Kazakh SSR, on railroad and 320 mi. SW of Karaganda; has copper smelter (fed by Dzhezkazgan mines), power plant.
Karsava (kär'sävä), Lettish *Kārsava*, Ger. *Karsau*, Rus. (until 1917) *Korsovka*, city (pop. 1,870), E Latvia, in Latgale, 23 mi. NE of Rezekne, near Russian SFSR border, in lumbering area. In Rus. Vitebsk govt. until 1920.
Karseong, India: see KURSEONG.
Karshi (kär'shē), city (1932 pop. estimate 20,400), ⊙ Kashka-Darya oblast, Uzbek SSR, on the Kashka Darya, on railroad and 250 mi. SW of Tashkent; 38°52'N 65°47'E. Center of fertile oasis (wheat, cotton, sericulture); food processing, distilling, wool washing, metalworking, light mfg. Rail branch to Kitab. Has 16th-cent. mausoleum and mosque. Named Bek-Budi from c.1925 to 1937. Karshi town, on railroad and 4 mi. S, absorbed c.1940.
Karsiang, India: see KURSEONG.
Karskiye Vorota (kär'skēü vŭrô'tŭ) [Rus.,=Kara gates], strait joining Barents (W) and Kara (E) seas of Arctic Ocean, off Russian SFSR, bet. Novaya Zemlya (N) and Vaigach Isl. (S); 30 mi. wide, 20 mi. long. Sometimes called Kara Strait.
Karsovai or **Karsovay** (kŭrsŭvī'), village, N Udmurt Autonomous SSR, Russian SFSR, 22 mi. ENE of Glazov; flax.
Kars River (kärs), NE Turkey, rises 18 mi. NW of Kagizman, flows 55 mi. NE, past Kars, to the Arpa Chai 31 mi. E of Kars.
Karst (kärst), Serbo-Croatian *Kras* (kräs), Ital. *Carso* (kär'zô), limestone plateau (up to 1,946 ft.) in Dinaric Alps, NW Yugoslavia and Free Territory of Trieste, N of Istria. Extends c.50 mi. bet. lower Isonzo R. (NW) and the N Kvarner (gulf; SE). A barren region, characterized by a sink (karst) topography interspersed with abrupt ridges, and by funnel-like caverns (notably POSTOJNA) and underground streams, the largest of which is the Reka (Timavo).
Karsun or **Karsun'** (kŭrsōōn'yŭ), town (1926 pop. 5,269), NW Ulyanovsk oblast, Russian SFSR, on Barysh R. (right tributary of Sura R.) and 55 mi. WSW of Ulyanovsk; road center; hemp milling.
Karszulkadriye, Turkey: see KADIRLI.
Kartaba, Lebanon: see QARTABA.
Kartabo (kärtä'bō), locality, Essequibo co., N central Br. Guiana, at confluence of Cuyuni and Mazaruni rivers, 4 mi. SW of Bartica. Starting point for near-by gold-mining region (Peter's Mine).
Kartal (kärtäl'), town (pop. 14,842), Istanbul prov., NW Turkey in Asia, on Gulf of Izmit, 14 mi. SE of Istanbul; grain market.
Kartalinia, Georgian SSR: see KARTLIA.
Kartaly (kŭrtä'lē), city (1933 pop. estimate 13,500), SE Chelyabinsk oblast, Russian SFSR, on left tributary of Tobol R., on S. Siberian RR and 70 mi. ESE of Magnitogorsk; rail junction (locomotive and car repair shops); chromium and anthracite mining; metalworking. Became city in 1944, absorbing anthracite mines of Poltavka (just N; 1926 pop. 2,982).
Kartarpur (kŭrtär'pŏŏr), town (pop. 12,150), Jullundur dist., central Punjab, India, 8 mi. NW of Jullundur; agr. market center (wheat, gram, cotton, maize); hand-loom weaving; known for carpentry (chairs, tables, boxes). Visited annually by Sikh pilgrims.
Karthalinian Range (kärthŭlĭ'nēŭn), S spur of the E Greater Caucasus, in NE Georgian SSR; extends in arc from Mt. Barbalo c.50 mi. SW and S to area NE of Tiflis; forms watershed bet. Iora and Aragva rivers.
Karthaus, Poland: see KARTUZY.
Kartlia (kärt'lēŭ) or **Kartalinia** (kärtŭlĭ'nēŭ), Rus. *Kartliya* or *Kartaliniya*, hilly central region of Georgian SSR, bet. Trialet Range (S) and outliers of the central Greater Caucasus; drained by middle Kura R. Grain, orchards. The heart of Georgia, it contains cities of Gori and Tiflis. Sometimes spelled Karthlia or Karthalinia.
Kartsa (kär'tsŭ), village (1939 pop. over 500), E North Ossetian Autonomous SSR, Russian SFSR, 3 mi. ENE of Dzaudzhikau; fruit and vegetable processing, woodworking. Until 1944 (in Chechen-Ingush Autonomous SSR), called Sholkhi.
Kartuzy (kärtōō'zĭ), Ger. *Karthaus* (kärt'hous), town (1946 pop. 5,991), Gdansk prov., N Poland, 18 mi. W of Danzig; mfg. of bricks, mineral water; sawmilling, brewing, tanning; resort center.
Karubwe (kärōō'bwä), township (pop. 22), Central Prov., Northern Rhodesia, on railroad and 20 mi. NNE of Lusaka; tobacco, wheat, corn; cattle, sheep, goats.
Karuizawa (kärōōē'zäwŭ), town (pop. 13,781), Nagano prefecture, central Honshu, Japan, 22 mi. E of Ueda; mtn. resort; dairying. Hot springs near by.
Karumai (kärōō'mī), town (pop. 8,011), Iwate prefecture, N Honshu, Japan, 13 mi. SSW of Hachinohe; rice, wheat, charcoal, lumber, livestock.
Karun, Birket, Egypt: see BIRKET KARUN.
Karun River (kärōōn'), biblical *Ulai*, anc. *Euloeus*, in Khuzistan, SW Iran, rises in the Kuh-i-Rang in the Bakhtiari country S of Khunsar, flows SE, W, and NW, through tortuous gorges of parallel Zagros ranges, enters Khuzistan plain at Shushtar, where it forms 2 arms which reunite further S, then flows past Ahwaz and Shadgan, to the Shatt al Arab at Khurramshahr on Iraq line; 500 mi. long. Navigable below Shushtar, though navigation is interrupted by rapids at Ahwaz, it is the chief navigable river of Iran; opened to foreign trade in 1888. Receives the Ab-i-Diz (right). Irrigation dam is projected at Shushtar.
Karur (kŭrōōr'). **1** Town, S Bombay, India: see KERUR. **2** City (pop. 27,575), Trichinopoly dist., S Madras, India, on Amaravati R. and 45 mi. WNW of Trichinopoly; road center in agr. area; cotton textiles, tobacco, plantain, chilis; peanut- and castor-oil extraction. Seasonal temple-festival markets. Industrial school and workshop (rattan furniture, smithery).
Karuvi, India: see KARWI.
Karuzi (kärōō'zē), village, central Ruanda-Urundi, in Urundi, 28 mi. NE of Kitega; cinchona and aleurite plantations; tropical plant nurseries.
Karvasaras, Greece: see AMPHILOCHIA.
Karvina or **Karvinna** (kär'vĭnä), Czech *Karviná* or *Karvinná*, Ger. *Karwin* (kär'vēn), Pol. *Karwina* (kärvē'nä), city (pop. 27,463), NE Silesia, Czechoslovakia, 8 mi. E of Ostrava; rail junction; major coal-mining center of OSTRAVA-Karvina coal basin. Part of TESCHEN territory. High-grade coal mined here has led to intensive local development of chemical industry (notably production of fertilizers), gasworks, and coke ovens. Also has iron mines and ironworks. Municipal area was enlarged in 1949 by inc. of former independent town of Frystat, Czech *Fryštát*, Ger. *Freistadt*, 4 mi. NE, on Olse R.
Karwar (kär'vär), town (pop. 15,812), ⊙ Kanara dist., S Bombay, India, port on Arabian Sea, on Karwar Bay (estuary), 305 mi. SSE of Bombay; market center for rice, fish, coconuts, timber; fish curing (mackerel, sardines, catfish), fruit canning, furniture mfg. English established factory near by (trade in pepper); used 1638 to 1752, when captured by Portuguese.
Karwendelgebirge (kärvĕn'dŭlgŭbĭrgŭ), range of Bavarian Alps, in Tyrol, W Austria, extending c.20 mi. WNW from the Inn at Schwaz to Ger. border at Scharnitz Pass; highest peak, Birkkar (9,042 ft.). Isar R. rises here.
Karwi (kŭr'vē), town (pop. 10,310), Banda dist., S Uttar Pradesh, India, on tributary of the Jumna and 40 mi. ESE of Banda; trade center (gram, jowar, wheat, cotton, oilseeds, rice). In 19th cent., residence of a Mahratta leader who built several temples. Sometimes called Karuri.
Karwin, Czechoslovakia: see KARVINA.
Karyagino (kŭryä'gēnŭ), city (1926 pop. 3,160), S Azerbaijan SSR, 28 mi. SSE of Agdam; wheat; clothing mfg. Formerly also called Sardar.
Karyai or **Kariai** (both: kärēä'), village (1928 pop. 305), ⊙ Mount Athos autonomous dist., Macedonia, Greece, on Akte prong of Chalcidice peninsula, 10 mi. NW of cape Akrathos.
Karymskoye (kŭrĭm'skŭyŭ), town (1948 pop. over 2,000), S central Chita oblast, Russian SFSR, on Trans-Siberian RR, on Ingoda R. and 45 mi. SE of Chita; cement plant. Tarski junction (rail branch to Manchuria) is just E.
Karystos or **Karistos** (both: kä'rĭstôs), Lat. *Carystus* (kurĭ'stŭs), town (pop. 2,901) SE Euboea, Greece, port on Bay of Karystos, 55 mi. SE of Chalcis; important marble quarries; sheep raising; fisheries. Site of anc. Carystus on slope of Mt. Oche (NE) is occupied by medieval ruins. Present town dates from Gr. war of independence.
Karystos, Bay of, or **Bay of Karistos,** inlet of Aegean Sea, in SE Euboea, Greece, bet. capes Mandeli (E) and Paximadi (W); 6 mi. long.
Karytaina or **Karitaina** (both: kŭrē'tĕnŭ), village (pop. 892), Arcadia nome, central Peloponnesus, Greece, on road and 8 mi. NW of Megalopolis; remains of noted 13th-cent. French castle.
Kas, river, Russian SFSR: see KAS RIVER.
Kas (käsh), Turkish *Kaş*, village (pop. 588), Antalya prov., SW Turkey, port on Mediterranean Sea 75 mi. SW of Antalya; wheat, barley, sesame, vetch. Formerly Andifli.
Kasaan (kŭsăn'), village (pop. 47), SE Alaska, on Kasaan Bay, on E shore of Prince of Wales Isl., 35 mi. WNW of Ketchikan; fishing; cannery. Haida Indian settlement.
Kasaan Bay, SE Alaska, inlet (35 mi. long, 2–8 mi. wide) of Clarence Strait, E Prince of Wales Isl., 25 mi. WNW of Ketchikan, near 55°31'N 132°25'W; fishing. Sparsely settled by Haida Indians. Kasaan village on N shore.
Kasaba, Turkey: see TURGUTLU.
Kasada. 1 Village, Mie prefecture, Japan: see INABE. **2** Town, Wakayama prefecture, Japan: see KASEDA.
Kasagi (kä"sä'gē), town (pop. 3,344), Kyoto prefecture, S Honshu, Japan, 21 mi. SSE of Kyoto; rice, wheat, lumber.
Kasai (käsī'), province (□ 124,111; 1948 pop. 1,882,385), central and S Belgian Congo, bounded S by Angola; ⊙ Lusambo. Drained by the Kasai and its tributaries. Savanna and wooded savanna in S, E, and W; N section is part of central Congo rain forest. Extensive cultivation of cotton, coffee, food staples (manioc, rice, yams, sweet potatoes, corn, plantains, groundnuts) for export to Katanga and Rhodesia. Cattle raising in Lomami region. The famous diamond fields of Tshikapa and Bushimaie rivers supply the international market with both the industrial diamonds and gems. There are 2 railroads: the Port-Francqui to Bukama line and a short section owned by the diamond mines (Charlesville–Makumbi). Kasai, Sankuru, Lukenie, and lower Lulua rivers are transport routes. Chief centers: Lusambo, Luluabourg, Luebo, Kabinda, Port-Francqui, Basongo. Prov. was called Lusambo, 1935–47.
Kasai, district, Belgian Congo: see LUEBO.
Kasai (käsī'), town (pop. 6,790), Shizuoka prefecture, central Honshu, Japan, 6 mi. NE of Hamamatsu; cotton textiles.
Kasai River, Port. *Cassai*, one of principal tributaries of Congo R., in S central Africa, rises on central plateau of Angola S of Alto Chicapa, flows E (parallel to Benguela RR) to Teixeira de Sousa area, then turns suddenly N, forming Angola–Belgian Congo border for c.250 mi., and arches NW across W Belgian Congo, past Tshikapa, Charlesville, Basongo, and Mushie to the Congo at Kwamouth. Total length, over 1,100 mi. An important trade artery, it is navigable from its mouth c.475 mi. to WISSMANN FALLS, and again bet. Makumbi and Mai Munene above the falls. Chief tributaries are the Lulua, Sankuru, and Fimi (right), and the Chicapa and Kwango (left). Lower course (below Mushie) known as the Kwa. Diamonds washed in Tshikapa region. Sometimes spelled Kasaï.
Kasai River, in Bihar and West Bengal, India, rises on E Chota Nagpur Plateau, W of Purulia; flows c.215 mi. generally SE, past Raipur and Midna-

pore, to Hooghly R. 15 mi. SW of Diamond Harbour. In lower course, called Haldi.

Kasaji (käsä'jē, käsäzhē'), village, Katanga prov., SE Belgian Congo, on railroad and 150 mi. SW of Kamina; trading center; rice processing. Protestant mission.

Kasama (kä"sä'mä), town (pop. 13,120), Ibaraki prefecture, central Honshu, Japan, 12 mi. W of Mito, in agr. area (rice, tobacco); pottery, bamboo ware, dyeing utensils.

Kasama (käsä'mä), township (pop. 1,383), ⊙ Northern Prov. (□ 53,000; pop. 450,000), NE Northern Rhodesia, 400 mi. NE of Lusaka, on Great North Road; 10°12'S 31°11'E. Corn, wheat; market gardening; cattle, sheep, goats. Airport. Chishimba Falls just NW. Was ⊙ former Awemba prov.

Kasamatsu (käsä'mätsōō), town (pop. 10,931), Gifu prefecture, central Honshu, Japan, on Kiso R. and 3 mi. S of Gifu; silk textiles.

Kasanga (käsäng'gä), town, Western Prov., SW Tanganyika, small port on S shore of L. Tanganyika, near Northern Rhodesia border, 45 mi. SW of Sumbawanga; fishing; tobacco, wheat, corn; cattle, sheep, goats. Known as Bismarckburg under Ger. rule.

Kasangulu (käsäng-gōō'lōō), village, Leopoldville prov., W Belgian Congo, on railroad and 18 mi. SSW of Leopoldville; native trade center; hardwood lumbering. R.C. and Protestant missions.

Kasaoka (käsä'ōkä), town (pop. 19,257), Okayama prefecture, SW Honshu, Japan, on Hiuchi Sea, 8 mi. E of Fukuyama; commercial center in agr. area (rice, wheat); cotton, textiles, raw silk.

Kasar, Cape (käsär'), headland of NE Africa on the Red Sea, marking border bet. Anglo-Egyptian Sudan and Eritrea; 18°2'N 38°34'E.

Kasaragod (kä'sŭrŭgōd), town (pop. 11,566), South Kanara dist., W Madras, India, on Malabar Coast of Arabian Sea, 27 mi. SSE of Mangalore; fish curing (sardines, mackerel); coconuts, mangoes, rice. Handicraft spinning and weaving 20 mi. SSE, at village of Nileshwar; pottery-clay pits. Sometimes spelled Kasargod.

Kasasa (kä"sä'sä) or **Kasasuna** (käsä'sōōnä), town (pop. 19,834), Kagoshima prefecture, S Kyushu, Japan, on SW Satsuma Peninsula, 24 mi. SW of Kagoshima, on E.China Sea; agr. center (rice, wheat); raw silk, livestock, timber.

Kasatka (kŭsät'kŭ), village (1948 pop. over 500), on E coast of Iturup Isl., S Kuriles, Russian SFSR, port on Hitokappu Bay (best-protected bay of isl.; 6 mi. long, 5 mi. wide), 17 mi. SW of Kurilsk; whale factory. Under Jap. rule (until 1945), called Toshimoe (tōshēmō'ē). From here Jap. fleet sailed (1941) to attack Pearl Harbor.

Kasauli (kŭsou'lē), town (pop., including cantonment area, 2,749), E Patiala and East Punjab States Union, India, 19 mi. SW of Simla; hill resort (alt. c.6,300 ft.) in Siwalik Range. Has Pasteur Inst., medical research institute, food laboratory. Distillery near by. Formerly in exclave of Ambala dist., Indian Punjab.

Kasawara (käsä'wärŏŏ), town (pop. 10,116), Gifu prefecture, central Honshu, Japan, 3 mi. SE of Tajimi; pottery making.

Kasba, E Pakistan: see JESSORE, town.

Kasbah Tadla, Fr. Morocco: see KASBA TADLA.

Kasba Lake (43 mi. long, 6-23 mi. wide), SW Keewatin Dist., Northwest Territories, near Mackenzie Dist. and Manitoba borders; 60°20'N 102°15'W. Drains N into Kazan R. through Ennadai L.

Kasba Tadla (käsbä' tädlä'), town (pop. 9,175), Casablanca region, W central Fr. Morocco, on the upper Oum er Rbia and 105 mi. SE of Casablanca, at foot of the Middle Atlas; 32°35'N 6°17'W. Road junction; agr. trade center (grain, livestock, lumber). Kasba Zidania Dam is 11 mi. SW. Town has one of Morocco's most imposing *casbahs*. Founded end of 17th cent. as a Berber fortress. Occupied by French in 1913, and served as hq. for pacification (1914–33) of the Middle Atlas region. Also spelled Kasbah Tadla.

Kasba Zidania Dam, Fr. Morocco: see OUM ER RBIA.

Kasbek, Mount, Georgian SSR: see KAZBEK, MOUNT.

Kaschau, Czechoslovakia: see KOSICE.

Kaseda (kä"sä'dä). **1** Town (pop. 22,494), Kagoshima prefecture, S Kyushu, Japan, on W Satsuma Peninsula, 18 mi. SW of Kagoshima; rice-producing center; sake breweries; raw silk, wheat. **2** or **Kasada** (kä"sä'dä), town (pop. 7,064), Wakayama prefecture, S Honshu, Japan, on W Kii Peninsula, 18 mi. ENE of Wakayama, in agr. area (rice, citrus fruit); raw silk; spinning.

Kasempa (käsĕm'pä), township (pop. 225), Western Prov., NW Northern Rhodesia, 220 mi. NW of Lusaka; corn, beeswax. Transferred 1946 from Kaonde-Lunda prov. Was ⊙ former Kasempa prov.

Kasenga (käsĕng'gä), village, Katanga prov., SE Belgian Congo, on Luapula R., on Northern Rhodesia border, and 120 mi. NE of Elisabethville; customs station and head of navigation on the Luapula; mfg. of ice; fisheries. R.C. mission.

Kasenyi (käsĕn'yē), village, Eastern Prov., E Belgian Congo, on L. Albert (Uganda border) and 30 mi. E of Irumu; terminus of lake navigation from Uganda side, customs station and fishing port. Has a research center for study of trypanosomiasis and is also known as tourist center and base for excursions to the alligator grounds of the Semliki. Bogoro agr. center with Protestant mission is 10 mi. W.

Kasese (käsĕ'sä), village, Kivu prov., E Belgian Congo, 295 mi. SE of Stanleyville; tin-mining center; also wolfram and tantalite mining.

Kasganj (käs'gŭnj), town (pop. 28,465), Etah dist., W Uttar Pradesh, India, 55 mi. NE of Agra; rail junction; trade center (wheat, pearl millet, barley, corn, jowar, mustard, cotton, sugar cane); sugar refining, coir-rope mfg.

Kasha, Al, Aden: see QASHA, AL.

Kashaf River (käshäf'), in Khurasan, NE Iran, rises in the Binalud Range 50 mi. NW of Meshed, flows 150 mi. SE, through Meshed valley, to the Hari Rud (Tedzhen R.) on USSR-Iranian border. Used for irrigation (wheat, barley).

Kashagawigamog Lake (10 mi. long, 1 mi. wide), S Ont., extends SW from Haliburton.

Kashan (gä'shän'), Mandarin *Chia-shan* (jyä'shän'), town (pop. 10,296), ⊙ Kashan co. (pop. 220,103), NE Chekiang prov., China, near Kiangsu line, 60 mi. NE of Hangchow, and on railroad to Shanghai; rice, wheat.

Kashan (käshän'), city (1939 pop. 44,994), Second Prov., N central Iran, 110 mi. S of Teheran across Namak L. salt flats; former ⊙ Kashan prov.; road and trade center on branch of Trans-Iranian RR; alt. 3,260 ft.; 33°59'N 51°27'E. Agr.: wheat, melons, figs. Noted for manufacture of fine Kashan rugs; copperware, silk; has cotton-spinning factory. Was once center of ceramic art in Iran. City is surrounded by gardens and orchards. Fine palace, 4 mi. SW, was 19th-cent. imperial summer residence. Kashan prov. was inc. (1938) into Iran's Second Prov. (see TEHERAN).

Kashar (kä'shär) or **Kashari** (kä'shärē), village (1930 pop. 795), W central Albania, on Tirana-Durazzo RR and 5 mi. W of Tirana; linked (since 1949) by 4-mi. rail spur with W industrial outskirts of Tirana.

Kashary (kŭshä'rē), village (1939 pop. over 2,000), N Rostov oblast, Russian SFSR, 30 mi. ENE of Millerovo; flour milling, metalworking.

Kashega (kŭshē'gŭ), village (1939 pop. 26), NW Unalaska Isl., Aleutian Isls., SW Alaska, 40 mi. SW of Dutch Harbor; sheep ranching. School.

Kashegelok (kŭshē'gŭlŏk), Eskimo village (1939 pop. 10), SW Alaska, on lower Holitna R. and 110 mi. SE of Holy Cross; trapping. Formerly spelled Kashegaluk.

Kashgar (kăsh'gär), Chinese *Shufu* (shōō'fōō') or *Su-fu* (sōō'fōō'), town (1945 pop. estimate 50,000) and oasis (1943 pop. 256,844), westernmost Sinkiang prov., China, near W edge of Taklamakan Desert, on Kashgar R. and 660 mi. WSW of Urumchi, 70 mi. from USSR border; 39°29'N 75°58'E. Caravan center of W Sinkiang at junction of routes from Aksu, Yarkand, and Khotan, and connected with Kirghiz SSR via Turugart Pass road (N) and Irkeshtam (W). Mfg. of cotton and wool textiles, rugs, gold and silver jewelry; flour milling, cheese processing, tanning. Visited c.1275 by Marco Polo, who spelled it Cascar, it passed 1760 to China. Opened to foreign trade in 1860. Was hq. of Yakub Beg, leader of the Moslem (Dungan) revolt (1861–78). It is sometimes called Kashgar Kona Shahr [Uigur, =Kashgar old town]. The new town (5 mi. SE) is known as YANGI SHAHR.

Kashgar Range, China: see MUZTAGH ATA RANGE.

Kashgar River, W Sinkiang prov., China, rises as the Kizil Su (Qizil Su) just across the USSR border in the Trans-Alai Range, flows 300 mi. E, past Kashgar, toward the Yarkand R., but disappears into the desert. Intermittent flow in lower course; irrigation.

Kashiagamiut (kăshēä'gŭmūt), Eskimo village (1939 pop. 33), SW Alaska, on Togiak R. and 60 mi. WNW of Dillingham; trapping.

Kashihara (käshē'härŏŏ) or **Kashiwara** (käshē'wärŏŏ), town (pop. 22,305), Osaka prefecture, S Honshu, Japan, 7 mi. E of Osaka; commercial center for agr. area (rice, wheat).

Kashii (käshē'), town (pop. 6,306), Fukuoka prefecture, N Kyushu, Japan, 5 mi. NNE of Fukuoka, on Hakata Bay; rail junction; rice, barley, wheat. Site of Shinto shrine dedicated to Empress Jingo (3d cent.).

Kashima (kä'shĭmä). **1** Town (pop. 4,809), Fukushima prefecture, N Honshu, Japan, 7 mi. SSE of Nakamura; rice, raw silk. **2** Agr. town (pop. 3,588), Ibaraki prefecture, central Honshu, Japan, 20 mi. NW of Choshi; on E shore of lagoon Kitaura. Has prefectural agr. school. Known for Shinto shrine said to have been founded in 7th cent. B.C. **3** Town (pop. 10,842), Saga prefecture, W Kyushu, Japan, on E Hizen Peninsula, 22 mi. ESE of Sasebo; rice, raw silk, charcoal.

Kashin (kä'shĭn), city (1939 pop. over 10,000), SE Kalinin oblast, Russian SFSR, on Kashinka R. (right affluent of the Volga) and 70 mi. ENE of Kalinin; distilling center; flax processing, clothing mfg., meat packing. Health resort (ferruginous springs, mud baths). Dates from 1237; passed (1486) to Moscow.

Kashing (gä'shĭng'), Mandarin *Chia-hsing* (jyä'shĭng'), town (pop. 53,374), ⊙ Kashing co. (pop. 420,252), N Chekiang prov., China, on Grand Canal and 50 mi. NE of Hangchow, and on railroad to Shanghai; commercial and silk center; mfg. (silk goods, gauze). Trades in rice, beans, poultry.

Kashino (käshē'nō), town (pop. 3,616), Okayama prefecture, SW Honshu, Japan, on Harima Sea, 12 mi. E of Okayama, in agr. area (rice, wheat, pears, peppermint); saltmaking.

Kashipur (kä'shēpŏŏr), town (pop. 13,223), Naini Tal dist., N Uttar Pradesh, India, on tributary of the Ramganga and 33 mi. SW of Naini Tal; rail and road junction; sugar milling; trades in rice, wheat, oilseeds, gram, corn, cloth. Anc. Hindu temple and fort ruins near by.

Kashira (kŭshē'rŭ), city (1939 pop. over 10,000), S Moscow oblast, Russian SFSR, on right bank of Oka R. and 65 mi. SSE of Moscow, in picturesque location. Industrial center; lumber, food products, clothing articles, metal goods. Mfg. of electric locomotives at Stupino, 5 mi. NNW; power plant near by, at KAGANOVICH. Founded (late-17th cent.) on left bank of river as fortress under Ivan the Terrible; later moved to present location. During Second World War, successfully defended (1941) against Ger. spearhead in Moscow campaign.

Kashirinskoye, Russian SFSR: see OKTYABRSKOYE, Chkalov oblast.

Kashirskoye (kŭshēr'skŭyŭ). **1** Fishing village (1939 pop. 607), NW Kaliningrad oblast, Russian SFSR, on Courland Lagoon, 17 mi. NNE of Kaliningrad. Until 1945, in East Prussia and called Schaaksvitte (shäks'vĭ"tŭ). **2** Village (1939 pop. over 2,000), central Voronezh oblast, Russian SFSR, 23 mi. SE of Voronezh; wheat.

Kashitu (käshē'tōō), township (pop. 45), Western Prov., N central Northern Rhodesia, on railroad and 50 mi. S of Ndola; tobacco, wheat, corn.

Kashiwa (kä"shē'wä), town (pop. 18,338), Chiba prefecture, central Honshu, Japan, 7 mi. NE of Matsudo; agr. (rice, wheat), poultry; raw silk.

Kashiwabara, Russian SFSR: see SEVERO-KURILSK.

Kashiwara, Japan: see KASHIHARA.

Kashiwazaki (kä"shĭwä'zäkē), city (1940 pop. 29,567; 1947 pop. 36,649), Niigata prefecture, central Honshu, Japan, on Sea of Japan, 47 mi. SW of Niigata; oil center; oil refining. Has agr. school. Sometimes spelled Kasiwazaki.

Kashka-Darya or **Kashka-Dar'ya** (käsh"kŭ-dŭryä'), oblast (□ 11,300; 1946 pop. estimate 300,000), SE Uzbek SSR; ⊙ Karshi. Bounded E by the Baisun-Tau; drained by the Kashka Darya. Cotton growing, orchards in Shakhrisyabz-Kitab area; wheat, cotton, sericulture in irrigated Karshi oasis; elsewhere, dry farming (wheat) and karakul sheep breeding. Kagan-Stalinabad RR passes NW–SE, with branch to Kitab. Pop.: Uzbeks, Tadzhiks. Formed 1943. An earlier oblast of this name existed 1924–26.

Kashka Darya or **Kashka-Dar'ya**, river in S Uzbek SSR, rises in W Gissar Range, flows c.200 mi. SW, past Kitab, and NW past Karshi, disappearing into sands of Kyzyl-Kum desert near Kagan. Stalinabad-Kagan RR runs along lower course.

Kashka-Su (käsh"kŭ-sōō'), village, central Tyan-Shan oblast, Kirghiz SSR, just W of Kum-Bel; tungsten mining.

Kashkatau, Russian SFSR: see SOVETSKOYE, Kabardian Autonomous SSR.

Kashlyk, USSR: see SIBIR.

Kashmar (käshmär'), town (1939 pop. 12,052), Ninth Prov., in Khurasan, NE Iran, on edge of salt desert, 110 mi. SW of Meshed; agr. (cotton, grain, raisins, fruit, opium). Produces silk. Originally called Sultanabad; later Turshiz or Torshiz. Present village of Sultanabad is 23 mi. E, on road to Turbat-i-Haidari.

Kashmir (kăshmēr', kăsh'mēr), officially **Jammu and Kashmir** (jŭ'mōō) or, formerly, **Kashmir and Jammu**, Sanskrit *Kasmir*, state (□ 82,258; 1941 pop. 4,021,616; 1950 pop. estimate 4,370,000) of the Indian subcontinent, S central Asia, the object, following partition of India in 1947, of conflicting Indian and Pakistani claims. Its traditional capitals have been Srinagar (summer) and Jammu (winter). Bordered E by Tibet, N by China (Sinkiang), NW by Afghanistan; E and N frontiers are undefined. Region is almost wholly mountainous and is dominated by some of world's highest peaks and largest alpine glaciers. INDUS RIVER, which crosses Kashmir from E to W, separates PUNJAB HIMALAYAS (S) from the great KARAKORAM mtn. system (N), both having a NW–SE axis. Along SW boundary, bet. Ravi and Jhelum rivers, is narrow stretch of outwash plain (1,000–1,500 ft.) sloping upwards to a series of low, broken ridges (2–4,000 ft.), including Siwalik Range in E. These hills in turn merge with the Lesser Himalayas, rising to 10–15,000 ft. in PIR PANJAL RANGE, a S spur of Great Himalayan range forming S border of Vale of Kashmir. This picturesque valley (85 mi. long, 20 mi. wide; alt. 5–6,000 ft.), known as Kashmir proper, comprises upper Jhelum R. basin and is floored with fertile fluvio-glacial and lacustrine deposits; WULAR LAKE, DAL LAKE, and city of Srinagar are situated here. Jhelum, Chenab, and Ravi rivers all flow S into W Pakistan, feeding Punjab's important irrigation canals. To the N, the Great Himalayan range extends from NANGA PARBAT (26,660 ft.) c.240 mi. SE to Indian border (19,000 ft.); Nunkun peak, in center, rises to 23,410 ft. The Indus valley forms a deep, narrow trench, 4,000 ft. high in W, where it bends around W end of the Himalayas, and 11,000 ft. high in E, where it separates ZASKAR RANGE (S) and LADAKH RANGE (N); main Indus affluents in Kashmir are Shyok, Suru, and Gilgit rivers. The Karakoram ranges, in N, averaging 20–23,000 ft., rise to 25,550 ft. in Rakaposhi, 26,470 ft. in Gasherbrum, and 28,250 ft. in K^2 (Mt. Godwin Austen) peaks and contain the great Baltoro, Biafo, and Siachen glaciers. NE corner of Kashmir is part of lofty Tibetan plateau, a desolate region (16–17,000 ft. high) dotted with numerous brackish lakes. State has great variety of climate, from semitropical submontane section in SW to alpine zones of the higher mtn. areas. Annual rainfall ranges from 51 in. in Punch and 40 in. in Udhampur to 5 in. in Gilgit; precipitation at higher altitudes is mostly snow. In Kashmir Valley temp. varies bet. 99°F. (July max.) and 11°F. (Jan. min.), while at Leh, in E Indus valley, max. summer temp. often reaches 120°F. and min. winter temp. drops below 0°F. Vegetation consists of scrub and bamboo below 5,000 ft., deodar, pine, fir, plane, and spruce bet. 6,000 and 11,000 ft., rhododendron and juniper at c.12,000 ft.; forests cover about ⅙ of total area. Because of mountainous terrain only 5% or some 2,300,000 acres of land is cultivated, mainly in SW valleys, where corn, wheat, rice, and barley are chief crops; buckwheat is grown at higher altitudes; in Ladakh a hardy type of barley is chief food staple. In Kashmir Valley fruitgrowing (apples, pears, peaches, cherries) is important. Sheep, goats, ponies, and yaks are raised, especially in remote frontier tracts of Ladakh, Baltistan, and Gilgit, where nomadic shepherds form bulk of sparse pop. Lumbering and sericulture are main non-agr. occupations, with wood carving and silk weaving the principal "cottage" industries. Other handicrafts for which Kashmir is famous include woolen textiles (cashmere shawls), carpets, papier-mâché, silverware, and leather goods. There are processing factories at SRINAGAR (silk, wool), JAMMU, MIRAN SAHIB (resin), BARAMULA (wood), and Nawanshahr (sugar). Mineral deposits (coal, iron ore, bauxite, indianite, slate, limestone, sapphires) are worked on a small scale. Tourism in the beautiful Vale of Kashmir is important source of revenue; Srinagar (houseboating on near-by lakes) and GULMARG (skiing) are well-known resorts. Polo is believed to have originated in NW Kashmir. Because of mountainous topography communications are poor. Access by road to Kashmir Valley is from Rawalpindi and Abbottabad (in W Pakistan) in the W and from Sialkot (Pakistan) and, since 1949, Pathankot (India) in the S; only rail line links Jammu with Sialkot; airport at Srinagar. Caravan routes to Gilgit and Leh cross the Himalayas through Burzil Pass and Zoji La respectively; Yarkand, in Sinkiang, is reached from LEH via Karakoram Pass (alt. 18,290 ft.). State's pop. (c.90% rural) is concentrated in the SW and is predominantly Moslem (77%); Hindus, mainly in Jammu prov., constitute 20%, Sikhs 1½%, and Buddhists, in E Ladakh, 1%. However, Kashmiris, Moslems and Hindus alike, belong to same cultural group and have many of same customs and local loyalties. Literacy is low (7%) and genuine political consciousness almost nonexistent. The Moslems may be grouped into Shaikhs, Sayids, Moguls, and Pathans, while the Hindus are mostly Brahmans, who are commonly called Pandits. S border country is home of Dogra community, a Rajput clan. Principal languages: Kashmiri, Punjabi, Western Pahari. In anc. Aryan times Kashmir was ruled by Brahman dynasties, but later came temporarily under control of Buddhist empires of Asoka (3d cent. B.C.) and the Kushans (1st cent. A.D.). During subsequent period (to early-14th cent.) of Hindu rule many fine 5th–10th-cent. temples were built, such as those at ANANTNAG and Awantipur; White Huns invaded the country in c.530; Hsüan-tsang visited (631) SW parts; several noted Sivaite philosophers lived in Kashmir in 9th and 10th cent. About 1339 a Moslem vizier seized power and became 1st sultan of Kashmir; in late-14th cent. Sikandar, the "idol-breaker," began oppressive rule, in which many Hindus were exiled or forcibly converted to Islam; his son, Zain-ul-abidin (1420–70), was an enlightened ruler and a patron of art and learning, both Moslem and Hindu. After region was annexed to Mogul empire in 1586, Vale of Kashmir became favorite resort of emperors Akbar, Jahangir, and Aurangzeb. Moguls were forced to cede Kashmir to Durrani Afghans in 1756, who, in turn, were driven out by the Sikhs under Ranjit Singh in 1819. For services rendered to the Sikhs, Gulab Singh, a Dogra, was made (1820) raja of Jammu; he soon acquired control over much of SW Kashmir, Ladakh, and Baltistan. At conclusion of 1st Anglo-Sikh War, during which he remained neutral, Gulab Singh received sovereignty, by treaty (1846) with British, over all mountainous country bet. Ravi and Indus rivers. With subjugation of Kashmir Valley and Gilgit all of Kashmir was united under the Dogra maharajas of Jammu and Kashmir. Permanent Br. Resident established (1885) at Srinagar. In 1947, after partition of India into dominions of India and Pakistan, a largely Moslem-supported revolt against the state govt. developed—upon maharaja's accession to India—into a civil war bet. "free Kashmir" insurgents aided by Pathan tribesmen and, later, by Pakistan army units infiltrating from NW Pakistan, and Kashmir govt. forces (mostly Dogras) and Indian troops, who had been flown in at the maharaja's request. In Jan., 1948, dispute was brought before U.N. Security Council, which proposed a cease-fire and certain truce terms; cease-fire took effect (Jan., 1949) along line running roughly parallel to W border from Mirpur dist. (S) to central Muzaffarabad dist., thence E into Ladakh mts.; N and W of line was Pakistan-held territory, while S and E was Indian-administered area. Both sides agreed in principle to a plebiscite, but working out of details caused breakdown in negotiations. State comprises JAMMU prov., consisting of Jammu, Kathua, Udhampur, Doda, Riasi (renamed Rajaori), and Mirpur dists. and Punch and Chineni dependencies; Kashmir prov., consisting of Anantnag, Baramula, and Muzaffarabad dists.; and frontier dists. of LADAKH, ASTOR, and GILGIT. Formerly also Cashmere.

Kashmir, province (□ 8,539; pop. 1,728,705) of Kashmir state; ⊙ Srinagar. Comprises dists. of Anantnag, Baramula, and Muzaffarabad.

Kashmir, Vale of, beautiful intermontane valley in the Himalayas, W Kashmir, drained by upper Jhelum (Veth) R.; 85 mi. long (NW–SE), c.20 mi. wide; average alt. 5,300 ft. Surrounded by lofty peaks (12–16,000 ft.) of Pir Panjal and main Himalayan ranges and containing a wealth of scenic grandeur, the valley is one of the garden spots of the East and a famous tourist attraction. Places of interest include SRINAGAR, largest city and ⊙ Kashmir, DAL LAKE (houseboating), WULAR LAKE, ANANTNAG (noted springs), Gulmarg (hill resort), and Vernag (source of Jhelum at near-by spring). Area is Kashmir's commercial and pop. center, noted for its wool and silk weaving and wood carving; fertile alluvial soil yields rice, corn, fruit (apples, pears), and vegetables. Main approaches to valley are by road over Banihal Pass (SE) from Jammu and through Jhelum gorge near Baramula (NW) from W Pakistan; airport at Srinagar. Long known for its beauty, the "happy valley" was visited by Mogul emperors, especially Jahangir, who built fine gardens and bldgs. here. Also called Kashmir Valley.

Kashmir North, district, Kashmir: see BARAMULA, district.

Kashmir South, district, Kashmir: see ANANTNAG, district.

Kashmor (kŭshmōr'), village, Upper Sind Frontier dist., N Sind, W Pakistan, 70 mi. ENE of Jacobabad; rail terminus; rice, millet; lacquerware.

Kasho-to, Formosa: see HWOSHAO ISLAND.

Kashpirovka, Russian SFSR: see SYZRAN.

Kashubia, region, Poland: see KASSUBIA.

Kasi, India: see BENARES, city.

Kasia (kŭs'yŭ), village, Gorakhpur dist., E Uttar Pradesh, India, 34 mi. E of Gorakhpur. Reputed site of anc. Kusangara or Kusinagara is 1 mi. W; scene of Buddha's death and cremation; one of 8 anc. great places of Buddhist pilgrimage. Buddhist remains include a large red sandstone image of the dying Buddha, carved at Mathura during Gupta period, and stupa ruins.

Kasibuggapalasa (käsēbŏŏ"gŭpŭlä'sŭ), town (pop. 9,214), Vizagapatam dist., NE Madras, India, 70 mi. NE of Vizianagaram; consists of 2 adjacent former villages of Kasibugga and Palasa. Trades in products (bamboo, tanning bark, lac) of forested hills (W); handmade paper. Salt pans SE, on Bay of Bengal.

Kasiglook (käsēg'lŏŏk), village (pop. 111), SW Alaska, near Bethel.

Kasilof (kŭsē'lŭf), fishing village (pop. 74), S Alaska, W Kenai Peninsula, on Cook Inlet, 65 mi. WNW of Seward. Site of Russian settlement, established 1786, called St. George.

Kasim, Saudi Arabia: see QASIM.

Kasimbazar, India: see COSSIMBAZAR.

Kasimov (kŭsē'mŭf), city (1926 pop. 13,007), NE Ryazan oblast, Russian SFSR, on Oka R. and 70 mi. ENE of Ryazan; linen milling, distilling, metalworking; clothing goods. Has several relics of Tatar domination (minaret, mausoleum of Tatar princes), regional mus. Dates from 12th cent. (then named Meshcherski Gorodets); passed 1393 to Moscow; chartered and named Kasimov (1467); was ⊙ Tatar principality (15th–17th cent.).

Kasindi (käsēn'dē), village, Kivu prov., E Belgian Congo, on N shore of L. Edward, 90 mi. NNE of Costermansville; customs station on Uganda border.

Kasioei, Indonesia: see WATUBELA ISLANDS.

Kasiui, Indonesia: see WATUBELA ISLANDS.

Kasiwazaki, Japan: see KASHIWAZAKI.

Kaskaskia (kăs"kă'skēŭ), village (pop. 112), Randolph co., SW Ill., on Kaskaskia Isl. (c.6 mi. long) in the Mississippi, at mouth of Kaskaskia R., 6 mi. W of Chester. On Mississippi bluffs near by is Fort Kaskaskia State Park (old earthworks and cemetery; Pierre Menard House, built 1802), which commemorates historic past of region. Jesuit missionaries established in 1703 a settlement (site now inundated by the Mississippi) at an Indian village; grew to be agr. community and French trading post, one of chief centers of the Illinois country. Fort Kaskaskia (built 1733 by the French) was destroyed in 1763 upon British occupation of region, which was in turn taken in 1778 for U.S. by George Rogers Clark. The turbulence following Clark's departure (1780) was succeeded by a period of growth when Kaskaskia became ⊙ Ill. Territory and, upon statehood (1818), ⊙ Ill. Shifting of capital to Vandalia in 1820 and disastrous floods in late-19th cent., which cut through peninsula to inundate town site and create present Kaskaskia Isl., ended existence of old town.

Kaskaskia River, central and SW Ill., rises near Urbana, flows c.320 mi. generally SW across state to the Mississippi just NW of Kaskaskia.

Kaskelen (kŭskyĭlyĕn'), village (1948 pop. over 500), SW Alma-Ata oblast, Kazakh SSR, 15 mi. W of Alma-Ata and on Kaskelen R. (left tributary of Ili R.); sawmilling.

Kasko (käsk'ŭ"), Swedish *Kaskö*, Finnish *Kaskinen* (käs'kĭnĕn), city (pop. 1,758), Vaasa co., W Finland, on Gulf of Bothnia, 50 mi. S of Vaasa; timber-shipping port; rail terminus. Pop. is largely Swedish-speaking. Founded 1785.

Kaskong (käs'kông'), town, Kampot prov., SW Cambodia, minor port on Gulf of Siam, 85 mi. NW of Kampot, near Thailand line; fishing center.

Kasli (käs'lyē), city (1936 pop. estimate 23,100), N Chelyabinsk oblast, Russian SFSR, in SE foothills of the central Urals, bet. 2 lakes, 55 mi. NW of Chelyabinsk; metallurgical center; ironware mfg.; corundum mining. Founded 1746 as copper-smelting plant; pig iron produced since 1770; became city in 1942. Formerly called Kaslinski Zavod.

Kaslo (kăz'lō), city (pop. 468), SE B.C., in Selkirk Mts., on Kootenay L., 35 mi. NNE of Nelson; silver, lead, zinc mining and smelting, lumbering (cedar), fruit ranching (noted for cherries). Resort.

Kasoda (kä'sōdŭ), town (pop. 6,947), East Khandesh dist., NE Bombay, India, 22 mi. SW of Jalgaon; local market for cotton, peanuts.

Kasongo (käsông'gō), town, ⊙ Maniema dist. (□ 39,279; 1948 pop. c.355,000), Kivu prov., E Belgian Congo, on Lualaba R. and 200 mi. SW of Costermansville; trading center for cotton, palm kernels, ground nuts, and African staples (manioc, yams, plantain); cotton ginning. Airport. Lualaba R. is navigable bet. here and Kibombo. R.C. mission of Kasongo-Saint-Charles, 7 mi. NE, built on site of Arab slave-traders' fort, still preserves remains of fortifications and cemetery of the Arab campaign (1890–94).

Kasongo Lunda (lōōn'dä), village, Leopoldville prov., SW Belgian Congo, on right bank of Kwango R. (Angola border) and 165 mi. SW of Kikwit; customs station; native trade; coffee, fibers.

Kasos (kä'sôs), Ital. *Caso* (kä'zō), Lat. *Casus* (kā'sŭs), Aegean island (□ 25; pop. 1,322) in the Dodecanese, Greece, SW of Karpathos and separated from E Crete by 30-mi.-wide Kasos Strait; 35°23'N 26°55'E; 8 mi. long, 4 mi. wide; rises to 1,972 ft. Sponge-fishing center; agr. (olives, fruit, barley, wine); gypsum deposits. Main town, Fry (Fri) or Kastro (pop. 410), is on NW shore. Participated in Greek War of Independence, conquered (1824) by the Egyptian navy.

Kasota (kŭsō'tŭ), village (pop. 600), LeSueur co., S Minn., on Minnesota R. and 9 mi. N of Mankato, in agr. area (corn, oats, barley, livestock, poultry). Limestone quarries here.

Kasperske Hory (kăsh'pĕrskä hô'rĭ), Czech *Kašperské Hory*, Ger. *Bergreichenstein* (bĕrk"rī'khŭnshtīn"), town (pop. 1,272), SW Bohemia, Czechoslovakia, 6 mi. SSE of Susice, in foothills of Bohemian Forest; lumbering; basketwork. Former gold-mining settlement. Rejstejn (rā'stān), known for toy making, is 2 mi. W, on Otava R.

Kaspi (käs'pē), town (1939 pop. over 2,000), central Georgian SSR, on railroad, on Kura R. and 22 mi. WNW of Tiflis; cement works.

Kaspichan (käspēchän'), village (pop. 1,534), Kolarovgrad dist., E Bulgaria, on Provadiya R. and 3 mi. S of Novi Pazar; rail junction; grain, truck.

Kaspisk, Kaspiisk, or **Kaspiysk** (kŭspēsk'), city (1947 pop. over 10,000), E central Dagestan Autonomous SSR, Russian SFSR, on Caspian Sea, 8 mi. SE of Makhachkala; industrial center (engine and machine mfg.). Developed in late 1930s; called (1936–47) Dvigatelstroi. Made city in 1947.

Kaspiski, Kaspiiski, or **Kaspiyskiy** (kŭspē'skē), town (1939 pop. over 2,000), SE Astrakhan oblast, Russian SFSR, on Caspian Sea, 70 mi. SW of Astrakhan; fish-canning center. Until 1944 (in Kalmyk Autonomous SSR), Lagan or Logan.

Kasplya (käs'plyŭ), village (1926 pop. 1,138), W Smolensk oblast, Russian SFSR, on Kasplya R. and 20 mi. NW of Smolensk, potatoes, flax.

Kasplya River, in W European Russian SFSR and Belorussian SSR, rises in Smolensk oblast ENE of Rudnya, flows SE, N, past Kasplya, and generally W, past Demidov (head of navigation), to Western Dvina R. at Surazh (Vitebsk oblast); 100 mi. long.

Kasr, for Arabic and Persian names beginning thus: see QASR.

Kasrik, Turkey: see GURPINAR.

Kas River or **Greater Kas River** (käs), Rus. *Bolshoi Kas* or *Bol'shoy Kas*, W Krasnoyarsk Territory, Russian SFSR, flows 165 mi. NE to Yenisei R. above Yartsevo. Receives the **Lesser Kas River,** Rus. *Maly Kas* or *Malyy Kas* (55 mi. long), which is connected with Ket R. (tributary of Ob R.) by OB-YENISEI CANAL SYSTEM.

Kassa, Czechoslovakia: see KOSICE.

Kassaba, Turkey: see TURGUTLU.

Kassala (käsä'lä, kă'sůlů), province (□ 134,450; 1948 pop. estimate 716,104), NE Anglo-Egyptian Sudan; ⊙ Kassala. Bordered NE by Red Sea, E by Eritrea, SE by Ethiopia. The Etbai, a massive mtn. range (up to 7,400 ft. high), borders Red Sea coast. Prov. is drained by Atbara R. and by lower courses of Barka and Gash rivers, which lose themselves in Nubian Desert. Irrigated agr. (especially cotton) near Kassala and Tokar. Nomadic stock grazing. Gold mining at Gebeit (near Red Sea). Pop. concentrated in sub-humid S scrublands. Chief towns are PORT SUDAN, Kassala, Gedaref, all on railroad to Sennar. Suakin harbor is falling into disuse.

Kassala, city (pop. 36,000), ⊙ Kassala prov., NE Anglo-Egyptian Sudan, on intermittent Gash R. (irrigation), near Eritrea border, on railroad to Port Sudan and Sennar, and 260 mi. E of Khartoum, at foot of the Jebel Kassala; 15°28'N 36°25'E. Commercial and agr. center, in major cotton zone; other crops are wheat, barley, corn, fruit. Trade in gum arabic, hides. Rail spur to Tessenei (Eritrea). Airport. Founded 1834 as Egyptian military camp. Held (1885–94) by Mahdists and later (1894–97) by Italy. Briefly occupied (1940–41) by Italians in unsuccessful invasion of Sudan during Second World War.

Kassala, Jebel (jĕ'bĕl), mountain, just NE of Kassala, E Anglo-Egyptian Sudan, near Eritrea border; rises to 4,415 ft.

Kassan (kŭsän'). **1** Village (1926 pop. 6,224), W Kashka-Darya oblast, Uzbek SSR, on railroad, on the Kashka Darya and 17 mi. NW of Karshi; silk milling, food processing. **2** Town, Namangan oblast, Uzbek SSR: see KASSANSAI.

Kassandra (kůsän'drů), anc. *Pallene* (pălē'nē), westernmost of the 3 arms of the Chalcidice peninsula, Greek Macedonia, on Aegean Sea, bet. Gulf of Salonika and Toronaic Gulf; 30 mi. long, 5 mi. wide; rises to 1,090 ft. Terminates in Capes Poseidion (SW) and Kanastraion (SE). On narrow isthmus at its base stood anc. Potidaea.

Kassandra, Cape, Greece: see POSEIDION, CAPE.

Kassandra, Gulf of, Greece: see TORONAIC GULF.

Kassansai or **Kassansay** (kŭsŭnsī'), town (1926 pop. 18,705), N Namangan oblast, Uzbek SSR, on S slope of Chatkal Range, 18 mi. NNW of Namangan, in cotton- and silkgrowing area; orchards. Until 1930s called Kassan. Orto-Tokoi reservoir, on the short Kassan-Sai, is N of here.

Kassel or **Cassel** (both: kă'sůl, Ger. kä'sůl), city (1939 pop. 216,141; 1946 pop. 127,568; 1950 pop. 161,322), ⊙ former Prussian prov. of Hesse-Nassau, W Germany, after 1945 in Hesse, on the Fulda (small harbor) and 90 mi. NNE of Frankfurt; 51°19'N 9°28'E. Rail hub and industrial center, mfg. (concentrated in N and E suburbs) locomotives, railroad coaches, cars, trucks, machinery, scientific and optical instruments, textiles (linen, wool, cotton, canvas), dyes, polish, paper, printed matter, pottery. Lignite mining in W outskirts. A center of Ger. airplane and tank production in Second World War, it was all but obliterated (75% destroyed) by Allied bombing, and none of its former handsome palaces, museums, theaters, and other public bldgs. escaped destruction or serious damage. Thousands perished in the ruins. Destroyed were the Ger. tapestry mus. (collection transferred to castle Wilhelmshöhe) and the baroque Karlskirche. Heavily damaged were: the 2 Gothic churches; baroque Orangerie castle in the Karlsaue, a large park in English style; monumental 20th-cent. town hall; the numerous museums, including the world-renowned picture gallery (most of the valuable collection of Flemish and Dutch paintings was saved). Large state library (founded 1586) and contents were burned down. Castle Wilhelmshöhe (near W suburb of WAHLERSHAUSEN) sustained light damage. First mentioned 913, Kassel was chartered in 12th cent. Was residence of landgraves of Hesse until 1567, when it became ⊙ HESSE-KASSEL. Occupied by French (1752–58). Was ⊙ kingdom of Westphalia (1807–13). City became (after 1866) ⊙ newly formed Prussian prov. of Hesse-Nassau and was retained as a residence of the Ger. emperors. Captured by U.S. troops in April, 1945.

Kasserine (kăs'ůrēn, Fr. käsrēn'), town (pop. 5,825), ⊙ Kasserine dist. (□ 3,597; pop. 123,035), W Tunisia, at foot of the Djebel Chambi, 40 mi. ESE of Tebessa (Algeria) and 135 mi. SW of Tunis; road and rail junction; center of newly irrigated agr. area. Zinc and lead deposits. Near by are ruins of anc. *Cillium*, including 2 Roman mausoleums. At **Kasserine Pass** (5 mi. NW; 2 mi. wide; crossed by road and rail), the spearhead of a German flanking attack (Feb., 1943) was contained by Allies in a decisive battle of the Tunisian campaign, in Second World War.

Kassidiares or **Kassidiaris,** Greece: see NARTHAKION.

Kasson, village (pop. 1,353), Dodge co., SE Minn., 15 mi. W of Rochester, in grain, livestock, potato area; dairy products, flour. Settled 1865, inc. 1870.

Kassubia (kăsōō'bēů, kŭ-) or **Kashubia** (kă-shōō'-bēů, kŭ-), Pol. *Kaszuby* (kä-shōō'bĭ), region in NW part of Gdansk prov., N Poland, extends inland from the Baltic and Hel Peninsula; centered on Gdynia, Wejherowo, and Kartuzy. Of ethnological importance, it is inhabited by Kashubes, a Slavonic people speaking Kassubian, a W Slavic language.

Kastamonu (kästä'mônōō), province (□ 5,491; 1950 pop. 411,576), N Turkey, on Black Sea; ⊙ Kastamonu. On S are Ilgaz Mts.; drained by Gok, Devrez, Arac, and Koca rivers. Coal and lignite in W, mercury, copper, chromium, and arsenic in scattered areas. Well forested. Wheat, oats, barley, rice, spelt, hemp, apples; mohair goats. Sometimes spelled Kastamuni.

Kastamonu, town (1950 pop. 13,688), ⊙ Kastamonu prov., N Turkey, near Gok R., 110 mi. NNE of Ankara; arsenic, textiles; wheat, hemp, mohair goats. Sometimes spelled Kastamuni.

Kastav (kä'stäf), Ital. *Castua* (kä'stōōä), village, NW Croatia, Yugoslavia, near Adriatic Sea, 6 mi. WNW of Rijeka (Fiume). Was ⊙ Liburnia, a dist. of anc. Illyria.

Kasteelbrakel, Belgium: see BRAINE-LE-CHÂTEAU.

Kastel (kästĕl'), former suburb (pop. 4,353) of MAINZ (connected by tramway), after 1945 inc. into Wiesbaden, Hesse, W Germany, on right bank of the Rhine (bridge) and 5 mi. SSE of Wiesbaden city center; watercraft repair shops. Built on site of Roman *Castellum Mattiacorum*.

Kastelanska Rivijera (kä'shtĕlänskä rĭvēyĕ'rä), Serbo-Croatian *Kaštelanska Rivijera*, Dalmatian resort area, S Croatia, Yugoslavia, extending c.6 mi. along Adriatic Sea, bet. Split and Trogir. Consists of 7 small villages or hamlets (including KASTEL SUCURAC), each named after a Venetian castle. Also called Kastela, Serbo-Croatian *Kaštela*, Ital. *Castèlli*, or Sedam Kastela, Serbo-Croatian *Sedam Kaštela* [=seven castles].

Kastelli (kůstĕ'lē), village (pop. 1,859), Canea nome, W Crete, port on Gulf of Kisamos, 14 mi. W of Canea; citrus fruits, wheat, carobs; olive oil, dairy products (milk, cheese). Sometimes called Kastellion; formerly Kisamos.

Kastellorizo (kästĕlô'rĭzô), Ital. *Castelrosso* (kästĕl-rôs'sō), easternmost island (□ 3.5; pop. 800) in the Dodecanese, Greece, in Mediterranean Sea, off small Turkish port of Kas; 36°8'N 29°35'E; 3.5 mi. long, 1.5 mi. wide. Olive oil, wine; sponge fishing. Occupied by France during First World War, it passed 1921 to Italy and was developed as a naval base. The near-by islets were ceded to Italy by Turkey in 1932. Awarded to Greece 1947–48. Sometimes spelled Castellorizo.

Kastell Paol, France: see SAINT-POL-DE-LÉON.

Kastel Sucurac (kă'stĕl sōō'tyōōräts), Serbo-Croatian *Kastel Sućurac*, village, S Croatia, Yugoslavia, in Dalmatia, on Adriatic Sea, on railroad and 3 mi. N of Split, in the Kastelanska Rivijera; mfg. (cement, plastics).

Kastl (kä'stůl), village (pop. 2,099), Upper Palatinate, central Bavaria, Germany, on small Lauerach R. and 12 mi. NE of Neumarkt; grain, livestock. Has former Benedictine abbey (1103–1803). Chartered 1323.

Kastoria (kästôrē'ů), nome (□ 667; pop. 63,935), Macedonia, Greece; ⊙ Kastoria. Bounded NW by Albania, SW by the Grammos, and NE by the Vernon, it contains L. Kastoria and is drained by upper Aliakmon R. Lumbering, charcoal burning; wheat, bean, and tobacco growing. Formed after Second World War.

Kastoria, Macedonian *Kostur*, anc. *Celethrum* or *Celetrum*, city (pop. 11,121), ⊙ Kastoria nome, Macedonia, Greece, in intermontane basin, 19 mi. SSW of Phlorina and 90 mi. W of Salonika, on peninsula extending into L. Kastoria (fisheries); known for its fur processing, trade center for wheat, wine, fruit, timber, charcoal, beans, skins. Bishopric. Remains of Byzantine architecture. Known as Kesrieh or Kesriyeh under Turkish rule.

Kastoria, Lake (□ 11.6), in Greek Macedonia, Greece, 16 mi. SSW of Phlorina; 4 mi. long 3 mi. wide; fisheries. Kastoria is on peninsula jutting out from W shore. Also called L. Orestias.

Kastornoye (kŭstôr'nŭyů), village (1948 pop. over 10,000), NE Kursk oblast, Russian SFSR, 45 mi. WNW of Voronezh; rail junction; site of sugar refinery.

Kastos (kästôs'), island (□ 2.7; pop. 285) in Ionian Sea, Greece, in Acarnania nome, 4 mi. off central Greek mainland (E); 38°35'N 20°55'E; 4½ mi. long, ½ mi. wide, rises to 520 ft.; oak trees; fisheries.

Kastri. 1 Village, Argolis, Greece: see HERMIONE. **2** Village, Phocis, Greece: see DELPHI.

Kastrikum, Netherlands: see CASTRICUM.

Kastron (kä'strôn), also **Kastro** or **Castro** (käs'trō), name of chief town of several Aegean isls. of Greece. **1** On Chios isl., Greece: see CHIOS, city. **2** Town (pop. 3,322), ⊙ and W coast port of Lemnos isl., Greece; 39°52'N 25°4'E. Formerly Lemnos. **3** On Lesbos isl., Greece: see MYTILENE.

Kastrop, Germany: see CASTROP-RAUXEL.

Kastrup (kä'strōōp), town (pop. 5,343), Copenhagen amt, Denmark, on E coast of Amager isl. and 4 mi. SSE of Copenhagen, on the Oresund; hardware mfg., shipbuilding; airport.

Kasu, Japan: see KAZO.

Kasuga, Mount, Japan: see NARA, city.

Kasugai (käsōō'gī), city (pop. 47,164), Aichi prefecture, central Honshu, Japan, just N of Nagoya; commercial center for agr. area (rice, wheat, poultry); raw silk, textiles. Formed in early 1940s by combining former town of Kachikawa (1940 pop. 11,032) and villages of Shinogi (1940 pop. 8,186) and Toriimatsu (1940 pop. 6,231).

Kasukabe (käsōō'käbā), town (pop. 14,866), Saitama prefecture, central Honshu, Japan, 9 mi. NE of Omiya, in agr. area (rice, wheat); woodworking.

Kasulu (käsōō'lōō), village, Western Prov., W Tanganyika, 40 mi. NE of Kigoma; millet, peanuts, corn, coffee.

Kasumbalesa (käsōōmbälĕ'sä), village, Katanga prov., SE Belgian Congo, on railroad and 40 mi. SSE of Elisabethville, near Northern Rhodesia border; iron mining.

Kasumi (kä"sōō'mē), town (pop. 7,937), Hyogo prefecture, S Honshu, Japan, on Sea of Japan, 25 mi. ENE of Tottori; fishing center; raw silk, rice, wheat; sawmilling.

Kasumi-ga-ura (–gä-ōō'rä), lagoon (□ 73), Ibaraki prefecture, central Honshu, Japan, 16 mi. S of Mito; 10 mi. long, 5 mi. wide; has 3 arms (largest 8 mi. long, 3 mi. wide). Connected with Tone R. Tsuchiura on W arm. Sometimes called Nishiura.

Kasum-Ismailovo (kŭsōōm"-ēsmē'lůvů), village (1939 pop. over 500), W Azerbaijan SSR, 25 mi. E of Kirovabad; cotton. Until c.1945, spelled Kasum-Izmailovo or Kasum-Izmaylovo.

Kasumkent (kŭsōōmkyĕnt'), village (1926 pop. 1,926), SE Dagestan Autonomous SSR, Russian SFSR, in foothills of the E Greater Caucasus, 3[illegible] mi. SSW of Derbent, in orchard area; fruit processing. Pop. largely Lezghian.

Kasumpti (kŭsōōmptī'), town (pop. 139), Simla dist., E Punjab, India, an E suburb of Simla town. Small area belongs to Himachal Pradesh and is administrative hq. of its Mahasu dist.

Kasungu (käsōōng'gōō), town, Central Prov., Nyasaland, on road and 55 mi. NW of Dowa; trade center; tobacco, cotton, corn. Has govt. experimental tobacco station, African hosp.

Kasungula or **Kazungula** (käzōōng-gōō'lä), village, Southern Prov., SW Northern Rhodesia, near Zambezi R., 40 mi. W of Livingstone; fishing; corn, millet; teak. Mission. Border meeting point of Northern Rhodesia, Southern Rhodesia, Caprivi strip of South-West Africa, and Bechuanaland Protectorate. Here David Livingstone first reached the Zambezi and later turned down the river to discover Victoria Falls in 1855.

Kasur (kŭsōōr'), city (pop. 53,101), Lahore dist., E Punjab, W Pakistan, 32 mi. SSE of Lahore; rail junction; trade center (grain, cotton, cloth fabrics, oilseeds, hides); cotton ginning, flour milling, mfg. of ice, glue, leather products; hand-loom weaving; slate works. A Pathan settlement in 17th and 18th cent.

Kaszaper (kŏ'sōpĕr), town (pop. 2,225), Csanad co., SE Hungary, 20 mi. SW of Bekescsaba; grain, potatoes, cattle, hogs.

Kaszuby, region, Poland: see KASSUBIA.

Kata, Japan: see KADA.

Katada (kä"tä'dä) or **Katata** (–tä'tä), town (pop. 7,482), Shiga prefecture, S Honshu, Japan, on SW shore of L. Biwa, 12 mi. NE of Kyoto; mfg. (dyes, rayon yarn).

Kataghan, Qataghan, or **Qatghan** (all: kätgän'), province (□ 10,000; pop. 800,000), NE Afghanistan, in Afghan Turkestan; ⊙ Baghlan. Situated on N slopes of the Hindu Kush, it extends N to Panj R. (USSR line) and is drained by Kunduz R. and its tributaries. Leading cotton-growing area of Afghanistan, with gins, cottonseed mills, and soap factories at Kunduz, Khanabad (former ⊙) and Taliqan. Sugar-beet production (refinery at Baghlan); wheat, barley, corn, rice. Cotton textile mill at Pul-i-Khumri. Prov. is linked by highways with Kabul and Mazar-i-Sharif. Pop. is largely Tadzhik (Tajik) and Uzbek. Long ruled by its own mirs, it absorbed Badakh-shan in 1840 and was conquered by Afghans in 1859. Badakhshan prov. was separated in mid-1940s.

Katagum (kätä'gōōm) town (pop. 1,918), Bauchi prov., Northern Provinces, N Nigeria, on Katagum R. (branch of the Komadugu Yobe) 25 mi. SE of Hadejia; peanuts, cotton, millet; cattle, skins.

Katahdin, Mount (kůtä'dĭn) (5,268 ft.), Piscataquis co., N central Maine; highest peak in state; 20 mi. NW of Millinocket, in Baxter State Park. N terminus of Appalachian Trail.

Katahdin Iron Works, village (pop. 8), Piscataquis co., central Maine, on Silver L. and 18 mi. NNE of Dover-Foxcroft in lumbering, recreational area; site of abandoned iron mines.

Kataisk or **Kataysk** (kŭtīsk'), city (1939 pop. over 2,000), NW Kurgan oblast, Russian SFSR, on Iset R., on Trans-Siberian RR and 40 mi. WNW of Shadrinsk; agr. center; metalworks, flour mill. In 18th and 19th cent., on main access route to Siberia.

Katakai (kätä'kī), town (pop. 11,891), Chiba prefecture, central Honshu, Japan, on E coast of Chiba Peninsula, 19 mi. ESE of Chiba; fishing center; beach resort.

Katakami (kätä'-kä'mē), town (pop. 6,281), Okayama prefecture, SW Honshu, Japan, on inlet of Harima Sea, 14 mi. ENE of Okayama; rice, wheat, raw silk.

K'a-ta-k'o, Tibet: see GARTOK.

Katako Kombe (kätä'kō kōm'bā), village, Kasai prov., central Belgian Congo, on headstream of Lukenie R. and 120 mi. NNE of Lusambo; trading center in cotton area; cotton ginning.

Katakolon (kŭtä'kôlôn), village (pop. 1,022), Elis nome, W Peloponnesus, Greece, port on Cape Katakolon at N end of Gulf of Kyparissia, 7 mi. W of Pyrgos (connected by rail), for which it is the port; exports Zante currants. Founded 1857.

Katalla (kŭtă'lŭ), village (1939 pop. 23), S Alaska, 50 mi. ESE of Cordova; 60°12'N 144°32'W; center of Katalla oil field. Had pop. of 5,000 in 1908.

Katamon (kätämōn'), residential SSW suburb of Jerusalem, E Israel.

Katana (kätä'nä), village, Kivu prov., E Belgian Congo, on W shore of L. Kivu, 20 mi. N of Costermansville; noted medical research center with hospitals for Europeans and natives. Has R.C. mission, various schools for natives (including medical assistants and teachers) and small seminary. Seat of vicar apostolic of Kivu. Katana is also known as Liége-Saint-Lambert (lyāzh-sē-lābâr'). Its port on the lake is Kakondo (käkōn'dō), an agr. center with coffee and cinchona plantations.

Katana, Syria: see QATANA.

Katanga (kätäng'gä, kätägä'), prov. (□ 191,827; 1948 pop. 1,258,185), in SE Belgian Congo; ⊙ Elisabethville. Bounded W and SW by Angola, partly along Kasai R.; S and SE by Northern Rhodesia, notably along Luapula R. and L. Mweru; E by L. Tanganyika. Drained by Lualaba, Lufira, Luvua, and Lukuga rivers. Most of the territory is the Katanga Plateau (alt. 3,000–6,000 ft.), descending NW and consisting of open or park-like savanna grasslands with occasional scrub-forest; extensive papyrus swamps are along L. Upemba and L. Kisale. Its tropical climate, with dry and wet seasons, is temperated by alt. It has a great copper-mining industry and also produces tin, cobalt, manganese, zinc, platinoids, and, at Shinkolobwe, uranium. Large copper and tin smelters, mfg. of explosives and chemicals, important food processing. Cattle farms are prominent in S and W; also notable are plantations growing citrus fruit and African food staples (manioc, yams, pulse, plantains). Hydroelectric plants at Mwadingusha and Piana-Mwanga. Rail lines to Angola and Northern Rhodesia; lake steamer to Tanganyika territory; boats ply the Lualaba R.; a fair road net is in SE. Principal centers are Elisabethville, Jadotville, Albertville, Kamina, Bukama, Kabalo, and Manono. When Katanga region was 1st reached by Port. explorer Lacerda in 1798, its copper deposits were already being mined by Swahilis from E African coast. During 19th cent. it was under the fierce rule of a native chief, M'Siri, whose resistance made Katanga the last part of Congo Free State to submit to European authority (1891). Prov. was called Elisabethville, 1935–47.

Katangi (kŭtăng'gē), village, Balaghat dist., central Madhya Pradesh, India, 25 mi. W of Balaghat; rail spur terminus; shipping point for manganese brought from mines near Ramrama Tola, 10 mi. NE, to Balaghat.

Katanino (kätänē'nō), township (pop. 31), Western Prov., N Northern Rhodesia, on railroad and 40 mi. SSE of Ndola; tobacco, wheat, corn.

Katanning (kŭtă'nĭng), town (pop. 2,456), SW Western Australia, 155 mi. SE of Perth; rail junction; agr. (wheat, oats); wool.

Katano, Japan: see KONO.

Katanohara (kätä'nō'härä) or **Katawara** (kätä'wärä), town (pop. 9,885), Aichi prefecture, central Honshu, Japan, on Atsumi Bay, 12 mi. W of Toyohashi; fishing center; textiles; poultry, raw silk.

Kataoka, Russian SFSR: see BAIKOVO.

Kataragama (kŭt'ŭrŭgŭm"ŭ), village (pop. 233), Uva Prov., SE Ceylon, 45 mi. SSE of Badulla; vegetable gardens. Hindu pilgrimage center. Isolated peak (1,390 ft.) of Kataragama is 2 mi. S.

Katarnian Ghat (kŭtŭr'nyän gät'), village, Bahraich dist., N Uttar Pradesh, India, on Girwa arm of Karnali (Gogra) R. and 60 mi. NNW of Bahraich; rail terminus; connected by road with RAJAPUR (Nepal).

Katas (kŭtäs'), village, Jhelum dist., N Punjab, W Pakistan, in Salt Range, 45 mi. WSW of Jhelum. Sacred pool (alt. c.2,200 ft.), connected with Sivaite legend, visited annually by pilgrims.

Katase (kä"tä'sä), town (pop. 9,313), Kanagawa prefecture, central Honshu, Japan, on N shore of Sagami Bay, bet. Fujisawa and Kamakura; tourist resort. Connected to city by a ½-mi. bridge is islet Eno-shima (½ mi. long), known for its Shinto shrine.

Katata, Japan: see KATADA.

Katav-Ivanovsk (kŭtäf"-ēvä'nŭfsk), city (1936 pop. estimate (16,600), W Chelyabinsk oblast, Russian SFSR, in S Urals, on left tributary of Yuryuzan R., on railroad and 50 mi. NNW of Beloretsk; metallurgical center, based on Bakal iron ores; cement mfg.; quartzite and marl quarrying. Mineral springs near by. Founded 1775; became city in 1939. Formerly called Katav-Ivanovski Zavod.

Katawara, Japan: see KATANOHARA.

Katayamazu (kätäyä'mäzōō), town (pop. 7,360), Ishikawa prefecture, central Honshu, Japan, 4 mi. NE of Daishoji, on small lagoon; silk and rayon textiles; lumbering, rice growing. Saline hot springs. Formed in early 1940s by combining of Sakumi and Shiotsu.

Kataysk, Russian SFSR: see KATAISK.

Katcha (kä'chä'), town (pop. 2,190), Niger prov., Northern Provinces, W central Nigeria, port on Niger R. opposite Eggan, on railroad, and 20 mi. S of Agaie; road center; shea-nut processing, rope- and sackmaking; roofing timber; cotton, cassava, yams, durra. Sometimes spelled Kacha.

Katchall Island (kă'chŭl), one of Nicobar Islands, in Bay of Bengal, 50 mi. NNW of Great Nicobar Isl.; 12 mi. long NW-SE, 5 mi. wide.

Kateng Ssu, Tibet: see GANDEN.

Katentania (kätĕntän'yä), village, Katanga prov., SE Belgian Congo, near railroad, 65 mi. NW of Jadotville; stock raising.

Katepwa Beach (kŭtĕp'wŭ), village, SE Sask., on the Fishing Lakes, 12 mi. N of Indian Head; resort.

Kater, Cape, NW extremity of Baffin Isl., E Franklin Dist., Northwest Territories, on Prince Regent Inlet; 73°53'N 90°11'W.

Katerban, Nepal: see KADARBANA.

Katerine or **Katerini** (both: kätĕrē'nē), city (1951 pop. 31,429), Salonika nome, Macedonia, Greece, on railroad 35 mi. SW of Salonika, near Gulf of Salonika; trading center for large agr. lowland, known as Pieria; wheat, vegetables, potatoes, beans; wine; charcoal, lumber.

Katerinky (kä'tĕrzhĭn-kĭ), Czech *Kateřinky*, NE-suburb (pop. 4,505) of Opava, Silesia, Czechoslovakia, on left bank of Opava R. Has 14th-cent. chapel.

Katerinopol or **Katerinopol'** (kŭtyĭrēnô'pŭl), village (1926 pop. 7,567), S Kiev oblast, Ukrainian SSR, 37 mi. ENE of Uman; metalworks. Also called Yekaterinopol.

Katernberg (kä'tŭrnbĕrk), industrial district (since 1929) of ESSEN, W Germany, near Rhine-Herne Canal, 3.5 mi. NNE of city center; coal mining.

Kates Needle, peak (10,002 ft.) on Alaska-B.C. border, in Coast Range, 40 mi. NE of Petersburg; 57°3'N 132°3'W.

Katghora (kŭtgō'rŭ), village, Bilaspur dist., E central Madhya Pradesh, India, 40 mi. NE of Bilaspur; rice, wheat, oilseeds. Coal mining 17 mi. NNW at village of Matin.

Katha (kŭ-thä'), district (□ 7,593; 1941 pop. 290,990), Sagaing div., Upper Burma; ⊙ Katha. Astride upper Irrawaddy R.; yearly rainfall: 58 in. Agr.: rice, tea, cotton, sesame; teak and bamboo forests in hills. Gem mine at Mogok, coal at Pinlebu, gold near Wuntho. Served by Myitkyina-Mandalay RR and Irrawaddy steamers. Pop. is 55% Burmese, 25% Thai, 15% Kachin.

Katha, village, ⊙ Katha dist., Upper Burma, on left bank of Irrawaddy R. and 105 mi. SW of Myitkyina; head of branch line to Mandalay-Myitkyina RR.

Katharinaberg, Czechoslovakia: see HORA SVATE KATERINY.

Katharinenstadt, Russian SFSR: see MARKS.

Katherina, Gebel, Jebel Katherina (gĕ'bĕl kăthŭrē'nŭ, jĕ'bĕl), **Jabal Katrinah** (kätrē'nŭ), **Mount Katherine,** or **Mount Catherine,** highest peak (8,651 ft.) of Sinai Peninsula and of Egypt, 57 mi. NNW of Ras Muhammed. Two mi. N is the peak Gebel MUSA, on whose slope is the famous convent of St. Catherine.

Katherine, settlement (dist. pop. 371), NW central Northern Territory, Australia, 165 mi. SE of Darwin, Darwin-Birdum RR; peanuts.

Kathgodam, India: see HALDWANI.

Kathiawar (kä'tyäwär, –vär), peninsula (□ c. 23,000) of W India, extending into Arabian Sea bet. Gulf of Cutch (W) and Gulf of Cambay (E). Coextensive with SAURASHTRA and with AMRELI and W Ahmadabad dists. of Bombay; DIU isl. (Port. India) lies off S coast. Adjoining Gujarat, of which it is often considered part, Kathiawar is noted for its important religious sites (particularly at Dwarka, Palitana, Girnar, Somnath). From Aryan times to mid-18th cent. known as Saurashtra (*Saurastrene* to anc. Greeks and Romans). Was part of Asokan empire in 3d cent. B.C. (rock edicts at foot of Girnar hill); visited by Mediterranean sea traders, 1st and 2d cent. A.D.; under Guptas, 4th–5th cent.; ruled c.480–790 by local *Vallabhipur* dynasty. Several Rajput tribes had settled in region and established petty kingdoms by the time Moslem invasions began in 11th cent.; celebrated temple of Somnath sacked c.1025 by Mahmud of Ghazni. From 14th to 16th cent., area under sultans of Gujarat; annexed (1570s) to Mogul empire. Mahrattas, who overran country in 18th cent., called it Kathiawar after name of territory of warlike Kathi Rajputs. By 1820, all states had made treaties with British; later grouped into various political agencies (WESTERN INDIA STATES agency formed 1924), except for detached areas of Baroda state (Amreli div.). Before merger of princely states into Saurashtra in 1948, Kathiawar was divided into some 450 separate political units (exclusive of almost as many isolated enclaves). Conflicting jurisdiction as well as semi-feudal nature of princely rule contributed to general backwardness of area.

Kathib, Ras, or **Ras Kethib** (both: räs' kĕthēb'), cape on Yemen coast of Red Sea, 10 mi. NNW of Hodeida, sheltering potential deepwater harbor.

Kathima, India: see BANBASA.

Kathiri (kăthērē'), sultanate (1946 pop. 49,337) of Eastern Aden Protectorate, and one of the Hadhramaut states; ⊙ Seiyun. Extends in a 30-mi.-wide belt from central main Hadhramaut valley (where pop. is concentrated) N toward the Rub' al Khali; farming, stock raising; handicraft industries (gold- and silverwork; limekilns). In power after c.1500, the Kathiri tribe had supremacy in the Hadhramaut until challenged by the rising Quaiti tribe in 19th cent. In the developing feud, the British sided with the Quaiti and the Kathiri lost control of the seacoast. The Quaiti-Kathiri agreement of 1918, concluded under British pressure, defined territorial control of each tribe and extended the British protectorate to the Kathiri state. This agreement was reaffirmed in 1939 and an adviser treaty concluded. Since 1945, the 2 Kathiri centers of Seiyun and Tarim, previously autonomous, have been under a single administration.

Kathiwara (kŭtĭvä'rŭ), former princely state (□ 68; pop. 6,689) of Central India agency, lying in W Vindhya Range. Since 1948, merged with Madhya Bharat.

Kathmandu, Nepal: see KATMANDU.

Katholisch-Hennersdorf, Poland: see HENNERSDORF.

Kathor (kä'tōr), town (pop. 5,597), Surat dist., N Bombay, India, on Tapti R. and 8 mi. NE of Surat; local market center for millet, cotton, rice; handicraft cloth weaving, calico printing. Sometimes spelled Kathore.

Kathryn, village (pop. 200), Barnes co., SE N.Dak., 18 mi. S of Valley City.

Kathua (kŭt'wŭ), district (□ 1,023; pop. 177,672), Jammu prov., SW Kashmir; ⊙ Kathua. Bounded SW by W Pakistan, S and E by Ravi R. and Indian Punjab; Siwalik Range crosses center (NW-SE). Agr.(wheat, rice, corn, bajra, barley, oilseeds, sugar cane, cotton, spices, tobacco). Main towns: Kathua, Parol, Basoli. Pop. 74% Hindu, 25% Moslem. Prevailing mother tongue, Dogri.

Kathua, town (pop. 5,586), ⊙ Kathua dist., SW Kashmir, near the Ravi, 45 mi. SE of Jammu; rice, wheat, corn, sugar cane, oilseeds.

Kati (kätē'), village, S Fr. Sudan, Fr. West Africa, on Dakar-Niger RR and 6 mi. NW of Bamako; peanuts, shea nuts, kapok, vegetables, fruit. Military school, R.C. mission.

Kati (kä'tē), village (pop. 468), N central Perak, Malaya, 7 mi. NNW of Kuala Kangsar, on road to Grik; rubber, rice.

Katif, Saudi Arabia: see QATIF.

Katigora or **Katigorha** (kŭtĭgō'rŭ), village, Cachar dist., S Assam, India, on Barak (Surma) R. and 15 mi. WNW of Silchar; rice, tea, cotton, rape and mustard; tea processing. Also spelled **Katigara.**

Katihar (kŭt'ĭhär), town (pop., including rail settlement, 26,326), Purnea dist., NE Bihar, India, on Ganges Plain, 17 mi. SSE of Purnea; rail and road junction; trade center (corn, tobacco, wheat, sugar cane); railroad workshops; rice, jute, oilseed and flour milling, match mfg.; sheep breeding. Formerly called Saifganj.

Katima Mulilo (kätē'mŭ mōōlē'lō), village in the CAPRIVI ZIPFEL of South-West Africa, on Zambezi R. and 110 mi. WNW of Livingstone, Northern Rhodesia; cattle. It is ⊙ East Caprivi Zipfel Dist., an area annexed 1939 by U. of So. Afr.

Katiola (kätyō'lä), town (pop. c.7,200), central Ivory Coast, Fr. West Africa, on railroad and 205 mi. NNW of Abidjan; sisal, cotton, rubber, coffee, tobacco, pepper. Airfield. R.C. mission.

Katipunan (kätēpōōnän'), town (1939 pop. 3,120; 1948 municipality pop. 38,230), Zamboanga prov., N Mindanao, Philippines, 45 mi. NNW of Pagadian; coconuts, corn, rice.

Katkol (kŭt'kōl), town (pop. 5,565), Belgaum dist., S Bombay, India, 45 mi. ENE of Belgaum; agr. market (cotton, wheat, peanuts). Sometimes spelled Katkola.

Katla, Iceland: see MYRDALSJOKULL.

Katlabug Lagoon or **Katlapug Lagoon** (kŭtlŭbōōk', –pōōk'), Rum. *Catlabug* or *Catlapug* (kätläbōōg', –pōōg'), S Izmail oblast, Ukrainian SSR, near Kiliya arm of the Danube, NE of Izmail; 17 mi. long, 4 mi. wide (S). Receives minor Katlabug R.

Katlacherra, India: see KATLICHERRA.

Katlanovo (kät'länôvô), village, N Macedonia, Yugoslavia, on Pcinja R. and 15 mi. SE of Skoplje. Katlanovska Banja, health resort with sulphur springs, is near by.

Katlicherra or **Katlacherra** (kŭtlĭchär'rŭ), village, Cachar dist., S Assam, India, on tributary of Barak (Surma) R. and 30 mi. SSW of Silchar; rice, tea, cotton, rape and mustard, sugar cane. Also spelled Katlichara.

Katmai National Monument (kăt'mī) (□ 4,214.9), S Alaska, near head of Alaska Peninsula, in Aleutian Range, bounded E by Shelikof Strait, 100 mi. WNW of Kodiak; volcanic region, slowly cooling, including KATMAI VOLCANO and the VALLEY OF TEN THOUSAND SMOKES. Scenery varies from wooded valleys to desolate volcanic areas and glacier-covered mts. Established 1918 by presidential proclamation following eruption (1912) of Katmai Volcano. Monument accessible only to well-equipped expeditions.

Katmai Volcano (7,000 ft.), S Alaska, in Katmai Natl. Monument, 100 mi. WNW of Kodiak; 58°16'N 154°59'W. Active volcano with crater 8 mi. in circumference and 3,700 ft. deep. Within crater are lake, small isl., and glacier-covered walls. Erupted June 5, 1912, desolated Kodiak Isl., covered □ 53 with sand and lava, created VALLEY OF TEN THOUSAND SMOKES, a fumarole field. Investigated in 1915 by Natl. Geographic Society expedition.

Katmandu or **Kathmandu** (kätmändōō'), city (1920 pop., including environs, 108,805), ⊙ Nepal, in Nepal Valley, on the Baghmati and 135 mi. N of Patna; 27°42'N 85°20'E; alt. 4,270 ft. Airfield (seasonal service). Most of its important temples (mainly Sivaite) are of Newar architecture, include temple of Katmandu (=wooden temple; built 1596) from which city receives its name (former name, Kantipura) and 5-storied royal shrine of Talijiu. Also has old royal palace (*Hanuman Dhoka*) and the *Kot* (military council chamber) in which almost all the country's leading men were massacred in 1846. Large, elaborate palace of the maharajadhiraja (king) and the maharaja (prime minister) in NE area. The city, founded 723, was a former petty kingdom ruled by Newars of Malla dynasty, who mostly recognized suzerainty of Bhadgaon; became independent in 1480, after division of valley; acquired Patan soon after. Captured 1768 by Gurkhas under Prithwi Narayan and has since remained ⊙ of the ruling Gurkha family (Sah) of Nepal. Damaged by earthquake of 1934. Pop. mainly Newar. Noted anc. Buddhist chaitya of Swayambhunath (supposedly built c.100 B.C.; frequently restored and enlarged), Buddhist pilgrimage center, is 2 mi. NE; approached by flight of some 600 steps faced by 3 large Dhyani Buddhas. At Nilkantha (also called Buda Nilkantha and Burhanilkantha), 6 mi. NNW, is a pool with anc., partially submerged statue of Narayan (avatar of Vishnu); Hindu pilgrimage site.

Katni (kŭt'nē) or **Murwara** (mōōrwä'rŭ), town (pop. 24,630), Jubbulpore dist., N Madhya Pradesh, India, 55 mi. NE of Jubbulpore; rail junction; industrial center; mfg. of cement, ordnance, pottery, paints, varnishes; fuller's-earth processing, rice milling. Industrial school. Important bauxite, limestone, and other workings near by.

Kato, Korea: see HADONG.

Kato Achaia or **Kato Akhaia** (both: kä'tô ŭkhä'yŭ), town (pop. 2,644), Achaea nome, N Peloponnesus, Greece, on Gulf of Patras, on railroad, and 13 mi. WSW of Patras; Zante currants, wine, wheat; livestock raising (cattle, sheep).

Kato Kleitoria or **Kato Klitoria** (both: kä'tô klētōrē'ŭ), town (pop. 1,727), Achaea nome, N Peloponnesus, Greece, in Ladon R. valley, 32 mi. SE of Patras; livestock raising (sheep, goats); tobacco.

Kato Kouphonesos or **Kato Koufonisos** (both: kä'tô kōōfōnē'sôs), Aegean island (□ 1.7; 1928 pop. 27) in the Cyclades, Greece, 3 mi. off the SE end of Naxos isl.; 34°55'N 26°10'E.

Katol (kä'tōl), town (pop. 12,097), Nagpur dist., central Madhya Pradesh, India, on tributary of Wardha R. and 33 mi. WNW of Nagpur; cotton ginning; millet, wheat, oilseeds; mango groves.

Katombora (kätōmbō'rä), village (pop. 131), Southern Prov., Northern Rhodesia, on Zambezi R. above Victoria Falls, and 25 mi. W of Livingstone; rail terminus; loading point for teak floated down Zambezi R.

Katonah (kŭtō'nŭ), residential village (1940 pop. 1,764), Westchester co., SE N.Y., 16 mi. NNE of White Plains, on a reservoir of Croton R. system, in agr. area.

Kato Neurokopion or **Kato Nevrokopion** (both: kä'tô nĕvrôkô'pēôn), town (pop. 3,290), Drama prov., Macedonia, Greece, 20 mi. NW of Drama, on road to Nevrokop, Bulgaria; tobacco center. Formerly called Zyrnovon or Zirnovon. Sometimes Kato Neurokopi (Nevrokopi).

Katon-Karagai or **Katon-Karagay** (kŭtôn"-kŭrŭgī'), village (1939 pop. over 2,000), E East Kazakhstan oblast, Kazakh SSR, near Bukhtarma R., in N foothills of Narym Range, 150 mi. SE of Ust-Kamenogorsk; mtn. tourist center.

Katoomba (kŭtōōm'bŭ), municipality (pop. 8,781), E New South Wales, Australia, 55 mi. WNW of Sydney, in Blue Mts.; tourist resort; orchards.

Kato Polemidhia, Cyprus: see POLEMIDHIA.

Katori (kä"tō'rē), town (pop. 5,905), Chiba prefecture, central Honshu, Japan, 2 mi. ESE of Sawara; rice, poultry, raw silk.

Kato Tzoumagia, Greece: see HERAKLEIA.

Katouna (kŭtōō'nŭ), town (pop. 3,167), Acarnania nome, W central Greece, 6 mi. SSW of Amphilochia; olive oil; wine; livestock.

Kato Vathia, Greece: see AMARYNTHOS.

Katowice (kätôvē'tsĕ), prov. (□ 3,807; 1946 pop. 2,482,851), S Poland; ⊙ Katowice. Borders S on Czechoslovakia; at N foot of the W Beskids; drained by upper Vistula, Klodnica (Klodnitz), and upper Warta rivers. Mining (coal, iron, zinc) and heavy-industry (steel furnaces and rolling mills, metalworking; mfg. of chemicals, glass, textiles) center of Poland. Largest cities are Katowice, Zabrze (Hindenburg), Chorzow, Czestochowa, Gleiwitz (Gliwice), Beuthen (Bytom), Sosnowiec, Bedzin, Dabrowa Gornica, Bielkso, and Myslowice. Created 1950 when Slask, Pol. *Śląsk* (shlōsk), prov., established 1945 and briefly called Slask Dabrowski, Pol. *Śląsk Dąbrowski*, was divided into Katowice prov. (E) and Opole prov. (W). W tip of prov. formed (until 1945) part of Ger. Upper Silesia prov., to which the entire territory had belonged until First World War.

Katowice, Ger. *Kattowitz* (kä'tōvĭts), city (1950 pop. c.170,000), ⊙ Katowice prov., S Poland, 40 mi. W of Cracow; rail center and one of chief Polish industrial centers; coal, iron, zinc, and lead mining; blast furnaces, zinc and lead foundries, rolling mills; mfg. of machinery, boilers, railroad cars, armatures, chemicals, dyes, phosphates, roofing materials, bricks, porcelain, leather goods, liqueur; sawmilling, mineral-oil refining, printing. Electrical, gas, and asphalt works. Inc. 1867, the city passed from Germany to Poland in 1921. Pop. was 14,000 in 1888; 44,000 in 1921. City damaged in Second World War. Bogucice (bôgōōtsē'tsĕ), Ger. *Bogutschütz* (bō'gōō-chüts), is a N suburb.

Kato Zodhia, Cyprus: see ZODHIA, KATO.

Katpadi, India: see VELLORE.

Katra (kŭ'trŭ). **1** Town, Gonda dist., Uttar Pradesh, India: see BIRPUR KATRA. **2** Town (pop. 2,379), Partabgarh dist., SE Uttar Pradesh, India, 5 mi. SSW of Bela; rice, barley, wheat, gram. Also called Katra Mehdunìganj. **3** Town, Shahjahanpur dist., Uttar Pradesh, India: see MIRANPUR KATRA.

Katra, town (pop. 1,005), Riasi dist., SW Kashmir, in Siwalik Range, 18 mi. NNE of Jammu; corn, wheat, rice, oilseeds.

Katrancik Dag (käträn jŭk'dä), Turkish *Katrancık Dağ*, peak (7,657 ft.), SW Turkey, 15 mi. W of Bucak.

Katrinah, Jabal, Egypt: see KATHERINA, GEBEL.

Katrine, Loch (lŏkh kă'trĭn), lake (8 mi. long, 1 mi. wide; 495 ft. deep), in Scotland, in SW Perthshire, bordering Stirling, at foot of Ben Venue, 5 mi. E of Loch Lomond and 10 mi. W of Callander, surrounded by hills and woods. It drains into Teith R. through Loch Achray (from which it is separated by the TROSSACHS) and Loch Vennachar. In 1859, when it became source of Glasgow water supply, its water level was raised, submerging the Silver Strand of Scott's *The Lady of the Lake* and reducing size of ELLEN'S ISLE, isl. at E end of loch.

Katrineholm (kä"trēnŭhôlm'), city (pop. 12,513), Sodermanland co., E Sweden, 25 mi. SSW of Eskilstuna; rail junction; mfg. of separators, pumps, ball bearings; foundries, sawmills, stone quarries. Has 17th-cent. castle, mus. Founded 1862, when railroad was constructed; inc. 1917.

Katschberg Pass (käch'bĕrk) (alt. 5,384 ft.), at E end of the HOHE TAUERN, S Austria, on Carinthia-Salzburg border, connecting Spittal an der Drau (S) with Mur R. valley (N).

Katscher, Poland: see KIETRZ.

Katsena Ala, Nigeria: see KATSINA ALA.

Katsepe, Madagascar: see MAJUNGA, town.

Katsina (kăchē'nä), province (□ 9,466; pop. 1,039,109), Northern Provinces, N Nigeria; ⊙ Katsina. In basin of upper Kebbi R.; bounded N by Fr. West Africa; savanna and scrub vegetation. Agr. (peanuts, cotton); cattle and skins. Chief centers: Katsina, Jibiya, Funtua. Pop. mainly Hausa. One of Hausa native states. Prov. formed in mid-1930s from N Zaria and Kano provs.

Katsina, town (pop. 22,347), ⊙ Katsina prov., Northern Provinces, N Nigeria, 90 mi. NW of Kano; 12°58'N 7°37'E. Road and trade center (peanuts, cotton, cattle, skins). Moslem teachers col., leper settlement, large mosque. Formerly an important seat of Hausa culture, it may have had a pop. of as much as 100,000 in 17th–18th cent. Came under Fulah rule in 19th cent.

Katsina Ala (ä'lä), town (pop. 1,138), Benue prov., Northern Provinces, E central Nigeria, on Katsina Ala R. and 55 mi. SW of Wukari; shea nuts, sesame, cassava, durra, yams. Also spelled Katsena Ala.

Katsina Ala River, E Nigeria, rises in Bamenda highlands in S Br. Cameroons, flows c.200 mi. NW, past Katsina Ala, to Benue R. just NE of Abinsi. Navigable for c.90 mi. below Katsina Ala.

Katsuki (kä"tsōō'kē), town (pop. 17,433), Fukuoka prefecture, N Kyushu, Japan, just W of Yawata; coal-mining center.

Katsumada (kätsōō'mädŭ) or **Katsumata** (–mätŭ), town (pop. 4,751), Okayama prefecture, SW Honshu, Japan, 7 mi. E of Tsuyama; rice, wheat, raw silk. Agr. and forestry school.

Katsumoto (kä'tsōōmō"tō), town (pop. 7,988), on N coast of Iki-shima, Nagasaki prefecture, Japan, 7 mi. N of Mushozu; fishing.

Katsunuma (kätsōō'nōōmä), town (pop. 4,212), Yamanashi prefecture, central Honshu, Japan, 9 mi. E of Kofu; spinning; raw silk, rice, wheat.

Katsusa (kä"tsōō'sä) or **Kazusa** (kä"zōō'sä), town (pop. 12,513), Nagasaki prefecture, W Kyushu, Japan, on S Shimabara Peninsula, 18 mi. ESE of Nagasaki across Tachibana Bay; summer resort in rice-growing area.

Katsushika, Japan: see FUNABASHI.

Katsuta (kä"tsō'tä), town (pop. 24,753), Ibaraki prefecture, central Honshu, Japan, 3 mi. E of Mito; agr. (rice, wheat).

Katsuura (kätsōō'rä). **1** Town (pop. 15,167), Chiba prefecture, central Honshu, Japan, on E coast of Chiba Peninsula, 29 mi. ENE of Tateyama; fishing port on the Pacific; canned and dried fish. **2** Town (pop. 5,651), Wakayama prefecture, S Honshu, Japan, port on Kumano Sea, on SE Kii Peninsula, 7 mi. SSW of Shingu; fishing center; dried bonito. Exports lumber, paper. Hot springs. Sometimes called Kii-katsuura.

Katsuyama (kätsōō'yämŭ), sometimes spelled Katuyama. **1** Town (pop. 6,377), Chiba prefecture, central Honshu, Japan, on W Chiba Peninsula, on Uraga Strait, 9 mi. N of Tateyama; dairying. **2** Town (pop. 16,991), Fukui prefecture, central Honshu, Japan, 16 mi. E of Fukui; textile milling, sake brewing. **3** Town (pop. 11,391), Okayama prefecture, SW Honshu, Japan, 17 mi. W of Tsuyama; commercial center in agr. area (rice, wheat, tobacco); inkstones, raw silk, charcoal, sake. Near by is Kanba Waterfall (300 ft. high) on small Asashi R.; hot springs. Sometimes called Chugoku-katsuyama.

Katta-Kurgan (kŭtä"-kōōrgän'), city 1932 pop. estimate 18,500), W Samarkand oblast, Uzbek SSR, on Trans-Caspian RR, near the Kara Darya (S arm of Zeravshan R.), and 40 mi. WNW of Samarkand, in cotton area. Cotton ginning, cottonseed-oil extraction, food processing. Just S is Katta-Kurgan storage reservoir (also known as Uzbek Sea; completed 1948), fed by canal from Zeravshan R. arm. Max. storage capacity: 500,000 acre-ft.

Katta-Kurganskoye Vodokhranilishche (–skŭyŭ vŭdŭkhrŭnyē'lyĭshchĭ) [Russ., =Katta-Kurgan reservoir], town (1947 pop. over 500), W Samarkand oblast, Uzbek SSR, just S of Katta-Kurgan, on Katta-Kurgan reservoir.

Kattefoss (kät'tŭfôs), waterfall (1,125 ft.) in Vest-Agder co., S Norway, 39 mi. N of Mandal, on the Skjerka at its influx into Mandal R.; hydroelectric plant.

Kattegat (kă'tĭgăt), strait (137 mi. long) bet. Sweden and Jutland, Denmark; joined N to the Skagerrak at Cape Skagen or The Skaw, Jutland, S to Baltic Sea by the Oresund or The Sound, the Great Belt, and the Little Belt. Width varies from 37 mi. at The Skaw to c.100 mi. near S end; max. depth, 410 ft. Isls. include Laeso, Anholt, and Samso, all Danish. Goteborg (Sweden) and Aarhus (Denmark) are important ports. Sometimes spelled Cattegat.

Kattenheim, France: see CATTENOM.

Kattiné, Syria: see QATTINE.

Kattowitz, Poland: see KATOWICE, city.

Kattumannarkoil, India: see MANNARGUDI, South Arcot dist.

Katugastota (kŭtōōgŭstō'tŭ), village, Central Prov., Ceylon, on Kandy Plateau, on the Mahaweli Ganga and 3 mi. N of Kandy; extensive cacao plantations; rubber, rice, vegetables.

Katul, Iran: see ALIABAD.

Katun or **Katun'** (kŭtōōn'yŭ), village (1939 pop. over 2,000), central Altai Territory, Russian SFSR, at confluence of Biya and Katun rivers, 10 mi. SSW of Bisk, in agr. area; stock-breeding farm.

Katun Alps or **Katun' Alps,** Rus. *Katunskiye Belki*, highest range of Altai Mts., SW Siberian Russian SFSR, in bend formed by upper Katun R.; 85 mi. long, 35 mi. wide; rise to 15,155 ft. at BELUKHA peak. Include 15 glaciers.

Katunayaka (kŭtōōnī'ŭkŭ), village (pop. 2,107), Western Prov., Ceylon, on Negombo Lagoon, 16 mi. N of Colombo; coir-rope mfg.; coconut palms, cinnamon, rice.

Katunga, Nigeria: see OLD OYO.

Katunitsa (kätōōnē'tsä), village (pop. 2,450), Plovdiv dist., S central Bulgaria, on Asenovitsa R. and 7 mi. ESE of Plovdiv; fruit (strawberries) and truck gardening, winegrowing; rice milling, liquor distilling.

Katunki (kŭtōōn'kē), town (1939 pop. over 500), W Gorki oblast, Russian SFSR, on Volga R. and 5 mi. N of Chkalovsk; garment mfg.

Katun River or **Katun' River** (kŭtōōn'yŭ), left headstream of Ob R., in SE Altai Territory, Russian SFSR, rises on S slopes of Belukha peak of Altai Mts.; flows W and N, around W end of Katun Alps, W, past Ust-Koksa, and N, past Elekmonar, joining Biya R. at Katun to form Ob R.; 386 mi. long. Navigable below Gorno-Altaisk. Receives Maima and Chuya rivers (right). Chuya highway passes through its lower valley.

Katuyama, Japan: see KATSUYAMA.

Katwa (kät'vŭ), town (pop. 11,282), Burdwan dist., central West Bengal, India, on Bhagirathi R., at Ajay R. mouth, and 33 mi. NNE of Burdwan; rail workshops; rice milling; rice, jute, gram, sugar cane. Here Vaishnava saint Chaitanya entered life of an ascetic.

Katwe (kä'twā), village, Western Prov., SW Uganda, on NE shore of L. Edward, 60 mi. SW of Fort Portal; salt-mining center; fishing; coffee, tea, bananas, corn.

Katwijk aan Zee (kät'vīk än zā'), town (pop. 16,680), South Holland prov., W Netherlands, on North Sea, at mouth of Old Rhine R., 5 mi. NW of Leiden; resort; ceramics, cement, chemicals, wood products, machinery, metalwork; fishing industry. Sometimes spelled Katwyk aan Zee. On the Old Rhine, 1 mi. SE, is village of Katwijk aan den Rijn (pop. 3,018).

Katy or **Katy Wroclawskie** (kä'tĭ vrôtswäf'skē), Pol. *Katy Wrocławskie*, Ger. *Kanth* (känt), town (1939 pop. 3,580; 1946 pop. 2,193) in Lower Silesia, after 1945 in Wroclaw prov., SW Poland, 12 mi. WSW of Breslau (Wroclaw); agr. market (grain, sugar beets, potatoes, livestock).

Katy, town (pop. 849), on Fort Bend-Harris-Waller co. line, S Texas, 25 mi. W of Houston.

Katyk (kŭtĭk'), town (1939 pop. over 2,000), E Stalino oblast, Ukrainian SSR, in the Donbas, 6 mi. W of Chistyakovo; coal. Called Zapadno-Gruppski until 1945.

Katymar (kŏ'tyŭmär), Hung. *Katymár*, town (pop. 4,992), Bacs-Bodrog co., S Hungary, on Kigyos R. and 16 mi. SE of Baja; flour mills; grain, paprika, cattle, hogs.

Katyn or **Katyn'** (kŭtĭn', Rus. kŭtĭn'yŭ), village (1926 pop. 68), W Smolensk oblast, Russian SFSR, 12 mi. W of Smolensk; leather goods. During Second World War, massacre of c.10,000 Pol. officers took place in near-by forest.

Katyshka, Russian SFSR: see GOLYSHMANOVO.

Katzbach (käts'bäkh), Pol. *Kaczawa* (kä-chä'vä), river in Lower Silesia, after 1945 in SW Poland, rises NE of Hirschberg (Jelenia Gora), flows N past Zlotoryja, and NE past Liegnitz (Legnica) and Prochowice, to Oder R. 3 mi. NE of Prochowice. In battle of the Katzbach (Aug., 1813), Blücher defeated French at Bremberg, 9 mi. S of Liegnitz.

Katzenbuckel (kä'tsŭnbŏŏ"kŭl), highest elevation (2,054 ft.) of the Odenwald, W Germany. Basalt quarried at Eberbach (W foot).

Katzenelnbogen (kä"tsŭnĕln'bō"gŭn), village (pop. 1,280), in former Prussian prov. of Hesse-Nassau, W Germany, after 1945 in Rhineland-Palatinate, 9 mi. SW of Limburg. Has ancestral castle of counts of Katzenellenbogen.

Katzhütte (käts'hü"tŭ), village (pop. 2,179), Thuringia, central Germany, in Thuringian Forest, on Schwarza R. and 15 mi. WSW of Saalfeld; china and glass mfg., woodworking. First Thuringian china works founded here in 1759.

Kaua (kou'ä), town (pop. 772), Yucatan, Mexico, 13 mi. WSW of Valladolid; henequen, corn.

Kauai (kou"wī'), county (□ 623; pop. 29,838), T.H., includes KAUAI Isl. and NIIHAU Isl.; ⊙ Lihue, Kauai.

Kauai, island (□ 551; pop. c.29,800), T.H., 4th in size of Hawaiian Isls., 98 naut. mi. NE of Honolulu, separated from Oahu by Kauai Channel; 22°5'N 159°31'W; ⊙ Lihue, principal town. Chief port is Nawiliwili Harbor. Roughly circular, isl. is 32 mi. in diameter. Kauai is oldest Hawaiian Isl. geologically; it has fertile valleys and deep fissures in a central mtn. mass; Kawaikini (5,170 ft.) is highest peak. WAIMEA CANYON is on Waialeale peak. Kauai was 1st isl. of Hawaii visited by Capt. Cook in 1778. WAIMEA harbor is on S coast. Chief products: sugar, rice, pineapples.

Kauai Channel, bet. Kauai and Oahu isls., T.H., 63 naut. mi. wide. Formerly Kaieiewahe Channel.

Kaub or **Caub** (both: koup), town (pop. 2,271), in former Prussian prov. of Hesse-Nassau, W Germany, after 1945 in Rhineland-Palatinate, on right bank of the Rhine and 16 mi. SSE of Oberlahnstein; wine. Slate-quarrying. Anc. fortress Gutenfels (restored 1886) towers above town. On a reef in the Rhine is the large castle of Pfalzgrafenstein or Pfalz, built in 14th cent. to protect the Rhine toll.

Kaufbeuren (kouf"boi'rŭn), city (1950 pop. 19,738), Swabia, SW Bavaria, Germany, on the Wertach and 18 mi. NE of Kempten; rail junction; mfg. of textiles, glass, jewelry, paper; brewing, metal- and woodworking; trades in dairy produce. Has two 15th-cent. churches. Chartered c.1220.

Kaufman (kôf'mŭn), county (□ 816; pop. 31,170), NE Texas; ⊙ Kaufman. Mainly rich blackland prairies, bounded W by Trinity R. and drained by its East Fork and other tributaries. Agr. (cotton; also corn, sorghums, hay, peanuts, fruit, truck), dairying, livestock (cattle, hogs, sheep, poultry). Some lumbering. Mfg., farm-products processing at Terrell, Kaufman. Formed 1848.

Kaufman, city (pop. 2,714), ⊙ Kaufman co., NE Texas, 30 mi. ESE of Dallas; market, trade, shipping center in rich blackland agr. area (cotton, dairy products, truck, cattle); cotton processing, mfg. of clothing, mattresses, beverages. Founded 1848, inc. 1873.

Kaufman, Mount, Tadzhik SSR: see LENIN PEAK.

Kauhajoki (kou'häyō"kē), village (commune pop. 17,139), Vaasa co., W Finland, 50 mi. SSE of Vaasa; road center in lumbering, grain-growing region.

Kauhava (kou'hävä), village (commune pop. 10,296), Vaasa co., W Finland, 45 mi. E of Vaasa, in lumbering region; mfg. of sheath knives.

Kauiki Head (kou-ē'kē), point, E coast of Maui, T.H., S of Hana; extinct crater; 20°45'N 155°58'W.

Kaukab or **Kawkab** (kou'käb), Fr. *Kaoukab*, village, Hama prov., W Syria, on railroad and 11 mi. NNE of Hama; cotton, cereals.

Kaukaban, Yemen: see SHIBAM.

Kaukauna (kôkô'nŭ), city (pop. 8,337), Outagamie co., E Wis., on Fox R. and 6 mi. E of Appleton; dairying center with large production of cheese; has railroad shops, stone quarries, paper mills, sulphate-processing plants, and breweries. Settled 1793 as fur-trading post; inc. 1885.

Kaukehmen, Russian SFSR: see YASNOYE.

Kauklahti, Finland: see KOKLAKS.

Kaukopää (kou'kōpä"), village in Ruokolahti commune (pop. 8,227), Kymi co., SE Finland, near USSR border, on E shore of L. Saimaa, 25 mi. ENE of Lappeenranta; lumber, pulp, and cellulose mills.

Kaula (kä-ōō'lŭ), rock isl. of Hawaiian group, c.20 mi. WSW of Niihau; light station for U.S. lighthouse service.

Kaulakahi Channel (kou'lŭkä'hē), bet. Kauai and Niihau isls., T.H., 15 naut. mi. wide. Formerly Kumukahi Channel.

Kaulille (kou'lēlŭ), town (pop. 2,011), Limburg prov., NE Belgium, 5 mi. ESE of Overpelt; gunpowder mfg. Formerly spelled Caulille.

Kauliranta (kou'lïrän"tä), village in Ylitornio commune (pop. 8,246), Lapi co., NW Finland, on Torne R. (Swedish border) and 45 mi. NNW of Tornio; rail head, starting point of roads to N Lapland.

Kaumajet Mountains, Labrador: see COD ISLAND.

Kaumalapau Harbor (kou'mŭlŭpou'), W Lanai, T.H.; port developed by pineapple company.

Kaunakakai (kou'nŭkäkī'), village (pop. 712), S Molokai, T.H.; principal port of isl.; exports pineapples.

Kaunas (kou'näs,–nŭs), Ger. *Kauen* (kou'ŭn), Pol. *Kowno* (kôv'nô), Rus. *Kovno* (kôv'nŭ), city (pop. 154,109), S central Lithuania, on Neman R., at mouth of the Viliya, and 55 mi. WNW of Vilna; 54°54'N 23°54'E. Industrial and commercial center; mfg. (agr. implements, central-heating equipment, nails, tin-metal goods, chemicals, prefabricated houses, rubber goods, plastics, oxygen, acetylene, cotton and woolen textiles, paper, tobacco, confectionery), meat packing, dairying, food canning. Has state univ. (1922), agr. col. (formerly at Dotnuva), school of decorative arts, conservatory. City consists of old town (castle ruins) at Neman-Viliya river confluence, rectilinear new town (E), and outlying industrial and residential suburbs of Vilijampole (N; on right Viliya R. bank), Aleksotas (SW; across Neman R.) with airport, and Sanciai and Panemune (S; on Neman R.). First mentioned in 13th cent.; medieval trade center and Lithuanian stronghold against Teutonic Knights; passed (1795) to Russia and became (1843) ⊙ Kovno govt. Though strongly fortified by Russians, it was captured (1915) by Germans in First World War. From 1918 to 1940, Kaunas was provisional ⊙ of Lithuania, Vilna (which Lithuania claimed as its rightful capital) being held by Poland until 1939. Following cession (1939) of Vilna to Lithuania by USSR, the capital was transferred there in 1940. Kaunas was occupied by German forces 1941–44. During German occupation the Jews of Kaunas (c.30% of pre-war population) were virtually exterminated. Before their evacuation at the approach of Russian troops the Germans destroyed much of the city. It became (1950) ⊙ newly created Kaunas oblast.

Kaunchi, Uzbek SSR: see YANGI-YUL.

Kauneonga Lake, N.Y.: see WHITE LAKE.

Kaunia (koun'yŭ), village, Rangpur dist., N East Bengal, E Pakistan, on Tista R. (rail bridge) opposite Tista village and 10 mi. ENE of Rangpur; rail junction; rice, jute, tobacco.

Kauniainen, Finland: see GRANKULLA.

Kaupanger, Norway: see SOGNDAL, Sogn og Fjordane co.

Kaur or **Kawr** (kour), granitic ranges in Aden hinterland, extending WSW-ENE along Yemen *status quo* line; consists of the Kaur al AUDHILLA (8-9,000 ft.) and the Kaur al AWALIQ (E).

Kaur or **Kau-ur** (kou'ōōr), town (pop. 532), Central Div., W central Gambia, on right bank of Gambia R. (wharf and ferry) and 85 mi. ENE of Bathurst; peanut-shipping point; palm oil and kernels, rice. Has elementary school.

Kaura Namoda (kourä' nämō'dä), town (pop. 13,068), Sokoto prov., Northern Provinces, NW Nigeria, 100 mi. ESE of Sokoto; rail terminus; cotton-shipping point; millet, peanuts; cattle raising. Gold and diamonds mined near by.

Kauriaganj (kour'yägŭnj), town (pop. 4,371), Aligarh dist., W Uttar Pradesh, India, 15 mi. E of Aligarh; wheat, barley, pearl millet, gram, cotton.

Kauriala Ghat (kour'yälŭ gät'), village, Kheri dist., N Uttar Pradesh, India, on Kauriala arm of Karnali (Gogra) R. and 27 mi. E of Palia; rail terminus; connected by road with RAJAPUR (Nepal).

Kauriala River, Nepal and India: see GOGRA RIVER.

Kausala (kou'sälä), village in Iitti commune (pop. 10,750), Kymi co., SE Finland, in lake region, 25 mi. ESE of Lahti; spool milling. Until 1949 in Uusimaa co.

Kausambi, India: see KOSAM.

Kaushany (kŭŏŏshä'nē), Rum. *Căușani* (kŭŏŏshän'), village (1941 pop. 5,437), SE Moldavian SSR, on Botna R., on railroad and 13 mi. SSW of Bendery; red-wine production center. Has 18th-cent. church with frescoes.

Kautenbach (kou'tŭnbäkh), village (pop. 205), N central Luxembourg, on Wiltz R., at mouth of Clerf R., and 8 mi. NNW of Ettelbruck; rail junction; mfg. of blast-furnace equipment.

Kautokeino (kou'tōkä"nō), Lapp village (pop. 270; canton pop. 1,372), Finnmark co., N Norway, near Finnish border, on Kautokeino R. (upper course of Alta R.) and 70 mi. S of Alta, 110 mi. ESE of Tromso. Airfield. First settled by Finns; church established 1701.

Kautokeino River, Norway: see ALTA RIVER.

Kau-ur, Gambia: see KAUR.

Kava or **Kyava,** Est. *Käva* (all: kă'vä), town, NE Estonia, just S of Kohtla-Jarve, in oil-shale mining area.

Kavadarci or **Kavadartsi** (both: kä'vädärtsē), village (pop. 6,053), Macedonia, Yugoslavia, in the Tikves, 50 mi. SSE of Skoplje; trade center for winegrowing and opium-producing region. Formerly also called Kavadar.

Kavajë (kävä'yŭ) or **Kavaja** (kävä'yä), Ital. *Cavaia*, town (1945 pop. 9,689), W central Albania, near the Adriatic, on railroad and 10 mi. SSE of Durazzo; agr. center (tobacco, cotton, oilseeds, corn). Agr. school (N).

Kavak (käväk'), village (pop. 1,576), Samsun prov., N Turkey, on railroad and 21 mi. SW of Samsun; cereals.

Kavakli, Greece: see HAGIOS ATHANASIOS.

Kavakli, Turkey: see MERIC.

Kavaklii, Bulgaria: see TOPOLOVGRAD.

Kavala, Greece: see KAVALLA.

Kavali (kä'vŭlē), town (pop. 11,969), Nellore dist., E Madras, India, 34 mi. N of Nellore, near Coromandel Coast of Bay of Bengal; cashew and Casuarina plantations; palmyra sugar. Laterite quarries near by.

Kavalla (kŭvä'lŭ), nome (□ 838; pop. 138,133) of Macedonia, Greece; ⊙ Kavalla. Situated on Aegean Sea bet. Mt. Pangaion (W) and Mesta R. mouth (E), it includes off-shore isl. of Thasos. Agr. (mainly in Khrysoupolis lowland) specializes in well-known Macedonian tobacco, exported through Kavalla. Corn and citrus fruit are also grown. Served by Drama-Xanthe highway.

Kavalla, anc. *Neapolis* (nēă'pŭlĭs), city (pop. 49,667), ⊙ Kavalla nome, Macedonia, Greece, port on promontory on Gulf of Kavalla of Aegean Sea and 75 mi. E of Salonika, opposite Thasos isl.; leading Greek tobacco center and, next to Salonika, most important artificial harbor in N Greece; processing and exporting of well-known Macedonian tobacco. Airport. Was embellished by Mohammed Ali (b. here 1769), Turkish viceroy of Egypt. Sometimes identified with anc. Neapolis, the port of Philippi, where St. Paul landed on way from Samothrace. Under Turkish rule, 15th cent. to Balkan Wars (1912–13). Sometimes spelled Kavala, Cavalla.

Kavaratti Island (kŭvŭrŭ'tē), coral island of Laccadive Isls., India, in Arabian Sea; 10°35'N 72°35'E. Administered by Malabar dist., Madras; coconuts.

Kavarna (kävär'nä), Rum. *Cavarna*, city (pop. 5,625), Stalin dist., NE Bulgaria, port (grain exports) on Black Sea, in S Dobruja, and 25 mi. NE of Stalin; flour milling. In Rumania (1913–40).

Kavathe Piran, India: see KAVTHA PIRAN.

Kaverino (kŭvyĕ'rĭnŭ), village (1939 pop. over 2,000), E Ryazan oblast, Russian SFSR, 12 mi. SSW of Sasovo; wheat, hemp, sugar beets.

Kaveripak (kä"värĭpäk') or **Kaveripakkam** (–kŭm), town (pop. 7,663), North Arcot dist., E central Madras, India, on Palar R. and 22 mi. E of Vellore, in canal-irrigated agr. area growing cotton, rice, peanuts.

Kaveripatnam (–pŭt'nŭm), town (pop. 7,058), Salem dist., W Madras, India, on Ponnaiyar R. and 8 mi. S of Krishnagiri; sesame- and castor-oil extraction.

Kaveri River, India: see CAUVERY RIVER.

Kavieng (kă'vē-ĕng'), port town, N New Ireland, Bismarck Archipelago, Territory of New Guinea, SW Pacific; chief town of isl.; airfield near by.

Kavirondo (kävērōn'dō), region in W Kenya along NE shore of L. Victoria; chief town, Kisumu. Inhabited by Nilotic Kavirondo tribe. Administratively divided into 3 dists. (North, Central, and South Kavirondo) of Nyanza prov.

Kavirondo Gulf, shallow NE inlet of L. Victoria, in SW Kenya; 35 mi. long, 15 mi. wide. Connected with lake via 3-mi.-wide strait. Its port is Kisumu. Navigable for 8-ft. draught.

Kavkazskaya (kŭfkä'skīŭ), village (1926 pop. 9,413), E Krasnodar Territory, Russian SFSR, on Kuban R. and 4 mi. E of KROPOTKIN (at Kavkazskaya rail junction); metalworking center; wheat, sunflowers, sugar beets.

Kavlinge (chĕv'lĭng-ŭ), Swedish *Kävlinge*, town (pop. 2,962), Malmohus co., S Sweden, on Kavlinge R. and 7 mi. NW of Lund; rail junction; sugar refining, tanning, mfg. of shoes, gloves.

Kavlinge River, Swedish *Kävlingeån* (–ûōn"), S Sweden, rises SE of Horby, flows 60 mi. generally W, past Ortofta and Kavlinge, to the Oresund 8 mi. N of Malmo.

Kavtha Piran (kou'tŭ pĭrän'), town (pop. 4,835), Satara South dist., S central Bombay, India, 6 mi. WNW of Sangli; local market for millet, sugar cane, cotton. Sometimes spelled Kavathe Piran.

Kaw or **Caux** (both: kō), town (commune pop. 105), N Fr. Guiana, on small Kaw R., near the Atlantic, on road, and 40 mi. SE of Cayenne; rubber gathering, hog raising. Diamond and platinum deposits near by.

Kaw, Okla.: see KAW CITY.

Kawa or **El Kawa** (ĕl kä'wŭ), town, Blue Nile prov., E central Anglo-Egyptian Sudan, in the Gezira, on right bank of the White Nile, on road and 20 mi. SSE of Dueim; cotton, barley, corn, sesame, durra; livestock.

Kawabara, Japan: see KAWAHARA.

Kawabe (kä"wä'bā), town (pop. 6,234), Gifu prefecture, central Honshu, Japan, 11 mi. NNW of Tajimi, in agr. area.

Kawachi (kä"wä'chē), former province in S Honshu, Japan; now part of Osaka prefecture.

Kawagoe (käwä'gōā), city (1940 pop. 38,407; 1947 pop. 50,294), Saitama prefecture, central Honshu, Japan, 23 mi. NW of Tokyo; mfg. (silk textiles). Has Buddhist temple founded in 9th cent.

Kawaguchi (käwä'gōōchē), city (1940 pop. 97,115; 1947 pop. 116,007), Saitama prefecture, central Honshu, Japan, just N of Tokyo; industrial center (ironworks, textile mills).

Kawahara (käwä'härŭ) or **Kawabara** (–bärŭ), town (pop. 2,950), Tottori prefecture, S Honshu, Japan, 6 mi. SSW of Tottori; rice, sake, raw silk.

Kawaharada (käwähä'rädŭ), town (pop. 3,501) on Sado Isl., Niigata prefecture, Japan, on W coast, 5 mi. SE of Aikawa; rice-growing center.

Kawaihae Bay (kŭwī'hī'), NW Hawaii, T.H.; landing for cattle shipment; fine bathing beach.

Kawaikini (käwī'kē'nē), peak (5,170 ft.), central Kauai, T.H., S of Waialeale; highest peak on isl.

Kawajiri (käwä'jērē), town (pop. 7,678), Hiroshima prefecture, SW Honshu, Japan, on Inland Sea, just E of Kure; mfg. (writing brushes, files, sake, soy sauce).

Kawakami, Russian SFSR: see SINEGORSK.

Kawakawa (kä'wŭkäwŭ), township (pop. 587), ⊙ Bay of Isls. co. (□ 613; pop. 10,409), N N.Isl., New Zealand, 110 mi. NNW of Auckland; agr. center.

Kawamata (käwä'mä'tä), town (pop. 9,697), Fukushima prefecture, N central Honshu, Japan, 10 mi. SE of Fukushima; raw silk, textiles.

Kawambwa (käwäm'bwä), township (pop. 758), Western Prov., N Northern Rhodesia, near Belgian Congo border, 170 mi. WNW of Kasama; corn, wheat; livestock. Has leper settlement. Transferred 1947 from Northern Prov.

Kawamoto (käwä'mōtō), town (pop. 4,673), Shimane prefecture, SW Honshu, Japan, 31 mi. SW of Izumo; lumber, charcoal, hemp. School of sericulture.

Kawanabe (käwä'nä'bā), town (pop. 22,371), Kagoshima prefecture, S Kyushu, Japan, on central Satsuma Peninsula, 16 mi. SW of Kagoshima; tobacco-producing center.

Kawanishi (käwä'nēshē). **1** Town (pop. 22,493), Hyogo prefecture, S Honshu, Japan, bet. Itami and Toyonaka; agr. center (rice, wheat, fruit); hatmaking. **2** Town (pop. 6,625), Tochigi prefecture, central Honshu, Japan, 24 mi. NE of Utsunomiya; rice, wheat, tobacco, silk cocoons.

Kawanoe (käwä'nōā), town and port (pop. 10,640), Ehime prefecture, N Shikoku, Japan, on Hiuchi Sea, 3 mi. NE of Mishima; paper-milling center. Exports paper, cotton thread, tobacco.

Kawanoishi (käwänō'ēshē), town (pop. 6,561), Ehime prefecture, W Shikoku, Japan, 33 mi. SW of Matsuyama; fishing.

Kawara (kä"wä'rä), town (pop. 5,149), Fukuoka prefecture, N Kyushu, Japan, 13 mi. SSE of Yawata; coal mining.

Kawarago, Japan; see TAGA, Ibaraki prefecture.

Kawardha (kŭvŭr'dŭ), town (pop. 6,210), Drug dist., E central Madhya Pradesh, India, 55 mi. N of Drug; cotton, wheat, oilseeds. Forested hills (W, N). Was ⊙ former princely state of Kawardha (□ 794; pop. 77,284), one of the Chhattisgarh States, since 1948 inc. into Drug dist.

Kawartha Lakes (kŭwôr'thŭ), group of 14 lakes, SE Ont., in Peterborough-Lindsay region; includes Sturgeon, Pigeon, Chemung, Scugog, Stony, Buckhorn, Clear, Deer, Cameron, Balsam, Katchiwano, Little Mud, Bald, Lovesick lakes. Popular resort region, formerly lumbering area.

Kawasaki (käwä'sä'kē). **1** Town (pop. 32,112), Fukuoka prefecture, N Kyushu, Japan, 24 mi. E of Fukuoka; commercial center for coal-mining and agr. area; rice, wheat, barley. **2** City (1940 pop. 300,777; 1947 pop. 252,923), Kanagawa prefecture, central Honshu, Japan, on Kwanto plain and on W shore of Tokyo Bay, bet. Tokyo (N) and Yokohama (S); forms part of urban belt. Industrial center (steel mills, shipyards, engineering works, sugar refineries, textile mills). Includes (since 1937) former town of Takatsu. Bombed (1945) in Second World War. **3** Town (pop. 15,602), Shizuoka prefecture, central Honshu, Japan, on W shore of Suruga Bay, 18 mi. SSW of Shizuoka; tea, rice. Formerly a port.

Kawashima (käwä'shĭmä). **1** Town (pop. 5,430), Kagawa prefecture, NE Shikoku, Japan, 5 mi. SE of Takamatsu; commercial center; sake, flour, straw mats, umbrellas, soy sauce. **2** Town (pop. 5,784), Tokushima prefecture, E Shikoku, Japan, on Yoshino R. and 13 mi. W of Tokushima; mulberry fields; supplies gravel.

Kawashiri, Japan: see KUMAMOTO, city.

Kawata (kä"wä'tä), town (pop. 8,390), Tokushima prefecture, E central Shikoku, Japan, on Yoshino R. and 19 mi. W of Tokushima, in forested area; charcoal; paper milling, sake brewing.

Kawatana (käwä'tänä). **1** Town (pop. 16,096), Nagasaki prefecture, W Kyushu, Japan, on NW coast of Hizen Peninsula, 10 mi. SE of Sasebo, on Omura Bay; fishing center. **2** Village (pop. 5,759), Yamaguchi prefecture, SW Honshu, Japan, 12 mi. N of Shimonoseki; hot-springs resort. Sometimes called Kawatana-onsen.

Kawauchi (käwä'ōōchē), town (pop. 8,585), Aomori prefecture, N Honshu, Japan, on Mutsu Bay, 13 mi. SW of Tanabu; lumbering.

Kawau Island (käwou'), in Hauraki Gulf, N N.Isl., New Zealand, 30 mi. NE of Auckland; 5 mi. long, 4 mi. wide; summer resort. Copper.

Kawawa, Japan: see YOKOHAMA.

Kaw City or **Kaw** (kô), city (pop. 561), Kay co., N Okla., within bend of Arkansas R., 15 mi. ENE of Ponca City, in agr. area; dried eggs; oil and gas wells.

Kaweah, Mount, Calif.: see SEQUOIA NATIONAL PARK.

Kaweah River (kŭwē'ŭ), central Calif., formed in Tulare co. by headstreams passing through Sequoia Natl. Park, flows 10 mi. SW to floor of San Joaquin Valley, where it divides into many channels, some of which reach Tulare L.; St. Johns R. (23 mi. long) is a distributary. Used for irrigation; site of proposed Terminus Dam (for flood control) of CENTRAL VALLEY project.

Kawhia (kä'fēŭ), town (pop. 261), ⊙ Kawhia co. (□ 330; pop. 1,985), W N.Isl., New Zealand, 80 mi. S of Auckland and on N shore of Kawhia Harbour (8 mi. long, 6 mi. wide); dairy products, limestone. Hot springs on beach.

Kawishiwi River (kŭwĭ'shŭwē), rises in cluster of lakes in Lake co., NE Minn., flows W through several small lakes, then forms 2 branches which join near White Iron L., and flow N, through Fall L., to chain of lakes on Ont. line. Total length, 60 mi. Used for logging and hydroelectric power. Drains part of Superior Natl. Forest.

Kawkab, Syria: see KAUKAB.

Kawkareik (kô'kŭrāk", Burmese kô'kŭlāk"), town (pop. 6,575), Amherst dist., Lower Burma, in Tenasserim, 40 mi. E of Moulmein, at foot of Dawna Range, on road to Myawaddy (Thailand border).

Kawlin (kô'lĭn"), village, Katha dist., Upper Burma, on railroad and 50 mi. SW of Katha, in rice-growing area.

Kawoela or **Kawula**, Indonesia: see LOMBLEM.

Kawr, Aden: see KAUR.

Kaw River, Kansas: see KANSAS RIVER.

Kaxipet, India: see KAZIPET.

Kay, county (□ 944; pop. 48,892), N Okla.; ⊙ Newkirk. Bounded N by Kansas line; intersected by Arkansas and Chikaskia rivers and by the Salt Fork of Arkansas R. Includes L. Ponca and Ponca Indian Reservation. Agr. (wheat, oats, corn, alfalfa), stock and poultry raising, dairying. Mfg. at Ponca City, Blackwell, and Tonkawa. Oil and natural-gas wells; extensive oil refining, gasoline mfg. Formed 1893.

Kaya (kä'yä), town (pop. c.3,600), central Upper Volta, Fr. West Africa, 55 mi. NNE of Ouagadougou. Growing and processing of shea nuts; stock raising (cattle, sheep, goats). R.C. and Protestant missions. Market.

Kaya (kä'yä), town (pop. 5,055), Kyoto prefecture, S Honshu, Japan, 14 mi. WNW of Maizuru; rail terminus; silk textiles; rice growing.

Kayakent (kīŭkyĕnt'), village (1926 pop. 2,166), E Dagestan Autonomous SSR, Russian SFSR, near Caspian coastal railroad, 33 mi. NNW of Derbent; wheat, cotton; fisheries. Hot sulphur springs, natural-gas deposits.

Kayak Island (kī'ăk) (20 mi. long, 1–2 mi. wide), S Alaska, in Gulf of Alaska, 65 mi. SE of Cordova in Chugach Natl. Forest; 59°55'N 144°26'W. Cape St. Elias is S extremity. Bering anchored off shore, 1741.

Kayalpatnam (kä"yŭlpŭt'nŭm), town (pop. 9,931), Tinnevelly dist., S Madras, India, port on Gulf of Mannar, 50 mi. ESE of Tinnevelly. Pop. (80% Moslem; descended from pre-Portuguese Arab settlers) trades in rice, coconuts, timber, betel, and local palmyra products. Numerous mosques. Salt factory at Arumuganeri, 2 mi. WNW.

Kayan (kŭyän'), village, Hanthawaddy dist., Lower Burma, 30 mi. E of Rangoon; on small Kayan R. (steamer service from Pegu R.) and on Thongwa-Pegu RR.

Kayangel (käyäng'ĕl), atoll, Palau, W Caroline Isls., W Pacific, 15 mi. N of Babelthuap; 4 wooded islets.

Kayankulam (kä'yŭngkōōlŭm), city (pop. 10,916), W Travancore, India, 20 mi. NNW of Quilon; trades in coir rope and mats, rice, cassava; cashew-nut processing. Also spelled Kayangulam.

Kayan River, Borneo: see KAJAN RIVER.

Kayasula or **Kayasulu** (kīŭsōōlä',–lōō'), village (1939 pop. over 500), NW Grozny oblast, Russian SFSR, 50 mi. SE of Budennovsk, in cotton- and sheep-raising area; metalworks.

Kayattar or **Kayatar** (kŭyŭtär'), town (pop. 5,192), Tinnevelly dist., S Madras, India, 15 mi. NNE of Tinnevelly; cotton, palmyra; weaving of grass mats. Also spelled Kayathar.

Kayayak, Alaska: see KAGUYAK.

Kaycee, town (pop. 211), Johnson co., N central Wyo., on headstream of Powder R. and 60 mi. NNW of Casper; alt. 4,660 ft.

Kaydee, Alta.: see GREGG RIVER.

Kaye, Cape, NW Baffin Isl., E Franklin Dist., Northwest Territories, on Prince Regent Inlet; 72°16'N 89°58'W.

Kayes (kāz), village, SW Middle Congo territory, Fr. Equatorial Africa, on the Atlantic at mouth of Kouilou R., 25 mi. NNW of Pointe-Noire; mfg. of starch and tapioca. Madingo (mädĭng-gō'), 30 mi. NW on the coast, has palm mills.

Kayes, town (pop. c.25,000), SW Fr. Sudan, Fr. West Africa, head of Senegal R. navigation (c.550 mi. upstream from Saint-Louis), on Dakar-Niger RR and c.400 mi. E of Dakar; 14°24'N 11°27'W. Trading center for agr. region (peanuts, millet, corn, potatoes, rice, manioc, vegetables, gum); livestock market. Kapok ginning, tanning. Has airport; R.C. mission, mosque; hippodrome, meteorological station. Its port can be reached in rainy season (July–Oct.) by ships drawing 15 ft.

Kayford, village (pop. 1,479, with near-by Acme), Kanawha co., W W.Va., 25 mi. SSE of Charleston.

Kayiankor, Gold Coast: see KANYANKAW.

Kaying, China: see MEIHSIEN, Kwangtung prov.

Kayjay, mining village (pop. c.450), Knox co., SE Ky., in the Cumberlands, 16 mi. NNW of Middlesboro, in bituminous-coal and timber area.

Kayl (kāl), town (pop. 3,063), S Luxembourg, 3 mi. E of Esch-sur-Alzette; iron mining; metal casting, mfg. (steel products, railroad equipment).

Kaymakchalan, mountain range, Greece and Yugoslavia: see KAJMAKCALAN.

Kaynar, Kazakh SSR: see KAINAR.

Kaynardzha, Bulgaria: see KAINARDZHA.

Kaynary, Moldavian SSR: see KAINARY.

Kaysatskoye, Russian SFSR: see KAISATSKOYE.

Kayseri (kī'sĕrē") or **Kaisaria** (kīsä'rēŭ), province (□ 5,090; 1950 pop. 404,650), central Turkey; ⊙ Kayseri. It is bordered E by Binboga Mts. Drained by the Kizil Irmak and headstreams of the Seyhan. Iron, lignite, salt; gum tragacanth, wool, dye plants, onions, garlic, chick-peas, rye, millet, raisins, apricots.

Kayseri or **Kaisaria**, anc. *Caesarea Mazaca*, city (1950 pop. 65,489), ⊙ Kayseri prov., Turkey, on railroad and 165 mi. ESE of Ankara, at N foot of Erciyas Dagi (Argaeus); alt. 3,422 ft.; 38°40'N 35°25'E. Cotton textile center; also tile making, rug mfg., meat curing; agr. trade (wheat, barley, rye, vetch, potatoes, onions, garlic, legumes, sugar beets). The anc. city was a center of Cappadocia and played an important part in history of Byzantine and Seljuk empires.

Kaysersberg (kāzĕrbâr', Ger. kī'zŭrsbĕrk), village (pop. 1,649), Haut-Rhin dept., E France, at E foot of the Vosges, 6 mi. NW of Colmar, in winegrowing area; cotton milling, cheese and pottery mfg. Its 12th–15th-cent. church, 16th-cent. town hall, and fortified bridge across the Weiss (tributary of Fecht R.) damaged in Second World War.

Kayshyadoris, Lithuania: see KAISIADORYS.

Kaysville, city (pop. 1,898), Davis co., N Utah, on Great Salt L., bet. Salt Lake City and Ogden, in irrigated truck-raising area; alt. 4,293 ft.; canning, flour milling. Settled 1849, inc. 1868.

Kayts (kāts), town (pop. 1,348), small seaport on N Velanai isl., Northern Prov., Ceylon, on Palk Strait shipping route; trades (mostly in grain, sugar) with India and Burma. Has 17th-cent. Du. fort.

Kayumi (kä"yōō'mē), town (pop. 5,411), Mie prefecture, S Honshu, Japan, 18 mi. W of Uji-yamada; raw silk, processed tea.

Kayuyak, Alaska: see KAGUYAK.

Kazabello Almaznyanka (kŭzŭbyĕ'lŭ-ŭlmŭznyän'-kŭ), town (1926 pop. 1,277), S Voroshilovgrad oblast, Ukrainian SSR, in the Donbas, SW of Rovenki; coal mines.

Kazachinskoye (kŭzä'chĭnskŭyŭ). **1** Village (1939 pop. over 500), E Irkutsk oblast, Russian SFSR, on Kirenga R. and 105 mi. S of Kirensk; agr., lumbering. **2** Village (1948 pop. over 2,000), S Krasnoyarsk Territory, Russian SFSR, 120 mi. N of Krasnoyarsk and on Yenisei R., in agr. area. Founded 1650 as a fort, Kazachi Lug.

Kazachka (kŭzäch'kŭ), village (1939 pop. over 500), SW Saratov oblast, Russian SFSR, 30 mi. E of Balashov; metalworks; wheat, sunflowers.

Kazachya Lopan or **Kazach'ya Lopan'** (kŭzä'chyŭ lô'pŭnyŭ), town (1926 pop. 5,745), N Kharkov oblast, Ukrainian SSR, on railroad and 25 mi. N of Kharkov; truck, fruit.

Kazachye or **Kazach'ye** (kŭzä'chyĭ), village (1948 pop. over 500), N Yakut Autonomous SSR, Russian SFSR, N of Arctic Circle, on Yana R., 60 mi. above its mouth; reindeer raising.

Kazakh (käzäk', kŭ-, Rus. kŭzäkh'), city (1936 pop. estimate 6,800), W Azerbaijan SSR, at N foot of the Lesser Caucasus, 5 mi. SW of Akstafa, near Armenian border; cotton, wheat, livestock; leather industry. Teachers col.

Kazakh Hills or **Kazakh Uplands**, Rus. *Kazakhskaya Skladchataya Strana* [=Kazakh folded region], eroded mtn. area, E central Kazakh SSR, extending from Chingiz-Tau (NE of L. Balkhash) NW to Ishim R.; dry steppes; rises to 4,800 ft. at peak Kyzyl-Rai, 135 mi. SE of Karaganda. Extensive coal deposits (Karaganda), copper, lead, zinc, tungsten, molybdenum.

Kazakhstan or **Kazakh Soviet Socialist Republic** (kä"zäkstän', Rus. kŭzŭkhstän'), second largest constituent republic (□ 1,063,200; 1947 pop. estimate 6,000,000) of the USSR, in Central Asia; ⊙ Alma-Ata. Bounded by Russian SFSR (N), China (E), Central Asian republics of Kirghizia, Uzbekistan, and Turkmenia (S), and Caspian Sea (W). Consists primarily of the dry Caspian and Turan lowlands, the arid plateau Ust-Urt, and the Kazakh Hills, bounded E and S by the highlands of Altai Mts., Tarbagatai Range, Dzungarian Ala-Tau, Trans-Ili Ala-Tau, and Kirghiz Range. Dry continental climate; mean temp. in Jan., 28°F. (S) to 0°F. (N), in July 86°F. (S) to 72°F. (N). Yearly precipitation, 8–12 in., with extremes of 20 in. on mtn. slopes and less than 4 in. near Aral Sea. Principal water bodies are the inland Aral Sea and L. Balkhash, and the peripheral Irtysh, Ural, Ili, and Syr Darya rivers. Pop. consists of Kazakhs (57%; a pastoral Turko-Mongolian group), Russians (20%), Ukrainians (13%), Uigurs, Dungans, Uzbeks, and Kirghiz. Administratively, republic falls into 16 oblasts: AKMOLINSK, AKTYUBINSK, ALMA-ATA, DZHAMBUL, EAST KAZAKHSTAN, GURYEV, KARAGANDA, KOKCHETAV, KUSTANAI, KZYL-ORDA, NORTH KAZAKHSTAN, PAVLODAR, SEMIPALATINSK, SOUTH KAZAKHSTAN, TALDY-KURGAN, WEST KAZAKHSTAN. The agr. economy is determined by latitudinal soil and vegetation differentiation. Black-earth wooded steppe (extreme N) is chief grain-growing area (hard-grained wheat, millet) and also has dairy farming; in chestnut-soil dry steppes (bet. 51° and 40°N), millet and fat-tailed sheep are important; semi-desert and desert are principal grazing areas (fat-tailed sheep, camels); on piedmont loess plains (S) irrigated agr. (sugar beets, tobacco, opium poppy, rubber-bearing plants, cotton, rice, orchards) predominates. Karakul sheep are raised in Kyzyl-Kum desert (SW). Industry based primarily on abundant mineral resources; chief centers are Balkhash and Dzhezkazgan (copper), Karaganda (coal), Leninogorsk, Tekeli, Achisai (lead, zinc), Temir-Tau (iron and steel milling), Emba petroleum dist., Chulak-Tau and Alga (phosphorite), Inderborski (borate); also agr. processing, machine mfg., textile milling. Chief urban centers (served by an extensive railroad net) are Alma-Ata, Karaganda, Aktyubinsk, Akmolinsk, Petropavlovsk, Chimkent, Semipalatinsk, and Guryev. Ancestral tribes of the Kazakh people (formerly called Kirghiz; later spelled Kazak) settled in the region in 13th–14th cents. and formed a distinct group in 15th cent. At first dominated by the Golden Horde, the region came (19th cent.) under Rus. rule and formed part of Rus. Turkestan. Kazakhs were first constituted (1920) within Russian SFSR as the Kirghiz (after 1925, Kazak) Autonomous SSR and (1936) as a constituent (Kazakh) republic within the USSR.

Kazakhstan, town (1948 pop. over 2,000), N West Kazakhstan oblast, Kazakh SSR, on railroad and 65 mi. E of Uralsk, in cattle-raising area.

Kazalinsk (kŭzŭlyēnsk'), city (1948 pop. over 10,000), NW Kzyl-Orda oblast, Kazakh SSR, on the Syr Darya and 5 mi. SW of Novo-Kazalinsk; rice; metalworking, meat packing. Former caravan center. Founded 1859 as Rus. military post.

Kazan, Bulgaria: see KOTEL.

Kazân, Rumania: see CAZANE DEFILE.

Kazan or **Kazan'** (kŭzän', -zăn', Rus. kŭzän'yŭ), city (1939 pop. 401,665; 1945 pop. estimate 500,000; 72% Russians, 24% Tatars), ⊙ Tatar Autonomous SSR, Russian SFSR, on Kazanka R., near left bank of the Volga, on railroad and 450 mi. E of Moscow; 55°47'N 49°7'E. Major industrial and commercial center; locomotive and car workshops; mfg. (aircraft, agr. combines, typewriters, musical instruments, synthetic rubber, gunpowder, films, furniture, building materials, glass, textiles, clothing, shoes, cosmetics); fur, wool, flax, and food (flour, meat, fish, hops) processing, sawmilling. Exports chemicals (glycerin, stearin, acids), furs, leather goods, grain. Leading cultural center of Volga region, with state university (established 1804), aviation, civil engineering, law, medical, veterinarian, chemical, finance, teachers, and agr. colleges, and branch of USSR Acad. of Sciences. Has noted Tatar mus. (established 1895), opera house, theaters, zoological garden, several monuments, old churches, and mosques. City's notable kremlin is site of 250-ft.-high Suyumbeka Tower, 19th-cent. palace with govt. offices, 16th-cent. cathedral, monastery, towers, and gates. Two railroad embankments (laid across Kazanka R. flood plain) link city with Volga R. waterfront (3 mi. WSW of the kremlin, at mouth of Kazanka R.; shipyards). City founded (1401) as ⊙ Kazan khanate; sacked (1552) by Ivan the Terrible; a Muscovite stronghold in 16th–17th cent. Developed as leather and textile mfg. center in 17th cent.; assaulted (1774) by peasant rebels under Pugachev. Major Rus. colonization outpost in 18th cent., producing gunpowder, chemicals, and felt boots. Was ⊙ Kazan govt. until 1920, when it became ⊙ Tatar Autonomous SSR; modernized and industrialized.

Kazandzhik (kŭzŭnjēk'), city (1932 pop. estimate 2,600), SW Ashkhabad oblast, Turkmen SSR, on Trans-Caspian RR and 175 mi. WNW of Ashkhabad; metalworking. Glauber's salt deposits near by.

Kazanka (kŭzän'kŭ), village (1926 pop. 11,650), NE Nikolayev oblast, Ukrainian SSR, 22 mi. WSW of Krivoi Rog; flour mill, metalworks.

Kazanka River, in Tatar Antonomous SSR, Russian SFSR, rises S of Baltasi, flows 60 mi. SW, past Arsk and Kazan, to Volga R. 3 mi. SW of Kazan.

Kazanlik (käzänlŭk'), city (pop. 19,386), Stara Zagora dist., central Bulgaria, in Kazanlik Basin, 18 mi. NW of Stara Zagora; horticultural and mfg. center (textiles, musical instruments, attar of roses); airport. Schools of aviation, applied mechanics. Developed as attar-of-roses mfg. center under Turkish rule in 17th cent. Ceded to Bulgaria 1877. Sometimes spelled Kazanlek or Kazanlak.

Kazanlik Basin (□ 216), part of Tundzha R. valley bet. central Balkan Mts. (N) and Sredna Gora (S), has mint and rose fields, chestnut groves, oak and elm forests.

Kazanovka (kŭzä'nŭfkŭ), town (1939 pop. over 500), E Tula oblast, Russian SFSR, on Don R. and 5 mi. S of Yepifan town, in Moscow Basin; lignite mining.

Kazan-retto: see VOLCANO ISLANDS.

Kazan River (kŭzän', -zăn'), Northwest Territories, rises in SE corner of Mackenzie Dist., flows NE into Keewatin Dist., through Ennadai and Yathkyed lakes, to Baker L. (which is drained by Chesterfield inlet); 455 mi. long.

Kazanshunkur (kŭzän"shoonkoor'), town (1943 pop. over 500), central Semipalatinsk oblast, Kazakh SSR, 45 mi. NNE of Zhangis-Tobe; gold mining.

Kazanskaya (kŭzän'skĭŭ), village (1926 pop. 664), N Rostov oblast, Russian SFSR, on Don R. and 60 mi. NE of Millerovo; flour mill, metalworks; wheat, sunflowers. Pop. largely Cossack.

Kazanskoye (-skŭyŭ). **1** Village (1939 pop. over 500), NE Mari Autonomous SSR, Russian SFSR, 60 mi. NE of Ioshkar-Ola; wheat, rye, oats. **2** Village (1948 pop. over 2,000), SE Tyumen oblast, Russian SFSR, on Ishim R. and 30 mi. S of Ishim, in agr. area (grain, livestock).

Kazarman (kŭzŭrmän'), village, W Tyan-Shan oblast, Kirghiz SSR, on E slope of Tergana Range, 50 mi. ENE of Dzhalal-Abad; grain, livestock.

Kazatin (kŭzä'tyĭn), city (1926 pop. 14,990), N Vinnitsa oblast, Ukrainian SSR, 37 mi. NNE of Vinnitsa; rail junction; meat packing; metalworks.

Kazaure (käzourā'), town (pop. 6,820), Kano prov., Northern Provinces, N Nigeria, 45 mi. NNW of Kano; agr. trade center; cotton, peanuts, millet; cattle, skins. Until 19th cent., seat of important native emirate.

Kazbeg (kŏzbĕk', Rus. kŭzbyĕk'), village (1932 pop. estimate 1,160), N Georgian SSR, in central Greater Caucasus, on Georgian Military Road, on Terek R. and 65 mi. N of Tiflis, at E foot of Mt. Kazbek. Until c.1940, spelled Kazbek.

Kazbek, Mount, peak (16,541 ft.) in the central Greater Caucasus, N Georgian SSR, 70 mi. NNW of Tiflis. Extinct volcano; its glaciers give rise to Terek R. Popular tourist and sports area. First scaled 1868. Sometimes spelled Kasbek. Village of Kazbeg is at E foot, on Georgian Military Road.

Kaz Dagi, Turkey: see IDA MOUNTAINS.

Kazenny Maidan or **Kazennyy Maydan** (kŭzyô'nē mīdän'), village (1926 pop. 2,531), S Mordvinian Autonomous SSR, Russian SFSR, 38 mi. WSW of Ruzayevka; grain, potatoes, hemp. Sometimes called Maidan Kazenny.

Kazerun (kä"zĕroon'), town (1940 pop. 23,697), Seventh Prov., in Fars, S Iran, on Shiraz-Bushire road and 55 mi. W of Shiraz; trade center; grain, opium, cotton, tobacco, rice. Ruins of anc. town of SHAPUR are 12 mi. NW.

Kazgorodok (käz"gŭrŭdôk'). **1** Village, Akmolinsk oblast, Kazakh SSR: see KURGALDZHINO. **2** Village, S Kokchetav oblast, Kazakh SSR, 5 mi. NNW of Stepnyak; cattle.

Kazhim (kŭzhēm'), town (1926 pop. 982), SW Komi Autonomous SSR, Russian SFSR, on Sysola R. (head of navigation) and 95 mi. SSE of Syktyvkar; iron mine; foundry (dating from 1756).

Kazi-Magomed (kŭzē"-mŭgŭmyĕt'), city (1939 pop. over 2,000), E Azerbaijan SSR, near Kura R., 50 mi. SW of Baku; rail junction; wheat, cotton. Until 1939, Adzhikabul.

Kazimayn, Al-, Iraq: see KADHIMAIN, AL.

Kazimierz or **Kazimierz Dolny** (käzē'myĕsh dôl'nĭ), Rus. *Kazimerzh* (kŭzē'mĭrzh), town (pop. 2,929), Lublin prov.; E Poland, port on the Vistula and 6 mi. S of Pulawy; tanning, flour milling; stone quarrying. Has 14th-cent. Gothic church. Castle ruins near by.

Kazim Pasa, Turkey: see OZALP.

Kazincbarcika (kŏ'zĕnts-bŏr"tsĕkŏ), town (pop. 1,314), Borsod-Gömör co., NE Hungary, on Sajo R. and 13 mi. NW of Miskolc; rail junction for Rudabanya iron mines. Construction of new industrial town with large lignite-fed power plant was begun near by in 1951. Formerly called Barcika.

Kazinga Channel (käzĭng'gä), SW Uganda, flows 25 mi. from L. George WSW to L. Edward.

Kazipet (kä'zēpāt), village, Warangal dist., E Hyderabad state, India, 3 mi. SW of Warangal. Major rail junction; branch to Chanda (140 mi. N) provides shortest rail route bet. Madras and Delhi. Formerly also spelled Kaxipet.

Kazo (kä'zō) or **Kasu** (-soo), town (pop. 7,963), Saitama prefecture, central Honshu, Japan, 12 mi. E of Kumagaya, in agr. area (rice, wheat); makes *tabi* (a kind of sock).

Kaztalovka (kŭstä'lŭfkŭ), village (1939 pop. over 2,000), NW West Kazakhstan oblast, Kazakh SSR, on Lesser Uzen R. and 25 mi. S of Aleksandrov-Gai; wheat, millet; cattle, camels.

Kazumba (käzoom'bä), village, Kasai prov., S Belgian Congo, 70 mi. SSE of Luebo; trading center in cotton-growing region.

Kazungula, Northern Rhodesia: see KASUNGULA.

Kazusa or **Kadzusa** (both: kä"zoo'sä), former province in central Honshu, Japan; now part of Chiba prefecture.

Kazusa, town, Japan: see KATSUSA.

Kazvin or **Qazvin** (kāzvēn'), city (1941 pop. 55,151), First Prov., N Iran, on highway and railroad and 90 mi. WNW of Teheran, at S foot of Elburz range; alt. 4,165 ft. Agr. and industrial center of former Kazvin prov.; rug weaving, distilling, wool and cotton weaving, oilseed and flour milling, soap mfg. Has 2 conspicuous mosques: the 18th-cent. Masjid-i-Jama, built by Harun al-Rashid, and the Masjid-i-Shah, originally built by Shah Tahmasp (16th cent.). Linked with Resht by highway across Elburz range; airfield. Reportedly founded by Shapur II (4th cent.), the city flourished under the Arabs, was ruined (13th cent.) by the Mongols, but revived under Shah Tahmasp, who made it (16th cent.) the capital of the Safavids. It continued to flourish under Abbas the Great, who transferred (1590) the capital to Isfahan. Pop. resisted Afghan raid (1723). Repeatedly destroyed by earthquakes. Kazvin prov. was inc. (1938) into Iran's First Prov. (see GILAN).

Kazym River (kŭzĭm'), in N Khanty-Mansi Natl. Okrug, Tyumen oblast, Russian SFSR, rises in swampy zone, flows c.350 mi. W, through reindeer-raising area, to an arm of the Ob 30 mi. E of Berezovo. Site of 16th-cent. Ostyak principality.

Kbely (ŭkbĕ'lĭ), village (pop. 4,425), central Bohemia, Czechoslovakia, on railroad and 7 mi. NW of Prague; site of military airport.

Kcynia (kŭtsĭ'nyä), Ger. *Exin* (ĕksēn'), town (pop. 4,099), Bydgoszcz prov., W central Poland, 23 mi. WSW of Bydgoszcz; rail junction; brick mfg., flour milling.

Kdyne (ŭkdĭ'nyĕ), Czech *Kdyně*, Ger. *Neugedein* (noi'gŭdīn), town (pop. 2,177), SW Bohemia, Czechoslovakia, 28 mi. SSW of Pilsen; textile mfg. (linen, woolen), lace making.

Kea, town and parish (pop. 1,649), W Cornwall, England, 2 mi. SW of Truro; agr. market.

Kea (kā'ŭ) or **Keos** (kā'ôs), Lat. *Cea* (sē'ŭ) or *Ceos* (sē'ŏs), northwesternmost island (□ 60; pop. 3,749) of the Cyclades, Greece, in Aegean Sea, 13 mi. off Cape Sounion (separated by Kea Strait); 37°35'N 24°20'E; 13 mi. long, 7 mi. wide, rises to 1,838 ft. in Mt. St. Elias. Produces cotton, silk, wine, citrus fruit, olive oil, figs, barley. Main town, Kea (pop. 2,869), is on N slope of mtn., on site of anc. Iulis. Its port is 2 mi. NW. The lyric poets Bacchylides and Simonides were b. here. Kea was a hiding place of pirates in Middle Ages, when it was also called Zea, Zia, or Tzia.

Keaau, T. H.: see OLAA.

Keady (kē'dē), urban district (1937 pop. 1,260; 1951 census pop. 1,463), W Co. Armagh, Northern Ireland, 7 mi. SSW of Armagh; linen milling.

Kealaikahiki Channel (kä'ulīkähē'kē), bet. Lanai and Kahoolawe isls., T. H., 16 naut. mi. wide.

Kealakekua Bay (kä'ŭlākākoo'ŭ), W Hawaii, T. H., in Kona dist.; Capt. James Cook, discoverer of the isls., was killed here 1779; monument to him stands on shore.

Kealia (kā'ŭlē'ŭ), coast village (pop. 655), E Maui, T.H.; sugar cane.

Keams Canyon, hamlet, Navajo co., NE Ariz., on high tableland (c.6,000 ft.), in Hopi Indian Reservation, c.65 mi. N of Holbrook. Reservation hq. here.

Keansburg, resort borough (pop. 5,559), Monmouth co., E N.J., on Raritan Bay and 9 mi. ESE of Perth Amboy, on Point Comfort; fishing, truck farming. Inc. 1917.

Kearney (kēr′nē), town (pop. 342), S Ont., 40 mi. ENE of Parry Sound; lumbering.

Kearney (kär′nē), county (□ 512; pop. 6,409), S Nebr.; ⊙ Minden. Agr. region bounded N by Platte R. Livestock, grain, dairy produce. Formed 1860.

Kearney (kär′nē). **1** (also kâr′nē) City (pop. 570), Clay co., W Mo., 23 mi. NNE of Kansas City; ships stock, grain; coal mines. **2** City (pop. 12,115), ⊙ Buffalo co., S central Nebr., 40 mi. WSW of Grand Island and on Platte R. Trade, processing, and rail center in Great Plains grain, livestock area. Produces mechanical appliances, cement products, alfalfa meal, beverages; ships potatoes, grain, livestock. State hosp. for tubercular, state teachers col. here. State industrial school for boys near by. Fort Kearney State Park, in vicinity, is on site of Fort Kearney, frontier outpost established 1848 to protect travelers on Oregon Trail.

Kearny (kär′nē), county (□ 853; pop. 3,492), SW Kansas; ⊙ Lakin. Gently rolling plain, drained by Arkansas R. Grain, livestock. Formed 1888.

Kearny, town (pop. 39,952), Hudson co., NE N.J., on Passaic R. E of Newark; contains much of tidal wastelands bet. Passaic and Hackensack rivers; shipyards, drydocks; mfg. (linoleum, aluminum ware, chemicals, batteries, electrical equipment, brushes, paint, varnish, wallboard, drugs, cosmetics, plastics, tools, clothing); gold, platinum refining. Includes industrial and residential Arlington. Inc. 1899. Shipyards here were greatly enlarged in 1941.

Kearsarge (kēr′särj″). **1** Locality, Inyo co., Calif.: see INDEPENDENCE. **2** Resort village in Conway town, E N.H., near North Conway.

Kearsarge, Mount, solitary peak (2,937 ft.) in Merrimack co., S central N.H., 7 mi. SE of New London.

Kearsarge Pass (alt. 11,823 ft.), E Calif., in the Sierra Nevada, c.10 mi. W of Independence.

Kearsley (kērz′lē), urban district (1931 pop. 9,737; 1951 census 10,675), SE Lancashire, England, on Irwell R. and 3 mi. SE of Bolton; cotton milling, coal mining, mfg. of chemicals, paper.

Keasbey, N.J.: see WOODBRIDGE.

Keats Island (□ 3), SW B.C., in Howe Sound, 18 mi. WNW of Vancouver, opposite Gibsons Landing; mixed farming.

Keban (kĕbän′), village (pop. 542), Elazig prov., E central Turkey, on Euphrates R. near mouth of Murat R., and 27 mi. WNW of Elazig; mines (lead ore with silver and gold).

Kebao Island (kä′bou′), triangular island (15 mi. long, 10 mi. wide) in Gulf of Tonkin, off Quangyen prov., N Vietnam, 110 mi. E of Hanoi; coal and iron-ore mines. Port Wallut, at NE end, is coal-loading port.

Kebbi River (kĕ′bē), N Nigeria, rises SE of Katsina, flows c.450 mi. NW, W, and SW, past Jibiya, Sokoto, and Birnin Kebbi, to the Niger at Gomba. Receives Sokoto and Zamfara rivers (left). Also called Rima R. Sometimes known as Sokoto R. below the Sokoto R. mouth.

Kébémer (kĕbĕmĕr′), village, W Senegal, Fr. West Africa, on Dakar–Saint-Louis RR and 22 mi. SW of Louga, in peanut-growing region.

Kébili (kăbēlē′), Saharan village, Southern Territories, S Tunisia, at E edge of Chott Djerid, 50 mi. ESE of Tozeur; 33°42′N 8°58′E. Largest of the Nefzaoua oases; date-growing center. Junction of caravan trails. Artesian wells. Airfield. Also spelled Kébilli.

Kebin, rivers, Kirghiz SSR: see KEMIN.

Kebnekaise (kĕb′nŭkī″sŭ), highest mountain (6,965 ft.) of Sweden, Norrbotten co., N Sweden, 45 mi. W of Kiruna, 25 mi. from Norwegian line; 67°54′N 18°35′E. Has several glaciers.

Keboemen, Indonesia: see KEBUMEN.

Kebrabassa Rapids, Mozambique: see QUEBRABASA RAPIDS.

Kebumen or **Keboemen** (both: kŭbōō″mĕn′), town (pop. 14,102), central Java, Indonesia, 50 mi. W of Jogjakarta, near S coast; trade center in agr. area (sugar, rice, corn); tile works.

Kecel (kĕ′tsĕl), town (pop. 11,622), Pest-Pilis-Solt-Kiskun co., S central Hungary, 33 mi. SW of Kecskemet; market center; flour mills; wheat, barley, tobacco, horses, cattle.

Kechi (kä′chē), town (pop. 5,925), on Tsushima, Nagasaki prefecture, Japan, on E coast, 5 mi. NNE of Izuhara, on Tsushima Strait; fishing.

Kech River, W Pakistan: see DASHT RIVER.

Keciborlu (kĕjĭ′bôrlōō), Turkish *Keçiborlu*, village (pop. 3,510), Isparta prov., W central Turkey, on railroad and 19 mi. NW of Isparta; attar of roses distillery; sulphur mines.

Kecoughtan, Va.: see PHOEBUS.

Kecskemet (kĕch′kĕmät), Hung. *Kecskemét*, city (1941 pop. 87,269), in, but independent of, Pest-Pilis-Solt-Kiskun co., central Hungary, 50 mi. SE of Budapest; rail, market, fruit-exporting center; airport. Mfg. (agr. implements, machines, chemicals, matches, shoes, furniture, baskets); vegetable and fruit preserves, rum, cognac, wine; flour mills, cement- and brickworks. Known for its fruit (apricots, apples, cherries, mahalebs). Grain, onions, potatoes, fruitgrowing, cattle raising near by. Several schools, academies, Calvinist Law School (library has 40,000 vols.), 17th- and 18th-cent. churches, mus. Town existed as far back as 4th cent. A.D. In administrative reorganization of 1950 the city lost its large rural area (and half its pop.) and became ⊙ newly formed Bacs-Kiskun co.

Keda (kyĕ′dŭ), village (1932 pop. estimate 370), central Adzhar Autonomous SSR, Georgian SSR, on Adzharis-Tskhali R. and 15 mi. E of Batum; tobacco, fruit.

Kedabek (kyĕdŭbyĕk′), town (1948 pop. over 2,000), W Azerbaijan SSR, on N slope of the Lesser Caucasus, 28 mi. WSW of Kirovabad; copper mine and smelter. Livestock (merino sheep), wheat, potatoes; lumbering.

Kedah (kădä′), state (□ 3,660; pop. 554,441; including transients, 554,581), NW Malaya, on Strait of Malacca; ⊙ Alor Star. Bounded NE by Thailand along Kalakhiri Range, NW by Perlis, and SE by Perak, it encloses (SW) the Penang enclave of Prov. Wellesley; includes Langkawi isl. group off Perlis. Drained by Kedah, Merbok, and Muda rivers, the state consists of N low-lying coastal belt (a leading rice-growing area of Malaya) and a hilly central and S part where rubber and tapioca are grown. Coconuts and tobacco are lesser crops. Tin and tungsten are mined (Karangan). W Kedah is served by W coast railroad, which links the rice center of Alor Star and the rubber hub of Sungei Patani. Pop. is 65% Malay, 20% Chinese, 9% Indian. Originally part of Srivijaya kingdom of Palembang, it passed (14th cent.) under Javanese rule, and accepted Islam in 15th cent. Portuguese contacts date from 1516, Dutch and Br. trade from 17th cent. Following Thai invasion (1821), Kedah lost Satun to Thailand and Perlis became a separate state. The Br. East India Company secured grant of Penang isl. (1786) and mainland Prov. Wellesley (1800). With the transfer (1909) of Thai rights to Great Britain, Kedah (ruled by a sultan) became one of the unfederated Malay states. After Second World War, when it was temporarily annexed (1943–45) by Thailand, it joined the Federation of Malaya.

Kedah Peak, isolated mountain (3,978 ft.) in W Kedah, Malaya, near Strait of Malacca, 25 mi. NNE of George Town; sanatorium; tin and iron-ore deposits. Also called Gunong Jerai.

Kedah River, short stream of Kedah, NW Malaya, formed at Alor Star by union of 2 longer headstreams, flows 10 mi. W to Strait of Malacca at Kuala Kedah. Navigable.

Kedainiai, Kedainyai, or **Kedaynyay** (kädī′nyī), Lith. *Kėdainiai*, Rus. *Keidany* or *Keydany*, city (pop. 8,662), central Lithuania, on Nevezis R. and 27 mi. N of Kaunas; rail and road junction; leather-working center; tanning; mfg. of shoes, furniture; metalworking, flour milling. Dates from 15th cent. In Rus. Kovno govt. until 1920.

Kedarnath (kā′därnät), village, Garhwal dist., N Uttar Pradesh, India, in central Kumaun Himalayas, 45 mi. NNE of Pauri. Noted Hindu pilgrimage center, with Sivaite temple. Kedarnath peak (22,770 ft.) is 5 mi. N.

Kedaynyay, Lithuania: see KEDAINIAI.

Kedesh or **Kedesh-Naphtali** (kē′dĕsh-năf′tūlē), anc. locality, Upper Galilee, N Palestine, on Lebanese border, 10 mi. N of Safad, on site of which is modern Qadas or Kades (both: kä′dĕs), Arab village. The home of Barak, it is repeatedly mentioned in the Bible. As *Cadasa* it was of some importance in Roman times; remains of synagogue in Roman style have been excavated.

Kediri (kŭdĭ′rē), town (pop. 48,567), E Java, Indonesia, on Brantas R. and 65 mi. SW of Surabaya, at foot of Willis Mts.; 7°49′S 112°1′E; trade center for agr. area (sugar, coffee, tobacco, rubber, rice, cassava). Textile and lumber mills, machine shops. Kediri was ⊙ Hindu-Javanese kingdom of Kediri which flourished 11th–13th cent. Sometimes spelled Kadiri.

Kedma, Israel: see QEDMA.

Kedoengwoeni, Indonesia: see KEDUNGWUNI.

Kédougou (kĕdōō′gōō), town (pop. c.800), SE Senegal, Fr. West Africa, near Fr. Guinea border, on Gambia R., and 380 mi. ESE of Dakar. Region produces shea-nut butter, kapok, beeswax, corn, peanuts, rice; sheep and goats. Airfield.

Kedowa (kĕdō′wä), village, Nyanza prov., W Kenya, on railroad and 5 mi. SSW of Londiani; coffee, tea, wheat, corn.

Kedungwuni or **Kedoengwoeni** (both: kŭdōōng-wōō′nē), town (pop. 10,677), N Java, Indonesia, 50 mi. W of Semarang; trade center for agr. area (sugar, rice, tobacco).

Kedzierzyn (kĕjĕ′zhĭn), Pol. *Kędzierzyn*, Ger. *Heydebreck* (hī′dŭbrĕk), commune (1939 pop. 6,331; 1946 pop. 4,866) in Upper Silesia, after 1945 in Opole prov., S Poland, near Klodnitz R. (Gliwice Canal), 18 mi. N of Ratibor (Raciborz); important rail junction; fertilizer mfg. Until 1934, called Kandrzin.

Keedysville (kē′dēzvĭl), town (pop. 417), Washington co., W Md., near Antietam Creek, 11 mi. S of Hagerstown, near Civil War battlefields of South Mtn. and Antietam.

Keegan, Maine: see VAN BUREN.

Keego Harbor, village (1940 pop. 2,554), Oakland co., SE Mich., 4 mi. SW of Pontiac. Cass L. is near by.

Keel, Ireland: see ACHILL ISLAND.

Keele Peak (c.8,500 ft.), W Mackenzie Dist., Northwest Territories; 63°27′N 130°20′W.

Keeline, village, Niobrara co., E Wyo., 15 mi. W of Lusk; alt. 5,289 ft. Trading point in grain and ranching area.

Keeling Islands, Singapore colony: see COCOS ISLANDS.

Keelung (kē′lōōng′), **Kilung**, or **Chilung** (both: jē′–), Jap. *Kiirun* or *Kirun* (both: kē′rōōn), city (1940 pop. 100,151; 1950 pop. 145,240), N Formosa, 15 mi. ENE of Taipei (linked by railroad and highway); 25°8′N 121°44′E. Leading port and naval base of Formosa, on well-sheltered Keelung harbor (an inlet of E.China Sea); exports tea, sugar, camphor. Major chemical industry (nitrate fertilizers, superphosphate); shipbuilding, cement mfg., food processing (flour, pineapples, fish products). City consists of older W section, and more recent E part developed under Jap. rule. First occupied by the Spaniards (1626), later by the Dutch (1641), Keelung passed in 1662 to Koxinga and in 1683 to the Manchus. Later contacts with the West date from c.1840. The port was opened to foreign trade in 1858 and was briefly held (1884) by the French during war with China. Captured 1895 by Jap. fleet, it remained under Jap. rule until 1945.

Keelung River, N Formosa, rises near N coast SE of Keelung, flows 40 mi. WSW, past Chitu, Shihchih, and Sungshan, to Tanshui R. in N outskirts of Taipei; coal mining in valley.

Keene. **1** Mfg. city (pop. 15,638), ⊙ Cheshire co., SW N.H., on Ashuelot R., at mouth of Beaver Brook, and 40 mi. W of Manchester. Trade center for agr., resort area; wood products, textiles, machinery, tools, shoes; railroad shops; granite quarries, feldspar and mica mines near by. State teachers col., summer theater, old bldgs. (Wyman Tavern, 1762; First Congregational Church, 1786). Settled 1736; town inc. 1753, city 1873. **2** Resort village (1940 pop. 538), Essex co., NE N.Y., in the Adirondacks, on East Branch of Ausable R. and 35 mi. SSW of Plattsburg. **3** Village (1940 pop. 606), Johnson co., N central Texas, 23 mi. S of Fort Worth, in agr. area; broom mfg. Grew up around Seventh Day Adventist acad., now Southwestern Jr. Col.

Keeneland, Ky.: see LEXINGTON.

Keenesburg (kēnz′bûrg), town (pop. 432), Weld co., NE Colo., 35 mi. NE of Denver; alt. 4,951 ft. Sugar beets, beans, wheat.

Keene Valley, resort village (pop. c.400), Essex co., NE N.Y., in scenic Keene Valley of the Adirondacks, on East Branch of Ausable R. and 39 mi. SSW of Plattsburg.

Keeney Knob (3,945 ft.), Summers co., SE W.Va., 11 mi. NE of Hinton; highest point of Keeney Mtn., a ridge of the Alleghenies.

Keensburg, village (pop. 302), Wabash co., SE Ill., 7 mi. SW of Mount Carmel, in agr. area.

Keeranur. **1** or **Kiranur** (both: kē′rŭnōōr), town (pop. 5,360), Madura dist., S Madras, India, 10 mi. N of Palni; rice, grain, tobacco. **2** Town, Trichinopoly dist., Madras, India: see KIRANUR.

Keerbergen (kär′bĕr-khŭn), village (pop. 4,204), Brabant prov., N central Belgium, 7 mi. E of Mechlin; agr., lumbering.

Keeseville (kēz′vĭl), village (pop. 1,977), on Clinton-Essex co. line, NE N.Y., on Ausable R. (bridged) and 13 mi. S of Plattsburg, in farm area (dairy products, apples, potatoes, hay); resort, with some mfg. (clothing, lumber and wood products). Settled 1806, inc. 1878. AUSABLE CHASM is near by.

Keesler Air Force Base, Miss.: see BILOXI.

Keeten, Netherlands: see MASTGAT.

Keetmanshoop (kĕt′mäns-hōōp″), town (pop. 4,477), S South-West Africa, 280 mi. SSE of Windhoek, 220 mi. NW of Upington; 26°35′S 18°8′E; chief town of Great Namaqualand. Karakul-sheep raising, pelt processing, commercial, and distributing center; railroad workshops. Airport. Near by is Berseba Hottentot Territory, a reserve (□ c.2,200).

Keewalik, Alaska: see KIWALIK.

Keewatin (kēwā′tĭn, –wä′tĭn), district of Canada, a provisional administrative division (land area □218,460, total □ 228,160) of the Northwest Territories, comprising E mainland part of the territory (except Melville and Boothia peninsulas) and all isls. in Hudson and James bays. Bounded by Mackenzie Dist. (W), Franklin Dist. (N), Hudson Bay (E), and Manitoba (S); includes isls. of Southampton, Coats, White, Mansel, Akimiski, and Charlton, and isl. groups of Belcher, Twin, Sleeper and Ottawa isls. Mainland surface consists (N) of a plateau, separated from Melville and Boothia peninsulas and from Roes Welcome Sound by coastal plains and extending S to Chesterfield Inlet. S of this inlet surface is low and level, comprising greater part of the BARREN GROUNDS (arctic prairie) region bet. Mackenzie R. basin and Hudson Bay. There are numerous lakes; largest are

Nueltin, Dubawnt, Baker, Yathkyed, Maguse, Aberdeen, Garry, Pelly, and Kaminuriak. Dist. is drained by Kazan, Thelon, Dubawnt, and Back rivers; coastline is deeply indented by Chantrey Inlet and the Gulf of Boothia (N), and Wager Bay and Chesterfield Inlet (E). Chief trading posts are Chesterfield Inlet, Baker Lake, Eskimo Point, Padlei, and Coral Harbour; latter is site of air base, established in Second World War on Southampton Isl. Fur trapping is chief occupation. Dist. was established 1876 and was administered by Man. govt. until annexed to Northwest Territories, 1905. Present boundaries were established 1912, when region S of 60th parallel was divided bet. Man. and Ont.

Keewatin, town (pop. 1,481), W Ont., on L. of the Woods, 4 mi. W of Kenora; lumber and flour milling; hunting and fishing center, noted for its scenic beauty.

Keewatin (kēwä'tĭn), village (pop. 1,807), Itasca co., NE Minn., on Mesabi iron range, 7 mi. WSW of Hibbing. Grew with exploitation of ore deposits after 1909.

Kef, Le (lü kĕf'), anc. *Sicca Veneria*, town (pop. 11,246), ⊙ Le Kef dist. (□ 2,043; pop. 163,617), NW Tunisia, near Algerian border, 90 mi. SW of Tunis; rail-spur terminus and road junction. Agr. trade center (grain, livestock, wool, camel hair); olive-oil and flour milling. Handicraft industries. Airfield. Iron mines near by. Built in amphitheater on S slope of a rocky height, Le Kef commands road to Algeria. Among anc. ruins is an early Christian basilica.

Kefallinia, Greece: see CEPHALONIA.

Kefalos, Greece: see KEPHALOS.

Kefar, for names in Israel beginning thus: see KFAR.

Kefermarkt (kā'fûrmärkt), village (pop. 1,718), NE Upper Austria, 16 mi. NE of Linz, N of the Danube.

Keffi (kĕ'fē), town (pop. 4,232), Benue prov., Northern Provinces, central Nigeria, 25 mi. NNE of Nasarawa; tin-mining center.

Keflavik (kĕp'lävēk"), Icelandic *Keflavík*, city (pop. 2,157), Gullbringu og Kjosar co., SW Iceland, on NW shore of Reykjanes Peninsula, on Faxa Bay, 20 mi. WSW of Reykjavik; 64°N 22°35'W; fishing port. Site of large international airport, serving transatlantic air lines bet. North America and Great Britain and Scandinavia; built by U.S. forces during Second World War. Air Force designation, Meeks Field.

Kef Mahmel (kĕf' mämĕl'), second highest peak (7,615 ft.) of Algeria and of the Aurès massif, in Constantine dept., 15 mi. SSE of Batna.

Kefri, Iraq: see KIFRI.

Kef-Sidi-Amar, Algeria: see OUARSENIS MASSIF.

Kega (kā'gä) or **Kiga** (kē'gä), town (pop. 11,476), Shizuoka prefecture, central Honshu, Japan, on NE shore of L. Hamana, 8 mi. NW of Hamamatsu, in rice-growing area; textiles, straw hats.

Kegalla (kĕgŭl'ŭ) or **Kegalle** (kĕgôl'), town (pop. 4,922), ⊙ Kegalla dist. (□ 642; pop., including estate pop., 402,557), Sabaragamuwa Prov., W central Ceylon, 20 mi. W of Kandy; rubber, vegetables, rice, coconuts. Graphite mines near by. Mining of dispersed precious and semi-precious stones in dist.

Keg Creek, SW Iowa, rises near Westphalia in Shelby co., flows c.60 mi. SW, past Glenwood, to Missouri R. 20 mi. S of Council Bluffs.

Kegeili or **Kegeyli** (kyĭgā'lyē), village, S Kara-Kalpak Autonomous SSR, Uzbek SSR, in the Amu Darya delta, 15 mi. N of Nukus; cotton, cattle.

Kegel, Estonia: see KEILA.

Kegen or **Kegen'** (kyĕ'gĭnyŭ), village (1939 pop. over 2,000), SE Alma-Ata oblast, Kazakh SSR, on Kegen R. and 115 mi. E of Alma-Ata; sheep.

Kegen River or **Kegen' River,** Alma-Ata oblast, Kazakh SSR, rises near China border, flows W past Kegen, and NE to Ili R.; c.180 mi. long. Used for irrigation.

Kegeyli, Uzbek SSR: see KEGEILI.

Keggum, Latvia: see KEGUMS.

Kegichevka (kyĕgĭchĕf'kŭ), village (1926 pop. 1,287), W Kharkov oblast, Ukrainian SSR, 15 mi. ESE of Krasnograd; sugar mill.

Kegonsa, Lake (kĭgŏn'sŭ), southernmost of the Four Lakes, Dane co., S Wis., 9 mi. SE of Madison; c.3 mi. long, 2½ mi. wide; drained by Yahara R.

Kegon Waterfall, Japan: see CHUZENJI, LAKE.

Kegulta, Russian SFSR: see SADOVOYE, Astrakhan oblast.

Kegums (tyā'gōōms), Lettish *Ķegums*, Ger. *Keggum*, village, central Latvia, in Vidzeme, on right bank of the Western Dvina (rapids) and 6 mi. SE of Ogre; large hydroelectric station.

Kegworth, town and parish (pop. 2,107), NW Leicester, England, on Soar R. and 5 mi. NW of Loughborough; hosiery and lace knitting; machine-tool works. Has 15th-cent. church.

Kehl (kāl), town (1939 pop. 12,199), S Baden, Germany, placed (1945) under Fr. administration, port on right bank of the Rhine (2 bridges), at mouth of Kinzig R., opposite STRASBOURG, France; rail junction; customs station. Mfg. of cellulose, briquettes, wool, felt hats; woodworking, paper milling. Active trade in large harbor (built 1842–1900), head of Rhine navigation for larger vessels. Founded as Fr. fortress in late-17th cent. Fr. occupation bridgehead 1919–30. Partly destroyed in Second World War. Following its transfer (1945) to Fr. administration, it was evacuated by Ger. pop. The suburbs of Sundheim and Kronenhof remained under Ger. administration and form SUNDHEIM village.

Kehlen (kā'lŭn), village (pop. 566), SW Luxembourg, 6 mi. NW of Luxembourg city; chalk quarrying.

Kehra or **Kekhra** (kĕkh'rä), town (pop. 236), N Estonia, 22 mi. ESE of Tallinn; sawmilling, sulphate-pulp mfgs.; oil-shale-based power plant.

Kehsi-Mansam (kā-shē' mänsäm'), N state (myosaship) (□ 551; pop. 21,809), Southern Shan State, Upper Burma, on the Nam Pang; ⊙ Kehsi Mansam, village 70 mi. S of Lashio. Forested hills, trading, cattle breeding.

Keidany, Lithuania: see KEDZINIAI.

Keighley (kēth'lē), municipal borough (1931 pop. 40,441; 1951 census 56,938), West Riding, W Yorkshire, England, on Aire R. and 8 mi. NW of Bradford; mfg. of woolens, silk, rayon, leather and leather goods, paper, sewing and washing machines, machine tools, and other metal products; stone quarries. Has early-English church, rebuilt 1710 and 1847. Textile industry introduced here 1780. In municipal borough (SW) is suburb of Ingrow, with leather-tanning industry.

Keihin, Japan: see TOKYO.

Kei Islands, Indonesia: see KAI ISLANDS.

Keijo, Korea: see SEOUL.

Keiki-do, Korea: see KYONGGI.

Keiko, Formosa: see KIHU.

Keila or **Keyla** (kā'lä), Ger. *Kegel*, city (pop. 969), NW Estonia, 15 mi. SW of Tallinn; rail junction; market center in potato, barley area; mfg. of woolens.

Keilberg, Czechoslovakia: see KLINOVEC.

Keilhau (kīl'hou), village (pop. 247), Thuringia, central Germany, 4 mi. W of Rudolstadt. Fröbel here founded (1817) the Universal German Educational Inst.

Keimoes (kā'mōōs), village (pop. 2,239), N Cape Prov., U. of So. Afr., on Orange R. and 25 mi. SW of Upington; wheat, peas, sultanas, lucerne.

Keisen (kā'sān), town (pop. 19,954), Fukuoka prefecture, N Kyushu, Japan, 16 mi. E of Fukuoka; coal-mining center.

Keiser (kī'zûr), town (pop. 522), Mississippi co., NE Ark., 22 mi. SSW of Blytheville; cotton. Inc. 1933.

Keisho-hokudo, Korea: see NORTH KYONGSANG.

Keisho-nando, Korea: see SOUTH KYONGSANG.

Keishu, Formosa: see KICHOW.

Keishu, Korea: see KYONGJU.

Keiskamahoek or **Keiskama Hoek** (kās"kämähōōk'), town (pop. 1,935), SE Cape Prov., U. of So. Afr., on Keiskama R. and 20 mi. NW of Kingwilliamstown, at foot of short Amatola Range; stock, fruit, grain. Seat of local native-affairs council, established 1928, with jurisdiction over Keiskamahoek dist. (□ 224; total pop. 18,391; native pop. 17,243), included in Ciskeian General Council.

Keiskama River (kās'kämä), SE Cape Prov., U. of So. Afr., rises in Amatola Range NE of Keiskamahoek, flows in winding course first SW, then SE, past Keiskamahoek, to the Indian Ocean 30 mi. SW of East London; 160 mi. long.

Keisyu, Korea: see KYONGJU.

Keitele, Lake (kā'tĕlä) (46 mi. long, 1–8 mi. wide), S central Finland, 50 mi. W of Kuopio. Drains S into L. Päijänne. Chief villages on lake are Äänekoski, Suolahti, and Viitasaari.

Keith (kēth), village (pop. 320), SE South Australia, 130 mi. SE of Adelaide and on railroad; wheat.

Keith, burgh (1931 pop. 4,424; 1951 census 4,365), central Banffshire, Scotland, on Isla R. (1609 bridge) and 18 mi. WSW of Banff; agr. market, with woolen milling, whisky distilling, mfg. of agr. machinery. Has R.C. church with altarpiece presented by Charles X of France, and remains of anc. Milton Tower, stronghold of the Oliphants. Just W, on opposite bank of Isla R., is Fife-Keith, formerly separate town. Just N of Keith is agr. village of Newmill; James Gordon Bennett b. here.

Keith, county (□ 1,072; pop. 7,449), SW central Nebr.; ⊙ Ogallala. Agr. region drained by N.Platte and S.Platte rivers. L. McConaughy (Kingsley Reservoir), on the N.Platte, was created by KINGSLEY DAM. Livestock, wheat, small grains. Formed 1873.

Keithsburg (kēths'bûrg), city (pop. 1,006), Mercer co., NW Ill., on the Mississippi at mouth of Pope Creek, and 32 mi. WNW of Galesburg, in agr. area; mfg. of pearl buttons. Inc. 1857.

Keitum (kī'tōōm), village (pop. 1,578), in Schleswig-Holstein, NW Germany, on Sylt isl., 3 mi. ESE of Westerland; orchards. Historic main village of Sylt.

Keizyo, Korea: see SEOUL.

Kej River, W Pakistan: see DASHT RIVER.

Kejser Franz Joseph Fjord, Greenland: see FRANZ JOSEF FJORD.

Kekaha (kākä'hä), town (pop. 1,984), SW Kauai, T.H., near Waimea Bay; sugar-cane cultivation.

Kekertak or **Qeqertaq** (both: kĕkĕkh'täk), fishing settlement (pop. 102), Ritenbenk dist., W Greenland, on small isl. in E arm of the Vaigat, near base of Nugussuak peninsula, 16 mi. N of Ritenbenk; 70°N 51°18'W.

Kekes, Rumania: see CHIOCHIS.

Kekes, Mount (kā'kĕsh), Hung. *Kékes*, in MATRA MOUNTAINS, Heves co., N Hungary, highest point (3,330 ft.) in Hungary. On SW slope is state-owned sanatorium (alt. 2,329 ft.).

Kekhra, Estonia: see KEHRA.

Kekkö, Czechoslovakia: see MODRY KAMEN.

Kekri (kā'krē), town (pop. 8,245), E Ajmer state, India, in detached area, 45 mi. SE of Ajmer; markets millet, cotton, wheat; cotton ginning, handloom weaving.

Keksgolm, Russian SFSR: see PRIOZERSK.

Keku Strait (kē'kōō, kē'–) (40 mi. long), SE Alaska, in Alexander Archipelago, extends N-S bet. Kupreanof Isl. (E) and Kuiu Isl. (W), W of Kake.

Kelâa des Srarhna, El (ĕl kĕlä-ä' dā srägnä'), town (pop. 6,833), Marrakesh region, W Fr. Morocco, 45 mi. NE of Marrakesh, in irrigated farm region; olive groves, orchards; trade in wool and olive-oil. Copper deposits in area.

Kelang (kŭläng'), island (10 mi. long, up to 8 mi. wide; pop. 1,025), S Moluccas, Indonesia, in Ceram Sea, just W of Ceram; 3°13'S 127°44'E. Wooded, hilly, rising to 2,641 ft.

Kelani Ganga (kā'lŭnē gŭng'gŭ), river, SW Ceylon, rises in S Ceylon Hill Country in 2 headstreams joining 11 mi. ESE of Yatiyantota; flows WNW past Yatiyantota, and generally W through extensive tea, rubber, and coconut-palm plantations, past Ruwanwella and Kelaniya, to Indian Ocean at Colombo.

Kelaniya (kĕlŭnē'ŭ), village (pop., including near-by villages, 3,719), Western Prov., Ceylon, on the Kelani Ganga and 4 mi. ENE of Colombo city center; coir-rope, pottery, and fertilizer mfg.; coconuts, rice, vegetables. Anc. Buddhist pilgrimage center; stupa (built 13th cent. A.D.; restored late-18th cent.). Historically, site of city built 3d cent. B.C. by Singhalese king. Also spelled Kalaniya.

Kelantan (kŭlŭn'tăn, Malay kŭlän'tän), state (□ 5,746; pop. 448,572; including transients, 448,-630), N Malaya, on South China Sea; ⊙ Kota Bharu. Bounded by Thailand (NW), and along high jungle-covered mts. by Perak (W), Pahang (S), and Trengganu (E); rises to 7,186 in the Gunong Tahan on Pahang line. NE monsoon climate. Drained by Kelantan R., it consists of densely populated coastal plain (coconuts, rice, rubber) and hilly interior with occasional estates (rubber, oil palm). Iron (near Temangan), manganese, tin, and gold are mined. Industry is concentrated in Kota Bharu and its port, Tumpat. In addition to dense road net in coastal plain, state is served by rail connection with Thailand (via Rantau Panjang) and E coast railroad (via Pasir Mas, Kuala Krai, Temangan; partly dismantled during Second World War). Pop. is 90% Malay, 7% Chinese, and includes nomadic aborigines in mtn. hinterland. Originally subject to Srivijaya state of Palembang, Kelantan passed (14th cent.) under Javanese rule. Ruled by a sultan; accepted Thai suzerainty in 1780 and passed to Great Britain in 1909 as an unfederated Malay state. After Second World War, when it was temporarily annexed (1943–45) by Thailand, it joined Federation of Malaya.

Kelantan River, chief river of Kelantan, N Malaya, rises in several branches (Galas, Nenggiri, Lebir) in mtn. borders of Kelantan, flows over 150 mi. N, past Kuala Krai, Pasir Mas, and Kota Bharu, to South China Sea at Tumpat. Navigable for launches for 80 mi. Its valley is used by E coast railroad.

Kelayres (kĕlârz'), village (pop. 1,059), Schuylkill co., E central Pa., 18 mi. NE of Pottsville.

Kelbadzhar or **Kel'badzhar** (kyĕlbŭjär'), village (1939 pop. over 500), SW Azerbaijan SSR, in the Lesser Caucasus, in the Kurdistan, on Terter R. and 70 mi. SW of Yevlakh; wheat, barley, livestock; lumbering.

Kelbra (kĕl'brä), town (pop. 3,438), in former Prussian Saxony prov., central Germany, after 1945 in Saxony-Anhalt, at N foot of the Kyffhäuser, in the Goldene Aue, on the Helme and 12 mi. ESE of Nordhausen; button mfg., brewing. Stone quarrying.

Këlcyrë (kŭlsü'rŭ) or **Këlcyra** (kŭlsü'rä), Serbo-Croatian *Klisura*, town (1945 pop. 710), S Albania, on Vijosë R. and 30 mi. SSE of Berat; road junction.

Kelebia (kĕ'lĕbĭŏ), town (pop. 4,133), Bacs-Bodrog co., S Hungary, 18 mi. S of Kiskunhalas, on Yugoslav frontier; wheat, corn, cattle, hogs.

Keles (kyĕ'lyĭs), village (1939 pop. over 500), N Tashkent oblast, Uzbek SSR, on Trans-Caspian RR, just NW of Tashkent; wool washing.

Kelford (kĕl'fûrd), town (pop. 405), Bertie co., NE N.C., 20 mi. NW of Windsor.

Kelham, village and parish (pop. 378), E Nottingham, England, on Trent R. and 2 mi. NW of Newark; beet-sugar refining. Has theological col. and 15th-cent. church. In the civil war bet. parliamentary and royalist forces, Charles I surrendered (1646) to Scots here.

Kelheim (kăl'hīm), town (pop. 10,108), Lower Bavaria, Germany, at confluence of Altmühl and Danube rivers, 12 mi. SW of Regensburg; rail terminus; mfg. of cellulose, sulphuric acid, textiles, paper; brewing, printing, woodworking, winegrowing. Has 15th-cent. church. Developed at site of Celtic, then Roman, settlement; chartered 1181. Marble quarried in area. On near-by hill (W) is the Befreiungshalle, a rotunda built (1842–63) by Louis I of Bavaria to commemorate the heroes of the War of Liberation from Napoleonic rule.

Kélibia (kālēbyä'), anc. *Clupea*, village, Grombalia dist., NE Tunisia, on the Mediterranean, near E tip of Cape Bon Peninsula, 50 mi. E of Tunis; muscat grapes.

Kelif (kyĭlēf'), village, SE Chardzhou oblast, Turkmen SSR, on the Amu Darya, on railroad and 70 mi. SE of Kerki; cotton.

Kelif Uzboi, Turkmen SSR: see KARA-KUM CANAL.

Kelkheim (kĕlk'hīm), town (pop. 6,944), in former Prussian prov. of Hesse-Nassau, W Germany, after 1945 in Hesse, on S slope of the Taunus, 10 mi. W of Frankfurt; wine.

Kelkit (kĕlkĭt'), village (pop. 2,444), Gumusane prov., NE Turkey, on Kelkit R. and 22 mi. S of Gumusane; wheat, barley. Also called Ciftlik.

Kelkit River, anc. *Lycus*, N Turkey, rises in Erzincan Mts., 16 mi. N of Erzincan, flows 220 mi. WNW, past Kelkit, Susehri, Koyulhisar, Resadiye, Niksar, and Erbaa, to the Yesil Irmak 6 mi. NW of Erbaa.

Kell, village (pop. 193), Marion co., S Ill., 12 mi. ESE of Centralia, in agr., oil, and bituminous-coal area.

Kellabine, Tunisia: see KERKENNAH.

Kellé (kĕlā'), village, central Middle Congo territory, Fr. Equatorial Africa, c.100 mi. WNW of Fort-Rousset.

Kellé, village, W Senegal, Fr. West Africa, on railroad and 65 mi. NE of Dakar; peanut growing.

Keller, village (1940 pop. 547), Tarrant co., N Texas, 14 mi. N of Fort Worth, in agr. area.

Kellerovka (kyĕ'lyĭrŭfkŭ), village, N Kokchetav oblast, Kazakh SSR, 40 mi. N of Kokchetav; wheat, cattle.

Kellerton, town (pop. 483), Ringgold co., S Iowa, 29 mi. SE of Creston, in livestock and grain area.

Kellerup or **Kjellerup** (kĕ'lûrŏŏp), town (pop. 2,207), Viborg amt, central Jutland, Denmark, 12 mi. S of Viborg; bricks, furniture, margarine.

Kellerwand (kĕ'lûrvänt), Ital. *Monte Coglians* (mōn'tĕ kôlyäns'), highest peak (9,219 ft.) of Carnic Alps, on Austro-Ital. border, 17 mi. SSE of Lienz, Austria.

Kellett Strait, Northwest Territories: see FITZWILLIAM STRAIT.

Kelley, town (pop. 244), Story co., central Iowa, 26 mi. N of Des Moines; livestock, grain.

Kelleys Island, village (pop. 324), Erie co., N Ohio, 10 mi. N of Sandusky, on **Kelleys Island** (2,888 acres) in L. Erie; summer resort, with limestone quarries, fishing, truck gardening, winegrowing. Glacial Grooves State Park is here. The name Wine Isls. is sometimes applied to Kelleys Isl. and neighboring isls.

Kelliher, village (pop. 351), SE Sask., in the Beaver Hills, 55 mi. W of Yorkton; mixed farming.

Kelliher, village (pop. 336), Beltrami co., N Minn., E of Lower Red L., 38 mi. NE of Bemidji, in dairying and truck-farming area; dairy products.

Kellinghusen (kĕ"lĭng-hŏŏ'zŭn), town (pop. 9,076), in Schleswig-Holstein, NW Germany, on the Stör (head of navigation) and 8 mi. ENE of Itzehoe; mfg. of textiles, leather goods, wood products, cigars; meat canning. Brickworks. Clay quarrying. Site (1765–1840) of noted faïence factory.

Kellmünz (kĕl'münts"), village (pop. 856), Swabia, SW Bavaria, Germany, on the Iller and 10 mi. NNW of Memmingen; textile mfg., dairying (cheese). Has late-Roman castrum (*Coelis Mons*).

Kello (kĕl'lō), village in Haukipudas commune (pop. 12,252), Oulu co., W Finland, on Gulf of Bothnia, 7 mi. NNW of Oulu; timber-shipping port; sawmills.

Kellogg. 1 City (pop. 4,913), Shoshone co., N Idaho, on fork of Coeur d'Alene R. and 60 mi. ESE of Spokane, Wash., in mining district of Coeur d'Alene Mts.; lead and zinc smelters and refineries, cadmium plant. Grew with development of Bunker Hill and Sullivan lead mines (discovered 1885, now combined as one of world's leading producers). Sunshine Mine is a leading U.S. silver producer. Founded as Milo 1893, renamed 1894, inc. 1913. **2** Town (pop. 670), Jasper co., central Iowa, on North Skunk R. and 38 mi. ENE of Des Moines; mfg. (washing machines, metal stampings, tools, dies). **3** Village (pop. 409), Wabasha co., SE Minn., near Mississippi R., 5 mi. SSE of Wabasha; dairy products. Wildlife refuge near by.

Kellokoski (kĕl'lōkōs"kē), village in Tuusula commune (pop. 16,079), Uusimaa co., S Finland, 25 mi. N of Helsinki; metalworking.

Kellomäki, Russian SFSR: see KOMAROVO, Leningrad oblast.

Kelloselkä (kĕl'lōsĕl"kă), village in Salla commune (pop. 8,588), Lapi co., NE Finland, border station 8 mi. WSW of Kuolayarvi (Kuolajärvi), USSR.

Kells (kĕlz). **1** Gaelic *Ceanannus Osraighe*, town (pop. 104), central Co. Kilkenny, Ireland, 8 mi. S of Kilkenny; agr. market (barley, potatoes; cattle). Has considerable remains of fortified monastery (c.1195). **2** Urban district, Co. Meath, Ireland: see CEANANNUS MÓR.

Kelly Air Force Base, Texas: see SAN ANTONIO.

Kelly Lake (40 mi. long, 2–4 mi. wide), NW Mackenzie Dist., Northwest Territories, 15 mi. NE of Norman Wells; 65°25'N 126°15'W.

Kelly's Ford, on Rappahannock R., N Va., and 20 mi. NW of Fredericksburg; scene (March 17, 1863) of an indecisive cavalry engagement bet. Union troops under W. W. Averell and Confederates under Fitzhugh Lee.

Kellyville, town (pop. 528), Creek co., central Okla., 20 mi. SW of Tulsa, in agr. and oil-producing area; cotton ginning.

Kelme (kĕl'mā), Lith. *Kelmė*, Rus. *Kelmy* or *Kel'my*, city (pop. 3,705), W central Lithuania, 25 mi. SW of Siauliai; mfg. (shoes, felt, bricks), flour milling, distilling. Has mus. In Rus. Kovno govt. until 1920.

Kelmentsy or **Kel'mentsy** (kĭlmyĕn'tsē), Rum. *Chelmenți* (kĕlmĕnts'), village (1941 pop. 4,204), E Chernovtsy oblast, Ukrainian SSR, in Bessarabia, 14 mi. ESE of Khotin, near Dniester R.; agr. center.

Kelmy, Lithuania: see KELME.

Kélo (kĕlō'), village, SW Chad territory, Fr. Equatorial Africa, 65 mi. NNW of Moundou; cotton ginning; millet, livestock.

Kelod (kā'lōd), town (pop. 5,596), Nagpur dist., central Madhya Pradesh, India, 25 mi. NW of Nagpur; cotton ginning; millet, wheat, oilseeds; mango groves. Manganese deposits near by.

Keloet, Indonesia: see KELUT.

Kelowna (kĭlō'nŭ), city (pop. 5,118), S B.C., on Okanagan L., 170 mi. ENE of Vancouver; center of fruit, vegetable, vineyard region, with canneries and packing plants; furniture mfg., dairying; stock, tobacco.

Kelpin or **Kelpin Bazar** (kĕlpĭn' bäzär'), Chinese *Koping* or *K'o-p'ing* (kŭ'pĭng'), town and oasis (pop. 15,275), W Sinkiang prov., China, 75 mi. SW of Aksu and on road to Kashgar; cattle raising; agr. products.

Kelsall (kĕl'sôl), village and parish (pop. 874), W Cheshire, England, 7 mi. E of Chester.

Kelsey City, Fla.: see LAKE PARK.

Kelseyville, village (pop. c.300), Lake co., NW Calif., near Clear L., 8 mi. SE of Lakeport; pear orchards.

Kelso, burgh (1931 pop. 3,855; 1951 census 4,119), NE Roxburgh, Scotland, on the Tweed at mouth of the Teviot, and 17 mi. ENE of Selkirk; agr. market. There are ruins of abbey, founded 1128 by David I, partially destroyed by English in 1545. In late 18th cent. the Ballantyne brothers established printing press here, publishing Scott's *Minstrelsy of the Scottish Border* in 1802. James Thomson was b. in village of Ednam, 2 mi. N of Kelso; commemorative obelisk.

Kelso. 1 Town (pop. 276), Scott co., SE Mo., near Mississippi R., 3 mi. SW of Illmo. **2** City (pop. 7,345), ⊙ Cowlitz co., SW Wash., on Cowlitz R. just N of Longview; fish, timber, dairy products, fruit. Settled 1847; inc. as town 1889, as city 1908; became ⊙ 1932.

Kelsterbach (kĕl'stûrbäkh), village (pop. 6,787), S Hesse, W Germany, in former Starkenburg prov., on left bank of the canalized Main and 7 mi. W of Frankfurt; mfg. of synthetic fiber.

Keltemashat or **Kel'temashat** (kĕltyĭmŭshät'), town (1945 pop. over 500), SE South Kazakhstan oblast, Kazakh SSR, in the Talas Ala-Tau, 7 mi. SE of Sas-Tyube; coal mining.

Keltma or **Kel'tma** (kĕlt'mŭ), name of two rivers in E European Russian SFSR. Northern Keltma R., in S Komi Autonomous SSR, is a left affluent of Vychegda R.; c.60 mi. long. In its upper course, 10-mi.-long Yekaterina [Rus.,=Catherine] Canal connects it with Southern Keltma R. (50 mi. long), a left affluent of upper Kama R. in N Molotov oblast. The waterway (built 1822) is in disuse.

Kelton, parish (pop. 3,621, including part of Castle Douglas burgh), S Kirkcudbright, Scotland.

Keltsy, Poland: see KIELCE, city.

Kelty, town in Beath parish, S Fifeshire, Scotland, 6 mi. NNE of Dunfermline; coal mining.

Keltys (kĕl'tēz), city (pop. 1,091), Angelina co., E Texas, just NW of Lufkin; lumber milling.

Kelut or **Keloet** (klŏŏt), active volcano (5,193 ft.) of central Java, Indonesia, SE of Kediri and NE of Blitar. Erupts at 20-year intervals, last in 1951.

Kelve, India: see MAHIM.

Kelvedon (kĕl'vûdŭn), town and parish (pop. 1,695), NE central Essex, England, on Blackwater R. and 9 mi. WSW of Colchester; agr. market. Has 13th–15th-cent. church.

Kelvin Grove, NW suburb of Brisbane, SE Queensland, Australia; rubber goods mfg.

Kelvington, town (pop. 698), E Sask., 80 mi. NW of Yorkton; dairying, lumbering; grain, stock.

Kelvin River, Stirling, Dumbarton, and Lanark, Scotland, rises in Kilsyth Hills 3 mi. NE of Kilsyth, flows 21 mi. SW to the Clyde in NW Glasgow.

Kelvinside, NW industrial suburb (pop. 23,348) of Glasgow, Lanark, Scotland, on Kelvin R.

Kem or **Kem'** (kĕm), Finnish *Kemi* (kĕ'mē), city (1941 pop. 16,700), E Karelo-Finnish SSR, on White Sea, at mouth of Kem R., on Murmansk RR and 215 mi. N of Petrozavodsk; sawmilling, mfg. of prefabricated houses, metalworking; fishing. Railroad shops. Its port is Rabocheostrovsk, 5 mi. ENE; linked by rail spur. Kem is center of Pomorye (White Sea coast), a dist. with large Rus. pop. One of oldest settlements of Karelia and a 15th-cent. trading center.

Ké-Macina (kā'-mäsēnä') or **Macina**, town (pop. c.1,000), S Fr. Sudan, Fr. West Africa, landing in fertile Macina depression of the Niger (irrigation), 70 mi. ENE of Ségou. Wool market; mfg. of woolen blankets. Airfield.

Kemah (kĕmä'), village (pop. 1,975), Erzincan prov., E central Turkey, on Euphrates R., on railroad, and 25 mi. WSW of Erzincan; silver; grain.

Kemajoran, Indonesia: see JAKARTA.

Kemaliye (kĕmä'lĭyĕ"), village (pop. 3,442), Erzincan prov., E central Turkey, on Euphrates R. and 85 mi. ESE of Sivas; grain. Formerly Egin.

Kemalpasa (kĕmäl'pä-shä), Turkish *Kemalpaşa*, village (pop. 3,450), Smyrna prov., W Turkey, 14 mi. E of Smyrna; raisins, tobacco. Formerly Nif (Nymphio).

Kemaman, town, Malaya: see CHUKAI.

Kemaman River (kŭmä'män), S Trengganu, Malaya, rises on Pahang border, flows 60 mi. ESE to South China Sea at Kuala Kemaman; iron and tin mining along course.

Kemanai (kāmä'nī), town (pop. 6,330), Akita prefecture, N Honshu, Japan, 11 mi. E of Odate; agr.; gold mining.

Kemanlar, Bulgaria: see ISPERIKH.

Kemasik or **Kemasek** (kŭmä'sĭk), village (pop. 1,298), S Trengganu, Malaya, on South China Sea, 65 mi. SSE of Kuala Trengganu; coconuts; fishing.

Kemayoran, Indonesia: see JAKARTA.

Kembé (kĕmbā'), village, S Ubangi-Shari, Fr. Equatorial Africa, on Kotto R. and 120 mi. SE of Bambari; cotton ginning.

Kemberg (kĕm'bĕrk), town (pop. 4,336), in former Prussian Saxony prov., central Germany, after 1945 in Saxony-Anhalt, 7 mi. S of Wittenberg; mfg. (cement products, barrels).

Kembs (kãs, Ger. kĕmps), village (pop. 726), Haut-Rhin dept., E France, on Huningue canal near the Rhine, and 9 mi. SE of Mulhouse. Dam and hydroelectric plant on the Rhine, 3 mi. S.

Kemchik River, Russian SFSR: see KHEMCHIK RIVER.

Kemecse (kĕ'mĕchĕ), town (pop. 4,465), Szabolcs co., NE Hungary, 9 mi. NNE of Nyiregyhaza; petroleum refinery, distilleries, flour mills; corn, wheat, sheep, cattle.

Kemer, Turkey: see BURHANIYE.

Kemer Dag (kĕmĕr' dä), Turkish *Kemer Dağ*, peak (10,660 ft.), NE Turkey, in Trebizond Mts., 38 mi. SSE of Trebizond.

Kemeri (tyā'mārē), Lettish *Ķemeri*, Ger. *Kemmern*, city (pop. 1,149), W central Latvia, in Vidzeme, 23 mi. W of Riga, near S shore of Gulf of Riga; major health resort; sulphur springs, mud baths.

Kemerovo (kĕ'mŭrŏ"vō, -rōvō"), Rus. kyĕ'myĭrŭvŭ, kyĕmyĭrō'vŭ), oblast (□ 36,900; pop. c.1,950,000) in S central Siberian Russian SFSR; ⊙ Kemerovo. Bet. Salair Ridge (W) and Kuznetsk Ala-Tau (E); drained by Tom and Kiya rivers; continental climate. Most highly developed industrial area of Siberia, based mainly on KUZNETSK BASIN coal and GORNAYA SHORIYA iron mines; includes ferrous metallurgy (STALINSK, GURYEVSK), chemical industry (fertilizer, artificial fiber, plastics), zinc metallurgy (BELOVO). The pop. (chiefly Russians and, in S, Tatars), concentrated along Trans-Siberian RR (N) and its branches, are also engaged in truck farming. In mountainous areas (E, S) there is gold mining (KIYA RIVER), lumbering, fur trapping, cattle raising. Formed 1943 out of Novosibirsk oblast.

Kemerovo, city (1926 pop. 21,726; 1939 pop. 132,978), ⊙ Kemerovo oblast, Russian SFSR, on branch of Trans-Siberian RR, on Tom R. and 2,000 mi. E of Moscow; 54°20'N 86°3'E. One of largest coal-mining centers of Kuznetsk Basin; extensive chemical industry (lead-zinc electrolysis, coking, sulphuric-acid and nitrate fertilizer production); glassworks, sawmills, power plant. Founded 1916; until c.1935, called Shcheglovsk.

Kemi (kĕ'mē), city (pop. 23,387), Lapi co., NW Finland, on Gulf of Bothnia, at mouth of Kemi R., 55 mi. NNW of Oulu; 65°48'N 24°28'E. Timber-shipping center, with major lumber and pulp mills. Airfield at Lautiosaari (4 mi. NNW). Inc. 1869. Karihaara (NW) is chief industrial suburb.

Kemi, Karelo-Finnish SSR: see KEM, city.

Kemigawa, Japan: see CHIBA, city.

Kemijärvi (kĕ'mēyăr"vē), Swedish *Kemiträsk* (kā'mētrĕsk"), village (commune pop. 11,147), Lapi co., N Finland, on L. Kemi, Finnish *Kemijärvi*, Swedish *Kemiträsk*, expansion (20 mi. long, 1–5 mi. wide) of Kemi R., 50 mi. ENE of Rovaniemi; commercial center of important lumbering region. Airfield (W).

Kemijoki: see KEMI RIVER; KEM RIVER.

Kemin (kyĕ'mĭn), name of 2 glacier-fed rivers in E Frunze oblast, Kirghiz SSR. Greater Kemin R.

rises on Kazakh-Kirghiz border, flows c.70 mi. WSW, bet. the Trans-Ili Ala-Tau and Kungei Ala-Tau, to Chu R. N of Boom Gorge. Lesser Kemin R. rises in the Trans-Ili Ala-Tau, flows c.35 mi. parallel to and N of the Greater Kemin, past Ak-Tyuz and Buruldai, to Chu R. 20 mi. E of Tokmak. Also called Kebin.

Kemi River, Finnish *Kemijoki* (kĕ'mĕyō"kē), Swedish *Kemiälv* (kā'mĕĕlv"), Lapland, N Finland, rises near USSR border S of L. Inari, near 68°15'N 26°30'E, flows 340 mi. in winding course generally S, through 20-mi.-long L. Kemi, past Rovaniemi, to Gulf of Bothnia at Kemi. Ounas R. is chief tributary. Longest river of Finland, it is important logging route; salmon fishing. There are several hydroelectric stations.

Kemitrask, Finland: see KEMIJÄRVI.

Kemlya (kyĕm'lyŭ), village (1926 pop. 1,620), NE Mordvinian Autonomous SSR, Russian SFSR, near Alatyr R., 38 mi. SE of Lukoyanov; distilling; wheat, hemp, potatoes.

Kemmanugundi, India: see BABA BUDAN RANGE.

Kemmarath, Thailand: see KHEMMARAT.

Kemmel Hill, Belgium: see PLOEGSTEERT.

Kemmerer (kĕ'mûrûr), town (pop. 1,667), ⊙ Lincoln co., SW Wyo., on Hams Fork, near Utah line, and 70 mi. WNW of Rock Springs; alt. c.6,900 ft. Shipping point for coal, cattle, sheep. Fossil fish beds near by. Settled 1897, inc. 1899.

Kemmern, Latvia: see KEMERI.

Kemnath (kām'nät), town (pop. 2,909), Upper Palatinate, NE Bavaria, Germany, at SW foot of the Fichtelgebirge, 15 mi. ESE of Bayreuth; textiles; printing, tanning. Chartered in 14th cent.

Kemnay (kĕm'nā), village and parish (pop. 1,468), central Aberdeen, Scotland, on Don R. and 4 mi. W of Kintore; granite quarrying. The 17th-cent. Castle Fraser is 2 mi. S.

Kemoedjan, Indonesia: see KARIMUNJAWA ISLANDS.

Kémo-Gribingui, Fr. Equatorial Africa: see FORT-SIBUT.

Kémo River (kĕmō'), S Ubangi-Shari, Fr. Equatorial Africa, rises 35 mi. E of Dekoua, flows 120 mi. S to Ubangi R. just E of Fort-de-Possel.

Kemp. 1 Town (pop. 158), Bryan co., S Okla., near Red R., 16 mi. S of Durant, in agr. area. Hendrix, sometimes called Kemp City, is 3 mi. W. **2** Town (pop. 881), Kaufman co., NE Texas, c.40 mi. SE of Dallas; trade center in cotton, corn area.

Kemp, Lake, Texas: see WICHITA RIVER.

Kemp City. 1 Town, Bryan co., Okla.: see HENDRIX. **2** Village, Wichita co., Texas: see KAMAY.

Kemp Coast, Antarctica, E of Enderby Land, on Indian Ocean, bet. head of Edward VIII Bay and William Scoresby Bay; 67°10'S bet. 56° and 59°40' E. Discovered 1833 by Peter Kemp, Br. captain.

Kempen, Belgium: see CAMPINE.

Kempen (kĕm'pŭn), town (pop. 9,827), in former Prussian Rhine Prov., W Germany, after 1945 in North Rhine-Westphalia, 6 mi. WNW of Krefeld; rail junction; textile mfg. Has Gothic church, 14th-cent. castle. First mentioned 890. Chartered 1294. St. Thomas à Kempis b. here.

Kempen, Poland: see KEPNO.

Kempendyai or **Kempendyay** (kĕmpĭndyī'), village (1948 pop. over 500), SW Yakut Autonomous SSR, Russian SFSR, on short Kempendyai R. (right affluent of the Vilyui) and 150 mi. SSW of Vilyuysk; salt mining.

Kemper, France: see QUIMPER.

Kemper, county (□ 757; pop. 15,893), E Miss., bordering E on Ala.; ⊙ De Kalb. Drained by small Sucarnoochee R. and small Okatibbee Creek. Agr. (cotton, corn), cattle raising, lumbering. Formed 1833.

Kemperle, France: see QUIMPERLÉ.

Kemp Newby, village (pop. 1,324), Wichita co., N Texas.

Kemp's Bay, town (pop. 268), W Bahama Isls., on SE shore of Andros Isl., 75 mi. S of Nassau; 24°1'N 77°33'W. Fishing, lumbering.

Kempsey, municipality (pop. 6,330), E New South Wales, Australia, on Macleay R. and 145 mi. NNE of Newcastle; dairying and agr. center. Silver-lead mines near by.

Kempston, urban district (1931 pop. 5,390; 1951 census 8,641), W central Bedford, England, on Ouse R. and 2 mi. SW of Bedford; leather and shoe industry. Has Norman church.

Kempten (kĕmp'tŭn), Lat. *Cambodunum*, city (1950 pop. 39,715), Swabia, SW Bavaria, Germany, on the Iller and 52 mi. SW of Augsburg; 47°43'N 10°19'E. Important rail junction; center of Allgäu dairy industry (butter, cheese); cotton mfg., metalworking (agr. tools, optical and precision instruments); cardboard, lumber, and paper milling; before 1945, seat of Ger. abrasives industry. Trades in dairy produce and cattle of Allgäu. On site of Romanesque abbey church, destroyed by Swedes, is mid-17th-cent. church. City's late-Gothic city hall was renovated in 1560 and 1874–76. Has baroque castle; early-18th-cent. Grain House now contains dairy exchange and local mus. An anc. Celtic settlement, Kempten became important Roman trade center. Flourished in Middle Ages; created free imperial city in 1525. Suffered great damage in Thirty Years War. Passed to Bavaria in 1802.

Kempt Lake (22 mi. long, 15 mi. wide), SW central Que., in the Laurentians, 120 mi. NW of Montreal; alt. 1,372 ft. Drained (W) by Lièvre R. Contains numerous isls.

Kempton, village (pop. 276), SE central Tasmania, 24 mi. NNW of Hobart; wheat.

Kempton. 1 Village (pop. 255), Ford co., E Ill., 22 mi. WSW of Kankakee, in rich agr. area. **2** Town (pop. 438), Tipton co., central Ind., near Cicero Creek, 14 mi. SSE of Kokomo, in agr. area.

Kempton Park, England: see FELTHAM.

Kempton Park, town (pop. 4,874), S Transvaal, U. of So. Afr., 8 mi. NNE of Germistown, at N edge of Witwatersrand and of gold-mining region; alt. 5,456 ft.; iron, brick, cement works. Jan Smuts international airport near by.

Kemptville, village (pop. 1,232), SE Ont., near Rideau R. and Rideau Canal, 28 mi. S of Ottawa; dairying center, lumbering. Site of Ont. govt. Kemptville Agr. School.

Kem River or **Kem' River** (kĕm), Finnish *Kemijoki* (kĕ'mĕyôkē), in central Karelo-Finnish SSR, rises SE of Kuusamo (Finland), flows 240 mi. E, through Kuito Lakes, to Onega Bay of White Sea at Kem; many rapids. Logging route. Frozen Nov.–Apr.

Kemujan, Indonesia: see KARIMUNJAWA ISLANDS.

Ken, Loch, Scotland: see NEW GALLOWAY.

Kena, Egypt: see QENA.

Kenadsa (kānädzä'), town (pop. 7,840), Aïn-Sefra territory, W Algeria, near Fr. Morocco border, 13 mi. WSW of COLOMB-BÉCHAR (linked by rail); coal-mining center. Also spelled Kénadza.

Kenai (kē'nī), Indian village (pop. 281), S Alaska, W Kenai Peninsula, on Cook Inlet, at mouth of Kenai R., 65 mi. SW of Anchorage; fishing, fish processing. Has Russian Orthodox church, Protestant mission. U.S. garrison here, 1869. Established 1791 by Russians who built Fort St. Nicholas here.

Kenai Lake (25 mi. long, 1 mi. wide), S Alaska, 20 mi. N of Seward, on Alaska RR; fishing, hunting.

Kenai Mountains, part of the Coast Ranges, S Alaska, extend 150 mi. along SE side of Kenai Peninsula; slope steeply to Gulf of Alaska; rise to c.7,000 ft. 35 mi.WSW of Seward. Largely unsurveyed, range has several glacier fields. Continued NE by Chugach Mts.

Kenai Peninsula, S Alaska, extends 150 mi. SW from Anchorage into the Gulf of Alaska, bet. Turnagain Arm (N), Cook Inlet (NW), and Prince William Sound (NE); 59°10'–61°N 148°–152°W. Kenai Mts. extend along SE coast, rise to c.7,000 ft. Coastal regions have mild climate, abundant rainfall, suitable for raising of grain, vegetables, potatoes. E part of peninsula is part of Chugach Natl. Forest; fisheries. Seward is largest town; villages include Homer, Seldovia, Kasilof. Peninsula is crossed by Alaska RR from Seward. Kenai Indians form native pop. Kenai Natl. Moose Range (established 1941) is in NW part of peninsula.

Kenansville (kē'nŭnzvĭl), town (pop. 674), ⊙ Duplin co., E N.C., 30 mi. SW of Kinston; sawmilling.

Kenaston (kĕ'nŭstŭn), village (pop. 235), S central Sask., 36 mi. WSW of Watrous; wheat, stock.

Kenberma, Mass.: see HULL.

Kenbridge, town (pop. 1,176), Lunenburg co., S Va., 45 mi. WSW of Petersburg; tobacco market.

Kencco, Peru: see CUZCO, city.

Kenco, Peru: see CUZCO, city.

Kendal (kĕn'dŭl), municipal borough (1931 pop. 15,577; 1951 census 18,543), S Westmorland, England, on Kent R. and 20 mi. N of Lancaster; mfg. of shoes, wool textiles, carpets, paper, soap, farm machinery; limestone quarrying near by. Has church dating from 13th–15th cent., ruins of 14th-cent. castle, and some 16th-cent. houses. It is birthplace of Catherine Parr, last wife of Henry VIII. Here died the painter Romney. Known in Middle Ages for mfg. of wool cloth known as "Kendal Green." Woolen industry introduced by Flemish immigrants in early 14th cent. Remains of a Roman station found here.

Kendal (kŭndäl'), town (pop. 13,804), N Java, Indonesia, near Java Sea, 15 mi. W of Semarang; trade center for agr. area (sugar, rice, peanuts, tobacco, coffee, kapok). Large Chinese settlement.

Kendall (kĕn'dŭl). **1** County (□ 320; pop. 12,115), NE Ill.; ⊙ Yorkville. Rich dairying and farming area (corn, oats, soybeans, wheat, livestock, poultry). Mfg.: dairy products, metal and bakelite products, batteries, plumbing supplies, tin cans. Drained by Fox R. Formed 1841. **2** County (□ 670; pop. 5,423), S central Texas; ⊙ Boerne. Generally broken area, on S edge of Edwards Plateau; drained by Guadalupe and Blanco rivers and Cibolo Creek; alt. c.1,000–1,600 ft. Chiefly sheep, goat ranching region (wool, mohair marketed); also beef and dairy cattle, poultry, agr. (corn, fruit, grain sorghums). Timber; clay, limestone deposits. Hunting, fishing, scenery, caves (Cascade Caverns, others) attract tourists. Formed 1862.

Kendall, village (pop. 558), Monroe co., W central Wis., 45 mi. E of La Crosse, in dairying and livestock region.

Kendall Green, Mass.: see WESTON.

Kendall Mountain (13,000 ft.), SW Colo., peak in San Juan Mts., just E of Silverton.

Kendall Peak (13,451 ft.), SW Colo., in San Juan Mts., 3 mi. ESE of Silverton.

Kendallville (kĕn'dŭlvĭl), city (pop. 6,119), Noble co., NE Ind., on Elkhart R. and 27 mi. NNW of Fort Wayne; shipping center in agr. area (especially onions); also dairy products, livestock, soybeans, grain. Mfg.: refrigerators, farm equipment, pumps, rivets and other metal products, artificial bait, brushes, brooms. Mulholland Mus. has Indian and pioneer relics. Settled 1833.

Kendangan, Indonesia: see KANDANGAN.

Kendangomuwa (kĕndŭng-gō'mōōvŭ), town (pop. 794), Sabaragamuwa Prov., SW central Ceylon, 15 mi. NNW of Ratnapura; vegetables, rice, rubber. Graphite mines near by. Also spelled Kendangamuwa.

Kendari (kĕndä'rē), town (dist. pop. 89,834), SE Celebes, Indonesia, port on inlet of Gulf of Tomini, 230 mi. ENE of Macassar; 3°58'S 122°35'E; trade center, shipping timber, resin, rattan. There is an important gold-ornament industry, carried on by Chinese. Has airport. In Second World War Kendari was major Jap. naval base.

Kenderes (kĕn'dĕrĕsh), town (pop. 6,434), Jasz-Nagykun-Szolnok co., E central Hungary, 13 mi. WSW of Karcag; corn, tobacco, hogs, sheep.

Kenderlyk River (kĕndyĭrlĭk'), East Kazakhstan oblast, Kazakh SSR, rises in Saur Range, flows 105 mi. NW to L. Zaisan; coal and oil shale deposits.

Kendrapara (kāndrä'pärŭ), town (pop. 11,880), Cuttack dist., E Orissa, India, 34 mi. E of Cuttack; center of large rice-growing area; biri mfg., palm-mat making, hand-loom weaving. Visited by Hindu pilgrims; Vishnuite shrine.

Kendrick. 1 Village (pop. 409), Latah co., W Idaho, 18 mi. SE of Moscow; agr. center; dairy products. **2** Town (pop. 172), Lincoln co., central Okla., 14 mi. S of Cushing, in agr. area.

Kendrick Peak (10,418 ft.), rises from high plateau in Coconino co., N central Ariz., 18 mi. NW of Flagstaff.

Kenduskeag (kĕndŭs'kēg), town (pop. 387), Penobscot co., S Maine, in agr., lake area, 10 mi. NW of Bangor.

Kenduskeag Stream, S Maine, rises in S Penobscot co., flows c.30 mi. SE to the Penobscot at Bangor.

Kenedy (kĕ'nĭdē), county (□ 1,407; pop. 632), extreme S Texas; ⊙ Sarita. Flat coastal plain, bordering E on Laguna Madre, protected from Gulf of Mexico by Padre Isl. Large-scale ranching area (cattle; also horses, sheep, goats, hogs, poultry), mostly included in huge King Ranch and others; little agr. Formed 1921 from parts of Willacy, Hidalgo, and Cameron counties.

Kenedy, city (pop. 4,234), Karnes co., S Texas, c.60 mi. SE of San Antonio; trade, processing center in oil, cotton, corn area; health resort (mineral wells); cottonseed milling, cotton and grain processing, mattress, cheese mfg. Holds annual flax festival. Founded 1882, inc. 1910.

Kenefick (kĕ'nŭfĭk), town (pop. 115), Bryan co., S Okla., 11 mi. N of Durant, in agr. area; cotton ginning.

Keneh, Egypt: see QENA.

Kenema (kĕnĕ'mä), town (pop. 3,571), ⊙ South-Eastern Prov. (□ 6,005; pop. 362,175), E Sierra Leone, on railroad and 40 mi. ESE of Bo; trade and road center; palm oil and kernels, cacao, coffee. Sawmilling. Hq. Kenema dist. Chromite mining at Hangha (7 mi. NNE).

Kenesaw (kĕn'ŭsô), village (pop. 584), Adams co., S Nebr., 15 mi. W of Hastings.

Kenga River, Russian SFSR: see PARABEL RIVER.

Kenge (kĕng'gā), village, Leopoldville prov., SW Belgian Congo, on Wamba R. and 120 mi. WNW of Kikwit; steamboat landing and center of native trade, palm-oil milling, fiber growing.

Kengere (kĕng-gā'rā), village, Katanga prov., SE Belgian Congo, near Northern Rhodesia border, 85 mi. WSW of Jadotville; lead mining.

Kenghung, China: see CHELI.

Kengir (kyĭn-gĕr'), village, W Karaganda oblast, Kazakh SSR, on railroad and 50 mi. E of Karsakpai; site of dam and reservoir on Kengir R. (tributary of the Sary-Su).

Kengkok (kĕng'kôk'), town, Savannakhet prov., central Laos, 30 mi. ESE of Savannakhet.

Kengma (gŭng'mä'), village (pop. 4,442), ⊙ Kengma dist. (pop. 28,121), SW Yunnan prov., China, 75 mi. SSW of Shunning, in mtn. region; rice, millet, beans, rapeseed. Formerly called Tachai.

Kengtung (kĕng'tōōng'), easternmost state (sawbwaship) (□ 12,405; pop. 225,894), Southern Shan State, Upper Burma; ⊙ Kengtung. The largest and most populous Shan state, bounded NE by Chinese Yunnan prov., E by Laos along Mekong R., S by Thailand, and W by Salween R.; rises to over 8,000 ft.; drained by the Nam Hkok (right affluent of the Mekong). Rice and sugar cane in valleys, tea and opium in hills, teak forests. Sericulture, weaving, pottery. Exports opium, cotton. Sometimes spelled Kentung.

Kengtung, town (pop. 5,508), ⊙ Kengtung state, Southern Shan State, Upper Burma, 165 mi. E of Taunggyi, on road to Lampang (Thailand); trading center. A walled and moated town, it has palace, pagodas, and monasteries. Founded 1819.

Kenhardt, town (pop. 2,010), NW Cape Prov., U. of So. Afr., on Hartebeest R. and 60 mi. S of Upington; agr. center (wheat, stock, fruit).

Kenhorst, borough (pop. 2,551), Berks co., SE central Pa., just S of Reading. Inc. 1931.

Kéniéba (kĕnyĕ'bä), village (pop. c.1,400), SW Fr. Sudan, Fr. West Africa, on Bafing R. and 125 mi. SE of Kayes; peanuts, rice, millet, livestock.

Kenilworth (kĕ'nĭl–, kĕ'nŭl–), urban district (1931 pop. 7,592; 1951 census 10,738), central Warwick, England, 5 mi. SW of Coventry; leather tanning; agr. market. Has ruins of Kenilworth Castle, founded by Geoffrey de Clinton c.1120. In 16th cent. Queen Elizabeth gave it to Robert Dudley, earl of Leicester, who lavishly entertained her here in 1575. The castle and this event are described in Scott's novel *Kenilworth.* In the Civil War the castle was partly dismantled by Parliamentary troops. Town also has ruins of an Augustinian priory founded 1122.

Kenilworth, residential town (pop. 810), NE Cape Prov., U. of So. Afr., in Griqualand West, N suburb of Kimberley; company-owned settlement for diamond-mine employees.

Kenilworth. 1 Village (pop. 2,789), Cook co., NE Ill., N suburb of Chicago, on L. Michigan, just N of Wilmette. Inc. 1896. Eugene Field is buried here. **2** Borough (pop. 4,922), Union co., NE N.J., 4 mi. NW of Elizabeth; mfg. (machinery, metal products, concrete pipes, paper and coal-tar products, plastics, brushes). Inc. 1907.

Kenimekh (kĕnyĕmyĕkh'), town (1939 pop. over 2,000), SE Bukhara oblast, Uzbek SSR, 30 mi. NE of Gizhduvan; cotton, livestock; food processing.

Kenisa, Jebel el, or **Jabal al-Kanisah** (both: jĕ'bĕl ĕl kĕnē'sü), Fr. *Kenisse,* mountain (6,660 ft.), Lebanon range, central Lebanon, 16 mi. ESE of Beirut.

Kénitra, Fr. Morocco: see PORT-LYAUTEY.

Kenjakura (kän'jŭkŏŏrü), village, Bankura dist., W West Bengal, India, 11 mi. W of Bankura; cotton weaving; rice, corn, wheat. Also spelled Kenjiakura.

Kenjiho, Korea: see KYOMIPO.

Kenley, England: see COULSDON AND PURLEY.

Kenly (kĕn'lē), town (pop. 1,129), Johnston co., central N.C., 15 mi. SW of Wilson; sawmilling.

Kenmar, village (pop. 2,984, with adjacent Faxon), Lycoming co., N central Pa.

Kenmare (kĕnmâr'), Gaelic *Neid in,* town (pop. 906), S Co. Kerry, Ireland, at head of Kenmare R., 13 mi. SSW of Killarney; small port; woolen milling, copper mining. Founded 1670 by Sir William Petty.

Kenmare (kĕn'mâr), city (pop. 1,712), Ward co., N N.Dak., 47 mi. NW of Minot and on Des Lacs R. near Des Lacs L. Lignite mines; grain farms; dairy produce, livestock, potatoes. Inc. 1903.

Kenmare River (kĕnmâr'), deep inlet of the Atlantic, bet. SW Co. Cork and S Co. Kerry, Ireland, extends 28 mi. inland bet. Lamb's Head (N) and Dursey Head (S), 2 to 6 mi. wide. At head of bay is Kenmare.

Kenmore (kĕnmôr'), agr. village and parish (pop. 962), N central Perthshire, Scotland, on the Tay, at E end of Loch Tay, 6 mi. WSW of Aberfeldy; resort. The 19th-cent. Taymouth Castle (now a hotel) is on site of 16th-cent. Castle of Balloch.

Kenmore (kĕn'môr), residential village (pop. 20,066), Erie co., W N.Y., just N of Buffalo; mfg. (chemicals, machinery; wood, metal, and rubber products; silk, electrical appliances); diversified farming. Inc. 1899.

Kennai, Korea: see HYONNAE.

Kennan, village (pop. 194), Price co., N Wis., 25 mi. ENE of Ladysmith; dairying.

Kennard. 1 (kĕ'nürd, kŭnärd', kĕnärd') Town (pop. 485), Henry co., E central Ind., 8 mi. W of New Castle, in agr. area. **2** (kĕ'närd) Village (pop. 273), Washington co., E Nebr., 20 mi. NNW of Omaha, near Missouri R.

Kennebago Lake (kĕnŭbā'gō), Franklin co., W Maine, lake (5 mi. long, 1 mi. wide) 10 mi. N of Rangeley L.; hunting, fishing.

Kennebec (kĕ'nŭbĕk), county (□ 865; pop. 83,881), S Maine; ⊙ Augusta, state capital. Mfg. (shoes, textiles, paper, wood and pulp products) at Hallowell, Waterville, and Gardiner on the Kennebec; dairying; canning and shipping of farm, orchard produce. Water power from Sebasticook and Kennebec rivers. Many resorts, notably in Belgrade and Kennebec lakes regions. Formed 1799.

Kennebec, town (pop. 374), ⊙ Lyman co., S central S.Dak., 40 mi. SE of Pierre and on Medicine Creek; trade center for farming region; dairy produce, livestock, poultry, grain. Dam and game preserve near by.

Kennebecasis River (kĕ"nĕbŭkā'sĭs, –kā'sĭs), S N.B., rises NE of Sussex, flows 60 mi. SW, past Sussex and Hampton, through 20-mi.-long estuary called Kennebecasis Bay (4 mi. wide) to St. John R. just above St. John.

Kennebec River (kĕ'nŭbĕk), Maine, flows from Moosehead L. in W central Maine c.150 mi. S to the Atlantic, furnishing power at Bingham, Skowhegan, Waterville, Augusta (head of navigation), and Gardiner; receives Androscoggin R. 25 mi. below Augusta to form Merrymeeting Bay; harbor at Bath is 12 mi. from the Atlantic. Explored by Champlain, 1604–05; 1st English settlement in Maine (Fort St. George) made at mouth in 1607.

Kennebunk (kĕ'nĭbŭngk, kĕnĭbŭngk'), town (pop. 4,273), York co., SW Maine, 22 mi. SSW of Portland and on Mousam and Kennebunk rivers, in resort area; wood products. Church bldg. (with Paul Revere bell, 1803) dates from Revolutionary times. Settled c.1650, inc. 1820. **Kennebunk Beach** village, resort, is on the coast 1 mi. W of Kennebunkport.

Kennebunkport or **Kennebunk Port** (both: kĕn"-ĭbŭngkpôrt', kĕn"ĭbŭngk'pôrt), town (pop. 1,522), York co., SW Maine, on the coast just SE of Kennebunk, at mouth of Kennebunk R.; summer resort, esp. for authors, artists, and actors. Summer playhouse opened 1933. Congregational church dates from 1764. Settled 1629; became shipping, shipbuilding center in 18th cent.; renamed from Arundel 1821. Forest fire (1947) did much damage in environs.

Kennebunk River (kĕ'nĭbŭngk, kĕnĭbŭngk'), SW Maine, rises in central York co., flows 15 mi. SE to the Atlantic at Kennebunkport.

Kennecott, Alaska: see KENNICOTT.

Kennedale (kĕ'nĭdāl), town (pop. 1,046), Tarrant co., N Texas, suburb 10 mi. SE of downtown Fort Worth. Inc. after 1940.

Kennedy, village (pop. 223), SE Sask., 30 mi. WSW of Moosomin; mixed farming.

Kennedy. 1 Town (pop. 393), Lamar co., W Ala., 35 mi. NW of Tuscaloosa. **2** Village (pop. 480), Kittson co., NW Minn., 9 mi. S of Hallock, in Red R. valley; shipping point for seed potatoes, in grain and livestock area; dairy products. **3** Village (1940 pop. 526), Chautauqua co., extreme W N.Y., on Conewango Creek and 8 mi. NE of Jamestown, in agr. area.

Kennedy Channel, sea passage (80 mi. long, 16–24 mi. wide), in the Arctic, bet. NE Ellesmere Isl. (Canada) and NW Greenland; 81°N 66°W. Opens N to the Arctic via Hall Basin, S to Kane Basin. Limited navigation in late summer and fall.

Kennedy Lake (20 mi. long, 1–3 mi. wide), SW B.C., on W Vancouver Isl., 30 mi. WSW of Port Alberni. Drains W into Tofino Inlet of Clayoquot Sound.

Kennedy Peak (7,540 ft.), SE Ariz., in Galiuro Mts., c.50 mi. NE of Tucson.

Kennedyville, village, Kent co., E Md., on the Eastern Shore 7 mi. NE of Chestertown; vegetable cannery. Near by is Shrewsbury Church, built 1832 on site of original church of late 1600s.

Kenner, town (pop. 5,535), Jefferson parish, SE La., on the Mississippi, just W of New Orleans; trading and shipping center for vegetable-growing area; mfg. (wood products, sheet metal, concrete products).

Kennesaw (kĕ'nŭsô), town (pop. 564), Cobb co., NW central Ga., 22 mi. NW of Atlanta. Kennesaw Mtn. Natl. Battlefield Park near by.

Kennesaw Mountain, peak in Cobb co., NW Ga., 15 mi. NW of Atlanta. Rises in 2 summits of 1,550 ft. and 1,809 ft. Kennesaw Mtn. Natl. Battlefield Park (□ 4.8; established 1947) is here, on site of battle of Kennesaw Mtn. (1864), decisive engagement of Civil War in which Union troops under Sherman made 2 unsuccessful attacks on Confederates led by Gen. J. E. Johnston, then forced retirement of Confederates by means of flanking tactics.

Kenneth, village (pop. 119), Rock co., SW Minn., 10 mi. NE of Luverne, in grain and potato area.

Kennet River, England, rises on Marlborough Downs in E Wiltshire, flows 44 mi. E into Berkshire, past Hungerford, to the Thames at Reading.

Kennett (kĕn'ŭt), city (pop. 8,685), ⊙ Dunklin co., extreme SE Mo., near St. Francis R., 42 mi. SE of Poplar Bluff; cotton gins and compresses; produces shirts. Founded c.1845.

Kennett Square, borough (pop. 3,699), Chester co., SE Pa., 12 mi. NW of Wilmington, Del.; mushrooms; canned goods, fiber products, machinery. Near by are famous Longwood Gardens. Settled c.1750, inc. 1855.

Kennewick (kĕ'nŭwĭk), city (1940 pop. 1,918; 1950 pop. 10,106), Benton co., S Wash., on Columbia R. (bridged) opposite Pasco; fruit, dairy products, wheat; river port (barges). Inc. 1904; pop. boomed during Second World War with influx of workers at atomic-energy installation near Richland (NW).

Kenney, village (pop. 409), De Witt co., central Ill., 17 mi. NNW of Decatur, in agr. area.

Kennicott (kĕ'nĭkŭt, –kŏt), village, S Alaska, 120 mi. NE of Cordova, at foot of Wrangell Mts.; site of formerly important Kennecott copper mine, discovered 1898, closed down 1938. Village now practically deserted. Formerly sometimes spelled Kennecott.

Kennington. 1 Town and parish (pop. 1,850), E central Kent, England, 2 mi. NE of Ashford; agr. market, with brickworks. Has Norman church. **2** District of Lambeth, London, England, on S bank of the Thames (here crossed by Vauxhall Bridge), 2 mi. S of Charing Cross. Here is the Oval, one of London's principal cricket grounds. On river embankment are famous Doulton pottery works. Kennington was site of Vauxhall Gardens, noted entertainment center of the Regency period.

Kennoway (kĕ'nŭwā), agr. village and parish (pop. 1,709), central Fifeshire, Scotland, 3 mi. NW of Leven.

Kenogami or **Kénogami** (kĕnŏ'gŭmē), town (pop. 6,579), S central Que., on Sable R. (tributary of Saguenay R.) and 8 mi. W of Chicoutimi; paper, pulp milling; dairying. Hydroelectric station.

Kenogami, Lake (17 mi. long, 1–5 mi. wide), central Que., on Chicoutimi R. and 10 mi. SW of Chicoutimi. Water reservoir for Chicoutimi-Arvida region.

Kenogami River, NW Ont., issues from N end of Long L., flows c.200 mi. E and N to Albany R. at 51°6'N 84°30'W.

Keno Hill (kē'nō), village, central Yukon, near Stewart R., 30 mi. NE of Mayo Landing; 63°55'N 135°19'W; silver and lead mining.

Kenora (kŭnô'rŭ), district (□ 153,220; pop. 33,372), W Ont., on L. of the Woods and on Man. border; ⊙ Kenora.

Kenora, town (pop. 7,745), ⊙ Kenora dist., W Ont., on L. of the Woods, 120 mi. E of Winnipeg; paper, pulp, lumber, and flour milling, boatbuilding, fur trading; in gold-mining, dairying, grain-growing region. Govt. fish hatchery; seaplane base. Resort center for hunting and fishing.

Kenosha (kĭnō'shŭ), county (□ 273; pop. 75,238), extreme SE Wis.; ⊙ Kenosha. Bordered E by L. Michigan, S by Ill. line; drained by Des Plaines and Fox rivers. Dairying and farming area (livestock, oats, corn). Mfg. at Kenosha. Lake resorts. Formed 1850.

Kenosha, industrial city (pop. 54,368), ⊙ Kenosha co., extreme SE Wis., port on L. Michigan, 28 mi. S of Milwaukee; mfg. (automobiles, mattresses, metal products, machinery, furniture, leather goods, rope, refrigerators, hosiery). Points of interest: Gilbert M. Simmons Library; civic center, with historical and art mus.; co. courthouse, with co. historical mus.; parks. First public school in Wis. established here (1849). Liberal German refugees came in 1850s. Settled c.1835; named Southport c.1837; inc. as Kenosha in 1850.

Kenosha Hills, central Colo., in Front Range, just N of Tarryall Mts., W of South Platte R. Rise 12,350 ft. in Kenosha Cones. Kenosha Pass crosses hills in NW tip.

Kenosha Pass (10,001 ft.), central Colo., in Kenosha Hills, Park co., c.45 mi. SW of Denver. Crossed by highway.

Kenova (kĭnō'vŭ), city (pop. 4,320), Wayne co., W W.Va., on the Ohio, at Big Sandy R. mouth, and 8 mi. W of Huntington, in bituminous-coal-mining area; sand and gravel pits; trade center; rail junction; lumber milling; mfg. of petroleum products, clay products, chemicals, cement, wood products, insulators. Inc. 1894.

Kenoza Lake (kŭnō'zŭ), resort village, Sullivan co., SE N.Y., on small Kenoza L., 12 mi. WSW of Liberty.

Ken River (kān), central India, rises in central Vindhya Range 15 mi. WNW of Katni (Murwara) in N Madhya Pradesh; flows c.235 mi. generally N, through central Vindhya Pradesh and S Uttar Pradesh, to Jumna R. 21 mi. SW of Fatehpur. Receives Sonar R. (left).

Kensal (kĕn'sŭl), village (pop. 376), Stutsman co., central N.Dak., 27 mi. N of Jamestown.

Kensal Green (kĕn'sŭl), famous cemetery in NW London, England, 4.5 mi. WNW of Charing Cross. Laid out 1832, it contains graves of Brunel, Thackeray, Trollope, John Owen, and Leigh Hunt.

Kensal Rise, England: see WILLESDEN.

Kenscoff (kĕnskôf'), town, Ouest dept., S Haiti, mtn. resort in the Massif de la Selle, 6 mi. SSE of Port-au-Prince; alt. c.4,400 ft.

Kensett (kĕn'sĭt). **1** Town (pop. 829), White co., central Ark., 4 mi. ESE of Searcy, in agr. area. **2** Town (pop. 424), Worth co., N Iowa, 14 mi. N of Mason City; livestock, grain.

Kensico Reservoir (kĕn'zĭkō) (2,218 acres), Westchester co., SE N.Y., a main unit of New York city water-supply system, impounded by Kensico Dam (307 ft. high; completed 1916) in Bronx R. c.3 mi. N of White Plains. Receives waters of Esopus and Schoharie creeks via CATSKILL AQUEDUCT, water from Delaware R. project through DELAWARE AQUEDUCT, and part of flow of Byram R.

Kensington (kĕn'zĭngtŭn), town (pop. 767), W central P.E.I., near Malpeque Bay, 10 mi. ENE of Summerside; agr. market in dairying, cattle-raising, potato-growing region.

Kensington, metropolitan and royal borough (1931 pop. 180,677; 1951 census 168,054) of London, England, N of the Thames, 3.5 mi. W of Charing Cross. A residential dist., it includes Kensington Gardens (274 acres), public park adjoining Hyde Park, originally the grounds of Kensington Palace. Features of gardens are Long Water (extension of the Serpentine), Orangery and Queen Anne's Alcove (designed by Wren), Round Pond, Dutch Garden, Flower Walk, and Broad Walk. Kensington Palace incorporates part of Nottingham House, with additions or alterations by Wren and William Kent. It became royal residence under William and Mary; Queen Anne, George II, and Queen Victoria (b. here) lived in it. It suffered air-raid damage in 1940. Holland House (N) was residence of the Fox family and of William Pitt. On S side of

Kensington Gardens are Albert Hall, Albert Memorial. South Kensington is col. and mus. center, with Victoria and Albert Mus., British Mus. of Natural History, Imperial Inst., Science Mus., Royal Col. of Art, Royal Col. of Science, and Royal Geographical Society.

Kensington. **1** Village, Hartford co., Conn.: see BERLIN. **2** City (pop. 635), Smith co., N Kansas, 13 mi. W of Smith Center, in corn belt; grain storage; metalworking. **3** Town (pop. 1,611), Montgomery co., central Md., NNW of Washington, on Rock Creek. **4** Village (pop. 354), Douglas co., W Minn., 18 mi. WSW of Alexandria; dairy products. Kensington Rune Stone, with anc. inscription describing journey of Swedish and Norwegian explorers, was found near by in 1898. **5** Town (pop. 542), Rockingham co., SE N.H., 12 mi. SW of Portsmouth. **6** Residential village (pop. 978), Nassau co., SE N.Y., near N shore of W Long Isl., just SSE of Great Neck, in summer-resort area.

Kensington and Norwood, E suburb (pop. 15,709) of Adelaide, SE South Australia; consists of 2 adjacent towns; cream of tartar factory.

Kensworth, agr. village and parish (pop. 583), S Bedford, England, 2 mi. SE of Dunstable; cement works. Has Norman church.

Kent. **1** County (□ 1,734; pop. 25,817), E N.B., on Northumberland Strait and Gulf of St. Lawrence; ⊙ Richibucto **2** County (□ 918; pop. 66,346), S Ont., on L. Erie, L. St. Clair, and Thames R.; ⊙ Chatham.

Kent, county (□ 1,524.9; 1931 pop. 1,219,273; 1951 census 1,563,286), SE England; ⊙ Maidstone. Bounded by Surrey (W), London (NW), Thames estuary (N), English Channel (E), and Sussex (SE). Drained by Thames, Medway, Stour, Darent, and Cray rivers. Off the Channel coast is roadstead of The Downs, protected by Goodwin Sands. Many lighthouses and lightships mark coastline. Co. includes Isle of THANET, Isle of SHEPPEY, and Isle of GRAIN, separated from mainland by narrow channels or rivers. The country is mostly flat, crossed by North Downs; in SE is drained ROMNEY MARSH; and in S the formerly wooded WEALD dist. Agr. includes hop, fruit, and grain growing, sheep raising, dairying. Chief industries are mfg. of paper, cement, brick, tile, leather; shipbuilding; brewing. Important coal deposits in NE. Besides Maidstone, other important towns are Canterbury; ports of Dover, Folkestone, and Gravesend; resorts of Ramsgate and Margate; naval base of Chatham; Rochester, Gillingham, Hythe, Deal, Tunbridge Wells, Tonbridge, Dartford, Bexley, Bromley. The co. formed Anglo-Saxon kingdom of Kent and played major part in early English history. There are many traces of Roman occupation, and many remains of the special culture of Kent in Anglo-Saxon times, commonly called Jutish culture.

Kent, village (1931 pop. 371), Sierra Leone colony, on Atlantic Ocean, on Cape Shilling of Sierra Leone Peninsula and 22 mi. S of Freetown; fishing.

Kent. **1** County (□ 595; pop. 37,870), central Del.; ⊙ Dover, state capital. Flat farming area, with some marshland; bounded N by Smyrna R., W by Md. line, S by Mispillion R., E by Delaware R. and Delaware Bay; drained by Leipsic, Choptank, Murderkill, and St. Jones rivers. Agr. (corn, vegetables, wheat, fruit, dairy products, poultry), fishing; oysters; fruit and vegetable canning, processing of dairy products; some mfg. at Dover. Formed 1683. **2** County (□ 284; pop. 13,677), E Md.; ⊙ Chestertown. Peninsula on Eastern Shore, bounded E by Del. line, W by Chesapeake Bay. Coastal plain agr. area (vegetables, fruit, corn, wheat, livestock, dairy products); large seafood industry (especially oysters); summer resorts; fishing, hunting. Includes many beautiful old churches and houses. Formed 1642. **3** County (□ 862; pop. 288,292), SW Mich.; ⊙ GRAND RAPIDS. Intersected by Grand R. and drained by Flat, Rogue, and Thornapple rivers. Fruitgrowing (apples, peaches); also agr. (livestock, poultry, truck, grain, corn, potatoes, beans; dairy products). Mfg. at Grand Rapids. Gypsum quarries, gravel pits. Lake resorts. Has a state fish hatchery. Organized 1836. **4** County (□ 172; pop. 77,763), W and central R.I., bounded E by Narragansett Bay, W by Conn. line; ⊙ East Greenwich. Industrial, resort and agr. area, producing chiefly textiles and textile machinery; also metal products, tools, chemicals; agr. (dairy products, poultry, corn, potatoes, fruit, mushrooms, truck); fisheries; lumbering. Many coast resorts. Includes state forests and parks. Drained by Pawtuxet, Moosup, Flat, and Wood rivers. Inc. 1750. **5** County (□ 901; pop. 2,249), NW Texas; ⊙ Clairemont. Rolling plains, with some broken areas; alt. 2,000–2,800 ft.; drained by Salt and Double Mtn. forks of Brazos R. Cattle-ranching region; also sheep, hogs, horses, poultry; agr. (corn, grain sorghums, oats, wheat, peanuts); beekeeping. Some oil; clay, sand, gravel. Formed 1876.

Kent. **1** Resort town (pop. 1,392), Litchfield co., W Conn., on Housatonic R. and N.Y. line, 19 mi. WSW of Torrington, in hilly region; agr., summer camps. Kent school for boys (1906) here. Includes South Kent village, seat of South Kent school (1923); 3 state parks. L. Waramaug is SE. Settled 1738, inc. 1739. **2** Town (pop. 169), Union co., S Iowa, near Little Platte R., 8 mi. SW of Creston. **3** Village (pop. 178), Wilkin co., W Minn., on Red R. and 32 mi. S of Fargo, N.Dak., in grain area. **4** City (pop. 12,418), Portage co., NE Ohio, 9 mi. NE of downtown Akron and on Cuyahoga R., within Akron metropolitan dist.; mfg. (motor vehicles, electrical apparatus, tools, wire products, machinery, furniture). Seat of Kent State Univ. Settled as Franklin Mills, which combined with Carthage and was renamed Kent in 1863; inc. as city in 1920. **5** City (pop. 3,278), King co., W central Wash., 15 mi. S of Seattle, near White R., in rich agr. valley; vegetables (especially lettuce), hops; canning and freezing plants. Founded 1860; inc. as town 1889, as city 1908.

Kent City, village (pop. 506), Kent co., SW Mich., 18 mi. NNW of Grand Rapids, in farm area.

Kentei, Khentei, or **Hentey** (all: khĕn'tā), aimak (□ 35,200; pop. 65,000), E central Mongolian People's Republic; ⊙ Undur Khan. Bounded N by Chita oblast of Russian SFSR, it extends from the wooded Kentei Mts. (NW) to the steppe (E) and is traversed by Kerulen R.

Kentei Mountains, Khentei Mountains, or **Hentey Mountains,** Mongolian *Henteyn Nuruu* (khĕn'tān nōō'rōō), in N Mongolian People's Republic, forming part of Transbaikalian mtn. system; extend 150 mi. NE from Ulan Bator; rise to 9,025 ft. in the Asaraltu, 45 mi. NE of Ulan Bator. Densely forested, the range forms a major watershed of the Iro, Khara, and Tola rivers of the Selenga-Baikal basin, and the Onon and Kerulen rivers of the Amur basin.

Kentfield, residential village (1940 pop. 1,352), Marin co., W Calif., just SW of San Rafael. Marin Jr. Col. is here.

Kentish Town, workers' residential district of St. Pancras, London, England, N of the Thames, 3 mi. NNW of Charing Cross.

Kent Island, E Md., largest (c.15 mi. long, 1–6 mi. wide) and most historic of Chesapeake Bay isls., in Queen Annes co., at S side of mouth of Chester R., E of Annapolis; separated from Eastern Shore mainland by narrow channel (bridged). Chester (1940 pop. 699; seafood packing) and Stevensville (pop. c.400; peach growing) are chief villages; others are Love Point (at N tip; lighthouse); Romancoke (rō'mŭnkōk) (S); Matapeake (mă'tŭpēk); Dominion; and Normans. Kent Point (S tip) has lighthouse. Isl. is E anchor of Chesapeake Bay Bridge. Large fishing and oystering fleet; seafood processing; tourist resort, with fishing (bluefish, rock and black bass), bathing, and duck hunting. William Claiborne established here (1631) 1st permanent English settlement in Md., claiming isl. for Va.; Lord Baltimore's grant of 1632 transferred it to Md., but conflicting claims remained unsettled until 1657. Near Stevensville is Kent Fort Manor (built c.1638–40).

Kentland, town (pop. 1,633), ⊙ Newton co., NW Ind., near Ill. line, 38 mi. NW of Lafayette, in dairying and farming area; makes cheese; ships seed. Settled 1860. George Ade was b. here.

Kenton. **1** Town and parish (pop. 1,837), S Devon, England, near Exe R. estuary, 6 mi. SSE of Exeter; agr. market. Has 15th-cent. church. **2** Suburb, Middlesex, England: see WEMBLEY.

Kenton, county (□ 165; pop. 104,254), extreme N Ky.; ⊙ Independence and Covington. Bounded N by Ohio R. (Ohio line), E by Licking R. Gently rolling upland area, in outer Bluegrass region. Includes part of metropolitan dist. of Cincinnati (N, across the Ohio). Mfg. and residential communities in N; some agr. (dairy products, poultry, livestock, corn, burley tobacco, alfalfa). Formed 1840.

Kenton. **1** Town (pop. 211), Kent co., W central Del., 9 mi. NW of Dover; canning. **2** City (pop. 8,475), ⊙ Hardin co., W central Ohio, 26 mi. ESE of Lima and on Scioto R.; trade center for agr. area; makes candy, machinery, tools, railroad equipment, toys. Limestone quarries. Platted 1833. **3** Village (pop. c.300), Cimarron co., extreme NW Okla., on high plains of the Panhandle, near N.Mex. line, 28 mi. NW of Boise City. Just NW is Black Mesa (4,978 ft.), highest point in Okla. **4** Town (pop. 899), Gibson and Obion counties, NW Tenn., on headstream (Rutherford Fork) of the Obion and 15 mi. S of Union City; trade center for farm area.

Kenton Vale, town (pop. 165), Kenton co., N Ky.

Kent Peninsula, NE Mackenzie Dist., Northwest Territories, on Dease Strait; 68°12'–68°56'N 104°55'–108°51'W. Extends 105 mi. W from narrow isthmus into Coronation Gulf; 7–29 mi. wide.

Kent Point, Md.: see KENT ISLAND.

Kent River, Westmorland, England, rises 9 mi. WSW of Shap, flows 20 mi. S, past Kendal, to its estuary on Morecambe Bay.

Kent's Cavern or **Kent's Hole,** England: see TORQUAY.

Kents Hill, Maine: see READFIELD.

Kentucky (kŭntŭ'kē, kĕn–), state (land □ 40,109; with inland waters □ 40,395; 1950 pop. 2,944,806; 1940 pop. 2,845,627), S central U.S., bordered N by Ohio and Ind., S by Tenn., E by W.Va., SE by Va., W by Ill., and SW by Mo.; 36th in area, 19th in pop.; admitted 1792 as 15th state; ⊙ Frankfort. The "Bluegrass State" is bounded by the Ohio (NW), the Big Sandy and Tug Fork (E), and the Mississippi (SW). It is c.425 mi. long E-W, c.180 mi. N-S. The state is hilly in the E (CUMBERLAND PLATEAU; Eastern Coal Field) and W (Western Coal Field); gently rolling in the center, whose N portion is in BLUEGRASS region and whose S part is the Pennyroyal plateau; flat in SW corner (the Purchase). The Eastern Coal Field is a forested, rugged, stream-dissected area bordered by sharp escarpments (Cumberland, Pine mts.) in the SE, where Big Black Mtn. rises to 4,150 ft., the highest point in the state. The rivers flow generally NW to Ohio R. The Licking, the Kentucky (and its tributary, the Dix), and Salt rivers drain E and N central Kentucky; the Cumberland and Green rivers flow through the W and S central parts; and the Tennessee demarcates the SW corner. There are several large lakes—Herrington, Wolf Creek, Dale Hallow, and Kentucky—formed by govt. (including TVA) and privately owned power dams. In the limestone regions many miles of subsurface stream channels, sinks, and caves (notably Mammoth Cave) have been dissolved in the bedrock. Originally most of the state was covered by hardwood forests; today c.45% of the area is timbered, especially in the E and, to a lesser extent, in the W. Kentucky has hot summers (average temp. c.75°F.) and short winters (c.36°F.) with 2 to 3 months of cold weather, when 10 to 20 inches of snow fall. The growing season is 176–197 days; average annual rainfall 45 inches. The state is primarily agricultural, with nearly 50% of the population living on farms and another 20% in rural towns. Erosion is widespread with c.45% of the state severely eroded and only c.5% of the area unaffected. Tobacco (especially burley) is the chief cash crop, although corn, hay, and pasture occupy the largest acreages. Wheat, other small grains, Irish and sweet potatoes are also grown. A major source of farm income is livestock (cattle, hogs, horses, mules, sheep, poultry). The best farm lands are the Bluegrass and Pennyroyal, which are separated by a chain of low hills called the Knobs. The Bluegrass region, the richest farm and livestock area in the state, is famed for its horse farms and distilleries (located here because of the quality of the water). Here are FRANKFORT, the capital, and the state's 3 largest cities—LOUISVILLE, where the Kentucky Derby is run, LEXINGTON, the heart of the region, and COVINGTON. Other important centers are Bardstown, Cynthiana, Danville, and Harrodsburg. In the Pennyroyal plateau are Bowling Green, Hopkinsville, Princeton, and Russellville. Mammoth Cave National Park, here, is a great tourist attraction. Kentucky is nationally important as a mineral producer, ranking 3d in bituminous coal, its chief mineral, and 2d in fluorspar and rock asphalt (both chiefly from the Pennyroyal). The state also produces petroleum and natural gas (from the coal fields and Pennyroyal), iron (Eastern Coal Field), limestone (Bluegrass, Pennyroyal), and clay. The Eastern Coal Field is the chief coal-mining region, with Harlan co. the leading producer. Iron is mined in the vicinity of ASHLAND, the chief city of E Kentucky. Sawmills (lumber, mine props), subsistence farms, and small towns are typical of the E, as is the isolation caused by a scanty transportation system geared chiefly to the needs of the mines. The W edge of the plateau is largely included in Cumberland Natl. Forest and contains natural bridges (Kentucky Natural Bridge, others). The Western Coal Field, bordered NW and N by the Ohio and enclosed on three sides by the Pennyroyal, resembles the E field in topography but is less rugged and therefore suitable for farming as well as mining. OWENSBORO, HENDERSON, and CENTRAL CITY are the chief towns. To the SW, beyond the Tennessee R., is the Purchase, so called because Andrew Jackson bought it from the Indians. This low plain is the chief clay-mining region, and also a farming area. PADUCAH and MAYFIELD are here. Kentucky's industries are based on the processing of its farm, mineral, and forest products. The principal manufactures are food and metal goods, textiles (especially clothing), lumber and furniture, chemicals, and tobacco products. Most of the mfg. centers—Louisville, Covington, Ashland, Maysville, Owensboro, and Paducah—are on the Ohio R., an important transportation artery. Land companies from Va. and N.C. promoted the early settlement of Kentucky. In 1750 an expedition headed by Dr. Thomas Walker entered the region through Cumberland Gap and explored the Big Sandy R. area. The 1st permanent settlement, Harrodsburg, was established 1774, and the next year Daniel Boone founded BOONESBORO. New settlers followed—some through the Gap and others down the Ohio. By 1794 the Indians had been decisively defeated. The pattern of small farms restricted the growth of slavery, although prior to the Civil War there were large markets here which supplied slaves for the lower South. Like other border states, Kentucky supplied men to both the North and South, a condition exemplified by the fact that Lincoln and Davis were both born here. Major engagements were fought at MILL SPRINGS.

Richmond, Munfordville, and Perryville. During the hard times after the war, the farmers turned to the Granger, Farmer's Alliance, and Populist movements. In the 1870s coal mining began on a large scale and was well established early in the 20th cent. After the boom of the First World War, unemployment and the continued poor living conditions resulted in a series of quarrels between the miners and operators. In the 1930s, when unionization was attempted in Harlan co., the violence reached its peak and the many killings resulted in a U.S. Senate subcommittee investigation in 1937. Peace was restored in 1939 when the United Mine Workers of America was finally recognized as a bargaining agent. Meanwhile a vast improvement of the highway system had been begun in the 1920s, the state government reorganized, and educational opportunities extended. The chief institutions of higher learning include the Univ. of Kentucky (at Lexington), Univ. of Louisville, and Berea Col. Fort Knox was a major training center in the Second World War. See also the articles on cities, towns, geographic features, and the 120 counties: Adair, Allen, Anderson, Ballard, Barren, Bath, Bell, Boone, Bourbon, Boyd, Boyle, Bracken, Breathitt, Breckinridge, Bullitt, Butler, Caldwell, Calloway, Campbell, Carlisle, Carroll, Carter, Casey, Christian, Clark, Clay, Clinton, Crittenden, Cumberland, Daviess, Edmonson, Elliott, Estill, Fayette, Fleming, Floyd, Franklin, Fulton, Gallatin, Garrard, Grant, Graves, Grayson, Green, Greenup, Hancock, Hardin, Harlan, Harrison, Hart, Henderson, Henry, Hickman, Hopkins, Jackson, Jefferson, Jessamine, Johnson, Kenton, Knott, Knox, Larue, Laurel, Lawrence, Lee, Leslie, Letcher, Lewis, Lincoln, Livingston, Logan, Lyon, McCracken, McCreary, McLean, Madison, Magoffin, Marion, Marshall, Martin, Mason, Meade, Menifee, Mercer, Metcalfe, Monroe, Montgomery, Morgan, Muhlenberg, Nelson, Nicholas, Ohio, Oldham, Owen, Owsley, Pendleton, Perry, Pike, Powell, Pulaski, Robertson, Rockcastle, Rowan, Russell, Scott, Shelby, Simpson, Spencer, Taylor, Todd, Trigg, Trimble, Union, Warren, Washington, Wayne, Webster, Whitley, Wolfe, Woodford.

Kentucky Dam, SW Ky., in Tennessee R., 22.4 river mi. above its mouth in Ohio R. at Paducah. Major TVA dam (206 ft. high, 8,422 ft. long; completed 1944); concrete construction, earthfill wings. Flood control, navigation (has lock 600 ft. long, 110 ft. wide, max. lift of 73 ft.), power. Forms **Kentucky Reservoir** (□ 247; 184 mi. long, 1–3 mi. wide; capacity 6,002,600 acre-ft.; sometimes known as Kentucky L.) in SW Ky. (Marshall, Calloway, Lyon, and Trigg counties) and W Tenn. (Henry, Benton, Decatur, Stewart, Houston, Humphreys, and Perry counties). Big Sandy R. enters reservoir near town of Big Sandy, Tenn., Duck R. near Waverly, Tenn. Recreation facilities at Kentucky Dam State Park just W of dam, and at Kentucky L. State Park in Marshall co. Kentucky Woodlands Natl. Wildlife Refuge on W shore of reservoir, in Trigg and Lyon counties. Nathan B. Forrest Memorial Park is near Camden, Tenn.

Kentucky Natural Bridge, Ky.: see Natural Bridge State Park.

Kentucky River, Ky., formed by junction of North and Middle forks 4 mi. ENE of Beattyville; flows 259 mi. generally NW, past Beattyville, Irvine, High Bridge (traverses deep gorge here), and Frankfort, to Ohio R. at Carrollton. Scenic Palisades and Chimney Rock are near Camp Nelson. Main tributaries are South Fork and Dix and Red rivers. Navigable for entire course by means of locks. North Fork rises in the Cumberlands in Letcher co. near Va. line, flows SW, then NW, past Jenkins, Whitesburg, Hazard, and Jackson; 168 mi. long. Middle Fork rises in the Cumberlands in Leslie co., flows 97 mi. generally N, past Hyden. South Fork rises in Bell co. in the Cumberlands, flows 75 mi. generally N past Booneville, to Kentucky R. at Beattyville.

Kentung, Burma: see Kengtung.

Kentville, town (pop. 3,928), ⊙ Kings co., N N.S., on Cornwallis R., near its mouth on the Minas Basin, and 50 mi. NW of Halifax; agr. market in fruitgrowing region; tourist resort. Mfg. of machinery.

Kentwood, town (pop. 2,417), Tangipahoa parish, SE La., 50 mi. NE of Baton Rouge, near Miss. line; strawberries, cotton, dairy products, truck; cotton ginning, lumber and grain milling. Settled in mid-19th cent.; inc. 1893.

Kenty, Poland: see Kety.

Kenvil, village (pop. 2,383, with near-by Succasunna), Morris co., N N.J., 4 mi. W of Dover; mfg. (explosives, concrete products); dairy products. Large powder plant here (founded 1871) nearly destroyed in 1940 by explosions that took 48 lives.

Kenvir (kĕn'vûr), mining village (pop. 3,420, with adjacent Redbud), Harlan co., SE Ky., in the Cumberlands, 9 mi. E of Harlan; bituminous coal.

Kenwood. 1 Suburban village (1940 pop. 4,771), Baltimore co., central Md., 5 mi. WSW of downtown Baltimore, near Catonsville. **2** Suburb of Oneida city, N.Y. **3** Village (pop. 4,124, with near-by Five Forks and Arlington), Prince George co., E Va., a suburb of Hopewell.

Kenwyn, village in Kenwyn rural parish (pop. 2,432), W Cornwall, England, just NW of Truro; agr. market. Site of bishop of Truro's palace. Has 15th-cent. church.

Kenya (kĕ'nyū, kē'nyū), British colony and protectorate (□ 224,960, including 5,230 sq. mi. of lake area; pop. 5,377,393), E Africa; ⊙ Nairobi. The protectorate is a 10-mi.-wide coastal strip (including offshore isls.) bet. Tanganyika border and mouth of Tana R. leased from Sultan of Zanzibar. Kenya is bounded N by Ethiopia, E by Ital. Somaliland, SE by Indian Ocean, S by Tanganyika, W by L. Victoria and Uganda, and NW by Anglo-Egyptian Sudan; it is crossed by the equator. Colony's N part (representing 3/5 of entire territory) is an arid region rising gradually from the coast toward outliers of Ethiopian massif (NW). S Kenya, in which almost entire pop. and economic production are centered, comprises a low, marshy coastal strip and a plateau raised to 3–10,000 ft. by volcanic action. The outstanding physiographic features, however, are the massive volcanic cones (Mt. Kenya, 17,040 ft.; Mt. Elgon, 14,178 ft.) which rise boldly above the tableland, and the Great Rift Valley which crosses W central Kenya N–S, cutting a trench 1,500–3,000 ft. deep. The valley here is 30–50 mi. wide; it is occupied by a string of alkaline lakes, including Rudolf (in N), Baringo, Nakuru, Naivasha, and Magadi (soda extraction); it is studded with extinct volcanoes; its flanks, in the shape of steep escarpments (Mau, Elgeyo, Kikuyu, Laikipia escarpments, Aberdare Range) are thickly forested. In extreme W, the plateau descends to the embayed shores of L. Victoria. The coastal strip has average temp. of 80°F., 40–50 in. annual rainfall (chiefly April–June). The arid N receives only 5 to 20 in. of precipitation. The S highlands enjoy a climate conducive to European colonization: average temp. is 70°F. at 4,000 ft., 52°F. at 10,000 ft. Temp. extremes at Nairobi are 57° and 78°F.; rainfall is 40–60 in. Because of its considerable alt. range, Kenya lends itself to a variety of agr. crops; above 5,000 ft. coffee, tea (Kericho dist.), corn, wheat, wattle bark, pyrethrum, deciduous fruits; at lower altitudes, sisal, cotton, oilseeds. Beans, potatoes, sorghum, pulse, coconuts, sugar cane, vegetables, and essential-oil plants are also grown. Cattle, hog, sheep, and poultry raising and dairying are becoming increasingly important for a growing local market. Only a small part of Kenya's varied mineral resources has been exploited; mining is limited to sodium carbonate (from L. Magadi), gold (Kakamega fields), kyanite, salt, and limestone. Industries (expanded since Second World War) include meat-packing, bacon mfg., flour milling, and processing of export crops. There are also canneries (at Nairobi, colony's chief mfg. center), and mfg. of tin cans, matches, clothing (at Thika), and cement (Sultan Hamud). Principal exports, shipped via Mombasa, are coffee, cotton, sisal, tea, soda, gold, hides and skins, wattle bark and extract, pyrethrum, rubber, elephant ivory, and tobacco. Kenya is served by the Kenya-Uganda RR (built 1901), linking Mombasa with Nairobi, L. Victoria (at Kisumu), and Kampala (Uganda); spurs lead into Tanganyika, to L. Magadi, and to foot of Mt. Kenya; NW of Nairobi railroad negotiates difficult crossing of Great Rift Valley. There are less than 2,000 mi. of improved roads, the Great North Road (a section of Cape-to-Cairo route) crossing the territory from Tanganyika to Uganda. Chief airports are at Nairobi (Eastleigh), Mombasa (Port Reitz), Naivasha, and Kisumu. Kenya is noted for the abundance of its game and bush animals (elephants, zebras, giraffes, antelopes). Tsavo and Nairobi natl. parks have recently been established. Over 12,000 sq. mi. of land may be set aside for settlement by European settlers; chief regions of colonization are the Uasin Gishu Plateau around Eldoret, the Great Rift Valley N of Nakuru, and Trans-Nzoia (around Kitale). In 1948, Kenya had 30,000 Europeans, almost 100,000 Indians, and over 24,000 Arabs (concentrated along coast). Native pop. includes various Bantu tribes, as well as the Nilotic Kavirondo, Nandi, Turkana, and Suk, and the Hamitic Masai, Somalis, and Galla. Swahili is the *lingua franca*. As early as 7th cent. A.D., the coastal strip was settled by Arab and Persian traders in ivory and slaves. The Portuguese controlled the area in 16th–17th cent. Great Britain, after having gained control through Br. East Africa Co. (chartered 1888), leased coastal strip from Sultan of Zanzibar, and extended its holdings to the interior. Boundaries with German East Africa (now Tanganyika) were fixed 1890. Territory was transferred (1895) to crown and organized as East Africa Protectorate. First Br. settlers (c.1900) were soon followed by other white settlers from England and South Africa, and by laborers from India. In 1920, the leased coastal strip was named Kenya Protectorate, while the remainder of the territory became a crown colony. Administratively the 2 areas are not differentiated, the protectorate being considered as part of Coast Prov. In 1923, Uganda's NE dist. adjoining L. Rudolf became part of Kenya, and in 1925 Jubaland was ceded to Italy. In Second World War, N Kenya was briefly occupied by Italians. Kenya is ruled by an appointed governor with the advice and consent of the legislative council on which representatives of the white settlers have a majority of the elective seats. There are 5 provinces (Nyanza, Rift Valley, Central (⊙ Nairobi), Coast Province, and Northern Frontier Province) and the Masai extra-provincial dist. The technical services (railroads, mail, statistical services, etc.) of Kenya are coordinated with those of neighboring Tanganyika and Uganda under an administrative body called the East Africa High Commission (established 1948), composed of the governors of the 3 territories; administrative hq. are at Nairobi.

Kenya, Mount, huge extinct volcanic cone (17,040 ft.) in central Kenya, rising boldly above E African plateau 70 mi. NNE of Nairobi; 0°10'S 37°18'E. Africa's 2d highest mtn. (Kilimanjaro is higher). Its base is 40 mi. in diameter; most of crater has been eroded, leaving a central core of rocky peaks; 15 glaciers (up to 1 mi. long) reach the 14,000 ft. level. Elevations bet. 5,000 and 12,000 ft. are forested (cedar, camphor, bamboo). Area above 11,000 ft. is a natl. park (□ 300). A scenic road circumscribes Mt. Kenya from Fort Hall (at S foot). Rail spur from Nairobi leads to Nanyuki (at NW foot), chief base for ascents. Discovered 1849 by Krapf, a German missionary; summit was 1st reached by Sir Halford Mackinder in 1899.

Kenyon. 1 Village (pop. 1,651), Goodhue co., SE Minn., on branch of Zumbro R. and 15 mi. E of Faribault, in grain, livestock, and poultry area; dairy products, canned corn. Settled 1856, inc. 1885. **2** Village, Washington co., R.I.: see Charlestown.

Kenzingen (kĕn'tsĭng-ŭn), village (pop. 3,152), S Baden, Germany, at W foot of Black Forest, on the Elz and 11 mi. SW of Lahr; tobacco mfg., metal- and woodworking. Has 16th-cent. town hall (formerly Capuchin monastery).

Keo (kē'ō), town (pop. 200), Lonoke co., central Ark., 18 mi. ESE of Little Rock, near Arkansas R.

Keokuk (kē'ùkŭk"), county (□ 579; pop. 16,797), SE Iowa; ⊙ Sigourney. Prairie agr. area (hogs, cattle, poultry, corn, oats, wheat) drained by Skunk, North Skunk, and South Fork English rivers. Limestone quarries, clay pits. Formed 1837.

Keokuk, city (pop. 16,144), a ⊙ Lee co., extreme SE Iowa, port on Mississippi R. (bridged here), at mouth of Des Moines R., and 32 mi. SSW of Burlington; rail junction; trade and mfg. center. Food, metal, and wood products; calcium carbide, blasting powder, shoes, overalls, paper containers, sponge rubber. Fishing. First cabin erected here in 1820; then in 1829 a trading post was established and named after Keokuk, Sac Indian chief. Platted 1837, inc. 1847. City's location at foot of the Des Moines rapids in the Mississippi led to its growth as a steamer transshipment point. In 1877, the U.S. govt. completed a ship canal (9 mi. long) around the rapids, which was superseded (1913) by Keokuk Dam (53 ft. high, 4,649 ft. long) with hydroelectric plant and large dry docks and lock for navigation. Dam forms L. Keokuk (sometimes called L. Cooper), which reaches to Burlington and covers the rapids and canal. The Natl. Cemetery (1861) has a monument to the Unknown Soldier; in Rand Park is the grave of Keokuk, with a monument. Mark Twain worked as a printer in Keokuk, and mementos of his sojourn are preserved.

Keonjhar (kyōn'jŭr), district (□ 3,206; pop. 529,786), N Orissa, India; ⊙ Keonjhargarh. Consists of hills (2–3,000 ft.) and lowland. Valuable deposits of manganese and iron ore (worked) in N area; sal, bamboo, and lac from forests. Formerly a princely state in Orissa States of Eastern States agency; merged 1948 with Orissa and made a dist.

Keonjhargarh (–gŭr), town (pop. 9,004), ⊙ Keonjhar dist., N Orissa, India, 80 mi. NNW of Cuttack; market center for rice, timber, lac, hides; hand-loom weaving. Formerly called Keonjhar.

Keonthal (kyōn'tŭl), former princely state (including dependencies, □ 295; pop. 51,645) of Punjab Hill States, India, S and E of Simla; ⊙ was Junga. Since 1948, merged with Himachal Pradesh.

Keos, Greece: see Kea.

Keosauqua (kēōsôk'wù, –sŏk'–), town (pop. 1,101), ⊙ Van Buren co., SE Iowa, on Des Moines R. and 30 mi. SE of Ottumwa; mfg. (dairy equipment, dairy products, feed). State park near by. Settled 1836, inc. 1851.

Keota (kēō'tù). **1** Town (pop. 21), Weld co., N Colo., 38 mi. NE of Greeley; alt. 5,000 ft. **2** Town (pop. 1,145), Keokuk co., SE Iowa, 14 mi. WNW of Washington; shipping point for dairy products and livestock. Settled 1871, inc. 1873. **3** Town (pop. 619), Haskell co., E Okla., 31 mi. WSW of Fort Smith (Ark.), in agr. area; cotton ginning.

Keowee River, S.C.: see Seneca River.

Kep (kĕp), town, Kampot prov., SW Cambodia, small deep-water port on Gulf of Siam, 12 mi. SE of Kampot, near Vietnam line; fisheries; seaside resort.

Kepa, peak, Yugoslavia: see MITTAGSKOGEL.

Kepala Batas (kŭpä'lŭ bä"täs'). **1** Town, Kedah, Malaya: see ALOR STAR. **2** Village, Prov. Wellesley, Penang, NW Malaya, 9 mi. NNE of Butterworth; coconuts, rice.

Kephallenia, Greece: see CEPHALONIA.

Kephalos or **Kefalos** (both: kĕ'fŭlôs), Ital. *Cefalo*, town (pop. 1,809), Kos isl., in the Dodecanese, Greece, 20 mi. WSW of Kos.

Kephart, Mount, Tenn. and N.C.: see GREAT SMOKY MOUNTAINS NATIONAL PARK.

Kephisia or **Kifisia** (both: kĭfĭsēä'), town (pop. 14,201), Attica nome, E central Greece, on spur of the Pentelikon, 9 mi. NE of Athens, in Athens metropolitan dist.; summer tourist and residential center; archaeological mus. Cherry orchards.

Kephisos River or **Kephissos River,** Greece: see CEPHISUS RIVER.

Kepno (kĕp'nô), Pol. *Kępno*, Ger. *Kempen* (kĕm'-pŭn), town (1946 pop. 7,810), Poznan prov., SW central Poland, 40 mi. ENE of Breslau (Wroclaw); rail junction; mfg. of cement, bricks, machinery, varnish; sawmilling.

Kepong (kĕpŏŏng'), town (pop. 1,751), central Selangor, Malaya, 6 mi. NW of Kuala Lumpur; tin mining; rubber; timber research laboratory.

Keppel Bay (kĕ'pŭl), inlet of Pacific Ocean, E Queensland, Australia; sheltered E by Curtis Isl.; 30 mi. long, 12 mi. wide. Port Alma (part of port of Rockhampton) is on SW shore, at mouth of Fitzroy R.

Keppel Harbor, deep-water channel of Singapore port area, bet. Tanjong Pagar section of Singapore city and Pulau Brani and Blakang Mati isls. (S). N side is lined with main Singapore harbor installations.

Keppel Island, Tonga: see NIUATOBUTABU.

Keradid, Fr. Morocco: see FOUCAULD.

Kerak, El Kerak, Al-Karak (all: kĕräk', ĕl), or **Krak,** town (pop. c.10,000), S central Jordan, on the Wadi Kerak (emptying into Dead Sea, 10 mi. W, at Mazra) and 50 mi. SSW of Amman; alt. 3,300 ft.; road junction, trade center; grain (barley, wheat). It was the anc. Kir Moab (also mentioned in the Bible as Kir Hareseth, Kir Haresh, and Kir Heres), citadel of the Moabites. In 1131 (1136?) the Knights Hospitalers built a huge castle (called Le Crac or Krak des Chavaliers) which still stands in an excellent state of preservation, one of the masterpieces of medieval military architecture. It was taken 1188 by Saladin. Kerak was the seat of an archbishop from the early Christian era until 1910, when the Turks massacred numbers of the Christian pop. and expelled the rest.

Kerakat, India: see KIRAKAT.

Keraksaan, Indonesia: see KRAKSAAN.

Kerala (kā'rŭlŭ), historical and linguistic region in extreme SW India, comprising roughly the present Travancore-Cochin state and Malabar dist. of Madras and thus including most of the MALABAR COAST; Malayalam—a Dravidian tongue—is the dominant language. Kerala or Chera (chā'rŭ) was an anc. Dravidian kingdom, dating back to Asoka's time (3d cent. B.C.). Conquered by Cholas in 10th cent. A.D., it later fell to Moslems (1310) and then to the Hindu Vijayanagar empire, which in turn was overthrown in 1565. In 1640 it was taken by sultan of Bijapur, in 1652 by king of Mysore.

Kerama-retto (kārä'mä-rāt-tō'), island group (□ 18; 1950 pop. 3,556) of Okinawa Isls., in Ryukyu Isls. in East China Sea, 15 mi. W of Okinawa. Comprises volcanic isls. of TOKASHIKI-SHIMA (largest), ZAMAMI-SHIMA, and several small coral islets. Mountainous, forested. Produces sugar cane, sweet potatoes. Fishing.

Keramos (kĕ'rŭmôs), village (pop. 254), N Chios isl., Greece, 17 mi. NW of Chios city; antimony mining.

Kerang (kŭrăng'), town (pop. 2,717), N Victoria, Australia, on Loddon R. and 150 mi. NNW of Melbourne; rail and commercial center for livestock, agr. area; dairy plant, flour mill.

Kerasun, Turkey: see GIRESUN.

Keratea (kĕrŭtā'ŭ), town (pop. 5,081), Attica nome, E central Greece, on railroad and 19 mi. SE of Athens; olive oil, wine; summer resort.

Keratsinion, Greece: see HAGIOS GEORGIOS KERATSINIOU.

Kerava (kĕ'rävä), Swedish *Kervo* (kĕr'vō), town (pop. 7,435), Uusimaa co., S Finland, 16 mi. NNE of Helsinki; rail junction; light industry.

Kerbela, Iraq: see KARBALA.

Kerbi, village, Russian SFSR: see POLINY OSIPENKO, IMENI.

Kerbi River, Russian SFSR: see AMGUN RIVER.

Kerch or **Kerch'** (kĕrch, kyĕrch), anc. *Panticapaeum*, city (1926 pop. 35,690; 1939 pop. 104,471), E Crimea, Russian SFSR, fortified port on inlet of Kerch Strait, at E end of Kerch Peninsula, 120 mi. ENE of Simferopol; 45°21'N 36°28'E. Rail terminus; major industrial center of Crimea; iron and steel mills supplied by coal and coke shipped from Zhdanov across Sea of Azov, and by iron ore from Kamysh-Burun mines (on rail spur; 6 mi. S of Kerch); coking plant, shipyards, railway shops; mfg. of leather goods, tobacco products, canned foods, biscuits; cotton ginning. Fishing port, with canneries. Limestone quarries near by. Port (floating, fishing, and petroleum docks; Genoese mole) exports iron ore, wine, grain, fish, caviar, leather, tobacco. City extends over 10 mi. along W coast of Kerch Strait, at foot of Mithridates hill (reached by stone stairway; excavations of anc. acropolis, fine views). Has 8th-cent. church of John the Baptist, archaeological, regional, and ichthyological museums. Archaeological remains found in catacombs and burial mounds near by. Mud baths in L. Chokrak, 9 mi. NW. Founded (6th cent. B.C.) as Gr. colony; became leading city of kingdom of Cimmerian Bosporus; passed (13th cent.) to Genoese and later to Turks; taken (1771) by Russia. During Second World War, held (1941–44) by Germans, except for brief Soviet raid (1941–42).

Kerchevski or **Kerchevskiy** (kyĕr'chĭfskē), town (1948 pop. over 2,000), N central Molotov oblast, Russian SFSR, on right bank of Kama R. and 30 mi. SSW of Cherdyn; lumbering; livestock, wheat.

Kerch Peninsula (kĕrch, kyĕrch), arid E section of Crimea, Russian SFSR, bet. Sea of Azov (N) and Black Sea (S); separated by Kerch Strait (E) from Taman Peninsula; 60 mi. long, 20–30 mi. wide. Connected with main part of Crimea by 10-mi.-wide isthmus. Irrigated agr. (wheat, cotton). Petroleum deposits; limestone, sulphur, and gypsum quarries. Kerch, with iron mines of Kamysh-Burun, is at E end.

Kerch Strait, anc. *Bosporus Cimmerius*, shallow channel in USSR connecting Sea of Azov and Black Sea; separates Crimea (W) from Taman Peninsula (E); 25 mi. long. Its Sea of Azov entrance (N) is narrowed to 2–3 mi. by narrow Chushka Spit; 9 mi. wide at Black Sea entrance. An arm, Taman Gulf, penetrates E into Taman Peninsula. Kerch (on the Crimea side) is principal port. Formerly known as Yenikale Strait.

Kerdous (kĕrdŏŏs'), village Agadir frontier region, SW Fr. Morocco, in SW spur of the Anti-Atlas, 27 mi. SE of Tiznit, on desert track and caravan route to Fr. West Africa; 29°33'N 9°19'W.

Kerdyllion or **Kerdhillion** (both: kĕrdhĭ'lēôn), mountain of Greek Macedonia, near Strymonic Gulf, W of Struma R. mouth; rises to 3,583 ft. 10 mi. SE of Nigrita.

Kerekegyhaza (kĕ'rĕkĕdyŭhä"zŏ), Hung. *Kerekegyháza*, town (pop. 6,020), Pest-Pilis-Solt-Kiskun co., central Hungary, 10 mi. WNW of Kecskemet; grain, cattle, apricots, apples.

Kerekere, Belgian Congo: see ZANI.

Kereli, Turkey: see KIRELI.

Kerema (kŭrē'mŭ), town, Territory of Papua, SE New Guinea, on Gulf of Papua, 140 mi. NW of Port Moresby; rubber.

Kerempe, Cape (kĕrĕmpĕ'), N Turkey, on Black Sea, 22 mi. W of Inebolu; 42°2'N 33°18'E.

Keren (kĕ'rĕn), Ital. *Cheren*, administrative division, N Eritrea; ⊙ Keren. Bordered by Anglo-Egyptian Sudan (N) and Red Sea (E). Difficult upland terrain and aridity render much of area useless. Nomadic stock raising (cattle, goats, camels); some agr. Sparsely settled, with chief villages on plateau.

Keren, Ital. *Cheren*, town (pop. 9,700), ⊙ Keren div., N Eritrea, on central plateau, near Anseba R., 45 mi. NW of Asmara (linked by rail); alt. 4,500 ft.; road junction. Agr. trade center (agave, tobacco, coffee, citrus fruit, vegetables); button mfg. (vegetable ivory), oilseed pressing, flour milling; incense industry. Gold mined near by. Has fort, churches, mosque, and school of arts and crafts. Occupied (1889) and administered by Italians until Second World War when it was taken (1941) by British.

Kerend, Iran: see KARIND.

Kerens (kĕr'ĭnz), town (pop. 1,198), Navarro co., E central Texas, 14 mi. E of Corsicana; cotton ginning. Settled 1881.

Kerensk, Russian SFSR: see VADINSK.

Kereny, Yugoslavia: see KLJAJICEVO.

Keresley (kärz'lē, kârz'–), town and parish (pop. 1,545), N central Warwick, England, 4 mi. NNW of Coventry; coal mining.

Keret or **Keret'** (kĕ'rĭtyŭ), Finnish *Kieretti*, village (1926 pop. 1,029), NE Karelo-Finnish SSR, lumber port on Kandalaksha Bay of White Sea, at mouth of Keret R., 65 mi. SSE of Kandalaksha; sawmilling.

Keret, Lake, or **Lake Keret',** Finnish *Kierettijärvi* (kyĕ'rĕt-tēyăr"vē), in NE Karelo-Finnish SSR, S of Loukhi; 20 mi. long; contains large isl. (□ 15) in S portion. Drains N into **Keret River,** which flows 35 mi. E to Kandalaksha Bay of White Sea at Keret.

Kerewan (kĕrĕ'wän), town (pop. 862), ⊙ Central Div., W Gambia, near Gambia R., on short right affluent (wharf and ferry) and 32 mi. E of Bathurst; fishing; peanuts, palm oil and kernels, rice. Has prison. New division hq. under construction at near-by Monsa Konko.

Kerfeunteun (kĕrfŭntŭn'), NE suburb (pop. 3,515) of Quimper, Finistère dept., W France; cider and flour milling, mfg. of agr. machinery.

Kergez (kyĭrgyĕs'), town (1945 pop. over 500) in Molotov dist. of Greater Baku, Azerbaijan SSR, 12 mi. SW of Baku; oil fields (developed 1933).

Kerguelen Islands (kûr'gŭlĕn), Fr. *Kerguélen* (kĕrgālĕn'), archipelago (□ c.2,700), outlying dependency of Madagascar, in the subantarctic zone of Indian Ocean, c.1,400 mi. off Antarctic mainland and 2,300 mi. off SE coast of Africa. Comprises over 300 isls. and islets lying bet. 48°40'S and 49°49'S and traversed by 70°E. Main isl., known sometimes as Desolation Isl., is 100 mi. long, of volcanic origin and has a deeply indented coast with numerous peninsulas, capes, and fjords. Cook Glacier (in W) covers ⅓ of isl. Mt. Ross (in S) rises to 6,422 ft. There are numerous glacial lakes, peat marshes, some lignite and guano deposits. Fauna includes fur seals, sea lions, penguins, wild hogs, wild dogs, rabbits, and many birds. Famous Kerguelen cabbage (*Pringlea antiscorbutica*), a formerly abundant native vegetable, is now on the decline. Discovered (1772) by French navigator Kerguélen-Trémarec, the isls. have since achieved note as seal-hunting grounds and whaling bases. Repeated attempts at sheep raising were also made and settlements were established, notably at Port-Couvreux (N center) and Port-Jeanne-d'Arc (S center), only to be given up (1932) before adverse conditions. In 1950, France sent a mission here to survey a site for the establishment of an air base on the route to Australia; new settlement was established at Port-des-Français, on NE peninsula.

Kerhonkson (kûrhŏngk'sŭn), resort village (1940 pop. 690), Ulster co., SE N.Y., on Rondout Creek and 19 mi. SW of Kingston, just W of the Shawangunk range; mfg. (wood products, machinery).

Keri (kĕrē'), village (pop. 605), SW Zante isl., Greece, 10 mi. SSW of Zante; mineral pitch deposits.

Kericho (kĕrē'chō), town (pop. c.3,000), W Kenya, on road from Lumbwa station and 40 mi. SE of Kisumu; colony's leading tea-growing center; wattle bark, coffee, flax, corn. Textile spinning and weaving school.

Kerinchi, Mount (kŭrĭn'chē), or **Indrapura Peak** (ĭndrŭpŏŏ'rŭ), highest peak (12,467 ft.) of Barisan Mts., W Sumatra, Indonesia, 85 mi. SE of Padang. Also spelled Kerintji, Kurinchi, and Koerintji.

Keriya (kĕrēyä'), Chinese *Yütien* or *Yü-t'ien* (both: yü'tyĕn'), town and oasis (pop. 73,298), S Sinkiang prov., China, on Keriya R. and 100 mi. E of Khotan, and on highway at S edge of Taklamakan Desert; 36°52'N 81°42'E. Salt-extracting center; carpet, silk-textile mfg.; wheat, cotton, corn, grapes, cattle, sheep; jade. Sometimes spelled Kaiya.

Keriya River, S Sinkiang prov., China, rises in the Kunlun mts. on Tibet border at 36°N 82°E, flows 300 mi. N, past Keriya, before disappearing into central Taklamakan Desert.

Kerka River, Yugoslavia: see KRKA RIVER, Croatia.

Kerk-Driel (kĕrk-drēl'), village (pop. 2,252), Gelderland prov., central Netherlands, on Maas R. and 6 mi. NNE of 's Hertogenbosch; mfg. of buttons, farm wagons, baskets. Also called Driel.

Kerkennah (kĕrkĕnä'), anc. *Cercina*, group of 7 islands (□ c.65; pop. 15,560), in Gulf of Gabès (central Mediterranean), off E coast of Tunisia (to which they belong), c.20 mi. E of Sfax; tunny and sponge fisheries, saltworks; some date palms. Mfg. of esparto products (baskets, cordage, footwear). Chief villages are Remla, Kellabine, and El-Attaia on Chergui isl. (largest), and Mellita (stone quarry) on Rharbi isl. (SW). Other isls. are uninhabited. Hannibal and Marius took refuge here. Also spelled Kerkenna.

Kerkheh River, Iran: see KARKHEH RIVER.

Kerkhoven (kûr'kō"vŭn), village (pop. 664), Swift co., SW central Minn., 14 mi. WNW of Willmar, in grain, livestock, and poultry area; dairy products, cattle feed.

Kerki (kyĭrkē'), city (1933 pop. estimate 14,200), SE Chardzhou oblast, Turkmen SSR, port on the Amu Darya, opposite Kerkichi, and 125 mi. SE of Chardzhou; metalworking, cotton ginning, food processing (meat and flour products). It was ⊙ former Kerki oblast (c.1943–47). Founded (late-19th cent.) as Rus. fort on Bukhara-Afghanistan trade-route.

Kerkichi (kyĕrkĭchē'), town (1941 pop. over 500), SE Chardzhou oblast, Turkmen SSR, on railroad, on the Amu Darya, opposite Kerki, and 125 mi. SE of Chardzhou; cotton-ginning center.

Kerkine or **Kerkini** (both: kĕrkē'nē), village (pop. 2,122), Serrai nome, Macedonia, Greece, 16 mi. W of Siderokastron. Formerly called Boutkovon or Butkovon. **Lake Kerkinitis** (kĕrkēnē'tĭs) (maximum □ 20), just E, is a natural flood reservoir for regulated Struma R.

Kerkine or **Kerkini,** Greece, Bulgaria, and Yugoslavia. **1** Mountain range: see BELASICA. **2** Its peak: see RADOMIR.

Kerkira, Greece: see CORFU.

Kerkrade (kĕrk'rädŭ), town (pop. 18,002; commune pop. 40,641), Limburg prov., SE Netherlands, 17 mi. E of Maastricht; coal-mining center on Ger. border. Coal mining dates from 1113. Near by (SE) is Rolduc Abbey with Romanesque church, consecrated 1108.

Kerkuk, Iraq: see KIRKUK, city.

Kerkyra, Greece: see CORFU.

Kerma or **Karma** (both: kĕr'mŭ), town, Northern Prov., Anglo-Egyptian Sudan, on right bank of the Nile (head of navigation above 3d cataract), and

30 mi. N of Dongola; cotton, wheat, barley, corn, fruits, durra; livestock. Harvard-Boston Expeditions carried out extensive excavations near here 1913–15.

Kermadec Deep, ocean depth (30,928 ft.) of South Pacific Ocean, E of Kermadec Isls. and S of Tonga Deep; discovered 1895.

Kermadec Islands (kûrmă'dĕk), volcanic group (□ 13; pop. 23), dependency of New Zealand, in S Pacific, 500 mi. NE of Auckland; 30°30'S 178°30'W. Include SUNDAY ISLAND, Macaulay Isl., Curtis Isls., L'Espérance Rock, and scattered islets. Mountainous, fertile. Annexed 1887 by New Zealand.

Kerman or **Kirman** (both: kĕrmän'), former province (□ 85,000; pop. 700,000) of SE Iran; ⊙ was Kerman. Bounded N by Khurasan, NW by Yezd, W by Fars, SE by Baluchistan, and E by Seistan; contains part of the SE Zagros ranges (S), and extends onto the central Iranian plateau (N), where it includes the salt desert Dasht-i-Lut. Agr. (mainly irrigated): wheat, barley, opium, cotton, and millet in higher, cooler regions; rice, corn, henna, dates and fruit (pomegranates, oranges) on warmer plains. Sheep and camel raising. Fine wool, which is the main export, also is the basis of the Kerman rug and shawl industry. Access to the Persian Gulf is through Bandar Abbas. Main inland centers are Kerman, Bam, Sirjan, and Rafsinjan. Main highways lead from Kerman to Yezd, Shiraz, and Zahidan. The anc. *Carmania*, it was traversed (325 B.C.) by Alexander the Great, and flourished under the Sassanids. It resisted Arab control, but was ravaged by the Afghans (17th cent.) and by Agha Mohammed Khan (18th cent.). Since 1938, the name Kerman is applied to the Eighth Province (□ 200,000; pop. 1,100,000), which includes Kerman, Seistan, and Iranian Baluchistan with its coastal dist. of Makran.

Kerman or **Kirman,** city (1941 pop. 50,048), ⊙ Eighth Prov., SE Iran, 500 mi. SE of Teheran and on Teheran-Zahidan road; alt. 5,600 ft.; 30°17'N 57°5'E. Largest city of SE Iran and of former Kerman prov.; major road and trading center; rug weaving (Kirman rugs); mfg. of shawls, artistic brasswork, cotton spinning. Has teachers col. Opium, cotton, grain, and oranges grown near by. Dominated by ruins of 3d-cent. Ardeshir and Dokhtar forts (E), the walled city contains citadel and 11th-cent. mosque (restored). The anc. *Carmana*, it was visited 325 B.C. by Craterus, one of Alexander the Great's generals; ruined (14th cent.) by Tamerlane and (18th cent.) by Agha Mohammed Khan, founder of Kajar dynasty. Modern development began in mid-18th cent.

Kerman (kûr'mŭn), city (pop. 1,563), Fresno co., central Calif., in San Joaquin Valley, 15 mi. W of Fresno; cotton, raisins, alfalfa. Inc. 1946.

Kermanshah (kĕrmänshä') or **Kermanshahan** (–shähän'), city (1940 pop. 88,622), ⊙ Fifth Prov., W Iran, 260 mi. WSW of Teheran, and on highway to Baghdad, near a headstream of Karkheh R.; alt. 4,860 ft.; 34°19'N 47°5'E. Major trade and transportation hub in W Iran and main city of former Kermanshah prov., in grain-producing area; beet-sugar refining, flour milling, rug weaving. Oil refinery for NAFT-I-SHAH oil field (linked by pipeline). Dating from 4th cent., Kermanshah was probably located nearer Taq-i-Bustan (E) during Sassanian times. It was then a secondary summer residence and retained this function under Harun al-Rashid. Flourished during Safavid dynasty (16th cent.) and again in 18th cent. Held by Turks in First World War. The prov. of Kermanshah, bounded W by Iraq, N by Kurdistan, E by Hamadan, and S by Luristan, was joined (1938) with Pusht Kuh, Kurdistan, Hamadan, and Malayer provs. to form Iran's Fifth Province (□ 30,000; 1940 pop. 1,827,591), to which the name Kermanshah is commonly applied. Sometimes spelled Kirmanshah.

Kerme, Gulf of, Turkey: see KOS, GULF OF.

Kermen (kĕrmĕn'), village (pop. 3,019), Yambol dist., E central Bulgaria, 13 mi. W of Yambol; grain, tobacco.

Kermine (kyĕrmĕnyĕ'), town (1932 pop. estimate 4,700), SE Bukhara oblast, Uzbek SSR, near Trans-Caspian RR, 35 mi. E of Gizhduvan; cotton-ginning center. Just S, at rail station, is town of Stantsiya Kermine [Rus.,=Kermine station].

Kermit. 1 Village (1940 pop. 23), Divide co., NW N.Dak., 13 mi. E of Crosby. **2** Town (pop. 6,912), ⊙ Winkler co., W Texas, 38 mi. NE of Pecos, near base of Cap Rock escarpment. Supply center for oil, natural-gas area, with cattle ranches; mfg. of oil-field supplies; carbon-black plants near by. Inc. 1938. **3** Town (pop. 964), Mingo co., SW W.Va., on Tug Fork (bridged) opposite Warfield, Ky.; natural gas, bituminous coal.

Kern, county (□ 8,170; pop. 228,309), S central Calif.; ⊙ Bakersfield. Includes S end of San Joaquin Valley, walled in by Tehachapi Mts. (S), the Sierra Nevada (E), and Coast Ranges (W). Part of MOJAVE DESERT (borax, tungsten, silver, gold mines) in E and SE. Kern R. used for hydroelectric power; irrigation water supplied by Friant-Kern Canal of Central Valley Project. Part of Sequoia Natl. Forest in N. Elk Hills Naval Petroleum Reserve is in W. Los Angeles Aqueduct cuts across E section. State's leading petroleum-producing co., with oil and natural-gas fields along W side of San Joaquin Valley and in Bakersfield dist. Irrigated agr. (since 1880s); potatoes, cotton, grain, alfalfa, grapes, citrus and deciduous fruit, truck; cattle and sheep ranching, hog and poultry raising, dairying. Cement-rock quarrying, gold, clay mining. Formed 1893.

Kern Canyon, Calif.: see KERN RIVER.

Kernersville (kûr'nŭrzvĭl), town (pop. 2,396), Forsyth co., N central N.C., 9 mi. E of Winston-Salem; hosiery, silk, and flour mills. Settled before 1770 by Germans.

Kern River, S central Calif., rises in the S Sierra Nevada in Sequoia Natl. Park just NW of Mt. Whitney, flows 155 mi. S and SW, past Bakersfield, to a reservoir in N part of what was Buena Vista L. (bwā'nŭ) (now nearly dry). In wet years, channels carry flood waters as far as Tulare L. (55 mi. NNW). Hydroelectric plants; supplies irrigation water to S San Joaquin Valley, with FRIANT-KERN CANAL of CENTRAL VALLEY project supplementing this supply. Projected site of Isabella Dam, another unit of project, is on the Kern. Receives South Fork (67 mi. long) 35 mi. NE of Bakersfield; above this point, main stream is sometimes called North Fork. Within Sequoia Natl. Park is its upper gorge, called Kern Canyon, a spectacular rift c.30 mi. long and up to 3,000 ft. deep, bet. main Sierra Nevada crest (E) and Great Western Divide of the range. Upper Kern is a famous trout stream.

Kerns (kĕrns), town (pop. 3,244), Obwalden half-canton, central Switzerland, 1 mi. E of Sarnen; health resort.

Kernstown, village, Frederick co., N Va., 3 mi. S of Winchester. In Civil War, Stonewall Jackson unsuccessfully attacked Union forces here, March 23, 1862.

Kéroman (kārômā'), S suburb of Lorient, Morbihan dept., W France, on an inlet of Bay of Biscay, and part of Lorient harbor; canning, shipbuilding, petroleum refining. An old fishing village, it was developed as a trawler port after 1920 and as a Ger. submarine base in Second World War.

Keros, Greece: see KAROS.

Kérouané (kĕrwä'nā), village, SE Fr. Guinea, Fr. West Africa, on road to Fr. Ivory Coast and 80 mi. S of Kankan; tobacco, rice; cattle. Airfield.

Kerpen (kĕr'pŭn), town (pop. 4,654), in former Prussian Rhine Prov., W Germany, after 1945 in North Rhine-Westphalia, 10 mi. NE of Düren. Has ruined castle.

Kerr (kûr), county (□ 1,101; pop. 14,022), SW Texas; ⊙ Kerrville. In scenic hill country of Edwards Plateau; alt. c.1,100–2,400 ft.; drained by Guadalupe R., rising in springs here. Ranching (sheep, goats, cattle) and vacation area, with camps, guest ranches, health resorts. Agr. (corn, grain, feeds, fruit, truck, pecans), dairying, poultry raising; hunting. Formed 1856.

Kerr, Lake, Marion co., N central Fla., in Ocala Natl. Forest, 23 mi. ENE of Ocala; c.5 mi. long, 2 mi. wide.

Kerrata (kĕrätä'), village, Constantine dept., NE Algeria, in Babor range of Little Kabylia, 22 mi. SE of Bougie; iron mines.

Kerr Dam, Mont.: see POLSON.

Kerrera (kĕ'rŭrŭ), island (pop. 79), W Argyll, Scotland, in the Firth of Lorne, opposite Oban across narrow Sound of Kerrera; 5 mi. long, 2 mi. wide; rises to 617 ft.

Kerreri, Anglo-Egyptian Sudan: see OMDURMAN.

Kerrick, village (pop. 81), Pine co., E Minn., 38 mi. SW of Duluth; dairying.

Kerrobert (kûrŏ'bûrt), town (pop. 711), W Sask., 30 mi. N of Kindersley; grain elevators, lumbering, dairying.

Kerrortussok or **Qerrortussoq** (both: kĕkhôkh'tŏŏshôk), fishing settlement (pop. 113), Holsteinsborg dist., SW Greenland, on Davis Strait, at mouth of Amerdlok Fjord (15 mi. long), 5 mi. E of Holsteinsborg; 66°54'N 53°30'W. Radio station.

Kerrville (kûr'vĭl), city (pop. 7,691), ⊙ Kerr co., SW Texas, in scenic hill country of Edwards Plateau, on Guadalupe R. and 55 mi. NW of San Antonio; resort center; important wool and mohair market for ranching region; also ships furs, dairy products, poultry. Seat of Schreiner Inst. (a jr. col.). State park and a veterans' hosp. are near. Settled 1847.

Kerry, Gaelic *Chiarraighe*, county (□ 1,815.2; pop. 133,893), Munster, SW Ireland, on the Atlantic; ⊙ Tralee. Bounded by Co. Cork (E and S), the Shannon (N), and Co. Limerick (NE). Coastline is deeply indented; main inlets, Kenmare R., Dingle Bay, Tralee Bay. Surface is generally mountainous, rising to 3,414 ft. on Carrantuohill in the Macgillycuddy's Reeks. Lakes of Killarney are noted for scenic beauty. Sea fisheries are important. Grain, potato growing; dairying. Some copper is mined (Kenmare); slate, flagstone, limestone are quarried. Industries include mfg. of agr. implements, shoes, hosiery, wood products, cattle feed, woolen milling. Towns are Tralee, Listowel, Killarney (tourist center), Dingle, Kenmare, Castleisland. Isl. of Valentia is E terminal of transatlantic cables. Other isls. are the Blaskets and Skelligs. There are numerous anc. castles, abbeys, round towers; noted are those of Muckross and Innisfallen. W part of co. was last region of Ireland to be evacuated by Danes. Irish is still spoken by many of the inhabitants.

Kerry, town and parish (pop. 1,626), SE Montgomery, Wales, 3 mi. ESE of Newtown; agr. market; sawmills. Has 14th-cent. church.

Kerry Head, cape, NW Co. Kerry, Ireland, at mouth of the Shannon, 14 mi. NW of Tralee; 52°25'N 9°57'W.

Kersal Moor (kûr'sŭl), NW suburb of Manchester, SE Lancashire, England, in Prestwich urban dist.; cotton milling, mfg. of chemicals, soap. Has 17th-cent. mansion of Kersal Cell.

Kersey (kûr'zē), agr. village and parish (pop. 360), S Suffolk, England, 2 mi. NW of Hadleigh. Has 15th-cent. church. The name *kersey*, a woolen cloth made in England in 13th cent., probably originates here. Just WNW is village of Lindsey, where *linsey-woolsey*, another woolen cloth, originated.

Kersey. 1 Town (pop. 304), Weld co., N Colo., on South Platte R. and 8 mi. ESE of Greeley; alt. 4,614 ft. **2** Village (pop. 1,070, with adjacent Dagus Mines), Elk co., N central Pa., 8 mi. SE of Ridgway.

Kershaw (kûrshô'), county (□ 786; pop. 32,287), N central S.C.; ⊙ CAMDEN. Contains part of Wateree R. and Wateree Pond; bounded E by Lynches R. Tourist area in Sand Hills; some agr. (peaches, pecans, sweet potatoes), timber. Formed 1791.

Kershaw, town (pop. 1,376), Kershaw and Lancaster counties, N S.C., 20 mi. N of Camden; lumber mills. Gold mine near by.

Kerspe, Germany: see RÖNSAHL.

Kert, territory, Sp. Morocco: see VILLA NADOR.

Kerteh (kûrtĕ'), village (pop. 1,071), S Trengganu, Malaya, on South China Sea, 60 mi. SSE of Kuala Trengganu; coconut and rubber plantations. Sometimes spelled Kretai.

Kertel, Estonia: see KARDLA.

Kerteminde (kĕr'tŭmĭnŭ), city (pop. 3,588) and port, Odense amt, Denmark, on E Fyn isl. and 11 mi. ENE of Odense, on Kerteminde Bay; fish canning, mfg. of agr. machinery.

Kertosono (kûrtōsō'nō), town (pop. 12,249), E Java, Indonesia, on Brantas R. and 50 mi. SW of Surabaya; trade center for agr. area (rice, cassava, corn, peanuts).

Kerulen, Mongolia: see CHOIBALSAN, city.

Kerulen River (kĕ'rŭlĕn) or **Herelen River** (khĕ'rĕlĕn), NE Mongolian People's Republic, rises on S slopes of the Kentei Mts. 120 mi. NE of Ulan Bator, flows 785 mi. S and ENE, past Undur Khan and Choibalsan, to lake Hulun Nor in China's Inner Mongolian Autonomous Region.

Kerur (kā'rōōr), town (pop. 6,988), Bijapur dist., S Bombay, India, 60 mi. SSW of Bijapur; cotton, millet, peanuts, wheat; handicraft cloth weaving. Sometimes spelled Karur.

Kerva (kyĕr'vŭ), town (1939 pop. over 500), E Moscow oblast, Russian SFSR, on small Svyatoye L., 4 mi. NNE of Shatura; peat works.

Kervo, Finland: see KERAVA.

Keryado (kĕryädō'), W suburb of Lorient, Morbihan dept., W France, a separate commune until 1947; dairying.

Kesach (kā'shät'), town, Soctrang prov., S Vietnam, 10 mi. N of Soctrang, near Bassac R. in highly irrigated area; rice center.

Kesan (kĕ-shän'), Turkish *Keşan*, town (pop. 8,320), Adrianople prov., Turkey in Europe, 55 mi. S of Adrianople; wheat, rice, barley. Some lignite near by. Sometimes spelled Keshan.

Kesap (kĕ-shäp'), Turkish *Keşap*, village (pop. 291), Giresun prov., N Turkey, on Black Sea, 6 mi. E of Giresun; hazelnuts, corn.

Kesarevo (kĕsä'rĕvô), village (pop. 3,597), Gorna Oryakhovitsa dist., N Bulgaria, on headstream of Bregovitsa R. and 14 mi. E of Gorna Oryakhovitsa; horticulture, truck, sugar beets.

Kesaria, Israel: see SDOT YAM.

Kesat (kā'shät'), village, Haiduong prov., N Vietnam, 25 mi. ESE of Hanoi; rice center.

Kesch, Piz, Switzerland: see PIZ KESCH.

Kesen (kā'sān), town (pop. 5,151), Iwate prefecture, N Honshu, Japan, 8 mi. NNE of Kesennuma; rice, wheat; charcoal.

Kesennuma (kāsān'nōōmä), town (pop. 21,218), Miyagi prefecture, N Honshu, Japan, fishing port on inlet of the Pacific, 36 mi. NNE of Ishinomaki; fish canning and drying.

Keshan, Turkey: see KESAN.

Keshena (kŭshē'nŭ), village (pop. c.800), Shawano co., NE Wis., on Wolf R. and 9 mi. WNW of Shawano, in the Menominee Indian Reservation. The Indian Agency bldgs. and a Catholic mission are here. Oshkosh clan burial plot is near by.

Keshi (kyĭshē'), W suburb of Ashkhabad, Turkmen SSR; residential section; parks.

Keshishkend, Armenian SSR: see MIKOYAN.

Keshm, Afghanistan: see KISHM.

Keshod (kā'shōd), town (pop. 7,500), SW Saurashtra, India, 20 mi. SW of Junagarh; local market for cotton, millet, oilseeds; hand-loom weaving. Airport.

Keshorai Patan (kā'shōrī pä'tŭn), town (pop. 3,149), SE central Rajasthan, India, on Chambal R. and 22 mi. SE of Bundi; local market for wheat, millet, oilseeds, gram. Also called Patan.

Kesi, India: see JHUSI.

Kesigi, India: see KOSIGI.

Kesis Dag (kĕ-shĭsh' dä), Turkish *Keşiş Dağ*, peak (11,604 ft.), E central Turkey, in Erzincan Mts., 15 mi. ENE of Erzincan.

Keskin (kĕskĭn'), village (pop. 4,698), Ankara prov., central Turkey, 45 mi. ESE of Ankara; wheat, barley; mohair goats. Formerly Maden.

Kesma or **Kes'ma** (kyĭsmä'), village (1926 pop. 513), NE Kalinin oblast, Russian SFSR, 45 mi. NNE of Bezhetsk; flax processing.

Kesmark, Czechoslovakia: see KEZMAROK.

Kesova Gora (kyĕ'sŭvŭ gŭrä'), village (1939 pop. over 500), E Kalinin oblast, Russian SFSR, 18 mi. NW of Kashin; flax processing.

Kesra, La (lä kĕsrä'), village, Maktar dist., central Tunisia, 9 mi. ESE of Maktar; Aleppo pine and oak forests. Olive-oil pressing. Also spelled La Kessera.

Kesrieh or **Kesriyeh,** Greece: see KASTORIA, city.

Kessel (kĕ'sŭl), town (pop. 4,297), Antwerp prov., N Belgium, 3 mi. ENE of Lierre; agr. market (vegetables, potatoes). Has 14th–15th-cent. church, object of pilgrimage.

Kessel, village (pop. 593), Limburg prov., SE Netherlands, on Maas R. and 8 mi. NNE of Roermond; bricks, roofing tiles; agr.

Kessel Falls, Austria: see KAPRUN.

Kessel-Lo (-lō'), town (pop. 14,170), Brabant prov., central Belgium, 2 mi. ENE of Louvain; metal industry; mfg. (railroad rolling-stock). Site of former Benedictine abbey founded in 12th cent. Formerly spelled Kessel-Loo.

Kesselsdorf (kĕ'sŭlsdôrf), village (pop. 1,053), Saxony, E central Germany, 7 mi. W of Dresden. Scene (Dec., 1745) of Prussian victory over Saxons in Second Silesian War.

Kessenich (kĕ'sŭnĭkh), agr. village (pop. 1,198), Limburg prov., NE Belgium, 5 mi. N of Maaseik near Netherlands border.

Kessera, La, Tunisia: see KESRA, LA.

Kessingland, fishing village and parish (pop. 1,799), NE Suffolk, England, near North Sea, 5 mi. SSW of Lowestoft; resort.

Kestenga or **Kesten'ga** (kyĕ'styĭnyŭgŭ), Finnish *Kiestinki*, village, N Karelo-Finnish SSR, on lake Topozero, 35 mi. WSW of Loukhi, on rail spur; woodworking.

Kestenholz, France: see CHÂTENOIS.

Kesteren (kĕs'tŭrŭn), village (pop. 1,039), Gelderland prov., central Netherlands, 7 mi. ENE of Tiel; rail junction; fruitgrowing, fruit-tree nurseries.

Kesteven, Parts of (kĕstē'vŭn, kĕ'stēvŭn), SW administrative division of Lincolnshire, England. See LINCOLN, county.

Keston, residential town and parish (pop. 1,728), NW Kent, England, 3 mi. S of Bromley. The park was site of Roman camp. Has 13th-cent. church.

Keswick (kĕ'zĭk), urban district (1931 pop. 4,635; 1951 census 4,868), S Cumberland, England, in the Lake District, on Greta R. near N shore of Derwentwater, and 22 mi. SSW of Carlisle; market town and tourist center, with some mfg. (lead pencils, bobbins for textile industry) and granite quarrying. Has church showing traces of Norman origin, and mus. in town hall. Keswick was scene of Shelley's honeymoon and attracted such poets and writers as Coleridge, Wordsworth, Southey, Lamb, and Ruskin. Robert Southey is buried here; Great Hall, his home, is preserved. Near by is the Druids' Circle.

Keswick (kĕz'wĭk), town (pop. 276), Keokuk co., SE Iowa, 24 mi. ENE of Oskaloosa; livestock, grain.

Keswick Dam, Calif.: see SACRAMENTO RIVER.

Keswick Lake, England: see DERWENTWATER.

Keszthely (kĕst'hĕĭ), resort town (pop. 11,987), Zala co., W Hungary, on L. Balaton and 25 mi. NNE of Nagykanizsa; breweries, brickworks. School of agr. and economics (the *Georgicon*) founded 1797. Winegrowing, horse breeding near by. Karl Goldmark b. here.

Kesztölc (kĕs'tûlts), town (pop. 2,664), Komarom-Esztergom co., N Hungary, 6 mi. SSE of Esztergom; vineyards, wheat, rye, cattle, horses.

Keta (kĕ'tä), town (pop. 11,373), Eastern Prov., SE Gold Coast colony, port on narrow strip of land bet. Keta Lagoon and Gulf of Guinea, 85 mi. ENE of Accra; fishing; saltworking, copra processing, cotton weaving. Danish trading post, founded 17th cent.; passed 1850 to British.

Keta Lagoon, SE Gold Coast, closed off from Gulf of Guinea by sandspit; 32 mi. long, 2–7 mi. wide; saltworks.

Ketama (kātä'mä), highest section of Rif Mts., central Sp. Morocco, with peaks (snow-covered in winter) rising over 7,000 ft. Here, in 1936, Franco began revolt which led to Sp. civil war.

Ketapang (kŭtäpäng'), town (pop. 4,385), W Borneo, Indonesia, port on Karimata Strait, 130 mi. SSE of Pontianak; 1°50'S 109°58'E; trade center, shipping rubber and rattan.

Ketchikan (kĕ'chĭkăn), town (pop. 5,305), SE Alaska, on S Revillagigedo Isl., Alexander Archipelago, on arm of Clarence Strait, opposite Gravina Isl., 230 mi. SSE of Juneau; 55°21'N 131°39'W. Trading center for fishing (notably salmon and halibut), fur-farming, logging area; has canneries, cold-storage plants, sawmill. With a good port on the Inside Passage, and with steamer and air connections to U.S., it is an important distribution and communications center. Port of entry to Alaska; has U.S. coast guard and lighthouse-service stations, and a federal bldg. Municipally owned public utilities. Developed as supply point for prospectors on way N during gold rush of the 1890s.

Ketchum (kĕ'chŭm). **1** Village, Blaine co., Idaho: see SUN VALLEY. **2** Town (pop. 254), Craig co., NE Okla., 10 mi. SE of Vinita, near L. of the Cherokees (just SE). Inc. 1938.

Ketegyhaza (kā'tĕdyŭhä"zŏ), Hung. *Kétegyháza*, town (pop. 4,520), Bekes co., SE Hungary, 8 mi. SW of Gyula; grain, melons, camomile; hogs.

Kete-Krachi (kĕ'tā-krä'chē), town (pop. 2,022), N Br. Togoland, administered as part of the Northern Territories of the Gold Coast, on Volta R. (ferry) and 150 mi. N of Accra; fishing and trade center; cacao, yams, palm oil and kernels. Emergency airfield. Hq. Krachi dist.

Ketereh (kŭtŭrĕ'), village (pop. 656), N Kelantan, Malaya, 12 mi. S of Kota Bharu; rice.

Kethely (kāt'hĕĭ), Hung. *Kéthely*, town (pop. 3,985), Somogy co., SW Hungary, 11 mi. SE of Keszthely; wine.

Kethib, Ras, Yemen: see KATHIB, RAS.

Keti Bandar (kā'tē bŭn'dŭr), village, Tatta dist., SW Sind, W Pakistan, small port in Indus R. delta mouth, near Arabian Sea, 55 mi. SSE of Karachi; coastal trade in rice, millet, oilseeds, cotton, firewood; fishing.

Ketmen-Tyube, Kirghiz SSR: see MUZTOR.

Ketoi Island or **Ketoy Island** (kyĭtoi') (□ 35), one of central main Kurile Isls. chain, Russian SFSR; separated from Ushishir Isls. (N) by Rikord Strait, from Simushir Isl. (S) by Diana Strait; 47°20'N 152°29'E; nearly circular (6 mi. in diameter); rises to 3,945 ft.

Ketoi-kaikyo, Russian SFSR: see RIKORD STRAIT.

Kétou (kĕ'tōō), village, S Dahomey, Fr. West Africa, 60 mi. N of Porto-Novo; palm kernels, palm oil. Customhouse. R.C. mission.

Ketovo (kyĕ'tŭvŭ), village (1939 pop. over 500), central Kurgan oblast, Russian SFSR, 6 mi. SE of Kurgan, across the Tobol, in agr. area.

Ketoy Island, Russian SFSR: see KETOI ISLAND.

Ket River or **Ket' River** (kĕ'tyŭ), in W Krasnoyarsk Territory and E Tomsk oblast, Russian SFSR, rises 60 mi. N of Krasnoyarsk, flows 842 mi. NW and W, past Bely Yar, to Ob R. 10 mi. S of Narym. Connected with Kas R. (tributary of Yenisei R.) by OB-YENISEI CANAL SYSTEM.

Ketrzyn (kĕ'chĭn), Pol. *Kętrzyn*, Ger. *Rastenburg* (rä'stŭnbōōrk), town (1939 pop. 19,634; 1946 pop. 5,468) in East Prussia, after 1945 in Olsztyn prov., NE Poland, in Masurian Lakes region, 40 mi. ENE of Allenstein (Olsztyn); agr. market (grain, sugar beets, livestock); sawmilling, brewing. Teutonic Knights founded castle here in early-14th cent. Formerly site of Ger. state stud farm. After Second World War, when it was c.50% destroyed, Ger. pop. left the town.

Ketsch (kĕch), village (pop. 4,696), N Baden, Germany, after 1945 in Württemberg-Baden, on an arm of the Rhine and 2.5 mi. SW of Schwetzingen; tobacco, sugar beets, strawberries.

Ketschendorf (kĕ'chŭndôrf), town (pop. 6,504), Brandenburg, E Germany, on the Spree and 2 mi. SSE of Fürstenwalde; mfg. of cables, tires, industrial belting; metalworking.

Kettering, municipal borough (1931 pop. 31,220; 1951 census 36,799), N central Northampton, England, on Ise R. and 14 mi. NE of Northampton; leather- and shoe-mfg. center, with woolen mills and mfg. of machine tools, agr. machinery, ball-bearings. Has 15th-cent. church, art gall., leather-trade school, library.

Kettle, parish (pop. 1,518), N central Fifeshire, Scotland, just S of Ladybank. Includes agr. villages of Kingskettle and Kettlebridge.

Kettle Falls, town (pop. 714), Stevens co., NE Wash., 8 mi. NE of Colville, near Roosevelt L. Town moved (1938–39) from site c.4 mi. S, now covered by lake.

Kettle Island, mining village (1940 pop. 748), Bell co., SE Ky., in the Cumberlands near Pine Mtn., 13 mi. NNE of Middlesboro; bituminous coal, lumber.

Kettleman Hills, S central Calif., low range (c.1,300 ft.) along W side of San Joaquin Valley, c.55 mi. SW of Fresno; important oil and natural-gas field here.

Kettle River, S B.C. and N Wash., rises in Canada in Monashee Mts. W of Upper Arrow L., flows S to vicinity of Grand Forks, where it crosses Wash. border twice, finally entering Columbia R. 13 mi. NW of Colville; 175 mi. long. Fertile agr. valley (fruits, vegetables).

Kettle River, village (pop. 223), Carlton co., E Minn., on Kettle R. and c.40 mi. SW of Duluth; dairy products. Sandstone quarried in vicinity.

Kettle River, rises in marshy area of Carlton co., E Minn., flows 80 mi. S, past villages of Kettle River and Willow River, to St. Croix R. in Pine co.

Kettlersville, village (pop. 172), Shelby co., W Ohio, 12 mi. NNW of Sidney. Also spelled Kettlerville.

Ketton, town and parish (pop. 966), Rutland, England, 4 mi. WSW of Stamford; cement and concrete works; stone quarrying. Church dates from 13th cent.

Kettwig (kĕt'vĭkh), town (pop. 14,125), in former Prussian Rhine Prov., W Germany, after 1945 in North Rhine-Westphalia, on Ruhr R. and 7 mi. SW of Essen, in the Ruhr; textile-mfg. center (fine cloth; spinning).

Ketung, Kotung, or **K'o-tung** (all: kŭ'dōōng'), town, ⊙ Ketung co. (pop. 73,293), central Heilungkiang prov., Manchuria, on road and 20 mi. SW of Pehan; soybeans, kaoliang, rye, indigo.

Kety (kĕ'tĭ), Pol. *Kęty*, Ger. *Kenty* (kĕn'tē), town (pop. 6,581), Katowice prov., S Poland, 34 mi. WSW of Cracow, near Sola R.; mfg. (furniture, cement products, woolen textiles), tanning, flour milling, sawmilling; iron foundry, brickworks. Monastery. Until 1951 in Krakow prov.

Ketzin (kĕ'tsĭn), town (pop. 5,107), Brandenburg, E Germany, on the Havel and 11 mi. NW of Potsdam; clay quarrying; brick mfg.; market gardening.

Keuka (kū'kŭ, kēū'kŭ), resort village, Steuben co., W central N.Y., on E shore of Keuka L., 27 mi. SSW of Geneva.

Keuka Lake, W central N.Y., one of the Finger Lakes, c.45 mi. SE of Rochester, in grape-growing, wine-making, and resort region; c.18 mi. long, ½–2 mi. wide, with 7-mi.-long W arm. Drains NE through short outlet into Seneca L. Penn Yan, at N end, and Hammondsport, at S end, are trade centers of region.

Keuka Park, village (pop. c.200), Yates co., W central N.Y., on Keuka L., 19 mi. SSW of Geneva. Seat of Keuka Col.

Keuruu (kā'ōōrōō), Swedish *Keuru* (kû'rü"), village (commune pop. 11,321), Vaasa co., S central Finland, on small lake, 13 mi. W of Jyväskylä, in lumbering region. Has 18th-cent. church.

Keustendil, Bulgaria: see KYUSTENDIL.

Kevelaer (kā'vŭlär), village (pop. 9,187), in former Prussian Rhine Prov., W Germany, after 1945 in North Rhine-Westphalia, in the Ruhr, near the Niers, 7 mi. SSE of Goch; mfg. (shoes, religious articles). Noted pilgrimage place with image of the Virgin.

Kevermes (kĕ'vĕrmĕsh), town (pop. 5,263), Csanad co., SE Hungary, 19 mi. SSE of Bekescsaba; grain, onions, cattle.

Kevevara, Yugoslavia: see KOVIN.

Kevil (kĕ'vŭl), town (pop. 202), Ballard co., SW Ky., 16 mi. W of Paducah, in agr. area; make brooms.

Kevin (kē'vŭn), town (pop. 351), Toole co., N Mont., 17 mi. NNW of Shelby; oil refining. Kevin-Sunburst oil field near by.

Kew (kū), municipality (pop. 30,859), S Victoria, Australia, 4 mi. ENE of Melbourne, in metropolitan area; residential.

Kew, residential district (pop. 3,101) in Richmond municipal borough, NE Surrey, England, on the Thames and 7 mi. W of London. Here are Kew Gardens, officially the Royal Botanical Gardens (288 acres), founded by dowager princess of Wales in 1760 and presented to nation as royal gift in 1840. There are thousands of plant species, 4 museums, laboratories, and hothouses. Rare plants were destroyed and hothouses damaged in 1940 air raids. Kew Palace was home of George III and of Queen Charlotte, who died here. Gainsborough is buried in graveyard of Church of St. Anne (1714). Kew Observatory (51°28'N 0°19'W) is a govt. station.

Kewagama Lake (10 mi. long, 5 mi. wide), W Que., 22 mi. E of Rouyn; alt. 958 ft. Drains W into L. Timiskaming.

Kewanee (kēwä'nē), industrial city (pop. 16,821), Henry co., NW Ill., 35 mi. ESE of Moline, in agr. and bituminous-coal-mining area; oil refining; mfg. of dairy products, boilers, pumps, farm machinery, steel building supplies, tools, safes, truck bodies, hardware, gloves. Inc. 1855, shortly after the railroad's coming; annexed residential Wethersfield (founded 1836) in 1924.

Kewanna (kŭwä'nŭ, kē–), town (pop. 680), Fulton co., N Ind., 20 mi. N of Logansport, in agr. area.

Kewaskum (kĭwô'skŭm), village (pop. 1,183), Washington co., E Wis., on branch of Milwaukee R. and 36 mi. NNW of Milwaukee, in dairy and farm area; mfg. (aluminum ware, concrete mixers, malt products, cheese, butter).

Kewaunee (kĭwô'nē), county (□ 331; pop. 17,366), E Wis.; ⊙ Kewaunee. Bounded E by L. Michigan, NW by Green Bay; situated near base of Door Peninsula. Partly wooded, hilly terrain, drained by several small streams. Farming, dairying, lumbering, woodworking. Formed 1852.

Kewaunee, city (pop. 2,583), ⊙ Kewaunee co., E Wis., on L. Michigan, on Door Peninsula, at mouth of small Kewaunee R., 25 mi. E of Green Bay, in dairying and stock-raising area; mfg. (furniture, wood and aluminum products); dairy plants, breweries. Ferry service to Frankfort and Ludington, Mich. A coast guard station is here. The North West Company set up a fur-trading post on site in 1795. Inc. 1883.

Keweenaw (kē′wĭnô), county (□ 544; pop. 2,918), NW Upper Peninsula, Mich.; ⊙ Eagle River. On NE KEWEENAW PENINSULA in L. Superior. Includes ISLE ROYALE NATIONAL PARK (NW). Copper-mining region, traversed by the Copper Range; also lumbering, some agr. (dairy products; potatoes). Resorts (hunting, fishing). Several lakes, 2 state parks in co. Formed and organized 1861.

Keweenaw Bay, NW Upper Peninsula, Mich., inlet of L. Superior lying to E of curving Keweenaw Peninsula, 55 mi. NW of Marquette. It is E terminus of Keweenaw Waterway. Baraga, Keweenaw Bay village, and L'Anse, all resorts with fisheries, are at its head.

Keweenaw Peninsula, Mich., curves c.60 mi. NE into L. Superior from NW Upper Peninsula; its base (c.30 mi. wide) is c.60 mi. WNW of Marquette. At its tip is Keweenaw Point. COPPER RANGE (here rising to 1,532 ft.) runs its length. Comprises Houghton and Keweenaw counties; principal cities are Hancock and Houghton. KEWEENAW WATERWAY crosses peninsula midway. Once famed as the "copper country" (peak production, 1916–17), now a resort area; has several state parks. Some copper mining; lumbering, farming, commercial fishing. Boat connections to Isle Royale Natl. Park.

Keweenaw Range, Mich.: see COPPER RANGE.

Keweenaw Waterway, NW Upper Peninsula, Mich., navigation channel (c.25 mi. long) intersecting Keweenaw Peninsula bet. Keweenaw Bay (SE) and L. Superior (NW). Consists of Portage L. (c.20 mi. long, 2 mi. wide), with a natural connection with Keweenaw Bay, and a land-cut ship canal (c.2 mi. long) across former portage bet. Portage L. and L. Superior. U.S. lighthouse at L. Superior entrance. Hancock, Houghton are ports.

Kew Gardens, England: see KEW.

Kew Gardens (kū), SE N.Y., a residential section of central Queens borough of New York city.

Kexholm, Russian SFSR: see PRIOZERSK.

Key, Lough (lŏkh), lake (3 mi. long, 3 mi. wide), N Co. Roscommon, Ireland, on Boyle R., 2 mi. NE of Boyle; noted for its scenic beauty. On isl. in lake are remains of Abbey of the Trinity; the *Annals of Lough Cé*, written here, are in Trinity Col. library, Dublin.

Keyaluvik or **Kioluvick** (kēŭlōō′vĭk), village (pop. 68), SW Alaska, near Bethel.

Keya Paha (kē′ŭ pä′hä), county (□ 769; pop. 2,160), N Nebr.; ⊙ Springview. Agr. area bounded N by S.Dak., S by Niobrara R.; drained by Keya Paha R. Livestock, grain. Formed 1884.

Keya Paha River, in S S. Dak. and N Nebr., rises in Todd co., S.Dak., flows 101 mi. ESE to Niobrara R. near Butte, Nebr.

Key Biscayne (bĭskān′) (c.5 mi. long), one of the Florida Keys, S Fla., in the Atlantic (E), 5 mi. SSE of Miami; partly shelters Biscayne Bay (W). At S end is Cape Florida, on Safety Valve Entrance.

Keyes, town (pop. 431), Cimarron co., extreme NW Okla., 15 mi. ENE of Boise City; livestock, grain.

Keyesport, village (pop. 438), on Bond-Clinton co. line, S central Ill., 16 mi. NNW of Centralia, in agr. and oil area.

Key Islands, Indonesia: see KAI ISLANDS.

Keyla, Estonia: see KEILA.

Key Largo (lär′gō), Monroe co., S Fla., largest island (28½ mi. long, 1–2 mi. wide) of the FLORIDA KEYS, 30 mi. S of Miami; over-ocean highway which links the keys passes to mainland from here. Commercial and sport fishing, citrus-fruit growing, limestone quarrying. Site of villages of Key Largo, Rock Harbor, Tavernier (tă′vürnēr″).

Keyling Inlet, Australia: see FITZMAURICE RIVER.

Keymer (kē′–, kī′–), agr. village and parish (pop. 1,491), central Sussex, England, 7 mi. N of Brighton. Church dates from 13th cent.

Keynsham (kān′shŭm), residential urban district (1931 pop. 4,251; 1951 census 8,277), NE Somerset, England, on the Avon and 5 mi. SE of Bristol; mfg. (chocolate, paper, chemicals, soap). Has 13th-15th-cent. church, remains of 3 Roman villas, and traces of anc. monastery.

Keyport, borough (pop. 5,888), Monmouth co., E N.J., 6 mi. SE of South Amboy; resort and fishing center with harbor on Raritan Bay; mfg. (boats, tile, cork products, rubber goods, clothing); agr. (truck, poultry, dairy products). Settled before 1700, inc. 1908.

Keyser (kī′zŭr). **1** Town, Moore co., N.C.: see ADDOR. **2** City (pop. 6,347), ⊙ Mineral co., NE W.Va., in Eastern Panhandle, on North Branch of the Potomac and 20 mi. SW of Cumberland, Md.; mfg. of woolen goods, beverages; lumber mills, railroad shops. Seat of Potomac State School of W.Va. Univ. An important supply base in Civil War. Settled 1802.

Keystone. 1 Town (pop. 438), Benton co., E central Iowa, 28 mi. W of Cedar Rapids, in agr. area. **2** Town (pop. 228), Pawnee co., N Okla., 16 mi. W of Tulsa, at junction of Cimarron and Arkansas rivers, in agr. area. **3** Village (pop. c.300), Pennington co., W S.Dak., 10 mi. SW of Rapid City, in Black Hills; alt. 4,342 ft. Feldspar mill and pottery market. Mt. Rushmore Natl. Memorial near by. **4** City (pop. 2,594), McDowell co., S W.Va., on Tug Fork 7 mi. E of Welch, in semibituminous-coal region; railroad yards. Inc. 1909.

Keystone Heights, town (pop. 307), Clay co., NE Fla., c.45 mi. W of St. Augustine; resort in lake region. Called Brooklyn until 1922.

Keysville. 1 Town (pop. 304), Burke co., E Ga., 21 mi. SW of Augusta and on Brier Creek; sawmilling. **2** Town (pop. 690), Charlotte co., S Va., 45 mi. SE of Lynchburg; rail junction; tobacco market; makes clothing; lumber.

Keytesville (kēts′vĭl), city (pop. 733), ⊙ Chariton co., N central Mo., near Missouri R., 28 mi. W of Moberly; grain; lumber products. Platted 1830.

Key West, city (pop. 26,433), ⊙ Monroe co., S Fla., occupying the isl. of Key West (c.4 mi. long, c.1½ mi. wide; westernmost of the FLORIDA KEYS), southernmost city of U.S., c.130 mi. SSW of Miami, c.100 mi. NNE of Havana, Cuba; 24°33′N 81°49′W. Resort; sponge-fishing center; port of entry. Has U.S. coast guard base (Fort Taylor, built 1844–46), naval station, and naval air station. Processes giant turtles for soup. Formerly a ship-salvage point and next a major cigar-mfg. center. Terminus of highway which in 1938 replaced railroad (completed 1912; destroyed in 1935 hurricane) spanning the keys from the mainland. Has lighthouse (1846), two Civil War forts, and an aquarium. Pop. is heterogeneous, including descendants of Cubans, Spaniards, Negroes, and Englishmen.

Kez (kyĕs), town (1942 pop. over 500), NE Udmurt Autonomous SSR, Russian SFSR, on railroad and 50 mi. ESE of Glazov; flax processing.

Kezar Falls, Maine: see PARSONSFIELD.

Kezar Lake (kē′zŭr). **1** In Oxford co., W Maine, in summer resort area near N.H. line; c.7.5 mi. long. Drains S, through Kezar Pond, to Saco R. **2** In Merrimack co., N.H.: see SUTTON.

Kezdivasarhely, Rumania: see TARGU-SACUESC.

Kezhma (kyĕzh′mŭ), village (1948 pop. over 2,000), SE Krasnoyarsk Territory, Russian SFSR, 235 mi. NE of Taishet and on Angara R.; lumbering. Founded 1665.

Kezi (kĕ′zē), village, Bulawayo prov., SW Southern Rhodesia, in Matabeleland, on road and 50 mi. SSW of Bulawayo; peanuts, corn; livestock. Cattle inspection station; police post.

Kezmarok (kĕzh′märôk), Slovak *Kežmarok*, Hung. *Késmárk* (kāzh′märk), town (pop. 7,216), N Slovakia, Czechoslovakia, in SE part of the High Tatra, on Poprad R., on railroad and 47 mi. NW of Kosice; long-established trade center; woodworking, linen mfg., embroidery making. Has picturesque castle, formerly of Tököly family, with 5 towers and 15th-cent. chapel; 15th-cent. Gothic church; 18th-cent. wooden church; Renaissance buildings; modern church with remains of Imre Tököly, brought from Turkey.

Kezmarske Zleby (kĕzh′märskā zhlĕ′bĭ), Slovak *Kežmarské Žleby*, village, N Slovakia, Czechoslovakia, at E foot of Lomnice Peak in the High Tatra, 7 mi. NW of Kezmarok; part of commune of Vysoke Tatry; summer resort (alt. 3,215 ft.) with sanatorium.

Kfar Aharon (kfär′ ähärōn′), settlement (pop. 200), W Israel, in Judaean Plain, 2 mi. NW of Rehovot; citriculture. Founded 1926. Also spelled Kefar Aharon.

Kfar Atta or **Kfar Ata** (ä′tä), settlement (pop. 2,300), NW Israel, in Zebulun Valley, 7 mi. E of Haifa; textile-milling center; tobacco processing; mixed agr. Founded 1925. Also spelled Kefar Atta or Kefar Ata.

Kfar Avraham (ävrähäm′), settlement (pop. 500), W Israel, in Plain of Sharon, just E of Petah Tiqva; mixed agr. Talmudic and trade schools. Founded 1932. Also spelled Kefar Avraham.

Kfar Azar (äzär′), residential settlement (pop. 450), W Israel, in Plain of Sharon, 4 mi. E of Tel Aviv; dairying, poultry; vegetable growing. Founded 1932. Also spelled Kefar Azar.

Kfar Barukh or **Kfar Baruch** (both: bärōōkh′), settlement (pop. 260), NW Israel, in Plain of Jezreel, near Kishon R., near railroad, 6 mi. WNW of Afula; grain, sunflowers. Founded 1926. Also spelled Kefar Barukh or Kefar Baruch.

Kfar Bialik, Israel: see QIRYAT BIALIK.

Kfar Bilu (bēlōō′), settlement (pop. 200), W Israel, in Judaean Plain, just SSE of Rehovot; citriculture, mixed farming. Large immigrants' reception camp near by. Founded 1932. Also Kefar Bilu.

Kfar Blum (blōōm), settlement (pop. 400), Upper Galilee, NE Israel, in Hula swamp region, 15 mi. NNE of Safad; clothespin mfg.; mixed farming; fish breeding. Founded 1943 on reclaimed soil. Also spelled Kefar Blum.

Kfar Brandeis (brändās′), settlement (pop. 170), W Israel, in Plain of Sharon, just SSE of Hadera; mixed farming. Founded 1928. Also spelled Kefar Brandeis.

Kfar Felix Warburg, Israel: see KFAR WARBURG.

Kfar Giladi or **Kfar Gil'adi** (gēl-ädē′), settlement (pop. 750), Upper Galilee, NE Israel, near Lebanese border, at S foot of Lebanon range, 19 mi. NNE of Safad; machine shops; agr. (fruit, olives); fish breeding. Founded 1916. Also spelled Kefar Giladi; sometimes spelled Kfar Gileadi or Kefar Gileadi. Absorbed (1926) settlement of Tel Hai (tĕl′ hī′), just S, noted for defense (1920) against Arab attack during which Trumpeldor was killed.

Kfar Glikson or **Kfar Glickson** (glĕk′sōn), settlement (pop. 250), W Israel, in Plain of Sharon, 7 mi. NE of Hadera; mixed farming, sheep raising. Founded 1939; repeatedly attacked by Arabs, 1948. Also spelled Kefar Glikson, Kefar Glickson.

Kfar ha Horesh or **Kfar Hahoresh** (hähōrĕsh′), settlement (pop. 250), Lower Galilee, N Israel, 2 mi. W of Nazareth; livestock, fruit; afforestation. Founded 1933. Also spelled Kefar ha Horesh or Kefar Hahoresh.

Kfar Haiyim (hä′yēm) or **Kfar Haim** (hīm′), settlement (pop. 375), W Israel, in Plain of Sharon, 3 mi. NE of Natanya; mixed farming, citriculture. Founded 1933. Also spelled Kefar Haiyim or Kefar Haim; sometimes spelled Kfar Hayim or Kefar Hayim.

Kfar ha Maccabi or **Kfar Hamaccabi** (hämäkäbē′), settlement (pop. 250), NW Israel, in Zebulun Valley, 7 mi. E of Haifa; mixed farming, banana growing; carp ponds. Founded 1936. Also spelled Kefar ha Maccabi or Kefar Hamaccabi.

Kfar ha Ro-e or **Kfar Haroeh** (härō′ā), settlement (pop. 650), W Israel, in Plain of Sharon, 4 mi. S of Hadera; mixed farming, citriculture. Has Talmudic and agr. col. Founded 1934. Also spelled Kefar ha Ro-e or Kefar Haroeh.

Kfar Hasidim or **Kfar Hassidim** (häsēdēm′), settlement (pop. 1,500), NW Israel, in Zebulun Valley, near Kishon R., 7 mi. ESE of Haifa; dairying, mfg. of ceremonial articles. Founded 1924. Also spelled Kefar Hasidim or Kefar Hassidim. Near by is orthodox youth village, with religious school.

Kfar Hess (hĕs), settlement (pop. 375), W Israel, in Plain of Sharon, 7 mi. SE of Natanya; citriculture, mixed farming. Founded 1933. Also spelled Kefar Hess.

Kfar Hittim (hētēm′), settlement (pop. 275), NE Israel, Lower Galilee, 2 mi. WNW of Tiberias; mixed farming, textile milling. Founded 1936. Also spelled Kefar Hittim.

Kfariye or **Kfariyah** (kfärē′yü), Fr. *Kfarié*, town, Latakia prov., W Syria, 20 mi. NE of Latakia; solid bitumen deposits exploited here.

Kfar Kisch (kfär′ kēsh′), settlement (pop. 150), Lower Galilee, N Israel, at ESE foot of Mt. Tabor, 9 mi. SW of Tiberias; mixed farming. Founded 1946. Also spelled Kefar Kisch; sometimes spelled Kfar kish or Kefar Kish.

Kfar Malal (mäläl′), settlement (pop. 450), W Israel, in Plain of Sharon, 3 mi. E of Herzliya; dairying, mixed farming. Founded 1911; destroyed in First World War and again 1921. Also spelled Kefar Malal.

Kfar Marmorek (mär′mōrĕk), residential settlement (pop. 1,000), W Israel, in Judaean Plain, just WSW of Rehovot. Has vocational training school. Founded 1931. Also spelled Kefar Marmorek.

Kfar Masaryk (mäsärēk′), settlement (pop. 400), NW Israel, in Zebulun Valley, 8 mi. NE of Haifa; mfg. of asphalt, bricks, dyes; mixed farming, fish breeding. Founded 1938 by Czech settlers. Also spelled Kefar Masaryk.

Kfar Menahem (mĕnähĕm′), settlement (pop. 350), W Israel, in Judaean Plain, 11 mi. S of Rehovot; grain, fruit. Founded 1937. Also spelled Kefar Menahem.

Kfar Nathan (nätän′) or **Beit Zera** (bĕt′ zĕ′rä), settlement (pop. 500), Lower Galilee, NE Israel, on the Jordan and 7 mi. SSE of Tiberias; mixed farming. Founded 1927. Also spelled Kefar Nathan or Bet Zera.

Kfar Ono (ōnō′), residential settlement (pop. 800), W Israel, in Plain of Sharon, 5 mi. E of Tel Aviv. Also spelled Kefar Ono, Shkhunat Ono, or Shchunat Ono.

Kfar Pines (pē′nĕs), settlement (pop. 400), W Israel, in Plain of Sharon, 4 mi. NE of Hadera; mixed farming. Has large Talmudic library. Founded 1933. Also spelled Kefar Pines.

Kfar Ruppin (rōō′pēn), settlement (pop. 230), NE Israel, on the Jordan (border of Kingdom of Jordan) and 4 mi. SE of Beisan; fish breeding, fruit-growing. Founded 1938. Also spelled Kefar Ruppin.

Kfar Sava (sä′vä) or **Kfar Saba** (sä′bä), settlement (1950 pop. estimate 8,000), W Israel, in Plain of Sharon, 11 mi. NE of Tel Aviv; agr. center (citriculture, vegetables, poultry); mfg. of knitted goods, rubber products; vacation resort. Has large hosp. Modern settlement founded 1903, destroyed during First World War, and again in subsequent Arab riots; resettled 1936. Also spelled Kefar Sava or Kefar Saba. Just N is site of anc. locality of *Capharsaba*, founded in era of Second Temple, fortified by Alexander Jannaeus.

Kfar Shmaryahu (shmäryähōō′), settlement (pop. 400), W Israel, in Plain of Sharon, near Mediterranean, 2 mi. NW of Herzliya; dairying; vegetables, poultry. Vacation resort. Founded 1936. Also spelled Kefar Shmaryahu.

Kfar Sirkin or **Kfar Syrkin** (sēr′kēn), settlement (pop. 650), W Israel, in Plain of Sharon, 3 mi. ESE of Petah Tiqva; poultry, fruit. Founded 1936. Also spelled Kefar Sirkin or Kefar Syrkin.

Kfar Szold (sōld), settlement (pop. 350), Upper Galilee, NE Israel, on Syrian border, at SW foot of Mt. Hermon, 18 mi. NE of Safad; woolen milling, woodworking, horticulture, olive growing; fish ponds. Founded 1942; withstood Arab attacks, 1948. Also spelled Kefar Szold.

Kfar Tavor (tävōr') or **Kfar Tabor** (täbōr'), settlement (pop. 300), Lower Galilee, N Israel, at E foot of Mt. Tabor, 7 mi. E of Nazareth; viticulture; grain, olives; dairying. Founded 1901. Also spelled Kefar Tavor or Kefar Tabor. Near by is Kadoorie agr. school.

Kfar Uriya or **Kfar Uria** (both: ōōrē'ä), settlement (pop. 200), W Israel, on W slope of Judaean Hills, 11 mi. E of Rehovot; grain, mixed farming. Founded 1909. Also spelled Kefar Uriya or Kefar Uria.

Kfar Vitkin (vēt'kēn), settlement (pop. 1,000), W Israel, in Plain of Sharon, near Mediterranean, 4 mi. NNE of Natanya; mixed farming; mfg. of citrus by-products. Founded 1933. Also spelled Kefar Vitkin. Adjoining is children's agr.-training school of Ben Shemen, moved here (1948) from former site near Lydda.

Kfar Warburg (vär'bōōrg), settlement (pop. 320), W Israel, in Judaean Plain, 13 mi. SSW of Rehovot; mixed farming, citriculture. Founded 1939. Shelled and bombed by Arabs, 1948. Also spelled Kefar Warburg; sometimes called Kfar Felix Warburg or Kefar Felix Warburg.

Kfar Yehezqel, Kfar Yehezkiel, or **Kfar Yehezkel** (all: yĕhĕzkĕl'), settlement (pop. 550), NE Israel, in E part of Plain of Jezreel, near railroad, 5 mi. ESE of Afula; citriculture; grain, vegetables. Founded 1921. Also spelled Kefar Yehezqel, Kefar Yehezkiel, or Kefar Yehezkel.

Kfar Yehoshua (yĕhōshōō'ä) settlement (pop. 600), NW Israel, at NW end of Plain of Jezreel, near Kishon R., 13 mi. SE of Haifa, near railroad; grain, fruit, poultry, dairying. Founded 1927. Also spelled Kefar Yehoshua.

Kfar Yona (yōnä'), settlement (pop. 600), W Israel, in Plain of Sharon, 5 mi. E of Natanya; citriculture, dairying. Founded 1932; withstood Arab attack, 1948. Also spelled Kefar Yona.

Kgalagadi (gälägä'dē), district (pop. 7,712), SW Bechuanaland Protectorate, bounded S by Cape Prov., U. of So. Afr.; ⊙ Tsabong. Dist. includes game reserve (□ 3,750) and bird sanctuary.

Kgatleng, Bechuanaland Protectorate: see BAKGATLA.

Khaapsalu, Estonia: see HAAPSALU.

Khabakhe (khäbäkhä'), Chinese *Hapaho* (hä'bähŭ'), town, ⊙ Khabakhe co. (pop. 13,520), northernmost Sinkiang prov., China, on Black Irtysh R. and 90 mi. W of Sharasume, near USSR border; livestock, agr. products.

Khabarovo (khŭbürô'vŭ), village, NE Nenets Natl. Okrug, Archangel oblast, Russian SFSR, on strait Yugorski Shar, opposite Vaigach Isl., 170 mi. NW of Vorkuta; trading post; reindeer raising.

Khabarovsk (khŭbürôfsk', khŭbä'rŭfsk), territory [Rus. *krai* or *kray*] (□ 965,400, 1946 pop. estimate 1,250,000) in E Siberian Russian SFSR; ⊙ Khabarovsk. Includes nearly all Soviet Far East, extending N along Okhotsk and Bering seas to E. Siberian and Chukchi seas, from 46°N to 70°N lat. Includes JEWISH AUTONOMOUS OBLAST, LOWER AMUR oblast, KAMCHATKA oblast. (Khabarovsk oblast, formed 1934, was dissolved 1939.) Mostly mountainous (Anadyr, Kolyma, Stanovoi, Bureya ranges), with tundra region in N. Chief agr. areas are along the middle Amur. Reindeer raising (N), seal hunting, fishing, and fur trapping important. Exports furs, fish, and lumber. Extensive gold fields along upper Kolyma and lower Amur rivers. Iron, coal, petroleum, and nonferrous metals abound and are increasingly exploited. Industry concentrated at Khabarovsk, Komsomolsk, and along Trans-Siberian RR. Chief ports: Sovetskaya Gavan, Nikolayevsk, Magaden, Petropavlovsk. Formed (1938) out of Far Eastern Territory.

Khabarovsk, city (1926 pop. 52,045; 1939 pop. 199,364; 1946 pop. estimate 300,000), ⊙ Khabarovsk Territory, Russian SFSR, on Trans-Siberian RR, on right bank of the Amur, just below mouth of Ussuri R., and 3,800 mi. ESE of Moscow; 48°28'N 135°3'E. Industrial and transportation center for Soviet Far East; oil refinery (for Sakhalin fields), shipbuilding docks, auto-assembly and aircraft plants, sawmilling, woodworking, meat packing, flour milling, agr. machinery mfg. Transfer point for Amur R. and Trans-Siberian RR traffic. Medical, teachers, and rail transport schools, archaeological and ethnological mus. Pop. includes Chinese and Korean elements. City consists of new section located on series of parallel ridges and 3-mi.-long old town nestling in hollows along the waterfront. Named for Rus. explorer Khabarov, who established fort here in 1652. Modern site dates from 1858, when it was founded as Rus. village of Khabarovka. Became administrative center of Rus. Far East in 1880; named Khabarovsk in 1883. Its importance increased following construction of Trans-Siberian RR section to Vladivostok (1897), Chita (1910s), and Khabarovsk (1937).

Khabary (khŭbä'rē), village (1926 pop. 2,296), W Altai Territory, Russian SFSR, on Burla R. and 55 mi. NE of Slavgorod, in agr. area.

Khabez (khŭbyĕs'), village (1948 pop. over 2,000), central Cherkess Autonomous Oblast, Stavropol Territory, Russian SFSR, on Little Zelenchuk R. and 20 mi. SW of Cherkessk; grain, livestock.

Khabis, Iran: see SHAHDAD.

Khabno or **Khabnoye,** Ukrainian SSR: see KAGANOVICHI PERVYE.

Khabour River, Syria: see KHABUR RIVER.

Khabura or **Khaburah** (khäbōō'rŭ), town (pop. 8,000), Batina dist., N Oman, port on Gulf of Oman, 35 mi. SE of Sohar.

Khabur River (khä'bōōr), largely in NE Iraq, rises in mts. of Turkish Kurdistan, flows c.100 mi. S and W into Iraq to the Tigris at the Syrian line 65 mi. NW of Mosul.

Khabur River, anc. *Habor,* Fr. *Khabour,* river of NE Syria, rising just over the border in mts. of SE Turkey, flows SE past El Haseke and S to the Euphrates 8 mi. N of Meyadin, S of Deir ez Zor; c.200 mi. long. Irrigates Jezire prov.

Khachbulag or **Khachbulakh** (khŭchbōōläk'), village (1939 pop. over 500), W Azerbaijan SSR, in the Lesser Caucasus, on N slope of the Shakh-Dag, 4 mi. WSW of Dashkesan city; alt. c.6,500 ft. Summer and health resort (mineral springs).

Khachmas (khŭchmäs'), city (1932 pop. estimate 3,280), NE Azerbaijan SSR, on railroad and 90 mi. NNW of Baku, near Caspian Sea coast (fisheries), in orchard dist. irrigated by Samur-Divichi Canal; fish canning.

Khachrod (käch'rōd), town (pop. 10,302), W Madhya Bharat, India, 36 mi. NW of Ujjain; market center for grain, cotton, tobacco; cotton ginning, hand-loom weaving; handicraft woodwork. Also spelled Khachraud.

Khadakavasla, India: see POONA, city.

Khadirabad, India: see JALNA.

Khadkhal or **Hadhal** (khäd'khäl), village (pop. over 2,000), Khubsugul aimak, NW Mongolian People's Republic, landing at S end of L. Khubsugul, at outlet of the Egin Gol, 55 mi. N of Muren; freight transshipment point on USSR-Mongolia trade route; woolwashing plant. Sometimes spelled Khatkhyl.

Khadyzhenski, Russian SFSR: see KHODYZHENSKI.

Khadzhi Dimitrovo (khäjē' dĭmē'trôvô), village (pop. 3,066), Pleven dist., N Bulgaria, 9 mi. SE of Svishtov; grain, stock, truck. Formerly Saryar.

Khadzhi Eles, Bulgaria: see PARVOMAY.

Khadzhi-Gasan, Azerbaijan SSR: see GADZHI-GASAN.

Khaf (khäf), town, Ninth Prov., in Khurasan, NE Iran, 70 mi. SE of Turbat-i-Haidari and on road to Afghan border, in fruitgrowing region (figs, grapes, melons).

Khafajiyeh, Iran: see SUSANGIRD.

Khafs Dhagara or **Khafs Daghra** (both: khäfs' dhä'gürü), well of Kharj oasis, E central Nejd, Saudi Arabia, 13 mi. SSE of Dilam; center of small model farm (developed in 1940s), irrigated from limestone pit; wheat, millet, vegetables, dates.

Khaga (kä'gŭ), town (pop. 3,304), Fatehpur dist., S Uttar Pradesh, India, 21 mi. ESE of Fatehpur; gram, barley, rice, jowar.

Khagaria (kŭg'ŭryŭ), town (pop. 15,559), Monghyr dist., NE central Bihar, India, on Burhi Gandak R. and 11 mi. NNE of Monghyr; road and trade (rice, wheat, corn, gram, barley, oilseeds) center.

Khagaul (kŭgoul'), town (pop. 8,795), Patna dist., N central Bihar, India, on Patna Canal and 7 mi. WSW of Patna; rice, gram, wheat, oilseeds, barley, corn. Large sugar-milling plant 10 mi. W, at Bihta.

Khaibar, W Pakistan: see KHYBER.

Khaibar or **Khaybar** (khī'bär), outlying town and oasis of Jebel Shammar prov., N Nejd, Saudi Arabia, 80 mi. NNW of Medina; dates, grain. Formerly considered part of Hejaz and spelled Kheibar.

Khaidarkan or **Khaydarkan** (khīdŭrkän'), town (1942 pop. over 500), W central Osh oblast, Kirghiz SSR, on N slope of Alai Range, 45 mi. SSE of Kokand; mercury- and antimony-mining center.

Khair (kīr), town (pop. 6,714), Aligarh dist., W Uttar Pradesh, India, 15 mi. WNW of Aligarh; road junction; wheat, barley, pearl millet.

Khairabad (khī'räbäd), town (pop. 13,643), Sitapur dist., central Uttar Pradesh, India, 6 mi. SE of Sitapur; durrie mfg.; wheat, rice, gram, barley, oilseeds. Founded 11th cent. by a pasi. Has 16th-cent. mosques. Annual fair.

Khairagarh (kī'rägŭr). **1** Town (pop. 5,015), Drug dist., E central Madhya Pradesh, India, 25 mi. NW of Drug; rice, wheat; biri mfg. Sometimes called Khairagarh Raj. Was ⊙ former princely state of Khairagarh (□ 931; pop. 173,713), one of the Chhattisgarh States, since 1948 inc. into Drug dist. **2** Village, Agra dist., W Uttar Pradesh, India, on Banganga R. and 20 mi. SSW of Agra; pearl millet, gram, wheat, barley. Also spelled Kherabgarh.

Khairan, Bandar Khairan, or **Bandar Khayran** (bändär' khīrän'), inlet of Gulf of Oman, in Oman, 13 mi. SE of Muscat; sheltered natural harbor.

Khairedin or **Khayredin** (khīrĕdēn'), village (pop. 4,177), Vratsa dist., NW Bulgaria, on Ogosta R. and 17 mi. SW of Oryakhovo; vineyards, grain, livestock. Formerly Yeredin.

Khairkhana Pass (khīrkhä'nŭ), in S outlier of the Hindu Kush, E Afghanistan, 7 mi. NW of Kabul, on highway to Samt-i-Shimali dist.

Khairpur (khīr'pōōr), princely state (□ 6,050; 1951 pop. 320,000), W Pakistan; ⊙ Khairpur. On W edge of Thar Desert; bounded NW by Indus R., NE, W, and S by Sind. Mainly a dry plain, broken by low sand hills, with fertile tract (NW); irrigated by left bank canals of Sukkur Barrage system. Agr. (millet, wheat, cotton, rice, oilseeds); handicraft work (cotton cloth, carpets, pottery, lacquer work, leather goods). Exports ghee, tobacco, cotton, grain, hides. Saline lakes (S) produce alkali salts (carbonates); large amount of fuller's earth mined; limestone deposits (N). Fishing (chiefly shad) in the Indus. In 1933, included in Punjab States agency; acceded to Pakistan in 1948.

Khairpur. 1 Town (pop. 5,964), Bahawalpur state, W Pakistan, 35 mi. NE of Bahawalpur; cotton, wheat, millet; handicraft cloth weaving and dyeing; leather goods, porcelain vessels. **2** Town (pop. 17,510); ⊙ Khairpur state, W Pakistan, in irrigated tract, 11 mi. SSW of Sukkur; trade center (grain, cotton, oilseeds, cloth fabrics); hand-loom weaving, pottery and lacquer-ware mfg. Industrial school. **3** Village, Sukkur dist., NE Sind, W Pakistan, 70 mi. ENE of Sukkur; millet, wheat, rice; handicrafts (cloth, pipe bowls, cooking pots).

Khait (khīēt'), village (1926 pop. 2,500), N Garm oblast, Tadzhik SSR, near Surkhab R., 30 mi. ENE of Garm; wheat.

Khajraho (kŭjrä'hō), village, W central Vindhya Pradesh, India, 21 mi. ESE of Chhatarpur, in Bundelkhand. Famous for its beautiful Brahman and Jain temples, built (A.D. 950–1050) of sandstone. Richly carved; contain fine sculptures and valuable inscriptions. Mus. (built 1919). Sometimes spelled Khajuraho.

Khajuha (kŭj'ōōhŭ), village, Fatehpur dist., S Uttar Pradesh, India, 3 mi. WNW of Bindki; gram, barley, rice, jowar. Formerly a town, founded 1659 by Aurangzeb.

Khajuraho, India: see KHAJRAHO.

Khakass Autonomous Oblast (khŭkäs'), administrative division (□24,000; 1939 pop. 270,665) of SW Krasnoyarsk Territory, Siberian Russian SFSR; ⊙ Abakan. Bet. upper Yenisei R. and Kuznetsk Ala-Tau mts.; drained by Abakan and Chulym rivers. Pop. half Khakass (a Siberian Turkic ethnic group), half Russian. Agr., dairy farming, lumbering. Rich in coal (Chernogorsk), gold (in Kuznetsk Ala-Tau), barite (Askiz), iron, copper, zinc. Served by S. Siberian RR and by Abakan-Achinsk branch. Formed 1930 out of Khakass okrug of former E.Siberian Territory.

Khakulabad, Uzbek SSR: see NARYN, Namangan oblast.

Khakurate, Russian SFSR: see TAKHTAMUKAI.

Khakurinokhabl or **Khakurinokhabl'** (khŭkōōrē"-nŭkhä'bŭl), village (1926 pop. 2,483), E Adyge Autonomous Oblast, Krasnodar Territory, Russian SFSR, on branch of Laba R. and 31 mi. NNE of Maikop; wheat, sunflowers, sunn and ambary hemp.

Khalach (khŭläch'), town (1939 pop. over 500), SE Chardzhou oblast, Turkmen SSR, on the Amu Darya and 25 mi. NW of Kerki; cotton; metalworks.

Khalandri, Greece: see CHALANDRI.

Khalari (kŭlä'rē), village, Ranchi dist., S Bihar, on Chota Nagpur Plateau, near tributary of the Damodar, 28 mi. NW of Ranchi; cement mfg.

Khalasa (khäläsä') or **Khalutza** (khälōōt'sä), anc. city, S Palestine, in the Negev, 12 mi. SW of Beersheba. In Roman times called *Elusa.* Sometimes spelled Khalasah.

Khalastra, Greece: see CHALASTRA.

Khalatse (kŭ'lŭtsä) or **Khalsi** (käl'sē), village, Ladakh dist., central Kashmir, at S foot of Ladakh Range, on the Indus (suspension bridge) and 40 mi. WNW of Leh; pulse, wheat, oilseeds. Brahmi and Karoshti inscriptions discovered here; has Dard and Tibetan castle ruins. Fighting here in 1948, during India-Pakistan struggle for control. Gold deposits NW. Noted 11th-cent. Buddhist monastery with frescoes, carvings, and sculptures is 18 mi. ESE, at Alchi or Alchi Gompa, village.

Khaldan (khŭldän'), village (1926 pop. 321), central Azerbaijan SSR, 7 mi. NE of Yevlakh; cotton, sericulture.

Khaldyvanbek (khŭldĭvŭnbyĕk'), village (1939 pop. over 500), W Andizhan oblast, Uzbek SSR, 4 mi. SW of Stalino; cotton; sericulture.

Khalifat Mountain (khŭlē'fŭt), N spur and one of highest points (11,434 ft.) of Central Brahui Range, in Sibi dist., NE central Baluchistan, W Pakistan, S of Ziarat; limestone deposits.

Khalil, El, Palestine: see HEBRON.

Khalilabad (kŭlē'läbäd), village, Basti dist., NE Uttar Pradesh, India, 17 mi. W of Gorakhpur; hand-loom cotton-weaving center; rice, wheat, barley.

Khalilovo (khŭlyē'lŭvŭ), town (1939 pop. over 2,000), E central Chkalov oblast, Russian SFSR, in S foothills of the S Urals, on railroad and 22 mi. NW of Orsk, in Orsk-Khalilovo industrial dist. Mining center, based on limonite deposits associated with titanium, vanadium, chromite, and nickel ores;

supplies Novo-Troitsk steel industry; mfg. (chemicals based on local magnesite, building materials). Developed in 1930s.

Khaljistan, Iran: see DASTGIRD.

Khalka River or **Khalkha River** (both: khälkhä'), Mongol *Khalkhin Gol* (khälkhēn' gōl'), Chinese *Ha-lo-hsin Ho* (hä'lô'shĭn' hŭ'), river on Manchuria-Mongolia line, rises in the Great Khingan Mts. E of Wenchüan, flows 145 mi. NW along international line to the lake Bor Nor, forming a delta. Nomonhan, on right bank, was scene (1939) of Soviet-Japanese border incident.

Khalkhal (khälkhäl'), town (1940 pop. 6,088), Third Prov., in Azerbaijan, NW Iran, 45 mi. SSE of Ardebil; grain, fruit; sheep raising; rugmaking. Copper and lead deposits. Also called Harauabad, Harowabad, or Herowabad; formerly Harau or Herau.

Khalkha River, Manchuria and Mongolia: see KHALKA RIVER.

Khalki, Greece: see CHALKE.

Khalkidiki, Greece: see CHALCIDICE.

Khalki Island, Turkey: see HEYBELI ISLAND.

Khalkis, Greece: see CHALCIS.

Khalmer-Sede or **Khal'mer-Sede** (khŭlmyĕr"-syĭdĕ'), village, Yamal-Nenets Natl. Okrug, Tyumen oblast, Russian SFSR, N of Arctic Circle, on Taz Bay, at mouth of Taz R., 330 mi. ENE of Salekhard, near site of anc. Mangazeya; trading post. Seaplane base. Until c.1930 called Tazovskoye.

Khalmer-Yu or **Khal'mer-Yu** (–yōō'), village (1939 pop. over 500), E Nenets Natl. Okrug, Archangel oblast, Russian SFSR, 40 mi. NE of Vorkuta; coal mines. Developed in 1940s.

Khalsi, Kashmir: see KHALATSE.

Khalturin (khŭltōō'rĭn), city (1926 pop. 4,722), central Kirov oblast, Russian SFSR, on Vyatka R. and 29 mi. W of Kirov; dairying, vegetable processing; handicrafts (furniture, mats). Dates from 15th cent.; chartered 1627; trading center until 19th cent. Called Orlov until 1923.

Khalutza, Palestine: see KHALASA.

Kham (käm), Chinese *Kang* or *K'ang* (käng), historical E province of Tibet, bet. c.93° and c.99°E (Yangtze R. line); main town, Chamdo. Although considered by the Chinese after 1914 as part of Sikang prov., it has remained under *de facto* Tibetan administration. Sometimes spelled Kam.

Khamar-Daban Range (khŭmär"-dŭbän'), in S Buryat-Mongol Autonomous SSR, Russian SFSR, S of L. Baikal; extension of Eastern Sayan Mts. E to Selenga R. Wooded slopes, rich in minerals, rise to 7,540 ft.

Khamba (käm'bä) or **Kampa** (–pä), Chinese *Kang-ma* (gäng'mä'), town [Tibetan *dzong*], S Tibet, on an India-Shigatse trade route and 75 mi. SSW of Shigatse; alt. 16,200 ft.

Khambha (kŭm'bŭ), town (pop. 2,726), Amreli dist., NW Bombay, India, 31 mi. S of Amreli; millet; cattle breeding.

Khambhaliya (kŭmbäl'yŭ), town (pop. 12,190), W Saurashtra, India, 32 mi. SW of Jamnagar; rail junction; trade center (millet, cotton, oilseeds, cloth fabrics, ghee, salt); cotton ginning, flour milling, peanut shelling; metalwork. Also spelled Khambhalia.

Khamgaon (käm'goun), town (pop. 26,402), Buldana dist. W Madhya Pradesh, India, 28 mi. W of Akola; rail spur terminus; road and cotton-trade center in major cotton tract; cotton ginning, oilseed milling; chemical works. Industrial school.

Kham-i-Ab (khŭm'-ĭ-äb'), village, Mazar-i-Sharif prov., N Afghanistan, on the Amu Darya, on USSR line, adjoining Bossaga (Uzbek SSR), and 55 mi. NE of Andkhui.

Khamir (khämĭr'), town, Huth prov., N central Yemen, on central plateau, 50 mi. NNW of Sana. Was stronghold of Imam during 2d Turkish occupation (1872–1918) of Sana.

Khami River (kä'mē), SW Southern Rhodesia, rises SW of Bulawayo, flows 55 mi. NW to Gwaai R. 50 mi. WNW of Bulawayo. Khami Dam, on upper course and 10 mi. W of Bulawayo, supplies city with water.

Khami Ruins, Southern Rhodesia: see BULAWAYO, city.

Khamis Mushait or **Khamis Mushayt** (khämēs' mōōshät'), town in Asir, Saudi Arabia, on plateau, 20 mi. ENE of Abha, in upper reaches of the Wadi Bisha; agr. center; dates, millet, sesame, olives.

Khammam (kŭm'mŭm) or **Khammamett** (–mät), town (pop. 18,982), Warangal dist., SE Hyderabad state, India, 65 mi. SSE of Warangal; agr. trade center; rice and oilseed milling. Sometimes spelled Khammameth.

Khammouane, province, Laos: see THAKHEK.

Khamseh (khämsĕ'), former province of NW Iran; main town, Zenjan. Bounded N by Azerbaijan, E by Gilan and Kazvin, S by Hamadan, and E by Garus; drained by Zenjan R. (tributary of the Qizil Uzun); vineyards; fruit, wine. Crossed by Teheran-Tabriz highway and railroad. Prov. was inc. 1938 into Iran's First Prov. (see GILAN)

Khamzoren, Bulgaria: see BEZMER.

Khanabad (khä'näbäd"), town (pop. 20,000), Kataghan prov., NE Afghanistan, in Afghan Turkestan; 110 mi. E of Mazar-i-Sharif; center of oasis irrigated by right tributary of Kunduz R.; cotton, rice. Linked by direct highway with Kabul. Former ⊙ Kataghan prov.

Khanabadski or **Khanabadskiy** (khŭnŭbät'skē), village (1926 pop. 2,313), E Andizhan oblast, Uzbek SSR, on the Kara Darya, on railroad and 30 mi. E of Andizhan; tanning center. Junction of rail spur to Kara-Tyube in Uzgen coal basin.

Khan al-Zabib, Jordan: see KHAN EL ZABIB.

Khanapur (kä'näpōōr), town (pop. 5,409), Belgaum dist., S Bombay, India, 14 mi. S of Belgaum; rice market; mfg. (tiles, bricks, pottery). Kaolin and laterite worked near by.

Khanaqin or **Khaniqin** (both: khä'nŭkēn), town, Diyala prov., E Iraq, near Iran border, on railroad and 90 mi. NE of Baghdad; site of oil refinery; dates, fruits, livestock. Customs station. Sometimes spelled Khanikin.

Khanbalik, China: see PEKING.

Khan Bela (khän' bä'lŭ), town (pop. 1,200), Bahawalpur state, W Pakistan, 65 mi. SW of Bahawalpur; wheat, rice.

Khan Cheykoun, Syria: see KHAN SHEIKHUN.

Khandagai, Manchuria: see KHANSHIRE.

Khandagaity or **Khandagayty** (khŭndŭgī'tē), village (1945 pop. under 500), S Tuva Autonomous Oblast, Russian SFSR, 125 mi. WSW of Kyzyl, near Mongolian border. Salt mining (E).

Khandaq, El (ĕl khän'dăk), town, Northern Prov., Anglo-Egyptian Sudan, on left bank of the Nile, on road, and 40 mi. S of Dongola.

Khandela (kŭndä'lŭ), town (pop. 9,484), E central Rajasthan, India, 50 mi. NNW of Jaipur; agr. (millet, gram, wheat); lacquered woodwork.

Khandesh, India: see EAST KHANDESH; WEST KHANDESH.

Khandgiri (kŭnd'gĭrē), village, Puri dist., E Orissa, India, 15 mi. SSW of Cuttack, 4 mi. WNW of Bhubaneswar. Old Buddhist and Jain caves in near-by hills of Khandgiri and Udayagiri; oldest from 1st to 2d cent. B.C.

Khandhar, India: see KANDAHAR.

Khandparagarh (kŭnd'pŭrägŭr), village, Puri dist., E Orissa, India, 50 mi. NW of Puri; timber trade. Formerly Khandpara. Was ⊙ former princely state of Khandpara (□ 229; pop. 87,341) in Orissa States, along right bank of Mahanadi R.; state inc. 1949 into Puri dist.

Khandwa (kŭnd'vŭ), town (pop. 38,493), ⊙ Nimar dist., W Madhya Pradesh, India, 185 mi. WNW of Nagpur; rail junction; cotton-trade center in agr. area (millet, wheat, oilseeds); cotton ginning, oilseed milling, sawmilling, ice mfg.; silk growing. Industrial school. Several 12th-cent. Jain temple ruins. Hemp growing near by.

Khan el Zabib, Khan ez Zabib, or **Khan al-Zabib** (all: khän' ĕz-zăbēb'), village, central Jordan, on Hejaz RR and 35 mi. SSE of Amman. Bedouin trade center; camel raising. Marble deposits (E). Sometimes spelled Khan ez Zebib.

Khanewal (känä'väl), town (pop. 17,036), Multan dist., S Punjab, W Pakistan, 27 mi. ENE of Multan; rail junction (workshops); trades in grain, oilseeds, fruit, cotton; oilseed and flour milling, cotton ginning, ice mfg., hand-loom weaving. Large forest plantation NE.

Khanfar (khänfär'), village, Fadhli sultanate, Western Aden Protectorate, on the Wadi Bana and 28 mi. WSW of Shuqra; agr. oasis. Mfg. of gunpowder. Saltpeter deposits near by.

Khangah Dogran (khäng'gä dō'grän), village, Sheikhupura dist., E central Punjab, W Pakistan, 22 mi. WNW of Sheikhupura; agr. market (wheat, cotton, millet); cotton ginning. Sometimes spelled Khangah Dogra.

Khangai Mountains or **Hangay Mountains** (khäng'-gī), major mountain massif in W central Mongolian People's Republic, extending c.500 mi. WNW-ESE, parallel to the Mongolian Altai; rises to 13,-225 ft. in the Otkhon Tengri, 35 mi. ESE of Uliassutai. The Dzabkhan, Selenga, and Orkhon rivers rise on massif's wooded slopes. At its foot are the centers of Uliassutai (W), Tsetserlik and Arbai Khere (E).

Khangarh (khän'gŭr), town (pop. 4,402), Muzaffargarh dist., SW Punjab, W Pakistan, near Chenab R., 10 mi. S of Muzaffargarh; market center for wheat, mangoes, dates, rice; cotton ginning, rice husking.

Khangmar, Tibet: see KANGMAR.

Khanguet-el-Hadjadj (kängĕt'-ĕl-häjäj'), village, Grombalia dist., NE Tunisia, 17 mi. SE of Tunis; winegrowing.

Khanguet-Kef-Tout (–kĕf'-tōōt') village, Béja dist., N Tunisia, 12 mi. NNW of Béja; calamine and galena mines.

Khanhhoa, province, Vietnam: see NHATRANG.

Khanhhoa (khä'nyŭ-hwä'), town, Khanhhoa prov., S central Vietnam, 6 mi. W of Nhatrang, on railroad; old Annamese prov. capital; citadel.

Khania, Crete: see CANEA.

Khaniadhana (kŭnyä'dänŭ), town, E Madhya Bharat, India, 40 mi. SE of Shivpuri. Was ⊙ former princely state of Khaniadhana (□ 101; pop. 20,124) of Gwalior Residency, India; in 1948, state was merged with Vindhya Pradesh and in 1950 was transferred to Madhya Bharat.

Khanikin, Iraq: see KHANAQIN.

Khanino (khä'nyĭnŭ), town (1926 pop. 1,589), W Tula oblast, Russian SFSR, 40 mi. W of Tula; metalworking center; distilling. During Second World War, briefly held (1941) by Germans in Moscow campaign.

Khaniqin, Iraq: see KHANAQIN.

Khanka, El, or **Al-Khanikah** (both: ĕl khăn'kŭ), village (pop. 12,572), Qalyubiya prov., Lower Egypt, 13 mi. NE of Cairo; cotton, flax, cereals, fruits. Has insane asylum.

Khanka, Lake, or **Lake Hanka** (both: khän'kŭ), Chinese *Hsing-k'ai Hu* (shĭng'kī' hōō'), lake (□ 1,700) on Manchuria-USSR border, 100 mi. N of Vladivostok; 60 mi. long, 45 mi. wide, 33 ft. deep. Fisheries. Inlets: Mo R., Lefu R. Outlet: Sungacha R., a tributary of the Ussuri. The Khanka lowland (S), in Maritime Territory of Russian SFSR, is one of the leading agr. dists. of Soviet Far East.

Khanka Plain, Rus. *Prikhankaiskaya Nizmennost*, low, fertile black-earth agr. area in SW Maritime Territory, Russian SFSR, E and S of L. Khanka; large Ukrainian pop. Chief crops: soybeans, kaoliang, millet, rice, sugar beets, fruit; truck gardening, beekeeping. Food processing at VOROSHILOV.

Khanki (kŭng'kē), village, Gujranwala dist., E Punjab, W Pakistan, on Chenab R. and 9 mi. SW of Wazirabad; wheat, rice. Headworks of Lower Chenab Canal irrigation system here.

Khanki (khŭn-kē'), village (1948 pop. over 2,000), E Khorezm oblast, Uzbek SSR, in Khiva oasis, on railroad and 10 mi. SE of Urgench; silk milling.

Khanlar (khŭnlär'). **1** City (1926 pop. 3,985), W Azerbaijan SSR, 6 mi. S of Kirovabad; rail spur terminus in orchard and winegrowing area; distilleries, wineries. Settled by Germans; until 1938, called Yelenendorf. **2** Town (1945 pop. over 500) in Stalin dist. of Greater Baku, E Azerbaijan SSR, c.5 mi. SSW of Baku.

Khanna (kŭn'nŭ), town (pop. 7,941), Ludhiana dist., central Punjab, India, 26 mi. SE of Ludhiana; agr. market (wheat, gram, cotton, oilseeds); cotton ginning, hosiery mfg., flour milling; steel rolling mills. Col. Sometimes called Khanna Kalan.

Khanozai (khä'nōzī), village, Quetta-Pishin dist., NE Baluchistan, W Pakistan, 32 mi. NNE of Quetta. Chromite mining near by.

Khan Piyesak, Yugoslavia: see HAN PIJESAK.

Khanpur (khän'pōōr), town (pop. 5,312), Bulandshahr dist., W Uttar Pradesh, India, 15 mi. NE of Bulandshahr; wheat, oilseeds, cotton, barley, corn, jowar. Also called Khanpur Gantu.

Khanpur, town (pop. 6,153), Bahawalpur state, W Pakistan, 80 mi. SW of Bahawalpur; rail junction; agr. trade center (wheat, rice, millet, cotton, dates); rice husking, cotton ginning, hand-loom weaving; metalware.

Khanqah Sharif (khän'kä shŭrēf'), town (pop. 1,480), Bahawalpur state, W Pakistan, 10 mi. SW of Bahawalpur.

Khan Sheikhun or **Khan Shaykhun** (khăn' shā-khōōn'), Fr. *Khan Cheykoun*, village, Aleppo prov., NW Syria, 60 mi. SSW of Aleppo; cotton, cereals. Here have been found remains dating back to 20th cent. B.C.

Khanshire (khänshĕrä') or **Khandagai** (khändägī'), village, N Inner Mongolian Autonomous Region, Manchuria, near Khalka R. (Mongolian border), 30 mi. WNW of Wenchüan, and on railroad.

Khantaak Island (kăn'tăk) (6 mi. long), SE Alaska, 3 mi. N of Yakutat; 59°36'N 139°46'W.

Khan Tengri (khŭn-tyĭngrē'), peak (22,949 ft.) in central Tien Shan mtn. system, on China-USSR border, 100 mi. E of Issyk-Kul (lake), Kirghiz SSR; 42°13'N 80°11'E. Thought to be highest peak of Tien Shan until discovery of POBEDA PEAK. Sometimes called Tengri Khan.

Khanty-Mansi National Okrug (khŭntē'-mŭnsē'), administrative division (□ 215,500; 1946 pop. estimate c.110,000) of central Tyumen oblast, NW Siberian Russian SFSR; ⊙ Khanty-Mansisk. On W.Siberian Plain; drained by lower Irtysh and Ob rivers. Pop. includes Russians, numbering c.80,000, along main streams, Mansi (Voguls) in W, and Khanty (Ostyaks) in E. Fishing, fur trapping, lumbering (sawmilling, match mfg.), livestock breeding (dairying) and, in N, reindeer raising. Large sable and beaver reserve on upper Konda R. One of first areas won in Rus. conquest of Siberia (16th cent.). Formed 1930 within former Ural oblast; passed 1934 to Omsk oblast, 1944 to Tyumen oblast. Until 1940, Ostyak-Vogul Natl. Okrug.

Khanty-Mansisk, Khanty-Mansiisk, or **Khanty-Mansiysk** (khŭntē"-mŭnsēsk'), city (1939 pop. over 2,000), ⊙ Khanty-Mansi Natl. Okrug, Tyumen oblast, Russian SFSR, on Ob R., at mouth of Irtysh R., and 300 mi. NNE of Tyumen; sawmilling, fish canning. Founded in early 1930s; until 1940 called Ostyako-Vogulsk.

Khanua (kän'wŭ), village, E Rajasthan, India, 13 mi. SSE of Bharatpur, near Banganga R. Site of decisive battle of 1527, when Moguls under Baber completely routed Rajput confederacy. Formerly also spelled Kanwa.

Khan Yunis (khăn' yōō'nĭs), village (1946 pop. estimate 12,350), SW Palestine, at NW edge of the Negev, near Mediterranean, on railroad and 15 mi. SW of Gaza. Has 13th-cent. mosque. Occupied by Egypt, 1948.

Khanzi, Bechuanaland Protectorate: see GHANZI.
Khapa (kä'pŭ), town (pop. 9,375), Nagpur dist., central Madhya Pradesh, India, on Kanhan R. and 20 mi. NNW of Nagpur; rail spur terminus, serving manganese mines bet. here and Soaner, 5 mi. SW.
Khapalu (kŭp'ŭlōō), village, Ladakh dist., N central Kashmir, in Ladakh Range, near Shyok R., 40 mi. ESE of Skardu; pulse, wheat. Residence of local raja. Small gold mines near by.
Khapcheranga (khŭpchĭrän'gŭ), town (1939 pop. over 2,000), SW Chita oblast, Russian SFSR, 175 mi. SSW of Chita, near Mongolian border; tin-mining center; sawmilling. Developed in 1930s.
Khara, river, Mongolia: see KHARA GOL.
Kharabali (khŭrŭbä'lyē), village (1926 pop. 5,261), E Astrakhan oblast, Russian SFSR, on left bank of Akhtuba R., on railroad and 80 mi. NNW of Astrakhan; fruit processing; wheat, livestock.
Kharaghoda (kä'rŭgōdŭ), village (pop. 4,771), Ahmadabad dist., N Bombay, India, on SE edge of Little Rann of Cutch, 55 mi. WNW of Ahmadabad; rail terminus; market center; salt mfg. (extensive brine deposits in the Rann); large magnesia works. Saltworks 6 mi. N, at Ooru.
Khara Gol or **Hara Gol** (khä'rä gōl'), river in N Mongolian People's Republic, rises in the Kentei Mts. 25 mi. WNW of Ulan Bator, flows 180 mi. generally N, past Mandal, to Orkhon R. 50 mi. SSW of Sukhe Bator. Used for logging for 100 mi.
Kharagouli, Georgian SSR: see ORDZHONIKIDZE, town, Georgian SSR.
Kharagpur (kŭrŭg'pŏŏr), city (□ 20; pop., including rail settlement, 87,185), Midnapore dist., SW West Bengal, India, 70 mi. WSW of Calcutta; rail junction (large workshops); mfg. of chemicals, shoes, silk cloth; rice milling; general engineering works; rice, pulse. Rail Inst. Shrine of saint venerated by Hindus and Moslems. Formerly spelled Kharakpur. Job Charnock's victory (1687) over Mogul army took place 4 mi. SW, at village of Hijili.
Kharal (khŭräl'), town (1945 pop. over 500), E central Tuva Autonomous Oblast, Russian SFSR, 45 mi. NE of Saryg-Sep; gold mining.
Kharan (kä'rän), princely state (□ 18,508; 1951 pop. 54,000), W Baluchistan, W Pakistan; ⊙ Kharan Kalat. Bordered by Iran (W), Ras Koh hills (N), and Siahan Range (S). Consists mainly of sandy desert wastes with low sand dunes and scant vegetation. Some millet and melons grown in NE section; thick brine-salt deposits (W). Formerly under suzerainty of Kalat; acceded independently in 1948 to Pakistan. Pop. 99% Moslem.
Kharan Kalat (kŭlät'), village, ⊙ Kharan state, N central Baluchistan, W Pakistan, on NE edge of sandy desert, 145 mi. SW of Quetta; caravan center; trades in millet, salt, wheat, melons; carpet weaving, palm-basket making. Sometimes called Kharan.
Khara Nor, Khara Nur, or **Hara Nuur** (all: khä'rä nōr', nŏŏr'), fresh-water lake (□ 200) in W Mongolian People's Republic, 60 mi. E of Kobdo; 18 mi. long, 15 mi. wide; alt. 3,622 ft. Connected by 15-mi.-long chain of lakes and straits with Durga Nor (S) and with Dzabkhan R. (E).
Kharar (kŭrär'). **1** Town (pop. 6,072), Ambala dist., E Punjab, India, 26 mi. NNW of Ambala; local market for wheat, corn, gram; woolen milling, cotton ginning. **2** Town (pop. 5,570), Midnapore dist., SW West Bengal, India, 31 mi. NE of Midnapore; cotton weaving, metalware mfg.; rice, pulse, potatoes, jute.
Kharari, India: see ABU ROAD.
Khara Usu or **Hara Usa** (ōō'sŭ), fresh-water lake (□ 680) in W Mongolian People's Republic, just E of Kobdo; 50 mi. long, 16 mi. wide; alt. 3,783 ft. Receives Kobdo R. Contains rocky Akbashi Isl. (□ 105). Formerly called Ikhe Aral Nor. A smaller lake (□ 21) of the same name, also called Namiriin Usa for Namir R. (a small tributary) is 80 mi. N of Kobdo.
Kharbin, Manchuria: see HARBIN.
Khardah (kŭr'dŭ), town (pop. 9,568), 24-Parganas dist., SE West Bengal, India, on the Hooghly and 11 mi. N of Calcutta city center; jute-milling center; woodworking. Vishnuite temple (pilgrimage center).
Kharfa or **Kharfah** (khär'fŭ), town and oasis, S Nejd, Saudi Arabia, in Aflaj dist., 6 mi. SSW of Laila; grain, vegetables, fruit; weaving.
Kharg or **Khark** (both: khärk), island in Persian Gulf, off SW Iran, 34 mi. NW of Bushire; 29°14'N 50°18'E; 4 mi. long, 2 mi. wide. Sparsely populated. Had Dutch fort and trading post (N), abandoned 1766.
Kharga, El Kharga (ĕl khär'gŭ), or **Al-Kharijah** (ĕl-khär'ĭjä), or **The Great Oasis,** large oasis (pop. 11,155), S central Egypt, in the Southern Desert prov., c.110 mi. WSW of Nag Hammadi, with which it is connected by rail; 25°N 30°35'E. Southernmost and largest of the Egyptian oases, it lies in a basin c.200 mi. long (N-S), 30 mi. wide (E-W). Apart from Faiyum, it is the only Egyptian oasis accessible by railroad. Also caravan routes to Dakhla oasis and the Nile valley. Most of the total cultivated area (□ 10) is around Kharga, the chief village (pop. 6,686) of the oasis, at 25°27'N 30°35'E. Dates, cotton, wheat, rice, barley, bananas, vines. Archaeological finds include axes of the Stone Age; there are also the ruins of the temples of Hibis (c.500 B.C.) and Nadura (A.D. c.150), a Christian necropolis, and a Christian convent.
Khargon (kŭrgōn'), town (pop. 14,851), ⊙ Nimar dist., SW Madhya Bharat, India, 65 mi. SSW of Indore; market center for cotton, millet, oilseeds, timber; cotton ginning, rice and oilseed milling. Sometimes spelled Khargone.
Khargu or **Kharku** (khärkōō'), island in Persian Gulf, off SW Iran, just N of Kharg isl. and 40 mi. NW of Bushire; quarantine station.
Khargupur (kŭr'gōōpŏŏr), town (pop. 1,947), Gonda dist., NE Uttar Pradesh, India, 17 mi. N of Gonda; rice, wheat, corn, gram, oilseeds.
Kharian (kär'yän), village, Gujrat dist., NE Punjab, W Pakistan, on railroad (workshop) and 20 mi. NW of Gujrat; wheat, millet, rice.
Khariar Road (kŭryär'), village, Kalahandi dist., W Orissa, India, on railroad and 80 mi. NW of Bhawanipatna; soap mfg., rice milling.
Kharifot or **Kharifut** (khärēfōt'), westernmost village of Dhofar dist. of Oman, 55 mi. WSW of Salala, near E limit of Aden Protectorate.
Kharijah, Al-, Egypt: see KHARGA.
Kharik (khä'rĭk), village, SW Irkutsk oblast, Russian SFSR, near Trans-Siberian RR (Kharik station; 5 mi. away), 50 mi. SE of Tulun, in agr. area (wheat, livestock); metalworks.
Kharimkotan Island (khŭrēmkŭtän'), Jap. *Harumukotan-to* (härōō"mōōkōtän'-tō') (□ 16), one of N main Kurile Isls. group, Russian SFSR, separated from Onekotan Isl. (N) by Sixth Kurile Strait and from Shiashkotan Isl. (S) by Severgin Strait; 49°7'N 154°32'E; 8 mi. long, 5 mi. wide. Rises to 3,976 ft. in volcanic Severgin Peak, Jap. *Harumukotan-dake.*
Kharj or **Al Kharj** (ăl khärj'), district of E central Nejd, Saudi Arabia, on railroad and 50 mi. SE of Riyadh; 24°N 47°E. One of chief agr. areas of Saudi Arabia, producing dates, wheat, alfalfa, and millet. Modern irrigation from limestone well pits was mechanized and a model farm set up in 1940s. Dist. was formerly called Yamamah or Yemamah.
Khark, Iran: see KHARG.
Kharkhira or **Hara Hira** (khär'khērä), outlying massif (13,504 ft.) of the Mongolian Altai, in W Mongolian People's Republic, 35 mi. SW of Ulankom.
Kharkho, Tibet: see GYANYIMA.
Kharkov or **Khar'kov** (kär'kŏf, Rus. khär'kŭf), oblast (□ 12,000; 1946 pop. estimate 2,500,000), NE Ukrainian SSR; ⊙ Kharkov. In SW outspurs of Central Russian Uplands; drained by Northern Donets, upper Orel, and lower Oskol rivers. Rich agr. area; sugar beets and *kok-sagyz* (NW and NE), wheat and sunflowers (S), truck produce and orchards in Kharkov metropolitan area. Rural industries based chiefly on agr. products (sugar refining in NW, flour milling in S, sunflower-oil extraction, distilling, dairying). Machine-building, food, and clothing industries in Kharkov and suburbs. Other major cities: Volchansk, Kupyansk, Izyum, Barvenkovo, Lozovaya, Krasnograd, Bogodukhov. Good rail network. Formed 1932.
Kharkov or **Khar'kov,** city (1926 pop. 417,342; 1939 pop. 833,432), ⊙ Kharkov oblast, Ukrainian SSR, at junction of Kharkov and Lopan rivers (tributaries of the Northern Donets), 400 mi. SSW of Moscow; 50°N 36°14'E. Fourth largest city (in 1939) of USSR; major industrial and transportation center of the Ukraine; junction of 6 rail lines and many highways, at gates to the Donbas coal basin and Krivoi Rog iron dist. Chief machine-mfg. hub of the Ukraine; produces tractors and other agr. machines, coal-mining and oil-drilling equipment, electrical goods, turbogenerators, locomotives, machine tools, ball bearings, precision instruments, cables, bicycles, glass, paper. Seat of univ. (1804), polytechnical institute, technological schools (engineering, mining, chemistry, aviation, rail transportation), agr., medical, law, and teachers colleges, scientific research institutions, agr., art, and historical museums. Civic center seat of Ukrainian govt. until 1934. Major suburbs include MEREFA (SW), LYUBOTIN (W), OLSHANY (NW). Pop. 50% Ukrainians, 30% Russians; the rest Jews, Poles, and others. Founded in early 17th cent. by Cossacks; became trade center in 18th cent.; grew rapidly after industrialization of S Ukraine in late 19th cent. Was ⊙ Ukrainian SSR (1920–34); succeeded by Kiev. In Second World War, held (1941–43) by Germans and heavily damaged by air bombing and shellfire.
Kharku, Iran: see KHARGU.
Kharlu (khär'lōō), Finnish *Harlu* (här'lōō), town (1940 pop. over 500), SW Karelo-Finnish SSR, on railroad and 10 mi. NE of Sortavala; paper-milling center. In Finland until 1940.
Kharmanlii or **Kharmanliy** (khär'mänlē), city (pop. 9,240), Khaskovo dist., SE Bulgaria, on right tributary of the Maritsa and 18 mi. E of Khaskovo; sericulture center; textiles (cotton, silk), tobacco processing. Has school of sericulture. Sometimes spelled Harmanli.
Kharovsk (khä'rŭfsk), town (1932 pop. estimate 2,830), central Vologda oblast, Russian SFSR, on Kubena R., on railroad and 50 mi. N of Vologda; sawmilling, glassworking. Formerly called Kharovskaya.
Kharput, Turkey: see HARPUT.
Kharsawan (kŭrsä'vän), village, Singhbhum dist., S Bihar, India, 23 mi. W of Jamshedpur; rice, oilseeds, corn, jowar, sugar cane; lac and silk growing. Sal, kusum, bamboo in forest area (W, N); a major cyanite and copper mining center. Was ⊙ former princely state of Kharsawan (□ 157; pop. 50,580) in Orissa States; state merged 1948 with Singhbhum dist.
Kharsia (kŭrs'yŭ), town (pop. 3,657), Raigarh dist., E Madhya Pradesh, India, 20 mi. WNW of Raigarh; rice, oilseeds. Sal forests, coal and iron-ore deposits near by. Formerly spelled Khursia.
Khartoum (kärtōōm', khär-), province (□ 5,700; 1948 pop. estimate 379,698), central Anglo-Egyptian Sudan; ⊙ Khartoum. The confluence of Blue and White Niles is chief physiographic feature. A strip ½–3 mi. wide on either river bank is cultivable. Crops: cotton, wheat, barley, corn, fruits, durra; cattle, sheep, goats. Main centers are Khartoum, Omdurman, Khartoum North.
Khartoum, city (□ 17; pop. 71,400), ⊙ Anglo-Egyptian Sudan and Khartoum prov., central Anglo-Egyptian Sudan, on left bank of the Blue Nile just above its junction with the White Nile, 1,000 mi. S of Cairo; 15°36'N 32°32'E. Major trade and communications center. A 710-yd. rail and road bridge (built 1908–10) extends across the Blue Nile to KHARTOUM NORTH, and a tramway across the White Nile (2,012-ft. bridge, built 1925–28) to OMDURMAN. A rail and river traffic center, it is terminus of rail lines from Wadi Halfa (N; Egyptian traffic), Port Sudan (NE; Red Sea port), and El Obeid (SW; in oilseed and gum-arabic region). From Mogren quays (railhead), just W of city, steamers ascend the Blue Nile to Roseires, and the White Nile to Juba. Seat of govt. offices, governor-general's palace, courts, Gordon Memorial Col. (1902), mus., zoological garden, Kitchener School of Medicine, military barracks. City has Anglican and R.C. cathedrals, Coptic, Maronite, and Greek Orthodox churches. Founded in 1820s by Mohammed Ali after his conquest of the Sudan, it developed rapidly as a trade depot (estimated 1882 pop., 70,000), sending slaves and goods to Egypt. Captured and destroyed by Mahdists in 1885, after a famous siege during which General Gordon, the Br. defender, was killed. Reoccupied 1898 by Lord Kitchener, it was rebuilt on modern town plan. Sometimes spelled Khartum.
Khartoum North, town (pop. 34,050), Khartoum prov., central Anglo-Egyptian Sudan, on right bank of the Blue Nile just above its junction with the White Nile, on railroad and opposite (N of) Khartoum (linked by bridge); commercial center; dockyard and marine workshops, with schools of marine and electrical engineering; cotton, wheat, barley, fruit; livestock. Has markets, commercial stores, military barracks.
Khartsyzsk (khŭrtsĭsk'), city (1939 pop. over 10,000), E central Stalino oblast, Ukrainian SSR, in the Donbas, 9 mi. E of Makeyevka; steel-pipe rolling, machinery works.
Khartum, Anglo-Egyptian Sudan: see KHARTOUM.
Khasab (khäsăb'), chief town of Ruus al Jibal dist., N Oman, at N tip of Oman Promontory, 80 mi. NE of Sharja; date groves; fisheries.
Khasan, Lake (khŭsän'), SW Maritime Territory, Russian SFSR, near intersection of USSR, Korea, and China, S of Posyet Bay. Zaozernaya Hill, Chinese *Changkufeng* or *Ch'ang-ku-feng* (W), was scene of Soviet-Japanese border fighting (1938).
Khasani, Greece: see ELLENIKON.
Khasavyurt (khŭsŭvyōōrt'), city (1939 pop. over 10,000), NW Dagestan Autonomous SSR, Russian SFSR, on railroad and 45 mi. WNW of Makhachkala; industrial center in cotton area; cotton ginning, fruit and vegetable canning, wine making, metalworking. Developed mainly after 1930.
Khash (khäsh), village, Farah prov., SW Afghanistan, on the Khash Rud and 75 mi. SE of Farah, in S Afghan desert.
Khash (khäsh), town (1940 pop. 9,291), Eighth Prov., in Baluchistan, SE Iran, on road and 90 mi. SSE of Zahidan; alt. 3,684 ft. Wheat, barley, cotton. Military post. Sometimes spelled Kwash or Khwash. Formerly called Vasht.
Khashdala (khŭshdŭlä'), village (1939 pop. over 500), SE Samarkand oblast, Uzbek SSR, on Trans-Caspian RR and 7 mi. ENE of Samarkand; cotton. Dzhambai village (1939 pop. over 500) is just E.
Khashm el Girba (khä'shŭm ĕl gĭr'bŭ), village, Kassala prov., NE Anglo-Egyptian Sudan, on left bank of Atbara R., on railroad, and 45 mi. SW of Kassala; cotton center.
Khash Rud (khäsh' rōōd'), river in SW Afghanistan, rises in outlier of the Hindu Kush 130 mi. NW of Kandahar, flows 250 mi. SW, past Dilaram, Khash, and Chakhansur, to Seistan lake depression on Iran line.
Khashuri (khŭshōō'rē), city (1939 pop. over 10,000), central Georgian SSR, on railroad, on Kura R. and 60 mi. WNW of Tiflis; junction for Surami (N) and Borzhomi (SW) health resorts; metalworks. Talc and marble quarries near by. Known as Mikhailovo before c.1920; known since

as Khashuri, except in early 1930s, when it was called Stalinissi.
Khasia, Greece: see CHASIA.
Khasi and Jaintia Hills or **United Khasi and Jaintia Hills** (kä'sē, jĭnt'yŭ), autonomous district (including KHASI STATES, □ 6,141; pop. 332,251), W Assam, India; ⊙ SHILLONG. Geographically within KHASI HILLS and JAINTIA HILLS (SHILLONG PLATEAU in central section); bordered W by Garo Hills, S by E Pakistan and Surma Valley, N by Brahmaputra valley; drained by tributaries of Surma and Kalang rivers. Agr. (rice, cotton, sesame, oranges, potatoes, betel nut); lac growing. Coal deposits near Maoflang, CHERRAPUNJI (world's heaviest rainfall record), Thanjinath, Lynkerdem, Maolong, Mustoh; limestone quarries near Shella. Original dist. (□ 2,353; 1941 pop. 118,665) enlarged 1948 by addition of former Khasi States.
Khasi Hills, range, W Assam, India, part of W Assam Range; rise sharply from Surma Valley (S) to Shillong Plateau (N) which separates them from Jaintia Hills; c.140 mi. long E-W; rise to c.6,370 ft. Average annual rainfall at Cherrapunji (southern slope), 450 in.
Khasi States or **Khasi Hill States,** former federation (□ 3,788; pop. 213,586) of 25 petty Assam States, India; ⊙ was Shillong. Situated largely in Khasi Hills, Assam. Acceded to India 1947 as a non-viable unit. In 1948, joined original Assam dist. of Khasi and Jaintia Hills to form united KHASI AND JAINTIA HILLS dist.
Khaskovo (khäs'kôvô), city (pop. 27,394), ⊙ Khaskovo dist. (formed 1949), S central Bulgaria, on right tributary of the Maritsa and 34 mi. S of Stara Zagora; major tobacco center; produces cigarettes, textiles (cotton, silk), rubber goods; sesame-oil extracting. Founded in 13th cent.; called Khaskoi (Chaskoi) under Turkish rule (15th–19th cent.); sometimes Haskovo.
Khaskovo Basin (□ 100; average alt. 550 ft.), S central Bulgaria, SE part of Thracian Plain, bet. Maritsa R. (N and E), Rhodope Mts. (S), and Plovdiv Basin (W). Chernozem and alluvial soils. Extensive agr. (cotton, silk, tobacco, sesame, vineyards). Main centers: Khaskovo, Kharmanlii.
Khatanga, India: see SURI.
Khatanga (khŭtän'gŭ), village, E Taimyr Natl. Okrug, Krasnoyarsk Territory, Russian SFSR, N of Arctic Circle, on Khatanga R. and 425 mi. ENE of Dudinka. Govt. observation post; airfield; hunting, fishing, reindeer raising.
Khatanga Gulf, inlet of Laptev Sea of Arctic Ocean, in NE Krasnoyarsk Territory, Russian SFSR, at mouth of Khatanga R.; 175 mi. long; extends along SE side of Taimyr Peninsula to Begichev Isl. Salt and petroleum deposits along coasts.
Khatanga River, NE Krasnoyarsk Territory, Russian SFSR, formed by union of Kotui (233 mi. long) and Moyero (312 mi. long) rivers in NE Evenki Natl. Okrug; flows N, past Khatanga, and NE to Khatanga Gulf of Laptev Sea; 412 mi. long. Abounds in fish. Name Kotui sometimes applied to river above Khatanga village.
Khatauli (kŭtou'lē), town (pop. 11,880), Muzaffarnagar dist., N Uttar Pradesh, India, on Upper Ganges Canal and 13 mi. S of Muzaffarnagar; trades in wheat, gram, sugar cane, oilseeds. Large Jain temples; serai built by Shah Jehan. Hydroelectric station (3,000 kw.) 5 mi. SSW, at village of Salawa.
Khatayevicha, Imeni Tovarishcha, Ukrainian SSR: see SINELNIKOVO.
Khategaon (kä'tāgoun), village, S Madhya Bharat, India, 12 mi. ESE of Kannod; cotton, wheat.
Khatkhyl, Mongolia: see KHADKHAL.
Khatra (kä'trŭ), village, Bankura dist., W West Bengal, India, 22 mi. SW of Bankura; lac trade center; rice, corn, wheat. Extensive lac growing near by.
Khatsapetovka (khŭtsŭpyĭtôf'kŭ), town (1939 pop. over 500), E Stalino oblast, Ukrainian SSR, in the Donbas, 7 mi. NNE of Yenakiyevo; rail junction.
Khattara, El, or **Al-Khattarah** (both: ĕl kät-tä'rŭ), village (pop. 7,226), Qena prov., Upper Egypt, on the Nile opposite Qus; cotton weaving, pottery making; cereals, sugar cane, dates.
Khattusas, Turkey: see BOGAZKOY.
Khatyrchi (khŭtĭrchē'), village (1926 pop. 2,343), SW Samarkand oblast, Uzbek SSR, on Zeravshan R., at confluence of its Kara Darya and Ak Darya arms, and 18 mi. WNW of Katta-Kurgan; cotton; metalworks.
Khaudag (khŭŏŏdäk'), town (1941 pop. over 500), S Surkhan-Darya oblast, Uzbek SSR, 30 mi. N of Termez; oil field.
Khaur (kour), village, Attock dist., NW Punjab, W Pakistan, on Potwar Plateau, 34 mi. SSE of Campbellpur; important petroleum deposits (wells in operation since 1917); oil pipe line to refinery at Rawalpindi, 45 mi. NE. Other wells at Dhulian, 8 mi. SW.
Khawak Pass (khŭwŭk') (alt. 11,640 ft.), in Hindu Kush, NE Afghanistan, at head of Panjshir valley, 90 mi. NNE of Kabul. Alexander the Great crossed here (327 B.C.).
Khawr [Arabic,=inlet], for Arabic names beginning thus: see under following part of the name.
Khawr 'Umayrah, Aden: see KHOR 'UMEIRA.
Khaybar, Saudi Arabia: see KHAIBAR.
Khaydarkan, Kirghiz SSR: see KHAIDARKAN.
Khayredin, Bulgaria: see KHAIREDIN.
Khazarasp (khŭzŭräsp'), village (1948 pop. over 2,000), S Khorezm oblast, Uzbek SSR, in Khiva oasis, on railroad and 30 mi. SSE of Urgench; cotton ginning.
Khed (kād). **1** Village (pop. 9,548), Poona dist., central Bombay, India, 23 mi. N of Poona; agr. market (millet, wheat). **2** Town (pop. 5,386), Ratnagiri dist., W Bombay, India, 50 mi. NNE of Ratnagiri; local rice market.
Kheibar, Saudi Arabia: see KHAIBAR.
Khekra (kā'krŭ), town (pop. 11,129), Meerut dist., NW Uttar Pradesh, India, 27 mi. WSW of Meerut; trade center (wheat, millet, sugar cane, oilseeds).
Khelat, W Pakistan: see KALAT.
Khelidonia, Cape, Turkey: see GELIDONYA, CAPE.
Khelmos, Greece: see AROANIA.
Khemarath, Thailand: see KHEMMARAT.
Khem-Belder, Russian SFSR: see KYZYL.
Khemchik River or **Kemchik River** (khyĕm'chĭk, kyĕm'–), W Tuva Autonomous Oblast, Russian SFSR, rises in Altai Mtn. system, flows 310 mi. NE, past Kyzyl-Mazhalyk, to the Yenisei 40 mi. WNW of Shagonar. Copper, asbestos along its course. Irrigates agr. area.
Khemissa (kĕmēsä'), village, Constantine dept., NE Algeria, 18 mi. SW of Souk-Ahras. Important remains of anc. *Thubursicum Numidarum* have been excavated here.
Khémisset (kāmēsĕt'), town (pop. 6,588), Rabat region, NW central Fr. Morocco, 30 mi. W of Meknès; agr. trade center (cereals, livestock, wool).
Khem Karan (kām' kŭr'ŭn), town (pop. 8,023), Amritsar dist., W Punjab, India, 37 mi. SSW of Amritsar; agr. market (wheat, gram, rice, oilseeds); hand-loom weaving. Sometimes Khem Karn.
Khemmarat (kām'mŭrät'), village (1937 pop. 3,481), Ubon prov., E Thailand, on right bank of Mekong R. (Laos line; rapids) and 60 mi. NNE of Ubon. Sometimes spelled Khemarath and Kemmarath.
Khenchela (kĕnshĕlä'), town (pop. 9,228), Constantine dept., NE Algeria, at NE foot of the Aurès massif, 70 mi. SSE of Constantine; rail-spur terminus from Aïn-Beïda; agr. market (sheep, wool, esparto, cereals). Livestock pastures and wheat fields in Tarf basin (N of the Aurès) are irrigated from Foum-el-Gueïss Dam (98 ft. high) on N slope of the Djebel Aïdel, 10 mi. W.
Khénifra (kānēfrä'), town (pop. 11,549), Meknès region, central Fr. Morocco, at N foot of the Middle Atlas, on the upper Oum er Rbia and 65 mi. S of Meknès; Berber commercial center; woodworking. Iron deposits (unexploited) in area. Lead mine (16 mi. N) near Aguelmous. Founded 17th cent. as Berber fortress; occupied 1914 by French.
Khentei, Mongolia: see KENTEI.
Khentsiny, Poland: see CHECINY.
Kherabgarh, India: see KHAIRAGARH, Uttar Pradesh.
Kheralu (kārä'lōō), town (pop. 8,141), Mehsana dist., N Bombay, India, 23 mi. NNE of Mehsana; agr. market (millet, pulse, wheat); oilseed milling.
Khéreddine (kārĕdēn'), village, Tunis dist., N Tunisia, on land tongue bet. Gulf of Tunis and L. of Tunis, just N of La Goulette; seaplane station.
Kheri (kā'rē), district (□ 2,972; pop. 1,024,025), N Uttar Pradesh, India; ⊙ Lakhimpur. Bounded E by Gogra R., N by Nepal; drained by Sarda and Gumti rivers. Agr. (rice, wheat, gram, corn, barley, oilseeds, sugar cane, millets, jute); extensive sal forest (N) containing *asaina* (*Terminalia tormentosa*). A major Indian sugar-milling dist.; cattle breeding. Main towns: Lakhimpur, Kheri, Muhamdi, Gola.
Kheri, town (pop. 8,210), Kheri dist., N Uttar Pradesh, India, 3 mi. S of Lakhimpur; rice, wheat, oilseeds, corn, millets. Has 16th-cent. Moslem tomb.
Kherla, fortress, India: see BETUL, town.
Kherson (khĕrsôn'), oblast (□ 10,600; 1946 pop. estimate 700,000), S Ukrainian SSR; ⊙ Kherson. Extends N of Crimea from Sea of Azov to Black Sea; drained by Dnieper R. (NW). Flat, dry steppe with cotton and wheat agr., truck produce, and orchards in area of Kherson, vineyards on the Dnieper below Kakhovka, dairy farming. Industry centered at Kherson, Kakhovka, Genichesk. Salt deposits along coasts. Chief ports: Kherson, Skadovsk, Khorly, Genichesk. SW area served by Dzhankoi-Tsyurupinsk RR (built during Second World War). Formed 1944.
Kherson, city (1939 pop. 97,186), ⊙ Kherson oblast, Ukrainian SSR, port on right bank of Dnieper R., 15 mi. from mouth, and 275 mi. SSE of Kiev; 46°38'N 32°37'E. Major rail and river-sea transportation center; shipyards and repair docks, agr.-machinery works; food industries (bakery products, canned foods, flour), clothing mills. Cathedral (with tomb of Potemkin), regional mus., agr. and teachers colleges. Founded 1778 as shipbuilding center and grain and wool port; declined after rise of Odessa and Nikolayev, but remained govt. capital until 1925. Deepening of river channel (1901) and development of Dnieper R. navigation (after 1932) provided new impetus to growth. Pop. 25% Jewish until Second World War, when city was held (1941–43) by Germans. It was once identified with Gr. colony of Chersonesus Heracleotica (Sevastopol), whence its name.
Khertseg Novi, Yugoslavia: see HERCEG NOVI.
Kherwara (kārvä'rŭ), town (pop. 1,489), S Rajasthan, India, 40 mi. S of Udaipur, in SE Aravalli Range.
Khetia (kāt'yŭ), village, SW Madhya Bharat, India, 32 mi. SW of Barwani, on Bombay border; cotton ginning.
Khetri (kā'trē), town (pop. 8,727), E Rajasthan, India, 75 mi. N of Jaipur, in N Aravalli Range; markets grain, cotton, oilseeds; hosiery and soap mfg. Copper, nickel, and cobalt deposits near by.
Khewra (kāv'rŭ), village, Jhelum dist., N Punjab, W Pakistan, in Salt Range, 5 mi. NW of Pind Dadan Khan, on rail spur; dispatching station for rock salt and coal mined near by; soda ash factory. Gypsum deposits, limestone quarries 10 mi. NE. Mayo salt mine known to have been worked by Moguls.
Khiav, Iran: see MISHKINSHAHR.
Khibinogorsk, Russian SFSR: see KIROVSK, Murmansk oblast.
Khibiny Mountains (khĭbē'nē), central Murmansk oblast, Russian SFSR, on Kola Peninsula bet. L. Imandra (W) and lake Umbozero (E); 25 mi. in diameter; rise to 3,930 ft. at Lyavochorr mtn. Rich deposits of apatite and nephelite (mines at Kirovsk and Kukisvumchorr). Over 60 elements found here, including titanium, vanadium, molybdenum, and rare earths.
Khiching (kĭching'), village, Mayurbhanj dist., N Orissa, India, 55 mi. W of Baripada. Archaeological mus. Was anc. ⊙ Mayurbhanj; has remains of c.10th-11th-cent. temples with fine sculptures.
Khidr, Al (äl khĭ'dŭr), or **Al-Khudur** (khōō'dōōr), village, Diwaniya prov., SE central Iraq, on the Euphrates, on railroad, and 65 mi. SE of Diwaniya; rice, dates.
Khiitola (khē'ĭtŭlŭ), Finnish *Hiitola* (hē'tôlä), village (1948 pop. over 500), SW Karelo-Finnish SSR, near L. Ladoga, 18 mi. NW of Priozersk; rail junction. In Finland until 1940.
Khilchipur (kĭl'chĭpōōr), town (pop. 6,663), N Madhya Bharat, India, 26 mi. NW of Narsinghgarh, 10 mi. W of Rajgarh; markets millet, cotton, wheat; cotton ginning; exports ochre and building stone. Was ⊙ former princely state of Khilchipur (□ 274; pop. 48,642) of Central India agency; since 1948, state merged with Madhya Bharat.
Khiliodromia, Greece: see HALONNESOS.
Khilly (khē'lē), village (1926 pop. 2,438), SE Azerbaijan SSR, on Kura R., 15 mi. from its mouth, and 45 mi. NNE of Lenkoran; cotton; metalworks.
Khilok (khēlôk'), town (1939 pop. over 10,000), SW Chita oblast, Russian SFSR, on Trans-Siberian RR, on Khilok R. and 140 mi. WSW of Chita; metalworks; truck produce.
Khilok River, SW Chita oblast and S Buryat-Mongol Autonomous SSR, Russian SFSR, rises in Yablonovy Range NW of Chita, flows SW, past Mogzon and Khilok, along Trans-Siberian RR, and N to Selenga R. below Novo-Selenginsk; 380 mi. long; abounds in fish.
Khimki (khēm'kē), city (1939 pop. over 10,000), central Moscow oblast, Russian SFSR, NW suburb of Moscow; port on Moscow Canal. Developed after 1937. Khimki Reservoir (S; on Moscow Canal) is N port for Moscow; 5 mi. long, 1 mi. wide.
Khingan (khĭng-gän'), Chinese *Hsingan* (shĭng'-än'), Mongolian league in central Inner Mongolian Autonomous Region, Manchuria, on SE slopes of the Great Khingan range; main town, Ulan Hoto. Separated from N Jerim league, it was part of South Hsingan prov. in Manchukuo; and was inc. 1946 into Liaopeh prov., and 1949 into Inner Mongolian Autonomous Region.
Khingan Mountains or **Great Khingan Mountains,** Chinese *Ta Hsingan Ling* (dä' shĭng'än' lĭng'), sometimes *Ta Khingan Shan*, Rus. *Bolshoi Khingan* (bŭlshoi' khĭn-gän'), range in W Manchuria, at E edge of Mongolian plateau, forming W limit of central Manchurian plain; mts. extend c.700 mi. SSW from great Amur R. bend to area of Tolun, where they join the Yin mtn. system; rise to 5,670 ft. in Shihwei peak, 70 mi. NNW of Solun. Densely forested, it forms divide bet. Argun and Nonni rivers and is crossed by Chinese Eastern RR. One of the more backward areas of Manchuria, it contains primitive Tungus tribes (Solon, Orochon, Daur), engaged in hunting. A NE offshoot, the ILKURI MOUNTAINS, is continued SE by the **Lesser Khingan Mountains** or **Little Khingan Mountains,** Chinese *Hsiao Hsingan Ling* (shyou), Rus. *Maly Khingan* (mä'-lē), forming the watershed bet. Amur and Sungari rivers. The Lesser Khingan rises to 4,665 ft. 80 mi. NW of Kiamusze, and is continued beyond the Amur in USSR by the BUREYA RANGE, to whose S section the name Lesser Khingan is sometimes applied.
Khios, Greece: see CHIOS.
Khiov, Iran: see MISHKINSHAHR.
Khipro (kĭp'rō), village, Thar Parkar dist., E central Sind, W Pakistan, 39 mi. NW of Umarkot;

local market (millet, rice, dates). Natural salt deposits SE, on W edge of Thar Desert; saltworks.

Khirasra (kĭrŭs'rŭ), town, central Saurashtra, India, 10 mi. WSW of Rajkot. Was ⊙ former Western Kathiawar state of Khirasra (□ 47; pop. 5,893) of Western India States agency; state merged 1948 with Saurashtra. Sometimes spelled Khirasara.

Khirbet Ruheiba, Palestine: see RUHEIBA.

Khirgis Nur, Mongolia: see KIRGIS NOR.

Khirpai (kĭrpī'), town (pop. 3,623), Midnapore dist., SW West Bengal, India, 27 mi. NE of Midnapore; rice, wheat, pulse.

Khisar Momina-banya (khēsär' mômē'nä-bä'nyä), village (pop. 4,109), Plovdiv dist., central Bulgaria, at S foot of central Sredna Gora, 11 mi. SSW of Karlovo; rail spur terminus; health resort (thermal springs); rye, livestock. Site of anc. Roman ruins. Village formed by union of Khisar and Momina-banya.

Khislavichi (khēslä'vēchē), town (1926 pop. 3,578), SW Smolensk oblast, Russian SFSR, on Sozh R. and 40 mi. S of Smolensk; distilling, hemp milling, garment mfg.

Khiuma, Estonia: see HIIUMAA.

Khiv (khēf), village, S Dagestan Autonomous SSR, Russian SFSR, in foothills of the E Greater Caucasus, 13 mi. WNW of Kasumkent; grain, sheep. Coal, mercury, and dolomite deposits. Pop. largely Lezghian.

Khiva (kē'vŭ, Rus. khē'vŭ, khēvä'), city (1932 pop. estimate 23,700), SW Khorezm oblast, Uzbek SSR, on Khiva oasis, near Kara-Kum desert, 18 mi. SW of Urgench; 41°24'N 60°30'E. Cotton milling, metalworking, carpet mfg. Has remains of khan's palace, minarets, shrines, and bazaar. After 7th cent., in Khorezm shahdom (anc. *Chorasmia*, Arabic *Khwarizm*), which controlled Persia in 13th cent. In late-16th cent. became ⊙ Khiva khanate, which fell to Russians in 1873, becoming Rus. protectorate, and later (1920–24), Khorezm Soviet People's Republic. In 1924 its territory (including Khiva oasis) was divided bet. Uzbek and Turkmen SSR.

Khizy (khēzē'), village (1939 pop. over 500), E Azerbaijan SSR, at SE end of the Greater Caucasus, 50 mi. NW of Baku; rug mfg.; livestock.

Khlebnikovo (khlyĕb'nyĭkŭvŭ), village (1939 pop. over 500), E Mari Autonomous SSR, Russian SFSR, 65 mi. NNE of Kazan; wheat, rye, oats.

Khledia (klĕdyä'), village, Tunis dist., N Tunisia, on railroad and 10 mi. S of Tunis; agr. (truck farming, fruit- and winegrowing).

Khlevnoye (khlyĕv'nŭyŭ), village (1926 pop. 3,967), NW Voronezh oblast, Russian SFSR, on Don R. and 36 mi. N of Voronezh; metalworks; wheat.

Khlong Toei (klông' tŭ'ē), SE suburb of Bangkok, Phra Nakhon prov., S Thailand, landing on Chao Phraya R., on railroad spur, and 5 mi. SE of city center; rail-river transfer wharf; seaplane base; oil refinery. Also spelled Klong Toi.

Khmelevitsy (khmĭlyô'vētsĕ), village (1926 pop. 466), NE Gorki oblast, Russian SFSR, 23 mi. ESE of Vetluga; flax, potatoes.

Khmelevoye (khmĕlyĭvoi'ŭ), village (1932 pop. estimate 3,780), W Kirovograd oblast, Ukrainian SSR, 40 mi. W of Kirovograd; wheat, sugar beets.

Khmelnik, Poland: see CHMIELNIK.

Khmelnik or **Khmel'nik** (khmĕl'nyĭk), town (1926 pop. 10,792), NW Vinnitsa oblast, Ukrainian SSR, on the Southern Bug and 32 mi. NW of Vinnitsa; cotton mill; dairying, food processing; metalworks, machine mfg.

Khobar or **Al Khobar** (ăl khō'bär), town in Hasa, E Saudi Arabia, small port on Persian Gulf, 5 mi. ESE of Dhahran, opposite Bahrein; fishing, pearling.

Khobdo, Mongolia: see KOBDO.

Khobi (khô'bē), village (1939 pop. over 2,000), W Georgian SSR, in Rion R. lowland, on railroad and 15 mi. NE of Poti; corn, livestock.

Khobotovo (khô'bŭtŭvŭ), village (1939 pop. over 500), W Tambov oblast, Russian SFSR, 12 mi. NNW of Michurinsk; flour milling, woodworking.

Khodavendikyar, Turkey: see BURSA, province.

Khodech, Poland: see CHODECZ.

Khodorov (khŭdŭrôf'), Pol. *Chodorów* (khôdô'rōōf), city (1931 pop. 7,646), NE Drogobych oblast, Ukrainian SSR, on tributary of the Dniester and 23 mi. NE of Stry; rail junction; agr. market; metalworking, food processing (sugar, meat, cereals, vegetable oils), sawmilling, tile and brick mfg. Has old monastery and palace. Passed from Poland to Austria (1772); reverted to Poland (1919); ceded to USSR in 1945.

Khodyzhenski or **Khodyzhenskiy** (khŭdĭzhĕn'skē), town (1926 pop. 2,224), S Krasnodar Territory, Russian SFSR, at N foot of the Greater Caucasus, 30 mi. WSW of Maikop; petroleum center linked by pipe line with Krasnodar; natural-gas wells. Sometimes spelled Khadyzhenski.

Khodzha-Akhrar (khŭjä"-ŭkhrär'), village (1939 pop. over 500), SE Samarkand oblast, Uzbek SSR, c.5 mi. from Samarkand.

Khodzhambas (khŭjŭmbäs'), town (1939 pop. over 500), SE Chardzhou oblast, Turkmen SSR, on the Amu Darya and 22 mi. NW of Kerki; cotton. Formerly spelled Khodzhambass.

Khodzheili or **Khodzheyli** (khŭjälyē'), city (1932 pop. estimate 4,820), W Kara-Kalpak Autonomous SSR, Uzbek SSR, on railroad, near the Amu Darya, and 10 mi. WSW of Nukus; cotton ginning, metalworking.

Khodzhent, Tadzhik SSR: see LENINABAD, city.

Khodzhiabad (khŭjĕŭbät'), village (1926 pop. 2,020), central Andizhan oblast, Uzbek SSR, 15 mi. SE of Andizhan; cotton, sericulture; metalworks.

Khoi or **Khoy** (khō'ē), town (1940 pop. 35,470), Fourth Prov., in Azerbaijan, northwesternmost Iran, 75 mi. WNW of Tabriz, off N end of L. Urmia; road and trade center, situated within 35–40 mi. of Turkish and Soviet borders; airfield. Grain, fruit, cotton; sheep raising; rug weaving. Armenian colony. Town withstood Russian siege (1827).

Khoiniki or **Khoyniki** (khoi'nyĭkē), town (1926 pop. 4,891), E Polesye oblast, Belorussian SSR, on rail spur and 33 mi. ESE of Mozyr; fruit and vegetable processing, sawmilling, wood distilling.

Khojak Pass, W Pakistan: see TOBA-KAKAR RANGE.

Khokand, Uzbek SSR: see KOKAND.

Khokhol (khŭkhôl'), village (1948 pop. over 10,000), W Voronezh oblast, Russian SFSR, 20 mi. WSW of Voronezh; wheat, sunflowers.

Kholbon (khŭlbôn'), town (1939 pop. over 500), central Chita oblast, Russian SFSR, on Trans-Siberian RR and 115 mi. E of Chita; power plant. Coal mines here and at near-by Arbogar.

Kholm, Poland: see CHELM.

Kholm (khôlm), city (1926 pop. 5,533), N Velikiye Luki oblast, Russian SFSR, on Lovat R. and 45 mi. NNW of Toropets; sawmilling center. Chartered 1471 under Novgorod; passed 1478 to Muscovy. During Second World War, held (1941–44) by Germans.

Kholmogory (khŭlmŭgô'rē), village (1948 pop. over 2,000), NW Archangel oblast, Russian SFSR, on Northern Dvina R., opposite mouth of the Pinega, and 40 mi. SE of Archangel; dairying (noted cattle breeds); bone-carving handicrafts. Chief port of region until rise of Archangel in 17th cent. Lomonosov b. near by.

Kholmsk (khôlmsk), city (1940 pop. 18,151), S Sakhalin, Russian SFSR, ice-free port on Sea of Japan, on W coast railroad and 33 mi. W of Yuzhno-Sakhalinsk; rail junction; industrial center; pulp and paper milling, fish canning, mfg. (soap, starch); cold-storage plant. Port developed in early 1920s. Under Jap. rule (1905–45), called Maoka (mäō'kä).

Kholmy (khŭlmĭ'), village (1926 pop. 2,920), NE Chernigov oblast, Ukrainian SSR, 28 mi. WSW of Novgorod-Severski; distilling.

Kholm-Zhirkovski or **Kholm-Zhirkovskiy** (khôlm"-zhĭrkôf'skē), village (1926 pop. 339), N Smolensk oblast, Russian SFSR, near Dnieper R., 37 mi. NW of Vyazma; dairying, flax retting. Formerly Kholm.

Kholodnaya Balka, Ukrainian SSR: see NOVO-VOIKOVO.

Kholomon, Greece: see CHOLOMON.

Kholopenichi (khŭlŭpyĕ'nyĭchē), town (1926 pop. 2,032), NE Minsk oblast, Belorussian SSR, 27 mi. NE of Borisov; clothing, shoes.

Kholui or **Kholuy** (khŭlōō'ē), town (1926 pop. 1,364), Ivanovo oblast, Russian SFSR, 7 mi. W of Yuzha; handicraft center (clothing, wood carving).

Khombole (khōmbō'lā), village, W Senegal, Fr. West Africa, on railroad and 50 mi. E of Dakar; peanut growing. Airfield.

Khomein or **Khomeyn,** Iran: see KHUMAIN.

Khomeir, Bandar, or **Bandar Khomeyr,** Iran: see BANDAR KHUMAIR.

Khomutovka (khŭmōō'tŭfkŭ), village (1926 pop. 1,730), NW Kursk oblast, Russian SFSR, 25 mi. SW of Dmitriyev-Lgovski; hemp processing. Formerly called Khomutovo.

Khomutovo (–tŭvŭ), village (1939 pop. over 500), central Orel oblast, Russian SFSR, 55 mi. E of Orel; hemp milling.

Khone (kônā'), village, Champassak prov., S Laos, 8 mi. SE of Khong and 180 mi. NNE of Pnompenh, at Cambodia line, on isl. in Mekong R. above Khone Falls. The isl., an extension of Dangrek Range, extends 9 mi. across river. A small railroad (c.5 mi. long) spans Khone isl. for transshipment of goods above falls.

Khong (kông), town, Champassak prov., S Laos, port on Khong Isl. (20 mi. long, 5 mi. wide) in Mekong R. and 65 mi. S of Pakse, at Cambodia line; trading center; imports cloth, exports rice, tobacco, lac, kapok, timber, cattle.

Khong, Se (sā'), river in Laos and Cambodia, rises in Annamese Cordillera SW of Hue at c.16°N, flows 300 mi. SSW, past Muong May and Siempang, and after receiving the Se San enters the Mekong at Stungtreng.

Khong Sedone (kông' sädôn'), town, Saravane prov., S Laos, 35 mi. N of Pakse, on the Se Done (left tributary of the Mekong).

Khoni, Georgian SSR: see TSULUKIDZE.

Khonkaen (kôn'kĕn'), town (1947 pop. 10,385), ⊙ Khonkaen prov. (□ 5,332; 1947 pop. 590,664), E Thailand, in Korat Plateau, 240 mi. NE of Bangkok and on railroad, near Chi R.; rice, corn; tobacco, horse raising. Sometimes spelled Konken.

Khonoma (kōnō'mŭ), village, Naga Hills dist., E Assam, India, in Naga Hills, 5 mi. WSW of Kohima; rice, cotton, oranges. Former stronghold of Naga tribes.

Khonsar, Iran: see KHUNSAR.

Khonu (khŭnōō'), village (1948 pop. over 500), NE Yakut Autonomous SSR, Russian SFSR, on Indigirka R. (head of navigation), at mouth of Moma R. (right tributary), and 265 mi. ESE of Verkhoyansk; trading post; reindeer farms.

Khoper River (khŭpyôr'), S central European Russian SFSR, rises SW of Penza, flows generally SW, past Balashov and Borisoglebsk, and S, past Novokhopersk and Uryupinsk, to Don R. just W of Serafimovich; 626 mi. long. Nonnavigable steppe river; frozen Dec.-March. Receives Vorona R. (right), Buzuluk R. (left). Extensive iron deposits near Uryupinsk.

Khopoli (kō'pōlē), village (pop. 962), Kolaba dist., W Bombay, India, 36 mi. ESE of Bombay; rail terminus. Hydroelectric plant (in operation since 1915) supplied by dams on 2 reservoirs just NE; powers (via Panvel) industries and railroad in Bombay and suburban areas.

Khor [Arabic,=inlet], for Arabic names beginning thus and not found here: see under following part of the name.

Khor, Iran: see KHUR.

Khor (khôr), town (1939 pop. over 500), S Khabarovsk Territory, Russian SFSR, on Khor R. (right tributary of Ussuri R.), near its mouth, on Trans-Siberian RR and 45 mi. S of Khabarovsk; sawmilling.

Khora, Greece: see CHORA.

Khoraiba, Aden: see KHOREIBA.

Khorasan, Iran: see KHURASAN.

Khora Sfakion, Crete: see SPHAKIA.

Khorat, Thailand: see NAKHON RATCHASIMA.

Khorat Plateau, Thailand: see KORAT PLATEAU.

Khoreiba, Khoraiba, Khuraiba, or **Khuraybah** (all: khōrā'bŭ), town, Quaiti state, in the upper Wadi Duan, 65 mi. NW of Mukalla, just SSW of 'Aura. Site of airfield, sometimes known as Qa' Ba Nua.

Khorezm (khŭrĕ'zŭm), oblast (□ 1,900; 1946 pop. estimate 300,000), NW Uzbek SSR; ⊙ Urgench. In Khiva oasis, on left bank of the Amu Darya, bet. Kara-Kalpak Autonomous SSR (NE) and Turkmen SSR (SW). Irrigated cotton region; sericulture; rice, cattle. Cotton-ginning, cotton and silk milling. Chief cities: Urgench and Khiva. Pop.: Uzbeks. Formed 1938. An earlier oblast of the same name existed 1924–26. See, also, KHIVA.

Khorgosh, Yugoslavia: see HORGOS.

Khorinsk (khô'rĭnsk), village (1948 pop. over 2,000), SE Buryat-Mongol Autonomous SSR, Russian SFSR, on Uda R. and 95 mi. ENE of Ulan-Ude, in agr. area (wheat, livestock).

Khoristi, Greece: see CHORISTE.

Khor Kalba or **Khawr Kalbah** (both: khōr' kăl'bŭ), village, Trucial Oman, in Fujaira sheikdom, on Gulf of Oman, 6 mi. S of Fujaira town; 25°N 56°20'E. Marks boundary bet. Trucial Oman and Oman sultanate.

Khorlovo (khôr'lŭvŭ), town (1939 pop. over 500), E central Moscow oblast, Russian SFSR, 9 mi. WSW of Yegoryevsk; cotton milling. Phosphorite deposits near by.

Khorly (khôr'lē), village (1926 pop. 1,350), S Kherson oblast, Ukrainian SSR, port on Karkinit Gulf of Black Sea, near Perekop Isthmus, 50 mi. SE of Kherson; ships cotton, grain.

Khormaksar (khōrmăk'sär), low isthmus linking rocky Aden peninsula to mainland; ¾ mi. wide at narrowest point; bounded N by small inlet Khor Maksar. Military reservation; air base.

Khormal, Iraq: see KHURMAL.

Khormuj, Iran: see KHURMUJ.

Khorog (khŭrôk'), city (1948 pop. over 2,000), ⊙ Gorno-Badakhshan Autonomous Oblast, Tadzhik SSR, in the Pamir, on Panj R. (Afghanistan border), at mouth of Gunt (here called Khorog) R., and 165 mi. SE of Stalinabad; 37°30'N 71°34'E. Terminus of highways from Stalinabad and Osh (Kirghiz SSR); airport; wheat, cattle, sheep.

Khorol (khŭrôl'). **1** City (1926 pop. 10,584), central Poltava oblast, Ukrainian SSR, near Khorol R. (right tributary of the Psel), 19 mi. SE of Lubny; flour milling, food processing, light mfg. Peat bogs (S). **2** or **Khorol'** (khŭrôl'yŭ), village (1939 pop. over 2,000), SW Maritime Territory, Russian SFSR, 45 mi. N of Voroshilov, on branch of Trans-Siberian RR, in rice-growing area; grain, soybeans; metalworks.

Khorol River, N Ukrainian SSR, rises WSW of Sumy, flows S, past Mirgorod and Khorol, and E to Psel R. 30 mi. NNE of Kremenchug; 130 mi. long.

Khoroshch, Poland: see CHOROSZCZ.

Khoroshevo (khŭrô'shĭvŭ), town (1926 pop. 2,673), N central Kharkov oblast, Ukrainian SSR, 9 mi. S of Kharkov city center; quarrying.

Khorostkov (khŭrŭstkôf'), Pol. *Chorostków* (khôrôst'kōōf), town (1931 pop. 7,330), E Ternopol oblast, Ukrainian SSR, on right tributary of Zbruch R. and 12 mi. SE of Terebovlya; flour milling, distilling; stud farm; stone quarry. Has old palace, Gothic church. Passed from Poland to Austria (1772); reverted to Poland (1919); ceded to USSR in 1945.

Khorramabad, Iran: see KHURRAMABAD.

Khorramshahr, Iran: see KHURRAMSHAHR.

Khorsabad (khôrsäbäd'), village, Mosul prov., NE Iraq, near the Tigris and 12 mi. NE of Mosul. Built on site of Dur Sharrukin, an Assyrian city (founded 8th cent. B.C. by Sargon), which covered one sq. mi. Its mounds were excavated by P. E. Botta in 1842 and in 1851, and statues of Sargon and of huge winged bulls which guarded the gates were taken to the Louvre. In 1932 there were discovered hundreds of cuneiform tablets in the Elamite language and a list of kings ruling from c.2200 B.C. to 730 B.C.

Khortiatis, Greece: see CHORTIATES.

Khortitsa, village, Ukrainian SSR: see VERKHNYAYA KHORTITSA.

Khortitsa Island (khôr'tyĭtsŭ), Ukrainian SSR, part of Zaporozhe city, bet. arms of Dnieper R., just below Dneproges dam; 6 mi. long, 2 mi. wide. Has important agr. research station and model truck and poultry farms. In 17th cent., hq. (*sech'*) of Zaporozhe Cossacks.

Khor 'Umeira or **Khawr 'Umayrah** (both: khōr' ŏŏmā'rŭ), village, ⊙ Barhimi sheikdom, Subeihi tribal area, Western Aden Protectorate, 60 mi. W of Aden, on the Khor 'Umeira (inlet of Gulf of Aden); airfield.

Khorzhele, Poland: see CHORZELE.

Khoseda-Khard (khŭsyĕ"dŭ-khärt'), village, S Nenets Natl. Okrug, Archangel oblast, Russian SFSR, in Bolshezemelskaya Tundra, 175 mi. ESE of Naryan-Mar; cultural center for Nentsy people; trading post; reindeer raising.

Khosravi or **Khosrovi,** Iran: see KHUSRAWI.

Khost, Afghanistan: see MATUN.

Khost (kōst), village, Sibi dist., NE central Baluchistan, W Pakistan, in Central Brahui Range, 50 mi. NNW of Sibi; coal mining.

Khosta (khŭstä'), town (1939 pop. over 2,000), S Krasnodar Territory, Russian SFSR, on Black Sea, on coastal railroad and 8 mi. SE of Sochi; subtropical health resort.

Khotan (kōtän'), Chinese *Hotien* (hō'tyĕn', hŭ'dyĕn'), town and oasis (pop. 134,220), SW Sinkiang prov., China, on the Yurung Kash (headstream of Khotan R.) and 270 mi. SE of Kashgar, and on anc. Silk Road skirting S edge of Taklamakan Desert; leading town of S Sinkiang, at N foot of Kunlun mts.; silkgrowing center. Mfg. of cotton and silk textiles, carpets, paper, leather goods. Jade found near by at KARA KASH. Khotan was visited c.1275 by Marco Polo, who spelled it Cotan. It became Chinese in 1878; formerly also called Ilchi.

Khotan River, S Sinkiang prov., China, rises in Kunlun mts. in 2 branches—the Kara Kash (left) and the Yurung Kash (right)—flows 400 mi. N, through Taklamakan Desert, but rarely reaching the Tarim, 60 mi. SE of Aksu.

Khoten or **Khoten'** (khŭtyĕn'yŭ), village (1926 pop. 3,810), E Sumy oblast, Ukrainian SSR, 11 mi. N of Sumy; metalworks.

Khotimsk (khŭtyēmsk'), town (1926 pop. 2,899), SE Mogilev oblast, Belorussian SSR, 40 mi. SSW of Roslavl; flax processing.

Khotin (khŭtyĕn'), city (1930 pop. 15,334; 1941 pop. 7,579), N Chernovtsy oblast, Ukrainian SSR, in Bessarabia, on Dniester R. and 30 mi. NE of Chernovtsy; agr. and commercial center; flour milling, oilseed processing, mfg. of alcohol, soap, bricks, tanning. Has remains of imposing 13th-cent. Genoese fortress (restored 18th cent. by Turks). Was a leading town of Moldavia, flourishing in 17th-18th cents. Passed (1812) to Russia. While in Rumania (1918–40; 1941–44), it was ⊙ Hotin dept. (□ 1,460; 1941 pop. 368,546).

Khotkovo or **Khot'kovo** (khôt'yŭkŭvŭ), city (1949 pop. over 2,000), NE Moscow oblast, Russian SFSR, 6 mi. SW of Zagorsk; cotton milling, mfg. (chemicals, electric insulators). Near by is Abramtsevo, 19th-cent. countryseat (now a mus.) of many literary figures (Aksakov, Gogol) and eminent painters.

Khotynets (khŭtĭnyĕts'), village (1926 pop. 746), W Orel oblast, Russian SFSR, 30 mi. WNW of Orel; hemp.

Khouribga (kōōrēbgä'), town (pop. 26,060), Casablanca region, W central Fr. Morocco, on railroad and 65 mi. SE of Casablanca; Morocco's chief phosphate-mining center, with mines extending to Boujniba (7 mi. E) and André Delpit (12 mi. ESE), all connected by rail spurs. Phosphate drying, superphosphate mfg. Construction of large workers' settlement at Khouribga began 1921.

Khovaling (khŭvŭlēnk'), village (1932 pop. estimate 880), N Kulyab oblast, Tadzhik SSR, 30 mi. NNE of Kulyab; wheat, horses.

Khovrino, Russian SFSR: see KRASNOOKTYABRSKI.

Khowai (kō'vī), village, Tripura, NE India, 20 mi. NNE of Agartala; trades in rice, cotton, tea, mustard, jute. Rail spur terminus at Balla station, just W; rice milling.

Khoy, Iran: see KHOI.

Khoyniki, Belorussian SSR: see KHOINIKI.

Khozdar, W Pakistan: see KHUZDAR.

Khram River (khräm), Georgian *Khrami*, S Georgian SSR, rises NE of Akhalkalaki in Trialet Range at 7,950 ft., flows 122 mi. ESE, past Tsalka (reservoir) and Molotovo (site of Khramges hydroelectric station), to Kura R. on Georgian-Azerbaijan SSR line, S of Rustavi.

Khrapunovo, Russian SFSR: see VOROVSKOGO, IMENI, Moscow oblast.

Khrenovoye (khryĕnŭvoi'ŭ), village (1926 pop. 9,813), central Voronezh oblast, Russian SFSR, 12 mi. E of Bobrov, in virgin steppe; woodworking. Large horse-breeding station (founded 1775) here. Formerly also called Khrenovo.

Khrisos, Greece: see CHRYSOS.

Khrisoupolis, Greece: see CHRYSOUPOLIS.

Khristinovka (khrĭstyē'nŭfkŭ), town (1926 pop. 2,618), SW Kiev oblast, Ukrainian SSR, 13 mi. NW of Uman; rail junction; metalworking, food processing.

Khristoforovo (khrēstŭfô'rŭvŭ), town (1943 pop. over 500), NW Kirov oblast, Russian SFSR, 13 mi. NW of Lalsk; peat.

Khrompik [Rus.,=dichromate], rail station, Russian SFSR: see PERVOURALSK.

Khrom-Tau (khrōm-tou'), town (1948 pop. over 2,000), N Aktyubinsk oblast, Kazakh SSR, on railroad and 37 mi. E of Aktyubinsk; chrome-mining center. Developed in early 1940s.

Khroub, Le (lŭ krōōb'), town (pop. 4,382), Constantine dept., NE Algeria, 8 mi. SE of Constantine; rail junction; agr. market in wheat-growing region. Flour milling. Has Constantine's airport.

Khroumirie (krōōmērē'), mountainous region of NW Tunisia, in the E Tell, bet. the Mediterranean (N) and Medjerda R. (S); extends from Algerian border (W) to Djebel-Abiod area (E). Has abundant rainfall and extensive cork-oak forests. Chief towns are Aïn-Draham and Tabarka (port). Also spelled Kroumirie. Berber pop.

Khroupista, Greece: see ARGOS ORESTIKON.

Khrustalnoye or **Khrustal'noye** (khrōōstäl'nŭyŭ), town (1926 pop. 2,540), S Voroshilovgrad oblast, Ukrainian SSR, in the Donbas, 3 mi. W of Krasny Luch; coal mines.

Khryplin (khrĭ'plyĭn), Pol. *Chryplin*, rail junction in central Stanislav oblast, Ukrainian SSR, 2 mi. SSE of Stanislav.

Khrysokhou Bay (khrēsôkhōō'), inlet of NW Cyprus, bounded W by Cape Arnauti; c.15 mi. long, up to 5 mi. wide. The Baths of Aphrodite are on its SW shore.

Khubsugul, Hubsugul, or **Höbsögöl** (all: khûb'sûgûl), aimak (□ 42,200; pop. 80,000), NW Mongolian People's Republic; ⊙ Muren. Bounded N and NW by USSR, the generally mountainous aimak contains L. Khubsugul in forested section (N) and a wooded steppe section (S) drained by Selenga R. Pop. includes Tuvinians. Agr. (S), hunting and yak raising (N). Graphite, gold, silver-lead, and copper deposits. Sometimes spelled Kosogol.

Khubsugul, Lake, or **Lake Hubsugul,** or **Lake Höbsögöl,** second-largest lake (□ 1,010), after Ubsa Nor, of Mongolian People's Republic, and its largest fresh-water body, situated near USSR line, 130 mi. from SW end of L. Baikal and 350 mi. NW of Ulan Bator; 80 mi. long (N–S), 20–25 mi. wide, 820 ft. deep; alt. 5,328 ft. Situated amid picturesque wooded mts., at S foot of E.Sayan Range, the lake has clear water and an abundance of fish. It is frozen Dec.–May; its outlet is the EGIN GOL. Steamer navigation bet. Turtu (N) and Khadkhal (S) forms part of a USSR-Mongolia trade route. Sometimes called Kosogol.

Khuchni (khōōch'nyē), village (1939 pop. over 500), SE Dagestan Autonomous SSR, Russian SFSR, on slope of the E Greater Caucasus, 19 mi. WSW of Derbent; woolen milling; orchards, grain, sheep. Tabasaran mtn. tribe of Dagestan inhabits dist.

Khudat (khōōdät'), town (1948 pop. over 2,000), NE Azerbaijan SSR, on railroad and 105 mi. NNW of Baku, near Caspian Sea coast; metalworks, vegetable and fish canning.

Khudian (kōōdyän'), town (pop. 4,969), Lahore dist., E Punjab, W Pakistan, 39 mi. S of Lahore; agr. market (wheat, cotton, oilseeds).

Khudur, Al, Iraq: see KHIDR, AL.

Khuitun, Mongolia: see TABUN BOGDO.

Khuldabad (kōōldäbäd'), village (pop. 4,070), Aurangabad dist., NW Hyderabad state, India, 13 mi. NW of Aurangabad; Moslem place of pilgrimage; site of Aurangzeb's tomb. Famous Ellora caves are just NW. Formerly also called Rauza.

Khulm, town, Afghanistan: see TASHKURGHAN.

Khulm River (khōōlm), in Afghan Turkestan, N Afghanistan, rises in the Hindu Kush at 35°35'N 68°10'E, flows 130 mi. N, past Haibak and Tashkurghan, and disappears into desert N of Tashkurghan. Used for irrigation in lower course.

Khulna (kōōl'nŭ), dist. (□ 4,805; 1951 pop. 2,079,000), East Bengal, E Pakistan, in Ganges Delta; ⊙ Khulna. Bounded E by Madhumati R., S by Bay of Bengal; drained by river arms of Ganges Delta; central portion of the Sundarbans in S (sundari timber; habitat of Bengal tigers, leopards, wild buffalo). Alluvial soil; extensive groves of date, betel- and coconut palms; rice, jute, oilseeds, sugar cane, tobacco. Rice, flour, and oilseed milling, cotton-cloth mfg. at Khulna (trade center for the Sundarbans) and Bagherhat; shipbuilding at Khulna; fishing. Ruins (15th-cent.) of Gaur kingdom at Bagherhat. Iswaripur was ⊙ 16th-cent. independent Moslem kingdom until defeated 1576 by Akbar's Hindu general. Part of former Br. Bengal prov., India, until inc. (1947) into new Pakistan prov. of East Bengal, following creation of Pakistan.

Khulna, town (pop. 31,749), ⊙ Khulna dist., SW East Bengal, E Pakistan, on river arm of Ganges Delta and 80 mi. SW of Dacca; rail terminus (spur to Bagherhat, just across river); trade center for the Sundarbans; rice, jute, oilseeds, sugar cane, betel- and coconuts, salt; rice, flour, and oilseed milling, cotton-cloth mfg., shipbuilding.

Khulo (khōōlô'), village (1932 pop. estimate 310), E Adzhar Autonomous SSR, Georgian SSR, 34 mi. E of Batum; tobacco, fruit.

Khum, Yugoslavia: see HUM.

Khumain, Khomein, or **Khomeyn** (all: khōmān'), town, Sixth Prov., in Gulpaigan, W central Iran, 20 mi. NW of Gulpaigan and on highway to Arak; wheat, barley, opium, cotton; wool weaving, rug-making.

Khumair, Bandar, Iran: see BANDAR KHUMAIR.

Khumalag (khōōmŭläk'), village (1926 pop. 3,740), central North Ossetian Autonomous SSR, Russian SFSR, 5 mi. WNW of Beslan, in hemp and soybean dist.

Khumarinski, Russian SFSR: see ORDZHONIKIDZEVSKI, Stavropol Territory.

Khungari (khōōn-gä'rē), town (1949 pop. over 500), S Khabarovsk Territory, Russian SFSR, on Khungari R. (right tributary of the Amur), on branch of Trans-Siberian RR and c.60 mi. ESE of Komsomolsk; sawmilling.

Khunsar or **Khonsar** (both: khōnsär'), town (1941 pop. 19,291), Sixth Prov., W central Iran, 15 mi. S of Gulpaigan and on highway to Isfahan; grain, tobacco, fruit, tamarisk.

Khun Tan Range (kōōn' tän'), N Thailand, bet. Ping and Wang rivers (headstreams of the Chao Phraya); rises to 6,601 ft. 30 mi. NE of Chiangmai. Crossed by Lampang-Chiangmai RR in 1-mi.-long tunnel.

Khunzakh (khōōnzäkh'), village (1948 pop. over 2,000), central Dagestan Autonomous SSR, Russian SFSR, in the E Greater Caucasus, near the Avar Koisu, on road and 30 mi. SW of Buinaksk; clothing handicrafts; grain, sheep. Pop. largely Avar. A former capital of Avar khanate; ruins of anc. palace and fortress.

Khur or **Khor** (khōr), village, Tenth Prov., in Yezd, central Iran, 135 mi. NNE of Yezd, in the Dasht-i-Kavir; barley, gums; camel breeding.

Khurai (kōōrī'), town (pop. 8,509), Saugor dist., N Madhya Pradesh, India, 30 mi. NW of Saugor; trades in wheat, oilseeds, millet; cattle market.

Khuraiba, Aden: see KHOREIBA.

Khurasan or **Khorasan** (both: khōräsän'), former province of NE Iran; main city, Meshed. Bounded N by Turkmen SSR of USSR, E by Afghanistan, S by Seistan and Kerman, and W by Gurgan, Shahrud, and Yezd. Contains the Turkmen-Khurasan ranges (N; Kopet Dagh, Ala Dagh, Hazar Masjid, and Binalud ranges), the arid E Iranian uplands, and in SW the margins of the closed desert basins of the Dasht-i-Kavir and Dasht-i-Lut. Agr. is restricted to the fertile valleys of the Atrek and Kashaf rivers (N) and the Qain and Birjand oases (E). Wheat, barley, rice, cotton, tobacco, sugar beets, and fruit are the main products. Saffron, pistachio nuts, and gums (asafetida) are gathered. The main centers—Meshed, Quchan, Bujnurd, Sabzawar, Nishapur, and Birjand—are linked by roads; a railroad runs from Teheran to Meshed. Food processing, rug weaving, and tanning are the chief industries; carpets, hides, wool, and canned goods the main exports. Khurasan originally had its capital at Mary (Merv) and included the great centers of Nishapur, Herat, and Balkh when the Arabs came in 7th cent. Home of Tahirid dynasty, which briefly ruled (820–872) E Persia under the Abbasid caliphate. Prov. was invaded (13th cent.) by the Mongols and flourished under Shah Abbas (17th cent.). Since 1938, Khurasan and its S dist., the Qainat, constitute the Ninth Province (□ 125,000; 1940 pop. 2,036,549) of Iran, to which the name Khurasan is commonly applied.

Khurda (kōōr'dŭ), village, Puri dist., E Orissa, India, 28 mi. NNW of Puri; road junction; market center (rice, forest produce); handicraft cloth weaving. Khurda Road, 5 mi. ESE, is rail junction (workshops); rice mill, biri factory.

Khurdalan (khōōrdŭlän'), town (1939 pop. over 500) in Kirov dist. of Greater Baku, Azerbaijan SSR, 7 mi. NW of Baku, on W Apsheron Peninsula; oil fields.

Khurd Kabul (khōōrd' kä'bōōl), village, Kabul prov., E Afghanistan, 15 mi. SE of Kabul; coal mining. The Khurd Kabul Pass (N), scene of massacre (1842) of British troops in 1st Afghan War, was formerly used by Peshawar-Kabul road.

Khurja (kōōr'jŭ), town (pop. 35,376), Bulandshahr dist., W Uttar Pradesh, India, 45 mi. SE of Delhi; road junction; trade center (wheat, oilseeds, barley, jowar, cotton, sugar cane, ghee); pottery mfg. Large Jain temple.

Khurma or **Khurmah,** Arabia: see TURABA, WADI.

Khurmal (khōōrmäl'), town, Sulaimaniya prov., NE Iraq, in Kurdistan, near Iran border, 35 mi. SE of Sulaimaniya; tobacco, fruit, livestock. Sometimes spelled Khormal.

Khurmuj or **Khormuj** (both: khōrmōōj'), town (1945 pop. estimate 2,500), Seventh Prov., in Fars, S Iran, 40 mi. ESE of Bushire; grain, cotton, tobacco.

Khurramabad or **Khorramabad** (both: khōrām"-äbäd'), town (1940 pop. 16,754), Sixth Prov., in Luristan, SW Iran, 150 mi. NNW of Ahwaz and 33 mi. SW of Burujird, and on Teheran-Khurramshahr road; market center; trades in wool, grain, fruit. Dominated by imposing medieval fortress atop rock in center of town. The capital of the atabegs of Luristan (12th–16th cent.), it was known as Diz-i-Siyah [Persian,=black fortress] until 14th cent.

Khurramshahr or **Khorramshahr** (–shä'hûr), town (1947 pop. estimate 20,000), Sixth Prov., in Khuzistan, SW Iran, Persian Gulf port on the Shatt al Arab (Iraq line), at mouth of Karun R., and 10 mi. NW of Abadan, 25 mi. E of Basra; leading overseas trade port of Iran, handling bulk of country's imports. Exports dates, rice, gums, cotton, tanning extracts, skins. Pop. is largely Arab. Situated on site of anc. port, Khurramshahr was occupied in 1841 by Persian troops. During Second World War, a modern port was built here, in 1943, to handle lend-lease to the USSR. It was connected by railroad with Ahwaz and thus partly supplanted the original S terminus of Trans-Iranian RR at Bandar Shahpur. Formerly known as Muhammerah, Mohammerah, or Mohammareh.

Khursia, India: see KHARSIA.

Khusf (khōosf), village, Ninth Prov., in Khurasan, NE Iran, 20 mi. WSW of Birjand.

Khushab (kōōshäb'), town (pop. 17,141), Shahpur dist., W central Punjab, W Pakistan, on Jhelum R. and 23 mi. NW of Sargodha; rail junction; trade center for cotton, grain, wool, ghee, cloth fabrics; wheat, millet, oilseeds; mfg. of drugs, perfume, felts; hand-loom weaving. Shipping point for rock salt and coal mined in Salt Range (N).

Khusrawi, Khosravi, or **Khosrovi** (all: khōsrōvē'), village, Fifth Prov., in Kermanshah, W Iran, 90 mi. W of Kermanshah and 6 mi. NE of Khanaqin; customs station on Iraq border, on main Teheran-Baghdad route.

Khust (khōōst), Czech *Chust* or *Husté* (khōōst, hōō'stā), Hung. *Huszt* (hōōst), city (1941 pop. 21,118), S Transcarpathian Oblast, Ukrainian SSR, near Tissa R., on railroad and 32 mi. SE of Mukachevo; trading center; mfg. (headwear, ceramics). Airfield. Ruins of 11th-cent. castle near by. A town of Austria-Hungary which passed 1920 to Czechoslovakia, 1939 to Hungary, and 1945 to USSR. In 1938–39 it was ⊙ autonomous Czech prov. called Carpatho-Ukraine.

Khutorok (khōōtûrôk'), town (1939 pop. over 500), E Krasnodar Territory, Russian SFSR, on railroad and 10 mi. NW of Armavir; processing of food products; wine, alcohol.

Khuzdar (khōōzdär'), village, Kalat state, E central Baluchistan, W Pakistan, 85 mi. S of Kalat, in Jhalawan div.; market center (wheat, millet, rice); palm-mat weaving. Antimony and lead-ore deposits 11 mi. NW, at Shekran. Sometimes spelled Khozdar.

Khuzhir (khōōzhēr'), town (1946 pop. over 500), SE Irkutsk oblast, Russian SFSR, on W shore of Olkhon Isl. in L. Baikal; fish processing. Founded 1942.

Khuzistan (khōōzĭstän') or **Khuzestan** (–ĕstän'), former province (□ 25,000; pop. 750,000) of SW Iran; ⊙ was Ahwaz. Bounded S by Persian Gulf, W by Iraq, N by Luristan, and E by Fars, it is situated at foot of the central Zagros highland on a plain forming part of the great Mesopotamian lowland. A subtropical region with hot, dry summers and cooler winters, it is irrigated by Karkheh, Karun, Zuhreh, and Ab-i-Diz rivers. Agr.: dates, grain; stock raising in foothills of the Zagros. Khuzistan is Iran's leading petroleum region, with fields at Lali, Masjid-i-Sulaiman, White Oil Springs, Naft Kel, Agha Jari, and Gach Saran—linked by pipe lines with Abadan refinery. Prov. is served by Trans-Iranian RR with maritime termini at Persian Gulf ports of Khurramshahr and Bandar Shahpur. Pop. contains important Arab elements. Main commercial centers are Ahwaz (transportation hub), Dizful, and Shushtar. The biblical ELAM, called *Susiana* in classical times and Arabistan in Middle Ages, it was formerly a flourishing agr. region, but declined with the neglect of the irrigation network. It revived in early-20th cent. with development of the oil fields and building of the Trans-Iranian RR. In 1938, Khuzistan, Gulpaigan, and Luristan were combined to form Iran's Sixth Province (□ 40,000; pop. 1,362,724), to which the name Khuzistan is also commonly applied.

Khvalynsk (khvŭlĭnsk'), city (1926 pop. 13,027), N Saratov oblast, Russian SFSR, grain port on right bank of Volga R. and 110 mi. NE of Saratov, in picturesque chalk hills; fruit and vegetable processing; flour and oilseed mills, tanning, sawmilling. Settled in 18th cent. by the Old Believers; chartered 1780.

Khvastovichi (khvä'stŭvēchē), village (1926 pop. 2,482), S Kaluga oblast, Russian SFSR, 23 mi. N of Karachev; hemp.

Khvatovka (khvä'tŭfkŭ), town (1926 pop. 2,986), N Saratov oblast, Russian SFSR, on railroad and 8 mi. NE of Bazarny Karabulak; glassworks.

Khvoinaya or **Khvoynaya** (khvoi'nīŭ), town (1939 pop. over 500), NE Novgorod oblast, Russian SFSR, 40 mi. NNE of Borovichi; dairying; metalworks.

Khvorostyanka (khvŭrŭstyän'kŭ). **1** Village (1926 pop. 4,254), SW Kuibyshev oblast, Russian SFSR, 40 mi. SW of Chapayevsk, metalworking; wheat, cattle, sheep. **2** Village (1926 pop. 1,244), NW Voronezh oblast, Russian SFSR, 16 mi. SE of Gryazi; wheat.

Khwae Noi River (kwä' noi') [Thai,=lesser Khwae], W central Thailand, rises in Tenasserim Range on Burma border near Three Pagodas Pass, flows 150 mi. SE through densely forested valley to Mae Klong R. at Kanchanaburi. Followed by Ban Pong–Thambyuzayat RR and road, built during Second World War.

Khwae Yai River, Thailand: see MAE KLONG RIVER.

Khwarizm, Uzbek SSR: see KHIVA.

Khwash, Iran: see KHASH.

Khyber (kī'bûr), tribal region (1951 pop. estimate 217,000), W North-West Frontier Prov., W Pakistan; comprises mountainous territory along Afghan border; crossed S by E Safed Koh Range, N by S offshoots of the Hindu Kush; contains most of Khyber Pass. Wheat, corn, barley grown in valleys; mica, marble, iron-ore deposits. Chief tribes are Mohmands and Afridis. Administered as political agency. Sometimes spelled Khaibar.

Khyber Pass, famous defile through Safed Koh Range, bet. Afghanistan and Pakistan, linking Kabul R. valley (W) with Peshawar (E); c.28 mi. long. Winds through barren, rugged cliffs; rises to c.3,500 ft. at highest point. Traversed by railway from Jamrud (E entrance) to Landi Khana (on Afghan border) and by 2 roads, one for motor transport, the other for caravans. An important trade route and strategic military area (has several fortified posts), Khyber Pass for centuries has been used by invaders of India, including Mahmud of Ghazni, Baber, Humayun, and Nadir Shah, although its difficult terrain and the presence of hostile Afridi tribes have made passage hazardous. British 1st entered pass in 1839 and by treaty of Gandamak (1879) secured control over most of it. Scene of several skirmishes during Afghan Wars (1838–42; 1878–80). Sometimes spelled Khaibar.

Khyrim (kī'rĭm), village, Khasi and Jaintia Hills dist., W Assam, India, on Shillong Plateau, 5 mi. S of Shillong; rice, sesame, cotton.

Khyrov (khĭ'rŭf), Pol. *Chyrów* (khĭ'rōōf), city (1931 pop. 3,864), W Drogobych oblast, Ukrainian SSR, on Stryyazh R. and 15 mi. W of Sambor; flour and sawmilling, brick mfg. Has 16th-cent. church, old monastery.

Khyulyulya (khyōōlū'lyä), Finnish *Helylä* (hĕ'lülă), town (1948 pop. over 500), SW Karelo-Finnish SSR, 3 mi. N of Sortavala; sawmilling, woodworking.

Kiachow, China: see KIAHSIEN, Shensi prov.

Kiafu (kyä'fōō), village, Leopoldville prov., W Belgian Congo, on railroad and 60 mi. N of Boma; agr. center; palm-oil milling, soap mfg.

Kiaho or **Chia-ho** (both: jyä'hŭ'), town, ⊙ Kiaho co. (pop. 133,991), S Hunan prov., China, 50 mi. WSW of Chenhsien; tin and arsenic mining.

Kiahsien or **Chia-hsien** (both: jyä'shyĕn'). **1** Town, ⊙ Kiahsien co. (pop. 201,332), NW central Honan prov., China, 45 mi. SSW of Chengchow; cotton weaving; wheat, corn, beans. **2** Town, ⊙ Kiahsien co. (pop. 13,280), N Shensi prov., China, 40 mi. ESE of Yülin and on Yellow R. (Shansi line); wheat, millet, cotton. Until 1913, Kiachow.

Kiakhta, Russian SFSR: see KYAKHTA.

Kiakiang or **Chia-chiang** (both: jyä'jyäng'), town (pop. 10,760), ⊙ Kiakiang co. (pop. 160,575), W Szechwan prov., China, 15 mi. NW of Loshan; paper milling, Chinese-wax processing; rice, millet.

Kiakiawang, China: see KIAWANG.

Kiali or **Chiali** (both: jyä'lē'), Jap. *Kari* (kä'rē), town (1935 pop. 7,947), W central Formosa, 11 mi. N of Tainan; rice, sugar cane.

Kiali or **Chia-li,** Tibet: see LHARI.

Kialinek Bay or **Kialineq Bay** (both: kyä'lĭnĕk), small inlet of Denmark Strait, SE Greenland; 66°55'N 33°5'W. Gives its name to surrounding region, known for its good hunting. Sometimes called Skraekken Bay (skrĕ'kŭn).

Kialing River (jyä'lĭng'), Chinese *Kialing Kiang* or *Chia-ling Chiang*, China, rises S of Tienshui in Shensi-Kansu border region, flows c.600 mi. S, past Lioyang (Shensi prov.), Langchung (head of junk navigation), Nanchung, and Hochwan (Szechwan prov.), to Yangtze R. at Chungking. Receives Chü R. (left) and Fow R. (right) near Hochwan.

Kiama (kīă'mŭ), municipality and port (pop. 2,256), E New South Wales, Australia, on coast, 55 mi. S of Sydney; exports dairy products. Coal mines near by.

Kiamari, W Pakistan: see KARACHI, city.

Kiambi (kyäm'bē), village, Katanga prov., SE Belgian Congo, on Luvua R. (head of navigation) and 130 mi. SW of Albertville; trading center in tin-mining region. Protestant mission.

Kiambu (kēäm'bōō), town (pop. c.1,000), S central Kenya, 5 mi. N of Nairobi; major coffee center; wheat, corn. Hq. of Gospel Mission.

Kiamichi River (kī"ŭmĭ'shē), SE Okla., rises near Ark. line in the Ouachita Mts., flows SW and S, past Pine Valley and Clayton, to Antlers, then SE to Red R. S of Fort Towson; c.165 mi. long. Site of Hugo Reservoir in river (for flood control in Red R. basin) is 7 mi. E of Hugo.

Kiamusze or **Chia-mu-ssu** (both: jyä'mōō'sŭ'), city (1947 pop. 168,000), N Sungkiang prov., Manchuria, 195 mi. NE of Harbin, and on right bank of Sungari R., opposite LIENKIANGKOW; rail terminus and major river port; wood pulp and sawmilling, brick and tile mfg.; flour and soybean mills, tanneries; power plant. A town of 20,000 pop. in 1931, Kiamusze developed greatly while in Manchukuo, when it became (1934) an independent municipality and ⊙ Sankiang prov. (1934–46). While under Nationalist rule, it was briefly (1946–49) ⊙ Hokiang prov.

Kian or **Chi-an** (both: jē'än'), city (1948 pop. 68,834), ⊙ but independent of Kian co. (1948 pop. 232,447), W Kiangsi prov., China, 110 mi. SW of Nanchang; major commercial port on Kan R.; trades in grain, tea, rice, ramie. Anthracite mines. Until 1914 called Luling. Became independent municipality in 1949.

Kiana (kīă'nŭ), village (pop. 178), NW Alaska, on lower Kobuk R. and 60 mi. E of Kotzebue, N of Selawik Lake; trapping; supply base for placer gold-mining operations. Scene of gold rush, 1910.

Kiandra (kīăn'drŭ), settlement, SE New South Wales, Australia, 50 mi. SSW of Canberra, in Great Dividing Range, near Muniong Range; alt. 4,600 ft.; snow falls May–Sept. Livestock.

Kiangan or **Chiang-an** (both: jyäng'än'), town (pop. 24,480), ⊙ Kiangan co. (pop. 240,271), SW Szechwan prov., China, 23 mi. WSW of Luhsien and on right bank of Yangtze R.; paper milling; rice, sweet potatoes, wheat, beans, kaoliang. Sulphur mines near by.

Kiangcheng or **Chiang-ch'eng** (both: jyäng'chŭng'), town, ⊙ Kiangcheng co. (pop. 18,160), S Yunnan prov., China, 55 mi. SE of Ningerh, near Laos border; alt. 4,150 ft.; rice, millet, beans. Until 1929 called Mangli.

Kiangchow, China: see JUICHENG.

Kiangchwan or **Chiang-ch'uan** (both: jyäng'chwän'), town (pop. 6,910), ⊙ Kiangchwan co. (pop. 55,479), SE central Yunnan prov., China, 45 mi. S of Kunming, on W shore of L. Fusien, in mtn. region; rice, wheat, beans.

Kianghsien or **Chiang-hsien** (both: jyäng'shyĕn'), town, ⊙ Kianghsien co. (pop. 59,590), S Shansi prov., China, 45 mi. S of Linfen; cotton weaving; wheat, beans, kaoliang, ramie, timber.

Kianghwa or **Chiang-hua** (both: jyäng'hwä'), town, ⊙ Kianghwa co. (pop. 199,523), S Hunan prov., China, near Kwangsi line, 70 mi. S of Lingling; tungsten, arsenic, and tin mining.

Kiangka, China: see NINGTSING, Sikang prov.

Kiangkow or **Chiang-k'ou** (both: jyäng'kō'). **1** Town (pop. 2,947), ⊙ Kiangkow co. (pop. 69,766), NE Kweichow prov., China, 35 mi. SE of Szenan; timber, wheat, millet, beans. Gold, antimony, and iron deposits, and gypsum quarry near by. Until 1913 called Tungjen. **2** Town, Szechwan prov., China: see PINGCHANG.

Kiangling or **Chiang-ling** (both: jyäng'lĭng'), town (pop. 15,389), ⊙ Kiangling co. (pop. 533,094), S Hupeh prov., China, 125 mi. W of Hankow and on left bank of Yangtze R.; an anc. walled city, one of the oldest of China, dating from c.1,000 B.C. Kiangling flourished until the rise of the near-by treaty port of SHASI after 1876. It was called Kingchow until 1912.

Kiangmen, China: see SUNWUI.

Kiangna, China: see YENSHAN, Yunnan prov.

Kiangnan or **Chiang-nan** (both: jyäng'nän'), former province of E China, on lower Yangtze R. Separated in 1667, in early Manchu dynasty, into Kiangsu and Anhwei.

Kiangning or **Chiang-ning** (both: jyäng'nĭng'), town (pop. 2,946), ⊙ Kiangning co. (pop. 433,056), S. Kiangsu prov., China, 7 mi. SSE of Nanking and on Chinhwai R.; rice, wheat, beans, kaoliang, corn. Iron and coal deposits near by. Called Tungshan until 1934.

Kiangpei or **Chiang-pei** (both: jyäng'bā'), town (pop. 16,128), ⊙ Kiangpei co. (pop. 532,041), S central Szechwan prov., China, on left bank of Yangtze R., at mouth of Kialing R., opposite Chungking; coal-mining center; iron mining. Sulphur deposits near by. Separated 1936 from Chungking. Sometimes spelled Kiangpeh.

Kiangpu or **Chiang-p'u** (both: jyäng'pōō'), town ⊙ Kiangpu co. (pop. 161,183), S Kiangsu prov., China, 8 mi. W of Nanking, across Yangtze R.; rice, wheat, beans.

Kiangshan or **Chiang-shan** (both: jyäng'shän'), town (pop. 11,506), ⊙ Kiangshan co. (pop. 266,-774), SW Chekiang prov., China, near Kiangsi line, 20 mi. SW of Chühsien, and on railroad; rice, wheat, beans, tung oil, indigo. Lead and coal mines, crystal quarries.

Kiangsi or **Chiang-hsi** (both: kyăng'sē', Chinese jyäng'shē'), province (□ 65,000; pop. 14,000,000) of S central China; ⊙ Nanchang. Bounded N by Anhwei and Hupeh (in part along Yangtze R.), W by Hunan, S by Kwangtung, and E by Fukien and Chekiang, Kiangsi is physiographically one of China's simplest provs. Low peripheral ranges (the South Yangtze hills) of red sandstone (W) and granite and porphyry (E) envelop the broad Kan R. valley extending N to Poyang L. basin, a natural flood reservoir of Yangtze R. The climate is temperate with high summer temperature and cool winters, and tends to become subtropical in extreme S. April and May have the greatest rainfall. Kiangsi is one of China's leading rice producers. Two crops are raised, mainly in Kan R. valley and Poyang L. basin. Sweet potatoes grow in drier areas; and beans, oilseed, and wheat are winter food crops. The main cash products are cotton (N), tea (in NW and NE hills), ramie (Wantsai), tobacco, sugar cane, and oranges. The prov. furnishes most of China's tungsten (center at Tayü) and has high-grade coking coal (at Pingsiang and Anyüan) and kaolin, which furnished the basis for the porcelain industry of Fowliang (Kingtehchen). Leading cities are Nanchang, Kiukiang (Yangtze port), Kanchow, Kian, Pingsiang, and Fuchow. They are served by railroads (N) radiating from Nanchang to Kiukiang, from Chekiang and Hunan, and by Kan R. navigation. Pop., concentrated in N, is largely Chinese, speaking the Kan (Kiangsi) variety of Mandarin. In the extreme N, lower Yangtze Mandarin is spoken; and in the S, adjoining Kwangtung, there is a large Hakka minority. Historically, Kiangsi has been China's main N-S corridor for migration and communication, linked with Kwangtung via Meiling Pass. Through the prov., along the Ambassadors' Route, passed the 19th-cent. Western envoys, from Canton to Peking. Traditionally known as Kan, Kiangsi [Chinese, = W of the river] is in reality S of Yangtze R. It is the W remainder of a prov. of the Tang dynasty (A.D. 618–906) known as Kiangnan [Chinese, = S of the river] and received its present name in the Southern Sung dynasty (1127–1280). During Mongol rule, it included E Kwangtung. Within its present boundaries, dating from Ming dynasty, prov. passed (1650) to Manchu rule. Most of Kiangsi was under Chinese Communist control (1927–34) after the split with the Kuomintang, and had its capital at Juikin. During Sino-Japanese War, prov. remained largely free of Jap. occupation, except for Nanchang area. It passed to Communists in 1949.

Kiangsu or **Chiang-su** (both: kyăng'sōō', Chinese jyäng'sōō'), province (□ 35,000; pop. 40,000,000) of E China, on Yellow Sea, at mouth of Yangtze R.; divided administratively since 1949 into North Kiangsu (Chinese *Supeh* or *Supei*) (□ 24,000; pop. 25,000,000; ⊙ Yangchow) and South Kiangsu (Chinese *Sunan*) (□ 11,000; pop. 15,000,000; ⊙ Wusih), respectively N and S of Yangtze R. Bounded N by Shantung along Lunghai RR, W by Anhwei, and S by Chekiang, Kiangsu prov. has a straight, low-lying coast, where sandbanks hinder navigation, and which is broken only by the 50-mi.-wide Yangtze estuary. Behind the coast, both N and S of the Yangtze, extends the flat, alluvial lowland, crisscrossed by rivers and canals, that has been formed over the centuries by the sediments of the Yangtze, Hwai, and Yellow rivers. Only in the SW, on Anhwei-Chekiang line, do low hills appear in the level landscape. Kiangsu contains some of the largest lakes of E China: Hungtze and Kaoyu lakes on Anhwei line (W) and Tai L. on Chekiang border (S). These lakes are linked by the Grand Canal, once a major N-S communication line. Climate varies from mild and humid in the S to more extreme temperatures and drier winters in the N. The densely populated rural area, engaged in intensive farming, produces grain (wheat, millets), beans, and peanuts in N; cotton in center (one of China's chief producing areas); and rice and silk in S. In the prov. as a whole, cotton and silk are by far the leading industrial crops, and are the basis of most of the country's industrial production, since Kiangsu's mineral resources are negligible. The main industrial centers are concentrated in South Kiangsu; here are Shanghai, Soochow, Wusih, Changchow, Chinkiang (former prov.), and Nanking. In North Kiangsu are Yangchow, Taichow, Nantung, and Hwaiyin. The S section is well served by Shanghai-Nanking RR; but N Kiangsu lacks railroads, and merely touches on Lunghai RR along Shantung border. In addition to textile production, Kiangsu's urban pop. is also engaged in trade along the lower Yangtze navigation route (accessible to ocean-going vessels). The lower Yangtze variety of Mandarin is spoken N of the Yangtze and in the Chinkiang-Nanking area, while the Wu dialect predominates in the Shanghai-Soochow dist. Northwesternmost Kiangsu falls into the N Mandarin zone. Originally part of the Wu kingdom, a name still applied as the traditional name of the prov., Kiangsu received its present name, derived from Kiangning (Nanking) and Suchow (Soochow), in 1667, when it was separated from the old prov. of Kiangnan. During Sino-Japanese War, it was held 1937–45 by the Japanese. Came under Communist control in 1949, when the NW zone, including Süchow, Sinhai, and Lienyün, passed to Shantung. An abbreviated form for Kiangsu is Su.

Kiangtsing or **Chiang-ching** (both: jyäng'jĭng'), town (pop. 21,516), ⊙ Kiangtsing co. (pop. 840,677), S Szechwan prov., China, 28 mi. SW of Chungking city and on right bank of Yangtze R.; ramie and silk textiles; winegrowing; rice, oranges, beans, wheat, kaoliang. Coal and rock-crystal mining, kaolin quarrying, oil deposits near by.

Kiangtu, China: see YANGCHOW.

Kiangyen or **Chiang-yen** (both: jyĕng'yĕn'), town, N Kiangsu prov., China, 13 mi. E of Taichow; commercial center.

Kiangyin or **Chiang-yin** (both: jyäng'yĭn'), town (pop. 56,623), ⊙ Kiangyin co. (pop. 772,470), S Kiangsu prov., China, 50 mi. ESE of Chinkiang, and on Yangtze R. (S), in rice region; silk and cotton weaving. Fort.

Kiangyu or **Chiang-yu** (both: jyäng'yōō'), town (pop. 15,305), ⊙ Kiangyu co. (pop. 207,542), NW Szechwan prov., China, on Fow R. and 55 mi. NNW of Santai, in mtn. region; medicinal plants, rice, sweet potatoes, indigo, wheat, millet.

Kianly (kēän'lē), coast town (1940 pop. 850), W Ashkhabad oblast, Turkmen SSR, fishing port on Caspian Sea, 12 mi. W of Krasnovodsk; canneries. Until c.1945, called Tarta.

Kiantone (kĭn'tōn, kī'ŭntōn), village in Kiantone town (1940 pop. 849), Chautauqua co., extreme W N.Y., 6 mi. SSE of Jamestown.

Kiaocheng or **Chiao-ch'eng** (both: jyou'chŭng'), town, ⊙ Kiaocheng co. (pop. 94,441), central Shansi prov., China, 30 mi. SW of Taiyüan; winegrowing center.

Kiaochow or **Chiao-chou** (both: kyou'chou', jyou'jō'), former German leased territory (□ 400) on S coast of Shantung prov., China, named for town of Kiaochow (present KIAOHSIEN). It included Kiaochow Bay (□ 200) of Yellow Sea, and the adjoining (E) TSINGTAO peninsula (□ 200). A neutral zone, 30 mi. in radius, surrounded the Ger. territory. Leased 1898 to Germany, the territory was seized by Japan in 1914, and returned to China in 1922.

Kiaochow Bay, Chinese *Kiaochow Wan* (wän), well-sheltered inlet (□ 200) of the Yellow Sea, in Shantung prov., China, 7 mi. SE of Kiaochow; 15 mi. wide, 20 mi. long. Tsingtao (deepwater harbor) is at entrance. Occupied 1898–1914 by Germany as part of Kiaochow lease, and 1914–22 by Japan.

Kiaoho or **Chiao-ho** (both: jyou'hŭ'). **1** Town, ⊙ Kiaoho co. (pop. 322,743), S Hopeh prov., China, 40 mi. N of Tehchow, near Grand Canal (Shantung line); wheat, kaoliang, millet. **2** Town, ⊙ Kiaoho co. (pop. 192,934), central Kirin prov., Manchuria, 40 mi. ESE of Kirin and on railroad; coal-mining center; lumbering.

Kiaohsien or **Chiao-hsien** (both: jyou'shyĕn'), town (1922 pop. estimate 50,000), ⊙ Kiaohsien co. (pop. 599,521), E Shantung prov., China, near Kiaochow Bay of Yellow Sea, 25 mi. NW of Tsingtao, and on railroad to Tsinan; wheat, millet, beans, kaoliang, peanuts. Until 1913 called Kiaochow, it was formerly a flourishing trade center.

Kiaokia or **Ch'iao-chia** (both: chyou'jyä'), town (pop. 12,739), ⊙ Kiaokia co. (pop. 142,724), NW Yunnan prov., China, 40 mi. NNW of Hweitseh and on right bank of Yangtze R. (Sikang line); alt. 2,575 ft.; iron smelting, tung-oil processing. Rice, buckwheat, millet, cotton. Copper and zinc deposits near by.

Kiaopanshan or **Chiao-pan-shan** (both: jyou'bän'shän'), Jap. *Habunsha* (häbōōn'shä), village, N Formosa, 6 mi. SE of Taki; alt. 1,400 ft.; aborigines village.

Kiashan or **Chia-shan** (both: jyä'shän'), town, ⊙ Kiashan co. (pop. 115,906), N Anhwei prov., China, 50 mi. NW of Nanking and on Tientsin-Pukow RR; wheat, beans, corn, kaoliang. Until 1932, Sankieh.

Kiashi, China: see FAIZABAD.

Kiasiang or **Chia-hsiang** (both: jyä'shyäng'), town, ⊙ Kiasiang co. (pop. 145,185), E Pingyuan prov., China, near Grand Canal (Shantung line), 50 mi. ENE of Hotseh; tobacco processing, cotton weaving; beans, medicinal herbs. Until 1949 in Shantung prov.

Kiating or **Chia-ting** (both: jyä'dĭng'). **1** Town (1935 pop. 73,030), ⊙ Kiating co. (1946 pop. 256,175), S Kiangsu prov., China, 18 mi. NW of Shanghai; cotton spinning and weaving; rice, wheat, beans. **2** Town, Szechwan prov., China: see LOSHAN.

Kiaton, Greece: see SIKYONIA.

Kiatzewan, China: see SINHSIEN, Shansi prov.

Kiawah Island (kē'ŭwä, -wô), Charleston co., SE S.C., one of Sea Isls., 11 mi. SW of Charleston; c.10 mi. long. Separated by narrow channel from Johns Isl. (N); Stono R. is E, Atlantic Ocean S.

Kiawang or **Chia-wang** (both: jyä'wäng'), iron-mining settlement, SW Shantung prov., China, 20 mi. NE of Süchow and on spur of Tientsin-Pukow RR. Sometimes called Kiakiawang.

Kiayi or **Chiayi** (both: jyä'yē'), Jap. *Kagi* (kä'gē), town (1940 pop. 92,428), W central Formosa, 35 mi. NNE of Tainan; major sugar-cane and lumbering center, in agr. area (rice, tobacco, pineapples, sweet potatoes); sugar milling, distilling, cement and tile mfg., sawmilling. Linked by railroad with Ali Shan lumbering dist. Radio station. Buddhist shrines, warm springs near by. Dates from 18th cent.

Kiayü or **Chia-yü** (both: jyä'yü'), town (pop. 17,598), ⊙ Kiayü co. (pop. 155,571), SE Hupeh prov., China, 45 mi. SW of Hankow and on Yangtze R.; tea, cotton, hemp; fisheries.

Kiayükwan or **Chia-yü-kuan** (jyä'yü'gwän'), town, NW Kansu prov., China, on Silk Road and 13 mi. WNW of Kiuchüan, across Peita R. and at W end of Great Wall; petroleum field near by.

Kibali-Ituri, district, Belgian Congo: see IRUMU.

Kibali River, Belgian Congo: see UELE RIVER.

Kibanga or **Kibanga Port** (kēbăng'gä), town, Buganda prov., S Uganda, small port on L. Victoria, 22 mi. SE of Kampala; cotton, coffee, sugar cane; fisheries.

Kibangou (kēbäng-gōō'), village, W Middle Congo territory, Fr. Equatorial Africa, on Niari R. and 50 mi. NNW of Dolisie.

Kibartai, Lithuania: see KYBARTAI.

Kibati, Belgian Congo: see GOMA.

Kibbi, Gold Coast: see KIBI.

Kibbutz Mahar, Israel: see GEVARAM.

Kibby Mountain (3,638 ft.), W Maine, peak in extreme N Franklin co., 8 mi. NE of Chain Lakes.

Kiberen, France: see QUIBERON.

Kibi (kē'bē), town (pop. 4,655), Eastern Prov., central Gold Coast colony, 25 mi. WNW of Koforidua; gold- and diamond-mining center. Sometimes spelled Kibbi.

Kibi (kē'bē), town (pop. 8,255), Okayama prefecture, SW Honshu, Japan, 4 mi. W of Okayama, in agr. area (rice, wheat, peppermint, fruit); dried mushrooms, insecticide. Formed 1937 by combining villages of Nazukawa and Niwase.

Kibigori (kēbēgō'rē), village, Nyanza prov., W Kenya, on railroad and 20 mi. E of Kisumu; sugar cane, cotton, peanuts, sesame, corn. Also spelled Kibigore.

Kibish River (kĭbĭsh'), rises in highlands of SW Ethiopia near Maji, flows S, forming part of boundary with Anglo-Egyptian Sudan, into N end of L. Rudolf; total length, c.135 mi.; generally dry.

Kibo, peak, Tanganyika: see KILIMANJARO.

Kibombo (kēbōm'bō), village, Kivu prov., central Belgian Congo, on the Lualaba, on railroad, and 55 mi. NW of Kasongo; agr. center (rubber, cotton, rice); lumbering, rice processing, cotton ginning. Has R.C. mission. Lualaba R. is navigable bet. here and Kasongo.

Kibondo (kēbōn'dō), village, Western Prov., W Tanganyika, near Ruanda-Urundi border, on road and 120 mi. NNE of Kigoma; cotton, peanuts, corn, coffee.

Kibongoto (kēbông-gō'tō), village, Northern Prov., Tanganyika, on SW slope of Kilimanjaro, 18 mi. NW of Moshi. Tuberculosis hosp.

Kibos (kē'bōs), village, Nyanza prov., W Kenya, on railroad and 8 mi. ENE of Kisumu; sugar-cane center; cotton, peanuts, sesame, corn. Area inhabited by Nilotic Kavirondo tribe.

Kibra, Russian SFSR: see KURATOVO.

Kibungu (kēbōōng'gōō), village, E Ruanda-Urundi, in Ruanda, 35 mi. ESE of Kigali; customs station near Tanganyika border; noted African game hunting grounds in vicinity.

Kiburg, Switzerland: see KYBURG.

Kibwezi (kēbwĕ'zē), town (pop. c.150), S central Kenya, on railroad and 110 mi. SE of Nairobi; rubber and sisal center; dairy farming.

Kicevo or **Kichevo** (both: kē'chĕvô), Serbo-Croatian *Kičevo*, village (pop. 7,099), W Macedonia, Yugoslavia, on Treska R., on narrow-gauge railroad and 40 mi. SW of Skoplje; market center for cattle region.

Kichha (kĭch'ŭ), village, Naini Tal dist., N Uttar Pradesh, India, 32 mi. S of Naini Tal; sugar processing; rice, wheat, mustard, gram.

Kichma (kēch'mŭ), village (1926 pop. 281), S Kirov oblast, Russian SFSR, 55 mi. NE of Ioshkar-Ola; coarse grain, flax.

Kichmengski Gorodok or **Kichmengskiy Gorodok** (kēch'myĭn-gskē-gŭrŭdôk'), village (1939 pop. over 500), E Vologda oblast, Russian SFSR, on Yug R., on Sharya-Kotlas road and 55 mi. SSW of Veliki Ustyug; flax processing.

Kichow. 1 Town, Hopeh prov., China: see KIHSIEN. **2** Town, Hupeh prov., China: see KICHUN.

Kichow, Chichou, or **Ch'i-chou** (all: chē'jō'), Jap. *Keishu* (kā'shōō), town (1935 pop. 5,523), W central Formosa, 23 mi. SSW of Taichung and on Choshui R.; sugar milling; rice, sugar cane, jute, sesame.

Kichun or **Ch'i-ch'un** (both: chē'chōōn'), town (pop. 32,085), ⊙ Kichun co. (pop. 487,924), SE Hupeh prov., China, 70 mi. SE of Hankow and on Yangtze R.; wheat, cotton, ramie, silk, medicinal herbs. Until 1912 called Kichow.

Kickamuit River (kĭkŭmū'ĭt), E R.I., rises in Warren town, near Mass.-R.I. line, flows c.4 mi. generally SE, bet. Bristol and Warren, to Mt. Hope Bay.

Kickapoo, Lake, Texas: see LITTLE WICHITA RIVER.

Kickapoo Creek. 1 In central Ill., rises in McLean co., flows c.60 mi. SW to Salt Creek SE of Lincoln.

2 In N central Ill., rises NW of Peoria, flows c.25 mi. SE to Illinois R. just below Peoria.

Kickapoo River, SW Wis., rises S of Tomah, flows c.90 mi. SSW to Wisconsin R. 13 mi. E of Prairie du Chien.

Kickelhahn, Germany: see ILMENAU.

Kicking Horse Pass (5,339 ft.), in Rocky Mts., on Alta.–B.C. border, 35 mi. NW of Banff; 51°27′N 116°18′W. Highest point on Canadian Pacific transcontinental route, it was discovered 1858 by Dr. Hector of the Palliser expedition.

Kidal (kēdäl′), village (pop. c.750), E Fr. Sudan, Fr. West Africa, at S foot of Adrar des Iforas, 170 mi. NE of Gao. Saharan post, radio and meteorological station.

Kidder, county (□ 1,377; pop. 6,168), central N.Dak.; ⊙ Steele. Agr. area watered by several small lakes, largest being Horsehead L. Grain refining; diversified farming (livestock, poultry, wheat, barley, rye). Formed 1873.

Kidder, town (pop. 222), Caldwell co., NW Mo., 29 mi. W of Chillicothe.

Kidderminster (kĭ′dŭrmĭnstŭr), municipal borough (1931 pop. 28,917; 1951 census 37,423), N Worcester, England, on Stour R. and 15 mi. N of Worcester; carpet-weaving center (since 1735); woolen milling; mfg. of textile machinery, electrical equipment, soap. Has 15th-cent. church and 17th-cent. almshouses.

Kidderpore (kĭd′ŭrpôr), section of Calcutta municipality, SE West Bengal, India, 2.5 mi. SW of city center; main dockyards of Calcutta; railroad workshop; general engineering works; hosiery mfg., sawmilling.

Kides, Finland: see KITEE.

Kidete (kēdē′tä), town, Eastern Prov., Tanganyika, on railroad and 18 mi. NW of Kilosa; cotton, sisal, rice, corn.

Kidira (kēdē′rä), village, E Senegal, Fr. West Africa, on Falémé R. (Fr. Sudan border), on Dakar-Niger RR, 50 mi. W of Kayes; hardwood, peanuts.

Kidlington, town and parish (pop. 1,683), central Oxfordshire, England, on Cherwell R. and 5 mi. N of Oxford; agr. market. Has 13th-cent. church.

Kidnappers, Cape, S extremity of Hawke Bay, E N.Isl., New Zealand, 15 mi. SE of Napier; 39°38′S 177°6′E; bird sanctuary.

Kidsgrove, urban district (1931 pop. 9,938; 1951 census 16,231), NW Stafford, England, 6 mi. NNW of Stoke-on-Trent; coal mining; has coke ovens and metalworks.

Kidugalo or **Kidugallo** (kēdōōgä′lō), village, Eastern Prov., Tanganyika, on railroad and 37 mi. E of Morogoro; sisal.

Kidwelly, Welsh *Cydweli* (both: kĭdwĕ′lē), municipal borough (1931 pop. 3,159; 1951 census 3,007), S Carmarthen, Wales, on Carmarthen Bay of Bristol Channel, 8 mi. S of Carmarthen; steel milling, tin smelting, brick mfg.; center of coal-mining dist. Has ruins of castle, built c.1106 by Bishop Roger of Salisbury, rebuilt c.1270. Church dates from 13th cent.

Kiedrich (kē′drĭkh), village (pop. 2,920), in former Prussian prov. of Hesse-Nassau, W Germany, after 1945 in Hesse, in the Rheingau, 7 mi. W of Wiesbaden; mineral spring. Noted vineyards on nearby Gräfenberg.

Kief (kēf), village (pop. 135), McHenry co., central N.Dak., 50 mi. ESE of Minot.

Kiefer (kē′fŭr), town (pop. 275), Creek co., central Okla., 15 mi. S of Tulsa, in agr. and oil area.

Kiefersfelden (kē′fŭrsfĕl″dŭn), village (pop. 4,324), Upper Bavaria, Germany, on E slope of the Bavarian Alps, on the Inn and 2 mi. N of Kufstein, on Austrian border; cement works; marble quarries.

Kiehchow, China: see WUTU.

Kiehsiu or **Chieh-hsiu** (both: jyĕ′shyō′), town, ⊙ Kiehsiu co. (pop. 123,108), S central Shansi prov., China, on Fen R., on railroad and 20 mi. SE of Fenyang; wheat, kaoliang, medicinal herbs.

Kiel (kēl), city (□ 25; 1939 pop. 273,735; 1946 pop. 214,335; 1950 pop. 253,857), ⊙ Schleswig-Holstein, NW Germany, Baltic harbor on Kiel Firth, at E end of Kiel Canal, 55 mi. NNE of Hamburg; until 1945, Germany's chief naval base; 54°20′N 10°9′E. Industry is concentrated at E bank dists. of Ellerbek, Gaarden, Wellingdorf, and NEUMÜHLEN-DIETRICHSDORF; mfg. of shipping and textile machinery, light metals, precision instruments, chemicals, textiles, garments, leather goods, ceramics; fish processing (smoked sprats), flour milling, brewing. The large shipyards were dismantled after 1945. Building of fishing boats; deep-sea fishing. Extensive harbor installations on inner firth. Airport at N suburb HOLTENAU (E end of Kiel Canal). Severe Second World War destruction included: naval base, situated at dists. of Wik (also free harbor) and Friedrichsort; univ. dist.; old town; 13th-cent. castle, where Tsar Peter III was born. Has noted univ. (founded 1665), with institute for world economy (1914), research institute for dairying (1925), teachers col. Town was chartered 1242. Was member of Hanseatic League. Treaty of Kiel (1814) transferred Norway from Denmark to Sweden, and Helgoland to England. Naval base established 1871. Became (1917) ⊙ Schleswig-Holstein. Ger. revolution of 1918 began with mutiny of fleet at Kiel.

Kiel, city (pop. 2,129), on Manitowoc-Calumet co. line, E Wis., on Sheboygan R. and 20 mi. NW of Sheboygan; trade center for dairying area; cheese processing, woodworking, mfg. of machinery. Inc. 1920.

Kiel Canal, NW Germany, connecting the North Sea (Elbe estuary at Brunsbüttelkoog) with the Baltic (at Kiel suburb of Holtenau); length 61 mi., depth 37 ft., surface width 338 ft.; locks at both ends; spanned by 7 bridges. Built 1887–95 to facilitate shifting of Ger. fleet bet. North Sea and the Baltic, and to connect Hamburg directly with Baltic trade. Enlarged 1907–14. Its international status (proclaimed by Treaty of Versailles) was repudiated by Hitler in 1936. Frequently bombed in Second World War. It was also called Kaiser Wilhelm Canal (for William II of Germany) until after First World War, and it is now also called the North Sea–Baltic Canal (Ger. *Nord-Ostsee-Kanal*).

Kielce (kyĕl′tsĕ), province [Pol. *województwo*] (□ 7,545; pop. 1,701,656), SE central Poland; ⊙ Kielce. Upland region with rolling hills rising to 2,004 ft. in Gory Swietokrzyskie range; drained by Vistula (S and E boundary), Pilica (N boundary), Nida, and Kamienna rivers. Textile milling, metalworking, mfg. of leather goods and trucks (Starachowice) are among chief industries. Principal crops are rye, potatoes, oats, wheat, barley, flax; livestock. Largest cities: Radom, Kielce, Ostrowiec, Wierzbnik, Skarzysko. Boundaries of pre-Second World War prov. (□ 9,880; 1931 pop. 2,935,697) were changed by transfer of territory to Katowice and Krakow provs. Includes greater part of former Keltsy (Kielce) and Radom govts. of Rus. Poland.

Kielce, Rus. *Keltsy* or *Kel′tsy* (kĕl′tsē), city (pop. 49,960), ⊙ Kielce prov., SE central Poland, 65 mi. NNE of Cracow, in Gory Swietokrzyskie. Rail junction; trade center; ironworks; mfg. of railroad cars, munitions, bricks; brewing, tanning, flour milling, food processing, sawmilling; lime and marble works; stone quarries. Known since 12th cent.; owned by bishops of Cracow until 1818. Passed 1795 to Austria, 1815 to Rus. Poland, where it was ⊙ Keltsy govt.; returned to Poland in 1919. Developed in late-19th cent. following building of railroad. In Second World War, a Ger. administrative hq.

Kieldrecht (kēl′drĕkht), agr. village (pop. 4,072), East Flanders prov., N Belgium, 9 mi. N of St-Nicolas, near Netherlands border.

Kiel Firth (kēl), Ger. *Kieler Förde* (kē′lŭr fûr′dŭ), estuarine inlet and best natural harbor of the Baltic, NW Germany; 10 mi. long, 4 mi. wide at mouth. Kiel city extends on both sides of inner firth (5 mi. long, 1.5 mi. wide, 26–52 ft. deep); industrial dists. with wharves are on E bank; free port (built 1924) and mouth of Kiel Canal are on W bank.

Kiembe Samaki (kyĕm′bä sämä′kē), village, near W coast of Zanzibar, 4 mi. SSE of Zanzibar town; fish market. Airport near by.

Kien, province, China: see KWEICHOW.

Kien, river, China: see KIEN RIVER.

Kienan or **Ch'ien-an** (both: chyĕn′än′), town, ⊙ Kienan co. (pop. 81,559), NW Kirin prov., Manchuria, 85 mi. NW of Changchun, at Heilungkiang line. The name Kienan was formerly applied to a town 50 mi. NW of Changchun.

Kienan (kyĕn′-än′), town, ⊙ Kienan prov. (□ 350; 1943 pop. 428,700), N Vietnam, in Tonkin, in Thaibinh R. delta, 55 mi. ESE of Hanoi; tobacco plantations; silk spinning, salt extraction. Meteorological observatory. Formerly called Phulien.

Kienchang or **Chien-ch'ang** (both: jyĕn′chäng′). **1** Town, ⊙ Kienchang co., N central Jehol prov., Manchuria, 20 mi. ENE of Chihfeng. Called Kienchangying until 1949. **2** Town, Jehol prov., Manchuria: see LINGYÜAN. **3** Town, Kiangsi prov., China: see NANCHENG.

Kiencheng or **Ch'ien-ch'eng** (both: chyĕn′chŭng′), town, ⊙ Kiencheng co. (pop. 89,460), W Hunan prov., China, near Kweichow-Szechwan line, 55 mi. N of Chihkiang; rice, wheat, beans. Coal and mercury mining. Called Kienchow until 1913, and Kienhsien, 1913–14.

Kienchow. 1 Town, Hunan prov., China: see KIENCHENG. **2** Town, Shensi prov., China: see KIENHSIEN. **3** Town, Szechwan prov., China: see KIENKO. **4** or **Kienchownan,** town, Szechwan prov., China: see KIENYANG.

Kienchwan or **Chien-ch'uan** (both: jyĕn′chwän′), town (pop. 4,907), ⊙ Kienchwan co. (pop. 54,551), NW Yunnan prov., China, 55 mi. NNW of Tali; alt. 7,447 ft.; rice, millet, beans, timber. Iron mines near by.

Kiengmai, Thailand: see CHIANGMAI.

Kienho or **Chien-ho** (both: jyĕn′hŭ′), town (pop. 2,156) ⊙ Kienho co. (pop. 64,450), E Kweichow prov., China, 35 mi. SSE of Chenyüan and on upper Yüan R.; cotton textiles, embroideries; timber, rice, millet, beans. Until 1914, Tsingkiang.

Kienhsien or **Ch'ien-hsien** (both: chyĕn′shyĕn′). **1** Town, Hunan prov., China: see KIENCHENG. **2** Town (pop. 8,877), ⊙ Kienhsien co. (pop. 162,687), SW Shensi prov., China, 45 mi. WNW of Sian and on road to Lanchow; commercial center; cattle raising, agr. Until 1913, Kienchow.

Kien Ki, China: see KIEN RIVER, Fukien prov.

Kienkiang or **Ch'ien-chiang** (both: chyĕn′jyäng′), town (pop. 11,321), ⊙ Kienkiang co. (pop. 136,306), SE Szechwan prov., China, on affluent of Kien R. and 85 mi. ESE of Fowling; rice, millet, wheat, tea, tobacco.

Kien Kiang, river, China: see KIEN RIVER, Kweichow prov.

Kienkiao or **Chien-ch'iao** (both: jyĕn′chyou′), town, N Chekiang prov., China, on railroad to Shanghai and 5 mi. NE of Hangchow, near estuary of Tsientang R.; airport; air force training center.

Kienko or **Chien-ko** (both: jyĕn′gŭ′), town (pop. 11,881), ⊙ Kienko co. (pop. 251,576), NW Szechwan prov., China, 40 mi. NW of Langchung; silk and cotton textiles, rice, sweet potatoes, wheat, rapeseed, peanuts, sugar cane. Until 1913 called Kienchow.

Kienli or **Chien-li** (both: jyĕn′lē′), town (pop. 19,534), ⊙ Kienli co. (pop. 487,176), S Hupeh prov., China, 55 mi. SE of Kiangling and on Yangtze R. (Hunan border); cotton-textile and pottery mfg.; rice, wheat, ramie, indigo, medicinal herbs.

Kiennan or **Ch'ien-nan** (both: chyĕn′nän′), town (pop. 5,546), ⊙ Kiennan co. (pop. 64,282), SW Kiangsi prov., China, 85 mi. SW of Kanchow, in Kiulien Mts., on Kwangtung line; rice, wheat, corn, beans. Tungsten mines (S).

Kienning. 1 or **Chien-ning** (jyĕn′nĭng′), town (pop. 7,511), ⊙ Kienning co. (pop. 50,038), W Fukien prov., China, near Kiangsi line, 80 mi. WNW of Nanping, and on tributary of Min R.; rice, sweet potatoes, peanuts, rapeseed. Until 1913, the name Kienning was also applied to KIENOW. **2** or **Ch'ien-ning** (chyĕn′nĭng′), town, ⊙ Kienning co. (pop. 1,419), E Sikang prov., China, 55 mi. NW of Kangting and on highway; gold center. Lamasery. Until 1945 called Taining.

Kienow or **Chien-ou** (both: jyĕn′ō′), town (pop. 12,286), ⊙ Kienow co. (pop. 77,850), N Fukien prov., China, 30 mi. NNE of Nanping and on Kien R. (tributary of Min R.); commercial center in major rice-growing region; wheat, sweet potatoes, sugar cane, peanuts. Copper, coal, gold, iron mines. Until 1913 called Kienning.

Kienping or **Chien-p'ing** (both: jyĕn′pĭng′). **1** Town, Anhwei prov., China: see LANGKI. **2** Town, ⊙ Kienping co. (pop. 206,999), E central Jehol prov., Manchuria, 45 mi. SE of Chihfeng; gold deposits; kaoliang, livestock, furs, skins, and hides. Formerly called Sintsiu.

Kien River. 1 Chinese *Kien Ki* or *Chien Ch'i* (both: jyĕn′chē′), NW headstream of Min R., in Fukien prov., China, formed by 3 headstreams in vicinity of Kienow, flows c.50 mi. S to Min R. at Nanping. Navigable for small vessels. **2** Chinese *Kien Kiang* or *Ch'ien Chiang* (both: chyĕn′ jyäng′), river whose upper course, known as Wu River (wōō) is chief stream of Kweichow prov., China; 700 mi. long. Rises in Weining area near Yunnan border, traverses entire prov. from W to E, past Szenan (head of navigation) and Yenho, and into SE Szechwan to the Yangtze at Fowling.

Kienshih or **Chien-shih** (both: jyĕn′shû′), town (pop. 14,918), ⊙ Kienshih co. (pop. 252,008), SW Hupeh prov., China, near Szechwan line, 30 mi. NNE of Enshih; sulphur mining; iron deposits.

Kienshui or **Chien-shui** (both: jyĕn′shwā′), town (pop. 27,618), ⊙ Kienshui co. (pop. 148,362), SE central Yunnan prov., China, on railroad and 100 mi. S of Kunming; alt. 4,836 ft.; cotton textile mfg., rice milling; wheat, millet, beans, sugar cane. Coal mines near by. Formerly called Linan.

Kiensi or **Ch'ien-hsi** (both: chyĕn′shē′), town (pop. 20,228), ⊙ Kiensi co. (pop. 181,918), W central Kweichow prov., China, 50 mi. NW of Kweiyang; millet-growing center; cotton textiles; lacquer, tung oil, tobacco, timber, rice.

Kienteh. 1 or **Chien-te** (both: jyĕn′dŭ′), town (pop. 12,408), ⊙ Kienteh co. (pop. 126,629), NW central Chekiang prov., China, 65 mi. SW of Hangchow, and on Tsientang R. at mouth of Sinan R. (affluent from Anhwei); commercial center; exports paper, timber, indigo, honey, beeswax. Until 1914 called Yenchow. **2** or **Ch'ien-te** (both: chyĕn′dŭ′), town and oasis (pop. 12,737), N central Sinkiang prov., China, just N of Urumchi and on highway; cattle raising; agr. products.

Kienwei or **Chien-wei** (both: jyĕn′wā′), town (pop. 18,481), ⊙ Kienwei co. (pop. 538,543), SW Szechwan prov., China, 30 mi. SSE of Loshan and on right bank of Min R.; Chinese-wax processing, match mfg.; rice, sweet potatoes, sugar cane, medicinal plants. Coal and iron mines, saltworks near by.

Kienyang. 1 or **Chien-yang** (both: jyĕn′yäng′), town (pop. 12,286), ⊙ Kienyang co. (pop. 77,850), N Fukien prov., China, 50 mi. N of Nanping and on tributary of Min R.; rice, wheat, sweet potatoes, beans; tobacco processing. **2** or **Ch'ien-yang** (chyĕn′yäng′), town, ⊙ Kienyang co. (pop. 213,812), W Hunan prov., China, on Yüan R. and 20 mi. SE of Chihkiang; commercial center. Gold, antimony, and coal mining near by. **3** or **Ch'ien-yang** (chyĕn′yäng′), town (pop. 2,859), ⊙ Kienyang co. (pop. 45,940), SW Shensi prov., China, 15 mi. N of Paoki; cotton weaving, furniture mfg.; winegrowing; grain. **4** or **Chien-yang** (jyĕn′yäng′), town (pop. 21,422), ⊙ Kienyang co. (pop. 986,870), W Szechwan prov., China, on railroad and 35 mi. SE of Chengtu, and on To R. (head of navigation); sugar-milling center; exports hog bristles; produces rice, cotton, sweet potatoes, kaoliang, millet, beans, wheat. Saltworks near by. Until 1913 called Kienchow or Kienchownan [Chinese, = Kienchow South].

Kierspe (kēr'spŏŏ), village (pop. 8,734), in former Prussian prov. of Westphalia, W Germany, after 1945 in North Rhine-Westphalia, 6 mi. SSW of Lüdenscheid; forestry.

Kierunavaara, Sweden: see KIRUNA.

Kiester (kē'stûr), village (pop. 541), Faribault co., S Minn., on branch of Blue Earth R., near Iowa line, and 21 mi. ESE of Blue Earth, in agr. area; dairy products, cattle feed.

Kieta (kyā'tä), town on SE coast of Bougainville isl., N Solomons, in Territory of New Guinea. Former ⊙ Kieta dist. (which comprised BOUGAINVILLE and Buka isls.), it has been replaced by SOHANO off Buka isl.

Kietrz (kyĕch), Ger. *Katscher* (kä'chûr), town (1939 pop. 8,914; 1946 pop. 4,679) in Upper Silesia, after 1945 in Opole prov., S Poland, near Czechoslovak border, 10 mi. W of Ratibor (Raciborz); woolen milling, gypsum quarrying.

Kietz (kēts), village (pop. 1,156), Brandenburg, E Germany, frontier station on left bank of the Oder and 3 mi. SW of Küstrin, at E edge of Oder Marshes.

Kiev or **Kiyev** (kē'ĕf', kē'ĕv, kē'ĕf, Rus. kē'ŭf), oblast (□ 15,900; 1946 pop. estimate 3,500,000), central Ukrainian SSR; ⊙ Kiev. In Dnieper Lowland (N) and Volyn-Podolian Upland (S); drained by Dnieper R. and its affluents, Teterev, Desna, and Ros rivers. Wooded steppe region, clearing toward S. Flax, potatoes, buckwheat, forests in N part; truck produce in Kiev metropolitan area; sugar beets and wheat basic crops in center and S; orchards in extreme S (Uman) and SE (Smela). Dairy-cattle raising. Peat cutting NW of Kiev and near Smela, lignite mining at Zvenigorodka. Extensive sugar refining throughout center and S; flour milling, distilling. Chief mfg. centers: Kiev, Cherkassy, Uman, Smela, Belaya Tserkov, Fastov. Formed 1932.

Kiev or **Kiyev**, city (1926 pop. 513,637; 1939 pop. 846,293), ⊙ Ukrainian SSR and Kiev oblast, on right bank of Dnieper R. and 460 mi. SW of Moscow; 50°27'N 30°30'E. Third-largest (in 1939) city of USSR; major transportation and mfg. center; junction of Dnieper R. traffic, 4 rail lines, and many highways. Mfg. of lathes, electric motors, fire-fighting equipment, agr. machines, rolling stock, cables, telephone and radio equipment, motorcycles; shipbuilding, silk and cotton milling, clothing and shoe mfg., flour milling. One of leading cultural centers of USSR; site of Ukrainian Acad. of Sciences, univ., polytechnic, engineering, and trade schools, medical, teachers, and agr. colleges. Has picture gall., theater of opera and ballet, ethnographical, historical, art, geological, and other museums, 1,000,000-volume natl. library, rubber and peat research institute, and numerous other technical and scientific institutes. Has Byzantine cathedral of St. Sophia (11th cent.), cathedral of St. Vladimir (completed 1896), church of St. Cyril (dating from Middle Ages), baroque church of St. Andrew (145 ft. high; built 1750 by Rastrelli), and monastery of St. Michael (11th cent.). Most important and oldest monastery is the former Lavra (now a mus. city), with 18th-cent. bell tower (302 ft. high), underground Pechersk monastery (11th cent.; consists of caves; formerly an important place of pilgrimage), 17th-cent. printing plant, and mus. of religious antiquities. Kiev includes Podol, the old commercial dist. on low Dnieper R. bank (N), old city (E center), hilly Pechersk-Lavra dist. (SE), govt. and administrative quarter (center), and railroad station and yards (W). Outlying residential and health resorts include Pushcha-Voditsa and Kurenevka (NW), and Svyatoshino and Belichi (W). Kiev has 3 bridges across Dnieper R.; includes left-bank suburb of Darnitsa, rail junction and site of many industries (car building, meat packing, lumber milling, rubber reclaiming, artificial-fiber mfg.). Located on great river trade route bet. Scandinavia and Byzantium, Kiev dates from 8th cent. First Slav inhabitants were absorbed by Varangians (862), and city became ⊙ Kievan Russia, flourishing in 11th cent. Declined in 12th cent.; overrun and plundered by Mongols (1240); successively under Lithuania and Poland; annexed (1667) to Russia. Developed as trading and industrial (sugar) center in 19th cent. Scene of early revolutionary struggles and pogrom (1905). Became (1917) ⊙ newly proclaimed Ukrainian SSR; remained seat of govt. except during repeated foreign occupations (1917–20) and when Kharkov was ⊙ (1920–34). In Second World War, held (1941–43) by Germans. After its liberation, only 200,000 of its pop. remained; Germans had massacred more than 50,000 Jews and wrecked large sections of the city before abandoning it. Reconstruction work began immediately and progressed swiftly; Kiev was soon reported to have again reached its pre-war pop.

Kiffa (kēf'fä), village, S Mauritania, Fr. West Africa, 150 mi. N of Kayes, Fr. Sudan; millet, gum arabic; sheep, goats, cattle; big game.

Kifisia, Greece: see KEPHISIA.

Kifisos River or **Kifissos River**, Greece: see CEPHISUS RIVER.

Kifrabhum, Syria: see KAFR BEHUM.

Kifri (kĭ'frē) or **Kufri** (kŏŏ'frē), village, Kirkuk prov., NE Iraq, 60 mi. SE of Kirkuk; barley, wheat, sheep raising. Sometimes spelled Kefri; also called Salahiya and Zeng Abad.

Kift, Egypt: see QIFT.

Kiga, Japan: see KEGA.

Kigali (kēgä'lē), town (1949 pop. 1,855), ⊙ Ruanda (□ 9,457; 1949 pop. 1,873,547), in Ruanda-Urundi, 110 mi. NNE of Usumbura; native trade center (cattle, hides, coffee, African food staples). Tin mined in vicinity. R.C. mission. Airport.

Kigezi, district, Uganda: see KABALE.

Kigi (kēyē'), Turkish *Kiği*, village (pop. 1,072), Bingol prov., E central Turkey, 30 mi. NNW of Bingol; grain.

Kigoma (kēgō'mä), town (pop. c.1,000), W Tanganyika, on L. Tanganyika, 220 mi. W of Tabora; rail-steamer transfer point at W terminus of Central RR from Dar es Salaam; 4°52'S 29°38'E. Lake navigation to Albertville (Belgian Congo; 75 mi. SSW) and Usumbura (Ruanda-Urundi; 100 mi. NNW). Exports rice, vegetable oils, cotton, cured and dried fish. An important settlement of Arab slave traders until end of 19th cent. Because of its excellent harbor, it became rail terminus (1914) in preference to neighboring UJIJI (4 mi. SE). Made a free port for Belg. vessels after First World War; Belg. customs and warehouses were established here. Declined in 1940s, owing to decrease in transit traffic (tin, gold) from Belgian Congo.

Kigombe (kēgōm'bā), village, Tanga prov., NE Tanganyika, on Pemba Channel of Indian Ocean, 15 mi. S of Tanga; copra; fisheries.

Kigwe (kē'gwā), village, Central Prov., central Tanganyika, on railroad and 18 mi. WNW of Dodoma; peanuts, gum arabic, beeswax.

Kihnu or **Kikhnu** (kēkh'nŏŏ), island (□ 7.5) of Estonia, in Gulf of Riga, 25 mi. SW of Parnu; 4.5 mi. long, 2 mi. wide.

Kihsien. 1 or **Ch'i-hsien** (both: chē'shyĕn'), town, ⊙ Kihsien co. (pop. 375,934), N Honan prov., China, 30 mi. SE of Kaifeng; road junction; winegrowing; cotton weaving, tobacco and vegetable-oil processing. **2** or **Chi-hsien** (jē'shyĕn'), town, ⊙ Kihsien co. (pop. 292,937), SW Hopeh prov., China, 40 mi. WNW of Tehchow; wheat, millet, kaoliang. Until 1913 called Kichow. **3** or **Chi-hsien** (jē'shyĕn'), town, ⊙ Kihsien co. (pop. 285,437), NE Hopeh prov., China, 50 mi. ENE of Peking, near Great Wall (Jehol line); cotton, wheat, kaoliang, millet. Monasteries. Until 1913 called Kichow. **4** or **Ch'i-hsien** (chē'shyĕn'), town, ⊙ Kihsien co. (pop. 121,909), central Shansi prov., China, on Fen R., on railroad, and 35 mi. SSW of Taiyüan; wheat, kaoliang, beans. **5** or **Chi-hsien** (jē'shyĕn'), town, ⊙ Kihsien co. (pop. 30,049), SW Shansi prov., China, 45 mi. W of Linfen, near Yellow R. (Shensi border); millet, beans.

Kihu, Chihu, or **Ch'i-hu** (all: chē'hŏŏ'), Jap. *Keiko* (kā'kō), town (1935 pop. 2,908), W central Formosa, 9 mi. SSW of Changhwa; sugar milling; rice, sweet potatoes, fruit, livestock.

Kii (kē), former province in S Honshu, Japan; now Wakayama prefecture and part of Mie prefecture.

Kii Channel, Jap. *Kii-suido*, Japan, strait connecting Osaka Bay (NE) and Harima Sea of Inland Sea (E) with Philippine Sea (S); bet. E coast of Shikoku and S coast of Honshu; c.30 mi. N–S, c.35 mi. E–W. Contains oyster beds.

Kii-katsuura, Japan: see KATSUURA, Wakayama prefecture.

Kii-kinomoto, Japan: see KINOMOTO, Mie prefecture.

Kiima, Kazakh SSR: see KIMA.

Kii Peninsula, Jap. *Kii-hanto*, S Honshu, Japan, bet. Kii Channel (W) and Kumano Sea (E); terminates S at Shio Point; comprises Wakayama prefecture and parts of Nara and Mie prefectures; 80 mi. E–W, 60 mi. N–S. Forested interior, drained by Kumano R. SE section is a resort area; contains Yoshino-kumano Natl. Park (□ 214; established 1936), with scenic rapids, waterfalls, and anc. temples and shrines. Hot springs in SW.

Kiirun, Formosa: see KEELUNG.

Kiirunavaara, Sweden: see KIRUNA.

Kii-tanabe, Japan: see TANABE, Wakayama prefecture.

Kijabe (kējä'bā), town, Central Prov., S central Kenya, on railroad and 25 mi. NNW of Nairobi, on E slope of Great Rift Valley; alt. 6,787 ft.; coffee, wheat, corn, fruits; dairy farming. Africa Inland Mission. Junction for road to Narok and Mara goldfields. Base for ascent of Longonot volcano.

Kijal (kējäl'), town (pop. 2,065), S Trengganu, Malaya, on South China Sea, 8 mi. NE of Chukai; coconuts; fisheries.

Kijo, Korea: see KUSONG.

Kikagati (kēkägä'tē), village, Western Prov., SW Uganda, on Kagera R. opposite Murongo (Tanganyika) and 30 mi. S of Mbarara; tin-mining center.

Kikai (kēkī'), largest town (1950 pop. 10,999) on Kikai-shima of isl. group Amami-gunto, in Ryukyu Isls., on SW coast; sugar cane, sweet potatoes.

Kikai-shima (kēkī'shĭmä) or **Kikaigashima** (kēkīgä'shĭmä), island (□ 24; 1950 pop. 18,363) of isl. group Amami-gunto, in Ryukyu Islands, in the Philippine Sea 15 mi. E of Amami-O-shima; 9 mi. long, 3.5 mi. wide; hilly; fertile (sugar cane, sweet potatoes). Chief town, Kikai (SW).

Kikerino (kē'kyĭrēnŭ), town (1939 pop. over 500), W Leningrad oblast, Russian SFSR, 6 mi. ENE of Volosovo; porcelain center (electrical appliances).

Kikhchik (kēkh'chĭk), town (1948 pop. over 500), Kamchatka oblast, Khabarovsk Territory, Russian SFSR, on W coast of Kamchatka Peninsula, on Sea of Okhotsk, 40 mi. N of Ust-Bolsheretsk; fish cannery.

Kikhnu, Estonia: see KIHNU.

Kikiang or **Ch'i-chiang** (both: chē'jyäng'), town (pop. 19,955), ⊙ Kikiang co. (pop. 405,290), SE Szechwan prov., China, 35 mi. S of Chungking city; iron-mining center; rice, sweet potatoes, wheat.

Kikiawan or **Ch'i-chia-wan** (chē'jyä'wän'), town, E Hupeh prov., China, 20 mi. NNW of Hankow and on Peking-Hankow RR; commercial center.

Kikinda (kē'kĭndä), Hung. *Nagykikinda* (nŏ'dyŭkĭk"ĭndŏ), city (pop. 28,070), Vojvodina, N Serbia, Yugoslavia, 50 mi. NE of Novi Sad, in the Banat. Rail junction (Belgrade, Budapest, Bucharest lines); major wheat-trading center; flour milling, mfg. of ceramic products. Until c.1947, called Velika Kikinda.

Kikladhes, Greece: see CYCLADES.

Kiknur (kĕk'nŏŏr), village (1926 pop. 470), SW Kirov oblast, Russian SFSR, 27 mi. W of Yaransk; flax.

Kikombo (kēkōm'bō), town, Central Prov., central Tanganyika, on railroad and 15 mi. ESE of Dodoma; cotton, peanuts, gum arabic, beeswax.

Kikonai (kēkō'nī), town (pop. 11,547), SW Hokkaido, Japan, on Tsugaru Strait, 16 mi. WSW of Hakodate; fishing, agr. (rice, potatoes, soybeans); dairying.

Kikondja (kēkōn'jä), village, Katanga prov., SE Belgian Congo, on W shore of L. Kisale, 100 mi. ENE of Kamina; trade in manioc, palm oil, fish. R.C. and Protestant missions.

Kikori (kēkô'rē), town, Territory of Papua, SE New Guinea, 245 mi. NW of Port Moresby; rubber, coconuts.

Kikow or **Ch'i-k'ou** (both: chē'kō'), town, NE Chekiang prov., China, 7 mi. W of Fenghwa; tea, peaches, timber, bamboo.

Kiku, Japan: see KOKURA.

Kikuma (kēkŏŏ'mä), town (pop. 9,593), Ehime prefecture, N Shikoku, Japan, on Iyo Sea, 9 mi. W of Imabari; commercial center for agr. area (rice, sweet potatoes, tobacco); sake, charcoal, tiles.

Kikungiri, Uganda: see KABALE.

Kikuyu (kēkŏŏ'yŏŏ), village, Central Prov., S central Kenya, on railroad and 10 mi. W of Nairobi; coffee, wheat, corn. Church of Scotland Mission.

Kikuyu Escarpment, section of E rim of Great Rift Valley, in S central Kenya, just W of Nairobi; extends 60 mi. N-S bet. Kijabe and Kajiado; alt. c.8,000 ft. Kikuyu Plateau (E) is densely settled and descends to 5,000 ft. in Nairobi area.

Kikvidze (kĭkvē'dzĕ), village (1939 pop. over 2,000), NW Stalingrad oblast, Russian SFSR, on Buzuluk R. and 22 mi. NE of Novo-Annenski; wheat, sunflowers. Until c.1935, Preobrazhenskaya.

Kikwit (kē'kwēt), town (1948 pop. 7,739), ⊙ Kwango dist. (□ 57,111; 1948 pop. c.1,139,000), Leopoldville prov., SW Belgian Congo, on left bank of Kwilu R. and 250 mi. ESE of Leopoldville; commercial center, terminus of steam navigation; palm-oil milling, fiber growing. Has R.C. missions, hosp. for Europeans, trade and native teachers' schools. Airport.

Kil (chēl), village (pop. 1,102), Varmland co., W Sweden, 10 mi. NW of Karlstad; railroad center: 1st Swedish railroad was built (1849) bet. here and Fryksta (frük'stä"), a village at S end of L. Fryk, 2 mi. NE of Kil.

Kila, for Afghan names beginning thus: see QALA.

Kila Didar Singh (kĭl'ŭ dē'där sĭng), town (pop. 6,127), Gujranwala dist., E Punjab, W Pakistan, 10 mi. W of Gujranwala; wheat, rice. Also spelled Qila Didar Singh and Killa Didar Singh.

Kilakarai (kēlŭkŭrī'), town (pop. 14,303; 80% Moslem), Ramnad dist., S Madras, India, port on Gulf of Mannar, 10 mi. SSW of Ramnad; fishing center; exports coconuts, coir products, coral.

Kilambé (kēlämbā'), peak (5,580 ft.) in N spur of Cordillera Isabelia, N Nicaragua, near Coco R., 25 mi. ENE of Quilalí.

Kilantai Lake or **Chi-lan-tai Lake** (both: jē'län'dī'), salt lake in Ningsia section of Inner Mongolia, China, near Kansu border, 100 mi. W of Yinchwan, in Alashan Desert; 38°N 104°E. Salt extraction.

Kila Saifulla, W Pakistan: see KILLA SAIFULLA.

Kilasevalpatti or **Kilasevvalpatti** (kĭlŭsā'vŭlpŭt-tē), town (pop. 2,458), Ramnad dist., S Madras, India, 7 mi. NE of Tiruppattur, in cotton area.

Kilauea (kē'läwä'ŭ), village (pop. 763), NE Kauai, T.H.; cooperative sugar plantation run by laborers owning homesteads.

Kilauea, crater (alt. 4,000 ft.), S central Hawaii, T.H., 23 mi. SW of Hilo, on SE slope of Mauna Loa in Hawaii Natl. Park; one of the largest active craters in world. Surrounded by volcanic rock 200–500 ft. high; circumference c.8 mi.; contains the fiery pit HALEMAUMAU.

Kilbagie (kĭlbā'gē), village in Clackmannan parish, Clackmannan, Scotland; paper milling.

Kilbaha, Gaelic *Cill Bheathach*, fishing village, SW Co. Clare, Ireland, on Kilbaha Bay, small inlet on N shore of the Shannon estuary, 17 mi. ESE of Kilrush.

Kilbarchan (kĭlbärkh'ŭn), town and parish (pop. 7,511), central Renfrew, Scotland, on Black Cart Water and 2 mi. W of Johnstone; mfg. of sewing cotton, leather, chemicals; handloomed woolens.

Kilbeggan (kĭlbĕ'gŭn), Gaelic *Cill Bheagáin*, town (pop. 685), S Co. Westmeath, Ireland, on Brosna R. and 7 mi. N of Tullamore; agr. market (dairying; cattle, potatoes); alcohol distilling.

Kilberry (kĭlbĕ'rē), Gaelic *Cill Bheara*, village (district pop. 296), W Co. Kildare, Ireland, on Barrow R. and 4 mi. NNW of Athy; peat-digging center. Has ruins of 12th-cent. Reban Castle and of anc. abbey.

Kilbirnie (kĭlbûr'nē), industrial town and parish (pop. 8,193), N Ayrshire, Scotland, on Garnock R. and 10 mi. N of Irvine; steel milling. Has noted church, built 1654. Just E is Kilbirnie Loch, a lake 1½ mi. long, ½ mi. wide. Parish includes steel-milling town of Glengarnock, at S end of lake.

Kilbourn, Wis.: see WISCONSIN DELLS.

Kilbourne (kĭl'bôrn), village (pop. 374), Mason co., central Ill., 30 mi. NW of Springfield, in agr. area.

Kilbrannan Sound (kĭlbră'nŭn) or **Kilbrennan Sound** (–brĕ'nŭn), arm of the Firth of Clyde, Scotland, extending c.25 mi. N–S, separating Kintyre peninsula (W) and Arran (E); 3–10 mi. wide.

Kilburn, England: see WILLESDEN.

Kilchberg (kĭlkh'bĕrk), town (pop. 4,547), Zurich canton, N Switzerland, on L. of Zurich and 4 mi. S of Zurich; cotton textiles.

Kilchoan, Scotland: see ARDNAMURCHAN.

Kilchu (kēl'chōō'), Jap. *Kisshu* or *Kissyu* (both: kēs'shōō), town (1944 pop. 30,026), N.Hamgyong prov., N Korea, 60 mi. SSW of Chongjin; commercial center for stock-raising, lumbering, and agr. area; makes celluloid products. Pulp milling, magnesite mining. Formerly sometimes Kilju.

Kilcolman Castle (kĭlkŏl'mŭn), castle ruins in N Co. Cork, Ireland, 2 mi. NE of Buttevant. Castle was Edmund Spenser's residence for 8 years; he here wrote 1st 3 books of the *Faerie Queene*. Castle was sacked and burned in 1598.

Kilconquhar (kĭlkŏng'kŭr), agr. village and parish (pop. 1,211), E Fifeshire, Scotland, near the Firth of Forth, 2 mi. N of Earlsferry.

Kilcormac, Ireland: see FRANKFORD.

Kilcrea (kĭl"krē'ŭ), village, S central Co. Cork, Ireland, 11 mi. WSW of Cork; agr. (dairying; potatoes, oats). Has remains of Franciscan abbey founded 1465 by Cormac MacCarthy, and of anc. castle of the MacCarthys.

Kilcreggan, Scotland: see COVE AND KILCREGGAN.

Kilcullen (kĭlkŭ'lŭn), Gaelic *Cill Chuillinn an Droichid*, town (pop. 614), central Co. Kildare, Ireland, on the Liffey (bridge dates from 1319) and 7 mi. E of Kildare, at E end of The Curragh; agr. market (cattle, horses; potatoes). Near by are remains of anc. round tower and abbey.

Kilcunda (kĭlkŭn'dŭ), village (pop. 243), S Victoria, Australia, on Bass Strait and 55 mi. SSE of Melbourne, near Wonthaggi; coal mine.

Kildare (kĭldâr'), Gaelic *Chill Dara*, county (□ 654.1; pop. 64,849), Leinster, E Ireland; ⊙ Kildare. Bounded by cos. Carlow (S), Laoighis and Offaly (W), Meath (N), Dublin (NE), and Wicklow (E). Drained by Barrow and Liffey rivers, crossed by Grand and Royal canals. Surface is generally low and level, with fertile soil, becoming hilly in E. In center of co. is the plain called The CURRAGH; part of Bog of Allan is in N. Marble quarries. Peat is exploited in Kilberry region (W). Mainly agr. area: cattle and horse raising; potatoes, wheat, barley, oats. Industries include paper, cotton, woolen milling; iron founding, brewing, whisky distilling, mfg. of shoes, rope. Besides Kildare, other towns are Naas, Athy, Droichead Nua, and Maynooth. There are many anc. castles, round towers, and earthworks. Naas was an old ⊙ Leinster.

Kildare, Gaelic *Cill Dara*, town (pop. 2,109), ⊙ Co. Kildare, Ireland, in E central part of co., 30 mi. WSW of Dublin; agr. market (cattle, horses; potatoes); paper mills. First church was established here 490 by St. Bridget; it was succeeded by many other religious establishments, which were attacked by Danes and, later, in the Elizabethan wars. Cathedral, built 1229, was destroyed 1641 by Cromwell and rebuilt 1683. Adjoining is an old round tower. There are remains of 13th-cent. castle and of anc. Carmelite monastery.

Kildare, town (pop. 155), Kay co., N Okla., 7 mi. N of Ponca City, in agr. area.

Kildare, Cape, NW P.E.I., on the Gulf of St. Lawrence, 6 mi. SE of Tignish; 46°53'N 63°58'W. Reputed landfall (1534) of Jacques Cartier.

Kildin Island or **Kil'din Island** (kĭldyēn'), in Barents Sea, in Murmansk oblast, Russian SFSR, off N Kola Peninsula, 20 mi. NE of Murmansk; 13 mi. long, 5 mi. wide. Kildin village at E end; fisheries.

Kildinstroi or **Kil'dinstroy** (kĭldyĭnstroi'), town (1948 pop. over 2,000), NW Murmansk oblast, Russian SFSR, on Kola Peninsula, on Kola R., on Murmansk RR and 12 mi. S of Murmansk; brickworks.

Kildonan (kĭldō'nŭn), village, SW B.C., on S central Vancouver Isl., on an inlet of Barkley Sound, 18 mi. SSW of Port Alberni; herring shipping; fish hatchery, cold-storage plant, cannery.

Kildonan (kĭldŏ'nŭn), village and parish (pop. 1,454), SE Sutherland, Scotland, on Helmsdale R. and 21 mi. NNE of Dornoch.

Kildonan (kĭldō'nŭn), village, Salisbury prov., N Southern Rhodesia, in Mashonaland, in Umvukwe Range, 45 mi. NW of Salisbury; rail terminus; chrome mining.

Kildorrery (kĭldô'rē), Gaelic *Cill Dairbhre*, town (pop. 207), NE Co. Cork, Ireland, on Funshion R. and 12 mi. NE of Mallow; agr. market (dairying; potatoes, oats). Bowen's Court is 2 mi. W.

Kilemary (kēlyĭmä'rē), village, NW Mari Autonomous SSR, Russian SFSR, on Greater Kundysh R. and 40 mi. WNW of Ioshkar-Ola; lumbering.

Kilembe (kēlĕm'bā), village, Western Prov., Uganda, on E slopes of the Ruwenzori, 35 mi. SSW of Fort Portal; rich copper deposits.

Kilfinane or **Kilfinnane** (kĭlfĭ'năn), Gaelic *Cill Fhionáin*, town (pop. 661), SE Co. Limerick, Ireland, 15 mi. SE of Tipperary; agr. market (dairying, cattle; grain, potatoes). Has notable anc. rath.

Kilfinnane, Ireland: see KILFINANE.

Kilgore (kĭl'gôr). **1** Village (pop. 189), Cherry co., N Nebr., 20 mi. W of Valentine, near S.Dak. line. **2** City (pop. 9,638), on Gregg-Rusk co. line, E Texas, 24 mi. E of Tyler; oil-producing and oil-field supply center, in East Texas field. Seat of a jr. col. Settled 1872, inc. 1931. Great boom followed oil discovery, 1930.

Kili (kē'lē), coral island (pop. 184), Ralik Chain, Majuro dist., Marshall Isls., W central Pacific, c.500 mi. SE of BIKINI; 5°38'N 169°7'E; 1 mi. long; coconuts. Bikini natives moved here in 1949 from UJELANG. Sometimes called Hunter Isl.

Kiliclar Dag (kĭlŭchlär'dä), Turkish *Kılıçlar Dağ*, peak (10,154 ft.), NE Turkey, 21 mi. ENE of Mesudiye.

Kilien or **Ch'i-lien** (both: chē'lyĕn'), town, ⊙ Kilien co. (pop. 6,116), NE Tsinghai prov., China, 90 mi. NW of Sining. Cattle raising, coal mines near by. Until 1939 called Papao. The Kilien Mts. (NW) are a range of the Nan Shan.

Kilifarevo (kēlĕfä'rĕvô), village (pop. 3,127), Gorna Oryakhovitsa dist., N Bulgaria, on branch of Yantra R. and 5 mi. SSW of Tirnovo; flour milling, vegetable canning; agr.-machinery workshops. Has 14th-cent. church, 19th-cent. monastery.

Kilifi (kēlē'fē), town (pop. c.2,000), SE Kenya, in coastal protectorate, small land-locked port on Indian Ocean, 30 mi. NNE of Mombasa; sisal center; cotton, copra. Fisheries.

Kilik Pass (kĭ'lĭk) (alt. 15,600 ft.), in N extension of Karakoram mtn. system, on Kashmir-China border (undefined), near Afghanistan panhandle, 21 mi. NNW of Misgar (Kashmir), on important trade route from Gilgit to Kashgar.

Kilimafeza, gold-mining town (1948 pop. c.150), Lake prov., N Tanganyika, 95 mi. SE of Musoma. Also spelled Kilmafeza.

Kilimanjaro (kĭ"lĭmŭnjä'rō), highest mountain (19,565 ft.) of Africa, in NE Tanganyika near Kenya border, 175 mi. WNW of Mombasa and 125 mi. SSE of Nairobi. A massive extinct volcanic cone rising boldly above the E African plateau, the Kilimanjaro culminates in 2 principal summits, the higher, snow-capped Kibo (W) and the Mawenzi (17,300 ft.), connected by a broad saddle. S slopes are densely populated. There are coffee and sisal plantations near base (3–6,000 ft.); corn, bananas, and papaws are also grown here. A belt of hardwood forests extends from 6,000 to 10,000 ft.; grasslands reach 12,000-ft. level. Moshi (at S foot) is chief trade center and base for ascent. First Europeans to see it were the missionaries Rebman and Krapf in 1848; Kibo summit was reached 1889 by Meyer and Purtscheller. Sometimes spelled Kilimandjaro.

Kilimli (kĭlĭmlē'), village (pop. 9,775), Zonguldak prov., N Turkey, on Black Sea, on railroad and 3 mi. NE of Zonguldak; coal mines.

Kilinailau (kē'lēnī'lou), atoll (pop. c.500), Solomon Isls., SW Pacific, 45 mi. NE of Buka; 7 isls. on reef 12 mi. in diameter; coconuts; governed as part of Australian Territory of New Guinea under U.N. trusteeship.

Kilindini, Kenya: see MOMBASA.

Kilindoni, Tanganyika: see MAFIA ISLAND.

Kilingi-Nomme or **Kilingi-Nymme**, Est. *Kilingi-Nõmme* (kē'lĭngē-nŭ'mā), Ger. *Kurkund*, city (pop. 1,445), SW Estonia, on railroad and 25 mi. SE of Parnu; agr. market; fodder crops, flax, livestock.

Kilinochchi (kĭlĭnō'chē), village (pop., including near-by villages, 1,997), Northern Prov., Ceylon, 32 mi. SE of Jaffna; agr. colony (irrigation project).

Kilis (kĭ'lĭs), city (pop. 27,048), Gaziantep prov., S Turkey, near Syrian line, 29 mi. SSW of Gaziantep; olives, grain, sesame, vetch, cotton.

Kiliya (kē'lyēŭ), Rum. *Chilia-Nouă* (kē'lyä-nō'ōōŭ) [=new Kiliya], city (1941 pop. 15,536), S Izmail oblast, Ukrainian SSR, in Bessarabia, port on Kiliya (N) arm (Rum. border) of Danube R. delta, 22 mi. ENE of Izmail; fishing center; flour milling, tanning, sawmilling. Across the Danube arm is Chilia-Veche [=old Kiliya], Rum. fishing village (1941 pop. 3,866) with ruins of 14th-cent. Moldavian fortress. Kiliya was (1941–44) ⊙ Rum. Chilia dept. (1941 pop. 136,469). Its cession to USSR in 1940 was confirmed 1947.

Kilju, Korea: see KILCHU.

Kilkee (kĭlkē'), Gaelic *Cill Chaoidhe*, town (pop. 1,804), SW Co. Clare, Ireland, on Moore Bay, small inlet of the Atlantic, 8 mi. WNW of Kilrush; seaside resort.

Kilkeel (kĭlkēl'), urban district (1937 pop. 2,549; 1951 census pop. 2,329), S Co. Down, Northern Ireland, on Irish Sea at mouth of Kilkeel R., 15 mi. ESE of Newry; fishing center, seaside resort.

Kilkenny (kĭlkĕ'nē), Gaelic *Chill Choinnigh*, county (□ 796; pop. 66,712), Leinster, SE Ireland; ⊙ Kilkenny. Bounded by cos. Waterford (S), Tipperary (W), Laoighis (N), and Carlow and Wexford (E). Drained by the Nore, Barrow, Suir rivers. Surface is generally hilly, rising to 1,694 ft. on Mt. Brandon, with fertile river valleys. Cattle raising; dairying; barley and potato growing are important. Coal (anthracite) is mined in Castlecomer region; marble and limestone are quarried. Industries include tanning, flour and woolen milling, brewing, mfg. of shoes, hosiery, furniture. Besides Kilkenny, other towns are Callan, Gorey, Thomastown, Castlecomer. Co. is generally coextensive with anc. kingdom of Ossory. There are several round towers, numerous ecclesiastical remains, and traces of anc. earthworks.

Kilkenny, Gaelic *Cill Choinnigh*, urban district (pop. 10,291), ⊙ Co. Kilkenny, Ireland, in N central part of co., on the Nore and 65 mi. SW of Dublin; woolen milling, brewing, mfg. of shoes, hosiery, furniture, cattle feed. Main part of Kilkenny, or Englishtown, is divided from district of Irishtown by small river; strife bet. the inhabitants of the 2 districts may have given rise to the stories of the Kilkenny Cats. Kilkenny Castle was built 1192 by earl of Pembroke on site of earlier fortress of Strongbow. In Irishtown are: Cathedral of St. Canice (13th cent.), seat of Protestant dioceses of Ossory, Ferns, and Leighlin; and R.C. Cathedral of St. Mary (1857), seat of R.C. diocese of Ossory. Among pupils of Protestant col. here were Swift, Congreve, and Bishop Berkeley. Other features of town are anc. round tower, St. John's Church (formerly chapel of hosp. founded c.1220), 13th-cent. St. Mary's Church, Shee's Almshouses (1594), and 1764 town hall. There are remains of 13th-cent. Dominican and Franciscan abbeys. Kilkenny was ⊙ kings of Ossory; c.1170 Strongbow established fortress here, and in 1202 episcopal see of Ossory was moved here from Aghab. In 14th, 16th, 17th cent. parliaments were held here. The Statute of Kilkenny (1367) prohibited intermarriage bet. English settlers and Irishmen. Town was hq. of the Confederates, 1642–48; in 1650 it was taken by Cromwell.

Kilkenny, village (pop. 174), Le Sueur co., S Minn., 15 mi. W of Faribault, in lake region; dairy products.

Kilkhampton, village and parish (pop. 856), NE Cornwall, England, 3 mi. NNE of Stratton; agr. market. Has 15th-cent. church.

Kilkich, Greece: see KILKIS.

Kilkieran Bay (kĭlkēr'ŭn), inlet (10 mi. long) of Galway Bay, SW Co. Galway, Ireland. Contains numerous isls., including Gorumna, Lettermore, and Lettermullen. At entrance is Mweenish isl.

Kilkis (kĭlkēs'), nome (□ 968; pop. 101,820), Macedonia, Greece; ⊙ Kilkis. Bordered N by Yugoslavia, W by the Paikon massif; is drained by Vardar R. Agr.: silkgrowing; cotton, tobacco, rice, wine, red peppers. Main centers are Kilkis and Goumenissa; served by railroads from Salonika to Belgrade and to Adrianople. Nome formed in 1930s.

Kilkis, Macedonian *Kukush*, city (pop. 10,201), ⊙ Kilkis nome, Macedonia, Greece, on highway and railroad, 25 mi. N of Salonika; road junction; trading center for cotton, tobacco, silk, wine. Called Kilkich under Turkish rule, 15th cent. to Balkan Wars (1912–13). Gr. victory here (1913) over Bulgarians.

Kilkivan, village (pop. 417), SE Queensland, Australia, 110 mi. NNW of Brisbane; mercury mine.

Killa Didar Singh, W Pakistan: see KILA DIDAR SINGH.

Killala (kĭlă'lŭ), Gaelic *Cill Alaidh*, town (pop. 414), NW Co. Mayo, Ireland, at head of Killala Bay, 25 mi. N of Castlebar; fishing port. It was formerly seat of bishopric, reputedly founded by St. Patrick; has cathedral dating from c.1670, and anc. round tower.

Killala Bay, inlet (7 mi. long, 6 mi. wide) of the Atlantic, bet. N Co. Mayo and NW Co. Sligo, Ireland. Receives Moy R. at head of bay; on SW shore is Killala.

Killaloe (kĭlŭlō′, –lōō′), Gaelic *Cill Dálua,* town (pop. 890), SE Co. Clare, Ireland, on the Shannon (bridged) at S end of Lough Derg, 13 mi. NE of Limerick; agr. market (potatoes, grain; dairying). Has cathedral, probably built 1182 by Donal O'Brien on site of church founded by St. Dalue in 7th cent.; former seat of a diocese. Killaloe or vicinity was site of Kincora, 10th-cent. palace of Brian Boru.

Killaloe Station (kĭlŭlōō′), village (pop. 628), SE Ont., near Golden L., 23 mi. SW of Pembroke; dairying, lumbering.

Killam (kĭ′lŭm), village (pop. 430), E Alta., 40 mi. ESE of Camrose; grain elevators.

Killamarsh, town and parish (pop. 4,906), NE Derby, England, 8 mi. SE of Sheffield; coal mining. Church has 15th-cent. tower.

Killarney (kĭlär′nē), town (pop. 1,091), SW Man., on Killarney L. (4 mi. long), 50 mi. SSE of Brandon; mfg. of agr. implements, cement; grain elevators; dairying, lumbering, stock raising. Resort. Site of experimental fruit farm.

Killarney, Gaelic *Cill Airne,* urban district (pop. 5,947)), central Co. Kerry, Ireland, near the Lakes of Killarney, 17 mi. SE of Tralee; tourist center in country noted for scenic beauty and mild climate; woolen milling, mfg. of shoes and lace, wood carving. Has R.C. cathedral built 1846 by Pugin, and palace of bishop of Kerry and Aghadoe diocese.

Killarney, Lakes of, 3 picturesque lakes in central Co. Kerry, Ireland, surrounded by mts. and famed for their beauty. Lough Leane (lŏkh lān′) or Lower Lake (5,000 acres; c.5 mi. long) contains Ross isl., with castle of the O'Donoghues, and Innisfallen isl., scene of Moore's poem and site of ruins of 6th-cent. abbey founded by St. Finian. On N shore of Muckross Lake, Middle Lake, or Lough Torc (680 acres) are remains of 15th-cent. Muckross Abbey. Upper Lake (430 acres) is S of Lough Leane. Macgillycuddy's Reeks tower over the lakes.

Killary Harbour (kĭlâ′rē), narrow inlet (12 mi. long) of the Atlantic, bet. Co. Mayo and Co. Galway, Ireland.

Killa Saifulla or **Qila Saifullah** (kĭl′ŭ sĭfōōl′lŭ), Zhob dist., NE Baluchistan, W Pakistan, near Zhob R., 80 mi. SW of Fort Sandeman; trades in wheat, millet, felts, carpets. Also spelled Kila Saifulla and Killa Saif-Ullah.

Killashandra, Ireland: see KILLESHANDRA.

Killashee (kĭlŭ-shē′), Gaelic *Cill na Sidhe,* agr. village (district pop. 394), W Co. Longford, Ireland, on the Royal Canal and 4 mi. SW of Longford; dairying; cattle, potatoes.

Killbuck, village (pop. 767), Holmes co., central Ohio, on Killbuck Creek and 33 mi. ESE of Mansfield.

Killbuck Creek, N Ohio, rises in region W of Akron, flows c.75 mi. S, past Wooster and Millersburg, to Walhonding R. 5 mi. NW of Coshocton.

Killburg, Germany: see KYLLBURG.

Killdeer, city (pop. 698), Dunn co., W central N.Dak., 33 mi. N of Dickinson and on Spring Creek; coal mines, livestock, dairy products, poultry, grain.

Killdeer Mountains, series of lofty buttes in W N.Dak.; they extend 10 mi. NE-SW and rise 600 ft. above surrounding countryside; alt. 3,000 ft.

Kill Devil Hill, N.C.: see KITTY HAWK.

Killeany (kĭlā′nē), town (pop. 161), SW Co. Galway, Ireland, on NE coast of Inishmore, Aran Isls., just SE of Kilronan; fishing port. In anc. times hq. of St. Enda or Eany, it has remains of several anc. churches and monastic establishments. Near by are Arkyn Castle and remains of anc. round tower and of prehistoric fort.

Killearnan (kĭlûr′nŭn), village and parish (pop. 705), SE Ross and Cromarty, Scotland, 6 mi. SSE of Dingwall. In parish is agr. village of Redcastle, on Beauly Firth, with castle built in 1179 by David, brother of William the Lion; reputedly the oldest inhabited castle in Scotland.

Killeen (kĭlēn′), city (pop. 7,045), Bell co., central Texas, c.45 mi. SW of Waco; market point in cotton, corn, livestock area. U.S. Fort Hood (formerly Camp Hood) and Gray Air Force Base are near. Settled 1882; inc. as city 1908.

Killegray (kĭ″lŭgrā′), island (pop. 5), Outer Hebrides, Inverness, Scotland, in the Sound of Harris, bet. Harris and North Uist; 2 mi. long, ½ mi. wide.

Killellan, Scotland: see HOUSTON.

Killeshandra or **Killashandra** (both: kĭ″lŭ-shăn′drŭ), Gaelic *Cill na Seanrátha,* town (pop. 427), W Co. Cavan, Ireland, on W shore of Lough Oughter, 7 mi. W of Cavan; agr. market (cattle, pigs; potatoes).

Killiecrankie, Pass of (kĭ″lēkrăng′kē), wooded defile through which flows Garry R. (a tributary of Tummel R.), NE Perthshire, Scotland, 3 mi. NW of Pitlochry. General Wade built road through the pass in 1732, and it is now used also by a railroad. At N end of pass was fought battle of Killiecrankie (1689), in which supporters of James II under John Graham of Claverhouse (Bonnie Dundee) defeated forces of William III under General Mackay. Claverhouse was killed here. Battle has been described by Scott and Macaulay.

Killik River, NW Alaska, rises in Brooks Range near 67°47′N 154°35′W, flows c.125 mi. N to Colville R. at 69°N 153°55′W; placer gold mining. Pop. of dist. in 1939 was 34.

Killin, town and parish (pop. 1,414), W central Perthshire, Scotland, at W end of Loch Tay, at mouth of Dochart R., 16 mi. N of Callander; woolen (tartan plaid) milling.

Killinek Island (20 mi. long, 2–9 mi. wide), SE Franklin Dist., Northwest Territories, at SE entrance of Hudson Strait, off N extremity of Labrador. NE extremity is Cape Chidley (60°23′N 64°26′W), usually considered to be N tip of Labrador. On W coast is Port Burwell trading post.

Killiney (kĭlĭ′nē), Gaelic *Cill Inghean Léinín,* residential town, SE Co. Dublin, Ireland, on small inlet of the Irish Sea, 3 mi. SSE of Dún Laoghaire. Has anc. stone monument. called Druid's Judgment Seat.

Killingly (kĭ′lĭnglē), town (1950 pop. 10,015), including industrial DANIELSON borough, Windham co., NE Conn., on Quinebaug R. and 18 mi. NE of Willimantic, on R.I. line. Mfg. (absorbent cotton, textiles, pins, insulation) at villages of East Killingly (1940 pop. 560), Goodyear (1940 pop. 700), Dayville (1940 pop. 715), and Attawaugan (1940 pop. 550); agr. (truck, dairy products, poultry). Includes South Killingly village. Settled c.1700, inc. 1708.

Killington Peak (4,241 ft.), S central Vt., E of Rutland, in recreational area; one of highest summits of Green Mts.

Killingworth, town (pop. 677), Middlesex co., S Conn., on Hammonasset R. and 20 mi. ENE of New Haven; dairy products, poultry. Has 18th-cent. houses, fine church (1817). State forest here.

Killini, Greece: see KYLLENE.

Killinkoski (kĭl′lĭn-kōs′kē), village in Virrat commune (pop. 12,428), Vaasa co., W Finland, in lake region, 60 mi. N of Tampere; lumber and pulp mills.

Killisnoo, Alaska: see HOOD BAY.

Killough (kĭlŏkh′), fishing village (pop. 1,143), SE Co. Down, Northern Ireland, on Killough Bay, small inlet of the Irish Sea, 6 mi. SSE of Downpatrick.

Killucan (kĭlōō′kŭn), Gaelic *Cill Lúcáin,* town (pop. 110), E Co. Westmeath, Ireland, 8 mi. E of Mullingar; agr. market (cattle, potatoes).

Kill Van Kull (kĭl″ văn kŭl′), NE N.J. and SE N.Y., narrow strait connecting Newark Bay and Upper New York Bay, bet. Staten Isl., N.Y., and Bayonne, N.J.; c.4 mi. long, ½ mi. wide. Spanned by Bayonne Bridge (1931).

Killybegs (kĭ″lēbĕgz′), Gaelic *Cealla Beaga,* town (pop. 742), S Co. Donegal, Ireland, on inlet of Donegal Bay, 15 mi. W of Donegal; fishing port.

Killyleagh (kĭlēlē′), town (pop. 1,778), E Co. Down, Northern Ireland, on W shore of Strangford Lough, 6 mi. NNE of Downpatrick; fishing port. Modern castle includes remains of anc. structure.

Kilmacolm (kĭlmŭkōm′), town and parish (pop. 5,402), N Renfrew, Scotland, 10 mi. W of Renfrew; resort.

Kilmafeza, Tanganyika: see KILIMAFEZA.

Kilmainham (kĭlmā′nŭm), Gaelic *Cill Mhaighneann,* W suburb (pop. c.15,000) of Dublin, Co. Dublin, Ireland. Parnell, confined in prison here, signed (1882) the Treaty of Kilmainham with Gladstone. Here also was hq. of commander of British forces in Ireland. In 7th cent. it was site of abbey.

Kilmallock (kĭlmă′lŭk), Gaelic *Cill Mocheallóg,* town (pop. 1,068), S Co. Limerick, Ireland, 18 mi. S of Limerick; agr. market (grain, potatoes; dairying). Two gates remain of anc. fortifications razed by Cromwell. Remains of old church incorporate a round tower. Town was once of great importance as hq. of the earls of Desmond. Near by are remains of 13th-cent. Dominican abbey.

Kilmarnock (kĭlmär′nŭk), burgh (1931 pop. 38,100; 1951 census 42,120), N Ayrshire, Scotland, on Kilmarnock Water (short tributary of Irvine R.) near its mouth on Irvine R., 19 mi. SSW of Glasgow; industrial center in mining area; mfg. of leather, shoes, carpets, agr. machinery, whisky, pharmaceuticals, oleomargarine; textile printing, woolen milling. McKie's library of Burnsiana and a Burns memorial are here. Burgh includes coal-mining suburb of KILMAURS (NW) and industrial suburb of RICCARTON (S).

Kilmarnock, town (pop. 689), Lancaster and Northumberland counties, E Va., near Chesapeake Bay, 50 mi. N of Newport News; fisheries, lumber mills, canneries (seafood, vegetables). Near-by Christ Church was built 1732.

Kilmartin (kĭlmär′tĭn), agr. village and parish (pop. 455), W Argyll, Scotland, 7 mi. NNW of Lochgilphead, in sheep-raising region. Near by are remains of 16th-cent. Carnassary Castle, built by Bishops of the Isles.

Kilmaurs (kĭlmôrz′), town and parish (pop. 4,396), N Ayrshire, Scotland, 2 mi. NW of Kilmarnock; coal mining. Near by is anc. Rowallan Castle, newest parts of which date from c.1560.

Kilmer, Camp, N.J.: see NEW BRUNSWICK.

Kilmersdon, town and parish (pop. 2,057), E Somerset, England, 2 mi. SSE of Radstock; coal mining. Has 15th-cent. church.

Kilmez or **Kil'mez'** (kēlmâs′), village (1926 pop. 1,249), SE Kirov oblast, Russian SFSR, on Kilmez R. and 50 mi. N of Vyatskiye Polyany; coarse grain; lumbering.

Kilmez River or **Kil'mez' River,** E central European Russian SFSR, rises 15 mi. W of Sergiyevski, flows 118 mi. SW and W, past Kilmez, to Vyatka R. opposite Shurma. Navigable for 75 mi.; lumber floating. Receives Loban (right) and Vala (left) rivers.

Kilmichael (kĭl″mī′kŭl), town (pop. 511), Montgomery co., central Miss., 10 mi. ESE of Winona.

Kilmorack (kĭlmô′rŭk), agr. village and parish (pop. 1,741), N Inverness, Scotland, on Beauly R. (Falls of Kilmorack) and 10 mi. W of Inverness. Near-by Beaufort Castle is seat of earls of Lovat, chiefs of Clan Fraser.

Kilmore (kĭlmôr′), town (pop. 1,328), S central Victoria, Australia, 36 mi. N of Melbourne; rail junction in livestock area; dairy plants.

Kilmuir, Scotland: see SKYE, ISLE OF.

Kilmun (kĭlmŭn′), fishing village, SE Argyll, Scotland, on Holy Loch (3-mi.-long inlet of the Firth of Clyde), 3 mi. N of Dunoon. There are remains of church founded 1442; 1st church was built here in 6th cent.

Kilnhurst, England: see RAWMARSH.

Kilo, Belgian Congo: see KILO-MINES; KILO-ÉTAT.

Kilo-État (kēlō′-ātä′) or **Kilo,** village, Eastern Prov., NE Belgian Congo, 28 mi. NE of Irumu; gold mining and trading center (alt. 3,280 ft.), with R.C. mission, school for native teachers. Lost its former importance through transfer (1919) of seat of gold operations to KILO-MINES. Sometimes called Vieux Kilo.

Kilofoss, Norway: see NAEROY FJORD.

Kilombero Valley, Tanganyika: see ITAKARA.

Kilómetro 100, Argentina: see CASTELLI, Chaco natl. territory.

Kilómetro 101, Argentina: see CONSCRIPTO BERNARDI.

Kilómetro 511, Argentina: see LLAJTA MAUCA.

Kilómetro 642 (kēlō′mātrō sāsyĕn′tōs kwärĕn′tä ē dōs′), village (pop. estimate 50), ⊙ Patiño dept. (□ c.9,000; 1947 pop. 23,489), central Formosa natl. territory, Argentina, on Bermejo R. and 190 mi. NW of Formosa; stock raising.

Kilómetro 924, Argentina: see ANGACO NORTE, town.

Kilómetro 1082, Argentina: see JOAQUÍN V. GONZÁLEZ.

Kilómetro 1172, Argentina: see CAMPO QUIJANO.

Kilómetro 1308, Argentina: see MUÑANO.

Kilo-Mines or **Kilo** (kēlō′, kē′lō), village, Eastern Prov., NE Belgian Congo, near right bank of Shari R. and 35 mi. NE of Irumu; alt. 3,936 ft. Center of major gold-mining and processing area employing c.13,000 native workers, with main gold fields at MONGBWALU, NIZI, TSI, ISURU, and KANGA. Power for smelting is supplied by 3 large hydroelectric plants on Shari R., notably at Soleniama (sōlĕnyä′mä), 8 mi. SSE. Kilo-Mines is also a commercial center and has several missions with educational institutions for natives, hosp. for Europeans. Gold was 1st discovered in area in 1895, mining started in 1905; seat of gold operations was transferred to Kilo-Mines from KILO-ÉTAT in 1919. Local activities are coordinated with those at WATSA into a single concern called Kilo-Moto. Kilo-Mines is also sometimes called Bambu (băm′bōō).

Kilosa (kēlō′sä), town (pop. c.2,500), E Tanganyika, on railroad and 160 mi. W of Dar es Salaam; agr. trade center; cotton, sisal, rice; gum arabic. An Arab settlement in middle 19th cent. Ilonga cotton experimental station is just NE. Tendigo swamp is E.

Kilpatrick, Scotland: see NEW KILPATRICK and OLD KILPATRICK.

Kilrenny (kĭlrĕ′nē), village (1931 pop. 2,122), E Fifeshire, Scotland, on the Firth of Forth, near its mouth on the North Sea, 9 mi. SE of St. Andrews; with adjacent Anstruther Easter and Anstruther Wester (see ANSTRUTHER), it forms one burgh (1931 pop. 3,325; 1951 census 2,991). Fishing port and seaside resort.

Kilronan (kĭlrō′nŭn), Gaelic *Cill Rónáin,* town (pop. 320), SW Co. Galway, Ireland, on NE coast of Inishmore, Aran Isls., 28 mi. WSW of Galway; fishing port. Near by are numerous remains of anc. churches, dating from early Christian era, and a large prehistoric fort.

Kilrush (kĭlrŭsh′), Gaelic *Cill Ruis,* urban district (pop. 3,351), SW Co. Clare, Ireland, on the Shannon estuary, 26 mi. SW of Ennis; 52°38′N 9°29′W; port and seaside resort, with dock installations; agr. market (grain, potatoes; dairying). Slate and flagstone are quarried near by. Off shore are Hog Isl. and Scattery Isl.

Kilsyth (kĭlsīth′), burgh (1931 pop. 7,551; 1951 census 9,915), S Stirling, Scotland, 7 mi. WSW of Denny and on Forth and Clyde Canal; coal and ironstone mining, hosiery knitting. The Wall of Antoninus passes town. Near by Montrose defeated the Covenanters under Baillie in 1645.

Kilsyth Hills, Scotland: see LENNOX HILLS.

Kiltamagh, Ireland: see KILTIMAGH.

Kiltan Island (kĭltăn′), coral island of Amin Divi group of Laccadive Isls., India, in Arabian Sea;

11°30′N 73°E. Administered by South Kanara dist., Madras; coconuts; mfg. of coir and copra. Lighthouse.

Kiltimagh or **Kiltamagh** (both: kĭltŭmä′), Gaelic *Coillte Amach*, town (pop. 1,105), E central Co. Mayo, Ireland, 13 mi. E of Castlebar; agr. market (cattle, potatoes).

Kiltyclogher (kĭltĭklŏkh′ŭr), Gaelic *Coillte Clochair*, town (pop. 150), N Co. Leitrim, Ireland, 16 mi. W of Enniskillen; agr. market (dairying; cattle, potatoes).

Kilung, Formosa: see KEELUNG.

Kilvey, Wales: see SWANSEA.

Kilwa (kēl′wä), village, Katanga prov., SE Belgian Congo, on SW bank of L. Mweru, at Northern Rhodesia line, 175 mi. NNE of Elisabethville; customs station, steamboat landing; fisheries. Franciscan mission.

Kilwa or **Kilwa Kivinje** (kēvēn′jä), town (pop. c. 3,000), SE Tanganyika, small port on Indian Ocean, just S of mouth of Matandu R., 135 mi. S of Dar es Salaam; exports copra, sisal, cotton, coffee. **Kilwa Kisiwani** (kēsēwä′nē), 16 mi. SSE on Kilwa Isl., is oldest town of Tanganyika; founded c.975 by Persians; was a prosperous slave- and ivory-trading center; preserves two 12th-cent. mosques.

Kilwinning (kĭlwĭ′nĭng), burgh (1931 pop. 5,325; 1951 census 6,553), N Ayrshire, Scotland, on Garnock R. and 3 mi. N of Irvine; machinery mills, ironworks, fireclay works. Traditional birthplace of Scottish freemasonry. There are remains of abbey founded 1140, dedicated to St. Winnin, who is reputed to have lived here. Town, long celebrated for archery meets, was formerly scene of annual shooting match, described in Scott's *Old Mortality*. In 1839 near-by Eglinton Castle was scene of tournament designed to revive ceremonies of anc. chivalry.

Kim (kēm), town (1926 pop. 1,029), NE Leninabad oblast, Tadzhik SSR, 6 mi. SSE of Kanibadam; oil field (producing since 1913). Until 1929, Santo.

Kim, village (pop. c.250), Las Animas co., SE Colo., 65 mi. E of Trinidad, near N.Mex. line; alt. 5,680 ft. Livestock, grain, beans.

Kima (kē′mä), village, Eastern Prov., E Belgian Congo, 170 mi. SSE of Stanleyville in tin-mining area; gold mining; also wolfram mining.

Kima, village, Central Prov., S central Kenya, on railroad and 60 mi. SE of Nairobi; sisal center; rubber, wheat, corn.

Kima, Kiima, or **Kiyma** (kē′mŭ), village (1939 pop. over 2,000), NW Akmolinsk oblast, Kazakh SSR, on Ishim R. and 35 mi. SW of Atbasar; cattle.

Kimamba (kēmäm′bä), village (pop. c. 1,000), E Tanganyika, on railroad and 10 mi. E of Kilosa; sisal center.

Kimba (kĭm′bŭ), village (pop. 314), S South Australia, on E central Eyre Peninsula, 115 mi. NNE of Port Lincoln, on Port Lincoln–Buckleboo RR; wheat, wool.

Kimball (kĭm′bŭl), county (□ 953; pop. 4,283), W Nebr.; ⊙ Kimball. Agr. area bordering on Colo. and Wyo.; drained by Lodgepole Creek. Livestock, wheat, small grains, potatoes. Formed 1888.

Kimball. 1 or **Kimball Prairie,** village (pop. 479), Stearns co., S central Minn., 19 mi. SSW of St. Cloud, in grain, livestock, poultry area; dairy products. **2** City (pop. 2,048), ⊙ Kimball co., W Nebr., 40 mi. S of Scottsbluff and on Lodgepole Creek; trade, grain-shipping center in Great Plains region; dairy and poultry produce, livestock, grain, potatoes. Inc. 1885. **3** City (pop. 952), Brule co., S central S.Dak., 20 mi. ESE of Chamberlain; livestock, poultry, dairy produce, grain. **4** City (pop. 1,359), McDowell co., S W.Va., on Tug Fork and 4 mi. E of Welch, in semibituminous-coal-mining, agr. (livestock, fruit, tobacco) region; railroad shops. State mine-rescue station here. Inc. 1911.

Kimball, Mount (9,680 ft.), E Alaska, in Alaska Range, 40 mi. W of Tanacross; 63°15′N 144°41′W.

Kimballton (kĭm′bŭltŭn), town (pop. 428), Audubon co., W central Iowa, 16 mi. N of Atlantic; dairy products.

Kimberley (kĭm′bŭrlē), city (pop. estimate 5,200), SE B.C., on St. Mary R. and 15 mi. NW of Cranbrook; alt. 3,662 ft.; one of Canada's largest silver-, lead-, and zinc-mining centers; site of Sullivan Mine. Inc. 1944.

Kimberley, town and parish (pop. 4,910), W Nottingham, England, 5 mi. WNW of Nottingham; coal mining; leather industry.

Kimberley, city (pop. 52,576; including suburbs 55,909), ⊙ Griqualand West dist., N Cape Prov., U. of So. Afr., near Orange Free State border, 280 mi. SW of Johannesburg; 28°44′S 24°46′E; alt. 4,012 ft. One of world's chief diamond-mining, cutting, and polishing centers. Mines, controlled by trust organized 1888 by Cecil Rhodes, include Dutoitspan, Wesselton, Bultfontein mines. The noted Kimberley Mine (abandoned 1915), originally called Colesberg Kopje or New Rush, was discovered 1871, reached 1,200 ft. in open-cast mining and was thence continued by shaft to depth of c.4,000 ft. The De Beers Mine is abandoned. Other industries include asbestos, manganese, gypsum mining, metalworking, mfg. of bricks, cement, furniture, clothing. City is a rail center in an important stock-raising region. Has technical col. and Perseverance Training School. Notable features include McGregor Mus. (1907), Duggan Cronin Bantu Gallery, Kimberley House (diamond-trade center), Vooruitgezigt farm, where 1st diamonds were found, and Anglican and R.C. cathedrals. Founded 1871, city developed rapidly with expansion of diamond mines. Reached 1885 by railroad from Cape Town. In early part of South African War it was besieged (Oct., 1899–Feb., 1900) by Boer forces under Piet Cronje until relieved by General French. Earlier efforts at relief were repulsed at near-by Modder River and Magersfontein. Suburbs include Kenilworth, Beaconsfield, and Ronaldsvlei (airport).

Kimberley. 1 Town (pop. 46), Pike co., SW Ark., 12 mi. NE of Nashville. **2** Village (1940 pop. 1,169), Fayette co., S central W.Va., near Kanawha R., 24 mi. SE of Charleston, in coal-mining region.

Kimberley Goldfield (□ 47,000), NE Western Australia; mining center is Hall's Creek. Gold discovered here 1882; area placed (1886) under govt. control and leased to mining interests.

Kimberly. 1 Village (pop. 1,347), Twin Falls co., S Idaho, 5 mi. ESE of Twin Falls; livestock, wheat, beans, potatoes. **2** Village (1940 pop. 507), White Pine co., E Nev., 8 mi. W of Ely; copper mines. **3** Village (pop. 3,179), Outagamie co., E Wis., on Fox R., just E of Appleton; paper milling. Inc. 1910.

Kimble, county (□ 1,274; pop. 4,619), W central Texas; ⊙ Junction. In scenic Edwards Plateau; alt. 1,800–2,300 ft.; drained by North Llano and South Llano rivers, here joining to form Llano R. Ranching (especially goats; also sheep, cattle); a leading U.S. co. in wool, mohair production. Some agr. (corn, oats, grain sorghums, wheat); pecan growing. Scenery, hunting, fishing attract tourist trade. Formed 1858.

Kimbolton (kĭmbōl′tŭn), town and parish (pop. 699), SW Huntingdon, England, 9 mi. WSW of Huntingdon; agr. market. Has 14th-cent. church and Kimbolton Castle (rebuilt 16th cent.), seat of duke of Manchester. Katherine of Aragon d. here.

Kimbolton, township (pop. 201), ⊙ Kiwitea co. (□ 359; pop. 2,182), S central N.Isl., New Zealand, 100 mi. NNE of Wellington; agr. center.

Kimbolton (kĭm′bŭltŭn), village (pop. 228), Guernsey co., E Ohio, 9 mi. N of Cambridge.

Kim Chuan (kĭm′ chōōän′), village (pop. 2,555), E central Singapore isl., 4 mi. NE of Singapore; rubber. Pop. is Chinese.

Kimen or **Ch'i-men** (both: chē′mŭn′), town, ⊙ Kimen co. (pop. 85,356), S Anhwei prov., China, 40 mi. W of Tunki; tea-growing center, known for the Keemun variety; tung oil. Kaolin quarries near by.

Kimi, Greece: see KYME.

Kimiidera, Japan: see WAKAYAMA, city.

Kimitsu (kēmē′tsōō), town (pop. 8,486), Chiba prefecture, central Honshu, Japan, on W Chiba Peninsula, on Tokyo Bay, just S of Kisarazu; rice growing, fishing, lumbering.

Kimkang, China: see TSINGMAI.

Kimmeria (kĭmĕ′rēŭ), town (pop. 4,276), Xanthe nome, W Thrace, Greece, 2 mi. E of Xanthe.

Kimmswick, town (pop. 207), Jefferson co., E Mo., on Mississippi R., S of mouth of the Meramec and 18 mi. S of St. Louis.

Kimolos (kē′mô̂lô̂s), Lat. *Cimolus* (sĭmō′lŭs), Aegean island (□ 15; pop. 1,900) in the Cyclades, Greece, just NE of Melos isl.; 5 mi. long, 4 mi. wide; produces wine, olive oil, wheat; chalk and iron ore mining; fisheries. Main town, Kimolos, is on SE shore. Formerly called Argentiera.

Kimovsk (kēmô̂fsk′), town (1948 pop. over 500), S Moscow oblast, Russian SFSR, in Moscow Basin, on Don R. and 12 mi. SE of Stalinogorsk; lignite mining. Until 1948, Mikhailovka.

Kimpangu (kēmpäng′gōō), village, Leopoldville prov., W Belgian Congo, on Angola boundary, 125 mi. E of Boma; customs station and center of native trade. R.C. mission.

Kimpersaiski, Kazakh SSR: see BATAMSHINSKI.

Kimpese (kēmpĕ′sä), village, Leopoldville prov., W Belgian Congo, on railroad and 90 mi. N of Boma; agr. center for native staples. Has R.C. and Baptist missions, mission schools, hosp. for Europeans.

Kimpolung, Rumania: see CAMPULUNG.

Kimpulung, Rumania: see CAMPULUNG.

Kimry (kēm′rē), city (1926 pop. 18,523), SE Kalinin oblast, Russian SFSR, on Volga R. (landing) and 50 mi. E of Kalinin; important center of shoe industry since 18th cent.; produces machinery.

Kimshan Cove (kĭm′shăm), village (1939 pop. 102), SE Alaska, on W Chichagof Isl., 50 mi. NW of Sitka; gold mining.

Kin, China: see KIN RIVER.

Kin, Norway: see KINN.

Kinabalu, Mount (kĭnŭbä′lōō), highest peak (13,455 ft.) of Borneo, in S Crocker Mts. of Br. N.Borneo, 35 mi. ENE of Jesselton; granite summit. Also spelled Kinibalu.

Kinabatangan River (kĭnŭbŭtăng′ŭn), largest river of Borneo, in Br. North Borneo, rises in central highlands of East Coast residency, flows c.350 mi. NE to Sulu Sea 30 mi. ESE of Sandakan; navigable for 75 mi. by small craft. Has wide delta.

Kinaion, Cape, Greece: see KYNAION, CAPE.

Kinak (kĭ′năk), Eskimo village (1939 pop. 36), W Alaska, on Kuskokwim R., near its mouth on Kuskokwim Bay, 40 mi. SW of Bethel; fishing, trapping.

Kinango (kēnäng′gō), village, Coast Prov., SE Kenya, on road and 26 mi. WSW of Mombasa; sugar cane, fruits.

Kinapusan Islands (kēnäpōōsän′) (□ .7; 1939 pop. 4,237), in Tawitawi Group, Sulu prov., Philippines, in Sulu Archipelago, 23 mi. E of Tawitawi Isl.; included in South Ubian municipality.

Kinards (kĭ′nŭrdz), town (1940 pop. 234), Newberry and Laurens counties, NW central S.C., 11 mi. NW of Newberry.

Kinaros, Greece: see KYNAROS.

Kinbrae (kĭnbrā′), village (pop. 85), Nobles co., SW Minn., 16 mi. NNE of Worthington, in grain and potato area. Small lakes near by.

Kinbuck (kĭnbŭk′), village, S Perthshire, Scotland, on Allan Water and 3 mi. N of Dunblane; cotton milling.

Kinburn Kosa (kēnbōōrn′ kŭsä″), W sandspit [Rus. *kosa*] extremity of peninsula in S Ukrainian SSR, jutting W into Black Sea and forming S shore of DNIEPER LIMAN. Westernmost tip (opposite Ochakov) was site of 18th-cent. Kinburn fortress.

Kincaid (kĭnkād′, kĭng-), village (pop. 271), SW Sask., 45 mi. W of Assiniboia; wheat.

Kincaid. 1 Village (pop. 1,793), Christian co., central Ill., on South Fork of Sangamon R. (bridged here) and 19 mi. SE of Springfield, in agr. and bituminous-coal area. Inc. 1915. **2** City (pop. 309), Anderson co., E Kansas, 30 mi. NW of Fort Scott, in livestock, grain, and dairy region. **3** Village (pop. 1,360, with adjacent Page), Fayette co., S central W.Va., 30 mi. SE of Charleston.

Kincardine (kĭn-kär′dĭn, kĭng-), town (pop. 2,507), S Ont., on L. Huron, 45 mi. SW of Owen Sound; knitting and woolen mills, furniture factory, saltworks; resort.

Kincardine, Kincardineshire (-shĭr), or **The Mearns** (mârnz), county (□ 382; 1931 pop. 39,865; 1951 census 47,341), E Scotland, on the North Sea; ⊙ Stonehaven. Bounded by Angus (S and W) and Aberdeen (N). Drained by the Dee and North Esk rivers. Surface is hilly in NW (Grampian Mts.), leveling toward central fertile tract of the Howe of the Mearns and the coast. Sheep grazing in uplands, sea fisheries, and salmon fishing (in the Dee) are important; some granite is quarried. There are extensive deer forests and grouse moors. Besides Stonehaven, other towns are Inverbervie, Laurencekirk, and Banchory. Among noted antiquities are Dunnottar Castle and anc. stone circles and tumuli. Co. includes small S sector of Aberdeen city.

Kincardine. 1 Town in Tulliallan parish (pop. 2,166), SW Fifeshire, Scotland, on the Firth of Forth (1936 road bridge), 5 mi. SE of Alloa; small port, with coal mines. Near by are remains of 15th-cent. Tulliallan Castle. **2** Agr. village and parish (pop. 962), NE Ross and Cromarty, Scotland, at head of Dornoch Firth, 12 mi. W of Dornoch.

Kincardine O'Neil, agr. village and parish (pop. 1,847), S Aberdeen, Scotland, on the Dee and 7 mi. WNW of Banchory. In parish, 3 mi. NE, is market and resort village of Torphins.

Kincardineshire, Scotland: see KINCARDINE, county.

Kinchafoonee River (kĭn″chŭfōō′nē), SW Ga., rises near Buena Vista, flows S and SE c.75 mi., past Preston, to Flint R. at Albany.

Kinchai or **Chin-chai** (both: jĭn′jī′), town, ⊙ Kinchai co. (pop. 265,761), W Anhwei prov., China, near Honan-Hupeh line, 45 mi. WSW of Liuan, N of Tapieh Mts.; rice, tea, hemp, sweet potatoes; papermaking. Originally called Kinkiachai, later (1933–49) Lihwang.

Kinchil (kēnchēl′), town (pop. 1,947), Yucatan, SE Mexico, 22 mi. W of Mérida; henequen.

Kinchinjunga, mountain, India and Nepal: see KANCHENJUNGA.

Kinchow, Manchuria: see CHINCHOW.

Kincraig (kĭnkrāg′), agr. village, E Inverness, Scotland, on the Spey near Loch Insh, and 4 mi. NE of Kingussie.

Kindat (kĭn′dät), village, Upper Chindwin dist., Upper Burma, on left bank of Chindwin R. and 6 mi. N of Mawlaik; low-water head of navigation.

Kindberg (kĭnt′bĕrk), town (pop. 5,477), Styria, E central Austria, on Mürz R. and 11 mi. NE of Bruck; ironworks, steelworks. Summer resort.

Kinde (kĭn′dē), village (pop. 571), Huron co., E Mich., 10 mi. N of Bad Axe, in farm area.

Kindelbrück (kĭn′dŭlbrük), town (pop. 2,610), in former Prussian Saxony prov., central Germany, after 1945 in Thuringia, on Wipper R. and 13 mi. SE of Sondershausen; fruit, vegetables, grain, sugar beets, livestock.

Kinder (kĭn′dŭr), town (pop. 2,003), Allen parish, SW La., near Calcasieu R., 28 mi. NE of Lake Charles city, in rice, cotton, and cattle-raising area; cotton gin; rice, lumber, and feed mills.

Kinderdijk (kĭn′dŭrdīk′), town (pop. 3,730), South Holland prov., W Netherlands, on Noord R. and 5 mi. NNW of Dordrecht; mfg. (bridging material, railroad rolling stock, machinery), shipbuilding. Sometimes spelled Kinderdyk.

Kinderhook (kĭn′dŭrhŏŏk″). **1** Village (pop. 299), Pike co., W Ill., 20 mi. SE of Quincy, in agr. area. **2** Resort village, Branch co., S Mich., 10 mi. S of Coldwater, near Ind. line, in lake area. **3** Village (pop. 853), Columbia co., SE N.Y., 17 mi. SSE of Albany, and on Kinderhook Creek, in diversified-farming area; mfg. (carbonated beverages, wood and metal products). Here are St. Paul's Church (1851), and the House of History (in early-19th-cent. mansion) of Columbia County Historical Society. Martin Van Buren was b. and is buried here; the Van Buren homestead is S of village. Settled before the Revolution; inc. 1838.

Kinderhook Creek, SE N.Y., rises in S Rensselaer co. in the Taconic Mts., flows c.45 mi. generally SW, past Valatie and Kinderhook, to the Hudson 4 mi. N of Hudson.

Kinder Scout, England: see PEAK, THE.

Kindersley, town (pop. 1,235), W Sask., 100 mi. NW of Swift Current; grain elevators, lumbering, stock raising.

Kindia (kĭn′dyŭ,–dēŭ), town (pop. c.11,600), W Fr. Guinea, Fr. West Africa, on railroad and 70 mi. ENE of Conakry; trading center for productive region; bananas, pineapples, manioc, rice, corn, indigo, rubber, honey, beeswax, cattle. Mfg. of food preserves. Has Pasteur Institute, experimental garden, school for native art, R.C. mission.

Kinding (kĭn′dĭng), village (pop. 576), Middle Franconia, central Bavaria, Germany, on the Altmühl and 12 mi. NE of Eichstätt; flour and lumber milling, brewing.

Kindred, village (pop. 504), Cass co., SE N.Dak., 20 mi. SSW of Fargo, near Sheyenne R.; grain, livestock, dairy.

Kindsbach (kĭnts′bäkh), village (pop. 1,785), Rhenish Palatinate, W Germany, 7 mi. WSW of Kaiserslautern; grain, potatoes.

Kindu (kĕn′dōō), town (1948 pop. 8,896), Kivu prov., central Belgian Congo, on both banks of the Lualaba and 115 mi. NNW of Kasongo; river port and commercial center. Important transshipment point, terminus of railroad from Albertville and head of steam navigation to Ponthierville. Shipyards, railroad workshops; rice and tin processing, pharmaceuticals mfg. Airport. Has R.C. mission and mission schools, including business school for natives; hosp. for Europeans. Also known as Kindu-Port-Empain (kĕndōō-pôrtăpē′).

Kinel or **Kinel′** (kēnyĕl′), city (1939 pop. over 10,000), central Kuibyshev oblast, Russian SFSR, near confluence of Greater Kinel and Samara rivers, 22 mi. E of Kuibyshev; rail junction (repair shops); petroleum-extracting center, developed during Second World War; gypsum quarrying, flour milling, brick mfg. Has agr. col. Became town in 1930, city in 1944.

Kinel-Cherkassy or **Kinel′-Cherkassy** (–chĭrkä′sē), village (1926 pop. 13,175), E Kuibyshev oblast, Russian SFSR, on Greater Kinel R., and 39 mi. ENE of Kinel city; agr. center (sugar beets, wheat, sunflowers); meat, dairy products; metalworking.

Kineo, Mount (kĭ′nēō). **1** Peak (1,806 ft.), Piscataquis co., central Maine, on peninsula extending W into Moosehead L. and 19 mi. NNW of Greenville; summer resort. **2** Peak (3,320 ft.) of White Mts., Grafton co., central N.H., E of Warren.

Kineshma (kē′nyĭshmŭ), city (1926 pop. 22,386; 1939 pop. 75,378), N Ivanovo oblast, Russian SFSR, port on Volga R. and 55 mi. NE of Ivanovo. Rail terminus; cotton- and lumber-milling center; felt-boot mfg., spinning, weaving, paper milling, sawmilling; ceramics, food processing. Phosphate fertilizer works at ZAVOLZHYE, across the Volga. Chartered 1539.

Kineton, town and parish (pop. 1,021), S Warwick, England, 9 mi. SSE of Warwick; agr. market. Has church with 14th-cent. tower. Here Charles I assembled his army (1642) before the battle of EDGEHILL.

King, China: see KING RIVER.

King. 1 County (☐ 944; pop. 870), NW Texas; ⊙ Guthrie. Rolling plains area; alt. 2,000–2,500 ft.; drained by tributaries of Wichita and Brazos rivers. Large-scale cattle ranching co., including parts of 3 of largest ranches in Texas (the Pitchfork, the 6666, and the Matador); also some agr. (grain sorghums, wheat, cotton); some sheep, horses, mules, hogs, poultry. Oil wells; lime, copper deposits. Formed 1876. **2** County (☐ 2,136; pop. 732,992), W central Wash.; ⊙ SEATTLE. Snoqualmie R. rises in Cascade Range in E. Includes part of Snoqualmie Natl. Forest. Lumber, clays, coal; fruit, nuts, dairy products, livestock, truck. Formed 1852.

King, Lake, lagoon (☐ 35), SE Victoria, Australia, 145 mi. E of Melbourne; separated from Tasman Sea by sandspit, with opening at town of Lakes Entrance; merges SW with L. Reeve and L. Victoria; 9 mi. long, 6 mi. wide; irregularly shaped. Contains small isl. Receives Mitchell R.

King, Mount (17,130 ft.), SW Yukon, near Alaska border, in St. Elias Mts., 190 mi. W of Whitehorse; 60°35′N 140°40′W.

King, Mount, or **Mount Clarence King,** E Calif., peak (12,909 ft.) of the Sierra Nevada, in Kings Canyon Natl. Park, 14 mi. W of Independence. Mt. STARR KING is in Yosemite Natl. Park.

Kingait, Northwest Territories: see META INCOGNITA.

King Alexander Canal, Yugoslavia: see NOVI SAD–MALI STAPAR CANAL.

Kingamyambo, Belgian Congo: see KOLWEZI.

King and Queen, county (☐ 318; pop. 6,299), E Va.; ⊙ King and Queen. In tidewater region; bounded W by Mattaponi and York rivers. Agr. (especially tomatoes, other truck; corn, wheat, tobacco, legumes, livestock). Oyster dredging. Formed 1691.

King and Queen, village, ⊙ King and Queen co., E Va., near Mattaponi R., 34 mi. ENE of Richmond.

Kingani River (kĭng-gä′nē), E Tanganyika, rises in Uluguru Mts. E of Morogoro, flows 125 mi. NE, past Ruvu, to Indian Ocean just NW of Bagamoyo, opposite Zanzibar isl. Called Ruvu R. in upper and middle course. Gold placers.

Kingaroy (kĭng′ŭroi), town (pop. 3,893), SE Queensland, Australia, 100 mi. NW of Brisbane; agr. center (wheat, corn).

King Channel, arm of the Pacific, in Chonos Archipelago, S Chile, at c.44°30′S; extends c.50 mi. E-W bet. the ocean and Moraleda Channel. Forms Chiloé-Aysén prov. line.

King Charles Islands, Svalbard: see KONG KARLS LAND.

King Charles South Land, Chile-Argentina: see TIERRA DEL FUEGO.

Kingcheng or **Ch′ing-ch′eng** (both: chĭng′chŭng′), town, ⊙ Kingcheng co. (pop. 165,739), SE Heilungkiang prov., Manchuria, on railroad and 85 mi. NNE of Harbin.

King Chiang Saen, Thailand: see CHIANG SAEN.

Kingchow. 1 Town, Hupeh prov., China: see KIANGLING. **2** Town, Kansu prov., China: see KINGCHWAN.

King Christian Island (17 mi. long, 9 mi. wide), N Franklin Dist., Northwest Territories, in Maclean Strait, off Ellef Ringnes Isl.; 77°45′N 102°10′W.

King Christian IX Land, Dan. *Kong Christian IX Land,* coastal region of SE Greenland; 65°–70°N.

King Christian X Land, Dan. *Kong Christian X Land,* coastal region of E Greenland; 70°–75°N.

Kingchwan or **Ching-ch′uan** (both: jĭng′chwän′), town, ⊙ Kingchwan co. (pop. 121,911), SE Kansu prov., China, on King R. and 105 mi. NE of Tienshui; felt making; sheepskins, hides, honey, wax, kaoliang, millet. Until 1913 called Kingchow.

King City. 1 City (pop. 2,347), Monterey co., W Calif., on Salinas R. and 45 mi. SE of Salinas; trade and shipping center near S end of rich irrigated Salinas valley; beans, grain, sugar beets, cattle. Founded 1868, inc. 1911. **2** City (pop. 1,031), Gentry co., NW Mo., 26 mi. NE of St. Joseph; agr. (corn, oats), livestock, poultry, dairy products, bluegrass seed.

King Cove, village (pop. 151), SW Alaska, near SW extremity of Alaska Peninsula, 10 mi. WSW of Belkofski; fish canneries; fishing, trapping. School.

King Edward, Mount (11,400 ft.), on Alta.–B.C. border, in Rocky Mts., on S edge of Jasper Natl. Park, 55 mi. SSE of Jasper; 52°9′N 117°31′W.

King Edward VII Land, Antarctica: see EDWARD VII PENINSULA.

King Edward VII Point, SE extremity of Ellesmere Isl., NE Franklin Dist., Northwest Territories, on Jones Sound; 76°8′N 81°9′W.

King Edward VIII Falls, central Br. Guiana, on affluent of the Mazaruni, and 30 mi. NW of Kaieteur Falls; 5°35′N 59°40′W. Drop 840 ft.

King Edward VIII Gulf, Antarctica: see EDWARD VIII BAY.

Kingfield, town (pop. 963), Franklin co., W central Maine, on the Carrabassett (water power) and 20 mi. N of Farmington; wood products. Settled 1805, inc. 1816.

Kingfisher, county (☐ 894; pop. 12,860), central Okla.; ⊙ Kingfisher. Intersected by Cimarron R. and Turkey Creek. Diversified agr. (wheat, cotton, oats, alfalfa, livestock, poultry). Processing of farm products is chief industry. Oil field. Formed 1890.

Kingfisher, city (pop. 3,345), ⊙ Kingfisher co., central Okla., 35 mi. NW of Oklahoma City, in rich agr. area (mainly wheat; also cotton, oats, alfalfa, livestock); flour and feed milling, dairying, cotton ginning. Founded 1889.

King Frederik VI Coast, Dan. *Kong Frederik VI Kyst,* coastal region of SE Greenland; 60°–65°N.

King Frederik VIII Land, Dan. *Kong Frederik den VIII Land,* coastal region of NE Greenland; 75°–81°N.

Kingfu. 1 or **Ching-fu** (jĭng′fōō′), town, Honan prov., China: see SINHSIEN. **2** or **Ch′ing-fu** (chĭng′fōō′), town (pop. 12,490), ⊙ Kingfu co. (pop. 171,380), SW Szechwan prov., China, 20 mi. S of Ipin; rice, sweet potatoes, sugar cane, millet, medicinal plants.

King George, county (☐ 178; pop. 6,710), E Va.; ⊙ King George. At base of Northern Neck peninsula; Potomac R. (bridged here to Md.) is N, Rappahannock R. (bridged to Caroline co.) is S. Rolling dairying and agr. region (truck, tobacco, hay); cattle, sheep. Game, commercial fishing. Includes U.S. naval proving ground at Dahlgren. Formed 1720.

King George, village (pop. c.100), ⊙ King George co., E Va., 16 mi. E of Fredericksburg, in agr. area; cannery.

King George, Mount (11,226 ft.), SE B.C., near Alta. border, 40 mi. S of Banff; 50°36′N 115°24′W.

King George IV Lake (6 mi. long, 5 mi. wide), SW N.F., on Lloyds R. and 55 mi. S of Corner Brook, at SW end of the Annieopsquotch Mts.

King George V Land, Antarctica: see GEORGE V COAST.

King George VI Falls, W Br. Guiana, near Brazil border, on affluent of the Mazaruni, and 45 mi. NW of Mt. Roraima; 5°44′N 61°8′W. Drop 1,600 ft.

King George VI Sound, Antarctica: see GEORGE VI SOUND.

King George Bay (c.20 mi. long, 2-7 mi. wide), inlet, West Falkland Isl.; 51°40′S 60°30′W.

King George Island (43 naut. mi. long, c.16 naut. mi. wide), South Shetland Isls., off Palmer Peninsula, Antarctica; 62°S 58°30′W. Meteorological station.

King George Islands, SE Keewatin Dist., Northwest Territories, group of 15 small isls. and islets in Hudson Bay off W Ungava Peninsula; 57°20′N 78°30′W. Covers area c.30 mi. long, 20 mi. wide.

King George Islands, Tuamotu Isls.: see TAKAROA.

King George's Falls, U. of So. Afr.: see AUGHRABIES FALLS.

King George Sound, inlet of Indian Ocean, SW Western Australia, bet. Bald Head (SW) and Cape Vancouver (NE); 5 mi. wide (at mouth, N-S), 10 mi. long (E-W). Princess Royal Harbour (W inlet) is site of Albany.

Kinghorn, burgh (1931 pop. 2,001; 1951 census 2,337), S Fifeshire, Scotland, on the Firth of Forth, 3 mi. SSW of Kirkcaldy; small port, with shipyards. Near by is monument to Alexander III, who was thrown by his horse and killed here. Just NNE, on the Firth of Forth, is coal-mining village of Seafield.

Kinghsien or **Ching-hsien** (both: jĭng′shyĕn′). **1** Town, ⊙ Kinghsien co. (pop. 207,664), S Anhwei prov., China, 40 mi. S of Wuhu; rice-growing center; wheat, tung oil. **2** Town, ⊙ Kinghsien co. (pop. 262,916), S Hopeh prov., China, near Shantung line, 15 mi. N. of Tehchow; cotton center; pears, jujubes, watermelons.

Kingigtok (kĭngĭkh′tôk), island (3 mi. long, 1 mi. wide), W Greenland, in Baffin Bay, 14 mi. NNW of Upernavik; 73°58′N 56°25′W. Stone with runic inscription (mid-14th cent.) found here. Also spelled Kingiktorssuak.

Kingisepp (kĭng′gĭsĕp, Rus. kēn-gĭsyĕp′), city (1926 pop. 5,003), SW Leningrad oblast, Russian SFSR, on Luga R. and 70 mi. WSW of Leningrad; sawmilling, dairying. Paper mills at Ivanovskoye and Sredneye Selo (SE). Founded (13th cent.) as fortress of Yam. Chartered 1703 following its recapture from Swedes. Estonian border station (1920–40). Called Yamburg until 1922, when it was renamed for an Estonian communist.

King Island (2.5 mi. long, 1.5 mi. wide; 1939 pop. 208), NW Alaska, in Bering Sea, SW of Seward Peninsula, 90 mi. WNW of Nome; 64°59′N 168°3′W; rises to 700 ft. Ukivok (ŭ′kĭvŏk), Eskimo village, on S shore. Each summer the Eskimos, noted primitive craftsmen, move to Nome to sell ivory carvings to tourists.

King Island, largest isl. (☐ 170) of Mergui Archipelago, Lower Burma, in Andaman Sea, 10 mi. W of Mergui town; 25 mi. long, 4–10 mi. wide; 12°36′N 98°19′E. Mountainous (highest point, 2,125 ft.); mangrove swamps on coast; rubber plantations on coastal plain (SE); manganese, galena, glass sands.

King Island (☐ 425; pop. 1,699), in Bass Strait, 55 mi. off NW coast of Tasmania; 39 mi. long, 16 mi. wide. Fertile plains; dairy plants. Tungsten mines at Grassy. Tin, zircons. Currie is its port and largest town.

King Karl Islands, Svalbard: see KONG KARLS LAND.

Kingking (kĭng″kĭng′), town (1939 pop. 2,748), center of Pantukan municipality (päntōō′kän) (1948 pop. 17,234), Davao prov., SE Mindanao, Philippines, 20 mi. ENE of Davao across Davao Gulf, opposite Samal Isl.; abacá, coconuts.

King Kirkland, village (pop. estimate 500), NE Ont., 4 mi. E of Kirkland Lake; gold mining.

Kingku or **Ching-ku** (both: jĭng′gōō′), town, ⊙ Kingku co. (pop. 33,935), SW Yunnan prov., China, 35 mi. NW of Ningerh; alt. 3,150 ft.; timber, tea, rice, millet, beans. Iron mines near by. Until 1914 called Weiyüan.

Kinglassie (kĭn-glă′sē), town and parish (pop. 2,427), central Fifeshire, Scotland, 5 mi. NW of Kirkcaldy; coal mining.

King Lear, Nev.: see JACKSON MOUNTAINS.

King Leopold Ranges, N Western Australia, extend 180 mi. SE from shores of Collier Bay. Mt. Broome (3,040 ft.), highest peak.

Kingman, county (☐ 865; pop. 10,324), S Kansas; ⊙ Kingman. Plains region, watered by Chikaskia R. and South Fork Ninnescah R. Wheat, livestock. Formed 1874.

Kingman. 1 Village (pop. 3,342), ⊙ Mohave co., W Ariz., E of Black Mts., 70 mi. SE of Hoover Dam in mining and livestock raising area. Gold, silver, lead, zinc, copper, and feldspar mines near by. Founded 1882. **2** Town (pop. 509), Fountain co., W Ind., 21 mi. WSW of Crawfordsville; agr.; bituminous-coal mines. **3** City (pop. 3,200), ⊙ Kingman co., S Kansas, on South Fork of Ninnescah R. and 40 mi. W of Wichita; market center for wheat region; flour milling. Founded c.1872, inc. 1883.

Kingman Reef, triangular islet, central Pacific, c.35 mi. NW of Palmyra; 6°24'N 162°24'W. Discovered 1874 by Americans; made U.S. naval reservation (1934) and air-line base (1937); later abandoned.

Kingmen or **Ching-men** (both: jĭng'mŭn'), town (pop. 12,037), ⊙ Kingmen co. (pop. 245,345), W central Hupeh prov., China, 30 mi. WSW of Chungsiang; road center; rice, wheat, cotton, beans.

King Mine, township (pop. 805), Victoria prov., SE central Southern Rhodesia, in Mashonaland, 4 mi. SE of Mashaba; asbestos-mining center.

King Mountain (c.3,000 ft.), W Texas, near Pecos R., 5 mi. N of McCamey. Was a pioneers' landmark.

King Mountains, Chinese *King Shan* or *Ching Shan* (both: jĭng' shän'), NW Hupeh prov., China, bet. Han and Yangtze rivers; rise to c.5,000 ft. 50 mi. NW of Kingmen.

Kingning or **Ching-ning** (both: jĭng'nĭng'), town (pop. 1,745), ⊙ Kingning co. (pop. 94,911), S Chekiang prov., China, 60 mi. W of Wenchow and on headstream of Wu R.; mfg. of straw mats and umbrellas; vegetable-oil processing. Rice, wheat, corn, tea.

Kingolwira (kĭng-gōlwē'rä), village, Eastern Prov., Tanganyika, on railroad and 8 mi. E of Morogoro; cotton, sisal. Mica deposits.

Kingombe, Belgian Congo: see KALIMA-KINGOMBE.

Kingoonya, village (pop. 143), S central South Australia, 220 mi. NW of Port Pirie, on Trans-Australian RR; wool, salt.

King Oscar Archipelago, group of islands in Greenland Sea, E Greenland, bet. Franz Josef Fjord (N) and King Oscar Fjord (S). Largest are TRAILL ISLAND, YMER ISLAND, and GEOGRAPHICAL SOCIETY LAND.

King Oscar Fjord, inlet (90 mi. long, 8-15 mi. wide) of Greenland Sea, E Greenland; 72°-73°N 22°15'-24°50'W. Extends NW bet. mainland (SW) and Traill Isl. (NE); from its head several arms radiate to edge of inland icecap and to Franz Josef Fjord. Mouth on Greenland Sea called Davy Sound.

King Oscar Land, NE Franklin Dist., Northwest Territories, SW part of Ellesmere Isl.

King Oscar Land, group of islands in Arctic Ocean, reported (1874) by Austrian explorer Payer as being NW of Franz Josef Land; proved to be nonexistent by Rus. Brusilov expedition (1912–13).

Kingpeng or **Ching-p'eng** (both: jĭng'pŭng'), town, ⊙ Kingpeng co. (pop. 35,691), S Inner Mongolian Autonomous Region, Manchuria, 100 mi. NW of Chihfeng; banner hq. in Jooda league. Founded 1914; in Jehol until 1949.

King Peter Canal, Yugoslavia: see DANUBE-TISZA CANAL.

Kingpo Lake or **Chingpo Lake,** Chinese *Kingpo Hu* or *Chingpo Hu* (both: jĭng'pô' hōō'), natural reservoir on upper Mutan R., E Manchuria, 50 mi. SW of Mutankiang; formed by lava flow across river course; 25 mi. long, 5 mi. wide. Hydroelectric station. Also called Pirton or Pilteng.

King Ranch, (area almost 1,000,000 acres), S Texas in several divisions S and W of Corpus Christi, and with hq. at Kingsville. Established c.1853 by Capt. Richard King, whose holdings were divided (1935) among his heirs, the central ranches still comprise one of world's largest cattle domains. Irrigated agr., petroleum production supplement raising of the noted Santa Gertrudis cattle developed here; fine cow ponies and race horses are also bred.

King River, Chinese *King Shui* or *Ching Shui* (both: jĭng' shwā'), NW central China, rises in the Liupan Mts. of Kansu prov., flows 200 mi. ESE, past Pingliang and Kingchwan, and into Shensi prov., past Changwu and Pinhsien, to Wei R. NE of Sian. Receives Wan R. (left).

Kings. 1 County (□ 1,374; pop. 21,573), S N.B., extending N from St. John, drained by St. John R.; ⊙ Hampton. **2** County (□ 842; pop. 28,920), NW N.S., on the Bay of Fundy; ⊙ Kentville. **3** County (□ 641; pop. 19,415), in E P.E.I.; ⊙ Georgetown.

King's, county, Ireland: see OFFALY.

Kings. 1 County (□ 1,395; pop. 46,768), S central Calif.; ⊙ Hanford. Level irrigated farm land of San Joaquin Valley, drained by Kings and Tule rivers. Tulare L. is in central part. Kettleman Hills (rich oil and natural-gas field here) are in SW. Cotton, grain, dairy products, beef cattle, raisin and table grapes, other fruit, nuts, olives, hay, flax, poultry. Farm-products processing and oil refining are chief industries. Gypsum quarrying Formed 1893. **2** County (□ 71; pop. 2,738,175), SE N.Y., coextensive with BROOKLYN borough of New York city. Formed 1683.

King Salmon River, S Alaska, on Alaska Peninsula, rises in SW part of Katmai Natl. Monument near 58°9'N 155°25'W, flows 90 mi. W to Bristol Bay at Egegik.

Kings Bay, Nor. *Kongsfjorden,* inlet (16 mi. long, 4–9 mi. wide) of the Arctic Ocean, NW West Spitsbergen, Spitsbergen group, 65 mi. NW of Longyear City; 78°57'N 12°0'E. Kings Glacier, Nor. *Kongsvegen,* empties into head of bay (SE). On S shore is Ny-Alesund (New Alesund) coal-mining settlement. Bay was stopping point of several polar flights, including those of Byrd and Bennett (May, 1926), Amundsen (May, 1926), and Nobile (May, 1928).

Kingsbridge, urban district (1931 pop. 2,987; 1951 census 3,153), S Devon, England, on inlet of the Channel, 10 mi. WSW of Dartmouth; agr. market known for breed of large cattle (South Devons), and scene of annual cattle fair; metal foundries. Has 17th-cent. grammar school, 15th-cent. church, 16th-cent. market house, and mus.

Kingsbridge, SE N.Y., a section of W Bronx borough of New York city, along Harlem R. opposite N Manhattan.

Kingsburg, city (pop. 2,310), Fresno co., central Calif., in San Joaquin Valley, near Kings R., 20 mi. SE of Fresno; ships melons; cotton ginning, cottonseed-oil extracting, wine making, fruit and vegetable canning. Settled in 1870s, inc. 1908.

Kingsbury. 1 Residential former urban district (1931 pop. 16,636), Middlesex, England, N suburb of London, just S of Hendon. Has 11th-cent. church, built with Roman bricks. Oliver Goldsmith lived here. Inc. 1934 in Wembley. **2** Town and parish (pop. 3,923), N Warwick, England, 11 mi. NE of Birmingham; coal mining. Church, with 14th-cent. tower, dates from Norman times.

Kingsbury, county (□ 819; pop. 9,962), E central S.Dak.; ⊙ De Smet. Agr. area watered by natural and artificial lakes. Dairy produce, livestock, poultry, grain; abundance of ducks and pheasants. Formed 1873.

Kingsbury. 1 Town (pop. 281), La Porte co., NW Ind., 6 mi. S of La Porte. **2** Plantation (pop. 35), Piscataquis co., central Maine, 21 mi. WSW of Dover-Foxcroft, in farming, lumbering, recreational area. **3** Village (pop. c.300), Guadalupe co., S central Texas, c.45 mi. ENE of San Antonio; rail point in agr. area (cotton, poultry, peanuts).

Kingsbury Episcopi, agr. village and parish (pop. 1,128), S Somerset, England, on Parrett R. and 8 mi. NW of Yeovil. Has 14th–15th-cent. church.

Kings Canyon National Park (□ 707.9; established 1940), E central Calif., c.55 mi. E of Fresno. Mtn. wilderness of massive peaks, glacial cirques, and impressive chasms of the Sierra Nevada; its E boundary is along Sierra crest, and it adjoins Sequoia National Park (S). Crossed by Middle Fork and South Fork of Kings R., which rise in NE and cut impressive gorges extending across W boundary of park. Canyon of Middle Fork (Tehipite Valley) is dominated by Tehipite Dome (7,713 ft.). Kings River Canyon along South Fork is more than 2,000 ft. deep and is overlooked from S by Grand Sentinel Dome or Sentinel Dome (9,127 ft.). Other features of scenic interest are in Evolution Valley (N), extending W from foot of Mt. Darwin (13,841 ft.) and drained by a headstream of San Joaquin R. General Grant Grove area (detached section of park on SW; known as General Grant Natl. Park until 1940) contains stands of giant sequoia trees, largest of which is General Grant Tree (267 ft. high, 3,500 yrs. old). Major peaks on park's E boundary include the Palisades peaks (Middle Palisade, 14,049 ft.; North Palisade or Mt. Sill, 14,254 ft., with Palisade Glacier on its flank); Split Mtn. (14,051 ft.). John Muir Trail crosses park in E and extends NW to Yosemite Natl. Park.

Kingsclere (kĭngz'klēr), town and parish (pop. 2,231), N Hampshire, England, 8 mi. NW of Basingstoke; agr. market. Has Norman church.

Kingscote (kĭngz'kōt), village (pop. 534), NE Kangaroo Isl., South Australia, on NW shore of Nepean Bay; tourist resort; sheep, barley, eucalyptus oil.

Kingscourt, Gaelic *Cabrach,* town (pop. 550), E Co. Cavan, Ireland, 18 mi. NNW of An Uaimh; agr. market (cattle, pigs; potatoes); China-clay mining, mfg. of gypsum products.

Kings Creek, village, Cherokee co., N S.C., 12 mi. E of Gaffney. Kings Mtn. Natl. Military Park is N.

Kingsey Falls, village (pop. 454), S Que., on Nicolet R. and 18 mi. E of Drummondville; paper milling, dairying; cattle, pigs.

Kingsford, city (pop. 5,038), Dickinson co., SW Upper Peninsula, Mich., suburb 2 mi. SW of Iron Mountain city, and on the Menominee; sawmill, drying kilns; mfg. (wooden auto parts, chemicals). Inc. as city 1947.

Kingsford Heights, village (pop. 1,104), La Porte co., NW Ind., 10 mi. S of La Porte.

Kingshan or **Ching-shan** (both: jĭng'shän'), town (pop. 18,645), ⊙ Kingshan co. (pop. 327,104), central Hupeh prov., China, 33 mi. ESE of Chungsiang; peanuts, cotton, medicinal herbs. Gypsum deposits near by.

King Shan, mountains, China: see KING MOUNTAINS.

King's Heath, England: see MOSELEY AND KING'S HEATH.

King Shui, China: see KING RIVER.

Kingsing or **Ching-hsing** (both: jĭng'shĭng'), town, ⊙ Kingsing co. (pop. 83,075), W Heilungkiang prov., Manchuria, 50 mi. WSW of Tsitsihar; soybeans, wheat, kaoliang, millet, corn, rye.

King's Island, Maldive Isls.: see MALE ISLAND.

Kingskettle, Scotland: see KETTLE.

Kingsland. 1 Town (pop. 337), Cleveland co., S central Ark., 29 mi. SW of Pine Bluff; rail point in agr. area. **2** City (pop. 1,169), Camden co., extreme SE Ga., 27 mi. SSW of Brunswick, near Fla. line; sawmilling. State park with ruins of Spanish mission (E). Founded 1894.

King's Langley, residential town and parish (pop. 3,335), SW Hertford, England, on Gade R. and 4 mi. NNW of Watford; mfg. of paper, pharmaceuticals; iron foundries, flour mills. Has 15th-cent. church.

Kingsley. 1 Town (pop. 1,098), Plymouth co., NW Iowa, near West Fork Little Sioux R., 22 mi. ENE of Sioux City; mfg. (livestock remedies, troughs, millwork products). Inc. 1884. **2** Town (pop. 488), Jefferson co., N Ky., just E of Louisville. **3** Village (pop. 425), Grand Traverse co., NW Mich., 13 mi. SSE of Traverse City.

Kingsley Dam, SW central Nebr., on N.Platte R. and c.50 mi. W of North Platte. PWA project completed 1941; earthfill dam c.¼ mi. thick at base, 162 ft. high. Used for power and irrigation; forms L. McConaughy (mŭkŏ'nŭgē) or Kingsley Reservoir, □ 50; 27 mi. long, average width 2 mi.; capacity 2,000,000 acre-ft. Water is diverted through conduit and canal to Sutherland Reservoir and power plant on S.Platte R., near North Platte city.

King's Lynn, Lynn, or **Lynn Regis** (lĭn', rē'jĭs), municipal borough (1931 pop. 20,583; 1951 census 26,173), W Norfolk, England, on Ouse R., near The Wash, and 38 mi. WNW of Norwich; 52°45'N 0°24'E; fishing port, with shipyards, beet-sugar refineries, metalworks; agr. market, with flour mills. Its importance dates from Saxon times; in Middle Ages it was one of England's chief ports. The church of St. Margaret, founded c.1100 by Bishop Losinga, contains noted brass. There is a Tudor guildhall, Customs House (1683), 15th-cent. Grey Friar's Tower, 1440 South Gate, and 1482 Red Mount Chapel. Fanny Burney and George Vancouver b. here. In municipal borough are residential suburbs of West Lynn (W) and Gaywood (E).

Kings Manor, village (pop. 1,710, with adjacent Swedesburg), Montgomery co., SE Pa., near Norristown.

Kingsmill Group: see GILBERT ISLANDS.

Kings Mills, village (1940 pop. 615), Warren co., SW Ohio, 22 mi. NE of Cincinnati and on Little Miami R.; produces communications equipment, chemicals, electrical equipment.

Kings Mountain, town (pop. 7,206), Cleveland co., SW N.C., 28 mi. W of Charlotte, near S.C. line; textile center. Inc. 1874. Kings Mtn., site of natl. military park, is just across state line.

Kings Mountain, isolated ridge (1,040 ft.) in York co., N S.C., near state line, 30 mi. WSW of Charlotte, N.C. Site of battle of Kings Mtn. (1780), Revolutionary War engagement in which frontiersmen surrounded and defeated Br. troops, is now included in Kings Mtn. Natl. Military Park (□ 6.3; established 1931). Large state park (recreational facilities) also here.

King's Norton, SW industrial suburb (pop. 22,811) of Birmingham, NW Warwick, England. Has 15th-cent. church and 16th-cent. grammar school.

King Sound, inlet of Indian Ocean, N Western Australia; Cape Leveque at E end of entrance; 40 mi. E-W, 80 mi. N-S; broken into small bays. Buccaneer Archipelago at NE entrance; Derby on S shore.

Kings Park, village (pop. 10,960), Suffolk co., SE N.Y., near N shore of W Long Isl., 9 mi. E of Huntington; agr. (truck, potatoes). A state hosp. is here. Near by is Sunken Meadow State Park (520 acres; bathing, hiking, picnicking).

Kings Peak (13,498 ft.), NE Utah, in Uinta Mts., 80 mi. E of Salt Lake City; highest point in state.

Kings Point, residential village (pop. 2,445), Nassau co., SE N.Y., on NW Long Isl., on Great Neck peninsula, 8 mi. N of Jamaica. A U.S. merchant marine acad. was established here in 1942. Inc. 1924.

Kingsport, industrial city (pop. 19,571), Sullivan co., NE Tenn., near Va. line, on Holston R. and 21 mi. NNW of Johnson City, in fertile agr. area of Great Appalachian Valley; book printing, mfg. of book cloth, paper, glass, chemicals, cement, bricks, cellulose acetate yarn, leather goods, hosiery. Was 1st city in Tenn. to adopt (1917) city-manager type of govt. City is on site of fort (built 1761) on old Wilderness Road.

Kings River. 1 In NW Ark. and SW Mo., rises in the Ozarks in SE Madison co. (Ark.), flows c.115 mi. N to White R. 15 mi. SE of Cassville, Mo. **2** In central Calif., rises in the Sierra Nevada in E Fresno co. as Middle and South branches, which flow through spectacular gorges in KINGS CANYON NATL. PARK before joining just W of park to form Kings R.; joined c.15 mi. hence by North Fork.

united stream flows c.125 mi. W and SW into San Joaquin Valley, and into Tulare L.; flood flows sometimes reach San Joaquin R. Pine Flat Dam, a flood-control unit of CENTRAL VALLEY project, was begun in 1947; dam, to be 440 ft. high, will impound reservoir of 1,000,000 acre-ft. capacity. **3** In NW Nev., rises in N Humboldt co. near Oregon line, flows c.40 mi. S to Quinn R. NE of Jackson Mts.

King's Seat, Scotland: see OCHIL HILLS.

King's Somborne, agr. village and parish (pop. 1,215), W Hampshire, England, 8 mi. W of Winchester. Church dates from 12th cent.

King's Stanley, town and parish (pop. 1,698), central Gloucester, England, near Frome R. 3 mi. WSW of Stroud; woolen milling. Church dates from Norman times. Roman remains found here; it was residence of a Mercian king.

Kingsteignton (kĭngz'tān'tŭn), town and parish (pop. 3,157), S Devon, England, on Teign R. and 2 mi. NE of Newton Abbot; clay quarrying. Has 15th-cent. church.

Kingsthorpe, England: see NORTHAMPTON.

Kingston, village and port (pop. 806), SE South Australia, on E shore of Lacepede Bay and 150 mi. SSE of Adelaide; rail terminus; dairy products, livestock. Sometimes called Port Caroline.

Kingston, city (pop. 30,126), ⊙ Frontenac co., SE Ont., at NE end of L. Ontario, at outlet of the St. Lawrence, at mouth of Cataraqui R., and 150 mi. ENE of Toronto; port, with one of the best harbors on the lake; S terminal of Rideau Canal from Ottawa. Mfg. of locomotives, machinery, chemicals, aluminum, nylon, textiles, leather, biscuits, food products, lumber; grain elevators. Seat of Queen's Univ. (1841), School of Mining and Agr., Royal Military Col. and Anglican and R.C. cathedrals. Frontenac built fort (1673) on site of Indian settlement of Cataraqui; subsequently La Salle became seigneur of fort and surrounding region and named it Fort Frontenac. Destroyed in King William's War, fort was rebuilt by Frontenac (1695). It was captured and destroyed (1758) by General John Bradstreet; present city was founded 1784 by United Empire Loyalists. Canadian naval base in War of 1812, Kingston was ⊙ United Canada, 1841–44. Extant are: bldg. which housed 1st govt. of Upper Canada; and Fort HENRY, built in War of 1812, rebuilt 1840–46. Just W of Kingston is suburb of Portsmouth, with prov. penitentiary and mental hosp.

Kingston, city (1943 pop. 109,056; 1947 estimate 120,000), largest city and ⊙ Jamaica, B.W.I., on SE coast, 500 mi. SE of Havana, 625 mi. NNE of Colón, Panama; 17°58'N 76°43'W. One of the most mportant ports in the West Indies, on an excellent deep bay of Kingston Harbour (protected by long sandspit, Palisadoes), and nestling at SW foot of the Blue Mts. Linked by rail with interior, NW, and SE Jamaica, it is in a fertile agr. area (sugar cane, coffee, coconuts, bananas). Average annual temp. 78.7°F. Among its industries are copra processing (lard, margarine, soap), brewing, fruit canning, slaughtering, tanning, woodworking; mfg. of ice, biscuits, confectionery, jam, cigars and cigarettes, clothing, footwear, furniture, drugs, cosmetics, matches. Center of coffee business, and port of call for steamship lines trading with adjacent isls., Europe, and the Americas. Kingston is also becoming known as a resort. The old colonial city, laid out in rectangular plan, has fine residential sections, and administrative and historic bldgs. such as St. Andrew parish church (rebuilt 1907), R.C. cathedral, Headquarters House (seat of govt.), the Inst. of Jamaica (with library, mus., and art gall.), theater. Kingston was founded in 1692 after Port Royal, on opposite peninsula, was destroyed by an earthquake. In early 18th cent. it became the isl.'s most important commercial center, but was not made permanent capital until 1872, replacing Spanish Town. The city has suffered from severe hurricanes and the disastrous 1907 earthquake. Residential sections are in adjoining hill area. Towards N and W, partly in St. Andrew parish, are workers' quarters. The governor's residence, called King's House, is at Half Way Tree suburb (N). Airport is c.3 mi. S on the opposite peninsula.

Kingston, village (pop. 43), S central S.Isl., New Zealand, on S shore of L. Wakatipu and 75 mi. N of Invercargill; rail terminus, lake port.

Kingston, principal village of NORFOLK ISLAND, S Pacific, on S coast; commercial and tourist center; produces citrus and passion fruit.

Kingston, fishing village, NE Moray, Scotland, on Spey Bay of Moray Firth, at mouth of the Spey, 8 mi. ENE of Elgin. Established 1784 by natives of Kingston-upon-Hull.

Kingston, town (pop. 379), SE Tasmania, 7 mi. S of Hobart and on Derwent R. estuary; orchards.

Kingston. 1 Town (pop. 675), Bartow co., NW Ga., 13 mi. E of Rome, near Etowah R.; mfg. (bedspreads, lumber). **2** Village (pop. 327), De Kalb co., N Ill., on South Branch of Kishwaukee R. (bridged here) and 20 mi. SE of Rockford, in rich agr. area. **3** Village (pop. c.150), Somerset co., SE Md., 22 mi. SSW of Salisbury; canning center in truck-farm area; lumber. **4** Town (pop. 3,461), including Kingston village (pop. 1,366), Plymouth co., SE Mass., on Plymouth Bay and 5 mi. NW of Plymouth; hardware, textiles. Settled 1620, inc. 1726. **5** Village (pop. 371), Tuscola co., E Mich., 38 mi. E of Saginaw, in agr. area. **6** City (pop. 338), ⊙ Caldwell co., NW Mo., 48 mi. NE of Kansas City; corn, oats. **7** Town (pop. 1,283), Rockingham co., SE N.H., 6 mi. SW of Exeter; agr. Josiah Bartlett's 18th-cent. home (remodeled). Includes Kingston Lake State Park, recreational center on Kingston L. Inc. 1694. **8** City (pop. 28,817), ⊙ Ulster co., SE N.Y., on W bank of the Hudson at mouth of Rondout Creek, and c.50 mi. S of Albany, in fruitgrowing area; mfg. (clothing, textiles, refrigerators, brick, metal products, machinery). Mushroom growing. The Senate House (1676), meeting place of the 1st New York state legislature, and adjoining mus. contain paintings and historical material. Ashokan Reservoir is 5 mi. NW. Settled 1652; inc. as village in 1805, as a city (union of Kingston and Rondout) in 1812. Coming (1828) of Delaware and Hudson Canal, of which it was E terminus, stimulated commercial growth. **9** Village (pop. 958), Ross co., S Ohio, 10 mi. NNE of Chillicothe; grain products; gas wells. **10** Town (pop. 677), Marshall co., S Okla., 27 mi. ESE of Ardmore, near L. Texoma; cotton ginning. **11** Industrial borough (pop. 21,096), Luzerne co., NE central Pa., on Susquehanna R. opposite Wilkes-Barre; mfg. (cigars, rayon, nylon); anthracite; railroad shops. Settled 1769, inc. 1857. **12** Residential village (pop. 2,156) in South Kingstown town, Washington co., S R.I., 24 mi. S of Providence, in agr. area. R.I. State Col. here. Has many historic 18th- and 19th-cent. houses. **13** Town (pop. 1,627), ⊙ Roane co., E Tenn., on arm of Watts Bar Reservoir of Clinch R. and 34 mi. WSW of Knoxville; makes hosiery. **14** Town (pop. 138), Piute co., S Utah, near Junction. **15** Village (pop. 1,098), Fayette co., S central W.Va., 31 mi. SE of Charleston, in coal-mining region. **16** Village (pop. 334), Green Lake co., central Wis., on Grand R. and 35 mi. W of Fond du Lac, in dairy and farm area.

Kingston-by-Sea, England: see SHOREHAM-BY-SEA.

Kingston Mines, village (pop. 404), Peoria co., central Ill., on Illinois R. (bridged here) and 12 mi. SW of Peoria, in agr. and bituminous-coal-mining area; gravel pits.

Kingston-on-Thames or **Kingston-upon-Thames** (tĕmz), municipal borough (1931 pop. 39,055; 1951 census 40,168), NE Surrey, England, on the Thames and 10 mi. SW of London, of which it is a residential suburb and resort; also has metalworking and mfg. of aircraft, leather, plastics, paint. Scene of Egbert's council meeting (838) and of Saxon coronations; the Coronation Stone is preserved in market place. Last battle of Civil War was fought here (1648). There is a 14th-cent. chapel.

Kingston-upon-Hull, England: see HULL.

Kingstown, Ireland: see DÚN LAOGHAIRE.

Kingstown, town (pop. 4,833; including suburbs 14,766), ⊙ SAINT VINCENT, Windward Isls., B.W.I., port on isl.'s SW shore, 100 mi. S of Fort-de-France, Martinique; 13°9'N 61°14'W. Situated on extensive Kingstown Bay, where vessels anchor ¼ mi. offshore. Exports arrowroot starch, cotton, sugar cane, molasses, cacao, tropical fruit. Arrowroot milling, cotton ginning. Has St. George's Cathedral, courthouse, and other public bldgs., botanical garden (established 1763) with Govt. House. Old Fort Charlotte is adjoining, NW of Kingstown Bay. Several beach resorts near by; Belair mineral springs 2 mi. E.

Kingstown, R.I.: see NORTH KINGSTOWN, SOUTH KINGSTOWN.

Kingstree, town (pop. 3,621), ⊙ Williamsburg co., E central S.C., on Black R. and 38 mi. S of Florence; trade center for tobacco, truck area; lumber milling, woodworking. Hunting and fishing resort. Settled 1732.

Kingsville, town (pop. 2,317), S Ont., on L. Erie, 25 mi. SE of Windsor; tobacco processing, fruit and vegetable canning; lake fisheries. Near by is large bird sanctuary.

Kingsville. 1 Hamlet, Baltimore co., N Md., 15 mi. NE of downtown Baltimore. Near-by Jerusalem Mills (begun 1772) are still operated. **2** Town (pop. 207), Johnson co., W central Mo., 18 mi. W of Warrensburg. **3** City (pop. 16,898), ⊙ Kleberg co., S Texas, 35 mi. SW of Corpus Christi. Hq. for huge KING RANCH and market, shipping, processing center for ranching, agr., petroleum-producing area; railroad shops, cotton-processing plants; large chemical plant near. Seat of Texas Col. of Arts and Industries. Settled 1902, inc. as town 1911, as city 1916.

Kingswood. 1 Urban district (1931 pop. 13,286; 1951 census 18,921), SW Gloucester, England, 4 mi. E of Bristol; leather and shoe center, with electrical-equipment works; coal mining. George Whitefield preached his 1st sermon here. **2** Town and parish (pop. 847), SW Gloucester, England, 15 mi. NE of Bristol; silk milling and mfg. of elastic. **3** Residential town and parish (pop. 2,289), central Surrey, England, 3 mi. N of Reigate; pharmaceuticals.

Kingtai or **Ching-t'ai** (both: jĭng'tī'), town, ⊙ Kingtai co. (pop. 34,155), central Kansu prov., China, near Yellow R., 80 mi. NNE of Lanchow; wheat, cattle and sheep raising. Until 1934 town was called Talutang, and co. was named Hungshui. The former co. seat, Hungshuipao (called Hungshui, 1913–34), is 30 mi. NW.

Kingteh or **Ching-te** (both: jĭng'dŭ'), town, ⊙ Kingteh co. (pop. 54,112), W Kwangsi prov., China, 30 mi. S of Poseh, near Yunnan line; cotton textiles; rice, beans, corn.

Kingtehchen, China: see FOWLIANG.

Kington, urban district (1931 pop. 1,742; 1951 census 1,890), NW Hereford, England, on Arrow R. and 17 mi. NW of Hereford; agr. market. Limestone quarries near by. Has 14th-cent. church.

Kingtung or **Ching-tung** (both: jĭng'dŏong'), town, ⊙ Kingtung co. (pop. 80,199), central Yunnan prov., China, 120 mi. WSW of Kunming; alt. 3,848 ft.; rice, wheat, millet, sugar cane, timber. Iron mines near by.

Kingtzekwan or **Ching-tzu-kuan** (both: jĭng'dzŭ'-gwän'), village, SW Honan prov., China, 95 mi. WNW of Nanyang, at Hupeh-Shensi border; commercial center at head of navigation on Tan R.

Kingussie (kĭng-yōō'sē, -gōō'sē), burgh (1931 pop. 1,067; 1951 census 1,067), E Inverness, Scotland, on the Spey and 29 mi. S of Inverness; health resort and tourist center with woolen mills. James Macpherson b. here. Kingussie is chief town of the wild BADENOCH dist. Just S of Kingussie, on the Spey, is Ruthven, with ruins of fortifications built against the Highlanders in 1718, destroyed by them in 1746. After 1745 battle of Culloden Moor the Highlanders assembled here for the last time.

King Wilhelm Land (vĭl'hĕlm), Dan. *Kong Wilhelms Land,* region, NE Greenland, on Greenland Sea, extends c.150 mi. N–S; 74°30'–76°30'N 22°W.

King William, county (□ 278; pop. 7,589), E Va.; ⊙ King William. In tidewater region; bounded SW by Pamunkey, NE by Mattaponi rivers, joining at SE tip of co. to form York R. Agr. (truck, tobacco, legumes, livestock, hay); pulpwood lumbering; fish and shellfish industries. Pulp and paper mfg. at West Point. Includes Pamunkey Indian Reservation. Formed 1702.

King William, village, ⊙ King William co., E Va., 27 mi. ENE of Richmond.

King William Island (110 mi. long, 100 mi. wide), S Franklin Dist., Northwest Territories, in the Arctic Ocean, separated from Keewatin Dist. mainland by Simpson and Rae straits, from Victoria Isl. (W) by Victoria Strait, and from Boothia Peninsula (NE) by James Ross Strait; 68°27'–69°55'N 95°10'–99°35'W. Irregular coast line. Discovered 1831 by Sir John Ross. On SE coast is Peterson Bay or Gjoa Haven; 68°38'N 95°55'W; trading post, site of winter quarters of Roald Amundsen's Northwest Passage expedition in 1903 and 1904. Sir John Franklin and most members of his expedition were lost on isl., 1847–48. Dr. J. Rae established (1854) its insularity.

Kingwilliamstown or **King Williams Town,** town (pop. 11,324), SE Cape Prov., U. of So. Afr., on Buffalo R. and 30 mi. WNW of East London; cotton milling, tanning, soap mfg.; center of stock-raising, grain-growing region. Commercial center for Transkeian Territories and the Ciskei; seat of Ciskeian General Council and of local native-affairs council, established 1927, with jurisdiction over Kingwilliamstown dist. (□ 819; total pop. 68,195; native pop. 57,213). Has Kaffrarian Mus. (1889), botanical gardens, training col. Founded 1825 as mission station, it was ⊙ British Kaffraria prov. until 1865. Popularly called simply King.

Kingwood, town (pop. 2,186), ⊙ Preston co., N W.Va., 19 mi. SE of Morgantown, in coal-mining, timber, limestone, agr. area; lumber milling. Founded 1811.

Kingyang. 1 or **Ch'ing-yang** (both: chĭng'yäng'), town, ⊙ Kingyang co. (pop. 72,810), SE Kansu prov., China, on Wan R. and 45 mi. N of Kingchwan; grain. **2** or **Ching-yang** (jĭng'yäng'), town (pop. 12,696), ⊙ Kingyang co. (pop. 113,536), S central Shensi prov., China, on King R. and 15 mi. N of Sian, and on railroad; cotton weaving; grain.

Kingyüan. 1 or **Ch'ing-yüan** (both: chĭng'yüän'), town (pop. 5,620), ⊙ Kingyüan co. (pop. 86,876), SW Chekiang prov., China, near Fukien line, 75 mi. SW of Lishui; timber, tea, rice, wheat. **2** Town, Kwangsi prov., China: see ISHAN. **3** or **Ching-yüan** (jĭng'yüän'), town, ⊙ Kingyüan co. (pop. 351,685), NW Shantung prov., China, near Hopeh line, 75 mi. S of Tientsin; wheat, kaoliang, millet, beans. Until 1949, called Yenshan, and in Hopeh prov.

Kingyün or **Ch'ing-yün** (both: chĭng'yün'), town, ⊙ Kingyün co. (pop. 155,291), NW Shantung prov., China, 65 mi. NE of Tehchow; wheat, millet, beans, kaoliang. Until 1949 in Hopeh prov.

Kinho, China: see KINPING, Yunnan prov.

Kinhsien, China: see YÜCHUNG.

Kinhwa or **Chin-hua** (both: jĭn'hwä'), town (pop. 23,427), ⊙ Kinhwa co. (pop. 252,129), central Chekiang prov., China, 80 mi. SSW of Hangchow and on right headstream of Tsientang R.; rail junction for Lanchi; commercial center; exports ham, dates, tea, sugar cane, rice. Lime quarries.

Kiniati (kĕnyä'tē), village, Leopoldville prov., W Belgian Congo, on railroad and 40 mi. NNW of

Boma; coffee, rubber, and cacao plantations; palm-oil milling, coffee processing.
Kinibalu, Mount, North Borneo: see KINABALU, MOUNT.
Kinigi, Ruanda-Urundi: see RUHENGERI.
Kinistino (kĭnĭ'stĭnô, –nō), village (pop. 610), central Sask., 35 mi. ESE of Prince Albert; grain elevators, mixed farming.
Kinkai, Korea: see KUMHAE.
Kinkala (kĭng-kälä'), town, ⊙ Pool region (□ 16,600; 1948 pop. 263,032), SE Middle Congo territory, Fr. Equatorial Africa, near railroad, 30 mi. WSW of Brazzaville; native trade center; food processing.
Kinkaseki, Formosa: see KINKWASHIH.
Kinki. 1 or **Chin-ch'i** (both: jĭn'chē'), town (pop. 5,603), ⊙ Kinki co. (pop. 75,699), E central Kiangsi prov., China, 30 mi. E of Fuchow; rice, wheat, fruit; exports timber, bamboo; papermaking. Graphite mines. **2** or **Chin-chi** (jĭn'gē'), town (pop. 3,669), ⊙ Kinki co. (pop. 49,390), SE Ningsia prov., China, 45 mi. SSW of Yinchwan, and on right bank of Yellow R., opposite Ningso; cattle raising; rice, wheat, millet.
Kinki, Japan: see HONSHU.
Kinkiachai, China: see KINCHAI.
Kin Kiang, China: see KIN RIVER.
Kin-ko, Korea: see KUM RIVER.
Kinkony, Lake (kĭngkōō'nē) (□ 55), Majunga prov., NW Madagascar, near the coast S of Mitsinjo; c.18 mi. wide, 10–15 mi. long; drains into Mahavavy R. Rice region.
Kinkwashih or **Chinkuashih** (both: jĭn'gwä'shŭ'), Jap. *Kinkaseki* (kēngkä'sākē), village (1935 pop. 9,549), N Formosa, on N coast, 7 mi. E of Keelung; major gold-mining center; silver and copper mining.
Kinlingchen or **Chin-ling-chen** (both: jĭn'lĭng'jŭn'), village, central Shantung prov., China, on Tsinan-Tsingtao RR and 7 mi. E of Changtien; iron-ore shipping point for Tiehshan (or T'ieh-shan) mines (on spur, 4 mi. N).
Kinloch (kĭn'lŏk), town (pop. 5,957), St. Louis co., E Mo.
Kinlochbervie (kĭn"lŏkh-bûr'vē), agr. village, NW Sutherland, Scotland, on Loch Inchard (5-mi.-long sea inlet), 13 mi. SW of Durness.
Kinlochleven (kĭn"lŏkh-lē'vŭn), town in Lismore and Appin parish (pop. 3,757), N Argyll, Scotland, at head of Loch Leven, at mouth of Leven R., and 9 mi. SE of Fort William; important hydroelectric station and aluminum works, with port facilities.
Kinloch Rannoch (kĭn'lŏkh rä'nŭkh), agr. village, N Perthshire, Scotland, on Tummel R., at E end of Loch Rannoch, and 13 mi. WNW of Aberfeldy.
Kinloss (kĭnlŏs'), fishing village and parish (pop. 778), NW Moray, Scotland, on Findhorn Bay of Moray Firth, 3 mi. NE of Forres. Has remains of Cistercian abbey founded 1150 by David I.
Kinmen, China: see QUEMOY.
Kinmount, village (pop. estimate 500), S Ont., 40 mi. NNW of Peterborough; dairying, farming.
Kinmundy (kĭn'mōōn"dē), city (pop. 912), Marion co., S central Ill., 22 mi. NE of Centralia, in bituminous-coal and oil-producing area; food processing (flour, cheese and other dairy products). Agr. (corn, wheat, livestock).
Kinn (chĭn), canton (pop. 2,685), Sogn og Fjordane co., W Norway, including over 50 small isls. in North Sea near Floro. On a small isl. 10 mi. WSW of Floro is a stone church (c.1200), with medieval furniture. Formerly spelled Kin.
Kinna (chĭ'nä), village (pop. 3,347), Alvsborg co., SW Sweden, on Viska R. and 17 mi. SW of Boras; woolen and cotton milling. Has old castle.
Kinnairds Head, Scotland: see FRASERBURGH.
Kinnarodden, Norway: see NORDKYN.
Kinnelon (kĕ'nŭlŭn, kĭ'–), borough (pop. 1,350), Morris co., N N.J., 12 mi. NW of Paterson.
Kinneret or **Kinnereth** (both: kēnĕ'rĕt), residential settlement (pop. 600), Lower Galilee, NE Israel, on SW shore of Sea of Galilee, 5 mi. SSE of Tiberias; lake shipping, mixed farming. Founded 1909.
Kinney, county (□ 1,391; pop. 2,668), SW Texas; ⊙ Brackettville. On S edge of Edwards Plateau and crossed E–W by Balcones Escarpment; Rio Grande (Mex. border) is SW boundary. Drained by tributaries of Nueces R. and the Rio Grande. Ranching area (cattle, sheep, goats); wool, mohair marketed; hunting. Formed 1850.
Kinney, village (pop. 336), St. Louis co., NE Minn., on Mesabi iron range, 9 mi. W of Virginia. Large open-pit mine near by.
Kinoe (kēnō'ā), largest town (pop. 4,861) on Osaki-kami-shima, Hiroshima prefecture, Japan, on E coast of isl.; boatyards.
Kinomoto (kēnō'mōtō). **1** Town (pop. 5,980), Mie prefecture, S Honshu, Japan, port on Kumano Sea, 13 mi. NNE of Shingu; fishing, agr. Exports lumber, fish. Sometimes called Kii-kinomoto. **2** Town (pop. 8,079), Shiga prefecture, S Honshu, Japan, on N shore of L. Biwa, 14 mi. SSE of Tsuruga; commercial center in agr. area (rice, tea, mushrooms); raw silk; artificial catgut, drugs; sawmilling.
Kinosaki (kēnō'säkē), town (pop. 3,958), Hyogo prefecture, S Honshu, Japan, 6 mi. N of Toyooka; hot-springs resort. Winter sports.
Kinping or **Chin-p'ing** (both: jĭn'pĭng'). **1** Town (pop. 4,473), ⊙ Kinping co. (pop. 76,403), E Kweichow prov., China, near Hunan line, 50 mi. SE of Chenyüan and on upper Yüan R.; paper mfg.; tobacco, tea, rice, wheat, millet. Gold washing near by. Until 1913 called Liping. **2** Town, ⊙ Kinping co. (pop. 30,040), S Yunnan prov., China, 40 mi. SW of Kaiyüan, near Vietnam border; cotton textiles; rice, millet, beans. Until 1936 called Kinho.
Kin River, Chinese *Kin Kiang* or *Chin Chiang* (both: jĭn' jyäng'), NW Kiangsi prov., China, rises near Hunan border, flows 130 mi. ENE, past Wantsai, Shangkao, and Kaoan, to Kan R. above Nanchang.
Kinross or **Kinross-shire** (–rŏs', –shĭr), county (□ 81.8; 1931 pop. 7,454; 1951 census 7,418), E Scotland; ⊙ Kinross. Bounded by Fifeshire (E and S), Clackmannan (W), and Perthshire (N). Drained by small Leven R. In center of co. is Loch Leven and adjoining central plain, surrounded by Ochil and Lomond hills. Limestone and sandstone are quarried; there are woolen and linen mills. Besides Kinross, Milnathort is only other important place. On isl. in Loch Leven is Lochleven Castle, scene of imprisonment of Mary Queen of Scots.
Kinross, burgh (1931 pop. 2,525; 1951 census 2,495), ⊙ Kinross-shire, Scotland, on W shore of Loch Leven, 13 mi. S of Perth; woolen and linen milling; agr. market.
Kinross (kĭn'rŏs), town (pop. 105), Keokuk co., SE Iowa, 14 mi. NE of Sigourney; livestock, grain.
Kinross-shire, Scotland: see KINROSS, county.
Kinsale (kĭnsāl'), Gaelic *Ceann Sáile*, urban district (pop. 2,087), S Co. Cork, Ireland, on Bandon R. estuary, 14 mi. S of Cork; 51°42'N 8°31'W; fishing port and seaside resort. Has 12th-cent. Church of St. Multose and 13th-cent. castle. Town was founded as Anglo-Norman settlement and in 1223 the de Courcys were made barons of Kinsale. In 1601 Spanish force under Don Juan del Aguila landed here and held town for 10 weeks. In 1689 James II landed at Kinsale to recover Ireland for Stuarts, leaving here after his defeat in 1690 when, after fall of Cork, Kinsale was retaken by Marlborough. Just SE of Kinsale is resort of Summer Cove, with Charles Fort (1677), several times object of siege.
Kinsale, village (pop. 450), W Montserrat, B.W.I., just SE of Plymouth; sea-island cotton, fruit.
Kinsale (kĭn'sāl), village (pop. c.300), Westmoreland co., E Va., on inlet of the Potomac, 50 mi. ESE of Fredericksburg; cans and ships seafood, vegetables.
Kinsarvik (chĭn'särvēk), village and canton (pop. 1,775), Hordaland co., SW Norway, on S shore of Hardanger Fjord, at mouth of Sor Fjord, 22 mi. NNE of Odda; terminus of ferry across Hardanger Fjord to Granvin. Has stone church (c.1290). Formerly spelled Kinservik.
Kinsen, Korea: see KUMCHON.
Kinservik, Norway: see KINSARVIK.
Kinsha or **Chin-sha** (both: jĭn'shä'). **1** Town, N Kiangsu prov., China, 14 mi. ENE of Nantung; commercial center. **2** Town (pop. 17,081), ⊙ Kinsha co. (pop. 170,431), NW Kweichow prov., China, 65 mi. NNW of Kweiyang; wheat, millet, timber. Coal deposits near by. Until 1932 called Sinchang.
Kinsha Kiang, China: see YANGTZE RIVER.
Kinshan or **Chin-shan** (both: jĭn'shän'), town (pop. 7,576), ⊙ Kinshan co. (pop. 167,926), S Kiangsu prov., China, near Chekiang line, 32 mi. SW of Shanghai, in canal dist.; rice, beans, rapeseed. Formerly called Chuking.
Kinshan or **Chin-shan,** Jap. *Kanayama* (känä'yämä), town (1935 pop. 5,005), N Formosa, near N coast, 12 mi. NW of Keelung; coal and sulphur mining; rice, sweet potatoes, tea. Fisheries.
Kinshasa, Belgian Congo: see LEOPOLDVILLE, city.
Kinshui or **Chinshui** (both: jĭn'shwā'), Jap. *Kinsui* (kēn'sōōē), village, NW Formosa, 13 mi. SSW of S Sinchu; 24°37'N 120°53'E. Natural-gas-producing center; benzine and carbon-black plants.
Kinsiang or **Chin-hsiang** (both: jĭn'shyäng'), town, ⊙ Kinsiang co. (pop. 263,812), SE Pingyuan prov., China, 45 mi. ESE of Hotseh; wheat, kaoliang, millet. Until 1949 in Shantung prov.
Kinsley, city (pop. 2,479), ⊙ Edwards co., SW central Kansas, on Arkansas R. and 35 mi. ENE of Dodge City; trade center for wheat and livestock region; flour milling, dairying, metalworking. Founded c.1875, inc. 1878. Santa Fe Trail passed through here.
Kinsman. 1 Village (pop. 147), Grundy co., NE Ill., 14 mi. ENE of Streator, in agr. and bituminous-coal area. **2** Village (1940 pop. 585), Trumbull co., NE Ohio, 18 mi. NE of Warren, near Pa. line; brass products, lumber, feed.
Kinsman Mountain, peak (4,363 ft.) of White Mts., W N.H., just N of Kinsman Notch and 8 mi. NW of North Woodstock village.
Kinsman Notch, Grafton co., W N.H., pass in White Mts. 5 mi. W of North Woodstock. Lost R. (part of small Moosilauke R.), running through caverns, is scenic feature. Wild Ammonoosuc R. rises here.
Kinston (kĭn'stŭn). **1** Town (pop. 312), Coffee co., S Ala., 20 mi. SE of Andalusia, near Pea R. **2** City (pop. 18,336), ⊙ Lenoir co., E central N.C., on Neuse R. (head of navigation) and 24 mi. SE of Goldsboro; tobacco market; tobacco-processing (stemming) center; mfg. of shirts, textiles, yarn, paper boxes, fertilizer; lumber mills. Large nylon plant near by. Settled 1740; town laid out 1762.
Kinsui, Formosa: see KINSHUI.
Kinta or **Chin-t'a** (both: jĭn'tä'), town, ⊙ Kinta co. (pop. 31,915), NW Kansu prov., China, on Peita R. and 30 mi. NE of Kiuchüan, near the Great Wall; alt. 4,199 ft.; wool, hides.
Kinta (kĭn'tŭ), town (pop. 283), Haskell co., E Okla., 12 mi. SSW of Stigler, in farm area; cotton ginning.
Kintail, parish (pop. 376), SW Ross and Cromarty, Scotland. Includes DORNIE. Kintail Forest, at head of Loch Duich, is a deer forest (□ c.40), at foot of Ben Fhada or Ben Attow (3,383 ft.).
Kintambo, Belgian Congo: see LEOPOLDVILLE, city.
Kintampo (kēntäm'pō), town, Ashanti, W central Gold Coast, on road and 35 mi. NE of Wenchi; hardwood, rubber, cacao.
Kintan or **Chin-t'an** (both: jĭn'tän'), town (pop. 17,531), ⊙ Kintan co. (pop. 274,733), S Kiangsu prov., China, 32 mi. SSE of Chinkiang; rice, wheat, rapeseed, cotton. Coal deposits near by.
Kintang or **Chin-t'ang** (both: jĭn'täng'). **1** Village, ⊙Kintang dist. (pop. 2,690), E Sikang prov., China, 25 mi. NE of Kangting; rice, wheat, corn, kaoliang, medicinal herbs. Called Shangyütung until 1932. Until 1938 in Szechwan. **2** Town (pop. 12,087), ⊙ Kintang co. (pop. 485,748), W Szechwan prov., China, 18 mi. NE of Chengtu; sugar-milling center; rice, sweet potatoes, wheat, beans, millet.
Kinta River (kĭn'tŭ), right affluent of Perak R., S central Perak, Malaya, rises in central Malayan range N of Cameron Highlands, flows 60 mi. W and S, past Tanjong Rambutan, Ipoh, and Batu Gajah, to Perak R., 10 mi. N of Telok Anson. The **Kinta Valley,** along middle course, bet. Kledang Range (W) and central Malayan range, is leading tin-mining area of Malaya.
Kintbury, agr. village and parish (pop. 1,784), SW Berkshire, England, on Kennet R. and 6 mi. W of Newbury; tile mfg. Has Norman church. Saxon burial ground found here.
Kintei, Korea: see KUMJE.
Kintinku (kēntĭng'kōō), town, Central Prov., central Tanganyika, on railroad and 40 mi. NW of Dodoma; cotton, peanuts, gum arabic, beeswax.
Kintla Peak, Mont.: see LEWIS RANGE.
Kintore (kĭntôr'), burgh (1931 pop. 755; 1951 census 870), E central Aberdeen, Scotland, on Don R. and 11 mi. WNW of Aberdeen; agr. market. Town Hall dates from 1740. Near by is Hallforest Castle of great antiquity.
Kintyre (kĭntīr'), peninsula of S Argyll, Scotland, bet. the sea (W) and Kilbrannan Sound (E), extending 42 mi. S from narrow isthmus bet. East Loch Tarbert and West Loch Tarbert; up to 10 mi. wide. Hilly, rising to 1,491 ft. At S extremity is the MULL OF KINTYRE, 13 mi. from Ireland. Chief town is CAMPBELTOWN, on E coast. The peninsula is sometimes spelled Cantyre.
Kinu or **Kin-u** (kĭn'ōō), village, Shwebo dist., Upper Burma, on railroad and 15 mi. WNW of Shwebo.
Kinvarra or **Kinvara** (both: kĭnvă'rŭ), Gaelic *Cinn Mhara*, town (pop. 351), S Co. Galway, Ireland, on inlet of Galway Bay, 11 mi. SE of Galway; fishing port, noted for its oysters.
Kinver, town and parish (pop. 3,220), S Stafford, England, 5 mi. WSW of Brierly Hill; mfg. of radio parts, metalworking. Has church dating from 14th cent. Just W is the hill of Kinver Edge (543 ft.) with remains of a Saxon camp.
Kinwat (kĭn'vŭt), village (pop. 4,277), Adilabad dist., N Hyderabad state, India, on Penganga R. and 22 mi. W of Adilabad; millet, rice; cotton ginning. Sometimes spelled Kinvat.
Kinyangiri, Tanganyika: see SINGIDA.
Kinyeti, Mount, Anglo-Egyptian Sudan: see IMATONG MOUNTAINS.
Kinzambi (kēnzäm'bē), village, Leopoldville prov., SW Belgian Congo, on Kwilu R. and 25 mi. NNW of Kikwit. Seat of R.C. mission, business school, seminary.
Kinzan, Korea: see KUMSAN.
Kinzhal (kēnzhäl'), peak (9,281 ft.) in N rocky front range of the central Greater Caucasus, Russian SFSR, 40 mi. W of Nalchik, to right of Malka R.
Kinzig River (kĭn'tsĭkh). **1** In Baden, S Germany, rises in the Black Forest 3 mi. SSE of Freudenstadt, flows SW, W, and NW, past Offenburg, to the Rhine at Kehl. Length, 60 mi. **2** In Hesse, W Germany, rises in the Rhön Mts., flows 45 mi. WSW to the Main at Hanau.
Kioa (kēō'ä), uninhabited volcanic island (□ 9), Fiji, SW Pacific, c.2 mi. E of Vanua Levu. Formerly Tate Isl.
Kioga, Cape, Japan: see KYOGA POINT.
Kioga, Lake, Uganda: see KYOGA, LAKE.
Kioluvick, Alaska: see KEYALUVIK.
Kionga, Mozambique: see QUIONGA.
Kion-Khokh (kēōn"-khōkh'), highest peak (11,230 ft.) in N rocky front range of the central Greater Caucasus, Russian SFSR, 35 mi. WSW of Dzaudzhikau, W of Ossetian Military Road.
Kioroshi (kyōrō'shē), town (pop. 5,214), Chiba prefecture, central Honshu, Japan, 9 mi. NW of Sakura; rice.

Kioshan or **Ch'iao-shan** (both: chyou'shän'), town, ⊙ Kioshan co. (pop. 236,413), S Honan prov., China, 45 mi. N of Sinyang and on Peking-Hankow RR; wheat, millet, beans. Iron deposits near by. Also written Chüehshan.

Kioto, Japan: see KYOTO, city.

Kiowa (kī'ůwů). **1** County (□ 1,792; pop. 3,003), E Colo.; ⊙ Eads. Wheat and livestock area, bordering on Kansas; watered by Big Sandy Creek and reservoirs in S. Formed 1889. **2** County (□ 720; pop. 4,743), S Kansas; ⊙ Greensburg. Rolling plain, watered by Rattlesnake Creek and by headstreams of Salt Fork of Arkansas R. and Medicine Lodge R. Grain, livestock. Formed 1886. **3** County (□ 1,032; pop. 18,926), SW Okla.; ⊙ Hobart. Bounded W by North Fork of Red R.; drained by Elk Creek. Part of low Wichita Mts. in SE. Agr. (wheat, cotton, oats, barley, livestock, poultry). Mfg. at Hobart. Granite and marble quarrying; oil wells. Formed 1901.

Kiowa. 1 Town (pop. 173), ⊙ Elbert co., central Colo., 40 mi. SE of Denver; alt. 6,400 ft. Dairy products, livestock, grain, beans. **2** City (pop. 1,561), Barber co., S Kansas, near Okla. line, 25 mi. WSW of Anthony, in cattle region; has machine shop. Inc. 1885. In 1900, Carry Nation damaged saloon here. **3** Town (pop. 802), Pittsburg co., SE Okla., 17 mi. SSW of McAlester, in agr. area (cotton, corn, oats); cotton ginning, lumber milling; foundry products.

Kiowa Creek, central Colo., rises in N El Paso co., flows intermittently 111 mi. N to South Platte R. near Fort Morgan.

Kiparissia, Greece: see KYPARISSIA.

Kipawa, town, Que.: see TIMISKAMING, town.

Kipchak (kēpchäk'), village (1948 pop. over 2,000), W Kara-Kalpak Autonomous SSR, Uzbek SSR, on the Amu Darya and 30 mi. SE of Nukus; metalworks.

Kipengere Range (kēpěng-gě'rä), Southern Highlands prov., S Tanganyika, N of L. Nyasa; rises to 9,000 ft.

Kipercheny (kēpyĭrchě'nē), Rum. *Chiperceni* (kēpěrchěn'), village (1941 pop. 3,064), E central Moldavian SSR, 10 mi. N of Orgeyev, in tobacco dist.

Kipfenberg (kĭp'fůnběrk), village (pop. 1,522), Middle Franconia, central Bavaria, Germany, on the Altmühl and 10 mi. ENE of Eichstätt; glassworks. Hops, cattle, hogs. Has early-17th-cent. baroque church. Towered over by ruins of medieval castle with 13th-cent. watchtower.

Kipili, Tanganyika: see KIRANDO.

Kipini (kēpē'nē), town, Coast Prov., SE Kenya, in coastal protectorate, small port at mouth of Tana R. on Indian Ocean, 120 mi. NNE of Mombasa; sisal center; cotton copra, sugar cane; fisheries.

Kipkabus (kēpkä'bōōs), village, Rift Valley prov., W Kenya, on Uasin Gishu Plateau, on railroad and 22 mi. SSE of Eldoret; coffee, wheat, corn, tea, wattle growing.

Kipkarren (kēpkä'rěn), village, Rift Valley prov., W Kenya, on railroad and 22 mi. WNW of Eldoret; coffee, tea, sisal, corn.

Kipling, village (pop. 404), SE Sask., 65 mi. NE of Weyburn; lumbering, mixed farming.

Kipnuk (kĭp'nōōk), village (pop. 185), W Alaska, near Bering Sea and Etolin Strait, 100 mi. SW of Bethel; fur farming; supply point.

Kippen, agr. village and parish (pop. 1,356), N Stirling, Scotland, near the Forth, 9 mi. W of Stirling. There are extensive vineyards.

Kippford, village in Colvend and Southwick parish, SE Kirkcudbright, Scotland, on small inlet of Solway Firth, 4 mi. S of Dalbeattie; seaside resort, with granite quarries.

Kippure (kĭpūr'), mountain (2,473 ft.), N Co. Wicklow, on Co. Dublin border, Ireland, 12 mi. S of Dublin.

Kip's Bay, SE N.Y., a district of Manhattan borough of New York city, along East R. S of 42d St.

Kipushi (kēpōō'shē), town (1948 pop. 15,400), Katanga prov., SE Belgian Congo, 15 mi. WSW of Elisabethville; major copper- and zinc-mining center, rail terminus, and customs station on Northern Rhodesia border. Has copper and zinc concentrating plants as well as chemical works producing sulphuric acid, glycerin, fatty acids, sodium chlorate, caustic soda, lubricants. Its noted Prince Leopold Mine is the only deep-shaft mine in Katanga. Benedictine mission.

Kiragawa (kērä'gäwů), town (pop. 5,524), Kochi prefecture, S Shikoku, Japan, on Tosa Bay, 35 mi. ESE of Kochi; agr. center (rice, sweet potatoes).

Kirakat (kĭrä'kůt), town (pop. 1,542), Jaunpur dist., SE Uttar Pradesh, India, on the Gumti and 16 mi. SE of Jaunpur; barley, rice, corn, wheat. Also spelled Kerakat.

Kiralyhaza, Ukrainian SSR: see KOROLEVO.

Kiraly Hegy, Czechoslovakia: see KRALOVA HOLA.

Kiraly Helmec, Czechoslovakia: see KRALOVSKY CHLMEC.

Kirando (kērän'dō), village, Western Prov., SW Tanganyika, small port on L. Tanganyika, just N of Kipili town, 75 mi. NW of Sumbawanga; fishing center; tobacco, wheat, corn.

Kiranur (kē'rŭnōōr). **1** Town, Madura dist., Madras, India: see KEERANUR. **2** Town, South Arcot dist., Madras, India: see ULUNDURPET. **3** Town (pop. 2,831), Trichinopoly dist., S Madras, India, 13 mi. N of Pudukkottai; millet, peanuts, rice. Also spelled Keeranur.

Kiraoli (kĭrou'lē), village, Agra dist., W Uttar Pradesh, India, 14 mi. WSW of Agra; pearl millet, gram, wheat, barley.

Kira Panayia, Greece: see PELAGONESI.

Kiratpur (kē'rŭtpōōr), town (pop. 19,415), Bijnor dist., N Uttar Pradesh, India, 10 mi. NNE of Bijnor; sugar refining; rice, wheat, gram, sugar cane. Ruins of 18th-cent. Pathan fort.

Kirby. 1 Village (pop. c.300), Pike co., SW Ark., 38 mi. WSW of Hot Springs; cinnabar mine. **2** Village (pop. 164), Wyandot co., N central Ohio, 21 mi. NW of Marion. **3** Town (pop. 257), Caledonia co., NE Vt., just NE of St. Johnsbury; agr. **4** Town (pop. 99), Hot Springs co., N central Wyo., on Bighorn R. and 12 mi. N of Thermopolis; alt. 4,270 ft.; coal-shipping point.

Kirby, Lake, W central Texas, impounded by dam in small Cedar Creek (a S tributary of Clear Fork of Brazos R.), just S of Abilene; c.2.5 mi. long; capacity 8,500 acre-ft.

Kirbyville, city (pop. 1,150), Jasper co., E Texas, near Neches R., c.40 mi. NNE of Beaumont; trade center for lumbering, agr. area; sawmill; cotton, fertilizer plants. Founded 1895, inc. 1926.

Kirchberg (kĭrkh'běrk), town (pop. 2,858), Tyrol, W Austria, 3 mi. W of Kitzbühel; summer resort; pilgrimage church.

Kirchberg. 1 Town (pop. 1,922), in former Prussian Rhine Prov., W Germany, after 1945 in Rhineland-Palatinate, in the Hunsrück, 22 mi. W of Bingen; wine. **2** Town (pop. 7,092), Saxony, E central Germany, at N foot of the Erzgebirge, 7 mi. S of Zwickau; mfg. of textiles (cotton, wool, rayon) and machinery; tanning. Granite quarrying. **3** or **Kirchberg an der Jagst** (än děr yäkst'), town (pop. 1,213), N Württemberg, Germany, after 1945 in Württemberg-Baden, on the Jagst and 6 mi. NW of Crailsheim; grain. Has 16th–18th-cent. castle.

Kirchberg. 1 Town (pop. 2,581), Bern canton, NW central Switzerland, on Emme R. and 11 mi. NE of Bern; metal- and woodworking, cotton textiles. **2** Town (pop. 5,311), St. Gall canton, NE Switzerland, 16 mi. W of St. Gall; embroideries, cotton textiles.

Kirchberg an der Pielach (än děr pē'läkh), town (pop. 2,596), central Lower Austria, 15 mi. SSW of Sankt Pölten; grain, cattle.

Kirchbichl (kĭrkh'bēkhůl), town (pop. 3,941), Tyrol, W Austria, on the Inn and 6 mi. SSW of Kufstein; summer resort. Lignite mined near by.

Kirchdorf (kĭrkh'dôrf). **1** or **Kirchdorf am Inn** (äm ĭn'), village (commune pop. 3,279), Upper Bavaria, Germany, on the Inn and 5 mi. S of Rosenheim. Paper milling at Redenfelden (pop. 853), 1 mi. NNE; chemical mfg. at Raubling (pop. 1,755), 1 mi. N. **2** or **Kirchdorf am Haunpold,** town, Bavaria, Germany: see BRUCKMÜHL. **3** Commune, Mecklenburg, N Germany: see POEL.

Kirchdorf an der Krems (än děr krěms'), town (pop. 2,606), SE central Upper Austria, 15 mi. E of Gmunden; brewery.

Kirchenlamitz (kĭr"khůnlä'mĭts), town (pop. 3,181), Upper Franconia, NE Bavaria, Germany, in the Fichtelgebirge, on small Lamitz R. and 8 mi. W of Selb; porcelain mfg., metalworking, tanning, flour and lumber milling. Clay pits in area.

Kirchen-Wehbach (kĭr'khůn-vā'bäkh), village (pop. 5,848), in former Prussian Rhine Prov., W Germany, after 1945 in Rhineland-Palatinate, on the Sieg and 7 mi. SW of Siegen; rail junction. Formed 1942 through unification of Kirchen and Wehbach.

Kirchhain (kĭrkh'hīn). **1** Town (pop. 7,636), Brandenburg, E Germany, in Lower Lusatia, 7 mi. W of Finsterwalde; sheepskin-tanning center; lignite mining; glass mfg., metalworking. Exploitation of coal deposits, discovered after Second World War, begun 1949. **2** or **Kirchhain im Bezirk Kassel** (ĭm bůtsĭrk" kä'sůl), town (pop. 4,284), in former Prussian prov. of Hesse-Nassau, W Germany, after 1945 in Hesse, near the Ohm, 6 mi. E of Marburg; grain.

Kirchhatten, Germany: see HATTEN.

Kirchheim (kĭrkh'hīm). **1** Village (pop. 1,624), Swabia, SW Bavaria, Germany, 24 mi. SW of Augsburg; dairying, brewing. Chartered 1490. **2** or **Kirchheim unter Teck** (ōōntůr těk'), town (pop. 18,700), N Württemberg, Germany, after 1945 in Württemberg-Baden, at N foot of the Teck, 9 mi. SE of Esslingen; textiles (cotton, cloth, knit goods, stockings); leather coats, gloves, and trousers; furniture; metalworking, paper milling. Has 14th-cent. church; and former ducal palace, now local mus. Chartered 1270.

Kirchheimbolanden (–bō'län"důn), town (pop. 4,650), Rhenish Palatinate, W Germany, 16 mi. W of Worms; wine. Brewing, lumber milling. Has 18th-cent. castle; pomological and viticultural school.

Kirchheim unter Teck, Germany: see KIRCHHEIM, Württemberg.

Kirchhellen (kĭrkh"hě'lůn), village (pop. 7,280), in former Prussian prov. of Westphalia, W Germany, after 1945 in North Rhine-Westphalia, in the Ruhr, 3 mi. NW of Gladbeck; dairying. Truck produce.

Kirchhörde (kĭrkh'hûr"dů), district (since 1929) of Dortmund, W Germany, 5 mi. S of city center; coal mining.

Kirchhundem (kĭrkh'hōōn"dům), village (pop. 9,398), in former Prussian prov. of Westphalia, W Germany, after 1945 in North Rhine-Westphalia, 15 mi. NNE of Siegen; forestry.

Kirchlengern (kĭrkh'lěng"ůrn), village (pop. 4,104), in former Prussian prov. of Westphalia, NW Germany, after 1945 in North Rhine-Westphalia, 6 mi. N of Herford; rail junction.

Kirchwärder, Germany: see VIERLANDE.

Kirchweyhe (kĭrkh'vī"ů), village (pop. 5,986), in former Prussian prov. of Hanover, NW Germany, after 1945 in Lower Saxony, 7 mi. SSE of Bremen.

Kirchzarten (kĭrkh'tsär'tůn), village (pop. 2,183), S Baden, Germany, in Black Forest, 5 mi. ESE of Freiburg; paper milling, woodworking. Summer resort.

Kirchzell (kĭrkh'tsěl"), village (pop. 1,380), Lower Franconia, W Bavaria, Germany, 7 mi. SW of Miltenberg; rye, hogs.

Kircubbin (kůrků'bĭn), fishing village (district pop. 1,349), NE Co. Down, Northern Ireland, on E shore of Strangford Lough, 10 mi. SE of Newtownards.

Kirda (kērdä'), town (1947 pop. over 500), N Tashkent oblast, Uzbek SSR; suburb of Yangi-Yul.

Kirdford, agr. village and parish (pop. 1,275), NW Sussex, England, 8 mi. WSW of Horsham. Has 13th-cent. church with noted glass. Had important glass industry in Middle Ages.

Kirdzhali (kērjä'lē), city (pop. 10,480), Khaskovo dist., S Bulgaria, in E Rhodope Mts., on Arda R. and 21 mi. SSW of Khaskovo; commercial center; tobacco and food processing, lead smelting. Sometimes spelled Kardzhali, Kirjali, or Krdzhali.

Kireli (kůrělē'), Turkish *Kireli*, village (pop. 862), Konya prov., W central Turkey, on E shore of L. Beysehir, 50 mi. W of Konya. Formerly also Kereli.

Kirenga River (kērĭn-gä'), in E central Irkutsk oblast, Russian SFSR, rises in Baikal Range, flows 340 mi. N, past Kazachinskoye, to Lena R. at Kirensk. Navigable for 90 mi. above mouth.

Kirensk (kērěnsk'), city (1939 pop. over 10,000), N central Irkutsk oblast, Russian SFSR, on Lena R., at mouth of Kirenga R., and 400 mi. NNE of Irkutsk, 150 mi. NNW of L. Baikal; shipbuilding; brickworks, distillery. Founded 1630.

Kiresun, Turkey: see GIRESUN, town.

Kireyevka (kērā'ůfků), town (1939 pop. over 500), E Tula oblast, Russian SFSR, 22 mi. SE of Tula; iron-mining center; lignite mining.

Kirghiz Autonomous Oblast, USSR: see KIRGHIZIA.

Kirghiz Autonomous Soviet Socialist Republic, USSR: see KAZAKHSTAN, republic; KIRGHIZIA.

Kirghizia (kĭrgē'zhů), **Kirghizstan** (kĭrgēstän'), or **Kirghiz Soviet Socialist Republic** (kĭrgēz', kûr'gēz, Rus. kĭrgēs'), constituent republic (□ 76,000; 1947 pop. estimate 1,490,000) of the USSR, in central Asia; ⊙ Frunze. Bounded by Kazakhstan (N), Uzbekistan (W), Tadzhikistan (SW), and China (SE). Essentially a mtn. country, located in the wide W section of the Tien Shan system with broad, grassy, highland valleys and E-W-oriented ranges converging (E) on Chinese border in glaciated mtn. hub rising to 24,406 ft. in Pobeda Peak. Chief agr. areas are the low-lying Chu and Talas river valleys (N), Fergana Valley (W), and Issyk-Kul basin (E). Pop. consists of Kirghiz or Kirgiz (67%; a pastoral Turko-Mongolian people), Russians, Ukrainians, and Uzbeks. Administratively, republic falls into oblasts: DZHALAL-ABAD, FRUNZE, ISSYK-KUL, OSH, TALAS, TYAN-SHAN. Republic has vertical vegetation zones: cold summer pastures of the short-grass alpine meadows (above 10,000 ft.; summer temp., 32°–50°F.); high-grass subalpine zone (6–10,000 ft.; summer temp. 50°–60° F.), which includes upper Naryn R. valley and constitutes the most important summer grazing area, with wooded slopes (N) and agr. (barley, oats, rye) in lower reaches; warm agr. zone (4–6,000 ft.; summer temp., 60°–72° F.), which has fall and winter pastures, irrigated agr., dry farming (wheat, corn, barley, opium poppy, tobacco) in Issyk-Kul basin, and wild-growing fruit and nut woods in Chatkal R. valley; and hot agr. zone (below 4,000 ft.; summer temp., 72°–82° F.), which produces cotton, silk, grapes, fruit in Fergana Valley and sugar beets, yellow tobacco, fiber crops in Chu and Talas river valleys. Industry based on mineral resources (mercury and antimony at Khaidarkan, Frunze, and Chauvai, coal at Tashkumyr, Kok-Yangak, Kizyl-Kiya, Uzgen, and Sulyukta, uranium at Tyuya-Muyun, petroleum at Changyrtash, tungsten, lead, and salt) and on agr. processing (sugar beets, cotton, grain, tobacco, silk, hides, meat). Cotton, coal, livestock, grain, and sugar are chief exports. Main industrial centers are Frunze, Dzhalal-Abad, and Osh. The Kirghiz people (formerly called Kara-Kirghiz; related to the Khakass, Tuvinian, and Oirot groups) migrated (largely in 16th cent.) to this region from the upper Yenisei. They were dominated (19th cent.) by the Kokand khanate. Region first constituted (1924) as Kara-Kirghiz Autonomous Oblast out of Turkestan Autonomous SSR; renamed (1925) Kirghiz Autonomous Oblast. Its status was raised (1926) to that of autonomous SSR within Russian SFSR and (1936) to that of constituent republic within the USSR.

Kirghiz Range, W branch of Tien Shan mtn. system, USSR; extends from Boom Gorge on Chu R. 225 mi. W to area of Dzhambul; forms part of Kazakh-Kirghiz border; rises to 14,800 ft. Most important passes: Merke, Kara-Balty, Shamsi. Gives rise to many affluents of Chu and Talas rivers. Kungei Ala-Tau forms E extension. Formerly called Alexander Range, Rus. *Aleksandrovskiy Khrebet.*

Kirghiz Steppe, USSR: see Steppes, The.

Kirgis Nor, Khirgis Nur, or **Hirgis Nuur** (all: khĕr′gēs nōr′, nōōr′), salt lake (□ 525) in W Mongolian People's Republic, 80 mi. SE of Ulankom; 52 mi. long, 20 mi. wide; alt. 3,392 ft. Situated in a semi-desert depression, the lake contains sodium sulphate and carbonate and magnesium chloride. Connected with Airik Nor (S).

Kirgiz-Miyaki (kĭrgĕs″-mēä′kē), village (1926 pop. 2,467), W Bashkir Autonomous SSR, Russian SFSR, 50 mi. W of Sterlitamak; grain, livestock.

Kiri, river, Albania: see Kiri River.

Kiriath-arba, Palestine: see Hebron.

Kirigalpotta (kĭrĭgŭlpŏt′ŭ), peak (7,857 ft.) in S central Ceylon, on Horton Plains, 11 mi. S of Nuwara Eliya; 2d-highest peak in Ceylon.

Kirikhan (kŭrŭk-hän′), Turkish *Kırıkhan,* village (pop. 3,690), Hatay prov., S Turkey, 23 mi. NNE of Antioch; grain.

Kirikkale (kŭrŭk′kälĕ), Turkish *Kırıkkale,* town (1950 pop. 15,695), Ankara prov., Turkey, near the Kizil Irmak, on railroad and 35 mi. E of Ankara; agr. and mfg. center; grain, fruit; mohair.

Kirillov (kĭrē′lŭf), city (1926 pop. 4,276), W central Vologda oblast, Russian SFSR, on Northern Dvina Canal and 65 mi. NW of Vologda, in flax and potato region; limestone quarry. Has 14th-cent. monastery, now mus. of old Rus. art. Chartered 1776.

Kirillovo (kĭrē′lŭvŭ), village (1947 pop. over 500), S Sakhalin, Russian SFSR, on W coast of Aniva Gulf, 20 mi. SSW of Aniva; fishing. Under Jap. rule (1905–45), called Uryu.

Kirin (kē′rĭn′), Chinese *Chi-lin* (jē′lĭn′), province (□ 45,000; pop. 7,000,000) of E central Manchuria; ⊙ Kirin. Extending 400 mi. NW-SE bet. the edge of Inner Mongolia and the USSR and Korea borders, Kirin is bounded N by Heilungkiang and Sungkiang provs. and S by Liaosi and Liaotung provs. It is drained W by upper Sungari R., whose basin is separated by the E Manchurian highlands from Tumen R. basin (E). Agr. (soybeans, wheat, millet, kaoliang, tobacco) is concentrated in Manchurian plain (W). Lumbering is important in the highlands, with center at Tunhwa. Mining is developed in Chientao, on USSR and Korea borders, with coal produced at Laotowkow, Towtaokow, and Santaokow, and nonferrous metals (copper, lead, zinc) at Tienpaoshan (near Laotowkow). Industry is powered partly by the Fengman hydroelectric station on Sungari R. The leading centers are Kirin and Changchun on the W agr. plain; the old trade center of Fuyü (Petuna) near Sungari-Nonni R. confluence; Tunhwa; and Yenki and Lungching (in Chientao). The name Kirin was originally applied to the easternmost prov. (□ 105,003; 1926 pop. estimate 5,633,186) of the 3 original Manchurian provs. (S of Sungari R.). It was reduced to nearly the present size in 1934 (□ 34,334; 1940 pop. 5,608,922), reorganized in 1946 (□ 28,060; pop. 7,315,123); and it absorbed Chientao in 1949.

Kirin, Chinese *Chi-lin,* city (1947 pop. 246,873), ⊙ Kirin prov., and ⊙ but independent of Yungki co. (1946 pop. 679,204), Manchuria, port on left bank of Sungari R. (head of navigation) and 60 mi. E of Changchun, 135 mi. S of Harbin; 43°51′N 126°32′E. Rail junction; industrial and commercial center, in tobacco-growing area; lumber products (paper and match mfg.), chemicals (synthetic rubber, calcium carbide), cement, brick and tiles; agr. processing (soybeans, flour, hemp, tobacco, medicinal herbs). Industry is powered by Sungari hydroelectric plant at Fengman (SE). Founded 1673 as a Chinese fortress, it developed an active tobacco, fur, and timber trade and became known as a junk-building center. Modern industrial development dates from 1912, when Kirin was reached by railroad from Changchun. A provincial capital since its founding, Kirin was called Yungki from 1929 until 1937, when it became an independent municipality.

Kirin (kĭrĭn′), village, Wallaga prov., W central Ethiopia, in Beni Shangul dist., 12 mi. WSW of Asosa; gold placers near by.

Kirindi Oya (kĭrĭn′dē ō′yŭ), river, S Ceylon, rises in S Uva Basin, just ESE of Bandarawela; flows N and S to Indian Ocean 6 mi. S of Tissamaharama; 73 mi. long. Land reclamation project (□ 37) on lower course, near Tissamaharama.

Kiri River (kē′rē), in N Albania, rises in North Albanian Alps, flows c.30 mi. SSW to the Drinassa (arm of the Drin) just S of Scutari.

Kirishi (kē′rĭshē), town (1939 pop. over 2,000), S Leningrad oblast, Russian SFSR, on Volkhov R. (landing) and 32 mi. SSW of Volkhov; rail junction; sawmilling center. During Second World War, briefly held (1941) by Germans.

Kirishima-yama (kērē′shĭmä-yämŭ), collective name for 2 volcanic peaks on Miyazaki-Kagoshima prefecture border, S Kyushu, Japan, near Takaharu, 33 mi. W of Miyazaki, in Kirishima Natl. Park (□ 83). Higher peak is Karakuni-dake (5,610 ft.), lower is Takachiho-dake (5,194 ft.). Hot springs on slopes of both peaks.

Kirit (kērēt′), village, central Br. Somaliland, on Haud plateau, on road and 55 mi. SE of Burao; camels, sheep, goats.

Kiriwina (kĭrĭwē′nŭ), volcanic island, largest of Trobriand Isls., Territory of Papua, SW Pacific, 95 mi. SE of New Guinea; 30 mi. long, 10 mi. wide. Chief town and port is Losuia, on W coast. Produces yams, pearl shell, pearls. In Second World War, site of Allied air base in 1943.

Kirjali, Bulgaria: see Kirdzhali.

Kirjath-arba, Palestine: see Hebron.

Kirjath-jearim, Palestine: see Abu Ghosh.

Kirkagac (kŭrkäch′), Turkish *Kırkağaç,* town (pop. 8,696), Manisa prov., W Turkey, on railroad and 36 mi. NNE of Manisa; raisins, tobacco, wheat, barley, vetch, chick-peas, cotton.

Kirkburton, urban district (1931 pop. 3,184; 1951 census 17,961), West Riding, S Yorkshire, England, 4 mi. SE of Huddersfield; woolen mills, chemical works. Absorbed near-by areas in 1938.

Kirkby (kûr′bē), village and parish (pop. 1,151), SW Lancashire, England, 6 mi. NE of Liverpool; mfg. of soap powder, chemicals, plastics, pottery; electrical engineering. Has modern church with 12th-cent. font.

Kirkby-in-Ashfield (kûr′bē), urban district (1931 pop. 17,797; 1951 census 20,131), W Nottingham, England, 2 mi. S of Sutton-in-Ashfield; coal mines, brickworks. Just E is brick-mfg. town of East Kirkby.

Kirkby Ireleth (kûr′bē ī′rlĕth), parish (pop. 1,366), N Lancashire, England. Includes slate-quarrying village of Grizebeck (grīz′bĕk), 5 mi. NNW of Ulverston; sheep raising, agr.

Kirkby Lonsdale (kûr′bē lŏnz′–), former urban district (1931 pop. 1,372), S Westmorland, England, near Lancashire boundary, on Lune R., and 10 mi. SE of Kendal; agr. market in cattle-raising and agr. area. Has remains of Stone Age graves and excavations of Roman camp.

Kirkby Moorside (kûr′bē mōōr′sīd), agr. market town and parish (pop. 1,843), North Riding, NE Yorkshire, England, on Dove R. and 11 mi. NNW of Malton; malt processing. Has 12th-13th-cent. church, rebuilt by Sir Gilbert Scott. George Villiers, 2d duke of Buckingham, died here (1687). Near by are several stone quarries. WSW 3 mi. is Kirkdale, site of cave discovered 1821 yielding remains of anc. species of animals and Stone Age implements and weapons.

Kirkby Stephen (kûr′bē stē′vŭn), village and parish (pop. 1,588), E Westmorland, England, on Eden R. and 8 mi. SSE of Appleby; cattle and sheep raising. Has many 17th-cent. houses, and church of Saxon and Norman origin with 16th-cent. tower.

Kirkcaldy (kŭrkô′dē,–kôl′dē), burgh (1931 pop. 43,874; 1951 census 49,037), S Fifeshire, Scotland, on the Firth of Forth, 12 mi. ENE of Dunfermline, 10 mi. N of Edinburgh; coal-shipping port and center of coal-mining region; also woolen milling, textile printing, mfg. of linoleum, boilers, and agr. machinery. Kirkcaldy's main street, running 4 mi. along coast, gave it the name "Lang Toun." Adam Smith b. here. Thomas Carlyle and Edward Irving were schoolmasters here at the same time. Burgh includes Dysart; Sinclairtown (N), with woolen and hosiery mills, machinery works; and Pathead (NE), with textile-bleaching works. In Pathead are ruins of 15th-cent. Ravenscraig Castle, the "Castle Ravenheugh" of Scott's *Rosabelle.* Just S of Kirkcaldy, on Firth of Forth, is woolen-milling suburb of Linktown, in former parish of Abbotshall, now included in Kirkcaldy burgh.

Kirkcolm (kûr′kŭm), agr. village and parish (pop. 1,388), NW Wigtown, Scotland, on the Rhinns of Galloway, near Loch Ryan, 5 mi. NNW of Stranraer. Sir John Ross b. near by.

Kirconnel (kŭrkŏ′nŭl), town and parish (pop. 3,962), NW Dumfries, Scotland, on Nith R. and 3 mi. WNW of Sanquhar; coal mining. Medicinal springs near by.

Kircowan (kŭrkōō′ŭn), town and parish (pop. 977), E central Wigtown, Scotland, on Tarff Water and 6 mi. WSW of Newton Stewart; woolen milling.

Kirkcudbright or **Kirkcudbrightshire** (kŭrkōō′brē, –shĭr), county (□ 898.7; 1931 pop. 30,341; 1951 census 30,742), S Scotland, on Solway Firth; ⊙ Kirkcudbright. Bounded by Wigtown (W), Ayrshire (W and NW), Dumfries (E and NE). Drained by Dee and Cree rivers. Surface is mountainous in NW (with several small lochs), sloping toward S. Co. forms E part of Galloway dist. Chief industries are sheep and cattle raising, fishing, woolen milling. Besides Kirkcudbright, other towns are Dalbeattie, Castle Douglas, Gatehouse, and New Galloway. Several small resorts on coast.

Kirkcudbright, burgh (1931 pop. 2,311; 1951 census 2,498), ⊙ Kirkcudbrightshire, Scotland, in S part of co., at head of Dee R. estuary, and 25 mi. SW of Dumfries; agr. market. There are traces of anc. wall and moat, and remains of Kirkcudbright Castle (1582) of McClellan family. The 16th-cent. courthouse is now factory. There are also slight remains of 13th-cent. church.

Kirkdale. 1 N suburb (pop. 40,389) of Liverpool, SW Lancashire, England; leather tanning and mfg.; engineering; mfg. of chemicals, soap. **2** In Yorkshire, England: see Kirkby Moorside.

Kirkden, village and parish (pop. 1,080), E Angus, Scotland. Includes Friockheim.

Kirkee (kĭr′kē), town (pop. 26,285), Poona dist., central Bombay, India, 2 mi. N of Poona; military station; large ordnance factories and workshops, chemical works; copper, brass, and iron products; dairy farm. Brewery 2 mi. NW. School of Military Engineering. Scene of Br. victory (1817) over Mahrattas.

Kirkenes (kĕr′kŭnĕs, Nor. chĭr′kŭnās), village (pop. c.2,100), Finnmark co., NE Norway, near USSR border, on Bok Fjord (S arm of Varanger Fjord), at mouth of Pasvik R., 160 mi. ESE of Hammerfest, 90 mi. NW of Murmansk; 69°43′N 30°3′E. Port and commercial center for Sor-Varanger canton, important iron-mining region. Seaplane base and airport; terminus of sea and air services from Bergen and of bus route from railhead at Lonsdal, Nordland co. Village grew since beginning (1910) of mining operations in region. German base in Second World War, it was largely destroyed by air raids. Captured by USSR (Oct., 1944) and occupied by the Russians until shortly after the end of hostilities.

Kirkersville, village (pop. 299), Licking co., central Ohio, 12 mi. SW of Newark.

Kirkfield, village (pop. estimate 400), S Ont., 20 mi. NW of Lindsay; dairying, mixed farming.

Kirkham (kûr′kŭm), urban district (1931 pop. 4,031; 1951 census 6,874), W Lancashire, England, 7 mi. W of Preston; cotton milling. A Roman road is town's main street.

Kirkheaton, former urban district (1931 pop. 2,610), West Riding, S Yorkshire, England, 3 mi. ENE of Huddersfield; woolen milling, chemical mfg. Inc. 1938 in Kirkburton.

Kirkhill (kŭrk′hĭl′), agr. village in N Inverness, Scotland, near Beauly Firth, 7 mi. W of Inverness.

Kirkhope, agr. village and parish (pop. 352), central Selkirk, Scotland, on Ettrick Water and 7 mi. SW of Selkirk. Has remains of Kirkhope Tower, 17th-cent. fort.

Kirkinner (kŭrkĭ′nŭr), agr. village and parish (pop. 1,004), SE Wigtown, Scotland, 3 mi. SSW of Wigtown.

Kirkintilloch (kŭrkĭntĭ′lŏkh), burgh (1931 pop. 11,817; 1951 census 14,824), in detached portion of Dumbarton, Scotland, 8 mi. NE of Glasgow; steel milling, coal mining, chemical mfg., textile milling. Gaelic name *Caerpentulach* [fort at the end of the ridge] refers to anc. fort at end of the Wall of Antoninus. The town was made a burgh in 1170.

Kirk-Kilissa, Turkey: see Kirklareli.

Kirkkonummi, Finland: see Kyrkslatt.

Kirkland, Scotland: see Maxwelton House.

Kirkland. 1 Village (pop. 685), De Kalb co., N Ill., on South Branch of Kishwaukee R. (bridged here) and 17 mi. SE of Rockford, in rich agr. area; makes cheese, tile. **2** Village (pop. c.500), Childress co., extreme N Texas, 10 mi. ESE of Childress, in cotton, wheat, livestock region. **3** Town (pop. 4,713), King co., W central Wash., on E shore of L. Washington and 8 mi. NE of Seattle; resort; hay, grain, fruit. Settled 1872, inc. 1905.

Kirkland Lake, town (pop. estimate 19,000), E Ont., on small Kirkland L., 65 mi. ESE of Timmins; center of one of the most important North American gold-mining regions.

Kirklar Dag (kĭrklär′ dä), Turkish *Kırklar Dağ,* peak (11,348 ft.), NE Turkey, in Rize Mts., 35 mi. S of Rize.

Kirklareli (kĭrklä′rĕlē″), Turkish *Kırklareli,* prov. (□ 2,599; 1950 pop. 192,333), Turkey in Europe; ⊙ Kirklareli. Bordered N by Bulgaria, E by Black Sea. Drained by Ergene R. Heavily forested. One of chief sugar-beet and canary-grass regions of Turkey; also wheat, rye. Sugar refinery at Alpullu.

Kirklareli, Turk. *Kırklareli,* town (1950 pop. 14,464), ⊙ Kirklareli prov., Turkey in Europe, 100 mi. NW of Istanbul, 34 mi. E of Edirne (Adrianople); rail terminus and trade center; market for local produce (grain, sugar beets, canary grass). Known for its numerous mosques and Greek churches. Here in the First Balkan War the Bulgarians defeated (1912) the Turks. Formerly Kirk-Kilissa, Kirk-Kilisseh.

Kirklees, village, West Riding, S Yorkshire, England, 4 mi. NNE of Huddersfield. Has remains of a Cistercian nunnery, built 1155. Legend states that Robin Hood died here.

Kirklin, town (pop. 734), Clinton co., central Ind., near Sugar Creek, 10 mi. SE of Frankfort, in agr. area.

Kirklington cum Upsland, agr. village and parish (pop. 249), North Riding, N central Yorkshire, England, 6 mi. N of Ripon.

Kirkliston (kŭrklĭ′stŭn), town and parish (pop. 3,975), E West Lothian, Scotland, 8 mi. W of Edinburgh; shale-oil mining center, whisky distilling.

Kirkmabreck (kûrk″mŭbrĕk′), parish (pop. 1,294), SW Kirkcudbright, Scotland. Parish includes CREETOWN.

Kirkmahoe, Scotland: see DUNCOW.

Kirkmaiden (kûrkmā′dŭn), agr. village and parish (pop. 1,554), SW Wigtown, Scotland, on the Rhinns of Galloway, 15 mi. SSE of Stranraer. Most southerly parish of Scotland.

Kirkman, town (pop. 131), Shelby co., W Iowa, on West Nishnabotna R. and 6 mi. NE of Harlan.

Kirkmansville, town (pop. 138), Todd co., S Ky., on Pond R. and 17 mi. NE of Hopkinsville.

Kirkmichael (–mī′kŭl). **1** Agr. village and parish (pop. 1,575), S Ayrshire, Scotland, 3 mi. ESE of Maybole. **2** Parish, Ross and Cromarty, Scotland: see RESOLIS.

Kirk Mountains, on Mozambique-Nyasaland border, NW of Blantyre, Nyasaland; extend c.40 mi. N-S bet. Ncheu and Neno; rise to 5,000 ft.

Kirknesvag, Norway: see STRAUMEN.

Kirknewton (kûrknū′tŭn), agr. village and parish (pop. 2,910), W Midlothian, Scotland, 9 mi. WSW of Edinburgh.

Kirk of Mochrum, Scotland: see MOCHRUM.

Kirk of Shotts, village in Shotts parish, NE Lanark, Scotland, 5 mi. ESE of Airdrie; coal, iron mining.

Kirkoswald (–ŏz′wŭld), village and parish (pop. 466), E Cumberland, England, 7 mi. NNE of Penrith; cattle, sheep; agr. Has remains of 12th-cent. castle and church of Norman origin.

Kirkoswald, agr. village and parish (pop. 1,802), S Ayrshire, Scotland, 4 mi. WSW of Maybole. Here are graves of Burns's Tam o' Shanter and Souter Johnnie, and the latter's cottage, housing Burns relics. On Firth of Clyde, 2 mi. W, is small seaside resort of Maidens, with the Shanter farm just S.

Kirkpatrick, village, S Alta., on Red Deer R. and 6 mi. WNW of Drumheller; coal mining.

Kirkpatrick, agr. village in Kirkpatrick-Fleming parish (pop. 1,069), S Dumfries, Scotland, 6 mi. ENE of Annan. Near by are medicinal springs.

Kirkpatrick, Mount (14,603 ft.), highest peak of Queen Alexandra Range, Antarctica, bet. Beardmore Glacier and head of Ross Shelf Ice; 84°20′S 167°E. Discovered 1908 by Sir Ernest Shackleton.

Kirksaeterora, Norway: see KYRKSAETERORA.

Kirk Sandall, town in Barnby Dun with Kirk Sandall parish (pop. 3,780), West Riding, S Yorkshire, England, 4 mi. NE of Doncaster; glass-mfg. center. Just NE is agr. village of Barnby Dun.

Kirkstall, town (pop. 19,582), in Leeds county borough, West Riding, S central Yorkshire, England, on Aire R. just NW of Leeds; woolen-milling and leather-tanning center; steel-rolling mills. Near by are ruins of Kirkstall Abbey (c.1150).

Kirkstead, England: see WOODHALL SPA.

Kirksville, city (pop. 11,110), ⊙ Adair co., N Mo., near Chariton R., 72 mi. NW of Hannibal; agr. center (grain, livestock, dairy products, poultry); shoe mfg.; coal. State teachers col., col. of osteopathy and surgery. Founded c.1841.

Kirkton, agr. village in Cavers parish, central Roxburgh, Scotland, 2 mi. E of Hawick.

Kirkton of Durris (dûr′ĭs), agr. village in Durris parish (pop. 731), N Kincardine, Scotland, on the Dee and 5 mi. E of Banchory.

Kirkton of Largo, Scotland: see UPPER LARGO.

Kirkton of Skene (skēn), agr. village in Skene parish (pop. 1,310), SE Aberdeen, Scotland, 9 mi. W of Aberdeen. Near by is the Loch of Skene (1 mi. long, 1 mi. wide).

Kirkton of Strathmartine (străth-mär′tĭn, strŭth–), agr. village in Mains and Strathmartine parish (pop. 1,643), S Angus, Scotland, NW of Dundee.

Kirktown of Alvah, agr. village in Alvah parish (pop. 1,101), NE Banffshire, Scotland, near Deveron R., 3 mi. S of Banff. Has chalybeate springs.

Kirkuk (kĭrkōōk′), province (□ 7,672; pop. 285,878), NE Iraq; ⊙ Kirkuk. It has agr. (barley, wheat, oranges, apples) and sheep raising, but it is now most important for its rich oilfields.

Kirkuk, city (pop. 69,035), ⊙ Kirkuk prov., NE Iraq, on railroad and 90 mi. SE of Mosul, 150 mi. N of Baghdad; 35°27′N 44°23′E. Although it is an important Kurdistan market town in an area producing wheat, barley, fruit, and sheep, it has developed since First World War as the center of a rich petroleum field. Oil pipe lines lead to the Mediterranean ports of Tripoli (Lebanon) and Haifa (Israel). Just NW is suburb of Baba Gurgur, with a refinery. Customs station. Kirkuk is built in an area whose settlement goes back at least to 3000 B.C. Sometimes spelled Karkuk, Kerkuk, Kurkuk, and Korkuk.

Kirkville, town (pop. 213), Wapello co., SE Iowa, 10 mi. NNW of Ottumwa; livestock, grain.

Kirkwall, burgh (1931 pop. 3,517; 1948 estimate 4,376), ⊙ ORKNEY co., Scotland, on E coast of POMONA isl., 35 mi. NE of Thurso; 58°59′N 2°57′W; largest town in the Orkneys, port and herring-fishing center, with woolen milling and whisky distilling. Chief exports: agr. produce, whisky, salted fish, cattle, pork, eggs; imports: coal, timber, salt, lime, fruit. Airfields near by. The Cathedral of St. Magnus was founded 1137 by Rognvald, earl of Orkney, and completed 1558; restored 1912–20. Ruins of Bishop's Palace date from 12th cent.; in 1263 king Haco or Haakon IV of Norway died here after battle of Largs. There are also remains of Earl's Palace (1607) and of 16th-cent. church of St. Olaf. Kirkwall early became a place of importance; in 1486 it was made royal burgh by James III.

Kirkwood, village (pop. 4,122), S Cape Prov., U. of So. Afr., on Sundays R. and 40 mi. NNW of Port Elizabeth; rail terminus; irrigated farming.

Kirkwood. 1 Village (pop. 747), Warren co., W Ill., 6 mi. SW of Monmouth, in agr. and bituminous-coal area. **2** City (pop. 18,640), St. Louis co., E Mo., suburb W of St. Louis; horticulture; lime, cement, lumber products. Laid out 1852, inc. 1865.

Kirlampudi, India: see SAMALKOT.

Kirloskarvadi (kĭrlōskŭrvä′dē), village, Satara South dist., S Bombay, India, 22 mi. NW of Miraj and on railroad; mfg. of agr. machinery.

Kirman, Iran: see KERMAN.

Kirmanshah, Iran: see KERMANSHAH.

Kirmasti, town, Turkey: see MUSTAFA KEMALPASA.

Kirmasti River (kûrmästŭ′), Turkish *Kırmastı*, anc. *Rhyndacus*, NW Turkey, rises 6 mi. NW of Simav, flows 115 mi. N, past Mustafa Kemalpasa, to L. Apulyont, then 5 mi. W to Simav R. at Karacabey. Also called Mustafa Kemalpasa; formerly also Adranos or Edrenos.

Kirmir River (kĭrmĭr′), N central Turkey, rises in Koroglu Mts., flows 75 mi. S and SW, past Kizilcahamam, to Sakarya R. 15 mi. SW of Beypazari.

Kirn (kĭrn), town (pop. 7,880), in former Prussian Rhine Prov., W Germany, after 1945 in Rhineland-Palatinate, on the Nahe and 18 mi. WSW of Bad Kreuznach; textile mfg., tanning.

Kirn (kûrn), resort on Firth of Clyde, in DUNOON burgh, E Argyll, Scotland.

Kiron (kī′rŭn), town (pop. 255), Crawford co., W Iowa, 13 mi. N of Denison, in agr. area.

Kirov (kē′rŭf), oblast (□ 47,000; 1946 pop. estimate 2,250,000), in N central European Russian SFSR; ⊙ Kirov. Rolling lowland in Vyatka R. basin; bordered N by the Northern Uvals; crossed N-S by the Vyatka Uval; continental climate; podsolic soils; forests and peat marshes (NE). Main mineral resources (NE): iron; phosphorites (mining at Rudnichny). Metallurgy in Omutninsk area, machine mfg. (Kirov), fur processing, tanning, shoe mfg. (Kirov-Slobodskoi area). Sawmills at river-rail intersections (Kirov, Kotelnich, Vyatskiye Polyany), match mfg., paper milling, wood distillation. Widespread handicraft industries (woodworking; toy, lace, and felt-boot mfg.). Flax grown on right bank, rye and oats on left bank, of Vyatka R.; dairy farming (Kirov-Kotelnich area). Trade oriented toward the Urals and Volga region. Originally constituted as Vyatka govt., inc. (1929) in Nizhegorod Territory and made, in 1936, a separate oblast.

Kirov. 1 City (1939 pop. over 10,000), SW Kaluga oblast, Russian SFSR, 80 mi. SW of Kaluga; metalworking center; iron foundry. Porcelain mfg. at near-by Fayansovy. Until 1936, Pesochnya. During Second World War, held (1941–42) by Germans. **2** City (1926 pop. 62,097; 1939 pop. 143,181), ⊙ Kirov oblast, Russian SFSR, on Vyatka R. and 260 mi. NE of Gorki, 480 mi. ENE of Moscow; 58°36′N 49°41′E. Industrial center; rail junction (railroad shops) of lines to the Urals, Kotlas, and Leningrad; mfg. of machine tools, agr. implements, matches, visual-teaching aids, shoes; fur processing, tanning, sawmilling, flour milling, meat packing, brewing, distilling. Has regional mus., pedagogic, agr., and veterinary institutes. Monument to A. I. Herzen. Old kremlin with 18th-cent. cathedral. Originally a Votyak settlement, founded (1174) by Novgorod colonists. Permanent Rus. colonization began in 14th cent. Called Khlynov after early 15th cent., Vyatka or Viatka after 1780. Flourishing trade center (17th–18th cent.) on road to Siberia; ⊙ Vyatka govt. until 1929. Place of political exile before revolution. Name changed (1934) to Kirov.

Kirov, W district of Greater Baku, Azerbaijan SSR, at base of Apsheron Peninsula, NW of Baku; oil fields. Main centers: Binagady, Geokmaly, Khurdalan.

Kirova, Imeni (ē′mĭnyē kē′rŭvŭ). **1** Town (1939 pop. over 500) in Ordzhonikidze dist. of Greater Baku, E Azerbaijan SSR, on central Apsheron Peninsula, c.10 mi. NE of Baku; vineyards, truck produce. **2** Town, SE Azerbaijan SSR: see BANK. **3** Town (1939 pop. over 500), central Leningrad oblast, Russian SFSR, on Mga R. (affluent of Neva R.), just SW of Mga; hydroelectric station. **4** Town (1945 pop. over 500), S Stalinabad oblast, Tadzhik SSR, in Vakhsh valley, 5 mi. ESE of Kurgan-Tyube, in long-staple-cotton area; cotton ginning. **5** Town (1939 pop. 500), N Stalino oblast, Ukrainian SSR, 6 mi. from Krasny Liman. **6** Town, central Stalino oblast, Ukrainian SSR: see ZHELEZNOYE. **7** Village, Uzbek SSR: see KIROVO, Fergana oblast.

Kirovabad (kē″rŭvŭbät′). **1** Second-largest city (1939 pop. 98,743) of Azerbaijan SSR, on Gandzha R. (right affluent of the Kura), on railroad and 110 mi. SE of Tiflis; industrial center; cotton milling, cottonseed-oil extraction (soaps, oils), metalworking; mfg. of copper sulphate, based on Chiragidzor and Kedabek mines; wine making, fruit canning. Oil deposits (SE). Site of 17th-cent. mosque. Agr. and teachers colleges, agr. experimental station. Located amid fruit and truck gardens, city proper is separated by industrial suburbs from the railroad (3 mi. N). An old city, destroyed in 12th cent. by earthquake and rebuilt on present site. Was ⊙ Gandzha or Ganja khanate until conquered (1804) by Russians, who named it Yelizavetpol and made it ⊙ Yelizavetpol govt. (until 1920). Became Gandzha again, after revolution; renamed Kirovabad (1935). Home of 12th-cent. Persian poet Nizami. **2** Town (1926 pop. 1,750), SE Stalinabad oblast, Tadzhik SSR, on Panj R. (Afghanistan border) and 45 mi. SSE of Kurgan-Tyube; cotton ginning. Formerly Sarai-Kamar, and later, until 1937, Baumanabad.

Kirovakan (kē″rŭvŭkän′), city (1934 pop. estimate 14,000), N Armenian SSR, on railroad and 35 mi. E of Leninakan; industrial center; chemical works (nitrate fertilizer); tanning, food processing, rug weaving. Until 1935, Karaklis.

Kirovgrad (kērŭvgrät′), city (1926 pop. 3,697; 1933 pop. estimate 34,700), SW central Sverdlovsk oblast, Russian SFSR, in E foothills of the central Urals, 45 mi. NNW of Sverdlovsk. Rail junction; a major copper-refining center, based on BELORECHKA, KARPUSHIKHA, and LEVIKHA mines; chemical processing, bronze mfg.; pyrite mining. Developed prior to First World War. Originally called Kalatinski Zavod and, later (1928–32), Kalata.

Kirov Gulf (kē′rŭf), inlet of Caspian Sea in SE Azerbaijan SSR, S of Salyany Steppe; enclosed by sandspits and low isls.; abounds in fish. Oil fields on shore. Formerly called Kyzyl-Agach Gulf.

Kirov Island, Russian SFSR: see SERGEI KIROV ISLANDS.

Kirovo (kē′rŭvŭ). **1** Village (1926 pop. 2,119), central Kurgan oblast, Russian SFSR, on Miass R. and 15 mi. NNW of Mishkino, in agr. area. Until 1939, Voskresenskoye. **2** City, Kirovograd oblast, Ukrainian SSR: see KIROVOGRAD, city. **3** Village (1926 pop. 4,874), W Fergana oblast, Uzbek SSR, on railroad (near Posyetovka station) and 18 mi. WSW of Kokand; cotton milling, metalworking. Formerly called Besh-Aryk and, later (1937–c.1940), Imeni Kirova.

Kirovo-Chepetski or **Kirovo-Chepetskiy** (–chĭpyĕt′skē), town (1942 pop. over 500), central Kirov oblast, Russian SFSR, on Vyatka R., at mouth of Cheptsa R., and 12 mi. E of Kirov; peat-fed power plant.

Kirovograd (kē″rŭvŭgrät′), oblast (□ 9,600; 1946 pop. estimate 1,100,000), central Ukrainian SSR; ⊙ Kirovograd. In W Volyn-Podolian Upland; bounded NE by Dnieper R.; drained by Ingul and Ingulets rivers. Chiefly agr. region, with wheat (basic crop), sugar beets (NW, E), sunflowers (S), and potatoes and flax in moist wooded region (N); livestock raising. Mfg. at Kirovograd, Aleksandriya (lignite mining), and Znamenka. Sugar refining, flour milling, dairying. Deposits of kaolin and refractory clays; granite quarries. Formed 1939.

Kirovograd, city (1939 pop. 100,331), ⊙ Kirovograd oblast, Ukrainian SSR, on Ingul R. and 150 mi. SE of Kiev; 48°31′N 32°17′E. Grain-trading, agr.-machinery mfg. center; metalworks; hemp and flour milling, distilling, clothing mfg. Lignite mine. Has natural history and revolutionary museums, agr.-machinery and pedagogic institutes. Founded 1754 as fortress; named (1775) Yelizavetgrad for Elizabeth Petrovna. Scene of pogroms (1881, 1905, 1919). Renamed Zinovyevsk (1924), Kirovo (1936), Kirovograd (1939). In Second World War, held (1941–43) by Germans.

Kirov Peak, Tadzhik SSR: see PETER THE FIRST RANGE.

Kirovsk (kē′rŭfsk). **1** Town (1945 pop. over 500), SE Azerbaijan SSR, near Caspian coast, 5 mi. NW of Lenkoran; subtropical agr. (tea). **2** Town (1939 pop. over 500), E Bobruisk oblast, Belorussian SSR, 14 mi. NE of Bobruisk; potatoes; chalk quarries. Until c.1940, Staritsy. **3** City (1939 pop. c.50,000), central Murmansk oblast, Russian SFSR, on Kola Peninsula, in Khibiny Mts., on spur of Murmansk RR 95 mi. S of Murmansk; major apatite-, nephelite- and titanium-mining center; concentrating plant, power works. Mines at Kukisvumchorr, 5 mi. N. Founded 1929, became city in 1931; called Khibinogorsk until 1934. **4** Town (1939 pop. over 500), SE Ashkhabad oblast, Turkmen SSR, on Tedzhen oasis, 25 mi. NNW of Tedzhen; wheat, cotton, cattle.

Kirovski or **Kirovskiy** (kē′rŭfskē). **1** Town (1939 pop. over 500) in Kirov dist. of Greater Baku, Azerbaijan SSR, on Apsheron Peninsula, 5 mi. N of Baku. **2** Town (1944 pop. over 500), central Taldy-Kurgan oblast, Kazakh SSR, 10 mi. SE of Taldy-Kurgan; irrigated agr. (sugar beets); sugar mill. Also called Imeni Kirova. **3** Town (1940 pop. over 500), NW Amur oblast, Russian SFSR, 40 mi. N of Skovorodino; gold mining. **4** Town (1948 pop. over 2,000), E Astrakhan oblast, Russian SFSR, on Kamyzyak arm of Volga R. delta mouth and 35 mi. S of Astrakhan; fish-processing center. 5 Town (1948 pop. over 500), Kamchatka oblast, Khabarovsk Territory, Russian SFSR, on W coast of Kamchatka Peninsula, on Sea of Okhotsk, 95 mi. N of Ust-Bolsheretsk; fish-processing plant. 6 Town (1939 pop. over 2,000), SW Maritime Territory, Russian SFSR, on Ussuri R., near Trans-Siberian RR, 120 mi. NE of Voroshilov, in agr. area (grain, soybeans, sugar beets, rice); metalworks. Prior to 1939, Uspenka or Uspenovka. 7 NW suburb (1926 pop. 5,289) of Dnepropetrovsk, Dnepropetrovsk oblast, Ukrainian SSR, on left bank of Dnieper R. and 10 mi. WNW of city center. Until 1938, Obukhovka.

Kirovskoye (kē'rŭfskŭyŭ). 1 Village (1939 pop. over 2,000), NW Talas oblast, Kirghiz SSR, on Talas R. and 32 mi. W of Talas; wheat, tobacco. Until 1937, Aleksandrovskoye. 2 Village (1939 pop. over 500), E. Crimea, Russian SFSR, on railroad and 15 mi. NW of Feodosiya; flour mill, metalworks; wheat, cotton. Until 1944, Islam-Terek. 3 Village (1948 pop. over 2,000), central N Sakhalin, Russian SFSR, 27 mi. ESE of Aleksandrovsk, in agr. area. Until 1937, Rykovskoye.

Kirriemuir (kĕrĕmūr'), burgh (1931 pop. 3,326; 1951 census 3,570), central Angus, Scotland, 5 mi. WNW of Forfar; agr. market, with linen mills. It is the "Thrums" of Sir James Barrie, b. here. Inverquharity Castle is 3 mi. NNE.

Kirrlach (kĭr'läkh"), village (pop. 5,670), N Baden, Germany, after 1945 in Württemberg-Baden, 8 mi. NNW of Bruchsal, in tobacco area; mfg. of cigars and cigarettes.

Kirrweiler (kĭr'vī"lŭr), village (pop. 1,304), Rhenish Palatinate, W Germany, at E foot of Hardt Mts., 8 mi. NNE of Landau; wine.

Kirs (kērs), town (1926 pop. 3,887), NE Kirov oblast, Russian SFSR, on railroad, on Vyatka R. and 45 mi. N of Omutninsk; steel milling (works in operation since 1728).

Kirsanov (kērsä'nŭf), city (1926 pop. 26,051), E Tambov oblast, Russian SFSR, near Vorona R. and 50 mi. E of Tambov; flour-milling center; metalworks; enameling, meat packing, vegetable drying. Chartered 1779.

Kirsehir (kŭr-shĕhĭr'), Turkish *Kırşehir*, province (□ 3,252; 1950 pop. 182,141), central Turkey; ⊙ Kirsehir. On NE is Delice R., on SW the Kizil Irmak. Forested. Grain, linseed, mohair goats.

Kirsehir, Turkish *Kırşehir*, anc. *Andrapa*, town (1950 pop. 14,168), ⊙ Kirsehir prov., Turkey, 85 mi. SE of Ankara; noted for its carpet mfg.; grain, linseed, mohair goats, vetch, potatoes. Sometimes spelled Kir-Shehr.

Kirthar Range (kēr'tŭr), mountain system along Sind-Baluchistan border, W Pakistan; from Mula R. in E Kalat extends c.220 mi. S to point NE of Karachi; c.20 mi. wide; rises to 7,430 ft. in N peak. Drained W by Hab R., E by seasonal streams. SE offshoots, including Lakhi Hills, form hilly region (Kohistan) in SW Sind. Range consists of limestone ridges with several hot springs, some having medicinal properties. Little cultivation, but ibex and mtn. sheep are found.

Kirtipur (kēr'tēpŏŏr), town, central Nepal, in Nepal Valley, on tributary of the Baghmati and 4 mi. SW of Katmandu city center. Originally under suzerainty of Patan kingdom; fell 1768 to Gurkha leader Prithwi Narayan after inflicting 2 severe defeats on the Gurkhas.

Kirtland Air Force Base, N.Mex.: see ALBUQUERQUE.

Kirtland Hills, village (pop. 235), Lake co., NE Ohio, 20 mi. ENE of Cleveland. Settled 1808–09, inc. 1926. The 1st Mormon Temple was built here (1833–36) by Joseph Smith and his followers.

Kirton-in-Lindsey, town and parish (pop. 1,601), Parts of Lindsey, NW Lincolnshire, England, 9 mi. NE of Gainsborough; agr. market, with limestone quarries, farm-tool plant, cement works. Has church dating from 13th cent.

Kirun, Formosa: see KEELUNG.

Kiruna (kē'rünä), city (1945 pop. 10,684; 1950 pop. 19,023), Norrbotten co., N Sweden, bet. Torne R. (N) and Kalix R. (S), 165 mi. WNW of Lulea, 80 mi. ESE of Narvik; 67°52'N 20°15'E. Overlooked by ore-bearing mts. of Luossavaara (lŏŏ'ôsävä"rä) (N) and Kiirunavaara or Kierunavaara (both: kē'rŏŏnävä"rä) (S), it is one of world's largest iron-mining centers, noted for purity of its ore (over 70% pure), which is shipped by rail to the Baltic port of Lulea and the Atlantic port of Narvik. Founded c.1900; ore shipments began (1902) with opening of Lapland railroad. Inc. 1948, when it absorbed mining villages of Jukkasjarvi (yŏŏ'-käsyĕr"vē), Swedish *Jukkasjärvi* (10 mi. E), Tuolluvaara (tŏŏ'ôlŏŏvä"rä) (2 mi. E), and Vittangi (vĭ'täng-ē) (40 mi. ESE), and became world's most extensive city (□ 5,458). Part of pop. consists of Lapp nomads.

Kirundu (kērŏŏn'dŏŏ), village, Eastern Prov., E Belgian Congo, on Lualaba R. and 90 mi. SSE of Stanleyville; steamboat landing and trading post; palm-oil milling. Has Protestant mission. Former hq. of Arab slave-traders. Congo Free State troops defeated the Arabs here, 1893.

Kirvin, town (pop. 152), Freestone co., E central Texas, 23 mi. SSE of Corsicana, in cotton, truck area.

Kirwin, city (pop. 374), Phillips co., N Kansas, on North Fork Solomon R. and 12 mi. ESE of Phillipsburg; corn, livestock.

Kirya or **Kiryah,** Israel: see HAKIRYA.

Kirya (kĕr'yŭ), town (1948 pop. over 2,000), S central Chuvash Autonomous SSR, Russian SFSR, on railroad and 20 mi. NE of Alatyr; sawmilling, woodworking.

Kiryat, for names in Israel beginning thus: see QIRYAT.

Kiryu (kĭrū'), city (1940 pop. 86,086; 1947 pop. 91,482), Gumma prefecture, central Honshu, Japan, 60 mi. NNW of Tokyo; major textile center (silk, rayon).

Kirzhach (kērzhäch'), city (1926 pop. 5,035), W Vladimir oblast, Russian SFSR, on Kirzhach R. (left affluent of the Klyazma) and 18 mi. SSE of Aleksandrov; mfg. (lighting equipment, auto parts), silk milling, agr. industries; power plant. Founded 1328.

Kirzhak, Russian SFSR: see UFA, city.

Kisa (kē'sä), town (pop. 7,210), Hiroshima prefecture, SW Honshu, Japan, 22 mi. NNW of Mihara; commercial center for agr. area; sake, soy sauce, raw silk; sawmilling.

Kisa (chē'sä"), village (pop. 1,671), Ostergotland co., SE Sweden, 25 mi. E of Tranas; sawmilling, metalworking. Has old church.

Kisac or **Kisach** (both: kē'säch), Serbo-Croatian *Kisač*, Hung. *Kiszács*, village (pop. 5,232), Vojvodina, N Serbia, Yugoslavia, 8 mi. NW of Novi Sad, in the Backa.

Kisagata, Japan: see KISAKATA.

Kisai (kēsī'), town (pop. 3,180), Saitama prefecture, central Honshu, Japan, 11 mi. ESE of Kumagaya; sake, rice, wheat.

Kisakata (kēsä'kätŭ) or **Kisagata** (–gätŭ), town (pop. 6,987), Akita prefecture, N Honshu, Japan, on Sea of Japan, 15 mi. SW of Honjo; rice growing; fishing; building-stone quarrying.

Kisale, Lake (kēsä'lā), expansion of Lualaba R. in SE Belgian Congo, N of L. Upemba; 10 mi. long, c.12 mi. wide. Swampy and overgrown with papyrus. Receives Lufira R. Its S and SE shores are part of Upemba Natl. Park.

Kis Alföld, Hungary and Czechoslovakia: see LITTLE ALFÖLD.

Kisamos, village, Crete: see KASTELLI.

Kisamos, Gulf of, or **Gulf of Kissamos** (both: kē'sŭmôs), Aegean inlet in E Crete, bet. capes Vouxa and Spatha; 6 mi. wide, 10 mi. long. Kastelli is on S shore.

Kisanga (kēsäng'gä), village, Katanga prov., SE Belgian Congo, 10 mi. NW of Jadotville; iron mining.

Kisangani, Belgian Congo: see STANLEYVILLE.

Kisangiro (kēsäng'gē'rō), village, Tanga prov., NE Tanganyika, 25 mi. SE of Moshi, on railroad; hardwood.

Kisantu (kēsän'tŏŏ, kēsätŏŏ'), village, Leopoldville prov., W Belgian Congo, on right bank of Inkisi R., on railroad, and 140 mi. ENE of Boma; major R.C. missionary center. Experimental farms and gardens, stock raising, various schools for natives, including junior college. Seat of vicar apostolic. In 1940s, Kisantu became, under sponsorship of several African welfare agencies, one of the main centers in Belgian Congo for training native agr. and medical assistants. Has hospitals for Europeans and natives.

Kisar (kēsär'), island (pop. 8,360), S Moluccas, Indonesia, 20 mi. NE of Timor; hilly. Coconut growing, fishing. Main town, Wonreli.

Kisarazu (kēsä'räzŏŏ), city (1940 pop. 16,288; 1947 pop. 37,675), Chiba prefecture, central Honshu, Japan, port on Tokyo Bay, on W Chiba Peninsula, 15 mi. E of Yokohama; agr. center; ships rice and market produce to Tokyo. Absorbed several villages since early 1940s.

Kisber (kĭsh'bār), Hung. *Kisbér*, town (pop. 4,075), Komarom-Esztergom co., N Hungary, 22 mi. SE of Györ; rail center; brickworks, flour mills. Stud farm established 1853.

Kisbey (kĭz'bē), village (pop. 295), SE Sask., near Moose Mountain Creek, 40 mi. NNE of Estevan; mixed farming.

Kis Duna, river, Czechoslovakia: see LITTLE DANUBE RIVER.

Kiselevsk (kēsĭ'lyôfsk'), city (1933 pop. estimate 13,000), W Kemerovo oblast, Russian SFSR, on railroad (Akchurla station) and 24 mi. NW of Stalinsk; coal-mining center in Kuznetsk Basin. Developed in 1930s.

Kiseljak or **Kiselyak** (both: kēsĕ'lyäk), village, S Bosnia, Yugoslavia, 5 mi. WSW of Visoko; mineral waters and baths.

Kisen, Korea: see HUICHON.

Kisenyi (kēsĕn'yē), village (1949 pop. 1,410), NW Ruanda-Urundi, in Ruanda, on NE shore of L. Kivu, near Belgian Congo border, 55 mi. WNW of Kigali; alt. 4,705 ft. Steamboat landing, center of tobacco trade; dairying region. Its scenery and lake beach make it popular as tourist center and resort. Has veterinary laboratory. Near by (4 mi. E) is R.C. mission of Nyundo (nyŏŏn'dō), sometimes spelled Nyondo, known for rug making; it was founded 1901.

Kis Fatra, mountains, Czechoslovakia: see LESSER FATRA.

Kish, anc. Sumerian city of Mesopotamia, whose site is near the Euphrates in central Iraq, in Hilla prov., 12 mi. E of city of Hilla (just NNE of which is site of Babylon), c.60 mi. S of Baghdad. Occupied from the most anc. times, it was a powerful and rich Sumerian city in the 4th millennium B.C. The site, 1st visited by a European in modern times in 1816, has been thoroughly excavated since 1922. The finds of the earliest level here are invaluable for understanding early Mesopotamia. Found also were a palace of Sargon of Agade and a great temple built by Nebuchadnezzar and Nabonidus in the later Babylonian period. There is also a complete sequence of pottery from the early Sumerian period to the time of Nebuchadnezzar.

Kish, Iran: see QAIS.

Kishan or **Ch'i-shan** (both: chē'shän'), town (pop. 1,456), ⊙ Kishan co. (pop. 146,034), SW Shensi prov., China, 80 mi. WNW of Sian and on road to Lanchow; cotton, grain.

Kishan, Chishan, or **Ch'i-shan,** Jap. *Kizan* (kē'zän), town (1935 pop. 8,527), S Formosa, 20 mi. N of Pingtung, in scenic location; sugar milling; camphor, rice, sweet potatoes. Noted park near by.

Kishanganga River (kĭshŭn'gŭng"gŭ), in W Kashmir, rises in several headstreams in main range of W Punjab Himalayas, flows WNW, SSW past Tithwal, and W to Jhelum R. at Muzaffarabad; c.150 mi. long. Also spelled Kishenganga.

Kishanganj (kĭsh'ŭngŭnj), town (pop. 10,424), Purnea dist., NE Bihar, India, near Mahananda R., 37 mi. NE of Purnea; trade center (rice, jute, corn, tobacco, rape and mustard, wheat); jute pressing. Annual livestock fair.

Kishangarh (kĭshŭn'gŭr), former princely state (□ 837; pop. 104,127) in Rajputana States, India; ⊙ was Kishangarh. Established in early-17th cent.; chiefs (Rathor Rajputs) entered Mogul service; treaty made with British in 1818. In 1948, merged with union of Rajasthan. Sometimes spelled Kishengarh.

Kishangarh, city (pop. 14,459), central Rajasthan, India, 65 mi. WSW of Jaipur; trades in cotton, millet, barley, oilseeds, cloth fabrics; mfg. of soap, woolen carpets and shawls; hand-loom weaving, dyeing, precious stone cutting. Founded 1611. Cotton mill at suburb of Madanganj, 1 mi. N. Mica, marble, and sandstone deposits worked in vicinity. Was ⊙ former Rajputana state of Kishangarh.

Kishanpur (kĭsh'ŭnpŏŏr), town (pop. 2,684), Fatehpur dist., S Uttar Pradesh, India, on the Jumna and 10 mi. SSW of Khaga; gram, barley, rice, jowar.

Kishegyes, Yugoslavia: see KRIVAJA.

Kishenganga River, Kashmir: see KISHANGANGA RIVER.

Kishengarh, India: see KISHANGARH, former princely state.

Kishenki or **Kishen'ki** (kē'shĭnyŭkē), town (1926 pop. 3,688), SE Poltava oblast, Ukrainian SSR, on Vorskla R., near its mouth at the Dnieper, and 35 mi. ESE of Kremenchug; wheat, corn.

Kishert, Russian SFSR: see UST-KISHERT.

Kishi (kē'shē), town, Oyo prov., Western Provinces, SW Nigeria, 60 mi. NW of Ilorin; cotton weaving, shea-nut processing, cattle raising.

Kishiku, Japan: see KISHUKU.

Kishimoto (kēshē'mōtō), town (pop. 2,116), Kochi prefecture, S Shikoku, Japan, on Tosa Bay, 12 mi. E of Kochi; textiles, soy sauce.

Kishinev (kĭ'shĭnĕv", kĭ"shĭnĕf', Rus. kĭshĕnyôf'), Rum. *Chişinău* (kĕshēnŭ'ŏŏ), city (1930 pop. 114,896; 1941 pop. 52,962; 1948 pop. estimate 102,500), ⊙ Moldavian SSR, in Bessarabia, on right bank of Byk R., on railroad, and 50 mi. NW of Odessa; 47°N 28°50'E. Economic and cultural center in rich agr. region (wine, fruit, corn); a major food-processing center producing canned goods, tobacco products, flour, vegetable oils, meat and dairy goods (cheese), white table wine, champagne, cognac, fruit juices; sawmilling, tanning, shoe and knitwear mfg.; cement mill, auto and motor repair shops, foundry. Has 19th-cent. Orthodox cathedral, mus. of natural history, univ., music school, teachers and agr. col. Consists of old lower town, Oriental in aspect, with crooked streets, on Byk R. bank adjoining railroad station, and of 19th-cent. upper city, rectilinear in layout. Pop., an ethnic mixture including Moldavians, Russians, Bulgarians, and Gypsies, was 40% Jewish until Second World War. First mentioned in 1436; did not develop greatly until its annexation by Russia in 1812 (pop. c.7,000); became (1818) ⊙ Bessarabia. Residence (1820–23) of Pushkin (commemorated by monument). City's growth was speeded following building of railroad in 1870s. An infamous pogrom took place here in 1903. Annexed (1918) to Rumania and was ⊙ Lapusna dept. (□ 1,614; 1941 pop. 367,890); returned in 1940 (confirmed 1947) to USSR. During Second World War, occupied (1941–44) by Rum. troops and suffered heavy destruction.

Kishiwada (kēshē'wädŭ), city (1940 pop. 46,486; 1947 pop. 88,654), Osaka prefecture, S Honshu, Japan, on Osaka Bay, 15 mi. SW of Osaka; collection center for agr. and marine products; textile mills. Includes (since early 1940s) former towns of

Haruki (1940 pop. 19,350) and Yamatae (1940 pop. 8,769). Sometimes spelled Kisiwada.

Kishkareny (kĕshkŭryĕ'nē), Rum. *Chişcăreni* (kĕshkŭrĕn'), village (1941 pop. 3,626), central Moldavian SSR, 15 mi. S of Beltsy; oilseed mill; corn, wheat, sugar beets.

Kishly (kĕsh'lē), suburb in Kishly dist. of Greater Baku, Azerbaijan SSR, on Apsheron Peninsula, on railroad and 3 mi. NE of Baku; food processing, sawmilling.

Kishm or **Keshm** (kĭ'shŭm), town (pop. over 2,000), Afghan Badakhshan, NE Afghanistan, 40 mi. SW of Faizabad, near road to Khanabad.

Kishm, Iran: see QISHM.

Kishon River or **Qishon River** (both: kĭ'shŏn, kĭ'-, kē'-, kĕshōn'), intermittent stream, NW Israel, rises in Mt. Gilboa E of Jenin, near Jordan border, flows 45 mi. in winding course generally NW, through Plain of Jezreel, then along NE slope of Mt. Carmel, to Bay of Acre of Mediterranean at Haifa. Connected with biblical stories of Sisera and Elija; in Bible also called Kison.

Kishorganj (kĭshōr'gŭnj), town (pop. 20,128), Mymensingh dist., E central East Bengal, E Pakistan, on tributary of the old Brahmaputra and 33 mi. SSE of Mymensingh; rice, jute, oilseeds; sugar milling. Large annual fair. Formerly noted for hand-woven muslins. Jute pressing near by. Also spelled Kishoreganj.

Kishtwar (kĭshtvär'), town (pop. 3,235), Doda dist., SW Kashmir, in Pir Panjal Range, near Chenab R., 45 mi. NNE of Udhampur; corn, wheat, barley, rice, fruit. Was ⊙ former independent Rajput raja. Shah Shuja stayed here, 1814–16, in his exile from Afghanistan. Important deodar forest near by.

Kishui. 1 or **Ch'i-shui** (chē'shwā'), town, Hupeh prov., China: see SISHUI. **2** or **Chi-shui** (jē'shwā'), town (pop. 5,369), ⊙ Kishui co. (pop. 150,826), W Kiangsi prov., China, 10 mi. NE of Kian and on Kan R.; commercial center; tea, rice; mfg. of bamboo paper. Anthracite mines.

Kishuku (kēshō'kōō), town (pop. 9,800) on Fukaeshima of isl. group Goto-retto, Nagasaki prefecture, Japan, on N coast of isl., 9.5 mi. N of Tomie; agr. center (rice, wheat, sweet potatoes). Sometimes called Kishiku.

Kishwaukee River (kĭsh"wô'kē), N Ill., rises in McHenry co., flows generally W and SW, past Belvidere, to Rock R. 6 mi. below Rockford; c.60 mi. long. Its South Branch rises near Shabbona in De Kalb co., flows c.56 mi. generally N and NW to Kishwaukee R. SE of Rockford.

Kisiaying, Suiyuan prov., China: see WUTUNG.

Kisielice (kē"shēlē'tsĕ), Ger. *Freystadt* (frī'shtät), town (1939 pop. 3,351; 1946 pop. 1,120) in East Prussia, after 1945 in Olsztyn prov., NE Poland, 17 mi. ESE of Marienwerder (Kwidzyn); grain and cattle market. Until 1919, in West Prussia prov.

Kisii (kēsē'), town, (pop. c.3,000) Nyanza prov., W Kenya, 40 mi. S of Kisumu; agr. and trade center; cotton, peanuts, sesame, corn. Soapstone deposits. Hq. of Seventh Day Adventists' mission.

Kisiklik, Greece: see NEOS SKOPOS.

Kisipidi (kēsē'pĭdē), village, central Nepal, in Nepal Valley, 5 mi. W of Katmandu. N terminus of 14-mi.-long aerial ropeway to Dharsing (S terminus); proposed extension to Katmandu.

Kisiwada, Japan: see KISHIWADA.

Kisjenö, Rumania: see CHISNEU-CRIS.

Kiska Island (kĭ'skŭ) (20 mi. long, 2–7 mi. wide), one of the Rat Isls., Aleutian Isls., SW Alaska, 200 mi. ESE of Attu Isl.; 52°N 177°30'E; rises to 3,996 ft. on Kiska Volcano (N). Air base; U.S. naval reserve. In Second World War it was occupied (1942) by Japanese and garrisoned by c.10,000 troops. Heavily bombed, and cut off by recapture (1943) of Attu, isl. was evacuated Aug., 1943, by Japanese just prior to U.S.-Canadian landing. Just off E coast is Little Kiska Isl. (3 mi. long).

Kiskalota, Rumania: see CALATELE.

Kiskapus, Rumania: see COPSA-MICA.

Kis Karpatok, Czechoslovakia: see LITTLE CARPATHIAN MOUNTAINS.

Kiskatom (kĭ'skŭtŏm"), resort village, Greene co., SE N.Y., in the Catskill foothills, 5 mi. WSW of Catskill.

Kiskiminetas River (kĭ"skĕmĭ'nĭtŭs), SW Pa., formed at Saltsburg by confluence of Conemaugh R. and Loyalhanna Creek; flows 27 mi. NW, past Vandergrift, to Allegheny R. opposite Freeport.

Kiskiralysag (kĭsh'kĭrĭ-shäg), Hung. *Kiskirályság*, town (pop. 2,650), Csongrad co., S Hungary, 15 mi. E of Szentes; grain, paprika, cattle.

Kiskittogisu Lake (□ 99), central Man., 18 mi. N of L. Winnipeg; 30 mi. long, 8 mi. wide. Drains N into Nelson R.

Kiskitto Lake (□ 65), central Man., 26 mi. N of L. Winnipeg; 20 mi. long, 6 mi. wide. Drains NW into Nelson R.

Kisko (kĭs'kō), village (commune pop. 4,082), Turku-Pori co., SW Finland, in lake region, 40 mi. ESE of Turku; mining region (copper, zinc, lead, silver).

Kiskörös (kĭsh'kûrûsh), Hung. *Kiskőrös*, town (pop. 12,875), Pest-Pilis-Solt-Kiskun co., central Hungary, 27 mi. SW of Kecskemet; rail junction; flour mills. Ger. pop. raises wheat, rye, apples, cherries. Birthplace of Petöfi.

Kisköszeg, Yugoslavia: see BATINA.

Kiskundorozsma (kĭsh'kōōndô"rô-zhmŏ), town (pop. 19,670), Csongrad co., S Hungary, 5 mi. WNW of Szeged; rail and market center; tobacco, cement, sawmills. Wheat, tobacco, sheep raised in vicinity.

Kiskunfelegyhaza (kĭsh'kōōnfā"lĕ-dyŭhä"zŏ), Hung. *Kiskunfélegyháza*, city (pop. 38,930), Pest-Pilis-Solt-Kiskun co., central Hungary, 15 mi. SSE of Kecskemet. Rail and agr. center; tobacco warehouses, flour mills, brickworks, stockyards; wheat, corn, apricots, apples. Also called Felegyhaza.

Kiskunhalas (kĭsh'kōōnhŏ'lŏsh), city (pop. 33,758), Pest-Pilis-Solt-Kiskun co., S central Hungary, 34 mi. SSW of Kecskemet; rail center; brickworks, flour mills. Trade in wheat, corn, cattle; Halas lace exported. Formerly called Halas. Small L. Halas near by.

Kiskunlachaza (kĭsh'kōōnlŏts"häzŏ), Hung. *Kiskunlacháza*, town (pop. 5,405), Pest-Pilis-Solt-Kiskun co., central Hungary, 21 mi. S of Budapest; flour mills; grain, cattle, hogs.

Kiskunmajsa (kĭsh'kōōnmoi"shŏ), town (pop. 18,282), Pest-Pilis-Solt-Kiskun co., S central Hungary, 29 mi. S of Kecskemet; flour mills; grain, tobacco, cattle raising.

Kiskunsag (–säg"), Hung. *Kiskunság* [little Cumania], section of the Alföld, S central Hungary, bet. the Danube and the Tisza. A section of sandy soils, largely anchored by vegetation. Rye and barley production.

Kislang (kĭsh'läng), Hung. *Kisláng*, town (pop. 3,239), Fejer co., W central Hungary, 16 mi. S of Szekesfehervar; grain, livestock.

Kislotny, Russian SFSR: see MOLOTOV, city.

Kislovodsk (kĕslŭvôtsk') [Rus., =acid water], city (1939 pop. 51,289), S Stavropol Territory, Russian SFSR, in the central Greater Caucasus, on Podkumok R. and 18 mi. SW of Pyatigorsk; alt. 2,693 ft. Rail terminus; noted health resort with carbonic springs, in wind-protected location. Has sanatoriums, rest homes, baths, physical-therapy institute, and parks. Mineral (Narzan) water bottling; dairying, meat packing, food processing. Founded in 18th cent. During Second World War, held (1942–43) by Germans.

Kismarja (kĭsh'mŏryŏ), town (pop. 2,564), Bihar co., E Hungary, on Berettyo R. and 13 mi. E of Berettyoujfalu; corn, dairy farming, poultry.

Kismarton, Austria: see EISENSTADT.

Kismayu (kēsmä'yōō), Ital. *Chisimaio*, town (pop. 10,000), in the Benadir, S Ital. Somaliland, port on Indian Ocean near mouth of Juba R., 250 mi. SW of Mogadishu; 0°22'S 42°33'E. Electric-power plant. Commercial center (livestock, hides, fish); mfg. of distilled water, ice; sawmill. Has mosques and fort (built 1872). Founded 1872 by Sultan of Zanzibar; taken by British in 1887; later became part of JUBALAND, the region ceded 1925 to Italy. Occupied (1941) by British in Second World War.

Kismet, city (pop. 180), Seward co., SW Kansas, 15 mi. NE of Liberal, in grain region.

Kisogawa (kēsō'gäwŭ), town (pop. 15,540), Aichi prefecture, central Honshu, on Kiso R. just NW of Ichinomiya; silk textiles, raw silk; poultry.

Kiso-koma-ga-take (kē'sō-kō'mä-gä-tä'kä), mountain (9,240 ft.), Nagano prefecture, central Honshu, Japan, 20 mi. NNW of Iida; thickly wooded. Sometimes called Koma-ga-take.

Kison River, Palestine: see KISHON RIVER.

Kiso River (kē'sō), Jap. *Kiso-gawa*, central Honshu, Japan, rises near On-take peak in Nagano prefecture, flows E, then generally SW, past Agematsu, Inuyama, Kasamatsu, and Oku, to Ise Bay 10 mi. WSW of Nagoya; 135 mi. long. Many hydroelectric stations provide power for industrial areas. Scenic rapids. Chief tributaries: Nagara and Ibi rivers.

Kisozi (kēsō'zē), village, S Ruanda-Urundi, in Urundi, 20 mi. WSW of Kitega; tropical research station with experimental plantations.

Kispest (kĭsh'pĕsht), city (pop. 65,149), Pest-Pilis-Solt-Kiskun co., N central Hungary, 5 mi. SE of Budapest city center. Chemicals, machinery, textiles (silk, cotton), stoves, electrical appliances, toys, brushes, porcelain; tile-, brickworks.

Kissamos, Gulf of, Crete: see KISAMOS, GULF OF.

Kissarmas, Rumania: see SARMAS.

Kissavos, Greece: see OSSA.

Kisseraing Island (kēsĕrĭng'), in central Mergui Archipelago, Lower Burma, in Andaman Sea, off Tenasserim coast, 45 mi. S of Mergui town; 20 mi. long, 10 mi. wide; irregular coast with mangrove swamps; forested hills.

Kisshu, Korea: see KILCHU.

Kissidougou (kēsēdōō'gōō), town (pop. c.4,050), SE Fr. Guinea, Fr. West Africa, in interior highland, near Sierra Leone, 100 mi. SW of Kankan; stock-raising (cattle, sheep, goats) and agr. center. Exports rice, palm oil, palm kernels, coffee, kola nuts. Experimental garden; R.C., Protestant missions.

Kissimmee (kĭsĭ'mē), city (pop. 4,310), ⊙ Osceola co., central Fla., 18 mi. S of Orlando, at N end of Tohopekaliga L.; resort and trade center for large cattle area (Kissimmee Prairies); citrus-fruit packing, sawmilling, box mfg.

Kissimmee, Lake, Osceola co., central Fla., c.40 mi. S of Orlando; c.15 mi. long, 5 mi. wide. Entered (NW) and drained (S) by Kissimmee R. Contains several small isls.

Kissimmee River, central Fla., rises in Tohopekaliga L. in Osceola co., flows c.140 mi. SSE to N end of L. Okeechobee 7 mi. SW of Okeechobee city. In upper course, connects chain of lakes (Tohopekaliga, Hatchineha, Kissimmee). River's valley has large cattle range (Kissimmee Prairies), some truck and citrus-fruit growing, and large wilderness tracts (muskrat trapping, naval-stores production).

Kissingen, Bad, Germany: see BAD KISSINGEN.

Kississing Lake (□ 141), W Man., near Sask. border, 24 mi. NE of Flin Flon; 17 mi. long, 16 mi. wide. Drains into Churchill R.

Kisslegg (kĭs'lĕk"), village (pop. 4,024), S Württemberg, Germany, after 1945 in Württemberg-Hohenzollern, in the Allgäu, 12 mi. E of Ravensburg; rail junction; dairying. Has 2 anc. castles, 18th-cent. church.

Kissos, Greece: see CHORTIATES.

Kissoué, Syria: see KISWE.

Kissy (kē'sē), town (1931 pop. 2,673), Sierra Leone colony, on Sierra Leone Peninsula, on railroad and 5 mi. ESE of Freetown; fishing; cassava, corn, ginger. Has insane asylum.

Kissyu, Korea: see KILCHU.

Kisszeben, Czechoslovakia: see SABINOV.

Kistanje (kēstä'nyĕ), Ital. *Chistagne* (kēstä'nyĕ), village, W Croatia, Yugoslavia, near Krka R., 17 mi. N of Sibenik, in Dalmatia.

Kistelek (kĭsh'tĕlĕk), town (pop. 8,916), Csongrad co., S Hungary, 17 mi. NNW of Szeged; market center.

Kistendei or **Kistendey** (kēstyĭndyā'), village (1939 pop. over 500), W Saratov oblast, Russian SFSR, on railroad and 11 mi. SSW of Rtishchevo; flour milling; wheat, fruit.

Kisterenye (kĭsh'tĕrĕnyĕ), town (pop. 4,699), Nograd-Hont co., N Hungary, on Zagyva R. and 7 mi. S of Salgotarjan; rail center; briquettes.

Kistler (kĭ'slŭr). **1** Borough (pop. 468), Mifflin co., central Pa., on Juniata R. opposite Mount Union. There is a village, Kistler, in Perry co., Pa. **2** Village (pop. 1,072), Logan co., SW W.Va., 9 mi. SE of Logan; coal mining.

Kistna (kĭst'nŭ), Hindi *Krishna* (krĭsh'nŭ), district (□ 3,469; pop. 1,444,294), NE Madras, India; ⊙ Masulipatam. Lies bet. Eastern Ghats (NW) and Bay of Bengal (SE); SW portion in Kistna R. delta. Agr.; rice, millet, oilseeds, tobacco, sugar cane, sunn hemp (jute substitute), cotton. Main towns: Bezwada, Masulipatam, Gudivada. E portion of original dist. separated (1925) to form West Godavari dist.

Kistna River or **Krishna River**, S India, rises in Western Ghats N of Mahabaleshwar, central Bombay, 40 mi. E of Arabian Sea; flows generally SE past Sangli, entering Hyderabad W of Raichur, thence generally ESE to Hyderabad-Madras border, ENE (for c.200 mi.) along border, into Madras, and ESE past Amaravati and Bezwada, to Bay of Bengal 40 mi. SW of Masulipatam; total length, 800 mi. Forms wide delta mouth with extensive navigable irrigation-canal system linked with that of Godavari delta (N) and with Buckingham Canal (S). Has 2 main tributaries: Bhima (left) and Tungabhadra (right) rivers. Main stream navigable (by coracle) only below Bezwada and near Tungabhadra confluence. Plans formulated in 1948 for large irrigation and hydroelectric project with headworks (dam begun 1949) at Siddeswaram, 23 mi. NE of Kurnool. River's mouth marks N boundary of Coromandel Coast.

Kisujszallas (kĭ'shōō"ĭsäl-läsh), Hung. *Kisújszállás*, city (pop. 14,461), Jasz-Nagykun-Szolnok co., E central Hungary, 11 mi. SW of Karcag; rail center; wheat, corn, hemp; cattle, horses.

Kisuki (kēsōō'gē) or **Kitsugi** (kētsōō'gē), town (pop. 4,616), Shimane prefecture, SW Honshu, Japan, 15 mi. SW of Matsue; commercial center for agr. area (rice, raw silk, sake).

Kisulu, Belgian Congo: see KAMPENE.

Kisumu (kēsōō'mōō), town (pop. 10,899), ⊙ Nyanza prov., W Kenya, port (marine workshops, drydock) on L. Victoria (at head of Kavirondo Gulf) and 165 mi. NW of Nairobi; 0°06'S 34°44'E; commercial, agr. and fishing center; cotton milling; coffee, corn, peanuts, sesame. Airport, seaplane base Hq. of L. Victoria steamboat administration. R.C. mission. Has European and native hosps. and a hosp. for infectious diseases; govt. and missionary primary and secondary schools. Formerly called Port Florence, it was reached 1901 by railroad from Mombasa; the rail connection is now a spur of Mombasa-Uganda RR.

Kisvarda (kĭsh'värdŏ), Hung. *Kisvárda*, town (pop 14,782), Szabolcs co., NE Hungary, 25 mi. NE of Nyiregyhaza; rail junction, market center. Petroleum refinery, foundry, metalworks, distilleries flour mills; hemp products. Teachers col. here Tobacco, corn, wheat, cattle, sheep near by.

Kiswe or **Kiswah** (kĭ'swŭ), Fr. *Kissoué*, village Damascus prov., SW Syria, 11 mi. SSW of Damascus; cereals, fruits.

Kiszacs, Yugoslavia: see KISAC.

Kiszetö, Rumania: see CHIZATAU.

Kiszombor (kĭsh'zômbôr), town (pop. 5,117), Csanad co., S Hungary, 4 mi. SW of Mako; market center for grain, cattle.

Kiszucaujhely, Czechoslovakia: see Kysucke Nove Mesto.

Kita (kētä'), town (pop. c.3,150), SW Fr. Sudan, Fr. West Africa, on Dakar-Niger RR and 100 mi. WNW of Bamako. Peanut-growing center; also shea-nut butter, rice, corn, potatoes, manioc, mango; goats, sheep, cattle.

Kitab (kē'tŭp), town (1932 pop. estimate 8,600), NE Kashka-Darya oblast, Uzbek SSR, 60 mi. ENE of Karshi, 3 mi. NE of terminus of rail spur from Karshi; cotton-ginning center in fertile oasis (cotton, rice, fruit). Has International Latitude Observatory (39°8'N).

Kita-daito-shima, Ryukyu Isls.: see Daito-shima.

Kitagata (kētä'gätō̤), town (pop. 4,851), Gifu prefecture, central Honshu, Japan, 4 mi. WNW of Gifu; persimmon growing; makes *geta* (wooden clogs).

Kitagi-shima (kētägē'shĭmä), island (□ 3; pop. 5,405), Okayama prefecture, Japan, in Hiuchi Sea, just off S coast of Honshu, 8 mi. E of Tomo; 2.5 mi. long, 2 mi. wide. Produces raw silk, wheat, sweet potatoes. Building-stone quarries.

Kitai or **Ch'i-t'ai** (both: chē'tī'), town and oasis (pop. 35,356), N Sinkiang prov., China, in the Dzungaria, 90 mi. E of Urumchi, and on highway N of the Tien Shan; junction for roads to N Dzungaria and Mongolia; trades in fur, skins, raisins, tea. Gold mines. Formerly called Kuchengtze. The old Kitai is 15 mi. SE.

Kitai Lagoon or **Kitay Lagoon** (kētī'), Rum. *Chitai* (kētī'), S Izmail oblast, Ukrainian SSR, near Kiliya arm of the Danube delta, NW of Kiliya; 13 mi. long, 1–2 mi. wide. Receives minor Kitai R. (N).

Kita-iwo-jima (kē'tä-ē'wō-jē'mä) [Jap.,=north sulphur island], island (□ 2; pop. 103), Volcano Isls., W Pacific, N of Iwo Jima, 110 naut. mi. SW of Chichi-jima, Bonin Isls. Submarine volcano is 2.5 mi. W of isl. Formerly San Alessandro Isl.

Kitakami River (kētä'kämē), Jap. *Kitakami-gawa*, N Honshu, Japan, in Iwate and Miyagi prefectures; rises in mts. 25 mi. N of Morioka, flows 152 mi. generally S, past Morioka, Hanamaki, Kurosawajiri, Mizusawa, and Tome, to Ishinomaki Bay at Ishinomaki. Waters extensive rice-growing area.

Kitakata (kētä'kätō̤), town (pop. 17,444), Fukushima prefecture, N central Honshu, Japan, 11 mi. NNW of Wakamatsu, in agr. area (rice, soybeans); raw silk, dyes, sake.

Kita-kozawa, Russian SFSR: see Telnovski.

Kitale (kētä'lā), town (pop. 6,338), Rift Valley prov., W Kenya, at E foot of Mt. Elgon, near Uganda border, 115 mi. NW of Nakuru; alt. 6,220 ft.; 0°58'N 34°57'E. Rail spur terminus; agr. trade center (coffee, pyrethrum, sisal, wheat, corn); cattle raising. Site of Stoneham Mus. and Research Center, European hosp. Airport. Center of Trans-Nzoia dist. (□ 1,155), a region of European settlement since 1920s. Starting point for Mt. Elgon ascents.

Kitami (kētä'mē), city (pop. 40,989), E Hokkaido, Japan, 75 mi. E of Asahigawa; rail junction; commercial center for agr. area (peppermint, rice, potatoes, hemp, soybeans); flour milling, dairying. Until early 1940s, called Nokkeushi (1940 pop. 32,849).

Kita-nayoshi, Russian SFSR: see Lesogorsk.

Kitano (kētä'nō), town (pop. 4,331), Fukuoka prefecture, N central Kyushu, Japan, 4 mi. NE of Kurume; rice, wheat.

Kita-oagari-shima, Ryukyu Isls.: see Daito-shima.

Kita-shiretoko-misaki, Russian SFSR: see Terpeniye, Cape.

Kitaura (kētä'ōō̤rä), town (pop. 7,291), Akita prefecture, N Honshu, Japan, on N Oga Peninsula, fishing port on Sea of Japan, 6 mi. NNW of Funakawaminato; agr. (rice, fruit).

Kita-uruppu-suido, Russian SFSR: see Boussole Strait.

Kitayama River, Japan: see Kumano River.

Kitay Lagoon, Ukrainian SSR: see Kitai Lagoon.

Kit Carson, county (□ 2,171; pop. 8,600), E Colo.; ⊙ Burlington. Grain and livestock area, bordering on Kansas. Drained by branches of Republican and Smoky Hill rivers. Formed 1889.

Kit Carson, town (pop. 379), Cheyenne co., E Colo., on Big Sandy Creek and 24 mi. W of Cheyenne Wells; alt. 4,273 ft. Inc. 1931.

Kit Carson Pass, Calif.: see Carson Pass.

Kit Carson Peak (14,100 ft.), S Colo., in Sangre de Cristo Mts., Saguache co.

Kitchener, city (pop. 35,657), ⊙ Waterloo co., S Ont., in Grand R. valley, 55 mi. W of Toronto; mfg. of trucks, trailers, machinery, domestic appliances, clocks, rubber products, radios, furniture, shoes, clothing; tanning, meat packing. Seat of St. Jerome's Jr. Col. (R.C.). Among noted features is Victoria Park. Founded 1806 by Ger. settlers from Pennsylvania, it was 1st called Sand Hills, then Mt. Pleasant. It received many Ger. immigrants c.1830 and was renamed Berlin. Name was changed 1916 to Kitchener. Adjoining (N) is town of Waterloo. Airport.

Kitchener, Mount (11,500 ft.), SW Alta., near B.C. border, in Rocky Mts., on S edge of Jasper Natl. Park, 55 mi. SE of Jasper; 52°13'N 117°20'W.

Kitchi, Mount (9,352 ft.), E B.C., in Rocky Mts., 100 mi. E of Prince George; 53°58'N 120°24'W.

Kitchioh Bay (kēt'jyĕ), Chinese *Chieh-shih*, inlet of S.China Sea, in Kwangtung prov., China, 65 mi. SW of Swatow; 15 mi. wide, 10 mi. long. Town and port of Kitchioh is on SE shore. Formerly called Hiechechin Bay.

Kite, town (pop. 447), Johnson co., E central Ga., 12 mi. WNW of Swainsboro and on Ohoopee R.

Kitee (kĭ'tā), Swedish *Kides* (kē'dĕs"), village (commune pop. 12,885), Kuopio co., SE Finland, near USSR border, in Saimaa lake region, 40 mi. SSE of Joensuu; lumbering, sawmilling.

Kitega (kētĕ'gä), town (1949 pop. 2,142), ⊙ Urundi (□ 10,658; 1949 pop. 2,015,511), in Ruanda-Urundi, 38 mi. E of Usumbura; trading center (hides, palm kernels, coffee, native food staples), communications point; mfg. of bricks and tiles; cinchona plantations in vicinity. Has R.C. mission, hospitals for Europeans and natives, veterinary laboratory. Airfield.

Kit Green, England: see Orrell.

Kitgum (kĭt'gōōm), town, Northern Prov., N Uganda, 50 mi. NE of Gulu; road center; cotton, peanuts, sesame, sweet potatoes, millet. Mission. Gold deposits.

Kithairon, Greece: see Cithaeron.

Kit Hill, England: see Callington.

Kithira, Greece: see Kythera.

Kithnos, Greece: see Kythnos.

Kiti (kē'tē), village (pop. 949), Larnaca dist., S Cyprus, near the Mediterranean, 6 mi. SW of Larnaca. Has noted Byzantine church with 6th-cent. mosaic of Madonna. Cape Kiti, sometimes called Cape Dades, is 2½ mi. SE at 34°49'N 33°37'E.

Kitimat or **Kitimat Mission** (kĭ'tĭmăt), Indian village, W B.C., at head of Douglas Channel (inlet of the Pacific) and 40 mi. SSW of Terrace. Aluminum plant projected near by.

Kition, Cyprus: see Citium.

Kitobola (kētōbō'lä), village, Leopoldville prov., W Belgian Congo, near railroad, 105 mi. ENE of Boma; agr. center (palms, sugar cane, cattle).

Kitoi or **Kitoy** (kētoi'), town (1941 pop. over 500), SE Irkutsk oblast, Russian SFSR, on Trans-Siberian RR and 30 mi. NW of Irkutsk; sawmilling.

Kitose, Russian SFSR: see Chkalovo, Sakhalin oblast.

Kitoy, Russian SFSR: see Kitoi.

Kitsap, county (□ 402; pop. 75,724), W Wash.; ⊙ Port Orchard. A peninsula bounded W by Hood Canal and E by Puget Sound; includes Port Madison Indian Reservation. Bremerton is important seaport and site of Puget Sound Navy Yard. Fruit, nuts, dairy products, poultry, truck, fish. Formed 1857.

Kitscoty, village (pop. 240), E Alta., near Sask. border, 21 mi. E of Vermilion; dairying, grain.

Kitseh or **Chi-tse** (both: jē'dzŭ'), town, ⊙ Kitseh co. (pop. 89,738), SW Hopeh prov., China, 22 mi. ESE of Singtai; wheat, kaoliang, chestnuts.

Kitsman or **Kitsman'** (kēts'mŭnyŭ), Ger. *Kotzman* (kôts'män), Rum. *Cozmeni* (kôzmĕn'), town (1941 pop. 3,855), N Chernovtsy oblast, Ukrainian SSR, in N Bukovina, 13 mi. NW of Chernovtsy; agr. center; flour, oilseeds. Agr. school.

Kitsu, Japan: see Kizu.

Kitsugi, Japan: see Kisuki.

Kitsuki (kētsōō'kē), town (pop. 16,424), Oita prefecture, NE Kyushu, Japan, on S Kunisaki Peninsula, 12 mi. N of Oita across Beppu Bay; agr. center (rice, wheat, barley, sweet potatoes).

Kitsuregawa (kētsōōrā'gäwō̤), town (pop. 9,874), Tochigi prefecture, central Honshu, Japan, 14 mi. NE of Utsunomiya; agr. center (rice, wheat, tobacco).

Kittam River (kētäm'), SW Sierra Leone, tidal inlet formed 30 mi. ESE of Bonthe by union of Waanje and Sewa rivers; flows c.30 mi. WNW, past Gbap, to Sherbro R. 7 mi. S of Bonthe. Its course forms N side of Turner's Peninsula. Sometimes called Bum R. or Bum Kittam R.

Kittanning (kĭtă'nĭng), borough (pop. 7,731), ⊙ Armstrong co., W central Pa., 35 mi. NE of Pittsburgh and on Allegheny R.; bituminous coal; mfg. (bricks, clay, metal, and leather products); gas, oil; limestone. Original site was an Indian village. Settled 1796, laid out 1804, inc. 1821.

Kittatinny Mountain (kĭ"tŭtĭ'nē), chiefly in NW N.J., ridge of the Appalachians extending SW, generally parallel to Delaware R., from Orange co., N.Y., where it joins Shawangunk Mtn., to Northampton co., Pa., where it joins Blue Mtn. At E base is Kittatinny Valley (a part of Great Appalachian Valley), which is continued NE by Wallkill Valley, SW by Lebanon Valley. High Point (alt. 1,801 ft.), in NW N.J. near N.Y. line, is highest point. Ridge traversed by Appalachian Trail; has resorts and recreational areas, including Stokes State Forest and High Point State Park. Delaware R. cuts ridge E of Stroudsburg, Pa., to form Delaware Water Gap.

Kittery (kĭ'tūrē), town (pop. 8,380), including Kittery village (pop. 6,692), York co., extreme SW Maine, at mouth of Piscataqua R. opposite Portsmouth, N.H. (connected by 2 bridges; 1923, 1940). U.S. (Portsmouth) Naval Base is on isls. in river. John Paul Jones's *Ranger*, 1st ship to fly Stars and Stripes, launched here 1777. Settled 1622 as Piscataqua; inc. 1647, 1st town in Maine. At **Kittery Point,** resort and fishing village (pop. 1,137), is old William Pepperell house (1682).

Kittigazuit, locality, NW Mackenzie Dist., Northwest Territories, on Refuge Cove, bay of the Beaufort Sea, at mouth of E channel of Mackenzie R. delta, 90 mi. NE of Aklavik; 69°21'N 133°43'W; U.S.-Canadian weather station. Site of Hudson's Bay Co. post, 1915–29.

Kittilä (kĭt'tĭlă), village (commune pop. 6,585), Lapi co., NW Finland, on Ounas R. and 80 mi. NNW of Rovaniemi; Lapp trading center. Near by are large iron deposits, centered on localities of Porkonen (pōr'kōnĕn) and Pahtavaara (pä'tävä"rä, päkh'tä–), 25 mi. E of Kittilä.

Kittim or **Chittim** (both: kĭ'tĭm), biblical term for Cyprus; also the name for the Cyprian port Citium.

Kittitas (kĭ'tĭtăs), county (□ 2,315; pop. 22,235), central Wash.; ⊙ Ellensburg. Mtn. area drained by Yakima R.; includes parts of Snoqualmie and Wenatchee natl. forests. Lumber, coal, gold, silica; livestock, dairy products, potatoes, apples. Formed 1883.

Kittitas, town (pop. 586), Kittitas co., central Wash., 6 mi. E of Ellensburg; silica mines, potatoes, peas, hay.

Kittrell (kĭ'trŭl), town (pop. 189), Vance co., N N.C., 8 mi. SSW of Henderson; plant nursery.

Kitts, mining village (pop. 1,431), Harlan co., SE Ky., in the Cumberlands, on Clover Fork of Cumberland R. and 29 mi. NE of Middlesboro; bituminous coal.

Kittsee (kĭt'sā), Hung. *Köpcsény* (kûp'chānyŭ), town (pop. 2,521), Burgenland, E Austria, 4 mi. S of Bratislava, Czechoslovakia; vineyards.

Kittson, county (□ 1,124; pop. 9,649), extreme NW Minn.; ⊙ Hallock. Agr. area drained by Two Rivers; bounded W by Red R. and N.Dak., N by Manitoba. Wheat, small grains, potatoes, livestock, dairy products. Formed 1878.

Kitty, town (pop., including adjoining Alexanderville, 8,927), Demerara co., N Br. Guiana, NE suburb of Georgetown, on the Atlantic, on railroad, in fertile agr. region (rice, sugar cane, coconuts, fruit, stock).

Kittybrewster, Scotland: see Aberdeen.

Kitty Hawk, village (pop. c.250), Dare co., NE N.C., on barrier beach bet. Atlantic Ocean and Kitty Hawk Bay (E end of Albemarle Sound), 32 mi. SE of Elizabeth City; Wright Memorial Bridge near by to Point Harbor. Kill Devil Hill Natl. Memorial (314.4 acres; established 1927) is 3 mi. S, near Kill Devil Hills village; here Wilbur and Orville Wright conducted glider experiments (1901–03) and made 1st sustained flights (1903) in airplane. A 60-ft. granite commemorative pylon was erected 1932 on dune from whose slopes flights were launched.

Kitui (kētōō'ē), town (1948 pop. c.750), S central Kenya, on road and 80 mi. E of Nairobi; agr. (coffee, sisal, wheat, corn).

Kitwe (kē'twā), township (pop. 2,993), Western Prov., N Northern Rhodesia, on rail spur and 30 mi. WNW of Ndola; commercial center for adjoining copper-mining center of Nkana. Govt. school. Township founded 1937 with modern facilities for European settlers.

Kityang (kĭt'yăng', Cantonese kĕt'yŭrn'), Mandarin *Chieh-yang* (jyĕ'yäng'), town (pop. 54,444), ⊙ Kityang co. (pop. 890,456), E Kwangtung prov., China, on coastal stream and 20 mi. WSW of Chaoan; tin-mining center; grass-cloth weaving, sugar refining.

Kitzbühel (kĭts'bü̇ŭl), town (pop. 7,282), Tyrol, W Austria, in Kitzbühel Alps, at S foot of Kitzbühler Horn, 50 mi. ENE of Innsbruck; winter sports center, summer resort. Copper deposits near by. Suspension railroad to Hahnenkamm (5,428 ft.), just S. Mineral spring near by.

Kitzbühel Alps, Ger. *Kitzbühler Alpen*, range of Eastern Alps in Tyrol and W Salzburg, W Austria, extending c.40 mi. E from Ziller R. to Saalach R., bounded S by the Pinzgau. Divided into 2 sections by Thurn Pass. W range rises to 8,366 ft. in the Kreuzjoch; E range to 7,762 ft. in the Gaisstein. Hahnenkamm (5,428 ft.) and Kitzbühler Horn (6,555 ft.) in N, Schmittenhöhe (6,457 ft.) in W are tourist and winter sports centers.

Kitzingen (kĭ'tsĭng-ŭn), city (1950 pop. 16,489), Lower Franconia, NW Bavaria, Germany, on the Main (canalized) and 11 mi. ESE of Würzburg; rail junction; wine-trading center; chemical mfg., lead and zinc smelting, lumber milling, woodworking, brewing, food processing, tanning. Has late-15th-cent. tower; mid-16th-cent. city hall; former Benedictine nunnery (founded c.750) with 17th-cent. church. Chartered mid-13th cent.; captured several times by Swedes in Thirty Years War.

Kitzmiller or **Kitzmillersville,** bituminous coal-mining town (pop. 652), Garrett co., W Md., in the Alleghenies, on North Branch of the Potomac (bridged to W.Va.), and 30 mi. SW of Cumberland. Near by are Potomac State Forest and Backbone Mtn.

Kitzscher (kĭ'chŭr), village (pop. 4,193), Saxony, E central Germany, 4 mi. NE of Borna, in lignite-mining region.

Kiu (kē'ōō), village, Central Prov., S central Kenya, on railroad and 50 mi. SSE of Nairobi; sisal, rubber, wheat, corn.

Kiuchüan or **Chiu-chüan** (both: jyō'jüän'), town, ⊙ Kiuchüan co. (pop. 128,377), N Kansu prov., China, on Peita R. and 120 mi. NW of Changyeh, near the Great Wall; commercial center on Silk Road to Sinkiang; wool, hides, grain. Gold deposits near by. Opened to foreign trade in 1881. Until 1913 called Suchow.

Kiuhsien or **Ch'iu-hsien** (both: chyō'shyĕn'), town, ⊙ Kiuhsien co. (pop. 81,904), S Hopeh prov., China, 60 mi. NE of Anyang, near Pingyuan line; cotton weaving; grain.

Kiukang (jyō'gäng') or **Chiu-chiang** (jyō'jyäng'), Jap. *Kyuko* (kyōō'kō), town (1935 pop. 1,127), NW Formosa, minor port on W coast, 3 mi. NNW of Sinchu; an outer harbor of Sinchu.

Kiukiang or **Chiu-chiang** (both: jyō'jyäng'), city (1948 pop. 120,555), ⊙ but independent of Kiukiang co. (1948 pop. 180,897), N Kiangsi prov., China, 110 mi. SE of Hankow, 75 mi. NNE of Nanchang; major river port on Yangtze R. (Hunan line), near Poyang L.; terminus of railroad from Nanchang; commercial center, in rice- and cotton-growing region. Exports tea, porcelain, paper, timber, ramie cloth. Spinning, weaving, and flour-milling industry. Iron and anthracite mines. City was held 1850–54 by Taipings in their rebellion against Manchu dynasty; was treaty port with British concession, 1861–1927. In Sino-Japanese War, was occupied by Japanese (1938–45). Just S is the wooded mtn. massif of Lü Shan with KULING resort and the WHITE DEER CAVE, where Chu Hsi (13th-cent. philosopher) lived and taught.

Kiukung Mountains, China: see MUFOW MOUNTAINS.

Kiulien Mountains or **Chiu-lien Mountains** (both: jyō'lyĕn'), section of the Nan Ling, on Kwangtung-Kiangsi border, China, extending c.50 mi. E–W along border in area of Tingnan (Kiangsi prov.). Mt. Kiulien, S of main range and 20 mi. ENE of Linping, rises over 2,000 ft.

Kiulung or **Chiu-lung** (both: jyō'lōōng'), town, ⊙ Kiulung co. (pop. 13,231), S Sikang prov., China, 80 mi. SSW of Kangting; wheat, millet, sweet potatoes. Asbestos found near by.

Kiulung Mountains, China: see TAPA SHAN.

Kiulung River (jyō'lōōng'), Chinese *Kiulung Kiang* or *Chiu-lung Chiang* (both: jyäng), Fukien prov., China, rises N of Lengyong, flows 120 mi. SE, past Changping, Hwaan, and Changtai, forming common estuary with Lung R. on Amoy Bay of Formosa Strait.

Kiungchow. 1 Town, Hainan, Kwangtung prov., China: see KIUNGSHAN. **2** Town, Szechwan prov., China: see KIUNGLAI.

Kiungchow Strait, China: see HAINAN STRAIT.

Kiunglai or **Ch'iung-lai** (both: chyōōng'lī'), town (pop. 18,728), ⊙ Kiunglai co. (pop. 361,119), W Szechwan prov., China, 40 mi. WSW of Chengtu, near Sikang line; rice, tea, sugar cane, wheat, rapeseed, medicinal plants. Until 1913, Kiungchow.

Kiunglang, pass, Tibet: see NITI PASS.

Kiungshan or **Ch'iung-shan** (both: chŭng'shän'), town, ⊙ Kiungshan co. (pop. 376,294), N Hainan, Kwangtung prov., China, port on Nantu R. near its mouth, 300 mi. SW of Canton; trading center; rice, coconuts, pineapple. Sugar milling, vegetable-oil extracting, cotton milling. Treaty port opened to foreign trade in 1858. Because shoals bar large vessels, most of trade passes through outer port of HOIHOW. Until 1912 called Kiungchow.

Kiungtung or **Ch'iung-tung** (both: chŭng'dōōng'), town, ⊙ Kiungtung co. (pop. 105,267), E Hainan, Kwangtung prov., China, 45 mi. SSE of Kiungshan; rattan cane, coconuts, sugar cane, rice, peanuts; poultry and hog raising. Graphite mined near by. Until 1914 called Hweitung.

Kiupeh or **Ch'iu-pei** (both: chyō'bā'), town (pop. 2,787), ⊙ Kiupeh co. (pop. 42,148), E Yunnan prov., China, 50 mi. N of Wenshan; alt. 5,203 ft.; rice, wheat, millet, beans, sugar cane. Antimony deposits near by.

Kiupu, China: see CHIHTEH.

Kiushiu, Japan: see KYUSHU.

Kiutai or **Chiu-t'ai** (both: jyō'tī'), town, ⊙ Kiutai co. (pop. 404,461), W central Kirin prov., Manchuria, 35 mi. NE of Changchun and on railroad; soybeans, grain. Until 1947 called Siakiutai.

Kiutiao Mountains, China: see TAPA SHAN.

Kivach Falls, Karelo-Finnish SSR: see SUNA RIVER.

Kivalina (kĭvŭlē'nŭ), Eskimo village (pop. 116), NW Alaska, on Chukchi Sea, 80 mi. NW of Kotzebue; reindeer herding. School.

Kivdinski or **Kivdinskiy** (kēvdyēn'skē), E suburb (1939 pop. over 2,000) of Raichikhinsk, SE Amur oblast, Russian SFSR, on spur of Trans-Siberian RR; lignite mines.

Kiverichi (kē'vyĭrēchē), village (1926 pop. 262), E central Kalinin oblast, Russian SFSR, 29 mi. S of Bezhetsk; flax.

Kivertsy (kē'vyĭrtsē), Pol. *Kiwerce* (kēvĕr'tsē), town (1931 pop. 3,650), SE Volyn oblast, Ukrainian SSR, 8 mi. NE of Lutsk; rail junction; saw-milling; grain, stock. Kivertsy village is 4 mi. SW.

Kivik (chē"vēk'), fishing village (pop. 601), Kristianstad co., S Sweden, on the Baltic, 10 mi. NNW of Simrishamn; seaside resort; noted for fruit grown here. Near by is site of Bronze Age grave.

Kivioli or **Kiviyli,** Est. *Kiviõli* (all: kē'vēulē) [=shale oil], city (1949 pop. over 2,000), NE Estonia, on railroad and 22 mi. E of Rakvere; oil-shale mining center.

Kivu (kē'vōō, kēvōō'), province (□ 88,860; 1948 pop. 1,532,172), E Belgian Congo; ⊙ Costermansville. Borders NE on Uganda (along Ruwenzori range and L. Edward), E on Ruanda-Urundi (along Virunga range, Ruzizi R., and N part of L. Tanganyika). Principal rivers are Lualaba, Lomami, Lowa, Elila, and Ulindi. Its eastern highlands (mean alt. 3,000–6,500 ft.), inhabited by pastoral Bantu tribes, are noted since 1928 as leading center of European agr. settlement in Congo; here are large coffee plantations and farms growing pyrethrum, derris, cinchona, citrus fruit, and temperate-climate vegetables. Tourists are attracted by incomparable scenery and Albert Natl. Park. W part of Kivu prov., in Congo basin, is covered with dense equatorial forest; cotton, palms, rice, and various African staples are grown by natives in scattered locations. Kivu also has a well-developed gold- and tin-mining industry (Shabunda, Kamituga, Kalima-Kingombe). Steamers ply L. Tanganyika, L. Kivu, and the lower Lualaba; railroads bet. Kindu and Kongolo and bet. Uvira and Kamaniola. Chief towns: Costermansville, Kasongo, Kindu, Uvira, Rutshuru. Prov. was called Costermansville, 1935–47.

Kivu, district, Belgian Congo: see COSTERMANSVILLE.

Kivu, Lake (□ c.1,100), E central Africa, on Belgian Congo and Ruanda-Urundi border, N of L. Tanganyika and W of L. Victoria; 60 mi. long, 30 mi. wide, c.1,600 ft. deep. Highest-lying lake (alt. 4,788 ft.) of the Albertine Rift, it drains into L. Tanganyika through Ruzizi R. Idjwi isl. occupies lake's center. Unlike other African lakes, it has no crocodiles and hippopotami, and its waters are scarce in fish; colonies of otters are abundant. L. Kivu area is the outstanding tourist region of Belgian Congo; many European settlers have established plantations on both shores. Main ports are Costermansville, Goma, Kisenyi. Discovered by Count von Gotzen, a Ger. explorer.

Kiwalik (kēwä'lĭk), village (1939 pop. 24), NW Alaska, on SE shore of Kotzebue Sound, N Seward Peninsula, at mouth of Kiwalik R. and 60 mi. SSE of Kotzebue; port and transfer point for Candle and Kiwalik R. valley. Sometimes spelled Keewalik.

Kiwalik River, NW Alaska, on N side of Seward Peninsula, rises near 65°20'N 161°30'W, flows c.60 mi. N, past Candle, to Kotzebue Sound at Kiwalik. Placer gold district.

Kiwerce, Ukrainian SSR: see KIVERTSY.

Kiwitea, New Zealand: see KIMBOLTON.

Kiyaly-Kurgancha (kēä'lē-kōōrgän'chŭ), village (1939 pop. over 500), NW Fergana oblast, Uzbek SSR, 4 mi. NW of Kokand; cotton; sericulture.

Kiyama (kēyä'mä). **1** Town (pop. 3,635), Kumamoto prefecture, W Kyushu, Japan, 6 mi. E of Kumamoto; rice, sweet potatoes. **2** Town (pop. 8,744), Saga prefecture, NW Kyushu, Japan, 7 mi. N of Kurume; rail junction; agr. center (rice, wheat); raw silk, sake. Mulberry trees, tallow trees (*sapium sebiferum*).

Kiyang or **Ch'i-yang** (both: chē'yäng'), town, ⊙ Kiyang co. (pop. 742,101), S Hunan prov., China, on Siang R. and 50 mi. SW of Hengyang; tea oil, tung oil, and colza oil. Coal mining near by.

Kiya River (kē'ŭ), in Kemerovo and Tomsk oblasts, Russian SFSR, rises in Kuznetsk Ala-Tau E of Pezas, flows N, past Mariinsk (on Trans-Siberian RR), and NW to Chulym R. at Zyryanskoye; 315 mi. long. Gold deposits along upper course, in Kemerovo oblast (Berikulski, Pervomaiski, Tsentralny mines).

Kiyasovo (kēä'sŭvŭ), village (1926 pop. 942), S Udmurt Autonomous SSR, Russian SFSR, 34 mi. S of Izhevsk; wheat, livestock.

Kiye, Turkey: see GEMLIK.

Kiyev, Ukrainian SSR: see KIEV.

Kiyevka (kē'ŭfkŭ), village (1948 pop. over 2,000), N Karaganda oblast, Kazakh SSR, near Nura R., 70 mi. NW of Karaganda, in cattle area.

Kiyma, Kazakh SSR: see KIMA.

Kiyomizu, Formosa: see TSINGSHUI.

Kiyosu (kēyō'sōō), town (pop. 7,528), Aichi prefecture, central Honshu, Japan, just NW of Nagoya; rice, poultry, market produce. Agr. experiment station.

Kizan, town, Formosa: see KISHAN.

Kizan Island, Formosa: see KWEISHAN ISLAND.

Kizel (kēzyĕl'), city (1933 pop. estimate 40,000), E central Molotov oblast, Russian SFSR, on left tributary of Yaiva R., on railroad and 80 mi. NE of Molotov. Leading coal-mining center of the Urals; mfg. (coal-mining machinery, clothing). Developed in 1890s, following building of railroad; became city in 1926. **Kizel** bituminous-coal basin (□ 560) extends c.40 mi. bet. Gremyachinsk (S) and Aleksandrovski (N). Extensive deposits (estimated reserves of 3,435,000,000 tons), known in 18th cent. and exploited since 1853, are suitable for coke production in combination with Kuzbas coal. Major mining centers: Kizel, Gubakha, Polovinka, Gremyachinsk, Kospash, Lunyevka, Nagornski, Usva.

Kizelstroi, Russian SFSR: see GUBAKHA.

Kizhinga (kēzhēn'gŭ), village, SE Buryat-Mongol Autonomous SSR, Russian SFSR, 95 mi. E of Ulan-Ude, in agr. area (wheat, livestock).

Kizil, in Rus. names: see also KIZYL, KYZYL, KZYL.

Kizil-agach, Bulgaria: see YELKHOVO.

Kizilcahamam (kŭzŭl"jähämäm'), Turkish *Kızılcahamam*, village (pop. 1,989), Ankara prov., central Turkey, on Kirmir R. and 38 mi. NNW of Ankara; hot springs; grain, fruit, chick-peas, vetch, mohair goats. Formerly Yabanabat and Chorba.

Kizil Dag (kŭzŭl' dä), Turkish *Kızıl Dağ*, peak (9,892 ft.), N central Turkey, 22 mi. W of Refahiye, near source of the Kizil Irmak.

Kizilhisar Dag (kŭzŭl"hĭsär' dä), Turkish *Kızılhisar Dağ*, peak (7,352 ft.), SW Turkey, in Mentese Mts. 10 mi. ESE of Tavas.

Kizil Irmak (kĭ'zĭl ĭrmäk', kĭzĭl', Turkish kŭzŭl' ĭrmäk') or **Kizil River,** Turkish *Kızıl Irmak* or *Kızılırmak* [=red river], anc. *Halys* (hā'lĭs), important river (715 mi. long) of Asia Minor, N central Turkey, rises near the Kizil Dag, N central Turkey, 12 mi. NW of Kurucay, E of Sivas, flows in a wide arc SW past Sivas, and NW, N, and NE to the Black Sea N of Bafra. Receives the Balaban, Devrez, and Gok Irmak (left), Delice R. (right).

Kizil Kum, USSR: see KYZYL-KUM.

Kizilskoye or **Kizil'skoye** (kēzēl'skŭyŭ), village (1926 pop. 2,578), SW Chelyabinsk oblast, Russian SFSR, on Ural R. and 50 mi. SSW of Magnitogorsk; rye, oats, sheep. Anthracite deposits. Formerly called Kizilski.

Kiziltash Liman (kēzēltäsh' lyĭmän'), lagoon of Black Sea, Krasnodar Territory, Russian SFSR, SE of Taman Peninsula; 12 mi. long, 6 mi. wide. Receives marshy Old Kuban arm of Kuban R.

Kiziltepe (kŭzŭl'tĕpĕ"), Turkish *Kızıltepe*, village (pop. 1,484), Mardin prov., SE Turkey, 11 mi. SW of Mardin; grain, legumes, mohair goats. Also called Kochisar.

Kizil-Yurt (kēzēl-yōōrt'), village (1939 pop. over 500), N central Dagestan Autonomous SSR, Russian SFSR, on Sulak R., on railroad and 35 mi. NW of Makhachkala; irrigated agr. (cotton, wheat, rice). Pop. largely Kumyk.

Kizimkasi (kēzēmkä'sē), village, near S tip of Zanzibar, 27 mi. SE of Zanzibar town; fishing center. Site of 12th-cent. Persian mosque. A former ⊙ Zanzibar isl.

Kizlyar (kēzlyär'), city (1932 pop. estimate 14,800), E Grozny oblast, Russian SFSR, in Caspian depression, on left bank of Terek R. and 60 mi. NE of Grozny, on railroad; alt. 45 ft. below sea level. Wine-making (cognac, liquors) center in cotton and fruitgrowing area. Founded 1735 as fortress, became important center for trade with Dagestan mtn. tribes. Acquired (c.1800) large Armenian pop. Rail terminus until construction, during Second World War, of extension to Astrakhan. Kizlyar area was part of Dagestan, 1922–38, passed (1938) to Stavropol (then Ordzhonikidze) Territory and (1944) to Grozny oblast.

Kizner (kēz'nyĭr), town (1948 pop. over 2,000), SW Udmurt Autonomous SSR, Russian SFSR, on railroad and 75 mi. SW of Izhevsk; wood cracking.

Kizu (kē'zōō) or **Kitsu** (kē'tsōō), town (pop. 8,227), Kyoto prefecture, S Honshu, Japan, 20 mi. SSE of Kyoto; rice growing.

Kizukuri (kēzōō'kōōrē), town (pop. 6,068), Aomori prefecture, N Honshu, Japan, 3 mi. W of Goshogawara; rice collection.

Kizu River, Japan: see YODO RIVER.

Kizyl, in Rus. names: see also KIZIL, KYZYL, KZYL.

Kizyl-Arvat (kēzĭl"-ŭrvät'), city (1932 pop. estimate 12,630), SW Ashkhabad oblast, Turkmen SSR, on Trans-Caspian RR and 130 mi. WNW of Ashkhabad; railroad shops; rug weaving; lime kilns, meat and flour products. Was the anc. Ferava, ruled (8th–9th cent.) by Arabs. Modern city founded 1881 by Russians.

Kizyl-Asker (–ä'skyĭr), village (1939 pop. over 2,000), N Frunze oblast, Kirghiz SSR, in Chu valley, just W of Frunze, on railroad (Pishpek station); sugar beets, orchards. Also spelled Kyzyl-Asker. Until 1944, Chalakazaki.

Kizyl-Atrek (–ŭtryĕk'), town (1948 pop. over 2,000), SW Ashkhabad oblast, Turkmen SSR, on Atrek R. (Iran border) and 195 mi. WSW of Ashkhabad; subtropical agr. (olives); wheat, cattle, camels.

Kizyl-Ayak (–läk'), town (1939 pop. over 500), SE Chardzhou oblast, Turkmen SSR, on the Amu Darya and 15 mi. SE of Kerki; cotton.

Kizyl-Kiya (–kē'ŭ), city (1939 pop. 15,104), N Osh oblast, Kirghiz SSR, in Fergana Valley, on rail spur and 38 mi. SW of Osh; important coal-mining center; power plant.

Kizyl-Kup (–kōōp'), town (1941 pop. over 500), W Ashkhabad oblast, Turkmen SSR, on S shore of Kara-Bogaz-Gol gulf, 65 mi. NE of Krasnovodsk; Glauber's salt is extracted here. There are also fish canneries.

Kizyl-Su (–sōō'), town (1939 pop. over 500), W Ashkhabad oblast, Turkmen SSR, on Caspian Sea sandspit, 15 mi. S of Krasnovodsk; fisheries; shipbuilding (fishing vessels).

Kjeller (chĕl′lůr), village (pop. 401) in Skedsmo canton, Akershus co., SE Norway, 10 mi. ENE of Oslo; site of military airfield. Has nuclear reactor.
Kjellerup, Denmark: see KELLERUP.
Kjelvik, Norway: see HONNINGSVAG.
Kjerknesvagen, Norway: see STRAUMEN.
Kjerkoy, Norway: see HVAL ISLANDS.
Kjerringsvik, Norway: see ULA.
Kjobenhavn, Denmark: see COPENHAGEN.
Kjoge, Denmark: see KOGE.
Kjopsvik (chûps′vĭk, –vēk), Nor. *Kjøpsvik,* village (pop. 785), in Tysfjord canton (pop. 3,680), Nordland co., N Norway, on Tys Fjord (inlet of Vest Fjord), 40 mi. SW of Narvik; cementworks. At Hundholmen (hōōn′hôlmůn) village, 4 mi. NNW, is feldspar quarry.
Kjosar, Iceland: see GULLBRINGU OG KJOSAR.
Kjosfoss (chōs′fôs), waterfall (722 ft.) in Sogn og Fjordane co., W Norway, in the Flamsdal just N of Myrdal; site of hydroelectric station.
Klabbeek, Belgium: see CLABECQ.
Kladanj, Kladan, or **Kladan'** (all: klä′dänyů), town (pop. 2,851), E Bosnia, Yugoslavia, on Drinjaca R. and 28 mi. NNE of Sarajevo; local trade in cereals, poultry.
Kladesholmen (klĕ″dŭs-hôl′mŭn), Swedish *Klädesholmen,* fishing village (pop. 769), Goteborg och Bohus co., SW Sweden, on isl. (410 acres) of same name in the Skagerrak, 4 mi. N of Marstrand.
Kladno (kläd′nô), city (pop. 19,166), W central Bohemia, Czechoslovakia, 15 mi. WNW of Prague; rail junction; center of coal-mining and metallurgical industries. Urban area (pop. 40,692), which includes towns of DUBI (NE), KROCEHLAVY (E), and ROZDELOV (W), produces high-grade alloys, steel, pig-iron, finished parts for machine industry, cables, bicycles, and semi-finished goods to be further processed at metallurgical works of CHOMUTOV. Its foundries and rolling mills are among the largest in Czechoslovakia. Has noted city hall, old chapel, 18th-cent. castle.
Kladovo (klä′dôvô), village (pop. 2,038), E Serbia, Yugoslavia, on the Danube, opposite (7 mi. W of) Turnu-Severin (Rumania); sturgeon fishing.
Klaeng (klăng), village (1937 pop. 2,088), Rayong prov., S Thailand, 26 mi. ENE of Rayong; fisheries (S) on Gulf of Siam.
Klafeld (klä′fĕlt), village (pop. 9,780), in former Prussian prov. of Westphalia, W Germany, after 1945 in North Rhine-Westphalia, 3 mi. N of Siegen; forestry.
Klaffenbach (klä′fůnbäkh), village (pop. 3,176), Saxony, E central Germany, at N foot of the Erzgebirge, 5 mi. S of Chemnitz; synthetic-oil plant.
Klagenfurt (klä′gůnfōōrt), Slovenian *Celovec,* city (1951 pop. 62,792), ⊙ Carinthia, S Austria, on Glan R. 60 mi. SW of Graz, in beautiful mtn.–lake area; rail center; metal, food, and chemical industries; mfg. (hats, umbrellas, clothing, leather goods, tobacco); breweries; soap- and candleworks. Well-known winter sports center. Seat of a bishop. Has theological seminary, Alpine mus., Rudolfinum mus., Landhaus (16th cent.), Lindwurmbrunnen (fountain of winged dragon; 1590). Became hq. of Br. occupation zone in 1945.
Klagshamn (kläks″hä′mŭn), village (pop. 945), Malmohus co., S Sweden, on the Oresund, 6 mi. SSW of Malmo; port; lime- and cementworks; limestone-quarrying region.
Klaipeda, Lithuania: see MEMEL, city.
Klaksvig (klägs′vēg), Faeroese *Klakksvík,* town (pop., with surrounding commune, 1,191) and port in Faeroe Isls., on SW Bordo isl., 16 mi. NNE of Thorshavn.
Klamath (klă′mŭth), county (□ 5,973; pop. 42,150), S Oregon, in Cascade foothills; ⊙ Klamath Falls. Agr. and lumbering area bordering on Calif. and drained in SW by Upper Klamath L. and Klamath R. Grain, alfalfa, potatoes, and livestock are raised in Klamath irrigation project, extending S from Lost R. into Siskiyou co., N Calif. Crater Lake Natl. Monument is in W. Klamath Indian Reservation occupies central portion. Formed 1882.
Klamath, village (pop. c.500), Del Norte co., NW Calif., 18 mi. SE of Crescent City, and on Klamath R. (here crossed by Douglas Memorial Bridge) near its mouth on the Pacific; game fishing. Lower Klamath Indian Reservation near by.
Klamath Agency, village (pop. c.100), Klamath co., S Oregon, 30 mi. NNW of Klamath Falls; alt. 4,170 ft. Hq. for Klamath Indian Reservation. Fish hatchery near by.
Klamath Falls, city (pop. 15,875), ⊙ Klamath co., S Oregon, at S tip of Upper Klamath L. (here connected by 1¼-mi. Link R.—entirely in city—with L. Ewauna), on E slope of the Cascades; alt. 4,105 ft. Lumbering (numerous sawmills) and rail center for farming (potatoes, grain, alfalfa) and sheep- and cattle-raising region. Resort center S of Crater Lake Natl. Park (40 mi. NNW) and near Klamath Indian Reservation. City settled c.1866 as Linkville, inc. 1889, renamed 1893, reinc. 1913. Growth stimulated by development of Klamath irrigation project (1900) and by arrival of railroad (1909).
Klamath Lake: see LOWER KLAMATH LAKE, Calif.; UPPER KLAMATH LAKE, Oregon.
Klamath Mountains, in N Calif. and SW Oregon, mountain knot which connects Coast Ranges of Oregon (N) with those of Calif. (W and S), and meets the Cascade Range (E) at N end of Central Valley of Calif.; extends c.250 mi. from foothills S of Willamette Valley, Oregon, to S extensions along W side of Central Valley. Subranges (N–S) are: Rogue River Range, Oregon; SISKIYOU MOUNTAINS; Scott Mts., Salmon Mts., Trinity Mts., South Fork Range (most southwesterly; sometimes considered one of Coast Ranges); and Bullychoop and Yolla Bolly or Yallo Bally mts., S extensions. Highest peaks: Mt. Eddy (9,038 ft.), c.15 mi. SW of Mt. Shasta; Thompson Peak (8,936 ft.), c.50 mi. SW of Mt. Shasta. Scenic Salmon-Trinity Alps (or Trinity Alps) region along Trinity-Siskiyou co. line in Calif. has been set aside as wilderness preserve. Klamath Mts. are drained by Coquille, Rogue, Klamath, and Trinity rivers and by a headstream of the Sacramento. Extensive lumbering (evergreen forests); dairying, fruitgrowing (notably along Rogue R.) in valleys; hunting, fishing, camping.
Klamath River, in S Oregon and N Calif., rises in Upper Klamath L. just above Klamath Falls, flows S as the 1¼-mi. Link R. to L. Ewauna, which it leaves as Klamath R., flowing generally SW through Klamath Mts., Calif., turning NW in Humboldt co., and emptying into the Pacific near Klamath, Calif.; 263 mi. long. River is connected by Klamath Strait (7 mi. long; largely in Oregon) with Lower Klamath L., in Calif. Supplies water for Klamath irrigation project, serving agr. area in Klamath co., Oregon, and Siskiyou co., Calif. Copco No. 1 Dam (227 ft. high, 415 ft. long; completed 1922), in Calif. section of stream, just S of Oregon line, is used for power. Trinity R., in Calif., is chief tributary.
Klampenborg, Sweden: see ESSVIK.
Klang (kläng), town (pop. 33,506), W Selangor, Malaya, on railroad and Klang R., 20 mi. WSW of Kuala Lumpur; sultan's residence; center of rubber- and fruitgrowing dist.; mfg. of rubber footwear, pineapple canning. Connaught Bridge (2 mi. E) is site of large steam power station.
Klang, Thailand: see SONG.
Klang Island, flat, mangrove island in Strait of Malacca, Selangor, Malaya, off Port Swettenham at Klang R. mouth; 8 mi. long and 4 mi. wide. North Klang Strait, bet. Klang Isl. and mainland, is chief access route to Port Swettenham.
Klang River, in Selangor, W Malaya, rises on Pahang line in central Malayan range, flows 60 mi. S and W, past Kuala Lumpur and Klang, to Strait of Malacca at Port Swettenham. Mangrove isls. (Klang Isl.) off mouth.
Klanjec (klä′nyĕts), village (pop. 1,015), N Croatia, Yugoslavia, on Sutla R. and 20 mi. NNW of Zagreb, on Slovenia border; local trade center. Several castles and monasteries near by.
Klappa (klĕ′pä), Swedish *Kläppa,* residential village (pop. 803), Gavleborg co., E Sweden, on Ljusna R., just SE of Ljusdal.
Klarentza, Greece: see KYLLENE.
Klar River, Swedish *Klarälven* (klär′ĕl″vůn), E Norway and W Sweden. Called Trysil R., Nor. *Trysilelv* (trü′sĭl-ĕlv″), in Norway, it issues from S end of Femund L., flows generally S, crosses into Sweden 35 mi. ENE of Elverum, and flows past Munkfors (head of navigation; power station) and Deje, to L. Vaner at Karlstad; c.200 mi. long. Important logging route and source of hydroelectric power.
Klasterec nad Ohri (klä′shtĕrĕts näd′ ôkhrē), Czech *Klášterec nad Ohří,* Ger. *Klösterle an der Eger* (klû′stůrlů än dĕr ā′gůr), village (pop. 1,618), W Bohemia, Czechoslovakia, on Ohre R., on railroad and 17 mi. NE of Carlsbad; porcelain mfg.
Klaster Hradiste, Czechoslovakia: see MNICHOVO HRADISTE.
Klaster Tepla, Czechoslovakia: see TEPLA.
Klastor pod Znievom (klä′shtôr pôd′ znyĕvôm), Slovak *Kláštor pod Znievom,* Hung. *Znióváralja* (znĭ′ōvä″rŏlyŏ), village (pop. 1,229), W central Slovakia, Czechoslovakia, on railroad and 17 mi. SSE of Zilina; known for its large trade in medicinal herbs.
Klaten (klä′tůn), town (pop. 12,039), central Java, Indonesia, 17 mi. ENE of Jogjakarta, at foot of Mt. Merapi; trade center for agr. area (tobacco, rice, peanuts); textile mills. Agr. experiment station and a branch of Jakarta meteorological station are here. There is Du. fort built 1807.
Klatovy (klä′tôvĭ), Ger. *Klattau* (klä′tou), town (pop. 13,236), SW Bohemia, Czechoslovakia, 24 mi. S of Pilsen; rail junction; noted tanning industry; produces chemicals, linen goods, leather goods, lace. Located in foothills of Bohemian Forest, it is a center of floriculture (annual exhibitions of carnations and roses) and point of departure for excursions into Sumava. Has 13th-cent. cathedral with 16th-cent. tower, 17th-cent. Jesuit church with catacombs, 16th-cent. city hall.
Klausberg, Poland: see MIKULCZYCE.
Klausen, Italy: see CHIUSA.
Klausenburg, Rumania: see CLUJ, city.
Klausen Pass (klou′zůn) (6,404 ft.), in Glarus Alps, Uri canton, central Switzerland. Klausen Road, over the pass, joins Linthal and Altdorf.
Klaustal-Zellerfeld, Germany: see CLAUSTHAL-ZELLERFELD.
Klavdiyevo-Tarasovo (kläv′dyēůvů-tůrä′sůvů), town (1926 pop. 730), N central Kiev oblast, Ukrainian SSR, 23 mi. WNW of Kiev.
Klavrestrom (klä′vrůstrûm″), Swedish *Klavreström,* village (pop. 612), Kronoberg co., S Sweden, 20 mi. NE of Vaxjo; foundry.
Klawak or **Klawock** (both: klůwäk′), village (1950 pop. 398), SE Alaska, on W coast of Prince of Wales Isl., 5 mi. N of Craig; fishing, fish processing. First salmon cannery in Alaska was located here.
Klawak Island (4 mi. long, 1 mi. wide; 1939 pop. 18), SE Alaska, in Alexander Archipelago, W of Klawak village on Prince of Wales Isl.; 55°33′N 133°6′W.
Klawock, village, Alaska: see KLAWAK.
Klaypeda, Lithuania: see MEMEL, city.
Klazienaveen (kläzē′nävān), town (pop. 3,897), Drenthe prov., NE Netherlands, 11 mi. ENE of Coevorden, near Ger. border; peat, strawboard center; chemicals.
Kléber (klābâr′), village (pop. 1,140), Oran dept., NW Algeria, 16 mi. NE of Oran; winegrowing.
Kleberg (klā′bûrg), county (□ 851; pop. 21,991), S Texas; ⊙ Kingsville. On Gulf coast, here protected by Padre Isl. and indented by Baffin Bay. Ranching area, including part of huge KING RANCH; beef cattle, horses, oil, natural gas; also sheep, goats, hogs, some agr. (feed, peanuts, cotton, some truck). Coast resorts (fishing, bathing). Formed 1913.
Klechev, Poland: see KLECZEW.
Kleck, Belorussian SSR: see KLETSK.
Klecko (kwĕts′kô), Pol. *Kłecko,* Ger. *Kletzko* (klĕts′kō), town (1946 pop. 1,532), Poznan prov., W central Poland, on railroad and 26 mi. NE of Poznan; brick mfg., flour milling.
Kleczew (klĕ′chĕf), Rus. *Klechev* (klĕ′chĭf), town (pop. 2,336), Poznan prov., W central Poland, 50 mi. E of Poznan.
Kledang Range (klĕ″däng′), in central Perak, Malaya, forming divide bet. Perak and Kinta rivers; 25 mi. long; rises to 3,469 ft. At E foot are the large Kinta Valley tin-mining centers of Tronoh, Batu Gajah, and Ipoh.
Kleidi, Greece: see RUPEL PASS.
Klein (klīn), village (pop. 1,995), Styria, SE Austria, 5 mi. SW of Leibnitz; grain, vineyards.
Klein, Kleine, Kleiner, Kleines, in German names: for features beginning thus and not found here, see under main part of name; e.g., for Kleines Schilthorn, see SCHILTHORN.
Klein (klīn), village (1940 pop. 638), Musselshell co., central Mont., on Musselshell R., opposite Roundup, in coal-mining area.
Kleinandelfingen, Switzerland: see ANDELFINGEN.
Klein-Auheim (klīn″-ou′hīm), village (pop. 4,719), S Hesse, W Germany, in former Starkenburg prov., on left bank of the canalized Main and 7 mi. E of Offenbach; paper milling.
Kleinbettingen (klīn″bĕ′tĭng-ůn), village (pop. 552), SW Luxembourg, 10 mi. WNW of Luxembourg city; frontier station on Belg. border; paints, varnishes, farinaceous food products.
Kleinblittersdorf (klīn″blĭ′tůrsdôrf), town (pop. 3,047), S Saar, on Saar R. (Fr. border) and 3 mi. NNW of Sarreguemines; clay quarrying; woodworking, flour milling. Opposite is Grossbliederstroff, France.
Klein Bonaire, Du. West Indies: see LITTLE BONAIRE.
Klein Curaçao, Du. West Indies: see LITTLE CURAÇAO.
Kleine Dommel River, Netherlands: see DOMMEL RIVER.
Kleine Emme River, Switzerland: see EMME RIVER, KLEINE.
Kleineislingen, Germany: see EISLINGEN.
Kleine Mühl River (klī′nů mül′), N Upper Austria, rises near Ger. border, flows 15 mi. S to the Danube 3 mi. W of Partenstein.
Kleinen, Bad, Germany: see BAD KLEINEN.
Kleinenberg (klī′nůnbĕrk), town (pop. 1,538), in former Prussian prov. of Westphalia, NW Germany, after 1945 in North Rhine-Westphalia, 9 mi. NW of Warburg.
Kleine Nete, Belgium: see PETITE NÈTHE RIVER.
Kleingartach (klīn″gär′täkh), town (pop. 1,021), N Württemberg, Germany, after 1945 in Württemberg-Baden, 11 mi. WSW of Heilbronn; wine.
Kleinheubach (klīn″hoi′bäkh), village (pop. 2,101), Lower Franconia, W Bavaria, Germany, on the Main (canalized) and 2 mi. NW of Miltenberg; hydroelectric station; textile mfg., metal- and woodworking, distilling, fruit conserving. Has early-18th-cent. baroque castle.
Kleinkamsdorf, Germany: see KAMSDORF.
Klein Kirchheim, Austria: see BAD KLEINKIRCHHEIM.
Kleinlangheim (klīn″läng′hīm), village (pop. 1,400), Lower Franconia, W Bavaria, Germany, 16 mi. ESE of Würzburg; wheat, barley, cattle. Has late-15th-cent. town hall.
Kleinlaufenburg, Germany: see LAUFENBURG.
Kleinmacher (klīn′mäkh-ůr), village (pop. 248), SE Luxembourg, on Moselle R., just SSW of Remich, on Ger. border; vineyards.
Klein Machnow (klīn″ mäkh′nō), residential village (pop. 11,792), Brandenburg, E Germany, on Teltow Canal and 10 mi. SW of Berlin city center; metalworking.

Klein Rosseln, France: see PETITE-ROSSELLE.
Klein-Schlatten, Rumania: see ZLATNA.
Klein Swartberg, U. of So. Afr.: see SWARTBERG.
Kleintettau (klīn″tĕ'tou), village (pop. 673), Upper Franconia, N Bavaria, Germany, 14 mi. SSW of Saalfeld; glass.
Klein Zwartberg, U. of So. Afr.: see SWARTBERG.
Klekovaca or **Klekovacha** (both: klĕ'kôvächä), Serbo-Croatian *Klekovača,* mountain in Dinaric Alps, W Bosnia, Yugoslavia; highest point, Velika Klekovaca (6,432 ft.), is 7 mi. NE of Drvar.
Klemme (klĕ'mē), town (pop. 555), Hancock co., N Iowa, 23 mi. WSW of Mason City; feed, millwork products.
Klenovnik (klĕ'nôvnĭk), hamlet, E Serbia, Yugoslavia, 5 mi. N of Pozarevac; lignite mine.
Klepp (klĕp), village and canton (pop. 4,678), Rogaland co., SW Norway, on railroad and 14 mi. S of Stavanger; quarries; exports kieselguhr and other insulation materials.
Kleppesto, Norway: see ASKOY.
Klerk (klyĕrk), town (1940 pop. over 500), SW Maritime Territory, Russian SFSR, on Peter the Great Bay, 38 mi. SE of Vladivostok; fish cannery.
Klerken (klĕr'kůn), agr. village (pop. 1,924), West Flanders prov., W Belgium, 3 mi. SSE of Dixmude. Formerly spelled Clercken.
Klerksdorp (klĕrks'dôrp), town (pop. 18,338), SW Transvaal, U. of So. Afr., on Schoon Spruit R., near its mouth on Vaal R., 100 mi. WSW of Johannesburg; alt. 4,347 ft.; rail junction; gold-mining and agr. center (corn, stock); grain elevator. Founded 1839; scene (March, 1902) of capture of Lord Methuen by Delarey in South African War. Mining operations begun 1933.
Kleshcheli, Poland: see KLESZCZELE.
Kleshchino Lake, Russian SFSR: see PLESHCHEYEVO LAKE.
Klesov (klyĕ'sůf), Pol. *Klesów* (klĕ'sōōf), town (1939 pop. over 2,000), NE Rovno oblast, Ukrainian SSR, 12 mi. E of Sarny; sawmilling; stone quarrying. Kaolin deposits near by.
Kleszczele (klĕsh-chĕ'lĕ), Rus. *Kleshcheli* (klĕsh-chĕ'lē), town (pop. 1,436), Bialystok prov., E Poland, on railroad and 40 mi. S of Bialystok, near Belorussian SSR border; pottery making, flour milling.
Kletnya (klyĭtnyä″), town (1939 pop. over 2,000), N Bryansk oblast, Russian SFSR, on rail spur and 25 mi. WSW of Zhukovka; lumber center; sawmills; woodworking (prefabricated houses).
Kletsk (klyĕtsk), Pol. *Kleck* (klĕtsk), city (1931 pop. 5,930), SE Baranovichi oblast, Belorussian SSR, 26 mi. ESE of Baranovichi; fruit canning, tanning, flax carding, woolen weaving; mfg. of rope, bricks; flour milling, sawmilling. Assaulted by Tatars (14th–16th cent.); passed (1793) from Poland to Russia; reverted (1921) to Poland; ceded to USSR in 1945.
Kletskaya (klyĕt'skīŭ), village (1926 pop. 2,622), W Stalingrad oblast, Russian SFSR, on right bank of Don R. and 75 mi. NW of Stalingrad; metalworks; wheat. Pop. largely Cossack.
Klettgau (klĕt'gou), land tract, Germany and Switzerland, along Wutach R., W of Schaffhausen.
Kletzko, Poland: see KLECKO.
Klevan or **Klevan'** (klyĭvän'yů), Pol. *Klewań* (klĕ'-vänyů), town (1931 pop. 1,780), W Rovno oblast, Ukrainian SSR, 13 mi. NW of Rovno; flour milling, sawmilling, lumbering, tanning; glassworks. Has old churches, ruins of 15th-cent. castle. Chartered in 1654.
Kleve, Germany: see CLEVES.
Klewan, Ukrainian SSR: see KLEVAN.
Klian Intan or **Intan** (klē"än' ĭntän'), town (pop. 1,694), northernmost Perak, Malaya, 37 mi. E of Sungei Patani, in Kalakhiri Range (Thailand line) and near Kedah border; tin mining.
Klichev (klyĕ'chĭf), town (1948 pop. over 2,000), NE Bobruisk oblast, Belorussian SSR, 25 mi. NNE of Bobruisk; dairy farming.
Klickitat (klĭ'kůtăt), county (□ 1,912; pop. 12,049), S Wash.; ⊙ Goldendale. Agr., lumbering area, rising toward Cascade Range in N; timber, wheat, fruit, dairy products, livestock. Drained by Columbia (S boundary) and Klickitat rivers. Includes part of Yakima Indian Reservation. Formed 1860.
Klickitat River, S Wash., rises in Cascade Range in Yakima Indian Reservation, flows c.85 mi. generally S to Columbia R. NW of The Dalles, Oregon. Receives West Fork (15 mi. long) from slopes of Mt. Adams.
Klidhi, Greece: see RUPEL PASS.
Klimkovice (klĭm'kôvĭtsĕ), Ger. *Königsberg* (kû'-nĭkhsbĕrk), town (pop. 2,710), central Silesia, Czechoslovakia, 7 mi. WSW of Ostrava, in sugar-beet and barley area; rail terminus.
Klimovichi (klyēmô'vēchē), city (1926 pop. 7,637), SE Mogilev oblast, Belorussian SSR, 45 mi. SW of Roslavl; food products, wood cracking, brick mfg.
Klimovo (klyĕ'můvů), town (1926 pop. 5,071), SW Bryansk oblast, Russian SFSR, 14 mi. SE of Novozybkov; dried vegetables, leather products. Formerly called Klimov.
Klimovsk (-můfsk), city (1939 pop. over 2,000), S central Moscow oblast, Russian SFSR, on railroad (Grivno station) and 5 mi. S of Podolsk; textile-machinery mfg. Called Klimovski after 1928, until it became city in 1940.
Klin (klyēn'), city (1939 pop. over 10,000), N Moscow oblast, Russian SFSR, 50 mi. NW of Moscow; mfg. (lathes, textiles, ceramic goods, artificial fiber); peat-fed power plant. Chartered 1318. Site of Tschaikowsky mus. (home of composer), damaged during Second World War, when Germans briefly held city (1941) in Moscow campaign.
Klinaklini River, SW B.C., rises in Coast Mts. near 51°50′N 125°W, flows 120 mi. in a wide arc SW and S to head of Knight Inlet.
Klin-Dmitrov Ridge (klyēn-dumē'trůf), E extension of Smolensk-Moscow Upland, in central European USSR; forms watershed bet. Volga and Klyazma rivers; rises to 960 ft. Crossed N-S by Moscow Canal.
Kline, town (pop. 230), Barnwell co., SW S.C., 40 mi. SW of Orangeburg.
Klinga, Norway: see BANGSUND.
Klinge, Netherlands: see CLINGE.
Klingenberg (klĭng'ůnbĕrk). **1** or **Klingenberg am Main** (äm mīn'), town (pop. 2,634), Lower Franconia, NW Bavaria, Germany, on the Main (canalized) and 13 mi. S of Aschaffenburg; textile mfg.; pottery works. Known for its red wine. Chartered 1276. Near-by ruined castle was built on Roman foundations. **2** Village (pop. 1,484), Saxony, E central Germany, in the Erzgebirge, on Wild Weisseritz R. (dam) and 8 mi. E of Freiberg.
Klingenbrunn (klĭng'ůnbrōōn'), village (commune pop. 2,759), Lower Bavaria, Germany, in Bohemian Forest, 8 mi. SE of Zwiesel; glass- and woodworking, food processing.
Klingenmünster (klĭng″ůnmün'stůr), village (pop. 2,381), Rhenish Palatinate, W Germany, at E foot of Hardt Mts., 6 mi. SW of Landau; wine.
Klingenthal (klĭng'ůntäl), town (pop. 6,652), Saxony, E central Germany, in the Erzgebirge, 18 mi. ESE of Plauen; frontier station on Czechoslovak border, opposite Kraslice; mouth-organ and accordion-mfg. center; embroidering, metalworking. Winter-sports center.
Klingnau (klĭng'nou), village (pop. 1,573), Aargau canton, N Switzerland, on Aar R. and 7 mi. NNW of Baden, near Ger. border; hydroelectric plant; plywood.
Klinovec (klē'nôvĕts), Czech *Klínovec,* Ger. *Keilberg* (kīl'bĕrk), highest peak (4,080 ft.) of the Erzgebirge, in W Bohemia, Czechoslovakia, near German border, 3 mi. NE of Jachymov; winter-sports center.
Klintehamn (klĭn″tůhä'můn), village (pop. 880), Gotland co., SE Sweden, on W coast of Gotland isl., on bay of the Baltic, 17 mi. S of Visby; seaside resort. Near by is 13th-cent. church.
Klintsovka (klyēntsôf'ků), village (1939 pop. over 500), E Saratov oblast, Russian SFSR, 29 mi. SE of Pugachev; metalworks; wheat, cattle, sheep.
Klintsy (klyēn'tsē), city (1926 pop. 22,229), W Bryansk oblast, Russian SFSR, 90 mi. SW of Bryansk; hemp-milling, woolen-cloth mfg. center; clothing mfg.; rope mills, tanneries, iron foundry. Has peat-fed power plant. Dates from 18th cent.; became city in 1925. During Second World War, held (1941–43) by Germans.
Klipheuvel (klĭp'hůvůl), village, SW Cape Prov., U. of So.Afr., 22 mi. NE of Cape Town; wireless transmitter.
Klippan (klĭ'pän), town (pop. 4,697), Kristianstad co., SW Sweden, near Ronne R., 18 mi. ENE of Halsingborg; rail junction; woolen and paper milling, tanning, brick making. First Swedish paper mill founded here, 1653.
Klipplaat (klĭp'lät), village (pop. 1,264), S Cape Prov., U. of So. Afr., on Doorn R. and 55 mi. S of Graaff Reinet; rail junction; stock, feed, fruit.
Klip River, W Natal, U. of So. Afr., formed 4 mi. WNW of Ladysmith by 2 short tributaries rising in Drakensberg range, flows 30 mi. SE, past Ladysmith, to Tugela R. 13 mi. SE of Ladysmith. Near Ladysmith is major power station.
Kliptown, residential town (pop. 3,531), S Transvaal, U. of So. Afr., on Witwatersrand, 10 mi. WSW of Johannesburg.
Klis (klēs), Ital. *Clissa* (klēs'sä), village, S Croatia, Yugoslavia, on railroad and 5 mi. NE of Split, in Dalmatia, at pass (alt. 1,200 ft.) on W slope of the Mosor. Has ruins of castle dating from Roman period, once a Turkish strongpoint menacing Venetian-held Split. First mentioned in Croat history in 850.
Klisura, Albania: see KËLCYRË.
Klisura (klēsōō'rä), city (pop. 2,019), Plovdiv dist., central Bulgaria, at E end of Koznitsa Pass, on Strema R. and 19 mi. W of Karlovo, on railroad; rose growing; livestock. Once a Turkish commercial town; declined after Bulg. uprising in 1876.
Klisura Pass, Bulgaria: see SAPAREVA-BANYA.
Kljajicevo or **Klyayichevo** (both: klyī'ĭchĕvô), Serbo-Croatian *Kljajićevo,* village (pop. 5,653), Vojvodina, N Serbia, Yugoslavia, 7 mi. E of Sombor, in the Backa. Until 1948, Krnjaja or Krnyaya [Hung. *Kerény*].
Kljuc or **Klyuch** (both: klyōōch), Serbo-Croatian *Ključ,* village (pop. 1,716), W Bosnia, Yugoslavia, on Sana R. and 26 mi. SW of Banja Luka; local trade center. First mentioned in 1325.
Klobouky (klô'bōkĭ), Ger. *Klobouk,* town (2,145), S Moravia, Czechoslovakia, on railroad and 18 mi. SE of Brno; agr. center (wheat, barley, sugar beets).
Klobuck (kwô'bōōtsk), Pol. *Kłobuck,* Rus. *Klobutsk* (klô'bōōtsk), town (pop. 6,533), Katowice prov., S Poland, 10 mi. NW of Czestochowa; tanning, sawmilling.
Klodawa (kwôdä'vä), Pol. *Kłodawa,* Rus. *Klodava* (klôdä'vů), town (pop. 4,062), Poznan prov., central Poland, 28 mi. ENE of Konin; brick mfg., flour milling.
Klodnica River (klôdnē'tsä), Ger. *Klodnitz* (klōt'-nĭts), in Upper Silesia, after 1945 in S Poland, rises SSW of Katowice, flows WNW past Gleiwitz (Gliwice) and Labedy, and W past Ujazd and Blachownia, to Oder R. just SE of Kozle; 47 mi. long. In lower course, beyond Gleiwitz, parallels Gleiwitz Canal.
Klodzkie, Gory, Poland: see KRALICKY SNEZNIK.
Klodzko, Poland: see GLATZ.
Kloengkoeng, Indonesia: see KLUNGKUNG.
Kloetinge (klōō'tĭng-ů), village (pop. 1,495), Zeeland prov., SW Netherlands, on South Beveland isl. and 1.5 mi. E of Goes; center of cherry-growing area; cement mfg.
Klokotnitsa (klôkôtnē'tsä), village (pop. 1,106), Khaskovo dist., S central Bulgaria, 5 mi. NW of Khaskovo; cotton, tobacco, vineyards. Theodore of Epirus defeated here (1230) by Bulg. king John Asen.
Klokoty, Czechoslovakia: see TABOR.
Klondike River (klŏn'dĭk), W Yukon, rises E of Dawson, flows 100 mi. W to Yukon R. at Dawson. Receives Bonanza Creek just SE of Dawson. Noted by Indians for its salmon. It gives its name to surrounding region. Gold was struck on Bonanza Creek, Aug. 17, 1896; subsequently other strikes were made in Klondike R. valley. Great influx of gold miners from the United States and Canada took place in 1897 and Dawson city grew up almost overnight with population of c.20,000 in 1898. Prospectors arrived at Skagway, traveled over White or Chilkoot passes to upper Yukon R., thence by boat to Dawson. Several other routes by overland trail were also used. Gold production in region has declined since 1900.
Klong Toi, Thailand: see KHLONG TOEI.
Klönthalersee or **Klöntalersee** (both: klůn'tälůrzā″), lake (□ 1), E central Switzerland, WSW of Glarus. Inlet: Klön R.; outlet: Löntsch R. The Glärnisch rises along S shore. Regulated by dam, lake feeds Löntsch hydroelectric plant.
Klos (klôs) or **Klosi** (klô'sē), village (1930 pop. 1,549), central Albania, near upper Mat R., 22 mi. SW of Peshkopi.
Kloster, Germany: see HIDDENSEE.
Klosterlausnitz, Bad, Germany: see BAD KLOSTERLAUSNITZ.
Klösterle an der Eger, Czechoslovakia: see KLASTEREC NAD OHRI.
Klostermansfeld (klō'stůrmänsfĕlt″), village (pop. 5,957), in former Prussian Saxony prov., central Germany, after 1945 in Saxony-Anhalt, at E foot of the lower Harz, 5 mi. NW of Eisleben; copper-slate mining. First mentioned in 10th cent.
Klosterneuburg (–noi'bōōrk), outer N district (□ 30; pop. 22,616) of Vienna, Austria, on right bank of the Danube, on N slope of the Wiener Wald. Formed (1938) through incorporation of 7 towns, including Kritzendorf and Klosterneuburg (pop. 13,710, 7 mi. N of city center), site of wealthy Augustinian monastery (consecrated 1136; oldest in Austria) which has Leopold's Chapel with altar of Verdun (1181), extensive library, large wine cellars.
Klosters (klō'stůrs), town (pop. 2,774), Grisons canton, E Switzerland, on Landquart R. and 16 mi. E of Chur; valley resort among mts.; hydroelectric plant. Klosters comprises villages of Platz (3,967 ft.), Brücke (3,874 ft.), Dörfli (3,697 ft.). Kloster Pass, 8 mi. E, leads to Austria.
Klosterwappen, Austria: see SCHNEEBERG.
Kloster Zinna (klō'stůr tsĭ'nä), village (pop. 1,829), Brandenburg, E Germany, 6 mi. SSW of Luckenwalde. Site of former Cistercian monastery (founded 1170 by monks from Cologne; dissolved 1547); extant bldgs. include 12th–13th-cent. church and 15th-cent. abbots' house.
Kloten (klō'tůn), town (pop. 2,019), Zurich canton, N Switzerland, 6 mi. NNE of Zurich; metal products. Site of Zurich overseas airport (opened 1948).
Klötze (klû'tsů), town (pop. 6,255), in former Prussian Saxony prov., central Germany, after 1945 in Saxony-Anhalt, 15 mi. S of Stendal; agr. market (grain, asparagus, hops, malt).
Klotzsche (klô'chů), town (pop. 9,848), Saxony, E central Germany, 6 mi. NNW of Dresden; mfg. of clothing, glass, pharmaceuticals, cosmetics; metal-working. Climatic health resort.
Klouto (klōō'tō), town, S Fr. Togoland, near Br. Togoland border, 70 mi. NW of Lomé. Agr. center (cacao, coffee, palm kernels and oil, cotton). Customhouse. Iron smelter.
Kluane, Indian village, SW Yukon, near Alaska border, on Kluane L., at foot of St. Elias Mts., 120 mi. W of Whitehorse, and on Alaska Highway; 61°2′N 138°24′W. Center of Kluane Game Sanctuary (established 1943).

Kluane Lake (□ 184), SW Yukon, near Alaska border, at foot of St. Elias Mts., 120 mi. W of Whitehorse; 61°15′N 138°44′W. It is 60 mi. long, 1–6 mi. wide; drains N into Yukon R.

Kluang (kloo͞′äng′), town (pop. 15,954), central Johore, Malaya, on railroad and 50 mi. NW of Johore Bharu; rubber and oil-palm plantations; airport.

Kluczbork (kloo͝ch′bôrk), Ger. *Kreuzburg* (kroits′-bo͝ork), town (1939 pop. 11,693; 1946 pop. 8,467) in Upper Silesia, after 1945 in Opole prov., S Poland, 25 mi. NNE of Oppeln (Opole); rail junction; linen milling, mfg. of machinery, leather, bricks. Novelist Freytag b. here.

Klukhori (klo͝okhô′rē), city (1939 pop. 5,829) NW Georgian SSR, on N slope of the Greater Caucasus, on Kuban R., at mouth of Teberda R., and 70 mi. NE of Sukhumi, on Sukhumi Military Road; brickworks, dairy plant. Founded c.1920; until 1943, called Mikoyan-Shakhar as ⊙ former Karachai Autonomous Oblast. During Second World War, held (1942–43) by Germans.

Klukhori Pass, in main range of the W Greater Caucasus, NW Georgian SSR, on Sukhumi Military Road (here a trail) and 45 mi. ENE of Sukhumi; alt. 9,239 ft.

Klukwan (klŭk′wän), village (pop. 91), SE Alaska, on Chilkat R. and 20 mi. NW of Haines, on Haines Cut-off to Alaska Highway; trading center. School.

Klundert (klŭn′dŭrt), town (pop. 2,472), North Brabant prov., SW Netherlands, 10 mi. NNE of Roosendaal; flax processing, shipbuilding, lumber milling.

Klungkung or **Kloengkoeng** (klo͝ong-ko͝ong′), town, SE Bali, Indonesia, 15 mi. NE of Denpasar; wood carving, metalworking. Near by are several Hindu temples. Was ⊙ Bali from 17th cent. to 1908.

Klüppelberg (klü′pŭlbĕrk), village (pop. 6,097), in former Prussian Rhine Prov., W Germany, after 1945 in North Rhine-Westphalia, 13 mi. SE of Remscheid.

Klutina River (klŭtē′nŭ), S Alaska, rises in Chugach Mts. near 61°44′N 145°45′W, flows 60 mi. NE, through Klutina L. (17 mi. long), to Copper R. at Copper Center.

Klütz (klüts), town (pop. 3,179), Mecklenburg, N Germany, near Wismar Bay of the Baltic, 13 mi. WNW of Wismar; center of wheat-growing region; chemical mfg. Has 13th-cent. church. Near by is 18th-cent. Bothmer castle.

Klyavlino (klyäv′lyĭnŭ), village (1932 pop. estimate 2,100), NE Kuibyshev oblast, Russian SFSR, on railroad and 35 mi. WSW of Bugulma; road center; flour milling; wheat, sunflowers.

Klyayichevo, Yugoslavia: see KLJAJICEVO.

Klyazma River or **Klyaz′ma River** (klyäz′mŭ), in central European Russian SFSR, rises on Klin-Dmitrov Ridge, E of Solnechnogorsk; flows 390 mi. E, through important textile-mfg. region, past Shchelkovo, Noginsk, Orekhovo-Zuyevo, Vladimir, Kovrov, and Vyazniki, to Oka R. WSW of Volodary. Navigable in lower course below Sobinka. Upper course connected with Moscow CANAL, which passes through Klyazma Reservoir (hydroelectric station at Pirogovski). Receives Ucha, Kirzhach, Nerl, Uvod, Teza (left) and Sudogda (right) rivers.

Klyuch, Yugoslavia: see KLJUC.

Klyuchevsk (klyo͞ochĕfsk′), town (1933 pop. estimate 5,500), S Sverdlovsk oblast, Russian SFSR, on railroad and 15 mi. NNE (under jurisdiction) of Berezovski; mfg. of ferro-alloys. Developed in 1930s; called Teply Klyuch until 1933.

Klyuchevskaya Sopka (klyo͞ochĭfskī′ŭ sôp′kŭ), highest active volcano (15,912 ft.) of Eurasian continent, in E mtn. range of Kamchatka Peninsula, Russian SFSR, on right bank of Kamchatka R., 220 mi. NNE of Petropavlovsk. Of perfect conic shape; has crater 650 ft. in diameter. Frequent eruptions.

Klyuchi (klyo͞ochē′). **1** Village (1926 pop. 3,116), W Altai Territory, Russian SFSR, on railroad and 55 mi. SSE of Slavgorod; flour mill. **2** Village (1947 pop. over 500), Kamchatka oblast, Khabarovsk Territory, Russian SFSR, on E central Kamchatka Peninsula, 60 mi. W of Ust-Kamchatsk and on Kamchatka R., at NE foot of Klyuchevskaya Sopka; sawmilling. Volcano research station.

Klyuchinski, Russian SFSR: see KRASNOMAISKI.

Klyuchishchi, Russian SFSR: see BOLSHIYE KLYUCHISHCHI.

Klyukvenny, Russian SFSR: see UYAR.

Knaben (kŭnä′bŭn), village (pop. 294) in Fjotland canton (pop. 1,503), Vest-Agder co., S Norway, 30 mi. NNE of Flekkefjord; mining center for near-by molybdenum mines. Sometimes spelled Knabbe.

Knabstrup (knäb′stro͞op), town (pop. 636), Holbaek amt, Zealand, Denmark, 7 mi. SW of Holbaek; pottery, peat, bricks.

Knapp (năp), village (pop. 424), Dunn co., W Wis., 12 mi. WNW of Menomonie, in dairying area.

Knapp Creek, village (pop. c.250), Cattaraugus co., W N.Y., 7 mi. SW of Olean, in oil-producing area on Pa. line.

Knared (kŭnâ′rŭd), Swedish *Knäred*, village (pop. 656), Halland co., SW Sweden, on Laga R. and 20 mi. ESE of Halmstad; grain, flax, sugar beets.

Knaresborough (nârz′bŭrŭ), urban district (1931 pop. 5,942; 1951 census 8,393), West Riding, central Yorkshire, England, on Nidd R. and 3 mi. ENE of Harrogate; linen milling; agr. market; resort. Has remains of castle built by Henry I, including 14th-cent. keep; church dating from 13th cent.; and "Dropping Well" with petrifying waters. In St. Robert's cave Eugene Aram hid the body of the murdered Daniel Clark in 1745.

Knaresborough Spa, England: see HARROGATE.

Knebworth (nĕb′wûrth), town and parish (pop. 2,183), central Hertford, England, 8 mi. NW of Hertford; agr. market. Knebworth House was home of Bulwer Lytton. Has 13th-cent. church.

Knee Lake (50 mi. long, 5 mi. wide), NE Man., on Hayes R.; 55°N 94°40′W.

Kneuttingen, France: see KNUTANGE.

Knezha (knĕzhä′), city (pop. 13,133), Vratsa dist., N Bulgaria, on small tributary of Iskar R. and 9 mi. ENE of Byala Slatina; agr. and livestock trading center. Has agr. school, experimental station. Formerly spelled Knizha.

Knezpolje or **Knezhpolye** (both: knĕsh′pôl″yĕ), Serbo-Croatian *Knežpolje*, hamlet, W Herzegovina, Yugoslavia, on road and 9 mi. W of Mostar, on NW border of Mostar L.; bauxite mine.

Knicanin or **Knichanin** (both: knē′chänĭn), Serbo-Croatian *Knićanin*, Hung *Rezsőháza* (rĕ′zhûházŏ), village (pop. 5,955), Vojvodina, N Serbia, Yugoslavia, on left bank of Tisa R., at Begej R. mouth opposite Titel, and 24 mi. E of Novi Sad, in the Banat.

Knielingen (kŭnē′lĭng-ŭn), NW district (since 1935) of Karlsruhe, Germany; paper milling.

Knierim (kŭnēr′ŭm), town (pop. 133), Calhoun co., central Iowa, 15 mi. WSW of Fort Dodge; wood products.

Knife Lake, in NE Minn. and W Ont., in chain of lakes on Can. line, in resort area of Superior Natl. Forest, 35 mi. NE of Ely; 10 mi. long, average width 1 mi.

Knife Point Mountain, Wyo.: see WIND RIVER RANGE.

Knife River, N.Dak., rises in Killdeer Mts., W central N.Dak., flows E 165 mi. to Missouri R. near Stanton.

Knightdale, town (pop. 461), Wake co., central N.C., 8 mi. E of Raleigh.

Knight Inlet, SW B.C., arm (75 mi. long, 1-4 mi. wide) of Queen Charlotte Strait, opposite Vancouver Isl.; receives Klinaklini R. at head.

Knight Island. 1 Island (25 mi. long, 2–9 mi. wide), S Alaska, in Prince William Sound, E of Kenai Peninsula, 40 mi. SE of Whittier; 60°20′N 147°44′W; rises to 3,261 ft. **2** Island (4 mi. long), SE Alaska, in Yakutat Bay, 10 mi. NW of Yakutat; 59°43′N 139°34′W.

Knight Island Passage (20 mi. long, 3–5 mi. wide), S Alaska, SW entrance to Prince William Sound, bet. Knight Isl. (E) and Kenai Peninsula and Chenega Isl. (W); 60°18′N 148°W.

Knighton, Welsh *Tref-y-clawdd* (trĕvŭkloudh′) [town of the dyke], urban district (1931 pop. 1,836; 1951 census 1,871), E Radnor, Wales, on Teme R. at English border, and 14 mi. W of Ludlow; woolen milling, shoe mfg. Just S is well-preserved section of Offa's Dyke.

Knightsbridge, road junction, E Cyrenaica, Libya, 28 mi. SW of Tobruk, near Bir Hacheim. Scene of major tank battles (1942) bet. Axis and British in Second World War.

Knights Landing, village (1940 pop. 649), Yolo co., central Calif., 20 mi. NW of Sacramento and on Sacramento R. (bridged here).

Knightstown, Ireland: see VALENTIA.

Knightstown, town (pop. 2,486), Henry co., E central Ind., on Big Blue R. and 34 mi. E of Indianapolis, in livestock and grain area; mfg. (canned goods, car bodies, furniture, fences). Home for orphans of soldiers and sailors. Settled 1825, inc. 1827.

Knightsville, town (pop. 678), Clay co., W Ind., just NE of Brazil, in agr. and bituminous-coal area.

Knightville Reservoir, Mass.: see WESTFIELD RIVER.

Knik (kŭnĭk′), village (1939 pop. 40), S Alaska, on W side of Knik Arm, 18 mi. N of Anchorage; supply point.

Knik Arm, N arm (30 mi. long, 2–6 mi. wide) of Cook Inlet, S Alaska; extends NE from Cook Inlet, just N of Anchorage.

Knin (knĭn), village (pop. 2,737), W Croatia, Yugoslavia, on Krka R. and 26 mi. NNE of Sibenik, in Dalmatia, near Bosnia line. Rail junction; road hub; local trade center; gypsum deposits. R.C. bishopric. Has mus. of Croatian art, old castle, old churches (some ruined), palace ruins. Former ⊙ medieval Croatia. Passed (1699) from Turkish rule to Venetian Dalmatia.

Kniphausen, Germany: see FEDDERWARDEN.

Knislinge (kŭnĭs′lĭng-ŭ), village (pop. 1,471), Kristianstad co., S Sweden, near Helge R., 11 mi. NNW of Kristianstad; textile milling, shoe mfg. Has 13th-cent. church. Sometimes spelled Knisslinge.

Knisslinge, Sweden: see KNISLINGE.

Knitsley (nĭts′lē), town and parish (pop. 2,276), NW central Durham, England, 11 mi. WNW of Durham; coal mining.

Knittelfeld (kŭnĭ′tŭlfĕlt), city (pop. 12,762), Styria, S central Austria, on Mur R. and 30 mi. NW of Graz; iron- and steelworks; summer resort, baths. Heavily bombed in Second World War.

Knittlingen (kŭnĭt′lĭng-ŭn), town (pop. 3,285), N Württemberg, Germany, after 1945 in Württemberg-Baden, 10 mi. SE of Bruchsal; grain, cattle. Traditional birthplace of Dr. Faust.

Knivskjellodden (kŭnēv′shĕl-lôd″dŭn) or *Knivskjerodden* (kŭnēv′shŭrôd″dŭn), low cape on Barents Sea of Arctic Ocean, on isl. of Mageroy, Finnmark co., N Norway, 60 mi. NE of Hammerfest; 71°11′8″N 25°43′E. The northernmost point of Europe, though NORTH CAPE, 4 mi. ESE, is popularly celebrated as such. NORDKYN is northernmost point on European mainland. Also spelled Knivskjelodden or Knivskjaerodden.

Knivsta (kŭnēv′stä″), village (pop. 807), Stockholm co., E Sweden, 10 mi. SE of Uppsala; metalwork.

Knizha, Bulgaria: see KNEZHA.

Knjazevac or **Knyazhevats** (both: knyä′zhĕväts), Serbo-Croatian *Knjaževac*, town (pop. 5,107), E Serbia, Yugoslavia, near Beli Timok R., on railroad and 24 mi. NE of Nis, near Bulg. border. Coal mines in vicinity.

Knobel (nō′bŭl), town (pop. 417), Clay co., extreme NE Ark., 19 mi. NNW of Paragould.

Knob Hill, village (pop. 3,612), El Paso co., E central Colo., just NE of Colorado Springs.

Knobly Mountain (nŏ′blē), E W.Va., a ridge of the Appalachians, in Eastern Panhandle; from North Branch of the Potomac opposite Cumberland, Md., extends c.50 mi. SW to a point W of Petersburg; rises to 2–3,000 ft., with knoblike summits to over 3,000 ft.

Knob Noster (nŏb′ nŏ′stŭr), city (pop. 585), Johnson co., W central Mo., near Blackwater R., 10 mi. E of Warrensburg; grain, livestock; coal.

Knockalongy (nŏ″kŭlŏng′ē), mountain (1,778 ft.) in W Co. Sligo, Ireland, 13 mi. WSW of Sligo; highest in the Slieve Gamph.

Knockanaffrin (nŏ″kŭnă′frĭn), mountain (2,504 ft.), N Co. Waterford, Ireland, 9 mi. SE of Clonmel; highest point of Comeragh Mts.

Knockando (nŏkăn′dō), town and parish (pop. 1,334), W Moray, Scotland, on the Spey and 5 mi. W of Aberlour; woolen milling, whisky distilling. Two mi. E, on the Spey, is whisky-distilling village of Carron.

Knockbain (nŏkbān′), parish (pop. 1,155), SE Ross and Cromarty, Scotland. Includes MUNLOCHY.

Knockbrett (nŏkbrĕt′) or **Knockbrit** (–brĭt′), Gaelic *Cnoc Briot*, agr. village, central Co. Tipperary, Ireland, 8 mi. E of Cashel; dairying; potatoes, beets.

Knocke, Belgium: see KNOKKE.

Knock Hill, Scotland: see GLENBARRY.

Knocklayd (nŏklăd′), mountain (1,695 ft.), N Co. Antrim, Northern Ireland, 3 mi. S of Ballycastle.

Knockmahon (nŏk′mŭho͞on′, –mŭhŏn′), village (district pop. 383), S Co. Waterford, Ireland, on the coast 12 mi. ENE of Dungarvan; copper mining.

Knockmealdown Mountains (–mēl′–), range in Munster, Ireland, extending 15 mi. E-W along border bet. NW Co. Waterford and SW Co. Tipperary; rises to 2,609 ft. 6 mi. N of Lismore.

Knocktopher, Gaelic *Cnoc an Tochair*, agr. village (district pop. 442), S central Co. Kilkenny, Ireland, 12 mi. S of Kilkenny; cattle; barley, potatoes. Remains of 14th-cent. Carmelite monastery.

Knokke (knô′kŭ), town (pop. 11,297), West Flanders prov., NW Belgium, near North Sea, 10 mi. NNE of Bruges. Formerly spelled Knocke. Near by, on North Sea, are popular seaside resorts: Knokke-sur-Mer (–sür-mâr′); Het Zoute (hĕt zou′tŭ), Fr. *Le Zoute* (lŭ zo͞ot′); and Albert-Plage (älbâr-plăzh′).

Knollwood Park, village (pop. 4,035, with adjacent Woodlawn Orchards), Jackson co., S Mich.

Knossos, Crete: see CNOSSUS.

Knott, county (□ 356; pop. 20,320), E Ky.; ⊙ Hindman. Drained by small Troublesome Creek, several other creeks. Mtn. coal-mining and agr. (livestock, fruit, tobacco) area, in Cumberland foothills. Formed 1884.

Knottingley, urban district (1931 pop. 6,839; 1951 census 9,989), West Riding, S Yorkshire, England, on Aire R. and 14 mi. SE of Leeds; glass- and chemical works.

Knowle (nōl), town and parish (pop. 2,982), NW central Warwick, England, 8 mi. SE of Birmingham; agr. market. Has 15th-cent. guildhall and church.

Knowles (nōlz), town (pop. 91), Beaver co., extreme NW Okla., 19 mi. ENE of Beaver, in wheat and livestock area.

Knowlton, village (pop. 972), ⊙ Brome co., S Que., at S end of Brome L., 16 mi. SE of Granby; dairying center; resort.

Knowsley (nōz′lē), residential and agr. village and parish (pop. 1,146), SW Lancashire, England, 3 mi. NW of Prescot. Site of Liverpool reservoir.

Knox. 1 County (□ 728; pop. 54,366), NW central Ill.; ⊙ Galesburg. Agr. (corn, wheat, oats, livestock, poultry, fruit; dairy products). Bituminous coal, clay, gravel. Diversified mfg., chiefly at Galesburg. Drained by Spoon R. and Pope and Henderson creeks. Formed 1825. **2** County (□ 517; pop. 43,415), SW Ind.; ⊙ Vincennes.

Bounded W by Wabash R. (here forming Ill. line), E by West Fork of White R., and S by White R.; drained by small Maria Creek and Deshee R. Agr. area (fruit, grain), producing also oil, natural gas, and bituminous coal. Mfg. at Vincennes; fruit-packing plants, nurseries, creameries. Formed 1790. **3** County (□ 373; pop. 30,409), SE Ky.; ⊙ Barbourville. In the Cumberlands; drained by Cumberland R. and several creeks. Includes Dr. Thomas Walker State Park. Bituminous-coal mining; agr. (livestock, fruit, vegetables, sorghum, corn, potatoes, hay, tobacco); timber, oil wells. Some mfg. at Corbin and Barbourville. Formed 1799. **4** County (□ 362; pop. 28,121), S Maine, on Penobscot Bay; ⊙ Rockland. Coastal and isl. area has resorts, fishing, shipping of seafood, cement, and lime. Inland agr. and lake area produces poultry, eggs, apples; has resorts, Lake St. George State Park. Drained by St. George R. Formed 1860. **5** County (□ 512; pop. 7,617), NE Mo.; ⊙ Edina. Drained by Salt R. and Middle and South Fabius rivers; corn, oats, hay, livestock; lumber. Formed 1845. **6** County (□ 1,124; pop. 14,820), NE Nebr.; ⊙ Center. Agr. area bounded N by Missouri R. and S.Dak.; drained by Niobrara R. Grain, livestock, dairy and poultry produce. Formed 1857. **7** County (□ 532; pop. 35,287), central Ohio; ⊙ Mount Vernon. Drained by Kokosing and Mohican rivers and North Fork of Licking R. Agr. area (livestock, dairy products, grain, fruit); mfg. at Mount Vernon; sand and gravel pits. Formed 1808. **8** County (□ 517; pop. 223,007), E Tenn.; ⊙ KNOXVILLE. In Great Appalachian Valley; drained by Tennessee R. (here formed by junction of Holston and French Broad rivers); bounded SW by Clinch R. Includes part of Fort Loudoun Reservoir. Livestock raising, dairying, agr. (corn, hay, tobacco, fruit). Zinc and bituminous-coal mines, marble quarries. Industry at Knoxville. Formed 1792. **9** County (□ 854; pop. 10,082), N Texas; ⊙ Benjamin. Plains area, drained by Brazos R., North and South forks of the Wichita. Agr., livestock-raising (cotton, grain sorghums, some fruit and truck; cattle, hogs, poultry; dairy products). Formed 1858.

Knox. 1 Town (pop. 3,034), ⊙ Starke co., NW Ind., on Yellow R. and 33 mi. SW of South Bend, in agr. area producing chiefly mint and onions; makes electrical appliances, clothing, pickles. **2** Town (pop. 445), Waldo co., S Maine, 11 mi. NW of Belfast, in agr., recreational area. **3** Village (pop. 190), Benson co., N central N.Dak., 27 mi. NW of Minnewaukan; dairy, livestock, wheat, oats. **4** Borough (pop. 1,213), Clarion co., W central Pa., 8 mi. WNW of Clarion; mfg. (bottles, fiber boxes, bricks, beverages, tools, butter); bituminous coal, oil, gas; timber. Name changed from Edenburg (ē'dŭnbûrg) 1933; Knox was long its post office.

Knox, Cape, W B.C., NW extremity of Graham Isl., on the Pacific, at SW end of Dixon Entrance; 54°11'N 132°54'W.

Knox, Fort, U.S. military reservation (33,000 acres), Hardin co., N Ky., 28 mi. SSW of Louisville. Established 1917 as a First World War training camp; made a permanent military post in 1932. U.S. Depository here (built 1936) contains bulk of the nation's gold bullion. In Second World War, the fort was again an important training center. Godman Air Force Base is here.

Knox Atoll, uninhabited atoll, Ratak Chain, Marshall Isls., W central Pacific, c.5 mi. SE of Mili; 10 islets.

Knox City. 1 Town (pop. 362), Knox co., NE Mo., bet. Middle and South Fabius rivers, 9 mi. E of Edina; grain, livestock; lumber. **2** Town (pop. 1,489), Knox co., N Texas, c.80 mi. WSW of Wichita Falls; rail, trade center in cotton, grain, cattle area. Inc. 1916.

Knox Coast, Antarctica, part of Wilkes Land, on Indian Ocean, bet. 104° and 109°E. Discovered 1840 by Charles Wilkes, U.S. explorer.

Knoxville. 1 Agr. village (pop. c.200), ⊙ Crawford co., central Ga., 20 mi. WSW of Macon. **2** City (pop. 2,209), Knox co., NW central Ill., 4 mi. SE of Galesburg, in agr. and bituminous-coal area; dairy products. Inc. 1832. **3** City (pop. 7,625), ⊙ Marion co., S central Iowa, 33 mi. ESE of Des Moines, near Whitebreast Creek; ships coal and livestock; mfg. (overalls, dairy and meat products, feed, concrete blocks). Limestone quarries near by. Has large U.S. veterans hosp. Settled 1845, inc. 1854. **4** Village (pop. c.400), Frederick co., W Md., on the Potomac, 15 mi. WSW of Frederick; railroad shops. **5** Borough (pop. 656), Tioga co., N Pa., 34 mi. WSW of Elmira, N.Y. **6** City (pop. 124,769), ⊙ Knox co., E Tenn., river port on Tennessee R. (head of navigation) and on hills above it, 100 mi. NE of Chattanooga, in Great Appalachian Valley bet. Great Smoky Mts. (E) and the Cumberlands (W). Tobacco and livestock market; an important industrial, commercial, distributing, and shipping center for a wide area; mfg. of textiles, clothing, furniture and other hardwood products, cement, iron products, food products, feed; flour milling; marble quarrying and working. Mining in region (coal, iron, zinc, copper, clays). Seat of divisions of Univ. of Tennessee and Knoxville Col., state school for deaf. Administrative hq. of TVA here. Norris Dam is c.20 mi. NW, Great Smoky Mts. Natl. Park c.20 mi. SE. Points of interest in city include graves of John Sevier, William Blount, and James White, Blount Mansion (1792), Chisholm Tavern (1791), and other old bldgs. Settled c.1786; laid out and named Knoxville in 1791. Was ⊙ "Territory South of the River Ohio" (1792–96) and state ⊙ (1796–1812; 1817–19). Knoxville, loyal to the Union in the Civil War, was held by Confederates until Sept., 1863, when it was abandoned to Federals under Gen. A. E. Burnside. Gen. James Longstreet's subsequent siege (Nov.–Dec., 1863) failed in attempt to recapture it.

Knuckles Group, extension of NE Ceylon Hill Country, S central Ceylon; irregular in shape; 25 mi. long (N-S), up to 15 mi. wide; rises to 6,112 ft. in Knuckles Peak, 9.5 mi. NE of Wattegama. Agr. (tea, rubber, rice, vegetables, cardamom); average rainfall, 100 to c.200 in.

Knutange (nütäzh'), Ger. *Kneuttingen* (knoi'tĭng-ŭn), town (pop. 4,567), Moselle dept., NE France, 7 mi. WSW of Thionville; iron mines, steel mills.

Knutsford (nŭts'fŭrd), urban district (1931 pop. 5,879; 1951 census 6,619), N central Cheshire, England, 11 mi. SW of Stockport; mfg. of leather goods, paper, agr. machinery. Has many 16th- and 17th-cent. houses, and a 17th-cent. Unitarian chapel. The town is the Cranford of Mrs. Gaskell.

Knutsholtind, Norway: see JOTUNHEIM MOUNTAINS.

Knyaginino (knyŭgē'nyĭnŭ), village (1926 pop. 1,297), E central Gorki oblast, Russian SFSR, 15 mi. S of Lyskovo; tanning center; leather products. Formerly called Knyaginin.

Knyazhaya Guba (knyä'zhŭ gōōbä'), village (1926 pop. 752), SW Murmansk oblast, Russian SFSR, on Kandalaksha Bay of White Sea, 20 mi. S of Kandalaksha; lumbering.

Knyazheva-polyana (knyä'zhĕvä-pôlyä'nä), village (pop. 3,124), Ruse dist., NE Bulgaria, 16 mi. ESE of Ruse; wheat, rye, sunflowers. Formerly Bei-alan.

Knyazhevats, Yugoslavia: see KNJAZEVAC.

Knyazhevo (knyä'zhĕvô), village (pop. 9,317, Sofia dist., W Bulgaria, SW suburb of Sofia; paper mfg., brewing; truck, dairying, poultry raising. Thermal springs. Formerly Bali-yefendi.

Knyazhpogost, Russian SFSR: see ZHELEZNODOROZHNY, Komi Autonomous SSR.

Knyaz Simeonovo (knyäs' sĭmĕô'nôvô), agr. village (pop. 3,856), Gorna Oryakhovitsa dist., N Bulgaria, 20 mi. NNW of Tirnovo.

Knysna (knĭs'nŭ), town (pop. 7,384), S Cape Prov., U. of So. Afr., on Knysna Harbour, on the Indian Ocean, 150 mi. W of Port Elizabeth, 35 mi. E of George; rail terminus; furniture-mfg. and lumbering center, boat building. Popular resort. Founded 1806.

Knyszyn (kŭnĭ'shĭn), Rus. *Knyshin* (kŭnyĭ'shĭn), town (pop. 2,780), Bialystok prov., NE Poland, 16 mi. NW of Bialystok, near railroad; mfg. of cement, bricks; tanning, flour milling.

Ko, Japan: see TOYOKAWA.

Ko [Thai, =island]: for names in Thailand beginning thus and not found here, see under following part of the name.

Kobarid, Yugoslavia: see CAPORETTO.

Kobata, Japan: see OBATA, Mie prefecture.

Kobayashi (kōbä'yä'shē), town (pop. 38,968), Miyazaki prefecture, S central Kyushu, Japan, 27 mi. WNW of Miyazaki; rice center; sawmills.

Kobbelbude, Russian SFSR: see SVETLOYE.

Kobbermine Bay (kô'bŭrmē"nŭ), Dan. *Kobberminebugt*, inlet (20 mi. long, 1-10 mi. wide) of Atlantic, SW Greenland, 70 mi. WNW of Julianehaab; 60°55'N 48°10'W. Copper formerly mined here.

Kobbo (kō'bō), village (pop. 360), Wallo prov., NE Ethiopia, near source of Golima R., on road and 17 mi. N of Waldia; cereals, corn.

Kobdo, Khobdo, or **Hobdo** (all: khōb'dō), aimak (□ 29,700; pop. 45,000), W Mongolian People's Republic; ⊙ Kobdo (Dzhirgalantu). Bounded S by China's Sinkiang prov., it is traversed by the Mongolian Altai, sloping N into the Khara Usu lake basin and S to Dzungarian Gobi desert. Pop. (largely West Mongol) engages in stock grazing and some irrigated agr.

Kobdo, Khobdo, or **Hobdo,** since 1928 officially **Dzhirgalantu** or **Jirgalanta** (jēr'gälāntŭ) [Mongolian, =happy (city)], city (pop. c.6,000), ⊙ Kobdo aimak, W Mongolian People's Republic, at N foot of the Mongolian Altai, 700 mi. W of Ulan Bator, W of lake Khara Usu and on small Buyantu R. (one on the lake's tributaries); alt. 4,000 ft.; 48°1'N 91°38'E. Main trading center of W Mongolia; processing of agr. and livestock products (skins, wool). Linked with USSR by Chuya highway. In appearance like the cities of Central Asia, Kobdo was founded in 1731 on Kobdo R. (N), but was moved in 1763 to present site because of floods. It developed as a center of trade with Russia and China.

Kobdo River, Khobdo River, or **Hobdo River,** W Mongolian People's Republic, rises on USSR line in the peak Tabun Bogdo of the Mongolian Altai, flows 330 mi. E, past Ulegei, and SE to lake Khara Usu near Kobdo city. High water in May and June.

Kobe (kō'bā), city (1940 pop. 967,234; 1947 pop. 607,079), ⊙ Hyogo prefecture, S Honshu, Japan, major port on Osaka Bay, 18 mi. W of Osaka; 34°41'N 135°10'E. City is sheltered N by Mt. Rokko (3,061 ft.), Mt. Maya (2,300 ft.), and several other hills. Rail junction; industrial center; shipbuilding, sugar refining, mfg. (chemicals, machinery, metal and rubber goods), flour milling. Exports textiles (cotton, silk, rayon), rubber goods, clothing. Site of Kansei Gakuin Univ., Univ. of Commerce, Nautical Col. Has anc. Buddhist temples, statue of Prince Hirobumi Ito, bronze image (38 ft. high) of Buddha. Winter sports in Mt. Rokko area. Anc. port of Hyogo (formerly spelled Hiogo; opened 1868 to foreign trade) became part of Kobe in 1878. City includes (since early 1940s) former town of Taruma (1940 pop. 23,140). Kobe is divided into 8 wards [Jap. *ku*]: Hyogo, Suma (fashionable beach resort), Nada, Fukiai, Kobe, Soto, Minato, Hayashida. Bombed (1945) in Second World War.

Kobelyaki (kŭbĭlyä'kē), city (1926 pop. 11,662), SE Poltava oblast, Ukrainian SSR, on Vorskla R. and 35 mi. SSW of Poltava; woolen milling, clothing mfg., metal- and woodworking; beer, malt.

Köben, Poland: see CHOBIENIA.

Kobenhavn, Denmark: see COPENHAGEN.

Kobenzl, Austria: see WIENER WALD.

Kobi, Formosa: see HUWEI.

Kobi (kō'bē), town (pop. 8,018), Gifu prefecture, central Honshu, Japan, on Kiso R. and 9 mi. NNW of Tajimi, in agr. area (rice, wheat, market produce); raw silk.

Kobi (kô'bē), town (1939 pop. over 2,000) in Molotov dist. of Greater Baku, Azerbaijan SSR, 7 mi. WNW of Baku, in oil-producing area.

Koblenz, Germany: see COBLENZ.

Koblenz (kō'blĕnts), village (pop. 748), Aargau canton, N Switzerland, on the Rhine (Ger. border; rail and road bridges) and 10 mi. NNW of Baden; watches; winegrowing.

Kobrin (kô'brĭn), Pol. *Kobryn* (kô'brĭn), city (1931 pop. 10,101), central Brest oblast, Belorussian SSR, on Mukhavets R. and 30 mi. ENE of Brest; grain- and sheep-trading center; flour milling, sawmilling, canning (meat, vegetables, fruit), dairying, brick mfg. Founded in 13th cent.; passed (1795) from Poland to Russia; reverted (1921) to Poland; ceded to USSR in 1945.

Kobrinskoye (kô'brĭnskŭyŭ), town (1949 pop. over 500), W central Leningrad oblast, Russian SFSR, 11 mi. S of Gatchina.

Kobroor or **Kobrur,** Indonesia: see ARU ISLANDS.

Kobryn, Belorussian SSR: see KOBRIN.

Kobuk (kō'bŭk), village (pop. 38), NW Alaska, on Kobuk R. and 6 mi. E of Shungnak; trapping, placer gold mining.

Kobuk River, NW Alaska, rises in Brooks Range near 67°5'N 154°15'W; flows c.300 mi. W, past Kobuk, Shungnak, Kiana, and Noorvik, to Hotham Inlet 20 mi. ESE of Kotzebue. Gold mining, trapping in valley.

Kobukuro (kō'bōōkōōrō), town (pop. 12,865), Fukuoka prefecture, N Kyushu, Japan, 17 mi. ENE of Fukuoka; coal mining; rice; vegetable wax.

Kobuleti (kŭbōōlyĕ'tyē), city (1932 pop. estimate 3,750), N Adzhar Autonomous SSR, Georgian SSR, on Black Sea, on railroad and 15 mi. NNE of Batum; sericulture; tea, essential oils, citrus fruit; distilling. Beach resort.

Koburg, Germany: see COBURG.

Kobuta (kŭbyōō'tŭ), village, Beaver co., W Pa., adjacent to Monaca; makes chemicals, especially synthetic-rubber components.

Kobyai or **Kobyay** (kŭbyī'), village (1948 pop. over 500), central Yakut Autonomous SSR, Russian SFSR, 130 mi. NW of Yakutsk, in agr. area.

Kobylin (kôbĭ'lēn), town (1946 pop. 2,464), Poznan prov., W Poland, 9 mi. W of Krotoszyn; rail junction; flour milling, sawmilling. Monastery.

Kocabas River, Turkey: see GRANICUS.

Kocaeli (kŏ'jää"lē), province (□ 3,257; 1950 pop. 474,716), NW Turkey; ⊙ Izmit. Bordered N by Black Sea, W by Sea of Marmara, S by Samanli Mts.; drained by lower course of Sakarya R. Rich in timber, especially beech. Deposits of lead, manganese, iron, copper, and zinc; cement; chestnuts, flax, cotton (Sakarya valley), corn, sugar beets, tobacco. Formerly Izmit or Ismid.

Kocane or **Kochane** (both: kô'chänĕ), Macedonian *Kocani* or *Kochani* (both: –nē), Serbo-Croatian *Kočane* or *Kočani*, village (pop. 6,358), Macedonia, Yugoslavia, near Bregalnica R., 50 mi. E of Skoplje, in fertile, rice-growing valley. Terminus of railroad to Titov Veles; commercial center for region producing poppies for opium and roses for attar.

Koca River (kôjä'). **1** In NW Turkey, rises 13 mi. SE of Burhaniye, flows NW past Balya to L. Manyas, then NW to Simav R. at Karacabey; 105 mi. long. **2** In N Turkey, rises in Kure Mts. 12 mi. SE of Kure, flows 55 mi. W and NW to Black Sea near Cide. **3** In SW Turkey, flows 75 mi. S to the Mediterranean. Near its mouth was anc. Xanthus, a name which was also given to the river.

Kocarli (kôchär'lŭ), Turkish *Koçarlı*, village (pop. 2,036), Aydin prov., W Turkey, on Buyuk Menderes R. and 10 mi. SW of Aydin; figs, olives.

Kocevje (kô'chĕvyĕ), Slovenian *Kočevje*, Ger. *Gottschee* (gôt'shā), village (pop. 3,425), S Slovenia, Yugoslavia, 34 mi. SSE of Ljubljana. Terminus of rail spur to Ljubljana; mfg. of woolen textiles; brown-coal mine. Until 1918, in Carniola.

Kocevski Rog, peak, Yugoslavia: see Rog.

Kocgiri, Turkey: see Zara.

Kochane or **Kochani,** Yugoslavia: see Kocane.

Kochang (kŭ'chäng'), Jap. *Kyosho*, town (1949 pop. 19,812), S.Kyongsang prov., S Korea, 40 mi. WSW of Taegu; rail junction; agr. center (rice, soybeans, hemp, cotton, ramie); makes grass linen.

Koch Bihar, India: see Cooch Behar, district.

Kochchi, India: see Cochin, administrative division.

Kochek, Tell, Syria: see Kojak, Tell.

Kochel (kô'khŭl), village (pop. 4,523), Upper Bavaria, Germany, on N slope of the Bavarian Alps, at NE tip of the Kochelsee, 11 mi. SW of Bad Tölz; rail terminus; metalworking, lumber milling; summer resort.

Kochelsee (kô'khŭlzā"), lake (□ 2.3), Upper Bavaria, Germany, on N slope of the Bavarian Alps, 11 mi. SW of Bad Tölz; 2.5 mi. long, 1.5 mi. wide, 213 ft. deep; alt. 1,968 ft. Fed and drained by the Loisach. Large hydroelectric plant on S shore; resort of Kochel at NE tip.

Kochendorf, Germany: see Bad Friedrichshall.

Kochenevo (kô'chĭnyĭvŭ), village (1926 pop. 2,057), E central Novosibirsk oblast, Russian SFSR, on Trans-Siberian RR and 25 mi. W of Novosibirsk; metalworks; flour milling.

Kocherinovo (kôchĕrē'môvô), village (pop. 3,316), Sofia dist., W Bulgaria, in Struma R. valley, 10 mi. S of Marek; rail junction; tobacco, fruit, vineyards, poppies. Paper mfg., sawmilling 2 mi. S, in Barakovo (pop. 937).

Kocher River (kô'khŭr), N Württemberg, Germany, rises 3 mi. S of Aalen, meanders generally NW, past Schwäbisch Hall, to the canalized Neckar at Bad Friedrichshall. Length, over 90 mi.

Kochetok (kŭchĭtôk'), town (1939 pop. over 500), N central Kharkov oblast, Ukrainian SSR, on the Northern Donets and 4 mi. NE of Chuguyev, in Kharkov metropolitan area; paper mill.

Kochetovka (kŭchĭtôf'kŭ), town (1926 pop. 3,545), W Tambov oblast, Russian SFSR, 8 mi. N of Michurinsk; machine mfg.

Kochevo (kô'chĭvŭ), village (1932 pop. estimate 600), central Komi-Permyak Natl. Okrug, Molotov oblast, Russian SFSR, 42 mi. NNW of Kudymkar; rye, oats, livestock.

Kochi (kō'chē), prefecture [Jap. *ken*] (□ 2,743; 1940 pop. 709,286; 1947 pop. 848,337), S Shikoku, Japan; chief port and ⊙ Kochi. Bounded S by Tosa Bay, SW by Hoyo Strait, SE by Philippine Sea; includes offshore isl. of Okino-shima. Mountainous, with fertile coastal plains; shores warmed by Japan Current. Niyodo and Shimando rivers drain large forested and rice-growing areas. Extensive forests (pine, Jap. cedar); orange trees, mulberry groves. Widespread cultivation of rice, tea, soybeans, sweet potatoes. Cattle raising, lumbering. Produces paper, silk textiles, sake, soy sauce, charcoal. Numerous fishing ports mainly produce dried bonito and ornamental coral. Kochi is only large center.

Kochi. 1 Town (1947 pop. 4,969), Hiroshima prefecture, SW Honshu, Japan, 25 mi. ENE of Hiroshima; livestock, rice. **2** City (1940 pop. 106,644; 1947 pop. 147,120), ⊙ Kochi prefecture, S Shikoku, Japan, port on inlet of Tosa Bay, 65 mi. WSW of Tokushima, at mouth of small Kagami R.; 33°33'N 133°33'E. Commercial center, known for marine products, principally dried bonito and ornamental coral; produces sake, raw silk. Exports dried bonito, paper, cement, lumber. Former castle town. Includes (since early 1940s) former town of Nagahama. Bombed (1945) in Second World War. Sometimes spelled Koti.

Ko-ch'iao, China: see Kokiao.

Kochino (kōchē'nō), town (pop. 20,713), Aichi prefecture, central Honshu, Japan, 12 mi. N of Nagoya; truck gardening; raw silk, bamboo ware; peach orchards. Sometimes spelled Kotino.

Kochisar. 1 Village, Ankara prov., Turkey: see Serefli Kochisar. **2** Village, Mardin prov., Turkey: see Kiziltepe. **3** Village, Sivas prov., Turkey: see Hafik.

Kochisarbala, Turkey: see Ilgaz.

Ko-chiu, China: see Kokiu.

Kochkar or **Kochkar'** (kŭchkär'), village (1926 pop. ,979), central Chelyabinsk oblast, Russian SFSR, mi. N of Plast; dairying; grain, livestock. Gold mines and placers near by. Formerly called Kochkarski.

Kochki (kôch'kē), village (1926 pop. 4,077), S Novosibirsk oblast, Russian SFSR, on Karasuk R. and 0 mi. S of Kargat; dairy farming.

Kochkorka (kŭchkôr'kŭ), village (1948 pop. over ,000), NE Tyan-Shan oblast, Kirghiz SSR, on Chu R. and 28 mi. SW of Rybachye; wheat; salt and coal mining.

Kochkurovo (kŭchkōōrô'vŭ), village (1926 pop. ,923), SE Mordvinian Autonomous SSR, Russian SFSR, 14 mi. SE of Saransk, in hemp area; bast-fiber processing.

Kochow, China: see Mowming.

Koch Peak, Mont.: see Madison Range.

Kochumdeka (kŭchōōmdyĕ'kŭ), village, Evenki Natl. Okrug, Krasnoyarsk Territory, Russian SFSR, 230 mi. W of Tura and on Lower Tunguska R.

Kochura (kŭchōō'rŭ), town (1939 pop. over 500), S Kemerovo oblast, Russian SFSR, in Gornaya Shoriya, 7 mi. SW of Tashtagol; iron mining.

Kock (kôtsk), Rus. *Kotsk* (kôtsk), town (pop. 2,381), Lublin prov., E Poland, on Tysmienica R., near its mouth, and 28 mi. N of Lublin; starch mfg., flour milling; brickworks. Before Second World War, pop. 75% Jewish.

Kockelscheuer, Luxembourg: see Luxembourg, city.

Kocs (kôch), town (pop. 3,071), Komarom-Esztergom co., N Hungary, 22 mi. ESE of Györ; wheat, tobacco, cattle, horses. Near-by springs contain sulphate of magnesium.

Kocsord (kô'chôrd), town (pop. 2,842), Szatmar-Bereg co., NE Hungary, 31 mi. E of Nyiregyhaza; grain, potatoes, hogs.

Kodachi, Japan: see Kotachi.

Kodaikanal (kōdĭkä'nŭl), city (pop. 9,724), Madura dist., S Madras, India, 50 mi. WNW of Madura. Climatic health resort (sanatorium) on scenic wooded plateau in Palni Hills; alt. c.7,000 ft. Fruit (orange, lemon, lime) and eucalyptus plantations. Site of solar photographic observatory (alt. 7,700 ft.), established 1899. Christian missionary colony.

Kodaikanal Road, India: see Ammayanakkanur.

Kodaira (kōdĭ'rä), town (pop. 16,976), Greater Tokyo, central Honshu, Japan, 5 mi. NE of Tachikawa; agr. (tea, rice, wheat); raw silk.

Kodake, Japan: see Kotake.

Kodali, India: see Kodoli.

Kodama (kōdä'mä), town (pop. 7,204), Saitama prefecture, central Honshu, Japan, 15 mi. WNW of Kumagaya; raw-silk center.

Kodangal (kō'dŭng-gŭl) or **Korangal** (kō'rŭng-gŭl), town (pop. 6,861), Gulbarga dist., SW central Hyderabad state, India, 35 mi. NW of Mahbubnagar; road center in millet and rice area.

Kodarma (kō'dŭrmŭ), village, Hazaribagh dist., central Bihar, India, 50 mi. WNW of Giridih, 33 mi. NNE of Hazaribagh; mica-mining center.

Koddiyar Bay (kŏd'dĭyŭr), NE Ceylon, semicircular inlet of Indian Ocean, bet. Foul Point (S) and Trincomalee promontory (N); 8 mi. long, 7 mi. wide. Trincomalee Inner Harbour (3 mi. long, 3 mi. wide) is N inlet; Tambalagam Bay (5 mi. long, 3 mi. wide; pearl banks) is W inlet. Lighthouse on isl. in middle of bay. Was much used by old-time sailing ships. Receives the Mahaweli Ganga (S).

Kodër (kô'dŭr) or **Kodra** (kô'drä), officially **Kodër Shëngjergj** or **Kodra Shëngjergjit**, Ital. *Kodra San Giorgio*, village, N Albania, 21 mi. NE of Scutari.

Kodiak (kō'dēăk, kŭ'dēăk), village (pop. 1,635), NE Kodiak Isl., S Alaska, on Chiniak Bay of Gulf of Alaska; 57°47'N 152°24'W; trade center for dairying, cattle- and sheep-raising, trapping, fur-farming region; fishing port, salmon canning. Numerous canneries in vicinity. Has Russian Orthodox church, Baptist orphanage. Russians under Shelekhov here moved (1792) their main settlement, originally established at Three Saints Bay, named it St. Pauls Harbor and later Kadiak or Kodiak. Hq. of Russian-America Co. before it was moved to Sitka. In Second World War Fort Greeley, major army supply base, was built near by. Womens Bay naval and naval air base is 10 mi. SW.

Kodiak Island (100 mi. long, 10–60 mi. wide), S Alaska, in Gulf of Alaska, separated from mainland by Shelikof Strait; 56°45'–58°N 152°9'–154°48' W. Coast is deeply indented, provides numerous fishing harbors. Generally hilly, rising to over 5,000 ft. near E coast; higher parts of isl. are heavily wooded. Lower regions are covered with grasses; dairying, cattle and sheep raising are important. Kodiak bear is native here and attracts many sportsmen. Fishing, fish canning, fur trapping, and farming are carried on. Kodiak village is on NE coast; near by is Womens Bay naval base. Isl. was discovered 1764 by Stepan Glotov, Russian fur trader; 1st settlement on isl., established 1784 by Grigorii Shelekhov (Gregory Shelekov) at Three Saints Bay (SE), was later moved to Kodiak, 1792. Isl. was blanketed with lava ash after Mt. Katmai eruption, June, 1912.

Kodiang (kōdē"äng'), village (pop. 382), N Kedah, Malaya, on railroad and 19 mi. NNW of Alor Star, on Perlis border; rice.

Kodinar (kō'dĭnär), town (pop. 8,442), Amreli dist., NW Bombay, India, on S Kathiawar peninsula, 65 mi. SSW of Amreli; rail terminus; trades in cotton, millet, ghee, oilseeds; handicraft cloth weaving and printing, cotton ginning. Pomfrets and Bombay duck caught in Arabian Sea (S).

Kodino (kô'dyĭnŭ), town (1939 pop. over 500), NW Archangel oblast, Russian SFSR, on railroad, on short Kodina R. and 45 mi. ESE of Onega; sawmilling. Developed after 1941.

Kodiyakadu, India: see Point Calimere, village.

Kodiyakkarai, India: see Point Calimere, village.

Kodjiger (kōjĕgĕr'), Chinese *Ningsi* or *Ning-hsi* (both: nĭng'shē'), town, ⊙ Kodjiger co. (pop. 27,925), W Sinkiang prov., China, 30 mi. W of Kuldja, on USSR border; cattle raising; agr.

Kodok (kō'dŏk), formerly **Fashoda** (fŭshō'dŭ), town, Upper Nile prov., S central Anglo-Egyptian Sudan, on left bank of White Nile, on road and 40 mi. NE of Malakal. Scene (1898) of the Fashoda Incident, which caused an Anglo-French diplomatic crisis. Area inhabited by Shilluk tribes.

Kodoli (kōdō'lē), town (pop. 6,749), Kolhapur dist., S Bombay, India, 12 mi. NNW of Kolhapur; market center for millet and rice. Sometimes spelled Kodali.

Kodor Range (kŭdôr'), S spur of the W Greater Caucasus, in NW Georgian SSR; extends c.50 mi. SW to Black Sea; rises to 10,856 ft. Forms left watershed of Kodor R.

Kodor River, Abkhaz Autonomous SSR, Georgian SSR, rises in the W Greater Caucasus, flows 45 mi. SW to Black Sea SSE of Sukhumi. Sukhumi Military Road passes through its mtn. valley.

Kodra, Albania: see Kodër.

Kodra (kô'drŭ), town (1926 pop. 2,045), W Kiev oblast, Ukrainian SSR, 40 mi. WNW of Kiev; ceramics; peat cutting.

Kodry (kŭdrē'), Rum. *Codri* (kôdrē') [=woods], forested, hilly region of central Moldavian SSR, bet. Kishinev and Ungeny; rises to 1,410 ft. Important wine- and fruitgrowing dist.

Kodumur or **Kodumuru** (kōdōōmōō'rōō), town (pop. 8,276), Kurnool dist., N Madras, India, 21 mi. SW of Kurnool; rice and oilseed (peanut) milling; millet, cotton, mangoes.

Kodur, India: see Rajampet.

Kodyma (kŭdĭ'mŭ), town (1926 pop. 5,329), NW Odessa oblast, Ukrainian SSR, 25 mi. WNW of Balta; fruit canneries; limestone works. In Moldavian Autonomous SSR (1924–40).

Koealakapoeas, Indonesia: see Kualakapuas.

Koealalangsa, Indonesia: see Langsa.

Koeandang, Indonesia: see Kuandang.

Koeantan River, Indonesia: see Indragiri River.

Koedoes, Indonesia: see Kudus.

Koedoespoort (kōō'dōōspōōrt), village, S central Transvaal, U. of So. Afr., 5 mi. E of Pretoria; important railroad workshops.

Koekelare (kōō'kŭlärŭ), agr. village (pop. 6,007), West Flanders prov., W Belgium, 6 mi. ENE of Dixmude. Formerly spelled Couckelaere.

Koekelberg (kōō'kŭlbĕrk), town (pop. 15,169), Brabant prov., central Belgium, residential and industrial NW suburb of Brussels; textile and flour mills.

Koemamba Islands, Netherlands New Guinea: see Kumamba Islands.

Koendoer, Indonesia: see Karimun Islands.

Koepang, Indonesian Timor: see Kupang.

K'o-erh-k'u-sha, Tibet: see Gar.

Koerich (kû'rĭkh), village (pop. 656), SW Luxembourg, 9 mi. WNW of Luxembourg city, near Belg. border; building-stone quarries, sawmills.

Koerintji, Mount, Indonesia: see Kerinchi, Mount.

Koeroedoe, Netherlands New Guinea: see Japen Islands.

Koersel (kōōr'sŭl), town (pop. 7,905), Limburg prov., NE Belgium, 10 mi. NNW of Hasselt; coal mining. Formerly spelled Coursel.

Koesfeld, Germany: see Coesfeld.

Koetai River, Borneo: see Mahakam River.

Koetaradja, Indonesia: see Kutaraja.

Koetoardjo, Indonesia: see Kutoarjo.

Koevorden, Netherlands: see Coevorden.

Kofa Mountains, Yuma co., SW Ariz., N of Gila R.; extend c.20 mi. E from Castle Dome Mts.; rise to 4,828 ft. in W tip.

Koffiefontein (kô'fēfôntān"), town (pop. 2,965), W Orange Free State, U. of So. Afr., on Riet R. and 50 mi. SSE of Kimberley; stock, grain, feed. Former diamond-mining center; mines closed 1932.

Köflach (kûf'läkh), town (pop. 4,866), Styria, S Austria, 16 mi. W of Graz; rail terminus; glassworks. Vineyards, lignite mines near by.

Koforidua (kōfōrēdōō'ä), town (pop. 17,715), ⊙ Eastern Prov. (□ 10,500; pop. 1,156,349), S central Gold Coast colony, on railroad and 40 mi. N of Accra; cacao-shipping center; palm oil and kernels, cassava, corn. Radio station.

Kofu (kō'fōō). **1** Town, Aichi prefecture, Japan: see Toyokawa. **2** City (1940 pop. 106,579; 1947 pop. 104,993), ⊙ Yamanashi prefecture, central Honshu, Japan, 70 mi. W of Tokyo, on large plain surrounded by mts.; collection center for silk cocoons and raw silk. Mfg. (silk textiles, crystal glassware), woodworking, sake brewing, wine making. Has remains of 16th-cent. castle. Sometimes spelled Kohu.

Koga (kō'gä). **1** Town (pop. 9,228), Fukuoka prefecture, N Kyushu, Japan, on Genkai Sea, 9 mi. NNE of Fukuoka; agr. center (rice, wheat, barley). Formerly Mushirouchi. **2** Town (pop. 30,265), Ibaraki prefecture, central Honshu, Japan, 27 mi. SSW of Utsunomiya; collection center for agr. and lumbering area; mfg. (dolls, yarn).

Kogalnik River or **Kogal'nik River** (kŭgäl'nyĭk), Rum. *Cogâlnic* (kōgŭl'nēk), Moldavian SSR and Izmail oblast, Ukrainian SSR, rises W of Strasheny, flows 120 mi. SSE, past Kotovskoye, Romanovka, and Artsiz, to Sasyk Lagoon at Tatarbunary. Intermittent in lower reaches. Also spelled Kogilnik.

Kogane (kōgä'nä), town (pop. 7,056), Chiba prefecture, central Honshu, Japan, 4 mi. NE of Matsudo; rice, wheat.

Koganei (kōgänā′), town (pop. 19,565), Greater Tokyo, central Honshu, Japan, 6 mi. E of Tachikawa, in agr. area (rice, wheat); raw silk. Known for cherry blossoms.

Kogarah (kŏ′gŭrŭ), municipality (pop. 39,298), E New South Wales, Australia, 10 mi. SW of Sydney, in metropolitan area; industrial center; aluminum ware, bricks.

Koge (kû′yû), Dan. *Køge*, city (1950 pop. 10,602), Copenhagen amt, Zealand, Denmark, port on Koge Bay of the Oresund and 22 mi. SSW of Copenhagen; 55°27′N 12°11′E. Mfg. (machinery, paint, cigars), woodworking, meat canning. Formerly spelled Kjoge.

Koge Bay, Dan. *Køge Bugt*, on E coast of Zealand isl., Denmark, on the Oresund; Amager isl. in N.

Kogen, Korea: see HONGWON.

Kogen-do, Korea: see KANGWON.

Kogala, Ceylon: see WELIGAMA.

Kogilnik River, USSR: see KOGALNIK RIVER.

Kogo (kō′gō), town (pop. 453), continental Sp. Guinea, landing on N bank of the Río Muni, diagonally opposite Cocobeach (Gabon), 50 mi. S of Bata; 1°4′N 9°43′E. Exports cabinet woods.

Kogota (kōgō′tä), town (pop. 3,805), Miyagi prefecture, N Honshu, Japan, 4 mi. WNW of Wakuya; rail junction; rice, raw silk, wheat. Agr. school.

Kogushi (kōgōō′shē), town (pop. 5,284), Yamaguchi prefecture, SW Honshu, Japan, 14 mi. N of Shimonoseki, on Hibiki Sea; fishing center; sake, soy sauce.

Koh [Persian,=mountain], for names in Afghanistan, Iran, and Pakistan beginning thus and not found here: see under KUH, or under following part of the name.

Koh [Thai,=island], for names in Thailand beginning thus and not found here: see under following part of the name.

Kohala Peninsula (kōhä′lŭ), N Hawaii, T.H. Rich in relics of anc. Hawaii. Sugar cane grown in fertile valleys. Kohala Mts. rise to 5,489 ft.

Kőhalom, Rumania: see RUPEA.

Kohama (kōhä′mä), village (pop. 14,628), Hyogo prefecture, S Honshu, Japan, just N of Nishinomiya, 13 mi. NW of Osaka. Known for Takarazuka, its entertainment dist., with several theaters and botanical gardens. Mineral springs. Orchards (peaches, pears).

Kohat (kō′hät), dist. (□ 2,707; 1951 pop. 305,000), North-West Frontier Prov., W Pakistan; ⊙ Kohat. Bordered NW by SE outliers of Safed Koh Range, NE by Indus R.; crossed E-W by broken hill ranges. Agr. (wheat, millet, corn, gram, barley); handicrafts (cloth, baskets, palm mats, leather goods); camel breeding. Hills (S center) have large deposits of rock salt (quarries at Bahadur Khel and Jatta Ismail Khel) and gypsum. Raided 1505 by Baber; under Sikh rule in early-19th cent. Dist. exercises political control over adjoining tribal area (pop. 134,000). Pop. 92% Moslem, 6% Hindu, 1% Sikh.

Kohat, town (pop. 34,316; including cantonment area, 44,977), ⊙ Kohat dist., E central North-West Frontier Prov., W Pakistan, 28 mi. S of Peshawar; military station, market center (wheat, millet, corn, rock salt); fodder milling, handicraft cloth weaving (silk turbans), palm-mat and basket making; ordnance factory (handmade rifles), engineering workshop.

Koheki, Formosa: see HOWPI.

Koh-i-Baba (kō′hĭbä′bŭ), W outlier of the Hindu Kush, in central Afghanistan, extends 125 mi. E-W along 34°40′N bet. 66°30′E and 68°30′E; rises to 16,872 ft. in the Shah Fuladi, 17 mi. SW of Bamian. Continued W by the Safed Koh and Siah Koh.

Koh-i-Dalil, volcano, W Pakistan: see DAMODIM.

Koh-i-Daman (kō′hĭdä′mŭn), district of Kabul prov., E Afghanistan, N of Kabul, beyond Khairkhana Pass, occupying S portion of the Samt-i-Shimali plain. Name is sometimes extended to entire plain.

Kohila or **Kokhila** (kôkh′ĕlä), town (pop. 952), NW Estonia, 19 mi. S of Tallinn; paper mfg.

Kohima (kōhē′mŭ), town (pop. 3,507), ⊙ Naga Hills dist., E Assam, India, in Naga Hills, 139 mi. E of Shillong; trades in rice, cotton, oranges, potatoes, lac. Northernmost point of Jap. penetration (1944) into India.

Koh-i-Malik Siah (kō′hĭmälēk′ sēä′) or **Kuh-i-Malik Siah** (kōō′hē–), peak (5,390 ft.) at junction of Pakistan, Iran, and Afghanistan borders; 29°51′N 60°52′E. Fixed as a frontier point in 1905.

Kohir (kō′hēr), town (pop. 6,768), Bidar dist., central Hyderabad state, India, 25 mi. SSE of Bidar; cotton, rice, sugar cane, mangoes.

Koh-i-Sabz, W Pakistan: see SIAHAN RANGE.

Kohistan (kō′hĭstän″), mountainous district of NE Afghanistan, on S slopes of the Hindu Kush and W of Nuristan.

Kohistan, district, E Patiala and East Punjab States Union, India; ⊙ Kandaghat.

Kohistan (kō′hĭstän″), hilly region in SW Sind, W Pakistan, comprising S offshoots of Kirthar Range; lies bet. Karachi (SSW) and Sehwan in Dadu dist. (NE); drained by Hab (W) and Baran (E) rivers. Lakhi Hills are E offshoot. Little cultivation; some sheep, goat, and camel breeding. Hot sulphur springs, small coal deposits.

Koh-i-Sultan (kō′ē-sōōltän′), extinct, oval-shaped volcano in Chagai dist., NW Baluchistan, W Pakistan, W of Chagai Hills; c.20 mi. long, 12 mi. wide; consists of 3 cones; rises to 7,650 ft. in Miri peak. Deposits of alum and sulphur ore on S slope; barite occurs in a dyke.

Kohler (kō′lŭr), village (pop. 1,716), Sheboygan co., E Wis., on Sheboygan R., just E of Sheboygan; garden city surrounding Kohler plumbing-fixtures plant. Inc. 1913.

Kohler Range (kō′lŭr), mountain range (alt. c.7,000 ft.) in Antarctica, extends along Walgreen Coast in 74°S bet. 102° and 114°W. Discovered 1940 by R. E. Byrd.

Kohlfurt, Poland: see WEGLINIEC.

Kohlgrub or **Bad Kohlgrub** (bät″ kōl′grōōp), village (pop. 2,052), Upper Bavaria, Germany, on N slope of the Bavarian Alps, 12 mi. N of Garmisch-Partenkirchen; climatic summer and winter resort (alt. 2,953 ft.), with mud baths.

Kohlsaat, Cape (kōl′zät), easternmost point of Franz Josef Land, Russian SFSR, in Arctic Ocean, on Graham Bell Isl.; 81°25′N 65°E.

Kohlscheid (kōl′shīt), coal-mining village (pop. 12,600), in former Prussian Rhine Prov., W Germany, after 1945 in North Rhine-Westphalia, near Dutch border, 4 mi. N of Aachen.

Kohren-Sahlis (kō′rŭn-zä′lēs), town (pop. 1,818), Saxony, E central Germany, 9 mi. SE of Borna; hosiery knitting, ceramics mfg.

Kohsan or **Kuhsan** (kōsän′), village (pop. over 500), Herat prov., NW Afghanistan, 60 mi. WNW of Herat, and on right bank of the Hari Rud, near Iran border. TIRPUL oil field is just SE.

Koh Sichang, Thailand: see SICHANG, Ko.

Kohtla or **Kokhtla** (kôkht′lä), town, NE Estonia, 6 mi. W of Johvi, in oil-shale mining area; rail junction (spur to Kohtla-Jarve); distilling plant.

Kohtla-Jarve or **Kokhtla-Yarve** (both: yăr′vä), Est. *Kohtla-Järve*, city (1947 pop. over 10,000), NE Estonia, 32 mi. E of Rakvere, on rail spur from Kohtla; oil-shale distilling center; produces shale oil, gas; power plant. Linked (1947) by gas pipe line to Leningrad. Developed largely after Second World War. Near by are oil-shale mines of Kava (S) and Kukruse (E).

Kohu, Japan: see KOFU, Yamanashi prefecture.

Koidanovo, Belorussian SSR: see DZERZHINSK, Minsk oblast.

Koide (kōē′dā), town (pop. 9,387), Niigata prefecture, central Honshu, Japan, 16 mi. SSE of Nagaoka; raw-silk collection.

Koigorodok or **Koygorodok** (koi″gŭrŭdôk′), village (1939 pop. over 500), SW Komi Autonomous SSR, Russian SFSR, on Sysola R. and 95 mi. SSE of Syktyvkar; flax, potatoes. Phosphorite deposits.

Koil, India: see ALIGARH, city.

Koilkuntla (kō″ĭlkōōnt′lŭ), town (pop. 6,141), Kurnool dist., N Madras, India, 45 mi. SSE of Kurnool; road center; cotton ginning; lacquer ware; millet, rice.

Koilovtsi or **Koylovtsi** (koi′lôftsē), agr. village (pop. 3,066), Pleven dist., N Bulgaria, 9 mi. NE of Pleven.

Koilpatti (kō″ĭlpŭt′tē) or **Kovilpatti** (kō″vĭl–), town (pop. 15,114), Tinnevelly dist., S Madras, India, 32 mi. NNE of Tinnevelly; major cotton-milling center.

Koina (koē′nä), easternmost village (pop. 7) of Gambia, near Fr. Senegal border, in Upper River div., head of navigation on Gambia R. (wharf) and 25 mi. ENE of Basse; peanuts, beeswax, hides and skins.

Koinadugu, district, Sierra Leone: see KABALA.

Koinare or **Koynare** (koinä′rĕ), village (pop. 7,349), Vratsa dist., N Bulgaria, on Iskar R. and 13 mi. SE of Byala Slatina; flour milling; truck, livestock, grain.

Koip or **Koyp** (koip), peak (3,707 ft.) in N Urals, Russian SFSR; 62°10′N. Pechora R. rises here.

Köi Sanjaq (kû′ē sän′jäk) or **Kuway Sandjaq** (kōōwī′), town, Erbil prov., N Iraq, in Kurdistan, 35 mi. ESE of Erbil; sesame, millet, corn.

Koisara or **Koysara** (koisŭrä′), village, NE Issyk-Kul oblast, Kirghiz SSR, on Issyk-Kul (lake) and 10 mi. NW of Przhevalsk; health resort.

Koisu or **Koysu** (koisōō′), name applied to several headstreams of Sulak R., in Dagestan Autonomous SSR, Russian SFSR. The **Andi Koisu** (än′dyē) rises on Mt. Barbalo in Georgian SSR, flows 100 mi. E and NE, past Agvali and Botlikh, joining the Avar Koisu (right) near Gimry to form Sulak R. The **Avar Koisu** (ŭvär′), rises on the Dyulty-Dag, flows NW past Tlyarata, and generally N to confluence with the Andi Koisu; 100 mi. long.

Koitash or **Koytash** (koitäsh′), town (1947 pop. over 500), NE Samarkand oblast, Uzbek SSR, 17 mi. NW of Gallya-Aral, at E end of the Nura-Tau; molybdenum and tungsten mining.

Koiva River or **Koyva River** (koi′vŭ), Molotov oblast, Russian SFSR, rises on W slopes of central Urals NW of Kosya, flows S, past Promysla and Teplaya Gora, and SW, past Biser, to Chusovaya R. 15 mi. ESE of Chusovoi; 112 mi. long.

Koivisto, Russian SFSR: see PRIMORSK, Leningrad.

Koizumi (kōēzōō′mē), town (pop. 9,785), Gumma prefecture, central Honshu, Japan, 11 mi. SSE of Kiryu; commercial center for agr. area (rice, wheat).

Koja (chû′yä), Swedish *Köja*, village (pop. 594) Vasternorrland co., NE Sweden, on Angerman R estuary, 20 mi. NNW of Harnosand; sawmills Includes Marieberg (märē″ŭbĕr′yŭ) village.

Kojak, Tell, or **Tall Kujak** (both: tĕl′ kō′jăk), Fr *Tell Kotchek*, town, Jezire prov., NE Syria, o Iraq line, on railroad, and 75 mi. ENE of El Ha seke; cereals. Also spelled Tell Kochek.

Koje Island (kŭ′jā′), Korean *Koje-do*, Jap. *Kyosai to* (□ 147; 1946 pop. 46,652), S.Kyongsang prov Korea, just off S coast, sheltering Chinhae Bay deeply indented W coast; 23 mi. long, 2–15 mi wide. Hilly, fertile. Fishing and agr. (rice, barley wheat, soybeans). Largest town, Changsungpo.

Kojetin (kô′yĕtyēn), Czech *Kojetín*, Ger. *Kojetein* town (pop. 5,292), central Moravia, Czechoslovakia, on Morava R and 17 mi. S of Olomouc rail junction; agr. center (wheat, barley, sugar beets, grapes).

Ko-jima (kō′jĭmä), volcanic island (□ 1.2; pop. 18(of isl. group Izu-shichito, Greater Tokyo, Japan, i Philippine Sea, just W of Hachijo-jima; 2 mi. long 1 mi. wide. Fishing, farming, stock raising; silkworm culture.

Kojo (kô′jŭ′). **1** Jap. *Kotei*, town (1944 pop 13,634), Kangwon prov., central Korea, N of 38°N on E.Korea Bay, 28 mi. SW of Wonsan; fishin port. Coal mined near by. **2** Town, Kangwo prov., Korea, SE of Wonsan: see KOSONG. **3** Town S.Chungchong prov., Korea: see HONGSONG.

Kojonup (kō′jŭnŭp), town (pop. 388), SW Wester Australia, 150 mi. SSE of Perth; wool and grai center.

Koka (kō′kŏ), Hung. *Kóka*, town (pop. 4,661), Pes Pilis-Solt-Kiskun co., N central Hungary, 23 mi. of Budapest; grain, cattle, horses.

Kokadjo (kōkă′jō, kô–), resort village, Piscataqu co., central Maine, on First Roach Pond (former Kokadjo L.) and 17 mi. NE of Greenville; huntin fishing.

Kokai, Korea: see KANGGYE.

Kokai-do, Korea: see HWANGHAE.

Kokaity or **Kokayty** (kŭkī′tē), oil town (1945 po over 500), S Surkhan-Darya oblast, Uzbek SS 25 mi. N of Termiz, on left bank of the Surkha Darya.

Kokalyane, Bulgaria: see STALIN DAM.

Kokan, Formosa: see KUNGKWAN.

Kokand (kōkănd′, Rus. kŭkänt′), city (1939 po 84,665), NW Fergana oblast, Uzbek SSR, in Fe gana Valley, on railroad, on Great Fergana Can and 40 mi. WNW of Fergana, in Sokh R. irrig tion fan. Cotton-ginning center; silk mill, cotto seed-oil press, sugar refinery, superphosphate a machine works. Junction for railroad to Nama gan. Has remains of khan's palace; womer teachers col. Of importance since 10th cen flourished in 18th cent. as ⊙ Kokand khanate, co quered (1876) by Russians. Seat of a counte revolutionary govt. (1917–18). Formerly al spelled Khokand.

Kokanee Peak (kōkă′nē) (9,400 ft.), SE B.C., Selkirk Mts., 18 mi. NNE of Nelson; 49°45′ 117°8′W.

Kokan-Kishlak (kŭkän″-kēshläk′), village (19 pop. 2,011), NE Andizhan oblast, Uzbek SSR, Tentyaksai rail station, 12 mi. NE of Andizha from which there is a rail spur; cotton ginning.

Koka-to, Korea: see KANGHWA ISLAND.

Kokava nad Rimavicou (kô′kävä näd′ rĭ″mävĭts Hung. *Rimakokova* (rĭ′mŏkô′kôvŏ), village (pc 5,350), S central Slovakia, Czechoslovakia, in foothills of Slovak Ore Mts., on railroad and 33 n ESE of Banska Bystrica.

Kokawa (kōkä′wä), town (pop. 8,573), Wakayar prefecture, S Honshu, Japan, on W Kii Peninsu 14 mi. ENE of Wakayama, in agr. area (citr fruit, bamboo shoots); charcoal.

Kokayty, Uzbek SSR: see KOKAITY.

Kok-Bulak (kôk″-bōōläk′), village (1939 pop. ov 500), E Kashka-Darya oblast, Uzbek SSR, c.25 r S of Shakhrizyabz; grain, livestock.

Kokcha River or **Kokchah River** (kōk′chŭ), Afghan Badakhshan, NE Afghanistan, rises in t Hindu Kush on Pakistan line at 36°N 71°10′ flows 200 mi. N and W, past Zebak and Faizaba to Panj R. (USSR line) 65 mi. W of Faizabad. Bu of region's pop. and irrigated agr. system is in valley, which also has salt and sulphur depos and, near its source, the noted lapis lazuli of B dakhshan.

Kokchetav (kŭkchĭtäv′), oblast (□ 28,600; 1946 pc estimate 300,000), N Kazakh SSR; ⊙ Kokcheta On wooded steppe merging (S) into picturesq hilly lake region (BOROVOYE). Chiefly agr. (whe oats, millet), with emphasis on livestock raisi (cattle, sheep) in E. Sunflowers grown arou Novo-Sukhotino. Trans-Kazakhstan RR cros oblast N-S. Pop. Russians, Ukrainians, Kazak Formed 1944.

Kokchetav, city (1926 pop. 11,060), ⊙ Kokchet oblast, Kazakh SSR, at S edge of wooded step on railroad and 770 mi. NNW of Alma-A 53°13′N 69°20′E. Agr.-processing center in whea cattle-, and sheep-raising area; meat, flo tanning, distilling; cattle market. Founded 18 in Rus. conquest of Kazakhstan.

Kokei, Korea: see KANGGYONG.

Kokemäki (kō'kĕmă"kē), Swedish *Kumo* (kü'mō), village (commune pop. 10,780), Turku-Pori co., SW Finland, on Kokemäki R. and 25 mi. SE of Pori, in lumbering region.

Kokemäki River, SW Finland, issues from L. Pyhä 8 mi. WSW of Tampere, flows 90 mi. in a wide arc generally W, through several small lakes, past Nokia (52-ft.-high Emä Rapids), Harjavalta (major power station), Nakkila, Ulvila, and Pori, to Gulf of Bothnia 5 mi. NW of Pori. With the Finnish generic for the word river, the name becomes *Kokemäenjoki* (kō'kĕmă"ĕnyō"kē).

Kokenhusen, Latvia: see KOKNESE.

Kokes, Turkey: see SERIK.

Kokez, Bulgaria: see SINI.

Ko Kha (kô' kä'), village (1937 pop. 2,715), Lampang prov., N Thailand, on Wang R. and 10 mi. SW of Lampang, in sugar-cane region; sugar mill.

Kokhanovo (kŭkhä'nŭvŭ), village (1926 pop. 1,249), S Vitebsk oblast, Belorussian SSR, 17 mi. WSW of Orsha; flax processing.

Kokhila, Estonia: see KOHILA.

Kokhma (kôkh'mŭ), city (1926 pop. 11,526), central Ivanovo oblast, Russian SFSR, on Uvod R. and 6 mi. SE of Ivanovo; cotton- and linen-milling center.

Kokhtla, Kokhtla-Yarve, Estonia: see KOHTLA, KOHTLA-JARVE.

Koki (kōkē'), village, Kandal prov., S Cambodia, on Mekong R. and 9 mi. SE of Pnompenh; corn, rice.

Kokiao or **Ko-ch'iao** (both: gŭ'chyou'), town, N Chekiang prov., China, 25 mi. SE of Hangchow and on railroad to Ningpo.

Kokilamukh, India: see JORHAT.

Kokiu or **Ko-chiu** (both: gŭ'jyō'), town (pop. 15,519), ⊙ Kokiu co. (pop. 53,403), S Yunnan prov., China, on railroad spur and 18 mi. W of Mengtsz; China's leading tin-mining center; concentrating plants, smelters.

Kokkinon (kô'kĭnôn), village (pop. 1,105), Boeotia nome, E central Greece, 11 mi. NNW of Thebes; iron mining.

Kokkinovrachos or **Kokkinovrakhos** (both: kôkĭnô'-vräkhôs), village (1928 pop. 183), Magnesia nome, SE Thessaly, Greece, 14 mi. E of Pharsala; chromite mining. Formerly called Ardouan or Arduan.

Kokkola (kŏk'kōlä), Swedish *Gamlakarleby* (gäm'läkärl'übü"), city (pop. 12,826), Vaasa co., W Finland, on Gulf of Bothnia, 70 mi. NE of Vaasa; seaport, shipping timber and wood products; rail junction. Woodworking; mfg. of machinery, leather products. Almost half of pop. speaks Swedish. Has 15th-cent. church, art museum. City founded 1620; attained considerable commercial importance in 18th cent. In Crimean War scene (1854) of unsuccessful British landing attempt. Ykspihlaja (W) is outport.

Kokkulam, India: see TIRUMANGALAM.

Kokla, Greece: see PLATAIAI.

Koklaks (chŭk'läks"), Swedish *Köklaks*, Finnish *Kauklahti* (kouk'lä"tē, läkh"tē), village in Esbo commune (pop. 21,496), Uusimaa co., S Finland, 13 mi. W of Helsinki, at E edge of Porkkala defense region; mfg. of glass, zinc-white.

Koknese (kŏk'näsä), Ger. *Kokenhusen*, village (commune pop. 3,024), S central Latvia, in Vidzeme, on right bank of the Western Dvina (scenic course) and 12 mi. W of Plavinas; tourist resort. Has castle ruins.

Koknur, India: see KUKNUR.

Koko, Formosa: see HUKOW.

Koko (kō'kō), town (pop. 860), Warri prov., Western Provinces, S Nigeria, port on Benin R. and 23 mi. SSW of Benin City; palm-oil processing; hardwood, rubber, cacao, kola nuts.

Kokoda (kōkō'dä, kŏkō'dŭ), town, Northern Territory of Papua, NE New Guinea, on Yodda R., 55 mi. NE of Port Moresby, near mtn. pass through Owen Stanley Range; rubber. In Second World War, taken 1942 by the Japanese in their unsuccessful drive on Port Moresby.

Koko Head (kō'kō'), 2 tufa craters (alt. 1,205 ft. and 644 ft.), SE Oahu, T.H.; contains Blow Hole, a salt-water geyser.

Kokolik River (kōkō'lĭk), NW Alaska, rises in NW Brooks Range near 68°35'N 162°W, flows c.150 mi. N to Chukchi Sea at 69°52'N 162°43'W.

Kokomo (kō'kŭmō", kō'kōmō"). **1** Town, Summit co., Colo.: see RECEN. **2** City (pop. 38,672), ⊙ Howard co., central Ind., on Wildcat Creek and 50 mi. N of Indianapolis; industrial and trading center in livestock, truck, and grain area. Mfg.: steel, iron, brass, and wire products; glass products, tools, automobile and tractor parts, plumbing equipment, ceramics, cutlery, radios, electrical machinery, stoves, canned goods, packed meat, furnaces, playground equipment, clothing, cosmetics. Founded c.1843, laid out 1844. First practical automobile was successfully tested here by inventor Elwood Haynes in 1894.

Koko Nor, province, China: see TSINGHAI.

Koko Nor or **Kuku Nor** (both: kōkō nōr'), Chinese *Tsing Hai, Ching Hai*, or *Ch'ing Hai* (all: chĭng' hī') [=blue sea], salt lake (□ 2,300) in NE Tsinghai prov., China, W of Sining; 65 mi. long, 40 mi. wide; alt. 10,115 ft. Shallow and brackish, it is of little economic value. Frozen Nov.-March.

Kokopo (kô'kôpô), town, NE New Britain, Bismarck Archipelago, Territory of New Guinea, SW Pacific, on Blanche Bay and 15 mi. SE of Rabaul; coconut plantations. Formerly Herbertshöhe, Ger. ⊙ archipelago.

Kokorevka (kô'kŭryĭfkŭ), town (1949 pop. over 500), SE Bryansk oblast, Russian SFSR, 20 mi. E of Trubchevsk; sawmilling.

Kokorin, Czechoslovakia: see MELNIK.

Kokosing River (kōkō'sĭng), central Ohio, rises in Morrow co., flows c.50 mi. generally SE, past Chesterville, Mount Vernon, and Gambier, joining Mohican R. to form Walhonding R. 16 mi. NW of Coshocton.

Kokpekty (kŭkpyĭktē'), village (1948 pop. over 500), E Semipalatinsk oblast, Kazakh SSR, on Kokpekty R. and 150 mi. SE of Semipalatinsk; livestock.

Kokpekty River, SE Semipalatinsk oblast, Kazakh SSR, rises in Kalba Range, flows c.100 mi. SE, past Kokpekty, to L. Zaisan; gold mining along upper course.

Kokrajhar (kō'krŭjŭr), village, Goalpara dist., W Assam, India, 23 mi. NE of Dhubri; rice, mustard.

Kokrines (kŏ'krĭnz), village (pop. 72), W Alaska, on Yukon R. and 80 mi. WSW of Tanana; trading post in fur-trapping and gold-mining region.

Kok River (kôk'), Thai *Mae Nam Kok*, Burmese *Nam Hkok*, Burma and Thailand, right affluent of Mekong R., rises S of Kengtung (Shan States), flows over 150 mi. S, E, and NE, past Chiangrai, to the Mekong SE of Chiang Saen.

Koksan (kôk'sän'), Jap. *Kokuzan*, township (1944 pop. 7,213), Hwanghae prov., central Korea, N of 38°N, 50 mi. ESE of Pyongyang, in tobacco-raising area.

Kokse Dag (kŭksĕ' dä), Turkish *Kökse Dağ*, peak (10,830 ft.), E Turkey, 12 mi. WNW of Aleskirt.

Kokshaal-Tau (kŭkshŭäl"tou'), branch of Tien Shan mountain system, on China-USSR (Kirghiz SSR) border; extends from Pobeda Peak 300 mi. SW to Chatyr-Kul (lake) area; rises to 17,380 ft. Main crossings are on China-USSR trade routes: Turugart Pass and Bedel Pass.

Kokshaga River, Russian SFSR: see GREATER KOKSHAGA RIVER; LESSER KOKSHAGA RIVER.

Koksijde (kôk'sīdŭ), town (pop. 4,297), West Flanders prov., W Belgium, near North Sea, 5 mi. SW of Nieuport. Seaside resort of Koksijde-Plage is 2 mi. NNW, on North Sea. Formerly spelled Coxyde.

Koksoak River (kŏk'sōäk, kōk'–), N Que., formed by Kaniapiskau and Larch rivers, 50 mi. SW of Fort Chimo, flows 90 mi. NE and N, past Fort Chimo, to Ungava Bay 30 mi. N of Fort Chimo; 3 mi. wide at mouth.

Koksovy or **Koksovyy** (kôk'sŭvē), town (1944 pop. over 10,000), W central Rostov oblast, Russian SFSR, on Northern Donets R. and 5 mi. NW of Belaya Kalitva; coal-mining center; rail terminus.

Kokstad (kŏk'stăt), town (pop. 6,584), ⊙ Griqualand East dist. of the Transkeian Territories, E Cape Prov., U. of So. Afr., on Umzimhlava R. and 90 mi. SW of Pietermaritzburg, in foothills of Drakensberg range; rail terminus; center of dairying, stock-raising region. Founded by Adam Kok III (d. 1875), last Griqua chief.

Koktal (kŭktäl'), village (1948 pop. over 2,000), SE Taldy-Kurgan oblast, Kazakh SSR, near China frontier, on highway from Sary-Uzek and 10 mi. W of Panfilov; irrigated agr. (cotton, opium); sheep.

Koktash (kŭktäsh'), town (1932 pop. estimate 2,200), central Stalinabad oblast, Tadzhik SSR, 8 mi. S of Stalinabad (linked by narrow-gauge railroad); wheat, horses; metalworks.

Kokubu (kōkōō'bōō). **1** Town (pop. 10,622), Kagoshima prefecture, S Kyushu, Japan, 16 mi. NE of Kagoshima; tobacco-producing center. Airfield bombed (1945) in Second World War. **2** Town (pop. 7,936), Osaka prefecture, S Honshu, Japan, 10 mi. SE of Osaka; agr. center (rice, wheat).

Kokubunji (kōkōōbōōn'jē), town (pop. 16,375), Greater Tokyo, central Honshu, Japan, 4 mi. E of Tachikawa, in agr. area (rice, wheat); raw silk.

Kokufu (kōkōō'fōō), town (pop 7,040), Tokushima prefecture, E Shikoku, Japan, just W of Tokushima; rice-growing center.

Kokui or **Kokuy** (kŭkōō'ē), town (1939 pop. over 500), central Chita oblast, Russian SFSR, on Shilka R. and 7 mi. W of Sretensk; shipbuilding.

Kokumbo (kōkōōm'bō), village, S central Ivory Coast, Fr. West Africa, 120 mi. NW of Abidjan; gold mining.

Kokura (kōkōō'rä), city (1940 pop. 173,639; 1947 pop. 168,119), Fukuoka prefecture, N Kyushu, Japan, port on Hibiki Sea, 40 mi. NE of Fukuoka, adjacent to Yawata (W), to Moji (NE), and to Tobata (NW). Industrial and rail center; steel mills, chemical plants, rice mill; mfg. (porcelain ware, cotton textiles). Exports coal. Horse racing. Site of feudal castle. Includes (since 1937) former town of Kiku, and (since early 1940s) former town of Sone (1940 pop. 12,335). Heavily bombed (1945) in Second World War.

Kokuzan, Korea: see KOKSAN.

Kok-Yangak (kôk"-yŭn-gäk'), city (1939 pop. 8,416), S Dzhalal-Abad oblast, Kirghiz SSR, in SW foothills of Fergana Range, 14 mi. NE of Dzhalal-Abad; coal-mining center; power plant; terminus (since 1932) of railroad from Karasu. Developed after 1930.

Kola, Indonesia: see ARU ISLANDS.

Kola (kô'lŭ), town (1926 pop. 614), NW Murmansk oblast, Russian SFSR, on Kola Peninsula, on Kola Gulf, on Murmansk RR and 6 mi. S of Murmansk; rail junction (spur to Polyarny); agr.; reindeer raising. Wooden 17th-cent. churches. One of oldest settlements on Kola Peninsula; founded 13th cent. by Novgorod.

Kolaba (kō'läbŭ), district (□ 2,677; pop. 807,122), W Bombay, India; ⊙ Alibag. Bordered W by Arabian Sea, E by Western Ghats; comprises central Konkan region; drained by small mtn. streams, including Ulhas R. (NE). Bombay Harbour is NW, with famous cave temples on Elephanta isl. A rugged belt of country, it grows rice and coconuts (along coast). Salt mfg. (NW), fishing (mackerel, pomfrets). Timber from E forests mostly exported; wood also used for local handicrafts. Panvel, Murud, and Mahad are chief towns; important hydroelectric plants at Khopoli, Bhivpuri, and Bhira. In 18th and early-19th cent., Mahratta pirates had strongholds on coast. Original dist. (□ 2,212; 1941 pop. 668,922) enlarged by inc. (1949) of former Deccan states of Janjira and (parts of) Bhor. Pop. 85% Hindu, 9% tribal, 4% Moslem.

Kolab River, India: see SABARI RIVER.

Kolachel, India: see COLACHEL.

Kola Gulf (kô'lŭ), narrow fjordlike ice-free inlet of Barents Sea, in NW Kola Peninsula, Russian SFSR; 50 mi. long, 1/2 mi. wide; receives Tuloma and Kola rivers. Kola and Murmansk on E shore. Inlet N of Polyarny (W shore) was formerly known as Yekaterina [Rus., =Catherine] Harbor.

Kolahun (kō'lähōōn), town, Western Prov., Liberia, 150 mi. NNE of Monrovia; palm oil and kernels, cotton, pineapples; cattle raising. Radio station.

Kolai, Russian SFSR: see AZOVSKOYE.

Kolambugan (kōlämbōō'gän), town (1939 pop. 6,667; 1948 municipality pop. 19,818), Lanao prov., W central Mindanao, Philippines, on Port Misamis (inlet of Iligan Bay) opposite Ozamiz (Misamis); port; has sawmill. Rice, corn.

Kolambur (kō'lŭmbōōr) or **Kalambur** (kä'–), town (pop. 9,450), North Arcot dist., E central Madras, India, on railroad (Arni Road station) and 5 mi. SW of Arni; trades in products (sandalwood, tanbark, tamarind) of Javadi Hills (W). Formerly called Aliyabad or Alliyabad.

Kolan or **K'o-lan** (kŭ'län'), town, ⊙ Kolan co. (pop. 39,900), NW Shansi prov., China, 45 mi. SW of Ningwu; kaoliang, beans. Coal mining near by.

Kolangui or **Kolanguy** (kŭlŭn-gōō'ē), town (1939 pop. over 500), SE Chita oblast, Russian SFSR, in Nerchinsk Range, 40 mi. E of Olovyannaya; tungsten mine.

Kola Peninsula (kô'lŭ), Rus. *Kol'skiy Poluostrov* (□ 50,000), in N European USSR, bet. Barents Sea (N) and White Sea (S); 250 mi. long, 150 mi. wide; consists of granite, gneiss, and other crystalline formations forming NE extension of Scandinavia. In MURMANSK oblast, Russian SFSR.

Kolapur, India: see KOLHAPUR, town, Hyderabad state.

Kolar (kō'lär), district (□ 3,187; pop. 970,813), E Mysore, India; ⊙ Kolar. On Deccan Plateau; undulating tableland, rising in W to c.4,800 ft. at Nandi, health resort. Agr. (silk, tobacco, sugar cane, cotton); dispersed kaolin and graphite workings. Tobacco curing, tanning, tile and match mfg., goldsmithing; handicrafts (silk, woolen, and cotton weaving, pottery, glass bangles, wickerwork). Chief towns: Kolar Gold Fields, Kolar, Chik Ballapur, Chintamani.

Kolar, town (pop. 19,006), ⊙ Kolar dist., E Mysore, India, 115 mi. NE of Mysore, 15 mi. NW of Kolar Gold Fields; road center; tobacco curing, tanning, hand-loom silk and cotton weaving, goldsmithing. Silk research station and sheep farm near by.

Kolaras (kōlä'rŭs), town (pop. 4,652), N Madhya Bharat, India, 14 mi. SSW of Shivpuri; millet, gram, wheat.

Kolar Gold Fields (kō'lär), city (□ 30; pop. 133,859), Kolar dist., E Mysore, India, 45 mi. E of Bangalore; rail spur terminus; goldsmithing, tanning, tobacco curing; slaughter house. Center of India's gold-mining industry; produces over 95% of India's gold (average annual output, 300,000 oz.) and some silver. Mines opened c.1885; powered since 1902 by hydroelectric works near SIVASAMUDRAM isl. (80 mi. SW). City limits include mining areas of Champion Reef (electrical transmission works), Nandidrug or Nandydroog (another Nandidrug, health resort, is near Chik Ballapur), and Oorgaum or Urigam, industrial area of Marikuppam (tile and brick mfg.), and residential area of Robertsonpet (commercial col.).

Kolarovgrad (kôlä'rŏvgrät), city (pop. 31,169), ⊙ Kolarovgrad dist. (formed 1949), E Bulgaria, in S part of Deliorman upland, 50 mi. W of Stalin (Varna); rail junction; mfg. and handicraft center with metal, leather, and woodworking industries. Has teachers col., technical school, mus. (prehistoric relics), 17th-cent. mosque (largest in Bulgaria), 19th-cent. churches, ruins of medieval fortress. Founded (927) by Bulg. tsar Simeon the

Great; later dominated by Byzantines. Under Turkish rule after 15th cent., called Shumla or Shumna; subjected to several Rus. assaults in 19th cent. Captured (1878) during Russo-Turkish war and ceded to Bulgaria, where it was called Shumen; renamed 1950.

Kolarov Peak (kôlä'rôf), peak (8,619 ft.) in E Rila Mts., W Bulgaria, 14 mi. SE of Samokov. Called Belmeken until 1949.

Kolasin or **Kolashin** (both: kôlä'shēn), Serbo-Croatian *Kolašin*, town (pop. 1,245), E Montenegro, Yugoslavia, on Tara R. and 30 mi. NNE of Titograd; local trade center; health and sport resort. The Bjelasica is NE of town. Under Turkish rule (until 1878), in Herzegovina.

Kolayat (kōlä'yŭt) or **Srikolayatji** (srēkōlä'yŭt-jē), village, N Rajasthan, India, 26 mi. SW of Bikaner; rail spur terminus.

Kolback (kōl'bĕk''), Swedish *Kolbäck*, village (pop. 973), Vastmanland co., central Sweden, on Kolback R., on Stromsholm Canal, and 8 mi. ENE of Koping; rail junction; agr. market; woodworking.

Kolback River, Swedish *Kolbäcksån* (kōl'bĕks''ōn''), central Sweden, rises NW of Ludvika, flows 100 mi. generally SE, past Ludvika, Smedjebacken, Fagersta, and Hallstahammar, to L. Malar 9 mi. E of Koping. Canalized below Smedjebacken, it forms Stromsholm Canal, Swedish *Strömsholmskanal* (strûms-hôlms'känäl'') (68 mi. long; built 1777–95, enlarged 1842–60); serves Bergslag mining region.

Kolba Range, Kazakh SSR: see KALBA RANGE.

Kolberg (kôl'bĕrk) or **Kolobrzeg** (kôwôb'zhĕk), Pol. *Kołobrzeg*, town (1939 pop. 36,616; 1946 pop. 2,816) in Pomerania, after 1945 in Koszalin prov., NW Poland, on the Baltic, at Prosnica R. mouth, 70 mi. NE of Stettin, 25 mi. W of Köslin (Koszalin); 54°11'N 15°35'E. Seaport; rail junction; seaside resort; chemical mfg. First mentioned c.1000; joined Hanseatic League in 1248; chartered 1255; cathedral built 1280. A salt-trading center in Middle Ages. Reformation introduced 1530. In Thirty Years War, captured (1631) and fortified by Gustavus Adolphus after prolonged siege. Passed 1648 to Brandenburg. In Seven Years War, thrice besieged, until captured (1761) by Russians. Withstood Fr. siege in 1807. Saltworks were closed in 1860; fortifications razed 1873. At end of First World War, last hq. (Jan.-Sept., 1919) of Ger. General Staff. After Second World War, when it was c.90% destroyed, its Ger. pop. was evacuated.

Kolbermoor (kôl'bûrmōr), W suburb (pop. 7,451) of Rosenheim, Upper Bavaria, Germany, on Mangfall R.; mfg. (electrical machinery and equipment; cotton).

Kolbuszowa (kôlbōō-shô'vä), town (pop. 2,124), Rzeszow prov., SE Poland, 17 mi. NNW of Rzeszow, flour milling, lumbering, distilling.

Kolchugino or **Kol'chugino** (kŭlchōō'gĭnŭ). **1** Town, Kemerovo oblast, Russian SFSR: see LENINSK-KUZNETSKI. **2** City (1926 pop. 11,639), W Vladimir oblast, Russian SFSR, on railroad (Peksha station) and 40 mi. WNW of Vladimir; nonferrous metallurgical center, based on the Urals copper ore; copper alloys, electrical equipment. Metallurgical school. Became city in 1931.

Kolda (kôl'dä), town (pop. c.4,000), S Senegal, Fr. West Africa, on upper Casamance R. and 90 mi. ENE of Ziguinchor; sisal and peanut growing. Clinic for sleeping sickness.

Kolding (kôl'dĭng), city (1950 pop. 31,017), Vejle amt, E Jutland, Denmark, port on Kolding Fjord 15 mi. S of Vejle. Commercial and industrial center; rail junction; hydroelectric plant; shipbuilding, cement and machinery mfg., dairy plant, fisheries. Ruins of Koldinghus, 13th-cent. castle with mus.

Kolding Fjord, inlet (c.8 mi. long) of the Little Belt, E Jutland, Denmark. Faeno isl. at mouth, Kolding city at head.

Koldyban or **Koldyban'** (kŭldĭ'bŭnyŭ), village (1926 pop. 2,203), S central Kuibyshev oblast, Russian SFSR, 23 mi. SE of Chapayevsk; wheat, cattle, sheep.

Kole (kō'lā), village, Kasai prov., central Belgian Congo, on Lukenie R. and 125 mi. NNW of Lusambo; steamboat landing; cotton ginning.

Koléa (kôlää'), town (pop. 10,282), Alger dept., N central Algeria, in the *sahel* (coastal area), 20 mi. SW of Algiers; agr. trade center (wine, fruits, vegetables); embroidering. Founded 1550, town is a Moslem pilgrimage center. Destroyed by earthquake in 1825.

Kolekole (kō'lākō'lā), peak (10,000 ft.), S Maui, T.H.

Koleno, Russian SFSR: see YELAN-KOLENOVSKI.

Kolenté River, Africa: see GREAT SCARCIES RIVER.

Kölesd (kû'lĕzhd), town (pop. 3,482), Tolna co., SW central Hungary, on Sio-Kapos Canal and 12 mi. NNW of Szekszard; wheat, corn, barley.

Kolguyev Island (kŭlgōō'yĭf) (□ 1,350; 1939 pop. c.300), in Barents Sea, forms part of Archangel oblast, Russian SFSR, 50 mi. off mainland, E of Kanin Peninsula; 47 mi. long, 35 mi. wide; tundra rises to over 400 ft.; 69°N 49°E. Pop. (90% Nentsy) engage in reindeer raising, fur trapping, collecting of birds' eggs and feathers. Main settlement, Bugrino, on S coast. Govt. observation station on N coast.

Kolhapur (kōl'häpōōr), former Deccan state (□ 3,219; pop. 1,092,046) in Bombay, India; ⊙ was Kolhapur. A strong Mahratta kingdom in 17th-18th cent. Inc. 1949 into newly-created dist. of Kolhapur and into Belgaum, Ratnagiri, and Satara South dists.

Kolhapur, district (created 1949), S Bombay, India; ⊙ Kolhapur. On W edge of Deccan Plateau; crossed N–S by Western Ghats; bounded N by Satara South dist., NE by Kistna R. A hilly region with extensive forests (teak, sandalwood, blackwood, myrobalan); agr. (rice, millet, sugar cane, tobacco, oilseeds); handloom weaving, pottery and hardware mfg. Iron-ore and bauxite deposits (N). Kolhapur is large trade center; other market towns are Ichalkaranji, Gad-Hinglaj, and Shirol. Formed out of most of former Kolhapur state.

Kolhapur. **1** City (pop., including cantonment area, 95,918), ⊙ Kolhapur dist., S Bombay, India, 180 mi. SSE of Bombay. Rail terminus; road junction; commercial center and agr. market (millet, rice, sugar cane, tobacco); trades in grain, cloth fabrics, timber; cotton, sugar, and oilseed milling, handloom weaving, mfg. of pottery, matches; tobacco factory, motion picture studios. Religious and cultural center; col.; law and technical schools. Was ⊙ former princely state of Kolhapur. **2** Town (pop. 5,588), Mahbubnagar dist., S Hyderabad state, India, near Kistna R., 50 mi. SE of Mahbubnagar; rice and oilseed milling. Also spelled Kolapur and Kollapur.

Kolhapur and Deccan States Agency, India: see DECCAN STATES.

Koliganek (kōlēgä'nĕk), village (pop. 90), SW Alaska, on Nushagak R. and 65 mi. NE of Dillingham; 59°49'N 157°26'W.

Kolijnsplaat, Netherlands: see NORTH BEVELAND.

Kolin (kô'lēn), Czech *Kolín*, city (pop. 19,820), central Bohemia, Czechoslovakia, on Elbe R. and 45 mi. E of Prague; industrial, railroad, and commercial center; important chemical industries (pitchblende processing, alcohol, lye, yeast, medicines, fertilizers); mfg. (scales, machines, cables, insulating materials, confectionery, soap, candles, footwear, furniture), food processing, (chocolate, sugar, coffee substitutes). Has large oil refinery. Noted for 13th- and 14th-cent. churches, 16th-cent. belfry, charnel house, baroque buildings, mus. Frederick the Great defeated near here (1757) by Field Marshal Daun. Coal and iron mining in vicinity.

Kolindros (kôlĭndrôs'), town (pop. 4,616), Salonika nome, Macedonia, Greece, 25 mi. WSW of Salonika; wheat, cotton, tobacco.

Kolka, Cape (kōl'kä), Lettish *Kolkasrags* (kōl'-käsrägs), Swedish *Domesnäs* (dō'mŭsnĕs), headland of W Latvia, on Gulf of Riga, at E end of Irbe Strait; 57°45'N 22°36'E.

Kolkhida, Georgian SSR: see COLCHIS.

Kolkhozabad (kŭlkhô''zŭbät'), village, S Kulyab oblast, Tadzhik SSR, on the Yakh-Su and 11 mi. SW of Kulyab; cotton, truck produce; salt deposits. Until c.1935, Paituk.

Kolkhoznoye (kŭlkhôz'nŭyŭ), village (1948 pop. over 2,000), NE Karaganda oblast, Kazakh SSR, on Nura R. and 30 mi. NE of Karaganda; wheat, cattle.

Kolki (kôl'kē), Pol. *Kołki* (kôw'kē), town (1931 pop. 2,150), E Volyn oblast, Ukrainian SSR, on Styr R. (head of navigation) and 30 mi. NNE of Lutsk; lumber-trading center; woodworking, pitch processing, brewing, flour milling.

Kollaimalai Hills (kŏl-lī'mŭlī''), outlier of S Eastern Ghats, S central Madras, India, SE of Salem, separated from Pachaimalai Hills (E) by river valley; 18 mi. long, 12 mi. wide; rise to over 4,600 ft. Magnetite mined here and in S outlying hill of Talamalai. Agr. products: rice, cotton, plantain, oranges.

Kollam, India: see QUILON.

Kollapur, India: see KOLHAPUR, town, Hyderabad.

Kölleda (kû'lädä), town (pop. 7,672), in former Prussian Saxony prov., central Germany, after 1945 in Saxony-Anhalt, 15 mi. NNW of Weimar; center for trade in medicinal herbs. Has Gothic church. Formerly spelled Cölleda.

Kollegal (kŏ'lĕgäl), town (pop. 15,101), Coimbatore dist., SW Madras, India, on Cauvery R. and 33 mi. ESE of Mysore; major silk-growing and -mfg. center; supplies raw silk to S Indian filatures; produces silk of parachute quality; gold-cloth mfg., cotton milling. Noted Cauvery Falls and hydroelectric works 9 mi. NE, at Sivasamudram.

Köllerbach (kû'lûrbäkh), town (pop. 5,417), SW Saar, 7 mi. NW of Saarbrücken; coal mining.

Kolleru Lake, India: see COLAIR LAKE.

Kölliken (kû'lĭkûn), town (pop. 2,535), Aargau canton, N Switzerland, 4 mi. S of Aarau; cotton textiles, tiles.

Kollipara (kŏ'lĭpŭrŭ), town (pop. 7,967), Guntur dist., NE Madras, India, in Kistna R. delta, 20 mi. E of Guntur; rice milling; tobacco.

Kollnau (kôl'nou), village (pop. 3,201), S Baden, Germany, in Black Forest, on the Elz and 1 mi. NE of Waldkirch; cotton mfg.

Kollum (kô'lŭm), village (pop. 2,338), Friesland prov., N Netherlands, 7 mi. ESE of Dokkum; dairying.

Kollur, India: see SATTENAPALLE.

Kolluru (kŏlōō'rōō), town (pop. 7,579), Guntur dist., NE Madras, India, in Kistna R. delta, on navigable irrigation canal and 25 mi. ESE of Guntur; rice milling; tobacco. Kolluru Road, rail station, is 3 mi. W. Also spelled Kollur.

Kolmar, France: see COLMAR.

Kolmar, Poland: see CHODZIEZ.

Kolmarden (kôlm'ōr''dŭn), Swedish *Kolmården*, village (pop. 424), Ostergotland co., SE Sweden, on N coast of Bra Bay, Swedish *Bråviken* (brō'vē''-kŭn), 30-mi.-long inlet of the Baltic, 8 mi. NE of Norrkoping; marble and limestone quarries, brickworks.

Kolmen Valtakunnan Kivi, Finland: see TRERIKSROYS, Norway.

Köln, Germany: see COLOGNE.

Kolno (kôl'nô), Rus. *Kolno* or *Kol'no* (both: kôl'-yŭnô), town (pop. 3,295), Bialystok prov., NE Poland, 18 mi. N of Lomza; rail spur terminus; flour milling, cement mfg.

Kolo (kō'lō), village, Leopoldville prov., W Belgian Congo, on railroad and 100 mi. ENE of Boma; agr. center with cattle farms, coffee and elaeis-palm plantations. R.C. mission. Airfield. Cattier (kätyā') railroad workshops are 10 mi. ENE.

Kolo (kô'wô), Pol. *Koło*, town (pop. 9,720), Poznan prov., central Poland, on Warta R. and 45 mi. NW of Lodz; rail junction; mfg. (cement, pottery, agr. machinery, roofing materials, hosiery, flour). In Second World War, under Ger. control, called Warthbrücken.

Koloa (kōlō'ü), village (pop. 1,464), SE Kauai, T.H.; Hawaii's oldest (1837) sugar plantation. Spouting Horn, a salt-water geyser, is here.

Kolob Canyon, Utah: see KOLOB TERRACE; ZION NATIONAL PARK.

Kolobovo (kô'lŭbŭvŭ), town (1941 pop. over 500), S Ivanovo oblast, Russian SFSR, near railroad (Ladyginskaya station), 10 mi. SSW of Shuya; cotton milling.

Kolobrzeg, Poland: see KOLBERG.

Kolob Terrace (kō'lŏb), SW Utah, deeply dissected plateau in Washington and Iron counties, extending W from Markagunt Plateau and S from Cedar City; bounded W by jagged 3,000-ft. escarpment. Rises to max. alt. of 9,000 ft. in N; includes colorful Kolob Canyon (1,500–2,500 ft.) and part of Zion Natl. Monument in S.

Kolocep Island (kô'lôchĕp), Serbo-Croatian *Koločep*, Ital. *Calamotta* (kälämôt'tä), anc. *Calaphodia*, Dalmatian island in Adriatic Sea, S Croatia, Yugoslavia, 5 mi. WNW of Dubrovnik; c.2 mi. long. Sometimes spelled Kolochep.

Kolodnya (kŭlô'dnyŭ), town (1948 pop. over 10,000), W central Smolensk oblast, Russian SFSR, 4 mi. E of Smolensk; metalworking center.

Kologriv (kŭlŭgrēf'), city (1926 pop. 3,108), N Kostroma oblast, Russian SFSR, on Unzha R. (landing) and 75 mi. ENE of Galich; sawmilling center. Chartered 1609.

Kolokani (kōlōkänē'), village (pop. c.1,400), S Fr. Sudan, Fr. West Africa, 60 mi. N of Bamako; peanuts, shea nuts, livestock. Mfg. of native pottery.

Kolomak (kô'lŭmŭk), village (1926 pop. 5,727), W Kharkov oblast, Ukrainian SSR, 40 mi. WSW of Kharkov; sugar refining.

Kolombangara (kôlômbäng'ärä), volcanic island, New Georgia, Solomon Isls., SW Pacific, 5 mi. W of main isl. of New Georgia, across Kula Gulf; 20 mi. long, 15 mi. wide; extinct volcanoes. In Second World War, Jap. air base at Vila in SE. Sometimes spelled Kulambangra.

Kolomea, Ukrainian SSR: see KOLOMYYA.

Kolomna (kŭlôm'nŭ), city (1926 pop. 30,767; 1939 pop. 75,139), SE Moscow oblast, Russian SFSR, on Moskva R., near its confluence with the Oka, and 65 mi. SE of Moscow; locomotive and car-building center since 1860s; shipyards; mfg. of textile machines, Diesel motors; flour, clothing, and sawmills. Teachers col. Has ruins of walls of kremlin (built 1585), cathedral (1672), 13th-14th-cent. church. Founded 1177; passed 1301 to Moscow. Played important role (until 16th cent.) in wars with Tatars as S fortified center of Moscow domain.

Kolomyya (kŭlŭmĭ'yŭ), Pol. *Kołomyja* (kôwômĭ'yä), Ger. *Kolomea* (kōlōmā'ä), city (1931 pop. 33,385), E Stanislav oblast, Ukrainian SSR, on Prut R. and 31 mi. SSE of Stanislav; transportation (4 rail lines) and mfg. center; petroleum refining, metal- and woodworking, mfg. (cement, chemicals, textiles, ceramics), agr. processing (hides, cereals, hops, fruit, vegetables). Has technical schools, mus., notable town hall, and numerous old churches. An old Pol. frontier town, frequently assaulted by Tatars and Walachians (15th-16th cent.). Passed to Austria (1772); reverted to Poland (1919); ceded to USSR in 1945.

Kolonedale, Indonesia: see KOLONODALE.

Kolonelsdiep (kôlônĕlz'dēp) or **Caspar Roblesdiep** (käs'pär rō'blŭzdēp), canal, Friesland prov., N Netherlands; extends 7 mi. E–W, bet. E shore of Bergum L. and the HOENDIEP at Stroobos (10 mi. ESE of Dokkum). Connects with the WIJDE EE at Bergum L.

Kolones, Cape, Greece: see SOUNION, CAPE.

Kolonja or **Kolonjë**, Albania: see ERSEKË.

Kolonnawa (kŏlŏnä′vŭ), E suburb (pop. 13,512) of Colombo, Western Prov., Ceylon, on tributary of the Kelani Ganga and 3 mi. E of Colombo city center; rice, vegetables, coconuts.

Kolonodale (kōlōnŏdä′lŭ), town, E Celebes, Indonesia, port at head of Tomori Bay (small inlet of Gulf of Tolo), 250 mi. NE of Macassar; 2°S 121°20′E; trade center, shipping resin and rattan. Sometimes spelled Kolonedale.

Kolosia (kōlōsē′ä), village, Northern Frontier Prov., W Kenya, 70 mi. NE of Kitale; stock raising; cotton, peanuts, sesame, corn.

Kolosjoki, Russian SFSR: see NIKEL, Murmansk oblast.

Kolosovka (kŭlŭsôf′kŭ). **1** Village (1926 pop. 1,032), central Omsk oblast, Russian SFSR, on Osha R. and 40 mi. SW of Tara; dairy farming. Until c.1940, Nizhne-Kolosovskoye. **2** Rail junction, Ukrainian SSR: see BEREZOVKA, Odessa oblast.

Kolozs, Rumania: see COJOCNA.

Kolozsborja, Rumania: see BORSA.

Kolozsvar, Rumania: see CLUJ, city.

Kolpakovski or **Kolpakovskiy** (kŭlpä′kŭfskē), town (1948 pop. over 500), Kamchatka oblast, Khabarovsk Territory, Russian SFSR, on W coast of Kamchatka Peninsula, on Sea of Okhotsk, 140 mi. N of Ust-Bolsheretsk; fish-processing plant.

Kolpakovskoye, Kazakh SSR: see DZERZHINSKOYE, Taldy-Kurgan oblast.

Kolpashevo (kŭlpŭshô′vŭ), city (1939 pop. over 10,000), central Tomsk oblast, Russian SFSR, on Ob R. and 145 mi. NW of Tomsk; fish canning, sawmilling; metalworks. Teachers col. Was ⊙ former Narym Okrug.

Kölpin Lake, Ger. *Kölpinsee* (kûl′pĭnzā″), lake (□ 8), Mecklenburg, N Germany, just NW of Müritz L., 3 mi. W of Waren; 5 mi. long, 1–3 mi. wide; greatest depth 100 ft., average depth 13 ft. Traversed by Elde R.

Kolpino (kôl′pēnŭ), city (1926 pop. 17,317), central Leningrad oblast, Russian SFSR, on Izhora R. and 17 mi. SE (under jurisdiction) of Leningrad; machine-mfg. center; site of Izhora naval construction works (founded 1722) producing machine tools and steam engines (since early 19th cent.) and ships (since 1863); steel-rolling mills. During Second World War, a fortified Rus. position in Ger. siege of Leningrad (1941–44).

Kolpny (kôlp′nē), village (1926 pop. 786), S Orel oblast, Russian SFSR, on Soska R. and 26 mi. SW of Livny; rail terminus; fruit and vegetable canning, hemp milling. Also called Kolpna.

Kolpur (kōl′pŏŏr), village, Bolan subdivision, NE central Baluchistan, W Pakistan, at W end of Bolan Pass, 21 mi. SSE of Quetta. Coal mined near by (E).

Kolsva (kôls′vä), village (pop. 2,349), Vastmanland co., central Sweden, 7 mi. NW of Koping; feldspar mines, iron- and steelworks (founded in 16th cent.); furniture mfg.

Koltakenges or **Kol'takenges** (kôl′täkĕng-gĕs), Finnish *Kolttaköngäs* (kōlt′täkŭng″äs), Lapp village, W Murmansk oblast, Russian SFSR, on Nor. border and the Paz R. (rapids), 25 mi. WNW of Pechenga; fishing.

Kolter (kŭl′tŭr), Faeroese *Koltur*, island (□ 1; pop. 22) of the W Faeroe Isls., separated from SW Stromo by Hesto Fjord. Highest point 1,568 ft.

Koltsovo or **Kol'tsovo** (kŭltsô′vŭ), town (1949 pop. over 500), S Sverdlovsk oblast, Russian SFSR, on railroad and 2 mi. N of Aramil; truck gardening, dairying.

Koltubanovski or **Koltubanovskiy** (kŭltŏŏbä′nŭfskē), town (1948 pop. over 2,000), W Chkalov oblast, Russian SFSR, near Samara R., on railroad (Koltubanka station) and 13 mi. NE of Buzuluk; sawmilling center.

Kolubara River (kôlŏŏ′bärä), W Serbia, Yugoslavia, rises SW of Valjevo, flows c.50 mi. NNE, past Obrenovac, to Sava R. 2 mi. E of Obrenovac. Kolubara co. (pop. 33,533; ⊙ Mionica) extends along upper course.

Koluk, Turkey: see KAHTA.

Kolumadulu Atoll (kō″lōōmŭdŏŏ′lōō), S central group (pop. 4,607) of Maldive Isls., in Indian Ocean, bet. 2°10′N and 2°34′N; coconuts; fishing.

Kolushkino, Russian SFSR: see YEFREMOVO-STEPANOVKA.

Koluszki (kôlŏŏsh′kē), Rus. *Kolyushki* (kôlyŏŏsh′-kē), town (pop. 5,627), Lodz prov., central Poland, 15 mi. E of Lodz; rail junction.

Koluton (kŭlŏŏtôn′), town (1945 pop. over 500), central Akmolinsk oblast, Kazakh SSR, on Koluton R. (tributary of the Ishim), on S.Siberian RR and 40 mi. E of Atbasar. Bauxite deposits near by.

Kolva River (kôl′vŭ), Molotov oblast, Russian SFSR, rises in the N Urals, on NW slope of Isherim mtn.; flows S and generally W, through coniferous taiga, and S, past Cherdyn, to Vishera R. just S of Cherdyn; c.290 mi. long. Lumber floating; seasonal tug navigation for c.160 mi. in lower course. Receives Visherka (right) and Berezovaya (left) rivers. Once part of trade route connecting Pechora and Kama rivers.

Kolwezi (kōlwĕ′zē), village (1948 pop. 17,889), Katanga prov., SE Belgian Congo, on railroad and 80 mi. WNW of Jadotville; alt. 4,679 ft. Center of major copper and cobalt producing area. Chief mines are at RUWE; MUSONOI; Dikuluwe (dĕkōō-lōō′wä), 10 mi. WSW; Kamoto (kämō′tō), 5 mi. W; and Kingamyambo (kĭng-gäm-yäm′bō), 7 mi. SE. Kolwezi is also a trading and tourist center. Has R.C. mission, hospitals, schools, and recreation facilities.

Kolybelskoye or **Kolybel'skoye** (kŭlĭbĕl′skŭyŭ), village (1926 pop. 3,960), SW Ryazan oblast, Russian SFSR, 11 mi. SSW of Chaplygin; coarse grain, tobacco.

Kolyberovo (kŭlĭbyĕ′rŭvŭ), town (1939 pop. over 10,000), E central Moscow oblast, Russian SFSR, on Moskva R., on railroad (Moskvoretskaya station) and 12 mi. N of Kolomna; cement-making center.

Kolyma Range (kŭlĭmä′) or **Gydan** (gĭdän′), N Khabarovsk Territory, Russian SFSR; extends from Magadan area 700 mi. NE to upper Anyui R.; forms divide bet. Kolyma R. basin and Sea of Okhotsk; rises to over 6,000 ft.

Kolyma River, in N Khabarovsk Territory and Yakut Autonomous SSR, Russian SFSR, rises in several branches (including Berelyakh R.) on SE Cherski Range, flows 1,335 mi. generally N, past Seimchan, Sredne-Kolymsk, and Nizhne-Kolymsk, to E.Siberian Sea, forming delta W of Ambarchik. In upper course traverses rich Kolyma gold-mining area (linked by highway with Magadan). Navigable (June–Oct.) for c.1,000 mi. Receives Omolon and Anyui (right) rivers.

Kolyshlei or **Kolyshley** (kŭlĭshlyā′), village (1948 pop. over 2,000), S Penza oblast, Russian SFSR, on railroad and 40 mi. SSW of Penza; flour milling; wheat, sunflowers.

Kolyubakino (kŭlyŏŏbä′kēnŭ), town (1939 pop. over 500), W central Moscow oblast, Russian SFSR, 5 mi. NNE of Tuchkovo; mfg. of needles. During Second World War, briefly held (1941) by Germans in Moscow campaign.

Kolyuchin Bay (kŭlyŏŏ′chĭn), inlet of Chukchi Sea in N Chukchi Peninsula, NE Siberia, Russian SFSR; 37 mi. long. **Kolyuchin Island**, site of govt. arctic station, is 25 mi. N, off bay entrance.

Kolyushki, Poland: see KOLUSZKI.

Kolyvan or **Kolyvan'** (kŭlĭvän′yŭ). **1** Town (1926 pop. 3,835), S Altai Territory, Russian SFSR, 60 mi. ESE of Rubtsovsk; silver-lead, copper, tungsten mining; polishing of precious stones mined here. One of oldest mines (founded 1726) in Siberia. **2** Village (1948 pop. over 500), NE Novosibirsk oblast, Russian SFSR, on Ob R. and 20 mi. N of Novosibirsk; river port. Founded 1713; a former commercial center on old Siberian Road at Ob R. crossing; declined after construction (1890s) of Trans-Siberian RR (S) and rise of Novosibirsk.

Kolyvan Lake, S Altai Territory, Russian SFSR, 15 mi. W of Kolyvan; 2.5 mi. long, 1.5 mi. wide; known for its picturesque granite cliffs.

Kom (kôm), peak (6,613 ft.) in Berkovitsa Mts., NW Bulgaria, 5 mi. SSW of Berkovitsa. Nisava R. rises at S foot.

Kom, Iran: see QUM.

Komadi (kô′mädē), Hung. *Komádi*, town (pop. 10,577), Bihar co., E Hungary, 36 mi. S of Debrecen; market center; hemp, flax mfg., brickworks.

Komadugu Yobe (kōmädŏŏ′gŏŏ yō′bā), river in NE Nigeria, formed NE of Gorgoram by union of Hadejia and Katagum rivers, flows over 200 mi. ENE, past Geidam, to L. Chad at Bosso. Forms border with Fr. West Africa in its lower course.

Koma-ga-take (kōmä′gä-täkē). **1** Volcanic peak (3,740 ft.), SW Hokkaido, Japan, near SW entrance to Uchiura Bay, 22 mi. SW of Muroran. Long thought to be extinct, it erupted violently in 1929. **2** Mountain, Honshu, Japan: see KISO-KOMA-GA-TAKE.

Komai, Tibet: see SANGA CHO.

Komaki (kōmä′kē), town (pop. 18,157), Aichi prefecture, central Honshu, Japan, 10 mi. N of Nagoya; agr. center (rice, wheat, medicinal herbs).

Komandorski Islands (kŭmŭndôr′skē) or **Commander Islands**, Rus. *Komandorskiye Ostrova*, group in SW Bering Sea, 110 mi. off Kamchatka Peninsula; part of Kamchatka oblast, Khabarovsk Territory, Russian SFSR; bet. 54°31′–55°20′N and 165°45′–168°E. Consist of BERING ISLAND, MEDNY ISLAND, and 2 islets off NW Bering Isl. Formed of tertiary volcanic rocks (andesite tuff, basalt), rising to over 2,000 ft. Group has foggy climate and frequent earthquakes. Habitat of arctic sea-cow (extinct since late 18th cent.), sea otter, and fur seal (preserves). Whaling base. Pop. is largely Aleut. Largest village, Nikolskoye. Named for 18th-cent. Rus. navigator, Bering, who died here, 1741.

Komarapalaiyam or **Kumarapalaiyam** (kŏŏmä″rŭpä′-lĭyŭm), town (pop. 6,961), Salem dist., S central Madras, India, on Cauvery R. (bridged) opposite Bhavani and 36 mi. WSW of Salem; rice, peanuts, castor beans. Corundum deposits near by. Also spelled Komarapalayam.

Komari (kō′mŭrē) or **Komariya** (–yŭ), village (pop. 637), Eastern Prov., Ceylon, on E coast, 50 mi. SSE of Batticaloa. Rice and coconut-palm plantations near by. Sangamankanda promontory, 1 mi. NNE, is easternmost point of Ceylon; formerly spelled Sankamankandimunai; lighthouse.

Komarichi (kŭmä′rēchē), village (1926 pop. 1,471), SE Bryansk oblast, Russian SFSR, 60 mi. SSE of Bryansk; wheat, sugar beets.

Komarin (kŭmä′rĭn), village (1926 pop. 963), SE Polesye oblast, Belorussian SSR, on Dnieper R. and 30 mi. W of Chernigov; agr. products, cloth milling.

Komarno (kô′märnô), Slovak *Komárno*, Ger. *Komorn* (kō′môrn), Hung. *Komárom* (kô′märôm), city on the Danube (Czechoslovak-Hung. border) and 55 mi. SE of Bratislava, 42 mi. NW of Budapest; partly in Czechoslovakia, partly in Hungary. Slovak **Komarno** (1947 pop. 15,461; 1941 pop. 21,892), rail, shipping, and trade center (lumber, coal), is on left bank of the Danube, at Vah R. mouth, at E extremity of Great Schütt isl.; mfg. of machinery and textiles (notably silk), shipbuilding, fishing, flour milling; still retains part of 15th–17th cent. fortifications. Hung. **Komarom** (1941 pop. 8,876), rail center and river port on right bank, has lumber yards, sawmills, textile mills; developed as suburb of Komarno. Originally an all-Hungarian autonomous city; noted in 18th cent. for its grain trade; divided by Treaty of Trianon (1920), reunited in 1939, divided again in 1945. Hung. novelist M. Jokai b. here.

Komarno (kŭmär′nŭ), city (1931 pop. 5,598), N Drogobych oblast, Ukrainian SSR, on left tributary of the Dniester, on artificial lake and 21 mi. NNE of Drogobych; agr. processing (cereals, potatoes, vegetable oils), brick mfg. Scene of defeat (1672) of Tatars by Pol. king John III Sobieski. The city passed from Poland to Austria in 1772, reverted to Poland in 1919, and was ceded to USSR in 1945.

Komarom, town, Hungary: see KOMARNO, Czechoslovakia.

Komarom-Esztergom (kô′märôm ĕs′tĕrgôm), Hung. *Komárom-Esztergom*, county (□ 765; pop. 199,391), N Hungary; ⊙ Esztergom. Mountainous in E (Gerecse Mts.), level in W (part of the Little Alföld); bounded N by the Danube. Industrial and mining region; coal, lignite mines near Esztergom and Tatabanya; limestone quarries at Labatlan, Felsögalla, Dorog. Industry, mainly cement, quicklime, starch, at Esztergom, Tata, and several small mining towns. Agr. (grain, potatoes), dairy farming. Stud farms at Babolna and Kisber. Area once Roman stronghold. Formed 1920 of Komarom and Esztergom counties.

Komarov (kô′märôf), Czech *Komárov*, village (pop. 1,403), W central Bohemia, Czechoslovakia, 32 mi. SW of Prague; rail terminus; ironworks.

Komarovka (kŭmŭrôf′kŭ). **1** Village (1926 pop. 4,450), central Chernigov oblast, Ukrainian SSR, 17 mi. NE of Nezhin; grain. **2** Town (1926 pop. 2,021), N central Kharkov oblast, Ukrainian SSR, 4 mi. N of Merefa, in Kharkov metropolitan area; woolen milling.

Komarovo (kŭmŭrô′vŭ). **1** Village, central Bashkir Autonomous SSR, Russian SFSR, just SW of Tukan, on rail spur, in Komarovo-Zigazinski iron dist. (extensive limonite and turgite deposits in the S Urals; mined at Inzer, Tukan, Verkhni Avzyan, and Zigazinski). **2** Town, N Leningrad oblast, Russian SFSR, on Gulf of Finland, just SE of Zelenogorsk; seaside resort. Called Kellomäki (kĕl′-lōmä″kē) while in Finland (until 1940) and, until 1948, in USSR. **3** Town (1943 pop. over 500), E central Novgorod oblast, Russian SFSR, near Msta R., 22 mi. NW of Borovichi; lignite mining.

Komatipoort (kōmä′tēpŏŏrt″), town (pop. 1,146), E Transvaal, U. of So. Afr., on Komati R. (Mozambique line), opposite Ressano Garcia, at influx of Crocodile R., 55 mi. NW of Lourenço Marques, near SE edge of Kruger Natl. Park. Airfield. Customs station on Johannesburg–Lourenço Marques RR. In South Africa War, occupation of Komatipoort (Oct., 1900) by British marked end of organized Boer resistance.

Komati River (kōmä′tē), Port. *Incomati* (ēngkômä-tē′), S Africa, in E Transvaal, Swaziland, and Mozambique, rises in N Drakensberg range N of Ermelo, flows in a winding course E through N Swaziland and NE to Komatipoort where it crosses into Mozambique; it continues NE and then turns sharply S to the Indian Ocean 15 mi. NE of Lourenço Marques; c.500 mi. long. Receives Crocodile R. (left).

Komatsu (kōmä′tsŏŏ). **1** Town (pop. 5,752), Ehime prefecture, N Shikoku, Japan, 20 mi. E of Matsuyama, in agr. area (rice, wheat); mulberry groves. **2** City (1940 pop. 19,139; 1947 pop. 61,898), Ishikawa prefecture, central Honshu, Japan, on Sea of Japan, 16 mi. SW of Kanazawa; silk-textile center; hot-springs resort; pottery making. Includes (since early 1940s) former town of Ataka (1940 pop. 7,965) and several smaller villages. Sometimes spelled Komatu. **3** Town (pop. 7,634), Yamagata prefecture, N Honshu, Japan, 7 mi. NNW of Yonezawa; collection center for raw silk and rice. Ski resort. **4** Town (pop. 5,829) on O-shima, Yamaguchi prefecture, Japan, port on NW coast of isl.; exports textiles, soy sauce, sake.

Komatsujima (kōmätsŏŏ′jĭmä), town (pop. 25,876), Tokushima prefecture, E Shikoku, Japan, port on Kii Channel, 5 mi. SSE of Tokushima; outer port of Tokushima. Exports textiles, raw silk, copper, fruit.

Komatu, Japan: see KOMATSU, Ishikawa prefecture.

Komavangard, Russian SFSR: see SOBINKA.

Komba (kŏm'bä), village, Eastern Prov., N Belgian Congo, 25 mi. WNW of Buta; rail junction in cotton area.

Kombai (kŏm'bī), town (pop. 9,344), Madura dist., S Madras, India, 7 mi. N of Cumbum, in Kambam Valley; cardamom, bamboo, turmeric in Cardamom Hills (W); grain, cattle raising. Cattle market at Virapandi village, 12 mi. NE. Sometimes spelled Combai.

Kombo Saint Mary (kŏm'bō), mainland district (□ 27; pop. 7,000) of GAMBIA colony, S of Gambia R. estuary and adjoining St. Mary's Isl. Here are truck gardens and the villages of Bakau and Fajara; pop. is largely Wollof. Since 1947 dist. is governed by Kombo Rural Authority. Adjoining it (S) is Kombo North dist. (□ 80; pop. 6,037), administered as part of Gambia protectorate's Western Div. Here are Yundum airport and poultry farm. Kombo St. Mary was acquired 1840 by British for settlement of liberated slaves. It is sometimes called British Kombo as opposed to Foreign Kombo (S) acquired 1894.

Komchén (kōmchĕn'), town (pop. 1,025), Yucatan, SE Mexico, 10 mi. N of Mérida; henequen.

Kom Dafana, Egypt: see TAHAPANES.

Kom el Ahmar, El, or **Al-Kum al-Ahmar** (both: ĕl kōōm' ĕl ä'mär), village (pop. 6,272), Qena prov., Upper Egypt, 6 mi. WNW of Nag Hammadi. Site of the extensive ruins and tombs of anc. Hieraconpolis.

Kom el Nur or **Kum al-Nur** (both: kōōm' ĕl nōōr'), village (pop., with adjoining village of Kafr el Dalil, 12,961), Daqahliya prov., Lower Egypt, 2 mi. NE of Mit Ghamr; cotton, cereals.

Komen, Belgium: see COMINES.

Komenda (kōmĕn'dä), town, Western Prov., S Gold Coast colony, on Gulf of Guinea, 15 mi. W of Cape Coast; fishing. Br. trading station in 19th cent. Formerly spelled Kommenda or Commenda.

Komenotsu (kōmā'nōtsōō), town (pop. 19,956), Kagoshima prefecture, W Kyushu, Japan, 38 mi. NNW of Kagoshima, on Yatsushiro Bay; agr. center (tobacco, rice, millet, sweet potatoes, tea).

Komgha (kôm'khù), town (pop. 1,190), SE Cape Prov., U. of So. Afr., near Great Kei R., 30 mi. N of East London, near Transkeian Territories boundary; stock, dairying, grain.

Kom Hamada or **Kum Kamadah** (both: kōōm hämă'dù), village (pop. 3,671), Beheira prov., Lower Egypt, on Rosetta branch of the Nile and 23 mi. SE of Damanhur; cotton, rice, cereals.

Komi Autonomous Soviet Socialist Republic (kō'mē, Rus. kô'mē), administrative division (□ 156,200; 1946 pop. estimate 450,000) of NE European Russian SFSR; ⊙ Syktyvkar. In sparsely populated basins of Pechora, Vychegda, and upper Mezen rivers; mountainous in extreme E (N Urals); Timan Ridge (center) divides forested, swampy lowland. Nearly half of area has permanently frozen soil; wooded tundra (N). Pop., concentrated in S, engaged mainly in lumbering, agr. (flax, potatoes; only along river valleys), and in livestock raising; in N, fur-trapping, reindeer raising, fishing are important. Coal mining in Pechora basin (Vorkuta, Inta), oil field at Ukhta, natural-gas wells and asphalt rock at Krutaya, grindstone works at Ust-Voya, iron mines and foundries at Nyuvchim and Kazhim. Sawmilling and wood distillation along Vychegda R. (Syktyvkar); chamois-leather plant at Ust-Tsilma, meat (game, fowl) packing at Ust-Usa. Construction (1940) of N.Pechora RR to Vorkuta boomed economy of region and led to expansion of oil fields and coal mines along railroad. Komi (formerly Zyryan or Zyrian) Autonomous Oblast (formed 1921) was part (1929–36) of Northern Territory, and became Autonomous SSR in 1936.

Kominato (kōmē'nä'tō). **1** Town (pop. 9,669), Aomori prefecture, N Honshu, Japan, on S Mutsu Bay, 13 mi. NE of Aomori; agr. (rice, soybeans), horse breeding, fishing. **2** Town (pop. 4,203), Chiba prefecture, central Honshu, Japan, on SE coast of Chiba Peninsula, 7 mi. W of Katsuura; fishing.

Koming (gō'mĭng'), Mandarin *Kaoming* (gou'mĭng'), town, ⊙ Koming co. (pop. 98,401), W central Kwangtung prov., China, 20 mi. SE of Koyiu; coal mining; rice, wheat, beans, sugar cane.

Komintern. **1** City, Russian SFSR: see NOVOSHAKHTINSK. **2** City, Ukrainian SSR: see MARGANETS.

Kominterna, Imeni (ĕ'mĭnyē kŭmēntyĕr'nŭ), town (1926 pop. 2,632), N Novgorod oblast, Russian SFSR, 8 mi. SE of Chudovo, across Volkhov R.; porcelain works. Until c.1930, Sosninskaya.

Kominternovski or **Kominternovskiy** (–nŭfskē), town (1939 pop. over 2,000), N central Kirov oblast, Russian SFSR; NE suburb of Kirov, across Vyatka R.; shoe mfg.

Kominternovskoye (–skŭyù), village (1939 pop. over 500), SE Odessa oblast, Ukrainian SSR, 25 mi. NNE of Odessa; wheat, cotton. Until 1930s, Antono-Kodintsevo.

Komi-Permyak National Okrug (kō'mē-pûrm'yăk, Rus. kô'mē-pĭrmyäk'), administrative division (□ 8,920; 1946 pop. estimate 300,000) of NW Molotov oblast, Russian SFSR; ⊙ Kudymkar. In W foothills of the central Urals; drained by Kama R. and its tributaries (Veslyana, Kosa, Inva). Humid continental climate (short summers). Peat deposits near Kudymkar. Heavily forested (N, W); flax, wheat, livestock (S); rye, oats, potatoes (center). Industries based on timber (wood distilling, pitch processing, woodworking, sawmilling) and agr. (flax processing, flour milling). Pop. 69% Permyaks; also Russians, Ukrainians. The Permyaks are a Finnic group of Rus. culture and Greek Orthodox religion; colonized by Russians in 15th cent. Area became administrative okrug in 1925; gained present status in 1929 within former Ural oblast; passed 1934 to Sverdlovsk oblast and 1938 to Molotov oblast.

Kom Ishqaw or **Kum Ishqaw** (both: kōōm' ĭsh'kou), village (pop. 6,051), Girga prov., central Upper Egypt, 7 mi. NW of Tahta; cotton, cereals, dates, sugar cane. Site of anc. Aphroditopolis.

Komiya, Japan: see HACHIOJI.

Komiza, Yugoslavia: see VIS ISLAND.

Komlo (kôm'lō), Hung. *Komló*, town (pop. 3,512), Baranya co., S Hungary, in Mecsek Mts., 8 mi. N of Pecs; coal mines.

Kommunar (kŭmōōnär'), town (1939 pop. over 10,000), W Khakass Autonomous Oblast, Krasnoyarsk Territory, Russian SFSR, in the Kuznetsk Ala-Tau, 90 mi. NW of Abakan; gold-mining center; boomed in early 1930s. Until 1932, Bogomdarovanny.

Komo, Tibet: see SANGA CHO.

Komodo (kōmō'dō), island (□ c.184; 20 mi. long, 12 mi. wide), Lesser Sundas, Indonesia, bet. Flores Sea (N) and Sumba Strait (S), bet. Flores (E) and Sumbawa (W); hilly; copra, fish.

Komoé River, Fr. West Africa: see COMOÉ RIVER.

Kom Ombo or **Kum Umbu** (both: kōōm' ōōm'bōō), village (1937 pop. 3,234; 1947 commune pop. 39,279), Aswan prov., S Egypt, on railroad and 27 mi. NNE of Aswan, near the Nile; sugar milling, cotton ginning. Site of ruins of several temples.

Komono, Fr. Equatorial Africa: see SIBITI.

Komono (kōmō'nō), town (pop. 5,894), Mie prefecture, S Honshu, Japan, 9 mi. W of Yokkaichi; rice growing. Hot springs.

Komorany (kô'mōrzhänĭ), Czech *Komořany*, village (pop. 3,014), NW Bohemia, Czechoslovakia, 3 mi. W of Most Litvinov; coal mines; power plants. Mining village of Trebusice (trĕ'bōōshĭtsĕ), Czech *Trebušice*, is just SE, on railroad.

Komori (kō'mōrē), town (pop. 2,454), Kyoto prefecture, S Honshu, Japan, 7 mi. N of Fukuchiyama; rail terminus; makes silk fabrics; rice growing. Sericulture school.

Komorn, Hungary and Czechoslovakia: see KOMARNO.

Komoro (kōmō'rō), town (pop. 17,338), Nagano prefecture, central Honshu, Japan, 11 mi. ESE of Ueda; lumbering and agr. center; sake, soy sauce, bean curd; raw silk.

Komoshtitsa (kômôshtē'tsä), village (pop. 3,037), Vidin dist., NW Bulgaria, 9 mi. SE of Lom; grain, legumes.

Komotau, Czechoslovakia: see CHOMUTOV.

Komotine or **Komotini** (both: kômôtēnē'), city (1951 pop. 31,906), ⊙ Greek Thrace and Rhodope nome, Greece, on railroad and 140 mi. ENE of Salonika; agr. trade center (tobacco, wheat, barley, vegetables, dairy products, cotton, silk). Lead-zinc mining (NE). Airport. Bishopric. Linked with Momchilgrad (Bulgaria) via Makaz Pass road. Under Turkish rule (until Balkan wars, 1912–13) called Gumuljina (Gumuldjina) or Gumurjina (Gumurdjina; Bulg. Gyumyurdzhina).

Komovi (kô'môvē), mountain in Dinaric Alps, E Montenegro, Yugoslavia, near Albania border, in the Brda. Highest point (8,148 ft.) is 8 mi. WSW of Andrijevica.

Kompaneyevka (kŭmpŭnyä'ŭfkŭ), village (1939 pop. over 500), S Kirovograd oblast, Ukrainian SSR, on road and 18 mi. S of Kirovograd; metalworks.

Kompong Bang (kômpông' bäng'), town, Kompong Chhnang prov., central Cambodia, on the Tonle Sap R. (opposite Kompong Chhnang) and 50 mi. NNW of Pnompenh.

Kompong Cham (chäm'), town, ⊙ Kompong Cham prov. (□ 3,900; 1948 pop. 570,761), S Cambodia, on right bank of Mekong R. (ferry) and 45 mi. NE of Pnompenh. Rubber-cultivation center; rice, corn, cotton, tobacco, sugar cane, indigo, sericulture; forestry and fisheries. Rubber factory, distillery (rice alcohol). Wat Nokor, 10th-cent. Brahman temple, near by.

Kompong Chhnang (shnäng'), town, ⊙ Kompong Chhnang prov. (□ 2,300; 1948 pop. 186,294), central Cambodia, at outlet of Tonle Sap, 50 mi. NNW of Pnompenh, on main highway; trade center; mfg. (bricks, pottery); distillery; cattle market. Head of navigation on Tonle Sap R. at low water.

Kompong Chrey (shrā'), town, Takeo prov., SW Cambodia, 50 mi. S of Pnompenh; rice center.

Kompong Kleang (klāäng'), town, Siemreap prov., W Cambodia, near lake Tonle Sap, 25 mi. SE of Siemreap; fisheries.

Kompong Luong (lōōäng'). **1** Village, Kandal prov., S Cambodia, on Tonle Sap R. (ferry) and 20 mi. NNW of Pnompenh; agr. market; distillery (rice alcohol). **2** or **Kompong Luong des Lacs** (dā läk'), village, Pursat prov., central Cambodia, on S shore of the Tonle Sap, 22 mi. E of Pursat; fishing.

Kompong Som Bay (sôm'), inlet of Gulf of Siam, SE Cambodia; 15–20 mi. wide, 35 mi. long; receives small Kompong Som R. (N).

Kompong Speu (spŭ'), town, Kompong Speu prov. (□ 2,700; 1948 pop. 176,469), S Cambodia, 25 mi. WSW of Pnompenh, at foot of Cardamom Mts.; sugar palm, rice; silk spinning, timber trading.

Kompong Thom (tôm'), town, ⊙ Kompong Thom prov. (□ 9,300; 1948 pop. 183,584), central Cambodia, 75 mi. N of Pnompenh, on the Stung Sen (affluent of lake Tonle Sap; navigable at high water), in densely forested (gum, gutta percha, lac) big-game region; iron-ore, jet, and gem deposits. Ruins of Sambor (anc. Isanapura), 15 mi. NE.

Kompong Trabek (träbĕk'), town, Preyveng prov., S Cambodia, on main highway to Saigon and 50 mi. SE of Pnompenh; rice, corn, fisheries.

Kompong Trach (träch'), town, Kampot prov., S Cambodia, 18 mi. ESE of Kampot, on small isolated ridge of Elephant Mts.; grottoes.

Kompong Tralach (träläch'), town, Kompong Chhang prov., central Cambodia, on Tonle Sap R. and 25 mi. NNW of Pnompenh, in forested (precious wood) area.

Komrat (kôm'rŭt), Rum. *Comrat* (kôm'răt), city (1941 pop. 11,943), S Moldavian SSR, on upper Yalpug R. and 50 mi. SSW of Kishinev, in wine-growing dist.; flour milling, wine making. Pop. largely Bulgarian and Gagauz (Turkish-speaking Christians).

Komsberg Escarpment (kôms'bĕrkh), SW Cape Prov., U. of So. Afr., extends c.60 mi. E–W in semicircle along SW edge of the Northern Karroo, bet. Roggeveld Escarpment (W) and Nieuwveld Range (E), 30 mi. N of Laingsburg; rises 2–3,000 ft. steeply from Great Karroo.

Komsomolabad (kŭmsùmôl"ŭbät'), village, W Garm oblast, Tadzhik SSR, on Vakhsh R. and 23 mi. SW of Garm; wheat, truck, cattle; gold placers. Until c.1935, Pombachi.

Komsomolets (kŭmsùmô'lyĭts), town (1943 pop. over 500), NW Kustanai oblast, Kazakh SSR, on railroad and 22 mi. SE of Troitsk.

Komsomolets Island, N island (□ 3,570) of Severnaya Zemlya archipelago, in Arctic Ocean, off Krasnoyarsk Territory, Russian SFSR; 65% covered by glaciers.

Komsomolsk or **Komsomol'sk** (kŭmsùmôlsk'). **1** Town (1948 pop. over 10,000), W central Ivanovo oblast, Russian SFSR, 22 mi. W of Ivanovo; flour milling. Has peat-fed Ivanovo power station (*Ivgres*). **2** Village (1939 pop. 906), W Kaliningrad oblast, Russian SFSR, on railroad and 11 mi. ESE of Kaliningrad, near Pregel R. Near by is 18th-cent. palace. Until 1945, in East Prussia and called Löwenhagen (lû'vùnhä"gùn). **3** or **Komsomolsk-on-Amur**, (–ämōōr'), Rus. *Komsomol'sk-na-Amure* (kŭmsùmôlsk' nŭ ùmōōr'yĭ), city (1939 pop. 70,746; 1946 pop. estimate 150,000), S Khabarovsk Territory, Russian SFSR, on left bank of Amur R. and 165 mi. NE of Khabarovsk, with which it is connected by railroad. Heavy-industry center for Soviet Far East: *Amurstal'* steel mills, shipbuilding, lumber, paper, and construction works, petroleum refining, aircraft mfg. Founded 1932 on site of village Permskoye by young Komsomol pioneers ("City of Youth"). From left-bank suburb of Pivan (railroad ferry), rail line leads to Sovetskaya Gavan, port on Tatar Strait. **4** Town, central Kuibyshev oblast, Russian SFSR, on left bank of Volga R., opposite Zhigulevsk, 33 mi. NW of Kuibyshev, at lower navigation locks of Kuibyshev Dam; founded 1950 adjoining Kuneyevka village. **5** City (1939 pop. over 10,000), central Stalino oblast, Ukrainian SSR, in the Donbas, 4 mi. NW (under jurisdiction) of Gorlovka; coal mines. **6** Village (1939 pop. over 500), S Samarkand oblast, Uzbek SSR, on road and 7 mi. SE of Samarkand; cotton, fruit. Until 1939, Tailak-Paion.

Komsomolskaya Pravda Islands or **Komsomol'skaya Pravda Islands** (kŭmsùmôl'skĭŭ präv'dŭ), in Laptev Sea of Arctic Ocean, 10–15 mi. off N Taimyr Peninsula, in Krasnoyarsk Territory, Russian SFSR; 77°15'N 107°E.

Komsomolskoye or **Komsomol'skoye** (–skŭyù). **1** Village (1939 pop. over 500), E Chuvash Autonomous SSR, Russian SFSR, on left tributary of Sviyaga R. and 18 mi. S of Kanash; wheat, livestock. Until 1939, Bolshoi Koshelei. **2** Village (1948 pop. over 2,000), SE Saratov oblast, Russian SFSR, 12 mi. SSE of Krasny Kut; flour milling; wheat, cattle. Until 1941 (in German Volga Autonomous SSR), Friedenfeld or Fridenfeld. **3** Town (1939 pop. over 500), SE Stalino oblast, Ukrainian SSR, in the Donbas, 12 mi. SW of Kuteinikovo; limestone-quarrying center. Until c.1945, Karakubstroi. **4** Village (1926 pop. 5,889), N Vinnitsa oblast, Ukrainian SSR, 34 mi. N of Vinnitsa; flour mill. Until c.1935, Makhnovka.

Komul, China: see HAMI.

Komyshnya (kŭmĭsh'nyŭ), village (1926 pop. 7,334), N Poltava oblast, Ukrainian SSR, near Khorol R., 32 mi. NE of Lubny; wheat, flax, mint. Formerly spelled Komyshna.

Kona (kō'nŭ), district of Hawaii co., W Hawaii, T.H.; region of coffee farms, cattle ranches, deep-sea fishing, health resorts. Capt. Cook died 1779 at Kealakekua Bay; 1st missionaries in Hawaii arrived 1820 at Kailua Bay.
Konada, India: see VIZIANAGARAM.
Konahuanui (kō'nähōō"ŭnōō'ē), peak (3,105 ft.), E Oahu, T.H., of Koolau Range; point near by reaches 3,150 ft.
Konakhkend (kŭnŭkhyĕnt'), village (1926 pop. 1,325), NE Azerbaijan SSR, at SE end of the Greater Caucasus, 20 mi. S of Kuba; wheat, livestock; rug mfg.
Konakovo (kŭnŭkô'vŭ), city (1939 pop. over 10,000), SE Kalinin oblast, Russian SFSR, on Volga Reservoir (landing) and 33 mi. ESE of Kalinin; porcelain center; vegetable processing, brickworking. Until mid 1930s, Kuznetsovo. It received the pop. evacuated (1936–37) from flooded former city of KORCHEVA.
Konakri, Fr. Guinea, Fr. West Africa: see CONAKRY.
Konan (kō'nä), town (pop. 12,301), Shiga prefecture, S Honshu, Japan, 25 mi. ESE of Kyoto; patent medicines. Formed in early 1940s by combining former villages of Tatsuike (1940 pop. 2,995), Terasho (1940 pop. 3,858), and 2 smaller villages.
Konan, Korea: see HUNGNAM.
Konanur (kō'nŭnōōr), town (pop. 2,981), Hassan dist., W Mysore, India, on Cauvery R. and 25 mi. S of Hassan; grain, rice; handicraft wickerwork.
Konar, Afghanistan: see KUNAR.
Konarak (kōnä'rŭk), village, Puri dist., E Orissa, India, 18 mi. ENE of Puri, near Bay of Bengal. Site of famous Black Pagoda, ruined 13th-cent. temple dedicated to sun god, whose chariot it represents; fine carvings of wheels and horses about base. Sometimes spelled Kanarak.
Konar River, India: see DAMODAR RIVER.
Kona Shahr (kōnä' shä'hûr) [Uigur,=old town], Chinese *Wensu* or *Wensuh* (wŭn'sōō'), town, ⊙ Kona Shahr co. (pop. 78,670), SW Sinkiang prov., China, 10 mi. N of Aksu; livestock, agr. products. Oil, coal mines, gypsum quarrying near by. The old town of Aksu, Kona Shahr is sometimes called Aksu Kona Shahr.
Konawa (kŏ'nŭwô, kŭnô'wŭ), town (pop. 2,707), Seminole co., central Okla., 15 mi. NNW of Ada; trade center and shipping point for agr. (cotton, corn, alfalfa; dairy products) and oil area; cotton ginning; mfg. of peanut products, furniture, mattresses.
Konda, India: see KONTA.
Kondagaon (kōn'dŭgoun), village, Bastar dist., SE Madhya Pradesh, India, 40 mi. NNW of Jagdalpur, in forest area (sal, bamboo, myrobalan; lac cultivation). Mica deposits (E). Formerly spelled Kondegaon.
Kondalwadi (kōn'dŭlvädē), town (pop. 7,708), Nander dist., N Hyderabad state, India, 37 mi. SE of Nander, 7 mi. W of Godavari-Manjra river confluence; millet, rice. Also spelled Kundalwadi.
Kondapalli or **Kondapalle** (kōn'dŭpŭlē), town (pop. 4,893), Kistna dist., NE Madras, India, near Kistna R., 8 mi. NW of Bezwada; rice, oilseeds, cotton; noted hand-carved wooden toys. Has 14th-cent. fortress taken 1687 by Aurangzeb and 1766, by English. Chromite mining in near-by forested hills (bamboo, myrobalan).
Konda River (kŭndä'), W Khanty-Mansi Natl. Okrug, Tyumen oblast, Russian SFSR, rises in swampy area, flows W, SSE, E, past Nakhrachi, and NE to Irtysh R. at Repolovo, 30 mi. SSE of Khanty-Mansisk; 715 mi. long. Large sable and beaver reserve in upper reaches.
Kondas (kŭndäs'), village (1939 pop. over 500), central Molotov oblast, Russian SFSR, on left bank of Kama R. and 9 mi. SW of Berezniki; lumbering; truck. Anc. metal relics found near by.
Kondavid, India: see GUNTUR, city.
Kondegaon, India: see KONDAGAON.
Kondi, W Pakistan: see NOK KUNDI.
Kondinskoye (kŭndyēn'skŭyŭ), village (1948 pop. over 2,000), NW Khanty-Mansi Natl. Okrug, Tyumen oblast, Russian SFSR, on Ob R. and 140 mi. NNW of Khanty-Mansisk; fish canning.
Kondoa (kōndō'ä), town (pop. c.2,000), central Tanganyika, on road and 85 mi. N of Dodoma; cotton, peanuts, gum arabic, beeswax.
Kondol or **Kondol'** (kŭndôl'), village (1939 pop. over 2,000), S central Penza oblast, Russian SFSR, 25 mi. S of Penza, in wheat-growing area.
Kondoma River (kŭndô'mŭ), SW Kemerovo oblast, Russian SFSR, rises in Abakan Range, flows 265 mi. N, through the Gornaya Shoriya, past Tashtagol and Kuzedeyevo, to Tom R. at Stalinsk. Lower course lies in Kuznetsk Basin.
Kondopoga (kôn'dŭpŭgŭ), Finnish *Kontupohja* (kôn'tōōpôyä), city (1941 pop. 14,000), S Karelo-Finnish SSR, on W shore of L. Onega, on Murmansk RR and 28 mi. N of Petrozavodsk; paper-milling center; pegmatite and glassworks; hydroelectric plant. In Second World War, held (1941–44) by Finns and Germans.
Kondoros (kôn'dôrôsh), town (pop. 7,483), Bekes co., SE Hungary, 15 mi. WNW of Bekescsaba; wheat, tobacco, hemp, cattle.
Kondowe, Nyasaland: see LIVINGSTONIA.
Kondrashevskaya, Ukrainian SSR: see STANICHNO-LUGANSKOYE.
Kondratyevskiy or **Kondrat'yevskiy** (kŭndrä'tyĭfskē), town (1939 pop. over 2,000), central Stalino oblast, Ukrainian SSR, in the Donbas, 6 mi. SE of Gorlovka; coal mines.
Kondrovo (kôn'drŭvŭ), city (1926 pop. 3,144), N central Kaluga oblast, Russian SFSR, 23 mi. NW of Kaluga; paper-milling center (mainly writing paper). Dates from 1800; became city in 1938.
Konduga (kŏndōō'gä), town (pop. 5,927), Bornu prov., Northern Provinces, NE Nigeria, 25 mi. SE of Maiduguri; cassava, millet, durra, gum arabic; cattle, skins.
Kondurcha River (kŭndōōr'chŭ), in SE European Russian SFSR, rises c.6 mi. E of Shentala, flows generally W, past Zubovka, and S, past Yelkhovka, to Sok R. at Krasny Yar (Kuibyshev oblast); 75 mi. long.
Koné (kōnā'), village (dist. pop. 2,185), W New Caledonia, 130 mi. NW of Nouméa; coffee, livestock. Nickel smelter at near-by Doniambo.
Koneshime, Japan: see NESHIME.
Konetspol, Poland: see KONIECPOL.
Konevo (kô'nyĭvŭ), village (1939 pop. over 500), SW Archangel oblast, Russian SFSR, on Onega R. and 50 mi. SW of Plesetsk; coarse grain.
Konfodah or **Konfudah,** Saudi Arabia: see QUNFIDHA.
Kong (kông), largely abandoned town, N Ivory Coast, Fr. West Africa, in uplands 260 mi. N of Abidjan, 70 mi. ESE of Korhogo. Was ⊙ anc. Kong kingdom. Founded in 11th cent. Has monument to commemorate Marchand mission (leading to Fashoda incident, 1898).
Konganevik Point (kŏng-gŭnē'vĭk), NE Alaska, on Camden Bay of Beaufort Sea, 100 mi. ESE of Beechey Point; 70°2'N 145°11'W. Eskimo settlement (1939 pop. 12) here.
Köngen (kŭng'ŭn), village (pop. 4,056), N Württemberg, Germany, after 1945 in Württemberg-Baden, on the Neckar and 4.5 mi. SE of Esslingen; wine. Has excavated Roman castrum.
Kongju (kông'jōō'), Jap. *Koshu,* town (1949 pop. 21,952), S.Chungchong prov., S Korea, on Kum R. and 19 mi. NW of Taejon; commercial center in gold-mining and agr. area (rice, soybeans); lumber, charcoal.
Kongka (kông'kä) or **Gongkar** (gông'kär), Chinese *Kung-k'a* (gōōng'kä') or *Kung-k'o* (gōōng'kô'), town [Tibetan *dzong*], S Tibet, on the Brahmaputra, opposite Kyi Chu river mouth, and 35 mi. SSW of Lhasa.
Kong Karls Land (kông kärls' län), **King Charles Islands,** or **King Karl Islands,** group of 3 islands and several islets (□ 128), part of the Norwegian possession Svalbard, in Barents Sea of Arctic Ocean, E of West Spitsbergen; 78°36'–79°N 26°20'–30°20'E. Largest isl. is Kongsoya (kôngs'ûyä), Nor. *Kongsøya,* at 78°54'N 28°50'E; 30 mi. long, 2–7 mi. wide; rises to 1,050 ft.
Konglu (kông-lōō'), village, Myitkyina dist., Kachin State, Upper Burma, 33 mi. E of Putao, on pack trail to Chinese Yunnan prov.
Kongmoon, China: see SUNWUI.
Kongolo (kông-gō'lō), town (1948 pop. 2,533), Katanga prov., E Belgian Congo, on Lualaba R., on railroad, and 160 mi. WNW of Albertville; transshipment point (steamer-rail) and market for native produce (manioc, yams, palm oil, plantains); cotton ginning. Airport. Has R.C. mission and schools. Seat of vicar apostolic of N Katanga.
Kongo-san, Korea: see DIAMOND MOUNTAINS.
Kongsberg (kôngs'băr), city (pop. 7,852), Buskerud co., SE Norway, on Lagen R. and 40 mi. WSW of Oslo; rail junction; center of fluorspar-quarrying region. Silver mining (since 1624); site of Norwegian mint. Firearms mfg., lumber and wood-pulp milling, brewing; hydroelectric plant. Has mining col. founded 1757.
Kongsfjorden, Spitsbergen: see KINGS BAY.
Kongsoya, Svalbard: see KONG KARLS LAND.
Kongsvinger (kôngs'vĭngûr), city (pop. 2,086), Hedmark co., SE Norway, near Swedish border, on Glomma R. and 50 mi. ENE of Oslo; rail junction; mfg. of furniture, ski, gloves. Has fortress, built 1683, demilitarized 1905 under Treaty of Karlstad.
Kongsvoll (kôngs'vôl), village in Opdal canton, Sor-Trondelag co., central Norway, on Driva R., on railroad and 22 mi. NE of Dombas; winter-sports center. Called Hullet until visit of Fredrik IV in 1704. Formerly spelled Kongsvold.
Kongwa (kông'gwä), village, Central Prov., central Tanganyika, 60 mi. E of Dodoma, on new rail spur from Msagali (40 mi. ESE of Dodoma); 6°12'S 36°25'E; center of peanut-growing scheme (ground 1st cleared 1947). Airfield.
Koni, Belgian Congo: see MWADINGUSHA.
Konia, Turkey: see KONYA.
Konice (kô'nyĭtsĕ), Ger. *Konitz* (kō'nĭts), town (pop. 1,792), W central Moravia, Czechoslovakia, on railroad and 16 mi. W of Olomouc; barley, oats.
Koniecpol (kônyĕts'pôl), Rus. *Konetspol* or *Konets-pol'* (both: kônyĕts'pôlyŭ), town (pop. 1,784), Lodz prov., S central Poland, on Pilica R. and 22 mi. SSE of Radomsko; copper rolling.
Konieh, Turkey: see KONYA.
König, Bad, Germany: see BAD KONIG.
Königgrätz, Czechoslovakia: see HRADEC KRALOVE.
Königinhof or **Königinhof an der Elbe,** Czechoslovakia: see DVUR KRALOVE.
Königreich (kû'nĭkhrĭkh"), village (pop. 1,704), in former Prussian prov. of Hanover, NW Germany, after 1945 in Lower Saxony, 11 mi. SE of Stade; building materials.
Königsbach (kû'nĭkhsbäkh"). **1** Village (pop. 3,399), N Baden, Germany, after 1945 in Württemberg-Baden, 6 mi. WNW of Pforzheim; wine. Has fortified Gothic church. **2** Village (pop. 843), Rhenish Palatinate, W Germany, on E slope of Hardt Mts., 2.5 mi. NNE of Neustadt; sandstone quarries.
Königsberg, Czechoslovakia: see KLIMKOVICE.
Königsberg or **Königsberg in Bayern** (–bĕrk" ĭn bī'ûrn), town (pop. 1,509), Lower Franconia, N Bavaria, Germany, 15 mi. ENE of Schweinfurt; mfg. (precision instruments, textiles). Regiomontanus, 15th-cent. astronomer, b. here.
Königsberg, former East Prussia: see KALININGRAD, city, Kaliningrad oblast, RSFSR.
Königsberg, Poland: see CHOJNA.
Königsberg an der Eger, Czechoslovakia: see KYNSPERK NAD OHRI.
Königsbronn (–brôn"), village (pop. 2,061), N Württemberg, Germany, after 1945 in Württemberg-Baden, 4 mi. NNW of Heidenheim; site of ironworks since 14th-cent.
Königsbrück (–brük"), town (pop. 5,100), Saxony, E central Germany, in Upper Lusatia, 17 mi. NNE of Dresden; metalworking, porcelain mfg. Spa. Granite quarries near by.
Königsee (kû'nĭkhzā"), town (pop. 4,387), Thuringia, central Germany, at foot of Thuringian Forest, 12 mi. W of Saalfeld; mfg. (machinery, glass, china, dolls). Formerly noted for its patent medicines.
Königsfeld, Czechoslovakia: see KRALOVO POLE.
Königshof, Czechoslovakia: see KRALUV DVUR.
Königshofen (kû"nĭkhs-hō'fŭn). **1** Town (pop. 1,413), N Baden, Germany, after 1945 in Württemberg-Baden, on the Tauber and 5 mi. NNW of Mergentheim; rail junction; wine. **2** or **Königshofen im Grabfeld** (ĭm gräp'fĕlt), village (pop. 3,122), Lower Franconia, N Bavaria, Germany, on the Franconian Saale and 19 mi. NE of Bad Kissingen; brewing, lumber and flour milling. Oats, cattle. Has late-Gothic church and late-16th-cent. town hall. Chartered in 11th cent. Gypsum and sandstone in area.
Königshütte, Poland: see CHORZOW.
Königslutter or **Königslutter am Elm** (–lōō'tŭr äm ĕlm'), town (pop. 8,639), in Brunswick, NW Germany, after 1945 Lower Saxony, 8 mi. WNW of Helmstedt; mfg. of tobacco products, machinery, furniture, shoes, toys; food processing (flour and dairy products, canned goods, sugar, beer, spirits). Has Romanesque basilica with tomb of Emperor Lothair II.
Königssee (kû'nĭkhs-zā") or **Bartholomäussee** (bär"-tōlōmā'ōōs-zā") [Ger., =Lake of St. Bartholomew], lake (□ 2), Upper Bavaria, Germany, in Salzburg Alps, 10 mi. SSE of Bad Reichenhall; 5 mi. long, 1–1½ mi. wide, 617 ft. deep; alt. 1.975 ft. One of Germany's most beautiful lakes, it lies amid magnificent Alpine scenery.
Königstadl, Czechoslovakia: see MESTEC KRALOVE.
Königstein (kû'nĭkh-shtīn"). **1** Village (pop. 941), Upper Palatinate, N central Bavaria, Germany, 15 mi. NW of Amberg; brewing. **2** or **Königstein im Taunus** (ĭm tou'nōōs), town (pop. 5,452), in former Prussian prov. of Hesse-Nassau, W Germany, after 1945 in Hesse, in the Taunus, 5 mi. W of Oberursel; summer resort and winter-sports center. On near-by hill (W) are ruins of 13th-cent. fortress, blown up by French in 1796. **3** Town (pop. 5,139), Saxony, E central Germany, in Saxonian Switzerland, on Elbe R. and 7 mi. ESE of Pirna; paper milling, metal- and woodworking; summer resort. Towered over by fortress built before 1150 by kings of Bohemia. Town passed 1406 to margraves of Meissen. Used in both World Wars as general-officers' prisoner-of-war camp. Gen. Henri Giraud escaped from here in 1942.
Königstuhl (–shtōōl"), massif (1,857 ft.), N Baden, Germany, at Heidelberg (NW foot; cable railway). Observatory; tower on summit affords excellent view of Neckar valley and Rhine plain.
Königswart, Czechoslovakia: see LAZNE KYNZVART.
Königswiesen (–wē"zŭn), town (pop. 2,774), NE Upper Austria, 26 mi. ENE of Linz, N of the Danube; summer resort (alt. 1,970 ft.).
Königswinter (–vĭn'tûr), town (pop. 6,118), in former Prussian Rhine prov., W Germany, after 1945 in North Rhine-Westphalia, in the Siebengebirge, at N foot of the Drachenfels (rack-and-pinion railroad), on right bank of the Rhine (landing) and 6 mi. SW of Bonn; summer resort, tourist center.
Königs Wusterhausen or **Königswusterhausen** (–vōōs"tûrhou'zŭn), town (pop. 6,614), Brandenburg, E Germany, on Dahme R. and 17 mi. SE of Berlin; has one of Germany's largest radio-broadcasting stations. Fur farming. Hunting lodge (18th cent.) was favorite retreat of Frederick William I.
Konin (kô'nĕn), town (pop. 11,197), Poznan prov., W central Poland, on Warta R. and 60 mi. NW of Lodz; rail junction; mfg. of bricks, furniture; brewing, flour milling, tanning.

Koningshooikt (kō'nĭngzoikt), village (pop. 3,212), Antwerp prov., N Belgium, 2 mi. SE of Lierre; agr., lumbering. Formerly spelled Koningshoyckt.

Konispol (kônēspôl') or **Konispoli** (kônēspô'lē), town (1945 pop. 1,813), in southernmost Albania, on Gr. line, 30 mi. S of Argyrokastron, near Channel of Corfu.

Konitsa (kô'nĭtsů), town (pop. 2,313), Ioannina nome, Epirus, Greece, near Albanian border, 27 mi. N of Ioannina, on Aoos R.; barley, corn; olive oil; timber; livestock (dairy products, meat, hides). Tourist center. Bishopric with Byzantine churches. Also spelled Konitza.

Konitz, Czechoslovakia: see KONICE.

Konitz, Poland: see CHOJNICE.

Konitza, Greece: see KONITSA.

Koniya (kōnē'yä), town (1950 pop. 11,987) on Amami-O-shima of isl. group Amami-gunto, in Ryukyu Isls., Japan, port on SW coast of isl.; agr. center (rice, wheat); raw silk. Until 1936, called Higashi-kata.

Köniz (kû'nĭts), town (1950 pop. 20,630), Bern canton, W central Switzerland, 2 mi. SSW of Bern; chemicals, beer, cement, watches; woodworking, printing. Old castle of the Teutonic Order.

Konjic or **Konyich** (both: kô'nyĭch), town (pop. 2,507), N Herzegovina, Yugoslavia, on the Neretva, on railroad and 28 mi. SW of Sarajevo; local trade center.

Konjice or **Slovenske Konjice** (slô'vĕnskē kô'nyĭtsē), Ger. *Gonobitz* (gô'nôbĭts), village, E Slovenia, Yugoslavia, on Dravinja R., on railroad and 11 mi. NE of Celje, in brown-coal area; health resort; leather industry. Castle ruins. First mentioned in 1146. Until 1918, in Styria.

Konjuh or **Konyukh** (both: kô'nyōōkh), mountain (4,356 ft.) in Dinaric Alps, E Bosnia, Yugoslavia, 9 mi. NW of Kladanj. Drinjaca R. rises on E slope.

Konkan (kōng'kŭn), coastal plain in W Bombay, India, bet. Western Ghats (E) and Arabian Sea (W); from Daman (N) extends c.330 mi. S, through dists. of Thana, Bombay Suburban (port of Bombay just S), Kolaba, and Ratnagiri, to Goa; 30–60 mi. wide. Has outliers of Western Ghats, including Matheran (health resort) and Jawhar; drained by several mtn. streams. Fertile coast (rice, coconuts, mangoes), with fishing centers (mackerel, pomfrets) at Bassein, Murud, Ratnagiri, and Malvan; inland rises to rocky and rugged spurs. Annual rainfall, over 100 in. Portuguese dominated coastal trade in 16th and 17th cent.; numerous creeks and harbors (as at Vijayadurg) were retreats for Mahratta pirates in 18th cent.

Konka River (kôn'kŭ) or **Konskaya River** (kôn'-skīŭ), left tributary of the Dnieper, in Zaporozhe oblast, Ukrainian SSR; rises in Azov Upland SE of Pologi, flows c.125 mi. generally W, past Pologi, Orekhov, and Kamyshevakha, to Dnieper R. E of Nikopol. Bet. its lower course and the Dnieper are extensive reed marshes (*plavni*). Formed (c.1770) Rus. defense line against Crimean Tatars.

Konken, Thailand: see KHONKAEN.

Konko (kōngkō'), town (pop. 12,113), Okayama prefecture, SW Honshu, Japan, 19 mi. WSW of Okayama; commercial center in rice-growing area; textiles, floor mats.

Konkouré (kôngkōō'rā), village, W central Fr. Guinea, Fr. West Africa, on Conakry-Kankan RR and 110 mi. ENE of Conakry; banana growing.

Konkouré River, Fr. Guinea, Fr. West Africa, rises in Fouta Djallon mts. W of Mamou, flows c.160 mi. generally W, past Ouassou, to the Atlantic at Sangaréa Bay, just N of Conakry.

Konnagar (kōn'nŭgŭr), town (pop., including RISHRA, 37,432), Hooghly dist., S central West Bengal, India, on Hooghly R. and 9 mi. N of Calcutta city center; mfg. of chemicals, glass; cotton milling, jute pressing, liquor distilling. Oilseed milling at Hatirkul, in N area.

Könnern (kû'nûrn), town (pop. 6,053), in former Prussian Saxony prov., central Germany, after 1945 in Saxony-Anhalt, near the Saxonian Saale, 9 mi. S of Bernburg; malting; brickworks. Market gardening; seed nurseries.

Konnersreuth (kô'nûrsroit″), village (pop. 1,766), Upper Palatinate, NE Bavaria, Germany, in the Fichtelgebirge, 4 mi. WNW of Waldsassen; rye, oats, cattle, hogs. Chartered 1468.

Konnerudkollen, Norway: see SKOGER.

Konnur (kōn'nōōr), town (pop. 12,491), Belgaum dist., S Bombay, India, 28 mi. NE of Belgaum; markets cotton, chili, millet; wool spinning. Noted cell tombs near by. Irrigation dam 1 mi. N, on Ghatprabha R.

Kono (kō'nō) or **Katano** (kätä'nō), town (pop. 7,651), Osaka prefecture, S Honshu, Japan, 12 mi. NE of Osaka; agr. center (rice, peaches, oranges).

Kono, district, Sierra Leone: see SEFADU.

Konobeyevo-Lesnoye, Russian SFSR: see LESNOYE KONOBEYEVO.

Konochti, Mount (kŭnŏk'tī), Lake co., NW Calif., peak (4,100 ft.) on W shore of Clear L., c.80 mi. N of San Francisco.

Konolfingen (kō'nôlfĭng″ŭn), town (pop. 3,343), Bern canton, W central Switzerland, 10 mi. ESE of Bern; canned goods, biscuits, chemicals; metal-and woodworking. Consists of Konolfingen proper, Stalden, and Gysenstein.

Konongo (kōnông'gō), town, Ashanti, S central Gold Coast, on railroad and 7 mi. WNW of Juaso; gold mining; cacao, cassava, corn.

Konopiste, Czechoslovakia: see BENESOV.

Konosha (kŭnô'shŭ), town (1939 pop. over 10,000), SW Archangel oblast, Russian SFSR, 90 mi. N of Vologda; junction of Moscow-Archangel and N. Pechora railroads; sawmilling center.

Kono-shima (kō'nō-shĭmä), island (□ 7; pop. 10,780), Okayama prefecture, Japan, in Hiuchi Sea, nearly connected with S coast of Honshu, near Kasaoka; 4 mi. long, 2 mi. wide. Produces rice, rushes.

Konosu (kō'nōsōō), town (pop. 13,540), Saitama prefecture, central Honshu, Japan, 10 mi. SE of Kumagaya; rice, wheat, raw silk.

Konotop (kŏnŭtôp', Rus. kŭnŭtôp'), city (1926 pop. 33,571), W central Sumy oblast, Ukrainian SSR, 70 mi. WNW of Sumy; rail junction; metalworks, agr.-machinery plant, flour mills, breweries. Teachers col. In Second World War, held (1941–43) by Germans.

Konoura (kōnō'rä), town (pop. 6,145), Akita prefecture, N Honshu, Japan, fishing port on Sea of Japan, 12 mi. SW of Honjo; building-stone quarrying.

Konovo or **Kon'ovo** (kô'nyôvô), village (pop. 2,063), Yambol dist., E central Bulgaria, 12 mi. SW of Yambol; horse-raising center; grain. Formerly Atloolu.

Konovo or **Kon'ovo Mountains** (kô'nyôvô), W Bulgaria; bordered by upper Struma R. (N, W, and S), and Dzherman R. (SE); c.25 mi. long, c.20 mi. wide; rise to 4,877 ft. at Mt. Viden, 9 mi. ENE of Kyustendil. Crossed by highway at **Konovo Pass** (alt. 3,412 ft.), 10 mi. NE of Kyustendil, on highway to Radomir.

Konradshof, Poland: see SKAWINA.

Konskaya River, Ukrainian SSR: see KONKA RIVER.

Konskie (kô'nyŭskyē), Pol. *Końskie*, Rus. *Konsk* (kônsk), town (pop. 7,386), Kielce prov., E central Poland, on railroad and 36 mi. WSW of Radom; mfg. of agr. machinery; tanning, sawmilling. Castle ruins near by.

Konstadt, Poland: see WOLCZYN.

Konstantinograd, Ukrainian SSR: see KRASNOGRAD.

Konstantinovka (kŭnstŭntyē'nŭfkŭ). **1** Town (1926 pop. 2,400), NW Kharkov oblast, Ukrainian SSR, 12 mi. NW of Kolomak; metalworks. **2** City (1926 pop. 25,303; 1939 pop. 95,087), central Stalino Oblast, Ukrainian SSR, in the Donbas, 37 mi. N of Stalino. Major metallurgical center; iron and steel mills; ceramics, superphosphate plants, glass and zinc works.

Konstantinov Kamen or **Konstantinov Kamen'** (kä'-mĭnyŭ), northernmost height (1,480 ft.) of the Urals, Russian SFSR, in NW Siberia, rising in isolated site amidst the tundra, 25 mi. from Baidarata Bay of the Kara Sea; 68°30'N 66°20'E.

Konstantinovo (–nŭvŭ), village (1939 pop. over 500), N Moscow oblast, Russian SFSR, 17 mi. NNW of Zagorsk; flax, wheat, dairy farming.

Konstantinovski or **Konstantinovskiy** (–nŭfskē). **1** Town (1926 pop. 976), S central Moscow oblast, Russian SFSR, 7 mi. E of Podolsk; woolen milling. **2** Town (1926 pop. 7,426), central Rostov oblast, Russian SFSR, on right bank of Don R. and 40 mi. E of Shakhty; flour milling, metalworks; orchards, vineyards. Until 1941, Konstantinovskaya. **3** Town (1926 pop. 1,870), E central Yaroslavl oblast, Russian SFSR, on Volga R. and 18 mi. NW of Yaroslavl; petroleum refinery; woodworking.

Konstantinovskoye (–nŭfskŭyŭ), village (1926 pop. 2,988), SE Amur oblast, Russian SFSR, on Amur R. and 50 mi. SSE of Blagoveshchensk, in agr. area (grain, soybeans). Formerly called Konstantinovka.

Konstantinovy Lazne, Czechoslovakia: see BEZDRUZICE.

Konstantynow or **Konstantynow Lodzki** (kônstäntĭ'-nōōf wōōts'kē), Pol. *Konstantynów Łódzki*, Rus. *Konstantinov* (kŭnstŭntyē'nŭf), town (pop. 6,694), Lodz prov., central Poland, on Ner R. and 6 mi. W of Lodz city center; cloth weaving and finishing, mfg. of dyes, shawls, tiles; flour milling.

Konstanz, Germany: see CONSTANCE.

Konta (kōn'tŭ), village, Bastar dist., SE Madhya Pradesh, India, on tributary of the Godavari and 60 mi. NNW of Rajahmundry; rice, oilseeds, mangoes. Sal forests near by. Formerly spelled Konda.

Kontagora (kōntä'gōōrä'), town (pop. 3,826), Niger prov., Northern Provinces, W Nigeria, 90 mi. NW of Minna; gold mining; shea-nut processing; cassava, millet, durra. Peanut growing scheme (S).

Kontich (kōn'tĭkh), residential town (pop. 9,298), Antwerp prov., N Belgium, 5 mi. SSE of Antwerp; agr. market. Formerly spelled Contich.

Kontiolahti (kōn'tēōlä″tē, –läkh″tē), Swedish *Kontiolaks* (kôn'tyôläks″), village (commune pop. 10,119), Kuopio co., SE Finland, on lake of Saimaa system, 10 mi. NNE of Joensuu, in lumbering region. Site of large tuberculosis sanitarium.

Kontiomäki (kōn'tēōmä″kē), village in Paltamo commune (pop. 8,201), Oulu co., central Finland, near E end of L. Oulu, 14 mi. NE of Kajaani; rail junction in lumbering region.

Kontum (kôn'tûm'), town, ⊙ Kontum prov. (□ 10,-500; 1943 pop. 157,200), central Vietnam, in Annam, in Moi Plateaus, 140 mi. SSE of Hue; alt. 1,720 ft. Trading center: hides, horses, wax, sesame; coffee, tea plantations. Big-game hunting. Pop. of area is largely Bahhar, one of Moi tribes.

Kontum Plateau, central Vietnam, one of the Moi Plateaus, W of Annamese Cordillera; c.70 mi. long, c.60 mi. wide; alt. c.2,000 ft., with basaltic formations rising up to 2,500 ft. Forests (big-game area) and grassy plains. Agr.: tea and coffee. Area of European colonization. Main town: Pleiku. Also called Jarai Plateau, for one of the Moi tribes.

Konuma, Russian SFSR: see NOVO-ALEKSANDROVSK.

Konya or **Konia** (kô'nyä), province (□ 18,796; 1950 pop. 740,595), S central Turkey; ⊙ Konya. On S are Taurus Mts.; it is on edge of the great plain of Asia Minor. Bordered NE by L. Tuz, W by lakes Aksehir and Beysehir and by Sultan Mts. Largest Turkish prov., highly productive despite big salt desert. Minerals include lead, silver, and gold from Bolkar Mts.; also mercury, salt, soda, magnesium sulphate. Produces charcoal, tiles, cotton goods, carpets, mohair. Much livestock (sheep, goats, horses, mules, camels, and, especially, mohair goats); wheat, barley, rye, oats, millet; potatoes, legumes, sugar beets; raisins, figs, apricots; opium. Formerly also spelled Konieh. The area of Konya was anciently part of the countries of Pamphylia and Cilicia on coast and Pisidia, Lycaonia, and Cappadocia farther north. Later, it was part of Karamania.

Konya or **Konia,** anc. *Iconium* (īkō'nēŭm), city (1950 pop. 64,509), ⊙ Konya prov., SW central Turkey, 145 mi. S of Ankara, and linked by rail with Smyrna, at SW edge of central plain of Asia Minor; alt. 3,363 ft.; 37°50'N 32°25'E. Mfg. of carpets, leather goods, and some cotton and silk goods; market for productive agr. (wheat, barley, rye, vegetables) and livestock area (known for its mohair and wool). Has anc. mosque, old walls, and the tomb of the founder of the whirling dervishes, of which Konya is an important center. Anc. Iconium was ⊙ of Lycaonia, became an important town of Roman Galatia, and was later visited by St. Paul. In 12th cent. it became a seat of the Seljuk Turks, under whom it reached its brilliant peak in early 13th cent. as seat of the sultanate of Iconium or Rum (so-called after Rome), which played an important part in the age of the Crusades. In late 13th cent. the Seljuks of Iconium were defeated by the allied Mongols and Armenians. Konya declined, passed to Karamania and (1472) to the Ottoman Turks. Most of the Armenians of the city, which had many, were deported in First World War.

Konyaereglisi, Turkey: see EREGLI.

Konyar (kôn'yär), Hung. *Konyár*, town (pop. 3,346), Bihar co., E Hungary, 14 mi. S of Debrecen; Konyar salt lake and baths near by.

Konyich, Yugoslavia: see KONJIC.

Konyshevka (kŭnĭshĕf'kŭ), village (1926 pop. 1,414), W Kursk oblast, Russian SFSR, 20 mi. SSE of Dmitriyev-Lgovski; hemp.

Konyukh, mountain, Yugoslavia: see KONJUH.

Konyukhovo (kô'nyōōkhŭvŭ), village, NE North Kazakhstan oblast, Kazakh SSR, c.70 mi. E of Petropavlovsk, in wheat area.

Konz (kônts), village (pop. 5,638), in former Prussian Rhine Prov., W Germany, after 1945 in Rhineland-Palatinate, at confluence of Saar and Mosel rivers, 5 mi. SW of Trier, near Luxembourg line; rail junction; wine. Has remains of Roman imperial villa. Formerly spelled Conz.

Konza (kōn'zä), town, Central Prov., S central Kenya, rail junction for Magadi, 40 mi. SE of Nairobi; alt. 5,427 ft.; wheat, corn; dairy farming.

Konzhakovski Kamen or **Konshakovskiy Kamen'** (kŭnzhŭkôf'skē kä'mĭnyŭ), highest peak (5,154 ft.) in central Urals, Russian SFSR; 59°40'N.

Koochiching (kōō'chĭ-chĭng), county (□ 3,129; pop. 16,910), N Minn.; ⊙ International Falls. Agr. and resort area bounded N by Ont. and Rainy R. and drained by Big Fork and Little Fork rivers. Grain, potatoes, dairy products; peat deposits. Lumber and paper milling at International Falls. Includes much of Nett L. and Nett Lake Indian Reservation in SE. State forests are in S and central areas; part of Rainy L. is in NE, on Ont. line. Marshland throughout. Formed 1906.

Koog aan de Zaan (kōkh' än dů zän'), town (pop. 7,184), North Holland prov., W Netherlands, on Zaan R. just NNW of Zaandam, in Zaanstreek industrial area; mfg. of cacao products, biscuits, glucose, cigars, dyes, brushes, machinery; linseed oil pressing; shipbuilding.

Koolan Island (kōō'lăn), uninhabited island of Buccaneer Archipelago, off N coast of Western Australia, in Yampi Sound bet. Collier Bay and King Sound, 70 mi. N of Derby; 7 mi. long, 2 mi. wide; rises to 670 ft. Valuable iron deposits.

Koolau Range (kō'ulou'), E Oahu, T.H., mountain chain extending NW–SE, rising to 3,150 ft. near Konahuanui peak (3,105 ft.); 2 mtn. passes, NUUANU PALI and WAIMANALO PALI, cut through the range.

Koolskamp (kōl'skämp), agr. village (pop. 2,068), West Flanders prov., W Belgium, 5 mi. W of Tielt. Formerly spelled Coolscamp.

Koorawatha (koor'ùwŏ'thù), village (pop. 522), SE central New South Wales, Australia, 155 mi. WSW of Sydney; rail junction; sheep and agr. center.
Kooringa, Australia: see BURRA.
Koosharem (kōō'shâ"rùm), town (pop. 300), Sevier co., central Utah, 20 mi. SE of Richfield; alt. 6,850 ft.; agr., livestock. Koosharem Indian Reservation near by. Sevier Plateau just W.
Kooskia, village (pop. 629), Idaho co., W central Idaho, 12 mi. SE of Nezperce, at junction of Middle Fork and South Fork of Clearwater R.; agr., lumber, livestock.
Kootenai (kōō'tĭnā, kōōt'nā), county (□ 1,256; pop. 24,947), N Idaho; ⊙ Coeur d'Alene. Rolling, wooded area bordering on Wash., watered by Coeur d'Alene L. and Spokane and Coeur d'Alene rivers. Lumbering, dairying, agr. (pears, cherries, apples, wheat). Includes part of Coeur d'Alene Mts., in Coeur d'Alene Natl. Forest. Formed 1864.
Kootenai, village (pop. 199), Bonner co., N Idaho, 3 mi. NE of Sandpoint and on N shore of Pend Oreille L.; lumber.
Kootenai River (in Canada, Kootenay), Canada, Mont., and Idaho, rises in SE British Columbia, flows S into NW Mont. near Eureka, turning W near Libby, thence NW through NE Idaho to S end of Kootenay L. in British Columbia, through which it is connected with Columbia R. Length, 448 mi., of which 276 mi. are in Canada. Passes through mining region in Rocky Mts. of Mont. Libby Dam (Mont.), for power and flood control, was authorized as a unit of Columbia R. basin development plan. The Kootenai was explored 1807 by David Thompson.
Kootenay Lake (kōō'tĭnā, kōōt'nā) (□ 191), S B.C., expansion of Kootenay R., 20 mi. E of Nelson; 64 mi. long, 1–4 mi. wide. Extending 22 mi. W and SW to Nelson is the West Arm of the lake, through which it is drained by Kootenay R. At S end of lake is Duck L. (8 mi. long, 3 mi. wide).
Kootenay National Park (□ 543), SE B.C., on Alta. border, in Rocky Mts., WSW of Banff and bordering on Banff Natl. Park; established 1920. Big-game sanctuary. High peaks include Stanley Peak and Foster Peak, over 10,000 ft. high. At SW edge of park is Radium Hot Springs, resort with radioactive springs.
Kootenay River, U.S. and Canada: see KOOTENAI RIVER.
Kootwijk (kōt'vīk), village, Gelderland prov., central Netherlands, 8 mi. WSW of Apeldoorn. Has radio-telegraph transmitter, with beam to Netherlands East Indies. Sometimes spelled Kootwyk.
Koo-wee-rup, town (pop. 1,135), S Victoria, Australia, 38 mi. SE of Melbourne; rail junction in agr. area; flax, potatoes.
Kop, Turkey: see BULANIK.
Kopaganj (kō'pägünj), town (pop. 8,649), Azamgarh dist., E Uttar Pradesh, India, 24 mi. E of Azamgarh; cotton weaving, saltpeter processing; trades in rice, barley, wheat, sugar cane.
Kopaigorod or **Kopaygorod** (kŭpī'gŭrùt), town (1926 pop. 2,938), W Vinnitsa oblast, Ukrainian SSR, 27 mi. N of Mogilev-Podolski; sugar beets, wheat, fruit.
Kopais, Lake, Greece: see COPAIS, LAKE.
Kopal, Kazakh SSR: see KAPAL.
Kopaonik (kô'pä-ônĭk), mountain range, S central Serbia, Yugoslavia, extends c.40 mi. S along right bank of middle Ibar R. and into the Kosovo. Highest point (6,616 ft.) is 13 mi. SW of Brus. Large lead, zinc, silver, and pyrite deposits mined at TREPCA, at S foot.
Kopargaon (kō'pŭrgoun), town (pop. 8,753), Ahmadnagar dist., E Bombay, India, on Godavari R. and 60 mi. NNW of Ahmadnagar; trade center for sugar, millet, cotton; sugar milling, gur mfg.
Kopatkevichi (kŭpùtkyĕ'vēchē), agr. town (1926 pop. 2,616), N central Polesye oblast, Belorussian SSR, on Ptich R. and 27 mi. NW of Mozyr; linseed press, brickworks.
Kopaygorod, Ukrainian SSR: see KOPAIGOROD.
Kopbal, India: see KOPPAL.
Köpcseny, Austria: see KITTSEE.
Kopeisk or **Kopeysk** (kŭpyäsk'), city (1926 pop. 8,820; 1936 pop. estimate 65,500), E Chelyabinsk oblast, Russian SFSR, just E of Chelyabinsk; major lignite-mining center; mfg. of excavators. Known prior to Bolshevik revolution as Ugolnye Kopi [Rus.,=coal mines]; subsequently called Goskopi [Rus.,=state mines] until 1928 and Kopi [Rus.,=mines], 1928–33; became city of Kopeisk in 1933. Absorbed town of Gornyak [Rus.,=miner] (c.3 mi. NNE of Kopeisk; developed in 1930s) during Second World War.
Köpenick (kû'pünĭk), district (1939 pop. 120,446; 1946 pop. 113,851), SE Berlin, Germany, on the Spree at mouth of Dahme R., and 10 mi. SE of city center. Mfg. of electrical equipment, cameras; metalworking. After 1945 in Soviet sector. Formerly spelled Cöpenick.
Koper, Free Territory of Trieste: see CAPODISTRIA.
Kopervik (kô'pürvēk), town (pop. 1,711), Rogaland co., SW Norway, on E shore of Karmoy, 9 mi. S of Haugesund; fishing center for herring and sardines; canneries. Health resort. Many Norse relics found in graves and barrows near by.
Kopet Dagh (kōpĕt' däg'), one of the Turkmen-Khurasan ranges, in SW Turkmen SSR and in Khurasan, NE Iran, extending c.200 mi. NW-SE bet. 56° and 60°E and along USSR-Iran line; rises to c.10,000 ft. Steppe vegetation in higher reaches. Soviet summer resort of Firyuza is on N slopes; and range is crossed by Ashkhabad-Quchan highway at Gaudan and Bajgiran frontier posts. Trans-Caspian RR hugs N foot in Turkmen SSR.
Kopeysk, Russian SFSR: see KOPEISK.
Kopi. 1 Mine, Chelyabinsk oblast, Russian SFSR: see KOPEISK. **2** Rail station, Russian SSR: see ALEKSANDROVSKI, Molotov oblast.
Koping, China: see KELPIN.
Koping (chû'pĭng"), Swed. *Köping,* city (1950 pop. 13,585), Vastmanland co., central Sweden, on small Koping R., Swedish *Köpingsån,* just above its mouth on L. Malar, 19 mi. WSW of Vasteras; inland port, shipping iron and other ores from Bergslag region; rail junction. Mfg. of machinery, fertilizer; woodworking. Limestone quarries near by. Has church (1702). An old trade center, chartered as city 1474. Residence (1775–89) of the chemist K. W. Scheele.
Kopingebro (chû"pĭng-ùbrōō'), Swedish *Köpingebro,* village (pop. 570), Malmohus co., S Sweden, near the Baltic, 5 mi. ENE of Ystad; sugar refining; grain, sugar beets, potatoes; cattle.
Kopisty (kô'pĭstĭ), Ger. *Kopitz* (kō'pĭts), mining town (pop. 7,052), NW Bohemia, Czechoslovakia, in urban area of MOST LITVINOV; coal, peat.
Kopjes or **Koppies** (both: kôp'yùs), town (pop. 2,020), N Orange Free State, U. of So. Afr., on Rhenoster R. and 35 mi. NE of Kroonstad; alt. 4,661 ft.; center of irrigated-farming region.
Koplik (kô'plēk) or **Kopliku** (kô'plēkōō), town (1930 pop. 1,388), N Albania, 10 mi. NNW of Scutari, near L. Scutari.
Kopmanholmen (chûp'mänhôl"mùn), Swedish *Köpmanholmen,* village (pop. 1,717), Vasternorrland co., NE Sweden, on Gulf of Bothnia, 9 mi. SW of Ornskoldsvik; lumber and pulp mills.
Kopomá (kōpōmä'), town (pop. 808), Yucatan, SE Mexico, 28 mi. SW of Mérida; henequen.
Kopondei, Point, Indonesia: see FLORES HEAD.
Koppa (kŏ'pù), town (pop. 1,478), Kadur dist., W Mysore, India, 37 mi. NW of Chikmagalur; rice milling. Coffee, cardamom, and pepper estates in near-by hills (bamboo, sandalwood).
Koppal or **Kopbal** (both: kōp'pŭl), town (pop. 13,970), Raichur dist., SW Hyderabad state, India, 55 mi. WNW of Bellary; oilseed milling, cotton ginning. Near-by hill fort remodeled 1786 by Fr. engineers under Tipu Sultan. Sometimes Kuppal.
Koppang (kôp'päng), village (pop. 656) in Stor-Elvdal canton (pop. 4,090), Hedmark co., E Norway, in the Osterdal, on Glomma R., on railroad and 40 mi. NE of Lillehammer; lumbering, agr.
Kopparberg (kô'pärbĕr"yù), county [Swedish *län*] (□ 11,648; 1950 pop. 267,019), central Sweden; ⊙ Falun. On Norwegian border, it is almost coextensive with Dalarna prov. Undulating surface rises toward mtn. range along Norwegian border; drained by Dal R. and its tributaries. Large L. Silja, in central part of co., is surrounded by agr. and dairying region. Grangesberg is center of one of Sweden's largest iron, copper, lead, and zinc mining regions. Steel industry is important. Other industries are lumbering, sawmilling, woodworking, tanning, textile milling. Cities are Falun, Ludvika, Borlange (with Domnarvet metalworks), Avesta, Hedemora, and Sater.
Kopparberg, town (pop. 2,031), Orebro co., S central Sweden, on Hork R. and 19 mi. SSW of Ludvika; copper and zinc mining and smelting center. Has 17th-cent. church.
Koppel (kŏ'pùl), borough (pop. 1,137), Beaver co., W Pa., 3 mi. SW of Ellwood City and on Beaver R.; sandstone; railroad-car mfg.
Köppelsdorf (kû'pùlsdôrf), town (pop. 3,760), Thuringia, central Germany, in Thuringian Forest, 2 mi. SE of Sonneberg; wood- and metalworking; mfg. of industrial ceramics, electrical appliances, phonographs, china, toys.
Koppenbrügge, Germany: see COPPENBRÜGGE.
Koppera, Norway: see MERAKER.
Kopperston, mining village (pop. 1,112), Wyoming co., S W.Va., 19 mi. W of Beckley, in coal region.
Koppies, U. of So. Afr.: see KOPJES.
Kopreinitz, Yugoslavia: see KOPRIVNICA.
Köprili, Yugoslavia: see TITOV VELES.
Koprinka, Bulgaria: see DIMITROV DAM.
Koprivnica (kô'prĭvnĭtsä), Hung. *Kapronca* (kŏp'-rôntsŏ), Ger. *Kopreinitz* (kôp'rīnĭts), town (pop. 9,105), N Croatia, Yugoslavia, in the Podravina, 25 mi. ESE of Varazdin, at NW foot of Bilo Gora, in Slavonia. Chemical center; mfg. of superphosphates and sulphuric acid. Petroleum deposits, lignite mine near by. First mentioned in 13th cent.; fortress during Turkish invasions (16th-17th cent.).
Koprivnice (kô'pŭrzhĭvnyĭtsĕ), Czech *Kopřivnice,* Ger. *Nesseldorf* (nĕ'sùldôrf), town (pop. 5,215), S central Silesia, Czechoslovakia, on railroad and 18 mi. SSW of Ostrava; major engineering works produce rolling stock, busses, trucks, automobiles.
Koprivshtitsa (kôprĕf'shtĕtsä), city (pop. 2,385), Plovdiv dist., W central Bulgaria, in Sredna Gora, on Topolnitsa R. and 13 mi. NE of Panagyurishte. Health resort; livestock center; dairying, meat preserving; carpet mfg. Has mus. and old bldgs. (Bulg. Renaissance). Important commercial center (cattle exports to Turkey and Egypt) under Turkish rule (15th–19th cent.). Declined following Bulg. uprising in 1876.
Kopro (kô'prù), village, S Yakut Autonomous SSR, Russian SFSR, on Chara R. (left affluent of Olekma R.) and 90 mi. SSW of Olekminsk; lumbering.
Köprülü, Yugoslavia: see TITOV VELES.
Kopru River (kû'prü), Turkish *Köprü,* anc. *Eurymedon,* S Turkey, rises ESE of Egridir, flows 97 mi. S to Mediterranean Sea 25 mi. E of Antalya (Adalia). Near its mouth, here in anc. Pamphylia, Cimon defeated (c.467 B.C.) the Persians.
Köpsen, Germany: see RÖSSULN.
Kopstal (kôps'täl), village (pop. 825), SW Luxembourg, 4 mi NNW of Luxembourg city; chalk quarrying; agr. (potatoes, wheat, oats, apples).
Koptelovo (kŭptyĕ'lùvŭ), village (1939 pop. over 500), S central Sverdlovsk oblast, Russian SFSR, on Rezh R. and 12 mi. SSE of Alapayevsk; lumbering; livestock.
Koptevo (kôptyĕ'vŭ), town (1949 pop. over 500), central Ivanovo oblast, Russian SFSR, near Teikovo.
Koptsevichi (kŭptsyĕ'vēchē), village (1926 pop. 1,056), W central Polesye oblast, Belorussian SSR, 45 mi. WNW of Mozyr; plywood mill.
Kopychintsy (kŭpĭchĕn'tsē), Pol. *Kopyczyńce* (kôpĭchĭn'yùtsĕ), city (1931 pop. 8,609), E Ternopol oblast, Ukrainian SSR, on left tributary of the Dniester and 8 mi. NE of Chortkov, in deciduous woodland; rail junction; agr.-trading center; starch mfg., flour milling, brickworking, lumbering. Has old castle. Passed from Poland to Austria (1772); reverted to Poland (1919); ceded to USSR in 1945.
Kopyczynce, Ukrainian SSR: see KOPYCHINTSY.
Kopyl or **Kopyl'** (kŭpĭl'), town (1926 pop. 3,924), NW Bobruisk oblast, Belorussian SSR, 22 mi. WNW of Slutsk; flour mill, brickworks.
Kopys or **Kopys'** (kô'pĭs), town (1926 pop. 3,577), S Vitebsk oblast, Belorussian SSR, on Dnieper R. and 15 mi. SSW of Orsha; cement.
Kor, river, Iran: see KUR RIVER.
Kora, India: see FATEHPUR, town, Fatehpur dist.
Korab (kô'räp), mountain in the Pindus system, on Yugoslav-Albanian border, bet. Radika R. and the Black Drin. Its peak (9,066 ft.), highest in Albania and 2d-highest in Yugoslavia, is 20 mi. W of Gostivar, Yugoslavia.
Korablino (kŭräb'lyĭnŭ), village (1926 pop. 868), central Ryazan oblast, Russian SFSR, 14 mi. N of Ryazhsk; wheat, tobacco.
Koraka, Cape (kôrä'kä), W Turkey, on Aegean Sea, 40 mi. SW of Smyrna; 38°5'N 26°37'E.
Koralpe (kōr'älpù), small range of Noric Alps on Styria-Carinthia border, Austria, extending 20 mi. N from Yugoslav line E of Lavant R; rises to 7,034 ft. in the Grosser Speikkogel. Continued N by Packalpe. Lignite mined at NE foot.
Korana River (kô'ränä), NW Croatia, Yugoslavia, rises in Plitvice Lakes, flows c.70 mi. N, past Slunj, to Kupa R. just NE of Karlovac. Receives Mreznica R. Hydroelectric plant near Karlovac.
Korangal, India: see KODANGAL.
Korangamite, Lake, Australia: see CORANGAMITE, LAKE.
Koraput (kō'rŭpōōt), district (□ 9,875; pop. 1,127,-862), SW Orissa, India; ⊙ Koraput. Bordered E by Madras, W by Madhya Pradesh; crossed (NE–SW) by Eastern Ghats. Plateaux and hill ranges (2–3,000 ft. average; several peaks over 4,000 ft.); thickly forested (sal, teak, bamboo). Rice is chief crop; some sugar cane and oilseeds grown. Trade centers: Jeypore, Gunupur. Area under Chola kings in 10th–11th cent. Formerly part of Vizagapatam dist., Madras; in 1936, transferred to newly-created Orissa prov. and inc. as separate dist.
Koraput, village, ⊙ Koraput dist., SW Orissa, India, in Eastern Ghats, 11 mi. ESE of Jeypore; rice, timber. Aluminum deposits near by (N).
Korat, Thailand: see NAKHON RATCHASIMA.
Korata (kō'rätä), Ital. *Quorata,* village, Begemdir prov., NW Ethiopia, on SE shore of L. Tana, 40 mi. WSW of Debra Tabor, in agr. region (coffee, legumes, citrus fruit); trade center. Seat of Jesuit mission in 17th cent. Also spelled Karata.
Koratagere (kō'rŭtŭgĭrē), town (pop. 2,979), Tumkur dist., E Mysore, India, 15 mi. NE of Tumkur; oilseeds, millet, rice; biri mfg., goldsmithing. Annual temple-festival market. Granite and corundum quarrying in near-by hills (sandalwood, lac).
Koratla (kō'rŭtlŭ), town (pop. 8,161), Karimnagar dist., NE central Hyderabad state, India, 13 mi. W of Jagtial; hand-made paper (bamboo forests).
Korat Plateau or **Khorat Plateau** (both: kō'rät'), saucer-shaped tableland of E Thailand, bounded by Mekong R. (Laos line; N and E), Petchabun and Dong Phaya Yen ranges (W), San Kamphaeng and Dangrek ranges (S); 250 mi. in diameter; mean alt. 600 ft., tilting toward SE. Drained by Mun, Chi, and Phao rivers, it has impermeable soils flooded during rainy season (Apr.–Nov.) and waterless during dry season. Agr. (rice, corn, cotton, hemp, peanuts); sericulture; cattle, horse, and hog raising. Served by railroad from Bangkok. The largest centers are Nakhon Ratchasima (Korat; SW), Udon (N), and Ubon (SE).

Korb (kôrp), village (pop. 3,302), N Württemberg, Germany, after 1945 in Württemberg-Baden, 2 mi. E of Waiblingen; wine.
Korba, India: see CHAMPA.
Korba (kôrbä'), village, Grombalia dist., NE Tunisia, on E shore of Cape Bon Peninsula, 40 mi. ESE of Tunis; olives, tobacco.
Korbach or **Corbach** (both: kôr'bäkh), town (pop. 10,402), in former Prussian prov. of Hesse-Nassau, W Germany, after 1945 in Hesse, 26 mi. W of Kassel; rail junction; mfg. (tires, metal furniture). Has 14th–15th-cent. church. Until 1929 in former Waldeck principality. Since 1942, ⊙ newly formed district [Ger. *Kreis*] of Waldeck.
Korbetta (kôrbĕ'tä), Ital. *Corbetta*, village (pop. 560), Tigre prov., N Ethiopia, 18 mi. NNE of Quoram, in agr. region (cereals, coffee, cotton); salt market.
Korbous (kôrbōōs'), village, Grombalia dist., NE Tunisia, on E shore of Gulf of Tunis, opposite Carthage, 21 mi. E of Tunis; bathing resort. Olive groves. Important stone quarries near by. Near hot springs are ruins of Roman bathhouses and modern hotels.
Korbu, Gunong (gōōnōōng' kōr'bōō), highest peak (7,160 ft.) of central Malayan range, Malaya, in E central Perak, 15 mi. NE of Ipoh.
Korça or **Korçë**, Albania: see KORITSA.
Korcheva (kŭrchĭvä'), former city (1926 pop. 1,976) of Kalinin oblast, Russian SFSR, on Volga R. and 40 mi. E of Kalinin. Pop. evacuated (1936–37) to KONAKOVO and city flooded by filling of VOLGA RESERVOIR.
Korcula Island (kôr'chōōlä), Serbo-Croatian *Korčula*, Ital. *Curzola* (kōōr'tsōlä), anc. *Corcyra Molaina*, Dalmatian island (□ 107) in Adriatic Sea, S Croatia, Yugoslavia; c.30 mi. long E–W, c.5 mi. wide; separated from Hvar Isl. (N) by Korcula Channel, Serbo-Croatian *Korčulski Kanal*. Marble quarries. Sometimes spelled Korchula. Chief village, Korcula (pop. 2,012), is on E shore, 50 mi. SSE of Split; seaside resort; wine trade; shipbuilding. Village has old walls and towers, cathedral believed to date from 12th cent., Venetian loggia, fortress, Dominican church and convent. Birthplace of Marco Polo. Contested in 13th-cent. Venetian-Genoese wars; declined in late-16th cent. Other villages: Blato, Velaluka.
Kordestan, Iran: see KURDISTAN.
Kordevan Dag (kôrdĕvän' dä), Turkish *Kordevan Dağ*, peak (10,000 ft.), NE Turkey, 23 mi. ESE of Artvin.
Kord Kuy, Iran: see KURD KUI.
Kordofan (kōrdōfăn'), province (□ 146,930; 1948 pop. estimate 1,568,704), central Anglo-Egyptian Sudan; ⊙ El Obeid. Undulating plateau (c.2,000 ft. high) with several isolated ranges rising to 4,000 ft. Vegetation ranges from savanna in S to steppe and scrub grass in N. Gum arabic (principal world source) and livestock are main resources. Some agr. (watermelons, corn, cotton, durra, oilseeds). Main centers are El Obeid and Nahud.
Kordun (kôr'dōōn), region in NW Croatia, Yugoslavia, bet. Slovenia (NW) and Bosnia (SE) borders. Devastated in Second World War. Chief center, VOJNIC.
Korea (kôrē'ù, kù–), Korean *Choson* or *Tae Han*, Jap. *Chosen* or *Tyosen*, peninsular country (□ 85,228; 1944 pop. 25,900,142, including offshore isls.; 1946 census of S Korea, only, showed pop. increase of 22% over 1944), E Asia, bounded N by Yalu and Tumen rivers (forming borders of Manchuria and Rus. Maritime Prov.), E by Sea of Japan, W by Korea Bay and Yellow Sea, S by Korea Strait; traditional ⊙ SEOUL; principal port, PUSAN. The Korean peninsula is c.480 mi. N–S, c.200 mi. E–W with deeply indented E and W coasts and a 5,000-mi. coast line. Relatively few good harbors are on the E coast, but there are many on W and S coasts. The largest of c.3,400 offshore isls. is CHEJU ISLAND; most of the isls. are rocky and uninhabited. Interior of the peninsula is largely mountainous, with principal mtn. range extending S from N border along E coast, forming backbone of peninsula and rising to 8,337 ft. in Mt. Kwanmo, highest peak of Korea. Forming part of the chain are the Diamond Mts., known for their scenic beauty. There are no large rivers or plains on E slopes of coastal range, while W side has fertile lowlands watered by large and navigable rivers (Taedong, Han, Kum, Somjin). The largest rivers, the Yalu and Tumen, are on the frontier; the largest in Korea proper is the Naktong in the S. There are many rivers with a short, swift course, particularly in N Korea where there are several hydroelectric plants. There are no lakes of any size. Mean annual temp. is 38°F. in N, 50°F. in central area, and 57°F. in S. The annual rainfall ranges from 37 to 53 in.; there are frequent floods. Despite favorable conditions for timber growth, Korea has very few virgin forests. Her valuable timber resources include pine, fir, alder, spruce, oak, birch, larch, maple, cypress, and bamboo. Flowering shrubs such as azalea, spirea, and syringa flourish on hillsides. Among the fauna are boars, deer, wolves, weasels, tigers, and leopards; birds include magpies, kites, herons, cranes, orioles, larks, and pheasants. There are few venomous snakes and numerous species of butterflies. Despite the comparatively limited farming area, the majority of Koreans are engaged in agr., particularly in S Korea. There are small but numerous rice paddies, many of them terraced on mtn. slopes. Other crops are barley, millet, rye, corn, soybeans, tobacco, fruit, and ginseng. Cotton (introduced in 1906 by the Japanese) is the most important of the fibrous plants; others of commercial value are hemp and ramie. Livestock (raised mostly in N) includes draft and dairy cattle, horses (a small native breed), hogs, sheep, goats, and rabbits. There is poultry farming and dairying on a small scale. The production of raw silk is widespread, but concentrated largely in the S, where there are several silk-reeling plants. With her extensive coast line, Korea has abundant fishing grounds. A branch of the Japan Current passing the E coast brings such warm-water fish as sardines and mackerel; the Okhotsk Current from the N brings herring and codfish. Other important marine products are edible seaweed of many varieties and shell fish. Principal mineral resources are gold, iron, tungsten, and coal. Other minerals occurring in smaller quantities are copper, silver, molybdenum, graphite, magnesite ore, zinc, and bauxite. Korea's heavy industry is largely centered in the N where there are chemical plants, steel foundries, and textile mills. There is some industrial activity also in the predominantly agr. S, at the major centers of Seoul and Pusan. Korea has long been known for its artisan industries: lacquer ware, metalwork, pottery, paper, textiles. Koreans belong to the Mongolian race and are therefore related to the Chinese and Japanese. Little is known about their language which is not clearly related to any other. The religion of most Koreans is a confused mixture of Shamanism, Buddhism, and Confucianism. The Christians who form a minority belong mostly to the upper classes. Buddhism and Confucianism were introduced in 4th cent.; Christianity, 1st preached by Korean scholars in 17th cent., was strengthened in 1780s by arrival of Fr. priests who were subsequently persecuted. After the 1st Christian mission was established in 1885, several colleges were founded by foreign Christian groups. Shintoism introduced during Jap. occupation did not gain many converts. Korea is divided into 14 provinces: NORTH HAMGYONG, SOUTH HAMGYONG, NORTH PYONGAN, SOUTH PYONGAN, HWANGHAE, KANGWON, KYONGGI, NORTH CHUNGCHONG, SOUTH CHUNGCHONG, NORTH KYONGSANG, SOUTH KYONGSANG, NORTH CHOLLA, SOUTH CHOLLA, and Cheju (comprising Cheju Isl., which until 1946 was included in S. Cholla prov.). Major centers in N Korea are PYONGYANG, HAMHUNG, CHONGJIN, SINUIJU, HAEJU, and the port cities of CHINNAMPO and WONSAN; centers in the S are Seoul, TAEJON, TAEGU, CHONJU, KWANGJU, CHONGJU, and the port cities of Pusan, CHEMULPO, MOKPO, and KUNSAN. There are naval bases at NAJIN (N) and CHINHAE (S). The mythical founder of the Korean state was Dankoon (Tangoon) a leader of nomadic tribes in N Korea in 24th cent. B.C. In 1122 B.C., the Chinese refugee scholar, Ki-tze (Kija), founded a colony at Pyongyang. Subsequently 3 kingdoms (Silla, Koguryu, and Pakche) were established; in the 7th cent. A.D., Silla with China's help absorbed the other 2 kingdoms. Silla decayed and in the 10th cent. the new kingdom of Koryu was established. Korea was occupied (1231–60) by Mongol forces. Succeeding the Koryu dynasty was the Yi dynasty, founded in 1392 with ⊙ at Seoul. In 1592 the Jap. military dictator Hideyoshi invaded Korea in his campaign to conquer China but was turned back at Pyongyang in 1596 by combined Chinese and Korean forces. A subsequent Jap. attempt to conquer Korea was thwarted largely by the use of iron-clad "turtle ships" which destroyed the Jap. fleet. Early in the 17th cent., Korea became a vassal state of China, and thereafter was known as the Hermit Kingdom because of her policy of strict isolation from the rest of the world (except China). The barrier to foreign influence was maintained until 1876 when Japan forced a trade treaty with Korea. Unsuccessful efforts had been made by the U.S. in 1866, 1871, and 1879 to obtain trade agreements; finally in 1882 a U.S.-Korean treaty was signed, opening the way for European countries. After the victory won in Sino-Jap. War (1894–95) fought on the Korean peninsula, Japan forced China to relinquish her control over Korea. N Korea was the battleground of Russo-Jap. War (1904–5); with Jap. victory, Korea became a protectorate which was annexed 1910. During the Second World War, Korea was promised independence "in due course" by the U.S., Great Britain, and China at the Cairo conference (1943). At the end of the war, Korea was occupied by Russia and the U.S., each governing roughly half of the peninsula (divided by the 38th parallel). Cooperation bet. the 2 zones proved impossible and in 1948 the division was formalized by the establishment of 2 regimes, the Republic of Korea in the southern zone, with ⊙ at Seoul; and the People's Republic of Korea in the northern zone, with ⊙ at Pyongyang. By mid-1949 all Russian and U.S. troops were withdrawn, but relations bet. the 2 parts of Korea were strained. On June 25, 1950, the North Korean army launched a surprise attack on South Korea. The United Nations Security Council (from which the USSR was voluntarily absent) declared North Korea an aggressor and directed that counter measures be taken. Surprise and superior forces carried the North Koreans swiftly down the peninsula until in Aug. the South Koreans and the newly-arrived U.N. forces (almost entirely U.S. troops from near-by Japan) stopped the drive, holding a perimeter defense 50 mi. from the port of Pusan. A counter-attacking drive, featured by a sea-borne invasion (Sept. 15) of Inchon, far behind the North Korean lines, carried the U.N. forces to the Manchurian border by early Nov. However, Chinese forces now entered the field for North Korea, and the U.N. forces were driven back far below the 38th parallel. The U.N. retreat continued into 1951, but again the Northern forces were stopped, and by early Feb., 1951, a U.N. counterattack had been mounted. Seoul was once more retaken by U.N. forces. Truce talks, begun in July, 1951, at Kaesong, were continued in the fall at near-by-Panmunjom. Whatever the outcome of the struggle on world political grounds, the real losers in the struggle were the Korean people, who suffered severe hardship and loss of life, and whose entire land, become a battlefield, suffered enormous devastation.
Korea (kōr'yä), former princely state (□ 1,647; pop. 126,874), one of Chhattisgarh States, India; ⊙ was Baikunthpur. Since 1948, inc. into Surguja dist. of Madhya Pradesh.
Korea Bay or **West Korea Bay** (kôrē'ù, kù–), Chinese *Hsi-ch'ao-hsien Wan* (shē'chou'shyĕn' wän'), Korean *Sojoson-man* (sō'jō'sŭn' män'), Jap. *Nishi-chosen-wan* (nēshē'-chō'sĕn'-wän'), inlet of Yellow Sea, bet. Liaotung peninsula of Manchuria (W) and NW Korea (E); receives Yalu R. Its main ports are Antung with its outer port of Tatungkow, and Chinnampo.
Korean Archipelago, collective name sometimes given to numerous isl. groups and isls. off SW coast of Korea, in Cheju Strait and Yellow Sea.
Korea Strait, Jap. *Chosen-kaikyo*, channel connecting Sea of Japan (NE) and East China Sea (S), bet. S coast of Korea (NW) and SW Japan (SE); c.110 mi. wide. The large isl. Tsushima divides strait into 2 sections, the E channel being TSUSHIMA STRAIT. The name Korea Strait sometimes indicates only the W channel (c.60 mi. wide).
Koregaon (kōrā'goun), village (pop. 5,717), Satara North dist., central Bombay, India, 12 mi. E of Satara; agr. market; peanut milling.
Koreiz (kŭrăēs'), town (1939 pop. over 500), S Crimea, Russian SFSR, Black Sea beach resort adjoining (W) Gaspra, 5 mi. SW of Yalta; winegrowing. At former Yusupov estate, now a sanatorium, Stalin lived during Yalta Conference, 1945.
Korelichi (kô'rĭl'ēchē), Pol. *Korelicze* (kôrĕlyē'tsĕ), village (1939 pop. over 500), N central Baranovichi oblast, Belorussian SSR, 13 mi. E of Novogrudok; lumbering; rye, oats, potatoes.
Korenevo (kô'rĭnyĭvŭ), town (1948 pop. over 2,000), W Kursk oblast, Russian SFSR, 15 mi. SE of Rylsk; flour-milling center.
Korenica, Yugoslavia: see TITOVA KORENICA.
Korenovskaya (kŭryĭnôf'skīŭ), village (1926 pop. 15,555), central Krasnodar Territory, Russian SFSR, on railroad and 38 mi. NNE of Krasnodar; agr. center in sugar-beet area; sugar and flour milling, sunflower-oil extraction.
Koren Pass, Austria and Yugoslavia: see WURZEN PASS.
Korets (kŭrĕts'), Pol. *Korzec* (kô'zhĕts), city (1931 pop. 3,956), E Rovno oblast, Ukrainian SSR, 38 mi. E of Rovno; cement mfg., sugar refining, flour milling, tanning; truck, fruitgrowing, beekeeping. Kaolin deposits near by. Flourished in 18th cent. as textile- and porcelain-mfg. center. Passed from Poland to Russia in 1793; reverted to Poland in 1921; ceded to USSR in 1945.
Korf or **Korff** (kôrf), town (1949 pop. over 500), NE Koryak Natl. Okrug, Kamchatka oblast, Khabarovsk Territory, Russian SFSR, 220 mi. NE of Palana and 10 mi. SW of Tilichiki, on NW shore of Korf Bay of Bering Sea; 60°20'N 165°50'E; lignite mining, fish canning.
Korgen (kôr'gùn), village (pop. 241; canton pop. 1,896), Nordland co., N central Norway, on Ros R. and 19 mi. SSW of Mo; lead, zinc mining.
Korhogo (kôrhō'gō), town (pop. c.5,700), N Ivory Coast, Fr. West Africa, road junction 125 mi. NNW of Bouaké, 300 mi. NNW of Abidjan; agr. center (rice, millet, cotton, sisal, kapok; beeswax, honey; sheep, goats). Cotton gin; animal husbandry; serum laboratory; R.C. mission.
Kori, Formosa: see HOWLI.
Kori (kō'rē), town (pop. 5,341), Fukushima prefecture, N Honshu, Japan, 7 mi. NNE of Fukushima; rice, raw silk.
Koribundu (kōrēbōōn'dōō), town (pop. 1,055), South-Western Prov., S central Sierra Leone, 17 mi. SSE of Bo; road center; palm oil and kernels, cacao, coffee.
Kori Creek, India: see LAKHPAT.

Korinthia, Greece: see Argolis and Corinthia.

Korinthos, Greece: see Corinth.

Köris, Mount (kû'rĭsh), Hung. *Kőrishegy* or *Kőröshegy,* highest point (2,339 ft.) in Bakony Mountains, NW central Hungary; heavily forested.

Koritnik (kô'rĭtnĭk), peak (7,854 ft.) in Sar Mts., on Yugoslav-Albania border, 13 mi. SW of Prizren, Yugoslavia.

Koritsa (kŭrĭt'sŭ), Albanian *Korçë* (kôr'chŭ) or *Korça* (kôr'chä), Ital. *Coriza* (kōrē'tsä), city (1945 pop. 24,035), SE Albania, 70 mi. SE of Tirana, at foot of Morava ridge; commercial and agr. center in fertile plain (grain, sugar beets); flour milling, dairying, distilling, brewing. Knitwear and cigarette mfg. Airport. Orthodox religious center of Albania, it also has large 15th-cent. mosque, modern govt. buildings. First mentioned 1280; destroyed 1440 by Turks. Developed again after 16th cent. Held (1912–13) by Greeks during Balkan Wars and (1916–20) by French during First World War.

Koriyama (kō'rēyämŭ). **1** City (1940 pop. 57,402; 1947 pop. 64,741), Fukushima prefecture, central Honshu, Japan, on Abukuma R. and 25 mi. SSW of Fukushima, in rice-growing area; mfg. (yarn, textiles, chemicals); building-stone quarrying. **2** Town (pop. 23,627), Nara prefecture, S Honshu, Japan, 3 mi. SW of Nara; goldfish-breeding center; knit goods.

Kork (kôrk), village (pop. 1,708), S Baden, Germany, 2 mi. E of Kehl; mfg. of chemicals.

Korkeakoski (kŏr'kääkōs"kē), village in Juupajoki commune (pop. 3,832), Häme co., SW Finland, 30 mi. NE of Tampere; shoe mfg.

Korkino (kôr'kēnŭ), city (1939 pop. over 2,000), E Chelyabinsk oblast, Russian SFSR, in E foothills of the S Urals, 17 mi. S of Chelyabinsk; rail spur terminus; lignite-mining center; light mfg. Became city in 1942.

Korkuk, Iraq: see Kirkuk, city.

Korkuteli (kôrkōō'tĕlē), village (pop. 4,000), Antalya prov., SW Turkey, on railroad and 30 mi. NNW of Antalya; wheat, barley. Sometimes spelled Korkudeli. Formerly Istanos.

Körlin, Poland: see Karlino.

Korlino, Poland: see Karlino.

Korlyaki (kŭrlyä'kē), village (1939 pop. under 500), SW Kirov oblast, Russian SFSR, 15 mi. NW of Sanchursk; flax, wheat.

Korma (kŭrmä'), town (1948 pop. over 2,000), N Gomel oblast, Belorussian SSR, near Sozh R., 50 mi. N of Gomel; food products; chalk quarries.

Kormakiti, Cape (kôrmäkē'tē), anc. *Crommyon,* N promontory of Cyprus, at NE gate of Morphou Bay, 30 mi. NW of Nicosia; lighthouse.

Kormantyn, Gold Coast: see Saltpond.

Körmend (kûr'mĕnd), town (pop. 7,472), Vas co., W Hungary, on Raba R. and 15 mi. S of Szombathely; rail center; flour mills, sawmills, brickworks. Battle against Turks, 1664.

Kormilovka (kŭrmē'lŭfkŭ), village (1948 pop. over 2,000), SE Omsk oblast, Russian SFSR, on Trans-Siberian RR, on Om R and 25 mi. E of Omsk; metalworking, flour milling.

Körmöcbanya, Czechoslovakia: see Kremnica.

Korna, Iraq: see Qurna, Al.

Kornat Island (kôr'nät), Ital. *Incoronata* (ēnkôrônä'tä), Dalmatian island in Adriatic Sea, W Croatia, Yugoslavia; 15 mi. long, up to 1.5 mi. wide; northernmost point 12 mi. WSW of Biograd. Venetian ruins, bathing beaches.

Kornburg (kôrn'bŏŏrk), village (pop. 870), Middle Franconia, W central Bavaria, Germany, 4 mi. ENE of Schwabach; rye hops, cattle, hogs.

Kornelimünster (kôrnā'lēmün'stŭr), village (pop. 5,635), in former Prussian Rhine Prov., W Germany, after 1945 in North Rhine-Westphalia, 5 mi. SE of Aachen. Has late-Gothic bldgs. of former abbey. Formerly also spelled Cornelimünster.

Korneshty (kŭrnyĕsh'tē), Rum. *Cornești* (kôrnĕsht'), village (1941 pop. 3,256), W Moldavian SSR, on railroad and 27 mi. S of Beltsy; corn, wheat; vineyards, orchards.

Kornet es Saouda, Lebanon: see Qurnet es Sauda.

Korneuburg (kôr"noi'bŏŏrk), town (pop. 7,558), E Lower Austria, on the Danube and 7 mi. N of Vienna; oil refinery; shipbuilding, dry docks.

Kornevo (kôr'nyĭvŭ), town (1939 pop. 5,800), W Kaliningrad oblast, Russian SFSR, on railroad and 20 mi. SSW of Kaliningrad, on Pol. line; resort; dairying, flour milling; mfg. (bricks, soap). Founded 1313. Until 1945, in East Prussia and called Zinten (tsĭn'tŭn).

Korneyevka (kŭrnyā'ŭfkŭ), village (1926 pop. 2,623), E Saratov oblast, Russian SFSR, 20 mi. S of Pugachev; wheat, cattle, sheep.

Kornik (kŏŏr'nēk), Pol. *Kórnik,* Ger. *Kurnik* (kŏŏr'nēk), town (1946 pop. 3,785), Poznan prov., W Poland, 13 mi. SSE of Poznan; flour milling, cider making, sawmilling. Castle with art treasures and noted library.

Kornin (kôr'nyĭn), town (1926 pop. 3,254), SE Zhitomir oblast, Ukrainian SSR, 38 mi. ESE of Zhitomir; sugar refining.

Kornok, Kôrnok, or **Qôrnok** (all: kŏr'nôk), settlement (pop. 143), Godthaab dist., SW Greenland, on NE shore of Bjorne Isl. (byôr'nŭ), Dan. *Bjørne* (17 mi. long, 4 mi. wide), in Godthaab Fjord, 30 mi. NE of Godthaab; 64°31'N 51°5'W; at foot of mtn. rising steeply to 4,116 ft. Fishing; meteorological and radio stations.

Kornoukhovo (kŭrnŭōō'khŭvŭ), village (1939 pop. over 500), W central Tatar Autonomous SSR, Russian SFSR, 33 mi. SE of Kazan; distilling; grain.

Kornsjo (kŏrn'shû), Nor. *Kornsjø,* village (pop. 213) in Idd canton (pop. 5,642), Ostfold co., SE Norway, frontier station on Swedish border, opposite Mon, 17 mi. SE of Halden.

Korntal (kôrn'täl), NW residential suburb (pop. 5,717) of Stuttgart, Germany.

Kornwestheim (kôrn"vĕst'hīm), town (pop. 15,686), N Württemberg, Germany, after 1945 in Württemberg-Baden, 2 mi. S of Ludwigsburg; rail junction; shoe-mfg. center; foundry; also mfg. of machinery. Chartered 1931.

Környe (kûr'nyĕ), town (pop. 2,819), Komarom-Esztergom co., N Hungary, 34 mi. W of Budapest; wheat, potatoes, horses. Ruins of Roman settlement near by.

Koro (kô'rō), volcanic island (□ 40; pop. 1,740), Fiji, SW Pacific, c.30 mi. S of Vanua Levu; 11 mi. long, 5 mi. wide. Densely wooded range rises to 1,850 ft. Copra, bananas.

Korobkovo, Russian SFSR: see Gubkin.

Korocha (kŭrô'chŭ), city (1926 pop. 14,139), SE central Kursk oblast, Russian SFSR, 30 mi. NE of Belgorod, in fruit area; fruit canning, flour milling, sunflower-oil extraction. Chartered 1638.

Koroglu Mountains (kûr'ōlōō"), Turkish *Köroğlu,* N central Turkey, extend 230 mi. W from Osmancik with Yenice and Devrez rivers to N and the Sakarya, Kirmir, and Kizil Irmak to S; rise to 7,802 ft. Towns of Nallihan, Beypazari, Kizilcahamam, Cankiri, and Iskilip on S slope. Copper in central area.

Korogwe (kōrō'gwā), town (pop. c.2,000), NE Tanganyika, on Pangani R., on railroad, and 45 mi. WSW of Tanga, at S foot of Usambara Mts.; center of extensive sisal-growing dist. A busy caravan center until mid-19th cent.

Koroit (kŭroit'), municipality (pop. 1,436), SW Victoria, Australia, 145 mi. WSW of Melbourne, near coast; rail junction; commercial center for livestock area; dairy plants.

Korolevo (kŭrŭlyô'vŭ), Czech *Královo nad Tisou,* Hung. *Királyháza,* village (1941 pop. 5,191), S Transcarpathian Oblast, Ukrainian SSR, on Tissa R. and 9 mi. SW of Khust; rail junction near Rum. border.

Koromo (kōrō'mō), town (pop. 30,564), Aichi prefecture, central Honshu, Japan, 15 mi. E of Nagoya; collection center for cotton and lacquer; textiles, glass.

Koronadal (kō"rōnädhäl'), village (1939 pop. 163; 1948 municipality pop. 53,563), Cotabato prov., S Mindanao, Philippines, 16 mi. WNW of Buayan, and NW of head of Sarangani Bay. In 1939 the Koronadal Valley was scene of resettlement project. Rice, coconuts.

Korone or **Koroni** (both: kôrô'nē), anc. *Asine* (ă'-sĭnē), town (pop. 2,270), Messenia nome, SW Peloponnesus, Greece, port on Gulf of Messenia, 17 mi. SSW of Kalamata. Developed (c.1300) as Venetian supply port of Coron, captured (c.1500) by Turks. Has ruins of Venetian castle. Anc. Corone was 10 mi. N, at site of modern village of Petalidhion or Petalidi (pop. 1,639)

Korone, Gulf of, Greece: see Messenia, Gulf of.

Koroneia, Lake, or **Lake Koronia** (both: kôrô'nēŭ), Lat. *Coronea,* lake (□ 22), in Greek Macedonia, at base of Chalcidice peninsula, 7 mi. ENE of Salonika; 8 mi. long, 3 mi. wide. Also called Lankada or Langadha.

Koronin-kaikyo, Russian SFSR: see Golovnin Strait.

Koronis, Lake (kŭrō'nĭs), Stearns and Meeker counties, SE central Minn., just S of Paynesville, 21 mi. NE of Willmar; 4 mi. long, 3 mi. wide. Boating and fishing resorts. Sometimes known as Cedar L. Fed and drained by North Fork Crow R.

Koronowo (kôrônô'vô), Ger. *Krone* or *Krone an der Brahe* (krō'nŭ än dĕr brä'ŭ), town (pop. 4,724), Bydgoszcz prov., N central Poland, on Brda R., 13 mi. NNW of Bydgoszcz; mfg. of bricks, ceramic products, furniture, mattresses; distilling, flour milling, sawmilling. Ger. name also spelled Crone or Crone an der Brahe.

Korop (kŏrôp'), town (1926 pop. 6,481), E Chernigov oblast, Ukrainian SSR, near Desna R., 27 mi. NNE of Bakhmach; hemp and food processing.

Koropets (kŭrŭpyĕts'), Pol. *Koropiec* (kôrô'pyĕts), village (1931 pop. 6,500), SW Ternopol oblast, Ukrainian SSR, on the Dniester and 12 mi. SW of Buchach; flour milling; grain, potatoes, livestock.

Koropi (kôrôpē'), town (pop. 7,066), Attica nome, E central Greece, on railroad and 9 mi. SE of Athens; wine center; vegetables, wheat, olive oil.

Koropiec, Ukrainian SSR: see Koropets.

Koror (kô'rôr), volcanic island (□ c.3), ⊙ Palau dist., W Caroline Isls., W Pacific, 1 mi. SW of Babelthuap; 7°20'N 134°30'E; c.3 mi. long; rises to 459 ft. Formerly Corrora.

Körös, village, Yugoslavia: see Krizevci.

Körösbanya, Rumania: see Baia-de-Cris.

Koro Sea (kô'rō), section of the Pacific, in Fiji isls.; bounded S by Viti Levu, N by Vanua Levu, E by Lau group.

Köröshegy (kû'rûsh-hĕ"dyŭ), Hung. *Köröshegy,* town (pop. 2,361), Somogy co., SW Hungary, 32 mi. N of Kaposvar; wheat, corn, wine. Resort of Balatonföldvar is near by.

Korosko or **Kurusku** (both: kōōrōōs'kōō), village (pop. 483), Aswan prov., S Egypt, on E bank of the Nile and 80 mi. NE of Wadi Halfa. Former trade center and starting point for caravans crossing the Nubian Desert.

Körösladany (kû'rûsh-lŏ"dänyŭ), Hung. *Köröslidány,* town (pop. 8,186), Bekes co., SE Hungary, on the Rapid Körös and 22 mi. E of Mezötur; brickworks, flour mills.

Körösmezö, Ukrainian SSR: see Yasinya.

Körös River (kû'rûsh), in Hungarian officially *Hármas Körös* [triple Körös] (här'mŏsh), Rum. *Criș* (krēsh), SE Hungary; formed by junction of the Rapid and the White Körös 7 mi. E of Gyoma; flows 50 mi. W and SW, past Kunszentmarton, to the Tisza just E of Csongrad. The **Rapid Körös,** Hung. *Sebes Körös* (shĕ'bĕsh), Rumanian *Crișul-Repede* (krē'shōōl-rā'pādā), rises in Transylvania just SE of Huedin, flows 120 mi. W, past Oradea and Körösladany, to join the White Körös. The **White Körös,** Hung. *Fehér Körös* (fĕ'hâr), Rumanian *Crișul-Alb* (-älb), rises near Zlatna, Rumania, in the Metalici Mts., flows 150 mi. WNW, past Brad and Bekes, to its junction with the Rapid Körös. Near Doboz the White receives the **Black Körös,** Hung. *Fekete Körös* (fĕ'kĕtĕ), Rumanian *Crișul-Negru* (-nā'grōō), which rises at Bihor Peak, Rumania, flows 85 mi. W, past Beius and Tinca.

Körösszegapati (kû'rûsh-sĕ"gŏpätē), Hung. *Körösszegapáti,* town (pop. 2,252), Bihar co., E Hungary, 33 mi. S of Debrecen; wheat, corn, cattle.

Köröstarcsa (kû'rûsh-tŏr"chŏ), town (pop. 5,444), Bekes co., SE Hungary, on the White Körös and 14 mi. N of Bekescsaba; flour mills; grain, tobacco.

Korosten or **Korosten'** (kŭrŭstyĕn'yŭ), city (1926 pop. 12,012), N central Zhitomir oblast, Ukrainian SSR, on Uzh R. and 45 mi. N of Zhitomir; rail junction; machine shops, porcelain plant. Dates from 9th cent.; originally called Iskorosten. Passed (14th cent.) to Lithuania, 1569 to Poland, and 1793 to Russia. Scene of civil war battles (1919–20). Until Second World War, when city was held (1941–43) by Germans, pop. was 50% Jewish.

Korostyshev (kŭrŭstĭ'shĭf), city (1939 pop. over 10,000), E Zhitomir oblast, Ukrainian SSR, on Teterev R. and 17 mi. E of Zhitomir, on main road from Kiev; paper milling, meat packing. Granite and limestone quarries.

Koroton, Formosa: see Fengyüan.

Korotovo (kŭrŭtô'vŭ), village (1926 pop. 487), SW Vologda oblast, Russian SFSR, on NW shore of Rybinsk Reservoir, 20 mi. SW of Cherepovets; flax, potatoes, wheat; fisheries.

Korotoyak (kŭrŭtŭyäk'), village (1939 pop. over 500), W central Voronezh oblast, Russian SFSR, on rail spur, on Don R. and 9 mi. NNE of Ostrogozhsk; sunflower-oil extraction, flour milling; chalk quarrying.

Korotych (kŭrô'tĭch), town (1926 pop. 2,636), NW Kharkov oblast, Ukrainian SSR, 9 mi. WSW of Kharkov city center.

Korovin Volcano (kô'rŭvĭn) (4,852 ft.), on E Atka Isl., Aleutian Isls., SW Alaska; 52°23'N 174°11'W. Active.

Korpilombolo (kôr'pēlôm"bôlō), village (pop. 589), Norrbotten co., N Sweden, near Finnish border, 60 mi. ESE of Gallivare; road junction; livestock.

Korpo (kôr'pō), Finnish *Korppoo* (kŏrp'pō), village (commune pop. 2,067), Turku-Pori co., SW Finland, on Korpo isl. (7 mi. long, 5 mi. wide) in strait bet. the Baltic and Gulf of Bothnia, 30 mi. WSW of Turku; fishing, limestone quarrying.

Korpona, Czechoslovakia: see Krupina.

Kor River, Iran: see Kur River.

Korsakov (kŭrsä'kŭf), city (1940 pop. 22,368), S Sakhalin, Russian SFSR, port on Aniva Gulf, 23 mi. S of Yuzhno-Sakhalinsk; a S terminus of E coast railroad; paper and pulp milling; fish canning, distilling (whisky, brandy). Chief port (opened 1909) of S Sakhalin; when icebound in winter, replaced by Kholmsk. First Rus. military post (founded 1853) of Sakhalin. Under Jap. rule (1905–45), called Otomari (ō'tōmärē). Was former ⊙ Karafuto.

Korsakovo (kŭrsä'kŭvŭ), village (1926 pop. 1,483), N Orel oblast, Russian SFSR, 31 mi. E of Mtsensk; distilling.

Korschenbroich (kôr'shŭnbroikh"), village (pop. 5,543), in former Prussian Rhine Prov., W Germany, after 1945 in North Rhine-Westphalia, 3 mi. E of Rheydt.

Korshev (kôr'shĭf), Pol. *Korszów* (kôr'shōōf), village (1939 pop. over 500), central Stanislav oblast, Ukrainian SSR, 8 mi. NNW of Kolomyya; wheat, rye, potatoes; lumbering.

Korsholm (kôrs"hōlm', kōsh"–), Finnish *Mustasaari* (mōōs'täsä"rē), village (commune pop. 6,565), Vaasa co., W Finland, on Gulf of Bothnia, 4 mi. SE of Vaasa. Formerly site of 14th-cent. castle (no remains). Just S was site of original city of Vaasa, destroyed (1852) by fire.

Korsnas (kôrs″nĕs′, kôsh″–), Swedish *Korsnäs*, village (pop. 1,255), Kopparberg co., central Sweden, at N end of 10-mi.-long Runn L. (rŭn), 3 mi. SE of Falun; lumber-milling center; paper mills.

Korsor (kôr′sûr), Dan. *Korsør*, city (pop. 10,667) and port, Soro amt, W Zealand, Denmark, on the Great Belt and 65 mi. WSW of Copenhagen; margarine, glass, machinery, bicycles; shipbuilding, fisheries. Ferry to Nyborg (Fyn).

Korsovka, Latvia: see KARSAVA.

Korsten, W residential suburb of Port Elizabeth, S Cape Prov., U. of So. Afr., on fringe of industrial section.

Korsun or **Korsun′** (kôr′sōōnyŏŏ). **1** City, Kiev oblast, Ukrainian SSR: see KORSUN-SHEVCHENKOVSKI. **2** Agr. town (1926 pop. 3,110), central Stalino oblast, Ukrainian SSR, in the Donbas, 6 mi. WSW of Yenakiyevo; truck.

Korsun-Shevchenkovski or **Korsun′-Shevchenkovskiy** (–shĭfchĕn′kŭfskē), city (1926 pop. 4,775), SE Kiev oblast, Ukrainian SSR, on Ros R. and 75 mi. SSE of Kiev; machine mfg., metalworking, flour milling, chemicals. Until c.1930, Korsun.

Korszow, Ukrainian SSR: see KORSHEV.

Kortemark (kōr′tŭmärk), town (pop. 5,225), West Flanders prov., W Belgium, 4 mi. SW of Torhout; agr. market; food canning. Has 13th-cent. church. Formerly spelled Cortemarck.

Kortes Dam (kôr′tĭs), S central Wyo., in canyon of North Platte R., bet. Seminoe Dam (S) and Pathfinder Dam (N), c.50 mi. SW of Casper. Power dam (240 ft. high, 440 ft. long) completed 1950.

Kortgene, Netherlands: see NORTH BEVELAND.

Korti (kōr′tē), town, Northern Prov., Anglo-Egyptian Sudan, on left bank of the Nile and 30 mi. SSW of Merowe; road junction; cotton, wheat, barley; livestock.

Kortkeros (kôrt′kyĭrŭs), village (1926 pop. 1,472), SW Komi Autonomous SSR, Russian SFSR, on Vychegda R. and 25 mi. ENE of Syktyvkar; flax. Formerly spelled Kortkeross.

Kortrijk, Belgium: see COURTRAI.

Koru (kō′rōō), village, Nyanza prov., SW Kenya, on railroad and 22 mi. W of Londiani; sugar cane, coffee, sisal, corn.

Korumburra (kŏrŭmbûr′ŭ), town (pop. 2,414), S Victoria, Australia, 65 mi. SE of Melbourne; livestock center; cheese factory. Coal mines near by.

Koru Mountains (kô′rōō) or **Kuru Mountains** (kōō′rōō), coast range, Turkey in Europe, extending c.20 mi. along shore of Gulf of Saros from Greek line; rise to 2,379 ft. in Koru Dag, 9 mi. S of Malkara.

Korvey, Germany: see HÖXTER.

Korwai (kōr′vī), village, E Madhya Bharat, India, on Betwa R. and 45 mi. NNE of Bhilsa; local agr. market (wheat, millet). Was ⊙ former princely state of Korwai (□ 142; pop. 29,544) of Central India agency; since 1948, state merged with Madhya Bharat. Sometimes spelled Kurwai.

Koryak National Okrug (kŭryäk′), administrative division (□ 151,740; pop. c.15,000) of Kamchatka oblast, Khabarovsk Territory, Russian SFSR, in NE Siberia; ⊙ Palana. Bordered by Kolyma and Koryak ranges; includes isthmus and N section of Kamchatka Peninsula; drained by Penzhina R.; tundra. Inhabited chiefly by Koryak (Nymylany; a paleo-Asiatic ethnic group); some Lamuts (NW). Reindeer raising, fishing, hunting. Lignite mining at Gizhiga and Tilichiki. Other centers: Kamenskoye, Olyutorskoye. Formed 1930 within former Far Eastern Territory.

Koryak Range, NE Khabarovsk Territory, Russian SFSR, extends from neck of Kamchatka Peninsula NNE to Anadyr Gulf; rises to c.4,500 ft.

Korycany (kô′rĭchänĭ), Czech *Koryčany*, Ger. *Koritschan* (kô′rĭchän), village (pop. 2,339), SE Moravia, Czechoslovakia, 24 mi. WSW of Gottwaldov; rail terminus; mfg. of bentwood furniture.

Koryo, Korea: see KANGNUNG.

Korytnica, Czechoslovakia; see RUZOMBEROK.

Koryu, Formosa: see HOWLUNG.

Koryukovka (kŭryōō′kŭfkŭ), town (1926 pop. 6,621), N Chernigov oblast, Ukrainian SSR, 45 mi. NE of Chernigov; sugar-refining center.

Korzec, Ukrainian SSR: see KORETS.

Kos (kŏs, kôs), Ital. *Coo*, Lat. *Cos*, second largest island (□ 111.4; pop. 18,545) of the Dodecanese, Greece, in Aegean Sea, off Turkish Bodrum peninsula (separated by narrow Channel of Kos), at entrance to Gulf of Kos (Turkey), 50 mi. NW of Rhodes; c.36°45′N bet. 26°55′ and 27°20′E; 26 mi. long (SW-NE), 5 mi. wide; rises to 2,870 ft. Largely low-lying, it produces wheat, barley, tobacco, olive oil, potatoes, tomatoes, chick-peas, figs, almonds, wine, grapes; stock raising. Lignite, lead, iron ore, and copper deposits; sulphur springs; sponge fisheries. Main city, Kos (pop. 7,955), is on NE shore. Probably colonized by Epidaurus, anc. Cos became a member of the Dorian Hexapolis. It was controlled in turn by Athens, Macedon, Syria and Egypt, and flourished as a literary center (led by Philetas and Theocritus) under the Ptolemies and remained prosperous under the Romans. Hippocrates was b. here c.460 B.C. There are remains of castles of the Knights Hospitalers, who held the isl. 1315–1523. Earthquakes are common, the last one in 1933.

Kos, Ital. *Coo*, Lat. *Cos*, main city (pop. 7,955) of Kos isl., in the Dodecanese, Greece, at NE end of isl., opposite Turkish Bodrum peninsula (across Channel of Kos); 38°54′N 27°16′E. Trade center for tobacco, olive oil, wine, figs; mfg. of tobacco products and brandy; sponge fisheries. Medieval castle.

Kos, Channel of, arm of Aegean Sea, in the Dodecanese, bet. Kos. isl. and Turkish Bodrum peninsula; 36°55′N 27°15′E; 2.5 mi. wide. Kos city is a port on S shore.

Kos, Gulf of, Gulf of Cos (both: kôs), **Gulf of Kerme** (kĕrmĕ′), or **Ceramic Gulf** (sûră′mĭk), anc. *Ceramicus Sinus* (sĕrŭmĭ′kŭs sī′nŭs), (60 mi. long, 18 mi. wide) of Aegean Sea, SW Turkey, N of Resadiye Peninsula. Isl. of Kos is at its mouth. The celebrated city of HALICARNASSUS (BODRUM is on the site) was located on N shore opposite Kos.

Kosa (kō′sä), town (pop. 6,928), Kumamoto prefecture, W Kyushu, Japan, 12 mi. SE of Kumamoto; agr. center (rice, millet, sweet potatoes); raw silk; spinning mill.

Kosa (kŭsä′). **1** Town, Kirov oblast, Russian SFSR: see KOSINO. **2** Village (1948 pop. over 2,000), E Komi-Permyak Natl. Okrug, Molotov oblast, Russian SFSR, 65 mi. NNE of Kudymkar; rye, oats, livestock; lumbering.

Kosai, Japan: see KOZAI.

Kosaka (kōsä′kä). **1** Town (pop. 13,060), Akita prefecture, N Honshu, Japan, 39 mi. ENE of Noshiro; mining center (copper, silver, gold, zinc); smelting. **2** Town, Osaka prefecture, Japan: see FUSE.

Kosala (kō′sŭlŭ), anc. Aryan kingdom in N India, roughly corresponding to region of OUDH in present Uttar Pradesh; ⊙ was AJODHYA; flourished 6th-4th cent. B.C.

Kosam (kō′sŭm), village, Allahabad dist., SE Uttar Pradesh, India, on the Jumna and 28 mi. WSW of Allahabad. Extensive anc. Hindu fort ruins; 11th-cent. Jain sculptures, coins covering entire period of India numismatics, stone carvings, and terracotta figures found here. Was ⊙ Hindu kingdom (1st or 2d cent. B.C.) founded by Kuru noble from Kurukshetra. Identified as famous anc. city of Kausambi. Important cave inscriptions found 5 mi. WNW, at Pabhosa. Name applied to 2 contiguous villages of Kosam Inam and Kosam Khiraj.

Kosaya Gora (kŭsī″ŭ gŭrä′), town (1939 pop. over 10,000), central Tula oblast, Russian SFSR, 6 mi. S of Tula; metallurgical center; iron- and steelworks; cement making; iron and lignite mines.

Koschagyl or **Koschagyl′** (kŭschŭgĭl′), oil town (1948 pop. over 2,000), N Guryev oblast, Kazakh SSR, on rail spur and 90 mi. SE of Guryev, in Emba oil fields; pipe line to Orsk. Until 1937, spelled Koshchagyl.

Koschmin, Poland: see KOZMIN.

Koscian (kôsh′chän), Pol. *Kościan*, Ger. *Kosten* (kô′stŭn), town (1946 pop. 10,800), Poznan prov., W Poland, On Obra R. and 25 mi. SSW of Poznan; rail junction; agr. trade center; beet-sugar and flour milling, mfg. of liqueur, furniture; sawmilling. Insane, deaf and dumb asylums.

Koscierzyna (kôsh-chĕ-zhĭ′nä), Pol. *Kościerzyna*, Ger. *Berent* (bĕ′rŭnt), town (1946 pop. 7,820), Gdansk prov., N Poland, 31 mi. SW of Danzig; rail junction; agr. center; lumbering, agr.-implements factory, tannery, brewery.

Kosciusko (kŏsēŭ′skō), county (□ 538; pop. 33,002), N Ind.; ⊙ Warsaw. Center of state's lake region; includes lakes Wawasee and Winona. Drained by Tippecanoe and Eel rivers and small Turkey Creek. Agr. (livestock, poultry; dairy products; grain, truck, soybeans); timber. Mfg. at Warsaw. Formed 1835.

Kosciusko, city (pop. 6,753), ⊙ Attala co., central Miss., c.45 mi. SE of Greenwood, in agr., dairying, and timber area; mfg. of textiles, chenille articles, cottonseed and dairy products; lumber milling. Settled in early 1830s on old Natchez Trace; inc. 1836.

Kosciusko, Mount (kŏ″zē-ŭ′skō), highest peak (7,305 ft.) of Australia, in SE New South Wales, 240 mi. SW of Sydney, in Muniong Range of Australian Alps; winter sports (May-Sept.). A near-by peak, Mt. TOWNSEND, was formerly called Mt. Kosciusko.

Kosciusko Island (25 mi. long, 5–12 mi. wide), SE Alaska, in Alexander Archipelago, W of Prince of Wales Isl., c.40 mi. NW of Craig, 56°3′N 133°30′W; fishing, lumbering.

Kose Dag (kûsĕ′ dä), Turkish *Köse Dağ*, peak (9,190 ft.; sometimes given as 11,735 ft.), N central Turkey, 13 mi. NE of Zara, near source of the Kizil Irmak.

Kosei, Korea: see KANGSO.

Kösely River (kû′shĕĭ), E Hungary, rises 5 mi. N of Debrecen, flows 100 mi. S and W, past Hajduszoboszlo and Nadudvar, to Hortobagy R. 5 mi. SW of Nadudvar.

Kösen, Bad, Germany: see BAD KÖSEN.

Kosgi (kōs′gē). **1** Town (pop. 9,965), Gulbarga dist., SW central Hyderabad state, India, 25 mi. NW of Mahbubnagar; millet, rice; hand-woven silk textiles. **2** Town, Madras, India: see KOSIGI.

Kosh, Iraq: see ALQOSH.

Kosh-Agach (kŭsh-ŭgäch′), village, SE Gorno-Altai Autonomous Oblast, Altai Territory, Russian SFSR, on Chuya R., on Chuya highway and 180 mi. SE of Gorno-Altaisk.

Koshan or **K′o-shan** (kŭ′shän′), town, ⊙ Koshan co. (pop. 183,710), N central Heilungkiang prov., Manchuria, 100 mi. NE of Tsitsihar and on railroad; soybeans, millet, kaoliang, rye, hemp, indigo. Until 1915 called Sanchan.

Koshchagyl, Kazakh SSR: see KOSCHAGYL.

Koshedary, Lithuania: see KAISIADORYS.

Koshekhabl or **Koshekhabl′** (kŭshĭkhä′bŭl), village (1926 pop. 2,500), E Adyge Autonomous Oblast, Krasnodar Territory, Russian SFSR, on Laba R and 30 mi. NE of Maikop; wheat, sunflowers, sunn and ambary hemp, essential oils (Kazanlik roses, coriander).

Koshigaya (kōshē′gäyŭ), town (pop. 7,138), Saitama prefecture, central Honshu, Japan, 8 mi. E of Urawa; peach orchards.

Koshiki-retto (kō′shĭkē-rāt′tō), island group (□ 47; pop. 24,503), Kagoshima prefecture, Japan, in E.China Sea off SW coast of Kyushu. Comprises SHIMO-KOSHIKI-SHIMA (largest isl.), KAMI-KOSHIKI-SHIMA, and scattered islets; mountainous. Agr (rice, wheat, sweet potatoes). Fishing.

Koshin, Korea: see KANGJIN.

Koshk, Afghanistan: see KUSHK.

Koshki (kôsh′kē), village (1926 pop. 2,773), NW Kuibyshev oblast, Russian SFSR, near Kondurcha R., 33 mi. WNW of Sergiyevsk; metalworking, flour milling; wheat, sunflowers.

Koshkonong (kŏsh′kŭnŏng). **1** Town (pop. 333), Oregon co., S Mo., near Spring R., 15 mi. SE of West Plains; grain, livestock. **2** Resort village, Jefferson co., S Wis., 12 mi. NNE of Janesville. Near by L. Koshkonong (widening of Rock R.) is c.6 mi. long, c.3 mi. wide.

Koshkonong, Lake, Wis.: see ROCK RIVER.

Kosh-Kupyr (kŭsh-kōōpĭr′), village (1939 pop. over 500), W Khorezm oblast, Uzbek SSR, in Khiva oasis, 14 mi. W of Urgench; cotton.

Koshtan-Tau (kŭshtän″-tou′), peak (16,880 ft.) in N front range of the central Greater Caucasus, in Kabardian Autonomous SSR, Russian SFSR, bet. 2 headstreams of upper Cherek R., 35 mi. SW of Nalchik.

Koshu. **1** Town, Hwanghae prov., Korea: see HWANGJU. **2** City, S.Cholla prov., Korea: see KWANGJU. **3** Town, S.Chungchong prov., Korea: see KONGJU.

Koshu-Kavak, Bulgaria: see KRUMOVGRAD.

Koshun, Formosa: see HENGCHUN.

Kosi (kō′sē), town (pop. 10,126), Muttra dist., W Uttar Pradesh, India, on Agra Canal and 25 mi. NW of Muttra; large cattle market; trades in gram, jowar, wheat, cotton, oilseeds. Has 16th-cent. serai.

Kosice (kô′shĭtsĕ), Slovak *Košice*, Ger. *Kaschau* (kä′shou), Hung. *Kassa* (kŏ′shŏ), city (pop. 51,689), ⊙ Kosice prov. (□ 2,873; pop. 461,938), SE Slovakia, Czechoslovakia, on Hornad R. and 190 mi. ENE of Bratislava; 48°74′N 21°16′E. Important rail junction; commercial and agr. center; 2d-largest town in Slovakia. Mfg. (woolen textiles, knit goods, machinery, chemicals, paper), food and tobacco processing, brewing, woodworking, embroidery making. Supreme Court, R.C. bishopric here. Magnesite mining in vicinity. The late-Gothic masterpiece St. Elizabeth cathedral (built in 14th–16th cent.; restored in 19th cent.) contains numerous art treasures, including 15th-cent. altar. Oldest city bldgs. are 14th-cent. Franciscan monastery and church, Levoca House. Several technical schools, broadcasting station, mus. with park and wooden Slovak chapel. Originally a fortress, chartered in 1235; became especially important in 15th cent. Held at different times by Austrians, Hungarians, Russians, and Turks; transferred (1920) from Hungary to Czechoslovakia by treaty of Trianon; again part of Hungary, 1938–45. Here Benes coalition government resided (April-May, 1945) and reorganized postwar Czechoslovak state. Health resorts with mineral springs in vicinity.

Ko Sichang, Thailand: see SICHANG, Ko.

Kosigi (kō′sĭgē), town (pop. 10,055), Bellary dist., NW Madras, India, 16 mi. N of Adoni; cotton ginning, peanut milling; tannery. Granite quarries near by. Also spelled Kosgi or Kesigi.

Kosikha (kŭsē′khŭ), village (1926 pop. 2,961), NE Altai Territory, Russian SFSR, 30 mi. E of Barnaul, in agr. area.

Kosino (kŭsēnō′). **1** Town (1939 pop. over 500), E Kirov oblast, Russian SFSR, 7 mi. ESE of Zuyevka; paper milling. Until 1938, Kosa. **2** Town (1939 pop. over 500), central Moscow oblast, Russian SFSR, 3 mi. NW of Lyubertsy; knitting mills.

Kosiorovo. **1** Town, Dnepropetrovsk oblast, Ukrainian SSR: see APOSTOLOVO. **2** Town, Voroshilovgrad oblast, Ukrainian SSR: see STANICHNO-LUGANSKOYE.

Kosi River, left tributary of the Ganges, in Nepal and India, formed by confluence of 3 headstreams (Sun or San Kosi, Arun, and Tamur rivers) 13 mi. WSW of Dhankuta (Nepal); flows S across India border, through N Bihar (here dividing into 2 main arms and many shifting channels, joining again E of Khagaria), and E to the Ganges 25 mi. SSW of Purnea; c.200 mi. long. In Nepal, also called Sapt Kosi. Projected dam (770 ft. high; will impound 6.9 million acre ft.) at BARAKAHSHETRA, below confluence of headstreams, and barrage at CHATRA; 2 canals extending from both banks will irrigate 3-4 million acres of land in Nepal and Bihar and also provide power, navigation, control of destructive floods in Bihar, drainage, malarial control, land reclamation, fish hatcheries, and recreation facilities.

Kosistek (kŭsēstyĕk'), village (1939 pop. over 500), N Aktyubinsk oblast, Kazakh SSR, 45 mi. NE of Aktyubinsk; wheat, cattle.

Kosisty, Cape, or **Cape Kosistyy,** Russian SFSR: see TIKSI.

Kosjeric or **Kosyerich** (both: kô'syĕrĭch), Serbo-Croatian *Kosjerić*, village (pop. 569), W Serbia, Yugoslavia, 10 mi. NNE of Titovo Uzice.

Koskullskulle (kô'skŭls"kŭ"lŭ), village (pop. 994), Norrbotten co., N Sweden, just E of Malmberget; iron mining.

Koslan (kŭslän'), village (1926 pop. 598), W Komi Autonomous SSR, Russian SFSR, on Mezen R. and 135 mi. NNW of Syktyvkar (linked by road); lumbering.

Koslanda (kōslän'dŭ), village (pop. 376), Uva Prov., S central Ceylon, in Ceylon Hill Country, 18 mi. SSW of Badulla; extensive tea and rubber plantations; rice, vegetables.

Köslin (kûs'lĭn) or **Koszalin** (kô-shä'lēn), town (1939 pop. 33,479; 1946 pop. 17,115) in Pomerania, after 1945 ⊙ Koszalin prov., NW Poland, near the Baltic, 85 mi. NE of Stettin; 54°12'N 16°12'E. Rail junction; woolen, linen, hemp, and paper milling, food canning, sawmilling, mfg. of chemicals, agr. machinery, bricks, soap, furniture; fruit processing. First mentioned in 1214; chartered 1266. Seat (1574–1622) of bishopric moved here from Kamien Pomorski. Suffered heavy destruction in Thirty Years War; passed 1648 to Brandenburg. Severely damaged by fire in 1718. After Second World War, during which it was c.50% destroyed, its Ger. pop. left.

Kosmach (kŭsmäch'), Pol. *Kosmacz* (kôs'mäch), town (1939 pop. over 2,000), S Stanislav oblast, Ukrainian SSR, in E Beskids, 17 mi. SW of Kolomyya; petroleum and natural-gas extraction. Pop. largely Guzuls; wood carving, weaving, sheep raising.

Kosmaj, Kosmai, or **Kosmay** (all: kôs'mī), mountain (2,060 ft.) in the Sumadija, central Serbia, Yugoslavia, 18 mi. S of Belgrade. Several lead mines date from Roman times.

Kosmet, oblast, Yugoslavia: see KOSOVO-METOHIJA.

Kosmonosy (kôs'mônôsĭ), village (pop. 3,000), N Bohemia, Czechoslovakia, 23 mi. SSW of Liberec; dyeing and weaving of cotton textiles.

Kosmynino (kŭsmĭ'nyĭnŭ), town (1939 pop. over 2,000), SW Kostroma oblast, Russian SFSR, 15 mi. SSW of Kostroma; peat working.

Kosogol, Mongolia: see KHUBSUGUL.

Kosolapovo (kŭsŭlä'pŭvŭ), village (1939 pop. over 500), E Mari Autonomous SSR, Russian SFSR, 65 mi. ENE of Ioshkar-Ola; wheat, rye, oats.

Kosong (kô'sŭng'), Jap. *Kojo*, town (1944 pop. 14,842), Kangwon prov., central Korea, N of 38°N, on Sea of Japan, 60 mi. SE of Wonsan, near Diamond Mts.; rice, soybeans, honey, livestock.

Kosov (kô'sŭf), Pol. *Kosów* (kô'so͞of), city (1931 pop. 5,653), SE Stanislav oblast, Ukrainian SSR, on right tributary of Prut R. and 15 mi. SSE of Kolomyya; summer resort; agr. processing (cereals, hides, fruit, vegetables), knitwear mfg.

Kosovo (kô'sôvô), region, W Croatia, Yugoslavia, in Dalmatia; extends 6 mi. N-S, bet. Knin and Drnis. Village of Kosovo is on railroad and 7 mi. NNE of Drnis.

Kosovo, Kosovo Polje, or **Kosovo Polye** (both: pô'lyĕ), [Serbian,=field of blackbirds], fertile valley in Dinaric Alps, S Serbia, Yugoslavia; since 1946 part of Kosovo-Metohija oblast. Drained by Sitnica R. and its tributary and (in S) by upper Southern Morava and Lepenac rivers. Lignite, magnesite, and asphalt deposits; lead and zinc mining in mts. N and E of valley. Largely agr. (wheat). Chief towns: PRISTINA, Kosovska MITROVICA. Kosovo Polje, rail station, 5 mi. WSW of Pristina, is junction of Belgrade-Skoplje and Pristina-Pec RRs; site of Turkish victories over Serbs (1389) and Hungarians (1448), with tombs of Turkish sultan Murad I and Serbian hero Milosh Obilich. Under Turkish rule (until 1913), valley was part of Kosovo (also spelled Kossovo) vilayet; capital was Prizren. W section of vilayet passed (1913) to Albania, where its main town is Kukës.

Kosovo-Metohija or **Kosovo-Metokhiya** (–mĕtô'-khēä), abbr. **Kosmet** (kôs'mĕt), Serbo-Croatian *Kosovo i Metohija* (ē mĕtô'hēä), autonomous oblast (□ 3,997; pop. 727,176), SW Serbia, Yugoslavia; ⊙ Pristina. Borders on Montenegro (NW), Albania (SW), and Macedonia (S); bet. North Albanian Alps and Mokra Planina (NW), the Kopaonik (N), Crna Gora (S) and Sar Mts. (SW); includes fertile valleys of Kosovo (center) and METOHIJA (W). Drained by Southern Morava, Ibar, and White Drin rivers and their tributaries. Chief crops are wheat, barley, and corn; vegetables (notably beans), tobacco, hemp, apples, grapes, chestnuts also grown. Stock raising, particularly sheep, is important; forestry is well developed. Lead, zinc, silver, gold, and chromium mining, notably at Trepca and Novo Brdo; pyrite, magnesite, and coal also mined. Home industry (embroideries, carpets) and handicrafts (metalworking) make up for lack of factories. Oblast is crossed by Lapovo-Skoplje and Nis-Pec RRs. Pop., mainly agricultural, is chiefly Albanian; some Serbs and Montenegrins. Besides Pristina, main towns are Prizren, Pec, and Mitrovica. Under Turkish rule (until 1913), part of Kosovo vilayet; partitioned (1913) bet. Serbia and Montenegro and again (1929) bet. Zeta, Morava, and Vardar banovinas of Yugoslavia; largely inc. (1941–44) into Italian-held Albania; reconstituted (1946) as autonomous oblast, based on predominantly Albanian pop.

Kosovska Mitrovica, Yugoslavia: see MITROVICA.

Kosow. 1 City, Belorussian SSR: see KOSSOVO. **2** City, Ukrainian SSR: see KOSOV.

Kospash (kŭspäsh'), city (1949 pop. over 10,000), E central Molotov oblast, Russian SFSR, 5 mi. E of Kizel; a major mining center in Kizel bituminous-coal basin. Developed in 1941; became city in 1949. Formerly Kospashski.

Kossa (kō'sä), Ital. *Cossa*, village, Kaffa prov., SW Ethiopia, in Enarea dist., 12 mi. NNE of Jimma; coffee growing.

Kosse (kŏ'sē), town (pop. 566), Limestone co., E central Texas, 35 mi. SE of Waco; trade point in farm area (cotton, cattle, corn).

Kosseir, Quseir (ko͞osār'), or **Al-Qusayr** (ĕl–), anc. *Leucus Limen*, town (1937 pop. 2,797; 1947 dist. pop. 5,388), E Egypt, port on the Red Sea, 95 mi. E of Qena (linked by road); 29°9'N 34°16'E. Exports the phosphate production of mines at near-by Bir Beida. S are lead and zinc deposits. In the Ptolemaic period a desert route from the Nile ended at anc. Kosseir (ruins 3 mi. N).

Kossovo (kô'sŭvŭ), Pol. *Kosów* (kô'so͞of), city (1937 pop. 3,700), NE Brest oblast, Belorussian SSR, 17 mi. NNE of Bereza; tanning, flour milling, brick mfg. Passed (1795) from Poland to Russia; reverted (1921) to Poland; ceded to USSR in 1945.

Kossovo, Yugoslavia: see Kosovo, valley.

Kossuth (kŭso͞oth'), county (□ 979; pop. 26,241), N Iowa, on Minn. line; ⊙ Algona. Rolling prairie agr. area (cattle, hogs, poultry, corn, oats, soybeans) drained by East Des Moines R. Has sand and gravel pits. State park near Algona. Formed 1851.

Kossuth (kŏ'sŭth), village (pop. 242), Alcorn co., NE Miss., 8 mi. WSW of Corinth, in agr. area.

Kosta (kôs'tä), village (pop. 855), Kronoberg co., S Sweden, 20 mi. E of Vaxjo; noted glass-mfg. center, founded 1731.

Kostajnica (kô'stĭnĭtsä), village (pop. 2,725), N Croatia, Yugoslavia, on Una R., on railroad and 20 mi. SSE of Sisak, on Bosnia border; trade center in plum-growing region. First mentioned in 13th cent. Village of Bosanska Kostajnica lies across the Una.

Kosta-Khetagurovo (kŭstä"-khyĕtŭgo͞o'rŭvŭ). **1** Village (1926 pop. 1,274), E North Ossetian Autonomous SSR, Russian SFSR, on railroad, on Sunzha R. and 15 mi. NNE of Dzaudzhikau; flour mill, metalworks; wheat, corn, vegetables. A Rus. fortress in Caucasian wars (18th–19th cent.). Until 1944 (in Chechen-Ingush Autonomous SSR), called Nazran. **2** Village (1926 pop. 2,614), SW Stavropol Territory, Russian SFSR, on Georgian border just N of Klukhori; coal mining near by (N) at Ordzhonikidzevski. Called Georgiye-Osetinskoye until c.1940; until 1943, in Karachai Autonomous Oblast.

Kostakoz, Tadzhik SSR: see CHKALOVSKI.

Kostandenets (kôstän'dĕnĕts), village (pop. 3,333), Ruse dist., NE Bulgaria, 20 mi. SSE of Ruse; wheat, rye, sunflowers.

Kostelec nad Cernymi Lesy (kô'stĕlĕts näd' chĕrnyē"mĭ lĕ'sĭ), Czech *Kostelec nad Černými Lesy*, town (pop. 3,341), W central Bohemia, Czechoslovakia, 20 mi. ESE of Prague; popular excursion center; earthenware mfg. Has sanatorium for tubercular patients. Fishing in vicinity, notably at Jevany (yĕ'vänĭ), 3 mi. SW, also known as summer and winter resort.

Kostelec nad Orlici (näd' ôr"lĭtsē), Czech *Kostelec nad Orlicí*, Ger. *Adlerkosteletz* (äd"lŭrkô'stŭlĕts), town (pop. 4,981), E Bohemia, Czechoslovakia, on Divocha Orlice R., on railroad and 18 mi. SE of Hradec Kralove; tanning, weaving, mfg. (leather goods, shoes, cotton textiles, linen).

Kosten, Poland: see KOSCIAN.

Kostenets, Bulgaria: see DIMITROVO.

Koster (kŏ'stŭr), town (pop. 2,010), SW Transvaal, U. of So. Afr., 25 mi. SW of Rustenburg, at foot of NW Witwatersrand; alt. 5,209 ft.; fruit, wheat, oats, cotton; grain elevator.

Kosterevo (kŭstyĭryô'vŭ), town (1939 pop. over 500), W Vladimir oblast, Russian SFSR, on Klyazma R. and 25 mi. ENE of Orekhovo-Zuyevo; woodworking center; linen mill.

Kostheim (kôst'hīm), former suburb (pop. 12,051) of MAINZ, after 1945 inc. into Wiesbaden, Hesse, W Germany, on right bank of the Rhine, at mouth of canalized Main R., and 6 mi. SSE of Wiesbaden city center; paper mfg.

Kosti (kō'stē), town (pop. 20,200), Blue Nile prov., E central Anglo-Egyptian Sudan, on left bank of the White Nile and 170 mi. S of Khartoum; 13°10'N 32°43'E. Rail-steamer transfer point for Khartoum (N), Juba (S), and El Obeid (W); agr. and trade center; cotton, wheat, barley, corn, fruits, durra, gum arabic; livestock. Airfield. Kosti Bridge (completed 1910, 2 mi. upstream; 470 yards long) carries rail and road traffic.

Kostinbrod (kô'stĭnbrôt), village (pop. 2,168), Sofia dist., W Bulgaria, on left tributary of Iskar R. and 9 mi. NW of Sofia; chemical center (fertilizers, soap, cosmetics); sunflower-oil extracting.

Kostino (kŭstyē'nŭ), city (1939 pop. over 2,000), N central Moscow oblast, Russian SFSR, on branch of Moscow Canal, 3 mi. E of Mytishchi and just S of Stalinski.

Kostolac or **Kostolats** (both: kôstô'läts), village, E Serbia, Yugoslavia, near Mlava R. and an arm of the Danube, 8 mi. N of Pozarevac; rail terminus; lignite mines.

Kostopol or **Kostopol'** (kŭstô'pŭl), city (1931 pop. 6,523), central Rovno oblast, Ukrainian SSR, 20 mi. NNE of Rovno; sawmilling center, producing plywood and prefabricated houses; iron smelting (deposits near by), mfg. of agr. machinery, glass-working, tanning, flour milling.

Köstritz, Bad, Germany: see BAD KÖSTRITZ.

Kostroma (kŭstrŭmä'), oblast (□ 22,400; 1946 pop. estimate 1,050,000) in N central European Russian SFSR; ⊙ Kostroma. Bordered N by the Northern Uvals; drained by left affluents of the Volga (Kostroma, Unzha, and upper Vetluga rivers); in forested region, partly cleared (W). Flax is main crop throughout region; wheat near Soligalich (N) and Nerekhta (SW), potatoes near Makaryev (S); dairy farming centered at Vokhma (NE). Lumbering is chief industry; sawmilling, veneering at Sharya, Manturovo, Neya, Galich, and Bui, along Vologda-Kirov RR. Woodworking, distilling, flax processing in rural areas; linen milling at Nerekhta. Kostroma (SW) is main industrial center. Formed 1944 out of Yaroslavl oblast.

Kostroma, city (1939 pop. 121,205), ⊙ Kostroma oblast, Russian SFSR, on high left bank of Volga R., at mouth of the Kostroma, and 190 mi. NE of Moscow, on railroad; 57°46'N 40°56'E. Major linen-milling center; mfg. of excavators, shoes; shipbuilding, paper- and sawmilling; flour, tobacco products, alcohol, flaxseed oil, starch, molasses. Peat-powered station. Has 14th-cent. Ipatyev monastery, scene of election (1613) of Michael, 1st tsar of Romanov dynasty, Uspenski cathedral (c.1250), and regional mus. Textile institute, teachers col. Founded 12th cent. on low right bank; transferred (1238) to present site after destruction by Tatars; developed into commercial center and became ⊙ 13th-cent. principality; annexed (1364) by Moscow. It was ⊙ Kostroma govt. before an administrative change in 1929.

Kostroma River, in Kostroma oblast, Russian SFSR, rises NW of Sudai in the Northern Uvals, flows W, past Soligalich, and S, past Bui (head of navigation), to the Volga at Kostroma; c.175 mi. long.

Kostrzyn (kôs'chĭn). **1** Ger. *Kostschin* (kôs'chĭn), town (1946 pop. 3,142), Poznan prov., W central Poland, 13 mi. E of Poznan; flour milling, sawmilling, gingerbread making. Also called Kostrzyn Wielkopolski. **2** Town, Zielona Gora prov., Poland: see KÜSTRIN.

Kostyukovichi (kŭstyo͞o'kŭvēchē), city (1926 pop. 3,242), SE Mogilev oblast, Belorussian SSR, 55 mi. SW of Roslavl; food processing. Marlpits.

Kostyukovka (–kŭfkŭ), town (1939 pop. over 500), S Gomel oblast, Belorussian SSR, 7 mi. NNW of Gomel; glassworks; peat.

Kosudo (kōso͞o'dō), town (pop. 11,296), Niigata prefecture, central Honshu, Japan, on Shinano R. and 12 mi. S of Niigata, in rice-growing area; cotton flannel.

Kosugi (kōso͞o'gē), town (pop. 8,016), Toyama prefecture, central Honshu, Japan, 7 mi. WNW of Toyama, in rice-growing area; patent medicines.

Kosulino (kŭso͞o'lyĭnŭ). **1** Village (1939 pop. over 500), S Kurgan oblast, Russian SFSR, 65 mi. SW of Kurgan, in agr. area. **2** Town, Sverdlovsk oblast, Russian SFSR: see VERKHNEYE DUBROVO.

Kosumberk, Czechoslovakia: see LUZE.

Kosva River or **Kos'va River** (kôs'vŭ), in Molotov oblast, Russian SFSR, rises in the central Urals c.10 mi. S of Kytlym, flows W, generally SW, past Gubakha, and W to Kama R. opposite (NE of) Chermoz; 190 mi. long. Lumber floating; seasonal navigation for c.60 mi. in lower course.

Kosya or **Kos'ya** (kô'syŭ), town (1939 pop. over 2,000), W Sverdlovsk oblast, Russian SFSR, in the central Urals, on left tributary of Tura R. and 13 mi. W of Is, near rail spur (Kryuchkovka station); gold and platinum placers.

Kosyerich, Yugoslavia: see KOSJERIC.

Kosyu, Korea: see KWANGJU.

Kos-Yu (kŭs-yo͞o'), river in Komi Autonomous SSR, Russian SFSR, rises in the N Urals at c.65°10'N, flows c.150 mi. NNE, through Pechora coal basin, to Usa R. at Kosya-Vom, 140 mi. SW of Vorkuta. Receives Kozhim and Inta rivers (right).

Koszalin (kô-shä'lēn), province [Pol. *województwo*] (□ 6,799; pop. 584,999), NW Poland; ⊙ Köslin

(Koszalin). Borders N on the Baltic; low level coast line; low rolling hills further inland, dotted with small lakes. Drained by Prosnica (Persante) and several smaller rivers. Agr. region; principal crops are rye, potatoes, barley, oats; livestock; fishing. Industries (mainly wood- and metalworking, paper milling) concentrated in cities of Köslin, Kolberg (Kolobrzeg; seaside resort, fishing port), Stolp (Slupsk), Szczecinek (Neustettin), and Bialogard (Belgard). Prov. created 1950 from territory detached from Szczecin prov.; until 1945, part of Ger. Pomerania prov. Ger. pop. expelled after 1945 and replaced by Poles.

Koszalin, town, Poland: see KÖSLIN.

Köszeg (kû'sĕg), Hung. *Kőszeg*, Ger. *Güns* (güns), city (pop. 10,321), Vas co., W Hungary, 11 mi. NNW of Szombathely, near Austrian line. Flour mills, sawmills; distilling, mfg. wool, cotton, rugs, soap, candles; brewery, brickworks. Heroic stand here, in 1532, against Turks.

Kota (kō'tŭ), town (pop., including adjacent railway settlement of Kargi Road, 4,352), Bilaspur dist., E central Madhya Pradesh, India, 17 mi. NNW of Bilaspur; match mfg., rice milling; sawmills.

Kotaagung or **Kotaagoeng** (both: kōtŭägōōng'), town (pop. 2,822), S Sumatra, Indonesia, port on Semangka Bay, 45 mi. W of Telukbetung; trade center shipping copra, pepper, coffee, timber.

Kotabaru or **Kotabaroe** (both: kō'tŭbä'rōō), town (pop. 3,756) on N coast of Pulu Laut, port on Macassar Strait, Indonesia, off SE coast of Borneo; coaling station; exports coal, rubber, pepper. Also called Kotabarupululaut.

Kota Bharu (kō'tŭ bä'rōō). **1** Town (pop. 22,765), ⊙ Kelantan, N Malaya, on right bank of Kelantan R., opposite rail station, 5 mi. from mouth and 210 mi. NNE of Kuala Lumpur, in densely populated coastal belt. Its port is TUMPAT. Residence of sultan and Br. adviser; sawmilling, match mfg., mfg. of cheroots; agr. station. Market gardening, rice, coconuts. Airport at Pengkalan Chepa (5 mi. NE). **2** or **Kota Bahru**, village (pop. 371), central Perak, Malaya, on railroad and 13 mi. S of Ipoh; rubber.

Kotachi (kō'tächē) or **Kodachi** (kō'dächē), town (pop. 4,156), Hiroshima prefecture, SW Honshu, Japan, 28 mi. NE of Hiroshima, in agr. area (rice, wheat).

Kotadaik, Indonesia: see LINGGA.

Kot Adu or **Kot Addu** (both: kōt' ŭd'ōō), town (pop. 6,960), Muzaffargarh dist., SW Punjab, W Pakistan, on railroad and 30 mi. NW of Muzaffargarh; wheat, millet, rice, dates. Technical and industrial schools.

Kotagiri (kō'tŭgĭrē), town (pop. 10,803), Nilgiri dist., SW Madras, India, in Nilgiri Hills, 11 mi. E of Ootacamund; scenic resort (sanatorium); eucalyptus-oil extraction; millet, barley, peas, potatoes. Tea and coffee estates near by.

Kotah (kō'tŭ), former princely state (□ 5,714; pop. 777,398) in Rajputana States, India; ⊙ was Kotah. Formed in early-17th cent. out of original Bundi state; treaty with British in 1817. In 1948, merged with union of Rajasthan.

Kotah, city (pop. 45,032), ⊙ Kotah dist., SE Rajasthan, India, on Chambal R. and 120 mi. S of Jaipur; trade center for wheat, cotton, millet, oilseeds, cloth fabrics; cotton and oilseed milling, hand-loom weaving (muslins); distillery, dairy farm; handicraft metalware. At rail junction, 3 mi. NE, are match factory and metalworks. Was ⊙ former Rajputana state of Kotah.

Kotaj (kōtoi), Hung. *Kótaj*, town (pop. 4,292), Szabolcs co., NE Hungary, 6 mi. N of Nyiregyhaza; distillery, vinegar mfg.; tobacco, corn, hogs.

Kotake (kōtä'kä) or **Kodake** (–dä'kä), town (pop. 13,967), Fukuoka prefecture, N Kyushu, Japan, 11 mi. S of Yawata; coal-mining and agr. (rice, wheat, barley) center.

Kota Kota (kō"tä kō'tä), town (pop. c.10,000), Central Prov., Nyasaland, port on L. Nyasa, 80 mi. NNE of Lilongwe; rice-growing center; also tobacco, cotton, corn; fishing. Largest native center in Nyasaland. African hosp., Anglican mission. Political center (seat of representative of Sultan of Zanzibar) in Arab slave-trade days (1880s, '90s).

Kota Kuala Muda, Malaya: see KUALA MUDA.

Kotaraja, Indonesia: see KUTARAJA.

Kota River, Fr. Equatorial Africa: see KOTO RIVER.

Kota Tinggi (kō'tŭ tĭng'gē), town (pop. 4,709), SE Johore, Malaya, 20 mi. NE of Johore Bharu, on Johore R.; center of rubber and pineapple (canning) dist. Tin mining (N). Became (1511) ⊙ Johore-Riouw kingdom.

Kotchandpur (kōtchänd'pōōr), town (pop. 6,418), Jessore dist., W East Bengal, E Pakistan, 21 mi. NNW of Jessore; trades in rice, jute, oilseeds, sugar cane.

Kotchek, Tell, Syria: see KOJAK, TELL.

Kotcho Lake (□ 90), NE B.C., near Alta. border; 59°4'N 121°9'W; 15 mi. long, 1–7 mi. wide. Drains S into Hay R.

Kot Chutta (kōt' chōōt'tŭ), town (pop. 3,064), Dera Ghazi Khan dist., SW Punjab, W Pakistan, 11 mi. S of Dera Ghazi Khan; wheat, millet, rice; handicraft woolen products. Sometimes spelled Kot Chhutta.

Kotda Sangani (kōt'dŭ säng'gänē), town, central Saurashtra, India, 18 mi. SSE of Rajkot. Was ⊙ former Western Kathiawar state of Kotda Sangani (□ 90; pop. 12,160) of Western India States agency; state merged 1948 with Saurashtra.

Kotdwara (kōt'dvärŭ), village, Garhwal dist., N Uttar Pradesh, India, on tributary of the Ramganga and 11 mi. SW of Lansdowne, at foot of Siwalik Range; rail spur terminus; trades in borax from Tibet, wheat, barley, sugar, rice, cloth, oilseeds.

Kötegyan (kû'tĕ-dyän), Hung. *Kötegyán*, town (pop. 2,764), Bihar co., E Hungary, 5 mi. E of Sarkad, near Rumanian line; rail junction; wheat, tobacco, dairy farming.

Kotei, Japan: see KOJO.

Kotel (kô'tĕl), city (pop. 3,671), Yambol dist., E central Bulgaria, in Kotel Mts., at S end of Kotel Pass, 15 mi. NNE of Sliven; carpet and woodworking shops. Health resort. Developed as wool-processing and cultural center under Turkish rule (15th-19th cent.), when it was called Kazan. Declined after Bulg. independence.

Kötelek (kû'tĕlĕk), Hung. *Kőtelek*, town (pop. 3,272), Jasz-Nagykun-Szolnok co., E central Hungary, on Tisza R. and 13 mi. ESE of Jaszladany; fishing, agr.

Kotel Mountains, E central Bulgaria, part of E Balkan Mts., extend c.12 mi. from Vratnik Pass E to Varbitsa Mts. Crossed by **Kotel Pass** (alt. 2,451 ft.), just N of Kotel, on highway to Omortag. On main road bet. the Danube and Constantinople during Turkish rule (15th-19th cent.), when it was called Kazan Pass.

Kotelnich or **Kotel'nich** (kŭtyĕl'nyĭch), city (1939 pop. over 10,000), W central Kirov oblast, Russian SFSR, on Vyatka R. and 50 mi. WSW of Kirov; rail junction of lines to Kirov, Vologda, and Gorki; food-processing center; shipyards; flour milling, dairying, metal- and woodworking. Founded 1181 as Cheremiss settlement of Koshkarov; Rus. colonization after 14th cent.

Kotelniki or **Kotel'niki** (kŭtyĕl'nyĭkē), town (1939 pop. over 500), central Moscow oblast, Russian SFSR, 2 mi. S of Lyubertsy; quartz quarries.

Kotelnikovo or **Kotel'nikovo** (–kŭvŭ), village, Leningrad oblast, Russian SFSR, 3 mi. SSW of Gatchina. Called Salyuzi until 1949.

Kotelnikovski or **Kotel'nikovskiy** (kŭtyĕl'nyĭkŭfskē), town (1939 pop. over 10,000), S Stalingrad oblast, Russian SFSR, on railroad (Kotelnikovo station) and 95 mi. SW of Stalingrad; flour mills, metalworks; wheat, mustard. Until 1929, Kotelnikovskaya.

Kotelnya or **Kotel'nya** (kŭtyĕl'nyŭ), village (1926 pop. 3,365), SE Zhitomir oblast, Ukrainian SSR, 14 mi. SE of Zhitomir; sugar beets.

Kotelny Island or **Kotel'nyy Island** (kōtĕl'nē, Rus. kŭtyĕl'nē), largest of Anjou group of NEW SIBERIAN ISLANDS, off Yakut Autonomous SSR, Russian SFSR; 100 mi. long, 60 mi. wide; rises to 1,150 ft. Arctic observation post on NW coast. Coastal creeks abound in fish. Discovered 1773 by Rus. merchant Lyakhov. Bunge Land, a low, sandy E extension of Kotelny Isl., is linked intermittently with Faddei Isl.

Kotelva or **Kotel'va** (kŭtyĕl'vŭ), village (1926 pop. 20,342), NE Poltava oblast, Ukrainian SSR, near Vorskla R., 35 mi. NNE of Poltava; flour milling, metal- and woodworking.

Koterbachy (kô'tĕrbäkhĭ), Hung. *Ötösbánya* (û'tûzhbä"nyŏ), village (pop. 1,625), E central Slovakia, Czechoslovakia, 6 mi. SE of Spisska Nova Ves; iron and copper mining. Markusovce iron mines are 3 mi. NW, on left bank of Hornad R.

Kotgarh (kōt'gŭr), village, central Himachal Pradesh, India, 24 mi. NE of Simla; wheat, corn, tea, barley; apple orchards.

Kothagudium, India: see KOTTAGUDEM.

Kothapet, India: see SIRPUR.

Kothapeta, India: see KOTTAPETA.

Köthen (kû'tŭn), city (pop. 42,588), in former Anhalt state, central Germany, after 1945 in Saxony-Anhalt, 13 mi. WSW of Dessau, 35 mi. NNW of Leipzig; 51°45'N 11°59'E. Rail junction; airport; lignite mining. Sugar refining, textile milling and knitting, machine-tool and paint mfg., metalworking. Center of market-gardening region. Site of technical col. and sugar-research institute. Has 15th-cent. church, 16th-cent. palace. First mentioned 1115. Until 1847, ⊙ duchy of Anhalt-Köthen. J. S. Bach was concertmaster here, 1717–23. Formerly spelled Cöthen.

Kother, Kashmir: see ANANTNAG, town.

Kothi (kō'tē), village, N central Vindhya Pradesh, India, 13 mi. NNW of Satna; markets millet, wheat; small ochre works. Was ⊙ former petty state of Kothi (□ 166; pop. 24,776) of Central India agency; since 1948, state merged with Vindhya Pradesh.

Koti, Japan: see KOCHI, city, Kochi prefecture.

Kotikovo (kô'tyĭkŭvŭ), village (1940 pop. 3,826), S Sakhalin, Russian SFSR, on E Terpeniye Gulf, 55 mi. ESE of Poronaisk, on narrow Terpeniye Peninsula; fisheries. Under Jap. rule (1905–45), called Chirie (chĭrē'ĕ).

Kotino, Japan: see KOCHINO.

Kotipalli, India: see COCANADA.

Kotka (kōt'kä), city (pop. 22,572), ⊙ Kymi co., SE Finland, near USSR border, on 2 small isls. (rail and road bridge to mainland) in Gulf of Finland, at mouth of Kymi R. (S part of Päijänne waterway), 70 mi. ENE of Helsinki; 60°28'N 26°55'E. Seaport, shipping paper, pulp, and lumber. Industrial center with lumber, pulp, cellulose, and flour mills, sugar refineries, machine shops, fertilizer- and glassworks. Fortified (c.1790) by Russians, city was virtually destroyed (1855) by British fleet. Modern city founded 1878.

Kot Kapura (kōt kŭpōō'rŭ), town (pop. 20,584), W Patiala and East Punjab States Union, India, 8 mi. SSE of Faridkot; rail junction; trade center (gram, wheat, cotton, oilseeds, millet); cotton ginning, oilseed pressing, hand-loom weaving. Formerly in princely state of Faridkot.

Kot Khai (kōt' kī'), village, central Himachal Pradesh, India, 22 mi. E of Simla; wheat, barley, potatoes; handicraft basket weaving.

Kotlas (kôt'lŭs), city (1939 pop. over 10,000), S Archangel oblast, Russian SFSR, on Northern Dvina R., at mouth of Vychegda R., on N.Pechora RR and 210 mi. NW of Kirov; junction of railroad to Kirov; sawmilling center; shipyards, lumber mills (mfg. of prefabricated houses), wood-cracking plants. Shipyards, pulp and paper mill at near-by LIMENDA. Chartered 1917.

Kotli (kōt'lē), town (pop. 2,761), Mirpur dist., W Kashmir, on tributary of the Jhelum and 24 mi. NNE of Mirpur; wheat, bajra, corn, pulse. Largely destroyed in 1947, during India-Pakistan struggle for control.

Kotlik (kŏt'lĭk), village (pop. 44), W Alaska, on SW shore of Norton Sound, 55 mi. SW of St. Michael; Eskimo fur-trading station.

Kotli Loharan (lōhä'rän), village, Sialkot dist., E Punjab, W Pakistan, 7 mi. NNW of Sialkot; metal products.

Kotlin Island, Russian SFSR: see KRONSTADT.

Kotlyarevskaya, Russian SFSR: see MAISKI, Kabardian Autonomous SSR.

Kot Moman (kōt' mō'mŭn), town (pop. 7,828), Shahpur dist., central Punjab, W Pakistan, 22 mi. ENE of Sargodha; wheat, millet; cattle breeding. Also spelled Kot Mumin and Kot Momin.

Kot Najibullah (kōt' nŭjē'bōōl-lŭ), town (pop. 5,315), Hazara dist., NE North-West Frontier Prov., W Pakistan, 24 mi. SW of Abbottabad; maize, wheat, barley. Sometimes written Kot Najib Ullah.

Koto, Korea: see KANGDONG.

Kotobuki, Formosa: see SHOW.

Kotohira (kōtō'hĕrä), town (pop. 8,231), Kagawa prefecture, N Shikoku, Japan, 7 mi. S of Marugame; rail junction; mfg. center (saws, files, bamboo products, towels, sake). Site of Kotohira-gu, one of most important Shinto shrines in Japan. Its grounds are densely wooded with cryptomeria, pine, and camphor.

Kotoni (kōtō'nē), town (pop. 16,221), SW Hokkaido, Japan, just W of Sapporo; agr. (rice, wheat, radishes); hemp clothmaking. Hokkaido agr. experiment station here. Hot springs near by.

Kotonu, Fr. West Africa: see COTONOU.

Kotor (kô'tôr). **1** Village, Croatia, Yugoslavia: see KOTORIBA. **2** Ital. *Cattaro* (kät-tä'rō), anc. *Ascrivium* and *Dekateron*, village (pop. 5,402), W Montenegro, Yugoslavia, on Bay of Kotor (SE inlet of Gulf of Kotor), at NW foot of the Lovcen, 25 mi. W of Titograd. Seaport, with naval base at TIVAT. Has 9th-cent. cathedral of St. Tryphon, old churches of St. Luke and St. Spiridione, medieval walls and fort. Founded by Romans; held by Venice from 15th cent. to 1797, when it passed to Austria. In Dalmatia until 1921. During Second World War, annexed (1941–44) by Italy.

Kotor, Gulf of, Serbo-Croatian *Boka Kotorska* (bô'kä kô'tôrskä), Ital. *Bocche di Cattaro* (bôk'kĕ dē kät-tä'rō), winding inlet of the Adriatic, SW Yugoslavia, largely in Montenegro, but touched (SW) by Dalmatia. Well-protected harbor; 25 to 50 ft. deep, up to c.20 mi. long from entrance channel; accommodates vessels of any size. Includes bays of Topla (NW), Tivat (S), Morinj and Risan (N), and Kotor (SE); all connected by channels. On its shores are HERCEG NOVI, RISAN, KOTOR, and TIVAT. The LOVCEN rises SE. Narrow-gauge railroad leads from Zelenika to Sarajevo; railroad via Pec to Belgrade planned.

Kotoriba (kô'tôrēbä), Hung. *Kotor* (kô'tôr), village, N Croatia, Yugoslavia, on Mura R. and 18 mi. E of Cakovec, in the Medjumurje, on Hung. border.

Koto River or **Kotto River** (kōtō'), in E and S Ubangi-Shari, Fr. Equatorial Africa, rises on Anglo-Egyptian Sudan border, flows 395 mi. S, SW, and again S, past Bria, to Ubangi R. 60 mi. E of Mobaye. Several rapids along its course. Sometimes called Kota.

Kotorosl River or **Kotorosl' River** (kŭtŭrôs'lyŭ), Yaroslavl oblast, Russian SFSR, formed by 2 headstreams just E of L. Nero, flows ENE, past Gavrilov-Yam, and N to the Volga at Yaroslavl; 72 mi. long. Logging.

Kotor Varos or **Kotor Varosh** (both: vä'rôsh), Serbo-Croatian *Kotor Varoš*, village (pop. 2,292), N central Bosnia, Yugoslavia, on Vrbanja R. and 15 mi. SSE of Banja Luka; local trade center.

Koto-sho, Formosa: see HUNGTOW ISLAND.

Kotoura (kōtō'rä), town (pop. 19,057), Okayama prefecture, SW Honshu, Japan, on strait bet. Hiuchi and Harima seas, 13 mi. SSW of Okayama; saltmaking center. Part of town is included in Inland Sea Natl. Park. Until 1907, Tanokuchi.

Kotovka (kô'tůfků), village (1926 pop. 4,559), N Dnepropetrovsk oblast, Ukrainian SSR, near Orel R., 45 mi. N of Dnepropetrovsk; wheat, sunflowers.

Kotovo (kô'tůvů), village (1926 pop. 3,508), N Stalingrad oblast, Russian SFSR, 30 mi. NW of Kamyshin; wheat, sunflowers.

Kotovsk (kô'tůfsk). **1** Industrial city (1939 pop. over 10,000), central Tambov oblast, Russian SFSR, on right bank of Tsna R. and 10 mi. SSE of Tambov city center, on rail spur (Tambov II station). A former industrial suburb of Tambov; developed around a chemical plant (mfg. of gunpowder, explosives). Called (after 1930) Krasny Boyevik, until it became (1940) the separate city of Kotovsk. **2** City (1926 pop. 10,007), W Odessa oblast, Ukrainian SSR, 14 mi. SSW of Balta; railroad shops, winery; light mfg., woodworking, food processing. Until c.1935, called Birzula. In Moldavian Autonomous SSR (1924–40), where it was temporary ⊙ (1928–30).

Kotovskoye (kô'tůfskůyů), town (1941 pop. 4,571), S central Moldavian SSR, 18 mi. SW of Kishinev; agr. center; flour and oilseed milling, distilling. Until 1944, called Gancheshty, Rum. *Hâncești*; renamed for Bolshevik military leader, Kotovski, b. here. Pop. 50% Jewish until Second World War.

Kot Putli (kōt' pōōt'lē), town (pop. 9,948), E Rajasthan, India, 60 mi. NNE of Jaipur; millet, oilseeds; marble sculpturing (quarries 8 mi. SW). Sometimes written Kotputli.

Kotra (kō'trŭ), town (pop. 943), S Rajasthan, India, 35 mi. WSW of Udaipur, in S Aravalli Range.

Kotrang (kō'trŭng), town (pop. 9,401), Hooghly dist., S central West Bengal, India, on Hooghly R. and 8 mi. N of Calcutta city center; mfg. of bricks, tiles, rope.

Kotri (kō'trē), town (pop. 9,979), Dadu dist., SW Sind, W Pakistan, on Indus R. (bridged) and 3 mi. W of Hyderabad; rail junction; trade center (overland and river traffic); grain market; handicraft cloth weaving, fishing, soap mfg.; distillery. Nearby irrigation barrage across the Indus under construction. Gypsum deposits (NW) are worked.

Kot Sabzal (kōt' sŭb'zŭl) or **Sabzal Kot**, town (pop. 1,410), Bahawalpur state, W Pakistan, near Sind border, 28 mi. SW of Rahimyar Khan; wheat, cotton.

Kot Samaba (sŭmä'bŭ), town (pop. 1,118), Bahawalpur state, W Pakistan, on railroad and 13 mi. NE of Rahimyar Khan; rice husking, cotton ginning. Other spellings: Kot Samba, Kotsamba, Kot Somaba.

Kötschach (kŭt'shäkh), town (pop. 2,105), Carinthia, S Austria, near Gail R., 15 mi. SE of Lienz. Has late-Gothic church.

Kotsk, Poland: see Kock.

Kotsuke (kō'tsōōkä) or **Kozuke** (kō'zōōkä), former province in central Honshu, Japan; now Gumma prefecture.

Kotsyubinskogo, Imeni (ē'mĭnyē kŭtsyōōbēn'skŭvŭ), NW suburb (1939 pop. over 500) of Kiev, Ukrainian SSR, 3 mi. N of Svyatoshino. Until 1941, Berkovets.

Kotta, Ceylon: see Kotte.

Kottagoda, Ceylon: see Kottegoda.

Kottagudem (kōt-tŭgōō'dăm) or **Kothagudium** (kōtŭgōōd'yōōm), town (pop. 9,669), Warangal dist., SE Hyderabad state, India, 75 mi. ESE of Warangal; mining center in Singareni coal field; served by rail branch (station, Bhadrachelam Road) from Dornakal, 32 mi. W. Mines opened in 1920s; center of operations moved here from Yellandlapad in 1941. Also called Kottaguda.

Kottai Malai (kŏt'tī mŭlī'), peak (6,624 ft.) in S Western Ghats, India, on Madras-Travancore border, 55 mi. WSW of Madura, 9 mi. E of Periyar L. Vaigai R. rises on N slope.

Kottaiyur (kōt-tī'yōōr), town (pop. 6,249), Ramnad dist., S Madras, India, 4 mi. NNE of Karaikudi; residence of Chetty merchant community.

Kottapatnam, India: see Alluru Kottapatnam.

Kottapeta or **Kothapeta** (kŏ'tŭpētŭ), town (pop. 6,985), East Godavari dist., NE Madras, India, on Gautami Godavari R., in Godavari delta, and 27 mi. SW of Cocanada; rice milling; sugar cane, tobacco, coconuts. Also called Kothapet.

Kottarakara (kŏtä'rŭkŭrŭ), town (pop. 6,953), SW Travancore, India, 15 mi. NE of Quilon; road center; cashew-nut processing; trades in coir rope and mats, rice, cassava.

Kottayam (kŏ'tŭyŭm), city (pop. 33,364), W Travancore, India, 50 mi. N of Quilon; processing and packing of rubber, mfg. of copra, coir rope and mats, plywood, tiles; engineering workshops (automobile repairing), sawmills; rice milling, cashew-nut processing. Col. (affiliated with Univ. of Travancore).

Kottbus, Germany: see Cottbus.

Kotte (kōt'tä), town (pop. 39,281), Western Prov., Ceylon, 5 mi. SE of Colombo city center; rice, vegetables, coconuts, cinnamon, rubber. Was ⊙ Kotte kingdom (15th-16th cent.); in 1565, abandoned and ⊙ moved to Colombo. Kotte urban council includes Nugegoda. Also spelled Cotta and Kotta.

Kottegoda or **Kottagoda** (kōt"tŭgō'dŭ), village (pop., including surrounding villages, 3,639), Southern Prov., Ceylon, on S coast, 7 mi. E of Matara; fishing center; vegetables, rice.

Kottingbrunn (kô'tĭngbrōōn), village (pop. 2,214), E Lower Austria, 4 mi. S of Baden; vineyards, orchards.

Kotto River, Fr. Equatorial Africa: see Koto River.

Kottuchcheri (kŏtōō'chĕrē), Fr. *Cotchéry* (kôchārē'), town (commune pop. 8,297), Karikal settlement, Fr. India, 3 mi. NW of Karikal. Also spelled Kottucheri.

Kottur (kŏ'tōōr). **1** Town (pop., including Malaiyandipattanam, 11,051), Coimbatore dist., SW Madras, India, 9 mi. SSW of Pollachi; cotton pressing; tea factory. Malaiyandipattanam adjoins (S). **2** Town, Bellary dist., Madras, India: see Kotturu.

Kotturu (kŏtōō'rōō), town (pop. 8,097), Bellary dist., NW Madras, India, 32 mi. SSW of Hospet; rail spur terminus; peanut milling, hand-loom cotton weaving. Bamboo, fiber, gum arabic in near-by forests. Sometimes spelled Kottur.

Kotui River, Russian SFSR: see Khatanga River.

Kotung, Manchuria: see Ketung.

Kotur, Iran: see Qutur.

Kotyuzhany (kŭtyōō'zhŭnē), Rum. *Cotiugenii-Mari* (kôtyōōjĕ'nē-mär), village (1941 pop. 4,642), NE Moldavian SSR, 30 mi. ENE of Beltsy; wheat, sunflowers.

Kotzebue (kŏt'sůbū), village (pop. 626), NW Alaska, at NW end of Baldwin Peninsula, on Kotzebue Sound, c.180 mi. NNE of Nome; 66°52'N 162°38'W; fur farming; asbestos, gold mining. Has Territorial Eskimo school, 2 missions. Air base and commercial airport. Formerly Eskimo trading center for arctic Alaska and Siberia.

Kotzebue Sound, NW Alaska, arm (100 mi. long, 70 mi. wide) of Chukchi Sea, on N side of Seward Peninsula, bounded E by Baldwin Peninsula; 66°40'N 163°W. Kotzebue, Kiwalik, and Deering villages on shores. Eschscholtz Bay is SE arm. Discovered 1816 by Count Otto von Kotzebue while searching for Northwest Passage. Knud Rasmussen here completed (1924) overland crossing from Repulse Bay, Northwest Territories.

Kotzenau, Poland: see Chocianow.

Kotzman, Ukrainian SSR: see Kitsman.

Kötzschenbroda, Germany: see Radebeul.

Kötzting (kŭts'tĭng), village (pop. 4,111), Lower Bavaria, Germany, in Bohemian Forest, on the White Regen and 24 mi. NNW of Deggendorf; mfg. of textiles, metal products, matches; brewing, lumber and flour milling; granite quarrying. Chartered before 1344.

Kou- or **K'ou**, for Chinese names beginning thus and not found here: see under Kow-.

Kouandé (kwän'dā), village (pop. c.800), NW Dahomey, Fr. West Africa, 16 mi. E of Natitingou; peanuts, shea nuts, livestock.

Kouango (kwäng-gō'), village, S Ubangi-Shari, Fr. Equatorial Africa, on Ubangi R. (Belgian Congo border) at mouth of Ouaka R. and 65 mi. SSW of Bambari; center of trade in cotton region.

Kouango River, Fr. Africa: see Ouaka River.

Kouba (kōōbä'), town (pop. 10,472), Alger dept., N central Algeria, an outer SE suburb of Algiers, adjoining (S) Hussein-Dey; boilermaking, woodworking, mfg. of vinegar, soap, ink, agr. equipment. Truck gardens, vineyards. View of Algiers Bay.

Kouchibouguac (kōō"shēbŏŏkwăk'), village, E N.B., on Kouchibouguac R., near its mouth on Northumberland Strait, 10 mi. NW of Richibucto; lumbering.

Kouchibouguac River, in E N.B., rises 30 mi. S of Newcastle, flows 45 mi. ENE to Northumberland Strait 12 mi. NNW of Richibucto.

Koudougou (kōōdōō'gōō), town (pop. c.25,900), central Upper Volta, Fr. West Africa, 55 mi. W of Ouagadougou (railroad under construction); agr. center (shea nuts, peanuts, millet, rice, manioc, onions). Shea-nut butter processing, cotton ginning; stock raising (cattle, sheep, goats). Has R.C. and Protestant missions; sleeping-sickness clinic. Some chromium and manganese deposits near by.

Koufalia, Greece: see Kouphalia.

Kouif, Djebel (jĕ'bĕl kwēf'), mountain in Constantine dept., NE Algeria, near Tunisia border, 13 mi. NE of Tebessa; site of Algeria's largest phosphate mine, linked by rail with Bône and Le Kef (Tunisia). Le Kouif is mining village.

Kouilou, region, Fr. Equatorial Africa: see Pointe-Noire.

Kouilou River or **Kwilu River** (kwēlōō'), S Middle Congo territory, Fr. Equatorial Africa, rises in Crystal Mts. 50 mi. SSW of Djambala, flows S, W past Loudima, NW, and SW past Kakamoeka, to the Atlantic 32 mi. NNW of Pointe-Noire; c.200 mi. long. Known as N'Douo (ŭndōō'ō) in its upper course, and as Niari (nyä'rē) in its middle course. Navigable in lower course for c.40 mi. below Kakamoeka. Many rapids. Niari R. basin is noted as mining area (copper, lead, zinc).

Kouinine (kwēnēn'), Saharan village, Touggourt territory, E Algeria, one of the Souf oases, 4 mi. NNW of El-Oued; Deglet Nur dates.

Koukdjuak, Great Plain of the, tundra region of SW Baffin Isl., SE Franklin Dist., Northwest Territories; c.120 mi. long, 60–90 mi. wide. N boundary is Koukdjuak R. (50 mi. long), which drains Nettilling L. into Foxe Basin.

Kouklia (kōōklēä'). **1** or **Old Paphos** (pā'fŏs), anc. *Palaepaphos*, village (pop. 791), SW Cyprus, 60 mi. SW of Nicosia and 10 mi. ESE of Paphos (New Paphos), linked by highway. Anc. city famous for its great, now ruined, temple to Aphrodite, who according to legend rose here from sea foam. After an earthquake, town was restored (15 B.C.) by Augustus. **2** Village (pop. 242), Famagusta dist., E Cyprus, 12 mi. W of Famagusta. Adjoined N by irrigation reservoir, fed by Pedias R.

Koukos, Greece: see Kallidromon.

Koulamoutou or **Koula-Moutou** (kōōlä-mōōtōō'), town, ⊙ Adoumas region (formed 1949; 1950 pop. 50,100), SE Gabon, Fr. Equatorial Africa, 215 mi. ESE of Port-Gentil; gold-mining center.

Koulikoro (kōōlēkō'rō), town (pop. c.4,350), S Fr. Sudan, Fr. West Africa, landing on Niger R. (irrigation area), terminus of Dakar-Niger RR and 32 mi. ENE of Bamako; trading and processing center (peanuts, shea nuts, kapok). Col.; cotton experiment station.

Kouloukia, Greece: see Chalastra.

Koulouri, Greece: see Salamis.

Koumac (kōō'mäk'), village (dist. pop. 3,055), New Caledonia, on NW coast, 180 mi. NW of Nouméa; agr. products, livestock; chrome mining.

Koumhané, Syria: see Qumkhane.

Koumi, Greece: see Kyme.

Koumra (kōōmrä'), village, S Chad territory, Fr. Equatorial Africa, 60 mi. WSW of Fort-Archambault; cotton ginning. Until 1946 in Ubangi-Shari colony.

Koungheul (kōōngûl'), village, S central Senegal, Fr. West Africa, on Dakar-Niger RR and 75 mi. WNW of Tambacounda; peanuts; stock.

Kounradski or **Kounradskiy** (kŏŏnrät'skē), town (1939 pop. over 2,000), SE Karaganda oblast, Kazakh SSR, 10 mi. N of Balkhash (linked by railroad); copper-mining center.

Kountze (kōōnts), city (pop. 1,651), ⊙ Hardin co., E Texas, 25 mi. NNW of Beaumont; lumber milling. Inc. after 1940.

Kouphalia or **Koufalia** (both: kōōfälēä'), town (pop. 5,317), Salonika nome, Macedonia, Greece, 21 mi. NW of Salonika; wheat, cotton, vegetables.

Kouphonesos or **Koufonisos** (both: kōōfônē'sôs), 2 Aegean islands in the Cyclades, Greece: see Ano Kouphonesos, Kato Kouphonesos.

Kourémalé (kōōrĕmä'lā), village (pop. c.300), S Fr. Sudan, Fr. West Africa, on Fr. Guinea border, 70 mi. SW of Bamako; gold fields.

Kourim (kōr'zhĭm), Czech *Kouřim*, town (pop. 2,398), central Bohemia, Czechoslovakia, 13 mi. WNW of Kutna Hora; rail terminus; noted for floriculture, fruit-tree nurseries, and preserves.

Kourou (kōōrōō'), town (commune pop. 582), N Fr. Guiana, on small Kourou R., on the coast, and 26 mi. NW of Cayenne; coffee, cacao, tropical fruit.

Kouroussa (kōōrōō'sä), town (pop. c.5,550), central Fr. Guinea, Fr. West Africa, road junction and landing on upper Niger (crossed by railroad) and 275 mi. ENE of Conakry, 190 mi. SW of Bamako, Fr. Sudan; trading and agr. center (rice, peanuts, shea nuts, rubber, honey, beeswax, cattle). Cotton gin. Gold and iron deposits in dist.

Kousseir, Syria: see Quseir, El.

Kousseri, Fr. Cameroons: see Fort-Foureau.

Kouteifé, Syria: see Quteife.

Koutiala (kōōtyä'lä), town (pop. c.2,900), S Fr. Sudan, Fr. West Africa, 170 mi. E of Bamako; millet, peanuts, cotton, kapok, shea-nut butter, cotton gin and research institute. Iron deposits near by.

Koutoumoula, Greece: see Coronea.

Kouts (kouts), town (pop. 718), Porter co., NW Ind., 11 mi. S of Valparaiso.

Kouvola (kō'vōlä), town (pop. 9,000), Kymi co., SE Finland, near Kymi R., 30 mi. NNW of Kotka; rail junction; pulp- and paper-milling center. Power station (NW).

Kovacica or **Kovachitsa** (both: kôvä'chētsä), Serbo-Croatian *Kovačica*, Hung. *Antalfalva* (ŏn'tŏlfŏlvŏ), village (pop. 6,070), Vojvodina, N Serbia, Yugoslavia, 21 mi. NNE of Belgrade, in the Banat; rail junction.

Kovacova, Czechoslovakia: see Zvolen.

Koval, Poland: see Kowal.

Kovaszna, Rumania: see Covasna.

Kovda (kôv'dŭ), Finnish *Kouta* (kō'tä), village (1939 pop. over 500), SW Murmansk oblast, Russian SFSR, lumber port on Kandalaksha Bay of White Sea, 35 mi. SSE of Kandalaksha. Pegmatite quarries near by. Sawmilling at Lesozavodski (N).

Kovda River, Finnish *Koutajoki* (kô'ōōtäyôkē), in Karelo-Finnish SSR, efflux of lake Topozero; flows N, through Pyaozero lake, and E, through Kovdozero lake, to Kandalaksha Bay of White Sea at Kovda; 137 mi. long. Frozen Oct.-May. Rapids along its course.

Kovdozero (kôvd'ō"zyĭrŭ), Finnish *Koutajärvi* (kô'ōōtäyärvē), lake (□ c.200) in SW Murmansk oblast, Russian SFSR, W of Kovda; 30 mi. long, 25 mi. wide; deeply dissected shores and isls. Traversed (W-E) by Kovda R.

Kovel or **Kovel'** (kô'vĭl), Pol. *Kowel* (kô'vĕl), city (1931 pop. 27,650), central Volyn oblast, Ukrainian SSR, on Turya R. and 43 mi. NW of Lutsk; rail junction (4 lines); agr.-processing (hides, grain, fruit, vegetables, tobacco) center; sawmilling, candlemaking, mfg. (knitwear, hosiery). Developed under Rus. rule in 19th cent.; passed to Poland (1921); ceded to USSR in 1945. Pop. largely Jewish prior to Second World War.

Kovernino (kŭvyĕr'nyĭnŭ), village (1948 pop. over 2,000), W Gorki oblast, Russian SFSR, 35 mi. NW of Semenov; woolen milling; flax processing.

Kovilj, Kovil, or **Kovil'** (kô'vĭl), Hung. *Kabol* (kŏ'bôl), village (pop. 5,179), Vojvodina, N Serbia, Yugoslavia, near the Danube, 9 mi. ESE of Novi Sad, in the Backa.

Koviljaca, Kovilyacha, Banja Koviljaca, or **Banya Kovilyacha** (all: bä'nyä, kôvē'lyächä), Serbo-Croatian *Banja Koviljača*, village, W Serbia, Yugoslavia, on the Drina (Bosnia border) and 3 mi. WSW of Loznica. Rail terminus; health resort with warm springs and hot mud; noted for treatment of rheumatism.

Kovilpatti, India: see KOILPATTI.

Kovilyacha, Yugoslavia: see KOVILJACA.

Kovin (kô'vĭn), Hung. *Kevevára* (kĕ'vĕvärŏ), village (pop. 8,376), Vojvodina, E Serbia, Yugoslavia, on the Danube and 24 mi. E of Belgrade, in the Banat; rail terminus.

Kovno, Lithuania: see KAUNAS.

Kovrov (kŭvrôv'), city (1939 pop. 67,163), N Vladimir oblast, Russian SFSR, on Klyazma R., near mouth of the Uvod, and 40 mi. ENE of Vladimir; machine-mfg. center (excavators, instruments, motorcycles); railway shops, cotton mills. Textile school. Limestone works near by. Chartered 1778.

Kovur (kŏvōōr'). **1** Town (pop. 10,601), Nellore dist., E Madras, India, 4 mi. N of Nellore; rice and oilseed milling; cashew and Casuarina plantations. Also spelled Kovvur or Kovvuru. **2** Town, West Godavari dist., Madras, India: see KOVVUR.

Kovvur (kŏvōōr'). **1** Town, Nellore dist., Madras, India: see KOVUR. **2** Town (pop. 8,933), West Godavari dist., NE Madras, India, on right bank of Godavari R. (rail bridge), at head of delta, and 4 mi. NW of (opposite) Rajahmundry; rice milling; silk growing. Building-stone quarries near by. Also spelled Kovur.

Kovylkino (kŭvĭl'kēnŭ), town (1948 pop. over 2,000), S Mordvinian Autonomous SSR, Russia SFSR, on Moksha R. and 40 mi. W of Ruzayevka; road and rail junction; flour milling, distilling.

Kovzha River (kôv'zhŭ), in Vologda oblast, Russian SFSR, issues from S Kovzha L. 25 mi. SW of Vytegra; flows 52 mi. S, past Annenski Most and Kovzhinski Zavod (sawmill) to lake Beloye Ozero at Kovzha village. Canalized lower course forms part of Mariinsk canal system; joined to Vytegra R. (NW) by Mariinsk Canal. Receives Shola R. (right).

Kowa (kō'wä), town (pop. 9,502), Aichi prefecture, central Honshu, Japan, on E Chita Peninsula, on Chita Bay, 8 mi. S of Handa; rice, raw silk, poultry. Fishing.

Kowai, New Zealand: see AMBERLEY.

Kowait, Arabia: see KUWAIT.

Kowal (kô'väl), Rus. *Koval* or *Koval'* (both: kô'vŭlyŭ), town (pop. 3,304), Bydgoszcz prov., central Poland, 9 mi. SSE of Wloclawek; brick mfg., sawmilling, flour milling.

Kowalewo (kôvälĕ'vô), Ger. *Schönsee* (shûn'zā"), town (pop. 3,326), Bydgoszcz prov., N central Poland, on railroad and 15 mi. NE of Torun; flour and beet-sugar milling, sawmilling.

Kowan or **K'ou-an** (both: kō'än'), town, N Kiangsu prov., China, 15 mi. S of Taichow and on Yangtze R.; commercial port.

Kowary (kôvä'rĭ), Ger. *Schmiedeberg* (shmē'dübĕrk), town (1939 pop. 6,638; 1948 pop. 6,923) in Lower Silesia, after 1945 in Wroclaw prov., SW Poland, near Czechoslovak border, at N foot of the Riesengebirge, 9 mi. SE of Hirschberg (Jelenia Gora); magnetite mining and smelting, woolen milling, metalworking, mfg. of carpets, china, industrial ceramics; health resort. Has 13th cent. church. After 1945, briefly called Krzyzatka, Pol. *Krzyżatka*.

Koweit, Arabia: see KUWAIT.

Kowel, Ukrainian SSR: see KOVEL.

Kowkong (gou'gông'), Mandarin *Chiu-chiang* (jyō' jyäng'), town, S Kwangtung prov., China, on West R. and 15 mi. SW of Namhoi; commercial center in silk growing dist.; exports silk and satin.

Kowloon (kou'lōōn', kō'lōōn'), Mandarin Chinese *Kiulung* or *Chiu-lung* (both: jyō'lōōng'), city (1931 pop. 264,675) of Hong Kong colony, on Kowloon peninsula of Chinese mainland, opposite Hong Kong city (Victoria) on Hong Kong isl. (ferry service). The colony's main industrial and trading center, Kowloon has most of its entrepôt trade (ocean-going ships dock on peninsula's W shore) and is the terminus of the railroad from Canton. Its industries include: cotton milling; cement, rubber-shoe, cigarette, and rope mfg.; and sugar milling. Greater Kowloon (1949 pop. estimate 700,000) consists of Kowloon proper or British Kowloon (on the peninsula; SW), and of New Kowloon on site of the old Chinese walled city of Kowloon (in the New Territories; adjoining NE). In NE outskirts, on reclaimed land, is Kaitak, Hong Kong's international airport. Kowloon peninsula (□ 3) was ceded by China in 1860, together with small near-by isls., and was inc. into the crown colony.

Kowno, Lithuania: see KAUNAS.

Kowpangtze or **Kou-pang-tzu** (both: gō'bäng'dzŭ'), town, SW Liaosi prov., Manchuria, 38 mi. NE of Chinchow; rail junction for lines to Mukden and Yingkow.

Koya (kō'yä), town (pop. 7,555), Wakayama prefecture, S Honshu, Japan, on N central Kii Peninsula, 24 mi. E of Wakayama, at foot of Mt. Koya (3,600 ft.) with 9th-cent. Buddhist monastery on summit; sawmilling. Produces *tofu* (bean curd). Sometimes called Koyasan.

Koyaguchi (kō'yägōōchē), town (pop. 6,579), Wakayama prefecture, S Honshu, Japan, on N central Kii Peninsula, 23 mi. ENE of Wakayama, in agr. area (rice, wheat, sweet potatoes); textiles (woolens, rayon, silk, cotton).

Koyama (kō'yämä). **1** Town (pop. 21,602), Kagoshima prefecture, S Kyushu, Japan, on central Osumi Peninsula, 28 mi. SE of Kagoshima; agr. center (tea, soybeans, sweet potatoes). Tropical trees (gum, camphor, lichee). **2** Town, Shizuoka prefecture, Japan: see OYAMA.

Koyambattur, India: see COIMBATORE.

Koyanose (kōyä'nōsā), town (pop. 6,807), Fukuoka prefecture, N Kyushu, Japan, 19 mi. NE of Fukuoka; rice; coal.

Koyasan, Japan: see KOYA.

Koycegiz (koijĕyĭz'), Turkish *Köyceğiz*, village (pop. 1,525), Mugla prov., SW Turkey, on N shore of L. Koycegiz, 25 mi. SE of Mugla; chromium, manganese, emery, asbestos mines; sesame, millet. Formerly Yuksekkum.

Koycegiz, Lake, Turkish *Köyceğiz* (□ 20), SW Turkey, 24 mi. SE of Mugla; 10 mi. long, 3 mi. wide.

Koygorodok, Russian SFSR: see KOIGORODOK.

Koyiu (gō'yē'ō), Mandarin *Kaoyao* (gou'you'), town (pop. 48,922), ⊙ Koyiu co. (pop. 466,353), W central Kwangtung prov., China, on left bank of West R. and 50 mi. W of Canton, in sugar-cane area; trading center; exports chinaware, tea, marble slabs. Kaolin and marble quarries near by. Until 1912 called Shiuhing or Chaoking.

Koylovtsi, Bulgaria: see KOILOVTSI.

Koynare, Bulgaria: see KOINARE.

Koyp, Russian SFSR: see KOIP.

Koysara, Kirghiz SSR: see KOISARA.

Koysu, Russian SFSR: see KOISU.

Koytash, Uzbek SSR: see KOITASH.

Koyuk (koi'ŭk), Eskimo village (pop. 134), W Alaska, on SE Seward Peninsula, at head of Norton Bay, at mouth of Koyuk R., 130 mi. ENE of Nome; fur trading; supply point for trappers and prospectors. Sometimes called Inglestat.

Koyuk River, W Alaska, rises on Seward Peninsula near 65°25'N 163°W, flows 120 mi. SE to Norton Bay at Koyuk.

Koyukuk (koi"ŭkŭk'), Indian village (pop. 80), W Alaska, on Yukon R. at mouth of Koyukuk R., and 170 mi. W of Tanana; 64°53'N 157°43'W; trapping, outfitting base for trappers. School; airfield.

Koyukuk River, village (pop. 48), W Alaska, on lower Koyukuk R., N of Nulato.

Koyukuk River, N central Alaska, rises on S slope of Brooks Range near 67°58'N 151°15'W, flows c.500 mi. generally SW, past Bettles, to Yukon R. at Koyukuk. Principal tributaries are Alatna R. and John R. Placer gold deposits on upper course. Partially explored (1855) by H. T. Allen.

Koyulhisar (kôyōōl'hĭsär"), village (pop. 2,116), Sivas prov., central Turkey, on Kelkit R. and 60 mi. NE of Sivas; lead mines yield ore with traces of silver. Formerly Misaz.

Koyva River, Russian SFSR: see KOIVA RIVER.

Koyvisto, Russian SFSR: see PRIMORSK, Leningrad.

Koyyeri, Turkey: see SARIZ.

Koza (kō'zä), town (pop. 3,876), Wakayama prefecture, S Honshu, Japan, on S Kii Peninsula, on Kumano Sea, 17 mi. SW of Shingu; fishing port.

Kozai (kō'zī) or **Kosai** (kō'sī), town (pop. 6,425), Kagawa prefecture, N Shikoku, Japan, port on Harima Sea, 3 mi. W of Takamatsu; agr. and fishing center; paper, pottery, sake, umbrellas. Exports apples, persimmons.

Kozakai (kōzä ī), town (pop. 11,037), Aichi prefecture, central Honshu, Japan, 3 mi. NW of Toyohashi; raw-silk center.

Kozaki (kōzä'kē), town (pop, 3,642), Chiba prefecture, central Honshu, Japan, 5 mi. WNW of Sawara; rice, wheat.

Kozak Mountains (kôzäk'), NW Turkey, extend 25 mi. NW from Dikili, rise to 4,390 ft. Silver, copper, antimony in W; lignite in E.

Kozakov (kô'zäkôf), Czech *Kozákov*, peak (2,437 ft.) in Lusatian Mts., N Bohemia, Czechoslovakia, 5 mi. ENE of Turnov; stone quarries, deposits of Bohemian garnets, agates, amethysts.

Kozan (kō'zä), town (pop. 3,671), Hiroshima prefecture, SW Honshu, Japan, 12 mi. N of Mihara, in rice-growing area; makes floor mats.

Kozan (kôzän'), town (pop. 6,821), Seyhan prov., S Turkey, 40 mi. NE of Adana; wheat, barley, oats, cotton. Has medieval church. Formerly Sis.

Kozane or **Kozani** (both: kôzä'nē), nome (□ 2,372; pop. 189,607), Macedonia, Greece; ⊙ Kozane. Bounded W by Pindus system, S by Thessaly, and E by Vermion and Pieria massifs, it is drained by Aliakmon R. (hydroelectric plant). Mainly agr.: wheat, tobacco, wine. Timber, charcoal. Livestock products (milk, cheese, skins). Lignite mining (N of Kozane). Main centers are Kozani, Ptolemais, Grevena, and Siatista.

Kozane or **Kozani,** city (pop. 14,022), ⊙ Kozane nome, Macedonia, Greece, 65 mi. WSW of Salonika; alt. 2,360 ft.; agr. trading center (wheat, barley, skins, livestock). Lignite mining (N). Hydroelectric plants (E) on Aliakmon R. Bishopric. Founded in Middle Ages; flourished under Turkish rule. Formerly called Kozhani.

Kozara Mountains (kô'zärä), in Dinaric Alps, NW Bosnia, Yugoslavia; c.15-mi. long NW–SE; partly bounded by Sava (W), Una (N), and Vrbas (SE) rivers. Highest peak (3,208 ft.) is 17 mi. NW of Banja Luka.

Kozato (kō'zätō), town (pop. 8,326), Tokushima prefecture, NE central Shikoku, Japan, 30 mi. W of Tokushima; commercial center in forested area; Paulownia, orange, and mulberry trees.

Kozel, Ukrainian SSR: see MIKHAILO-KOTSYUBINSKOYE.

Kozelets (kŭzĕ'lyĭts), town (1926 pop. 3,476), SW Chernigov oblast, Ukrainian SSR, 40 mi. S of Chernigov; road junction; quarrying; peat bogs.

Kozelshchina or **Kozel'shchina** (kŭzyĕl'shchĭnŭ), town (1926 pop. 1,961), SE Poltava oblast, Ukrainian SSR, 22 mi. NE of Kremenchug; wheat, livestock. Lignite deposits.

Kozelsk or **Kozel'sk** (kŭzyĕlsk'), city (1948 pop. over 10,000), E Kaluga oblast, Russian SFSR, on Zhizdra R. and 37 mi. SSW of Kaluga, in orchard area; metalworks, fruit cannery, starch plant. Berezichi glassworks (S). Near by is former hermit monastery of Optina Pustyn, now a sanatorium. City dates from 1149; was ⊙ principality (13th–16th cent.) before it passed to Moscow.

Kozenitsy, Poland: see KOZIENICE.

Kozhani, Greece: see KOZANE.

Kozhevnikovo (kŭzhĕv'nyĭkŭvŭ), village, NE Taimyr Natl. Okrug, Krasnoyarsk Territory, Russian SFSR, N of Arctic Circle, port on Kozhevnikov Bay (NE inlet of Khatanga Gulf), 200 mi. NE of Khatanga. Supply point on Arctic sea route; govt. polar station. Until 1943, called Nordvik, a name since applied to salt and petroleum center 40 mi. NE. **2** Village (1939 pop. over 2,000), S Tomsk oblast, Russian SFSR, on Ob R. and 40 mi. WSW of Tomsk, in flax-growing area.

Kozhuf, Kozhukh, mountain, Yugoslavia and Greece: see KOZUF.

Kozhva (kôzh'vŭ), village (1948 pop. over 500), E central Komi Autonomous SSR, Russian SFSR, on left bank of Pechora R. opposite Kanin, on N. Pechora RR and 145 mi. NE of Ukhta; reindeer farms. Formerly also called Ust-Kozhva.

Koziakas, Greece-Yugoslavia: see KOZJAK.

Kozienice (kô-zhĕnē'tsĕ), Rus. *Kozenitsy* (kŭ-zhĕnē'tsē), town (pop. 4,099), Kielce prov., E central Poland, 21 mi. NE of Radom, near the Vistula. Rail spur terminus; horse-breeding station; flour milling, sawmilling, mfg. of bricks, hats, wooden cartons. Kozienice Forest, Pol. *Puszcza Kozienicka*, is SW.

Kozi Hradek, castle, Czechoslovakia: see TABOR.

Kozin (kô'zĭn), village (1931 pop. 1,020), SW Rovno oblast, Ukrainian SSR, 16 mi. SW of Dubno; grain processing, tile mfg.

Kozi Rtarij, Albania-Yugoslavia: see DJERAVICA.

Kozjak or **Kozyak** (both: kô'zyäk). **1** Gr. *Koziakas* (kôzyä'kŭs), mountain on Greek-Yugoslav border, in Macedonia; rises to 5,951 ft. 11 mi. NW of Ardea, 65 mi. SSE of Skoplje. **2** Mountain, N Macedonia, Yugoslavia, along left bank of Pcinja R.; rises to 4,212 ft. 15 mi. NE of Kumanovo, 32 mi. NE of Skoplje.

Kozlany (kŏzh'länĭ), Czech *Kožlany*, village (pop. 1,082), W Bohemia, Czechoslovakia, 12 mi. SW of Rakovnik, 25 mi. WSW of Prague. Eduard Benes b. here.

Kozle (kôzh'lĕ), Pol. *Koźle*, Ger. *Cosel* (kō'zŭl), town (1939 pop. 13,337; 1946 pop. 8,277) in Upper Silesia, after 1945 in Opole prov., S Poland, port on the Oder, just opposite Klodnica R. mouth, near W end of Gleiwitz (Gliwice) Canal, and 25 mi. SSE of Oppeln (Opole); sugar refining, paper and flour milling, metal- and woodworking. N terminus of canal (under construction) bet. the Oder and the Danube. In Seven Years War, withstood several Austrian sieges.

Kozlikha, Russian SFSR: see SITNIKI.

Kozlodui or **Kozloduy** (kôzlōdōō'ē), village (pop. 7,422), Vratsa dist., NW Bulgaria, on the Danube and 11 mi. WNW of Oryakhovo; vineyards, truck; fisheries. Monument marks landing (1876) of Bulg. revolutionary troops led by Khristo Botev against the Turks.

Kozlov (kŭzlôf'). **1** City, Crimea, Russian SFSR: see YEVPATORIYA. **2** City, Tamblov oblast, Russian SFSR: see MICHURINSK. **3** Pol. *Kozlów* (kôz'wōōf), village (1931 pop. 4,070), central Ternopol oblast, Ukrainian SSR, on left tributary of Strypa R. and 11 mi. W of Ternopol; grain, livestock.

Kozlovets (kôz'lôvĕts), village (pop. 4,337), Pleven dist., N Bulgaria, 7 mi. S of Svishtov; grain, livestock, truck. Formerly Tursko Slivo.

Kozlovka (kŭzlôf'kŭ). **1** Town (1932 pop. estimate 1,060), NE Chuvash Autonomous SSR, Russian SFSR, on right bank of the Volga (landing), opposite Volzhsk, and 30 mi. W of Kazan; egg-shipping center; woodworking. Limestone deposits near by. **2** Village (1926 pop. 1,535), NE Mordvinian Autonomous SSR, Russian SFSR, 16 mi. SW of Ardatov, in hemp area; wheat, potatoes. **3** Village (1926 pop. 10,873), E Voronezh oblast, Russian SFSR, 38 mi. NW of Borisoglebsk; wheat, sunflowers.

Kozlovo (kŭzlô'vŭ). **1** Town, Buryat-Mongol Autonomous SSR, Russian SFSR: see NIZHNE-ANGARSK. **2** Village (1939 pop. over 500), central Kalinin oblast, Russian SFSR, 33 mi. E of Vyshni Volochek; flax.

Kozlovshchina (kŭzlôf'shchĭnŭ), Pol. *Kozlowszczyzna* (kôzwôfshchĭ'nä), village (1939 pop. over 500), W Baranovichi oblast, Belorussian SSR, 16 mi. N of Slonim; rye, oats, potatoes.

Kozlow, Ukrainian SSR: see KOZLOV, Ternopol oblast.

Kozlowszczyzna, Belorussian SSR: see KOZLOVSHCHINA.

Kozlu (kôzlōō'), town (pop. 14,122), Zonguldak prov., N Turkey, 6 mi. SW of Zonguldak; coal mines; power plant.

Kozluk (kôzlŏŏk'), village (pop. 1,634), Siirt prov., SE Turkey, 30 mi. NW of Siirt; grain. Formerly Hazo.

Kozluk (kôz'lŏŏk), village (pop. 5,347), E Bosnia, Yugoslavia, on Drina R. (Serbia border) and 7 mi. N of Zvornik.

Kozmin (kôzh'mēn), Pol. *Koźmin*, Ger. *Koschmin* (kôsh'mĭn), town (1946 pop. 5,559), Poznan prov., W central Poland, 45 mi. SSE of Poznan; rail junction; mfg. of agr. machinery, flour milling, sawmilling; trades in cattle and grain. Sanatorium; monastery.

Kozmodemyansk or **Koz'modem'yansk** (kŭz"mŭdyĭmyänsk'), city (1936 pop. estimate 12,900), SW Mari Autonomous SSR, Russian SFSR, port on right bank of the Volga, near mouth of Vetluga R. (lumber floating), and 55 mi. WSW of Ioshkar-Ola; major lumber-trading center; sawmilling, woodworking, mfg. (furniture, muscial instruments), vegetable processing. Has natl. Mari mus. Founded 1583 as Muscovite stronghold.

Koznitsa Pass (kôznē'tsä) (alt. 3,542 ft.), central Bulgaria, bet. central Balkan Mts. (N) and Sredna Gora (S), 4 mi. W of Klisura; crossed by highway to Pirdop, connecting Karlovo Basin (E) and Zlatitsa Basin (W).

Kozoji (kō'zō'jē), town (pop. 10,932), Aichi prefecture, central Honshu, Japan, 12 mi. NE of Nagoya; mining center (lignite, quartz crystal).

Kozovo (kô'zŭvŭ), Pol. *Kozowa* (kôzô'vä), village (1931 pop. 6,064), W Ternopol oblast, Ukrainian SSR, 10 mi. E of Berezhany; flour milling, brickworking; stone quarrying.

Kozu (kō'zōō), town (pop. 6,226), Kanagawa prefecture, central Honshu, Japan, port on NW shore of Sagami Bay, 4 mi. NE of Odawara; exports rice.

Kozuchow (kô-zhōō'khōōf), Pol. *Kożuchów*, Ger. *Freystadt* (frī'shtät), town (1939 pop. 6,669; 1946 pop. 2,385) in Lower Silesia, after 1945 in Zielona Gora prov., W Poland, 14 mi. SSE of Grünberg (Zielona Gora); textile milling (linen, hemp, jute). Chartered 1291. One of 6 churches of Grace allowed Silesian Protestants under Treaty of Altranstädt (1707) established here in 18th cent. In Second World War, c. 50% destroyed.

Kozuf or **Kozhuf** (kô'zhōōf), Serbo-Croatian *Kožuf*, mountain massif on Yugoslav-Greek border, W of Vardar R.; highest peak (7,013 ft.) is 18 mi. W of Djevdjelija. Also called Kozuh or Kozhukh, Serbo-Croatian *Kožuh*.

Kozuke, Japan: see KOTSUKE.

Kozulka or **Kozul'ka** (kŭzōōl'kŭ), village (1948 pop. over 2,000), SW Krasnoyarsk Territory, Russian SFSR, 55 mi. W of Krasnoyarsk and on Trans-Siberian RR; lumber milling.

Kozu-shima (kō'zōō-shĭmä), island (□ 7; pop. 2,423) of isl. group Izu-shichito, Greater Tokyo, Japan, in Philippine Sea, 35 mi. SSW of O-shima; 3 mi. long, 1–3.5 mi. wide. Hilly, with extinct volcano rising to 1,971 ft. Produces raw silk, camellia oil; fishing, farming. Formerly sometimes called Kantsu.

Kozyak, Greece; Yugoslavia: see KOZJAK.

Kpandae or **Kpandai** (kŭpändī'), town, N Br. Togoland, administered as part of the Northern Territories of the Gold Coast, 45 mi. N of Kete-Krachi, on main N–S road; shea nuts, durra, millet, yams. Hq. of Br. Togoland section of Gonja dist.

Kpandu (kŭpän'dōō), town, S Br. Togoland, administered as part of Eastern Prov., Gold Coast colony, near Volta R., 30 mi. NNW of Ho; cacao center; pottery making, ivory and ebony carving. Sometimes spelled Kpando.

Kpong (kŭpông'), town, Eastern Prov., SE Gold Coast colony, 6 mi. NW of Akuse; road junction; cacao, palm oil and kernels, cassava.

Kra, village, Thailand: see KRABURI.

Kra, Isthmus of (krä), neck of land in S Thailand bet. Gulf of Siam (E) and Pakchan R. estuary (inlet of Andaman Sea; W), connecting Malay Peninsula with Asian mainland, at 10°N; 25–30 mi. wide (at narrowest point) bet. Kraburi (for which it is named) and Chumphon. A canal across the isthmus was planned 1881, but abandoned.

Kraaifontein (krī'fôntän"), town (pop. 2,932), SW Cape Prov., U. of So. Afr., 18 mi. ENE of Cape Town; rail junction; agr. market (grain, fruit).

Krab, Albania: see KRRAB.

Kraba, Albania: see KRRABË.

Krabbendijke (krä'bŭndī"kŭ), village (pop. 2,292), Zeeland prov., SW Netherlands, on South Beveland isl., 11 mi. ESE of Goes; vegetable canning, flax spinning. Sometimes spelled Krabbendyke.

Krabë, Albania: see KRRABË.

Krabi, Albania: see KRRAB.

Krabi (krä'bē'), town (1947 pop. 1,447), ⊙ Krabi prov. (□ 1,531; 1947 pop. 59,483), S Thailand, in Malay Peninsula, port on Strait of Malacca, 130 mi. NW of Songkhla; coconuts. Coal and tin mining near by. Linked by road with rail station of Huai Yot.

Krabin or **Krabinburi,** Thailand: see KABINBURI.

Kraburi (krä'bōōrē'), village (1937 pop. 2,053), Ranong prov., S Thailand, in Isthmus of Kra, 30 mi. WSW of Chumphon (linked by road across isthmus), at head of Pakchan R. estuary (Burma border). Sometimes called Kra.

Krachi, Br. Togoland: see KETE-KRACHI.

Kragero (krä'gŭrû), Nor. *Kragerø*, city (pop. 4,016) and port, Telemark co., S Norway, at mouth of Toke R. on small inlet of the Skagerrak, 70 mi. NE of Kristiansand; lumbering center, with shipyards, sawmills, and mfg. of wood pulp and knit goods. City founded in 17th cent. Surrounding Skatoy or Skaatoy canton (Nor. *Skåtøy*) has feldspar and quartz quarries.

Kragujevac or **Kraguyevats** (both: krä'gōōyĕväts), city (pop. 32,528), ⊙ Kragujevac oblast (formed 1949), central Serbia, Yugoslavia, on railroad and 60 mi. SSE of Belgrade. Economic and cultural center of the Sumadija; munitions industry; vegetable canning, flour milling; ships plums. First mentioned in 17th cent.; seat (1818–39) of Milosh Obrenovich I and the cultural and political center of Serbia.

Krai, Malaya: see KUALA KRAI.

Kraiburg (krī'bōōrk), village (pop. 2,493), Upper Bavaria, Germany, on the Inn and 6 mi. SW of Mühldorf; glass and textile mfg., metalworking, lumber milling.

Kraichbach (krīkh'bäkh), river in N Baden, Germany, rises 1.5 mi. SE of Sulzfeld, flows 35 mi. NW, past Hockenheim, to an arm of the Rhine just SW of Ketsch.

Krain, former crownland, Yugoslavia: see CARNIOLA.

Krainburg, Yugoslavia: see KRANJ, village.

Krainka (krī'ĭnkŭ), town (1939 pop. over 500), W Tula oblast, Russian SFSR, 7 mi. E of Chekalin; health resort (mineral springs).

Krainovka or **Kraynovka** (krī'nŭfkŭ), village (1939 (pop. over 500), E Grozny oblast, Russian SFSR, on Caspian Sea, at mouth of N (Old Terek) arm of Terek R. delta, 35 mi. ENE of Kizlyar; cotton, livestock raising. Fisheries.

Kraishte, highland, Bulgaria and Yugoslavia: see KRAJISTE.

Krajenka (kräyĕn'kä), Ger. *Krojanke* (krōyäng'kŭ), town (1939 pop. 3,227; 1946 pop. 1,856) in Pomerania, after 1945 in Koszalin prov., NW Poland, 15 mi. NE of Schneidemühl (Pila); grain and cattle market; woodworking. Until 1938, in former Prussian prov. of Grenzmark Posen–Westpreussen.

Krajiste or **Krayishte** (both: krī'ĭshtĕ), Serbo-Croatian *Krajište*, Bulg. *Kraishte* (krī'shtĕ), highland in W Bulgaria and SE Yugoslavia, bet. Besna Kobila mtn. (W) and upper Struma R. (E), S of Trin; includes Milevo Mts. Scattered magnetite, galena, zinc, gold, and lignite deposits. Highest area in Yugoslavia; rises to 5,686 ft. in Milevo Mts., on border. Deforested; little vegetation.

Krak, Jordan: see KERAK.

Krakatoa (krä"kŭtō'ŭ) or **Krakatau** (kräkätou'), volcanic islet, Indonesia, in Sunda Strait bet. Java and Sumatra, 90 mi. W of Jakarta; 6°9'S 105°27'E; roughly circular, 3 mi. in diameter. Has active volcano (alt. 2,667 ft.). Its awesome eruption of August, 1883, one of the most catastrophic ever recorded, destroyed part of isl., altered the boundaries of Sunda Strait, scattered debris as far as Madagascar, and formed new islets from the outpouring of lava. The explosion was heard as far as the Philippines and Japan. There have been subsequent minor eruptions. Also spelled Krakatoea; sometimes called Rakata.

Krakau, city, Poland: see CRACOW.

Krakeroy, Norway: see FREDRIKSTAD.

Krakor or **Anlongthnot** (kräkôr', änlôngt-nôt'), village, Pursat prov., central Cambodia, on road and 22 mi. ESE of Pursat, near lake Tonle Sap (its port is Kompong Luong des Lacs).

Krakovets (krä'kŭvyĭts), Pol. *Krakowiec* (kräkô'vyĕts), town (1931 pop. 1,706), W Lvov oblast, Ukrainian SSR, on Pol. border, 10 mi. W of Yavorov; sawmilling; grain.

Krakow or **Krakow am See** (krä'kō äm zā'), town (pop. 3,553), Mecklenburg, N Germany, on Krakow L. (□ 6.1; 7 mi. long, 1–2 mi. wide), 11 mi. SSE of Güstrow; agr. market (grain, potatoes, stock); sawmilling, distilling. Tourist resort.

Krakow (krä'kō, krä'kou), Pol. *Kraków* (krä'kōōf), province [Pol. *województwo*] (□ 5,901; pop. 2,005,-779), S Poland; ⊙ Cracow. From upper Vistula R. valley rises steeply (S) to the W Beskids range and the High Tatra; highest point, the Rysy (8,212 ft.), is on Czechoslovak border. Wood- and metalworking, lumbering, mfg. of machinery, railroad cars, and chemicals are principal industries. Hydroelectric power plants. Major salt mines at Wieliczka and Bochnia. Iron, lead, zinc, and coal are worked. Chief crops are rye, oats, potatoes, wheat; livestock. Principal towns: Cracow, Tarnow, Nowa Huta (metallurgical center), Nowy Sacz. Zakopane, Krynica, and Rabka are popular health and winter-sports resorts. Boundaries of the pre-Second World War prov. (□ 6,710; 1931 pop. 2,297,802) were changed by transfer of territory to Rzeszow prov. Before First World War, prov. was part of Austro-Hungarian Galicia prov.

Krakow, city, Poland: see CRACOW.

Krakowiec, Ukrainian SSR: see KRAKOVETS.

Kraksaan or **Kraksan** (both: kräksän'), town (pop. 4,738), E Java, Indonesia, on Madura Strait, 60 mi. SE of Surabaya; trade center for agr. area (sugar, rice, corn). Also spelled Keraksaan.

Kralendijk (krä"lŭndīk'), chief town of Bonaire, Du. West Indies, on W inlet of the isl., guarded by Little Bonaire isl., 45 mi. E of Willemstad, Curaçao. Shipbuilding. The region produces divi-divi, aloes, salt, wool.

Kralice or **Kralice na Hane** (krä'lĭtsĕ nä hä'nĕ), Czech *Kralice na Hané*, Ger. *Kralitz* (krä'lĭts), village (pop. 1,144), central Moravia, Czechoslovakia, just E of Prostejov, in the Hana region. The main Bohemian version of the Bible was 1st printed here in 16th cent.

Kralicky Sneznik (krä'lĭtskē snyĕzh'nĭk), Czech *Králický Sněžník*, Ger. *Glatzer Schneegebirge* (glä'-tsŭr shnā'gŭbĭr"gŭ), Pol. *Góry Kłodzkie* (gōō'rĭ kwôts'kyĕ), mountain group of the Sudetes, in NE Bohemia and Lower Silesia, on Czechoslovak-Pol. border, NW of Stare Mesto; highest peak (4,672 ft.) is Kralicky Sneznik, Ger. *Glatzer Schneeberg*, Pol. *Śnieżnik*. Important watershed; Glatzer Neisse and Morava rivers rise on S slope.

Kraliky (krä'lēkĭ), Czech *Králíky*, Ger. *Grulich* (grōō'lĭkh), village (pop. 2,493), E Bohemia, Czechoslovakia, in SSE foothills of the Adlergebirge, 34 mi. ENE of Pardubice, near Pol. border; rail junction; woodworking, toy mfg.; oat growing.

Kralingen (krä'lĭng-ŭn), South Holland prov., W Netherlands, an E suburb of Rotterdam, on New Maas R.

Kraljevica (krä'lyĕvētsä), Ital. *Porto Re* (pôr'tô rā'), village, NW Croatia, Yugoslavia, on Adriatic Sea, 8 mi. ESE of Rijeka (Fiume), on channel leading to Bay of Bakar; shipbuilding; fishing. Bathing resort near wooded hills; sanatorium. Has 2 castles.

Kraljevo, Yugoslavia: see RANKOVICEVO, town.

Kralova Hola (krä'lyôvä hô'lyä), Slovak *Kráľova Hoľa*, Hung. *Király Hegy* (kĭ'rī hĕ'dyŭ), second-highest peak (6,373 ft.) of the Low Tatra, in central Slovakia, Czechoslovakia, 23 mi. NW of Roznava. Hron R. rises on SE, Cierny Vah R. on N slopes.

Kralovany (krä'lyôvänĭ), Slovak *Kraľovany*, Hung. *Kralován* (krŏ'lôvän), village (pop. 622), N Slovakia, Czechoslovakia, on Vah R., at Orava R. mouth, and 19 mi. ESE of Zilina; rail junction; excursion center. Summer and winter health resort of Lubochna (lŏŏ'bôchnyä), Slovak *Lubochňa*, is c.3 mi. SE, along left bank of Orava R.

Kralovice (krä'lôvĭtsĕ), Ger. *Kralowitz* (krä'lōvĭts), town (pop. 1,997), W Bohemia, Czechoslovakia, on railroad and 17 mi. NNE of Pilsen, in barley- and oat-growing region.

Kralovo nad Tisou, Ukrainian SSR: see KOROLEVO.

Kralovo Pole (krä'lôvô pô'lĕ), Czech *Královo Pole*, Ger. *Königsfeld* (kû'nĭkhsfĕlt), town (pop. 23,082), S Moravia, Czechoslovakia, on railroad and 2 mi. NNW of Brno; part of Greater Brno. Mfg. of machinery (notably for sawmills and plywood factories); sugar refining.

Kralovske Vinohrady (krä'lôfskā vĭnôhrädĭ), Czech *Královské Vinohrady*, E district (pop. 93,865) of Prague, central Bohemia, Czechoslovakia; business and residential area.

Kralovsky Chlmec (krä'lyôfskē khŭl'mĕts), Slovak *Kráľovský Chľmec*, Hung. *Királyhelmec* (kĭ'rīhĕl"-mĕts), town (pop. 3,410), SE Slovakia, Czechoslovakia, on railroad and 38 mi. SE of Kosice; agr. center (wheat, sugar beets, corn, grapes, tobacco). In Hungary, 1938–45.

Kralupy nad Vltavou (krä'lŏŏpĭ näd'vŭltävō"), town (pop. 9,167), N central Bohemia, Czechoslovakia, on Vltava R. and 12 mi. NNW of Prague; rail hub; large oil refinery; mfg. of dyes and drugs, beer brewing, food processing. Coal mines near by.

Kraluv Dvur (krä'lōōf dvōōr"), Czech *Králův Dvůr*, Ger. *Königshof* (kû'nĭkhshōf), village (pop. 3,390), central Bohemia, Czechoslovakia, on railroad and 3 mi. SW of Beroun; iron foundries, steel mills, large cement works.

Kralyevo, Yugoslavia: see RANKOVICEVO, town.

Kram, Le (lŭ kräm'), residential N suburb of La Goulette, Tunis dist., N Tunisia, on W shore of Gulf of Tunis, 8 mi. ENE of Tunis; bathing resort.

Kramatorsk (krŭmŭtôrsk′), city (1926 pop. 12,348; 1939 pop. 93,350), N Stalino oblast, Ukrainian SSR, in the Donbas, 50 mi. NNW of Stalino. Major machine-building center; iron and steel mills; mfg. (mining and metallurgical machinery, heavy machine tools, cement). Formerly called Kramatorskaya.

Krambruk, Australia: see APOLLO BAY.

Kramer, village (pop. 198), Bottineau co., N N.Dak., 15 mi. SW of Bottineau. Large cooperative grain elevator is here.

Kramfors (kräm″fôrs′, –fôsh′), village (1945 pop. 1,651; 1950 pop. 13,865), Vasternorrland co., NE Sweden, on Angerman R. estuary, 20 mi. NNW of Harnosand; lumber and pulp milling, woodworking; sulphite works.

Krammer (krä′mŭr), SW Netherlands, in Zeeland, part of S arm of Waal and Maas estuary, bet. Overflakkee isl. and Sint Philipsland. Formed by branching of the Hollandschdiep into the Volkerak (vōl′kûräk), which extends W as the Krammer, and farther W as the Grevelingen (grā′vŭlĭng″ŭn), to the North Sea.

Kramsach (kräm′säkh), town (pop. 2,840), Tyrol, W Austria, on the Inn and 26 mi. NE of Innsbruck; glass mfg.; summer resort.

Kranach, Germany: see KRONACH.

Kranenburg (krä′nŭnbŏŏrk), village (pop. 4,065), in former Prussian Rhine Prov., W Germany, after 1945 in North Rhine-Westphalia, 5 mi. W of Cleves; customs station near Dutch border. Until 1936, spelled Cranenburg.

Krange (krông′ŭ), Swedish *Krånge,* village (pop. 914), Vasternorrland co., NE Sweden, on Fax R., Swedish *Faxälven* (fäks′ĕl″vŭn), tributary of Angerman R., 25 mi. NE of Solleftea; market center in lumbering, dairying region.

Krangede (krông′ŭdŭ), Swedish *Krångede,* locality, Jamtland co., N central Sweden, on Indal R. and 35 mi. W of Solleftea; major hydroelectric station.

Kranichfeld (krä′nĭkhfĕlt), town (pop. 3,729), Thuringia, central Germany, on Ilm R. and 10 mi. SW of Weimar; woodworking, china and electrical-equipment mfg. Has 2 medieval castles.

Kranidion or **Kranidhion** (both: kränē′dhēōn), town (pop. 4,588), Argolis and Corinthia nome, E Peloponnesus, Greece, on Argolis Peninsula, 23 mi. SE of Nauplia; olive-oil production; fisheries and sponge fishing.

Kranj, crownland, Yugoslavia: see CARNIOLA.

Kranj (krī′nyŭ), Ger. *Krainburg* (krīn′bŏŏrk), anc. *Carnium,* village (pop. 15,640), N Slovenia, Yugoslavia, on Sava R. and 15 mi. NNW of Ljubljana; rail junction; mfg. of woolen textiles, electrotechnical and precision instruments, leather. Site of former castle of dukes of Carniola. Until 1918, in Carniola.

Kranjska Gora (krīn′skä gô′rä), Ger. *Kronau* (krō′nou), village, NW Slovenia, Yugoslavia, on the Sava Dolinka, on railroad and 25 mi. WNW of Jesenice, at N foot of Julian Alps; climatic resort and sports center. Hydroelectric plant. Until 1918, in Carniola.

Kranz, Russian SFSR: see ZELENOGRADSK.

Kra Peninsula: see MALAY PENINSULA.

Krapina (krä′pēnä), village (pop. 1,760), N Croatia, Yugoslavia, on railroad and 25 mi. N of Zagreb, near Slovenia border; local trade center; brown-coal mine; sulphur deposits. First mentioned in 1193. Krapinske Toplice, 5 mi. SSW, is health resort with mineral springs.

Krapina River, N Croatia, Yugoslavia, rises 11 mi. SSW of Varazdin, flows c.40 mi. SW to Sava R. near Podsused.

Krapivino (krŭpē′vĭnŭ), village (1948 pop. over 2,000), central Kemerovo oblast, Russian SFSR, in Kuznetsk Basin, on Tom R. and 30 mi. NE of Leninsk-Kuznetski, in agr. area; coal mining.

Krapivna (krŭpēv′nŭ), village (1926 pop. 6,051), central Tula oblast, Russian SFSR, on Upa R. and 25 mi. SW of Tula; flour milling, metal- and woodworking.

Krapkowice (kräpkôvē′tsĕ), Ger. *Krappitz* (krä′pĭts), town (1939 pop. 5,559; 1946 pop. 2,826) in Upper Silesia, after 1945 in Opole prov., SW Poland, on the Oder and 13 mi. S of Oppeln (Opole); cellulose mfg., sawmilling, limestone quarrying. After 1945, briefly called Chrapkowice.

Krapotkin, Russian SFSR: see KROPOTKIN.

Krappfeld (kräp′fĕlt), Carinthia, S Austria, fertile region bet. Althofen and Sankt Veit an der Glan, drained by Gurk R.

Krappitz, Poland: see KRAPKOWICE.

Kra River, Thailand-Burma: see PAKCHAN RIVER.

Kras, plateau, Yugoslavia: see KARST.

Krasavino (krŭsä′vēnŭ), city (1926 pop. 2,963), NE Vologda oblast, Russian SFSR, on Lesser Northern Dvina R. and 14 mi. NNE of Veliki Ustyug; linen-milling center.

Krasic (krä′shĭch), Serbo-Croatian *Krašić,* village, N Croatia, Yugoslavia, near Kupa R., 10 mi. N of Karlovac.

Krasilov (krŭsē′lŭf), village (1926 pop. 4,925), central Kamenets-Podolski oblast, Ukrainian SSR, 16 mi. N of Proskurov; sugar refining, metalworking.

Krasivka (krŭsēf′kŭ), village (1926 pop. 2,234), E Tambov oblast, Russian SFSR, on Vorona R. and 25 mi. SSW of Kirsanov; wheat.

Kraskino (kräs′kēnŭ). **1** Settlement on S coast of S isl. of Novaya Zemlya, Archangel oblast, Russian SFSR; 70°45′N 54°30′E. Trading post. **2** Town (1948 pop. over 2,000), SW Maritime Territory, Russian SFSR, on Posyet Bay, 65 mi. SW of Vladivostok; terminus of branch of Trans-Siberian RR; lignite mines. Formerly Novokiyevskoye.

Kraslava (krä′slävä), Lettish *Krāslava,* Ger. *Kraslau,* Rus. (until 1917) *Kreslavka,* city (pop. 4,276), SE Latvia, in Latgale, on right bank of the Western Dvina and 25 mi. E of Daugavpils; flour milling, wool processing; rye, flax. In Rus. Vitebsk govt. until 1920.

Kraslice (krä′slĭtsĕ), Ger. *Graslitz* (gräs′lĭts), town (pop. 6,294), W Bohemia, Czechoslovakia, on railroad and 18 mi. WNW of Carlsbad, near Ger. border opposite Klingenthal; mfg. of musical toys and wind instruments, lace, embroidery, woolen textiles. Tungsten mining at Rolava (rô′lävä), Ger. *Sauersack* (zou′ûrzäk), 6 mi. NE. Tin mining at Prebuz (pûrzhĕ′bŏŏs), Czech *Přebuz,* Ger. *Frühbuss* (frü′bŏŏs), 5 mi. ENE.

Krasna Horka, Czechoslovakia: see ROZNAVA.

Krasna Lipa (krä′snä lē′pä), Czech *Krásná Lípa,* Ger. *Schönlinde* (shûn′lĭndĕ), village (pop. 3,487), N Bohemia, Czechoslovakia, in W Sudetes, 27 mi. NE of Usti nad Labem; rail junction; dyeing, tanning, mfg. (clothing, textiles, knit goods). Founded in 13th cent. by Ger. colonists.

Krasnaya [Rus.,=red], in Rus. names: see also KRASNO- [Rus. combining form], KRASNOYE, KRASNY, KRASNYE.

Krasnaya Armiya Strait (krä′snīŭ är′mēŭ) [Rus.,= Red Army], joins Kara and Laptev seas of Arctic Ocean, at c.80°N., in Krasnoyarsk Territory, Russian SFSR; separtes Komsomolets and Pioner isls. from Oktyabrskaya Revolyutsiya Isl. of Severnaya Zemlya archipelago; 90 mi. long, 5–10 mi. wide.

Krasnaya Gora (gŭrä′), village (1948 pop. over 2,000), W Bryansk oblast, Russian SFSR, 30 mi. NW of Klintsy; tobacco.

Krasnaya Gorbatka (gŭrbät′kŭ), town (1939 pop. over 2,000), E Valdimir oblast, Russian SFSR, 23 mi. NNW of Murom; paper-milling center. Selivanovo village (sawmilling) is 2 mi. NNW.

Krasnaya Gorka (gôr′kŭ). **1** Village (1926 pop. 3,193), NE Bashkir Autonomous SSR, Russian SFSR, on Ufa R. (landing) and 45 mi. NE of Ufa, in woodland; lumbering; livestock. **2** Town (1942 pop. over 500), W Gorki oblast, Russian SFSR, 5 mi. W of Volodary.

Krasnaya Kamenka, Ukrainian SSR: see CHERVONAYA KAMENKA.

Krasnaya Pakhra (päkh′rŭ), village (1939 pop. over 500), S central Moscow oblast, Russian SFSR, on Pakhra R. and 10 mi. W of Podolsk; truck produce, poultry, fruit.

Krasnaya Polyana (pŭlyä′nŭ). **1** Village (1926 pop. 1,207), S Krasnodar Territory, Russian SFSR, on S slope of the W Greater Caucasus, near Mzymta R., 22 mi. NNE of Adler (connected by road); climatic mtn. resort (alt. c.2,500 ft.). Mineral springs near by. **2** Town (1926 pop. 4,360), central Moscow oblast, Russian SFSR, 20 mi. NNW of Moscow; cotton mill.

Krasnaya Rechka (ryĕch′kŭ), town (1939 pop. over 500), S Khabarovsk Territory, Russian SFSR, on Trans-Siberian RR and 8 mi. S of Khabarovsk; flour milling.

Krasnaya Shapochka (shä′pŭchkŭ), hill on E slopes of central Urals, Russian SFSR; 60°10′N. Bauxite mining was begun here (c.1940) at SEVEROURALSK.

Krasnaya Sloboda (slŭbŭdä′). **1** NW suburb (1945 pop. over 500) of Kuba, NE Azerbaijan SSR; orchards; fruit canning. **2** Town (1926 pop. 2,111), W Bobruisk oblast, Belorussian SSR, 29 mi. SW of Slutsk; dairying, flour milling. **3** Town (1939 pop. over 10,000), E Stalingrad oblast, Russian SFSR, on left bank of Volga R., opposite Stalingrad (ferry); metalworks.

Krasnaya Yaruga (yä′rŏŏgŭ), village (1926 pop. 4,109), S Kursk oblast, Russian SFSR, 40 mi. WNW of Belgorod; sugar refinery.

Krasnaya Zarya (zŭryä), village (1939 pop. over 500), central Orel oblast, Russian SFSR, 34 mi. WNW of Yelets; grain.

Krasnaya Zvezda (zvyĭzdä′), N suburb (1926 pop. 3,193) of Chistyakovo, E Stalino oblast, Ukrainian SSR; coal mines.

Krasne. **1** Town, Belorussian SSR: see KRASNOYE, Molodechno oblast. **2** Village, Ukrainian SSR: see KRASNOYE, Lvov oblast.

Krasnik (kräsh′nĕk), Pol. *Kraśnik,* town (pop. 9,158), Lublin prov., E Poland, 27 mi. SSW of Lublin, on medieval route from Lithuania to Cracow; flour milling, tanning; brickworks. Before Second World War, pop. 40% Jewish.

Krasno (krä′snô), Czech *Krásno,* Ger. *Schönfeld* (shûn′fĕlt), village (pop. 1,171), W Bohemia, Czechoslovakia, 19 mi. ENE of Cheb; tungsten mining. Other tungsten works at near-by Cista (chĭ′stä), Czech *Čistá,* Ger. *Lauterbach* (lou′tûrbäkh); until c.1946 called Mesto Litrbachy.

Krasno-[Rus. combining form,=red], in Rus. names: see also KRASNAYA, KRASNOYE, KRASNY, KRASNYE.

Krasnoarmeisk or **Krasnoarmeysk** (krä″snŭ-ŭrmyäsk′). **1** City (1926 pop. 4,444), E Moscow oblast, Russian SFSR, on rail spur and 31 mi. NE of Moscow; cotton-milling center. Until 1928, called Voznesenkaya Manufaktura and later (until 1947), Krasnoarmeiski. **2** City (1926 pop. 12,241), S Saratov oblast, Russian SFSR, 37 mi. SSW of Saratov, near Volga R.; industrial center; cotton milling, mfg. (apparel, shoes), food processing. Originally called Goly Karamysh; known as Baltser or Balzer (1920–41), while in German Volga Automonous SSR. **3** S suburb of Stalingrad, Stalingrad oblast, Russian SFSR, on the Volga and 14 mi. S of Stalingrad city center, at N end of Sarpa Lakes valley; shipbuilding; locomotive- and car-building works. Dist. known for mustard production. Founded c.1770 as Ger. colony; called Sarepta until 1920.

Krasnoarmeiskaya or **Krasnoarmeyskaya** (–ŭrmyā′skīŭ), village (1926 pop. 14,306), W Krasnodar Territory, Russian SFSR, 45 mi. WNW of Krasnodar; flour mill, metalworks; rice, cotton, vineyards. Until 1930s, Poltavskaya.

Krasnoarmeiski Rudnik or **Krasnoarmeyskiy Rudnik** (–ŭrmyā′skē rŏŏdnyĭk′), town (1926 pop. 570), W Stalino oblast, Ukrainian SSR, in the Donbas, 14 mi. NNW of Krasnoarmeiskoye; coal mines. Formerly Svyatogorovski Rudnik.

Krasnoarmeiskoye or **Krasnoarmeyskoye** (–skŭyŭ). **1** Village (1939 pop. under 500), N central Chuvash Autonomous SSR, Russian SFSR, 25 mi. S of Cheboksary; wheat, livestock. Until 1939, Peredniye Traki. **2** Village (1926 pop. 13,010), S Grozny oblast, Russian SFSR, 14 mi. SSW of Grozny and on right branch of Sunzha R.; wheat, corn. Until 1944, Urus-Martan. **3** City (1926 pop. 11,377), W Stalino oblast, Ukrainian SSR, in the Donbas 35 mi. NW of Stalino; rail junction; coal-mining center; metalworks. Until c.1935, Grishino. **4** Town, Zaporozhe oblast, Ukrainian SSR: see CHERVONOARMEISKOYE.

Krasnoborsk (krŭsnŭbôrsk′), village (1926 pop. 989), SE Archangel Oblast, Russian SFSR, on Northern Dvina R. and 30 mi. NW of Kotlas; dairying.

Krasnodar (krŭsnŭdär′), territory [Rus. *krai* or *kray*] (□ 32,800; 1946 pop. estimate 3,000,000) in S European Russian SFSR, on Sea of Azov and Black Sea; ⊙ Krasnodar. Astride forested NW end of the Greater Caucasus; extends N into level treeless Kuban lowland; includes ADYGE AUTONOMOUS OBLAST. Drained by Kuban R. and its affluents, Belaya and Laba rivers. Main agr. dist. in Kuban Steppe, with large areas under spring wheat and sunflowers. Lesser crops are winter wheat, barley, corn, tobacco, and, near Sea of Azov, cotton, hemp, soy- and castor beans. Seed selection and seed export important. Rice grown along reclaimed lower Kuban R. Intensive livestock raising for dairy products, hides, and meat. Subtropical Black Sea littoral (at S foot of the Greater Caucasus) produces garden crops, citrus fruit, essential oils, tea, and wine; site of such important health resorts as Sochi, Matsesta, and Anapa. Industry (centered at Krasnodar, Kropotkin, and Armavir) based on agr. processing (vegetable oils, canned goods, tobacco, flour). Petroleum industry; production centers at Apsheronsk and Neftegorsk, in Maikop oil fields; refining at Krasnodar and Tuapse, a major petroleum port. Fish-processing (from Sea of Azov fisheries) plants at Yeisk, Primorsko-Akhtarskaya, and Temryuk. Cement mills at Novorossisk. Formed 1937 out of Azov-Black Sea Territory. Occupied (1942–43) by Germans during Second World War, except for Black Sea littoral.

Krasnodar, city (1939 pop. 203,946) ⊙ Krasnodar Territory, Russian SFSR, port on right bank of lower Kuban R. and 150 mi. SSW of Rostov, 73 mi. S of Moscow; 45°1′N 38°59′E. Rail hub and major industrial center in black-earth zone; petroleum refining (pipe line from Maikop oil fields), mfg. (machinery, tractor parts), railroad repair shops, repair docks; steel foundry. Processes agr. products (tobacco, dairy goods, alcohol, flour, meat, vegetable oils), hides, and skins. Has agr., medical and teachers colleges, research institute for oil-bearing plants, regional mus. Founded 1794 under Catherine II (commemorated by monument) and called Yekaterinodar (or Ekaterinodar); became ⊙ Kuban oblast and hq. of Kuban Cossacks. Renamed Krasnodar in 1920. During Second World War, held (1942–43) by Germans.

Krasnodon (–dôn′), city (1939 pop. over 10,000), SE Voroshilovgrad oblast, Ukrainian SSR, in the Donbas, on the Bolshaya Kamenka (right affluent of the Northern Donets) and 30 mi. SE of Voroshilovgrad; coal-mining center. Formerly Sorokinsk Rudnik or Sorokino.

Krasnodonetskaya, Russian SFSR: see SINEGORSKI.

Krasnodonski or **Krasnodonskiy** (–skē), town (1926 pop. 7,227), SE Voroshilovgrad oblast, Ukrainian SSR, in the Donbas, 9 mi. WNW of Krasnodon; coal mines. Formerly Krasnodonetski Rudnik.

Krasnofarforny or **Krasnofarfornyy** (krŭsnŭfär′fûrnē), town (1939 pop. over 500), N Novgorod oblast, Russian SFSR, on Volkhov R. and 6 mi. N of Chudovo; porcelain mfg.

Krasnogorka (–gôr′kŭ), village (1948 pop. over 500), SE Dzhambul oblast, Kazakh SSR, in Chu-Ili Mts., 90 mi. W of Alma-Ata; grain, sheep.

Krasnogorodskoye (krä"snŭgŭrôt'skŭyŭ), village (1939 pop. over 500), NW Velikiye Luki oblast, Russian SFSR, 17 mi. NW of Opochka, near Latvian border; flax processing. Also Krasnogorodsk.

Krasnogorovka (krŭsnŭgô'rŭfkŭ), city (1926 pop. 1,861), central Stalino oblast, Ukrainian SSR, in the Donbas, 14 mi. W of Stalino; quartzite and gypsum quarries; fire bricks; formerly Krasnogorski Rudnik.

Krasnogorsk (–gôrsk'). **1** City (1939 pop. over 10,000), central Moscow oblast, Russian SFSR, residential NW suburb of Moscow, on left bank of Moskva R.; metalworking; optical goods. Until c.1935, Pavshino or Banki. Arkhangelskoye, 5 mi. SW, was 18th-cent. countryseat of Prince Golitsyn; now a mus. **2** City (1940 pop. 17,417), on W coast of S Sakhalin, Russian SFSR, at SW foot of mtn. Krasnaya Gora, 45 mi. N of Tomari; fisheries. Under Jap. rule (1905–45), called Chinnai (chĕn'nĭ).

Krasnogorski or **Krasnogorskiy** (–gôr'skē), town (1938 pop. over 500), S Mari Autonomous SSR, Russian SFSR, on Ilet R. and 40 mi. SSE of Ioshkar-Ola, on rail spur; sawmilling center. Wood cracking, soap mfg. near by. Until 1938, Ilet.

Krasnogorskoye (–skŭyŭ), village, W Udmurt Autonomous SSR, Russian SFSR, 30 mi. SSW of Glazov; flax processing. Until 1938, Baryshnikovo.

Krasnograd (krŭsnŭgrät'), city (1926 pop. 12,695), W Kharkov oblast, Ukrainian SSR, 50 mi. SW of Kharkov, flour-milling center; fruit and vegetable canning, dairying. Formerly Konstantinograd.

Krasnogrigoryevka, Ukrainian SSR: see CHERVONO-GRIGOROVKA.

Krasnogvardeisk or **Krasnogvardeysk** (krä"snŭgvŭrdyäsk'). **1** City, Leningrad oblast, Russian SFSR: see GATCHINA. **2** Town (1948 pop. over 2,000), S Samarkand oblast, Uzbek SSR, on Trans-Caspian RR and 18 mi. ENE of Samarkand; sugar beets, wheat, cotton; metalworks, sugar refinery. Until 1930s, Rostovtsevo.

Krasnogvardeiski or **Krasnogvardeyskiy** (–dyä'skē). **1** Town (1926 pop. 2,598), S central Sverdlovsk oblast, Russian SFSR, on Irbit R. (right tributary of Nitsa R.) and 37 mi. SSE of Alapayevsk, on railroad (Taly Klyuch station); metallurgical center (steel); peat. Founded 1776; until 1938, Irbitski Zavod. **2** Town (1948 pop. over 500), E Tula oblast, Russian SFSR, near Bolokhovo, in Moscow Basin; lignite mining.

Krasnogvardeiskoye or **Krasnogvardeyskoye** (–skŭyŭ), village (1939 pop. over 500), N central Crimea, Russian SFSR, on railroad and 15 mi. SSW of Dzhankoi; flour milling, metalworks; wheat, cotton, livestock. Until 1944, Kurman-Kemelchi.

Krasnokamsk (krŭsnŭkämsk'), city (1936 pop. estimate 29,300), central Molotov oblast, Russian SFSR, port on right bank of Kama R. and 20 mi. W of Molotov, near railroad. Center of newly developed petroleum dist.; oil cracking, mfg. (paper, cellulose, agr. machinery, fishing nets, ethyl alcohol, chemicals); woodworking; peat digging. Developed in 1936 around paper mill; became city in 1938. Exploitation of extensive Devonian oil fields began in 1937. Chief oil-drilling settlements are Strelka (just E, on right Kama R. bank), Severokamsk (NW; linked by 10-mi.-long pipe line), and Maiski.

Krasnokholm, Russian SFSR: see KRASNY KHOLM, Chkalov oblast.

Krasnokokshaisk, Russian SFSR: see IOSHKAR-OLA.

Krasnokutsk (krŭsnŭkōōtsk'), town (1926 pop. 9,941), NW Kharkov oblast, Ukrainian SSR, 45 mi. W of Kharkov; flour milling.

Krasnokutskoye (–kōōt'skŭyŭ), agr. village (1939 pop. over 500), central Pavlodar oblast, Kazakh SSR, 55 mi. NNW of Pavlodar.

Krasnolesny or **Krasnolesnyy** (–lyĕ'snē), town (1948 pop. over 2,000), N central Voronezh oblast, Russian SFSR, 20 mi. NE of Voronezh; rail junction (Grafskaya station); lumber mill.

Krasnomaiski or **Krasnomayskiy** (–mī'skē), town (1926 pop. 1,332), W central Kalinin oblast, Russian SFSR, on railroad (Leontyevo station) and 6 mi. NW of Vyshni Volochek; glassworking center. Until 1940, Klyuchinski.

Krasnooktyabrski or **Krasnooktyabr'skiy** (krä"snŭŭktyä'bŭrskē). **1** Town (1941 pop. over 500), NW Frunze oblast, Kirghiz SSR, in Chu valley, just NE of Kaganovich; beet-sugar refinery. **2** Town (1926 pop. 1,441), central Moscow oblast, Russian SFSR, adjoining Moscow (NW); brickworks. Until 1928, Khovrino.

Krasnoostrovski or **Krasnoostrovskiy** (–ŭstrôf'skē), town (1940 pop. over 500), NW Leningrad oblast, Russian SFSR, just SE of Primorsk, on Karelian Isthmus; cellulose and paper milling. Called Byerkski, 1940–48.

Krasno-Perekopsk (–pĕrĭkôpsk'), town (1939 pop. over 500), N Crimea, Russian SFSR, on Perekop Isthmus, on railroad and 8 mi. SSE of Armyansk; bromine works.

Krasnopolye or **Krasnopol'ye** (krŭsnŭpô'lyĭ). **1** Town (1926 pop. 2,549), S Mogilev oblast, Belorussian SSR, 60 mi. SE of Mogilev; flax processing. **2** S suburb (1926 pop. 5,079) of Dnepropetrovsk, Dnepropetrovsk oblast, Ukrainian SSR, 6 mi. SW of city center. **3** Village (1926 pop. 8,170), SE Sumy oblast, Ukrainian SSR, 22 mi. ESE of Sumy; bldg. stone. **4** Town (1939 pop. over 2,000), SW Voroshilovgrad oblast, Ukrainian SSR, in the Donbas, 5 mi. S of Kadiyevka; coal mines. Formerly Krasnopolski Rudnik.

Krasnoselkup or **Krasnosel'kup** (krä"snŭsĕlkōōp'), village, E Yamal-Nenets Natl. Okrug, Tyumen oblast, Russian SFSR, on Taz R. and 180 mi. SW of Igarka, in reindeer-raising area; trading post. Pop. largely Selkups.

Krasno-selo, Bulgaria: see SOFIA, city.

Krasnoselsk or **Krasnosel'sk** (krŭsnŭsĕlsk'), village (1939 pop. over 2,000), E Armenian SSR, near E shore of L. Sevan, 50 mi. ESE of Kirovakan, near Azerbaijan border; livestock, potatoes.

Krasnoshchekovo (krŭsnŭshchô'kŭvŭ), village (1939 pop. over 2,000), S Altai Territory, Russian SFSR, on Charysh R. and 65 mi. E of Rubtsovsk; agr.

Krasnoslobodsk (krä"snŭslŭbôtsk'), city (1926 pop. 7,176), W central Mordvinian Autonomous SSR, Russian SFSR, on Moksha R. and 60 mi. WNW of Saransk, in hemp area; bast-fiber-processing center; flour milling. Founded 1571.

Krasnostav, Poland: see KRASNYSTAW.

Krasnotorka (krŭsnŭtôr'kŭ), town (1939 pop. over 500), N Stalino oblast, Ukrainian SSR, in the Donbas, 2 mi. S of Kramatorsk.

Krasnoturansk (–tōōränsk'), village (1926 pop. 3,242), S Krasnoyarsk Territory, Russian SFSR, 35 mi. N of Minusinsk and on Yenisei R.; dairy farming. Formerly Abakanskoye.

Krasnoturinsk or **Krasnotur'insk** (–rēnsk'), city (1926 pop. 5,602; 1946 pop. estimate 45,000), W Sverdlovsk oblast, Russian SFSR, in NE foothills of the central Urals, on railroad (Turinskiye station) and 18 mi. NW of Serov. 5 mi. E of Karpinsk, major aluminum-refining center, based on SEVEROURALSK, CHEREMUKHOVO, and KALYA bauxite mines; cellulose mfg.; copper and zinc mining. Largely developed after construction of aluminum works in 1940. Until 1944, Turinski or Turinski Rudnik.

Krasnoufimsk (–ōōfēmsk'), city (1936 pop. estimate 21,600), SW Sverdlovsk oblast, Russian SFSR, in SW foothills of the central Urals, on right bank of Ufa R. and 110 mi. WSW of Sverdlovsk, on railroad (repair shops); mfg. center (machine tools, caterpillar tread, fireproof bricks, pottery, starch). Founded 1736 as stronghold; chartered 1781.

Krasnouralsk or **Krasnoural'sk** (krä"snŭōōrälsk'), city (1936 pop. estimate 35,000), W Sverdlovsk oblast, Russian SFSR, in E foothills of the central Urals, 30 mi. N of Nizhni Tagil; rail spur terminus; a major copper-mining and -refining center; pyrite mining; mfg. of sulphuric acid. Developed in 1920s. Called Uralmedstroi until 1931; became city in 1932.

Krasnouralski Rudnik, Russian SFSR: see NOVOASBEST.

Krasnousolski or **Krasnousol'skiy** (–ōōsôl'skē), town (1948 pop. over 10,000), central Bashkir Autonomous SSR, Russian SFSR, 30 mi. NNE of Sterlitamak; glass-mfg. center. Quartz sand near by.

Krasnovishersk (krŭsnŭvē'shĭrsk), city (1935 pop. estimate over 14,000), N Molotov oblast, Russian SFSR, on Vishera R. (landing) and 55 mi. NNE of Solikamsk; major paper-mfg. center. Became city in 1942.

Krasnovo (krä'snôvô), village (pop. 2,164), Plovdiv dist., W central Bulgaria, at S foot of central Sredna Gora, 25 mi. NNW of Plovdiv; health resort; rye, potatoes, livestock. Formerly Krastovo.

Krasnovodsk (krŭsnŭvôtsk'), city (1939 pop. 23,600), W Ashkhabad oblast, Turkmen SSR, port on Krasnovodsk Gulf of Caspian Sea, 320 mi. WNW of Ashkhabad; W terminus of Trans-Caspian RR. Important trading center for transshipment of oil, cotton, salt, grain, timber. Petroleum refining (pipe line from Nebit-Dag), metalworking, food processing, fish canning; gypsum works. Founded (1869) 40 mi. NW of Rus. fortress of Mikhailovsk, base for conquest of Turkmenia (1877–85) and original terminus of Trans-Caspian RR. Krasnovodsk developed following extension of railroad in 1895. Was ⊙ former Krasnovodsk oblast, 1939–47.

Krasnoyarka (krŭsnŭyär'kŭ), village (1926 pop. 1,109), S Omsk oblast, Russian SFSR, on Irtysh R. and 25 mi. NNW of Omsk; metalworks.

Krasnoyarsk (krŭsnŭyärsk'), territory [Rus. *krai* or *kray*] (□ 928,000; 1939 pop. 1,940,002; 1946 pop. estimate 2,100,000) in central Siberian Russian SFSR; ⊙ Krasnoyarsk. Extends from Sayan Mts. (S) through wooded steppe, forests, and tundra to Kara and Laptev seas of Arctic Ocean (N); drained by the Yenisei and its tributaries, which are important transportation routes. Includes TAIMYR NATIONAL OKRUG, EVENKI NATIONAL OKRUG, and KHAKASS AUTONOMOUS OBLAST. Krasnoyarsk proper is hilly in extreme S and E of the Yenisei. Continental climate; rivers are frozen Nov.–May. N of Angara R. there are extensive forests, gold mines (Yenisei Ridge), coal (Tunguska Basin) and graphite (Kureika R.) deposits. Southernmost arable section (17% of total area; 94% of pop.) is traversed by Trans-Siberian and S.Siberian RRs; has chief industrial centers (Krasnoyarsk, Kansk, Achinsk, Minusinsk). Chief seaport (on the lower Yenisei), Igarka. Wheat, sugar-beet, and dairy farming along Trans-Siberian RR and in Minusinsk area. Lumber, gold, agr. products are chief exports. Formed in 1934 out of E.Siberian Territory. Area was part of Yeniseisk govt. from 1822 to 1925.

Krasnoyarsk, city (1926 pop. 72,261; 1939 pop. 189,999; 1946 pop. estimate 300,000), ⊙ Krasnoyarsk Territory, Russian SFSR, on Yenisei R., on Trans-Siberian RR and 2,100 mi. E of Moscow; 56°N 92°50'E. Transportation center; machinery construction (locomotives, agr. combines, drilling equipment, oil pumps); cement, lumber, and paper industries; textile and flour mills, refrigerating plants. City proper is located on left (W) bank of Yenisei R. After 1930s, a new industrial section developed on right river bank. Seat of Yenisei regional mus., teachers, medical, and timber-industry schools, and scientific research institutes. Founded 1628 as a fort, Krasny Yar. Became (1822) ⊙ Yeniseisk govt.; developed rapidly following construction of Trans-Siberian RR.

Krasnoye [Rus.,=red], in Rus. names: see also KRASNAYA, KRASNO- [Rus. combining form], KRASNY, KRASNYE.

Krasnoye (krä'snŭyŭ). **1** Pol. *Krasne* (krä'snĕ), town (1931 pop. 4,000), SE Molodechno oblast, Belorussian SSR, on Usha R. (left tributary of Viliya R.) and 12 mi. ESE of Molodechno; tanning, flour milling, sawmilling, tile and brick mfg. **2** Village (1939 pop. over 2,000), W Astrakhan oblast, Russian SFSR, 30 mi. E of Stepnoi; sheep raising; millet, mustard. Until 1944 (in Kalmyk Autonomous SSR), Ulan-Erge. **3** Village (1926 pop. 2,195), NE Orel oblast, Russian SFSR, 19 mi. NE of Yelets; distilling. **4** Village (1926 pop. 2,803), W Smolensk oblast, Russian SFSR, 28 mi. WSW of Smolensk; dairy center. Formerly called Krasny. **5** Village (1939 pop. over 2,000), W Voronezh oblast, Russian SFSR, 17 mi. WNW of Ostrogozhsk; woodworking. Also called Krasnoye Ukolovo or Krasnoye Ukolovskoye. **6** Pol. *Krasne,* village (1939 pop. over 500), central Lvov oblast, Ukrainian SSR, 25 mi. ENE of Lvov; rail junction; sawmilling, flour milling. Has ruins of 18th-cent. castle and church.

Krasnoye Ekho (ĕ'khŭ), town (1940 pop. over 500), S central Vladimir oblast, Russian SFSR, 11 mi. N of Gus-Khrustalny; glassworks.

Krasnoye on Volga (vŏl'gŭ), Rus. *Krasnoye na Volge,* village (1926 pop. 4,453), SW Kostroma oblast, Russian SFSR, on Volga R. and 20 mi. SSE of Kostroma; metalworking, flax processing; handicrafts (jewelry).

Krasnoye Selo (syĭlô'). **1** SE suburb (1945 pop. over 500) of Kirovabad, Azerbaijan SSR. **2** City (1939 pop. over 10,000), central Leningrad oblast, Russian SFSR, 15 mi. SSW of Leningrad; paper milling. Palaces at near-by NAGORNOYE and ROPSHA. Chartered 1654; called Krasny for few years after revolution. During Second World War, held (1941–44) by Germans in siege of Leningrad.

Krasnoye Ukolovo, Russian SFSR: see KRASNOYE, Voronezh oblast.

Krasnoye Vereshchagino, Russian SFSR: see VERESHCHAGINO.

Krasnoye Znamya (znä'myŭ), town (1948 pop. over 500), S Mary oblast, Turkmen SSR, 60 mi. SE of Mary, on Kushka RR and Murgab R.; irrigated agr.

Krasnozavodsk (krä"snŭzŭvôtsk'), city (1940 pop. over 2,000), NE Moscow oblast, Ukrainian SSR, 10 mi. NNE of Zagorsk; chemical works. Developed in late 1930s; until 1940, called Zagorski.

Krasnozerskoye (krŭsnŭzyôr'skŭyŭ), village (1939 pop. over 2,000), S Novosibirsk oblast, Russian SFSR, on Karasuk R. and 50 mi. ENE of Karasuk; dairying, flour milling.

Krasnoznamensk (–nä'myĭnsk), city (1939 pop. 2,066), NE Kaliningrad oblast, Russian SFSR, on Sheshupe R. and 22 mi. N of Nesterov, on narrow-gauge railroad; agr. market. Until 1945, in East Prussia where it was called Lasdehnen (läsdā'nŭn) and, later (1938–45), Haselberg (hä'zŭlbĕrk).

Krasny or **Krasnyy** [Rus.,=red], in Rus. names: see also KRASNAYA, KRASNO- [Rus. combining form], KRASNOYE, KRASNYE.

Krasny. **1** Village, Smolensk oblast, Russian SFSR: see KRASNOYE. **2** City, Tuva oblast, Russian SFSR: see KYZYL. **3** City, Udmurt Autonomous SSR, Russian SFSR: see MOZHGA.

Krasny Bazar or **Krasnyy Bazar** (krä"snē bŭzär'), town (1947 pop. over 500), S Nagorno-Karabakh Autonomous Oblast, Azerbaijan SSR, 14 mi. SE of Stepanakert; wine. Also called Karmir Bazar.

Krasny Bogatyr or **Krasnyy Bogatyr'** (bŭgŭtĭr'), town (1926 pop. 545), central Vladimir oblast, Russian SFSR, 11 mi. ENE of Sudogda; glassworks.

Krasny Bor or **Krasnyy Bor** (bôr'). **1** Town (1926 pop. 3,623), central Leningrad oblast, Russian SFSR, 22 mi. SE of Leningrad, glassworking center; chemicals. **2** Village (1939 pop. over 500), NE Tatar Autonomous SSR, Russian SFSR, on Kama R. and 11 mi. N of Menzelinsk; grain, livestock. Bronze relics (5th–7th cent.) excavated near by. Formerly called Pyany Bor.

Krasny Boyevik, Russian SFSR: see KOTOVSK, Tambov oblast.

Krasny Chetai or **Krasnyy Chetay** (chĭtī′), village (1948 pop. over 2,000), W Chuvash Autonomous SSR, Russian SFSR, 16 mi. NW of Shumerlya; wheat, rye, oats. Until c.1937, Krasnyye Chetai.

Krasny Chikoi or **Krasnyy Chikoy** (chĭkoi′), village (1948 pop. over 2,000), SW Chita oblast, Russian SFSR, on Chikoi R. and 60 mi. S of Petrovsk; gold mining; tanning.

Krasnye or **Krasnyye** [Rus.,=red], in Rus. names: see also KRASNAYA, KRASNO- [Rus. combining form], KRASNOYE, KRASNY.

Krasnye Baki or **Krasnyye Baki** (krä″snēŭ bä′kē), town (1926 pop. 3,077), N central Gorki oblast, Russian SFSR, on Vetluga R. and 70 mi. NE of Gorki; wood-cracking center.

Krasnye Okny or **Krasnyye Okny** (ôk′nē), village (1926 pop. 3,644), W Odessa oblast, Ukrainian SSR, 28 mi. SSW of Balta; wines; metalworks. Until c.1935, Okny.

Krasnye Tkachi or **Krasnyye Tkachi** (tŭkŭchē′), town (1926 pop. 1,366), N central Yaroslavl oblast, Russian SFSR, on Kotorosl R. and 10 mi. SSW of Yaroslavl; linen weaving.

Krasny Gorodok, Ukrainian SSR: see RAIGORODOK.

Krasny Kholm or **Krasnyy Kholm** (krä″snē khôlm′). **1** Village (1926 pop. 6,923), S Chkalov oblast, Russian SFSR, near Ural R., 40 mi. WSW of Chkalov; metalworking; wheat, livestock. Until c.1940, called Krasnokholm or Krasnokholmski. **2** City (1926 pop. 4,680), E Kalinin oblast, Russian SFSR, near Mologa R., 25 mi. NE of Bezhetsk; flax processing; metalworks, clothing mill. Chartered 1627.

Krasny Klyuch or **Krasnyy Klyuch** (klyōōch′), town (1948 pop. over 2,000), NE Bashkir Autonomous SSR, Russian SFSR, on Ufa R. (landing) and 13 mi. N of Krasnaya Gorka, in woodland; paper mfg.

Krasny Kut or **Krasnyy Kut** (kōōt′). **1** Town (1939 pop. over 10,000), S Saratov oblast, Russian SFSR, on Yeruslan R. and 50 mi. SE of Engels; rail junction; metalworks, flour mill. Agr. selection station. Kumiss resort. Until 1941, in German Volga Autonomous SSR. **2** Town (1926 pop. 2,942), S Voroshilovgrad oblast, Ukrainian SSR, in the Donbas, 7 mi. NW of Krasny Luch; coal mines.

Krasny Liman or **Krasnyy Liman** (lyĭmän′). **1** Village (1939 pop. over 2,000), central Voronezh oblast, Russian SFSR, 30 mi. ESE of Voronezh; wheat. **2** City (1939 pop. over 10,000), N Stalino oblast, Ukrainian SSR, in the Donbas, 65 mi. N of Stalino; rail junction; metalworks. Until c.1940, Liman.

Krasny Luch or **Krasnyy Luch** (lōōch′), city (1926 pop. 7,029; 1939 pop. 50,829), S Voroshilovgrad oblast, Ukrainian SSR, in the Donbas, 34 mi. SSW of Voroshilovgrad; coal-mining center; metal- and glassworks.

Krasny Mayak or **Krasnyy Mayak** (mŭyäk′), town (1926 pop. 684), E central Vladimir oblast, Russian SFSR, 22 mi. S of Kovrov; glassworks.

Krasny Oktyabr or **Krasnyy Oktyabr′** (ŭktyä′bŭr). **1** Town (1944 pop. over 500), central Kurgan oblast, Russian SFSR, on Trans-Siberian RR (Kosobrodsk station) and 22 mi. NW of Kurgan; sawmilling. **2** Town (1942 pop. over 500), W Vladimir oblast, Russian SFSR, 3 mi. SE of Kirzhach. **3** Town (1926 pop. 860), N Vladimir oblast, Russian SFSR, 19 mi. SSE of Kovrov; glassworks. **4** Town (1939 pop. over 2,000), E Stalino oblast, Ukrainian SSR, in the Donbas, 2 mi. NW of Yenakiyevo; coal mines. Formerly Narniyevski Rudnik.

Krasny Profintern or **Krasnyy Profintern** (prŭfĭntyĕrn′). **1** Town (1948 pop. over 2,000), E Yaroslavl oblast, Russian SFSR, on Volga R. and 21 mi. ENE of Yaroslavl; sirup factory. Until c.1926, Ponizovkino. **2** Town (1926 pop. 4,089), central Stalino oblast, Ukrainian SSR, in the Donbas, 2 mi. NW of Yenakiyevo; coal mines. Formerly called Verovski Rudnik.

Krasnystaw (kräsnĭ′stäf), Rus. *Krasnostav* (krŭsnŭstäf′), town (pop. 10,579), Lublin prov., E Poland, on Wieprz R. and 30 mi. SE of Lublin; tanning, flour milling, sawmilling, hat mfg.; bricks.

Krasny Steklovar or **Krasnyy Steklovar** (krä″snē styĕklŭvär′), town (1926 pop. 639), SE Mari Autonomous SSR, Russian SFSR, near Ilet R., 45 mi. SE of Ioshkar-Ola; glassworks.

Krasny Stroitel or **Krasnyy Stroitel′** (strŭē′tyĭl), town (1946 pop. over 500), central Moscow oblast, Russian SFSR, 3 mi. SW of Lenino; woolen milling.

Krasny Sulin or **Krasnyy Sulin** (sōōlyēn′), city (1933 pop. estimate 30,600), SW Rostov oblast, Russian SFSR, 45 mi. NNE of Rostov, in E Donets Basin; metallurgical center; iron- and steelworks, firebrick mfg. Coal-fed power plant. Originally called Sulin or Sulinovskoye.

Krasny Tekstilshchik or **Krasnyy Tekstil′shchik** (tyĭkstyēl′shchĭk), town (1939 pop. over 2,000), central Saratov oblast, Russian SFSR, on right bank of Volga R. and 15 mi. SW (under jurisdiction) of Engels, across river; cotton milling. Until 1929, Shakhmatovo, Saratovskaya Manufaktura.

Krasny Tkach or **Krasnyy Tkach** (tŭkäch′), town (1939 pop. over 500), SE Moscow oblast, Russian SFSR, 6 mi. NNE of Yegoryevsk; cotton mill.

Krasny Ural, Russian SFSR: see URALETS.

Krasny Uzel, Russian SFSR: see ROMODANOVO.

Krasny Yar or **Krasnyy Yar** (yär′). **1** Village (1939 pop. over 2,000), E Astrakhan oblast, Russian SFSR, on Buzan arm of Volga R. delta mouth and 20 mi. NE of Astrakhan; metalworking; fisheries; cotton, fruit. **2** Village (1926 pop. 3,144), central Kuibyshev oblast, Russian SFSR, on Sok R. (landing), opposite mouth of the Kondurcha, and 25 mi. NE of Kuibyshev; metalworking; wheat, sunflowers. **3** Village (1926 pop. 4,600), central Saratov oblast, Russian SFSR, near Volga R., 15 mi. NE of Engels; flour mill, metalworks; wheat, tobacco. **4** Village (1926 pop. 7,337), N Stalingrad oblast, Russian SFSR, on railroad, on Medveditsa R. and 50 mi. NW of Kamyshin; metalworks; wheat, sunflowers. Limestone quarries (SE). **5** Village (1939 pop. over 2,000), S Stalingrad oblast, Russian SFSR, c.20 mi. S of Stalingrad. **6** NE suburb (1939 pop. over 500) of Voroshilovgrad, Ukrainian SSR, on the Northern Donets, and 8 mi. NE of city center; truck produce.

Krasnyye Chetai, Russian SFSR: see KRASNY CHETAI.

Krastets Pass (krä′stĕts) (alt. 2,066 ft.), central Bulgaria, in S spur of Kalofer Mts., at Kalofer; railroad connects Karlovo (W) and Kazanlik (E) basins.

Kraszna, village, Rumania: see CRASNA.

Kraszna River (krŏz′nŏ), Rum. *Crasna* (kräs′nä), in NW Rumania and NE Hungary, rises on N slopes of Apuseni Mts. 14 mi. SW of Zalau, flows 125 mi. N and NNW, past Simleul-Silvanici, to Somes R. just below its confluence with Tisa R. Partly canalized. Forms S boundary of Ecsed Marsh NE of Carei.

Krathis River (krä′thēs), Lat. *Crathis* (krā′thĭs), rises in Aroania mts., N Peloponnesus, Greece, flows c.15 mi. N to Gulf of Corinth below Akrata; site of hydroelectric plants.

Kratie (krätyā′), town, ⊙ Kratie prov. (□ 9,600; 1948 pop. 64,532), central Cambodia, on left bank of Mekong R. (head of regular navigation) and 95 mi. NE of Pnompenh, in forested (hardwoods, big game) region; agr. center; corn, tobacco, rubber, cotton, castor beans, rice, kapok; trade in timber, horns, and hides. Slate quarries near by.

Kratke Range (krät′kŭ), NE New Guinea; rises to c.10,000 ft.

Kratovo (krä′tôvô), village (pop. 3,269), Macedonia, Yugoslavia, 38 mi. E of Skoplje, at W foot of Osogov Mts.; home industry (candles, tar). Copper and lead mines; also traces of gold, silver, iron, and zinc. Mining center in Roman times.

Kratske, Russian SFSR: see PODCHINNY.

Kratsovon, Greece: see CHASIA.

Krattske, Russian SFSR: see PODCHINNY.

Kratzau, Czechoslovakia: see CHRASTAVA.

Kratzke, Russian SFSR: see PODCHINNY.

Kraubath (krou′bät), village (pop. 1,263), Styria, SE central Austria, near Mur R., 8 mi. NE of Knittelfeld; processes magnesite.

Krauchmar (krouchmär′), village, Kompong Cham prov., central Cambodia, port on left bank of Mekong R. and 20 mi. NE of Kompong Cham, in forested (hardwoods) and agr. (cotton, tobacco, corn, peanuts) area; rice, alcohol distillery.

Kraulshavn (krouls′houn″), hunting settlement (pop. 83), Upernavik dist., W Greenland, on peninsula in Baffin Bay, 100 mi. NNW of Upernavik; 74°8′N 57°5′W.

Krauthausen, Germany: see LENDERSDORF-KRAUTHAUSEN.

Krautheim (krout′hīm), town (pop. 1,122), N Baden, Germany, after 1945 in Württemberg-Baden, on the Jagst and 9 mi. SW of Mergentheim; wheat. Has medieval fortifications.

Krauthem, Luxembourg: see CRAUTHEM.

Kravasta Lagoon or **Karavasta Lagoon** (krävä′stä, kä″rä–), Albanian *Kenët′ e Karavastas*, coastal lagoon in W central Albania, on the Adriatic, bet. Durazzo and Valona; 9 mi. long, 3 mi. wide. Delta of Seman R. (S).

Krawang (kräwäng′), town (pop. 18,227), W Java, Indonesia, 32 mi. ESE of Jakarta; trade center for rice-growing region; machine shops. Near by are major irrigation works of Chitarum R.

Kray (krī), industrial district (since 1929) of ESSEN, W Germany, 3 mi. E of city center; brickworks. Coal mining.

Krayishte, highland, Bulgaria and Yugoslavia: see KRAJISTE.

Kraynovka, Russian SFSR: see KRAINOVKA.

Krbava (kûr′bävä), region in W Croatia, Yugoslavia, bet. Adriatic Sea and Bosnia border, E of the Lika. **Krbava River** rises near Ubina, flows c.5 mi. NW, disappearing into the karst.

Krebs, city (pop. 1,532), Pittsburg co., SE Okla., 3 mi. E of McAlester, in agr. area. Once a coal-mine boom town, settled c.1880, inc. 1903; coal industry has since declined.

Krechevitsy (krĭchĕ′vĭtsē), town (1939 pop. over 500), NW Novgorod oblast, Russian SFSR, on Volkhov R. and 7 mi. NNE of Novgorod; building materials.

Krefeld (krā′fĕlt), city (□ 43; 1939 pop. 170,968; 1946 pop. 150,354; 1950 pop. 170,482), in former Prussian Rhine Prov., W Germany, after 1945 in North Rhine-Westphalia, port on left bank of the Rhine and 12 mi. NW of Düsseldorf; 51°20′N 6°22′E. Rail hub; airport (NE outskirts). Major center of Germany's silk and velvet industry. Produces quality steels; mfg. of machinery, dyes; food processing (margarine; sugar refining, distilling, flour milling). Site of textile school (founded 1855). Krefeld, chartered 1373, was an important linen-weaving center until it passed (1702) to Prussia. Silk industry, encouraged by a monopoly given to town by Frederick the Great, soon superseded linen weaving. During last few decades the mfg. of artificial silk gained in prominence and now comprises about 4/5 of city's silk industry. In 1929 Krefeld (formerly also spelled Crefeld) and neighboring (W) Uerdingen (or Ürdingen) were united and called Krefeld-Uerdingen until 1940. Subjected to severe Allied bombing (1943–45); total damage about 70%. Captured by U.S. troops in March, 1945.

Kreider, Le (lŭ krādâr′), village, Oran dept., NW Algeria, in the High Plateaus, at N edge of the Chott ech Chergui, on railroad to Colomb-Béchar and 50 mi. S of Saïda. Military post.

Kreiensen (krī′ŭnzŭn), village (pop. 3,185), in Brunswick, NW Germany, after 1945 in Lower Saxony, on the Leine and 3 mi. WSW of Bad Gandersheim; rail junction; metalworking.

Kreka (krĕ′kä), village, NE Bosnia, Yugoslavia, just W of Tuzla, on railroad; lignite and salt mines; saltworks (evaporating plant, built 1892); stone quarry.

Kremaste or **Kremasti** (both: krĕmästē′), Ital. *Cremasto*, town (pop. 1,859), N Rhodes isl., Greece, on NW shore, 6 mi. SW of Rhodes.

Kremenchug (krĕmĭnchōōk′), city (1939 pop. 89,553), S Poltava oblast, Ukrainian SSR, on left bank of Dnieper R. and 60 mi. SW of Poltava. River-rail and industrial center; metalworking, machine mfg. (agr. machinery, road-building equipment), motor repair shops, lumber mills; food processing (flour, meat, bakery and dairy products). Includes Kryukov (left-bank suburb) with large car-building works. Granite quarries and Stone Age tumuli near by. In Second World War, held (1941–43) by Germans.

Kremenets (krĕmĭnyĕts′), Pol. *Krzemieniec* (kshĕmyĕ′nyĕts), city (1931 pop. 19,997), N Ternopol oblast, Ukrainian SSR, in Kremenets Hills, 38 mi. N of Ternopol, in Volhynia. Rail spur terminus; grain-trading and agr.-processing (cereals, honey, fruit, hops) center; mfg. (milling machinery, transmission belts, cement, lubricating oil), tanning, hatmaking; lignite mining, peat extracting, chalk quarrying; ceramics. Has teachers col., 16th-cent. bldgs. An old Slavic settlement, assaulted by Mongols in 13th cent.; successively dominated (14th–15th cent.) by Lithuania and Poland. Developed in 15th cent. as residence of Pol. queen Bona Sforza. Sacked (1648) by Cossacks. Site of noted Pol. lyceum established by 19th-cent. historian Thaddeus Czacki. City passed to Russia in 1795, reverted to Poland in 1919, ceded to USSR in 1945. Pol. poet Julius Slowacki b. here (1809).

Kremenets Hills, Pol. *Góry Krzemienieckie*, in Volyn-Podolian Upland, W Ukrainian SSR, extend c.45 mi. SW-NE, from Ikva R. near Kremenets to Goryn R. near Ostrog; average alt. 1,000 ft. Chalk and peat deposits.

Kremennaya (krĭmyĕ′nĭŭ), city (1939 pop. over 10,000), W Voroshilovgrad oblast, Ukrainian SSR, in the Donbas, near the Northern Donets, 6 mi. NW of Rubezhnoye; coal mining, woodworking. Formerly also called Novo-Glukhov.

Kremikovtsi (krĕmē′kôftsē), village (pop. 1,515), Sofia dist., W Bulgaria, at S foot of Murgash Mts., 10 mi. NE of Sofia; livestock, truck. Has 15th-cent. convent, church with 11th-cent. paintings.

Kremlin (krĕm′lĭn), town (pop. 143), Garfield co., N Okla., 10 mi. N of Enid, in agr. area.

Kremlin-Bicêtre, Le (lŭ krĕmlē′-bēsĕ′trŭ), town (pop. 12,475), Seine dept., N central France, an immediate S suburb of Paris, 3 mi. from Notre Dame Cathedral, bet. Gentilly (W) and Ivry-sur-Seine (E); mfg. (chemicals, heating equipment). Its hosp., founded 1632, is now known as the Bicêtre insane asylum.

Kremmen (krĕ′mŭn), town (pop. 3,605), Brandenburg, E Germany, near small Kremmen L., 9 mi. W of Oranienburg; mfg. (bricks, pottery); peat digging.

Kremmling, town (pop. 623), Grand co., N central Colo., on Colorado R., just N of Gore Range, and 80 mi. WNW of Denver; alt. 7,322 ft. Market center for livestock, hay, vegetable region; sawmill. Routt Natl. Forest near by.

Kremnica (krĕm′nyĭtsä), Ger. *Kremnitz* (krĕm′nĭts), Hung. *Körmöcbánya* (kûr′mûtsbä′nyŏ), town (pop. 4,979), W central Slovakia, Czechoslovakia, in S spur of the Great Fatra, on railroad and 11 mi. WSW of Banska Bystrica; old mining center, still working gold and silver deposits (also lead, zinc, and antimony); tanning, woodworking, ceramics mfg., lace making. Noted for picturesque surroundings; still retains much of 14th-cent. fortifications; has Gothic church, 15th-cent. castle chapel, square market place. Old gold mint, underground hydroelectric power plant, hot radioactive spring, and mus. also here. Skiing facilities in vicinity.

Krempe (krĕm'pü), village (pop. 3,158), in Schleswig-Holstein, NW Germany, 4 mi. NE of Glückstadt; mfg. of leather goods.

Krems or **Krems an der Donau** (krĕms' än dĕr dō'nou), city (1951 pop. 20,359), Lower Austria, on the Danube, at mouth of Krems R., and 35 mi. WNW of Vienna; metal industry; leather goods, tobacco, mustard, fruit preserves; excellent wine. Municipal mus. opened 1889. Stein an der Donau (with 14th-cent. church) and Mautern (on site of anc. Roman camp) became part of city in 1938.

Kremsier, Czechoslovakia: see KROMERIZ.

Kremsmünster (krĕmz'münstür), town (pop. 5,370), E central Upper Austria, on Krems R. and 13 mi. W of Steyr. Notable Benedictine abbey (founded 777) has large library and observatory.

Krems River (krĕms), E Upper Austria, rises 13 mi. E of L. Traun, flows c.35 mi. N, past Kremsmünster, to Traun R. 2 mi. E of Traun. Grapes and fruit raised in valley.

Krenau, Poland: see CHRZANOW.

Krenitsyn Peak, Russian SFSR: see ONEKOTAN ISLAND.

Krenitsyn Strait, Russian SFSR: see KURILE STRAIT.

Krenitzin Islands (krünĭt'sĭn), group of 5 isls. of the Fox Isls., E Aleutian Isls., SW Alaska, bet. Unalaska (SW) and Unimak (ENE); 54°1'N 165°23'W. Main isls. are Akutan and Akun.

Kreole, village (pop. 1,106), Jackson co., SE Miss., 3 mi. NE of Pascagoula.

Kreslavka, Latvia: see KRASLAVA.

Kress, village (pop. c.500), Swisher co., NW Texas, in Llano Estacado, 12 mi. N of Plainview, in agr. and cattle area.

Kressbronn or **Kressbronn am Bodensee** (krĕs' brôn" äm bō'dünzā"), village (pop. 4,032), S Württemberg, Germany, after 1945 in Württemberg-Hohenzollern, on N shore of L. of Constance, 7 mi. SE of Friedrichshafen; hops.

Krestena, Greece: see SELINOUS.

Krestovaya Guba (krĭstô'vīŭ gōōbä') [Rus.,=bay of the cross], settlement and bay on W coast of N isl. of Novaya Zemlya, Russian SFSR; 74°5'N 55°40'E. Trading post.

Krestovy Pereval, Georgian SSR: see CROSS, PASS OF THE.

Kresttsy (krĭstsē'), town (1926 pop. 3,249), central Novgorod oblast, Russian SFSR, 50 mi. ESE of Novgorod; rail-spur terminus; dairying, sawmilling; clothing.

Kretai, Malaya: see KERTEH.

Krete, Greece: see CRETE.

Kretinga (krĕ'tĭng-gä), Ger. *Krottingen,* city (pop. 5,255), W Lithuania, 13 mi. NNE of Memel; rail and road junction; mfg. (linen goods, woolens, candles, furniture), oilseed pressing, flour milling, sawmilling. Dates from 13th cent.; became Russo-Prussian frontier town after 1795; in Rus. Kovno govt. until 1920.

Kretsa or **Kritsa** (both: krētsä'), town (pop. 3,237), Lasethi nome, E Crete, 4 mi. SW of Hagios Nikolaos; carobs, raisins, olive oil.

Kreuth (kroit), resort (commune pop. 2,760), Upper Bavaria, Germany, in Bavarian Alps, 11.5 mi. SE of Bad Tölz; alt. 2,533 ft. Wildbad Kreuth (pop. 68; alt. 2,717 ft.), 1.5 mi. S, has mineral springs known since 16th cent.

Kreuz, Poland: see KRZYZ.

Kreuz, Yugoslavia: see KRIZEVCI.

Kreuzberg (kroits'bĕrk), residential district (1939 pop. 332,635; 1946 pop. 204,867), S central Berlin, Germany. Mfg. of electrical equipment and paper products; printing. After 1945 in U.S. sector.

Kreuzberg Pass, Italy: see CROCE DI COMELICO, PASSO DI MONTE.

Kreuzburg, Latvia: see KRUSTPILS.

Kreuzburg, Poland: see KLUCZBORK.

Kreuzburg, Russian SFSR: see SLAVSKOYE.

Kreuzen (kroi'tsün), town (pop. 2,013), NE Upper Austria, 23 mi. E of Linz, N of the Danube.

Kreuzingen, Russian SFSR: see BOLSHAKOVO.

Kreuzjoch, Austria: see KITZBÜHEL ALPS.

Kreuzlingen (–lĭng"ün), town (1950 pop. 10,071), Thurgau canton, NE Switzerland, on L. of Constance, S of and adjacent to Constance, Germany; shoes, knit goods, aluminum, foodstuffs, soap; woodworking. Former 17th-cent. abbey with church noted for wood carvings.

Kreuznach, Bad, Germany: see BAD KREUZNACH.

Kreuzwald, France: see CREUTZWALD-LA-CROIX.

Kreuzwertheim (kroits'vârt'hīm), village (pop. 1,652), Lower Franconia, NW Bavaria, Germany, on the Main (canalized) and 18 mi. W of Würzburg; woodworking, brewing.

Krian (krē"än'), coastal district (□ 331; pop. 98,588) of NW Perak, Malaya, on Penang and Kedah (Krian R.) borders; one of Malaya's leading rice-producing dists.; watered by Kuran R. with irrigation headworks at Bukit Merah. Coconuts along Strait of Malacca coast. Main centers are Parit Buntar and Bagan Serai.

Krian River, on Kedah-Perak line, NW Malaya, flows 60 mi. SW along boundary, past Selama, Parit Buntar, Bandar Bharu, and Nibong Tebal, to Strait of Malacca in S Prov. Wellesley. Forms N border of rich Krian rice dist.

Kria Vrisi, Greece: see KRYA VRYSE.

Krib, Le (lü krēb'), town (pop. 1,026), Teboursouk dist., N central Tunisia, 10 mi. SSW of Teboursouk; French agr. settlement; grain, cattle. Zinc and lead mines near by.

Kribi (krē'bē), administrative region (□ 4,700; 1950 pop. 48,683), SW Fr. Cameroons, on Gulf of Guinea; ⊙ Kribi. Bounded S by Sp. Guinea. Lies in tropical rain-forest zone. Principal exports are hardwoods, coffee, cacao, rubber, palm oil.

Kribi, town, ⊙ Kribi region, SW Fr. Cameroons, on Gulf of Guinea, 80 mi. S of Douala; lumber-shipping and fishing port, trading center. Also exports coffee and cacao. Lighthouse, hydroelectric plant.

Krichev, (krē'chĭf), city (1926 pop. 6,367), E Mogilev oblast, Belorussian SSR, on Sozh R. and 55 mi. E of Mogilev; rail and road center; mfg. (cement, ceramics, fertilizer, waterproof cloth); chalk works.

Krichim (krē'chĭm), village (pop. 6,016), Plovdiv dist., S central Bulgaria, at N foot of W Rhodope Mts., on Vacha R. (power plant) and 16 mi. WSW of Plovdiv; fruit and vegetable canning, vegetable-oil extracting, winegrowing.

Krichim Gara (gä'rä) [Bulg.,=Krichim station], village (pop. 3,216), Plovdiv dist., S central Bulgaria, on Vacha R. and 10 mi. W of Plovdiv; rail junction, fruit and truck center; exports grapes.

Krichim River, Bulgaria: see VACHA RIVER.

Krieglach (krēg'läkh), town (pop. 4,261), Styria, E central Austria, on Mürz R. and 24 mi. NE of Leoben; ironworks; summer resort. Peter Rosegger buried here.

Kriekouki, Greece: see ERYTHRAI.

Kriens (krē-ĕns'), town (pop. 8,772), Lucerne canton, central Switzerland, 2 mi. SW of Lucerne; metal products (notably lamps), silk textiles, chemicals, foodstuffs.

Kriewen, Poland: see KRZYWIN.

Krilon, Russian SFSR: see CRILLON, CAPE.

Krim (krēm), peak (3,632 ft.) in Dinaric Alps, W Slovenia, Yugoslavia, 10 mi. SSW of Ljubljana.

Krimmitschau, Germany: see CRIMMITSCHAU.

Krimml (krĭ'mül), village (pop. 679), Salzburg, W central Austria, near Tyrol border, 30 mi. WSW of Zell am See, on the Krimml R., a short tributary of the upper Salzach; just S are the noted Krimml Falls, dropping 1,250 ft. in 3 sections.

Krimpen aan den Ijssel (krĭm'pün än dün ī'sül), town (pop. 6,672), South Holland prov., W Netherlands, on Hollandsche Ijssel R. and 5 mi. E of Rotterdam; asphalt and coal-tar mfg., metal products, woven mats; shipbuilding.

Krimpen aan den Lek (–lĕk'), town (pop. 3,373), South Holland prov., W Netherlands, on Lek R., at mouth of Noord R., and 7 mi. ESE of Rotterdam; bricks, woodwork, industrial belting; copper foundry; shipbuilding.

Kringsja (krĭng'shô), Nor. *Kringsjå,* waterfall (43 ft.) on Otra R., Vest-Agder co., S Norway, 11 mi. N of Kristiansand; hydroelectric plant. Sometimes called Paulenfoss.

Krinichki (krĭnyĕch'kē), village (1926 pop. 8,451), central Dnepropetrovsk oblast, Ukrainian SSR, 12 mi. SW of Dneprodzerzhinsk; truck produce. Formerly called Krinichevatoye.

Krinichnaya (–nīŭ), town (1939 pop. over 500), central Stalino oblast, Ukrainian SSR, in the Donbas, 8 mi. NNE of Makeyevka; cement works.

Krio, Cape (krēō'), SW Turkey, on Aegean Sea; tip of Resadiye Peninsula, at entrance to Gulf of Kos; 36°39'N 26°58'E. Site of anc. CNIDUS.

Krioneri, Greece: see KRYONERI.

Krionero, Albania: see VALONA.

Krishna, India: see KISTNA.

Krishna Gandaki River, Nepal: see KALI GANDAKI RIVER.

Krishnagar (krĭsh'nŭgŭr), town (pop. 32,016), ⊙ Nadia dist., E West Bengal, India, on the Jalangi and 55 mi. N of Calcutta; trade center (rice, jute, linseed, sugar cane, wheat); mfg. of clay figures, sugar milling. Col. Also spelled Krishnanagar.

Krishnagiri (krĭsh'nŭgĭrē), town (pop. 15,311), Salem dist., W Madras, India, 50 mi. SE of Bangalore; road and trade center in agr. area; castor-, peanut-, and sesame-oil extraction, tanning; grapes, mangoes.

Krishnanagar, India: see KRISHNAGAR.

Krishnarajasagara (krĭsh"nŭrä"jŭsŭ'gŭrŭ) or **Kannambadi** (kŭn-nŭm'bŭdē), village, Mandya dist., SW Mysore, India, near Cauvery R., 10 mi. NW of Mysore city center. Krishnaraja Sagara, reservoir (□ 50; 14 mi. long, up to 7 mi. wide), lies just NW; impounded by masonry dam (140 ft. high, 8,600 ft. long) across the Cauvery; dam, crossed by motor road, was begun 1911 and completed in present form in 1931. Reservoir supplies IRWIN CANAL (important irrigation system) and furnishes auxiliary water supply to major hydroelectric works near SIVASAMUDRAM isl. Brindavan Gardens, below the dam, are famous for their landscaped terraces with diversiform fountains (floodlit at night), which have made the place a popular tourist resort.

Krishnarajnagar (krĭshnŭräj'nŭgŭr), town (pop. 4,741), Mysore dist., SW Mysore, India, on Cauvery R., at its entrance into Krishnaraja Sagara (reservoir), and 20 mi. NW of Mysore; rice, tobacco, millet; handicrafts (biris, pottery). Also spelled Krishnarajanagar. Formerly Yedatore.

Krishnarajpet (krĭshnŭräj'pĕt), town (pop. 3,127), Mandya dist., S central Mysore, India, 28 mi. WNW of Mandya; trades in millet, sugar cane, rice; hand-loom weaving. Also spelled Krishnarajpete. Formerly called Attikuppa.

Krishna River, India: see KISTNA RIVER.

Kristdala (krĭst'dä"lä), village (pop. 945), Kalmar co., SE Sweden, 13 mi. NW of Oskarshamn, sawmilling, metalworking.

Kristiania, Norway: see OSLO.

Kristianopel (krĭs"tyänōō'pül), town (pop. 97), Blekinge co., S Sweden, on Baltic, at S end of Kalmar Sound, 18 mi. ENE of Karlskrona; fishing port. Founded in 17th cent. as Danish fortress opposite Kalmar; has old walls, 17th-cent. church.

Kristians, county, Norway: see OPLAND.

Kristiansand (krĭs'chŭnsănd", Nor. krĭstyänsän'), city (pop. 24,343), ⊙ Vest-Agder co., S Norway, on small inlet of the Skagerrak, at mouth of Otra R., on railroad and 150 mi. SW of Oslo; 58°9'N 8°1'E. Port, protected by isls., has important lumber and fish trade; point of call for transatlantic liners. Seaplane base (NE). Has shipyards, copper and nickel smelter, woolen mills; tobacco-, leather-, soap-, metalworks; canneries, breweries. Lutheran episcopal see, moved here from Stavanger in 1682. Naval station. Car ferry to Hirtshals, Denmark. Has 19th-cent. cathedral. Founded 1641 by Christian IV of Denmark and Norway; rebuilt after destructive fire (1892). Formerly also spelled Christiansand.

Kristianstad (krĭstyän'städ), county [Swedish *län*] (□ 2,485; 1950 pop. 258,895), S Sweden; ⊙ Kristianstad. Part of SKANE prov.; extends NW-SE bet. Skalder Bay of Kattegat and Hano Bay of Baltic. Low undulating surface is drained by Helge, Ronne, and several smaller streams. Fertile soil produces grain, sugar beets, potatoes, some tobacco; cattle. Fishing is important. Industries include stone quarrying, mfg. of bricks, furniture, leather goods, textiles. Chief cities are Kristianstad, Hassleholm (railroad center), Angelholm, and Simrishamn. Numerous old castles and country seats.

Kristianstad, city (1950 pop. 24,036), ⊙ Kristianstad co., S Sweden, on Helge R., on N Hammar L., Swedish *Hammarsjön* (5 mi. long, 2 mi. wide), 55 mi. NE of Malmo; 56°2'N 14°10'E; railroad, industrial, and commercial center, with woolen, cardboard, and flour mills, sugar and oil refineries; machinery, brick, and food-canning plants. Site of technical col.; has 17th-cent. church, mus. Residence (1711–14) of King Stanislaus of Poland. Founded (1612) as Danish fortress on Swedish border; chartered 1614. Conquered 1658 by Sweden, seized 1676 by the Danes, regained 1678 by Sweden. Formerly spelled Christianstad. Its seaport, Ahus, is 9 mi. SE, on Baltic.

Kristiansten, Norway: see TRONDHEIM.

Kristiansund (krĭstyänsōōn'), city (pop. 13,152), ⊙ More og Romsdal co., W Norway, on 4 small isls. (Kirklandet, Inlandet, Nordlandet, and Skorpen) in North Sea which enclose the port, 85 mi. WSW of Trondheim; 63°6'N 7°47'E. Fishing center, with Norway's largest trawler fleet. Has extensive fish-drying grounds, fish canneries, cod-liver-oil refineries, boat yards, and plants processing fish meal, glue, soap, margarine; ferroalloy works. Inc. 1742. Shelled by British in 1808. Heavily damaged by bombing in Second World War, when it was German supply base. Formerly also Christiansund.

Kristiinankaupunki, Finland: see KRISTINESTAD.

Kristina, Finland: see RISTIINA.

Kristineberg (krĭ'stēnübĕr"yü), village (pop. 925), Vasterbotten co., N Sweden, 70 mi. WNW of Skelleftea; mining center (copper, zinc, silver, gold, sulphur). Cable railroad (60 mi. long) takes ore to Boliden for shipment to smelters at Ronnskar.

Kristinehamn (krĭ"stĭnühä'mün), city (1950 pop. 19,084), Varmland co., W Sweden, on NE L. Vaner, 20 mi. E of Karlstad; major lake port, serving iron mines of W Bergslag region; rail junction. Iron works, flour mills, mfg. of machinery, storage batteries, brushes, chocolate. Has old church, mus. Trading center in Middle Ages; ironworks established (1572) by Charles IX. Inc. 1642. Suffered destructive fires 1777 and 1893. Formerly spelled Christinehamn.

Kristinestad (krĭstē'nüstäd"), Finnish *Kristiinankaupunki* (krĭs'tēnän-kou"pōōngkē), city (pop. 2,797), Vaasa co., W Finland, on Gulf of Bothnia, 55 mi. S of Vaasa; timber-shipping port; rail terminus. Pop. is largely Swedish-speaking. Founded 1649. Formerly spelled Christinestad.

Kriti, Greece: see CRETE.

Kritsa, Crete: see KRETSA.

Kritzendorf (krĭt'sündôrf), town (pop. 2,204), after 1938 in Klosterneuburg dist. of Vienna, Austria, on the Danube and 9 mi. NNW of city center; popular summer resort; vineyards.

Krivaja or **Krivaya** (both: krē'väyä), village (pop. 6,714), Vojvodina, N Serbia, Yugoslavia, 10 mi. N of Vrbas, in the Backa. Until 1947, called Mali Idjos or Mali Idyosh, Serbo-Croatian *Mali Idoš,* Hung. *Kishegyes.*

Krivaja River or **Krivaya River,** E Bosnia, Yugoslavia, rises in 2 headstreams joining 9 mi. SW of Kladanj, flows c.50 mi. NW to Bosna R. at Zavidovici. Zavidovici–Han Pijesak RR follows its course, including right headstream.

Krivandino (krēvän'dyĭnŭ), village (1939 pop. over 500), E Moscow oblast, Russian SFSR, 7 mi. E of Shatura; rail junction; glassworks.

Krivan Peak (krĭ'vänyŭ), Slovak *Kriváň*, Hung. *Kriván* (krĭ'vän), Pol. *Krywan* (krĭ'vän), one of highest peaks (8,186 ft.) of the High Tatra, N Slovakia, Czechoslovakia, 15 mi. NW of Poprad, near Pol. border. Strba L. is on SE slope.

Kriva Palanka (krē'vä pä'län-kä), Turkish *Eğridere*, village, (pop. 2,956), Macedonia, Yugoslavia, on the Kriva Reka and 50 mi. ENE of Skoplje, at N foot of Osogov Mts.; local trade center, linked via Velbazh Pass with Kyustendil (Bulgaria). First mentioned in 1633.

Kriva Reka (rĕ'kä) [Serbo-Croatian,=crooked river], river, Macedonia, Yugoslavia, rises on N slope of Osogov Mts., 6 mi. SE of Kriva Palanka; flows c.45 mi. W, past Kriva Palanka, to Pcinja R. 6 mi. E of Kumanovo.

Krivaya, Yugoslavia: see KRIVAJA.

Krivichi (krēvĭchē'), Pol. *Krzywicze* (kshĭvē'chĕ), village (1939 pop. over 500), E Molodechno oblast, Belorussian SSR, 22 mi. NE of Vileika; rye, oats, flax; lumbering.

Krivoi Rog or **Krivoy Rog** (krēvoi' rôk'), city (1926 pop. 31,285; 1939 pop. 197,621), SW Dnepropetrovsk oblast, Ukrainian SSR, on Ingulets R., at mouth of Saksagan R., and 85 mi. SW of Dnepropetrovsk; 47°54'N 33°20'E. Center of important iron-mining region (reserves of over 1 billion tons); iron foundry, coking plant, machinery and food industries. Mining and teachers colleges. Within city limits, extending c.20 mi. N-S, are iron-mining suburbs of Imeni ARTEMA, Imeni KARLA LIBKNEKHTA, Imeni OKTYABRSKOI REVOLYUTSII, and Imeni LENINA, and large rail junction of DOLGINTSEVO (E of city). In Second World War, held (1941–44) by Germans, who destroyed most of the industrial installations.

Krivoklat (kûrzhĭ'vôklät), Czech *Křivoklát*, town (pop. 768), W central Bohemia, Czechoslovakia, on Berounka R., on railroad and 24 mi. W of Prague. Has noted 12th-cent. castle, (now a mus.); burned down in 1422 and later rebuilt; royal hunting residence in medieval times.

Krivorozhye or **Krivorozh'ye** (krēvurô'zhyĭ). **1** Village (1926 pop. 2,256), W central Rostov oblast, Russian SFSR, on Kalitva R. and 17 mi. ESE of Millerovo; flour mill, metalworks; wheat, sunflowers, livestock. **2** Town (1939 pop. over 10,000), SW Voroshilovgrad oblast, Ukrainian SSR, in the Donbas, 3 mi. SE of Kadiyevka; coal mines. Formerly Krivorozhski Rudnik.

Krivoshchekovo (krēvŭshchô'kuvŭ, –shchĕ'–), industrial section of NOVOSIBIRSK, Novosibirsk oblast, Russian SFSR, on left bank of Ob R.; machine building, sawmilling, food processing.

Krivosheino (–shā'ĭnŭ), village (1948 pop. over 2,000), SE Tomsk oblast, Russian SFSR, on Ob R. and 70 mi. NNW of Tomsk, in flax-growing area.

Krivoye Ozero (krēvoi"ŭ ô'zyĭrŭ), town (1926 pop. 4,174), N Odessa oblast, Ukrainian SSR, 24 mi. WSW of Pervomaisk; metalworks.

Kriz (krēz), village, Tozeur dist., SW Tunisia, in El-Oudiane oasis, at N edge of the Chott Djerid, 9 mi. NE of Tozeur; dates.

Krizevci (krē'zhĕftsē), Serbo-Croatian *Križevci*, Hung. *Körös* (kû'rûsh), Ger. *Kreuz* (kroits), village (pop. 5,248), N Croatia, Yugoslavia, 16 mi. WNW of Bjelovar, in Slavonia; trade and rail center for winegrowing region. Agr. and forestry school. Orthodox Eastern bishopric. Known since 1253.

Krk (kûrk), Ital. *Veglia* (vĕl'lyä), village (pop. 2,745), NW Croatia, Yugoslavia, on W coast of Krk Isl. on Adriatic Sea, 22 mi. S of Rijeka (Fiume); seaport; bathing resort; fishing. Winegrowing in vicinity. Has medieval walls and castle, 13th-cent. cathedral, and many Venetian houses. First mentioned (3d cent. B.C.) as Greek *Kurikta;* later known as Roman *Curicum;* became R.C. bishopric in 9th cent.

Krk, mountain (3,608 ft.) in Dinaric Alps, E Bosnia, Yugoslavia, 10 mi. ESE of Srebrenica; surrounded on 3 sides by Drina R.

Krka River (kûr'kä). **1** In W Croatia, Yugoslavia, in Dalmatia, rises N of Knin, flows 46 mi. SSW, past Knin, Skradin, and Sibenik, to Adriatic Sea just below Sibenik. Navigable for 31 mi.; links Sibenik with sea. Forms series of small lakes in lower course; on isl. in one of its lakes is a Franciscan convent. Forms 50 waterfalls (up to 280 ft. high, up to 300 ft. wide) utilized by hydroelectric plants, including one at Skradin. Receives Cikola R. Formerly called Kerka. **2** In S Slovenia, Yugoslavia, rises 7 mi. SE of Grosuplje, flows c.60 mi. E, past Novo Mesto, to Sava R. opposite Brezice.

Krk Island (kûrk), Ital. *Veglia* (vĕ'lyä), largest (□ 165) of Yugoslav islands, in N Adriatic Sea, NW Croatia, S of Rijeka (Fiume); separated from mainland by narrow channel; highest point (1,774 ft.) is 5 mi. ESE of Krk; bauxite deposits. Known for vineyards and olive groves. Several bathing resorts, including Krk, Omisalj, Malinska, Baska, and Vrbnik. Formerly part of Istria; passed (1918) to Yugoslavia.

Krkonose, Czechoslovakia and Poland: see RIESENGEBIRGE.

Krn (kûrn), Ital. *Nero* (nā'rô), peak (7,365 ft.) in Julian Alps, NW Slovenia, Yugoslavia, 4 mi. ENE of Kobarid. Until 1947, in Italy.

Krndija Planina (kûrn'dēä plänē'nä), mountain, N Croatia, Yugoslavia, 11 mi. W of Nasice; rises to 2,296 ft., sloping c.10 mi. ESE from peak.

Krnjaja, Yugoslavia: see KLJAJICEVO.

Krnjevo or **Krnyevo** (both: kûr'nĕyô), village (pop. 5,520), central Serbia, Yugoslavia, 5 mi. NE of Palanka.

Krnov (kûr'nôf), Ger. *Jägerndorf* (yā'gûrndôrf"), town (pop. 16,335), NW Silesia, Czechoslovakia, on Opava R. and 30 mi. NW of Ostrava, on Pol. border; important rail junction; noted for organ-building and textile (mainly broadcloth) industries. Popular summer resort and winter-sports center. Has town hall with 166-ft. tower; castle.

Krnyaya, Yugoslavia: see KLJAJICEVO.

Krobia (krô'byä), Ger. *Kröben* (krû'bûn), town (1946 pop. 2,659), Poznan prov., W Poland, 8 mi. S of Gostyn; machinery mfg., sawmilling, flour milling. Cannery near by.

Krocehlavy (krô'chĕkhlävĭ), Czech *Kročehlavy*, town (pop. 10,917), W central Bohemia, Czechoslovakia, 14 mi. WNW of Prague, in urban area of KLADNO.

Kroderen (krû'drûn), Nor. *Krøderen*, lake expansion (□ 16) of Drammen R., SE Norway, at S end of the Hallingdal, 35 mi. NW of Oslo; 27 mi. long, 1-2 mi. wide. Drains S into Drammen R. Fisheries. Sometimes called Kroren, Nor. *Krøren.*

Krodsherad, Norway: see NORESUND.

Kroh (krō), town (pop. 1,099), northernmost Perak, Malaya, 35 mi. ENE of Sungei Patani, in Kalakhiri Mts. (Thailand line) and near Kedah border; tin mining. Malay border post on highway to Betong (Thailand).

Krojanke, Poland: see KRAJENKA.

Krokeai (krôkēä'), Lat. *Croceae* (krōsē'ē), (pop. 3,012), Laconia nome, S Peloponnesus, Greece, 15 mi. SSE of Sparta; citrus fruits, olives, wheat. Formerly called Levetsova.

Kroken, Sweden: see BJORNEROD.

Krokom (kroo'kôm), village (pop. 1,303), Jamtland co., N central Sweden, on NE arm of Stor L., at outflow of Indal R., 11 mi. NW of Ostersund; lumber and pulp milling, metalworking. Includes Hissmofors (hĭs"moofôrs', –fôsh') village.

Krolevets (krŭlyĕ'vyĭts), city (1926 pop. 12,580), W Sumy oblast, Ukrainian SSR, 22 mi. NNE of Konotop; cotton and flour milling, metalworking. Phosphorite deposits near by.

Krolewska Huta, Poland: see CHORZOW.

Krolewski, Kanal, Belorussian SSR: see DNIEPER-BUG CANAL.

Krolewszczyzna, Belorussian SSR: see KRULEVSHCHIZNA.

Kromdraai (krôm'drī"), town (pop. 2,670), SE Transvaal, U. of So. Afr., 10 mi. SE of Standerton; alt. 5,291 ft.; stock, potatoes, oats, mealies.

Kromeriz (krô'myĕrzhēsh), Czech *Kroměříž*, Ger. *Kremsier* (krĕm'zēr), town (pop. 17,626), W central Moravia, Czechoslovakia, on Morava R. and 21 mi. SSE of Olomouc, in barley, wheat, and sugar-beet region. Rail junction; mfg. (generators, gasoline engines, footwear), malt processing. Has 13th-cent. church, 18th-cent. summer palace (with extensive library) of archbishop of Olomouc, art gall., and ceremonial hall where 1st Austrian Constituent Parliament met in 1848.

Krommenie (krô'mûnē), town (pop. 6,698), North Holland prov., W Netherlands, 5 mi. NNW of Zaandam, in Zaanstreek industrial area; mfg. of linoleum, jute, food cans, cacao products, furniture, foundry products. Rail station Krommenie-Assendelft also serves Assendelft, 2 mi. SSW.

Kromme Rijn River, Netherlands: see CROOKED RHINE RIVER.

Krompachy (krôm'päkhĭ), Hung. *Korompa* (kô'rômpô), village (pop. 3,340), E central Slovakia, Czechoslovakia, on Hornad R., on railroad and 22 mi. NW of Kosice; iron and copper mining; former iron foundries. Ironworks at Margecany (6 mi. ESE), Slovinky (4 mi. S), Zakarovce (4 mi. SE).

Kromy (krô'mē), village (1926 pop. 5,126), W Orel oblast, Russian SFSR, 21 mi. SW of Orel; hemp milling.

Kronach (krō'näkh), town (pop. 8,929), Upper Franconia, N Bavaria, Germany, on small Hasslach R. and 24 mi. NW of Bayreuth; rail junction; noted for Rosenthal porcelain; mfg. of heavy machinery, textiles, chemicals; leather and woodworking, lumber and flour milling, brewing, printing, tanning. Has 14th–16th-cent. walls; Gothic church. Cranach, the elder, b. here. On hill (N) is 15th–18th-cent. castle Rosenberg, with 13th-cent. watchtower. Formerly also spelled Kranach.

Kronau (krō'nou), village (pop. 3,014), N Baden, Germany, after 1945 in Württemberg-Baden, on the Kraichbach and 7 mi. N of Bruchsal; tobacco, asparagus.

Kronau, Yugoslavia: see KRANJSKA GORA.

Kronberg (krōn'bĕrk), town (pop. 5,678), in former Prussian prov. of Hesse-Nassau, W Germany, after 1945 in Hesse, on S slope of the Taunus, 9 mi. NW of Frankfurt; fruit. Winter-sports center. Has anc. castle, rebuilt 1897–1900. Sometimes spelled Cronberg.

Krondorf-Kyselka, Czechoslovakia: see CARLSBAD.

Krone, Poland: see KORONOWO.

Kronenberg, Germany: see CRONENBERG.

Kronenhof, Germany: see KEHL.

Krongjawng Pass, India-Burma: see KUMJAWNG PASS.

Kronoberg (kroo'noobĕr"yŭ), county [Swedish *län*] (□ 3,826; 1950 pop. 157,751), S Sweden; ⊙ Vaxjo. Forms S part of SMALAND prov. Rolling area of woods, marshland, and numerous lakes (Asne and Mockel lakes are largest); drained by Morrum, Helge, Laga, and many smaller rivers. Lumbering, sawmilling, woodworking, and paper milling are chief industries; Orrefors and Kosta are well-known glass-mfg. centers. Vaxjo and Ljungby are cities.

Kronotskaya River (krŭnôt'skŭŭ), E central Kamchatka Peninsula, Khabarovsk Territory, Russian SFSR, rises in Kronotskoye L., flows 30 mi. SE to Kronotski Gulf of the Pacific. Receives Bogachevka R., site of extensive petroleum deposits.

Kronotskaya Sopka (sôp'kŭ), active volcano (11,909 ft.) on E Kamchatka Peninsula, Khabarovsk Territory, Russian SFSR; terminates (S) on **Kronotski Gulf** or **Kronotskiy Gulf** of the Pacific, which is separated from Kamchatka Gulf (N) by **Kronotski Peninsula,** 50 mi. wide. W of the volcano is **Kronotskoye Lake** (–skŭyŭ) (□ 73; 420 ft. deep; alt. 1,430 ft.), out of which flows Kronotskaya R.

Kronprins Christian Land, Greenland: see CROWN PRINCE CHRISTIAN LAND.

Kronprinsen Islands (krōn'prĭns"ŭn), Dan. *Kronprinsens Ejlande*, group of 7 islets (pop. 59), W Greenland, in Davis Strait, at mouth of Disko Bay. Chief settlement is Imerigsoq (ĭmĕrĭkh'sôk), 70 mi. SSE of Godhavn; 69°1'N 53°18'W.

Kronprinzenkoog (krōn"prĭn'tsŭnkōk"), village (pop. 2,444), in Schleswig-Holstein, NW Germany, near the North Sea, 23 mi. WNW of Itzehoe, in the S Dithmarschen; cattle. Built on reclaimed (1788) polder land.

Kronshagen (krōns'hä"gŭn), village (pop. 5,810), in Schleswig-Holstein, NW Germany, 2 mi. W of Kiel city center; mfg. (metal goods, textiles, cosmetics, furniture).

Kronstadt, Rumania: see STALIN (Brasov), city.

Kronstadt (krōn'shtät), Rus. *Kronshtadt* (krŭnshtät'), city (1939 pop. c.50,000) and naval fortress, Leningrad oblast, Russian SFSR, on SE Kotlin Isl. (7.5 mi. long, 1 mi. wide) in E Gulf of Finland, 14 mi. W (under jurisdiction) of Leningrad; lumber milling, clothing and shoe industries. Naval base of Baltic fleet; site of extensive arsenal, docks, and shipyards. Has early-18th-cent. Ital. palace, admiralty building, 18th-cent. cathedral. Naval fortifications (forts, floating gun batteries) command sea approach to Leningrad. Founded (1703) by Peter the Great as fortress of Kronslot; named Kronstadt (1721). Flourished as commercial port for St. Petersburg until dredging (1875–93) of 17-mi. deep-sea canal, enabling direct access to St. Petersburg by ocean-going vessels. Scene of naval revolts (1905–06). Garrison was active in Bolshevik revolution (1917) and in defense of Petrograd (1919); staged counter-revolutionary revolt (1921). During Second World War, its fortifications played major role in resisting Leningrad siege (1941–44) and maintaining Rus. Lomonosov bridgehead.

Kronte (krûn'tŭ), peak (10,203 ft.) in Alps of the Four Forest Cantons, central Switzerland, 7 mi. ESE of Engelberg.

Kroonenburg (krō'nûbûrkh), village (pop. 1,504), Commewijne dist., N Du. Guiana, on Commewijne R. and 11 mi. ENE of Paramaribo; sugar, coffee, rice.

Kroonstad (kroon'stät), town (pop. 21,151), N Orange Free State, U. of So. Afr., on Valsch R. (tributary of Orange R.) and 120 mi. NE of Bloemfontein; alt. 4,489 ft.; rail junction with important switching yards; motor assembly, metalworking, clothing mfg.; grain elevator, flour mills. Center of stock-raising, grain-growing region. Site of branch of Bloemfontein technical col., railroad training institute, govt. agr. experimental station. Founded 1859, it was ⊙ Orange Free State Republic March 13th-May 11, 1900, after fall of Bloemfontein. Near by are coal and diamond mines (closed at present).

Kropachevo (krŭpuchĕ'vŭ), town (1939 pop. over 2,000), W Chelyabinsk oblast, Russian SFSR, in the S Urals, on railroad and 27 mi. E of Asha; machine mfg.

Kröpelin (krû'pulĭn), town (pop. 4,839), Mecklenburg, N Germany, near Mecklenburg Bay of the Baltic, 14 mi. W of Rostock; agr. market (grain, potatoes, sugar beets, stock).

Kropotkin (krŭpôt'kĭn). Formerly spelled Krapotkin. **1** Town (1948 pop. over 500), NE Irkutsk oblast, Russian SFSR, 60 mi. NE of Bodaibo; gold mining. **2** City (1926 pop. 30,963), E Krasnodar Territory, Russian SFSR, on right bank of Kuban R. and 80 mi. ENE of Krasnodar, on Rostov-Baku RR (Kavkazskaya station); rail center with branches to Stavropol, Krasnodar, and Novorossisk; railroad workshops; agr. processing (flour, vegetable oils, meat, canned goods); iron foundry. Originally a village called Romanovski Khutor; became city in 1926.

Kropp (krôp), village (pop. 3,653), in Schleswig-Holstein, NW Germany, 7 mi. S of Schleswig; woodworking.

Kroppenstedt or **Croppenstedt** (both: krô'pŭn-shtĕt), town (pop. 3,355), in former Prussian Saxony prov., central Germany, after 1945 in Saxony-Anhalt, 8 mi. SE of Oschersleben; agr. market (sugar beets, grain, vegetables).

Kroren, Norway: see KRODEREN.

Kroscienko, Poland: see PIENINY.

Krosniewice (krôsh"nyĕvē'tsĕ), Pol. *Krośniewice,* Rus. *Krosnevitse* (krŭsnyĭvē'tsĕ), town (pop. 3,250), Lodz prov., central Poland, 8 mi. W of Kutno; brick mfg., flour milling.

Krosno (krôs'nô). **1** Town (pop. 13,873), Rzeszow prov., SE Poland, on Wislok R., on railroad, and 26 mi. SSW of Rzeszow. Center of region producing petroleum and natural gas (gas pipe line to Ostrowiec, Radom, and Sandomierz); petroleum refinery; mfg. of machinery, glass, rubber footwear; flour mills, sawmills, brickworks; airport. **2** or **Krosno Odrzanskie** (ôjä'nyŭskyĕ), Pol. *Krosno Odrzańskie,* Ger. *Crossen* (krô'sŭn), town (1939 pop. 10,794; 1946 pop. 2,224) in Brandenburg, after 1945 in Zielona Gora prov., W Poland, port on the Oder, at Bobrawa R. mouth, and 18 mi. ENE of Guben, in Lower Lusatia; woolen milling, metal- and woodworking; grape growing. First mentioned c.1000; chartered 1201; passed 1482 to Brandenburg. After Second World War, during which it was c.50% destroyed, its Ger. pop. left.

Krotoszyn (krôtô'shĭn), Ger. *Krotoschin* (krō'tō-shĭn), town (1946 pop. 13,748), Poznan prov., W central Poland, 12 mi. WNW of Ostrow; rail junction; mfg. of bricks, furniture, ceramics, roofing materials, agr. machinery; brewing, distilling, flour milling, fruit canning.

Krotovka (krô'tŭfkŭ), village (1939 pop. over 2,000), E central Kuibyshev oblast, Russian SFSR, near Greater Kinel R., 22 mi. ENE of Kinel; rail junction; wheat, sunflowers. Recently-developed petroleum wells at Mukhanovo station, 9 mi. NE.

Krottingen, Lithuania: see KRETINGA.

Krotz Springs, village (pop. 866), St. Landry parish, S central La., 20 mi. E of Opelousas, and on Atchafalaya R., in oil and natural-gas area.

Kroumirie, Tunisia: see KHROUMIRIE.

Krousson (kroosôn'), town (pop. 2,707), Herakleion nome, central Crete, 11 mi. SSW of Candia; carobs, raisins, olive oil.

Krozingen, Bad, Germany: see BAD KROZINGEN.

Krrab (kräb) or **Krrabi** (krä'bē), mountain massif (5,413 ft.) in N Albania, 7 mi. NE of Pukë. Also spelled Krab or Krabi.

Krrabë (krä'bŭ) or **Krraba** (krä'bä), mountain region of central Albania bet. Shkumbî and Arzen rivers; crossed by Elbasan-Tirana highway. Coal mining at Peqin (SW). Also spelled Krabë or Kraba.

Krsko (kŭrsh'kô), Slovenian *Krško,* Ger. *Gurkfeld* (goork'fĕlt), village (pop. 1,961), S Slovenia, Yugoslavia, on Sava R., on railroad and 45 mi. E of Ljubljana; center of winegrowing region; health resort. First mentioned in 895. Until 1918, in Carniola.

Krstaca or **Krstacha** (both: kŭr'stächä), Serbo-Croatian *Krstača,* mountain in Dinaric Alps, Yugoslavia, on Serbia-Montenegro border; highest point (5,756 ft.) is 10 mi. W of Tutin.

Kruë, Albania: see KRUJË.

Kruger National Park (kroo'gŭr) (□ c.8,000), NE Transvaal, U. of So. Afr., bounded by Crocodile R. (S), Mozambique (E), Southern Rhodesia (N); 210 mi. long, 25-50 mi. wide. Park, crossed by 1,200 mi. of roads, is reserve for almost all species of game found in So. Afr., including lions, buffaloes, elephants, zebras, giraffes, hippopotamuses, crocodiles, leopards, hyenas, cheetahs, warthogs, and large variety of antelopes, monkeys, small game, and birds. There are several tourist camps. Founded 1898 as Sabie Game Reserve by President Kruger, park was subsequently enlarged; became Union property, 1926.

Krugersdorp (kroo'gŭrzdôrp, Afrikaans krü'yŭrs-dôrp"), town (pop. 71,885), S Transvaal, U. of So Afr., at W end of Witwatersrand, 20 mi. WNW of Johannesburg; alt. 5,709 ft.; rail junction; gold- and manganese-mining center; tanning, metalworking, mfg. of chemicals, paint. Site of technical col. Town named for Paul Kruger, last president of Transvaal republic. Near by are Paardekraal, scene (1880) of meeting at which South African Republic was restored; Sterkfontein, site of discovery of prehistoric human remains; and Doornkop, scene (1886) of surrender of Dr. Jameson.

Krugloye (kroog'lŭyŭ), town (1926 pop. 1,344), NW Mogilev oblast, Belorussian SSR, 33 mi. NW of Mogilev; flax processing.

Kruglyakov (kroogly̆ä'kŭf), village (1939 pop. over 500), S Stalingrad oblast, Russian SFSR, on railroad (near Zhutovo station) and 65 mi. SW of Stalingrad; wheat, sunflowers.

Kruibeke (kroi'bĕkŭ), town (pop. 5,953), East Flanders prov., N Belgium, on Scheldt R. and 5 mi. SW of Antwerp; agr. market (dairying, vegetables). Has 18th-cent. church. Sometimes spelled Cruybeke.

Kruiningen (kroi'nĭng-ŭn), town (pop. 1,735), Zeeland prov., SW Netherlands, on South Beveland isl., 7 mi. ESE of Goes, on the Western Scheldt; extensive oyster beds; synthetic fertilizer.

Kruisfontein (krois'fôntān"), town (pop. 1,935), S Cape Prov., 50 mi. W of Port Elizabeth, 3 mi. NW of Humansdorp; stock, wheat, fruit, vegetables.

Kruishoutem (krois'houtŭm), agr. village (pop. 4,734), East Flanders prov., W central Belgium, 5 mi. NNW of Oudenaarde. Formerly spelled Cruyshautem.

Krujë (kroo'yŭ) or **Kruja** (kroo'yä), Ital. *Croia* (kroi'yä), Turkish *Akche Hissar,* town (1945 pop. 5,542), N central Albania, 12 mi. N of Tirana, situated picturesquely on 2,000-ft. mtn. spur above Ishm R. valley; handicraft industry (metals, pottery, wood, natl. costumes); olive groves. Bauxite deposits near by. Pop. is largely Moslem. The 14th-15th-cent. fortress was (1443–68) the center of Scanderbeg's resistance against Turks. Was bishopric (1246–1694). Also spelled Kruë.

Krukenitsa (kroo'kyĭnyĕtsŭ), Pol. *Krukienice* (krookyĕnyē'tsĕ), village (1939 pop. over 500), NW Drogobych oblast, Ukrainian SSR, 13 mi. NNW of Sambor; potatoes, oats, rye; lumbering.

Krulevshchizna (kroolyĭfshchē'znŭ), Pol. *Królewszczyzna* (kroolĕfshchĭ'znŭ), rail junction in S Polotsk oblast, Belorussian SSR, 9 mi. SSE of Glubokoye.

Krumbach (kroom'bäkh), town (pop. 5,826), Swabia, SW Bavaria, Germany, on small Kamlach R. and 20 mi. SE of Ulm; mfg. of textiles, chemicals, metal and leather products; brewing, dairying. Has rococo church. Mineral springs near by. Chartered 1380.

Krummau, Czechoslovakia: see CESKY KRUMLOV.

Krummhübel, Poland, see KARPACZ.

Krumovgrad (kroo'môvgrät), city (pop. 1,249), Khaskovo dist., S Bulgaria, in E Rhodope Mts., on tributary of Arda R., and 18 mi. SE of Kird zhali; market center (tobacco, woolen cloth). Chrome, lead, and zinc deposits N. Until 1934, Koshu-Kavak.

Krumovo (kroo'môvô), village (pop. 1,374), Plovdiv dist., S central Bulgaria, 6 mi. SE of Plovdiv; rail junction; tobacco, rice, sugar beets. Formerly Pashamakhla.

Krumpa (kroom'pä), village (pop. 2,241), in former Prussian Saxony prov., central Germany, after 1945 in Saxony-Anhalt, 8 mi. SW of Merseburg; lignite mining. In 1938 it inc. Lützkendorf (lüts'kŭndôrf), just N, with synthetic-oil plant.

Krumpendorf (kroomp'ŭndôrf), town (pop. 2,191), Carinthia, S Austria, on N shore of the Wörthersee and 4 mi. W of Klagenfurt; summer resort.

Krung Kao, Thailand: see AYUTTHAYA.

Krung Thep, Thailand: see BANGKOK.

Krupa or **Bosanska Krupa** (bô'sänskä kroo'pä), village (pop. 3,829), NW Bosnia, Yugoslavia, on Una R. and 15 mi. NE of Bihac, on railroad; bauxite mining; lumbering.

Krupanj, Krupan, or **Krupan'** (all: kroo'pänyŭ), village (pop. 847), W Serbia, Yugoslavia, 26 mi. W of Valjevo; antimony smelter. Two antimony mines near by. Center of lead-mining dist., with mines dating from Middle Ages.

Krupets (kroopyĕts'), village (1939 pop. over 500), W Kursk oblast, Russian SFSR, 14 mi. WNW of Rylsk; metalworks, distillery.

Krupina (kroo'pĭnä), Ger. *Karpfen* (kärp'fŭn), Hung. *Korpona* (kôr'pônŏ), town (pop. 5,330), S Slovakia, Czechoslovakia, on railroad and 27 mi. S of Banska Bystrica; fruit-trade center. Magnesite mined near by.

Krupka (kroop'kä), Ger. *Graupen* (grou'pŭn), village (pop. 2,165), NW Bohemia, Czechoslovakia, in the Erzgebirge, 3 mi. NNE of Teplice; tin, antimony, and tungsten mining. Vrchoslav (vŭr'-khôsläf) metalworks are just SSW, on railroad.

Krupki (kroop'kē), town (1926 pop. 2,080), NE Minsk oblast, Belorussian SSR, 25 mi. ENE of Borisov; sawmilling, mfg. (matches, pottery).

Krupp, town (pop. 98), Grant co., E central Wash., 25 mi. ENE of Ephrata, in Columbia basin agr. region.

Krusadi Island (kroosŭd'ē), Tamil *Krusadi Tivu* (kooroosŭ'dĭ tĭ'voo), in Gulf of Mannar, off SW coast of Rameswaram Isl., S Madras, India, 29 mi. E of Kilakarai; 1½ mi. long, ¼ mi. wide. Marine research station; pearl farm.

Kruschwitz, Poland: see KRUSZWICA.

Krusenstern, Cape (kroo'zŭnstŭrn), N Mackenzie Dist., Northwest Territories, on Coronation Gulf, at E end of Dolphin and Union Strait; 68°23'N 113°55'W; trading post.

Krusenstern Island, Alaska: see LITTLE DIOMEDE ISLAND.

Krusenstern Strait, Russian SFSR: see KRUZENSHTERN STRAIT.

Krusevac or **Krushevats** (both: kroo'shĕväts), Serbo-Croatian *Kruševac,* town (pop. 14,104), S central Serbia, Yugoslavia, on Rasina R., just above its influx into the Western Morava, on railroad and 95 mi. SSE of Belgrade. Mfg. of rolling stock, chemicals, munitions; hydroelectric plant. Chromium deposits and mineral waters in vicinity. Medieval seat of a Serbian ruler.

Krusevo or **Krushevo** (both: kroo'shĕvô), Serbo-Croatian *Kruševo,* village (pop. 3,442), W Macedonia, Yugoslavia, 45 mi. S of Skoplje; marketing center; homemade carpets. Pop. of Roman provincial origin; uses a Romance dialect.

Krushovene (krooshôvĕ'nĕ), village (pop. 4,582), Vratsa dist., N Bulgaria, on Iskar R. and 23 mi. ESE of Oryakhovo; wheat, corn, livestock.

Krushovitsa (kroo'shôvĕtsä). **1** Village (pop. 2,997), Pleven dist., N Bulgaria, 13 mi. WSW of Pleven; grain, livestock. **2** Village (pop. 4,378), Vratsa dist., NW Bulgaria, on Skat R. and 10 mi. SSW of Oryakhovo; vineyards, grain, truck.

Krusne Hory, Czechoslovakia: see ERZGEBIRGE.

Krustpils (kroost'pēls), Ger. *Kreuzburg,* city (pop. 3,658), S central Latvia, in Latgale, on right bank of the Western Dvina, opposite Jekabpils, and 75 mi. ESE of Riga; rail junction; mfg. (leather, knitwear), sugar refining. In Rus. Vitebsk govt. until 1920.

Kruszwica (kroosh-vē'tsä), Ger. *Kruschwitz* (kroosh'-vĭts), town (pop. 4,822), Bydgoszcz prov., central Poland, on W shore of L. Goplo, 9 mi. S of Inowroclaw; beet-sugar and flour milling.

Krut, Ban, Thailand: see BAN KRUT.

Krutaya (krootĭ'ŭ), village, central Komi Autonomous SSR, Russian SFSR, on Izhma R. and 50 mi. SSE of Ukhta; asphalt rock; natural-gas wells.

Krutikha (krootyē'khŭ), village (1926 pop. 4,314), NW Altai Territory, Russian SFSR, near Ob R., 13 mi. N of Kamen; dairy farming.

Krutinka (krootyēn'kŭ), village (1939 pop. over 2,000), W Omsk oblast, Russian SFSR, on small L. Ik, 30 mi. N of Novo-Nazyvayevka; dairy farming.

Kru Town, Sierra Leone: see FREETOWN.

Kruzenshtern Island, Alaska: see LITTLE DIOMEDE ISLAND.

Kruzenshtern Strait or **Krusenstern Strait** (krooz-ĭnshtyĕrn'), Jap. *Mushiru-kaikyo* (mooshē'roo-kī'kyō'), in N main Kurile Isls. group, Russian SFSR, bet. Lovushki Isls. (N) and Raikoke Isls. (S); 31 mi. wide. Name sometimes extended to entire strait bet. Shiashkotan and Raikoke isls., including Fortuna Strait.

Kruzof Island (kroo'zôf) (23 mi. long, 8 mi. wide), SE Alaska, in Alexander Archipelago, 10 mi. W of Sitka; 57°10'N 135°42'W; rises to 3,271 ft. on Mt. Edgecumbe (S); fishing.

Krya Vryse or **Kria Vrisi** (both: krē'ŭ vrē'sē), village (pop. 2,914), Pella nome, Macedonia, Greece, 16 mi. SE of Edessa, near drained L. Giannitsa; cotton, wheat; wine. Also spelled Krya Vrissi.

Krylbo (krül'boo"), town (pop. 2,410), Kopparberg co., central Sweden, on Dal R. and 2 mi. SE of Avesta; rail junction; foundries, flour mills.

Krylovskaya (krĭlôf'skŭ), village (1926 pop. 9,427), N Krasnodar Territory, Russian SFSR, 45 mi. WNW of Tikhoretsk; metalworks, flour mill; dairying; wheat, sunflowers, sunn hemp, essential oils.

Krym, Russian SFSR: see CRIMEA.

Krymskaya (krĭm'skŭ), village (1926 pop. 14,502), W Krasnodar Territory, Russian SFSR, at N foot of the Greater Caucasus, 17 mi. NE of Novorossisk; rail junction; agr. center; canned goods, wine, tobacco.

Krynica (krĭnē'tsä), town (pop. 2,649), Krakow prov., S Poland, in the Carpathians, 18 mi. SSE of Nowy Sacz, near Czechoslovak border. Rail spur terminus; health and winter-sports center (alt. 1,922 ft.) with mineral springs and hot baths; dry-ice processing. Sometimes called Krynica Zdroj, Pol. *Krynica Zdrój.* During Second World War, under Ger. rule, called Bad Krynica.

Kryoneri or **Krioneri** (both: krēônĕ'rē), village (pop. 647), Acarnania nome, W central Greece, deep-water port of Missolonghi on Gulf of Patras, 10 mi. ESE of Missolonghi (linked by rail); fisheries.

Krypton (krĭp'tŭn), village (1940 pop. 606), Perry co., SE Ky., in Cumberland foothills on North Fork Kentucky R. and 8 mi. WNW of Hazard, in bituminous-coal-mining area.

Krystynopol (krĕstyēnô'pŭl), village, N Lvov oblast, Ukrainian SSR, on Bug R. and 7 mi. SSW of Sokal; rail junction. Until 1951 in Poland.

Kryuchkovka, Russian SFSR: see KOSYA.

Kryukov, Urkainian SSR: see KREMENCHUG.

Kryukovo (kryoo'kŭvŭ), town (1926 pop. 957), central Moscow oblast, Russian SFSR, 23 mi. NW of Moscow; glass, clothing. During Second World War, reached (1941) by advance Ger. units in Moscow campaign.

Kryulyany (kryoolyä'nē), Rum. *Criuleni* (kryoolĕn'), town (1941 pop. 1,852), E Moldavian SSR, on the Dniester, just below Reut R. mouth, and 20 mi. NE of Kishinev, in fruitgrowing dist.

Krywan, peak, Czechoslovakia: see KRIVAN PEAK.

Kryzhopol or **Kryzhopol'** (krĭzhô'pŭl), town (1926 pop. 2,986), S Vinnitsa oblast, Ukrainian SSR, 50 mi. E of Mogilev-Podolski; metal-, woodworking.

Krzemieniec, Ukrainian SSR: see KREMENETS.

Krzepice (kshĕpē'tsĕ), Rus. *Krzhepitse* (kshĕpē'tsĕ), town (pop. 4,343), Katowice prov., S Poland, 20 mi. NW of Czestochowa; flour milling.

Krzeszowice (kshĕ"shôvē'tsĕ), town (pop. 2,837), Krakow prov., S Poland, on railroad and 15 mi. WNW of Cracow. Health resort with sulphur springs and hot baths; stone and clay quarrying;

mfg. of chemicals, distilling. Has castle with park and art works.

Krzhepitse, Poland: see KRZEPICE.

Krzhizhanovsk, Russian SFSR: see GUBAKHA.

Krzna River (kŭshnä'), Lublin prov., E Poland, rises just W of Lukow, flows c.40 mi. generally E, past Lukow, Miedzyrzec, and Biala Podlaska, to Bug R. 8 mi. WNW of Brest.

Krzywicze, Belorussian SSR: see KRIVICHI.

Krzywin, Pol. *Krzywiń* (kshĭ'vēnyů) or *Krzywin* (kshĭ'vēn), Ger. *Kriewen* (krē'vůn), town (1946 pop. 1,498), Poznan prov., W Poland, on Obra R. and 11 mi. SE of Koscian; flour milling, cement.

Krzyz (kshĭsh), Pol. *Krzyż*, Ger. *Kreuz* (kroits), town (1939 pop. 4,956; 1946 pop. 3,299) in Pomerania, after 1945 in Poznan prov., W central Poland, near Notec R., 35 mi. WSW of Schneidemühl (Pila); rail junction. Founded 1850 during construction of Berlin–East Prussia RR; chartered 1936. Until 1939, Ger. frontier station on Pol. border, 50 mi. NW of Poznan. Until 1938, in former Prussian prov. of Grenzmark Posen–Westpreussen.

Krzyzatka, Poland: see KOWARY.

Ksar el Kebir, El, Sp. Morocco: see ALCAZARQUIVIR.

Ksar-es-Souk (ksär'-ĕs-so͝ok'), town (pop. 5,484), Meknès region, S central Fr. Morocco, oasis on the Oued Ziz, at S foot of the High Atlas, 150 mi. SSE of Meknès; alt. 2,950 ft.; 31°56'N 4°26'W. Junction of roads from Marrakesh (W), Figuig (E), Fez (N), and Tafilalet oasis (S). Trade center (wool, esparto, dates, olive oil). Fine date-palms, olive and fig trees mark the oasis. Agr. experiment station. Occupied by French since 1916.

Ksar-Hellal (–hĕl-läl'), village, Sousse dist., E Tunisia, near the Mediterranean, 18 mi. SE of Sousse; silk and cotton cloth-mfg. center (artisan industry); olive-oil pressing.

Ksel, Djebel (jĕ'bĕl ksĕl'), highest peak (6,588 ft.) of the Djebel Amour (range of the Saharan Atlas) in N central Algeria, just NE of Géryville.

Ksenyevka or **Ksen'yevka** (ksĕ'nyĭfkŭ), town (1939 pop. over 2,000), NE Chita oblast, Russian SFSR, on Trans-Siberian RR and 240 mi. NE of Chita, in gold-mining area.

Kseur, El- (ĕlksûr'), village (pop. 3,232), Constantine dept., NE Algeria, in Oued Soummam valley, on railroad and 14 mi. SW of Bougie; olive and winegrowing; oil pressing. Iron mining in vicinity.

Kshen, Russian SFSR: see SOVETSKI, Kursk oblast.

Kshtut, Tadzhik SSR: see TAKFAN.

Ksiaz or **Ksiaz Wielkopolski** (kshōsh' vyĕlkôpôl'-skē), Pol. *Książ Wielkopolski*, Ger. *Xions* (ksyōns), town (1946 pop. 1,699), Poznan prov., W Poland, 27 mi. SSE of Poznan.

Ksiba, El (ĕlksēbä'), agr. village, Meknès region, central Fr. Morocco, on W slope of the Middle Atlas, 15 mi. E of Kasba Tadla; grain; oak forests. Hill resort.

Ksibet-el-Mediouni (ksēbĕt'-ĕl-mĕdyo͞onē'), village, Sousse dist., E Tunisia, near the Mediterranean, 15 mi. SE of Sousse; olive-oil pressing; limekiln.

Ksour (kso͞or), village, Le Kef dist., W central Tunisia, 18 mi. W of Maktar; grain and wool market.

Ksour-Essaf (–ĕsäf'), town (pop. 9,925), Mahdia dist., E Tunisia, near the Mediterranean, 34 mi. SE of Sousse; olive-oil pressing. Artisan industries.

Ksour Mountains, range of the Saharan Atlas, in W Algeria, extending c.100 mi. NE from the Fr. Morocco border at Figuig, bet. the High Plateaus (N) and Sahara Desert (S). Highest peaks are Djebel Aïssa (7,336 ft.) just N of Aïn-Sefra, and Djebel Mzi (6,988 ft.). Traversed at Aïn-Sefra by narrow-gauge railroad to Colomb-Béchar.

Kstovo (kstô'vů), village (1939 pop. over 500), central Gorki oblast, Russian SFSR, on Volga R. and 12 mi. SE of Gorki, on rail spur; sawmilling.

Ktima, N suburb of PAPHOS, Cyprus.

Ktypas or **Ktipas** (both: ktĭpäs'), mountain in Boeotia nome, E central Greece, near Gulf of Euboea, rises to 3,350 ft. 6 mi. W of Chalcis. Sometimes called Messapion.

Kua-, for Chinese names beginning thus and not found here: see under KWA-.

Kuah (ko͞oä'), village (pop. 1,226) and port on S shore of Langkawi Isl., Kedah, Malaya; 6°10'N 99°50'E; fisheries.

Kuala Belait (kwä'lů bůlĭt'), town (pop. 3,981) in W section of Brunei, NW Borneo, near S.China Sea, on small Belait R. (20 mi. long) and 55 mi. SW of Brunei town; 4°35'N 114°11'E; supply center for Seria oil fields (10 mi. E). Agr. (cassava, sago), stock raising, fishing. Town has modern facilities.

Kuala Besut or **Besut** (bĕso͞ot'), town (pop. 3,475), N Trengganu, Malaya, South China Sea port at mouth of the small Besut R., 50 mi. NW of Kuala Trengganu; coconuts, rice; fisheries.

Kuala Brang (brăng'), village (pop. 555), E central Trengganu, Malaya, on road and Trengganu R., 20 mi. SW of Kuala Trengganu.

Kuala Dungun or **Dungun** (do͞on"go͞on'), town (pop. 4,256), E central Trengganu, Malaya, South China Sea port at mouth of small Dungun R., 40 mi. SSE of Kuala Trengganu; sawmilling, boatbuilding; ships iron ore from Bukit Besi mine (15 mi. W).

Kuala Gula (go͞o'lä), village (pop. 1,077), NW Perak, Malaya, minor fishing port on Strait of Malacca, 19 mi. WNW of Taiping; coconuts.

Kuala Kangsar (käng"sär'), town (pop. 8,350), N central Perak, Malaya, on railroad and 14 mi. ESE of Taiping, on Perak R.; sultan's residence; road center in rice and rubber dist.; Malay col. Former residence of high commissioner of Federated Malay States.

Kualakapuas or **Koealakapoeas** (kwälůkäpwäs'), town (pop. 8,682), S Borneo, Indonesia, on Barito delta, 28 mi. NW of Banjermasin; trade center for rubber-growing region.

Kuala Kedah (kā'dä), town (pop. 3,364), N Kedah, Malaya, Strait of Malacca port at mouth of Kedah R., 5 mi. W of Alor Star; coconuts, rice; fisheries.

Kuala Kemaman (kůmä'män), town (pop. 2,419), S Trengganu, Malaya, South China Sea port at mouth of Kemaman R., just E of Chukai, 75 mi. SSE of Kuala Trengganu; fisheries.

Kuala Ketil (kĕtĕl'), village (pop. 645), S central Kedah, Malaya, on Muda R. at mouth of small Ketil R., and 11 mi. E of Sungei Patani; rubber plantations.

Kuala Klawang (klä"wäng'), town (pop. 1,367), N Negri Sembilan, Malaya, 18 mi. NNE of Seremban; main town of Jelebu; rice-growing center.

Kuala Krai or **Krai** (krī), town (pop. 2,326), N central Kelantan, Malaya, on Kelantan R. and 40 mi. S of Kota Bharu, on E coast railroad; rubber plantations.

Kuala Kubu Bharu or **Kuala Kubu Bahru** (ko͞o'bo͞o bä'ro͞o), town (pop. 2,794), NE Selangor, Malaya, on Selangor R., 29 mi. N of Kuala Lumpur and on railroad (Kuala Kubu Road station); road-rail transfer point for Fraser's Hill and Pahang via Semangko Gap. Original town of Kuala Kubu, located 2 mi. SSW on lower ground, was abandoned (early 1930s) for present site because of floods.

Kuala Kurau (ko͞orou'), village (pop. 3,815), NW Perak, Malaya, minor fishing port on Strait of Malacca, 24 mi. NW of Taiping, at mouth of Kurau R.; coconuts, rice.

Kualalangsa, Indonesia: see LANGSA.

Kuala Lipis (lēpēs'), town (pop. 5,204), ⊙ Pahang, Malaya, on E coast railroad and on road, 75 mi. NNE of Kuala Lumpur, on Jelai R. (a headstream of Pahang R.); Br. residence; rubber, rice, gutta percha.

Kuala Lumpur (kwä'lů lo͝om'po͝or), city (pop. 175,961), ⊙ Federation of Malaya and ⊙ Selangor state, on Klang R. and 200 mi. NW of Singapore; 3°10'N 101°42'E. Administrative and communications hub on W coast railroad, at junction of roads to Port Swettenham (its ocean port on Strait of Malacca) and to Pahang via Semangko Gap; airport; center of tin-mining and rubber-growing dist.; has govt. offices, public buildings, mus. Railroad workshops at Sentul, N suburb. Pop. is 65% Chinese, 18% Indian. A village at time (1870s) of Br. arrival, Kuala Lumpur had a rapid growth and became (1895) ⊙ Federated Malay States. After Second World War, it was made ⊙ Federation of Malaya.

Kuala Muda or **Kota Kuala Muda** (kō'tů kwä'lů mo͞o'dů), village (pop. 624), SW Kedah, Malaya, on Strait of Malacca, at mouth of Muda R. (Penang line), 10 mi. SW of Sungei Patani; fisheries, rice.

Kuala Nerang (nůräng'), village (pop. 562), N Kedah, Malaya, on road and 20 mi. NE of Alor Star; rice.

Kuala Paka or **Paka** (pä'ků), village (pop. 1,698), E central Trengganu, Malaya, on South China Sea at mouth of small Paka R., 50 mi. SSE of Kuala Trengganu; coconuts, fisheries.

Kuala Perlis (pĕrlĭs'), village, Perlis, NW Malaya, minor port on Strait of Malacca at mouth of Perlis R., 5 mi. SW of Kangar, near Thailand line; fisheries.

Kuala Pilah (pēlä'), second largest town (pop. 7,305) of Negri Sembilan, SW Malaya, 21 mi. E of Seremban, near Muar R., in rice and rubber-growing area.

Kualapuu (ko͞o'äläpo͞o'o͞o), village (pop. 607), N Molokai, T.H., near Kalaupapa leper settlement; pineapples grown here.

Kuala Sedili (sůdē'lē), village (pop. 901), E Johore, Malaya, on South China Sea, 40 mi. NE of Johore Bharu; fisheries.

Kuala Selama (sůlä'mů), village (pop. 742), S Kedah, Malaya, 27 mi. SE of George Town, on Krian R. (Perak line) opposite Selama, at mouth of Small Selama R.; rubber.

Kuala Selangor (sůläng'ôr), village (pop. 1,483), W Selangor, Malaya, fishing port on Strait of Malacca, 35 mi. NW of Kuala Lumpur, at mouth of Selangor R., in rubber and coconut dist.

Kuala Trengganu (kwä'lů trĕng-gä'no͞o), town (pop. 27,004), ⊙ Trengganu, NE Malaya, port on South China Sea at mouth of Trengganu R. and 180 mi. NE of Kuala Lumpur; 5°20'N 103°8'E; residence of sultan and Br. adviser; coastwise trade; domestic weaving industry (silk sarongs, cotton goods). Sometimes called Trengganu.

Kuan- or **K'uan-,** for Chinese names beginning thus and not found here: see under KWAN-.

Kuan (gwän), town, ⊙ Kuan co. (pop. 195,432), N Hopeh prov., China, 35 mi. S of Peking and on Yungting R.; willow plaiting; chestnuts, wheat, kaoliang, millet.

Kuandang, Kwandang, or **Koeandang** (all: kwändäng'), town (dist. pop. 7,178), N Celebes, Indonesia, port on inlet of Celebes Sea, 25 mi. NNW of Gorontalo; ships timber, resin, rattan, hides, copra, kapok.

Kuang- or **K'uang-,** for Chinese names beginning thus and not found here: see under KWANG-.

Kuang-chi, China: see KWANGTSI.

Kuang-chou, China: see CANTON.

Kuang-hsi, China: see KWANGSI.

Kuang-hsin Chiang, China: see KWANGSIN RIVER.

Kuang-ning, China: see KWONGNING.

Kuan-hsi, Formosa: see KWANSI.

Kuantan (kwäntän'), largest town (pop. 8,084) of Pahang, Malaya, port on South China Sea, at mouth of minor Kuantan R. and 90 mi. ESE of Kuala Lipis (linked by highway); chief port of Pahang; ships tin (from Sungei Lembing), rubber, copra. Airport.

Kuantan River, Indonesia: see INDRAGIRI RIVER.

Kuanza River, Angola: see CUANZA RIVER.

Kuba (ko͞o'bä), town (pop. 3,906), Hiroshima prefecture, SW Honshu, Japan, on Hiroshima Bay, 16 mi. SW of Hiroshima, in agr. area (rice, wheat). Fishing.

Kuba (ko͞obä'). **1** City (1936 pop. estimate 21,024), NE Azerbaijan SSR, on N slope of the Greater Caucasus, 95 mi. NW of Baku, in orchard dist.; fruit and vegetable canning, sawmilling, rug mfg. Teachers col. **2** Village (1926 pop. 2,848), N Kabardian Autonomous SSR, Russian SFSR, on Malka R. and 27 mi. NNW of Nalchik; wheat, corn, sunflowers; horse and cattle raising.

Kuban (ko͞obän'yů), former oblast of Russia, in the Northern Caucasus; ⊙ was Yekaterinodar. Coextensive with the Kuban R. basin, it was merged (1920) with the Black Sea govt. to form the Kuban–Black Sea oblast. This, in turn, was inc. (1924) into the Northern CAUCASUS Territory.

Kuban River or **Kuban' River,** longest stream (584 mi.) of the N Caucasus, in Georgian SSR and Russian SFSR, rises in Georgian section of the Greater Caucasus, on W slope of Mt. Elbrus; flows in wide arc N, past Klukhori, Cherkessk, Nevinnomyssk, and Armavir, and W, past Kropotkin city, Ust-Labinskaya (head of navigation), and Krasnodar, entering Sea of Azov in a swampy, lagoon-filled delta mouth with 2 main arms, the Kuban proper at Temryuk and the Protoka (right) at Achuyevo. The Old Kuban [Rus. *Staraya Kuban*] arm (left; dry after c.1900; reclaimed c.1950) empties into Black Sea via Kiziltash Liman. A typical mtn. river with gorges in upper course, the Kuban becomes a slow, meandering, steppe stream in lower reaches, draining dry Kuban Steppe, one of major grain-growing dists. of USSR. Navigable for 150 mi.; regular steamer service bet. Krasnodar and Temryuk. Receives all affluents (Teberda, Zelenchuk, Urup, Laba, and Belaya rivers) on left (Caucasus) side. Connected with Yegorlyk R. by NEVINNOMYSSK CANAL.

Kubatly (ko͞obät'lē), village (1939 pop. over 500), S Azerbaijan SSR, in Kurdistan, 20 mi. S of Lachin; livestock, wheat, rice.

Kübelberg (kü'bůlbĕrk), village (pop. 1,112), Rhenish Palatinate, W Germany, 9 mi. W of Landstuhl; diamond grinding.

Kubena River (ko͞o'byĭnŭ), in NW European Russian SFSR, rises near Konosha, flows 215 mi. SE and SW, past Kharovsk, to Kubeno L., forming delta mouth below Ustye. Formerly spelled Kubina.

Kubeno Lake (ko͞o'byĭnŭ), Rus. *Kubenskoye Ozero* (□ 143), in Vologda oblast, Russian SFSR, NNW of Vologda; 37 mi. long, 2–7 mi. wide, 43 ft. deep; receives Porozovitsa R. (N; part of NORTHERN DVINA CANAL system) and Kubena R. (E). Sukhona R. is outlet (SE). Formerly spelled Kubino, Rus. *Kubinskoye*.

Kubenskoye (ko͞o'byĭnskŭyů), village (1939 pop. over 2,000), S Vologda oblast, Russian SFSR, on SW shore of Kubeno L. and 16 mi. NW of Vologda; dairying.

Kubikenborg (kübē'kůnbôr"yů), ESE suburb of Sundsvall, Vasternorrland co., NE Sweden, on inlet of Gulf of Bothnia, opposite Alno isl.; aluminum-milling center.

Kubina River, Russian SFSR: see KUBENA RIVER.

Kubino Lake, Russian SFSR: see KUBENO LAKE.

Kubi Tsangpo River, Tibet: see BRAHMAPUTRA RIVER.

Kubkub (ko͞obko͞ob'), Ital. *Cub Cub*, village, Keren div., N Eritrea, 25 mi. SE of Nagfa, in stock-raising region; road junction.

Küblis (kü'blĭs), village (pop. 660), Grisons canton, E Switzerland, on Landquart R. and 12 mi. ENE of Chur; alt. 2,685 ft.; hydroelectric plant. Has 15th-cent. church.

Kubokawa (ko͞obō'käwů), town (pop. 10,941), Kochi prefecture, S Shikoku, Japan, 34 mi. SW of Kochi; commercial center in agr. area (rice, wheat, tea).

Kucevo or **Kuchevo** (both: ko͞o'chĕvô), Serbo-Croatian *Kučevo*, village (pop. 3,404), E Serbia, Yugoslavia, 26 mi. ESE of Pozarevac; rail terminus. Gold and silver mines near by.

Kucha (ko͞ochä'), Chinese *Kuche* or *K'u-ch'e* (both: ko͞o'chŭ'), town and oasis (pop. 103,865), W central Sinkiang prov., China, 140 mi. ENE of Aksu, and on highway S of the Tien Shan; petroleum cen-

ter; mfg. of cotton and silk textiles, carpets, hats; tanning. Sericulture; livestock.
Kuchan, Iran: see QUCHAN.
Kuchan, Manchuria: see HUMA.
Kuchang. 1 (gōō'jäng') Town, ⊙ Kuchang co. (pop. 65,022), NW Hunan prov., China, 20 mi. NW of Yüanling; rice, wheat. Iron, lead, and zinc mining near by. **2** or **Ku-ch'ang** (gōō'chäng'), industrial SE suburb of Kunming, Yunnan prov., China, ⊙ Kuchang co. (pop. 172,821), on NE shore of lake Tien Chih. Coal mines, mineral pigments and bauxite deposits near by. Until 1945 Kwantu.
Kuchawan (kōōchä'vŭn) or **Kuchaman** (kōōchä'mŭn), town (pop. 11,653), N central Rajasthan, India, 130 mi. ENE of Jodhpur; trades in salt, metal, millet; handicraft sword making. Brine-salt deposits in small lake, just S. Kuchawan Road, rail station, is 12 mi. SE, on Sambhar L.
Kuch Bihar, India: see COOCH BEHAR, district.
Kuche, China: see KUCHA.
Kuchen (kōō'khŭn), village (pop. 3,419), N Württemberg, Germany, after 1945 in Württemberg-Baden, on the Fils and 2 mi. NW of Geislingen; grain, cattle.
Kucheng or **Ku-ch'eng** (gōō'chŭng'). **1** Town, ⊙ Kucheng co. (pop. 124,668), S Hopeh prov., China, on Grand Canal and 10 mi. SW of Tehchow; cotton, grain. **2** Town (pop. 19,667), ⊙ Kucheng co. (pop. 319,891), NW Hupeh prov., China, on right bank of Han R., across from Kwanghwa, and 35 mi. NW of Siangyang; cotton weaving; beans, wheat, mushrooms, sesame. Asbestos and gypsum deposits near by.
Kuchengtze, China: see KITAI.
Kuchesfahan, Iran: see KUCH-I-ISFAHAN.
Kuchevo, Yugoslavia: see KUCEVO.
Kuch-i-Isfahan or **Kuchesfahan** (both: kōōch'ĕsfähän'), town, First Prov., in Gilan, N Iran, 10 mi. E of Resht, and on W bank of the Sefid Rud and 10 mi. from Caspian Sea; agr. center; rice, berries, tobacco; silk.
Kuching (kōōchĭng'), city (pop. 37,954), ⊙ SARAWAK, in W Borneo, port on Sarawak R., 18 mi. above its mouth on S.China Sea, c.450 mi. E of Singapore; 1°34'N 110°21'E; largest city and chief commercial center of colony. Small-scale mfg.: matches, soap, alcohol. Livestock trading; fisheries. Exports sago flour, pepper, jelutong (jungle rubber). Residence of Br. governor and Sarawak Mus. (1878) are here. Has Anglican and R.C. cathedrals. There is a large Chinese quarter. Formerly sometimes called Sarawak.
Kuchino (kōō'chĭnŭ), residential town (1935 pop. over 500), E central Moscow oblast, Russian SFSR, 13 mi. E of Moscow; brickworks. Has geophysical observatory.
Kuchinotsu (kōōchē'nōtsōō), town (pop. 10,915), Nagasaki prefecture, W Kyushu, Japan, on S tip of Shimabara Peninsula, 20 mi. ESE of Nagasaki across Tachibana Bay; rice, fish, raw silk.
Kuchki (kōōch'kē), village (1926 pop. 2,418), central Penza oblast, Russian SFSR, 25 mi. SW of Penza, in wheat-growing area.
Kuchl (kōōkhŭl), town (pop. 3,042), Salzburg, W Austria, on the Salzach and 13 mi. SSE of Salzburg; rye, cattle.
Küchow or **Ch'ü-chou** (both: chü'jō'). **1** Town, Chekiang prov., China: see CHÜHSIEN. **2** Town, ⊙ Küchow co. (pop. 213,686), SW Hopeh prov., China, 30 mi. SE of Singtai; cotton, wheat, beans, kaoliang, peanuts.
Kuchow, Kweichow prov., China: see JUNGKIANG.
Kuchuk Kainarji, Bulgaria: see KAINARDZHA.
Kuchuk Lake, Russian SFSR: see KULUNDA STEPPE.
Kuckerneese, Russian SFSR: see YASNOYE.
Kuçovë (kōōchô'vŭ) or **Kuçova** (kōōchô'vä), city, S central Albania, on Devoll R. and 8 mi. NNW of Berat; petroleum center, linked by pipeline with Valona; refinery, power plant, airport. A small village until after Second World War, when it was developed as an industrial center. Renamed Stalin or Qyteti Stalin (City of Stalin) in 1950.
Kucukcekmece (küchük'chĕkmĕjĕ"), Turkish *Küçükçekmece*, lake (□ 5), Turkey in Europe, 9 mi. W of Istanbul; 5 mi. long, 3 mi. wide. Connected with Sea of Marmara.
Kucuk Menderes River (küchük' mĕndĕrĕs'), Turkish *Küçük Menderes* [=little Menderes or little Maeander]. **1** anc. *Scamander* or *Xanthus*, NW Turkey, rises 19 mi. E of Bayramic, flows 60 mi. W across the Trojan Plain, past Bayramic and Ezine, to the Dardanelles 4 mi. NW of site of Troy. **2** anc. *Caystrus* or *Cayster*, W Turkey, N of Buyuk Menderes R. (anc. Maeander), rises in Boz Mts. 20 mi. E of Odemis, flows 85 mi. W to Gulf of Kusada S of Smyrna, passing the ruins of anc. Ephesus.
Kucukyozgat, Turkey: see ELMADAGI.
Kuda (kōōd'ŭ), village, N Saurashtra, India, on S edge of Little Rann of Cutch, 35 mi. NNW of Wadhwan; rail spur terminus; saltworks.
Kudal (kōōdäl'), town (pop. 4,885), Ratnagiri dist., W Bombay, India, 70 mi. SSE of Ratnagiri; rice, coconuts, cashew nuts. Sometimes spelled Kudol.
Kudali (kōō'dŭlē), village, Shimoga dist., NW Mysore, India, 7 mi. NE of Shimoga, at confluence of Tunga and Bhadra rivers to form the Tungabhadra. Annual cattle fair.
Kudalur, India: see CUDDALORE.
Kudamatsu (kōōdä'mätsōō), city (1940 pop. 33,212; 1947 pop. 38,515), Yamaguchi prefecture, SW Honshu, Japan, just SE of Tokuyama, port on Suo Sea. Industrial center; engineering works (locomotive engines, oil refinery); salt- and sake making; woodworking. Exports mineral oil, machinery. Bombed (1945) in Second World War.
Kudara (kōōdŭrä'). **1** Village (1948 pop. over 2,000), S Buryat-Mongol Autonomous SSR, Russian SFSR, near L. Baikal, 50 mi. NW of Ulan-Ude; wheat, livestock. Petroleum and natural-gas deposits near by. **2** Village, SE Buryat-Mongol Autonomous SSR, Russian SFSR: see KUDARA-SOMON.
Kudara-Somon (-sŭmôn'), village (1948 pop. over 2,000), SE Buryat-Mongol Autonomous SSR, Russian SFSR, near Chikoi R. and Mongolia border, 45 mi. SE of Kyakhta, in agr. area; grain. Until 1948, Kudara or Bolshaya Kudara.
Kudat (kōōdät'), town (pop. 3,800, including environs), West Coast residency, Br. North Borneo, port on NW shore of Marudu Bay, 70 mi. NE of Jesselton; 6°54'N 116°50'E; trade center for area producing rubber and copra.
Kudecha (kōōdyĭchä'), town (1940 pop. over 500), E Chita oblast, Russian SFSR, 30 mi. SW of Mogocha; molybdenum and gold mining.
Kudever or **Kudever'** (kōōdyĕ'vĭr), village (1926 pop. 230), NW Velikiye Luki oblast, Russian SFSR, on Bezhanitsy Upland, 18 mi. S of Novorzhev; flax.
Kudinovo, Russian SFSR: see ELEKTROUGLI.
Kudligi (kōōd'lĭgē), village, Bellary dist., NW Madras, India, 25 mi. S of Hospet; road center; peanuts, tamarind; silk growing.
Kudol, India: see KUDAL.
Kudowa Zdroj (kōōdô'vä zdrōō'ē), Pol. *Kudowa Zdrój*, Ger. *Bad Kudowa* (bät" kōōdō'vä), town (1939 pop. 1,981; 1946 pop. 2,326) in Lower Silesia, after 1945 in Wroclaw prov., SW Poland, on Czechoslovak border, at W foot of Heuscheuer Mts., 20 mi. W of Glatz (Klodzko); health resort; cotton milling. Mineral springs known since 16th cent. Chartered after 1945.
Kudoyama (kōōdō'yämŭ), town (pop. 7,310), Wakayama prefecture, S Honshu, Japan, on W Kii Peninsula, 23 mi. ENE of Wakayama, in agr. area (rice, citrus fruit); raw silk.
Kuds, El, Palestine: see JERUSALEM.
Kudus or **Koedoes** (both: kōōdōōs'), town (pop. 54,524), central Java, Indonesia, 30 mi. ENE of Semarang, at foot of Mt. Muria; trade center for agr. area (sugar, rice, cassava); textile mills.
Kudymkar (kōōdĭmkär'), city (1935 pop. estimate 10,200), ⊙ Komi-Permyak Natl. Okrug, Molotov oblast, Russian SSR, on Inva R. (short right tributary of Kama R.) and 90 mi. NE of Molotov; agr. center; flax processing, flour milling. Has regional mus., technical schools. Developed after First World War; became city in 1938.
Kudzsir, Rumania: see CUGIR.
Kuei-, for Chinese names beginning thus and not found here: see under KWEI-.
Kuei-ch'i, China: see KWEIKI.
Kuenlun, China: see KUNLUN.
Kuerhlei, China: see KURLA.
K'u-erh-lo, China: see KURLA.
Kues, Germany: see BERNKASTEL-KUES.
Kufa, Al Kufa, or **Al-Kufah** (äl kōō'fŭ), town, Karbala prov., central Iraq, on the Shatt Hindiya (branch of the Euphrates) and 45 mi. SE of Karbala, 90 mi. S of Baghdad. An old Mesopotamian city, founded 638, it soon rivaled Basra in size. It was for a time seat of the Abbasid caliphate and became a great educational and cultural center. Was repeatedly plundered by the Karmathians in 9th and 10th cent. and lost its importance. Its tombs, its history, and its proximity to NAJAF (7 mi. S, joined by horse-drawn train across the desert) attract Moslem pilgrims.
Kufara, Cyrenaica: see KUFRA.
Küfow or **Ch'ü-fou** (both: chü'fō'), town, ⊙ Küfow co. (pop. 185,804), SW Shantung prov., China, 10 mi. ENE of Tzeyang, near railroad; silk weaving, straw plaiting; wheat, millet, rice. Home of Confucius (551–478 B.C.) and of his descendants (the K'ung family). Has large Confucianist temple.
Kufra (kōō'frä), Arabic *Kufara*, Ital. *Cufra*, group of oases in an elliptical basin (□ 457; 1950 pop. 3,800), near center of the Libyan Desert, S Cyrenaica, Libya, 575 mi. SE of Benghazi; 30 mi. long (NE-SW), 12 mi. wide; 24°N 23°E. Chief oasis is El Giof. Agr. (dates, barley, olives, grapes) and camel breeding. Local industries; olive-oil pressing, weaving (carpets, baskets), leatherworking, silverworking. Center for caravan trade bet. the coast, Fr. Equatorial Africa, and Tibesti Mts. Was stronghold of the Senusi. Occupied by Italians 1931.
Kufre, Turkey: see SIRVAN.
Kufri, Iraq: see KIFRI.
Kufstein (kōōf'shtīn), city (pop. 11,844), Tyrol, W Austria, near Ger. border, on the Inn and 41 mi. NE of Innsbruck, bet. the Kaisergebirge and Bavarian Alps. Customs station; mfg. (machines, guns, explosives), breweries, soap and cement works; summer resort, winter sports center. Fortress of Geroldseck, built by Maximilian I in early 16th cent., has powerful organ (*Heldenorgel*). Economist List buried here. Limestone quarries near by.
Kuft, Egypt: see QIFT.
Kuga (kōō'gä). **1** Town (pop. 7,582), Yamaguchi prefecture, SW Honshu, Japan, 7 mi. SW of Iwakuni; agr. center (rice, wheat); sake, soy sauce, textiles. Coal mines near by. **2** Town, O-shima, Yamaguchi prefecture, Japan: see KUKA.
Kugaly (kōōgä'lē), village (1948 pop. over 2,000), SE Taldy-Kurgan oblast, Kazakh SSR, in the Dzungarian Ala-Tau, 37 mi. SSE of Taldy-Kurgan; irrigated agr. (wheat, opium).
Kug-Aral, Kazakh SSR: see ARAL SEA.
Kuge, Japan: see KUMAGAYA.
Kugesi (kōōgyĕ'sē), village (1939 pop. over 500), N Chuvash Autonomous SSR, Russian SFSR, 8 mi. SSE of Cheboksary; wheat, rye, oats.
Kugeta (kōōgā'tä), town (pop. 7,919), Tochigi prefecture, central Honshu, Japan, 14 mi. SSE of Utsunomiya; rice, cocoons.
Kugitang (kōōgĕtän-k'), town (1945 pop. over 500), SE Chardzhou oblast, Turkmen SSR, in the Kugitang-Tau (S spur of Baisun-Tau), 70 mi. E of Kerki; coal mining.
Kugulta or **Kugul'ta** (kōōgōōl'tŭ), village (1926 pop. 10,173), central Stavropol Territory, Russian SFSR, 30 mi. NE of Stavropol; wheat, cotton, livestock.
Kuh (kōō) [Persian,=mountain], for names in Afghanistan, Iran, and Pakistan beginning thus and not found here: see under KOH, or under following part of the name.
Kühbach (kü'bäkh), village (pop. 1,318), Upper Bavaria, Germany, 20 mi. NW of Dachau; brewing. Has 17th-cent. church.
Kuhbanan or **Kuhbenan** (both: kōōbänän'), town, Eighth Prov., in Kerman, SE Iran, 90 mi. NNW of Kerman, at foot of Kuh Banan mts., one of the S Iranian ranges.
Kuh-e-Dasht, Iran: see KUH-I-DASHT.
Kuh-e-Rang, Iran: see KUH-I-RANG.
Kuh Ghizar (kōō' gĭzär') governorship (pop. 8,512) in Gilgit Agency, NW Kashmir; comprises feudatory states of Kuh (□ 480) and Ghizar (□ 1,500); ⊙ Gupis. In trans-Indus extension of N Punjab Himalayas traversed (W-E) by Gilgit (Ghizar) R. Held since 1948 by Pakistan.
Kuh-i-Dasht or **Kuh-e-Dasht** (kōō'hĕdäsht'), town, Sixth Prov., in Luristan, SW Iran, 45 mi. W of Khurramabad, in mountainous tribal region.
Kuh-i-Malik Siah: see KOH-I-MALIK SIAH.
Kuh-i-Rang or **Kuh-e-Rang** (-räng'), mountain (alt. 14,000 ft.) in Zagros ranges, SW Iran, in Bakhtiari country, 100 mi. W of Isfahan and S of Khunsar; divide bet. Zaindeh and Karun rivers.
Kühlungsborn or **Ostseebad Kühlungsborn** (ôst'zäbät" kü'lōōngsbôrn"), town (pop. 9,851), Mecklenburg, N Germany, on Mecklenburg Bay of the Baltic, 16 mi. WNW of Rostock; seaside resort. Includes (since 1937) seaside resort of Arendsee. Called Brunshaupten until 1938, when it was chartered.
Kuhmo (kōō'mō, kōōkh'mō), village (commune pop. 11,734), Oulu co., E Finland, near USSR border, in lake region, 55 mi. E of Kajaani; lumbering.
Kuhpayeh or **Qohpayeh** (both: kōpäyĕ'), town, Tenth Prov., in Isfahan, W central Iran, 45 mi. E of Isfahan and on Isfahan-Yezd road; wheat, opium, cotton, madder root, almonds.
Kuhsan, Afghanistan: see KOHSAN.
Kuibyshev or **Kuybyshev** (kwē'bĭshĕf, Rus. kōō'ēbĭshĭf), oblast (□ 20,800; 1946 pop. estimate 1,950,000) in SE European Russian SFSR; ⊙ Kuibyshev. In middle Volga R. valley, at Samara Bend (W), with Obshchi Syrt foothills of the S Urals (E); drained by Samara, Sok, Greater Kinel, and Greater Irgiz rivers. Humid continental (N; short summers) and steppe (S) climate. Mineral resources: petroleum (Zhiguli Mts., Syzran, Stavropol, Pokhvistnevo, Kinel, Mukhanovo), asphalt (Zhiguli Mts., Syzran, Alekseyevka town), oil shale (Syzran), gypsum, phosphorite, sulphur, cement rock, limestone, quartz sand. Extensive agr., with rye, oats, barley, potatoes, sunflowers; wheat (S), truck (around Kuibyshev), sugar beets (around Timashevo), orchards (Volga, Sok, and Greater Kinel river valleys), coriander (NW). Lightly forested. Industries based on agr. (tanning, food processing, flour and sugar milling) and quarrying (mfg. of building materials). Metal- and woodworking and light mfg. in main urban centers (Kuibyshev, Syzran, Chapayevsk). Well developed rail and road net; commercial traffic on the Volga facilitates exports (petroleum, building materials, machinery, chemicals, grain, livestock). Formed 1934 out of Middle Volga Territory; first named (1934) Samara Territory and (1935) Kuibyshev Territory; contained Mordvinian Autonomous SSR until 1936, when it became an oblast. Separation (1943) of Ulyanovsk oblast was last of a series of territorial changes. Developed as important petroleum region in Second World War.
Kuibyshev or **Kuybyshev. 1** City (1939 pop. 253,655; 1946 pop. estimate 600,000), ⊙ Kuibyshev oblast, Russian SFSR, port on left bank of the Volga, on Samara Bend, at mouth of Samara R., and 530 mi. ESE of Moscow; 53°12'N 19°47'E. Major industrial, commercial (grain and livestock exports), and transportation (river- and rail-transshipment)

center; airport. Mfg. (aircraft, locomotives, rail cars, ballbearings, spinning machinery, tractors, carburetors, batteries, cables, movie projectors, synthetic rubber, textiles, shoes, paper), agr. processing (hides, grain, meat, sunflower oil), woodworking; petroleum refining (pipelines from Pokhvistnevo and Zhiguli Mts. oil wells), quarrying (alabaster, gypsum, sulphur). Cultural center; aviation, engineering, medical, economic, and teachers colleges, research institutes. Has 2 cathedrals, old churches, museums, and several monuments. City center lies at confluence of Volga and Samara rivers. During Second World War, Kuibyshev expanded c.15 mi. N, forming a narrow urbanized strip bet. Volga R. waterfront (extensive shipyards) and slopes of near-by hills. Resorts and extensive orchards on N and E outskirts. Founded 1586 as Muscovite stronghold; assaulted by Nogai Tatars (1615) and Kalmyks (1644); opened gates to Cossack rebels under Stenka Razin in 1670. Grain-, livestock-, and tallow-trading center in 17th cent. Chartered 1688; became ⊙ Samara govt. in 1851; largely developed after building of railroads to Siberia (1896) and Central Asia (1906). Boom town with estimated pop. of 800,000 during Second World War; govt. offices and diplomatic corps located here (1941–43) following German assault on Moscow. Originally called Samara; renamed (1935) for Soviet leader V. V. Kuibyshev. **2** City (1939 pop. over 10,000), central Novosibirsk oblast, Russian SFSR, on Baraba Steppe, on Om R. and 5 mi. N of Barabinsk (linked by rail spur); agr. center; distilling, tanning, flour milling, metalworking. Founded 1722; once a commercial transit center on old Siberian Road; now supplanted by Barabinsk on Trans-Siberian RR. Until 1935, called Kainsk; renamed for Soviet leader exiled here 1907, 1909. **3** City (1936 pop. estimate 5,300), SW Tatar Autonomous SSR, Russian SFSR, near Volga R., 50 mi. SSE of Kazan; flour-milling center. Peat deposits near by. Chartered 1781; until 1935, Spassk.

Kuibysheva, Imeni, Uzbek SSR: see KUIBYSHEVO, Fergana oblast.

Kuibyshevabad, Tadzhik SSR: see KUIBYSHEVSK.

Kuibyshev Dam, on middle Volga R., Russian SFSR, 30 mi. NW of Kuibyshev, on N side of Samara Bend. Construction project (begun 1950; planned completion, 1955) includes right-bank hydroelectric plant (2,000,000 kw capacity) near ZHIGULEVSK, main earth dam section (85 ft. high) and left-bank concrete spillway with navigation canal and locks. The Volga, whose level at the dam is raised 80 ft., is backed up 300 mi. and reaches a width of 25 mi. upstream. A multi-purpose project, the dam improves navigation of the middle Volga, furnishes power to Moscow, Kuibyshev, and Saratov, and activates irrigation pumps for the dry lands E of the Volga.

Kuibyshevka, Kuybyshevka, Kuibyshevka-Vostochnaya, or **Kuybyshevka-Vostochnaya** (kōō'ēbĭshĭfkŭ-vŭstŏch'nīŭ) [Rus.,=eastern Kuibyshevka], city (1939 pop. over 10,000), SE Amur oblast, Russian SFSR, rail junction on Trans-Siberian RR and 60 mi. NNE of Blagoveshchensk (linked by railroad); agr. center in wheat area; flour milling, dairying, tractor repair. Originally called Bochkarevo; later known (1926–35) as Aleksandrovka.

Kuibyshevo or **Kuybyshevo** (kōō'ēbĭshĭvŭ). **1** Village, S Guryev oblast, Kazakh SSR, on Mangyshlak Peninsula, on road and 75 mi. ESE of Fort Shevchenko. Coal mining near by. **2** Village (1939 pop. over 500), S Crimea, Russian SFSR, on Belbek R. and 8 mi. S of Bakhchisarai; tobacco, fruit, berries. Until 1944, Albat. Sometimes called Kuibyshevskoye. **3** Village, Kemerovo oblast, Russian SFSR: see STALINSK, city. **4** Village (1926 pop. 5,536), SW Rostov oblast, Russian SFSR, on Mius R. and 40 mi. N of Taganrog; flour mill, metalworks; wheat, sunflowers, castor beans. Until c.1936, Golodayevka or Golodayevskoye. **5** Fishing village (1940 pop. 2,350), Sakhalin oblast, Russian SFSR, on Iturup Isl., S Kurile Isls., on W coast, 12 mi. SW of Kurilsk. Under Jap. rule (until 1945), called Rubetsu. **6** Village, central Mary oblast, Turkmen SSR, on railroad (Talkhatan-Baba station) and 20 mi. SE of Mary; cotton. Until c.1940, Talkhatan-Baba. **7** Village (1926 pop. 5,696), E Zaporozhe oblast, Ukrainian SSR, 40 mi. NNW of Osipenko; wheat. Until c.1935, called Tsarekonstantinovka. Tsarekonstantinovka station is at Kanysh-Zarya, just SE. **8** Village (1926 pop. 5,424), SW Fergana oblast, Uzbek SSR, 20 mi. SE of Kokand; cotton, sericulture; metalworks. Formerly called Rishtan and, 1937–c.1940, Imeni Kuibysheva.

Kuibyshevsk or **Kuybyshevsk** (kōō'ēbĭshĭfsk), town (1939 pop. over 500), S Stalinabad oblast, Tadzhik SSR, in Vakhsh valley, 8 mi. N of Kurgan-Tyube; cotton; metalworks. Formerly Aral and (c.1935–40) Kuibyshevabad.

Kuibyshevski Zaton or **Kuybyshevskiy Zaton** (–skē zŭtŏn'), town (1926 pop. 2,478), Tatar Autonomous SSR, Russian SFSR, port on left bank of Volga R. and 6 mi. WNW of Kuibyshev; winter anchorage; freight depot; shipyards. Until 1935, Spasski Zaton.

Kuik, Netherlands: see CUYK.

Kuilenburg, Netherlands: see CULEMBORG.

Kuils River (koilz), Afrikaans *Kuilsrivier* (koilsrĭfēr'), village (pop. 1,581), SW Cape Prov., U. of So. Afr., 15 mi. E of Cape Town; fruit, tobacco, viticulture; tin deposits.

Kuilyuk or **Kuylyuk** (kōōēlyŏŏk'), village (1939 pop. over 500), N Tashkent oblast, Uzbek SSR, on Chirchik R., just SE of Tashkent; food processing (fruits, vegetables).

Kuinjipad, India: see KURINJIPADI.

Kuito Lakes or **Kuyto Lakes** (kōō'ētŭ), Finnish *Kuittijärvi* (kōō'ētĭyăr"vē), chain of lakes in W Karelo-Finnish SSR, 75 mi. W of Kem; 70 mi. long, up to 6 mi. wide. Include Upper Kuito L. (W), Middle Kuito L. (Ukhta on N shore), and Lower Kuito L. (E). Crossed W-E by Kem R. Frozen Nov.-Apr. Formerly called Kutnozero.

Kuitun or **Kuytun** (kōōētōōn'), village (1948 pop. over 2,000), SW Irkutsk oblast, Russian SFSR, on Trans-Siberian RR and 40 mi. ESE of Tulun, in agr. area.

Kuiu Island (kōō'yōō) (65 mi. long, 6–23 mi. wide), SE Alaska, in Alexander Archipelago, bet. Kupreanof Isl. (E) of Baranof Isl. (W), 30 mi. W of Petersburg; 56°28'N 134°1'W; rises to c.3,000 ft. Fishing, zinc mining.

Kuivastu or **Kuyvastu** (kōō'ēvästōō), village, on E coast of Muhu isl., Estonia, 6 mi. SE of Muhu village; connected by ferry across Muhu Sound with Virtsu on mainland.

Kujak, Tall, Syria: see KOJAK, TELL.

Kujawy (kōōyä'vĭ), region, N central Poland, in SE Bydgoszcz and NW Warszawa provs., along left bank of the Vistula; centered on Inowroclaw and Wloclawek. Dotted with lakes, it is noted for its fertility. Principal crops are rye, potatoes, oats, wheat, sugar beets; stock raising. Sometimes called Cuyavia.

Kuji (kōō'jē). **1** Town (pop. 10,793), Ibaraki prefecture, central Honshu, Japan, on the Pacific, 7 mi. SSW of Hitachi; fishing port; agr. (rice, wheat). **2** Town (pop. 8,970), Iwate prefecture, N Honshu, Japan, port on the Pacific, 27 mi. SE of Hachinohe; fishing, agr.; exports charcoal, lumber.

Kuju (kōōjōō'), town (pop. 3,170), Oita prefecture, central Kyushu, Japan, 23 mi. SW of Oita; rice, lumber, charcoal, livestock; sake brewery. Mt. Kuju is near by.

Kuju, Mount, Jap. *Kuju-san,* highest peak (5,850 ft.) of Kyushu, Japan, in Oita prefecture, 24 mi. WSW of Oita, in Aso Natl. Park; winter sports. Hot-springs resorts in NE foothills.

Kuka (kōō'kä) or **Kuga** (kōō'gä), town (pop. 8,203) on O-shima, Yamaguchi prefecture, Japan, on N coast of isl.; boatbuilding, woodworking; sake, soy sauce.

Kukarka, Russian SFSR: see SOVETSK.

Kukawa (kōō'käwä") or **Kuka** (kōō'kä), town (pop. 3,282), Bornu prov., Northern Provinces, NE Nigeria, 80 mi. NNE of Maiduguri, 15 mi. from L. Chad; cassava, millet, gum arabic; cattle raising; saltworking. In 19th cent. was ⊙ Bornu and a major native commercial center with pop. of c.60,000. After its destruction (1894), capital was moved to Dikwa; returned here (1902) after rebuilding of Kukawa by British. Capital finally transferred (1908) to Maiduguri.

Kukenaam (kōō"kŭnäm') or **Cuquenán** (kōōkänän'), mountain and waterfalls (drop c.2,000 ft.) on Br. Guiana–Venezuela border, just NW of Mt. Roraima.

Kukës (kōō'kŭs) or **Kukësi** (kōō'kŭsē), town (1945 pop. 1,095), N Albania, near Yugoslav border, 45 mi. E of Scutari and on Drin R. where it is formed by union of White Drin and Black Drin; commercial center of Albanian Kosovo; airport. Iron and chrome deposits near by.

Kukes, Turkey: see SERIK.

Küki or **Ch'ü-ch'i** (both: chü'chē'), town, ⊙ Küki co. (pop. 38,881), SE central Yunnan prov., China, 70 mi. S of Kunming, in mtn. region; rice, timber.

Kuki (kōō'kē), town (pop. 8,130), Saitama prefecture, central Honshu, Japan, 17 mi. ESE of Kumagaya; mfg. (cotton goods, noodles, sake).

Kukisvumchorr (kōō'kēsvōōmchŭr), town (1948 pop. over 2,000), central Murmansk oblast, Russian SFSR, on Kola Peninsula, in Khibiny Mts., 5 mi. N of Kirovsk; apatite and nephelite mines.

Kukkus, Russian SFSR: see PRIVOLZHSKOYE.

Kuklen (kŏŏk'lĕn), village (pop. 4,747), Plovdiv dist., S central Bulgaria, at N foot of W Rhodope Mts., 5 mi. WNW of Asenovgrad; wine making; tobacco, sericulture. Site of old monastery.

Kukmor (kōōkmôr'), town (1936 pop. estimate 7,900), N Tatar Autonomous SSR, Russian SFSR, near Vyatka R., on railroad and 8 mi. WSW of Vyatskiye Polyany; felt-boot mfg. center; woolen-weaving handicrafts.

Kuknur or **Kuknoor** (kōōknōōr'), town (pop. 5,424), Raichur dist., SW Hyderabad state, India, 15 mi. NW of Koppal; millet, cotton; oilseed milling. Also spelled Koknur.

Kukoboi or **Kukoboy** (kōōkŭboi'), village, N Yaroslavl oblast, Russian SFSR, 31 mi. NE of Poshekhonye-Volodarsk; flax.

Kükong (kŏk'gông'), Mandarin *Ch'ü-chiang* (chü'jyäng'), town (pop. 72,963), ⊙ Kükong co. (pop. 226,456), N Kwangtung prov., China, port (head of navigation) on North R. (formed here by union of Wu and Cheng rivers), on railroad to Hankow and 120 mi. N of Canton; trading center for lumber, salt, tobacco, cattle, and for cotton goods. Paper milling, tanning, furniture mfg. Near by are extensive coal, antimony, tungsten, and bismuth mines. Until 1912, Shiuchow or Shaochow.

Kükoshakia, China: see KWEITEH, Tsinghai prov.

Kükow, China: see KUNGHO.

Kukruse (kōō'krōōsä), town, NE Estonia, on rail spur and 3 mi. E of Kohtla-Jarve, in oil-shale mining area.

Kuks (kŏŏks), village (pop. 279), NE Bohemia, Czechoslovakia, 4 mi. SE of Dvur Kralove; former bathing resort. Has church with notable sculptures and paintings. Rock-sculptures depicting biblical scenes near by.

Kukshi (kŏŏk'shē), town (pop. 7,114), SW Madhya Bharat, India, 45 mi. SW of Dhar; markets maize, wheat, cotton, millet; cotton ginning. Sometimes spelled Kuksi.

Kukshik, Russian SFSR: see PERVOMAISKI, Bashkir Autonomous SSR.

Kuku, Ethiopia: see ALGA.

Kuku Hoto, China: see KWEISUI.

Kuku Nor, China: see KOKO NOR.

Kukup (kōōkōōp'), village (pop. 941), S Johore, Malaya, on Strait of Malacca, 22 mi. WSW of Johore Bharu; fisheries; coconuts.

Kula (kōō'lä), city (pop. 5,566), Vidin dist., NW Bulgaria, 19 mi. SW of Vidin, near Yugoslav border; agr. center (grain, livestock, truck). Linked with Zajecar (Yugoslavia) by Vrashka-chuka Pass.

Kula (kōōlä'), town (pop. 9,180), Manisa prov., W Turkey, 65 mi. E of Manisa; carpets, wool; wheat, barley, tobacco.

Kula (kōō'lä), village (pop. 10,476), Vojvodina, NW Serbia, Yugoslavia, on Danube-Tisa Canal and 27 mi. NNW of Novi Sad, in the Backa; rail junction; woolen and felt hatmaking.

Kulachi (kōōlä'chē), town (pop. 8,840), Dera Ismail Khan dist., S North-West Frontier Prov., W Pakistan, 26 mi. WNW of Dera Ismail Khan; trades in wheat, millet, ghee; handicraft cloth weaving, camel breeding.

Kulagino (kōōlä'gĭnŭ), village (1939 pop. over 500), N Guryev oblast, Kazakh SSR, on Ural R. and 85 mi. N of Guryev; cattle.

Kula Gulf (kōō'lä), Solomon Isls., SW Pacific, 5 mi. wide, bet. Kolombangara (W) and main isl. of New Georgia (E). In Second World War, scene of 2 naval battles won by U.S. over Japan.

Kulai (kōōlī'), town (pop. 3,256), S Johore, Malaya, on railroad and 18 mi. NNW of Johore Bharu; rubber, timber, pineapples.

Kula Kangri (kōōlä' kängrē'), peak (24,780 ft.) in main range of W Assam Himalayas, on undefined Bhutan-Tibet border, at 28°14'N 90°37'E. Kangri peak (24,740 ft.) is 16 mi. SSW, also on border.

Kulal, Mount (kōōläl'), volcano (7,520 ft.), N Kenya, at E rim of Great Rift Valley, near S tip of L. Rudolf; 3°20'S 36°54'E. Cone is split into 2 sections by a cleft 3,000 ft. deep.

Kulambangra, Solomon Isls.: see KOLOMBANGARA.

Kulanak (kōōlŭnäk'), village (1939 pop. over 500), central Tyan-Shan oblast, Kirghiz SSR, on Naryn R. and 23 mi. W of Naryn; wheat.

Kulang (gōō'läng'), town, ⊙ Kulang co. (pop. 39,144), central Kansu prov., China, on Silk Road to Sinkiang, and 30 mi. S of Wuwei, at the Great Wall; alt. 6,856 ft.; wheat, millet.

Kulangar (kōōlŭng-gär'), village, Kabul prov., E Afghanistan, on Logar R. and 35 mi. S of Kabul, on road to Gardez.

Kulanghsü or **Kulangsü,** China: see AMOY.

Kulasekharapatnam (kōōlŭsä"kŭrŭpŭt'nŭm), town (pop. 11,900), Tinnevelly dist., S Madras, India, port on Gulf of Mannar, 35 mi. SE of Tinnevelly; produces alcohol, sugar, salt; exports palmyra fiber, oils and oil cake, jaggery, tobacco. R.C. village of Manapad (formerly Manappadu), reputed residence (1540s) of St. Francis Xavier, and lighthouse are on headland 2 mi. S. Formerly spelled Kulasekarapatnam.

Kulata (kōō'lätä), village (pop. 1,532), Gorna Dzhumaya dist., SW Bulgaria, rail station on Gr. border, 7 mi. E of Petrich; tobacco, oil-bearing plants. Customhouse is just N, in Chuchuligovo (chōōchōōlē'gôvô) (pop. 601).

Kulaura (kōōlou'rŭ), village, Sylhet dist., E East Bengal, E Pakistan, 27 mi. SSE of Sylhet; rail junction (spur to Sylhet); rice, tea, oilseeds. Tea processing near by.

Kulautuva (kōōloutōōvä'), town, S central Lithuania, on right bank of the Neman and 12 mi. WNW of Kaunas; summer resort; sanatorium.

Kuldiga (kōōl'dēgä), Lettish *Kuldīga,* Ger. *Goldingen* (gōl'dĭng-ŭn), city (pop. 7,180), W Latvia, in Kurzeme, on Venta R. (head of navigation) and 45 mi. NE of Liepaja, on railroad; road hub in timber region; mfg. (matches, veneers, leather goods, woolen and silk textiles); machine shops. Has castle ruins.

Kuldiha (kōōl'dĭhŭ), village, Mayurbhanj dist., NE Orissa, India, on railroad and 38 mi. WNW of Baripada; pottery mfg. Iron ore mined in near-by hills (SE).

Kuldja or **Kulja** (kōōl'jä), Chinese *Ining* (yē'nĭng'), until 1913 *Ningyüan,* town, ⊙ Kuldja co. (pop.

149,069), W Sinkiang prov., China, on Ili R. and 300 mi. E of Urumchi, near USSR border; 43°55'N 81°20'E. Leading center of ILI dist., trading in tea, cattle; tanning, wool-textile mfg. Iron, coal mines. Sometimes called Ili.

Kuldur or **Kul'dur** (kōōldōōr'), health resort, NW Jewish Autonomous Oblast, Khabarovsk Territory, Russian SFSR, 15 mi. N of Birakan; hot alkaline-sulphur springs.

Kulebaki (kōōlyĭbä'kē), city (1926 pop. 15,142), SW Gorki oblast, Russian SFSR, 22 mi. ESE of Murom; steel-milling center, based on scrap and Krivoi Rog iron ore, produces locomotive and railway car parts; flour mills, sawmills. Became city in 1932.

Kulebovka (kōōlyĭbôf'kŭ), SW suburb (1926 pop. 5,206) of Novo-Moskovsk, N Dnepropetrovsk oblast, Ukrainian SSR.

Kulemborg, Netherlands: see CULEMBORG.

Kulevi (kōōlyĕ'vē), village (1926 pop. 872), W Georgian SSR, on Black Sea, in Colchis lowland, 9 mi. N of Poti; woodworking (hardwoods).

Kulgam (kōōlgäm'), village, Anantnag dist., SW central Kashmir, in Vale of Kashmir, near the Jhelum, 10 mi. SW of Anantnag; rice, corn, oilseeds, wheat.

Kuli (kōōlyē'), village (1926 pop. 2,430), S Dagestan Autonomous SSR, Russian SFSR, in the E Greater Caucasus, 12 mi. SSE of Kumukh; hardy grain, sheep. Pop. largely Lak.

Kuliang (gōō'lyäng') or **Kuling** (-lĭng'), town, NE Fukien prov., China, 5 mi. E of Foochow and N of Min R. mouth; alt. 4,000 ft. Summer resort.

Kuligi (kōōlyē'gē), village, NE Udmurt Autonomous SSR, Russian SFSR, 40 mi. ENE of Glazov; flax; lumbering.

Kulikov (kōōlyĭkôf'), Pol. *Kulików* (kōōlyē'kōōf), town (1931 pop. 3,390), central Lvov oblast, Ukrainian SSR, 9 mi. N of Lvov; wheat, rye, oats.

Kulikovka (-kŭ), village (1926 pop. 2,828), central Chernigov oblast, Ukrainian SSR, 16 mi. ESE of Chernigov; hemp.

Kulikovo, Russian SFSR: see KURKINO.

Kulikow, Ukrainian SSR: see KULIKOV.

Kulim (kōōlĭm'), town (pop. 9,481), S Kedah, Malaya, 15 mi. E of George Town, near Penang line; rubber-growing center.

Kulin (gōō'lĭn'), town (pop. 11,576), ⊙ Kulin co. (pop. 321,654), southernmost Szechwan prov., China, 60 mi. SSE of Luhsien, on Kweichow border; sugar cane, rice, millet. Sulphur mines, coal deposits near by.

Kuling (gōō'lĭng'). **1** Town, Fukien prov., China: see KULIANG. **2** Noted hill resort of N Kiangsi prov., China, in Lü Shan massif, 4 mi. S of Kiukiang. Opened 1895 to foreign residence.

Kulithura (kōōlĭ'tōōrŭ) or **Kuzhittura** (kōōzhĭ'-tōōrŭ), city (pop. 8,853), S Travancore, India, 20 mi. SE of Trivandrum; coir rope and mats, palmyra jaggery. Monazite workings near by.

Kulittalai or **Kulitalai** (both: kōōlĭt'ŭlī), town (pop. 9,242), Trichinopoly dist., S Madras, India, on Cauvery R. opposite Musiri (ferry) and 18 mi. WNW of Trichinopoly; rice, plantain, coconut palms; cotton textiles, wicker coracles.

Kuliyapitiya (kōōlĭyŭpĭt'ĭyŭ), town (pop., including adjacent Dandagamuwa, 2,159), North Western Prov., Ceylon, 22 mi. W of Kurunegala; vegetables, rice, coconut palms.

Kulja, China: see KULDJA.

Kulladakurichi, India: see KALLIDAIKURICHI.

Kullen (kŭ'lŭn), peninsula, SW Sweden, extends 15 mi. into the Kattegat at mouth of the Oresund, 15 mi. NNW of Halsingborg; 1–10 mi. wide; forms S shore of Skalder Bay. Hilly surface rises to 617 ft. (N). At extremity (56°18'N 12°27'E) is Kullen lighthouse. Molle and Arild are seaside resort.

Kulluk, Turkey: see GULLUK.

Kulm, Czechoslovakia: see CHLUMEC.

Kulm, Poland: see CHELMNO.

Kulm (kŭlm), city (pop. 707), La Moure co., S N.Dak., 32 mi. W of La Moure; livestock, grain, dairy products.

Kulmbach (kōōlm'bäkh), city (1950 pop. 24,159), Upper Franconia, N Bavaria, Germany, on the White Main and 12 mi. NNW of Bayreuth; 50°6'N 11°27'E. Rail junction; malt-mfg. and -brewing center; textile (spinning, weaving; plush, stockings), food (meat canning; yeast), and metal industries (trucks, precision instruments). Also lumber and paper milling, printing. Has Gothic and 16th-cent. churches, baroque city hall. First mentioned 1035, Kulmbach was chartered before 1248. Was residence of margraves of Kulmbach (1340–1603). Almost completely destroyed by imperial troops in 1533. Passed to Bavaria in 1810. Captured by U.S. troops in April, 1945. Hans von Kulmbach b. here. On near-by hill is old fortress Plassenburg (1st mentioned in early-12th cent.; rebuilt in Renaissance style after disaster of 1533), since 1808 a prison.

Kulmsee, Poland: see CHELMZA.

Kuloi or **Kuloy** (kōōloi'), town (1945 pop. over 500), S Archangel oblast, Russian SFSR, on railroad and 5 mi. S of Velsk; sawmilling. Developed in early 1940s.

Kuloi River or **Kuloy River**, 2 streams in Archangel oblast, Russian SFSR. **1** Rises NW of Totma in Vologda oblast, flows c.100 mi. N to Vaga R. near Velsk. **2** Rises near Pinega, flows c.150 mi. N to Mezen Bay of White Sea at Dolgoshchelye. Called Sotka R. in upper course. Connected by canal with Pinega R.

Kulomzino, Russian SFSR: see OMSK, city.

Kulotino (kōōlô'tyĭnŭ), town (1926 pop. 3,042), E central Novgorod oblast, Russian SFSR, 20 mi. W of Borovichi; linen milling.

Kuloy, in Rus. names: see KULOI.

Kulp (kōōlp), village (pop. 1,184), Diyarbakir prov., E Turkey, 60 mi. NE of Diyarbakir; cereals. Formerly Pasur.

Külpenberg (kül'pŭnbĕrk), highest point (1,565 ft.) of the Kyffhäuser, central Germany, 11 mi. WSW of Sangershausen.

Kulpmont, borough (pop. 5,199), Northumberland co., E central Pa., 17 mi. ESE of Sunbury; anthracite; clothing mfg. Settled 1905, inc. 1916.

Kulsary or **Kul'sary** (kōōlsä'rē), oil town (1945 pop. over 500), N Guryev oblast, Kazakh SSR, 10 mi. NE of Koschagyl, in Emba oil fields.

Külsheim (küls'hīm), town (pop. 2,300), N Baden, Germany, after 1945 in Württemberg-Baden, 6 mi. S of Wertheim; fruit, grain.

Kultbaza Alygdzher, Russian SFSR: see ALYGDZHER.

Kulti (kōōl'tē), town (pop. 19,423), Burdwan dist., W West Bengal, India, in Damodar Valley and Raniganj coal field, 9 mi. WNW of Asansol; a major iron- and steelworks center; brick and tile mfg. Coal-mining centers at Dishergarh (2½ mi. S) and Salanpur (3 mi. NE) villages.

Kultuk (kōōltōōk'), town (1948 pop. over 2,000), SE Irkutsk oblast, Russian SFSR, on Trans-Siberian RR, at SW end of L. Baikal, 4 mi. N of Slyudyanka, on highway to Kyren and Turtu; metalworks.

Külu or **Chü-lu** (both: jü'lōō'), town, ⊙ Külu co. (pop. 139,768), SW Hopeh prov., China, 30 mi. ENE of Singtai; cotton, wheat, kaoliang, millet, peanuts.

Kulu (kōōl'ōō), central subdivision of Kangra dist., NE Punjab, India, in Punjab Himalayas; bordered N by Lahul, E by Spiti, S by Saraj subdivisions. Forests and mtn. wastes, with fertile, picturesque valley of upper Beas R. (called Kulu valley). Wheat, corn, barley, potatoes; hand-loom weaving, beekeeping. Kulu valley noted for tea and fruit-growing; willow plantation. Strong Rajput state in Middle Ages.

Kulu, village, Kangra dist., NE Punjab, India, on Beas R. and 50 mi. ESE of Dharmsala; trades in grain, wool, fruit, tea, honey, timber; hand-loom weaving, basket making. Formerly Sultanpur.

Kuludzhunski or **Kuludzhunskiy** (kōōlōōjōōn'skē), town (1948 pop. over 2,000), W East Kazakhstan oblast, Kazakh SSR, 15 mi. WNW of Samarskoye; gold mining.

Kulukak (kŭlōō'kŭk), Eskimo village (1939 pop. 55), SW Alaska, on Kulukak Bay, N arm (7 mi. long, 4–6 mi. wide) of Bristol Bay, 50 mi. W of Dillingham; fishing. School.

Kulun, Mongolia: see ULAN BATOR.

Kulunda (kōōlōōndä'), town (1944 pop. over 500), W Altai Territory, Russian SFSR, on S.Siberian RR and 33 mi. SSE of Slavgorod; rail junction; Glauber's-salt deposits.

Kulunda Lake, largest (□ 230) of salt lakes in Kulunda Steppe, NW Altai Territory, Russian SFSR, 40 mi. E of Slavgorod; up to 13 ft. deep. Salt deposits in narrow inlets. Smaller Kuchuk L. is just S. **Kulunda River**, which rises near Ob R., flows 125 mi. generally SW, past Sharchino and Bayevo, to Kulunda L.

Kulunda Steppe, S extension of Baraba Steppe, in SW Siberian Russian SFSR, bet. Ob R. and E Pavlodar oblast, Kazakh SSR; 50–250 mi. (E-W) by 200 mi. (N-S); average alt. 330 ft. Has several small fresh-water lakes (e.g., Topolnoye L.) and many salt-water lakes (e.g., KULUNDA LAKE, Kuchuk L.). Glauber's salts and soda are extracted. Chief cities: Pavlodar, Slavgorod, Kamen.

Kulunkai, Manchuria: see SUITUNG.

Kuluri, Greece: see SALAMIS.

Kuluyevo (kōōlōō'yĭvŭ), village (1926 pop. 377), central Chelyabinsk oblast, Russian SFSR, on Miass R. and 25 mi. NE of Miass; grain, livestock. Gold placers near by.

Kulyab (kōōlyäp'), oblast (□ 4,600; 1946 pop. estimate 200,000), SE Tadzhik SSR; ⊙ Kulyab. Bounded by Panj R. (S, E); drained by the Kyzyl-Su and Yakh-Su; Darvaza Range in NE. Agr. (wheat, truck produce); cotton in lower valleys. Livestock (sheep, goats, cattle) on mtn. slopes; extensive walnut forests (N). Industry (cotton ginning, cottonseed-oil extraction) at Kulyab, Parkhar. Gold placers along rivers. Pop.: Tadzhiks, Uzbeks. Formed 1939.

Kulyab, city (1932 pop. estimate 6,700), ⊙ Kulyab oblast, Tadzhik SSR, on the Yakh-Su and 70 mi. SE of Stalinabad; 37°55'N 69°46'E. In cotton area; cotton ginning, cottonseed-oil extraction; metalworking. Salt deposits.

Kum, Iran: see QUM.

Kum (kōōm), Ger. *Kumberg* (kŭm'bĕrk), peak (3,998 ft.) in Dinaric Alps, Slovenia, Yugoslavia, 27 mi. E of Ljubljana.

Kuma (kōō'mä), town (pop. 7,480), Ehime prefecture, W central Shikoku, Japan, 15 mi. SE of Matsuyama; agr. center in forested area; rice, wheat, tea.

Kumagaya (kōōmä'gäyŭ), city (1940 pop. 39,412; 1947 pop. 63,267), Saitama prefecture, central Honshu, Japan, 22 mi. NW of Tokyo; mfg. (silk textiles, dyes, flour, cement, sake, soy sauce). Includes (since early 1940s) former town of Kuge (1940 pop. 1,939).

Kumai (kōōmī'), village, Darjeeling dist., N West Bengal, India, 35 mi. E of Darjeeling; tea, rice, corn, millet, cardamom. Limestone deposits near by. Coal and copper pyrite deposits 7 mi. WNW, near Daling.

Kumait, Al, or **Al-Kumayt** (äl kōōmīt'), town, 'Amara prov., E Iraq, on Tigris R. and 22 mi. NW of 'Amara; dates, rice, corn, millet, sesame.

Kumak (kōōmäk'), town (1926 pop. 2,678), E Chkalov oblast, Russian SFSR, on Kumak R. (left tributary of Ural R.) on railroad and 13 mi. NE of Orsk, in Orsk-Khalilovo industrial dist.; metalworking, fireproof-clay quarrying; truck gardening.

Kumamba Islands (kōōmäm'bŭ), Netherlands New Guinea, in the Pacific, just off N coast, 150 mi. WNW of Hollandia; 1°40'S 138°47'E. Consists of Liki (4 mi. long) and Nirumoar or Niroemoar (both: nērōōmwär'), 3 mi. long. In Second World War, isls. were taken May, 1944, by U.S. forces. Also spelled Koemamba.

Kumamoto (kōōmä'mōtō), prefecture [Jap. *ken*] (□ 2,872; 1940 pop. 1,368,179; 1947 pop. 1,765,726), W central Kyushu, Japan; ⊙ KUMAMOTO. Mainland bounded W by the Ariakeno-umi, Shimabara Bay, and Yatsushiro Bay; prefecture includes SHIMO-JIMA, KAMI-SHIMA, OYANO-SHIMA, and scattered islets of AMAKUSA ISLANDS. Principal port, YATSUSHIRO. Mountainous terrain rises to 5,240 ft. in volcanic Aso-san in Aso Natl. Park. Hot springs in NE area. Drained by Kuma and Chikugo rivers. Primarily agr., producing rice, sweet potatoes, fruit (oranges, pears, plums). Extensive lumbering in interior. Products include cotton textiles, porcelain ware, paper, dolls, camellia oil, cement. Principal centers (all on W coast): Kumamoto, Yatsushiro, HITOYOSHI, ARAO.

Kumamoto, city (1940 pop. 194,139; 1947 pop. 245,841), ⊙ Kumamoto prefecture, W Kyushu, Japan, 560 mi. WSW of Tokyo and on Shirakawa R., on large plain; 32°48'N 130°44'E. Commercial and cultural center; mfg. (cotton textiles, tiles). Seat of Kumamoto Medical Univ., school of pharmacy. Suizenji Park (opened 1532) contains a lake 4 mi. in circumference. Was great castle town in 16th cent. Includes (since early 1940s) former town of Kawashiri. Bombed (1945) in Second World War.

Kumane (kōō'mänĕ), Hung. *Kumán* (kōō'män), village (pop. 5,022), Vojvodina, N Serbia, Yugoslavia, 14 mi. NW of Zrenjanin, in the Banat.

Kumano (kōōmä'nō), town (pop. 9,355), Hiroshima prefecture, SW Honshu, Japan, 8 mi. SE of Hiroshima; commercial center in agr. and livestock area; produces writing brushes.

Kumano River, Jap. *Kumano-gawa*, on Kii Peninsula, S Honshu, Japan; rises in mts. near Yoshino, flows generally S, past Hongu, and SE to Kumano Sea at Shingu; 100 mi. long. Log drives; navigable for c.30 mi. by excursion motorboats to Hongu. Called Totsu R. in upper course. Known for scenic Toro (or Doro) Gorge on its main (left) tributary, Kitayama R. (40 mi. long).

Kumano Sea, Jap. *Kumano-nada*, N arm of Philippine Sea; forms wide bight along E coast of Kii Peninsula, S Honshu, Japan; c.80 mi. long.

Kumanosho (kōōmä"nōshō'), town (pop. 5,536), Kumamoto prefecture, W Kyushu, Japan, 5 mi. S of Kumamoto; rice, wheat, raw silk; spinning mill. Airfield.

Kumanovo (kōō'mänôvô), town (pop. 19,798), N Macedonia, Yugoslavia, on railroad and 17 mi. ENE of Skoplje; trade center for tobacco-growing region; handicrafts. Health resort near by. First mentioned in 1660; site of decisive Serbian victory over Turks in 1912.

Kumaon, India: see KUMAUN.

Kumara (kōō'mŭrŭ), borough (pop. 420), W S.Isl., New Zealand, 11 mi. SSE of Greymouth; gold dredging.

Kumara (kōōmŭrä'), village (1948 pop. over 500), SE Amur oblast, Russian SFSR, on Amur R. and 95 mi. NNW of Blagoveshchensk, in agr. area (wheat, livestock). Cossack village, founded 1858.

Kumarapalaiyam, India: see KOMARAPALAIYAM.

Kumardhubi, India: see KUMHARDHUBI.

Kumarhata, India: see HALISAHAR.

Kuma River (kōō'mä), Jap. *Kuma-gawa*, Kumamoto prefecture, W Kyushu, Japan; rises in mts. 25 mi. E of Yatsushiro, flows SSW, past Hitoyoshi, W, and N to Yatsushiro Bay at Yatsushiro; 75 mi. long. Scenic rapids.

Kuma River (kōō'mŭ, kōōmä'), in the N Caucasus, Russian SFSR, rises on N slope of the central Greater Caucasus, ENE of Klukhori; flows 360 mi. generally ENE, past Suvorovskaya, Mineralnye Vody, Soldato-Aleksandrovskoye, Budennovsk, and Levokumskoye, losing itself on Astrakhan-Grozny oblast border, in swamps and reed lakes, c.50 mi. from Caspian Sea, which it reaches only during spring floods and in years of heavy precipitation. Low water level, in lower course, caused by dry climate, evaporation, and loss through irrigation (vineyards, cotton, fruit) in Budennovsk area. Receives Zolka and Podkumok rivers (right). Lower course to be used by MANYCH CANAL.

Kumarkhali (kōōmär'kälē), town (pop. 5,582), Kushtia dist., W East Bengal, E Pakistan, on upper Madhumati (Garai) R. and 8 mi. ESE of Kushtia; trade center (rice, jute, linseed, sugar cane). Until 1947, in Nadia dist. of Br. Bengal.

Kumashkino (kōōmä'shkēnŭ), village (1948 pop. over 2,000), SW East Kazakhstan oblast, Kazakh SSR, on Kurchum R. and 110 mi. SSE of Ust-Kamenogorsk; agr., cattle breeding.

Kumasi (kōōmä'sē), city (pop. 70,705), ⊙ Ashanti, S central Gold Coast, rail terminus 125 mi. NW of Accra, 125 mi. N of Takoradi; 6°43'N 1°37'W. Major communication and commercial center in cacao area, at junction of S rail and N trunk-road network; cacao market (storage sheds); livestock and poultry trade. Sawmilling (hardwood); processing and shipping of cacao, kola nuts, rubber. Agr. experiment station. Airfield. Has Br. fort (1898), markets, St. Augustine's and Wesley colleges. Residence of Chief of Ashanti Confederacy. Developed (17th cent.) as ⊙ Ashanti; center of Ashanti military power in 18th and 19th cent. Occupied and destroyed (1874) by British. Its modern development as 2d city of Gold Coast dates from 2d Br. occupation (1896) and subsequent construction of railroads from Sekondi (1903) and Accra (1923). Besieged (1900) during a native revolt. Formerly spelled Coomassie.

Kumaun (kōōmoun'), division (□ 18,273; pop. 1,978,631), N Uttar Pradesh, India; ⊙ Naini Tal. Comprises Naini Tal, Almora, Garhwal, and Tehri dists. Former div. (□ 13,757; 1941 pop. 1,581,262) was enlarged 1949 by inc. of former princely state of Tehri. Largely within Kumaun Himalayas (N) and Siwalik Range (S). Also spelled Kumaon.

Kumaun Himalayas (hĭmä'lŭyŭz, hĭmŭlā'yŭz), W central subdivision of the HIMALAYAS, S central Asia, extending from upper Sutlej R. in SW Tibet and Himachal Pradesh (India) c.200 mi. ESE to Kali (Sarda) R. on India-Nepal border (E). Paralleled S by SIWALIK RANGE. In W section, paralleled by N lateral range, considered part of ZASKAR RANGE, rising in SE to KAMET mtn. (25,447 ft.) and containing important Shipki, Mana, and Lipu La passes. Major peaks of Kumaun Himalayas are NANDA DEVI (25,645 ft.; highest), Trisul (23,360 ft.), Badrinath (23,190 ft.), and Kedarnath (22,270 ft.). Give rise to several sacred Indian rivers, including the Bhagirathi (Ganges) rising in Gangotri glacier, the Jumna, and the Alaknanda. Of many lakes, Naini Tal is most noted. Main range bifurcates at Badrinath peak and at Sutlej R. Has noted Indian hill stations of Simla, Almora, Naini Tal, Mussoorie, Dehra Dun, and Lansdowne. Hindu pilgrimage centers include Kedarnath, Badrinath, Jamnotri, Gangotri, Devaprayag, Rikhikesh, and, at foot of Siwalik Range, Hardwar. Also spelled Kumaon.

Kumawu (kōōmä'wōō), town, Ashanti, S central Gold Coast, 27 mi. NE of Kumasi; cacao, kola nuts, hardwood, rubber.

Kumayt, Al-, Iraq: see KUMAIT, AL.

Kumba (kōōm'bä), town (pop. 7,882), S Br. Cameroons, administered as part of Eastern Provinces of Nigeria, on road and 38 mi. NNE of Buea; trade center; cacao, bananas, palm oil and kernels. Has hosp. Called Johann-Albrechtshöhe by Germans.

Kumbakonam (kōōmbŭkō'nŭm), city (pop. 67,008), Tanjore dist., SE Madras, India, on arm of Cauvery R. delta and 20 mi. NE of Tanjore; road center; rice milling, silk and cotton weaving; musical instruments, gold and silver jewelry, gold thread, copperwork (gold and silver inlay); betel and mulberry farms. Brahmanic cultural center; Sanskrit library (founded 9th cent. A.D.); Sanskrit schools; aggregate Sivaite and Vishnuite temples; site of duodecennial pilgrimage. Govt. col., industrial school. Became ⊙ Chola kingdom in 7th cent. A.D. Was a major city of successive Hindu kingdoms until ceded by Mahrattas to English in 1799. Formerly also spelled Combaconum.

Kum-Bel or **Kum-Bel'** (kōōm-bĕl'), town (1945 pop. over 500), central Tyan-Shan oblast, Kirghiz SSR, on Naryn-Rybachye highway and 25 mi. NNW of Naryn; tungsten mining; smelter. Until 1945, Kara-Unkurt.

Kumberg (kōōm'bĕrk), town (pop. 2,064), Styria, SE Austria, 7 mi. NE of Graz; summer resort.

Kumbhalgarh (kōōm'bŭlgŭr), walled hill fortress in Aravalli Range, S Rajasthan, India, 40 mi. NNW of Udaipur; alt. c.3,500 ft. Built in mid-15th cent.

Kumbher, Nepal: see BARDIA.

Kumbhkaran Lungur, mountain, Nepal and India: see KANCHENJUNGA.

Kumbhraj (kōōmbräj'), village, W Madhya Bharat, India, 25 mi. SW of Guna; wheat, millet, corn, gram.

Kumbo (kōōm'bō), town (pop. 4,368), S Br. Cameroons, administered as part of Eastern Provinces of Nigeria, in Bamenda hills, 40 mi. NE of Bamenda; cattle raising; durra, millet. Exports hides. Chief town of Banso tribal dist.

Kumbum (kōōmbōōm'), large lamasery in Hwangchung, NE Tsinghai prov., China, SW of Sining; pilgrimage center. Founded c.1400. Sometimes spelled Gumbum. Its living Buddha became the 10th Panchen Lama (see TASHI LUMPO, Tibet).

Kumbungu (kōōmbōōng'gōō), town, Northern Territories, N central Gold Coast, 13 mi. NW of Tamale; shea nuts, cotton; cattle, skins.

Kumchon (kōōm'chŭn'), Jap. *Kinsen*. **1** Township (1944 pop. 9,437), Hwanghae prov., central Korea, N of 38°N, 50 mi. NW of Seoul, in coal-mining area. **2** Town (1949 pop. 51,328), N.Kyongsang prov., S Korea, 40 mi. NW of Taegu; rail junction; commercial center for gold-mining and agr. area (rice, soy beans, barley, cotton); paper, raw silk.

Kumeny (kōō'myĭnē), village (1939 pop. over 500), central Kirov oblast, Russian SFSR, 35 mi. SSE of Kirov; wood cracking.

Kume-shima (kōōmä'shĭmä), westernmost island (□ 26; 1950 pop. 16,086) of Okinawa Isls., in Ryukyu Isls., in East China Sea, 55 mi. W of Okinawa; 26°21'N 126°47'E; 8 mi. long, 7 mi. wide. Volcanic, mountainous; rises to 1,102 ft. Pine and oak forests. Produces sugar cane, charcoal, rice.

Kum-gang, Korea: see KUM RIVER.

Kumgang-san, Korea: see DIAMOND MOUNTAINS.

Kumhae (kōōm'hă'), Jap. *Kinkai*, town (1949 pop. 33,213), S.Kyongsang prov., S Korea, 11 mi. NW of Pusan; commercial center for agr. area (rice, barley, soy beans, cotton); raw silk.

Kumhardhubi or **Kumardhubi** (kōōmŭr'dōōbē), village, Manbhum dist., E Bihar, India, 13 mi. WNW of Asansol; firebrick and general engineering works, iron- and steel-rolling mill.

Kumharsain (kōōmhär'sĭn), village, central Himachal Pradesh, India, near Sutlej R., 22 mi. NE of Simla. Was ⊙ former princely state of Kumharsain (□ 84; pop. 13,983) of Punjab Hill States, India; since 1948, state merged with Himachal Pradesh.

Kumher (kōōm'hăr), town (pop. 5,556), E Rajasthan, India, 9 mi. NW of Bharatpur; agr. (millet, oilseeds, gram).

Kumi, Greece: see KYME.

Kumi (kōō'mē), town, Eastern Prov., Uganda, on railroad and 27 mi. SE of Soroti near L. Kyoga; cotton, peanuts, sesame, rice; livestock.

Kumihama (kōōmē'hämŭ), town (pop. 2,772), Kyoto prefecture, S Honshu, Japan, on Sea of Japan, 10 mi. NE of Toyooka, in rice-growing area; sake, bamboo ware; woodworking.

Kumilla, E Pakistan: see COMILLA.

Kumisheh, Iran: see SHAHRIZA.

Kum Ishqaw, Egypt: see KOM ISHQAW.

Kumjawng Pass (kōōn'joung") or **Krongjawng Pass** (krông'joung) (alt. 9,613 ft.), on India-Burma border, 35 mi. NNW of Putao; 27°50'N 97°10'E. Difficult route, rarely used by local pop.

Kumje (kōōm'jā'), Jap. *Kintei*, town (1949 pop. 25,989), N.Cholla prov., S Korea, 10 mi. SE of Kunsan, in agr. area (rice, barley, soy beans, cotton, hemp); rice milling.

Kumkale or **Kum Kale** (kōōm kälĕ'), village (pop. 404), Canakkale prov., NW Turkey, at Aegean entrance to the Dardanelles, on Asiatic side. In First World War its fortifications were stormed by the Allies in Gallipoli campaign.

Kumla (kŭm'lä), city (pop. 7,450), Orebro co., S central Sweden, 10 mi. S of Orebro; rail junction; shoe-mfg. center. Inc. 1942 as city.

Kummerow Lake or **Cummerow Lake** (both: kōō'mŭrō), Ger. *Kummerower See* or *Cummerower See* (both: kōō'mŭrō"vŭr zā'), lake (□ 13), Mecklenburg, N Germany, 3 mi. NE of Malchin; 7 mi. long, 2–3 mi. wide, greatest depth 98 ft. Drained by Peene R. Connected by canal with Malchin L., 7 mi. SW.

Kumo, Finland: see KOKEMÄKI.

Kumon Range (kōōmôn'), in Kachin State, Upper Burma, extends 100 mi. N of Myitkyina bet. Hukawng Valley (W) and Mali headstream of the Irrawaddy; rises to 11,190 ft., 20 mi. WNW of Sumprabum.

Kumrabai Mamila (kōōmräbī' mämē'lä), village (pop. 550), Northern Prov., central Sierra Leone, 15 mi. SW of Magburaka, on railroad; terminus of road from Bo; palm oil and kernels, rice, cacao, coffee. Sometimes spelled Kumrabai Mamilla. Kumrabai Matuku (mätōō'kōō), village (pop. 800), is 1 mi. SW.

Kum River (kōōm), Korean *Kum-gang*, Jap. *Kinko*, S Korea, rises in mts. c.25 mi. SE of Chonju, flows N, turns NW and generally SW past Kongju, Puyo, and Kanggyong to Yellow Sea at Kunsan; 247 mi. long; navigable c.80 mi. by small craft. Drains agr. and gold-mining area.

Kumsan (kōōm'sän'), Jap. *Kinzan*, town (1949 pop. 15,929), N.Cholla prov., S Korea, 45 mi. ENE of Kunsan; agr. center (rice, barley, soy beans, cotton); silk cocoons. Gold mined near by.

Kumsi (kōōm'sē), town (pop. 2,608), Shimoga dist., NW Mysore, India, on railroad and 15 mi. NW of Shimoga. Near-by manganese mines and limestone quarries supply steel plant at Bhadravati.

Kumta (kōōm'tŭ), town (pop. 12,466), Kanara dist., S Bombay, India, port on Arabian Sea, 32 mi. SSE of Karwar; trade center for rice, betel nuts, coconuts, gur, cotton, spices; fish-curing yards (mackerel, sardines, catfish). Lighthouse (NW).

Kumukahi, Cape (kōō'mōōkä'hē), E extremity of Hawaii, T.H.; 19°31'N 154°48'W.

Kumukahi Channel, T.H.: see KAULAKAHI CHANNEL.

Kumukh (kōōmōōkh'), village (1948 pop. over 2,000), S Dagestan Autonomous SSR, Russian SFSR, in the E Greater Caucasus, 45 mi. S of Buinaksk; clothing handicraft; hardy grain, sheep. Pop. largely Lak.

Kumul, China: see HAMI.

Kum Umbu, Egypt: see KOM OMBO.

Kumyan (gŭm'yŭn'), Mandarin *Kanen* (gän'ŭn'), town, ⊙ Kumyan co. (pop. 35,131), W Hainan, Kwangtung prov., China, port of Gulf of Tonkin on coastal railroad and 125 mi. SW of Kiungshan; fisheries, saltworks. Hog raising. Exports hides and melon seeds.

Kumylzhenskaya (kōōmĭlzhĕn'skīŭ), village (1926 pop. 1,336), W Stalingrad oblast, Russian SFSR, on Khoper R. and 30 mi. SW of Mikhailovka; wheat, sunflowers.

Kuna (kōō'nŭ), village (pop. 534), Ada co., SW Idaho, 15 mi. SW of Boise, in grain and livestock area; flour, feed.

Kunagota (kōō'nägôtō), Hung. *Kunágota*, town (pop. 6,426), Csanad co., SE Hungary, 18 mi. S of Bekescsaba; onions, grain, cattle, poultry.

Kunar or **Konar** (kōōnŭr'), town (pop. over 2,000), Eastern Prov., Afghanistan, 27 mi. NE of Jalalabad and on left bank of Kunar R., near Pakistan line; center of irrigated oasis (rice, corn, fruit); furniture handicrafts based on Nuristan timber.

Kunar River or **Konar River**, in W Pakistan and E Afghanistan, rises in the E Hindu Kush in Chitral state, flows 250 mi. SW, past Mastuj, Chitral, and into Afghanistan, past Asmar and Kunar, to Kabul R. just below Jalalabad. Used for logging and for irrigation in lower course. Called Chitral R. in upper reaches.

Kunashak (kōōnŭshäk'), village (1926 pop. 4,919), NE Chelyabinsk oblast, Russian SFSR, 35 mi. NNE of Chelyabinsk, near railroad; wheat, rye, oats, livestock.

Kunashiri-kaikyo, Russian SFSR: see YEKATERINA STRAIT.

Kunashir Island (kōōnŭshēr'), Jap. *Kunashiri-shima* (kōōnä'shĭrē'shmä), southernmost and 2d largest (□ 1,548) of main Kurile Isls. chain, Russian SFSR; separated from Iturup Isl. (NE) by Yekaterina Strait, from Hokkaido, Japan (SW), by Nemuro Strait; 44°20'N 146°E. Consists of 5 volcanic massifs connected by lower ridges; rises to 5,978 ft. in the volcano Tyatya, 2d-highest of the Kuriles. Fishing, sealing, fish processing, lumbering, hunting, and sulphur mining are chief economic activities; some garden farming. Main centers: Yuzhno-Kurilsk, Golovnino, Tyatino. Isl. already known to Japanese when visited (1713) by Russians. Jap. colonization began in mid-18th cent.; formalized in 1855.

Kunbaja (kōōm'boi-ŏ), town (pop. 2,920), Bacs-Bodrog co., S Hungary, 25 mi. ESE of Baja; grain, potatoes, cattle, hogs.

Kunch (kōōnch), town (pop. 18,530), Jalaun dist., S Uttar Pradesh, India, 20 mi. W of Orai; rail spur terminus; trade center (gram, wheat, oilseeds, jowar, rice, ghee).

Künchow, China: see KÜNHSIEN.

Kund (kōōnd), village, Gurgaon dist., SE Punjab, India, on railroad and 14 mi. WSW of Rewari; metalworks. Slate quarried near by.

Kunda (kōōn'dä), city (pop. 1,863), N Estonia, port on Gulf of Finland, 12 mi. NNE of Rakvere (linked by rail spur); cement-milling center.

Kunda (kōōn'dŭ), village, Partabgarh dist., SE Uttar Pradesh, India, on railroad and 27 mi. WNW of Allahabad; rice, barley, wheat, gram, mustard. Rail station called Harnamganj.

Kundalwadi, India: see KONDALWADI.

Kundapur, India: see COONDAPOOR.

Kundarkhi (kōōn'dŭrkē), town (pop. 5,111), Moradabad dist., N central Uttar Pradesh, India, 11 mi. S of Moradabad; wheat, rice, pearl millet, sugar.

Kundeling, Tibet: see LHASA.

Kundgol (kōōnd'gōl), town (pop. 6,902), Dharwar dist., S Bombay, India, 22 mi. SE of Dharwar; local cotton center; handicraft cloth weaving.

Kundi, W Pakistan: see NOK KUNDI.

Kundla (kōōnd'lŭ), town (pop. 17,181), S Saurashtra, India, 60 mi. SW of Bhaunagar; agr. market (cotton, millet, wheat); cotton ginning, handicraft cloth weaving. Sometimes called Savar Kundla.

Kundravy (kōōndrä'vē), village (1926 pop. 2,278), W Chelyabinsk oblast, Russian SFSR, 11 mi. SSE of Miass; flour milling; grain, livestock.

Kunduk Lagoon, Ukrainian SSR: see SASYK LAGOON.

Kundur, Indonesia: see KARIMUN ISLANDS.

Kunduz or **Qunduz** (kōōndōōz'), town (pop. 10,000), Kataghan prov., NE Afghanistan, in Afghan Turkestan, 15 mi. WNW of Khanabad; center of oasis (cotton, rice) irrigated by Kunduz R.; cotton ginning, cottonseed-oil milling, soap mfg., rice and flour milling.

Kunduz River or **Qunduz River**, in Afghan Turkestan, NE Afghanistan, known as **Surkhab** (sōōr-khäb'), in upper course; rises W of Bamian in the Hindu Kush, flows 250 mi. E, through Bamian valley, then N, through Shikari Pass, past Doab

Mekh-i-Zarin, Doshi, Pul-i-Khumri, Baghlan, and Kunduz, to the Amu Darya (USSR line) near mouth of Vakhsh R. Important cotton and sugar-beet irrigation along lower course. Middle course, where it joins Saighan, Kamard, and Andarab valleys, is used by Kabul–Mazar-i-Sharif highway.

Kundysh River, Russian SFSR: see GREATER KUNDYSH RIVER; LESSER KUNDYSH RIVER.

Kuneitra, Syria: see QUNEITRA, EL.

Kunene River, SW Africa: see CUNENE RIVER.

Kunersdorf (kōō'nûrsdôrf) or **Kunowice** (kōōnôvē'tsē), village in Brandenburg, after 1945 in Zielona prov., W Poland, 4 mi. E of Frankfurt. In Seven Years War, scene (Aug., 1759) of critical defeat of Prussians under Frederick the Great by Austrians under Loudon and Russians under Soltikov.

Kunetice, Czechoslovakia: see PARDUBICE.

Kuneyevka, Russian SFSR: see KOMSOMOLSK, Kuibyshev oblast.

Kung, China: see KUNG RIVER.

Kungalv (kŭng'ĕlv"), Swedish *Kungälv*, city (pop. 3,632), Goteborg och Bohus co., SW Sweden, on Nordre R., near Gota R., 11 mi. N of Goteborg; glass and shoe mfg., metalworking. On isl. in river are remains of early 14th-cent. Bohus Castle. Of importance since 9th cent., city was called Konghelle in Middle Ages and is mentioned in sagas. Fortified 1120; plundered 1135 by Wends. Captured 1368 by Hanseatic League; later suffered Danish attacks. Came to Sweden 1612.

Kungan (gōōng'än'), town (pop. 19,104), ⊙ Kungan co. (pop. 243,379), S Hupeh prov., China, near Hunan line, 28 mi. SSW of Kiangling; rice, tea, beans.

Kungchang, China: see LUNGSI.

Kungcheng or **Kung-ch'eng** (both: gōōng'chŭng'), town, ⊙ Kungcheng co. (pop. 126,763), NE Kwangsi prov., China, 45 mi. SE of Kweilin, near Hunan line; rice, wheat, beans. Tin, tungsten mines near by.

Kungchenkiao, China: see HANGCHOW.

Kung-chiao, Tibet: see GONJO.

Kung-chüeh, Tibet: see GONJO.

Kungchuling (gōōng'jōō'lĭng'). **1** Town (1938 pop. 33,643), W Kirin prov., Manchuria, on South Manchuria RR and 40 mi. SW of Changchun, at Liaosi line; commercial center. Developed in 1900s with railroad construction. **2** Town, W central Liaotung prov., Manchuria, 30 mi. NE of Anshan; iron-mining center, yielding 35–40% ore for Anshan steel mill.

Kungei Ala-Tau or **Kungey Ala-Tau** (kōōn-gyā' ŭlä"-tou'), branch of Tien Shan mountain system, Kirghiz SSR; extends E of Kirghiz Range, from Boom Gorge on Chu R. 180 mi. E to area of Kegen, Kazakh SSR; forms section of Kirghiz-Kazakh border; rises to 16,300 ft. The lake Issyk-Kul is S.

Kungha (gōōng'hä'), town, ⊙ Kungha co. (pop. 43,176), W Sinkiang prov., China, on tributary of upper Ili R. and 60 mi. E of Kuldja; livestock, agr. products. Gold, lead, and iron mines near by.

Kunghit Island (kŭng'gĭt) (□ 83), W B.C., southernmost of the Queen Charlotte Isls., 140 mi. NW of Vancouver Isl., separated from Moresby Isl. (N) by Houston Stewart Channel (1–2 mi. wide); 15 mi. long, 1–8 mi. wide. At S extremity is Cape St. James (51°56'N 131°1'W). Rose Harbour (N) is whaling station.

Kungho (gōōng'hŭ'), town, ⊙ Kungho co. (pop. 16,015), E Tsinghai prov., China, 70 mi. SW of Sining and on Yellow R.; wheat, millet, beans, medicinal plants. Gold washing near by. Until 1931 called Kükow.

Kunghsien (gōōng'shyĕn'). **1** Town, ⊙ Kunghsien co. (pop. 113,342), N Honan prov., China, on Lo R. near its mouth on Yellow R., on Lunghai RR (N) and 28 mi. E of Loyang; cotton weaving; millet, wheat, kaoliang, indigo. **2** Town (pop. 12,549), ⊙ Kunghsien co. (pop. 141,112), SW Szechwan prov., China, 35 mi. SSE of Ipin; rice, millet, sweet potatoes, wheat. Gypsum quarrying, sulphur mining near by.

Kunghsien, Tibet: see GONJO.

Kungipu, China: see KUNGYIFOW.

Kung-k'a or **Kung-k'o,** Tibet: see KONGKA.

Kungka Shan, China: see MINYA KONKA.

Kung-kuan, Formosa: see KUNGKWAN.

Kungkwan or **Kung-kuan** (gōōng'gwän'), Jap. *Kokan* (kō'kän), town (1935 pop. 2,912), NW Formosa, 4 mi. S of Miaoli; oranges, persimmons.

Kungliu (gōōng'lyō'), town, ⊙ Kungliu co. (pop. 32,432), N Sinkiang prov., China, 60 mi. SE of Kuldja, and on Kunges R. (headstream of the Ili R.); cattle raising; agr. products. Gold mines near.

Kungpeh, China: see LAPPA.

Kungpei, China: see LAPPA.

Kungrad (kōōn-grät'), town (1926 pop. 3,125), central Kara-Kalpak Autonomous SSR, Uzbek SSR, in the Amu Darya delta, 55 mi. NW of Nukus; cotton. Terminus of railroad (built in late 1940s) from Chardzhou.

Kungribingri, pass, Tibet-India border: see ANTA DHURA.

Kung River, Chinese *Kung Shui* (gōōng'shwā'), right headstream of Kan R., in Kiangsi prov., China, rises on Fukien line, flows 130 mi. W, past Hweichang and Yütu, joining Tsang R. at Kanchow to form Kan R.

Kungsbacka (kŭngs'bäkä), city (pop. 2,478), Halland co., SW Sweden, near the Kattegat, 15 mi. SSE of Goteborg; woolen milling, furniture mfg. Radio station for overseas telegraph traffic. Has old wooden church. Chartered 1557.

Kungsgarden (kŭngs'gōr"dŭn), Swedish *Kungsgården*, village (pop. 692), Gavleborg co., E Sweden, on N shore of Stor L., 5 mi. WSW of Sandviken; grain, flax, potatoes, stock.

Kungshan (gōōng'shän'), village, ⊙ Kungshan dist. (pop. 6,261), northwesternmost Yunnan prov., China, on right bank of Salween R. and 200 mi. N of Paoshan, near Sikang line; timber, rice, millet, beans; mica deposits. Until 1935 called Tala; formerly also known as Chamutang.

Kung Shui, China: see KUNG RIVER.

Kungsor (kŭngsûr'), Swedish *Kungsör*, town (pop. 2,849), Vastmanland co., central Sweden, at W end of L. Malar, at mouth of Arboga R., 6 mi. SE of Koping; lake port. Has 17th-cent. royal hunting lodge.

Kungtsing, China: see TZEKUNG.

Kungtung Island, China: see CHEFOO.

Kungur (kōōn-gōōr'), city (1936 pop. estimate 27,700), SE Molotov oblast, Russian SFSR, on Sylva R., on railroad and 45 mi. SSE of Molotov; center of leather industry; mfg. (shoes, excavators, cement mixers, clothing, knitwear), metal- and woodworking, stone-cutting handicrafts. Gypsum quarries 9 mi. WNW, at Yergach station; alabaster-walled ice caves near by. Founded 1648 as fortress; developed as trading town in 18th cent.

Kungur Massif, China: see MUZTAGH ATA RANGE.

Kungutas (kōōng-gōō'täs), town, Southern Highlands prov., S Tanganyika, in Lupa goldfield, 12 mi. WNW of Chunya.

Kungwe, Mount (kōōng'gwā), peak (8,250 ft.), W Tanganyika, overlooking L. Tanganyika, opposite Albertville (Belgian Congo).

Kungyangon (kōōn"jäng-gōn'), village, Hanthawaddy dist., Lower Burma, in Irrawaddy delta, 25 mi. SSW of Rangoon, near Andaman Sea.

Kungyifow (gōōng'yĭk'fou'), Mandarin *Kungipu* (gōōng'yē'pōō'), town, S Kwangtung prov., China, port on Tam R., on railroad and 13 mi. N of Toishan; commercial center.

Kungyüan, Manchuria: see PENKI.

Kunhegyes (kōōn'hĕ-dyĕsh), town (pop. 10,769), Jasz-Nagykun-Szolnok co., E central Hungary, 14 mi. NW of Karcag; flour mill; wheat, corn, cattle.

Künhsien or **Chün-hsien** (both: jün'shyĕn'), town (pop. 21,392), ⊙ Künhsien co. (pop. 190,626), NW Hupeh prov., China, 20 mi. ESE of Yünhsien and on right bank of Han R.; tobacco-growing center; exports tung oil, mushrooms, wheat, beans, millet. Until 1912 called Künchow.

Kuniamuthem, India: see KUNIYAMUTHUR.

Kunie, New Caledonia: see PINES, ISLE OF.

Kunigal (kōō'nĭgŭl), town (pop. 5,846), Tumkur dist., central Mysore, India, 22 mi. SSW of Tumkur; silk growing, rice milling, handicrafts (woolen blankets, biris, pottery); horse-breeding farm. Kaolin worked near by.

Kunihar (kōōnĭhär'), former princely state (□ 7; pop. 2,399) of Punjab Hill States, India, W of Simla. Since 1948, merged with Himachal Pradesh.

Kunisaki (kōōnē'säkē) or **Kunizaki** (-zäkē), town (pop. 11,062), Oita prefecture, NE Kyushu, Japan, on E Kunisaki Peninsula, 24 mi. NNE of Oita, on Iyo Sea; agr. center (rice, wheat, barley); sake.

Kunisaki Peninsula, NE Kyushu, Japan, in Oita prefecture, bet. Suo Sea (N) and Beppu Bay (S); 24 mi. N-S, 18 mi. E-W. Mountainous; rises to 2,365 ft. Kitsuki on S coast. Fertile coastal strip produces grain.

Kuniyamuthur or **Kuniyamuttur** (kōōnĭyŭ'mōōtōōr), town (pop. 6,843), Coimbatore dist., SW Madras, India, suburb (3 mi. S) of Coimbatore; cotton milling. Sometimes called Kuniamuthem.

Kuniyoshi (kōōnē'yōshē), town (pop. 4,485), Chiba prefecture, central Honshu, Japan, on E Chiba Peninsula, 5 mi. NW of Ohara; agr. (rice, wheat), poultry raising; raw silk.

Kunizaki, Japan: see KUNISAKI.

Kunjabangarh (kōōn'jŭbŭng-gŭr"), village, Puri dist., central Orissa, India, 75 mi. WNW of Puri; markets timber, rice, bamboo. Was ⊙ former princely state of Daspalla. Formerly called Kunjaban.

Kunjah (kōōnjä'), town (pop. 8,873), Gujrat dist., NE Punjab, W Pakistan, 7 mi. SW of Gujrat; wheat, millet, cotton, rice.

Kunkels Pass (kōōnk'ŭls) (4,432 ft.), in the Glarus Alps, E Switzerland, 6 mi. W of Chur; road over the pass leads along Tamina R. valley to Rhine valley.

Künlien (jün'lyĕn') or **Yün-lien** (yün'–), town (pop. 15,262), ⊙ Künlien co. (pop. 77,899), SW Szechwan prov., China, 40 mi. SSW of Ipin, on Yunnan border; rice, wheat, millet, sugar cane, ramie.

Kunlong (kōōn'lông'), village, North Hsenwi state, Northern Shan State, Upper Burma, on left bank of Salween R. (ferry) and 65 mi. NE of Lashio, on route to Chinese Yunnan prov.

Kunlun, Chinese *K'un-lun* (kōōn'lōōn'), one of the great mountain systems of central Asia, China, bet. the Himalayas and the Tien Shan; separates high Tibetan plateau (S) from Tarim basin of Sinkiang prov. (N), to which it drops abruptly. Extends over 1,000 mi. W-E from the Pamir mtn. knot, where the Kunlun is separated from Karakoram mtn. system by Yarkand R., to central Tsinghai prov., where it branches into the complex ranges of W central China. The highest peak is Ulugh Muztagh (25,340 ft.), at 36°30'N 87°20'E. The Altyn Tagh is an important N branch. Sometimes spelled Kuenlun and Kwenlun.

Kunmadaras (kōōn'mŏdŏrŏsh), town (pop. 8,232), Jasz-Nagykun-Szolnok co., E central Hungary, 10 mi. NNW of Karcag; corn, tobacco, horses, sheep.

Kunming or **K'un-ming** (both: kōōn'mĭng'), city (pop. 300,297), ⊙ Yunnan prov., China, 390 mi. SW of Chungking, 340 mi. NW of Hanoi, on N shore of lake Tien Chih; alt. 6,299 ft.; 25°4'N 102°41'E. A leading commercial and cultural center of SW China, at junction of important transportation routes; terminus of railroad from Hanoi and of Burma Road. Mfg. of silk and cotton textiles, chemicals, machinery; iron and copper smelting, food processing. Seat of univ. and teachers col. Kunming consists of old walled city, modern commercial suburb (S), and residential and univ. section (N). It developed as a communications hub in 19th cent., but reached its greatest prosperity following construction (1910) of railroad from Hanoi. During Second World War, it expanded further as vital supply point and air ferry base at E end of Burma Road, and was refuge of several Chinese universities. Called Yunnan or Yunnanfu until 1913, it became a municipality in 1935.

Kunnamkulam (kōōnŭm'kōōlŭm), town (pop. 12,207), NW Cochin, India, 45 mi. NNW of Ernakulam; coir products (rope, mats), copra; rice and oilseed milling.

Kuno (kōō'nû), Dan. *Kunø*, Faeroese *Kunoy*, island (□ 14; pop. 197) of the NE Faeroe Isls.; c.8 mi. long, 2 mi. wide. Mountainous (highest point 2,726 ft.); fishing, sheep raising.

Kunoura (kōōnō'rä), town (pop. 3,021), Oita prefecture, NE Kyushu, Japan, on NE Kunisaki Peninsula, 27 mi. NNE of Oita; rice, wheat, barley; straw mats.

Kunowice, Poland: see KUNERSDORF.

Kunsan (kōōn'sän'), Jap. *Gunzan*, city (1949 pop. 74,447), N.Cholla prov., S Korea, port at mouth of Kum R. on Yellow Sea, 27 mi. WNW of Chonju; rail terminus; rice-collection center; rice refining, sake brewing. Near by are copper refineries. Exports rice, soy beans, leather, gold, sake.

Kunshan or **K'un-shan** (kōōn'shän'), town, ⊙ Kunshan co. (1946 pop. 281,046), SE Kiangsu prov., China, 34 mi. WNW of Shanghai and on Shanghai-Nanking RR; rice and flour milling, oil pressing, silk spinning; rice, wheat, beans, cotton.

Kunstat (kōōn'shtät), Czech *Kunštát*, Ger. *Kunstadt* (kōōn'shtät), town (pop. 1,150), W Moravia, Czechoslovakia, 22 mi. NNW of Brno; oats; graphite mining.

Kunszentmarton (kōōn'sĕntmär"tôn), Hung. *Kunszentmárton*, town (pop. 11,986), Jasz-Nagykun-Szolnok co., E central Hungary, on the Körös and 28 mi. S of Szolnok; sawmill; wheat, barley, cattle, sheep.

Kunszentmiklos (kōōn'sĕntmĭ"klôsh), Hung. *Kunszentmiklós*, town (pop. 7,748), Pest-Pilis-Solt-Kiskun co., central Hungary, 28 mi. WNW of Kecskemet; rail junction; flour mills. Calvinist acad. here.

Kuntaur or **Kunta-ur** (kōōntä'ōōr), town (pop. 302), MacCarthy Isl. div., central Gambia, on Gambia R. (wharf and ferry) 12 mi. NW of Georgetown; peanut-shipping point; palm oil and kernels, rice.

Kuntsevo (kōōn'tsyĭvŭ), city (1926 pop. 9,978; 1939 pop. 60,963), central Moscow oblast, Russian SFSR, adjoining (WSW of) Moscow; woolen-milling, metalworking center; aluminum products.

Küntu or **Chün-tu** (both: jün'dōō'), village, W Shansi prov., China, 20 mi. W of Lishih, and on Yellow R. (Shensi line), opposite Wupu; road ferry.

Kuntzig, Luxembourg: see CLÉMENCY.

Kunvald (kōōn'vält), village (pop. 1,255), E Bohemia, Czechoslovakia, in foothills of the Adlergebirge, 30 mi. ESE of Hradec Kralove; former hq. of Bohemian-Moravian church assembly (1457).

Kunya or **Kun'ya** (kōōn'yŭ), village (1939 pop. over 500), central Velikiye Luki oblast, Russian SFSR, 17 mi. E of Velikiye Luki; dairying, flax processing; brickworks.

Kunyang or **K'un-yang** (both: kōōn'yäng'), town (pop. 1,121), ⊙ Kunyang co. (pop. 63,844), E central Yunnan prov., China, 25 mi. SSW of Kunming, on SW shore of lake Tien Chih; alt. 6,552 ft.; iron smelting; rice, wheat, beans. Iron and coal mines near by.

Kunyang Hu, China: see TIEN CHIH.

Kunya-Urgench (–ōōrgyĕnch'), town (1948 pop. over 2,000), N Tashauz oblast, Turkmen SSR, on NW Khiva oasis, 55 mi. NW of Tashauz; cotton, saltpeter. Has remains of 11th-cent. minaret. On site of anc. Urgench, capital of old Khorezm kingdom; abandoned in late-16th cent. when the Amu Darya changed its course and capital was transferred to Khiva.

Kunzak (kōōn'zhäk), Czech *Kunžak*, village (pop. 1,218), S Bohemia, Czechoslovakia, on railroad and

9 mi. ESE of Jindrichuv Hradec, in fish-pond region; hosiery mfg.

Künzelsau (kün'tsůlsou), town (pop. 5,559), N Württemberg, Germany, after 1945 in Württemberg-Baden, on the Kocher and 15 mi. SSW of Mergentheim; wine.

Kuo-, for Chinese names beginning thus and not found here: see under Kwo-.

Kuokkala, Russian SFSR: see REPINO.

Kuolayarvi (kōō'ůlůyär"vē), Finnish *Kuolajärvi* (kōō'ôläjăr"vē), city (1939 pop. over 2,000), NW Karelo-Finnish SSR, on Finnish border, on railroad and 90 mi. W of Kandalaksha, on road; agr.; reindeer raising. Called Salla (1937–40); ceded (1940) by Finland to USSR and Finnish pop. resettled in Kursu (Finland), which was renamed SALLA.

Kuop (kōō'ôp), atoll, E Caroline Isls., W Pacific, 2 mi. S of Truk; 11 mi. long, 4 mi. wide; 4 coral islets. Generally classed as one of Truk isls. Formerly Royalist Isl.

Kuopio (kōō'ôpēō), county [Finnish *lääni*] (□ 13,844; including water area, □ 16,533; pop. 464,960), E Finland; ⊙ Kuopio. Bounded E by USSR, it forms part of Karelia region. Surface is generally marshy, partly wooded; among numerous lakes are lakes Pielinen and Kalla, and N part of Saimaa lake system. Agr. (rye, oats, barley, potatoes), stock raising, dairying. Lumbering and woodworking industries (mfg. of plywood, wallboard, spools, bobbins) are important. Finland's chief copper mines at Outokumpu; molybdenum and asbestos mines, limestone quarries. Cities are Kuopio, Joensuu, and Iisalmi.

Kuopio, city (pop. 31,274), ⊙ Kuopio co., S central Finland, on L. Kalla, at head of Saimaa lake system, 200 mi. NE of Helsinki; 62°53'N 27°40'E. Woodworking center (processing of lumber, plywood, wallboard, doors, spools, and bobbins); machine shops, flour mills. Inland-navigation, tourist, and fishing center. Airfield. Seat of Lutheran bishopric. Radio station. Founded 1782. S suburb of Haapaniemi has large bobbin mills. Puijo hill (771 ft.), 2 mi. N, is tourist and skiing center.

Kuortane (kōō'ôrtänä), village (commune pop. 6,034), Vaasa co., W Finland, in lake region, 60 mi. ESE of Vaasa; quartz and feldspar quarries. Noted for its folk music.

Kupang (kōōpäng'), village (pop. 702), E Kedah, Malaya, on road and 5 mi. WSW of Baling; rubber plantation.

Kupang or **Koepang** (both: kōōpäng'), town (pop. 7,171), ⊙ Indonesian TIMOR, near SW tip of isl., port on small Kupang Bay of Savu Sea; 10°10'S 123°34'E; bunker station and trade center; ships copra, hides, sandalwood, pearls, trepang. Its airport is on Java-Australia route.

Kupa River (kōō'pä), NW Croatia, Yugoslavia, rises 16 mi. NE of Rijeka (Fiume), flows 184 mi. generally E, past Brod na Kupi, Karlovac, and Petrinja, to Sava R. at Sisak. Navigable for 84 mi. In upper course forms part of Croatia-Slovenia border; POKUPJE region extends along middle course. Hydroelectric plant at Ozalj, 7 mi. N of Karlovac. Receives Dobra Korana, and Glina rivers.

Kuparuk River (kōōpä'růk), N Alaska, rises in N Brooks Range, near 68°40'N 149°W, flows c.140 mi. N to Beaufort Sea of Arctic Ocean at 70°23'N 148°47'W.

Kupavna, Russian SFSR: see STARAYA KUPAVNA.

Kupehkow, Kupeikow, or **Ku-pei-k'ou** (gōō'bā'kō'), town, N Hopeh prov., China, on railroad and 70 mi. NE of Peking, at gate in Great Wall (Jehol line).

Kupferdreh (kŏop'fůrdrā), industrial suburb (since 1929) of ESSEN, W Germany, on Ruhr R. and 5 mi. SE of city center; metalworking center; coal mining.

Kupino (kōō'pēnŭ), city (1948 pop. over 10,000), SW Novosibirsk oblast, Russian SFSR, on railroad and 75 mi. SE of Tatarsk; metalworking, dairying. Industrialized after c.1935.

Kupiskis or **Kupishkis** (kōōpēshkēs'), Lith. *Kupiškis*, Rus. *Kupishki*, city (pop. 3,296), NE Lithuania, 25 mi. ENE of Panevezys; flour milling; concrete ware. In Rus. Kovno govt. until 1920.

Kup-Koi, Greece: see PROTE.

Kuppal, India: see KOPPAL.

Kuppam (kōō'pŭm), town (pop. 5,377), Chittoor dist., W Madras, India, 60 mi. SW of Chittoor; processing of essential oil (sandalwood, lemon grass), silk growing; exports chrysanthemum and jasmine flowers.

Kuppenheim (kōō'půnhīm), village (pop. 3,103), S Baden, Germany, on the Murg and 3 mi. SE of Rastatt; leather-, metal-, and woodworking; flour and lumber milling, cement mfg. Has early-18th-cent. town hall.

Kupreanof Island (kōōprēă'nŏf, kōō'prĭnŏf) (52 mi. long, 20–30 mi. wide), SE Alaska, in Alexander Archipelago, W of Petersburg; 56°48'N 133°25'W; rises to 3,984 ft. (NE). Lindenberg Peninsula (30 mi. long, 12 mi. wide) is separated from SE side of isl. by Duncan Canal. Fishing, fish processing, lumbering. Kake village is in NW. Isl. named after Capt. Kupreanov, governor of Russian America who succeeded (1836) Baron Wrangell.

Kupreanof Point, promontory, SW Alaska, on SW Alaska Peninsula, on E side of Stepovak Bay; 55°34'N 159°37'W.

Kupreanof Strait (20 mi. long, 2–3 mi. wide), S Alaska, bet. Kodiak Isl. (S) and Raspberry Isl. (N), connects Gulf of Alaska (E) and Shelikof Strait (W), 25 mi. WNW of Kodiak.

Küps (küps), village (pop. 2,116), Upper Franconia, N Bavaria, Germany, on the Rodach and 4 mi. SW of Kronach; porcelain mfg., metal- and woodworking, brewing.

Kupyansk (kōōpyänsk'), city (1926 pop. 15,156), E Kharkov oblast, Ukrainian SSR, on Oskol R. and 60 mi. ESE of Kharkov; wood- and metalworking; dairying, sugar refining, flour milling. Rail junction of Kupyansk-Uzlovoi (1926 pop. 3,162) is 5 mi. SSE.

Kur, river, Iran: see KUR RIVER.

Kura, Turkey and USSR: see KURA RIVER.

Kuragano (kōōrä'gä'nō), town (pop. 6,568), Gumma prefecture, central Honshu, Japan, just SE of Takasaki; raw silk, rice, wheat.

Kuragino (kōōrä'gēnŭ), village (1926 pop. 3,986), S Krasnoyarsk Territory, Russian SFSR, 40 mi. ENE of Minusinsk and on Tuba R.; lumbering, dairy farming.

Kurahashi-jima (kōōrä'-hä'shē-jĭmä), island (□ 30; pop. 42,090), Hiroshima prefecture, Japan, at E side of entrance to Hiroshima Bay, just SE of Nomi-shima and opposite Kure; 9 mi. long. Mountainous, fertile. Produces rice, building stone.

Kuraima, Jordan: see KUREIMA.

Kurakh (kōōräkh'), village (1948 pop. over 10,000), S Dagestan Autonomous SSR, Russian SFSR, in the E Greater Caucasus, on road and 20 mi. WSW of Kasumkent; hardy grain, sheep. Pop. largely Lezghian.

Kurakhovka (kōōrä'khůfkŭ), town (1939 pop. over 500), central Stalino oblast, Ukrainian SSR, in the Donbas, on Volchya R. and 20 mi. WNW of Stalino; coal mines. Just N lies Kurakhovstroi, site of large coal-fed power works.

Kura Lowland (kōōrä'), extensive plain in SE Azerbaijan SSR and NW Iran, on Caspian Sea, bet. the Greater and Lesser Caucasus; embraces valleys of lower Kura and Aras rivers; 150 mi. long, 90 mi. wide. Major portion below sea level; formed by fluvial sediments. Rich irrigated cotton region. Rivers divide it into Shirvan Steppe (N of Kura R.), Mili Steppe (bet. Kura and Aras rivers), Mugan Steppe (S of Aras and Kura rivers), and Salyany Steppe (bet. Kura R. and Caspian Sea).

Kurama, Mount (kōōrä'mä), Jap. *Kurama-yama* (1,800 ft.), Kyoto prefecture, S Honshu, Japan, 10 mi. N of Kyoto. Site of Buddhist temple founded in 8th cent.

Kurama Range (kōōrä'mŭ), branch of Tien Shan mountain system, on Uzbek-Tadzhik SSR border; extends c.100 mi. SW from Chatkal Range to the Syr Darya; rises to 7,550 ft. Rich in mineral deposits, mainly lead, zinc, antimony, tungsten, and radioactive ores.

Kurandvad (kŏor'ŭndväd), town (pop. 9,026), Satara South dist., S central Bombay, India, near Kistna R., 12 mi. S of Sangli; agr. market (millet, cotton, wheat, oilseeds, sugar cane); handicraft cloth weaving. Also spelled Kurundwad, Kurundvad. Was ⊙ former Deccan state of Kurandvad Senior.

Kurandvad Junior, former princely state (□ 126; pop. 46,609) in Deccan States, Bombay, India; ⊙ was Maindargi. Inc. 1949 into Sholapur and Belgaum dists.

Kurandvad Senior, former princely state (□ 200; pop. 52,552) in Deccan States, Bombay, India; ⊙ was Kurandvad. Inc. 1949 into Satara South, Belgaum, and Bijapur dists., Bombay.

Kuraoli, India: see KURAULI.

Kura River (kōōrä'), anc. *Cyrus*, chief river of Georgian and Azerbaijan SSRs, in Transcaucasia; 940 mi. long. Rises WNW of Kars, Turkey, at 6,500 ft.; flows generally NE, past Ardahan and Borzhomi, and ESE, past Gori, Tiflis, Yevlakh, and Salyany, to Caspian Sea 75 mi. SSW of Baku, forming small delta mouth. Lower, diked course flows in sediments rising above surrounding Kura Lowland. Delta rich in fisheries. Navigation begins at Yevlakh, 300 mi. above mouth. Chief hydroelectric works at Zemo-Avchala 8 mi. N of Tiflis, and at Mingechaur—at E end of Mingechaur Reservoir (40 mi. long). Irrigates cotton region. Main tributaries: Aragva and Alazan (left), Khram, Terter, and Aras (right) rivers. Formerly also Kur R.

Kurashasaiski or **Kurashasayskiy** (kōōrŭshŭsī'skē), town (1943 pop. over 500), N Aktyubinsk oblast, Kazakh SSR, 12 mi. WNW of Aktyubinsk; coal mining.

Kurashiki (kŏorä'shĭkē), city (1940 pop. 32,228; 1947 pop. 48,133), Okayama prefecture, SW Honshu, Japan, 10 mi. WSW of Okayama. Rail junction; mfg. (textiles, floor mats), wood- and metalworking; agr. (rice, wheat, peppermint, watermelons).

Kuratovo (kŭrä'tůvŭ), village, SW Komi Autonomous SSR, Russian SFSR, 20 mi. from Vizinga. Until c.1940 called Kibra.

Kurauli (kōōrou'lē), town (pop. 5,315), Mainpuri dist., W Uttar Pradesh, India, on distributary of Lower Ganges Canal and 12 mi. NNW of Mainpuri; wheat, gram, pearl millet, corn, barley. Also spelled Kuraoli.

Kurau River (kōōrou'), NW Perak, Malaya, rises E of Taiping, flows 50 mi. W, through rich Krian rice dist., to Strait of Malacca at Kuala Kurau. Irrigation headworks at Bukit Merah.

Kuraymah, Jordan: see KUREIMA.

Kurayoshi (kōōrä'yōshē), town (pop. 20,559), Tottori prefecture, SW Honshu, Japan, 23 mi. WSW of Tottori; transportation center; cotton-textile, spinning mills; rice, raw silk.

Kurba (kŏor'bŭ), village (1926 pop. 1,076), E central Yaroslavl oblast, Russian SFSR, 15 mi. WSW of Yaroslavl; potatoes, tobacco.

Kurba River, central Buryat-Mongol Autonomous SSR, Russian SFSR, rises in E extension of Khamar-Daban Range, flows c.110 mi. SW to Uda R., below Unegytei. Extensive iron-ore deposits along upper course (Balbagar mines).

Kurbat (kōōrbät'), village (pop. 3,309), Ruse dist., NE Bulgaria, 25 mi. E of Ruse; market center; grain, sunflowers. Until 1934, Balbunar.

Kurca (kŏor'chŏ), by-channel of Tisza R., S Hungary, leaving it near Csongrad; flows S, past Szentes, rejoining Tisza R. above Mindszent; 20 mi. long. Formerly spelled Kurcza.

Kurchum River (kŏorchōōm'), East Kazakhstan oblast, Kazakh SSR, rises in Narym Range N of Marka-Kul, flows 125 mi. W, past Kumashkino, through narrow, wooded valley, to lower Irtysh R.; gold mining.

Kurdistan (kûr'dĭstăn", kŏor"dĭstän') [Persian,= country of the Kurds], indefinite plateau and mountain region, shared by Turkey, Iraq, and Iran, and inhabited by the Kurds, a strongly Sunni Moslem, seminomadic pastoral people speaking an Iranian language. Known as fierce and predatory, the Kurds have traditionally resisted subjugation by other nations in spite of their tribal political organization. Living primarily in the mts. of SE Anatolia and of the NW Zagros system, the Kurds migrate bet. summer mtn. pastures, and winter valley quarters where they engage in rug weaving and some agr. Commonly identified with the anc. *Corduene*, inhabited by the Carduchi (mentioned by Xenophon), Kurdistan was converted to Islam (7th cent.) by the Arabs, held by the Seljuk Turks (11th cent.) and the Mongols (13th–15th cent.); and was disputed by Turkey and Persia, during 19th cent., with Turkey holding the greater part. Kurdish claims for natl. autonomy were reaffirmed after First World War at the Paris Peace Conference, and the Treaty of Sèvres (1920) provided for an autonomous Kurdistan; however, the Treaty of Lausanne (1923), which superseded it, failed to mention Kurdistan. Subsequent revolts, particularly in 1925 and 1930 in Turkey, and in 1946 in Iran, were suppressed. Total Kurdish pop. of Kurdistan is estimated at 2,500,000–3,000,000, including 1,000,000–1,500,000 in SE Turkey, 600,000 in NE Iraq, and 700,000 in NW Iran. Most of Iranian Kurdistan (or Kordestan), unlike the Turkish and Iraqi sections, constitutes a political administrative unit (formerly called Ardelan); it was inc. in 1938 into Iran's Fifth Prov. (see KERMANSHAH), and its main centers are at Sanandaj and Saqqiz. The remainder of the Iranian Kurd country forms part of Fourth Prov. (W AZERBAIJAN and GARUS), with chief towns Mehabad and Bijar. Name of Kurdistan is also applied to a small mtn. dist. (chief town, Lachin) of SW Azerbaijan SSR in Soviet Transcaucasia; and Kurds are settled on the slopes of Mt. Aragats in Soviet Armenia.

Kurd Kui or **Kord Kuy** (both: kōrd' kōōē'), town, Second Prov., in Gurgan, NE Iran, 20 mi. WSW of Gurgan, near Caspian Sea; road junction. Formerly called Kurd Mahalleh.

Kurduvadi or **Kurduwadi** (kŏordōōvä'dē), town (pop., including SW suburb of Kurdu, 10,513), Sholapur dist., E central Bombay, India, 45 mi. NW of Sholapur; rail junction (workshops); trades in millet, cotton, wheat, peanuts; cotton ginning.

Kurdyum, Russian SFSR: see SARATOV, city.

Kure (kōō'rā). **1** City (1940 pop. 238,195; 1947 pop. 185,740), Hiroshima prefecture, SW Honshu, Japan, on Hiroshima Bay, 12 mi. SSE of Hiroshima, opposite Nomi-shima and Kurahashi-jima. Major naval base and commercial port; shipbuilding. Other mfg.: fountain pens, sake, Western-style clothing. Exports sake, cotton yarn, pens, machinery, rice. Heavily bombed (1945) in Second World War. Includes, since early 1940s, former town of Nigata (1940 pop. 7,207). **2** Town (pop. 7,065), Kochi prefecture, S Shikoku, Japan, on Tosa Bay, 24 mi. SW of Kochi; fishing and agr. center; charcoal, rice, raw silk. Sometimes called Tosa-kure.

Kure (kürĕ'), Turkish *Küre*, village (pop. 1,191), Kastamonu prov., N Turkey, 30 mi. N of Kastamonu; grain, sugar beets.

Kure Beach (kyŏor), town (pop. 228), New Hanover co., SE N.C., on the coast 17 mi. S of Wilmington; bathing resort. Bromine-extracting plant near by.

Kureika or **Kureyka** (kōōrā'kŭ), village (1939 pop. over 500), N Krasnoyarsk Territory, Russian SFSR, on Kureika R. and 65 mi. SE of Igarka, N of Arctic Circle. Graphite mines near by. Stalin exiled here, 1913–16.

Kureika River or **Kureyka River,** N Krasnoyarsk Territory, Russian SFSR, rises in Putorana Mts., flows 500 mi. W to Yenisei R. at Ust-Kureika. Passes through graphite-mining region 60 mi. above its mouth.

Kureima or **Kuraymah** (both: kōōrā'mù), village, N Jordan, 18 mi. NNW of Salt; vineyards, citrus fruits. Also spelled Kuraima.

Kure Island (kōō'rā), circular atoll, N Pacific, in NW part of Hawaiian Isls., c.50 mi. NW of Midway. Annexed 1886 by Hawaii and worked for guano, placed (1936) under U.S. navy. Sometimes written Curé; formerly Ocean Isl.

Kure Mountains (kürĕ'), Turkish *Küre,* N Turkey, extend 150 mi. E-W along the Black Sea N of Kastamonu, bet. Yenice R. (W) and Kizil Irmak (E); rise to 6,514 ft. in Yaraligoz Dag. Coal, lignite, and some chromium in W, arsenic and mercury in center, copper and chromium in E. Sometimes called Isfendiyar.

Kurenets (kōōryĭnyĕts'), Pol. *Kurzeniec* (kōōzhĕ'nyĕts), town (1939 pop. over 500), central Molodechno oblast, Belorussian SSR, 5 mi. NNE of Vileika; lumbering; rye, oats, potatoes.

Kuressaare or **Kuressare** (kōō'rĕsärä), Ger. and Swedish *Arensburg* (ä'rĕnsbōōrk), city (pop. 4,478), port on S shore of Saare isl., Estonia, on Gulf of Riga, 75 mi. W of Parnu. Exports grain, fish, livestock; fish processing, tanning, mfg. of furniture, cardboard. Health resort (mud baths). Founded 1227 by Livonian Knights. Has 14th-cent. episcopal castle (now regional mus.). Formerly spelled Kuresaare. In Rus. Livonia until 1920.

Kureyka, Russian SFSR: see KUREIKA.

Kurg, India: see COORG.

Kurgaldzhin, Lake, or **Lake Kurgal'dzhin** (kōōrgŭljĕn'), salt lake (□ c.200), Akmolinsk oblast, Kazakh SSR, just E of Tengiz (lake), on dry steppe. Nura R. flows through.

Kurgaldzhino or **Kurgal'dzhino** (–jēnô'), village (1939 pop. over 500), SW Akmolinsk oblast, Kazakh SSR, on Nura R. and 70 mi. SW of Akmolinsk, in agr. and cattle area. Until 1937, Kazgorodok.

Kurgan (kōōrgän'), oblast (□ 27,500; 1946 pop. estimate c.900,000) in SW Siberian Russian SFSR; ⊙ Kurgan. In SW part of W.Siberian Plain; drained by middle Tobol, Iset, and Miass rivers; steppe vegetation (occasional drought). Economy mainly agr., with emphasis on wheat and dairy farming. Chief towns (Kurgan, Shadrinsk, Shchuchye) engage in food processing (flour milling, meat packing, tanning, dairying). Served by Trans-Siberian RR, forming 2 branches W of Kurgan. Formed 1943 out of Chelyabinsk oblast.

Kurgan, city (1939 pop. 53,224), ⊙ Kurgan oblast, Russian SFSR, on Tobol R., at junction of 2 branches of Trans-Siberian RR, and 155 mi. E of Chelyabinsk, 1,075 mi. E of Moscow; 55°25'N 65°20'E. Center of rich agr. area; mfg. of agr. and dairy machinery, distilling, meat packing, flour milling, tanning, butter making. Agr. col. Founded 1616; chartered 1782.

Kurgannaya (–nīyù), village (1926 pop. 13,713), E Krasnodar Territory, Russian SFSR, 25 mi. W of Armavir, near Laba R.; rail junction; meat packing, flour and rice milling; metalworks.

Kurganovka (–gä'nùfkù), town (1948 pop. over 2,000), NW Kemerovo oblast, Russian SFSR, on railroad and 18 mi. N of Kemerovo; gold mining. Called Zaboishchik until 1944.

Kurgan-Tyube (kōōrgän"-tyōōbyĕ'), city (1936 pop. estimate 6,000), S Stalinabad oblast, Tadzhik SSR, in Vakhsh valley, 50 mi. S of Stalinabad (linked by narrow-gauge railroad); major cotton-ginning center; cottonseed-oil extraction, food processing, metalworking. Was ⊙ former Kurgan-Tyube oblast (1943–47).

Kurhessen, Germany: see HESSE-KASSEL.

Kuri, Russian SFSR: see SUKHOI LOG.

Kuria (kōō'rēä), island (□ 4.9; pop. 315), N Gilbert Isls., W central Pacific; 14°N 173°24'E. Formerly Woodle Isl.

Kuria Muria Bay (kōō'rēù mōō'rēù), inlet of Arabian Sea, on SE Oman coast, bet. capes Ras Nus (SW) and Ras Sharbatat (NE); 80 mi. wide. Contains Kuria Muria Isls.

Kuria Muria Islands, Arabic *Jaza'ir Bin Ghalfan* (jăză'ĭr bĭn gălfăn'), group of 5 islands (□ 28; 1947 pop. c.70) in Kuria Muria Bay of Arabian Sea, off SE Oman coast, considered part of British colony of Aden; 17°30'N, bet. 55°30' and 56°30'E. The isls., of granite formation and extending 50 mi. E–W, are the summits of a submarine ridge. They are (from W to E): HASIKIYA, SUDA, HALLANIYA, QIBLIYA, and GHARZAUT. Hallaniya, the largest, is the only inhabited isl. Depopulated (1818) following pirate raids from Trucial Oman, the group was seized by the Bin Ghalfan family of the Arab Mahra (Mahrah) tribe on adjoining mainland. The group later passed to the sultan of Oman, who ceded it (1854) to Britain for purposes of a cable station. Guano was worked here 1857–59 and a telegraph station operated temporarily 1859–60.

Kuriate (küryät'), small island group (□ 1.5) in the central Mediterranean, off E coast of Tunisia, 22 mi. E of Sousse; lighthouse. Tunny fisheries. No permanent pop.

Kurichchi (kōōrĭ'chē), town (pop. 14,228), Coimbatore dist., SW Madras, India, on Noyil R. and 3 mi. S of Coimbatore; cotton milling. Another Kurichchi, near Cauvery R., is 9 mi. N of Bhavani.

Kurigram (kōōrĭgräm'), town (pop. 6,339), Rangpur dist., N East Bengal, E Pakistan, on Dharla (Jaldhaka) R. and 26 mi. ENE of Rangpur; terminus of rail spur from Tista village; trades in rice, jute, tobacco, oilseeds, sugar cane.

Kurihara, Japan: see ONOMICHI.

Kurihashi (kōōrē'-hä'shē), town (pop. 11,715), Saitama prefecture, central Honshu, Japan, 18 mi. E of Kumagaya, in agr. area (rice, wheat); silk.

Kurile Islands or **Kuril Islands** (both: kōōrēl', kōō'rĭl), also **Kuriles** or **Kurils,** Rus. *Kurilskiye Ostrova,* Jap. *Chishima-retto,* island chain (□ 5,700; 1940 pop. 17,549) in Sakhalin oblast, Russian SFSR, bet. N Pacific and Sea of Okhotsk; extend from S tip (Cape Lopatka) of Kamchatka Peninsula to Hokkaido, Japan; 650 mi. long, bet. 50°26'N (Alaid Isl.) and 43°26'N (Shuishio Isl.). Volcanic in origin; includes 30 large isls., 20 lesser isls., and numerous reefs and rocks. Principal isls. (N to S; Shumshu, Paramushir, Onekotan, Simushir, Urup, Iturup, Kunashir) are located in main (volcanic) Kurile chain. A lesser, non-volcanic group extends c.65 mi. ENE of Hokkaido, parallel to (S of) Kunashir Isl.; includes Shikotan, Shibotsu, and Shuishio isls. Many volcanic mts. (including 16 active volcanoes), rising to 7,657 ft. in Alaid volcano; hot springs are abundant. Sulphur mined mainly on Kunashir and Iturup isls.; iron, copper, and gold also found. Humid climate, with cold, snowy winters and cool, foggy summers. Economy based on fishing, whaling, sealing, crabbing, lumbering, hunting of fur-bearing animals, production of iodine and agar-agar, and sulphur mining. Agr. restricted to grain and truck gardens. Main centers: Severo-Kurilsk on Paramushir Isl., Kurilsk on Iturup Isl., Yuzhno-Kurilsk on Kunashir Isl. Pop. is Russian since 1945, when Jap. pop. was largely repatriated. Original Ainu pop. died out under Jap. rule. Kuriles first visited (1643) by Du. navigator De Vries; penetrated from S by Japan (after 1643) and from N by Russia (after 1711). After setting of boundary (1854) of Rus. and Jap. spheres of influence at Friz (Vries) Strait, entire group passed (1875) to Japan (when Russia assumed full control of Sakhalin) and became part of Hokkaido prefecture. Occupied (1945) by Soviet troops, the Kuriles became (1947) part of Sakhalin oblast of Russian SFSR.

Kurile Lake, crater lake near S tip of Kamchatka Peninsula, Russian SFSR, 130 mi. SSW of Petropavlovsk; 7 mi. in diameter; 1,004 ft. deep.

Kurile Strait or **Kuril Strait.** Name applied to 6 straits in N section of main Kurile Isls. group, Russian SFSR, connecting Sea of Okhotsk and Pacific Ocean. **First Kurile Strait,** Jap. *Shimushu-kaikyo* (7.7 mi. wide), separates Shumshu Isl. from Cape Lopatka (S extremity of Kamchatka Peninsula). **Second Kurile Strait,** Jap. *Paramushiru-kaikyo,* narrowest (little over 1 mi. wide) of entire group, separates Shumshu and Paramushir isls. **Third Kurile Strait,** Jap. *Shirinki-kaikyo* (5.5 mi. wide), separates Paramushir and Shirinki isls. **Fourth Kurile Strait,** Jap. *Onnekotan-kaikyo* (27 mi. wide), separates Paramushir and Shirinki isls. (N) from Onekotan and Makanru isls. (S). **Fifth Kurile Strait,** Jap. *Yamato-suido* (17 mi. wide), separates Onekotan and Makanru isls. **Sixth Kurile Strait** or **Krenitsyn Strait,** Jap. *Harumukotan-kaikyo* (9 mi. wide), separates Onekotan and Kharimkotan isls. Straits first reached and named in numerical order in early-18th cent. by Rus. Cossack explorers from Kamchatka.

Kurilo (kōōrē'lô), village (pop. 1,743), Sofia dist., W Bulgaria, in Sofia Basin, near S end of Iskar R. gorge, 9 mi. N of Sofia; summer resort; lead smelting. Lignite mining N.

Kurilovka (kōōrē'lùfkù). **1** Village, N Saratov oblast, Russian SFSR: see VYAZOVKA. **2** Town (1939 pop. over 2,000), central Dnepropetrovsk oblast, Ukrainian SSR, on left bank of Dnieper R. and 20 mi. W of Dnepropetrovsk.

Kurilsk or **Kuril'sk** (kōōrēlsk'), city (1940 pop. 1,600), Sakhalin oblast, Russian SFSR, on W coast of Iturup Isl., S Kuriles; 45°14'N 147°53'E; fish-processing center; whale-oil factory. Under Jap. rule (until 1945), called Shana.

Kurinchi, Mount, Indonesia: see KERINCHI, MOUNT.

Ku-ring-gai (kōōrĭng'gī), N suburb (pop. 39,874) of Sydney, E New South Wales, Australia. Here is scenic natl. park (35,000 acres).

Kurinjipadi or **Kurinjippadi** (kōōrĭnjĭpä'dē), town (pop. 8,620), South Arcot dist., SE Madras, India, 16 mi. SW of Cuddalore; rice milling, cotton and silk weaving. Cashew plantations near by. Also called Kuinjipad.

Kurino (kōōrē'nō), town (pop. 14,223), Kagoshima prefecture, S Kyushu, Japan, 27 mi. NNE of Kagoshima; rail junction; mining center (gold, silver); rice, raw silk, livestock.

Kurische Aa, Latvia: see LIELUPE RIVER.

Kurische Nehrung, Kurisches Haff, USSR: see COURLAND LAGOON.

Kurk, Turkey: see SIVRICE.

Kurkino (kōōr'kēnŭ), village (1926 pop. 2,578), SE Tula oblast, Russian SFSR, 35 mi. SE of Bogoroditsk; distilling. Small Nepryadva R., 15 mi. N, near its confluence with the Don, was scene (1380) of battle of Kulikovo (kōōlyĭkô'vù), which marked defeat of Tatars by Russians under Dmitri Donskoi.

Kurkuk, Iraq: see KIRKUK, city.

Kurkund, Estonia: see KILINGI-NOMME.

Kurla (kōōrlä'), Chinese *Kuerhlei* or *K'u-erh-lo* (both: kōōr'lŭ'), town and oasis (pop. 23,690), central Sinkiang prov., China, on highway S of the Tien Shan, and 160 mi. SW of Urumchi; junction for caravan track to Charkhlik; sericulture; carpets; cotton, cattle.

Kurla (kōōr'lŭ), town (pop. 39,066), Bombay Suburban dist., W Bombay, India, on Salsette Isl., 10 mi. NNE of Bombay city center; rail junction; cotton milling, dyeing, mfg. of matches, ink, rope, binding tape; automobile assembly factory, glass- and metalworks. Old Kurla (N) has tanneries. First electric railway in India built 1925 from Bombay to Kurla.

Kurland, Latvia: see COURLAND.

Kurleya (kōōrlyä'ŭ), town (1939 pop. over 2,000), E Chita oblast, Russian SFSR, on Gazimur R. and 60 mi. E of Sretensk; agr., lumbering.

Kurlovski or **Kurlovskiy** (kōōr'lŭfskē), town (1926 pop. 2,193), S Vladimir oblast, Russian SFSR, 12 mi. SSW of Gus-Khrustalny; glassworking center; woodworking. Also called Kurlovo.

Kurmanayevka (kōōrmŭnī'ŭfkŭ), village (1939 pop. over 500), W Chkalov oblast, Russian SFSR, on Buzuluk R. and 20 mi. SSW of Buzuluk; wheat, livestock. Oil-shale, phosphorite deposits near by.

Kurman-Kemelchi, Russian SFSR: see KRASNOGVARDEISKOYE.

Kurmenty (kōōrmyĕn'tē), village, NE Issyk-Kul oblast, Kirghiz SSR, on NE shore of Issyk-Kul (lake), 7 mi. NNW of Tyup; cement works (built late 1940s); limestone quarrying.

Kurmuk (kōōr'mōōk), village, Blue Nile prov., S central Anglo-Egyptian Sudan, on Ethiopian border, 90 mi. SSW of Roseires; livestock. Police post.

Kurmysh (kōōrmĭsh'), village (1926 pop. 2,183), E Gorki oblast, Russian SFSR, on Sura R. and 42 mi. ESE of Lyskovo; wheat, potatoes. Founded at end of 14th cent. as Muscovite frontier town.

Kurna, El, Egypt: see QURNA, EL.

Kurnik, Poland: see KORNIK.

Kurnool (kŭrnōōl'), district (□ 7,893; pop. 1,190,842), N Madras, India; ⊙ Kurnool. On Deccan Plateau; crossed (E) by Eastern Ghats. Agr.: oilseeds (extensive peanut growing), millet, cotton, rice, chili. Barite, ocher, and slate mines. Timber, bamboo, dyewood (red sandalwood), and fibers in dispersed forests. Main towns: Kurnool, Nandyal. Original dist. (□ 7,634; pop. 1,146,250) enlarged 1948 by inc. of former Madras State of Banganapalle.

Kurnool, city (pop. 45,250), ⊙ Kurnool dist., N Madras, India, on Tungabhadra R. and 240 mi. NW of Madras; trade center in agr. area; cotton ginning, rice and oilseed milling; tannery. Handloom weaving institute. Ruined 16th-cent. fort. Dams across the Tungabhadra at villages of Sunkesula (14 mi. WNW; fishery, saltworks) and SIDDESWARAM. Barite, ocher, and slate mining 27 mi. SSE, near Betamcherla rail station.

Kurobane (kōōrō'-bä'nā), town (pop. 8,641), Tochigi prefecture, central Honshu, Japan, 25 mi. NE of Utsunomiya; rice, tobacco; lumber, charcoal.

Kurobe River (kōōrō'bā), Toyama prefecture, central Honshu, Japan; rises in mts. NW of peak Yari-ga-take, flows 60 mi. N and NNW to Toyama Bay 8 mi. WSW of Tomari; forms delta mouth. Several hydroelectric plants. Known for scenic gorge.

Kurogi, Japan: see KUROKI.

Kuroi (kōōrō'ē), town (pop. 3,630), Hyogo prefecture, S Honshu, Japan, 9 mi. S of Fukuchiyama; rice, wheat, raw silk, charcoal.

Kuroishi (kōōrō'ēshē), town (pop. 10,073), Aomori prefecture, N Honshu, Japan, 7 mi. ENE of Hirosaki; largely residential; sake brewing. Agr. experiment station.

Kuroiso (kōōrō'ēsō), town (pop. 10,849), Tochigi prefecture, central Honshu, Japan, 30 mi. NNE of Utsunomiya; commercial center for agr. area (tobacco, wheat); charcoal collection.

Kuroki (kōōrō'kē) or **Kurogi** (-gē), town (pop. 3,614), Fukuoka prefecture, N central Kyushu, Japan, 11 mi. SE of Kurume; rice, wheat, barley. Site of feudal castle.

Kurort Oberwiesenthal, Germany: see OBERWIESENTHAL.

Kurosaka (kōōrō'säkù), town (pop. 3,461), Tottori prefecture, S Honshu, Japan, 16 mi. S of Yonago, in forested area; timber, charcoal; rice, wheat, silk.

Kurosawajiri (kōōrō'säwŭjērē), town (pop. 13,661), Iwate prefecture, N Honshu, Japan, on Kitakami R. and 29 mi. S of Morioka; rail junction; commercial center for horse-breeding area.

Kuroshio: see JAPAN CURRENT.

Kurovskoye (kōō'rŭfskŭyù), town (1939 pop. over 10,000), E Moscow oblast, Russian SFSR, 50 mi. ESE of Moscow; rail junction; cotton milling.

Kurow (kōōrou'), township (pop. 434), E S.Isl., New Zealand, 45 mi. SW of Timaru and on Waitaki R.; rail terminus; wool, grain. Site of hydroelectric plant.

Kurrajong (kŏŏr'ŭjŏng), town (pop. 555), E New South Wales, 40 mi. NW of Sydney; rail terminus; orchards; citrus fruit.

Kurram (kŏŏr'rŭm), tribal region (□ 738; 1951 pop. 163,000), W North-West Frontier Prov., W Pakistan; hq. at Parachinar. Bordered W by Afghanistan (separated by Durand Line), N by Safed Koh Range; drained by Kurram R. Agr. (wheat, rice, corn, barley); fruitgrowing (apples, pears, peaches); hand-loom weaving. Administered as political agency. Ceded 1879 to Britain.

Kurram River, in E Afghanistan and S North-West Frontier Prov., W Pakistan, rises in W Safed Koh Range, SSE of Kabul (Afghanistan); flows c.200 mi. SE, past Thal and Bannu, to Indus R. 10 mi. W of Mianwali. Drains valley of Kurram agency and plain of Bannu dist.; waters wheat, corn, and rice fields.

Kurri Kurri (kûr'ē kûrē), town (pop. 5,440), E New South Wales, Australia, 16 mi. WNW of Newcastle; coal-mining center.

Kur River or **Kor River** (both: kōr), anc. *Cyrus*, in Zagros ranges of S central Iran, rises 120 mi. NW of Shiraz, flows 200 mi. SE, past Ramjird (irrigation headworks), to Niriz L. Receives Pulvar R. (left) on Marvdasht plain. Called Bandamir R. in lower course.

Kur River (kŏŏr), in Khabarovsk Territory, Russian SFSR, rises in E outlier of Bureya Range, flows c.250 mi. S, past Novo-Kurovka, and E, past Volochayevka II, to Amur R. just below Khabarovsk. Lumber floating.

Kurru, Anglo-Egyptian Sudan: see KURU.

Kursavka (kŏŏr'sŭfkŭ), village (1932 pop. estimate 2,180), W Stavropol Territory, Russian SFSR, on Stavropol Plateau, on railroad and 30 mi. ESE of Nevinnomyssk; road center; wheat, sunflowers; sheep.

Kursenai, Kurshenai, or **Kurshenay** (kōŏrshä'nī), Lith. *Kuršėnai*, Rus. *Kurshany*, city (pop. 3,819), N central Lithuania, on Venta R. and 15 mi. WNW of Siauliai; sugar refinery, brickworks, flour mill. In Rus. Kovno govt. until 1920.

Kurseong (kûrs'yŭng), town (pop. 8,495), Darjeeling dist., N West Bengal, India, 11 mi. S of Darjeeling, in SE Nepal Himalayan foothills; health resort; trades in tea, rice, corn, cardamom, oranges, jute; tea processing; general-engineering factory. Also spelled Karseong; formerly Karsiang.

Kurshany, Lithuania: see KURSENAI.

Kurshenai, Lithuania: see KURSENAI.

Kursk (kōōrsk), oblast (□ 19,615; 1946 pop. estimate 3,000,000) in SW European Russian SFSR; ⊙ Kursk. In Central Russian Upland; drained by upper Seim, Psel, Vorskla, and Oskol rivers; black-earth steppe; moderate, humid climate. Important agr. region, with sugar beets (W) and winter wheat (E) basic crops; main sugar producer of Russian SFSR. Also hemp (NW), potatoes (extreme NE), truck produce, orchard products near cities, legumes. Raising of hogs (based on sugar-refining by-products) and poultry important. Industry (flour milling, sugar refining, distilling, tanning, fruit canning, meat packing) based on agr. Mineral industries: phosphates (Shchigry), bricks, tiles, chalk (Belgorod), and limestone. Dist. of Kursk magnetic anomaly, an extensive iron-ore region (90 mi. long, 10 mi. wide), bet. Shchigry (NW) and Valuiki (SE), was developed after opening (1939) of mine at Gubkin. Main industrial centers: Kursk, Belgorod, Shchigry, Stary Oskol. Formed 1934 out of Central Black-Earth Oblast.

Kursk, city (1939 pop. 119,972), ⊙ Kursk oblast, Russian SFSR, on Seim R. at mouth of Tuskor R. (left tributary), and 280 mi. SSW of Moscow; 51°44'N 36°11'E. Rail junction; industrial center; mfg. (agr. and spinning machines, electrical goods, calculating machines, electric batteries, conveyor belts, clothing, shoes, tobacco products), flour mills, distilleries, tanneries. Medical and teachers colleges, regional mus. Has 18th-cent. cathedral. Founded in 9th cent.; chartered 1095; became (11th cent.) ⊙ principality. Completely destroyed (1238) during Tatar invasion; remained in ruins until 16th cent., when it was rebuilt (1586) as a military outpost of Moscow domain. Was ⊙ Kursk govt. until 1928. During Second World War, held (1941–43) by Germans.

Kurskaya (kŏŏr'skīŭ), village (1926 pop. 2,008), SE Stavropol Territory, Russian SFSR, 23 mi. NNW of Mozdok, on small Kura R. (flowing c.70 mi. into steppe; used for irrigation); cotton, wheat, rice.

Kurski Zaliv, USSR: see COURLAND LAGOON.

Kurslak, Germany: see VIERLANDE.

Kursu, Finland: see SALLA.

Kursumlija or **Kurshumliya** (both: kŏŏrshōōm'lyēä), Serbo-Croatian *Kuršumlija*, village, S Serbia, Yugoslavia, on Toplica R., on railroad and 34 mi. WSW of Nis. Kursumlijska Banja, health resort, is 6 mi. S.

Kursunlu (kŏŏr-shōōnlōō'), Turkish *Kurşunlu*, village (pop. 2,288), Cankiri prov., N central Turkey, on railroad, near Devrez R., and 24 mi. NW of Cankiri; grain, mohair goats.

Kurtalan (kōōrtälän'), village (pop. 1,591), Siirt prov., SE Turkey, 17 mi. W of Siirt; rail terminus; grain. Formerly Ayinkasir.

Kurtamysh (kōōrtŭmĭsh'), town (1926 pop. 5,732), S Kurgan oblast, Russian SFSR, 50 mi. SW of Kurgan; metalworks, flour mill.

Kurtik Dag (kŏŏrtĭk' dä), Turkish *Kurtik Dağ*, peak (8,822 ft.), E central Turkey, in Bitlis Mts., 6 mi. SSW of Mus. Sometimes called Hacres Dag.

Kürtös, Rumania: see CURTICI.

Kurtovo Konare (kŏŏr'tôvô kônä'rĕ), village (pop. 2,946), Plovdiv dist., S central Bulgaria, on Vacha R. and 13 mi. WSW of Plovdiv; tomato- and pepper-growing center; tobacco, rice.

Kuru or **Kurru** (kōō'rōō), village, Northern Prov., Anglo-Egyptian Sudan, on right bank of the Nile and 8 mi. S of Kareima. Site of pyramid field with tombs of Ethiopian kings (after 7th cent. B.C.).

Kuru (kōō'rōō), village (commune pop. 5,333), Häme co., SW Finland, on NW shore of L. Näsi, 25 mi. N of Tampere; granite quarries.

Kurudu, Netherlands New Guinea: see JAPEN ISLANDS.

Kurukshetra (kōōrōōkshā'trŭ), village, Karnal dist., E Punjab, India, 20 mi. NNW of Karnal; rail junction; important Hindu pilgrimage center. Large sacred tank just W attracts several thousands of bathers during solar eclipses; also a wild fowl sanctuary. In 1947, large refugee camp set up here to accommodate non-Moslems migrating from W Pakistan. Near-by area, extending roughly SW to Jind (Patiala and East Punjab States Union), was one of earliest Aryan settlements in India (c.2000–1500 B.C.) and is associated with legends of Mahabharata.

Kuruman (kōō'rōōmän), town (pop. 3,639), Bechuanaland dist., Cape Prov., U. of So. Afr., in Kuruman Hills, on upper Kuruman R. and 120 mi. NW of Kimberley; stock-raising, dairying center. Founded 1838 as mission station. Near by is noted spring, called "Eye of Kuruman."

Kuruman Hills, N Cape Prov., U. of So. Afr., N extension of ASBESTOS MOUNTAINS.

Kuruman River, intermittent stream, N Cape Prov., U. of So. Afr., rises in Kuruman Hills SE of Kuruman, flows 250 mi. in a wide arc NW and W, past Kuruman, parallel to S border of Bechuanaland Protectorate, to Molopo R. at 26°57'S 20°40'E.

Kurume (kōōrōō'mā), city (1940 pop. 89,490; 1947 pop. 90,999), Fukuoka prefecture, N central Kyushu, Japan, on Chikugo R. and 20 mi. SSE of Fukuoka. Rail junction; mfg. and commercial center in rice-growing area; rubber goods, lacquer ware, cotton textiles. Seat of Kurume Medical Col. Includes (since early 1940s) town of Mii.

Kurumkan (kōōrōōmkän'), village (1948 pop. over 500), NW Buryat-Mongol Autonomous SSR, Russian SFSR, on Barguzin R. and 200 mi. NNE of Ulan-Ude; dairy products.

Kuru Mountains, Turkey: see KORU MOUNTAINS.

Kurundu, W New Guinea: see JAPEN ISLANDS.

Kurundwad, India: see KURANDVAD, town.

Kurunegala (kōōrōōnä'gŭlŭ), anc. *Hathigiripura* [Singhalese, =city of the elephant rock], town (pop. 13,510), ⊙ North Western Prov. and Kurunegala dist. (□ 1,846; pop., including estate pop., 485,329), Ceylon, 23 mi. NW of Kandy, at foot of noted ELEPHANT ROCK. Road junction; trade (coconuts, rice, cacao, rubber, vegetables, fruit) center. Was ⊙ Ceylon in early-14th cent., under Singhalese kings.

Kurupukari (kōōrōōpōōkä'rē), village, Essequibo co., S Br. Guiana, on upper Essequibo R. and 115 mi. S of Bartica; ferry and govt. station, where the Rupununi cattle trail from Dadanawa crosses the Essequibo toward Takama on Berbice R.

Kurupung (kōōrōōpōōng'), diamond mine, Essequibo co., W Br. Guiana, on Mazaruni R., at 6°13'N 60°10'W.

Kururi (kōōrōō'rē), town (pop. 6,281), Chiba prefecture, central Honshu, Japan, on central Chiba Peninsula, 10 mi. SE of Kisarazu; rice, raw silk; poultry raising, lumbering.

Kurusku, Egypt: see KOROSKO.

Kuruwita (kōōrōōvĭt'ŭ), town (pop. 123), Sabaragamuwa Prov., SW central Ceylon, 7 mi. NNW of Ratnapura; precious-stone mining (notably star sapphires); rice, vegetables, rubber.

Kurvelesh or **Kurveleshi,** Albania: see GUSMAR.

Kurwai, India: see KORWAI.

Kurya or **Kur'ya** (kōōr'yŭ), village (1926 pop. 5,515), S Altai Territory, Russian SFSR, 45 mi. E of Rubtsovsk; dairy farming.

Kurzeme (kōōr'zāmā) [Lettish, =Courland], former province (□ 5,100; 1935 pop. 292,659) of W Latvia; ⊙ Liepaja. Originally ruled by Livonian Knights; became (1561–1795) part of duchy of Courland, which passed in 1795 to Russia and in 1920 to independent Latvia.

Kurzeniec, Belorussian SSR: see KURENETS.

Kus, Egypt: see QUS.

Kusa (kōō'sŭ), city (1936 pop. estimate 16,600), W Chelyabinsk oblast, Russian SFSR, in the S Urals, 13 mi. NW of Zlatoust, near railroad; metalworking center; mfg. (boilers, household equipment); charcoal burning, iron foundries, woodworking. Founded 1787 as iron-mining and -working settlement. Developed as mfg. center prior to First World War; became city in 1943. Formerly called Kusinski Zavod. Village of Petropavlovski (1939 pop. over 500) is 5 mi. NW, on Ai R.; distilling.

Kusada (kōōsī'dä), town (pop. 4,232), Katsina prov., Northern Provinces, N Nigeria, 50 mi. NW of Kano; peanuts, cotton; cattle, skins.

Kusadak (kōō'sädäk), village (pop. 6,789), central Serbia, Yugoslavia, 8 mi. WNW of Palanka.

Kusadasi (kōō"shädäsŭ'), Turkish *Kuşadası*, town (pop. 5,442), Smyrna prov., W Turkey, port on Gulf of Kusadasi 38 mi. S of Smyrna; olives, tobacco, figs. Site of anc. Ephesus is near by. Formerly Scalanuova, Scalanova, or Selcuk.

Kusadasi, Gulf of, inlet of Aegean Sea in W Turkey, S of Smyrna, 32 mi. W of Aydin; 25 mi. wide, 19 mi. long. Town of Kusadasi on E shore. Isl. of Samos on its S side. Formerly Gulf of Scalanuova.

Kusaie or **Kuseie** (kōōsī'ĕ), volcanic island (□ c.42; pop. 1,652), easternmost of Caroline Isls., Ponape dist., W Pacific, 780 mi. ESE of Truk; 5°19'N 162°59'E; 8 mi. in diameter. Small islets are offshore. The central mass, called Ualan, has 2 peaks, higher being Mt. Crozer (2,079 ft.). Lele Harbor in NE is best of 4 harbors. Site of ruins of anc. stone walls, dikes. Guano deposits in caves. Chief product is copra. In Second World War, site of Jap. air base; isl. surrendered with defeat of Japan.

Kusakabe (kōōsä'-kä'bā). **1** Town (pop. 4,985), on Shodo-shima, Kagawa prefecture, Japan, on S coast of isl.; salt, soy sauce, tobacco. **2** Town (pop. 5,713), Yamanashi prefecture, central Honshu, Japan, 7 mi. ENE of Kofu; rice, wheat, raw silk.

Kusanagara, India: see KASIA.

Kusano (kōōsä'nō), town (pop. 4,284), Fukuoka prefecture, N central Kyushu, Japan, 7 mi. E of Kurume; rice, wheat.

Kusary (kōōsä'rē), city (1948 pop. over 10,000), NE Azerbaijan SSR, on N slope of the Greater Caucasus, 7 mi. NW of Kuba; orchards; rug mfg.

Kusatsu (kōōsä'tsōō). **1** Town (pop. 7,393), Gumma prefecture, central Honshu, Japan, 23 mi. E of Nagano; sulphur mining. Hot-springs resort, known since 12th cent. **2** Town (pop. 10,498), Shiga prefecture, S Honshu, Japan, near SE shore of L. Biwa, 11 mi. E of Kyoto; rail junction; knit goods, sailcloth, sake, soy sauce, *mochi* (glutinous-rice cakes). Agr. experiment station.

Kuse (kōō'sä), town (pop. 9,201), Okayama prefecture, SW Honshu, Japan, 14 mi. W of Tsuyama, in agr. area (rice, wheat, persimmons, peppermint); raw silk, charcoal. Tobacco factory.

Kuseie, Caroline Isls.: see KUSAIE.

Kusel (kōō'zŭl), town (pop. 4,586), Rhenish Palatinate, W Germany, 17 mi. NW of Kaiserslautern; mfg. of cloth and agr. machinery; tanning, brewing.

Kush, in the Bible: see CUSH.

Kushagi, Russian SFSR: see UST-TARKA.

Kushalgarh (kōōshäl'gŭr), town (pop. 3,520), S Rajasthan, India, 23 mi. S of Banswara; maize, millet, rice; hand-loom weaving. Was ⊙ former petty state of Kushalgarh (□ 340; pop. 41,153) in Rajputana States, India; a dependency of Banswara state. In 1948, state merged with union of Rajasthan.

Kushalino, Russian SFSR: see BOLSHOYE KUSHALINO.

Kushan (gōō'shän'), town, ⊙ Kushan co., S Liaotung prov., SW Manchuria, 45 mi. WSW of Antung, on Yellow Sea; soybeans, kaoliang, wild silk; fish and salt. Until 1947 called Takushan.

Kushchevskaya (kōōshchĕf'skīŭ), village (1926 pop. 11,862), N Krasnodar Territory, Russian SFSR, on Yeya R. and 45 mi. S of Rostov; rail junction; flour mill, metalworks.

Kushchi (kōō'shchē), village (1939 pop. over 500), W Azerbaijan SSR, 4 mi. N of Dashkesan; terminus of rail spur (from Alabashly station on main Baku-Tiflis RR) for Dashkesan magnetite mines.

Kushevat (kōōshĭvät'), village (1939 pop. under 500), W Yamal-Nenets Natl. Okrug, Tyumen oblast, Russian SFSR, on right arm of Ob R. and 100 mi. S of Salekhard.

Kushh, El, or **Al-Kushh** (both: ĕl kōōsh'), village (pop. 7,114), Girga prov., central Upper Egypt, 5 mi. E of El Balyana; cotton, cereals, dates, sugar.

Kushigahama, Japan: see TOKUYAMA.

Kushih (gōō'shŭ'), town, ⊙ Kushih co. (pop. 510,577), SE Honan prov., China, near Anhwei line, 90 mi. E of Sinyang; cotton weaving; bamboo articles, ramie, peanuts. Coal mines near by.

Kushikino (kōō"shĭkē'nō), town (pop. 31,920), Kagoshima prefecture, SW Kyushu, Japan, on NW Satsuma Peninsula, 19 mi. NW of Kagoshima, on E.China Sea; commercial center in agr. area (rice, wheat); raw silk, livestock, timber. Fishery.

Kushimoto (kōōshē'mōtō), town (pop. 8,934), Wakayama prefecture, S Honshu, Japan, on Kumano Sea, on S Kii Peninsula, 21 mi. SW of Shingu, near Shio Point; whaling port. Harbor is sheltered by O-shima (E).

Kushira (kōōshē'rä), town (pop. 17,749), Kagosima prefecture, S Kyushu, Japan, on central Osumi Peninsula, 27 mi. ESE of Kagoshima; commercial center in agr. area (rice, wheat, sweet potatoes); raw silk, livestock, timber.

Kushiro (kōōshē'rō), city (1940 pop. 63,180; 1947 pop. 61,421), SE Hokkaido, Japan, port on the Pacific, 110 mi. SE of Asahigawa; principal commercial center for E Hokkaido; fishing center (fish oil, canned fish). Exports coal (mined near by), lumber, paper, marine products. Sometimes spelled Kusiro.

Kushk or **Koshk** (ko͝oshk), town (pop. 10,000), Herat prov., NW Afghanistan, on Kushk R. and 40 mi. NE of Herat, 30 mi. SE of Soviet rail terminus of Kushka; alt. 3,800 ft. Ships cotton and dried fruit. Pop. is largely Jamshidi.

Kushka (ko͞osh'kŭ), southernmost town (1932 pop. estimate 3,450) of USSR, in S Mary oblast, Turkmen SSR, on Kushka R. (left affluent of Murgab R.), on Afghanistan border and 160 mi. S of Mary (connected by railroad); 35°38'N 62°19'E. Wheat; pistachio woods. Founded in late-19th cent. as Rus. fort; reached (1898) by railroad.

Kushka River, Afghanistan and USSR: see Kushk River.

Kushk-i-Nakhud (ko͝oshk'-ĭ-nŭkho͞od'), town, Kandahar prov., S Afghanistan, on highway to Girishk and 40 mi. W of Kandahar, on Kushk-i-Nakhud R. (right tributary of the Arghandab); oasis center; irrigated agr. Maiwand (NE) was scene of severe defeat (1880) of British by Afghan faction.

Kushk River (ko͝oshk), Rus. *Kushka* (ko͞osh'kŭ), in NW Afghanistan and SE Turkmen SSR, rises in Paropamisus Mts. 55 mi. ENE of Herat, flows 150 mi. NW, past Kushk, then N, past Kushka, and NNE, along Kushka rail branch, to Murgab R. at Tashkepristroi (dam). Irrigation along middle course.

Kushmurun (ko͞oshmo͝oro͞on'), town (1943 pop. over 500), NE Kustanai oblast, Kazakh SSR, 60 mi. SE of Kustanai and on S.Siberian RR, at S end of **Lake Kushmurun** (□ c.400; formerly L. Ubagan). Bauxite deposits near by.

Kushnarenkovo (ko͞oshnä'ryĭnkŭvŭ), village (1939 pop. over 2,000), central Bashkir Autonomous SSR, Russian SFSR, on Belaya R. (landing) and 38 mi. NW of Ufa; flour milling. Called Topornino until 1930s.

Kushnitsa, Greece: see Pangaion.

Kushrabad (ko͞oshrŭbät'), village (1939 pop. over 500), central Samarkand oblast, Uzbek SSR, c.35 mi. from Katta-Kurgan.

Kushtagi (ko͞osh'tŭgē), village (pop. 4,802), Raichur dist., SW Hyderabad state, India, 28 mi. N of Koppal; millet, oilseeds.

Kushtia (ko͞osht'yŭ), district (□ c.1,300; 1951 pop. 895,000), W East Bengal, E Pakistan; ⊙ Kushtia. In Ganges Delta; bounded N by Padma R., W by West Bengal, India; drained by distributaries of the delta. Alluvial plain (rice, jute, linseed, sugar cane, wheat, tobacco, chili, turmeric); scattered swamps (bamboo, Moringa, and areca palm groves). Large sugar-processing factory near Chuadanga; sugar milling at Kushtia; food canning, liquor distilling, cotton-cloth weaving, brick and hosiery mfg. Originally part of Sen kingdom, overcome in 13th cent. by Afghans. Formed 1947 from E area of Nadia dist., Br. Bengal prov., following creation of Pakistan.

Kushtia, town (1941 pop. 13,842), ⊙ Kushtia dist., W East Bengal, E Pakistan, on upper Madhumati (Garai) R. and 11 mi. WSW of Pabna; sugar milling, cotton-cloth weaving, textile mfg.; trades in rice, jute, linseed, sugar cane, wheat. Until 1947, in Nadia dist.

Kushugum (ko͞osho͝ogo͞om'), town (1926 pop. 2,255), NW Zaporozhe oblast, Ukrainian SSR, 5 mi. S of Zaporozhe.

Kushunnai, Russian SFSR: see Ilinski.

Kushva (ko͞osh'vŭ), city (1926 pop. 14,274; 1936 pop. estimate 35,200), W Sverdlovsk oblast, Russian SFSR, at SW foot of Blagodat mtn., 27 mi. NNW of Nizhni Tagil, on railroad; metallurgical center (steel, pig iron); metalworking. Founded 1739 following discovery of Blagodat mtn. magnetite deposits; became city in 1926. Rail junction of Goroblagodatskaya is just SW.

Kusial Bharu (ko͞osyäl' bä'ro͞o), village (pop. 702), N central Kelantan, Malaya, on Kelantan R. at mouth of small left tributary Sungei Kusial and 26 mi. SSW of Kota Bharu, on E coast railroad; rubber and rice plantations. Also called Sungei Kusial.

Kusieh, El, Egypt: see Qusiya, El.

Kusinagara, India: see Kasia.

Kusinski Zavod, Russian SFSR: see Kusa.

Kusiro, Japan: see Kushiro.

Kusiyara River (ko͞osĭyä'rŭ), arm of lower Surma R. in E Assam (India) and E Pakistan, leaves the Surma 15 mi. W of Silchar, flows c.90 mi. WSW, past Karimganj and Fenchuganj, dividing into numerous arms and returning to lower Surma (Kalni) R.

Kuskokwim Bay (kŭ'skŭkwĭm) (100 mi. long, 100 mi. wide at mouth), SW Alaska, NW of Bristol Bay; center near 59°30'N 162°30'W; receives Kuskokwim R.

Kuskokwim Mountains, SW Alaska, W of Alaska Range, SE of Yukon R.; extend 250 mi. NE-SW; 61°–64°N 155°–159°W; rise to c.4,000 ft. Placer gold region.

Kuskokwim River, W Alaska, rises in 4 branches on W slope of Alaska Range. North Fork, East Fork, and South Fork join at Medfra (63°6'N 154°43'W); West Fork joins river 11 mi. downstream. River thence flows generally SW, past McGrath, Sleetmute, Napamiute, Akiak, Bethel, and Napakiak, to Kuskokwim Bay of the Bering Sea; c.600 mi. long. Navigable to McGrath.

Kuskovo, Russian SFSR: see Perovo, Moscow oblast.

Kusluyan, Turkey: see Golkoy.

Kusma (ko͞os'mŭ), town, central Nepal, on the Kali Gandaki and 18 mi. W of Pokhara; rice, wheat, millet, vegetables. Extensive colored mica and corundum deposits near by.

Küsnacht (küs'näkht), town (pop. 7,228), Zurich canton, N Switzerland, on L. of Zurich and 4 mi. SSE of Zurich; metal products; woodworking, printing.

Kusong (ko͞o'sŭng'), Jap. *Kijo*, township (1944 pop. 11,191), N.Pyongan prov., N Korea, 45 mi. ESE of Sinuiju, in agr. area (rice, millet, soy beans). Gold mines near by.

Kussabat, Tripolitania: see Cussabat.

Küssnacht (küs'näkht), town (pop. 5,152), Schwyz canton, central Switzerland, on N arm of L. of Lucerne, at NW foot of the Rigi, and 6 mi. ENE of Lucerne; year-round resort; leather, glass. Scene of traditional exploits of William Tell, with commemorative chapel and statue. Memorial chapel for Belgian Queen Astrid, who died here.

Küssnacht, Lake of, Switzerland: see Lucerne, Lake of.

Kustanai or **Kustanay** (ko͞ostŭnī'), oblast (□ 76,700; 1946 pop. estimate 400,000), NW Kazakh SSR; ⊙ Kustanai. Drained by Tobol and Ubagan rivers (N), by Turgai R. (S); steppe plateau with black earth (N), dry steppe (center), and desert (S). Wheat, millet, and oats grown N of S.Siberian RR; cattle and sheep raising in S. Gold mining at Dzhetygara. Meat and grain processed at Kustanai. Pop.: Ukrainians, Kazakhs, Russians. Formed 1936.

Kustanai or **Kustanay**, city (1936 pop. estimate 38,900), ⊙ Kustanai oblast, Kazakh SSR, on Tobol R., on branch of S.Siberian RR., and 160 mi. SE of Chelyabinsk, 900 mi. NW of Alma-Ata; 53°13'N 63°35'E. Agr.-processing center (meat, flour) in wheat-, cattle-, and hog-raising area; metalworks; cattle and grain market. Teachers col. Founded 1879–81.

Kustendil, Bulgaria: see Kyustendil.

Küstendje, Rumania: see Constanta, city.

Küsten Kanal, Germany: see Ems-Hunte Canal.

Küstenland (kü'stŭnlänt') [Ger.,=coastland],former province (□ 3,077; 1910 pop. 893,797) of Austria, consisting of Istria, Görz-Gradisca, and Trieste; ⊙ was Trieste. Created in 1849, it passed to Italy in 1919.

Kusto, Finland: see Kuusisto.

Küstrin (küstrēn') or **Kostrzyn** (kôs'chĭn), town (1939 pop. 23,711; 1946 pop. 634) in Brandenburg, after 1945 in Zielona Gora prov., W Poland, on the Oder (German border), at Warta R. mouth, and 18 mi. NNE of Frankfurt; paper and pulp milling; frontier station. First mentioned in early-13th cent.; passed 1445 to Brandenburg. Fortified in 16th cent. Frederick the Great, as crown prince, was imprisoned here (1730) by his father. In Seven Years War, heavily shelled (1758) by Russians; subsequently rebuilt by Frederick the Great. Occupied, 1806–14, by French. Admiral Tirpitz b. here. After Second World War, during which it was virtually obliterated, it was evacuated by its Ger. pop. Formerly spelled Cüstrin.

Kusu (ko͞o'so͞o). **1** Town (pop. 8,526), Mie prefecture, S Honshu, Japan, on W shore of Ise Bay, 4 mi. S of Yokkaichi; rice, raw silk, poultry; sake, wool. **2** Town (pop. 7,255), Oita prefecture, N central Kyushu, Japan, 28 mi. W of Oita; rice-growing center; sake; lumber.

Kusumapura, India: see Patna, city.

Kusune, Japan: see Fuse.

Kusung (go͞o'so͞ong'), town (pop. 13,954), ⊙ Kusung co. (pop. 107,954), S Szechwan prov., China, 40 mi. SSW of Luhsien; rice, sweet potatoes, wheat, beans, millet. Sulphur mines, copper deposits near by.

Kusye-Aleksandrovskoye or **Kus'ye-Aleksandrovskoye** (ko͞o"syĭ-ŭlyĭksän'drŭfskŭyŭ), town (1926 pop. 1,875), E Molotov oblast, Russian SFSR, on Koiva R. and 19 mi. E (under jurisdiction) of Chusovoi; iron mining, charcoal burning. Until 1946, Kusye-Aleksandrovski Zavod.

Kut (ko͞ot), province (□ 6,188; pop. 224,792), E Iraq, on the Tigris; ⊙ Kut or Kut al Imara. Agr. area: dates, rice, millet, sesame, cotton.

Kut, Kut al Imara, or **Kut al-Amarah** (ko͞ot äl ŭmä'rŭ), city (pop. 56,294), ⊙ Kut prov., E Iraq, on the Tigris (here throwing off a branch, the Shatt al Gharraf), on railroad, and 100 mi. SE of Baghdad; licorice processing; rice, corn, millet, sesame, dates. A barrage is on the Tigris just upstream.

Kut, Ko (kô' ko͞ot'), southernmost Thai isl. on E coast of Gulf of Siam, in Trat prov., SE Thailand, 15 mi. off coast; 11°40'N 102°35'E; rises to 1,007 ft.

Kuta (ko͞otä'), town (pop. 5,107), Niger prov., Northern Provinces, W central Nigeria, 20 mi. NNE of Minna, near railroad; major gold-mining center; shea-nut processing; ginger, cassava, durra.

Kutahya (kütä'yä), Turk. *Kütahya*, prov. (□ 5,889; 1950 pop. 419,100), W Turkey; ⊙ Kutahya. Bordered NE by Ulu Mts., NW by Demirci Mts. Drained by Simav, Porsuk, Gediz, and Buyuk Menderes rivers. Chromium, copper, mercury, magnesite, iron, lignite, potter's clay. Mohair goats; cotton, sugar beets, apples, pears, plums, figs, raisins, valonia. Sometimes spelled Kutaiah and Kutaya.

Kutahya, Turk. *Kütahya*, town (1950 pop. 19,547), ⊙ Kutahya prov., W Turkey, on railroad, on Porsuk R., and 160 mi. WSW of Ankara, 75 mi. SE of Bursa; ceramic industry (tiles, faïence) from local clay; magnesite, copper, lignite; cotton factory, mfg. of carpets; wheat, barley trade. Meerschaum in vicinity. Sometimes spelled Kutaiah and Kutaya.

Kutai River, Borneo: see Mahakam River.

Kutais (ko͞otŭēs'), town (1945 pop. over 500), S Krasnodar Territory, Russian SFSR, at N foot of the Greater Caucasus, 37 mi. W of Maikop; oil wells. Developed after Second World War.

Kutaisi (ko͞otŭē'sē) or **Kutais** (ko͞otŭēs'), largest city (1939 pop. 81,479) of W Georgian SSR, on Rion R., on rail spur and 110 mi. WNW of Tiflis; road and air line hub; S terminus of Ossetian Military Road from Alagir. Important mfg. center amid citrus farms and market gardens; produces automobile trucks, coal-mining equipment, chemicals (sulphuric acid, lithopone), textiles (woolen, cotton, and silk goods), shoes, leather goods. Sawmilling, fruit canning, vegetable-oil pressing. Industry is powered by Rion hydroelectric station. Has ruins of old Imeritian castle and 11th-cent. cathedral (destroyed in 17th cent. by Turks). Teachers col., agr. school with tree nursery and botanical garden. Founded 6th cent. B.C.; Kutaisi became ⊙ Imeretia. Passed (1804) to Russia; was ⊙ Kutais govt. until 1921. After 1936 the Georgian form (Kutaisi) of Kutais became official.

Kut al Imara, Iraq: see Kut, city.

Kutami (ko͞otä'mē), town (pop. 5,842), Kumamoto prefecture, W Kyushu, Japan, 13 mi. N of Kumamoto; rice, wheat. Has artisan fan industry.

Kutang I, peak, Nepal: see Manaslu.

Kutaraja, Kutaradja, or **Koetaradja** (all: ko͞oturä'-jŭ), town (pop. 10,724), N Sumatra, Indonesia, on Achin R. and 270 mi. NW of Medan; 5°32'N 95°20'E; trade center for agr. area (copra, pepper). Town is connected by railroad with its port, Ule-Lue, 3 mi. W. There is a large mosque (1881). Also spelled Kotaraja or Kotaradja.

Kutaya, Turkey: see Kutahya.

Kutch, India: see Cutch.

Kutchan (ko͞ochä'), town (pop. 15,135), SW Hokkaido, Japan, 14 mi. ESE of Iwanai; rail junction; iron and sulphur mining; agr. (hemp, potatoes), horse breeding.

Kutcharo, Lake (ko͞ochä'rō), Jap. *Kutcharo-ko* (□ 31), E Hokkaido, Japan, 22 mi. S of Abashiri; 9 mi. long, 5 mi. wide; hot springs on shores. Sometimes spelled Kuttyaro. Lake is in Akan Natl. Park (□ 340), known for virgin forests and active volcanoes.

Kutchuk Kainarji, Bulgaria: see Kainardzha.

Kutdligssat or **Qutdligssat** (both: ko͞otlĭkh'shät), settlement (pop. 616), Ritenbenk dist., W Greenland, on NE Disko isl., 60 mi. NNE of Godhavn; 70°4'N 53°W. Lignite mining. Meteorological and radio stations.

Kute (ko͞o'tā), town (pop. 6,488), Shimane prefecture, SW Honshu, Japan, on Sea of Japan, 37 mi. WSW of Matsue, in agr. and livestock area; silk textiles, soy sauce; rice, sweet potatoes.

Kuteinikovo or **Kuteynikovo** (ko͞otyä'nyĭkŭvŭ), town (1926 pop. 1,213), SE Stalino oblast, Ukrainian SSR, in the Donbas, 8 mi. W of Amvrosiyevka; rail junction.

Kuthanallur, India: see Kuttanallur.

Kuthar (ko͞otär'), former princely state (□ 21; pop. 4,970) of Punjab Hill States, India, SW of Simla. Since 1948, merged with Himachal Pradesh.

Kuther, Kashmir: see Anantnag, town.

Kutien or **Ku-t'ien** (both: go͞o'tyĕn'), town (pop. 15,515), ⊙ Kutien co. (pop. 153,717), NE Fukien prov., China, 45 mi. NW of Foochow and on small Kutien R. (tributary of Min R.); sweet potatoes, rice, wheat, tobacco. Iron, copper, silver, and lead mines.

Kutina (ko͞o'tēnä), village (pop. 4,663), N Croatia, Yugoslavia, on railroad and 20 mi. E of Sisak, in Slavonia; local trade center; mfg. (carbon black, enamel ware).

Kutiyana (ko͞otĭyä'nŭ), town (pop. 18,949), SW Saurashtra, India, on Bhadar R. and 32 mi. WNW of Junagarh; agr. market center (millet, cotton, wheat, oilseeds, sugar cane); handicrafts (cotton cloth, metalware).

Kutkai (ko͞ot'kī), village, North Hsenwi state, Northern Shan State, Upper Burma, on Burma Road and 35 mi. NNE of Lashio; airport.

Kutkashen (ko͞otkŭshĕn'), village (1932 pop. estimate 2,470), N Azerbaijan SSR, on S slope of the Greater Caucasus, 45 mi. NNE of Yevlakh; orchards.

Kutlu-Bukash (ko͞otlo͞o"-bo͞okäsh'), village (1939 pop. over 500), central Tatar Autonomous SSR, Russian SFSR, 18 mi. N of Chistopol; wheat, livestock. Sometimes written Kutlubukash.

Kutna Hora (ko͞ot'nä hô'rä), Czech *Kutná Hora*, Ger. *Kuttenberg* (ko͞o'tŭnbĕrk), town (pop. 12,119), central Bohemia, Czechoslovakia, on Elbe R., on railroad and 39 mi. ESE of Prague, in wheat and sugar-beet region; organ-building. Famous medieval silver mines, which supplied treasury of Bohemian kings, here. Has noted architectural treasures: Bohemian-Gothic St. Barbara cathedral (late-14th cent.); 14th-cent. St. James cathedral; 16th-cent. church of St. Marie; "Italian Court" (*Vlassky dvur*), a former royal residence and silver mint; 15th-cent. Gothic fountain; stone cistern; 17th-cent. Jesuits' col. (now used as barracks); baroque Ursuline convent; mus. with medieval collections. Founded in 13th cent.; fell to Hussites in 1422, the silver mines having been set on fire; remained a Protestant center for 200 years. Mining ceased to be profitable at end of 18th cent.

Kutno (kōōt'nô), city (pop. 20,066), Lodz prov., central Poland, 33 mi. N of Lodz. Rail junction; trade center; mfg. of agr. machinery and tools, cement, bricks, soap; beet-sugar and flour milling, chicory drying, sawmilling, distilling, brewing. Lignite deposits in vicinity. Before Second World War, pop. was 50% Jewish. Near by, Poles fought (1939) one of longest and bloodiest battles against Germans.

Kutnozero, Karelo-Finnish SSR: see KUITO LAKES.

Kutoarjo, Kutoardjo, or **Koetoardjo** (all: kōōtōär'jō), town (pop. 11,496), central Java, Indonesia, near Indian Ocean, 30 mi. W of Jogjakarta; trade center for agr. area (rice, sugar, peanuts).

Kütsing or **Ch'ü-ching** (both: chü'jĭng'), town (pop. 15,003), ⊙ Kütsing co. (pop. 100,687), E Yunnan prov., China, on railroad and 80 mi. ENE of Kunming; alt. 6,330 ft.; ham-producing center; stone carving; rice, millet, beans. Kaolin quarrying near by.

Kuttalam (kōōt-tä'lŭm). **1** Town (pop. 6,848), Tanjore dist., SE Madras, India, on arm of Cauvery R. delta and 4 mi. WSW of Mayavaram; rice, peanuts, millet. **2** Village (pop. 2,168), Tinnevelly dist., S Madras, India, on Chittar R. (falls) and 3 mi. SW of Tenkasi. Health resort (sanatorium) at E foot of Western Ghats; cool climate caused by SW monsoon blowing through gap in mts.

Kuttanallur or **Kuthanallur** (kōōtä'nŭl-lōōr), town (pop. 9,805), Tanjore dist., SE Madras, India, in Cauvery R. delta, 9 mi. SW of Tiruvarur; rice, coconut palms, bamboo; mat weaving.

Kuttawa (kŭtô'wŭ), town (pop. 794), Lyon co., SW Ky., on Cumberland R. and 27 mi. E of Paducah, in agr., limestone-quarry, hardwood-timber area. Near by are ruins of William Kelly's iron furnace. Kuttawa Mineral Springs Park, Kentucky Dam, and Kentucky Woodlands Wildlife Refuge are also near.

Kuttejou or **Kyutteyyu,** Est. *Küttejõu* (all: kü'tĕyŭōō), town (1949 pop. over 500), NE Estonia, 2 mi. E of Kivioli; oil-shale mining.

Kuttenberg, Czechoslovakia: see KUTNA HORA.

Küttigen (kü'tĭgŭn), town (pop. 2,129), Aargau canton, N Switzerland, 2 mi. N of Aarau; silk textiles.

Kuttyaro, Lake, Japan: see KUTCHARO, LAKE.

Kutu (kōō'tōō), village (1946 pop. c.2,500), Leopoldville prov., W Belgian Congo, on right bank of Fimi R. at outlet of L. Leopold II, 55 mi. SSW of Inongo; trading and agr. center, steamboat landing; rice, palm products, copal. R.C. mission.

Kutubu, Lake (kōōtōō'bōō), in central highlands of Territory of Papua, SE Guinea; 6°24'S 143°20'E; 12 mi. long, 2–3 mi. wide; alt. 2,700 ft. Government patrol post, mission station on shore. Pop. in area, 400.

Kutulik (kōōtōōlyĭk'), town (1939 pop. over 500), SW Ust-Orda Buryat-Mongol Natl. Okrug, Irkutsk oblast, Russian SFSR, on Trans-Siberian RR and 18 mi. NW of Cheremkhovo, in agr. area; grain elevator; metalworks.

Kutum (kōōtōōm'), town, Darfur prov., W Anglo-Egyptian Sudan, on road and 60 mi. NW of El Fasher; trade center; gum arabic; corn, durra; livestock.

Kutur, Iran: see QUTUR.

Kutuzovo (kōōtōō'zŭvŭ), town (1939 pop. 1,090), E Kaliningrad oblast, Russian SFSR, on Sheshupe R. (Lith. line) opposite Naumiestis, and 15 mi. NE of Nesterov; agr. market. First mentioned 1563; chartered 1725. Until 1945, in East Prussia (Germany's easternmost town) and called Schirwindt (shĭr'vĭnt).

Kutuzov-Volodarsk, Ukrainian SSR: see VOLODARSK-VOLYNSKI.

Kuty (kōō'tē), Slovak *Kúty,* Hung. *Jókút* (yō'kōōt), village (pop. 3,348), W Slovakia, Czechoslovakia, 9 mi. SE of Breclav; sugar beets; rail junction.

Kuty (kōō'tē), town (1931 pop. 5,393), SE Stanislav oblast, Ukrainian SSR, on Cheremosh R. and 20 mi. SSE of Kolomyya, in coniferous woodland; sawmilling; extraction of pitch, turpentine, tar, colophony, resin; tanning, fur processing; horse raising. A Pol.-Rumanian frontier town (after 1920); passed to USSR following occupation of E Poland in 1939.

Kutztown (kōōts'toun), borough (pop. 3,110), Berks co., E central Pa., 14 mi. NNE of Reading; textiles, metal products; limestone. Has state teachers col. Crystal cave near here. Settled 1733 by Germans, inc. 1815.

Kuuli-Mayak (kōōōōlyē"-mīäk'), town (1932 pop. estimate 680), W Ashkhabad oblast, Turkmen SSR, port on Caspian Sea, 22 mi. NNW of Krasnovodsk; fish canneries; salt extraction.

Kuurne (kür'nŭ), town (pop. 8,530), West Flanders prov., NW Belgium, NE suburb of Courtrai.

Kuusamo (kōō'sämō), village (commune pop. 14,413), Oulu co., NE Finland, near USSR border, in lake region, 100 mi. ESE of Rovaniemi; road center in lumbering region. Tourist resort. Site of people's col.

Kuusankoski (kōō'sän-kōs"kē), village (commune pop. 17,560), Kymi co., SE Finland, on Kymi R. (rapids) and 4 mi. NW of Kouvola; rail terminus; pulp, cellulose, and paper mills. Hydroelectric station. Until 1949 in Uusimaa co.

Kuusisto (kōō'sĭstō), Swedish *Kustö* (küst'û"), island (6 mi. long, 1–2 mi. wide), Turku-Pori co., SW Finland, in inlet of Gulf of Bothnia, 6 mi. SE of Turku. Site of remains of 14th-cent. castle of R.C. bishops of Finland, destroyed (1528) by Gustavus Vasa.

Kuusjärvi (kōōs'yăr"vē), village (commune pop. 11,804), Kuopio co., SE Finland, in Saimaa lake region, 25 mi. WNW of Joensuu; asbestos quarrying, lumbering. Near by are Outokumpu copper mines.

Kuva (kōōvä'), village (1926 pop. 5,907), E Fergana oblast, Uzbek SSR, 18 mi. NE of Fergana near railroad (Fedchenko station); cotton-ginning center; sericulture.

Kuvakino (kōōvä'kēnŭ), village (1926 pop. 2,999), SW Chuvash Autonomous SSR, Russian SFSR, 12 mi. NNW of Alatyr; wheat, livestock.

Kuvam River, India: see COOUM RIVER.

Kuvandyk (kōōvŭndĭk'), town (1939 pop. over 10,000), N Chkalov oblast, Russian SFSR, in S foothills of the S Urals, on Sakmara R. and 10 mi. NW of Mednogorsk, in Orsk-Khalilovo industrial dist.; machine mfg., metalworking, flour milling.

Kuvasai or **Kuvasay** (kōōvŭsī'), town (1939 pop. over 2,000), SE Fergana oblast, Uzbek SSR, on rail spur and 12 mi. SE of Fergana; cement works, power plant.

Kuvshinovo (kōōfshē'nŭvŭ), city (1939 pop. over 10,000), W central Kalinin oblast, Russian SFSR, 30 mi. W of Torzhok; paper-milling center. Has power station based on Rantsevo peat works (SW).

Kuwait, Kuweit (both: kōōwīt', kōōwāt'), or **Al-Kuwayt** (ăl–), independent Arab state (□ 6,000; 1949 pop. estimate 170,000) under British protection, on NE Coast of Arabian Peninsula, at head of Persian Gulf; ⊙ Kuwait. Bounded N and W by Iraq and S by Saudi Arabia and the Kuwait–Saudi Arabia neutral zone (□ 1,800; established 1922), the state surrounds Kuwait Bay (small inlet of Persian Gulf) and includes Bubiyan, Failaka, and some smaller isls. Largely desert, gravelly (N) and sandy (S), Kuwait has some irrigated agr. around Jahra producing grain, vegetables, dates. Precipitation is 4–5 inches yearly, mostly in the cooler winter (Dec.–March), while the summer is very hot. Fishing and pearling are important industries, and Kuwait builds Arab dhows and pearling craft on the basis of imported teak (from Burma) and fibers. Large-scale oil production, begun 1946 at BURGAN field, made Kuwait the 6th world oil producer by 1949, and was followed by the founding of the oil tank farm of AHMADI and the loading port of MENA AL-AHMADI. State trades in livestock with interior of Saudi Arabia and Iraq and in fish and pearls with Persian Gulf ports. Owing to its good harbor, it is a collecting center and transshipment point for goods from smaller gulf ports. Pop. is largely Sunni Arab, with some Persians (10%) and Negro slaves. The state developed in early-18th cent. around the town of Kuwait, and the reigning dynasty was founded in 1756. Growth was fostered by Kuwait's role in the gulf trade and by its consideration (19th cent.) as a possible terminus of the Baghdad railroad. The state was included nominally in the Ottoman prov. of Basra until 1899, when the ruling sheik accepted British protection (confirmed by a 1914 agreement). A joint U.S.-British oil concession granted in 1934 resulted in exploratory drilling in late 1930s, but large-scale production began only in 1946. Concession (to U.S. company) was also granted in 1948–49 in the Kuwait–Saudi Arabia neutral zone. Formerly called Qurein, Grane, or Grain, for islet in Kuwait Bay; sometimes spelled Kowait and Koweit.

Kuwait, Kuweit, or **Al-Kuwayt,** chief town (1948 pop. estimate 80,000) of Kuwait state, port on S shore of Kuwait Bay of Persian Gulf, just NE of its suburban port Shuwaikh and 80 mi. S of Basra; 29°22'N 48°E. Commercial center, serving as entrepôt for Persian Gulf coastal trade and for caravans to interior; shipbuilding industry provides Arab dhows for coastwise shipping. Exports pearls, hides, skins. Residence of sheik and British political agent; U.S. mission (1912). Founded in early-18th cent.; considered (19th cent.) as possible rail terminus of Baghdad railroad; ringed (1921) by wall as defense against Wahabis; expanded in late 1940s following oil development in state. Formerly called Qurein, Grane, or Grain, for a near-by islet; sometimes spelled Kowait and Koweit.

Kuwana (kōōwä'nä), city (1940 pop. 41,848; 1947 pop. 35,890), Mie prefecture, S Honshu, Japan, on N shore of Ise Bay, 15 mi. SW of Nagoya; mfg. center (cotton textiles, machinery, vegetable oil). Includes (since 1937) former town of Nishi-kuwana.

Kuwano (kōōwä'nō), town (pop. 5,784), Tokushima prefecture, E Shikoku, Japan, 13 mi. SSE of Tokushima; rice center.

Kuwayrah, Jordan: see KUWEIRA.

Kuway Sandjaq, Iraq: see KOI SANJAQ.

Kuwayt, Al-, Arabia: see KUWAIT.

Kuweira or **Kuwayrah** (both: kōōwā'rŭ), village, S Jordan, on road and 38 mi. SW of Ma'an; fruit, sheep, and goat raising. Airfield. Sometimes spelled Quweira.

Kuweit, Arabia: see KUWAIT.

Küwo or **Ch'ü-wo** (both: chü'wô'), town, ⊙ Küwo co. (pop. 86,037), S Shansi prov., China, on road and 30 mi. S of Linfen; wheat, beans, corn.

Kuxhaven, Germany: see CUXHAVEN.

Kuyahoora Lake, N.Y.: see WEST CANADA CREEK.

Kuya-Mazar (kōōyä"mŭzär'), village (1939 pop. under 500), S Bukhara oblast, Uzbek SSR, on Bukhara oasis, 15 mi. NE of Bukhara. Just E, on edge of desert, is large reservoir (completed 1947); stores Zeravshan R. overflow for irrigation of Sverdlovsk, Alat, and Karakul areas.

Küyang or **Ch'ü-yang** (both: chü'yäng'), town, ⊙ Küyang co. (pop. 163,645), W Hopeh prov., China, 40 mi. N of Shihkiachwang; cotton, wheat, kaoliang, beans.

Kuyang (gōō'yäng'), town (pop. 5,755), ⊙ Kuyang co. (pop. 37,178), central Suiyan prov., China, in Tatsing Mts., 35 mi. N of Paotow; wheat, oats, cattle. Coal mining near by.

Kuybyshev, in Rus. names: see KUIBYSHEV.

Kuyeda (kōōyĭdä'), village (1939 pop. over 500), S Molotov oblast, Russian SFSR, on railroad and 60 mi. S of Osa; flax processing; wheat, clover, livestock.

Küyeh or **Chü-yeh** (both: jü'yĕ'), town, ⊙ Küyeh co. (pop. 345,993), E Pingyuan prov., China, 38 mi. ENE of Hotseh; cotton and silk weaving; peanuts, tobacco. Until 1949 in Shantung prov.

Kuyi, China: see SANKIANG.

Kuylyuk, Uzbek SSR: see KUILYUK.

Kuyto Lakes, Karelo-Finnish SSR: see KUITO LAKES.

Kuytun, Russian SFSR: see KUITUN.

Kuyüan (gōō'yüăn'). **1** Town, Chahar prov., China: see PAOYÜAN. **2** Town, ⊙ Kuyüan co. (pop. 128,345), SE Kansu prov., China, 50 mi. NNW of Pingliang; alt. 6,600 ft.; cattle-raising center; grain; coal mines.

Küyung or **Chü-yung** (both: jü'yōōng'), town (pop. 7,281), ⊙ Küyung co. (pop. 302,895), S Kiangsu prov., China, 20 mi. ESE of Nanking; rice, wheat, beans; cement mfg. Also written Chüjung.

Kuyunjik, Iraq: see NINEVEH.

Kuyvastu, Estonia: see KUIVASTU.

Kuzbas or **Kuzbass,** Russian SFSR: see KUZNETSK BASIN.

Kuzedeyevo (kōōzyĭdyä'ŭvŭ), village (1939 pop. over 2,000), SW Kemerovo oblast, Russian SFSR, in Kuznetsk Basin, on Kondoma R., on railroad and 30 mi. S of Stalinsk, in agr. area.

Kuzhener (kōōzhĭnyĕr'), village (1939 pop. over 500), E Mari Autonomous SSR, Russian SFSR, 40 mi. ENE of Ioshkar-Ola; wheat, rye, oats.

Kuzhenkino (kōōzhĕn'kēnŭ), town (1939 pop. over 500), NW Kalinin oblast, Russian SFSR, 9 mi. SSW of Bologoye; road center.

Kuzhittura, India: see KULITHURA.

Kuzino (kōō'zēnŭ), town (1936 pop. estimate 5,000), SW Sverdlovsk oblast, Russian SFSR, in the central Urals, 20 mi. NW of Pervouralsk (where pop. is employed); rail junction; truck gardening.

Kuznechikha (kōōznyĕ'chĭkhŭ), village (1926 pop. 3,069), S Tatar Autonomous SSR, Russian SFSR, 25 mi. SSE of Kuibyshev; grain, livestock.

Kuznetsk (kōōznyĕtsk'). **1** City, Kemerovo oblast, Russian SFSR: see STALINSK, city. **2** City (1936 pop. estimate 41,000), E Penza oblast, Russian SFSR, 65 mi. E of Penza; tanning center (sheepskins); mfg. (shoes, leather goods, rope, farm implements). An 18th-cent. robbers' nest; chartered 1780.

Kuznetsk Ala-Tau (ŭlä"-tou'), mountain system in SW Siberian Russian SFSR, along borders of Khakass Autonomous Oblast (Krasnoyarsk Territory) and Kemerovo oblast; extends from Teletskoye L. NE and N to Trans-Siberian RR. Rises to 6,890 ft. in central portion. S section, N to Tom R. source, is known as ABAKAN RANGE. Formed of erosion-resistant rocks (granite, gneiss). Gold, iron, manganese are important mineral resources.

Kuznetsk Basin (kōōznĕtsk', Rus. kōōznyĕtsk') abbr. **Kuzbas,** Rus. *Kuznetski Bassein* or *Kuznetskiy Basseyn,* abbr. *Kuzbass,* richest coal basin (□ 10,000) of USSR, in Kemerovo oblast, Russian SFSR, bet. Kuznetsk Ala-Tau (E) and Salair Ridge (W); 150 mi. long (N–S), 65 mi. wide. Coal reserves (400–450 billion tons), in thick seams to 4,500 ft. in depth, are of high quality and great variety. Main mines at Anzhero-Sudzhensk (oldest; developed late 19th cent.), Kemerovo, Leninsk-Kuznetski, Prokopyevsk, Kiselevsk, Osinniki. Site of greatest industrial development in Asiatic USSR: heavy metallurgy (Stalinsk), zinc metallurgy (Belovo), chemical industry (Kemerovo).

Kuznetskoye (kōōznyĕt'skŭyŭ), village (1926 pop. 5,387), N central Chelyabinsk oblast, Russian SFSR, on small lake, 15 mi. SSE of Kyshtym; wheat, rye, oats, livestock.
Kuznetsovo, Russian SFSR: see KONAKOVO.
Kuznica (kōōzh-nē'tsä), Pol. *Kuźnica,* village, Bialystok prov., NE Poland, frontier station on Belorussian SSR line, on Warsaw-Leningrad railroad and 9 mi. NE of Sokolka, 13 mi. SE of Grodno.
Kuzomen or **Kuzomen'** (kōōzŭmyĕn'yŭ), village (1926 pop. 533), S Murmansk oblast, Russian SFSR, port on White Sea, on Kola Peninsula, 135 mi. ESE of Kandalaksha; fisheries.
Kuzovatovo (kōōzŭvä'tŭvŭ), village (1926 pop. 3,741), central Ulyanovsk oblast, Russian SFSR, 22 mi. ESE of Barysh; sawmilling.
Kuzu or **Kuzuu** (both: kōō"zōō'), town (pop. 10,808), Tochigi prefecture, central Honshu, Japan, 7 mi. WNW of Tochigi; agr. (rice, wheat); silk cocoons; limestone.
Kuzumaki (kōōzōō'mäkē), town (pop. 6,742), Iwate prefecture, N Honshu, Japan, 28 mi. NE of Morioka; charcoal, livestock.
Kuzutsuka (kōōzōō'tsŏokä), town (pop. 10,119), Niigata prefecture, central Honshu, Japan, 9 mi. E of Niigata; rice, silk cocoons, cotton textiles.
Kuzuu, Japan: see KUZU.
Kvaenang Fjord (kvăn'äng), Nor. *Kvaenangenfjord,* inlet (45 mi. long, 1–12 mi. wide) of Norwegian Sea, Troms co., N Norway, 60 mi. ENE of Tromso. At mouth are several isls., including Skiervoy.
Kvaloy (kväl'ûü), Nor. *Kvaløy.* **1** Island (□ 127; pop. 4,153) in Norwegian Sea, Finnmark co., N Norway; 17 mi. long, 10 mi. wide; rises to 2,047 ft. HAMMERFEST city is on W coast, near Fuglnes cape. **2** Island (□ 284; pop. 3,283) in Norwegian Sea, Troms co., N Norway, 6 mi. W of Tromso, from which it is separated by arm of Tromso Sound; 30 mi. long, 2–14 mi. wide; rises to 3,392 ft. in Skitntind mtn. (W). Hillesoy (hĭl'lŭs-ûü) (Nor. *Hillesøy*) fishing village (canton pop. 2,572) is on SW coast, 20 mi. W of Tromso.
Kvalsund (kväl'sōōn), fishing village (pop. 248; canton pop. 1,877), Finnmark co., N Norway, on narrow Kval Sound, which separates Kvaloy from mainland, opposite Stallogargo (ferry), 13 mi. SW of Hammerfest.
Kvalvik, Norway: see FREI.
Kvam, canton, Norway: see ALVIK.
Kvam (kväm), village in Nord-Fron canton, Opland co., S central Norway, in the Gudbrandsdal, on Lagen R., on railroad and 50 mi. NW of Lillehammer; talc and slate quarries. In Second World War, scene (April, 1940) of fighting bet. Anglo-Norwegian and German forces.
Kvanum (kvĕ'nŭm"), Swedish *Kvänum,* village (pop. 528), Skaraborg co., SW Sweden, 10 mi. SW of Skara; hosiery knitting, brick mfg., woodwork.
Kvareli (kvŭrĕ'lyē), village (1926 pop. 5,571), NE Georgian SSR, in Kakhetia, on S slope of the Greater Caucasus, near Alazan R., 17 mi. E of Telavi; wine center.
Kvarkeno (kvär'kyēnŭ), village (1948 pop. over 500), NE Chkalov oblast, Russian SFSR, in E foothills of the S Urals, on right tributary of Ural R. and 75 mi. NE of Orsk; metalworking. Gold deposits near by.
Kvarner (kvär'nĕr), Ital. *Quarnero* (kwärnĕ'rô), *Quarnaro* (kwärnä'rô), or *Carnaro* (kärnä'rô), gulf of Adriatic Sea, NW Croatia, Yugoslavia, bet. Istria (W) and Cres and Krk isls. (E); Rijeka (Fiume) on NE shore. Mali Kvarner, Ital. *Quarnerolo* (kuärnĕrô'lô), *Quarnarolo* (kuärnärô'lô), or *Carnarolo* (kärnärô'lô), a smaller gulf, lies bet. Cres and Lsoinj (W) and Krk, Rab, and Pag (E) isls.
Kvarnsveden (kvärns'vä"dŭn), village, Kopparberg co., central Sweden, on Dal R. and 2 mi. NW of Borlange; paper and lumber-milling center.
Kvasnikovka (kvŭsnyē'kŭfkŭ), village (1926 pop. 3,700), central Saratov oblast, Russian SFSR, near Volga R., 10 mi. SSW of Engels; wheat, tobacco.
Kvernaes, Norway: see KVERNES.
Kvernaland (kvăr'nälän), village (pop. 343) in Time canton (pop. 4,899), Rogaland co., SW Norway, 14 mi. S of Stavanger; mfg. of agr. tools and machinery.
Kvernes (kvăr'nās), village and canton (pop. 812), More og Romsdal co., W Norway, on E tip of Averoy, 7 mi. S of Kristiansund; fishing, lumbering. Has medieval stone church. Formerly spelled Kvernaes.
Kvichak Bay (kwē'jăk) (50 mi. long, 30 mi. wide), S Alaska, NE arm of Bristol Bay, on E side of base of Alaska Peninsula; 58°40'N 157°34'W. Base for Bristol Bay salmon fleet. Receives Kvichak R.
Kvichak River, S Alaska, at base of Alaska Peninsula, issues from Iliamna L., flows 65 mi. SW to head of Kvichak Bay.
Kvidinge (kvē'dĭng-ŭ), village (pop. 858), Kristianstad co., SW Sweden, 15 mi. ENE of Halsingborg; paper milling; grain, potatoes, stock.
Kvikne (kvĭk'nŭ), agr. village and canton (pop. 1,372), Hedmark co., E Norway, on small Orkla R. (tributary of Glomma R.) and 35 mi. W of Roros. Bjornson (Nor. *Bjørnson*) was b. here; his house is natl. monument. Has 17th-cent. church.
Kvillsfors (kvĭls"fôrs', –fôsh'), village (pop. 588), Jonkoping co., S Sweden, on Em R. and 15 mi. E of Vetlanda; woodworking.
Kvina River (kvē'nä), Vest-Agder co., S Norway, rises in Ruven Mts., flows 45 mi. S to inlet of North Sea 10 mi. E of Flekkefjord; forms several falls, including Trelandsfoss.
Kvindherred, Norway: see SUNDE.
Kvinesdal (kvē'nŭsdäl), village and canton (pop. 3,515), Vest-Agder co., S Norway, on the Kvina 3 mi. from its mouth, and 11 mi. E of Flekkefjord. Lumber milling near by. Sometimes called Liknes.
Kvineshei Tunnel (kvē'nŭs-hā) (9,913 yards long), Vest-Agder co., S Norway, on Kristiansand-Stavanger RR and 30 mi. WNW of Kristiansand; extends W from Snartemo. Adjoining Haegebostad Tunnel (hăg'ŭbôstä) (9,267 yards long) extends E from Snartemo.
Kvinnherad, Norway: see SUNDE.
Kvirila River (kvērē'lŭ), W Georgian SSR, rises in the central Greater Caucasus W of Dzhava, flows SW, past Sachkhere and Chiatura, and W, past Zestafoni, to Rion R. S of Kutaisi; 80 mi. long. Rapids.
Kvirily, Georgian SSR: see ZESTAFONI.
Kvissle, Sweden: see NOLBY.
Kviteseid (kvē'tŭs-äd), village and canton (pop. 3,277), Telemark co., S Norway, 41 mi. WNW of Skien, on Kviteseid L. on Bandak-Norsja Canal; fishing, lumbering; large tourist traffic.
Kviteseid Lake, Telemark co., S Norway, 35 mi. WNW of Skien; part of Bandak-Norsja Canal; 6 mi. long, 1½ mi. wide, 692 ft. deep; alt. 236 ft. Fishing; tourist resort.
Kvitingsoy, Norway: see KVITSOY.
Kvitoya (kvēt'ûyä), Nor. *Kvitøya,* island (□ 102) of the Norwegian possession Svalbard, in Barents Sea of Arctic Ocean, bet. Northeast Land of Spitsbergen group (W) and Franz Josef Land (E); 80°9'N 32°30'E. Isl. is 26 mi. long (ENE–WSW), 3–5 mi. wide; rises to 886 ft. S. A. Andrée and 2 companions perished here (autumn, 1897) after crashing in attempt to reach North Pole by balloon; bodies recovered in 1930.
Kvitsoy (kvĭts'ûü), Nor. *Kvitsøy,* island (□ 1; pop. 657), in North Sea at entrance to Bokn Fjord, Rogaland co., SW Norway, 14 mi. NW of Stavanger. Fishing village of Leiasundet (NE) produces herring meal and oil. Formerly called Kvitingsoy.
Kwa, Belgian Congo: see KASAI RIVER.
Kwaadmechelen (kwäd'mākh"ŭlŭn), town (pop. 3,056), Limburg prov., NE Belgium, near junction of Albert Canal and Canal d'Embranchement, 9 mi. NNE of Diest; chemicals (sulphuric acid, superphosphates). Formerly spelled Quaedmechelen.
Kwachow or **Kua-chou** (gwä'jō'), town, N Kiangsu prov., China, 10 mi. SSW of Yangchow, and on Yangtze R. at mouth of Grand Canal; commercial center.
Kwa Ibo River (kwä ē'bō), SE Nigeria, in forest belt, rises near Ikot Ekpene, flows 70 mi. SSE to Gulf of Guinea below Eket.
Kwajalein (kwä'jälän, kwä'jŭlĕn), atoll (□ 6; pop. 832), largest of Marshall Isls., in Ralik Chain, W central Pacific; 8°43'N 167°44'E; 97 islets on lagoon c.60 mi. long. Largest islet is Kwajalein, ⊙ Marshall Isls. div. of U.S. Trust Territory of Pacific Isls. In Second World War, U.S. conquest of the Marshalls (Jap. stronghold) began here 1944 with taking of Kwajalein and its islets Roi (site of airfield) and Namur. U.S. naval and air bases established 1945; site of radio beacon. Sometimes spelled Kwajalong.
Kwakoegron (kwäkōōgrôn'), village (pop. 63), Surinam dist., N Du. Guiana, on Saramacca R., on Paramaribo-Dam RR and 40 mi. SSW of Paramaribo.
Kwaksan (kwäk'sän'), Jap. *Kakuzan,* township (1944 pop. 9,339), N.Pyongan prov., N Korea, 46 mi. SE of Sinuiju; agr., gold mining.
Kwakwani (kwäkwä'nē), village, Berbice co., NE Br. Guiana, on Berbice R. and 85 mi. SSW of New Amsterdam; bauxite mining.
Kwale (kwä'lā), town (pop. c.300), SE Kenya, on road and 17 mi. WSW of Mombasa; copra, sugar cane, fruits.
Kwale (kwälĕ'), town (pop. 1,591), Warri prov., Western Provinces, S Nigeria, on headstream of Benin R. and 35 mi. NE of Warri; road center; palm oil and kernels, hardwood, rubber, cacao, kola nuts.
Kwall (kwôl), town (pop. 2,164), Plateau Prov., Northern Provinces, central Nigeria, 18 mi. WSW of Jos, E of Kwall falls (800 ft. high). Tin-mining center.
Kwamouth (kwämōōt'), village, Leopoldville prov., SW Belgian Congo, on left bank of Congo R. (Fr. Equatorial Africa border) at mouth of the Kwa and 180 mi. SW of Inongo; trading center, steamboat landing; palm products.
Kwancheng or **Kuan-ch'eng** (gwän'chŭng'). **1** or **Kwanchengtze,** city, Kirin prov., Manchuria, China: see CHANGCHUN. **2** Town, ⊙ Kwancheng co. (pop. 75,109), N Pingyuan prov., China, 65 mi. ESE of Anyang, near Hopeh line; cotton weaving, mfg. of straw articles; wheat, rice, millet, beans. Until 1949 in Shantung prov.
Kwandang, Indonesia: see KUANDANG.
Kwando River (kwän'dō), Port. *Cuando,* S central Africa, rises on central plateau of Angola, flows SE, forming S section of Angola–Northern Rhodesia border, then crosses Caprivi Strip of South-West Africa, and loses itself in marshes along Bechuanaland Protectorate border near 18°30'S 23°30'E. Length, c.500 mi. Also called Linyanti. CHOBE RIVER is usually considered an extension of the Kwando, beyond the marshes.
Kwandruma, Belgian Congo: see NIOKA.
Kwang or **Kuang** (gwäng'), ancient province of S China. First formed in 3d cent. A.D., it was divided (14th cent.) into Kwangsi (W) and Kwangtung (E).
Kwangan or **Kuang-an** (both: gwäng'än'), town (pop. 18,207), ⊙ Kwangan co. (pop. 569,166), E central Szechwan prov., China, 38 mi. NE of Hochwan and on Chü R.; paper-milling center, match mfg.; rice, sweet potatoes, sugar cane, wheat, beans.
Kwangchang or **Kuang-ch'ang** (both: gwäng'chäng'). **1** Town, Hopeh prov., China: see LAIYÜAN. **2** Town (pop. 5,091), ⊙ Kwangchang co. (pop. 67,259), E Kiangsi prov., China, 80 mi. S of Fuchow and on upper Fu R.; rice-growing center; tea oil, sugar, tobacco; ramie weaving. Tungsten mining.
Kwangchon (kwäng'chŭn'), Jap. *Isen,* town (1949 pop. 17,488), S.Chungchong prov., S Korea, 35 mi. NNW of Kunsan; gold mining.
Kwangchow. 1 Town, Honan prov., China: see HWANGCHWAN. **2** City, Kwangtung prov., China: see CANTON.
Kwangchowan, China: see CHANKIANG.
Kwangchow Bay (gwäng'jō'), Chinese *Kwangchow Wan* or *Kuang-chou Wan* (wän'), inlet of S.China Sea, in SW Kwangtung prov., China, at NE base of Luichow Peninsula. Contains Tunghai and Siungchow isls. These isls. and a coastal strip, leased 1898–1945 to France, now constitute the municipality of CHANKIANG.
Kwangchowwan, China: see CHANKIANG.
Kwangfeng or **Kuang-feng** (both: gwäng'fŭng'), town (pop. 18,497), ⊙ Kwangfeng co. (pop. 298,195), NW Kiangsi prov., China, near Fukien-Chekiang line, 18 mi. ESE of Shangjao; tobacco, rice. Anthracite mine.
Kwanghan or **Kuang-han** (both: gwäng'hän'), town (pop. 22,480), ⊙ Kwanghan co. (pop. 274,996), NW Szechwan prov., China, 24 mi. NNE of Chengtu; rice, wheat, rapeseed, millet. Until 1913, Hanchow.
Kwanghwa or **Kuang-hua** (both: gwäng'hwä'), until 1947 **Laohokow** or **Lao-ho-k'ou** (lou'hŭ'kō'), town (pop. 29,333), ⊙ Kwanghwa co. (pop. 153,259), NW Hupeh prov., China, near Honan line, 200 mi. NW of Hankow, and on Han R. (head of regular navigation); major trade center serving NW Hupeh, SW Honan, and SE Shensi; cotton weaving, tung-oil processing; wheat, millet, kaoliang. A mission center originally named Laohokow, it was renamed (1947) when Kwanghwa co. seat was moved here from near-by village.
Kwangjao or **Kuang-jao** (both: gwäng'rou'), town, ⊙ Kwangjao co. (pop. 344,861), N Shantung prov., China, 45 mi. NW of Weifang; wheat, millet, peanuts, cotton. Until 1914 called Loan.
Kwangju (kwäng'jōō'), Jap. *Koshu* or *Kosyu* (both: kō'shōō), city (1949 pop. 138,883), ⊙ S.Cholla prov., S Korea, 165 mi. S of Seoul; 35°8'N 126°54'E; rail junction; textile center (cotton, silk). Has anc. temples and royal tombs.
Kwangling or **Kuang-ling** (both: gwäng'lĭng'), town, ⊙ Kwangling co. (pop. 84,914), SW Chahar prov., China, 50 mi. ESE of Tatung; millet, kaoliang. Until 1949 in Shansi.
Kwangnan or **Kuang-nan** (both: gwäng'nän'), town, ⊙ Kwangnan co. (pop. 104,035), southeasternmost Yunnan prov., China, near Kwangsi border, 65 mi. NE of Wenshan; alt. 4,511 ft.; cotton textiles; rice, millet, wheat, beans, sugar cane, timber. Antimony deposits near by.
Kwangning, Manchuria: see PEHCHEN.
Kwango, district, Belgian Congo: see KIKWIT.
Kwango River (kwäng'gō), Port. *Cuango,* principal left tributary of Kasai R., in N Angola and SW Belgian Congo, rises in central plateau of Angola S of Alto Chicapa, flows c.300 mi. NW, then, turning NNW, forms Angola–Belgian Congo border for over 200 mi., and flows N in Belgian Congo to the Kasai just below Banningville. Total length, c.700 mi. Navigable from Senga (just below Guillaume and François-Joseph Falls). Receives Wamba and Kwilu rivers (right).
Kwangping or **Kuang-p'ing** (both: gwäng'pĭng'), town, ⊙Kwangping co. (pop. 84,257), SW Hopeh prov., China, 45 mi. SSE of Singtai; cotton, wheat, beans, corn, kaoliang. Until 1913, the name Kwangping was applied to YUNGNIEN.
Kwangshan or **Kuang-shan** (both: gwäng'shän'), town, ⊙ Kwangshan co. (pop. 249, 048), SE Honan prov., China, 50 mi. ESE of Sinyang; rice, wheat, beans, kaoliang.
Kwangshui or **Kuang-shui** (both: gwäng'shwā'), town, E Hupeh prov., China, near Honan line, 75 mi. NNW of Hankow, and on Peking-Hankow RR; commercial center.
Kwangsi or **Kuang-hsi** (both: kwăng'sē', gwäng'shē') [Chinese,=W section of the Kwang], prov-

ince (□ 85,000; pop. 15,000,000) of S China; ⊙ Kweilin. Bounded SW by N Vietnam, W by Yunnan, N by Kweichow and Hunan along the Nan Ling range, and E by Kwangtung, the prov. is separated from the Gulf of Tonkin (S) by the W panhandle of Kwangtung. A SE continuation of the Kweichow-Yunnan tableland, Kwangsi consists of weathered limestone and sandstone formations, which are frequently striking scenery, dissected deeply by the headstreams (Kwei, Liu, Hungshui, Yü, Li rivers) of West R., one of China's major streams, whose upper basin Kwangsi occupies. The climate is temperate (N) and tropical (S); the latter is conditioned by a long, wet summer (April–Oct.) and monsoon rainfall. Agr. is largely confined to low-lying fields where 1–2 crops of rice are grown. In higher areas, sugar cane, cotton, corn, and tobacco are raised. Fruit, nuts (litchi, walnuts), ramie (Kwei R. valley) are also produced. Among Kwangsi's exports are cassia (or Chinese cinnamon), camphor, and tung oil. Mineral resources (gold, silver, tin, antimony) are little exploited. Trade proceeds mainly along river valleys (Yü branch of West R. system). There is a good road net and the prov. is connected by rail with Hunan, Kweichow, and N Vietnam. The leading cities are Liuchow (rail hub), Wuchow (E trade focus and steamer port on West R.), Nanning (center for trade with Vietnam), Kweilin, and Poseh (trade center near Yunnan border). Pop. is composed of Chinese (Mandarin-speaking Hunan immigrants in N and Cantonese element in S), Hakka (extreme E), Yao (in the Yao Shan area), and the Thai-speaking aborigines known as Ikias or Dioi (W). Originally combined with Kwangtung in anc. Kwang prov., Kwangsi was separated in 14th cent. It passed in 1650 to Manchu rule. During Second World War, it was partly occupied in 1944–45 by Japanese, and came under Communist control in 1949–50. The traditional name of prov. is Kwei, the Chinese word for cassia.

Kwangsi, town, China: see LUSI, Yunnan prov.

Kwangsin, town, China: see SHANGJAO.

Kwangsin River (gwäng'shĭn'), Chinese *Kwangsin Kiang* or *Kuang-hsin Chiang* (both: jyäng), NE Kiangsi prov., China, rises on Chekiang border, flows 180 mi. SW and W, past Yüshan, Shangjao (formerly Kwangsin), Kweiki, and Yükiang, to S Poyang L.

Kwangteh or **Kuang-te** (gwäng'dŭ'), town, ⊙ Kwangteh co. (pop. 159,164), S Anhwei prov., China, near Kiangsu-Chekiang line, 60 mi. ESE of Wuhu; mfg. of paper; rice, silk.

Kwangtseh or **Kuang-tse** (both: gwäng'dzŭ'), town (pop. 7,662), ⊙ Kwangtseh co. (pop. 53,576), NW Fukien prov., China, 65 mi. WNW of Kienow, on Kiangsi line; rice, wheat, tea; coal mines. Part of Kiangsi prov., 1934–47.

Kwangtsi or **Kuang-chi** (both: gwäng'jē'), town (pop. 23,253), ⊙ Kwangtsi co. (pop. 241,806), SE Hupeh prov., China, 17 mi. ENE of Kichun; rice, cotton, tobacco, peanuts.

Kwangtsung or **Kuang-tsung** (both: gwäng'dzŏŏng'), town, ⊙ Kwangtsung co. (pop. 103,156), SW Hopeh prov., China, 35 mi. E of Singtai; cotton, wheat, beans, chestnuts.

Kwangtung or **Kuang-tung** (both: gwäng'dŏŏng') [Chinese,=E section of the Kwang], southernmost province (□ 85,000; pop. 32,000,000) of China, on S.China Sea; ⊙ Canton. Includes prov. proper on Chinese mainland, HAINAN isl., and the SOUTH CHINA SEA isls. and reefs (Pratas, Paracel, and Nansha isls.) under Chinese sovereignty. The only remaining foreign enclaves in China, MACAO and HONG KONG, are on Kwangtung's coast. Mainland Kwangtung is bounded NE by Fukien, N by Kiangsi and Hunan along the Nan Ling system, NW by Kwangsi, and touches in extreme W on N Vietnam. Generally mountainous, Kwangtung's relief consists of low sandstone formations inland and of granitic hills along the indented isl.-studded shore. The coast line, the longest of any Chinese prov., is broken only by the alluvial flatlands of the CANTON RIVER DELTA, the economic heart of the prov., and the Han R. delta. The Luichow Peninsula, opposite Hainan isl., is the most prominent coastal feature. Physiographically, Kwangtung is divided into the Mei-Han R. valley (E) oriented toward Swatow; the central valleys of East, North, and West rivers, converging on Canton; and the W coastal strip extending to the Vietnam border bet. Kwangsi and the sea. Traversed by the Tropic of Cancer, Kwangtung has, except for the cooler interior mts., a tropical monsoon climate of high humidity. The rainy spring and summer (when occasional typhoons occur) are followed by a clear, cool, and dry winter (Oct.–Feb.) and a short, muggy, variable transition period (March–April). Yearly rainfall varies from 50 inches (W) to 70 inches (E). Agr. (mainly wet farming) is restricted to the river valleys and delta lowlands, whose alluvium is in contrast to the poor soils of the bare hillsides. In the lowlands, 2 crops of rice and 1 crop of fruit and vegetables supply the main food products, but the prov. remains a rice-deficit area. Sugar cane, tobacco, wheat are produced in Swatow area, bananas near Tungkun, tangerines along coast. Silk is the premier cash crop and the prov.'s leading export. Grass matting (Tungkun) and palm-leaf fans (Sunwui) are other important export products. Timber is floated down North R. to Namhoi, and bamboo grows along Sui R. The chief mineral resources are tungsten, manganese, coal, and iron. The leading industrial centers are Canton and its satellite town of Namhoi, Swatow (E), Kükong (N), and Chankiang (SW). Transportation depends mainly on West, North, East, and Mei-Han rivers; on railroads radiating from Canton to Samshui, Kükong (on N–S line to Hankow), and Kowloon, and on the Chaoan-Swatow and Sunwui-Towshan lines. The leading ports are Canton, Pakhoi, Hoihow (on Hainan isl.), Chankiang, Swatow, in addition to Hong Kong, which handles the bulk of Kwangtung's overseas trade. Canton and its outer port of Whampoa are accessible only to shallow-draught river steamers. The Cantonese, the original Chinese immigrants, who are settled chiefly in Canton R. delta and in West R. basin, constitute the bulk of the pop., which is overwhelmingly non-Mandarin speaking. Later Chinese immigration brought the Hakka from Kiangsi into the upper North and East river valleys, and the Hoklo from Fukien to the Swatow area, Luichow Peninsula, and Hainan isl. Among the few remaining aborigines are the Yao (SW; descendants of the region's original Thai pop.) and the Ikias or Chungkias on the Hunan (NW) line. The region, originally known as Yüeh, came under Chinese suzerainty after 211 B.C. under the Tsin dynasty. The region, 1st known as Nanhai, became part of anc. prov. of Kwang under the Three Kingdoms (A.D. 220–280), and was separated (14th cent.) as Kwangtung under the Ming dynasty. It passed to Manchu control in 1650. Kwangtung was the main scene of China's early foreign contacts, chiefly through Canton, having been regularly visited for centuries by Arab, Hindu, and Parsi traders. First European contact was (16th cent.) with the Portuguese; and Canton was, prior to 1842, the only port open to foreign trade. During 19th cent., a large-scale Chinese overseas emigration began in Kwangtung; HONG KONG was ceded to Britain, MACAO to Portugal, and Kwangchowwan (CHANKIANG; returned to China in 1945) to France. Isolated from the rest of China, Kwangtung nevertheless was also a scene of unrest during the Chinese revolution (1911). Here the Kuomintang was formed (1912) under the leadership of Sun Yat-sen, and here Chiang Kai-shek began his drive (1920s) for the unification of the country. During Sino-Japanese War, the prov. was partly occupied during 1938–45 by the Japanese. It passed to Chinese Communist control in 1949.

Kwangtung or **Kuang-t'ung** (both: gwäng'tŏŏng'), town, ⊙ Kwangtung co. (pop. 29,520), central Yunnan prov., China, 15 mi. NE of Tsuyung; alt. 6,299 ft.; rice, wheat, millet, beans. Coal mines near by.

Kwangwu. **1** or **Kuang-wu** (gwäng'wōō'), town, ⊙ Kwangwu co. (pop. 74,103), N Honan prov., China, 20 mi. NW of Chengchow, near Yellow R.; agr. products. **2** or **K'uang-wu** (kwäng'wōō'), town, ⊙ Kwangwu co. (pop. 148,664), NW Shantung prov., China, 20 mi. ESE of Tehchow; grain, peanuts, melons. Until 1949 called Linghsien.

Kwangyüan or **Kuang-yüan** (both: gwäng'yüän'), town (pop. 30,575), ⊙ Kwangyüan co. (pop. 197,739), N Szechwan prov., China, on Kialing R. and 60 mi. N of Langchung, near Shensi line; match mfg., tobacco processing; mushrooms, rice, sweet potatoes, wheat, millet. Gold, iron, sulphur, coal, graphite, and rock crystal found near by.

Kwanhsien or **Kuan-hsien** (both: gwän'shyĕn'). **1** Town, ⊙ Kwanhsien co. (pop. 211,844), N Pingyuan prov., China, on main road and 65 mi. NE of Anyang, near Hopeh line; cotton weaving; wheat, millet, sesame, peanuts. Until 1949 in Shantung prov. **2** Town (pop. 47,025), ⊙ Kwanhsien co. (pop. 296,766), N Szechwan prov., China, 35 mi. NW of Chengtu, and on Min R., where it splits into the irrigation arms of the Chengtu plain; trades in tea and medicinal plants. Agr.: rice, wheat, beans, rapeseed. Coal mines, iron, gold deposits near by.

Kwania, Lake (kwä'nyä), central Uganda, NW arm of L. Kyoga; c.40 mi. long. Partly filled with papyrus-reed swamps.

Kwanling or **Kuan-ling** (both: gwän'lĭng'), town (pop. 3,464), ⊙ Kwanling co. (pop. 111,701), SW Kweichow prov., China, 35 mi. SW of Anshun; alt. 3,806 ft.; grain, hides; asbestos mining.

Kwanmo, Mount (kwän'mô'), Jap. *Kambo-ho*, Korean *Kwanmo-bong*, peak (8,337 ft.), N.Hamgyong prov., N Korea, 30 mi. WSW of Chongjin. Sometimes spelled Kanbo.

Kwansi, Kuansi, or **Kuan-hsi** (all: gwän'shē'), Jap. *Kansai* (kän'sī), village (1935 pop. 3,453), NW Formosa, 13 mi. E of Sinchu; tea, oranges, livestock; wood products.

Kwantao or **Kuan-t'ao** (both: gwän'tou'), town, ⊙ Kwantao co. (pop. 224,051), S Hopeh prov., China, on Wei R. and 85 mi. W of Tsinan; cotton weaving; wheat, kaoliang, beans.

Kwantien or **K'uan-tien** (both: kwän'dyĕn'), town, ⊙ Kwantien co. (pop. 264,267), SE Liaotung prov., Manchuria, 45 mi. NNE of Antung; railroad terminus; mica, copper, and lead-zinc deposits.

Kwanto or **Kanto** (both: kän'tō'), largest and most densely populated plain (□ c.5,000) of Japan, in central Honshu; contains Tokyo-Yokohama industrial belt. Rural area produces rice, tea, dry grains, and tobacco.

Kwantu, China: see KUCHANG, Yunnan prov.

Kwantung or **Kuan-tung** (both: kwăn'tŏŏng', Chinese gwän'dŏŏng'), Jap. *Kanto* (kän'tō'), former Japanese leased territory (□ 1,337; 1941 pop. 1,493,491) in S Manchuria, on S tip (Kwantung peninsula) of Liaotung peninsula. Dairen was its ⊙ (after 1937), free port, and economic center; Port Arthur, its naval base. The territory included the peninsula S of 39°30'N and the adjacent isls., notably the Changshan Isls. Kwantung began to be developed by the Chinese in the 1880s, and was leased in 1898 by the Russians from China for 25 years as the S exit of the Chinese Eastern RR, then under construction. After the Russo-Japanese war, the Kwantung lease was transferred (1905) to Japan, which in 1915 obtained from China an extension of the original lease for 99 years, i.e., until 1997. Following the Second World War, however, the greater part of Kwantung was inc. (1945) into the PORT ARTHUR naval base dist.

Kwantzeling or **Kuan-tzu-ling** (both: gwän'dzû'-lĭng'), Jap. *Kanshirei* (känshē'rā), village (1935 pop. 996), W central Formosa, 9 mi. E of Howpi (linked by rail), 10 mi. SSE of Kiayi; health resort with carbonated springs.

Kwanyang or **Kuan-yang** (both: gwän'yäng'), town, ⊙ Kwanyang co. (pop. 122,042), NE Kwangsi prov., China, 50 mi. ENE of Kweilin, near Hunan line; rice, wheat, beans. Tungsten mines near by.

Kwanyün or **Kuan-yün** (both: gwän'yün'), town (pop. 65,029), ⊙ Kwanyün co. (pop. 434,950), N Kiangsu prov., China, near Shantung line, 8 mi. SE of Sinhai, and on Yen R.; salt-producing center; wheat, beans, kaoliang. Until 1912, Panpu.

Kwanza River, Angola: see CUANZA RIVER.

Kwa River, Belgian Congo: see KASAI RIVER.

Kwash, Iran: see KHASH.

Kwatsang Mountains, Chinese *Kua-ts'ang Shan* (gwä'tsäng' shän'), SE Chekiang prov., China, near coast, bet. Ling (N) and Wu (S) rivers; rises to 4,655 ft. SW of Linhai.

Kwatta (kwä'tä), village (pop. 2,037), Surinam dist., N Du. Guiana, 6 mi. W of Paramaribo; coffee, rice, sugar cane.

Kwei, province, China: see KWANGSI.

Kwei, river, China: see KWEI RIVER.

Kweichih or **Kuei-ch'ih** (both: gwā'chû'), town, ⊙ Kweichih co. (pop. 132,866), S Anhwei prov., China, 25 mi. ENE of Anking and on right bank of Yangtze R.; rice, cotton, wheat, rapeseed, silk. Coal mining near by. Until 1912, Chihchow.

Kweichow or **Kuei-chou** (both: kwā'chou', gwā'jō') [Chinese,=valuable region], province (□ 65,000; pop. 11,000,000) of SW China; ⊙ Kweiyang. Bounded N by Szechwan, W by Yunnan, S by Kwangsi, and E by Hunan, Kweichow forms a continuation of the E Yunnan plateaus, sloping from 4,000 ft. (W) to 2,000 ft. (E). Its tableland, located on Yangtze-West R. watershed, is cut on its periphery by the access valleys of the Ho or Chihshui (N), the Wu (Kweichow's chief river, which bisects the prov.), the upper Yüan (E), and the Hungshui and Liu (headstreams of West R.; S). Its less-dissected, central portion, around Kweiyang, forms the economic heart of Kweichow. The climate is influenced by summer monsoon rains (June–Sept.) and unhealthy, tropical conditions in the S valleys. Poor soil and steep, narrow valleys reduce agr. to a subsistence level. Rice (in the valleys) and corn, wheat, beans (on the plateau) are the chief food crops. Some cotton, tobacco, and tea are produced. The wealth of the prov. lies in its forest resources, yielding tung oil and lacquer, and construction timber (conifers, oak, chestnut) floated down the numerous access rivers, notably the Yüan. Of its mineral resources, only mercury is mined for export, at Yüping (on Hunan border) and near Hingi (SW). Coal, tungsten, bauxite, and copper are also found. The chief city is Kweiyang (center), where highways from the adjoining provs. converge. Kweiyang is also the center of the projected rail network of which only the S line from Kwangsi existed in 1950. Other towns are Tsunyi (the N gateway), Pichieh (NW), Anshun (W central), Hingi (SW), Chenyüan (the leading E trade center), and Szenan (NE). Pop. is 80% Chinese, settled largely in the urban centers and the peripheral access valley. The rural plateau areas are inhabited chiefly by the Miao aborigines (SE; known for their embroidery work), the Chungkias or Ikias (S; descendants of 10th-cent. Chinese settlers, speaking a Thai dialect), and the Lolos (SW). Under China's suzerainty since 10th cent., Kweichow became a prov. in 17th cent. under the Ming dynasty, but the Miao pop. was not completely subdued until c.1870. Prov. remained in Chinese hands during Sino-Japanese War (1937–45) and passed in 1950 to Communist control. The traditional name of Kweichow is Kien or Ch'ien, so called for Kien R., the main stream of prov.

Kweichow. **1** Town, Hupeh prov., China: see TZEKWEI. **2** Town, Szechwan prov., China: see FENGKIEH.

Kweichu or **Kuei-chu** (both: gwā'jōō'), town (pop. 10,754), ⊙ Kweichu co. (pop. 145,726), central Kweichow prov., China, 7 mi. S of Kweiyang; pottery center; cotton-textile mfg., tobacco processing, mat and embroidery making; rice, wheat, beans. Bauxite deposits and coal mines near by. Called Kwaki until 1930, when co. govt. was transferred here from KWEIYANG.

Kweihsien or **Kuei-hsien** (both: gwā'shyĕn'), town, ⊙ Kweihsien co. (pop. 467,436), SE Kwangsi prov., China. 35 mi. SW of Kweiping and on Yü R.; grain, beans, sugar cane, peanuts. Coal, silver, and zinc mines near by.

Kweihwa. 1 Town, Fukien prov., China: see MINGKI. 2 Town, Kweichow prov., China: see TZEYÜN. 3 Town, Suiyuan prov., China: see KWEISUI.

Kweiki or **Kuei-ch'i** (both: gwā'chē'), town (pop. 5,592), ⊙ Kweiki co. (pop. 179,085), NE Kiangsi prov., China, 50 mi. WSW of Shangjao and on Kwangsin R.; junction on Chekiang-Kiangsi RR; papermaking. Soapstone and coal mining.

Kwei Kiang, China: see KWEI RIVER.

Kweilin or **Kuei-lin** (both: gwā'lĭn'), city (1946 pop. 142,202; 1947 pop. 130,790), ⊙ Kwangsi prov., S China, on right bank of Kwei R. and 250 mi. NW of Canton; 25°20'N 110°10'E. Cultural and commercial center on Hunan-Kwangsi RR; cotton-textile mfg. (spinning, weaving, dyeing); processing of sugar, tung oil, paper; exports rice, wheat, beans, ramie, timber. Has univ. and medical col. Situated in amphitheater dominated by grotesque mtn. formations, city consists of right-bank walled town linked by bridge with left-bank commercial suburb. A municipality under provincial jurisdiction since 1930, it has been ⊙ Kwangsi except for temporary transfer (1913–36) to Nanning. A U.S. air base in Second World War, city was briefly occupied (1944–45) by Japanese.

Kweiping or **Kuei-p'ing** (both: gwā'pĭng'), town, ⊙ Kweiping co. (pop. 474,129), SE Kwangsi prov., China, on Sün R. section of West R., at confluence of Yü and Hungshui rivers, and 85 mi. W of Wuchow; rice, wheat, beans, millet. Manganese and coal deposits near by. Until 1913 called Sünchow.

Kwei River, Chinese *Kwei Kiang* or *Kuei Chiang* (both: gwā'jyäng'), W Kwangsi prov., China, rises near Hunan border, flows 200 mi. SE, past Kweilin, Pinglo, and Chaoping, joining Sün R. section of West R. at Wuchow to form West R. proper. Navigable for junks in entire course, it is linked in upper reaches by canal with Hunan's Siang R.

Kweishan Island or **Kuei-shan Island** (both: gwā'shän'), Jap. *Kizan* (kē'zän), volcanic island (1935 pop. 590) off NE Formosa, 13 mi. NE of Ilan; sulphur deposits; fisheries. Has caves and warm springs.

Kweishun, China: see TSINGSI.

Kweisui or **Kuei-sui** (gwā'swā'), city (1948 pop. 110,142), ⊙ Suiyuan prov., N China, on railroad and 250 mi. W of Peking, at foot of Tatsing Mts.; 40°47'N 111°37'E. Major commercial center, in grain and livestock area; flour milling, wool weaving (rugs), fur and hide processing, soap mfg. City consists of 2 sections, 1.5 mi. apart, known as Kweihwa (SW) and Suiyuan (NE). Kweihwa (called Kuku Hoto until 16th cent.) is a Mongolian political and religious center dating from 9th cent. It was the seat of the Grand Lama until his removal (1664) to Urga (Ulan Bator). The newer Chinese walled city of Suiyuan is the commercial and administrative center. In N Shansi until 1914, the 2 towns were combined in 1914 to form Kweisui, the ⊙ Suiyuan prov.; city became an independent municipality in 1948. Controlled by Japanese during 1937–45, it was (as Hohohoto) ⊙ Jap. puppet state of MENGKIANG.

Kweiteh or **Kuei-te** (both: gwā'dŭ'). 1 Town, Honan prov., China: see SHANGKIU. 2 Town, ⊙ Kweiteh co. (pop. 37,299), NE Tsinghai prov., China, 45 mi. SSW of Sining and on Yellow R.; center of fur and wool trade. Until 1928 in Kansu prov., and called Kükoshakia.

Kweiting or **Kuei-ting** (both: gwā'dĭng'), town (pop. 9,825), ⊙ Kweiting co. (pop. 105,401), central Kweichow prov., China, on railroad and 30 mi. E of Kweiyang; alt. 3,222 ft.; cotton-textile mfg., tobacco processing; wheat, millet, beans. Coal deposits near by. Projected rail junction.

Kweitung or **Kuei-tung** (both: gwā'dōōng'), town, ⊙ Kweitung co. (pop. 84,927), SE Hunan prov., China, near Kiangsi line, 65 mi. ENE of Chenhsien; tungsten and tin mining.

Kweiyang or **Kuei-yang** (both: gwā'yäng'). 1 Town, ⊙ Kweiyang co. (pop. 349,816), S Hunan prov., China, 30 mi. W of Chenhsien; rice, wheat, cotton. Antimony, copper, graphite, and arsenic found near by. Until 1913, the name Kweiyang was applied to JUCHENG. 2 City (1946 pop. 262,740; 1948 pop. 239,571), ⊙ Kweichow prov., China, 200 mi. S of Chungking; alt. 3,592 ft.; 26°35'N 106°43'E. Communications and industrial center; mfg. of cotton and silk textiles, glass, matches, ink, paper, chemicals; winegrowing; tobacco processing. Exports grain, hides, vegetable oil, pharmaceutical products. Coal mines near by. Has univ., teachers and medical colleges. Was ⊙ KWEICHU co. until it became municipality under provincial jurisdiction in 1930. A major hosp. center in Sino-Japanese War.

Kweneng (kwĕ'nĕng), district (pop. 40,126), SE Bechuanaland Protectorate; ⊙ Molepolole; co-extensive with Bakwena tribal reserve, established 1908.

Kwenlun, China: see KUNLUN.

Kwethluk (kwĭth'lōōk), Eskimo village (pop. 242), SW Alaska, on Kuskokwim R. and 12 mi. E of Bethel; base for trappers. Formerly spelled Quithlook.

Kwidjwi Island, Belgian Congo: see IDJWI ISLAND.

Kwidzyn, Poland: see MARIENWERDER.

Kwigamiut (kwĭ'gümūt), village (1939 pop. 12), W Alaska, at S end of Nunivak Isl.; 59°48'N 166°5'W; primitive native culture; carving, fishing.

Kwigillingok (kwĭgĭ'lĭn-gŏk), village (pop. 244), SW Alaska, on N side of Kuskokwim Bay, 65 mi. NW of Platinum; 59°43'N 162°52'W; outfitting point for trappers and prospectors. Formerly sometimes spelled Quillingok.

Kwiguk (kwē'zhŭk), village (1939 pop. 25), W Alaska, on Yukon R., 30 mi. NE of its mouth, 120 mi. SSE of Nome; fishing, fish processing, trapping.

Kwilu River (kwē'lōō), Port. *Cuilo* (kwē'lōō), right tributary of Kwango R. in N Angola and S Belgian Congo, rises near Alto Chicapa, flows c.650 mi. generally NNW, past Gungu and Kikwit (head of navigation), to the Kwango 8 mi. SSW of Banningville.

Kwilu River, Fr. Equatorial Africa: see KOUILOU RIVER.

Kwinhagak (kwĭ'nŭgăk, kwĭ'nŭk), Eskimo village. (pop. 194), SW Alaska, on E shore of Kuskokwim Bay, 50 mi. N of Platinum; 59°45'N 161°52'W; fishing and trapping. Site of Moravian mission. Formerly also spelled Quinhagak.

Kwisa River (kvē'sä), Ger. *Queis* (kvīs), in Lower Silesia, after 1945 in SW Poland, rises in the Isergebirge WSW of Hirschberg (Jelenia Gora), flows 65 mi. generally N, past Gryfow Slaski, Lesna (irrigation dam 2 mi. E), and Luban, to Bobrawa R. 5 mi. ESE of Sagan (Zagan).

Kwo, China: see KWO RIVER.

Kwo Ho, China: see KWO RIVER.

Kwohsien or **Kuo-hsien** (both: gwô'shyĕn'), town, ⊙ Kwohsien co. (pop. 238,654), N Shansi prov., China, on upper Huto R. and 25 mi. ESE of Ningwu, and on railroad; mat weaving; pear orchards. Coal mining near by.

Kwoliochen, China: see LINGPAO.

Kwongning (gwông'nĭng'), Mandarin *Kuang-ning* (gwäng'nĭng'), town (pop. 5,485), ⊙ Kwongning co. (pop. 254,653), W Kwangtung prov., China, near the Sui (a branch of North R.), 40 mi. NW of Samshui, in hilly region; grain. Gold mining.

Kwo River, Chinese *Kwo Ho* or *Kuo Ho* (gwô' hŭ'), N Anhwei prov., China, rises near Kaifend in Honan prov., flows 220 mi. SE, past Kihsien and Checheng in Honan prov., and Pohsien and Mengcheng in Anhwei prov., to Hwai R. at Hwaiyüan.

Kwoteh or **Kuo-te** (both: gwô'dŭ'), town, ⊙ Kwoteh co. (pop. 64,886), SW Kwangsi prov., China, 60 mi. NW of Nanning and on Yü R.; cotton textiles; rice, beans, corn, indigo.

Kwoyang or **Kuo-yang** (both: gwô'yäng'), town, ⊙ Kwoyang co. (pop. 469,499), N Anhwei prov., China, near Honan line, 45 mi. NE of Fowyang, and on Kwo R.; wheat, beans, kaoliang, buckwheat.

Kyabé (kyäbā'), village, S Chad territory, Fr. Equatorial Africa, 45 mi. ENE of Fort-Archambault; cotton ginning. Until 1946 in Ubangi-Shari colony.

Kyabram (kĭă'brŭm), town (pop. 2,137), N Victoria, Australia, 105 mi. N of Melbourne; fruitgrowing center; canned and dried fruit.

Kyaiklat (chĭk'lăt), town (pop. 10,658), Pyapon dist., Lower Burma, on Bogale R. (arm of Irrawaddy delta) and 40 mi. SW of Rangoon.

Kyaikpi (chĭkpē'), village, Myaungmya dist., Lower Burma, in Irrawaddy delta, 25 mi. SW of Maubin.

Kyaikto (chĭk'tō), town (pop. 6,611), Thaton dist., Lower Burma, on left bank of Sittang R. estuary and 70 mi. NW of Moulmein, on Pegu-Martaban RR; rice-growing area.

Kya-in Seikkyi (chä-ĭn"sākchē'), village, Amherst dist., Lower Burma, in Tenasserim, 45 mi. SE of Moulmein, on Ataran R. (head of navigation). Also spelled Kya-in Seikgyi.

Kyakhta (kyäkh'tŭ), city (1936 pop. estimate 12,300), SE Buryat-Mongol Autonomous SSR, Russian SFSR, on Ulan-Ude–Ulan-Bator highway, 115 mi. SSW of Ulan-Ude, on Mongolian border opposite Altan Bulak (Mongolia). Transit point for USSR-Mongolian trade; brickmaking, meat plants, shoe mfg. Regional mus., teachers col. Founded 1728 as Rus. fortress on the then Chinese frontier and named Troitskosavsk; developed with adjacent Kyakhta village (S) as major commercial center for Russo-Chinese trade (tea, leather, furs). Declined after 1860s. Entire city named Kyakhta c.1935. Sometimes Kiakhta.

Kyakisalmi, Russian SFSR: see PRIOZERSK.

Kyangin (chăng'gĭn), town (pop. 6,780), Henzada dist., central Lower Burma, on right bank of Irrawaddy R. and 35 mi. S of Prome; head of railroad to Henzada.

Kyardla, Estonia: see KARDLA.

Kyaring Tso or **Kyaring Tsho** (both: kyä'rĭng tsō'), Chinese *Cha-lin Hu* (jä'lĭn' hōō'), lake in central Tibet, on Chang Tang plateau, 180 mi. NW of Lhasa; 31°10'N 88°15'E; 40 mi. long, 10 mi. wide.

Kyaukme (chouk'mĕ), village, Hsipaw state, Northern Shan State, Upper Burma, on Mandalay-Lashio RR and 55 mi. SW of Lashio.

Kyaukmedaung (choukmĕdoung'), village, Tavoy dist., Lower Burma, in Tenasserim, on road and 15 mi. ENE of Tavoy, on ridge of central Tenasserim Range; mining center for tin, tungsten, molybdenum.

Kyaukmyaung (chouk-myoun'), village, Shwebo dist., Upper Burma, on right bank of Irrawaddy R. and 15 mi. E of Shwebo; handles Shwebo river trade.

Kyaukpadaung(chouk"pŭdoung'),village,Myingyan dist., Upper Burma, 35 mi. S of Pakokku; head of railroad to Pyinmana, on N plateau of Pegu Yoma, at SW foot of Mt. Popa. Sesame, palm sugar. Pagoda is site of yearly pilgrimage.

Kyaukpyu (chouk'pyōō), central district (□ 4,793; 1941 pop. 252,281) of Arakan div., Lower Burma; ⊙ Kyaukpyu. Bet. Bay of Bengal and Arakan Yoma; includes Ramree and Cheduba isls. Drained by An R.; mostly hilly and forested; narrow coastal strip is cut up by many isls. in mangrove swamps. Petroleum on main off-shore isls. Pop. is 90% Burmese, 8% Chin. Served by coastal steamers and An Pass route.

Kyaukpyu, town (pop. 4,232), ⊙ Kyaukpyu dist., Lower Burma, in Arakan, on N end of Ramree Isl.; one of best natural harbors on Arakan coast, linked by steamer with Akyab, Cheduba, Sandoway, and lower An R.; rice trade.

Kyaukse (chouk'sĕ'), district (□ 1,241; 1941 pop. 152,506), Mandalay div., Upper Burma; ⊙ Kyaukse. In dry zone (annual rainfall 30 in.), it lies S of Myitnge R. in Samon R. plain and Shan hills. Irrigated agr.: rice (2–3 crops yearly), sesame, beans. Served by Rangoon-Mandalay RR. Pop. is 90% Burmese.

Kyaukse, town (pop. 7,353), ⊙ Kyaukse dist., Upper Burma, on Rangoon-Mandalay RR and 20 mi. S of Mandalay; trade with Shan State. Pagoda built 1028.

Kyauktan (chouk-tän'), village, Hanthawaddy dist., Lower Burma, near Rangoon R., 14 mi. SE of Rangoon.

Kyauktaw (chouk'tô), village, Akyab dist., Lower Burma, in Arakan, on Kaladan R. and 45 mi. N of Akyab.

Kyaunggon (choung-gōn'), village, Bassein dist., Lower Burma, in Irrawaddy delta, 35 mi. NE of Bassein.

Kyava, Estonia: see KAVA.

Kybartai, Kibartai, or **Kibartay** (kēbär'tī), Pol. and Rus. *Kibarty*, city (pop. 7,337), S Lithuania, on railroad (VIRBALIS station) and 3 mi. NW of Virbalis city, adjoining Chernyshevskoye (Kaliningrad oblast); foundry, tin-metal works; mfg. of knitwear, shoes, furniture, chemicals; sawmilling, oilseed pressing. Developed in 19th cent. around railroad customs station on East Prussian border; in Rus. Suvalki govt. until 1920.

Kyburg or **Kiburg** (both: kē'bōōrk), village (pop. 362), Zurich canton, N Switzerland, 3 mi. S of Winterthur. Medieval castle (now historical mus.) of counts of Kyburg.

Kyebogyi (chăbōjē'), former Karenni state (□ 790; pop. 14,282) of Upper Burma; ⊙ was Kyebogyi, village 20 mi. S of Loikaw. Pop: Red Karens. Since 1947, part of the Karenni State.

Kyeintali (chān'tŭlē), village, Sandoway dist., Lower Burma, on Arakan coast, 30 mi. S of Sandoway.

Kyelang (kyā'lŭng), village, Kangra dist., NE Punjab, India, in Punjab Himalayas (alt. c.10,200 ft.), on Bhaga R. (headstream of the Chenab) and 50 mi. NE of Dharmsala.

Kyerong, Kyirong (kyē'rông), or **Girang** (gē'räng), Chinese *Chi-lung* (jē'lōōng'), town, S Tibet, in N Nepal Himalayas, on Trisuli R. and 50 mi. N of Katmandu (Nepal); 28°26'N 85°18'E; alt. 9,100 ft. Hot spring near by.

Kyffhäuser (kĭf'hoi"zŭr), small wooded mountain range, central Germany, N of Bad Frankenhausen, separated from the lower Harz by the Goldene Aue; rises to 1,565 ft. in the Külpenberg. Ruined castles of Rothenburg (7th cent.) and Kyffhausen (12th cent.) are WSW of Sangerhausen. According to legend, Emperor Frederick I (Frederick Barbarossa) sleeps in limestone cave here and will arise to restore German greatness. Originally applied to Emperor Frederick II, legend was popularized in poems by Rückert, Uhland, and Heine.

Kyi Chu or **Kyi Chhu** (chē' chōō'), river, SE Tibet, chief left tributary of upper Brahmaputra R., rises in E central Nyenchen Tanglha range in several headstreams joining 40 mi. NNE of Lhasa; flows SE and SW, past Ganden, Dechen, and Lhasa, to the Brahmaputra 4 mi. N of Kongka; 195 mi. long. Used as transportation (mainly yak-hide coracles) artery for Lhasa.

Kyjov (kĭ'yôf), Ger. *Gaya* (gä'yä), town (pop. 4,870), S Moravia, Czechoslovakia, on railroad and 26 mi. ESE of Brno; glass mfg., wine making, flour milling, lignite mining, natural-gas production. Extensive orchards and vineyards in vicinity. Picturesque regional folkways attract many tourists. Has ethnographic mus.

Kyklades, Greece: see CYCLADES.

Kyk-over-all (kĭk), islet in N Br. Guiana, at confluence of Cuyuni and Mazaruni rivers, 4 mi. SW of Bartica. One of 1st Du. settlements and once a flourishing trading post. Old fort.

Kyle, village (pop. 234), SW Sask., 40 mi. NNW of Swift Current; wheat.

Kyle or **Kyle of Lochalsh** (kīl, lŏkh-ălsh'), fishing village in Lochalsh parish (pop. 1,525), SW Ross and Cromarty, Scotland, at mouth of Loch Alsh, 60 mi. WSW of Inverness. It is terminal of car ferry to Kyleakin, Skye. In narrow entrance to Loch Alsh from the Inner Sound (N), called Kyle Akin, is small Gillean Isl. (pop. 3), site of lighthouse (57°18'N 4°44'W).

Kyle, town (pop. 888), Hays co., S central Texas, near Blanco R., 21 mi. SSE of Austin; trade point in agr. area; creamery, cotton gin.

Kyle of Lochalsh, Scotland: see KYLE.

Kyle of Sutherland, Scotland: see OYKELL RIVER.

Kyle of Tongue, Scotland: see TONGUE.

Kyle Rhea, Scotland: see ALSH, LOCH.

Kyles of Bute (kīlz, būt), 10-mi.-long arm (c.1 mi. wide) of the Firth of Clyde, Scotland, extending around N part of Isle of Bute, separating it from Cowal peninsula of S Argyll.

Kyllburg (kül'bŏŏrk), village (pop. 1,225), in former Prussian Rhine Prov., W Germany, after 1945 in Rhineland-Palatinate, 19 mi. N of Trier; tourist center in the Eifel. Has Gothic church. Formerly also spelled Killburg.

Kyllene or **Killini** (both: kĭlē'nē), Lat. *Cyllene* (sĭlē'nē), village (pop. 744), Elis nome, on Westernmost Peloponnesus, Greece, Ionian Sea port 23 mi. NW of Pyrgos; rail terminus. Remains of 13th-cent. French castle. It is on **Cape Kyllene** (37°56'N 21°9'E) at S end of **Gulf of Kyllene**, a broad but slight inlet of Ionian Sea, 20 mi. wide. Sometimes spelled Kyllini. These features were formerly called Glarentza or Klarentza (Ital. *Chiarenza*).

Kyllene Mountains or **Killini Mountains**, Lat. *Cyllene*, in Argolis and Corinthia nome, N Peloponnesus, Greece; 15 mi. long; rise to 7,792 ft., 27 mi. NW of Argos. Formerly called Zeria or Ziria.

Kyme or **Kimi** (both: kē'mē), Lat. *Cyme* (sī'mē), town (pop. 4,071), E central Euboea, Greece, port on Aegean Sea, 29 mi. ENE of Chalcis; figs, walnuts, wines. Lignite deposits (S) and near Andronianoi, 3 mi. WNW. Cape Kyme is 3 mi. ENE at 38°38'N 24°10'E. Also spelled Kymi; formerly Koumi or Kumi.

Kymi (kü'mē), Swedish *Kymmene* (kü'mŭnŭ), county [Finnish *lääni*] (□ 4,146; including water area, □ 4,863; pop. 305,080), SE Finland; ⊙ Kotka. On Gulf of Finland (S) and on USSR border (E). Includes S part of Saimaa lake system. Drained by Kymi, Vuoksi, and several smaller rivers, and by Saimaa Canal. Noted falls and major hydroelectric station at Imatra. Agr. (rye, oats, barley), cattle raising, dairying. Kymi R. valley is industrial center; lumbering, timber processing, and woodworking are important. Other industries are metalworking, iron and steel milling, textile milling; mfg. of glass, cement, bricks. Granite and limestone quarries. Cities are Kotka, Lappeenranta, and Hamina. Co. was created 1945, comprising the part of former Viipuri co. not ceded to USSR.

Kymi, Swedish *Kymmene*, village (commune pop. 25,193), Kymi co., SE Finland, on Kymi R. and 5 mi. N of Kotka; rail junction; pulp and paper mills, insulating-material works.

Kymi, Greece: see KYME.

Kymi River, Finnish *Kymijoki* (kü'mēyō"kē), Swedish *Kymmene älv* (kü'mŭnŭ ĕlv"), SE Finland, issues from SE end of L. Päijänne, flows through several small lakes in winding course generally SE to Kuusankoski (rapids), thence flows S, over several rapids, past Inkeroinen, Anjala, and Kymi, to Gulf of Finland at Kotka; 90 mi. long. Provides hydroelectric power for one of Finland's chief industrial regions.

Kymmene, Finland: see KYMI.

Kyn (kĭn), town (1939 pop. over 500), E Molotov oblast, Russian SFSR, near Chusovaya R., 33 mi. SE (under jurisdiction) of Lysva, near railroad; bituminous-coal mining.

Kynaion, Cape, or **Cape Kinaion** (both: kĭnā'ôn), NW extremity of Euboea, Greece, bet. N Gulf of Euboea (E) and Maliaic Gulf (W). Formerly called Cape Lithada.

Kynance Cove (kī'năns), inlet of the Channel, W Cornwall, England, just NW of Lizard Head; site of interesting caves and serpentine rocks.

Kynaros or **Kinaros** (kē'nărô), Ital. *Chinaro* (kē'närô), Aegean island (□ 1.6; 1928 pop. 10) of the Dodecanese, Greece, NE of Amorgos; 36°59'N 26°17'E. It was considered part of Greece during Ital. rule of the Dodecanese.

Kyneton (kĭn'tŭn), town (pop. 3,081), S central Victoria, Australia, on Campaspe R. and 50 mi. NNW of Melbourne; livestock; flour, woolen mills; dairy plant. Gold mines near by.

Kynsperk nad Ohri (kĭn'shpĕrk näd' ôkhrē), Czech *Kynšperk nad Ohří*, Ger. *Königsberg an der Eger* (kû'nĭkhsbĕrk än dĕr ā'gŭr), village (pop. 2,045), W Bohemia, Czechoslovakia, on Eger R., on railroad, and 7 mi. NE of Cheb; woodworking; lumbering school.

Kynzvart, Czechoslovakia: see LAZNE KYNZVART.

Kyoga, Lake, or **Lake Kioga** (kyō'gä), many-armed lake (c.80 mi. long; alt. 3,390 ft.) in central Uganda, N of L. Victoria, formed by the Victoria Nile in its middle course. Has swampy papyrus-reed shores and long arms, including L. KWANIA (NW), L. Salisbury (NE), Mpologoma R. (SE), and Sezibwa R. (S). Shallow-draught navigation, especially bet. Namasagali and Masindi Port (only navigable section of Victoria Nile). Regulator dam (at lake's W end) is planned as part of Nile harnessing scheme.

Kyoga Point (kyō'gä), Jap. *Kyoga-misaki*, in Kyoto prefecture, S Honshu, Japan, in Sea of Japan; forms W side of entrance to Wakasa Bay; 35°47'N 135°14'E; lighthouse. Sometimes called Cape Kioga.

Kyogle (kīō'gŭl), town (pop. 2,686), NE New South Wales, 80 mi. S of Brisbane; dairying and agr. center; bananas.

Kyojo, Korea: see KYONGSONG.

Kyomipo (kyŭm'ē'pô'), Jap. *Kenjiho*, town (1944 pop. 53,035), Hwanghae prov., central Korea, N of 38°N, on Taedong R. and 20 mi. SSW of Pyongyang; mining center (iron, coal). Has steel mills and chemical plants.

Kyondo (chŏn'dō; Burmese chōng'gŭdō"), village, Amherst dist., Lower Burma, in Tenasserim, on Gyaing R. (head of navigation) and 27 mi. ENE of Moulmein.

Kyong (chông), W state (ngegunhmu) (□ 24; pop. 2,571), Southern Shan State, Upper Burma; ⊙ Kyong, village 25 mi. W of Taunggyi; grassy downs.

Kyonggi (kyông'gē'), Korean *Kyonggi-do*, Jap. *Keiki-do*, province [Jap. and Korean *do*] (□ 4,947; 1944 pop. 3,089,888), central Korea, bounded W by Yellow Sea; ⊙ SEOUL. Its port is CHEMULPO. Includes KANGHWA ISLAND and several other offshore isls. Hilly and generally forested terrain, drained by Han R. Stockraising, agr. (ginseng, tobacco), iron and gold mining. Seoul and Chemulpo are industrial centers. The major part of the prov. is S of 38°N.

Kyongju (kyŭng'jōō'), Jap. *Keishu* or *Keisyu*, town (1949 pop. 36,348), N.Kyongsang prov., S Korea, 35 mi. E of Taegu; rail junction, in coal-mining area; tourist center. There are mus. containing historical relics, 7th-cent. temple, 6th-cent. monastery, and anc. observatory. Near by is a cave with walls sculptured in 8th cent.; Kyongju was ⊙ (57 B.C.–A.D.935) of kingdom of Silla.

Kyongsang-namdo, Korea: see SOUTH KYONGSANG.

Kyongsang-pukdo, Korea: see NORTH KYONGSANG.

Kyongsong (kyŭng'sŭng'). **1** City, Kyonggi prov., Korea: see SEOUL. **2** Jap. *Kyojo*, town (1944 pop. 25,925), N.Hamgyong prov., N Korea, 10 mi. SW of Chongjin and just S of Nanam; agr. center (raw silk, tobacco). Has agr. school. Provincial ⊙ until 1920, preceding Nanam.

Kyonpyaw (chōnpyô'), town (pop. 5,866), Bassein dist., Lower Burma, on Daga R. (arm of Irrawaddy delta) and 45 mi. NE of Bassein; head of navigation for steamers.

Kyosai-to, Korea: see KOJE ISLAND.

Kyosho, Korea: see KOCHANG.

Kyoto (kyō'tō), prefecture [Jap. *fu*] (□ 1,784; 1940 pop. 1,729,993; 1947 pop. 1,739,084), S Honshu, Japan; ⊙ Kyoto. Bounded N by Sea of Japan; L. Biwa is just E. Principally urban, with major part of pop. centered in Kyoto area. Scattered rice fields; lumbering in mountainous interior. Mfg. (textiles, rubber goods), woodworking. Kyoto city is center of artistic crafts. Other centers: FUKUCHIYAMA, MAIZURU.

Kyoto, third largest city (□ 111; 1940 pop. 1,089,726; 1947 pop. 999,660) of Japan, ⊙ Kyoto prefecture, S Honshu, on Kamo R. (branch of Yodo R.) and 230 mi. WSW of Tokyo; 35°N 135°45'E. Anc. cultural center of Japan; artisan industries (cloisonné, porcelain, and lacquer ware, silk fabrics, bronzes, damascene work, dolls). YODO is its port. Kyoto is connected with L. Biwa by canal (7.5 mi. long) which supplies city with hydroelectric power. A center of Buddhism, Kyoto has many anc. temples (a few dating from 6th cent.), and a 58-ft. wooden image of Buddha. Seat of Doshisha Univ. (founded 1873 as Amer. mission col.) and Kyoto Imperial Univ. (1897). Site of tombs of Meiji, Hideyoshi, and Emperor Kwammu (founder of city). Has anc. imperial palace and 2 imperial villas. There are *kabuki* and *no* theaters; Nishijin mus. (1915) has textile collection. City founded in 8th cent. as Uda. Given the poetic name Heian-kyo [Jap.,=capital of peace and tranquillity] when it became ⊙ Japan in 794; was popularly called Kyoto and Miyako. In 1868, ⊙ was shifted to Tokyo [Jap.,=eastern capital], and Kyoto came to be known popularly as Saikyo [Jap.,=western capital]. In Second World War, only major Jap. city that escaped bombing. Formerly sometimes spelled Kioto.

Kyparissia or **Kiparissia** (both: kēpärĭsē'ŭ), Lat. *Cyparissiae* (sĭpŭrĭsĭ'ē), town (pop. 5,586), Messenia nome, SW Peloponnesus, Greece, port and rail head on Gulf of Kyparissia, 28 mi. WNW of Kalamata. Fisheries; wheat, olive oil. Lignite mine just NE. Castle on cliff above town. Known as Arcadia from Middle Ages until destruction (1825) by Turks.

Kyparissia, Gulf of, inlet of Ionian Sea, in SW Peloponnesus, Greece, SE of Cape Katakolon; 35 mi. wide, 10 mi. long. Kyparissia village is on SE shore. Formerly called Gulf of Arcadia.

Kypros: see CYPRUS.

Kyra (kĭrä'), village (1926 pop. 1,371), SW Chita oblast, Russian SFSR, 185 mi. SSW of Chita, near Mongolian border; gold mines.

Kyra Panagia, Greece: see PELGONESI.

Kyrchany (kĭrchä'nē), village (1939 pop. over 500), S central Korov oblast, Russian SFSR, 10 mi. NE of Molotovsk; leather products.

Kyren (kĭrĕn'), village (1948 pop. over 2,000), SW Buryat-Mongol Autonomous SSR, Russian SFSR, on Irkut R. and 95 mi. WSW of Irkutsk, on Irkutsk-Jibhalanta highway, in agr. and stock-raising area.

Kyrenia (kĭrē'nyŭ), district (□ 247; pop. 28,174), N Cyprus, on the Mediterranean; ⊙ KYRENIA. Traversed W-E by the Kyrenia Mts., which rise in W above 3,300 ft. Has a narrow coastal strip. Predominantly agr., producing carobs, olives, almonds, citrus fruit, oats, barley; stock raising (sheep, goats). Principal agr. center is LAPITHOS. There are several medieval castles.

Kyrenia, town (pop. 2,916), ⊙ Kyrenia dist., N Cyprus, 12 mi. N of Nicosia. Minor Mediterranean port and popular winter resort. Towered over by 12th-cent. castle; 4 mi. E is the Abbey of Bella Paise, noted for its Gothic architecture. Other ruined castles near by, among them 10th-cent. Ayios Hilarion (3 mi. SSW).

Kyrenia Mountains, N Cyprus, extend c.100 mi. along Mediterranean coast from Cape Kormakiti (W) to Cape Andreas (E) on Karpas Peninsula. Rise in W above 3,300 ft.; the lower E section on Karpas Peninsula is sometimes called Karpas or Karpass Mts. Bounds the fertile interior Messaoria basin.

Kyritz (kü'rĭts), town (pop. 8,679), Brandenburg, E Germany, 25 mi. N of Rathenow; mfg. of machinery, starch; flour milling. Has late-Gothic church, many half-timbered houses. Swedes under Torstensson here defeated (1635) Saxons.

Kyrkebyn (chür'kŭbün"), village (pop. 521), Varmland co., W Sweden, near NW shore of L. Vaner, 17 mi. WSW of Karlstad; pulp mills.

Kyrkerud, Sweden: see SAFFLE.

Kyrkesund (chür'kŭsŭnd'), fishing village (pop. 275), Goteborg och Bohus co., SW Sweden, on Haron (hâr'ûn"), Swedish *Härön*, isl. (2 mi. long) in the Skagerrak, 18 mi. S of Lysekil.

Kyrkjebo, Norway: see HOYANGER.

Kyrksaeterora (chürk'sătŭrŭ"rä), Nor. *Kyrksæterøra* (formerly *Kirksæterøra*), village (pop. 300) in Hemne (formerly Hevne) canton (pop. 2,132), Sor-Trondelag co., central Norway, at head of Hemne Fjord (12-mi. inlet of North Sea), 40 mi. WSW of Trondheim; animal husbandry; fishing; boatbuilding, shoe mfg.

Kyrkslatt (chürk'slĕt"), Swedish *Kyrkslätt*, Finnish *Kirkkonummi* (kĭrk'kōnŏŏm"mē), village in Soviet-leased defense region of Porkkala, S Finland, 17 mi. W of Helsinki. Has 14th-cent. church.

Kyrock (kī'rŏk), village, Edmonson co., central Ky., on Nolin R. and 21 mi. NNE of Bowling Green; rock asphalt mining.

Kyröskoski (kü'rûkôs"kē), Swedish *Kyröfors* (chü"-rûfôrs', -fôsh'), village in Hämeenkyrö commune (pop. 10,056), Turku-Pori co., SW Finland, in lake region, 20 mi. NW of Tampere; pulp, paper mills.

Kyserike (kī'zŭrĭk), resort village, Ulster co., SE N.Y., on Rondout Creek and 12 mi. SW of Kingston. Also called Alligerville (ă'lĭgŭrvĭl).

Kyshtovka (kĭshtôf'kŭ), village (1926 pop. 1,430), NW Novosibirsk oblast, Russian SFSR, on Tara R. (head of navigation) and 85 mi. N of Chany; dairy farming.

Kyshtym (kĭshtĭm'), city (1926 pop. 15,988; 1936 pop. estimate 38,400), N Chelyabinsk oblast, Russian SFSR, on SE slope of the central Urals, bet. several small lakes, 50 mi. NW of Chelyabinsk. Rail junction; leading copper-refining and -smelting center, based on Karabash deposits; mfg. (copper-refining machinery, boilers); mining and processing of cobalt, corundum, emery, barite, graphite, kaolin, and quartzite. Founded 1757 as ironworks of Verkhni Kyshtym. Industry shifted from ferrous to copper metallurgy after First World War. Became city in 1934; absorbed town of Severny (N) in 1948.

Kysibl-Kyselka, Czechoslovakia: see CARLSBAD.

Kysucke Nove Mesto (kĭ'sŏŏtskä nô'vä mĕ'stô), Slovak *Kysucké Nové Mesto*, Hung. *Kiszucaújhely* (kĭ'sŏŏkouĕhā"), town (pop. 2,318), NW Slovakia, Czechoslovakia, 5 mi. NNE of Zilina; lumbering.

Kyte River, N Ill., rises in E Lee co., flows c.40 mi. generally NW to Rock R. 3 mi. S of Oregon.

Kythera or **Kithira** (both: kē'thērä), Lat. *Cythera* (sĭthēr'ŭ), Ital. *Cerigo* (chārē'gō), island (□ 108.5; pop. 7,932), in Mediterranean Sea at mouth of Gulf of Laconia, part of Attica nome, Greece, 15 mi. SW of Cape Malea (SE Peloponnesus) across

Elaphonesi Channel; 36°20'N 22°58'E; 18 mi. long, 11 mi. wide. Olive oil, wine, figs, raisins, almonds, grain; sheep and goat raising; fisheries. On S shore lies the chief village, Kythera (pop. 1,235), formerly called Kapsali. Anc. Cythera was a center of the cult of Aphrodite and was noted for its purple-yielding murices, for which it was called Porphyrousa. Under Spartan and Athenian control in antiquity, its medieval history is that of the Ionian Isls., in which it is sometimes included.

Kythnos or **Kithnos** (both: kēth'nôs), Lat. *Cythnus* (sĭth'nŭs), Aegean island (□ 38; pop. 2,688) in the Cyclades, Greece, bet. Kea and Seriphos, W of Syros isl.; 37°25'N 24°28'E; 11 mi. long, 4 mi. wide; rises to 965 ft. Produces barley, wine, almonds, figs, olive oil. Hematite deposits. Main town, Kythnos (pop. 1,243) is near E shore. Colonized by Ionians. Ruled (1537–1832) by Turkey. Also called Thermia for hot springs on E coast.

Kythrea (kēthrā'ä), town (pop. 2,818), Nicosia dist., N Cyprus, at S foot of Kyrenia Mts., 8 mi. NE of Nicosia; wheat, citrus fruit, carobs, olives; cattle, hogs, sheep. Noted for its healthful climate.

Kytlym (kĭtlĭm'), town (1936 pop. estimate 6,500), W Sverdlovsk oblast, Russian SFSR, in the central Urals, on Lobva R. (left tributary of Lyalya R.) and 50 mi. NNW of Is; platinum-mining center; gold placers.

Kytmanovo (kĭtmä'nŭvŭ), village (1926 pop. 2,081), NE Altai Territory, Russian SFSR, on Chumysh R. and 70 mi. E of Barnaul, in agr. area.

Kyuko, Formosa: see KIUKANG.

Kyulyunken (kyōōlyōōnkyĕn'), village (1948 pop. over 500), E Yakut Autonomous SSR, Russian SFSR, on Tompo R. (right affluent of the Aldan) and 260 mi. NNE of Yakutsk; trading post; reindeer raising.

Kyunam La, pass, India: see ANTA DHURA.

Kyunhla (chōōnhŭlä'), village, Shwebo dist., Upper Burma, on Mu R. and 60 mi. NNW of Shwebo.

Kyurdakhany (kyōōrdŭkhä'nē), town (1939 pop. over 500) in Mashtagi dist. of Greater Baku, Azerbaijan SSR, near N shore of Apsheron Peninsula, 13 mi. NNE of Baku; vineyards.

Kyurdamir (kyōōrdŭmēr'), city (1932 pop. estimate 2,580), central Azerbaijan SSR, on railroad and 85 mi. W of Baku, in cotton and wheat dist.; wine making; metalworking, carpet weaving.

Kyushu (kyōō'shōō), island (□ 13,770; including offshore isls.: □ 14,990; 1940 pop. 8,963,715; 1947 pop. 11,398,976), Japan, bet. E.China Sea and Philippine Sea, just S of Honshu across Shimonoseki Strait, 115 mi. SE of Korea across Korea and Tsushima straits; 210 mi. long, 120 mi. wide. Southernmost, 3d largest, and most densely populated of 4 major isls. of Japan. Mountainous terrain rises to 5,850 ft. at Mt. Kuju in Oita prefecture. Volcanic Aso-san and hot springs are in Aso Natl. Park in the interior. There are hot springs in Unzen Natl. Park (on W peninsula) and Kirishima Natl. Park (S), but the greatest concentration is in NE area, with Beppu as the major center. Chikugo R. (largest river of isl.) drains extensive rice-growing area. Generally mild climate; mean annual temp. 60°F. Rainfall (88 in. annually) is especially heavy on E coast. Subtropical flora in S includes gum, palm, banana, camphor, and lichee trees. Most of its extensive forests are state-owned; trees include pine, Japan cedar, tallow trees (*sapium sebiferum*), bamboo. Greater production of rice in N, and of cereals and sweet potatoes in S. Tobacco, soybeans, and tea are grown everywhere; oranges, pears, and plums in E area. Extensive production of raw silk; numerous fisheries. Chikuho (principal coal field of Japan) is near major industrial centers of YAWATA, WAKAMATSU, and KOKURA; MOJI is principal coal-loading port, connected by a tunnel with Shimonoseki. Gold, silver, and iron are mined in S, tin in NE. Kyushu is known for its fine porcelain (Satsuma and Hizen ware). Principal exports: agr. products, lumber, tobacco, pottery. Isl. contains 7 prefectures: NAGASAKI (W), SAGA (NW), FUKUOKA (N), OITA (NE), KUMAMOTO (W), MIYAZAKI (E), KAGOSHIMA (S). Sometimes spelled Kiushiu and Kyusyu.

Kyustendil (kyōōstĕndēl'), anc. *Pautalia*, city (pop. 19,309), Sofia dist., W Bulgaria, on E slope of Osogov Mts., on right tributary of the Struma and 43 mi. SW of Sofia. Health resort; market and horticultural center in Kyustendil Basin (□ 54; average alt. 1,500 ft.; fruit, vineyards, truck, tobacco); fruit preserving, plum-brandy distilling, textile mfg.; vegetable hothouses, tobacco warehouses. Site of curative baths. Has teachers col., technical schools, archaeological mus., ruins of Roman temple. Once a Thracian settlement; became a health resort under Roman rule. Successively under First Bulg. Kingdom (until 1018) and Byzantium (1018–1186); site of defeat (1330) of Bulgarians by Serbs during Second Bulg. Kingdom. Under Turkish rule from 14th cent.; captured (1878) by Russians and ceded to Bulgaria. Called Pautalia and Ulpianum by Romans; renamed Velbuzhd by Bulgarians and Justiniana Secunda by Byzantines; known as Kyustendil since 15th cent. Sometimes spelled Keustendil or Kustendil.

Kyusyu, Japan: see KYUSHU.

Kyusyur (kyōōsyōōr'), village (1948 pop. over 2,000), N Yakut Autonomous SSR, Russian SFSR, on Lena R., opposite Bulun, and 260 mi. NW of Verkhoyansk; trading post; fishing; reindeer farms.

Kyutteyyu, Estonia: see KUTTEJOU.

Kywebwe (chwĕbwĕ'), village, Toungoo dist., Lower Burma, on Rangoon-Mandalay RR and 17 mi. S of Toungoo; road to ferry across Sittang R., 2 mi. E.

Kyzas (kĭzäs'), town (1939 pop. over 2,000), SW Khakass Autonomous Oblast, Krasnoyarsk Territory, Russian SFSR, 125 mi. SW of Abakan; gold mines.

Kyzyl, in Rus. names: see also KIZIL, KIZYL, KZYL.

Kyzyl (kĭzĭl') [Turkic,=red], city (1939 pop. over 10,000), ⊙ Tuva Autonomous Oblast, Russian SFSR, on Yenisei R. (here formed by junction of the Greater and Lesser Yenisei) and 305 mi. S of Krasnoyarsk, 2,300 mi. ESE of Moscow, on highway from Minusinsk; 51°40'N 94°25'E. Tanning, sheepskin mfg., woodworking. Coal mining near by. Called Belotsarsk before 1917; since then successively known as Krasny, Khem-Belder, Kyzyl-Khoto.

Kyzyl-Art Pass, Tadzhik SSR: see TRANS-ALAI RANGE.

Kyzyl-Burun (kĭzĭl"-bōōrōōn'), town (1946 pop. over 500), NE Azerbaijan SSR, on railroad and 60 mi. NNW of Baku, near Caspian Sea coast (fisheries); cotton.

Kyzyl-Dzhar, Kazakh SSR: see PETROPAVLOVSK, North Kazakhstan oblast.

Kyzyl-Khoto, Russian SFSR: see KYZYL.

Kyzyl-Kum (-kōōm'), extensive desert area in Kazakh and Uzbek SSR, extending SE from Aral Sea, bet. the Amu Darya and the Syr Darya; rises to 3,380 ft. in center; partially covered with sand dunes. Semi-nomadic raising of karakul sheep (S).

Kyzyl-Mazhalyk (-mŭzhŭlĭk'), village (1945 pop. under 500), SW Tuva Autonomous Oblast, Russian SFSR, on Khemchik R. and 160 mi. WSW of Kyzyl, on road, in agr. area.

Kyzyl-Rai, Kazakh SSR: see KAZAKH HILLS.

Kyzyl-Su (-sōō'). **1** River in S Osh oblast, Kirghiz SSR; rises in E Alai Range, flows c.130 mi. W, through fertile Alai valley (wheat, pastures), past Daraut-Kurgan, into Tadzhik SSR, joining the Muk-Su to form Surkhab R. 28 mi. ENE of Khait. **2** River in Kulyab oblast, Tadzhik SSR; rises in several branches N of Boldzhuan, flows c.120 mi. S, past Boldzhuan and Kzyl-Mazar, to Panj R. below Parkhar. Receives the Yakh-Su.

Kzyl, in Rus. names: see also KIZIL, KIZYL, KYZYL.

Kzyl-Kuga (ksĭl-kōōgä'), village (1939 pop. under 500), NW Guryev oblast, Kazakh SSR, 100 mi. NNW of Guryev; cattle breeding.

Kzyl-Mazar (-mŭzär'), village (1939 pop. over 500), W Kulyab oblast, Tadzhik SSR, on the Kyzyl-Su and 15 mi. NW of Kulyab; wheat growing, livestock raising.

Kzyl-Orda (-ŭrdä') [Kazakh,=red capital], oblast (□ 88,900; 1946 pop. estimate 300,000), SW Kazakh SSR; ⊙ Kzyl-Orda. On Aral Sea, in Turan Lowlands; drained by the Syr Darya; includes sandy deserts (Aral Kara-Kum and Kyzyl-Kum). Irrigated agr. (chiefly rice) in the Syr Darya valley; sheep and camel raising in desert. Extensive saltpeter, salt, and phosphorite deposits. Fisheries along Aral Sea coast (cannery at Aralsk). Trans-Caspian RR runs along the Syr Darya. Pop. chiefly Kazakh. Formed 1938.

Kzyl-Orda, city (1939 pop. over 30,000), ⊙ Kzyl-Orda oblast, Kazakh SSR, on the Syr Darya, on Trans-Caspian RR and 585 mi. WNW of Alma-Ata; 44°52'N 65°27'E. Rice processing, metalworking, meat packing. Teachers col. Near by is Tas-Buget, site of Kzyl-Orda irrigation reservoir. Originally the Kokand fortress of Ak-Mechet; stormed by Russians (1853) and renamed Perovsk; again named Ak-Mechet (c.1920) and Kzyl-Orda (1925); was ⊙ Kazak Autonomous SSR (1925–29).

Kzyl-Tepe, Uzbek SSR: see BUSTON.

Kzyl-Tuu (-tōōōō'), village (1939 pop. over 500), NE Kokchetav oblast, Kazakh SSR, 120 mi. ENE of Kokchetav, in cattle area. Until 1940, spelled Kzyl-Tu.

L

Laa an der Thaya (lä' än dĕr tä'yä), town (pop. 5,324), N Lower Austria, near Czechoslovak border, 17 mi. ESE of Znojmo, Czechoslovakia; old border town; market center.

La Adela, Argentina: see Río COLORADO, La Pampa natl. territory.

Laage (lä'gŭ), town (pop. 3,824), Mecklenburg, N Germany, on the Recknitz and 12 mi. NE of Güstrow; agr. market (grain, potatoes, stock). Entirely destroyed (1637–38) in Thirty Years War.

Laagen River, Norway: see LAGEN RIVER.

La Aguada (lä ägwä'dä), suburb (pop. 1,175) of Corral, Valdivia prov., S central Chile.

Laakirchen (lä'kĭrkhŭn), town (pop. 5,738), S Upper Austria, in the Salzkammergut, on Traun R. and 4 mi. N of Gmunden; paper mill.

Laaland, Denmark: see LOLLAND.

La Altagracia (lä ältägrä'syä), province (□ 1,429; 1935 pop. 55,032; 1950 pop. 71,045), SE Dominican Republic; ⊙ La Romana. At E tip of Hispaniola isl. Off S coast are Catalina and Saona isls. Tropical lowlands with some outliers of Cordillera Central. Sugar cane is grown extensively in SW. Cattle raising. Products include bananas, coffee, rice, cacao, corn, hides, timber. La Romana has large sugar mill. Higüey is known for its shrine. Prov. was set up 1944; formerly part of Seibo prov.

La Angostura (lä äng-göstōō'rä). **1** Village, Neuquén natl. territory, Argentina: see VILLA LA ANGOSTURA. **2** Village (pop. estimate 700), W Río Negro natl. territory, Argentina, 100 mi. NE of San Carlos de Bariloche; fruitgrowing; livestock (sheep, goats).

Laanke, Norway: see LANKE.

Laar (lär), village (pop. 523), in former Prussian prov. of Hanover, NW Germany, after 1945 in Lower Saxony, on the Vechte and 18 mi. NW of Nordhorn, on Dutch border. Rail station is called Laarwald (lär'vält).

Laardal, Norway: see LARDAL.

La Arena (lä ärä'nä), village (pop. 1,095), Herrera prov., S central Panama, in Pacific lowland, on branch of Inter-American Highway and 1.5 mi. WNW of Chitré. Indian handicrafts, pottery. Corn, rice, beans, livestock.

La Arena, town (pop. 2,172), Piura dept., NW Peru, on coastal plain, near Piura R., 11 mi. SSW of Piura, in irrigated cotton area.

Laarne (lär'nŭ), town (pop. 4,875), East Flanders prov., NW Belgium, 6 mi. ESE of Ghent; textile industry; agr. market. Has 16th-cent. Gothic church. Formerly spelled Laerne.

Laarwald, Germany: see LAAR.

Laas, Italy: see LASA.

Laasphe (läs'fŭ), town (pop. 5,071), in former Prussian prov. of Westphalia, W Germany, after 1945 in North Rhine-Westphalia, on the Lahn and 17 mi. NW of Marburg; iron mining. Summer resort. Has 18th-cent. castle.

La Asunción (läsōōnsyōn') or **Asunción**, city (1941 pop. 4,061; 1950 census 4,502), ⊙ Nueva Esparta state, NE Venezuela, on Margarita Isl. (E), in fertile interior valley, 210 mi. ENE of Caracas; 11°2'N 63°52'W. Agr. region (cotton, sugar cane, yuca, coconuts); cotton ginning, corn and sugar milling, *aguardiente* distilling. First Sp. settlement 1524.

Laatefoss, Norway: see LATEFOSS.

Laatokka, USSR: see LADOGA, LAKE.

La Azulita (lä sōōlē'tä), town (pop. 655), Mérida state, W Venezuela, in Andean spur, 20 mi. WNW of Mérida; alt. 3,724 ft.; sugar cane, coffee, grain.

La Baie, Que.: see BAIE, LA.

La'ban (läbăn'), village, S central Jordan, 16 mi. S of Kerak. Poultry and vegetable farm is just S. Copper deposits (W).

Laband, Poland: see LABEDY.

La Banda (lä bän'dä), town (1947 pop. 17,017), ⊙ La Banda dept. (□ 1,285; 1947 census pop. 61,248), W central Santiago del Estero prov., Argentina, 5 mi. NNE of Santiago del Estero across Río Dulce (irrigation area); rail junction; commercial and agr. center (alfalfa, corn, wheat, cotton, fruit); cotton gin, grain mill, textile factory.

La Barca (lä bär'kä), city (pop. 13,427), Jalisco, central Mexico, E of L. Chapala, on Lerma R. and 60 mi. SE of Guadalajara; agr. center (grain, vegetables, oranges, livestock); dairying, tanning; bottling of mineral waters.

Laba River (lä'bŭ), Krasnodar Territory, Russian SFSR, rises in main range of the W Greater Caucasus in 2 headstreams, the Great Laba (E) and Little Laba (W), joining SSE of Mostovskoye; flows NW, past Labinsk and Koshekhabl, and W, past Temirgoyevskaya, to Kuban R. at Ust-Labinskaya. Length (including Great Laba branch), 219 mi. Has braided middle and lower course.

La Barra (lä bä'rä), resort, Tamaulipas, NE Mexico, on Gulf at mouth of Pánuco R., 6 mi. NE of Tampico.

Labarthe-Inard (läbärt'-ēnär'), village (pop. 263), Haute-Garonne dept., S France, near Garonne R., 5 mi. E of Saint-Gaudens; paper milling, sugar-beet processing.

Labasa, Fiji: see LAMBASA.

Labasheeda (lăbŭ-shē'dŭ), Gaelic *Leaba Síoda*, town (pop. 147), SW Co. Clare, Ireland, on the Shannon and 10 mi. E of Kilrush; fishing port.

Labastide-Clairence (läbästēd'-klärãs'), agr. village (pop. 290), Basses-Pyrénées dept., SW France, 12 mi. ESE of Bayonne. Medieval stronghold built 1314.

Labastide-Murat (–mürä'), village (pop. 444), Lot dept., SW France, in the Causse de Gramat, 15 mi. NNE of Cahors; sheep. Joachim Murat b. here.

Labastide-Rouairoux (–rōōärōō'), town (pop. 2,422), Tarn dept., S France, on Thoré R. and 22 mi. ESE of Castres; woolen mills, fertilizer factory.

Labatlan (lä'bŏtlŏn), Hung. *Lábatlan*, town (pop. 1,645), Komarom-Esztergom co., N Hungary, on the Danube and 12 mi. W of Esztergom; cement works; quicklime. Limestone quarry near by.

La Baye, Grenada, B.W.I.: see GRENVILLE.

Labaznoye (lŭbäz'nŭyŭ), village, SW Chukchi Natl. Okrug, Kamchatka oblast, Khabarovsk Territory, Russian SFSR, on Greater Anyui R. and 450 mi. WNW of Anadyr; lumbering.

Labe, Czechoslovakia and Germany: see ELBE RIVER.

Labé (läbā'), town (pop. c.3,450), N Fr. Guinea, Fr. West Africa, in Fouta Djallon mts., near Gambia R. source and 160 mi. NE of Conakry. Produces rice, essential oil (from oranges), honey, beeswax, pepper, rubber, cattle. Slate quarrying. Airfield; Protestant mission; sleeping-sickness clinic.

Labedy (wäbē'dĭ), Pol. *Łabędy*, Ger. *Laband* (lä'bänt), commune (1939 pop. 8,152; 1946 pop. 12,219) in Upper Silesia, after 1945 in Katowice prov., S Poland, on Klodnica R. (Gliwice Canal) and 5 mi. NW of Gleiwitz (Gliwice), in coal-mining region; rail junction; steel milling.

Labégude (läbāgüd'), village (pop. 1,270), Ardèche dept., S France, on the Ardèche, 2 mi. NW of Aubenas; glass-bottle works for near-by Vals-les-Bains mineral waters.

Labelle (läbĕl'), county (□ 2,392; pop. 22,974), SW Que., on L. Baskatong; ⊙ Mont Laurier.

Labelle, village (pop. 709), S Que., in the Laurentians, 27 mi. NW of Ste. Agathe des Monts, in garnet-mining region; dairying.

La Belle (lù bĕl', lä). **1** City (pop. 945), ⊙ Hendry co., S Fla., on Caloosahatchee R. and 27 mi. ENE of Fort Myers; shipping center for sugar-cane, cattle, and watermelon area. **2** City (pop. 840), Lewis co., NE Mo., near Middle Fabius R., 30 mi. WNW of Quincy, Ill.; corn, soy beans, hogs; lumber.

La Belle Lake, Wis.: see LAC LA BELLE.

Laberge, Lake (□ 87), S Yukon, expansion of Lewes R., 20 mi. N of Whitehorse; 30 mi. long, 1–4 mi. wide.

Laberinto de las Doce Leguas, Cuba: see DOCE LEGUAS, CAYOS DE LAS.

Labes, Poland: see LOBEZ.

Labette (lùbĕt'), county (□ 654; pop. 29,285), SE Kansas; ⊙ Oswego. Level area, bordering S on Okla.; drained in E by Neosho R. Stock raising, dairying, general agr. Oil and gas fields; coal deposits. Formed 1867.

Labette, city (pop. 145), Labette co., extreme SE Kansas, 9 mi. SSE of Parsons; dairying, agr.

Labiau, Russian SFSR: see POLESSK.

Labin (lä'bēn), Ital. *Albona d'Istria* (älbô'nä dē'strēä), village (pop. 5,654), NW Croatia, Yugoslavia, 23 mi. SSW of Rijeka (Fiume), in Istria. RASA coal mine near by.

Labine Point, Northwest Territories: see PORT RADIUM.

Labinot (läbē'nôt) or **Labinoti** (läbē'nôtē), village (1930 pop. 831), central Albania, on railroad and 5 mi. NE of Elbasan, on Shkumbi R.; chrome and iron mining.

Labinsk (lä'bĭnsk), city (1926 pop. 28,831), SE Krasnodar Territory, Russian SFSR, on Laba R. and 30 mi. SW of Armavir, on rail spur from Kurgannaya, in grain area; agr. center; canned goods, sunflower-oil, essential oils, flour; lumber milling. Became city in 1947.

Labis (lùbĭs'), town (pop. 1,567), NW Johore, Malaya, on railroad and 17 mi. SE of Segamat; rubber.

Labiszyn (wäbē'shĭn), Pol. *Łabiszyn*, Ger. *Labischin* (läbē'shĭn), town (pop. 2,201), Bydgoszcz prov., W central Poland, on Notec R. and 13 mi. SSW of Bydgoszcz; brick mfg., distilling, flour milling.

La Blanca (lä bläng'kä), town (pop. 1,384), Zacatecas, N central Mexico, 30 mi. SE of Zacatecas; cereals, maguey, livestock; silver deposits.

Labná, Mexico: see OXKUTZCAB.

Labo (läbō'), town (1939 pop. 2,548; 1948 municipality pop. 14,977), Camarines Norte prov., SE Luzon, Philippines, 9 mi. WNW of Daet; agr. center (coconuts, rice, abacá); garnet mining.

La Boca (lä bō'kä), SE section of Buenos Aires, Argentina, on the Río de la Plata; oldest section of the city, still preserving the character of old port and fishing village.

La Boca. 1 or **Boca Bío-Bío** (bō'kä bē'ō-bē'ō), village (1940 pop. 276), Concepción prov., S central Chile, at mouth of Bío-Bío R. on the Pacific, 2 mi. inland 5 mi. W of Concepción; minor port and seaside resort. **2** Village (1930 pop. 181), Santiago prov., central Chile, minor port on the Pacific at mouth of Maipo R., 3 mi. S of San Antonio; rail terminus. Sometimes Boca de Maipo.

La Boca (lù bō'kù), town (pop. 4,246), Balboa dist., S Panama Canal Zone, at Pacific entrance of the Panama Canal (crossed by ferry of Inter-American Highway), just SW of Balboa.

Labod (lä'bôd), Hung. *Lábod*, town (pop. 1,881), Somogy co., SW Hungary, 19 mi. SW of Kaposvar; starch mfg.

Laboe (lä'bō), village (pop. 4,064), in Schleswig-Holstein, NW Germany, at mouth of Kiel Firth, 7 mi. NNE of Kiel city center; seaside resort. Site of modernistic navy memorial (280 ft. high) of First World War.

Laboeandeli, Indonesia: see LABUAN DELI.

Laboeha, Indonesia: see LABUHA.

Laboehandeli, Indonesia: see LABUAN DELI.

La Bolt, town (pop. 164), Grant co., E S.Dak., 12 mi. S of Milbank.

La Bonanza, Nicaragua: see BONANZA.

Labor, La, Honduras: see LA LABOR.

L'Abord à Plouffe (läbôr' ä plōōf'), village (pop. 1,773), S Que., on R. des Prairies, on SW shore of Jesus Isl., 8 mi. WNW of Montreal; truck gardening, tomato canning.

Laborde (läbōr'dā), town (pop. 3,136), SE Córdoba prov., Argentina, 60 mi. SSE of Villa María; wheat, flax, corn, oats, livestock; dairying, flour milling.

Laborec River (lä'bôrĕts), Hung. *Laborc* (lŏ'bôrts), E Slovakia, Czechoslovakia, rises on S slope of E Beskids, near Pol. border, 24 mi. ENE of Bardejov; flows 80 mi. S, past Humenne and Michalovce, to Latoritsa R. 12 mi. E of Trebisov.

Labores, Las (läs lävō'rĕs), town (pop. 991), Ciudad Real prov., S central Spain, near Toledo prov. border, 30 mi. NE of Ciudad Real; olives, grain, grapes; olive-oil extracting.

Laborie (lăbûrē'), village (pop. 844), S St. Lucia, B.W.I., 17 mi. S of Castries; sugar growing.

Labouheyre (läbōōär'), village (pop. 1,877), Landes dept., SW France, 30 mi. NW of Mont-de-Marsan; wood industry (railroad ties, pit-props, turpentine, wood pulp). Freight yards.

Laboulaye (läbōlä'yä), town (pop. 9,548), ⊙ Presidente Roque Sáenz Peña dept. (pop. 29,565), S Córdoba prov., Argentina, 90 mi. SE of Río Cuarto. Rail junction on Buenos Aires–Mendoza line. Agr. center (grain, flax, alfalfa, sunflowers, sheep and cattle); dairying, flour milling. Cement.

Labourd (läbōōr'), small historical region of SW France, surrounding Bayonne (Basses-Pyrénées dept.), in the Basque country. Was a dependency of Gascony.

Labourdonnais, Mauritius: see MAPOU.

Labourse (läbōōrs'), outer SE suburb (pop. 2,207) of Béthune, Pas-de-Calais dept., N France; coal.

Laboutarié (läbōōtärēä'), village (pop. 150), Tarn dept., S France, on Dadou R. and 10 mi. S of Albi; tanning.

Labra, Peña (pā'nyä lä'vrä), massif in the Cantabrian Mts., Santander and Leon provs., N Spain, 15 mi. WNW of Reinosa; the Pico de las Aguas (7,136 ft.) is highest point. The Cordillera Ibérica extends SE from this mtn. knot. It is also the source of Ebro R., flowing SE to the Mediterranean, and of Pisuerga R., flowing S to the Douro (Duero) and thus to the Atlantic.

Labrador (lă'brùdôr), territory (□ 110,000; pop. 5,528), E Canada, a dependency of Newfoundland; ⊙ Battle Harbour. The name was sometimes considered to include the whole peninsula known as UNGAVA, most of which is part of Quebec prov. The Labrador territory is now the Atlantic coastal strip, roughly bet. 52°N–60°N and 55°W–68°W. Its bleak coastline, swept by the cold Labrador Current, is deeply indented, rocky, and barren, becoming mountainous toward N, where peaks rise to 5,000 ft. SW part of territory contains innumerable lakes that drain into the Atlantic through Hamilton and Naskaupi rivers. On Hamilton R. are the noted Grand Falls. Near coast (SE) is large L. Melville. Settlement is confined to coast, where lumbering (spruce) and fishing (cod, salmon) are chief occupations; the coast fisheries were formerly heavily exploited. Of the inhabitants c.1,300 are Eskimos; there are also a few Algonquian Indians. Besides Battle Harbour, other important settlements are Cartwright, Rigolet, Hopedale, Nain. In Second World War major Canadian air base was established at Goose Bay, on L. Melville; later converted to civilian use. Iron deposits have been discovered in the territory, and mining is carried on at Burnt Creek Camp, on Que. border. Some believe the Northmen (11th cent.), John Cabot (1498), and Corte Real (1500) visited Labrador. It is known that Sebastian Cabot (1508?) and Jacques Cartier (1534) skirted the coast. Treaty of Paris (1763) assigned territory to Great Britain, and it came under jurisdiction of governor of Newfoundland; transferred to Canada (1774), it was returned to Newfoundland in 1809, but boundary with Que. was in dispute until settled by decision of the British Privy Council (1927). Settlement did not begin until 19th cent., when several fishing stations and Moravian mission were established. At end of 19th cent. Sir Wilfred Grenfell established his noted medical missions in territory.

Labrador Current, cold ocean current formed off Labrador coast by currents descending from Baffin Bay and W Greenland, flows S along Labrador coast and E Newfoundland, meets Gulf Stream off the Grand Banks; meeting of cold and warm streams results in the fogs for which this region is noted. Labrador Current carries ice into main shipping lanes bet. America and Europe. Also called Arctic Current or Arctic Stream.

Labrador Sea, part of North Atlantic Ocean, bet. Labrador and SW Greenland, linked by Davis Strait with Baffin Bay. The West Greenland Current flows N along the Greenland coast, and the Labrador Current S along the Labrador Coast.

Labrang, China: see SIAHO.

Labranzagrande (läbrän″sägrän'dä), town (pop. 905), Boyacá dept., central Colombia, in valley of Cordillera Oriental, 28 mi. ESE of Sogamoso; alt. 3,750 ft.; coffeegrowing.

Lábrea (lä'brēù), city (pop. 1,156), S Amazonas, Brazil, on right bank of Purus R. (navigable) and 120 mi. NNW of Pôrto Velho; rubber, mica, iron. Founded 1871.

La Brea (lä brā'ä), village (pop. 365), Valle dept., S Honduras, minor Pacific port on Gulf of Fonesca, 7 mi. SW of Nacaome; saltworks.

La Brea, village (pop. 36), Piura dept., NW Peru, in W outliers of Cordillera Occidental, E of Negritos and 10 mi. ESE of Talara. Petroleum production center. Petroleum is shipped via pipe line through TALARA.

La Brea (lä brē'ù), village (pop. 2,616), SW Trinidad, B.W.I., on the Gulf of Paria, 10 mi. WSW of San Fernando; adjoins famous Pitch Lake, where asphalt is worked and then exported through La Brea pier at Pitch Point (10°15'N 61°37'W). Petroleum deposits near by. Sir Walter Raleigh here calked his ships with asphalt (1595).

La Brea, Calif.: see LOS ANGELES, city.

Labrède (läbrĕd'), village (pop. 473), Gironde dept., SW France, 11 mi. S of Bordeaux; sawmilling winegrowing. Montesquieu b. here.

Labrit (läbrē'), village (pop. 259), Landes dept., SW France, 15 mi. N of Mont-de-Marsan; resinous products. Was ⊙ former duchy of Albret which became part of Gascony prov. in 1607. Formerly called Albret.

Labruguière (läbrügyâr'), town (pop. 2,152), Tarn dept., S France, on Thoré R. 5 mi. S of Castres; mfg. of textiles (hosiery, fezzes), furniture, tanning extracts; dairying.

Labuan (läbōōän'), island (□ 35; pop. 8,603) off NW Borneo, in S.China Sea, at entrance to Brunei Bay, belongs to Interior and Labuan residency of Br. NORTH BORNEO, 20 mi. NE of Brunei town; 5°20'N 115°12'E; roughly triangular, 11 mi. long, 8 mi. wide at base. Low-lying. Chief products: rubber, sago, copra. Stock raising, fishing. Chief town and port (linked by ferry with Weston) is Victoria, on SE shore. Ceded 1846 to Great Britain by sultan of Brunei, isl. became crown colony in 1848. Included (1890–1906) in Br. North Borneo; inc. 1907 into Straits Settlements as part of Singapore; became 1912 a separate settlement. Occupied by the Japanese during Second World War. In July, 1946, it became part of newly created Br. colony of North Borneo.

Labuan Deli or **Laboehandeli** (both: läbōōän″dä'lē), town (dist. pop. 31,921, including near-by Belawan), NE Sumatra, Indonesia, port on Deli R. near its mouth on Strait of Malacca, 10 mi. N of Medan; ships rubber, tobacco, fibers, palm oil, spices, tea, copra, gambir. Formerly important as harbor for Medan, it was superseded by near-by Belawan and is now subsidiary port. Railroad connection with Medan and Belawan. Also spelled Laboeandeli.

Labuha or **Laboeha** (both: läbōō'ä), chief port of BACHAN isl., Indonesia, on W coast, on inlet of Molucca Passage; 0°49'N 127°18'E; exports timber, resin, bamboo, copra, spices. In Second World War, Jap. naval base was here.

Labuissière (läbwēsyâr'), village (pop. 1,239), Hainaut prov., S Belgium, on Sambre R. and 14 mi. WSW of Charleroi; marble quarrying. Sometimes spelled La Buissière.

Labuk Bay (lùbōōk'), inlet (30 mi. long, 20 mi. wide) of Sulu Sea, NE Borneo, NW of Sandakan.

Labuk River, NE Borneo, rises in mts. S of Mt. Kinabalu, flows 200 mi. generally ENE to Labuk Bay (inlet of Sulu Sea), 40 mi. WNW of Sandakan; navigable 30 mi. by small craft.

Labun or **Labun'** (lä'bōōnyù), village (1926 pop. 2,593), NE Kamenets-Podolski oblast, Ukrainian SSR, 17 mi. SE of Shepetovka.

Labutta (lùbōō'tä), village, Myaungmya dist., Lower Burma, in Irrawaddy delta, 45 mi. S of Bassein.

L'Acadie (läkädē'), village (pop. estimate 500), S Que., on Richelieu R. and 5 mi. W of St. Jean; dairying; grain, cattle.

Lacahahuira River (läkähäwē'rä), in Oruro dept., W Bolivia; rises in marshes SW of L.Poopó, which it drains; flows intermittently 70 mi. W across the Altiplano, to L. Coipasa. Sometimes spelled Lacajahuira.

Lacalahorra (läkäläô'rä), town (pop. 1,738), Granada prov., S Spain, 9 mi. SSE of Guadix; cereals, potatoes, sugar beets. Its 16th-cent. castle, with

4 round corner towers, is decorated in Italian Renaissance style.

La Caldera, Argentina: see CALDERA.

La Calera (lä kälā'rä) or **Calera,** town (pop. estimate 1,500), NW central Córdoba prov., Argentina, 10 mi. WNW of Córdoba; rail junction, resort and mining center; granite quarries; cement and lime factories. Dam on Río Primero near by provides hydroelectric power.

La Calera, town (pop. 262), Cundinamarca dept., central Colombia, 12 mi. NNE of Bogotá; alt. 8,917 ft.; cement plant.

La Campana (lä kämpä'nä), village (pop. 302), Panama prov., central Panama, off Inter-American Highway, 3 mi. SSW of Capira; gold mines; orange groves; stock raising.

La Cañada (lä känyä'dä), town (pop. estimate 1,000), ⊙ Figueroa dept. (□ 2,540; 1947 pop. 21,060), central Santiago del Estero prov., Argentina, on railroad and 30 mi. ENE of Santiago del Estero; corn, alfalfa, cotton, livestock; flour milling, lumbering.

La Cañada, Mexico: see EL MARQUÉS.

La Canada (lä kúnä'dú), unincorporated residential town (1940 pop. 2,334), Los Angeles co., S Calif., in foothills of San Gabriel Mts., 11 mi. N of downtown Los Angeles.

La Candelaria, Argentina: see CANDELARIA, Salta prov.

Lacandón River, Guatemala, Mexico: see LACANTÚN RIVER.

La Canoa (lä känō'ä), town (pop. 921), Baja Verapaz dept., central Guatemala, on Motagua R. and 18 mi. SSW of Salamá; coffee, sugar cane, grain. Gold placers near by.

Lacantún River (läkäntōōn') or **Lacandón River** (läkändōn'), in Guatemala and Mexico, rises in several branches in Cuchumatanes Mts., flows c.100 mi. NW to Usumacinta R., receives Jataté R. in Chiapas.

Lacapelle-Marival (läkäpĕl'-märēväl'), village (pop. 666), Lot dept., SW France, 10 mi. NNW of Figeac; cattle, lumber; mineral springs.

La Capilla (lä käpē'yä), town (pop. estimate 800), central Entre Ríos prov., Argentina, 12 mi. SE of Villaguay; wheat, corn, flax, livestock.

La Capilla, village (pop. 1,416), Piura dept., NW Peru, on coastal plain, near Chira R., 13 mi. NNE of Paita, in irrigated area; cotton, fruit.

Lacar, department, Argentina: see SAN MARTÍN DE LOS ANDES.

Lacar, Lake (läkär') (□ 20; alt. 2,103 ft.), in the Andes, SW Neuquén natl. territory, Argentina, in Argentinian lake dist., E of Ilpela Pass; extends 16 mi. E from Chile border to San Martín de los Andes.

La Carlota (lä kärlō'tä), town (pop. 4,616), ⊙ Juárez Celman dept. (□ c.5,200; pop. 39,304), S central Córdoba prov., Argentina, on the Río Cuarto and 70 mi. S of Villa María; rail junction, agr. center (grain, alfalfa, sunflowers, cattle); luggage mfg.

La Carlota, town (1939 pop. 5,213; 1948 municipality pop. 45,789), Negros Occidental prov., W Negros isl., Philippines, 17 mi. S of Bacolod; sugar milling.

Lacarne, Ohio: see PORT CLINTON.

La Carrasquilla (lä käräskē'yä), residential town (pop. 1,614), Panama prov., central Panama, 4 mi. NNE of Panama city; highway junction.

La Carrera (lä kärä'rä), village (pop. estimate 300), SE Catamarca prov., Argentina, on the Río de Valle and 12 mi. NNE of Catamarca. Hydroelectric station; grain farming and stock raising in irrigated area.

La Carrière, Trinidad, B.W.I.: see POINTE-À-PIERRE.

La Castellana (lä kästāyä'nä, -lyä'nä), town (1939 pop. 3,975; 1948 municipality pop. 24,654), Negros Occidental prov., W central Negros isl., Philippines, 14 mi. NE of Binalbagan; agr. center (rice, sugar cane).

Lacaune (läkōn'), village (pop. 1,271), Tarn dept., S France, in the Monts de Lacaune, 24 mi. ENE of Castres; health resort. Wool spinning. Slate quarries near by.

Lacaune, Monts de (mō'dú-), low range of S Massif Central, Tarn dept., S France, extending c.25 mi. E of Castres; rises to 4,153 ft. Sheep and cattle grazing, dairying.

Lac au Saumon (läk ō sōmō'), village (pop. 1,703), E Que., on Salmon L., 30 mi. SSE of Matane; lumbering, dairying. Lake was formerly salmon spawning ground.

Lac aux Sables (läk ō sä'blú), village (pop. estimate 500), S central Que., on Batiscan R., at S end of L. aux Sables (3 mi. long), 22 mi. NE of Grand'Mère; dairying; cattle, pig, poultry raising.

Lacave (läkäv'), village (pop. 184), Ariège dept., S France, on the Salat and 9 mi. WNW of Saint-Girons; slaked-lime mfg.

Lac Beauport (läk bōpôr'), resort village, S Que., on small L. Beauport, 10 mi. NNW of Quebec.

Lac Bouchette (läk bōō-shĕt'), village (pop. 624), S central Que., on Bouchette L. (5 mi. long), on Ouiatchouanish R., and 17 mi. SSE of Roberval; alt. 1,135 ft.; quartz mining.

Laccadive Islands (lă'kúdīv), Sanskrit *Laksha divi* [=100,000 isls.], group of 14 coral isls. and reefs (pop. 18,355) in Arabian Sea, c.200 mi. off Malabar Coast, part of Madras, India; bet. 8°15'–12°N and 72°–74°E. The Indian census gives their area as □ c.10, but an estimate of □ 80 has long been used; the actual area is probably bet. these figures. Comprise 2 main groups: Amin Divi Isls. (N of 11°N; pop. 6,177; administered by South Kanara dist.); Laccadives proper (pop. 12,178; administered by Malabar dist.; formerly also called Cannanore Isls.), which include Androth, Kavaratti, and Minicoy (southernmost; separated from others by Nine Degree Channel). Main products: coir, copra (traded for rice from the coast), fish. Colonized (9th cent. A.D.) by Malabar Coast Hindus who were converted to Islam by an Arab saint in 13th cent. Discovered by Portuguese in 1499; the Amin Divis came, c.1785, under Tippoo Sahib of Mysore and the Laccadives proper under East India Co. in 1791; both groups assigned to Madras by early-19th cent. Pop. still almost entirely Moslem. Language (except in MINICOY ISLAND), Malayalam.

Lacchiarella (läk-kyärĕl'lä), village (pop. 2,756), Milano prov., Lombardy, N Italy, 10 mi. S of Milan; foundry, cotton dyeworks.

Lacco Ameno (läk'kô ämä'nô), village (pop. 1,423), Napoli prov., Campania, S Italy, on NW coast of Ischia isl.; resort with warm mineral springs and baths.

Lac-d'Issarlès, Le (lú läk-dēsärlĕs'), village (pop. 136), Ardèche dept., S France, near the upper Loire, 18 mi. SE of Le Puy; alt. 3,271 ft. Resort on deep-crater lake.

Lac du Flambeau (lăk' dú flăm'bō), Indian village (pop. 686), Vilas co., N Wis., on small Lac du Flambeau, 33 mi. NW of Rhinelander, in lake-resort area of the Lac du Flambeau Indian Reservation. Near by is a fish hatchery.

Lacedaemon, Greece: see LACONIA and SPARTA.

Lacedonia (lächĕdô'nyä), town (pop. 6,253), Avellino prov., Campania, S Italy, 19 mi. ESE of Ariano Irpino, in cereal-growing region. Bishopric. Heavily damaged by earthquakes (1456, 1930).

La Ceiba, Dominican Republic: see HOSTOS.

La Ceiba (lä sā'bä), city (pop. 12,185), ⊙ Atlántida dept., N Honduras, major Caribbean port, 70 mi. E of Puerto Cortés; 15°47'N 86°52'W. Industrial and agr. center; mfg. of footwear, cigars, soap, coconut oil, jams; flour and sawmilling, brewing, tanning. Has hospitals, col., radio stations, airfield. Exports mainly coconuts, abacá fiber, oranges. Developed in late 19th cent.; a major banana port until destruction (1930s) of plantations by leaf-spot disease.

La Ceiba, town (pop. 223), Trujillo state, W Venezuela, landing on L. Maracaibo, 33 mi. WNW of Valera; terminus of railroad from Motatán; sugar milling.

La Ceja (lä sā'hä), town (pop. 4,801), Antioquia dept., NW central Colombia, in Cordillera Central, 18 mi. SSE of Medellín; alt. 7,273 ft. Agr. center (coffee, corn, beans, sugar cane, yucca, stock); dairying, tanning. Notable church.

La Center. 1 Town (pop. 593), Ballard co., SW Ky., 21 mi. W of Paducah, in agr. area; lumber, concrete products. **2** Town (pop. 204), Clark co., SW Wash., on East Fork of Lewis R. and 15 mi. N of Vancouver, in agr. region.

Lacepede Bay (lă'süpēd), bight of Indian Ocean, SE South Australia, bet. Cape Jaffa (SW) and Granite Rocks; 19 mi. long. Kingston on E shore.

Laces (lä'chĕs), Ger. *Latsch*, village (pop. 1,367), Bolzano prov., Trentino–Alto Adige, N Italy, near the Adige, 15 mi. WSW of Merano, in fruitgrowing region; woodworking.

Lac Etchemin (läk ĕchmĕ'), village (pop. estimate 1,500), S Que., on L. Etchemin (3 mi. long), 45 mi. SE of Quebec; dairying, lumbering, pig raising.

Laceyville, borough (pop. 505), Wyoming co., NE Pa., 31 mi. WNW of Scranton and on Susquehanna R.; sawmill, gristmill; flagstone quarrying.

Lacha, Lake (lä'chŭ) (□ 133), SW Archangel oblast, Russian SFSR, 50 mi. WNW of Konosha; 22 mi. long, 6 mi. wide; low, marshy banks; frozen Nov.-May. Receives Svid R (S). Outlet: Onega R., at Kargopol. Fisheries.

La Chamiza, Chile: see CHAMIZA.

Lachanokepos or **Lakhanokipos** (both: läkhänô'-kĭpôs), town (pop. 3,049), Salonika nome, Macedonia, Greece, on railroad (junction) and 6 mi. NW of Salonika; cotton, wheat, silk. Formerly called Araple or Arapli.

Lachapelle-aux-Pots (läshäpĕl'-ō-pō'), village (pop. 639), Oise dept., N France, 8 mi. W of Beauvais; pottery and Camembert cheese mfg.

Lâchar (lä'chär), village (pop. 1,456), Granada prov., S Spain, on Genil R. and 13 mi. W of Granada; sugar mill. Olive oil, cereals, lumber, livestock.

La Charqueada, Uruguay: see GENERAL ENRIQUE MARTÍNEZ.

Lachay Point, Peru: see SALINAS POINT.

Lachen (lä'khún), town (pop. 3,226), Schwyz canton, NE central Switzerland, on L. of Zurich and 15 mi. NNE of Schwyz; silk textiles; wood- and metalworking. Rococo church. Hydroelectric plants of Etzel and Siebnen are near by.

Lachen Chu (lächĕn' chōō'), river, Tibet and India, rises in SE Tibet, on NE slope of Singalila Range; flows c.35 mi. SSE, joining Lachung Chu at Chungtang (India) to form Tista R.

Lachen-Speyerdorf (lä'khún-shpī'úrdôrf), village (pop. 2,849), Rhenish Palatinate, W Germany, 3 mi. SW of Neustadt; wine; also grain, tobacco.

Lachhmangarh (lŭch'mŭngŭr), town (pop. 15,044), E Rajasthan, India, 15 mi. NNW of Sikar; trades locally in millet, cattle, hides. Sometimes spelled Lachmangarh.

Lachin (lä'chĭn), city (1932 pop. estimate 680), S Azerbaijan SSR, in the Lesser Caucasus, in the Kurdistan, 75 mi. SSW of Yevlakh; livestock, wheat. Formerly called Abdalyar.

Lachine (lú-shēn'), city (pop. 20,051), S Que., on S shore of Montreal Isl., at E end of L. St. Louis, SW terminal of Lachine Canal, 6 mi. SW of Montreal; iron, steel founding; mfg. of tires, wire, tiles, phonograph records. Settled 1675, it was scene of massacre (1689) by Iroquois Indians.

Lachine Canal, on the St. Lawrence, S Que., extends 9 mi. SW–NE bet. the St. Lawrence at Montreal and L. St. Louis at Lachine, by-passing Lachine Rapids. Opened c.1825, later enlarged; there are 5 locks.

Lachine Rapids, on the St. Lawrence, S Que., at S end of Montreal Isl., bet. S part of Montreal and Lasalle; 3 mi. long, with total drop of 42 ft. At E end of rapids is Heron islet. Rapids are by-passed by Lachine Canal. Hydroelectric power.

Lachinovo (lä'chĭnŭvŭ), village (1939 pop. over 500), NE Kursk oblast, Russian SFSR, 35 mi. N of Stary Oskol; sugar beets.

Lachish (lā'kĭsh), biblical locality, S Palestine, in Judaean Hills, near N edge of the Negev, 25 mi. SW of Jerusalem, 15 mi. W of Hebron. Site, now called Tell ed Duweir or Tell ad-Duweir, was scene (1932–38) of important excavations; archives of Judah in anc. Hebrew script were among the archaeological finds.

Lachlan River (lăk'lún), S central New South Wales, Australia, rises in Great Dividing Range N of Gunning, flows NW, past Wyangala (dam), Cowra, Forbes, and Condobolin, thence SW, past Lake Cargelligo and Hillston, to Murrumbidgee R. 40 mi. NE of Balranald. Length, 922 mi.

La Chorrera (lä chōrā'rä), town (pop. 4,345), Panama prov., central Panama, in Pacific lowland, on Inter-American Highway and 16 mi. WSW of Panama city; road and agr. center (coffee; orange groves); stock raising. Its port on Gulf of Panama is Puerto Caimito.

Lachowicze, Belorussian SSR: see LYAKHOVICHI.

Lachung (lä'chōōng), village, E Sikkim, India, on the Lachung Chu and 27 mi. NNE of Gangtok, in extreme W Assam Himalayas; corn, pulse, oranges; apple orchards. Weaving school. Buddhist monastery near by.

Lachung Chu (chōō'), river in Sikkim, India, rises in NW Dongkya Range, flows c.30 mi. S, past Lachung, joining Lachen Chu at Chungtang to form Tista R.

Lachute (lúshōōt'), town (pop. 5,310), ⊙ Argenteuil co., SW Que., on North R. (waterfalls) and 40 mi. WNW of Montreal; woolen and paper milling, lumbering, butter and cheese making, mfg. of felt, veneer; resort. Adjoining is Lachute Mills.

La Ciénaga (lä syā'nägä), village (pop. estimate 500), S central Catamarca prov., Argentina, 10 mi. N of Belén; dam near Belén R.; grain, alfalfa, wine, livestock.

La Ciénaga, town (pop. 756), Falcón state, NW Venezuela, 3 mi. SSE of Puerto Cumarebo; yuca, divi-divi. Petroleum deposits near by.

Lac Île-à-la-Crosse (läk-ēl-ä-lä-krôs'), NW central Sask., expansion (60 mi. long, 5 mi. wide) of Churchill R., 180 mi. NW of Prince Albert.

Lackawanna (lăkúwä'nú), county (□ 454; pop. 257,396), NE Pa.; ⊙ Scranton. Anthracite-mining and industrial region, drained by Lackawanna and Susquehanna rivers. Hilly upland lies N, Pocono plateau S, of Lackawanna R. valley, anthracite center of world. Mfg. (textiles, clothing, food products, paints); printing; electrical, plastic, rubber, steel, and tobacco products; agr. (vegetables, poultry, dairy products). Formed 1878.

Lackawanna, city (pop. 27,658), Erie co., W N.Y., just S of Buffalo; mfg. (iron, steel, wood products, cement, concrete); stone quarries. Site of the basilica and charitable institutions of Our Lady of Victory. Inc. 1909.

Lackawanna River, NE Pa., formed by E and W branches joining just below Union Dale, Susquehanna co.; flows c.35 mi. SW, through rich anthracite region, past Carbondale and Scranton, to Susquehanna R. at NE end of Wyoming Valley, just N of Pittston.

Lackawaxen (lăkúwăk'sún), village (pop. c.500), Pike co., NE Pa., on the Delaware at mouth of Lackawaxen R. and 18 mi. WNW of Port Jervis, N.Y.

Lackawaxen River, NE Pa., formed by headstreams joining above Honesdale; flows 25 mi. SE, past Honesdale, to Delaware R. at Lackawaxen.

Lackey, mining town (pop. 452), Floyd co., E Ky., in Cumberland foothills, 17 mi. W of Pikeville, in bituminous-coal, oil, and gas area.

Lackhausen, Germany: see OBRIGHOVEN-LACKHAUSEN.
Lackland Air Force Base, Texas: see SAN ANTONIO.
Lac La Belle, resort village (pop. 174), Waukesha co., SE Wis., on small La Belle L., near Oconomowoc.
Lac la Biche (läk lä bēsh'), village (pop. 642), E Alta., on Lac la Biche, 50 mi. E of Athabaska; tanning, lumber and flour milling, dairying.
Laclede (lŭklēd'), county (□ 770; pop. 19,010), S central Mo.; ⊙ Lebanon. In the Ozarks; drained by Gasconade R. Dairy region; wheat, corn, hay; oak timber. Part of Mark Twain Natl. Forest is here. Formed 1849.
Laclede, city (pop. 544), Linn co., N central Mo., 5 mi. W of Brookfield; Pershing State Park is here.
Laclubar (lŭklōōbär'), town, Portuguese Timor, in central Timor, 27 mi. SE of Dili; agr. (wheat, fruit), cattle raising. Formerly Vila de Ourique.
Lac Masson, Que.: see SAINTE MARGUERITE.
Lacobriga, Portugal: see LAGOS.
La Cocha (lä kō'chä), town (pop. estimate 1,500), SW Tucumán prov., Argentina, 70 mi. SSW of Tucumán; rail terminus; industrial, lumbering, and agr. center. Mfg.: alcohol, charcoal, and other wood products. Corn, alfalfa, sugar cane, tobacco, cotton, olives, fruit, livestock. Tobacco research station.
Lacock (lā'kŏk), town and parish (pop. 1,105), NW Wiltshire, England, on the Avon and 3 mi. S of Chippenham; agr. market in dairying region. Has abbey (dating from 13th cent.; now private residence), 14th-15th-cent. church, many 15th-cent. houses.
Lacolle (läkôl'), village (pop. 874), SW Que., near Richelieu R., 17 mi. SSW of St. Jean; dairying. U.S. force under General Wilkinson was defeated here (1814) by the British.
La Colmena (lä kōlmā'nä), town (dist. pop. 4,078), Paraguarí dept., S Paraguay, 70 mi. SE of Asunción; fruit, livestock; lumbering. Sometimes Colonia La Colmena.
La Colorada (lä kōlōrä'dä), town (pop. 993), Sonora, NW Mexico, 32 mi. SE of Hermosillo; copper-mining center; silver, lead, zinc, graphite.
La Colorada, village (pop. 609), Veraguas prov., W central Panama, in Pacific lowland, 5 mi. S of Santiago, in gold-mining area; coffee, sugar cane, livestock.
Lacombe (lŭkōm'), town (pop. 1,808), S central Alta., near Gull L., 14 mi. N of Red Deer; rail junction; grain elevators; lumber, flour, grist mills; dairying. Dominion experimental farm.
Lacon (lā'kŭn), city (pop. 2,020), ⊙ Marshall co., N central Ill., on Illinois R. (bridged) and 24 mi. NNE of Peoria, in agr. and bituminous-coal area; grain elevator, woolen mills. Laid out as Columbia in 1826; inc. 1839.
Lacona (lŭkō'nŭ). **1** Town (pop. 430), Warren co., S central Iowa, 30 mi. SSE of Des Moines. **2** Village (pop. 540), Oswego co., N central N.Y., 25 mi. NE of Oswego; summer resort; mfg. (furniture, wood products, feed); sand, gravel pits.
La Concepción (lä kōnsĕpsyōn'), town (1950 pop. 1,670), Masaya dept., SW Nicaragua, 7 mi. WSW of Masaya; coffee and sugar-cane center.
La Concepción, Panama: see CONCEPCIÓN.
La Concepción or **Concepción,** town (pop. 2,816), Zulia state, NW Venezuela, on N shore of L. Maracaibo, 16 mi. SSW of Maracaibo; oil drilling and refining.
La Concordia (lä kōng-kôr'dyä), town (pop. 1,405), Chiapas, S Mexico, in N plain of Sierra Madre, 18 mi. SSW of Venustiano Carranza; cereals, sugar cane, fruit, stock.
La Concordia, town (1950 pop. 609), Jinotega dept., W Nicaragua, 13 mi. WNW of Jinotega; sugar cane, coffee, corn.
La Concordia, village, La Paz dept., S Salvador, minor port on Jaltepeque Lagoon, just off Pacific Ocean, and 24 mi. SE of San Salvador; coastal trade in salt and lumber. Sometimes called Puerto de la Concordia.
Laconi (lä'kônē), village (pop. 2,113), Nuoro prov., central Sardinia, 45 mi. N of Cagliari; clay, lignite deposits.
Laconia or **Lakonia** (lŭkō'nēŭ), nome (□ 1,453; pop. 144,156), SE Peloponnesus, Greece; ⊙ SPARTA. Consists of Taygetus and Parnon mtn. ranges enclosing the Eurotas R. valley and terminating S in capes Matapan and Malea on Aegean Sea. Mainly agr.: subtropical fruits (citrus fruits, figs), wheat, olives, cotton; livestock raising (sheep, goats); fisheries along coast. Tourist trade. Industry centered at Sparta. Main port, Gytheion. The anc. region of Laconia was settled by Dorians and came under the sway of Sparta, whose history it shared. Alternate names are Laconica (lŭkŏ'nĭkŭ) and Lacedaemon (lăsŭdē'mŭn).
Laconia. 1 Town (pop. 82), Harrison co., S Ind., near Ohio R., 23 mi. SW of New Albany, in agr. area. **2** City (pop. 14,745), ⊙ Belknap co., central N.H., 23 mi. N of Concord and on Winnipesaukee R. Industrial (hosiery, textiles, textile machinery, metal products, skis, boats), trade center for agr., resort area (near by: L. Winnipesaukee, Winnisquam L., L. Paugus). Resort suburbs: LAKEPORT, THE WEIRS. Its radio station was 1st in state (1922). Set off from Meredith 1855, inc. as city 1893.
Laconia, Gulf of, in SE Peloponnesus, Greece, inlet of Ionian Sea, bet. capes Matapan and Malea; 35 mi. wide, 30 mi. long. Gytheion (formerly Marathonisi) is on NW shore. Formerly called Gulf of Marathonisi.
La Conner, town (pop. 594), Skagit co., NW Wash., 7 mi. WSW of Mt. Vernon and on Puget Sound; agr. (hay, grain, seeds); salmon, wood products.
La Conquista (lä kōng-kē'stä), town (1950 pop. 367), Carazo dept., SW Nicaragua, 6 mi. S of Jinotepe, in sugar-cane zone.
La Consulta (lä kōnsōōl'tä), town (pop. estimate 1,000), NW central Mendoza prov., Argentina, in Tunuyán R. valley (irrigation area), on railroad and 60 mi. SSW of Mendoza; fruit, wine, potatoes.
La Convención, province, Peru: see QUILLABAMBA.
Lacoochee, village (pop. 1,792), Pasco co., W central Fla., 7 mi. N of Dade City.
La Cordillera (lä kôrdĭyä'rä), department (□ 1,910; pop. 158,990), central Paraguay; ⊙ Caacupé. Bounded W by Paraguay R., it is largely in the Cordillera de los Altos, hilly forested outliers of Brazilian plateau. In SW is L. Ypacaraí. Has subtropical, humid climate. Fertile agr. region: maté, tobacco, sugar cane, oranges, livestock, timber. Lumbering and processing concentrated at Caacupé, Atyrá, Altos, Arroyos y Esteros, Eusebio Ayala, Caraguatay, Piribebuy. San Bernardino on L. Ypacaraí is a popular resort. Dept. was called Caraguatay until 1944.
Lacorne (lŭkôrn'), village (pop. estimate 250), W Que., 18 mi. SE of Amos; molybdenum, lithium mining.
Lacosta Island (lŭkŏ'stŭ), SW Fla., narrow barrier island (c.7 mi. long) in Gulf of Mexico, N of Captiva Pass, at entrance to Charlotte Harbor and Pine Island Sound. Sometimes called Cayo Costa (kī'ō).
Lacoste (lŭkōst'), village, SW Que., near L. Nominingue, 30 mi. ESE of Mont Laurier; mica mining.
Lac-ou-Villers (läk-ōō-vēlâr'), village (pop. 1,777), Doubs dept., E France, on the Doubs and 4 mi. W of Le Locle (Switzerland) in the E Jura; customhouse on Swiss border; watchmaking, cheese mfg. Sanatorium. L. of BRENETS is 2 mi. NE. Sometimes called Villers-le-Lac.
Lacovia (lŭkō'vēŭ), town (pop. 1,750), St. Elizabeth parish, SW Jamaica, on Black R. and 36 mi. WNW of May Pen, in agr. region (cassava, corn, vegetables, spices, stock).
Lacq (läk), village (pop. 406), Basses-Pyrénées dept., SW France, 15 mi. NW of Pau and on the Gave de Pau; oil deposits.
Lac qui Parle (lă"kē pärl'), county (□ 773; pop. 14,545), SW Minn.; ⊙ Madison. Agr. area bordering S.Dak., bounded N and E by Minnesota R. (flowing through Lac qui Parle), and drained in SE by Lac qui Parle R. Corn, oats, barley, livestock. Formed 1871.
Lac qui Parle, enlargement of Minnesota R. bet. Lac qui Parle and Chippewa counties, SW Minn., 10 mi. NW of Montevideo; 8 mi. long, 1 mi. wide. Receives Lac qui Parle R. at SE end.
Lac qui Parle River, rises in small lake in Deuel co., E S.Dak., enters SW Minn. near Canby, flows NE, past Dawson, to Minnesota R. at SE end of Lac qui Parle; c.70 mi. long.
La Crescent, village (pop. 1,229), Houston co., extreme SE Minn., on Mississippi R. opposite La Crosse, Wis., in agr. area (grain, potatoes, fruit); dairy products.
La Crescenta (lä krŭsĕn'tŭ), unincorporated residential town (1940 pop. 3,623), Los Angeles co., S Calif., in La Crescenta Valley, in foothills of San Gabriel Mts., 12 mi. N of downtown Los Angeles.
Lacret (läkrā'), town (pop. 1,511), Matanzas prov., W Cuba, on railroad and 23 mi. ESE of Cárdenas; sugar cane, fruit, sisal.
La Croix, Lac (lăk lŭ kroi'), in NE Minn. and W Ont., large body of water in chain of lakes on Can. line, 30 mi. N of Ely; c.30 mi. long, max. width 4 mi. In resort area and bounded S by Superior Natl. Forest.
Lacroix-Saint-Ouen (läkrwä'-sĕtōōä'), village (pop. 1,671), Oise dept., N France, at W edge of Forest of Compiègne, 5 mi. SSW of Compiègne; sawmilling, woodworking (furniture, toys, boxes). Sometimes written La Croix-Saint-Ouen.
Lacroma, island, Yugoslavia: see DUBROVNIK.
La Crosse (lŭ krôs'), county (□ 469; pop. 67,587), W Wis.; ⊙ La Crosse. Fertile farming, dairying, stock-raising area. Lumber milling, processing of dairy products; other mfg. at La Crosse. Drained by La Crosse and Black rivers. Formed 1851.
La Crosse. 1 Town (pop. 146), Alachua co., N Fla., 14 mi. NNW of Gainesville, in truck-farming area. **2** Town (pop. 618), La Porte co., NW Ind., 30 mi. SE of Gary, in agr. area. **3** City (pop. 1,769), ⊙ Rush co., W central Kansas, 30 mi. WNW of Great Bend; shipping point for wheat and livestock. Oil and gas wells near by. Founded 1876, inc. 1886. **4** Town (pop. 675), Mecklenburg co., S Va., 2 mi. SE of South Hill; rail junction in agr. area (tobacco); lumber. **5** City (pop. 47,535), ⊙ La Crosse co., W Wis., on the Mississippi (bridged here), at confluence of Black and La Crosse rivers, and c.125 mi. WNW of Madison, at foot of bluffs; distributing and industrial center for dairying area; mfg. of farm equipment and implements, machinery, air-conditioning systems, rubber footwear, beer, automobile accessories, metal products; lumber milling. Rock quarries. Has state teachers col., Viterbo Col. City's park contains U.S. fish hatchery, Indian mound, and zoo. Site of Fr. fur-trading post in late-18th cent.; lumbering caused early growth, but was replaced in importance by other mfg. after depletion of forests in 1900s. Inc. 1856.
Lacrosse, town (pop. 457), Whitman co., SE Wash., 32 mi. WNW of Pullman; ships wheat.
La Crosse River, W Wis., rises in Monroe co., flows c.50 mi. generally SW, past Sparta, to the Mississippi at La Crosse.
La Cruz (lä krōōs'), town (pop. estimate 2,000), ⊙ San Martín or General San Martín dept. (□ c.5,400; pop. 26,321), E Corrientes prov., Argentina, port on Uruguay R. (Brazil border) and 90 mi. E of Mercedes; livestock and agr. center (corn, rice, manioc, peanuts, maté, olives, watermelons, tobacco, citrus fruit). Founded 1630 by Jesuits.
La Cruz, town (pop. 3,818), Valparaiso prov., central Chile, on railroad, on Aconcagua R. and 28 mi. NE of Valparaiso; agr. (grain, fruit, wine, hemp, tobacco, livestock).
La Cruz. 1 Town (pop. 2,614), Nariño dept., SW Colombia, in Cordillera Central, on road, and 33 mi. NE of Pasto; alt. 9,252 ft.; coffee, cereals, potatoes, cacao, sugar cane, livestock. **2** Town, Norte de Santander dept., Colombia: see ABREGO.
La Cruz, village (dist. pop. 5,566), Guanacaste prov., NW Costa Rica, on Inter-American Highway, near Nicaragua border, and 33 mi. NNW of Liberia. Stock raising. Its port is Puerto Soley.
La Cruz. 1 Town (pop. 776), Chihuahua, N Mexico, on Conchos R., on railroad and 75 mi. SE of Chihuahua; cotton, corn, beans, cattle. **2** Town (pop. 1,618), Sinaloa, NW Mexico, on Elota R., in coastal lowland, on railroad and 70 mi. SE of Culiacán; lumbering and agr. center (corn, chick-peas, fruit); dye-extract factory.
La Cruz or **La Cruz del Río Grande** (dĕl rē'ō grän'dā), town (1950 pop. 173), Zelaya dept., E Nicaragua, port on Río Grande and 85 mi. NNW of Bluefields; banana center; livestock. Banana plantation of El Gallo (W).
La Cruz (lä krōōs'), town (pop. 2,000), Florida dept., S central Uruguay, in the Cuchilla Grande Inferior, on railroad and 13 mi. NNW of Florida; viticulture center.
La Cruz del Río Grande, Nicaragua: see LA CRUZ.
La Cruz de Taratara (dā tärätä'rä), town (pop. 922), Falcón state, NW Venezuela, on S slopes of Sierra de San Luis, 25 mi. S of Coro; coffee, cacao.
Lac Saint Jean Est (läk sē zhänĕst'), county (□ 905; pop. 25,245), S central Que., on L. St. John; ⊙ St. Joseph d'Alma.
Lac Saint Jean Ouest (zhä wĕst'), county (□ 22,818; pop. 39,061), central Que., on L. St. John; ⊙ Roberval.
Lac Saint Louis, Que.: see MELOCHEVILLE.
La Cuchilla, Uruguay: see RÍO BRANCO.
La Cuesta (lä kwĕ'stä), village (dist. pop. 363), Puntarenas prov., S Costa Rica, near Panama border, 14 mi. N of Puerto Armuelles. Rice, beans, manioc, bananas; hog raising.
La Cueva (lä kwä'vä), village, Mora co., N N.Mex., on Mora R. and 5 mi. SE of Mora, in Sangre de Cristo Mts., in irrigated agr. region; alt. 7,634 ft.; livestock, fruit, grain, vegetables.
Lacui Peninsula (lä'kwē), NW headland of Chiloé Isl., S Chile, on the Pacific, just NW of Ancud. Huechucuicui Point is its NW tip. The peninsula was fiercely disputed during war of independence and has ruins of Sp. forts.
Laculete (lŭ'kōōlätsä), Rum. *Lăculeţe*, village (pop. 1,426), Prahova prov., S central Rumania, near Ialomita R., on railroad and 10 mi. N of Targoviste; lignite mining, gunpowder mfg., gypsum quarrying.
Lacul-Rosu, Rumania: see GHEORGHENI.
La Cumbre (lä kōōm'brä). **1** Town (pop. 3,968), NW Córdoba prov., Argentina, on SW slope of Sierra Chica, 35 mi. NW of Córdoba; tourist resort in N Córdoba hills; alt. 4,000 ft. Marble quarrying and stock raising. Adjoining is health resort of Cruz Chica. **2** Village, San Luis prov., Argentina: see JUAN W. GEZ.
La Cumbre, pass, Argentina-Chile: see USPALLATA PASS.
La Cumbre, town (pop. 1,619), Valle del Cauca dept., W Colombia, in Cordillera Occidental, on railroad and 14 mi. NNW of Cali; alt. 5,184 ft.; sugar cane, tobacco, coffee, fruit, cattle.
Lacu-Sarat (lä'kōō-sŭ'rät), Rum. *Lacu-Sărat*, resort, Galati prov., SE Rumania, 6 mi. SW of Braila; noted saline, iodine, and sulphurous springs.
Lacus Palicorum, Sicily: see PALAGONIA.
Lac Vieux Desert (lăk vū" dĭzâr'), lake (□ c.10) on Wis.-Mich. line, largely in Vilas co., N Wis., and partly in Gogebic co., W Upper Peninsula, Mich., in forested area; c.4 mi. long, 2 mi. wide; muskellunge fishing. Drained by Wisconsin R.
La Cygne (lŭ sēn'), city (pop. 794), Linn co., E Kansas, on Marais des Cygnes R. and 32 mi. N of

Fort Scott; stock and poultry raising, general agr. Oil wells and coal mines near by.

Lacy Isles, Australia: see Nuyts Archipelago.

Lada (lä'dŭ), village (1926 pop. 2,872), NE Mordvinian Autonomous SSR, Russian SFSR, on Insar R. and 30 mi. NNE of Saransk; grain, potatoes. Oil-shale deposits near by. Formerly also Lady.

Ladakh (lŭdäk'), district (□ 45,762; pop. 195,431), E Kashmir; ⊙ Leh. Comprises Ladakh, Kargil, and Skardu tahsils; bounded N by China, E by Tibet; drained by Indus (separates Karakoram mtn. system from Punjab Himalayas) and Shyok rivers. In W lies Baltistan tract, with highest peaks of the Karakoram, including K^2, Gasherbrum I, and Broad Peak. Agr. (pulse, wheat, oilseeds, corn). Main towns: Leh, Skardu. Essentially an area allied ethnologically and geographically with Tibet and hence sometimes called Indian Tibet. Buddhism prevails in E area, with important monasteries, including Himis Gompa, Lamayuru, and Alchi; following advent of Islam in Kashmir, W area became Moslem. Invaded periodically by Moslems after 1531, while nominally a dependency of Tibet; in mid-19th cent. annexed to Kashmir by Gulab Singh. Area N of Kargil held since 1948 by Pakistan. Prevailing mother tongues, Balti and Ladakhi. Pop. 79% Moslem, 20% Buddhist.

Ladakh Range, trans-Shyok lateral range of Karakoram mtn. system, E Kashmir; from Shyok R. mouth extends c.230 mi. SE, parallel with right bank of the Indus (which separates it from Zaskar Range), to Tibet (border undefined); rises to crest line of c.20,000 ft. Deosai Mts., a W section of Punjab Himalayas, are sometimes regarded as a trans-Indus extension of Ladakh Range.

Ladan (lä'dŭn), town (1926 pop. 2,786), SE Chernigov oblast, Ukrainian SSR, on Udai R. and 10 mi. SE of Priluki; peat digging.

Ladário (lŏdä'ryōō), town (pop. 2,577), W Mato Grosso, Brazil, on right bank of Paraguay R. and 3 mi. E of Corumbá; federal naval station for river flotilla; ship-repair yards. Loading point for manganese and iron ore from Morro do Urucum (10 mi. S). Built and fortified in 1873.

Ladce (lä'tsĕ), Hung. *Lédec* (lā'dĕts), village (pop. 1,724), W Slovakia, Czechoslovakia, near Vah R., on railroad and 24 mi. SW of Zilina; major cement works; large hydroelectric plant.

Ladd, village (pop. 1,224), Bureau co., N Ill., 4 mi. N of Spring Valley, in agr. and bituminous-coal area; mfg. (dairy products, furniture). Inc. 1890.

Ladder of Tyre, Palestine and Lebanon: see Ras en Naqura.

Ladd Field, U.S. air base and commercial airport for Fairbanks, central Alaska, near Tanana R., 5 mi. E of Fairbanks; 64°49'N 147°38'W. Important in Second World War, it was on air ferry route to Russia. Connected with Alaska RR.

Laddonia (lŭdō'nyŭ), city (pop. 599), Audrain co., NE central Mo., 13 mi. ENE of Mexico; grain, livestock, lumber.

Lade (lä'dŭ), industrial area in Sor-Trondelag co., central Norway, on Trondheim Fjord, on railroad just E of Trondheim; produces sheet metal, radiators, brick, construction stone, drainage pipes. Has teachers col. Was 10th-cent. seat of Viking kings, when it was called Hladir (Old Norse *Hlaðir*); church is preserved.

Ladek Zdroj (lō'dĕk zdrōō'ē), Pol. *Lądek Zdrój*, Ger. *Bad Landeck* (bät" län'dĕk), town (1939 pop. 4,861; 1946 pop. 5,804) in Lower Silesia, after 1945 in Wroclaw prov., SW Poland, near Czechoslovak border, at W foot of Reichenstein Mts., 11 mi. SE of Glatz (Klodzko); health resort.

Ladelle (lŭdĕl'), town (pop. 38), Drew co., SE Ark., 11 mi. S of Monticello.

La Democracia, Guatemala: see Democracia.

La Democracia (lä dāmōkräs'yä), town (pop. 964), Miranda state, N Venezuela, 37 mi. SSE of Caracas; coffee, cacao, sugar cane.

Ladenburg (lä'dŭnbŏŏrk), anc. *Lopodunum*, town (pop. 6,799), N Baden, Germany, after 1945 in Württemberg-Baden, on the canalized Neckar and 6 mi. E of Mannheim, in tobacco area; metal (turbines, machinery) and tobacco (cigars, cigarettes) industries; pharmaceuticals, textiles. Hydroelectric station. Has early-Gothic church. Of Celtic-Roman origin; has retained medieval appearance.

Ladendorf (lä'dŭndôrf), village (pop. 1,485), NE Lower Austria, 5 mi. SW of Mistelbach; corn, vineyards.

La Descubierta (lä dĕskōōbyĕr'tä), town (1950 pop. 1,637), Bahoruco prov., SW Dominican Republic, on N shore of L. Enriquillo, 15 mi. W of Neiba; coffee, grapes, fruit, timber.

Ladesti (lŭdĕsht'), Rum. *Lădeşti*, village (pop. 510), Valcea prov., S central Rumania, 20 mi. SW of Ramnicu-Valcea; agr. center; orchards.

Ladhiqiya, El, Syria: see Latakia.

Ladhon River, Greece: see Ladon River.

Ladies Island, Beaufort co., S S.C., one of Sea Isls., c.35 mi. NE of Savannah, Ga., bet. St. Helena Isl. (SE) and Port Royal Isl. (W), with highway bridges to both; c.10 mi. long. Wilkins village on NE shore. Oyster and vegetable canning.

La Digue Island (lä dēg') (2,500 acres; pop. 1,412), one of the Seychelles, in Indian Ocean, 35 mi. NE of Victoria (on Mahé Isl.); 4°22'S 55°50'E; 4 mi. long, 2 mi. wide; of granite formation. Agr.: vanilla, copra, essential oils; fisheries. Hosp.

Ladik (lädĭk'), Turkish *Lâdik*, anc. *Laodicea Combusta*, village (pop. 4,844), Samsun prov., N Turkey, 33 mi. SW of Samsun; cereals.

Ladislao Cabrera, Bolivia: see Salinas de Garci Mendoza.

Ladismith (lā'dē–), town (pop. 1,751), SW Cape Prov., U. of So. Afr., 55 mi. W of Oudtshoorn, at foot of Seven Weeks Poort mtn.; rail terminus; agr. center (dairying; grain, fruit, sheep, ostriches); brandy distilling.

Ladner, town (pop. estimate 2,000), SW B.C., near mouth of S branch of Fraser R. delta on Strait of Georgia, 11 mi. S of Vancouver; dairying, milk, fruit, vegetable, and fish canning, lumbering.

Ladnun (läd'nōōn), town (pop. 16,446), N central Rajasthan, India, 125 mi. NE of Jodhpur; local trade in hides, cattle, wool, grain, salt; hand-loom weaving; gold ornaments, leather work. Sandstone quarried 1 mi. S.

Lado (lä'dō), village, Equatoria prov., S Anglo-Egyptian Sudan, on left bank of the Bahr el Jebel (White Nile), on road, and 10 mi. N of Juba; cotton, sesame, corn, durra; livestock. Founded 1874 by Gordon; was ⊙ Lado Enclave (□ c.15,000, now in S Anglo-Egyptian Sudan and N Uganda), leased (1894–1910) to Belgian Congo.

Ladoeiro (lŭdwā'rōō), village (pop. 1,980), Castelo Branco dist., central Portugal, 12 mi. E of Castelo Branco, in region growing olives, vegetables, and fruits (especially melons).

Lado Enclave, Anglo-Egyptian Sudan and Uganda: see Lado.

Ladoga (lŭdō'gŭ), town (pop. 912), Montgomery co., W central Ind., on Raccoon Creek and 11 mi. SSE of Crawfordsville; canned foods.

Ladoga, Lake (lä'dŭgŭ), Rus. *Ladozhskoye Ozero*, Finnish *Laatokka* (lä'tŏk-kä), largest (□ 7,100) lake in Europe, in NW European USSR, bet. Karelian (W) and Olonets (E) isthmuses; 130 mi. long, 80 mi. wide, max. depth 732 ft.; alt. 17 ft. Low, marshy shores (S); rocky, indented shores (N). Valaam Isl. (N) has Greek Orthodox monastery. Autumn storms and ice-cover (4 months in S, 2 months in N) render navigation difficult. Receives Svir R. (E) from L. Onega, Vuoksi R. (W) from L. Saimaa. Discharges W, through Neva R., into Gulf of Finland. S portion of lake and the Ladoga Canals (100 mi. long parallel to its S coast bet. Svir and Neva rivers) form part of White Sea–Baltic, Vyshnevolotsk, Tikhvin, and Mariinsk canal systems. Main ports are Priozersk and Sortavala (N), Petrokrepost and Novaya Ladoga (S). Until 1940, Soviet-Finnish border passed NE–SW through center of lake.

Ladol (lä'dōl), town (pop. 6,202), Mehsana dist., N Bombay, India, 22 mi. E of Mehsana; local trade in millet, pulse, wheat; tanning.

Ladonia (lŭdō'nēŭ), town (pop. 1,104), Fannin co., NE Texas, 27 mi. SW of Paris; trade point in agr. area (cotton, grain, hay); cotton gins.

Ladon River or **Ladhon River** (both: lä'dhôn), in central Peloponnesus, Greece, rises in Aroania mts., flows c.40 mi. SW and S to the Alpheus 10 mi. ESE of Olympia. Hydroelectric plant. Formerly known as Roufias, Rouphia, or Ruphia R., a name then also applied to lower course of the Alpheus.

Ladora, town (pop. 273), Iowa co., E central Iowa, 31 mi. WSW of Cedar Rapids; livestock, grain.

La Dorada (lä dōrä'dä), town (pop. 5,965), Caldas dept., central Colombia, river port on the Magdalena and 70 mi. NW of Bogotá; head of navigation of the lower Magdalena and transfer point to railroads to Bogotá, Girardot, and Honda, avoiding the rapids which render the Magdalena here unnavigable. Trading and communication center. Airport.

La Dormida (lä dōrmē'dä), town (pop. estimate 1,500), NE Mendoza prov., Argentina, on railroad, on Tunuyán R. (irrigation) and 60 mi. SE of Mendoza; wine, fruit, grain; wine making, sawmilling.

Ladozhskaya (lä'dŭshskīŭ), village (1926 pop. 11,805), E Krasnodar Territory, Russian SFSR, on Kuban R. and 32 mi. WSW of Kropotkin; flour mill, metalworks.

Ladrone Islands (lŭdrōn'), Chinese *Wanshan*, in S. China Sea, Kwangtung prov., China, off Canton R. estuary, 18 mi. SE of Macao. Include Great Ladrone and Little Ladrone isls.

Ladrone Islands: see Marianas Islands.

La Due (lŭ dōō', dū'). **1** Town (1940 pop. 42), Crawford co., central Mo., in the Ozarks, adjacent to Cuba. **2** Hamlet, Henry co., W central Mo., 7 mi. SW of Clinton.

Ladue (lŭdōō', lŭdū'), city (pop. 5,386), St. Louis co., E Mo., just W of St. Louis. Inc. 1936 as consolidation of former Ladue, Deer Creek, and McKnight towns.

Ladushkin (lä'dōōshkĭn), city (1939 pop. 1,252), W Kaliningrad oblast, Russian SFSR, near Courland Lagoon, 16 mi. SW of Kaliningrad; summer resort. Until 1945, in East Prussia and called Ludwigsort (lōōt"vĭkhsôrt').

Ladva (läd'vŭ), village, S Karelo-Finnish SSR, 30 mi. SSE of Petrozavodsk; lumbering; grain.

Lady, Russian SFSR: see Lada.

Ladybank or **Ladybank and Monkston,** burgh (1931 pop. 1,128; 1951 census 1,149), N central Fifeshire, Scotland, 5 mi. SW of Cupar; agr. market, with asphalt works.

Ladybrand, town (pop. 6,004), S Orange Free State, U. of So. Afr., near Basutoland border, 75 mi. E of Bloemfontein; alt. 5,241 ft.; agr. center (dairying, wheat, rye, oats, potatoes); freestone quarrying. Airfield. Near by are numerous caves with old Bushman paintings.

Lady Evelyn Lake (20 mi. long, 4 mi. wide), SE central Ont., 16 mi. W of Cobalt; alt. 930 ft. Drains S into L. Timagami. Fishing resort.

Lady Franklin, Cape, NE extremity of Bathurst Isl., N central Franklin Dist., Northwest Territories, at N end of Queens Channel; 76°40'N 98°42'W.

Lady Franklin Bay, NE Ellesmere Isl., NE Franklin Dist., Northwest Territories, inlet (25 mi. long, 6–10 mi. wide) of Robeson Channel, at NW end of Hall Basin; 81°40'N 65°W. On N shore, near entrance of bay, is small inlet of Discovery Harbour, site of Fort Conger, both of importance in late-19th-cent. exploration of the Arctic.

Lady Franklin Point, SW extremity of Victoria Isl., SW Franklin Dist., Northwest Territories, on Coronation Gulf, at E entrance of Dolphin and Union Strait; 68°31'N 113°9'W.

Lady Frere (frēr'), town (pop. 740), E Cape Prov., U. of So. Afr., in Stormberg range, on tributary of White Kei R. and 25 mi. NE of Queenstown; stock, dairying, grain. It is ⊙ Glen Grey dist. (□ 929; total pop. 66,688; native pop. 65,957), administered by dist. council, a form of native self-govt., established 1894.

Lady Grey, town (pop. 2,074), E Cape Prov., U. of So. Afr., in Witteberge mts., 30 mi. E of Aliwal North; stock, dairying, grain.

Lady Isle, islet in Firth of Clyde, off coast of Ayrshire, Scotland, 3 mi. WSW of Troon; lighthouse (55°32'N 4°45'W).

Lady Lake, town (pop. 331), Lake co., central Fla., c.40 mi. NNW of Orlando, in citrus-fruit and watermelon area; packs fruit.

Ladysmith, city (pop. 1,706), SW B.C., on SE Vancouver Isl., on inlet of Strait of Georgia, 13 mi. SSE of Nanaimo; rail-water transfer point for mainland traffic; port and shipping point for nearby fishing, logging area and coal mines; fruitgrowing, dairying, oyster culture.

Ladysmith, town (pop. 14,221), W Natal, U. of So. Afr., on Klip R. and 85 mi. NNW of Pietermaritzburg, at foot of Drakensberg range; rail junction; distributing center for N Natal, Orange Free State, and Transvaal; cotton milling; center of stock-raising region. Airfield. Named for wife of Sir Harry Smith, a governor of Cape Colony. In South African War British forces here were besieged by Boers from Nov., 1899, until relieved (Feb. 28, 1900) by troops under Sir Redvers Buller. Near town are battlefields of Colenso, Spion Kop, Wagon Hill, and Nicholsons Nek.

Ladysmith, city (pop. 3,924), ⊙ Rusk co., N Wis., on Flambeau R. and c.50 mi. NE of Eau Claire, in lake-resort area; dairy products, paper, woodenware, canned vegetables. A large cooperative creamery is here. Has hydroelectric plant. Inc. 1905.

Ladyzhinka (lŭdĭzhĕn'kŭ), village (1926 pop. 3,501), SW Kiev oblast, Ukrainian SSR, 13 mi. S of Uman; sugar beets.

Ladzhene, Bulgaria: see Velingrad.

Lae (lī), atoll (pop. 138), Ralik Chain, Kwajalein dist., Marshall Isls., W central Pacific, 75 mi. SW of Kwajalein; 17 islets on lagoon c.5 mi. long.

Lae, town and harbor, Morobe dist., Territory of New Guinea, NE New Guinea, on Huon Gulf and 180 mi. N of Port Moresby; founded 1927 to serve air transport lines into gold fields. In Second World War, occupied 1942 by Japanese, taken 1943 by Allies.

Laeken, Belgium: see Laken.

Laem Sing (lăm'sĭng'), village (1937 pop. 1,612), Chanthaburi prov., S Thailand, port at mouth of Chanthaburi R., on Gulf of Siam, serving as deep-water harbor for Chanthaburi (9 mi. N); rice milling.

La Encarnación (lä ĕng-kärnäsyōn'), town (pop. 853), Ocotepeque dept., W Honduras, on W slope of Sierra del Merendón, 20 mi. NNE of Nueva Ocotepeque; tobacco, rice.

Laerdal (lâr'däl), valley and canton (pop. 1,925), Sogn og Fjordane co., W Norway, drained by Laerdal R., and extending from W part of the Hemsedalsfjell c.15 mi. W to head of Laerdals Fjord, a 5-mi.-long arm of Sogne Fjord. Laerdalsoyri (lâr'dälsûürē), Nor. *Laerdalsøyri*, village (pop. 714) at head of fjord, is tourist center and was road terminus for traffic to Oslo before completion of Bergen RR.

Laerne, Belgium: see Laarne.

La Esmeralda (lä ĕzmäräl'dä), village (pop. c.250), Tarija dept., SE Bolivia, in the Chaco, on Pilcomayo R. and 80 mi. SE of Villa Montes; meeting point of Bolivia-Argentina-Paraguay borders is here.

La Esmeralda, Cuba: see Esmeralda.

Laeso (lâ'sû), Dan. *Læsø*, island (□ 44; pop. 3,400), Denmark, in the Kattegat, 12 mi. E of NE Jutland; 13 mi. long, 4 mi. wide; highest point, 79 ft. Cliffs along N coast, flat in S.

La Esperanza (lä ĕspärän'sä), town (pop. 3,894), SE Jujuy prov., Argentina, 30 mi. E of Jujuy; sugar-refining center.

La Esperanza, Cuba: see PUERTO ESPERANZA.

La Esperanza, town (1950 pop. 296), Quezaltenango dept., SW Guatemala, 2 mi. NW of Quezaltenango; alt. 7,831 ft. Corn, wheat, fodder grasses, livestock raising. Site of Quezaltenango airport.

La Esperanza, city (pop. 1,327), ⊙ Intibucá dept., SW Honduras, in Sierra de Opalaca, 75 mi. WNW of Tegucigalpa; 14°18'N 88°19'W; alt. 4,951 ft. Commercial center in fruitgrowing area (peaches, quinces, figs); produces peach liquor; fruit processing. Founded in early 19th cent., next to old Indian town of Intibucá (adjoining; N).

La Estrella (lä ĕstrĕ'yä), former river port, Santa Cruz dept., central Bolivia, 65 mi. NNW of Portachuelo. Abandoned 1929 following flood and change of course of Río Grande.

La Estrella or **Estrella,** village (1930 pop. 332), Colchagua prov., central Chile, near the coast, 45 mi. NW of San Fernando; grain, peas, potatoes, fruit, wine, livestock.

La Estrella, village, Limón prov., E Costa Rica, on Estrella R. (a 35 mi.-long Caribbean coastal stream), on railroad and 18 mi. SSE of Limón; bananas. Sometimes called Estrella.

Lafa or **Lafachan** (lä'fä'jän'), town, central Kirin prov., Manchuria, 40 mi. E of Kirin; rail junction.

La Fábrica (lä fä'brēkä), village (1930 pop. 366), Llanquihue prov., S central Chile, resort on S shore of L. Llanquihue, 10 mi. NNE of Puerto Montt.

La Falda (lä fäl'dä), town (pop. 2,900), NW Córdoba prov., Argentina, 30 mi. NW of Córdoba; popular tourist resort in N Córdoba hills; alt. 3,000 ft. Quarrying (granite, marble, lime) and stock-raising center. Picturesque setting. Grottoes and waterfalls near by.

Lafarge, France: see VIVIERS.

La Farge (lù färj'), village (pop. 905), Vernon co., SW Wis., on Kickapoo R. and 35 mi. SE of La Crosse, in dairying and tobacco-growing area; timber; cheese.

La Fargeville (lù färj'vĭl), village (1940 pop. 616), Jefferson co., N N.Y., 16 mi. N of Watertown, in timber area.

Lafayette (läfäyĕt'), village (pop. 2,282), Constantine dept., NE Algeria, in Little Kabylia, 20 mi. NW of Sétif; cereals. Cork-oak forests and olive groves (N). Zinc deposits.

Lafayette, Brazil: see CONSELHEIRO LAFAIETE.

Lafayette or **Central Lafayette,** locality, SE Puerto Rico, just N of Arroyo, 3½ mi. E of Guayama; sugar mill.

Lafayette. 1 (lä"fēĕt') County (□ 537; pop. 13,203), SW Ark.; ⊙ Lewisville. Bounded S by La. line, W by Red R.; drained by Bodcau Creek. Oil and agr. area (cotton, corn, potatoes, hay); cotton ginning, lumber milling; sulphur plant. Timber; gravel. Formed 1827. **2** (lă'fāĕt", lùfā'ĭt) County (□ 543 pop. 3,440), N Fla., bounded E and NE by Suwannee R.; ⊙ Mayo. Swampy flatwoods area, with many small lakes. Farming (corn, peanuts, tobacco), cattle raising, lumbering. Limestone and phosphate deposits. Formed 1856. **3** (lä"fäĕt') Parish (□ 283; pop. 57,743), S La.; ⊙ Lafayette. Bounded N by short Bayou Carencro, drained by Vermilion R. (navigable). Agr. (cotton, sugar cane, rice, sweet potatoes, corn, hay, livestock). Lumber; oil, natural gas; fisheries. Processing of farm products, other mfg. Formed 1823. **4** (lä"-fāĕt', lùfā'ĭt) County (□ 679; pop. 22,798), N Miss.; ⊙ Oxford. Drained by Yocono and Tallahatchie rivers; Sardis Reservoir is in NW. Agr. (cotton, corn, dairy products, poultry, truck); pine, hardwood timber. Formed 1836. **5** (lă"fēĕt', lä'-fēĕt) County (□ 634; pop. 25,272), W central Mo.; ⊙ Lexington. Bounded N by Missouri R. Agr. (wheat, corn, oats, apples), cattle, poultry, hogs; coal mines, rock quarries; mfg. at Higginsville. Formed 1834. **6** (lă'fāĕt") County (□ 643; pop. 18,137), S Wis., bordered S by Ill.; ⊙ Darlington. Drained by Pecatonica and Galena rivers. Farming, dairying, stock raising; zinc mining. Area formerly had important lead-mining industry. Contains First Capital State Park. Formed 1846.

La Fayette. 1 or **Lafayette** (lù fā'ĭt), city (pop. 4,884), ⊙ Walker co., NW Ga., 31 mi. NNW of Rome; textile mfg. (hosiery, overalls, cloth). Founded 1835. **2** (lă'fāĕt") Village (pop. 301), Stark co., N central Ill., 10 mi. SSW of Kewanee, in agr. and bituminous-coal area. **3** or **Lafayette** (both: läfā'ĭt), town (pop. 246), Christian co., SW Ky., near Tenn. line, 17 mi. SW of Hopkinsville.

Lafayette. 1 (lùfā'ĭt) City (pop. 2,353), ⊙ Chambers co., E Ala., 65 mi. NE of Montgomery, in cotton, corn, and potato area; textile and lumber milling. Settled 1883. **2** (lă"fēĕt') Residential village (1940 pop. 1,227), Contra Costa co., W Calif., 10 mi. ENE of Oakland; fruit, nuts. **3** (lä"fēĕt') Town (pop. 2,090), Boulder co., N central Colo., 20 mi. NNW of Denver, in coal, grain, and sugar-beet area; alt. 5,176 ft. Inc. 1890. **4** (lä'fēĕt", lă"fēĕt') City (pop. 35,568), ⊙ Tippecanoe co., W central Ind., on the Wabash and c.60 mi. NW of Indianapolis; market for grain and livestock; coal-mining center, with railroad shops, meat-packing plants. Mfg. also of rubber, paper, wire and foundry products, gears, tools, electrical appliances, building materials, drugs, soap, beer, soybean oil, safes, plumbing and mill supplies. Seat of Purdue Univ. Has a historical mus. and an art mus. Settled 1825, inc. 1853. A monument marks site of Indian trading post 7 mi. W of the city. Battle of Tippecanoe fought in 1811 at near-by BATTLE GROUND. **5** (lä"fäĕt') City (pop. 33,541), ⊙ Lafayette parish, S La., c.50 mi. WSW of Baton Rouge and on Vermilion R.; mfg., commercial, and shipping center for agr. and mineral area; machine and railroad shops, sugar refineries, cotton- and cottonseed-processing plants, canneries, creameries. Agr. (rice, sugar cane, cotton, corn, oats, potatoes, truck, livestock). Oil and gas fields, salt and sulphur mines. Seat of Southwestern Louisiana Inst. First inc. 1836, reincorporated 1869; renamed 1884; and inc. 1914 as a city. Here are several historic landmarks and old houses, a R.C. cathedral (1916), and a Carmelite monastery. **6** (lă'fēĕt", lă"fēĕt') Village (pop. 438), Nicollet co., S Minn., on branch of Minnesota R. and 28 mi. NW of Mankato, in agr. area (grain, sugar beets, livestock, poultry); dairy products. **7** (lä"fāĕt', lă"fēĕt') Village (pop. 444), Allen co., W Ohio, 8 mi. E of Lima, near Ottawa R.; limestone quarrying. **8** (lä'fēĕt", lă'–) City (pop. 662), Yamhill co., NW Oregon, 5 mi. NE of McMinnville and on Yamhill R.; grain, truck. **9** (lă'fēĕt") Residential and mfg. village (1940 pop. 527) in North Kingstown town, Washington co., S central R.I., 18 mi. S of Providence; woolens. **10** (lă'fāĕt") Town (pop. 1,195), ⊙ Macon co., N Tenn., 50 mi. NE of Nashville; trade center for farm area; produces hardwood flooring, underwear, packed meat. Inc. since 1940.

Lafayette, Fort, N.Y.: see FORT HAMILTON.

Lafayette, Mount, N.H.: see FRANCONIA MOUNTAINS.

Lafayette National Park, Maine: see ACADIA NATIONAL PARK.

Lafayette Springs (lä"fāĕt', lùfā'ĭt), village (1940 pop. 151), Lafayette co., N Miss., 15 mi. E of Oxford, in agr. and timber area; lumber milling.

La Feria (lù fĕr'ēù), city (pop. 2,952), Cameron co., extreme S Texas, 27 mi. NW of Brownsville, in lower Rio Grande valley; trade, shipping point in rich irrigated citrus, truck, cotton area; cotton ginning, fruit, vegetable packing.

Laferrière (läfĕryâr'), village (pop. 4,239), Oran dept., NW Algeria, 4 mi. NNE of Aïn-Témouchent; winegrowing, distilling.

Laferté-sur-Amance (läfĕrtā'-sür-ämãs'), village (pop. 254), Haute-Marne dept., NE France, 17 mi. E of Langres; grows oysters.

Lafia (läfē'ä), town (pop. 6,594), Benue prov., Northern Provinces, central Nigeria, on railroad and 50 mi. N of Makurdi; lignite-mining center. Sometimes called Lafia Beriberi.

Lafiagi (läfyä'jē), town (pop. 7,134), Ilorin prov., Northern Provinces, W central Nigeria, near the Niger, 60 mi. NE of Ilorin; agr. trade center; sheanut processing, cotton weaving; cassava, yams, corn; cattle, skins. Limestone deposits.

Lafitte (lùfēt'), village (1940 pop. 665), Jefferson parish, extreme SE La., on Gulf Intracoastal Waterway and 12 mi. S of New Orleans; shrimp fishing, canning. Lafitte Village, on site of old settlement of Lafitte's 19th-cent. pirate band, is 5 mi. SSE; shrimp fisheries; hunting, fishing clubs.

Laflèche or **La Flèche** (lä flĕsh'), village (pop. 474), S Sask., 27 mi. W of Assiniboia; grain elevators, flour mills.

Laflin, borough (pop. 258), Luzerne co., NE central Pa., 4 mi. ENE of Wilkes-Barre.

La Florencia (lä flōrĕn'syä), village, ⊙ Matacos dept., W Formosa natl. territory, Argentina, on Bermejo R. and 110 mi. WNW of Las Lomitas; corn and rice growing, lumbering.

La Floresta (lä flōrĕ'stä), town (pop. 2,000) Canelones dept., S Uruguay, beach resort at mouth of the Río de la Plata, on railroad and 29 mi. ENE of Montevideo. Sometimes called Costa Azul for an adjoining resort. La Floresta station is 7 mi. NNW, near Soca.

La Florida (lä flōrē'dä), town (pop. 2,980), Valle del Cauca dept., W Colombia, in Cauca valley, 20 mi. ESE of Cali; agr. center (sugar cane, coffee, tobacco, corn, cattle).

Lafnitz River (läf'nĭts), SE Austria and SW Hungary, rises in SE Fischbach Alps, flows c.50 mi. S to Raab R. at Szentgotthard, Hungary, just over Hung. border.

La Follette (lù fŏ'lĭt), city (pop. 5,797), Campbell co., NE Tenn., near Norris Reservoir, 30 mi. NNW of Knoxville, in E foothills of the Cumberlands; coal-mining center; mfg. of shirts, wagons; lumbering. Inc. 1897.

La Fonciere, Paraguay: see PUERTO FONCIERE.

La Fontaine (lä foun'tùn), town (pop. 627), Wabash co., NE central Ind., near Mississinewa R., 8 mi. NNW of Marion, in agr. area.

Laforce (läfôrs'), village (pop. 430), Dordogne dept., SW France, near the Dordogne, 5 mi. W of Bergerac; winegrowing.

Lafourche (läfōōsh'), parish (□ 1,157; pop. 42,209), extreme SE La.; ⊙ Thibodaux. Bounded S by Gulf of Mexico, SW by Bayou Pointe au Chien, E partly by Barataria Bay; intersected by Bayou Lafourche (navigable); crossed by Gulf Intracoastal Waterway and Southwestern Louisiana Canal. Agr. (sugar cane, corn, potatoes, hay, truck). Natural gas, oil. Mfg., including sugar refining. Formed 1805.

La Fourche, Bayou (bī'ō"), NE La., rises in Morehouse parish, flows generally S c.75 mi. to Boeuf R. c.13 mi. W of Winnsboro. There is a Bayou Lafourche in SE La.

Lafourche, Bayou, SE La., formerly a right-bank distributary of the Mississippi, from which it is now cut off by dam at Donaldsonville; extends 107 mi. SE, through Assumption and Lafourche parishes, to Gulf of Mexico bet. Timbalier and Caminada bays. Navigable to Napoleonville; main traffic is oil barges. Crossed at Leeville by Southwestern Louisiana Canal, and at point c.25 mi. N by Gulf Intracoastal Waterway. There is a Bayou La Fourche in NE La.

Lafragua, Mexico: see SALTILLO, Puebla.

Lafrançaise (läfrãsĕz'), village (pop. 717), Tarn-et-Garonne dept., SW France, near the Tarn, 9 mi. NW of Montauban; flour milling, fruit and vegetable growing.

La France, textile village (1940 pop. 964), Anderson co., NW S.C., 10 mi. NNW of Anderson; upholstery fabrics.

La Francia (lä frän'syä), town (pop. estimate 1,500), E Córdoba prov., Argentina, 32 mi. W of San Francisco; wheat, flax, oats, stock; dairy products.

Laga, Monti della (môn'tē dĕl-lä lä'gä), mountain group, S central Italy, NW of Gran Sasso d'Italia, bet. Tronto and Vomano rivers. Chief peaks, Monte Gorzano (8,040 ft.) and Pizzo de Sevo (7,946 ft.).

Lagadia, Greece: see LANGADIA.

La Gaiba, Bolivia: see GAIBA, LAKE.

La Gallareta (lä gäyärä'tä), town (pop. estimate 1,000), N central Santa Fe prov., Argentina, on railroad and 70 mi. NE of San Cristóbal; agr. (corn, flax, wheat, livestock) and lumbering center; tannin factory.

Lagan, Russian SFSR: see KASPISKI.

Lagan River (lă'gùn), Northern Ireland, rises 4 mi. SW of Ballynahinch, Co. Down, flows past Dromore, turns N and flows NE along border of cos. Antrim and Down, past Lisburn, to Belfast Lough at Belfast; 45 mi. long. Canal joins it to Lough Neagh.

Lagares (lùgä'rĭsh), village (pop. 1,392), Coimbra dist., N central Portugal, 34 mi. ENE of Coimbra; corn, grain, beans, wine; pine forests. Also called Lagares da Beira.

Lagarfljot (lä'gärfùlyōt"), Icelandic *Lagarfljót*, river, E Iceland, rises at E edge of Vatnajokull, flows c.100 mi. NE to Atlantic 30 mi. NNW of Seydisfjordur. Lower course is navigable.

Lagarina, Val (väl lägärē'nä), valley of Adige R., N Italy; extends from Calliano S to Rivoli Veronese. Agr. (grapes, raw silk, fruit, tobacco). Chief centers: Rovereto, Mori, Ala.

Laga River, Swedish *Lagan* (lä'gän"), SW Sweden, rises S of Jonkoping, flows S, past Varnamo and Ljungby, to Markaryd; thence flows W, past Laholm, to the Kattegat 4 mi. WNW of Laholm; 170 mi. long. Hydroelectric plants at Knared and Traryd; salmon fishing.

Lagartera (lägärtä'rä), town (pop. 2,491), Toledo prov., central Spain, 20 mi. W of Talavera de la Reina; cereals, vegetables, grapes, olives, cattle, sheep. Known for its old Toledan customs.

Lagarto (lùgär'tōō), city (pop. 3,328), central Sergipe, NE Brazil, 40 mi. W of Aracaju; coffee, tobacco, sugar, cotton.

Lagarto (lägär'tō), village (pop. 306), Colón prov., central Panama, just S of Nuevo Chagres, at road junction to Escobal and at mouth of Lagarto R. (small coastal stream). Corn, rice, beans, coconuts, livestock.

Lagartos Lagoon (lägär'tōs), inlet of Gulf of Mexico, on Yucatan-Quintana Roo border, N Yucatan Peninsula, 60 mi. NE of Valladolid; linked with ocean by narrow, 12-mi. channel.

Lagash (lā'găsh) or **Shirpurla** (shĭrpōōr'lù), anc. Sumerian city, S Babylonia, whose site is at Telloh, SE Iraq, in Muntafiq prov., bet. the Tigris and the Euphrates, 40 mi. N of Nasiriya. Flourished c.3000 B.C. and for a time controlled a large part of S Babylonia, its power extending over Nippur. Excavations begun 1877 revealed ruins of a palace on site of much older temple (c.2700 B.C.). The notable Stele of the Vulture was found and some 30,000 inscribed tablets were recovered, revealing city rivaled Kish and Umma, was destroyed, and rose to new supremacy under Gudea, c.2450 B.C.

Lage (lä'gù), town (pop. 9,901), in former Lippe, NW Germany, after 1945 in North Rhine-Westphalia, at N foot of Teutoburg Forest, on the Werre and 5 mi. NW of Detmold; rail junction; mfg. of machine tools.

Lage (lä'hā), town (pop. 1,134), La Coruña prov., NW Spain, fishing port on the Atlantic, 31 mi. WSW of La Coruña; lumbering, cattle raising; cereals, vegetables, fruit. Kaolin quarries near by.

Lageado, Brazil: see LAJEADO.
Lage Island (lä'zhī), low islet in entrance to Guanabara Bay, SE Brazil, 4 mi. from center of Rio de Janeiro. Ship channel is E of it.
Lagen River (lô'gŭn), Nor. *Lågen*. **1** In SE Norway, rises in the E Hardangervidda N of Rodberg, flows 210 mi. generally SSE, through the NUMEDAL, past Rodberg, Kongsberg, and Sandsvaer, to the Skagerrak at Larvik. Below Rodberg it falls over 1,150 ft. into expansion of Norefjord (10 mi. long); major power station here supplies Oslo and Tonsberg. Sometimes spelled Laagen; sometimes called Numedalslagen (nōō'mŭdäls-lô"gŭn), Nor. *Numedalslågen*. **2** In Opland co., S central Norway, rises on N slope of Jotunheim Mts., flows 125 mi. generally SE, through the Gudbrandsdal, past Dombas, Dovre, Otta, Kvam, Vinstra, Ringebu, and Tretten, to L. Mjosa 4 mi. NNW of Lillehammer. Receives Otta and Vinstra rivers (right). Sometimes spelled Laagen; sometimes called Gudebrandslagen, Nor. *Gudebrandslågen*.
Lagens, Azores: see LAJES.
Lagens do Pico, Azores: see LAJES DO PICO.
Lägerdorf (lā'gūrdôrf), village (pop. 4,638), in Schleswig-Holstein, NW Germany, 4 mi. SE of Itzehoe; limestone quarrying.
Lageri (lä'gyĭrē), town (1926 pop. 3,815), central Kharkov oblast, Ukrainian SSR, near the Northern Donets, 2 mi. WNW of Balakleya.
Lägern (lā'gūrn), extreme E spur of the Jura, N Switzerland. Burghorn, its highest peak (2,830 ft.), is 2 mi. E of Baden.
Lages, in Brazilian and Portuguese names: see LAJES.
Lage Tatra, Czechoslovakia: see LOW TATRA.
Lage Zwaluwe (lä'khū zvä'lüvū), town (pop. 2,418), North Brabant prov., SW Netherlands, on the Hollandschdiep and 8 mi. NNW of Breda; rail junction near S end of Moerdijk Bridge. Sometimes spelled Lagezwaluwe.
Laggan (lă'gŭn). **1** Agr. village and parish (pop. 621), S Inverness, Scotland, on the Spey and 10 mi. WSW of Kingussie. Loch Laggan (7 mi. long, 1 mi. wide) is 6 mi. SW on Spean R.; has 2 islets, on one of which are ruins of very old castle. Just W of the loch is a new 4-mi.-long reservoir connected by tunnel with Loch Treig, forming part of the LOCHABER hydroelectric power system. **2** Agr. village, central Inverness, Scotland, on Caledonian Canal, at head of Loch Lochy, and 9 mi. SW of Fort Augustus. Site of canal locks, and scene (1541) of the Battle of the Shirts, bet. the Frasers and Macdonalds.
Laghman (lŭgmän'), town (pop. over 2,000), Eastern Prov., Afghanistan, 20 mi. NW of Jalalabad; center of irrigated valley formed by Alishang and Alinghar rivers, which rise in the Hindu Kush and join Kabul R. (S).
Laghouat (lägwät'), town (pop. 11,010) and Saharan oasis, ⊙ Ghardaïa territory, N central Algeria, at S foot of the Djebel Amour (Saharan Atlas), 65 mi. SSW of Djelfa; 33°49'N 2°53'E; alt. 2,600 ft. Junction of roads from Oran and Algiers, and N terminus of trans-Saharan auto track to Zinder (Fr. West Africa). Military station. Oasis grows dates, citrus fruit, figs, vegetables. Occupied 1852 by French after a costly siege.
Lagich (lä'gĭch), town (1926 pop. 4,082), NE Azerbaijan SSR, on S slope of the Greater Caucasus, 20 mi. NW of Shemakha; livestock, wheat.
La Gloria (lä glōr'yä), town (pop. 1,331), Magdalena dept., N Colombia, port on Magdalena R. and 30 mi. SSE of El Banco; trading post and airport; coffee, cacao, stock.
La Gloria, Texas: see PREMONT.
Lagnieu (länyû'), village (pop. 1,902), Ain dept., E France, at foot of the S Jura, near Rhone R., 19 mi. NW of Belley; drawplate mfg., wiredrawing, glass making.
Lagny (länyē'), town (pop. 7,613), Seine-et-Marne dept., N central France, on left bank of the Marne (canalized) and 16 mi. E of Paris; tanning center; mfg. (photographic equipment, optical instruments, vinegar), metalworking, printing. Has unfinished 13th-cent. abbatial church.
Lago (lä'gô), village (pop. 1,672), Cosenza prov., Calabria, S Italy, 11 mi. SW of Cosenza.
Lago, district, Mozambique: see VILA CABRAL.
Lagoa (lùgō'ù), town (pop. 6,412), Ponta Delgada dist., E Azores, on S shore of São Miguel Isl., 5 mi. E of Ponta Delgada; agr. center (wine, pineapples, sugar beets); alcohol distilling, flour milling, pottery mfg.
Lagoa, town (pop. 2,462), Faro dist., S Portugal, 5 mi. E of Portimão, in fertile agr. region (almonds, figs, carobs, wine, vegetables); cork processing, pottery mfg.
Lagoa dos Gatos (dōōs gä'tōōs), city (pop. 1.951), E Pernambuco, NE Brazil, 22 mi. W of Palmares; cotton, sugar.
Lagoa Dourada (dōrä'dù), city (pop. 1,954), S central Minas Gerais, Brazil, 19 mi. NE of São João del Rei; tin deposits.
Lago Argentino, town, Argentina: see EL CALAFATE.
Lagoa Santa (sän'tù), city (pop. 2,667), S central Minas Gerais, Brazil, on fine lake of same name, 18 mi. N of Belo Horizonte. Extensive excavations conducted here uncovered skeleton of paleolithic *homo brasiliensis*.
Lagoa Vermelha (vĕrmā'lyù), city (pop. 2,339), NE Rio Grande do Sul, Brazil, in the Serra Geral, 30 mi. E of Passo Fundo; livestock slaughtering, by-products processing. Pinewoods lumbering (N).
Lago Buenos Aires (lä'gō bwā'nōs ī'rās), village (pop. estimate 1,500), SW Comodoro Rivadavia, Argentina, 8 mi. E of L. Buenos Aires, on road to Chile, and 100 mi. W of Colonia Las Heras; resort and sheep-raising center. Airport. Lead mines near by. Formerly Río Fenix.
Lagodei, El, Ital. Somaliland: see GARDO.
Lagodekhi (lŭgùdyĕ'khē), town (1948 pop. over 2,000), E Georgian SSR, in Kakhetia, on S slope of the Greater Caucasus, 40 mi. E of Telavi, near Azerbaijan border; tobacco center.
La Gomera (lä gōmā'rä), town (1950 pop. 392), Escuintla dept., S Guatemala, in coastal plain, 23 mi. SW of Escuintla; livestock.
Lagonegro (lägōnā'grô), town (pop. 4,729), Potenza prov., Basilicata, S Italy, 22 mi. SSE of Sala Consilina; mfg. (woolen textiles, tower clocks).
Lagonoy (lägōnoi', lägō'noi), town (1939 pop. 2,481; 1948 municipality pop. 22,604), Camarines Sur prov., SE Luzon, Philippines, near Lagonoy Gulf, 24 mi. ENE of Naga; chrome-ore mining and agr. center (abacá, rice).
Lagonoy Gulf, large inlet of Philippine Sea, SE Luzon, bet. Rungus Point peninsula and Catanduanes isl. in N and San Miguel, Cagraray, Batan, and Rapu-Rapu isls. in S; c.50 mi. E-W, c.20 mi. N-S. Merges N with Maqueda Channel.
Lagoon Islands: see ELLICE ISLANDS.
Lagor (lägôr'), village (pop. 327), Basses-Pyrénées dept., SW France, on the Gave de Pau and 9 mi. SE of Orthez; orchards, vineyards; cattle and horse raising.
Lago Ranco (lä'gō räng'kō), village (1930 pop. 68), Valdivia prov., S central Chile, on S shore of L. Ranco, in Chilean lake dist., 55 mi. SE of Valdivia; rail terminus, tourist resort; fishing, lumbering.
Lagos or **Lagos de Moreno** (lä'gōs dā mōrā'nō), city (pop. 12,490), NE Jalisco, central Mexico, in Sierra Madre Occidental, on railroad and 23 mi. NW of León; alt. 6,371 ft. Resort; silver mining and agr. center (beans, chili, corn, stock); dairy industry, shoe mfg. Colonial churches.
Lagos (lä'gùs, lā'gŏs), Yoruba *Eko*, town (pop. 90,193; township pop. 126,108), ⊙ Nigeria, on Lagos Isl., at W end of Lagos Lagoon just off Gulf of Guinea, 75 mi. SW of Ibadan, 260 mi. ENE of Accra (Gold Coast); 6°26'N 3°23'E. Chief port of Nigeria, accessible (since 1907, when entrance channel was dredged) to ocean-going vessels drawing 27 ft. Exports palm oil and kernels, hardwood, cacao, rubber, peanuts, cotton, hides, shea products, tin, copra, piassava fiber and gums. Apapa, on mainland opposite city, is terminus of railroad to the interior (Ibadan, Kano) and has modern harbor facilities. Sawmilling and brewing are chief industries. Lagos is residence of governor of Nigeria. Has customs wharf, govt. bldgs., hosps., churches, mosques, and racecourse. Site of King's Col., Queen's Col. Lagos township includes all of Lagos Isl. (5 mi. long, 1 mi. wide; Lagos at W end; Ikoyi in E), Iddo Isl. (linked with Lagos by Carter Bridge; with mainland by railroad and road bridge), and, on mainland, Apapa (port), Ebutte Metta, and Yaba (residential towns). Site named *lagos* by Port. navigators in 15th cent. Settled by Yorubas c.1700. A notorious slave market until mid-19th cent. Off Lagos, in 1759, Admiral Boscowen defeated French fleet. City was occupied by British in 1851; ceded to the crown in 1861. Colony of Lagos (formed 1862) was administered as part of Sierra Leone after 1866, and as part of Gold Coast 1874–86. In 1886, Lagos and surrounding territory were separated from Gold Coast and erected into self-governing colony and protectorate, which in turn were amalgamated (1906) with protectorate of Southern Nigeria, to form colony and protectorate of Southern Nigeria. Today, the colony (□ 1,381; pop. 325,020) is one of Nigeria's 4 major administrative divisions, governed by a commissioner residing at Lagos.
Lagos (lä'gōōsh), city (pop. 6,938), Faro dist., S Portugal, port on the Atlantic (S coast), 19 mi. ENE of Cape St. Vincent; rail terminus; sardine and tuna fisheries and canneries; pottery mfg. Once a favorite residence of Prince Henry the Navigator, it was laid in ruins by earthquake of 1755. Anc. Lacobriga, a Roman port, was near by.
Lagos, Los, department, Argentina: see NAHUEL HUAPÍ.
Lagos, Los, Chile: see LOS LAGOS.
Lago Santo (lä'gô sän'tô), village (pop. 2,664), Ferrara prov., Emilia-Romagna, N central Italy, 5 mi. NNW of Comacchio, on a lagoon of the Adriatic; fishing.
Lagos de Moreno, Mexico: see LAGOS.
Lagos Lagoon (lä'gùs, lā'gŏs), W part of coastal lagoon, SW Nigeria, N of Lagos; 11 mi. long, 5 mi. wide. Opens into Gulf of Guinea S of Lagos. Receives Ogun R.
Lagosta, island, Yugoslavia: see LASTOVO ISLAND.
La Grande (lä grănd'), city (pop. 8,635), ⊙ Union co., NE Oregon, 40 mi. SE of Pendleton and on Grande Ronde R., at foot of Blue Mts., W of Wallowa Mts.; alt. 2,786 ft. Railroad shops, lumber and flour mills, meat-packing plants; trade and shipping point for livestock, fruit, lumber area. Seat of Eastern Oregon Col. of Education. Founded 1861, inc. 1886.
La Grande Dam, Wash.: see NISQUALLY RIVER.
La Grandeza (lä grändā'sä), town (pop. 860), Chiapas, S Mexico, in Sierra Madre, 11 mi. N of Motozintla; sugar cane, fruit.
Lagrange (lùgrānj'), county (□ 379; pop. 15,347), NE Ind.; ⊙ Lagrange. Bounded N by Mich. line; drained by Pigeon and Short Little Elkhart rivers. Dairying, farming (soybeans, grain), stock raising; poultry hatcheries; processing of dairy products. Formed 1832.
La Grange (lù grānj'). **1** City (pop. 25,025), ⊙ Troup co., W Ga., 39 mi. N of Columbus, near Ala. line. Textile-center; mfg. (tire-cord fabrics, yarn, overalls, cloth); sawmilling. La Grange Col. here. Many old classic-revival houses. Inc. 1828. **2** Residential village (pop. 12,002), Cook co., NE Ill., W suburb of Chicago, 23 mi. E of Aurora, in diversified-farming area; mfg. (transportation equipment, aluminum products); limestone quarries. Has jr. col. Settled in 1830s; inc. 1879. **3** Town (pop. 1,558), ⊙ Oldham co., N Ky., 25 mi. ENE of Louisville, in agr. area (burley tobacco, dairy products, oats, corn). In 1940, succeeded Frankfort as seat of state reformatory and penitentiary. **4** or **Lagrange**, town (pop. 511), Penobscot co., central Maine, 20 mi. E of Dover-Foxcroft; agr., lumbering. **5** City (pop. 1,106), Lewis co., NE Mo., on the Mississippi, at mouth of Wyaconda R., and 6 mi. S of Canton; agr. (grain, livestock); iron foundry. Platted 1830. **6** Town (pop. 1,852), Lenoir co., E central N.C., 12 mi. SE of Goldsboro; agr. trade center; mfg. of metal products; lumbering. Inc. 1869. **7** Town (pop. 241), Fayette co., SW Tenn., near Wolf R., 45 mi. E of Memphis. **8** City (pop. 2,738), ⊙ Fayette, S central Texas, on Colorado R. and c.55 mi. ESE of Austin; trade, shipping, processing center for cotton, dairy, truck area; milk processing, mattress plants; hatcheries; cotton ginning. State park here has monument on tomb of men killed in Texans' expedition (1842) against Mier, Mexico, and those slain (1842) by Mexican invaders near San Antonio. **9** Town (pop. 221), Goshen co., SE Wyo., on Horse Creek, near Nebr. line, and 48 mi. NE of Cheyenne; alt. 4,560 ft.
Lagrange. **1** Town (pop. 1,892), ⊙ Lagrange co., NE Ind., on Pigeon R. and 28 mi. E of Elkhart; dairying center; poultry hatcheries. Platted 1836, inc. 1855. **2** Town, Maine: see LA GRANGE. **3** Village (pop. 712), Lorain co., N Ohio, 8 mi. S of Elyria, in agr. area.
La Grange Park, village (pop. 6,176), Cook co., NE Ill., W suburb of Chicago, just N of La Grange, in diversified-farming area. Inc. 1892.
Lagrasse (lägräs'), village (pop. 573), Aude dept., S France, in the Corbières, 16 mi. SE of Carcassonne; winegrowing. Has ruins of medieval abbey founded by Charlemagne.
La Grita (lä grē'tä), town (pop. 3,918), Táchira state, W Venezuela, in Andean spur, 31 mi. NE of San Cristóbal; alt. 4,715 ft.; agr. center (potatoes, wheat, cacao, coffee, sugar cane, cattle).
Lagro (lùgrō'), town (pop. 545), Wabash co., NE central Ind., on Wabash R. opposite mouth of Salamonie R., and 5 mi. ENE of Wabash; rock-wool products.
La Guaira (lä gwī'rä), town (pop. 10,103), Federal Dist., N Venezuela, port on the Caribbean, at foot of steep coastal range, 7 mi. N of Caracas (linked by highway and railroad over mts.); 10°36'N 66°56'W. Has hot, tropical climate. Venezuela's principal port for exports, and 2d for imports; almost all trade for central part of republic passes through here. Has one of world's most beautiful harbors, which can accommodate ships of any size. Exports coffee, cacao, tobacco, hides, skins, lumber. Mfg. includes breweries, soap and candle factories, sawmills, tanneries. Fishing center and resort. Customhouse, airport. Has old colonial bldgs., including a fort and fine churches. Founded 1577. Seaside resort of Macuto is 2½ mi. E.
La Guajira, commissary, Colombia: see GUAJIRA.
Laguardia (lägwär'dhyä), town (pop. 2,053), Álava prov., N Spain, 9 mi. NW of Logroño; winegrowing center; also flour mills; cereals, olive oil, fruit. Has remains of medieval walls.
La Guardia Field (lù gwär'dēù), SE N.Y., New York city municipal airport (558 acres) in N Queens borough, along Flushing Bay. Seaplane, landplane facilities; part of Port of New York. Opened 1939.
La Guayra (lä gwī'rä), village (pop. 63), Colón prov., central Panama, minor port on Caribbean Sea, 7.5 mi. NE of Portobelo; bananas, abacá, cacao, livestock.
Laguépie (lägäpē'), village (pop. 777), Tarn-et-Garonne dept., SW France, on the Aveyron at mount of the Viaur, and 14 mi. SSW of Villefranche-de-Rouergue; shoe mfg., wool spinning.
Laguiole (lägyôl'), village (pop. 833), Aveyron dept., S France, on W slope of Monts d'Aubrac, 26 mi. SE of Aurillac; cheese making; mfg. of cutlery, wool spinning. Winter sports.
Laguna (lùgōō'nù), city (pop. 8,498), SE Santa Catarina, Brazil, on the Atlantic near entrance to a

shallow inlet (lagoon), 65 mi. SSW of Florianópolis; coal-shipping port serving mines in Tubarão area (just SW; linked by rail). Coal goes to Rio de Janeiro for Volta Redonda steel mill. Loading facilities greatly improved since 1945. Also ships timber, skins, clay, alcohol. Founded c.1720. Hq. of 1893 insurrection.

Laguna (lägōō'nä), village (pop. 969), Alajuela prov., W central Costa Rica, on San Carlos road, and 1 mi. N of Zarcero; potatoes, fruit, flowers.

Laguna (lūgōō'nū, Sp. lägōō'nä), province (□ 465; 1948 pop. 321,247), S Luzon, Philippines, bounded N by Laguna de Bay; ⊙ SANTA CRUZ. Fertile terrain, drained by many small streams; rises in S to 3,750 ft. at Mt. Makiling, and in SE to 7,177 ft. at Mt. Banahao on border of Quezon prov. Agr. (rice, coconuts, sugar cane), fishing. SAN PABLO city is in, but independent of, the prov.

Laguna (lūgōō'nū), pueblo (□ 660.8), Valencia co., W central N.Mex. Laguna village (1948 pop. 2,932) is on San Jose R. and c.45 mi. W of Albuquerque; alt. 5,786 ft. Inhabitants are Pueblo Indians of several linguistic stocks, but Keresan and English are generally spoken. Fiesta is that of San José (Sept. 19). San José de Laguna Church dates from 1699. Village settled 1697, established as pueblo 1699. San Mateo Mts. are near by.

Laguna, La (lä lägōō'nä), city (pop. 10,485), Tenerife, Canary Isls., 4 mi. WNW of Santa Cruz de Tenerife (linked by tramway). Beautifully situated university and cathedral town with a benign climate, attracting many visitors. Chiefly agr. trade (grapes, cereals, tomatoes, onions, potatoes). Mfg. of chocolate, soft drinks, meat products, ceramics, tiles, tobacco goods, photographic film. An old city, once chief town of the isls., it was superseded in importance by its port Santa Cruz de Tenerife.

Laguna Beach (lūgōō'nū), residential and resort city (pop. 6,661), Orange co., S Calif., on the Pacific, 30 mi. SE of Long Beach; artists' colony; known for scenic bays, cliffs, canyons. Inc. 1927.

Laguna Blanca (lägōō'nä bläng'kä). **1** Village (pop. 1,000), E Chaco natl. territory, Argentina, on railroad and 30 mi. NW of Resistencia; cotton, livestock center; cotton ginning. **2** Town (pop. estimate 1,000), ⊙ Pilagá dept. (□ c.1,500; 1947 census pop. 4,371), E Formosa natl. territory, Argentina, 38 mi. WNW of Asunción (Paraguay). Stock-raising center; farming, lumbering. Site of Franciscan mission.

Laguna Dam, Ariz. and Calif.: see IMPERIAL DAM.

Laguna de Bay, Philippines: see BAY, LAGUNA DE.

Laguna de Duero (dhä dhwä'rō), town (pop. 1,687), Valladolid prov., N central Spain, near the Duero, 5 mi. S of Valladolid, and on edge of salt-water lagoon; cattle raising, lumbering.

Laguna del Perro (lūgōō'nū dĕl pĕ'rō), lake in Torrance co., central N.Mex., E of Manzano Range, just SE of Estancia; 12 mi. long, 1 mi. wide; surrounded by numerous small, half-evaporated lakes.

Laguna de Negrillos (nāgrē'lyōs), town (pop. 1,617), Leon prov., NW Spain, 26 mi. SSW of Leon; beans, cereals, wine.

Laguna de Yaxhá, Guatemala: see YASHÁ.

Laguna District [Span. *laguna*=lake, so-called from shallow lakes on plain], irrigated area (c.900,000 acres) under cultivation mainly in W Coahuila, partly in E Durango, Mexico. Water comes from NAZAS RIVER. Formerly consisted of large estates owned by Sp. and Br. settlers; land reapportioned 1936 as part of agrarian reform of Cárdenas and distributed to Mex. farmers on *ejido* system, a kind of cooperative. Major crops: cotton and wheat. TORREÓN and GÓMEZ PALACIO are chief centers. Lakes Mayrán and Viesca are principal basins.

Laguna Larga (lär'gä), town (pop. 2,704), central Córdoba prov., Argentina, 33 mi. SE of Córdoba; peanuts, corn, wheat, fruit, vegetables, livestock.

Laguna Madre (lūgōō'nū mä'drē), NE Mexico and S Texas, narrow, shallow lagoon along Gulf coast; from Corpus Christi Bay, Texas, it extends c.120 mi. S to mouth of the Rio Grande, whose delta interrupts it for c.40 mi., then continues c.100 mi. to point 10 mi. N of mouth of Soto la Marina R., Tamaulipas. Sheltered from the Gulf by narrow barrier isls. (notably Padre Isl., Texas). U.S. section is traversed by Gulf Intracoastal Waterway.

Laguna Mountains, S Calif., wooded range in central San Diego co., extends c.35 mi. NW from Mexico border (N end of Sierra Juárez); max. alt. c.6,300 ft. Recreational region; largely in Cleveland Natl. Forest. Carrizo Gorge is at SE end.

Laguna Paiva (lägōō'nä pī'vä), town (pop. c.1,500), E Santa Fe prov., Argentina, 22 mi. N of Santa Fe; rail junction (with workshops) and agr. center (flax, corn, sunflowers, wheat, livestock). Has theater.

Lagunas (lägōō'näs), village (pop. 111), Tarapacá prov., N Chile, on railroad and 60 mi. SE of Iquique. Salt deposits near by.

Lagunas, town (pop. 1,548), Loreto dept., N central Peru, landing on Huallaga R., in Amazon basin, and 50 mi. NE of Yurimaguas; 5°20'S 75°40'W; bananas, yucca, forest products (rubber, timber).

Lagundo (lägōōn'dô), Ger. *Algund*, village (pop. 458), Bolzano prov., Trentino-Alto Adige, N Italy, on Adige R. and 1 mi. NW of Merano; sawmills.

Lagunilla (lägōōnē'lyä), village (pop. 1,876), Salamanca prov., W Spain, 12 mi. WSW of Béjar; olive-oil processing; livestock, chestnuts, wine.

Lagunillas (lägōōnē'yäs), town (pop. c.2,100), ⊙ Cordillera prov., Santa Cruz dept., SE Bolivia, 135 mi. SSW of Santa Cruz, on road; subtropical fruit (oranges, melons, bananas), corn.

Lagunillas, town (pop. 865), San Luis Potosí, N central Mexico, 37 mi. SE of Río Verde; grain, fruit, livestock.

Lagunillas, **1** Town (pop. 1,160), Mérida state, W Venezuela, in Andean spur, on transandine highway and 17 mi. WSW of Mérida; alt. 3,540 ft. Sugar cane, coffee, fruit, grain. The mineral urao (for treating tobacco) is extracted from lake near by. **2** or **Ciudad Ojeda** (syōōdädh' ōhā'dä), town (pop. 1,567; municipio pop. 19,391), Zulia state, NW Venezuela, on E shore of L. Maracaibo, 40 mi. SE of Maracaibo; petroleum center in what is considered the largest oil-producing field in South America; some oil derricks are in lake. Terminus of oil pipe line from fields near by.

Lagunita, Argentina: see BERMEJO, town.

Lagunitas, Peru: see LAGUNITOS.

Lagunitas (lägūnē'tūs), resort village (pop. c.375), Marin co., W Calif., 10 mi. W of San Rafael, and on Lagunitas Creek, which rises on N slope of Mt. Tamalpais, flows generally NW c.30 mi. to Tomales Bay. Dam impounds Alpine L. (c.2 mi. long; for water supply) 5 mi. W of San Rafael.

Lagunitas, Venezuela: see LIBERTAD, Cojedes state.

Lagunitos (lägōōnē'tōs), village (pop. 2,396), Piura dept., NW Peru, on coastal plain, SE of Negritos and 7 mi. SSE of Talara; petroleum production center. Petroleum is shipped via pipe line through TALARA. Also Lagunitas.

La Habana, Cuba: see HAVANA.

La Habra (lä hä'brū), city (pop. 4,961), Orange co., S Calif., just N of Fullerton, near oil fields; ships citrus fruit, avocados. Inc. 1925.

Lahad Datu (lū-äd' dä'tōō), town (pop. 3,000, including environs), East Coast residency, Br. North Borneo, on N shore of Darvel Bay, 55 mi. S of Sandakan; hemp-, tobacco-growing center; fisheries.

Lahaina (lūhī'nū), coast city (pop. 4,025), W Maui, T.H.; important port, formerly for whalers, now for sugar export; early (1810–1845) ⊙ Hawaiian Isls., until shift to Honolulu. First white settlement in Hawaiian Isls. Site of Lahainaluna School (established 1831).

Lahar (lūhär'), village, NE Madhya Bharat, India, 50 mi. E of Lashkar; gram, millet.

La Harpe (lū härp'). **1** City (pop. 1,295), Hancock co., W Ill., 17 mi. WNW of Macomb, in agr. area (grain, soybeans, livestock; dairy products); poultry hatchery. Inc. 1859. **2** City (pop. 511), Allen co., SE Kansas, 6 mi. E of Iola; livestock, grain; dairying.

Laharpur (lä'hŭrpōōr), town (pop. 13,218), Sitapur dist., central Uttar Pradesh, India, 17 mi. NE of Sitapur; trades in wheat, rice, gram, barley, oilseeds. Founded 1374 by Firoz Shah Tughlak. Raja Todar Mal, Akbar's finance minister and general, b. here.

Lahasusu, Manchuria: see TUNGKIANG, Sungkiang prov.

Lahat (lūhät'), town (pop. 1,438), central Perak, Malaya, 4 mi. SW of Ipoh; tin mining.

Lahave River (lūhāv'), W N.S., issues from small Lahave L. 30 mi. ENE of Annapolis Royal, flows 60 mi. SE, through several small lakes, past Bridgewater, to the Atlantic 7 mi. SSW of Lunenburg. Navigable below Bridgewater. Important salmon fisheries.

La Haye, Netherlands: see HAGUE, THE.

Lahdenpohja, Karelo-Finnish SSR: see LAKHDENPOKHYA.

Lahej or **Lahj** (lä'hūj), town (pop. 10,000), ⊙ Abdali sultanate, Western Aden Protectorate, 20 mi. WNW of Aden, in fertile agr. area irrigated by the Wadi Tiban; principal commercial center in Aden hinterland, trading with tribal areas; entrepôt on caravan route to Yemen; native handicrafts (metalwork). Imposing sultan's palace on town's S edge. Held by Turks during First World War, Lahej was later temporarily linked by railroad with Aden.

Laheria-Sarai, India: see DARBHANGA, city.

La Herradura or **Puerto Herradura** (lä, pwĕr'tō, ĕrädōō'rä), village (1930 pop. 252), Coquimbo prov., N central Chile, S suburb of Coquimbo, minor port on small inlet of Pacific; resort.

La Herradura, Peru: see CHORRILLOS.

La Herradura, village, La Paz dept., S Salvador, on Jaltepeque Lagoon, 28 mi. SE of San Salvador; resort (hunting, fishing). Salt extraction near by.

La Higuera (lä ēgā'rä), village (1930 pop. 678), Coquimbo prov., N central Chile, near the coast, 28 mi. NNW of La Serena; copper and silver mining.

Lahijan (lähējän'), town (1941 pop. 16,520), First Prov., in Gilan, N Iran, 23 mi. E of Resht and E of the Sefid Rud; trade center; known for its tea, rice, silk, oranges.

Lahinch or **Lehinch** (both: lūhĭnch'), Gaelic *Leacht Ui Chonchubhair*, town (pop. 354), W Co. Clare, Ireland, on Liscannor Bay, 2 mi. W of Ennistymon; seaside and golfing resort.

Lahj, Aden: see LAHEJ.

Lähn, Poland: see WLEN.

Lahn River (län), W Germany, rises on the Ederkopf, flows 160 mi. E, S, and W, past Marburg, Giessen (head of navigation), Wetzlar, Limburg, and Bad Ems, to the Rhine at Oberlahnstein. Receives the Dill (right). Iron mined in valley bet. Giessen and Limburg.

Laholm (lähôlm'), city (pop. 2,724), Halland co., SW Sweden, on Laga R. (falls), near its mouth on the Kattegat, 13 mi. SE of Halmstad; light industries; salmon fishing. Hydroelectric station. Has remains of 17th-cent. castle, on site of earlier fortification. Trade center in Middle Ages; suffered heavily in 17th-cent. Swedish-Danish wars.

Lahoma (lūhō'mū), town (pop. 190), Garfield co., N Okla., 12 mi. W of Enid, in agr. area.

La Honda (lä hŏn'dū), resort hamlet (pop. c.200), San Mateo co., W Calif., 11 mi. SSW of Redwood City, in a canyon among redwood groves.

Lahontan, Lake (lūhŏn'tūn), prehistoric body of water (□ c.8,400) which once covered much of NW Nev. and part of NE Calif. Some features of its irregular shoreline are still preserved. Greatest depth was 886 ft. Chief remnants are Pyramid, Walker, and Winnemucca lakes and Carson Sink. Part of its basin around Fallon now irrigated by Carson and Truckee rivers.

Lahontan Dam, Nev.: see CARSON RIVER.

Lahore (lūhôr'), dist. (□ 2,191; 1951 pop. 1,894,000), E Punjab, W Pakistan; ⊙ Lahore. In Bari Doab, bet. Ravi R. (NW) and Sutlej R. (SE); bordered E by Indian Punjab; irrigated by Upper Bari Doab and (S) by Dipalpur canal systems. Agr. (wheat, cotton, gram, oilseeds, rice); hand-loom weaving, cotton ginning. Trade centers: Lahore, Kasur, Chunian. Original dist. (□ 2,595; 1941 pop. 1,695,375) was divided in 1947 bet. East Punjab (India) and West Punjab (Pakistan).

Lahore, city (1951 pop., including cantonment area, 849,000), ⊙ Punjab prov. and Lahore dist., W Pakistan, near left bank of Ravi R., 640 mi. NE of Karachi and 270 mi. NW of New Delhi; 31°35'N 74°18'E. One of Pakistan's largest cities. Important trade and communications center, linked by rail, road, and air with Rawalpindi and Peshawar (NW), Multan and Karachi (SW), and New Delhi via Punjab, India (SE). Large industrial and financial center; agr. market (wheat, cotton, oilseeds, gram, rice, sugar cane). Chief industries are cotton, flour, and oilseed milling; general and electrical engineering, fruit canning, mfg. of matches, ice, glass, woolen goods, chemicals, machinery, agr. implements, sewing machines, tools, surgical instruments, furniture; metalworks, printing presses, motion picture studios, sawmills, salt refinery. Handicrafts include cotton and silk cloth, metalware, cutlery, pottery, soap, leather goods, tongas. Pakistan mint located here. City proper is NW; govt. bldgs., commercial houses, and residences are in W and S sections. Architectural landmarks are of Mogul period, notably Badshahi Masjid, Moti Masjid (Pearl Mosque) of white marble, fort area, and Shalamar Gardens (E) with terraces, canals, and fountains. Mus. has Greco-Buddhist sculptures, Mogul paintings, coins, and W Pakistan handicrafts. Educational institutions include Punjab Univ. (founded 1882) with medical, law, and technical cols.; Mayo School of Arts; and Aitchison's Chiefs' Col. Industrial suburbs are Badami Bagh (N; metalworks, flour and varnish factories), Moghalpura (E; large railroad workshops), and Model Town (S; engineering and metalworks, celluloid and vulcanite products). Lahore cantonment (formerly called Mian Mir) is SE, across branch of Upper Bari Doab Canal, and has ordnance factory and maintenance units. During most of 11th and 12th cent., city was ⊙ Ghaznevid dominions E of the Indus. Flourished under Mogul rule (16th–17th cent.) and for short time served as seat of the emperors. After period of decline in 18th cent., it regained prominence under Sikhs; passed to British in 1849; was ⊙ former Br. prov. of Punjab prior to partition of India (1947).

Lahorighat (lähō'rĭgät), village, Nowgong dist., central Assam, India, 22 mi. WNW of Nowgong; rice, jute, rape and mustard, tea.

Lahou Lagoon (lähōō'), along coast of Ivory Coast, Fr. West Africa, 70 mi. W of Abidjan. Separated from ocean by narrow spit. At its entrance (Bandama R. mouth) is GRAND-LAHOU.

Lahr (lär), town (pop. 16,944), S Baden, Germany, at W foot of Black Forest, 22 mi. N of Freiburg; noted for its paper. Tobacco industry; mfg. of chemicals, textiles; leather-, metal-, and woodworking; printing, food processing. Has 12th- and 13th-cent. churches and 16th-cent. town hall (rebuilt 1855).

Lahri (lä'rē), village, Kalat state, E Baluchistan, W Pakistan, 100 mi. SE of Quetta, on Kachhi plain; local market for millet, wheat, rice; hand-loom weaving; camel and horse breeding.

Lahti (lä'tē, läkh'tē), Swedish *Lahtis* (lä'tĭs), city (pop. 42,364), Häme co., S Finland, at S end of Päijänne lake system, 60 mi. NNE of Helsinki; rail junction; center of Finnish furniture industry. Lumber, plywood, and spool mills, machine shops; mfg. of glass, matches, shoes. Site of chief Finnish radio transmitter. Has folk mus., town hall (1912) by Saarinen. Scene of annual ski competitions. Founded 1878; inc. 1905. Lake port of Vesijärvi, just N, serves city.

La Huaca (lä wä'kä), town (pop. 2,012), Piura dept., NW Peru, on coastal plain, on Chira R., on Paita-Piura RR and 16 mi. NE of Paita, in irrigated area; cotton, fruit.

La Huacana (lä wäkä'nä), town (pop. 1,414), Michoacán, W Mexico, 35 mi. S of Uruapan; cereals, sugar cane, fruit; silver deposits.

La Huerta (lä wĕr'tä) or **Laprida** (läprē'dä), village, SE San Juan prov., Argentina, at SE foot of Sierra de la Huerta, 80 mi. ENE of San Juan; sulphur deposits.

Lahul (lä'hōōl), N subdivision of Kangra dist., NE Punjab, India, in Punjab Himalayas (several peaks rise to over 20,000 ft.); bordered by Chamba (W; Himachal Pradesh), Kashmir (N), and Spiti (E) and Kulu (S) subdivisions. Consists of rugged mtn. ridges, snow fields, and glaciers; some barley grown in lower valleys. Antimony ore deposits near Shigri (SE).

Lahun, El, Egypt: see ILLAHUN.

La Hune, Cape (lů hōōn'), S N.F., on E side of La Hune Bay (extending 7 mi. inland), 40 mi. E of Burgeo; 47°32'N 56°32'W. Opposite is fishing village of La Hune; salmon canning.

Lahuy Island (lä'wē) (□ 7; 1939 pop. 2,112), Camarines Sur prov., Philippines, in Philippine Sea, just off S coast of Luzon, 15 mi. NW of Rungus Point; 6 mi. long, 2 mi. wide; rises to 613 ft. Gold mining.

Lai (lä'), village, SW Chad territory, Fr. Equatorial Africa, on Logone R. and 60 mi. NNE of Moundou; center of rice cultivation. Former military outpost. Until 1946, in Ubangi-Shari colony.

Laian (lī'än'), town, ⊙ Laian co. (pop. 127,894), N Anhwei prov., China, near Kiangsu line, 30 mi. NW of Nanking; rice, wheat, beans, kaoliang, corn.

Laiatico (läyä'tēkô), village (pop. 762), Pisa prov., Tuscany, central Italy, 8 mi. NW of Volterra.

Laibach, Yugoslavia: see LJUBLJANA.

Laichau (lī'chou'), town (1936 pop. 1,173), ⊙ Laichau prov. (□ 7,800; 1943 pop. 67,300), N Vietnam, in Tonkin, on Black R. (head of navigation) and 60 mi. SW of Laokay.

Laichingen (lī'khĭng-ŭn), village (pop. 3,399), S Württemberg, Germany, after 1945 in Württemberg-Hohenzollern, in Swabian Jura, 15 mi. NW of Ulm; linen.

Laichow, China: see YEHSIEN, Shantung prov.

Laidlaw, village, S B.C., on Fraser R. and 19 mi. NE of Chilliwack; lumbering, dairying.

Laidley, town (pop. 1,309), SE Queensland, Australia, 40 mi. W of Brisbane; dairying, agr. (corn, sugar cane).

Laie (lä'yä), village (pop. 842), Oahu, T.H., on NE coast; has largest Mormon temple outside of Salt Lake City.

Laifeng (lī'fŭng'), town (pop. 13,850), ⊙ Laifeng co. (pop. 117,362), SW Hupeh prov., China, on Hunan line, 50 mi. S of Enshih; copper and iron deposits.

Laigle (lĕ'glü), town (pop. 5,021), Orne dept., NW France, on the Risle and 17 mi. N of Mortagne; pin and needle-mfg. center; other mfg. (furniture, footwear, hardware, corsets). Cider, grain, lumber, and cattle trade. Damaged in Second World War. Sometimes spelled L'Aigle.

Laignes (lĕ'nyü), village (pop. 980), Côte-d'Or dept., E central France, 10 mi. W of Châtillon-sur-Seine; dairying.

Laigneville (lĕnyůvēl'), village (pop. 1,410), Oise dept., N France, 9 mi. NW of Senlis; metalworks, stone quarries.

Laiguegiia (līgwā'lyä), village (pop. 1,220), Savona prov., Liguria, NW Italy, port on Gulf of Genoa and 10 mi. NE of Imperia; sea bathing; fish canneries.

Laihka (lī'kä''), central state (sawbwaship) (□ 1,559; pop. 36,319), Southern Shan State, Upper Burma; ⊙ Laihka, village on Hsipaw-Loilem road and 55 mi. NW of Taunggyi. Mtn. range (W) and plateau (E). Iron ore, lacquer.

Laijun, Aden: see GHEIL BA YAMIN.

Laikipia Escarpment (līkĕpē'ä), section of E rim of Great Rift Valley, in W central Kenya, bet. Thomson's Falls and Baringo. Laikipia Plateau is E.

Laikovats, Yugoslavia: see LAJKOVAC.

Laila or **Laylah** (lā'lů), town and oasis, S Nejd, Saudi Arabia, in Aflaj dist., 170 mi. S of Riyadh; grain (sorghums, barley), dates, alfalfa, vegetables, fruit.

Lainate (līnä'tĕ), village (pop. 3,660), Milano prov., Lombardy, N Italy, 10 mi. NNW of Milan; mills (silk, cotton, flax).

La Independencia (lä ĕndāpăndān'syä), town (pop. 870), Chiapas, S Mexico, in Sierra Madre, E of Comitán; corn, fruit.

La India or **Mina La India** (mē'nä lä ēn'dyä), village, León dept., Nicaragua, 7 mi. SE of Santa Rosa; gold- and silver-mining center.

Laindon (lān'dŭn), residential town and parish (pop. 4,552), S Essex, England, 11 mi. E of Romford; machinery works. Church has 15th-cent. priest's house. Just S is residential town and parish (pop. 2,103) of Langdon Hills or Laindon Hills.

Laingsburg (lăngz'bûrg), town (pop. 1,836), S Cape Prov., U. of So. Afr., in Wittebergen mts., on Buffels R. and 80 mi. WNW of Oudtshoorn; stock, fruit.

Laingsburg (lăngz'bûrg, lāngz'-), village (pop. 942), Shiawassee co., S central Mich., 15 mi. NE of Lansing, in farm area (livestock, poultry, grain, corn, hay; dairy products).

Laing's Nek or **Langsnek** (both: lăngz'nĕk), locality, NW Natal, U. of So. Afr., near Transvaal border, 7 mi. S of Volksrust, in Drakensberg range; alt. 5,399 ft.; scene (Jan. 28, 1881) of battle in Transvaal revolt. Sometimes written Laingsnek.

Lainsitz River, Czechoslovakia and Austria: see LUZNICE RIVER.

Laipin (lī'bĭn'), town, ⊙ Laipin co. (pop. 151,388), central Kwangsi prov., China, on Hungshui R. and 40 mi. S of Liuchow, and on railroad; rice, wheat, beans. Coal mines near by.

Laipo (lī'pō'), Mandarin *Li-p'u* (lē'pōō'), town, ⊙ Laipo co. (pop. 147,483), NE Kwangsi prov., China, 60 mi. ENE of Liuchow; wheat, rice, beans. Tin deposits near by.

Laird (lârd), village (pop. 329), central Sask., 40 mi. N of Saskatoon; mixed farming, dairying.

Lairg (lârg), agr. village and parish (pop. 1,065), S Sutherland, Scotland, at SE end of Loch Shin 18 mi. NW of Dornoch; angling resort.

Lais (līs, lä'ēs), town (1939 pop. 8,185), Davao prov., S Mindanao, Philippines, 50 mi. S of Davao, on Davao Gulf; abacá, coconuts.

La Isabela, Cuba: see ISABELA DE SAGUA.

La Isabela, Dominican Republic: see ISABELA.

Laish, Palestine: see DAN.

Laishevo (lŭē'shĭvŭ), village (1926 pop. 3,783), W central Tatar Autonomous SSR, Russian SFSR, on right bank of Kama R. (landing) and 32 mi. SSE of Kazan; food processing (sago, potatoes); grain, livestock. Founded 1555–57; one of oldest Rus. settlements in lower Kama R. valley. Until c.1928, Laishev (city).

Laishi, department, Argentina: see HERRADURA.

Laisholm, Estonia: see JOGEVA.

Laishui (lī'shwā'), town, ⊙ Laishui co. (pop. 123,318), N Hopeh prov., China, 50 mi. SW of Peking and on spur of Peking-Hankow RR; cotton, wheat, kaoliang.

Laiski Zavod, Russian SFSR: see LAYA.

La Isla or **San Antonio la Isla** (sän äntō'nyō lä ē'slä), town (pop. 1,289), Mexico state, central Mexico, 11 mi. SSE of Toluca; grain, livestock.

Laissac (lĕsäk'), village (pop. 1,065), Aveyron dept., S France, near Aveyron R., 13 mi. E of Rodez; dairying.

Laitec Island (lītäk') (□ 12.7; pop. 368), off SE coast of Chiloé Isl., Chiloé prov., S Chile, 50 mi. SSE of Castro; 43°13'S; 8 mi. long, c.1 mi. wide.

Laithieu (lī'tyō'), village, Thudaumot prov., S Vietnam, 10 mi. N of Saigon, on railroad; pottery.

Laitlyngkot (lĭt'lĭngkōt), village, Khasi and Jaintia Hills dist., W Assam, India, in Khasi Hills, 9 mi. SSW of Shillong; trades in rice, cotton, betel nuts.

Laitung, China: see LAIYANG.

Laives (lī'vĕs), Ger. *Leifers*, Bolzano prov., Trentino-Alto Adige, N Italy, near Adige R., 5 mi. S of Bolzano; porphyry quarries.

Laivung (lī'vōōng'), town, Sadec prov., S Vietnam, on Bassac R. and 12 mi. WSW of Sadec; rice.

Laiwu (lī'wōō'), town, ⊙ Laiwu co. (pop. 403,448), W central Shantung prov., China, in Tai Mts., 45 mi. SE of Tsinan; cotton weaving; rice, wheat, beans, peanuts.

Laiyang (lī'yäng'), town, ⊙ Laiyang co. (pop. 909,436), E Shantung prov., China, 70 mi. N of Tsingtao; pears, peanuts, kaoliang, wheat; silk trade. Until 1949, the name Laiyang was applied to Laitung, 20 mi. ESE of present site.

Laiyüan (lī'yüän'), town, ⊙ Laiyüan co. (pop. 94,462), NW Hopeh prov., China, in Taihang Mts., beyond Great Wall, 50 mi. NW of Paoting, near Chahar line; cotton, wheat, melons. Until 1914 called Kwangchang.

Laja (lä'hä), town (pop. c.6,900), La Paz dept., W Bolivia, in the Altiplano, 17 mi. WSW of La Paz; potatoes, barley, sheep.

Laja, department, Chile: see LOS ANGELES.

Laja, town (pop. 1,368), Bío-Bío prov., S central Chile, at confluence of Bío-Bío R. and Laja R., on railroad and 22 mi. NW of Los Angeles. Agr. center (wheat, rye, wine, fruit); flour milling; lumber.

Laja, La, Argentina: see LA LAJA.

Laja, La, Panama: see LA LAJA.

Laja, Lake (□ 40), in Bío-Bío and Ñuble provs., S central Chile, in the Andes near Argentina line, 50 mi. E of Los Angeles; 20 mi. long. Antuco Volcano on W shore.

La Jalca (lä häl'kä) or **Jalca**, town (pop. 1,189), Amazonas dept., N Peru, in E Andean foothills, 20 mi. SSE of Chachapoyas; sugar growing.

Lajamina (lähämē'nä), village (pop. 579), Los Santos prov., S central Panama, in Pacific lowland, 4 mi. SSW of Pocrí; sugar cane, coffee, livestock.

Lajão, Brazil: see CONSELHEIRO PENA.

La Jara (lů hä'rů), town (pop. 912), Conejos co., S Colo., on branch of Rio Grande, E of San Juan Mts., and 14 mi. SSW of Alamosa, in San Luis Valley; alt. 7,600 ft. Livestock, grain, dairy, truck, poultry products. U.S. farm resettlement project near by.

Laja River (lä'hä), S central Chile, rises in L. Laja in the Andes near Argentina border, flows c.100 mi. W, past Antuco and Tucapel, along Ñuble-Bío-Bío and Concepción-Bío-Bío prov. borders, to Bío-Bío R. at San Rosendo. Has several rapids, of which the best known is Salto del Laja (45 mi. SE of Concepción), a noted tourist site. It is used for hydroelectric power, supplying coal mines and steel mills of Concepción prov.

Laja River, Guanajuato, central Mexico, rises near Doctor Hernández Alvarez in Sierra Madre Occidental, flows c.85 mi. S, past Comonfort and San Miguel Octopan, to Apaseo R. (affluent of Lerma R.) 3 mi. SE of Celaya.

Lajas or **Santa Isabel de las Lajas** (sän'tä ēsäbä'lä dā läs lä'häs), town (pop. 4,781), Las Villas prov., central Cuba, on railroad and 21 mi. W of Santa Clara; agr. center (sugar cane, fruit). The sugar central of Caracas is SE.

Lajas (lä'häs), town (pop. 1,147), SW Puerto Rico, near the coast, on railroad and 11 mi. SSE of Mayagüez; mfg. (cigars, needlework). Coffee and breadfruit are grown in vicinity. Large slate deposits near by.

Lajas, Las, Argentina: see LAS LAJAS.

Lajas, Las, Panama: see LAS LAJAS.

Lajeado (lůzhēä'dōō). **1** City, Mato Grosso, Brazil: see GUIRATINGA. **2** City (pop. 3,590), E central Rio Grande do Sul, Brazil, head of navigation on Taquari R. and 4 mi. N of Estrêla; agr. center (wheat, potatoes, poultry); hog raising, lard mfg. Amethysts and agates found near by. Formerly spelled Lageado.

Lajeosa (lůzhĭō'zů), village (pop. 1,094), Viseu dist., N Portugal, 10 mi. SSW of Viseu; wine, oranges, corn, rye.

Lajes (lä'zhĭsh) or **Lagens** (lůzhĕnsh'), village (pop. 2,171), Angra do Heroísmo dist., central Azores, on NE shore of Terceira Isl., 10 mi. NE of Angra do Heroísmo. Site of Allied air base built during Second World War; 38°45'N 27°6'W.

Lajes. 1 City, Rio Grande do Norte, Brazil: see ITARETAMA. **2** City (pop. 7,603), central Santa Catarina, Brazil, in the Serra do Mar, 110 mi. WSW of Florianópolis, and on Curitiba-Pôrto Alegre highway; cattle-raising center supplying Rio Grande do Sul meat-processing plants. Founded 17th cent. by Portuguese. Formerly Lages.

Lajes, Ribeirão das, Brazil: see RIBEIRÃO DAS LAJES.

Lajes das Flores (dāsh flō'rĭsh), town (pop. 955), Horta dist., W Azores, on S shore of Flores Isl., 6 mi. SSW of Santa Cruz; 39°22'N 31°11'W. Cattle raising, dairying, whaling. Exports sperm-oil. Formerly spelled Lages or Lagens das Flores.

Lajes do Pico (dōō pē'kōō), town (pop. 629), Horta dist., central Azores, on S coast of Pico Isl., 22 mi. SE of Horta (on Faial Isl.); 38°24'N 28°16'W. Whaling; dairying, grain milling. Formerly spelled Lagens do Pico.

Lajkovac, Laikovats, or **Laykovats** (all: lī'kôväts), village, central Serbia, Yugoslavia, on Kolubara R. (railroad bridge) and 15 mi. ENE of Valjevo.

La Jolla (lů hoi'yů), resort and residential community, San Diego co., S Calif., N suburb within city limits of San Diego; ocean beaches, caves, cliffs. Scripps Institution of Oceanography of Univ. of Calif. is here.

La Jose, Pa.: see NEWBURG, Clearfield co.

Lajoskomarom (loi'ôsh-kômärôm), Hung. *Lajoskomárom*, town (pop. 2,748), Veszprem co., W central Hungary, 24 mi. S of Szekesfehervar; wheat, corn, cattle, hogs.

Lajosmizse (loi'ôsh-mĭ-zhĕ), town (pop. 12,689), Pest-Pilis-Solt-Kiskun co., central Hungary, 10 mi. NNW of Kecskemet; distilleries, flour mills; grain, cattle, apricots, apples.

La Joya (lä hoi'ä), town (pop. c.1,900), Oruro dept., W Bolivia, in the Altiplano, on Desaguadero R. and 30 mi. NW of Oruro; alt. 12,542 ft.; potatoes, sheep.

Lajta River, Austria, Hungary: see LEITHA RIVER.

La Junta (lä hōōn'tä), village, Limón prov., E Costa Rica, rail junction on Reventazón R. and 2 mi. NW of Siquirres; abacá, rubber, bananas, cacao.

La Junta (lů hōōn'tů, hŭn'tů), city (pop. 7,712), ⊙ Otero co., SE Colo., on Arkansas R. and 60 mi. ESE of Pueblo; alt. 4,100 ft. Trade and railroad center, with repair shops, in grain and sugar-beet region; dairy and meat products, flour, melons. Fort Bent Mus. has fossils and scale model of Bent's Fort, noted trading post which flourished near by on the Arkansas from 1820s to 1850s. City founded 1875, inc. 1881.

Lakagigar, Iceland: see LAKI.

Lakamti, Ethiopia: see NAKAMTI.

La-kang, Tibet: see LHAKHANG.

Lakatnik (läkät'nĭk), village (pop. 2,292), Sofia dist., W Bulgaria, in Iskar R. gorge, 26 mi. N of Sofia; livestock, sheep. Karstlike land formations and caves attract tourists. Scattered copper and zinc deposits near by (E).

Lake, New Zealand: see QUEENSTOWN.

Lake. 1 County (□ 1,256; pop. 11,481), NW Calif.; ⊙ Lakeport. Mtn. and valley region, in the Coast Ranges; drained by Cache Creek and headstreams of Eel R. Natural features: Clear L. (largest fresh-water lake in Calif.), L. Pillsbury, Blue Lakes, Hull Mtn. (6,954 ft.), Mt. Konochti (4,100 ft.). Part of Mendocino Natl. Forest in N. Fruitgrowing, especially Bartlett pears; also dairying, stock raising (sheep, poultry), farming (alfalfa, grain, vegetables, nuts). Scenic recreational region; fishing, hunting, camping; mineral and hot springs (resorts); mineral-water bottling. A leading quicksilver-producing co. of Calif.; also sand and gravel quarrying. Several small Indian reservations. Formed 1861. **2** County (□ 380; pop. 6,150), central Colo.; ⊙ Leadville. Mining, dairying, and livestock-grazing area, drained by headwaters of Arkansas R. Gold, silver, lead, copper, zinc. Molybdenum mines at Climax. Has large part of Cochetopa Natl. Forest. Sawatch Mts. extend N–S; include Mt. Massive and Mt. Elbert (14,431 ft.; highest point in Colo.). Formed 1861. **3** County (□ 996; pop. 36,340), central Fla., bounded NE by St. Johns R.; ⊙ Tavares. Rolling terrain with hundreds of lakes, including Harris, Griffin, Dora, Eustis, Yale, and part of Apopka. Ocala Natl. Forest extends into NE corner. Citrus-fruitgrowing area, with canneries and many packing houses; also truck produce, watermelons, corn, peanuts, cotton, and poultry. Has concrete plants and sawmills. Diatomite mines, sand pits, peat deposits. Formed 1887. **4** County (□ 457; pop. 179,097), extreme NE Ill., bounded E by L. Michigan and N by Wis. line; ⊙ Waukegan. Drained by Fox and Des Plaines rivers. Includes many N suburbs of Chicago; diversified mfg. Sand, gravel, stone deposits. Dairying, agr. (livestock, poultry, corn, oats, wheat; nursery products). Contains many resort lakes and Chain-O'-Lakes State Park; fishing, duck hunting. Formed 1839. **5** County (□ 514; pop. 368,152), extreme NW Ind.; ⊙ Crown Point. Bounded N by L. Michigan, W by Ill. line, S by Kankakee R.; traversed by Grand Calumet and Little Calumet rivers. Heavily industrialized CALUMET region, part of metropolitan area of Chicago, is one of world's most important steel-mfg. centers. Harbors at Gary and East Chicago (Indiana Harbor). Agr. areas of co. produce truck, dairy products, poultry, soybeans, corn. Formed 1836. **6** County (□ 572; pop 5,257), W central Mich.; ⊙ Baldwin. Drained by Pere Marquette and Little Manistee rivers, and small South Branch of Manistee R. Livestock, dairy products, poultry, potatoes, truck, grain. Resort area (hunting, fishing). Part of Manistee Natl. Forest is in N. Organized 1871. **7** County (□ 2,132; pop. 7,781), NE Minn.; ⊙ Two Harbors. Extensively watered area bounded S by L. Superior, N by chain of lakes along Ont. line. Dairy products, poultry, grain, potatoes; peat deposits. S half of co. is drained by small streams, N half by many lakes, including Knife, Snowbank, Basswood, and Bald Eagle. Area lies within Superior Natl. Forest and is part of famous recreational region known as "Arrowhead Country." Formed 1866. **8** County (□ 1,500; pop. 13,835), NW Mont.; ⊙ Polson. Mtn. region drained by Flathead and Swan rivers. Livestock, sugar beets, grain. Flathead Indian Reservation throughout, Flathead L. in N. Formed 1893. **9** County (□ 232; pop. 75,979), NE Ohio; ⊙ Painesville. Bounded N by L. Erie; drained by Grand and Chagrin rivers. Fruitgrowing (especially apples, grapes); also truck, poultry. Mfg. at Painesville, Wickliffe, and Willoughby. Salt production; commercial fisheries; lake resorts. Formed 1840; smallest co. in Ohio. **10** County (□ 8,270; pop. 6,649), S Oregon; ⊙ Lakeview. Mtn. area containing Summer L., Abert L., and part of Goose L.; borders on Calif. and Nev. Lumber, livestock, dairying. Fremont Natl. Forest in S and W. Part of Great Sandy Desert in N. Formed 1874. **11** County (□ 571; pop. 11,792), E S.Dak.; ⊙ Madison; agr. area. Has lakes Madison and Herman. Livestock, dairy produce, poultry, corn. Formed 1873. **12** County (□ 164; pop. 11,655), extreme NW Tenn.; ⊙ Tiptonville. Bounded N by Ky., W by the Mississippi (Mo. line), NE by Reelfoot L. (hunting, fishing). Timber, livestock, agr. (corn, soybeans, alfalfa, cotton). Formed 1870.

Lake, town (pop. 345), Scott co., central Miss., 35 mi. W of Meridian; paint, lumber.

Lake Alfred, city (pop. 1,270), Polk co., central Fla., 6 mi. W of Haines City, in lake region; citrus-fruit shipping center, with packing houses, canneries, and experiment station. Mfg. of citrus oil, pulp feed, and molasses; fertilizer, insecticides.

Lake Almanor Dam, Calif.: see ALMANOR, LAKE.

Lake Alpine, Calif.: see ALPINE, LAKE.

Lake Andes (ăn'dēz), city (pop. 1,851), ⊙ Charles Mix Co., S S.Dak., 90 mi. WSW of Sioux Falls, near L. ANDES; fishing resort; trading point for agr. area; wheat, alfalfa, livestock.

Lake Angelus, village (pop. 123), Oakland co., SE Mich., just NW of Pontiac, on small L. Angelus.

Lake Ann, village (pop. 99), Benzie co., NW Mich.. on small lake, 12 mi. SW of Traverse City.

Lake Arrowhead, Calif.: see ARROWHEAD, LAKE

Lake Arthur. 1 Town (pop. 2,849), Jefferson Davis parish, SW La., on L. Arthur (widening of navigable Mermentau R.), 34 mi. ESE of Lake Charles city, in rice and livestock area; rice and lumber milling. Oil wells, and fishing and hunting near by. Inc. 1909. **2** Town (pop. 380), Chaves co., SE N.Mex., on Pecos R. and 29 mi. SSE of Roswell.

Lake Benton, village (pop. 863), Lincoln co., SW Minn., on L. Benton, near S.Dak. line, 18 mi. N of Pipestone, in grain and poultry area; dairy products.

Lake Beulah (bū'lŭ), resort village, Walworth co., SE Wis., near small L. Beulah (c.4 mi. long), 10 mi. NNW of Burlington.

Lake Bluff, village (pop. 2,000), Lake co., extreme NE Ill., N suburb of Chicago, near L. Michigan, 17 mi. NNW of Evanston. Great Lakes Naval Training Station is just N. Inc. 1895.

Lake Bonaparte, N.Y.: see BONAPARTE, LAKE.

Lake Borgne Canal (bôrn) or **Violet Canal**, SE La., canal (c.7 mi. long) joining L. Borgne with the Mississippi at Violet (lock here), 10 mi. ESE of New Orleans.

Lake Bronson, Minn.: see BRONSON.

Lake Butler, city (pop. 1,040), ⊙ Union co., N Fla., 25 mi. N of Gainesville; naval-stores center.

Lake Cargelligo (kärjĕ'lĭgō), town (pop. 986), S central New South Wales, Australia, on Lachlan R. and 210 mi. NW of Canberra, near L. Cargelligo (3 mi. long, 1.5 mi. wide); rail terminus; sheep and agr. center.

Lake Carmel, village (pop. 1,055), Putnam co., SE N.Y.

Lake Charles, city (pop. 41,272), ⊙ Calcasieu parish, SW La., 55 mi. E of Beaumont (Texas), and on L. Charles (widening of Calcasieu R.); port of entry on deepwater channel to Gulf of Mexico; rail- and ocean-shipping center for oil, lumber, rice, and cotton region. Rice and lumber milling, oil refining and gasoline extracting, boatbuilding, meat packing, cotton ginning; mfg. of turpentine, fertilizer, food products, chemicals, synthetic rubber, oil-well supplies, concrete and machine-shop products, bricks. Has jr. col. Settled c.1852; inc. as town in 1867, as city in 1904.

Lake Charles Canal (c.25 mi. long), SW La., deepwater E–W land cut connecting Sabine R. just below Orange (Texas) with Calcasieu R. c.15 mi. below Lake Charles city; section of Gulf Intracoastal Waterway.

Lake City. 1 Town (pop. 783), a ⊙ Craighead co., NE Ark., 12 mi. E of Jonesboro, near St. Francis R., in area of sunken lands caused by 1811 earthquakes. **2** Resort town (pop. 141), ⊙ Hinsdale co., SW central Colo., on branch of Gunnison R., in San Juan Mts., and 45 mi. SE of Montrose; alt. 8,500 ft. Uncompahgre Peak 8 mi. WNW. **3** City (pop. 7,571), ⊙ Columbia co., N Fla., c.60 mi. W of Jacksonville; trade center (tobacco, lumber, naval stores). Here are a U.S. veterans hosp. and the hq. of near-by Osceola Natl. Forest. Founded as a military post in the 1830s. **4** City (pop. 2,308), Calhoun co., central Iowa, 33 mi. WSW of Fort Dodge; creamery, rendering works; wood and concrete products. Sand and gravel pits near by. Inc. 1887. **5** City (pop. 719), ⊙ Missaukee co., N central Mich., 11 mi. NE of Cadillac, on L. Missaukee (c.3 mi. long, 2 mi. wide), in resort and farm area. Indian earthworks and a state park are near by. Inc. 1932. **6** City (pop. 3,457), Wabasha co., SE Minn., on L. Pepin (natural widening of Mississippi R.) and 15 mi. SE of Red Wing; resort and milling point in grain, poultry, and livestock area; butter, ice cream, beverages, flour, feed; foundry products. Tree nurseries here, wildlife refuge near by. Platted 1856, inc. 1872. **7** Town (pop. 5,112), Florence co., E central S.C., 25 mi. S of Florence; market for tobacco, truck; lumber, wood products. **8** Town (pop. 110), Marshall co., NE S.Dak., 17 mi. ESE of Britton, just W of Sisseton Indian Reservation; surrounded by lakes; supply point for hunters and fishermen. **9** Town (pop. 1,827), Anderson co., E Tenn., 21 mi. NW of Knoxville, near Norris Reservoir, in coal-mining region. Until 1939, called Coal Creek.

Lake Clear Junction, resort village, Franklin co., NE N.Y., on L. Clear (c.2 mi. long) in the Adirondacks, 5 mi. NW of Saranac Lake village; rail point.

Lake Cowichan (kou'ĭchŭn, kou-ĭ'chŭn), village (pop. estimate 500), SW B.C., on S Vancouver Isl., on Cowichan L. at outlet of Cowichan R., 40 mi. NW of Victoria, in lumbering region.

Lake Crystal, city (pop. 1,430), Blue Earth co., S Minn., on small lake, near Watonwan R., and 12 mi. SW of Mankato; resort; agr. trading point in agr. area; dairy products, cattle feed. Platted 1857, inc. as village 1870, as city 1930.

Lake Delton, resort village, Sauk co., S central Wis., 9 mi. NNW of Baraboo, on L. Delton, near the Dells of the Wisconsin.

Lake Denmark, N.J.: see DOVER.

Lake District, beautiful lake and mountain region in N Lancashire, W Westmorland, and S Cumberland, NW England. It is c.30 mi. in diameter and includes part of Furness peninsula. In it are 15 lakes, including Coniston Water, Ullswater, Derwentwater, Buttermere, Windermere, Grasmere, Thirlmere, Crummock Water, and Ennerdale, several beautiful falls, and the mts. of Scafell, Skiddaw, and Helvellyn. Numerous prehistoric relics remain, such as the Druids' Circle near Keswick, and there are ruins of anc. castles and churches and remains of Roman occupation. The area is favored by artists and writers; Wordsworth, Coleridge, and Southey were known as "the Lake Poets," and Gray, Ruskin, Keats, Shelley, Tennyson, and many others lived in the area. Chief resorts are Ambleside, Windermere, and Keswick.

Lake Elmo, village (pop. 386), Washington co., E Minn., near L. St. Croix (in St. Croix R.), 11 mi. E of St. Paul; dairying.

Lake Elmore, Vt.: see ELMORE.

Lakefield, village (pop. 1,349), S Ont., on small Katchiwano L., at mouth of Otonabee R., 9 mi. NNE of Peterborough; dairying, woodworking, lumbering, granite quarrying.

Lakefield, village (pop. 1,651), Jackson co., SW Minn., at SE tip of Heron L., near Iowa line, 10 mi. WNW of Jackson; agr. trading point in grain, livestock, and poultry area; dairy products. Settled 1879, inc. 1887.

Lake Forest, beautiful residential city (pop. 7,819), Lake co., extreme NE Ill., N suburb of Chicago, on L. Michigan, 16 mi. NNW of Evanston. Seat of Lake Forest Col. and Barat Col. of the Sacred Heart. Settled 1835, platted 1856, inc. 1861.

Lake Fork, stream rising in Uinta Mts. near Tokewanna Peak, NE Utah; flows c.50 mi. SE to Duchesne R. 8 mi. SW of Roosevelt. Moon Lake Dam (110 ft. high, 1,108 ft. long; completed 1938) is chief unit in Moon L. irrigation project, which supplies water to 70,000 acres in NE Utah.

Lake Frances, town (pop. 15), Benton co., extreme NW Ark., 21 mi. WNW of Fayetteville.

Lake Fremont, Minn.: see ZIMMERMAN.

Lake Geneva (jŭnē'vŭ), resort and residential city (pop. 4,300), Walworth co., SE Wis., on NE shore of L. Geneva at its outlet (White R.), 38 mi. SW of Milwaukee; year-round lake sports. Has many estates of residents of Chicago, and a hotel designed by Frank Lloyd Wright. Bird sanctuary of Univ. of Chicago is near by. Settled before 1845, inc. 1883.

Lake George, resort village (pop. 1,005), ⊙ Warren co., E N.Y., in the Adirondacks, at S end of L. George, 9 mi. NNW of Glens Falls; year-round sports center, and trading point for lumbering and dairying area. Inc. 1903. Here are vestiges of Fort William Henry, built 1756, captured and demolished by Montcalm in 1757 in French and Indian War. In Lake George Battleground Park (S) are a monument commemorating a colonial victory (1755) over French forces; and ruins of Fort George, which was erected in 1759 and later figured in the Revolution.

Lake Hamilton, town (pop. 604), Polk co., central Fla., 4 mi. S of Haines City, on L. Hamilton (2 mi. long); citrus-fruit packing houses.

Lake Harbor, village (1940 pop. 1,097), Palm Beach co., SE Fla., 8 mi. W of Belle Glade, at S tip of L. Okeechobee, in truck-farming area.

Lake Harbour, trading post, S Baffin Isl., SE Franklin Dist., Northwest Territories, at head of North Bay, inlet of Hudson Strait; 62°15'N 69°53'W; radio station, Royal Canadian Mounted Police post. Site of Anglican mission. Fur-trading post was established 1911.

Lake Helen, city (pop. 926), Volusia co., NE Fla., 20 mi. SW of Daytona Beach, in citrus-fruit growing area.

Lake Henry, village (pop. 97), Stearns co., central Minn., 32 mi. WSW of St. Cloud, in grain, stock, poultry area.

Lake Hopatcong, N.J.: see HOPATCONG, LAKE.

Lake Huntington, resort village, Sullivan co., SE N.Y., near Pa. line, on small L. Huntington, 15 mi. W of Monticello.

Lakehurst, borough (pop. 1,518), Ocean co., E N.J., 8 mi. SW of Lakewood; site of U.S. naval air station with facilities for dirigibles. The *Shenandoah*, 1st American-built airship, made its initial flight here (1923). American terminal for transatlantic airships from 1924 until burning of the *Hindenburg* here, 1937.

Lake Jackson, city (pop. 2,897), Brazoria co., S Texas, on Brazos R. and 9 mi. NW of Freeport, in Brazosport industrial area (sulphur, chemicals). Inc. after 1940.

Lake Junaluska (jōō"nŭlŭ'skŭ), resort village, Haywood co., W N.C., 3 mi. NNE of Waynesville, on small lake. Summer session of Duke Univ. meets here.

Lake June, town (pop. 1,517), Dallas co., N Texas, a suburb of Dallas. Inc. after 1940.

Lakeland. 1 City (pop. 30,851), Polk co., central Fla., 30 mi. ENE of Tampa; trade and citrus-fruit-shipping center, with packing houses and canneries; mfg. of packing and canning machinery, boats, trailers, millwork, candy, fertilizer, leather goods. Hq. of Florida Citrus Commission; has frost forecasting laboratory. Resort with many small lakes in and near the city. Florida Southern Col. is here. Settled in 1870s, inc. 1885. **2** City (pop. 1,551), ⊙ Lanier co., S Ga., 19 mi. NE of Valdosta, bet. Alapaha R. and Banks L.; agr. center; mfg. of naval stores. **3** Town (pop. 2,172), La Porte co., NW Ind., near L. Michigan, just SE of Michigan City. Inc. 1937. **4** Village, Jefferson co., N Ky., 11 mi. E of Louisville; seat of Central State Hosp. Near by is Ormsby Village, an institution for children.

Lake Landing, resort village, Hyde co., E N.C., 29 mi. E of Belhaven, on Mattamuskeet L.
Lakeland Junction, Fla.: see WINSTON.
Lakeland Shores, village (pop. 43), Washington co., E Minn., c.15 mi. E of St. Paul.
Lake Lansing, Mich.: see HASLETT.
Lake Lenore (lŭnôr'), village (pop. 241), central Sask., near Lenore L. (17 mi. long, 4 mi. wide), 15 mi. NE of Humboldt; resort.
Lake Leopold II, district, Belgian Congo: see INONGO.
Lake Lillian, village (pop. 358), Kandiyohi co., S central Minn., on small lake, 15 mi. SE of Willmar; dairy products.
Lake Linden, village (pop. 1,462), Houghton co., NW Upper Peninsula, Mich., 9 mi. NE of Houghton, on Torch L., in copper region; stamping- and sawmills. Inc. 1885.
Lakeline, village (pop. 183), Lake co., NE Ohio, on L. Erie, 17 mi. NE of Cleveland.
Lake Louise, village (pop. estimate 100), SW Alta., near B.C. border, in Rocky Mts., in Banff Natl. Park, on Bow R. and 30 mi. NW of Banff; alt. 5,050 ft. Famous tourist resort, with several large hotels, heated swimming pools, and extensive entertainment and sports facilities. Near foot of Mt. Victoria, 2 mi. SW, is small L. Louise.
Lake Loveland Dam, Calif.: see SWEETWATER RIVER.
Lake Lure, resort town (pop. 174), Rutherford co., SW N.C., 23 mi. SE of Asheville and on Broad R., here dammed to form 3-mi.-long lake; hydroelectric plant.
Lake Luzerne or **Luzerne** (lōozûrn'), year-round resort village (1940 pop. 505), Warren co., E N.Y., in the Adirondacks, bet. the Hudson and small L. Luzerne. Ski trails near by.
Lake Manawa (mă'nùwä), resort village (1940 pop. 660), Pottawattamie co., SW Iowa, on L. Manawa (c.2 mi. long), just S of Council Bluffs. Lake Manawa State Park is here.
Lake Maude, village (pop. 1,429), Polk co., central Fla.
Lakemba (läkĕm'bä), volcanic island (□ 22; pop. 1,833), Lau group, Fiji, SW Pacific; 5 mi. long. Central mtn. range rises to 720 ft.; fertile coast. Site (1835) of 1st missionary settlement in Fiji. Sometimes spelled Lakeba.
Lake Mills. 1 Town (pop. 1,560), Winnebago co., N Iowa, near Minn. line, 25 mi. NW of Mason City; vegetable cannery, feed mill. Inc. 1880. Rice Lake State Park is SE. **2** City (pop. 2,516), Jefferson co., S Wis., on Rock L., 24 mi. E of Madison, in dairying, farming, and resort region; mfg. (dairy equipment, shoes, canned vegetables, powdered milk). A U.S. fish hatchery is here. Settled c.1836, inc. 1905. Near-by Aztalan Mound Park contains remains of prehistoric Indian village, rare platform mounds, and a mus. with anc. Indian relics.
Lake Milton, village (1940 pop. 123), Mahoning co., NE Ohio, 16 mi. W of Youngstown, on E shore of Milton Reservoir. Inc. 1930, disincorporated 1947.
Lake Minchumina (mĭn"chōomē'nù), village (pop. 41), E central Alaska, on L. Minchumina, 150 mi. SW of Fairbanks; airfield.
Lake Minnewaska (mĭnùwŏ'skù), resort, Ulster co., SE N.Y., on small L. Minnewaska, in the Shawangunk range, 17 mi. SW of Kingston.
Lake Mohawk, N.J.: see SPARTA.
Lakemont, summer resort (pop. c.100), Rabun co., extreme NE Ga., 6 mi. S of Clayton, near L. Rabun, in the Blue Ridge.
Lakemore, village (pop. 2,463), Summit co., NE Ohio, 6 mi. SE of downtown Akron. Inc. 1920.
Laken (lä'kùn), town, Brabant prov., central Belgium, N suburb of Brussels; petroleum refinery. Site of royal palace (built by Napoleon for Josephine) and large surrounding park. Formerly spelled Laeken.
Lake Nebagamon (nĭbă'gùmùn), resort village (pop. 340), Douglas co., NW Wis., on small L. Nebagamon, 22 mi. SE of Superior. Was lumbering center in late 1800s.
Lakenham, England: see NORWICH.
Lakenheath, agr. village and parish (pop. 1,656), NW Suffolk, England, 5 mi. SW of Brandon. Has medieval church. Large air base.
Lake Norden, city (pop. 373), Hamlin co., E S.Dak., 23 mi. S of Watertown, near L. Norden.
Lake Odessa (ōdĕ'sù), village (pop. 1,596), Ionia co., S central Mich., 30 mi. W of Lansing, in lake-resort and agr. area; cannery, grain elevator. Settled c.1870, inc. 1889.
Lake of the Cherokees, Okla.: see GRAND RIVER DAM.
Lake of the Ozarks (ō'zärks), central Mo., formed by impounding of Osage R. by BAGNELL DAM; with irregular, wooded shores and many arms, it winds through the Ozarks for c.130 mi. State park; recreational facilities; fishing.
Lake of the Woods, county (□ 1,308; pop. 4,955), NW Minn.; ⊙ Baudette. Agr. region bounded NE by Rainy R. and extending N bet. Can. provinces of Man. and Ont.; includes Northwest Angle, northernmost land in continental U.S. Potatoes, dairy products. Includes extensive state forests, much marshland, and part of Lake of the Woods. Formed 1922.
Lake of the Woods (□ 1,485), in N Minn., SE Man., and W Ont., WNW of International Falls, Minn., in pine-forest region; c.70 mi. long, c.60 mi. wide. Was once part of glacial L. Agassiz. Receives Rainy R. in S and has N outlet, at city of Kenora, Ont., into Winnipeg R. Shore line is extremely irregular. Largest of many peninsulas is Aulneau (c.30 mi. long, 18 mi. wide) extending W. Just S of it are Bigsby Isl. and Big Isl. (12 mi. long, max. width 8.5 mi.), largest of some 14,000 islands and islets. SW corner of lake, in U.S., separates part of Lake of the Woods co. from rest of Minn. This area (the Northwest Angle), a peninsula and islets, is northernmost land in continental U.S.; roadless and inaccessible, region is site of settlements of Penasse, Angle Inlet, and Oak Isl. Lake has abundance of fish and game and many fishing, boating, and bathing resorts. Village of Warroad is on SW shore, in Minn.
Lake Okeechobee-Cross Florida Waterway, Fla.: see OKEECHOBEE WATERWAY.
Lake Orion (ō'rēùn, ô'rēŏn"), resort village (pop. 2,385), Oakland co., SE Mich., 11 mi. NNE of Pontiac, on small L. Orion. Market center for agr. area (grain, potatoes, corn, beans, poultry; dairy products). Inc. 1859. Formerly Orion.
Lake Orion Heights, village (pop. 1,075), Oakland co., SE Mich., near Lake Orion.
Lake Park. 1 Town (pop. 489), Palm Beach co., SE Fla., 5 mi. N of West Palm Beach, on L. Worth lagoon. Formerly Kelsey City. **2** Town (pop. 334), Lowndes co., S Ga., 11 mi. SE of Valdosta, near Fla. line. **3** Town (pop. 924), Dickinson co., NW Iowa, 23 mi. NNW of Spencer, in resort area; mills (lumber, feed), creamery; harnesses, canvas products. State park, sand and gravel pits near by. **4** Village (pop. 689), Becker co., W Minn., 13 mi. WNW of Detroit Lakes, in grain, livestock, poultry area; dairy products, cattle feed. Small lakes near.
Lake Peekskill, resort village, Putnam co., SE N.Y., on Peekskill L. (c.½ mi. long), 5 mi. NE of Peekskill.
Lake Placid. 1 City (pop. 417), Highlands co., S central Fla., 15 mi. S of Sebring, in lake region; citrus fruit. **2** Resort village (pop. 2,999), Essex co., NE N.Y., in the Adirondacks, on small Mirror L. and at S end of L. Placid (4 mi. long, c.½ mi. wide; alt. 1,859 ft.), c.40 mi. SW of Plattsburg; noted eastern winter-sports center and summer resort. Scene of 1932 Olympic winter games. Mt. Van Hoevenberg (văn hō'vùnbûrg), with noted bobsled run, is SE. Northwood School for boys is in village. Near by (at North Elba) are farm and grave of John Brown. Settled c.1850, inc. 1900.
Lake Pleasant. 1 Village, Franklin co., Mass.: see MONTAGUE. **2** Resort village, ⊙ Hamilton co., E central N.Y., on L. Pleasant (□ c.2; 3½ mi. long), 50 mi. NE of Utica, in the Adirondacks; summer and winter resort; lumbering.
Lake Pleasant Dam, Ariz.: see AGUA FRIA RIVER.
Lakeport. 1 Town (pop. 1,983), ⊙ Lake co., NW Calif., on Clear L., c.45 mi. NNW of Santa Rosa; resort, farm trade center; pears, beans, walnuts. Founded 1861, inc. 1888. **2** Village, Belknap co., central N.H., suburb of Laconia, on L. Paugus; lumber mills, mfg. (machinery, bldg. materials). Terminus for mail boats operating on L. Winnipesaukee.
Lake Preston, city (pop. 957), Kingsbury co., E S.Dak., 9 mi. E of De Smet, near L. Preston; trade point for farming region; livestock, dairy produce, poultry, grain.
Lake Providence, town (pop. 4,123), ⊙ East Carroll parish, extreme NE La., on Mississippi R. and 36 mi. NNW of Vicksburg (Miss.), in cotton-growing area; cotton ginning, wood-products mfg., flour milling. Commercial fisheries. One of oldest towns in La.; settled c.1812, inc. 1876. L. Providence (c.5 mi. long; fishing), an oxbow lake formed by the Mississippi, is just N. During Civil War, Grant attempted construction of canal (remains extant) bet. lake and the Mississippi.
Lake Province (□ 39,134; pop. 1,835,326), NW Tanganyika; ⊙ Mwanza. Includes portion of L. Victoria S of 1°S. Mainly cultivable grasslands with some bush forest and thicket. Chief crops: coffee, cotton, peanuts, rice, millet; sisal and coffee especially along lake shore; tobacco in SW. Densely populated along Tabora-Mwanza RR and on lake shore. Important mining region: goldfields near Musoma and SW of Mwanza (Geita mine); diamond mines near Shinyanga; tin mines at Murongo.
Lake Range, W Nev., largely in Pyramid Lake Indian Reservation, bet. Pyramid L. (W) and Winnemucca and Mud lakes (E). Rises to 8,174 ft. in Tohakum Peak and to 7,800 ft. in Pah-rum Peak.
Lake Ronkonkoma (rŏngkŏng'kùmù), resort village (1940 pop. 770), Suffolk co., SE N.Y., on central Long Isl., 7 mi. NW of Patchogue, on L. Ronkonkoma (c.¾ mi. in diameter).
Lakes, The, urban district (1948 pop. estimate 5,207), W Westmorland, England, in the Lake District, 10 mi. NW of Kendal; formed 1935 out of Ambleside and Grasmere.
Lakes Entrance, town (pop. 1,044), Victoria, Australia, on SE coast, 165 mi. E of Melbourne, at entrance to L. King; seaside resort.
Lakeshire, town (pop. 295), St. Louis co., E Mo.
Lake Shore, village (pop. 326), Cass co., central Minn., 15 mi. NW of Brainerd, near Gull L.
Lakeside. 1 Village (1940 pop. 786), San Diego co., S Calif., 17 mi. NE of San Diego, on small lake; resort; agr. **2** W suburb (pop. 46) of Denver, Jefferson co., N central Colo. **3** Village, Litchfield co., Conn.: see MORRIS. **4** Resort town (pop. 219), Buena Vista co., NW Iowa, just SE of Storm L. Inc. 1933. **5** or **Lakeside Park,** town (pop. 988), Kenton co., N Ky., 8 mi. SW of Covington, within Cincinnati metropolitan dist. Inc. 1930. **6** Resort village (pop. c.300), Berrien co., extreme SW Mich., 21 mi. SSW of St. Joseph, on L. Michigan. **7** Village (pop. 1,209, with adjacent Bayport Park), Genesee co., E central Mich. **8** Resort village (pop. 1,034), Ottawa co., N Ohio, on Marblehead Peninsula in L. Erie, 7 mi. NNW of Sandusky. **9** Town (1940 pop. 134), Coos co., SW Oregon, 12 mi. N of North Bend. **10** Resort town (pop. 288), Chelan co., central Wash., 15 mi. N of Waterville and on L. Chelan.
Lakes of the Clouds, N.H.: see PRESIDENTIAL RANGE.
Lake Solai (sōlī'), village, Rift Valley prov., W central Kenya, 22 mi. N of Nakuru; rail spur terminus in Great Rift Valley. Settled after 1909 by cattle breeders and corn farmers. Also called Solai.
Lake Spaulding Dam, Calif.: see YUBA RIVER.
Lake Stevens, village (pop. 2,586), Snohomish co., NW Wash., on small lake and 5 mi. E of Everett.
Lake Success, village (pop. 1,264), Nassau co., SE N.Y., near N shore of W Long Isl., 7 mi. NE of Jamaica. Became temporary hq. of the United Nations, 1946–51. Mfg. of aerial and naval instruments.
Lake Tara, town (pop. 224), Clayton co., NW central Ga.
Laketown, town (pop. 217), Rich co., N Utah, at S end of Bear L., 28 mi. ENE of Logan.
Lake View. 1 Resort town (pop. 1,158), Sac co., W Iowa, 19 mi. NNW of Carroll, near Black Hawk L. (state park here); popcorn, seed corn; concrete. Gravel pits in vicinity. Settled 1875, inc. 1887. **2** Plantation (pop. 23), Piscataquis co., central Maine, on Schoodic L. and 19 mi. NE of Dover-Foxcroft, in recreational area. **3** Residential village (1940 pop. 3,271), Nassau co., SE N.Y., on W Long Isl., just SW of Hempstead. A state park is near by.
Lakeview. 1 Village (pop. 13,161, with adjacent Springfield Place), Calhoun co., S Mich. **2** Village (pop. 975), Montcalm co., central Mich., 38 mi. NNE of Grand Rapids, on small Tamarack L. (resort), in agr. area (livestock, poultry, potatoes, sugar beets, beans; dairy products); gas wells. **3** Resort village (pop. 966), Logan co., W central Ohio, 12 mi. NW of Bellefontaine, on Indian L. **4** Town (pop. 2,831), ⊙ Lake co., S Oregon, N of Goose L. in livestock and forest area; alt. 4,800 ft. Sawmills, woodworking plants; dairying. Hq. of near-by Fremont Natl. Forest. Founded 1876, inc. 1884. **5** Town (pop. 653), Dillon co., NE S.C., 35 mi. ENE of Florence, near N.C. line. Formerly Pages Mill. **6** Town (pop. 287), Hall co., NW Texas, 32 mi. NW of Childress, in cotton, truck, and fruit area. **7** Town (pop. 3,091), Jefferson co., SE Texas, NE suburb of Port Arthur. Inc. 1938. **8** Village (1940 pop. 589), McLennan co., E central Texas, 6 mi. N of Waco.
Lake Villa, village (pop. 824), Lake co., extreme NE Ill., 13 mi. WNW of Waukegan, in dairying and lake-resort area.
Lake Village, town (pop. 2,484), ⊙ Chicot co., extreme SE Ark., 14 mi. WSW of Greenville (Miss.), on L. Chicot; cotton ginning, feed- and sawmilling, woodworking, commercial fishing; resort. Founded in 1850s, inc. 1901.
Lakeville. 1 Resort village (1940 pop. 1,309) in Salisbury town, Litchfield co., NW Conn., on L. Wononskopomuc; fishing tackle, dairy products, poultry. Hotchkiss school for boys (1892). Ethan Allen made Revolutionary munitions here. **2** Town (pop. 736), St. Joseph co., N Ind., 11 mi. S of South Bend; resort, with lakes near by. **3** Plantation (pop. 50), Penobscot co., E central Maine, 40 mi. NE of Old Town, in hunting, fishing area. **4** Agr. town (pop. 2,066), Plymouth co., SE Mass., on Assawompsett Pond and 15 mi. N of New Bedford. Settled 1717, inc. 1853. Long, Great Quittacas, and Snipatuit ponds are near. **5** Village (pop. 628), Dakota co., SE Minn., near small lake, 22 mi. SSW of St. Paul, in grain, potato, livestock area; dairy products. **6** Village (pop. 3,432), Ashtabula co., NE Ohio, surrounding city of Conneaut. Inc. 1944. **7** Hamlet, Holmes co., central Ohio, near Mohican R., 27 mi. ESE of Mansfield.
Lake Waccamaw (wŏ'kùmô", –ä"), resort town (pop. 575), Columbus co., SE N.C., 10 mi. E of Whiteville, on L. Waccamaw (c.5 mi. long, 3 mi. wide); hunting, fishing.
Lake Wales, city (pop. 6,821), Polk co., central Fla., c.55 mi. E of Tampa; citrus-fruit shipping center; packing houses, large cannery, tannery; sand and gravel pits. A noted resort, with IRON MOUNTAIN near by. Platted 1911.
Lake Washington Ship Canal, Wash.: see WASHINGTON, LAKE.

Lake Wilson, village (pop. 434), Murray co., SW Minn., on Des Moines R. near its source and 10 mi. W of Slayton, in grain, livestock, poultry area.

Lake Windermere, village, B.C.: see ATHALMER.

Lakewood. 1 Town (1940 pop. 123), Walton co., NW Fla., near Ala. line, 23 mi. NE of Crestview. **2** Village (pop. 393), McHenry co., NE Ill., on Crystal L., 12 mi. N of Elgin, in dairying and resort area. **3** Village, Somerset co., Maine: see SKOWHEGAN. **4** Township (pop. 9,970), Ocean co., E N.J., on South Branch Metedeconk R. and 13 mi. SSE of Freehold; winter resort on small L. Carasaljo. Georgian Court Col., Maryknoll Jr. Col., and boys' school here; former Rockefeller estate, now a state reserve, near by. Settled 1786. **5** Village (pop. c.100), Eddy co., SE N.Mex., on L. McMillan and 17 mi. NNW of Carlsbad, in irrigated region; grain, cotton, sugar beets, fruit. Wildlife refuge near by. **6** Resort village (pop. 3,013), Chautauqua co., extreme W N.Y., on Chautauqua L., 5 mi. W of Jamestown; machine tools, dies. Settled 1809, inc. 1893. **7** City (pop. 68,071), Cuyahoga co., N Ohio, just W of Cleveland, on L. Erie; mainly residential, with mfg. of metal products, machinery, chemicals, tools, millinery, electrical apparatus. Settled as East Rockport; renamed 1889; inc. 1911. **8** Village, Kent co., R.I.: see WARWICK.

Lakewood Bluff, Wis.: see MAPLE BLUFF.

Lakewood Village, Calif.: see LONG BEACH.

Lake Worth. 1 Resort city (pop. 11,777), Palm Beach co., SE Fla., just S of West Palm Beach, on resort-bordered L. Worth, a straight narrow lagoon (c.22 mi. long; part of Intracoastal Waterway) opening into the Atlantic through Lake Worth Inlet (dredged) at N end of Palm Beach barrier beach. Inc. 1913, reincorporated 1925. **2** Village (pop. 2,351), Tarrant co., N Texas, suburb just NW of Fort Worth, near L. Worth. Inc. after 1940.

Lake Zurich (zōō'rĭk), village (pop. 850), Lake co., NE Ill., 17 mi. SW of Waukegan, in agr. and lake-resort area.

Lakhanokipos, Greece: see LACHANOKEPOS.

Lakhaoti, India: see AURANGABAD SAIYID.

Lakhapani, India: see LIKHAPANI.

Lakhdenpokhya or **Lakhdenpokh'ya** (läkh'dyĭnpŭkhyŭ), Finnish *Lahdenpohja* (lä'dĕnpôyä), city (1945 pop. 1,832), SW Karelo-Finnish SSR, port on NW shore of L. Ladoga, on railroad and 20 mi. SW of Sortavala; plywood mill. Steamer connection to Valaam Isl. Until 1940, in Finland.

Lakheri (lŭkā'rē), town (pop. 6,260), E Rajasthan, India, 37 mi. NE of Bundi; markets wheat, millet, barley, gram; large cement works.

Lakhi Hills (lŭ'kē), most easterly offshoot of Kirthar Range, in Dadu dist., W Sind, W Pakistan; narrow ridge extending c.70 mi. S from Indus R., 5 mi. S of Sehwan; 1,500–2,000 ft. high. S end drained by Baran R. Little vegetation; hot sulphur springs (N) noted for medicinal properties.

Lakhimpur (lŭkĭm'pōōr), district (□ 4,153; pop. 894,842), NE Assam, India; ⊙ Dibrugarh. Mainly in Brahmaputra valley; bounded N by Dafla and Abor hills, W by Subansiri R., E by undefined India-Burma border (Patkai Range); traversed by Brahmaputra R. Mainly alluvial soil; tea (major Assam tea garden dist.), rice, jute, sugar cane, rape and mustard; silk growing; cotton trees in forest area, E. Major Indian oil field near Digboi (petroleum refineries). Important Assam coal-field centers at Margherita and Likhapani. Extensive tea processing, rice and oilseed milling, cement and tin-can mfg.; railroad workshops; sawmills. N terminus of Ledo (Stilwell) Road at Ledo; steamer terminus at Dibrugarh. Suffered greatly in 1950 earthquake. Pop. 55% Hindu, 37% Animist tribes (including Shans and Miris).

Lakhimpur, town (pop. 21,235), ⊙ Kheri dist., N Uttar Pradesh, India, on tributary of the Sarda and 75 mi. N of Lucknow; road junction; trade center (rice, wheat, gram, corn, barley, oilseeds, sugar cane); sugar milling. Dist. hq. since 1859.

Lakhipur (lŭk'ĭpōōr), village, Goalpara dist., W Assam, India, on left tributary of the Brahmaputra and 22 mi. E of Dhubri; rice, mustard, jute.

Lakhisarai, India: see LUCKEESARAI.

Lakhna (lŭk'nŭ), town (pop. 3,360), Etawah dist., W Uttar Pradesh, India, on Lower Ganges Canal and 12 mi. SSE of Etawah; pearl millet, wheat, barley, corn, gram, cotton.

Lakhnadon (lŭknä'dōn), village, Chhindwara dist., central Madhya Pradesh, India, 36 mi. N of Seoni; sunn-hemp retting, essential-oil extraction (*rosha* or Andropogon); wheat, rice, oilseeds. Cattle raising, lac cultivation in near-by forested hills.

Lakhnau, district, India: see LUCKNOW.

Lakhnau. 1 Village, Aligarh dist., Uttar Pradesh, India: see HATHRAS. **2** City, Lucknow dist., Uttar Pradesh, India: see LUCKNOW.

Lakhpat (lŭk'pŭt), village, W Cutch, India, at head of Kori Creek (inlet of Arabian Sea; c.35 mi. long), on SW edge of Rann of Cutch, 70 mi. NW of Bhuj; trades in salt, wheat.

Lakhsetipet, India: see LAKSHETTIPET.

Lakhtar (lŭk'tŭr), town (pop. 6,741), NE Saurashtra, India, 13 mi. NNE of Wadhwan; agr. market (millet, cotton); cotton ginning, oilseed milling. Was ⊙ former Eastern Kathiawar state of Lakhtar (□ 247; pop. 26,780) of Western India States agency; state merged 1948 with Saurashtra.

Lakhtinski or **Lakhtinskiy** (läkh'tyĭnskē), town (1926 pop. 1,229), NW Leningrad oblast, Russian SFSR, on Gulf of Finland, 7 mi. NW of Leningrad; peat works.

Laki (lä'kē) or **Skafta** (skäft'ou"), Icelandic *Skaftá*, volcano (2,684 ft.), S Iceland, at SW edge of Vatnajokull; 64°3'N 18°17'W. Major eruption (1783) was one of most devastating volcanic eruptions on record. Surrounding crater are the Lakagigar (lä'kägē"kär), Icelandic *Lakagígar*, series of c.100 volcanic rifts. Surrounding lava field (□ 220) is called Skaftareldahraun (skäft'our"ĕl"tähürû"-ün), Icelandic *Skaftáreldahraun*.

Lakiashih, China: see TUNGTEH.

Laki Marwat (lŭk'ē mŭrvät') or **Lakki** (lŭk'kē), town (pop. 10,141), Bannu dist., SE North-West Frontier Prov., W Pakistan, 32 mi. SE of Bannu; rail junction; markets wheat, gram, corn; handicraft cloth weaving.

Lakin (lā'kĭn), city (pop. 1,618), ⊙ Kearny co., SW Kansas, on Arkansas R. and 21 mi. W of Garden City; grain, cattle. Gas wells near by. L. McKinney is irrigation reservoir just NE.

Lakinski or **Lakinskiy** (lŭkēn'skē), town (1926 pop. 2,300), W Vladimir oblast, Russian SFSR, 19 mi. WSW of Vladimir, near railroad (Undol station); cotton-milling center. Formerly Imeni Lakina.

Lakmos (läk'môs), massif in central Pindus Mts., S Epirus, Greece, rises to 7,529 ft. in the Peristeri, 15 mi. E of Ioannina.

Laknauti, India: see GAUR.

Lakonia, Greece: see LACONIA.

Lakor (lŭkôr'), island (pop. 1,576), Leti Isls., S Moluccas, Indonesia, in Banda Sea, just E of Moa, 55 mi. ENE of Timor; 10 mi. long, 5 mi. wide. Coconut growing, fishing.

Lakota (läkō'tä), village (pop. c.700), S Ivory Coast, Fr. West Africa, 65 mi. NW of Grand-Lahou; coffee, cacao, palm kernels.

Lakota (lŭkō'tŭ). **1** Town (pop. 443), Kossuth co., N Iowa, 22 mi. NNE of Algona; dairy products. **2** City (pop. 1,032), ⊙ Nelson co., NE central N.Dak., 60 mi. W of Grand Forks; livestock, wheat, flax.

Laksam, E Pakistan: see LAKSHAM.

Laksapana Falls, Ceylon: see LAXAPANA FALLS.

Laksevag (läk'sûvôg), Nor. *Laksevåg*, village (pop. 8,755; canton pop. 11,565), Hordaland co., SW Norway, on Pudde Fjord, just WSW of Bergen; shipbuilding, mfg. of wire fencing. Coastal fortifications. At Oldernes (E) is production of candied fruit; at Simonsvik (½ mi. E) is rolling mill producing steel and tin plate.

Laksha divi, India: see LACCADIVE ISLANDS.

Laksham (läk'shäm), village, Tippera dist., SE East Bengal, E Pakistan, on tributary of Meghna R. and 16 mi. SSW of Comilla; rail junction (lines to Chittagong, Chandpur, and Noakhali); rice, jute, oilseeds. Also spelled Laksam.

Lakshettipet or **Lakshattipet** (both: lŭkshŭt'ĭpĕt), village (pop. 3,145), Adilabad dist., NE Hyderabad state, India, on Godavari R. and 70 mi. SSE of Adilabad; millet, oilseeds, rice. Sawmilling near by. Sometimes spelled Luxhattipet; formerly spelled Lakhsetipet.

Lakshmantirtha River (lŭkshmŭntēr'tŭ), in SE Coorg and S Mysore, India, rises in Western Ghats SE of Mercara, flows c.70 mi. NNE, past Hunsur, to Krishnaraja Sagara (reservoir on Cauvery R.) 16 mi. NW of Mysore.

Lakshmeshwar (lŭkshmā'shvŭr), town (pop. 10,369), Dharwar dist., S Bombay, India, 38 mi. SE of Dharwar; road center; cotton market; cotton ginning, handicraft cloth weaving. Annual fair. Also spelled Lakshmeshvar or Laxmishwar.

Lakshmikantapur, India: see JAYNAGAR, West Bengal.

Lakshmipur (lŭksh'mēpōōr), village, Noakhali dist., SE East Bengal, E Pakistan, near Meghna R., 19 mi. WNW of Noakhali; trades in rice, jute, oilseeds; cotton-cloth mfg.

Laktasi or **Laktashi** (both: läk'täshē), Serbo-Croatian *Laktaši*, village, NW Bosnia, Yugoslavia, near Vrbas R., 11 mi. NNE of Banja Luka; hot baths.

Lal (läl), town, Kabul prov., central Afghanistan, on Lal R. (tributary of the Hari Rud) and 45 mi. W of Panjao, and on central Kabul-Herat highway, in the Hazarajat.

La Labor (lä läbōr'), town (pop. 454), Ocotepeque dept., W Honduras, 7 mi. NW of San Marcos; corn, beans.

Lalaghat, India: see HAILAKANDI.

Lalaguda, India: see HYDERABAD, city.

La Laguna, Canary Isls.: see LAGUNA, LA.

La Laja (lä lä'hä), village, S San Juan prov., Argentina, at S foot of Sierra de Villicún, 15 mi. NNE of San Juan; resort, with mineral springs. Marble, travertine quarries in mts. near by. Sometimes called Baños de la Laja.

La Laja, village (pop. 609), Los Santos prov., S central Panama, in Pacific lowland, 1 mi. S of Las Tablas; sugar cane, coffee, livestock.

La Lama, village (pop. 7,866, with near-by Airport), Stanislaus co., central Calif.

Lala Musa (lä'lŭ mōō'sŭ), town (pop. 12,163), Gujrat dist., NE Punjab, W Pakistan, 11 mi. NW of Gujrat; rail junction (workshop); wheat, millet; cotton-cloth handicrafts.

Lalapanzi (läläpän'zē), village, Gwelo prov., central Southern Rhodesia, in Matabeleland, on railroad and 25 mi. ENE of Gwelo; alt. 4,907 ft. Chrome mining.

Lalapasa (lälä'pä-shä), Turkish *Lalapaşa*, village (pop. 647), Adrianople prov., Turkey in Europe, 15 mi. NE of Adrianople; wheat, rice, rye, sugar beets. Sometimes spelled Lalapasha.

La Lata, Uruguay: see CARDONA.

Lalbagh, India: see MURSHIDABAD, town.

Lalbenque (lälbăk'), village (pop. 428), Lot dept., SW France, in the Causse de Limogne, 9 mi. SE of Cahors; woodworking; tobacco and truffles.

Laleham, England: see STAINES.

Laleston, town in Tythegston Higher parish (pop. 2,370), S Glamorgan, Wales, 7 mi. S of Maesteg; stone quarrying.

Lalevade-d'Ardèche (lälüväd'-därdĕsh'), village (pop. 1,072), Ardèche dept., S France, on the Ardèche and 5 mi. NW of Aubenas; tanning extract processing, sawmilling.

Lalganj (läl'gŭnj). **1** Town (pop. 9,481), Muzaffarpur dist., N Bihar, India, on Gandak R. and 23 mi. SW of Muzaffarpur; river-trade center; rice, wheat, barley, corn, sugar cane, oilseeds, hides. Basarh, anc. *Vaisali*, village, 7 mi. NW, was ⊙ kingdom of Magadha period; one of 8 great anc. Buddhist pilgrimage centers; clay seals discovered here. **2** Town (pop. 2,280), Rae Bareli dist., central Uttar Pradesh, India, 16 mi. WSW of Rae Bareli; rice, wheat, barley, gram.

Lalguda, India: see HYDERABAD, city.

Lalgudi (läl'gōōdē), town (pop. 7,314), Trichinopoly dist., S Madras, India, 9 mi. ENE of Trichinopoly; rice, plantain, coconut palms, millet. Agr. experimental farm. Cement factory 10 mi. NE, at village of Dalmiapuram.

Lali (lälē'), oil town, Sixth Prov., in Khuzistan, SW Iran, on Karun R. and 20 mi. NE of Shushtar, 140 mi. NNE of Abadan (linked by pipeline); oil field opened 1948.

La-li, Tibet: see LHARI.

Lalian (läl'yän), town (pop. 5,216), Jhang dist., central Punjab, W Pakistan, 45 mi. NNE of Jhang-Maghiana; wheat, cotton; cotton ginning.

Lalibala (lä'lēbälä), town (pop. 3,000), Wallo prov., NE Ethiopia, near Abuna Josef mtn., 75 mi. NW of Dessye; 12°N 39°4'E. A major religious and pilgrimage center with 10 famous monolithic churches built in 12th cent.

La Libertad (lä lēbĕrtädh'), village, Guayas prov., W Ecuador, port on S shore of Santa Elena Bay, on Santa Elena Peninsula, just E of Salinas and 75 mi. W of Guayaquil. Petroleum-drilling and -refining center. Connected by rail and pipe line with Ancón oil wells, 10 mi. SE.

La Libertad, town (1950 pop. 632), Petén dept., N Guatemala, 18 mi. SW of Flores; sugar cane, grain, livestock.

La Libertad, town (pop. 398), Chiapas, S Mexico, in lowland, on affluent of Usumacinta R. and 4 mi. SSE of Emiliano Zapata; rubber, fruit.

La Libertad, town (1950 pop. 1,972), Chontales dept., S Nicaragua, 20 mi. NE of Juigalpa; gold- and silver-mining center. Near by are San Juan and Esmeralda mines.

La Libertad, department, Peru: see LIBERTAD.

La Libertad, department (□ 843; pop. 165,202), W central Salvador, on the Pacific; ⊙ Nueva San Salvador. Bounded N by Lempa R.; crossed E-W by coastal range (center); contains volcano San Salvador. Agr. (coffee, sugar cane, grain), livestock raising; balsam of Peru extraction and hardwood lumbering near coast. N part served by rail lines and Inter-American Highway. Main centers are Nueva San Salvador, Quezaltepeque, and major Pacific port of La Libertad. Formed 1865.

La Libertad, town (pop. 2,219), La Libertad dept., SW Salvador, 2d largest port of Salvador, on the Pacific, 13 mi. S of Nueva San Salvador (connected by road); 13°29'N 89°19'W. Fisheries; grain, livestock raising; popular all-year resort. Exports coffee, sugar, balsam of Peru, hardwood. Developed in 19th cent.

La Ligua (lä lē'gwä) or **Ligua,** town (pop. 3,178), ⊙ Petorca dept. (□ 1,909; pop. 33,997), Aconcagua prov., central Chile, on Ligua R. and 50 mi. NNE of Valparaiso; rail and agr. center (beans, potatoes, oats).

La Lima (lä lē'mä), town (pop. 6,128), Cortés dept., NW Honduras, on Chamelecón R. and 7 mi. SE of San Pedro Sula, in banana zone. Consists of old commercial section (left bank) and new residential section (right bank; hq. of near-by banana plantations).

Lalin (lä'lĭn'), town, ⊙ Lalin co., W Sungkiang prov., Manchuria, 40 mi. SSE of Harbin, and on railroad, near Lalin R. (short affluent of Sungari R.; Kirin line); soybean pressing, lumbering.

Lalín (lälēn'), town (pop. 1,136), Pontevedra prov., NW Spain, in Galicia, 26 mi. SE of Santiago; agr. trade (cereals, potatoes, livestock). Tin mines and lignite deposits near by.

Lalinde (lälĕd'), village (pop. 1,029), Dordogne dept., SW France, on the Dordogne and 12 mi. E of

Bergerac; paper milling, food processing (*pâté de foie gras* and truffles). Two hydroelectric plants near by on Dordogne R.

La Línea, Spain: see LÍNEA, LA.

Lalitpur (lŭlĭt′pŏŏr), town (pop. 16,881), Jhansi dist., S Uttar Pradesh, India, on tributary of the Betwa and 55 mi. S of Jhansi; road junction; trade center (jowar, oilseeds, wheat, gram, dried beef, hides, ghee). Hindu and Jain temples. Wrested from Gonds by Bundela Rajput leader in 16th cent.; battle here, c.1800, bet. Bundelas and Mahrattas. Was ⊙ former Chanderi dist. in 1844; gave its name to dist. in 1861; in 1891, Jhansi and Lalitpur dists. merged. Jain ruins, including large slab dated A.D. 907, are 11 mi. NW, near Siron village. Projected 40-ft.-high irrigation dam near by, on tributary of the Betwa.

Lallaing (lälē′), residential town (pop. 3,729), Nord dept., N France, on the Scarpe (canalized) and 4 mi. ENE of Douai; truck gardening.

Lalla Khadidja, Algeria: see LELLA KHEDIDJA.

Lalla-Marnia, Algeria: see MARNIA.

Lalla Takerkoust, Fr. Morocco: see N'FIS, OUED.

La Llave (lä yä′vä), village (pop. 1,320), Querétaro, central Mexico, on railroad and 27 mi. ESE of Querétaro; grain, sugar, vegetables, fruit, stock; opal cutting.

Lal-lo (läl″lō′), town (1939 pop. 4,565; 1948 municipality pop. 10,730), Cagayan prov., N Luzon, Philippines, on Cagayan R. and 11 mi. S of Aparri; agr. center (rice, tobacco).

Lalmanir Hat (läl′mŭnĭr hät′), town (pop., including rail settlement, 10,796), Rangpur dist., N East Bengal, E Pakistan, 16 mi. NE of Rangpur; rail workshops; rice and oilseed milling, soap mfg.; trades in rice, jute, tobacco, oilseeds. Also called Lalmonirhat.

La Loma, Dominican Republic: see LOMA DE CABRERA.

Lalone Island (lŭlōn′), St. Lawrence co., N N.Y., in the St. Lawrence, at Ont. line, just S of Cardinal, Ont.; c.½ mi. in diameter.

Lalouvesc (lälōōvĕk′), village (pop. 543), Ardèche dept., S France, in the Monts du Vivarais, 11 mi. SW of Annonay; alt. 3,450 ft. Pilgrimage center. Produces religious articles. Sometimes spelled La Louvesc.

Lalsanga, India: see CHAMOLI.

Lalsk or **Lal'sk** (lälsk), village (1926 pop. 1,784), NW Kirov oblast, Russian SFSR, on Luza R. and 45 mi. SE of Kotlas; dairying. Paper-milling town of Lalsk (1926 pop. 1,430) is just W.

Lalsot (läl′sōt), town (pop. 6,685), E Rajasthan, India, 40 mi. SE of Jaipur; markets millet, barley, gram. In near-by battle (1787), combined forces of Jaipur and Jodhpur defeated Mahrattas.

Laluque (lälük′), village (pop. 311), Landes dept., SW France, 10 mi. N of Dax; tile factory, sawmills. Lignite mining.

La Luz (lä lōōs′), mining settlement (pop. 611), Guanajuato, central Mexico, in Sierra Madre Occidental, 7 mi. WNW of Guanajuato; alt. 7,644 ft.; mercury mining.

La Luz, Nicaragua: see SIUNA.

Lam (läm), village (pop. 2,836), Lower Bavaria, Germany, in Bavarian Forest, on the White Regen and 25 mi. N of Deggendorf; woodworking, glass grinding; pyrite mining. Has mid-18th-cent. pilgrimage church.

Lam (läm), town, Bacgiang prov., N Vietnam, 50 mi. NE of Hanoi.

Lama dei Peligni (lä′mä dä pĕlē′nyē), village (pop. 2,253), Chieti prov., Abruzzi e Molise, S central Italy, near Maiella mts., 17 mi. SSW of Lanciano. Largely destroyed in Second World War.

Lamadelaine (lämädlĕn′), Ger. *Rollingen* (rô′lĭng-ün), town (pop. 1,059), SW Luxembourg, just ESE of Rodange, near Fr. frontier; iron-mining center.

Lamadrid, for Argentine names not found here: see under GENERAL LAMADRID.

La Madrid (lä mädrēd′), town (pop. estimate 1,000), S Tucumán prov., Argentina, on Marapa R. and 55 mi. S of Tucumán; rail junction and agr. center (corn, alfalfa, wheat, livestock). Sometimes Lamadrid and General Lamadrid.

Lamadrid, town (pop. 1,807), Coahuila, N Mexico, 135 mi. NW of Monterrey; cereals, cattle.

La Magdalena or **Magdalena Tetela** (lä mägdälä′nä, tĕtä′lä), town (pop. 1,782), Puebla, central Mexico, 18 mi. E of Puebla; cereals, maguey, stock.

La Magdalena Contreras, Mexico: see CONTRERAS.

Lamagistère (lämäzhĕstâr′), village (pop. 764), Tarn-et-Garonne dept., SW France, on the Garonne and 12 mi. ESE of Agen; fruit preserving and shipping, tanning, sawmilling.

Lama-Kara (lä′mä-kä′rä), town (pop. 3,205), N Fr. Togoland, 40 mi. N of Sokode; cotton, peanuts, shea nuts; cattle, sheep and goat raising. R.C. missions. Sleeping sickness clinic.

Lamalou-les-Bains (lämälōō′-lä-bē′), village (pop. 1,070), Hérault dept., S France, in the Monts de l'Espinouse, near the Orb, 15 mi. SW of Lodève; spa with mineral springs.

Lamamiao, China: see TOLUN.

Lamancha (lŭmăng′kŭ), agr. village in Newlands parish (pop. 614), N Peebles, Scotland, 9 mi. NNW of Peebles. Lamancha House was built in 1663 by earl of Dundonald.

La Mancha, Spain: see MANCHA, LA.

Lamangan, Indonesia: see LAMONGAN.

La Mansión (lä mänsyōn′), village (dist. pop. 9,184), Guanacaste prov., NW Costa Rica, 6 mi. ESE of Nicoya; grain, sugar cane, livestock.

La Manzanilla (lä mänsänē′yä), town (pop. 1,704), Jalisco, central Mexico, in Sierra Madre Occidental, 30 mi. NE of Sayula; grain, beans, fruit, livestock.

La Mar, province, Peru: see SAN MIGUEL, Ayacucho dept.

Lamar (lŭmär′). **1** County (□ 605; pop. 16,441), W Ala.; ⊙ Vernon. Level region bordering on Miss., drained by Buttahatchee R. Cotton, timber, mules, bees. Formed 1867. **2** County (□ 181; pop. 10,242), W central Ga.; ⊙ Barnesville. Piedmont agr. (peaches, pecans, cotton, corn, truck, livestock) and timber area; textile mfg. at Barnesville. Formed 1920. **3** County (□ 500; pop. 13,225), SE Miss.; ⊙ Purvis. Drained by Black and Red creeks. Agr. (cotton, corn, pecans); extensive lumbering (pine). Formed 1904. **4** County (□ 906; pop. 43,033), NE Texas; ⊙ Paris. Bounded N by Red R. (here the Okla. line), S by North Fork of Sulphur R. Diversified agr.: cotton, corn, hay, grains, peanuts, pecans, fruit, truck; dairying; livestock (cattle, hogs, sheep, horses, mules, poultry); some beekeeping; timber. Mfg., farm-products processing at Paris. Includes game sanctuary. Formed 1840.

Lamar. 1 Town (pop. 555), Johnson co., NW Ark., 14 mi. NW Russellville, near Arkansas R. **2** City (pop. 6,829), ⊙ Prowers co., SE Colo., on Arkansas R. and 50 mi. ENE of La Junta; food-processing center for grain and livestock region; flour, condensed milk, meal. Has a jr. col. Madonna of the Trail Monument here. Inc. 1886. **3** Village (1940 pop. 68), Benton co., N Miss., 13 mi. NNE of Holly Springs, in agr. area. **4** City (pop. 3,233), ⊙ Barton co., SW Mo., on branch of Spring R. and 32 mi. NNE of Joplin; wheat, corn, hay, poultry; coal. Founded c.1856. Harry S. Truman b. here 1884. **5** Village (pop. 81), Chase co., S Nebr., 17 mi. W of Imperial, near Colo. line. **6** Town (pop. 180), Hughes co., central Okla., 16 mi. E of Holdenville, in agr. area. **7** Village (pop. c.250), Clinton co., N central Pa., 9 mi. SW of Lock Haven. U.S. fish hatchery here. **8** Town (pop. 958), Darlington co., NE central S.C., 17 mi. W of Florence.

Lamarche (lämärsh′), village (pop. 941), Vosges dept., E France, in the Monts Faucilles, 20 mi. SSE of Neufchâteau; metalworking, winegrowing.

Lamarche-sur-Saône (–sür-sōn′), village (pop. 1,263), Côte-d'Or dept., E central France, on Saône R. and 17 mi. E of Dijon; mfg. of explosives.

La Marina (lä märē′nä), village, Alajuela prov., N Costa Rica, 4 mi. ENE of Villa Quesada; road terminus; lumbering; stock; potatoes, sugar cane.

La Mariscala, Uruguay: see MARISCALA.

Lamarmora, Punta, Sardinia: see GENNARGENTU, MONTI DEL.

Lamarque (lŭmärk′), village (pop. 7,359), Galveston co., S Texas, 12 mi. NW of Galveston; strawberries, truck; oil fields near.

Lamas (lä′mäs), city (pop. 5,625), ⊙ Lamas prov. (□ c.770; enumerated pop. 29,247, plus estimated 4,000 Indians), San Martín dept., N central Peru, near Mayo R., in E Andean outliers, 45 mi. SE of Moyobamba, 11 mi. WNW of Tarapoto. Agr. center in fertile region (cotton, sugar cane, tobacco, coffee, coca, cacao, rice).

Lamas, Cerro, Argentina: see PUNTIAGUDO, CERRO.

Lamastre (lämä′strü), town (pop. 2,256), Ardèche dept., S France, on the Doux and 13 mi. SW of Tournon; jewelry and hosiery mfg., lumbering. Cattle, fruit, and chestnut market.

Lamativie (lämätēvē′), village (pop. 39), Lot dept., SW France, near the Cère, 20 mi. W of Aurillac; hydroelectric plant.

La Matriz, Ecuador: see GUANO.

La Maya (lä mī′ä), town (pop. 2,900), Oriente prov., E Cuba, on railroad and 17 mi. NE of Santiago de Cuba; fruit, cattle.

Lamayuru or **Lamayuru Gompa** (lä′mŭyōōrōō gôm′-pä), village, Ladakh dist., central Kashmir, in NW Zaskar Range, near left tributary of the Indus, 45 mi. WNW of Leh; pulse, wheat. Large Buddhist monastery, founded 9th or 10th cent.; former center of Bon religion. Fotu La, pass (alt. 13,432 ft.) in Zaskar Range, is 4 mi. W, on Kargil-Leh trade route.

Lamb, county (□ 1,022; pop. 20,015), NW Texas; ⊙ Littlefield. On the Llano Estacado; alt. c.3,500 ft. Drained by intermittent Double Mtn. Fork of Brazos R. Rich agr. and livestock region, with irrigated areas; leads in Texas production of grain sorghums; also grows cotton, corn, truck, some fruit; dairying; poultry, livestock (beef cattle, hogs, sheep). Oil, natural-gas wells; potash deposits. Formed 1876.

Lambach (läm′bäkh), town (pop. 2,866), central Upper Austria, on Traun R. and 7 mi. SW of Wels; textiles. Benedictine abbey (founded 1032) with large library.

Lambaesis, Algeria: see LAMBÈSE.

Lamballe (lābäl′), town pop. 4,901), Côtes-du-Nord dept., W France, 12 mi. ESE of Saint-Brieuc; rail and road junction; hosiery and footwear mfg., printing. Stud farms. Site of Norman Gothic church of Notre Dame, originally part of castle.

Lambaré (lämbärā′), S suburb (pop. 7,089) of Asunción, Paraguay, near Paraguay R.; liquor distilling; saltworks.

Lambaréné (lāmbärĕnā′), village, W Gabon, Fr. Equatorial Africa, on Ogooué R. and 100 mi. E of Port-Gentil; trading and lumbering center (sawmills, notably for *okume* wood); steamboat landing. Hq. of Protestant missions in Fr. Equatorial Africa. Famous hospital for natives, directed by Albert Schweitzer, is here. Also R.C. mission.

Lambari (lāmbŏŏrē′), city (pop. 5,438), S Minas Gerais, Brazil, on railroad and 32 mi. N of Itajubá; alt. 2,965 ft. Resort noted for its cool, dry climate and mineral springs. Tourist season: Feb.–April. Old spelling Lambary. Formerly also called Aguas Virtuosas.

Lambasa or **Labasa** (both: lämbä′sä), town (pop. 1,106), N Vanua Levu, Fiji, SW Pacific; Indian settlement on S bank of Lambasa R.; sugar center. Also called Nasea.

Lambayeque (lämbī′ā′kā), department (□ 4,615; pop. 199,660), NW Peru; ⊙ Chiclayo. Bordered by the Pacific (W) and Cordillera Occidental (E). Includes deserts of Mórrope and Olmos, and Lobos Isls. Situated mainly on coastal plain, and having very little rainfall, it is drained by Leche, Lambayeque, Eten, and Saña rivers and Taimi Canal, which feed numerous irrigation channels. Dept. is Peru's chief rice producer and one of its main sugar-cane areas; also produces cotton, corn, vegetables; cattle and goat raising; apiculture. Sugar milling and distilling (Cayaltí, Tumán), rice milling (Chiclayo, Pucalá, and Ferreñafe). Served by rail system radiating from Chiclayo to the ports Pimentel and Puerto Eten and to the inland centers Lambayeque and Ferreñafe.

Lambayeque, city (pop. 6,846), ⊙ Lambayeque prov. (□ 3,615; pop. 90,306), Lambayeque dept., NW Peru, on coastal plain, on Lambayeque R. and 7 mi. NW of Chiclayo, on Pan American Highway and Chiclayo–Ferreñafe RR. Trade center for irrigated rice area; rice milling, cotton ginning, distilling; sugar cane, cotton, corn, cattle.

Lambayeque River, Lambayeque dept., NW Peru, formed by confluence of CHANCAY RIVER and Cumbil R. 9 mi. ENE of Chongoyape, flows 70 mi. W through major sugar-cane region, past Lambayeque, to the Pacific 5 mi. SW of Lambayeque. Feeds numerous irrigation channels in middle and lower course. Called Chongoyape R. in upper course up to area where Taimi Canal and Eten R. branch off.

Lambay Island (lăm′bā) (2 mi. long, 1 mi. wide; rises to 418 ft.), in the Irish Sea, 8 mi. ENE of Swords, NE Co. Dublin, Ireland. Has remains of 16th-cent. fortifications. It is now bird sanctuary and coastguard station.

Lamberhurst, town and parish (pop. 1,521), SW Kent, England, 6 mi. ESE of Tunbridge Wells; agr. market. Has 14th-cent. church and remains of Premonstratensian abbey (1260).

Lambermont (lābĕrmō′), town (pop. 2,676), Liége prov., E Belgium, near Vesdre R., just W of Verviers; wool spinning and weaving.

Lambersart (lābĕrsär′), NW suburb (pop. 17,225) of Lille, Nord dept., N France; mfg. (electrical equipment, tiles, furniture, perfumes), textile dyeing, meat processing.

Lambert. 1 Town (pop. 1,023), Quitman co., NW Miss., 15 mi. E of Clarksdale, in cotton-growing area. **2** Town (pop. 39), Scott co., SE Mo., near Mississippi R., just SE of Benton. **3** Village (pop. c.200), Richland co., NE Mont., on branch of Yellowstone R. and 22 mi. W of Sidney; grain, livestock. **4** Town (pop. 55), Alfalfa co., N Okla., 15 mi. ESE of Alva, in grain-growing area.

Lamberton, agr. village in Mordington parish, E Berwick, Scotland, near English border, 4 mi. NW of Berwick-on-Tweed.

Lamberton, village (pop. 1,208), Redwood co., SW Minn., on Cottonwood R. and c.40 mi. WSW of New Ulm, in grain and livestock area; dairy products.

Lambert's Bay, Afrikaans *Lambertsbaai* (–bī′), village (pop. 1,605), W Cape Prov., U. of So. Afr., on the Atlantic, 130 mi. N of Cape Town; resort, fishing port; crayfish canning. Just offshore is Bird Isl., islet with guano deposits.

Lambertville, city (pop. 4,477), Hunterdon co., W N.J., 14 mi. NW of Trenton and on Delaware R. (bridged here) opposite New Hope, Pa.; mfg. (metal products, silverware, rubber goods, clothing, paper, luggage, sausage); stone quarries; livestock, poultry, truck farming. Founded 1732, inc. 1849.

Lambesc (lābĕsk′), village (pop. 1,418), Bouches-du-Rhône dept., SE France, 13 mi. NW of Aix-en-Provence; canning.

Lambèse (lābĕz′), village (pop. 1,814), Constantine dept., NE Algeria, on N slope of the Aurès massif, 7 mi. SE of Batna. Has penitentiary. Here are extensive ruins (amphitheater, temples, baths) of Roman *Lambaesis* or *Lambessa*, the camp of the third Augustan legion (2d-4th cent. A.D.).

Lambessa, Algeria: see LAMBÈSE.

Lambeth (lăm′bŭth), metropolitan borough (1931 pop. 296,147; 1951 census 230,105) of London,

England, on S bank of the Thames (here crossed by Vauxhall, Lambeth, Westminster, and Waterloo bridges), just SW of Charing Cross. Here are Waterloo Station, important railroad station for Southampton and SW England; Lambeth Palace (dating from 15th cent.), chief residence of Archbishop of Canterbury since 1197 and scene of decennial conferences of bishops of the Church of England; 9th-cent. St. Thomas's Hosp.; St. George's Cathedral (R.C.), built by Pugin; the Oval, important cricket ground. Lambeth was formerly site of Vauxhall Gardens, famous amusement center of the Regency Period, and of Bethlem Royal Hosp. (popularly called Bedlam), 1st English insane asylum, now moved to a locality bet. Croydon and Beckenham. At S end of Westminster Bridge is County Hall, modern administrative bldg. of the London County Council. Lambeth Palace was damaged and its chapel destroyed in air raids 1940–41.

Lambézellec (lãbāzělěk'), N dist. of city of Brest, Finistère dept., W France, until 1945 a separate commune; mfg. (chemicals, soap, oxygen); lumber.

Lambourn, town and parish (pop. 2,316), W Berkshire, England, 6 mi. N of Hungerford; agr. market. Has 12th–15th-cent. church and anc. market cross.

Lambrama (lämbrä'mä), town (pop. 606), Apurímac dept., S central Peru, in Andean spur, 18 mi. SSE of Abancay; sheep, cattle, and horse grazing.

Lambrecht (läm'brěkht), village (pop. 4,216), Rhenish Palatinate, W Germany, in Hardt Mts., on the Speyer and 3 mi. WNW of Neustadt; foundries. Mfg. of machinery, cloth, felt; brewing. Has textile school.

Lambres (lã'brů), industrial suburb (pop. 583) of Aire, Pas-de-Calais dept., N France; mfg. (fertilizer, sugar, bricks). Also called Lambres-lès-Aire.

Lambro River (läm'brô), Lombardy, N Italy, rises bet. 2 arms of L. Como, 5 mi. S of Bellagio; flows 80 mi. SSE, past Monza, Melegnano, and Sant'Angelo Lodigiano, to Po R. 9 mi. NW of Piacenza.

Lamb's Head, promontory on the Atlantic, SW Co. Kerry, Ireland, on N shore of entrance to Kenmare R., 26 mi. WSW of Kenmare; 51°44'N 10°8'W. Offshore are Hog Isls.

Lambsheim (lämps'hīm), village (pop. 5,876), Rhenish Palatinate, W Germany, at NE foot of Hardt Mts., 3 mi. WSW of Frankenthal; wine. Remains from Stone Age excavated near by.

Lambton, W suburb of Newcastle, New South Wales, Australia; coal-mining center.

Lambton (lăm'tůn), county (□ 1,124; pop. 56,925), S Ont., on L. Huron and on St. Clair and Thames rivers, on Mich. border; ⊙ Sarnia.

Lambton, village (pop. 581), S Que., near L. St. Francis, 20 mi. NNW of Megantic; lumbering, dairying. Near by is dam across S end of L. St. Francis.

Lambton, Cape, S extremity of Banks Isl., SW Franklin Dist., Northwest Territories, on Amundsen Gulf; 71°4'N 123°9'W.

Lambton Mills, W suburb of Toronto, S Ont.

Lambunao (lämbōō'nou), town (1939 pop. 1,668; 1948 municipality pop. 26,099), Iloilo prov., central Panay isl., Philippines, 25 mi. NNW of Iloilo; rice-growing center.

Lambusart (lãbüzär'), town (pop. 2,896), Hainaut prov., S central Belgium, 6 mi. NE of Charleroi; coal mining.

Lame Deer, village, Rosebud co., SE Mont., on branch of Yellowstone R. and 45 mi. S of Forsyth, in livestock region. Hq. of Tongue River Indian Reservation.

Lamego (lůmā'gōō), city (pop. 10,698), Viseu dist., Trás-os-Montes e Alto Douro prov., N Portugal, near left bank of the Douro, 45 mi. E of Oporto; commercial center in winegrowing region producing fine port wines; figs, almonds, olives. Its cathedral retains part of original Romanesque tower and has Gothic façade (c.1500). Overlooking city is ruined Moorish castle. Lamego was taken from the Moors by Ferdinand I of Castile in 1057. Scene of Cortes of 1143.

La Mendieta (lä měndyä'tä), town (1947 pop. 2,234), SE Jujuy prov., Argentina, on railroad, on the Río Grande de Jujuy and 22 mi. ESE of Jujuy; sugar-refining center.

Lamentin (lämãtẽ'), town (commune pop. 9,423), NE Basse-Terre, Guadeloupe, 6 mi. WNW of Pointe-à-Pitre, in sugar-growing region; mfg. of alcohol.

Lamentin (lämãtẽ'), town (pop. 3.995), W Martinique, at head of Fort-de-France Bay, 3 mi. E of Fort-de-France; trade center on fertile plain (sugar cane, bananas, cacao); sugar milling, rum distilling; limekiln.

Lamentin, Plain of, W Martinique, along Fort-de-France Bay, only extensive level land on the isl.; sugar-growing area.

La Merced (lä měrsědh'). **1** Village (pop. estimate 500), ⊙ Paclín dept. (□ 255; pop. 4,499), SE Catamarca prov., Argentina, 23 mi. NNE of Catamarca, in cattle and tobacco area. **2** Town (pop. estimate 1,000), central Salta prov., Argentina, on railroad and 13 mi. SSW of Salta; agr. center (peas, corn, tobacco, livestock); lime works.

La Merced, town (pop. 831), Junín dept., central Peru, on Chanchamayo R., on road, and 32 mi. NE of Tarma; coffee, sugar cane, cotton, fruit; lumbering in surrounding forests. Founded 1635 by Sp. missionaries.

Lameroo, village (pop. 427), SE South Australia, 115 mi. ESE of Adelaide; wheat.

La Mesa (lä mā'sä), town (pop. 3,444), Cundinamarca dept., central Colombia, on W slopes of Cordillera Oriental, 27 mi. W of Bogotá; alt. 4,330 ft. Resort and trading center in agr. region (coffee, sugar cane, tobacco, fruit, stock); produces honey. Cattle and horse shows.

La Mesa, village (pop. 596), Veraguas prov., W central Panama, in San Pablo R. valley, 13 mi. WNW of Santiago; coffee; gold and iron mines.

La Mesa (lů mā'sů), city (pop. 10,946), San Diego co., S Calif., just E of San Diego; citrus fruit, avocados, truck, poultry. Inc. 1912.

Lamesa (lůmē'sů), city (pop. 10,704), ⊙ Dawson co., NW Texas, 40 mi. NW of Big Spring, on S Llano Estacado; commercial, shipping, processing center for cattle, oil, agr. region (cotton, grain, soybeans); cottonseed-oil mills, cotton gins and compress; mfg. of dried eggs, feed, mattresses, dairy products. Settled 1903, inc. 1917.

La Mesa (lä mā'sä), town (pop. 667), Trujillo state, W Venezuela, in Andean spur, 20 mi. SSW of Valera; alt. 5,715 ft.; wheat, corn, potatoes.

La Mesa, cinnabar mines in Lara state, NW Venezuela, in Segovia Highlands, 55 mi. WNW of Barquisimeto. Development began 1942.

Lamesley (lāmz'lē), town and parish (pop. 7,343), NE Durham, England, 4 mi. S of Newcastle-upon-Tyne; coal mining.

Lamhult (läm'hůlt"), village (pop. 1,071), Kronoberg co., S Sweden, on small Lam L., Swedish *Lammen,* 20 mi. E of Varnamo; grain, potatoes.

Lamia (lä'mēů, Gr. lůmē'ů), city (1951 pop. 25,843), ⊙ Phthiotis nome, E central Greece, on railroad and 95 mi. NW of Athens, near mouth of Spercheios R.; 38°54'N 22°26'E; road center; cotton milling, tobacco processing; trade in wheat, olive oil, oranges, melons. Bishopric; medieval citadel. Its port on Malian Gulf is STYLIS (linked by railroad). Founded c.5th cent. B.C., it was chief city of anc. Malis and developed as an Athenian ally. It gave its name to the Lamian War (323–22 B.C.), waged by the confederate Greeks against the Macedonian general Antipater, who took refuge in the city and was besieged there for several months. Lamia suffered some damage in the Second World War. It was known as Zituni or Zeitun from Middle Ages to the 19th cent.

Lamia, Gulf of, Greece: see MALIAN GULF.

Lamiaco, Spain: see LEJONA.

Lamine River (lůmīn'), central Mo., rises in several branches in Morgan and Pettis counties, flows c.70 mi. N to the Missouri 6 mi. W of Boonville.

Lamington, Mount, volcano, SE New Guinea, in Owen Stanley Range, 75 mi. NE of Port Moresby; 8°58'S 148°8'E. Erupted violently Jan., 1951, killing many thousands.

La Misión (lä mēsyōn') or **Misión,** town (pop. 460), Hidalgo, central Mexico, 7 mi. NNE of Jacala; grain, beans, stock.

Lamitan (lämē'tän), town (1939 pop. 7,701), on Basilan Isl., Zamboanga prov., Philippines, off SW tip of Mindanao.

Lamlash (lůmlăsh'), village on E coast of ARRAN isl., Buteshire, Scotland, 4 mi. S of Brodick; fishing port and resort. Holy Isl. shelters the bay.

Lamma (lä'mä'), Chinese *Pokliu Chau* (pôk'lyōō' jou'), island of the New Territories of Hong Kong colony, separated from Hong Kong isl. (NE) by 1-mi.-wide East Lamma Channel, and from Lan Tao isl. by 6-mi.-wide West Lamma Channel; 4½ mi. long, 2½ mi. wide; mountainous; barren.

Lamma Bar (lä'mä bär'), village (pop. 400), Harar prov., SE Ethiopia, in the Ogaden, near Ital. Somaliland border, 50 mi. E of Callafo, in camel- and sheep-raising region.

Lamme Fjord, Denmark: see ISE FJORD.

Lammermuir Hills or **Lammermoor Hills** (lămůrmūr', –mōōr', –mōr', lăm'–), range in Scotland, extends 25 mi. ENE along East Lothian–Berwick border to North Sea WNW of St. Abb's Head; c.12 mi. wide. Highest peaks: Meikle Says Law (1,750 ft.), 5 mi. SE of Gifford; and Lammer Law (1,733 ft.), 4 mi. SSE of Gifford.

Lamoille (lůmoil'), county (□ 475; pop. 11,388), N central Vt., with Green Mts. in W; ⊙ Hyde Park. Dairying; mfg. (machinery, wood products, textiles); granite, asbestos; lumber; maple sugar. Includes Mt. Mansfield (winter sports), highest peak of Green Mts. Drained by Lamoille R. Organized 1835.

La Moille (lů moil'). **1** Village (pop. 505), Bureau co., N Ill., on Bureau Creek and 17 mi. NNW of La Salle, in agr. and bituminous-coal area. **2** Village (pop. c.150), Marshall co., central Iowa, 7 mi. W of Marshalltown; feed.

Lamoille River, NW Vt., rises near Hardwick, flows c.70 mi. generally W, through the range, past Morrisville (power dam forms L. Lamoille here), to L. Champlain 10 mi. N of Burlington. Receives North Branch (c.20 mi. long) near Cambridge.

Lamoine (lůmoin'), fishing and resort town (pop. 443), Hancock co., S Maine, on Frenchman Bay just N of Mt. Desert Isl.

La Moine River (lů moin'), W Ill., rises in SW Warren co., flows c.100 mi. SW, S, and SE, to Illinois R. below Beardstown.

Lamoka Lake (lůmō'ků), Schuyler co., W central N.Y., in Finger Lakes region, 10 mi. W of Watkins Glen; 1½ mi. long. Connected by stream to Waneta L. (N).

Lamon Bay (lämōn'), arm of Philippine Sea, in Philippines, bounded W by E coast of Luzon, N by Polillo Isls., and S by Alabat Isl.; merges NW with Polillo Strait; c.50 mi. long, c.25 mi. wide. Its S arms are Lopez and Calauag bays.

Lamone River (lämō'ně), N central Italy, rises in Etruscan Apennines 6 mi. SW of Marradi, flows NNE, past Marradi and Faenza, and E to the Adriatic at Marina di Ravenna; c.60 mi. long. Canalized in lower course; used for irrigation.

Lamongan (lůmông-än'), town (pop. 11,012), NE Java, Indonesia, 24 mi. WNW of Surabaya; trade center for agr. area (tobacco, rice, corn, cassava); textile mills. Oil fields near by. Also Lamangan.

Lamoni (lůmō'nī, –nē), town (pop. 2,196), Decatur co., S Iowa, near Mo. line c.70 mi. SSW of Des Moines; concrete blocks, dairy products. Has Graceland jr. col. Platted 1879, inc. 1885.

Lamont (lůmŏnt'), village (pop. 468), central Alta., 30 mi. ENE of Edmonton; grain elevators, lumbering. Gateway to Elk Island Natl. Park (S).

Lamont. 1 Village (pop. 3,571), Kern co., S central Calif., 9 mi. SE of Bakersfield; agr. (cotton, potatoes). **2** Town (pop. 574), Buchanan co., E Iowa, near Maquoketa R., 35 mi. E of Waterloo. Sand and gravel pits near by. **3** Town (pop. 594), Grant co., N Okla., 26 mi. NE of Enid, in agr. area; grain elevator, poultry hatchery. **4** Town (pop. 101), Whitman co., SE Wash., 40 mi. SW of Spokane, in agr. region.

La Monte (lů mŏnt'), city (pop. 502), Pettis co., central Mo., 11 mi. WNW of Sedalia.

Lamorandière (lämôrãdyâr'), village, W Que., 22 mi. ENE of Amos; gold mining.

Lamoricière (lämôrēsyâr'), village (pop. 1,994), Oran dept., NW Algeria, in Tlemcen Mts., on railroad and 15 mi. E of Tlemcen; agr. market (olive oil, wine, truck, cereals).

Lamothe-Capdeville (lämôt'-käpdůvēl'), village (pop. 169), Tarn-et-Garonne dept., SW France, on the Aveyron and 4 mi. N of Montauban; pottery mfg., winegrowing.

Lamothe-Montravel (–mõrävěl'), village (pop. 511), Dordogne dept., SW France, on the Dordogne and 14 mi. ESE of Libourne in well-known winegrowing area (wines for liqueurs). Montaigne b. in near-by 14th–16th-cent. castle.

Lamotrek (lä'mōtrěk), atoll (pop. 134), Yap dist., W Caroline Isls., W Pacific, c.560 mi. ESE of Yap; 7°28'N 146°23'E; 8 mi. long, 3.5 mi. wide; 3 wooded islets on triangular reef. Formerly Swede Isl.

La Mott, Pa.: see CHELTENHAM.

La Motte or **Lamotte,** town (pop. 280), Jackson co., E Iowa, 15 mi. S of Dubuque, in agr. area.

La Motte, Isle, Vt.: see ISLE LA MOTTE.

Lamotte-Beuvron (lämôt'-bûvrõ'), town (pop. 2,825), Loir-et-Cher dept., N central France, in the Sologne on Beuvron R. and 21 mi. SSE of Orléans; agr. trade center; sawmilling, broommaking, resin processing. Attracts huntsmen.

La Moure (lůmōōr'), county (□ 1,137; pop. 9,498), SE central N.Dak.; ⊙ La Moure. Rich agr. area drained by James R. Grain, livestock, dairy products. Formed 1873.

La Moure, city (pop. 1,010), ⊙ La Moure co., SE central N.Dak., 43 mi. SSE of Jamestown and on James R.; livestock, dairying. Settled 1883, inc. 1906.

Lampa (läm'pä), town (pop. 1,065), Santiago prov., central Chile, 15 mi. NW of Santiago; agr. center (alfalfa, grain, fruit, wine, livestock); stone quarries. Anc. Inca settlement. Formerly a gold-mining town.

Lampa, town (pop. 3,039), ⊙ Lampa prov. (□ 2,853; pop. 32,744), Puno dept., SE Peru, on the Altiplano, 41 mi. NW of Puno; alt. 12,648 ft. Silver and copper mining; barley, potatoes, livestock.

Lampang (läm'päng'), town (1947 pop. 22,405), ⊙ Lampang prov. (□ 4,833; 1947 pop. 332,276), N Thailand, on Wang R., on railroad, and 45 mi. SE of Chiangmai, E of Khun Tan Range, in forested area; highway N to Kengtung (Burma). Teak-extraction center; cotton weaving, tanning; sugar mill at Ko Kha (SW); rice, sugar cane, tobacco, coffee. Copper, lead, and iron deposits near by. Airport. Original city, founded 6th-7th cent., was located 10 mi. SW of present site.

Lampasas (lămpă'sůs), county (□ 726; pop. 9,929), central Texas; ⊙ Lampasas. Bounded W by Colorado R.; drained by Lampasas R. Livestock (cattle, sheep, goats, poultry); wool, mohair shipped; agr. (cotton, grain sorghums, corn, oats, barley, wheat, pecans, fruit). Clay, glass-sand mining; fur trapping. Mineral springs (health resort) at Lampasas. Formed 1856.

Lampasas, city (pop. 4,869), ⊙ Lampasas co., central Texas, on a tributary of Lampasas R. and c.60 mi. NNW of Austin; market for pecans, wool, mohair; also ships livestock, furs, dairy products. Health resort; Hancock Springs are here. Settled 1854, inc. 1874.

Lampasas River, central Texas, rises in Hamilton co., flows c.110 mi. SE and E to join Leon R. c.9 mi. S of Temple, to form Little R.

Lampazos (lämpä'sōs), officially Lampazos de Naranjo, city (pop. 2,820), Nuevo León, N Mexico, on railroad and 70 mi. SW of Nuevo Laredo; agr. center (cotton, wheat, stock); iron ore. Old colonial town; former Sp. mission.

Lampedusa (lämpĕdōō'zä), anc. *Lopadusa*, largest island (□ 8; pop. 3,146) of PELAGIE ISLANDS, in Mediterranean Sea bet. Malta and Tunis, 135 mi. SW of Licata, Sicily; 35°30'N 12°35'E. Is 7 mi. long, 2 mi. wide; rises to 436 ft.; long dry season. Fisheries (sponges, coral, sardines); agr. (grapes, wheat). Long a site of exile colony. Chief port, Lampedusa (pop. 1,977), on SE coast; sardine canneries. Heavily bombed (1943) in Second World War.

Lampertheim (läm'pĕrt-hīm), town (pop. 14,384), Rhenish Hesse, W Germany, after 1945 in Hesse, on an arm of the Rhine and 7 mi. N of Mannheim; rail junction; mfg. of small Diesel motors, electric rectifiers, furniture, cement, cigars; woodworking.

Lampeter (läm'pĭtŭr), municipal borough (1931 pop. 1,742; 1951 census 1,800), S Cardigan, Wales, on Teifi R. and 25 mi. E of Cardigan; agr. market, with woolen mills and tanneries. Site of St. David's Col., founded 1822, affiliated with Oxford and Cambridge. Just SSE, on Teifi R., is village of Cwmann (kōōmän'), with tanneries.

Lamphun (läm'pōōn'), town (1947 pop. 7,896), ⊙ Lamphun prov. (□ 1,740; 1947 pop. 180,781), N Thailand, near Ping R., on railroad and 15 mi. S of Chiangmai, in wide valley, E of Thanon Thong Chai Range; teak and agr. center (rice, lac, tobacco); cotton weaving. Silver deposits (SW). One of oldest cities of N Thailand (founded c.6th cent.), it flourished until rise of Chiangmai in 13th cent. Sometimes spelled Lampoon.

Lampman, village (pop. 253), SE Sask., 20 mi. NE of Estevan; railroad junction; grain elevators.

Lampoeng Bay, Indonesia: see LAMPUNG BAY.

Lampong Bay, Indonesia: see LAMPUNG BAY.

Lampoon, Thailand: see LAMPHUN.

Lamporecchio (lämpôrĕk'kyô), village (pop. 642), Pistoia prov., Tuscany, central Italy, 8 mi. S of Pistoia; macaroni, artificial fruit and flowers.

Lamprechtshausen (läm'prĕkhts-houzŭn),town (pop. 2,900), Salzburg, W Austria, 14 mi. N of Salzburg, near Ger. border; rail terminus; wheat, rye, fruit.

Lamprey River, Rockingham co., SE N.H., rises near Deerfield, flows c.35 mi. SE and E, past Newmarket (water power), to Great Bay.

Lampsacus (lămp'sŭkŭs), anc. Greek city-state of Mysia, NW Asia Minor, on the Hellespont (Dardanelles) opposite Callipolis (modern Gallipoli); on its site is modern village of Lapseki, Turkey, 20 mi. NE of Canakkale. Known as Pityusa before its colonization by Ionian Greeks from Phocaea and Miletus. The Persian king assigned it to Themistocles to provide him with wine. Flourished under Greeks and Romans. Was seat of cult of Priapus.

Lampung Bay or **Lampoeng Bay** (both: lämpōōng'), inlet (25 mi. N–S, 35 mi. E–W) of Sunda Strait, Indonesia, at S end of Sumatra, opposite Java. Telukbetung is at head of bay; Hog Point is at E side of entrance. Also spelled Lampong Bay.

Lamskoye (läm'skŭyŭ), village (1939 pop. over 500), NE Orel oblast, Russian SFSR, 12 mi. SSW of Yefremov; coarse grain.

Lamspringe (läm'shprĭng"ŭ), village (pop. 4,035), in former Prussian prov. of Hanover, NW Germany, after 1945 in Lower Saxony, 8 mi. ESE of Alfeld; mfg. of chemicals; sawmilling, woodworking.

Lamstedt (läm'shtĕt), village (pop. 2,133), in former Prussian prov. of Hanover, NW Germany, after 1945 in Lower Saxony, 15 mi. WNW of Stade; mfg. of chemicals.

Lamtar (lämtär'), village (pop. 1,505), Oran dept., NW Algeria, 12 mi. SW of Sidi-bel-Abbès; cereal- and winegrowing.

Lamu (lä'mōō), town (pop. 5,707), Coast Prov., SE Kenya, in coastal protectorate, on SE shore of Lamu Isl. in Indian Ocean just off coast and 150 mi. NNE of Mombasa; minor shipping center; native shipbuilding, shark-liver processing; sisal (rope and bag making); cotton, copra, sugar cane; fisheries. Once a Persian colony and a possession of sultan of Zanzibar, it rivaled Mombasa as an entrepôt of gold, ivory, spice, and slaves until end of 19th cent. Large Arab pop. The Lamu archipelago includes Lamu, Manda, and Patta isls.

Lamud (lämōōdh'), city (pop. 2,406), ⊙ Luya prov. (in 1940: □ 3,289; pop. 30,943), Amazonas dept., N Peru, in E Andean foothills, 7 mi. NNW of Chachapoyas; agr. (corn, potatoes, alfalfa, sugar, cattle); alcohol distilling.

Lamure-sur-Azergues (lämür'-sür-äzärg'), village (pop. 516), Rhône dept., E central France, in the Monts du Beaujolais, 12 mi. NW of Villefranche; cotton weaving, woodworking.

Lamuria (lämōōrē'ä), village, Rift Valley prov., W Kenya, on road and 55 mi. ENE of Nakuru; coffee, tea, wheat, corn.

Lamy (lämē'), village (pop. 873), Constantine dept., NE Algeria, in the Medjerda Mts., 17 mi. NNE of Souk-Ahras; cork stripping.

Lamy (lā'mē), village (pop. c.200), Santa Fe co., N central N.Mex., in foothills of Sangre de Cristo Mts., 16 mi. S of Santa Fe; alt. c.6,460 ft.; livestock. Rail station for Santa Fe. Santa Fe Natl. Forest near by.

Lan, China: see LWAN RIVER.

Lana (lä'nä), town (pop. 5,393), Bolzano prov., Trentino–Alto Adige, N Italy, 3 mi. S of Merano, near Adige R.; lumber and paper mills, fruit cannery, chemical works.

Lanaeken, Belgium: see LANAKEN.

Lanagan (lă'nĭgŭn), town (pop. 368), McDonald co., extreme SW Mo., on branch of Elk R., 19 mi. S of Neosho; sulphur water.

Lanagh Lough, Ireland: see CASTLEBAR.

Lanai (lünī'), island (□ 141; pop. 3,131), T.H., c.7 mi. W of Maui, across Auau Channel; 18 mi. long, 10 mi. wide; Mt. Palawai (3,370 ft.) is highest point. Used for cattle grazing until 1922, when isl. was bought by pineapple company and was transformed into modern plantation. Port developed at Kaumalapau Harbor and modern Lanai City built.

Lanai City, town (pop. 2,746), central Lanai, T.H.; founded 1922 by a pineapple company.

Lanaja (länä'hä), town (pop. 2,158), Huesca prov., NE Spain, 25 mi. SSE of Huesca; sawmilling; agr. trade (wine, cereals, livestock, honey).

Lanaken (lä'näkŭn), town (pop. 6,368), Limburg prov., NE Belgium, near Meuse R. and the Zuid-Willemsvaart, 3 mi. NNW of Maastricht, frontier station near Netherlands border; market center. Formerly spelled Lanaeken.

Lanalhue, Lake (länäl'wā) (□ 25), Arauco prov., S central Chile, at W foot of Cordillera de Nahuelbuta, 25 mi. SE of Lebu; c.10 mi. long; resorts.

Lanao (länä'ō, länou'), province (□ 2,575; 1948 pop. 343,918), W central Mindanao, Philippines, on Iligan Bay; ⊙ Dansalan. Rice and corn area. Moro country. In it are L. Lanao and the active volcano Mt. Ragang.

Lanao, Lake (□ 131), W central Mindanao, Philippines, S of Iligan Bay; 20 mi. long, 10 mi. wide. Dansalan near N shore.

Lanark (lă'nŭrk), county (□ 1,138; pop. 33,143), SE Ont., on Ottawa R. and on Rideau L.; ⊙ Perth.

Lanark, village (pop. 663), SE Ont., on Clyde R. and 10 mi. NW of Perth; knitting and lumber mills; dairying.

Lanark or **Lanarkshire** (lă'nŭrk, –ärk, –shĭr), county (□ 853.1; 1931 pop. 1,586,047; 1951 census 1,614,125), S Scotland; ⊙ Lanark. Bounded by Ayrshire and Renfrew (W), Dumbarton and Stirling (N), West Lothian (NE), Midlothian and Peebles (E), and Dumfries (S). Drained by the Clyde and its tributaries. N part of co. is flat and fertile; central section is undulating, rising to 2,335 ft. in Tinto Hills, with pastures, woodlands, and famous Clydesdale orchards; S part is mountainous and barren, rising to the Lowther Hills. Coal is extensively mined; lead (in Lowther Hills), iron, shale, and clay are also worked. Raising of cattle, sheep, and Clydesdale workhorses; there is large dairying industry. Industry is centered on Glasgow; there are shipyards, steel mills, machinery, textile, and brickworks. GLASGOW, largest city in Scotland and 3d-largest in Great Britain, is center of population and chief port. Other towns are Hamilton, Rutherglen, Motherwell and Wishaw, Coatbridge, Airdrie, Biggar, and Carstairs. There are numerous old castles and sites of battles of Langside, Bothwell Bridge, and Drumclog.

Lanark, burgh (1931 pop. 6,178; 1951 census 6,219), ⊙ Lanarkshire, Scotland, in center of co., on the Clyde and 23 mi. SE of Glasgow; agr. market, with woolen mills. Has 12th-cent. church of St. Kentigern. William Wallace lived here for some time and, in 1297, overpowered English garrison of Lanark. Just E, on Lanark Moor, is racecourse. Falls of Clyde, a series of 4 waterfalls, are 2 mi. S of Lanark. Just S is cotton-milling town of New Lanark, founded 1785 by David Dale and Richard Arkwright, scene of industrial and social experiments of Robert Owen.

Lanark (lă'närk, lŭnärk'), city (pop. 1,359), Carroll co., NW Ill., near Rock Creek, 16 mi. SW of Freeport; trade and shipping center in rich agr. area (grain, livestock, poultry); mfg. of dairy and canned foods, feed milling. Inc. 1867.

Lanarkshire, Scotland: see LANARK, county.

Lancashire (lăng'kŭshĭr, –shŭr) or **Lancaster** (lăng'kŭstŭr), county (□ 1,877.9; 1931 pop. 5,039,455; 1951 census 5,116,013), W England; ⊙ Lancaster. Bounded by Irish Sea and Morecambe Bay (W), Cumberland and Westmorland (N), Yorkshire (E), and Cheshire (S). Drained by Mersey, Ribble, Lune, Wyre, and Irlam rivers. Has low coastline, the E and N are hilly, and the S is low moorland. Fertile agr. land in W. Lancashire is a great mfg. area and the most populous co. in England. Humid climate, good water transportation, and coal deposits have favored development of the major industry, cotton spinning and weaving, concentrated in SE part of co. and centered on Manchester. There are also deposits of iron, lead, copper, clay, and limestone. Other major industries are shipbuilding (Liverpool, Barrow-in-Furness); mfg. of chemicals, paper, glass, rayon, rubber goods; engineering, leather tanning, iron mining (Furness peninsula). Chief cities are Lancaster, Manchester, Liverpool, Blackburn, Blackpool (resort), Barrow-in-Furness, Bolton, Bootle, Burnley, Bury, Oldham, Preston, Rochdale, St. Helens, Salford, Southport (resort), Warrington, Wigan. The co. also constitutes a duchy, vested in the sovereign; its chancellorship is frequently a nondepartmental cabinet post.

Lancaster (lăng'kŭstŭr), village (pop. 684), SE Ont., on the St. Lawrence and 15 mi. NE of Cornwall; dairying, mixed farming.

Lancaster, county, England: see LANCASHIRE.

Lancaster, municipal borough (1931 pop. 43,383; 1951 census 51,650), ⊙ Lancashire, England, in N part of county, on Lune R. and 20 mi. N of Preston; textile industry (rayon spinning and weaving, carpet weaving); mfg. of agr. machinery, linoleum, soap; engineering, milling. Has 13th-cent. castle on site of Roman camp; remains of Roman basilica and of Viking crosses found. The castle has Norman tower built 1170. St Mary's church dates mostly from 15th cent. and has 18th-cent. tower. In Lancaster are Royal Albert asylum, Ripley orphanage, and large memorial to Victorian era with bas-relief figures of its outstanding personalities.

Lancaster, village, Bulawayo prov., S central Southern Rhodesia, in Matabeleland, 22 mi. N of Filabusi; tobacco, corn; cattle, sheep, goats.

Lancaster. **1** (lăng'kă"stŭr, lăng'kĭstŭr) County (□ 845; pop. 119,742), SE Nebr.; ⊙ Lincoln, the state capital. Commercial and agr. region drained by small tributaries of Missouri R. Industry and mfg. at Lincoln; feed; livestock, field crops. Formed 1859. **2** (lăng'kĭstŭr) County (□ 945; pop. 234,717), SE Pa.; ⊙ Lancaster. One of richest agr. counties in U.S.; bounded W by Susquehanna R. First settled 1709 by Swiss and French, later by Germans, Welsh, English, and Scotch-Irish. Conestoga wagon and Kentucky rifle were early products. Agr. (tobacco, cattle, small grains); mfg. (linoleum, textiles, lumber, leather); limestone, slate. Formed 1729. **3** (lăng'kĭstŭr) County (□ 504; pop. 37,071), N S.C.; ⊙ Lancaster. Bounded W by Catawba R., N by N.C. Agr. area (cotton, corn, wheat, oats, hay, tobacco), timber mfg. at Lancaster. Formed 1785. **4** (lăng'kĭstŭr) County (□ 142; pop. 8,640), E Va.; ⊙ Lancaster. On S shore of Northern Neck peninsula; bounded W and S by the Rappahannock, which enters Chesapeake Bay (E) at S tip of co.; shores indented by many inlets. Fish, oysters, crabs caught and canned; agr. (especially tomatoes and other canning crops; tobacco, poultry, livestock); lumbering (pine). Summer resorts. Formed 1652.

Lancaster. **1** (lăn'kă"stŭr, lăng'–) Unincorporated town (pop. 3,594), Los Angeles co., S Calif., in Antelope Valley (W Mojave Desert), c.45 mi. N of Los Angeles; chief trade center for irrigated agr. area (alfalfa, sugar beets, grain). Seat of Antelope Valley Jr. Col. **2** (lăng'kă"stŭr, lăng'kĭstŭr) City (pop. 200), Atchison co., NE Kansas, 10 mi. W of Atchison, near corn belt. **3** (lăn'kĭstŭr) City (pop. 2,402), ⊙ Garrard co., central Ky., near Herrington L. (Dix R.), 31 mi. S of Lexington, in Bluegrass agr. region (burley tobacco, corn, wheat, hay); mfg. of work clothing; flour and feed mills. Cottage industry (hooked rugs) in vicinity. Near by is site of Kennedy House, where Harriet Beecher Stowe is said to have visited while gathering material for *Uncle Tom's Cabin*, and of Gilbert's Creek Meeting House, 1st Baptist church in Ky., erected 1781 by Traveling Baptist Church. Settled 1798. **4** (lăng'kă"stŭr, lăng'kĭstŭr) Town (pop. 3,601), Worcester co., N central Mass., on Nashua R. and 15 mi. NNE of Worcester, N of Wachusett Reservoir. Luther Burbank b. here. Has fine Bulfinch church (1817). Settled 1643, inc. 1653. Includes South Lancaster village (pop. 1,462). **5** (lăn'kă"-stŭr) Village (pop. 536), Kittson co., NW Minn., near Man. line, on fork of Two Rivers, and 8 mi. NE of Hallock; dairy products. **6** (lăng'kĭstŭr) City (pop. 856), ⊙ Schuyler co., N Mo., near Chariton R., 23 mi. N of Kirksville; grain, poultry. Inc. 1856. **7** (lăng'kă"stŭr, lăng'kĭstŭr) Town (pop. 3,113), including Lancaster village (pop. 2,296), ⊙ Coos co., NW N.H., on Connecticut R., at mouth of Israel R., 30 mi. NNE of Woodsville. Agr. trade center near White Mts. resorts; mfg. (wood products, machinery, drugs), timber, dairy products. Inc. 1764. **8** (lăn'kă"stŭr) Village (pop. 8,665), Erie co., W N.Y., 8 mi. E of Buffalo; mfg. (steel, wood and glass products, aircraft parts, machinery); stone quarries; dairying. Settled 1810, inc. 1849. **9** (lăn'kă"stŭr, lăng'–) City (pop. 24,180), ⊙ Fairfield co., central Ohio, 26 mi. SE of Columbus and on Hocking R.; trade center for agr. area. Mfg.: flint glass, farm machinery, electrical products, foundry products, carbon, chemicals. State Industrial School for boys is near by. William Tecumseh Sherman and Thomas Ewing were b. here. Founded 1800. **10** (lăng'kĭstŭr) City (pop. 63,774), ⊙ Lancaster co., SE Pa., 70 mi. W of Philadelphia. Commercial center for one of richest agr. counties in nation, with one of largest stockyards in East. Tobacco products, linoleum, watches, umbrellas, candy, metal products, textiles, clothing, leather products, machine tools, radio parts.

Franklin and Marshall Col. here. Munitions center in 18th cent., famous for Kentucky rifle. Continental Congress met here briefly 1777; state ⊙ 1799–1812. Home of Robert Fulton and Thaddeus Stevens; "Wheatland," near-by home of James Buchanan, dedicated 1937 as historic memorial. Settled c.1721, laid out 1730, inc. as borough 1742, as city 1818. **11** (lăng'kĭstûr) Town (pop. 7,159), ⊙ Lancaster co., N S.C., 23 mi. SE of Rock Hill, near the Wateree; large textile mill and finishing plant; lumber, fertilizer, cottonseed-oil, and grist mills. Courthouse and jail date from 1823. Bordered by several mill villages. **12** (lăng'kă"stûr) City (pop. 2,632), Dallas co., N Texas, 13 mi. S of Dallas, in cotton, truck area. Mfg. of garments, insulation. Settled 1846, inc. 1886. **13** (lăng'kĭstûr) Village (pop. c.150), ⊙ Lancaster co., E Va., 55 mi. N of Newport News; cans seafood, vegetables. **14** (lăn'kă"stûr) City (pop. 3,266), ⊙ Grant co., extreme SW Wis., 23 mi. N of Dubuque (Iowa), in livestock and dairy area; dairy products, canned foods, beverages, veterinary remedies, feed, timber; ships livestock. Settled before 1840, inc. 1878.

Lancaster Bay, England: see Morecambe Bay.

Lancaster Mills (lăng'kĭstûr), village (pop. 4,313, with adjacent Springdale), Lancaster co., N S.C., just W of Lancaster; textile milling.

Lancaster Sound, E Franklin Dist., Northwest Territories, arm (c.200 mi. long, 40 mi. wide) of Baffin Bay, extending W, bet. Devon Isl. and Baffin and Somerset isls.; 74°N 85°W. Leads via Barrow Strait to Beaufort Sea of the Arctic Ocean. Discovered (1616) by William Baffin.

Lance Amour, Labrador: see Anse Amour, L'.

Lance au Loup, Labrador: see Anse au Loup, L'.

Lance Creek, village (1940 pop. 676), Niobrara co., E Wyo., 21 mi. NNW of Lusk, in highly productive oil field.

Lancerota, Canary Isls.: see Lanzarote.

Lancheng, China: see Lwancheng.

Lanchi, Lanki, or **Lan-ch'i** (all: län'chē'), town (pop. 27,988), ⊙ Lanchi co. (pop. 295,552), W central Chekiang prov., China, on rail spur and 12 mi. NW of Kinhwa, and on Tsientang R. (formed here by its 2 main headstreams); communications center; ham, vegetable oil, berries, tea, rice.

Lanchin (län'chĭn), Pol. *Łanczyn* (wōōän'chĭn), town (1939 pop. over 500), S central Stanislav oblast, Ukrainian SSR, on Prut R. and 14 mi. W of Kolomyya; health resort with mineral springs; saltworks; lumbering.

Lanchkhuti (lŭnchkhōō'tyē), town (1926 pop. 3,709), W Georgian SSR, in Colchis lowland, on railroad and 15 mi. WSW of Samtredia; tea, tung oil; sawmilling. Until 1936, spelled Lanchkhuty.

Lanchow or **Lan-chou** (both: län'jō'), city (1947 pop. 156,468), ⊙ Kansu prov., China, c.700 mi. WSW of Peking and on right bank of Yellow R.; 36°3'N 103°41'E. One of leading economic cities of NW China, at W terminus of Lunghai RR; here begins the Silk Road to Sinkiang. Trade and cultural center; cotton and wool weaving, alcohol distilling, metalworking (foundry), soap and match mfg., tobacco processing. City has univ., veterinary and teachers col., and libraries. Historically the chief crossing of the upper Yellow R. (bridged here, 1910) on the trade route to the West and to Tibet, Lanchow developed as a major communications center. As seat of the Kaolan co. govt., it was sometimes called Kaolan until 1946, when it became an independent municipality.

Lanciano (länchä'nô), anc. *Anxanum*, town (pop. 10,654), Chieti prov., Abruzzi e Molise, S central Italy, 6 mi. from the Adriatic, 15 mi. SE of Chieti, on 3 hills, 2 of them connected by a Roman bridge. Mfg. (linen, cotton, and woolen textiles, agr. machinery, furniture, shoes, pottery, chemicals, macaroni). Archbishopric. Has Roman ruins (aqueduct, theater), cathedral (rebuilt 18th cent.), and 12th-cent. church. Badly damaged by heavy fighting (1943–44) in Second World War.

Lancié, (lāsyā'), village (pop. 365), Rhône dept., E central France, 12 mi. N of Villefranche; aluminum reducing.

Lancing, England: see South Lancing.

Lanco (läng'kō), town (pop. 2,793), Valdivia prov., S central Chile, on railroad and 37 mi. NE of Valdivia; agr. center (wheat, barley, peas, potatoes, livestock); lumbering, dairying, flour milling.

Lancones (läng-kō'nās), village (pop. 516), Piura dept., NW Peru, on Chira R. and 25 mi. NE of Sullana; sugar cane; vineyards.

Lancut (wä'nyŭtsōōt), Pol. *Łańcut*, town (pop. 9,106), Rzeszow prov., SE Poland, on railroad and 10 mi. E of Rzeszow, near Wislok R.; distilling, brewing, tanning, flour milling, ether mfg. Castle.

Lancy (lāsē'), town (pop. 5,042), Geneva canton, SW Switzerland, SW of and adjacent to Geneva.

Lanczyn, Ukrainian SSR: see Lanchin.

Landa, village (pop. 132), Bottineau co., N N.Dak., 21 mi. W of Bottineau.

Landaburu, Spain: see Baracaldo.

Landaff, town (pop. 342), Grafton co., NW N.H., on Ammonoosuc R. and 30 mi. NW of Plymouth, in mtn. recreational area.

Landak Tso, Tibet: see Rakas Lake.

Lândana (län'dŭnŭ), town (pop. 819), Cabinda dist. (exclave of Angola), on the Atlantic, 24 mi. N of Cabinda. Ships palm oil and kernels, cacao; sawmilling.

Landau (län'dou). **1** or **Landau an der Isar** (än dĕr ē'zär), town (1946 pop. 6,035), Lower Bavaria, Germany, on the Isar and 16 mi. SSE of Straubing; textile mfg.; brick- and tileworks; brewing, printing, woodworking. Has rococo church. Chartered c.1224. **2** Town (1946 pop. 1,097), in former Prussian prov. of Hesse-Nassau, W Germany, after 1945 in Hesse, 17 mi. W of Kassel. Until 1929 in former Waldeck principality. **3** Town (1950 pop. 22,870), Rhenish Palatinate, W Germany, on the Queich and 19 mi. NW of Karlsruhe; 49°12'N 8°7'E. Rail junction; iron foundry; tobacco industry. Mfg. of machinery, furniture; food processing (cheese, spirits). Wine trade. Second World War damage (c.30%) included 15th-cent. church. Chartered 1274. Under Fr. occupation, 1680–1815. Captured by U.S. troops in March, 1945.

Landeck (län'dĕk), town (pop. 5,534), Tyrol, W Austria, on the Inn and 40 mi. WSW of Innsbruck, at N end of Rhaetian Alps; cotton mills, carbide mfg.; health resort. Old Landeck castle on near-by height.

Landeck. 1 Town, Pomerania: see Ledyczek, Koszalin prov., Poland. **2** or **Bad Landeck**, town, Lower Silesia: see Ladek Zdroj, Wroclaw prov., Poland.

Landegem (län'dŭ-khĕm), agr. village (pop. 1,953), East Flanders prov., NW Belgium, 6 mi. W of Ghent.

Landen (län'dŭn), town (pop. 3,997), Liége prov., E central Belgium, 23 mi. WNW of Liége; rail junction; sugar-refining center.

Lander, county (□ 5,621; pop. 1,850), N central Nev.; ⊙ Austin. Reese R. flows N bet. Toiyabe Range and Shoshone Mts.; Humboldt R. flows across N part of co. Gold, silver, lead, copper; ranches. Formed 1863.

Lander, town (pop. 3,349), ⊙ Fremont co., W central Wyo., on Popo Agie R., just E of Wind River Range, and 120 mi. W of Casper; alt. c.5,360 ft. Resort and trade center for Popo Agie valley; hq. for Washakie Natl. Forest; livestock, dairy products, timber, fruit. Oil wells, gold and coal mines in vicinity. Agr. experiment station of state univ., Wind R. Indian Reservation near by. Settled in 1870s around military post, inc. 1890.

Landerneau (lādĕrnō'), town (pop. 9,175), Finistère dept., W France, on Elorn R. and 12 mi. ENE of Brest; road center and livestock market; mfg. (chemicals, fertilizer, bricks and tiles, umbrellas), brewing, wood- and leatherworking.

Landero y Cos (ländā'rō ē kōs'), town (pop. 750), Veracruz, E Mexico, 15 mi. NE of Jalapa; fruit, corn.

Landes (lād), department (□ 3,615; pop. 248,395), in Gascony, SW France, occupying 75% of the Landes region; ⊙ Mont-de-Marsan. Bounded by Bay of Biscay (W) and foothills of W Pyrenees (S). Drained by the Adour and its tributaries (Midouze, Luy, Gave de Pau). Only the Chalosse (S of Adour R.) has intensive agr. (corn, tobacco, poultry and hogs). Some lignite is mined. Chief industries are lumber milling and the preparation of resinous products and cork. Main towns are Mont-de-Marsan and Dax (commercial center and noted spa). Capbreton, Vieux-Boucau-les-Bains, and Mimizan-les-Bains are small seaside resorts.

Landes, sparsely populated region (□ c.4,600) in Gironde, Landes, and Lot-et-Garonne depts., SW France, extends c.150 mi. N–S along the Bay of Biscay from the Pointe de Grave (N) to Adour R. (S), and reaches inland up to 70 mi. (apex at Nérac). Originally a sandy and marshy waste, it has been reclaimed through extensive planting of pine and oak forests. The straight coastline, indented only by the Arcachon Basin, is paralleled by a belt of sand dunes (up to 10 mi. wide, 200 ft. high), which separate a series of marshy lagoons and tidal lakes from the sea. The dunes have been fixed by pine forests. Lumbering and processing of resins and cork are chief occupations. Agr. is still of minor importance. Main inland towns are Mont-de-Marsan and Dax. Arcachon is the leading bathing resort.

Landes de Lanvaux (lād dŭ lāvō'), wooded ridge in Morbihan dept., W France, 30 mi. long, 3 mi. wide, extending WNW–ESE across dept. c.15 mi. from Atlantic Ocean. Rises to 525 ft.; grazing, hunting.

Landes du Méné (dü mānā'), chain of hills, part of Armorican Massif, in Côtes-du-Nord dept., W France, c.15 mi. SSE of Saint-Brieuc, extending NW–SE. Provide panoramic view of Channel coast. Rise to 1,115 ft. Sometimes spelled Ménez.

Landeshut, Poland: see Kamienna Gora.

Landete (ländā'tā), town (pop. 1,778), Cuenca prov., E central Spain, 40 mi. ESE of Cuenca; grain, sheep; apiculture; flour milling, mfg. of plaster and tiles.

Landgrove, town (pop. 80), Bennington co., S central Vt., in Green Mts., 19 mi. W of Springfield.

Landhi (län'dē), village, Karachi administration area, W Pakistan, 13 mi. E of Karachi; saltworks; pharmaceutical works; radio transmitting station.

Landi Khana (lŭn'dē khän'ŭ), fort and village in Khyber Pass, W North-West Frontier Prov., W Pakistan, 27 mi. WNW of Peshawar, on Afghan border opposite Torkham; rail terminus.

Landi Kotal (kō'tŭl), fort and village in Khyber Pass, W North-West Frontier Prov., W Pakistan, 25 mi. WNW of Peshawar, near Afghan border.

Landi Muhammad Amin Khan (lŭn'dē mōōhŭm-mŭd' ŭmēn' khän'), town and oasis, Kandahar prov., S Afghanistan, on Helmand R. and 100 mi. SSW of Girishk; irrigated agr. Hq. of Garmsel or Garmser dist., for which it is sometimes named.

Landing, resort village, Morris co., N N.J., at S end of L. Hopatcong, 6 mi. W of Dover; boating. State park near by.

Landingville, borough (pop. 230), Schuylkill co., E central Pa., 7 mi. SE of Pottsville and on Schuylkill R.

Landis (lăn'dĭs), town (pop. 1,827), Rowan co., central N.C., 11 mi. SW of Salisbury; cotton yarn.

Landisburg, borough (pop. 279), Perry co., S central Pa., 24 mi. WNW of Harrisburg.

Landisville, village (pop. c.750), Atlantic co., S N.J., 6 mi. NE of Vineland; macaroni, clothing; poultry, truck.

Landivisiau (lādēvēzyō'), town (pop. 3,417), Finistère dept., W France, 21 mi. ENE of Brest; horse-breeding center; mfg. (glue, carved furniture), tanning, beekeeping.

Landivy (lādēvē'), village (pop. 447), Mayenne dept., W France, 12 mi. NE of Fougères; wooden shoes; apple orchards.

Landkirchen (länt'kĭr"khŭn), village (pop. 3,228), in Schleswig-Holstein, NW Germany, on Fehmarn isl., 2 mi. WNW of Burg; grain, potatoes, cabbage, beets.

Landl (län'dŭl), village (pop. 1,763), Styria, central Austria, near Enns R., 25 mi. NW of Leoben; dairy farming.

Land O'Lakes, village (pop. c.200), Vilas co., N Wis., on Wis.-Mich. line, 37 mi. NNE of Rhinelander; resort center in wooded lake region.

Landon, village (pop. 1,853, with adjacent West Gulfport), Harrison co., SE Miss., 9 mi. N of Gulfport.

Landour (lŭn'dour), town (pop. 1,206), Dehra Dun dist., N Uttar Pradesh, India, in W Kumaun Himalaya foothills, 10 mi. NNE of Dehra; residential suburb of Mussoorie.

Landover Hills, town (pop. 1,661), Prince Georges co., central Md., an E suburb of Washington. Inc. after 1940.

Landport, England: see Portsmouth.

Landquart or **Landquart Dorf** (länt'kvärt dôrf'), hamlet of Igis commune, Grisons canton, E Switzerland, on the Rhine above Bad Ragaz, at mouth of the Landquart; paper milling, metalworking.

Landquart River, E Switzerland, rises in Silvretta Group, flows WNW through the Prätigau to the Rhine at Landquart.

Landrail Point, village, S Bahamas, on NW Crooked Isl., 8 mi. NW of Colonel Hill; 22°50'N 74°20'W.

Landrecies (lādrŭsē'), town (pop. 2,281), Nord dept., N France, port on the Sambre, at N terminus of Oise-Sambre Canal, and 11 mi. W of Avesnes; industrial center (decorative tiles, parchment paper, glass) in dairying area.

Landres (lā'drŭ), village (pop. 471), Meurthe-et-Moselle dept., NE France, 8 mi. NW of Briey; iron mining.

Landriano (ländrēä'nô), village (pop. 2,065), Pavia prov., Lombardy, N Italy, 10 mi. NNE of Pavia.

Landrienne (lādrēĕn'), village (pop. estimate 500), W Que., 8 mi. E of Amos; gold mining.

Landrum, town (pop. 1,333), Spartanburg co., NW S.C., 22 mi. NW of Spartanburg, at N.C. line; lumber, hosiery, textiles.

Landsberg (länts'bĕrk). **1** City (1950 pop. 11,718), Upper Bavaria, Germany, at S tip of the Lechfeld, on the Lech and 22 mi. S of Augsburg; textile mfg., metalworking, printing, lumber and paper milling, brewing. Has medieval gate, the Bayertor (1425); late-Gothic church; late-17th-cent. city hall. Chartered 1315. While imprisoned in fortress here, Hitler wrote *Mein Kampf*. Sometimes called Landsberg am Lech. **2** Town (1946 pop. 3,089), in former Prussian Saxony prov., central Germany, after 1945 in Saxony-Anhalt, 9 mi. ENE of Halle; sugar refining, malting; porphyry quarrying. Towered over by remains of 12th-cent. castle. In 12th cent., chief town of a margraviate; passed to Meissen in early 13th cent., to Prussia in 1815.

Landsberg. 1 or **Landsberg an der Warthe** (än dĕr vär'tŭ) or **Gorzow Wielkopolski** (gô'zhōōf vyĕlkô-pôl'skē), Pol. *Gorzów Wielkopolski*, town (1939 pop. 48,053; 1946 pop. 19,796) in Brandenburg, after 1945 in Zielona Gora prov., W Poland, on Warta (Warthe) R. and 60 mi. SE of Stettin, in lignite-mining region. Rail junction; textile milling, metal- and woodworking, mfg. of soap, chocolate, bricks. Seat of R.C. bishop. Chartered 1257 by Ascanian margraves of Brandenburg; became trade center. In Thirty Years War, fell 4 times to Swedes and was destroyed. Town rose again in 18th cent. Besieged 1813 by Russians. In Second World War, c.50% destroyed. Pop. now entirely Polish. **2** Town, East Prussia: see Gorowo Ilaweckie, Olsztyn prov., Poland. **3** or **Landsberg in Oberschlesien**, town, Silesia: see Gorzow, Opole prov., Poland.

Landsbro (länts'brōō"), village (pop. 1,218), Jonkoping co., S Sweden, 7 mi. WSW of Vetlanda; woodworking.

Land's End or **Lands End**, anc. *Bolerium* or *Bellerium*, promontory, W Cornwall; extreme SW point of England, 9 mi. WSW of Penzance; 50°4'N 5°43'W. Formed of granite cliffs 60–100 ft. high. In the Atlantic, 1 mi. W, is rocky islet of Carn Bras, with Longships lighthouse.

Land's End, Calif.: see SAN FRANCISCO.

Landser (läsâr', Ger. länt'sûr), village (pop. 302), Haut-Rhin dept., E France, 5 mi. SSE of Mulhouse.

Landshut, Czechoslovakia: see LANZHOT.

Landshut (länts'hōōt), city (1950 pop. 47,179), ⊙ Lower Bavaria, Germany, on the Isar and 38 mi. NE of Munich; 48°32'N 12°9'E. Rail transshipment point; industrial center; food-processing (canned food, flour, beer), metal products (foundries; machinery, radios, condensers), chemicals (pharmaceuticals, dyes, lacquer). Other products: furniture, glass, ceramics, snuff. Lumber milling. Hops trade. Late-12th-cent. castle Trausnitz, until 1503 the residence of dukes of Bavaria-Landshut, has 13th-cent. chapel. Among many noteworthy churches are late-Gothic St. Martin; and rococo church of Cistercian nunnery Seligenthal (founded 1232) containing 13th–16th-cent. tombs of Wittelsbach family. Founded 1204, Landshut was chartered 1279. Ducal residence (1255–1340; 1392–1503). Suffered heavily in Thirty Years War. From 1800 to 1826 was site of Bavarian univ. (founded 1472 at Ingolstadt; since 1826 situated at Munich). Scene of Napoleon's victory over Archduke Charles (1809). Captured by U.S. troops in spring, 1945. Second World War destruction (about 15%) included ducal town residence (1536–43).

Landskron (länts'krōn), town (pop. 7,524), Carinthia, S Austria, 3 mi. NNE of Villach; summer resort. Fortress ruins near by.

Landskron, Czechoslovakia: see LANSKROUN.

Landskrona (läntskrōō'nä), city (1950 pop. 25,089), Malmohus co., S Sweden, on the Oresund, 19 mi. NNW of Malmo; 55°52'N 12°51'E. Port, with shipyards, sugar refineries, flour mills; mfg. of machinery, arms, metalware, fertilizer. Has 15th-cent. citadel and baroque church. Chartered 1413, city, then herring-fishing center, was burned 1428 by Hanseatic League; fortified in mid-15th cent. Sacked in wars in 16th and 17th cent. Offshore, Swedes won (1677) naval victory over Danes. Near by, in the Oresund, is Ven Isl.

Lands Lokk, island (20 mi. long, 8 mi. wide), NE Franklin Dist., Northwest Territories, in the Arctic Ocean, at N end of Nansen Sound, off NW Ellesmere Isl.; 81°45'N 91°45'W.

Landstrasse (länt'shträsû), district (□ 3; pop. 114,950) of Vienna, Austria, just SE of city center.

Landstuhl (länt'shtōōl), town (pop. 6,281), Rhenish Palatinate, W Germany, 9 mi. W of Kaiserslautern; rail junction; brewing, malting, tanning. Has ruined ancestral castle of Franz von Sickingen, who was killed here during a siege in 1523.

Landsweiler-Reden (länts'vī"lûr-rā'dûn), town (pop. 6,121), central Saar, 12 mi. NNW of Saarbrücken; coal mining; coke ovens; mfg. of chemicals, wood and tobacco products. Called Landsweiler until 1937.

Landusky (lăndŭ'skē), village (pop. c.150), Phillips co., N central Mont., in Lewis and Clark Natl. Forest, 50 mi. SW of Malta. Gold mines near by.

Landwarow, Lithuania: see LENTVARIS.

Lane. 1 County (□ 720; pop. 2,808), W central Kansas; ⊙ Dighton. Rolling plain, with low hills in E and NE. Grain, livestock. Formed 1886. **2** County (□ 4,594; pop. 125,776), W Oregon, on Pacific coast; ⊙ Eugene. Mtn. area in Coast and Cascade ranges; crossed by Willamette and Siuslaw rivers. Agr. (fruit, truck, grain, poultry), dairying, lumber milling, quicksilver mining. Natl. forests in W and E. Formed 1851.

Lane. 1 City (pop. 200), Franklin co., E Kansas, on Pottawatomie Creek and 16 mi. SE of Ottawa; livestock, grain. **2** Town (pop. 580), Williamsburg co., E central S.C., 10 mi. S of Kingstree; lumber. **3** Town (pop. 145), Jerauld co., SE central S.Dak., 8 mi. E of Wessington Springs; large school is here.

Lane Cove, municipality (pop. 19,817), E New South Wales, Australia, 4 mi. NW of Sydney across Port Jackson, in metropolitan area; mfg. (chemicals, fountain pens); tanneries.

Lane Island, Knox co., S Maine, in Carvers Harbor; bridged to Vinalhaven isl.; ½ mi. long.

Lanesboro. 1 Town (pop. 280), Carroll co., W central Iowa, near Raccoon R., 12 mi. NE of Carroll. **2** or **Lanesborough**, agr. town (pop. 2,069), Berkshire co., NW Mass., 5 mi. N of Pittsfield, near Pontoosuc L.; resort. Settled c.1753, inc. 1765. Includes state forest and villages of Berkshire and Balance Rock. **3** Resort village (pop. 1,100), Fillmore co., SE Minn., on branch of Root R. and 32 mi. SE of Rochester; grain, potato, dairy area. **4** Borough (pop. 591), Susquehanna co., NE Pa., on Susquehanna R. just above Susquehanna Depot.

Lanesville. 1 Town (pop. 314), Harrison co., S Ind., 10 mi. WSW of New Albany, in agr. area. **2** Village, Essex co., Mass.: see GLOUCESTER. **3** Resort village, Greene co., SE N.Y., in the Catskills, 20 mi. NW of Kingston.

Lanett (lûnĕt'), city (pop. 7,434), Chambers co., E Ala., on Chattahoochee R. and 30 mi. NNW of Columbus, Ga., in truck and dairying area; mfg. and processing of cotton fabrics. Inc. 1893.

Laneuveville-à-Bayard (lănûvēl'-ä-bäyär'), village (pop. 103), Haute-Marne dept., NE France, on Marne R. and Marne-Saône Canal, and 9 mi. SE of Saint-Dizier. Iron foundries at near-by Bayard.

Laneuveville-devant-Nancy (–dùvā-nāsē'), outer SE suburb (pop. 1,927) of Nancy, Meurthe-et-Moselle dept., NE France, at junction of Marne-Rhine Canal and Canal de l'Est; mfg. (soda, cartons). Salt mines near by.

Lanezi Lake (12 mi. long, 1 mi. wide), E B.C., in Cariboo Mts., 65 mi. E of Quesnel, S of Issac L. Drained W by Cariboo R. through Sandy L. (5 mi. long) into Quesnel R.

Lanfeng (län'fŭng'), town, ⊙ Lanfeng co. (pop. 97,484), N Honan prov., China, on Lunghai RR and 27 mi. E of Kaifeng; salt-producing center; peanuts, beans, ramie, wheat.

Lang, village (pop. 278), S Sask., 40 mi. SSE of Regina; wheat.

Langaa (läng'ô), town (pop. 1,830), Viborg amt, N Jutland, Denmark, 19 mi. ESE of Viborg; chemical works, machine shops.

Langa de Duero (läng'gä dhā dhwā'rō), town (pop. 1,399), Soria prov., N central Spain, on Duero or Douro R., on railroad and 17 mi. ESE of Aranda de Duero; cereals, grapes, sugar beets, potatoes, beans, fruit, livestock. Flour milling, soap mfg.

Langadha, Lake, Greece: see KORONEIA, LAKE.

Langadhas, town, Greece: see LANKADAS.

Langadia, Langadhia, or **Lankadia** (all: läng-gä'dhēü), town (pop. 3,333), Arcadia nome, central Peloponnesus, Greece, 23 mi. NW of Tripolis; summer resort; livestock (goats, sheep), wine. Also spelled Lagadia.

Langana, Lake (läng'gänä) (□ c.80), S central Ethiopia, in Great Rift Valley, bet. lakes Zwai and Shala, and parallel to L. Hora Abyata (2 mi. W), 90 mi. S of Addis Ababa; 7°40'N 38°45'E; 13 mi. long, 9 mi. wide. Receives many short tributaries (W, S); during flood periods overflows into L. Hora Abyata. Its water is saline.

Langanes (loung'gänĕs"), peninsula, NE Iceland, extends 30 mi. NE into Greenland Sea, bet. Thistil Fjord (NW) and Bakka Bay (SE); 66°15'N 15°W. Rises to 2,359 ft. Thorshofn fishing village (SW).

Langar cum Barnstone (lăng'gûr), agr. parish (pop. 469), SE Nottingham, England. Includes dairying and cheese-making villages of Langar, 3 mi. SSE of Bingham, and (NE) Barnstone. Langar has 13th-cent. church. Samuel Butler b. in Langar.

Langarud (längärōōd'), town, First Prov., in Gilan, N Iran, 31 mi. E of Resht, near Caspian Sea; subtropical agr.

Langatabbetje (läng"ütä'bĕtyù), landing in Marowijne dist., E Du. Guiana, on upper Marowijne or Maroni R. (Fr. Guiana border) and 40 mi. NE of Dam, in tropical forests (timber, balata); 5°N 54°31'W.

Langat River (läng"ät'), Selangor, W Malaya, rises in central Malayan range at Pahang-Negri Sembilan line, flows 100 mi. SW and W, past Kajang, to Strait of Malacca SW of Port Swettenham. Mangrove isls. off mouth.

Langbiang Plateau (läng'bēäng'), S central Vietnam, one of the Moi Plateaus, W of Annamese Cordillera; c.30 mi. wide, c.30 mi. long, average alt. c.5,400 ft. Covered with pine forests; healthful climate. Dalat is main town.

Langchen Khambab, river, Tibet: see SUTLEJ RIVER.

Lang-ch'i, China: see LANGKI.

Langchu, China: see NINGLANG.

Langchung (läng'jōōng'), town (pop. 20,753), ⊙ Langchung co. (pop. 387,858), N Szechwan prov., China, 55 mi. N of Nanchung and on left bank of Kialing R.; sweet potatoes, rice, wheat, beans. Gold mines, saltworks near by. Until 1913 called Paoning.

Langdale, village (pop. 2,721), Chambers co., E Ala., on Chattahoochee R. (dammed here) and 25 mi. NNW of Columbus, Ga.: cotton fabrics.

Langdale Fell, mountain area of the Pennines, England, in NW Yorkshire, on Westmorland border, 5 mi. N of Sedbergh.

Langdale Pikes, two Cumbrian peaks of the Lake District, at NW border of Westmorland, England, 7 mi. WNW of Ambleside. Harrison Stickle is 2,401 ft., Pike o' Stickle 2,323 ft.

Langdon. 1 City (pop. 128), Reno co., S central Kansas, 26 mi. SW of Hutchinson, in wheat region. Fish hatchery here. **2** Town (pop. 378), Sullivan co., SW N.H., 5 mi. NE of Bellows Falls, Vt. **3** City (pop. 1,838), ⊙ Cavalier co., NE N.Dak., 85 mi. NW of Grand Forks. Grain-distribution center, dairy products, livestock. Seat of state agr. experiment station. Inc. 1888.

Langdon Hills, England: see LAINDON.

Langeac (lāzhäk'), town (pop. 4,382), Haute-Loire dept., S central France, bet. Montagnes de la Margeride (W) and Monts du Velay (E), on the Allier and 19 mi. W of Le Puy; road and market center; fruit and vegetable processing, coal and fluorspar mining, stone quarrying.

Langeais (lāzhā'), village (pop. 1,925), Indre-et-Loire dept., W central France, on Loire R. and 14 mi. WSW of Tours; mfg. (agr. implements, building materials). Vineyards. Has 15th-cent. feudal castle which was scene of marriage (1491) of Charles VIII and Anne of Brittany. Bequeathed to French Institute in 1904. Slightly damaged during Second World War.

Langeberg (läng'ùbĕrkh"), mountain range, SW Cape Prov., U. of So. Afr., extends 130 mi. E from Hex River Mts. near Worcester to Gouritz R. valley S of Calitzdorp. E part of range parallels Indian Ocean coast. Rises to 6,809 ft. on Keeromsberg at W end of range, 11 mi. NE of Worcester. Continued E by Outeniqua Mts.

Langed (lông'äd), Swedish *Långed*, village (pop. 574), Alvsborg co., SW Sweden, on Dalsland Canal and 16 mi. WSW of Amal; pulp and paper mills, hydroelectric station.

Langeh, Iran: see LINGEH.

Langeland (läng'ùlăn), island (□ 110; pop. 20,354), Denmark, in Baltic Sea, bet. Fyn and Lolland isls; N tip extends into the Great Belt; 33 mi. long, 3 mi. wide; grain farming. Chief city, Rudkobing. Tranekjaer, NE of Rudkobing, is 13th-cent. castle.

Langeland Belt (c.8 mi. wide), Denmark, strait bet. Langeland (W) and Lolland (E) isls.; joins the Great Belt (N) and Baltic Sea (S).

Langeloth (lăng'lŏth"), village (pop. 1,068), Washington co., SW Pa., 16 mi. NW of Washington.

Langelsheim (läng'ùls-hīm), village (pop. 6,381), in Brunswick, NW Germany, after 1945 in Lower Saxony, at NW foot of the upper Harz, on the Innerste and 3 mi. NW of Goslar; rail junction; mfg. of chemicals, machinery, furniture, shoes; sawmilling.

Langemark (läng'ùmärk), village (pop. 4,459), West Flanders prov., W Belgium, 5 mi. NNE of Ypres. Site of battle (1914) in First World War. Formerly spelled Langemarck.

Langen (läng'ùn), village (pop. 689), Vorarlberg, W Austria, 25 mi. E of Feldkirch; winter sports center (alt. 3,992 ft.). W entrance to ARLBERG TUNNEL.

Langen. 1 Village (pop. 3,316), in former Prussian prov. of Hanover, NW Germany, after 1945 in Lower Saxony, 4 mi. N of Bremerhaven; woodworking. **2** Town (pop. 12,097), S Hesse, W Germany, in former Starkenburg prov., 8 mi. N of Darmstadt; mfg. of iron, steel, and metal goods; leatherworking, tanning, paper milling.

Langenargen (läng'ùnär"gùn), village (pop. 3,439), S Württemberg, Germany, after 1945 in Württemberg-Hohenzollern, on N shore of L. of Constance, 5 mi. SE of Friedrichshafen; hops. Has institute for lake research, founded 1920. On near-by small peninsula is Montfort castle, built 1858 in Moorish style.

Langenau (läng'ùnou), town (pop. 6,016), N Württemberg, Germany, after 1945 in Württemberg-Baden, 8 mi. NE of Ulm; grain, cattle. Has Gothic-baroque church.

Langenberg (läng'ùnbĕrk). **1** Town (pop. 13,911), in former Prussian Rhine Prov., W Germany, after 1945 in North Rhine-Westphalia, 3 mi. E of Velbert; mfg. of machinery and silk ribbon. **2** Town (pop. 5,277), Thuringia, central Germany, on the White Elster and 4 mi. NNW of Gera; china mfg.

Langenbielau, Poland: see BIELAWA.

Langenbruck (läng'ùnbrōōk), village (pop. 849), Basel-Land half-canton, N Switzerland, 6 mi. W of Olten; health resort (alt. 2,339 ft.) on the Oberhauenstein; watches.

Langenbrücken (läng'ùnbrü"kùn), village (pop. 1,950), N Baden, Germany, after 1945 in Württemberg-Baden, 6 mi. NNE of Bruchsal; furniture mfg. Sulphur springs.

Langenburg (lăng'ùnbûrg), village (pop. 405), SE Sask., 40 mi. SE of Yorkton, near Man. border; mixed farming.

Langenburg (läng'ùnbōōrk), town (pop. 1,840), N Württemberg, Germany, after 1945 in Württemberg-Baden, on the Jagst and 12 mi. NW of Crailsheim; grain. Has Renaissance castle, renovated in 17th cent.

Langendamm (läng'ùndäm), village (commune pop. 12,620), in Oldenburg, NW Germany, after 1945 in Lower Saxony, just W of Varel town. Commune is called Varel-Land (fä'rùl-länt").

Langendorf, Rumania: see SATULUNG.

Langendorf (läng'ùndôrf), town (pop. 2,143), Solothurn canton, NW Switzerland, adjacent to Solothurn; watches, metal products.

Langendreer (läng"ùndrâr'), district (since 1929) of Bochum, W Germany, 5 mi. ESE of city center; coal mining.

Langeness, Germany: see NORDMARSCH-LANGENESS.

Langenfeld (läng'ùnfĕlt), town (pop. 20,761), in former Prussian Rhine Prov., W Germany, after 1945 in North Rhine-Westphalia, 7 mi. SW of Solingen; mfg. (Solingen steelware, iron pipes and fittings, textiles, leather clothing, glass, flash bulbs, cardboard); hothouse vegetables grown. Called Richrath-Reusrath until 1936. Chartered 1948.

Langenhagen (läng"ùnhä'gùn), village (pop. 9,341), in former Prussian prov. of Hanover, W Germany, after 1945 in Lower Saxony, 5 mi. N of Hanover city center; mfg. of electrical machinery and equipment, chemicals (oxygen, nitric acid).

Langenhorn (läng'ùnhôrn), village (pop. 3,113), in Schleswig-Holstein, NW Germany, near the North

Sea, 14 mi. NNW of Husum, in North Friesland; grain, cattle.

Langenlois (läng'ŭnlois), town (pop. 4,839), central Lower Austria, near Kamp R., 5 mi. NE of Krems; wine.

Langensalza (läng"ŭnzäl'tsä), town (pop. 16,013), in former Prussian Saxony prov., central Germany, after 1945 in Thuringia, on small Salza R. near its mouth on the Unstrut, and 11 mi. SE of Mühlhausen; machinery mfg., cotton and paper milling, knitting, tanning, printing, metalworking, tobacco processing. Has remains of medieval town walls; two 14th-cent churches; 13th-cent. Dryburg castle (rebuilt); 18th-cent. town hall. Chartered 1212. Town was center of Teutonic Order in 13th cent. Passed to Prussia in 1815. Scene (June, 1866) of battle in which Prussians defeated Hanoverians. Just NE is the spa Bad Langensalza.

Langenschwalbach, Germany: see BAD SCHWALBACH.

Langenselbold (läng"ŭnzĕl'bôlt), village (pop. 8,001), in former Prussian prov. of Hesse-Nassau, W Germany, after 1945 in Hesse, on the Kinzig and 6 mi. ENE of Hanau; mfg. (machinery, rubber goods, household articles). Has 18th-cent. castle.

Langensteinbach (läng"ŭn-shtīn'bäkh), village (pop. 3,095), N Baden, Germany, after 1945 in Württemberg-Baden, 8 mi. SE of Karlsruhe; sulphur springs. Has remains of 14th-cent. chapel.

Langenthal, Rumania: see VALEA-LUNGA.

Langenthal (läng'ŭntäl), town (pop. 8,036), Bern canton, NW central Switzerland, on Langeten R. and 12 mi. E of Solothurn; textiles (linen, woolen), porcelain, flour, beer; metal- and woodworking, printing.

Langenwang (läng'ŭnväng), town (pop. 3,387), Styria, E central Austria, on Mürz R. and 28 mi. ENE of Leoben; tannery.

Langenweddingen (läng"ŭnvĕ'dĭng-ŭn), village (pop. 4,111), in former Prussian Saxony prov., central Germany, after 1945 in Saxony-Anhalt, 8 mi. SW of Magdeburg; flour milling, food canning; market gardening.

Langenzenn (läng'ŭntsĕn"), town (pop. 3,816), Middle Franconia, N central Bavaria, Germany, on small Zenn R. and 8 mi. WNW of Fürth; brickworks; beer. Has 15th-cent. church and former Augustine monastery. Chartered 1442.

Langenzersdorf (längĕnt'sŭrsdôrf), town (pop. 4,146), after 1938 in Floridsdorf dist. of Vienna, Austria, 7 mi. N of city center; vineyards, vegetables.

Langeoog (läng"ŭōk'), North Sea island (□ 6.9; pop. 1,678) of East Frisian group, Germany, 7 mi. N of Esens; 7 mi. long (E–W), c.1 mi. wide (N–S). Nordseebad Langeoog (W) is resort.

Langerbrugge (läng'ŭrbrŭ'khŭ), town, East Flanders prov., NW Belgium, on Ghent-Terneuzen Canal and 4 mi. N of Ghent; mfg. (newsprint, cyanamide), petroleum refining; electric-power station.

Langerfeld (läng'ŭrfĕlt), district (since 1922) of Barmen, W Germany.

Langerwehe (läng'ŭrvā"ŭ), village (pop. 2,427), in former Prussian Rhine Prov., W Germany, after 1945 in North Rhine-Westphalia, 5 mi. WNW of Düren; mfg. of needles.

Langesund (läng'ŭsōōn), town (pop. 2,056), Telemark co., S Norway, at mouth of Langesund Fjord, 16 mi. SSE of Skien; shipbuilding; fishing. Important lumber-shipping center in 16th cent.

Langesund Fjord, Telemark co., S Norway, inlet of the Skagerrak at Langesund; from its isl.-dotted mouth it extends inland in 2 branches, Frier Fjord (7 mi. long) and Erdanger Fjord (4 mi. long). Brevik is on it.

Langevin (lăzhvē') or **SaintJustine** (sĕt zhüstēn'), village (pop. estimate 550), SE Que., 50 mi. SE of Quebec; dairying; pigs.

Langewiesen (läng"ŭvē'zŭn), town (pop. 5,008), Thuringia, central Germany, at foot of Thuringian Forest, on Ilm R. and 3 mi. ESE of Ilmenau; mfg. of china, glass, chemicals, cardboard; woodwork.

Langfjell (läng'fyĕl), collective name applied to an almost continuous range of mountains in W Norway, including Jotunheim, Jostedalsbre, Hardangerfjell, Hardangervidda, Haukelifjell, Bykle Mts.

Langford (lăng'fŭrd), agr. village and parish (pop. 1,147), E central Bedford, England, on Ivel R. and 2 mi. S of Biggleswade. Has 14th-cent. church.

Langford, town (pop. 456), Marshall co., NE S.Dak., 14 mi. S of Britton; dairy produce, livestock, poultry, grain.

Langford Station, village (pop. estimate 500), SW B.C., on SE Vancouver Isl., 6 mi. W of Victoria; lumbering, mixed farming, fruitgrowing.

Langham (lăng'ŭm), town (pop. 311), central Sask., near North Saskatchewan R., 20 mi. NW of Saskatoon; grain elevators, dairying, ranching.

Langhara or **Langhera** (lŭng'gŭrŭ), village and oasis, Farah prov., SW Afghanistan, 95 mi. ESE of Farah and on road to Kandahar; irrigated agr.

Langhirano (läng-gērä'nô), town (pop. 1,669), Parma prov., Emilia-Romagna, N central Italy, on Parma R. and 13 mi. S of Parma; sausage, canned tomatoes.

Langhit (läng'hĭt'), village, Thainguyen prov., N Vietnam, 9 mi. N of Thainguyen; zinc-mining center.

Langholm (lăng'ŭm), burgh (1931 pop. 2,448; 1951 census 2,403), E Dumfries, Scotland, on Esk R., and 18 mi. N of Carlisle; agr. market, with woolen mills (tweed) and tanneries; large sheep fairs. Near by are remains of anc. Wauchope Castle.

Langhorne, borough (pop. 1,579), Bucks co., SE Pa., 20 mi. NE of Philadelphia; mfg. (rugs, wallpaper, textiles); agr. Laid out 1783, inc. 1874.

Langhorne Manor, borough (pop. 781), Bucks co., SE Pa., just S of Langhorne.

Langisjor (loung'gĭsyōr"), Icelandic *Langisjór*, 2 lakes, S Iceland, on SW edge of Vatnajokull. Larger lake (64°11'N 18°17'W) is 10 mi. long, 1 mi. wide. Drained SW by Skafta R.

Langjokull (loung'yû"kütŭl), Icelandic *Langjökull*, extensive glacier, W Iceland, 50 mi. NE of Reykjavik; 40 mi. long, 5–15 mi. wide; rises to 4,757 ft. at 64°36'N 20°36'W.

Lang-k'a or **Lang-k'a-tzu,** Tibet: see NAGARTSE.

Langkawi Island (längkä'wē), main island of Langkawi group (□ 203; pop. 13,969), in Strait of Malacca, Malaya, on Thailand line, 15 mi. off Perlis, but administered as part of Kedah; 18 mi. long, 10 mi. wide; rises to 2,888 ft.; coconuts, rubber; tin and lead mining. Main village of Kuah is on S shore.

Langkha Tuk (läng'kä tōōk'), peak (4,173 ft.), S Thailand, on Malay Peninsula, 50 mi. WNW of Suratthani.

Langki or **Lang-ch'i** (both: läng'chē'), town, ⊙ Langki co. (pop. 127,340), S Anhwei prov., China, near Kiangsu line, 45 mi. ESE of Wuhu; rice, wheat, rapeseed. Until 1914, Kienping.

Langkiung, China: see ERHYÜAN.

Langlade, village, W central Que., 60 mi. ESE of Senneterre; garnet mining.

Langlade, Saint Pierre and Miquelon: see MIQUELON.

Langlade (lăng'lād), county (□ 858; pop. 21,975), NE Wis.; ⊙ Antigo. Drained by Wolf and Eau Claire rivers. Wooded lake region; contains section of Nicolet Natl. Forest. Lumbering and dairying are chief industries; farming is limited to potato growing. Formed 1879.

Langley. 1 Town, Buckingham, England: see SLOUGH. **2** Town in Macclesfield municipal borough, E Cheshire, England; silk mills.

Langley. 1 Town (pop. 204), Mayes co., NE Okla., 13 mi. SSE of Vinita. Grand River Dam is just E. Inc. 1939. **2** Village (pop. 3,696, with near-by Bath), Aiken co., W S.C., 7 mi. WSW of Aiken; textiles. **3** Town (pop. 427), Island co., NW Wash., on Whidbey Isl. and 10 mi. WNW of Everett; resort; trade center for agr. area (poultry, dairy products, livestock, berries, nuts).

Langley, Mount (14,042 ft.), E Calif., in the Sierra Nevada, c.5 mi. SSE of Mt. Whitney and on E boundary of Sequoia Natl. Park. Formerly Mt. Corcoran.

Langley Air Force Base, Va.: see HAMPTON.

Langley Marish (mă'rĭsh), town and parish (pop. 1,180), SE Buckingham, England, 2 mi. E of Slough. Has 12th-cent. church.

Langley Point, promontory on the Channel bet. Pevensey Bay and Beachy Head, SE Sussex, England, 2 mi. NE of Eastbourne.

Langley Prairie, town (pop. estimate 1,200), SW B.C., in lower Fraser R. valley, 20 mi. SE of Vancouver, in lumbering, dairying, fruit- and hop-growing region.

Langley View, village (pop. 1,176), Elizabeth City co., SE Va., a suburb of Hampton.

Langli, China: see CHANGSHA.

Langnau in Emmental (läng'nou ĭm ĕ'mĕntäl) or **Langnau,** town (pop. 8,726), Bern canton, W central Switzerland, in the EMMENTAL, on Ilfis R. and 16 mi. E of Bern; export center of Emmental cheese; textiles (linen, woolen, cotton), pottery, flour; metalworking, canning, tanning.

Lango, district, Uganda: see LIRA.

Langogne (lăgô'nyŭ), town (pop. 3,742), Lozère dept., S France, near the Allier, 22 mi. NE of Mende; railroad junction; meat processing, sawmilling. Summer resort.

Langon (lăgō'), town (pop. 4,151), Gironde dept., SW France, on left bank of Garonne R. and 26 mi. SE of Bordeaux; wine trade; distilling, flour- and sawmilling; orchards near by.

Langoy (läng'ûü), Nor. *Langøy* [=long island], island (□ 332; pop. 15,675) in North Sea, Nordland co., N Norway, in the Vesteralen group, separated from Hinnoy (E) by narrow strait; 35 mi. long (NNE–SSW), 25 mi. wide. Deeply indented (SE) by Vesteral Fjord. Has important fisheries. Chief villages: Eidsfjord, Sortland.

Langport, town and parish (pop. 686), central Somerset, England, on Parrett R. and 12 mi. E of Taunton; agr. market in dairying and flower-growing region. Has 15th-cent. church with "hanging chapel." Walter Bagehot b. here.

Langquaid (läng'kvīt), village (pop. 1,889), Lower Bavaria, Germany, on Great Laaber R. and 13 mi. S of Regensburg; mfg. of chemicals. Hops, wheat, cattle, hogs.

Langreo (läng-grä'ō), mining region, Oviedo prov., NW Spain, in Nalón valley, 10 mi. SE of Oviedo; bituminous coal, iron. Chief towns: La Felguera and Sama de Langreo.

Langres (lă'grŭ), anc. *Andematunum*, fortress town (pop. 5,624), Haute-Marne dept., NE France, 19 mi. SSE of Chaumont, on rocky spur of Plateau of Langres. Overlooks Marne R., Canal de l'Est, and rail junction (1.5 mi. NNE) with which it is connected by rack-and-pinion railway. Produces cutlery, grindstones, cheese; grain, wine, horse, sheep trade. Has 12th-cent. cathedral of Saint-Mamès (damaged in Second World War), mus. of Gallo-Roman antiquities, citadel (1 mi. S), 19th-cent. ramparts built on Roman and medieval foundations. An early Roman stronghold, it became episcopal see in 3d cent.; ruled by count-bishops (12th–18th cent.). Diderot b. here.

Langres, Plateau of, forested limestone tableland of E central France, in N Côte-d'Or and S Haute-Marne depts. Extends c.50 mi. from Dijon (S) to beyond Langres (N), forming watershed bet. Seine and Saône river systems. Rises to c.1,800 ft. Continued by CÔTE D'OR (S), Côtes de MOSELLE (N), and Monts FAUCILLES (NE). Sheep raising, cheese mfg. Traversed by Paris-Dijon and Paris-Belfort RR lines, and by Marne-Saône Canal. Seine, Aube, Marne, and Meuse rivers rise here.

Langrune or **Langrune-sur-Mer** (lăgrün"-sür-mâr'), village (pop. 1,112), Calvados dept., NW France, beach resort on English Channel, 10 mi. N of Caen. Has 13th-cent. church (damaged in Allied Normandy landings of June, 1944).

Langsa (läng'sŭ), town (pop. 4,749), NE Sumatra, Indonesia, near Strait of Malacca, 80 mi. NW of Medan, on Medan-Kutaraja railroad; trade center for rubber-growing area. Its port, Kualalangsa or Koealalangsa (both: kwä"lŭläng'sŭ), is 4 mi. NE on the Strait; exports rubber, resin, palm oil.

Langsele (lông'sā"lŭ), Swedish *Långsele*, village (pop. 1,231), Vasternorrland co., NE Sweden, on Fax R., Swedish *Faxälven* (fäks'ĕl"vŭn), near its mouth on Angerman R., 7 mi. W of Solleftea; rail junction in lumbering, dairying region. Has old church. Hydroelectric station (S).

Langshan (läng'shän'), town (pop. 3,570), ⊙ Langshan co. (pop. 39,664), W Suiyuan prov., China, 45 mi. W of Wuyüan, in Howtao oasis; cattle raising; grain, licorice. Until 1942, Yunganpao.

Langshyttan (lôngs"hü'tän"), Swedish *Långshyttan*, village (pop. 2,788), Kopparberg co., central Sweden, 19 mi. SE of Falun; iron and steel mills.

Langside (lăng'sīd), S suburb (pop. 17,980) of Glasgow, Lanark, Scotland. In 1568 the Regent Moray here defeated troops of Mary Queen of Scots; site is marked by memorial.

Langsnek, U. of So. Afr.: see LAING'S NEK.

Langson (läng'shŭn'), town (1936 pop. 7,400), ⊙ Langson prov. (□ 2,400; 1943 pop. 213,100), N Vietnam, in Tonkin, near China border, on Hanoi-Nacham RR and 85 mi. NE of Hanoi, on the Song Kikong (right headstream of Li R.); commercial center and military post; sericulture; aromatic produce. Copper, lead, zinc, and oil-shale deposits near by. Chinese fort (15th cent.). Captured 1885 by French and 1950 by the Vietminh.

Langston, England: see HAVANT.

Langston, town (pop. 685), Logan co., central Okla., 10 mi. ENE of Guthrie. Seat of Langston Univ. Oil field near by.

Langstone Harbour or **Langston Harbour,** Hampshire, England, bet. Portsea and Hayling isls.; 4 mi. long.

Lang Suan (läng' sōōän'), town (1937 pop. 3,138), Chumphon prov., S Thailand, in Isthmus of Kra, port on Gulf of Siam, on railroad and 40 mi. S of Chumphon; tin mining; fruit gardening, fishing. Sometimes spelled Langsuen.

Langtai (läng'dī'), town (pop. 8,844), ⊙ Langtai co. (pop. 122,105), SW Kweichow prov., China, 40 mi. W of Anshun; cotton-textile mfg., pottery- and papermaking. Arsenic mines, coal deposits near by.

Langton Bay, Northwest Territories: see FRANKLIN BAY.

Langtry (lăng'trē), village, Val Verde co., SW Texas, on the Rio Grande near mouth of the Pecos and c.50 mi. NW of Del Rio. Near by, at old town of Langtry, Judge Roy Bean, "the law west of the Pecos," meted out justice in his frontier saloon.

Languard, Piz, Switzerland: see PIZ LANGUARD.

Langue (läng'gä), town (pop. 2,832), Valle dept., S Honduras, on Inter-American Highway and 11 mi. WNW of Nacaome; commercial center; beverage mfg., rope milling; henequen, livestock. Has noted church (1804).

Languedoc (lăgŭdôk'), region and former province, S France, bounded roughly by the foothills of E Pyrenees (S), the Gulf of Lion (SE), the lower Rhone (E), and the Massif Central (W). It extends in a great arc from Toulouse (SW) to Annonay (NE), occupying the E portion of the Aquitaine Basin, the lowlands at the foot of the Cévennes, and part of E escarpment of the Massif Central. It is now administratively divided into AUDE, TARN, HÉRAULT, GARD, LOZÈRE, and ARDÈCHE depts., and part of HAUTE-GARONNE and HAUTE-LOIRE depts. Languedoc is France's chief wine-growing region. Principal cities are Toulouse (historical capital), Montpellier, Nîmes, Bèziers, Carcassonne, Narbonne, and Albi. It roughly corresponds to Narbonensis prov. of Roman Gaul. Its history from Frankish conquest (completed 8th cent.) until incorporation into French royal domain (1271) is largely that of the counts of Toulouse. Languedoc [language using *oc*, i.e., "yes"] was named from a familiar term for Provençal, the language of the region; the opposed term, for French, was Langue d'Oïl [language using *oïl*]. Under the old régime Languedoc had its own *parlement* sitting at Toulouse. In 1790 the prov. was broken up into present depts.

L'Anguille River (lăng″gē'lē, lăn″gēl'), E Ark., rises in Craighead co., flows S and SE, past Marianna, to St. Francis R. in Lee co.; c.110 mi. long.

Languiñeo, department, Argentina: see TECKA.

Languiñeo (läng-gēnyä'ō), village (pop. estimate 500), W Chubut natl. territory, Argentina, 50 mi. SE of Esquel; sheep, cattle.

Langulya River, India: see NAGAVALI RIVER.

Langwathby, village and parish (pop. 287), E Cumberland, England, on Eden R. and 4 mi. ENE of Penrith; paper mfg.; cattle and sheep raising.

Langwedel (läng'vā″dŭl), village (pop. 1,940), in former Prussian prov. of Hanover, NW Germany, after 1945 in Lower Saxony, 4 mi. N of Verden; rail junction; mfg. of leather goods and tobacco products.

Lanham (lă'nŭm), village (1940 pop. 705), Prince Georges co., central Md., ENE of Washington.

Lan Ho, China: see LWAN RIVER.

Lan-hsi, Manchuria: see LANSI.

Lanhsien (län'shyĕn'). **1** Town, Hopeh prov., China: see LWANHSIEN. **2** Town, ⊙ Lanhsien co. (pop. 72,398), NW Shansi prov., China, 60 mi. NW of Taiyüan; wheat, chestnuts, beans.

Lanier, Cuba: see LIGUANEA.

Lanier (lŭnēr'), county (□ 167; pop. 5,151), S Ga.; ⊙ Lakeland. Coastal plain area intersected by Alapaha R. Agr. (corn, sweet potatoes, tobacco, fruit, livestock) and forestry (lumber, naval stores). Formed 1919.

Lanigan, town (pop. 336), S central Sask., 70 mi. ESE of Saskatoon; grain elevators, lumbering.

Lanikai (lä'nĕkī'), village, E Oahu, T.H., 14 mi. N of Honolulu.

Lanildut (lānēldü'), village (pop. 31), Finistère dept., W France, 13 mi. NW of Brest; pink-granite quarries.

Lanín Volcano (länēn'), Andean peak (c.12,300 ft.) on Argentina-Chile border, S of Mamuil-Malal Pass; 39°38'S. Site of natl. park.

Lanjarón (länhärōn'), town (pop. 4,749), Granada prov., S Spain, on S slope (alt. 2,300 ft.) of the Sierra Nevada, 19 mi. SSE of Granada; olive-oil processing, flour milling, liqueur mfg. Oranges and other fruit, chestnuts, vegetables. Has famous mineral springs. Dominated by anc. castle. Gypsum quarries near by.

Lanka, Asia: see CEYLON.

Lankada, Lake, Greece: see KORONEIA, LAKE.

Lankadas or **Langadhas** (both: läng-gädhäs'), town (pop. 5,859), Salonika nome, Macedonia, Greece, 10 mi. NE of Salonika; wheat, cotton, citrus fruits, silk. Sulphur springs.

Lankadia, Greece: see LANGADIA.

Lankao (län'gou'), town (pop. 1,256), ⊙ Lankao co. (pop. 70,198), S Shensi prov., China, in the Tapa Shan, 22 mi. SSW of Ankang; wheat, rice, beans, millet. Until 1913 called Chwanping.

Lankatilaka, Ceylon: see GADALADENIYA.

Lanke (lông'kŭ), Nor. *Lånke*, village and canton (pop. 1,695), Nord-Trondelag co., central Norway, on Stjordal R., on railroad and 21 mi. E of Trondheim; quarries slate and lime; produces bricks, drainage pipes. Sometimes spelled Laanke.

Lankershim, Calif.: see NORTH HOLLYWOOD.

Lanki, China: see LANCHI.

Lankin, village (pop. 287), Walsh co., NE N.Dak., 25 mi. WSW of Grafton, near branch of Forest R.

Lanmeur (lāmûr'), village (pop. 849), Finistère dept., W France, 7 mi. NE of Morlaix; dairying, woodworking.

Lannemezan (länmŭzä'), town (pop. 2,655), Hautes-Pyrénées dept., SW France, at S end of Lannemezan Plateau, 12 mi. ENE of Bagnères-de-Bigorre; industrial and commercial center (livestock and dairy market); electrometallurgical (aluminum, steel) and electrochemical works (cyanamide, fertilizer). Chief distribution point of electricity generated in Pyrenees.

Lannemezan Plateau, tableland (average alt. 2,000 ft.) of SW France, occupying part of Hautes-Pyrénées, Gers, and Haute-Garonne depts. Bounded by Adour R. (W), Neste R. and foothills of central Pyrenees (S), and upper Garonne R. (SE). From the terminal moraine near Lannemezan (S) numerous streams (Baïse, Gers, Gimone, Save) drain N and NE to the Garonne. Armagnac brandy originates here. Horse breeding.

Lannepax (länŭpäks'), village (pop. 280), Gers dept., SW France, 13 mi. SW of Condom; white wines, Armagnac brandy.

Lannilis (länēlēs'), village (pop. 1,945), Finistère dept., W France, 13 mi. N of Brest; fruits and vegetables; pottery. Has 17th-cent. castle of Kérouartz.

Lannion (lányō'), town (pop. 6,136), Côtes-du-Nord dept., W France, 40 mi. WNW of Saint-Brieuc; flax processing, woodworking, printing, cider milling. Megalithic monument near by.

Lannon, village (pop. 438), Waukesha co., SE Wis., 14 mi. NW of Milwaukee, in dairy and farm area.

L'Annonciation (länōsēäsēō'), village (pop. 632), SW Que., in the Laurentians, 40 mi. NW of Ste. Agathe des Monts; dairying.

Lannoy (länwä'), outer SE suburb (pop. 1,318) of Roubaix, Nord dept., N France, near Belg. border; textile mills (blankets, quilts, rugs, spreads).

Lanoraie (länôrā'), village (pop. estimate 1,000), S Que., on the St. Lawrence and 35 mi. NNE of Montreal; dairying; resort.

La Noria (lä nō'ryä), village (pop. 49), Tarapacá prov., N Chile, 5 mi. W of the Salar de Pintados, 22 mi. SE of Iquique. Former nitrate-mining center. Flourished c.1900.

Lanouaille (länwī'), village (pop. 569), Dordogne dept., SW France, 25 mi. NE of Périgueux; road junction; mfg. of agr. tools. Paper mill (packing paper) near by.

Lanovtsy (lä'nŭftsē), Pol. *Łanowce* (ŏŏänôf'tsĕ), village (1931 pop. 730), NE Ternopol oblast, Ukrainian SSR, on right tributary of Goryn R. and 24 mi. SE of Kremenets; flour milling, brickworking, hatmaking.

Lanping or **Lan-p'ing** (both: län'pĭng'), town (pop. 2,220), ⊙ Lanping co. (pop. 30,894), NW Yunnan prov., China, near Mekong R., 65 mi. NW of Tali; alt. 10,138 ft.; timber, rice, millet, beans. Lead mines near by.

Lanques-sur-Rognon (lăk'-sür-rônyō'), village (pop. 235), Haute-Marne dept., NE France, 11 mi. E of Chaumont; cutlery mfg.

Lanrivain (lārēvē'), village (pop. 337), Côtes-du-Nord dept., W France, 15 mi. S of Guingamp. Has 16th-cent. calvary. In near-by Toul-Goulic gorge Blavet R. flows partially underground.

Lan River, China: see LWAN RIVER.

Lans, Isère dept., France: see LANS-EN-VERCORS.

Lans, Montagnes de, France: see VERCORS.

Lansallos (lănsă'lŭs), agr. village and parish (pop. 570), E Cornwall, England, on the Channel and 3 mi. E of Fowey. Has 15th-cent. church.

Lansdale, borough (pop. 9,762), Montgomery co., SE Pa., 21 mi. N of Philadelphia; clothing, metal products, tiles, radio tubes, glue. Settled 1857, inc. 1872.

Lansdowne, village (pop. estimate 500), SE Ont., 27 mi. ENE of Kingston; dairying, mixed farming.

Lansdowne (lănz'doun), cantonment town (pop. 6,174), Garhwal dist., N Uttar Pradesh, India, 32 mi. SSE of Hardwar; alt. 5,026 ft.; wheat, barley, rice. Founded 1887. Sometimes written Lansdown.

Lansdowne (lănz'doun). **1** Industrial suburb, Baltimore co., central Md., 5 mi. WSW of downtown Baltimore; makes radios, whisky. **2** Borough (pop. 12,169), Delaware co., SE Pa., SW suburb of Philadelphia; metal products, paper, dyes, abrasives. Inc. 1893.

Lansdown Hill, ridge, NE Somerset, England; extends 5 mi. NW from Bath; rises to 780 ft. Noted for its breed of sheep.

L'Anse (lăns), resort village (pop. 2,376), ⊙ Baraga co., NW Upper Peninsula, Mich., 27 mi. SSE of Houghton, at head of Keweenaw Bay, in farm and lumber area; fisheries. L'Anse Indian Reservation is E. Inc. 1873.

Lanse, village (pop. 1,085, with adjacent Winburne), Clearfield co., central Pa., 16 mi. ESE of Clearfield.

L'Anse Amour, Labrador: see ANSE AMOUR, L'.

Lans-en-Vercors (lās-ā-vĕrkôr'), village (pop. 114), Isère dept., SE France, in Dauphiné Pre-Alps, 8 mi. SW of Grenoble; resort. Until 1947, Lans.

Lansford. 1 City (pop. 352), Bottineau co., N N.Dak., 30 mi. N of Minot; dairy products, poultry, wheat, livestock. **2** Borough (pop. 7,487), Carbon co., E Pa., 8 mi. WSW of Mauch Chunk; anthracite; clothing mfg. Founded 1846, inc. 1877.

Lanshan (län'shän'), town, ⊙ Lanshan co. (pop. 127,847), S Hunan prov., China, near Kwangtung line, 70 mi. SW of Chenhsien; tin mining.

Lansi or **Lan-hsi** (both: län'shē'), town, ⊙ Lansi co. (pop. 194,745), S Heilungkiang prov., Manchuria, 35 mi. NW of Harbin, near Sungkiang line; soybeans, kaoliang, rye, millet, corn. Formerly called Shwangmiaotze.

Lansing (lăn'sĭng). **1** Village (pop. 8,682), Cook co., NE Ill., S suburb of Chicago, at Ind. line, just S of Calumet City; bottling works; dairy, grain, truck farms. Founded in 1860s; inc. 1893. **2** Town (pop. 1,536), Allamakee co., extreme NE Iowa, at foot of bluffs on Mississippi R. (bridged here), 28 mi. ENE of Decorah; mfg. (pearl buttons, metal toys). Fisheries, timber, limestone quarries, lead and zinc deposits near by. Large group of Indian effigy mounds and a state fish hatchery are in vicinity. Laid out 1851, inc. 1867. **3** Village (1940 pop. 733), Leavenworth co., NE Kansas, 4 mi. S of Leavenworth, near Missouri R., in general agr. region. State prison for women is here. **4** City (pop. 92,129), ⊙ Mich., in Ingham co., S central Mich., c.80 mi. NW of Detroit, and on Grand R. at mouth of Red Cedar R.; 42°44'N 84°33'W; alt. c.850 ft. Important automobile-mfg. center, and market for rich S Mich. agr. area. Also makes buses, trucks, automotive parts, construction machinery, tools, metal products, gas engines, fire-fighting equipment, chemicals, paints, canvas, wood and cement products, sugar. The capitol (1878) houses a mus.; the state office bldg. contains the state library and state historical commission. City also has a state school for the blind and a vocational school for boys. Mich. State Col. of Agr. and Applied Science is at adjacent East Lansing. Settled 1837; selected as state capital in 1847, when still a wilderness hamlet, it grew to pop. of c.4,000 by 1859, when it was inc. as city. Industrial development came with railroads (1870s); carriage and wagon factories flourishing by late 19th cent. were succeeded in importance after 1901 by the automobile industry. **5** Village (pop. c.300), Mower co., SE Minn., on Cedar R. and 6 mi. N of Austin; dairy products. **6** Town (1940 pop. 274), Ashe co., NW N.C., 31 mi. NW of North Wilkesboro, near Va. line. **7** Village (1940 pop. 1,374), Belmont co., E Ohio, 5 mi. NNW of Bellaire, and on small Wheeling Creek, in coal-mining area, near W.Va. line; mfg. (toys, burial vaults).

Lansing, Lake, Mich.: see HASLETT.

Lanskroun (länsh'krōn), Czech *Lanškroun*, Ger. *Landskron* (länts'krōn), town (pop. 4,952), E Bohemia, Czechoslovakia, 40 mi. SE of Hradec Kralove; rail terminus; mfg. (cotton textiles, paper), tobacco processing.

Lanslebourg (lālŭbōōr'), village (pop. 406), Savoie dept., SE France, in upper Maurienne valley of Savoy Alps, on the Arc and 13 mi. NW of Susa (Italy); road junction for Mont Cenis Pass (2 mi. SSE) and Col de l'Iseran (12 mi. NE). Asbestos quarries. Winter sports.

Lanta (lātä'), village (pop. 239), Haute-Garonne dept., S France, 11 mi. ESE of Toulouse; horse raising, agr.

Lanta, Ko (kô' län'tä'), island (1937 pop. 6,499) of Krabi prov., S Thailand, in Gulf of Siam, off coast of Malay Peninsula, 30 mi. SSE of Krabi; 15 mi. long, 5 mi. wide.

Lantadilla (läntä-dhē'lyä), town (pop. 1,124), Palencia prov., N central Spain, on Pisuerga R. and 27 mi. NE of Palencia; wheat, wine, sheep.

Lantana (lăntă'nŭ), resort town (pop. 773), Palm Beach co., SE Fla., 9 mi. S of West Palm Beach, on L. Worth lagoon.

Lan Tao or **Lan Tau** (both: län'dou'), island of the New Territories of Hong Kong colony, separated from Hong Kong isl. (E) by 6-mi.-wide West Lamma Channel; 15 mi. long, 6 mi. wide. Lead (Silver Mine Bay) and tungsten deposits.

Lanteglos (lăntĕg'lŏs, –tăg'–), agr. village and parish (pop. 1,368), E Cornwall, England, on Fowey R., opposite Fowey. Has 15th-cent. church.

Lanteira (läntā'rä), town (pop. 1,323), Granada prov., S Spain, on N slope of the Sierra Nevada, 9 mi. S of Guadix; flour mills. Chestnuts, lumber. Mineral springs. Iron mines near by.

Lantejuela, La (lä läntāhwā'lä), town (pop. 2,368), Seville prov., SW Spain, in a lake dist., 40 mi. E of Seville; olives, cereals, livestock. Sulphur spa near by.

Lantien or **Lan-t'ien** (län'tyĕn'), town (pop. 4,453), ⊙ Lantien co. (pop. 218,522), SE Shensi prov., China, 20 mi. ESE of Sian; cotton weaving; indigo, ramie, beans, wheat, potatoes.

Lantosque (lātôsk'), village (pop. 905), Alpes-Maritimes dept., SE France, in Vésubie valley of Maritime Alps, and 19 mi. N of Nice; resort.

Lantsang or **Lan-ts'ang** (both: län'tsäng'), town (pop. 483), ⊙ Lantsang co. (pop. 93,759), SW Yunnan prov., China, near Burma border, 60 mi. WSW of Ningerh, in mtn. region, W of the Mekong; rice, millet, beans. Until 1914 called Chenpien.

Lantsang Chiang China: see MEKONG RIVER.

Lanús (länōōs'), city (pop. estimate 165,000), ⊙ Cuatro de Junio dist. (□ 17; pop. 247,613), in Greater Buenos Aires, Argentina, 6 mi. S of Buenos Aires. Major industrial center; armaments, textiles, paper, chemicals, wire, vegetable oils, lubricants, shoes, rubber goods, haberdashery; canning plants and tanneries. Has technical schools.

Lanusei (länōōzā'), village (pop. 4,045), Nuoro prov., E Sardinia, 33 mi. SSE of Nuoro; wine, fruit.

Lanuvio (länōō'vyō), village (pop. 2,157), Roma prov., Latium, central Italy, in Alban Hills, 4 mi. W of Velletri; macaroni mfg. Occupies site of anc. Lanuvium and has Roman ruins. Largely destroyed by air and artillery bombing in Second World War. Formerly Civita Lavinia.

Lanuza (länōō'sä), town (1939 pop. 4,949; 1948 municipality pop. 8,559), Surigao prov., NE Mindanao, Philippines, at head of Lanuza Bay, on inlet of Philippine Sea, 55 mi. SE of Surigao.

Lanvollon (lāvôlō'), village (pop. 752), Côtes-du-Nord dept., W France, 13 mi. NW of Saint-Brieuc; apple orchards.

Lany (lä'nĭ), Czech *Lány*, village (pop. 1,407), central Bohemia, Czechoslovakia, on railroad and 6 mi. WSW of Kladno. Has 18th-cent. hunting lodge, park, and game preserve. Summer residence of Thomas G. Masaryk, who is buried here.

Lanywa (län'yŭwä″), village, Pakokku dist., Upper Burma, on right bank of Irrawaddy R. and 30 mi. SW of Pakokku; petroleum center (1st well sunk 1927) in Singu oil fields.

Lanz (länts), village (pop. 829), Brandenburg, E Germany, 8 mi. NW of Wittenberge. Friedrich Ludwig Jahn b. here.

Lanza (län′sä), town (pop. c.4,100), La Paz dept., W Bolivia, on E slopes of Eastern Cordillera of the Andes, 20 mi. SSE of Inquisivi; potatoes, grain. Until c.1945, Mohoza.

Lanzahita (län-thäē′tä), town (pop. 1,313), Ávila prov., central Spain, in the Sierra de Gredos, 32 mi. SSW of Ávila; olives, grapes, livestock; olive-oil pressing, flour milling.

Lanzarote (län-thärō′tä), anc. *Capraria*, northernmost and smallest island (□ 307; pop. 27,476) of the larger Canary Isls., in Las Palmas prov., Spain, in the Atlantic, bet. Fuerteventura (S) and Graciosa Isl. (N), c.110 mi. NE of Las Palmas and 80 mi. NW of Cape Juby on coast of Sp. Morocco. Chief town and port is Arrecife. Isl. extends 35 mi. NE-SW from 29°14′N 13°28′W to 28°52′N 13°51′W; up to 12 mi. wide. Deeply indented, Lanzarote is composed of volcanic rocks, rising in the Famara Massif to 2,215 ft. Still active is the Montaña de Fuego or Montañas del Fuego. The climate is generally mild and tropical. Although water is scarce, crops are raised for export, chiefly onions, cereals, potatoes, grapes, chick-peas, fruit. Some stock raising. Fish—canned or dried—is another important source of income. There are several saltworks. Minor industries are processing, quarrying, embroidery mfg. Practically all foreign trade passes through Arrecife. Among other towns are Haría, San Bartolomé, and Teguise. Rich in associations with early Sp. and Port. discoveries, Lanzarote was variously known as Torçusa, Isla del Infierno, Tierra del Fuego, Lancelot, etc. Large volcanic eruptions were recorded 1730–36 and 1824–25. Sometimes called Lancerota.

Lanzhot (länsh′hôt), Czech *Lanžhot*, Ger. *Landshut* (länts′ho͝ot), village (pop. 3,650), SE Moravia, Czechoslovakia, on railroad and 4 mi. SE of Breclav, near Austrian border; barley, wheat. Retains colorful regional costumes and customs.

Lanzo Torinese (län′tsô tôrēnā′zĕ), resort village (pop. 1,925), Torino prov., Piedmont, NW Italy, 17 mi. NNW of Turin; textile industry. Antimony, talc mines near by.

Laoag (läwäg′), city (1939 pop. 21,236; 1948 municipality pop. 44,406), ⊙ Ilocos Norte prov., NW Luzon, Philippines, on small Laoag R. near its mouth on S.China Sea, 125 mi. N of Baguio; 18°12′N 120°35′E. Trade center for rice area.

Laoang Island (läwäng′) (7 mi. long, 3 mi. wide), Samar prov., Philippines, in Philippine Sea, near Batag Isl., nearly connected to N coast of Samar isl. Coconut growing, fishing. On SW coast is Laoang town (1939 pop. 4,782; 1948 municipality pop. 29,748, including adjacent isls.). Formerly Calamutang Isl.

Laodicea (lāō″dĭsē′ù), name of several Greek cities of Asia and Asia Minor founded by the Seleucids. The most important was **Laodicea ad Lycum** (ăd lī′kùm), in W Asia Minor, near present-day DENIZLI, SW Turkey, on a tributary of the Maeander. It withstood wars and earthquakes and was important in Hellenistic and Roman times. It was an early Christian center, the seat of one of the "seven churches in Asia." There are extensive ruins. **Laodicea ad Mare** (ăd mâ′rē) was seaport of Syria S of Antioch, the modern LATAKIA, and flourished under the Romans with exports of wine and fruit. **Laodicea Combusta** (kŏmbŭ′stù) was an anc. town of N Asia Minor; its site is present-day town of LADIK, Turkey, 33 mi. SW of Samsun.

Laoet. 1 Island, Indonesia: see NORTH NATUNA ISLANDS. **2** Island, Indonesia: see PULU LAUT.

Laohokow, China: see KWANGHWA.

Laoighis (lā′ĭsh) or **Leix** (lāks), formerly Queen's, county (□ 663.9; pop. 49,697), Leinster, central Ireland; ⊙ Port Laoighise (Maryborough). Bounded by cos. Kilkenny (S), Tipperary (SW), Offaly (W and N), Kildare (E), and Carlow (SE). Drained by Nore and Barrow rivers. Surface is flat, level, partly boggy, in center, becomes hilly in SE and rises to 1,733 ft. in the Slieve Bloom mts. in NW. Coal is mined in S, peat is exploited near Portarlington and Timahoe. Cattle raising, wheat, barley, potato, beet growing are important. Industries include woolen milling, malting, agr.-implement mfg. Besides Port Laoighise, other towns are Abbeyleix, with 12th-cent. abbey, Durrow, and Stradbally. Antiquities include anc. round tower (Timahoe) and fortress of Dunamase, anc. stronghold of kings of Leinster and of Strongbow.

Laokay (lou′kī′), town, ⊙ Laokay prov. (□ 2,300; 1943 pop. 69,500), N Vietnam, in Tonkin, on Red R. (China frontier), opposite Hokow, on Hanoi-Kunming RR and 160 mi. NW of Hanoi; trading center. Phosphate and graphite deposits; cardamom.

Laolung (lou′lo͝ong′), town, E Kwangtung prov., China, on East R. (head of navigation) and 5 mi. NE of Lungchün; commercial center.

Laon (lã), town (pop. 14,868), ⊙ Aisne dept., N France, on a rocky height 330 ft. above surrounding plain, 29 mi. NW of Rheims; rail center. Mfg. (agr. equipment, stoves, furniture, sugar). Fortified since Roman times, it is accessible only through medieval gates by zigzagging roads and rack-and-pinion streetcar from railroad station. Dominating town is vast 12th-13th-cent. church (former cathedral) of Notre Dame. The former abbatial church of St. Martin was burned in 1944. Episcopal see from 6th cent. to French Revolution. During Middle Ages, torn by struggles bet. bishops and burghers who ultimately had their charter recognized. Often besieged in Hundred Years War. Occupied by Germans through most of First World War, Laon remained virtually undamaged, but was heavily hit in Second World War. Jacques Marquette b. here.

Laona (lāō′nù), resort village (pop. 1,113), Forest co., NE Wis., 36 mi. ESE of Rhinelander, in lake region; lumbering.

Lao River (lou), S Italy, rises in the Apennines 7 mi. E of Lauria, flows 25 mi. SSW to Tyrrhenian Sea 3 mi. S of Scalea. Formerly also Laino.

La Oroya (lä ōroi′ä) or **Oroya,** town (pop. 14,494), ⊙ Yauli prov. (□ 1,321; pop. 33,617), Junín dept., central Peru, in Cordillera Central of the Andes, on Mantaro R. at mouth of the Yauli, and 80 mi. ENE of Lima (connected by rail and highway); alt. 12,178 ft. Rail and road junction of lines to Cerro de Pasco and Huancayo. Metallurgical center (copper, silver, zinc, lead); ore smelting, electrolytic copper refining. Hydroelectric power station (fed by Pomacocha reservoir). Produces bismuth, arsenic, and cadmium as by-products. Ships minerals, grain, livestock. Receives ores from Cerro de Pasco, Morococha, and Casapalca mines; connected with Pachachaca power plant.

Laos (lā′ōs, lāōs′), kingdom (□ 91,400; 1947 pop. 1,169,000), NW Indochina, a state associated with France within the French Union; administrative ⊙ at Vientiane; royal residence at Luang Prabang. Bounded N by Yünnan prov. (China), E by Vietnam, S by Cambodia, and W by Burma and Thailand (along Luang Prabang Range and Mekong R.), the Laos consists of the broad upper Laos (N), a dissected region of wooded ranges and plateaus cut by narrow valleys and gorges, and the narrow lower Laos (S), a region of more arid limestone terraces, sparsely forested, descending from the Annamite Cordillera toward the Mekong. A wet summer (May-Oct.) with rainfall up to 80 in. is succeeded by a dry season, in turn cool (Nov.-Feb.) and hot (Feb.-May). Largely agricultural, Laos grows rice (chief food crop), corn, vegetables, cotton, cardamoms, and tobacco. Coffee (Boloven Plateau), benzoin, opium, and lac are the chief export items. Cattle and teak (N) are also exported. The least developed of the Indochina states, Laos has little modern industry (rice mill at Savannakhet), tin being the only mineral mined (at Boneng and Phontiou). Native industry produces woven goods and metal art objects. The principal centers (Vientiane, Luang Prabang, Thakhek, Savannakhet, and Pakse) lie along the Mekong (which remains, in spite of rapids, the chief transportation route) and are linked by highways with Vinh and Dongha (near Quangtri) in Vietnam. Pop. includes chiefly the Lao (50%) and other Thai groups, indigenous hill aborigines (Kha; 20%), Chinese aborigines (Man and Miao). Little is known about the Laos until the 14th cent., when a unified Lao kingdom of Lanxang was reconstituted astride Mekong R. This was divided (late 17th cent.) into the two kingdoms of Vientiane (annexed 1827 by Siam, or Thailand) and Luang Prabang (which acknowledged Siamese suzerainty shortly thereafter) The Laos passed from Siam to France in 1893 (left-bank section) and 1904 (right-bank section), the Vientiane kingdom coming under direct Fr. administration and Luang Prabang as a French protected state. During Second World War, the right-bank section passed temporarily (1941–46) to Thailand. The Laos was reunited (1947) as a constitutional monarchy under the dynasty of Luang Prabang and joined (1948–50) the French Union as an associated state recognized by the U.S.

Lao Shan (lou′ shän′), mountain (3,707 ft.) in E Shantung prov., China, overlooking Yellow Sea, 20 mi. NE of Tsingtao.

Laotieh Shan or **Lao-t'ieh Shan** (lou′tyĕ′ shän′), southernmost headland of Liaotung peninsula, S Manchuria, overlooking the Strait of Chihli, 6 mi. SW of Port Arthur; 38°46′N 121°10′E.

Laotowkow or **Lao-t'ou-kou** (both: lou′tō′gō′), town, E Kirin prov., Manchuria, 25 mi. W of Yenki; coal-mining center. Nonferrous metals (copper, lead, zinc, silver) mined at Tienpaoshan (SW).

Laoyao, China: see LIENYÜN.

Laoyatan, China: see YENTSING, Yunnan prov.

Lapa (lä′pù). **1** City, Bahia, Brazil: see BOM JESUS DA LAPA. **2** City (pop. 4,324), SE Paraná, Brazil, on railroad and 35 mi. SW of Curitiba; flour milling, maté processing; rye, tobacco, cattle. Sand deposits, clay quarries.

Lapa, La (lä lä′pä), town (pop. 639), Badajoz prov., W Spain, 38 mi. SE of Badajoz; olives, cereals, vegetables, livestock; tiles, pottery.

Lapa, Serra da (sĕ′rù dù lä′pù), mtn. range (3,100 ft.) of N central Portugal, in Viseu and Guarda dists., NW of Trancoso; Vouga R. rises here.

Lapachito (läpächē′tō), village (pop. estimate 500), E Chaco natl. territory, Argentina, 23 mi. NW of Resistencia; rail junction; cotton and lumber center; sawmills, cotton gins.

Lapac Island (läpäk′) (□ 15.6; 1939 pop. 5,804), in Tapul Group, Sulu prov., Philippines, in Sulu Archipelago, just W of Siasi Isl., 25 mi. SW of Jolo Isl.

Lapalisse or **La Palisse** (lä pälēs′), town (pop. 2,283), Allier dept., central France, on the Besbre and 27 mi. SSE of Moulins; road center and agr. market; mfg. (leather goods, knitwear, buttons, padlocks, and food preserves); flour- and sawmilling. Has 16th-cent. castle.

La Palma (lä päl′mä), town (pop. 2,730), Cundinamarca dept., central Colombia, on W slopes of Cordillera Oriental, 25 mi. NE of Honda; alt. 4,796 ft. Agr. center (sugar cane, coffee, tobacco, fruit).

La Palma, saddle depression (alt. 6,000 ft.) in the Central Cordillera, central Costa Rica, bet. Barba (W) and Irazú (E) volcanoes, NE of San José. Admits rain-bearing Caribbean air masses to central plateau. Crossed by Carrillo–San José road.

La Palma or **Consolación del Norte** (kōnsōläsyōn′ dĕl nôr′tä), town (pop. 1,885), Pinar del Río prov., W Cuba, 25 mi. NNE of Pinar del Río, in agr. region (sugar cane, tobacco); mfg. of cigars, lumbering. The Niagára sugar mill is 5 mi. NE.

La Palma, town (pop. 3,199), Michoacán, central Mexico, on SE shore of L. Chapala, 14 mi. S of Ocotlán; cereals, vegetables, fruit, stock.

La Palma. 1 Village (pop. 1,103), ⊙ Darién prov., E Panama, port on Tuira R. estuary, on San Miguel Gulf, 90 mi. SE of Panama city. Agr. (plantains, corn, rice); stock raising; sawmilling. **2** Village (pop. 1,544), Los Santos prov., S central Panama, in Pacific lowland, 4 mi. SE of Las Tablas; sugar cane, coffee, livestock.

La Paloma (lä pälō′mä), town, Rocha dept., SE Uruguay, port on the Atlantic adjoining Cape Santa María, 16 mi. SE of Rocha, on railroad. Bathing and fishing resort. Sometimes called Puerto La Paloma.

La Paloma, town (pop. 671), Zulia state, NW Venezuela, in Maracaibo lowlands, 28 mi. SW of Encontrados. Petroleum drilling in the Tarra oil field, served by local railroad and by pipe line along Escalante R. (NE) to L. Maracaibo.

Lapaluoto, Finland: see RAAHE.

La Pampa (lä päm′pä), interior province (□ 55,103; pop. 169,480), central Argentina; ⊙ Santa Rosa. Low, grassy area (dry Pampa), sloping gradually E from Mendoza prov. border (NW). Bordered S by the Río Colorado, watered by Atuel R. and the Río Salado, which reach the central marshes. Contains a number of salt marshes and salt deposits. Climate is generally dry and temperate. Mostly stock raising (cattle, sheep, goats, horses). Agr. in N and E: barley, wheat, alfalfa, corn, oats, rye, sunflowers. In NE is lumbering of hardwood (cedar, carob, oak). Also salt mining, dairying. Meat packing at Santa Rosa; flour milling at Santa Rosa, General Pico, General San Martín. Established as a natl. territory 1884, became a province 1951.

La Panza Range (lä pŏn′sù), San Luis Obispo co., SW Calif., one of the Coast Ranges, extends c.30 mi. NW-SE bet. Santa Lucia Range (W) and Temblor Range (E); rises to 4,054 ft. 24 mi. E of San Luis Obispo.

La Para (lä pä′rä), town (pop. estimate 1,500), N Córdoba prov., Argentina, on the Río Primero near the Mar Chiquita, and 80 mi. NE of Córdoba; rail junction and agr. center. Wheat, flax, alfalfa, cotton; dairying, stock raising; meat-packing plant.

La Paragua (lä pärä′gwä), town (pop. 155), Bolívar state, SE Venezuela, on Paragua R. and 100 mi. SSE of Ciudad Bolívar (highway connection), in tropical forest region (gums); some rice growing. Formerly Barceloneta.

La Parida, Venezuela: see BOLÍVAR, CERRO.

Lapas (lä′pùsh), village (pop. 1,069), Santarém dist., central Portugal, a suburb of Torres Novas, 19 mi. NNE of Santarém; alcohol distilling.

Lapas, Las, Canary Isls.: see FRONTERA.

Lapataia (läpätī′ä), village, SW Tierra del Fuego natl. territory, Argentina, port on inlet of Beagle Channel, near Chile border, and 10 mi. W of Ushuaia. Small sheep-raising settlement.

La Paz, department, Argentina: see SAN ANTONIO, Catamarca prov.

La Paz (lù päz′, Sp. lä päs′). **1** Town (1947 pop. 15,138), ⊙ La Paz dept. (□ 2,685; 1947 pop. 57,698), NW Entre Ríos prov., Argentina, on Paraná R. and 80 mi. NE of Paraná; rail terminus, port, and agr. center (corn, oats, alfalfa, rice, olives, fruit, livestock). Lime factory, flour mills. Has theater, natl. col. Group of picturesque isls. in Paraná R. is popular resort area. **2** Town (pop. estimate 1,500), ⊙ La Paz dept. (□ 2,650; 1947 census 5,498), E Mendoza prov., Argentina, on Tunuyán R. (irrigation) and 85 mi. SE of Mendoza; rail junction, lumbering and farming center (fruit, wine, alfalfa, livestock); wine making.

La Paz, department (□ 51,605; 1949 pop. estimate 1,276,500), W Bolivia; ⊙ La Paz. Bordered W by Peru, in extreme SW by Chile. Includes E part of L. Titicaca. The Eastern Cordillera of the Andes (with its peaks ILLAMPU and ILLIMANI) crosses dept. NW-SE, separating the Altiplano or high plateau (S; 13,000–14,500 ft.) from the Yungas and tropical lowlands (N). The Altiplano is drained by Desaguadero R., tropical lowlands by Beni R. and its affluents, La Paz, Kaka, Tuichi, and Madidi rivers. Grain, potatoes, sheep and llama raised on plateau, tropical agr. (coffee, cacao, quina, coca, fruit) in lowlands. Rubber plantations along Beni and Madre de Dios rivers (N). Mining centers include Corocoro (copper), Cordillera de Tres Cruces (tin, tungsten, antimony), Tipuani R. (gold). Main industrial centers are La Paz and Viacha (rail junction), with rail connection to Arica (Chile) and rail-steamer service to Puno (Peru). Roads cross Eastern Cordillera into lowlands where river transportation prevails. Archaeological sites at Tiahuanaco and Titicaca and Coati isls.

La Paz, city (1949 pop. estimate 319,600), ⊙ La Paz dept., W Bolivia, on W slopes of Cordillera de La Paz, near Illimani peak, in canyon formed by La Paz R., and 50 mi. E of SE end of L. Titicaca, 200 mi. E of Pacific coast at Arica (Chile); 16°29'S 68°7'W. Highest large city in the world; alt. 11,909 ft. Although Sucre is legal ⊙ Bolivia, La Paz has been since c.1900 seat of govt. and de facto ⊙ Bolivia. Political and commercial center of Bolivia; head of railroads to Arica and Antofagasta (Chile), Villazón (Argentine border), Cochabamba, Potosí-Sucre, L. Titicaca, and the Yungas. Site of major Bolivian industries: tanning, brewing, distilling, flour milling, mfg. (textiles, shoes, pharmaceuticals, paper and cardboard goods, soap, furniture, silver articles, metalware). Chief trade center for agr. products of the Yungas (coca, bananas, oranges, coffee) and the Altiplano (potatoes, sheep, wool). In center of city are govt. palace (residence of the President), legislative palace (Congress), city hall, cathedral (bishopric). Has univ., public library, Tiahuanaco mus. of archaeology. Chief suburbs: Obrajes (SE); El Alto on the Altiplano (SW; alt. 13,395 ft.), site of rail station and airport, connected with La Paz by highway. City founded (1548) by Spaniards as a commercial center and named Nuestra Señora de La Paz; scene of several Indian revolts, including siege of 1781; center of revolutionary movement (1809–1824). City's full name changed (1827) to La Paz de Ayacucho in honor of decisive battle for independence. Because of better transportation facilities, La Paz developed more rapidly than Sucre.

La Paz, department (□ 1,247; 1950 pop. 56,341), SW Honduras, on Salvador border; ⊙ La Paz. Astride continental divide; includes Sierra de Guajiquiro (W), upper Goascorán R. valley (SE), upper Comayagua R. valley (NE). Coffee, wheat in highlands (Marcala, Opatoro), henequen (La Paz); cattle raising. Ropemaking, palm-hat mfg., ceramics are local industries. Main centers: La Paz (oriented toward Comayagua), Marcala (linked by road with La Esperanza). Formed 1869.

La Paz, city (pop. 3,681), ⊙ La Paz dept., SW Honduras, in Comayagua R. valley, 10 mi. SSW of Comayagua; 14°16'N 87°40'W; alt. 2,461 ft. Commercial center; ropemaking; henequen, coffee, livestock. Founded 1792; known as La Paz since 1851.

La Paz. 1 City (pop. 10,401), ⊙ Southern Territory, Lower California, NW Mexico, port at head of La Paz Bay on Gulf of California, 265 mi. NW of Mazatlán; 24°9'N 110°18'W. Pearl-fishing center; agr. (sugar cane, dates, corn, livestock); fish canning, tanning. Port of call for steamers running bet. Mazatlán and U.S. West Coast. Founded as Jesuit mission 1720. Captured briefly in 1853 by the Amer. filibuster William Walker. **2** Town (pop. 5,071), San Luis Potosí, N central Mexico, at E foot of Sierra Catorce, 5 mi. NW of Matehuala; rail terminus; mining center (silver, gold, copper, zinc).

La Paz or **La Paz de Oriente** (dā ōryĕn'tā), town (1950 pop. 921), Carazo dept., SW Nicaragua, 5 mi. ESE of Jinotepe, in sugar-cane zone.

La Paz. 1 Town (1939 pop. 2,228; 1948 municipality pop. 13,784), E Leyte, Philippines, 25 mi. S of Tacloban; agr. center (rice, coconuts, corn). **2** Town (1939 pop. 3,294; 1948 municipality pop. 18,395), Tarlac prov., central Luzon, Philippines, 10 mi. ESE of Tarlac; agr. center (coconuts, rice, sugar cane).

La Paz, department (□ 909; pop. 129,276), S Salvador, on the Pacific; ⊙ Zacatecoluca. Slopes from coastal range S to the Pacific; drained by Jiboa R. Includes part of L. Ilopango (NW) and SW slopes of volcano San Vicente (NE). Grain, livestock raising. Salt extraction (at Jaltepeque Lagoon) and hardwood lumbering are important. Main centers: Zacatecoluca, San Juan Nonualco, Santiago Nonualco; linked by road with San Salvador. Formed 1833. Scene of Nonualco Indian revolt, 1843.

Lapaz or **La Paz** (lŭpăz'), town (pop. 512), Marshall co., N Ind., 16 mi. S of South Bend, in agr. area.

La Paz (lä päs'). **1** Town, Canelones dept., S Uruguay, on railroad and 10 mi. N of Montevideo; winegrowing, granite quarrying. **2** Town (pop. 1,000), Colonia dept., SW Uruguay, urban nucleus of the COLONIA VALDENSE agr. settlement, 32 mi. ENE of Colonia. Sometimes Colonia Piamontesa, a name also applied to the Colonia Valdense.

La Paz, Cordillera de (kôrdĭyâ'rä dā lä päs'), highest range in the Eastern Cordillera of the Andes, W Bolivia; extends 170 mi. SE from Nudo de Apolobamba on Peru border to La Paz R. Rises to 21,490 ft. in the Ancohuma, a peak of the ILLAMPU. Tungsten deposits at SE ft. of peak Illimani. Also called Cordillera Real.

La Paz Bay, large sheltered, deep-water inlet of Gulf of California, on SE coast of Lower California, NW Mexico, bordered E by Espíritu Santo Isl.; 50 mi. long NW-SE, c.20 mi. wide. City of La Paz is at its head.

La Paz Central or **La Paz Centro** (lä päs' sĕnträl', –sĕn'trō), town (1950 pop. 3,527), León dept., W Nicaragua, near L. Managua, on railroad and 16 mi. SE of León; brick- and tile-making center; pottery mfg.; corn, sesame. Old town of La Paz Viejo is on railroad, 2 mi. NW.

La Paz de Oriente, Nicaragua: see LA PAZ.

La Paz River, La Paz dept., W Bolivia, rises in 2 branches (Choqueyapu and Chuquiaguillo rivers) on the Chacaltaya, 10 mi. N of La Paz; flows c.100 mi. SE and NE, through Eastern Cordillera of the Andes, past La Paz, Obrajes, and Mecapeca, joining Tamampaya R. 20 mi. ENE of Chulumani to form BOPI RIVER. Receives Palca R. (left), Luribay R. (right). Considered chief headstream of Beni R.

Lapeer (lŭpēr'), county (□659; pop. 35,794), E Mich.; ⊙ Lapeer. Drained by Flint and Belle rivers and by short Mill Creek. Stock raising, dairying, agr. (fruit, grain, sugar beets, beans, potatoes, celery, onions). Mfg. at Lapeer. Numerous small lakes. Organized 1833.

Lapeer, city (pop. 6,143), ⊙ Lapeer co., E Mich., 20 mi. E of Flint and on South Branch of Flint R., in dairying and grain-growing area; mfg. (foundry products, aircraft parts, furniture, insect exterminators). Has state home and school for mentally ill. Settled 1831, inc. as city 1869.

Lapeer Heights, village (pop. 1,722), Genesee co., SE central Mich.

Lapel (lŭpĕl'), town (pop. 1,389), Madison co., E central Ind., 26 mi. NE of Indianapolis, in livestock and grain area; canned goods, glass jars.

La Pelada (lä pālä'dä), town (pop. estimate 1,000), central Santa Fe prov., Argentina, 55 mi. NNW of Santa Fe; rail junction, agr. center (corn, flax, wheat, livestock, poultry).

La Peña (lä pā'nyä), village (pop. 792), Veraguas prov., W central Panama, near Inter-American Highway, 4 mi. NW of Santiago, in gold-mining area; sugar cane, livestock.

La Pérade, Que.: see SAINTE ANNE DE LA PÉRADE.

La Perla (lä pĕr'lä), town (pop. 819), Veracruz, E Mexico, at SE foot of Pico de Orizaba, 13 mi. WNW of Córdoba; fruit.

La Perla, Peru: see BELLAVISTA, Callao constitutional prov.

La Perouse, Mount (lă pŭrōōs') (10,750 ft.), SE Alaska, in Fairweather Range, near Gulf of Alaska, 100 mi. W of Juneau, in Glacier Bay Natl. Monument; 58°34'N 137°5'W.

La Perouse Pinnacle, T.H.: see FRENCH FRIGATE SHOAL.

La Pérouse Strait (lä pārōōz'), Rus. *Proliv La-peruza*, joins Sea of Japan (W) and Sea of Okhotsk (E); separates capes Soya and Noshappu of Hokkaido, Japan, and Cape Crillon of Sakhalin, Russian SFSR; 26 mi. wide, up to 220 ft. deep. Sometimes called Soya Strait, Jap. *Soya-kaikyo* (sō'yä-kīkyō').

Lapeza (läpā'thä), town (pop. 1,945), Granada prov., S Spain, 18 mi. ENE of Granada; olive oil, cereals, fruit, sugar beets.

Lapi, county, Finland: see LAPLAND.

La Piedad or **La Piedad Cavadas** (lä pyādädh' kävä'däs), city (pop. 12,369), Michoacán, central Mexico, on central plateau, on Lerma R. (Guanajuato border) and 90 mi. ESE of Guadalajara; mfg. and agr. center (cereals, sugar cane, fruit, vegetables, livestock); tanneries, rayon mills; mfg. (native shawls, sweets). Radio station. Railroad station 2½ mi. NNE.

Lapinin Island (läpēnēn') (1939 pop. 5,350), Bohol prov., Philippines, in Canigao Channel, just off NE coast of Bohol isl.; c.3 mi. long; 10°6'N 124°33'E. Flat, and fringed with mangrove trees. Coconut growing, fishing.

La Pintada (lä pēntä'dä), village (pop. 192), Coclé prov., central Panama, in Coclé Mts., 6 mi. NNW of Penonomé; road terminus; rice, corn, beans, livestock.

Lapithos (lä'pēthôs), town (pop. 3,327), Kyrenia dist., N Cyprus, near Mediterranean coast, 15 mi. NW of Nicosia; agr. center; citrus fruit, almonds, carobs, olive oil; sheep, goats. Reform school for juvenile delinquents.

Laplace (lŭpläs'), village (pop. 2,352), St. John the Baptist parish, SE La., on E bank (levee) of the Mississippi and 25 mi. WNW of New Orleans, in sugar-cane and truck-farming area.

La Plaine (lä plān'), village (pop. 464), SE Dominica, B.W.I., 10 mi. ENE of Roseau; limes. Agr. demonstration center.

Lapland (lăp'lănd"), Finnish *Lapi* or *Lappi* (both: läp'pē), Nor. *Lapland* (läp'län), Swedish *Lappland* (läp'länd), vast region of N Europe, on Barents Sea of Arctic Ocean, largely within the Arctic Circle. Bounded W by Norwegian Sea of the Atlantic, it covers N parts of Norway, Sweden, and Finland, and NW extremity of the USSR to E tip of Kola Peninsula. S limit of Lapp settlement or habitation is generally 65°N. Mountainous in Norway and Sweden, it becomes a lake-strewn tundra region in Finland and USSR. High mts. are Kebnekaise (6,965 ft.), Sweden, and Mt. Haltia (4,343 ft.), on Finnish-Norwegian border. Coast line is irregular and deeply indented by Lyng, Porsanger, and Varanger fjords (Norway), and by Kandalaksha Bay of the White Sea (USSR). Lapland is drained by Alta, Tana, Pats (Paz), and Tuloma rivers, emptying into Arctic Ocean, and by Lule, Kalix, Torne, Muonio, and Kemi rivers, emptying into Gulf of Bothnia. Lakes Imandra (USSR), Inari (Finland), and Torne (Sweden) are largest of the region. S part of Lapland, especially in Sweden and Finland, is densely forested (chiefly spruce, pine, and birch); toward N vegetation becomes progressively sparser and is generally confined to reindeer lichen. Rye, barley, and potatoes are grown in S Lapland; there is some cattle raising, but the reindeer is mainstay of Lapp economy, both as source of food and as pack animal. Fishing is important in coastal region and L. Inari, Finland; whitefish, trout, and redbelly form bulk of catch. Lapland is rich in minerals; iron mines at KIRUNA, Gallivare, and Malmberget (Sweden) are among the richest in the world; those in Sor-Varanger canton of Norway are also important. Copper pyrites are mined at Sulitjelma, Norway; nickel mines at Nikel and Salmiyarvi, in Pechenga region (USSR); apatite is worked at Kirovsk (USSR). Alluvial gold found in many rivers. Chief ports of Lapland are Narvik, Tromso, and Kirkenes (Norway), Lulea and Haparanda (Sweden); Tornio and Kemi (Finland), and Pechenga and Murmansk (USSR). Railroads include Swedish iron-ore line bet. Lulea and Narvik, serving Gallivare and Kiruna, with connection to Stockholm, and to Finland via Haparanda and Tornio. Finnish Arctic Highway (330 mi. long) bet. Rovaniemi and Pechenga, was completed 1929. Norwegian Lapland also has road connection with railhead at Lonsdal. Murmansk is USSR rail terminus. All larger rivers in Lapland are transportation and logging routes. Indigenous pop. consists of c.30,000 Lapps or Lapplanders; the majority is concentrated in Norway, where they are called Finns. While most Lapps are nomads who follow their reindeer herds, wintering in the lowlands and summering in the mts. and on isls. off NW Norway, many Lapps are settled in villages, especially fisher Lapps. Lapp language belongs to W division of Finno-Ugric branch of the Uralic group. Language is subdivided into several geographically-defined dialects; among these are Norwegian Lappish, Lule Lappish (Lulea region of Sweden), and Kola Lappish (Kola Peninsula, USSR). It is believed that the Lapps came from central Asia and are closely related to the Samoyeds. In prehistoric times region settled by Lapps covered most of present Finland and N Russia, extending E to L. Onega. They were pushed to N extremity of Europe by migrations of the Finns, Scandinavians, and Slavs. In the 14th cent. trade with Lapland was opened up by Finnish traders, especially those from Pirkkala. Creation of new national boundaries hindered Lapps' traditional annual migrations and their special rights in this respect were not recognized until end of 19th cent. Nominally conquered by Swedes and Norwegians in Middle Ages, Christianization of Lapps was begun (13th cent.) by Norwegians. For a short time in 16th and 17th cent. Swedish kings held title of "King of the Lapps," renounced (1613) by Gustavus II. In 18th cent. a literary Lapp language was created by Swedes; spoken Lapp was codified (1780) in the Swedish *Lexicon Lapponicum.* Though Christianization of Lapland was generally completed by 18th cent. through efforts of Scandinavian and Russian missionaries, Shamanism and pagan rites survived until late 19th cent. Bear hunting was, until recently, one of chief Lapp ceremonial occasions, and the bear is object of many important taboos; among others, circumscriptions are used when speaking of it. Administratively, Lapland is divided into Norwegian counties of FINNMARK, TROMS, and N part of NORDLAND; Swedish prov. [Swedish *landskap*] of Lappland (□ 42,349; pop. 126,521), which is included in counties of Vasterbotten and Norrbotten; Finnish co. [Finnish *lääni*] of Lapi or Lappi (□ 38,274; pop. 162,698), ⊙ Rovaniemi, created (1938) in N part of Oulu co.; and MURMANSK oblast, Russian SFSR.

La Plata (lä plä'tä), city (pop. 217,738), ⊙ Buenos Aires prov. and La Plata dist. (□ 455; pop. 303,633), Argentina, 35 mi. SE of Buenos Aires, 5 mi. inland from ENSENADA, its suburban port on the Río de la Plata; 34°55'S 57°58'W. Administrative, commercial, and industrial center; meat packing, cold storage, petroleum refining; cement works, textile-, flour-, and sawmills. Exports *pampa* products (grain, meat, wool) through Ensenada. A modern, well-planned city, it is laid out in form of a 3-mi. square centered on Plaza Moreno (site of cathedral). Parks (NE) include the Parque Iraola, which contains zoological gardens, observatory, mus. of natural history (noted for ethnological and paleontological collections). Govt. bldgs. include govt. palace, legislature, and ministry of treasury. City has univ., natl. col., natl. library, and prov. mus. of fine arts. Its suburbs include Ensenada, BERISSO, Tolosa (N outskirts; residential), and bathing resort of Punta Lara (20 mi. NNW). Founded 1882 as provincial capital after Buenos Aires had been federalized (1880) as natl. capital.

La Plata, Bolivia: see SUCRE.

La Plata, town (pop. 1,897), Huila dept., S central Colombia, on affluent of upper Magdalena R., in E foothills of Cordillera Central, and 55 mi. SW of Neiva; alt. 3,458 ft. Cacao, coffee, rice, silk, livestock. Silver mines, worked since pre-Sp. days.

La Plata (lù plä'tù), county (□ 1,689; pop. 14,880), SW Colo.; ⊙ Durango. Livestock-grazing area, bordering on N.Mex.; bounded W by La Plata Mts.; drained by Animas R. and branches of San Juan R. Gold, silver, lead, and coal mines near Durango. Includes parts of San Juan and Montezuma natl. forests. Formed 1874.

La Plata. 1 (lù plă'tù) Town (pop. 780), ⊙ Charles co. (since 1895), S Md., 25 mi. S of Washington; tobacco market, with large warehouses. Near by is "La Grange," built in 1760s. **2** (lù plā'tù) City (pop. 1,331), Macon co., N central Mo., 20 mi. N of Macon; grain, dairy cattle, poultry. Laid out 1855.

La Plata Island, off Pacific coast of Manabí prov., W Ecuador, 20 mi. SW of Cape San Lorenzo; 1°20'S 81°5'W.

La Plata Mountains (lù plä'tù), SW Colo. and NW N.Mex., spur of San Juan Mts. extending N-S bet. La Plata and Animas rivers. Highest points: Helmet Peak (11,976 ft.), HESPERUS PEAK (13,225 ft.). Gold, silver, coal mined.

La Plata Peak (14,342 ft.), central Colo., in Sawatch Mts., 18 mi. SW of Leadville.

La Plata River, Argentina and Uruguay: see PLATA, RÍO DE LA.

La Plata River or **Río de la Plata** (rē'ō dā lä plä'tä), E central Puerto Rico, rises in the Sierra de Cayey S of Caguas, flows c.45 mi. NW and N, past Comerío, Toa Alta, Toa Baja, and Dorado, to the Atlantic 9 mi. W of San Juan. Near its source is the artificial L. Carite, the water of which is diverted to S coast, serving 3 hydroelectric plants N of Guayama.

La Plata River (lù plä'tù), in SW Colo. and NW N.Mex., rises in La Plata Mts., Colo.; flows c.70 mi. S to San Juan R. just W of Farmington, N.Mex.

Lapleau (läplō'), agr. village (pop. 402), Corrèze dept., S central France, 9 mi. WNW of Mauriac. Dam (295 ft. high, 902 ft. long) and hydroelectric plant of L'Aigle 4 mi. SE on the Dordogne.

Laplume (läplüm'), village (pop. 423), Lot-et-Garonne dept., SW France, 8 mi. SSW of Agen; wine, grains, tobacco.

La Pointe (lù point'), fishing village (pop. c.200), SW Madeline Isl., in APOSTLE ISLANDS, Ashland co., N Wis., on narrow channel of L. Superior, on W side of entrance to Chequamegon Bay. A French fortified trading post was built here in 1693, evacuated 1698, and reoccupied 1718–59. In early-19th cent., site of an American Fur Company post.

La Poma (lä pō'mä), village (pop. estimate 500), ⊙ La Poma dept. (□ 1,770; 1947 pop. 1,833), W central Salta prov., Argentina, on Calchaquí R. and 50 mi. WNW of Salta, in grain and livestock area; flour milling.

La Porte (lù pôrt'), county (□ 608; pop. 76,808) NW Ind., bounded NW by L. Michigan, N by Mich. line, partly S by Kankakee R.; ⊙ La Porte. Resorts on L. Michigan and other lakes in co. Mfg. especially at Michigan City and La Porte; agr. (grain, livestock); lake shipping; fisheries; timber. Formed 1832.

La Porte. 1 City (1950 pop. 17,882; 1951 special census pop. 20,414), ⊙ La Porte co., NW Ind., on Pine L. (c.1¼ mi. long), 33 mi. E of Gary; produces industrial and farm machinery, road-building materials, furniture, metal doors, auto equipment, heating and ventilating equipment, baby carriages, woolen goods, clothing, shoes, florists' supplies. Has U.S. ordnance plant. Resort, with many lakes near by; timber. Settled 1830; inc. as town in 1835, as city in 1852. **2** Town (pop. 4,429), Harris co., S Texas, 21 mi. ESE of Houston near Houston Ship Channel and Galveston Bay. Summer resort; oil wells, refineries; insecticide plant. Settled 1889, inc. 1892.

Laporte (lùpôrt'). **1** Village (pop. c.250), Larimer co., N Colo., in lake region E of Front Range, 4 mi. NW of Fort Collins; alt. 5,069 ft.; supply point. Cement plant near by. **2** Resort village (pop. 189), Hubbard co., N central Minn., near Leech L. and Leech Lake Indian Reservation, 20 mi. SSE of Bemidji, in grain and potato area. **3** Resort borough (pop. 199), ⊙ Sullivan co., NE Pa., 32 mi. ENE of Williamsport, in mts.

La Porte City, town (pop. 1,770), Black Hawk co., E central Iowa, on Wolf Creek near its mouth on Cedar R., and 15 mi. SSE of Waterloo; canned tomatoes and corn, dairy products, feed, concrete blocks. Limestone quarry near by. Inc. 1871.

Laposbanya, Rumania: see BAITA.

Lapoutroie (läpōōtrwä'), Ger. *Schnierlach* (shnēr'läkh), village (pop. 1,003), Haut-Rhin dept., E France, in the Vosges, 10 mi. NW of Colmar, on road to Col du Bonhomme (W); cotton milling, alcohol and cheese mfg. Formerly spelled La Poutroye.

Lapovo (lä'pôvô), village (pop. 7,512), central Serbia, Yugoslavia, 15 mi. NE of Kragujevac, near the Morava; rail junction. Silk growing in vicinity.

Lappa (läp'pä), Chinese *Kungpeh* or *Kungpei* (gōōng'bā'), town, S Kwangtung prov., China, port on Lappa isl., just W of Macao (across channel of Canton R. delta); commercial center. Opened to foreign trade in 1871.

Lappeenranta (läp'pānrän"tä), Swedish *Villmanstrand* (vĭl"mänstränd'), city (pop. 16,362), Kymi co., SE Finland, near USSR border, on S shore of L. Saimaa, 60 mi. NE of Kotka, 30 mi. NW of Vyborg; lake port and industrial center, with chemical, lime, and cement works, lumber and cellulose mills, machinery works. Health resort. Has church (1794). Its economic importance dates from Middle Ages. Destroyed (1741) by Russians; passed to Russia (1743) and became important border fortress. Formerly called Lapperanda.

Lappi, county, Finland: see LAPLAND.

Lappland, province, Sweden: see LAPLAND.

Lappo, Finland: see LAPUA.

Laprairie (läprâ'rē), county (□ 170; pop. 13,730), S Que., on the St. Lawrence, just S of Montreal; ⊙ Laprairie.

Laprairie, town (pop. 2,936), ⊙ Laprairie co., S Que., on the St. Lawrence, near E end of the Lachine Rapids, opposite Montreal; brick mfg., fruit canning and freezing; truck gardening. Settled 1673, it was site of fort built by Frontenac; attacked (1691) by New Englanders under Peter Schuyler. First railroad in Canada was built (1836) to St. Jean.

La Prairie (lù prâ'rē). **1** Village (pop. 142), Adams co., W Ill., 26 mi. ENE of Quincy, in agr. area. **2** Village (pop. 88), Itasca co., N central Minn., on Mississippi R. and just E of Grand Rapids, in grain area.

Laprida (läprē'dä). **1** Town (pop. 3,246), ⊙ Laprida dist. (□ 1,334; pop. 8,584), S central Buenos Aires prov., Argentina, 50 mi. SSW of Olavarría; agr. center: oats, wheat, sheep, cattle; flour milling. **2** Village, San Juan prov., Argentina: see LA HUERTA.

La Protección, Honduras: see PROTECCIÓN.

La Providence, Que.: see PROVIDENCE, LA.

La Providencia (lä prōvēdĕn'syä), village (pop. estimate 200), central Buenos Aires prov., Argentina, 9 mi. SSE of Olavarría; railhead and limestone-quarrying center.

Laprugne (läprü'nyù), village (pop. 348), Allier dept., central France, in the Bois Noirs, 13 mi. NE of Thiers; copper mining; mineral springs.

La Pryor (lù prī'ùr), village (1940 pop. 863), Zavala co., SW Texas, 18 mi. N of Crystal City, in spinach-growing area; also ships asphalt.

Lapseki (lăp'sĕkē"), Turkish *Lâpseki*, anc. *Lampsacus*, village (pop. 3,384), Canakkale prov., NW Turkey in Asia, on E shore of Dardanelles, opposite Gallipoli, 20 mi. NE of Canakkale; coal, iron, lead deposits; cereals, lentils. Formerly also Lapsaki.

Laptevo (läp'tyĭvŭ), town (1926 pop. 654), N Tula oblast, Russian SFSR, 19 mi. N of Tula; agr.-machine mfg.

Laptev Sea (läp'tyĭf), Rus. *More Laptevykh*, section of Arctic Ocean, in Russian SFSR; bounded S by coast of E Siberia, W by Severnaya Zemlya, N by border of continental shelf (c.80°N lat.) to 139°E long., E by New Siberian Isls. Receives Khatanga, Anabar, Olenek, Lena, and Yana rivers. Up to 330 ft. deep; navigable only during ice-free Aug.-Sept. Main ports: Nordvik, Tiksi. Named for Khariton and Dmitri (or Dmitriy) Laptev, 18th-cent. Rus. navigators. Formerly called Nordenskjöld or Nordenskiöld Sea [Rus. *More Nordenshelda*], named for 19th-cent. Swedish explorer.

Laptev Strait, Russia: see DMITRI LAPTEV STRAIT.

Lapua (lä'pōō-ä), Swedish *Lappo* (lä'pō), village (commune pop. 15,871), Vaasa co., W Finland, on 100-mi.-long Lapua R., Finnish *Lapuan joki*, 45 mi. E of Vaasa; metalworking; lumbering region. Near by is scene (1808) of Finnish victory over Russians.

La Puerta (lä pwĕr'tä). **1** Village (pop. estimate 600), ⊙ Ambato dept. (□ 933; pop. 3,667), SE Catamarca prov., Argentina, on the Río del Valle and 22 mi. N of Catamarca; mixed farming; lime pit. **2** Town (pop. estimate 1,500), N Córdoba prov., Argentina, 75 mi. NE of Córdoba; wheat, flax, corn, cotton, peanuts; stock raising, dairying.

La Puerta, town (pop. 640), Trujillo state, W Venezuela, in Andean spur, 16 mi. SSW of Valera, on highway; alt. 5,768 ft.; wheat, corn, potatoes.

La Punta (lä pōōn'tä), village (pop. estimate 500), SW Santiago del Estero prov., Argentina, at S foot of Sierra de Guasayán, on railroad and 50 mi. SW of Santiago del Estero. Stock-raising and lumbering center; gypsum works.

La Punta, W suburb (pop. 3,589) of Callao, W central Peru, situated on spit of land stretching out into the Pacific, 2 mi. W of Callao (linked by electric trains). Fashionable bathing resort. Seat of naval school.

Lapurdum, France: see BAYONNE.

La Purga, Mexico: see MANLIO FABIO ALTAMIRANO.

La Purísima (lä pōōrē'sēmä), town (pop. 598), Southern Territory, Lower California, NW Mexico, in valley 180 mi. NW of La Paz; some agr. (grain, livestock).

La Purisima Concepcion, Mission, Calif.: see LOMPOC.

Lapush (lùpōōsh'), fishing village, Clallam co., NW Wash., on Pacific coast, at mouth of Quillayute R. and 25 mi. S of Cape Flattery; hq. of Quillayute Indian Reservation.

Lapushna (lä'pōōshnŭ), Rum. *Lăpuşna* (lùpōōsh'nä), village (1941 pop. 3,714), W Moldavian SSR, 22 mi. WSW of Kishinev; wine, corn.

Lapusna, department, Rumania: see KISHINEV.

Lapusna, village, Moldavian SSR: see LAPUSHNA.

Lapwai (lăp'wā), village (pop. 480), Nez Perce co., W Idaho, 10 mi. E of Lewiston; trade center and agency hq. for Coeur d'Alene and Nez Perce Indian reservations in Idaho, and for Kalispel Indian Reservation in Wash. Sanitarium and school are here.

Lapy (wä'pĭ), Pol. *Łapy*, town (pop. 4,842), Bialystok prov., NE Poland, on Narew R. and 15 mi. SW of Bialystok; rail junction (repair shops).

La Quebrada (lä kābrä'dä), town (pop. 525), Trujillo state, W Venezuela, in Andean spur, 10 mi. SSE of Valera; alt. 4,659 ft.; wheat, corn, potatoes.

La Quemada, Mexico: see QUEMADA.

Laqueville (läkvēl'), village (pop. 220), Puy-de-Dôme dept., central France, in Monts Dore, 19 mi. WSW of Clermont-Ferrand; blue cheese.

La Quiaca (lä kēä'kä), town (1947 pop. 6,722), ⊙ Yaví dept. (□ 1,330; 1947 pop. 13,113), N Jujuy prov., Argentina, on Bolivia border opposite Villazón across a small stream, 155 mi. NNW of Jujuy; alt. 11,300 ft. Customhouse. Trade and mining center, with ocher and antimony deposits. Meteorological station.

Laquinhorn (läkvēn'hôrn), peak (13,036 ft.) in Pennine Alps, S Switzerland, 11 mi. S of Brig.

Lar (lär), town (pop. 6,356), Gorakhpur dist., E Uttar Pradesh, India, 50 mi. SSE of Gorakhpur; trades in rice, wheat, barley, oilseeds, sugar cane.

Lar (lär), town (1940 pop. 13,010), Seventh Prov., S Iran, 170 mi. SE of Shiraz and Shiraz–Bandar Abbas road; main town of Laristan; tobacco, cotton, dates, mustard seed.

Lara (lä'rä), inland state (□ 7,640; 1941 pop. 332,975; 1950 census 370,030), N Venezuela; ⊙ BARQUISIMETO. Mountainous region, containing NE section of great Andean spur (S), outliers of coastal range (E), and arid Segovia Highlands. Drained by Tocuyo R. Climate dry and tropical, with rains generally in fall. Predominantly agr. region, producing coffee, cacao, sugar cane, corn, cotton, tobacco, bananas, sisal; and wheat, barley, potatoes at higher altitudes. Cattle grazing on well-watered plains around Carora, goat grazing in arid uplands.

Larache (lärä'chä), Arabic *El Araish* (ĕl ärīsh'), city (pop. 41,286), ⊙ Lucus territory (□ 1,202; 1945 pop. 233,997), W Sp. Morocco, port on the Atlantic at mouth of Lucus R., 45 mi. SSW of Tangier; 35°12'N 6°10'W. Spanish Morocco's 2d-largest city (after Tetuán) and terminus of rail spur (narrow gauge) from Alcazarquivir (20 mi. SE). Commercial center for irrigated Lucus R. valley (orchards, truck gardens). Ships grain, skins, wool, fruit, hardwoods. Boat-building yards. Harbor obstructed by sand bar. The crowded old dist. has a 16th-cent. castle and a picturesque market square. Ruins of anc. *Lixus*, a Phoenician settlement and later a Roman colony, are 2 mi. NE, on right bank of the Lucus. City was held by Spaniards 1610–89, until recaptured by Sultan Ismail. Under Sp. protectorate since 1912. One fourth of city's pop. is Spanish.

Laragne (lärä'nyù), village (pop. 1,376), Hautes-Alpes dept., SE France, on the Buëch and 10 mi. NW of Sisteron; brickworks; flour milling, lavender essence distilling; sericulture, orchards.

Larak, Iran: see LARK.

La Ramada (lä rämä'dä), town (pop. estimate 700), NE Tucumán prov., Argentina, on railroad and 20 mi. NE of Tucumán; lumbering and agr. center (corn, sugar cane, livestock).

La Ramada, town (pop. c.4,600), Cochabamba dept., central Bolivia, on S slopes of Cordillera de Cochabamba, on road and 8 mi. E of Tapacarí; barley, corn; livestock.

Laramie (lă'rùmē), county (□ 2,703; pop. 47,662), SE Wyo.; ⊙ Cheyenne. Agr. area bordering on Colo. and Nebr.; watered by Chugwater, Horse, and Lodgepole creeks. Livestock, grain, sugar beets. Formed 1867.

Laramie, city (pop. 15,581), ⊙ Albany co., SE Wyo., on Laramie R., W of Laramie Mts., and 42 mi. WNW of Cheyenne; alt. 7,145 ft. Transportation and industrial center in cattle and sheep region; railroad repair shops; cement, bricks and tiles, timber. Settled 1868 with arrival of railroad, inc. 1874. City grew with development of livestock industry. It was early advocate of woman suffrage, allowing women to serve (1870) on juries. Hq. of Medicine Bow Natl. Forest, seat of Univ. of Wyo. Points of interest: St. Matthews Cathedral (Protestant), newspaper office used by Edgar Wilson (Bill) Nye, humorist and editor. Near by are agr. experiment station of state univ., Sheep Mtn. Game Refuge, and site of Fort Sanders, established 1866 to protect travelers on Overland stage route and workers on Union Pacific RR.

Laramie, Fort, Wyo.: see FORT LARAMIE.

Laramie Basin, Wyo.: see LARAMIE PLAINS.

Laramie Mountains, a range of the Rockies, N extension of Front Range, Colo.; reach into SE Wyo. as far as Casper and N.Platte R.; flank Laramie Plains on E and NE. Highest point, Laramie Peak (10,274 ft.).

Laramie Peak (10,274 ft.), highest point in Laramie Mts., SE Wyo., 65 mi. N of Laramie.

Laramie Plains or **Laramie Basin** (7–8,000 ft.), in Albany and Carbon counties, SE Wyo.; high plateau drained by Medicine Bow and Laramie rivers; bounded E and NE by Laramie Mts., W by Medicine Bow Mts.; cattle-grazing area.

Laramie River, in N Colo. and SE Wyo., rises in Front Range, Colo., flows 216 mi. N and NE, past Laramie, Wyo., through Laramie Plains and Wheatland reservoirs, to N.Platte R. at Fort Laramie. Supplies water to Cache la Poudre R. in N Colo. through Laramie-Poudre, or Greeley-Poudre, Tunnel (c.2 mi. long; finished 1911), unit in irrigation project.

Laranda, Turkey: see KARAMAN.

Laranjal Paulista (lŏorāzhäl' poulē'stŏŏ), city (pop. 3,170), S central São Paulo, Brazil, on railroad and 21 mi. SSW of Piracicaba; mfg. of pottery and agr. implements, distilling; agr. (coffee, sugar, fruit). Until 1944, Laranjal.

Laranjeiras (lŏorāzhā'rŏŏs). **1** City, Paraíba, Brazil: see ALAGOA NOVA. **2** City (pop. 4,007), E Sergipe, NE Brazil, on Cotingüiba R., on railroad and 12 mi. NW of Aracaju; sugar-growing and -milling center. Ships sugar, coffee, cotton, salt.

Laranjeiras do Sul (dŏŏ sōōl'), city (pop. 638), SW central Paraná, Brazil, on road, and 50 mi. W of Guarapuava; maté collecting, cattle raising. Until 1944, called Laranjeiras; and, 1944–48, Iguaçu. Was ⊙ Iguaçu territory, 1943–46.

Larantoeka, Indonesia: see FLORES.

Larantuka, Indonesia: see FLORES.

Laraos (lärä'ōs), town (pop. 1,023), Lima dept., W central Peru, in Cordillera Occidental, 12 mi. ENE of Yauyos; weaving of native textiles; grain, potatoes, livestock.

Larap (läräp'), town (1939 pop. 7,773) in Jose Pañganiban municipality, Camarines Norte prov., SE Luzon, Philippines, just W of Jose Pañganiban, 55 mi. NW of Naga, at base of small peninsula in Philippine Sea; iron-mining center.

Laraquete (lärākā'tā), village (1930 pop. 234), Concepción prov., S central Chile, minor port on Pacific coast, on railroad and 26 mi. SSW of Concepción; swimming and fishing resort.

Larat, Indonesia: see TANIMBAR ISLANDS.

Larbert (lär'bŭrt), town and parish (pop. 13,028), E Stirling, Scotland, 3 mi. NW of Falkirk; coal mining, steel milling.

Larche (lärsh), village (pop. 401), Corrèze dept., S central France, in Brive Basin, on the Vézère and 6 mi. WSW of Brive-la-Gaillarde; metalworks.

Larche Pass: see MADDALENA PASS.

Larchmont (lärch'mŏnt"), suburban residential village (pop. 6,330), Westchester co., SE N.Y., on harbor on Long Island Sound, bet. New Rochelle (SW) and Mamaroneck; yachting center (annual regattas). Mfg.: furniture, metal products. Joyce Kilmer lived here. Developed c.1845, inc. 1891.

Larch River, N Que., issues from Lower Seal Lakes, just N of Clearwater L., flows 270 mi. NE to confluence with Kaniapiskau R., 50 mi. SW of Fort Chimo, here forming Koksoak R., which flows NE to Ungava Bay. Numerous rapids.

Larchwood, town (pop. 415), Lyon co., extreme NW Iowa, near Minn. line, 13 mi. W of Rock Rapids. State park and site of large Indian village are near by.

Lardal (lôr'däl), Nor. *Lårdal*, village and canton (pop. 1,466), Telemark co., S Norway, on Bandak lake, 55 mi. WNW of Skien; cattle breeding. Molybdenite mine at Dalen, 6 mi. WNW of village. Tourist hotels. Quarries in vicinity. Lastein, ½ mi. E of Dalen, is NW extremity of Bandak-Norsja Canal. Sometimes spelled Laardal.

Larderello (lärdĕrĕl'lō), village (pop. 352), Pisa prov., Tuscany, central Italy, on small affluent of Cecina R. and 12 mi. S of Volterra. Has *soffioni* used to produce boric acid and electricity. Factories, badly damaged in Second World War, have been repaired.

Larder Lake, town (pop. 1,464), E Ont., on Larder L., 45 mi. N of Haileybury; gold mining. Inc. 1938.

Lardero (lär-dhā'rō), village (pop. 1,101), Logroño prov., N Spain, 3 mi. S of Logroño; fruit, olive oil, wine, vegetables, cattle, sheep.

Lardier, Cape (lärdyā'), on the Mediterranean, in Var dept., SE France, formed by a spur of Monts des Maures, 8 mi. S of Saint-Tropez; 43°10'N 6°37'E.

Lardin, Le (lŭ lärdē'), village (pop. 547), Dordogne dept., SW France, on Vézère R. and 15 mi. W of Brive-la-Gaillarde; paper mill.

Lardizábal, Mexico: see TEPETITLA.

L'Ardoise (lärdwäz'), fishing village (pop. estimate 450), E N.S., on S coast of Cape Breton Isl. 30 mi. E of Port Hawkesbury. In mid-18th cent. it was important center of Acadian fishing and slate-quarrying region, with active fur trade. Zinc is mined near by.

Lardosa (lärdō'zŭ), village (pop. 1,472), Castelo Branco dist., central Portugal, on railroad and 12 mi. NNE of Castelo Branco; grain, corn, olives, horse beans.

Larecaja, Bolivia: see SORATA, town.

Laredo (lärā'dō), village (pop. 4,952), Libertad dept., NW Peru, on irrigated coastal plain, on railroad and 4 mi. ENE of Trujillo; sugar-milling center; distilling.

Laredo, town (pop. 4,881), Santander prov., N Spain, fishing and ore-shipping port on Bay of Biscay, 20 mi. E of Santander; fish processing (salmon, sardines, anchovies), boatbuilding, sawmilling; chemical works. Corn, potatoes, lemons, cattle in area. Bathing resort.

Laredo (lŭrā'dō). **1** City (pop. 426), Grundy co., N Mo., 10 mi. ESE of Trenton. **2** Village (pop. c.150), Hill co., N Mont., on branch of Milk R. and 12 mi. SW of Havre; grain-shipping point; livestock. **3** City (pop. 51,910), ⊙ Webb co., SW Texas, on the Rio Grande (bridged) opposite Nuevo Laredo, Mexico, and c.140 mi. SSW of San Antonio. An important port of entry, internatl. commercial center, and tourist gateway, connected by rail and the Inter-American Highway (opened 1936) with Mexico City (570 mi. S). Center for ranching, irrigated agr. area (cattle, truck, fruit), with oil and natural-gas wells; city has oil refinery, antimony smelter, foundries, meat-packing plant, canneries; mfg. of hats, brooms, Mex. novelties, clothing, brick; railroad shops. Seat of a jr. col., occupying former Fort McIntosh (1849). Holds annual Pan-American Fair and internatl. celebration of Washington's birthday. Founded in 1750s as Sp. settlement; grew as port on road to Texas settlements; held by Mexico after Texas Revolution, area was disputed until cession to U.S. after Mexican War. With coming of railroads in 1880s, city's commercial importance began; later, irrigated farming (in 1890s) and discovery of gas (1908) and oil (1921) caused further growth.

La Reforma (lä rāfōr'mä), town (1950 pop. 300), San Marcos dept., SW Guatemala, in Pacific piedmont, 10 mi. S of San Marcos; alt. 3,800 ft., coffee, sugar cane, grain, livestock.

La Reforma, Mexico: see REFORMA.

La Reina, Nicaragua: see SAN RAMÓN.

Laren (lä'rŭn), village (pop. 11,076), North Holland prov., W central Netherlands, 3 mi. NE of Hilversum; residential area, with lumber mills; agr.

Lares (lä'rĕs), town (pop. 581), Cuzco dept., S central Peru, on upper Urubamba R. and 15 mi. N of Cuzco, in agr. region (coca, cacao, sugar cane); thermal spring. Silver mines near by. N is the Lares Pass (14,711 ft.).

Lares, town (pop. 3,836), W Puerto Rico, on Guajataca R. and 15 mi. SW of Arecibo; alt. 1,125 ft.; coffee center; resort.

Largeau (lärzhō'), town, ⊙ Borkou-Ennedi-Tibesti region (□ 223,175; 1950 pop. 41,800), N Chad territory, Fr. Equatorial Africa, 480 mi. NE of Fort-Lamy; 17°30'N 19°E. Military outpost and oasis in SE Sahara; desert road junction; dates, millet. Also known as Faya.

Largentière (lärzhãtyâr'), village (pop. 1,228), Ardèche dept., S France, 7 mi. SW of Aubenas; silk throwing and spinning, winegrowing.

Largo, parish (pop. 2,299), SE Fifeshire, Scotland. Includes LOWER LARGO and UPPER LARGO.

Largo (lär'gō), city (pop. 1,547), Pinellas co., W Fla., 3 mi. S of Clearwater; packs and ships citrus fruit.

Largo, Cayo (kī'ō lär'gō), narrow islet (15 mi. long NE–SW), off S Cuba, on Jardines Bank, 65 mi. WSW of Cienfuegos.

Largs (lärgz), burgh (1931 pop. 6,134; 1951 census 8,606), N Ayrshire, Scotland, on Firth of Clyde, 11 mi. SSW of Greenock; 55°48'N 4°54'W; port, agr. market, and seaside resort. In Firth of Clyde, 2 mi. W, is GREAT CUMBRAE ISLAND. At battle of Largs (1263) Alexander III of Scotland defeated attempted invasion of Scotland by Haakon IV of Norway. Sir Thomas Brisbane b. in near-by Brisbane House.

Lari (lä'rē), village (pop. 1,032), Pisa prov., Tuscany, central Italy, 14 mi. SE of Pisa; macaroni mfg.; marble quarrying.

Larimer (lă'rĭmŭr), county (□ 2,619; pop. 43,554), N Colo.; ⊙ Fort Collins. Irrigated agr. area, bordering on Wyo.; drained by Cache la Poudre and Laramie rivers. Sugar beets, beans, livestock. Includes part of Rocky Mtn. Natl. Park in SW and of Front Range in W. Roosevelt Natl. Forest extends throughout. Feature of irrigation system is Laramie-Poudre, or Greeley-Poudre, Tunnel, connecting Laramie and Cache la Poudre rivers; used to irrigate 125,000 acres in Larimer and Weld counties. Formed 1861.

Larimer, village (pop. 1,057), Westmoreland co., SW Pa., 15 mi. SE of Pittsburgh.

Larimna, Greece: see LARYMNA.

Larimore, city (pop. 1,374), Grand Forks co., E N.Dak., 28 mi. W of Grand Forks; dairy, poultry products, livestock, grain, potatoes. Inc. 1883.

Laringovi, Greece: see ARNAIA.

Larino (lärē'nō), town (pop. 4,872), Campobasso prov., Abruzzi e Molise, S central Italy, 21 mi. NNE of Campobasso; macaroni, flour, olive oil, wine. Bishopric. Has cathedral (completed 1319) and several palaces. Near by are ruins (amphitheater) of anc. Larinum.

Larino (lä'rēnŭ), town (1939 pop. over 500), central Stalino oblast, Ukrainian SSR, in the Donbas, 8 mi. SE (under jurisdiction) of Stalino; limestone quarries; building materials.

Larinski, Russian SFSR: see NEVER.

La Rioja (lä ryō'hä), province (□ 35,691; pop. 110,746), W Argentina; ⊙ La Rioja. Bounded NW by the Andes where it borders Chile. Drained by headwaters of Bermejo R. On E border is the Salinas Grandes. Contains the Sierra Punilla (W), Sierra de Famatina (N), Sierra de Velasco (center), and Sierra de los Llanos (SE). The fertile, inhabited valleys enjoy Mediterranean climate. Among its mineral resources are zinc and lead (Guandacol), copper, silver, nickel, gold (Sierra de Famatina, Cumbre de la Mejicana), tungsten (Sierra de Velasco), barium sulphate (Nonogasta), coal (Sierra de Velasco). Agr. activity in irrigated subandean valleys (Vinchina, Famatina, Guandacol): alfalfa, corn, wine, wheat, olives, citrus fruit, cotton; stock raising, primarily of goats. Lumbering (quebracho, carob) in lower mtn. areas (center and SE). Rural industries: mining, charcoal burning, lumbering, flour milling, wine making. Mfg.: olive oil (Aimogasta), plaster (Chamical), wine (Nonogasta), canned food (Chilecito), textiles (La Rioja). Major resort is Chilecito in S Famatina Valley. Separated from Córdoba prov. in 1816.

La Rioja, town (pop. 23,164), ⊙ La Rioja prov. and La Rioja dept. (□ 5,770; 1947 pop. 26,924), W Argentina, on the small Rioja R. at E foot of Sierra de Velasco, on railroad and 90 mi. SW of Catamarca, 600 mi. NW of Buenos Aires; 29°24'S 66°53'W; alt. 1,620 ft. Farming, lumbering, and trading center. Sawmills, textile mills. Agr. products: olives, fruit, grain, livestock. An old colonial city, founded 1591, it has modern administrative bldgs., natl. col., archaeological mus., seismographic station. Severely damaged by earthquake in 1894. The dam on the Rioja, completed in 1930 and irrigating and supplying power to the area, is near by.

Larisa, Greece: see LARISSA.

Larissa or **Larisa** (lŭrĭ'sŭ, Gr. lä'rēsŭ), nome (□ 2,080; pop. 190,080), E Thessaly, Greece; ⊙ Larissa. Bounded N by Olympus and Kamvounia mts., and extending S to the Orthys, it contains the fertile Larissa lowland drained by Peneus R. Its 30-mi.-long Aegean coast line, astride Mt. Ossa, is devoid of ports. Agr.: wheat, vegetables, tobacco, olives, almonds, citrus fruit; livestock raising. Chromite mining E of Pharsala. Traversed by Salonika-Athens RR; main centers are Larissa, Tyrnavos, Pharsala, and Hagia.

Larissa or **Larisa,** city (1951 pop. 41,163), ⊙ Thessaly and Larissa nome, Greece, on bank of Peneus R., on railroad and 135 mi. NW of Athens. Road hub, linked by rail with its Aegean port, Volos; center of a large agr. lowland, producing wheat, barley, vegetables, silk, tobacco, citrus fruit and olives. Airport. Bishopric. The anc. ⊙ of the Pelasgians, Larissa became (6th cent. B.C.) one of the leading cities of anc. Thessaly under the ruling Aleuadae family. An ally of Athens in Peloponnesian War, it was later rivaled by Crannon and Pherae, but continued as ⊙ Thessalian League under Roman rule (after 196 B.C.). Under the Turks (after 15th cent.) it was known as Yeni-Shehr or Yeni-Shehr-Fanar. Was hq. of Ali Pasha in Gr. war of independence, and passed 1881 to Greece. It suffered from bombings (1940–41) during Second World War.

Laristan (lärēstän'), former province of S Iran, in SE Fars; main town, Lar. Situated in central Zagros ranges, it was once quasi-independent, became part of Iran under Abbas I in early-17th cent., and flourished in early-18th cent. with the prosperity of near-by port of Bandar Abbas. Since 1938, it forms part, with Fars, of Iran's Seventh Prov., commonly known as Fars.

Larius Lacus, Italy: see COMO, LAKE.

Lark (lärk), Persian Gulf island of SE Iran, in Strait of Hormuz, 20 mi. S of Bandar Abbas and off NE tip of Qishm isl.; 7 mi. long, 5 mi. wide; fishing, pearling. Also spelled Larak.

Larkana (lärkä'nŭ), district (□ 2,857; pop. 511,208), NW Sind, W Pakistan; ⊙ Larkana. Bounded W by N Kirthar Range, E by Indus R.; irrigated by right-bank canals of Sukkur Barrage system. Fertile area (rice, wheat, millet, rape-seed); mangoes, dates cultivated. Rice milling, handicrafts (cotton and woolen fabrics, metalwork, leather goods). Sheep grazing in W hills; shad fishing in the Indus. Prehistoric remains at Mohenjo-Daro. Sometimes spelled Larkhana.

Larkana, town (pop. 28,085), ⊙ Larkana dist., NW Sind, W Pakistan, in canal-irrigated tract near Indus R., 200 mi. NNE of Karachi; rail junction;

trade center (rice, wheat, millet, gram, handicraft cloth); rice and flour milling; metalwork, leather goods. Agr. research station. Mangoes and dates grown near by.

Larkhall, town in Dalserf parish, N Lanark, Scotland, on Avon Water, near the Clyde, 3 mi. S of Motherwell; coal mining, light-metals production.

Lark River, Suffolk, England, rises in several branches 4 mi. S of Bury St. Edmunds, flows 26 mi. NW, past Bury St. Edmunds and Mildenhall, to Ouse R. 3 mi. NE of Ely.

Larkspur, residential town (pop. 2,905), Marin co., W Calif., 13 mi. N of San Francisco, near Mt. Tamalpais (SW). Inc. 1908. Larkspur Canyon near by has redwood grove.

Larksville, borough (pop. 6,360), Luzerne co., NE central Pa., on Susquehanna R. opposite Wilkes-Barre; anthracite. Inc. 1909.

Larnaca (lär'nůkü), district (□ 435; pop. 52,189), SE Cyprus, on the Mediterranean; ⊙ LARNACA. Mostly lowland, except for outliers of the Olympus Mts. in N. Predominantly agr.: oats, vetches, almonds, carobs, wine, olive oil; sheep, goats. Fishing. Salt and terra umbra (Turkey umber) are extracted. Pyrite mines at KALAVASO. Main port and processing center is Larnaca. Among other towns are ATHIENOU and LEFKARA. Anc. city of CITIUM is now partly occupied by Larnaca.

Larnaca, city (pop. 14,772), ⊙ Larnaca dist., SE Cyprus, port on Larnaca Bay (c.14 mi. long, 8 mi. wide) of the Mediterranean, 23 mi. SE of Nicosia. Trades in carobs, wines, almonds, barley, olive oil; mules, donkeys. Mfg. of brandy, cigarettes, soap, leather, buttons, artificial teeth. Along harbor are modern Scala and Marina sections, which partly occupy anc. Phoenecian CITIUM (Chittim of Old Testament), where Stoic philosopher Zeno was born, commemorated by statue. Port facilities include 450-ft. metal pier. City has ruined fort and churches. Airport is 2 mi. S. The medieval town was built c.1 mi. inland, because of pirate incursions. SW of Larnaca are 2 salt lakes, from which salt is extracted. Bet. the 2 lakes is cypress-lined Turkish monastery which contains a Moslem shrine with grave of Tekké Umn Haran, kinswoman of the Prophet. Stavrovouni monastery is 11 mi. W. Sometimes spelled Larnaka.

Larne (lärn), municipal borough (1937 pop. 11,090; 1951 census 11,976), E Co. Antrim, Northern Ireland, on Lough Larne, near its mouth on the North Channel, 18 mi. N of Belfast; 54°51'N 5°48'W; seaport and tourist center, terminal of mail steamers from Stranraer, Scotland. Exports bauxite, iron ore, beef, potatoes; principal imports: coal, wood pulp, china clay, flour, grain, manufactured products. Industries include bauxite refining, linen milling, clothing mfg. Harbor is sheltered by Curran Peninsula, site of remains of anc. Olderfield Castle.

Larned (lär'nĭd), city (pop. 4,447), ⊙ Pawnee co., SW central Kansas, on Arkansas R., at mouth of Pawnee R., and 22 mi. SW of Great Bend; trade center for agr. area (wheat, alfalfa, sugar beets); flour milling, agr. equipment mfg., dairying. Hosp. for insane is near by. Site of Fort Larned (established 1859 to protect travelers on Santa Fe Trail; abandoned 1878) is in vicinity. Laid out 1873, inc. 1886.

Laroche, Belgium: see ROCHE-EN-ARDENNE, LA.

Laroche-Migennes, France: see LAROCHE-SAINT-CYDROINE.

Laroche-Saint-Cydroine (lärôsh'-sē-sēdrwän'), village (pop. 927), Yonne dept., N central France, at junction of Yonne R. and Burgundy Canal, 12 mi. NNW of Auxerre. Important railroad station and yards at Laroche-Migennes (1 mi. E).

Larochette (lärôshĕt'), Ger. *Fels* (fĕls), village (pop. 927), E central Luxembourg, 7 mi. SE of Ettelbruck; woolen textiles, brushes; market center for fruitgrowing area (apples, pears).

Laroles (lärō'lĕs), village (pop. 1,427), Granada prov., S Spain, 22 mi. SSE of Guadix; olive-oil processing, flour milling. Ships chestnuts, nuts, figs. Sericulture.

La Romana (lä rōmä'nä), city (1935 pop. 10,912; 1950 pop. 11,587), ⊙ La Altagracia prov., SE Dominican Republic, sugar port on the Caribbean, opposite Catalina Isl., 60 mi. E of Ciudad Trujillo; 18°30'N 68°57'W. Sugar-refining center; produces coffee, tobacco, cattle, beeswax, hides; corn milling; mfg. of shoes, soap, furniture; fishing. Airfield.

Laropi (lärō'pē), village, Northern Prov., NW Uganda, on the Albert Nile and 9 mi. SSE of Moyo; cotton, peanuts, sesame, millet. Seaplane landing.

Laroque (lärôk'), village (pop. 328), Hérault dept., S France, 7 mi. SE of Le Vigan; silk mfg.

Laroquebrou (lärôkbrōō'), village (pop. 1,226), Cantal dept., S central France, on the Cère and 12 mi. W of Aurillac; mfg. of footwear, draperies, pottery. Has ruins of a feudal castle and an ornate 14th-15th-cent. Gothic church.

Laroque-d'Olmes (lärôk'-dôlm'), village (pop. 1,966), Ariège dept., S France, 13 mi. E of Foix; textile milling.

Laroque-Timbaut (-tēbō'), village (pop. 469), Lot-et-Garonne dept., SW France, 9 mi. NE of Agen; wheat, cattle.

La Rosa (lä rō'sä), town (pop. 1,602), Zulia state, NW Venezuela, on NE shore of L. Maracaibo, 3 mi. SE of Cabimas, in petroleum field extending into lake.

La Rose, village (pop. 178), Marshall co., central Ill., near small Crow Creek, 25 mi. NE of Peoria, in agr. area.

Larose, village (pop. 1,286), Lafourche parish, SE La., 30 mi. SW of New Orleans.

Larrabee, town (pop. 158), Cherokee co., NW Iowa, 8 mi. N of Cherokee.

Larraga (lärä'gä), town (pop. 2,228), Navarre prov., N Spain, near Arga R., 12 mi. SE of Estella; olive oil, wine, cereals.

Larrainzar (lärīnsär'), town (pop. 593), Chiapas, S Mexico, in Sierra de Hueytepec, 12 mi. NW of San Cristóbal de las Casas; wheat, fruit.

Larreynaga (lärānä'gä), town (1950 pop. 1,374), León dept., W Nicaragua, on railroad and 20 mi. NE of León; livestock; sesame, corn.

Larroque or **Villa Larroque** (vĭ'yä lärō'kä), town (pop. estimate 2,000), SE Entre Ríos prov., Argentina, on railroad and 29 mi. W of Gualeguaychú; agr. center (grain growing, stock raising, dairying).

Larroudé, Argentina: see BENJAMÍN LARROUDÉ.

Larsa (lär'sů), biblical *Ellasar*, anc. city of S Babylonia, bet. the lower Tigris and Euphrates; its site is in SE Iraq, in Muntafiq prov., on left bank of the Euphrates, 13 mi. SE of site of Erech and 30 mi. WNW of Nasiriya. In time of Abraham, Arioch, king of Larsa, invaded Canaan. The city, dedicated to the sun-god Shamash, was ⊙ of a Semitic dynasty and later, under the Elamites (who subdued Ur, to SE of Larsa), conquered N Babylonia, becoming, in turn, subject to Babylon. Its ruins have yielded important finds. The excavation site is called Senkerah or Senkereh.

Lars Christensen Coast (lärz' krĭ'stĭnsĭn), Antarctica, on Indian Ocean, extends from Cape Darnley on Bjerk Peninsula to Mt. Caroline Mikkelsen at head of Sandefjord Bay, bet. 69°30' and 74°E. Discovered 1931 by Norwegian whalers.

Larsen Bay, S Alaska, S arm (20 mi. long) of Uyak Bay, inlet of Shelikof Strait, W Kodiak Isl., 60 mi. WSW of Kodiak; 57°32'N 154°3'W; salmon canning. Larsen Bay village (pop. 54) is on shore.

Larson, village (pop. 59), Burke co., NW N.Dak., 30 mi. WNW of Bowbells.

Larson Air Force Base, Wash.: see MOSES LAKE.

Larto, Lake (lär'tō), Catahoula parish, E central La., oxbow lake (c.10 mi. long) formed by a cutoff of Ouachita R., 30 mi. E of Alexandria; fishing.

Larue, county (□ 260; pop. 9,956), central Ky.; ⊙ Hodgenville. Bounded E and NE by Rolling Fork; drained by Nolin R. Rolling agr. area (livestock, burley tobacco, corn); limestone quarries, gas wells, timber. Includes ABRAHAM LINCOLN NATIONAL PARK near Hodgenville. Formed 1843.

La Rue, village (pop. 793), Marion co., central Ohio, 13 mi. W of Marion and on Scioto R.; duck hatchery; tile plant.

Laruns (lärŭ'), village (pop. 1,232), Basses-Pyrénées dept., SW France, on the Gave d'Ossau, in Ossau valley of central Pyrenees, and 17 mi. SE of Oloron-Sainte-Marie; road junction on trans-Pyrenean highway to Spain via Pourtalet pass (12 mi. S). Woodworking, slate quarrying. Near by are the spas of Les EAUX-CHAUDES and Les EAUX-BONNES.

Larussell, city (pop. 82), Jasper co., SW Mo., on Spring R. and 14 mi. E of Carthage.

Larvik (lär'vēk), city (pop. 9,824), Vestfold co., SE Norway, at head of Larvik Fjord, at mouth of Lagen R., on railroad and 65 mi. SSW of Oslo; 59°3'N 10°3'E. Fishing, whaling, shipping, and industrial center, with ironworks, lumber mills, woodworking plants; also mfg. of rock wool, insulating materials, knit goods, soap; brewing, tobacco processing. Seaside resort. Car ferry to Frederikshavn, Denmark. Granite quarried near by. Town founded in 17th cent. Just N is Farris Lake (□ 8.5), 15 mi. long, 1-2 mi. wide, 430 ft. deep.

Larwill (lär'wĭl), town (pop. 316), Whitley co., NE Ind., 26 mi. WNW of Fort Wayne, in agr. area.

Laryak or **Lar'yak** (lŭryäk'), village, SE Khanty-Mansi Natl. Okrug, Tyumen oblast, Russian SFSR, on Vakh R. and 370 mi. E of Khanty-Mansisk; fish canning, reindeer raising.

Larymna or **Larimna** (lůrĭm'nů, Gr. lä'rĭmnů), village (pop. 704), Phthiotis nome, E central Greece, on Gulf of Euboea, 16 mi. N of Thebes; limonite and nickel mining. In anc. times, a major port at old mouth of Cephisus R.

Larzac, Causse du, France: see CAUSSES.

Lasa (läsä'), town, westernmost Yunnan prov., China, 55 mi. WSW of Lungling, near Burma border. Officially known as Juili (rwā'lē) in summer and fall seasons, when JUILI dist. seat, moved from MENGMAO (28 mi. S), is situated here.

Lasa (lä'sä), Ger. *Laas*, village (pop. 1,659), Bolzano prov., Trentino-Alto Adige, N Italy, in Val Venosta, on Adige R. and 22 mi. WSW of Merano; marble quarries.

La-sa, Tibet: see LHASA.

La Sábana (lä sä'bänä), village (pop. estimate 800), ⊙ Tapenagá dept. (pop. 26,928), S Chaco prov., Argentina, on railroad and 65 mi. SW of Resistencia, in livestock area; sawmills.

Las Acequias (läs äsä'kyäs), town (pop. estimate 1,500), S central Córdoba prov., Argentina, 24 mi. SE of Río Cuarto; wheat, flax, cattle.

La Sal, village (pop. c.300), San Juan co., SE Utah, near Colo. line, 25 mi. SE of Moab, in La Sal Mts.; alt. 7,125 ft.; copper refining.

La Salle (lůsăl', Fr. läsäl'). **1** Residential town (pop. 951), S Ont., on Detroit R. and 8 mi. SW of Windsor. **2** or **Lasalle,** residential town (pop. 4,651), S Que., on S shore of Montreal Isl., at W end of the Lachine Rapids, 7 mi. SW of Montreal. Inc. 1912. Also called Ville La Salle.

Lasalle (läsäl'), village (pop. 900), Gard dept., S France, in the Cévennes, 12 mi. SW of Alès; men's clothing. Iron and zinc mining at Saint-Félix-de-Pallières (4 mi. SE) and Thoiras (4 mi. ENE).

La Salle (lů săl'). **1** County (□ 1,153; pop. 100,610), N Ill.; ⊙ Ottawa. Drained by Illinois, Fox, Vermilion, and Little Vermilion rivers. Includes Illinois and Starved Rock state parks, part of Illinois and Michigan Canal Parkway. Agr. (corn, oats, soybeans, wheat, livsetock, poultry; dairy products). Bituminous-coal mines; limestone, silica, clay, shale, cement-rock deposits. Diversified mfg., chiefly at La Salle, Peru, Ottawa. Formed 1831. **2** Parish (□ 638; pop. 12,717), central La.; ⊙ Jena. Bounded W by Little R. Includes Catahoula and Saline lakes (fishing, waterfowl hunting). Oil fields; timber. Agr. (sugar cane, rice, cotton, corn, hay). Some mfg., including cotton ginning and lumber milling. Formed 1908. **3** County (□ 1,501; pop. 7,485), S Texas; ⊙ Cotulla. Drained by Nueces and Frio rivers. Mainly cattle-ranching area; partly in irrigated Winter Garden truck, citrus region; dairying. Oil wells. Formed 1858.

La Salle. 1 Town (pop. 797), Weld co., N Colo., on South Platte R. and 5 mi. S of Greeley, in irrigated grain and sugar-beet region; alt. 4,700 ft. **2** City (pop. 12,083), La Salle co., N Ill., on Illinois R. (bridged here), adjoining Peru, and 12 mi. W of Ottawa; trade, industrial, and shipping center; cement-rock, silica-sand deposits; mfg. (meat products, clocks, glass, cement, zinc, vehicles, sulphuric acid, steel wheels, boiler plates). Agr. (corn, wheat, oats, soybeans, livestock, poultry; dairy products), and bituminous-coal mines in region. Seat of a jr. col. Near by is Starved Rock State Park. Laid out 1837, inc. 1852. Developed as important water transportation center after opening of Illinois and Michigan Canal (1848). **3** Village (pop. 144), Watonwan co., S Minn., on Watonwan R. and 7 mi. NNE of St. James; dairy products.

La Sal Mountains, range in La Sal Natl. Forest, San Juan and Grand counties, E Utah, bet. Colorado R. and Colo. line. Chief peaks: Mt. Tomasaki (12,271 ft.), Mt. Waas (12,586 ft.), and Mt. PEALE (13,089 ft.). Copper deposits.

La Salud (lä sälōōdh'), town (pop. 2,701), Havana prov., W Cuba, on railroad and 18 mi. SSW of Havana; tobacco, oranges, vegetables.

Las Animas (läs ä'nēmäs) or **Animas,** town (pop. 1,159), Valdivia prov., S central Chile, 2 mi. ESE of Valdivia; suburb in agr. area (cereals, potatoes, fruit, livestock); lumbering. An old Sp. fort in colonial times.

Las Animas (läs ä'nēmäs, ă'nĭ-), county (□ 4,794; pop. 25,902), SE Colo.; ⊙ Trinidad. Coal-mining and livestock-grazing area, bordering on N.Mex.; drained by Purgatoire and Apishapa rivers. Part of Sangre de Cristo Mts. and San Isabel Natl. Forest in W. Formed 1866.

Las Animas, city (pop. 3,223), ⊙ Bent co., SE Colo., on Arkansas R. and 75 mi. E of Pueblo; alt. 4,100 ft. Trade center in irrigated grain and sugar-beet area; beet sugar, flour, cantaloupes, poultry. Near-by Fort Lyon has Kit Carson Mus. (in cabin where the scout died) and U.S. veterans' hosp. City founded 1869, moved to present site 1873 to be on railroad, inc. 1886.

Las Anod (läs' änōd'), town, SE Br. Somaliland, in Haud plateau, on road and 235 mi. ESE of Hargeisa; stock-raising center. Hq. Las Anod dist.

La Sarre, Que.: see SARRE, LA.

Las Banderas (läs bändä'räs), village, Managua dept., SW Nicaragua, 25 mi. NE of Managua; road junction; corn, beans.

Las Barrancas (läs bäräng'käs). **1** Town (pop. estimate 2,000) in Greater Buenos Aires, Argentina, seaside resort on the Río de la Plata, adjoining San Isidro, and 13 mi. NW of Buenos Aires. **2** or **Barrancas,** village (pop. estimate 500), N Mendoza prov., Argentina, in Mendoza R. valley (irrigation area), 15 mi. SSE of Mendoza, in agr. area (wine, corn, alfalfa); oil fields, asphalt deposits.

Las Bela (lŭs' bä'lŭ), princely state (□ 7,043; 1951 pop. 76,000), SE Baluchistan, W Pakistan; ⊙ Bela. Bounded E by Kirthar Range, SE by Hab R.; crossed N-S by Pab Range; central lowland drained by Porali R.; S coast lies along Sonmiani Bay, with long strip extending W bet. Arabian Sea and Makran Coast Range. Agr. (millet, rice, oilseeds, dates); fishing (catfish), salt panning, handicrafts (woolen carpets, leather goods, crochet work). Chief towns: Bela, Sonmiani, Ormara. Crossed 325 B.C. by part of army of Alexander the Great on return to Persia, while fleet cruised offshore; visited by Arab traders in Middle Ages. Formerly under suzerainty of Kalat; acceded independently in 1948 to Pakistan. Pop. 97% Moslem. Sometimes spelled Lus Bela.

Las Bela, town, W Pakistan: see Bela.

Lasberg (läs'bĕrk), town (pop. 2,061), NE Upper Austria, 3 mi. SSE of Freistadt, N of the Danube; linen mfg.

Las Bonitas (läs bōnē'täs), town (pop. 288), Bolívar state, SE Venezuela, landing on Orinoco R. and 40 mi. ENE of Caicara; 7°53'N 65°40'W; stock raising.

Las Breñas (läs brā'nyäs), town (1947 census 2,559), SW Chaco natl. territory, Argentina, on railroad and 45 mi. SW of Presidencia Roque Sáenz Peña; agr. (cotton, corn, alfalfa, flax, peanuts), lumbering, cotton ginning.

Las Cabras (läs kä'bräs), town (pop. 1,032), O'Higgins prov., central Chile, on Cachapoal R. and 38 mi. WSW of Rancagua; rail terminus and agr. center (grain, alfalfa, fruit, potatoes, livestock).

Lascahobas (läskäō'bäs), town (1950 census pop. 2,191), Ouest dept., S central Haiti, on Artibonite Plain, 32 mi. NE of Port-au-Prince, linked by road to Elías Piña (Dominican Republic).

Las Cañas (läs kä'nyäs), village (pop. estimate 600), SE Catamarca prov., Argentina, 40 mi. NE of Catamarca, in corn, livestock, and lumber area.

Las Cañas, village (1930 pop. 412), Coquimbo prov., N central Chile, on railroad and 8 mi. SSW of Illapel; lead mining and smelting.

Lascano (läskä'nō), town (pop. 4,100), Rocha dept., SE Uruguay, trading center on highway, and 29 mi. SSE of Treinta y Tres, in stock-raising region (cattle, sheep).

Las Carabelas, Argentina: see Carabelas.

Las Carolinas, Argentina: see Carolina.

Las Casas, Mexico: see San Cristóbal de las Casas.

Las Casuarinas (läs käswärē'näs), town (pop. estimate 1,000), S San Juan prov., Argentina, in San Juan R. valley (irrigation area), on railroad and 23 mi. SE of San Juan; viticulture center.

Las Catitas (läs kätē'täs), town (pop. estimate 1,000), NE Mendoza prov., Argentina, on railroad, on Tunuyán R. (irrigation) and 55 mi. SE of Mendoza; lumbering and agr. center (fruit, wine, grain, livestock). Formerly José Néstor Lencinas.

Las Cejas (läs sā'häs), town (pop. estimate 700), E Tucumán prov., Argentina, 30 mi. E of Tucumán; rail junction; stock-raising and lumbering center; mfg. of charcoal.

Las Colonias, department, Argentina: see Esperanza.

Las Coloradas (läs kōlōrä'däs), village (pop. estimate 100), ⊙ Catán-Lil dept., S Neuquén natl. territory, Argentina, in foothills of the Andes, 55 mi. SSW of Zapala; sheep-raising center.

Las Conchas, Argentina: see Tigre.

Las Condes (läs kōn'dĕs), village (1930 pop. 494), Santiago prov., central Chile, in Andean foothills, 9 mi. NE of Santiago; copper mining (Disputada mine; 1930 pop. 191); agr. (cereals, fruit, cattle).

Las Cotorras, islands, Trinidad and Tobago, B.W.I.: see Five Islands.

Las Cruces (läs kroō'sās), village (pop. 282), Retalhuleu dept., SW Guatemala, 6 mi. WSW of Retalhuleu and on Tilapa R.; rail junction of branch to Champerico; coffee, sugar cane.

Las Cruces (läs kroō'sĭs), town (pop. 12,325), ⊙ Dona Ana co., S N.Mex., on Rio Grande and 40 mi. NNW of El Paso, Texas; trade center for livestock and irrigated agr. region; cotton, grain, sugar beets, fruit, vegetables; cotton ginning. Founded 1848, inc. as town 1907. Near by are historic village of Mesilla and old Indian community of Tortugas (pop. c.500). Organ Needle is 14 mi. E, in Organ Mts. N.Mex. Col. of Agr. and Mechanic Arts just SE. White Sands Proving Grounds are NE, near Alamogordo.

Las Cruces (läs kroō'sās), town (pop. 1,093), Zulia state, NW Venezuela, in Maracaibo lowlands, 32 mi. SSW of Encontrados; petroleum drilling in the Tarra oil field, served by local railroad.

Las Cuevas (läs kwā'väs), village (pop. estimate 100), NW Mendoza prov., Argentina, 70 mi. W of Mendoza, on Transandine RR (Mendoza-Valparaiso), at Chile frontier near Uspallata Pass. Custom house. Copper deposits near by.

Las Cuevas, Mexico: see Villa Matamoros.

Las Daua, Ital. Somaliland: see Laz Daua.

Lasdehnen, Russian SFSR: see Krasnoznamensk.

Las Delicias (läs dālē'syäs), village (pop. estimate 600), W Entre Ríos prov., Argentina, on railroad and 16 mi. SSE of Paraná; wheat, flax, livestock. Agr. school.

Las Dureh (läs' doō'rā), village, NE Br. Somaliland, in Ogo highland, on road and 55 mi. NNE of Burao; gums; camels, sheep, goats.

Lasea (lăsē'ŭ), anc. town, Crete, S of Candia, mentioned in the Bible; was near the harbor where Paul landed. Some ruins remain.

Lasem (lŭsĕm'), town (pop. 15,731), NW Java, Indonesia, near Java Sea, near Rembang, 95 mi. WNW of Surabaya; trade center for agr. area (rice, corn, cassava, peanuts); batik printing. Sometimes spelled Lassem.

La Serena (lä sārā'nä), city (1940 pop. 21,742, 1949 estimate 23,130), ⊙ Coquimbo prov. and La Serena dept. (□ 2,578; 1940 pop. 42,011), N central Chile, at mouth of Elqui R., near the Pacific (Coquimbo Bay), 8 mi. NE of Coquimbo (its port), 250 mi. NNW of Santiago, on railroad; 29°54'S 71°16'W. Resort; commercial and agr. center. Trades in dried fruit, and barley, flowers, fruit, livestock. Exports mineral ores (copper, silver, gold, manganese). Tanning, brewing, soap making, olive-oil processing. Hydroelectric plant. A city of Old-World charm, La Serena is known for its cathedral, fine bldgs., gardens, and orchards. Has mining school. Founded 1544, it was declared a city in 1552. Heavily damaged in 1922 earthquake. Its seaside resort Peñuelas is 4 mi. SW on Coquimbo Bay.

Las Esperanzas (läs ĕspärän'säs), mining settlement (pop. 2,524), Coahuila, N Mexico, in Sabinas coal dist., on railroad and 12 mi. SE of Múzquiz.

Lasethi or **Lasithi** (both: lŭsē'thē), nome (□ 738; pop. 71,172), E Crete, E of Mt. Dikte; ⊙ Hagios Nikolaos. Agr.: olives, carobs, raisins, wheat, olive oil; stock raising (sheep, goats); fisheries. Main ports are Hagios Nikolaos, Seteia, and Hierapetra.

Las Flores (läs flō'rĕs). **1** Town (pop. 8,955), ⊙ Las Flores dist. (□ 1,290; pop. 22,646), E central Buenos Aires prov., Argentina, 110 mi. SSW of Buenos Aires. Rail junction; agr. center (corn, sunflowers, wheat, livestock). Formerly Carmen de las Flores. **2** Town, Santa Fe prov., Argentina: see Piquete.

Las Flores or **Flores,** town, Maldonado dept., S Uruguay, on railroad and 21 mi. WNW of Maldonado, in agr. region (sugar beets, grain, stock). Adjoining S is a beach resort.

Las Garzas (läs gär'säs), town (pop. estimate 1,000), NE Santa Fe prov., Argentina, 30 mi. NNE of Reconquista; agr. center (corn, flax, livestock).

Las Guabas (läs gwä'bäs), town (pop. 467), Los Santos prov., S central Panama, in Pacific lowland, 8 mi. SW of Los Santos; bananas, sugar cane, livestock.

Lashburn, village (pop. 349), W Sask., 20 mi. SE of Lloydminster, near Alta. border; wheat.

Las Heras (läs ā'räs). **1** Town, Comodoro Rivadavia military zone, Argentina: see Colonia Las Heras. **2** Town (1947 pop. 14,865), ⊙ Las Heras dept. (□ 4,290; 1947 pop. 38,896), N Mendoza prov., Argentina, on railroad, in Mendoza R. valley (irrigation area), just N of Mendoza. Agr. and mfg. center. Produces cement, pottery, dried fruit, wine; has sawmills, lime quarries. Agr. products: wine, fruit, potatoes, alfalfa. Airport. Some uranium has been found in the area.

Lashgarak or **Lashkarak** (both: läshkäräk'), village, Second Prov., in Teheran, N Iran, 13 mi. NE of Teheran, in Elburz mts.; popular skiing resort.

Lashio (lăsh'yō, lŭsh-yō', Burmese lä'-shō'), town (pop. 4,638), ⊙ Shan State and Northern Shan State, Upper Burma, 120 mi. NE of Mandalay; 22°56'N 97°45'E; communications center at terminus of railroad from Mandalay and head of Burma Road to Chinese Yunnan prov.; airfield. In Second World War recaptured 1944 from Japanese by Chinese forces.

Lash-Jawain or **Lash-Juwain** (lŭsh'-jŭwīn'), town (pop. over 2,000), Farah prov., SW Afghanistan, on the lower Farah Rud and 55 mi. SW of Farah, near Iran line, at edge of Seistan lake depression. Consists of 2 sections that developed around anc. forts: Lash on right bank, and Jawain on left bank.

Lashkar (lŭsh'kŭr), city (pop. 113,718; including S cantonment and town of Gwalior, 156,834), winter ⊙ Madhya Bharat (summer ⊙ at Indore) and ⊙ Gird Gwalior dist., India, 175 mi. SSE of New Delhi. Rail and road junction; commercial center; agr. market (wheat, millet, gram, cotton, oilseeds); trades in cloth fabrics, grain, ghee, building stone, iron ore; mfg. of pottery, soap, pen nibs, hosiery, playing cards, tobacco products, toiletries; engineering and metalworks, distillery. Contains fine palace, Victoria, Col., mus., and technical institute. Near Maharajpur village, 6 mi. NE, are airport and agr. farm; seaplane base on reservoir 8 mi. W. Surrounding country well forested (big game hunting). Founded 1810 by Daulat Rao Sindhia as military camp (Urdu, = *lashkar*); soon became ⊙ Mahratta state of Gwalior. Combined area of Gwalior and Lashkar cities is often called Gwalior.

Lashkarak, Iran: see Lashgarak.

Lashma (läsh'mŭ), town (1939 pop. over 2,000), N Ryazan oblast, Russian SFSR, on Oka R. and 8 mi. W of Kasimov; metalworks.

Las Hortensias (läs ōrtĕn'syäs) or **Hortensias,** village (1930 pop. 679), Cautín prov., S central Chile, on railroad and 25 mi. SE of Temuco, in agr. area (cereals, vegetables, potatoes, livestock).

Lashva, Yugoslavia: see Lasva.

La Sierra (lä syĕ'rä), town (dist. pop. 3,162), Guanacaste prov., NW Costa Rica, on Abangares R. and 3 mi. ENE of Las Juntas; gold-mining center in Abangares dist. Mines are at Gongolona and Tres Hermanos.

La Sierra (lä sēē'rŭ), village (pop. 3,802), Riverside co., S Calif., 16 mi. SW of Riverside.

La Sierra (lä syĕ'rä), town (pop. 500), Maldonado dept., S Uruguay, on railroad and 40 mi. ENE of Montevideo, in sugar-beet region; large sugar refinery. Also wheat and cattle raising.

Lasin (wä'shēn), Pol. *Łasin*, Ger. *Lessen* (lĕ'sŭn), town (pop. 2,141), Bydgoszcz prov., N Poland, 14 mi. E of Grudziadz; rail spur terminus; mfg. of agr. machinery, sawmilling, flour milling. Monastery.

Lasinja (lä'sēnyä), village, N Croatia, Yugoslavia, on Kupa R. and 20 mi. S of Zagreb, in the Pokupje; health resort.

Lasithi, nome, Crete: see Lasethi.

Lasithi, Mount, Crete: see Dikte, Mount.

Las Juntas (läs' hoōn'täs), town (1950 pop. 803), ⊙ Abangares canton, Guanacaste prov., NW Costa Rica, on Abangares R. and 40 mi. SE of Liberia, in Abangares gold-mining area; trading center; grain, livestock; lumbering.

Las Junturas (läs hoōntoō'räs), town (pop. estimate 1,500), central Córdoba prov., Argentina, 55 mi. SE of Córdoba; wheat, corn, flax, livestock.

Lask (wäsk), Pol. *Łask*, town (pop. 3,819), Lodz prov., central Poland, 18 mi. SW of Lodz; tanning, distilling, mfg. of caps, slippers.

Läskelä, Karelo-Finnish SSR: see Lyaskelya.

Lasker, town (pop. 177), Northampton co., NE N.C., 21 mi. ESE of Roanoke Rapids.

Las Khoreh (läs khō'rā), locality, NE Br. Somaliland, on Gulf of Aden, 70 mi. NE of Erigavo; gums (frankincense, myrrh); fisheries.

Lasko (läsh'kô), Slovenian *Laško*, Ger. *Tüffer* (tüf'ŭr), village, central Slovenia, Yugoslavia, on Savinja R., on railroad and 35 mi. E of Ljubljana, in brown-coal area; brewery. Health resort with radioactive warm springs. Until 1918, in Styria.

Las Lajas (läs lä'häs), town (pop. estimate 1,500), ⊙ Picunches dept. (1947 pop. 5,819), central Neuquén natl. territory, Argentina, on the Río Agrio, in Andean foothills, and 30 mi. NW of Zapala; road center on route to Pino Hachado Pass (Chile border). Stock raising.

Las Lajas, town (pop. 1,027), Chiriquí prov., W Panama, in Pacific lowland, 38 mi. ESE of David, on Inter-American Highway; hardwood lumbering, stock raising.

Las Lomas (läs lō'mäs), village (pop. 397), Chiriquí prov., W Panama, 1 mi. E of David, on Inter-American Highway; coffee, bananas, livestock.

Las Lomas, village (pop. 701), Piura dept., NW Peru, in W foothills of Cordillera Occidental, 45 mi. NE of Piura; vineyards, orchards; sugar cane.

Las Lomitas (läs lōmē'täs), town (pop. estimate 1,000), central Formosa natl. territory, Argentina, on railroad and 180 mi. NW of Formosa; stock-raising center; lumbering. Airport.

Las Maderas (läs mädä'räs), village, Managua dept., SW Nicaragua, on Inter-American Highway and 31 mi. NE of Managua; lumbering.

Las Manos (läs mä'nōs), village, Nueva Segovia dept., NW Nicaragua, 12 mi. N of Ocotal. Frontier station on Honduras border, on road to Danlí (Honduras).

Las Margaritas (läs märgärē'täs), town (pop. 1,383), Chiapas, S Mexico, in Sierra Madre, 11 mi. ENE of Comitán; sugar cane, cereals, fruit, stock.

Las Marías (läs märē'äs), town (pop. 562), W Puerto Rico, 10 mi. ENE of Mayagüez; coffee center.

Las Matas or **Las Matas de Farfán** (läs mä'täs dā färfän'), town (1950 pop. 1,818), Benefactor prov., W Dominican Republic, in irrigated San Juan Valley, on highway, and 20 mi. W of San Juan; coffee, bananas, vegetables, cereals.

Las Mercedes (läs mĕrsā'dĕs), town (pop. estimate 1,000), S Entre Ríos prov., Argentina, 25 mi. SW of Gualeguaychú, in grain and stock area; dairying.

Las Mercedes, town (pop. 1,495), Guárico state, central Venezuela, 28 mi. WSW of Valle de la Pascua; cattle raising. Oil wells.

Las Minas (läs mē'näs), town (pop. 195), Veracruz, E Mexico, 19 mi. NW of Jalapa.

Las Minas. 1 Village, Colón prov., Panama: see Puerto Pilón. **2** Village (pop. 433), Herrera prov., S central Panama, 20 mi. WSW of Chitré; gold-mining center; stock raising.

Las Palmas (läs päl'mäs). **1** Town (pop. estimate 3,000), N Buenos Aires prov., Argentina, 8 mi. W of Zárate; cattle-raising and meat-packing center. **2** Town (1947 pop. 4,319), E Chaco natl. territory, Argentina, on railroad and 30 mi. NNE of Resistencia; processing and agr. center. Vegetable-oil refineries (cottonseed, peanut, sunflower, spurge), sugar refineries, tannin works, sawmills, cellulose factories, cotton gins. Agr. (sugar cane, cotton, citrus fruit, livestock). Its port is 4 mi. SE on Paraguay R.

Las Palmas, Canary Isls.: see Palmas, Las.

Las Palmas, village (pop. 640), Veraguas prov., W central Panama, 30 mi. W of Santiago; gold-mining center; magnesium mining. It is situated on Las Palmas Peninsula, a S projection of Panama, bet. Tabasará and San Pablo rivers, and forming W side of Montijo Gulf.

Las Paredes (läs pärā'dĕs), town (pop. estimate 500), central Mendoza prov., Argentina, on railroad (Capitán Montoya station) and 7 mi. W of San Rafael, near Diamante R. (irrigation area); wine, potatoes, fruit; wine making, dried-fruit processing.

Las Parejas (läs pärē'häs), town (pop. estimate 2,500), S central Santa Fe prov., Argentina, 55 mi. WNW of Rosario; agr. center (wheat, corn, sunflowers, flax, livestock); dairying.

Las Peñas (läs pā'nyäs), town (pop. estimate 1,000), N Córdoba prov., Argentina, 60 mi. NNE of Córdoba; corn, alfalfa, livestock; quarrying, woodcutting.
Las Peñas, Mexico: see PUERTO VALLARTA.
Las Perdices (läs pĕrdē'sĕs), town (pop. estimate 1,000), central Córdoba prov., Argentina, 32 mi. SW of Villa María; grain, livestock.
Las Petas (läs pā'täs), village, Santa Cruz dept., E Bolivia, 120 mi. E of San Ignacio, near Brazil border.
Las Piedras (läs pyā'dräs), town (pop. c.100), ⊙ Madre de Dios prov., Pando dept., N Bolivia, on Madre de Dios R. and 5 mi. W of Riberalta; rubber, cacao, coffee.
Las Piedras, town (pop. 3,150), E Puerto Rico, 3 mi. NW of Humacao; sugar cane, tobacco, coffee.
Las Piedras, town (pop. 15,000), Canelones dept., S Uruguay, on railroad and 9 mi. NNW of Montevideo, in winegrowing and ostrich-farming dist. Known for its race track. Has Gothic chapel of the Salesians. Site of decisive victory (1811) of Artigas over the Spanish.
Las Piedras, village (pop. 939), Falcón state, NW Venezuela, on W shore of Paraguaná Peninsula, 26 mi. WSW of Pueblo Nuevo; petroleum shipping point; refinery. Sometimes Amuay (ämwī').
Las Piedrecitas, Nicaragua: see MANAGUA, city.
Las Pilas (läs pē'läs), W Nicaragua, volcano (3,514 ft.) in Cordillera de los Marabios, 14 mi. ENE of León.
Las Piñas (läs pē'nyäs), town (1939 pop. 3,493; 1948 municipality pop. 9,280), Rizal prov., S Luzon, Philippines, on Manila Bay, on railroad and 8 mi. S of Manila; agr. center (rice, fruit).
Las Plumas (läs plōō'mäs), village (pop. estimate 100), ⊙ Mártires dept., E central Chubut natl. territory, Argentina, on Chubut R. and 115 mi. WSW of Rawson; rail junction; stock raising, fishing.
Las Quebradas (läs kābrä'dhäs), town, Izabal dept., E Guatemala, 6 mi. SE of Morales, in gold-placer dist.; lumbering; plywood factory.
Las Quemas or **Las Quemas del Salto** (läs kā'mäs dĕl säl'tō), village (1930 pop. 343), Llanquihue prov., S central Chile, on Maullín R. and 14 mi. NW of Puerto Montt, in agr. area (wheat, flax, potatoes, livestock); dairying, lumbering.
Lasqueti Island (lăskĕ'tē) (□ 26), SW B.C., in Strait of Georgia just S of Texada Isl., 50 mi. WNW of Vancouver; 10 mi. long, 3 mi. wide. Copper and gold mining in N central area. Village of Lasqueti is on W shore.
Las Rosas (läs rō'säs), town (pop. estimate 5,000), ⊙ Belgrano dept. (□ 940; 1947 pop. 30,155), S central Santa Fe prov., Argentina, 65 mi. NW of Rosario; rail junction and agr. center (wheat, corn, flax, alfalfa, fruit, livestock).
Las Rosas, town (pop. 5,712), Chiapas, S Mexico, at SW foot of Sierra de Hueytepec, 29 mi. SE of San Cristóbal de las Casas; agr. center (cereals, sugar cane, coffee, fruit, livestock, timber). Pinola until 1934.
Lassan (lä'sän), town (pop. 3,217), in former Prussian Pomerania prov., N Germany, after 1945 in Mecklenburg, on Peene R. estuary near its mouth on the Baltic, opposite Usedom isl., 10 mi. NE of Anklam; fishing port; woodworking.
Lassay (läsā'), village (pop. 1,028), Mayenne dept., W France, 11 mi. NNE of Mayenne; tanning, flour milling. Has 15th-cent. castle.
Lassem, Indonesia: see LASEM.
Lassen (lă'sun), county (□ 4,548; pop. 18,474), NE Calif.; ⊙ Susanville. On high volcanic plateau (here above 4,000 ft.) extending E from Cascade Range, whose southernmost summit (Lassen Peak) is near SW corner of co.; the Sierra Nevada is along SW and S borders. Highest alt. (over 8,000 ft.) in co. at Warner Mts. (NE). Includes part of LASSEN VOLCANIC NATIONAL PARK. Much of co. is in Modoc, Plumas, and Tahoe natl. forests. Eagle L. and HONEY LAKE are here. Drained by Pit and Susan rivers. Densely forested (pine, fir, cedar); logging and lumber milling are chief industries. Stock grazing (cattle, sheep); farms (some irrigation) produce hay, potatoes, dairy products, fruit, chiefly in Honey L. valley. Fishing, hunting, camping, winter sports attract vacationers. Region resisted with arms (1863) California's jurisdiction until Lassen co. was formed in 1864.
Lassen Peak or **Mount Lassen** (10,453 ft.), N Calif., at S end of Cascade Range, N of the Sierra Nevada, c.50 mi. E of Redding. Only active volcano in U.S., discovered (probably 1821) by Luis Argüello, later named for Peter Lassen, pioneer and guide. Most violent eruptions 1914–15; intermittently active until 1921. Peak is in **Lassen Volcanic National Park** (□ 161.6; established 1916), area of spectacular lava formations, hot sulphur springs, and other remnants of volcanic action. Skiing facilities in SW corner of park; small lakes in E, with facilities for camping and fishing.
Lasseube (läsûb'), village (pop. 303), Basses-Pyrénées dept., SW France, 7 mi. ENE of Oloron-Sainte-Marie; winegrowing.
Lassigny (läsēnyē'), agr. village (pop. 672), Oise dept., N France, 12 mi. N of Compiègne. Scene of heavy fighting (1914, 1917–18) in First World War.
Lassing (lä'sĭng), village (pop. 1,488), Styria, central Austria, 34 mi. NW of Knittelfeld; dairy farming.
Lassiter Shelf Ice (lă'sĭtûr), narrow belt of shelf ice in Antarctica, along Edith Ronne Land at head of Weddell Sea; extends c.400 naut. mi. S of Richard Black Coast in 78°S bet. 40° and 61°45'W. Discovered 1948 by U.S. expedition led by Finn Ronne.
L'Assomption (läsōpsyō'), county (□ 247; pop. 17,-543), S Que., on the St. Lawrence, N of Montreal; ⊙ L'Assomption.
L'Assomption, town (pop. 1,829), ⊙ L'Assomption co., S Que., on L'Assomption R. and 22 mi. NNE of Montreal; lumbering, woodworking, mfg. of shoes; market in tobacco-growing, dairying region. Site of Dominion Experimental Farm.
L'Assomption River, S Que., rises in the Laurentians in Mont Tremblant Park, flows SE to Joliette, thence S, past L'Assomption, to the St. Lawrence at N end of Montreal Isl.; 100 mi. long.
Lasswade, Scotland: see BONNYRIGG AND LASSWADE.
Las Tablas (läs tä'bläs), town (1950 pop. 2,711), ⊙ Los Santos prov., central Panama, in Pacific lowland, on branch of Inter-American Highway 90 mi. SW of Panama city. Commercial center; agr. (sugar cane, corn, rice, yucca, coffee, beans; horse raising). Formerly a gold-mining town. Its port is Mensabé.
Lastarria (lästär'yä), village (1930 pop. 560), Cautín prov., S central Chile, on railroad and 35 mi. S of Temuco, in agr. area (wheat, barley, peas, potatoes, livestock).
Lastarria Volcano, Argentina-Chile: see AZUFRE VOLCANO.
Lastein, Norway: see LARDAL.
Las Tejerías (läs tāhārē'äs), town (pop. 952), Aragua state, N Venezuela, on Tuy R., on railroad and highway, and 25 mi. SW of Caracas; coffee, cacao, corn, fruit.
Las Termas, Argentina: see TERMAS DEL RÍO HONDO.
Lástimas, Cerro (sĕ'rō läs'tēmäs), Andean peak (10,-000 ft.), Linares prov., S central Chile, 25 mi. SE of Linares.
Last Mountain (2,275 ft.), S central Sask., 50 mi. NNW of Regina. Near by is Last Mountain L.
Last Mountain Lake (□ 89), S central Sask., 22 mi. NW of Regina; 58 mi. long, 3 mi. wide. Drains S into Qu'Appelle R.
Las Toscas (läs tō'skäs), town (pop. estimate 2,000), NE Santa Fe prov., Argentina, on railroad and 60 mi. NNE of Reconquista; agr. center (sugar; also flax, corn, potatoes, rice, tobacco, livestock); sugar refineries.
Las Toscas, beach resort, Canelones dept., S Uruguay, on the Río de la Plata and 25 mi. ENE of Montevideo, near Atlántida.
Lastours (lästōōr'), village (pop. 221), Aude dept., S France, 8 mi. N of Carcassonne; blanket mfg. Silver and arsenic mining.
Lastoursville or **Lastourville** (lästōōr vēl'), village, S Gabon, Fr. Equatorial Africa, on Ogooué R. and 30 mi. NE of Koulamoutou.
Lastovo Island (lä'stôvô), Ital. *Lagosta* (lägô'stä), Dalmatian island in Adriatic Sea, S Croatia, Yugoslavia, 60 mi. W of Dubrovnik; 6 mi. long, 3 mi. wide; winegrowing. In Zara prov., Italy, 1920–47. Village of Lastovo is on N shore. Lastovo Channel, Serbo-Croatian *Lastovski Kanal*, separates it from Korcula Isl. (N).
Lastra a Signa (lä'strä ä sē'nyä), town (pop. 2,060), Firenze prov., Tuscany, central Italy, on Arno R. and 8 mi. W of Florence; mfg. (straw hats, pottery).
Lastras de Cuéllar (lä'sträs dhā kwĕ'lyär), town (pop. 1,320), Segovia prov., central Spain, 23 mi. N of Segovia; cereals, grapes; resins; livestock. Lumbering; flour milling, pottery mfg.
Lastres (lä'strĕs), village (pop. 1,520), Oviedo prov., NW Spain, fishing port on Bay of Biscay, and 20 mi. E of Gijón; fish processing, flour milling. Apple orchards in area. Coal shipping.
Lastres, Cape, Oviedo prov., NW Spain, on Bay of Biscay, and 18 mi. E of Gijón; 43°34'N 5°18'W.
Las Trincheras (läs trēnchä'räs), town (pop. 1,554), Carabobo state, N Venezuela, 9 mi. NNW of Valencia; health resort with radioactive thermal springs.
Lastrup (läs'trōōp), village (commune pop. 9,233), in Oldenburg, NW Germany, after 1945 in Lower Saxony, 8 mi. WSW of Cloppenburg; mfg. of agr. machinery.
Lastrup (lă'strŭp), village (pop. 158), Morrison co., central Minn., 17 mi. ENE of Little Falls; dairy products.
Las Tunas, Cuba: see VICTORIA DE LAS TUNAS.
La Suiza (lä swē'sä), village, Cartago prov., central Costa Rica, 6 mi. SE of Turrialba, in coffee area; stock raising.
Lasva or **Lashva** (both: läsh'vä), Serbo-Croatian *Lašva*, hamlet, central Bosnia, Yugoslavia, on Bosna R., at mouth of Lasva R., and 5 mi. S of Zenica, in Sarajevo coal area; rail junction.
Las Vacas (läs vä'käs), village (1930 pop. 74), Coquimbo prov., N central Chile, on railroad and 18 mi. SW of Illapel, in agr. area (fruit, grain, livestock); gold mining.
Las Varillas (läs värī'yäs), town (pop. 5,958), E Córdoba prov., Argentina, 50 mi. SW of San Francisco; rail junction and agr. center (wheat, flax, corn, livestock); produces casein, cheese, candy, flax fibers, agr. implements.
Lasva River or **Lashva River,** central Bosnia, Yugoslavia, rises NNE of Donji Vakuf, at S foot of Vlasic Mts.; flows 30 mi. ESE, past Travnik (hydroelectric plant), to Bosna R. at Lasva.
Las Vegas, Cuba: see VEGAS.
Las Vegas (läs vā'gŭs). **1** City (1940 pop. 8,422; 1950 pop. 24,624), ⊙ Clark co., SE Nev., 25 mi. WNW of Hoover Dam, c.225 mi. NE of Los Angeles, Calif.; alt. 2,033 ft.; second-largest city in state. Resort center in mining and truck-farming area; dairy products, beverages. Nellis Air Force Base. Atomic Energy Commission installations c.40 mi. NW, near Indian Springs. Site of city was watering place on trail to S Calif. Settled 1855 by Mormons, abandoned 1857. Fort Baker, U.S. military post, was established here 1864. City was resettled 1905, when railroad arrived; inc. 1911. The city is famous for its gambling casinos and divorce courts. **2** City (pop. 7,494), ⊙ San Miguel co., N central N.Mex., on Gallinas R., in Sangre de Cristo Mts., and 40 mi. ESE of Santa Fe, in irrigated region; alt. 6,398 ft. Forms one community with town (pop. 6,269) of Las Vegas, settled c.1833 on Santa Fe Trail and sometimes known as West Las Vegas. Las Vegas is mtn. and health resort, shipping center for livestock, lumber, wool, and hides in grain and livestock area. N.Mex. Highlands Univ. and state hosp. for insane are here. Hot springs 6 mi. N; ruins of Fort Union (1851–91), dude ranches, and Santa Fe Natl. Forest in vicinity.
Las Vigas (läs vē'gäs), town (pop. 3,888), Veracruz, E Mexico, in Sierra Madre Oriental, on railroad and 13 mi. NW of Jalapa; alt. 7,943 ft.; agr. center (cereals, coffee, fruit).
Las Villas (läs vē'yäs), province (□ 8,267; pop. 938,-581), central Cuba; ⊙ Santa Clara. Bet. Matanzas prov. (W) and Camagüey prov. (E), bounded by Nicholas Channel (N) and the Caribbean (S). Its indented coastline includes marshy Zapata Peninsula and is fringed by numerous keys. Rivers include Sagua la Grande, Agabama, and Zaza. Hilly ranges in center and E, rising in the Pico San Juan (Sierra de San Juan) to 3,793 ft. The scenic mts. near Trinidad have become a tourist area. Swamps in SW, where tropical hardwood and wildlife thrive. Immensely fertile region; sugar-cane growing and milling is principal industry; and there are more than 50 centrals, served by a dense rail net. Other products: tobacco, coffee, cacao, corn, fruit, cereals, vegetables. Excellent pastures. Gold, copper, iron, manganese, asphalt, and petroleum deposits. Leading ports: Caibarién (N), also sponge-fishing hq.; Cienfuegos (SW), on a fine sheltered bay. Other important centers: Sagua la Grande (N), Placetas (center), Sancti-Spíritus (E), Trinidad (S). Santa Clara is one of the isl.'s chief communications hubs. Prov. is traversed by the Central Highway. Formerly called Santa Clara prov.
Laswari (lŭsvä'rē), village, E Rajasthan, India, 20 mi. E of Alwar. In 1803, British under General Lake defeated Mahrattas in near-by battle.
Las Yaras (läs yä'räs), town (pop. 430), Tacna dept., S Peru, on Sama R. (irrigation) and 25 mi. NW of Tacna; sugar cane, cotton, corn; alcohol distilling.
Lata, La, Uruguay: see CARDONA.
Lataband Pass (lŭtŭbŭnd') (alt. 5,900 ft.), in N outlier of the Safed Koh, E Afghanistan, 21 mi. E of Kabul and on highway from Khyber Pass.
La Tablada, Argentina: see TABLADA.
Latacunga (lätäkōōng'gä), city (1950 pop. 10,340), ⊙ Cotopaxi prov., N central Ecuador, in the Andes, on Pan American Highway, on Quito-Guayaquil RR, on upper Patate R. and 50 mi. S of Quito; 0°56'S 78°35'W; alt. 9,055 ft. It is surrounded by ten snow-capped peaks, among them Cotopaxi (20 mi. NNE). Has a cool climate. Commercial center for a cattle-and-farming region, with flour mills, dairy plants, potteries, iron foundry. Large airport. The city dates back to pre-colonial times and was visited by the Incas for its thermal springs. Kaolin and saltpeter deposits in vicinity. Frequently shaken by earthquakes, it was destroyed in 1797 and severely hit in the 1949 earthquake.
La Tagua (lä tä'gwä), village, Caquetá commissary, SE Colombia, on Caquetá R. and 130 mi. SSE of Florencia; rice, cacao, sugar cane, gums. Until 1950 in Amazonas.
Latah (lā'tô, lätô'), county (□ 1,090; pop. 20,971), N Idaho; ⊙ Moscow. Long, rolling hills, drained by Palouse and Potlatch rivers. Borders on Wash. Lumber, livestock, wheat, cherries, pears. Includes part of St. Joe Natl. Forest in N. Formed 1888.
Latah, town (pop. 244), Spokane co., E Wash., 28 mi. SE of Spokane; grain, peas, livestock.
Latakia (lătŭkē'ŭ, lätū-), Arabic *El Ladhiqiya* or *Al-Laziqiyah*, Fr. *Lattaquié*, province (□ 2,433; 1946 pop. 471,673), W Syria, on the Mediterranean, bounded E by the Orontes; ⊙ Latakia. A region of tobacco, cotton, cereals, olives, figs, and sericulture. After First World War and under the French mandate of Syria, the area had a semi-autonomous status as the territory of the Alawites or Alaouites until it was inc. into the newly formed Syrian republic in 1942.

Latakia, Arabic *El Ladhiqiya* or *Al-Laziqiyah,* Fr. *Lattaquié,* Lat. *Laodicea ad Mare,* city (pop. c.35,000), ⊙ Latakia prov., W Syria, port on the Mediterranean opposite Cyprus, 110 mi. N of Beirut; 35°30'N 35°46'E. Only sheltered Syrian port deep enough for small seagoing ships. Famous for the tobacco (Latakia), which it exports; also trade in cotton, sericulture, cereals, olives, figs. An anc. Phoenician city, it later prospered under the Romans. Remained in Byzantine hands until captured (1103) by the Crusaders under Tancred. It throve in 12th cent. until taken (1188) by Saladin. Has some Roman remains.

Latchford, town (pop. 587), E Ont., on Montreal R. and 12 mi. SW of Haileybury, in mining region (silver, cobalt, nickel, antimony, mercury, bismuth, arsenic).

Latchford Without, parish (pop. 1,266), N Cheshire, England. Includes residential town of Latchford, on Mersey R., on Manchester Ship Canal (locks are here), just SE of Warrington; has steel mills.

Late (lä'tā'), uninhabited island (□ 6), N Tonga, S Pacific, W of Vavau group; rises to 1,700 ft.; dormant volcano.

Latefoss (lô'tüfôs), Nor. *Låtefoss,* waterfall (538 ft.) in Hordaland co., SW Norway, 8 mi. S of Odda; tourist attraction. Sometimes spelled Laatefoss.

Latera (lä'tĕrä), village (pop. 1,589), Viterbo prov., Latium, central Italy, near L. Bolsena, 16 mi. WSW of Orvieto; sulphur mining.

Laterina (lätĕrē'nä), village (pop. 689), Arezzo prov., Tuscany, central Italy, near the Arno, 9 mi. WNW of Arezzo.

Laterrière or **La Terrière** (lätĕrēâr'), village (pop. 512), S central Que., 9 mi. SSW of Chicoutimi; lumbering, dairying.

Laterza (lätĕr'tsä), town (pop. 10,022), Ionia prov., Apulia, S Italy, 10 mi. ESE of Matera, in agr. region (olives, grapes, cereals). Has castle and cathedral.

Latgale (lät'gälä), **Latgalia,** or **Latgallia** (lătgăl'yů, -ēü), former province (□ 6,054; 1935 pop. 567,163) of E Latvia; ⊙ Daugavpils. Inhabited chiefly by R.C. Latgals, related to Lutheran Letts. Originally ruled by Livonian Knights; passed in 1561 to Poland-Lithuania and in 1772 to Russia. Part of Rus. Vitebsk govt. until 1920, when it passed to independent Latvia. The northernmost, predominantly Rus. section (□ c.500), including Kachanovo and Pytalovo, was originally in Pskov principality (absorbed 1510 by Russia), later in Rus. Pskov govt. until 1920, when it joined independent Latvia; in 1945, it was again attached to Pskov oblast of Russian SFSR.

Latham (lā'thům). **1** Village (pop. 387), Logan co., central Ill., 13 mi. NW of Decatur, in agr. and bituminous-coal area. **2** City (pop. 218), Butler co., SE Kansas, 35 mi. ESE of Wichita, in cattle region. **3** Town (pop. 172), Moniteau co., central Mo., 8 mi. SW of California.

Latheron (lă'dhürůn), fishing village and parish (pop. 3,276), S Caithness, Scotland, on Moray Firth, 15 mi. SW of Wick.

Lathi (lä'tē), town (pop. 6,603), SE Saurashtra, India, 50 mi. W of Bhaunagar; local agr. market (millet, cotton). Was ⊙ former Eastern Kathiawar state of Lathi (□ 48; pop. 10,812) of Western India States agency; stage merged 1948 with Saurashtra.

Lathrop (lā'thrŭp). **1** Village (pop. c.300), San Joaquin co., central Calif., 9 mi. S of Stockton; U.S. army supply depot here. **2** City (pop. 888), Clinton co., NW Mo., 30 mi. SE of St. Joseph; agr., mule market.

Latiano (lätyä'nô), town (pop. 9,496), Brindisi prov., Apulia, S Italy, 13 mi. SW of Brindisi; agr. center (wine, olive oil, figs, cereals).

Latimer, county (□ 737; pop. 9,690), SE Okla.; ⊙ Wilburton. Drained by small Gaines Creek; part of Ouachita Mts. in SE. Cattle raising, lumbering, coal mining; natural-gas wells; some agr. Includes a state park. Formed 1907.

Latimer. 1 Town (pop. 434), Franklin co., N central Iowa, 28 mi. SSW of Mason City, in livestock and grain area. **2** City (pop. 34), Morris co., E central Kansas, 20 mi. S of Junction City; grazing, farming.

Latina (lätē'nä), until 1947 **Littoria** (lēt-tô'rēä), province (□ 868; pop. 237,333), Latium, S central Italy; ⊙ Latina. Borders on Tyrrhenian Sea, with reclaimed PONTINE MARSHES on coast, surrounded by Apennine hills. Agr. (cereals, grapes, olives, citrus fruit, sugar beets); stock raising (cattle, sheep). Fishing (Gaeta, Terracina). Mfg. at Formia. Formed 1934 from Roma prov.

Latina, until 1947 **Littoria,** town (pop. 2,577), ⊙ Latina prov., Latium, S central Italy, 37 mi. SE of Rome; 41°28'N 12°54'E. A modern agr. town; beet-sugar refinery, fruit and vegetable cannery, soap and glass factories; 1st center founded (1932) by Mussolini in the reclaimed Pontine Marshes. Became ⊙ prov. in 1934. Damaged (1943-44) in Second World War.

Latin America, collective term for the countries S of the Rio Grande speaking languages derived from Latin. It includes the 20 republics: Argentina, Bolivia, Brazil, Chile, Colombia, Costa Rica, Cuba, Dominican Republic, Ecuador, Guatemala, Haiti, Honduras, Mexico, Nicaragua, Panama, Paraguay, Peru, Salvador, Uruguay, Venezuela. Except for French-speaking Haiti and Portuguese-speaking Brazil, Spanish is the official language in all of them. The term is sometimes also used to include Puerto Rico (a U.S. territory), the French West Indies (including French Guiana), and other isls. of the West Indies where a Romance tongue is spoken.

Latin Way, Lat. *Via Latina,* anc. Roman road extending from Rome SE past Tusculum to the Appian Way near Capua.

Latir Peak (12,723 ft.), Sangre de Cristo Mts., N N.Mex., near Colo. line, 9 mi. NE of Questa.

Latisana (lätēzä'nä), town (pop. 3,563), Udine prov., Fruili-Venezia Giulia, NE Italy, on Tagliamento R. and 23 mi. SSW of Udine; agr. center; wine making.

Latium (lā'shům), Ital. *Lazio* (lä'tsyô), region (□ 6,634; pop. 2,654,924), central Italy; ⊙ Rome. Bordered by Tuscany (N), Campania (S), Umbria and Abruzzi e Molise (E), and Tyrrhenian Sea (W). Comprises 5 provs.: FROSINONE, LATINA, RIETI, ROMA, VITERBO. Includes Pontine (or Ponza) Isls. Consists of coastal plain (narrow in N) extending c.140 mi. bet. Fiora (N) and Liri (Garigliano; S) rivers, enclosed by Apennine hills and mts. which cover most of inland area. Contains volcanic hills (Alban, Tolfa) and crater lakes (Albano, Bolsena, Bracciano, Nemi, Vico). Watered by lower Tiber, Aniene, Liri, Marta, Rapido, Sacco, and Velino rivers. Rainfall chiefly in spring and autumn. Agr. (wheat, corn, fodder, grapes, olives, fruit, vegetables) and stock raising (sheep, cattle) predominate; area expanded by reclamation work in CAMPAGNA DI ROMA and PONTINE MARSHES. Fishing (Gaeta, Civitavecchia, Terracina, Anzio), forestry, mining (alum, asphalt), and quarrying (marble, alabaster, volcanic stone) also carried on. Hydroelectric plants along Aniene and Liri rivers. Has resorts in Alban Hills (Albano Laziale, Frascati), the Apennines (Fiuggi), and along coast (Lido di Roma, Gaeta). Its few industries include paper (Isola del Liri, Subiaco, Tivoli), chemicals (Allumiere), furniture (Viterbo), textiles (Rieti, Sora), and ironworking (Civitavecchia). Rome is the chief commercial and industrial center, CIVITAVECCHIA the main port. Anciently Latium included limited area E and S of the Tiber to Alban Hills; Latins lived here, with Etruscans N of the Tiber. Conquered by Romans in 3d cent. B.C.; after 8th cent. the duchy of Rome, including most of modern Latium, belonged to the popes. Most of it remained part of Papal States until its annexation (1870) to Italy. In Second World War suffered widespread damage (1943–44) from heavy fighting (ANZIO, Nettuno, CASSINO) and air bombs.

Latiyan (lätēyän'), village, Second Prov., in Teheran, N Iran, in Elburz mts., 15 mi. NE of Teheran, and on the river Jaj Rud; site of irrigation and hydroelectric project.

Lat Lum Kaeo (lät' lo͝om' kăo͞o), village (1937 pop. 3,992), Pathumthani prov., S Thailand, 20 mi. NE of Bangkok, in irrigated area; rice-milling center.

Latnaya (lät'nīŭ), town (1944 pop. over 500), W Voronezh oblast, Russian SFSR, 14 mi. W of Voronezh; brickworks. Refractory-clay and quartzite quarries.

La Toma, Argentina: see CUATRO DE JUNIO.

La Toma (lä tō'mä), resort, Trujillo Valdez prov., S Dominican Republic, 15 mi. W of Ciudad Trujillo.

La Toma, Ecuador: see LOJA, city.

Latonia Race Track, Ky.: see COVINGTON.

Latopolis, Egypt: see ISNA.

Latoritsa River (lä'tŭrētsŭ), Czech *Latorica* (lä'-tôrĭtsä), Hung. *Latorca* (lŏ'tôrkŏ), in W Transcarpathian Oblast, Ukrainian SSR, and SE Slovakia, Czechoslovakia; rises on S slope of the Beshchady 13 mi. WNW of Veretski Pass, flows S and W, past Svalyava and Mukachevo, joining Ondava R. 31 mi. SE of Kosice, Czechoslovakia, to form Bodrog R.; length, c.95 mi.

Latouche (lătōōsh'), village (1939 pop. 40), S Alaska, NW Latouche Isl., 55 mi. E of Seward; 60°3'N 147°54'W; supply point for farming, copper mining, fishing, fish processing.

Latouche Island (12 mi. long, 2–4 mi. wide), S Alaska, in Gulf of Alaska, at entrance of Prince William Sound, off E coast of Kenai Peninsula, 50 mi. E of Seward; 60°N 147°55'W; rises to 2,064 ft. Copper mining, fishing, fur farming. Named by Vancouver in 1794. Latouche village, NW.

Latour (lätōōr'), town (pop. 880), Luxembourg prov., SE Belgium, 2 mi. ESE of Virton; railroad shops. Medieval castle ruins.

Latour or **Latour-d'Auvergne** (-dōvâr'nyů), village (pop. 473), Puy-de-Dôme dept., central France, in Monts Dore, 25 mi. SW of Clermont-Ferrand; resort; cheese making.

Latour (lůtōōr'), town (pop. 80), Johnson co., W central Mo., 21 mi. WSW of Warrensburg.

Latour-d'Auvergne, France: see LATOUR.

Latour-de-Carol (-dů-kärôl'), village (pop. 358), Pyrénées-Orientales dept., S France, in CERDAGNE, on Sp. border 3 mi. NW of Puigcerdá; trans-Pyrenean RR junction and frontier station, just S of Puymorens tunnel. Sometimes spelled La Tour-de-Carol.

Latour-de-France (-dů-frãs'), village (pop. 1,007), Pyrénées-Orientales dept., S France, on Agly R. and 13 mi. WNW of Perpignan; winegrowing, honey making, feldspar processing.

Latrabjarg (lou'träbyärk"), Icelandic *Látrabjarg,* steep rocky cape, W extremity of Iceland, at tip of Vestfjarda Peninsula, on Denmark Strait; 65°30'N 24°32'W. Lighthouse. Scene of many shipwrecks.

La Trappe, France: see SOLIGNY-LA-TRAPPE.

La Trinidad, Argentina: see VILLA LA TRINIDAD.

La Trinidad (lä trēnēdhädh'), town (1950 pop. 1,282), Estelí dept., W Nicaragua, 16 mi. SSE of Estelí, on Inter-American Highway; rice, corn; livestock, poultry. Exports eggs.

La Trinidad (lů trĭ'nĭdăd", Sp. lä trēnēdhädh') or **Trinidad,** village (1939 pop. 1,195; 1948 municipality pop. 7,994), Benguet sub-prov., Mountain Prov., N Luzon, Philippines, 4 mi. N of Baguio; truck gardening.

La Trinitaria (lä trēnētär'yä), town (pop. 2,279), Chiapas, S Mexico, in Sierra Madre, 10 mi. SSE of Comitán; alt. 5,262 ft.; cereals, sugar cane, tobacco, fruit, livestock. Customhouse. Zapaluta until 1934.

Latrobe (lůtrōb'), town (pop. 1,716), N Tasmania, 40 mi. WNW of Launceston, near mouth of Mersey R.; cattle; flax mill, sawmill.

Latrobe, borough (pop. 11,811), Westmoreland co., SW central Pa., on Loyalhanna Creek and 33 mi. ESE of Pittsburgh; bituminous coal; mfg. (metal products, ceramics, plastics, textiles); agr. St. Vincent Col. here. Inc. 1854.

Latrobe, Mount, Australia: see WILSON'S PROMONTORY.

Latronico (lätrô'nēkô), town (pop. 3,093), Potenza prov., Basilicata, S Italy, 13 mi. ESE of Lagonegro; wine, olive oil. Marble quarries and sulphur baths near by.

Latronquière (lätrōkyâr'), village (pop. 376), Lot dept., SW France, 14 mi. N of Figeac; cattle, sheep.

Latrun (lätro͞on'), village of Palestine, after 1948 in W Jordan, in Judaean Hills, 15 mi. WNW of Jerusalem; road center. After 1945 site of large British detention camp. In 1948 Arab stronghold athwart road from coast to Jerusalem; blowing up of pumping station here cut Jerusalem's water supply.

Latsch, Italy: see LACES.

Latta, town (pop. 1,602), Dillon co., NE S.C., 21 mi. NE of Florence; trading and shipping center for tobacco and cotton; cannery.

Lattaquié, Syria: see LATAKIA.

Lattimore (lă'tůmōr), town (pop. 286), Cleveland co., S N.C., 6 mi. W of Shelby.

Lattingtown, summer-resort village (pop. 745), Nassau co., SE N.Y., on N shore of W Long Isl., just NE of Glen Cove.

Latty, village (pop. 272), Paulding co., NW Ohio, 17 mi. SW of Defiance, in agr. area; grain milling.

La Tuque, Que.: see TUQUE, LA.

Latur (lä'to͞or), town (pop. 24,985), Osmanabad dist., W Hyderabad state, India, 39 mi. ENE of Osmanabad; rail spur terminus; cotton-ginning and grain trade (chiefly wheat, millet, rice) center. Ships cotton to Barsi mills, 60 mi. W, by rail. Latur Road station is on another railroad, 19 mi. ENE.

Latvia (lăt'vēů), Lettish *Latvija* (lät'vĭyä), Ger. *Lettland,* Pol. *Łotwa,* Rus. *Latviya,* one of the Baltic States of NE Europe, since 1940 a constituent (Soviet Socialist) republic (□ 24,900; 1947 pop. estimate 1,800,000; 1935 pop. 1,950,502), of the USSR, but in 1951 still unrecognized as such by the U.S.; ⊙ RIGA. Borders on Estonia (N), Lithuania (S), Baltic Sea (with sand-dune lined Gulf of Riga; W), and Russian SFSR (E). Chiefly a lowland centered on fertile Riga-Jelgava plain, with glacial ridges in Courland and Livonia (LIVONIAN SWITZERLAND) rising to 1,017 ft.; drained by Gauja, Western Dvina (Daugava), Lielupe, and Venta rivers, used chiefly for timber floating. Forests (N, W) cover 20% of area, grasslands 14%, marshes 12%. Moderate humid continental climate; mean temp., 20°–23°F. (Jan.), 62°–65°F. (July); yearly precipitation, 22–26 in. Pop. consists of Latvians or Letts (76%; a Baltic ethnic group of Lutheran religion), Latgals (15%; related to Latvians, but of R.C. religion), Russians, Jews. Administratively, Latvia is divided (since 1950) into independent cities and raions. Dairy-cattle and hog raising is chief agr. occupation, based on fodder grasses (clover, timothy), root crops, and potatoes. Grain (oats, rye, barley), fiber flax, sugar beets, tobacco, and hops also grown, and, S of the Western Dvina, pears, plums, berries. Leading industries (food processing, textile milling, mfg. of chemicals, lumber products, and machinery) in Riga, LIEPAJA, DAUGAVPILS, JELGAVA, and VENTSPILS. Power is furnished by peat-based power stations and KEGUMS hydroelectric plant. Herring, salmon, and cod fisheries along coast. Principal exports: butter, cheese, bacon, fish products, linen, cotton and rubber goods, matches, paper, telephone and radio equipment. Latvia falls into 4 regions: N of the Western Dvina are VIDZEME and LATGALE (parts of historic Livonia); S of river are KURZEME and ZEMGALE (parts of historic Courland). The Lettish tribes were conquered by Livonian Knights and christianized in early 13th cent.; after dissolution (1561) of the Order, LIVONIA (N of the Western Dvina) passed to Poland-Lithuania, while COURLAND (S of the Western Dvina) became a duchy under Pol. suzerainty. In 1629, Sweden conquered Livonia (except Latgale), losing it to Russia in 1721. With 1st (1772) and 3d (1795) partitions of Poland, Latgale and Courland also passed to Russia. Under Rus. rule, the German "Baltic barons" retained their power and Latvia attained great economic prosperity by 1900, handling c.20% of Rus. exports. Latvia was devastated in First World War. The modern Latvian state (proclaimed 1918 an independent republic; recognized 1920 by USSR) was formed out of Rus. Courland (except Palanga) and S Livonia govts., as well as portions of govts. of Vitebsk (Latgale) and Pskov (Pytalovo). Granting (1939) by Latvia of military bases to USSR paved the way for its annexation in 1940. During Second World War, Latvia was held (1941–44) by Germans, who also held a Courland bridgehead until end of war in 1945. In 1945 the extreme NE section (largely Russian pop.) of Latvia passed to Pskov oblast of Russian SFSR.

La-tzu, Tibet: see LHATSE.

Lau (lou), group of limestone islands of Fiji, SW Pacific, 150 mi. E of Viti Levu; 17°S 178°30'W; enclosed within barrier reef (circumference, 77 mi.). Includes VANUA MBALAVU (largest isl.), KANATHEA, MANGO, THITHIA, MOALA, TOTOYA, MATUKU, KAMBARA, and several smaller isls. Named Exploring Isls. by U.S. expedition (1840).

Lau, town, Adamawa prov., Northern Provinces, E Nigeria, landing on Benue R. and 21 mi. NNW of Jalingo; cassava, millet, durra; cattle raising.

Lau, Uad (wädh' lou'), river of NW Sp. Morocco, rises in Rif Mts. S of Xauen, flows 40 mi. NNE to the Mediterranean at Uad Lau village. On its middle course is Sp. Morocco's only hydroelectric plant.

Laubach (lou'bäkh), town (pop. 2,999), central Hesse, W Germany, in former Upper Hesse prov., 13 mi. ESE of Giessen; lumber milling. Has Renaissance castle.

Lauban, Poland: see LUBAN.

Laucala, Fiji: see LAUTHALA.

Lauca River (lou'kä), in Omro dept., W Bolivia, rises in the Andes on Chilean line, flows 120 mi. SE, across high plateau, to L. Coipasa 29 mi. SSE of Huachacalla. Receives Turco R.

Laucha (lou'khä), town (pop. 3,655), in former Prussian Saxony prov., central Germany, after 1945 in Saxony-Anhalt, on the Unstrut and 8 mi. NW of Naumburg; noted for its bell foundry. Has 15th-cent. church and remains of old town walls.

Lauchhammer (loukh'hä"mŭr), town (pop. 6,401), in former Prussian Saxony prov., central Germany, after 1945 in Saxony-Anhalt, 9 mi. W of Senftenberg; lignite mining; bronze casting (since 1725). Power station.

Lauchheim (loukh'hīm), town (pop. 1,533), N Württemberg, Germany, after 1945 in Württemberg-Baden, on the Jagst and 7 mi. ENE of Aalen; grain.

Lauch River (lōk, Ger. loukh), Haut-Rhin dept., E France, rises in the Vosges at foot of the Ballon de Guebwiller, flows E, past Guebwiller, then N in Alsatian lowland, to the Thur 3 mi. above Colmar; c.20 mi. long.

Lauchstädt, Bad, Germany: see BAD LAUCHSTÄDT.

Lauda (lou'dä), town (pop. 4,235), N Baden, Germany, after 1945 in Württemberg-Baden, on the Tauber and 7 mi. NNW of Mergentheim; rail junction; mfg. of musical instruments; metal- and woodworking. Has 16th-cent. bridge.

Laudar, Aden: see LODAR.

Lauder (lô'dŭr), burgh (1931 pop. 628; 1951 census 623), W Berwick, Scotland, in Lauderdale, on Leader Water and 8 mi. NNE of Galashiels; agr. market. Has 17th-cent. church. Near by is 17th-cent. Thirlestane Castle, seat of earl of Lauderdale.

Lauderdale, Scotland: see LEADER WATER.

Lauderdale (lô'dŭrdāl). **1** County (□ 688; pop. 54,179), extreme NW Ala.; ⊙ Florence. Cotton-growing area bordering on Miss. and Tenn., drained in S by Pickwick Landing Reservoir, L. Wilson, and Wheeler Reservoir. Wilson and Wheeler dams provide hydroelectric power for industries at Florence. Formed 1918. **2** County (□ 721; pop. 64,171), E Miss., bordering E on Ala.; ⊙ MERIDIAN. Drained by affluents of Chickasawhay R. Agr. (cotton, corn, sweet potatoes), dairying, stock raising (beef cattle, hogs); lumbering. Formed 1833. **3** County (□ 487; pop. 25,047), W Tenn.; ⊙ Ripley. Bounded W by the Mississippi, N by Forked Deer R., S by Hatchie R. Timber and agr. area (cotton, corn, livestock, truck). Formed 1835.

Lauderdale, village (pop. 1,033), Ramsey co., E Minn., NW suburb of St. Paul.

Lauderdale-by-the-Sea, town (pop. 234), Broward co., S Fla., 7 mi. N of Fort Lauderdale.

Laudun (lōdŭ'), village (pop. 935), Gard dept., S France, 13 mi. NW of Avignon; winegrowing.

Lauenburg or **Lauenburg an der Elbe** (lou'ŭnbŏŏrk än dĕr ĕl'bŭ), town (pop. 10,613), in Schleswig-Holstein, NW Germany, harbor on right bank of Elbe R., at mouth of Elbe-Trave Canal, and 10 mi. NE of Lüneburg; mfg. of chemicals, furniture, matches, barrels; weaving. Has many 16th- and 17th-cent. paneled bldgs. Chartered c.1260.

Lauenburg, Poland: see LEBORK.

Lauenburg, Duchy of, Germany: see RATZEBURG.

Lauenburg an der Elbe, Germany: see LAUENBURG.

Lauenförde (lou"ŭnfûr'dŭ), village (pop. 2,816), in former Prussian prov. of Hanover, W Germany, after 1945 in Lower Saxony, on right bank of the Weser and 12 mi. S of Holzminden; woodworking.

Lauenstein (lou'ŭn-shtīn), town (pop. 1,286), Saxony, E central Germany, in the Erzgebirge, 14 mi. SSW of Pirna, near Czechoslovak border; woodworking, toy mfg., straw plaiting. Has old castle.

Lauerz, Lake of, and **Lauerzersee**, Switzerland: see LOWERZ, LAKE OF.

Lauf (louf), town (pop. 9,868), Middle Franconia, N central Bavaria, Germany, on the Pegnitz and 10 mi. ENE of Nuremberg; mfg. of porcelain, bronze products, stoves, precision instruments, chemicals; woodworking, printing, tanning, brewing. On isl. in the Pegnitz is early-15th-cent. castle.

Laufen (lou'fŭn), town (pop. 4,324), Upper Bavaria, Germany, on the Salzach and 14 mi. ENE of Traunstein, on Austrian border; lumber milling, printing, tanning. Has mid-14th-cent. church. Chartered c.1041.

Laufen, town (pop. 2,797), Bern canton, NW Switzerland, on Birs R. and 10 mi. SSW of Basel; metal products, cement, tiles, silk textiles, flour, pastry; woodworking.

Laufenburg (–bŏŏrk), village (pop. 2,006), S Baden, Germany, at S foot of Black Forest, on the Rhine (Swiss border; bridge, lock) and 5 mi. E of Säckingen; hydroelectric plant; mfg. (textiles, chemicals). Formerly called Kleinlaufenburg.

Laufenburg, village (pop. 1,531), Aargau canton, N Switzerland, on the Rhine (Ger. border; bridge) and 12 mi. N of Aarau; hydroelectric plant; knit goods, chemicals, woodworking. Late-Gothic church, ruined castle. Formerly Grosslaufenburg.

Lauffen or **Lauffen am Neckar** (lou'fŭn äm nĕ'kär), town (pop. 6,365), N Württemberg, Germany, after 1945 in Württemberg-Baden, on the canalized Neckar and 5 mi. SW of Heilbronn; rail junction; mfg. (shoes, cigars, Portland cement, chemicals). Has Gothic church. Poet Hölderlin b. here.

Laugharne (lärn), town and parish (pop. 880), SW Carmarthen, Wales, on Taf R. estuary and 9 mi. SW of Carmarthen; agr. market and small port. Has remains of castle, built c.1100, taken 1647 by Parliamentarians. Church dates from 15th cent.

Lauingen (lou'ĭng"ŭn), town (pop. 7,547), Swabia, W Bavaria, Germany, on the Danube and 23 mi. ENE of Ulm; grain and hog market; machinery and textile mfg.; bell foundries; woodworking, brewing. Has remains of medieval town wall; tower (1478); late-Gothic church, and late-18th-cent. town hall. Chartered c.1156, it was 2d capital of small principality of Pfalz-Neuburg. Albertus Magnus (1193?–1280) b. here.

Laujar de Andarax (louhär' dhä ändäräks'), town (pop. 3,348), Almería prov., S Spain, 11 mi. NNE of Berja; olive-oil processing, flour milling, knit-goods mfg. Ships grapes. Wine, cereals, fruit, vegetables, sugar beets in area. Mineral springs.

Laukaa (lou'kä), Swedish *Laukas* (lou'käs), village (commune pop. 14,518), Vaasa co., S central Finland, in lake region, 14 mi. NNE of Jyväskylä; lumbering region.

Laumes-D'Alésia, Les, France: see VENAREY.

Laun, Czechoslovakia: see LOUNY.

Launay (lōnā'), village, W Que., 20 mi. WNW of Amos; gold mining.

Launceston (lôn'stŭn, län'–, lô'stŭn, lä'–), municipal borough (1931 pop. 4,071; 1951 census 4,467), E Cornwall, England, on Kensey R. and 20 mi. NE of Bodmin; agr. market; tanneries, agr.-equipment works. Has ruins of Norman castle and of early-12th-cent. Augustinian priory. Granite church dates from 14th cent.

Launceston (lôn'sĕstŭn, lŏn'–), city and port (pop. 37,717; metropolitan Launceston 40,442), N Tasmania, 2d largest city of Tasmania, at head of Tamar R., at confluence of N.Esk and S.Esk rivers; 41°45'S 147°6'E. Steamship service to South Australia and Victoria; agr. and commercial center; butter, flour, oatmeal; woolen goods, lock- and brassworks, sporting-goods factories, sawmills. Cataract Cliff Gardens, Royal Park, Queen Victoria Mus. Scenic gorge near. Founded 1805.

Launes, Norway: see LAUVSNES.

Launglon (loung-lōn'), village, Tavoy dist., Lower Burma, on peninsula, 10 mi. SW of Tavoy.

Laungowal (loung-gō'väl), town (pop. 6,848), central Patiala and East Punjab States Union, India, 45 mi. WSW of Patiala; gram, wheat. Sometimes spelled Longowal.

La Unión (lä ōōnyōn'), town (pop. 7,234), ⊙ La Unión dept. (□ 1,242; pop. 30,315), Valdivia prov., S central Chile, 38 mi. SSE of Valdivia, in lake dist. Rail junction, commercial and agr. center (cereals, sugar beets, livestock); sawmills, flour mills, distilleries, tanneries, linen mills. Founded 1821.

La Unión, town (pop. 2,626), Nariño dept., SW Colombia, on Pasto-Popayán highway, in Cordillera Central, 28 mi. NNE of Pasto; alt. 5,856 ft. Cereals, cacao, coffee, sugar cane, potatoes, fruit, livestock.

La Unión. 1 Town, Cartago prov., Costa Rica: see TRES RÍOS. **2** Village (dist. pop. 4,192), Puntarenas prov., W Costa Rica, 4 mi. NW of Miramar; gold mining, lumbering.

La Unión. 1 City, San Marcos dept., Guatemala: see SAN MARCOS city. **2** Town (1950 pop. 1,447), Zacapa dept., E Guatemala, in highlands, 11 mi. SSE of Gualán; coffee, sugar cane, livestock. Until c.1920, Monte Oscuro.

La Unión. 1 Town (pop. 749), Copán dept., W Honduras, on E slope of Sierra del Gallinero, 7 mi. SW of Santa Rosa, in tobacco area; cigar mfg.; sugar cane, livestock. **2** Town (pop. 888), Lempira dept., W Honduras, in Sierra de Atima, 17 mi. NE of Gracias; tobacco, grain. **3** Town (pop. 352), Olancho dept., central Honduras, on upper Yaguale R. (right affluent of Aguán R.) and 11 mi. NNW of Salamá; sugar milling; coffee, sugar, rice. Airfield.

La Unión, town (pop. 767), Guerrero, SW Mexico, in Pacific lowland, 75 mi. SW of Huetamo, 145 mi. NW of Acapulco; rice, sugar cane, fruit. Silver deposits near by.

La Unión, province, Peru: see COTAHUASI.

La Unión. 1 City (pop. 1,799), ⊙ Dos de Mayo prov. (□ 2,306; pop. 65,522), Huánuco dept., central Peru, on E slopes of Cordillera Blanca of the Andes, near Marañón R., 40 mi. WNW of Huánuco. Barley, potatoes; sheep raising. **2** Town (pop. 3,232), Piura dept., NW Peru, on coastal plain, on Piura R. and 15 mi. SSW of Piura, in irrigated cotton area.

La Union, province (□ 530; 1948 pop. 237,340), N central Luzon, Philippines, bounded W by S.China Sea and Lingayen Gulf; ⊙ SAN FERNANDO. Largely mountainous terrain, drained by many small streams. Rice is principal product.

La Unión, department (□ 883; pop. 123,591), E Salvador; ⊙ La Unión. Bounded N by Honduras, E by Nicaragua (along Goascorán R.), SE by Gulf of Fonseca of the Pacific; mountainous (W), sloping E to coastal lowland; contains volcano Conchagua. Agr. (grain, coffee, sugar cane), livestock raising. Fisheries, salt production, and tortoise-shell collection along coast. Gold and silver mining (San Sebastián). Main centers are La Unión and Santa Rosa, served by railroad and Inter-American Highway. Formed 1865.

La Unión, city (pop. 6,757), ⊙ La Unión dept., E Salvador, port on La Unión Bay (NW inlet of Gulf of Fonseca), on spur of Inter-American Highway and railroad, and 95 mi. ESE of San Salvador, at N foot of volcano Conchagua; 13°20'N 87°51'W. Main Pacific port of Salvador, handling c.50% of country's ocean trade; exports coffee, indigo, sugar, cotton, henequen, silver, and gold. Tortoise-shell industry, fisheries, livestock raising. Most harbor facilities at port of Cutuco (1.5 mi. E); developed beach resorts near by.

La Unión (lä ōōnyōn'), town (pop. 1,186), Barinas state, W Venezuela, landing on Portuguesa R., at mouth of Guanare R., and 55 mi. SSW of Calabozo; cattle raising.

Laupahoehoe (lou'pähoi'hoi"), village (pop. 398), E Hawaii, T.H., on leaf-shaped point; site of lighthouse.

Laupen (lou'pŭn), town (pop. 1,314), Bern canton, W Switzerland, on Saane R., at mouth of Sense R., and 10 mi. WSW of Bern.

Lauperswil (lou'pŭrsvēl), town (pop. 2,812), Bern canton, W central Switzerland, in the EMMENTAL, 14 mi. E of Bern.

Laupheim (loup'hīm), town (pop. 6,708), S Württemberg, Germany, after 1945 in Württemberg-Hohenzollern, 12 mi. SW of Ulm; textile mfg., woodworking. Has 17th-cent. church.

Laur (lour), town (1939 pop. 2,187; 1948 municipality pop. 16,964), Nueva Ecija prov., central Luzon, Philippines, 16 mi. ENE of Cabanatuan; agr. center (rice, corn). Manganese deposits.

Laura. 1 Settlement, NE Queensland, Australia, 125 mi. NW of Cairns; terminus of railroad from Cooktown; fruit, cattle. **2** Town (pop. 594), S South Australia, 17 mi. E of Port Pirie; wheat, fruit, dairy products.

Laura, village (pop. 380), Miami co., W Ohio, 15 mi. SW of Piqua, in agr. area; cannery.

Lauragais (lōrägā'), small region and former dist. of Languedoc prov., S France, now in Tarn, Haute-Garonne, and Aude depts.; ⊙ Castelnaudary. Wheat growing.

Lauragais, Col de, France: see NAUROUZE, COL DE.

Laurahütte, Poland: see SIEMIANOWICE.

Laurana, Yugoslavia: see OPATIJA.

La Urbana (lä ōōrbä'nä), town (pop. 388), Bolívar state, SE Venezuela, landing on Orinoco R. (Apure state border) and 65 mi. SW of Caicara; 7°18'N 66°57'W; forest products (rubber, balata gum), livestock.

Laureana di Borrello (lourĕä'nä dē bôr-rĕl'lō), town (pop. 4,800), Reggio di Calabria prov., Calabria, S Italy, 16 mi. NE of Palmi; olive pressing, sawmilling; mfg. of wagon wheels.

Laurel, county (□ 448; pop. 25,797), SE Ky.; ⊙ London. Bounded W by Rockcastle R., S by Laurel R.; drained by several creeks. Mtn. agr. area, in Cumberland foothills; livestock, poultry, dairy products, tobacco, corn, wheat, fruit; coal mines, timber. Includes Levi Jackson Wilderness

Road State Park and part of Cumberland Natl. Forest. Formed 1825.

Laurel. 1 Town (pop. 2,700), Sussex co., SW Del., 15 mi. N of Salisbury, Md., and on Laurel R.; canning, packing, and shipping center for truck products; lumber, fertilizer. Laid out 1802, inc. 1883. **2** Town (pop. 680), Franklin co., SE Ind., 10 mi. SSE of Connersville, in agr. area. **3** Town (pop. 257), Marshall co., central Iowa, 12 mi. S of Marshalltown, in agr. area. **4** Town (pop. 4,482), Prince Georges co., central Md., on Patuxent R. and 18 mi. NE of Washington, in agr. area (tobacco, corn, wheat, truck). Large race track. Fort George G. Meade is near by. Site was patented in late 17th cent. **5** City (pop. 25,038), a ⊙ Jones co., SE Miss., on Tallahala Creek and 27 mi. NNE of Hattiesburg; trade, rail, and processing center for pine-timber and agr. area; mfg. of textiles, fiberboard, chemicals, farm tools, sweet-potato starch, cotton and cottonseed products, clothing; meat packing, naval-stores processing. Lauren Rogers Library here has a mus. of art. A U.S. Indian school and Bogue Homo Indian Reservation are near by. Town founded 1881 as lumber camp. **6** City (pop. 3,663), Yellowstone co., S Mont., on Yellowstone R., near mouth of Clarks Fork, and 16 mi. SW of Billings; oil refinery; shipping point for copper, zinc, lumber, grain, livestock, wool. Rail junction with yards and repair shops. Dairy products, sugar beets. Inc. 1908. **7** Village (pop. 944), Cedar co., NE Nebr., 35 mi. W of Sioux City, Iowa, and on Logan Creek; livestock, grain. **8** Village (pop. 1,165, with near-by Inman and Linden), Wise co., SW Va., near Big Stone Gap.

Laureldale, borough (pop. 3,585), Berks co., SE central Pa., 3 mi. N of Reading; textiles. Settled 1902, inc. 1930.

Laureles (lourä'lĕs), town (dist. pop. 3,027), Ñeembucú dept., S Paraguay, near Paraná R., 65 mi. ESE of Pilar; stock raising.

Laureles, village, Tacuarembó dept., N Uruguay, on railroad and 25 mi. NNE of Tacuarembó.

Laureles, Los, Chile: see LOS LAURELES.

Laurel Heights, village, Snohomish co., NW Wash., 3 mi. S of Everett.

Laurel Hill. 1 Town (pop. 327), Okaloosa co., NW Fla., near Ala. line, c.60 mi. NE of Pensacola. **2** Village (pop. c.400), Scotland co., S N.C., 5 mi. WNW of Laurinburg; mfg. of textiles, yarn.

Laurel Hill. 1 Ridge (2,400–2,900 ft.) of the Alleghenies, in SW Pa., runs 55 mi. NE from S Fayette co. to just W of Nanty Glo. Youghiogheny R. cuts through just below Confluence, Conemaugh R. just W of Johnstown. Bituminous coal, limestone, sandstone, clay, shale. **2** Ridge in W.Va.: see LAUREL RIDGE.

Laurel Hollow, village (pop. 169), Nassau co., SE N.Y., on N shore of Long Isl., 3 mi. W of Huntington, in summer-resort and diversified-farming area. Until 1935, called Laurelton.

Laurel Park, town (pop. 302), Henderson co., W N.C., just W of Hendersonville.

Laurel Ridge or **Laurel Hill,** N W.Va., a ridge of the Alleghenies; from Cheat R. W of Rowlesburg extends 32 mi. SSW to Tygart R. W of Elkins; rises to c.3,300 ft. Rich Mtn. is its S continuation. Scene (July 8, 1861) of Civil War engagement (battle of Laurel Hill) E of Belington, in which Confederate troops were forced to retreat.

Laurel River. 1 In SW Del., navigable tidal stream formed at Laurel by junction of short headstreams, flows c.7 mi. W to Nanticoke R. near Md. line. Sometimes called Broad Creek. **2** In SE Ky., rises in the Cumberlands in E Laurel co., flows 38 mi. generally SW to Cumberland R. 11 mi. W of Corbin.

Laurel Run, borough (pop. 858), Luzerne co., NE central Pa., 3 mi. SE of Wilkes-Barre.

Laurel Springs, borough (pop. 1,540), Camden co., SW N.J., 10 mi. SE of Camden; makes signal fuses, flares. Inc. 1913.

Laurelton (lô'rültŭn). 1 Village, Nassau co., N.Y.: see LAUREL HOLLOW. **2** A residential section of SE Queens borough of New York city, SE N.Y.

Laurelville, village (pop. 482), Hocking co., S central Ohio, 16 mi. NE of Chillicothe, in agr. area; grain products, lumber.

Laurencekirk, burgh (1931 pop. 1,316; 1951 census 1,485), S Kincardine, Scotland, 13 mi. SW of Stonehaven; agr. market. In 18th cent. it was noted for its snuff boxes.

Laurens (lõrã'), village (pop. 1,014), Hérault dept., S France, 13 mi. N of Béziers; marble quarries.

Laurens. 1 (lô'rŭnz, lŏ'-) County (□ 811; pop. 33,123), central Ga.; ⊙ Dublin. Coastal plain agr. (cotton, corn, peanuts, livestock) and lumbering area intersected by Oconee R. Formed 1807. **2** (lŏ'rŭns) County (□ 713; pop. 46,974), NW central S.C.; ⊙ Laurens. Bounded SW by Saluda R., NE by Enoree R.; part of L. Greenwood is in S. Includes part of Sumter Natl. Forest. Agr. (especially cotton; also grain, vegetables, peanuts), dairying; mfg. (chiefly textiles). Formed 1785.

Laurens. 1 (lûrĕnz') Town (pop. 1,556), Pocahontas co., N central Iowa, c.40 mi. NW of Fort Dodge; mfg. of hoists, loaders, wagons; poultry packing, feed milking. Inc. 1890. **2** (lô'rŭnz) Village (pop. 261), Otsego co., central N.Y., 4 mi. N of Oneonta, in dairying area. Near by is Gilbert Lake State Park. **3** (lŏ'rŭns) City (pop. 8,658), ⊙ Laurens co., NW central S.C., 33 mi. S of Spartanburg and on tributary of the Saluda. Trade and mfg. center in agr. area; textiles, hosiery, glass, grain products, cottonseed oil, beverages.

Laurensberg (lou'rŭnsbĕrk), village (pop. 5,457), in former Prussian Rhine Prov., W Germany, after 1945 in North Rhine-Westphalia, 2 mi. NNW of Aachen.

Laurentian Mountains (lôrĕn'shŭn) or **Laurentides** (lô'rŭntīdz, Fr. lõrãtēd'), range in S Quebec, Canada, extending NE from Ottawa R. along N edge of St. Lawrence valley. Rises to over 3,800 ft. in Laurentides Park, N of Quebec, and to 3,150 ft. on Mt. Tremblant in Montagne Tremblant Park, NW of Montreal; just S of Laurentides Park, NE of Quebec, it rises to 3,905 ft. Near mouth of Saguenay R. it forms steep escarpment above St. Lawrence R.; forms watershed bet. Hudson Bay and the St. Lawrence. In the areas adjoining Montreal and Quebec are numerous winter and summer resorts. Laurentian Mts. constitute SE edge of the Precambrian **Laurentian Plateau** or **Canadian Shield,** which covers over ½ of Canada in the shape of a horseshoe, its S boundary running roughly from Labrador coast, around Hudson Bay, through Que. and Ont. and through lakes Winnipeg, Great Slave, and Great Bear, to the Arctic near mouth of Mackenzie R.; extends S into the U.S. to include the Adirondack Mts., Upper Michigan Peninsula, N Wis., and NE Minn. It has thousands of lakes and extensive marshy areas, remnants from the Pleistocene continental glacier. The area has enormous coniferous forest resources, hydroelectric potential, and mineral deposits, but remains largely undeveloped except for mining towns, lumbering camps, and fur-trading posts.

Laurentides (lô'rŭntīdz, Fr. lõrãtēd'), town (pop. 1,342), SW Que., 25 mi. NNW of Montreal; woodworking, truck gardening, dairying, tobacco growing and processing. Sir Wilfrid Laurier b. here. It was called St. Lin until inc. 1883.

Laurentides, range, Canada: see LAURENTIAN MOUNTAINS.

Laurentides Park, provincial park (□ 4,000), S central Que., on the Laurentian Plateau, N of Quebec and S of L. St. John; 80 mi. long, 60 mi. wide; rises to 3,800 ft. (S). Public recreation ground and game reserve, park contains c.1,600 lakes and vast network of streams. Chicoutimi R. rises in center of park. Established 1895.

Laurenzana (lourĕntsä'nä), town (pop. 4,059), Potenza prov., Basilicata, S Italy, 15 mi. SE of Potenza; meat and dairy products, wine.

Lauria (lou'rēä), commune (pop. 11,097), Potenza prov., Basilicata, S Italy, 11 mi. ESE of Sapri; agr. (cereals, fruit, potatoes), livestock raising. Chief villages, Lauria Inferiore (pop. 2,611) and just N, Lauria Superiore (pop. 2,158).

Lauricocha, Lake (lourēkō'chä), small Andean lake (c.4 mi. long; alt. 14,270 ft.), Huánuco dept., central Peru, 38 mi. NE of Cerro de Pasco. Feeding upper Marañón R., it is sometimes considered the source of the Amazon.

Laurie Island (lô'rē) (125 naut. mi. long, 1–3 naut. mi. wide), South Orkney Isls., in the South Atlantic, E of Coronation Isl.; 60°45'S 44°35'W. Discovered 1821. Claimed by Britain, but Argentina maintains a meteorological and radio station here.

Laurier (lô'rēŭr), village, Ferry co., NE Wash., port of entry at international line, 11 mi. ESE of Grand Forks, British Columbia.

Laurière (lõrēâr'), village (pop. 434), Haute-Vienne dept., W central France, 19 mi. NNE of Limoges; cattle.

Laurierville (lô'rēävĭl), village (pop. 383), S Que., 22 mi. NW of Thetford Mines; dairying.

Laurin (lûrā'), village (pop. c.100), Madison co., SW Mont., on Ruby R. and 50 mi. SSE of Butte, in livestock region.

Laurinburg (lŏ'rĭnbûrg), town (pop. 7,134), ⊙ Scotland co., S N.C., 37 mi. SW of Fayetteville, near S.C. line; mfg. of cotton yarn, textiles, cottonseed oil, fertilizer, plywood, veneer; flour and lumber mills. Seat of Laurinburg Industrial Inst. Inc. 1877.

Laurino (lourē'nō), town (pop. 1,826), Salerno prov., Campania, S Italy, 8 mi. NNE of Vallo della Lucania.

Laurion or **Lavrion** (both: läv'rēōn), Lat. *Laurium* (lô'rēŭm), city (1940 pop. 6,680), Attica nome, E central Greece, port on Gulf of Petalion opposite Makronesos isl., on railroad (terminus) and 26 mi. SE of Athens. Major smelting and shipping center for complex ores of lead-zinc, iron, and silver mined at Kamariza (1928 pop. 1,003), 2.5 mi. W, included in Laurion municipality. Anc. Laurium was important for its silver mines which contributed to growth of Athens. Mining ceased 400 B.C. and was resumed 1864 by French and 1875 by Greeks. Formerly called Ergasteria. Near by are ruins of a temple of Poseidon.

Laurito (lourē'tō), village (pop. 1,562), Salerno prov., Campania, S Italy, 8 mi. SE of Vallo della Lucania.

Lauritsala (lou'rĭtsä"lä), town (pop. 9,977), Kymi co., SE Finland, near USSR border, on S shore of L. Saimaa, at NW end of Saimaa Canal, 3 mi. ENE of Lappeenranta; lumber, cellulose, plywood, and bobbin mills.

Laurium, Greece: see LAURION.

Laurium (lô'rēŭm), village (pop. 3,211), Houghton co., NW Upper Peninsula, Mich., 9 mi. NE of Houghton, in copper-mining region. Inc. 1889.

Lauriya Nandangarh, India: see BETTIAH.

Lauro (lou'rō), village (pop. 1,316), Avellino prov., Campania, S Italy, 16 mi. NW of Salerno.

Lauro, Monte (môn'tĕ), highest peak (3,231 ft.) in Monti Iblei and in Siracusa prov., SE Sicily; source of Irminio, Acate, and Anapo rivers.

Lauro Müller (läoo'roo mooler'), town (pop. 1,266), SE Santa Catarina, Brazil, rail terminus 40 mi. W of Laguna; coal mining. Named for 1st governor of state after establishment of republic (1889).

Lausanne (lõzăn', Fr. lõzän'), city (1950 pop. 107,225, including the port Ouchy), ⊙ Vaud canton, W Switzerland, on L. Geneva, on S slopes of Mt. Jorat; large year-round resort (mainly fall and summer). Originally a Celtic settlement (Roman *Lausonium*), Lausanne was SW of its present location until destroyed (c.379) and moved to the hill of the Cité. An episcopal see since late 6th cent., Lausanne was ruled by its prince-bishops and later by Bern; it accepted the Reformation in 1536. Became ⊙ Vaud in 1803. Mfg. (radios, leather and metal products, clothes, pastry, biscuits, beer, chemicals); printing, woodworking; wine trade. A hilly city, Lausanne is divided by short Flon and Louve rivers into 3 parts: Cité (oldest), Bourg, and St. Laurent; has 3 bridges. Univ. (founded 1891) has valuable library, museums of art and science. Cathedral (consecrated 1275) is in early Gothic style; tower (14th cent.) of bishop's old palace contains historical mus.; castle (15th cent.) is occupied by cantonal govt.; town hall dates from 1458. Lausanne is seat of Swiss Supreme Court of Justice (which until 1927 was housed in Fr.-Renaissance Palace of Justice) and of International Olympic Committee; scene of Lausanne Conference of 1922–23. The Signal de Lausanne (2,122 ft.) is reached by cable railway. OUCHY, on the lake, is the port of Lausanne.

Lauscha (lou'shä), town (pop. 6,506), Thuringia, central Germany, in Thuringian Forest, 8 mi. N of Sonneberg; glass-mfg. center (artificial eyes, ornaments); woodworking. Climatic health and winter-sports resort. Has glass-trade school. Glass industry introduced in late 16th cent.

Lausick, Bad, Germany: see BAD LAUSICK.

Lausitz, region, Germany and Poland: see LUSATIA.

Lausitzer Gebirge, Germany: see LUSATIAN MOUNTAINS.

Lausitzer Neisse River, Germany: see NEISSE RIVER.

Laussedat, Mount (lõsdä') (10,035 ft.), SE B.C., near Alta. border, in Rocky Mts., in Hamber Park, 65 mi. WNW of Banff; 51°35'N 116°58'W.

Laut, Indonesia: see NORTH NATUNA ISLANDS; PULU LAUT.

Lauta (lou'tä), town (pop. 8,316), Brandenburg, E Germany, in Lower Lusatia, 5 mi. SE of Senftenberg; lignite mining; aluminum smelting and refining. Power station.

Lautaret, Col du (kôl dü lõtärā'), pass (alt. 6,752 ft.) bet. Cottian Alps (NNE) and Massif du Pelvoux (S), in Hautes-Alpes dept., SE France, connecting upper valleys of the Romanche (W) and of the Guisane (which flows to the Durance). On Grenoble-Briançon road (completed 1804), and junction for Col du GALIBIER road. Winter sports.

Lautaro (loutä'rō), town (pop. 9,602), ⊙ Lautaro dept. (□ 798; pop. 41,762), Cautín prov., S central Chile, on Cautín R., on railroad and 16 mi. NNE of Temuco; agr. center (wheat, oats, peas, potatoes, sheep, cattle); flour milling, lumbering, tanning. Salmon hatcheries near by. Founded 1881 as fort against Araucanian Indians.

Lautem, district, Portuguese Timor: see LOSPALOS.

Lautem (loutĕm'), town, Portuguese Timor, in E Timor, on Wetar Strait, 80 mi. ENE of Dili; fishing.

Lautenbach (lõtābäk', Ger. lou'tŭnbäkh), village (pop. 913), Haut-Rhin dept., E France, in SE Vosges Mts., on the Lauch and 4 mi. NW of Guebwiller; sewing thread mfg., sawmilling. The Ballon de Guebwiller is 4 mi. SW.

Lautenburg, Poland: see LIDZBARK.

Lautenthal (lou'tŭntäl), town (pop. 3,146), in former Prussian prov. of Hanover, W Germany, after 1945 in Lower Saxony, in the upper Harz, on Innerste R. and 4 mi. NNW of Clausthal-Zellerfeld; summer resort with mineral baths; metal- and woodworking, brewing.

Lauter (lou'tŭr), village (pop. 6,738), Saxony, E central Germany, in the Erzgebirge, 3 mi. SE of Aue, near Czechoslovak border, in uranium-mining region; textile milling; mfg. of machinery, paper, enamelware; woodworking.

Lauteraar Glacier, Switzerland: see AAR RIVER.

Lauteraarhorn or **Gross Lauteraarhorn** (grōs lou'tŭrär'hôrn), peak (13,272 ft.) in Bernese Alps, S central Switzerland, 5 mi. SE of Grindelwald.

Lauterach (lou'tŭräkh), town (pop. 2,770), Vorarlberg, W Austria, 2 mi. S of Bregenz; soap, embroidery; corn, potatoes.

Lauterbach, Czechoslovakia: see KRASNO.

Lauterbach (lou'tůrbäkh), town (pop. 8,463), central Hesse, W Germany, in former Upper Hesse prov., 13 mi. WNW of Fulda; rail junction; artificial-silk and linen mfg. Has 2 castles. Basalt quarry near by.

Lauterberg im Harz, Bad, Germany: see BAD LAUTERBERG.

Lauterbourg (lōtĕrbōōr'), Ger. *Lauterburg* (lou'tůrbōōrk), village (pop. 1,054), Bas-Rhin dept., E France, on the Lauter (Ger. border) near its mouth on the Rhine; customs station; esparto processing, woodworking. Formerly fortified. Easternmost Fr. commune, 48°58'N 8°11'E.

Lauterbrunnen (lou'tůr brōō'nůn), town (pop. 2,819), Bern canton, S central Switzerland, in the Lauterbrunnental of Bernese Alps, on White Lütschine R. and 6 mi. S of Interlaken; year-round resort near many Alpine peaks. River valley is here known as the **Lauterbrunnental;** bounded by cliffs (1,000–1,500 ft.) and noted for numerous Alpine streams and their waterfalls (e.g., STAUBBACH, TRÜMMELBACH, SCHMADRIBACH).

Lauterburg, France: see LAUTERBOURG.

Lauterecken (lou"tůrĕ'kůn), town (pop. 2,313), Rhenish Palatinate, W Germany, on the Glan, at mouth of Lauter R., and 16 mi. NNW of Kaiserslautern; furniture mfg., leatherworking, tanning. Chartered before 1384.

Lauterhofen (lou"tůrhō'fůn), village (pop. 2,055), Upper Palatinate, central Bavaria, Germany, 9 mi. NE of Neumarkt; rye, oats, wheat, cattle. Chartered before 1159.

Lauter River (lou'tůr). **1** In W Germany and E France, formed by several mtn. streams 6 mi. ESE of Pirmasens, flows 35 mi. generally SE to the Rhine 2 mi. E of Lauterbourg. Forms French-German border below Wissembourg. **2** In Rhenish Palatinate, W Germany, rises 4 mi. SE of Kaiserslautern, flows 25 mi. NNW, past Kaiserslautern, to the Glan at Lauterecken.

Lauthala or **Laucala** (both: loudhä'lä), volcanic island (□ 5; pop. 66), Fiji, SW Pacific, 10 mi. E of Taveuni; 4 mi. long; copra.

Lauthala Bay or **Laucala Bay,** SE Viti Levu, Fiji, SW Pacific, E of Suva; 4 mi. E–W, 2 mi. N–S.

Lautiosaari (lou'tēōsä"rē), village in Kemi rural commune (pop. 4,982), Lapi co., NW Finland, on Kemi R. (major railroad and road bridge) and 4 mi. NNW of Kemi. Site of Kemi airfield.

Lautoka (loutō'kä), port town (pop. 2,225), NW Viti Levu, Fiji, SW Pacific; 2d largest port of Fiji; center of sugar industry; agr. school. Airfield.

Lautrec (lōtrĕk'), agr. village (pop. 481), Tarn dept., S France, 9 mi. NW of Castres.

La Uvita (lä ōōvē'tä), village, Puntarenas prov., SW Costa Rica, small Pacific port 16 mi. NW of Puerto Cortés; tobacco exports.

Lauvsnes (loufs'nās), village in Flatanger canton (pop. 1,912), Nord-Trondelag co., central Norway, on the North Sea, 18 mi. W of Namsos; wood-pulp production, fishing. Sometimes spelled Launes, Lauvnes, or Lovsnes.

Lauwe (lou'wů), town (pop. 7,157), West Flanders prov., W Belgium, on Lys R. and 3 mi. WSW of Courtrai, in flax-growing area; brick mfg.

Lauwers Zee (lou'ůrzā), inlet of the Waddenzee bet. Friesland and Groningen provs., N Netherlands, E of Dokkum; 6 mi. long, 5 mi. wide. Port of Oostmahorn on W shore.

Lauzerte (lōzârt'), village (pop. 738), Tarn-et-Garonne dept., SW France, 15 mi. N of Castelsarrasin; fruits, vegetables.

Lauzès (lōzĕs'), village (pop. 150), Lot dept., SW France, 10 mi. NE of Cahors; sheep, cattle.

Lauzet, Le (lů lōzā'), Alpine village (pop. 234), Basses-Alpes dept., SE France, on the Ubaye and 11 mi. WNW of Barcelonnette, at SW foot of the Montagne de Parpaillon; stock raising, lumbering.

Lauzon (lōzō'), town (pop. 7,877), S Que., on the St. Lawrence, just NE of Lévis, opposite SW end of Île d'Orléans; shipbuilding, lumbering; has large dry dock. Seat of a commercial col. and a convent. Settled 1647.

Lauzoua (lōzwä'), village (pop. c.3,300), S Ivory Coast, Fr. West Africa, on NW shore of a coastal lagoon, 20 mi. W of Grand-Lahou; cacao; coffee, palm kernels, rubber.

Lauzun (lōzū'), village (pop. 417), Lot-et-Garonne dept., SW France, 15 mi. S of Bergerac; food canning, furniture mfg.

Lava Beds National Monument (□ 71.9; alt. 4,000–5,000 ft.; established 1925), N Calif., 30 mi. SE of Klamath Falls, Oregon. Area of volcanic formations, including crater-pitted cinder cones, deep chasms, and lava caves. Pictographs have been found on walls of caves, petroglyphs on Petroglyph Cliff, in small detached section of park just NE. Region was scene of Modoc War (1872–73), in which Modoc Indians twice defeated numerically superior forces of U.S. troops.

Lavaca (lůvă'ků), county (□ 975; pop. 22,159), S Texas; ⊙ Hallettsville. In coastal plains region; drained by Lavaca and Navidad rivers. Agr. (cotton, corn, grain sorghums, peanuts, hay, fruit, truck); poultry raising, also cattle, hogs. Oil, natural-gas fields; sand, gravel, clay deposits. Formed 1846.

Lavaca, town (pop. 373), Sebastian co., W Ark., 13 mi. ESE of Fort Smith, near Arkansas R.

Lavaca Bay, Texas: see MATAGORDA BAY.

Lavaca River, S Texas, rises in Fayette co., flows 100 mi. generally SSE to Lavaca Bay, the NW arm of Matagorda Bay. Receives Navidad R. 11 mi. above mouth.

Lavadores (lävä-dhō'rĕs), SE suburb (pop. 7,065) of Vigo, Pontevedra prov., NW Spain in Galicia; fish processing, boatbuilding, flour milling, metal stamping, mfg. of paper and soap.

Lavagna (lävä'nyä), town (pop. 5,422), Genova prov., Liguria, N Italy, port on Gulf of Rapallo, separated from Chiavari by small stream; cotton and silk mills, shipyards; resort. Noted for slate quarries. Pope Innocent IV b. here.

Lava Hot Springs, village (pop. 591), Bannock co., SE Idaho, 25 mi. SE of Pocatello and on Portneuf R.; alt. 5,060 ft. Several natatoriums, sanitarium use mineral waters, here.

Lavak, Pristan, Turkmen SSR: see PRISTAN LAVAK.

Laval (läväl'), former co. of S Que., now Île Jésus co., coextensive with JESUS ISLAND.

Laval, village, Que.: see SAINTE ANGÈLE DE LAVAL.

Laval. 1 Town (pop. 28,171), ⊙ Mayenne dept., W France, on both banks of Mayenne R. and 45 mi. E of Rennes; communication and textile center with linen and cotton mills. Other mfg.: leather goods, shoes, furniture, cheese, and cider. Old quarter on right bank has 11th–12th-cent. feudal castle, 16th-cent. Renaissance château (now the Palais de Justice), both damaged in Second World War, and a 16th-cent. cathedral. Known for its linen since 14th cent. Here Vendeans defeated Republicans in 1793. **2** Village, Vosges dept., France: see LAVAL-SUR-VOLOGNE.

Laval-de-Cère (läväl'-dů-sâr'), village (pop. 412), Lot dept., SW France, 23 mi. W of Aurillac; hydroelectric installation on Cère R.

Laval des Rapides (dā räpēd'), residential town (pop. 3,242), S Que., on SW shore of Jesus Isl., 8 mi. W of Montreal.

Lavalle. 1 District, Buenos Aires prov., Argentina: see GENERAL LAVALLE, town. **2** Department, Corrientes prov., Argentina: see SANTA LUCÍA.

Lavalle (lävä'yä). **1** Town, Corrientes prov., Argentina: see PUERTO LAVALLE. **2** Town (pop. estimate 1,000), ⊙ Lavalle dept. (□ 3,665; 1947 pop. 17,081), NE Mendoza prov., Argentina, on railroad and 18 mi. NE of Mendoza; wine and fruit center; stock raising, wine making. **3** Village (pop. estimate 500), W Santiago del Estero prov., Argentina, at W foot of Sierra de Gausayán, on Catamarca prov. border, on railroad and 32 mi. N of Frías, in stock-raising and lumbering area; sulphur springs; sawmills.

La Valle (lů văl'), village (pop. 448), Sauk co., S central Wis., on Baraboo R. and 21 mi. WNW of Baraboo, in dairy and livestock region.

Lavalleja (läväyä'hä), department (□ 4,820; pop. 115,864), SE Uruguay; ⊙ Minas. Bounded by the Cuchilla Grande Principal (W); drained (N) by Cebollatí R. Principally a cattle- and sheep-raising area; agr. products: wheat, corn, oats. Lead deposits and quarries near Minas. Main centers: Minas, José Batlle y Ordóñez, Solís. Dept. was formed 1816. Formerly called Minas.

Lavalleja or **Colonia Lavalleja** (kōlōn'yä –), village (pop. 3,000), Salto dept., NW Uruguay, on road, and 55 mi. ENE of Salto; agr. center (cereals; cattle, sheep, horses).

Lavallette (lävůlĕt'), resort borough (pop. 567), Ocean co., E N.J., on peninsula bet. Barnegat Bay and the Atlantic, 7 mi. NE of Toms River.

Laval sur le Lac (läväl' sür lů läk'), town (pop. 312), S Que., at SW end of Jesus Isl., on L. of the Two Mountains, 15 mi. W of Montreal; resort.

Laval-sur-Vologne (–vôlô'nyů), village (pop. 574), Vosges dept., E France, in the W Vosges, 12 mi. E of Épinal; paper mill. Until 1937, called Laval.

Lavaltrie (lävältrē'), village (pop. 415), SW Que., on the St. Lawrence and 9 mi. SW of Sorel; dairying. Just E, in the St. Lawrence, is islet of Lavaltrie.

Lavamünd (lä'fämünt), town (pop. 2,488), Carinthia, S Austria, on the Drau, at mouth of the Lavant, near Yugoslav border, and 15 mi. S of Wolfsberg; customs station; hydroelectric plant.

Lavancia (lävăsyä'), village (pop. 14), Jura dept., E France, on the Brienne and 10 mi. SW of Saint-Claude; hydroelectric plant.

Lavandou, Le (lů lävădōō'), village (pop. 1,162), Var dept., SE France, fishing port on the Mediterranean, 22 mi. E of Toulon, at foot of the Monts des Maures; resort on Fr. Riviera, damaged in Allied landings (Aug., 1944) in Second World War.

Lavansaari (lä'vŭnsüärē), town (1941 pop. over 500), on island Lavansaari in Gulf of Finland, Leningrad oblast, Russian SFSR, 80 mi. W of Leningrad and 40 mi. NNW of Narva; naval fortifications. Beach resort under Finnish rule (until 1940). During Second World War, held (1941–44) by Finns.

Lavans-lès-Saint-Claude (lävă'-lā-sē-klōd'), village (pop. 626), Jura dept., E France, on the Brienne and 4 mi. WSW of Saint-Claude; produces fountain pens, plastic buttons and toys. Wood turning.

Lavant River (lä'fänt), S Austria, rises S of Judenburg, flows 50 mi. S, past Wolfsberg, to Drau R. at Lavamünd. Excellent cattle (Lavanttaler Rind) bred in upper valley; extensive wheat growing, fruit cultivation below Wolfsberg.

Lavapié Point (läväpyā'), Pacific cape at entrance to Arauco Gulf, S central Chile, 37 mi. SW of Concepción; 37°8'S.

Lavara (lä'vůrů), town (pop. 3,116), Hevros nome, W Thrace, Greece, on railroad and 30 mi. SSW of Adrianople (Edirne), on Maritsa R. (Turkish line).

Lavarande (lävärăd'), village (pop. 226), Alger dept., N central Algeria, in the Chéliff valley, 3 mi. W of Affreville; mfg. of explosives.

Lavardac (lävärdäk'), village (pop. 1,671), Lot-et-Garonne dept., SW France, on the Baise and 4 mi. NNW of Néroc; cork-mfg. center; ARMAGNAC brandy distilling and shipping, sawmilling, hog raising. Lumber trade.

Lavardin (lävärdē'), village (pop. 189), Loir-et-Cher dept., N central France, on Loir R. and 9 mi. WSW of Vendôme. Has ruined castle inhabited (11th–13th cent.) by counts of Vendôme.

Lavaufranche (lävōfrăsh'), village (pop. 232), Creuse dept., central France, 16 mi. W of Montluçon; tin deposits near by.

Lavaur (lävōr'), town (pop. 4,783), Tarn dept., S France, on Agout R. and 20 mi. ENE of Toulouse; commercial center. Metalworking, printing, flour milling, brush mfg. Has 13th–14th-cent. Gothic church. Stronghold of Albigenses, captured (1211) by Simon de Montfort. Episcopal see (1317–1790).

Lavaux (lävō'), district (pop. 10,185), Vaud canton, W Switzerland, on L. Geneva just E of Lausanne. Largest town, Lutry.

Lavaveix-les-Mines (lävävĕ'-lā-mēn'), village (pop. 1,386), Creuse dept., central France, near Creuse R., 9 mi. NNW of Aubusson; coal mining.

Lavayén River (läväyān'), left headstream of San Francisco R., in Salta and Jujuy provs., Argentina, flows c.75 mi. NE, joining the Río Grande de Jujuy near San Pedro to form the San Francisco.

La Vega (lä vā'gä), town (pop. 1,114), Cundinamarca dept., central Colombia, on W slopes of Cordillera Oriental, 30 mi. NW of Bogotá, in agr. region (sugar cane, coffee, tobacco, fruit, livestock); alt. 3,986 ft.

La Vega, province (□ 1,337; 1935 pop. 134,541; 1950 pop. 193,015), central Dominican Republic; ⊙ La Vega. A mountainous interior prov., bounded by Cordillera Central (S) and Cordillera Setentrional (N); drained by the Yaque del Norte and Camú R., which here forms La Vega Real valley, part of the Republic's most fertile and densely populated Cibao region. Main crops: tobacco, cacao; also coffee, rice, corn, cattle; wheat in the uplands. Constanza and Jarabacoa, with near-by Jimenoa falls, are mtn. resorts. The region was visited 1492 by Columbus, who built a fort. Became a prov. 1845.

La Vega, officially Concepción de la Vega, city (1935 pop. 9,339; 1950 pop. 14,445), ⊙ La Vega prov., central Dominican Republic, in fertile La Vega Real valley (Cibao), on Camú R. and 65 mi. NW of Ciudad Trujillo; 19°14'N 70°31'W. Rail terminus; trading, processing, lumbering, and agr. center (cacao, coffee, tobacco, rice, fruit, cattle). Airfield. Old colonial city in one of most populous regions of the Republic. Founded by Bartholomew Columbus in 1495 at foot of Concepción fortress, built 1 year earlier by Christopher Columbus. Site of city was moved after 1564 earthquake to right bank of Camú R. At Santo Cerro, 4 mi. N, stands church and shrine where the Virgin appeared to Columbus during Vega Real battle.

La Vega (lä vä'gä), town (pop. 5,207), Federal Dist., N Venezuela, on Guaire R. and on railroad, SW suburb of Caracas; lime-quarrying and cement-milling center.

La Vega Real (rääl'), valley, NE Dominican Republic, fertile lowland, E section of the CIBAO along Camú and Yuna rivers, extending c.60 mi. E from La Vega city to Sánchez. Main crops: cacao, coffee, rice, corn, tropical fruit.

La Vela or **La Vela de Coro** (lä vā'lä dā kō'rō), town (pop. 3,639), Falcón state, NW Venezuela, port on the Caribbean, at base of Isthmus of Médanos leading N to Paraguaná Peninsula, 8 mi. ENE of Coro (linked by highway, and by narrow-gauge railroad built in 1893). Exports hides, coffee, dividivi; and ships corn, lard, salted meat, and cattle to Dutch West Indies. Customhouse.

La Vela de Coro, Venezuela: see LA VELA.

Lavelanet (lävůlänā'), town (pop. 5,364), Ariège dept., S France in the Plantaurel range, 13 mi. E of Foix; textile-milling center; mfg. of hosiery, dyes, combs. Bauxite mines near by.

Lavello (lävĕl'lô), town (pop. 11,291), Potenza prov., Basilicata, S Italy, 8 mi. NE of Melfi; macaroni, wine, olive oil, cement.

Lavena (läfä'nä), gorge and hydroelectric plant, S Liechtenstein, near Swiss border, 5 mi. SSE of Vaduz.

Lavenham (lă'vůnům), town and parish (pop. 1,451), W Suffolk, England, 6 mi. NE of Sudbury; agr. market. Has 15th–16th-cent. church with tall tower, 16th-cent. guildhall, and anc. market cross. Lavenham was a center of medieval East Anglia cloth industry.

L'Avenir (lävnēr'), village (pop. 310), S Que., near St. Francis R., 12 mi. SE of Drummondville; dairying; cattle, pigs.

Laveno (lävā'nô), village (pop. 2,545), Varese prov., Lombardy, N Italy, port on E shore of Lago Maggiore, 12 mi. NW of Varese. Resort; pottery works, alcohol distillery, glue factory. Feldspar quarries near by.

La Venta (lä vän'tä), village, W Tabasco, Mexico, in coastal mangrove swamps, 30 mi. E of Coatzacoalcos, near Tonalá R. (Veracruz border). Colossal basalt heads, dating from A.D. 500–800, were excavated here in 1942.

Laventie (lävãtē'), village (pop. 1,643), Pas-de-Calais dept., N France, 9 mi. NE of Béthune; parquetry and footwear mfg. Potatoes, sugar beets. British First World War military cemeteries near by.

Laver (lä'vûr), village (pop. 242), Norrbotten co., N Sweden, 40 mi. WSW of Boden; copper mines.

La Verde (lä věr'dā), town (pop. estimate 1,000), E Chaco natl. territory, Argentina, 35 mi. NW of Resistencia; agr. center (corn, cotton, tobacco, livestock); sawmills, cotton gins.

Laverie, La (lä lävrē'), village, Tunis dist., N Tunisia, 15 mi. SSE of Tunis; lead-mining settlement on slope of the Djebel Ressas.

La Verkin, town (pop. 387), Washington co., SW Utah, 20 mi. NE of St. George and on Virgin R.; fruit.

Laverlochère (lävĕrlôshâr'), village (pop. estimate 800), W Que., 16 mi. W of Haileybury; gold mining.

La Verne (lù vûrn'), city (pop. 4,198), Los Angeles co., S Calif., 27 mi. E of Los Angeles, in citrus-fruit region. La Verne Col. here. Inc. 1906.

Laverne, town (pop. 1,269), Harper co., NW Okla., 33 mi. NW of Woodward, in agr. area (wheat, sorghums, alfalfa, corn); oil and natural-gas wells.

La Vernia or **Lavernia** (both: lùvûr'nēù), village (pop. c.500), Wilson co., S Texas, 24 mi. ESE of San Antonio, in agr. area.

Laverton (lā'vûrtùn), town (pop. 153), S central Western Australia, 155 mi. NNE of Kalgoorlie; terminus of railroad from Kalgoorlie. Gold mines at near-by Mt. Margaret.

La Veta (lù vē'tù), town (pop. 701), Huerfano co., S Colo., in E foothills of Sangre de Cristo Mts., 15 mi. WSW of Walsenburg; alt. 7,024 ft. Resort and trading point in agr. and coal-mining region; livestock, grain, truck and dairy products. Part of San Isabel Natl. Forest near by. **La Veta Pass** (9,382 ft.), in Sangre de Cristo Mts., W of La Veta, is crossed by railroad.

Lavezares (lävāsä'rās), town (1939 pop. 4,492; 1948 municipality pop. 18,508), NW Samar isl., Philippines, on San Bernardino Strait, 65 mi. NW of Catbalogan; agr. center (corn, rice, coconuts).

Laviano (lävyä'nô), village (pop. 2,043), Salerno prov., Campania, S Italy, in the Apennines, 30 mi. ENE of Salerno.

La Victoria (lä vēktōr'yä), town (pop. 2,234), Valle del Cauca dept., W Colombia, in Cauca valley, on railroad and 18 mi. SW of Cartago; tobacco, sugar cane, coffee, cacao, bananas, corn, cattle. Silver, gold, and platinum mined near by.

La Victoria, Nicaragua: see NIQUINOHOMO.

La Victoria, E suburb (pop. 55,134) of Lima, Lima dept., W central Peru; industrial suburb (mfg. of textiles; food processing). Inc. 1940 into Lima proper.

La Victoria, town (pop. 8,554), Aragua state, N Venezuela, on Aragua R., in valley of coastal range, on Pan-American Highway, on railroad and 36 mi. WSW of Caracas; trading and agr. center (coffee, cacao, sugar cane, tobacco, vegetables, cereals, grapes); mfg. (soap, cigars). Former ⊙ Aragua state.

Lavigérie (lävēzhrē'), village (pop. 904), Alger dept., N central Algeria, on the Chéliff and 11 mi. ESE of Affreville; cereal, tobacco, wine.

La Viña (lä vē'nyä), village (pop. estimate 500), ⊙ La Viña dept. (□ 840; 1947 pop. 4,128), S Salta prov., Argentina, on railroad (Castañares station) and 50 mi. S of Salta; agr. center (alfalfa, wheat, corn, oats, wine, livestock); flour milling.

La Viña, village (pop. 541), Lambayeque dept., NW Peru, in W foothills of Cordillera Occidental, 8 mi. E of Saña; rail terminus; rice, corn.

Lavina (lùvī'nù), town (pop. 195), Golden Valley co., S central Mont., on Musselshell R. and 40 mi. NW of Billings.

Lavínia (lùvē'nyù), city (pop. 1,976), NW São Paulo, Brazil, on railroad and 38 mi. W of Araçatuba; cattle raising.

La Virgen (lä vēr'hĕn), village, Heredia prov., N Costa Rica, on Sarapiquí R. and 27 mi. N of Heredia; bananas, fodder crops, livestock.

La Virtud (lä vērto͞odh'), town (pop. 751), Lempira dept., W Honduras, near Lempa R. (Salvador border), 6 mi. SW of Candelaria; grain, livestock.

Lavis (lä'vēs), village (pop. 2,231), Trento prov., Trentino–Alto Adige, N Italy, 5 mi. N of Trent and on Avisio R., near its confluence with the Adige; wine.

Lavit (lävē'), village (pop. 576), Tarn-et-Garonne dept., SW France, 11 mi. SW of Castelsarrasin; wheat, cattle. Sometimes called Lavit-de-Lomagne.

Lavizzara, Val, Switzerland: see VALLEMAGGIA.

Lavongai (lävông'ī, lävùng-gī'), volcanic island (□ c.460; pop. 5,000), New Ireland dist., Bismarck Archipelago, Territory of New Guinea, SW Pacific, 20 mi. W of New Ireland across Byron Strait; 32 mi. long, 20 mi. wide. Highest peak of Lavongai (Tirpitz) Range is c.2,800 ft.; mangroves. Formerly New Hannover, later New Hanover.

Lavonia, city (pop. 1,766), Franklin co., NE Ga., near S.C. line, 16 mi. SE of Toccoa; mfg. (yarns, work clothes, lumber).

Lavon Reservoir, Texas: see TRINITY RIVER.

Lavoûte-Chilhac (lävo͞ot'-shēyäk'), village (pop. 353), Haute-Loire dept., S central France, on NE slope of Montagnes de la Margeride, on the Allier and 10 mi. S of Brioude; antimony mining at near-by Ally (5 mi. W) and Mercoeur (5 mi. NW).

Lavoy (lùvoi'), village (pop. 127), central Alta., 9 mi. ESE of Vegreville; grain, dairying.

Lavra, Cape, Greece: see AKRATHOS.

Lavras (lä'vrùs). **1** City (pop. 11,075), S Minas Gerais, Brazil, on railroad and 45 mi. W of São João del Rei; textile milling, distilling; ships coffee, tobacco, cattle. Has agr. col. established 1908 by American Presbyterian Church. **2** City, Rio Grande do Sul, Brazil: see LAVRAS DO SUL.

Lavras da Mangabeira (dä mãng-gùbā'rù), city (pop. 1,913), SE Ceará, Brazil, on Fortaleza-Crato RR and 45 mi. NE of Crato, in semiarid cattle-raising area. Until 1944, called Lavras.

Lavras do Sul (do͞o so͞ol'), city (pop. 2,718), S central Rio Grande do Sul, Brazil, 35 mi. NNE of Bagé; rice, wheat, wine. Gold mining. Copper deposits. Until 1944, called Lavras.

Lavrentiya (lŭvrĕn'tyēŭ), settlement, NE Chukchi Natl. Okrug, Kamchatka oblast, Khabarovsk Territory, Russian SFSR, on Lavrentiya [Rus.,=(St.) Lawrence] Bay of Bering Sea, 350 mi. ENE of Anadyr; govt. arctic station, airfield.

Lavrion, Greece: see LAURION.

La Vuelta (lä vwāl'tä), village, Chocó dept., W Colombia, landing on affluent of Atrato R. and 18 mi. SSE of Quibdó; hydroelectric plant supplies power for gold and platinum mines.

Law, town in Carluke parish, N Lanark, Scotland, 2 mi. SE of Wishaw; coal-mining center.

Lawa (lä'vŭ), village, E central Rajasthan, India, 18 mi. NW of Tonk; local agr. market (millet, cotton, gram). Was ⊙ former petty state of Lawa (□ 20; pop. 2,808); in 1948, state merged with union of Rajasthan.

Lawar (lä'vŭr), town (pop. 5,435), Meerut dist., NW Uttar Pradesh, India, 9 mi. NNE of Meerut; wheat, gram, jowar, sugar cane, oilseeds.

Lawa River, Du. and Fr. Guiana: see MARONI RIVER.

Lawas (lùwäs'), town (pop. 1,008), N Sarawak, NW Borneo, near Brunei Bay, on Lawas R. (24 mi. long) 32 mi. E of Brunei; rubber, stock raising, fishing.

Lawdar, Aden: see LODAR.

Lawiczka, Poland: see RESKO.

Lawit, Gunong (go͞ono͞ong' läwĭt'), highest peak (4,978 ft.), of Trengganu, NE Malaya, 40 mi. WNW of Kuala Trengganu; 5°25'N 102°35'E. Sometimes called Gunong Batil.

Lawksawk (lôksôk'), NW state (sawbwaship) (□ 2,362; pop. 30,102), Southern Shan State, Upper Burma; ⊙ Lawksawk, village 35 mi. NW of Taunggyi and on Zawgyi R. Parallel mtn. ranges extend S with wide plateau (alt. 3,500 ft.) in center. Teak forests.

Lawler, town (pop. 539), Chickasaw co., NE Iowa, 26 mi. E of Charles City, in corn, hog, and dairy area.

Lawley, England: see WELLINGTON.

Lawn, town (pop. 311), Taylor co., W central Texas, 21 mi. S of Abilene, in cotton, cattle area.

Lawndale. **1** Unincorporated residential town (1940 pop. 4,019), Los Angeles co., S Calif., 13 mi. SW of downtown Los Angeles and adjacent to Hawthorne. **2** Town, San Mateo co., Calif.: see COLMA. **3** Textile town (pop. 964), Cleveland co., S N.C., 8 mi. N of Shelby.

Lawnside, borough (pop. 1,566), Camden co., SW N.J., 7 mi. SE of Camden. Site bought by abolitionists for Negroes (1840), and 1st called Free Haven. Inhabitants mostly Negroes. Inc. 1926.

Lawoe, Mount, Indonesia: see LAWU, MOUNT.

Lawra (lô'rä), town, Northern Territories, NW Gold Coast, on Black Volta R. (Fr. West Africa border) and 50 mi. NNW of Wa; road junction; shea nuts, millet, durra, yams; cattle, skins.

Lawrence, borough (pop. 573), ⊙ Tuapeka co. (□ 1,388; pop. 4,002), SE S.Isl., New Zealand, 40 mi. W of Dunedin; agr. center; gold mines.

Lawrence. **1** County (□ 686; pop. 27,128), NW Ala.; ⊙ Moulton. Drained in N by Wheeler Reservoir (in Tennessee R.). Part of Wm. B. Bankhead Natl. Forest is in S. Cotton, corn, poultry; deposits of coal, limestone, and asphalt. Formed 1818. **2** County (□ 592; pop. 21,303), NE Ark.; ⊙ Walnut Ridge and Powhatan. Bounded E by Cache R.; intersected by Black R., and drained by Spring and Strawberry rivers and by small Village Creek. Agr. (cotton, corn, rice, hay, livestock); timber. Formed 1815. **3** County (□ 374; pop. 20,539), SE Ill., bounded E by Wabash R.; ⊙ Lawrenceville. Drained by Embarrass R. Agr. area, with oil and natural-gas wells; poultry, livestock, soybeans, corn, wheat. Oil refineries; also other mfg. at Lawrenceville. Formed 1821. **4** County (□ 459; pop. 34,346), S Ind.; ⊙ Bedford. Drained by Salt Creek and East Fork of White R. Large limestone quarries; agr. (fruit, grain); mfg. at Bedford, Mitchell. Formed 1818. **5** County (□ 425; pop. 14,418), NE Ky.; ⊙ Louisa. Bounded E by Big Sandy R. and its Tug Fork (both form W.Va. line here); drained by Levisa Fork and small Blaine Creek. Mtn. agr. area (dairy products, livestock, poultry, corn, sorghum, tobacco, fruit); oil and gas wells, coal mines, fireclay and sand pits; timber. Formed 1821. **6** County (□ 433; pop. 12,639), S central Miss.; ⊙ Monticello. Drained by Pearl R. Agr. (cotton, corn); lumbering. Formed 1874. **7** County (□ 619; pop. 23,420), SW Mo.; ⊙ Mount Vernon. In the Ozarks; drained by Spring R. Agr. (wheat, corn, oats, strawberries), poultry, dairying; mfg., especially dairy and grain products; lead, zinc mines, limestone deposits. Formed 1845. **8** County (□ 456; pop. 49,115), S Ohio; ⊙ Ironton. Bounded S by Ohio R., here forming boundary with Ky. and W.Va.; drained by small Symmes Creek. Agr. (dairy products; grain, livestock, fruit, tobacco, truck, hay); mfg. (especially steel and iron) at Ironton; coal and iron mining, limestone quarrying. Formed 1816. **9** County (□ 367; pop. 105,120), W Pa.; ⊙ New Castle. Mfg. and mining area, drained by Shenango, Mahoning, and Beaver rivers. Iron center in mid-19th cent. Metal products, glass, clay and stone products, cement; dairying. Formed 1849. **10** County (□ 800; pop. 16,648), W S.Dak., on Wyo. line; ⊙ DEADWOOD. Farming and mining region in Black Hills. Tourist trade; gold, quartz, timber, livestock, grain. Development of co. parallels growth of Homestake Mining Co. at LEAD. Part of Black Hills Natl. Forest in S; Terry Peak is near Lead. Formed 1875. **11** County (□ 634; pop. 28,818), S Tenn.; ⊙ Lawrenceburg. Bounded S by Ala.; drained by upper Buffalo River and Shoal Creek. Upland agr. region; cotton, corn, livestock, dairy products; timber; phosphate mining. Formed 1817.

Lawrence. **1** Residential town (pop. 1,951), Marion co., central Ind., on West Fork of White R., just NE of Indianapolis. **2** City (pop. 23,351), ⊙ Douglas co., NE Kansas, on Kansas R. and 32 mi. WSW of Kansas City, Kansas; processing and shipping center for grain-growing and truck-farming region. Flour and alfalfa milling, dairying, canning; mfg. of paper products, pipe organs. Army ordnance works. Founded 1854 by New England Emigrant Aid Society; inc. 1858. Became political center for Free Staters; raided (1856) by proslavery group, sacked (1863) by guerrilla band under William Quantrill. Territorial legislature convened here during late 1850s, though Lecompton was nominal capital. Grew as trade and educational center. Seat of University of Kansas (opened 1866) and Haskell Inst. (opened 1884; Indian). N part of city damaged by great flood of July, 1951. **3** Industrial city (pop. 80,536), a ⊙ Essex co., NE Mass., on Merrimack R. (water power) and 9 mi. NNE of Lowell; one of world's greatest woolen-textile centers; cotton goods, paper products, shoes, clothing, feed, malt liquors, plastic fabrics, rubber products, soap, radio equipment, machinery. Port of entry. Settled 1655, laid out as industrial town 1845, set off from Andover and Methuen 1847, inc. as city 1853. A granite dam on the Merrimack dates from c.1845. **4** Village (pop. 679), Van Buren co., SW Mich., 24 mi. WSW of Kalamazoo and on Paw Paw R., in fertile truck- and fruit-growing area; mfg. (flour, crates, canned foods). **5** Village (pop. 376), Nuckolls co., S Nebr., 20 mi. SSE of Hastings; dairying; grain, livestock, poultry. **6** Residential village (pop. 4,681), Nassau co., SE N.Y., on S shore of W Long Isl., 9 mi. SE of Jamaica, in resort area; mfg. (toys, clothing, towel racks). Inc. 1897. **7** or **Lawrence Hills**, village (pop. 1,162), Washington co., SW Pa., 12 mi. NE of Washington.

Lawrence, Cape, NE Ellesmere Isl., NE Franklin Dist., Northwest Territories, on Kennedy Channel; 80°21'N 69°15'W.

Lawrenceburg. **1** City (pop. 4,806), ⊙ Dearborn co., SE Ind., on Ohio R. and 50 mi. S of Richmond, in agr. area; mfg. (whisky, feed, flour, machinery, lumber, shoes, caskets, pharmaceuticals). Port of entry. Prehistoric fortifications found near here. Laid out 1802. Inundated by flood in 1937. **2** City (pop. 2,369), ⊙ Anderson co., central Ky., 22 mi. W of Lexington; trade center in Bluegrass agr. region (dairy products, poultry, horses, burley tobacco, corn, hay); mfg. of industrial cotton thread, whisky, pork products, cheese, feed, brooms, stone products. Settled 1776; inc. 1820. **3** City (pop. 5,442), ⊙ Lawrence co., S Tenn., on Shoal Creek (water power) and 70 mi. SSW of Nashville, in timber, livestock-raising, dairying, cotton-growing area; lumber milling; shirts, cheese. Founded c.1815.

Lawrence Hills, Pa.: see LAWRENCE.

Lawrencetown, village (pop. estimate 600), W N.S., on Annapolis R. and 20 mi. NE of Annapolis Royal; apple packing, barrel mfg.; fishing, hunting center. Site of Prov. Forest Nursery.

Lawrenceville, village (pop. 360), SW Que., 19 mi. E of Granby; dairying, lumbering, woodworking.

Lawrenceville. **1** City (pop. 2,932), ⊙ Gwinnett co., N central Ga., 26 mi. ENE of Atlanta; mfg. (shoes, clothing, feed, lumber). Inc. 1821. **2** Industrial city (pop. 6,328), ⊙ Lawrence co., SE Ill., on Embarrass R. near the Wabash, and 8 mi. WNW of Vincennes (Ind.), in oil, natural-gas, and agr. area. Oil refineries; mfg. of oil-well and telephone equipment, chemicals, barrels, asphalt products. Poultry, livestock, soybeans, corn, wheat. Founded 1821, inc. 1835. Oil was discovered here in 1906. **3** Village (pop. 1,056), Mercer co., W N.J., 5 mi. NNE of Trenton; agr. (potatoes, corn, hay); stone quarries. Has transoceanic radio-telephone transmitting station. Lawrenceville School for boys (1810) here. Settled 1692. **4** Village (pop. 191), Clark co., W central Ohio, 5 mi. NNW of Springfield. **5** Borough (pop. 479), Tioga co., N Pa., on Tioga R. and 17 mi. WSW of Elmira, N.Y., at N.Y. line. **6** Town (pop. 2,239), ⊙ Brunswick co., S Va., near Meherrin R., 40 mi. SW of Petersburg; tobacco market; trade center for agr. area (tobacco, grain, cotton); railroad shops; mfg. of chairs, clay products, clothing. Seat of St. Paul's Polytechnic Inst. Founded 1814; inc. 1874.

Laws, Calif.: see BISHOP.

Lawson, city (pop. 486), Ray co., NW Mo., 16 mi. NW of Richmond; corn, livestock.

Lawson Air Force Base, Ga.: see COLUMBUS.

Lawsonia (lôsō'nēŭ), village (1940 pop. 1,745), Somerset co., SE Md., on the Eastern Shore near Tangier Sound, 31 mi. SSW of Salisbury, in truck-farm and fishing region.

Lawtey, city (pop. 576), Bradford co., N Fla., 30 mi. NE of Gainesville; shipping point (strawberries, pecans, grapes).

Lawton. 1 Town (pop. 254), Woodbury co., W Iowa, 11 mi. E of Sioux City, in agr. area. **2** Village (pop. 1,206), Van Buren co., SW Mich., 16 mi. SW of Kalamazoo, in area of vineyards and small lakes; mfg. (wine, grape juice, tools, bearings, foundry products, baskets). **3** Village (pop. 211), Ramsey co., NE N.Dak., 25 mi. NE of Devils Lake. **4** City (pop. 34,757), ⊙ Comanche co., SW Okla., on Cache Creek and c.50 mi. N of Wichita Falls (Texas), near SE end of the Wichita Mts.; commercial, industrial center for agr. area (cotton, livestock, wheat), with oil wells near by. Cottonseed oil, dairy products, packed meat, flour, feed, leather goods, concrete products, mattresses, wood products, tile, patent medicines. Granite, limestone quarries; sand, gravel, asphalt pits. Cameron State Agr. Col. and an Indian hosp. are here. Near by are huge U.S. Fort Sill military reservation (established 1868), Fort Sill Boarding School (for Indians), a wildlife refuge, and Medicine Park (resort). Founded 1901.

Lawton, Fort, Wash.: see SEATTLE.

Lawtonka, Lake (lôtông'kŭ), Comanche co., SW Okla., 12 mi. NW of Lawton, and at edge of Wichita Mts.; water supply for Lawton and Fort Sill. Medicine Park (resort) and a wildlife refuge are here.

Lawu, Mount, or **Mount Lawoe** (both: lä'wōō) (10,712 ft.), central Java, Indonesia, 25 mi. E of Surakarta.

Laxa (läks'ō"), Swedish *Laxå*, town (pop. 2,449), Orebro co., S central Sweden, 30 mi. SW of Orebro; rail junction; steel, paper, and lumber mills, sulphite works. Has 17th-cent. manor house.

Laxapana Falls or **Laksapana Falls** (lŭksŭpä'nŭ), waterfall in Hatton Plateau, S central Ceylon, on left headstream of the Kelani Ganga and 7 mi. W of Hatton; hydroelectric project, begun 1920. Also called Laxapanagala and Raksapana.

Laxenburg (läk'sŭnbŏŏrk), town (pop. 1,331), after 1938 in Mödling dist. of Vienna, Austria, on Schwechat R., 10 mi. S of city center. Has former imperial castles, large park.

Laxey, village district (1939 pop. 1,312), E coast of Isle of Man, England, 7 mi. NE of Douglas; seaside resort, with woolen milling. Lead was formerly mined here. Garwick Glen, smugglers' cave, is celebrated in Scott's *Guy Mannering*.

Laxmishwar, India: see LAKSHMESHWAR.

Laxou (läshōō'), W suburb (pop. 6,305) of Nancy, Meurthe-et-Moselle dept., NE France; copper smelting; mfg. of toys, chocolate, gingerbread.

Laya (lī'ŭ), village (1926 pop. 3,577), W Sverdlovsk oblast, Russian SFSR, on railroad and 10 mi. NNW (under jurisdiction) of Nizhni Tagil; truck gardening. Former site of ironworks called Laiski Zavod.

Layang Layang (līäng" līäng'), town (pop. 1,061), S Johore, Malaya, on railroad and 30 mi. NW of Johore Bharu; rubber and oil-palm plantations.

Lay Dam, central Ala., in Coosa R., 20 mi. SW of Sylacauga. Privately built power dam (104 ft. high, 1,603 ft. long) completed 1914; forms small reservoir (□ 9.3). Hydroelectric plant.

La Yesca (lä yĕs'kä), town (pop. 453), Nayarit, W Mexico, on Jalisco border, 55 mi. ESE of Tepic; corn, tobacco, cattle. Gold, silver mines near by.

Laykovats, Yugoslavia: see LAJKOVAC.

Laylah, Saudi Arabia: see LAILA.

Layon River (läyō'), Maine-et-Loire dept., W France, rises 3 mi. SW of Vihiers, flows 60 mi. NE and NW, past Thouarcé, to the Loire at Chalonnes-sur-Loire.

Layopolis (lāō'pŭlĭs), town (pop. 273), Gilmer co., central W.Va., 5 mi. SE of Glenville.

Layou (läyōō'), town (pop. 779), W St. Vincent, B.W.I., 4 mi. NW of Kingstown; sugar cane, cotton, arrowroot; fishing.

Layou River, W central Dominica, B.W.I., flows c.10 mi. W, through Layou Plateau, to the coast.

Layrac (lārăk'), village (pop. 1,100), Lot-et-Garonne dept., SW France, on the Gers near its mouth on the Garonne, and 5 mi. SSE of Agen; brickworks; agr.-equipment mfg., fruit shipping.

Lay River (lĕ), Vendée dept., W France, rises 4 mi. N of La Châtaigneraie, flows 80 mi. SW, past Mareuil, to the Pertuis Breton of the Bay of Biscay 10 mi. SW of Luçon. Receives the Yon (right), which flows past La Roche-sur-Yon.

Laysan (läsăn'), sand island, N Pacific, c.790 mi. NW of Honolulu T.H.; 25°46'N 171°44'W; known for its numerous birds. Annexed 1857 by Hawaiian kingdom; now U.S. possession.

Layton, town (pop. 3,456), Davis co., N Utah, 13 mi. S of Ogden, bet. Great Salt L. and Wasatch Range; alt. 4,356 ft.; lumbering, agr. area (sugar beets, truck); beet sugar, canned foods, flour.

Laytona, town (pop. 405), Davis co., N Utah, contiguous to Layton.

Laytonsville, town (pop. 132), Montgomery co., central Md., 23 mi. NNW of Washington; truck, dairy products.

Laza (lä'sä), town (pop. c.3,100), La Paz dept., W Bolivia, in the Yungas, 3 mi. NNE of Irupana; subtropical agr. (coffee, cacao, quina).

Lazarev, Port, Korea: see YONGHUNG BAY.

Lazarevac or **Lazarevats** (both: lä'zärĕväts), village (pop. 5,214), central Serbia, Yugoslavia, on railroad and 30 mi. SSW of Belgrade, in the Sumadija.

Lazarevo (lä'zŭryĭvŭ), village (1939 pop. over 500), central Tula oblast, Russian SFSR, 25 mi. S of Tula; truck produce.

Lazarevskaya (lŭzŭryĕf'skīŭ), village (1948 pop. over 500), S Krasnodar Territory, Russian SFSR, on Black Sea coastal railroad, 18 mi. SE of Tuapse, in subtropical agr. area (tea, citrus fruit). A fortified point in 19th-cent. Rus. wars against Circassians.

Laz Daua (läz' dä'wä), Ital. *Las Daua*, village in the Mijirtein, N Ital. Somaliland, at Br. Somaliland border, 55 mi. S of Bender Kassim; road junction.

Lazdijai, **Lazdiyai**, or **Lazdiyay** (läz'dĭyī), Pol. *Łozdzieje*, city (pop. 3,029), S Lithuania, 23 mi. SSE of Marijampole, near Pol border; road junction; shoe mfg., flour milling. Passed in 1795 to Prussia, in 1815 to Rus. Poland; in Suvalki govt. until 1920.

Lazi (lä'sē), town (1939 pop. 1,927; 1948 municipality pop. 13,840), on S Siquijor isl., Negros Oriental prov., Philippines, on small inlet of Mindanao Sea; rice growing, fishing.

Laziali, Colli, Italy: see ALBAN HILLS.

Lazio, Italy: see LATIUM.

Laziqiyah, Al-, Syria: see LATAKIA.

Lazise (lätsē'zō), village (pop. 854), Verona prov., Veneto, N Italy, port on SE shore of Lago di Garda, 13 mi. NW of Verona; sausage factory.

Laziska Gorne (wä-zhē'skä gōŏr'), Pol. *Łaziska Górne*, village, Katowice prov., S Poland, 11 mi. SW of Katowice; large coal-fed power plant.

Lazistan, Turkey: see RIZE.

Lazne Belohrad (läz'nyĕ byĕ'lôhrät), Czech *Lázně Bělohrad*, village (pop. 2,233), NE Bohemia, Czechoslovakia, on railroad and 10 mi. W of Dvur Kralove; health resort (alt. 915 ft.) with peat baths and ferruginous springs. Has Renaissance castle, baroque church, mus. Just SW is Mlazovice (mlä'zôvĭtsĕ), Czech *Mlázovice*, another health resort.

Lazne Kunratice (kōŏn'drätyĭtsĕ), Czech *Lázně Kundratice*, Ger. *Kunnersdorf* (kōō'nŭrsdôrf), village (pop. 435), N Bohemia, Czechoslovakia, 7 mi. SW of Liberec; health resort with mineral baths.

Lazne Kynzvart (kĭnzh'värt), Czech *Lázně Kynžvart*, Ger. *Bad Königswart* (bät" kû'nĭkhsvärt), town (pop. 1,144), W Bohemia, Czechoslovakia, on railroad and 4 mi. NW of Marienbad; health resort (alt. 1,935 ft.) with carbonated mineral springs and baths. Fine castle. Prameny (prä'mĕnĭ), formerly Sangerberg, another health center (alt. 2,300 ft.) is 5 mi. NE.

Lazne Libverda, Czechoslovakia: see HEJNICE.

Lazne Podebrady, Czechoslovakia: see PODEBRADY.

Lazo (lä'zŭ). **1** Village (1939 pop. over 500), SE Maritime territory, Russian SFSR, on short Sudzukhe R. and 45 mi. ENE of Suchan; lumbering. Until 1949, called Vangou. **2** S suburb (1939 pop. over 2,000) of Iman, W Maritime Territory Russian SFSR, on Trans-Siberian RR; metalworks. Formerly Muravyev-Amurski.

Lazonby (lā'zŭnbē), village and parish (pop. 667), E Cumberland, England, on Eden R. and 6 mi. NNE of Penrith; cattle, sheep, agr.

Lazorki (lŭzôr'kē), village (1939 pop. over 500), NW Poltava oblast, Ukrainian SSR, 15 mi. WNW of Lubny; wheat.

Lbishchensk, Kazakh SSR: see CHAPAYEVO.

Lea (lē), village in Lea, Ashton, Ingol and Cottam parish (pop. 1,802), W Lancashire, England, on Lancaster Canal and 3 mi. WNW of Preston; dairying.

Lea (lē), county (□ 4,393; pop. 30,717), extreme SE N.Mex., in Llano Estacado; ⊙ Lovington. Livestock-grazing region; bounded S and E by Texas. Petroleum, natural-gas fields. Formed 1917.

Leach, industrial village, Boyd co., NE Ky., on Big Sandy R. and 10 mi. WSW of Huntington, W.Va.; makes chemicals, plastics, petroleum products.

Leach River, England: see THAMES RIVER.

Leachville (lēch'vĭl), town (pop. 1,230), Mississippi co., NE Ark., 20 mi. W of Blytheville, near Mo. line, in cotton, corn, and soybean area; cotton ginning and compressing.

Lead (lēd), city (pop. 6,422), Lawrence co., W S.Dak., 33 mi. NW of Rapid City, in Black Hills; alt. 5,320 ft. Gold-mining and tourist center; timber, livestock. Homestake Mine, largest gold mine in U.S., is here; maintains company hosp. and recreation facilities. Platted 1876, following discovery of gold here; inc. 1890.

Leadbetter Island (lĕd'bĕtŭr), Knox co., S Maine, in Penobscot Bay just W of Vinalhaven Isl.; 1 mi. long, ½ mi. wide.

Leadenham (lĕ'dŭnŭm), town and parish (pop. 550), Parts of Kesteven, W Lincolnshire, England, 13 mi. S of Lincoln; ironstone quarrying. Has late-14th-cent. church.

Leader (lē'dŭr), town (pop. 716), SW Sask., 45 mi. SSW of Kindersley; railroad junction; grain elevators, flour mills.

Leader Water (lē'dŭr), river in East Lothian and Berwick, Scotland, rises on Lammer Law, flows 21 mi. SSE, past Lauder and Earlston, to the Tweed 2 mi. E of Melrose. Lower course forms Berwick-Roxburgh boundary. Its valley, noted for scenic beauty and angling resorts, is called Lauderdale.

Leadgate, England: see CONSETT.

Lead Hill (lĕd), town (pop. 110), Boone co., N Ark., 17 mi. NE of Harrison, in the Ozarks, near Mo. line.

Leadhills, village in Crawford parish, S Lanark, Scotland, in Lowther Hills 6 mi. SW of Crawford; alt. 1,350 ft.; lead mining. Allan Ramsay, poet, b. here. Just SW, in Dumfries, is lead-mining village of WANLOCKHEAD.

Leadon River (lĕ'dŭn), Hereford, England, rises 7 mi. WNW of Great Malvern, flows 22 mi. SE, past Ledbury, to the Severn just NW of Gloucester.

Leadore (lē'ŭdôr), town (pop. 159), Lemhi co., E Idaho, on Lemhi R. and c.45 mi. SSE of Salmon.

Leadville (lĕd'vĭl), city (pop. 4,081), ⊙ Lake co., central Colo., on headstream of Arkansas R., in Sawatch Mts., and 75 mi. SW of Denver; alt. c.10,190 ft. Tourist and mining center in ranching and dairying area; smelting, refining. Gold, silver, lead, copper, zinc, molybdenum mines in vicinity. Early history of city is one of booms. First occurred c.1860, when Abe Lee, among others, found gold in California Gulch. Second took place in 1877 with discovery of lead carbonate lodes having high silver content. First known as Oro City, later as New Oro City; inc. 1878 as Leadville. By 1880, peak year for silver production, had pop. of c.35,000. Its fame attracted such celebrities as General Grant, General Sherman, and Oscar Wilde. Decline started 1893, with fall in price of silver and beginning of depression; late in 1890s there was another revival because of opening of rich gold mines near by. More than $600,000,000 worth of silver, gold, lead, zinc, and copper has been extracted from region. Fortunes were made, some —like that of H. A. W. Tabor—to be squandered, others—like that of Meyer Guggenheim—to persist. During 1930s industry was stimulated by development of molybdenum deposits at Climax, 10 mi. NE, and by reopening of old mines. Near by is Yak tunnel (c.4 mi. long), built to drain mines in vicinity. Mt. Elbert, highest point in Colo., is 12 mi. SW.

Leadwood, village (pop. 1,479), St. Francois co., E Mo., in St. Francois Mts. 5 mi. S of Bonne Terre; lead mining.

Leaf River, N Que., issues from L. Minto, flows 300 mi. NE, through tidal Leaf L. (30 mi. long, 15 mi. wide), to Ungava Bay 65 mi. NNW of Fort Chimo.

Leaf River, village (pop. 444), Ogle co., N Ill., on Leaf R. and 19 mi. WSW of Rockford, in rich agr. area.

Leaf River. 1 In N Ill., rises S of Freeport, flows c.25 mi. generally SE to Rock R. N of Oregon. **2** In W and W central Minn., rises in Otter Tail co., flows 50 mi. E, past Bluffton, to Crow Wing R. 10 mi. NNW of Staples. **3** In S central and SE Miss., rises in Scott co., flows S to Hattiesburg, thence SE, joining Chickasawhay R. to form Pascagoula R. in N George co.; c.180 mi. long.

Leagrave, England: see LUTON.

League City, village (pop. 1,341), Galveston co., S Texas, 23 mi. SE of Houston, in agr. area (truck, fruit); oil wells near.

Leake (lēk), county (□ 586; pop. 21,610), central Miss.; ⊙ Carthage. Drained by Pearl and Yockanookany rivers and Lobutcha Creek. Includes 2 small Indian reservations. Agr. (cotton, corn), cattle raising, lumbering. Formed 1833.

Leakesville, town (pop. 893), ⊙ Greene co., SE Miss., 45 mi. ESE of Hattiesburg and on Chickasawhay R.; makes clothing.

Leakey (lā'kē), village (pop. c.500), ⊙ Real co., SW Texas, 36 mi. N of Uvalde and on Frio R.; trade center for ranching area (goats, sheep, cattle). The scenic Frio Canyon (frē'ō) is visited by tourists.

Leaksville (lēks'–), town (pop. 4,045), Rockingham co., N N.C., 11 mi. NNW of Reidsville and on Dan R.; mfg. of bedding, curtains, rugs, woolens. Residential New Leaksville village (pop. 1,528) is just S. Laid out 1797; inc. 1874.

Leal, village (pop. 72), Barnes co., E central N.Dak., 19 mi. NW of Valley City.

Leales (lā-ä'lĕs), village (pop. estimate 700), ⊙ Leales dept. (□ c.900; 1947 pop. 25,686), central Tucumán prov., Argentina, at confluence of the Río Colorado and Salí R., on railroad and 27 mi. SSW of Tucumán, in agr. area (corn, alfalfa, sugar cane, cotton, livestock); apiculture.

Lealui, Northern Rhodesia: see MONGU.

Leaminburg (lē'mĭnbûrg), village (pop. 1,146, with adjacent Cascade), Yakima co., S Wash., near Yakima.

Leamington (lē'mĭngtŭn, lĕ'–), town (pop. 5,858), S Ont., on L. Erie, 28 mi. SE of Windsor; port; agr. center (fruit, vegetables, tobacco), with canneries. Resort.

Leamington (lĕ'mĭngtŭn), officially **Royal Leamington Spa,** municipal borough (1931 pop. 29,669; 1951 census 36,345), central Warwick, England, on Leam R. and 8 mi. S of Coventry. Health resort (largely of 19th-cent. growth) with mineral springs, it features Royal Pump Room and large gardens. Also has foundries, metalworks, leather and brickworks. Borough officially became Royal Leamington Spa in 1838, after a visit of Princess Victoria.

Leamington (lē'mĭngtŭn), town (pop. 214), Millard co., W central Utah, 20 mi. NE of Delta and on Sevier R.

Leam River (lĕm), Northampton and Warwick, England, rises 5 mi. SW of Daventry, flows 25 mi. W, past Leamington, to Avon R. E of Warwick.

Leander (lēăn'dŭr), village (pop. c.400), Williamson co., central Texas, 22 mi. NNW of Austin, in cotton, corn, livestock area; limestone quarries.

Leandro N. Alem, district, Argentina: see VEDIA.

Leandro N. Alem (lā-än'drō ĕ'nā älām'), town (pop. estimate 2,500), S Misiones natl. territory, Argentina, 40 mi. SE of Posadas. Agr. center (corn, tobacco, cotton, maté, tung, potatoes, jute, tea, citrus fruit, grapes); lumbering; maté and tobacco processing.

Leane, Lough, Ireland: see KILLARNEY, LAKES OF.

Leán River (lāän'), N Honduras, rises on Yoro dept. border in Sierra de Nombre de Dios, flows c.50 mi. NNE to Caribbean Sea 10 mi. ENE of Tela. Called Río Colorado in lower course.

Leão, Brazil: see BUTIÁ.

Lea River (lē), SE England, rises just N of Luton, flows 46 mi. SE and S, through Hertford, along Essex-Middlesex boundary, and past Hatfield, Hertfield, and Ware, to the Thames at Blackwall. Receives Stort R. just E of Hoddesdon.

Learned (lûr'nĭd), town (pop. 126), Hinds co., W Miss., 22 mi. WSW of Jackson.

Leary, town (pop. 721), Calhoun co., SW Ga., 20 mi WSW of Albany; lumber, peanut products.

Leasburg, town (pop. 178), Crawford co., E central Mo., in the Ozarks, near Meramec R., 9 mi. N of Steelville; alt. 1,024 ft.; caverns near by.

Leaside (lē'sīd), residential town (pop. 6,183), S Ont., NE suburb of Toronto; mfg. of trucks.

Leask (lēsk), village (pop. 258), central Sask., 40 mi. WSW of Prince Albert; farming, dairying.

Leatherhead, residential urban district (1931 pop. 6,916; 1951 census 27,203), central Surrey, England, on Mole R. and 17 mi. SW of London; mfg. of electric cables and equipment. Has 12th-cent. church and several old houses.

Leatherman Peak, Idaho: see LOST RIVER RANGE.

Leaton, Fort, Texas: see PRESIDIO.

Léau, Belgium: see ZOUTLEEUW.

Leavenworth (lĕ'vŭnwûrth), county (□ 465; pop. 42,361), NE Kansas; ⊙ Leavenworth. Gently rolling to hilly area, bounded E by Missouri R. and Mo., S by Kansas R. Grain growing, stock raising, dairying. Formed 1855.

Leavenworth. 1 Town (pop. 358), Crawford co., S Ind., near Ohio R., 29 mi. W of New Albany, in agr. area. Moved (1937–38) to higher ground from flood-ravaged former site. **2** City (pop. 20,579), ⊙ Leavenworth co., NE Kansas, on Missouri R. (here forming Mo. line) and 20 mi. NW of Kansas City, Kansas; trade and industrial center for diversified-farming and coal-mining area. Mfg. of furniture, sashes and doors, mattresses, canvas goods; flour milling, meat packing, metalworking (structural-steel products, milling equipment). Federal penitentiary is here. Sherman Air Force Base near by. City was settled 1854 by proslavery Missourians near Fort Leavenworth (3 mi. N; built 1827 for protection of traffic on Santa Fe Trail; now seat of command and general staff school); inc. 1855. Grew as supply point for travelers to West. Points of interest are Cathedral of the Immaculate Conception (R.C.) and Fort Leavenworth. **3** City (pop. 1,503), Chelan co., central Wash., 20 mi. NW of Wenatchee and on Wenatchee R.; copper; fruit, dairy products; lumber. Camping, fishing, winter sports in near-by Leavenworth Recreation Area. Site of large U.S. salmon hatchery. Inc. 1906.

Leavitt Peak (lĕ'vĭt) (11,575 ft.), E Calif., in the Sierra Nevada, 32 mi. NW of Mono L.

Leavittsburg (lĕ'vĭtsbûrg), village (pop. 2,533), Trumbull co., NE Ohio, 3 mi. W of Warren and on Mahoning R.

Leawood, city (pop. 1,167), Johnson co., E Kansas, a suburb of Kansas City. Inc. after 1940.

Leba (wĕ'bä), Pol. *Łeba,* Ger. *Leba* (lā'bä), town (1939 pop. 2,846; 1946 pop. 3,021) in Pomerania, after 1945 in Gdansk prov., N Poland, on Leba R., near the Baltic, and 18 mi. NNW of Lebork; rail spur terminus; fishing port; fish canning and smoking. Founded 14th cent. by Teutonic Knights; chartered 1357.

Lebach (lā'bäkh), town (pop. 3,163), central Saar, on Theel R. and 10 mi. NE of Saarlouis; rail junction; agr. market (grain, stock); flour milling.

Lebadea, Greece: see LEVADIA.

Lebane (lĕ'bänĕ), village (pop. 4,095), S Serbia, Yugoslavia, 12 mi. SW of Leskovac.

Lebanon (lĕ'bŭnŭn), Fr. *Liban* (lēbã'), republic (□ 3,927; 1946 pop. 1,165,208), SW Asia, at E end of the Mediterranean, bordering S on Palestine and E and N on Syria; ⊙ BEIRUT. Largely mountainous, with the Lebanon mts. extending the length of the country close to and parallel with the coast. Bet. these mts. and the Anti-Lebanon (on E border with Syria) is the BEKAA, a high fertile valley watered by the Litani (anc. Leontes), the agr. heart of Lebanon. Lebanon grows grain, vegetables, corn, apples, oranges, pears, nuts, cotton. Mulberry trees sustain silk culture, and there are extensive olive groves and vineyards; tobacco is also important. There are cotton and silk weaving industries; also shoe mfg. The iron mines, worked since ancient times, are no longer productive, but lignite is still mined. The famed Cedars of Lebanon are reduced to some 400 trees at the foot of the Dahr el Qadib, 16 mi. SE of Tripoli, just NE of Bsherri. In the cool Lebanon mts. are numerous summer resorts. Beirut is a busy transit port, but the famous old coast cities of TRIPOLI, SAIDA (Sidon), and TYRE have only recently regained some importance; Tripoli is terminus of an oil pipe line from Kirkuk (Iraq), and Saida of one from Abqaiq (Saudi Arabia). In ancient times, the great Phoenician cities established a virtual commercial empire in this area. The cities fell to the Assyrians and the Persians. The region is historically connected with Syria, with which it came under Roman domination and was included in Byzantine Empire until part of it fell to the Arabs in the 7th cent. Before this, however, the Maronites—a Christian sect—had established itself in Lebanon while Syria was becoming Moslem. The Druses also settled in part of Lebanon in regions adjacent to Syria, and trouble bet. them became a constant strain in regional history. The Crusaders were active in Lebanon, and the Lebanese Christians lent them some aid. After that time Lebanon was under Ottoman control until the First World War. Massacres of Maronites by the Druses in 1841 and 1860 led to pressure from the European governments and forced the sultans to grant some autonomy to Great, or Greater, Lebanon as the region was then called. After First World War, the Levant States (Syria and Lebanon) were put under French mandate. Lebanon became a republic (1926) under the mandate and in 1936 a treaty with France (not ratified, however, by the French) provided for independence after a 3-yr. transition period. In Second World War the French Vichy govt. retained control until a British and Free French force conquered (June–July, 1941) the Lebanese coast. The Free French proclaimed Lebanon a republic, but this did not become an accomplished fact until Jan. 1, 1944.

Lebanon, Lat. *Libanus,* mountain range of Lebanon, close to the Mediterranean, extending c.100 mi. NNE–SSW almost the whole length of Lebanon; rises to 10,131 ft. in the Qurnet es Sauda; at foot of the Dahr el Qadib (c.10,000 ft.) are the remains of the Cedars of Lebanon. Both peaks are snow-capped. Bet. the Lebanon and the Anti-Lebanon (on Syrian line) is the fertile BEKAA, a high valley. Beirut-Damascus RR crosses range. There are numerous summer resorts. Also called Jebel el Gharbi.

Lebanon, county (□ 363; pop. 81,683), SE central Pa.; ⊙ Lebanon. Industrial, mining, and agr. area, drained by Swatara Creek. Blue Mtn. is in N part, Lebanon Valley in S. Settled c.1710 by Germans. Stiegel glassware made here in 18th cent. Indiantown Gap Military Reservation, 10 mi. NW of Lebanon, established 1935. Metal products, food products; magnetite, limestone; dairying, agr. (poultry, corn). Formed 1813.

Lebanon. 1 Town (pop. 1,654), New London co., E central Conn., 11 mi. NW of Norwich; farming. Revolutionary War Office (1727), Gov. Trumbull house (1740; now historical mus.), other 18th-cent. houses here. Inc. 1700. **2** City (pop. 2,417), St. Clair co., SW Ill., on Silver Creek and 17 mi. E of East St. Louis, in agr. area (corn, wheat, poultry; dairy products); mfg. of flour, cigars, harvest hats. Seat of McKendree Col.; an old inn (1830) is here. Settled in early-19th cent.; inc. 1857. **3** City (pop. 7,631), ⊙ Boone co., central Ind., 25 mi. NW of Indianapolis, in dairying and farming area; mfg. (oil-refining and farm equipment, bus bodies, auto parts, concrete products, tools, kitchen equipment, condensed milk). Laid out 1832. **4** City (pop. 610), Smith co., N Kansas, 12 mi. ENE of Smith Center; corn, livestock. Geographic center (39° 50'N 98°35'W) of U.S. is 2 mi. NW. **5** City (pop. 4,640), ⊙ Marion co., central Ky., 28 mi. WSW of Danville, in outer Bluegrass agr. region (burley tobacco, corn, hay); mfg. of whisky, wood products, packed meat, crushed limestone, clothing; feed and lumber mills; airport. Natl. cemetery and St. Mary's Col. (W; at St. Mary) near by. **6** Town (pop. 1,499), York co., SW Maine, near Salmon Falls R. above Berwick. Settled 1738, inc. 1767. **7** City (pop. 6,808), ⊙ Laclede co., S central Mo., in the Ozarks, 47 mi. NE of Springfield; shipping center for grain and dairy products; food-processing plants, overall factory. State park near by. Founded c.1849. **8** Village (pop. 213), Red Willow co., S Nebr., 20 mi. SE of McCook and on Beaver Creek, near Kansas line. **9** Town (pop. 8,495), including Lebanon village (pop. 4,614), Grafton co., W N.H., on Mascoma R., near junction with the Connecticut, and 4 mi. S of Hanover. Mfg. (textiles, wood, leather and metal products); printing; dairy products, poultry; winter sports. Includes West Lebanon (pop. 1,737), railroad center, on Connecticut R. (bridged). Founded 1761. **10** Borough (pop. 752), Hunterdon co., W N.J., 18 mi. ESE of Phillipsburg; machinery mfg.; dairying. **11** Village (pop. 4,618), ⊙ Warren co., SW Ohio, 28 mi. NE of Cincinnati and on small Turtle Creek; trade center in agr. area; food products, shoes, stove parts, metal products; poultry hatcheries. Near by is Fort Ancient State Memorial Park. Laid out 1802. **12** City (pop. 5,873), Linn co., W Oregon, on South Santiam R. and 12 mi. SE of Albany in fruit and grain area noted for strawberries; lumber and paper milling, dairying. Platted 1851, inc. 1878. **13** City (pop. 28,156), ⊙ Lebanon co., SE central Pa., 23 mi. ENE of Harrisburg, in central Lebanon Valley; iron and steel products, heating equipment, clothing, chemicals, textiles, food products, paper boxes, shoes; railroad shops. Lebanon Valley, rich limestone-soil agr. area, extends for c.50 mi., approximately bet. Harrisburg (W) and Schuylkill R. (E); lying bet. mtn. ridges, it is part of Great Appalachian Valley. Lebanon settled c.1720, laid out 1750, inc. as borough 1821, as city 1868. **14** Town (pop. 215), Potter co., N central S.Dak., 10 mi. ENE of Gettysburg. **15** Town (pop. 7,913), ⊙ Wilson co., N central Tenn., 28 mi. E of Nashville, in timber, tobacco, livestock area; mfg. of trousers, woolen blankets, pencils and other wood products, dairy products. Seat of Cumberland Univ; Castle Heights Military Acad. Sam Houston practiced law here. Fine ante-bellum homes near by, include the HERMITAGE. Founded c.1802. **16** Town (pop. 672), ⊙ Russell co., SW Va., 22 mi. NNE of Bristol; timber, agr. Rail station at Cleveland, 5 mi. NW.

Lebanon Independent, borough (pop. 2,778), Lebanon co., SE central Pa., just N of Lebanon. Inc. 1912.

Lebanon Junction, town (pop. 1,243), Bullitt co., N Ky., near Rolling Fork, 29 mi. S of Louisville, in agr. area.

Lebanon Valley, Pa.: see LEBANON, city.

Leba River (wĕ'bä), Pol. *Łeba,* Ger. *Leba* (lā'bä), NW Poland, in Pomerania, rises W of Kartuzy, flows N, W, past Lebork, and N, through Leba L., past Leba town, to the Baltic just N of Leba; 80 mi. long. **Leba Lake** (□ 29), is just W of the town, on Koszalin-Gdansk prov. border, separated from the Baltic by a narrow spit; 10 mi. long, 2–5 mi. wide.

Lebbeke (lĕ'bākŭ), town (pop. 12,053), East Flanders prov., N Belgium, 3 mi. SSE of Dendermonde; wool weaving; agr. market.

Lebda, Tripolitania: see HOMS.

Lebec (lŭbĕk'), village (pop. c.275), Kern co., S central Calif., in Tehachapi Mts., 37 mi. S of Bakersfield; oil refining.

Lebedin (lyĕbĭdyēn'), city (1926 pop. 19,301), S Sumy oblast, Ukrainian SSR, near Psel R., 26 mi. SSW of Sumy; flour-milling center; brickworks, sawmills. Teachers col.

Lebedinovskoye, Kirghiz SSR: see VOROSHILOVSKOYE.

Lebedyan or Lebedyan' (lyĕbĭdyän'yŭ), city (1926 pop. 12,155), SW Ryazan oblast, Russian SFSR, on Don R. and 36 mi. NE of Yelets, in rich agr. region (grain, hemp, rubber-bearing plants, fruit). Chartered 1617.

Lebenstedt (lā'bŭn-shtĕt"), N district of WATENSTEDT-SALZGITTER, NW Germany; potash mines, oil wells.

Lebeny (lā'bānyŭ), Hung. *Lébény,* Ger. *Leiden,* town (pop. 3,507), Györ-Moson co., NW Hungary, 12 mi. WNW of Györ. Noted Romanesque church.

Leberau, France: see LIEPVRE.

Lebo (lē'bō), city (pop. 575), Coffey co., E Kansas, 16 mi. E of Emporia, in livestock, poultry, and grain region.

Lebombo Mountains (lĕbŏm'bō), hill range of SE Africa, extending c.100 mi. along Transvaal-Mozambique border NNW of Lourenço Marques.

Lebong (lā'bông), town (pop. 446), Darjeeling dist., N West Bengal, India, N suburb of (1,000 ft. higher than) Darjeeling. Former Br. cantonment.

Lebork (lĕ'bôrk), Pol. *Lębork*, Ger. *Lauenburg* (lou'ùnbŏŏrk), town (1939 pop. 19,114; 1946 pop. 10,954) in Pomerania, after 1945 in Gdansk prov., N Poland, on Leba R. and 30 mi. ENE of Stolp (Slupsk); rail junction; linen milling, food canning, woodworking, agr.-implement mfg. Founded 1341 by Teutonic Knights, who built castle. Passed 1657 to Brandenburg.

Lebret (lùbrĕt'), village (pop. 309), SE Sask., on the Fishing Lakes, 16 mi. N of Indian Head; mixed farming, fishing.

Lebrija (lāvrē'hä), town (pop. 1,372), Santander dept., N central Colombia, 5 mi. W of Bucaramanga; coffeegrowing center; tobacco, sugar cane, rice, corn, pineapples, cattle. Petroleum deposits in vicinity. Cerro de Palonegro near by was site of revolutionary battle.

Lebrija, city (pop. 12,598), Seville prov., SW Spain, in Andalusia, in lower basin of the Guadalquivir, on railroad and 32 mi. S of Seville. Processing and trading center for agr. products of fertile region (grapes, olives, cereals, livestock). Mining of aluminum silicate, which is exported. Flour mills, potteries. Its outstanding bldgs., in Mozarabic style, include 12th-cent. church (formerly a mosque), ruins of Moorish castle and Carthusian convent, and 18th-cent. tower modeled after the Giralda of Seville. Of anc. origin, Lebrija was the Roman *Nerissa Veneria*, where Venus was worshiped. Birthplace of the Sp. humanist Antonio de Nebrija and the navigator Díaz de Solís.

Lebrija River, N central Colombia, rises in Cordillera Oriental NW of Bucaramanga, flows N c.100 mi. to Magdalena R. at Bodega Central.

Lebu (lā'bōō), town (pop. 3,827), ⊙ Arauco prov. and Lebu dept. (□ 419; pop. 14,279), S central Chile, on the Pacific, and 65 mi. SSW of Concepción; 37°38'S 73°41'W. Port, rail terminus, coal-mining center; beach resort. Fishing grounds along coast. Also agr. products: grain, leguminous vegetables; stock raising. Founded 1862 by Cornelio Saavedra.

Lebus (lā'bōōs), town (pop. 1,498), Brandenburg, E Germany, on left bank of the Oder and 6 mi. N of Frankfurt; sugar beets, grain, potatoes; starch mfg. Until 1385 seat of bishopric, later moved to Fürstenwalde.

Lebyazhye or **Lebyazh'ye** (lyĭbyä'zhyĭ). **1** Village (1939 pop. under 500), SE Pavlodar oblast, Kazakh SSR, on Irtysh R. and 65 mi. SSE of Pavlodar, in agr. area; cattle. **2** Village, SW Altai Territory, Russian SFSR, on small bitter-salt lake, 40 mi. N of Rubtsovsk; health resort (baths). **3** Village (1926 pop. 282), S Kirov oblast, Russian SFSR, on Vyatka R. and 18 mi. SW of Molotovsk; coarse grain, wheat. **4** Town (1926 pop. 2,307), E Kurgan oblast, Russian SFSR, near Trans-Siberian RR, 45 mi. ESE of Kurgan; health resort; flour mill.

Lebyazhye or **Lebyazh'ye,** mountain of the central Urals, W Sverdlovsk oblast, Russian SFSR, near Vysokaya mtn. and Nizhni Tagil. Phosphorous-iron mines, limestone-crushing works, supplying metallurgical plants of Nizhni Tagil.

Leça da Palmeira (lā'sù dä pälmā'rù), town (pop. 6,805), Pôrto dist., N Portugal, at mouth of small Leça R. on the Atlantic and 6 mi. NW of Oporto (linked by trolley); seaside resort. With adjoining Matozinhos (SE) it encloses artificial harbor of LEIXÕES. Has 17th-cent. fortress.

Le Cap, Haiti: see CAP-HAÏTIEN.

Lecce (lĕt'chĕ), province (□ 1,065; pop. 526,553), Apulia, S Italy; ⊙ Lecce. Bet. Adriatic Sea and Gulf of Taranto; forms S extremity of "heel" of Ital. peninsula. Plain in N; low, hilly terrain in S, rising to 659 ft. Watered by few small streams. Leads Italy in production of olive oil and tobacco. Other major crops are grapes, figs, cereals, citrus fruit. Livestock raising; fishing. Mfg. at Lecce and Gallipoli. Area reduced to form provs. of Ionio (1923) and Brindisi (1927).

Lecce, city (pop. 42,622), ⊙ Lecce prov., Apulia, S Italy, on "heel" of Ital. peninsula, 50 mi. ESE of Taranto; 40°21'N 18°9'E. Agr. and commercial center; olive oil, wine, alcohol, flour, tobacco products, mfg. of toys, glass, pottery, wax, hosiery, furniture. Bishopric. Noted for its baroque architecture; has 17th-cent. cathedral, seminary, many fine churches and palaces. A Greek and later Roman town; semi-independent from 1053 to 1463; flourished in 16th and 17th cent.

Lecce nei Marsi (nā mär'sē), village (pop. 1,868), Aquila prov., Abruzzi e Molise, S central Italy, 16 mi. SE of Avezzano; bauxite mining.

Lecco (lĕk'kô), town (pop. 19,784), Como prov., Lombardy, N Italy, port on L. of Lecco (SE arm of L. Como), at efflux of Adda R., 15 mi. ENE of Como. Resort and industrial center; iron- and steelworks, silk and paper mills, lime kilns, nail factories, food canneries, chromolithographic plant; mfg. of textile machinery, plastics, wine. A major market and exporter of cheese, especially Gorgonzola. Has picturesque medieval bridge (14th cent.; partly modernized) over the Adda and mus. of natural history.

Le Center, village (pop. 1,314), ⊙ Le Sueur co., S Minn., c.45 mi. SSW of Minneapolis, in agr. area (corn, oats, barley, potatoes, livestock, poultry); dairy products. Log cabin on co. fairgrounds contains pioneer relics. Settled 1864, inc. 1876. Known as Le Sueur Center (lù sōōr') until 1931.

Lécera (lā'thärä), town (pop. 2,066), Saragossa prov., NE Spain, 30 mi. SSE of Saragossa, in fertile agr. area (cereals, wine, saffron).

Lech (lĕkh), village (pop. 715), Vorarlberg, W Austria, on Lech R. and 25 mi. E of Feldkirch; winter sports center (alt. 4,485 ft.) near the Arlberg.

Lechaina or **Lekhaina** (both: lĭkhīnä'), town (pop. 3,473), Elis nome, W Peloponnesus, Greece, on railroad and 20 mi. NW of Pyrgos; livestock market (cattle, sheep); Zante currants, figs, wheat, wine. Also spelled Lechena and Lekhaena.

Leche Lagoon (lā'chā) (7 mi. long, up to 5 mi. wide), Camagüey prov., E Cuba, 3 mi. N of Morón, and bounded N by Turiguanó Isl. Linked by tidal marshes with the sea (inlets of Old Bahama Channel). Its milky color is due to lime sulphates.

Lechemti, Ethiopia: see NAKAMTI.

Lechena, Greece: see LECHAINA.

Lechenich (lĕ'khùnĭkh), town (pop. 4,722), in former Prussian Rhine Prov., W Germany, after 1945 in North Rhine-Westphalia, 12 mi. SW of Cologne. Has 13th-cent. castle, destroyed 1689.

Léchère-les-Bains, La, France: see NOTRE-DAME-DE-BRIANÇON.

Leche River (lā'chā), Lambayeque dept., NW Peru, rises on Lambayeque–Cajamarca dept. border in Cordillera Occidental 25 mi. ENE of Salas, flows 80 mi. W through agr. region (rice, cotton, corn), past Illimo, to area of Mórrope 10 mi. from the Pacific, where it dries up before reaching the sea. Receives Motupe R. near Jayanca; called Mórrope R. below confluence. Feeds numerous irrigation channels in middle course.

Lechfeld (lĕkh'fĕlt"), plain in Bavaria, Germany, S of Augsburg, drained by the Lech. Emperor Otto I here decisively defeated the Hungarians (955).

Lechiguanas Islands (lächēgwä'näs), in Paraná R. delta, E Argentina, bounded by Paraná Pavón and Paraná Ibicuy arms (N) and main Paraná R. channel (S); extend c.70 mi. from Villa Constitución (Santa Fe prov.) to Ibicuy. Subject of dispute bet. Buenos Aires and Entre Ríos provs.

Lechinta (lĕkēn'tsä), Rum. *Lechința*, Ger. *Lechnitz* (lĕkh'nĭts), Hung. *Szászlekence* (säs'lĕkĕntsĕ), village (pop. 2,474), Rodna prov., N central Rumania, on railroad and 10 mi. SW of Bistrita; agr. center. In Hungary, 1940–45.

Lechkhumi Range (lyĕch-khōō'mē), S spur of the central Greater Caucasus, in NW Georgian SSR, forming watershed bet. the Tskhenis-Tskali and upper Rion rivers; rises to 11,844 ft.

Lechlade, England: see FAIRFORD.

Lechnitz, Rumania: see LECHINTA.

Lech River (lĕkh), in Austria and Germany, rises 10 mi. E of Bludenz (Austria), flows NE to Ger. border, then N, past Füssen, Landsberg, and Augsburg, to the Danube 3 mi. N of Rain. Length c.175 mi. Regulated in lower course. Receives the Wertach (left).

Lechtal Alps (lĕkh'täl), in Tyrol, W Austria, extend 35 mi. NE from the Arlberg, rising to 9,965 ft. in the Parseierspitze; pastures, cattle. The Lechtal, valley of upper Lech R., parallels range on N; the Stanzertal and the valley of the Inn (below Landeck) parallel it on S.

Lechuguilla Island (lächōōgē'yä) (□ 13), narrow alluvial islet in SE Gulf of California, off coast of Sinaloa, NW Mexico, at mouth of Río del Fuerte, 28 mi. W of Los Mochis; 12 mi. long, 1–2 mi. wide.

Leciñena (lā-thēnyä'nä), village (pop. 1,855), Saragossa prov., NE Spain, 16 mi. NE of Saragossa; cereals, wine, sheep, lumber.

Leck (lĕk), village (pop. 4,310), in Schleswig-Holstein, NW Germany, 18 mi. W of Flensburg, in North Friesland; market center for cattle region.

Le Claire (lù klâr'), town (pop. 1,124), Scott co., E Iowa, on Mississippi R. and 12 mi. ENE of Davenport; metal products.

Leclercville (lùklârk'vĭl), village (pop. 544), S Que., on the St. Lawrence and 30 mi. NE of Trois Rivières; lumbering, dairying.

L'Écluse, Netherlands: see SLUIS.

Lecompte (lùkŏmpt'), town (pop. 1,443), Rapides parish, central La., 15 mi. S of Alexandria in agr. area (cotton, sugar cane); cotton gins, sugar mills. Settled c.1855.

Lecompton (lĕkŏmp'tùn), city (pop. 263), Douglas co., NE Kansas, on Kansas R. and 13 mi E of Topeka, in fertile farming region. Was ⊙ Kansas Territory, 1855–58; proslavery constitution, written here (1858) in Constitution Hall, was later rejected by territorial electorate.

Le Conte, Mount (lù kŏnt') (6,593 ft.), in Great Smoky Mts., Sevier co., E Tenn., 6 mi. SE of Gatlinburg; tourist lodge here.

Lectoure (lĕktōōr'), town (pop. 2,185), Gers dept., SW France, on Gers R. and 12 mi. E of Condom; agr. market (wheat, cattle, wine); Armagnac brandy distilling, furniture mfg., brewing. Has two 15th–17th cent. churches and ruined castle of counts of Armagnac. Seat of a bishop until 1790.

Leczna (wĕch'nä), Pol. *Łęczna*, Rus. *Lenchna* (lĕnch'nù), town (pop. 2,126), Lublin prov., E Poland, on Wieprz R. and 14 mi. ENE of Lublin; flour milling, mfg. of soap, cotton wads; horse trading.

Leczyca (wē-chĭ'tsä), Pol. *Łęczyca*, Rus. *Lenchitsa* (lyĭn-chē'tsù), town (pop. 6,755), Lodz prov., central Poland, on Bzura R. and 23 mi. NNW of Lodz; flour milling, brewing, mfg. of cement, starch. Romanesque church, built 1161, was restored 1951. During Second World War, under Ger. rule, called Lentschütz.

Ledaña (lā-dhä'nyä), town (pop. 2,704), Cuenca prov., E central Spain, 27 mi. NNE of Albacete; saffron, cereals, grapes, olives, vegetables, livestock.

Ledang, Gunong, Malaya: see OPHIR, MOUNT.

Leda River, Germany: see EMS-HUNTE CANAL.

Ledava River, Yugoslavia: see LENDAVA RIVER.

Ledbury, urban district (1931 pop. 3,284; 1951 census 3,689), E Hereford, England, on Leadon R. and 12 mi. E of Hereford; agr. market. Has Norman church, 17th-cent. market house, and several old inns. John Masefield b. here.

Lede (lā'dù), agr. village (pop. 8,729), East Flanders prov., N central Belgium, 4 mi. NW of Alost.

Ledeberg (lā'dùbĕrkh), town (pop. 12,203), East Flanders prov., NW Belgium, on Scheldt R., just S of Ghent; coke plants.

Ledec nad Sazavou (lĕ'dĕch näd' säzävō), Czech *Ledeč nad Sázavou*, Ger. *Ledetsh an der Sazawa*, town (pop. 2,439), W Bohemia, Czechoslovakia, on Sazawa R., on railroad and 14 mi. NW of Havlickuv Brod; barley, oats, timber.

Ledegem (lā'dù-khùm), agr. village (pop. 3,997), West Flanders prov., W Belgium, 6 mi. W of Courtrai. Formerly spelled Ledeghem.

Ledengskoye, Russian SFSR: see BABUSHKINA, IMENI.

Ledesma (lā-dhāz'mä), town (1947 pop. 4,414), ⊙ Ledesma dept. (□ 1,122; 1947 pop. 25,865), SE Jujuy prov., Argentina, on railroad and 40 mi. NE of Jujuy; lumbering and agr. center (sugar cane, alfalfa, fruit, vegetables, livestock). Sugar refineries, alcohol distilleries, sawmills. Lead mines near by.

Ledesma, town (pop. 2,234), Salamanca prov., W Spain, on Tormes R. and 20 mi. NW of Salamanca; flour- and sawmilling, tanning, woolen-cloth mfg.; cereals, livestock. Mineral springs.

Ledetsch an der Sazawa, Czechoslovakia: see LEDEC NAD SAZAVOU.

Lédignan (lādēnyä'), village (pop. 743), Gard dept., S France, in the Garrigues, 9 mi. S of Alès; wine-growing.

Lednice (lĕd'nyĭtsĕ), Ger. *Eisgrub* (īs'grōōp), village (pop. 1,550), S Moravia, Czechoslovakia, on Dyje R. and 28 mi. SSE of Brno, in agr. area (grapes, tobacco, wheat); rail terminus. Has picturesque castle, part of former domain of Prince Liechtenstein, with valuable collections and extensive park.

Lednicke Rovne (lĕd'nyĭtskā rôv'nĕ, Slovak *Lednické Rovne*, Hung. *Lednicróna* (lĕd'nĭkrōnō), village (pop. 1,649), W Slovakia, Czechoslovakia, in NE foothill of the White Carpathians, on Vah R. and 23 mi. SW of Zilina; rail terminus; large glass-works.

Ledo (lē'dō), village, Lakhimpur dist., NE Assam, India, on Burhi Dihing R. and 55 mi. ESE of Dibrugarh; rail terminus; India terminus of Ledo (Stilwell) Road; brick- and pottery works.

Ledo Road (lē'dō) or **Stilwell Road,** military highway linking Assam (India) and Burma, built during Second World War. Begun in Dec., 1942, from railhead of Ledo, Assam, into Burma, it crossed Patkai Range in Pangsau Pass and followed Hukawng Valley track via Shinbwiyang and Maingkwan and along Mogaung R. valley to Mogaung station. In 1944, a connection was built via Myitkyina and Bhamo to Burma Road near Muse. Originally called Ledo Road and renamed for Gen. J. W. Stilwell, U.S. commander in Burma, the road ceased to be an important route after the war.

Ledrada (lādh-rä'dhä), village (pop. 1,150), Salamanca prov., W Spain, 6 mi. NNE of Béjar; meat processing; cereals, wine.

Ledrae, Cyprus: see NICOSIA.

Leduc (lùdōōk'), town (pop. 920), central Alta., 20 mi. S of Edmonton, near oil fields; rail junction; grain elevators; lumber, flour mills; dairying. Founded 1890 as telegraph station.

Ledyard (lĕd'yùrd). **1** Town (pop. 1,749), New London co., SE Conn., bet. Thames and Mystic rivers, 7 mi. SSE of Norwich; farming. Site of Fort Decatur (built in War of 1812) is marked. Includes Gales Ferry village, site of training quarters for Yale Univ. boat crews. Settled c.1653, inc. 1836. **2** Town (pop. 327), Kossuth co., N Iowa, near Minn. line, 34 mi. E of Estherville.

Ledyczek (lĕdĭ'chĕk), Pol. *Lędyczek*, Ger. *Landeck* (län'dĕk), town (1939 pop. 1,010; 1946 pop. 266) in Pomerania, after 1945 in Koszalin prov., NW Poland, 16 mi. SSE of Szczecinek; dairying; grain, livestock. Until 1938, in former Prussian prov. of Granzmark Posen–Westpreussen.

Lee. 1 County (□ 612; pop. 35,766), E Ala.; ⊙ Opelika. Piedmont area leveling off to flat farm lands below Fall Line; bounded on E by Chattahoochee R. and Ga. Cotton, corn, truck; textiles. Granite, dolomite, manganese. Formed 1866. **2** County (□ 620; pop. 24,322), E Ark.; ⊙ Marianna. Bounded E by the Mississippi; drained by St. Francis and L'Anguille rivers. Agr. (cotton, corn, soybeans); timber. Industries at Marianna. Co.

has U.S. soil-conservation project and a state univ. cotton experiment station. Formed 1873. **3** County (□ 786; pop. 23,404), SW Fla., on Gulf of Mexico (W); ⊙ Fort Myers. Lowland area, swampy in SE, drained by Caloosahatchee R. Bordered by a chain of barrier isls. (Lacosta, Captiva, Sanibel, and Estero isls.) sheltering several lagoons (Pine Island Sound, San Carlos Bay, Estero Bay) and Pine Isl. Agr. (gladioli growing; citrus fruit, vegetables), cattle raising, and fishing. Formed 1887. **4** County (□ 355; pop. 6,674), SW central Ga.; ⊙ Leesburg. Bounded E by Flint R.; drained by Kinchafoonee R. and Muckalee Creek. Coastal plain agr. (peanuts, pecans, corn, livestock) and timber area. Formed 1826. **5** County (□ 17,729; pop. 36,451), N Ill.; ⊙ Dixon. Agr. (corn, wheat, oats, soybeans, livestock, poultry). Mfg. (dairy products, farm machinery, cement and clay products, shoes, metal and wire goods, caskets, gasoline). Sand, gravel pits. Drained by Rock, Green, and Kyte rivers, and Bureau Creek. Formed 1839. **6** County (□ 522; pop. 43,102), extreme SE Iowa; ⊙ Fort Madison and Keokuk. Bounded NE by Skunk R., E by Mississippi R. (forms Ill. line here), and S by Des Moines R. (forms Mo. line here). Prairie agr. area (hogs, cattle, poultry, corn, oats, soybeans); limestone quarries, coal deposits. Industry at Fort Madison and Keokuk. Formed 1836. **7** County (□ 210; pop. 8,739), E central Ky.; ⊙ Beattyville. In the Cumberlands; drained by Kentucky R. and its North, Middle, and South forks. Mtn. agr. area, (livestock, fruit, tobacco, corn, potatoes); coal mines, oil wells; hardwood timber. Includes part of Cumberland Natl. Forest. Formed 1870. **8** County (□ 455; pop. 38,237), NE Miss.; ⊙ Tupelo. Drained by tributaries of the Tombigbee. Agr. (cotton, corn, dairy products, cattle); timber. Includes Ackia Battleground Natl. Monument, Brices Cross Roads Natl. Battlefield Site (near Baldwin), and Tupelo Natl. Battlefield Site. Formed 1866. **9** County (□ 255; pop. 23,522), central N.C.; ⊙ Sanford. Forested piedmont (N) and sand-hill (S) area; bounded N by Cape Fear and Deep rivers. Farming (especially tobacco; cotton, corn), sawmilling; mfg. at Sanford. Formed 1907. **10** County (□ 409; pop. 23,173), NE central S.C.; ⊙ Bishopville. Drained by Lynches and Black rivers. Agr. area (cotton, sweet potatoes, peanuts, cucumbers); timber. Lee State Park (c.2,840 acres) is along Lynches R. near Bishopville. Formed 1902. **11** County (□ 644; pop. 10,144), S central Texas; ⊙ Giddings. Drained by Yegua Creek. Diversified agr., livestock area: cotton, peanuts, corn, grain sorghums, hay, pecans, fruit, truck, cattle, goats, sheep (wool, mohair marketed), hogs, poultry; dairying. Formed 1874. **12** County (□ 434; pop. 36,106), extreme SW Va., in angle formed by Ky. (N) and Tenn. (S); ⊙ Jonesville. Mtn. and valley region, with Cumberland Mts. along Ky. line, Cumberland Gap at SW tip, and part of Powell Mtn. in E; includes part of Jefferson Natl. Forest. Drained by Powell R. Agr. (tobacco, grain, truck, fruit), livestock raising; extensive bituminous-coal mining, limestone quarrying, lumbering. Limestone caves. Formed 1792.

Lee. **1** Town (pop. 228), Madison co., N Fla., 7 mi. ESE of Madison, in agr. and lumbering area. **2** Village (pop. 251), on Lee-De Kalb co. line, N Ill., 13 mi. SW of De Kalb, in rich agr. area. **3** Town (pop. 610), Penobscot co., E central Maine, 36 mi. NNE of Old Town, in hunting, fishing area. **4** Town (pop. 4,820), including Lee village (pop. 2,847), Berkshire co., W Mass., in the Berkshires, on Housatonic R. and 9 mi. S of Pittsfield; resort; paper and lumber mills; marble quarries. Settled 1760, set off from Great Barrington and Washington 1777. Includes state forest, villages of East Lee, South Lee, and Jacobs Pillow. **5** Town (pop. 575), Strafford co., SE N.H., on Lamprey R. and 9 mi. SW of Dover.

Lee, Fort, Va.: see PETERSBURG.

Lee, Lake, Washington co., W Miss., oxbow lake (c.8 mi. long) near Mississippi R., 8 mi. S of Greenville.

Leechburg, borough (pop. 4,042), Armstrong co., W central Pa., 24 mi. NE of Pittsburgh and on Kiskiminetas R.; mfg. (strip steel, beverages); bituminous coal; agr. Laid out 1828, inc. 1850.

Leech Lake (□ 251), Cass co., N central Minn., SE of Bemidji, largely in Leech Lake Indian Reservation; 20 mi. long, max. width 15 mi. Fishing, bathing, and boating resorts. Drains through Leech R. (c.30 mi. long; dammed just W of Federal Dam village) into Mississippi R. Bear Isl. (3.5 mi. long, 1 mi. wide) is in SE; village of Walker is on SW shore. Lake is surrounded by Chippewa Natl. Forest and used as reservoir.

Lee City, town (pop. 120), Wolfe co., E central Ky., in the Cumberlands, 50 mi. ESE of Winchester.

Leedey, town (pop. 558), Dewey co., W Okla., 39 mi. S of Woodward, in agr. area; cotton ginning.

Leeds, county (□ 900; pop. 36,042), SE Ont., on the St. Lawrence and on N.Y. border; ⊙ Brockville.

Leeds. **1** Agr. village and parish (pop. 643), central Kent, England, 4 mi. ESE of Maidstone. Has Norman church. Castle, dating from Saxon times, was rebuilt in Norman and Tudor eras. As a princess, Elizabeth was imprisoned here. **2** County borough (1931 pop. 482,809; 1951 census 504,954) and city, West Riding, central Yorkshire, England, on Aire R. and 40 mi. NE of Manchester; 53°48′N 1°32′W; industrial and communications center, with good rail and water (river and canal) connections to both coasts. Woolen milling (dating from 14th cent.) is important, and manufactures include: clothing, locomotives, machinery, airplane parts and other metal products, leather goods, chemicals, pottery, glass; printing industry. Site of: Leeds Univ. (1904), formerly Yorkshire Col. (1874); Corinthian town hall (1858), scene of triennial music festivals; Cathedral of St. Anne; St. Peter's Church; St. John's Church (1634); Coliseum; several libraries and museums. Dr. John Priestley was pastor at Mill Hill Chapel. In the county borough are industrial suburbs of ARMLEY AND NEW WORTLEY, BEESTON, FARNLEY AND WORTLEY, HOLBECK, KIRKSTALL, and HUNSLET CARR AND MIDDLETON.

Leeds. **1** City (pop. 3,306), on Jefferson-St. Clair co. line, N central Ala., 10 mi. E of Birmingham, in coal, iron, and limestone area; lumber and steel wire products, cement. Founded 1881. **2** Town (pop. 797), Androscoggin co., SW Maine, on the Androscoggin and 15 mi. NE of Auburn; vegetables canned. **3** Village, Hampshire co., Mass.: see NORTHAMPTON. **4** Resort village, Green co., SE N.Y., 3 mi. NW of Catskill and on Catskill Creek. Has 18th-cent. stone bridge. **5** City (pop. 778), Benson co., N central N.Dak., 30 mi. WNW of Devils Lake.

Leedstown, hamlet, Westmoreland co., E Va., on the Rappahannock and 30 mi. SE of Fredericksburg. Here, in 1766, were drawn up the Leedstown Resolutions, embodying points later included in Declaration of Independence.

Leefdaal (lāf′däl), agr. village (pop. 2,188), Brabant prov., central Belgium, 5 mi. SW of Louvain. Romanesque 12th-cent. church and chapel. Formerly spelled Leefdael.

Leegebruch (lā′gubro͝okh″), village (pop. 5,554), Brandenburg, E Germany, 3 mi. SW of Oranienburg; market dairying.

Lee Hall, hamlet, Warwick co., SE Va., near the James, 18 mi. NNW of Newport News; rail station for U.S. Fort Eustis (ū′stĭs), just SW.

Leek (lēk), urban district (1931 pop. 18,567; 1951 census 19,358), N Stafford, England, near the Churnet, 10 mi. NE of Stoke-on-Trent; silk-milling center; mfg. of textile machinery and machine tools. Has remains of a Cistercian abbey founded 1214. Parish church has 14th-cent. tower and 4 Saxon crosses in churchyard.

Leek (lāk), town (pop. 1,338), Groningen prov., N Netherlands, 8 mi. WSW of Groningen, near small lake; cattle raising, dairying; meat packing.

Leelanau (lē′lunô), county (□ 349; pop. 8,647), NW Mich.; ⊙ Leland. A peninsula (Leelanau Peninsula) bounded W by L. Michigan and E by Grand Traverse Bay. Agr.: fruitgrowing (especially cherries); also poultry, truck, potatoes; dairy products. Sawmills, fisheries. Resorts on Leelanau and Glen lakes. It is a former lumber region. Lighthouse at tip of peninsula. Organized 1863.

Leelanau, Lake, Leelanau co., NW Mich., on Leelanau Peninsula, just E of Leland; c.4½ mi. long; resort. Connected to Lower Leelanau L. (c.9 mi. long; just S) by short stream.

Leelanau Peninsula, Mich.: see LEELANAU, county.

Leende (lān′dů), village (pop. 1,560), North Brabant prov., S Netherlands, 7 mi. SSE of Eindhoven; silver-fox breeding; mfg. (strawboard, cigars); cattle raising, agr.

Lee-on-the-Solent, England: see GOSPORT.

Leeper, Mount (8,800 ft.), S Alaska, in Chugach Mts., 20 mi. NE of Cape Yakataga; 60°17′N 142°5′W.

Leer (lâr), town (pop. 18,100), in former Prussian prov. of Hanover, NW Germany, after 1945 in Lower Saxony, port on right bank of the Ems, at mouth of Leda R. (W end of Ems-Hunte Canal), and 13 mi. SE of Emden; rail junction; base of herring fleet; foundry; flax mills. Food processing (chocolate, cacao, condensed milk, milk sugar). Other products: soda, soap, tobacco, porcelain. Cattle markets. Has 16th-cent. castle, 17th- and 18th-cent. churches. Founded c.790. Chartered 1823.

Leerdam (lār′däm), town (pop. 3,365), South Holland prov., W Netherlands, 14 mi. S of Utrecht; glassworking center; ceramics, crates, boxes; lumber mill; dairying.

Lee River. **1** In Co. Cork, Ireland, rises in Shehy Mts., flows 50 mi. E, past Macroom and Cork, to Lough Mahon, NW reach of Cork Harbour. **2** In Co. Kerry, Ireland, rises ENE of Tralee, flows 10 mi. SW, past Tralee, to Tralee Bay.

Leers (lârs), town (pop. 2,789), Nord dept., N France, 3 mi. ESE of Roubaix, near Belg. border; customhouse; textile milling.

Lees, urban district (1931 pop. 4,738; 1951 census 4,160), SE Lancashire, England, 2 mi. E of Oldham; cotton milling.

Leesburg. **1** City (pop. 7,395), Lake co., central Fla., 35 mi. NW of Orlando, bet. lakes Griffin and Harris; head of navigation on OKLAWAHA RIVER system. Shipping center (citrus fruit, truck produce, watermelons); packing houses, citrus-fruit canneries, crate factory. Has watermelon laboratory. Settled 1856, inc. 1875. **2** City (pop. 659), ⊙ Lee co., SW central Ga., 10 mi. N of Albany, near Kinchafoonee R., in agr. area. **3** Town (pop. 428), Kosciusko co., N Ind., 31 mi. SE of South Bend, in agr. area. **4** Village (pop. c.600), Cumberland co., S N.J., on Maurice R. and 10 mi. SSE of Millville, in truck farming area. State prison farm here. **5** Village (pop. 841), Highland co., SW Ohio, 10 mi. NNE of Hillsboro, in stock-raising and farming area. **6** Town (pop. 1,703), ⊙ Loudoun co., N Va., near the Potomac, 30 mi. WNW of Washington, D.C.; trade center in region known for livestock breeding (horses, cattle); grain growing, dairying. Limestone quarrying. Near by, on the Potomac, Civil War engagement of Ball's Bluff was fought (Oct., 1861); a Confederate victory. Settled 1749; inc. 1758.

Lees Summit, city (pop. 2,554), Jackson co., W Mo., 18 mi. SE of Kansas City. Agr. center, dairying; meat products. Laid out 1865.

Leest (lāst), agr. village (pop. 1,864), Antwerp prov., N central Belgium, 3 mi. W of Mechlin.

Lee State Park, S.C.: see LEE, county.

Leeste (lā′stů), village (pop. 5,914), in former Prussian prov. of Hanover, NW Germany, after 1945 in Lower Saxony, 7 mi. S of Bremen.

Leeston (lē′stůn), town (pop. 612), ⊙ Ellesmere co. (□ 230; pop. 2,788), E S.Isl., New Zealand, 23 mi. SW of Christchurch; grain, sheep.

Leesville. **1** Village, Middlesex co., Conn.: see EAST HADDAM. **2** Town (pop. 4,670), ⊙ Vernon parish, W La., 50 mi. WSW of Alexandria; lumber milling, cotton ginning; livestock, cotton, corn, sweet potatoes. Inc. 1899. U.S. Camp Polk, a state park, and Kisatchie Natl. Forest are near by. **3** Village (pop. 297), Carroll co., E Ohio, 24 mi. SSE of Canton. Flood-control dam near by impounds Leesville Reservoir (capacity 37,400 acre-ft.) in a small tributary of Tuscarawas R. **4** Town (pop. 1,453), Lexington co., W central S.C., 27 mi. WSW of Columbia, adjacent to Batesburg; caskets, cottonseed oil, ice.

Lees Wharf, Md.: see WOODLAND BEACH.

Leete's Island, Conn.: see GUILFORD.

Leeton, town (pop. 3,912), S New South Wales, Australia, 165 mi. WNW of Canberra; dairying center; vineyards.

Leeton, town (pop. 372), Johnson co., W central Mo., 12 mi. S of Warrensburg.

Leetonia. **1** Village (1940 pop. 396), St. Louis co., NE Minn., on Mesabi iron range just W of Hibbing; iron mines near by. **2** Village (pop. 2,565), Columbiana co., E Ohio, 15 mi. S of Youngstown; makes pretzels, tools, truck bodies, machinery; coal mines. Laid out 1866.

Leetsdale, residential borough (pop. 2,411), Allegheny co., W Pa., 15 mi. NW of Pittsburgh and on Ohio R.; steel products. Settled 1796, inc. 1904.

Leeuwarden (lā′üvärdůn), Frisian *Lieuwert*, anc. *Leovardia*, city (pop. 57,923; including suburb of Huizum, 72,008), ⊙ Friesland prov., N Netherlands, at junction of the Harlinger Trekvaart and the Wijde Ee, 70 mi. NNE of Amsterdam; 53°12′N 5°46′E. Rail junction; major dairying and agr. center, noted for its cattle market; mfg. (clothing, artificial silk, paper). Airport. Has 16th-cent. chancellery and other 16th- and 17th-cent. buildings, Frisian Mus. (housed in 18th-cent. mansion), 18th-cent. town hall. Chartered in 1435, it was center of gold and silver industry in 16th–18th cent.

Leeuwin, Cape (lo͞o′ĭn), SW Western Australia, in Indian Ocean, at W end of Flinders Bay, in area known for treacherous currents and gales; 34°22′S 115°8′E; lighthouse.

Leeuw-Saint-Pierre, Belgium: see SINT-PIETERS-LEEUW.

Leeville, village, Lafourche parish, extreme SE La., on navigable Bayou Lafourche at intersection with Southwestern Louisiana Canal, in marshy region bet. Caminada and Timbalier bays, c.50 mi. S of New Orleans; center of oil field.

Leevining (lē″vī′nĭng), village (pop. c.200), Mono co., E Calif., in the Sierra Nevada, near Mono L., in mining and recreational region. Canyon of Leevining Creek (W) has hydroelectric plant.

Leeward Islands (lo͞o′ůrd, lū′-, lē′-), N chain of islands of the Lesser Antilles, E West Indies, extending SE from Puerto Rico to the Windward Isls., bet. 15°40′–18°45′N and 61°40′–65°5′W. The principal isls. are: the VIRGIN ISLANDS of the U.S. and Great Britain (geologically a part of the Greater Antilles); the Fr. isl. of GUADELOUPE and its dependencies; the Du. isls. of SAINT EUSTATIUS and SABA; SAINT MARTIN, divided bet. France and Holland; and the Br. colony of the **Leeward Islands** (□ 422.5; pop. 108,838), a federation of 4 presidencies, ANTIGUA (with BARBUDA and REDONDA), SAINT KITTS-NEVIS (with ANGUILLA and SOMBRERO), MONTSERRAT, and the Br. Virgin Isls., the last separated from the rest of the colony by 40-mi.-wide Anegada Passage. St. Kitts, Nevis, Montserrat, and SW Antigua are part of the volcanic formation of the Lesser Antilles, while N and E Antigua, and Anguilla and Barbuda are of coral limestone. The climate varies but is generally dry and healthful. Annual temp. about 80°F.; somewhat cooler in the Virgin Isls. Rainfall 40–60 inches; rainy season Aug.-Jan. Hurricanes occur occasionally, and the volcanic isls. are subject to earth tremors. Isls. are of great fertility; their mainstay has been sugar cane (and mfg. of molasses and rum), now largely replaced by sea-island cotton; also produce limes, coconuts, tobacco, vegetables, livestock, dairy products. Industries: sugar refining, rum distilling, cotton ginning, mfg. of citrus products, charcoal burning, fishing. The isls. are visited by tourists in winter. Leading ports and commercial and processing centers are SAINT JOHN'S (Antigua), BASSETERRE (St. Kitts), Plymouth (Montserrat). Discovered 1493 by Columbus on his 2d voyage; actual settlement began in 17th cent., when Sir Thomas Warner arrived (1623) at St. Kitts and was made governor of the as yet uncolonized neighboring isls. Nevis, Antigua, Montserrat, and Barbuda were settled from St. Kitts. Fr. colonists arrived at St. Kitts in 1625. The isls. were merged under a general legislature. Br. possession was contested by France and Spain; Spain soon abandoned the struggle, but the isls. were pawns in French-British conflicts for many years; almost every treaty bet. the countries made some disposition of isls. in the Leewards until the end of the Napoleonic Wars in 1815, when their final disposition was accomplished. The isl. of Dominica, united with the Leewards in 1833, was transferred to Windward Isls. in 1940 (Imperial Act passed 1938). The pop. of the Leewards is now predominantly Negro.

Leeward Islands, Fr. Oceania: see SOCIETY ISLANDS.

Leffe (lĕf'fĕ), village (pop. 2,666), Bergamo prov., Lombardy, N Italy, 12 mi. NE of Bergamo; bedcover factories, cotton mills. Lignite mines near by.

Leffrinckoucke (lĕfrĕkōōk', Fl. lĕf'rĭnkōkŭ), village (pop. 1,221), Nord dept., N France, 4 mi. E of Dunkirk; steel milling.

Lefka or **Leuka** (both: lĕf'kä), town (pop. 3,752), Nicosia dist., NW Cyprus, near Morphou Bay, in agr. region (citrus fruit, olives; sheep, goats). Has copper-reducing plants. Near by in Evrykhou Valley are important Mavrovouni and Skouriotissa pyrite mines. Its port Karavostasi or Xeros, 2 mi. NE, ships minerals and citrus fruit.

Lefkara or **Pano Lefkara** (pä'nō lĕf'kärä), town (pop. 2,598), Larnaca dist., S Cyprus, 18 mi. W of Larnaca; olive oil, wine, carobs; sheep, goats. Lace making.

Lefkas, Greece: see LEUKAS.

Lefkimmi, Greece: see LEUKIMME.

Lefkoniko (lĕfkô'nēkō), town (pop. 2,596), Famagusta dist., NE Cyprus, 25 mi. ENE of Nicosia, in agr. region (wheat, barley, vetches, olives, almonds; sheep, cattle, hogs).

Lefkosha, Cyprus: see NICOSIA.

Leflore (lŭflôr'), county (□ 588; pop. 51,813), W central Miss.; ⊙ Greenwood. Tallahatchie and Yalobusha rivers unite here to form Yazoo R. Cotton growing. Greenwood is market, processing center. Formed 1871.

Le Flore (lù flôr'), county (□ 1,575; pop. 35,276), SE Okla.; ⊙ Poteau. Bounded N by Arkansas R., E by Ark. line; drained by Poteau and Kiamichi rivers; includes part of Ouachita Mts. Lumbering, agr. (corn, cotton, livestock, vegetables); coal mining; natural-gas wells. Part of Ouachita Natl. Forest is in co. Formed 1907.

Leforest (lùfôrā'), town (pop. 4,518), Pas-de-Calais dept., N France, 5 mi. N of Douai; coal mining.

Lefors (lē'fûrz), town (pop. 577), Gray co., extreme N Texas, in the Panhandle, 65 mi. ENE of Amarillo and on North Fork of Red R.; a trade center for oil, gas, and cattle area; makes carbon black.

Lefroy, Mount (lŭfroi') (11,230 ft.), on Alta.-B.C. border, in Rocky Mts., on W edge of Banff Natl. Park, 35 mi. WNW of Banff; 51°22'N 116°16'W.

Leftwich, residential town and parish (pop. 1,021), central Cheshire, England, on Weaver R. just S of Northwich; leather tanning.

Legal (lùgăl'), village (pop. 445), central Alta., near Manawan L. (4 mi. long), 28 mi. N of Edmonton; grain elevators, mixed farming. French-Canadian settlement, founded 1898.

Leganés (lāgänās'), town (pop. 5,064), Madrid prov., central Spain, 7 mi. SSW of Madrid (linked by tramways); cereals, truck produce, livestock; mfg. of toys and soft drinks. Mineral springs. Insane asylum.

Leganiel (lāgänyĕl'), town (pop. 1,169), Cuenca prov., central Spain, 40 mi. ESE of Madrid; cereals, grapes, olives, sheep.

Legaspi (lùgä'spē, Sp. lägä'spē), city (1939 pop. 15,780; 1948 metropolitan area pop. 78,828), ⊙ Albay prov., SE Luzon, Philippines, on Albay Gulf, 210 mi. ESE of Manila; 13°8'N 123°44'E. Chief port of E Luzon, shipping copra and abacá. Pulp milling, abacá processing; machine shops. The metropolitan area originally comprised 2 municipalities (organized 1903)—Legaspi and Albay. These were combined in 1907 and called Legaspi in 1925. Near-by Daraga municipality (därä'gä) (1939 pop. 29,484) was combined in early 1940s with Legaspi municipality to form Legaspi city. In Second World War, city was occupied by the Japanese, Dec., 1941–April, 1945.

Legazpia (lāgäth'pyä), town (pop. 1,737), Guipúzcoa prov., N Spain, 14 mi. WSW of Tolosa; metalworking; mfg. of paper, celluloid articles, fireworks. Lead and zinc mines near by.

Légé (lā-zhā'), village (pop. 892), Loire-Inférieure dept., W France, 23 mi. S of Nantes; woodworking, hog raising.

Legge Tor (lĕg' tôr'), highest peak (5,160 ft.) in Tasmania, in Ben Lomond range. Sometimes called Legge's Peak.

Leghorn (lĕg'hôrn), Ital. *Livorno* (lēvôr'nô), city (pop. 109,067), ⊙ Livorno prov., Tuscany, central Italy, on Ligurian Sea, 50 mi. WSW of Florence; 43°33'N 10°20'E. Chief W coast port of Italy, after Genoa and Naples. Has major shipyards; seat of Ital. naval acad. Exports wine, olive oil, textiles, marble. Industrial center; metallurgical plants (copper), iron- and steelworks, mineral-oil refinery, alcohol distilleries, glass factories; mfg. of automobile chassis, electric motors, cables, aluminum products, chemicals, paint, lubricants, macaroni. Also noted as a bathing resort. Bishopric. A fortified castle in Middle Ages; developed under the Medici into a flourishing town. Suffered severe air bombing (1943–44) in Second World War, with destruction of many bldgs., including cathedral (completed 1595), synagogue (1591), library; heavy damage to industries and port installations.

Legi Oberskie, Poland: see OBRA RIVER.

Legio Maximianopolis, Palestine: see MEGIDDO.

Legion, village, Kerr co., SW Texas, a SE suburb of Kerrville; U.S. veterans' hosp. here.

Legion Mine, village, Bulawayo prov., SW Southern Rhodesia, in Matabeleland, 27 mi. SSE of Antelope; gold-mining center.

Legnago (lĕnyä'gô), town (pop. 4,528), Verona prov., Veneto, N Italy, on Adige R. and 23 mi. SE of Verona; rail junction. Mfg. (agr. and woodworking machinery, buttons, fertilizer, castor oil). Large beet-sugar refinery. Was SE fortress of the "Quadrilateral" in 16th cent. and again after 1814.

Legnano (lĕnyä'nô), city (pop. 31,959), Milano prov., Lombardy, N Italy, on Olona R. and 16 mi. NW of Milan. Industrial center; foundries, cotton and flour mills, dyeworks, shoe factories; mfg. of machinery, engines, soap, candles, liquor. Lombard League defeated (1176) Frederick Barbarossa near by.

Legnica, Poland: see LIEGNITZ.

Legnickie Pole, Poland: see WAHLSTATT.

Legnone, Monte (môn'tĕ lĕnyô'nĕ), highest summit (8,563 ft.) in L. Como region, Lombardy, N Italy, 17 mi. NNE of Lecco.

Legoendi, Indonesia: see LEGUNDI.

Legoniel, Northern Ireland: see LIGONIEL.

Legostayevo (lyĕgŭstī'ŭvŭ), village (1948 pop. over 2,000), E Novosibirsk oblast, Russian SFSR, 15 mi. E of Iskitim; dairy farming.

Legrad (lĕ'grät), Hung. *Légrád* (lā'gräd), village, N Croatia, Yugoslavia, on Drava R., at Mura R. mouth, and 25 mi. E of Varazdin, on Hung. border; trade center for agr. (poultry, dairy products) area.

Legrand (lùgrã'), village (pop. 538), Oran dept., NW Algeria, 12 mi. E of Oran; winegrowing.

Le Grand, town (pop. 393), Marshall co., central Iowa, near Iowa R., 7 mi. ESE of Marshalltown. Limestone quarries near by.

Leg River (wĕk), Pol. *Łeg,* Rzeszow prov., SE Poland, rises 11 mi. N of Rzeszow, flows c.50 mi. N to Vistula R. 3 mi. E of Sandomierz. Another Leg R., Ger. *Lyck* (lĭk), right tributary of Biebrza R., is in Bialystok prov.

Leguan Island (□ 17.4; pop. 4,295), Essequibo co., N Br. Guiana, in Essequibo R. estuary, on the Atlantic, E of Wakenaam Isl., 18 mi. WNW of Georgetown; 8 mi. long. Rice growing. Its settlement, Leguan, is ⊙ Essequibo Isls. dist.

Légué, Le (lù lāgā'), N suburb and fishing port (pop. 1,200) of Saint-Brieuc, Côtes-du-Nord dept., W France.

Léguevin (lāgvē'), village (pop. 430), Haute-Garonne dept., S France, 10 mi. W of Toulouse; horse raising, agr.

Leguízamo or **Puerto Leguízamo** (pwĕr'tō lāgē'sāmō), town, Casanare intendancy, S Colombia, on Putumayo R. (Peru line) and 140 mi. SE of Florencia. Formerly called Caucayá; until 1950 in Amazonas.

Legundi or **Legoendi** (both: lùgōōn'dē), islet (5 mi. long), Indonesia, in Sunda Strait, just off S coast of Sumatra, at entrance to Lampung Bay, 25 mi. S of Telukbetung. Wooded, hilly, rising to 1,125 ft. Coconuts. The British established settlement here in 1624, but withdrew in 1625.

Leh (lā), town (pop. 3,372), ⊙ Ladakh dist. and Ladakh tahsil (□ 29,848; pop. 36,307), E central Kashmir, in Ladakh Range, near the Indus, 150 mi. E of Srinagar; pulse, wheat. Has palace of former rajas (defeated by Dogras in 1834), fort, Buddhist monastery; Dard graves (1st–6th cent. A.D.) unearthed. First visited in 1715 by a European. Fighting here in 1948, during India-Pakistan struggle for control.

Lehavoth Habashan, Israel: see MA'ALE HAB BASHAN.

Lehe, Germany: see BREMERHAVEN.

Lehesten (lā'ŭstùn), town (pop. 1,933), Thuringia, central Germany, in Thuringian Forest, 13 mi. SSE of Saalfeld; slate-quarrying center (since 13th cent.), with paper mills. Climatic health and winter-sports resort.

Lehi (lē'hī), city (pop. 3,627), Utah co., N central Utah, 25 mi. S of Salt Lake City, near Wasatch Range; alt. 4,550 ft. Trading point for agr. area (alfalfa, sugar beets); flour, feed, beet sugar; clay products. Settled by Mormons 1850; inc. 1852. Surrounding region is irrigated by water from Utah L. (just S) and Provo R. Formerly Lehi City.

Lehigh (lē'hī), county (□ 347; pop. 198,207), E Pa.; ⊙ Allentown. Industrial and farm area, drained by Lehigh R. Potatoes; limestone, slate; cement, motor vehicles, textiles. Formed 1812.

Lehigh. 1 Town (pop. 881), Webster co., central Iowa, on Des Moines R. and 12 mi. SSE of Fort Dodge; brick and tile plant. Clay, sand, gravel pits near by. State park is NW. **2** City (pop. 240), Marion co., central Kansas, 45 mi. N of Wichita, in grain-, stock-, and oil-producing region. **3** Village, Stark co., W N.Dak., 5 mi. E of Dickinson and on branch of Heart R. Lignite briquettes and creosote are made here. **4** City (pop. 352), Coal co., S central Okla., 5 mi. S of Coalgate; coal mining.

Lehigh River, E Pa., rises in SW Wayne co., flows 103 mi. S and E, past Mauch Chunk, through industrial area (power dams), past Allentown and Bethlehem, to Delaware R. at Easton. Scenic Lehigh Gap is gorge cut through Blue Mtn. near Palmerton.

Lehighton (lēhī'tùn), borough (pop. 6,565), Carbon co., E Pa., 20 mi. NW of Allentown and on Lehigh R., clothing, textiles, cement products, chemicals, beverages; timber; agr. Settled 1746, inc. 1866.

Lehinch, Ireland: see LAHINCH.

Lehliu (lĕkh'lēōō), village (pop. 2,645), Ialomita prov., SE Rumania, 32 mi. NW of Calarasi.

Lehman Caves National Monument (lē'mùn) (640 acres; alt. 7,000 ft.; established 1922), E Nev., on E flank of Wheeler Peak in Snake Range, and 40 mi. ESE of Ely; monument hq. at Baker, 5 mi. E. Subterranean chambers and tunnels, containing a variety of stalactites and stalagmites. Caves were used as burial ground by prehistoric Indians.

Lehmann (lā'män), town (pop. estimate 1,000), central Santa Fe prov., Argentina, 60 mi. NW of Santa Fe; agr. center (alfalfa, wheat, flax, livestock); dairying.

Lehnin (lānēn'), village (pop. 3,978), Brandenburg, E Germany, 10 mi. SE of Brandenburg; climatic health resort. Has remains of Cistercian monastery (founded 1180; dissolved 1542).

Lehr (lâr), city (pop. 394), Logan and McIntosh counties, S N.Dak., 17 mi. N of Ashley.

Lehrberg (lâr'bĕrk), village (pop. 1,706), Middle Franconia, W Bavaria, Germany, on the Franconian Rezat and 4 mi. NW of Ansbach; rye, oats, wheat, hops.

Lehre (lā'rù), village (pop. 2,121), in Brunswick, NW Germany, after 1945 in Lower Saxony, 7 mi. NE of Brunswick; flour products; sugar beets.

Lehrte (lâr'tù), town (pop. 16,397), in former Prussian prov. of Hanover, NW Germany, after 1945 in Lower Saxony, 10 mi. E of Hanover; rail center; potash mining. Foundries; mfg. of oil-drilling machinery, electrical equipment, chemicals, wood products; food processing (flour products, canned goods, grain starch, beverages, spirits). Cattle market.

Lehua (lähōō'ù), small island off N coast of Niihau, T.H.; light station of U.S. lighthouse service.

Lehututu (lähōōtōō'tōō), village (pop. 1,366), N Kgalagadi dist., SW Bechuanaland Protectorate, in Kalahari Desert, 280 mi. NW of Mafeking; 23°59'S 21°53'E; hq. of the Bakalagadi Hottentots; road junction.

Lei, China: see LEI RIVER.

Leiah (lā'yŭ), town (pop. 13,087), Muzaffargarh dist., SW Punjab, W Pakistan, on railroad and 65 mi. NNW of Muzaffargarh; market center for wheat, millet, rice, dates; hand-loom weaving, woolen-blanket mfg.; ivory products.

Leiasundet, Norway: see KVITSOY.

Leibnitz (līp'nĭts), town (pop. 5,920), Styria, SE Austria, near Mur R., 20 mi. S of Graz; mfg. (machines, leather goods); vineyards.

Leicester or **Leicestershire** (lĕ'stùr, -shĭr), county (□ 831.9; 1931 pop. 541,861; 1951 census 630,893), central England; ⊙ Leicester. Bounded by Warwick (SW), Stafford (W), Derby (NW), Nottingham (N), Lincolnshire and Rutland (E), and Northampton (SE). Drained by Soar R. and Wreak R. Low undulating country, with fertile pastures; dairying (Melton Mowbray region). There are coal (W) and ironstone (NE) deposits. Chief industries are hosiery knitting, leather and shoe mfg., and metalworking. Important towns are Leicester, Loughborough, Melton Mowbray, Ashby-de-la-Zouch, Hinckley, and Coalville.

Leicester, county borough (1931 pop. 239,169; 1951 census 285,061) and city, ⊙ Leicestershire, England, in center of co., on Soar R. and 90 mi. NW of London; 52°38'N 1°7'W. One of England's more modern industrial centers, specializing in a number of lighter industries, such as leather tanning and mfg. of shoes and hosiery. Also makes chemicals, aniline dyes, paint, pharmaceuticals, textiles, textile machinery, light-metal products, rubber products. Leicester is site of the Roman settlement of *Ratae Coritanorum*, or *Ratae*, on the anc. road Fosse Way; it was also an anc. Br. settlement and one of the "Five Boroughs" of Danish times. Site of an artificial mound, on which was built an anc. castle. Near the Jewry Wall, a Roman structure 20 ft. high and 75 ft. long, extensive Roman remains have been found. There are also remains of Norman castle; ruins of an abbey founded 1143, scene of death of Cardinal Wolsey; 2 city gates; 14th-cent. Trinity Hosp.; an Elizabethan grammar school; several old churches; and many modern public bldgs., including University Col., founded 1921. Town was of industrial importance as early as 14th cent. Richard III was buried here after battle of Bosworth Field. It sustained 2 sieges in Civil War.

Leicester, village (1931 pop. 219), Sierra Leone colony, on Sierra Leone Peninsula, at NE foot of Leicester Peak, 2 mi. SSE of Freetown; cassava, corn.

Leicester. 1 Residential town (pop. 6,029), Worcester co., central Mass., just W of Worcester; printing. Has a jr. col. Settled 1713, inc. 1722. Includes villages of Leicester Center (pop. 1,465), Cherry Valley (1940 pop. 1,007), and Rochdale (1940 pop. 936). **2** Village (pop. 364), Livingston co., W central N.Y., 32 mi. SSW of Rochester; canned foods. **3** Town (pop. 511), Addison co., W Vt., near L. Dunmore, in Green Mts., 11 mi. S of Middlebury.

Leicester Peak (1,952 ft.), in Sierra Leone colony, on Sierra Leone Peninsula, 2.5 mi. S of Freetown.

Leicestershire, England: see LEICESTER, county.

Leichhardt (līk'härt), municipality (pop. 29,462), E New South Wales, Australia, on S shore of Port Jackson, 3 mi. WSW of Sydney, in metropolitan area; mfg. center (soap, shoes, furniture, celluloid goods), iron foundries.

Leichhardt Range, E spur of Great Dividing Range, E Queensland, Australia; extends c.130 mi. SSE from Home Hill; rises to 4,190 ft. (Mt. Dalrymple).

Leichhardt River, N Queensland, Australia, rises in hills SW of Dobbyn, flows 300 mi. NNW to Gulf of Carpentaria; shallow. Alexandra R., main tributary.

Leichlingen (līkh'lĭng"ŭn), town (pop. 10,327), in former Prussian Rhine Prov., W Germany, after 1945 in North Rhine-Westphalia, on the Wupper and 5 mi. SE of Solingen; textile mfg.; summer resort.

Leiden, Hungary: see LEBENY.

Leiden or **Leyden** (lī'dŭn), anc. *Lugdunum Batavorum*, city (pop. 86,914), South Holland prov., W Netherlands, on Old Rhine R. and 10 mi. NE of the Hague; rail junction. Renowned for its univ. (founded 1575), largest in the Netherlands and one of most famous in Europe. Also mfg. center (cloth, blankets, machinery, boilers, surgical apparatus, artificial leather, soap, perfume, fireworks, candy, canned food). In 14th cent., influx of weavers from Ypres, Belgium, made it a leading textile center until 18th cent. Became famous as printing center after Elzevir family established its press here in 1580. Leiden was for 11 years the home of the Pilgrim Fathers before they embarked for America. In 17th and 18th cent. Univ. of Leiden was celebrated both as a center of Protestant theological learning and of science and medicine. Here the Leyden jar was invented and Boerhaave taught. John of Leiden and the painters Jan van Goyen, Rembrandt, and Jan Steen b. here. Site of an observatory, 14th-cent. *Pieterskerk*, 15th-cent. *Hooglandsche Kerk*, Natl. Ethnographic Mus., Natl. Mus. of Antiquities, Municipal Mus., and many laboratories and 17th-cent. bldgs. Played an important part in revolt of the Netherlands against Sp. rule. Besieged and reduced to famine in 1574, it was saved from surrender when William the Silent ordered the flooding of the surrounding land by cutting the dikes, thus enabling the fleet of the Beggars of the Sea to sail to its relief across the countryside.

Leiderdorp (lī'dŭrdôrp), village (pop. 4,549), South Holland prov., W Netherlands, on Old Rhine R., just ESE of Leiden; ropemaking center.

Leidy, Mount (lī'dē) (10,317 ft.), peak in Rocky Mts., NW Wyo., 40 mi. NE of Jackson.

Leie River, France and Belgium: see LYS RIVER.

Leifers, Italy: see LAIVES.

Leigh (lē), municipal borough (1931 pop. 45,317; 1951 census 48,714), S Lancashire, England, 11 mi. W of Manchester; textile industry (cotton and rayon spinning and weaving); coal mining, metalworking, mfg. of cables, paint, oleomargarine. Has public library containing major collection of Restoration literature; 19th-cent. church with 15th-cent. tower.

Leigh (lē), village (pop. 551), Colfax co., E Nebr., 20 mi. NNW of Schuyler; livestock, grain, poultry.

Leigh Creek (lē), village (pop. 223), E central South Australia, 170 mi. N of Port Pirie; wool, livestock. Lignite mine.

Leighlin, Ireland: see OLD LEIGHLIN.

Leighlinbridge (lē'lĭnbrĭj), Gaelic *Leithghlinn an Droichid*, town (pop. 394), W Co. Carlow, Ireland, on Barrow R. and 7 mi. SSW of Carlow; agr. market (sheep; potatoes, wheat, beets). Has remains of Black Castle, built 1181 by Hugh de Lacy.

Leigh-on-Sea, England: see SOUTHEND-ON-SEA.

Leigh Smith Island, in S Franz Josef Land, Russian SFSR, in Arctic Ocean, E of Hooker Isl.; 80°15'N 54°E. Discovered 1880 by Br. explorer Leigh Smith.

Leighton. 1 (lē'tŭn) Town (pop. 1,080), Colbert co., NW Ala., 10 mi. E of Tuscumbia. **2** (lā'tŭn) Town (pop. 118), Mahaska co., S central Iowa, 8 mi. WNW of Oskaloosa, in bituminous-coal-mining area.

Leighton Buzzard (lā'tŭn), urban district (1931 pop. 7,030; 1951 census 9,023), SW Bedford, England, 11 mi. WNW of Luton; agr. market, with farm-implement works, silica-sand quarries, cement works. Has 15th-cent. market cross and 13th-cent. church.

Leigné-sur-Usseau (lĕnyā'-sür-üsō'), agr. village (pop. 107), Vienne dept., W central France, 7 mi. NNW of Châtellerault.

Leijun, Aden: see GHEIL BA YAMIN.

Leikanger, Norway: see HERMANSVERK.

Leimbach (līm'bäkh), town (pop. 3,165), in former Prussian Saxony prov., central Germany, after 1945 in Saxony-Anhalt, at E foot of the lower Harz, on the Wipper and 7 mi. NW of Eisleben; copper-slate mining and smelting.

Leimebamba (lāmĕbäm'bä), town (pop. 550), Amazonas dept., N Peru, on Utcubamba R. and 32 mi. S of Chachapoyas; sugar, fruit.

Leimen (lī'mŭn), village (pop. 5,447), N Baden, Germany, after 1945 in Württemberg-Baden, 4 mi. S of Heidelberg; mfg. of cigars, cigarettes, cement; metalworking.

Leimun Pass or **Lyemun Pass** (both: lā'yü'mōōn', Mandarin lē'yü'mŭn), strait in Hong Kong colony at E end of Hong Kong harbor, bet. Hong Kong isl. (S) and mainland (N); ¼–½ mi. wide.

Leina Canal, Germany: see GOTHA.

Leine River (lī'nŭ), NW Germany, rises near Worbis, flows W, then generally N, past Göttingen and Hanover (head of navigation), to the Aller 11 mi. NW of Wietze; c.120 mi. long. Receives the Innerste (right).

Leinster (lĕn'stŭr, lĭn'–), province (□ 7,580.2; pop. 1,281,117), E and central Ireland, including cos. Carlow, Dublin, Kildare, Kilkenny, Laoighis, Longford, Louth, Meath, Offaly, Westmeath, Wexford, and Wicklow.

Leinster, Mount (2,610 ft.), on border bet. cos. Wexford and Carlow, Ireland, 12 mi. NW of Enniscorthy; highest point of Blackstairs Mts.

Leintwardine, town and parish (pop. 810), N Hereford, England, on Teme R. and 7 mi. W of Ludlow; agr. market. Has 13th–14th-cent. church.

Leipe, Poland: see LIPNO.

Leipheim (līp'hīm), town (pop. 2,911), Swabia, W Bavaria, Germany, on the Danube and 3 mi. W of Günzburg; grain, livestock. Chartered c.1330.

Leiping or **Lei-p'ing** (lā'pĭng'), town, ⊙ Leiping co. (pop. 75,666), SW Kwangsi prov., China, 60 mi. WSW of Nanning; rice, wheat, corn, tobacco.

Leipnik, Czechoslovakia: see LIPNIK NAD BECVOU.

Leipo (lā'bō'), town (pop. 12,379), ⊙ Leipo co. (pop. 40,057), southwesternmost Szechwan prov., China, 65 mi. WSW of Ipin, near Yangtze R. (Yunnan line); rice, wheat, beans, sugar cane.

Leipsic, Germany: see LEIPZIG.

Leipsic. 1 (lĭp'sĭk) Town (pop. 253), Kent co., central Del., 6 mi. N of Dover and on Leipsic R., which rises just N, flows c.12 mi. E, through marshy region (hunting, fishing), to Delaware Bay. **2** (lĭp'sĭk) Village (pop. 1,706), Putnam co., NW Ohio, 18 mi. WNW of Findlay, in grain-growing area; food and dairy products, brooms, clay and cement products.

Leipson or **Lipson** (both: lēpsōn'), village (pop. 1,660), Arta nome, S Epirus, Greece, 20 mi. NE of Arta, at foot of the Tzoumerka; barley, almonds, peaches; olive oil.

Leipsos or **Lipsos** (both: lēp'sôs), Ital. *Lisso* (lēs'sô), Aegean island (□ 6; pop. 873) in the Dodecanese, Greece, E of Patmos; 37°18'N 26°45'E; 4 mi. long, 1 mi. wide, rises to 900 ft.; wheat, figs, raisins; sponge fisheries.

Leipzig (lĭp'sĭg, Ger. līp'tsĭkh), city (1939 pop. 707,365; 1946 pop. 607,655), Saxony, E central Germany, on the White Elster where it receives the Pleisse and Parthe rivers and 65 mi. WNW of Dresden, 90 mi. SW of Berlin; 51°20'N 12°23'E. Largest city of Saxony and its chief commercial, industrial, and cultural center; also a communications center (rail and road hub; airports at Mockau and Schkeuditz). Until Second World War it was the center of Ger. book and music publishing and of the European fur trade; its 2 great yearly industrial fairs were resumed after Second World War. Leipzig is a textile-mfg. center and has mfg. of steel products, machinery (especially printing presses), automobiles, electrical equipment, musical and precision instruments, light metals, plastics, chemicals, leather and glass products; food processing. The Univ. of Leipzig was founded 1409. City is seat of Mendelssohn Acad. (state col. of music, formerly the conservatory), acad. of graphic and book arts, art col. First psychological laboratory established here in 1879 by Wundt. Has church of St. Nicholas, 1st mentioned 1017; 13th-cent. church of St. Thomas (where J. S. Bach was cantor, 1723–50); the Gewandhaus (1884), originally a merchants-guild house, since 1743 scene of the Gewandhaus concerts; 13th-cent. Pauline church. There is also the old town hall (1558); old stock exchange (1682); 17th-cent. church of St. John, with graves of J. S. Bach and Gellert; Auerbach's Keller, an inn in which a part of Goethe's *Faust* is laid. The Brühl, with house where Wagner was born, is one of city's main streets, formerly center of fur trade. Leipzig was heavily bombed in air raids during Second World War, and badly damaged bldgs. included Ger. Natl Library (1916); former Ger. supreme court (Reichsgericht; established here in 1879); railroad station (1916), one of Europe's largest. In 10th cent., Emperor Henry I destroyed anc. Slav settlement of Lipsk and erected fort around which town grew. Chartered 1174, it rapidly developed into a commercial center at intersection of N–S and E–W trade routes. In early Middle Ages its fairs were introduced, and the printing industry here dates from c.1480. Accepted Reformation in 1539. In Thirty Years War, 2 major battles were fought at Breitenfeld, 5 mi. NW. Leibniz was b. here (1646) and studied at univ. In 18th cent., Gottsched, Gellert, Lessing, Schiller, and others made Leipzig a literary center; young Goethe was student here. In 19th and 20th cent. Leipzig also developed as a music center; Mendelssohn and Schumann lived and worked here. Monument commemorates battle of Leipzig (Oct. 16–19, 1813), in which Napoleon was defeated by Allies. In Second World War, captured by U.S. troops in April, 1945; later placed in Soviet zone of occupation. Among chief suburbs are: Mockau, Gohlis, Eutritzsch (N); Möckern (NW); Lindenau, Plagwitz (W); Connewitz (S); Stötteritz (SE); Reudnitz, Volkmarsdorf (E); Schönefeld (NE); and Wahren (ENE). Sometimes spelled Leipsic in English and French.

Leirfosse (lār'fôs-sŭ), 2 waterfalls (105 ft. and 92 ft.) on Nid R., in Sor-Trondelag co., central Norway, 4 mi. S of Trondheim; hydroelectric plants supply power for Trondheim's industries. Formerly spelled Lerfosse.

Leiria (lārē'ŭ), district (□ 1,307; pop. 353,675), W central Portugal, divided bet. Beira Litoral (N) and Estremadura (S) provinces; ⊙ Leiria. Extends along Atlantic coast from Cape Carvoeiro (S) almost to mouth of Mondego R. at Figueira da Foz. Includes Portugal's largest pine forest W of Leiria. Chief towns are Leiria, Caldas da Rainha (spa), Peniche (fish-processing center), Alcobaça (noted for its abbey), Nazaré and Marinha Grande (glass mfg.). Here also are battlefield of Aljubarrota, and the Dominican monastery of Batalha.

Leiria, anc. *Collippo*, city (pop. 7,208), ⊙ Leiria dist., Beira Litoral prov., W central Portugal, on small Liz R., on railroad and 40 mi. SSW of Coimbra; agr. trade center (wine, olives, corn, livestock); tanneries, cementworks; woodworking. Episcopal see. Has well-preserved Moorish castle (rebuilt c.1300), and a small Romanesque church (built after town was recaptured from the Moors in 1140). A printing press (established here in mid-15th-cent. was noted for its Hebrew works. Bet. Leiria and the Atlantic coast (12 mi. W) lies Portugal's largest pine forest (23,000 acres) planted to check landward advance of sand dunes.

Lei River, Chinese *Lei Shui* (lā' shwā'), right tributary of Siang R., in Hunan prov., China, rises near Kweitung on Kiangsi line, flows c.200 mi. SW and NW, past Jucheng, Yunghing, and Leiyang, to Siang R. at Hengyang.

Leirvik (lār'vĭk, –vēk), village (pop. 1,247) in Stord canton, Hordaland co., SW Norway, port on SE Stord isl., 26 mi. NNE of Haugesund; herring fishing and curing; boatbuilding. Sometimes spelled Lervik.

Leisar, Wadi, Aden: see DUAN, WADI.

Leisenring (lī'zŭnrĭng), village (1940 pop. 769), Fayette co., SW Pa., 2 mi. W of Connellsville; rail junction.

Leishan (lā'shän'), town (pop. 1,476), ⊙ Leishan co. (pop. 34,669), SE Kweichow prov., China, 30 mi. NNW of Jungkiang; embroideries; tobacco, wheat, millet, kaoliang. Until 1943 called Tankiang.

Lei Shui, China: see LEI RIVER.

Leisnig (līs'nĭkh), town (pop. 10,077), Saxony, E central Germany, on the Freiberger Mulde and 9 mi. WNW of Döbeln; woolen milling, metal- and woodworking; mfg. of textile machinery, electrical equipment, furniture, toys, cigars. Old Mildenstein castle towers over town.

Leiston (lā'stŭn), town in Leiston cum Sizewell urban district (1931 pop. 4,184; 1951 census 4,055), E Suffolk, England, 20 mi. NE of Ipswich; agr. market. Near by are remains of 14th-cent. Premonstratensian abbey. On North Sea, 2 mi. E, is village of Sizewell.

Leitches Creek (lē'chĭz), village (pop. estimate 150), NE N.S., NE Cape Breton Isl., on Sydney Harbour, 6 mi. WNW of Sydney; silica mining.

Leitchfield (lĭch'fēld), town (pop. 1,312), ⊙ Grayson co., W central Ky., 36 mi. NNE of Bowling Green, in agr. (dairy products, poultry, burley tobacco corn, hay), asphalt- and coal-mining, stone-quarrying area; mfg. of clothing, concrete products, dairy products, soft drinks; lumber, flour, and feed mills; airport.

Leitersburg (lī'tůrzbûrg), village (pop. c.250), Washington co., W Md., 6 mi. NE of Hagerstown. Grain mill here has operated since 1792. Near by is Mennonite church, used since 1835.

Leith (lēth), port and former burgh, Scotland, just N of Edinburgh proper, on S shore of the Firth of Forth, at mouth of Water of Leith; 55°59'N 3°11'W. Since 1920 inc. in Edinburgh, of which it forms several wards (pop. 82,934). It is 2d-largest seaport of Scotland, with shipping lines to E coast ports of Britain and to Scandinavia, the Baltic, NW Europe, and America. It is also an important fishing center; fish curing is a leading industry. Other industries include shipbuilding, flour milling, brewing, whisky distilling, tanning, sugar refining, mfg. of paper, shoes, chemicals, biscuits, ropes, sails. Notable features are Trinity House, founded 1555 as institution for seamen, now housing pilots' corporation, and Leith Fort (1779), now disused. Leith was sacked by the English in 1544 and 1547. In 1561 Mary Queen of Scots landed here on her return from France. Mary of Guise here repulsed attacks of the Lords of the Congregation (1559–60). The citadel, built 1650 by Cromwell, was seized and destroyed by Jacobites in 1715 uprising; there are some slight remains. Just W of Leith, on Firth of Forth, are fishing ports of Newhaven and Granton.

Leith (lēth). **1** Village (pop. 160), Grant co., S N.Dak., 50 mi. SW of Bismarck. **2** Village (pop. 2,018), Fayette co., SW Pa., just S of Uniontown.

Leith, Water of (lēth), river, Midlothian, Scotland, rises 5 mi. SE of West Calder, flows 23 mi. NE, past Balerno and Edinburgh, to Firth of Forth at Leith.

Leitha Mountains (lī'tä), E Austria, on Burgenland–Lower Austria border, extend from Parndorf c.20 mi. SW, along NW shore of Neusiedler L., rising to 1,584 ft. in the Sonnenberg. Large limestone quarries; vineyards, orchards (cherries, peaches) on lower slopes. Eisenstadt at S foot.

Leitha River, Hung. *Lajta* (loi'tŏ), E Austria and NW Hungary, formed in Austria just NE of Erlach by Schwarza and Pitten rivers; flows NE and E, past Bruck an der Leitha, Austria, thence SE to an arm of the Danube near Mosonmagyarovar, Hungary; length, 112 mi. Once part of old historic boundary bet. Austria and Hungary, dividing Cisleithania on W from Transleithania on E.

Leith Hill (lēth), hill (965 ft.) of North Downs, S central Surrey, England, 4 mi. SSW of Dorking, with tower from which, on clearest days, can be seen St. Paul's in London (NNE) and the Channel (S), each distant c.20 mi.

Leitmeritz, Czechoslovakia: see LITOMERICE.

Leitomischl, Czechoslovakia: see LITOMYSL.

Leitrim (lē'trĭm), Gaelic *Liathdroma*, county (□ 588.7; pop. 44,591), Connacht, NW Ireland; ⊙ Carrick-on-Shannon. Bounded by cos. Roscommon (SW), Sligo (NW), Donegal Bay and Co. Donegal (N), cos. Fermanagh and Cavan (E), and Longford (S). Drained by the Shannon and its tributaries. Surface is hilly and barren in N, rising to 2,113 ft. on Truskmore, becoming level and partly boggy in S. Climate is notably damp. There are numerous lakes, largest of which is Lough Allen. Iron, lead, coal are mined (Drumshambo, Slieve Anierin), limestone is quarried. Dairying, cattle raising, potato growing are chief occupations. Industries include iron founding; woolen and linen milling. Besides Carrick-on-Shannon, other towns are Ballinamore, Manorhamilton, Drumshambo, Dromahair, Drumkeerin, Mohill, and Carrigallen. In anc. times co. was part of dist. of Breffni O'Rourke. There are monastic and castle ruins.

Leitrim, Gaelic *Liathdruim*, town (pop. 96), SW Co. Leitrim, Ireland, on the Shannon and 3 mi. NNE of Carrick-on-Shannon; agr. market (dairying; cattle, potatoes). Has slight remains of castle of Prince of Breffni.

Leiva (lā'vä), village (pop. 876), Boyacá dept., N central Colombia, in Cordillera Oriental, on road from Chiquinquirá, and 14 mi. NW of Tunja; alt. 7,050 ft. Wheat, corn, divi-divi bark, stock. Emerald mines. Silver deposits near by. An early congress (1812) was held here.

Leivadion or **Livadhion** (both: lēvä'dhēôn), town (pop. 3,200), Larissa nome, N Thessaly, Greece, 36 mi. NNW of Larissa, at W foot of Olympus; olives, livestock products. Passed to Greece in 1913. Also spelled Livadion.

Leivadostra, Bay of, Greece: see LIVADOSTRA, BAY OF.

Leix, Ireland: see LAOIGHIS.

Leixlip (lāks'lĭp), Gaelic *Léim an Bhradáin*, town (pop. 467), NE Co. Kildare, Ireland, on the Liffey, on the Royal Canal, and 9 mi. W of Dublin; agr. market (cattle, horses; potatoes). Near by are 1308 bridge across the Liffey and a 13th-cent. castle.

Leixões (lāshō'ĭsh), artificial harbor of Oporto, N Portugal, on the Atlantic at mouth of small Leça R. and 5 mi. NW of city. Consists of 2 curved moles (¾ mi. and 1 mi. long) at the base of which are twin towns of Leça da Palmeira and Matozinhos. Harbor was completed 1890, to accommodate vessels unable to ascend Douro R. (sand bar at mouth) to Oporto. Chief export, port wine. Also called Pôrto de Leixões.

Leiyang (lā'yäng'), town, ⊙ Leiyang co. (pop. 448,698), SE Hunan prov., China, on Lei R., on Hankow-Canton RR and 38 mi. SSE of Hengyang, in mining region (coal, manganese).

Lejasciems or **Leyastsiems** (lĕ'yästsyĕms), village (pop. 466), NE Latvia, in Vidzeme, on Gauja R. and 10 mi. NW of Gulbene; lumbering.

Lejeune, Camp, N.C.: see JACKSONVILLE.

Lejía, Cerro (sĕ'rō lāhē'ä), peak (17,585 ft.) of N Chile, in Antofagasta prov., in the Puna de Atacama; 23°33'S 67°48'W.

Lejona (lāhō'nä), suburban commune (pop. 5,255) NW of Bilbao, Vizcaya prov., N Spain; metal foundries. Chief village, Lamiaco (pop. 2,371), on Nervión R., has glassworks and distilleries.

Leka, Austria: see LOCKENHAUS.

Leka (lā'kä), island (□ 22; pop. 865) in North Sea, Nord-Trondelag co., W Norway, just off mainland, 40 mi. N of Namsos; 10 mi. long, 1–6 mi. wide. Leka fishing village (pop. 129) on E shore; sometimes called Leknes. Isl. sometimes called Leko, Nor. *Lekø*.

Lekemti, Ethiopia: see NAKAMTI.

Leketi River, Fr. Equatorial Africa: see ALIMA RIVER.

Lekhaina, Greece: see LECHAINA.

Lekhchevo (lĕkhchĕ'vô), village (pop. 3,999), Vratsa dist., NW Bulgaria, on Ogosta R. and 18 mi. NE of Mikhailovgrad; grain, legumes, livestock.

Lekhta (lyĕkh'tŭ), Finnish *Lehto* (lĕ'tô), village, central Karelo-Finnish SSR, 23 mi. WSW of Belomorsk; dairying.

Lekir (lĕkĭr'), village (pop. 327), W Perak, Malaya, on Strait of Malacca, 8 mi. SE of Lumut; coconuts, rubber.

Lekkerkerk (lĕ'kůrkĕrk), town (pop. 2,837), South Holland prov., W Netherlands, on Lek R. and 8 mi. E of Rotterdam; mfg. (ropes, wires, rubber, basalt bricks), shipbuilding; meat packing, truck gardening.

Lekki (lĕ'kē), town, Nigeria Colony, on Gulf of Guinea, 50 mi. E of Lagos; fisheries; palm oil and kernels. Lekki Lagoon (N) is E part of coastal lagoon paralleling Gulf of Guinea.

Leknes, Norway: see LEKA.

Leko, Norway: see LEKA.

Lékoni (lĕkōnē'), village, SE Gabon, Fr. Equatorial Africa, 50 mi. E of Franceville.

Lek River (lĕk), central Netherlands, N arm of the Rhine delta; branches off LOWER RHINE RIVER at Wijk bij Duurstede; flows 40 mi. WSW, past Culemborg, Vreeswijk, Vianen, and Lekkerkerk, joining Noord R. ½ mi. W of Krimpen aan den Lek to form NEW MAAS RIVER. Crossed by Merwede Canal near Vreeswijk and Vianen; Hollandsche Ijssel R. branches off just WSW of Vreeswijk. Entire length navigable.

Leksand (lāk'sänd") or **Leksands Noret** (lāk"sänts nōō'rŭt), village (pop. 1,503), Kopparberg co., central Sweden, on East Dal R., at SE end of L. Silja, 20 mi. WNW of Falun; shoe mfg.; tourist resort. Has church (c.1700) and art mus. Scene of Dalecarlian mid-summer festival.

Leksha, Lake, Karelo-Finnish SSR: see LEKSOZERO.

Leksmond, Netherlands: see LEXMOND.

Leksozero (lyĕks'ô"zyĭrŭ), Finnish *Lieksajärvi* (lyĕk'säyärvē), lake in W Karelo-Finnish SSR, 5–10 mi. from Finnish border; 25 mi. long, 8 mi. wide. Reboly village on NW shore. Formerly spelled Leksha and Lyeksa.

Leksura, Georgian SSR: see LENTEKHI.

Leland (lē'lůnd). **1** Village (pop. 537), La Salle co., N Ill., 26 mi. WSW of Aurora, in agr. and bituminous-coal area; feed milling. **2** Town (pop. 209), Winnebago co., N Iowa, on Lime Creek, and 25 mi. WNW of Mason City. **3** Village (pop. c.400), ⊙ Leelanau co., NW Mich., 19 mi. NNW of Traverse City, bet. L. Leelanau (E) and L. Michigan, in dairy and fruit area; commercial fisheries. Resort. Mich. State Col. holds summer art classes here. **4** City (pop. 4,736), Washington co., W Miss., 10 mi. E of Greenville, and on small Deer Creek, in rich cotton-growing and truck-farming area; cottonseed products, lumber. Agr. experiment station near by. Settled 1847, laid out 1884.

Leland, Mount (7,434 ft.), on Alaska-B.C. border, in St. Elias Mts., 40 mi. W of Skagway; 59°22'N 136°29'W.

Lelang Lake, Swedish *Lelången* (lä'lông"ŭn), W Sweden, near Norwegian border, 2 mi. W of Bengtsfors; 28 mi. long, 1 mi. wide. Connected N with Fox and Stora Le lakes; drained E into L. Vaner.

Lelchitsy or **Lel'chitsy** (lyĕl'chĭtsĕ), town (1948 pop. over 2,000), SW Polesye oblast, Belorussian SSR, in Pripet Marshes, 45 mi. SW of Mozyr; lumber milling.

Lelekovka (lyĭlyĕ'kŭfkŭ), town (1926 pop. 4,198), central Kirovograd oblast, Ukrainian SSR, 5 mi. NNW of Kirovograd; truck produce.

Leleque (lĕlā'kā), village (pop. estimate 600), ⊙ Cushamén dept., NW Chubut natl. territory, Argentina, 37 mi. NNE of Esquel; oats, wheat, alfalfa, sheep, cattle.

Lelija or **Leliya** (both: lĕ'lēä), mountain (6,665 ft.) in Dinaric Alps, Yugoslavia, on Bosnia-Herzegovina line, along right bank of upper Neretva R., 5 mi. S of Kalinovik.

Lella Khedidja (lĕlä' kĕdējä'), highest peak (7,572 ft.) in the Djurdjura range of Great Kabylia, N central Algeria, 70 mi. ESE of Algiers, and culminating point of Algeria's coastal Tell ranges. Also spelled Lalla Khadidja and Lella Kredidja.

Lelydorp (lā'lēdôrp), village (pop. 6,327), Surinam dist., N Du. Guiana, on Paramaribo-Dam RR and 10 mi. S of Paramaribo; coffee, rice, fruit.

Lely Mountains (lā'lē), NE spur of the Guiana Highlands in E Du. Guiana, 100 mi. SSE of Paramaribo; extend c.40 mi. along Tapanahoni and Maroni rivers near Brazil border; rise to 2,428 ft.

Lemahabang (lůmähäbäng'), town (pop. 12,940), central Java, Indonesia, near Java Sea, 10 mi. SE of Cheribon; trade center for agr. area (sugar, rice, peanuts); textile mills.

Le Maire Strait (lů mâr'), channel in the South Atlantic bet. SE tip of main isl. of Tierra del Fuego and Staten Isl., S Argentina; 18 mi. wide. Named for the Dutch navigator Le Maire, who discovered it 1616.

Lema Islands (lā'mä), Chinese *Lima* (lē'mä), group in S.China Sea, Kwangtung prov., China, S of Hong Kong. Consist of 4 main isls. extending 15 mi. ENE–WSW; 22°N 114°10'E. Include Tamkan Isl., Mandarin *Tankan* (E; largest of group; 7 mi. long, 1 mi. wide), and Ye Chow, Mandarin *Erh Chou* (center; rises to 1,253 ft.).

Leman, Lake, Switzerland: see GENEVA, LAKE.

Le Mars (lů märz'), city (pop. 5,844), ⊙ Plymouth co., NW Iowa, on Floyd R. and 23 mi. NNE of Sioux City; agr.-trade and mfg. center; overalls factory, foundry, rendering plant, grain mill (cereals, feed), creameries, cement work. Sand and gravel pits near by. Westmar Col. (coeducational; 1890) is here. Founded in late 1870s; inc. 1881.

Lembang (lĕmbäng'), health resort in Preanger region, W Java, Indonesia, 7 mi. N of Bandung; alt. 4,091 ft.; hot springs. During Second World War, Lembang was briefly (early 1942) hq. of Allied Far East Command.

Lembeek (lĕm'bāk), town (pop. 6,133), Brabant prov., central Belgium, on Charleroi-Brussels Canal and 2 mi. SSW of Hal; chemicals, ceramics. Formerly spelled Lembecq.

Lembeni (lĕmbĕ'nē), village, Tanga prov., NE Tanganyika, in Pare Mts., on railroad and 35 mi. SE of Moshi; hardwood.

Lemberg, town (pop. 456), SE Sask., 24 mi. NE of Indian Head; grain-shipping center; grain elevators; dairying, stock raising.

Lemberg (läbâr', Ger. lĕm'bĕrk), village (pop. 1,347), Moselle dept., NE France, in the N Vosges, 16 mi. SE of Sarreguemines; crystal works.

Lemberg (lĕm'bĕrk), village (pop. 3,138), Rhenish Palatinate, W Germany, 3 mi. SE of Pirmasens; glass.

Lemberg, highest peak (3,330 ft.) of Swabian Jura, SW Germany, 5 mi. ESE of Rottweil.

Lemberg, Ukrainian SSR: see LVOV, city.

Lembeye (läbā'), village (pop. 714), Basses-Pyrénées dept., SW France, 17 mi. NE of Pau; high-grade wines; cereals, poultry, hogs.

Lembongan (lĕmbông"än'), island (pop. 4,176), Indonesia, in Lombok Strait, just W of Penida isl., near Bali; lighthouse.

Leme (lā'mĭ), city (pop. 4,434), E central São Paulo, Brazil, on railroad and 50 mi. NNW of Campinas; pottery mfg., processing of macaroni; agr. (coffee, cotton).

Lemery (lāmārē'), town (1939 pop. 5,293; 1948 municipality pop. 23,879), Batangas prov., S Luzon, Philippines, on Balayan Bay, 30 mi. WSW of San Pablo; fishing and agr. center (rice, sugar cane, corn, coconuts).

Lemeshenski, Russian SFSR: see ORGTRUD.

Lemeshkino (lyĕ'myĭshkēnŭ), village (1939 pop. over 500), N Stalingrad oblast, Russian SFSR, 31 mi. E of Yelan; flour mill, metalworks.

Lemessos, Cyprus: see LIMASSOL.

Lemfu (lĕm'fōō), village, Leopoldville prov., W Belgian Congo, on right bank of Inkisi R. and 145 mi. ENE of Boma; R.C. missionary center with small seminary and convents for native nuns and monks; also center of native trade (manioc, yams, bananas, plantains, palm products).

Lemgo (lĕm'gō), town (pop. 17,984), in former Lippe, NW Germany, after 1945 in North Rhine-Westphalia, 11 mi. SE of Herford; mfg. of furniture, textiles, cigars; leatherworking. Has 2 Gothic churches, 14th–17th-cent. town hall. Was member of Hanseatic League.

Lemhi (lĕm'hī), county (□ 4,585; pop. 6,278), E Idaho; ⊙ Salmon. Mtn. and valley area drained by Salmon R. and tributaries and bounded on E by Bitterroot Range and Mont. Livestock raising, mining (gold, tungsten, lignite, coal); manganese deposits. Salmon River and Yellowjacket mts. are in NW, Lemhi Range in E. Formed 1869.

Lemhi Range, E Idaho, NW–SE chain bet. Salmon city and Snake River Plain, in Salmon Natl. Forest. Portland Mtn. (10,821 ft.) is highest point.

Lemhi River, formed by confluence of several forks in Lemhi co., E Idaho, near Mont. line, flows 70 mi.

NNW, bet. Bitterroot and Lemhi ranges, to Salmon R. at Salmon.

Lemington, England: see NEWBURN.

Lemington (lĕ'mĭngtŭn), town (pop. 105), Essex co., NE Vt., on the Connecticut and 20 mi. N of Guildhall, in hunting, fishing region. Monadnock Mtn. is here.

Lemland (lĕm'lănd"), fishing village (commune pop. 1,448), Aland co., SW Finland, on Lemland isl. (□ 42), one of Aland group, 6 mi. ESE of Mariehamn.

Lemmer (lĕ'mŭr), town (pop. 4,237) and port, Friesland prov., N Netherlands, on the Ijsselmeer, near N edge of North East Polder, and 12 mi. SW of Heerenveen; fishing; herring curing. Drainage pumping station for North East Polder here.

Lemmi (lĕm'mē), town (pop. 4,812), Bauchi prov., Northern Provinces, E central Nigeria, on road and 45 mi. WNW of Bauchi; major tin-mining center.

Lemmon, city (pop. 2,760), Perkins co., NW S.Dak., 140 mi. NW of Pierre, on N.Dak. line; trading point for large grain and livestock region in N.Dak. and S.Dak.; coal mines; wheat, alfalfa. Near by is Petrified Wood Park.

Lemmon, Mount (9,185 ft.), SE Ariz., highest peak in Santa Catalina Mts., 17 mi. NNE of Tucson. Sometimes Lemmon Mtn.

Lemnos or **Limnos** (lĕm'nŏs, Gr. lēm'nôs), Greek Aegean island (□ 186; pop. 23,842), in Lesbos nome, NW of Lesbos; 39°54'N 25°21'E. Of irregular coastline, it is deeply indented N and S; its longest dimension is 25 mi. (SW-NE), its shortest, 2.5 mi., at central isthmus. It rises 1,411 ft. in deforested volcanic formations, whose lava flows have created fertile soils producing grain, fruit, figs, grapes, almonds, cotton, silk, and tobacco. Sheep raising is important. The noted Lemnian bole (earth) was formerly used as an astringent. The chief centers are Kastron and Moudros, with its strategic gulf. In legend, Lemnos was sacred to Hephaestus, who was hurled here from Olympus by Zeus; it is associated with the stories of Hypsipyle and Philoctetes. Conquered (510 B.C.) by Athenian general Miltiades, it remained in possession of Athens through antiquity. In the Middle Ages it was controlled by the Genoese from Lesbos, passed 1464 to Venice, 1478 to the Turks, and 1913 to Greece.

Lemona (lāmō'nä), commune (pop. 1,906), Vizcaya prov., N Spain, 8 mi. ESE of Bilbao; cement works; mfg. of leather belts. Anaiba (pop. 537) is seat of commune.

Lemon Fair River, W Vt., rises near Shoreham, flows c.20 mi. N to Otter Creek near Weybridge.

Lemon Grove or **Lemongrove**, village (1940 pop. 2,100), San Diego co., S Calif., just E of San Diego; citrus-fruit packing, shipping.

Lemont (lŭmŏnt'), village (pop. 2,757), Cook co., NE Ill., SW of Chicago, on Des Plaines R. and Sanitary and Ship Canal, and 10 mi. NNE of Joliet. Argonne Natl. Laboratory (for atomic research) and Argonne Forest Preserve (recreational area) are near by. Oil refining; mfg. of aluminum products, beverages, clothing; limestone quarries. Ships petroleum, stone. Inc. 1873.

Lemonweir River, W Wis., rises in Jackson co., flows c.60 mi. SE, past New Lisbon and Mauston, to Wisconsin R. 11 mi. E of Mauston.

Lemoore (lŭmôr'), city (pop. 2,153), Kings co., S central Calif., in farm and orchard region of San Joaquin Valley, 30 mi. S of Fresno; dairy products. Inc. 1900.

Lemos (lā'mōs), town (pop. 2,852), Valle del Cauca dept., W Colombia, in Cauca valley, 22 mi. SW of Cartago; sugar cane, tobacco, corn, bananas, yucca, corn, rice, stock.

Lemovices, France: see LIMOGES.

Lemoyne (lŭmoin'), residential borough (pop. 4,605), Cumberland co., S central Pa., on Susquehanna R. opposite Harrisburg. Northernmost point of Confederate advance, 1863.

Lempa River (lĕm'pä), in central America, rises near Esquipulas (Guatemala), flows S through W extremity of Honduras, past Nueva Ocotepeque, and into Salvador at Citalá. In Salvador, the Lempa winds S, E, and S, past San Marcos (rail and road bridge) to the Pacific 38 mi. ESE of La Libertad; c.200 mi. long. Navigable for small craft in lower course.

Lempira (lĕmpē'rä), department (□ 1,295; 1950 pop. 100,000), W Honduras, on Salvador border; ⊙ Gracias. Astride main Andean divide; bounded S by Lempa and Sumpul rivers; drained N by Jicatuyo R. branches, S by Mocal R. Mainly agr. (coffee, tobacco, rice, wheat, indigo); cattle, hogs; alcohol distilling. Rich opal deposits near Erandique were formerly exploited. Main centers: Gracias, Erandique, Candelaria, Guarita. Formed 1825; called Gracias until 1943.

Lempster, agr. town (pop. 309), Sullivan co., SW N.H., 9 mi. S of Newport.

Lemro River (lĕm'rō', Burmese lĕ'myō), in the Arakan, Lower Burma, rises in S Chin Hills at 22°N, flows S c.180 mi., through Arakan Hill Tracts and Akyab dist., past Myaungbwe (head of navigation) and Minbya, to Bay of Bengal at Myebon. Navigable 30 mi. above mouth.

Lemsal, Latvia: see LIMBAZI.

Lemui Island (lām'wē) (□ 49; pop. 4,902), off E coast of Chiloé Isl., Chiloé prov., S Chile, 10 mi. SE of Castro; 42°37'S; 9 mi. long, 3-5 mi. wide. Puqueldón, on N shore, is chief village. Also spelled Lemuy.

Lemvig (lĕm'vē), city (pop. 5,245) and port, Ringkobing amt, W Jutland, Denmark, on Lim Fjord and 31 mi. N of Ringkobing; fishing, meat packing, shipbuilding, machinery mfg.

Lemyethna (lĕmyĕt'nä), village, Henzada dist., Lower Burma, on right bank of Bassein R. and 22 mi. WSW of Henzada.

Lena (lē'nŭ). **1** Town (pop. 1,227), Stephenson co., N Ill., near Wis. line, 11 mi. NW of Freeport, in agr. area; processes dairy products. Inc. 1869. **2** Town (pop. 353), Leake co., central Miss., 10 mi. SSW of Carthage. **3** Village (pop. 526), Oconto co., NE Wis., 30 mi. N of Green Bay; flour milling; has cooperative cheese factory and creamery.

Lena Beach, fishing village (pop. 52), SE Alaska, on Lynn Canal, 15 mi. NW of Juneau and on Glacier Highway; 58°24'N 134°45'W.

Lenakel, New Hebrides: see TANNA.

Lenapah (lĕ'nŭpô), town (pop. 328), Nowata co., NE Okla., 20 mi. ENE of Bartlesville, in cotton and livestock area.

Lena River (lā'nä) or **Caudal River** (kou-dhäl'), Oviedo prov., NW Spain, rises in the Cantabrian Mts. near Pajares Pass, flows 30 mi. NNW across rich coal- and iron-mining region, past Mieres, to Nalón R. 3 mi. SSW of Oviedo.

Lena River (lē'nŭ, Rus. lyĕ'nŭ), easternmost and longest (2,648 mi.) of great rivers of Siberian Russian SFSR; rises near L. Baikal in W Baikal Range (Irkutsk oblast) at c.4,700 ft.; flows NE, through Central Siberian Plateau, past Ust-Kut, Kirensk, and Vitim, receiving (right) Kirenga and Vitim rivers. Entering Yakut Autonomous SSR, its valley widens progressively as it passes Peledui, Olekminsk, Pokrovsk, and Yakutsk (here flowing N) and receives (right) Olekma, Botoma, and Aldan rivers. Here turning NW, the Lena flows parallel to and 100-150 mi. W of Verkhoyansk Range, reaching its greatest width of 8.5 mi. above Zhigansk; receives Vilyui R. (left). Valley narrows again as the Lena flows bet. Bulun and Kyusyur, entering Laptev Sea through a 150-mi.-wide delta mouth; Olenek, Bykov, and Trofimov are main mouth branches. Navigation, mainly for lumber and grain, upstream to Ust-Kut (2,135 mi. from mouth; May-Nov.); at high water ships go to Kachuga, 310 mi. further upstream. At Yakutsk (915 mi. from mouth) river is ice-free June-Oct., at delta, July-Sept. Coal, oil, and chiefly gold are found along the Lena and its tributaries (Vitim, Aldan). Reached by Russians 1630.

Lenarue (lĕ'nŭrōō), mining village, Harlan co., SE Ky., in the Cumberlands c.5 mi. SE of Harlan; bituminous coal.

Lenauheim (lā'nouhīm"), Hung. *Csátad* (chä'lŏt), village (pop. 2,618), Timisoara prov., W Rumania, 20 mi. NW of Timisoara. Austrian poet N. Lenau b. here.

Lenawee (lĕ'nŭwē), county (□ 754; pop. 64,629), SE Mich.; ⊙ Adrian. Bounded S by Ohio line; drained by Raisin R. and its branches, and by Tiffin R. Agr. area (grain, corn, beans, truck, livestock; dairy products). Mfg. at Adrian, Hudson, Morenci, and Tecumseh. Hatcheries. Sand, gravel. Chrysanthemum raising. Lake resorts. Organized 1826.

Lenchitsa, Poland: see LECZYCA.

Lenchna, Poland: see LECZNA.

Lencloître (lāklwä'trŭ), village (pop. 1,213), Vienne dept., W central France, 10 mi. W of Châtellerault; truck gardening (chiefly asparagus), dairying.

Lençóis (lĕnsois'). **1** City (pop. 3,633), central Bahia, Brazil, at foot of the Chapada Diamantina, 17 mi. NNW of Andaraí; old diamond-mining center, highly productive until end of 19th cent. Semiprecious stones also found here. Formerly spelled Lençoes. **2** City, São Paulo, Brazil: see LENÇÓIS PAULISTA.

Lençóis Paulista (poulē'stŭ), city (pop. 2,125), central São Paulo, Brazil, on railroad and 26 mi. SE of Bauru; cotton, manioc, and rice processing; distilling. Until 1944, Lençóis; and,1944–48,Ubirama.

Lend (lĕnt), town (pop. 2,112), Salzburg, W central Austria, on the Salzach, near mouth of the Gasteiner Ache, and 11 mi. SW of Bischofshofen; aluminum plant. Hydroelectric station SE, in Gastein Valley.

Lendava (lĕn'dävä). **1** or **Dolnja Lendava** (dôl'nyä), Serbo-Croatian *Donja Lendava* (dô'nyä), Hung. *Alsólendva* (ŏl'sŭlĕndvŏ), village (pop. 3,868), NE Slovenia, Yugoslavia, on Lendava R., on railroad and 38 mi. E of Maribor, on Hung. border; local trade center; umbrella mfg. Petroleum deposits near by. **2** or **Gornja Lendava** (gôr'nyä), Hung. *Felsőlendva* (fĕl'sŭlĕndvŏ), village (1941 pop. 1,083), NE Slovenia, Yugoslavia, 23 mi. NW of Dolnja Lendava.

Lendava River, Hung. *Lendva* (lĕnd'vŏ), in Austria and NE Slovenia, Yugoslavia, rises in Austria 7 mi. SSE of Feldbach, flows c.50 mi. SE, through the Prekmurje, past Murska Sobota and Dolnja Lendava, to Mura R. on Hung. border, 9 mi. SE of Dolnja Lendava. Sometimes called Ledava.

Lendelede (lĕn'dŭlādŭ), town (pop. 4,515), West Flanders prov., W Belgium, 5 mi. NNW of Courtrai; textiles; agr. market.

Lendersdorf-Krauthausen (lĕn'dŭrsdôrf"-krout'-hou"zŭn), village (pop. 3,076), in former Prussian Rhine Prov., W Germany, after 1945 in North Rhine-Westphalia, 2 mi. S of Düren; paper mfg.

Lendinara (lĕndēnä'rä), town (pop. 4,995), Rovigo prov., Veneto, N Italy, 9 mi. W of Rovigo; mfg. (agr. machinery, fertilizer, jute products, vinegar, beet sugar).

Lendringsen (lĕn'drĭng-sŭn), village (pop. 7,163), in former Prussian prov. of Westphalia, W Germany, after 1945 in North Rhine-Westphalia, 2 mi. SE of Menden; forestry.

Lendva, Yugoslavia: see LENDAVA.

Lene, Lough (lŏkh lēn'), lake (3 mi. long, 1 mi. wide), NE Co. Westmeath, Ireland, 3 mi. E of Castlepollard.

Lenexa (lĕnĕk'sŭ), city (pop. 803), Johnson co., E Kansas, 12 mi. SSW of Kansas City (Kansas), in dairying and general agr. area.

L'Enfant Jésus, Que.: see VALLÉE JONCTION.

Lenga (lĕng'ŭ), village (pop. 241), NW Johore, Malaya, 22 mi. NE of Bandar Maharani and on Muar R.; rubber plantations.

Lengau (lĕng'ou), town (pop. 3,742), SW Upper Austria, 16 mi. NE of Salzburg, in Hausruck Mts.; dairy farming.

Lengby, village (pop. 206), Polk co., NW Minn., just N of White Earth Indian Reservation, 35 mi. WNW of Bemidji; dairy products.

Lengede (lĕng'ŭdŭ), village (pop. 3,135), in former Prussian prov. of Hanover, NW Germany, after 1945 in Lower Saxony, 8 mi. SSE of Peine; limonite mining.

Lengefeld (lĕng'ŭfĕlt"), town (pop. 3,901), Saxony, E central Germany, in the Erzgebirge, 14 mi. SE of Chemnitz; cotton milling, hosiery knitting, toy mfg., wood- and metalworking.

Lengenfeld (lĕng'ŭnfĕlt), town (pop. 8,168), Saxony, E central Germany, in the Erzgebirge, on Göltzsch R. and 12 mi. NE of Plauen; cotton and woolen milling, curtain mfg. Wolframite mined near by.

Lenger (lyĭn-gyĕr'), city (1945 pop. over 10,000), SE South Kazakhstan oblast, Kazakh SSR, on spur of Turksib RR and 15 mi. SE of Chimkent; lignite-mining center, supplying Chimkent lead works.

Lengerich (lĕng'ŭrĭkh), town (pop. 17,799), in former Prussian prov. of Westphalia, NW Germany, after 1945 in North Rhine-Westphalia, in Teutoburg Forest, 10 mi. SW of Osnabrück; rail junction; mfg. of machinery, motorcycles, cables, stoves; woodworking. Cement and lime works, paper mills. Chartered 1727.

Lenggeng (lĕng"gĕng'), village (pop. 228), W Negri Sembilan, Malaya, 9 mi. N of Seremban; timber, rubber.

Lenggong (lĕng"gōōng'), village (pop. 1,563), N Perak, Malaya, 23 mi. NE of Taiping, on road to Grik, near Perak R., in forested dist.; rice, rubber.

Lenggries (lĕng'grēs), village (pop. 6,389), Upper Bavaria, Germany, in Bavarian Alps, on the Isar and 5 mi. S of Bad Tölz; rail terminus; brewing. Summer resort (alt. 2,228 ft.).

Lengnau (lĕng'nou), town (pop. 2,377), Bern canton, NW Switzerland, 6 mi. ENE of Biel; watches.

Lengsfeld, Germany: see STADTLENGSFELD.

Lengua de Pájaro, Cuba: see NICARO.

Lengua de Vaca, Punta (pōōn'tä lĕng'gwä dā vä'kä), cape on Pacific coast, Coquimbo prov., N central Chile, at W end of Tongoy Bay; 30°14'S 71°38'W.

Lengua de Vaca Pass, on Michoacán–Mexico state border, central Mexico, on highway from Toluca to Zitácuaro, 45 mi. W of Toluca; alt. 9,348 ft.

Lengwethen, Russian SFSR: see LUNINO, Kaliningrad oblast.

Lengyeltoti (lĕn'dyĕltōtē), Hung. *Lengyeltóti*, town (pop. 2,906), Somogy co., SW Hungary, 22 mi. NNW of Kaposvar; wheat, wine.

Lengyong (lĕng'yông'), Mandarin *Ningyang* (nĭng'-yäng'), town (pop. 2,071), ⊙ Lengyong co. (pop. 21,686), SW central Fukien prov., China, 65 mi. ESE of Changting; rice, sugar cane.

Lenham (lĕ'nŭm), town and parish (pop. 2,166), central Kent, England, 9 mi. NW of Ashford; agr. market. Has 14th-cent. church.

Lenhartsville, borough (pop. 229), Berks co., E central Pa., 16 mi. N of Reading.

Lenhovda (lăn"hōōv'dä), village (pop. 1,100), Kronoberg co., S Sweden, 19 mi. ENE of Vaxjo; metalworking, glass mfg., sawmilling. Has 14th-cent. prison.

Lenin (lĕ'nĭn, Rus. lyĕ'nyĭn), district of Greater Baku, Azerbaijan SSR, on central Apsheron Peninsula, NE of Baku. Its oil fields in exploitation since 1870–80. Main centers: Balakhany, Sabunchi, Romany.

Lenin, town (1948 pop. over 2,000), E Pinsk oblast, Belorussian SSR, on Sluch R. and 30 mi. ENE of Luninets, on former USSR-Pol. border; flour milling, sawmilling.

Lenina, Imeni (ē'mĭnyē lyĕ'nyĭnŭ), N iron-mining suburb (1926 pop. 1,860) of Krivoi Rog, Dnepropetrovsk oblast, Ukrainian SSR, 14 mi. NNE of city center and on right bank of Saksagan R. Until c.1926, called Kalachevski Rudnik.

Lenina, Imeni V. I., town (1939 pop. over 2,000), W Ulyanovsk oblast, Russian SFSR, 12 mi. SSW of Barysh; woolen-milling center. Until c.1938, Rumyantsevo.

Leninabad (lyĕ"nyĭnŭbät'), oblast (□ 9,400; 1946 pop. estimate 550,000), NW Tadzhik SSR; ⊙ Leninabad. Area along Zerafshan R. (S) and projecting across Turkestan Range NE to W Fergana Valley at the Syr Darya and Kurama Range; bounded S by Gissar Range, N by Uzbek and Kirghiz SSR. Agr. chiefly in Fergana Valley, along rivers, and on lower mtn. slopes (wheat, cotton, grapes); silkworm breeding, fruitgrowing, sheep and goat raising. Cotton and silk processing, silk weaving, fruit canning, cottonseed-oil extracting; wine making. Extensive mining area on S slope of Kurama Range: lead and zinc at Kansai and Kara-Mazar, radioactive ores and vanadium at Taboshar, bismuth at Adrasman, arsenic at Takeli, tungsten at Chorukh-Dairon; coal mining at Shurab, oil fields at Kim and Nefteabad. Fergana Valley RR runs along the Syr Darya, past Nau, Proletarsk, Leninabad, and Kanibadam, chief urban centers. Pop.: Tadzhiks, Uzbeks. Formed 1939.

Leninabad, city (1939 pop. c.45,900), ⊙ Leninabad oblast, Tadzhik SSR, on the Syr Darya, at its exit from Fergana Valley, on railroad and 125 mi. NNE of Stalinabad; 40°17'N 69°37'E. Cotton and silk center; cotton ginning, silk spinning and milling, clothing and shoe mfg., food canning, auto repair shops. Has teachers col., theater, house of culture. An old city, captured (c.329 B.C.) by Alexander the Great; fell to Russians in 1866. Largest Tadzhik city until rise (1930s) of Stalinabad. Called Khodzhent until 1936. At the railroad station, 7 mi. SE, is town of Leninabad (1939 pop. over 500).

Leninakan (–ŭkän'), city (1939 pop. 67,707), NW Armenian SSR, on Shiraki Steppe, on the Western Arpa-Chai, on railroad and 55 mi. NW of Erivan, near Turkish border; junction of railroad to Erzurum, Turkey. Textile center, with cotton and knitwear mills; bicycle mfg., lumber milling; penicillin, meat, and sugar-beet processing. Trade in silk, cloth, and rugs. Pumice and tuff quarries near by. Teachers col. Founded 1837 as Rus. fortress Aleksandropol on site of old village of Gumri. Named Leninakan in early 1920s. Destroyed in 1926 earthquake.

Leninakan Steppe, Armenian SSR: see SHIRAKI STEPPE.

Lenindzhol (–jôl'), village (pop. over 500), SE Dzhalal-Abad oblast, Kirghiz SSR, in Fergana Valley, 21 mi. WNW of Dzhalal-Abad; cotton. Formerly called Massy.

Leningori (–gô'rē), village (1932 pop. estimate 730), SE South Ossetian Autonomous Oblast, Georgian SSR, 30 mi. NW of Tiflis; orchards.

Leningrad (lĕ'nĭngrăd, Rus. lyĕnyĭngrät'), oblast (□ 32,850; 1946 pop. estimate 4,800,000) in NW European Russian SFSR; ⊙ Leningrad. In moraine region bordering on Gulf of Finland and on lakes Peipus, Ladoga, and Onega; watered by Luga, Neva, Volkhov, and Svir rivers; includes Karelian Isthmus (N part acquired 1944 from Karelo-Finnish SSR). Temperate continental climate. Mineral resources include oil shale (Slantsy, Veimarn), peat (near Leningrad), bauxite (Boksitogorsk), marble and dolomite (Volosovo), brick clays, and building stone. Hydroelectric plants on Svir R. (Svirstroi, Podporozhye), on Volkhov R. (Volkhov), and on Vuoksi R. (Svetogorsk); peat-fed power stations supply industries of Leningrad and aluminum refinery at Volkhov. Lumbering (chiefly in NE) supplies extensive sawmilling, paper-milling, woodworking, and wood-distilling industries. Agr. (truck farming, dairy-cattle raising, potatoes, fodder crops, coarse grain, wheat). Oblast has dense rail network and waterways connecting with Volga R. and White Sea. In addition to Leningrad, major urban centers are Volkhov, Tikhvin, Vyborg, and Priozersk. Formed 1927 out of govts. of Leningrad, Murmansk, Novgorod, Pskov, and Cherepovets. During Second World War, partly occupied (1941–44) by Germans and Finns.

Leningrad, city (1926 pop. 1,690,065; 1939 pop. 3,191,304), ⊙ Leningrad oblast, Russian SFSR, major Baltic Sea port on Gulf of Finland, at mouth of Neva R., at S end of Karelian Isthmus, 400 mi. NW of Moscow; 59°57'N 30°18'E. Second-largest city of the USSR and the world's northernmost city with over a million habitants, Leningrad is also the foremost machine- and electrical-goods mfg. center of the Soviet Union and a leading rail hub. Mfg. accounts for 10% of total USSR output; includes special steels (based largely on scrap metal), heavy and electrical machine tools, electrical machinery (turbines, generators, transformers, Diesel motors, high-frequency installations), railroad cars, cranes, textile machines, linotype machines, light bulbs, telephone and radio equipment. A noted shipbuilding center; also produces chemicals (caustic soda, superphosphate, reagents, paints, cosmetics, drugs), rubber goods (footwear, tires, industrial belting); cotton, woolen, and silk textiles, leather shoes, cigarettes, paper; annual international fur auction. The extensive harbor installations, largely in SW portion, make Leningrad the best-equipped Soviet port, connected (1875–93) by 17-mi. deep-water canal with Kotlin Isl. (site of outer port and naval base of KRONSTADT). During navigation season (Apr.-Nov.) lumber, grain, and chemicals are exported. Electric power supplied to city by local peat and coal-based steam-electric plants and by hydroelectric stations on Vuoksi, Volkhov, and Svir rivers, and (since 1947) oil-shale gas power by pipe line from Kohtla-Jarve (Estonia). Leading cultural center of the USSR, with univ., polytechnical col., acad. of arts, industrial and trade schools, maritime, arctic, and meteorological institutes, and many historical bldgs., such as the fortress of Sts. Peter and Paul, St. Isaac cathedral, admiralty bldg., and Winter Palace. Leningrad consists of mainland portions N and S of Neva R. and of isls. bounded by the Neva's delta arms (Greater and Lesser Neva, Greater, Middle and Lesser Nevka). Erected on a swampy site, the city had to be built laboriously on reclaimed land, still subject to floods by Neva waters backed up by strong W autumn winds. The principal section of the city, bounded by the Greater Neva (N) and the Fontanka, a curving, 50-yd.-wide connecting canal (S), is in turn divided by lesser Moika and Griboyedov canals. On the Neva bank stands the 850-yd.-long admiralty bldg. (completed 1823; naval offices) surmounted by a 230-ft. spire. It is surrounded SW by former senate (palace of justice) and holy synod bldgs. (now museums) facing the equestrian statue of Peter the Great (1775) by Falconet; S by St. Isaac cathedral (1817–58; now a mus.) with its 330-ft.-high gilded dome; E by spacious Uritski (former Palace) Square which contains the 100-ft.-high monolithic granite Alexander column (1834) and is bounded S by imposing bldg. of former tsarist General Staff. NE of the admiralty bldg., bet. Neva R. and Uritski Square, is the former baroque Winter Palace (built 1754–62 by Rastrelli; now a mus.), and beyond is the Hermitage (1840–52), with one of the world's leading collections of W European painting and sculpture, and of classical, Egyptian, and Scythian antiquities. From the admiralty bldg., the *Nevski prospekt* (Leningrad's chief thoroughfare) extends E to the Moscow railroad station, past Kazan cathedral (1801–11) with Corinthian colonnade and tomb of Kutuzov, Gostiny Dvor (a shopping center), Saltykov-Shchedrin public library, Pushkin (former Alexandra) theater (1828–35), and 18th-cent. Pioneer's (former Anichkov) palace. Upstream, along the Neva, beyond the Hermitage, are the marble palace (1768–85), Kirov bridge (longest across the Neva), the Field of Mars with its monument to the 1917 October Revolution and the adjoining Summer Garden with the Summer Palace (1710–12) of Peter the Great. Farther E, along the Neva and facing the suburb of Okhta, is noted Smolny Inst.(1806–08), 1st hq. (1917) of the Soviet govt. On E end of Vasili isl. (largest of Neva R. delta isls.), opposite the Admiralty, are the city's leading cultural institutions: univ., acad. of arts, mining institute (1773), former Exchange, and former seat of Acad. of Sciences (since 1934 in Moscow). Near by on a little isl. in Neva R. is the fortress of Sts. Peter and Paul, oldest bldg. of the city and a political prison in tsarist days. Other Neva R. isls. are Petrograd isl. (residential and industrial), Apothecary isl. (botanical gardens), Krestovski, Yelagin, and Kamenny isls. (parks, playgrounds, stadiums). The leading industrial sections of the city are the Vyborg quarter (N of the Neva) and the S side, where greater urban expansion is taking place. In addition to the Moscow station, city is served by 4 rail termini, the Baltic, Warsaw, and Vitebsk stations (on S side) and the Finland station (on N side). Building of a subway was begun in 1946. Administered by a city council and divided into *raions* (*rayons*), Leningrad is (since 1931) an independent city subordinate directly to the Russian SFSR govt. It has jurisdiction over the suburban cities of KOLPINO, KRONSTADT, PETRODVORETS, and PUSHKIN. Since 1946 Leningrad includes within its city limits the former cities of Sestroretsk and Zelenogorsk and adjoining seaside resorts. Founded 1703 by Peter the Great on the site of a former Swedish strong point, the city was laid out as a modern capital, a "window looking on Europe," Western European in character, built entirely of stone and on a grand classical scale and named St. Petersburg; it succeeded (1713) Moscow as ⊙ Russia. Under Peter and his successors, St. Petersburg became one of Europe's brilliant capitals, a center of art and culture, with sumptuous imperial residences in the city and in near-by cities of Pushkin, Petrodvorets, Gatchina, and Pavlovsk. During the late-19th cent., it developed as a leading industrial city, linked (1848–51) by rail with Moscow and based chiefly on imported raw materials, and site of large Putilov (now Kirov) engineering works. Its numerous workers precipitated the Rus. revolution of 1905 and the revolution of Feb. and Oct., 1917. Under the Soviets, Leningrad remained the economic and cultural rival of Moscow, although it lost much of its former splendor, and the capital was returned (1918) to Moscow. Called Petrograd (1914–1924) prior to its renaming for Lenin. During the first Five-Year plan, its factories pioneered in the establishment of many new Rus. industries. In Second World War a major Ger. objective, the city was cut off by land from the rest of the USSR by the fall of Petrokrepost (Aug., 1941). The siege (accompanied by daily shelling and air raids) was lifted partially (Jan., 1943) and entirely (Jan., 1944).

Leningradskaya (–skīŭ), village (1926 pop. 20,728), N Krasnodar Territory, Russian SFSR, 20 mi. SW of Kushchevskaya; flour mill, metalworks. Until 1930s, called Umanskaya.

Lenino (lyĕ'nyĭnŭ). **1** N suburb (1926 pop. 9,365) of Irkutsk, Irkutsk oblast, Russian SFSR, on left bank of Angara R., at Irkutsk II station of Trans-Siberian RR; rail repair shops. Formerly called Innokentyevskaya; inc. 1930 into Irkutsk. **2** Town (1939 pop. over 10,000), central Moscow oblast, Russian SFSR, adjoining (S of) Moscow; glass- and brickworks; food products. Excursion center. Has ruins of castle of Catherine II, amidst English gardens. Formerly called Tsaritsyno. **3** City, W central Kemerovo oblast, Russian SFSR: see LENINSK-KUZNETSKI.

Leninogorsk (lyĕ"nyĭnŭgôrsk'), city (1926 pop. 9,469; 1939 pop. c.50,000), NE East Kazakhstan oblast, Kazakh SSR, in NW Altai Mts., near Ulba R., 50 mi. NE of Ust-Kamenogorsk. Rail terminus; major lead-zinc mining center; lead smelter; power works. Mines in exploitation since 1784. Until 1940, called Ridder.

Lenin Peak (lĕ'nĭn, Rus. lyĕ'nyĭn), highest peak (23,382 ft.) in Trans-Alai Range, USSR, on Kirghiz-Tadzhik SSR border, 85 mi. S of Osh. Formerly called Mt. Kaufman. Was considered highest point of USSR until 1932–33, when STALIN PEAK was found to be higher.

Leninpol or **Leninpol'** (lyĕnyĭnpôl'), village (1948 pop. over 2,000), N Talas oblast, Kirghiz SSR, 15 mi. W of Talas; wheat.

Leninsk (lyĕ'nyĭnsk). **1** Town (1946 pop. over 500), W central Chelyabinsk oblast, Russian SFSR, near Miass city. **2** City, Leningrad oblast, Russian SFSR: see PETRODVORETS. **3** City, Moscow oblast, Russian SFSR: see TALDOM. **4** Village (1926 pop. 14,808), E Stalingrad oblast, Russian SFSR, on Akhtuba R., on railroad and 30 mi. E of Stalingrad; metalworks, canneries. **5** City (1939 pop. over 10,000), SW Andizhan oblast, Uzbek SSR, in Fergana Valley, on railroad (Assake Station) and 10 mi. SW of Andizhan, in cotton area; cotton ginning, cottonseed-oil extracting. Oil fields of Palvantash and Andizhan (town) near by (E). Pipe line to Vannovski. Formerly called Assake and, later in middle 1930s, Zelensk.

Leninskaya Sloboda (–skīŭ slŭbŭdä'), town (1939 pop. over 500), central Gorki oblast, Russian SFSR, on Volga R. and 24 mi. SE of Gorki.

Leninski or **Leninskiy** (–skē). **1** Town (1941 pop. over 500), W Mari Autonomous SSR, Russian SFSR, on Vetluga R. (landing) and 25 mi. NW of Kozmodemyansk; glassworking center. Until 1941, Marino. **2** Town (1939 pop. over 500), central Tula oblast, Russian SFSR, on railroad (Obidimo station) and 8 mi. NW of Tula; asphalt works. Until 1939, Domman-Asfaltovy Zavod. **3** Town (1939 pop. over 500), SE Voroshilovgrad oblast, Ukrainian SSR, in the Donbas, near Sverdlovsk; coal mines.

Leninsk-Kuznetski or **Leninsk-Kuznetskiy** (–kōōz-nyĕt'skē), city (1926 pop. 19,645; 1939 pop. 81,980), W central Kemerovo oblast, on Inya R., on branch of Trans-Siberian RR and 18 mi. S of Kemerovo; one of large coal-mining centers of Kuznetsk Basin; power plant, brickworks, flour mills, sawmills. Originally called Kolchugino; later Lenino, until 1925, when it became a city.

Leninskoye (–skŭyŭ). **1** Village (1939 pop. over 500), S South Kazakhstan oblast, Kazakh SSR, 30 mi. N of Tashkent; cotton, cattle; metalworks. **2** Village (pop. under 500), NE Osh oblast, Kirghiz SSR, in Fergana Valley, 23 mi. NE of Osh; cotton, silk. Until 1937, Pokrovka. **3** Village (1939 pop. over 500), S Jewish Autonomous Oblast, Khabarovsk Territory, Russian SFSR, on Amur R. and 60 mi. S of Birobidzhan (with which it is connected by railroad), in agr. area. Formerly Mikhailovo-Semenovskoye and, until 1939, Blyukherovo. **4** Town (1939 pop. over 2,000), W Kirov oblast, Russian SFSR, on railroad (Shabalino station) and 45 mi. W of Kotelnich; flax. Formerly called Shabalino; since c.1940, also Leninski.

Leninsk-Turkmenski, Turkmen SSR: see CHARDZHOU, city.

Lenjan, Iran: see LINJAN.

Lenk (lĕngk), village (pop. 1,752), Bern canton, SW central Switzerland, on Simme R. and 22 mi. SSW of Thun; health resort, winter sports center.

Lenkersheim (lĕng'kŭrs-hīm), village (pop. 754), Middle Franconia, W Bavaria, Germany, on Aisch R. and 2 mi. E of Windsheim; oats, wheat, hops, sheep. Chartered 1199.

Lenkoran or **Lenkoran'** (lyĕnkŭrän'yŭ), city (1936 pop. estimate 24,000), SE Azerbaijan SSR, port on Caspian Sea, on railroad and 120 mi. SSW of Baku,

20 mi. N of Iran border, in Lenkoran Lowland; sawmilling, food canning; fisheries; tea-drying plant. Humid, subtropical climate; agr. (tea, citrus fruit, tung oil). Was ⊙ former Talysh khanate, conquered (1813) by Russians.

Lenkoran Lowland, Caspian coastal belt (40 mi. long) in SE Azerbaijan SSR, on Iran border, at foot of wooded Talysh Mts.; marked by humid, subtropical climate. Agr.: tangerines, lemons, tea, tung oil, figs, pomegranates, bamboo, rice. Fisheries. Main centers: Lenkoran, Astara.

Lennep (lĕ'nĕp), outer district (since 1927) of REMSCHEID, W Germany, 3 mi. E of city center; textile mfg. Röntgen b. here.

Lenne River (lĕ'nü), W Germany, rises on the Kahle Asten, flows c.60 mi. NW, past Altena and Hohenlimburg, to the Ruhr just NW of Hagen.

Lennick-Saint-Quentin (lĕ'nĭk-sē-kātē'), village (pop. 3,934), Brabant prov., central Belgium, 10 mi. WSW of Brussels; agr. center (cherries, potatoes). Village of Lennick-Saint-Martin (–märtē') (pop. 1,655) is just ENE.

Lenningen (lĕ'nĭng-ün), village (pop. 290), SE Luxembourg, 4 mi. N of Remich; vineyards; liquor distilling.

Lenno, Poland: see WLEN.

Lennonville, village, W central Western Australia, 210 mi. ENE of Geraldton and on Geraldton-Wiluna RR; mining center in Murchison Goldfield.

Lennox, Scotland: see DUMBARTON, county.

Lennox. 1 Unincorporated town (1940 pop. 10,526), Los Angeles co., S Calif., suburb 10 mi. SSW of downtown Los Angeles, in industrial, and truck- and dairy-farming dist. **2** City (pop. 1,218), Lincoln co., SE S.Dak., 15 mi. SW of Sioux Falls; livestock center; animal feed, meat products, dairy produce, poultry, grain. Co. fair takes place here. Settled 1879, inc. 1906.

Lennox and Addington, county (□ 1,170; pop. 18,469), SE Ont., on L. Ontario; ⊙ Napanee.

Lennox Hills, hill range, S Stirling, Scotland, extends 15 mi. along Dumbarton and Lanark border. W part is called Campsie Fells, E part Kilsyth Hills. Highest points are Earl's Seat (1,896 ft.), 3 mi. N of Strathblane, and Meikle Bin (1,870 ft.), 4 mi. NW of Kilsyth.

Lennox Island (□ 51.3), in Tierra del Fuego, just E of Navarino Isl., 20 mi. S of main isl. of the archipelago; c.9 mi. long, 9 mi. wide. Disputed by Chile and by Argentina, which claims Cape Carolina (55°33'S 66°56'W) as its southernmost point.

Lennoxtown, town in Campsie parish, S Stirling, Scotland, 8 mi. N of Glasgow; coal mining, textile printing.

Lennoxville, residential town (pop. 2,150), S Que., on St. Francis R., at mouth of Massawippi R., 3 mi. SE of Sherbrooke; mfg. of asbestos products, hosiery, lumbering, dairying. Site of Bishop's Col., Bishop's Col. School for Boys, and Dominion Experimental Farm.

Leno (lā'nô), town (pop. 3,942), Brescia prov., Lombardy, N Italy, near Mella R., 12 mi. S of Brescia; mfg. of electrical apparatus. Has Benedictine convent founded 758.

Lenoir (lünôr'), county (□ 391; pop. 45,953), E central N.C.; ⊙ Kinston. On coastal plain; drained by Neuse R. Agr. (especially tobacco; corn, cotton); sawmilling. Industry at Kinston. Formed 1791.

Lenoir, town (pop. 7,888), ⊙ Caldwell co., W central N.C., in Blue Ridge foothills; 17 mi. NW of Hickory; furniture-making center; mfg. of veneer, cotton yarn, clothing, mirrors, paper and metal products; lumber milling. Summer resort. Inc. 1851.

Lenoir City, city (pop. 5,159), Loudon co., E Tenn., on Tennessee R. and 23 mi. SW of Knoxville, in timber and agr. area; mfg. of hosiery, chairs, railroad cars, canned goods; lumbering. Fort Loudon Dam and Reservoir (water power) near by. Founded 1840.

Lenola (lā'nôlä), village (pop. 2,154), Latina prov., Latium, S central Italy, 15 mi. NNW of Gaeta.

Lenora, Czechoslovakia: see VIMPERK.

Lenora, city (pop. 511), Norton co., NW Kansas, on North Fork Solomon R. and 16 mi. SSW of Norton; wheat, corn, alfalfa.

Lenore Lake (17 mi. long, 3–7 mi. wide), central Sask., 17 mi. NNE of Humboldt.

Lenox (lĕ'nüks). **1** Town (pop. 789), Cook co., S Ga., 12 mi. SSE of Tifton. **2** Town (pop. 1,171), Taylor co., SW Iowa, 15 mi. SW of Creston; shipping point in livestock, grain, poultry area. Inc. 1875. **3** Resort town (pop. 3,627), including Lenox village (pop. 1,604), Berkshire co., W Mass., in the Berkshires, 7 mi. S of Pittsfield. Scene of annual Berkshire Symphonic Festival (begun 1934) at "Tanglewood," a former estate, mainly in adjoining Stockbridge town. Hawthorne's cottage, burned in 1890, was rebuilt and dedicated as shrine in 1948. Lenox is noted for its many estates. Settled c.1750, set off from Richmond 1767. Includes state forest and villages of New Lenox and Lenox Dale (1940 pop. 562).

Lens (lãs), agr. village (pop. 1,782), Hainaut prov., S Belgium, on Dender R. and 7 mi. NNW of Mons. Has 18th-cent. monastery bldgs.

Lens, town (pop. 34,134), Pas-de-Calais dept., N France, 17 mi. SW of Lille; center of France's most productive coal field (mines at Billy-Montigny, Avion, Liévin, Hénin-Liétard, Harnes, Fouquières-lès-Lens), surrounded by numerous miners' suburbs known as *cités* or *corons*. Rail hub with metalworks (cable and wire mfg., copper and bronze founding), coke ovens, and glassworks. Here Louis II of Condé defeated (1648) imperialists in last important battle of Thirty Years War. Held by Germans through most of First World War, Lens suffered heavily from proximity of battle front at near-by Hill 70 (NW) and Vimy Ridge (SSW). Again very seriously damaged in Second World War. Large Polish pop.

Lenskoye (lyĕn'skŭyü), village (1947 pop. over 500), E central Sverdlovsk oblast, Russian SFSR, on Tura R. and 20 mi. WNW of Turinsk; wheat, livestock.

Lent, village (pop. 2,321), Gelderland prov., E Netherlands, on Waal R., opposite Nijmegen; cherries; cattle raising; agr.

Lentekhi (lyĭntyĕ'khē), village (1939 pop. over 500), NW Georgian SSR, in Svanetia, 35 mi. N of Kutaisi; stock, grain. Until 1938, called Leksura.

Lenthe (lĕn'tü), village (pop. 697), in former Prussian prov. of Hanover, W Germany, after 1945 in Lower Saxony, 5 mi. W of Hanover city center. Inventor Siemens b. here.

Lenti (lĕn'tē), town (pop. 2,370), Zala co., W Hungary, 20 mi. SW of Zalaegerszeg; agr.; hogs, cattle.

Lentini (lĕntē'nē), anc. *Leontini*, town (pop. 23,511), Siracusa prov., E Sicily, near L. Lentini, 16 mi. S of Catania, in citrus-fruit area. Produces citrus syrups, macaroni, glass, lime, cement. Exports citrus fruit. One of oldest Greek settlements in Sicily; founded 729 B.C. on site of anc. Siculian fortress by Chalcidians from Naxos. Overwhelmed (498 B.C.) by Hippocrates; further colonized (476 B.C.) by Hieron of Syracuse. Stormed by Romans (A.D. 214), Saracens (A.D. 848). Largely destroyed by earthquake of 1693. Gorgias b. here.

Lentini, Lake, largest permanent lake (□ c.4) in Sicily, in Siracusa prov., 2 mi. NW of Lentini; partly artificial; waterfowl, fish. Its vapors make Lentini unhealthy in the summer. Also called Biviere di Lentini.

Lentschütz, Poland: see LECZYCA.

Lentvaris (lĕntvärēs'), Pol. *Landwarów*, city (1930 pop. 1,242), SE Lithuania, 9 mi. WSW of Vilna; rail junction; mfg. (nails, screws); stone quarries. In Rus. Vilna govt. until it passed to Poland in 1921, to Lithuania in 1939.

Lenva, Russian SFSR: see BEREZNIKI.

Leny, Pass of (lĕ'nē), narrow mountain pass in SW Perthshire, Scotland, 2 mi. WNW of Callander, in valley of short Leny R. which drains Loch Lubnaig into Teith R.

Lenzburg (lĕnts'bŏŏrk), town (pop. 4,266), Aargau canton, N Switzerland, on Aa R. and 7 mi. E of Aarau; flour, pastry, biscuits, canned goods, paper products; metalworking, printing. Castle (mentioned in 1040) is E.

Lenzburg (lĕnz'bûrg), village (pop. 431), St. Clair co., SW Ill., 27 mi. SE of East St. Louis, in bituminous-coal and agr. area.

Lenzen (lĕn'tsün), town (pop. 3,840), Brandenburg, E Germany, near the Elbe, 14 mi. NW of Wittenberge; flax, grain, potatoes, stock. Has late-Gothic church, anc. castle.

Lenzerheide (lĕnt'sürhī'dü), Romansh *Planüra* (plänü'rä), health resort (alt. 4,843 ft.), Grisons canton, E Switzerland, 8 mi. S of Chur; winter sports (notably skiing). The Lenzerhorn (9,550 ft.) is near by.

Lenzing (lĕn'tsĭng), town (pop. 4,371), S central Upper Austria, in the Salzkammergut, on Ager R. and 9 mi. NW of Gmunden; pulp and rayon milling.

Lenzkirch (lĕnts'kĭrkh), village (pop. 1,856), S Baden, Germany, in Black Forest, on the Wutach and 3 mi. SSW of Neustadt; mfg. of musical instruments, metalworking, lumber milling. Climatic health resort, winter-sports center (alt. 2,657 ft.).

Lenzspitze, Switzerland: see MISCHABELHÖRNER.

Léo (lā'ō), town (pop. c.2,100), S Upper Volta, Fr. West Africa, near Gold Coast border, 90 mi. SSW of Ouagadougou; shea nuts, peanuts; cattle, sheep, goats. Customhouse.

Leoben (lāō'bün), city (pop. 35,785), Styria, SE central Austria, on Mur R. and 26 mi. NNW of Graz; rail junction. Industrial center in coal-mining area; large ironworks; textile mills, breweries. School of mining. Donawitz (dō'nüvĭts) and Göss, suburbs, became part of Leoben in 1939. At Donawitz is a large steel mill.

Leobersdorf (lāō'bürsdôrf''), town (pop. 3,566), E Lower Austria, on Triesting R. and 6 mi. S of Baden; rail junction; mfg. of industrial machinery.

Leobschütz, Poland: see GLUBCZYCE.

Leodium, Belgium: see LIÉGE, city.

Léogane (lāōgän'), town (1950 census pop. 3,608), Ouest dept., S Haiti, port on NE coast of Tiburon Peninsula, 18 mi. W of Port-au-Prince; sugar-growing and -loading center. Has grotto.

Leogang (lā'ōgäng), village (pop. 2,094), Salzburg, W central Austria, 17 mi. E of Kitzbühel. Bad Leogang, with mineral springs, near by.

Léognan (lāônyã'), village (pop. 1,064), Gironde dept., SW France, 8 mi. S of Bordeaux; dry white wines.

Léojac (lāôzhäk'), commune (pop. 326), Tarn-et-Garonne dept., SW France, 4 mi. E of Montauban; strawberries.

Leola (lēō'lü). **1** Town (pop. 313), Grant co., central Ark., 33 mi. W of Pine Bluff. **2** City (pop. 772), ⊙ McPherson co., N S.Dak., 28 mi. NW of Aberdeen; shipping point for grain and hogs; duck hunting in vicinity.

Leominster (lĕm'stûr), municipal borough (1931 pop. 5,707; 1951 census 6,289), N Hereford, England, on Lugg R. and 12 mi. N of Hereford; agr. market, with agr.-machinery works. Has 11th-cent. minster, restored in 1866, and many old half-timbered bldgs.

Leominster (lĕ'mĭnstür), city (pop. 24,075), Worcester co., N Mass., on N branch of Nashua R., just SSE of Fitchburg; mfg. (plastics, machinery, tools, paper, toys, clothing). Set off from Lancaster 1740, inc. as city 1915.

León (lāōn'), village (pop. estimate 500), S Jujuy prov., Argentina, on railroad, on the Rio Grande de Jujuy and 13 mi. NW of Jujuy, in fruitgrowing, stock-raising, and mining area. Limestone, lead, silver deposits.

León, province, Ecuador: see COTOPAXI, province.

Léon (lāõ'), village (pop. 491), Landes dept., SW France, 17 mi. NW of Dax; cork mfg., turpentine extracting, winegrowing.

León (lāōn'), officially León de los Aldamas, city (pop. 74,155), Guanajuato, central Mexico, in fertile Río Turbio valley, 85 mi. SW of San Luis Potosí; alt. 6,086 ft. Commercial, industrial, silver-mining, and agr. center (potatoes, cereals, chickpeas, fruit, livestock). Mfg. (leather goods, shoes, hats, shawls, pottery, gold and silver work, jewelry); tanneries, flour and textile mills, cement plant. Gold, silver, copper, lead, and tin deposits near by. Has impressive cathedral, municipal palace, theater, airport. Founded 1576; once 2d largest city in Mexico. Frequent floods, especially that of 1888, destroyed its prominence; a dam protects it now.

León, department (□ 2,355; 1950 pop. 124,189), W Nicaragua, on the Pacific; ⊙ León. Bounded E by L. Managua; includes volcanic range of Cordillera de los Marabios (volcanoes Telica, Rota, Cerro Negro, Las Pilas), and Momotombo volcano. Agr.: corn, sesame, beans, cotton, coffee, sugar cane (mills near Quezalguaque), cacao; livestock; cheese production. Gold and silver mining at El Limón, La India, and Valle de las Zapatas. Mfg. concentrated in León. Main centers (served by railroad): León, La Paz Central, Nagarote, El Sauce.

León, city (1950 pop. 31,008), ⊙ León dept., W Nicaragua, on short León R. (hydroelectric station), on railroad and 45 mi. NW of Managua; 12°26'N 86°54'W. Second largest city of Nicaragua and its intellectual center; mfg. (matches, furniture, footwear, leather goods, soap, candles, perfume); cheese and wine making. Site of univ. (1813; constituted Natl. Univ. of Nicaragua in 1951), theological seminary, several colleges, cathedral (built 1746–79), and episcopal palace. A city of colonial appearance, it has several colonial churches, the oldest (Subtiava church) dating from 1560, hosp., and hippodrome. Home of poet Rubén Darío (died here 1916). Connected by road with seaside resort of Poneloya. Founded 1524 at foot of volcano Momotombo; moved (1610) to present site (adjoining Indian town of Subtiava) following destruction of original city. First bishopric of Nicaragua; became capital of Sp. prov. of Nicaragua and (until 1857) of the republic.

Leon, town (1939 pop. 3,343; 1948 municipality pop. 21,805), Iloilo prov., SE Panay isl., Philippines, 14 mi. WNW of Iloilo; rice growing.

Leon (lē'ŏn), Sp. *León* (lāōn'), region (□ 20,594; pop. 1,732,082) and former kingdom, NW Spain, consisting of provs. of Leon, PALENCIA, SALAMANCA, VALLADOLID, and ZAMORA. Bounded by Asturias (N), Old Castile (E), Estremadura (S), Galicia and Portugal (W). Comprises NW part of central plateau of Spain, bounded by the Cantabrian Mts. (N), Leon Mts. (NW), Sierra de Gredos (S). Drained by the Duero (Douro), traversing region E-W, and its tributaries (Pisuerga, Valderaduey, Esla, Tormes). Has irrigation canals, reservoirs, and some power plants: great hydroelectric works under construction (Saltos del Duero). Large barren plateau dissected by fertile valleys. Some sections yield large crops of wheat (Tierra de Campos, Tierra del Pan) and wine (Tierra del Vino). Other crops: rye, barley, oats, potatoes, vegetables, flax, sugar beets; also fruitgrowing. Extensive forests and pastures on S slopes of Cantabrian Mts.; cattle (N Leon prov.), hog and sheep raising (Zamora and Salamanca). Transhumance. Rich mineral resources in Cantabrian Mts., chiefly anthracite and bituminous coal. Iron, zinc, tungsten, and manganese are also mined. Slate, limestone quarries; sand pits; mineral springs. Industries limited to processing of agr. and forest products. Traditional woolen industry is now greatly reduced, while linen mfg. has regained importance. Coal and dairy products are only exports. Chief cities are capitals of provs.; Valladolid and Salamanca are most important. Region was reconquered (8th-9th cent.) from Moors by kings of Asturias; kingdom of Asturias and Leon (⊙ Leon city) was established in 10th cent. and comprised also Galicia and parts of Castile, Navarre, and Vizcaya. After Castile became (1035) an autonomous kingdom, Leon and Castile were repeatedly united and separated through confused dynastic struggles, until permanent union was achieved (1230) under Ferdinand III.

Leon, Sp. *León,* province (□ 5,432; pop. 493,258), NW Spain, in Leon region; ⊙ Leon. Bounded by crest of Cantabrian Mts. (N) and crossed by their offshoots; rest of prov. is part of central high plateau. Drained by Esla R. and its tributaries and by Sil R. Sufficient rainfall in N and W, where are extensive forests and pastures (cattle and sheep raising; transhumance) and fertile valleys; barren, cold areas on plateau. Essentially agr.: cereals, potatoes, wine, vegetables, sugar beets, flax, some fruit. Leading Sp. prov. for anthracite (about 70% of total) and 2d for bituminous-coal production from mines in Cantabrian Mts. (Villablino, Tremor, Toreno, Pola de Gordón); also iron (Ponferrada), zinc (Picos de Europa), barite, and some tungsten mines. Clay and limestone quarries. Few industries, mostly derived from agr.: dairy-products and meat processing, tanning, flour and sugar milling, linen mfg., brandy distilling; also makes coal briquettes, ceramics, candy, soap. Chief cities: Leon, Astorga, Ponferrada.

Leon, Sp. *León,* city (pop. 43,260), ⊙ Leon prov. and region, Spain, at confluence of Bernesga R. and small Torio R., at foot of S slopes of the Cantabrian Mts., 180 mi. NW of Madrid; 42°36'N 5°35'W. Communications and agr. trade center (livestock, wine, cereals, sugar beets, vegetables); tanneries, brewery, watch factory, flour and sugar mills. Mfg. of coal briquettes, linen and woolen textiles, pharmaceuticals, ceramics, glass, chocolate; dairy-products and meat processing. Episcopal see. Has narrow, crooked streets and is partly circled by Roman walls and towers (3d cent. A.D.). Has 13th-cent. cathedral (later restored), one of finest examples of Fr.-Gothic architecture in Spain, with beautiful stained-glass windows and cloisters; Romanesque church of San Isidro (11th cent.; restored) containing former royal mausoleum, partly destroyed; 16th-cent. convent of St. Marks (originally a pilgrim's hospice, now in part a barracks), housing provincial mus. with Roman antiquities. Also notable are the town hall and the Casa de los Guzmanes (both 16th cent.). City owes its name to Roman legion encamped here. Taken by Visigoths (6th cent.) and Moors (8th cent.); liberated (882) by Alfonso III. Became ⊙ kingdom of Leon (10th cent.); prospered in 12th-13th cent., but declined with rise of Castile and never recovered.

Leon. 1 (lē'ŭn) County (□ 685; pop. 51,590), NW Fla., on Ga. line (N), and bounded W by Ochlockonee R. and L. Talquin; ⊙ Tallahassee. Rolling terrain in N, coastal plain in S; includes many lakes and part of Apalachicola Natl. Forest. Agr. (corn, peanuts, cotton, vegetables, cattle, hogs, poultry; dairy products), and forestry (lumber, naval stores). Industry at Tallahassee. Formed 1824. **2** (lē'ōn) County (□ 1,099; pop. 12,024), E central Texas; ⊙ Centerville. Bounded W by Navasota R., E by Trinity R. Agr., lumbering, livestock; oil, natural-gas wells. Cotton, corn, grain sorghums, peanuts, potatoes, truck (especially watermelons), fruit; hogs, cattle, goats, sheep, poultry; dairying. Lumber milling, farm-products processing. Hunting, fishing. Formed 1846.

Leon (lē'ŭn, lē'ōn). **1** City (pop. 2,139), ⊙ Decatur co., S Iowa, c.60 mi. S of Des Moines; dairy products, concrete blocks. Settled 1840, inc. 1867. **2** City (pop. 518), Butler co., SE Kansas, 27 mi. E of Wichita, in cattle and grain area. Oil wells near by. **3** Village (pop. c.250), Cattaraugus co., W N.Y., 17 mi. NE of Jamestown; dairy products. **4** Town (pop. 122), Love co., S Okla., near Red R., 26 mi. SW of Ardmore, in farm area. **5** Village (pop. 244), Mason co., W W.Va., on Kanawha R. and 12 mi. SE of Point Pleasant.

León, Pico El (ĕl pē'kō lāōn'), Andean peak (15,561 ft.), Mérida state, W Venezuela, in Sierra Nevada de Mérida, 11 mi. SSE of Mérida, SW of La Columna.

Leona (lēō'nŭ), city (pop. 130), Doniphan co., NE Kansas, 25 mi. W of St. Joseph, Mo.; agr. (chiefly apples).

Leona Mines, village (pop. 1,486, with near-by Benedict), Lee co., extreme SW Va., 13 mi. WSW of Big Stone Gap, in bituminous-coal region.

Leonard (lĕ'nŭrd). **1** Village (pop. 391), Oakland co., SE Mich., 18 mi. NE of Pontiac. **2** Village (pop. 88), Clearwater co., NW Minn., 21 mi. NW of Bemidji; dairy products. **3** Town (pop. 165), Shelby co., NE Mo., on branch of Salt R., 10 mi. NW of Shelbyville. **4** Town (pop. 1,211), Fannin co., NE Texas, 9 mi. S of Bonham; market, trade point in cotton, corn, truck area; grain milling, cotton ginning, mfg. of rubber mats; poultry hatchery. Settled c.1880.

Leonardo (lēŭnär'dō), village (pop. 1,887), Monmouth co., E N.J., near Sandy Hook Bay, 4 mi. N of Red Bank.

Leonardtown (lĕ'nŭrdtoun), town (pop. 1,017), ⊙ St. Marys co. (since 1710), S Md., c.45 mi. SSE of Washington and on navigable estuary entering the Potomac; ships tobacco, lumber. Has 18th-cent. buildings. Near by are St. Francis Xavier Church (built 1767 on site of church erected c.1654), and site of St. Ignatius Chapel, built 1662 by Jesuits. Laid out 1708.

Leonardville (lĕ'nŭrdvĭl), city (pop. 320), Riley co., NE Kansas, 20 mi. NW of Manhattan; trading point in livestock and grain region.

Leonard Wood, Fort, Mo.: see NEWBURG.

Leona River (lēō'nŭ), S central Texas, rises N of Uvalde, flows c.75 mi. generally SE, through livestock-ranching area, to the Frio 10 mi. S of Pearsall.

Leonberg (lā'ōnbĕrk), town (pop. 10,329), N Württemberg, Germany, after 1945 in Württemberg-Baden, 7 mi. WNW of Stuttgart; mfg. of machinery, tools, precision instruments, chemicals, gypsum, shoes; metal- and woodworking, food processing, lumber milling. Has 13th-cent. church, Renaissance castle. Schelling b. here.

Leonding (lā'ōndĭng), town (pop. 6,619), N central Upper Austria, 3 mi. SW of Linz; truck farming (poultry, fruit).

Leone (lāō'nā), village (pop. 711), W Tutuila, American Samoa.

Leone, Monte (mōn'tĕ lĕō'nĕ), highest peak (11,683 ft.) of Lepontine Alps, on Italo-Swiss border, 7.5 mi. SE of Brig. Pierced by Simplon Tunnel. Simplon Pass is just W.

Leones (lāō'nĕs), town (pop. 4,870), E Córdoba prov., Argentina, 12 mi. W of Marcos Juárez; agr. center (wheat, flax, corn, alfalfa, potatoes, vegetables, cattle); dairying, tanning.

Leones, Cerro, or **Cerro Alto de los Leones** (sĕ'rō äl'tō dā lōs), Andean peak (19,455 ft.) in Aconcagua prov., central Chile, just S of 33°S.

Leones Islands, small archipelago in the Atlantic, belonging to Argentina, 2 mi. off coast of Comodoro Rivadavia military zone, 20 mi. SSE of Camarones. Guano deposits.

Leonessa (lĕōnĕs'sä), town (pop. 1,526), Rieti prov., Latium, central Italy, 12 mi. NNE of Rieti, in livestock and agr. (cereals, potatoes) region; woodworking.

Leonfelden (lā'ōnfĕldŭn), town (pop. 2,676), N Upper Austria, 15 mi.N of Linz, near Czechoslovak line; breweries; resort (alt. 2,457 ft.) with mineral springs.

Leonforte (lĕōnfôr'tĕ), town (pop. 15,700), Enna prov., central Sicily, near source of Dittaino R., 8 mi. NE of Enna; rail terminus. Sulphur mines are S. Scene of heavy fighting (1943).

Leongatha (lēŭn-gă'thŭ), town (pop. 1,990), S Victoria, Australia, 70 mi. SE of Melbourne, in livestock, agr. area; cheese; potatoes, flax.

Leonia (lēō'nyŭ), residential borough (pop. 7,378), Bergen co., NE N.J., 3 mi. ESE of Hackensack, near W approach to George Washington Bridge. Inc. 1894.

Leonidas (lēŭnī'dŭs), village (pop. 88), St. Louis co., NE Minn., on Mesabi iron range, just W of Eveleth; iron mines near by.

Leonidion or **Leonidhion** (both: lāōnē'dhēōn), town (pop. 3,452), Arcadia nome, SE Peloponnesus, Greece, near Gulf of Argolis, 24 mi. ENE of Sparta; wine, almonds. Anc. Doric dialect still spoken here. Formerly also Leonidi.

Leonidovo (lyăŭnyē'dŭvŭ), town (1947 pop. over 500), S Sakhalin, Russian SFSR, on E coast railroad and 12 mi. WNW of Poronaisk; rail junction; coal mining. Under Jap. rule (1905–45), called Kami-shikuka.

Leonine City (lē'ōnīn), part of Rome W of the Tiber; site of the Vatican.

León Island, Sp. *Isla de León* (ē'slä dhā lāōn'), or **San Fernando Island** (sän fĕrnän'dō), offshore island (c.10 mi. long) on Atlantic coast of Cádiz prov., SW Spain, separated from mainland by narrow canals. Irregularly shaped, it encloses (S and W) the Bay of Cádiz. On it are the cities of Cádiz and San Fernando. Several saltworks. Isl. was named for Juan Ponce de León, to whom Henry IV of Castile ceded it.

Leon Mountains (lē'ōn), Sp. *León* (lāōn'), S offshoots of the Cantabrian Mts., Leon prov., N Spain, covering W part of prov., bet. the Órbigo (E) and the Sil (W) valleys. Highest peak, Teleno (6,950 ft.).

León Muerto, Sierra (syĕ'rä lā-ōn' mwĕr'tō), subandean mountain range in Catamarca and Salta provs., Argentina, E of Antofagasta; extends E-W c.20 mi.; rises to c.17,500 ft.

Leonora (lēŭnō'rŭ), town (pop. 452), S central Western Australia, on spur of Kalgoorlie-Laverton RR and 130 mi. N of Kalgoorlie; gold mining.

Leonora, village (pop. 4,518), Demerara co., N Br. Guiana, near Atlantic coast, on railroad and 10 mi. WNW of Georgetown; sugar cane, rice, stock.

Leonore (lē'ŭnôr), village (pop. 204), La Salle co., N Ill., 12 mi. SW of Ottawa, in agr. and bituminous-coal area.

León River (lāōn'), Antioquia dept., NW Colombia, rises on W slopes of Serranía de Abibe near Chocó intendancy border, flows c.75 mi. NNW to the Caribbean at Gulf of Urabá.

Leon River (lē'ōn), central Texas, rises in several branches in Comanche co., flows c.145 mi. generally SE, past Gatesville, joining Lampasas R. to form Little R. c.9 mi. S of Temple. Dam impounds L. Brelsford (capacity 4,900 acre-ft.)in Eastland co.; recreation area (bathing, fishing) here.

Leontes, Lebanon: see LITANI RIVER.

Leontini, Sicily: see LENTINI.

Leonville (lēōn'vĭl), village (pop. 514), St. Landry parish, S central La., 7 mi. SE of Opelousas and on Bayou Teche; agr. (truck, sweet potatoes, sugar cane, cotton); moss gathering and curing.

Leopold II, Lake (□ 900), W Belgian Congo, E of Congo R. and SSE of Tumba L.; 90 mi. long, up to 25 mi. wide; empties S into the Kasai by Fimi R. Shallow in depth and of irregular shape, with low, forested shores, it increases in size by 2 or 3 times in rainy season. Main port, Inongo. Lake was discovered 1882 by Stanley.

Leopold and Astrid Coast, Antarctica, on Indian Ocean, extends bet. 81° and 86°E. Discovered 1934 by Lars Christensen, Norwegian.

Leopold Canal, Germany: see DREISAM RIVER.

Leopoldina (līōpōldē'nŭ). **1** City, Alagoas, Brazil: see COLÔNIA LEOPOLDINA. **2** Town, Goiás, Brazil: see ARUANÃ. **3** City (pop. 7,261), SE Minas Gerais, Brazil, near Rio de Janeiro border, 50 mi. NE of Juiz de Fora; rail-spur terminus; agr. trade center (coffee, sugar, dairy products, tobacco) with processing plants. **4** City, Pernambuco, Brazil: see PARNAMIRIM.

Leopold Island (7 mi. long), E Franklin Dist., Northwest Territories, in Davis Strait, off Cape Mercy, SE Baffin Isl., near entrance of Cumberland Sound; 64°59'N 63°18'W. Steep cliffs rise to c.2,000 ft.

Leopoldov, Czechoslovakia: see HLOHOVEC.

Leopoldsberg, Austria: see WIENER WALD.

Leopoldsburg, Belgium: see BOURG-LÉOPOLD.

Leopoldsdorf or **Leopoldsdorf im Marchfelde** (lā'ôpôltsdôrf ĭm märkh'fĕldŭ), village (pop. 1,594), E Lower Austria, 15 mi. E of Vienna; sugar refinery.

Leopoldshall, Germany: see STASSFURT.

Leopoldstadt (lā'ôpôlt-shtät"), district (□ 7; pop. 101,411) of Vienna, Austria, on isl. formed by the Danube and Danube Canal, just E of city center; porcelain mfg. Has large amusement park, the well-known Prater. Designated (17th cent.) official ghetto of Vienna.

Leopoldville (lē'ōpōldvĭl), Fr. *Léopoldville* (lāōpôld-vēl'), province (□ 140,017; 1948 pop. 2,378,629), in W and SW Belgian Congo; ⊙ Leopoldville. Bounded S by Angola (partly along estuary of Congo R.), W by the Atlantic and Cabinda (an exclave of Angola) along Shiloango R., N by Fr. Equatorial Africa (mostly along Congo R.). Drained by Congo, Kasai, and Kwango rivers. Has both equatorial rain forest and parklike savanna, with baobabs. In SE are grown palm products, fibers, sesame; in NE, hardwood, copal, rice, groundnuts. Along lower Congo sugar, cattle, and native food staples (manioc, yams, plantains) are raised. Most productive region is the Mayumbe, with coffee, cacao, and banana plantations, elaeis-palm groves, gold mines, and wild-rubber and tropical hardwood forests. Boma-Tshela and Matadi-Leopoldville railroads in W; river traffic in E. Principal centers: Leopoldville, Boma, Matadi, Thysville, Kikwit, Inongo.

Leopoldville, Fr. *Léopoldville,* city (1948 pop. 126,115; 1938 pop. 35,946), ⊙ Belgian Congo, Leopoldville prov., and Middle-Congo dist. (□ 10,996; 1948 pop. c.325,000), in W Belgian Congo, on left bank of Congo R. bet. Stanley Pool and the 1st rapids of Livingstone Falls, opposite Brazzaville (Fr. Equatorial Africa); 4°19'S 15°18'E. Leading commercial center and largest city of Belgian Congo; important industrial center. Plays a prominent part as a hub of African air services connected both with Europe over the Sahara and with North America via Brazil; also the main base of navigation on Congo R. and terminus of railroad from Matadi on the lower Congo. Industries include mfg. of cotton and jute textiles, footwear, iron and steel structures, bicycle parts, construction materials, furniture, chemicals, pharmaceuticals, soap, palm oil, beer, carbonated drinks, printed matter; food processing; shipbuilding (mainly steamer tugs and barges). A fast-growing city, it is built on modern architectural lines amidst tropical palms and colorful gardens. Comprises several sections (total □ 20) spanned by wide tree-lined avenues. The European city (1948 pop. 7,244) extends N along Congo R. shore for c.10 mi. and includes Kinshasa (kēnshä'sä, kēnshä-sä') or Leopoldville East, the commercial and industrial dist. with the harbor and main railroad station; Kalina (kälē'nä, kälēnä'), with the administrative and government quarters; and Leopoldville West, also known as Kintambo (kēntäm'-bō), chiefly residential but also terminus of oil pipe line from Matadi and site of another railroad station. Kinshasa, an important transit point for Fr. Equatorial Africa, is connected with Brazzaville by launch. Farther inland to S of the European zone sprawls the African city (1948 pop. 118,871), a conglomerate of clay and adobe houses surrounded by wattle fences; a large military camp separates its E and W parts. In E section is Queen Astrid stadium for natives and N'dolo or Dolo, the city airport. Other notable features of the capital are a mus. of African life, zoological gardens, race course, and a well-known short-wave radio broadcasting station. Among the educational institutions are the weavers', carpenters', ironsmiths', river pilots', and machinists' schools for natives, 2 junior colleges for Europeans, and a noted research institute of tropical medicine. Leopoldville is also hq. of R.C. Belgian missions and of Protestant missions in the Congo, and seat of vicar apostolic. Founded in 1887 by Henry Stanley, it succeeded Boma as ⊙ Belgian Congo in 1926. During Second World War a large contingent of U.S. troops was stationed here and war industries were developed.

Leopolis, Ukrainian SSR: see Lvov, city.

Leoti (lēō'tī), city (pop. 1,250), ⊙ Wichita co., W Kansas, c.45 mi. NW of Garden City; shipping point for grain and cattle area.

Leovardia, Netherlands: see LEEUWARDEN.

Leoville (lē'ōvĭl"), village (pop. 408), W central Sask., 70 mi. NE of North Battleford; mixed farming, dairying.

Leovo (lyăô'vŏŏ), Rum. *Leova* (lĕô'vä), city (1930 pop. 6,539; 1941 pop. 2,654), SW Moldavian SSR, on Prut R. (head of navigation) and 45 mi. SW of Kishinev, on Rum. border; agr. center; flour and oilseed milling, lumbering.

Lepaera (lāpää'rä), town (pop. 775), Lempira dept., W Honduras, in Sierra de Atima, 14 mi. N of Gracias; tobacco, coffee, corn.

Lepakshi, India: see HINDUPUR.

Lépanges (lāpäzh'), village (pop. 1,286), Vosges dept., E France, 11 mi. E of Épinal; textile milling.

Lepanto (lāpän'tō), town (dist. pop. 6,416), Puntarenas prov., W Costa Rica, small port on Gulf of Nicoya of the Pacific, on Nicoya Peninsula, 12 mi. W of Puntarenas (across the gulf); lumbering.

Lepanto, Greece: see NAUPAKTOS.

Lepanto (lĭpăn'tō), town (pop. 1,638), Poinsett co., NE Ark., 26 mi. SE of Jonesboro, in agr. area; cotton ginning and compressing, lumber milling. Inc. 1909.

Lepanto, Gulf of, Greece: see CORINTH, GULF OF.

Lepanto, Strait of, Greece: see RION STRAIT.

Lepar (lĕpär'), island (□ c.75; 13 mi. long, 10 mi. wide), Indonesia, in Java Sea, just off SE coast of Bangka.

Lepaterique (lāpätārē'kā), town (pop. 546), Francisco Morazán dept., S central Honduras, in Sierra de Lepaterique, 16 mi. WSW of Tegucigalpa; alt. 4,659 ft.; pottery making, tanning; livestock, corn, wheat, beans.

Lepaterique, Sierra de, section of main Andean range in S central Honduras, SW of Tegucigalpa; extends from Lepaterique c.20 mi. SE; forms divide bet. upper Choluteca (N) and upper Nacaome (S) rivers; rises to 5,636 ft. in Hule peak.

Lepaya, Latvia: see LIEPAJA.

Lepe (lā'pā), town (pop. 7,399), Huelva prov., SW Spain, near the Atlantic, 14 mi. W of Huelva; summer resort and agr. center (olives, cereals, fruit, stock). Processing of figs and chicory, flour milling, lumbering, fish salting.

Lepel or **Lepel'** (lyĕ'pĭl), city (1926 pop. 6,776), W Vitebsk oblast, Belorussian SSR, on Ulla R., on small Lepel L., and 65 mi. WSW of Vitebsk; rail terminus; food processing, brick mfg.

Lepenac River or **Lepenats River** (both: lĕ'pĕnäts), SW Yugoslavia, rises 7 mi. E of Prizren, flows E and SSE, past Kacanik, through Kacanik defile, to Vardar R. 3 mi. WNW of Skoplje.

Leper Island, New Hebrides: see AOBA.

Lépi (lĕ'pē), town (pop. 2,450), Benguela prov., W central Angola, on Benguela RR and 27 mi. WSW of Nova Lisboa.

Lépine or **L'Épine** (lāpēn'), village (pop. 246), Marne dept., N France, on the Vesle and 5 mi. ENE of Châlons-sur-Marne; pilgrimage center. Has noted 15th–16th-cent. church.

L'Épiphanie (lāpēfänē"), village (pop. 1,941), S Que., 4 mi. NW of L'Assomption; woodworking; mfg. of furniture, packing cases; dairying.

Lepoglava (lĕ'pôglävä), village, N Croatia, Yugoslavia, on railroad and 16 mi. WSW of Varazdin, at W foot of Ivanscica mtn., in lignite-mining area.

Lepontine Alps (lŭpŏn'tīn), Fr. *Alpes Lépontiennes*, Ital. *Alpi Lepontine*, division of Central Alps, along Italo-Swiss border (but mostly in Ticino and Grisons cantons, Switzerland); extend from Pennine Alps at Simplon Pass (WSW) to Rhaetian Alps at Splügen Pass (ENE). Bounded N by upper Rhone and Vorderrhein valleys, S by Ital. lake dist. (Lago Maggiore, Lugano and Como lakes). Highest peak, Monte Leone (11,683 ft.). Include ADULA and SAINT GOTTHARD groups. Deep Leventina and Mesolcina valleys on S slope. Important passes: Simplon, St. Gotthard, Lukmanier, San Bernardino.

Leppävirta (lĕp'pävĭr"tä), village (commune pop. 14,278), Kuopio co., S central Finland, in Saimaa lake region, 25 mi. S of Kuopio; agr. market in grain-growing, lumbering region. Lake port.

Lepreau, Point (lŭprō'), promontory on the Bay of Fundy, S N.B., 24 mi. SW of St. John; 45°3'N 66°28'W; lighthouse. Iron is mined here.

Lepreum (lĕ'prēŭm), anc. city in Elis nome, W Peloponnesus, Greece, 22 mi. SE of Pyrgos. Remains include acropolis and small temple. Originally independent, the city was ruled by Elis (c.450–400 B.C.), later allied with Arcadia, and became a member of Achaean League. Just S is modern village of Lepreon (pop. 762), formerly Strovitsi.

Lepsa River (lyĕp'sŭ), Taldy-Kurgan oblast, Kazakh SSR, rises in the Dzungarian Ala-Tau, flows 210 mi. NW, past Lepsinsk, to E end of L. Balkhash; used for irrigation.

Lepseny (lĕp'shänyŭ), Hung. *Lepsény*, town (pop. 2,540), Veszprem co., W central Hungary, 17 mi. ESE of Veszprem; rail junction; wheat, corn, vineyards, cattle, poultry.

Lepsinsk (lyĕp'sĭnsk), village (1926 pop. 4,353), NE Taldy-Kurgan oblast, Kazakh SSR, in the Dzungarian Ala-Tau, on Lepsa R. and 115 mi. NE of Taldy-Kurgan, in wheat area; distillery.

Lepsy (lyĕp'sē), town (1948 pop. over 2,000), N Taldy-Kurgan oblast, Kazakh SSR, on Turksib RR, on Lepsa R. and 85 mi. NNE of Taldy-Kurgan, in desert area.

Leptis Magna, Tripolitania: see HOMS.

Lepton, former urban district (1931 pop. 3,323), West Riding, S Yorkshire, England, 4 mi. E of Huddersfield; coal mining, woolen milling. Inc. 1938 in Kirkburton.

Lepuix or **Lepuix-Gy** (lŭpwē'-zhē'), industrial village (pop. 708), Territory of Belfort, E France, at foot of the Ballon d'Alsace, 9 mi. N of Belfort; cotton weaving, ski mfg.

Lequeitio (lĕkā'tyō), village (pop. 1,237), Coahuila, N Mexico, in Laguna Dist., 25 mi. NE of Torreón; cotton, wheat, corn, grapes, vegetables. Cooperative settlement.

Lequeitio (lĕkā'tyō), town (pop. 4,062), Vizcaya prov., N Spain, fishing port on Bay of Biscay, 22 mi. ENE of Bilbao; fish processing, boatbuilding, sawmilling. Cereals, fruit, cattle, lumber in area. Bathing resort.

Lequile (lā'kwēlĕ), village (pop. 3,202), Lecce prov., Apulia, S Italy, 3 mi. SSW of Lecce.

Le Raysville, agr. borough (pop. 310), Bradford co., NE Pa., 14 mi. ENE of Towanda.

Lerberget (lâr'bĕr"yŭt), fishing village (pop. 509), Malmohus co., SW Sweden, on the Kattegat, 10 mi. NNW of Halsingborg; seaside resort.

Lercara Friddi (lĕrkä'rä frēd'dē), town (pop. 12,070), Palermo prov., central Sicily, 18 mi. S of Termini Imerese, in grape- and cereal-growing region; macaroni. Many sulphur mines near by.

Lerdal (lâr'däl"), village (pop. 853), Kopparberg co., central Sweden, on E shore of L. Silja, 25 mi. NE of Falun; lumbering, dairying; grain, livestock.

Lerdo or **Ciudad Lerdo** (syōōdädh' lĕr'dō), city (pop. 9,349), Durango, N Mexico, in fertile irrigated area, 4 mi. W of Torreón, across Nazas R. Rail terminus; processing and agr. center (cotton, grain, wine, fruit, vegetables, sugar cane, tobacco); cotton ginning, flour milling, fruit canning, wine and liquor making; foundries.

Lerdo de Tejada (lĕr'dō dā tāhä'dä), town (pop. 3,494), Veracruz, SE Mexico, on peninsula bet. Alvarado Lagoon and Gulf of Campeche, opposite mouth of Papaloápam R., 8 mi. SE of Alvarado; agr. center (coffee, sugar cane, fruit, cattle).

Léré (lārā'), village (pop. 497), Cher dept., central France, on Loire Lateral Canal and 5 mi. NNW of Cosne; mfg. of carburetants.

Léré, village, SW Chad territory, Fr. Equatorial Africa, on Mayo-Kebbi R. near Fr. Cameroons boundary, and 90 mi. SW of Bongor; cotton ginning; millet, stock. Cotton weavers' school.

Lere, Nigeria: see LERI.

Lerez River (lārĕth'), Pontevedra prov., NW Spain, rises in Cantabrian Mts. 8 mi. WSW of Lalín, flows 27 mi. WSW to Pontevedra Bay at Pontevedra.

Lerfosse, Norway: see LEIRFOSSE.

Leri (lā'rē), town (pop. 12,232), Bauchi prov., Northern Provinces, E central Nigeria, 55 mi. SW of Bauchi; tin-mining center. Sometimes spelled Lere.

Leribe (lĕrē'bā), village, ⊙ Leribe dist. (pop. 98,269, with absent laborers 112,498), N Basutoland, near Caledon R., on main N–S road and 45 mi. NE of Maseru. Formerly called Hlotse.

Lerici (lā'rēchē), town (pop. 4,148), La Spezia prov., Liguria, N Italy, port on Gulf of Spezia and 5 mi. SE of Spezia, in agr. region (olives, grapes, citrus fruit); sea mussels, oysters. Sea bathing, winter resort. Has 12th-cent. Pisan castle (now a marine observatory).

Lérida (lā'rē-dhä), town (pop. 1,928), Tolima dept., W central Colombia, in Magdalena valley, 6 mi. S of Armero; bananas, yucca, corn, coffee, cotton, rice, tobacco, sugar cane, sheep.

Lérida, province (□ 4,659; pop. 297,440), NE Spain, in Catalonia; ⊙ Lérida. Bounded by France (frontier along crest of central Pyrenees) and Andorra (N). Occupied by S slopes and spurs of the Pyrenees (with several peaks of c.10,000 ft.), by the valley de Arán, by the CERDAÑA, and by the Urgel plain. Drained by the Segre and its tributaries (numerous hydroelectric plants); prov. is greatest producer of hydroelectric energy in Spain. Lignite and some zinc deposits. Predominantly agr.: cereals, olive oil, wine, sugar beets, alfalfa, livestock. Mfg.: cement, hats, soap. Chief towns: Lérida, Balaguer, Borjas Blancas, Cervera, Seo de Urgel.

Lérida, anc. *Ilerda*, fortified city (pop. 35,061), ⊙ Lérida prov., NE Spain, in Catalonia, on Segre R. and 48 mi. NW of Tarragona, in strategic position on Urgel plain, near head of Segre and Cinca valleys, at foot of the central Pyrenees; 41°37'N 0°37'E. Communications and trade center. Mfg. of arms, chemicals (hydrochloric, sulphuric, and nitric acid; copper sulphate), soap, liqueurs, furniture, flour products; olive-oil and wine processing, canning (tomatoes, pepper, fruit), sawmilling. Agr. trade (livestock, cereals, sugar beets, alfalfa, forage). Bishopric. Dominated by castle-crowned hill; within castle's ramparts is Romanesque cathedral (13th cent.), now used as a barracks. Has new cathedral (18th cent.), 13th-cent. church of San Lorenzo, Romanesque town hall, episcopal palace. Of Iberian origin, town was captured (49 B.C.) by Caesar; taken (714) by Moors, liberated (1149) by Christians. Univ. founded here c.1300 by James II of Aragon was transferred in 1717 to Cervera by Philip V. Strategically located, Lérida was the key to Aragon and Catalonia and saw much military action. It was taken by the French in 1707 and 1810. In Sp. civil war, it capitulated to the Nationalists in April, 1938.

Lerik (lyĕ'rĭk), village (1932 pop. estimate 780), SE Azerbaijan SSR, on N slope of Talysh Mts., 23 mi. W of Lenkoran; livestock, wheat, potatoes.

Lerín (lārēn'), town (pop. 2,854), Navarre prov., N Spain, on Ega R. and 13 mi. SSE of Estella; flour milling; sugar beets, cereals, wine.

Lérins, Îles de (ēl dŭ lārē'), island group in the Mediterranean, just off Cap de la Croisette, SE France, administratively in Alpes-Maritimes dept. Consists of Sainte-Marguerite isl. (□ 4/5; 2 mi. long; 3 mi. SE of Cannes) with 17th-cent. fort in which "The Man in the Iron Mask" and Marshal Bazaine were imprisoned; Saint-Honorat isl. (□ 1/4; 4 mi. SE of Cannes) with oldest monastery in W Europe, founded c.400 by St. Honoratus; and 2 minor islets.

Lerma (lĕr'mä), officially Lerma de Villada, city (pop. 1,174), Mexico state, central Mexico, on upper Lerma R. and 28 mi. WSW of Mexico city, 8 mi. E of Toluca, on railroad; alt. 8,780 ft. Cereals, livestock; trout fishing.

Lerma, town (pop. 2,127), Burgos prov., N Spain, on Arlanza R. (affluent of the Duero), on Burgos-Madrid highway and 20 mi. S of Burgos, in fertile region (grapes, cereals, vegetables, livestock); tanning, flour milling, mfg. of chocolate and charcoal. Airfield. Historic town has superb palace (built in early 17th cent. by Cardinal Duke Francisco Gómez de Sandoval), noted col., and convents.

Lerma River, central Mexico, rises on central plateau in Mexico state 15 mi. SE of Toluca, flows NW and W, past Lerma and Ixtlahuaca, and into Guanajuato state, past Acámbaro, Salvatierra, Salamanca, and Pueblo Nuevo, and along Michoacán–Guanajuato border, to E shore of L. Chapala 15 mi. WSW of La Barca. Together with SANTIAGO RIVER (outlet of L. Chapala), considered a continuation of the Lerma, it forms the largest Mexican river system, finally reaching the Pacific. Length to L. Chapala, c.350 mi.; length with the Santiago, c.600 mi. Used extensively for irrigation and hydroelectric power; not navigable. Among its many affluents are Laja R., Apaseo R., the Río Turbio. Linked with L. Yuriria (Guanajuato) and L. Cuitzeo (Michoacán).

Lerma Valley, subandean valley in central Salta prov., Argentina, along Toro R. (irrigation), extending c.30 mi. S from Salta. Grain, fruit, and tobacco are grown. Main centers: Salta, Rosario de Lerma, Cerrillos, Chicoana.

Lerna, village (pop. 304), Coles co., E central Ill., 7 mi. SE of Mattoon, in rich agr. area.

Leros (lĕ'rôs, lē'rŏs), Ital. *Lero* (lā'rō), Aegean island (□ 21.2; pop. 6,131) in the Dodecanese, Greece, just NW of Kalymnos; 37°10'N 26°50'E; 8 mi. long, 1–4 mi. wide. Produces wheat, barley, potatoes, tomatoes, carobs, olives, fruit, wine; livestock raising (sheep, goats). Main town, Leros (pop. 3,010), is on E shore. Isl., used as a naval base by Italians in Second World War, was bombed and bombarded by the British.

Lérouville (lārōōvēl'), village (pop. 1,273), Meuse dept., NE France, on the Canal de l'Est and 3 mi. NW of Commercy; furniture mfg., stone quarrying.

Leroy (lŭroi'), village (pop. 213), S central Sask., 22 mi. SE of Humboldt; mixed farming, dairying.

Le Roy. **1** or **Leroy,** city (pop. 1,820), McLean co., central Ill., 14 mi. SE of Bloomington; trade and processing center in rich agr. area; canned corn, dairy products. Inc. 1857. **2** Town (pop. 91), Decatur co., S Iowa, 20 mi. WSW of Chariton, in livestock area. **3** City (pop. 695), Coffey co., E Kansas, on Neosho R. and 30 mi. NNW of Chanute, in grain area. Walnut timber in vicinity. **4** Village (pop. 243), Osceola co., central Mich., 14 mi. S of Cadillac, in stock-raising area; lake resorts. **5** Village (pop. 959), Mower co., SE Minn., on small affluent of Mississippi R., near Iowa line, and 26 mi. ESE of Austin, in grain, livestock, poultry area; dairy and calcium products. Limestone deposits near by. **6** Village (pop. 4,721), Genesee co., W N.Y., 10 mi. E of Batavia, in rich farm area; mfg. of patent medicines, insulators, machinery, gelatin, textiles, metal and stone products; canning. Salt mines, gypsum quarries. Agr. (dairy products; poultry, fruit). Near by is an egg-laying test farm sponsored by Cornell Univ. Settled 1793, inc. 1834.

Leroy, village (pop. 320), Medina co., N Ohio, 23 mi. WSW of Akron, in dairying area.

Leroy Johnson, Camp, La.: see NEW ORLEANS.

Lerum (lā'rŭm''), residential village (pop. 2,548), Alvsborg co., SW Sweden, on Save R. and 13 mi. ENE of Goteborg; dyeworks. Includes Aspenas (äs'pūnĕs''), Swedish *Aspenäs*, and Hedefors (ha''dūfôrs', -fôsh'), villages.

Lervik, Norway: see LEIRVIK.

Lerwick (lûr'wĭk), burgh (1931 pop. 4,221; 1951 census 5,538), ⊙ Shetland Islands, Scotland, on E coast of Mainland isl., on Bressay Sound, sheltered by Bressay isl.; 60°9'N 1°10'W; port and fishing center (herring, cod, haddock, ling, halibut); hand-knitting industry. Chief exports: butter, cattle, eggs, fish, hides, ponies, sheep, woolen clothing; imports: coal, grain, timber, food products. Town is chief market for the Shetlands. There is a seaplane base. Fort Charlotte, naval reserve station, was built by Cromwell, rebuilt 1665 by Charles II, destroyed 1673 by the Dutch, repaired 1781. Lerwick is scene of annual regatta and of *Uphellya* festival, when the New Year is celebrated by fancy-dress torchlight procession. N of Lerwick is promontory of Easter Rova Head, with lighthouse (60°11'N 1°9'W), marking N entrance to Lerwick harbor.

Lesa (lā'zä), village (pop. 884), Novara prov., Piedmont, N Italy, port on SW shore of Lago Maggiore, 3 mi. S of Stresa, in fruitgrowing region.

Lesaca (läsä'kä), town (pop. 2,104), Navarre prov., N Spain, in Bidassoa valley, 7 mi. SSE of Irún; corn, beans, apples. Iron mines near by.

Lesbos (lĕs'bŏs, lĕz'bŏs) or **Lesvos** (lĕs'vôs), also called **Mytilene** or **Mitilini** (both: mĭtĭlē'nē), for its chief city, Greek Aegean island (□ 632; pop. 134,054) off Asia Minor, athwart entrance to Gulf of Edremit and separated from Turkish mainland by Mytilene (E) and Muselim Remma (N) channels; 39°10'N 25°50'E. Forms, with Lemnos and Hagios Eustratios isls., the nome of Lesbos (□ 836; pop. 159,031; ⊙ Mytilene). Lesbos isl. is roughly triangular (38 mi. long, 22 mi. wide), but deeply indented on S coast by the landlocked gulfs of Gera and Kallone. It rises to 3,176 ft. in the Lepetymnos (Lepetimnos; N) and to 3,175 ft. in the Olympus (S). These forested heights are separated by fertile lowlands, producing grain (mainly wheat), olives, vegetables, citrus fruit, wine, silk, figs, and almonds; livestock raising, sardine and sponge fisheries. Sulphur springs. Mytilene and Plomarion are the chief cities. Airport. Settled by Aeolians, it was known in antiquity as Pentapolis, for its 5 large cities of Mytilene, Methymna, Eresus, Antissa, and Pyrrha, of which the first two contested for leadership. The isl. flourished in late 7th and early 6th cent. as a brilliant center of civilization that produced such figures as the lyric poets Alcaeus and Sappho, the statesman Pittacus, and, in 4th cent., the philosopher Theophrastus. Lesbos joined the Delian League and declined after an unsuccessful revolt against Athens (428–427 B.C.) at the start of the Peloponnesian War. Passed 1354 from Byzantine Empire to Genoese and 1462 to Turks. It joined Greece in 1913.

Lescar (lĕskär'), anc. *Bencharnum*, village (pop. 1,238), Basses-Pyrénées dept., SW France, 4 mi. NW of Pau; produces Basque berets, furniture, woolens; horse breeding. Has large 12th-cent. Romanesque church (cathedral until 1790).

Les Cayes, Haiti: see CAYES, LES.

Les Cheneaux Islands (lā'' shŭnō'), Mich., group of 35 small wooded isls. in L. Huron, just S of SE Upper Peninsula and NE of the Straits of Mackinac; locally called "The Snows." Resort area (boating, fishing, hunting); annual regatta. Commercial fisheries. Largest of group is Marquette Isl. (märkĕt'), c.5 mi. long.

Leschkirch, Rumania: see NOCHRICH.

Leschnitz, Poland: see LESNICA.

Lesconil (lĕskônēl', lākŏnē'), town (pop. 2,482), Finistère dept., W France, on Bay of Biscay, 14 mi. SW of Quimper; sardine, lobster canning; lace making.

Les Coteaux (lā kōtō'), village (pop. 1,002), SW Tobago, B.W.I., 3 mi. N of Scarborough; cacao.

Lescure-d'Albigeois (lĕskür'-dälbēzhwä'), village (pop. 387), Tarn dept., S France, on Tarn R. and 2 mi. NNE of Albi; fruit and vegetable shipping. Until 1941 called Lescure.

Lese (lĕ'shĕ), Slovenian *Leše*, Ger. *Liescha* (lē'shä), hamlet, N Slovenia, Yugoslavia, just SW of Prevalje, near Meza R.; brown-coal mines.

Leseru (lĕsĕ'rōō), town, Rift Valley prov., W Kenya, rail junction for Kitale, 10 mi. NW of Eldoret; alt. 6,489 ft.; coffee, wheat, corn, tea, wattle growing; dairy farming. Sometimes spelled Lesuru.

Lesh (lĕsh) or **Leshi** (lĕ'shē), Ital. *Alessio* (älĕs'sēō), anc. *Lissus*, town (1945 pop. 1,047), N Albania, on left bank and near mouth of old Drin R. arm, 20 mi. SSE of Scutari, on main Tirana-Scutari road. Linked by road with its Adriatic port, Shengjin. Copper mining at Rrubig (7 mi. E). Has ruins of 15th-cent. Venetian citadel with tomb (desecrated by Turks) of Scanderbeg (d. here 1468). Founded (4th cent. B.C.) as a Syracusan colony; held (1393–1478) by Venetians. Sometimes spelled Lezh, Leshë, or Lesha.

Leshara (lŭshâ'rŭ), village (pop. 61), Saunders co., E Nebr., 25 mi. W of Omaha and on Platte R.

Leshem, Palestine: see DAN.

Leshi, Albania: see LESH.

Leshnitsa, Yugoslavia: see LESNICA.

Leshukonskoye (lyĕshŏŏkôn'skŭyŭ), village (1939 pop. over 500), S central Archangel oblast, Russian SFSR, on Mezen R. (head of navigation) and 150 mi. ENE of Archangel; lumbering. Until 1929 also called Ust-Vashka.

Lesichovo (lĕ'sēchôvô), village (pop. 3,112), Plovdiv dist., W central Bulgaria, on Topolnitsa R. and 14 mi. NW of Pazardzhik; vineyards, rice, truck.

Lesignano de' Bagni (lēsēnyä'nô dĕbä'nyē), village (pop. 259), Parma prov., Emilia-Romagna, N central Italy, 11 mi. S of Parma. Hot mineral springs.

Lesima, Monte (môn'tĕ lĕzē'mä), peak (5,656 ft.) in Ligurian Apennines, N central Italy, 9 mi. SSE of Varzi.

Lesina, Yugoslavia: see HVAR; HVAR ISLAND.

Lesina, Lago di (lä'gô dē lā'zēnä), shallow lagoon (□ 20) on N coast of Gargano promontory, S Italy; separated from the Adriatic by a sand bar (2 canals in E); 14 mi. long, 2 mi. wide; fishing; bird hunting. On SW shore is town of Lesina (pop. 3,608).

Lesja (lā'shä), village and canton (pop. 3,107), Opland co., S central Norway, at head of the Gudbrandsdal, on Lagen R., on railroad and 80 mi. SSE of Kristiansund; lumber and flour mills; livestock. Church built 1748. Lesjaverk (lā'shävärk) village, 10 mi. WNW, was site (1650–1812) of iron foundry.

Lesjofors (lā''shû''fôrs', -fôsh'), Swedish *Lesjöfors*, village (pop. 1,763), Varmland co., W Sweden, in Bergslag region, 18 mi. N of Filipstad; iron- and steelworks, lumber mills. Iron-mining region.

Lesken River, Russian SFSR: see STARY LESKEN.

Lesko (lĕ'skô), Ger. *Lisko* (lĭ'skō), town (pop. 2,129), Rzeszow prov., SE Poland, on San R., 8 mi. SE of Sanok.

Leskovac or **Leskovats** (both: lĕ'skôväts), city (pop. 21,765), SE Serbia, Yugoslavia, on railroad and 23 mi. S of Nis, near the Southern Morava; textile mfg. Quince and hemp growing near by; vineyards. Dates from early-19th cent.; under Turkish rule until 1878.

Leskovec, Bulgaria: see LYASKOVETS.

Leskovik (lĕskô'vēk) or **Leskoviku** (lĕskô'vēkōō), village (1945 pop. 1,342), S Albania, 34 mi. SSW of Koritsa, near Gr. border; sulphur springs near.

Leslau, Poland: see WLOCLAWEK.

Leslie, burgh (1931 pop. 2,477; 1951 census 2,612), central Fifeshire, Scotland, 7 mi. NNW of Kirkcaldy; agr. market; paper milling, flax spinning.

Leslie (lĕs'lē), county (□ 412; pop. 15,537), SE Ky.; ⊙ Hyden. In the Cumberlands; drained by Middle Fork Kentucky R. and small Cutshin Creek. Mtn. agr. area, (corn, hay, truck, livestock, fruit, tobacco); timber; bituminous-coal mines. Formed 1878.

Leslie. **1** Town (pop. 610), Searcy co., N Ark., c.50 mi. N of Conway and on Middle Fork of Little Red R.; cooperage. **2** Agr village (pop. 417), Sumter co., SW central Ga., 12 mi. SE of Americus. **3** Village (pop. 1,543), Ingham co., S central Mich., 14 mi. N of Jackson, in agr. area (livestock, poultry, fruit, grain, sugar beets, corn). Settled 1836, inc. 1869. **4** Town (pop. 114), Franklin co., E central Mo., in Ozark region, 15 mi. SW of Washington.

Lesmahagow (lĕsmŭhā'gō), town and parish (pop. 11,661), central Lanark, Scotland, on Nethan R. and 5 mi. SW of Lanark; coal mining. Monks of Lesmahagow introduced Clydeside fruitgrowing industry. Sometimes called Abbey Green, after abbey founded here c.1140 (no remains).

Lesmo (lĕs'mô), village (pop. 1,023), Milano prov., Lombardy, N Italy, near Lambro R., 5 mi. NE of Monza; furniture factory, flax mill.

Lesna (lĕsh'nä), Pol. *Leśna*, Ger. *Marklissa* (märk''-lĭ'sä), town (1939 pop. 2,201; 1946 pop. 1,632) in Lower Silesia, after 1945 in Wroclaw prov., SW Poland, in Upper Lusatia, on Kwisa R. (irrigation dam 2 mi. E) and 15 mi. SE of Görlitz; cotton milling.

Lesna River (lyĕs'nŭ), Pol. *Leśna* (lĕsh'nä), in W Belorussian SSR, rises in 2 branches in Bialowieza Forest joining NW of Kamenets, flows c.90 mi. generally SW, past Kamenets, to Bug R. 9 mi. NW of Brest; logging.

Lesnaya Volchanka, Russian SFSR: see VOLCHANKA.

Lesneven (lĕsnüvĕ'), town (pop. 3,708), Finistère dept., W France, 15 mi. NNE of Brest; market center; horse breeding, woodworking.

Lesnica (lĕsh-nē'kä), Pol. *Leśnica*, Ger. *Bergstadt* (bĕrk'shtät), town (1939 pop. 3,323; 1946 pop. 2,122) in Upper Silesia, after 1945 in Opole prov., S Poland, on Bystrzyca R. and 20 mi. SSE of Oppeln (Opole); leather mfg. Until 1937, called Leschnitz.

Lesnica or **Leshnitsa** (both: lĕsh'nĭtsä), Serbo-Croatian *Lešnica*, village, W Serbia, Yugoslavia, on railroad and 21 mi. SW of Sabac.

Lesnoi or **Lesnoy** (lyĭsnoi'), town (1939 pop. over 2,000), S Murmansk oblast, Russian SFSR, port on Kandalaksha Bay of White Sea, on Kola Peninsula, 60 mi. SE of Kandalaksha; sawmilling, fish canning.

Lesnoye (-noi'ŭ), village (1948 pop. over 2,000), N Kalinin oblast, Russian SFSR, 22 mi. SSW of Pestovo; flax.

Lesnoye Konobeyevo (kŭnŭbyā'ŭvŭ), village (1926 pop. 3,697), E Ryazan oblast, Russian SFSR, on Tsna R. and 17 mi. NE of Shatsk; wheat, hemp. Also called Konobeyevo-Lesnoye.

Lesnyaki or **Lisnyaki** (lyĭsnyä'kē), town (1926 pop. 4,774), NW Poltava oblast, Ukrainian SSR, 55 mi. WNW of Lubny, just S of Yagotin; sugar-refining center.

Lesogorsk (lyĕsŭgôrsk'), city (1940 pop. 18,618), S Sakhalin, Russian SFSR, on Tatar Strait, 100 mi. S of Aleksandrovsk; coal mining; sawmill, fisheries. Hot springs near by. Under Jap. rule (1905–45), called Nayoshi or Kita-nayoshi (kē'tä-näyō'shē).

Lesogorski or **Lesogorskiy** (-gôr'skē), town (1940 pop. over 500), NW Leningrad oblast, Russian SFSR, on Vuoksi R. and 23 mi. NNE of Vyborg; sawmilling, pulp milling, artificial-silk mfg. Its Finnish name was Jääski, Rus. *Yaski;* town passed to USSR in 1940 and in 1948 was renamed.

Lesopilnoye or **Lesopil'noye** (lyĕsŭpēl'nŭyŭ), town (1948 pop. over 2,000), S Khabarovsk Territory, Russian SFSR, on Trans-Siberian RR (Zvenyevoi station), on Bikin R. and 5 mi. SE of Bikin; sawmilling.

Lesozavodsk (lyĕs''ŭzŭvôtsk'), city (1936 pop. estimate 10,500), W Maritime Territory, Russian SFSR, on Trans-Siberian RR (Ussuri station), on Ussuri R. (head of navigation) and 135 mi. NNE of Voroshilov; sawmilling center. Railroad shops in Ruzhino, its N suburb. Developed in 1930s.

Lesozavodski or **Lesozavodskiy** (-vôt'skē). **1** Town (1939 pop. over 2,000), central Kirov oblast, Russian SFSR, on Vyatka R. and 5 mi. SSE of Kirov; sawmilling center. Until 1939, Grukhi. **2** Town (1941 pop. over 500), SW Murmansk oblast, Russian SFSR, on isl. in Kandalaksha Bay of White Sea, 2 mi. N of Kovda; sawmilling.

Lesparre-Médoc (lĕspär'-mādôk'), village (pop. 1,837), Gironde dept., SW France, 37 mi. NNW of Bordeaux; market center (wines, fruits, vegetables); distilling, fertilizer mfg. Formerly named Lesparre.

Lesparrou (lĕspärōō'), village (pop. 194), Ariège dept., S France, 17 mi. E of Foix; plaster, combs.

L'Esperance (lĕspärāns'), village on W coast of Mahé Isl., Seychelles, on the Anse à la Mouche (inlet of Indian Ocean), 8 mi. S of Victoria; copra, essential oils; fisheries.

L'Espérance Rock, New Zealand: see KERMADEC ISLANDS.

Lesquin (lĕskē'), S suburb (pop. 3,361) of Lille, Nord dept., N France; steel milling, meat salting. Airport.

Lessay (lĕsā'), village (pop. 390), Manche dept., NW France, near the Channel, 13 mi. NNW of Coutances; dairying, sawmilling. Airport. The 11th–12th-cent. Romanesque church of abbey founded c.1050 damaged in Second World War.

Lesse, river, Belgium: see LESSE RIVER.

Lessebo (lĕ'sŭbōō''), town (pop. 2,277), Kronoberg co., S Sweden, on small L. Lae, Swedish *Laen* (lä'ĕn), 20 mi. ESE of Vaxjo; paper, pulp, and sawmilling.

Lessen, Belgium: see LESSINES.

Lessen, Poland: see LASIN.

Lessenbosch, Belgium: see BOIS-DE-LESSINES.

Lesser, in Rus. names: see also MALAYA, MALOMALOYE, MALY, MALYE.

Lesser Antilles, West Indies: see ANTILLES.

Lesser Anyui River, Russian SFSR: see ANYUI.

Lesser Balkhan Range, Turkmen SSR: see BALKHAN.

Lesser Cheremshan River, Russian SFSR: see GREATER CHEREMSHAN RIVER.

Lesser Fatra or **Lesser Fatra Mountains** (fä'trä), Slovak *Malá Fatra* (mä'lä), Hung. *Kis Fátra* (kĭsh fä'trŏ), mountain range of the Carpathians, NW Slovakia, Czechoslovakia; extend c.40 mi. NE-SW, along both banks of upper Vah R., SE of Zilina; rise to 5,612 ft. in Maly Krivan.

Lesser Irgiz River, Russian SFSR: see IRGIZ, rivers.

Lesse River (lĕs), SE Belgium, rises just W of Libramont, flows 50 mi. NW, past Han-sur-Lesse and Wanlin, to Meuse R. just S of Dinant. Its course near Han is subterranean, traversing series of limestone caves.

Lesser Kas River, Russian SFSR: see KAS RIVER.

Lesser Kemin River, Kirghiz SSR: see KEMIN.

Lesser Khingan Mountains, Manchuria: see KHINGAN MOUNTAINS.

Lesser Kinel River, Russian SFSR: see GREATER KINEL RIVER.

Lesser Kokshaga River (kŭkshŭgä'), Rus. *Malaya Kokshaga*, in Mari Autonomous SSR, Russian SFSR, rises 17 mi. WNW of Novy Toryal, flows c.125 mi. S, past Ioshkar-Ola, to the Volga 8 mi. ESE of (opposite) Mariinski Posad; lumber floating. Receives Lesser Kundysh R. (left). Also called Kokshaga.

Lesser Kundysh River (kŏŏndĭsh′), Rus. *Maly Kundysh*, in Mari Autonomous SSR, Russian SFSR, rises 13 mi. S of Novy Toryal, flows c.50 mi. SW to Lesser Kokshaga R. 20 mi. S of Ioshkar-Ola; lumber floating. Also called Lower Kundysh, Rus. *Nizhni Kundysh*, or simply Kundysh.

Lesser Northern Dvina River (dvēnä′), Rus. *Malaya Severnaya Dvina*, NW European Russian SFSR; formed by junction of Sukhona and Yug rivers at Veliki Ustyug; flows N, past Krasavino, joining Vychegda R. at Kotlas to become Northern Dvina R. proper. The name Sukhona is sometimes applied to the Lesser Northern Dvina.

Lesser Slave Lake (□ 461), central Alta., 130 mi. NNW of Edmonton; 60 mi. long, 3–12 mi. wide. Drains E to Athabaska R. by short Lesser Slave R.

Lesser Sundas, Indonesia: see SUNDA ISLANDS.

Lesser Tsivil River, Russian SFSR: see TSIVIL.

Lesser Uzen River, Russian SFSR: see UZEN.

Lesser Walachia, Rumania: see WALACHIA.

Lesser Yenisei River, Russian SFSR: see YENISEI RIVER.

Lessines (lĕsēn′), Flemish *Lessen* (lĕ′sŭn), town (pop. 9,906), Hainaut prov., SW central Belgium, on Dender R. and 6 mi. NNE of Ath; porphyry-quarrying center; mfg. (matches, electric lamps); processing of chicory, medicinal herbs.

Lessini, Monti (môn′tē lĕs-sē′nē), mountain group, N Italy, separated from Monte Baldo group by Adige R. Rises to 7,424 ft. in Cima Carega. Marble and limestone quarries.

Lessudden, Scotland: see SAINT BOSWELLS.

Lesten, Poland: see CZERNINA.

Lester. 1 Town (pop. 217), Lyon co., NW Iowa, 8 mi. W of Rock Rapids; livestock, grain. **2** Town (pop. 780), Raleigh co., S W.Va., 7 mi. WSW of Beckley; semibituminous-coal area.

Lester Prairie, village (pop. 663), McLeod co., S central Minn., on South Fork Crow R. and 16 mi. E of Hutchinson; dairy products.

Lesterville, town (pop. 192), Yankton co., SE S.Dak., 15 mi. NW of Yankton.

Lestock, village (pop. 316), SE central Sask., 65 mi. NNE of Regina; wheat, dairying.

Le Sueur (lŭ sŏŏr′), county (□ 441; pop. 19,088), S Minn.; ⊙ Le Center. Agr. area bordered W by Minnesota R. Livestock, corn, oats, barley, dairy products. Formed 1853.

Le Sueur, city (pop. 2,713), Le Sueur co., S Minn., on Minnesota R. and c.45 mi. SW of Minneapolis; trading center in grain, livestock, poultry area; food processing (dairy products, canned corn and peas, cattle feed); cement products. Settled 1852.

Le Sueur Center, Minn.: see LE CENTER.

Le Sueur River, rises in Freeborn co., S Minn., flows 80 mi. N and W, past St. Clair, to Blue Earth R. just S of Mankato.

Lesuru, Kenya: see LESERU.

Lesvos, Greece: see LESBOS.

Leswalt (lĕswôlt′), agr. village and parish (pop. 2,376, including part of Stranraer burgh), W Wigtown, Scotland, on the Rhinns of Galloway, just NW of Stranraer.

Leszno (lĕsh′nô), Ger. *Lissa* (lĭ′sä), city (pop. 20,820), Poznan prov., W Poland, 40 mi. SSW of Poznan. Rail junction; trade center; mfg. of machinery, railroad cars, pianos, candy; flour milling, brewing, sawmilling, tanning; grain and cattle trade. Chalk quarries, lignite deposits near by. City passed (1793, 1815) to Prussia; returned to Poland in 1919.

L'Étang du Nord, Que.: see ÉTANG DU NORD.

Letcher, county (□ 339; pop. 39,522), SE Ky.; ⊙ Whitesburg. In the Cumberlands; bounded E and SE by Va.; drained by North Fork Kentucky R. and Poor Fork of Cumberland R. Includes part of Pine Mtn. Important bituminous-coal mining area; clay, sand, and gravel pits, stone quarries, timber; some agr. (dairy products, poultry, livestock, corn, soybeans, apples, sweet and Irish potatoes, tobacco). Formed 1842.

Letcher, town (pop. 291), Sanborn co., SE central S.Dak., 15 mi. NNW of Mitchell; trade center for diversified farming region; corn, hogs, poultry.

Letchworth, urban district (1931 pop. 14,454; 1951 census 20,321), N Hertford, England, 14 mi. NNW of Hertford; planned industrial garden city founded 1903 by Sir Ebenezer Howard. Has varied light industries (light metals, machine tools, silk, scientific instruments, food products, pharmaceuticals). Its printing and book-mfg. industry is important. Has 15th-cent. church.

Letchworth State Park, N.Y.: see GENESEE RIVER.

Letchworth Village, N.Y.: see HAVERSTRAW.

Letea, Rumania: see BACAU, city.

Letea Island (lĕ′tyä) or **Leti Island** (lĕ′tē), marshy island (c.40 mi. long, 18 mi. wide) in Danube delta on Black Sea coast of Rumania, formed by Kiliya arm (N) and Sulina arm (S).

Letellier (lŭtĕlyā′, lŭtĕl′yă), village (pop. estimate 800), SE Man., on Marais R. and 11 mi. NW of Emerson; grain, stock.

Letenye (lĕ′tĕnyĕ), town (pop. 4,348), Zala co., W Hungary, 13 mi. W of Nagykanizsa; potatoes, grain, hogs.

Lethbridge (lĕth′brĭj), city (pop. 16,522), S Alta., near Mont. border, on Oldman R. and 100 mi. SE of Calgary, in foothills of the Rockies; coal-mining center and distributing point for S Alta. and SE B.C., in irrigated farming, ranching, and lumbering region. Has grain elevators, canneries, dehydrating plants, cereal-food, clothing, and knitting mills. Royal Canadian Mounted Police hq. for Alta. Site of Dominion experimental station and technical school. SW of city is Blood Indian reservation. In early 1870s coal mining was begun here, supplying fuel to Fort Macleod; subsequent mining settlement was called Coalbanks. Name was changed 1885 to Lethbridge.

Lethem (lĕ′thŭm), village, ⊙ Rupununi dist., Essequibo co., S Br. Guiana, on Brazil border, 45 mi. NNW of Dadanawa, on Rupununi cattle trail. Airfield. Formerly called Bon Success.

Leti (lĕ′tē), island (□ 48; pop. 6,078), Leti Isls., S Moluccas, Indonesia, in Banda Sea, just W of Moa, 25 mi. E of Timor; 11 mi. long, 5 mi. wide; coconut growing, fishing.

Letichev (lyĭtyē′chĭf), town (1926 pop. 7,160), E Kamenets-Podolski oblast, Ukrainian SSR, on the Southern Bug and 28 mi. E of Proskurov; food processing, cotton milling.

Leticia (lātēs′yä), town (pop. 1,674), ⊙ Amazonas commissary, extreme SE Colombia, on upper Amazon R., at Peru and Brazil borders, and 665 mi. SE of Bogotá, 300 mi. E of Iquitos (Peru), 3 mi. NNW of Sapurara (Brazil). Only Colombian port on the Amazon, it is military outpost and airfield in forested tropical lowlands at S tip of the *Leticia Trapezium*. This area, bet. Amazon and Putumayo rivers, confirmed as Colombian territory by a treaty (1922) with Peru, was seized Sept. 1, 1932, by Peruvian irregulars; the resulting dispute was settled by the League of Nations, which in 1934 restored the territory to Colombia.

Leti Island, Rumania: see LETEA ISLAND.

Leti Islands or **Letti Islands** (both: lĕ′tē), group (□ c.290; pop. c.11,300), S Moluccas, Indonesia, in Banda Sea, off E tip of Timor; 8°20′S 127°57′E. Comprise MOA (largest isl.), LAKOR, LETI, and several islets. Isls. are hilly and forested. Cattle raising, agr. (rice, tobacco), copra producing, fishing.

Letiny, Czechoslovakia: see BLOVICE.

Letka (lyĕt′kŭ), village (1948 pop. over 500), SW Komi Autonomous SSR, Russian SFSR, on Letka R. (right affluent of upper Vyatka R.) and 70 mi. N of Kirov; flax, potatoes.

Letmathe (lāt′mä″tŭ), town (pop. 10,538), in former Prussian prov. of Westphalia, W Germany, after 1945 in North Rhine-Westphalia, on the Lenne and 4 mi. W of Iserlohn; rail junction; limestone works. Zinc mining.

Letnany, Czechoslovakia: see CAKOVICE.

Letnerechenski or **Letnerechenskiy** (lyĕ″tnyĭryĕ′chĭnskē), town (1939 pop. over 500), E Karelo-Finnish SSR, on Murmansk RR (Letni station) and 18 mi. SW of Belomorsk; sawmilling; mfg. of prefabricated houses.

Letnitsa (lĕt′nĕtsä), village (pop. 5,253), Pleven dist., N Bulgaria, on Vit R. and 5 mi. SW of Levski; flour milling; livestock, poultry.

Letnyaya Stavka (lyĕt′nyŭ stäf′kŭ) [Rus.,=(nomad) summer hq.], village (1926 pop. 362), central Stavropol Territory, Russian SFSR, 20 mi. N of Blagodarnoye; cattle and sheep raising. Pop. largely Turkmen.

Letoianni (lĕtŏyän′nē), village (pop. 2,135), Messina prov., E Sicily, port on Ionian Sea, 3 mi. NNE of Taormina; citrus extracts.

Letona (lŭtō′nŭ), town (pop. 164), White co., central Ark., 9 mi. NW of Searcy.

Letopolis, Egypt: see AUSIM.

Letovice (lĕ′tôvĭtsĕ), Ger. *Lettowitz* (lĕ′tōvĭts), village (pop. 3,357), W Moravia, Czechoslovakia, on Svitava R., on railroad, and 24 mi. N of Brno; woolen, cotton textiles. Graphite mining near by.

Letpadan (lĕtpŭdän′), town (pop. 12,160), Tharrawaddy dist., Lower Burma, on Rangoon-Mandalay RR and 70 mi. NNW of Rangoon; head of railroad to Tharrawaw.

Letras, Costa Rica: see PUERTO LETRAS.

Letrini, Greece: see PYRGOS.

Letrinoi, Greece: see PYRGOS.

Let River, Swedish *Letälven* (lāt′ĕl″vŭn), S central Sweden, rises S of Vansbro, flows 100 mi. generally S, through L. Mockel, past Degerfors, to L. Skager 10 mi. WNW of Laxa.

Lettelingen, Belgium: see PETIT-ENGHIEN.

Letter (lĕ′tŭr), village (pop. 5,581), in former Prussian prov. of Hanover, W Germany, after 1945 in Lower Saxony, bet. Leine R. and Weser-Elbe Canal, 4 mi. NW of Hanover city center.

Letterkenny (lĕ″tŭrkĕ′nē), Gaelic *Leitir Ceanainn*, urban district (pop. 2,848), E central Co. Donegal, Ireland, at head of Lough Swilly, at mouth of Swilly R., 17 mi. W of Londonderry; fishing port, agr. market (flax, oats, potatoes; cattle, sheep). Has cathedral completed 1901.

Lettermore (lĕ″tŭrmôr′), Gaelic *Leitir Mór*, island (2,253 acres; 4 mi. long, 1½ mi. wide) in Kilkieran Bay, inlet of Galway Bay, SW Co. Galway, Ireland, 25 mi. W of Galway, just N of Gorumna isl.

Lettermullen or **Lettermullan** (both: lĕ″tŭrmŭ′lŭn), Gaelic *Leitir Mealláin*, island (829 acres; 3 mi. long, 2 mi. wide), in Kilkieran Bay, inlet of Galway Bay, SW Co. Galway, Ireland, 28 mi. W of Galway, just W of Gorumna isl.

Letti Islands, Indonesia: see LETI ISLANDS.

Lettland: see LATVIA.

Letts, town (pop. 404), Louisa co., SE Iowa, 12 mi. WSW of Muscatine; livestock, grain.

Letur (lātŏŏr′), town (pop. 1,861), Albacete prov., SE central Spain, 25 mi. WSW of Hellín; olive-oil processing, flour milling, basket mfg. Honey, esparto, cereals.

Letzeburg, Luxembourg: see LUXEMBOURG, city.

Leubnitz (loip′nĭts), village (pop. 5,495), Saxony, E central Germany, just S of Werdau; textile milling (cotton, wool, silk).

Leubus (loi′bŏŏs) or **Lubiaz** (lŏŏ′byŏsh), Pol. *Lubiąż*, village in Lower Silesia, after 1945 in Wroclaw prov., SW Poland, on the Oder and 14 mi. ENE of Liegnitz (Legnica). Has former Cistercian monastery, founded c.1175, rebuilt 18th cent., secularized 1810. Sacked 1432 by Hussites and (1639), in Thirty Years War, by Swedes.

Leucadia, island, Greece: see LEUKAS.

Leucadia, Cape, Greece: see DOUKATO, CAPE.

Leucallec Island, Chile: see GUAITECAS ISLANDS.

Leucas, Greece: see LEUKAS.

Leucate (lûkät′), village (pop. 1,009), Aude dept., S France, near the coast, 16 mi. NNE of Perpignan; distilling. Leucate lagoon, extending 9 mi. S into Pyrénées-Orientales dept., is swampy area regularly flooded by seawater.

Leucayec Island, Chile: see GUAITECAS ISLANDS.

Leuchars (lŏŏkh′ŭrz), town and parish (pop. 3,221), NE Fifeshire, Scotland, near Eden R. estuary, 5 mi. NW of St. Andrews; agr. market. Has 12th-cent. church with 17th-cent. belfry. On Eden R., 2 mi. S, is paper-milling village of Guard Bridge.

Leuchtenberg (loikh′tŭnbĕrk), village (pop. 686), Upper Palatinate, E Bavaria, Germany, in Bohemian Forest, 7 mi. SE of Weiden; grain, livestock. Has ruins of 14th-cent. castle.

Leuctra (lŏŏk′trŭ), anc. city of Boeotia, Greece, 9 mi. SW of Thebes. Here the Thebans, under Epaminondas, defeated the Spartans in 371 B.C. and assumed hegemony over Greece. On site is modern village of Leuktra or Levktra (pop. 1,202), formerly called Parapoungia.

Leuk (loik), Fr. *Loèche* (lôĕsh′), town (pop. 2,242), Valais canton, S Switzerland, on the Rhone and 14 mi. ENE of Sion. Resort village of Leukerbad is 4 mi. N.

Leuka, Cyprus: see LEFKA.

Leuka, Mount, or **Mount Levka** (both: lĕf′kŭ), highest peak (8,045 ft.) of W Crete, 15 mi. S of Canea. Also called Madares.

Leukas or **Levkas** (lū′kŭs, Gr. lĕf′kŭs), Lat. *Leucas* or *Leucadia* (lūkā′dēŭ), Ital. *Santa Maura* (sän′tä mou′rä), island (□ 114; pop. 28,980) of Ionian group, Greece, in Ionian Sea, off Acarnania; forms (with isls. of ITHACA and MEGANESI) a nome (□ 214; pop. 39,476) of Epirus-Corfu div.; ⊙ Leukas. Separated (NE) by a narrow channel (⅓–3 mi. wide) from mainland, isl. is 20 mi. long, 8 mi. wide; rises to 3,743 ft. in limestone ridge terminating S in Cape Doukato. Agr.: currants, wine, olive oil; tobacco. Salines near Leukas, chief urban center (NE). Sometimes identified with anc. Ithaca, Leukas was settled (7th cent. B.C.) by Corinth, sided with Corinth in Peloponnesian War, and joined (3d cent. B.C.) the Acarnanian League. Passed to Rome 197 B.C. In early Middle Ages it was ruled with Cephalonia and Zante by various Ital. families (Orsini, Tocco) and became known as Santa Maura. It was seized 1477 by the Turks and passed 1684 to Venice. Its later history is that of the Ionian Isls. Sometimes spelled Lefkas.

Leukas or **Levkas**, Lat. *Leucas*, town (pop. 5,816), ⊙ Leukas nome, Greece, on NE end of Leukas isl., on channel separating isl. from Acarnanian mainland; trade center; salines. Connected by road across lagoon with Venetian fort of Santa Maura. Seat of Gr. metropolitan. Site of anc. city was 2 mi. S.

Leukerbad (loi′kŭrbät), Fr. *Loèche-les-Bains* (lôĕsh′-lā-bē′), village (pop. 514), Valais canton, S Switzerland, on short Dala R., 4 mi. N of Leuk; mtn. resort (alt. 4,630 ft.) noted for curative thermal springs. Gemmi Pass is N.

Leukimme or **Levkimmi** (both: lĕfkē′mē), town (pop. 3,043), S Corfu isl., Greece, 17 mi. SSE of Corfu city; olive oil, wine, citrus fruits. Also spelled Lefkimmi.

Leukosia, Cyprus: see NICOSIA.

Leuna (loi′nä), town (pop. 9,918), in former Prussian Saxony prov., central Germany, after 1945 in Saxony-Anhalt, near the Saxonian Saale, 3 mi. S of Merseburg; integrated synthetic-chemical mfg. center (oil, nitrogen, nitrates, sulphuric acid, fibers); lignite mining. Power station. First Ger. synthetic-nitrogen plant (Haber-Bosch process) established here in 1916. Chemical installations heavily bombed in Second World War; subsequently repaired.

Leutenberg (loi′tŭnbĕrk), town (pop. 2,278), Thuringia, central Germany, in Thuringian Forest, 7 mi. SE of Saalfeld; woodworking, paper and cardboard milling; slate quarrying. Towered over by ruins of Friedensburg castle (15th–17th cent.).

Leutersdorf (loi′tŭrsdôrf), village (pop. 3,925), Saxony, E central Germany, in Upper Lusatia, in Lusatian Mts., 8 mi. NW of Zittau, near Czechoslovak border; cotton and linen milling.

Leutershausen (loi″tůrs-hou′zůn). **1** Village (pop. 3,013), N Baden, Germany, after 1945 in Württemberg-Baden, 8 mi. E of Mannheim; wine. **2** Town (pop. 2,075), Middle Franconia, W Bavaria, Germany, on the Altmühl and 7 mi. W of Ansbach; mfg. of metal products and textiles; tanning, brewing, lumber and flour milling. Grain, hops.

Leuthen (loi′tůn) or **Lutynia** (lōōtĭn′yä), village in Lower Silesia, after 1945 in Wroclaw prov., SW Poland, 11 mi. W of Breslau (Wroclaw). Here, in 1757, Austrians defeated by Prussians under Frederick the Great. After 1945, briefly called Litom.

Leutkirch (loit′kĭrkh″), town (pop. 5,601), S Württemberg, Germany, after 1945 in Württemberg-Hohenzollern, 19 mi. ENE of Ravensburg; rail junction; dairying.

Leutschau, Czechoslovakia: see LEVOCA.

Leuven, Belgium: see LOUVAIN.

Leuze (lûz), town (pop. 6,569), Hainaut prov., W Belgium, on branch of Dender R. and 10 mi. E of Tournai; artificial silk, textiles.

Leva, Czechoslovakia: see LEVICE.

Levack, town (pop. 895), SE central Ont., 21 mi. WNW of Sudbury; nickel and copper mining.

Levadia, Levadeia, or **Levadhia** (all: lĕvä′dhēů), Lat. *Lebadea* (lĕbůdē′ů) city (pop. 12,368), ⊙ Boeotia nome, E central Greece, on railroad and NW of Athens, 38°25′N 22°54′E. Cotton and woolen milling center; trade in wheat, cotton, tobacco, wine. Anc. Lebadea was the site of the oracle of Trophonios, a Boeotian god. It flourished in Middle Ages and was an administrative center of central Greece under Turkish rule. Sometimes spelled Livadia.

Levallois-Perret (lůvälwä′-pĕrā′), city (pop. 61,348), Seine dept., N central France, just NW of Paris, 4 mi. from Notre Dame Cathedral, on right bank of Seine R.; industrial center mfg. automobile and electrical equipment, arms, precision instruments, pharmaceuticals, perfumes; rail yards, workshops.

Leval-Trahegnies (lůväl-trähĕnyē′), town (pop. 6,230), Hainaut prov., Belgium, 10 mi. W of Charleroi; coal mining; glass mfg., metal industry.

Levan (lůvăn′), town (pop. 521), Juab co., central Utah, 10 mi. SSW of Nephi; alt. 5,163 ft.; dry farming.

Levanger (lăväng′ůr), town (pop. 1,678), Nord-Trondelag co., central Norway, port on E shore of Trondheim Fjord, on railroad and 35 mi. NE of Trondheim; manufactures textiles, mirrors; exports lumber. Has teachers col. Mentioned in 1247 as Lifangr; inc. 1836; rebuilt after fire in 1897. Alstadhaug church (4 mi. SW) antedates 1250.

Levanna, Monte (mōn′tā lävän′nä), peak (12,070 ft.) in Graian Alps, on French-Italian border, SW of the Gran Paradiso; 45°24′N 7°10′E.

Levant (lůvănt′) [=east], a name applied to the countries along the E shore of the Mediterranean and including all the bordering countries, i.e., Greece, Turkey, Syria, Lebanon, Palestine, and Egypt. In a more restricted sense it refers only to the non-European coastlands. The parts of the former Fr. mandate over Syria and Lebanon were called the Levant States.

Levant (lĕvănt′), agr. town (pop. 706), Penobscot co., S Maine, 8 mi. NW of Bangor.

Levant, Île du (ēl dü lůvä′), island (5 mi. long, 1 mi. wide), easternmost of Hyères isls., in Mediterranean off S coast of France, 18 mi. ESE of Hyères; a rocky and barren hogback. Reached from Le Lavandou (9 mi. NNW). Captured in Allied assault landing, Aug., 1944.

Levanto (lä′väntô), town (pop. 2,948), La Spezia prov., Liguria, N Italy, port on Gulf of Genoa and 12 mi. NW of Spezia, in olive- and grape-growing region; resort. Has Gothic church (1232), Franciscan convent (1449). Marble, sandstone, serpentine quarries near by.

Levanzo (lä′väntsô), anc. *Phorbantia* (□ 2; pop. 330), one of Egadi Isls., in Mediterranean Sea off W Sicily, 9 mi. W of Trapani; 3 mi. long; rises to 912 ft. Major tunny fisheries. Chief port, Levanzo, on S coast.

Levashi (lyĕvůshē′), village (1926 pop. 1,614), E central Dagestan Autonomous SSR, Russian SFSR, in Gimry Range, on road and 30 mi. SSE of Buinaksk; grain, sheep. Pop. largely Darghin.

Levasy (lĕ′vůsē), town (pop. 139), Jackson co., W Mo., 25 mi. NE of Kansas City.

Levaya Rossosh or **Levaya Rossosh'** (lyĕ′vĭů rô′-sůsh), village (1926 pop. 4,145), central Voronezh oblast, Russian SFSR, 25 mi. SSE of Voronezh; wheat, sunflowers.

Level Island, Chile: see CHONOS ARCHIPELAGO.

Levelland (lĕ′vůlănd″), town (pop. 8,264), ⊙ Hockley co., NW Texas, on the Llano Estacado, 30 mi. W of Lubbock; trade, shipping, processing center for cotton, grain, fruit, truck, dairying, livestock region, with oil wells; oil refinery. Founded 1921, inc. 1926.

Levelock, village (pop. 76), SW Alaska, near Naknek.

Level Park, village (pop. 1,364, with adjacent Oak Park), Calhoun co., S Mich., 7 mi. NW of Battle-creek.

Levels, New Zealand: see TIMARU.

Leven (lē′vůn), burgh (1931 pop. 7,411; 1951 census 8,868), E Fifeshire, Scotland, on the Firth of Forth at mouth of Leven R., 19 mi. NNE of Edinburgh; coal-shipping port and seaside resort, with steel and paper mills, metallurgical, chemical engineering works.

Leven, Loch (lŏkh). **1** Sea inlet bet. Argyll and Inverness, Scotland, extending 9 mi. E from Loch Linnhe at Ballachulish; up to 1 mi. wide. Receives Coe R. and, at Kinlochleven, at head of loch, the canalized Leven R. (16 mi. long), which supplies hydroelectric power station at Kinlochleven. On S shore is GLENCOE. **2** Lake (□ 8) in E Kinross, Scotland; 4 mi. long, 3 mi. wide. Among its isls. are Castle Isl., 2 mi. E of Kinross, with remains of 15th-cent. Lochleven Castle, scene of imprisonment of Mary Queen of Scots in 1567–68, and St. Serf's Isl., with ruins of anc. priory. The loch is noted for its pink trout. Outlet: Leven R.

Leven River (lē′vůn), Westmorland and Lancashire, England, rises in L. Windemere, flows 11 mi. SW and S to Morecambe Bay just E of Ulverston.

Leven River. 1 In Dumbarton, Scotland, issues from S end of Loch Lomond at Balloch, flows 7 mi. S, past Jamestown, Alexandria, and Bonhill, to the Clyde at Dumbarton. Its valley is center of textile printing and dyeing industry. **2** In Kinross and Fife, Scotland, rises at SE end of Loch Leven, flows 15 mi. E to Firth of Forth at Leven.

Leven River, N Tasmania, rises SE of Waratah, flows 50 mi. NE to Bass Strait at Ulverstone, on N coast.

Levens (lĕ′vůnz), village and parish (pop. 733), S Westmorland, England, on Kent R. and 4 mi. SSW of Kendal; sheep raising, agr.

Levens (lăvās′), village (pop. 361), Alpes-Maritimes dept., SE France, near the Vésubie, 11 mi. N of Nice; olive-oil processing.

Levenshulme (lē′vůnz-hūm), SE suburb (pop. 19,869) of Manchester, SE Lancashire, England; cotton milling, carpet weaving, mfg. of machine tools, chemicals, soap, pharmaceuticals.

Leventina (lāvĕntē′nä), district (pop. 9,046), Ticino canton, S Switzerland. The Valle Leventina, Ger. *Livinental,* follows Ticino R. from Airolo to Biasca. Main town, Faido.

Leventué, Argentina: see VICTORICA.

Leveque, Cape (lůvĕk′), N Western Australia, in Indian Ocean, at W end of King Sound; 16°23′S 122°55′E; lighthouse.

Leverano (lĕvĕrä′nô), town (pop. 6,546), Lecce prov., Apulia, S Italy, 10 mi. WSW of Lecce; agr. center (wine, olive oil, cheese, wheat, tobacco).

Leverburgh, Scotland: see HARRIS.

Leverett, town (pop. 791), Franklin co., N central Mass., 11 mi. NNE of Northampton.

Leverger, Brazil: see SANTO ANTÔNIO DO LEVERGER.

Levering (lĕ′vůrĭng), village (pop. c.325), Emmet co., NW Mich., 11 mi. SSW of Mackinaw City, in lake region; ships farm produce.

Leverington (lĕv′rĭngtůn), town and parish (pop. 1,981), in Isle of Ely, N Cambridge, England, just NW of Wisbech; agr. market in fruitgrowing region, with flour mills. Has 13th-cent. church.

Leverkusen (lā″vůrkōō′zůn), town (pop. 64,758), in former Prussian Rhine Prov., W Germany, after 1945 in North Rhine-Westphalia, port on right bank of the Rhine, at mouth of Wupper R., and 16 mi. SE of Düsseldorf; 51°1′N 7°E. A center of Ger. chemical industry, mfg. dyes (basic, direct, acid, alizarin, vat), sulphuric and nitric acid, chlorine, pharmaceuticals, explosives, fertilizer. Ironworks and -foundries (machinery, fire extinguishers, electrical measuring devices, scythes); textiles. Formed 1930 through incorporation of town of Wiesdorf and 4 neighboring villages.

Leverville (lāvârvēl′), village, Leopoldville prov., SW Belgian Congo, on left bank of Kwenge R. and 13 mi. NNW of Kikwit; major palm-products center; palm-oil milling. Has R.C. missions, hospitals for Europeans and natives, mechanical and other trade schools for natives.

Levet (lůvā′), village (pop. 517), Cher dept., central France, 11 mi. S of Bourges; livestock, grains; woodworking; minor iron deposits near by.

Levetsova, Greece: see KROKEAI.

Lévézou (lāvāzōō′), barren mountain range of Aveyron dept., S France, in Massif Central, extends c.15 mi. S–N bet. Tarn and Aveyron rivers just W of Millau. Rises to 3,800 ft. Sheep raising. Sometimes spelled Lévezou.

Levi, village (1940 pop. 1,442), Kanawha co., W W.Va., on Kanawha R. and 6 mi. SE of Charleston, in bituminous-coal region.

Lévi, Cape (lāvē′), headland of NW France, on the Channel, on N shore of Cotentin Peninsula, Manche dept., 8 mi. NE of Cherbourg; 49°42′N 1°28′W. Lighthouse.

Levice (lĕ′vĭtsĕ), Hung. *Léva* (lā′vŏ), town (pop. 11,749), S Slovakia, Czechoslovakia, 25 mi. ESE of Nitra; rail junction; major grain and cattle market. Has picturesque 18th-cent. castle ruins. Several villages in vicinity are noted for colorful regional costumes. In Hungary, 1938-45.

Levico (lā′vēkô), village (pop. 3,454), Trento prov., Trentino–Alto Adige, N Italy, 10 mi. SE of Trent, in Valsugana, near Lago di Levico (1.5 mi. long; a source of Brenta R.). Resort (alt. 1,660) with mineral springs.

Levidi or **Levidhi** (both: lĭvē′dhē), anc. *Elymia* (ĕlĭ′mēů), town (pop. 3,142), Arcadia nome, central Peloponnesus, Greece, 13 mi. NNW of Tripolis; wheat, tobacco, livestock (sheep, goats). Scene of Gr. victory over Turks (1821). Sometimes Levidhion or Levidion.

Levie (lůvē′), town (pop. 2,715), S central Corsica, 10 mi. NE of Sartène.

Levier (lůvyā′), village (pop. 1,146), Doubs dept., E France, in the Jura, 12 mi. WNW of Pontarlier; lumbering, cheese mfg.

Levikha (lyĕ′vĭkhů), town (1935 pop. estimate 2,100), SW central Sverdlovsk oblast, Russian SFSR, 12 mi. NNW (under jurisdiction) of Kirovgrad; rail-spur terminus; copper- and zinc-mining center, supplying Kirovgrad refinery; sawmilling.

Levin, Czechoslovakia: see USTEK.

Levin (lůvĭn′), borough (pop. 3,259), ⊙ Horowhenua co. (□ 544; pop. 7,754), S N.Isl., New Zealand, 50 mi. NNE of Wellington; dairies, sawmills.

Lévis (lē′vĭs, Fr. lāvē′), county (□ 272; pop. 38,119), S Que., on the St. Lawrence, just S of Quebec; ⊙ Lévis.

Lévis, city (pop. 11,991), ⊙ Lévis co., S Que., on the St. Lawrence, opposite Quebec (ferry); port with drydocks; shipbuilding, woodworking, mfg. of trucks, domestic appliances, chemicals, soap, paint cigars, furniture. Site of arsenal and of fortifications built 1865–71 and 1914. Base (1759) for Wolfe's siege of Quebec.

Levisa Bay (lāvē′sä), small inlet (8 mi. long, 4 mi wide) of the Atlantic in Oriente prov., E Cuba, on N coast, 7 mi. E of Mayarí; connects with sea through narrows. Nicaro is on S shore.

Levisa Fork (lůvī′sů), river in SW Va. and E Ky. rises in E Buchanan co., Va.; flows NW past Grundy, into Pike co., Ky., past Pikeville and Prestonsburg, and N, joining Tug Fork at Louisa to form Big Sandy R.; 164 mi. long. Partially navigable; has locks, dams. Main tributary, RUSSELL FORK.

Levitha (lĕ′vētů), Ital. *Levita* (lā′vētä), uninhabited island (□ 4) in the Dodecanese, Greece; 37°N 26°30′E. It was considered part of Greece during Ital. rule of the Dodecanese.

Levittown (lĕ′vĭtoun″), residential village (1949 estimated pop. c.40,000), Nassau co., SE N.Y., on W Long Isl., just SW of Hicksville. Begun 1947 a private housing development for veterans' families

Levka, Mount, Crete: see LEUKA, MOUNT.

Levkas, Greece: see LEUKAS.

Levkimmi, Greece: see LEUKIMME.

Levkosia, Cyprus: see NICOSIA.

Levoca (lĕ′vôchä), Slovak *Levoča,* Ger. *Leutschau* (loit′shou), Hung. *Lőcse* (lû′chĕ), town (pop 7,427), N central Slovakia, Czechoslovakia, 36 mi NW of Kosice; rail terminus. Old cultural center famous for its late-Gothic and Renaissance architecture: St. James's cathedral, begun in 13th cent. with remarkable woodwork and 15 altars; 14th-cent. Franciscan monastery and church; 16th-cent. town hall, now mus.; medieval burghers' houses remains of fortifications. Wood carving blossomed here in Middle Ages, printing in 16th cent.

Levokumskoye (lyĕvůkōōm′skůyů), village (1926 pop. 6,206), E Stavropol Territory, Russian SFSR, on left bank of Kuma R. and 25 mi. E of Budennovsk; wine making, flour milling, metalworking fruit, vegetables.

Lévrier Bay (lāvrēā′), Sp. *Bahía del Galgo,* deep inlet of the Atlantic, W Mauritania, Fr. West Africa, bet. Cap Blanc Peninsula and mainland; 28 mi. long, up to 20 mi. wide. On its W shore is Port-Étienne. The bay is an important fishing ground, mainly for lobster.

Levroux (lůvrōō′), town (pop. 2,448), Indre dept., central France, 12 mi. NNW of Châteauroux; tanning, mfg. (shirts, labels, biscuits). Has fine 13th-cent. church of Saint-Sylvain built atop ruins of a Gallo-Roman palace.

Levshino, Russian SFSR: see MOLOTOV, city.

Levski (lĕf′skē), city (pop. 5,085), Pleven dist., N Bulgaria, near Osam R., 26 mi. ESE of Pleven; rail junction; grain-trading, poultry-raising center. Formerly Kara Agach.

Levski, Peak, Bulgaria: see AMBARITSA.

Lev Tolstoi or **Lev Tolstoy** (lyĕf″ tŭlstoi′), town (1926 pop. 2,191), SW Ryazan oblast, Russian SFSR, 22 mi. W of Chaplygin; rail junction; metal-works. Station room, where L. N. Tolstoi died (1910), now a mus. Until 1927, called Astapovo.

Levuka (lĕvōō′kä), port town (pop. 1,944), E Ovalau, Fiji, SW Pacific; ⊙ colony (1874-82); site of 1st white settlement in Fiji. Bananas, pineapples. Former sandalwood center.

Levunovo (lĕvōō′nôvô), village (pop. 1,034), Gorna Dzhumaya dist., SW Bulgaria, on Struma R. and 8 mi. NE of Petrich; trades in tobacco, rice, cotton, truck.

Levy (lē′vē), county (□ 1,103; pop. 10,637), N Fla., bounded by Gulf of Mexico (S,W) and by Suwannee (W) and Withlacoochee (S) rivers; ⊙ Bronson. Flatwoods area, with many small lakes and some swamps. Stock raising (hogs, cattle), farming (corn, vegetables, peanuts), lumbering, fishing, and some quarrying (limestone, dolomite). Formed 1845.

Levy, Ark.: see NORTH LITTLE ROCK.

Levye Lamki, Vtorye, Russian SFSR: see VTORYE LEVYE LAMKI.

Lewarae (lo͞o'ûrā''), town (pop. 479), Richmond co., S N.C., 4 mi. W of Rockingham.

Lewe (lĕ'wĕ), village, Yamethin dist., Upper Burma, 10 mi. SW of Pyinmana and on railroad.

Lewellen (lo͞oĕ'lĭn), village (pop. 510), Garden co., W Nebr., 10 mi. ESE of Oshkosh and on N. Platte R.; livestock, grain, sugar beets.

Lewes (lo͞o'ĭs, lo͞o'ĭz), municipal borough (1931 pop. 10,784; 1951 census 13,104), SE central Sussex, England, on Ouse R. and 8 mi. ENE of Brighton, ⊙ Sussex co. and administrative co. of East Sussex; agr. market, with some mfg. (shoes, agr. machinery). Has remains of anc. castle, Sussex archaeological mus., several old churches (including one dating from Norman times and one from 12th cent.), libraries, and science and art schools. There are remains of Cluniac priory (1078); William de Warenne and his wife, Gundrada, are buried here. In 1264 Lewes was scene of victory of Simon de Montfort over Henry III. Thomas Paine was an excise officer here. There is 15th-cent. mansion, residence of Anne of Cleves.

Lewes (lo͞o'ĭs, lū'–), resort town (pop. 2,904), Sussex co., SE Del., 15 mi. NE of Georgetown, just W of Cape Henlopen, on harbor protected by Delaware Breakwater on Delaware Bay; deep-sea fishing; fish processing and canning, hosiery mfg.; sand and gravel pits. Port of entry. Lewes and Rehoboth Canal passes to SW. Fort Miles near by. Settled by Dutch in 1631 as 1st white settlement along the Delaware; inc. 1857.

Lewes and Rehoboth Canal (rĭhō'bŭth), SE Del., waterway (c.15 mi. long) connecting Delaware Bay and N end of Rehoboth Bay; passes SW of Cape Henlopen; for small craft. Has 2 N entrances: at mouth of Broadkill R. and at inlet NW of Lewes. S entrance is c.2 mi. S of Rehoboth Beach.

Lewes River (lo͞o'ĭs, lū'–), S Yukon, the upper course of Yukon R., issues from Tagish L. on B.C. border, flows N, through Marsh L., past Whitehorse (head of navigation), through L. Laberge, and NW past Carmacks, to confluence with Pelly R. at Fort Selkirk, forming Yukon R. proper; 338 mi. long. Receives Teslin R.

Lewin (lĕ'vēn), Ger. *Hummelstadt* (ho͝o'mŭl-shtät), town (1939 pop. 1,051; 1946 pop. 1,362) in Lower Silesia, after 1945 in Wroclaw prov., SW Poland, near Czechoslovak border, at SW foot of Heuscheuer Mts., 16 mi. WSW of Glatz (Klodzko); health resort. Until 1938, Ger. name was Lewin.

Lewin Brzeski (lĕ'vēn bzhĕ'skē), Ger. *Löwen* (lû'vŭn), town (1939 pop. 3,978; 1946 pop. 2,241) in Lower Silesia, after 1945 in Opole prov., SW Poland, on the Glatzer Neisse (head of navigation) and 10 mi. SE of Brieg (Brzeg); sugar refining, tile mfg., sawmilling. After 1945, briefly called Lubien, Pol. *Lubień*.

Lewis, Scotland: see LEWIS WITH HARRIS.

Lewis. 1 County (□ 478; pop. 4,208), W Idaho; ⊙ Nezperce. Agr. area bounded on E by Clearwater R. Wheat, potatoes, grain, beans, lumber. Includes part of Nez Perce Indian Reservation. Formed 1911. **2** County (□ 485; pop. 13,520), NE Ky.; ⊙ Vanceburg. Bounded N by Ohio R. (Ohio line); drained by North Fork Licking R. and several creeks. Rolling agr. area (dairy products, livestock, burley tobacco, grain, truck); some mfg. (especially leather and wood products) at Vanceburg. Formed 1806. **3** County (□ 505; pop. 10,733), NE Mo.; ⊙ Monticello. Bounded E by Mississippi R.; drained by Wyaconda R. and North and Middle Fabius rivers. Corn, wheat, oats, soy beans, livestock; lumber. Formed 1832. **4** County (□ 1,293; pop. 22,521), N central N.Y.; ⊙ Lowville. Rises to foothills of the Adirondacks in E; drained by Black R. (water power). Dairying area, with mfg. of paper, wood products, textiles, clothing, cheese; lumbering. Formed 1805. **5** County (□ 285; pop. 6,078), central Tenn.; ⊙ Hohenwald. Drained by Buffalo R. and small Swan Creek. Lumbering, dairying, livestock raising, some agr. (corn, hay, cotton). Contains Meriwether Lewis Natl. Monument. Formed 1843. **6** County (□ 2,447; pop. 43,755), SW Wash.; ⊙ Chehalis. Includes parts of Snoqualmie and Columbia natl. forests and small sec. of Mt. Rainier Natl. Park (NE); drained by Cowlitz and Chehalis rivers. Timber; quicksilver; dairy products, poultry, grain, truck; food processing. Formed 1845. **7** County (□ 392; pop. 21,074), central W.Va.; ⊙ Weston. On Allegheny Plateau; drained by the West Fork (a headstream of the Monongahela). Agr. (livestock, fruit, tobacco); natural-gas and oil wells; timber. Formed 1816.

Lewis 1 Town (pop. 511), Cass co., SW Iowa, on East Nishnabotna R. and 8 mi. SSW of Atlantic, near Cold Springs State Park, in rich agr. region; limestone quarry. **2** City (pop. 475), Edwards co., S central Kansas, 9 mi. E of Kinsley, in grain area. Oil wells. **3** Lumbering village, Essex co., NE N.Y., in the Adirondacks, 30 mi. SSW of Plattsburg.

Lewis, Fort, Wash.: see TACOMA.

Lewis and Clark, county (□ 3,478; pop. 24,540), W central Mont.; ⊙ Helena. Mtn. region crossed by Continental Divide; drained by Missouri and Blackfoot rivers. Livestock, grain; gold. Sections of Helena Natl. Forest in SE and NW. Willow Creek Bird Reservation and Reservoir in N. Formed 1867.

Lewis and Clark Cavern National Monument, Mont.: see MORRISON CAVE STATE PARK.

Lewisberry, borough (pop. 299), York co., S Pa., 9 mi. S of Harrisburg.

Lewisburg. 1 Town, Jefferson co., Ala.: see FULTONDALE. **2** Town (pop. 496), Logan co., S Ky., near Mud R., 28 mi. W of Bowling Green, in agr. and timber area. **3** Village (pop. 1,230), Preble co., W Ohio, 21 mi. WNW of Dayton and on small Twin Creek; trade center for farm and orchard area; nurseries; limestone quarries. **4** Borough (pop. 5,268), ⊙ Union co., central Pa., 20 mi. SSE of Williamsport and on West Branch of Susquehanna R.; textiles, lumber products, furniture; limestone; grist mills. Federal penitentiary, Bucknell Univ. here. Laid out 1785, inc. 1813. **5** Town (pop. 5,164), ⊙ Marshall co., central Tenn., 50 mi. S of Nashville; trade, shipping, processing center for prosperous livestock-raising, dairying, grain-growing, and hardwood-timber region; mfg. of shoes, stoves, pencils, cheese, butter; lumber. U.S. dairy experiment station near by. Inc. 1837. **6** Town (pop. 2,192), ⊙ Greenbrier co., SE W.Va., near Greenbrier R., 25 mi. ENE of Hinton; resort (alt. c.2,300 ft.) in farm and livestock region; limestone quarrying. Seat of Greenbrier Jr. Col. for Women, Greenbrier Military School. Old stone church (1796) and site of Fort Savannah (later Fort Union) here. Inc. 1782.

Lewis Cass, Mount (6,864 ft.), on Alaska-B.C. border, in Coast Range, 50 mi. E of Wrangell; 56° 24'N 131°5'W.

Lewisham (lo͞o'ĭ-shŭm), metropolitan borough (1931 pop. 219,953; 1951 census 227,551) of London, England, S of the Thames, 6 mi. SE of Charing Cross; residential dist., with some market gardens and factories. Suffered air-raid damage, 1940–41.

Lewis Hills, range in W N.F., extending 40 mi. SSW-NNE along the Gulf of St. Lawrence bet. Port au Port Bay (S) and the Bay of Islands (N); rises to 2,673 ft. N part is called Blomidon Range.

Lewisport, town (pop. 656), Hancock co., NW Ky., on left bank (levee) of the Ohio and 17 mi. NE of Owensboro, in agr., coal, and oil region.

Lewis Range, E front range of Rocky Mts. in NW Mont., extends c.160 mi. SSE from near Waterton L. on Alta. line, through GLACIER NATIONAL PARK, to Blackfoot R. NW of Helena; forms part of Continental Divide. Within park is highest portion of range, including some of most spectacular summits of the Rockies; chief peaks are Mt. Cleveland (10,448 ft., highest in range and park), Mt. Stimson (10,165 ft.), Kintla Peak (kĭnt'lŭ) (10,110 ft.), Mt. Jackson (10,033 ft.), Mt. Siyeh (sī'ŭ) (10,014 ft.), Going-to-the-Sun Mtn. (9,604 ft.). Within park, range is crossed by Marias and Logan passes.

Lewis River. 1 In NW U.S., the old name of SNAKE RIVER. **2** In SW Wash., rises on NW slopes of Mt. Adams in Cascade Range, flows c.95 mi. generally SW to Columbia R. c.20 mi. below Vancouver. Receives East Fork (c.30 mi. long) near mouth. Privately-owned hydroelectric developments include Ariel Dam (313 ft. high, 1,250 ft. long; completed 1931), forming L. Merwin (c.12 mi. long), and new Yale Dam (300 ft. high, 1,500 ft. long), upstream from L. Merwin; their power supplements output from Bonneville and Grand Coulee projects. **3** In NW Wyo., rises in mtn. region of Yellowstone Natl. Park, flows c.30 mi. S, through Shoshone L., to Snake R. near S boundary of park.

Lewis Run, borough (pop. 694), McKean co., N Pa., 5 mi. S of Bradford.

Lewiston. 1 City (pop. 12,985), ⊙ Nez Perce co., W Idaho, on Snake R. (forming part of Wash. line) at mouth of Clearwater R., and 90 mi. SSE of Spokane, Wash.; one of lowest points (alt. 941 ft.) in state. Shipping point (at head of Snake R. navigation) for livestock and irrigated fruit area; food processing (flour, canned fruits and vegetables, meat and dairy products, beverages), lumber milling, mfg. of tents, awnings, paint. Has state normal school. Hydroelectric plant. Site was visited (1805) by Lewis and Clark expedition. Mission settlement was established (1836) near by. City founded 1861 after discovery of gold on Clearwater R. Grew as supply and shipping point during gold rush. Had 1st newspaper (*The Golden Age*, 1862) in Idaho; was first capital (1863–64) of Idaho Territory. **2** Industrial city (pop. 40,974), Androscoggin co., SW Maine, on E bank of Androscoggin R. (here crossed by several bridges) opposite AUBURN; 2d-largest city in Maine; textile-milling center (from early 19th cent.), with power from river's 50-ft. falls; shoes, shoe manufacturers' supplies, wood products, bricks, metal products, printing. Seat of Bates Col., state armory, state fairgrounds. Settled 1770, town inc. 1795, city 1861. **3** Village (pop. c.500), Montmorency co., N Mich., c.45 mi. SW of Alpena near Twin Lakes (each c.2 mi. long), in hunting, fishing, and agr. region. **4** Village (pop. 786), Winona co., SE Minn., near Mississippi R., 13 mi. WSW of Winona, in grain, livestock, poultry area; dairy products. **5** Village (pop. 94), Pawnee co., SE Nebr., 15 mi. NW of Pawnee City. **6** Village (pop. 1,626), Niagara co., W N.Y., on Niagara R. (bridged here to Queenston, Ont.), just N of Niagara Falls and 20 mi. NNW of Buffalo; chemicals, crushed stone; silica deposits. Settled c.1796, inc. 1822. **7** Town (pop. 339), Bertie co., NE N.C., 15 mi. NW of Windsor; mfg. of farm machinery; lumber. **8** City (pop. 1,533), Cache co., N Utah, at Idaho line, 17 mi. N of Logan, near Bear R., in Cache Valley, in dairying and irrigated agr. area (alfalfa, sugar beets, truck); beet-sugar refining; alt. 4,505 ft. Settled 1870 by Mormons, inc. 1904.

Lewiston Orchards, village (pop. 4,494), Nez Perce co., W Idaho, 6 mi. SE of Lewiston. Sometimes Orchards.

Lewistown. 1 City (pop. 2,630), ⊙ Fulton co., central Ill., 36 mi. WSW of Peoria, in agr. and bituminous-coal-mining area; corn, wheat, poultry, livestock, dairy products. Settled 1821, inc. 1857. City was the home of Edgar Lee Masters; and the territory, its people, and legends are reflected in his *Spoon River Anthology.* Lincoln and Douglas delivered speeches here. Dickson Mounds State Park is near by. **2** Village (pop. c.300), Frederick co., N Md., 9 mi. N of Frederick. State fish hatchery. United Brethren in Christ church was organized (1800) near by. **3** Town (pop. 415), Lewis co., NE Mo., near Middle Fabius R., 24 mi. WNW of Quincy, Ill.; agr. **4** City (pop. 6,573), ⊙ Fergus co., central Mont., on branch of Judith R. and 90 mi. ESE of Great Falls; trade center for agr. and mining region; coal, gold mines; oil and cement products, bricks and tiles, flour; livestock, grain, dairy produce. Fish hatchery here. Gypsum and cement plant at near-by village of Heath. Laid out as Reed's Fort 1882, inc. as Lewistown 1899. **5** Borough (pop. 13,894), ⊙ Mifflin co., central Pa., 43 mi. NW of Harrisburg and on Juniata R., in agr., dairying area. Viscose, metal products, clothing; sand. Settled 1754, laid out 1790, inc. 1811.

Lewistown Junction, village (pop. 1,259), Mifflin co., central Pa.

Lewisville. 1 Town (pop. 1,237), ⊙ Lafayette co., SW Ark., 27 mi. E of Texarkana, near Red R. (bridged), in agr. area (cotton, corn, potatoes); cotton ginning, sawmilling. **2** Village (pop. 402), Jefferson co., SE Idaho, 5 mi. WNW of Rigby; alt. 4,790 ft.; grain, potatoes, sugar beets. **3** Town (pop. 591), Henry co., E Ind., near Flatrock Creek, 9 mi. S of New Castle, in agr. area. **4** Village (pop. 362), Watonwan co., S Minn., 27 mi. SW of Mankato; dairy products. **5** Village (pop. 217), Monroe co., E Ohio, 15 mi. S of Barnesville, in agr. area. **6** Borough (pop. 495), Potter co., N Pa., 15 mi. NE of Coudersport, near source of Genesee R. **7** Town (pop. 1,516), Denton co., N Texas, 22 mi. NNW of Dallas, in farm area; cotton ginning, broom mfg.

Lewis with Harris, island (□ 825.2; pop. 28,042), largest and most northerly of the Outer Hebrides, Scotland, separated from the mainland by The Minch. N part, Lewis, is in Ross and Cromarty co., smaller S part, HARRIS, is in Inverness-shire. The whole isl. is sometimes called simply Lewis, and sometimes, with the offshore islets, The Lews. Isl. is 60 mi. long and up to 28 mi. wide. Coast has steep cliffs and is deeply indented, notably by Loch Roag (W). Surface is hilly, specially in Harris; highest elevation is Clisham (2,622 ft.), 5 mi. N of Tarbert. There are peat bogs, marshes, wasteland, and numerous fresh-water and salt-water lochs. Little land is under cultivation; chief industries are fishing, stock raising, crofting, and spinning and hand-weaving of tweeds (Harris tweeds). Tourists are attracted by good salmon and trout fishing. Chief town, STORNOWAY, on E coast. At CALLERNISH or Callanish is fine prehistoric monument. Fishing ports include Carloway, on NW coast, 15 mi. WNW of Stornoway, and Port of Ness, near N extremity of isl., 21 mi. NNE of Stornoway. E of Stornoway is Eye Peninsula, 7 mi. long, up to 3 mi. wide, connected with isl. by narrow isthmus. Chief navigational landmark is Butt of Lewis, promontory at N extremity of isl., site of lighthouse (58° 33'N 6°16'W). Airfield at Stornoway.

Lews, The, Scotland: see LEWIS WITH HARRIS.

Lexington, county (□ 716; pop. 44,279), central S.C.; ⊙ Lexington. Bounded NE by Congaree R., SW by North Fork of the Edisto; drained by Saluda R. (dammed to form L. Murray) in N. In Sand Hill belt; some agr. (cotton, asparagus, peaches). Residential and mfg. suburbs of Columbia in E. Formed 1785.

Lexington. 1 Town (pop. 514), ⊙ Oglethorpe co., NE Ga., 17 mi. ESE of Athens, in farm and timber area. **2** City (pop. 1,181), McLean co., central Ill., 15 mi. NE of Bloomington; trade and shipping center in rich agr. area; corn, oats, wheat, soybeans, livestock, poultry, dairy products. Settled 1828, inc. 1867. **3** City (pop. 55,534), ⊙ Fayette co., central Ky., 75 mi. ESE of Louisville; 38°2'N 84°30'W. In heart of the BLUEGRASS region; 3d-largest city (after Louisville and Covington) in Ky.; the U.S. center for raising of thoroughbred horses; an important market for looseleaf burley tobacco, livestock (horses, cattle, lambs), bluegrass seed, wool, and grain. Rail junction; shipping center for E Ky.; railroad shops; airport. Meat-packing, coffee-roasting, tobacco-processing, and printing plants, distilleries; mfg. of clothing, limestone products, cutting tools, sheet-metal products, furniture, toys, electrical equipment, auto parts; flour milling. Seat of Univ. of Kentucky, Transylvania Col. (opened

1785 at Danville; moved here 1787; oldest col. W of the Alleghenies), and Col. of the Bible. Natl. cemetery (1861), U.S. hosp. for treatment of drug addicts, U.S. veterans' hosp., state hosp. for the insane, and U.S. military supply depot here. In Lexington cemetery are graves of Henry Clay, John Hunt Morgan, John C. Breckinridge, and James Lane Allen. Public library (founded 1795; oldest circulating library W of Alleghenies) has complete file of John Bradford's *Kentucky Gazette*, founded 1787. Among the fine old homes in Lexington are: "Ashland," home of Henry Clay (designed 1806 by Latrobe); "Hopemont," home of Confederate Gen. John Hunt Morgan, with a mus.; Thomas Hart house (1794); home of Mary Todd Lincoln. Known for its near-by estates and horse farms, including Faraway Farm, home of famous stallion Man O'War. City's trotting track dates from 1873; Keeneland track was opened 1936. City holds an annual horse show (July), a tobacco carnival, and a farm and home convention (Nov.). City was named (1775) by group of hunters (including Simon Kenton) encamped here when they heard news of Revolutionary battle of Lexington; founded 1779; chartered 1782; inc. 1832. **4** Residential town (pop. 17,335), Middlesex co., E Mass., 10 mi. NW of Boston; printing, publishing; agr. (truck, nursery produce). First skirmish of Revolution fought here April 19, 1775; site marked by monument on triangular green. Has fine 17th- and 18th-cent houses. Settled c.1640, inc. 1713. **5** Resort village (pop. 594), Sanilac co., E Mich., 21 mi. NNW of Port Huron, on L. Huron; fisheries; lumber. **6** City (pop. 3,198), ⊙ Holmes co., central Miss., 29 mi. SSE of Greenwood, in agr. and timber area; lumber, dairy products, sand and gravel; cotton ginning. Inc. 1836. **7** City (pop. 5,074), ⊙ Lafayette co., W central Mo., on Missouri R. and 35 mi. E of Kansas City; agr.; coal mines, rock quarries. Wentworth Military Col. (jr.) here. Laid out 1822, inc. 1845. **8** City (pop. 5,068), ⊙ Dawson co., S central Nebr., 35 mi. W of Kearney and on Platte R.; flour, feed; grain, sugar beets, livestock, dairy and poultry produce. Near by is a diversion dam, part of tri-co. project to develop power and irrigation. Laid out as Plum Creek (on the Oregon Trail) 1872, changed to Lexington 1889. **9** Resort village, Greene co., SE N.Y., in the Catskills, on Schoharie Creek and 24 mi. NW of Saugerties. **10** City (pop. 13,571), ⊙ Davidson co., central N.C., 19 mi. S of Winston-Salem, near High Rock L.; trade center for agr. and dairying area; furniture factories, cotton, rayon, and lumber mills, creameries. Settled 1775; inc. 1828. **11** Village (pop. 739), Richland co., N central Ohio, 6 mi. SW of Mansfield and on Clear Fork of Mohican R.; makes vegetable oil, agr. machinery, wooden containers. **12** Town (pop. 1,176), Cleveland co., central Okla., 33 mi. SSE of Oklahoma City, near Canadian R.; trading point in agr. area (cotton, wheat, oats, livestock); cotton ginning, mfg. of leather goods and beverages. Settled 1889. **13** City (pop. 237), Morrow co., N Oregon, 9 mi. NW of Heppner and on Willow Creek; ships wheat. **14** Town (pop. 1,081), ⊙ Lexington co., central S.C., 12 mi. W of Columbia, near L. Murray, in agr. area; textiles, lumber, caskets, agr. produce. **15** Town (pop. 3,566), ⊙ Henderson co., W Tenn., 24 mi. E of Jackson, in cotton, corn, truck-farming area; work shirts, lumber. Natchez Trace Forest State Park is near by. **16** Town (pop. 603), Lee co., S central Texas, c.40 mi. ENE of Austin, in agr. area (cotton, cattle, corn). **17** Town (pop. 5,976), ⊙ Rockbridge co., W Va., in Shenandoah Valley, on North R. and 30 mi. NNW of Lynchburg, in scenic resort and agr. area. Seat of Va. Military Institute, Washington and Lee Univ. Robert E. Lee and Stonewall Jackson buried here. Laid out 1777; inc. 1841; reinc. 1874. Damaged in Civil War.

Lexington Park, village, St. Marys co., S Md., 10 mi. E of Leonardtown. Near by are Patuxent Naval Air Test Center and several colonial houses. Called Jarboesville until 1950.

Lexmond or **Leksmond** (lĕks'mōnt), village (pop. 707), South Holland prov., W central Netherlands, near Lek R., 3 mi. SW of Vianen; dairying, basket-making, cattle raising.

Lexourion or **Lixourion** (both: lĭksōō'rēōn), town (pop. 5,077), on SW peninsula of Cephalonia isl., Greece, 2 mi. W of Argostoli, across Argostoli Bay; trade in currants, olive oil, wine. Fisheries. Also called Lexuri, Lixuri, or Lixouri. The anc. *Pale* (just N) was one of leading cities of Cephalonia.

Leyastsiems, Latvia: see LEJASCIEMS.

Leyburn (lā'bûrn), town and parish (pop. 1,440), North Riding, NW Yorkshire, England, near Ure R., 7 mi. SSW of Richmond.

Leyden, Netherlands: see LEIDEN.

Leyden (lī'dŭn), agr. town (pop. 306), Franklin co., NW Mass., on Green R. and 8 mi. N of Greenfield.

Leyland (lā'lŭnd), urban district (1931 pop. 10,571; 1951 census 14,722), W central Lancashire, England, 5 mi. S of Preston; steel industry (blast furnaces, rolling mills); mfg. of heavy vehicles (trucks and buses), tires, paint; textile industry (cotton, rayon). Has Elizabethan mansion, 17th-cent. inn.

Leyre River (lâr'), Landes and Gironde depts., SW France, rises near Sabres, flows 50 mi. NW to the Arcachon Basin of the Bay of Biscay. Navigable in Gironde dept.

Leysin (lāzē'), town (pop. 3,240), Vaud canton, SW Switzerland, 22 mi. SE of Lausanne; year-round health resort (alt. 4,592 ft.) with numerous sanatoria for the tubercular.

Leyte (lā'tē, Sp. lā'tā), island (□ 2,785; 1939 pop. 835,532) of Visayan Isls., E central Philippines, bet. Luzon and Mindanao, bounded W by Visayan and Camotes seas, E by Leyte Gulf and Surigao Strait, N by Samar Sea, S by Mindanao Sea, and separated from Samar isl. (NE) by San Juanico Strait; 10°–11°34'N 124°17'–125°15'E. Extremely irregular coast line, with several deep bays (Sogod, Ormoc, and Carigara). Isl. is mountainous, rising to 4,426 ft. in central area. There are manganese and oil deposits; sulphur is mined. Agr.: coconuts, rice, sugar cane, hemp, corn. TACLOBAN and MACARTHUR (formerly Ormoc) are chief centers. Leyte province (□ 3,084; 1948 pop. 1,006,891) includes Leyte isl. and adjacent isls. (PANAON ISLAND, BILIRAN ISLAND, MARIPIPI ISLAND); ⊙ Tacloban. In Second World War, U.S. troops landed at Leyte on Oct. 20, 1944. Fighting was bitter on land and on sea, but after the battle of Leyte Gulf, the Japanese were crushed.

Leyte, town (1939 pop. 1,269; 1948 municipality pop. 20,559), N Leyte, Philippines, at head of Leyte Bay (small inlet of Biliran Strait; 7 mi. long, 2 mi. wide), 36 mi. WNW of Tacloban; agr. center (rice, sugar cane).

Leyte Gulf, large inlet of Philippine Sea bet. Leyte and Samar, Philippines. Homonhon Isl. guards the entrance, and Surigao Strait opens S to Mindanao Sea; a narrow channel in N, bet. Leyte and Samar, leads to Samar Sea and the inland waters. In Second World War, here was fought the battle of Leyte Gulf (also called 2d battle of the Philippine Sea) on Oct. 23–26, 1944. The battle, bet. almost all of the Jap. fleet and the U.S. Third and Seventh Fleets, resulted in a great U.S. victory, which definitively destroyed Japan's sea power. The action was fought in 3 general areas: in Surigao Strait; off Samar; and off Cape Engaño.

Leyton (lā'tŭn), residential municipal borough (1931 pop. 128,313; 1951 census 105,183), SW Essex, England, 7 mi. NE of London. In municipal borough (E) is residential town of Leytonstone (pop. 13,454).

Lezajsk (lĕ'zhĭsk), Pol. *Leżajsk*, town (pop. 4,957), Rzeszow prov., SE Poland, on railroad and 24 mi. NE of Rzeszow, near San R.; brick- and cement-works; tanning, distilling. Cloister.

Lézardrieux (lāzärdrēû'), village (pop. 616), Côtes-du-Nord dept., W France, on estuary of Trieux R. and 17 mi. ENE of Lannion; agr. (early potatoes), fishing, cattle raising.

Lezay (lŭzā'), village (pop. 923), Deux-Sèvres dept., W France, 22 mi. ESE of Niort; dairying.

Lezh, Albania: see LESH.

Lezha (lyĕ'zhŭ), town (1939 pop. over 500), S Vologda oblast, Russian SFSR, on Lezha R. (right affluent of the Sukhona), on railroad and 38 mi. SE of Vologda; flax processing, dairying.

Lezhnevo (lyĕzh'nyĭvŭ), town (1926 pop. 4,076), S Ivanovo oblast, Russian SFSR, 16 mi. S of Ivanovo; cotton milling. Tobacco, potatoes grown in vicinity.

Lézignan-Corbières (lāzēnyã'-kôrbyâr'), town (pop. 6,510), Aude dept., S France, 12 mi. W of Narbonne; wine-trading center. Mfg. of casks and equipment for winegrowers.

Lézinnes (lāzēn'), village (pop. 797), Yonne dept., N central France, on Armançon R. and Burgundy Canal, and 7 mi. SE of Tonnerre; stone cutting.

Lezo (lā'thō), town (pop. 1,310), Guipúzcoa prov., N Spain, 4 mi. E of San Sebastián; chemical works (fertilizers, dyes); rubber processing.

Lezoux (lŭzōō'), town (pop. 2,076), Puy-de-Dôme dept., central France, in the Limagne, 8 mi. WSW of Thiers; agr. market. Produced ceramics in Gallo-Roman times.

Lez River (lĕ). **1** In Drôme and Vaucluse depts., SE France, rises in Dauphiné Pre-Alps, drains Tricastin region, and enters Rhone R. 6 mi. below Bollène; c.35 mi. long. **2** In Hérault dept., S France, rises in the Monts Garrigues, flows c.20 mi. S, past Montpellier, to Gulf of Lion at Palavas-les-Flots.

Lezuza (lā-thōō'thä), town (pop. 2,636), Albacete prov., SE central Spain, 27 mi. W of Albacete; flour mills; cereals, saffron, sheep, goats.

Lgov or **L'gov** (ŭlgôf'), city (1948 pop. over 10,000), W Kursk oblast, Russian SFSR, on Seim R. and 38 mi. W of Kursk; agr. center; metalworks; flour milling, sugar refining, distilling. Chartered 1849; a center (1905) of peasant revolt. Rail junction of Lgov, with adjacent town of Lgovski (1939 pop. over 500), lies 4 mi. S.

Lhakhang (lä'käng), Chinese *La-kang* (lä'gäng'), town [Tibetan *dzong*], S Tibet, in central Assam Himalayas, near undefined Tibet-Bhutan border, on tributary of Manas R. and 110 mi. S of Lhasa; alt. 9,850 ft.

Lhanbryde or **Lhanbryd** (lăn'brīd), agr. village, N Moray, Scotland, 4 mi. E of Elgin.

Lhari, Lharigo, or **Lhariguo** (lä'rēgō), Chinese *La-li* (lä'lē'), after 1913 *Kiali* or *Chia-li* (both: jyä'lē'), town, E Tibet, in Kham prov., 250 mi. NE of Lhasa and on road to Chamdo; farming, stock raising. Hot springs near by.

Lhasa (lä'sŭ, lă'sŭ), Chinese *La-sa* (lä'sä'), town (pop. c.20,000), ⊙ Tibet, on right bank of the Kyi Chu and 250 mi. NE of Darjeeling, 25 mi. N of the Brahmaputra; 30°39'N 91°8'E; alt. 12,087 ft. The center of Lamaism and the main Tibetan trade center (wool, grain, furs, brick tea, musk, salt, gold, spices, drugs, carpets); handicrafts (woolen weaving; gold- and silverware). Reached by roads from Kalimpong and Udalguri (India), Leh (Kashmir), Kangting and Jyekundo (China), and Katmandu (Nepal). Main entry (W) is through large gateway surmounted by a chorten called Pargo Kaling. Circular in form, city is located amid mts. It is overlooked (NW) by the Potala, a spectacular bldg. over 400 ft. high and 1,200 ft. long, begun 1641 by 5th Dalai Lama on site of former (7th cent.) fortress; contains winter residence (in central section; called red palace) and audience chambers of the Dalai Lama, govt. offices, monks' quarters, and mausoleums of past Dalai Lamas. W of the Potala is Chakpori temple, main Tibetan medical col. In center of city is 3-storied temple of Jokang (built A.D. 652; frequently enlarged), the most sacred shrine in Tibet and a Buddhist pilgrimage center. Regents who rule Tibet during the minority of a Dalai Lama are generally chosen from the 4 royal lamaseries of Lhasa, Kundeling and Tengyeling (W), Chomoling (NW), and Tsomoling (S), although the near-by 3 great lamaseries (DREPUNG, SERA, GANDEN) exert tremendous influence in govt. affairs. There are many spacious parks; Norbu Linga [=Jewel Park], the finest, lies W of city on small lake and has summer residence of Dalai Lama. Town holds many annual fairs, largest being New Year festival lasting 15 days. Became ⊙ Tibet in 7th cent., probably succeeding early Ladakh capital. First important European contact was British expedition of 1904 under Younghusband. Occupied 1910–12 by Chinese. Remoteness of city and traditional hostility of Tibetan clergy toward foreigners has led Lhasa to be called the Forbidden City.

Lhatse (lä'tsĕ), Chinese *La-tzu* (lä'dzŭ'), town [Tibetan *dzong*], S Tibet, on the Brahmaputra, on main Leh-Lhasa trade route and 75 mi. W of Shigatse; alt. 13,010 ft. Lamasery.

Lho Sumawe or **Lhoseumawe** (both: lō' sŭmä'wā), town, NE Sumatra, Indonesia, port on Strait of Malacca, 130 mi. ESE of Kutaraja on Medan-Kutaraja RR; 5°11'N 97°8'E; trade center for agr. area, shipping resin, copra, spices, coffee, tea. Also spelled Lho Somawe.

Lhotse, peak, Tibet and Nepal: see E[1].

Lhuis (lwē'), village (pop. 293), Ain dept., E France, near the Rhone, 8 mi. W of Belley; cattle, lumber area.

Li, China: see LI RIVER.

Liabygda (lē'äbüg"dä) or **Liabygd,** village in Stranda canton, More og Romsdal co., W Norway, port on N side of entrance to Norddal Fjord (arm of Stor Fjord), 30 mi. ESE of Alesund; manufactures upholstered furniture.

Liakoura or **Liakura,** Greece: see PARNASSUS.

Liampo, China: see NINGPO, Chekiang prov.

Lian (lēän'), town (1939 pop. 2,700; 1948 municipality pop. 10,702), Batangas prov., S Luzon, Philippines, near Nasugbu, 45 mi. SW of Manila; agr. center (rice, sugar cane, corn, coconuts).

Liancourt (lēäkōōr'), town (pop. 3,328), Oise dept., N France, 10 mi. NW of Senlis; agr. market (beans); mfg. (agr. tools, footwear, cartons, furniture). Has 15th–17th-cent. church.

Lianga (lēäng'gä), town (1939 pop. 2,952; 1948 municipality pop. 15,872), Surigao prov., Philippines, on E coast of Mindanao, at head of Lianga Bay (deep inlet of Philippine Sea).

Liangcheng or **Liang-ch'eng** (lyäng'chŭng'), town (pop. 12,977), ⊙ Liangcheng co. (pop. 166,429), E Suiyuan prov., China, 45 mi. SE of Kweisui; cattle raising; millet, grain. Until 1914 in N Shansi, and during 1914–28 in Chahar.

Liangchow, China: see WUWEI, Kansu prov.

Liangho (lyäng'hŭ'), village, ⊙ Liangho dist. (pop. 35,799), W Yunnan prov., China, 18 mi. S of Tengchung; silk, rice, millet, beans. Until 1935 called Tachang.

Liang-hsiang, China: see LIANGSIANG.

Liangshan (lyäng'shän'). **1** Town, ⊙ Liangshan co., E Pingyuan prov., China, 70 mi. SW of Tsinan; wheat, peanuts, millet. Until 1949 in Shantung prov. **2** Town (pop. 18,321), ⊙ Liangshan co. (pop. 388,027), E Szechwan prov., China, 35 mi. WSW of Wanhsien; paper milling; exports tung oil, medicinal plants; produces rice, sugar cane, sweet potatoes, millet, beans, wheat.

Liangsiang or **Liang-hsiang** (both: lyäng'shyäng'), town, ⊙ Liangsiang co. (pop. 67,865), N Hopeh prov., China, 15 mi. SW of Peking and on Peking-Hankow RR; winegrowing; chestnuts, wheat, millet, kaoliang. Coal mining near by.

Liangtang (lyäng'däng'), town, ⊙ Liangtang co. (pop. 205,105), SE Kansu prov., China, 45 mi. SE of Tienshui, near Shensi border; rice, wheat, millet.

Liao, Manchuria: see LIAO RIVER.

Liaocheng or **Liao-ch'eng** (lyou'chŭng'), town, ⊙ Liaocheng co. (pop. 230,256), NE Pingyuan prov., China, on Grand Canal and 60 mi. WSW of Tsinan; cotton and wool weaving, straw-mat mfg.; medicinal herbs. Has noted library. Called Tungchang until 1913. Until 1949 in Shantung prov.

Liaochow, China: see TSOCHÜAN.

Liaochung (lyou'jŏŏng'), town, ⊙ Liaochung co. (pop. 330,759), SE Liaosi prov., Manchuria, on Liao plain, 45 mi. SW of Mukden, and on left bank of lower Liao R.; raw cotton, soybeans, wheat, kaoliang.

Liao Ho, Manchuria: see LIAO RIVER.

Liao-hsi, Manchuria: see LIAOSI.

Liaohsien, China: see TSOCHÜAN.

Liaoning (lyou'nĭng') [Chinese,=peace of the Liao], former southernmost province (□ 100,246; 1926 pop. 13,775,559) of the 3 original provs. of Manchuria; ⊙ was Mukden. Known under the Manchu dynasty as Fengtien or Shengking (for Mukden's former Chinese names), it was divided (1934) under Manchukuo regime into Antung, Fengtien (see MUKDEN), Chinchow, and South Hsingan provs. It was reconstituted briefly (1946–49) as prov. (□ 26,372; pop. 9,943,315) by the Nationalists after Second World War, before being divided (1949) by the Communists into Liaosi and Liaotung provs.

Liaopeh or **Liaopei** (both: lyou'bā'), former province (□ 46,949; pop. 4,904,399) of SW Manchuria; ⊙ was Liaoyüan (Shwangliao). Formed 1946 from South Hsingan prov. and sections of Fengtien, Kirin, and Lungkiang provs. of Manchukuo. Its Mongol section (W) passed 1949 to Inner Mongolian Autonomous Region, while the Chinese portion (E) was inc. into newly formed Heilungkiang, Kirin, and Liaosi provs.

Liao River (lyou), Chinese *Liao Ho* (lyou' hŭ'), chief river of S Manchuria, formed SE of Shwangliao by the union of its E (left) and W (right) headstreams. The W or main branch of the Liao (Mongolian *Shira Muren* or *Shara Muren*) rises on the Inner Mongolian plateau 90 mi. WNW of Chihfeng, flows E along N border of Jehol, past Tungliao and Shwangliao, to confluence with the lesser E branch, which rises in area of Sian. The combined stream flows S, past Tiehling and Liaochung, through the alluvial Liao plain to Gulf of Liaotung at Yingkow. Total length, including W branch, 900 mi. Frozen Dec.–March. Although silting and sudden level fluctuations reduce its navigability, the Liao was the chief access route to S Manchuria, serving the old Chinese centers of settlement in the Liao valley, until the coming of the railroad. During 19th cent., its river-mouth port was progressively shifted downstream from Newchwang to Tienchwangtai, and then to Yingkow. The lower course forms Liaosi-Liaotung prov. border.

Liaosi or **Liao-hsi** (both: lyou'shē') [Chinese,=W of the Liao], province (□ 25,000; pop. 7,000,000) of SW Manchuria, W of Liao R.; ⊙ Chinchow. Bounded W by Jehol and the Inner Mongolian Autonomous Region, N by Heilungkiang and Kirin, and W by Liaotung (in part along Liao R.), Liaosi prov. is situated on N shore of the Gulf of Liaotung of the Yellow Sea. Its area comprises essentially the vast alluvial lowland formed by lower Liao R. A major agr. region, it produces soybeans, kaoliang, millet, corn. In the E outliers of the Jehol plateau are the coal-mining centers of Fusin, Heishan, Ihsien, and Chinsi. Near Chinsi, lead and molybdenum are mined. The main urban centers are the rail city of Szeping (formerly Szepingkai) and the Mongolian trade center of Shwangliao (formerly Liaoyüan) in the N, Chinchow and the port of Hulutao in the S. Liaosi is traversed by the Peking-Mukden RR. Prov. was formed 1949 out of W Liaoning and SE Liaopeh provs.

Liaotung (lyou'dŏŏng') [Chinese,=E of the Liao], province (□ 40,000; pop. 11,000,000) of S Manchuria, E of Liao R.; ⊙ Antung. Bounded SE by Korea along Yalu R., N by Kirin, and NE by Liaosi along Liao R., Liaotung prov. juts S into the Yellow Sea as a peninsula, separating Korea Bay (E) and the Gulf of Liaotung (W), and approaching within 60 mi. of the Shantung peninsula. The tip of the Liaotung peninsula formed during 1905–45 the Japanese-leased territory of KWANTUNG and since 1945 is the PORT ARTHUR naval-lease dist. Liaotung is comprised essentially of a mountainous outlier of the E Manchurian highlands, forming the divide bet. Liao and Yalu rivers. While agr. is limited to staple grain, tobacco, soybeans, and wild silk, Liaotung is Manchuria's chief industrial area, containing the Mukden complex of Fushun (coal, oil shale), Anshan and Penki (steel), as well as the Tungpientao iron and coal dist., a potential metallurgical base, with center at Tunghwa. Hydroelectric power is furnished by the Supung station on the Yalu. Ports are Antung (with its outer port Tatungkow, on Korea Bay), and Yingkow on the Gulf of Liaotung; however, politically separate Dairen handles most of Liaotung's maritime trade. The prov. was formed 1949 out of E Liaoning and Antung provs.

Liaotung, Gulf of, N arm of the Gulf of Chihli, in SW Manchuria, bet. Shanhaikwan corridor of Liaosi prov. (W) and Liaotung peninsula (E); 100 mi. long, 60 mi. wide. Receives Liao R. (N). Its main ports are Yingkow and Hulutao.

Liaoyang (lyou'yäng'). **1** City (1940 pop. 102,478), ⊙ but independent of Liaoyang co. (1946 pop. 830,134), W Liaotung prov., Manchuria, China, 40 mi. SSW of Mukden, in Manchuria's chief cotton-growing area; rail junction on South Manchuria RR.; commercial center; cotton and silk weaving, soybean and flour milling. One of oldest towns of Manchuria, Liaoyang dates from Pohai kingdom (7th–10th cent.). It was later the E capital of the Liao (Kitan) dynasty and continued as an administrative center until the Manchu dynasty. Scene of Russian defeat (1904) during Russo-Japanese War. The city became an independent municipality in 1932; revived 1949. **2** Town, Shensi prov., China: see LIOYANG.

Liaoyüan, Manchuria: see SHWANGLIAO.

Liard River (lē'ärd"), W Canada, rises in S Yukon E of White Horse, flows ESE, crossing into B.C., to Nelson Forks (where it receives Fort Nelson R.), thence generally N into Mackenzie Dist., past Fort Liard (head of navigation, c.165 mi. upstream), to Mackenzie R. at Fort Simpson; 570 mi. long.

Liari (lyä'rē), village, Las Bela state, SE Baluchistan, W Pakistan, 39 mi. SSE of Bela; local market for salt, rice, fish, millet.

Liat (lēät'), island (8 mi. long, 6 mi. wide), Indonesia, in Java Sea, 35 mi. E of SE coast of Bangka.

Lib (lĕb), coral island (pop. 84), Ralik Chain, Marshall Isls., W central Pacific, c.60 mi. SW of Kwajalein.

Liban (lĭ'bänyŭ), Czech *Libáň*, town (pop. 1,872), N Bohemia, Czechoslovakia, 28 mi. SSE of Liberec, in sugar-beet area; rail terminus.

Liban, Lebanon: see LEBANON.

Líbano (lē'bänō), town (pop. 7,659), Tolima dept., W central Colombia, at E foot of Nevado del Ruiz in Cordillera Central, 30 mi. SW of Honda; alt. 5,200 ft. Mining (silver, gold) and agr. center (coffee, potatoes, wheat, corn, bananas, sugar cane, yucca, vegetables, cattle, hogs); flour milling, coffee roasting, mfg. of soap and chocolate. Named for majestic cedars near by.

Líbano, village (dist. pop. 2,168), Guanacaste prov., NW Costa Rica, 4 mi. SSE of Tilarán; coffee, grain, sugar cane, livestock. Gold mining near by.

Libanovon, Greece: see AIGINION.

Libanus, Lebanon: see LEBANON, mountains.

Libau, Latvia: see LIEPAJA.

Libava or **Mesto Libava** (mĕ'shtô lĭ'bävä), Czech *Město Libavá*, Ger. *Liebau* or *Stadt Liebau* (shtät lē'bou), town (pop. 3,265), N central Moravia, Czechoslovakia, 15 mi. NE of Olomouc, in oat-growing area.

Libava, Latvia: see LIEPAJA.

Libby, city (pop. 2,401), ⊙ Lincoln co., NW Mont., 60 mi. WNW of Kalispell and on Kootenai R., just NE of Cabinet Mts.; trade center for lumbering, mining, agr. area; large sawmill; dairy products, livestock, grain. Gold, silver, lead, zinc, vermiculite mines near by. Fish hatchery here. Founded as mining village in 1860s, inc. 1910.

Libby Dam, Mont.: see KOOTENAI RIVER.

Libbyville, Alaska: see NAKNEK.

Liben (lĭ'bĕn), Czech *Libeň*, N mfg. suburb of Prague, Czechoslovakia.

Libenge (lĕbĕng'gä), town (1946 pop. c.3,000), Equator Prov., NW Belgian Congo, on Ubangi R. (Fr. Equatorial Africa border) opposite Mongoumba and 225 mi. NW of Lisala; customs station, river port, and trading center; cotton ginning. Airport. Coffee and rubber plantations; extensive farming of African staples (manioc, yams, plantains) in vicinity. Libenge has Capuchin and Augustinian missions, trade schools for natives, hosp. for Europeans.

Liberal. **1** City (pop. 7,134), ⊙ Seward co., SW Kansas, near Okla. line, 65 mi. SW of Dodge City; trade and shipping center for grain and livestock area; grain milling. Gas fields near by. Inc. 1888. **2** City (pop. 739), Barton co., SW Mo., 15 mi. NE of Pittsburg, Kansas; agr.; coal.

Liberalitas Julia, Portugal: see ÉVORA.

Liberator Village, Texas: see WHITE SETTLEMENT.

Libercourt (lĕbĕrkōōr'), town (pop. 6,170), Pas-de-Calais dept., N France, 8 mi. ENE of Lens, in coal-mining dist.; tar processing. Damaged in First World War.

Liberdade (lĕbĕrdä'dĭ), city (pop. 1,027), S Minas Gerais, Brazil, in the Serra da Mantiqueira, on railroad and 45 mi. NW of Barra do Piraí (Rio de Janeiro); nickel mining; electrometallurgy.

Liberec (lĕ'bĕrĕts), Ger. *Reichenberg* (rī'khŭnbĕrk), city (pop. 29,690; urban commune pop. 52,798), ⊙ Liberec prov. (□ 1,636; pop. 479,874), N Bohemia, Czechoslovakia, on Lusatian Neisse R. and 55 mi. NNE of Prague, in the Sudetes bet. Lusatian Mts. and the Isergebirge; 50°13'N 15°49'E. Rail hub; major center of textile industry (cotton, linen, silk, woolen); mfg. (textile-processing machinery, footwear, dyes, pianos, embroidery), food processing, printing. Airport. Has Gothic church, 16th-cent. castle, Renaissance town hall, large zoo, museums. Though founded in 13th cent., its development began in 1823, upon establishment of 1st textile factory. Formerly had large Ger. pop. Lignite deposits in vicinity. Cable railway leads up Jested Mtn., 3 mi. SW.

Liberia (lībē'rēŭ), Africa's only republic (□ c.43,000; 1949 pop. estimate 1,600,000), at SW edge of the continent's great bulge, nearest to South America; ⊙ Monrovia. Bounded NW by Sierra Leone (British), N by Fr. Guinea, NE and E by Ivory Coast (British). From a marshy, lagoon-studded shore line (370 mi. long) on the Grain Coast, the country rises in a series of ill-defined plateaus toward the inland border ranges 4–6,000 ft. high. Territory extends inland 100–160 mi. Short streams (Mano, Lofa, St. Paul, St. John, Cess, Cavalla), flowing to the Atlantic generally at right angles to the coast, have steep gradients and are navigable only in lower reaches for flat barges. Rainy tropical climate is marked by uniformly high temperatures (daily mean c.80°F.). Monsoon-type precipitation (averaging bet. 150 and 170 in. per year) is concentrated in rainy season (April–Nov.), during which relative humidity is high and rainfall occurs daily. The influence of the Saharan harmattan is felt in dry season. Agr. (excepting plantations) is of the primitive type; it is carried on in clearings under a "bush rotation" system requiring constant burning of the natural vegetation from the encroaching jungle. Chief native crops are rice and cassava (manioc). Coffee is cultivated by the Westernized element of the pop. Principal sources of cash income for natives are palm kernels and palm oil, and piassava fiber. Minor export crops are cacao, kola nuts, peanuts, and calabar beans. Overshadowing all economic activity is the 80,000-acre Firestone rubber plantation (hq. at Harbel on Farmington R.), developed after 1926. Rubber (exported via Marshall until 1950; later also via Monrovia) provides almost 90% of export value. Gold is also shipped from alluvial dredgings. There is no industry outside of native crafts. Exploitation of extensive hardwood forests lacks capital and transport. There are 700 mi. of roads, including one linking Monrovia with Fr. Guinea. All ports (outside of Monrovia) require lighterage from ship to shore. About 95% of pop. still retains tribal customs and govt. The principal ethnological groups are the Kru, Gola, and the Moslem Mandingo. Some 28 dialects are spoken by the natives, few of whom speak English, the official language. The term "Americo-Liberians" has been applied to the descendants of American Negroes (c.15–20,000) who until recently were the only literate inhabitants and represented the governing group. The Westernized element has however grown to c.60,000 through intermarriage. Economic development (with exception of rubber plantations) dates from Second World War, when the U.S. undertook the defense of strategically located Liberia by building a deep-water port at Monrovia (free port, opened 1948, is accessible to vessels drawing 28 ft.; cold-storage plant, rubber warehouses, bunkering facilities) and Roberts Field airport (30 mi. ESE of Monrovia; now used by transatlantic air lines). Other projects include exploitation of the Bomi Hills iron mine (linked 1950 by a railroad with Monrovia), and modern cacao plantings. Advances in public health and education are also under way. Institutions of advanced learning are Liberia col., Col. of West Africa (at Monrovia), and the Booker T. Washington agr. and technical inst. at Kakata. Relations bet. Liberia and the U.S. have been close ever since establishment (1822) by the American Colonization Society of a small colony of freed slaves near present site of Monrovia. It survived its early hardships mainly because of the efforts of Jehudi Ashmun and Ralph Gurley. A free and independent republic was proclaimed in 1847, its govt. and constitution patterned on that of the U.S. and the right of property ownership limited to "persons of African descent." Throughout 19th and early 20th cent., the aegis of the U.S. protected Liberia from encroachments by France and England. Financial hardships resulting in bankruptcy placed Liberia under virtual U.S. protectorate in 1909. The 99-yr. lease on over 1,000,000 acres granted the Firestone Co. in 1926 marked the beginning of economic development. The coastal strip (c.40 mi. deep) of Liberia is administratively divided into 5 counties (Grand Bassa, Sinoe, Maryland, Grand Cape Mount, Montserrado) and Marshall territory; the hinterland, inhabited by tribal natives, is divided into Eastern, Central, and Western provinces.

Liberia (lēbär'yä), city (1950 pop. 3,390), ⊙ Guanacaste prov., NW Costa Rica, on Inter-American Highway, on Liberia R. (left affluent of Tempisque R.) and 105 mi. NW of San José; agr. center (livestock, fruit, grain, sugar cane).

Liberta (lĭbĕrtä'), village (pop. 1,660), S Antigua, B.W.I., 6 mi. SSE of St. John's; sugar cane, sea-island cotton. Founded after emancipation of slaves (1834).

Libertad (lĕbĕrtädh'), town (pop. 2,109), NE Buenos Aires prov., Argentina, 3 mi. SE of Merlo; cattle raising, dairying, fruitgrowing; plant nurseries; railroad workshops.

Libertad or **La Libertad,** department (□ 10,209; pop. 404,024), NW Peru; ⊙ Trujillo. Bordered by the Pacific (W) and Cordillera Central of the Andes (E). Includes in E section the Cordillera Occidental, separated from Cordillera Central by Marañón R. Its coastal region, drained by Jequetepeque, Chicama, and Virú rivers, contains a large irrigation system, one of Peru's main sugar-cane dists., also producing rice and cotton. Barley and wheat are cultivated in mts., where cattle and sheep are also raised. Coca grows on E and W slopes of the Andes. Gold, silver, copper mined at Salpo and Quiruvilca. Dept. is crossed by Pan American Highway and served by several railroads connecting the agr. centers with seaports (Pacasmayo, Puerto Chicama, Salaverry). Other centers: Trujillo, San Pedro, Santiago de Chuco, Otusco.

Libertad, town (pop. 2,900), San José dept., S Uruguay, on highway, and 30 mi. NW of Montevideo, in agr. region (cereals, livestock); flour milling.

Libertad. **1** Town (pop. 1,047), Barinas state, W Venezuela, on Masparro R. and 45 mi. ESE of Barinas; cattle. **2** Town (pop. 378), Cojedes state, N Venezuela, in llanos, 25 mi. S of San Carlos; cattle raising. Sometimes Lagunitas. **3** Town (pop. 728), Táchira state, W Venezuela, in Andean spur, 8 mi. NW of San Cristóbal; alt. 4,416 ft.; coffeegrowing.

Libertad, La, in Latin America: see LA LIBERTAD.

Libertador (lēbĕrtädōr'), province (□ 356; 1935 pop. 27,239; 1950 pop. 25,513), NW Dominican Republic, on Haiti border; ⊙ Dajabón. Drained by Massacre R. Main products: rice, coffee, corn, fruit, stock, hides, beeswax, honey, timber. Highway to Haiti. The area was heavily disputed during struggles against Spain and Haiti. Formerly part of Monte Cristi prov.; set up 1938 as a separate prov.

Libertador, village, Dominican Republic: see PEPILLO SALCEDO.

Liberton, SE suburb (pop. 10,901) of Edinburgh, Scotland; coal mines.

Liberty. **1** County (□ 838; pop. 3,182), NW Fla., bounded by Ochlockonee (E) and Apalachicola (W) rivers; ⊙ Bristol. Forestry (lumber, naval stores) and agr. (livestock, corn, peanuts). S half of co. included in Apalachicola Natl. Forest. Formed 1855. **2** County (□ 510; pop. 8,444), SE Ga.; ⊙ Hinesville. Bounded SE by the Atlantic, NE by Canoochee R. Includes St. Catherines Isl. Coastal plain agr. (corn, sugar cane, rice, truck, livestock), forestry (lumber, naval stores), and fishing area. Camp Stewart military reservation in NW part of co. Formed 1777. **3** County (□ 1,459; pop. 2,180), N Mont.; ⊙ Chester. Agr. area bordering on Alta.; drained in S by Marias R. Grain, livestock. Formed 1920. **4** County (□ 1,173; pop. 26,729), E Texas; ⊙ Liberty. S part is on Gulf coastal plain; N is rolling, wooded. Drained by Trinity R. (shallow-draft navigation to Liberty). Agr. (rice, wheat, cotton, corn, truck, pecans); livestock (especially hogs; also cattle, sheep, goats, poultry); dairying. Lumbering (chiefly pine), lumber milling; oil wells, oil refining; sulphur production. Formed 1836.

Liberty. **1** Village (pop. 172), White co., SE Ill., 29 mi. WSW of Mount Carmel, in grain and livestock region. **2** Town (pop. 1,730), ⊙ Union co., E Ind., 13 mi. S of Richmond, in agr. area (livestock; dairy products; grain); makes agr. implements, paint; ships grain. Settled 1822. **3** City (pop. 185), Montgomery co., SE Kansas, on Verdigris R. and 9 mi. N of Coffeyville; stock raising, agr. Oil and gas fields near by. **4** Town (pop. 1,291), ⊙ Casey co., central Ky., on Green R. and 22 mi. SSW of Danville, in agr., timber, stone-quarry area; lumber mills; mfg. of wood products, seat covers, packed meat. Settled 1791. **5** Resort town (pop. 497), Waldo co., S Maine, 14 mi. WSW of Belfast; wood and metal products. Includes part of Lake St. George State Park. **6** Town (pop. 683), ⊙ Amite co., SW Miss., c.45 mi. SE of Natchez; lumber milling. **7** City (pop. 4,709), ⊙ Clay co., W Mo., 14 mi. NE of Kansas City. Agr. (corn, wheat, blue grass, tobacco); grain elevators; railroad yards. William Jewell Col. here. Founded 1822. **8** Village (pop. 246), Gage co., SE Nebr., 18 mi. SE of Beatrice and on branch of Big Blue R., near Kansas line. **9** Vacation and health-resort village (pop. 4,658), Sullivan co., SE N.Y., in the Catskills, 30 mi. NW of Middletown. Tuberculosis sanitarium here. Neversink Reservoir near by. Settled 1793, inc. 1870. **10** Town (pop. 1,342), Randolph co., central N.C., 18 mi. SE of Greensboro; mfg. of furniture, veneer, brooms, hosiery. **11** Borough (pop. 1,900), Allegheny co., SW Pa., on Youghiogheny R. opposite McKeesport. Inc. c.1912. **12** Borough (pop. 271), Tioga co., N Pa., 23 mi. N of Williamsport. **13** Town (pop. 2,291), Pickens co., NW S.C., 17 mi. WSW of Greenville; agr., cotton mills, quarry. **14** Town (pop. 314), De Kalb co., central Tenn., 22 mi. SE of Lebanon. **15** City (pop. 4,163), ⊙ Liberty co., E Texas, on Trinity R. at head of shallow-draft navigation and 40 mi. NE of Houston; trade center in agr. (rice, cotton, corn, hogs), lumbering, oil-producing area; tool mfg.; sulphur plant near. Founded c.1830.

Liberty, Mount, N.H.: see FRANCONIA MOUNTAINS.

Liberty Cap, Calif.: see YOSEMITE NATIONAL PARK.

Liberty Center, village (pop. 816), Henry co., NW Ohio, 7 mi. ENE of Napoleon, near Maumee R.; makes sauerkraut.

Liberty Hill, village (pop. c.750), Williamson co., central Texas, 29 mi. NNW of Austin; ships cotton, cedar.

Libertytown, village (pop. c.600), Frederick co., N Md., 10 mi. ENE of Frederick; highway junction in agr. area.

Libertyville. **1** Village (pop. 5,425), Lake co., extreme NE Ill., on Des Plaines R. (bridged here) and 7 mi. SW of Waukegan, in dairy and farm area; mfg. (food products, upholstery fabrics, wire fence, machine-shop products). Stone, gravel pits. Named 1837, inc. 1882. **2** Town (pop. 311), Jefferson co., SE Iowa, 6 mi. SW of Fairfield, in bituminous-coal-mining and livestock area.

Libia, N Africa: see LIBYA.

Libin (lēbē'), village (pop. 1,123), Luxembourg prov., SE Belgium, 7 mi. NW of Libramont, in the Ardennes; kaolin-earth quarrying.

Libiola, Italy: see SESTRI LEVANTE.

Liblar (lē'blär), village (pop. 4,833), in former Prussian Rhine Prov., W Germany, after 1945 in North Rhine-Westphalia, near the Erft, 10 mi. SW of Cologne; rail junction.

Libmanan (lēbmä'nän), town (1939 pop. 3,275; 1948 municipality pop. 43,482), Camarines Sur prov., SE Luzon, Philippines, on Sipocot R. (tributary of Bicol R.), on railroad and 10 mi. NW of Naga; trade center for agr. area (rice, abacá, corn).

Libochovice (lĭ'bôkhôvĭtsĕ), Ger. *Libochowitz,* town (pop. 2,609), W central Bohemia, Czechoslovakia, on Ohre R. and 28 mi. NW of Prague; rail junction; sugar milling.

Libohovë (lēbôhô'vù) or **Libohova** (lēbôhô'vä), town (1945 pop. 1,472), S Albania, near Gr. border, 7 mi. SE of Argyrokastron; agr. center. Has early 19th-cent. castle built by Ali Pasha.

Libon (lē'bōn), town (1939 pop. 2,895; 1948 municipality pop. 23,931), Albay prov., SE Luzon, Philippines, near L. Bato, 23 mi. WNW of Legaspi; agr. center (abacá, rice, coconuts).

Libos, France: see FUMEL.

Libourne (lēbōōrn'), town (pop. 14,563), Gironde dept., SW France, port on the Dordogne at mouth of Isle R. (head of ocean navigation) and 17 mi. ENE of Bordeaux; commercial and winegrowing center; iron foundry, glass works; hosiery and footwear mfg., distilling. Has 16th-cent. town hall and 15th-cent. church. Founded 1286 as a bastide by Edward I of England. Residence of Edward the Black Prince and birthplace of Richard II.

Libramont (lēbrämō'), town (pop. 1,955), Luxembourg prov., SE central Belgium, 16 mi. WSW of Bastogne, in the Ardennes; rail junction; highest point (1,570 ft.) of Brussels-Luxembourg RR.; agr. and cattle market. Recogne (rùkōny'ù), 1 mi. W, was refuge of Napoleon III after battle of Sedan (1871).

Library, village (pop. 2,124), Allegheny co., W Pa., 10 mi. SSW of downtown Pittsburgh.

Librazhd (lēbräzhd') or **Librazhdi** (lēbräzh'dē), village (1930 pop. 500), central Albania, on Shkumbi R. and 14 mi. ENE of Elbasan; road center. Also spelled Librash or Librashi.

Libres, Argentina: see PASO DE LOS LIBRES.

Libres (lē'brĕs), town (pop. 1,403), Puebla, central Mexico, 45 mi. NE of Puebla; alt. 7,792 ft.; cereals, maguey, stock.

Libreville (lēbrùvēl'), town (1950 pop. 9,900), ⊙ Gabon territory and of Estuaire region (□ 7,340; 1950 pop. 36,300), W Gabon, Fr. Equatorial Africa, on Gulf of Guinea, on N shore of mouth of Gabon R., 510 mi. NW of Brazzaville; 0°26'N 9°25'E. Lumber and cabotage port, shipping chiefly mahogany, ebony, Gabon walnut, *okume* wood, cacao, rubber, palm products; sawmilling. Airport. Has military camp, large hosp., several schools, R.C. mission dating from 1843. Seat of vicar apostolic of Gabon. Founded 1849 with Negroes from slave ship. Shelled and occupied by Free French and British forces in 1940. Before development of Pointe-Noire (1934–46), it was the main port of Fr. Equatorial Africa.

Librilla (lēvrē'lyä), town (pop. 1,888), Murcia prov., SE Spain, 15 mi. SW of Murcia; sandal mfg., olive-oil processing, flour milling; ships grapes.

Libus (lĭ'bōōsh), Czech *Libuš,* village (pop. 1,021), central Bohemia, Czechoslovakia, 6 mi. SSE of Prague; goose breeding; feather trade.

Libya (lĭ'bēù), Ital. *Libia,* former Italian colony (□ c.680,000; 1938 pop. 888,401; 1947 pop. estimate 1,166,000), N Africa, on the central Mediterranean; ⊙ Tripoli. Bounded NW by Tunisia, W by Algeria, S by Fr. West Africa and Fr. Equatorial Africa, SE by Anglo-Egyptian Sudan, and E by Egypt. From a desert coast line (over 1,000 mi. long, deeply indented by the Gulf of Sidra) Libya extends deep into the Sahara. Because the climate is arid and torrid throughout, Libya's useful land is limited to a string of coastal oases and to small dists. near the Mediterranean where yearly rainfall reaches 15 in. The country consists of 3 historical regions, 1st amalgamated under Ital. rule in 1912. They are TRIPOLITANIA, in NW along coast, CYRENAICA, E of the Gulf of Sidra, and FEZZAN, SW, in the Sahara. Tripoli and Benghazi are the only deep-water ports. Other towns (Homs, Misurata, Barce, Cyrene, Derna, Tobruk) are strung out along or near the shore linked by a coastal highway which extends from the Tunisian to the Egyptian border. Short rail lines link Tripoli with Azizia and Garian in immediate hinterland, and with Zuara along coast; in Cyrenaica, Benghazi is served by short railroad from Barce and Soluch. In the Gebel el Akhdar region of Cyrenaica and in the Tripoli area, agr. settlements, established by Italians during 1930s, have greatly contributed to the local food supply. Chief crops are barley, wheat, olives, grapes, citrus fruit, almonds, vegetables, and dates. Stock raising (goats, sheep, camels) is widespread among nomadic and seminomadic Berbers and Arabs. Mineral deposits, apart from salt along NW coast, are negligible. Industry (mostly agr. processing) is limited to Tripoli and Benghazi; handicrafts include carpet weaving, metal- and leatherworking. While in 1938 the total pop. included 89,098 Italians, only 44,419 remained in 1947, all concentrated in Tripolitania; in 1947, there remained 33,186 Jews. Libya was the old Greek name for N Africa. Under the Romans, region was divided into Marmarica or lower Libya (E) and Cyrenaica or upper Libya (W). The name was revived by Italians who, as a result of Turco-Italian War (1911–12), annexed territory bet. Tunisia and Egypt. Present boundaries were established after First World War, but effective occupation was not completed until 1931, with the conquest of Kufra oases (stronghold of the Senusi). Little effort to develop the colony was made until 1930s, when Italians undertook their vaunted road-building program, and also erected civic bldgs. and hosps. In 1934, coastal areas were administratively divided into Tripoli, Misurata, Benghazi, and Derna provs. and became (1939) an integral part of Italy. Libya was one of the chief battlegrounds of North Africa during Second World War. After 2 years of seesaw battles, it was occupied by British in 1942–43; Tripolitania and Cyrenaica came under Br. military administration, Fezzan under Fr. rule. Italy having renounced all claims to its former colony, the future of Libya was determined (1949) by the U.N. A U.N. commissioner was appointed to prepare the country for independence by Jan. 1, 1952. With the proclamation (1950) of the ruler of the Senusi as king of Libya, the way was paved for a federal state uniting Tripolitania, Cyrenaica, and Fezzan on an equal representation basis, with 2 capitals, after independence, Tripoli and Benghazi.

Libyan Desert (lĭb'yùn, lĭ'bēùn), easternmost part of the Sahara, extending E and S through Cyrenaica (in Libya), Egypt, and NW Anglo-Egyptian Sudan. Its E limit is the Nile valley. Its Egyptian and Libyan area is also known as the WESTERN DESERT, and here, in the N, was fought (1940–42) a critical phase of the Second World War. One of the most forbidding areas of the Sahara, the Libyan Desert knows no rain for years at a time, temperatures are extreme, and there are violent winds. Among its oases are: KUFRA in Libya, SIWA, FARAFRA, KHARGA, Dakhla, and Bahariya in Egypt.

Libyssa (lĭbĭ'sù), anc. town of Bithynia, NW Asia Minor, whose ruins are on N shore of Gulf of Izmit, just E of Gebze, 35 mi. ESE of Istanbul, Turkey; scene of Hannibal's suicide.

Licab (lĕkäb'), town (1939 pop. 1,676; 1948 municipality pop. 7,854), Nueva Ecija prov., central Luzon, Philippines, 12 mi. ENE of Tarlac; rice, corn.

Licancábur Volcano (lēkäng-kä'bōōr), Andean peak (19,455 ft.) in Antofagasta prov., N Chile, at Bolivia line; 22°50'S. Sometimes Licancaur.

Licania (lĕkùnē'ù), city (pop. 1,755), N Ceará, Brazil, 15 mi. NNE of Sobral; tannins, carnauba wax, hides, cotton. Until 1944, called Santana, also spelled Sant' Anna.

Licanray (lĕkänrī'), village, Valdivia prov., S central Chile, on N shore of L. Calafquén, in Chilean lake dist., 65 mi. NE of Valdivia; resort; fishing, lumbering. Founded in early 1940s.

Licantén (lĕkäntĕn'), village (pop. 869), ⊙ Mataquito dept. (□ 690; pop. 16,922), Curicó prov., central Chile, on Mataquito R. and 45 mi. W of Curicó; grain, goats.

Licata (lĕkä'tä), town (pop. 30,641), Agrigento prov., S Sicily, port on Mediterranean Sea, at mouth of Salso R., 28 mi. S of Caltanissetta; sulphur mining and refining, mfg. (cement, macaroni). Exports sulphur, cheese, wool, hides. Near by is site of anc. Phintias (built 3d cent. B.C.) on hilly promontory of Sant'Angelo, anc. *Ecnomus,* off which Romans defeated (256 B.C.) the Carthaginian fleet in the Punic wars. Bombed (1943) in Second World War, Licata was one of initial Allied invasion points, July 9–10.

Licciana Nardi (lēt-chä'nä när'dē), village (pop. 540), Massa e Carrara prov., Tuscany, central Italy, 13 mi. NNW of Carrara; macaroni. Formerly Licciana.

Lice (lĭjĕ'), town (pop. 5,457), Diyarbakir prov., E Turkey, bet. Tigris and Batman rivers, 45 mi. NNE of Diyarbakir; wheat.

Lich (lĭkh), town (pop. 4,409), central Hesse, W Germany, in former Upper Hesse prov., 7 mi. SE of Giessen; lumber milling. Has 16th-cent. church, 18th-cent. castle.

Licheng or **Li-ch'eng** (both: lē'chŭng'). **1** Town, ⊙ Licheng co. (pop. 77,542), SE Shansi prov., China, on road and 36 mi. NE of Changchih, near Hopeh line; wheat, millet, kaoliang, corn, ramie. **2** Town, ⊙ Licheng co. (pop. 437,852), N Shantung prov., China, 10 mi. ENE of Tsinan and on Tsingtao-Tsinan RR; cotton weaving; wheat, millet, peanuts. Called Wangshejenchwang until 1935, when co. seat was moved here from Tsinan.

Lichfield, municipal borough (1931 pop. 8,507; 1951 census 10,624), E Stafford, England, 12 mi. SW of Burton-on-Trent; a peaceful market town famous for its 3-spired cathedral and its close associations with Dr. Johnson. The cathedral, dating from 13th and 14th cent., replaced the original church built by St. Chad, who founded the see in 7th cent.; badly damaged by Parliamentary forces in the Civil War, it was not completely restored until 19th cent. The house where Dr. Johnson was born and lived is now a museum containing many relics of his life and works. At the old grammar school (founded 1495) Johnson, Addison, and Garrick studied. In 18th cent. a literary circle which included Erasmus Darwin, Thomas Day, and Anna Seward was known as the Lichfield group. In Second World War town was site of large U.S. army camp.

Li-chiang, town, China: see LIKIANG.

Li Chiang, river, China: see LI RIVER, Kwangsi.

Li-ching, China: see LITSING.

Lichow, China: see LIHSIEN, Hunan prov.

Lichtenau (lĭkh'tŭnou), town (pop. 1,877), in former Prussian prov. of Westphalia, NW Germany, after 1945 in North Rhine-Westphalia, 9 mi. SE of Paderborn.

Lichtenau, Hessisch, Germany: see HESSISCH LICHTENAU.

Lichtenberg, France: see INGWILLER.

Lichtenberg (lĭkh'tŭnbĕrk). **1** Town (pop. 1,411), Upper Franconia, NE Bavaria, Germany, in the Franconian Forest, 12 mi. NW of Hof; weaving, paper milling. Chartered 1466. **2** District (1939 pop. 196,811; 1946 pop. 157,721), E Berlin, Germany, on the Spree and 5 mi. E of city center. Mfg. (machinery, electrical equipment, paint). After 1945 in Soviet sector. **3** NW district of WATENSTEDT-SALZGITTER, in Brunswick, NW Germany, after 1945 in Lower Saxony; potash mining.

Lichtenburg (lĭkh'tŭnbûrkh"), town (pop. 7,927), SW Transvaal, U. of So. Afr., 120 mi. W of Johannesburg; rail terminus; center of mining (diamonds, gold) and agr. (corn) region; cement mfg.

Lichtenfels (lĭkh'tŭnfĕls"), town (pop. 10,143), Upper Franconia, N Bavaria, Germany, on the Main and 19 mi. NNE of Bamberg; rail junction; mfg. of clothing, chemicals; leather- and woodworking, printing, lumber milling, tanning, basket weaving. Has 15th-cent. church and 18th-cent. town hall. Chartered 1206.

Lichtenfels (lĭkh'tŭnfĕls), locality, Godthaab dist., SW Greenland, on small Irkens Havn inlet of the Atlantic, 2 mi. SW of Fiskenaesset; site (1758–1900) of Moravian mission. Church extant.

Lichtenstein or **Lichtenstein in Sachsen** (lĭkh'tŭnshtīn" ĭn zäk'sŭn), town (pop. 13,407), Saxony, E central Germany, 7 mi. ENE of Zwickau, in coal-mining region; textile industry (cotton, rayon, and silk milling, knitting, and dyeing); paper milling. Includes former commune of Callnberg (S). Formerly called Lichtenstein-Callnberg.

Lichtental (lĭkh'tŭntäl), E suburb of Baden-Baden, S Germany, on the Oos. Site of Cistercian nunnery, founded 1245.

Lichtentanne (lĭkh"tŭntä'nŭ), village (pop. 5,134), Saxony, E central Germany, on Pleisse R. and 4 mi. WSW of Zwickau, in coal-mining region.

Lichtenvoorde (lĭkh'tŭnvōrdŭ), town (pop. 3,526), Gelderland prov., E Netherlands, 7 mi. W of Winterswijk; leather tanning; mfg. (shoes, brushes), woodworking, meat products.

Lichtenwörth (lĭkh'tŭnvûrt), town (pop. 2,676), E Lower Austria, on Leitha R. and 3 mi. NE of Wiener Neustadt; orchards.

Lichterfelde (lĭkh"tŭrfĕl'dŭ), residential section of Steglitz dist., SW Berlin, Germany, on Teltow Canal and 7 mi. SW of city center. Formerly site of officers-training school. After 1945 in U.S. sector.

Lichtervelde (lĭkh'tŭrvĕldŭ), agr. village (pop. 6,679), West Flanders prov., W Belgium, 3 mi. SSE of Torhout.

Li-ch'uan, Hupeh prov., China: see LICHWAN.

Lichüan or **Li-ch'üan** (lē'chüän'), town (pop. 6,389), ⊙ Lichüan co. (pop. 123,946), S central Shensi prov., China, 30 mi. NW of Sian; rice, wheat, corn.

Lichwan or **Li-ch'uan** (both: lē'chwän'). **1** Town (pop. 20,950), ⊙ Lichwan co. (pop. 226,525), SW Hupeh prov., China, on Szechwan line, 35 mi. W of Enshih; rice, wheat, beans, cotton. **2** Town (pop. 13,069), ⊙ Lichwan co. (pop. 88,916), E Kiangsi prov., China, 55 mi. SE of Fuchow, in the Bohea Hills; tobacco, hemp, watermelons, bamboo. Until 1914 called Sincheng.

Lick Branch, W.Va.: see SWITCHBACK.

Licking, county (□ 686; pop. 70,645), central Ohio; ⊙ NEWARK. Drained by Licking R. and Raccoon Creek. Includes part of Buckeye L. (recreation). Agr. area (livestock, dairy products, grain); mfg. at Newark; sand and gravel pits. Formed 1808.

Licking, town (pop. 733), Texas co., S central Mo., in the Ozarks, 32 mi. S of Rolla; alt. 1,277 ft.; grain, lumber products.

Licking River. 1 In E Ky., rises in S Magoffin co., flows 320 mi. generally NW, past Salyersville and Falmouth, to Ohio R. bet. Covington and Newport, opposite Cincinnati. Partly navigable. North Fork rises in NE Ky. in Lewis and Fleming counties, flows c.80 mi. generally W to the Licking 10 mi. SW of Falmouth. South Fork rises in N central Ky. in Bourbon co., flows c.90 mi. generally N, past Paris and Cynthiana, to the Licking at Falmouth. River was early travel route for Indians and pioneers, and later a busy trade artery; George Rogers Clark's frontiersmen gathered at its mouth in 1780 for their march up the Little Miami, and the battle of Blue Licks (at BLUE LICKS SPRINGS) occurred in Licking R. valley in 1782. **2** In central Ohio, formed by North and South forks and Raccoon Creek at Newark, flows c.40 mi. E and SE to the Muskingum at Zanesville. North Fork rises in Knox co., flows c.35 mi. E and S. South Fork rises in Licking co., flows SE and NE for c.30 mi. Raccoon Creek (c.25 mi. long), entirely within Licking co., flows SE to junction with the other headstreams.

Lick River, S Ind., rises in E Orange co., flows c.25 mi. NW, past Paoli, to Lost R. near West Baden Springs.

Licodia Eubea (lēkô'dyä ĕōōbā'ä), village (pop. 5,970), Catania prov., SE Sicily, on SW slope of Monti Iblei, 12 mi. ESE of Caltagirone; wine, olive oil, cement, tobacco products. Built on ruins of anc. Eubea (founded 7th cent. B.C. by Lentini).

Licosa, Punta (pōōn'tä lēkô'zä), promontory, S Italy, at SE end of Gulf of Salerno, 20 mi. W of Vallo della Lucania; 40°15'N 14°54'E.

Licq-Athérey (lēk'-ätärā'), village (pop. 195), Basses-Pyrénées dept., SW France, near Sp. border, on Saison R. and 16 mi. SW of Oloron-Sainte-Marie; customhouse; cattle and lumber market. Hydroelectric station.

Lida (lyē'dŭ), city (1931 pop. 19,490), NE Grodno oblast, Belorussian SSR, 55 mi. S of Vilna, 60 mi. ENE of Grodno; rail junction (repair shops); mfg. center (agr. machinery, textiles, rubber and leather shoes, cement, tiles, soap); agr. processing (flaxseed, grain, hops), sawmilling. Has ruins of old castle. Founded 1323 by Lith. duke Gedymin; sacked (1392) by Teutonic Knights. Developed as flax- and livestock-trading center in 16th cent. Passed (1795) from Poland to Russia; reverted (1919) to Poland; ceded to USSR in 1945.

Lida, Lake (lī'dŭ) (□ 10), Otter Tail co., W Minn., just S of L. Lizzie, 19 mi. NNE of Fergus Falls; 4 mi. long, 2.5 mi. wide. Resorts.

Lidcombe (lĭd'kŭm), municipality (pop. 20,281), E New South Wales, Australia, 11 mi. W of Sydney, in metropolitan area; rail junction; knitting and textile mills, meat-packing plants.

Liddel Water, river, Roxburgh and Dumfries, Scotland, rises 11 mi. SE of Hawick, flows 27 mi. SW, past Newcastleton, to Esk R. 2 mi. S of Canonbie.

Lidderdale, town (pop. 180), Carroll co., W central Iowa, 6 mi. NE of Carroll; feed milling.

Lidgerwood, city (pop. 1,147), Richland co., SE N.Dak., 30 mi. SW of Wahpeton; dairy products, poultry, grain. Inc. 1901.

Lidhorikion, Greece: see LIDORIKION.

Lidhult (lēd'hŭlt"), village (pop. 488), Kronoberg co., S Sweden, near L. Bolm, 19 mi. W of Ljungby; woodworking, furniture mfg.

Lidice (lĭ'dĭtsĕ), village (1941 pop. c.500), W central Bohemia, Czechoslovakia, 4 mi. E of Kladno. As a reprisal for the assassination of Reinhard Heydrich, Ger. Protector of Bohemia and Moravia, the Germans "liquidated" (June, 1942) Lidice by killing all the men, deporting the women and children, and razing the village to the ground. In 1947, a new village of Lidice was begun near by; site of the old village was set aside as a natl. memorial.

Lidice (lĭ'dĭsē, lē'dĭ-shä), village (pop. 4,311, with adjacent Raynor Park), Will co., NE Ill., just NW of Joliet.

Lidingo (lē'dĭng-û"), Swedish *Lidingö,* city (1950 pop. 20,798), Stockholm co., E Sweden, on the isl. (□ 12) of same name in the Baltic, separated from mainland by narrow sound (bridge), 3 mi. NE of Stockholm city center; seaside resort. Mfg. of gas and electrical equipment; shipbuilding. Inc. 1926 as city.

Lidkoping (lēd'chû"pĭng), Swedish *Lidköping,* city (pop. 13,031), Skaraborg co., SW Sweden, on S shore of L. Vaner, at mouth of Lida R. (lē'dä"), Swedish *Lidan* (50 mi. long), 35 mi. ENE of Trollhattan; rail junction; sugar refining, sawmilling, metalworking, stone quarrying; mfg. of matches, porcelain. Tourist resort. Has old town hall. Chartered 1446.

Lido (lē'dô) [Ital.,=beach], N Italy, resort on sandy island chain separating Lagoon of Venice from the Adriatic. Principal isl. (Lido or Lido di Venezia) is 7.5 mi. long and narrow; has a beautiful beach only 20 minutes by boat from Venice; one of most fashionable bathing resorts in Europe. Chief channels bet. isls. are those of Lido, Malamocco, and Chioggia.

Lido di Roma (lē'dô dē rô'mä), town (pop. 5,295), Roma prov., Latium, central Italy, on Tyrrhenian Sea, near mouth of the Tiber, 15 mi. SW of Rome; bathing resort.

Lido Isle, Calif.: see NEWPORT BEACH.

Lidorikion or **Lidhorikion** (both: lēdhôrē'kēôn), village (pop. 1,611), Phocis nome, W central Greece, 9 mi. W of Amphissa; sheep and goat raising.

Lidzbark (lēdz'bärk), Ger. *Lautenburg* (lou'tŭnbōōrk), town (pop. 3,720), Olsztyn prov., N Poland, on railroad and 15 mi. W of Dzialdowo; mfg. of chemicals, mineral water; tanning, distilling, lumbering. Also called Lidzbark Welski.

Lidzbark Warminski (värmē'nyŭskē), Pol. *Lidzbark Warmiński,* Ger. *Heilsberg* (hīls'bĕrk), town (1939 pop. 11,787; 1946 pop. 4,201) in East Prussia, after 1945 in Olsztyn prov., NE Poland, on Lyna R. and 25 mi. N of Allenstein (Olsztyn); grain and cattle market; sawmilling. Radio station. Seat (1350–1772) of bishops of Ermland. Has remains of 15th-cent. town walls. In Second World War, c.50% destroyed.

Liebau, Czechoslovakia: see LIBAVA.

Liebau, Poland: see LUBAWKA.

Liebenau (lē'bŭnou), town (pop. 2,243), NE Upper Austria, 14 mi. E of Freistadt, near Czechoslovak line; vineyards.

Liebenau or **Liebenau an der Diemel** (än dĕr dē'mŭl), town (pop. 982), in former Prussian prov. of Hesse-Nassau, W Germany, after 1945 in Hesse, on the Diemel and 4 mi. W of Hofgeismar.

Liebenau bei Schwiebus, Brandenburg: see LUBRZA, Poland.

Liebenburg (lē'bŭnbōōrk), village (pop. 2,591), in Brunswick, NW Germany, after 1945 in Lower Saxony, 8 mi. N of Goslar; sawmilling. Has 18th-cent. castle. Until 1941 in former Prussian prov. of Hanover.

Liebenfelde, Russian SFSR: see ZALESYE.

Liebenstein, Bad, Germany: see BAD LIEBENSTEIN.

Liebenthal, Poland: see LUBOMIERZ.

Liebenthal (lē'bŭn-thäl), city (pop. 211), Rush co., W central Kansas, 15 mi. S of Hays, in wheat and livestock area.

Liebenwalde (lē'bŭnväl"dŭ), town (pop. 3,708), Brandenburg, E Germany, on the Havel at junction of Voss and Finow canals, and 25 mi. N of Berlin, 11 mi. NE of Oranienburg; market gardening, lumbering; wire and rope mfg.

Liebenwerda, Bad, Germany: see BAD LIEBENWERDA.

Liebenzell, Bad, Germany: see BAD LIEBENZELL.

Lieberose (lē'bŭrō"zŭ), town (pop. 2,495), Brandenburg, E Germany, in Lower Lusatia, NE of Spree Forest, 16 mi. N of Cottbus; flax, vegetables, stock. Has late-Gothic church, 18th-cent. palace.

Lieberwolkwitz (lē"bŭrvôlk'vĭts"), village (pop. 5,966), Saxony, E central Germany, 5 mi. SE of Leipzig, in lignite-mining region; metalworking, cement mfg. Scene (Oct., 1813) of opening engagement of battle of Leipzig.

Liebig or **Liebigs,** village, Río Negro dept., W Uruguay, on railroad and 8 mi. ESE of Fray Bentos. A settlement of workmen for meat-packing factory in Fray Bentos. Agr. produce (wheat, wine, cattle, sheep).

Liebstadt (lēp'shtät), town (pop. 1,100), Saxony, E central Germany, in Saxonian Switzerland, 8 mi. SSW of Pirna, near Czechoslovak border; grain, livestock.

Liebwerda, Czechoslovakia: see HEJNICE.

Liechtenstein (lĭkh'tŭnshtīn"), sovereign principality (□ 62; pop. 11,218), central Europe, bet. Switzerland (W) and Austria (E), bordered by the Rhine not far from its influx into L. of Constance; ⊙ VADUZ. It is 15 mi. long (N–S), 5 mi. wide. The tiny country, beautifully set amid the Alps, has a narrow alluvial belt on the Rhine (partly canalized), but is predominantly mountainous, forming part of the Rhätikon spur, which rises in Naafkopf on Austro-Swiss-Liechtenstein border to c.8,440 ft. Principally a pastoral and agr. region, it grows corn, potatoes, wheat, vegetables, wine. Cattle raising and dairying are its chief activity; hogs, goats, and sheep are also raised. There are marble deposits. Industries include some textile (cotton) milling, lumbering, mfg. of pottery and leather goods. Much revenue is derived from issuance of postage stamps. A hydroelectric plant has been built in Lavena valley (S). Its N section is crossed at SCHAAN by the Arlberg Express to Vienna via Buchs (Switzerland) and Feldkirch (Austria). The German-speaking pop. is largely R.C. The principality was created (1719) when the county of Vaduz and barony of Schellenberg were merged under the house of Liechtenstein. It remained a part of the Holy Roman Empire until 1806, when it became a sovereign member within Confederation of the Rhine. Belonged to German Confederation 1815–66. Until end of First World War it was oriented toward Austria, but now maintains closer links with Switzerland, whose currency it adopted (1921) and with whom it joined (1924) in a customs union. It is also represented abroad through the Swiss govt. Its democratic constitution of 1921 provides for an elected diet of 15 members. It has had no army since 1868. Because of its smallness, Liechtenstein was overlooked in the upheavals of the past century and a half. It was also neutral during Second World War.

Liedekerke (lē'dŭkĕrkŭ), town (pop. 7,838), Brabant prov., central Belgium, 13 mi. W of Brussels; agr. market (fruit, vegetables, poultry, dairying). Has ruins of anc. Carmelite monastery.

Liedolsheim (lē'dôls-hīm), village (pop. 2,707), N Baden, Germany, after 1945 in Württemberg-Baden, 10 mi. N of Karlsruhe; asparagus, strawberries, tobacco.

Liége (lyĕzh), Flemish *Luik* (loik), province (□ 1,526; pop. 973,911), E Belgium; ⊙ Liége. Bounded by Limburg prov. (N), Brabant and Namur provs. (W), Luxembourg prov. and grand duchy of Luxembourg (S), Germany (E). Drained by Meuse, Amblève, Ourthe, and Vesdre rivers. Food crops and sugar beets grown in N, around Waremme; fruitgrowing and dairying in Herve region (NE) and in S. Industrial area along Meuse and Vesdre rivers: heavy machine mfg., armaments, electrical equipment; coal mining (centers: Liége, Huy, Seraing); wool textiles (Verviers, Pepinster). Spa is a noted resort. Prov. mainly French-speaking, except in area along Ger. border (Eupen-Malmédy), which is German-speaking. Liége was for over a thousand years an independent church-state ruled by prince-bishops of Liége. After years of struggle for liberty it passed to the Netherlands in 1815 and to Belgium in 1830.

Liége, Flemish *Luik*, anc. *Leodium*, city (pop. 156,664; with suburbs 432,471), ⊙ Liége prov., E Belgium, on Meuse R., at mouth of Ourthe R., and 55 mi. ESE of Brussels; 50°40'N 5°34'E. Vital communications center at S end of Albert Canal and Liége-Maastricht Canal, and road and rail center for traffic with Germany. Major industrial city and the commercial hub of industrial Meuse valley, including suburbs of Herstal, Seraing, Ougrée, Jemeppe. Mfg. of machinery, machine tools, armaments, bicycles; leather tanning; processing of aluminum, rubber, zinc; brewing, flour milling, paper milling. Has univ. founded 1817, with fine engineering and mining faculty; cathedral of St. Paul, partly dating from 13th cent.; 10th-cent. church of St. Denis; 16th-cent. Gothic Palace of Justice, formerly residence of prince-bishops of Liége; 2 art museums; archaeological mus. Until 1792 city was ruled by prince-bishops of Liége, the last of whom was expelled by the French under Dumouriez. Liége is the cultural center of French-speaking Belgium and an episcopal see. In early stage of First World War its important fortress of Eben Emael fell only after heavy bombardment, but in Second World War it was rapidly captured by Germans; liberated (1944) by U.S. 9th Army; thereafter bombed by Ger. rocket weapons, but it survived without major damage to its principal bldgs. and streets.

Liege (lēj), town (pop. 77), Montgomery co., E central Mo., 9 mi. E of Montgomery City.

Liége Island (lyĕzh) (8 naut. mi. long, 6 wide), Antarctica, NE of Brabant Isl., off Palmer Peninsula; 64°4'S 61°50'W. Discovered 1898 by Adrien de Gerlache, Belgian explorer.

Liége-Maastricht Canal (–mäs'trĭkht) (16 mi. long), E Belgium; section of Albert Canal bet. Liége (Belgium) and Maastricht (Netherlands).

Liége-Saint-Lambert, Belgian Congo: see KATANA.

Liegnitz (lēg'nĭts) or **Legnica** (lĕgnē'tsä), trading and mfg. town (1939 pop. 83,681; 1946 pop. 24,357; 1950 pop. estimate 56,000) in Lower Silesia, after 1945 in Wroclaw prov., SW Poland, on the Katzbach and 40 mi. W of Breslau (Wroclaw). Rail junction; commercial center; textile milling and knitting, mfg. of chemicals, paints, pharmaceuticals, gypsum products, pianos. Has 11th-cent. castle (rebuilt 1835), baroque church of St. John (earlier structure has tombs of the Piasts), remains of 14th-cent. town walls. First mentioned c.1000; chartered 1252. Was (1163–1675) ⊙ duchy of Liegnitz under branch of Piast dynasty, then passed to the Hapsburgs. Reformation introduced 1522. Treaty of Liegnitz (1537) was basis for Frederick the Great's claim to Silesia. In Thirty Years War, scene (1634) of Saxon victory over imperial forces. Passed 1742 to Prussia after War of the Austrian Succession. Heavily damaged in Second World War. Near by were fought the historic battles of WAHLSTATT, BREMBERG (battle of the Katzbach), and PANTEN.

Lieksa (lē'ĕksä), town (pop. 3,542), Kuopio co., E Finland, near USSR border, on E shore of L. Pieli, 50 mi. N of Joensuu; sawmilling, woodworking. Pielisjärvi molybdenum mines near by.

Lieksajärvi, Karelo-Finnish SSR: see LEKSOZERO.

Lielahti (lē'ĕlä"tē, –läkh"tē), suburb of Tampere, Häme co., SW Finland, bet. lakes Näsi (N) and Pyhä (S), 2 mi. W of city center; lumber, pulp, cellulose, and paper mills.

Lielupe River (lyĕ'lōōpā), Ger. *Aa* or *Kurische Aa* [=Courland Aa], also *Bolderaa*, in W central Latvia, formed at Bauska by union of Memele and Musa rivers; flows NW past Jelgava, N and ENE to Gulf of Riga, joining mouth of Western Dvina R. bet. Daugavgriva and Bolderaja; 74 mi. long; including either headstream, c.190 mi. long. Parallels coast of Gulf of Riga in lower course, forming a sandspit on which is Rigas Jurmala. Navigable for entire course.

Lien. 1 River, Kiangsu prov., China: see YEN RIVER. **2** River, in Kwangsi and Kwangtung provs., China: see LIM RIVER.

Liénart (lyānär'), village, Eastern Prov., N Belgian Congo, 50 mi. ENE of Buta; rail junction and trading post in cotton-growing area.

Liencheng or **Lien-ch'eng** (lyĕn'chŭng'), town (pop. 15,939), ⊙ Liencheng co. (pop. 107,741), SW Fukien prov., China, 25 mi. E of Changting; rice, sweet potatoes, wheat. Coal mines near by.

Lien-chiang. 1 Town, Fukien prov., China: see LIENKONG. **2** Town, Kwangtung prov., China: see LIMKONG.

Lien Chiang, river, China: see LIM RIVER.

Lien-chiang-k'ou, Manchuria: see LIENKIANGKOW.

Lienchow, China: see HOPPO.

Lienchow, Kiang, China: see LINCHOW RIVER.

Lienen (lē'nŭn), village (pop. 6,988), in former Prussian prov. of Westphalia, NW Germany, after 1945 in North Rhine-Westphalia, in Teutoburg Forest, 9 mi. SSW of Osnabrück; grain.

Lienhsien, China: see LINHSIEN.

Lienhwa or **Lien-hua** (both: lyĕn'hwä'), town (pop. 4,170), ⊙ Lienhwa co. (pop. 78,757), W Kiangsi prov., China, near Hunan line, 65 mi. W of Kian; rice, tea, tobacco, hemp. Anthracite mines; iron and sulphur deposits.

Lien Kiang, China: see LIM RIVER.

Lienkiangkow or **Lien-chiang-k'ou** (both: lyĕn'-jyäng'kō'), N suburb of Kiamusze, Sungkiang prov., Manchuria, on N bank of Sungari R.; rail terminus for Hingshan coal mines and Suihwa.

Lienkong (lyĕn'gông'), Mandarin *Lien-chiang* (–jyäng'), town (pop. 11,415), ⊙ Lienkong co. (pop. 217,656), E Fukien prov., China, 15 mi. ENE of Foochow, on E.China Sea; rice, sweet potatoes, sugar cane, rapeseed. Talc quarrying. Former port, now silted.

Liennan, China: see LINNAM.

Lien-p'ing, China: see LINPING.

Lien River, China: see YEN RIVER.

Lienshan (lyĕn'shän'). **1** Town, Kwangtung prov., China: see LINSHAN. **2** Town, Liaosi prov., Manchuria, China: see CHINSI. **3** Village, ⊙ Lienshan dist. (pop. 13,849), W Yunnan prov., China, 40 mi. SW of Tengchung, near Burma border; rice, wheat, millet, beans. Until 1935, Chanta or Tsanta.

Lienshui (lyĕn'shwā'), town (pop. 4,870), ⊙ Lienshui co. (pop. 59,662), N Kiangsu prov., China, 18 mi. NE of Hwaiyin and on Yen R. (also called Lien R.); wheat, corn, beans, kaoliang, cotton. Until 1914 called Antung.

Lienyün (lyĕn'yün'), town (1947 pop. 76,941), ⊙ Lienyün co., S Shantung prov., China, 105 mi. SW of Tsingtao, 20 mi. NE of Sinhai; major port on Yellow Sea, and E terminus of Lunghai RR; commercial center; exports wheat, kaoliang, corn, beans, wine. Has saltworks and fisheries. Developed in 1930s as deepwater port bet. Shanghai and Tsingtao. Called Laoyao until 1935. It was an independent municipality from 1935 until 1949, when it was merged with SINHAI in the municipality of Sinhailien. Until 1949 in Kiangsu prov.

Lienz (lē'ĕnts), town (pop. 10,085), ⊙ East Tyrol, S Austria, on the Drau, at mouth of Isel R., and 75 mi. W of Klagenfurt; mfg. (waterproof cloth, leather goods). Wheat, rye, fruit grown in surrounding fertile basin. Has 2 Gothic churches, 16th-cent. castle. Lienz is at N foot of Lienz Dolomites (W group of Gailtal Alps).

Lienz Dolomites (dō'lŭmīts), sub-range of the Gailtal Alps, S Austria, along East Tyrol–Carinthia line, S of Drau R. Highest peak, Sandspitze (9,391 ft.). At its N foot lies Lienz.

Liepaja or **Lepaya** (lyĕ'päyä), Lettish *Liepāja*, Ger. *Libau* (lē'bou), Rus. (until 1917) *Libava* (lē'bävä), second-largest city (pop. 57,098) of Latvia, in Kurzeme, ice-free Baltic port, 120 mi. WSW of Riga; 56°31'N 21°E. Rail terminus; major industrial center; steel mills (rolled steel, ingots); mfg. of wire, nuts, bolts, agr. machinery, explosives, paints, linoleum, cork and leather goods; shipbuilding (naval installations), rail car repair; timber industry (pulpwood, matches, paper, cardboard); food processing (sugar, meat, tobacco), fish canning. Exports timber, steel products, linoleum, matches. Noted health resort (baths). Has city theater, city hall. On 1.5-mi.-wide isthmus bet. Baltic Sea and small Liepaja L. (10 mi. long, 2 mi. wide), joined by 300-ft.-wide city canal which separates old city (S) from new city (N). Extensive artificial port installations include old commercial harbor (in city canal), winter harbor (at W end of canal), and fortified naval harbor (in city's N outskirts). City dates from 1263; chartered (1625) in duchy of Courland; passed (1795) to Russia. Reached (1871) by railroad; developed rapidly as one of Russia's chief ice-free Baltic ports. Occupied and served as Ger. naval base (1915–18) during First World War and again (1941–45) during Second World War. In independent Latvia (1920–40), it was ⊙ Kurzeme.

Liepvre (lēē'vrŭ), Ger. *Leberau* (lā'bŭrou), village (pop. 1,228), Haut-Rhin dept., E France, in the Vosges, 8 mi. W of Sélestat; woolen milling. Also spelled Lièpvre.

Lier, Belgium: see LIERRE.

Lier (lē'ŭr), village (pop. 614; canton pop. 13,507), Buskerud co., SE Norway, on Lier R., on railroad and 3 mi. NNE of Drammen; market gardening, lumber milling, cement mfg.; fruit-distributing point. Just E is insane asylum.

Liernais (lyĕrnā'), village (pop. 315), Côte-d'Or dept., E central France, in the Monts du Morvan, 17 mi. N of Autun; cattle, vegetables.

Lierneux (lyĕrnû'), village (pop. 3,122), Liége prov., E Belgium, 25 mi. SSE of Liége; agr., lumbering. Site of lunatic rehabilitation colony.

Lierre (lyâr), Flemish *Lier* (lēr), town (pop. 29,129), Antwerp prov., N Belgium, at confluence of Grande Nèthe R. and Petite Nèthe R. (here forming Nèthe R.), 9 mi. SE of Antwerp; lock, tool, and cutlery center; lace making. Has 15th-cent. church of St. Gommarius, 17th–18th-cent. town hall with 14th-cent. belfry.

Lier River (lē'ŭr), Buskerud co., SE Norway, rises near S side of Tyri Fjord, flows c.25 mi. S to head of Drammen Fjord 3 mi. E of Drammen. Valley is one of SE Norway's most fertile regions.

Liers (lyârs), village (pop. 1,055), Liége prov., E Belgium, 4 mi. N of Liége; beet-sugar refining.

Liesing (lē'zĭng), outer SW district (□ 51; pop. 53,255) of Vienna, Austria. Formed (1938) through incorporation of 13 towns, including Atzgersdorf, Erlaa, Inzersdorf, Kaltenleutgeben, Mauer, Perchtoldsdorf, Rodaun, Siebenhirten, Vösendorf, and Liesing (pop. 6,013; 6 mi. SW of city center; mfg. of aluminum alloys; brewing).

Liesse (lēĕs'), village (pop. 1,004), Aisne dept., N France, 9 mi. ENE of Laon. Its 14th–15th-cent. church of Notre-Dame-de-Liesse (with 12th-cent. image of the Virgin) has been goal of pilgrimage since the Crusades.

Liestal (lēs'täl), town (pop. 7,211), ⊙ Basel-Land half-canton, N Switzerland, on Ergolz R. and 8 mi. SE of Basel; textiles (woolen, silk), knit goods, chemicals, metal products; printing. Has old town hall, cantonal mus.

Liétor (lyā'tōr), town (pop. 2,449), Albacete prov., SE central Spain, on Mundo R. and 15 mi. W of Hellín; esparto processing, flour milling; olive oil, honey, fruit. Large reservoir near by. Tripoli mines.

Lietuva: see LITHUANIA.

Lietzenburg, Germany: see CHARLOTTENBURG.

Lieuwert, Netherlands: see LEEUWARDEN.

Lievenhof, Latvia: see LIVANI.

Lievestuore (lē'ĕvĕstōō"ôrä), village in Laukaa commune (pop. 14,518), Vaasa co., S central Finland, on small lake near N end of L. Päijänne, 14 mi. E of Jyväskylä; pulp mill, wood-alcohol plant.

Liévin (lyävē'), town (pop. 15,272), Pas-de-Calais dept., N France, 3 mi. WSW of Lens; important coal-mining center with numerous miners' residential districts. Just S rises Vimy Ridge of First World War fame.

Lièvre River (lē'vŭr) or **Rivière du Lièvre** (rēvyâr dü lyĕ'vrŭ), SW Que., issues from Kempt L., in the Laurentians, 120 mi. NW of Montreal, flows c.225 mi. S, through several lakes and past Mont Laurier, Buckingham, and Masson, to Ottawa R. 4 mi. S of Buckingham; 22 mi. NNW of Buckingham are 130-ft. High Falls.

Lièvres, Île aux, Que.: see HARE ISLAND.

Lieze, Belgium: see LIXHE.

Liezen (lē'tsŭn), town (pop. 4,687), Styria, central Austria, near Enns R., 36 mi. NW of Knittelfeld; resort. Peat bogs in vicinity.

Lifake, Belgian Congo: see DJOLU.

Lifan, China: see LIHSIEN, Szechwan prov.

Liff and Benvie (bĕnvē'), parish (pop. 2,141), SW Angus, Scotland. Includes agr. villages of Liff, 4 mi. WNW of Dundee, and Benvie, just S of Liff.

Liffey River (lĭ'fē), Ireland, rises on SW slope of Kippure mtn., N Co. Wicklow, flows generally W into Co. Kildare to Droichead Nua (Newbridge), where it turns NE to Leixlip at Co. Dublin line and E through Dublin to Dublin Bay (inlet of Irish Sea); c.50 mi. long.

Liffol-le-Grand (lēfôl'-lŭ-grä'), village (pop. 1,732), Vosges dept., E France, 6 mi. SW of Neufchâteau; furniture carving.

Lifford, Gaelic *Leithbhearr*, town (pop. 476), ⊙ Co. Donegal, Ireland, in E part of co., at confluence of Mourne and Finn rivers, here forming Foyle R., opposite Strabane (Northern Ireland), and 110 mi. NNW of Dublin; mfg. of shirts, furniture. It was scene (1600) of battle bet. Hugh Roe O'Donnell and English garrison of Londonderry.

Liffré (lēfrā'), village (pop. 785), Ille-et-Vilaine dept., W France, 10 mi. NE of Rennes; mfg. of wooden shoes.

Lifu (lē'fōō'), Fr. *Lifou*, coral island, (pop. c.6,300), largest of Loyalty Isls., SW Pacific, 60 mi. E of New Caledonia; roughly semicircular, c.40 mi. long, 10 mi. wide; copra. Chépénéhé is chief town.

Lifudzin (lyĭfōō'dzĭn), town (1946 pop. over 500), SE Maritime Territory, Russian SFSR, on shore Lifudzin R. and c.50 mi. W of Tetyukhe; lead, zinc, tin mining.

Lifuka (lēfōō'kä), coral island (pop. 1,000), Haabai group, central Tonga, S Pacific; c.5 mi. long. Seat of Pangai, ⊙ Haabai group; port of entry.

Liganga (lēgäng'gä), locality, Southern Highlands prov., S Tanganyika, near N end of L. Nyasa, 40 mi. SSE of Njombe; iron deposits (titaniferous magnetite).

Ligao (lēgä'ō, lēgou'), town (1939 pop. 5,084; 1948 municipality pop. 37,331), Albay prov., SE Luzon, Philippines, on railroad and 15 mi. WNW of Legaspi; trade center for agr. area (abacá, rice); gypsum.

Ligatne (lē'gätnā), Lettish *Līgatne*, town, N central Latvia, on railroad and 6 mi. ENE of Sigulda. Large paper mill on Gauja R., 3 mi. N.

Liger, France: see LOIRE RIVER.

Liggett, mining village, Harlan co., SE Ky., in the Cumberlands, 8 mi. SSW of Harlan; bituminous coal.

Lighthouse Island, Northern Ireland: see OLD LIGHTHOUSE ISLAND.

Lighthouse Island, Mass.: see BREWSTER ISLANDS.

Lightning Ridge, village (pop. 286), N New South Wales, Australia, 335 mi. NW of Newcastle; opal mines.

Light River, SE South Australia, rises in Mt. Lofty Ranges, flows 100 mi. SW, past Kapunda and Hamley Bridge, to Gulf St. Vincent 20 mi. N of Port Adelaide.

Ligné (lēnyā'), village (pop. 346), Loire-Inférieure dept., W France, 16 mi. NE of Nantes; coal deposits near by.

Lignières (lēnyâr'), village (pop. 1,623), Cher dept., central France, on Arnon R. and 16 mi. W of Saint-Amand-Montrond; road center and agr. market.

Lignite, village (1939 pop. 13), S central Alaska, NE of Mt. McKinley Natl. Park, 5 mi. N of Healy, on Alaska RR; sub-bituminous coal deposits.

Lignite, village (pop. 230), Burke co., NW N.Dak., 15 mi. WNW of Bowbells, near lignite-mining center.

Lignon River (lēnyō'). **1** Left tributary of Loire R., in Loire dept., SE central France, rises in Monts du Forez 7 mi. W of Saint-Georges-en-Couzan; flows 37 mi. E, past Boën-sur-Lignon, to the Loire below Feurs. Sometimes called Lignon du Forez. **2** Right tributary of the Loire, in Haute-Loire dept., central France, rises near Mont Mézenc 9 mi. E of Le Monastier, flows 60 mi. N, past Fay-sur-Lignon and Tence, to the Loire above Monistrol-sur-Loire. Sometimes called Lignon du Velay.

Ligny (lēnyē'), village (pop. 1,965), Namur prov., central Belgium, 14 mi. WNW of Namur; chalk quarrying. In battle here (1815) French under Napoleon defeated Prussians under Blücher 2 days before battle of Waterloo.

Ligny-en-Barrois (–ā-bärwä'), town (pop. 4,351), Meuse dept., NE France, on the Ornain and Marne-Rhine Canal, and 9 mi. SE of Bar-le-Duc; woodworking center (furniture, toys, measuring devices). Mfg. of lenses, magnifying glass, footwear; fruit preserving.

Ligny-en-Cambrésis (–kābrāsē'), town (pop. 2,042), Nord dept., N France, 8 mi. SE of Cambrai; fine fabrics.

Ligny-le-Châtel (–lů-shätěl'), village (pop. 786), Yonne dept., N central France, on Serein R. and 11 mi. NE of Auxerre, in winegrowing area.

Ligon (lĭ'gůn), mining village (1940 pop. 785), Floyd co., E Ky., in Cumberland foothills, 14 mi. SW of Pikeville; bituminous coal.

Ligoniel or **Legoniel** (lĭgůněl'), NW suburb of Belfast, S Co. Antrim, Northern Ireland.

Ligonier. 1 (lĭ'gůnėr, lĭgůnēr') City (pop. 2,375), Noble co., NE Ind., on Elkhart R. and 37 mi. SE of South Bend; trade center in dairying and poultry-raising area; mfg. (furniture, refrigerators, pipes, culverts, work clothes, bedding, flour). **2** (lĭgůnēr') Borough (pop. 2,160), Westmoreland co., SW Pa., on Loyalhanna Creek and 17 mi. ESE of Greensburg; agr.; bituminous coal; mfg. (drugs, beverages), timber; resort. Fort Ligonier built c.1758. Laid out 1817, inc. 1834.

Ligovo (lyē'gůvů), town (1939 pop. over 2,000), central Leningrad oblast, Russian SFSR, adjoins URITSK (E), which was formerly (until 1925) named Ligovo.

Ligua, Chile: see LA LIGUA.

Liguanea (lēgwänā'ä) or **Lanier,** swamps, Isle of Pines, Cuba, extending c.25 mi. E-W across central part of isl.

Liguanea Plain (lĭ'gůnē', lĭ'gůnē), fertile lowland in SE Jamaica, on coast around Kingston. Vere Plain continues it W.

Ligua River, Sp. *Río de la Ligua* (rē'ō dā lä lē'gwä), Aconcagua prov., central Chile, rises in the Andes at c.32°15'N, flows c.70 mi. W, past Cabildo and La Ligua, to the Pacific N of Papudo.

Liguasan Marsh (lĭgwůsän', lĭgwä'sän), large swampy area (25 mi. long, 20 mi. wide) in S central Mindanao, Philippines, along Pulangi R., SE of Cotabato.

Ligueil (lēgû'ē), village (pop. 1,436), Indre-et-Loire dept., W central France, 20 mi. NE of Châtellerault; dairying; limekilns near by.

Ligugé (lēgü-zhā'), village (pop. 1,005), Vienne dept., W central France, 5 mi. S of Poitiers; paper mill.

Liguria (lĭgūr'ēů, Ital. lēgōō'rēä), region (□ 2,098; pop. 1,466,810), NW Italy; ⊙ Genoa. Borders Piedmont and Emilia-Romagna (N), Ligurian Sea (S), Tuscany (E), and France (W). Comprises 4 provs.: GENOVA, IMPERIA, LA SPEZIA, SAVONA. Consists chiefly of S slope of Ligurian Alps (W) and Ligurian Apennines (E), extending in an arc around Gulf of Genoa (Ligurian Sea), bet. Roya (W) and Magra (E) river basins. Has narrow, indented coastal strip, the Ital. RIVIERA, noted for its picturesque scenery, mild winter climate (mean temp. 50°F.), and luxuriant vegetation. Rainfall along coast ranges from under 30 in. (W of Savona) to 60 in. (around Spezia); increases to 80 in. along crest of mts. Summers are dry and have a mean temp. of 75°F. Forests cover 50%, pastures 20% of area. The Riviera, though celebrated primarily as a winter resort area (San Remo, Bordighera, Rapallo, Santa Margherita Ligure, Portofino), also contains most of the region's pop. (over 40% in Greater Genoa alone), commerce, industry, and agr. Chief centers of commerce and industry: Greater Genoa, Savona, Spezia, Imperia, Vado Ligure, Chiavari, Sarzana. Principal industries: shipbuilding, iron- and steelworks, chemical plants, olive-oil refining. Leads Italy in production of flowers. Other major crops: olives, grapes, vegetables, fruit (especially peaches), mushrooms, chestnuts. Has quarries of marble (Palmaria, Portovenere, Levanto), slate (Lavagna, Cicagna, Uscio), and limestone, and copper mines (Libiola). Livestock raising (cows, sheep). Fishing. Its anc. inhabitants, the Ligures, were driven by Celtic migrations from mts. and by Phoenician, Greek, and Carthaginian colonization from coast. Region conquered by Romans in 2d cent. B.C. From 16th cent. until its annexation (1815) to kingdom of Sardinia, controlled by Genoa. Republic of Genoa, established by French in 18th cent., was also called Ligurian Republic. A small mtn. area (□ 15; pop. 527) in W (vicinity of Monte Saccarello) went to France in treaty of 1947.

Ligurian Alps (lĭgūr'ēůn), Ital. *Alpi Liguri*, E division of Maritime Alps, NW Italy; extend 60 mi. W from Ligurian Apennines at Cadibona Pass to Tenda Pass; rise to 8,697 ft. in Monte Marguareis, and to 7,218 ft. in Monte Saccarello. W end forms part of Fr.-Ital. border.

Ligurian Apennines (ă'pěnīnz), Italy, W division of N Apennines, extend 100 mi. bet. Maritime Alps at Cadibona Pass (W) and Etruscan Apennines at La Cisa pass (E). Chief peaks: Monte Maggiorasca (5,915 ft.), Monte Bue (5,840 ft.), Monte Antola (5,243 ft.), and Monte Beigua (4,222 ft.). Passes include GIOVI PASS, Passo del TURCHINO, and Colle della SCOFFERA. In N is source of Orba, Scrivia, Taro, and Trebbia rivers; in S, of Lavagna and Vara rivers.

Ligurian Sea, arm of Mediterranean Sea indenting NW coast of Italy; extends from Liguria (N) to Corsica (S), and from Tuscany (E) to French boundary (W). Connects with Tyrrhenian Sea (SE) in Tuscan Archipelago. More than 9,300 ft. deep NW of Corsica. N portion is called Gulf of GENOA.

Lihir Islands (lē'hĭr), small volcanic group (□ c.70; pop. c.3,600), New Ireland dist., Bismarck Archipelago, Territory of New Guinea, SW Pacific, 30 mi. NE of New Ireland; comprise c.5 isls. Largest isl., Lihir, is c.12 mi. long, rises to 1,640 ft.

Lihou (lēōō'), island (38 acres), one of Channel Isls., just off W coast of Guernsey. Has remains of anc. priory.

Lihsien (lē'shyěn'). **1** Town, ⊙ Lihsien co. (pop. 201,633), W central Hopeh prov., China, 25 mi. S of Paoting; cotton, wheat, beans, kaoliang. **2** Town, ⊙ Lihsien co. (pop. 543,575), N Hunan prov., China, on Li R. and 40 mi. NNE of Changteh, and on road to Yangtze port of Shasi; rice, wheat, beans, cotton. Coal mining near by. Until 1913 called Lichow. Commercial port of Tsingshih is 7 mi. E. **3** Town, ⊙ Lihsien co. (pop. 156,809), SE Kansu prov., China, 45 mi. WSW of Tienshui; wool textiles; tobacco processing; wheat, licorice. **4** Town (pop. 3,968), ⊙ Lihsien co. (pop. 23,002), NW Szechwan prov., China, on tributary of Min R. and 70 mi. NW of Chengtu, in mtn. region; medicinal plants, millet, wheat. Until 1945, Lifan. **5** Town, Yunnan prov., China: see HWANING.

Li-hua, China: see LIHWA.

Lihue (lēhōō'ā), coast town (pop. 3,870), ⊙ Kauai co., SE Kauai, T.H., near Nawiliwili Harbor.

Lihuel Calel, dept., Argentina: see CUCHILLO-CÓ.

Lihula or **Likhula** (lē'khōōlä), town (pop. 749), W Estonia, on railroad and 20 mi. SSE of Haapsalu; agr. market; fodder crops, barley, potatoes.

Lihwa or **Li-hua** (both: lē'hwä'), town, ⊙ Lihwa co. (pop. 8,053), W Sikang prov., China, 105 mi. W of Kangting; gold-mining center; cattle raising. Lamasery. Until 1913 called Litang. Placed 1950 in Tibetan Autonomous Dist.

Lihwang, China: see KINCHAI.

Liinahamari, Russian SFSR: see LINAKHAMARI.

Lija (lē'jä), village (parish pop. 1,950), central Malta, 3½ mi. W of Valletta. Lija and near-by BALZAN and ATTARD are called the "Three Villages." Orange-growing dist. Has many fine churches.

Lika (lē'kä), karst region in W Croatia, Yugoslavia, bet. Adriatic Sea and Bosnia border; stock raising. Chief town, GOSPIC. Scene of operations by Yugoslav partisans in Second World War; greatly devastated. **Lika River** rises 12 mi. ESE of Gospic, flows c.35 mi. NW, disappearing into the karst 18 mi. NNW of Gospic.

Likati (lēkä'tē), village, Eastern Prov., N Belgian Congo, on a tributary of Itimbiri R., on railroad and 65 mi. NW of Buta; center of rice and cotton area; cotton ginning. Has R.C. mission. Coffee and aleurite plantations in vicinity.

Likenai or **Likenay** (lēkā'nī), Lith. *Likėnai*, town, N Lithuania, 9 mi. W of Birzhai; summer resort.

Likeri, mountain, Greece: see PARNASSUS.

Likeri, Lake, Greece: see HYLIKE, LAKE.

Likhapani (lĭkŭpä'nē), village, Lakhimpur dist., NE Assam, India, on Burhi Dihang R. and 60 mi. ESE of Dibrugarh; rail spur terminus; coal-mining center. Also spelled Lakhapani.

Likhaya, Russian SFSR: see LIKHOVSKOI.

Likhma (lĭk'mŭ), village, Raipur dist., E Madhya Pradesh, India, 50 mi. SSE of Dhamtari; terminus of lumber railway; sawmilling.

Likhoslavl or **Likhoslavl'** (lyĭkhůslä'vůl), city (1926 pop. 2,962), central Kalinin oblast, Russian SFSR, 25 mi. NW of Kalinin; rail junction; clothing mill; flax processing, metalworking. Was ⊙ former Karelian Natl. Okrug (1937–39).

Likhovka (lyĭkhôf'ků), village (1926 pop. 6,248), W Dnepropetrovsk oblast, Ukrainian SSR, 18 mi. WNW of Verkhne-Dneprovsk; truck produce.

Likhovskoi or **Likhovskoy** (lyēkhŭfskoi'), town (1944 pop. over 10,000), W Rostov oblast, Russian SFSR, 12 mi. S of Kamensk; rail center; machine mfg., food processing; coal mining. Until 1930, Likhaya.

Likhula, Estonia: see LIHULA.

Likhvin, Russian SFSR: see CHEKALIN.

Liki, New Guinea: see KUMAMBA ISLANDS.

Likiang or **Li-chiang** (both: lē'jyäng'), town (pop. 8,651), ⊙ Likiang co. (pop. 90,511), NW Yunnan prov., China, near Yangtze R., 75 mi. N of Tali; alt. 8,136 ft.; horse-breeding center; cotton textiles; timber, rice, millet, beans. Gold and iron mines near by.

Li Kiang, river, China: see LI RIVER, Kwangsi prov.

Likiep (lē'kēěp), atoll (□ 4; pop. 503), Ratak Chain, Majuro dist., Marshall Isls., W central Pacific, 125 mi. NE of Kwajalein; 64 islets on lagoon 26 mi. long. Sometimes spelled Likieb.

Likimi (lēkē'mē), village, Equator Prov., NW Belgian Congo, on Mongala R. and 65 mi. NW of Lisala; agr. (cotton, sesame) and trading center.

Likino-Dulevo (lyē'kēnů-dōō'lyĭvů), city (1939 pop. over 10,000), E Moscow oblast, Russian SFSR, 7 mi. S of Orekhovo-Zuyevo; formed c.1930 by union of Likino (N; cotton textiles, lumber machines) and Dulevo (S; porcelain works).

Likodhimos, Greece: see LYKODIMOS.

Likoma Island (lēkō'mä), Northern Prov., E Nyasaland, in L. Nyasa, off E shore, 40 mi. ESE of Chinteche; 5 mi. long, 4 mi. wide. Likoma, village (pop. 3,172), is on SE shore; fishing; rice, corn. Hq. of Universities Mission to Central Africa (Church of England).

Likorema (lēkô'rēmů), uninhabited Aegean island (□ 1.2) in Northern Sporades, Magnesia nome, Greece, off NE coast of Halonnesos isl.; 39°14'N 24°E. Also called Peristeri and Xeronesi (Xeronisi).

Likouala, region, Fr. Equatorial Africa: see IMPFONDO.

Likouala-aux-herbes River (lēkwälä'-ō-ârb'), N Middle Congo territory, Fr. Equatorial Africa, rises c.60 mi. WNW of Dongou, thence meanders c.300 mi. S, past Epéna and through a region of swamps, to Sanga R. 10 mi. W of Liranga. Navigable c.150 mi. in middle and lower course. Also called Likouala-Essoubi (–ěsōōbē').

Likouala-Mossaka, region, Fr. Equatorial Africa: see FORT-ROUSSET.

Likouala River or **Likouala-Mossaka River** (mōsä-kä'), central Middle Congo territory, Fr. Equatorial Africa, formed by several headstreams 40 mi. W of Makoua, flows c.325 mi. E, past Makoua, and SSE to Congo R. at Mossaka (also point of confluence of Sangha R.). Forms extensive swamps in lower course and is connected by a network of side streams with the lower Sangha. Navigable for c.250 mi. below Makoua. Was explored (1878) by de Brazza.

Lil, Oued el (wěd' ěl lēl'), river of N Tunisia, rises in the Medjerda Mts., flows 30 mi. SE to the Medjerda near Souk-el-Khemis. Irrigation and flood-control dam under construction (1950).

Lila Lake (lī'lů), Hamilton co., NE central N.Y., in the Adirondacks, 21 mi. SW of Tupper Lake village; c.2½ mi. long, ½–1½ mi. wide.

Lilas, Les (lā lēlä'), town (pop. 17,401), Seine dept., N central France, just ENE of Paris, 3.5 mi. from Notre Dame Cathedral; metalworks; mfg. (shoes, rubber goods, office furniture, hosiery, umbrellas, candy).

Lilayi (lĭlä'yē), township, Central Prov., Northern Rhodesia, on railroad and 7 mi. S of Lusaka; tobacco, corn, wheat, potatoes, truck; livestock.

Lilbourn (lĭl'bûrn), city (pop. 1,361), New Madrid co., extreme SE Mo., near Mississippi R., 5 mi.W of New Madrid; cotton gins, lumber mills. Inc. as city 1910.

Lilesville (līlz'vĭl), town (pop. 605), Anson co., S N.C., 5 mi. E of Wadesboro, in agr. and lumber area; concrete-pipe mfg.

Lilia (lĭl'yŭ), town (pop. 3,861), S Saurashtra, India, 55 mi. WSW of Bhaunagar; millet, cotton, oilseeds, sugar cane.

Lilibeo, Cape, Sicily: see BOEO, CAPE.

Lilienfeld (lē'lyŭnfĕlt), town (pop. 2,922), S central Lower Austria, on Traisen R. and 13 mi. S of Sankt Pölten; mfg. (scythes, cutlery). Cistercian abbey.

Lilienthal (lēl'yŭntäl), village (pop. 5,309), in former Prussian prov. of Hanover, NW Germany, after 1945 in Lower Saxony, 5 mi. NNE of Bremen; mfg. of chemicals. Has church of former Cistercian nunnery.

Liling (lē'lĭng'), town, ⊙ Liling co. (pop. 566,050), E Hunan prov., China, near Kiangsi line, 45 mi. SE of Changsha, and on railroad; porcelain-mfg. center. Kaolin quarrying near by.

Lilio (lēlē'ō), town (1939 pop. 3,918; 1948 municipality pop. 7,977), Laguna prov., S Luzon, Philippines, 8 mi. ENE of San Pablo; agr. center (rice, coconuts, sugar cane).

Lilla Edet (lĭl'ä" ā'dŭt), village (pop. 2,198), Alvsborg co., SW Sweden, on Gota R. (falls; navigation lock) and 12 mi. SW of Trollhattan; paper mills, hydroelectric station, foundry.

Lillafüred (lĭl'lōfürĕd), year-round resort (pop. 111), Borsod-Gömör co., NE Hungary, on L. HAMOR, 7 mi. W of Miskolc, in Bükk Mts.; large tourist trade.

Lille (lēl), Flemish *Ryssel* or *Rijssel* (rī'sŭl), city (pop. 179,778), ⊙ Nord dept., N France, on canalized Deûle R. and 130 mi. NNE of Paris, forming a major industrial conurbation (pop. c.600,000) together with ROUBAIX (6 mi. NE), TOURCOING (8 mi. NNE), and a ring of suburban communities; 50°38'N 3°1'E. A leading textile center especially known for its lisle (the name was derived from an old spelling of Lille), it has numerous flax, hemp, jute, cotton, and woolen mills. Has important metallurgical industry (locomotives built at Fives-Lille; auto chassis, bicycles, miscellaneous machinery, electrical equipment), chemical works, breweries, beet-sugar refineries, and print shops. Also produces candies and biscuits, chicory, lubricants and industrial oils, starch, soap, tobacco products. Large industrial establishments are powered by coal from near-by coal-mining dist. (largest in France). Intensive agr. (partly irrigated) and dairying are carried on in area. Commercial activity culminates in well-known yearly fair (June). Chief suburbs: La Madeleine (NNE), Hellemmes-Lille (E), Ronchin (SE), Loos (SW), Lambersart (NW), Marquette and Saint-André (N). Lille is regularly laid out, in triangular shape. Of its 17th-cent. fortifications (built by Vauban) a large citadel remains. Has a 17th-cent. stock exchange; several churches containing paintings of Flemish school; and an unfinished cathedral (begun 1854). Its art mus. (damaged and looted in Second World War; paintings since restored) has outstanding collection of Flemish, Dutch, French, and Spanish masters. Seat of univ. (since 1887), of Catholic seminary, and of bishopric (since 1913). Chief city of medieval county of Flanders; residence of 15th-cent. dukes of Burgundy, and (after 1668) ⊙ French Flanders. Taken (1708) by Eugene of Savoy and Marlborough after costly siege; restored to France by Peace of Utrecht (1713). Occupied by Germans, 1914–18, and heavily damaged by Allied air raids in Second World War. Formerly spelled L'Isle and Lisle. De Gaulle b. here.

Lillebo, Norway: see LITLABO.

Lillebonne (lēlbôn'), anc. *Juliobona,* town (pop. 5,046), Seine-Inférieure dept., N France, near Seine R. estuary, 19 mi. E of Le Havre; cotton-milling center. Has ruins of a Roman theater (A.D. c.120) and of a castle built by William the Conqueror. Castle of TANCARVILLE is 4 mi. SW. Port-Jérôme, 3 mi. S, on right bank of the Seine opposite Quillebeuf, has France's largest petroleum refinery.

Lille Dimon, Faeroe Isls.: see SUDERO FJORD.

Lillehammer (lĭl'lŭhäm"mŭr), city (pop. 6,565), ⊙ Opland co., SE Norway, at N end of L. Mjosa near mouth of Lagen R., at SE end of the Gudbrandsdal, on railroad and 85 mi. N of Oslo; 61°6'N 10°29'E. Commercial and tourist center for the Gudbrandsdal; summer and winter-sports resort, noted for its healthful climate; pipe-mfg. center. Has textile, lumber, and flour mills, and breweries; mfg. of furniture, prefabricated houses, cheese. Inc. 1827. In SE part of city is Maihaugen (mī'hougŭn), which contains folk mus. consisting of old bldgs. of the region, including a 12th-cent. church and Peer Gynt's hut.

Lille Koldewey, Greenland: see GREAT KOLDEWEY.

Lillerod (lĭ'lŭrûdh), Dan. *Lillerød,* town (pop. 2,321), Frederiksborg amt, Zealand, Denmark, 5 mi. SSE of Hillerod; orchards; chemical works, fountain-pen mfg.

Lillers (lēlâr'), town (pop. 5,658), Pas-de-Calais dept., N France, 8 mi. WNW of Béthune, in fertile agr. dist. (wheat, sugar beets, tobacco, vegetables); sugar refining, metalworking (agr. equipment), shoe and fertilizer mfg. Has 12th-cent. church damaged (1918) in First World War. First artesian well said to have been sunk here.

Lillesand (lĭl'lŭsän), town (pop. 1,089), Aust-Agder co., S Norway, on an inlet of the Skagerrak, on railroad and 15 mi. ENE of Kristiansand; shipping and shipbuilding; tanning, mfg. of glassware; exports timber, feldspar, quartz.

Lille Sotra, Norway: see STORE SOTRA.

Lillestrom (lĭl'lŭstrûm) Nor. *Lillestrøm,* village and canton (pop. 7,784), Akershus co., SE Norway, on N shore of Oyeren L. and 10 mi. ENE of Oslo; rail junction; lumber milling; mfg. of plastics, prefabricated houses, knit goods.

Lillhagen (lĭl'hä"gŭn), residential village (pop. 917), Goteborg och Bohus co., SW Sweden, near Gota R., 4 mi. N of Goteborg; site of large hosp.

Lillington (lĭ'lĭngtŭn), town (pop. 1,061), ⊙ Harnett co., central N.C., 28 mi. SSW of Raleigh and on Cape Fear R.; agr. trade center; mfg. of bricks, wood products.

Lillo (lē'lō), village (pop. 1,326), Antwerp prov., N Belgium, on Scheldt R. and 9 mi. NW of Antwerp; beet-sugar refining. Formerly spelled Lilloo.

Lillo (lē'lyō), town (pop. 3,659), Toledo prov., central Spain, road center in upper La Mancha, 27 mi. SE of Aranjuez, in fertile region (cereals, potatoes, sugar beets, saffron, olives, grapes, truck produce, fruit, sheep). Cheese processing, olive-oil pressing.

Lillooah, India: see LILUAH.

Lillooet (lĭ'lōōĕt), village (pop. estimate 500), S B.C., on Fraser R., near Seton L., 70 mi. W of Kamloops, in gold-mining and mixed-farming region; hydroelectric power.

Lillooet Lake (21 mi. long, 1–2 mi. wide), SW B.C., expansion of Lillooet R., in Coast Mts., 40 mi. SW of Lillooet.

Lillooet River, SW B.C., rises in Coast Mts. at foot of Mt. Dalgleish, W of Lillooet, flows 130 mi. SE, through Lillooet L., to NW end of Harrison L., which drains into Fraser R.

Lilly. 1 Town (pop. 177), Dooly co., central Ga., 6 mi. WNW of Vienna. **2** Borough (pop. 1,898), Cambria co., SW central Pa., 21 mi. ENE of Johnstown; bituminous coal.

Lilly Grove, village (pop. 1,023), Mercer co., S W.Va.

Liloan (lēlō'än, lēlōän'), town (1939 pop. 2,087; 1948 municipality pop. 12,292), central Cebu isl., Philippines, on Camotes Sea, 10 mi. NE of Cebu city; agr. center (corn, coconuts).

Lilongwe (lēlông'gwä), town (pop. 1,515), ⊙ Central Prov. (□ 14,045; pop. 751,384), Nyasaland, on road and 130 mi. NW of Zomba, on Lilongwe R. (flows E to L. Nyasa); 14°S 33°48'E. Tobacco-processing center. Airfield.

Liloy (lē'loi), town (1939 pop. 11,562) in Sindañgan municipality, Zamboanga prov., W Mindanao, Philippines, on Sulu Sea, 55 mi. WNW of Pagadian; fishing; coconuts, rice, corn.

Liluah (lĭl'wä), N suburb of Howrah, Howrah dist., S West Bengal, India, near Hooghly R., 2.5 mi. N of Howrah, 3.5 mi. NNW of Calcutta city center; large railroad workshops; extensive iron and steel rolling works; mfg. of chemicals, brass and copper sheets, silk and cotton cloth, hosiery, rubber goods, pottery, cement, soap, paint; oilseed milling. Also spelled Lillooah.

Lily. 1 Mining village (1940 pop. 515), Laurel co., SE Ky., in Cumberland foothills, on Laurel R. and 35 mi. NW of Middlesboro; bituminous coal. **2** Town (pop. 139), Day co., NE S.Dak., 13 mi. SW of Webster; trading point.

Lilybaeum, Sicily: see MARSALA.

Lily Bay, village (pop. 16), Piscataquis co., central Maine, on Moosehead L. and 11 mi. NNE of Greenville; hunting, fishing.

Lilydale, town (pop. 2,072), S Victoria, Australia, 20 mi. ENE of Melbourne; rail junction; fruit-growing center; wineries. Limestone quarries.

Lilydale, town (pop. 448), N Tasmania, 13 mi. NNE of Launceston; agr. center; lavender farms, orchards.

Lily Dale, resort village (pop. c.100), Chautauqua co., extreme W N.Y., 9 mi. S of Dunkirk, on Cassadaga Lakes, in agr. area. A center of spiritualism since organization of Lily Dale Assembly, 1879.

Lily Lake. 1 Hamlet, Kane co., NE Ill., 15 mi. NNW of Aurora. **2** Village (1940 pop. 47), McHenry co., NE Ill., near Fox R., 19 mi. W of Waukegan.

Lilypons (lĭ'lēpŏnz"), village, Frederick co., central Md., 10 mi. S of Frederick; grows aquatic plants, ornamental fish.

Lim, China: see LIM RIVER.

Lima (lē'mä), town (pop. 2,151), N Buenos Aires prov., Argentina, 11 mi. WNW of Zárate; agr. center; cattle raising, dairying, seed production.

Lima, town (dist. pop. 2,122), San Pedro dept., central Paraguay, on an affluent of the Jejuí-guazú and 45 mi. NE of San Pedro; stock-raising center in maté and lumber area.

Lima, department (□ 15,052; pop. 849,171), W central Peru, on the Pacific; ⊙ Lima. Includes Don Martín, San Lorenzo, and Hormigas de Afuera isls. The Cordillera Occidental of the Andes crosses dept. N-S. Drained by Chancay, Huaura, Mala, and Rímac rivers. Sugar and cotton plantations o irrigated coastal plain; wheat, corn, potatoes; cof fee, and sheep raising in mts. Fisheries (Callao Huacho). Mining of copper at Casapalca; salt a Huacho and Chilca; coal fields at Oyón. Mfg. i Lima, Callao, and suburbs. Beach resorts in Lim metropolitan area, thermal baths at Churín an Chilca. Ruins of pre-Incan and Incan times a Pachacamac and Cajamarquilla. Served by rail road and air lines, and crossed by Pan-America Highway. Main centers: Lima, Callao, Huacho Cañete. Callao constitutional prov., set up 1836 forms a separate administrative unit.

Lima, largest city (pop. 533,645) and ⊙ Peru an Lima dept., W central Peru, on lower Rímac R., o Pan-American Highway, and 7 mi. E of its Pacifi port Callao (linked by railroads and boulevards) 12°3'S 77°3'W; alt. c.500 ft. Situated in an ari coastal zone, it has a dry, semitropical climate with an average temp. of 66°F. and with almost n rain, but with winter fogs. Over the city towers Sa Cristóbal hill. Lima is Peru's administrative, com mercial, industrial, and cultural center. From i radiate highways, air lines, and railroads, an through it pass most of its imports and exports Major industries include textile mills (cotton wool), tanneries, foundries, oil refineries, lumbe and flour mills, breweries, auto-assembly plant mfg. of cement, glassware, silver articles, soap pharmaceuticals, cosmetics, candles, clothing, shoes rubber goods, cigarettes, cottonseed oil, chocolate The surrounding irrigated plains produce cotton sugar, grain, fruit, vegetables. Modern Lima ha tall office bldgs., fine apartment houses, banks, an hotels; yet its historical past remains dominant. O the impressive Plaza de Armas stands the Cathedra (the cornerstone of which was laid by Pizarro whose mummy is preserved there), the archbishop' palace, the Natl. Palace, municipal bldg., etc. T its cultural heritage testify more than 50 churches such as Santo Domingo, San Francisco, La Mer ced, San Agustín, Sanctuary of St. Rose of Lim (1st Amer. saint). There are also numerous monas teries and convents. Since early colonial times i has been a city of the arts and sciences, and its Sa Marcos Univ. (founded 1551) is one of the oldest i the Americas. Other institutions of higher learnin include a R.C. univ., a school of engineering, natl. library (founded 1821 by San Martín), muse ums, learned societies, and theaters. Founded 153 by Pizarro as the "City of the Kings" on the bank of the Rímac, its name is a corruption of th river's. For nearly 3 cents. it was the seat of Sp sovereignty and the wealthiest and most famou city in the New World. During the struggle for independence Lima was long a stronghold of Sp. resistance, until San Martín made his triumphal entrance (1821). The constituent congress met one year later. During the War of the Pacific it was occupied by Chilean forces (1881–83), who looted some priceless art treasures and documents. The 8th International Conference of American States (1938) met here. Lima has been often subject to earthquakes (notably in 1687 and 1746) and has had to be rebuilt several times. After 1940, when its boundaries included c.270,000 people, the city absorbed several suburbs, thus almost doubling its pop. Among these new sections—most of them in S and SE—are fashionable beach and residential resorts, such as Chorrillos, Barranco, Miraflores, Magdalena del Mar, San Miguel. The Limatambo airport is in SE outskirts. In the city's vicinity are many Incan and pre-Incan remains, of which the most renowned are Pachacamac (SE) and Cajamarquilla (ENE).

Li-ma, Tibet: see RIMA.

Lima (lī'mŭ). **1** Village (pop. 154), Adams co., W Ill., 16 mi. N of Quincy, in agr. area. **2** Town (pop. 483), Beaverhead co., extreme SW Mont., 40 mi. S of Dillon, near Idaho line, and on Red Rock R. in Jefferson R. system; livestock, grain. Near-by Lima Reservoir used for irrigation and fishing. **3** Village (pop. 1,147), Livingston co., W central N.Y., 18 mi. S of Rochester; makes insulators. Site of Genesee Jr. Col. **4** City (pop. 50,246), ⊙ Allen co., W Ohio, c.70 mi. SSW of Toledo and on Ottawa R.; rail hub, trade and mfg. center. Mfg. of locomotives, Diesel engines, and other railroad equipment; electrical goods, steel castings, machine-shop products, tobacco products, food products, heating apparatus, enameled goods, power shovels, electric motors; oil refining. Limestone quarries. Has state hosp. for criminally insane; military ordnance depot. Laid out 1831, inc. 1842. **5** Town (pop. 99), Seminole co., central Okla., 6 mi. WNW of Wewoka, in agr. area. **6** Village, Greenville co., NW S.C., in the Blue Ridge, on North Saluda R. and 17 mi. N of Greenville.

Lima, La, Honduras: see LA LIMA.

Lima, La (lä lē'mä), village (pop. 429), Pistoia prov., Tuscany, central Italy, on Lima R. and 12 mi. NW of Pistoia; paper mill.

Limache (lēmä'chä), town (pop. 3,836), Valparaiso prov., central Chile, in Aconcagua R. valley (on Limache R.), 20 mi. E of Valparaiso. Agr. center (cereals, fruit, wine, beans, cattle) and resort. Copper, silver, and gold deposits near by. Just NW is San Francisco de Limache.

Lima Duarte (lē'mū dwär'tĭ), city (pop. 2,503), S Minas Gerais, Brazil, in the Serra da Mantiqueira, 30 mi. W of Juiz de Fora; rail-spur terminus; low-grade rutile deposits.

Limagne (lēmä'nyū), fertile lowland in Puy-de-Dôme and Allier depts., central France; bounded by volcanic Auvergne Mts. (W) and granitic Monts du Forez (E). Traversed lengthwise by Allier R.; c.60 mi. long, 10–25 mi. wide; occupies bottom of a tertiary lake. On its alluvial soil (enriched by lava flows) wheat, sugar beets, fruit trees, vegetables, and tobacco are intensively cultivated. Wine is grown on W slopes. Although primarily agr., Limagne contains an important industrial dist. centered on Clermont-Ferrand and Thiers. Other towns: Vichy, Gannat, Riom, Issoire.

Liman (lyĭmän'). **1** Village (1939 pop. over 500), SE Astrakhan oblast, Russian SFSR, near indented Caspian Sea coast, 55 mi. SW of Astrakhan; millet, cotton; sheep raising. Until 1944 (in Kalmyk Autonomous SSR), called Dolban. **2** City, Stalino oblast, Ukrainian SSR: see KRASNYY LIMAN.

Liman, Mount, Indonesia: see WILLIS MOUNTAINS.

Limanowa (lēmänô'vä), town (pop. 1,963), Krakow prov., S Poland, on railroad and 14 mi. WNW of Nowy Sacz; tanning. In Second World War, under Ger. rule, called Ilmenau (ĭl'mūnou).

Lima Reservoir (lī'mū), SW Mont., in Beaverhead co., just S of Snowcrest Mts., near Idaho line, in Red Rock R.; 8 mi. long, 1 mi. wide. Irrigates livestock region. Town of Lima 12 mi. W.

Limarí River (lēmärē'), Coquimbo prov., N central Chile, rises in the Andes near Argentina border, flows 125 mi. W, past Sotaquí and Ovalle, to the Pacific 30 mi. WSW of Ovalle. Irrigates fruitgrowing area. Not navigable.

Lima River (lē'mä), Tuscany, central Italy, rises in Etruscan Apennines E of Passo dell'Abetone, flows S, past La Lima, and W, to Serchio R. 1 mi. SW of Bagni di Lucca; 20 mi. long.

Lima River (lē'mū), Sp. *Limia* (lē'myä), in NW Spain and N Portugal, rises in Antela L. (Orense prov.), flows 70 mi. SW, past Ponte da Barca (head of navigation), to the Atlantic at Viana do Castelo. Hydroelectric plant W of Lindoso.

Limassol (lĭmūsôl'), Gr. *Lemessos* (lĕmĕsôs'), district (□ 537; pop. 75,421), S and SW Cyprus; ⊙ Limassol. In N the Olympus Mts. slope down towards coast. AKROTIRI PENINSULA juts S into Mediterranean bet. Episkopi and Akrotiri bays. Predominantly agr.: grain, carobs, grapes, olives, almonds, citrus fruit; sheep, goats, cattle. Fishing. Chromite, asbestos, and ocher are mined. Processing industries centered at Limassol, one of isl.'s principal ports. Several summer resorts in the wooded mts., among them Pano PLATRES and TROODOS. Dist. contains ruins of anc. cities AMATHUS and CURIUM.

Limassol, Gr. *Lemessos,* city (pop. 22,799), ⊙ Limassol dist., S Cyprus, on Akrotiri Bay of the Mediterranean, 38 mi. SW of Nicosia. One of isl.'s leading ports (open roadstead). In fertile region (wine, citrus fruit, carobs, almonds, olives, barley; livestock), it ships agr. products and minerals (chromite, asbestos, ocher) from Olympus Mts. Local industries include mfg. of brandy, beer, perfumes, cigarettes, food preserves. Has 12th-cent. Venetian castle (now jail) in whose court is a turret with chapel, where the marriage of Richard I (Richard Lion-Heart) to Berengaria of Navarre in 1191 is said to have taken place. Near by is site of anc. Phoenician city of Amathus.

Limatola (lēmä'tôlä), village (pop. 919), Benevento prov., Campania, S Italy, near the Volturno, 6 mi. NE of Caserta.

Limavady (lĭmūvă'dē), urban district (1937 pop. 2,772; 1951 census 3,179), N Co. Londonderry, Northern Ireland, on Roe R. and 15 mi. ENE of Londonderry; agr. market (flax, potatoes oats).

Limaville (lī'mūvĭl), village (pop. 209), Stark co., E central Ohio, 17 mi. NE of Canton.

Limay (lēmā'), town (pop. 3,134), Seine-et-Oise dept., N central France, on right bank of the Seine opposite Mantes-Gassicourt; foundry, cement-works; baskets. Damaged in Second World War.

Limay or **San Juan de Limay** (sän hwän' dā lēmī'), town (1950 pop. 1,224), Estelí dept., W Nicaragua, 21 mi. WNW of Estelí; hammock mfg.; coffee; livestock. Gold and silver deposits at old Grecia mine, 4 mi. E.

Limay (lēmī'), town (1939 pop. 2,608; 1948 municipality pop. 4,509), Bataan prov., S Luzon, Philippines, on W Bataan Peninsula, on Manila Bay, 27 mi. W of Manila; sugar cane, rice.

Limay Mahuida (lēmī' mäwē'dä), village (pop. estimate 200), ⊙ Limay Mahuida dept. (pop. 1,674), W central La Pampa prov., Argentina, on the Río Salado and 120 mi. W of General Acha, in stock-raising area.

Limay River (lēmī'), in Neuquén and Río Negro natl. territories, Argentina, rises in L. Nahuel Huapí at Nahuel Huapí in Argentinian lake dist., flows c.260 mi. NE, past Piedra del Aguila, Picún-Leufú, and Plottier, to join Neuquén R. at Neuquén, forming the Río Negro. Its lower course is used for irrigation (fruitgrowing, viticulture) and water power. Receives Collón Curá R. and Arroyo Picún-Leufú.

Limbach (lĭm'bäkh), town (pop. 17,693), Saxony, E central Germany, 8 mi. WNW of Chemnitz; hosiery-knitting center; mfg. of machinery, gloves, cardboard, pharmaceuticals; textile dyeing. Was 1st center of Saxon knitting industry in 18th cent.

Limbach, town (pop. 2,431), SE Saar, on Blies R. and 3 mi. W of Homburg; clay quarrying; agr. market (grain, stock).

Limbadi (lēmbä'dē), village (pop. 2,431), Catanzaro prov., Calabria, S Italy, near Gulf of Gioia, 1 mi. W of Nicotera; wine, olive oil, dried fruit, silk.

Limbang (lĭmbäng'), town (pop. 2,894), N Sarawak, NW Borneo, on Limbang R. (122 mi. long), near its mouth on Brunei Bay, 10 mi. SSE of Brunei, on narrow strip separating 2 sections of sultanate of Brunei; trade center for area producing rubber, rice, livestock; fisheries.

Limbara, Monte (môn'tĕ lēmbä'rä), highest point (4,468 ft.) in Sassari prov., N Sardinia, 33 mi. ENE of Sassari.

Limbazi or **Limbazhi** (lēm'bä-zhē), Lettish *Limbaži,* Ger. *Lemsal,* city (pop. 2,870), N Latvia, in Vidzeme, 45 mi. NNE of Riga, in timber and potato dist.; mfg. of leather goods, woolens, flour, metalworks. Castle ruins. Was Hanseatic town in 14th cent.

Limbdi (lĭm'būdē), town (pop. 13,474), NE Saurashtra, India, on Kathiawar peninsula, 12 mi. SE of Wadhwan; agr. market (cotton, millet, wheat); cotton ginning, handicrafts (cloth fabrics, ivory bangles, metalware). Was ⊙ former princely state of Limbdi (□ 344; pop. 44,024) of Western India States agency; state merged 1948 with Saurashtra.

Limbé (lēbā'), town (1950 census pop. 3,212), Nord dept., N Haiti, 12 mi. WSW of Cap-Haïtien; rice, coffee, sugar cane. Old colonial town.

Limbe (lēm'bā), town (pop. 8,869), Southern Prov., Nyasaland, in Shire Highlands, on railroad and 5 mi. SE of Blantyre; alt. 3,800 ft. Major commercial and transportation center; mfg. (cigarettes, soap); tea, tobacco, tung. Hq. of Nyasaland railways, customs. Anglican and R.C. cathedrals, Marist Fathers mission. Has tung experimental station. Became township in 1909.

Limberg Dam, Austria: see KAPRUN.

Limbiate (lēmbyä'tē), village (pop. 3,333), Milano prov., Lombardy, N Italy, 10 mi. N of Milan; machinery mfg.

Limbourg, province, Belgium: see LIMBURG.

Limbourg (lĭm'bûrg, Fr. lēbōōr'), Flemish *Limburg* (lĭm'bûrkh), town (pop. 4,188), Liége prov., E Belgium, on Vesdre R. and 4 mi. ENE of Verviers; wool spinning and weaving. Has church with 16th-cent. apse. Until 1648, ⊙ duchy of Limburg, now divided bet. Belgium and the Netherlands. Destroyed by French under Condé in 1675.

Limburg (lĭm'bûrg, Flemish lĭm'bûrkh) or **Limbourg** (Fr. lēbōōr'), province (□ 930; pop. 475,716), NE Belgium, bordering E and N on the Netherlands; ⊙ Hasselt. Bounded by Antwerp prov. (NW), Brabant prov. (W), Liége prov. (S). Level moorland; drained by Meuse R., Albert Canal, Scheldt-Meuse Junction Canal, and the Zuid-Willemsvaart. Largely agr. (potato growing, cattle raising), with coal mining principally in Campine area, W. Mfg. of chemicals, nonferrous metals, glass, bricks. Important towns: Hasselt, St-Trond, Tongres, Genk (coal mining), Tessenderloo (chemicals), Maaseik. Prov. is largely Flemish-speaking. Most of the region was included until 1792 in the prince-bishopric of Liége. It became (1815) part of the Dutch prov. of Limburg, which was divided bet. Netherlands and Belgium in 1839.

Limburg, town, Belgium: see LIMBOURG.

Limburg or **Limburg an der Lahn** (lĭm'bûrg, Ger. lĭm'bōōrk än dĕr län'), town (pop. 13,554), in former Prussian prov. of Hesse-Nassau, W Germany, after 1945 in Hesse, on the Lahn and 22 mi. NNW of Wiesbaden; road-building machinery, metal goods. Pottery works. R.C. bishopric since 1827. Has 13th-cent. cathedral, built on site of 10th-cent. church. Belonged to electors of Trier 1420-1803.

Limburg (lĭm'bûrg, Du. lĭm'bûrkh), prov. (□ 839.7; pop. 684,105), SE Netherlands; ⊙ Maastricht. Bounded by Belgium (W and S), Germany (E), North Brabant and Gelderland provs. (N). Crossed by Maas R. Hills in S are site of chief Netherlands coal deposits, centered on Heerlen. Engineering industries, some textile mfg., pottery- and brick-making; agr. (fruit, rye, oats, some winter wheat, potatoes, beans, sugar beets, green fodder). Chief towns: Maastricht, Heerlen, Sittard, Roermond, and Venlo, all important traffic centers. Predominantly Roman Catholic. It takes its name from former duchy of Limburg, which comprised S part of modern prov., including Maastricht, and E portion of modern Liége prov., Belgium. The small town of Limbourg, E of Liége, was its capital. In the Peace of Westphalia (1648) the duchy was divided bet. the United Netherlands (which received Maastricht), and the Spanish Netherlands. It was united (1815) under the kingdom of the Netherlands. Limburg prov., as established in 1815, no longer corresponded to the borders of the old duchy. It was contested after the establishment (1831) of an independent Belgium. The Dutch-Belgian treaty of 1839 divided the territory, which was inc. with the Dutch and Belgian provs. of Limburg.

Limbury, England: see LUTON.

Limchow, China: see HOPPO.

Lime Creek, rises in small lake in Freeborn co., S Minn., flows S into Winnebago co., N Iowa, then E, past Mason City, to Shell Rock R. at Rockford; 78 mi. long.

Lime Hall, town (pop. 1,300), St. Ann parish, N Jamaica, 2½ mi. S of St. Ann's Bay, in agr. region (citrus fruit, corn, pimento, coffee, cattle).

Limehouse, district of Stepney, London, England, on N bank of the Thames, 4 mi. E of Charing Cross. It is London's Chinese district, with workers' residences, docks, wharves, warehouses, and factories —heavily damaged in 1940–41 air raids.

Limeil-Brévannes (lēmā'-brāvän'), town (pop. 4,387), Seine-et-Oise dept., N central France, a SE suburb of Paris, 10 mi. from Notre Dame Cathedral. Hospitals, sanatorium.

Limeira (lēmā'rū). **1** City, Santa Catarina, Brazil: see JOAÇABA. **2** City (1950 pop. 27,962), E central São Paulo, Brazil, on railroad 32 mi. NW of Campinas; orange-growing center; produces cotton gins and coffee-processing machinery, apiary supplies, hats; has meat-packing plant. Sericulture and apiculture in area.

Lime Kiln, village (pop. c.200), Frederick co., N Md., near Monocacy R., 4 mi. S of Frederick; cement, lime works.

Limekilns, fishing village, SW Fifeshire, Scotland, on the Firth of Forth, 3 mi. S of Dunfermline.

Lime Lake, Cattaraugus co., W N.Y., resort lake (c.1 mi. long), 25 mi. N of Olean. Lime Lake village is on N shore; Machias is just SW.

Limen, Greece: see THASOS.

Limena (lēmā'nä), village (pop. 1,042), Padova prov., Veneto, N Italy, on Brenta R. and 5 mi. N of Padua; wine machinery.

Limenda (lyĭmyĕn'dŭ), town (1947 pop. over 500), S Archangel oblast, Russian SFSR, on railroad and 25 mi. S of Kotlas; pulp, paper mill; building of river tugs.

Limen Vatheos or **Limin Vatheos** (both: lĭmĕn' văthā'ôs) [Gr.,=Vathy harbor], town (pop. 7,143), ⊙ Samos nome, Greece, port for VATHY, on Vathy Bay of NE Samos isl.; exports wine, olive oil, figs, tobacco. A modern town, it became ⊙ Samos in 19th cent.

Limerick, village (pop. 281), S Sask., 13 mi. W of Assiniboia; wheat.

Limerick (lĭm'–), Gaelic *Luimneach,* county (□ 1,037.4; pop. 142,559), Munster, SW Ireland; ⊙ Limerick. Bounded by cos. Cork (S), Kerry (W), Clare (N), and Tipperary (E). Drained by the Shannon and its tributaries. Surface is mountainous along S border, leveling to undulating plain toward the Shannon. Grain crops and potatoes are grown; dairying and stock raising are important. Salmon fisheries in the Shannon. Clay, slate, sandstone are quarried. Industries include woolen, paper, flour milling, tobacco processing, mfg. of agr. implements, cattle feed, food products. Besides Limerick, other towns are Newcastle, Croom, Bruff, Bruree, Adare, Glin, Foynes. Most of co. was controlled by O'Donovans until 12th cent. There are remains of numerous abbeys and castles in the co.

Limerick, Gaelic *Luimneach,* county borough (pop. 42,970), ⊙ Co. Limerick, Ireland, in N part of co., at head of Shannon estuary, 110 mi. WSW of Dublin; 52°40'N 8°38'W; seaport with quays and floating and graving docks; railroad shops; tanning, food canning, dairying, salmon fishing, bacon and ham curing, tobacco processing; mfg. of agr. implements, cement, clothing, lace, rope, fish nets, biscuits, cattle feed. City is divided into 3 sections: English Town, dating from King John's time, on King's Isl. in the Shannon; Irish Town (S); and Newtown Pery (S), founded 1769. Features are Protestant Cathedral of St. Mary, founded c.1179 by Donal O'Brien, restored 1860; Norman castle of King John; St. Munchin's Church, founded in 7th cent.; 1691 Treaty Stone; custom house (1769); library and mus.; and several fortified mansions. Founded by Danes in 9th cent., Limerick was taken by Brian Boru and became ⊙ kingdom of Munster. In 1316 it was taken by Edward Bruce. It was besieged in 1641, 1651, and 1690, when it was defended by Patrick Sarsfield until its surrender in 1691. Surrender treaty, granting political and religious liberty to Roman Catholics, was broken by William III and Queen Anne, and Limerick became known as the "City of the Violated Treaty." Limerick was the last stronghold of James II in Ireland.

Limerick, town (pop. 961), York co., SW Maine, 25 mi. W of Portland; yarn mills. Settled c.1775, inc. 1787.

Lime Ridge, village (pop. 183), Sauk co., S central Wis., 21 mi. W of Baraboo, in dairy and livestock region.

Limerlé, Belgium: see GOUVY.

Lime Rock. 1 Village, Litchfield co., Conn.: see SALISBURY. **2** Village, Providence co., R.I.: see LINCOLN.

Lime Springs, town (pop. 551), Howard co., NE Iowa, near Upper Iowa R., 10 mi. NW of Cresco; feed and flour milling. Limestone quarries, sand and gravel pits near by.

Limestone. 1 County (□ 545; pop. 35,766), N Ala.; ⊙ Athens. Bounded N by Tenn., drained by Wheeler Reservoir (on Tennessee R.) and Elk R. Cotton, timber, corn; phosphate. First Ala. co. invaded in Civil War, 1862. Formed 1818. 2 County (□ 932; pop. 25,251), E central Texas; ⊙ Groesbeck. Drained by Navasota R. Agr. (cotton, corn, grain sorghums, legumes, hay, fruit, truck, pecans), dairying, livestock (cattle, poultry, hogs, sheep, horses, mules). Oil, natural gas, clay; some lumbering. Farm-products processing, mfg. at Groesbeck, Mexia. Includes a state park. Formed 1846.

Limestone. 1 Town (pop. 2,427), Aroostook co., NE Maine, 10 mi. ENE of Caribou, at N.B. line, in potato country; port of entry; terminus of Bangor and Aroostook RR. With construction here of large U.S. air base (begun 1947), the town has boomed. Settled 1849, inc. 1869. 2 Village (pop. 601), Cattaraugus co., W N.Y., on Allegheny R. and 10 mi. WSW of Olean, in oil and natural-gas area. 3 Village, Cherokee co., S.C.: see EAST GAFFNEY.

Lim Fjord (lĭm′fyôr), strait (c.110 mi. long) across N Jutland, Denmark, connecting North Sea with the Kattegat. Cuts off Vendsyssel (N) and Thy (NW) regions from mainland. Irregular in form with many inlets; opens into 15-mi.-wide lagoon in its middle course. Shallow in parts (max. depth, 50 ft.); deepened to aid navigation. Largest isl., Mors. Before 1825, W part was a number of fresh-water lakes, drained into the Kattegat by E part; breakthrough to North Sea caused an unusual combination of salt- and fresh-water flora and fauna. Chief ports: Aalborg, Norre Sundby, Logstor, Nykobing, Thisted.

Limia River, Spain and Portugal: see LIMA RIVER.

Limin, Greece: see THASOS.

Limingen Lake (lē′mĭng-ŭn) (□ 36), Nord-Trondelag co., central Norway, extends 15 mi. SE from Gjersvika; 4 mi. wide.

Limington (lĭ′mĭngtŭn), town (pop. 851), York co., SW Maine, on Saco R. and 20 mi. WNW of Portland; wood products.

Limin Vatheos, Greece: see LIMEN VATHEOS.

Limite sull'Arno (lē′mētĕ sōōlär′nô), village (pop. 1,362), Firenze prov., Tuscany, central Italy, on the Arno and 2 mi. NE of Empoli; boatbuilding.

Limko (lŭm′gō′), Mandarin *Linkao* (lĭn′gou′), town, ⊙ Limko co. (pop. 164,341), N Hainan, Kwangtung prov., China, 40 mi. W of Kiungshan, in sugar-growing area. Tin mining near by.

Limkong (lĕm′gông′), Mandarin *Lien-chiang* (lyĕn′jyäng′), town (pop. 3,845), ⊙ Limkong co. (pop. 396,581), SW Kwangtung prov., China, 30 mi. NNW of Chankiang; sugar cane. Until 1914 called Shekshing.

Lim Kong, river, China: see LIM RIVER.

Limmared (lĭ′märād″), village (pop. 1,048), Alvsborg co., SW Sweden, 20 mi. SE of Boras; rail junction; glassworks (founded 1740). Has ruins of 14th-cent. fortress.

Limmat River, Switzerland: see LINTH RIVER.

Limmen Bight (lĭ′mŭn), in Gulf of Carpentaria, indentation of NE coast of Northern Territory, Australia, bet. Groote Eylandt (N) and Sir Edward Pellew Isls. (S); 85 mi. NW-SE. Receives Roper and Limmen Bight rivers.

Limmen Bight River, NE Northern Territory, Australia, rises in N hills of Barkly Tableland, flows 140 mi. NNE to Limmen Bight of Gulf of Carpentaria.

Limmer (lĭ′mŭr), village (pop. 1,371), in former Prussian prov. of Hanover, NW Germany, after 1945 in Lower Saxony, 3 mi. W of Alfeld; asphalt quarries.

Limne or **Limni** (both: lĭm′nē), anc. *Aegae* (ē′jē), town (pop. 3,398) NW Euboea, Greece, port on N Gulf of Euboea, 25 mi. NNW of Chalcis; magnesite deposits (S); fisheries.

Limnos, Greece: see LEMNOS.

Limoeiro (lēmwā′rōō), city (pop. 12,493), E Pernambuco, NE Brazil, on railroad and 40 mi. WNW of Recife; sugar milling, alcohol distilling; ships cotton and livestock.

Limoeiro de Anadia (dĭ änŭdē′ŭ), city (pop. 901), central Alagoas, NE Brazil, 20 mi. S of Palmeira dos Índios; cotton, sugar, tropical fruit. Until 1944, called Limoeiro.

Limoeiro do Norte (dōō nôr′tĭ), city (pop. 2,954), E Ceará, Brazil, on Jaguaribe R., near Rio Grande do Norte border, and 45 mi. SSW of Aracati; cotton, cattle; ships carnauba wax. Until 1944, Limoeiro.

Limoges (lĭmōzh′, Fr. lēmôzh′), anc. *Augustoritum Lemovicensium*, later *Lemovices*, city (pop. 99,535), ⊙ Haute-Vienne dept., W central France, on right bank of Vienne R. and 220 mi. SSW of Paris; chief center of French porcelain industry, using locally quarried kaolin. Other industries include tanning and shoe mfg., paper milling, printing and bookbinding (especially prayer books). Limoges also produces cotton and woolen textiles, furniture, automobile chassis, bicycle accessories, machinery and tools for mining and ceramics industry, perfumes, dyes, and food preserves. City has a 13th–16th-cent. cathedral (with 19th-cent. additions), a notable ceramics mus., an art gall. containing works by Renoir (b. here), and 2 old bridges over the deeply entrenched Vienne. Old city walls have been converted into circular boulevards. Of Gallic origin, Limoges was Christianized (3d cent.) by St. Martial. In 10th cent. it became seat of a viscountship and in 1589 ⊙ of Limousin prov. Often visited by war, pestilence (10th and 17th cent.), and famine. Richard Coeur de Lion was killed 1199 in battle near Limoges. In 1371 Edward the Black Prince burned the city and massacred its population. Famous Limoges enamel industry (which dates back to Merovingian times) flourished in 13th cent. but declined when city was once more devastated in Wars of Religion. Turgot, who was intendant of Limoges in mid-18th cent., introduced celebrated china manufactures.

Limogne (lēmô′nyŭ), village (pop. 346), Lot dept., SW France, in the Causse de Limogne, 17 mi. ESE of Cahors.

Limogne, Causse de, France: see CAUSSES.

Limón (lēmōn′), province (□ 3,600; 1950 pop. 41,360) of E Costa Rica, on Caribbean Sea; ⊙ Limón. Extends from San Juan R. (Nicaragua border) S to Sixaola R. (Panama border), and is drained by Tortuguero, Parismina, and Reventazón rivers. Largely swampy, malarial lowland along N coast, it becomes mountainous near the Andean divide (Cordillera de Talamanca; SW). Agr.: cacao, coconuts, abacá, rubber and bananas (formerly the chief products). Main food crops are beans, corn, fruit. Fodder crops support some livestock. Prov. is served by coastal shipping (ports of Limón, Barra de Colorado, Cahuita, Puerto Viejo, Sixaola) and railroads (Limón-San José RR and plantation lines). Main centers are Limón, Siquirres, Matina, and Guápiles. Pop. is largely Jamaican Negro.

Limón or **Puerto Limón** (pwĕr′tō), city (1950 pop. 11,310), ⊙ Limón prov., E Costa Rica, major port and railhead on Caribbean Sea, 70 mi. E of San José; 10°N 83°2′W. Commercial center, exporting bananas, coffee, cacao, coconuts. Has considerable passenger traffic on route to San José. Site of cathedral and Vargas Park. Has large Negro pop. in its suburbs of Yumecatón (corruption of Jamaica Town; NW) and Cieneguita (SE). Located on site of anc. Indian village visited (1502) by Columbus, Limón was formerly Costa Rica's main banana-shipping center, now largely replaced by Quepos and Golfito.

Limón, village, Santiago-Zamora prov., S central Ecuador, on E slopes of the Andes, 50 mi. SSW of Macas; timber, fruit, stock.

Limón, town (pop. 1,082), Colón dept., N Honduras, in Mosquitia, on Caribbean Sea, at mouth of small Limón R., 30 mi. E of Trujillo; coconuts, corn, beans; livestock. Sometimes called Barra de Limón.

Limon (lĭ′mŭn), town (pop. 1,471), Lincoln co., E central Colo., on Big Sandy Creek and 80 mi. SE of Denver; alt. 5,280 ft. Trade and shipping point in grain and livestock region; poultry, beans. Founded 1888, inc. 1909.

Limón, El, Mexico: see EL LIMÓN.

Limón, El, Nicaragua: see EL LIMÓN.

Limonade (lēmônäd′), town (1950 census pop. 1,209), Nord dept., N Haiti, near the Atlantic, 8 mi. SE of Cap-Haïtien; sugar cane, bananas, citrus fruit. Magnesite deposits near by.

Limonar (lēmōnär′), town (pop. 2,595), Matanzas prov., W Cuba, on Central Highway, on railroad and 12 mi. ESE of Matanzas, in sugar-growing region. Also apiculture, cattle raising. Near by are refineries and centrals of Triunfo (NE) and Limones (S), the latter affiliated with Havana Univ.

Limonar, E residential section of Málaga, S Spain.

Limon Bay (lēmōn′), Sp. *Bahía Limón* (bäē′ä lēmōn′), inlet of Caribbean Sea, in Panama Canal Zone, at N end of Panama Canal; c.4½ mi. long, c.2½ mi. wide. Entrance protected by breakwaters. On E shore are Colón, Cristobal, and Telfers Isl. At NW gate are Toro Point and Fort Sherman.

Limone Piemonte (lēmô′nĕ pyĕmôn″tĕ), village (pop. 839), Cuneo prov., Piedmont, NW Italy, in Maritime Alps, N of Tenda Pass, 13 mi. S of Cuneo; customs station. Tourist resort (alt. 3,248 ft.), especially for winter sports. Has natl. ski school.

Limones or **Central Limones** (sĕnträl′ lēmō′nĕs), sugar-mill village (pop. 853), Matanzas prov., W Cuba, 13 mi. SE of Matanzas. Affiliated with Havana Univ.

Limones, Ecuador: see VALDEZ.

Limonest (lēmônā′), village (pop. 351), Rhône dept., E central France, 7 mi. NNW of Lyons; tileworks.

Limonum, France: see POITIERS.

Limours (lēmōōr′), agr. village (pop. 984), Seine-et-Oise dept., N central France, 11 mi. SSW of Versailles.

Limousin (lēmōōzē′), former province of S central France, now forming Corrèze and part of Haute-Vienne depts.; ⊙ Limoges. Traversed by 2 outlying ranges (Monts du Limousin and Monts de la Marche) of the Massif Central, region has infertile uplands (cattle raising, dairying; buckwheat, rye, potatoes), and several river valleys and basins (notably around Brive-la-Gaillarde) where fruit and vegetables are grown. Numerous hydroelectric plants. Kaolin quarries supply the Limoges ceramics industry. Chief towns: Limoges, Brive-la-Gaillarde, Tulle. In 1152 Limousin passed under English domination. It was fought over by Philip II of France and Richard I (who fell in 1199 near Limoges), and was finally ceded to England (1259) by Louis IX. Ravaged during the Hundred Years War; Du Guesclin reconquered it for France. As the viscountship of Limoges held by the Bourbon-Vêndome family, it was not incorporated into royal domain until 1589, when Henry IV became king of France. Economic development of Limousin lagged until Turgot introduced his reforms (1761–74). In 1790 prov. was divided into present depts.

Limousin, Monts du (mō dü), W offshoots of Auvergne Mts., in Massif Central, central France, extending c.60 mi. SW–NE across parts of Haute-Vienne, Corrèze, and Creuse depts., and c.30 mi. wide bet. Aubusson and Ussel. Rise to 3,200 ft. Important cattle-raising dist. Locally named Montagne Limousine.

Limoux (lēmōō′), town (pop. 5,694), Aude dept., S France, on Aude R. and 13 mi. SSW of Carcassonne; known for its sparkling white wines (*blanquette de Limoux*); honey and nougat mfg., woodworking. Brickworks, limekilns. Has 14th–16th-cent. church and 15th-cent. bridge.

Limpia Canyon, Texas: see DAVIS MOUNTAINS.

Limpias (lēm′pyäs), town (pop. 1,526), Santander prov., N Spain, 20 mi. ESE of Santander; corn, potatoes, citrus and other fruit. Shrine here is place of pilgrimage.

Limpio (lēm′pyō), town (dist. pop. 5,432), Central dept., S Paraguay, 12 mi. NE of Asunción; stock-raising and meat-packing center; apiculture. Founded 1785.

Limpopo River (lĭmpō′pō) or **Crocodile River,** U. of So. Afr., Bechuanaland Protectorate, Southern Rhodesia, and Mozambique, rises in S Transvaal on the Witwatersrand N of Johannesburg, flows NNW, past Brits, to Bechuanaland Protectorate border, turns NE and E, forming border bet. Transvaal on S and Bechuanaland Protectorate and Southern Rhodesia border on N, past Beitbridge (bridge), to enter Mozambique at 22°25′S 31°19′E; here it turns SE, flowing to Indian Ocean 80 mi. NE of Lourenço Marques. It is c.1,000 mi. long, navigable for c.60 mi. above its mouth. Receives Shashi, Magalakwin, Bubye, and Olifants rivers. On upper course is extensive irrigation scheme. Named Rio do Espiritu Santo (1497) by Vasco da Gama.

Limpsfield, residential town and parish (pop. 3,167), E Surrey, England, 9 mi. E of Reigate. Has 12th-cent. church.

Lim River (lĕm), Mandarin *Lien Kiang* or *Lien Chiang* (both: lyĕn′ jyäng′), Cantonese *Lim Kong* (lĕm′ gông′), S China, rises in SE Kwangsi prov., flows 135 mi. SW, past Watlam and Pokpak (Kwangsi), and Hoppo (Kwantung), to Gulf of Tonkin, forming delta N of Pakhoi. In connection with portage linking it with Jung R., it was former Kwangtung-Kwangsi trade route.

Lim River (lēm), S Yugoslavia, longest (right) affluent of the Drina, rises in Plav L. in North Albanian Alps, flows 136 mi. NNW, past Andrijevica, Berane, Bijelo Polje, Prijepolje, and Priboj, to Drina R. 5 mi. SW of Visegrad. Navigable for 104 mi. The POLIMLJE extends along its upper course.

Limsta (lĕm′stä″), village (pop. 3,338), Vasternorrland co., NE Sweden, on Angerman R. estuary, 20 mi. N of Harnosand; sawmilling, woodworking. Includes Brunne (brŭ′nŭ) village.

Limuru (lēmōō′rōō), town, Central Prov., S central Kenya, on railroad and 18 mi. NW of Nairobi; alt. 7,340 ft. Health resort and agr. center; coffee and tea plantations, truck farms. One of 1st Kenya dists. settled by Europeans.

Linakhamari (lyē′nŭkhŭmŭrē), Finnish *Liinahamari* (lē′nähä″märē), village, NW Murmansk oblast, Russian SFSR, port on W shore of Pechenga Fjord, 7 mi. N of Pechenga; ice-free deepwater harbor; fish processing.

Linan (lĭn′än′). 1 Town (pop. 3,929), ⊙ Linan co. (pop. 84,480), NW Chekiang prov., China, 28 mi. W of Hangchow, S of Tienmu Mts.; rice, wheat, tea, silk, bamboo. 2 Town, Yunnan prov., China: see KIENSHUI.

Linao (lēnou′), village (1930 pop. 403), Chiloé prov., S Chile, on NE coast of Chiloé Isl., 15 mi. SE of Ancud; minor port in agr. area (potatoes, wheat, livestock); fishing, lumbering.

Linapacan Island (lēnäpä′kän) (1939 pop. 1,245; 10 mi. long), one of the Calamian Isls., Palawan prov., Philippines, 15 mi. off N tip of Palawan, and separated from Culion Isl. by 12-mi.-wide Linapacan Strait leading to S. China Sea. Coconuts. Fishing.

Linard, Piz, Switzerland: see PIZ LINARD.

Linares, Bolivia: see PUNA.

Linares (lēnä′rĕs), province (□ 3,792; 1940 pop. 134,968; 1949 estimate 135,355), S central Chile, bordering on the Andes; ⊙ Linares. Fertile agr. area in the central valley, watered by Longaví, Loncomilla, and Perquilauquén rivers. Wheat, corn, beans, lentils, chick-peas, fruit, wine, cattle. Lumbering, flour milling, wine making; some dairying.

Main centers: Linares, Parral, San Javier. Spas and resorts: Quinamávida, Panimávida, Catillo. There are several volcanoes. Prov. was set up 1873.

Linares, town (pop. 17,108), ⊙ Linares prov. and Linares dept. (□ 2,525; pop. 67,328), S central Chile, in the central valley, 175 mi. SW of Santiago; 35°52'S 71°37'W. Rail junction, commercial and agr. center (grain, wine, fruit, vegetables, livestock). Dairies, tanneries, flour mills, brick factory. Artillery school. Town founded 1755.

Linares, town (pop. 3,069), Nariño dept., SW Colombia, in S Cordillera Occidental, 23 mi. WNW of Pasto; alt. 5,036 ft.; corn, wheat, cacao, coffee, sugar, stock.

Linares, city (pop. 9,918), Nuevo León, N Mexico, at foot of Sierra Madre Oriental, on railroad, on Inter-American Highway and 75 mi. SE of Monterrey; trading center in rich farming (sugar cane, oranges, cotton, cereals) and grazing dist. Old colonial churches.

Linares, city (pop. 31,720), Jaén prov., S Spain, in Andalusia, rail center at foot of the Sierra Morena, 25 mi. NNE of Jaén; major lead-mining center. Metalworks (tubes, wires, ammunition), chemical works (lubricants, insecticides, paints and varnishes, soap); other mfg.: asphalt, pottery, tiles, mirrors, liqueurs, and candy. Cereals, olive oil, truck produce in area. Mineral springs. Two mi. S are ruins of Iberian settlement of *Cástulo.*

Linares de la Sierra (dhä lä syĕ'rä), town (pop. 729), Huelva prov., SW Spain, 3½ mi. WSW of Aracena; olives, acorns, corn, fruit, cereals, sheep, hogs; timber. Charcoal burning.

Linares de Riofrío (rē"ōfrē'ō), town (pop. 1,565), Salamanca prov., W Spain, 16 mi. NW of Béjar; flour- and sawmilling; livestock, cereals, nuts, vegetables. Limestone quarries and anthracite deposits near by.

Linas, Monte (môn'tĕ lē'näs), highest point (4,045 ft.) in Cagliari prov., SW Sardinia, 11 mi. NNE of Iglesias.

Linby, village and parish (pop. 575), W Nottingham, England, 7 mi. NNW of Nottingham; coal mining. Church is of Norman origin.

Lince (lēn'sä), S central residential section (pop. 25,636), of Lima, Lima dept., W central Peru. Inc. 1940 into Lima proper.

Lincheng or **Lin-ch'eng** (lĭn'chŭng'), town, ⊙ Lincheng co. (pop. 80,235), SW Hopeh prov., China, 40 mi. S of Shihkiachwang and on spur of Peking-Hankow RR; coal-mining center; wheat, millet, kaoliang.

Lin-chiang, Manchuria: see LINKIANG.

Lin-chin, China: see LINTSIN.

Lin-ch'ing, China: see LINTSING.

Linchow, town, China: see LINHSIEN, Kwangtung prov.

Linchow River (lĕn'jou'), Mandarin *Lienchow Kiang* or *Lien-chou Chiang* (both: lyĕn'jō' jyäng'), N Kwangtung prov., China, rises on Hunan-Kwangtung border N of Linhsien, flows 100 mi. SE, past Linhsien and Yeungshan, to North R. S of Yingtak.

Linchü or **Lin-ch'ü** (both: lĭn'chü'), town, ⊙ Linchü co. (pop. 425,116), central Shantung prov., China, 13 mi. SSE of Yitu; tobacco center; silk, wheat, millet.

Linchüan or **Lin-ch'üan** (lĭn'chüăn'), town, ⊙ Linchüan co. (pop. 729,360), N Anhwei prov., China, near Honan line, 27 mi. WNW of Fowyang; wheat, cotton, beams, kaoliang, sweet potatoes. Until 1934 called Shenkiu, a name now applied to a town in Honan, just across the border.

Lin-ch'uan, Kiangsi prov., China: see FUCHOW.

Linchwan, China: see FUCHOW.

Lincoln, city (pop. 12,515), ⊙ Lincoln dist. (□ 2,381; pop. 40,532), N Buenos Aires prov., Argentina, 38 mi. SW of Junín; rail junction and agr. center (grain, cattle and sheep raising); meat packing, dairying.

Lincoln, county (□ 332; pop. 65,066), S Ont., on L. Ontario and on Niagara R., on N.Y. border; ⊙ St. Catharines.

Lincoln or **Lincolnshire** (-shĭr), county (□ 2,663; 1931 pop. 624,589; 1951 census 706,574), NE England; ⊙ Lincoln. Bounded by Leicester and Nottingham (W), Yorkshire (NW and N), North Sea (E), Norfolk (SE), Cambridge, Northampton, and Rutland (S). Drained by Humber, Trent, Witham, Welland, and Bain rivers. Mostly fertile lowland, with chalky Wold hills in NE. The extensive fenland areas are drained by numerous canals. Administratively the co. is divided into Parts of Lindsey (1951 census pop. 473,463) in N, Parts of Kesteven (1951 census pop. 131,566) in SW, and Parts of Holland (1951 census pop. 101,545) in SE. Besides Lincoln, important towns are Grimsby, Boston (important fishing ports), Scunthorpe (steel industry), Grantham (machinery), Spalding, Wisbech (fruit and vegetable centers), and Gainsborough. Many parts of the co. show traces of Roman occupation. Shortened form is Lincs.

Lincoln, county borough (1931 pop. 66,243; 1951 census 69,412) and city, ⊙ Lincolnshire, England, in Parts of Lindsey and in W central part of co., on Witham R. at mouth of Till R., and 125 mi. N of London; 53°13'N 0°32'W; water and rail transportation center, with railroad shops; mfg. of radios, machinery, light metal products, automobile parts, feed cakes, flour, and food products. Lincoln Cathedral, built 1075–1501 and restored (1922–32) with help of American contributions, has 271-ft. central tower containing the famous bell "Great Tom of Lincoln." Lincoln castle was begun by William the Conqueror in 1086; it was besieged by Parliamentarians in 1644. The town was burned in 12th cent.; scene of 5 parliaments in 14th cent. Horse races and fairs have been held here for centuries. Lincoln was an anc. British fort and the Roman *Lindum* or *Lindum Colonia.* In co. borough (E) is ironstone-quarrying town of Greetwell.

Lincoln, township (pop. 587), E S.Isl., New Zealand, 11 mi. SW of Christchurch; rail junction; agr. center. Canterbury Col. of Agr. here.

Lincoln. 1 County (□ 565; pop. 17,079), SE Ark.; ⊙ Star City. Bounded NE by Arkansas R.; drained by Bayou Bartholomew. Agr. (cotton, truck, corn, fruit); cotton ginning, lumber milling. Formed 1871. **2** County (□ 2,593; pop. 5,909), E central Colo.; ⊙ Hugo. Agr. area, drained by Big Sandy Creek. Wheat, livestock. Formed 1889. **3** County (□ 253; pop. 6,462), NE Ga.; ⊙ Lincolnton. Bounded E by S.C. line, formed here by Savannah R., and S by Little R. Piedmont agr. (cotton, corn, hay, truck, fruit) and sawmilling area. Formed 1796. **4** County (□ 1,203; pop. 4,256), S Idaho; ⊙ Shoshone. Livestock-raising and agr. area in Snake River Plain; watered by Big Wood and Little Wood rivers. Irrigated region in SW, around Shoshone, produces sugar beets, potatoes, dry beans. Formed 1895. **5** County (□ 726; pop. 6,643), central Kansas; ⊙ Lincoln. Rolling prairie region, drained by Saline R. Livestock, grain. Formed 1870. **6** County (□ 340; pop. 18,668), central Ky.; ⊙ Stanford. Drained by Dix and Green rivers and small Fishing Creek. Rolling upland agr. area, partly in outer Bluegrass region; dairy products, livestock, burley tobacco, corn, wheat, fruit, timber. Formed 1780 from Kentucky co., Va., it was one of 3 original counties of Kentucky dist. of Va. **7** Parish (□ 469; pop. 25,782), N La.; ⊙ Ruston. Drained by Middle Fork of Bayou D'Arbonne. Agr. (cotton, corn, hay, fruit, peanuts, sweet potatoes); dairying; some mfg. Natural gas. Formed 1873. **8** Coastal county (□ 457; pop. 18,004), S Maine; ⊙ Wiscasset. Fishing and resort area, with some agr. in N part; boatbuilding, shipping and canning of sea food. Resorts dot its rugged coast and isls. Sheepscot and Eastern rivers, Damariscotta and Medomak inlets. Formed 1760. **9** County (□ 540; pop. 10,150), SW Minn.; ⊙ Ivanhoe. Agr. area bordering on S.Dak. Corn, oats, barley, livestock. Includes part of Coteau des Prairies. Formed 1873. **10** County (□ 586; pop. 27,899), SW Miss.; ⊙ Brookhaven. Drained by Bogue Chitto. Agr. (cotton, corn), dairying, cattle raising, lumbering. Formed 1870. **11** County (□ 629; pop. 13,478), E Mo.; ⊙ Troy. Bounded E by Mississippi R., drained by the Cuivre. Wheat, corn, apples, livestock; coal, limestone. Formed 1818. **12** County (□ 3,715; pop. 8,693), extreme NW Mont.; ⊙ Libby. Mtn. region bordering on British Columbia and Idaho; drained by Kootenai R. Livestock, dairy products, lumber; lead, silver, gold. Kootenai Natl. Forest in NW, Cabinet Mts. in SW, Whitefish Range in NE. Formed 1909. **13** County (□ 2,525; pop. 27,380), SW central Nebr.; ⊙ North Platte; agr. area. The S.Platte and N.Platte rivers join here to form the Platte. Livestock, grain. Formed 1860. **14** County (□ 10,649; pop. 3,837), SE Nev.; ⊙ Pioche. Mtn. region bordering on Ariz. and Utah, watered by Meadow Valley Wash. Mining (lead, zinc), ranching. Part of Egan Range is in N. Formed 1866. **15** County (□ 4,859; pop. 7,409), S central N.Mex.; ⊙ Carrizozo. Stock-grazing, coal-mining area, watered by Rio Hondo. Parts of Lincoln Natl. Forest in center and N; ranges of Sacramento Mts. extend N–S. Formed 1869. **16** County (□ 308; pop. 27,459), W central N.C.; ⊙ Lincolnton. In piedmont area; bounded E by Catawba R. Agr. (cotton, corn, wheat, hay, poultry, dairy products), textile mfg., sawmilling. Formed 1779. **17** County (□ 973; pop. 22,102), central Okla.; ⊙ Chandler. Intersected by the Deep Fork. Diversified agr. (cotton, corn, sorghums, pecans); dairying, stock and poultry raising, beekeeping. Oil and natural-gas wells; oil refineries, gasoline plants. Formed 1890. **18** County (□ 1,006; pop. 21,308), W Oregon; ⊙ Toledo. Bounded W by Pacific Ocean, drained by Alsea and Yaquina rivers. Lumber, dairying, truck, fruit. Part of Siuslaw Natl. Forest in N. Formed 1893. Small portion of co. in S transferred (1949) to Benton co. (E). **19** County (□ 576; pop. 12,767), SE S.Dak., on Iowa line; ⊙ Canton. Rolling prairie region bounded E by Big Sioux R. Livestock, dairy products, poultry, grain. Formed 1862. **20** County (□ 581; pop. 25,624), S Tenn.; ⊙ Fayetteville. Bounded S by Ala.; crossed by Elk R. Timber, livestock, corn, grain, tobacco, dairy products. Some industry at Fayetteville. Formed 1809. **21** County (□ 2,317; pop. 10,970), E Wash.; ⊙ Davenport. Spokane R. enters Columbia R., dammed into Roosevelt L., on N boundary. Wheat, fruit, livestock. Formed 1883. **22** County (□ 438; pop. 22,466), W W.Va.; ⊙ Hamlin. On Allegheny Plateau; drained by Guyandot, Mud, and Coal rivers and tributaries. Agr. (livestock, fruit, tobacco); oil and natural-gas wells; bituminous-coal field. Formed 1867. **23** County (□ 900; pop. 22,235), N central Wis.; ⊙ Merrill. Drained by Wisconsin R. Wooded lake region in N is resort area; dairying and farming in S part. Paper milling and some other mfg. at Merrill and Tomahawk. Contains Council Grounds State Forest. Formed 1874. **24** County (□ 4,101; pop. 9,023), W Wyo.; ⊙ Kemmerer. Grain, livestock area bordering Utah and Idaho; watered by Salt and Greys rivers. Coal, oil. Salt River Range and Bridger Natl. Forest extend N–S. Formed 1911.

Lincoln. 1 Town (pop. 547), Talladega co., E central Ala., 18 mi. W of Anniston, near Coosa R. **2** Town (pop. 771), Washington co., NW Ark., 17 mi. WSW of Fayetteville, in the Ozarks, near Okla. line; strawberries, grain, poultry. **3** City (pop. 2,410), Placer co., central Calif., 25 mi. NNE of Sacramento, in Sacramento Valley; ships fruit, grain; makes pottery, clay products. Inc. 1890. **4** City (pop. 14,362), ⊙ Logan co., central Ill., 28 mi. NNE of Springfield; shipping and industrial center in agr. and bituminous-coal-mining area; corn, wheat, livestock, poultry; mfg. (china, cigars, dairy products, caskets). Seat of Lincoln Col., and a state school for the feeble-minded. Settled near by as Postville in the 1830s; platted and promoted, with the aid of Abraham Lincoln, in 1853; inc. 1857. Lincoln practiced law here, 1847–59. A Lincoln chautauqua has been held annually since 1902. **5** Town (pop. 194), Tama co., central Iowa, 18 mi. NE of Marshalltown, in agr. area. **6** or **Lincoln Center,** city (pop. 1,636), ⊙ Lincoln co., N central Kansas, on Saline R. and 32 mi. WNW of Salina; shipping center for grain and livestock area; limestone quarrying; flour milling. Founded 1871, inc. 1879. **7** Plantation (pop. 71), Oxford co., W Maine, on Magalloway R. and c.35 mi. NW of Rumford. **8** Town (pop. 4,030), including Lincoln village (pop. 2,548), Penobscot co., central Maine, on the Penobscot and c.45 mi. N of Bangor, on Mattanawcook Pond; agr. center, with wood products, textile mills. Settled c.1825, inc. 1829. **9** Residential town (pop. 2,427), Middlesex co., E Mass., 14 mi. WNW of Boston; agr. Settled c.1650, inc. 1754. **10** Village (pop. 409), Alcona co., NE Mich., 26 mi. S of Alpena, near L. Huron. Small lakes (resorts) near by. **11** Town (pop. 316), Benton co., central Mo., near L. of the Ozarks, 22 mi. S of Sedalia. **12** City (pop. 98,884), ⊙ Nebr. and Lancaster co., SE Nebr., 50 mi. SW of Omaha and on Salt Creek of Platte R., in prairie region, 45 mi. W of Missouri R.; 40°49'N 96°42'W; alt. 1,148 ft. Is 2d largest city and the educational center of state, trade, rail, and industrial center for extensive grain and livestock region; oil refining, food processing, mfg. (concrete products; farm, printing, and office equipment; machine parts, plumbing accessories, windmills, bricks; flour, feed, dairy and cold-storage products). Modern state capitol, with 400-ft. central tower, was designed by B. E. Goodhue and completed 1934; contains sculpture and mural decoration by Lee Lawrie and other artists; houses various govt. departments, historical society and mus. City is seat of Univ. of Nebr. and Col. of Agr., Union Col., and Nebr. Wesleyan Univ. Has numerous churches, orphans' home, orthopedic hosp., veterans' hosp., insane asylum, penitentiary, municipal park, and 3 airports. Founded as Lancaster 1864, chosen to be state capital and replatted as Lincoln 1867, inc. 1869, made city of 1st class 1887. **13** Town (pop. 1,415), Grafton co., N central N.H., 17 mi. SE of Woodsville, in White Mts., S of Franconia Notch, and on the Pemigewasset; paper, pulp mills; lumbering. Inc. 1764. **14** Village (pop. c.300), Lincoln co., S central N.Mex., on headstream of Rio Hondo, just S of Capitan Mts., 50 mi. WNW of Roswell; alt. c.5,600 ft.; agr.; livestock. Center of Lincoln co. cattle war, 1877–78. State mus., formerly co. courthouse, contains historical and archaeological collection. Billy the Kid imprisoned here 1881. Parts of Lincoln Natl. Forest near by. **15** Village (pop. 2,722, with adjacent Cool Ridge Heights), Richland co., N central Ohio. **16** Village (1940 pop. 607), Lancaster co., SE Pa., just NW of Ephrata, in rich agr. area. **17** Town (pop. 11,270), Providence co., NE R.I., on Blackstone R. and 7 mi. N of Providence; mfg. (textiles, bakery products, bleaches); limestone quarries. Includes villages of Lime Rock, MANVILLE, and SAYLESVILLE, and parts of ALBION and LONSDALE. Lincoln Woods Reservation (state park); pre-Revolutionary houses. Set off from Smithfield and inc. 1871. **18** Town (pop. 577), Addison co., W central Vt., on New Haven R. and 11 mi. NE of Middlebury, in Green Mts.; wood and dairy products. Settled 1795 by Quakers.

Lincoln, Mount. 1 Highest peak (14,284 ft.) in Park Range, central Colo., 12 mi. NE of Leadville. Gold, silver, lead, copper, zinc, molybdenum mines in vicinity. **2** Peak in N.H.: see FRANCONIA MOUNTAINS.

Lincoln City, village (pop. c.250), Spencer co., SW Ind., 34 mi. ENE of Evansville. Laid out 1872 on site of farm of Thomas Lincoln. Lincoln State Park (just S) includes memorial at grave of Nancy

Hanks Lincoln, and site of Lincoln cabin built in 1816.

Lincoln Gardens, village (pop. 2,049, with adjacent College Heights), Madison co., SW Ill.

Lincoln Heights, residential city (pop. 5,531), Hamilton co., extreme SW Ohio, suburb 10 mi. N of downtown Cincinnati. Inc. 1946.

Lincoln Highway, in U.S., road extending for more than 3,300 mi. from New York city to San Francisco; built 1913–27.

Lincoln Homestead State Park, Ky.: see SPRINGFIELD.

Lincoln Island, Chinese *Howu* (hŭ'wōō'), easternmost of Paracel Isls., China, in S.China Sea; 16°40'N 112°44'E; 1¼ mi. long. ½ mi. wide.

Lincoln Log Cabin State Park (86 acres), E central Ill., 8 mi. S of Charleston, on site of last Lincoln family homestead in Ill.; contains reconstruction of Lincoln cabin built in 1837.

Lincoln Mountain, W central Vt., in Green Mts., 15 mi. NE of Middlebury; 1 of its summits, Mt. Ellen (4,135 ft.), is 3d highest in range.

Lincoln Park. 1 Village (pop. 1,345), Fremont co., S central Colo., near Canon City. **2** Village (pop. 1,575), Upson co., W central Ga., near Thomaston. **3** City (pop. 29,310), Wayne co., SE Mich., residential suburb 10 mi. SW of downtown Detroit. Inc. as village 1921, as city 1925. **4** Borough (pop. 3,376), Morris co., N N.J., 7 mi. W of Paterson; truck farming; summer resort; mfg. of plumbing fixtures, hardware, machinery; nursery. Inc. 1922. **5** Village (pop. 1,527), Ulster co., SE N.Y.

Lincoln Sea, part of the Arctic Ocean off NE Ellesmere Isl. (Canada) and NW Greenland.

Lincolnshire, England: see LINCOLN, county.

Lincolnton. 1 Town (pop. 1,315), ⊙ Lincoln co., NE Ga., 34 mi. NW of Augusta, near Savannah R.; sawmilling center (lumber, pulpwood); clothes mfg. **2** Town (pop. 5,423), ⊙ Lincoln co., W central N.C., 28 mi. NW of Charlotte, in farm area; mfg. of cotton textiles, yarn, hosiery, furniture; flour and lumber mills. Inc. 1785.

Lincoln Tunnel, vehicular tunnel under Hudson R. bet. midtown Manhattan borough of New York city and Weehawken, N.J. Opened 1937, it is 8,215 ft. long (portal to portal) and nearly 100 ft. below surface of the river.

Lincoln University, village, Chester co., SE Pa., 20 mi. W of Wilmington, Del. Seat of Lincoln Univ., founded 1854 as one of 1st U.S. universities for Negroes.

Lincolnville. 1 City (pop. 228), Marion co., E central Kansas, 10 mi. NNE of Marion, in grain and livestock region. **2** Resort town (pop. 881), Waldo co., S Maine, on Penobscot Bay and 10 mi. S of Belfast. **3** Town (pop. 278), Charleston co., SE S.C., 20 mi. NW of Charleston.

Lincolnwood, village (pop. 3,072), Cook co., NE Ill., suburb just N of Chicago. Until 1935 called Tessville.

Lincs, England: see LINCOLN, county.

Lincura (lĭngkōō'rä), town (pop. 1,094), Ñuble prov., S central Chile, 18 mi. SSW of Bulnes, on Hata R.

Lind, town (pop. 796), Adams co., SE Wash., 15 mi. SW of Ritzville, in Columbia basin agr. region; wheat, livestock, poultry.

Linda (lyĕn'dŭ), village, W Gorki oblast, Russian SFSR, on railroad and 13 mi. SW of Semenov; flax.

Lindal, England: see PENNINGTON.

Lindale. 1 Village (pop. 3,234, with Silver Creek), Floyd co., NW Ga., 4 mi. S of Rome; textile mfg. **2** Town (pop. 1,105), Smith co., E Texas, 13 mi. NNW of Tyler, near Sabine R.; canning, shipping center in fruit, truck, area; brick, tile.

Lindas (lĭn'dōs"), Swedish *Lindås,* village (pop. 599), Kalmar co., SE Sweden, 15 mi. SW of Nybro; motor and machinery works.

Lindau (lĭn'dou). **1** Town (1946 pop. 1,603), in former Anhalt State, central Germany, after 1945 in Saxony-Anhalt, 6 mi. N of Zerbst; spa; brick mfg. **2** Town (1946 pop. 17,915), Swabia, SW Bavaria, Germany, after 1945 under Württemberg-Hohenzollern, on an isl. in L. of Constance, 16 mi. SSE of Ravensburg, 4 mi. NW of Bregenz (Austria); connected with shore by rail causeway (NW) and bridge (NE). Customs station (steamers to Austria and Switzerland); machinery mfg., woodworking. Summer resort and tourist center. Has 15th-cent. town hall (renovated in 19th cent.). On E mole of small harbor is a large carved lion, the landmark of the town. Created free imperial city in 1275. Passed to Bavaria in 1803. After Second World War, although Swabia, along with most of Bavaria, was placed in U.S. zone of occupation, Lindau town and district [Ger. *Kreis*] (□ 120; 1946 pop. 52,621, including displaced persons 52,853; 1950 pop. 57,970) were placed under Württemberg-Hohenzollern in Fr. occupation zone. **3** Village (1946 pop. 2,298), in former Prussian prov. of Hanover, W Germany, after 1945 in Lower Saxony, 12 mi. NE of Göttingen; woodworking, spinning.

Linden (lĭn'dŭn). **1** W industrial district (since 1920) of Hanover, in former Prussian prov. of Hanover, W Germany, after 1945 in Lower Saxony, on left bank of the Leine; long noted for its velvet. A short canal leads 8 mi. W to Weser-Elbe Canal. **2** District (since 1929) of Bochum, in former Prussian prov. of Westphalia, W Germany, after 1945 in North Rhine-Westphalia, on the Ruhr, and 4 mi. SW of city center; coal mining.

Linden. 1 Town (pop. 1,363), ⊙ Marengo co., W Ala., c.45 mi. WSW of Selma, in cotton and corn area; lumber milling, cotton ginning. Founded 1823. **2** Town (pop. 590), Montgomery co., W Ind., 17 mi. S of Lafayette, in agr. area. **3** Town (pop. 290), Dallas co., central Iowa, 34 mi. W of Des Moines, in agr. area; feed. **4** Village (pop. 933), Genesee co., SE central Mich., 14 mi. SSW of Flint, in lake and farm area; flour mill, grain elevator, creamery. Summer resort. **5** City (pop. 30,644), Union co., NE N.J., 3 mi. SW of Elizabeth; large oil refinery, auto assembly plant; mfg. (chemicals, pharmaceuticals, clothing, machinery, beverages, concrete blocks, paints, phonograph records, sports equipment); lead refining at Grasselli (just E). Site bought from Lenni-Lenape Indians 1664, inc. 1924. **6** Town (pop. 194), Cumberland co., S central N.C., 15 mi. NNE of Fayetteville; brick mfg. **7** Town (pop. 854), ⊙ Perry co., W central Tenn., on Buffalo R. and 70 mi. SW of Nashville; trade center for lumbering and agr. area. **8** Town (pop. 1,744), ⊙ Cass co., NE Texas, 33 mi. N of Marshall; trade center for truck-farming, lumbering area; cotton plants; woodworking. Founded c.1850. **9** Village, Warren co., Va.: see MANASSAS GAP. **10** Village (pop. 1,165, with near-by Inman and Laurel), Wise co., SW Va., near Big Stone Gap. **11** Village (pop. 463), Iowa co., SW Wis., 8 mi. SW of Dodgeville, in dairying and hog-raising area.

Lindenau (lĭn'dŭnou), W suburb of Leipzig, Saxony, E central Germany; textile milling (cotton, wool, carpets).

Lindenberg (lĭn'dŭnbĕrk). **1** or **Lindenberg im Allgäu** (ĭm äl'goi), town (pop. 5,748), in LINDAU dist., SW Bavaria, Germany, in the Allgäu, 10 mi. NE of Lindau, near Austrian border; rail junction; mfg. of straw and felt hats; dairying. Summer resort. **2** Village (pop. 938), Brandenburg, E Germany, 35 mi. SE of Berlin, 6 mi. WNW of Beeskow; site of aerological observatory; 52°12'N 14°7'E.

Lindenberg, mountain range (2–3,000 ft.), N Switzerland, E of the Baldeggersee and Hallwilersee.

Lindenfels (lĭn'dŭnfĕls), village (pop. 2,001), S Hesse, W Germany, in former Starkenburg prov., 7 mi. E of Bensheim, picturesquely situated in the Odenwald; syenite polishing. Tourist center. Has ruined castle.

Lindenhurst, village (pop. 8,644), Suffolk co., SE N.Y., near S shore of W Long Isl., 2 mi. W of Babylon, in resort area; mfg. (electrical apparatus, cabinets, machinery, metal products, aircraft parts, marine equipment, beer, buttons, textiles, clothing). Settled 1869, inc. 1923.

Lindenows Fjord (lĭn'dŭnōz), inlet (35 mi. long, 1–3 mi. wide) of the Atlantic, SE Greenland, 60 mi. E of Julianehaab; 60°32'N 43°45'W. Extends inland to edge of icecap, which rises steeply to 7,500 ft. on N shore. Ruins of medieval Scandinavian settlement found here.

Lindenthal (lĭn'dŭntäl), industrial town (pop. 5,626), Saxony, E central Germany, 5 mi. NW of Leipzig city center. Includes (since 1913) former village of BREITENFELD.

Lindenwold (lĭn'dŭnwōld"), borough (pop. 3,479), Camden co., SW N.J., 11 mi. SE of Camden. Settled 1742, laid out 1885, inc. 1929.

Lindesay, Mount (4,064 ft.), E Australia, in McPherson Range, on Queensland–New South Wales border, 60 mi. SSW of Brisbane.

Lindesberg (lĭn'dŭsbĕr"yŭ), city (pop. 4,782), Orebro co., S central Sweden, on Hork R. and 20 mi. N of Orebro; mfg. of locomotives, tractors, washing machines, shoes; woodworking. Has medieval church, mus. Trade center since Middle Ages; chartered 1642.

Lindesnes, Lindesnaes (both: lĭn'nŭsnās, lĭn'dŭsnās), or **The Naze,** cape at S extremity of Norway, at entrance to the Skagerrak; 57°59'N 7°3'E. Powerful beacon light here, emplaced 1650, was 1st in Norway. An old spelling is Lyndesnas.

Lindfield, town and parish (pop. 3,488), central Sussex, England, on Ouse R., just N of Haywards Heath; agr. market. Has 14th-cent. church.

Lindhos, Greece: see LINDOS.

Lindi (lĭn'dē), town (pop. 8,577), ⊙ Southern Prov. (□ 55,223; pop. 888,278), SE Tanganyika, port on Lindi Bay of Indian Ocean, at mouth of navigable Lukuledi R., 225 mi. SSE of Dar es Salaam; 9°59'S 39°43'E. Sisal-shipping center. Also exports copra, cotton, tobacco, mangrove bark, beeswax; fisheries. Airfield. Terminus of road leading W to Masasi, Tunduru, and Songea, and of river-rail route to Nachingwa peanut scheme area. Salt, copal, limestone deposits in area.

Lindi River (lēn'dē), E Belgian Congo, rises 35 mi. SW of Lubero, flows c.375 mi. NW, W, and SW, past Makala and Bafwasende, through dense equatorial forest, to Congo R. 5 mi. WNW of Stanleyville. Numerous rapids in lower course.

Lindisfarne, England: see HOLY ISLAND.

Lind Island, Canada: see JENNY LIND ISLAND.

Lindlar (lĭnt'lär), village (pop. 10,352), in former Prussian Rhine Prov., W Germany, after 1945 in North Rhine-Westphalia, 8 mi. W of Gummersbach.

Lindley, England: see HUDDERSFIELD.

Lindley, town (pop. 2,285), E Orange Free State, U. of So. Afr., on Valsch R. and 35 mi. NW of Bethlehem; agr. center (grain, stock, dairying).

Lindóia (lēndô'yŭ), city (pop. 540), E São Paulo, Brazil, 36 mi. NE of Campinas, near Minas Gerais border; alt. 3,100 ft. Resort with hot springs (developed after 1920).

Lindon, town (pop. 801), Utah co., N central Utah, 7 mi. NNW of Provo; alt. 5,640 ft.; berries, truck. Served by Provo R. irrigation project.

Lindos or **Lindhos** (lĭn'dŭs, Gr. lĭn'dhôs), Ital. *Lindo,* Lat. *Lindus,* village (pop. 793), Rhodes isl., Greece, on E shore, 26 mi. S of Rhodes. One of the leading city-states of anc. Rhodes and a member of the Dorian Hexapolis, Lindos was noted for its shrine to Athena. Has small Crusaders' church and collections of 17th-cent. oriental faïence. The apostle Paul landed here on his voyage to Rome.

Lindoso (lēndō'zōō), village, Viana do Castelo dist., N Portugal, 26 mi. NE of Braga; customhouse on Sp. border. Hydroelectric plant 3 mi. W on Lima R.

Lindow (lĭn'dō), town (pop. 3,414), Brandenburg, E Germany, on small lake, 9 mi. ENE of Neuruppin; potatoes, grain, stock; dairying; forestry. Has remains of 17th-cent. Premonstratensian monastery.

Lindsay, town (pop. 8,403), ⊙ Victoria co., S Ont., 60 mi. NE of Toronto; woolen milling and knitting, flour and lumber milling; mfg. of machinery, chemicals, milk food, crayons. Site of Dominion Arsenal.

Lindsay (lĭn'zē). **1** City (pop. 5,060), Tulare co., S central Calif., 55 mi. SE of Fresno, in Sierra Nevada foothills; packs and ships oranges, cans olives, processes olive oil. Inc. 1910. **2** Village (pop. 247), Platte co., E central Nebr., 23 mi. NW of Columbus and on branch of Platte R.; grain, stock. **3** Town (pop. 3,021), Garvin co., S central Okla., 23 mi. SE of Chickasha, and on Washita R., in agr. area; ships broomcorn; cotton ginning; mfg. of flour, feed, brooms.

Lindsborg (lĭnz'bôrg), city (pop. 2,383), McPherson co., central Kansas, on Smoky Hill R. and 19 mi. S of Salina; trade center for wheat and livestock area; flour. Festival of religious music is presented here annually during Holy Week in cooperation with Bethany Col. (Lutheran; founded 1881) and features famous chorus. Founded 1868, inc. 1879.

Lindsey, Suffolk, England: see KERSEY.

Lindsey (lĭn'zē), village (pop. 512), Sandusky co., N Ohio, 7 mi. NW of Fremont, in agr. area; metal stampings, meat products.

Lindsey, Parts of, N administrative division of LINCOLNSHIRE, England.

Lindstrom, resort village (pop. 729), Chisago co., E Minn., on small lake, near St. Croix R., and 33 mi. NNE of St. Paul, in agr. area (grain, potatoes, livestock, poultry); dairy products, flour.

Lindum or **Lindum Colonia,** England: see LINCOLN.

Lindus, Greece: see LINDOS.

Línea, La, or **La Línea de la Concepción** (lä lē'nää, dhä kōn-thĕpthyōn'), city (pop. 35,101), Cádiz prov., S Spain, port on isthmus at Algeciras Bay, on Sp. border just N of neutral zone which separates it from Gibraltar (Br. colony), and 55 mi. ESE of Cádiz. Strategically placed, it is a modern, active trading center supplying Gibraltar with fruit and vegetables. Produces also grapes, strawberries, wine, liquor, fish preserves, cement products. Has customhouse and fortifications.

Line Islands, coral group in central and S Pacific; 5°53'N–11°25'S 151°48'–162°4'W. Include FLINT ISLAND, VOSTOK ISLAND, CAROLINE ISLAND, STARBUCK ISLAND, MALDEN ISLAND, JARVIS ISLAND, PALMYRA, CHRISTMAS ISLAND, FANNING ISLAND, WASHINGTON ISLAND. Last 3 isls. belong to Br. colony of Gilbert and Ellice Isls.; Palmyra and Jarvis Isl. belong to U.S.; both countries have claims on the other isls. Once worked for guano, isls. are now important as potential air bases. Sometimes called Equatorial Isls.

Linekin Neck (lĭ'nĭkĭn), Lincoln co., S Maine, peninsula E of Boothbay Harbor, terminating in Ocean Point; resort villages.

Linesville, borough (pop. 1,246), Crawford co., NW Pa., 14 mi. W of Meadville, on Pymatuning Reservoir; poultry, potatoes, corn, oats. Inc. 1862.

Lineville. 1 Town (pop. 1,548), Clay co., E Ala., 25 mi. S of Anniston; lumber, clothing. **2** Town (pop. 482), Wayne co., S Iowa, at Mo. line, 33 mi. SSW of Chariton; livestock, grain.

Linfen (lĭn'fŭn'), town, ⊙ Linfen co. (pop. 161,994), S Shansi prov., China, on Fen R., on railroad and 135 mi. SSW of Taiyüan; agr. and industrial center in one of Shansi's main irrigated farming dists. (wheat, cotton, wine); mfg. of paper, porcelain; flour milling. Traditionally the residence of Yao, one of China's legendary emperors (2357–2255 B.C.), Linfen is an anc. market center, called Pingyang until 1912.

Linfield, village (1940 pop. 610), Montgomery co., SE Pa., 5 mi. SE of Pottstown; grain mill, distilling.

Ling, China: see LING RIVER.

Linga (lĭng'gŭ), islet of the Shetlands, Scotland, just off NE coast of Mainland isl.

Lingampalli, India: see SANGAREDDIPET.

Lingayen (lĭng-gī'ŭn, -gä'ŭn), town (1939 pop. 5,329; 1948 municipality pop. 36,806), ⊙ Pangasinan prov., central Luzon, Philippines, port on

S shore of Lingayen Gulf, on Agno delta, 7 mi. W of Dagupan; agr. center (rice, corn, copra).

Lingayen Gulf, large inlet of S.China Sea, central Luzon, Philippines, bet. Santiago Isls. (W) and San Fernando Point (E); 26 mi. wide at entrance, extends c.35 mi. inland. Contains Cabarruyan and Santiago isls. In Second World War, the Japanese landed here in Dec., 1941, and U.S. forces in Jan. 1945.

Lingbo (lĭng'bōō"), village (pop. 958), Gavleborg co., E Sweden, 20 mi. SW of Soderhamn; metal- and woodworking.

Ling Chiang, China: see LING RIVER.

Ling-ch'iu, China: see LINGKIU.

Lingchow, China: see LINGWU.

Lingchwan or **Ling-ch'uan** (both: lĭng'chwän'). **1** Town, ⊙ Lingchwan co. (pop. 11,650), NE Kwangsi prov., China, on upper Kwei R., on railroad and 12 mi. NNE of Kweilin; rice, wheat, beans, timber, tea. Silver, copper, iron, tin deposits near by. **2** Town, ⊙ Lingchwan co. (pop. 136,238), SE Shansi prov., China, 35 mi. SSE of Changchih, in Taihang Mts.; rice, wheat, beans, timber.

Lingeh or **Bandar Lingeh** (bändär' lĭng-gĕ'), town (1940 pop. 9,617), Seventh Prov., in Fars, S Iran, port on Persian Gulf, 95 mi. WSW of Bandar Abbas; pearl trade. Airfield. Sometimes spelled Langeh.

Lingen (lĭng'ŭn), town (pop. 15,442), in former Prussian prov. of Hanover, NW Germany, after 1945 in Lower Saxony, on Dortmund-Ems Canal, near Ems R., and 17 mi. NNW of Rheine; rail junction; textile mfg., metalworking. Oil wells. Has 17th-cent. town hall.

Lingenfeld (lĭng'ŭnfĕlt"), village (pop. 2,641), Rhenish Palatinate, W Germany, on an arm of the Rhine and 6 mi. SW of Speyer; rail junction; wheat, tobacco, sugar beets.

Lingfield, town and parish (pop. 5,214), SE Surrey, England, on Eden R. and 3 mi. N of East Grinstead; agr. market. Has 15th-cent. church. Site of racecourse.

Lingga (lĭng'gŭ), island (□ c.360; 40 mi. long, up to 20 mi. wide), Lingga Archipelago, Indonesia, in S.China Sea, off E coast of Sumatra and S of Riouw Archipelago, just N of Singkep, 100 mi. SSE of Singapore; 0°9'S 104°39'E. Generally low, with hills rising to 3,266 ft. in SW. Agr. and forest products: sago, copra, gambier, pepper, rattan, timber. Fishing. Chief town and port is Kotadaik (kōtŭdīk') or Daik (dīk) on S coast of isl.

Lingga Archipelago, island group (□ 842; pop. 30,524), Indonesia, in S.China Sea, off E coast of Sumatra and S of Riouw Archipelago; 0°9'S 104°39'E; comprises numerous isls., largest being LINGGA and SINGKEP. Bet. Lingga and Singkep is small but important islet of Penuba or Penoeba (7 mi. long, 3 mi. wide), site of Penuba, chief town and port of Lingga group. N of Lingga are smaller isls. of Sebangka (20 mi. long, 4 mi. wide), Bakung or Bakoeng (10 mi. long, 3 mi. wide), and Temiang (8 mi. long, 2 mi. wide). Isls. are generally low and of coral formation. Chief products: tin (mined on Singkep), sago, copra, gambier, pepper, rattan. Lumbering, fishing.

Linggadjati, Indonesia: see CHERIBON.

Linggajati, Indonesia: see CHERIBON.

Linggi River (lĭng'gē), W Negri Sembilan, Malaya, rises in central Malayan range NW of Seremban, flows 40 mi. S, past Seremban, to Strait of Malacca on Malacca border below Pengkalan Kempas.

Linghed (lĭng'hād"), village (pop. 1,141), Kopparberg co., central Sweden, 17 mi. NE of Falun; sawmilling center. Iron mined near by.

Linghsien. 1 Town, Hunan prov., China: see NINGHSIEN. **2** Town, Shantung prov., China: see KWANGWU.

Ling Kiang, China: see LING RIVER.

Lingkiu or **Ling-ch'iu** (both: lĭng'chō'), town, ⊙ Lingkiu co. (pop. 116,530), SW Chahar prov., China, in Wutai Mts., 65 mi. SE of Tatung, near Shansi-Hopeh line; cattle raising; wool weaving; wheat, kaoliang, beans. Until 1949 in Shansi.

Lingle, town (pop. 403), Goshen co., SE Wyo., on N.Platte R. and 9 mi. NW of Torrington in irrigated region; alt. 4,165 ft. Shipping point for sugar beets, livestock, potatoes.

Lingling (lĭng'lĭng'), town, ⊙ Lingling co. (pop. 418,774), S Hunan prov., China, on Siang R. and 80 mi. SW of Hengyang, and on rail spur; tung oil, hemp, rice, wheat. Coal mining (N). Until 1913 called Yungchow.

Lingmell, England: see SCAFELL.

Lingnan, Manchuria: see TSINGPING, Jehol prov.

Lingolsheim (lĕgôlzĕm', Ger. lĭng'ôls-hīm), outer SW suburb (pop. 4,802) of Strasbourg, Bas-Rhin dept., E France; tanning.

Lingpao (lĭng'bou'), town, ⊙ Lingpao co. (pop. 132,378), NW Honan prov., China, near Lunghai RR and Yellow R., 24 mi. E of Tungkwan; cotton textiles; hides, dates, melons. Until c.1947 called Kwoliochen. The old Lingpao was 8 mi. NNE on Lunghai RR.

Lingpi (lĭng'bē'), town, ⊙ Lingpi co. (pop. 556,534), N Anhwei prov., China, near Kiangsu line, 45 mi. NNE of Pengpu; wheat, beans, kaoliang, tobacco.

Ling River, Chinese *Ling Kiang* or *Ling Chiang* (both: lĭng' jyäng'), Chekiang prov., China, rises in 2 branches which join at Linhai, flows 35 mi. SE, past Haimen, to Taichow Bay of E.China Sea.

Lingshan (lĭng'shän'), town (pop. 4,156), ⊙ Lingshan co. (pop. 405,426), SW Kwangtung prov., China, on Yam R. and 65 mi. ESE of Nanning; cotton, rice, wheat, beans.

Lingshi (lĭng'shē), fortified village [Bhutanese *dzong*], NW Bhutan, 33 mi. NW of Punakha; alt. 12,590 ft. **Lingshi La,** pass (alt. 16,118 ft.) in main range of W Assam Himalayas, is 2.5 mi. NNW of village.

Lingshih (lĭng'shû'), town, ⊙ Lingshih co. (pop. 81,835), S central Shansi prov., China, on Fen R. and 30 mi. S of Fenyang, and on railroad; wheat, millet, beans.

Lingshow or **Ling-shou** (lĭng'shō'), town, ⊙ Lingshow co. (pop. 124,131), SW Hopeh prov., China, 20 mi. NNW of Shihkiachwang and on Huto R.; rice, wheat, beans.

Lingshui (lĭng'shwā'), town, ⊙ Lingshui co. (pop. 50,583), SE Hainan, Kwangtung prov., China, 110 mi. SSW of Kiungshan; poultry, hogs, and cattle raising; saltworks and fisheries. Exports eggs, hides, hemp.

Lingsugur (lĭngsōōgōōr'), village (pop. 2,618), Raichur dist., SW Hyderabad state, India, 55 mi. W of Raichur; millet, oilseeds; cotton ginning. Was ⊙ former Lingsugur dist. (divided 1905 bet. Raichur and Gulbarga dists.).

Lingtai or **Ling-t'ai** (lĭng'tī'), town, ⊙ Lingtai co. (pop. 110,650), SE Kansu prov., China, 35 mi. SSE of Kingchwan, near Shensi border; wheat, millet, kaoliang, beans.

Linguaglossa (lēng'gwäglôs'sä), village (pop. 6,905), Catania prov., E Sicily, on NE slope of Mt. Etna, 16 mi. N of Acireale; wine.

Linguère (lĕgâr'), town (pop. c.1,300), N central Senegal, Fr. West Africa, rail terminus 160 mi. ENE of Dakar; exports peanuts and gums. Corn growing, stock raising.

Linguetta, Cape (lĭng-gwĕ'tŭ), Albanian *Kep i Gjuhëzës*, promontory of SW Albania, on the Strait of Otranto; 40°25'N 19°17'E. Forms NW tip of mountainous Karaburun (or Acroceraunia) peninsula, which closes off the Bay of Valona. Also called Cape Glossa and Cape Acroceraunia.

Lingwu (lĭng'wōō'), town (pop. 3,722), ⊙ Lingwu co. (pop. 82,918), SE Ningsia prov., China, 25 mi. S of Yinchwan, across Yellow R.; cattle raising; grain; saltworks. Until 1913, Lingchow.

Lingyüan (lĭng'yüăn'), town, ⊙ Lingyüan co. (pop. 234,635), S Jehol prov., SW Manchuria, 75 mi. ENE of Chengteh and on railroad; commercial center; furs, agr. products, livestock. Trade with Mongols. Originally called Tatzekow, later Kienchang (1738–1914), and briefly Takow in 1914.

Lingyün (lĭng'yün'), town, ⊙ Lingyün co. (pop. 70,095), W Kwangsi prov., China, 30 mi. N of Poseh; wheat, millet, beans. Until 1913, Szecheng.

Linhai (lĭn'hī'), town (pop. 25,669), ⊙ Linhai co. (pop. 530,804), E Chekiang prov., China, on small Ling R. and 65 mi. NNE of Wenchow, 25 mi. from Taichow Bay of E.China Sea; mfg. of bamboo articles; exports salt and fish. Rice, wheat, cotton grown near by. Until 1912, Taichow.

Linhares (lēnyä'rĭsh), city (pop. 733), N central Espírito Santo, Brazil, on the swampy lower Rio Doce and 65 mi. N of Vitória; cacao, coffee. Animal reserve established near by in 1943.

Linhares, village (pop. 585), Guarda dist., N central Portugal, 10 mi. W of Guarda. Its 12th-cent. castle played part in Moorish wars.

Linhcam (lĭng'käm'), town, Hatinh prov., N central Vietnam, 12 mi. SW of Vinh; road center. Agr. (tea, corn, beans); sericulture. Forestry (hard woods, rattan). Sulphur springs.

Linho (lĭn'hŭ'), town (pop. 2,852), ⊙ Linho co. (pop. 62,193), W Suiyuan prov., China, near Yellow R., on railroad and 135 mi. W of Paotow, in Howtao oasis; cattle raising; wheat, beans, licorice.

Lin-hsi, Manchuria: see LINSI.

Lin-hsia, China: see LINSIA.

Lin-hsiang, China: see LINSIANG.

Linhsien. 1 (Cantonese lĕn'yün'), Mandarin *Lienhsien* (lyĕn'shyĕn'), town (pop. 20,796), ⊙ Linhsien co. (pop. 211,865), N Kwangtung prov., China, on Linchow R. and 70 mi. W of Kükong; tin and coal mining. Until 1912 called Linchow. **2** (lĭn'shyĕn') Town, ⊙ Linhsien co. (pop. 364,355), NW Pingyuan prov., China, 30 mi. W of Anyang, at E foot of Taihang Mts.; walnuts, peppers. Until 1949 in Honan prov. **3** (lĭn'shyĕn') Town, ⊙ Linhsien co. (pop. 206,541), W Shansi prov., China, 32 mi. NNW of Lishih; cotton weaving; wheat, beans, ramie, medicinal herbs.

Linhwaikwan or **Lin-huai-kuan** (lĭn'hwī'gwän'), town, N Anhwei prov., China, 20 mi. E of Pengpu, on Hwai R. and Tientsin-Pukow RR; commercial center.

Linhwang, Manchuria: see LINTUNG.

Lini (lĭn'yē'). **1** Town (1922 pop. estimate 100,000), ⊙ Lini co. (1946 pop. 157,233), S Shantung prov., China, on I River and 135 mi. SE of Tsinan; commercial and road center of S Shantung; silk weaving; peanuts, grain, melons. Has noted monasteries. Until 1913 called Ichow. **2** Town, Shantung prov., China: see LINYI.

Linière (lēnyâr') or **Saint Côme** (sē kōm'), village (pop. 695), S Que., on affluent of Chaudière R., 40 mi. NNE of Megantic; lumbering, dairying.

Liniers (lēnyĕrs'), W industrial section of Buenos Aires, Argentina; textile mills, railroad shops.

Linjan or **Lenjan** (both: lĕnjän'), agr. district (1932 pop. estimate 85,000) in Tenth Prov., W central Iran, just SW of Isfahan, along Zaindeh R.; one of the chief rice-producing regions of Iran; also grows cotton, opium, millet.

Linju (lĭn'rōō'), town, ⊙ Linju co. (pop. 238,889), NW Honan prov., China, on road and 40 mi. SSE of Loyang; wheat-growing center; millet, beans, kaoliang. Until 1913 called Juchow.

Linkao, China: see LIMKO.

Linkenheim (lĭng'kŭnhīm), village (pop. 3,218), N Baden, Germany, after 1945 in Württemberg-Baden, 8 mi. N of Karlsruhe; asparagus, strawberries, tobacco.

Linkiang or **Lin-chiang** (both: lĭn'jyäng'). **1** Town, Kiangsi prov., China: see TSINGKIANG. **2** Town, ⊙ Linkiang co. (pop. 153,922), E Liaotung prov., Manchuria, China, 50 mi. E of Tunghwa and on upper Yalu R. (Korea border); mining center in Tungpientao dist. Coal and iron mining near by.

Linkinhorne, agr. village and parish (pop. 1,208), E Cornwall, England, 7 mi. S of Launceston. Has Elizabethan manor house and church.

Linkoping (lĭn'chŭ"pĭng), Swedish *Linköping*, city (1950 pop. 54,552), ⊙ Ostergotland co., SE Sweden, on Stang R., near its mouth on L. Rox (Gota Canal route), 100 mi. SW of Stockholm; 58°24'N 15°37'E. Rail junction and industrial center, with steel mills, railroad shops, sugar refineries, breweries; textile milling, hosiery knitting, tobacco processing, woodworking. See of Lutheran bishop. Has cathedral (begun 1230), 13th-cent. castle, noted episcopal library, Church of St. Lars, and county mus. Bishopric established 1120; in Middle Ages city attained great commercial importance; fell into decline after destructive fire (1700). Scene (1598) of decisive defeat of King Sigismund III of Poland by Swedish Protestant forces; Sigismund's remaining supporters were massacred (1600) in the city. Its industrial development stems from construction of Gota and Kinda canals.

Linkow or **Lin-k'ou** (lĭn'kō'), town, ⊙ Linkow co. (pop. 65,000), central Sungkiang prov., Manchuria, 60 mi. NE of Mutankiang; rail junction and graphite-mining center.

Link River, small stream (1¼ mi. long), S Oregon, at city of Klamath Falls. Connects Upper Klamath L. with L. Ewauna, which is drained by Klamath R. Small dam on it.

Linktown, Scotland: see KIRKCALDY.

Linli (lĭn'lē'), town, ⊙ Linli co. (pop. 199,760), N Hunan prov., China, 25 mi. N of Changteh; rice, wheat, sugar cane, cotton. Until 1914 called Anfu.

Linlin Island (lēn'lēn) (□ 3.2; pop. 686), just off E coast of Chiloé Isl., S Chile; 42°23'S 73°26'W.

Linlithgow, county, Scotland: see WEST LOTHIAN.

Linlithgow (lĭnlĭth'gō), burgh (1931 pop. 3,666; 1951 census 3,929), ⊙ West Lothian (formerly Linlithgowshire), Scotland, in NW part of co., near S end of Loch Linlithgow (1 mi. long), 16 mi. W of Edinburgh; leather, shoe, paper mfg., whisky distilling; agr. market. It is noted for its many fountains; has 12th-cent. Church of St. Michael, founded by David I, and remains of Linlithgow Palace, on high ground above the loch, begun in early 14th cent. by Edward I. James V and Mary Queen of Scots b. here. Palace was burned in 1746. In 1570 the Regent earl of Murray (or Moray) was murdered in Linlithgow. Edinburgh Univ. was transferred here during 1645–46 plague epidemic, and in 1646 last Scottish National Parliament met here.

Linlithgowshire, Scotland: see WEST LOTHIAN.

Linn. 1 County (□ 713; pop. 104,274), E Iowa; ⊙ Cedar Rapids. Prairie agr. area (hogs, cattle, poultry, corn, oats) drained by Cedar and Wapsipinicon rivers and Buffalo Creek. Many limestone quarries, sand and gravel pits. Has state park. Industry at Cedar Rapids. Formed 1837. **2** County (□ 607; pop. 10,053), E Kansas; ⊙ Mound City. Gently sloping to rolling area, bordering E on Mo.; drained (NE) by Marais des Cygnes R. Stock raising, general agr. Oil and gas fields; coal, lead, zinc deposits. Formed 1855. **3** County (□ 624; pop. 18,865), N central Mo.; ⊙ Linneus. Agr. (corn, wheat, oats, hay), livestock; coal; mfg. at Brookfield. Formed 1837. Gen. Pershing b. here 1860. **4** County (□ 2,294; pop. 54,317), W Oregon; ⊙ Albany. Level farm land rising E to Cascade Range; bounded W by Willamette R. Dairying, agr. (fruit, truck, grain, seeds, hay), logging. Part of Willamette Natl. Forest in W. Formed 1847.

Linn. 1 City (pop. 395), Washington co., N Kansas, 40 mi. NW of Manhattan; shipping point in grain and livestock region; dairying, poultry and produce packing. **2** City (pop. 758), ⊙ Osage co., central Mo., near Missouri R., 19 mi. ESE of Jefferson City; agr.; clay pits.

Linnam (lĕn'näm'), Mandarin *Liennan* (lyĕn'nän'), town, ⊙ Linnam co. (pop. 75,640), NW Kwangtung prov., China, 20 mi. S of Linhsien; grain. Lead mine. Called Chaikang until 1942.

Linn Creek, town (pop. 162), Camden co., central Mo., in the Ozarks, near L. of the Ozarks, 48 mi. SW of Jefferson City.

Linndale, village (pop. 399), Cuyahoga co., N Ohio, a SW suburb of Cleveland.

Linne (lĭ'nü), village (pop. 1,707), Limburg prov., SE Netherlands, on Maas R. and 3 mi. SW of Roermond; chemicals.

Linné, Cape (lĭnā'), W West Spitsbergen, Spitsbergen group, on Arctic Ocean, on S side of mouth of Is Fjord, 30 mi. WSW of Longyear City; 78°3'N 13°35'E. Meteorological observatory (established 1933), radio station, lighthouse, radio beacon.

Linneus (lĭ'nēus). **1** Town (pop. 777), Aroostook co., E Maine, 8 mi. SW of Houlton, in agr., hunting, fishing area. **2** City (pop. 513), ⊙ Linn co., N central Mo., 8 mi. NW of Brookfield; grain, livestock.

Linn Grove, town (pop. 320), Buena Vista co., NW Iowa, on Little Sioux R. and 18 mi. N of Storm Lake; concrete blocks, feed, tankage. Sand and gravel pits near by. State park is W.

Linnhe, Loch (lŏkh lĭ'nē), inlet (35 mi. long, 1–5 mi. wide) on W coast of Scotland, bet. Inverness and Argyll. At its head is Fort William, where it joins the 7-mi.-long Loch Eil (ēl') at right angles, and where the Caledonian Canal begins. At mouth of Loch Linnhe is LISMORE isl.

Linnich (lĭ'nĭkh), town (pop. 1,963), in former Prussian Rhine Prov., W Germany, after 1945 in North Rhine-Westphalia, on the Rur and 6 mi. NW of Jülich; metalworking.

Linntown, village (pop. 1,131), Union co., central Pa., near Lewisburg.

Liñola (lēnyō'lä), town (pop. 1,924), Lérida prov., NE Spain, 16 mi. ENE of Lérida, in irrigated agr. area (sweet sherry, olive oil, cereals, alfalfa); sheep raising; gravel.

Linosa (lēnô'zä), anc. *Aegusa*, island (□ 2; pop. 336), one of PELAGIE ISLANDS, in Mediterranean Sea bet. Malta and Tunis, 105 mi. SW of Licata, Sicily; 2 mi. long; rises to 640 ft. Fisheries; vineyards, orchards. Chief port, Linosa (S).

Linping. 1 or **Lin-p'ing** (lĭn'pĭng'), town, N Chekiang prov., China, 13 mi. NE of Hangchow and on railroad to Shanghai. **2** (lĕn'pĭng'), Mandarin *Lien-p'ing* (lyĕn'pĭng'), town (pop. 4,165), ⊙ Linping co. (pop. 90,130), E central Kwangtung prov., China, 70 mi. SE of Kükong, near Kiangsi prov. border; rice, wheat, fruit, sugar cane. Coal mining near by.

Linpu or **Lin-p'u** (lĭn'pōō'), town, N Chekiang prov., China, 8 mi. S of Siaoshan and on Chekiang-Kiangsi RR.

Lins (lēns), city (1950 pop. 24,170), W central São Paulo, Brazil, on railroad, 60 mi. NW of Bauru; coffeegrowing and -processing center; sawmilling, furniture and pottery mfg. Ships coffee, manioc, rice, dairy produce. Bishopric. Has business school (established 1943). Formerly called Albuquerque Lins.

Linselles (lĕsĕl'), town (pop. 4,112), Nord dept., N France, 6 mi. N of Lille; textiles (flax, cotton).

Linsen (lĭn'sŭn'), town, ⊙ Linsen co. (pop. 546,034), E Fukien prov., China, on Min R. and 5 mi. NW of Foochow. Until c.1945 called Hungshankiao.

Linshan (lĕn'sän'), Mandarin *Lienshan* (lyĕn'shän'), town (pop. 626), ⊙ Linshan co. (pop. 42,573), NW Kwangtung prov., China, 13 mi. SW of Linhsien; lumbering; bamboo, rice. Gold and molybdenum mines near by.

Linshui (lĭn'shwā'), town (pop. 6,464), ⊙ Linshui co. (pop. 360,231), E central Szechwan prov., China, 50 mi. NNE of Chungking city; tung-oil trading center; millet, sweet potatoes, rice, sugar cane, wheat, beans. Sulphur mines, coal deposits near by.

Lin Shui, river, China: see PEITA RIVER.

Linsi or **Lin-hsi** (both: lĭn'shē'), town, ⊙ Linsi co. (pop. 36,321), S Inner Mongolian Autonomous Region, Manchuria, 95 mi. NNW of Chihfeng, in Jooda league. Founded 1908; in Jehol until 1949.

Linsia or **Lin-hsia** (both: lĭn'shyä'), town, ⊙ Linsia co. (pop. 205,105), SE Kansu prov., China, 45 mi. SW of Lanchow; tobacco processing; wheat. Pop. is largely Moslem. Until 1913 named Hochow; called Taoho, 1913–28.

Linsiang or **Lin-hsiang** (both: lĭn'shyäng'), town, ⊙ Linsiang co. (pop. 204,103), northeasternmost Hunan prov., China, on Canton-Hankow RR and 20 mi. ENE of Yoyang, near Hupeh line; tea, rice, fish. Gold and zinc mining. Until 1936, Linsiang was a town on the Yangtze R. 17 mi. WNW of its present site; it was moved here following completion of the railroad.

Linslade, urban district (1931 pop. 2,433; 1951 census 3,269), E Buckingham, England, on Ouzel R. and just W of Leighton Buzzard; agr. market. Has 15th-cent. church.

Linstead (lĭn'stĭd, lĭn'stĕd''), town (pop. 2,254), St. Catherine parish, central Jamaica, on railroad and 12 mi. NNW of Spanish Town; annatto, tropical fruit, coffee, stock.

Lintan or **Lin-t'an** (lĭn'tän'), town, ⊙ Lintan co. (pop. 48,084), SE Kansu prov., China, 90 mi. S of Lanchow; cattle and sheep raising. Until 1913 called Taochow. The old town of Taochow is 20 mi. W.

Lintao or **Lin-t'ao** (lĭn'tou'), town, ⊙ Lintao co. (pop. 146,937), SE Kansu prov., China, 45 mi. S of Lanchow and on Tao R.; tobacco processing; exports wool, hides, licorice, timber. Pop. is largely Moslem. Until 1928 called Titao.

Lintelermarsch, Germany: see NORDDEICH.

Lintfort, Germany: see KAMP-LINTFORT.

Lintgen (lĭnt'gŭn), town (pop. 1,065), S central Luxembourg, on Alzette R. and 7 mi. N of Luxembourg city; agr. machinery, metal castings, cement and paper products. Just SW is agr. village of Prettingen or Pretten.

Linthal (lĭn'täl), town (pop. 1,708), Glarus canton, E central Switzerland, on Linth R. and 9 mi. SSW of Glarus; cotton textiles. Road leads to Klausen Pass (SW).

Linth Canal (lĭnt), NE Switzerland, 11 mi. long; Linth R. flows through from L. of Wallenstadt to L. of Zurich.

Linthicum or **Linthicum Heights** (lĭn'thĭkŭm), suburban village (pop. c.1,000), Anne Arundel co., central Md., 7 mi. SSW of downtown Baltimore. Friendship International Airport (opened 1950) is near by.

Linth River, N Switzerland, formed by 2 headstreams 4 mi. S of Linthal; flows N, past Glarus, through Escher Canal, to L. of Wallenstadt (its old bed by-passes L. of Wallenstadt), thence through Linth Canal to L. of Zurich. Emerges from L. of Zurich at Zurich as Limmat R. (lĭ'mät); flows NW, past Baden, to Aar R. NE of Brugg. Length of Linth-Limmat R., 87 mi. Hydroelectric plant at Wettingen.

Linthwaite, former urban district (1931 pop. 9,688), West Riding, SW Yorkshire, England, on Colne R. and 3 mi. WSW of Huddersfield; woolen mills, pharmaceutical works.

Lintien (lĭn'dyĕn'), town, ⊙ Lintien co. (pop. 110,119), SW central Heilungkiang prov., Manchuria, 45 mi. ESE of Tsitsihar; kaoliang, soybeans, corn, millet, rye. Called Tungtsichen until 1917.

Lintin Island (lĭntĭn'), Chinese *Lingting* (lĭng'dĭng'), in Canton R. estuary, Kwangtung prov., China, 22 mi. NE of Macao, near Hong Kong border. Noted for conical peak rising to 833 ft.

Linton. 1 Town and parish (pop. 1,402), S Cambridge, England, on Cam R. and 10 mi. SE of Cambridge; agr. market, with flour mills. Has 15th-cent. church and village col. **2** Town and parish (pop. 1,791), S Derby, England, 4 mi. SSE of Burton-upon-Trent; coal mining.

Linton. 1 City (pop. 5,973), Greene co., SW Ind., 32 mi. SSE of Terre Haute, in agr. area; mfg. (machine-shop products, beverages); bituminous-coal mines; poultry hatcheries. Laid out 1830; inc. as town in 1886, as city in 1900. **2** City (pop. 1,675), ⊙ Emmons co., S N.Dak., 45 mi. SSE of Bismarck and on Beaver Creek, 15 mi. E of Missouri R.; farming center, grain, livestock. Inc. 1916.

Lintseh or **Lin-tse** (both: lĭn'dzŭ'), town, ⊙ Lintseh co. (pop. 47,771), N Kansu prov., China, on Silk Road to Sinkiang, 30 mi. NW of Changyeh, and on Hei R., at the Great Wall; wheat, millet. Until 1913 called Fuyi.

Lintsin or **Lin-chin** (both: lĭn'jĭn'), town, ⊙ Lintsin co. (pop. 75,956), SW Shansi prov., China, 22 mi. NE of Yüngtsi, near Yellow R.; cotton weaving, pottery mfg.; wheat, beans, fruit.

Lintsing or **Lin-ch'ing** (both: lĭn'chĭng'), town (1934 pop. estimate 50,000), ⊙ Lintsing co. (1946 pop. 275,692), S Hopeh prov., China, near Pingyuan line, on Grand Canal, at mouth of Wei R., and 70 mi. W of Tsinan; cotton-textile, carpet, brick, and pottery mfg.; vegetable-oil processing; grain, fruit. Flourished prior to Taiping Rebellion.

Lintung. 1 (lĭn'dōōng') Town, ⊙ Lintung co. (pop. 16,137), S Inner Mongolian Autonomous Region, Manchuria, 120 mi. N of Chihfeng; banner hq. in Jooda league. Founded 1925; in Jehol until 1949. Near by is ruined Mongol city of Borohoto or Borokhoto, Chinese *Linhwang*, the N capital of the Liao (Khitan) dynasty (937–1125). **2** or **Lin-t'ung** (lĭn'tōōng'), town (pop. 4,122), ⊙ Lintung co. (pop. 212,406), SE central Shensi prov., China, 18 mi. ENE of Sian and on Lunghai RR; cotton weaving; kaoliang, millet.

Lintze or **Lin-tzu** (both: lĭn'dzŭ'), town, ⊙ Lintze co. (pop. 174,364), N central Shantung prov., China, 14 mi. NNW of Yitu, near Tsingtao-Tsinan RR; cotton weaving, tobacco processing; silk cocoons; wheat, beans.

Lintzford, England: see WHICKHAM.

Linville (lĭn'vĭl), summer resort (pop. c.500), Avery co., NW N.C., 24 mi. NNW of Morganton, and on Linville R. Near by are Linville Dam and Linville Falls (S) and Linville Caverns (12 mi. SSW), with stalactite and stalagmite formations.

Linville River, NW N.C., rises in the Blue Ridge in Avery co., flows S, past Linville, to L. James (backed up in Catawba R.); c.30 mi. long. Linville Falls, 2 cascades 10 mi. S of Linville, are scenic attractions. On upper course is Linville Dam (160 ft. high, 1,326 ft. long; for hydroelectric power; completed 1919).

Linwood, village (pop. 500), S Ont., 15 mi. NW of Kitchener; dairying, mixed farming.

Linwood, town in Kilbarchan parish, NE Renfrew, Scotland, on Black Cart Water and 3 mi. W of Paisley; paper milling.

Linwood. 1 Town (pop. 858), Walker co., NW Ga., just NW of La Fayette. **2** City (pop. 261), Leavenworth co., NE Kansas, on Kansas R. and 20 mi. WSW of Kansas City, Kansas; general agr. **3** Village, Worcester co., Mass.: see NORTHBRIDGE. **4** Village (pop. 168), Butler co., E Nebr., 43 mi. NNW of Lincoln, near Platte R. **5** City (pop. 1,925), Atlantic co., SE N.J., 7 mi. W of Atlantic City. Inc. as borough 1889, as city 1931. **6** Village (1940 pop. 3,108), Delaware co., SE Pa., near Delaware R., 17 mi. SW of Philadelphia.

Linwu (lĭn'wōō), town, ⊙ Linwu co. (pop. 125,615), S Hunan prov., China, on Wu R. and 45 mi. SW of Chenhsien, near Kwangtung line. Tin and tungsten mining at Sianghwaling, 5 mi. N.

Linxe (lēks), village (pop. 657), Landes dept., SW France, 17 mi. NW of Dax; lumber trade.

Linyanti River, Angola and Bechuanaland Protectorate: see KWANDO RIVER.

Linyi or **Lini** (both: lĭn'yē'), town, ⊙ Linyi co. (pop. 870,000), NW Shantung prov., China, 35 mi. N of Tsinan; cotton weaving; wheat, millet, rice, kaoliang.

Linying (lĭn'yĭng), town, ⊙ Linying co. (pop. 240,664), N central Honan prov., China, on Ying R., on Peking-Hankow RR and 15 mi. NNW of Yencheng; sesame, wheat, beans, kaoliang.

Linyü (lĭn'yü'), town, ⊙ Linyü co. (pop. 212,803), NE Hopeh prov., China, 15 mi. WSW of Shanhaikwan. Called Haiyang until 1949, when co. seat was moved here from SHANHAIKWAN.

Linyu (lĭn'yōō'), town (pop. 968), ⊙ Linyu co. (pop. 36,996), W Shensi prov., China, 45 mi. NE of Paoki, in mtn. region; cotton weaving; wheat, millet, beans.

Linyüan (lĭn'yüän'), Jap. *Rinken* (rēn'hān), village, S Formosa, near W coast, 8 mi. SSE of Fengshan, near mouth of Lower Tanshui R.; sugar cane, pineapples.

Linz (lĭnts), anc. *Lentia*, city (1951 pop. 185,177), ⊙ Upper Austria, on the Danube, 100 mi. W of Vienna; rail, commercial, and mfg. center, large river port. Iron- and steelworks, large hydroelectric plant, mfg. of machines, textiles, nitric acid, fertilizer, tobacco; shipyards, flour and paper mills. Bishopric, with old and new cathedral; Francisco-Carolineum mus.; Franz Joseph Square with marble column from early 18th cent. Near by is 8th-cent. Benedictine abbey. Urfahr (ōōr'fär), large suburb on left bank of the Danube, is connected to city by bridge.

Linz town (pop. 5,566), in former Prussian Rhine Prov., W Germany, after 1945 in Rhineland-Palatinate, on right bank of the Rhine (landing) and 14 mi. SE of Bonn; rail junction; basalt quarrying and trade. Has late-Romanesque–Gothic church. Red wine grown in vicinity.

Linzee, Cape, westernmost point of Cape Breton Isl., NE N.S., on Gulf of St. Lawrence, 3 mi. NNW of Port Hood; 46°3'N 61°32'W.

Lion, Gulf of, or **Gulf of Lions,** Fr. *Golfe du Lion* (gôlf dü lēõ'), anc. *Sinus Gallicus*, wide bay of the Mediterranean, washing most of S coast of France; extends from Fr.-Sp. border (W) to Toulon (E). Its varied coastline includes easternmost spurs of the Pyrenees, shallow lagoons, the Rhone delta, and limestone hills flanking Marseilles. Receives (E–W) Tech, Têt, Aude, Orb, Hérault, Vidourle, Petit Rhône, and Grand Rhône rivers. Principal capes: Cerbère, Couronne, Croisette, Sicié, and Cap de l'Aigle. Gulf of Fos (which receives outlet from Étang de Berre) and Marseilles bay are chief indentions. Marseilles and Sète are main ports.

Lion-d'Angers, Le (lù lēõ'-däzhā'), village (pop. 1,299), Maine-et-Loire dept., W France, on Oudon R. and 13 mi. NW of Angers; road center; copper and bronze foundry; cattle raising. Has a partly Romanesque 11th–15th-cent. church.

Lioni (lēō'nē), town (pop. 4,728), Avellino prov., Campania, S Italy, on Ofanto R. and 21 mi. NE of Salerno.

Lions, Gulf of, France: see LION, GULF OF.

Lions Head, village (pop. 368), S Ont., on Saugeen Peninsula, on Georgian Bay, 33 mi. NNW of Owen Sound; dairying, mixed farming.

Lion's Head, Ireland: see HOWTH, HILL OF.

Lion-sur-Mer (lēõ'-sür-mâr'), village (pop. 1,171), Calvados dept., NW France, beach resort on the Channel, 9 mi. N of Caen; fishing.

Liopesi, Greece: see PAIANIA.

Lioran, Le (lù lēōrã'), village, Cantal dept., S central France, on N slope of Plomb du Cantal, 17 mi. WNW of Saint-Flour; alt. 3,783 ft. Winter sports. Road and rail tunnel across Massif du Cantal just W.

Lioyang or **Liaoyang** (both: lyou'yäng'), town (pop. 2,135), ⊙ Lioyang co. (pop. 80,325), SW Shensi prov., China, on Kialing R. and 65 mi. WNW of Nancheng, in mtn. region; commercial center; exports sugar, tobacco. Mercury deposits near by. Sometimes written Lüehyang.

Liozno (lēōz'nü), town (1926 pop. 2,601), E Vitebsk oblast, Belorussian SSR, 28 mi. SE of Vitebsk; linen milling.

Lipa (lēpä'), city (1939 pop. 7,687; 1948 metropolitan area pop. 49,884) in but independent of Batangas prov., S Luzon, Philippines, 14 mi. SW of San Pablo, near railroad; trade center for agr. area (rice, sugar cane, corn, coconuts); cutlery mfg.

Lipanos, Bolsón de los (bōlsōn′ dā lōs lēpä′nōs), arid depression in N outliers of Sierra Madre Oriental of Coahuila, N Mexico, on Chihuahua border, NE of Bolsón de Mapimí; alt. c.3,000 ft.

Lipany, Czechoslovakia: see CESKY BROD.

Lipari (lĭ′pərē, Ital. lē′pärē), anc. *Lipara,* island (□ 14.4; pop. 10,342), largest of Lipari Isls., in Tyrrhenian Sea off NE Sicily, bet. Salina (NW) and Vulcano (S), 22 mi. NW of Milazzo, in Messina prov.; 38°29′N 14°56′E. Is 6 mi. long, 4 mi. wide; rises to 1,978 ft. in Monte Chirica (N). Pumice industry centered at Canneto (pop. 2,686), on E coast; quarries on Campo Bianco, a near-by mtn. slope. Agr. (capers, grapes, figs, olives); lobster fisheries. Chief port, Lipari (pop. 4,530), on SE coast; commercial center of isls.; mfg. of pumice soap; exports pumice, currants, malmsey wine. Resort with sulphur baths. Bishopric since 1400; has Norman cathedral, restored 1654. Long a place of exile.

Lipari Islands or **Aeolian Islands** (ēō′lēŭn), anc. *Aeoliae Insulae,* group (□ 44; pop. 17,697) in Tyrrhenian Sea bet. 38°22′N and 38°49′N, 14–34 mi. off Cape Milazzo, NE Sicily, in Messina prov. Comprise volcanic isls. of LIPARI, SALINA, VULCANO (active), STROMBOLI (active), FILICUDI, PANARIA, ALICUDI, and 10 islets, including uninhabited Basiluzzo (□ .1). Isls. are elevated summits of submarine mtn. chain rising to 3,156 ft. on Salina. Mild climate and low rainfall. Agr. (grapes, olives, figs, barley); livestock raising (asses, sheep); lobster fishing. Exports malmsey wine, raisins, figs, fish, pumice. Steamer service to Milazzo and Messina. Colonized in late 6th cent. B.C. Antiquities include obsidian artifacts, sepulchers.

Lipcani, Moldavian SSR: see LIPKANY.

Lipetrén, Sierra (syĕ′rä lēpātrĕn′), low pre-Andean range in S Río Negro natl. territory, Argentina, S of L. Carri Laufquén; extends to Chubut border in arid Patagonian plateau.

Lipetsk (lyē′pyĭtsk), city (1926 pop. 21,416; 1939 pop. 66,625), NW Voronezh oblast, Russian SFSR, on Voronezh R. and 65 mi. NNE of Voronezh. Iron-mining and metallurgical center; old and new metallurgical works (pig-iron production), pipe foundry, tractor works; mfg. (radiators, calcium-carbide, silicate bricks). Near by is health resort (chalybeate mineral springs, mud baths). Center of Lipetsk iron-ore dist. (□ 2,000) extending N and NW of Lipetsk, with reserves of 170,000,000 tons. City has metallurgical, teachers, and medical schools. Founded 1707 on right Voronezh R. bank as iron-milling center under Peter the Great; chartered 1779. New industrial section developed in Soviet times on left bank, around blast furnaces, steel mills, and ferroalloy plant.

Lípez, Cordillera de (kōrdēyä′rä dā lē′pĕs), range in the Andes, southernmost part of the Eastern Cordillera, SW Bolivia; extends c.160 mi. SW from Portugalete (at S end of Cordillera de Chichas) to Mt. Zapaleri on Bolivia-Chile-Argentina border; rises to 19,225 ft. Forms watershed bet. Río Grande de Lípez (W) and San Juan R. (E).

Liphook, England: see BRAMSHOTT.

Lipiany (lēpyä′nĭ), Ger. *Lippehne* (lĭp″ä′nū), town (1939 pop. 4,374; 1946 pop. 3,380) in Brandenburg, after 1945 in Szczecin prov., NW Poland, on small lake, 25 mi. S of Stargard; agr. market (grain, sugar beets, potatoes, livestock); potato and fruit processing, furniture mfg. After 1945, briefly called Lipiny.

Lipik (lē′pĭk), village, Croatia, Yugoslavia, on Pakra R., on railroad and 2 mi. SW of Pakrac, at W foot of the Psunj, in Slavonia; health resort, with waters rich in iodine. Petroleum, natural gas, and lignite in vicinity.

Lipin-Bor (lyē′pĭn-bôr″), village (1939 pop. over 500), W Vologda oblast, Russian SFSR, on lake Beloye Ozero and 32 mi. NNW of Kirillov; flax, wheat.

Liping or **Li-p'ing** (lē′pĭng′). **1** Town (pop. 5,326), ⊙ Liping co. (pop. 143,179), SE Kweichow prov., China, 150 mi. ESE of Kweiyang, near Hunan-Kwangsi line; cotton textiles, embroideries; timber, wheat, millet. **2** Town, Kweichow prov., China: see KINPING.

Lipiny, Poland: see LIPIANY.

Lipitsy (lyē′pĭtsē), village (1939 pop. over 500), S Tula oblast, Russian SFSR, 30 mi. ENE of Mtsensk; wheat.

Lipiya (lyē′pēŭ), town (1945 pop. over 500), SW Gorki oblast, Russian SFSR, near Oka R., 7 mi. ESE of Murom. Shipyards near by.

Lipkany (lyēp′kŭnē), Rum. *Lipcani* (lĭpkän′), town (1941 pop. 3,652), N Moldavian SSR, on Prut R., on railroad and 40 mi. E of Chernovtsy, on Rum.–Ukrainian SSR border. Agr. center; flour milling; gypsum quarry. Until Second World War, pop. largely Jewish.

Lipnik nad Becvou (lĭp′nyĕk näd′ bĕchvō), Czech *Lipník nad Bečvou,* Ger. *Leipnik* (līp′nĭk), town (pop. 6,887), NE central Moravia, Czechoslovakia, on Becva R., on railroad and 15 mi. ESE of Olomouc; mfg. (machinery, machine tools, matches, textiles, soap, candles), cheese making. Has 13th-cent. church, rebuilt in 18th cent., 16th-cent. castle, Jewish cemetery and synagogue, 17th-cent. Renaissance belfry.

Lipno (lēp′nô), town (pop. 8,389), Bydgoszcz prov., central Poland, on railroad and 14 mi. NNE of Wloclawek; cement mfg., tanning, flour milling. During Second World War, Ger. administrative hq., called Leipe.

Lipo (lē′pŭ′), town (pop. 4,319), ⊙ Lipo co. (pop. 79,745), S Kweichow prov., China, 55 mi. SW of Jungkiang; alt. 1,453 ft.; tobacco-growing center; cotton textiles, embroideries; wheat, millet. Coal deposits near by.

Lipotvar, Czechoslovakia: see HLOHOVEC.

Lipova (lĭ′pôvä), Czech *Lipová,* village (pop. 1,052), N Bohemia, Czechoslovakia, on railroad and 28 mi. NE of Usti nad Labem; mfg. (basketwork, brushes, brooms). Until 1947, Hanspach, Czech *Hanšpach,* Ger. *Hainspach.*

Lipova (lē′pôvä), Hung. *Lippa* (lēp′pŏ), town (1948 pop. 6,556), Arad prov., W Rumania, in Banat, on left bank of Mures R. opposite Radna, on railroad and 32 mi. NE of Timisoara; health resort with mineral springs; also trading (notably in livestock) and processing center (brewing, flour milling); mfg. of carbonated waters, tiles and bricks; granite quarrying. Has 13th-cent. castle remains and a fine Orthodox church built originally in Byzantine style (14th cent.) and repeatedly restored.

Lipovaya Dolina (lyē′pŭvŭ dŭlyē′nŭ), village (1926 pop. 4,283), SW Sumy oblast, Ukrainian SSR, on Khorol R. and 18 mi. SE of Romny; metalworks.

Lipovets (–vyĭts), town (1939 pop. over 10,000), E Vinnitsa oblast, Ukrainian SSR, 25 mi. E of Vinnitsa; cotton milling.

Lippa, Rumania: see LIPOVA.

Lippe (lĭ′pŭ), former state (□ 469; 1939 pop. 187,220), NW Germany, after 1945 included in North Rhine-Westphalia; ⊙ was Detmold. Situated bet. Teutoburg Forest and Weser R., it was surrounded by former Prussian provs. of Hanover and Westphalia. Lordship of Lippe was raised (16th cent.) to a county. From the various divisions of the county in 17th cent., 2 counties (after 18th cent., principalities) emerged—Lippe or Lippe-Detmold, and Schaumburg-Lippe. Lippe joined German Confederation in 1815; sided with Prussia in Austro-Prussian War; joined (1871) German Empire. In 1897 the contested succession was awarded to the collateral branch of Lippe-Biesterfeld. After abdication (1918) of ruling prince, Lippe joined Weimar Republic. A local electoral victory (Jan., 1933) of National Socialists helped Hitler into power.

Lippehne, Poland: see LIPIANY.

Lippe Lateral Canal, Ger. *Lippe-Seitenkanal* (lĭ′pŭ-zī′tŭnkänäl″), W Germany, a major transportation artery of the Ruhr connecting Rhine R. and Dortmund-Ems Canal (at DATTELN); extends 66 mi. bet. Wesel (W) and Hamm (E); 8 locks; navigable for vessels up to 1,000 tons. Parallels lower course of Lippe R.

Lippe River, W Germany, rises in Teutoburg Forest 6 mi. NE of Bad Lippspringe, flows 147 mi. W, past Lippstadt (head of navigation), Hamm, and Lünen, to the Rhine at Wesel. Canalized in lower course. Paralleled by Lippe Lateral Canal bet. Hamm and Wesel. Forms N border of Ruhr industrial region.

Lippe-Seitenkanal, Germany: see LIPPE LATERAL CANAL.

Lippspringe, Bad, Germany: see BAD LIPPSPRINGE.

Lippstadt (lĭp′shtät), town (pop. 28,377), in former Prussian prov. of Westphalia, W Germany, after 1945 in North Rhine-Westphalia, on the Lippe (head of navigation) and 17 mi. W of Paderborn; rail junction; iron foundries, wire mills; textile mfg., metalworking. Has 12th- and 13th-cent. churches. Founded 1170. Joined Hanseatic League in 1280. In Second World War, U.S. troops met here (April, 1945), completing encirclement of the Ruhr.

Lipscomb (lĭp′skŭm), county (□ 934; pop. 3,658), extreme N Texas; ⊙ Lipscomb. In NE corner of the Panhandle; alt. 2,000–2,500 ft. In W, high plains broken by deep valley of Wolf Creek; in E, rolling hills. Grain (wheat, grain sorghums, barley, oats, corn, alfalfa); some fruit, truck; beef and dairy cattle, hogs, sheep, poultry. Hunting for quail, wild turkey, deer. Formed 1876. Acquired part of Ellis co., Okla., in relocation of 100th meridian (1930).

Lipscomb. 1 Town (pop. 2,550), Jefferson co., N central Ala., just S of Birmingham. Settled c.1890, inc. 1910. **2** Village (pop. c.200), ⊙ Lipscomb co., extreme N Texas, on edge of high plains of the Panhandle, c.55 mi. WSW of Woodward and on Wolf Creek; retail center for farm, livestock area.

Lipson, Greece: see LEIPSON.

Lipsos, Greece: see LEIPSOS.

Lipton, village (pop. 320), SE central Sask., 45 mi. NE of Regina; grain elevators, lumbering, mixed farming.

Liptovsky Hradok (lĭp′tôfskē hrä′dôk), Slovak *Liptovský Hrádok,* Hung. *Liptóujvár* (lĭp′tō-ōōēvär), town (pop. 1,395), N Slovakia, Czechoslovakia, on Vah R., on railroad and 19 mi. ESE of Ruzomberok; large sawmill.

Liptovsky Svaty Mikulas (svä′tē mĭ′kōōläsh), Slovak *Liptovský Svätý Mikuláš,* Hung. *Liptószentmiklós* (lĭp′tōsĕntmĭ′klōsh), town (pop. 5,578), N Slovakia, Czechoslovakia, on right bank of Vah R., on railroad and 14 mi. E of Ruzomberok; lumbering center; tanning, tawing, linen mfg. Has 13th-cent. church, restored in 18th cent. Former cultural center of Slovak Protestants; 1st popular demonstration for Slovak independence, here, in 1848.

Liptrap, Cape, S Victoria, Australia, in Bass Strait, just W of Waratah Bay; 38°55′S 145°55′E. Its face is nearly perpendicular, rising to 297 ft.; lighthouse.

Liptsy (lyēp′tsē), village (1926 pop. 7,634), N Kharkov oblast, Ukrainian SSR, 15 mi. NNE of Kharkov; truck produce.

Li-p'u, China: see LAIPO.

Lipu La (lēpōō′ lä), pass (alt. c.17,000 ft.) in SE Zaskar Range of Kumaun Himalayas, SW Tibet, 9 mi. WSW of Taklakot, on pilgrimage route to Manasarowar L., at 30°14′N 81°2′E. Also called Lipu Lekh; sometimes written Lipulekh.

Liquiça (lēkē′sŭ), town, Portuguese Timor, in central Timor, on Ombai Strait, 17 mi. W of Dili; fishing; copra. Sometimes spelled Liquissa.

Lira (lē′rä), town, Northern Prov., central Uganda, 50 mi. SE of Gulu; agr. trade center (cotton, peanuts, sesame). Hq. Lango dist., inhabited by Nilotic Lango tribe.

Liranga (lēräng-gä′), village, central Middle Congo territory, Fr. Equatorial Africa, on Congo R. (Belgian Congo border), just below its confluence with Ubangi R., and 60 mi. ESE of Fort-Rousset; banana plantations, palm groves. R.C. mission.

Lircay (lērkī′), city (pop. 2,184), ⊙ Angaraes prov. (in 1940: □ 1,281; pop. 64,263), Huancavelica dept., S central Peru, in Cordillera Occidental of the Andes, 26 mi. ESE of Huancavelica (connected by highway); alt. 8,904 ft. Wheat, alfalfa; cattle, sheep. Silver mining near by. In 1943 Acobamba prov. was formed from part of Angaraes prov.

Liria (lē′ryä), city (pop. 10,451), Valencia prov., E Spain, 17 mi. NW of Valencia; olive- and cotton-seed-oil processing, flour milling, brandy and liqueur distilling, ham curing. Other mfg.: cement pipes, ceramics, silk textiles, burlap. Wine, truck produce, esparto in area. Kaolin quarries. Has 14th-cent. church and Renaissance palace of duke of Berwick, who was invested (18th cent.) with city by Philip V.

Liri River (lē′rē), anc. *Liris,* S central Italy, rises in the Apennines 8 mi. WSW of Avezzano, flows SSE and S, past Sora and Isola del Liri, ESE, past Pontecorvo, and S to Gulf of Gaeta 9 mi. E of Gaeta; 98 mi. long. Receives outlet of reclaimed Lago Fucino and Rapido R. (right), Sacco R. (left). Used for hydroelectric power. In lower course, below mouth of Rapido R., called Garigliano R.; forms Latium-Campania boundary. In Second World War, the lower Liri R. valley (Garigliano), traversed by Ger. Gustav line, was scene of heavy fighting (1943–44) during Allied advance to Rome.

Li River. 1 Chinese *Li Shui* (lē′ shwā′), river in NW Hunan prov., China, rises on Hupeh line, flows 250 mi. SE and E, past Tzeli, Lihsien, and Tsingshih, to Tungting L. near Ansiang. **2** Chinese *Li Kiang* or *Li Chiang* (both: lē′ jyäng′), river in SW Kwangsi prov., China, rises in N Vietnam in 2 headstreams—the Song Banggiang (left) and the Song Kikong (right)—which join at Lungtsin (head of steamer navigation), flows c.100 mi. ENE, past Tsungshan, to Yü R. above Nanning. Important route for N Vietnam trade. Also called Tso River (tsô), Chinese *Tso Kiang* or *Tso Chiang.*

Liro River (lē′rô), Sondrio prov., N Italy, rises in small lake 1 mi. W of Splügen Pass, flows 15 mi. S to Mera R. 1 mi. SW of Chiavenna. Dammed 1 mi. S of Pass to form reservoir (1 mi. long) which supplies large Mese hydroelectric plant near CHIAVENNA.

Lirquén (lērkĕn′), town (pop. 1,126), Concepción prov., S central Chile, on Concepción Bay, on railroad and 8 mi. NNE of Concepción; coal-mining center; glass mfg.

Lisac or **Lisats** (both: lē′säts), mountain (6,344 ft.), Macedonia, Yugoslavia, 14 mi. WNW of Titov Veles.

Lisala (lēsä′lä), town (1946 pop. c.2,500), ⊙ Congo-Ubangi dist. (□ 66,862; 1948 pop. c.920,000), Equator Prov., NW Belgian Congo, on right bank of Congo R. and 270 mi. NE of Coquilhatville; commercial center, notably for native produce (copal, cotton, palm kernels, raphia); palm-oil milling. Has medical and accounting schools for natives, hosp. for Europeans, R.C. missions. Airfield. Seat of vicar apostolic of Nouvelle-Anvers. Upoto Baptist mission is 3 mi. SW. Umangi R.C. mission is 12 mi. W.

Lisa Mountains (lē′sä), E central Bulgaria, N spur of E Balkan Mts.; extend N from Kotel Mts.; rise to over 3,000 ft.; forested. Form watershed bet. Golyama Kamchiya and Yantra rivers. Sometimes called Sakar Balkan Mts.

Lisan, El, or **Al-Lisan** (both: ĕl-lĭsăn′), peninsula on Dead Sea, in S central Jordan, WNW of Kerak; 10 mi. wide, 5 mi. long. Airfield. Wheat, barley, vegetables, fruits. Bitumen, salt, potash deposits.

Lisats, mountain, Yugoslavia: see LISAC.

Lisbellaw (lĭs″bulô′), town (pop. 624), central Co. Fermanagh, Northern Ireland, 5 mi. ESE of Enniskillen; woolen milling.

Lisboa (lēzhbō′ŭ), district (□ 1,061; pop. 1,070,103), W central Portugal, in Estremadura and W part of

Ribatejo provinces; ⊙ Lisbon. Bounded by the Atlantic (W and S), by lower Tagus R. and its estuary (SE). Contains Europe's westernmost point at Cape Roca. Winegrowing. Besides Lisbon, Cintra and the Port. Riviera resorts of Estoril and Cascais attract tourists.

Lisbon (lĭz'bŭn), Port. *Lisboa* (lēzhbō'ŭ), anc. *Olisipo*, later *Felicitas Julia*, important commercial city (1940 pop. 709,179; 1950 pop. 783,919), ⊙ Portugal, Estremadura prov., and Lisboa dist., seaport on right bank of Tagus estuary at a point where Lisbon Bay narrows to a channel (8 mi. long, 2 mi. wide) leading to the Atlantic Ocean; continental Europe's westernmost capital (38°42'N 9°10'W), it became a hub of transoceanic air transport during Second World War. Noted for its magnificent situation along terraced hills overlooking one of the continent's best natural harbors, Lisbon is Portugal's largest city, its administrative, commercial, and industrial center, and the nation's showplace geared to transient and tourist trade. Although a sand bar obstructs mouth of Tagus R. 9 mi. WSW of Lisbon, large vessels can reach city's docks along 5-mi.-long waterfront and find commodious anchorage in Lisbon Bay. City exports agr. and forest products (wine, olive oil, fruit, cork, resins), salt, small quantities of nonferrous ores, and canned fish (especially sardines). The port is particularly important for its entrepôt and transshipping activities. Industries of Lisbon area (including S bank of Tagus estuary) are chiefly of the light and consumer class. They include mfg. of textiles, chemicals (dyes, fertilizer), paper, tobacco products, pottery, soap, and perfume. There are flour mills, sugar refineries, miscellaneous metalworks (including ship-repair yards), and a govt. armaments and explosives factory. City is linked by rail with N, central, and E Portugal (several lines cross into Spain). Ferries across Lisbon Bay to Barreiro connect with railroad to S Portugal. There is a short electric rail line to Cascais (W) serving the near-by Port. Riviera. Portela international airport is 4 mi. NNE of city center. Lisbon has a mild west coast marine climate, with a mean annual temp. of 60°F., a winter mean of 51°F. (almost no snow), and average yearly rainfall of 30 inches. In its layout, Lisbon falls naturally into 3 main divisions: the centrally located lower city (*Cidade Baixa*) occupying a broad valley bet. hills, the old city (E), and the modern residential section (W and NW). The *Cidade Baixa*, the heart of Lisbon, was entirely rebuilt by the marques de Pombal after the earthquake of 1755. It faces the Tagus at the Praça do Comércio (commonly called Terreiro do Paço; nicknamed Black Horse square by English), a spacious square flanked on 3 sides by arcaded public bldgs. housing the post office, various ministries, the stock exchange, and the customhouse. A triumphal arch at its N end gives on Rua Augusta, a commercial artery leading N to Rossio square (also called Praça de Dom Pedro IV), at city's geographical center. At square's NW corner, flanked by central railroad station and natl. theater, begins the 300-ft.-wide Avenida da Liberdade; over 1 mi. long, with a double row of trees dividing it into 3 traffic lanes, this attractive avenue is Lisbon's chief promenade. The old town, to the E, built on site of Phoenician and Roman settlements, is topped by a Moorish citadel (castle of St. George). S of citadel lies the crowded and picturesque Alfama dist. clustered around the cathedral (founded 12th cent. by Alfonso I; wrecked by 2 earthquakes and rebuilt; contains relics of St. Vincent, Lisbon's patron saint). In modern W Lisbon is the secularized convent of São Bento, which has been occupied since 1834 by both houses of parliament. The former royal residence (Palacio das Necessidades) is now the foreign ministry. Beyond it are the W suburbs of Alcántara and Belém (now part of Lisbon city). The latter is noted for its Hieronymite convent and for the white tower of Belém, a famous Port. landmark. Lisbon has a univ. (originally founded here in 1290; permanently transferred to Coimbra in 1537; re-established 1911), and a technical univ. (founded 1930). City's many cultural institutions also include museums of anc. and contemporary art, the noteworthy artillery mus., and the coach exhibit in Belém. The Renaissance monastery of São Vicente de Fora contains tombs of the Braganza kings, and the church of São Roque has a sumptuous chapel (built 18th-cent. by John V). Lisbon receives its water supply from the Serra de Sintra (200-year-old aqueduct over Alcántara valley in W suburbs) and from Alcanena area (60 mi. NNE). City's W outskirts, especially the Port. Riviera at Estoril and Cascais and the Cintra region, attract numerous foreign tourists. While 1st permanent settlement dates from Phoenician times, and Caesar, renaming it *Felicitas Julia*, raised it to a municipality, Lisbon's true importance dates from 1147, when Alfonso I recaptured it from the Moors with the help of Crusaders. Alfonso III transferred his court here from Coimbra c.1260. City's great prosperity came in 16th cent. with establishment of Port. empire in Africa and India. Bet. 1580 and 1640, Lisbon was a prov. city under Sp. rule, and in 1588 the Sp. Armada sailed from here. In 1755, a disastrous earthquake destroyed most of city. Occupied by Fr. for 1 year during Peninsular War, it was subsequently fortified by Wellington. Camões (b. 1524) is Lisbon's greatest son.

Lisbon. 1 Farming town (pop. 1,282), New London co., SE Conn., on Quinebaug R. and 4 mi. NE of Norwich. Inc. 1786. **2** Village (pop. 183), Kendall co., NE Ill., 20 mi. SSW of Aurora, in rich agr. area. **3** Town (pop. 952), Linn co., E Iowa, near Cedar R., 15 mi. ESE of Cedar Rapids; dairy products, feed. Limestone quarries near by. **4** Town (pop. 4,318), Androscoggin co., SW Maine, on the Androscoggin and 7 mi. SE of Lewiston. Mfg. (lineolum, textiles, gypsum products) at Lisbon Falls (pop. 2,155) and Lisbon Center villages. In Bowdoin until inc. 1799. **5** Village (1940 pop. 51), on Kent-Ottawa co. line, SW Mich., 14 mi. NW of Grand Rapids, in farm area. **6** Town (pop. 2,009), including Lisbon village (pop. 1,372), Grafton co., NW N.H., on the Ammonoosuc and 10 mi. SSW of Littleton. Wood and metal products, lumbering, agr.; winter sports. Iron, gold, other minerals formerly mined. Includes village of Sugar Hill, summer resort. Settled 1753, renamed from Concord 1824. **7** City (pop. 2,031), ⊙ Ransom co., SE N.Dak., 57 mi. SW of Fargo and on Sheyenne R.; agr., dairy products. Site of state soldiers' home. Settled 1878, inc. 1883. **8** Village (pop. 3,293), ⊙ Columbiana co., E Ohio, 22 mi. SSW of Youngstown, in coal, clay, and limestone area; makes ceramics, electrical appliances, leather goods, sales books. Founded as New Lisbon in 1802.

Lisbon, Rock of, Portugal: see ROCA, CAPE.

Lisbon Bay or **Mar da Palha** (mär' dä pä'lyŏŏ), upper section of Tagus estuary, W central Portugal, forming a lake (7 mi. wide, 12 mi. long) just above city of Lisbon. Its E shore is low and marshy, while the higher W shore is lined with Lisbon's N suburbs and part of its harbor installation. The bay is linked with the Atlantic by a channel (c.2 mi. wide) extending 8 mi. W from Lisbon.

Lisbon Falls, Maine: see LISBON.

Lisburn (lĭs'bûrn), urban district (1937 pop. 13,042; 1951 census 14,778), S Co. Antrim, Northern Ireland, on Lagan R. and 8 mi. SW of Belfast; linen-milling center, with mfg. of thread and furniture. Christ Church, founded 1622, is cathedral of Protestant diocese of Down, Connor, and Dromore; town is seat of R.C. bishop of Down and Connor. Jeremy Taylor was bishop and died here 1667. In 1627 Charles I granted town to the Conways, who built castle, burned down 1707. Linen industry was introduced 1694 by French Huguenots. In 1930 Lisburn was scene of serious religious riots during which over 300 bldgs. were burned. Near by are Elizabethan Castle Robin, round tower, and rath.

Lisburne, Cape (lĭz'bûrn), NW Alaska, on Chukchi Sea, 40 mi. NNE of Point Hope; 68°53'N 166°4'W. Here are large rookeries. Coal deposits near by.

Liscannor (lĭskă'nŭr), Gaelic *Lios Ceanúir*, town (pop. 170), W Co. Clare, Ireland, on Liscannor Bay (4 mi. wide, 5 mi. deep) of the Atlantic, 4 mi. W of Ennistymon; fishing port. Has remains of anc. castle of the O'Briens.

Liscard, England: see WALLASEY.

Lischanna, Piz, Switzerland: see PIZ LISCHANNA.

Lischau, Czechoslovakia: see LISOV.

Liscomb (lĭ'skŭm), town (pop. 278), Marshall co., central Iowa, near Iowa R., 11 mi. NNW of Marshalltown; feed milling.

Lisen (lē'shĕnyŏŏ), Czech *Líšeň*, Ger. *Lösch* (lûsh), village (pop. 7,683), S Moravia, Czechoslovakia, c.4 mi. E of Brno; part of Greater Brno; rail terminus; fruit and poultry trade.

Lisets (lyĭsyĕts'), Pol. *Łysiec* (ŏŏĭ'syĕts), town (1931 pop. 1,560), central Stanislav oblast, Ukrainian SSR, 7 mi. SW of Stanislav; tanning, industrial-glue mfg., flour milling, sawmilling.

Lishan (lē'shän'), town (pop. 26,865), ⊙ Lishan co. (pop. 278,790), E Hupeh prov., China, near Honan line, 65 mi. N of Hankow; rice, wheat, beans.

Lishih (lē'shû'), town, ⊙ Lishih co. (pop. 154,586), W Shansi prov., China, 45 mi. WNW of Fenyang, and on main road to Yellow R. crossing at Küntu; coal mining, lumbering, wheat growing. Until 1912 called Yungning.

Lishu (lē'shōō'), town, ⊙ Lishu co. (pop. 467,073), N Liaosi prov., Manchuria, 10 mi. N of Szeping; soybeans, kaoliang, millet, wheat. An old Manchurian town, 1st mentioned in 18th cent., it was largely eclipsed by the newer rail city of Szeping.

Lishuchen, Manchuria: see MULING.

Lishui (lē'shwā'). **1** Town (pop. 17,243), ⊙ Lishui co. (pop. 119,958), S central Chekiang prov., China, 55 mi. NW of Wenchow and on headstream of Wu R.; commercial center; mfg. (cotton textiles, matches, firecrackers); tung oil, timber, bamboo, tea, fruit. Iron, silver mining near by. Until 1913 called Chuchow. **2** Town (pop. 10,549), ⊙ Lishui co. (pop. 194,460), S Kiangsu prov., China, 35 mi. SSE of Nanking and on Chinhwai R.; rice, wheat, beans, rapeseed.

Li Shui, river, China: see LI RIVER, Hunan prov.

Lishukow, Manchuria: see MULING.

Lisianski Inlet (lĭsēăn'skē), SE Alaska, long narrow fjord on NW coast of Chichagof Isl., opening into Cross Sound at 58°7'N 136°28'W; 25 mi. long.

Lisianski Island (lĭsyăn'skē), N Pacific, c.900 mi. NW of Honolulu, T.H.; 26°4'N 173°58'W; level, sandy. Annexed 1857 by Hawaiian kingdom, now owned by U.S. Sometimes written Lisyanski.

Lisichansk (lyĭsĕchänsk'), city (1939 pop. over 10,000), W Voroshilovgrad oblast, Ukrainian SSR, on the Northern Donets, in the Donbas, and 7 mi. SSE of Rubezhnoye; coal-mining center; metallurgical works, sawmills. Near-by are industrial centers of Proletarsk (glass, coal) and Verkhneye (soda chemicals, glass). Liskhimstroi or Liskhimstroy, a chemical center under construction, is near Lisichansk.

Lisieux (lēzyû'), anc. *Noviomagus*, town (pop. 11,-569), Calvados dept., NW France, on the Touques and 27 mi. E of Caen; communications and textile center (flannels, cotton goods); cider distilling, petroleum refining, Camembert cheese mfg. One of oldest towns in Normandy, rich in 16th-cent. houses. Town center, including 2 old churches (12th cent. and 15th cent.), seriously damaged during Normandy campaign (June-July, 1944) of Second World War. Shrine of St. Theresa of the Child Jesus (canonized 1925) has become major place of pilgrimage. New basilica (on hill just SE) was dedicated 1937.

Lisimakhia, Lake, Greece: see LYSIMACHIA, LAKE.

Lisina Mountain (lē'sēnä), in Dinaric Alps, W Bosnia, Yugoslavia; highest point, Lisina (4,812 ft.) is 9 mi. SW of Mrkonjic Grad.

Lisi Nos or **Lisiy Nos** (lyē'sē nôs"), town (1948 pop. over 500), W Leningrad oblast, Russian SFSR, on Gulf of Finland, opposite Kronstadt, 12 mi. NW of Leningrad.

Liska (lē'skä), mountain (6,262 ft.) in Macedonia, Yugoslavia, 12 mi. S of Kicevo.

Liskeard (lĭskärd'), municipal borough (1931 pop. 4,268; 1951 census 4,391), E Cornwall, England, bet. Looe and Seaton rivers, 11 mi. E of Bodmin; agr. market town; woolen mills; former mining center. Has 15th-cent. church. Just S is Well of St. Keyne, celebrated in poem by Southey.

Liskhimstroi, Ukrainian SSR: see LISICHANSK.

Liski (lyē'skē), city (1939 pop. 25,500), central Voronezh oblast, Russian SFSR, on left bank of Don R. and 45 mi. SSE of Voronezh; rail junction (repair shops); meat-packing center; flour milling. Called Svoboda (1928–41). Became city in 1937. Liski village (1926 pop. 3,324), across Don R., was absorbed and give the new city its name in 1943.

Lisko, Poland: see LESKO.

Liskovec (lē'skôvĕts), Czech *Lískovec*, town (pop. 2,819), E Silesia, Czechoslovakia, on Ostravice R., on railroad and 9 mi. SSE of Ostrava; part of commune of FRYDEK-Mistek. Has strip mills producing sheet iron, steel girders.

L'Isla, Malta: see SENGLEA.

Lisle, France: see LILLE.

Lisle. 1 (lĭl, lĭ'ŭl) Village (1940 pop. 552), Du Page co., NE Ill., W of Chicago. Seat of St. Procopius Col. **2** Village (pop. 221), Broome co., S N.Y., on Tioughnioga R. and 18 mi. NNW of Binghamton, in dairying area.

Lisle-en-Rigault (lēl-ā-rēgō'), village (pop. 577), Meuse dept., NE France, on the Saulx and 7 mi. SW of Bar-le-Duc; paper mill.

Lisle-sur-Tarn (lēl-sür-tärn'), village (pop. 999), Tarn dept., S France, on Tarn R. and 17 mi. WSW of Albi; wine trade.

L'Islet (lēlā'), county (□ 773; pop. 20,589), S Que., on the St. Lawrence and on Maine border; ⊙ St. Jean Port Joli.

L'Islet or **Bon Secours** (bō sŏŏkōōr'), village (pop. 699), SE Que., on the St. Lawrence and 14 mi. NE of Montmagny; lumbering, woodworking, dairying, metal casting.

Lisman (lĭs'mŭn), town (pop. 606), Choctaw co., SW Ala., near Miss. line, 28 mi. SE of Meridian, Miss.; lumber.

Lismore (lĭz'môr, lĭzmôr'), municipality and river port (pop. 15,214), NE New South Wales, Australia, 95 mi. S of Brisbane and on N.Arm of Richmond R.; exports dairy foods, sugar cane, bananas. R.C. cathedral.

Lismore (lĭzmôr'), Gaelic *Lios Mór Mochuda*, town (pop. 1,174), W Co. Waterford, Ireland, on the Blackwater and 14 mi.WNW of Dungarvan; agr. market (dairying, cattle raising, potato growing); fertilizer mfg. In 7th cent. St. Carthagh founded monastery and bishopric here; it became a renowned religious and academic center. Cathedral dates from 1633, a previous bldg. having been destroyed c.1600. Lismore Castle, built 1185 by King John, was modernized in 19th cent. In 1753 it passed to duke of Devonshire. Valuable medieval Irish MS, the *Book of Lismore*, is preserved here. Robert Boyle, Roger Boyle (earl of Orrery), and William Congreve b. in Lismore.

Lismore, island (pop. 280), N Argyll, Scotland, at mouth of Loch Linnhe; 9 mi. long, 1½ mi. wide; rises to 417 ft. Among ruins of several old castles on isl. is former residence of bishops of Argyll. Part of 13th-cent. cathedral (restored) is now used as parish church. The 16th-cent. Gaelic *Book of the Dean of Lismore*, composed by Dean James McGregor and his brother Duncan, is one of oldest and most valuable collections of Gaelic poetry. Just off SW extremity of isl. is Musdile or Musdale, islet with lighthouse (56°24'N 5°35'W).

Lismore (lĭz′môr), village (pop. 317), Nobles co., SW Minn., 21 mi. NW of Worthington, in grain and potato area.

Lisnaskea (lĭs″nŭskē′), town (pop. 751), S Co. Fermanagh, Northern Ireland, near Upper Lough Erne, 10 mi. SE of Enniskillen; agr. market (potatoes, cattle).

Lisnyaki, Ukrainian SSR: see LESNYAKI.

Lisov (lĭ′shôf), Czech *Lišov*, Ger. *Lischau* (lĭ′shou), town (pop. 2,447), S Bohemia, Czechoslovakia, 6 mi. NE of Budweis; barley, oats, rye; furniture.

Lispeszentadorjan (lĭsh′pĕsĕntŏdôryän″), Hung. *Lispeszentadorján* town (pop. 1,000), Zala co., W Hungary, 15 mi. WNW of Nagykanizsa. Extraction of petroleum and natural gas near by begun 1937. Gas pipe line to Budapest completed 1949. Includes former hamlet of Lispe.

Liss, town and parish (pop. 2,407), E Hampshire, England, 4 mi. NNE of Petersfield; agr. Has 14th-cent. church.

Lissa, Czechoslovakia: see LYSA NAD LABEM.

Lissa, Poland: see LESZNO.

Lissa, Yugoslavia: see VIS ISLAND.

Lisse (lĭ′sŭ), town (pop. 8,600), South Holland prov., W Netherlands, 9 mi. S of Haarlem, near the Ringvaart; flower-bulb-growing center; mfg. (bulb-sorting machinery, crates, boxes), meat processing, food canning.

Lissewege (lĭ′sŭwā-khŭ), agr. village (pop. 2,192), West Flanders prov., NW Belgium, on Bruges-Zeebrugge Canal and 6 mi. N of Bruges. Has 13th-cent. church. Formerly spelled Lisseweghe.

Lisso, Greece: see LEIPSOS.

Lissone (lēs-sô′nĕ), town (pop. 13,627), Milano prov., Lombardy, N Italy, 2 mi. NW of Monza. Furniture mfg. center; cotton mills, glass factories, foundry; textile machinery, cosmetics, sausage.

Lissoy, Ireland: see AUBURN.

Lissus, Albania: see LESH.

List (lĭst), village (pop. 3,693), in Schleswig-Holstein, NW Germany, on Sylt isl., 9 mi. NNE of Westerland; North Sea resort. Formerly noted for its oyster culture. Was site of 2 schools for fliers until 1945.

Lista (lĭs′tä), peninsula (□ c.54) in Vest-Agder co., S Norway, on the North Sea and flanked by 2 fjords; flat, partly forested area, c.12 mi. long, 10 mi. wide. Many farmers here are repatriated American immigrants. Sometimes called Lister or Listerland.

Liste-Guba, Karelo-Finnish SSR: see MASELSKAYA.

Lister, Germany: see OLPE.

Lister, Norway: see LISTA.

Lister, Mount (13,350 ft.), in Royal Society Range, Antarctica, W of McMurdo Sound, along W shore of Ross Sea; 78°5′S 163°E. Discovered 1902 by R. F. Scott, Br. explorer.

Listerhill, Ala.: see SHEFFIELD.

Listerland, Norway: see LISTA.

Listerland, Swedish *Listerlandet* (lĭs′tŭrlän″dŭt), peninsula (7 mi. long, 6 mi. wide), S Sweden, on the Baltic at N end of Hano Bay, 20 mi. E of Kristianstad; 56°2′N 14°40′E. At base is Solvesborg city; Hallevik and Horvik are fishing ports.

Lister og Mandals, county, Norway: see VEST-AGDER.

Listopadovka (lyĕstŭpä′dŭfkŭ), village (1948 pop. over 2,000), E Voronezh oblast, Russian SFSR, 25 mi. W of Borisoglebsk; wheat, sunflowers.

Listowel (lĭstō′ŭl), town (pop. 3,013), S Ont., on Middle Maitland R. and 24 mi. N of Stratford; textile milling, dairying, furniture mfg.

Listowel (lĭstoul′), Gaelic *Lios Tuathail*, urban district (pop. 3,311), NE Co. Kerry, Ireland, on Feale R. and 16 mi. NE of Tralee; agr. market (grain, potatoes; dairying). There are slight remains of anc. castle of the Desmonds.

Listvyanka (lyĕst′vyŭn-kŭ), town (1939 pop. over 2,000), S Irkutsk oblast, Russian SFSR, port on L. Baikal, near Angara R. outlet, 37 mi. SE of Irkutsk; shipbuilding, fishing. Formerly Listvenichnoye.

Listvyanski or **Listvyanskiy** (–skē), town (1948 pop. over 500), SE Novosibirsk oblast, Russian SFSR, 15 mi. ESE of Cherepanovo; coal mining.

Lisyanka, Ukrainian SSR: see LYSYANKA.

Lisyanski Island, T.H.: see LISIANSKI ISLAND.

Litakovo (lĭtä′kôvô), village (pop. 3,035), Sofia dist., W Bulgaria, in Botevgrad Basin, 7 mi. WNW of Botevgrad; dairying, hog raising, fruit, truck.

Litang, China: see LIHWA.

Litani River, Du. and Fr. Guiana: see ITANY RIVER.

Litani River (lētä′nē), anc. *Leontes*, in Lebanon, rises near Baalbek and flows SSW through the fertile BEKAA valley, bet. Lebanon and Anti-Lebanon ranges, turning abruptly W 6 mi. SW of Merj ʻUyun to enter the Mediterranean 5 mi. N of Tyre; 90 mi. long. The short westward section in its lower course is called the Qasimiye or Qasimiyah (both: käsē′mĭyŭ).

Litchfield, county (□ 938; pop. 98,872), NW Conn., on Mass. and N.Y. lines; ⊙ Winsted and Litchfield. Agr., resorts, mfg.; includes Torrington, a brass center, and clock-making centers of Thomaston and Winsted. Diversified mfg. (hardware, electrical equipment, typewriters, silverware, machinery, glass and plastic products, sports equipment, textiles, clothing, tools, furniture, hatters' fur); agr. (dairy products, truck, fruit, tobacco, poultry). Many resorts on lakes and in Litchfield Hills; Bear Mtn., highest point in Conn., is near Salisbury. Includes part of L. Candlewood, and Waramaug, Wononskopomuc, Highland, and Bantam lakes, several state parks and forests; winter sports center at Mohawk Mtn. State Park. Drained by Housatonic, Naugatuck, Shepaug, Farmington, Pomperaug, and Still rivers. Constituted 1751.

Litchfield. 1 Town (pop. 4,964), a ⊙ Litchfield co., W Conn., just SW of Torrington; includes boroughs of Litchfield (pop. 1,174; inc. 1879) and Bantam (pop. 940; inc. 1915). Agr. (poultry, fruit, dairy products), mfg. (electrical equipment, lumber, metal furniture). Resorts on Bantam L. (S); has state parks. First U.S. school exclusively for law students here, 1784–1833. Ethan Allen, Henry Ward Beecher, Harriet Beecher Stowe b. here. Inc. 1719. **2** City (pop. 7,208), Montgomery co., SW central Ill., c.40 mi. S of Springfield; trade center for bituminous-coal-mining and agr. area (corn, wheat, soybeans, livestock). Mfg. (shoes, radiators, metal products, dairy products, beverages). Inc. 1859. Oil was here 1st commercially produced in Ill. in 1880s. **3** Town (pop. 953), Kennebec co., S Maine, 7 mi. W of Gardiner in farming, resort region. **4** Village (pop. 882), Hillsdale co., S Mich., 10 mi. NW of Hillsdale and on St. Joseph R., in dairy-farming area; mfg. (auto parts, playground equipment, butter). **5** Village (pop. 4,608), ⊙ Meeker co., S central Minn., on small lake, c.65 mi. W of Minneapolis; trading point in grain, livestock, poultry area; dairy products, woolen goods. Settled 1856, platted 1869, inc. 1872. **6** Village (pop. 337), Sherman co., central Nebr., 12 mi. SW of Loup City and on Mud Creek; grain, livestock, poultry. **7** Town (pop. 427), Hillsboro co., S N.H., on the Merrimack below Manchester.

Litchfield Hills, NW Conn., S extension of the Berkshires running E of Housatonic R., in NW Litchfield co.

Litchfield Park, resort village (pop. c.1,000), Maricopa co., S central Ariz., near Agua Fria R., 17 mi. W of Phoenix in cotton, grain, and alfalfa area; cotton ginning.

Litchurch, England: see DERBY, city.

Litchville, village (pop. 408), Barnes co., SE N.Dak., 22 mi. SSW of Valley City; cattle, dairy products, poultry.

Lith or **Al Lith** (ăl lēth′), town, S Hejaz, Saudi Arabia, minor Red Sea port 120 mi. SE of Jidda; agr.: sorghum, dates, rice, vegetables, fruit.

Lithada, Cape, Greece: see KYNAION, CAPE.

Litherland (lĭ′dhŭrlŭnd), residential and mfg. urban district (1931 pop. 15,959; 1951 census 22,197), SW Lancashire, England, 4 mi. N of Liverpool; leather-tanning center; also tin smelting, mfg. of chemicals, soap.

Lithgow (lĭth′gō), municipality (pop. 14,461), E New South Wales, Australia, in Blue Mts. and 70 mi. WNW of Sydney; coal-mining center; ironworks, steel and woolen mills; bricks, pottery.

Lithinon, Cape (lēthĭnôn), headland of S Crete, on Mediterranean Sea; 34°55′N 24°44′E. Southernmost point of Crete.

Lithium (lĭ′thēŭm), town (pop. 57), Perry co., E Mo., near Mississippi R., 8 mi. N of Perryville.

Lithonia (lĭthō′nēŭ), city (pop. 1,538), De Kalb co., NW central Ga., 16 mi. ESE of Atlanta; granite-quarrying center; mfg. (clothing, light fixtures).

Lithopolis (lĭth-ŏ′pŭlĭs), village (pop. 350), Fairfield co., central Ohio, 15 mi. SE of Columbus.

Lithuania (lĭ″thŭwā′nyŭ, –thŭā′nēŭ), Lith. *Lietuva* (lyĕtōō′vä), Pol. *Litwa* (lēt′vä), Rus. *Litva* (lēt′vä), southernmost of Baltic States of NE Europe; since 1940 a constituent (Soviet Socialist) republic (□ 25,200; 1947 pop. estimate 2,700,000) of the USSR, but in 1951 still unrecognized as such by the U.S.; ⊙ VILNA. Borders on Latvia (N), Belorussia (SE), Poland and Kaliningrad oblast (former East Prussia) of Russian SFSR (SW), and Baltic Sea (with shallow COURLAND LAGOON; W). Mainly a lowland, with glacial moraine ridges (up to 961 ft.) in SE and Samogitian hills in W central portion; largely deforested (woods cover 19% of area); extensive marsh and lake dists. Main rivers are the Neman (timber floating; regular navigation below Kaunas) and its right tributaries (Viliya, Nevezys, and Dubysa rivers). Moderate humid continental climate; mean temp., 24°–28°F. (Jan.), 62°–66°F. (July); yearly precipitation, 20–24 in. Pop. consists of Lithuanians (80%; Baltic ethnic group of R.C. religion), Russians, Jews, Poles. Administratively, since 1950 Lithuania falls into oblasts of Vilnius (Vilna), Kaunas, Klaipeda (Memel), and Siauliai, further subdivided into independent cities and raions. Mainly an agr. area (rye, oats, potatoes, flax, sugar beets, forage grasses); dairy cattle (butter and cheese exports), hogs, poultry. Peat is chief domestic and industrial fuel (power stations); amber is dug on Baltic coast (Palanga). Industry (agr. and lumber products, cotton textiles, leather goods, machinery) concentrated in Vilna, KAUNAS, MEMEL (Klaipeda), SIAULIAI, and PANEVEZYS. Handicraft articles are amber ornaments, folk costumes, knitwear, and woodcarvings. Exports dairy and meat products, linen, timber, and furniture. A grand duchy (centered on Vilna) from early 13th cent., Lithuania expanded rapidly during 14th cent., and at its greatest extent (mid-15th cent.) reached from the Baltic to Black Sea and included all Belorussia, a large part of the Ukraine, and sections of Great Russia. The early Greek-Catholic Rus. influence was replaced by R.C. Polish culture after Lithuania joined Poland in 1386 (dynastic union) and in 1569 (Union of Lublin) in a single commonwealth. Area now constituting Lithuania was acquired by Russia and Prussia during 3d Polish partition of 1795; Prussian section later (1815) joined Rus. Poland. Occupied by Germans during First World War; modern Lithuanian state (proclaimed 1918; recognized 1920 by USSR) was formed out of greater part of Rus. Kovno govt., sections of Vilna and Suvalki govts., and SW tip of Courland (Palanga). Area was reduced (1920) by Poland's seizure of Vilna (which caused rupture of relations bet. the 2 countries until 1938) and enlarged (1923) by Lithuanian occupation of Memel Territory, which was again lost (1939) to Germany. Following Soviet occupation of E Poland, Vilna was transferred (1939) to Lithuania. Military bases were granted to USSR, who occupied the country, and Lithuania became a constituent republic of the USSR in 1940. During Second World War, when Lithuania was occupied (1941–44) by Germans, the considerable Jewish minority (7%) was largely exterminated. In 1945 Lithuania regained Memel.

Lithuanian-Belorussian Upland, Rus. *Litovsko-Belorusskaya Vozvyshennost*, moraine region in Poland, the Baltic States, and Belorussian SSR; extends c.300 mi. from Masurian Lakes in Poland NE to Western Dvina R.; forms divide bet. Baltic Sea and Black Sea drainage areas. Rises to 1,140 ft.; gives rise to Viliya R. (N), Berezina, Ptich, and Sluch rivers (S); crossed by Neman R.

Litija (lē′tēyä), Ger. *Littai* (lĭt′ī), village, central Slovenia, Yugoslavia, on Sava R., on railroad and 16 mi. E of Ljubljana; lead mine (worked since 1870); lead smelter; mfg. of textiles (woolen, cotton). Until 1918, in Carniola.

Litin (lyē′tyĭn), town (1926 pop. 8,382), W Vinnitsa oblast, Ukrainian SSR, 18 mi. WNW of Vinnitsa; sawmills, metalworks.

Lititz (lĭ′tĭts), borough (pop. 5,568), Lancaster co., SE Pa., 8 mi. N of Lancaster; chocolate, pretzels, shoes, textiles. Linden Hall Jr. Col. here. Settled c.1740 by Moravians, laid out 1757, inc. 1759.

Litlabo (lĭt′läbŭ), Nor. *Litlabø*, village in Stord canton, Hordaland co., SW Norway, on SW shore of Stord isl., 26 mi. NNE of Haugesund; mines pyrites (with low copper content), shipped via Sagvag. Sometimes spelled Lillebo, Nor. *Lillebø*.

Litochoron or **Litokhoron** (both: lētô′khôrôn), town (pop. 5,032), Salonika nome, Macedonia, Greece, 32 mi. N of Larissa, at foot of the Olympus, which is ascended from here; tourist trade.

Litom, Poland: see LEUTHEN.

Litomerice (lĭ′tômyĕrzhĭtsĕ), Czech *Litoměřice*, Ger. *Leitmeritz* (līt′mŭrĭts), town (pop. 14,402), N Bohemia, Czechoslovakia, on the Elbe, opposite Ohre R. mouth, on railroad and 9 mi. SSE of Usti nad Labem. River port; noted for tanning industry; food processing. Extensive vineyards and orchards (peaches, apricots) in vicinity. Has 16th-cent. town hall, 16th-cent. building with cup-shaped tower (now a mus.). Seat of R.C. bishop.

Litomysl (lĭ′tômĭshŭl), Czech *Litomyšl*, Ger. *Leitomischl*, town (pop. 6,384), E Bohemia, Czechoslovakia, 27 mi. SE of Pardubice; rail terminus; noted for cotton mfg. and embroidery making. Has 14th-cent. church, 16th-cent. Renaissance castle with art gall., 18th-cent. Piarist church, town hall with extensive library, Moorish-style synagogue, remains of medieval forts. Smetana b. here.

Litovel (lĭ′tôvĕl), Ger. *Littau* (lĭ′tou), town (pop. 4,092), N central Moravia, Czechoslovakia, on Morava R., on railroad and 11 mi. NW of Olomouc, in agr. area (sugar beets, oats, barley); brewing, distilling, sugar refining, ceramics making.

Litovko (lyĭtôf′kŭ), town (1948 pop. over 2,000), S Khabarovsk Territory, Russian SFSR, on branch of Trans-Siberian RR and 115 mi. SSW of Komsomolsk; sawmilling.

Litsing or **Li-ching** (both: lē′jĭng′), town, ⊙ Litsing co. (pop. 176,169), NW Shantung prov., China, 75 mi. NW of Weifang, and on Yellow R. at head of its delta; cotton weaving; peanuts, potatoes. Saltworks near by.

Litsingtien, China: see NANCHAO.

Littai, Yugoslavia: see LITIJA.

Littau, Czechoslovakia: see LITOVEL.

Littau (lĭ′tou), town (pop. 5,131), Lucerne canton, central Switzerland, 2 mi. W of Lucerne; silk textiles, chemicals, metalworks, printing. Includes part of EMMENBRÜCKE.

Little Abaco Island (ă′bŭkō), Abaco dist., N Bahama Isls., just NW of Great Abaco Isl., NE of Grand Bahama Isl., 125 mi. N of Nassau; hemp.

Little Aden (ā′dŭn, ä′dŭn), W volcanic peninsula (□ 15) of Aden Colony, separated from Aden peninsula (E) by Aden Bay; rocky and barren; rises to 1,218 ft. Has 2 Arab fishing villages: Fukum (1946 pop. 276) on W shore and Bureika (1946 pop. 944) on E shore. Adjoining the isthmus (N) is the settlement of Little Aden saltworks (1946 pop. 378). Peninsula was inc. 1868 into Aden Colony.

Little Alföld (ŏl'fûld), Hung. *Kis Alföld* (kĭsh), Czech *Podunajská nížina* (pô'dōōnĭskä nyē'zhĭnä), Czechoslovakia and NW Hungary; fertile plain (□ c.3,860), bounded S and E by Bakony and Vertes mts., W by Austrian border, N by spurs of the Carpathians. Drained by Danube, Raba, and Vah rivers; Hansag swamps are SW. Agr. (wheat, rye, barley, corn, sugar beets, potatoes, vegetables, fodder crops), large-scale dairy farming, breeding of riding horses, orchards, vineyards, tobacco. Main cities: Györ, Komarno, Novy Zamky. Great Schütt isl., with large, prosperous villages, and Little Schütt isl. occupy its central and NE parts.

Little America, Antarctica, a base for exploring expeditions, located on the Ross Shelf Ice S of Bay of Wales; 78°34'S 163°56'W; c.80 ft. above sea level. First established and named 1929 by R. E. Byrd and used by him also in his expeditions of 1933–35 and 1946–47.

Little Andaman Island (ăn'dŭmŭn, –măn), southernmost of Andaman Isls., in Bay of Bengal, separated from main group by Duncan Passage, from Car Nicobar Isl. (S) by Ten Degree Channel; 26 mi. long N-S, 16 mi. wide.

Little Arkansas River (ärkăn'zŭs, är'kŭnsô), S central Kansas, formed by confluence of 2 headstreams in Rice co. ENE of Lyons, flows 90 mi. SE to Arkansas R. at Wichita.

Little Armenia: see CILICIA.

Little Auglaize River (ôglāz'), W Ohio, rises W of Lima, flows c.45 mi. generally N to the Auglaize just N of Melrose.

Little Bahama Bank (bŭhā'mŭ, bŭhä'mŭ), shoal, NW Bahama Isls., N of Grand Bahama Isl., 60 mi. E of West Palm Beach (across Straits of Florida); c.150 mi. long NW-SE, c.50 mi. wide. Surrounded by many cays and isls.

Little Barrier Island, uninhabited volcanic island in S Pacific, 50 mi. NNE of Auckland, New Zealand; 5 mi. long, 3 mi. wide. 2,400 ft. high; bird sanctuary.

Little Bassa, Liberia: see MARSHALL.

Little Basses, Singhalese *Kuda Ravana Kotuwa* [=Little Ravana's Rocks], small group of rocks off SE coast of Ceylon; 6°24'N 81°44'E; lighthouse.

Little Bay, SE N.J., small inlet just S of Great Bay; protected from the Atlantic by isls.; traversed by Intracoastal Waterway channel.

Little Bay De Noc (dŭ nŏk'), a N arm of Green Bay indenting SW shore of Delta co., Upper Peninsula, Mich.; c.16 mi. long N–S, 1–4 mi. wide. Escanaba is on W shore. Peninsula separates it from Big Bay De Noc (E).

Little Bay Island (□ 2; pop. 697), E N.F., in Notre Dame Bay, 25 mi. SW of Cape St. John; 49°39'N 55°50'W. Fishing.

Little Bear Mountain (14,040 ft.), S Colo., in Rocky Mts., Costilla co.

Little Bear River, rises in Wasatch Range NNE of Ogden, N Utah, flows 50 mi. generally N, past Hyrum and Wellsville, to Bear R. 8 mi. NW of Logan. Hyrum Dam (98 ft. high, 540 ft. long; completed 1935), just SW of Hyrum, is used for irrigation.

Little Beaver River, in E Ohio and W Pa., formed by Middle, West, and North forks in SE Columbiana co., Ohio, flows c.7 mi. SE to the Ohio just across Pa. line. Main headstream (Middle Fork) rises in Mahoning co., flows SE c.35 mi.

Little Belt, Dan *Lille Bælt* (lĭ'lŭ bĕlt'), Denmark, strait connecting the Kattegat with Baltic Sea, bet. Jutland and Als isl. (W) and Fyn and Aero isls. (E); c.30 mi. long, ½-c.20 mi. wide, min. depth c.50 ft. Chief ports: Middelfart and Assens on Fyn isl.; Fredericia on Jutland.

Little Belt Mountains, range of Rocky Mts. in central Mont., rise SE of Great Falls, extend c.40 mi. SE to Musselshell R. Lie within Lewis and Clark Natl. Forest. Highest point, Big Baldy Mtn. (9,191 ft.). Silver, lead, gold, sapphires, zinc mined.

Little Bernera, Scotland: see GREAT BERNERA.

Little Bighorn River, in Wyo. and Mont., rises in Bighorn Mts., N Wyo., flows c.90 mi. NE and N, past Lodge Grass, S Mont., to Bighorn R. at Hardin. On right bank and 15 mi. SE of Hardin is site of battle of Little Bighorn, in which detachment of U.S. soldiers under command of Gen. George A. Custer was wiped out (June 25, 1876) by Indians (largely Sioux, among whom were chiefs Crazy Horse, Gall, and Sitting Bull). Battleground was proclaimed natl. reservation in 1886; named Custer Battlefield Natl. Monument (765.3 acres) in 1946.

Little Bitter Lake, Egypt: see BITTER LAKES.

Little Blue River, in S Nebr. and N Kansas, rises in Kearney co., flows ESE, past Hebron and Fairbury, Nebr., thence SSE to Big Blue R. at Blue Rapids, Kansas; 206 mi. long.

Little Boars Head, N.H.: see GREAT BOARS HEAD.

Little Bonaire (bônâr'), Du. *Klein Bonaire,* islet (2 mi. long, 1½ mi. wide) just off W coast of Bonaire isl., Du. West Indies, 40 mi. E of Willemstad; 12°10'N 68°19'W.

Littleborough, urban district (1931 pop. 12,028; 1951 census 10,982), SE Lancashire, England, on Roch R. and 14 mi. NNE of Manchester; cotton, wool, rayon milling, leather tanning, mfg. of chemicals and pharmaceuticals. Has 16th-cent. Stubbley Old Hall, one of oldest mansions of the region.

Little Brewster Island, Mass.: see BREWSTER ISLANDS.

Little Broughton, England: see BROUGHTON.

Little Burro Mountains, N.Mex.: see BIG BURRO MOUNTAINS.

Little Calumet River, Ill. and Ind.: see CALUMET RIVER.

Little Cape Mount River, Liberia: see LOFA RIVER.

Little Captain Island, SW Conn., two small isls. joined by reefs, in Long Isl. Sound, 2 mi. offshore, S of Greenwich; public recreation center here.

Little Carleton, England: see CARLETON.

Little Carpathian Mountains (kärpā'thēŭn), Slovak *Malé Karpaty* (mä'lā kär'pătĭ), Hung. *Kis Karpatok* (kĭsh kŏr'pŏtôk), range in SW Slovakia, Czechoslovakia; extend c.55 mi. NE-SW, bet. Nove Mesto nad Vahom (N) and Devin (S); rise to 2,473 ft. Best-known mtn. is Bradlo (1,784 ft.). Broadleaf forests, extensive vineyards, limestone and granite quarries. Pyrite mined in W foothills, at Malacky.

Little Cayman (kā'mŭn, kīmän'), island (□ 9.24; pop. 63) of Cayman Isls., dependency of Jamaica, B.W.I., separated by narrow channel from Cayman Brac (E) and 60 mi. ENE of Grand Cayman; 19°40'N 80°5'W; c.9 mi. long, 1 mi. wide. Exports turtle shells and coconuts.

Little Cedar River. 1 In SW Upper Peninsula, Mich., rises NW of Hermansville in Menominee co., flows c.40 mi. S, past Hermansville and Daggett, to Menominee R. 8 mi. S of Stephenson. **2** In Minn. and Iowa, rises in Mower co., SE Minn., flows 60 mi. S, into N Iowa, past Stacyville, to Cedar R. at Nashua.

Little Chazy River (shā''zē'), NE N.Y., rises in E central Clinton co., flows c.20 mi. E and NE, past Chazy, to L. Champlain 6 mi. S of Rouses Point.

Little Chebeague Island (shĭbēg'), SW Maine, in Casco Bay off Portland; c.¾ mi. long.

Little Chester, England: see DERBY, city.

Little Choptank River, E Md., tidal arm (c.15 mi. long) of Chesapeake Bay, penetrating the Eastern Shore in Dorchester co., just N of Taylors Isl.

Little Chuckawalla Mountains, Calif.: see CHUCKAWALLA MOUNTAINS.

Little Chute (shōōt), residential village (pop. 4,152), Outagamie co., E Wis., opposite Kimberly, on Fox R. and 5 mi. ENE of Appleton; inhabited largely by paper-mill workers of Kimberly. A dam is here. Settled 1850, inc. 1899.

Little City, town (pop. 101), Marshall co., S Okla.

Little Colinet Island, N.F.: see GREAT COLINET ISLAND.

Little Colorado River (kŏlŭrä'dō, –rā'dō), largely in Ariz., rises in Catron co., W N.Mex., near Ariz. line, flows 315 mi. generally NW through Ariz., past St. Johns and Holbrook and along Painted Desert, to Colorado R. in the Grand Canyon, 21 mi. NE of Grand Canyon village. Stream is dammed for irrigation near St. Johns.

Little Compton, town (pop. 1,556), Newport co., SE R.I., bet. Sakonnet R. and Mass. line, and bounded S by the Atlantic; agr., fishing, resort area. Includes villages of Adamsville, Little Compton, and SAKONNET. Inc. as a Plymouth Colony town in 1682, passed to R.I. 1746. John and Priscilla Alden's daughter Elizabeth lived and is buried here; Benjamin Church also lived here. Rhode Island Red fowl originated in the town.

Little Courland Bay, Tobago: see MOUNT IRVINE BAY.

Little Creek, town (pop. 266), Kent co., E Del., 4 mi. E of Dover; fishing resort on short Little Creek; oysters.

Little Cumbrae (kŭmbrā'), island (pop. 21) of Buteshire, Scotland, in the Firth of Clyde, just S of Great Cumbrae; 2 mi. long, 1 mi. wide; rises to 406 ft. Off E coast is Castle Isl., small islet with ruins of old tower.

Little Curaçao (kūrŭsō', kōōräsou'), Du. *Klein Curaçao,* islet in Du. West Indies, 20 mi. ESE of Willemstad, Curaçao; 12°N 68°40'W. Lighthouse

Little Current, town (pop. 1,088), S central Ont., on N Manitoulin Isl., on North Channel of L. Huron, 70 mi. SW of Sudbury; fishing port, lumbering, woodworking; yachting resort. Railroad bridge to mainland.

Little Cypress Creek or **Little Cypress Bayou** (bī'ō), NE Texas, rises in several streams N of Gilmer, flows c.50 mi. generally E to Cypress Bayou c.6 mi. E of Jefferson.

Little Danube River (dă'nūb), Slovak *Malý Dunaj* (mä'lē dōō'nī), Hung. *Kis Duna* (kĭsh' dōō'nŏ), arm of the Danube, SW Slovakia, Czechoslovakia; branches off main stream 2 mi. SE of Bratislava, meanders SE, joining Vah R. at Guta; encloses, together with the Vah and the Danube, Great Schütt isl.

Little Diomede Island (dī'ŭmēd) (2 mi. long, 1 mi. wide; pop. 103), Diomede Isls., NW Alaska, in Bering Strait, 20 mi. WNW of Cape Prince of Wales (Seward Peninsula), 27 mi. SE of Cape Dezhnev (Siberia), and 4.5 mi. E of Rus. isl. of Ratmanov; 65°45'N 168°57'W; rises to 1,200 ft. On W coast is Diomede village; school. Chukchi inhabitants noted for skill as seamen. Just W is international boundary bet. U.S. and USSR. Discovered by Bering, St. Diomede's Day, 1728. Also known as Kruzenshtern (Krusenstern) and Ignaluk.

Little Downham, England: see DOWNHAM.

Little Dragoon Mountains, Ariz.: see DRAGOON MOUNTAINS.

Little Duchrae, Scotland: see NEW GALLOWAY.

Little Dunkeld (dŭnkĕld'), agr. village and parish (pop. 2,182), E central Perthshire, Scotland, on the Tay, just S of Dunkeld. Parish includes BIRNAM.

Little Dunmow, England: see DUNMOW.

Little Eaton, town and parish (pop. 1,261), S Derby, England, on Derwent R. and 4 mi. N of Derby; paper milling.

Little Eau Pleine River (ō plān'), central Wis., rises NW of Marshfield near Clark-Marathon co. line, flows c.40 mi. generally SE to Wisconsin R. 12 mi. NNW of Stevens Point.

Little Edisto Island, S.C.: see EDISTO ISLAND.

Little Egg Harbor, SE N.J., inlet of the Atlantic E of Tuckerton; sheltered from ocean by S end of Long Beach isl.; c.6 mi. long, 4 mi. wide. Link in Intracoastal Waterway, entering from Manahawkin Bay (N) and continuing into Great Bay (S). Beach Haven Inlet, S of Beach Haven, and Little Egg Inlet are entrances from the Atlantic.

Little Exuma Island (ĕksōō'mŭ, ĕgzōō'mŭ), central Bahama Isls., southernmost (apart from small Hog Cay) of the Exuma isls., and adjoining Great Exuma Isl., 150 mi. SE of Nassau; 13 mi. long, c.1 mi. wide. It is crossed by the Tropic of Cancer. Main settlement is Williams Town.

Little Falls. 1 City (pop. 6,717), ⊙ Morrison co., central Minn., on Mississippi R. and 30 mi. NNW of St. Cloud; resort and trade center for grain, livestock, poultry, and truck-farming area; food processing (dairy products, flour, beverages); mfg. (roofing material, boats, clothing). Granite quarry near by. Point of interest is Lindbergh State Park, surrounding flier's childhood home. Settled 1855, inc. as village 1879, as city 1889. Grew with establishment of mills that used falls in river as source of water power. **2** Township (pop. 6,405), Passaic co., NE N.J., on Passaic R. and 3 mi. SW of Paterson; has large laundry plant; mfg. (rugs, metal products, hosiery, athletic goods, concrete products, bricks); poultry, truck, dairy products. Includes Singac (sĭng'găk'') village (resort). Settled 1711. **3** City (pop. 9,541), Herkimer co., central N.Y., 18 mi. ESE of Utica, at falls of Mohawk R. (water power) and on the Barge Canal (locks here); mfg. (clothing, footwear; paper, felt, and wood products; food products, feed, machinery, bicycles, furniture). Summer resort. Settled c.1725; inc. as city in 1895.

Little Ferry, borough (pop. 4,955), Bergen co., NE N.J., on Hackensack R. and 4 mi. ESE of Paterson; mfg. (machinery, building materials, metal products, buttons, woven labels); truck farming. Settled 1636, inc. 1894.

Littlefield, city (pop. 6,540), ⊙ Lamb co., NW Texas, on the Llano Estacado, 35 mi. NW of Lubbock; trade, shipping, processing center for agr. and livestock; grain sorghums, cotton, poultry, dairy products; cotton gins and compress, grain elevator, cottonseed-oil mill, creamery, hatchery. Lakes near by (hunting, fishing). Settled 1911, inc. 1925; became co. seat 1946.

Little Fogo Islands (fō'gō), group of 10 islets at entrance of Notre Dame Bay, E N.F., 5 mi. N of Fogo. Northernmost isl. has lighthouse (49°49'N 54°7'W).

Littlefork, village (pop. 671), Koochiching co., N Minn., on Little Fork R. and 16 mi. SW of International Falls, in grain and potato area; dairy products.

Little Fork River, formed by confluence of 2 forks in St. Louis co., N Minn., flows 150 mi. NW, past Littlefork village, to Rainy R. (on Ont. line) 10 mi. SW of International Falls.

Little Goose Creek, N Wyo., rises in Bighorn Mts. near Cloud Peak, flows c.30 mi. N to Goose Creek at Sheridan.

Little Grand Lake (10 mi. long, 1 mi. wide), W N.F., 23 mi. S of Corner Brook; drains into Grand L.

Little Gull Island, N.Y.: see GULL ISLANDS.

Little Gunpowder Falls, stream, rises in N Md., flows c.25 mi. SE, forming part of Baltimore-Harford co. line, to Gunpowder R. (estuary), c.15 mi. ENE of Baltimore.

Littlehampton, urban district (1931 pop. 10,178; 1951 census 13,948), SW Sussex, England, on the Channel at mouth of Arun R., 8 mi. W of Worthing; resort. In Middle Ages it was port for near-by Arundel. In urban dist. (N) is Wick.

Little Horton, England: see BRADFORD.

Little Hulton, former urban district (1931 pop. 7,874), S Lancashire, England, 4 mi. S of Bolton; cotton milling, coal mining. Inc. 1932 in Worsley.

Little Humboldt River (hŭm'bōlt), N Nev., intermittent stream formed in E Humboldt co., flows c.60 mi. W and SW to Humboldt R. just N of Winnemucca.

Little Inagua Island (ĭnä'gwŭ), S Bahama Isls., just NE of Great Inagua Isl., SW of Caicos Isls., 360 mi. SE of Nassau; roughly 10 mi. long, up to 10 mi. wide. Practically uninhabited.

Little Irchester, England: see IRCHESTER.

Littlejohn Island, SW Maine, resort isl. 1 mi. long, in Casco Bay off Yarmouth; bridge connects with Cousins Isl.

Little Juniata River, Pa.: see JUNIATA RIVER.

Little Kai, Indonesia: see NUHU ROWA.

Little Kanawha River (kŭnô'wŭ), W W.Va., rises in S Upshur co., flows generally W past Burnsville, and NW past Grantsville, to Ohio R. at Parkersburg; c.160 mi. long.

Little Karroo, U. of So. Afr.: see SOUTHERN KARROO.

Little Kentucky River, N Ky., rises in Henry co., flows c.35 mi. generally N to Ohio R just W of Carrollton.

Little Khingan Mountains, Manchuria: see KHINGAN MOUNTAINS.

Little Kiska Island, Alaska: see KISKA ISLAND.

Little Koldewey, Greenland: see GREAT KOLDEWEY.

Little Lake. **1** In extreme SE La., tidal inlet of Gulf of Mexico, c.25 mi. SSW of New Orleans; c.10 mi. long. Joined to Barataria Bay (SE) and L. Salvador and the Gulf Intracoastal Waterway (N) by navigable waterways. **2** In N.Y.: see WANETA LAKE.

Little Lever (lē'vŭr), urban district (1931 pop. 4,944; 1951 census 4,703), SE Lancashire, England, 3 mi. ESE of Bolton; cotton weaving, coal mining; mfg. of paper, ebonite, and chemicals for textile industry.

Little Loch Broom, Scotland: see BROOM, LOCH.

Little London, town (pop. 2,080), Westmoreland parish, SW Jamaica, in coastal lowland, 5 mi. WNW of Savanna-la-Mar; sugar, rice, breadfruit, stock.

Little Lost River, E Idaho, rises in Lemhi Range, flows c.60 mi. SSE, disappearing into depression ENE of Arco in E part of Butte co.

Little Machipongo Inlet, Va.: see HOG ISLAND.

Little Madawaska River (mădŭwäs'kŭ), NE Maine, rises in NE Aroostook co., flows c.35 mi. NE and SE to the Aroostook near Caribou.

Little Makin (mä'kĭn), atoll (□ 2.8; pop. 969), northernmost of Gilbert Isls., W central Pacific; 3°17'N 172°58'E; copra. Also called Makin Meang.

Little Malad River (mŭläd', mŭlăd'), formed by confluence of 2 forks in Oneida co., SE Idaho, flows c.45 mi. S, joining Deep Creek and Devil Creek near Malad City to form Malad R.

Little Malvern, England: see MALVERN.

Little Manistee River (mănĭstē'), W Mich., rises near Luther in Lake co., flows c.50 mi. NW to Manistee L. at Manistee.

Little Marlow, agr. village and parish (pop. 1,110), S Buckingham, England, on the Thames and 2 mi. ENE of Marlow. Has Norman church.

Little Martinique, Grenadines, B.W.I.: see PETITE MARTINIQUE.

Little Marton, England: see MARTON.

Little Meadows, borough (pop. 196), Susquehanna co., NE Pa., 17 mi. NW of Montrose.

Little Miami River (mīă'mŭ, –mē), SW Ohio, rises in Clark co., flows generally SW for 95 mi., past Waynesville, Morrow, South Lebanon, and Loveland, and through suburbs of Cincinnati, to the Ohio in E Cincinnati. East Fork rises in Clinton co., flows c.80 mi. SW and NW to join the Little Miami near Milford. Another E tributary is Todd Fork (c.35 mi. long).

Little Minch, Scotland: see MINCH, THE.

Little Missenden (mĭ'sŭndŭn), agr. village and parish (pop. 1,769), S central Buckingham, England, 5 mi. NE of High Wycombe. Has Norman church and Elizabethan manor house.

Little Missouri River. **1** In SW Ark., rises W of Norman in the Ouachita Mts., flows c.145 mi. SE to Ouachita R. 27 mi. above Camden; 7 mi. NNW of Murfreesboro is site of Narrows Dam (for flood control, power production). **2** In NW U.S., rises in NE Wyo., flows NE through Mont., S.Dak., and N.Dak. to Missouri R. NW of Bismarck. Not navigable, not used extensively for irrigation; 560 mi. long.

Little Moose Mountain (3,630 ft.), Hamilton co., NE central N.Y., in the Adirondacks, 15 mi. NW of Speculator. Little Moose L. (c. 1 mi. long) is just NE.

Littlemore, residential town and parish (pop. 2,387), S Oxfordshire, England, near the Thames 2 mi. SE of Oxford; site of co. mental hosp. It was site of 12th-cent. convent(16th-cent. bldg. remains).

Little Mountain, town (pop. 213), Newberry co., NW central S.C., 24 mi. WNW of Columbia; lumber, food products.

Little Muddy River, S Ill., rises in SE Washington co., flows c.60 mi. generally S into Big Muddy R. W of Hurst.

Little Muskegon River (mŭskē'gŭn), central Mich., rises in small lakes in Mecosta co., flows c.35 mi. SW, past Morley, to Muskegon R. 7 mi. E of Newaygo.

Little Muskingum River (mŭskĭng'gŭm, mŭskĭng'ŭm), SE Ohio, rises in Monroe co., flows generally SW c.65 mi., through Washington co., to Ohio R. 3 mi. SE of Marietta.

Little Namaqualand, U. of So. Afr.: see NAMAQUALAND.

Little Narragansett Bay (nărŭgăn'sĭt), on R.I.–Conn. line, inlet of the Atlantic at mouth of Pawcatuck R.; sheltered by curving peninsula, site of WATCH HILL village; yachting.

Little Neck, SE N.Y., a residential section of NE Queens borough of New York city, on Little Neck Bay.

Little Neck Bay, SE N.Y., inlet of Long Island Sound indenting N shore of W Long Isl., bet. Queens borough (W) and Great Neck peninsula in Nassau co. (E); c.1½ mi. wide at entrance, 2½ mi. long. U.S. Fort Totten is at W side of entrance.

Little Nemaha River (nĕ'mŭhä, –hô), SE Nebr., rises near Lincoln, flows c.75 mi. SE, past Syracuse and Auburn, to Missouri R. near Nemaha; channel straightened in parts.

Little Niangua River (nīăng'gwŭ), central Mo., rises in the Ozarks in Dallas co., flows c.40 mi. NE to arm of L. of the Ozarks in Camden co.

Little Nicobar Island: see NICOBAR ISLANDS.

Little Ocmulgee River (ōkmŭl'gē), S central Ga., rises in S Twiggs co., flows c.70 mi. SE, past McRae, to Ocmulgee R. just SE of Lumber City.

Little Osage River (ō'sāj), in W Mo. and E Kansas, rises near Moran, Kansas, flows 68 mi. E, joining Marais des Cygnes R. to form Osage R. SE of Rich Hill, Mo.

Little Ossipee Pond (ŏs'ĭpē), SW Maine, center of Waterboro resort area; 2.5 mi. long; drains N into **Little Ossipee River** (17 mi. long), which enters the Saco at Limington.

Little Pamir, Afghanistan: see WAKHAN.

Little Paternoster Islands, Indonesia: see BALABALAGAN ISLANDS.

Little Patuxent River (pŭtŭk'sŭnt), central Md., rises in N Howard co., flows c.35 mi. SE, past Fort George G. Meade, to the Patuxent 4 mi. ESE of Bowie.

Little Peconic Bay (pĕkŏ'nĭk, pĭ–), SE N.Y., bet. N and S peninsulas of E Long Isl. and E of Great Peconic Bay; c.6 mi. long, 4½ mi. wide.

Little Pee Dee River (pē'dē), E S.C., formed by small headstreams in E Marlboro co. near N.C. line; flows c.90 mi. generally SE and S to Pee Dee R. 18 mi. W of Myrtle Beach.

Little Pendulum Island, Greenland: see PENDULUM ISLAND.

Little Platte River (plăt), in SW Iowa and NW Mo., rises near Creston, Iowa, and flows generally S c.170 mi. to Missouri R. below Leavenworth, Kansas. Sometimes called Platte River.

Little Popo, Fr. Togoland: see ANÉCHO.

Little Popo Agie River, Wyo.: see POPO AGIE RIVER.

Littleport, town and parish (pop. 4,709), in Isle of Ely, N Cambridge, England, on Ouse R. and 4 mi. NNE of Ely; agr. market.

Littleport, town (pop. 139), Clayton co., NE Iowa, on Volga R. and 7 mi. S of Elkader, in corn, hog, dairy region.

Little Powder River, in Wyo. and Mont., rises in Campbell co., NE Wyo., flows c.100 mi. N to Powder R. near Broadus, SE Mont.

Little Prespa Lake (prĕ'spä), Albanian *Liqen i Prespës së vogël* (lēkyĕn' ē prĕ'spŭs sŭ vô'gŭl), Greek *Limni Mikre* (or *Mikri*) *Prespa* (□ 19), on Albanian-Greek border, near Yugoslav line, just S of L. Prespa (separated by 1.5-mi.-long sandspit); 12 mi. long, 4 mi. wide; c.16 ft. deep. Fisheries. A former inlet of L. Prespa, it is gradually drying out.

Little Red River, N central Ark., formed by Middle and South forks at Edgemont, flows c.105 mi. SE, past Pangburn and Judsonia, to White R. 8 mi. SSW of Augusta. Just E of Heber Springs is site of Greers Ferry Dam (for flood control). Middle Fork rises in S Searcy co., flows c.55 mi. SE, past Leslie and Shirley, to union with South Fork (c.60 mi. long; rises in W Van Buren co.).

Little Rich Mountain (3,100 ft.), in the Blue Ridge, NW S.C., c.25 mi. NNW of Greenville, near N.C. line.

Little River, township (pop. 315), ⊙ Wairewa co. (□ 170; pop. 895), E S.Isl., New Zealand, on Banks Peninsula, 17 mi. SSE of Christchurch; rail terminus; dairy products.

Little River, county (□ 544; pop. 11,690), extreme SW Ark.; ⊙ Ashdown. Bounded W by Texas, S by Red R., N and E by Little R. Agr. (fruit, cotton, truck, corn, hay, livestock). Cotton ginning, lumber milling, mfg. of wood products. Timber; sand, gravel. Formed 1867.

Little River. **1** City (pop. 635), Rice co., central Kansas, on Little Arkansas R. and 24 mi. N of Hutchinson, in wheat area. Salt mines and oil wells near by. **2** Summer resort, Horry co., E S.C., 25 mi. E of Conway and on tidal Little R., here followed by Intracoastal Waterway.

Little River. **1** In NE Ala., formed by confluence of 2 headstreams in Lookout Mtn., NE Ala., flows c.30 mi. SW to Chattooga R. 5 mi. NNE of Centre. **2** In E Conn., rises N of Hampton, flows c.25 mi. S to Shetucket R. 5 mi. NNE of Norwich. **3** In E Ga., rises near Maxeys, meanders c.75 mi. E to Savannah R. 20 mi. NW of Augusta. **4** In S Ga.: see WITHLACOOCHEE RIVER. **5** In NE Ind., rises in W Allen co., flows c.30 mi. SW, past Huntington, to the Wabash c.2 mi. W of Huntington. **6** In SW Ky., formed in Christian co. S of Hopkinsville by junction of its forks, flows c.70 mi. generally W, past Cadiz, to Cumberland R. 8 mi. W of Cadiz. **7** In central La., formed just above Rochelle by junction of Dugdemona R. and Bayou Castor, flows SE to Catahoula L., thence ENE to Ouachita R. (Black R.) at Jonesville; c.90 mi. long. **8** In SE Mo., rises near Delta, flows c.70 mi. S to the Mississippi flood-plain drainage development near Wardell. **9** In central Okla., rises SE of Oklahoma City, flows 90 mi. generally SE, past Moore and Macomb, to Canadian R. in Hughes co., c.5 mi. S of Holdenville. **10** In Okla. and Ark., rises S of Pine Valley in Ouachita Mts. in Okla., flows SW, then SE, past Wright City, into Ark., joining Red R. just W of Fulton, Ark.; c.220 mi. long. Site of Millwood Reservoir (for flood control) is c.10 mi. NW of Fulton. Mountain Fork (c.40 mi. long) rises in W Ark., enters main stream from N in McCurtain co., Okla. **11** In E Tenn., rises in Great Smoky Mts. Natl. Park, on Clingmans Dome, near N.C. line; flows c.50 mi. NW past Elkmont, Townsend, and Walland, to Fort Loudoun Reservoir (Tennessee R.) 8 mi. S of Knoxville. **12** In central Texas, formed by Leon and Lampasas rivers 9 mi. S of Temple, flows c.75 mi. generally SE and E to Brazos R. c.5 mi. W of Hearne. **13** In N Va., rises in NE Fauquier co., flows c.30 mi. NE to Goose Creek (a tributary of the Potomac) in Loudoun co., 3 mi. SE of Leesburg. **14** In SW Va., rises in NE Floyd co., flows c.50 mi. S and WNW, forming part of Floyd-Montgomery and Pulaski-Montgomery co. lines, to New R. 3 mi. S of Radford. **15** In central Va., rises in E Louisa co., flows c.40 mi. SE to North Anna R. 5 mi. NNW of Hanover.

Little Rocher (lĭ'tŭl rŏsh''), village, SE N.B., on Chignecto Bay, 18 mi. SW of Hopewell Cape; gypsum quarrying.

Little Rock. **1** City (pop. 102,213), ⊙ Arkansas and Pulaski co., central Ark., on Arkansas R. (navigable) and c.130 mi. W of Memphis, Tenn.; largest city and commercial center of state, near its geographical center, in foothills of Ouachita Mts.; alt. 300 ft.; 34°43'N 92°16'W. Rail and highway focus, market and distribution center for rich agr. (cotton), mining (bauxite, coal, clay), timber, oil, and natural-gas region. Woodworking plants (furniture, lumber, staves), chemical, flour, feed, and cottonseed-products plants; mfg. of clothing, building materials, paper boxes, canvas products, foundry products; in adjoining North Little Rock are stockyards, railroad shops, timber-creosoting plants, cottonseed-oil mills. Seat of Philander Smith and Ark. Baptist colleges for Negroes, St. John's Seminary, 2 jr. colleges, Univ. of Ark. School of Medicine, R.C. (1882) and Episcopal (1888) cathedrals, state schools for the deaf and blind, and a mus. of fine arts. Points of interest include War Memorial Bldg. (the capitol, 1836–1911; designed by Gideon Shryock); the present capitol, designed by Cass Gilbert; Joe T. Robinson Memorial Auditorium; Albert Pike House (1840). Near by are a U.S. veterans' hosp., U.S. Camp Joseph T. Robinson (Camp Pike in First World War), a fish hatchery, a natl. cemetery, and corrective institutions. Laid out 1820, chartered 1831. Captured 1863 by Federal troops under Gen. Frederick Steele. Gen. Douglas MacArthur b. here. **2** Town (pop. 533), Lyon co., NW Iowa, on Little Rock R. and 19 mi. N of Sheldon, in livestock and grain area.

Little Rock River, rises in Nobles co., SW Minn., flows 40 mi. SW into NW Iowa, past Little Rock village, to Rock R. just S of Doon.

Little Ross Island, islet in Solway Firth at mouth of Kirkcudbright Bay and Wigtown Bay, S Kirkcudbright, Scotland, 5 mi. SSW of Kirkcudbright. Lighthouse (54°48'N 4°5'W).

Little Russia, USSR: see UKRAINE.

Little Sac River (sôk), SW central Mo., rises in the Ozarks N of Springfield, flows c.45 mi. NW to Sac R. in Cedar co.

Little Saint Bernard Pass (bŭrnärd'), Fr. *Petit-Saint-Bernard* (pŭtē'-sē-bĕrnär'), Ital. *Piccolo San Bernardo* (pēk'kôlô sän bĕrnär'dô), Alpine pass (alt. 7,178 ft.), bet. Mont Blanc massif (N) and Graian Alps (SSE), in Savoie dept., SE France, ½ mi. SW of Ital. border, on road bet. Bourg-Saint-Maurice (7 mi. SW) and Morgex (10 mi. NE), connecting Tarentaise valley (France) with Val d'Aosta (Italy). Numerous serpentines on Fr. slope. Hospice (just SW of pass), founded 10th cent. by St. Bernard of Menthon, damaged in Second World War. Until 1947, pass formed Fr.-Ital. border.

Little Saint Lawrence, village (pop. 166), SE N.F., on SW side of Placentia Bay, on Burin Peninsula, 22 mi. ESE of Grand Bank; hydroelectric station supplies power for near-by fluorspar mines.

Little Salkehatchie River, S.C.: see COMBAHEE RIVER.

Little Salkeld (sôl'kĕld), village and parish (pop. 91), E Cumberland, England, on Eden R. and 5 mi. NE of Penrith; paper mfg. Near by is an anc. burial ground with stones of the Stonehenge type.

Little Salmon River, W Idaho, rises in mtn. region S of New Meadows, flows 40 mi. N, through deep canyon, to Salmon R. in SW corner of Idaho co.

Little San Bernardino Mountains (săn bŭrnŭrdē'nō) (c.4,000–5,500 ft.), S Calif., SE continuation of

San Bernardino Mts., extend c.40 mi. NW–SE along E side of Coachella Valley. Partly (E slope) within Joshua Tree Natl. Monument.

Little Sandy River, NE Ky., rises in central Elliott co., flows c.90 mi. generally NNE, past Grayson, to Ohio R. at Greenup.

Little San Salvador (săn″ săl′vùdôr), islet, central Bahama Isls., just W of N Cat Isl., 95 mi. ESE of Nassau; a narrow, bifurcated bar, c.6 mi. long W–E. San Salvador or Watling Isl., where Columbus made his 1st landfall, is 95 mi. ESE, on the other side of Cat Isl.

Little Satilla River, Ga.: see SATILLA RIVER.

Little Scarcies River (skär′sēz), W Africa, largely in Sierra Leone, rises SW of Dabola, S central French Guinea, flows c.170 mi. SW, past Mange, and forms common estuary with the Great Scarcies 25 mi. N of Freetown. Navigable for 22 mi. below Mange. Also called Kaba R.

Little Schütt, Hungary: see SCHÜTT.

Little Schuylkill River, Pa.: see SCHUYLKILL RIVER.

Little Scioto River (sīō′tù), S Ohio, rises in Jackson co., flows c.40 mi. S through Scioto co. to the Ohio 6 mi. E of Portsmouth.

Little Sea, Poland: see PUCK BAY.

Little Sebago Lake (sĭbā′gō), SW Maine, in central Cumberland co., E of Sebago L.; 6 mi. long, ½–1 mi. wide. Drains SSW into Presumpscot R.

Little Shelford, England: see GREAT SHELFORD.

Little Silver, borough (pop. 2,595), Monmouth co., E N.J., just SE of Red Bank. U.S. Fort Monmouth near by. Inc. 1923.

Little Sioux (sōō), town (pop. 349), Harrison co., W Iowa, on Little Sioux R. near its mouth on Missouri R., and 16 mi. SSE of Onawa.

Little Sioux River, rises in Jackson co., SW Minn., flows 221 mi. S and SW, through NW Iowa, past Spencer and Cherokee, to Missouri R. near Little Sioux town. Irrigates rich agr. area. Included in flood-control and soil-conservation program affecting extensive areas in NW Iowa. Tributaries are West Fork (74 mi. long), Maple R., and Ocheyedan R.

Little Skellig, Ireland: see SKELLIGS, THE.

Little Smoky River, Alta., rises in Rocky Mts. N of Jasper Natl. Park, flows 185 mi. E and N to Smoky R. 60 mi. NE of Grande Prairie.

Little Snake River, in NW Colo. and S Wyo., rises in N tip of Park Range, Colo.; flows W, along Wyo. line, past Dixon and Baggs, S Wyo., and SW into Colo. to Yampa R. near Dinosaur Natl. Monument; c.150 mi. long.

Little Sodbury, England: see OLD SODBURY.

Little Sodus Bay (sō′dùs), Cayuga co., W central N.Y., inlet of L. Ontario, 12 mi. E of Sodus Bay; c.2 mi. long, ½–¾ mi. wide. Fair Haven (resort) and a state park are here.

Little Somes River, Rumania: see SOMES RIVER.

Little Sound, Bermuda: see PORT ROYAL BAY.

Little Squam Lake, N.H.: see SQUAM LAKE.

Little Stour River, England: see GREAT STOUR RIVER.

Littlestown, borough (pop. 2,635), Adams co., S Pa., 10 mi. SE of Gettysburg. Laid out 1765, inc. 1864.

Little Sugar Loaf, mountain (1,120 ft.), NE Co. Wicklow, Ireland, 3 mi. SSW of Bray.

Little Switzerland, summer resort (pop. c.200), McDowell co., W N.C., 12 mi. NNW of Marion, in the Blue Ridge.

Little Tallahatchie River, Miss.: see TALLAHATCHIE RIVER.

Little Tallapoosa River (tălùpōō′sù), in W Ga. and E Ala., rises in N Carroll co., flows c.90 mi. SW, past Carrollton, into Ala. to Tallapoosa R. 6 mi. W of Wedowee.

Little Tancook Island, islet in Mahone Bay, S N.S., 8 mi. SE of Chester; 44°28′N 64°8′W.

Little Tennessee River, in Ga., N.C., and Tenn., rises in the Blue Ridge N of Clayton, NE Ga.; flows N into N.C., past Franklin, and WNW around Great Smoky Mts., into Tenn., to Tennessee R. opposite Lenoir City, just below Fort Loudoun Dam. FONTANA and CHEOAH dams in N.C. course of river, CALDERWOOD DAM in Tenn. portion.

Little Thurrock, residential town and parish (pop. 4,428), S Essex, England, near Thames R., just E of Grays Thurrock.

Little Tibet, Kashmir: see BALTISTAN.

Little Tobago Island (tùbā′gō, tō–), islet (c.500 acres) off NE Tobago, B.W.I., 18 mi. NE of Scarborough; 11°13′N 60°30′W. Noted as reserve for birds of paradise, introduced from Du. New Guinea in 1909. The isl. was presented to govt. of Trinidad and Tobago in 1929. Sometimes called Bird of Paradise Isl.

Littleton, Gaelic *Baile Dáith*, village, central Co. Tipperary, Ireland 4 mi. SE of Thurles; peat-digging center.

Littleton. **1** Town (pop. 3,378), ⊙ Arapahoe co., N central Colo., on South Platte R. just S of Denver, E of Front Range; alt. 5,362 ft. Trade center for irrigated grain area; dairy, poultry, truck products; mfg. (flour, trucks, fire extinguishers, cameras). Inc. 1890. **2** Village (pop. 215), Schuyler co., W Ill., 16 mi. S of Macomb, in agr. and bituminous-coal area. **3** Town (pop. 1,001), Aroostook co., E Maine, 8 mi. N of Houlton in potato-growing area. Inc. 1856. **4** Rural town (pop. 2,349), Middlesex co., NE central Mass., 13 mi. SW of Lowell; poultry, dairying, apples; elastic products, telegraph instruments, preserves, chair frames. Settled on site of "praying Indian" village of Nashoba, established c.1686; inc. 1715. Includes village of Littleton Common (pop. 1,017). **5** Town (pop. 4,817), including Littleton village (pop. 3,819), Grafton co., NW N.H., on Ammonoosuc R. (235-ft. drop) and 15 mi. NNE of Woodsville, bet. Connecticut R. and White Mts. Resort trade center, mfg. (gloves, shoes, wood products), pulpwood, dairy products; winter sports. Settled 1769, inc. 1784. **6** Town (pop. 1,173), Warren and Halifax counties, N N.C., 15 mi. W of Roanoke Rapids, in lumber, truck-farming area. Founded before 1775. **7** Town (pop. 448), Wetzel co., NW W.Va., 28 mi. W Morgantown.

Littleton-upon-Severn, village and parish (pop. 179), SW Gloucester, England, near Severn R., 3 mi. W of Thornbury; brick- and tileworks. Has 14th-cent. church.

Little Traverse Bay (tră′vûrs), NW Mich., inlet of L. Michigan c.15 mi. NE of Grand Traverse Bay; c.10 mi. long, 5 mi. wide. Bay View, Petoskey, Harbor Springs, and resort villages are on its shores; fishing.

Little Truckee River (trŭ′kē), E Calif., rises in small lake in the Sierra Nevada, flows c.30 mi. E and S to Truckee R. 6 mi. NE of Truckee, near Nev. line. Boca Dam (1,629 ft. long, 116 ft. high; completed 1939 by Bureau of Reclamation) is on lower course near mouth. Forms small reservoir (capacity 40,900 acre-ft.) and is chief unit in Truckee storage project. Water from reservoir is released into Truckee R. and used for irrigation of 30,000 acres in Washoe and Storey counties, W Nev., and to supplement CARSON and TRUCKEE rivers in supplying Newlands irrigation project in vicinity of Fallon, W Nev.

Little Tupper Lake, N.Y.: see TUPPER LAKE.

Little Unadilla Lake, N.Y.: see MILLERS MILLS.

Little Urswick, England: see URSWICK.

Little Valley, village (pop. 1,287), ⊙ Cattaraugus co., W N.Y., 7 mi. NNW of Salamanca; mfg. of cutlery, dairy products, feed; printing; lumber milling. Agr. (grain, potatoes). Inc. 1876.

Little Vermilion River, in E Ill. and W Ind., rises in SE Champaign co., Ill., flows c.55 mi. generally E to the Wabash just E of Newport, Ind.

Little Wabash River (wô′băsh), E central and SE Ill., rises near Mattoon, flows c.200 mi. S and SE to the Wabash near New Haven. Dam impounds small Paradise L. (or L. Mattoon) near Mattoon; fish hatchery here.

Little Walsingham (wôl′sĭng-ùm), town and parish (pop. 716), N Norfolk, England, 5 mi. N of Fakenham, site of Walsingham Abbey, one of the great shrines of medieval England. There are ruins of Augustinian priory founded 1149. The sacred shrine of Our Lady of Walsingham, built c.1061, became a center of medieval pilgrimages; there are no remains, but the priory chapel was restored in 1921 and the wayside Slipper Chapel (where pilgrims left their shoes) in 1934. There is a 15th-cent. church. Just NE is agr. village and parish (pop. 396) of Great Walsingham, with 14th-cent. church.

Little Washita River (wŏ′shĭtô, wä′–), S Okla., rises in SE Caddo co., flows SE and then NE, through Grady co., to Washita R. just SE of Chickasha; c.30 mi. long.

Little Watts Island, Va.: see WATTS ISLAND.

Little Wellington Island, Chile: see SERRANO ISLAND, Aysén prov.

Little Wichita River (wĭ′chĭtô), N Texas, rises in Archer co., flows c.50 mi. generally NE to Red R. 14 mi. ENE of Henrietta. Dam impounds L. Kickapoo (capacity 105,000 acre-ft.) WNW of Archer City.

Little Wood River, rises in Pioneer Mts., S central Idaho, flows S, past Richfield, then W, past Shoshone, to Big Wood R. just W of Gooding; 90 mi. long. Dam in upper course.

Little York. **1** Village (pop. 324), Warren co., NW Ill., 20 mi. W of Galesburg, in agr. and bituminous-coal area. **2** Town (pop. 146), Washington co., S Ind., 29 mi. N of New Albany, in agr. area.

Little Zab, Iraq and Iran: see ZAB, LITTLE.

Little Zelenchuk River, Russian SFSR: see ZELENCHUK.

Littoinen (lĭt′toinĕn), Swedish *Littois* (lĭ′tois), suburb of Turku, Turku-Pori co., SW Finland, 4 mi. ENE of city center; woolen mills.

Litton, agr. village and parish (pop. 823), NW Derby, England, 7 mi. ENE of Buxton; former lead-mining center. Ancestral home of the Lytton family (Bulwer-Lytton).

Littoral Province or **Littoral Territory**, Russian SFSR: see MARITIME TERRITORY.

Littoral Range, Russian SFSR: see BAIKAL RANGE.

Littoria, Italy: see LATINA.

Littry (lētrē′), village (pop. 1,043), Calvados dept., NW France, 9 mi. WSW of Bayeux; dairying (cheese and casein mfg.). Coal mining at Bernesq, 4 mi. NNW.

Lituya Bay (lĭtōō′yù), SE Alaska, inlet (9 mi. long, 2 mi. wide) of Gulf of Alaska, 100 mi. SE of Yakutat, SSW of Mt. Fairweather; 58°38′N 137°34′W. At head of bay mts. rise to 12,000 ft. Discovered 1786 by Count de la Pérouse, who named it Port des Français.

Litva (lĭt′vä), town, Bosnia, Yugoslavia, near Tuzla, on slope of Mt. Konjuh; coal-fed power station.

Litvino, Russian SFSR: see SOSNOVOBORSK.

Litvinov (lĭt′vēnôf), Czech *Litvínov*, Ger. *Leutensdorf* (loi′tùnzdôrf), town (pop. 12,587), NW Bohemia, Czechoslovakia, in NE foothills of the Erzgebirge, 5 mi. NNW of Most; gas, electrical, and chemical works; power plant; synthetic fuel plant. Intensive lignite mining in vicinity. Formed, c.1948, by union of Horni Litvinov, Ger. *Oberleutensdorf*, and Dolni Litvinov.

Litvinovka (lyĭtvē′nùfkù), village (1939 pop. over 500), W central Rostov oblast, Russian SFSR, on Kalitva R. and 15 mi. NNE of Belaya Kalitva; wheat, sunflowers, cattle.

Litzmannstadt, Poland: see LODZ, city.

Litz Manor, village (pop. 4,846, with adjacent Highland Park), Sullivan co., NE Tenn., just SE of Kingsport.

Litzner or **Gross Litzner** (grōs′ lĭts′nùr), peak (10,208 ft.), in Silvretta Group of the Rhaetian Alps, on Swiss-Austrian border, 7 mi. E of Klosters. Klein Litzner peak is N.

Liu, China: see LIU RIVER.

Liuan (lyō′än′), town, ⊙ Liuan co. (pop. 102,306), N Anhwei prov., China, 45 mi. W of Hofei and on Pi R.; center of tea (sunglo type) and hemp cultivation; rice, cotton, wheat, tung oil, lacquer.

Liucheng or **Liu-ch'eng** (both: lyō′chŭng′), town, ⊙ Liucheng co. (pop. 121,511), N central Kwangsi prov., China, 10 mi. NNW of Liuchow and on Liu R.; rice, wheat, beans. Coal mines near by.

Liu-chiang, town, China: see LIUKIANG.

Liu Chiang, river, China: see LIU RIVER.

Liu-ch'iu, islands: see RYUKYU ISLANDS.

Liuchow or **Liu-chou** (both: lyō′jō′, lyōō′–), city (1946 pop. 208,447), ⊙ but independent of Liukiang (until 1937, Maping) co. (1946 pop. 237,345), central Kwangsi prov., China, 90 mi. SW of Kweilin; largest city of Kwangsi; railroad- and air-transportation center. Railroad shops; mfg. of alcohol and machinery. Has aviation school. Developed rapidly after construction of Hunan-Kwangsi RR. Was U.S. air base in Second World War. Became a municipality under provincial jurisdiction in 1946.

Liuho (lyō′hŭ′). **1** Town, S Kiangsu prov., China, 25 mi. NW of Shanghai and on Yangtze R.; commercial center; cotton, rice, beans. **2** Town, Kiangsu prov., China: see LUHO. **3** Town, ⊙ Liuho co. (pop. 180,029), NE Liaotung prov., S Manchuria, China, 40 mi. NNW of Tunghwa and on railroad; soybeans, kaoliang, rice, tobacco, medicinal herbs.

Liuhokow or **Liu-ho-kou** (lyō′hŭ′gō′), town, NW Pingyuan prov., China, at E foot of Taihang Mts., 20 mi. NW of Anyang, on Hopeh line; coal mining.

Liukiang or **Liu-chiang** (both: lyō′jyăng′), Cantonese *Liukong* (lyōō′gông′), town, ⊙ Liukiang co. (pop. 58,966), NE central Kwangsi prov., China, 35 mi. ENE of Liuchow, near railroad; rice, wheat, corn, beans.

Liu Kiang, river, China: see LIU RIVER.

Liukiu, islands: see RYUKYU ISLANDS.

Liukong, China: see LIUKIANG.

Liukung Island, China: see WEIHAI.

Liupa (lyō′bä′), town (pop. 1,020), ⊙ Liupa co. (pop. 22,014), SW Shensi prov., China, 40 mi. N of Nancheng; rice, wheat, beans, millet. Iron deposits near by.

Liupan Mountains, Chinese *Liu-p'an Shan* (lyō′pän′ shän′), SE Kansu prov., China, separate Wan-King R. basin (SE) from rest of Kansu; rise to c.10,000 ft. 10 mi. NNE of Lungteh.

Liu River, Chinese *Liu Kiang* or *Liu Chiang* (both: lyō′ jyăng′), in SE Kweichow and NE Kwangsi provs., China, rises SE of Kweiyang, flows 300 mi. E and S, past Santu (head of junk navigation), Junghsien, and Liuchow, to the Hungshui above Mosün. Used for logging.

Liushun (lyō′shōōn′), town, ⊙ Liushun co. (pop. 17,869), S Yunnan prov., China, 25 mi. SW of Ningerh, in mtn. region; cotton textiles; rice, millet.

Liuyang (lyō′yăng′), town, ⊙ Liuyang co. (pop. 699,301), NE Hunan prov., China, 38 mi. E of Changsha; ramie-producing center; mfg. (cotton textiles, paper, firecrakers). Tungsten, arsenic, and salt found near by.

Livadhion, Greece: see LEIVADION.

Livadhostra, Bay of, Greece: see LIVADOSTRA, BAY OF.

Livadia, Greece: see LEVADIA.

Livadica or **Livaditsa** (both: lē′vädĭtsä), peak (8,170 ft.) in Sar Mts., Yugoslavia, on Serbia-Macedonia border, 13 mi. NNE of Tetovo.

Livadion, Greece: see LEIVADION.

Livadiya (lyĭvä′dyēŭ). **1** Town (1939 pop. over 500), S Crimea, Russian SFSR, resort on Black Sea, 1.5 mi. SSW of Yalta; winegrowing. Site of white Ital. Renaissance palace (built 1910–11), former summer residence of Nicholas II, now a sanatorium. Residence of President Roosevelt and Big Three meeting place during Yalta Conference, 1945. **2** Town (1941 pop. over 500), SW Maritime Territory, Russian SFSR, on Sea of Japan, near Nakhodka; fish canning.

Livadostra, Bay of, Bay of Leivadostra, or **Bay of Livadhostra** (all: lēvŭ-dhô′strŭ), inlet of Gulf of Corinth, in E central Greece, on N side of Megara peninsula; 10 mi. wide, 15 mi. long.

Livani or **Livany** (lē′vänē), Lettish *Līvāni*, Ger. *Lievenhof*, city (pop. 3,527), SE Latvia, in Latgale, on right bank of the Western Dvina and 35 mi. NNW of Daugavpils; wool processing, weaving. In Rus. Vitebsk govt. until 1920.

Livarot (lēvärō′), village (pop. 1,914), Calvados dept., NW France, on the Vie and 10 mi. SSW of Lisieux; butter and cheese mfg., cider distilling.

Livazeny, Rumania: see LIVEZENI.

Livengood (lĭ′vŭngo͝od), village (pop. 28), central Alaska, 50 mi. NNW of Fairbanks, at N end of Elliott Highway from Fairbanks; placer gold mining; outfitting center for prospectors. Airfield.

Livenza River (lēvĕn′tsä), NE Italy, rises 4 mi. N of Sacile, flows 70 mi. SE, across Venetian plain, past Sacile and Motta di Livenza, to the Adriatic near Caorle. Navigable for 30 mi.

Live Oak, county (□ 1,072; pop. 9,054), S Texas; ⊙ George West. Drained by Frio, Atascosa, and Nueces rivers. Cattle ranching, agr. (grain sorghums, broomcorn, corn, cotton, flax, truck, citrus); oil, natural-gas wells; glass sand, clay mined and processed. Formed 1856.

Live Oak. 1 City (pop. 1,770), Sutter co., N central Calif., in Sacramento Valley, near Feather R., 10 mi. N of Yuba City; trade and shipping center for agr. area (fruit, nuts, truck). Inc. 1947. **2** City (pop. 4,064), ⊙ Suwannee co., N Fla., c.80 mi. E of Tallahassee; rail junction; chief bright-leaf tobacco market of the state; lumber milling; mfg. of naval stores, clothing. Florida Memorial Col. (preparatory; Negro) is here.

Liverdun (lēvĕrdŭ′), village (pop. 1,827), Meurthe-et-Moselle dept., NE France, on the Moselle and Marne-Rhine Canal, and 7 mi. NW of Nancy; mfg. (pumps, brushes), fruit preserving.

Livermore (lĭ′vŭrmôr). **1** City (pop. 4,364), Alameda co., W Calif., 30 mi. ESE of Oakland, in Livermore Valley (noted for wines), amid the Coast Ranges; wheat, cattle, poultry; magnesite mines. U.S. veterans' hosp. and co. hosp. for tubercular here. Holds annual rodeo. Inc. as town in 1876, as city in 1930. **2** Town (pop. 615), Humboldt co., N central Iowa, near East Des Moines R., 26 mi. N of Fort Dodge; feed milling. **3** Town (pop. 1,441), McLean co., W Ky., on Green R., at Rough R. mouth, and 23 mi. ENE of Madisonville, in agr., coal-mining, timber area; makes wood products. **4** Town (pop. 1,313), Androscoggin co., SW Maine, 20 mi. N of Auburn; farming, mfg. (gloves, wood and pulp products). Seat of "The Norlands," home of the Washburns. Inc. 1795. **5** Borough (pop. 57), Westmoreland co., SW central Pa., 4 mi. WNW of Blairsville and on Conemaugh R.

Livermore, Mount (8,382 ft.), extreme W Texas, 24 mi. NNW of Marfa; highest peak in DAVIS MOUNTAINS and 2d-highest in state. Sometimes called Baldy Peak or Old Baldy.

Livermore Falls, town (pop. 3,359), Androscoggin co., SW Maine, 25 mi. N of Lewiston and on the Androscoggin; paper mills, canneries. Settled 1786, inc. 1843. Called East Livermore until 1930.

Livernon (lēvĕrnō′), village (pop. 153), Lot dept., SW France, in the Causse de Gramat, 9 mi. WNW of Figeac.

Liverpool (lĭ′–), municipality (pop. 12,642), E New South Wales, Australia, 17 mi. WSW of Sydney; woolen mills; poultry, dairy products.

Liverpool, town (pop. 3,170), ⊙ Queens co., SW N.S., at head of Liverpool Bay (5 mi. long) of the Atlantic, at mouth of Mersey R., 70 mi. SW of Halifax; 44°2′N 64°43′W; fishing center; shipbuilding; paper-, pulp-, sawmilling; yeast mfg.

Liverpool, county borough (1931 pop. 856,072; 1951 census 789,532) and city, SW Lancashire, England, on the Mersey near its mouth, and 180 mi. NW of London; 53°23′N 3°0′W. Great industrial city and 2d-largest port of Great Britain, serving important Lancashire, Midland, and Yorkshire industrial area, with regular shipping lines to all parts of world. Docks over 7 mi. long line the Mersey up to Bootle; there are 90 basins and docks (largest are Gladstone Docks, with 1,050-ft. graving dock), with water area of 477 acres and 29 mi. of quays. Ocean liners use Prince's Landing Stage, 2,534-ft. floating quay. Liverpool and Birkenhead docks are under administration of Mersey Docks and Harbour Board (established 1858). There is an airport at SPEKE. Tunnels under the Mersey connect city with Birkenhead. Chief imports: cotton, grain, timber, tobacco; chief exports: textiles and machinery. Industries include large flour mills and tobacco factories. Liverpool is Europe's leading cotton market, but its importance declined considerably after Second World War. In 1207 King John gave city 1st charter and established castle here; mainly used as port for shipping to Ireland. In 1229 Henry III confirmed it as free borough. It was severely affected by the plague in 16th and 17th cent.; in 1644 it surrendered to Prince Rupert after several sieges. It subsequently became important slave-trading port, and in 1709 1st wet dock in Great Britain was built here. Later Liverpool acquired most of Bristol's trade and is now Britain's largest port of registration. Points of interest: Liverpool Cathedral, which will be largest in England upon completion; R.C. cathedral (also under construction); St. George's Hall, part of group of bldgs. including libraries and art gall.; Bluecoat School (1714); Royal Liver Bldg., 17-story landmark; Cunard Bldg., modeled on Farnese Palace in Rome; Town Hall, built 1754 by John Wood of Bath; Cotton Exchange; and Liverpool Univ., founded 1881, independently chartered 1903. Richard Mather, father of Increase and grandfather of Cotton, was minister here. Francis Bacon was member of Parliament for Liverpool, 1588–92. In Second World War concentrated air raids (1940–41) caused heavy damage and many casualties in Liverpool and surrounding areas. Chief suburbs: Allerton (ôl′–, ăl′–), Speke, Garston, West Derby (där′bē), and Wavertree.

Liverpool. 1 Resort village (pop. 2,933), Onondaga co., central N.Y., on Onondaga L., just N of Syracuse; mfg. of machinery; agr. (dairy products; poultry, truck). Inc. 1830. **2** Borough (pop. 654), Perry co., central Pa., 22 mi. NNW of Harrisburg and on Susquehanna R.

Liverpool, Cape, N Bylot Isl., E Franklin Dist., Northwest Territories, on Baffin Bay, at E end of Lancaster Sound; 73°45′N 77°45′W.

Liverpool, Curiche (ko͞orē′chä) [Sp.,=Liverpool lagoon], marshy lake in Santa Cruz dept., NE Bolivia, 120 mi. N of Concepción; 15 mi. long, 13 mi. wide. Affluent and outlet: San Martín R. Formerly called Lake Rey.

Liverpool Coast, region, E Greenland, on Greenland Sea, extends 80 mi. N from mouth of Scoresby Sound; 71°N 21°30′W. Rugged and indented, noted for its dangerous currents and scene of numerous shipwrecks.

Liverpool Range, E central New South Wales, Australia, part of Great Dividing Range extending E–W bet. Coonabarabran and Murrurundi; rises to 4,500 ft. (Oxley's Peak).

Liversedge, England: see SPENBOROUGH.

Livesey (lĭv′zē, lĭv′zē), parish (pop. 1,970), central Lancashire, England. Includes village of Feniscowles (fĕ′nĭskōlz), 3 mi. SW of Blackburn, with silk industry and mfg. of paper and chemicals.

Livet-et-Gavet (lēvā′-ā-gävā′), commune (pop. 2,657), Isère dept., SE France, in Oisans (along deep Alpine gorge of Romanche R.), 11 mi. SE of Grenoble. Bet. Livet and Gavet (4 mi. apart) are electrochemical (chlorates, calcium carbide, explosives) and electrometallurgical (steel, ferroalloys) works of Livet, Les Clavaux, and Rioupéroux powered by 17 hydroelectric plants (near Rioupéroux, Gavet, and La Salignière).

Livets River, Poland: see LIWIEC RIVER.

Livet Water, Scotland: see GLENLIVET.

Livezeni (lēvăzĕn′), Hung. *Livázeny* (lĕ′väzĕnyŭ), village (pop. 2,788), Hunedoara prov., W central Rumania, on headstream of Jiu R. and 2 mi. S of Petrosani; rail junction, lignite-mining center. Sometimes spelled Livazeni.

Livindo River, Fr. Equatorial Africa: see IVINDO RIVER.

Lívingston (lē′vēng-stōn), town (1950 pop. 2,602), Izabal dept., E Guatemala, minor port on Bay of Amatique (inlet of Caribbean Sea), at mouth of Río Dulce, and 11 mi. WNW of Puerto Barrios; 15°49′N 88°55′W. Supply point for L. Izabal region; boatbuilding, mahogany working; customhouse. Exports bananas, rubber, sarsaparilla, lumber. Until rise of Puerto Barrios, leading Atlantic port of Guatemala; until 1920, ⊙ Izabal dept.

Livingston, village and parish (pop. 4,415), S West Lothian, Scotland, 4 mi. E of Bathgate; shale-oil mining.

Livingston. 1 County (□ 1,043; pop. 37,809), E central Ill; ⊙ Pontiac. Agr. (corn, oats, wheat, soybeans, livestock, poultry; dairy products). Bituminous coal, clay, stone. Diversified mfg. Drained by Vermilion R. Formed 1837. **2** County (□ 318; pop. 7,184), SW Ky.; ⊙ Smithland. Bounded W and N by Ohio R. (Ill. line), S by Tennessee R.; crossed by Cumberland R. KENTUCKY DAM and Kentucky Reservoir are on S border. Gently rolling agr. area (burley tobacco, livestock, corn); fluorspar mines, stone quarries. Formed 1798. **3** Parish (□ 665; pop. 20,054), SE La.; ⊙ Livingston. Bounded W and S by Amite R., partly E by Natalbany, SE by L. Maurepas; drained by Tickfaw R. Agr. (strawberries, vegetables, corn, cotton, sweet potatoes, hay, livestock); pine timber (pulpwood). Sand, gravel. Hunting, fishing. Formed 1832. **4** County (□ 571; pop. 26,725), SE Mich.; ⊙ Howell. Drained by Red Cedar, Huron, and Shiawassee rivers. Livestock, poultry, grain, beans, sugar beets, potatoes; dairy products. Mfg. at Howell. Summer resorts; numerous small lakes. Organized 1836. **5** County (□ 533; pop. 16,532), N central Mo.; ⊙ Chillicothe. Drained by Grand R. Agr. (corn, wheat, oats), livestock; mfg. at Chillicothe. Formed 1837. **6** County (□ 638; pop. 40,257), W central N.Y.; ⊙ Geneseo. Drained by Genesee R. and by Canaseraga and Honeoye creeks. Situated in Finger Lakes region; Conesus and Hemlock lakes are in co. Dairying and farming area (fruit, truck, grain, potatoes, hay, poultry); some mfg. at Avon, Geneseo, Dansville, Mount Morris. Salt mines; gypsum and limestone quarries. Includes part of Letchworth State Park. Formed 1821.

Livingston. 1 Town (pop. 1,681), ⊙ Sumter co., W Ala., 55 mi. SW of Tuscaloosa, bet. Tombigbee R. and Miss. line; lumber milling, cotton ginning. Founded c.1833. Has state teachers col. **2** City (pop. 1,502), Merced co., central Calif., in San Joaquin Valley, near Merced R., 14 mi. NW of Merced; fruit packing and shipping. **3** Village (pop. 999), Madison co., SW Ill., 14 mi. NE of Edwardsville, in agr. and bituminous-coal area. Inc. 1905. **4** Town (pop. 378), Rockcastle co., central Ky., on Rockcastle R. and 27 mi. NE of Somerset, in Cumberland Natl. Forest; coal mining, agr., limestone quarries. Hunting and fishing in vicinity. **5** Village (pop. c.400), ⊙ Livingston parish, SE La., 25 mi. E of Baton Rouge, in lumbering area. Founded 1918. **6** City (pop. 7,683), ⊙ Park co., S Mont., 20 mi. E of Bozeman and on Yellowstone R., N of Yellowstone Natl. Park and just NW of Absaroka Range; railroad, tourist, trade center for agr. and mining area; arsenic, silver, gold mines; marble, granite; railroad shops; cigars, feed, flour; dairy products, livestock, grain. Annual frontier celebration takes place here. Founded 1882, inc. 1889. **7** Village (pop. c.3,000), Essex co., NE N.J., near Passaic R., 8 mi. NW of Newark; nursery products, beverages; poultry, dairy products. **8** Town (pop. 210), Orangeburg co., W central S.C., 15 mi. W of Orangeburg. **9** Town (pop. 2,082), ⊙ Overton co., N Tenn., 85 mi. ENE of Nashville, in coal, timber agr. (poultry, corn, hay) area; lumber; wood products, clothing. Standing Stone State Park and Dale Hollow Reservoir are near by. **10** Town (pop. 2,865), ⊙ Polk co., E Texas, 45 mi. S of Lufkin; trade, shipping center in oil, timber, agr. area; lumber milling, mfg. of wood products, machine-shop products, furniture; sand quarrying. Alabama-Coushatta Indian Reservation is c.15 mi. E. **11** Village (pop. 452), Grant and Iowa cos., SW Wis., 11 mi. N of Platteville, in diversified-farming area.

Livingston, Fort, La.: see GRAND TERRE ISLAND.

Livingstone (lĭ′vĭngstŭn), municipality (pop. 7,899), ⊙ Southern Prov. (□ 27,000; pop. 180,000), S Northern Rhodesia, near Victoria Falls of Zambezi R., on railroad and 230 mi. SW of Lusaka; alt. 3,000 ft. Port of entry, industrial, agr., and livestock center; sawmilling, woodworking, furniture making, tobacco processing (warehouses, grading sheds), leatherworking and tanning; blanket factory, iron foundry. Agr. (tobacco, corn, wheat, potatoes, truck), dairy products. Has govt. and convent schools, European and African hospitals. Site of Rhodes-Livingstone Mus. (collection of native weapons and implements and of relics of the explorer after whom city is named). Tourist center for Victoria Falls. New internatl. airport and game park near by. Was ⊙ Northern Rhodesia (1911–35) until its removal to Lusaka, and ⊙ former Batoka prov.

Livingstone, Fort, post of North West Mounted Police, W Man., near town of Swan River. From 1875 to 1877, ⊙ Northwest Territories and hq. of Mounted Police.

Livingstone Falls, 32 cataracts of lower Congo R., partly in W Belgian Congo, partly along Fr. Equatorial Africa border, extending bet. Matadi and Leopoldville. Here Congo R. cuts a narrow gorge through Crystal Mts. and falls 850 ft. in c.220 mi. An 80-mi.-long placid stretch exists in the rapids bet. Manyanga and Isangila. Unsuccessful ascent of the cataracts was attempted (1816) by Brit. explorer Capt. J. K. Tuckey. Henry M. Stanley conquered the falls (1877) at the end of his journey down Congo R. In 1890–98, Matadi-Leopoldville RR was built to circumvent the falls.

Livingstone Memorial, Northern Rhodesia: see CHITAMBO.

Livingstone Mountains, S Tanganyika, on NE shore of L. Nyasa, N of Manda; rise to 7,000 ft.

Livingstonia (lĭvĭngstō′nyŭ), village, Northern Prov., NE Nyasaland, on E edge of Nyika Plateau, on road and 15 mi. SW of Deep Bay; alt. 4,500 ft. Hq. of Church of Scotland mission (established 1894), with technical, vocational, and teachers training schools, hosp. Coal deposits near by. Formerly called Kondowe. Its port is Florence Bay, 5 mi. NE, on L. Nyasa.

Livingston Island (37 naut. mi. long, 5–19 naut. mi. wide), South Shetland Isls., off Palmer Peninsula, Antarctica; 62°35′S 60°35′W.

Livingston Manor, village (1940 pop. 1,373), Sullivan co., SE N.Y., in the Catskills, on small Willowemoc Creek and 8 mi. NW of Liberty; mfg. of chemicals, wood products; lumber milling. Summer and winter (skiing) resort.

Livitaca (lēvētä′kä), town (pop. 407), Cuzco dept., S Peru, in the Andes, 60 mi. SSE of Cuzco; mfg. of woolen goods; marble deposits.

Livland, Latvia and Estonia: see LIVONIA.

Livländische Aa, Latvia: see GAUJA RIVER.

Livno (lĕv′nô), town (pop. 3,286), SW Bosnia, Yugoslavia, 36 mi. NE of Split; handicraft center. Brown-coal mine near by. Town has been known since 9th cent.

Livny (lyĕv'nē), city (1926 pop. 19,873), S Orel oblast, Russian SFSR, on Sosna R. and 70 mi. SE of Orel; metalworking (irrigation machinery); mfg. of synthetic rubber, flour milling, distilling, fruit canning. Stone and gravel quarries near by. Chartered 1586. During Second World War, briefly held (1941) by Germans.

Livonia (lĭvō'nēŭ), Ger. *Livland* (lēf'länt), region and former Russian govt., comprising larger S section of present Estonia and N part (VIDZEME) of Latvia. Borders W on Gulf of Riga of Baltic Sea; separated by Western Dvina R. (S) from Courland. Agr. (flax, grain) and wooded hill land, drained by Gauja and Parnu rivers. Chief centers are Riga (its historic capital), Tartu, Parnu, Viljandi, Valmiera, and Cesis. Originally inhabited by Livs or Livonians, an extinct Finno-Ugric group; region was ruled (13th cent.) by German Livonian Knights, who extended their rule, in union with the Teutonic Knights, to N Estonia, Courland, and Latgale. After dissolution (1561) of the Livonian Order, greater Livonia was contested by Poland-Lithuania, Russia, and Sweden. COURLAND (SW) became a duchy under Polish suzerainty; LATGALE (SE) passed to Poland; Livonia proper was annexed first by Poland, then (1629) by Sweden, which also held N ESTONIA. The Swedish share was conquered (1710) by Peter I of Russia, who kept it at Peace of Nystad (1721). In 1783 Livonia was constituted a separate Rus. govt., which was divided equally (1918; confirmed 1920) bet. independent Latvia (Vidzeme prov.) and Estonia.

Livonia. **1** Town (pop. 185), Washington co., S Ind., 31 mi. NW of New Albany, in agr. area. **2** City (pop. 17,534), Wayne co., SE Mich., just W of Detroit. **3** Town (pop. 193) Putnam co., N Mo., on Chariton R. and 15 mi. E of Unionville. **4** Village (pop. 837), Livingston co., W central N.Y., near Conesus L., 23 mi. S of Rochester, in agr. area; summer resort; mfg. (cement blocks, leather goods).

Livonian Switzerland, scenic resort dist. in central Latvia, NE of Riga, in Vidzeme, on middle Gauja R.; has wooded hills, caves, grottoes. Its center is Sigulda.

Livorno (lēfôr'nō), village (pop. 1,579), Surinam dist., N Du. Guiana, on Surinam R. and 3 mi. S of Paramaribo; rice, coffee, fruit.

Livorno (lēvôr'nō), province (□ 471; pop. 249,468), Tuscany, central Italy; ⊙ LEGHORN. Borders on Ligurian Sea; comprises narrow, 50-mi.-long coastal strip enclosed by Apennine hills. Includes isls. of ELBA, Capraia, Pianosa, Gorgona, and Monte Cristo. Watered by Cecina R. and small streams. Agr. (grapes, olives, cereals, fruit), livestock raising; fishing; mining. Chief producer of Italy's iron ore, on Elba. Other mines (tin, copper, iron) at Campiglia Marittima. Mfg. at Leghorn, Piombino, Portoferraio, and Cecina. Area increased by addition of territory from Pisa prov. in 1925.

Livorno, city, Italy: see LEGHORN.

Livorno Ferrais (fĕr-rīs'), village (pop. 2,610), Vercelli prov., Piedmont, N Italy, 17 mi. WSW of Vercelli.

Livradois, Massif du (mäsēf' dü lēvrädwä'), granitic mtn. range of the Massif Central, central France, bet. Allier and Dore river valleys in Puy-de-Dôme and Haute-Loire depts. Average alt. 3,000 ft. Several extinct volcanoes near Vic-le-Comte and Brassac-les-Mines. Grazing.

Livramento (lēvrämĕn'tōō). **1** City, Mato Grosso, Brazil: see NOSSA SENHORA DO LIVRAMENTO. **2** Town, Minas Gerais, Brazil: see OLIVEIRA FORTES. **3** City, Piauí, Brazil: see JOSÉ DE FREITAS. **4** City (1950 pop. 29,906), SW Rio Grande do Sul, Brazil, in the Coxilha de Santana, on Uruguay border, adjoining Rivera (Uruguay) and 250 mi. WSW of Pôrto Alegre. Custom station on chief rail line to Uruguay; airport. Livestock center with meat-packing and -canning plants; processing of animal by-products, leatherworking; exports lumber and maté. Amethysts and agates exploited just NW. Formerly called Santa Ana (old spellings: Santa Anna, Sant' Ana, Sant' Anna) do Livramento.

Livramento do Brumado (dōō brōōmä'dōō), city (pop. 819), central Bahia, Brazil, 65 mi. SSW of Andaraí; gold mining. Until 1944, Livramento.

Livron or **Livron-sur-Drôme** (lēvrō'-sür-drōm'), village (pop. 1,768), Drôme dept., SE France, on the Drôme near its mouth into the Rhone, and 11 mi. S of Valence; rail junction; mfg. (chemicals, pharmaceuticals, agr. tools), silk milling.

Livry-Gargan (lēvrē'-gärgã'), town (pop. 20,556), Seine-et-Oise dept., N central France, an outer ENE suburb of Paris, 10 mi. from Notre Dame Cathedral; metalworks; mfg. (plaster, hardware). Its abbey, founded 1186 and destroyed in French Revolution, was rebuilt 19th cent.

Liwa (lĭwă'), town (pop. 3,500), Batina dist., N Oman, on Gulf of Oman, 14 mi. NW of Sohar.

Liwale (lēwä'lā), town, Southern Prov., SE Tanganyika, 125 mi. SW of Kilwa; agr. and road center; tobacco, wheat, peanuts, corn; livestock.

Liwiec River (lē'vyĕts), Rus. *Livets* (lē'vyĭts), E Poland, rises 3 mi. S of Mordy, flows 72 mi. NW, past Wegrow, to Bug R. 4 mi. E of Wyszkow.

Liwonde (lēwŏn'dā), center in native village area, Southern Prov., Nyasaland, on left bank of Shire R., on road and 20 mi. NNW of Zomba; tobacco, cotton, tung, corn, rice; livestock.

Lixha or **Lixhë,** Albania: see LLIXHË.

Lixhe (lĭks), Flemish *Lieze* (lē'zü), village (pop. 1,249), Liége prov., E Belgium, on Meuse R., near Liége-Maastricht Canal, just NNW of Visé; cement making.

Lixourion, Greece: see LEXOURION.

Lixuri, Greece: see LEXOURION.

Lixus, Sp. Morocco: see LARACHE.

Liyang (lē'yäng'), town (pop. 20,673), ⊙ Liyang co. (pop. 342,926), SW Kiangsu prov., China, near Anhwei-Chekiang line, 50 mi. S of Chinkiang; rice, wheat, beans; oil pressing, rice milling.

Lizard, The, promontory, SW Cornwall, England, on the Channel, 15 mi. SSW of Falmouth. The whole peninsula S of Helford R. is sometimes called The Lizard, and its S extremity (southernmost point of Great Britain; 49°58'N 5°13'W) Lizard Point or Lizard Head; site of 2 lighthouses. Coast has colored serpentine rocks, inlets, caves, islets, and dangerous reefs.

Lizard Head Peak, Wyo.: see WIND RIVER RANGE.

Lizton (lĭz'tŭn), town (pop. 276), Hendricks co., central Ind., 22 mi. WNW of Indianapolis, in agr. area.

Lizy-sur-Ourcq (lēzē'-sür-ōōrk'), village (pop. 1,222), Seine-et-Marne dept., N central France, on the Ourcq near its influx into the Marne, and 8 mi. NE of Meaux; ferronickel mfg., sugar milling.

Lizzanello (lētsänĕl'lō), village (pop. 3,644), Lecce prov., Apulia, S Italy, 4 mi. SSE of Lecce.

Lizzano (lētsä'nō), town (pop. 4,555), Ionio prov., Apulia, S Italy, 13 mi. ESE of Taranto; wine, olive oil, cheese.

Lizzano in Belvedere (ēn bĕlvĕdā'rĕ), village (pop. 440), Bologna prov., Emilia-Romagna, N central Italy, in Etruscan Apennines, 4 mi. W of Poretta Terme; resort (alt. 2,100 ft.).

Lizzie, Lake (□ 8), Otter Tail co., W Minn., just N of L. Lida, 22 mi. N of Fergus Falls; 4 mi. long, 3 mi. wide. Resorts. Fed and drained by Pelican R., flowing from Pelican L., just N.

Ljeskovec, Bulgaria: see LYASKOVETS.

Ljosafoss (lyō'säfôs"), Icelandic *Ljósafoss,* waterfall, SW Iceland, on Sog R. 25 mi. E of Reykjavik. Power station here is largest in Iceland.

Ljubelj Pass, Yugoslavia and Austria: see LOIBL PASS.

Ljubija or **Lyubiya** (both: lyōō'bēä), village, NW Bosnia, Yugoslavia, 30 mi. WNW of Banja Luka; center of iron-mining area. Mines opened in 1916.

Ljubinje or **Lyubinye** (both: lyōō'bĭnyĕ), village, S Herzegovina, Yugoslavia, on Mostar-Trebinje road and 30 mi. SSE of Mostar; local trade center.

Ljubisnja, Velika, and **Ljubisnja, Mala,** Yugoslavia: see VELIKA LJUBISNJA.

Ljubljana (lyōō'blyänä), Ger. *Laibach* (lī'bäkh), Ital. *Lubiana* (lōōbēä'nä), anc. *Æmona* or *Emona,* city (pop. 120,994), ⊙ Slovenia and Ljubljana oblast (formed 1949), Yugoslavia, on Ljubljanica R., on Zagreb-Trieste RR and 70 mi. WNW of Zagreb, among low hills. Major trade, transportation, and industrial center; terminus of highway to Belgrade (constructed 1947–50); airport. Mfg. of machinery, chemicals, tobacco and tobacco products, leather and leather goods, furniture, paper, textiles, beer, and foodstuffs; woodworking. Slovenian cultural center; has univ. (1596), academies of science, art, music, drama, and pedagogy, natl. theater of drama and opera, natl. gall. and library, museums, churches, monasteries, and parks. Seat of R.C. archbishop. Remains of anc. Roman city still exist. First mentioned as Ljubljana in 1144; flourished (13th cent.) under dukes of Carinthia. Under Hapsburg rule from c.1280; was successively ⊙ Illyrian Provs. (1809–13), Austrian kingdom of Illyria (1816–49) and Carniola. Seat of Congress of Laibach (1821), which widened the rift within the Quadruple Alliance. During Second World War, it was capital (1941–43) of an autonomous Ital. prov.; occupied (1943–45) by Germans. Much changed since 1895 earthquake.

Ljubljanica River (lyōō'blyänĭtsä), Ger. *Laibach* (lī'bäkh), W Slovenia, Yugoslavia, rises near Vrhnika, flows c.20 mi. ENE, past Vrhnika and Ljubljana, to Sava R. just ENE of Ljubljana.

Ljubostinja or **Lyubostinya** (both: lyōō'bôstĭnyä), monastery, central Serbia, Yugoslavia, 17 mi. WNW of Krusevac, near the Western Morava.

Ljuboten or **Lyuboten** (both: lyōō'bôtĕn), peak (8,187 ft.) in Sar Mts., SW Yugoslavia, 16 mi. NNE of Tetovo, above Kacanik defile. Near-by Ljuboten mines produce chromium processed at RADUSA.

Ljubovija or **Lyuboviya** (both: lyōō'bôvēä), village (pop: 602), W Serbia, Yugoslavia, on Drina R. (Bosnia border) and 26 mi. W of Valjevo.

Ljubusa Mountains or **Lyubusha Mountains** (both: lyōō'bōōshä), Serbo-Croatian *Ljubuša Planina,* in Dinaric Alps, SW Bosnia, Yugoslavia; c.10 mi. long. Highest peak, Ljubusa (5,894 ft.), is 12 mi. WSW of Prozor.

Ljubuski or **Lyubushki** (both: –kē), Serbo-Croatian *Ljubuški,* town (pop. 4,089), W Herzegovina, Yugoslavia, 16 mi. SW of Mostar, near Dalmatian border; center of tobacco-growing region.

Ljugarn (yü'gärn"), village (pop. 264), Gotland co., SE Sweden, on E coast of Gotland isl., 25 mi. SE of Visby; seaside resort; grain, sugar beets, potatoes, flax. Has archaeological mus.

Ljunga River, Swedish *Ljungan* (yŭng'än"), N Sweden, rises near Norwegian border SE of Trondheim, flows 200 mi. generally ESE, through several small lakes, past Ange, Ljungaverk (power station), and Matfors, to Gulf of Bothnia 4 mi. SE of Sundsvall. Important logging route; salmon fishing.

Ljungaverk (yŭng"ävĕrk'), village (pop. 2,091), Vasternorrland co., NE Sweden, on Ljunga R. and 40 mi. W of Sundsvall; chemical-industry center (mfg. of ammonia, ammonium sulphate, calcium carbide, lime), with large hydroelectric station.

Ljungby (yŭng'bü"), city (pop. 6,138), Kronoberg co., S Sweden, on Laga R. and 30 mi. W of Vaxjo; rail junction; foundries, mechanical works; furniture and shoe mfg. Inc. 1936.

Ljungbyhed (yŭng"bühād'), village (pop. 1,337), Kristianstad co., S Sweden, 20 mi. E of Halsingborg; grain, potatoes, livestock. Site of military flying school.

Ljungskile (yŭngs"chē'lü), village (pop. 1,169), Goteborg och Bohus co., SW Sweden, on narrow channel of the Skagerrak, opposite Orust isl., 8 mi. S of Uddevalla; seaside resort.

Ljusdal (yüs'däl"), town (pop. 2,322), Gavleborg co., E Sweden, on Ljusna R. and 30 mi. W of Hudiksvall; rail junction; agr. market (grain, flax, potatoes, berries, livestock). Tourist center. Has old manor house.

Ljusfors, Sweden: see SKARBLACKA-LJUSFORS.

Ljusna River, Swedish *Ljusnan* (yüs'nän"), N central Sweden, rises in Norwegian border mts. W of Roros, flows 270 mi. in winding course generally SE, past Sveg, Ljusdal, and Bollnas, to Gulf of Bothnia at Ljusne. Logging route; salmon fishing. Hydroelectric stations. Receives Voxna R.

Ljusne (yüs'nü), village (pop. 3,261), Gavleborg co., E Sweden, on Gulf of Bothnia at mouth of Ljusna R., 6 mi. SE of Soderhamn; lumber-milling center, with plywood and wallboard works, foundries; chain mfg. Hydroelectric station. Includes Ala (ä'lä") village.

Ljutomer (lyōō'tômĕr), Ger. *Luttenberg* (lōōt'ŭnbĕrk), village (pop. 1,638), NE Slovenia, Yugoslavia, 26 mi. E of Maribor, at SE foot of the Slovenske Gorice; rail junction; winegrowing; trade in wine and horses. Has castle. First mentioned in 1265. Formerly called Lotmerk. Until 1918, in Styria.

Llagostera (lyägōstā'rä), town (pop. 2,130), Gerona prov., NE Spain, 11 mi. SSE of Gerona; road center; cork processing; cereals, fruit.

Llaillai, Chile: see LLAY-LLAY.

Llaima (yī'mä), village (1930 pop. 51), Cautín prov., S central Chile, on railroad and 32 mi. ENE of Temuco; cereals, stock.

Llaima Volcano, Andean peak (10,040 ft.), Cautín prov., S central Chile, 45 mi. ENE of Temuco; active volcano. Winter sports.

Llajta Mauca (wī'tä mou'kä), town (pop. 3,055), E Santiago del Estero prov., Argentina, 20 mi. NW of Añatuya. Formerly called Kilómetro 511.

Llallagua (yäyä'gwä), town (pop. c.9,500), Potosí dept., W central Bolivia, on E slopes of Cordillera de Azanaques 3 mi. NNW of Uncía and on Machacamarca-Uncía RR; alt. 13,297 ft. Formerly chief tin-mining center of Bolivia; gradually being replaced by new CATAVI mines, 2 mi. NE.

Llama (yä'mä), town (pop. 1,212), Cajamarca dept., NW Peru, in Cordillera Occidental, 32 mi. WNW of Chota; wheat, corn.

Llambrión, Torre de (tô'rā dhā lyämbrēōn'), peak (8,586 ft.) of Cantabrian Mts., N Spain, in Picos de Europa (massif), 12 mi. NE of Riaño.

Llamellín (yämĕyēn'), town (pop. 1,072), Ancash dept., W central Peru, on E slopes of Cordillera Blanca, near Marañón R., 25 mi. NE of Huari; wheat, corn, livestock.

Llanaber, Wales: see BARMOUTH.

Llanaelhaiarn (lănīl-hī'ärn), agr. village and parish (pop. 1,654), W Caernarvon, Wales, on Lleyn Peninsula, 6 mi. N of Pwllheli.

Llanarth (lă'närth), agr. village and parish (pop. 1,444), W Cardigan, Wales, 3 mi. SE of New Quay.

Llanarthney (lănärth'nē), town and parish (pop. 3,857), central Carmarthen, Wales, on Towy R. and 8 mi. E of Carmarthen; agr. market.

Llanasa (lănä'sä), town and parish (pop. 3,230), Flint, Wales, 3 mi. ESE of Prestatyn; agr. market. Has 15th-cent. church.

Llanbadrig (lănbä'drĭg), village and parish (pop. 707), N Anglesey, Wales, on Irish Sea, 11 mi. NE of Holyhead; stone quarrying, brick mfg. Has anc. church. Just ENE is Llanlliana (lăn-thlēä'nŭ) promontory, northernmost point of Wales; 53°25'N 4°25'W.

Llanbedr (lănbĕ'dŭr), town and parish (pop. 324), NW Merioneth, Wales, near Cardigan Bay of Irish Sea, 7 mi. NNW of Barmouth; manganese mining.

Llanbedrog (lănbĕ'drôg), village and parish (pop. 633), on Lleyn Peninsula, SW Caernarvon, Wales, 4 mi. SW of Pwllheli; granite quarrying. Has 15th-cent. church.

Llanberis (lănbĕ'rĭs), town and parish (pop. 2,370), central Caernarvon, Wales, 8 mi. ESE of Caernarvon, at S end of Padarn lake (2 mi. long); slate quarrying. Terminal of rack-and-pinion railroad to SNOWDON summit. Near by is 13th-cent. Dolbadarn Castle. Just ENE is slate-quarrying village of Dinorwic (dĭnôr'wĭk).

Llanboidy (lănboi'dē), town and parish (pop. 1,205), W Carmarthen, Wales, 12 mi. WNW of Carmarthen; woolen milling. Near by is anc. Druidical circle.

Llanbrynmair (lănbrĭnmīr'), town and parish (pop. 1,025), W central Montgomery, Wales, 9 mi. E of Machynlleth; lead mining. Has 15th-cent. church.

Llancanelo, Lake, or **Lake Llancanello** (yängkänā'lō), salt lake (□ 185), S Mendoza prov., Argentina, 75 mi. SW of San Rafael, in N part of a salt desert.

Llancynfelyn, Wales: see BORTH.

Llandaff (lăn'dăf'), suburb (pop. 27,762) of Cardiff, SE Glamorgan, Wales, on Taff R. and 3 mi. WNW of Cardiff. Cathedral, dating from 1120, is built on site of church founded in late 6th or early 7th cent. by St. Dubricius. Has Protestant theological col. and remains of palace built by Bishop Urban. Cathedral severely damaged in Second World War.

Llandanwg (lăndă'nŏŏg), village and parish (pop. 1,103), NW Merioneth, Wales, on Cardigan Bay, 2 mi. SSW of Harlech.

Llandarcy, Wales: see SWANSEA.

Llanddarog (lăn-dhă'rôg), agr. village and parish (pop. 1,013), S central Carmarthen, Wales, 10 mi. N of Llanelly.

Llanddeiniolen (lăn-dhīnyō'lŭn), town and parish (pop. 4,779), N Caernarvon, Wales, 5 mi. NE of Caernarvon; agr. market. Just NW, on Menai Strait, is slate-shipping port of Port Dinorwic (dĭnôr'wĭk), linked by rail with slate quarries at LLANBERIS.

Llanddetty (lăn-dhĕ'tē), agr. village and parish (pop. 398), SE Brecknock, Wales, on Usk R. and 7 mi. SE of Brecknock.

Llanddeusant (lăn-dhī'sŭnt), village and parish (pop. 396), E Carmarthen, Wales, 6 mi. S of Llandovery; woolen milling.

Llandebie, Wales: see LLANDYBIE.

Llandefeilog (lăndĭvī'lôg), agr. village and parish (pop. 1,020), S Carmarthen, Wales, 5 mi. S of Carmarthen.

Llandegai (lăndŭgī'), residential town and parish (pop. 2,603), N Caernarvon, Wales, just SE of Bangor; model cottage estate for slate-industry workers. Has 16th-cent. church. Just N is 18th-cent. Penrhyn Castle.

Llandilo (lăndī'lō), urban district (1931 pop. 1,886; 1951 census 2,003), E central Carmarthen, Wales, on Towy R. and 13 mi. E of Carmarthen; agr. market and resort, with shoe mfg. Has 13th-cent. church. Just W is Dynevor Park, with ruins of 13th-cent. Dynevor Castle.

Llandinam (lăndē'nŭm), town and parish (pop. 1,246), S Montgomery, Wales, on Severn R. and 5 mi. NE of Llanidloes.

Llandore, Wales: see SWANSEA.

Llandovery (lăndŭ'vrē, -dō'vŭrē), municipal borough (1931 pop. 1,980; 1951 census 1,856), NE Carmarthen, Wales, on Towy R. and 12 mi. NE of Llandilo; agr. market. Has ruins of Norman castle. Site of Llandovery Col. (founded 1848), a public school.

Llandrillo-yn-Rhos, Wales: see COLWYN BAY.

Llandrindod Wells (lăndrĭn'dŏd), urban district (1931 pop. 2,925; 1951 census 3,213), W Radnor, Wales, 17 mi. WSW of Knighton; resort with mineral springs; woolen milling, shoe mfg. Urban dist. includes Cefnllys (kĕvŭn-thlēs') (pop. 1,904).

Llandudno (lăndŭd'nō, -dĭd'-), urban district (1931 pop. 13,679; 1951 census 16,712), NE Caernarvon, Wales, on a peninsula on Colwyn Bay of Irish Sea, 4 mi. N of Conway; seaside resort, with beach, marine drive, pier, and pavilion. Promontory of GREAT ORMES HEAD is 2 mi. NW; just E is promontory of Little Ormes Head.

Llandwrog (lăndōō'rŏg), agr. town and parish (pop. 3,317), W central Caernarvon, Wales, 5 mi. SSW of Caernarvon.

Llandybie or **Llandebie** (both: lăndĭbē'ă), town and parish (pop. 8,877), central Carmarthen, Wales, 4 mi. SSW of Llandilo; coal mining.

Llandyssul (lăndĭ'sĭl), town and parish (pop. 2,590), S Cardigan, Wales, on Teifi R. and 12 mi. SW of Lampeter; woolen milling. Its 13th-cent. church, with Norman tower, contains 6th-cent. inscribed stone. Woolen-milling village of Capel Dewi (kăp'ĕl dū'ē) is 2 mi. ENE.

Llanedy (lănĕ'dē), town and parish (pop. 4,280), SE Carmarthen, Wales, on Loughor R. and 7 mi. NE of Llanelly; agr. market.

Llanegwad (lănĕg'wŭd), agr. village and parish (pop. 1,161), central Carmarthen, Wales, on Towy R. and 7 mi. E of Carmarthen.

Llanelly (lănĕ'lē, -ĕ'thlē). **1** Town and parish (pop. 3,437), SE Brecknock, Wales, 4 mi. ENE of Brynmawr; paper milling. **2** Municipal borough (1931 pop. 38,416; 1951 census 34,329), SE Carmarthen, Wales, on Burry Inlet of Carmarthen Bay, at mouth of Loughor R., and 10 mi. WNW of Swansea; 51°41'N 4°9'W; steel- and tinplate-milling center; mfg. of copper, chemicals, bricks, and pottery; coal-shipping port. Has 13th-cent. church. In municipal borough (NE) is Felinfoel (vĕlĭnvōl'), with automobile factory.

Llanengan (lănĕng'găn), agr. village and parish (pop. 1,162), SW Caernarvon, Wales, on Lleyn Peninsula, 7 mi. SW of Pwllheli. Has 15th-cent. church.

Llanerch, Pa.: see HAVERFORD.

Llanerchydol, Wales: see WELSHPOOL.

Llanerchymedd (lănŭrkh-ŭmădh'), town and parish (pop. 730), N central Anglesey, Wales, 5 mi. SSW of Amlwch; agr. market, noted for cattle fairs.

Llanes (lyä'nĕs), town (pop. 2,953), Oviedo prov., NW Spain, in Asturias, fishing port on Bay of Biscay, 50 mi. W of Santander; fish salting, boatbuilding; dairy-products mfg. Has 15th-cent. Gothic church and remains of medieval walls. Mineral springs.

Llanfachreth (lănvăkh'rĕth), village and parish (pop. 316), W Anglesey, Wales, 4 mi. E of Holyhead; woolen milling.

Llanfaelog (lănvī'lŏg), agr. village and parish (pop. 1,307), W Anglesey, Wales, 8 mi. SE of Holyhead.

Llanfaes, Wales: see BRECKNOCK, city.

Llanfair Caereinion (lăn'vīr kärīn'yôn), town and parish (pop. 1,665), central Montgomery, Wales, 8 mi. W of Welshpool.

Llanfair Clydogau, Wales: see LLANGYBI.

Llanfairfechan (lănvīr-vĕkh'ŭn), urban district (1931 pop. 3,162; 1951 census 3,163), N Caernarvon, Wales, on Conway Bay of Irish Sea, 7 mi. ENE of Bangor at base of Penmaenmawr; seaside resort.

Llanfair-is-Gaer (lăn'vīr-ēs-gīr'), town and parish (pop. 1,471), N Caernarvon, Wales, on Menai Strait, 2 mi. NE of Caernarvon; brickworks.

Llanfairpwll or **Llanfairpwllgwyngyll** (lăn'vīrpōōl, -gwĭn'gĭl), town and parish (pop. 912), SE Anglesey, Wales, near Menai Strait, 2 mi. W of Menai Bridge; agr. market.

Llanfihangel Aberbythych (lănvĕhăng'ŭl ăbŭrbĭ'thĭkh), agr. village and parish (pop. 1,284), E central Carmarthen, Wales, near Towy R., 3 mi. SW of Llandilo.

Llanfihangel Abercowin (ăbŭrkou'ĭn), town and parish (pop. 940), SW Carmarthen, Wales, 7 mi. WSW of Carmarthen; woolen milling.

Llanfihangel ar Arth or **Llanfihangel ararth** (—är-ärth'), town and parish (pop. 1,752), N Carmarthen, Wales, on Teifi R. and 9 mi. E of Newcastle Emlyn; woolen milling. Just ENE is woolen-milling village of Maesycrugiau (mīsĭkrĭg'yī).

Llanfihangel Pontymoel, England: see PANTEG.

Llanfor (lănvôr'), agr. village and parish (pop. 1,019), E central Merioneth, Wales, on the Dee just NE of Bala.

Llanfrechfa Lower (lănvrĕkh'vä), agr. parish (pop. 1,440), S Monmouth, England. Includes village of Llanfrechfa, 3 mi. N of Newport.

Llanfrechfa Upper, former urban district (1931 pop. 4,482), S central Monmouth, England. In it is steel-milling town of Pontnewydd (pŏntnū'wĭdh), 3 mi. SSE of Pontypool. Urban dist. inc. (1935) in Cwmbran.

Llanfwrog, Wales: see RUTHIN.

Llanfyllin (lănvŭ'thlĭn), municipal borough (1931 pop. 1,449; 1951 census 1,419), N Montgomery, Wales, 9 mi. NNW of Welshpool; agr. market. Once noted for ale brewing.

Llanfynydd (lănvŭ'nĭdh), town and parish (pop. 1,602), Flint, Wales, 6 mi. NW of Wexham; coal mining.

Llangadock (lăn-gă'dôk), town and parish (pop. 1,441), E Carmarthen, Wales, on Towy R. and 6 mi. NE of Llandilo; agr. market. Near by is prehistoric camp of Carn Goch, covering c.15 acres.

Llanganates, Cordillera de los (kōrdĭyä'rä dā lōs yäng-gänä'tĕs), E Andean massif, central Ecuador, E of Ambato; includes several volcanic peaks, highest of which is Cerro Hermoso (15,216 ft.). The region is rich in minerals (vanadium, molybdenum, chromium, iron, phosphorus, arsenic).

Llangefni (lăn-gĕv'nē), urban district (1931 pop. 1,782; 1951 census 2,225), central Anglesey, Wales, 8 mi. N of Caernarvon; agr. market.

Llangeler (lăn-gĕ'lŭr), town and parish (pop. 1,722), S Cardigan, Wales, on Teifi R. and 4 mi. E of Newcastle Emlyn; woolen-milling center. Parish includes woolen-milling villages of Drefach (drĕ-väkh'), Velindre (vĕlĭn'drā), and Pentrecwrt (pĕn-trĕkōōrt').

Llangelynin (lăn-gĕlŭ'nĭn), town and parish (pop. 1,247), SW Merioneth, Wales, on Cardigan Bay of Irish Sea, 4 mi. NNW of Towyn; seaside resort.

Llangendeirne (lăn-gĕndīrn'), town and parish (pop. 3,350), S Carmarthen, Wales 5 mi. SE of Carmarthen; agr. market.

Llangennech (lăn-gĕ'nĕkh), town and parish (pop. 2,845), SE Carmarthen, Wales, on Loughor R. and 4 mi. ENE of Llanelly; tinplate milling.

Llangiwg, Wales: see YSTALYFERA.

Llanglydwen (lăn-glĭd'wĕn), village and parish (pop. 248), W Carmarthen, Wales, on Taf R. and 3 mi. NW of Llanboidy; woolen milling. Just N is woolen-milling village of Hebron.

Llangoedmor (lăn-goid'môr), village and parish (pop. 677), SW Cardigan, Wales, near Teifi R., just E of Cardigan; woolen milling.

Llangollen (lăn-gŏ'lĭn, lăn-gō'thlĭn), urban district (1931 pop. 2,937; 1951 census 3,275), SE Denbigh, Wales, on the Dee (14th-cent. bridge) in Vale of Llangollen, and 18 mi. SE of Denbigh; agr. market, with leather mfg. and woolen (flannel) milling; tourist and fishing resort. Has Norman church. Near by are many antiquities, including Dinas Bran or Crow Castle, Eliseg's Pillar (9th-cent. stone monument), and Valle Crucis Abbey (c.1200). Near-by Plas Newydd (pläs nū'wĭdh) was residence of Lady Eleanor Butler and Sarah Ponsonby, "Ladies of the Vale" or "Ladies of Llangollen," noted 18th-cent. eccentric recluses.

Llangorse Lake (lăn-gôrs'), Welsh *Llyn Safaddan* (lĭn sävä'dhăn), E central Brecknock, Wales, 5 mi. ESE of Brecknock; 1 mi. long, 1 mi. wide; drained by short tributary of Wye R. At N end is village of Llangorse.

Llangybi (lăn-gŭ'bē), village and parish (pop. 235), S Cardigan, Wales, 4 mi. NNE of Lampeter; woolen milling. Just SE is Llanfair Clydogau (lăn'vīr klĭdō'gī), with silver mines dating from Roman times.

Llangyfelach (lăn-gŭvĕ'lŭkh), town (pop. 1,763) in Llwchwr urban dist., W Glamorgan, Wales, 3 mi. N of Swansea; coal mines.

Llangynwyd Middle (lăn-gŭ'nōōĭd), agr. parish (pop. 1,955), SW central Glamorgan, Wales, 2 mi. S of Maesteg.

Llanharan (lănhă'rŭn), town and parish (pop. 2,551), SE central Glamorgan, Wales, 7 mi. ENE of Bridgend; coal mining. Site of mineral spring.

Llanhilleth, England: see ABERTILLERY.

Llanidan, Wales: see BRYN SIENCYN.

Llanidloes (lănĭd'lois), municipal borough (1931 pop. 2,356; 1951 census 2,341), S Montgomery, Wales, on Severn R. and 11 mi. WSW of Newtown; agr. market; leather mfg., woolen (flannel) milling. Has 13th-cent. church. A center of Chartist riots (1839). Formerly lead-mining center.

Llanitos, Los (lōs yänē'tōs), peak (9,452 ft.), Guanajuato, central Mexico, in Sierra Madre Occidental, 10 mi. NNE of Guanajuato.

Llanlliana, Wales: see LLANBADRIG.

Llanllwchaiarn, Wales: see NEWTOWN.

Llanllyfni (lăn-thlŭv'nē), town and parish (pop. 4,520), W central Caernarvon, Wales, 7 mi. S of Caernarvon; woolen milling; agr. market.

Llannon (lănôn'), town and parish (pop. 5,599), SE Carmarthen, Wales, 6 mi. NNE of Llanelly; coal mining.

Llano (lă'nō), county (□ 947; pop. 5,377), central Texas; ⊙ Llano. Hilly area on E Edwards Plateau; alt. c.650–1,800 ft.; bounded E by Colorado R. and L. Buchanan, drained by Llano R. and tributaries. Ranching (cattle, sheep, goats, hogs, horses, some poultry); also agr. (peanuts, corn, pecans, grain sorghums, oats, fruit). Granite quarrying. Scenery, hunting, fishing attract tourists. Formed 1856.

Llano, town (pop. 2,954), ⊙ Llano co., central Texas, on Edwards Plateau, c.65 mi. NW of Austin and on Llano R.; rail terminus in ranching, agr. area; granite quarrying and cutting, cotton ginning, dairying; ships wool, mohair. Tourist trade (hunting, fishing). L. Buchanan is c.12 mi. E. Inc. 1901.

Llano, El, Mexico: see EL LLANO.

Llano, El, Panama: see EL LLANO.

Llano Estacado (lä'nō ĕstŭkä'do, lă'nō) or **Staked Plain,** in E N.Mex. and W Texas, vast, semiarid, almost level S portion of the Great Plains, extending over most of Texas Panhandle and over the part of N.Mex. E of Pecos R from SE corner of N.Mex. to region N of Clovis; alt. in N c.4,000 ft.; in S, c.2,500 ft. In Texas, Cap Rock escarpment (300–1,000 ft. high), facing E and SE and curving from NE corner of the Panhandle towards the SW, marks transition bet. the Llano Estacado and the prairies to E; on SE, Edwards Plateau adjoins. Sometimes subdivided into High (or Panhandle) Plains in N, centering on Amarillo, and the South Plains around Lubbock. Flat, wind-swept grasslands are varied only by "breaks" or canyons of streams heading near its boundary and contributing to the Canadian, Red, Brazos, and Colorado rivers. Region was formerly devoted to large-scale cattle ranching; important natural-gas and oil fields and irrigated and dry-farm agr. now supplement stock raising as chief activities.

Llano River (lă'nō), central Texas, formed at Junction by North Llano and South Llano rivers, both rising on Edwards Plateau; flows c.105 mi. generally E to the Colorado 16 mi. SE of Llano.

Llanos (yä'nōs) [Sp.,=plains], Spanish American term for prairies, specifically those of the Orinoco basin in Venezuela and part of E Colombia. Shunned by man before the Spaniards came and supporting little wild life except egrets, whose plumes once were a valuable export, the region is a vast, hot, sparsely-populated savanna broken by low-lying interfluvial mesas, scrub forest, and scattered palms. Elevation above sea level never reaches more than a few hundred feet. Plagues of insects, often deadly, make human and animal life almost intolerable. During the dry season (Nov.–April) the land is sere and baked, the grass brown, brittle, and inedible; during the rains much of the area is inundated. Still, until the recurrent revolutions of the 19th cent., the llanos supported several million head of cattle, herded by the hard-riding, tough *llanero*, an expert horseman comparable to the *gaucho* of the Argentine pampas. The *llanero* has played an important role in Venezuelan history as an ardent henchman of successive revolutionary *caudillos*. Today the cattle industry is being revived and agr. encouraged.

Llanos, Los (lōs lyä'nōs), city (pop. 1,541), Palma, Canary Isls., 9 mi. WSW of Santa Cruz de la Palma, in agr. region (bananas, tomatoes, tobacco, almonds, grapes, sugar cane, potatoes, livestock). Flour milling, cheese processing, wine making; mfg. of tobacco goods, embroidery.

Llanos, Los, Dominican Republic: see LOS LLANOS.

Llanos, Sierra de los (syĕ'rä dā lōs yä'nōs), pampean mountain range in SE La Rioja prov., Argentina, SE of Patquia; c.25 mi. long (N-S).

Llanpumpsaint (lănpĭmp'sĭnt), village and parish (pop. 645), W central Carmarthen, Wales, 6 mi. N of Carmarthen; woolen milling.

Llanquihue (yäng-kē'wā), province (□ 7,107; 1940 pop. 117,225; 1949 estimate 117,609), S central Chile; ⊙ PUERTO MONTT. Located bet. the Pacific (W), the Andes (E), and Gulf of Ancud (S), just N and NE of Chiloé Isl., it embraces part of the Chilean lake dist., notably L. Llanquihue and L. Todos los Santos, over which tower Osorno and Calbuco volcanoes. Numerous isls. in Gulf of Ancud and Reloncaví Sound include: Maillén, Guar, Calbuco, Puluqui, Quenu. Has temperate, humid climate. It is a predominantly lumbering, dairying, and agr. region (wheat, barley, flax, potatoes, apples, sheep, cattle), with fisheries in the gulfs and in the fresh-water lakes. Fish canneries concentrated at Calbuco; at Puerto Montt are breweries, lumber mills, dry docks. A noted tourist country with fine scenery, its major resorts are: Puerto Varas, Ensenada, Petrohué, Peulla.

Llanquihue, department, Chile: see PUERTO MONTT.

Llanquihue, village (1930 pop. 703), Llanquihue prov., S central Chile, on SW shore of L. Llanquihue, on railroad and 16 mi. N of Puerto Montt; dairying, lumbering.

Llanquihue, Lake (□ 300), in Osorno and Llanquihue provs., S central Chile, in Chilean lake dist., 10 mi. N of Puerto Montt; 22 mi. long, 25 mi. wide. Bounded by the volcanoes Osorno (E) and Calbuco (SE) and by wooded subandean hills, it is a well-known resort, bordered by villages of Puerto Octay (N), Frutillar (W), Puerto Varas (S), Ensenada (E). Lumbering, fishing; sports. Depths of almost 5,000 ft. have been measured. Outlet: Maullín R.

Llanrhaiadr (lănrī'ädůr), agr. village in Llanrhaiadr-yn-Cinmerch (-ŭn-kĭn'mĕrkh) parish (pop. 1,124), N Denbigh, Wales, 2 mi. SE of Denbigh. Has 15th-cent. church.

Llanrhidian Higher, Wales: see PENCLAWDD.

Llanrhydd, Wales: see RUTHIN.

Llanrug (lănrēg'), town and parish (pop. 2,617), N Caernarvon, Wales, 3 mi. E of Caernarvon; agr. market. Just W is radio station of Bryn Bras.

Llanrwst (lănrōōst'), urban district (1931 pop. 2,372; 1951 census 2,592), W Denbigh, Wales, on Conway R. (17th-cent. bridge), and 11 mi. SSW of Colwyn Bay; agr. market, with leather mfg. Has 15th-cent. church, reputed to contain tomb of Llewellyn the Great. Formerly famous for mfg. of Welsh harps.

Llansá (lyänsä'), town (pop. 1,430), Gerona prov., NE Spain, 12 mi. NE of Figueras, near the Mediterranean; olive-oil and wine processing. Small port of Puerto de Llansá is 1 mi. NNE.

Llansamlet, Wales: see SWANSEA.

Llansantffraid Deythur, Wales: see LLANSANTFFRAID-YM-MECHAINT.

Llansantffraid Glyn Ceiriog (lănsăntfrīd' glĭn' kī'rēōg), town and parish (pop. 1,058), S Denbigh, Wales, 3 mi. S of Llangollen; woolen milling, slate quarrying.

Llansantffraid-ym-Mechaint (-ŭm-mĕkh'īnt), agr. village in Llansantffraid Pool parish (pop. 717), NE Montgomery, Wales, on Vyrnwy R. and 8 mi. N of Welshpool. It is frequented by anglers. Just S is agr. village and parish of Llansantffraid Deythur (dī'thōōr) (pop. 346).

Llansilin (lănsĭ'lĭn), agr. village and parish (pop. 1,081), S Denbigh, Wales, 9 mi. S of Llangollen.

Llanstephan (lănstĕ'făn), town and parish (pop. 974), SW Carmarthen, Wales, on Towy R. estuary and 7 mi. SW of Carmarthen; agr. market, with woolen mills. Site of remains of noted 11th–13th-cent. castle. Has Norman church.

Llanta (yän'tä), mining settlement (1930 pop. 316), Atacama prov., N Chile, on railroad and 55 mi. E of Chañaral, on the Quebrada del Salado; copper mining.

Llanta Apacheta, Bolivia: see MILLARES.

Llantarnam (lăntär'nŭm), residential former urban district (1931 pop. 7,283), S Monmouth, England, 3 mi. N of Newport. Inc.(1935) in Cwmbran.

Llantilio Pertholey (lăntĭ'lyō pŭrthō'lē), agr. village and parish (pop. 1,182), N Monmouth, England, just NE of Abergavenny. Has 14th-cent. church.

Llantrisant (lăntrĭ'sănt), town and parish (pop. 22,276), E Glamorgan, Wales, 10 mi. WNW of Cardiff; agr. market. Has remains of 13th-cent. castle. On near-by hill are anc. earthworks.

Llantwitfardre (lăn'twĭtvär'drā), town and parish (pop. 3,633), E Glamorgan, Wales, 3 mi. NE of Llantrisant; agr. market.

Llantwit Major (lăn'twĭt), town and parish (pop. 1,541), S Glamorgan, Wales, near Bristol Channel, 8 mi. SE of Bridgend; agr. market. Has 13th-cent. church, built on site of 5th-cent. monastery, containing anc. Celtic cross of Illtyd.

Llanwenog (lănwĕ'nōg), agr. village and parish (pop. 1,285), S Cardigan, Wales, 5 mi. WSW of Lampeter.

Llanwnda (lănōōn'dŭ), town and parish (pop. 1,850), W Caernarvon, Wales, 3 mi. S of Caernarvon; agr. market.

Llanwrda (lănōōr'dä), village and parish (pop. 461), E Carmarthen, Wales, on Towy R. and 4 mi. SW of Llandovery; woolen milling.

Llanwrtyd Wells (lănōōr'tĭd), village in Llanwrtyd urban district (1931 pop. 742; 1951 census 560), NW Brecknock, Wales, 15 mi. NW of Brecknock; resort with sulphur spring; agr. market; woolen milling.

Llanybyther (lănbī'thĕr), town and parish (pop. 1,100), N Carmarthen, Wales, on Teifi R. and 4 mi. WNW of Lampeter; agr. market, with woolen milling. Site of sanitarium.

Llao-Llao (you-you'), village (pop. estimate 250), SW Río Negro natl. territory, Argentina, on L. Nahuel Huapí, 15 mi. WNW of San Carlos de Bariloche; fashionable resort with numerous hotels.

Llardecáns (lyärdäkäns'), town (pop. 1,094), Lérida prov., NE Spain, 17 mi. SSW of Lérida; soap mfg., olive-oil processing; sheep raising.

Llaretas, Cordón de las (kōrdōn' dā läs yärā'täs), Andean range in W central Mendoza prov., Argentina; rises to over 16,000 ft.

Llata (yä'tä), city (pop. 1,873), ⊙ Huamalíes prov. (□ 1,220; enumerated pop. 36,425, plus estimated 4,000 Indians), Huánuco dept., central Peru, on E slopes of Cordillera Blanca of the Andes, near Marañón R., 50 mi. NW of Huánuco; alt. 11,246 ft. Weaving of native textiles; agr. products (wheat, corn, potatoes); sheep raising.

Llaucán River (youkän'), Cajamarca dept., NW Peru, rises in Cordillera Occidental 10 mi. WNW of Celendín, flows 70 mi. NW and NNE, past Bambamarca, to Marañón R. 7 mi. SE of Cujillo.

Llaurí (lyourē'), village (pop. 1,696), Valencia prov., E Spain, 6 mi. E of Alcira; rice, oranges.

Llavalol (yävälōl'), town (pop. estimate 3,000) in Greater Buenos Aires, Argentina, 12 mi. SSW of Buenos Aires; residential dist.; textile mfg.

Llay (lā), town and parish (pop. 3,627), E Denbigh, Wales, on Alyn R. and 3 mi. N of Wrexham; coal mining.

Llay-Llay (yī-yī'), town (pop. 4,137), Valparaiso prov., central Chile, on Aconcagua R. and 37 mi. NE of Valparaiso; rail junction and agr. center (grain, wine, hemp, fruit, cattle). Mfg. of pharmaceuticals. Sometimes Llaillai.

Llefiá (lyäfyä'), SW suburb (pop. 1,892) of Badalona, Barcelona prov., NE Spain.

Llera (yä'rä), officially Llera de Canales, town (pop. 1,050), Tamaulipas, NE Mexico, in E outliers of Sierra Madre Oriental, 30 mi. SSE of Ciudad Victoria; silver, gold, lead mining.

Llera (lyä'rä), town (pop. 1,959), Badajoz prov., W Spain, 15 mi. N of Llerena; mining (lead, pitchblende, calamine) and agr. (wheat, barley, sheep).

Llerena (lyārā'nä), city (pop. 7,510), Badajoz prov., W Spain, in Estremadura, in NW Sierra Morena (rich in minerals), on railroad to Seville and 70 mi. SE of Badajoz. Processing, stock-raising (sheep, hogs), and agr. center (cereals, olives, grapes, honey, wax, acorns; apiculture). Liquor distilling, olive-oil extracting, flour milling, brewing; potteries, limekilns. Coal deposits in vicinity. Noted plateresque church with Mudejar tower. The old historic city was the Roman *Degina Turdulorum.* Heavily disputed by Moors, it was finally taken (1241) by the Knights of the Order of Santiago, who made it their hq. Sacked by French during Peninsular War.

Lleu-Lleu, Lake (yĕ'ōō-yĕ'ōō) (□ 27), Arauco prov., S central Chile, within 5 mi. of the Pacific, at W foot of Cordillera de Nahuelbuta, 40 mi. SE of Lebu. Has several long, narrow arms; c.10 mi. long. Tourist site.

Llewellyn (lōōĕ'lĭn), village (1940 pop. 576), Schuylkill co., E central Pa., 4 mi. W of Pottsville, in anthracite region.

Lleyn Peninsula or **The Lleyn** (lĭn), hilly peninsula in Wales, bet. Cardigan Bay and Caernarvon Bay of Irish Sea, constituting the SW part of Caernarvon; c.30 mi. long, 5–15 mi. wide. Chief town, Pwllheli. At SW extremity is promontory of BRAICH-Y-PWLL.

Llica (yē'kä), town, Potosí dept., SW Bolivia, in Cordillera de Llica, on NW shore of Salar de Uyuni and 40 mi. WSW of Salinas de Garci Mendoza; alt. 12,027 ft.; quinoa, alpaca.

Llica, Cordillera de, spur of the western Cordillera of the Andes, Oruro dept., SW Bolivia; extends 60 mi. E from Cordillera de Sillajhuay to Salinas de Garci Mendoza; separates Salar de Coipasa (N) and Salar de Uyuni (S).

Llico (yē'kō). **1** Village (1930 pop. 282), Arauco prov., S central Chile, on the Pacific (Arauco Gulf) 32 mi. N of Lebu; agr. (grain, beans, livestock); fishing. **2** Village (1930 pop. 193), Curicó prov., central Chile, on the coast, near Vichuquén Lagoon, 55 mi. NW of Curicó; resort.

Llifén (yēfĕn'), village (1930 pop. 80), Valdivia prov., S central Chile, on E bank of L. Ranco, in Chilean lake dist., 60 mi. SE of Valdivia. Resort; lumbering. Thermal springs.

Llinás (lyēnäs'), town (pop. 1,312), Barcelona prov., NE Spain, 7 mi. NNW of Mataró; knitwear mfg. Cork, wine, lumber in area. Summer resort.

Llingua Island (yĭng'gwä) (□ 2.3; pop. 396), just off E coast of Chiloé Isl., S Chile; 42° 25'S 73°27'W.

Lliuco (yēōō'kō), village (1930 pop. 835), Chiloé prov., S Chile, on NE coast of Chiloé Isl., 22 mi. SE of Ancud, in agr. area (potatoes, wheat, livestock); lumbering.

Llivia (lyē'vyä), town (pop. 637), part of Gerona prov., NE Spain, in an enclave (□ 5; pop. 723) located in Pyrénées-Orientales dept., S France, 4 mi. NE of Puigcerdá (Spain). Smuggling. Grazing and subsistence agr. Was ⊙ Cerdaña until 12th cent. The enclave resulted from the Peace of the Pyrenees (1659), which also provided for a neutral road across Fr. territory to Puigcerdá.

Llixhë (lē'jù) or **Llixha** (lē'jä), village, central Albania, 6 mi. SE of Elbasan; hot sulphur springs. Also spelled Lixhë or Lixha.

Lloa (yō'ä), village, Pichincha prov., N central Ecuador, in the Andes, 7 mi. WSW of Quito. Starting point for ascent of Cerro Pichincha.

Llobregat River (lyōvrägät'), Barcelona prov., NE Spain, rises in Sierra de Cadí of E Pyrenees, flows 105 mi. S and SE to the Mediterranean S of Barcelona. Receives Cardoner R. Irrigates fertile Llobregat coastal plain. Vineyards and several hydroelectric plants along its course.

Llocllapampa (yōkyäpäm'pä), town (pop. 705), Junín dept., central Peru, on railroad, on Mantaro R. and 8 mi. WSW of Jauja; thermal baths.

Llodio (lyō'dhyō), village (pop. 1,181), Álava prov., N Spain, on Nervión R. and 8 mi. SSW of Bilbao; metalworks; glass mfg., flour- and sawmilling. Cereals, potatoes, cattle, hogs. Locally called Plaza.

Llogora Pass (lôgô'rä) (3,461 ft.), in Acroceraunia, S Albania, on Valona-Himarë, road and 9 mi. NW of Himarë, at foot of Mt. Çikë. Also spelled Logora.

Llolleo (yōyā'ō), town (pop. 3,891), Santiago prov., central Chile, on the Pacific at mouth of Maipo R., just S of San Antonio; beach resort.

Llombay (lyōmbī'), town (pop. 2,088), Valencia prov., E Spain, 17 mi. SW of Valencia; olive-oil processing, flour milling; wine, raisins, oranges. Gypsum quarries. Marquisate belonged to Osuna family.

Llorente (yōrān'tā, lyō–), town (1939 pop. 2,664; 1948 municipality pop. 13,955), SE Samar isl., Philippines, on Philippine Sea, 50 mi. SE of Catbalogan; agr. center (coconuts, hemp).

Lloret de Mar (lyōrĕt' dhā mär'), town (pop. 2,829), Gerona prov., NE Spain, 19 mi. SSE of Gerona; bathing resort on the Mediterranean; cork, wine, olive oil.

Lloret de Vista Alegre (vē'stä älĕ'grä), town (pop. 795), Majorca, Balearic Isls., 18 mi. E of Palma; cereals, vegetables, figs, apricots, poultry, livestock; lumbering.

Llosa de Ranes (lyō'sä dhā rä'nĕs), village (pop. 2,495), Valencia prov., E Spain, 3 mi. N of Játiva; olive oil, cereals, truck produce; sericulture.

Lloseta (lyōsā'tä), town (pop. 2,560), Majorca, Balearic Isls., on railroad and 15 mi. NE of Palma; olives, almonds, carobs, grapes; food canning, shoe and tile mfg.; gravel quarrying.

Lloyd Barrage, W Pakistan: see SUKKUR BARRAGE.

Lloyd Dam, Poona dist., central Bombay, India, on upper Nira R. and 22 mi. S of Poona; 5,300 ft. long, 190 ft. high; in operation since 1928. Impounds reservoir (□ 14½) powering hydroelectric plant and supplying Nira R. canal irrigation system (headworks 16 mi. E).

Lloydell, village (pop. 2,560, with adjacent Beaverdale), Cambria co., W central Pa., 12 mi. E of Johnstown.

Lloyd George, Mount (10,000 ft.), N central B.C., in Rocky Mts.; 57°51'N 124°57'W.

Lloyd Harbor, resort village (pop. 945), Suffolk co., SE N.Y., on N shore of Long Isl., on Lloyd Neck near Lloyd Harbor (arm of Long Island Sound), 2 mi. NW of Huntington.

Lloyd Harbor, SE N.Y., an arm of Long Island Sound indenting E shore of Lloyds Neck in N Long Isl.; extends c.2½ mi. W from its mouth on Huntington Bay N of Huntington; ¼–1 mi. wide.

Lloydminster (loid'mĭnstůr), town (pop. 1,833), on Sask.-Alta. line, 80 mi. NW of North Battleford; oil and natural-gas center; grain elevators, lumbering, dairying. Until merged in 1930, Sask. and Alta. parts of town were separate municipalities.

Lloyd Neck, SE N.Y., peninsula on N shore of Long Isl., bet. Oyster Bay (W) and Huntington Bay (E); c.5 mi. long, 1½–3½ mi. wide. E shore is deeply indented by Lloyd Harbor. Lloyd Point is at tip.

Lloyd Place, suburb (pop. 4,687, with near-by Jericho and Pleasant Hill) of Suffolk, Nansemond co., SE Va.

Lloyd Point, N.Y.: see LLOYD NECK.

Lloyd Shoals Reservoir, central Ga., formed by Lloyd Shoals Dam (c.100 ft. high, 500 ft. long; built 1910 for power) in Ocmulgee R., 7 mi. E of Jackson. Reservoir is c.10 mi. long, 1 mi. wide, and receives Alcovy, Yellow, and South rivers (N), whose former confluence was source of Ocmulgee R. Also called Jackson Lake.

Lloyds Lake (12 mi. long, 1 mi. wide), SW N.F., on Lloyds R. and 45 mi. SSE of Corner Brook. On S shore are Annieopsquotch Mts.

Lloyds River, SW N.F., upper course of Exploits R., flows 60 mi. ENE, through King George IV L., Lloyds L., and Red Indian L., where it becomes Exploits R. proper.

Llubí (lyōōvē′), town (pop. 2,424), Majorca, Balearic Isls., 21 mi. ENE of Palma; capers, apricots, almonds, grapes, stock. Liquor distilling, wine making, vegetable canning, flour milling, barrel mfg.

Lluchmayor (lyōōchmīôr′) or **Llummayor** (lyōōmīôr′), inland city (pop. 9,347), Majorca, Balearic Isls., on railroad and 14 mi. ESE of Palma; industrial center in agr. region (cereals, grapes, carobs, almonds, fruit, sheep, hogs). Liquor distilling, wine making, textile milling; mfg. of shoes, felt, lace, paper. Gravel quarries.

Llullaillaco, Cerro (sĕ′rō yōōyīyä′kō), one of highest peaks (22, 015 ft.) of the Andes, an extinct, snow-capped volcano on Argentina-Chile border, 145 mi. WSW of San Antonio de los Cobres; 24°43′S. Socompa Pass, with railroad, is N.

Llummayor, Spain: see LLUCHMAYOR.

Llusco (yōō′skō), town (pop. 612), Cuzco dept., S Peru, in Andean valley, 55 mi. S of Cuzco; gold washing; mfg. of woolen goods.

Lluta River (yōō′tä), N Chile, rises in the Andes at N foot of Cerro de Tacora on Peru border, flows c.100 mi. S and WSW, through arid subandean plateaus, to the Pacific 5 mi. N of Arica. In its lower irrigated reaches cotton and fruit are grown.

Llwchwr or **Loughor** (both: lōōkh′ûr), urban district (1931 pop. 26,752; 1951 census 25,737), W Glamorgan, Wales, on Loughor R. estuary and 6 mi. WNW of Swansea; coal-mining, tin-smelting center. Has remains of Norman castle, built on site of Roman station. In urban dist. are towns of PONTARDULAIS, GORSEINON, GOWERTON, and LLANGYFELACH.

Llwchwr, river, Wales: see LOUGHOR RIVER.

Llwynypia, Wales: see RHONDDA.

Llyn Cwellyn (lĭn kwĕ′lĭn) or **Lake Quellyn,** lake in central Caernarvon, Wales, at foot of SNOWDON, 7 mi. SE of Caernarvon; 1 mi. long, ½ mi. wide.

Llyn Gwynant (lĭn gwĭ′nŭnt), lake in central Caernarvon, Wales, 3 mi. SE of SNOWDON summit; 1 mi. long.

Llyn Llydaw (lĭn lĭ′dou), lake in central Caernarvon, Wales, just E of SNOWDON summit; 1 mi. long.

Llyn Safaddan, Wales: see LLANGORSE LAKE.

Llyn Tegid, Wales: see BALA LAKE.

Llysfaen, Wales: see COLWYN BAY.

Lo (lō), village (pop. 1,356), West Flanders prov., NW Belgium, 6 mi. WSW of Dixmude; agr., cattle raising, dairying. Fortified in 1167; had important textile industry in Middle Ages. Formerly Loo.

Lo, China: see LO RIVER.

Lo, New Hebrides: see TORRES ISLANDS.

Loa, department, Chile: see CALAMA.

Loa, river, Chile: see LOA RIVER.

Loa (lō′ŭ), town (pop. 437), ⊙ Wayne co., S central Utah, 35 mi. SE of Richfield and on Fremont R.; alt. 7,000 ft.

Lo Aguirre (lō ägē′rā) or **Aguirre,** village (1930 pop. 119), Santiago prov., central Chile, 12 mi. W of Santiago; copper mining.

Loaiza, Bolivia: see LURIBAY.

Loami (lōă′mē), village (pop. 439), Sangamon co., central Ill., 13 mi. SW of Springfield, in agr. and coal area.

Loan (lô′än′). **1** Town (pop. 8,396), ⊙ Loan co. (pop. 89,870), central Kiangsi prov., China, 45 mi. ENE of Kian; coal mining; rice, wheat, cotton. **2** Town, Shantung prov., China: see KWANGJAO.

Loanda, Angola: see LUANDA, city.

Loango (lwäng-gō′), town, SW Middle Congo territory, Fr. Equatorial Africa, on the coast, on Loango Bay, 10 mi. NNW of Pointe-Noire (of which it is now a part); former port and caravan terminus noted throughout 19th and early 20th cent. for its trade in tropical commodities. Seat of vicar apostolic of Loango. French factories in Loango area existed as early as 17th cent. Formal occupation of Loango by France dates from 1882.

Loangwa River, Northern Rhodesia: see LUANGWA RIVER.

Loanhead, burgh (1931 pop. 3,939; 1951 census 4,886), central Midlothian, Scotland, on North Esk R. and 6 mi. SSE of Edinburgh; coal mining, limestone quarrying.

Loano (lôä′nô), village (pop. 2,539), Savona prov., Liguria, NW Italy, port on Gulf of Genoa and 6 mi. N of Albenga, in agr. region; fish canning; shoe mfg. Resort on Riviera di Ponente. Has palace (built 1578; now town hall).

Loan River (lô′än′), Chinese *Loan Kiang* or *Loan Chiang* (both: jyäng), NE Kiangsi prov., China, rises on Anhwei-Chekiang line, flows 130 mi. W, past Loping, joining Chang R. to form short Po R. at Poyang, on Poyang L.

Loa River (lō′ä), in Antofagasta and Tarapacá provs., N Chile, rises in the Andes at N foot of Miño Volcano near Bolivia border, flows c.275 mi. in U-shape S, W, and N, through the Atacama Desert, past Chiuchiu, Calama, and Toco, to the Pacific 45 mi. N of Tocopilla. Longest of Chilean rivers (Baker R., in extreme S, is about as long), it is not navigable, but it furnishes drinking water for Antofagasta, irrigates Calama and neighboring oases, and supplies hydroelectric power for nitrate and copper works.

Loay (lōī′), town (1939 pop. 1,774; 1948 municipality pop. 10,694), SW Bohol isl., Philippines, on Mindanao Sea, 11 mi. ESE of Tagbilaran; agr. center (rice, coconuts).

Loayza, Bolivia: see LURIBAY.

Loba, Brazo de, Colombia: see BRAZO DE LOBA.

Lobatera (lōbätā′rä), town (pop. 804), Táchira state, W Venezuela, in Andean outliers, 12 mi. N of San Cristóbal; coffeegrowing.

Lobato (lōōbä′tōō), N suburb of Salvador, E Bahia, Brazil, on Todos os Santos Bay; site of Brazil's 1st major oil field (discovered 1939), sometimes called Lobato-Joanes field.

Lobatsi (lōbä′tsē), town, ⊙ Lobatsi dist. (pop. 8,354), SE Bechuanaland Protectorate, near U. of So. Afr. border, 45 mi. N of Mafeking, on railroad; dairying. Hq. of Baralong tribe; hosp. Dist. includes Lobatsi block of farms (proclaimed crown land, 1904, now held by British South Africa Co.) and Baralong Farms native reserve (established 1895).

Lobau (lô′bou′), island, Lower Austria, in the Danube at Vienna. Scene (1809) of noted battle bet. Fr. and Austrian troops.

Löbau (lû′bou), town (pop. 15,361), Saxony, E central Germany, in Upper Lusatia, at NE foot of Lusatian Mts., 14 mi. WSW of Görlitz; rail junction; woolen and cotton milling, sugar refining, stone polishing; mfg. of pianos, glass, shoes, flour products. Has several late-Gothic churches. First mentioned 1221. Was member of Lusatian League, founded here in 1346.

Löbau, Poland: see LUBAWA.

Lobaye, Fr. Equatorial Africa: see M'BAÏKI.

Lobaye River (lōbäyā′), W and SW Ubangi-Shari, Fr. Equatorial Africa, rises just E of Bouar, flows 275 mi. SE and E to Ubangi R. just N of Mongoumba. Navigable c.40 mi. upstream.

Lobberich (lô′bûrĭkh), village (pop. 8,254), in former Prussian Rhine Prov., W Germany, after 1945 in North Rhine-Westphalia, 4 mi. NW of Süchteln; velvet mfg.

Lobbes (lôb), town (pop. 3,329), Hainaut prov., S Belgium, on Sambre R. and 9 mi. WSW of Charleroi; barge mfg.

Lobburi, Thailand: see LOPBURI.

Löbejün (lû′bûyün), town (pop. 3,918), in former Prussian Saxony prov., central Germany, after 1945 in Saxony-Anhalt, 11 mi. N of Halle, in coal-mining region; porphyry quarrying.

Loben, Poland: see LUBLINIEC.

Lobendava (lô′bĕndävä), Ger. *Lobendau* (lō′bûndou), village (pop. 687), N Bohemia, Czechoslovakia, 28 mi. NNE of Usti nad Labem, near Ger. border; mfg. of artificial flowers, feather ornaments.

Lobenstein (lō′bûn-shtīn), town (pop. 4,194), Thuringia, central Germany, in Franconian Forest, near the Thuringian Saale, 15 mi. NW of Hof; woodworking, cigar mfg. Spa.

Lobería (lōbārē′ä), town (pop. 7,865), ⊙ Lobería dist. (□ 2,010; pop. 27,825), S Buenos Aires prov., Argentina, 27 mi. N of Necochea; agr. center (grain, flax, cattle, sheep); flour milling.

Loberod (lû′bûrûd″), Swedish *Löberöd*, village (pop. 608), Malmohus co., S Sweden, 18 mi. ENE of Lund; grain, potatoes, sugar beets, stock.

Lobez (wô′bĕs), Pol. *Łobez*, Ger. *Labes* (lä′bûs), town (1939 pop. 7,322; 1946 pop. 2,064) in Pomerania, after 1945 in Szczecin prov., NW Poland, on the Rega and 30 mi. NE of Stargard; metalworking, limestone quarrying, flour milling, potato processing, mfg. of agr. implements. In Second World War, c.50% destroyed.

Lobith or **Lobit** (both: lō′bĭt), town (pop. 1,233), Gelderland prov., E Netherlands, 12 mi. SE of Arnhem, near Ger. border. Near by, on Rhine R., is border check point for river traffic to and from Germany.

Lobito (lōōbē′tōō), city (pop. 13,592), Benguela prov., W Angola, on Lobito Bay of the Atlantic, 240 mi. S of Luanda and 950 mi. W of Elisabethville (Belgian Congo); 12°21′S 13°32′E. W terminus of Benguela RR (crossing S central Africa to Beira on Indian Ocean, via the Rhodesias and S Belgian Congo) and one of best ports on W African coast. Bay is sheltered by a sandspit (3 mi. long, 400 yds. wide) along which modern town is expanding. Harbor, at bay's head, has ½ mi. of docking facilities for vessels drawing 30 ft. First harbor works date from 1905, recent improvements from Second World War. Exports include coffee, sisal, cotton, beeswax, hides and skins (from Angola's central plateau), and copper and allied minerals from Belgian Congo's Katanga prov. (for which Benguela RR is most direct route of access). Lobito is also important distributing center for European agr. settlements on plateau along railroad. Airport. Dry tropical climate. Development dates from completion of railroad (1929). Has cement plant, castor-oil processing.

Lobitos (lōbē′tōs), town (pop. 4,168), Piura dept., NW Peru, port on the Pacific, 8 mi. N of Talara, in petroleum area; oil-shipping center; petroleum storage. Power plant, machine shops; fisheries. Administration center for surrounding oil fields of EL ALTO, RESTÍN, CABO BLANCO.

Lob Nor or **Lop Nor** (both: lōb′ nôr′, lôp′ nôr′), Chinese *Lo-pu-no-erh*, marshy salt-lake depression, E Sinkiang prov., China, at E end of Tarim basin; c.40°N 90°E. Once occupied by the anc. Lop Nor (lake), it is now largely dried out, with only small periodic lakes receiving the shifting channels of Tarim R. The apparent wandering of the lake (the Lob Nor "problem"), caused by shifts in the lower course of the Tarim, was observed by the Russian explorer Przhevalski (1876–77) and Sven Hedin (1899–1902). In his last expedition (1928), Sven Hedin found lake at 40°30′N 90°30′E, occupying at times max. area 60 mi. long, 15–25 mi. wide.

Lobnya (lôb′nyŭ), town (1947 pop. over 500), N central Moscow oblast, Russian SFSR, 18 mi. NNW of Moscow; brickworks.

Lobón (lōvōn′), town (pop. 1,612), Badajoz prov., W Spain, on the Guadiana and 16 mi. WSW of Mérida; olives, cereals, grapes, asparagus; stock.

Lobos (lō′vōs), town (pop. 8,574), ⊙ Lobos dist. (□ 666; pop. 21,882), NE Buenos Aires prov., Argentina, 55 mi. SW of Buenos Aires; rail hub and agr. center (grain, flax, livestock); mfg.: canned milk, butter, cheese, footwear.

Lobos, Isla de (ē′slä dā lō′vōs), volcanic islet (□ 2.4; c.2 mi. long), Canary Isls., in La Bocayna channel, just off NE Fuerteventura. Supports a few fishermen. Lighthouse.

Lobos, Point (lō′bōs). **1** Promontory on S side of Golden Gate, at entrance to San Francisco Bay, W Calif. **2** Promontory on S shore of Carmel Bay, W Calif., S of Monterey Bay; state park.

Lobos, Punta de (pōōn′tä), cape, Montevideo dept., S Uruguay, on N bank of the Río de la Plata, guarding W gate of the port of Montevideo; 34°54′S 56°15′W.

Lobos Cay, Bahama Isls.: see CAY LOBOS.

Lobos Island (lō′vōs). **1** Island (□ 5½), in Gulf of California, off coast of Sonora, NW Mexico, 45 mi. SSE of Guaymas; low and sandy, 12 mi. long, c.1 mi. wide. Lighthouse on W coast, at Point Lobos (27°22′N 110°38′W). **2** Island, off Gulf coast of Veracruz, E Mexico, 10 mi. SE of Cabo Rojo; 21°28′N 97°13′W. Small coral reef.

Lobos Island. 1 Island off coast of Maldonado dept., S Uruguay, at mouth of the Río de la Plata, 10 mi. SSE of Maldonado city; 35°2′S 54°53′W. Said to have most powerful lighthouse in South America. Seals hunted on large scale. **2** Island at confluence of the Río Negro and Uruguay R., SW Uruguay, just SW of Vizcaíno Isl.; 1½ mi. wide, 3 mi. long.

Lobos Islands or **Seal Islands,** two groups of guano islands off Pacific coast of Lambayeque dept., NW Peru, 35 mi. apart. Largest and northernmost is Isla Lobos de Tierra (ē′slä lō′vōs dā tyĕ′rä) [Sp.,=landward seal island], 75 mi. NW of Puerto Eten and 10 mi. offshore; 6°28′S 80°52′W; 2 mi. wide, 6 mi. long. To S are the Islas Lobos de Afuera (äfwä′rä) [Sp.,=seaward seal islands], consisting of 2 isls. (each c.2 mi. long, 1½ mi. wide), separated by a narrow channel, 55 mi. W of Puerto Eten and 40 mi. offshore; 6°57′S 80°43′W.

Lobositz, Czechoslovakia: see LOVOSICE.

Lobsens, Poland: see LOBZENICA.

Lobster House, mountain (1,916 ft.), W central N.F., 14 mi. NNW of Buchans.

Lobster Lake, Piscataquis co., W central Maine, 27 mi. N of Greenville, just E of Moosehead L., in recreational area; irregularly shaped; 4 mi. long, 2 mi. wide.

Löbtau (lûp′tou), W suburb of Dresden, Saxony, E central Germany.

Loburg (lō′bōōrk), town (pop. 4,051), in former Prussian Saxony prov., central Germany, after 1945 in Saxony-Anhalt, 14 mi. SE of Burg; tanning, flour milling. Has old town gate, 18th-cent. town hall, remains of early-Gothic castle.

Loburn (lō′bûrn), village (pop. 256), ⊙ Ashley co. (□ 309; pop. 613), E S.Isl., New Zealand, 21 mi. NNW of Christchurch; sheep, fruit.

Lobutcha Creek (lōbōō′chŭ), central Miss., rises in NW Winston co., flows c.50 mi. SW to Pearl R. near Carthage.

Lobva (lôb′vŭ), town (1936 pop. estimate 5,200), W Sverdlovsk oblast, Russian SFSR, on Lobva R. (left tributary of Lyalya R.) and 10 mi. NNW (under jurisdiction) of Novaya Lyalya, on railroad; woodworking, sawmilling. Until 1928, Lobvinski Zavod.

Lobzenica (wôb″zhĕnē′tsä), Pol. *Łobżenica*, Ger. *Lobsens* (lôp′zûns), town (pop. 1,776), Bydgoszcz prov., NW Poland, 32 mi. WNW of Bydgoszcz; brewing, cement mfg.

Locarno (lōkär′nō), Ger. *Luggarus* (lōōgä′rōōs), town (1950 pop. 7,747), Ticino, S Switzerland, on Lago Maggiore, near mouth of Maggia R., 11 mi. W of Bellinzona; resort (mainly spring and fall) noted for its mild climate. Jewelry, chemicals, beer, flour, pastry; woodworking, printing. Italian-style architecture. Locarno Conference (1925) was held here. Old castle of dukes of Milan has town mus. Hills of Madonna del Sasso (1,165 ft.), with 15th-cent. church, and Monti della Trinità (1,325 ft.), with chapel, are N. Muralto and Minusio are E of town.

Locate Triulzi (lōkä'tĕ trēōōl'tsē), village (pop. 2,159), Milano prov., Lombardy, N Italy, 7 mi. S of Milan; meat and dairy products.

Locbinh (lŏk'bĭng'), town, Langson prov., N Vietnam, 12 mi. SE of Langson, on the Song Kikong (right headstream of Li R.); lignite mining.

Loccum (lô'kōōm), village (pop. 3,073), in former Prussian prov. of Hanover, W Germany, after 1945 in Lower Saxony, 13 mi. S of Nienburg. Has former Cistercian monastery (founded 1163), with Romanesque church.

Lochaber (lŏkh-ä'bûr), mountainous district of S Inverness, Scotland, bet. Great Glen of Scotland and Perthshire and Argyll. Includes Ben Nevis and numerous lochs, now connected by water tunnels, supplying power stations which form part of the Lochaber hydroelectric system. District, of noted scenic beauty, is celebrated in Allan Ramsay's *Farewell to Lochaber*.

Lo Chacón (lō chäkōn'), town (pop. 1,061), Santiago prov., central Chile, 3 mi. SW of El Monte, near Maipo R.

Lochalsh, Scotland: see KYLE.

Lo-ch'ang, China: see LOKCHONG.

Lochauer Heide, Germany: see MÜHLBERG.

Lochboisdale (lŏkh-boiz'dāl), fishing port, chief town of SOUTH UIST, Inverness, Scotland, at head of Loch Boisdale (4 mi. long, up to 2 mi. wide), on SE coast of isl. Site of radio station.

Lochbroom, parish (pop. 2,004), NW Ross and Cromarty, Scotland. Includes ULLAPOOL.

Lochbuie (lŏkh-bū'ē), village on MULL, Scotland.

Lochcarron (lŏkh-kă'rŭn) or **Jeantown**, fishing village and parish (pop. 967), W Ross and Cromarty, Scotland, at head of Loch Carron (15-mi.-long inlet of the Inner Sound), 13 mi. NE of Kyle.

Lochee, Scotland: see DUNDEE.

Lochem (lō'khŭm), town (pop. 6,531), Gelderland prov., E Netherlands, on Berkel R., on Twente Canal and 9 mi. E of Zutphen; meat packing, leather tanning, mfg. of industrial belting, chemicals, dyes, fertilizer, organs; dairy products.

Lo-ch'eng, China: see LOSHING.

Loches (lôsh), town (pop. 4,102), Indre-et-Loire dept., W central France, on Indre R. and 23 mi. SE of Tours; agr. trade center (vegetables, mushrooms, fruits). An unusually picturesque old town with tortuous streets and wooden houses. Has a feudal castle (important medieval stronghold and residence of early kings of France) which encloses part of the old dist. within its walls and contains tomb of Agnès Sorel; its dungeon became a dreaded state prison under Louis XI. Alfred de Vigny b. here.

Lochfoot, Scotland: see LOCHRUTTON.

Loch Garman, Ireland: see WEXFORD.

Lochgelly (lŏkh-gĕ'lē), burgh (1931 pop. 9,298; 1951 census 9,102), S central Fifeshire, Scotland, 6 mi. W of Kirkcaldy; coal mining.

Lochgilphead (lŏkh-gĭlp'hĕd), burgh (1931 pop. 974; 1951 census 1,229), central Argyll, Scotland, at head of Loch Gilp (1-mi.-long inlet of Loch Fyne), on Crinan Canal, and 20 mi. WNW of Dunoon, agr. market in sheep-raising region.

Lochgoilhead (lŏkh-goil'hĕd), cod-fishing village, SE Argyll, Scotland, at head of Loch Goil, 15 mi. N of Dunoon.

Lo-chiang, China: see LOKIANG.

Lochih (lô'jŭ'), town (pop. 45,496), ⊙ Lochih co. (pop. 423,475), central Szechwan prov., China, 60 mi. ESE of Chengtu; cotton textiles; rice, sweet potatoes, wheat, beans, indigo. Saltworks near by.

Lo-ch'ing, China: see YOTSING.

Lochinver (lŏkh-ĭn'vûr), village (pop. c.200), SW Sutherland, Scotland, on Loch Inver (3-mi.-long sea inlet), 18 mi. N of Ullapool; tourist and angling resort.

Loch Lynn Heights, Md.: see LOCK LYNN.

Lochmaben (lŏkh-mā'bŭn), burgh (1931 pop. 1,014; 1951 census 1,127), central Dumfries, Scotland, 8 mi. NE of Dumfries; agr. market. Has ruins of 14th-cent. castle of Robert Bruce. Near by are several small lakes.

Lochmaddy, Scotland: see NORTH UIST.

Lochmoor, Mich.: see GROSSE POINTE WOODS.

Lochnagar (lŏkh-nŭgär'), peak (3,768 ft.) of Grampian Mts., SW Aberdeen, Scotland, 7 mi. ESE of Braemar.

Loch Ness, Scotland: see NESS, LOCH.

Loch Raven Dam (lŏk″ rā'vŭn), N Md., in Gunpowder Falls (stream) near Cub Hill; 75 ft. high, 650 ft. long, completed 1922. It impounds Loch Raven Reservoir (c.10 mi. long) for water supply to Baltimore.

Lochristi (lō-khrĭ'stē), village (pop. 5,193), East Flanders prov., NW Belgium, 6 mi. NE of Ghent; vegetables, flowers; tree nurseries. Formerly spelled Loochristi or Loochristy.

Lochrutton (lŏkh-rŭ'tŭn), parish (pop. 453), E Kirkcudbright, Scotland. Includes agr. village of Lochfoot, at N end of Lochrutton Loch (1 mi. long, ½ mi. wide), 5 mi. WSW of Dumfries.

Lochsa River, Idaho: see CLEARWATER RIVER.

Loch Sheldrake (lŏk″ shĕl'drāk), resort village, Sullivan co., SE N.Y., on small Loch Sheldrake, 5 mi. SE of Liberty.

Lo-ch'uan, China: see LOCHWAN.

Lochwan or **Lo-ch'uan** (both: lŭ'chwän'), town, ⊙ Lochwan co. (pop. 59,770), N central Shensi prov., China, 50 mi. S of Yenan, near Lo R.; petroleum fields, saltworks.

Lochwinnoch (lŏkh-wĭ'nŭkh), town and parish (pop. 3,868), W Renfrew, Scotland, at SW end of Castle Semple Loch (2 mi. long), 6 mi. SW of Johnstone; silk milling and printing. Near by is 16th-cent. Peel Castle. Black Cart Water rises in Castle Semple Loch.

Lochy, Loch (lŏkh lŏkh'ē), lake (10 mi. long, 1½ mi. wide; 531 ft. deep), SW Inverness, Scotland, bet. lochs Oich (NE) and Linnhe (SW); forms part of Caledonian Canal.

Lockbourne (lŏk'bûrn), village (pop. 376), Franklin co., central Ohio, 10 mi. S of Columbus. Lockbourne Air Force Base here.

Locke, village (pop. c.400), Cayuga co., W central N.Y., in Finger Lakes region, 20 mi. SSE of Auburn; feed, lumber. Millard Fillmore was b. here.

Locke, Mount, Texas: see DAVIS MOUNTAINS.

Locke Mills, Maine: see GREENWOOD.

Lockenhaus (lôk'ŭnhous), Hung. *Léka* (lā'kō), village (pop. 1,127), Burgenland, E Austria, 15 mi. NNW of Szombathely, Hungary; furniture mfg.

Lockeport (lŏk'pôrt), town (pop. 1,084), SW N.S., on Lockeport Harbour (8 mi. long) of the Atlantic, 50 mi. ESE of Yarmouth; herring-fishing center; fish canneries.

Lockerbie (lŏ'kûrbē), burgh (1931 pop. 2,574; 1951 census 2,623), S central Dumfries, Scotland, 10 mi. ENE of Dumfries; agr. market, with woolen mills; scene of large sheep and cattle fairs. Near-by Dryfe Sands was scene of last clan fight (1593) on border. Lockerbie is surrounded by extensive agr. parish of Dryfesdale (pop. 3,343).

Lockesburg, town (pop. 714), Sevier co., SW Ark., 10 mi. ESE of De Queen, in truck-farm area.

Lockhart, town (pop. 898), S New South Wales, Australia, 135 mi. W of Canberra; sheep and agr. center.

Lockhart. 1 Town (pop. 819), Covington co. S Ala., 22 mi. SSE of Andalusia, near Fla. line; woodworking. **2** Village (pop. 1,685), Union co., NW S.C., on Broad R. and 18 mi. ESE of Spartanburg; textile mills. **3** City (pop. 5,573), ⊙ Caldwell co., S central Texas, 27 mi. S of Austin, in dairying, agr. area (cotton, truck, corn); mfg. (mattresses, clothing, furniture, leather products, dairy products). Oil fields near. Lockhart State Park (just NE) is on site of battle of Plum Creek (1840), Texan victory over Comanche Indians. Founded 1848, inc. 1870.

Lock Haven, city (pop. 11,381), ⊙ Clinton co., N central Pa., 20 mi. WSW of Williamsport and on West Branch of Susquehanna R.; mfg. (airplanes, paper, textiles, furniture, chemicals, metal products, bricks); railroad shops, tannery; clay pits. State teachers col. here. Settled 1769, laid out c.1833, inc. as borough 1840, as city 1870.

Lockington, village (pop. 245), Shelby co., W Ohio, on Great Miami R. and 4 mi. N of Piqua.

Lockland, city (pop. 5,736), Hamilton co., extreme SW Ohio, just NNE of Cincinnati; produces airplane engines, paving and roofing materials, insulation, electrical machinery, containers, furniture, pulp and paper, steel castings, chemicals, fertilizer. Platted 1828, inc. 1865.

Lock Lynn or **Loch Lynn Heights** (lŏk″ lĭn'), town (pop. 415), Garrett co., W Md., in the Alleghenies just SE of Oakland.

Lockney, town (pop. 1,692), Floyd co., NW Texas, on the Llano Estadaco, c.45 mi. NE of Lubbock, near White R.; market, processing, shipping point for alfalfa, wheat, cotton area; cottonseed-oil and feed mills. Settled 1894, inc. 1907.

Löcknitz (lûk'nĭts), village (pop. 3,623), in former Prussian Pomerania prov., N Germany, after 1945 in Mecklenburg, 13 mi. W of Stettin; tobacco, sugar beets, grain, stock.

Lockport. 1 City (pop. 4,955), Will co., NE Ill., 5 mi. N of Joliet, at locks connecting Sanitary and Ship Canal with Des Plaines R.; locks of old Illinois and Michigan Canal are also here. In agr. and bituminous-coal area; mfg. (cereal, petroleum products). Seat of Lewis Col. of Science and Technology. The state prison is near by. Laid out 1837, inc. 1853. **2** Town (pop. 102), Henry co., N Ky., on Kentucky R. and 18 mi. NNW of Frankfort. Zinc and lead mines near. **3** Village (pop. 1,388), Lafourche parish, SE La., 34 mi. SW of New Orleans and on Bayou Lafourche; sugar milling; mfg. of concrete and machine-shop products, beverages. **4** Industrial city (pop. 25,133), ⊙ Niagara co., W N.Y., on the Barge Canal and 20 mi. NNE of Buffalo; trade center with varied mfg., including radiators, paper products, flour, textiles, steel, automobile parts, machinery, hardware, chemicals, canned foods, vending machines, cider and vinegar; leather, wood, and glass products, cosmetics, wallboard, thermostats; also printing; stone products. Settled 1816; inc. as village in 1829, as city in 1865. Grew around locks in old Erie Canal.

Lockridge, town (pop. 233), Jefferson co., SE Iowa, 11 mi. E of Fairfield, in coal-mining area.

Lock Springs, town (pop. 137), Daviess co., NW Mo., near Grand R., 12 mi. WNW of Chillicothe.

Lockstedter Lager (lôk'shtĕ″tûr lä'gûr), town (pop. 4,632), in Schleswig-Holstein, NW Germany, 5 mi. NE of Itzehoe, at S end of noted former military training camp. Developed industrially after 1946. Mfg. of chemicals, textiles, shoes, metal and leather goods, tobacco products; woodworking.

Lockwood, England: see HUDDERSFIELD.

Lockwood, city (pop. 791), Dade co., SW Mo., near Sac R., 38 mi. NE of Joplin; agr.; limestone quarries, coal mines.

Lockwood, Cape, W Ellesmere Isl., NE Franklin Dist., Northwest Territories, on Greely Fjord; 80°29′N 82°55′W.

Lockwood Island (6 mi. long, 5 mi. wide), in Arctic Ocean, just off Peary Land region, N Greenland; 83°23′N 39°30′W; rises to 2,461 ft. Discovered (May, 1882) by Lockwood and Brainard of Greely expedition.

Locle, Le (lŭ lô'klŭ), town (1950 pop. 12,058), Neuchâtel canton, W Switzerland, 9 mi. NW of Neuchâtel, 2 mi. from Fr. border, in the Jura; alt. 3,040 ft. Large watch mfg. center; chocolate, biscuits, metalworking. Art gall., historical mus.

Locmariaquer (lôkmärēäkâr'), village (pop. 654), Morbihan dept., W France, 11 mi. SW of Vannes; oyster beds. Numerous megalithic monuments, including well-preserved dolmens and a giant menhir, attract tourists.

Locminé (lôkmēnā'), town (pop. 2,337), Morbihan dept., W France, 16 mi. NNW of Vannes; cattle market; hosiery and lingerie mfg.

Locninh (lŏk'nĭng'), town, Thudaumot prov., S Vietnam, railroad terminus 75 mi. N of Saigon, near Cambodia line rubber plantations.

Loco (lō'kō), city (pop. 236), Stephens co., S Okla., 20 mi. SE of Duncan, in agr. area.

Locorotondo (lô″kôrôtôn'dô), town (pop. 3,845), Bari prov., Apulia, S Italy, 14 mi. SSE of Monopoli; wine making.

Locri (lô'krē), town (pop. 5,259), Reggio di Calabria prov., Calabria, S Italy, port on Ionian Sea, 3 mi. SSW of Siderno Marina; bathing resort; olive oil refining, wine making, mfg. (furniture, bricks). Lignite and barite mines, hot mineral baths near by. Town badly damaged by earthquakes (1907–08). Called Gerace Marina until 1934. Has archaeological mus. with finds from anc. Locri Epizephyrii, a colony of Greek Locris, founded in 7th cent. B.C. Its ruins, 2 mi. SW, on coast, include temples, town walls, extensive necropolis.

Locris (lō'krĭs), anc. state of E central Greece, in existence before the coming of the Phocians. The rise of Doris and Phocis split the original region into W and E portions. Western (Ozolaean or Ozolian) Locris extended along N coast of Gulf of Corinth, W of the Parnassus. Its chief centers were Amphissa and Naupactus. Eastern Locris, along the Malian Gulf and Gulf of Euboea bet. Thermopylae and Larymna, was split (6th cent. B.C.) by Phocis into Epicnemedian (Hypoenemedian; W) and Opuntian (E) Locris. Largely hemmed in by stronger states, the Locrians played a minor role in Greek history. However, they founded one of the earliest Greek colonies in S Italy, Locri Epizephyrii (modern Locri).

Locroja (lōkrō'hä), town (pop. 1,300), Huancavelica dept., S central Peru, in Cordillera Central, 41 mi. ENE of Huancavelica; grain, sugar cane, cattle.

Löcse, Czechoslovakia: see LEVOCA.

Loctudy (lôktüdē'), village (pop. 1,307), Finistère dept., W France, fishing port on N Bay of Biscay, 13 mi. SSW of Quimper; iodine mfg. Bathing resort.

Locumba (lōkōōm'bä), town (pop. 634), Tacna dept., S Peru, on Locumba R. and 40 mi. NW of Tacna; winegrowing, stock raising; wine and liquor distilling. Until 1929, ⊙ Tacna dept.

Locumba River, Tacna dept., S Peru, rises at S foot of Tutupaca Volcano, flows c.100 mi. SW, past Curibaya and Locumba, to the Pacific 30 mi. SE of Ilo. Used for irrigation.

Locust, town (pop. 216), Stanly co., S central N.C., 23 mi. E of Charlotte.

Locust Creek, in S Iowa and N Mo., rises 10 mi. SE of Corydon in Wayne co. (Iowa), flows c.85 mi. S, into Mo., to Grand R. 2 mi. W of Sumner.

Locust Fork, stream, rises near Boaz, NE Ala., flows c.110 mi. SW to Mulberry Fork c.20 mi. W of Birmingham, forming Black Warrior R.

Locust Gap, village (pop. 1,041), Northumberland co., E central Pa., 14 mi. NW of Pottsville.

Locust Grove. 1 Town (pop. 405), Henry co., N central Ga., 11 mi. NE of Griffin. **2** Town (pop. 730), Mayes co., NE Okla., 45 mi. E of Tulsa, in stock-raising and agr. area.

Locust Valley, residential village (1940 pop. 2,534), Nassau co., SE N.Y., near N shore of W Long Isl., 3 mi. E of Glen Cove, in resort area; mfg. (cables, wire).

Lod, Palestine: see LYDDA.

Loda (lō'dŭ), village (pop. 559), Iroquois co., E Ill., 15 mi. SE of Bloomington; agr. (grain, poultry).

Lodar, Laudar, or **Lawdar** (all: lōdär'), chief town of Audhali sultanate, Western Aden Protectorate, on road and 40 mi. NNE of Shuqra; airfield; market center. Sultan's residence is at town of Zara, 3 mi. SSW.

Loddington, village and parish (pop. 307), N central Northampton, England, 3 mi. W of Kettering; ironstone quarrying. Has 13th-cent. church.

Loddon, town and parish (pop. 1,017), SE Norfolk, England, 11 mi. SE of Norwich; agr. market. Has flint church, built c.1480.

Loddon River (lŏ'dŭn), central Victoria, Australia, rises in Great Dividing Range, near Creswick, flows 155 mi. N, past Bridgewater and Kerang, to Murray R. 20 mi. E of Swan Hill; used for irrigation; frequently dry.

Loddon River, Hampshire and Berkshire, England, rises at Basingstoke, flows 30 mi. NE to the Thames at Wargrave. Receives Blackwater R.

Lodeinoye Pole or **Lodeynoye Pole** (lŭdyā'nŭyŭ pô'lyĭ), city (1939 pop. over 10,000), NE Leningrad oblast, Russian SFSR, on Svir R. and 125 mi. ENE of Leningrad; railroad shops, machine works, sawmills. Site of Olonets shipyards (founded 1702 by Peter the Great), in operation until 1830s. Chartered 1785. During Second World War, a Rus. front-line position (1941–44).

Lodelinsart (lôdlĕsär'), town (pop. 11,275), Hainaut prov., S central Belgium, 2 mi. N of Charleroi; glass mfg.

Löderburg (lû'dûrbŏŏrk), village (pop. 4,182), in former Prussian Saxony prov., central Germany, after 1945 in Saxony-Anhalt, 3 mi. NW of Stassfurt; lignite and potash mining.

Loderup (lû'dûrŭp"), Swedish *Löderup*, village (pop. 585), Kristianstad co., S Sweden, near Baltic, 12 mi. SW of Simrishamn; grain, sugar beets, potatoes, stock.

Lodève (lôdĕv'), anc. *Luteva* and *Forum Neronis*, town (pop. 5,908), Hérault dept., S France, at foot of the Cévennes, 27 mi. N of Béziers; woolen-milling center; fertilizer mfg., metalworking, olive-oil pressing. Has 14th-cent. church. Was one of chief towns of Septimania. Episcopal see from 4th cent. to 1790.

Lodeynoye Pole, Russian SFSR: see LODEINOYE POLE.

Lodge, town (pop. 316), Colleton co., S central S.C., 30 mi. S of Orangeburg; lumber.

Lodge Grass, town (pop. 536), Big Horn co., S Mont., on Little Bighorn R. and 30 mi. SSE of Hardin; trading point for ranching region.

Lodgepole, village (pop. 555), Cheyenne co., W Nebr., 20 mi. E of Sidney and on Lodgepole Creek; dairying, livestock, grain.

Lodgepole Creek, in Wyo., Nebr., and Colo.; rises in SE Wyo. at alt. of 8,000 ft.; flows 212 mi. E, past Kimball, Sidney, and Chappell, W Nebr., to S. Platte R. near Julesburg, Colo.

Lodhran (lō'drän), village, Multan dist., S Punjab, W Pakistan, 45 mi. SSE of Multan; rail junction; wheat, millet, dates; cotton ginning, oilseed milling, soap mfg.

Lodi (lôdē'), village (pop. 521), Alger dept., N central Algeria, on railroad and 3 mi. W of Médéa; winegrowing. Plaster mfg. at Mouzaïa-les-Mines (4 mi. NNW).

Lodi (lô'dē), town (pop. 23,305), Milano prov., Lombardy, N Italy, on Adda R. and 18 mi. SE of Milan. Agr. and industrial center; dairy and meat products, cattle feed, fertilizer, farm machinery, furniture, bricks; flour, rice, and textile mills, tanneries. Bishopric. Has 12th-cent. cathedral and 15th-cent. church of the Incoronata. Founded by Frederick Barbarossa in 1158, after destruction of old Lodi (Lodi Vecchio) by Milan in 1155. Here in 1796 Napoleon defeated Austrians.

Lodi (lō'dī). **1** City (pop. 13,798), San Joaquin co., central Calif., on Mokelumne R. and 13 mi. N of Stockton, at N tip of San Joaquin Valley; wine center in grape-producing area; also fruit and vegetable packing and canning; mfg. of olive oil, machinery, pumps, concrete. Inc. 1906. **2** Industrial borough (pop. 15,392), Bergen co., NE N.J., just NE of Passaic; dye works, mfg. (machinery, metal cloth, chemicals, textiles, clothing, toys, confectionery). Has a jr. col. **3** Village (pop. 362), Seneca co., W central N.Y., in Finger Lakes region, 20 mi. NW of Ithaca, near Seneca L.; summer resort. **4** Village (pop. 1,523), Medina co., N Ohio, 27 mi. WSW of Akron and on East Branch of Black R.; trade center for agr. area; dairy products, fertilizer, wheelbarrows, wood novelties. **5** City (pop. 1,416), Columbia co., S central Wis., on small Spring Creek and 18 mi. NNW of Madison, in diversified-farming area; cheese, chocolate, canned foods. Inc. as village in 1872, as city in 1941.

Lodi Vecchio (lô'dē vĕk'kyô), anc. *Laus Pompeia*, village (pop. 2,730), Milano prov., Lombardy, N Italy, 4 mi. W of LODI; cheese factories, flour and rice mills.

Lodja (lō'jä), village, Kasai prov., central Belgian Congo, on right bank of Lukenie R. and 100 mi. N of Lusambo; terminus of steamboat navigation; trading center; cotton ginning, rice milling. Has R.C. mission, hosp. for Europeans.

Lodomeria, Ukraine: see VLADIMIR-VOLYNSKIY.

Lodore, Canyon of, Colo.: see DINOSAUR NATIONAL MONUMENT.

Lodore, Falls of, England: see DERWENTWATER.

Lodosa (lō-dhō'sä), town (pop. 3,970), Navarre prov., N Spain, on the Ebro and 20 mi. E of Logroño, in irrigated agr. area (cereals, wine, fruit, pepper). Sawmilling, olive-oil processing, tanning; mfg. of soap, fertilizers, brandy, plaster. Hydroelectric plant near by. Cave dwellings in area.

Lodosa Canal, in Navarre and Saragossa prov., N Spain, parallels the Ebro for c.50 mi.; used for irrigation.

Lods (lō), village (pop. 402), Doubs dept., E France, on the Loue and 11 mi. NNW of Pontarlier, in the central Jura; forges.

Lodwar (lō'dwär), village, Northern Frontier Prov., NW Kenya, on Turkwell R., on road, and 150 mi. NNE of Kitale; 3°12'N 35°46'E; stock raising; peanuts, sesame, corn. Airfield. Hq. Turkana dist. (since 1946 in Northern Frontier Prov.), formerly extra-provincial dist. along W shore of L. Rudolf.

Lodz (lōdz, lŏdz, lŏŏj), Pol. *Łódź* (wŏŏj), Rus. *Lodz* or *Lodz'* (both: lô'tsyŭ), province [Pol. *województwo*] (□ 6,503; 1946 pop., minus Lodz city, 1,518,447), central Poland; ⊙ Lodz. Hilly plateau in S, sloping to undulating plain (N); drained by Warta, Pilica, Prosna, and Bzura rivers. Cotton milling, principal industry of prov., is concentrated in larger cities (Lodz, Piotrkow, Pabianice, Tomaszow, Zgierz). Principal crops are rye, potatoes, oats, barley, rapeseed; stock raising is important. Boundaries of pre-Second World War prov. (□ 7,349; 1931 pop. 2,632,010) were changed by transfer of territory to Kielce, Poznan, and Warszawa provs. Includes greater part of former Petrokov (Piotrkow) and Kalish (Kalisz) govts. of Rus. Poland. Lodz city has status of autonomous prov.

Lodz, Pol. *Łódź*, Rus. *Lodz* or *Lodz'*, city (□ 80; 1950 pop. estimate 622,500), central Poland, ⊙, but independent of, Lodz prov., 75 mi. WSW of Warsaw; 51°46'N 19°25'E. Second-largest city of Poland; rail junction; airport; center of Pol. textile industry; mfg. of clothing, dyes, leather goods, electrical goods, metalware, machinery, paper, bldg. material; food and tobacco processing, sawmilling, printing. Has univ. (1945). Its checkerboard pattern of narrow streets hinders traffic; large stone buildings stand next to falling wooden houses and only its S sections have villas and parks. The youngest of the large Pol. cities, inc. in early-15th cent.; passed (1793) to Prussia and (1815) to Russia. In 1827, pop. was 339; city developed rapidly when govt. brought Ger. weavers here and to surrounding towns. Although situated on a watershed, far from large rivers, the presence of small but fast-flowing streams (used to move machinery) and forests (used for fuel) favored its industrial growth. Steam engines installed in mid-19th cent., railroad built in 1866. In First World War, after battle fought near by, fell to Germans in 1914; restored to Poland in 1919. In Second World War, Lodz again fell (1939) to Germans, who included it in Wartheland and named it Litzmannstadt. Although it had a Ger. pop. of less than 9%, it was subjected to ruthless Germanization; it is estimated that 250,000 Jews and 150,000 Poles were evacuated and 150,000 Germans (of whom 24,321 remained in 1946) moved in. City suffered relatively little war damage.

Loe Band (lō'ā bänd'), village, Zhob dist., NE Baluchistan, W Pakistan, 110 mi. W of Fort Sandeman, on Afghan border; control post for traveling merchants.

Loèche, Switzerland: see LEUK.

Loèche-les-Bains, Switzerland: see LEUKERBAD.

Loeches (lōĕ'chĕs), town (pop. 835), Madrid prov., central Spain, 15 mi. E of Madrid; noted spa with several mineral springs. Has gypsum quarries. Region produces olives, cereals, grapes, livestock.

Loe Dakka, Afghanistan: see DAKKA.

Loei or **Loey** (lû'ē), town (1947 pop. 4,717), ⊙ Loei prov. (□ 4,344; 1947 pop. 134,202), N central Thailand, on NW edge of Korat Plateau, on Loei R. (minor affluent of the Mekong) and 100 mi. NW of Khonkaen; rice, cotton, lac. Gold mining at Chiang Khan (N).

Loemadjang, Indonesia: see LUMAJANG.

Loenen (lōō'nŭn), village (pop. 841), Utrecht prov., W central Netherlands, on Vecht R. and 9 mi. NNW of Utrecht, on Merwede Canal, in Loosdrechtsche Plassen lake area; lake fishing, water sports; limekilns.

Loenhout (lōōn'hout), agr. village (pop. 2,713), Antwerp prov., N Belgium, near Netherlands border, 16 mi. NE of Antwerp.

Loen Lake (lō'ŭn), Nor. *Loenvatn*, lake (□ 4) in a fissure of the glacier Jostedalsbre, Sogn og Fjordane co., W Norway; extends c.7 mi. SE from Loen village (pop. 137) at head of Nord Fjord in Stryn canton, 65 mi. ENE of Floro. Tourist area. Landslide in 1905 caused waves that threw a steamer 300 ft. onto a mountainside, where it still reposes. Near by, 8 mi. SE, is highest point of the Jostedalsbre (6,700 ft.).

Loevestein, Netherlands: see BOMMELWAARD.

Loey, Thailand: see LOEI.

Lofao Mountains (lô'fou'), Mandarin *Lofu* (lŭ'fōō'), S Kwangtung prov., China, extend 60 mi. SW from Hoyün to Tsengshing bet. Tseng and East rivers. Rises to over 1,300 ft. at Mt. Lofao (SW), site of numerous temples. Sometimes spelled Lohfau.

Lofa River (lō'fä), W Liberia, rises on Fr. Guinea border, flows c.200 mi. SW to the Atlantic 30 mi. WNW of Monrovia. Forms boundary bet. Grand Cape Mount and Montserrado counties. Sometimes spelled Loffa; sometimes called Little Cape Mount R.

Lofer (lō'fûr), village (pop. 1,411), Salzburg, W Austria, on river Saalach and 22 mi. SW of Salzburg, near Ger. border; furniture mfg., brewery; summer resort (alt. 2,096 ft.).

Loffa River, Liberia: see LOFA RIVER.

Löffingen (lû'fĭng-ŭn), village (pop. 1,524), S Baden, Germany, in Black Forest, 6 mi. ESE of Neustadt; woodworking, lumber milling. Summer resort (alt. 2,638 ft.) and pilgrimage center.

Lofley, Cape, S point of Alexandra Land, Franz Josef Land, Russian SFSR, in Arctic Ocean; 80°27'N 45°30'E.

Lofoten Islands (lōfō'tŭn, Nor. lōō'fōōtŭn), group (□ c.550; pop. c.30,000) in the North Sea, Nordland co., N Norway, 1–50 mi. off the mainland, entirely within the Arctic Circle, and just S of the VESTERALEN group; 67°25'-68°29'N 11°53'-15°11'E. Isls. include Austvagoy, Vestvagoy, Moskenesoy, Flakstadoy, Vaeroy, and Rost; separated from mainland by Vest Fjord. Straits bet. isls. are noted for violent tidal currents, especially in the Maelstrom or Moskenstraum. Washed by North Atlantic Drift, isls. have unusually mild climate. Surface is mountainous, rising to c.3,000 ft.; there are extensive marsh regions. Offshore shoals provide one of world's richest cod- and herring-fishing grounds. The numerous Lofoten fishing villages have extensive fish-drying and -curing establishments. Chief town: Svolvaer, on Austvagoy. The Lofotens are sometimes considered, in a larger sense, to include the Vesteralen group.

Loftus, urban district (1931 pop. 7,631; 1951 census 7,423), North Riding, NE Yorkshire, England, 8 mi. ESE of Redcar; iron and steel mills.

Lofty, Mount, Australia: see MOUNT LOFTY RANGES.

Lofu Mountains, China: see LOFAO MOUNTAINS.

Log, Russian SFSR: see LOGOVSKI.

Loga (lō'gä), village (pop. 306) in Nes canton (pop. 2,310), Vest-Agder co., S Norway, on railroad and 2 mi. N of Flekkefjord; textile milling. At Fjeldsa (fyĕlt'sä) (Nor. *Fjeldså*, *Fjelså*, or *Fjeldse*) village (pop. 142), 3 mi. SSW, leather tanning. At Drangeid (dräng'ād) village (pop. 393), 1 mi. S, mfg. of wood products.

Logan, Russian SFSR: see KASPISKI.

Logan (lō'gŭn). **1** County (□ 727; pop. 20,260), W Ark.; ⊙ Booneville and Paris. Bounded N by Arkansas R.; drained by Petit Jean R. Agr. (fruit, truck, cotton, corn, potatoes, livestock; dairy products); timber. Coal mining, sawmilling, cotton ginning. Hunting, fishing. Magazine Mtn. is in co. Formed 1873 as Sarber co., renamed 1874. **2** County (□ 1,827; pop. 17,187), NE Colo.; ⊙ Sterling. Irrigated agr. area, bordering on Nebr.; drained by South Platte R. Sugar beets, beans, livestock. Formed 1887. **3** County (□ 622; pop. 30,671), central Ill.; ⊙ Lincoln. Agr. (corn, wheat, soybeans, hay, oats, livestock, poultry). Bituminous-coal mining; timber. Some mfg. (china, cigars, dairy products, caskets). Drained by Salt and Kickapoo creeks and small Sugar Creek. Formed 1839. **4** County (□ 1,073; pop. 4,206), W Kansas; ⊙ Russell Springs. Farming and grazing area, drained by Smoky Hill R. Formed 1887. **5** County (□ 563; pop. 22,335), S Ky.; ⊙ Russellville. Bounded S by Tenn.; drained by Mud and Red rivers and several creeks. Rolling agr. area (dark tobacco, corn, wheat, livestock, poultry, dairy products). Bituminous coal and asphalt mines, timber, stone quarries. Some mfg. at Russellville. Formed 1792. **6** County (□ 570; pop. 1,357), central Nebr.; ⊙ Stapleton; farming area. Livestock, grain. Formed 1885. **7** County (□ 1,003; pop. 6,357), S N.Dak.; ⊙ Napoleon; agr. area watered by Beaver Creek. Livestock, grain, dairy products. Formed 1873. **8** County (□ 461; pop. 31,329), W central Ohio; ⊙ Bellefontaine. Drained by Great Miami and Mad rivers and small Mill and Rush creeks. Includes Indian Lake State Park (resort) and Campbell Hill (1,550 ft.), state's highest point. Agr. area (livestock, dairy products, grain); mfg. at Bellefontaine; limestone quarries, sand and gravel pits. Formed 1817. **9** County (□ 747; pop. 22,170), central Okla.; ⊙ Guthrie. Intersected by Cimarron R. and by small Ephraim and Cottonwood creeks. Diversified agr. (grain, cotton, fruit); stock raising; dairying. Some mfg. at Guthrie. Oil and gas wells; gasoline mfg. Formed 1890. **10** County (□ 456; pop. 77,391), SW W.Va.; ⊙ Logan. On Allegheny Plateau; drained by Guyandot R. Bituminous coal-mining region; natural-gas fields; timber; some agr. (livestock, fruit, tobacco). Formed 1824.

Logan. **1** Village, Franklin co., Ill.: see HANAFORD. **2** Town (pop. 1,550), ⊙ Harrison co., W Iowa, on Boyer R. and 26 mi. N of Council Bluffs; mfg. of school supplies. Settled as Boyer Falls; named Logan 1864; inc. 1876. **3** City (pop. 859), Phillips co., N Kansas, on North Fork Solomon R. and 15 mi. WSW of Phillipsburg, in grain, cattle area; farm equipment. **4** Village (pop. c.150), Gallatin co., SW Mont., on Gallatin R., near Missouri R., and 25 mi. NW of Bozeman, in grain region. **5** Village, Quay co., E N.Mex., on Canadian R., near Texas line, and 21 mi. NE of Tucumcari; trading point in ranching region. **6** City (pop. 5,972), ⊙ Hocking co., S central Ohio, 34 mi. SW of Zanesville, and on Hocking R., in rich agr. area; shoes, foundry products, pottery, tools, flour, lumber. Coal mines, oil and gas wells. Founded 1816, inc. 1839. **7** City (pop. 16,832), ⊙ Cache co., N Utah, on branch of Little Bear R. and 35 mi. N of Ogden, in Cache Valley; alt. 4,535 ft. Trade and industrial center for irrigated agr. area (sugar beets, truck, grain); food-processing (flour, condensed milk, feed, beverages, candy), mfg. of textiles, mattresses, foundry products; oil refining. State agr. col., Mormon tabernacle, Logan Temple (also Mormon; completed 1884), and hq. of near-by Cache Natl. Forest are here. Logan Canyon and Logan Peak (9,713 ft.) are in Wasatch Range, just E. City laid out 1859 by Mormons, inc. 1866. **8** City (pop. 5,079), ⊙ Logan co., SW W.Va., on Guyandot R. and 40 mi. SW of Charleston, in coal-mining, lumbering, agr. (fruit, tobacco, livestock) region; trade center; ships coal; gas wells, lumber mills.

Logan, Mount. 1 Peak (3,700 ft.), E Que., on NW Gaspé Peninsula, in Shickshock Mts., 40 mi. E of Matane. **2** Peak (19,850 ft.), SW Yukon, near Alaska border, in St. Elias Mts., highest peak of Canada and 2d highest in North America, 180 mi. W of Whitehorse, N of the Seward Glacier; 60°34′N 140°24′W. Climbed 1925 by party headed by A. H. McCarthy and H. F. Lambert.

Logan Creek, E Nebr., rises in Wayne co., flows 112 mi. SSE and S, past Wakefield, Pender, and Lyons, to Elkhorn R. near Hooper.

Logan Glacier, S Alaska, in St. Elias Mts. glacier system, extends 65 mi. WNW from Mt. Logan, near 60°50′N 141°W; 3 mi. wide. Flows into Chitina R.

Logan Pass (alt. 6,664 ft.), NW Mont., in Lewis Range, near center of Glacier Natl. Park, on Continental Divide; crossed by Going-to-the-Sun Highway. Near-by points of interest are Hidden L. and Hanging Gardens (with colorful displays of wildflowers).

Logan Peak, Utah: see LOGAN, city.

Logansport. 1 City (pop. 21,031), ⊙ Cass co., N central Ind., on the Wabash at mouth of Eel R., and 36 mi. NE of Lafayette; industrial and shipping center in agr. area (livestock, grain, truck, fruit, poultry). Produces fire apparatus, radiators, farm equipment, buttons, clothing, beer, packed meat, oxygen and acetylene gas, fishing tackle. Nurseries; timber. A state mental hospital is near by. Settled c.1826. **2** Town (pop. 1,270), De Soto parish, NW La., 40 mi. SSW of Shreveport and on Sabine R. (here forming Texas line); cotton, corn, truck, poultry, livestock. Cotton ginning; mfg. of canned foods, sauces; lumber milling. Founded in 1830s.

Loganton, borough (pop. 346), Clinton co., central Pa., 10 mi. SE of Lock Haven.

Loganville. 1 City (pop. 699), Walton and Gwinnett cos., N central Ga., 29 mi. ENE of Atlanta. **2** Borough (pop. 569), York co., S Pa., 8 mi. SSE of York. **3** Village (pop. 250), Sauk co., S central Wis., on small Narrows Creek and 15 mi. W of Baraboo, in dairy and livestock region.

Logaros Lagoon (lôgûrôs′) (□ 11.6), in Arta nome, S Epirus, Greece, on N shore of Gulf of Arta 7 mi. SW of Arta; 5 mi. long, 3 mi. wide; fisheries.

Logar River (lō′gûr), E Afghanistan, rises in SW outliers of the Hindu Kush at 34°N 68°E, flows 150 mi. E, past Shaikhabad and Baraki Rajan, and N, past Kulangar, to Kabul R. E of Kabul. Used for timber floating. Also spelled Lohgar and Lohgard. Called Wardak R. in middle course. Chrome mining in valley.

Loggerhead Key, Fla.: see DRY TORTUGAS.

Loggia, La (lä lôd′jä), peak (10,095 ft.) in Lepontine Alps, S Switzerland, 9 mi. NNE of Biasca.

Loggieville, village (pop. estimate c.450), NE N.B., on Miramichi R. estuary and 5 mi. NE of Chatham; lumber port.

Loggiovano, Yugoslavia: see LOZOVAC.

Logie-Pert (lō′gē), agr. village and parish (pop. 903), E Angus, Scotland, 5 mi. NW Montrose.

Logierait (lō″gērāt′), agr. village and parish (pop. 1,452), NE Perthshire, Scotland, on the Tay and 8 mi. ENE of Aberfeldy. It was seat of dukes of Atholl, who held quasi-regal court here. In 1717 Rob Roy escaped from local jail.

Login, Wales: see CILYMAENLLWYD.

Logishin (lō′gĭshĭn), Pol. *Lohiszyn* (lôhē′shĭn), village (1931 pop. 2,638), central Pinsk oblast, Belorussian SSR, 17 mi. NNW of Pinsk; agr. processing (flaxseed, grain), brick mfg.

Logoisk or **Logoysk** (lŭgoisk′), town (1926 pop. 2,172), W central Minsk oblast, Belorussian SSR, 25 mi. NNE of Minsk; woodworking, starch making, dairying, brick mfg.

Logone, region, Fr. Equatorial Africa: see MOUNDOU.

Logone River (lōgōn′, lōgō′nä, lōgōnä′), main tributary of Shari R. in W Chad territory, Fr. Equatorial Africa, and along Fr. Cameroons border; formed by M'Béré R. (W branch of Logone) and Pendé R. (E branch of Logone) 28 mi. SSE of Laï, flows 240 mi. NW and N, past Laï and Bongor, to join with the Shari at Fort-Lamy and form a wide delta entering L. Chad to S. Its length with M'Béré R. (sometimes considered as main headstream) is c.500 mi. Forms extensive swamps through most of its course and at times of high water is linked with Benoué R. (Benue) through Fianga and Tickem swamps and Mayo-Kebbi R. Navigable for small steamers part of the year below Bongor. Fishing is important.

Logora Pass, Albania: see LLOGORA PASS.

Logovski or **Logovskiy** (lô′gŭfskē), village (1939 pop. over 2,000), central Stalingrad oblast, Russian SFSR, on railroad (Log station) and 20 mi. SSE of Frolovo; food processing.

Logroño (lōgrō′nyō), province (□ 2,044; pop. 221,160), N Spain, in Old Castile; ⊙ Logroño. Comprises fertile agr. region (most of La Rioja) sloping from central plateau to Ebro R., bet. Burgos and Navarre. Copper, tin, lead, and coal deposits only partly exploited. Essentially agr., noted for its wine and fruit; produces also cereals, vegetables, olive oil, sugar beets, sheep, and some cattle and hogs. Wine production is chief industry; others, derived from agr., are canning (vegetables, fruit), meat processing, distilling (alcohol, brandy), mfg. of wool fabrics and leather goods. Chief cities: Logroño, Calahorra, Haro, and Santo Domingo de la Calzada.

Logroño, city (pop. 43,709), ⊙ Logroño prov., N Spain, in Old Castile, on fertile plain, on right bank of Ebro R. and 160 mi. NE of Madrid; 42°28′N 2°26′W. Industrial and communications center, with active trade in wines of La Rioja dist. Canning (fruit, vegetables), meat processing, flour- and sawmilling; mfg. of furniture, mechanical presses (for wine and olive oil), knit goods, woolen fabrics, perfumes and cosmetics, insecticides, tiles, candy, and flour products. Wine, vegetables, fruit, olive oil in area. Has twin-towered collegiate church (15th cent.) with tomb of Gen. Espartero, Romanesque church of Santa María de Palacio (11th–12th cent.), and 13th–14th cent. Gothic church of San Bartolomeo; 2 bridges span the Ebro. Founded by Celtiberians, was liberated in 10th cent. from the Moors by the kings of Navarre and annexed to Castile in 1173. Unsuccessfully besieged by the French in 1521; was repeatedly in Fr. hands during Peninsular War, 1808–13).

Logrosán (lōgrōsän′), town (pop. 5,505), Cáceres prov., W Spain, 23 mi. SE of Trujillo; chemical-fertilizer processing, flour milling; agr. trade (cereals, livestock, lumber). Mineral springs. Phosphate mines and limestone quarries.

Logstor (lûkstûr′), Dan. *Løgstør,* city (pop. 3,193), Aalborg amt, N Jutland, Denmark, on Lim Fjord and 25 mi. W of Aalborg; fisheries, meat cannery, lime kilns.

Logtak Lake, India: see LOKTAK LAKE.

Logumkloster (lû′khûmklô″stûr), Dan. *Løgumkloster,* town (pop. 1,784), Tonder amt, S Jutland, Denmark, 12 mi. NE of Tonder. Site of 12th-cent. Lygum Monastery.

Lohardaga (lōhär′dŭgŭ), town (pop. 7,400), Ranchi dist., SW Bihar, India, on Chota Nagpur Plateau, 41 mi. W of Ranchi; rail terminus; trades in rice, oilseeds, corn, cotton; mfg. of brass utensils.

Loharu (lōhä′rōō), town (pop. 4,023), Hissar dist., S Punjab, India, 50 mi. S of Hissar; local market center for millet, cotton, salt, oilseeds. Was ⊙ former princely state of Loharu (□ 226; pop. 27,892) of Punjab States, India; since 1948, state inc. into Hissar dist.

Lohawat (lōhä′vŭt), town (pop. 6,027), W central Rajasthan, India, 55 mi. NNW of Jodhpur; local market for hides, salt, woolen handicrafts.

Loheia, Luhaiya, or **Luhayyah** (all: lōhä′yŭ), town (pop. 6,000), Hodeida prov., W Yemen, minor port on Red Sea, 65 mi. N of Hodeida; dhow trade in coffee; rock-salt deposits.

Lohfau Mountains, China: see LOFAO MOUNTAINS.

Lohfelden (lō′fĕl″dŭn), village (pop. 4,406), in former Prussian prov. of Hesse-Nassau, W Germany, after 1945 in Hesse, 4 mi. SSE of Kassel; paper milling.

Lohgar or **Lohgard,** river, Afghanistan: see LOGAR RIVER.

Lohiszyn, Belorussian SSR: see LOGISHIN.

Lohja (lō′yä, lōkh′yä), Swedish *Lojo* (lōō′yōō″), town (pop. 6,748), Uusimaa co., S Finland, in lake region, 30 mi. W of Helsinki; pulp, lumber, cellulose, and plywood mills, cement works, limestone quarries. Has 14th-cent. church.

Lohmann (lō′mŭn), town (pop. 123), Cole co., central Mo., near Missouri R., 11 mi. W of Jefferson City.

Lohne (lō′nŭ), town (pop. 11,409), in Oldenburg, NW Germany, after 1945 Lower Saxony, 27 mi. NNE of Osnabrück; mfg. of agr. machinery, cotton goods, cigars, cork; meat processing (ham), distilling (brandy).

Löhne (lû′nŭ), village (pop. 4,783), in former Prussian prov. of Westphalia, NW Germany, after 1945 in North Rhine-Westphalia, on the Werre and 5 mi. N of Herford; rail junction.

Lohner or **Gross Lohner** (grōs lō′nŭr), peak (10,013 ft.), in Bernese Alps, SW central Switzerland, 3 mi. SE of Adelboden. Klein Lohner peak is NNW.

Lohnsburg (lōns′bŏŏrk), town (pop. 2,271), W Upper Austria, 28 mi. W of Wels; wheat, rye, cattle.

Loho, China: see LOTIEN, Kweichow prov.

Lohpu, China: see LOP.

Lohr (lōr), town (pop. 10,499), Lower Franconia, NW Bavaria, Germany, on the Main (canalized) and 19 mi. E of Aschaffenburg; rail junction; hydroelectric plant; mfg. of metal products, textiles, glass, pottery; printing, woodworking; cider. Chartered 1333. Has Gothic church. Sandstone and heavy spar in area.

Lohrville (lôr′vĭl). **1** Town (pop. 698), Calhoun co., central Iowa, 25 mi. SW of Fort Dodge; metal products, feed. **2** Village (pop. 206), Waushara co., central Wis., 29 mi. W of Oshkosh, in dairy and farm area.

Lo-hui, China: see LOKWEI.

Lohumbo (lōhōōm′bō), village, Lake Prov., NW Tanganyika, on railroad and 28 mi. SW of Shinyanga; cotton, peanuts, corn, rice; livestock. Gold and limestone deposits. Also called Didia.

Lohwei, China: see LOKWEI.

Loibl Pass (loi′bŭl) or **Ljubelj Pass** (lyōō′bŭlyŭ), in the Karawanken, on Austro-Yugoslav frontier, 5 mi. N of Trzic; alt. 4,494 ft. Crossed by Klagenfurt-Ljubljana road.

Loigny-la-Bataille (lwänyē′-lä-bätī′), village (pop. 252), Eure-et-Loir dept., N central France, in the Beauce, 17 mi. NNW of Orléans. Here (1870) Germans defeated French in Franco-Prussian War.

Loikaw (loi′kô′), town, ⊙ Karenni State, Upper Burma, on the Nam Pilu and 70 mi. NE of Toungoo, on road; 19°40′N 97°13′E. Timber center.

Loilem (loi′lĕm′), village (pop. 2,070), Mongnai state, Southern Shan State, Upper Burma, on Thazi-Kentung road and 35 mi. ENE of Taunggyi; head of road (N) to Hsipaw.

Loilong (loilông′), SW state (myosaship) (□ 1,098; pop. 37,163), Southern Shan State, Upper Burma, on the Nam Pilu; ⊙ Pinlaung, village 45 mi. SW of Taunggyi. Hilly (highest point, 6,124 ft.), forested.

Loimaa (loi′mä″), town (pop. 3,322), Turku-Pori co., SW Finland, 40 mi. NE of Turku; metal-working, leather-goods mfg.

Loimwe (loi′mŭwĕ″), village, Kengtung state, Southern Shan State, Upper Burma, 13 mi. SE of Kengtung, on road to Lampang (Thailand).

Loing Canal (lwē), Loiret and Seine-et-Marne depts., N central France, formed by junction of ORLÉANS CANAL and BRIARE CANAL just below Montargis, paralleling Loing R. to its mouth on the Seine below Moret-sur-Loing.

Loing River, Yonne, Loiret, and Seine-et-Marne depts., N central France, rises near Saint-Sauveur, flows c.100 mi. N, past Montargis and Nemours, to the Seine below Moret-sur-Loing. Paralleled by BRIARE CANAL (bet. Rogny and Montargis), and by Loing Canal to its mouth. Receives the Ouanne (right).

Loino or **Loyno** (loi′nŭ), village (1939 pop. over 500), NE Kirov oblast, Russian SFSR, on Kama R. (head of navigation) and 75 mi. NNE of Omutninsk; coarse grain, flax. Ships phosphorite from near-by Rudnichny field.

Loir, river, France: see LOIR RIVER.

Loire (lwär), department (□ 1,853; pop. 631,591), in Lyonnais, E central France; ⊙ Saint-Étienne. Lies wholly within the Massif Central, bounded by the Monts du Forez (W), Monts du Beaujolais (NE), Monts du Lyonnais (E), Mont Pilat and Rhone R. (SE). Drained (S-N) by the Loire, which alternately flows through narrow gorges and level basins (FOREZ Plain, Roanne basin). Agr. (rye, wheat, wine, potatoes, colza, vegetables) in the lowlands; sheep, cattle, and hogs in the uplands. One of France's leading industrial depts. The Saint-Étienne dist., extending from Unieux on the Loire (W) through the Gier valley (JAREZ) to Rive-de-Gier (E), has important coal mines (Firminy, Roche-la-Molière, La Ricamarie), numerous metallurgical mills (Saint-Étienne, Firminy, Saint-Chamond, Unieux, Rive-de-Gier, Izieux), and textile plants (Saint-Chamond). The Roanne dist., extending from Riorges (W) into the RHINS RIVER valley to Thizy and Tarare (E), is a cotton-textile mfg. center. Feurs was ⊙ Loire dept., 1793–1801, followed by Montbrison (1801–56) and Saint-Étienne.

Loire, village (pop. 979), Rhône dept., E central France, on right bank of Rhone R. and 4 mi. NW of Vienne; ships cherries, apricots, pears.

Loire, river, France: see LOIRE RIVER.

Loire, Haute-, France: see HAUTE-LOIRE.

Loire-Inférieure (ĕfārēûr′), department (□ 2,693; pop. 665,064), S Brittany, W France; ⊙ Nantes. On Bay of Biscay, bisected by widening Loire R. estuary; level region drained by lower Loire R. and its tributaries, the Erdre (right) and the Sèvre Nantaise (left). Numerous depressions are filled with salt marshes, peat bogs, and shallow lagoons (La Grande-Brière, L. of Grand-Lieu). Extensive livestock raising and dairying; vineyards, apple orchards, truck gardens. Chief crops: wheat, buckwheat, potatoes, sugar beets, forage. Fisheries. Iron deposits near Châteaubriant. Chief industrial dist. of W France (shipbuilding, oil refining, wood- and leatherworking, food processing) is centered on NANTES and SAINT-NAZAIRE, which also carry on important trade with Africa and America. Densely populated N bank of Loire estuary has several bathing resorts (especially La Baule) at its E end.

Loire Lateral Canal, Fr. *Canal latéral à la Loire,* parallels middle course of Loire R. bet. Roanne (S terminus) and Briare (Loiret dept.). Total length, c.150 mi. Built 1822–56, it spans the Allier on an aqueduct 5 mi. SW of Nevers. Chief towns on canal are Digoin (junction with Canal du CENTRE), Decize (junction with NIVERNAIS Canal), Nevers, and Sancerre. At Marseille-les-Aubigny it is joined by Berry Canal. At Briare (N terminus) navigation continues on the Loire proper and on BRIARE Canal towards the Seine. Building material, lumber, wine shipments.

Loire River, anc. *Liger,* longest stream (625 mi.) in France. Rises in SE at 4,430 ft. near Mont Gerbier de Jonc in Massif Central, Ardèche dept., 20 mi. WNW of Privas; flows N, then W to the Atlantic (Bay of Biscay) at Saint-Nazaire. In its upper torrential course it traverses basaltic gorges and small basins (in Velay), and 2 Tertiary lake bottoms (Forez Plain, Roanne basin). Leaving the Massif Central above Nevers, it enters the Paris Basin, flanked by the vineyards of Sancerre and Pouilly-sur-Loire, and forms the Orléans bend around the SOLOGNE (S). Flowing W in a wider valley (known successively as Val de Loire, Val d'Orléans, Val de Touraine, Val d'Anjou), it passes by well-known vineyards (Vouvray, Rochecorbon, Montlouis-sur-Loire) and the noted châteaux (Chaumont-sur-Loire, Amboise, Langeais). Below Les Ponts-de-Cé, it limits the Armorican Massif (N) and forms an estuary (35 mi. long) below Nantes. The Loire has a seasonally fluctuating volume, subject to heavy floods, and is only intermittently navigable (except in lower course). Extensive dykes have been built bet. Orléans and Angers since Middle Ages. Its chief tributaries are the Allier, Cher, Indre, Vienne (which receives the Creuse), Sèvre Nantaise (left), and the Nièvre, Maine, Erdre (right). The Loire Lateral Canal follows the river from Roanne to Briare. Other canals (Berry, Centre, Nivernais, Briare, Orléans) connect it with the Seine and Rhone drainage systems and with industrial centers (Bourges, Vierzon, Montluçon, Le Creusot). Chief towns on the Loire are Roanne, Nevers, Gien, Orléans, Blois, Amboise, Tours, Saumur, Nantes (with its industrial dist.), and Saint-Nazaire.

Loiret (lwärā'), department (□ 2,630; pop. 346,918), in former Orléanais prov., N central France; ⊙ ORLÉANS. Generally flat, it is traversed E-W by the Loire. Also drained by Loing and Essonne rivers, tributaries of the Seine. The Orléans, Briare, and Loing canals connect the Seine with the Loire. Primarily agr., dept. contains S part of the wheat-growing BEAUCE (N and NW), the Gâtinais region (E) known for its honey, part of the poorly drained SOLOGNE (S of the Loire), and the vast Forest of Orléans. Chief crops are wheat, barley, saffron, sugar beets, colza, and vegetables. There are apple and cherry orchards, and vineyards (Beaugency, Saint-Jean-de-Braye). Food processing (vinegar, cider, honey, sugar, candies, and biscuits) is principal industry. Wool is made into blankets at Orléans. Other mfg. centers are Montargis (clothing, rubber), Pithiviers (sugar refining, pastry mfg.), and Gien (faïence).

Loir-et-Cher (lwär-ā-shâr'), department (□ 2,479; pop. 242,419), part of Orléanais, N central France; ⊙ Blois. Generally level region well drained by the Loire in its central portion and by 2 important tributaries, the Loir (N) and the Cher (S), which give dept. its name. Cattle raising and wheat growing in N; poorer SOLOGNE region has rye, corn, vegetables, fowl. Light industry is concentrated in the principal towns: Blois Romorantin (blankets, cottons), Vendôme (gloves). The châteaux of the Loire (Blois, Chambord, Chaumont, Cheverny) attract numerous tourists.

Loiret River (lwärā'), Loiret dept., N central France, rises in 2 abundant springs (resurgence of Loire R. waters lost by seepage) 3 mi. ESE of Olivet, flows 7 mi. W to the Loire 5 mi. below Orléans.

Loiron (lwärō'), village (pop. 329), Mayenne dept., W France, 7 mi. W of Laval; limekilns.

Loir River (lwär), NW central France, rises N of Illiers (Eure-et-Loir dept.), flows 193 mi. generally WSW, past Châteaudun, Vendôme, Château-du-Loir (head of navigation), and La Flèche, to the Sarthe above Angers. Traverses wheat-growing Little Beauce in upper course, then a deep and fertile alluvial valley.

Loisach River (loi'zäkh), Bavaria, Germany, rises W of Ehrwald (Austria), flows 62 mi. NNE, past Garmisch-Partenkirchen, through the Kochelsee, to the Isar 1 mi. N of Wolfratshausen.

Loitz (loits), town (pop. 6,895), in former Prussian Pomerania prov., N Germany, after 1945 in Mecklenburg, on the Peene and 14 mi. SW of Greifswald; agr. market (grain, sugar beets, potatoes, stock); woodworking.

Loíza (lôē'sä), town (pop. 2,872), NE Puerto Rico, near Loíza R., on railroad and 15 mi. ESE of San Juan, in sugar-growing region; sugar milling, cigar making. Just N is sugar-mill locality (pop. 2,950) of Canóvanas (känō'vänäs), a name formerly applied to town of Loíza. Loíza Aldea, N, was also formerly known simply as Loíza.

Loíza Aldea (äldā'ä), village (pop. 1,740), NE Puerto Rico, at mouth of Loíza R., 15 mi. E of San Juan, in sugar-growing and cattle-raising region. Settled 1511 at site of a pre-Columbian village. Frequently attacked during 19th cent. by Carib Indians. It was formerly known simply as Loíza, the name now applied to a town a few mi. S.

Loíza River or **Río Grande de Loíza** (rē'ō grän'dā dā), river, E Puerto Rico, rises in the Sierra de Cayey S of San Lorenzo, flows c.40 mi. N and NE, through fertile Caguas valley, past San Lorenzo, Caguas, Trujillo Alto, and Carolina, to the Atlantic at Loíza Aldea. Used for irrigation.

Loja (lō'hä), prov. (□ 4,536; 1950 pop. 215,585), S Ecuador, bordering on Peru; ⊙ Loja. Situated in the Andes, intersected by the Río Grande or Catamayo R. Climate is semitropical; main rainy season Dec.-April; there are large arid sections. The region around Loja city is rich in gold, silver, copper, iron, kaolin, and marble deposits, little exploited. Primarily agr.: cereals, potatoes, sugar cane, coffee, subtropical fruit, fiber plants. Considerable cattle, sheep, and mule raising. The prov. was in colonial times the chief source for cinchona bark. Woolen goods (blankets, carpets) are made at most of its trading centers, such as Loja and Gonzanamá. The international border with Peru was adjusted in 1942.

Loja, city (1950 pop. 18,200), ⊙ Loja prov., S Ecuador, in the Andes at NW foot of Cordillera de Zamora, on Pan-American Highway and 270 mi. SSW of Quito; 4°1'S 79°12'W; alt. c.7,300 ft. With a humid, though pleasant, subtropical climate, it is a trading center in fertile agr. region (sugar cane, coffee, tobacco, cereals, potatoes, pomegranates, cinchona, livestock); exports cattle to NW Peru. Tanning; mfg. of textile goods (woolens, blankets, carpets). An old colonial city (founded 1546), with a law school. It was formerly the world's center for cinchona production. Near by are gold, silver, copper, iron, kaolin, and marble deposits, little exploited. Its airport, La Toma, is 10 mi. W.

Loja, city (pop. 11,023), Granada prov., S Spain, in Andalusia, on the Genil and 30 mi. W of Granada; mfg. of footwear, felt hats, soap, chocolate, flour products; olive-oil processing, flour milling; marble cutting. Cereals, sugar beets, vegetables, almonds; livestock; lumber. White-marble quarries. Has remains of Moorish castle and two 16th-cent. churches. Played important role in Christian conquest of kingdom of Granada as one of keys to city; fell to Catholic Kings in 1488. Near here is picturesque gorge of Los Infernos, through which flows the Genil.

Lojo, Finland: see LOHJA.

Lojung, China: see LOYUNG.

Lokachi (lŭkŭchē'), Pol. *Łokacze* (wôkä'chĕ), town (1931 pop. 1,790), S Volyn oblast, Ukrainian SSR, 30 mi. W of Lutsk; grain-trading center; flour milling, brick mfg.

Lokandu (lōkän'dōō), village, Kivu prov., central Belgian Congo, on Lualaba R. and 150 mi. NNW of Kasongo; steamboat landing, trading center in rice-growing area. Also center of training for native troops. Has R.C. mission, hosp. for Europeans. Lokandu was built on former site of Riba-Riba, a noted Arab slave-traders' camp razed in 1893.

Lok-Batan (lôk-bŭtän'), town (1945 pop. over 500) in Molotov dist. of Greater Baku, Azerbaijan SSR, on Caspian Sea, 8 mi. SW of Baku; oil wells.

Lokchong (lôk'chŭrn'), Mandarin *Lo-ch'ang* (lŭ'-chäng'), town (pop. 16,694), ⊙ Lokchong co. (pop. 92,969), N Kwangtung prov., China, on Wu R. and 37 mi. NW of Kükong, and on Canton-Hankow RR; paper and pottery mfg., tung-oil and vegetable-oil extracting; hemp, rice, timber. Tungsten, tin, and coal mining near by.

Lokeren (lō'kürŭn), town (pop. 25,575), East Flanders prov., NW Belgium, 12 mi. ENE of Ghent; mfg. (cotton, linen, lace, leather, shoes, furniture). Has church with carved 18th-cent. pulpit.

Loket (lô'kĕt), Ger. *Elbogen* (ĕl'bōgŭn), town (pop. 2,038), W Bohemia, Czechoslovakia, on Ohre R., on railroad and 5 mi. E of Falknov; glass and porcelain industries; lignite mining. Has 12th-cent. castle, church (1701–34) with Gothic Madonna, and mus.

Lokhvitsa (lôkh'vētsŭ), city (1926 pop. 10,834), N Poltava oblast, Ukrainian SSR, near Sula R., 26 mi. NNE of Lubny; distilling center; woolen and flour mills. Sugar refinery near by, at Stalinka.

Loki, Mount (lō'kē) (9,090 ft.), SE B.C., in Selkirk Mts., 35 mi. NE of Nelson; 49°51'N 116°45'W.

Lokiang or **Lo-chiang** (both: lô'jyäng'), town (pop. 15,779), ⊙ Lokiang co. (pop. 156,969), NW Szechwan prov., China, 50 mi. NE of Chengtu; cotton textiles; rice, sugar cane, sweet potatoes, wheat, beans.

Lokitaung (lōkētoung'), village, Northern Frontier Prov., northwesternmost Kenya, near borders of Anglo-Egyptian Sudan and Ethiopia, on road and 80 mi. N of Lodwar, near L. Rudolf; stock raising; peanuts, sesame, corn, wild coffee.

Lokken (lŭ'kŭn), Dan. *Løkken,* town (pop. 1,765), Hjorring amt, N Jutland, Denmark, on the Skagerrak and 12 mi. SW of Hjorring; fisheries.

Lokken, Norway: see MELDAL.

Loknya (lôk'nyŭ), town (1948 pop. over 2,000), N Velikiye Luki oblast, Russian SFSR, 35 mi. NNW of Velikiye Luki; flax processing.

Loko (lō'kō), town (pop. 2,343), Benue prov., Northern Provinces, central Nigeria, on Benue R. and 38 mi. SSE of Nasarawa; shea nuts, cassava, durra.

Lokoja (lōkōjä'), town (pop. 8,085), ⊙ Kabba prov., Northern Provinces, S central Nigeria, on right bank of Niger R. at mouth of Benue R., and 200 mi. ENE of Ibadan; alt. 320 ft.; 7°48'N 6°44'E. Agr. trade center; shea-nut processing, cotton weaving, palm oil industry; cassava, yams, durra. Iron-ore deposits. First Br. consulate in Nigeria opened here (1859) by Scottish explorer William Baikie. Important Br. commercial center in late 19th cent.

Lokot or **Lokot'** (lô'kŭtyŭ). **1** Village (1926 pop. 5,675), S Altai Territory, Russian SFSR, near Alei R., 20 mi. S of Rubtsovsk, near junction of Turksib RR and branch line to Leninogorsk; metalworks. **2** Town (1926 pop. 3,260), SE Bryansk oblast, Russian SFSR, 45 mi. SSE of Bryansk; sawmilling, distilling, machine mfg.; hemp mill. Brasovo village is just NE.

Lokrum Island, Yugoslavia: see DUBROVNIK.

Loksa (lôk'sä), town (pop. 537), N Estonia, port on Gulf of Finland, 35 mi. ENE of Tallinn; ship repair dock, sawmill, tile works; bathing beach.

Loks Land, island (20 mi. long, 15 mi. wide), E Franklin Dist., Northwest Territories, in Davis Strait, off SE Baffin Isl., at entrance of Frobisher Bay; 62°27'N 64°35'W.

Loktak Lake (lŏk'tăk, lōk'tŭk), large marshy lake (c.25 mi. long, N-S; 4–13 mi. wide), S central Manipur, India, S of Imphal; drained by Manipur (or Imphal) R. Sometimes spelled Logtak.

Loktung (lôk'dōōng'), Mandarin *Lotung* (lŭ'dōōng'), ⊙ Loktung co. (pop. 49,840), SW Hainan, Kwangtung prov., China, 25 mi. N of Aihsien; sweet potatoes, millet, corn. Lead mining near by.

Lokva (lôk'vä), mountain, Macedonia, Yugoslavia, near right bank of Vardar R.; highest peak (4,238 ft.) is 13 mi. NNW of Djevdjelija.

Lokwei (lôk'wā'), Mandarin *Lo-hui* (lŭ'hwā'), town, ⊙ Lokwei co. (pop. 105,466), E Hainan, Kwangtung prov., China, at mouth of Wanchuan R., 60 mi. S of Kiungshan; rattan cane; hog and cattle raising. Fisheries. Sometimes spelled Lohwei.

Lola (lō'lä), village, SE Fr. Guinea, Fr. West Africa, near Liberia border, 20 mi. E of N'zérékoré; coffee, rice, kola nuts; livestock.

Lola, Mount (lō'lŭ) (9,160 ft.), Nevada co., E Calif., peak of the Sierra Nevada N of Donner Pass and 30 mi. W of Reno, Nev.

Lolgorien, Kenya: see MARA.

Loling (lô'lĭng'), town, ⊙ Loling co. (pop. 318,448), N Shantung prov., China, 75 mi. NNE of Tsinan, near Hopeh line; cotton and silk weaving, straw plaiting; peanuts.

Loliondo (lōlēōn'dō), village, Northern Prov., Tanganyika, near Kenya border, 120 mi. NW of Arusha, on road; red ochre and gold deposits. Airfield.

Lolland or **Laaland** (lô'län), island (□ 479; pop. 87,150), Denmark, in Baltic Sea, separated from S Zealand by Smaalandsfarvand strait and from Ger. Fehmarn isl. by Fehmarn Belt. Irregular coastline; c.35 mi. wide (E-W), c.17 mi. long (N-S). Dikes in marshy S coastal regions prevent flooding. Highest point, 97 ft. Coast broken N by Sakskobing Fjord, W by Nakskov Fjord. Largest lake is Maribo L. Forests in N and E. Sugar beets are chief crop. Maribo, ⊙ MARIBO amt, and Nakskov are its important cities.

Lolodorf (lō'lōdôrf"), village, Kribi region, SW Fr. Cameroons, 60 mi. ENE of Kribi; road junction; cacao plantations.

Lolog, Lake (lō'lôkh) (□ 13; alt. 3,146 ft.), in the Andes, SW Neuquén natl. territory, Argentina, in Argentinian lake dist., 15 mi. SW of Junín de los Andes; extends c.15 mi. E (1–2 mi. wide) from a point 4 mi. E of Chile border.

Lolo Pass, Idaho and Mont.: see BITTERROOT RANGE.

Lolotla (lōlō'tlä), town (pop. 657), Hidalgo, central Mexico, 50 mi. N of Pachuca; cereals, beans, fruit, stock.

Lom (lôm), city (pop. 15,182), Vidin dist., NW Bulgaria, port on right bank of the Danube (Rum. border), at mouth of Lom R., and 45 mi. NNW of Vratsa. Rail terminus; commercial center; light mfg.; ceramics, foodstuffs, leather industries. Winegrowing and truck gardening near by. Lignite deposits just S, at Momin-brod (pop. 940). Has ruins of Roman camp and Turkish fortress. Founded 1st cent. A.D. as Roman fortress of Almus. Was small commercial town under Turkish rule (15th-19th cent.); developed as major river port following building of Sofia-Vratsa-Lom RR. Formerly called Lom Palanka.

Lom (lôm), village and canton (pop. 3,027), Opland co., S central Norway, on Otta R., at N foot of the Jotunheim Mts., 80 mi. NW of Lillehammer; stock raising, lumbering. Has 11th-cent. stave church and several notable old wooden bldgs. Knut Hamsun b. here.

Loma (lō'mŭ). **1** Village, Mesa co., W Colo., near Colorado R. and Utah line, 15 mi. NW of Grand Junction, in irrigated agr. and livestock region; alt. 4,515 ft. **2** Village (pop. 53), Cavalier co., NE N.Dak., 10 mi. SSW of Langdon.

Loma, Point (lō'mŭ), S Calif., S tip of high rugged peninsula sheltering San Diego Bay from the Pacific, W of San Diego; lighthouse. Old light house (1855) on crest near tip is included in Cabrillo Natl. Monument (kŭbrē'ō) (½ acre; established 1913), set aside in memory of Juan Rodríquez Cabrillo, who discovered the bay (1542). U.S. Fort Rosecrans (rō'zĭkrănz") and Point Loma residential dist. (part of San Diego) are on peninsula.

Loma Alta (lō'mä äl'tä), village, Pando dept., N Bolivia, on Beni R. and 16 mi. NNE of Riberalta; rubber.

Loma Bonita (lō'mä bōnē'tä), town (pop. 2,707), Oaxaca, S Mexico, near Tuxtepec; pineapple-growing center, developed in 1930s.

Loma de Cabrera (lō'mä dā käbrā'rä), town (1950 pop. 1,417), Libertador prov., NW Dominican Republic, on Massacre R., near Haiti border, and 6 mi. SSE of Dajabón; agr. center (coffee, rice, goats, hides, beeswax, honey). Formerly La Loma.

Loma de Tierra (tyĕ'rä), town (pop. 1,160), Havana prov., W Cuba, on Central Highway and 10 mi. SE of Havana, in sugar-growing and dairying region.

Lomagundi, district, Southern Rhodesia: see SINOIA.

Loma Linda (lō"mŭ lĭn'dŭ), village (1940 pop. 1,589), San Bernardino co., S Calif., 5 mi. W of Redlands; seat of a sanatorium and of Col. of Medical Evangelists.

Lomami River (lōmä'mē), left tributary of Congo R. in SE and central Belgian Congo; rises in Katanga highlands 15 mi. W of Kamina, flows N in wide curves parallel to the Lualaba, past Tshofa and Opala, to Congo R. at Isangi; c.900 mi. long. Navigable for barges in lower course for 245 mi. below Benakamba. Upper Lomami region is cattle-raising area.

Loma Mountains (lō'mä), NE Sierra Leone, c.40 mi. N of Sefadu; c.20 mi. long. Rise to 6,390 ft. in the Bintimane, highest peak in Sierra Leone. The Niger rises just E.

Loma Negra (lō'mä nä'grä), town (pop. estimate 1,000), central Buenos Aires prov., Argentina, 7 mi. SSE of Olavarría; railhead and cement-milling center; clay and limestone quarries.

Lomas (lō'mäs), town (pop. 500), Arequipa dept., S Peru, landing on the Pacific, on Pan-American Highway and 55 mi. S of Nazca (Ica dept.). Outlet for cattle and cotton region.

Lomas, Las, Panama: see LAS LOMAS.

Lomas, Las, Peru: see LAS LOMAS.

Lomas de Zamora (lō'mäs dā sämō'rä), city (pop. 40,110), ⊙ Lomas de Zamora dist. (□ 38; pop. 127,-570), in Greater Buenos Aires, Argentina, 9 mi. SSW of Buenos Aires. Major industrial center: meat packing, dairying, lumbering; plastics, paper bags, ceramics, chemical products, rubber goods, shoes. Stock and poultry raising. Has agr. school, art gall.

Loma Tina, Dominican Republic: see TINA, MONTE.

Lomax (lō'măks), village (pop. 490), Henderson co., W Ill., on the Mississippi and 9 mi. S of Burlington, Iowa; agr. (grain; dairy products; livestock).

Lomazzo (lômät'sō), village (pop. 3,586), Como prov., Lombardy, N Italy, 8 mi. SSW of Como; shoes, textile machinery, candy.

Lombard (lŏm'bärd), residential village (pop. 9,817), Du Page co., NE Ill., W suburb of Chicago, 4 mi. E of Wheaton, in farm and dairy area; mfg. of women's clothing; lilac nurseries. Settled 1834, inc. 1869.

Lombardy (lŏm'bŭrdē, lŭm'–), Ital. *Lombardia* (lômbär'dyä), region (□ 9,190; pop. 5,836,479), N Italy; ⊙ Milan. Bordered by Switzerland (N), Emilia-Romagna (S), Trentino–Alto Adige and Veneto (E), and Piedmont (W). Comprises 9 provs.: BERGAMO, BRESCIA, COMO, CREMONA, MANTOVA, MILANO, PAVIA, SONDRIO, VARESE. Extends S c.120 mi. from Lepontine and Rhaetian Alps (over 13,000 ft.) to Po R. (alt. 35 ft.), and W c.160 mi. from Mincio R. to Ticino R. Mtn. and hill terrain in N covers c.50% of area, with Lombard plain in S half. Area c.20% forested. Drained by the middle Po and its tributaries, Adda, Oglio, Chiese, Lambro, Serio, and Mella rivers. Richest lake region of Italy; contains lakes Como, Idro, Iseo, and Varese, and part of Garda, Lugano, and Maggiore. Continental type climate, modified in Alpine margins by lakes. Average annual rainfall 79 in. (mtn.), 39–49 in. (hills), 23.5–29.5 in. (plain). Leading industrial region of Italy. Chief industries: textiles (cotton, silk), iron and steel, chemicals, publishing, paper, tanning (shoes), rubber. Has 2d largest number of hydroelectric plants (222) in country. Commerce greatly favored by international routes over such important Alpine passes as Simplon, St. Gotthard, Bernina, Splügen, Stelvio, San Bernardino, and Maloja, which converge on Lombard plain, especially at Milan. Has largest railroad mileage in the country. Leading cities are Milan, chief Ital. industrial and commercial center, the prov. capitals, and Monza, Sesto San Giovanni, Lecco, Lodi, Vigevano, Voghera, Busto Arsizio, and Gallarate. Agr. ranks almost with industry and commerce in importance, aided by widespread irrigation (c.55% of Lombard plain). Basic crops are wheat, corn, fodder, raw silk, rice, potatoes. Industrial plants include sugar beets, flax, and hemp. Leads Italy in raising cattle, swine, and horses, with 20% of area in pasture; large dairy industry. Lombardy became part of Roman Empire in 3d cent. B.C. Suffered heavily from barbaric invasions, and in 569 became center of kingdom of Lombards. Passed to Charlemagne in 774. The 11th cent. was marked by gradual transfer of power from feudal lords to autonomous communes, and by economic revival. Lombard League defeated Frederick I at Legnano (1176). Dominated by Visconti and Sforza dukes of Milan in 14th and 15th cent. Came under rule of Spain (1535–1713), Austria (1713–96), and France (1796–1814). Liberated in 1859 and passed to Italy.

Lombe (lōm'bā), village, Malange prov., NW Angola, on railroad and 14 mi. WNW of Malange; corn, rice, beans.

Lombez (lōbā'), village (pop. 635), Gers dept., SW France, on the Save and 20 mi. SE of Auch; brick- and ironworks; orchards. Has 14th-cent. former cathedral.

Lomblem (lŏmblĕm'), **Kawula**, or **Kawoela** (both: käwōō'lŭ), largest island (□ 499; pop. 17,761) of Solor Isls., Lesser Sundas, Indonesia, bet. Flores Sea (N) and Savu Sea (S), 25 mi. E of Flores, just W of Adonara; 8°25'S 123°32'E. Irregular in shape, 50 mi. long, 20 mi. wide; mountainous, rising to 5,394 ft. Agr., fishing.

Lombok (lŏmbŏk'), island (□ 1,826; pop. 701,290), Lesser Sundas, Indonesia, bet. Java Sea (N) and Indian Ocean (S), 20 mi. E of Bali across Lombok Strait, 10 mi. W of Sumbawa across Alas Strait; 8°12'–9°1'S 115°46'–116°40'E. Roughly circular (c.50 mi. in diameter) with small SW peninsula. Generally mountainous, rising to 12,224 ft. in Mt. Rinjani (N). In S area is a fertile plain separated from steep coast by rocky range. Chief products: rice, coffee, corn, sugar, cotton, tobacco. Chief town is MATARAM; principal port is AMPENAN. Natives are principally Sassaks or Sasaks (Mohammedan Malayan group related to the Javanese); some Balinese live in W part. Zoologically Lombok represents transitional point bet. Asiatic fauna (found in W isls. of Indonesia) and Australian fauna (in E isls.). First visited 1674 by the Dutch who began trade with isl. in following year. Controlled by rulers of near-by Bali from late-18th to mid-19th cent.

Lombok, Peak of, Indonesia: see RINJANI, MOUNT.

Lombo Kangra (lôm'bō käng'grä), highest peak (23,165 ft.) in Kailas Range, S Tibet, 40 mi. NW of Saka.

Lombok Strait, channel (50 mi. long, 20–40 mi. wide) connecting Indian Ocean (S) and Java Sea (N), bet. Bali (W) and Lombok (E); contains Penida isl. Its W arm (bet. Bali and Penida) is BADUNG PASSAGE. Alfred R. Wallace, English naturalist, noted that Lombok Strait formed part of dividing line bet. fauna of Australia and that of Asia.

Lomé (lō'mā, lōmā'), city (commune pop. 30,264), ⊙ and chief port of Fr. Togoland, on Slave Coast of Gulf of Guinea, 100 mi. ENE of Accra (Gold Coast) and 100 mi. WSW of Porto-Novo (Dahomey); 6°7'N 1°13'E. Residence of High Commissioner. Commercial and shipping center with railroads to rich agr. hinterland (Palimé, Blitta) and to Anécho on coast. Exports chiefly cacao, palm oil and kernels, cotton. Cotton ginning; ice mfg. Airport; primary and secondary schools; hosps. and medical laboratories; R.C. and Protestant missions.

Lomela (lōmĕ'lä), village, Kasai prov., central Belgian Congo, on right bank of Lomela R. and 180 mi. N of Lusambo; terminus of steam navigation; trading center; cotton ginning, rice fields.

Lomela River, central Belgian Congo, rises 10 mi. N of Katako Kombe, flows c.500 mi. NW and WNW, past Lomela, to join Tshuapa R. just W of Boende, forming the Busira. Navigable for 400 mi. below Lomela village.

Lomellina (lômĕl-lē'nä), region (□ 410) of Po plain, Pavia prov., Lombardy, N Italy; extends c.20 mi. N of the Po, bet. lower courses of Ticino (E) and Sesia (W) rivers. Fertile and highly irrigated; produces large quantities of rice (chief crop), cereals, and vegetables. Cattle raising widespread. Clay, saltpeter, and potash quarries. Chief town, Mortara.

Lomello (lômĕl'lō), village (pop. 2,308), Pavia prov., Lombardy, N Italy, on Agogna R. and 18 mi. WSW of Pavia, in rice-growing region.

Lometa (lōmē'tŭ), town (pop. 951), Lampasas co., central Texas, near the Colorado, c.50 mi. SE of Brownwood; trade point in livestock, agr. area; ships pecans, wool.

Lom et Kadéï (lōm' ā kädā'), administrative region (□ 36,680; 1950 pop. 128,400), SE and E Fr. Cameroons; ⊙ Batouri. Borders E and S on Fr. Equatorial Africa. Drained by Lom, Kadéï, N'Goko and Sanga rivers. In tropical rain-forest zone; coffee production. Also hardwoods, rubber, palm kernels, gold.

Lomié (lōmē'ā), village, Haut-Nyong region, S Fr. Cameroons, 65 mi. SSE of Abong-M'Bang; coffee plantations. Occupied by Belgian colonial troops 1915.

Lomira (lōmī'rŭ), village (pop. 746), Dodge co., E Wis., 13 mi. S of Fond du Lac, in dairying region; cannery; lime works.

Lo Miranda (lō mērän'dä), town (pop. 1,242), O'Higgins prov., central Chile, on Cachapoal R., on railroad and 7 mi. WSW of Rancagua; agr. center (grain, alfalfa, beans, potatoes, fruit, wine, cattle); flour milling, dairying.

Lomita (lōmē'tŭ), unincorporated town (1940 pop. 5,639), Los Angeles co., S Calif., suburb 18 mi. S of downtown Los Angeles, near Torrance and San Pedro.

Lomita Park, suburban village (1940 pop. 1,328), San Mateo co., W Calif., near San Francisco Bay, 13 mi. S of San Francisco; dairying.

Lomitas, Las, Argentina: see LAS LOMITAS.

Lomma (lōō'mä"), village (pop. 2,917), Malmohus co., S Sweden, on the Oresund, 5 mi. NE of Malmo; brick-, tile-, cement-, and metalworks.

Lommatzsch (lô'mäch), town (pop. 5,832), Saxony, E central Germany, 8 mi. WNW of Meissen; center of vegetable- and fruitgrowing region; mfg. (agr. machinery, glass, mirrors). Has late-Gothic church.

Lomme (lôm), outer W suburb (pop. 18,113) of Lille, Nord dept., N France; textile milling (sewing thread, cotton and linen cloth), metalworking (agr. tools), dairying, mfg. of tiles, bricks, soap, brushes, shoes.

Lommel (lô'mŭl), town (pop. 13,705), Limburg prov., NE Belgium, 20 mi. N of Hasselt; zinc and lead processing.

Lomnica River, Ukrainian SSR: see LOMNITSA RIVER.

Lomnice nad Luznic (lôm'nyĭtsĕ näd' lōōzh-nyĭtsĕ), Czech *Lomnice nad Lužnicí*, Ger. *Lomnitz an der Linde* (lôm'nĭts än dĕr lĭn'dŭ), town (pop. 1,675), S Bohemia, Czechoslovakia, on Luznice R., on railroad and 13 mi. NE of Budweis, in region of large fish ponds; carp breeding and fishing, mostly for export; also tench, pike, and perch fishing.

Lomnice nad Popelkou (näd' pôpĕlkō), town (pop. 4,875), N Bohemia, Czechoslovakia, on railroad and 21 mi. SE of Liberec; sugar refining, textiles.

Lomnice Peak, Slovak *Lomnický Štít* (lôm'nyĭtskē shtyēt"), Ger. *Lomnitzer Spitze* (lôm'nĭtsŭr shpĭ'-tsŭ), Hung. *Lomnici Csúcs* (lôm'nĭtsĭ chōōch), second-highest peak (8,639 ft.) of the High Tatra, N Slovakia, Czechoslovakia, 10 mi. NNW of Poprad; has cable railway. Meteorological observatory on top. Tatranska Lomnica is at SE, Kezmarske Zleby at E foot.

Lomnitsa River (lôm'nyĭtsŭ), Pol. *Łomnica* (wômnyē'tsä), Stanislav oblast, Ukrainian SSR, formed 13 mi. SSW of Pereginsko by confluence of headstreams rising in the Gorgany; flows N, past Peregìnsko, and NE to Dniester R. just NW of Galich; length, 73 mi.

Lomnitz an der Linde, Czechoslovakia: see LOMNICE NAD LUZNICI.

Lomnitzer Spitze, Czechoslovakia: see LOMNICE PEAK.

Lomo de Arico, Canary Isls.: see ARICO.

Lomond (lō'mŭnd), village (pop. 138), S Alta., 50 mi. N of Lethbridge; coal mining; wheat.

Lomond, Loch (lŏk, lŏkh), lake (4 mi. long, 1 mi. wide), S N.B., 10 mi. NE of St. John. Graphite mined near by.

Lomond, Loch (lŏkh), lake bet. Dumbarton and Stirling, Scotland, extends N-S bet. Balloch (S) and Ardlui (N); 23 mi. long; 5 mi. wide near its outlet (Leven R.) at S end, where there are numerous wooded isles; narrows to 1 mi. toward N; alt. 23 ft.; max. depth 623 ft. The largest lake in Scotland, it is noted for scenic beauty and is celebrated in song and poetry. Chief riparian villages are Balloch, Ardlui, Tarbert, and Inversnaid. Inlets include the Endrick and the Luss. Several castles are on shore of lake and on isls. Receives outlet of Loch Sloy (hydroelectric plant was opened here in 1950).

Lomond Hills, mountain range in Fifeshire and Kinross, Scotland, extends 6 mi. E-W. Highest points are East Lomond (1,471 ft.), just SSW of Falkland, and West Lomond (1,713 ft.), 4 mi. W of Falkland.

Lomonosov (lŭmŭnô'sŭf), city (1939 pop. over 10,000), central Leningrad oblast, Russian SFSR, on Gulf of Finland, opposite Kronstadt, 18 mi. WSW of Leningrad; metal- and brickworks, lumber mills, shoe factory. Site of palace (built 1714 under Peter the Great) and Chinese palace (built 1768 under Catherine the Great). Summer resort with boat landing. Here Lomonosov founded (1752) noted glass- and mosaic works. Chartered 1780; until 1948, called Oranienbaum. During siege of Leningrad (1941–44), center of Rus. bridgehead on Gulf of Finland.

Lomont (lômō'), narrow range forming N escarpment of the Jura, in Doubs dept., E France, extending c.25 mi. bet. Baume-les-Dames (W) and Swiss border (E); rises to 2,746 ft. Traversed by the Doubs at Pont-de-Roide.

Lom Palanka, Bulgaria: see LOM.

Lompobatang, Mount (lômpôbätäng'), or **Bonthain Peak** (bŏntīn') (9,419 ft.), Celebes, Indonesia, at S end of SW peninsula, 40 mi. ESE of Macassar.

Lompoc (lŏm'pōk), city (pop. 5,520), Santa Barbara co., SW Calif., c.45 mi. WNW of Santa Barbara, and on Santa Ynez R., in coastal valley (Lompoc Valley; c.25 mi. long, up to 10 mi. wide) noted for flower-seed growing. Kieselguhr quarries and oil field near by. Mission La Purisima Concepcion (founded 1787; now a state historic monument) and U.S. Camp Cooke are in vicinity. Founded 1874, inc. 1888.

Lom River (lôm), NW Bulgaria, formed by confluence of streams rising in Sveti Nikola Mts. near Sveti Nikola Pass; flows 58 mi. NE to the Danube at Lom.

Lom River (lōm), left headstream of Sanaga R. in E Fr. Cameroons, rises near Fr. Equatorial Africa border 40 mi. ENE of Meiganga, flows generally SW, joining another headstream 90 mi. NW of Batouri to form the Sanaga.

Lom Sak (lôm′ säk′), town (1937 pop. 6,243), Petchabun prov., central Thailand, on Pa Sak R. and 25 mi. N of Petchabun; gold mining. Airport.

Lom u Mostu (lôm″ ŏŏ′ môstŏŏ), Ger. *Bruch* (brŏŏkh), town (pop. 5,353), NW Bohemia, Czechoslovakia, on railroad and 5 mi. N of Most Litvinov; deep-shaft coal mining.

Lomza (lŏm′zhä, -zü), Pol. *Łomża* (wôm′zhä), Rus. *Lomzha* (lôm′zhŭ), town (pop. 13,772), Bialystok prov., NE Poland, on Narew R. and 45 mi. W of Bialystok. Rail junction; trade center; mfg. of railroad cars, electrical goods, bricks, soap, artificial woolen, vinegar, gingerbread; tanning, flour milling, brewing, sawmilling. Peat deposits near by. Probably founded in earliest period of Pol. kingdom. Passed (1795) to Prussia; in Rus. Poland, 1815–1921, and ⊙ Lomzha govt. Before Second World War, pop. ⅓ Jewish; in Second World War, town was under administration of East Prussia.

Lonaconing (lōnŭkō′nĭng), mining town (pop. 2,289), Allegany co., W Md., in the Alleghenies and 14 mi. WSW of Cumberland, in bituminous-coal area. Big Savage Mtn. and Savage R. State Forest are just W. Settled c.1835.

Lonan (lŭ′nän′), town (pop. 3,721), ⊙ Lonan co. (pop. 195,829), SE Shensi prov., China, near Honan line, 65 mi. E of Sian, in mtn. region; wheat, beans, kaoliang. Iron and coal deposits near by.

Lonar, India: see MEHKAR.

Lonate Pozzolo (lônä′tĕ pôtsô′lô), village (pop. 3,721), Varese prov., Lombardy, N Italy, near Ticino R., 5 mi. WSW of Busto Arsizio; cotton mills, foundry, shoe factory.

Lonato (lônä′tô), village (pop. 1,960), Brescia prov., Lombardy, N Italy, near SW shore of Lago di Garda, 14 mi. ESE of Brescia; silk industry center. Peat fields near by. Noted for victory (1796) of Napoleon over Austrians.

Lonauli (lōnou′lē) or **Lonavla** (lōnäv′lŭ), town (pop. 10,876), Poona dist., central Bombay, India, in Western Ghats, 36 mi. NW of Poona; rail station (workshops). Just NW are 2 reservoirs supplying Khopoli hydroelectric plant.

Loncoche (lōng-kō′chā), town (pop. 5,109), ⊙ Villarrica dept. (□ 1,710; pop. 53,966), Cautín prov., S central Chile, on railroad and 45 mi. S of Temuco; agr. and commercial center. Wheat, barley, peas, potatoes, livestock. Tanning, flour milling, dairying, lumbering.

Loncomilla, department, Chile: see SAN JAVIER.

Loncomilla River (lōnkōmē′yä), Linares prov., S central Chile, formed by union of Longaví R. and Perquilauquén R. 10 mi. WNW of Linares, flows c.20 mi. N, past San Javier, to Maule R.; used for irrigation.

Loncopué (lōngkōpwā′), village (pop. estimate 1,000), ⊙ Loncopué dept. (1947 pop. 3,499), W central Neuquén natl. territory, Argentina, on the Río Agrio and 65 mi. NW of Zapala; stock-raising center.

Londe-les-Maures, La (lä lōd-lā-mōr′), village (pop. 1,236), Var dept., SE France, near Rade d'Hyères of the Mediterranean, 5 mi. ENE of Hyères, at foot of Monts des Maures; cork mfg., winegrowing. Silver-bearing lead mined 2 mi. SE.

Londerzeel (lŏn′dŭrzāl), agr. village (pop. 7,445), Brabant prov., central Belgium, 11 mi. NW of Brussels. Has 13th-cent. church.

Londiani (lōndēä′nē), town, Nyanza prov., W Kenya, on railroad and 60 mi. E of Kisumu; alt. 7,533 ft.; agr. and trade center; coffee, tea, wheat, corn; dairying.

Londinières (lōdēnyâr′), agr. village (pop. 814), Seine-Inférieure dept., N France, 16 mi. SE of Dieppe.

Londinium, England: see LONDON.

Londoko (lŭndŭkô′), town (1939 pop. over 500), NW Jewish Autonomous Oblast, Russian SFSR, on Trans-Siberian RR and 45 mi. W of Birobidzhan; cementworks.

London, city (pop. 78,264), ⊙ Middlesex co., S Ont., on Thames R. and 100 mi. SW of Toronto; commercial, industrial, and financial center of rich agr. area (fruit, vegetables, dairying, grain); tanneries, rolling mills, knitting and hosiery mills, aircraft-assembly plants, breweries; mfg. of radios, electrical equipment, boilers, hardware, enamel and brass products, leather, shoes, cardboard boxes, cereal foods, biscuits, cigars. Site of Univ. of Western Ontario, Huron Col., several other educational institutions, and prov. mental hosp.; seat of Anglican and R.C. bishops. Airport. Site was selected (1792) by Simcoe as future ⊙ Upper Canada, but settlement was not begun until 1826. Inc. 1848, London's growth was rapid after middle of the cent. Until 1885 it was center of Ont. oil industry, later superseded by Sarnia and Petrolia. British garrison was stationed here, 1838–53.

London, anc. *Londinium,* city and administrative county (□ 116.9; 1931 pop. 4,397,003; 1951 census 3,348,336), England, ⊙ United Kingdom and chief city of the British Empire, on both banks of the Thames, near its mouth on the North Sea; 51°30′48″N 0°5′48″W (St. Paul's Cathedral). Mean temp.: Jan. 39.4°F., July 61.1°F.; annual rainfall 27.91 inches. Greater London (□ 692.9; 1931 pop. 8,203,942; 1951 census 8,346,137) includes sections of the home counties, Essex, Kent, Hertford, Middlesex, and Surrey. Administrative co. of London consists of City of London (□ 1; 1931 pop. 10,999; 1951 census 5,268) administered by a corporation headed by the Lord Mayor, and the 28 metropolitan boroughs: Battersea, Bermondsey, Bethnal Green, Camberwell, Chelsea, Deptford, Finsbury, Fulham, Greenwich, Hackney, Hammersmith, Hampstead, Holborn, Islington, Kensington, Lambeth, Lewisham, St. Marylebone, Paddington, Poplar, St. Pancras, Stepney, Shoreditch, Southwark, Stoke Newington, Wandsworth, Westminster, and Woolwich (see individual articles); each borough has its own mayor and borough council, responsible to the London County Council. London is commercial, financial, industrial, and cultural center and largest port of the United Kingdom, with world-wide banking and insurance interests. Commercial center is in the City, where banks (including the Bank of England in Threadneedle Street), financial houses, and insurance companies (Lloyd's of London is famous) have their offices. Port of London, administered by the Port of London Authority, extends from Teddington (W) to Tilbury (E) (ocean-going vessels can go as far as the Tower Bridge) and consists of a vast system of docks on the Thames (largest are the Royal Victoria, Royal Albert, King George V, and Surrey Commercial docks), and has trade with all parts of the world. London's chief airports are London Airport or Heath Row, for intercontinental traffic, and Northolt, for European and internal lines. Univ. of London, of which London School of Economics, Univ. Hosp., and several extension colleges form part, is one of largest in the country. Westminster Palace (see WESTMINSTER) is meeting place of the Houses of Parliament; adjoining it is WHITEHALL, street in which most govt. offices are located; Downing Street (off Whitehall) has residence of the prime minister. Sovereign's London residence (since 1837) is Buckingham Palace, built 1703 by the duke of Buckingham, purchased (1761) by George III, remodeled (1825) by Sir John Nash, the E façade being added by Edward Blore, 1847. The palace contains a noted collection of paintings. In Second World War palace sustained damage from air raids (1940–41) and from a robot bomb (1944). St. James's Palace, built by Henry VIII on site of St. James's Hosp., was a royal residence from burning of Whitehall (1697) to Victoria's time. It is now used for ceremonial functions. British court is still officially designated the Court of St. James's. Parts of palace suffered considerable damage in 1941 air raid. Of administrative importance are also County Hall, seat of London County Council, and Transport House, trade union hq. Of numerous theaters, the Royal Opera House at COVENT GARDEN, the Old Vic, and Sadler's Wells (ballet) are best known. Famous are British Mus., Victoria and Albert Mus., various specialized museums in South KENSINGTON, National Gall. (in Trafalgar Square), Tate Gall., and Wallace Collection. Within each borough separate districts bear individual names; BLOOMSBURY is the academic, intellectual, and publishing center; MAYFAIR is fashionable residential district. Among London's streets, famous are: Fleet (newspaper center), Regent, Bond, Oxford (fashionable shopping centers), Lombard (financial center), PICCADILLY, PALL MALL, and the STRAND. Largest of the many parks are HYDE PARK, KENSINGTON Gardens, and Regent's Park (372 acres). Notable churches are Westminster Abbey (see WESTMINSTER) and St. Paul's. St. Paul's Cathedral, designed by Wren, is a noted example of Renaissance church architecture. An early church was destroyed by fire c.1080; c.1280 a successor cathedral was completed. Toward mid-17th cent. it was restored by Inigo Jones but was almost wholly destroyed in 1666 fire. Present church was begun 1675, opened for worship 1697, and finally completed 1710. Resembling St. Peter's in Rome, it is in form of a Latin cross, 500 ft. long and 118 ft. wide, with 250-ft.-long transept. Outer dome is 364 ft. high. In 1940–41 air raids St. Paul's sustained considerable damage, while surrounding area was almost wholly destroyed. St. Martin's in the Fields was built (1722–26) by James Gibbs; its crypt provides night asylum to the homeless. Church sustained air-raid damage in 1940. Notable are the Temple (one of the Inns of Court); the Old Bailey (central criminal court, on site of former Newgate prison); and the Tower of London (anc. fortress and royal castle built c.1078 by Gundulf, bishop of Rochester), used now mainly as an arsenal, mus., and prison for military prisoners. The Tower's N bastion was destroyed (1940) in air raids. A vast variety of mfg. industries are carried on in London and immediate vicinity; there is also important trade in imported produce (nonferrous metals, wines, tobacco, etc.). Little is known of London prior to A.D. 61, where, according to Tacitus, followers of Queen Boadicea slaughtered the inhabitants of fort of *Londinium* after the departure of Roman governor Suetonius. Roman authority was restored and 1st city walls (of which there are extant remnants) were built. In early 5th cent. Romans withdrew finally, and London is mentioned next in 866, when it was under control of Alfred the Great, who rebuilt defenses and gave it a form of govt. Town grew under Edward the Confessor and Harold, and William the Conqueror treated with London as separate entity after his conquest. William built White Tower, nucleus of the Tower of London. In reign of Richard I City of London obtained its present form of govt. In 13th and 14th cent. the guilds gained great power. The Inns of Court and original structures of St. Paul's and Westminster Abbey were built. Religious and civil life in London inspired *Piers Plowman* and Chaucer's *Canterbury Tales.* Strife was provoked by Wyclif (14th cent.), Wat Tyler (1381), Jack Cade (1450) uprisings. Reformation resulted in destruction or conversion to other uses of religious bldgs. by Henry VIII, who founded several grammar schools for the poor. London rose to unprecedented wealth, power, and cultural influence under Elizabeth; its life inspired works of Shakespeare, Spenser, Nashe, Greene, Peele, Kyd, and Marlowe. Stuart period brought struggle with the crown for London democratic privileges, culminating in the Civil War. In 1665 the Great Plague claimed c.75,000 lives, and in 1666 the Great Fire, lasting 5 days, virtually destroyed the city, including St. Paul's. Subsequent rebuilding gave London its many famous bldgs. by Wren. The Restoration revived London life; theaters (closed under Commonwealth) flourished, with contributions by Dryden, Congreve, Wycherley, and others. The 17th and 18th cent. saw rise of coffee houses as places for business transactions, later growing into commodity and other exchanges. Further architectural contributions were made by Nash. In 1750 Westminster Bridge supplemented London Bridge (hitherto the only Thames bridge); other bridges were added later (Blackfriars, 1770; Southwark, 1819; Tower Bridge, 1894). London was scene of many international conferences: 1830 conference on Greece; 1839 treaty recognizing Belgian independence and neutrality; 1852 conference; 1933 naval conference, 1933 world monetary and economic conference; 1944 convention on war criminals; and 1946 U.N. General Assembly meeting. Olympic Games were held here in 1948. In Second World War London suffered severe damage and heavy casualties from German air raids (mainly 1940–41), and from rocket bombs in 1944–45. E part of London and the City suffered most heavily and many famous bldgs. were destroyed or damaged.

London. 1 Town (pop. 353), Pope co., N central Ark., 8 mi. WNW of Russellville and on Arkansas R. **2** City (pop. 3,426), ⊙ Laurel co., SE Ky., in Cumberland foothills, 29 mi. E of Somerset; trade center for agr. (poultry, dairy products, tobacco, corn, wheat), coal, timber area; mfg. of buckets, textiles, fertilizer; sawmills, bottling works. Seat of Sue Bennet Col. (jr.; 1896). Near by are Sublimity Farms (a U.S. Forest Service land-use project), Levi Jackson Wilderness Road State Park, and Cumberland Natl. Forest. **3** Village (pop. 5,222), ⊙ Madison co., central Ohio, 24 mi. WSW of Columbus, in livestock and grain area; metal products. State prison farm near by. Founded 1811, inc. 1831. **4** Village (pop. 1,796, with adjacent Hugheston), Kanawha co., W.Va., on Kanawha R. and c.18 mi. SE of Charleston.

London Bridge, 5-arched granite bridge over the Thames in E central London, England, 1.5 mi. E of Charing Cross; 928 ft. long, it was designed by Rennie and built 1825–31, replacing several earlier structures; 1st of these was wooden bridge (963–75), replaced (1176–1209) by stone bridge with houses and a chapel. Until construction of Westminster Bridge (1739) it was only Thames bridge in London. Buildings were removed 1756–62.

Londonderry or **Derry** (lŭn″dŭndĕ′rē, dĕ′rē), county (□ 804.3; 1937 pop. 94,923; 1951 census 105,421, excluding Londonderry co. borough), Ulster, NW Northern Ireland; ⊙ Londonderry. Bounded by Co. Tyrone (S) and Co. Donegal (W), Ireland; the Atlantic (N); and Co. Antrim (E). Drained by Bann, Roe, and Foyle rivers. Surface is generally hilly, except for river valleys and narrow coastal strip; highest elevation is Sawel (2,240 ft.) in Sperrin Mts. (S). Some bog iron is worked. Chief agr. occupations are flax, oats, potato, barley growing, cattle and poultry raising, dairying. Sea fisheries are important. Linen milling is leading industry; other industries are mfg. of shoes, shirts, furniture, agr. implements; alcohol distilling, food canning. Beef cattle and eggs are exported. Besides Londonderry, towns are Coleraine, Limavady, and Port Stewart. Co. is associated with St. Columba. During reign of James I it was intensively colonized by the English, land being granted to corporations of City of London. In 1689 town of Londonderry was scene of famous siege. Excavations

(1932–36) by archaeologists revealed traces of occupation c.2000 B.C.

Londonderry or **Derry,** Gaelic *Dhoire,* county borough (1937 pop. 47,813; 1951 census 50,099), ⊙ Co. Londonderry, Northern Ireland, in W part of co., on a hill above Foyle R. (5 mi. above its mouth on Lough Foyle), and 65 mi. NW of Belfast; 55°N 7°20′W; seaport, with extensive quays, drydocks, shipyards, exporting chiefly cattle. Industries include linen and flour milling, tanning, iron founding, alcohol distilling, mfg. of shoes, agr. implements, shirts, hosiery, dairy products; bacon and ham curing. Town is also fishing center and agr. market. Notable features: town walls (1609), with 6 gates; Protestant cathedral (1628–33; restored 1886–87); R.C. cathedral; monastery church founded 1164; and Protestant bishops' palace. St. Columba founded abbey here 545; it was burned 812 by the Danes, who occupied site until 11th cent. In 1311 town was granted to Richard de Burgh; in 1566 the English here defeated Shane O'Neill, earl of Tyrone. Town was burned in 1608 and handed over to the corporations of the City of London, who changed name from Derry to Londonderry and settled Protestant colony here. In 1689 Londonderry was besieged by James II and held out under leadership of the Rev. George Walker until relieved after 105 days. A triumphal arch, one of town gates, and column commemorate event. In 1939 and 1940 Londonderry was scene of I.R.A. disturbances. It was a U.S. naval base in Second World War. Across the Foyle (bridged) is suburb of Waterside.

Londonderry. 1 Agr. town (pop. 1,640), Rockingham co., SE N.H., just SE of Manchester. Early settlers introduced potato growing, flax raising, linen making; now produces wood products, fruit, dairy products, poultry. Settled by Scotch-Irish 1719, chartered 1722. **2** Town (pop. 953), Windham co., S central Vt., on West R. and 28 mi. NW of Brattleboro; lumber, wood and dairy products. Partly in Green Mtn. Natl. Forest.

Londonderry, Cape, northernmost point of Western Australia, in Timor Sea, on NE coast at W end of Joseph Bonaparte Gulf; 13°45′S 126°55′E.

Londonderry Island (27 mi. long), Tierra del Fuego, Chile, on the Pacific, SW of main isl. of the archipelago; 55°S 71°W. Just off SW coast is small Treble Isl.

London Mills, village (pop. 581), on Fulton-Knox co. line, W central Ill., on Spoon R. (bridged here) and 16 mi. NW of Canton, in agr. and bituminous-coal-mining area; feed milling.

Londres (lōn′drĕs), town (pop. estimate 1,000), S central Catamarca prov., Argentina, 6 mi. SW of Belén; agr. (cereals, alfalfa, wine, walnuts, olives, livestock). Tungsten and tin mines near by.

Londrina (lōndrē′nụ), city (1940 pop. 10,531; 1950 census pop. 33,707), N Paraná, Brazil, on railroad and 190 mi. NW of Curitiba; chief trade center of N Paraná pioneer settlement zone, processing coffee, cotton, rice, fruit, and livestock; furniture mfg., paper milling, distilling. Founded 1932. Has large German and Slavic pop.

Londza River (lôn′jä), Serbo-Croatian *Londža,* N Croatia, Yugoslavia, in Slavonia; rises 5 mi. SSW of Nasice, flows c.30 mi. SW to Orljava R. just S of Pleternica.

Lone Cone, peak (12,761 ft.) in San Juan Mts., SW Colo., bet. San Miguel and Dolores counties.

Lone Elm, city (pop. 82), Anderson co., E Kansas, 13 mi. S of Garnett; livestock, grain; dairying.

Lonely Island, Russian SFSR: see UYEDINENIYE ISLAND.

Lonely Mine, township (pop. 88), Bulawayo prov., central Southern Rhodesia, in Matabeleland, 45 mi. NNE of Bulawayo (linked by road); gold mining. Declined since 1930s.

Lone Mountain, Nev.: see INDEPENDENCE MOUNTAINS.

Lone Oak. 1 Town (pop. 120), Meriwether co., W Ga., 14 mi. NE of La Grange. **2** Town (pop. 571), Hunt co., NE Texas, near Sabine R., 14 mi. SE of Greenville, in agr. area.

Loneoak, village (1940 pop. 868), McCracken co., SW Ky., 5 mi. SW of Paducah.

Lone Pine, village (pop. 1,415), Inyo co., E Calif., in Owens Valley, c.55 mi. S of Bishop; mining (lead, silver); stock raising. Gateway to Mt. Whitney recreational areas (W), Death Valley (E).

Lone Rock. 1 Town (pop. 188), Kossuth co., N Iowa, 11 mi. NNW of Algona; dairy products. **2** Village (pop. 570), Richland co., SW Wis., on Wisconsin R. and 14 mi. SE of Richland Center, in timber and agr. area; lumber, cheese.

Lonerock, city (pop. 38), Gilliam co., N Oregon, 24 mi. SW of Heppner.

Lone Tree, town (pop. 639), Johnson co., E Iowa, 13 mi. SSE of Iowa City; feed milling.

Lonevag (lō′nụvôg), Nor. *Lonevåg,* village (pop. 137) in Haus canton, Hordaland co., SW Norway, on W Osteroy, 11 mi. NNE of Bergen; leather mfg.

Lone Wolf, town (pop. 660), Kiowa co., SW Okla., 8 mi. WSW of Hobart, in cotton, grain, livestock area; cotton ginning, flour and feed milling.

Long, village (1939 pop. 28), W Alaska, 24 mi. S of Ruby; placer gold mining. Airfield.

Long, county (□ 403; pop. 3,598), SE Ga.; ⊙ Ludowici. Bounded SW by Altamaha R. Coastal plain agr. (corn, truck, livestock) and forestry (lumber, naval stores) area. Formed 1920.

Long, Loch (lŏkh), inlet of Firth of Clyde, bet. Dumbarton and Argyll, Scotland, extends 17 mi. N from Firth of Clyde to Arrochar. Loch Goil (5 mi. long) is a NW branch.

Longa Island (lŏng′gụ), at mouth of Gairloch, W Ross and Cromarty, Scotland; 1 mi. long, ½ mi. wide; rises to 229 ft.

Longares (lōng-gä′rĕs), town (pop. 1,336), Saragossa prov., NE Spain, 24 mi. SW of Saragossa; wine, cereals, sheep.

Longá River (lōng-gä′), Piauí, NE Brazil, rises S of Campo Maior, flows 150 mi. N to Parnaíba R. 25 mi. above Parnaíba city. Not navigable.

Longarone (lông-gärō′nĕ), village (pop. 1,040), Belluno prov., Veneto, N Italy, on Piave R. and 9 mi. NNE of Belluno; commercial center; sawmills, cardboard factory.

Long Ashton, residential town and parish (pop. 2,606), N Somerset, England, 3 mi. WSW of Bristol. Site of large orthopedic hosp. and 15th-cent. Ashton Court.

Longatico Inferiore, Yugoslavia: see DOLENJI LOGATEC.

Longaví (lōng-gävē′), town (pop. 1,561), Linares prov., S central Chile, on railroad and 10 mi. SW of Linares; health resort in agr. area (wheat, vegetables, fruit, wine, livestock). Thermal springs.

Longaví, Nevado (nävä′dō), Andean peak (10,600 ft.), Linares prov., S central Chile, 35 mi. SE of Linares.

Longaví River, Linares prov., S central Chile, rises in the Andes 12 mi. WNW of Dial Pass (Argentina border), flows c.60 mi. NW to join Perquilauquén R. 10 mi. WNW of Linares, forming Loncomilla R.

Longay (lŏng′gā), island (½ mi. long, ½ mi. wide), Inner Hebrides, Inverness, Scotland, just E of Scalpay; rises to 221 ft.

Long Barn, winter-sports resort, Tuolumne co., central Calif., in the Sierra Nevada, c.65 mi. ENE of Stockton.

Long Beach. 1 City (pop. 250,767), Los Angeles co., S Calif., 20 mi. S of downtown Los Angeles; has deepwater Long Beach Harbor (adjacent to Los ANGELES HARBOR) on San Pedro Bay. Year-round resort, with 8½-mi. bathing beach, a horseshoe-shaped pleasure pier, amusement zone, municipal auditorium, yacht harbor (on Alamitos Bay), fine parks. U.S. naval base (with dry docks). Port ships petroleum and cement, receives minerals, copra, timber; bulk of commerce is coastwise, but foreign trade is substantial. Shipyards; fishing fleet; includes E part of Terminal Isl. Large oil field (discovered 1921) at SIGNAL HILL (independent city surrounded by Long Beach). Mfg. of aircraft, tires, soap; oil refining, automobile assembling, fish and fruit canning. Has municipal airport, Air Force and naval air bases, and a city col. (jr.). Lakewood Village (pop. c.1,800) is a N suburb. Founded in 1880s, inc. 1888. **2** Resort town (pop. 1,103), La Porte co., NW Ind., on L. Michigan, 4 mi. NE of Michigan City. **3** Resort village (pop. 181) and W suburb of Glenwood, Pope co., W Minn., on L. Minnewaska. Fish hatchery near by. **4** Resort town (pop. 2,703), Harrison co., SE Miss., just W of Gulfport, on Mississippi Sound. Seat of Gulf Park Col. **5** Resort and residential city (pop. 15,586), Nassau co., SE N.Y., on barrier isl. off S shore of W Long Isl. (rail, highway connections), 8 mi. SE of Jamaica; mfg. (clothing, machinery, umbrellas), fisheries. A terminus of Long Isl. RR. Inc. 1922. **6** Town (pop. 783), Pacific co., SW Wash., on coast, just N of mouth of the Columbia, and 15 mi. NW of Astoria, Oregon; resorts, agr. experiment station.

Long Beach, narrow island (c.19 mi. long), E N.J., sheltering Little Egg Harbor, Manahawkin Bay, and S end of Barnegat Bay from the Atlantic. Barnegat City is at Barnegat Inlet at N end, Beach Haven and Beach Haven Inlet are at S end. Other resorts: Harvey Cedars, Surf City, Ship Bottom (bridge to mainland here).

Longbenton, urban district (1931 pop. 14,074; 1951 census 28,071), SE Northumberland, England, 3 mi. NNE of Newcastle-upon-Tyne; steel milling, coal mining. In urban dist. (3 mi. N) is coal-mining town of Burradon.

Longboat Key, SW Fla., narrow barrier island (c.10 mi. long), in Gulf of Mexico, sheltering Sarasota Bay.

Long Branch, residential town (pop. 5,172), S Ont., on L. Ontario; SW suburb of Toronto; resort.

Long Branch (lông′ brănch″). **1** Resort city (pop. 23,090), Monmouth co., E N.J., on the coast 5 mi. N of Asbury Park. Noted resort since early 19th cent.; mfg. (silk, fur goods, clothing, boats, rubber goods, dental goods); seafood; nursery products, truck. Has jr. col. Presidents Grant and Garfield had homes here. Settled 1740, inc. 1904. Includes communities of Elberon (estates; fishing), North Long Branch, and West End (estates; resort; whaling before 1860). **2** Borough (pop. 450), Washington co., SW Pa., 3 mi. S of Charleroi.

Long Buckby, town and parish (pop. 2,326), W Northampton, England, 10 mi. WNW of Northampton; shoe industry. Has 13th–14th-cent. church.

Long Cay (kā, kē) or **Fortune Island,** islet (10 mi. long NE-SW, c.1 mi. wide) and district (□ 8; pop. 101), S Bahama Isls., just W of Crooked Isl., 250 mi. SE of Nassau. Main settlement, Albert Town (center). Produces sisal, stock (goats, pigs, sheep), and salt.

Long Clawson, agr. village and parish (pop. 664), NE Leicester, England, 6 mi. NNW of Melton Mowbray; cheese making. Has 13th-cent. church.

Long Creek, town (pop. 288), Grant co., NE central Oregon, 50 mi. SE of Heppner; alt. 3,754 ft.

Longdale, town (pop. 277), Blaine co., W central Okla., 21 mi. NNW of Watonga, in agr. area (cotton, grain, livestock).

Longdendale, urban district (1951 census pop. 4,590), NE Cheshire, England, NE of Stockport; cotton and rayon milling. Formed 1936 from Hollingworth and Mottram.

Long Ditton, England: see ESHER.

Long Eaton, urban district (1931 pop. 22,345; 1951 census 28,638), SE Derby, England, near Trent R. 9 mi. E of Derby; cotton milling; major railroad switching yards. Site of Trent Col. Has Norman church, rebuilt in 14th cent.

Longeau (lōzhō′), village (pop. 272), Haute-Marne dept., NE France, on Plateau of Langres, 7 mi. S of Langres; cheese mfg.

Longeville-lès-Metz (lōzhvēl′-lā-mĕs′), W suburb (pop. 2,910) of Metz, Moselle dept., NE France, on left bank of Moselle R.

Long Falls Dam, Maine: see DEAD RIVER.

Longfellow-Evangeline Memorial State Park, S central La., along Bayou Teche just N of St. Martinville; established 1934 to commemorate supposed real-life heroine of Longfellow's poem *Evangeline.*

Longford, England: see COVENTRY.

Longford, Gaelic *Longphuirt,* county (□ 403; pop. 36,218), Leinster, Ireland; ⊙ Longford. Bounded by cos. Westmeath (SE and S), Roscommon (W), Leitrim (NW), and Cavan (NE). Drained by the Shannon and its tributaries; served by the Royal Canal. Surface is generally level, partly boggy, and becomes hilly on NW border. There are several lakes; co. is bounded by Lough Ree (SW). Limestone and marble are quarried. Dairying and butter making, cattle raising, potato growing are main occupations. Industries include linen and woolen milling. Besides Longford, other towns are Granard, Ballymahon, Drumlish, and Edgeworthstown. Pallas, near Ballymahon, is reputed birthplace of Oliver Goldsmith. On isls. in Lough Ree are noted monastic ruins.

Longford, Gaelic *Longphort,* urban district (pop. 4,020), ⊙ Co. Longford, Ireland, in W central part of co., on Camlin R., on branch of the Royal Canal, and 70 mi. WNW of Dublin; agr. market in dairying, cattle-raising, potato-growing region. The 19th-cent. St. Mel's Cathedral is seat of R.C. bishop of Ardagh. A 17th-cent. castle replaces earlier fort of the O'Farrells.

Longford, town (pop. 1,085), NE central Tasmania, 12 mi. S of Launceston and on S.Esk R.; livestock.

Longford, city (pop. 178), Clay co., N central Kansas, 27 mi. NNE of Salina; grain, livestock.

Longforgan (lŏng-fôr′gụn), agr. village and parish (pop. 2,106), SE Perthshire, Scotland, near Firth of Tay, 6 mi. W of Dundee. Site of Castle Huntly, begun c.1450.

Longframlington, town and parish (pop. 552), E central Northumberland, England, 8 mi. SSW of Alnwick; coal mining.

Long Grove, town (pop. 156), Scott co., E Iowa, 11 mi. N of Davenport, in agr. area.

Long Hill, Conn.: see TRUMBULL.

Long Hope, Scotland: see HOY.

Longhorn Cavern, Texas: see BURNET, town.

Longhorn Village, town (pop. 41), Crawford co., E central Mo.

Longhurst (lông′hûrst), village (pop. 1,539), Person co., N N.C., 3 mi. N of Roxboro; cotton-yarn mfg.

Long Island (15 mi. long, 2–6 mi. wide), SE Alaska, in Cordova Bay, N arm of Dixon Entrance, 55 mi. SW of Ketchikan; 54°51′N 132°42′W. Fishing at Howkan village (W) and in Elbow Bay region (NE). Sometimes called Howkan Isl.

Long Island, long, narrow island (65 mi. long, 1–3 mi. wide) and district (□ 130; pop. 4,564), S central Bahama Isls., bet. Exuma isls. (NW) and Crooked Isl. (SE), separated from the latter by Crooked Island Passage, and 150 mi. SE of Nassau. Crossed by the Tropic of Cancer. Main industries: salt panning, hemp growing, and stock raising (goats, pigs, sheep). Among the settlements are Clarence Town (S), Deadman's Cay (adjoining W), and Simms' (W). The isl., discovered by Columbus (Oct. 16, 1492), was originally inhabited by Indians. It was largely settled by Amer. loyalists in 1783; they introduced cotton, but left after abolition of slavery. Long Cay is 35 mi. SE.

Long Island. 1 Island (□ 13; pop. 671), SE N.F., in Placentia Bay, 65 mi. W of St. John's; 15 mi. long, 2 mi. wide; 47°35′N 54°5′W. On SE coast is fishing settlement of Harbour Buffet. **2** Island (6 mi. long, up to 4 mi. wide), E N.F., in Notre Dame Bay, 25 mi. SSW of Cape St. John; 49°35′N

55°40'W. **3** In Hermitage Bay, N.F.: see GAULTOIS ISLAND. **4** Island (12 mi. long, 2 mi. wide), in the Atlantic, W N.S., at entrance to Bay of Fundy, forming SW shore of St. Mary Bay, 30 mi. SW of Digby. At its extremities are Boar Head (N) and Dartmouth Point (S).

Long Island, volcanic island (□ 160; pop. c.250), Madang dist., Territory of New Guinea, SW Pacific, 30 mi. NE of New Guinea; copra. Has 2 craters; higher is Reumur Peak (4,278 ft.).

Long Island, New Zealand: see MUTTON BIRD ISLANDS; DUSKY SOUND.

Long Island, Scotland, name applied sometimes to the whole chain of the Outer HEBRIDES and sometimes just to LEWIS WITH HARRIS.

Long Island. 1 City (pop. 247), Phillips co., N Kansas, on Prairie Dog Creek, near Nebr. line, and 21 mi. ENE of Norton; corn, livestock. **2** Plantation (pop. 97), Hancock co., S Maine, on Long Isl. (c.2 mi. diameter; site of Frenchboro village), and on smaller Placentia, Black, Great Duck (lighthouse), and Little Duck (bird sanctuary) isls.; c.8 mi. S of Mt. Desert Isl., near entrance to Blue Hill Bay. **3** Village (pop. 2,147), Sullivan co., NE Tenn., just S of Kingsport.

Long Island. 1 Resort, fishing, and farming island (c.900 acres) off Portland, Maine, in Casco Bay. **2** Island (c.1½ mi. long), E Mass., in Boston Bay SE of downtown Boston. Connected to mainland by bridge (¾ mi. long) opened 1951, it is site of city hosp. and almshouse and a lighthouse. **3** Island (□ 1,401; 1940 pop. 4,600,022; 1950 pop. 5,237,909), SE N.Y.; it is 118 mi. long, 12–20 mi. wide, and extends ENE from mouth of the Hudson, generally parallel to N.Y. and Conn. shore (N), from which it is separated by LONG ISLAND SOUND; separated from Staten Isl. (W) by the Narrows of New York Bay, from Manhattan and Bronx boroughs of New York city by EAST RIVER. Its counties (W to E) are Kings (coextensive with BROOKLYN borough), Queens (coextensive with QUEENS borough), NASSAU, and SUFFOLK. Surface is generally a plain composed of glacial outwash, sloping gently S from higher N shore (max. alt. of bluffs, c.200 ft.) to low S shore; 2 ridges (100-c.400 ft. high), terminal moraines of glaciers, run length of isl., one near N shore and one near its center; in E, each is backbone of a long, fluke-like peninsula. The N fluke (c.27 mi. long) terminates at Orient Point; S fluke (c.43 mi. long) extends to Montauk Point, easternmost point of N.Y. Indented N shore of isl. has many bays and harbors in W, which are separated by moderately high, wooded peninsulas here called "necks"; resorts, residential communities; known for yachting. Along c.75 mi. of S shore is a barrier beach pierced by several inlets and sheltering large shallow bays (Jamaica, Great South, Moriches, Shinnecock) from the Atlantic. Here are shore resorts (Coney Isl., the Rockaway Peninsula, Long Beach, Jones Beach, Fire Isl.), residential and fishing communities. E Long Isl., more thinly settled than W, is known for the rural charm of its old villages, most of which are summer resorts. Fine country estates are scattered over isl. Its many potato and truck farms are an important source of supply for New York city; poultry raising (especially ducks), fisheries, and oyster culture (especially in Great South Bay) are important. Nassau co. and Suffolk counties are included in New York city metropolitan area; pop. of their residential communities increased greatly after Second World War. Isl. is served by Long Isl. RR net; has fine system of highways and landscaped parkways giving access to its many state parks and recreational areas. Site of La Guardia Field (New York municipal airport) and New York International Airport (at Idlewild). First occupied in 1636 by white men; Dutch and English colonies were established before the English gained control in 1664. Battle of Long Island (a British victory) was fought in W on Aug. 27, 1776. The isl. long remained a semi-rural region of farmers, whalers, and fishermen; pop. increased rapidly only after the growth of New York city created a vast market for its products, and after railroads and highways were built.

Long Island City, SE N.Y., an industrial and administrative center (with a co. courthouse) of Queens borough of New York city, on East R. opposite Manhattan; contains many industries, making food products, pianos, machinery, paint, shoes, cut stone, furniture, optical goods, aircraft parts; oil refining. Large railroad yards, express terminal. Extensive water front on East R. Connected to Manhattan by Queensboro Bridge, Queens-Midtown Vehicular Tunnel. Formerly a city of Queens co.; became part of borough in 1898.

Long Island Sound, N.Y. and Conn., sheltered arm of the Atlantic bet. N shore of Long Isl. and N.Y.-Conn. shore (N); c.90 mi. long, 3–20 mi. wide. Joined by East R. to Upper New York Bay; connects with Block Island Sound SW of New London, Conn. Important coastal shipping route; has extensive fisheries and shellfish beds. Its shores have many fine residential communities and yachting centers.

Longjumeau (lõ-zhümō'), town (pop. 2,758), Seine-et-Oise dept., N central France, on small Yvette R. and 11 mi. S of Paris; tanneries, glassworks; mfg. of chemicals, pharmaceuticals. In 1568, a treaty bet. Catholics and Protestants signed here.

Long Key, Pinellas co., W Fla., narrow barrier island (c.6 mi. long) and resort area, in Gulf of Mexico, near mouth of Tampa Bay, 7 mi. WSW of St. Petersburg; connected by causeway with near-by mainland. There is also a Long Key in FLORIDA KEYS chain.

Longlac (lông'lăk), village (pop. estimate 250), central Ont., on Long L., 150 mi. NE of Port Arthur; alt. 1,035 ft.; gold mining.

Long Lake. 1 Lake (□ 3; 6 mi. long, 1 mi. wide), N central N.B., 40 mi. E of Grand Falls. **2** Lake (□ 75), central Ont., 150 mi. NE of Port Arthur; 45 mi. long, 2 mi. wide; drains S into L. Superior. At N end is Longlac.

Long Lake. 1 Village (pop. 2,637), Lake co., NE Ill., 15 mi. W of Waukegan. **2** Resort village (pop. 399), Hennepin co., E Minn., just N of L. Minnetonka, 15 mi. W of Minneapolis; cheese. **3** Resort village, Hamilton co., NE central N.Y., in the Adirondacks, on E shore of Long L. (14 mi. long, c.1 mi. wide), c.75 mi. NE of Utica. Has seaplane port. Lake receives and discharges Raquette R.

Longlake or **Long Lake,** town (pop. 175), McPherson co., N S.Dak., 18 mi. NW of Leola.

Long Lake. 1 In NE Calif., in the Sierra Nevada at base of Mt. Elwell, 14 mi. SW of Portola; campgrounds; fishing. **2** In Aroostook co., N Maine, lake in course of the Allagash, in recreational area 68 mi. W of Presque Isle; 4 mi. long. **3** In Aroostook co., N Maine, most easterly of FISH RIVER LAKES. **4** Cumberland co., SW Maine, center of resort area; 13.5 mi. long, .5–1 mi. wide. Discharges S through Songo R. into Sebago L. Seaplane, steamboat service. **5** In Alpena and Presque Isle counties, NE Mich., 7 mi. N of Alpena, near L. Huron; c.8 mi. long, 1 mi. wide; resort. **6** In Grand Traverse co., NW Mich., c.6 mi. SW of Traverse City, in forested resort area; c.4 mi. long, 1 mi. wide. **7** In Crow Wing co., central Minn., lake (□ 10) in state forest, just E of Gull L., 4 mi. N of Brainerd; 6.5 mi. long. Resorts. **8** In Hubbard co., W Minn., just E of Park Rapids; 6 mi. long, 1 mi. wide. Fishing, boating, and bathing resorts. Drains through small stream into Crow Wing R. **9** In S central N.Dak., 30 mi. E of Bismarck; 20 mi. long. Used as migratory waterfowl refuge. **10** In Washburn co., NW Wis., 11 mi. SE of Spooner, in resort area; narrow lake, c.13 mi. long, and bordered by spruce trees.

Long Lake Dam, Wash.: see SPOKANE RIVER.

Longlaville (lõlävēl'), NE suburb (pop. 2,918) of Longwy, Meurthe-et-Moselle dept., NE France, on Chiers R., at Luxembourg border, in Longwy iron-mining and metallurgical dist. Customhouse.

Longlier (lõlēā'), village (pop. 1,178), Luxembourg prov., SE Belgium, in the Ardennes, just NE of Neufchâteau; agr., lumbering.

Long Marston, England: see MARSTON MOOR.

Longmeadow, residential town (pop. 6,508), Hampden co., S Mass., on Connecticut R. just S of Springfield. Settled 1644, inc. 1783.

Long Melford, town and parish (pop. 2,525), S Suffolk, England, on Stour R. and 3 mi. N of Sudbury; agr. market; pharmaceutical and agr.-implement works. Has 15th-cent. inn, 2 moated Elizabethan mansions.

Longmire, Wash.: see MOUNT RAINIER NATIONAL PARK.

Longmont, city (pop. 8,099), Boulder co., N Colo., on St. Vrain Creek, near Front Range and 30 mi. N of Denver; alt. 5,000 ft. Trade and food-processing center for sugar-beet and grain region; beet sugar, flour, canned vegetables, dairy products; bricks, tiles. Coal mines in vicinity. Longs Peak 28 mi. W. Founded c.1870, inc. as town 1873, as city 1885.

Longmy (loung'mē'), town, Rachgia prov., S Vietnam, 27 mi. WNW of Loctrang; rice.

Longny-au-Perche (lõnyē'-ō-pârsh'), village (pop. 1,000), Orne dept., NW France, 9 mi. E of Mortagne, in the Perche hills; horse fairs.

Longobardi (lông-gōbär'dē), village (pop. 1,556), Cosenza prov., Calabria, S Italy, near Tyrrhenian Sea, 12 mi. WSW of Cosenza.

Longobucco (lông-gôbōōk'kô), town (pop. 5,526), Cosenza prov., Calabria, S Italy, near Trionto R., 9 mi. S of Rossano, in fruitgrowing region; domestic weaving.

Longonjo (lông-gōn'jō), town, Benguela prov., W Angola, on Benguela RR and 35 mi. WSW of Nova Lisboa; alt. 4,650 ft. Brick and tile works.

Longonot (lông-gō'nōt), village, Rift Valley prov., W central Kenya, in Great Rift Valley at foot of Longonot volcano (alt. 9,350 ft.), on railroad and 10 mi. SSE of Naivasha; wheat-growing center; coffee, sisal, corn, fruits.

Longorien, Kenya: see MARA.

Longos, peninsula, Greece: see SITHONIA.

Longosa, Bulgaria: see KAMCHIYA RIVER.

Longotoma (lōng-gōtō'mä), village (1930 pop. 2,956), Aconcagua prov., central Chile, on railroad and 9 mi. NW of La Ligua; agr. (potatoes, oats, livestock).

Longowal, India: see LAUNGOWAL.

Long Pine, city (pop. 567), Brown co., N Nebr., 8 mi. E of Ainsworth; resort; livestock, truck produce. Recreation park and dam near by.

Long Point, peninsula, S Ont., extends 20 mi. E into L. Erie, ESE of Port Rowan; 1–4 mi. wide.

Long Point, village (pop. 286), Livingston co., N central Ill., 16 mi. WNW of Pontiac, in agr. and bituminous-coal area.

Long Point, SE Mass., sandspit on N tip of Cape Cod; curves SE to shelter Provincetown harbor. Has lighthouse (42°2'N 70°12'W).

Long Pond, village (pop. 89), Somerset co., W Maine, on Long Pond (8 mi. long, 1 mi. wide) and 27 mi. NW of Greenville, in lumbering, hunting, fishing area.

Long Pond. 1 Lake in Plymouth co., SE Mass., 9 mi. SE of Taunton, in lake region; c.3.5 mi. long. Joined by stream to Assawompsett Pond (NE). **2** Lake in N.Y.: see WILLSBORO.

Longport, England: see STOKE-ON-TRENT.

Longport, borough (pop. 618), Atlantic co., SE N.J., on the coast 5 mi. SW of Atlantic City.

Long Prairie, village (pop. 2,443), ⊙ Todd co., central Minn., on Long Prairie R. and 25 mi. W of Little Falls; trading point in grain, livestock, and poultry area; flour, dairy, and wood products; printing. Platted 1867, inc. 1883. Winnebago Indian Agency here 1848–55.

Long Prairie River, rises in cluster of lakes in Douglas co., W Minn. flows 120 mi. E and N, past long Prairie village, to Crow Wing R. at Motley.

Longpré-les-Corps-Saints (lõprā'-lā-kôr-sē'), village (pop. 1,147), Somme dept., N France, near the Somme, 9 mi. SE of Abbeville; varnishes and paints.

Long Range Mountains, extend 120 mi. NNW from Bonne Bay along NW coast of N.F. Highest peak is Gros Morne (2,666 ft.), 45 mi. NNE of Corner Brook. Other peaks are Gros Pate (2,115 ft.) and Blue Mtn. (2,085 ft.)

Longreach, town (pop. 3,282), central Queensland, Australia, 240 mi. NW of Charleville; chief wool-producing center of state.

Longridge, urban district (1931 pop. 4,158; 1951 census 4,314), N central Lancashire, England, 6 mi. NE of Preston; cheese processing, stone quarrying. Site of Preston reservoirs.

Long Sault Island (lông' sōō'), St. Lawrence co., N N.Y., in the St. Lawrence (Long Sault rapids here), at Ont. line, 3 mi. N of Massena; c.4½ mi. long, ¼–1 mi. wide.

Long Sault Rapids (sōō'). **1** In the St. Lawrence, SE Ont., 12 mi. WSW of Cornwall; 9 mi. long. Bypassed by Cornwall Canal (11 mi. long). **2** Two series of waterfalls in Ottawa R. bet. SW Que. and E Ont. At the first, below Timiskaming, river drops 194 ft. over distance of 8 mi. At the second, bet. Montreal and Ottawa, opposite Hawkesbury, a small French force under Dollard des Ormeaux, attempting to save Ville Marie (Montreal), was overpowered by large Iroquois force, May, 1660.

Longside, agr. village and parish (pop. 2,321), NE Aberdeen, Scotland, on Ugie R. and 6 mi. W of Peterhead.

Longs Peak (14,255 ft.), N Colo., in Front Range of Rocky Mts., 10 mi. SSW of Estes Park town. Peak is highest point in Rocky Mtn. Natl. Park; from summit, reached by 2 trails, there is spectacular view of peaks of Rocky Mts.

Longstone Island, England: see FARNE ISLANDS.

Long Stop Hill or **Djebel el Athmera** (jĕ'bĕl ĕl ätmĕrä'), height (alt. 951 ft.) in N Tunisia, near left bank of Medjerda R., 6 mi. N of Medjez-el-Bab. Scene of bitter fighting in last phase of Tunisian campaign (April–May, 1943) in Second World War.

Long Strait or **De Long Strait,** joins E.Siberian and Chukchi seas at 70°N lat., separating Wrangel Isl. from mainland of NE Siberian Russian SFSR; 85 mi. wide. Named for U.S. explorer De Long, who first navigated here, 1867.

Longstreet, village (pop. 224), De Soto parish, NW La., 31 mi. SSW of Shreveport, in agr. area.

Long Sutton, former urban district (1931 pop. 2,902), Parts of Holland, SE Lincolnshire, England, 5 mi. E of Holbeach; agr. market in fruit-growing region. Has church of Norman origin with 15th-cent. additions.

Longthanh (loung'tä'nyů), town, Bienhoa prov., S Vietnam, 17 mi. E of Saigon; rubber plantations; airport. Center of Caodaist cult.

Long Tom River, W Oregon, rises in Lane co., on E slope of Coast Range, flows 50 mi. N to Willamette R. S of Corvallis. Fern Ridge Dam, 10 mi. WNW of Eugene, consists of earth embankment (10,860 ft. long, 44 ft. high) and concrete sec. (294 ft. long, 49 ft. high); total length 11,154 ft. Completed 1941 by U.S. Army Engineers as storage unit in flood-control and navigation project in Willamette R. basin. Reservoir has max. capacity of 102,000 acre-ft.

Longton. 1 Village and parish (pop. 3,205), W Lancashire, England, 5 mi. WSW of Preston; dairy farming, agr. **2** Town in the Potteries district, NW Stafford, England, since 1910 part of STOKE-ON-TRENT.

Longton, city (pop. 478), Elk co., SE Kansas, on Elk R. and 21 mi. WNW of Independence; shipping and trading point in grain and cattle area. Oil and gas wells near by.

Longtown, agr. market town in parish of Arthuret (pop. 2,145), N Cumberland, England, on Esk R., on Scottish border, and 8 mi. N of Carlisle. N, 3 mi., is E end of Scot's Dyke, a wooded fortified line 3 mi. long, built in 1552.

Longtown, town (pop. 139), Perry co., E Mo., 6 mi. SE of Perryville.

Long Trail, Vt.: see GREEN MOUNTAINS.

Longué (lõgā'), town (pop. 2,034), Maine-et-Loire dept., W France, 9 mi. N of Saumur; furniture mfg., food preserving, winegrowing.

Longueau (lõgō'), outer SE suburb (pop. 2,770) of Amiens, Somme dept., N France, on the Avre near its mouth on the Somme; rail junction.

Longue Island or **Long Island,** one of the Seychelles, in Mahé group, off NE coast of Mahé Isl., 4 mi. E of Victoria, 4°37'S 55°31'E; ½ mi. long, ¼ mi. wide. Quarantine station.

Longue Pointe (lŏng point', Fr. lõg pwĕt'), NE suburb of Montreal, S Que., on the St. Lawrence, on E side of Montreal Isl.

Longueuil (lõgû'ē), residential city (pop. 7,087), ⊙ Chambly co., SW Que., on the St. Lawrence, opposite Montreal (ferry). Settled 1657, inc. 1874.

Longueville (lõgvēl'), village (pop. 934), Seine-et-Marne dept., N central France, 4 mi. SW of Provins; mfg. of copper tubing; peat extracting, cementworks.

Longueville-sur-Scie (–sür-sē'), village (pop. 622), Seine-Inférieure dept., N France, 9 mi. S of Dieppe; powdered-milk mfg., flour milling.

Longuyon (lõgēō'), town (pop. 4,519), Meurthe-et-Moselle dept., NE France, on Chiers R. and 9 mi. SW of Longwy; rail center; mfg. (hosiery, vinegar), metalworking. Damaged in Second World War.

Long Valley Reservoir, Calif.: see OWENS RIVER.

Long View, village (pop. 239), Champaign co., E Ill., 18 mi. SSE of Champaign, in agr. area.

Longview. 1 Village (1940 pop. 227), Oktibbeha co., E Miss., 7 mi. WSW of Starkville. **2** Town (pop. 2,291), Catawba co., W central N.C., just W of Hickory. **3** City (pop. 24,502), ⊙ Gregg co., E Texas, near Sabine R., c.55 mi. W of Shreveport, La.; principal supply, trade, industrial center of rich East Texas oil field; pipeline terminus; oil refining, mfg. (steel, chemicals, tools, lumber, oil-field, farm, and bldg. machinery, cottonseed oil, food products). Seat of Le Tourneau Technical Inst. Settled 1865, inc. 1872; boomed after discovery of oil, 1930. **4** City (pop. 20,339), Cowlitz co., SW Wash., near Kelso and at junction of the Cowlitz with Columbia R., spanned here by cantilever interstate bridge, one of country's longest (center span, 1,200 ft.). Lumber-milling and wood-processing center (pulp, paper, plywood) and deep-water port (c.50 mi. from the Pacific); port of entry. Aluminum plant; fish canneries, food-processing plants. Has a jr. col. Founded 1923 as the Northwest's 1st "planned city."

Longville, village (pop. 116), Cass co., N central Minn., c.45 mi. N of Brainerd, SE of Leech L.

Longwood, England: see HUDDERSFIELD.

Longwood, Gaelic *Magh Dearmhaighe,* town (pop. 115), S Co. Meath, Ireland, on the Royal Canal and 9 mi. SW of Trim; agr. market (cattle, horses; potatoes).

Longwood, locality, central SAINT HELENA, in S Atlantic, on interior plateau, 2.5 mi. SE of Jamestown. Famed as residence (1815–21) of Napoleon, who was confined here by the British until his death. His body was removed (1840) to France. Site of govt.-owned flax-fiber mill.

Longwood, town (pop. 717), Seminole co., E central Fla., 11 mi. N of Orlando, in citrus-fruit area.

Longwood Park, village (pop. 1,585), Richmond co., S N.C., 3 mi. N of Hamlet.

Longwy (lõwē'), town (pop. 12,064), Meurthe-et-Moselle dept., NE France, on Chiers R. and 18 mi. WSW of Luxembourg city, near Belg. and Luxembourg border; customs station. Major center of important Longwy iron-mining and metallurgical dist.; blast furnaces, steel mills, boiler works. Also produces porcelain, ceramic refractories. Comprises Longwy-Bas (alt. 740 ft.; pop. 4,796), business and mfg. dist.; residential Longwy-Gouraincourt (pop. 2,848); and Longwy-Haut (alt. 1,265 ft.; pop. 4,420), an old stronghold fortified by Vauban. Unsuccessfully defended by French in 1815, 1870, and 1914. Industrial area and rail yards damaged in Second World War.

Longxuyen (loung'sōōyĕn'), town, ⊙ Longxuyen prov. (□ 1,000; 1943 pop. 280,200), S Vietnam, in Cochin China, on right bank of Bassac R. and 90 mi. WSW of Saigon, in highly irrigated area; major rice and agr. (sugar cane, corn, beans, peanuts, tobacco, fruit) center; sericulture. Former Khmer territory; passed (18th cent.) to Annamese.

Longyear City, Nor. *Longyearbyen* (lông'yērbü'ŭn), chief settlement (pop. 633) and port of West Spitsbergen, Spitsbergen group, in central part of isl., at head of Advent Bay (small S arm of Is Fjord); 78°13'N 15°35'E. Seat of governor of the Norwegian possession Svalbard; coal-mining center; radio station. Port ice-free from July to late Sept. during which time the pop. is increased. Founded 1906 by the American miner Longyear. In Second World War, settlement was evacuated, then occupied (1941) by Germans; recaptured (1942) by Free Norwegian forces; destroyed (July, 1943) by German navy; later rebuilt.

Loni (lō'nē), town (pop. 3,275), Meerut dist., NW Uttar Pradesh, India, 7 mi. NNE of Delhi; wheat, gram, jowar, sugar cane, oilseeds.

Lonigo (lônē'gô), town (pop. 5,303), Vicenza prov., Veneto, N Italy, at SW foot of Monti Berici, 13 mi. SW of Vicenza. Agr. center; mfg. (metalworking machinery, cable, electric drills, leather goods, buttons, silk and cotton textiles). Noted for its annual horse fair.

Loning (lô'nĭng'), town, ⊙ Loning co. (pop. 167,197), NW Honan prov., China, on Lo R. and 55 mi. WSW of Loyang; cotton weaving; kaoliang, millet, beans. Until 1914 called Yungning.

Löningen (lû'nĭng-ŭn), village (commune pop. 10,002), in Oldenburg, NW Germany, after 1945 in Lower Saxony, 14 mi. SW of Cloppenburg; mfg. of agr. machinery, wool; brewing, distilling (brandy).

Lonja River (lô'nyä), N Croatia, Yugoslavia, rises 9 mi. SSW of Varazdin, flows c.100 mi. S, past Ivanic Grad, to Sava R. 9 mi. S of Kutina; forms W boundary of Slavonia. Called Lojnica in upper course, in lower course, Trebes, Serbo-Croatian *Trebeš.* Receives Cazma, Ilova, and Pakra rivers.

Lonkin (lōngkĭn'), village, Myitkyina dist., Kachin State, Upper Burma, on Uyu R. (left affluent of Chindwin R.) and 60 mi. WNW of Myitkyina, jade-mining center, linked by road with Mogaung.

Lonmay (lŏnmā'), agr. village and parish (pop. 1,812), NE Aberdeen, Scotland, 5 mi. S of Fraserburgh.

Lonneker (lô'nŭkŭr), town (pop. 14,204), Overijssel prov., E Netherlands, 2 mi. NE of Enschede; center of cooperative agr. movement; cattle feed, synthetic fertilizer, butter; mfg. of cement, plastics, spring mattresses; stone quarrying.

Lonnerstadt (lô'nŭr-shtät), village (pop. 1,173), Upper Franconia, N Bavaria, Germany, 19 mi. W of Forchheim; brewing.

Lonoke (lō'nōk), county (□ 800; pop. 27,278), central Ark.; ⊙ Lonoke. Bounded N by small Cypress Bayou; drained by small Plum, Meto, and Two Prairie bayous. Agr. (rice, cotton, truck, fruit, livestock). Mfg. of wood products, cheese and other dairy products; feed; cotton ginning, rice milling, sawmilling. Has state fish hatchery. Formed 1873.

Lonoke, city (pop. 1,556), ⊙ Lonoke co., central Ark., 21 mi. E of Little Rock; trade center and shipping point for area producing rice, cotton, pecans, strawberries; cotton ginning, sawmilling. Has state fish hatchery.

Lonoli (lōnō'lē), village, Equator Prov., central Belgian Congo, near Tshuapa R., 50 mi. ESE of Boende; palm-oil milling, hardwood lumbering.

Lonquimay (lōngkēmī'), town (pop. estimate 1,000), E La Pampa natl. territory, Argentina, on railroad and 40 mi. ENE of Santa Rosa; grain and livestock center. Mfg. of insecticides, liquor, dairy products.

Lonquimay, village (1930 pop. 19), Malleco prov., S central Chile, 95 mi. SE of Angol, on trans-Andean road to Zapala, Argentina; health resort; wheat, livestock. Lonquimay Volcano (9,480 ft.) is 20 mi. NW.

Lonsboda (lŭns'bōō"dä), Swedish *Lönsboda,* village (pop. 799), Kristianstad co., S Sweden, 25 mi. N of Kristianstad; stone quarrying.

Lonsdal (lŭns'däl), Nor. *Lønsdal,* village in Saltdal canton, Nordland co., N central Norway, in the Lonsdal (valley), within Arctic Circle, on tributary of Salt R. and 40 mi. SE of Bodo; tourist resort. Terminus of railroad under construction (in 1950) to Bodo. Starting point of bus routes to Bodo, Narvik, Tromso, and Kirkenes.

Lonsdale (lŏnz'dāl). **1** Town (pop. 91), Garland co., central Ark., 14 mi. E of Hot Springs. **2** Village (pop. 510), Rice co., S Minn., 35 mi. SSW of St. Paul, in grain, livestock, poultry area. **3** Industrial village (1940 pop. 1,680) in Cumberland and Lincoln towns, Providence co., NE R.I., on Blackstone R. (bridged here) and 6 mi. N of Providence; textiles, bakery goods. Trappist monastery near by. **4** or **Jordania** (jôrdā'nēŭ), mill village (pop. 1,533), Oconee co., NW S.C.; suburb of Seneca; textiles.

Lonsdale, Point (lŏnz'dāl), S Victoria, Australia, in Bass Strait; forms W side of entrance to Port Phillip Bay; 38°18'S 144°37'E. Surrounded by reefs; lighthouse.

Lons-le-Saunier (lō-lŭ-sōnyā'), town (pop. 14,247), ⊙ Jura dept., E France, at the foot of the Jura, 45 mi. NW of Geneva; commercial center with extensive trade in Gruyère cheese and sparkling wines. Mfg. (chocolates, soap, fountain pens). Saltworks near by. Thermal station with brine wells known since Roman times. Rouget de Lisle b. here.

Lontué, department, Chile: see MOLINA.

Lontué (lōntwā'), town (pop. 1,212), Talca prov., central Chile, near Lontué R., 4 mi. NNE of Molina, on railroad; wine, wheat, barley, livestock. Hydroelectric station near by.

Lontué River, central Chile, rises in the Andes near Argentina border, flows c.75 mi. along Curicó and Talca prov. borders to join Teno R. 5 mi. WNW of Curicó, forming Mataquito R. The upper course is called Río Colorado. Used for hydroelectric power and irrigation. Known for wine grown along its valley.

Lontzen, Belgium: see HERBESTHAL.

Lonya (lō'nyŏ), Hung. *Lónya,* town (pop. 2,161), Szatmar-Bereg co., NE Hungary, 35 mi. NE of Nyiregyhaza; potatoes, tobacco, apples, pears.

Loo, Belgium: see Lo.

Loo, Het, Netherlands: see APELDOORN.

Looc (lō-ōk'), town (1939 pop. 1,317; 1948 municipality pop. 14,830), SW Tablas Isl., Romblon prov., Philippines, on Looc Bay (inlet of Tablas Strait); agr. center (rice, coconuts).

Loo-choo: see RYUKYU ISLANDS.

Loochristi or **Loochristy,** Belgium: see LOCHRISTI.

Looe (lōō), urban district (1931 pop. 2,877; 1951 census 3,801), E Cornwall, England, on Looe Bay of the Channel, at mouth of Looe R., and 14 mi. SE of Bodmin. Includes fishing ports, agr. markets, and tourist resorts of East Looe, on E bank of Looe R., and West Looe, opposite. West Looe has 16th-cent. inn, former pirates' and smugglers' resort, and 14th-cent. church. Just offshore is small Looe Isl.

Loogootee (lŭgō'tē, lō–), city (pop. 2,424), Martin co., SW Indiana, near East Fork of White R., 14 mi. E of Washington, in agr. area (wheat, corn, hay); lumber milling; mfg. of veneer, tile, brick, buttons, shirts. Bituminous-coal mines, gas and oil wells.

Lookeba (lōō'kŭbô, lōō'–), town (pop. 206), Caddo co., W central Okla., 25 mi. WSW of El Reno, in agr. area; cotton ginning.

Lookingglass River, S central Mich., rises near Shiawassee-Livingston co. line, flows c.65 mi. N and W, past De Witt, to Grand R. at Portland.

Lookout, village (pop. c.1,000), Pike co., E Ky., in the Cumberlands, 14 mi. NE of Jenkins, in bituminous-coal region.

Lookout, Cape, N Ont., on Hudson Bay, 65 mi. W of entrance of James Bay; 55°18'N 83°55'W.

Lookout, Cape. 1 In E N.C., headland at meeting of 2 barrier Isls. (Core Banks and Shackleford Banks), c.70 mi. SW of Cape Hatteras; lighthouse at 34°37'N 76°31'W. **2** In NW Oregon, coastal promontory c.10 mi. SW of Tillamook.

Lookout, Point, low headland, St. Marys co., S Md., at N side of mouth of the Potomac on Chesapeake Bay; lighthouse (built 1830). Resort (beach; duck shooting, fishing). Cemetery here is on site of Civil War fort where some 3,000 Confederate prisoners died.

Lookout Creek, in Ala., Ga., and Tenn., rises near Valley Head, Ala., flows c.50 mi. NE, through extreme NW Ga., to Tennessee R. just W of Chattanooga.

Lookout Heights, town (pop. 603), Kenton co., N Ky., just SW of Covington.

Lookout Mountain, residential town (pop. 1,675), Hamilton co., SE Tenn., along N ridge of Lookout Mtn. at Ga. line, 3 mi. SW of Chattanooga; reached by road and cable railway from Chattanooga. Has limestone caves, interesting rock formations, Adolph S. Ochs Observatory and Mus. (dedicated 1940). Civil War "Battle above the Clouds" fought here. Part of surrounding area is in Chickamauga and Chattanooga Natl. Military Park.

Lookout Mountain. 1 Peak (6,505 ft.) in Sierra Ancha, central Ariz., c.60 mi. NE of Phoenix. **2** Peak (7,375 ft.) in Front Range, just W of Denver, N central Colo. On summit is grave of William F. Cody (Buffalo Bill). **3** Peak (9,110 ft.) in W N. Mex., in Zuni Mts., 34 mi. SE of Gallup. **4** Narrow ridge (c.2,000 ft.) of the Cumberland Plateau in Tenn., Ga., and Ala., parallel to Sand Mtn.; from Moccasin Bend of Tennessee R. near Chattanooga, Tenn., extends c.75 mi. SSW, across NW corner of Ga., to Gadsden, Ala.; coal mining. Cable railway and road ascend NE end (alt. 2,392 ft.), a popular tourist area with a magnificent view, interesting limestone caverns, notable Rock City Gardens, and Adolph S. Ochs Observatory and Mus. This portion of ridge contains residential town of Lookout Mountain, was site (1863) of Civil War Battle of Lookout Mountain ("Battle above the Clouds"), and is partly included in Chickamauga and Chattanooga Natl. Military Park.

Lookout Point Dam, Oregon: see MIDDLE FORK.

Lookout Shoals Lake, N.C.: see CATAWBA RIVER.

Loomis. 1 Village (pop. c.525), Placer co., central Calif., in Sacramento Valley, 23 mi. NE of Sacramento; ships fruit. **2** Village (pop. 218), Phelps co., S Nebr., 6 mi. WNW of Holdrege.

Loon (lō-ōn'), town (1939 pop. 1,430; 1948 municipality pop. 29,683), W Bohol isl., Philippines, on Bohol Strait, 11 mi. NNW of Tagbilaran; agr. center (rice, coconuts, hemp).

Loon Lake, resort village, Franklin co., NE N.Y., on Loon Lake (c.2 mi. long), 31 mi. WSW of Plattsburg.

Loon Lake, Piscataquis co., NW Maine, 47 mi. N of Greenville, in wilderness recreational area; 4.5 mi. long.

Loon op Zand (lōn' ôp sänt'), town (pop. 2,489), North Brabant prov., S Netherlands, 5 mi. N of Tilburg; leather tanning.

Loop Head, promontory on the Atlantic, SW Co. Clare, Ireland, on N shore of mouth of the Shannon, 20 mi. WSW of Kilrush; lighthouse (52°34'N 9°56'W).

Loos (lōs). **1** WSW suburb (pop. 12,240) of Lille, Nord dept., N France; chemical works (dyes, fertilizer, waxes), textile mills. Its old Cistercian abbey is now a prison. **2** Town, Pas-de-Calais dept., France: see LOOS-EN-GOHELLE.

Loos, Îles de, Fr. West Africa: see LOS ISLANDS.

Loosahatchie River (lo͞osŭhă′chē), SW Tenn., rises SW of Hardeman, flows c.65 mi. W past Somerville, to Mississippi R. near Memphis; upper course canalized.

Loosdorf (lōs′dôrf), town (pop. 2,567), central Lower Austria, near the Danube, 10 mi. W of Sankt Pölten; grain, cattle, orchards.

Loosdrechtsche Plassen (lōs′drĕkhtsů plä′sůn), group of shallow lakes in Utrecht prov., W central Netherlands, 6 mi. NNW of Utrecht; 4 mi. long, 3 mi. wide. Lake fishing, water sports.

Loosduinen (lōs′doinůn), village (pop. 6,238), South Holland prov., W Netherlands, 4 mi. SSW of The Hague; grows vegetables and flowers, chiefly marketed in The Hague.

Loose, residential town and parish (pop. 2,173), central Kent, England, 2 mi. S of Maidstone; stone quarries near by.

Loos-en-Gohelle (lōs-ā-gôĕl′), town (pop. 3,170), Pas-de-Calais dept., N France, 3 mi. NW of Lens, in coal-mining dist. Recaptured by British during costly battle of Loos (Sept.–Oct., 1915) in First World War. Near-by Double Crassier (a shale hill) and Hill 70 were scene of desperate fighting. Several Br. cemeteries in area. Named Loos until 1937.

Looz, Belgium: see BORGLOON.

Lop (lŏp), Chinese *Lohpu* or *Lo-p'u* (both: lŭ′po͞o′), town and oasis (pop. 123,608), SW Sinkiang prov., China, 20 mi. SE of Khotan and on highway; silk-milling center; cotton textiles, carpets; corn, wheat, fruit; jade.

Lopadusa, Pelagie Isls.: see LAMPEDUSA.

Lopandino (lôpŭndyĕnů), town (1948 pop. over 500), SE Bryansk oblast, Russian SFSR, 4 mi. NNE of Komarichi; sugar refining.

Lopasnya (lŭpäs′nyů), village (1948 pop. over 2,000), S Moscow oblast, Russian SFSR, 19 mi. S of Podolsk; dairying.

Lopatin (lŭpä′tyĭn). **1** Town (1947 pop. over 500), N Dagestan Autonomous SSR, Russian SFSR, fishing port on Caspian Sea, on N tip of Agrakhan Peninsula, 60 mi. N (under jurisdiction) of Makhachkala; fish processing. **2** Pol. *Łopatyn* (wôpä′tĭn), village (1931 pop. 3,427), NE Lvov oblast, Ukrainian SSR, 15 mi. NW of Brody; agr. processing (grain, vegetables, hops).

Lopatino (lŭpä′tĭnů). **1** Village, Mari Autonomous SSR, Russian SFSR: see VOLZHSK. **2** Village, Moscow oblast, Russian SFSR: see VOSKRESENSK. **3** Village (1939 pop. over 2,000), SE Penza oblast, Russian SFSR, 26 mi. NE of Petrovsk; metal-works; wheat, sunflowers.

Lopatka, Cape (lŭpät′kŭ), S extremity of Kamchatka Peninsula, NE Siberian Russian SFSR; 50°52′N 156°40′E. Separated by First Kuril Strait from Shumshu Isl., northernmost of the Kuriles.

Lopatki (lŭpät′kē), village (1926 pop. 2,255), SE Kurgan oblast, Russian SFSR, 20 mi. S of Lebyazhye, in agr. area; metalworks.

Lopatyn, Ukrainian SSR: see LOPATIN, Lvov oblast.

Lopburi (lôp′bo͝orē′), town (1947 pop. 7,779), ⊙ Lopburi prov. (□ 2,511; 1947 pop. 203,313), S Thailand, on Lopburi R., on railroad, and 75 mi. N of Bangkok; rice center. Has 17th-cent. royal palace (built by Fr. architects), with archaeological mus.; remains of Khmer temples and shrines. The anc. Lavo, it was ruled (7th–8th cent.) by the Mon dynasty and (10th–13th cent.) by the Khmers. During the Ayutthaya period, it was (after 1665) royal summer residence and alternate capital. Declined after fall of Ayutthaya. Sometimes spelled Lobburi.

Lopburi River, S Thailand, a left arm of Chao Phraya R., branches off below Singburi; flows 75 mi. S, past Lopburi and Ayutthaya (where it receives Pa Sak R.), and rejoins Chao Phraya R. at Ratchakhram.

Lopeh or **Lopei** (both: lô′bā′), town, ⊙ Lopeh co. (pop. 45,000), N Sungkiang prov., Manchuria, 25 mi. NE of Kiamusze and on right bank of Amur R. (USSR line); gold and coal deposits; wheat, rice, kaoliang, tobacco.

Lopera (lōpā′rä), town (pop. 5,644), Jaén prov., S Spain, 10 mi. SW of Andújar; olive-oil processing, soap mfg. Cereals, melons, wine, and tobacco in area. Has ruins of Moorish castle.

Lopevi (lōpā′vē), volcanic island (pop. c.150), New Hebrides, SW Pacific, 10 mi. SSE of Ambrym; c.4 mi. long; rises to 4,755 ft.

Lopez (lō′pās), town (1939 pop. 4,816; 1948 municipality pop. 22,935), Quezon prov., S Luzon, Philippines, near Lopez Bay, 45 mi. E of Lucena; copra center. Its port is Hondagua (1939 pop. 1,415), just N, on SE shore of Lopez Bay.

Lopez (lō′pĕz), village (1940 pop. 699), Sullivan co., NE Pa., 34 mi. W of Scranton.

Lopez, Cape, low, forested headland in W Gabon, Fr. Equatorial Africa, on the Gulf of Guinea at the extremity of an isl. formed by 2 mouths of Ogooué R. and just NNW of Port-Gentil; 0°38′S 8°42′E. Mangroves, guano deposits. It is the southernmost limit of Bight of Biafra.

López, Cerro (sĕ′rō lō′pās), Andean peak (6,890 ft.) in SW Río Negro natl. territory, Argentina, on S shore of L. Nahuel Huapí, 15 mi. W of San Carlos de Bariloche; popular skiing ground.

Lopez Bay, S arm of Lamon Bay, Philippines, bet. Alabat Isl. (E) and S coast of Luzon (W and S); 36 mi. long, 3–11 mi. wide. Cabalete Isl. is at entrance; Atimonan is on SW shore.

López de Filippis, Paraguay: see MARISCAL ESTIGARRIBIA.

Lopez Island, Wash.: see SAN JUAN ISLANDS.

Lopez Point (lō′pĕz), W Calif., coastal promontory c.40 mi. SSE of Monterey.

Loping or **Lo-p'ing** (lô′pĭng′). **1** Town (pop. 17,894), ⊙ Loping co. (pop. 205,084), NE Kiangsi prov., China, 30 mi. ESE of Poyang and on Loan R. (left headstream of Po R.); commercial center; coal mining; indigo, cotton, medicinal herbs, sugar cane. **2** Town (pop. 9,031), ⊙ Loping co. (pop. 77,059), E Yunnan prov., China, near Kweichow line, 50 mi. SE of Kütsing; alt. 6,561 ft.; rice, wheat, millet, beans. Sulphur mines near by.

Lop Nor, China: see LOB NOR.

Lopori River (lōpō′rē), W Belgian Congo, rises 70 mi. S of Yakuma, flows c.380 mi. NW and W, past Simba, Lokolenge, and Bongandanga, to join Maringa R. at Basankusu, forming the Lulonga. Navigable for 280 mi. downstream from Simba.

Lo-p'u, China: see LOP.

Lopud Island (lô′po͞ot), Ital. *Mezzo* (mĕt′sô), anc. *Delaphodia,* Dalmatian island in Adriatic Sea, S Croatia, Yugoslavia; 2 mi. long. Chief village, Lopud, is 8 mi. WNW of Dubrovnik, in tourist area. Ruins of chapels and Venetian forts.

Lo-pu-no-erh, China: see LOB NOR.

Lora, La (lä lō′rä), tableland in NW Burgos prov., N Spain, along Santander prov. border; Sedano is its agr. center.

Lora de Estepa (lō′rä dhā ĕstā′pä), town (pop. 1,235), Seville prov., SW Spain, in outliers of the Cordillera Penibética, 16 mi. E of Osuna; olives, cereals, esparto, onions.

Lora del Río (dhĕl rē′ō), town (pop. 9,786), Seville prov., SW Spain, on the Guadalquivir, on railroad and 31 mi. NE of Seville; trading and processing center in agr. region (olives, cereals, fruit, livestock). Vegetable canning, flour milling, olive-oil pressing. Has graphite, sand, and granite quarries. Near by are ruins of old fortress. The anc. town is of Iberian origin and has been identified with the Roman *Axatiana,* mentioned by Pliny. The town was taken (1243) from the Moors by Ferdinand III. Ruins of Setefillas castle are 3 mi. NE.

Lorado (lůrā′dō), village (pop. 1,087), Logan co., SW W.Va., 15 mi. ESE of Logan, in coal-mining region.

Lorain (lôrān′), county (□ 495; pop. 148,162), N Ohio; ⊙ Elyria. Bounded N by L. Erie; drained by Black and Vermilion rivers. Agr. area (dairy products, grain, poultry, livestock, fruit); mfg. at Lorain, Elyria, Wellington. Commercial fishing; sandstone quarries; lake resorts. Formed 1824.

Lorain. 1 City (pop. 51,202), Lorain co., N Ohio, port at mouth of Black R. and L. Erie, 25 mi. W of Cleveland; important transshipment point, unloading L. Superior iron ore, and shipping coal; industrial and shipbuilding center. Mfg. of iron and steel (especially pipe), machinery, chemicals, steam shovels, cranes, heating equipment, clothing, electrical equipment; railroad shops. Commercial fisheries. Sandstone quarries. Lake View Park, and U.S. coast guard station are here. Resorts. Settled 1807; inc. 1836 as Charleston; rechartered 1876 as Lorain. **2** Borough (pop. 1,406), Cambria co., SW central Pa., just SE of Johnstown; steel.

Loraine (lôrān′). **1** Village (pop. 370), Adams co., W Ill., 18 mi. NNE of Quincy, in agr. area. **2** Village (pop. 70), Renville co., N N.Dak., 8 mi. N of Mohall. **3** Town (pop. 1,045), Mitchell co., W Texas, 8 mi. E of Colorado City; dairy-products processing and shipping point. Inc. 1907.

Loralai (lō′rŭlī), dist. (□ 7,375; 1951 pop. 97,000), Baluchistan, W Pakistan; ⊙ Loralai. Bordered E by Sulaiman Range, S by Central Brahui Range; drained by several seasonal streams and (W) by upper course of Nari R. Wheat, millet grown in valleys, olives in Sulaiman Range (E). Limestone deposits in hills (center, NE); some gypsum (SE). Handicrafts (felts, felt coats, mats, saddlebags); cattle raising (Barkhan noted for its horses). Pop. 95% Moslem, 3% Hindu, 1% Sikh.

Loralai, town (1941 pop., with cantonment area, 5,095), ⊙ Loralai dist., NE Baluchistan, W Pakistan, near Nari (Loralai) R., 95 mi. E of Quetta; agr. (wheat, rice, barley); handicrafts (mats, felts, handbags); cattle raising.

Loralai River, W Pakistan: see NARI RIVER.

Loramie, Lake, Ohio: see LORAMIE CREEK.

Loramie Creek (lô′rŭmē), W Ohio, rises in Shelby co., flows SW, past Botkins, to L. Loramie or Loramie Reservoir (c.5 mi. long) just SE of Minster, then SE to Great Miami R. just N of Piqua; c.40 mi. long.

Loranca del Campo (lōräng′kä dhĕl käm′pō), town (pop. 708), Cuenca prov., E central Spain, 31 mi. W of Cuenca; cereals, grapes, olives, saffron, chick-peas, honey, sheep.

Lorca (lôr′kä), city (pop. 24,491), Murcia prov., SE Spain, 40 mi. SW of Murcia; industrial and agr. trade center. Mfg. of chemical fertilizers, woolen cloth and blankets, footwear, rugs, leather goods, pottery, candy; sulphur refinery, tanneries, flour- and sawmills, brandy distilleries. Ships grapes, figs, and other fruit; also olive oil, cereals, and esparto, grown in surrounding garden region partly irrigated by water from Puentes reservoir 8 mi. NW (1st built in 18th cent.; dam burst in 1802; repaired in 1886). Sulphur and iron mines, gypsum quarries near by. City is built on slope of hill crowned by Moorish castle (12th cent.; restored). Has St. Patrick's collegiate church (16th–18th cent.) and other baroque churches, fine old mansions, and 17th–18th-cent. town hall. Flourished under Romans; taken (8th cent.) by Moors; liberated (1243) by Christians. Was base of operations of Catholic Kings against Granada (15th cent.).

Lorcé (lôrsā′), village (pop. 359), Liége prov., E Belgium, near Amblève R., 17 mi. SSE of Liége; manganese mining.

Lorch, Austria: see ENNS.

Lorch (lôrkh). **1** Town (pop. 2,939), in former Prussian prov. of Hesse-Nassau, W Germany, after 1945 in Hesse, on right bank of the Rhine and 19 mi. W of Wiesbaden; wine. Has Gothic church. **2** Town (pop. 4,931), N Württemberg, Germany, after 1945 in Württemberg-Baden, on the Rems and 5 mi. W of Schwäbisch Gmünd; mfg. of autos, chassis, furniture, canes, paper; weaving, food processing. Has Benedictine monastery (founded c.1100, partly destroyed 1525), with Romanesque church. On site of Roman castrum.

Lorcha (lôr′chä), town (pop. 1,330), Alicante prov., E Spain, 11 mi. SW of Gandía; olive-oil processing; cereals, wine, sheep.

Lörchingen, France: see LORQUIN.

Lord Hood Island, Gambier Isls.: see MARUTEA.

Lord Howe Island, volcanic island (□ 5; pop. 179) in S Pacific, 435 mi. NE of Sydney; dependency of New South Wales, Australia; 31°33′S 159°5′E. Rocky, hilly; 7 mi. long, 1 mi. wide; Mt. Gower (2,840 ft.), highest peak; dense vegetation. Chief product is Kentia palm seed. Summer resort. Discovered 1788 by British.

Lord Howe Island, Solomon Isls.: see ONTONG JAVA.

Lordsburg, village (pop. 3,525), ⊙ Hidalgo co., SW N.Mex., 39 mi. SW of Silver City, near Ariz. line; alt. c.4,240 ft. Trade center, resort; livestock, truck. Copper, silver, gold, lead mines in vicinity. Southwest N.Mex. fair and livestock show take place here. Part of Gila Natl. Forest near by.

Loreauville (lō′růvĭl), village (pop. 478), Iberia parish, S La., 6 mi. NE of New Iberia, and on Bayou Teche, in agr. area; sugar milling.

Lore City, village (pop. 495), Guernsey co., E Ohio, 7 mi. ESE of Cambridge, in coal-mining area.

Lorelei (lô′rŭlī, Ger. lō′rŭlī) or **Lurlei** (lo͝or′lī), cliff (433 ft. high) on right bank of the Rhine (dangerous narrows), W Germany, just S of Sankt Goarshausen; large winter harbor at foot; hotel on summit. The legend connected with it has been popularized by Brentano's romance (1800) and Heine's poem (1823).

Lorena (lo͞orā′nů), city (pop. 10,040), SE São Paulo, Brazil, on Paraíba R. and 110 mi. NE of São Paulo; rail junction on Rio de Janeiro–São Paulo RR (spur to Minas Gerais). Sugar milling, alcohol distilling, meat drying, dairying; plant nursery. Trades in coffee, rice, corn. Talc quarries.

Lorengau (lôrĕng-ou′), main town of Admiralty Isls. and ⊙ Manus dist., Territory of New Guinea, on E coast of Manus isl.; 2°5′S 147°20′ E. After Second World War, briefly replaced as administrative center by Inrim plantation, 10 mi. W.

Lorentzweiler (lō′rĕntswī″lůr), village (pop. 539), S central Luxembourg, on Alzette R. and 6 mi. N of Luxembourg city; lumbering.

Lorenzo (lůrĕn′zō), town (pop. 939), Crosby co., NW Texas, on the Llano Estacado, 20 mi. ENE of Lubbock; shipping point in grain, cotton area.

Loreo (lôrā′ô), town (pop. 2,008), Rovigo prov., Veneto, N Italy, 6 mi. E of Adria; beet-sugar mill.

Lorestan, Iran: see LURISTAN.

Loreto (lōrā′tō). **1** Town (pop. estimate 1,000), N Corrientes prov., Argentina, 100 mi. ESE of Corrientes; agr. center (alfalfa, sugar cane, cotton, livestock). **2** Town (pop. estimate 1,000), ⊙ Loreto dept. (□ 1,115; 1947 pop. 13,602), SW Santiago del Estero prov., Argentina, on railroad and 55 mi. S of Santiago del Estero; agr. center (wheat, corn, alfalfa, cotton, grapes, livestock).

Loreto, town (pop. c.1,400), ⊙ Marbán prov., Beni dept., NE Bolivia, in the llanos, 34 mi. SSE of Trinidad; cattle, tropical agr. products (cotton, cacao, bananas).

Loreto (lo͞orā′to͞o), city (pop. 609), S central Maranhão, Brazil, on Balsas R. and 50 mi. NE of Balsas (connected by road); hides, rubber, resins; cattle raising. Airfield.

Loreto (lōrā′tō), village (1930 pop. 128), Magallanes prov., S Chile, on N Brunswick Peninsula, 4 mi. NW of Punta Arenas (linked by short rail line); coal mining.

Loreto (lůrĕ′tō, It. lôrā′tô), town (pop. 3,310), Ancona prov., The Marches, central Italy, near the Adriatic, 14 mi. SSE of Ancona; mfg. (religious articles, harmoniums, harmonicas). Bishopric. Noted pilgrimage center. Has famous Santa Casa (according to tradition, the Holy House of the Virgin; transported here from Nazareth at end of 13th cent.) with a marble screen by Bramante. Over it was built a church (begun 1468; bomb damage restored) with fine bronze doors; has frescoes by Michelozzo da Forti and Luca Signorelli. Jesuit col. Formerly also spelled Loretto.

Loreto (lōrā'tō). **1** Town (pop. 912), Southern Territory, Lower California, NW Mexico, port on Gulf of California, 145 mi. NW of La Paz; 26°N 111°20'W; sugar cane, dates, figs. Formerly a Jesuit mission, founded 1697. **2** Town (pop. 1,688), Zacatecas, N central Mexico, on railroad and 50 mi. SE of Zacatecas; grain, livestock.

Loreto, town (dist. pop. 4,713), Concepción dept., central Paraguay, 13 mi. NE of Concepción; stock-raising and agr. center (corn, alfalfa, vegetables, maté).

Loreto, department (□ 119,301; enumerated pop. 181,341, plus estimated 140,000 Indians), NE and E Peru, just S of the equator; ⊙ IQUITOS. Borders NW on Ecuador, NE (Putumayo R.) and E (Javarí R.) on Brazil. The largest administrative div. of Peru, covering approximately ⅓ of the country. Bounded W by E outliers of the Andes, it is entirely within the Amazon basin, here frequently called montaña. A vast network of streams, tributary to the Amazon, intersect the region; among them are the Ucayali and Marañón, which form the Amazon S of Iquitos. The climate is humid and tropical with little variation; main rainy season Nov.–May. In spite of its rich vegetation, the dept. is little developed; clearings have been made only along the rivers, where cotton, sugar cane, rice, cacao, coca, yucca, beans, chick-peas, corn, and tropical fruit of all kinds thrive. Once predominantly a rubber-producing region, its virgin forests yield rubber, balata, chicle, cascarilla, tagua nuts, tanning barks, aromatic and medicinal plants, and a variety of fine timber. There are gold, petroleum, salt, and gypsum deposits. Its large navigable rivers serve as main lines of communication, and its trade via Amazon R. is oriented toward the Atlantic. Iquitos, its leading inland port and trading and processing center, can be reached by ocean-going vessels. Formerly a part of old Maynas prov., it was set up as a separate dept. 1861. It included, until 1906, San Martín dept. The international boundaries were settled in 1943.

Loreto, province, Peru: see NAUTA.

Loreto Aprutino (lôrā'tô äprōōtē'nô), town (pop. 3,091), Pescara prov., Abruzzi e Molise, S central Italy, 12 mi. WSW of Pescara; olive-oil refining. Damaged in Second World War.

Lorette (lôrĕt'), town (pop. 3,429), Loire dept., SE central France, in the Jarez, on Gier R., and 11 mi. ENE of Saint-Étienne; steel milling. Quartzite quarries near by.

Loretteville (lôrĕt'vĭl), village (pop. 2,564), S central Que., on short Nelson R. and 8 mi. NW of Quebec; mfg. of gloves, skis, canoes. Huron settlement began here 1697; village was known as Indian Lorette or Jeune Lorette. Near by is Ancienne Lorette.

Loretto. 1 Village (pop. c.400), Marion co., central Ky., 27 mi. E of Elizabethtown; makes whisky; flour and feed mills. Seat of Loretto Convent (mother house of its order), with acad. and jr. col. **2** Village (pop. 179), Hennepin co., E Minn., 19 mi. W of Minneapolis. **3** Borough (pop. 863), Cambria co., SW central Pa., 5 mi. ENE of Ebensburg. St. Francis Col. here. **4** Town (pop. 706), Lawrence co., S Tenn., 13 mi. SSW of Lawrenceburg; lumbering; truck and fruit farming.

Lorgues (lôrg), village (pop. 1,619), Var dept., SE France, in Provence Alps, 6 mi. SW of Draguignan; mfg. (corks, olive oil).

Lorica (lōrē'kä), town (pop. 6,146), Bolívar dept., N Colombia, in Caribbean lowlands, on navigable Sinú R. and 33 mi. N of Montería; agr. center (rice, corn, bananas, sugar cane, livestock); fishing. Airport.

Lorient (lôrēä'), town (1946 pop. 10,764; 1936 pop. 40,753), Morbihan dept., W France, on inlet of Bay of Biscay formed by estuaries of Scorff and Blavet rivers, 80 mi. WSW of Rennes; fortified naval station and fishing port with fine natural harbor; shipbuilding, fish canning, oyster breeding, kaolin quarrying (at near-by Ploëmeur). Founded 1664 by French East India Company for trade with Orient, it was bought by Fr. govt. in 1782 and became a leading naval station under Napoleon II. In Second World War, it became Ger. submarine base and was frequently bombed (1943–44) by Allies, suffering virtually complete destruction. Bet. Aug., 1944, and May, 1945, its Ger. garrison withstood an Allied siege. Formerly spelled L'Orient.

Loriga (lōōrē'gù), village (pop. 2,363), Guarda dist., N central Portugal, in Serra da Estrêla, 28 mi. SW of Guarda; wool spinning, dairying.

L'Orignal (lôrnĕl', Fr. lôrēnyäl'), village (pop. 1,118), ⊙ Prescott and Russell cos., SE Ont., on Ottawa R. and 50 mi. ENE of Ottawa; lumbering center, dairying; resort.

Lorimor (lôr'ùmùr), town (pop. 505), Union co., S Iowa, 17 mi. ENE of Creston; metal products.

Lőrinci (lû'rĭntsē), Hung. *Lőrinci*, town (pop. 4,929), Nograd-Hont co., N Hungary, on Zagyva R. and 32 mi. NE of Budapest; sugar refineries, cement works, flour mills. Limestone quarry near by.

Loring (lô'rĭng), fishing village, SE Alaska, on W side of Revillagigedo Isl., 20 mi. N of Ketchikan.

Loriol or **Loriol-sur-Drôme** (lôrēôl'-sür-drōm'), village (pop. 1,383), Drôme dept., SE France, near the Drôme, 13 mi. SSW of Valence; mfg. (nougats, pharmaceuticals, fertilizer), silk milling.

Loris (lō'rĭs), town (pop. 1,614), Horry co., E S.C., 17 mi. NNE of Conway, near N.C. line; strawberry and tobacco market; lumber.

Lori Steppe (lô'rē), in the Lesser Caucasus, on Georgian-Armenian SSR border, NE of Leninakan; livestock, wheat, potatoes. Its center is Kalinino.

Lo River, Chinese *Lo Shui* (lô' shwā'). **1** In NW Honan prov., China, rises in mts. on Shensi line, flows c.200 mi. ENE, past Lushih, Loning, Yiyang, and Loyang, to Yellow R. below Kunghsien. Valley is center of earliest recorded Chinese civilization. **2** In Shensi prov., China, rises in northwesternmost Shensi at Suiyuan-Ningsia line, flows 250 mi. SSE, past Kanchüan, Fuhsien, and Tali, to Wei R. just above its confluence with Yellow R.

Lormes (lôrm), village (pop. 1,442), Nièvre dept., central France, 18 mi. SE of Clamecy; lumber and livestock trade.

Lormont (lôrmō'), NE industrial suburb (pop. 3,350) of Bordeaux, Gironde dept., SW France, section of port of Bordeaux on right bank of Garonne R.; Portland cement, inlaid woodwork.

Lorn, Scotland: see LORNE.

Lorne, village (pop. 1,028), S Victoria, Australia, 75 mi. SW of Melbourne and on Bass Strait; seaside resort.

Lorne or **Lorn,** mountainous district of W Argyll, Scotland, bounded W by the Firth of Lorne, N by Loch Leven, NW by Loch Linnhe, E by Perthshire, and S by Loch Awe; c.25 mi. long, 20 mi. wide. Chief town, Oban.

Lorne or **Lorn, Firth of,** arm of the sea, W Argyll, Scotland, separating Mull isl. from mainland; c.16 mi. long, 5 mi. wide.

Loros, Chile: see LOS LOROS.

Loroux-Béconnais, Le (lù lôrōō'-bākônā'), village (pop. 662), Maine-et-Loire dept., W France, 16 mi. WNW of Angers; dairying, winegrowing; granite quarries near by.

Loroux-Bottereau, Le (–bôtrō'), village (pop. 1,003), Loire-Inférieure dept., W France, 10 mi. E of Nantes; mfg. of slippers, winegrowing.

Lorquí (lôrkē'), town (pop. 2,899), Murcia prov., SE Spain, on Segura R. and 10 mi. NW of Murcia; fruit-conserve mfg., pepper processing, sawmilling. Agr. trade (fruit, saffron, cereals, peanuts); sericulture. Near here the Roman generals Publius and Gnaeus Scipio were defeated (212 B.C.) by the Numidian Masinissa.

Lorquin (lôrkē'), Ger. *Lörchingen* (lûrkh'ĭng-ùn), village (pop. 1,033), Moselle dept., NE France, on NW slopes of the Vosges, 5 mi. SW of Sarrebourg; cotton spinning, embroidering, sawmilling. Gallo-Roman remains in area.

Lörrach (lû'räkh), town (pop. 19,294), S Baden, Germany, at SW foot of Black Forest, 4 mi. NNE of Basel, on Swiss border; 47°37'N 7°40'E. Rail junction; textile (calico, cloth, cotton, silk ribbons) industry; foundries. Machinery mfg., metal- and woodworking, food processing (chocolate), lumber and paper milling. Trades in wine, fruit, timber. Has ruined castle, formerly residence of counts of Hachberg; 15th-cent. church; 19th-cent. chalet and church. Obtained market rights in 1403; chartered 1682.

Lorrain (lôrān'), village, E Ont., on Montreal R. and 5 mi. WSW of Cobalt; silver and cobalt mining.

Lorrain (lôrē'), town (pop. 1,803), NE Martinique, on the Atlantic, and 15 mi. N of Fort-de-France; sugar milling, rum distilling. Sometimes called Le Lorrain.

Lorraine (lùrān', Fr. lôrĕn'), Ger. *Lothringen* (lō'trĭng-ùn), region and former province of E France, old ⊙ Nancy. Borders on Belgium and Luxembourg (N), the Saar (NE), Alsace (E), and Champagne (W). Now administratively divided into Moselle, Meurthe-et-Moselle, Meuse, and Vosges depts. Physically, it consists of a slightly accidented tableland, poorly drained in spots, cut by valleys of the Moselle and the Meuse (flowing S–N), and by ridges (Côtes de Moselle, Côtes de Meuse) paralleling rivers. In E, Lorraine plateau slowly rises to wooded crest of the Vosges. Though it has diversified agr. (including hop- and winegrowing districts), greatest wealth lies in extensive iron fields, concentrated in Briey, Longwy, Thionville, and Nancy basins. The iron-processing and steel-making industry of Lorraine must depend upon coking coal from the Ruhr, N France, and the adjoining Saar. Some coal is mined in S extension of Saar basin, near Forbach and Saint-Avold. Chief cities are Nancy, Metz, Verdun, Toul, Bar-le-Duc, Épinal, Thionville, and Lunéville. Before 10th cent. Lorraine was part of Kingdom of Lotharingia. Became duchy under Holy Roman Empire. Several 13th-cent. fiefs (county of Bar, bishoprics of Metz, Toul, and Verdun) escaped dukes' control, and 3 bishoprics were annexed by France in 1552. René II of Lorraine helped (1477) to defeat (at Nancy) Charles the Bold of Burgundy, who had seized most of duchy. Under Duke Charles II, Lorraine prospered, while the Guise family (cadet branch of house of Lorraine) gained great influence in France. Occupied by France in Thirty Years War. In 1697 Leopold I was again recognized in possession of duchy. His heir became emperor of Austria by marriage to Maria Theresa, and founded house of Hapsburg-Lorraine. In 1735, Lorraine was exchanged for Tuscany with Louis XV of France, and given to Stanislaus I, ex-king of Poland, upon whose death (1766) it passed to France, becoming a prov. In 1871, as result of Franco-Prussian War, area of present Moselle dept. was ceded to Germany and united with Alsace as imperial land (*Reichsland*) of Alsace-Lorraine. It reverted to France in 1918; was again annexed to Germany, 1940–44. Lorraine suffered in both world wars. In the first, Verdun was scene of heavy fighting which caused over a million casualties. In 1944, during Allied sweep to Ger. border, Germans put up stiff resistance at Metz and along roads to the Vosges passes. Only in Moselle dept. is German widely spoken.

Lorraine, city (pop. 195), Ellsworth co., central Kansas, 40 mi. WSW of Salina; wheat, cattle.

Lorrainville (lôrān'vĭl), village (pop. 562), W Que., 16 mi. ESE of Haileybury; dairying, cattle raising; gold-mining region.

Lorrez-le-Bocage (lôrā'-lù-bôkäzh'), village (pop. 498), Seine-et-Marne dept., N central France, 15 mi. SE of Fontainebleau.

Lorris (lōrē'), village (pop. 1,525), Loiret dept., N central France, 13 mi. SW of Montargis; livestock market. Has Renaissance town hall.

Lorsch (lôrsh), village (pop. 7,763), S Hesse, W Germany, in former Starkenburg prov., 3 mi. SW of Bensheim; apricots, peaches. Has ruins of one of most powerful abbeys of Germany, founded in 8th cent.; passed to archbishops of Mainz in 1232. Louis the German and Louis the Younger buried here. Mentioned in Nibelungenlied as burial place of Siegfried.

Lorsica (lôr'sēkä), village (pop. 294), Genova prov., Liguria, N Italy, 6 mi. N of Rapallo; slate quarries.

Lorton, village (pop. 75), Otoe co., SE Nebr., 10 mi. WSW of Nebraska City and on branch of Little Nemaha R.

Los Alamitos (lōs ălùmē'tōs, –tùs), village (1940 pop. 937), Orange co., S Calif., 6 mi. ENE of Long Beach; citrus fruit.

Los Alamos (lōs ä'lämōs), village (1930 pop. 578), Arauco prov., S central Chile, 11 mi. E of Lebu; coal mining; also agr. (grain, vegetables, livestock).

Los Alamos (lōs ă'lùmōs), county (□ c.110; pop. 10,476), N N.Mex.; ⊙ Los Alamos. High plateau area largely within Valle Grande Mts. Atomic research at Los Alamos. Formed 1949 from parts of Sandoval and Santa Fe counties.

Los Alamos. 1 Village (pop. c.400), Santa Barbara co., SW Calif., 16 mi. SSE of Santa Maria; oil field near. **2** Community (pop. 9,934), ⊙ Los Alamos co., N N.Mex., in Valle Grande Mts., near Rio Grande, 24 mi. NW of Santa Fe; alt. c.7,500 ft. In the atomic-energy laboratories here the atomic bomb was made; tested (July 16, 1945) in desert region just W of SIERRA OSCURA, c.50 mi. NW of Alamogordo.

Los Aldamas (lōs äldä'mäs), town (pop. 679), Nuevo León, N Mexico, in lowland, on San Juan R. and 75 mi. ENE of Monterrey; cotton, corn, sugar cane.

Los Alerces (lōs älĕr'sĕs), Argentinian national park in W Chubut natl. territory, Argentina, in the Patagonian lake dist.; comprises lakes of Epuyén, Puelo, Menéndez, and Futalaufquén. Tourist resort; lumbering and fishing dist. Established 1937.

Los Altos (lōs ăl'tùs), residential village (1940 pop. 1,171), Santa Clara co., W Calif., 6 mi. S of Palo Alto, in foothills of Santa Cruz Mts.

Los Altos (lōs äl'tōs), town (pop. 982), Sucre state, NE Venezuela, near Caribbean coast, 21 mi. SW of Cumaná; cacao, coffee, sugar cane.

Los Amates (lōs ämä'tĕs), town (1950 pop. 628), Izabal dept., E Guatemala, on Motagua R., on railroad, and 45 mi. SW of Puerto Barrios, in banana area; grain, livestock, lumbering.

Los Andes (lōs än'dĕs), former national territory (□ 24,186) of NW Argentina. Formed 1910; dissolved 1943, when Jujuy received the N part (Susques dept.), Salta the center (San Antonio de los Cobres and Pastos Grandes depts.), and Catamarca the S (Antofagasta de la Sierra dept.).

Los Andes, Bolivia: see PUCARANI.

Los Andes, town (pop. 12,409), ⊙ Los Andes dept. (□ 1,222; pop. 34,747), Aconcagua prov., central Chile, in the Andes, on Aconcagua R. and 45 mi. N of Santiago, on Transandine RR; alt. 2,700 ft. Agr. (cereals, wine, hemp, livestock) and industrial center, with copper mining and marble quarrying. Mfg. of cordage, bags, food preserves, canned milk, wine. Tourist resort. Formerly Santa Rosa de los Andes.

Los Ángeles (lōs än'hālĕs), city (1940 pop. 20,979, 1949 estimate 18,826), ⊙ Bío-Bío prov. and Laja dept. (□ 2,642; 1940 pop. 84,931), S central Chile, on a tributary of the Bío-Bío, in S part of the central valley, and 60 mi. SE of Concepción, 300 mi. SSW of Santiago; 37°28'S 72°22'W. Rail terminus and agr. center (wheat, fruit, wine, peas); flour milling, wine making, lumbering. Founded 1739, the town was several times destroyed by Indians. Formerly spelled Los Ánjeles.

Los Ángeles, town (pop. 1,767), Sonora, NW Mexico, on San Miguel R. and 30 mi. NE of Hermosillo; cotton, corn, wheat, fruit, livestock.

Los Angeles (lŏs ăng'gûlŭs, ăn'jûlŭs, –lēz), county (□ 4,071; 1940 pop. 2,785,643; 1950 pop. 4,151,687), S Calif.; ⊙ LOS ANGELES. The fertile Los Angeles basin, a plain reaching to the Pacific on W, is almost surrounded by mts. covering c.½ of co.'s surface; in the basin and in tributary San Fernando Valley are the scores of cities of the metropolitan area, many of them virtually part of Los Angeles, and all including large suburban and semirural areas. Largest (all over 50,000 pop.) are LONG BEACH, PASADENA, GLENDALE, BURBANK, SANTA MONICA, ALHAMBRA, SOUTH GATE. San Gabriel Mts. (NE wall of basin) have peaks over 10,000 ft.; coastal ranges (including Santa Monica Mts., Santa Susana Mts.) are lower. Antelope Valley (part of Mojave Desert; irrigated agr.) is in N. Off coast, which is indented by San Pedro Bay (Los Angeles Harbor here) and Santa Monica Bay, are isls. (including Santa Catalina, noted resort) of Santa Barbara group. Intermittent Los Angeles and San Gabriel rivers and their tributaries have flood-control works. Co.'s mediterranean climate and its resorts have long attracted winter residents and year-round tourists. Has some of nation's most valuable farmland (irrigation required; c.½ of farms under 10 acres), important industries (motion pictures, at HOLLYWOOD, Culver City, Burbank; oil refining, automobile assembling; mfg. of aircraft, tires and tubes, steel, foundry products, clothing, furniture, food products), rich oil fields, ocean fisheries (tuna, sardines, mackerel). Chief farm products (whose value generally leads all U.S. counties) are citrus fruit, dairy products, deciduous and subtropical fruit, nuts, vegetables, poultry and rabbits, field crops (especially alfalfa hay, beans), cattle, horses, and hogs; nursery stock and cut flowers are extensively grown. Formed 1850.

Los Angeles, city (□ 452.2; 1950 pop. 1,970,358; 1940 pop. 1,504,277), ⊙ Los Angeles co., S Calif., on the Pacific coast, c.350 mi. SSE of San Francisco; 34°3'N 118°14' W; alt. rises from sea level to c.2,800 ft. Largest city of Calif., 4th largest in pop. of U.S., and 1st in U.S. in area as result of frequent annexations of neighboring towns, it extends for c.50 mi. N–S from the San Fernando Valley (N) to Los Angeles Harbor, and for 30 mi. from the San Gabriel Mts. (E) to the sea. It has long been a tourist resort and winter residential city because of its sunny mediterranean climate (Jan. average 55°F., July average 71°F.; annual rainfall c.15 in., mainly Nov.-April), which also helped make it the world's motion-picture production center. Los Angeles has become a major seaport and port of entry (since dredging 1912–14 of artificial LOS ANGELES HARBOR), and an aviation center, with many aircraft factories and several airports, notably Burbank and an international terminal at Culver City. It is terminus of 3 transcontinental rail lines, and the commercial, financial, distribution, and market center of S Calif. Among industries in city and environs, aircraft mfg., oil production and refining, and motion-picture production (at Hollywood, Culver City, West Los Angeles, Burbank) lead in importance, followed by automobile assembling, mfg. of rubber products (chiefly tires and tubes), furniture, and clothing, food processing (sea food canning, packing and canning of fruits and vegetables, meat packing), mfg. of machinery (including oil-field machinery), electrical machinery and equipment, household appliances, glassware, pottery, tile, building materials, brass products, chemicals, pharmaceuticals, soap, paint; also steel fabricating, shipbuilding, printing and publishing, brewing, flour milling, coffee roasting, and spice grinding. Enormous tourist trade is attracted by near-by beach, mtn., and desert resorts and scenery, the motion-picture studios, the orange groves, old missions, and other near-by points of interest. Educational institutions here include Univ. of California at Los Angeles, Univ. of Southern Calif., Occidental Col., Loyola Univ. of Los Angeles, Chapman Col., George Pepperdine Col., Mt. St. Mary's Col., Immaculate Heart Col., Southwestern Univ., Bible Inst. of Los Angeles, Col. of Medical Evangelists, Col. of Osteopathic Physicians and Surgeons, Otis and Chouinard art schools, other colleges, and junior colleges, theological seminaries, and professional and technical schools. The sprawling city is notable for its many shopping and business centers outside of the downtown dist. In its growth it has annexed many communities which retain a measure of separate identity—among them HOLLYWOOD, the harbor cities of WILMINGTON and SAN PEDRO, Venice, Eagle Rock, Highland Park, Playa del Rey, and most of the SAN FERNANDO VALLEY communities, including Canoga Park, Chatsworth, Encino, North Hollywood, Tujunga, Universal City, and Van Nuys. In addition, its metropolitan area embraces scores of independent communities whose interests are closely bound with those of Los Angeles—among them ALHAMBRA, Altadena, Baldwin Park, Bell, Bellflower, Bell Gardens, Belvedere, BEVERLY HILLS, BURBANK, Clearwater, Compton, CULVER CITY, Downey, Duarte, East Los Angeles, El Monte, Flintridge, Florence, Gardena, GLENDALE, Glendora, Hawthorne, HUNTINGTON PARK, Hynes, INGLEWOOD, La Canada, La Crescenta, La Verne, Lawndale, Lennox, Lomita, LONG BEACH, Lynwood, Maywood, Monrovia, Montebello, Monterey Park, Montrose, Norwalk, PASADENA, Pico, San Dimas, San Fernando, San Gabriel, San Marino, SANTA ANA, SANTA MONICA, Sierra Madre, SOUTH GATE, South Pasadena, Temple City, TORRANCE, Verdugo City, Vernon, Willowbrook. Downtown dist., c.15 mi. from the coast, contains the civic center, including City Hall, only skyscraper (32 stories) in Southern Calif., Federal Bldg., State Bldg., and county courthouse; also the old Plaza (laid out 1815); old Plaza Church (1818), the Lugo house (1840), Olvera St., a reproduction (on original site) of a street of old Mex. city; Avila Adobe (c.1818; oldest house in city), Casa la Golondrina (1850–65), new "China City," replacing old Chinatown demolished to make way for Union Passenger Terminal; St. Vibiana's Cathedral (R.C.); Pico House (1868–69); "Little Tokyo" dist., containing Buddhist temples; a large public market; picturesque Angel's Flight funicular railroad up Bunker Hill; the Philharmonic Auditorium (1906; remodeled 1938), home of Los Angeles Symphony Orchestra; Pershing Square; large central public library; the stock exchange. To E of downtown dist. lie old residential sections (including Boyle Heights); to SE and S along the Los Angeles R. lies the principal industrial dist., extending along a "shoestring strip" of city territory to the harbor. To NE of downtown dist. is Pasadena; to N, beyond Elysian Park (600 acres; site of Naval and Marine armory) are Glendale and Griffith Park (□ 5 of foothills and canyons, containing a zoo, the Greek Theater, Griffith Observatory and Planetarium, established 1935, and extensive recreational facilities). Beyond is San Fernando Valley, northernmost part of city. NW Los Angeles includes Echo Park dist., centering on 31-acre park, Silver L. dist. (reservoir here), and Hollywood, site of huge, open-air Hollywood Bowl. W from downtown Los Angeles stretches Wilshire Blvd., along which lies the Wilshire dist. of fine shops, stores, offices, hotels, and residential streets; blvd. passes through several parks, including Hancock Park, which contains La Brea (lŭ brā'ŭ) tar pits, from which prehistoric animals' skeletons have been recovered in huge numbers. After passing through Beverly Hills (residential, fine shops, hotels), blvd. continues W through Westwood (site of Univ. of California at Los Angeles), residential West Los Angeles (site of U.S. veterans' home), skirts residential Brentwood, and passes into Santa Monica, where it meets the coast highway. Along the Pacific S of Santa Monica are Venice and Playa del Rey, both parts of Los Angeles. Other points of interest in city include Shrine Civic Auditorium, Exposition Park (has fine rose garden), Los Angeles County Mus. of History, Science, and Art, containing many reconstructed animal specimens from La Brea tar pits; Los Angeles Coliseum (seats 105,000), which was scene of 1932 Olympic Games; the Figueroa adobe house (1847), Hollenbeck Park, county general hosp. (2,500 beds), Los Angeles Orthopaedic Hosp., ostrich, alligator, and lion farms, Sycamore Grove and Lincoln parks; Southwest Mus., with extensive Indian collections. There are many large churches. Los Angeles has large communities of Chinese, Japanese, Mexican, and Negro descent. Exotic plants flourish here, and residential dists. are made colorful by jacaranda, acacia, eucalyptus, oleander, and citrus trees, bougainvillea and other subtropical vines, and flowers and shrubs remaining in bloom the year around. City's water supply is brought from great distances by Los Angeles Aqueduct (233 mi. long) from Owens R., and by Colorado Aqueduct (392 mi. long) from the Colorado R.; power from Hoover Dam is supplied to city. Large flood-control works in canyons of surrounding mts. and on Los Angeles R. protect the Los Angeles basin from rainy-season violence of its intermittent streams. Site of Los Angeles was visited by Gaspar de Portolá in 1769, and in 1781 El Pueblo Nuestra Señora la Reina de los Angeles de Porciuncula (the town of Our Lady Queen of Angels of Porziuncola) was founded. It was several times capital of Alta California, and was a center of cattle ranching in Spanish and Mexican days. In 1846 it was taken by U.S. forces, and it was inc. 1850. Expansion was stimulated by coming of railroads (Southern Pacific in 1876, Santa Fe in 1885) and discovery of oil in early 1890s. Further impetus was given by development here of the motion-picture industry early in the 20th cent., and the growth of aircraft mfg. after early 1920s. From 1900 to 1940, the pop. increased c.1,535%. With Calif., it has shared a particularly marked increase in pop. and in industry since the Second World War.

Los Angeles Aqueduct, Calif.; see OWENS RIVER.

Los Angeles Harbor, S Calif., man-made port of Los Angeles city, on San Pedro Bay, 20 mi. S of city's center, at SAN PEDRO and WILMINGTON. Consists of 2 major parts: outer harbor (U.S. navy's chief Pacific coast anchorage) in San Pedro Bay, sheltered by breakwater (in 2 sections; 4½ mi. long), extending E from Point Fermin; inner harbor, consisting of channels and turning basins dredged in former mudflats and of TERMINAL ISLAND (largely artificial) lying bet. inner and outer harbors. Communicates with Long Beach Harbor (E) via Cerritos Channel. Port generally ranks high in U.S., and 1st on Pacific coast, in volume of cargo, most of which is outgoing (foreign and coastwise). Ships oil and petroleum products, manufactured goods, citrus and other fruit, canned fish, vegetables, cotton, borax, potash, soda ash, cement; receives iron, steel, lumber, bananas, copra, jute, hemp, fertilizers, rubber, sugar, spices, coffee, tea, newsprint, wool. Harbor dist. (Wilmington, San Pedro, Harbor City) is served by 120-mi. belt-line railroad, connecting with 3 transcontinental lines. Port has c.25 mi. of dock frontage, oil terminals and refineries, shipyards, dry docks, a foreign trade zone (free port) opened in 1949, a naval operating base and other naval and coast guard installations, a fishing port (at Terminal Isl.; has large canneries, by-products plants) which generally leads Calif. in catches (tuna, mackerel, sardines); also passenger terminals (at Wilmington); and automobile-assembling and other industrial plants. Harbor's modern development began in 1899, when breakwater was begun in exposed anchorage which had been in use as port since 1850s, and which had been connected (1869) by railroad to Los Angeles; Los Angeles annexed San Pedro and Wilmington in 1909, and formed a harbor dist. to coordinate development; dredging of inner harbor was done 1912–14. Opening in 1914 of Panama Canal, and the accelerating agr. and commercial growth of Southern California, as well as development of area's great oil fields, stimulated trade of port and led to subsequent improvements.

Los Angeles River, S Calif., intermittent stream heading in San Fernando Valley, flows E along N base of Santa Monica Mts., then S, past E end of range and through downtown Los Angeles, its S industrial dist., and SE suburbs, to San Pedro Bay at Long Beach; c.50 mi. long. Torrential rainy-season flows are controlled by masonry embankments and huge catchment basins on upper river and tributaries (Pacoima R., Tujunga Creek, short Rio Hondo).

Los Ánjeles, Chile: see LOS ÁNGELES.

Los Antiguos (lōs äntē'gwōs), village (pop. estimate 300), SW Comodoro Rivadavia military zone, Argentina, on S shore of L. Buenos Aires, on Chile border, 130 mi. W of Colonia Las Heras; stock-raising (sheep, goats) and lumbering area. Customhouse, airport.

Losap (lō'säp), atoll (pop. 682), Truk dist., E Caroline Isls., W Pacific, 75 mi. SE of Truk; 5 mi. long; 17 islets on triangular reef.

Los Arabos (lōs ärä'bōs), town (pop. 2,771), Matanzas prov., W Cuba, on Central Highway and 60 mi. ESE of Matanzas; rail junction in agr. region (sugar cane, bananas). The refinery and central of Zorrilla is NE.

Losarcos, Spain: see ARCOS, LOS.

Losar de la Vera (lōsär' dhä lä vā'rä), town (pop. 3,113), Cáceres prov., W Spain, 27 mi. ENE of Plasencia; olive-oil processing, flour milling; stock raising; ships pepper and fruit.

Los Asientos (lōs äsyĕn'tōs), village (pop. 383), Los Santos prov., S central Panama, in Pacific lowland, 3 mi. NW of Pedasí; sugar cane, coffee, corn, livestock.

Los Bajos (lōs bä'hōs), village (1930 pop. 141), Llanquihue prov., S central Chile, on headland at W shore of L. Llanquihue, 28 mi. N of Puerto Montt; dairying, lumbering.

Los Banos (lŏs bă'nŭs), city (pop. 3,868), Merced co., central Calif., in San Joaquin Valley, 40 mi. S of Modesto; dairying, irrigated farming; powdered-milk plant.

Los Cerrillos, Chile: see SANTIAGO, city.

Los Cerrillos, Uruguay: see CERRILLOS.

Lösch, Czechoslovakia: see LISEN.

Los Chiles (lōs chē'lĕs), village, Alajuela prov., N Costa Rica, near Nicaragua border, in tropical Guatuso Lowland, on the Río Frío and 8 mi. SSE of San Carlos (Nicaragua). Stock raising, lumbering; ipecac root, cacao. Airfield.

Loschwitz (lôsh'vĭts), E suburb of Dresden, Saxony, E central Germany, on Elbe R.; climatic health resort. Frequently visited by Schiller during his stay in Dresden, 1785–87.

Los Coconucos (lōs kōkōnōō'kōs), volcanic massif, SW Colombia, in Cordillera Central, 20 mi. SE of Popayán; has 2 major peaks, rising to 14,908 ft.

Los Cóndores (lōs kōn'dōrĕs), village, N San Luis prov., Argentina, 60 mi. NE of San Luis; tungsten.

Los Corralitos (lōs kōrälē'tōs), town (pop. estimate 500), N Mendoza prov., Argentina, in Mendoza R. valley (irrigation area), 10 mi. ESE of Mendoza, in fruitgrowing area.

Los Duranes (lōs dōōrä'nĭs), village (pop. 2,873), Bernalillo co., central N.Mex., NW suburb of Albuquerque, near Old Albuquerque.

Los Encuentros (lōs ĕng-kwĕn′trōs), village (pop. 689), Sololá dept., SW central Guatemala, on Inter-American Highway and 4.5 mi. N of Sololá; alt. 8,038 ft.; road center.

Losenstein (lō′zŭnshtīn), village (pop. 1,838), SE Upper Austria, on Enns R. and 8 mi. S of Steyr; scythes, knives.

Loser (lō′zŭr), peak (6,024 ft.) of the Totes Gebirge, Styria, W central Austria, overlooking Altaussee in the Salzkammergut. Excellent view.

Loser, Mount (11,092 ft.), N Sumatra, Indonesia, in N Barisan Mts., near W coast, 110 mi. W of Medan.

Losevo (lô′syĭvŭ), village (1926 pop. 9,483), S central Voronezh oblast, Russian SFSR, on Bityug R. and 38 mi. NNE of Rossosh; wheat, sugar beets.

Los Fresnos (lŏs frĕz′nŭs), town (pop. 1,113), Cameron co., extreme S Texas, 12 mi. N of Brownsville; rail point in rich irrigated truck area of lower Rio Grande valley. Inc. after 1940.

Los Gatos (lŏs gă′tŭs), residential town (pop. 4,907), Santa Clara co., W Calif., 8 mi. SW of San Jose, in foothills of Santa Cruz Mts.; health resort; fruit cannery, wineries. Oil field, quicksilver mines near by. Inc. 1887.

Loshan (lô′shän′). **1** Town, ⊙ Loshan co. (pop. 184,157), S Honan prov., China, 23 mi. E of Sinyang; rice, wheat, kaoliang, beans. **2** Town (pop. 32,038), ⊙ Loshan co. (pop. 339,525), SW Szechwan prov., China, 75 mi. SSW of Chengtu and on right bank of Min R.; indigo-producing center; paper milling, cotton spinning and weaving, match mfg.; medicinal herbs, Chinese wax, rice, millet, wheat. Coal mines, oil and iron deposits, saltworks near by. The sacred mtn. OMEI SHAN is c.20 mi. W. Until 1913, Kiating.

Losheim (lōs′hīm), town (pop. 2,962), NW Saar, 7 mi. NE of Merzig; stock, grain. Formerly in Prussian Rhine Prov.; annexed to Saar in 1946.

Los Herreras (lōs ĕrā′räs), town (pop. 1,421), Nuevo León, N Mexico, on railroad, on Pesquería R. and 60 mi. ENE of Monterrey; cotton, sugar cane, cereals, fruit.

Loshing (lô′shĭng′), Mandarin *Lo-ch'eng* (lô′chŭng′), town, ⊙ Loshing co. (pop. 122,488), N Kwangsi prov., China, 40 mi. NW of Liuchow; lumbering. Coal deposits near by.

Lo Shui, China: see LO RIVER.

Losice (wôsē′tsĕ), Pol. *Łosice*, Rus. *Lositsy* (lôsē′tsyĭ), town (pop. 2,933), Lublin prov., E Poland, 19 mi. E of Siedlce.

Losingtah, China: see PAGODA.

Losinj Island (lô′shĭnyŭ), Serbo-Croatian *Lošinj*, Ital. *Lussino* (lo͞os-sē′nô), island (□ 30) in Adriatic Sea, W Croatia, Yugoslavia; 19 mi. long N–S; rises (N) to c.1,930 ft.; linked with Cres Isl. by bridge. Southernmost point 40 mi. NW of Zadar. Stock raising, agr., fishing; tourist trade. Part of Istria; passed (1918) to Italy and (1947) to Yugoslavia. Chief village, Mali Losinj, Serbo-Croatian *Mali Lošinj*, Ital. *Lussinpiccolo* (pop. 3,393), is on S part of isl.; resort. Near-by Veli Losinj, Serbo-Croatian *Veli Lošinj*, Ital. *Lussingrande*, village, also called Velo Selo, is small seaport; cathedral.

Losinoostrovskaya, Russian SFSR: see BABUSHKIN, Moscow oblast.

Losino-Petrovski or **Losino-Petrovskiy** (lŭsē″nŭ-pētrôf′skē), town (1926 pop. 2,621), E central Moscow oblast, Russian SFSR, on Klyazma R. and 9 mi. W of Noginsk; cotton mill. Until 1928, Petrovskaya Sloboda.

Losinovka (lŭsē′nŭfkŭ), village (1926 pop. 9,782), S Chernigov oblast, Ukrainian SSR, 14 mi. S of Nezhin; grain farming.

Losiny or **Losinyy** (lŭsē′nē), town (1942 pop. over 500), S Sverdlovsk oblast, Russian SFSR, on railroad (Adui station) and 17 mi. NNE (under jurisdiction) of Berezovski; gold mining.

Los Islands (lôs), Fr. *Îles de Los* or *Îles de Loos* (ēl′ dŭ lô-ôs′), group of Atlantic islets just off Conakry, Fr. Guinea, Fr. West Africa; 9°30′N 13°50′W. There are 5 larger isls., among them Tamara and Factory isls. Bauxite deposits. Turtles abound. Have prison, lighthouse, beaches, fisheries. Principal villages are Fotoba and Kassa. Ceded 1904 by Gr. Britain to France.

Lositsy, Poland: see LOSICE.

Los Lagos, department, Argentina: see NAHUEL HUAPÍ, village.

Los Lagos (lōs lä′gōs), town (pop. 2,106), Valdivia prov., S central Chile, on Calle-Calle R. and 23 mi. E of Valdivia; rail junction and tourist resort in agr. area (cereals, potatoes, peas, livestock); flour milling, lumbering. It is a gateway to L. Riñihue in Chilean lake dist.

Loslau, Poland: see WODZISLAW.

Los Laureles (lōs lourā′lēs), town (pop. 1,401), Cautín prov., S central Chile, on railroad and 18 mi. ESE of Temuco; agr. center (wheat, barley, peas, potatoes, livestock); flour milling, lumbering.

Los Llanos (lōs yä′nōs), officially Villa de San José de Los Llanos, town (1950 pop. 892), San Pedro de Macorís prov., SE Dominican Republic, 28 mi. ENE of Ciudad Trujillo, in sugar-growing and cattle-raising region. Quisqueya sugar mill is SE.

Los Loros or **Loros** (lōs lō′rōs), village (1930 pop. 357), Atacama prov., N central Chile, on Copiapó R. (irrigation), on railroad, and 40 mi. SE of Copiapó; alfalfa, clover, corn, subtropical fruit, goats.

Los Lunas (lŏs lo͞o′nŭs), village (pop. 889), ⊙ Valencia co., central N.Mex., on Rio Grande and 20 mi. S of Albuquerque; alt. c.4,850 ft. Trade center, livestock-shipping point in irrigated grain and truck-farming area. Isleta Pueblo Indian village is just N, Manzano Range E.

Los Menucos (lōs mänōō′kōs), village (pop. estimate 500), S central Río Negro natl. territory, Argentina, on railroad and 45 mi. NE of Maquinchao; alfalfa, fruit, sheep, goats.

Los Millanes (lōs mēyä′nās), town (pop. 921), on Margarita Isl., Nueva Esparta state, NE Venezuela, 7 mi. W of La Asunción; corn, sugar cane, fruit.

Los Mochis (lōs mō′chēs) or **Mochis**, city (pop. 12,937), Sinaloa, NW Mexico, in coastal lowland, near Gulf of California, on railroad and 120 mi. NW of Culiacán. Resort; sugar-growing and -refining center; tomatoes, chick-peas, corn, fruit; cannery.

Los Molles (lōs mô′yēs), village (pop. estimate 500), SW Mendoza prov., Argentina, on tributary of Atuel R. and 100 mi. WSW of San Rafael; health resort with hot springs.

Los Muermos (lōs mwĕr′mōs), village (1930 pop. 649), Llanquihue prov., S central Chile, 27 mi. WNW of Puerto Montt; wheat, potatoes, flax, livestock; dairying, lumbering.

Los Negros Island, Bismarck Archipelago: see ADMIRALTY ISLANDS.

Los Nietos (lŏs nēē′tŭs), unincorporated town (1940 pop. 1,837), Los Angeles co., S Calif., suburb 12 mi. SE of downtown Los Angeles, near Whittier; oil wells, citrus-fruit groves.

Losonc, Czechoslovakia: see LUCENEC.

Lososinoye (lŭsŭsē′nŭyŭ), village, S Karelo-Finnish SSR, 10 mi. SW of Petrozavodsk; sawmilling, ski mfg.

Los Palacios (lōs pälä′syōs), town (pop. 4,008), Pinar del Río prov., W Cuba, on Los Palacios R., on railroad and 30 mi. ENE of Pinar del Río, in agr. region (sugar cane, tobacco, pineapples, cattle). Mfg. of cigars. The Central La Francia is 6 mi. SSE, linked by rail.

Lospalos (lo͞osh-pä′lo͞osh), town, ⊙ Lautem dist. (□ 1,266; pop. 33,754), Portuguese Timor, in E Timor, 95 mi. E of Dili; copra, tobacco, hardwood.

Los Pinos (lōs pē′nōs), village (pop. estimate 500), SE Buenos Aires prov., Argentina, 8 mi. SW of Balcarce, in pine woods supplying timber for Mar del Plata paper mills; quartzite quarries.

Los Pinos, town (pop. 4,984), Havana prov., W Cuba, on railroad and 5 mi. S of Havana, in dairying region.

Los Pinos River, in SW Colo. and NW N.Mex., rises in San Juan Mts. near Rio Grande Pyramid, flows c.75 mi. S, past Bayfield and Ignacio (Colo.), to San Juan R. in San Juan co., N.Mex. Sometimes called Pine R. Vallecito Dam (162 ft. high, 4,010 ft. long; completed 1941) is 10 mi. N of Bayfield; creates Vallecito Reservoir (capacity 129,700 acre-ft.), used to irrigate 33,100 acres.

Los Planes or **Planes de Renderos** (lōs, plä′nēs dā rĕndā′rōs), village, San Salvador dept., S central Salvador, in coastal range, 5 mi. S of San Salvador (linked by road); residential mtn. resort; tuberculosis sanatorium.

Los Pozos (lōs pō′sōs), village (pop. 380), Herrera prov., S central Panama, 20 mi. SW of Chitré; gold-mining center; stock raising.

Los Queltehues, Chile: see QUELTEHUES.

Los Quirquinchos (lōs kērkēn′chōs), town (pop. estimate 2,000), SW Santa Fe prov., Argentina, 70 mi. SW of Rosario; agr. center (wheat, corn, alfalfa, flax, livestock, poultry; apiculture); flour milling.

Los Ralos (lōs rä′lōs), town (pop. estimate 1,000), central Tucumán prov., Argentina, on railroad and 14 mi. ESE of Tucumán; agr. center (sugar cane, corn, alfalfa, livestock); sugar refinery.

Los Ramones (lōs rämō′nēs), town (pop. 1,452), Nuevo León, N Mexico, on railroad, on Pesquería R. and 40 mi. E of Monterrey; cotton, sugar cane, grain.

Los Reyes (lōs rā′ēs). **1** Residential town (pop. 1,639), Federal Dist., central Mexico, 6 mi. S of Mexico city. **2** Town (pop. 1,826), Mexico state, central Mexico, 12 mi. SE of Mexico city; rail junction; agr. center (cereals, maguey, livestock). **3** Town (pop. 1,592), Mexico state, central Mexico, 40 mi. WNW of Mexico city; cereals, livestock. **4** Officially Los Reyes de Salgado, town (pop. 5,452), Michoacán, central Mexico, at W foot of Sierra de los Terascos, 30 mi. SSW of Zamora; agr. center (corn, sugar cane, tobacco, fruit, livestock). **5** Officially San Francisco de los Reyes, town (pop. 2,508), Michoacán, central Mexico; 12 mi. WSW of El Oro; cereals, livestock. **6** Town (pop. 2,851), Puebla, central Mexico, on railroad and 28 mi. ESE of Puebla; agr. center (cereals, maguey, fruit).

Los Ríos (lōs rē′ōs), province (□ 2,295; 1950 pop. 137,077), W central Ecuador; ⊙ Babahoyo. Inland, bounded E by the Andes, it consists almost entirely of densely forested lowlands traversed by numerous rivers tributary to the Guayas. Has a humid, tropical climate with considerable rainfall Dec.-June. A leading cacao-growing region, it also produces coffee, sugar cane, rice, coconuts, melons, oranges, bananas, yucca. The luxuriant forests yield balsa wood, cedar, laurel, tagua nuts, *toquilla* straw, rubber, etc. Some cattle and horse raising. The region's products are shipped via Guayas R. to Guayaquil, Vinces, and Babahoyo, which serve as main river ports.

Los Saenz, Texas: see ROMA.

Los Santos (lōs sän′tōs), province (□ 1,411; 1950 pop. 61,174), central Panama, on Pacific coast; ⊙ Las Tablas. Occupies SE part of Azuero Peninsula. Agr. (plantains, coffee, sugar cane, corn, rice, beans, yucca); poultry raising is important. There are deposits of nickel, cobalt, sulphur. Prov. is served by a branch of Inter-American Highway on the E coast. Main centers are Las Tablas and Los Santos. Formed 1855 out of old Azuero prov.

Los Santos, town (pop. 1,953), Los Santos prov., S central Panama, in Pacific lowland, on branch of Inter-American Highway and 14 mi. NW of Las Tablas. Commercial and industrial center; distilling, saltworking. Agr. (bananas, corn, rice, beans, coffee, livestock). Founded 1555.

Los Santos Peninsula, Panama: see AZUERO PENINSULA.

Los Sauces, Argentina: see SAN BLAS.

Los Sauces (lōs sou′sēs), town (pop. 2,158), Malleco prov., S central Chile, 14 mi. SSW of Angol; rail junction and agr. center (wheat, oats, apples, wine, peas, livestock); flour milling, lumbering.

Losser (lô′sŭr), town (pop. 3,366), Overijssel prov., E Netherlands, 9 mi. E of Hengelo, near Ger. border; cotton, wooden shoes, sandstone, bricks.

Lossiemouth (lŏsēmouth′), burgh (1931 pop. 3,915; 1951 census 5,596), N Moray, Scotland, on Moray Firth, at mouth of Lossie R., 5 mi. N of Elgin; fishing port, seaside resort. James Ramsay MacDonald b. and lived here. Burgh includes fishing port of Branderburgh.

Lossie River, Moray, Scotland, rises 10 mi. W of Aberlour, flows 31 mi. NE, past Elgin, to Moray Firth at Lossiemouth.

Lössnitz (lûs′nĭts), town (pop. 7,786), Saxony, E central Germany, in the Erzgebirge, 3 mi. NNE of Aue, in mining region (uranium, magnesium silicate); wood carving, metalworking, cotton milling, shoe and leather mfg.

Los Surgentes (lōs so͞orhän′tēs), town (pop. estimate 2,000), E Córdoba prov., Argentina, on the Río Tercero and 20 mi. S of Marcos Juárez; wheat, corn, alfalfa; horticulture; stock raising.

Lostant (lô′stŭnt, lō′stănt), village (pop. 432), La Salle co., N Ill., 13 mi. S of La Salle, in agr. and bituminous-coal area.

Los Taques (lōs tä′kās), town (pop. 790), Falcón state, NW Venezuela, on W coast of Paraguaná Peninsula, 25 mi. WSW of Pueblo Nuevo; fishing.

Lost Cabin, town (pop. 73), Fremont co., central Wyo., on branch of Bighorn R. and 75 mi. WNW of Casper.

Lost Creek. **1** Village (1940 pop. 1,678), Schuylkill co., E central Pa., just SW of Shenandoah, in anthracite region. **2** Town (pop. 798), Harrison co., N W.Va., 8 mi. S of Clarksburg.

Los Telares (lōs tālä′rēs), village (pop. estimate 500), S Santiago del Estero prov., Argentina, 30 mi. NNE of Ojo de Agua, in agr. (corn, alfalfa), fruit-growing, stock-raising, and lumbering (quebracho, carob) area; charcoal burning.

Los Teques (lōs tā′kās), city (1941 pop. 11,101; 1950 census 16,351), ⊙ Miranda state, N Venezuela, in coastal range, on highway and railroad to Caracas and 13 mi. SW of Caracas; 10°30′N 67°2′W; alt. 3,864 ft. Trading center in agr. region (coffee, sugar cane, cacao, grain); sawmilling. Popular residential area and resort for citizens of Caracas; noted for beautiful parks.

Lostice (lôsh′tyĭtsĕ), Czech *Loštice*, village (pop. 2,454), NW central Moravia, Czechoslovakia, on railroad and 18 mi. NW of Olomouc; noted for its cheese pastry; earthenware mfg., tanning. Bouzov castle mus. is 3 mi. SW.

Lostine (lŏstēn′), town (pop. 178), Wallowa co., NE Oregon, 9 mi. NW of Enterprise.

Lost Mine Peak, Texas: see CHISOS MOUNTAINS.

Lost Nation, town (pop. 557), Clinton co., E Iowa, 32 mi. NNW of Davenport; feed milling.

Los Toldos (lōs tōl′dōs), town (pop. 5,234), ⊙ General Viamonte dist. (□ 828; pop. 19,965), N central Buenos Aires prov., Argentina, 30 mi. S of Junín, in agr. zone (grain, livestock); dairying (butter, cheese).

Lost Park Mountain, peak (11,800 ft.) in Front Range, Park co., central Colo.

Lost River, village (pop. 37), Custer co., central Idaho, c.65 mi. SE of Challis. Lost River atomic-energy plant is near Arco (SE).

Lost River. **1** In Calif. and Oregon, flows NW from Clear Lake Reservoir, N Calif., into Klamath co., S Oregon, then W past Bonanza, and S to Tule L., Calif., 4 mi. S of state line; c.70 mi. long. Dam at reservoir and system of small diversion dams and canals along middle course are units in Klamath irrigation project, supplying water to agr. area in Siskiyou co., Calif., and Klamath co., Oregon. **2** In S Ind., rises in W Washington co., flows c.75 mi. W (partly in subterranean channel), past West Baden Springs, to East Fork of White R. in S Martin co. **3** In N.H.: see KINSMAN NOTCH. **4** In W.Va.: see CACAPON RIVER.

Lost River Range, in Custer and Butte counties, E Idaho, bet. Big Lost and Little Lost rivers, in part of Challis Natl. Forest. Chief peaks: BORAH PEAK (12,655 ft.; highest point in state), Dorion Peak (12,016 ft.), Leatherman Peak (12,230 ft.), Invisible Peak (11,343 ft.), Dickey Peak (11,140 ft.).

Lost Springs. 1 City (pop. 184), Marion co., central Kansas, 7 mi. S of Herington, in grain-, stock-, and oil-producing area. **2** Town (pop. 9), Converse, co., E Wyo., 23 mi. E of Douglas; alt. 4,995 ft. Coal mines and oil field near by. Formerly Lost Spring.

Los Tuxtlas, Mexico: see SAN ANDRÉS TUXTLA.

Lostwithiel (lŏswĭ'dhēŭl, –th–, lŏstwĭ'–), municipal borough (1931 pop. 1,327; 1951 census 2,165), E Cornwall, England, on Fowey R. (14th-cent. bridge) and 5 mi. SSE of Bodmin; agr. market and fishing port. Has 13th-cent. church and remains of 14th-cent. Duchy Palace. Just N is 13th-cent. Restormel Castle.

Losuia (lōsōō'yŭ), chief town of Trobriand Isls., Territory of Papua, port on W coast of Kiriwina isl.; 8°30'S 151°5'E.

Los Vilos (lōs vē'lōs), village (1930 pop. 832), Coquimbo prov., N central Chile, minor port on the Pacific and 30 mi. SW of Illapel; rail terminus, beach resort, and agr. center (grain, fruit, livestock). Silver and manganese deposits near by.

Lot (lôt), department (□ 2,018; pop. 154,897), in Quercy, SW France; ⊙ Cahors. Slopes NE-SW from the Massif Central to the Garonne valley. Center and SE occupied by the CAUSSES. Drained (E-W) by the Dordogne, Cère, Lot, and Célé rivers. Agr. (wine, fruits, vegetables, tobacco, cereals) in river valleys. Sheep in the Causses. Truffle cultivation (chiefly in Martel area); hog, goose, and turkey raising. Little industry aside from food processing and *pâté de foie gras* canning. Chief towns are Cahors and Figeac (agr. and trade centers).

Lot, river, France: see LOT RIVER.

Lota (lō'tä), city (1940 pop. 31,087, 1949 estimate 28,108), Concepción prov., S central Chile, port on the Pacific coast (Arauco Gulf), on railroad and 20 mi. SSW of Concepción; 37°6'S 73°8'W. Major coal-mining and shipping center, with coal and copper mines, copper smelters, ceramics factories, breweries. Also a seaside resort with a famed botanical garden on a hill above the city. The business and hotel section is called Lota Baja. Lota is adjoined NE by Lota Alta, a coal-mining suburb.

Lotbinière (lôtbēnyâr'), county (□ 726; pop. 26,664), S Que., on the St. Lawrence; ⊙ Ste. Croix.

Lotbinière, village (pop. 531), S Que., on the St. Lawrence and 35 mi. WSW of Quebec; lumbering, dairying.

Loten, Norway: see ADALSBRUK.

Lot-et-Garonne (lôt-ā-gärôn'), department (□ 2,079; pop. 265,449), SW France, in former Guienne and Gascony provinces; ⊙ Agen. Lies in Aquitaine Basin, bounded by LANDES (SW); drained SE-NW by the middle Garonne and its tributaries (Lot, Dropt, Gers, Baïse). Rich agr. valleys (wheat, corn, tobacco, plums, wine, and vegetables); cattle and poultry raising. Brandy distilling (Nérac area), lumbering (Landes). Iron mining near Fumel. Chief towns are Agen (fruit-preserving center), Villeneuve-sur-Lot (canning), Marmande (distilling, tomato shipping), and Nérac (cork and brandy trade).

Lotfabad, Iran: see LUTFABAD.

Loth, (lŏth), agr. village and parish (pop. 343), SE Sutherland, Scotland, near Moray Firth, 5 mi. SW of Helmsdale. Memorial marks site of killing of last Scottish wolf, c.1700.

Lothair. 1 (lō'thâr) Mining village (pop. 1,313), Perry co., SE Ky., in Cumberland foothills, on North Fork Kentucky R. just SE of Hazard; bituminous coal. **2** (lō'thâr, lō'thŭr) Village, Liberty co., N Mont., 12 mi. W of Chester, in gas and oil region.

Lotharingia (lŏthŭrĭn'jŭ), former W European kingdom; it comprised, roughly, the present Netherlands, Belgium, Luxembourg, Lorraine, Alsace, and NW Germany, including Aachen and Cologne. Originated in Treaty of Verdun (843) when N portion of Carolingian Empire was assigned to Lothair I. Later (959) divided into duchies of Lower Lorraine (N) and Upper Lorraine (S).

Lothersdale, town and parish (pop. 450), West Riding, W Yorkshire, England, 4 mi. SW of Skipton; woolen and cotton milling.

Lothians, The (lō'dhēŭnz), division of SE Scotland, including counties of EAST LOTHIAN, MIDLOTHIAN, and WEST LOTHIAN. In anc. times the district extended bet. the Tweed (S) and the Firth of Forth (N); part of kingdom of Northumbria, 547-1018.

Lothringen, France: see LORRAINE.

Lotien. 1 or **Lo-t'ien** (lŭ'tyĕn'), town (pop. 14,158), ⊙ Lotien co. (pop. 196,800), E Hupeh prov., China, 75 mi. ENE of Hankow; silk, tung oil, timber. **2** (lô'dyen') Town (pop. 1,978), ⊙ Lotien co. (pop. 76,646), S Kweichow prov., China, 80 mi. S of Kweiyang; cotton textiles; tobacco processing; wheat, rice, millet. Saltworks near by. Until 1930 called Loho.

Lotikovo (lô'tyēkŭvŭ), town (1926 pop. 1,625), S central Voroshilovgrad oblast, Ukrainian SSR, in the Donbas, 7 mi. NE of Voroshilovsk; coal mines. Formerly Lotikovski Rudnik.

Loting. 1 or **Lo-t'ing** (lô'tĭng'), town, ⊙ Loting co. (pop. 339,452), NE Hopeh prov., China, 40 mi. ESE of Tangshan, near Lwan R., on Gulf of Chihli; salt-producing center. **2** (lŭ'dĭng') Town (pop. 5,470), ⊙ Loting co. (pop. 308,814), W Kwangtung prov., China, 55 mi. S of Wuchow; indigo processing. Gold and tin mines near by.

Lo-to-k'o, Tibet: see RUDOK.

Lotoshino (lŭtŭshē'nŭ), village (1939 pop. over 500), NW Moscow oblast, Russian SFSR, 17 mi. NW of Volokolamsk; distilling, dairying.

Lot River (lôt), anc. *Oltis*, S and SW France, rises near Mont Lozère 3 mi. NE of Le Bleymard, flows 300 mi. W, past Mende, Espalion, Cahors, Fumel, and Villeneuve-sur-Lot, to the Garonne at Aiguillon (Lot-et-Garonne dept.). Traverses the CAUSSES in deep gorge. Has vineyards and orchards in lower valley. No longer navigable since removal of locks. Receives Truyère and Célé rivers (right).

Lötschberg Tunnel (lûch'bĕrk), S Switzerland, 3d longest (9 mi.) in the Alps. Used by Lötschberg Railway; leads from Thun (Bern canton) to Brig (Valais canton); lies under Lötschen Pass; built 1911; max. alt. 4,078 ft.

Lötschen Pass (lû'chŭn) (8,836 ft.), in Bernese Alps, S Switzerland, 1 mi. ESE of the Balmhorn; leads from S Bern canton into Valais canton.

Lötschental (lû'chŭntäl), valley, S Switzerland, extending from Bernese Alps to the Rhone valley; watered by short Lonza R., which flows SW and S to the Rhone at Gampel.

Lotsing, China: see YOTSING.

Lotsmano-Kamenka (lôt'smŭnŭ-kä'myĭn-kŭ), SE suburb (1926 pop. 4,734) of Dnepropetrovsk, Dnepropetrovsk oblast, Ukrainian SSR, on right bank of Dnieper R. (landing) and 4 mi. SSE of city center.

Lot's Wife, barren rock of isl. group Izu-shichito, Greater Tokyo, Japan, in Philippine Sea, c.150 mi. N of Chichi-jima of Bonin Isls.; 29°48'N 140°21'E. Also called Sofu-gan and Yamome-iwa.

Lott, city (pop. 956), Falls co., E central Texas, near Brazos R., 25 mi. S of Waco; shipping, trade center in cotton, corn area.

Lottefors (lô"tŭfôrs', –fôsh'), village (pop. 557), Gavleborg co., E Sweden, on Ljusna R. and 5 mi. N of Bollnas; lumber and pulp mills.

Lotu (lô'dōō), town, ⊙ Lotu co. (pop. 88,150), NE Tsinghai prov., China, 35 mi. ESE of Sining and on Sining R.; wheat, cattle raising. Until 1928 in Kansu prov., and called Ningpo.

Lotung, China: see LOKTUNG.

Lotung (lô'dōōng'), Jap. *Rato* (rä'tō), town (1935 pop. 6,498), N Formosa, 5 mi. S of Ilan; rail junction; industrial center; lumber milling; ferroalloy metallurgy (carbide, manganese, ferrosilicon, steel alloys); camphor and camphor-oil processing, sugar milling. Hydroelectric plant near by.

Lotus Island, St. Lawrence co., N N.Y., in the St. Lawrence, at Ont. line, just SE of Cardinal, Ont.; c.½ mi. in diameter.

Lotze or **Lo-tz'u** (both: lô'tsŭ'), town (pop. 3,171), ⊙ Lotze co. (pop. 36,884), NE central Yunnan prov., China, 28 mi. NW of Kunming; alt. 6,403 ft.; timber, rice, wheat, millet, beans, peanuts. Coal mines near by.

Lötzen, Poland: see GIZYCKO.

Louann (lōō'ăn"), town (pop. 291), Ouachita co., S Ark., 15 mi. NW of El Dorado.

Loubi, Czechoslovakia: see DECIN.

Loucna nad Desnou (lōk'nä näd dĕ'snō), Czech *Loučná nad Desnou*, formerly *Vizmberk*, Ger. *Wiesenberg* (vē'zŭnbĕrk), village (pop. 1,309), N Moravia, Czechoslovakia, in the Jeseniky, on railroad and 9 mi. NNE of Sumperk; paper mills. Mfg. of agr. machinery in near-by Sobotin (sô'-bôtyēn), Czech *Sobotín*, 4 mi. S.

Loudéac (lōōdāäk'), town (pop. 2,801), Côtes-du-Nord dept., W France, 12 mi. NE of Pontivy; rail and road junction; woodworking.

Loudes (lōōd), village (pop. 409), Haute-Loire dept., S central France, 7 mi. WNW of Le Puy; cattle trading.

Loudias River or **Loudhias River** (both: lōōdhē'ŭs), in Macedonia, Greece, rises in the Paikon, flows 25 mi. SE, through drained L. Giannitsa, to the Gulf of Salonika in delta 15 mi. WSW of Salonika.

Loudima (lōōdēmä'), village, S Middle Congo territory, Fr. Equatorial Africa, on Niari R., on railroad, and 150 mi. W of Brazzaville; agr. center (groundnuts, tobacco, corn, soya, sweet potatoes), site of experimental station for mechanized tropical farming.

Loudon (lou'dŭn), county (□ 240; pop. 23,182), E Tenn.; ⊙ Loudon. In Great Appalachian Valley; crossed by Tennessee and Little Tennessee rivers; bounded NW by Clinch R. Includes part of Fort Loudoun Reservoir. Agr. (corn, tobacco, hay, fruit), livestock raising, dairying; large timber tracts (pine, oak). Mfg. at Loudon and Lenoir City. Formed 1870.

Loudon. 1 Town (pop. 1,012), Merrimack co., S central N.H., on Soucook R. just NE of Concord. **2** Town (pop. 3,567), ⊙ Loudon co., E Tenn., on Tennessee R. and 28 mi. SW of Knoxville; trade, shipping center for timber and farm area; makes hosiery, chairs. Near by is site of Fort Loudon (built 1756), which fell to the Cherokees in 1760 after a long siege. Fort Loudoun Dam and Reservoir are NE. Settled 1828; inc. 1927.

Loudon, Mount (lou'dŭn) (10,550 ft.), SW Alta., near B.C. border, in Rocky Mts., near Banff Natl. Park, 65 mi. NW of Banff.

Loudonville (lou'dŭnvĭl). **1** Village (1940 pop. 732), Albany co., E N.Y., 3 mi. N of downtown Albany. Seat of St. Bernardine of Siena Col. **2** Village (pop. 2,523), Ashland co., N central Ohio, 17 mi. ESE of Mansfield and on Black Fork of Mohican R.; produces motor vehicles, foodstuffs, greases, oils. Mohican State Forest is near by. Laid out 1814.

Loudoun (lou'dŭn), parish (pop. 7,570), N Ayrshire, Scotland, including parts of burghs of DARVEL, GALSTON, and NEWMILNS AND GREENHOLM.

Loudoun, county (□ 517; pop. 21,147), N Va.; ⊙ Leesburg. Rolling piedmont region, rising to the Blue Ridge along NW border; bounded NE by the Potomac (Md. line); drained by Little R. and short Goose Creek. Agr. and country-estate area, known for horse and cattle breeding, fox hunting; wheat, corn, forage crops, tobacco, apples; dairying, poultry raising. Timber, limestone. Formed 1757.

Loudoun Hill, Scotland: see DARVEL.

Louds Island, S Maine, island (3 mi. long, c.½ mi. wide), in Muscongus Bay, just E of Bristol. Sometimes called Muscongus Isl.

Loudun (lōōdŭ'), town (pop. 4,587), Vienne dept., W central France, 19 mi. SSE of Saumur; road center and cattle market; mfg. of agr. implements; lacemaking. Town suffered from revocation (1685) of Edict of Nantes.

Loudwater, town in parish of Chepping Wycombe Rural (pop. 3,130), S Buckingham, England, on the Wye and 3 mi. SE of High Wycombe; paper-milling center.

Loué (lwā'), village (pop. 1,075), Sarthe dept., W France, 16 mi. W of Le Mans; cattle raising.

Louellen, mining village, Harlan co., SE Ky., on Clover Fork of Cumberland R. and 13 mi. ENE of Harlan; bituminous coal.

Loue River (lōō), Doubs and Jura depts., E France, rises in the central Jura 7 mi. NNW of Pontarlier (underground connection with upper Doubs R.), flows c.80 mi. generally W, past Ornans and Quingey, to the Doubs 5 mi. SSW of Dôle. Used for hydroelectric power.

Louga (lōō'gä), town (pop. c.4,100), NW Senegal, Fr. West Africa, rail junction 100 mi. NE of Dakar; agr. center (peanuts, gums, cotton, millet, corn, manioc; livestock). Vegetable-oil extracting; native handicrafts. Agr. school and experimental station.

Loughborough (lŭf'bŭrŭ), municipal borough (1931 pop. 26,945; 1951 census 34,731), N Leicester, England, near Soar R., 10 mi. NNW of Leicester; mfg. of hosiery, leather, shoes, electrical switch-gear and appliances, boilers, lace, pottery, pharmaceuticals. There are bell foundries (the great bell of St. Paul's in London was cast here 1881, and Loughborough's First World War memorial has a carillon of 47 bells). Has 14th-cent. church and a technical col.

Loughbrickland (lŏkhbrĭk'lŭnd), agr. village (district pop. 1,086), W Co. Down, Northern Ireland, 10 mi. SW of Dromore; flax, oats; sheep. Just S is small Lough Brickland.

Lougheed (lŏhēd', lŏ'hēd), village (pop. 171), E Alta., 30 mi. WSW of Wainwright; grain elevators, stockyards.

Lougheed Island, largest (□ 504) of the Findlay Isls., NW Franklin Dist., Northwest Territories, in the Arctic Ocean, N of Bathurst Isl. and separated from Borden Isls. (W) by Prince Gustav Adolph Sea and from Ellef Ringnes Isl. (NE) by Maclean Strait; 77°30'N 105°W. Isl. is 50 mi. long, 12–15 mi. wide.

Loughgall (lŏkh-gôl'), agr. village (district pop. 1,081), NW Co. Armagh, Northern Ireland, 4 mi. NNE of Armagh; fruitgrowing center.

Loughor, urban district, Wales: see LLWCHWR.

Loughor River, Welsh *Llwchwr* (both: lŏŏkh'ŭr), Glamorgan, Wales, rises 3 mi. NE of Ammanford, flows 15 mi. SW, past Ammanford, Pontardulais, Llwchwr, Llanelly, and Burry Port, to Bristol Channel 2 mi. W of Burry Port.

Loughrea (lŏkhrā'), Gaelic *Baile Locha Riach*, town (pop. 2,887), S Co. Galway, Ireland, on Lough Rea (2-mi. lake), 21 mi. ESE of Galway; agr. market (sheep; potatoes, beets). There are remains of castle and Carmelite friary, both founded c.1300 by Richard de Burgh.

Loughton (lou'tŭn), residential former urban district (1931 pop. 7,390), SW Essex, England, 3 mi. NE of Chingford, at E end of Epping Forest; electrical-equipment works. Just N are remains of anc. Br. earthworks. Inc. 1933 in Chigwell.

Louhans (lōōä'), town (pop. 3,683), Saône-et-Loire dept., E central France, on the Seille and 16 mi. WSW of Lons-le-Saunier; agr. market; poultry shipping.

Louhossoa (lōō-ôsôä'), village (pop. 206), Basses-Pyrénées dept., SW France, in W Pyrenees, near Nive R., 14 mi. SSE of Bayonne; winegrowing, sheep and cattle raising. Feldspar quarrying. Basque pop.

Louin (lo͞o′ĭn), town (pop. 478), Jasper co., E central Miss., 38 mi. WSW of Meridian, in agr. and timber area.

Louisa. 1 (lo͞oē′zŭ, lo͞oī′zŭ) County (□ 403; pop. 11,101), SE Iowa, on Ill. line (E; here formed by Mississippi R.); ⊙ Wapello. Prairie agr. area (cattle, hogs, poultry, corn, oats, wheat) drained by Iowa R. Fertile E section (bet. the Iowa and the Mississippi) is artificially drained (pumping stations, ditches). Limestone quarries. Formed 1836. **2** (lŭwē′zŭ, lŭwī′zŭ) County (□ 514; pop. 12,826), central Va.; ⊙ Louisa. Bounded N and NE by North Anna R.; drained by South Anna R. Agr. (tobacco, grain, hay), dairying, livestock, poultry; some timber. Formed 1742.

Louisa. 1 (lo͞oē′zŭ) Town (pop. 2,015), ⊙ Lawrence co., NE Ky., on Big Sandy R. (here formed by junction of Levisa and Tug forks) and 26 mi. S of Ashland; toll bridge to Fort Gay, W.Va. Trade and shipping center for mtn. agr. (dairy products, livestock, poultry, corn, sorghum, tobacco) area; also oil and gas wells, coal mines, fireclay and sand pits, timber; mfg. of artificial limbs, soft drinks; lumber, flour, and feed mills. The Big Sandy is dammed here. First settlement in this area made 1789. **2** (lŭwē′zŭ, lŭwī′zŭ) Town (pop. 344), ⊙ Louisa co., central Va., 26 mi. E of Charlottesville; trade point in agr., timber area; clothing mfg.; lumber.

Louisburg or **Louisbourg** (lo͞o′ĭsbûrg), town (pop. 1,012), NE N.S., on E coast of Cape Breton Isl., 20 mi. SE of Sydney; swordfish fishing center. Just SW was site of great French fortress of Louisburg (or Louisbourg), built 1720–40 and named for Louis XIV. It became one of the strongest French bases in North America, guarding entrance to the Gulf of St. Lawrence. Near by grew a large city of nearly 10,000 inhabitants. Its port became major naval base and fishing center. In 1745 Louisburg was captured by a New England force under William Pepperrell, with help of fleet under Commodore Warren. It was returned to France in 1748 by the Treaty of Aix-la-Chapelle, in exchange for Madras, India. In 1758 Louisburg was finally taken by British land force under Gen. Jeffrey Amherst and naval force under Admiral Boscawen. In 1759 it became base for Wolfe's operations against Quebec, and in 1760 fortress and town were razed by the British. Site became (1928) a natl. historic park (340 acres), containing ruins of fortress, city, and military cemetery. Other relics are contained in small mus.

Louisburg. 1 City (pop. 677), Miami co., E Kansas, near Mo. line, 32 mi. S of Kansas City, Kansas; shipping point for livestock. Gas and oil wells. **2** Village (pop. 93), Lac qui Parle co., SW Minn., near Minnesota R., 11 mi. N of Madison, in grain area. **3** Town (pop. 2,545), ⊙ Franklin co., N central N.C., on Tar R. and 28 mi. NE of Raleigh; trade center for tobacco and cotton area; sawmilling. Seat of Louisburg Col. Settled 1758.

Louisburgh (lo͞o′ĭsbûrŭ), Gaelic *Cluain Chearbán*, town (pop. 302), SW Co. Mayo, Ireland, on S shore of Clew Bay, 12 mi. WSW of Westport; fishing port.

Louisburgh, Scotland: see WICK.

Louise, town (pop. 479), Humphreys co., W Miss., 15 mi. SSW of Belzoni, in cotton area.

Louise, Lake (1½ mi. long), SW Alta., near B.C. border, in Rocky Mts., in Banff Natl. Park, 2 mi. SW of Lake Louise town; alt. 5,680 ft. Resort, noted for its scenic beauty; on shore is large hotel. Drains E into Bow R.

Louise Island (□ 105), W B.C., Queen Charlotte Isls., in Hecate Strait, E of N Moresby Isl.; 15 mi. long, 2 mi. wide. Rises to 3,550 ft.

Louisenfels, Germany: see OBERKREUZBERG.

Louiseville (lo͞oēz′vĭl), town (pop. 3,542), ⊙ Maskinonge co., S Que., on R. du Loup, near its mouth on the St. Lawrence, 20 mi. WSW of Trois Rivières; silk milling, lumbering, butter making; mfg. of clothing, shirts. Founded 1714.

Louis Gentil (lwē zhātēl′), town (pop. 4,835), Marrakesh region, W Fr. Morocco, on railroad and 40 mi. E of Safi; phosphate mining since 1930s.

Louisiade Archipelago (lo͞oē′zēăd′, lo͞o″ĭzēăd′), E.Central Div., Territory of Papua, SW Pacific, 125 mi. SE of New Guinea; 11°30′S 152°E. Comprises c.10 volcanic isls. and numerous coral reefs. Chief isls.: TAGULA (largest), ROSSEL ISLAND, MISIMA, DEBOYNE ISLANDS. Mountainous; highest peak (2,645 ft.) on Tagula. Gold on most of volcanic isls. Papuan natives. Bwagaoia on Misima is chief town. In Second World War, Deboyne Isls. were site of Jap. seaplane base; battle of Coral Sea (1942) was fought near Misima.

Louisiana (lŭwē″zēă′nŭ, lo͞oē″–), state (land □ 45,177; with inland waters □ 48,523; 1950 pop. 2,683,516; 1940 pop. 2,363,880), S U.S.; 30th in area, 21st in pop.; admitted 1812 as 18th state; ⊙ Baton Rouge. Fronting S on Gulf of Mexico, La. is bounded N by Ark., E by Miss. (partly on Mississippi R., partly on Pearl R.), and W by Texas (mostly along Sabine R.). Extreme dimensions of the "Pelican State" (or "Creole State") are 275 mi. N–S, 300 mi. E–W. La. is a part of the Gulf coastal plain and has the lowest mean alt. (100 ft.) of all the states. DRISKILL MOUNTAIN (N) is the highest point (535 ft.) and New Orleans (SE), the lowest (5 ft. below sea level). Levees line the Mississippi and other rivers, and there are many miles of floodways. The low rolling uplands in the N descend gradually to the flatlands in the S and to low bluffs in the E bordering the wide Mississippi alluvial plain. The uplands have mixed pine and hardwood forests (oak, gum, ash, hickory) in the N, while the central hills and flatlands have pine woods. There is some prairie land in SW. Hardwood forests, cypress and tupelo swamps, and oxbow lakes are typical of the Mississippi alluvial plain and river valleys. The timber lands (c.50% of the state) make wood processing (lumbering, pulp and paper milling) the largest industry in La. The wide belt of tidal marshes are dotted by thousands of shallow lakes and lagoons and cut by numerous bayous and other sluggish streams, many of them navigable for small craft. The INTRACOASTAL WATERWAY traverses the marshes, where dry land is largely limited to low canecovered ridges and hammocks. W of the great Mississippi delta, the coast is marked by straight sandy beaches. Fishing, trapping, hunting, and, to a lesser extent, moss gathering are important in the coastal belt, but are far surpassed by the vast mineral wealth (oil, natural gas, salt, sulphur). Large areas have been set aside as wildlife sanctuaries. Shrimp, oysters, and crabs are caught in large quantities, while the marshes are the habitat of fur-bearing animals (notably muskrats), alligators, bullfrogs, and birds. La. is the leading U.S. producer of furs and frogs, and a major source of shrimp. Upper La. drains S and SE to the Mississippi through the meandering Red and Ouachita rivers and their tributaries. Along the Red R., which bisects the state, are a number of lakes, including Caddo, Bistineau, and Black in NW La. and Catahoula and Iatt in the central part. Chief cities of upper La. are SHREVEPORT (NW) and ALEXANDRIA (central) on Red R., and MONROE (NE) on the Ouachita. Chief rivers of lower La. are the Atchafalaya, the Calcasieu, Bayou Teche, and Bayou Lafourche. Some of the larger water bodies in the coastal strip are Barataria and Atchafalaya bays, and lakes Pontchartrain, Borgne, Maurepas, Salvador, Grand, White, and Calcasieu. The major cities of lower La. are the 3 deepwater ports (BATON ROUGE and NEW ORLEANS on the Mississippi, and LAKE CHARLES on the Calcasieu), and Lafayette, New Iberia, and Bogalusa. Farming, the chief occupation, is favored by the humid subtropical climate, characterized by long, hot summers (July average temp. 82°F.) and short, mild winters (Jan. average temp. 48°F. in N, 53°F. in S). The growing season ranges from 220–250 days in upper La. to 250–320 days in lower La., and the rainfall averages c.55 in. annually. Farm tenancy is high (c.50%), and animals (mules, horses) are still widely used for farm work. Mechanization is most advanced on the large rice and sugar plantations in the S. La. produces almost all of the U.S. sugar cane, and ranks 2d (after Texas) in rice. The "Sugar Bowl" of La. is inland from the coastal marshes bet. the Mississippi delta in the SE and the rice-growing (under irrigation) and cattle-raising prairies in the SW. The S is also the chief region for truck crops (grown especially around New Orleans), Easter lily bulbs, strawberries, sweet potatoes, oranges, tung and pecan nuts. Cotton, the chief crop, is grown mostly in upper La., which also produces corn, oats, Irish potatoes, and hay. Livestock (cattle, hogs, poultry, sheep) is a major source of farm income. Important processing industries are sugar refining, milling (rice, cotton, cottonseed), canning (shellfish, vegetables), and packing (meat, dairy, and poultry products). The refineries and chemical plants are based on the state's mineral wealth. La. ranks 2d as a U.S. producer of natural gas and sulphur, 3d in petroleum (its chief mineral), and 4th in salt. The Gulf coast is the richest mineral region, producing large quantities of oil (recently also obtained from offshore wells), sulphur (from the Grande Ecaille area and Jefferson Isl.), and salt (from large salt domes called the FIVE ISLANDS. There are also important oil fields in the NW part of the state, while the NE is the major natural-gas region. Louisiana State Univ. (near Baton Rouge) and Tulane Univ. (at New Orleans) are the principal educational institutions. After earlier Sp. explorations from Florida, La Salle descended the Mississippi to its mouth in 1682 and claimed all of its drainage basin for France, naming it Louisiana after Louis XIV. Natchitoches, the oldest settlement in present La., grew from a fort built by the French in 1714. Rhenish Germans settled above New Orleans (founded 1718) on what is still the Ger. Coast. Negroes were brought in great numbers as slaves. The French and Indian War saw the cession of old La. W of the Mississippi to Spain (1762) and the part E of the river to Great Britain (1763). Descendants of the French and Spanish are called Creoles. About 5,000 French deported from Acadia arrived by 1800 and settled in the "Cajun" (Acadian) or Teche country (named after Bayou Teche). The French regained the Sp. portion in 1800, but Napoleon, fearing he could not hold it, sold it to the U.S. (the Louisiana Purchase) in 1803 for $15,000,000; after various boundary adjustments in the region and U.S. occupation of portion E of the Mississippi in 1810 state's present boundaries were set. Fr. influence remained, not only in the Creole and "Cajun" elements but in the civil law and the division of the state into parishes rather than counties. The 19th cent. saw the development of great sugar and cotton plantations as settlers poured in from other southern states. By 1840 New Orleans became a great river and ocean port, and ranked 2d to New York. The port fell to the Federal forces in 186[2] during the Civil War. The Reconstruction period was marked by bitter disputes bet. the Democrats and Republicans, and by race riots. The plantation economy was greatly modified by an increase in farm tenancy. Oil and natural gas were discovered in early 1900s, and the old curse of yellow fever epidemics was ended in 1905. After the disastrous Mississippi flood of 1927, the Federal govt undertook a vast control program. In 1928 a virtual political revolution occurred when the dictatorial Huey P. Long was elected governor. The Long machine continued in power (after his assassination in 1935) until 1939–40, and again after 1948. Traditionally Democratic, La. bolted in the 194[8] presidential election to the States Rights party candidate, an upholder of "white supremacy." Since Reconstruction the issue of Negro rights has been a bitter one in the state, where Negroes constitute c.⅓ of the pop. The Negroes live primarily in S La. and in the E, where they are partially blended into the old Creole culture, which persists in New Orleans even today. The descendants of the Acadians also preserve some of their distinctive culture, including Roman Catholicism and Fr. customs. Completely different is the Protestant white culture of N La. See also articles on cities, towns, geographic features, and the 64 parishes: ACADIA, ALLEN, ASCENSION, ASSUMPTION, AVOYELLES, BEAUREGARD, BIENVILLE, BOSSIER, CADDO, CALCASIEU, CALDWELL, CAMERON, CATAHOULA, CLAIBORNE, CONCORDIA, DE SOTO, EAST BATON ROUGE, EAST CARROLL, EAST FELICIANA, EVANGELINE, FRANKLIN, GRANT, IBERIA, IBERVILLE, JACKSON, JEFFERSON, JEFFERSON DAVIS, LAFAYETTE, LAFOURCHE, LA SALLE, LINCOLN, LIVINGSTON, MADISON, MOREHOUSE, NATCHITOCHES, ORLEANS, OUACHITA, PLAQUEMINES, POINTE COUPEE, RAPIDES, RED RIVER, RICHLAND, SABINE, SAINT BERNARD, SAINT CHARLES, SAINT HELENA, SAINT JAMES, SAINT JOHN THE BAPTIST, SAINT LANDRY, SAINT MARTIN, SAINT MARY, SAINT TAMMANY, TANGIPAHOA, TENSAS, TERREBONNE, UNION, VERMILION, VERNON, WASHINGTON, WEBSTER, WEST BATON ROUGE, WEST CARROLL, WEST FELICIANA, WINN.

Louisiana, city (pop. 4,389), Pike co., E Mo., on Mississippi R. (here spanned by Champ Clark Bridge) and 25 mi. SE of Hannibal; agr. (grain, orchard and nursery products); mfg. (gloves, buttons, tools). Ammonia plant has been converted for study and production of synthetic fuels. Laid out 1818.

Louisiana Point, extreme SW point of La., on Gulf coast at E side of Sabine Pass entrance, 14 mi. SSE of Port Arthur, Texas. Sabine Pass lighthouse (29°43′N 93°51′W) is 2 mi. N.

Louis Napoleon, Cape, E Ellesmere Isl., NE Franklin Dist., Northwest Territories, on Kane Basin, 79°38′N 72°17′W; at end of Darling Peninsula (20 mi. long). Shoreline was explored by Shackleton, 1935.

Louis Philippe Peninsula (lwē fēlēp′), Antarctica, in South Pacific, the extreme N tip of Palmer Peninsula, extending c.80 naut. mi. NE from Charcot Bay and Sjögren Fiord. Discovered 1838 by Dumont d'Urville, Fr. navigator. Chile established in 1949 a military base on W coast at 63°20′S 57°54′W. Sometimes called Trinity (Sp. *Trinidad*) Peninsula.

Louis Trichardt (lo͞o′ē trĭ′khärt), town (pop. 5,671), N Transvaal, U. of So. Afr., at foot of Zoutpansberg mts., 65 mi. NE of Pietersburg; stock, grain. Airfield.

Louisville. 1 (lo͞o′ĭsvĭl) Town (pop. 622), Barbour co., SE Ala., 25 mi. WSW of Eufaula; lumber. **2** (lo͞o′ĭsvĭl) Town (pop. 1,978), Boulder co., N central Colo., just E of Front Range, 15 mi. NNW of Denver; alt. 5,350 ft. Coal-mining point in grain, sugar-beet region. Inc. 1892. **3** (lo͞o′ĭsvĭl) City (pop. 2,231), ⊙ Jefferson co., E Ga., on Ogeechee R. and c.40 mi. SW of Augusta; mfg. (clothes, fertilizer, furniture). Has old slave market (built before 1800), and several late-18th-cent. houses. Laid out 1786 as the prospective capital of Ga. State bldgs. completed 1795; seat of govt. until 1804, when Milledgeville became capital. **4** (lo͞o′ĭsvĭl) Village (pop. 970), ⊙ Clay co., S central Ill., 22 mi. W of Olney, in agr., oil, and natural-gas area; corn, wheat, fruit, poultry, truck; flour mill. **5** (lo͞o′ĭsvĭl) City (pop. 190), Pottawatomie co., NE Kansas, on small affluent of Kansas R. and 34 mi. WNW of Topeka; livestock, grain. **6** (lo͞o′ēvĭl, lū′–) City (□ 40.8; pop. 369,129), ⊙ Jefferson co., N Ky., along left bank (levee) of the Ohio at its falls and

90 mi. SW of Cincinnati; 38°15'N 85°46'W; alt. 380–540 ft. Largest city of state and a principal commercial, industrial, financial, and educational center of the South; port of entry. Rail junction (repair shops); important tobacco market and processing center, making most of Ky. output of tobacco products; its large distilleries (famed especially for bourbon whisky) produce a large part of U.S. supply. Has stockyards, meat-packing and wood-working plants, foundries, machine shops, flour mills, and plants processing other foodstuffs, petroleum, and metals; mfg. of farm equipment, clothing, textiles, plumbers' and builders' supplies, leather goods, electrical goods, furniture, paint, plastics, synthetic rubber, chemicals, gases, cement products, and industrial, air-filtering, heating, and refrigeration equipment. Its hinterland, mainly in the BLUEGRASS agr. region, produces burley tobacco, grain, vegetables, livestock, phosphate, fluorspar, limestone, clay. Louisville is situated on flood plain at a bend of the Ohio, which is spanned by bridges to New Albany and Jeffersonville, Ind. Univ. of Louisville (includes Louisville Municipal Col. for Negroes), Louisville Presbyterian Theological Seminary, Southern Baptist Theological Seminary, Jefferson School of Law, Univ. of Ky. col. of pharmacy; Nazareth Col., Ursuline and Sacred Heart jr. colleges, state school for the blind (1842), and American Printing House for the Blind (1858), which produces Braille books, are here. Has R.C. cathedral, army medical depot. In outskirts, city is circled by parks (Shawnee, Chickasaw, Iroquois, and Cherokee), state fairgrounds (annual fair in Sept.), Churchill Downs race track, scene (since 1875) of annual Kentucky Derby, most famous U.S. horse-racing event. Points of interest in city also include Filson Club (founded 1884; has historical library and mus.), J. B. Speed art mus., public library, memorial auditorium, old Cave Hill Cemetery, with grave of George Rogers Clark and a natl. cemetery, old Grayson House (built before 1810), Federal fish hatchery, state forest nursery, and the Haymarket (a farmers' market). U.S. dam (completed 1928) in the Ohio and the Louisville and Portland Canal (2 mi. long; 1st opened 1830, rebuilt 1927) aid navigation here around Falls of the Ohio, which are used for power; only inland coast guard station in U.S. is here. Has municipal airport (Bowman Field). Near city are home and tomb of Zachary Taylor. Settlement here was laid out 1773, on site chosen because of its strategic location at portage around falls. George Rogers Clark led 1st party of settlers here in 1778 and built a fort. Va. legislature named settlement (1780) in honor of Louis XVI. Fort Nelson (1782) was Clark's supply base for conquest of the Old Northwest Territory. Served as portage place for river cargo until opening (1830) of canal made possible the through navigation of the Ohio to Pittsburgh. Arrival of railroads in 1850s further stimulated commerce. After Civil War, in which city's loyalties were sharply divided, although it was a Union supply base, Louisville made a successful bid for the Southern trade. Its early populace was drawn from the South, from New England, and from France, and in 1840s many Germans came. Despite extensive protection work, periodic floods of the Ohio have done much damage; the most destructive (in 1937) caused enormous losses. Inc. 1828. **7** (lo͞o'ĭsvĭl) City (pop. 5,282), ⊙ Winston co., E central Miss., 45 SW of Columbus, in agr., dairying, and timber area; lumber, creosoted-wood products, dairy products. State park near by. Inc. 1836. **8** (lo͞o'ĭsvĭl) Village (pop. 1,014), Cass co., E Nebr., 20 mi. SW of Omaha and on Platte R.; cement and pottery products; grain. Recreation grounds near by. **9** (lo͞o' ĭs vĭl) Village (pop. 3,801), Stark co., E central Ohio, 6 mi. ENE of Canton; mfg. (foundry products, clothing).

Loukhi (lô'o͝okhē), Finnish *Louhi* (lō'hē), village (1948 pop. over 2,000), N Karelo-Finnish SSR, on Murmansk RR and 75 mi. S of Kandalaksha; junction of rail spur to Kestenga. Pegmatite quarries.

Loukkos River, Sp. and Fr. Morocco: see LUCUS RIVER.

Loukoléla (lo͞okōlĕlä'), village, central Middle Congo, Fr. Equatorial Africa, on Congo R. opposite Lukolela (Belgian Congo) and 250 mi. NNE of Brazzaville; sawmills.

Loulay (lo͞olā'), village (pop. 644), Charente-Maritime dept., W France, 7 mi. N of Saint-Jean-d'Angély; mule market.

Loulé (lōlĕ'), town (pop. 5,442), Faro dist., S Portugal, 10 mi. NW of Faro; light-mfg. center; produces soap, pottery, burlap, baskets. Exports carob, figs, and almonds. Ruins of Moorish fortifications.

Louny (lō'nĭ), Ger. *Laun* (loun), town (pop. 11,447), NW Bohemia, Czechoslovakia, on Ohre R. and 33 mi. NW of Prague; rail junction; ironworks; mfg. of porcelain goods, sugar milling. Annual fairs. Wheat, hops, rape seed, and fruitgrowing in vicinity. Once a royal seat, it retains 16th-cent. church and castle ruins. Jaroslav Vrchlicky b. here.

Loup (lo͞op), county (□ 574; pop. 1,348), central Nebr.; ⊙ Taylor. Agr. region drained by Calamus and N.Loup rivers. Livestock, grain. Formed 1883.

Loup City, city (pop. 1,508), ⊙ Sherman co., central Nebr., 40 mi. NW of Grand Island and on Middle Loup R.; dairy products, grain. Settled 1873.

Loupe, La (lä lo͞op'), town (pop. 1,889), Eure-et-Loir dept., NW central France, 14 mi. NE of Nogent-le-Rotrou; agr. trade center; mfg. (plumbing fixtures, baby carriages, agr. equipment); horse breeding.

Loupiac (lo͞opyäk'), village (pop. 85), Gironde dept., SW France, on right bank of the Garonne and 20 mi. SE of Bordeaux; sauterne wines.

Loupmont (lo͞omõ'), village (pop. 120), Meuse dept., NE France, 6 mi. ESE of Saint-Mihiel, at foot of Loupmont ridge (Ger. stronghold in First World War).

Loup River (lo͞o), Alpes-Maritimes dept., SE France, rises in Provence Alps, flows 25 mi. SE, through narrow gorge near Le Bar, to the Mediterranean S of Cagnes-sur-Mer. Hydroelectric plant.

Loup River (lo͞op), E central Nebr.; formed by North and Middle Loup rivers in Howard co., near St. Paul; flows 68 mi. E, past Fullerton, Genoa, and Columbus, to Platte R. at Columbus. Its tributaries flow SE: North Loup rises in Cherry co., flows 212 mi., past Ord, to join the Middle Loup, which also rises in Cherry co. and flows 221 mi., past part of Nebr. Natl. Forest and Loup City; the South Loup rises in Logan co., flows 152 mi., past Ravenna, to the Middle Loup near Boelus. Calamus R. joins the North Loup, Dismal R. the Middle Loup, and Cedar R. the main stream. Diversion dam SW of Genoa is unit in Loup R. power project, directing water through a canal to generators at Monroe and Columbus.

Lourches (lo͞orsh), town (pop. 5,834), Nord dept., N France, on the Escaut (canalized) and 2 mi. SW of Denain; coal-mining center; chemical- and metal-works.

Lourdes (lo͞ordz, lo͞ord, Fr. lo͞ord), town (pop. 12,421), Hautes-Pyrénées dept., SW France, at foot of the central Pyrenees, on Gave de Pau R. and 11 mi. SSW of Tarbes; a leading Catholic place of pilgrimage and well-known tourist center; produces religious articles and jewelry. Chalk, slate, and ophite are quarried in area. Near by is the grotto where Our Lady of Lourdes appeared to St. Bernadette in 1858. The miraculous cures worked here since then have attracted millions of pilgrims and invalids.

Lourdes (lōr'dās), village (1939 pop. 1,026; 1948 municipal dist. pop. 10,249) Misamis Oriental prov., N Mindanao, Philippines, 14 mi. WNW of Cagayan; corn, coconuts; chromite deposits.

Lourenço Marques (lôrĕn'sō mär'kĕs, Port. lōrān'-so͞o mär'kĭsh), city (1950 commune pop. 93,516), ⊙ Mozambique, on DELAGOA BAY, an inlet of the Indian Ocean, near Port. colony's S border, 300 mi. E of Johannesburg and NNE of Durban (U. of So. Afr.); 25°58'S 32°33'E. Administrative center and largest city of Mozambique, and important outlet for the Transvaal, linked by rail since 1895. A rail spur to Goba (30 mi. SW) provides access to Swaziland. Has one of S Africa's best harbors. Modern facilities include cold-storage warehouse, coaling and oil-fueling station, drydock. Chief exports are coal and livestock products from U. of So. Afr., cotton, sugar, sisal, oil seeds, copra, hardwoods. Processing industries include textile mill and ironworks. Climate is healthful, especially in winter (May-Sept.). Mean yearly temp. is 71°F.; average rainfall 26 in. (Oct.-March). City has regular layout; its development dates from beginning of 20th cent. Chief public bldgs. are a new general hosp., cathedral, town hall, and govt. offices. Airport. Bay 1st visited 1502 by António do Campo. Region explored by a trader, Lourenço Marques, after whom settlement was named. Officially superseded Mozambique city as ⊙ Portuguese East Africa in 1907. Also ⊙ Lourenço Marques dist. (□ 4,008; 1950 pop. 199,423).

Loures (lō'rĭsh), town (pop. 1,306), Lisboa dist., central Portugal, 7 mi. N of Lisbon; sugar refining, chemical fertilizer mfg., textile dyeing.

Louriçal (lōrēsäl'), village (pop. 306), Leiria dist., W central Portugal, 19 mi. NNE of Leiria; wine, rice, resin (from near-by pine woods). Has 17th-cent. convent.

Lourinhã (lōrē'nyů), town (pop. 1,126), Lisboa dist., central Portugal, near the Atlantic and 9 mi. SSE of Peniche; distilling; wine, olives, almonds.

Lourmel (lo͞ormĕl'), town (pop. 3,818), Oran dept., NW Algeria, on railroad and 24 mi. SW of Oran, at W end of the Oran Sebkha; winegrowing.

Louros River (lo͞o'rôs), in S Epirus, Greece, rises in the Tomaras, flows 47 mi. S to the Gulf of Arta of Ionian Sea 13 mi. SW of Arta. Hydroelectric plant.

Louroujina (lo͞oro͞oyē'nä), village (pop. 1,816), Nicosia dist., S central Cyprus, 13 mi. SSE of Nicosia; wheat, barley, oats; sheep, hogs.

Lousa (lō'zů), village (pop. 1,651), Bragança dist., N Portugal, 30 mi. ESE of Vila Real, near right bank of the Douro, vineyards (for port wine).

Lousã (lōzã'), town (pop. 1,152), Coimbra dist., N central Portugal, on railroad and 12 mi. SE of Coimbra, at N foot of Serra da Lousã (3,950 ft.; SW outlier of Serra da Estrêla); mfg. (paper, rugs, blankets, hats); sawmilling.

Lousada (lōzä'dů), town (pop. 604), Pôrto dist., N Portugal, on railroad and 18 mi. ENE of Oporto; agr. trade (corn, beans, olives, figs); winegrowing.

Lousal (lōzäl'), town (pop. 1,131), Setúbal dist., S central Portugal, on railroad and 13 mi. SE of Grândola; copper mining. Also called Mina do Lousal.

Louth (louth), municipal borough (1931 pop. 9,682; 1951 census 11,128), Parts of Lindsey, NE central Lincolnshire, England, on Lud R. and 23 mi. ENE of Lincoln; agr. market with agr.-machinery and chemical works and metal foundries. Has 16th-cent. grammar school which Tennyson attended; parish church dating from late 12th or early 13th cent., with 300-ft. 16th-cent. spire; and, near by, ruins of Cistercian Louth Park Abbey, founded 1139. For centuries Louth was an important religious center, site (1536) of a meeting of partisans of the Pilgrimage of Grace.

Louth (loudh, louth), Gaelic *Lughbhaidh*, county (□ 316.9; pop. 66,194), Leinster, E Ireland; ⊙ Dundalk. Smallest co. in Ireland, bounded by cos. Meath (S and SW), Monaghan (W), and Armagh (N), and by Carlingford Lough (N) and the Irish Sea (E). Drained by the Boyne (navigable to Drogheda), Dee, Fane, and Castletown rivers. Surface is generally low and level, becoming hilly in NW and mountainous in NE. Coastline is low and sandy; chief inlets are Carlingford Lough and Dundalk Bay. Sea fisheries are important; oyster beds in Carlingford Lough. Cattle raising; wheat, barley, potato growing are chief occupations. Industries include linen milling, brewing, tanning, iron founding, mfg. of railroad equipment, machinery, clothing, shoes, lace, chemicals, soap, cattle feed, fertilizer, agr. implements, furniture. Beef and cattle are exported. Besides Dundalk, other towns are Drogheda, Ardee, Carlingford, Greenore, Dunleer. Co. was formerly part of lordship of Oriel and is associated with legend of Cuchulain. It was N border of Anglo-Norman region of Ireland. There are remains of anc. abbeys, round towers, and earthworks; monastic remains of Monasterboice are notable.

Louth, Gaelic *Lughbhadh*, town (pop. 172), central Co. Louth, Ireland, 6 mi. WSW of Dundalk; agr. market (wheat, barley, potatoes; cattle). It is former ⊙ Co. Louth. St. Patrick founded religious house here, which became center of learning; in 9th cent. it was pillaged by Danes. There are remains of abbey founded 1148.

Louth Bay (louth), inlet of Spencer Gulf, South Australia, on SE Eyre Peninsula, bet. Boston Point (S) and Point Bolingbroke (N); 12 mi. long, 7 mi. wide. Sheltered by Sir Joseph Banks Isls.

Loutra Aidepsou or **Loutra Aidhipsou** (both: lo͞oträ' ā-dhĭpso͞o') [Gr.,=spa of Aidepsos], city (pop. 6,461), NW Euboea, Greece, port on N Gulf of Euboea, 40 mi. NW of Chalcis. Health resort with sulphur springs, frequented since anc. times; fisheries. The municipality (formed c.1940) includes villages of Aidepsos, Aidhipsos, or Aedipsos, 2 mi. N, Hagios or Ayios, 4 mi. N, Gialtra or Yialtra, 4 mi. W across Gulf of Aidepsos, and Gourgouvitsa, 2 mi. ENE.

Loutrakion (lo͞oträ'kēôn), city (pop., including Perachora, 6,282), Argolis and Corinthia nome, NE Peloponnesus, Greece, port on Bay of Corinth, 4 mi. NE of Corinth; summer resort (alkaline springs). Includes town of Perachora or Perakhora (both: pĭrůkhô'rů), 4 mi. NW, and POSEIDONIA, 2.5 mi. S. Formerly called Loutraki.

Loutro, Crete: see PHOENIX.

Louvain (lo͞ovē'), Flemish *Leuven* (lû'vůn), city (pop. 37,188), Brabant prov., central Belgium, on Dyle R. and 15 mi. E of Brussels; cultural and industrial center. Rail junction; brewing, distilling, mfg. of machinery, shoes and other leather goods, chemicals. Its fame is largely due to its univ. (founded 1423 by John IV of Brabant), which became celebrated throughout Europe and is one of the world's leading centers of Catholic learning. Louvain's fine bldgs. include Hôtel de Ville (magnificent Gothic structure built 1447–63), Church of St. Peter (begun 1423) and several other early churches, 14th-cent. cloth hall (Louvain was a medieval textile center). In 1914, when the city was set afire by Germans, among its losses was the fine univ. library. In 1928 a new library (gift of American people) was dedicated; this was destroyed by the Germans in 1940. Louvain antedates the Middle Ages; was capital of duchy of Brabant until Brussels replaced it in 15th cent.; became a medieval trade center. Its declining economic importance was offset by growth and influence of its univ.

Louveigné (lo͞ovĕnyā'), agr. village (pop. 2,007), Liége prov., E central Belgium, 9 mi. SE of Liége.

Louvemont (lo͞ovmō'), village (pop. 363), Haute-Marne dept., NE France, on Blaise R. and 6 mi. S of Saint-Dizier; foundries. Sand quarries.

Louvesc, La, France: see LALOUVESC.

Louvicourt (lo͞ovēko͞or'), village, W Que., 11 mi. ENE of Val d'Or; gold and copper mining.

Louvière, La (lä lo͞ovyâr'), town (pop. 22,225), Hainaut prov., S central Belgium, on Canal du Centre and 12 mi. WNW of Charleroi; steel-mfg. center; coal mining; mfg. (locomotives, cement, ceramics, colored glass). Canal du Centre has major hydraulic elevator here.

Louviers (lōōvyā'), town (pop. 8,720), Eure dept., NW France, on left bank of braided Eure R. and 16 mi. SSE of Rouen; woolen-mfg. center; woodworking, iron founding, rubber vulcanizing. Has 12th–16th-cent. church (damaged in Second World War). Town center was severely hit in 1940 fighting.

Louviers (lōōvērz'), village (pop. c.400), Douglas co., central Colo., on Plum Creek, near South Platte R., and 15 mi. S of Denver; alt. c.5,800 ft.; mine explosives.

Louvigné-du-Désert (lōōvēnyā'-dü-dāzâr'), town (pop. 2,065), Ille-et-Vilaine dept., W France, 10 mi. NNE of Fougères; granite-quarrying center. Numerous megalithic monuments near by.

Louvres (lōō'vrů), village (pop. 1,893), Seine-et-Oise dept., N central France, 14 mi. NNE of Paris; chemical works.

Louvroil (lōōvrwäl'), heavy industrial SSE suburb (pop. 4,748) of Maubeuge, Nord dept., N France, on the Sambre; forges, foundries, rolling mills. Mfg. of machine-tools, iron and steel tubes, sandstone pipes, tiles. Woodworking.

Lovagny (lōvänyē'), village (pop. 133), Haute-Savoie dept., SE France, near the Fier, 5 mi. W of Annecy; asphalt mines.

Lo Valdés (lō väldĕs'), ski resort, Santiago prov., central Chile, in the Andes, near Argentina frontier, 40 mi. SE of Santiago.

Lovanger (lův'ông"ůr), Swedish *Lövånger*, village (pop. 503), Vasterbotten co., N Sweden, on small lake near Gulf of Bothnia, 30 mi. SSE of Skelleftea; cattle; dairying. Noted for cheese made here. Has 15th-cent. church.

Lovango Cay (lōvăng"gō kā', kē'), islet (118 acres; alt. 255 ft.), U.S. Virgin Isls., off NW St. John Isl., 8 mi. E of Charlotte Amalie; 18°22'N 64°47'W.

Lovasbereny (lô'vŏsh-bĕ"rānyů), Hung. *Lovasberény*, town (pop. 3,249), Fejer co., N central Hungary, 10 mi. NE of Szekesfehervar; corn, cattle, horses.

Lovaszi (lô'väsē), Hung. *Lovászi*, village (pop. 751), Zala co., W Hungary, 20 mi. WNW of Nagykanizsa; center of natural-gas field; power plant.

Lovat River or **Lovat' River** (lůvät'yů), in W European Russian SFSR, rises SE of Nevel on Russian SFSR–Belorussian SSR line, flows 335 mi. N, past Velikiye Luki and Kholm, to L. Ilmen, forming a joint delta mouth with Pola R. Receives Kunya (right) and Polist (left) rivers. Navigable for 40 mi. in lower course. Part of anc. Baltic–Black Sea water route.

Lovcen or **Lovchen** (both: lôf'tyĕn), Serbo-Croatian *Lovćen*, basaltic mountain in Dinaric Alps, SW Montenegro, Yugoslavia, on Gulf of Kotor; highest point (5,737 ft.) is 3 mi. SE of Kotor. Crossed by scenic serpentine road connecting Kotor on Adriatic coast with Titograd, via Cetinje (at E foot). Was refuge of Serbian nobles after battle of Kosovo (1389) and center of Montenegrin resistance against Turks.

Love, village (pop. 274), E central Sask., 10 mi. NW of Nipawin; wheat, dairying.

Love, county (□ 503; pop. 7,721), S Okla.; ⊙ Marietta. Bounded S by Red R., here forming Texas line. Includes part of L. Murray (with state park) and part of L. Texoma. Agr. area (livestock, cotton, grain, corn). Cotton ginning. Oil and natural-gas wells. Formed 1907.

Lovea (lōvä'ä), town, Battambang prov., W Cambodia, 16 mi. S of Sisophon. In Thailand, 1941–46.

Lovech (lô'vĕch), city (pop. 11,730), Pleven dist., N Bulgaria, on Osam R. and 19 mi. S of Pleven; agr., tanning center. Leathercraft school. Once a Roman settlement; became important stronghold under Turkish rule (15th–19th cent.).

Lovejoy. 1 or **Lovejoys Station**, town (pop. 204), Clayton co., N central Ga., 21 mi. S of Atlanta. **2** Village, St. Clair co., Ill.: see BROOKLYN.

Lovelady, city (pop. 541), Houston co., E Texas, 13 mi. S of Crockett, in agr. area.

Loveland (lŭv'lůnd). **1** City (pop. 6,773), Larimer co., N Colo., on Thompson R., in lake region, and 45 mi. N of Denver; alt. 4,982 ft. Tourist stop; food-processing center; beet sugar, canned fruits and vegetables, dairy products. Experimental farm of state col. of agr. near by. Rocky Mtn. Natl. Park 23 mi. W. Founded 1877, inc. 1881. **2** Village (pop. 2,149), on Clermont-Hamilton-Warren co. line, SW Ohio, 18 mi. NE of Cincinnati, and on Little Miami R., in truck, fruit, and dairying area; makes fireworks, candy. Settled 1825, inc. 1876. **3** Town (pop. 96), Tillman co., SW Okla., 15 mi. ESE of Frederick, in agr. area (cotton, grain).

Loveland, Lake, Calif.: see SWEETWATER RIVER.

Loveland Pass (11,992 ft.), N central Colo., in Front Range, c.55 mi. W of Denver. Winter sports. Construction of vehicular tunnel beneath pass was started 1941; pioneer bore (5,484 ft. long) completed 1943. Grays Peak is just E.

Lovell (lŭ'vůl). **1** Town (pop. 640), Oxford co., W Maine, on Kezar L. and 31 mi. SW of Rumford, in resort area; wood products. **2** Town (pop. 73), Logan co., central Okla., 17 mi. NW of Guthrie, in oil-producing and agr. area. **3** Town (pop. 2,508), Big Horn co., N Wyo., on Shoshone R., near Mont. line, and 65 mi. S of Billings, Mont.; supply and processing point in irrigated sugar-beet and grain region; oil refineries; beet sugar, beans, clay products. Oil wells in vicinity. Laid out 1900 by Mormons.

Lovelock, city (pop. 1,604), ⊙ Pershing co., W central Nev., on Humboldt R., bet. Trinity and Humboldt ranges, and c.75 mi. NE of Reno; alt. 3,977 ft.; trade center for Humboldt irrigation project (alfalfa, livestock; dairying). Gold, silver, copper, lead, and kieselguhr are mined in vicinity. Lovelock Cave, containing anc. artifacts, is near by. Settled 1860, inc. 1917.

Lovendegem (lōvĕn'dů-khům), agr. village (pop. 4,827), East Flanders prov., NW Belgium, on Bruges-Ghent Canal and 5 mi. NW of Ghent.

Lovenia, Mount, Utah: see UINTA MOUNTAINS.

Lövenich (lû'vůnĭkh), village (pop. 11,840), in former Prussian Rhine Prov., W Germany, after 1945 in North Rhine-Westphalia, 5 mi. W of Cologne; sugar beets.

Love Point, Md.: see KENT ISLAND.

Lovere (lô'vĕrĕ), town (pop. 4,653), Bergamo prov., Lombardy, N Italy, port on N shore of Lago d'Iseo, 21 mi. NE of Bergamo; resort; silk mill, scale factory.

Lovero Valtellino (lô'vĕrō vältĕl-lē'nô), village (pop. 862), Sondrio prov., Lombardy, N Italy, in the Valtellina, on Adda R. and 3 mi. ENE of Tirano; hydroelectric plant.

Loves Park, city (pop. 5,366), Winnebago co., N Ill., on Rock R., just NE of Rockford. Inc. 1947.

Lovestad (lû'vůstäd"), Swedish *Lövestad*, village (pop. 509), Malmohus co., S Sweden, on Kavlinge R. and 15 mi. NNE of Ystad; grain, sugar beets, potatoes, cattle.

Lövete, Rumania: see LUETA.

Lovett (lŭ'vĭt), town (pop. 80), Laurens co., central Ga., 11 mi. NE of Dublin, in agr. area.

Lovettsville, town (pop. 341), Loudoun co., N Va., near the Potomac, 16 mi. SW of Frederick, Md.

Lovewell Mountain, peak (2,473 ft.), SW N.H., on Sullivan-Merrimack co. line, near Washington.

Lovewell Pond, Oxford co., W Maine, near Fryeburg; 2 mi. long. Monument marks site of victory over Indians, 1725.

Lovich, Poland: see LOWICZ.

Lovilia (lōvĭ'lů) town (pop. 619), Monroe co., S Iowa, near Cedar Creek, 9 mi. NW of Albia, in bituminous-coal-mining and livestock area; mfg. (feed, concrete blocks).

Loving (lŭ'vĭng), county (□ 647; pop. 227), W Texas; ⊙ Mentone. High rolling prairies; bordered N by N.Mex. line, W by Pecos R.; alt. c.2,500–3,000 ft. Cattle ranching; also horses, mules, some poultry. Some oil produced. Includes part of Red Bluff L. (irrigation, recreation). Formed 1887.

Loving, village (pop. 1,487), Eddy co., SE N.Mex., near Pecos R., 13 mi. SSE of Carlsbad, in irrigated cotton and alfalfa region; potash refineries, cottonseed-oil plant. Carlsbad Caverns are WSW.

Lovingston (lŭ'vĭngstůn), village (pop. c.350), ⊙ Nelson co., central Va., 29 mi. NE of Lynchburg, in apple-growing area. Rail station at Shipman, 4 mi. SE; apple-shipping point.

Lovington (lŭ'vĭngtůn). **1** Village (pop. 1,152), Moultrie co., central Ill., 17 mi. ESE of Decatur; corn, wheat, soybeans, livestock, dairy products. Inc. 1873. **2** Town (pop. 3,134), ⊙ Lea co., SE N.Mex., on Llano Estacado, near Texas line, 20 mi. NW of Hobbs; trade center in livestock, grain, truck region; dairy and poultry products, cotton. Potash mines and oil wells in vicinity. Rodeo and co. fair take place here in August. Founded 1908.

Lovisa (lōōvē'sä"), Finnish *Loviisa* (lō'vēsä), city (pop. 4,362), Uusimaa co., S Finland, at head of small bay of Gulf of Finland, 50 mi. ENE of Helsinki; fishing port; rail terminus. Seaside resort. Pop. is largely Swedish-speaking. Founded (1745) as Degerby, renamed 1752. Nearby fortifications destroyed (1855) by British.

Lovni-dol (lôvnē'-dôl"), village (pop. 2,100), Gorna Oryakhovitsa dist., N central Bulgaria, on N slope of Balkan Mts., 8 mi. ESE of Sevliyevo; horse-raising center; horticulture. Formerly Chiflik.

Lovo, island, Sweden: see DROTTNINGHOLM.

Lovosice (lô'vôsĭtsĕ), Ger. *Lobositz* (lō'bōzĭts), town (pop. 4,962), N Bohemia, Czechoslovakia, on Elbe R. and 10 mi. S of Usti nad Labem; rail junction; noted rayon industry; food processing (edible oils, chocolate, chicory, canned fruit); production of fertilizers. Garnet deposits near by. Frederick the Great defeated Austrians here in 1756.

Lovozero (lôv'ô"zyĭrů), village (1948 pop. over 2,000), central Murmansk oblast, Russian SFSR, on Kola Peninsula, on lake Lovozero (30 mi. long, 3 mi. wide), 85 mi. SE of Murmansk; lumbering, reindeer raising. Rare earths and diatomite deposits (S).

Lovran, Yugoslavia: see OPATIJA.

Lovsnes, Norway: see LAUVSNES.

Lovushki Islands (lůvōōsh'kē), Jap. *Mushiru-retsugan* (mōōshē'rōō-rĕtsōōgän'), group of reefs in N main Kurile Isls. group, Russian SFSR; separated from Shiashkotan Isl. (N) by Fortuna Strait, from Raikoke Isl. (S) by Kruzenshtern Strait; 48°33'N 153°50'E.

Low, Cape, S extremity of Southampton Isl., E Keewatin Dist., Northwest Territories, on Hudson Bay; 63°7'N 85°18'W.

Lowa (lō'wä), village, Eastern Prov., E Belgian Congo, on Lualaba R. opposite mouth of Lowa R., and 135 mi. SSE of Stanleyville; steamboat landing, trading center. R.C. mission. Airfield.

Low Archipelago: see TUAMOTU ISLANDS.

Lowa River (lō'wä), E tributary of the Lualaba, in E Belgian Congo, formed by several headstreams rising on N and NW slopes of the Kahusi range c.25 mi. W of Bobandana, flows generally W, past Walikale and through dense equatorial forest, to Lualaba R. opposite Lowa village; c.275 mi. long. Drains important tin-mining area.

Low Countries, region of NW Europe comprising the Netherlands, Belgium, and grand duchy of Luxembourg. The N parts of the Netherlands and Belgium form a low plain bordering on North Sea, but S Belgium and Luxembourg are part of the Ardennes. The name Low Countries thus is a political and historic rather than a strictly geographic concept. One of the wealthiest areas of medieval and modern Europe, it also has been a chronic theater of war. For the geography and history, see articles on the individual countries and on their provinces.

Low Crosby, England: see CROSBY-ON-EDEN.

Lowden (lou'důn), town (pop. 642), Cedar co., E Iowa, 28 mi. NW of Davenport; dairy products. Limestone quarries near by.

Lowdham, agr. village and parish (pop. 1,103), central Nottingham, England, 7 mi. NE of Nottingham. Has church dating mainly from 15th cent. Site of experimental reform school.

Lowe, Mount (lō) (5,650 ft.), Los Angeles co., S Calif., in San Gabriel Mts., N of Pasadena and just NW of Mt. Wilson. Astronomical observatory (built 1894). Formerly had incline railway to summit.

Lowell (lō'ůl). **1** Copper-mining village (pop. 1,136, with near-by South Bisbee), Cochise co., SE Ariz., in Mule Mts., near Mex. line, 3 mi. SE of Bisbee; alt. 5,250 ft. **2** Town (pop. 341), Benton co., extreme NW Ark., 14 mi. N of Fayetteville, in the Ozarks. **3** Town (pop. 1,621), Lake co., NW Ind., 22 mi. S of Gary; brushes, dairy products, nursery stock. Settled 1849. **4** Town (pop. 192), Penobscot co., central Maine, 21 mi. NNE of Old Town, in hunting, fishing area. **5** City (pop. 97,249), a ⊙ Middlesex co., NE Mass., on the Merrimack (water power), at mouth of Concord R., and 24 mi. NW of Boston. Great textile center (cloth, clothing, textile machinery); mfg. (leather products, electrical wire and equipment, beverages, gas, shoes, bakery products, metal products), printing. Textile mills begun 1822. Lowell Textile Inst., state teachers col. here. Settled 1653, inc. as town 1826, as city 1836. **6** (also lōl) Village (pop. 2,191), Kent co., SW Mich., 17 mi. E of Grand Rapids and on Grand R. at mouth of Flat R., in agr. area; mfg. (furniture, flour, feed); hatcheries. Resort. Settled 1821, inc. 1859. **7** Textile town (pop. 2,313), Gaston co., S N.C., 4 mi. E of Gastonia; mfg. of cotton yarn, rayon. **8** Village (pop. 638), Washington co., SE Ohio, 8 mi. NNW of Marietta and on Muskingum R., in agr. area. **9** Town (pop. 643), Orleans co., N Vt., on Missisquoi R. and 16 mi. SW of Newport; wood products, asbestos. **10** Village, Snohomish co., NW Wash., 3 mi. S of Everett; paper mill. **11** Village (pop. 319), Dodge co., S central Wis., 8 mi. S of Beaver Dam, in dairying region.

Lowell, Lake, Idaho: see DEER FLAT RESERVOIR.

Lowellville, village (pop. 2,227), Mahoning co., E Ohio, 8 mi. SE of downtown Youngstown, and on Mahoning R., near Pa. line; steel mills; chemicals, dairy products. Limestone quarries. Settled c.1800, inc. 1836.

Löwen, Poland: see LEWIN BRZESKI.

Löwenberg, Poland: see LWOWEK SLASKI.

Löwenhagen, Russian SFSR: see KOMSOMOLSK, Kaliningrad oblast.

Löwenstein (lû'vůn-shtīn), town (pop. 1,454), N Württemberg, Germany, after 1945 in Württemberg-Baden, 8 mi. SE of Heilbronn; grain. Has ruined castle. Mineral springs near by.

Löwentin Lake, Poland: see NIEGOCIN, LAKE.

Lower, in Rus. names: see also NIZHNE-, NIZHNEYE, NIZHNI, NIZHNIYE, NIZHNYAYA.

Lower Allithwaite (ă'lĭthwāt"), parish (pop. 1,121), N Lancashire, England. Includes village of Allithwaite, near Morecambe Bay, 6 mi. E of Ulverston; sheep raising, agr. Has Wraysholme Tower, a 15th-cent. fort.

Lower Alps, France: see BASSES-ALPES.

Lower Ammonoosuc River, N.H.: see AMMONOOSUC RIVER.

Lower Amur (ămōōr'), Rus. *Nizhne-Amur*, oblast (□ 202,700; 1946 pop. estimate 150,000) in central Khabarovsk Territory, E Siberian Russian SFSR; ⊙ Nikolayevsk. On Sea of Okhotsk; extends from Tatar Strait and lower Amur R. (51°N) to SE Cherski Range (64°N); Dzhugdzhur Range rises in central section parallel to coast. Area of lower Amur R. and Tatar Strait (SE) inhabited by Russians engaged in fishing, gold mining, and lumbering. Evenki (Tungus) and Eveni (Lamuts) fish and raise reindeer in sparsely populated N section, centered on Ayan and Okhotsk. Formed 1934 within former Far Eastern Territory; included 1938 in Khabarovsk Territory.

Lower Arrow Lake, B.C.: see ARROW LAKES.

Lower Aulaqi, Aden: see AULAQI.

Lower Austria, Ger. *Niederösterreich* (nē'dûrû"-stûrīkh"), autonomous province [Ger. *Bundesland*] (□ 7,097; 1951 pop. 1,249,610), NE Austria; borders Czechoslovakia (N, E), Burgenland (SE), Styria (S), and Upper Austria (W); ⊙ VIENNA. Hilly region, including spurs of Eastern Alps (S) and the WIENER WALD (E central); drained by the Danube. Agr. (grain, potatoes in NW, sugar beets in E), cattle, truck farming along Danube and in Vienna area, wine in NE and E. Over half of Austrian industry centers in and around Greater Vienna and WIENER NEUSTADT (machinery, textiles); ironworks, tool mfg. in W (Waidhofen an der Ybbs, Amstetten); oil fields around Zistersdorf (NE). Tourist trade in Vienna, Baden, and mtn. region. Prov. once part of Roman Noricum; given by Charlemagne to the Babenbergs after creation of Ostmark; created duchy 1156; passed to Hapsburgs in 14th cent. Placed (1945) in Soviet occupation zone.

Lower Avon River, England: see AVON RIVER.

Lower Bann River, Northern Ireland: see BANN RIVER.

Lower Bavaria (bûvâ'rēû), Ger. *Niederbayern* (nē'dûrbī"ûrn), administrative division [Ger. *Regierungsbezirk*] (□ 4,153; 1946 pop. 1,084,450; 1950 pop. 1,080,815) of E BAVARIA, Germany; ⊙ Landshut. Bounded N by Upper Palatinate, W and S by Upper Bavaria, SE and E by Austria, NE by Czechoslovakia. Includes Bohemian Forest (NE). Drained by Danube, Inn, and Isar rivers. Wheat (S of Danube only), barley, rye, cabbage; livestock; intensive hop growing around Landshut. Industries (metals, wood, beer) at Landshut, Passau, and Straubing. Glassworking in Bohemian Forest (Frauenau, Zwiesel).

Lower Bebington, England: see BEBINGTON.

Lower Beeding, agr. village and parish (pop. 1,322), central Sussex, England, 4 mi. SE of Horsham.

Lower Bentham, England: see BENTHAM.

Lower Buchanan, Liberia: see BUCHANAN.

Lower Burma: see BURMA.

Lower California, Sp. *Baja California* (bä'hä kälēfôr'nyä), peninsula (c.760 mi. long, 30–150 mi. wide), NW Mexico, separating Gulf of California from the Pacific. The land area (□ 55,634) is divided by the 28°N parallel into almost 2 equal parts: Northern Territory (□ 27,655; 1940 pop. 78,907; 1950 pop. 226,871; ⊙ Mexicali) and Southern Territory (□ 27,979; 1940 pop. 51,471; 1950 pop. 60,495; ⊙ La Paz). Except for 2 large coastal plains on the Pacific side, it consists largely of rugged mtn. ranges, such as Sierra Juárez, Sierra San Pedro Mártir (rises to 10,063 ft.), and Sierra de la Giganta (averaging c.5,000 ft.). Numerous small isls. off coast. Generally desolate and arid, it has a Mediterranean climate in N, similar to S California (U.S.), with mild temperatures all year and light winter rains; the S region is considerably warmer and has a rainy period in summer. The dry gulf coast is considered to be one of the world's hottest areas. Only isolated sections in extreme NW and SE and several interior valleys and highlands are inhabited, although much of the peninsula's soil, water supply permitting, is fertile. Lower California is rich in minerals: silver, lead, gold at San Antonio and El Triunfo (SE); copper at Santa Rosalía and Mulegé (E center); magnesite at Santa Margarita Isl. There are also known deposits of good iron ore, kaolin, and nitrates; guano is found on Pacific isls. The SE gulf coast has been a noted pearl-fishing ground since early colonial days; fishing (sharks, seals, whales, barracuda, corvina, tuna, sardines, lobsters) is still a major source of income. Agr. crops in irrigated area are mainly cotton, wheat, wine, tomatoes, beans, alfalfa (N); sugar cane, corn, tropical fruit (SE). Some stock raising (cattle, goats in highlands and SE; goats are raised on Guadalupe Isl. (NW). Processing plants at Mexicali, Ensenada, La Paz. Lower California was visited in 1539 by Francisco de Ulloa, a Cortés lieutenant. Sebastián Vizcaíno in 1596 undertook the 1st real land exploration. Attempts at colonization of the forbidding interior, even those by the intrepid mission fathers, were largely unsuccessful; most of the area is still inhabited by primitive Indians. Lower California was occupied (1847–48) by U.S. forces in the Mexican War; and the filibuster William Walker attempted in 1853–54 to wrest it from Mexico. After Mexican War, irrigation was introduced in the N; the extension of the Imperial Valley (California, U.S.) irrigation scheme into Mexico has increased agr. production. In Dec., 1951, Lower California became a state; ⊙ Tijuana.

Lower Canada: see QUEBEC, city.

Lower Chateaugay Lake, N.Y.: see CHATEAUGAY LAKE.

Lower Chindwin (chĭnd'wĭn'), district (□ 3,676; 1941 pop. 427,340), Sagaing div., Upper Burma; ⊙ Monywa. Astride lower Chindwin R., in dry zone (annual rainfall, 31 in.); irrigated agr.: rice, cotton, beans. Teak forests, gold placers. Pop. is nearly entirely Burmese. Dist. is served by Mandalay-Yeu RR and Chindwin R. navigation.

Lower Congo, district, Belgian Congo: see BOMA.

Lower Darwen, England: see ECCLESHILL.

Lower Don, physiographic region of S European USSR, on lower Don R., roughly coextensive with Rostov oblast.

Lower Dutton, England: see DUTTON.

Lower Falls of Yellowstone River, Wyo.: see YELLOWSTONE NATIONAL PARK.

Lower Fox River, Wis.: see FOX RIVER.

Lower Franconia (frăngkō'nēû), Ger. *Unterfranken* (ŏŏn'tûrfräng"kûn), administrative division [Ger. *Regierungsbezirk*] (□ 3,277; 1946 pop. 984,395; 1950 pop. 1,038,748) of NW Bavaria, Germany; ⊙ Würzburg. Bounded by Hesse (W, N), Thuringia (N), Upper and Middle Franconia (E), Württemberg-Baden (S). Hilly region including The Spessart and part of Rhön Mts.; drained by the Main. Agr. (wheat, rye, barley) and stock raising; winegrowing in river valleys. Industrial centers at historic towns of Würzburg (machine tools), Schweinfurt (dyes), and Aschaffenburg (textiles, paper). Bad Kissingen is noted resort. Part of old historic region of FRANCONIA. Called Mainfranken (mīn'fräng"kûn), 1938–45.

Lower Galilee, Palestine: see GALILEE.

Lower Ganges Canal, India: see GANGES CANALS.

Lower Holker (hŏŏ'kûr), parish (pop. 1,425), N Lancashire, England. Includes village of Holker, 5 mi. E of Ulverston; sheep raising, agr.

Lower Hutt (hŭt'), city (pop. 31,254), S N.Isl., New Zealand, 8 mi. NE of Wellington; mfg. (paint, textiles, tile). Many govt. housing developments.

Lower Kalskag (kăl'skăg), village (pop. 88), SW Alaska, near Kalskag, on Kuskokwim R.

Lower Klamath Lake (klă'mûth), sump in NE corner of Siskiyou co., N Calif., at state line, c.20 mi. S of Klamath Falls, Oregon. Has variable area. Serves as catch basin for surplus irrigation water, which is pumped (NW) into Klamath R. through Klamath Strait (7 mi. long; largely in Oregon) and used to generate power at Copco No. 1 Dam on Klamath R. in Calif. U.S. bird refuge (c.82,000 acres) occupies N half of Lower Klamath L. and extends N into Klamath co., Oregon.

Lower Kundysh River, Russian SFSR: see LESSER KUNDYSH RIVER.

Lower Lake, village (pop. c.850), Lake co., NW Calif., at S end of Clear L., 20 mi. SE of Lakeport; farm center. Mineral springs (resorts) near by.

Lower Largo, fishing village in Largo parish, E Fifeshire, Scotland, on Largo Bay of Firth of Forth, 3 mi. ENE of Leven.

Lower Leelanau Lake, Mich.: see LEELANAU, LAKE.

Lower Loire, France: see LOIRE-INFÉRIEURE.

Lower Lusatia, region, Germany and Poland: see LUSATIA.

Lower MacNean (mûknēn'), lake (2 mi. long, 1 mi. wide), SW Co. Fermanagh, Northern Ireland, 8 mi. WSW of Enniskillen.

Lower Matecumbe Key, Fla.: see FLORIDA KEYS.

Lower Merion (mĕ'rēûn), urban township (pop. 48,745), Montgomery co., SE Pa., residential W suburb of Philadelphia. Includes Haverford village (1940 pop. 2,529), seat of Haverford Col., adjacent to HAVERFORD township; ARDMORE (chief center of township); BALA-CYNWYD; part of BRYN MAWR, seat of Bryn Mawr Col.; Gladwyne (glăd'wĭn) (1940 pop. 1,025); MERION or Merion Station (some mfg.); Penn Wynne (1940 pop. 2,037); WEST MANAYUNK; Wynnewood or Wynwood (1940 pop. 2,055); and part of ROSEMONT, seat of Rosemont Col.

Lower Merwede River, Du. *Beneden Merwede* (bûnā'dû mĕr'vādû), SW Netherlands; outlet of Waal and Maas rivers formed by forking of UPPER MERWEDE RIVER into Lower Merwede R. and New Merwede R. 4.5 mi. W of Gorinchem; flows 9 mi. W, past Sliedrecht and Papendrecht, dividing to form Old Maas R. and Noord R. 1 mi. N of Dordrecht. Entire length navigable.

Lower Navarre or **French Navarre** (nûvär'), Fr. *Basse Navarre* or *Navarre Française*, small historical region of SW France, in Basses-Pyrénées dept., in the Basque country; its old ⊙ was Saint-Jean-Pied-de-Port. Consists of section of old kingdom of Navarre on N slope of the Pyrenees. It was annexed to France by Henry IV in 1589.

Lower Paia (päē'û), village (pop. 1,138), N Maui, T.H., 8 mi. ENE of Wailuku; sugar cane.

Lower Palatinate, Germany: see RHENISH PALATINATE.

Lower Pyrenees, France: see BASSES-PYRÉNÉES.

Lower Red Lake, Minn.: see RED LAKE.

Lower Red Rock Lake, Mont.: see RED ROCK LAKES.

Lower Rhine, France: see BAS-RHIN.

Lower Rhine River, Du. *Neder Rijn* (nā'dûr rīn'), central Netherlands; arm of the Rhine formed by forking of Rhine R. into Lower Rhine R. and Waal R. near Millingen (8 mi. ENE of Nijmegen); flows 17 mi. WNW, past Arnhem, Oosterbeek, and Rhenen, to Wijk bij Duurstede, here forming LEK RIVER. Ijssel R. branches from it 2.5 mi. SE of Arnhem. Course bet. the Rhine and Arnhem is canalized and is also known as Pannerden Canal. Entire length navigable.

Lower Richardson Lake, Maine: see RANGELEY LAKES.

Lower Saint Mary Lake, Mont.: see GLACIER NATIONAL PARK.

Lower Saint Regis Lake, N.Y.: see SAINT REGIS RIVER.

Lower Salem (sā'lûm), village (pop. 126), Washington co., SE Ohio, 10 mi. NNE of Marietta.

Lower Saranac Lake, N.Y.: see SARANAC LAKES.

Lower Savage Islands, group of 3 small isls., SE Franklin Dist., Northwest Territories, off SE Baffin Isl., in Gabriel Strait (arm of Hudson Strait); 61°48'N 65°48'W.

Lower Saxony (săk'sûnē), Ger. *Niedersachsen* (nē'dûrzäk"sûn), state (□ 18,231; 1939 pop. 4,539,520; 1946 pop. 6,277,561, including displaced persons 6,432,793; 1950 pop. 6,795,128), NW Germany; ⊙ Hanover. Formed after 1945 through incorporation of former states of OLDENBURG, SCHAUMBURG-LIPPE, most of BRUNSWICK, and former Prussian prov. of HANOVER. Situated on North Sea and occupying W portion of N German lowlands, it is bordered by the Netherlands (W), North Rhine-Westphalia (S, SW), Hesse and Thuringia (S), Saxony-Anhalt (E), Mecklenburg and Schleswig-Holstein (NE); Bremen (N) forms complete enclave, Hamburg (NE) forms partial enclave. Mountainous (Harz, Weser Mts.) in extreme S; includes East Frisian Isls. Drained by navigable Ems, Weser, Aller, and Elbe rivers. Heath and moors (peat cutting) form central belt; cattle raising and some grain growing in N polders; sugar beets and asparagus grown near Hanover and Brunswick cities. Oil wells in the Emsland (W) and Celle-Peine region (E); large iron-ore deposits at Watenstedt-Salzgitter; salt at Lüneburg and Stade; potash at Fallersleben and Lehrte; coal mined in the Deister and in Osnabrück area, lignite near Helmstedt; varied ore deposits in the Rammelsberg. Industry (iron and steel, textiles, chemicals) is centered in Brunswick, Celle, Delmenhorst, Goslar, Hameln, Hanover, Lüneburg, Nordhorn, Osnabrück, Stade, and Watenstedt-Salzgitter. Major ports are Emden, Wilhelmshaven, and Cuxhaven. Univ. at Göttingen. Area has had no historic unity since 1180, when Emperor Frederick I broke up duchy of Henry the Lion of Saxony, to which it had belonged. Term Lower Saxony continued as a geographic expression; was used to designate (16th cent.–1806) a circle of Holy Roman Empire which also included Mecklenburg, Holstein, and Bremen. After capture (1945) by British, Canadian, and U.S. troops, Lower Saxony was constituted as new state in Br. occupation zone. Because of influx of displaced persons and of refugees from E Germany, pop. of region increased 40% over 1939 figure. Joined (1949) the German Federal Republic (the West German state).

Lower Seine, France: see SEINE-INFÉRIEURE.

Lower Silesia, province, Germany: see SILESIA.

Lower Tallassee Dam, Ala.: see THURLOW DAM.

Lower Tanshui River, Formosa: see TANSHUI RIVER.

Lower Tunguska River (tŏŏn-gŏŏ'skû), Rus. *Nizhnyaya Tunguska*, in Irkutsk oblast and Krasnoyarsk Territory, Russian SFSR, rises on Central Siberian Plateau, N of Ust-Kut; flows N, past Yerbogachen, and WNW, past Tura, to Yenisei R. at Turukhansk; 1,587 mi. long. Navigable May–Oct. for 1,100 mi. below Tura. In its upper course, approaches within 18 mi. of Lena R. Receives Kochechuma (right) and Taimura (left) rivers.

Lower Volga Territory, Rus. *Nizhne-Volzhskiy Kray*, former administrative division of S European Russian SFSR; ⊙ was Saratov. Formed 1928 out of govts. of Astrakhan, Stalingrad, and Saratov, it also included Kalmyk Autonomous Oblast and German Volga Autonomous SSR; dissolved 1934 into Stalingrad and Saratov territories (after 1936, oblasts).

Lower Yafa, Aden: see YAFA.

Lower Yosemite Fall, Calif.: see YOSEMITE NATIONAL PARK.

Lowerz, Lake of, or **Lake of Lauerz** (both: lou'ûrts), Ger. *Lowerzersee* or *Lauerzersee* (–ûrzā"), Schwyz canton, central Switzerland, WNW of Schwyz, at foot of the Rossberg; □ 1. Lowerz or Lauerz, village (pop. 485), is on W shore. Schwanau, an isl. with ruined castle, is in lake.

Lowes, Loch of the, Scotland: see SAINT MARY'S LOCH.

Lowestoft (lō'stôft,–stŭf), municipal borough (1931 pop. 41,769; 1951 census 42,837), NE Suffolk, England, on North Sea and on Oulton Broad, 22 mi. ESE of Norwich; major fishing port, seaside resort, and yachting center. On North Sea is Lowestoft Ness (52°29'N 1°46'E), most easterly point of England. Just N are Lowestoft Denes, an open stretch, with esplanade and golf course. Lowestoft has 14th-cent. church. North Sea cables from Zandvoort, Netherlands, terminate here. Mfg. (electrical equipment, motor coaches; shipbuilding and fish packing). China industry was formerly important; town gives its name to a type of china. South Lowestoft (S; pop. 11,408) is separated from old town by L. Lothing. Just W is resort town of Oulton Broad (pop. 4,651), on stretch of water of that name. Cromwell took Lowestoft in 1643, and in 1665 the English under duke of York here defeated Dutch under van Wassenaer.

Loweswater (lōz'–), small lake in the Lake District, W Cumberland, England, 6 mi. S of Cockermouth; 1½ mi. long. On SE shore is agr. village and parish of Loweswater (pop. 262).

Low Fell, England: see GATESHEAD.

Low Harrogate, England: see HARROGATE.

Low Head, headland, N Tasmania, in Bass Strait, at E end of Port Dalrymple (mouth of Tamar R.); 41°2'S 146°46'E; lighthouse.

Low Hesket, England: see HESKET IN THE FOREST.

Lowicz (wô'vĭch), Pol. *Łowicz*, Rus. *Lovich* (lô'vĭch), town (pop. 13,764), Lodz prov., central Poland, on Bzura R. and 45 mi. WSW of Warsaw. Rail junction; mfg. of agr. machinery, wheels, bricks, tiles, cement, kitchen articles, carpets, vinegar, candy; weaving and spinning, brewing, flour milling. Has 2 monasteries. Castle ruins near by.

Low Island (9 naut. mi. long, 5 naut. mi. wide), South Shetland Isls., off Palmer Peninsula, Antarctica; 63°18'S 62°10'W.

Low Moor, town (pop. 279), Clinton co., E Iowa, 9 mi. WSW of Clinton, in agr. area.

Lowndes (lounz, loundz). **1** County (□ 716; pop. 18,018), S central Ala.; ⊙ Hayneville. In the Black Belt; bounded N by Alabama R.; drained by its tributaries. Cotton, corn; dairying, lumber milling. Formed 1830. **2** County (□ 506; pop. 35,211), S Ga.; ⊙ Valdosta. Bounded S by Fla. line; drained by Withlacoochee R. Coastal plain agr. (tobacco, cotton, peanuts, corn, watermelons, livestock) and forestry (naval stores, lumber) area; mfg. at Valdosta. Formed 1825. **3** County (□ 508; pop. 37,852), E Miss.; ⊙ COLUMBUS. Bordered E by Ala.; drained by Tombigbee R., small Oktibbeha R., and Luxapalila R. Agr. (cotton, corn, hay), dairying, stock raising, lumbering. Formed 1830.

Lowndesville (lounz'vĭl), town (pop. 252), Abbeville co., NW S.C., 27 mi. W of Greenwood.

Low Point, cape, NE N.S., on NE Cape Breton Isl., 9 mi. N of Sydney; 46°16'N 60°7'W; lighthouse.

Low Row, England: see NETHER DENTON.

Lowry (lou'rē). **1** Village (pop. 285), Pope co., W Minn., 7 mi. NW of Glenwood; dairy products. **2** Town (pop. 70), Walworth co., N central S.Dak., 13 mi. S of Selby; grain elevators here.

Lowry Air Force Base, Colo.: see DENVER.

Lowry City, city (pop. 493), St. Clair co., W Mo., near Osage R., 7 mi. N of Osceola.

Lowrys (lou'rĭz), town (pop. 368), Chester co., N S.C., 15 mi. SW of Rock Hill.

Low Tatra or **Low Tatra Mountains** (tä'trŭ), Slovak *Nízké Tatry* (nyēz'kā tä'trĭ), Ger. *Lage Tatra* (lä'gŭ tä'trä), Hung. *Alacsony Tátra* (ŏ'lŏchônyŭ tä'trŏ), Pol. *Tatry Niżne* (tä'trĭ nyĭzh'nĕ), section of the Carpathians in central Slovakia, Czechoslovakia, parallel to and S of the High Tatra; extend c.65 mi. E–W, bet. the Greater Fatra (W), Hornad and Vah rivers (N), Hron R. (S), and Vondrisel (E). Rise to 6,707 ft. in Dumbier, to 6,373 ft. in Kralova Hola peaks. Extensively forested; noted for picturesque scenery, underground rivers, and stalactite caverns in limestone formations to N (Demanova Caves); trout fishing in streams to S. Cierny Vah, Hornad, and Hron rivers rise here.

Lowther Hills (lou'dhŭr), mountain range on Lanark-Dumfries border, Scotland, extending 20 mi. in semicircle, and continuing E in Moffat Hills. Highest peaks: Queensberry (2,285 ft.) in Dumfries, 7 mi. SW of Moffat; and Green Lowther (2,403 ft.) in Lanark, 2 mi. E of Wanlockhead.

Lowther Island (17 mi. long, 2–6 mi. wide), central Franklin Dist., Northwest Territories, in Barrow Strait, bet. Bathurst Isl. and Prince of Wales Isl.; 74°35'N 97°35'W.

Lowton, parish (pop. 3,851), S Lancashire, England Includes village of Lowton Common, 6 mi. NNE of Warrington; cotton mills.

Lowville (lou'vĭl), village (pop. 3,671), ⊙ Lewis co., N central N.Y., on Black R. and 25 mi. SE of Watertown; summer resort; trade center in dairying area; mfg. of cheese, heating pads, feed, wood products; cold-storage plants; timber. Inc. 1871.

Loxstedt (lôks'shtĕt), village (pop. 2,189), in former Prussian prov. of Hanover, NW Germany, after 1945 in Lower Saxony, 5 mi. SE of Bremerhaven; food processing.

Loxton, village (pop. 1,238), SE South Australia, 120 mi. ENE of Adelaide and on Murray R., near Victoria border; rail terminus; sheep, some fruit.

Loyada (lōyä'dä), village, Fr. Somaliland, on S coast of Gulf of Tadjoura, 12 mi. SE of Djibouti; police post on Br. Somaliland border; fisheries.

Loyal, 1 Town (pop. 125), Kingfisher co., central Okla., 13 mi. NW of Kingfisher, in agr. area. Inc. 1930. **2** City (pop. 1,104), Clark co., central Wis., 17 mi. WNW of Marshfield, in dairying region; cheese, canned vegetables. Inc. as city in 1948.

Loyalhanna, village, Westmoreland co., SW Pa., just E of Latrobe.

Loyalhanna Creek, SW Pa., rises in S Westmoreland co., flows c.50 mi. NE and NW, joining Conemaugh R. to form Kiskiminetas R at Saltsburg. Flood-control dam and reservoir 4.5 mi. above mouth.

Loyall, town (pop. 1,548), Harlan co., SE Ky., in the Cumberlands, on Cumberland R. and 26 mi. NE of Middlesboro; bituminous coal. Inc. 1928.

Loyalsock Creek, N central Pa., rises in NE Sullivan co., flows c.60 mi. SW to West Branch of Susquehanna R. at Montoursville.

Loyalton. 1 Town (pop. 911), Sierra co., NE Calif., in Sierra Valley of the Sierra Nevada, 20 mi SE of Portola; dairying, farming, lumber milling, stock raising. **2** Town (pop. 57), Edmunds co., N central S.Dak., 16 mi. SW of Ipswich.

Loyalty Islands, coral group (□ 800; pop. 11,854), SW Pacific, 60 mi. E of New Caledonia, of which they are a dependency; comprise 3 large isls. (LIFU, MARÉ, UVEA), and many islets; export copra.

Loyang (lō'yăng', lô'yăng'), city (1935 pop. 77,159), NW Honan prov., China, on Lo R. near its mouth on Yellow R., on Lunghai RR and 100 mi. W of Kaifeng; road junction; agr. and stock-raising center; hides, sheepskins, agr. products. Has engineering col. The center of earliest recorded Chinese settlement (1900 B.C.), Loyang is situated near or at the site of some of China's earliest capitals. Loyang itself was capital of the Chou dynasty (770–255 B.C.) and Eastern Han dynasty (c.100 A.D.). It continued intermittently as imperial residence and administrative center until eclipsed by Kaifeng under the Mongol dynasty (13th cent.). It was (1932) temporary ⊙ China, when the Nationalist govt. briefly moved here from Nanking. Scene of fighting (1944) during Sino-Japanese War. Called Honan until 1913. Became a separate municipality in 1949. The noted LUNGMEN caves are 12 mi. SW.

Loyeh (lô'yĕ'), town, ⊙ Loyeh co. (pop. 51,149), W Kwangsi prov., China, 60 mi. N of Poseh, near Hungshui R. (Kweichow line); wheat, corn, potatoes. Until 1936 called Loya.

Loyev (loi'ŭf), town (1926 pop. 4,212), S Gomel oblast, Belorussian SSR, on Dnieper R. (landing), at mouth of the Sozh, and 35 mi. SSW of Gomel; quartz and crystal works; chemicals.

Loyno, Russian SFSR: see LOINO.

Loyola, Spain: see AZPEITIA.

Loyüan (lô'yüăn'), town (pop. 3,980), ⊙ Loyüan co. (pop. 98,423), NE Fukien prov., China, 30 mi. NNE of Foochow, on E. China Sea coast; rice, sweet potatoes, wheat, sugar cane.

Loyung (lô'yŏŏng'), town, ⊙ Loyung co. (pop. 43,514), NE central Kwangsi prov., China, 20 mi. NE of Liuchow and on railroad; rice, wheat, beans, cotton. Also written Lojung.

Lozdzieje, Lithuania: see LAZDIJAI.

Lozère (lôzâr'), department (□ 2,000; pop. 90,523), in former Languedoc prov., S France; ⊙ Mende. Wholly within Massif Central; traversed by Monts d'Aubrac (NW), Montagnes de la Margeride (N), and the Cévennes (SE) which culminate in the Mont Lozère (5,584 ft.). CAUSSES in center and SW. Drained by the Allier (NE), Truyère (NW), Lot and Chassezac (center), and Tarn rivers. Soils infertile. Sheep raising, dairying, and cultivation of fruit and mulberry trees. Some lead and antimony mining. Chief towns: Mende (textiles), Marvejols, and Saint-Chély-d'Apcher (electrometallurgy). One of France's least populous depts. Caves in the Causses and the remarkable Tarn R. gorge are tourist attractions.

Lozère, Mont (mô), granitic massif in E central Lozère dept., S France, in the CÉVENNES; extends c.15 mi. E-W bet. Florac and Villefort. Rises to 5,584 ft. at Finiels signal c.14 mi. ESE of Mende. Tarn, Lot, and Cèze rivers rise here. Lead mines.

Lozhan (lô'zhän) or **Lozhani** (lô'zhänē), village (1930 pop. 380), SE Albania, 14 mi. WNW of Koritsa, on Devoll R.

Loznica or **Loznitsa** (both: lôz'nĭtsä), village pop.) 3,377), ⊙ Jadar co., W Serbia, Yugoslavia, on railroad and 27 mi. SW of Sabar, near the Drina (Bosnia border); ships plums; antimony smelter. Antimony mines near by.

Lozno-Aleksandrovka (lôz'nŭ-ŭlyĭksän'drŭfkŭ), village (1926 census pop. 2,888), NW Voroshilovgrad oblast, Ukrainian SSR, 40 mi. NNW of Starobelsk; metalworks. Until mid-1930s called Alexandrovka.

Lozon (lôzõ'), village (pop. 54), Manche dept., NW France, 8 mi. WNW of Saint-Lô. Heavy fighting during American Saint-Lô offensive (July, 1944) of Second World War.

Lozovac (lô'zôväts), Ital. *Loggiovano* (lôj-jôvä'nô), village, W Croatia, Yugoslavia, on Krka R. opposite Skradin, in Dalmatia; bauxite mine; mfg. of aluminum.

Lozovaya (lŭzŭvī'ŭ), city (1926 pop. 13,198), S Kharkov oblast, Ukrainian SSR, 75 mi. S of Karkov; rail junction; metalworks, flour mills.

Lozovaya Pavlovka (päv'lŭfkŭ), town (1926 pop. 6,383), SW Voroshilovgrad oblast, Ukrainian SSR, in the Donbas, 5 mi. SE of Kadiyevka; coal mining, woodworking.

Lozovik (lô'zôvĭk), village (pop. 6,394), N central Serbia, Yugoslavia, near the Morava, 10 mi. NE of Palanka.

Lozoya (lō-thoi'ä), town (pop. 552), Madrid prov., central Spain, on Lozoya R., on E slopes of Sierra de Guadarrama, 37 mi. N of Madrid; potatoes, rye, livestock; apiculture; lumbering.

Lozoya Canal, Spain: see ISABEL II CANAL.

Lozoya River, Madrid prov., central Spain, rises in the Sierra de Guadarrama near Segovia prov. border, flows c.50 mi. NE and E, past Rascafría and Buitrago del Lozoya, to Jarama R. 6 mi. NE of Torrelaguna. Near its mouth are several reservoirs, which feed the Isabel II or Lozoya Canal supplying Madrid with fresh water.

Lozoyuela (lō-thoiwā'lä), town (pop. 669), Madrid prov., central Spain, 35 mi. N of Madrid; rye, potatoes, cattle, sheep. Granite quarries.

Lozva River or **Loz'va River** (lôz'vŭ), Sverdlovsk oblast, Russian SFSR, rises in the central Urals at 61°50'N, flows 265 mi. generally SE, joining Sosva R. 8 mi. N of Gari to form Tavda R. Navigable below Ivdel; logging. Receives Ivdel R. (right).

Lozzo Cadore (lôt'tsô kädô'rĕ), village (pop. 1,784), Belluno prov., Veneto, N Italy, 26 mi. NNE of Belluno; mfg. (celluloid, spectacles).

Lu, province, China: see SHANTUNG.

Lu. 1 River, in Sikang and Yunnan provs., China: see SALWEEN RIVER. **2** River, Szechwan prov., China: see To RIVER.

Lu (lōō), village (pop. 2,464), Alessandria prov., Piedmont, N Italy, 9 mi. NW of Alessandria.

Luabo (lwä'bō), sugar mill, Zambézia prov., S central Mozambique, on lower Zambezi R. and 22 mi. NW of Chinde.

Lualaba, district, Belgian Congo: see JADOTVILLE.

Lualaba River, Belgian Congo: see CONGO RIVER.

Luan-, for Chinese names beginning thus and not found here: see under LWAN-.

Luan, town, China: see CHANGCHIH.

Luana (lōōă'nŭ), town (pop. 220), Clayton co., NE Iowa, 15 mi. N of Elkader, in corn, livestock, dairying region.

Luana Point (lōōă'nŭ), cape, SW Jamaica, 4 mi. W of Black River town; 18°3'N 77°55'W.

Luanco (lwäng'kō), town (pop. 2,201), Oviedo prov., NW Spain, fishing port and bathing resort on Bay of Biscay, 8 mi. NW of Gijón; fish salting, boat building. Iron mines near by.

Luanda, province, Angola: see CONGO.

Luanda (lwän'dä), formerly **Loanda** and **São Paulo de Loanda** (sãō pou'lōō dĭ lwän'dŭ), city (pop. 61,028), ⊙ Angola, port on the Atlantic, 35 mi. N of Cuanza R. estuary and 330 mi. SSW of Leopoldville (Belgian Congo); 8°50'S 13°15'E. The Portuguese colony's largest city, its administrative center (since 1627), and its 2d seaport (after Lobito). Exports coffee, corn, sugar, beeswax, cotton, palm oil and kernels, sisal, diamonds. Linked to fertile interior by railroad (to Malange) and several roads. Airport. Growing secondary industries include processing of cotton and sugar grown in coast area, mfg. of soap and tobacco products, woodworking (veneers); also textile plant, paper mill, shoe factory. Improved harbor has ½ mi. of docks (alongside depth, 34 ft.). Governor's palace, old fortress of São Miguel (overlooking port and sandy Luanda isl.), cathedral, modern hosp. Mean annual temp. 77°F.; yearly rainfall c.25 in. City was founded 1575 by Portuguese. Was important center of slave trade bet. Africa and Brazil in 17th–18th cent. Until 1946, ⊙ Luanda prov. (now Congo prov.). City's European pop. c.10,000.

Luanda (lōōän'dä), village, Nyanza prov., W Kenya, on railroad and 12 mi. SSE of Butere; cotton, peanuts, sesame, corn.

Luang, village, Thailand: see CHOM THONG.

Luanginga River (lwäng-gĭng'gä), SW central Africa, right tributary of the Zambezi, rises on central plateau of Angola, flows c.250 mi. SE into Barotseland (Northern Rhodesia) and to the Zambezi below Kalabo.

Luang Prabang (lōōäng' präbäng'), city, ⊙ Luang Prabang prov. (□ 14,400; 1947 pop. 142,000), Laos, port on spit of land at confluence of Mekong R. and the small Nam Khan, at alt. 1,148 ft., 130 mi. NNW of Vientiane and 235 mi. WNW of Vinh (linked by highways); 19°53'N 102°8'E. Residence of king of Laos; trades in catechu, benzoin, lac, teak, cloth; salt mines, fisheries. Big-game hunting. Airport. A site inhabited in prehistoric times, it was original ⊙ Lanxang (Lao) Kingdom.

Luang Prabang Range, Thai *Luang Phra Bang*, on Thailand-Laos line, extending along (W of) Mekong R. to Phetchabun Range (S); densely forested (teak), it rises to 6,735 ft.

Luang River, Thailand: see TAPI RIVER.

Luangwa, former Province, Northern Rhodesia: see BROKEN HILL.

Luangwa River (lwäng'gwä), E Northern Rhodesia, rises on Nyasaland border NE of Isoka, flows c.500 mi. SSW, along E side of Muchinga Mts., to Zambezi R. bet. Feira and Zumbo. Forms Northern Rhodesia-Mozambique border in lower course. The Great East Road (bet. Lusaka and Fort Jameson) crosses river at Luangwa or Beit Bridge, 45 mi. N of Feira. Formerly spelled Loangwa.

Luanshya (lwänsh'yä), township (pop. 2,318), Western Prov., N Northern Rhodesia, 20 mi. SW of Ndola; rail-spur terminus; commercial center for adjoining Copper-mining center of Roan Antelope. Has govt. and convent schools, European and native hospitals.

Luapula River (lōōŭpōō'lŭ), E central Africa, along Belgian Congo–Northern Rhodesia border, issues from S end of L. Bangweulu, flows c.350 mi. S, NW, and N, past Kasenga, to L. Mweru. Navigable below Kasenga. Together with Chambezi R. (with which it merges in swamps SE of L. Bangweulu),

Luapula R. is considered the upper course of the Luvua (which issues from N end of L. Mweru), so that the Luvua-Luapula system represents E headstream of the Congo.

uarca (lwär'kä), town (pop. 4,180), Oviedo prov., NW Spain, fishing port and bathing resort on Bay of Biscay, and 35 mi. WNW of Oviedo; fish and meat processing, tanning, furniture mfg.; also makes dairy products. Coal shipping.

ua River (lōō'ä), NW Belgian Congo, rises 40 mi. ESE of Bosobolo, flows for c.190 mi. SSW and SW to Ubangi R. at Dongo. Navigable for c.80 mi. downstream from Mogale.

uashi (lwä'shē), village, Katanga prov., SE Belgian Congo, on Angola boundary, 200 mi. W of Jadotville; customs station and trading post in cotton area. R.C. and Protestant missions.

ubaczow (lōōbä'chōōf), Pol. *Lubaczów*, town (pop. 4,986), Rzeszow prov., SE Poland, on Lubaczowka R. and 30 mi. NNE of Przemysl, near USSR border; flour milling; lumber mill.

ubaczowka River (lōōbä-chōōf'kä), Pol. *Lubaczówka*, Rus. *Lyubachovka* (lūbŭ-chôf'kŭ), W Ukrainian SSR and SE Poland, rises SE of Nemirov (Ukrainian SSR), flows c.50 mi. generally W, past Lubaczow (Poland), to San R. 7 mi. N of Jaroslaw.

ubaga (lōōbä'gä), village, Lake Prov., NW Tanganyika, on N tip of Ukerewe Isl. (in L. Victoria), 40 mi. N of Mwanza; cotton, peanuts, mixed farming. Agr. experiment station.

uban (lōō'bänyŭ), Pol. *Lubań*, Ger. *Lauban* (lou'bän), town (1939 pop. 17,353; 1946 pop. 8,149) in Lower Silesia, after 1945 in Wroclaw prov., SW Poland, in Upper Lusatia, on Kwisa R. and 14 mi. E of Görlitz, in lignite-mining region; cotton milling, metalworking. In Second World War, heavily damaged (c.65% destroyed). In Middle Ages, a member of Lusatian League (founded 1346).

ubana Lake (lōō'bänä), Lettish *Lubāna*, largest lake (□ 34) of Latvia, 23 mi. NW of Rezekne; 10 mi. long, 5 mi. wide. Outlet: Aiviekste R.

ubang Islands (lōōbäng'), small group (1948 pop. 14,581), Mindoro prov., Philippines, in S.China Sea, SW of Luzon, just off NW coast of Mindoro isl. across Calavite Passage (c.6 mi. wide); comprises Lubang Isl. (largest), Ambil Island, Golo Island, Cabra Island, and several islets. Generally mountainous. Rice growing, stock raising. Inhabited by Tagalogs. Lubang Isl. (□ 74; 1939 pop. 10,606) is 12 mi. off NW coast of Mindoro isl.; 18 mi. long, 6 mi. wide; rises to 1,967 ft. Lubang (1939 pop. 2,688), on N coast of isl., is chief town of group.

ubango, Angola: see Sá da Bandeira.

ubao (lōōbä'ō, lōōbou'), town (1939 pop. 2,557; 1948 municipality pop. 36,574), Pampanga prov., central Luzon, Philippines, on railroad and 9 mi. SW of San Fernando; sugar-growing center. Sugar mill and distillery at near-by village of Del Carmen (dĕl kär'mān).

ubarika, Belgian Congo: see Luvungi.

ubartow (lōōbär'tōōf), Pol. *Lubartów*, Rus. *Lyubartov* (lyōōbär'tŭf), town (pop. 5,542), Lublin prov., E Poland, on railroad and 15 mi. N of Lublin, near Wieprz R.; mfg. (glass, vinegar, concrete blocks, beer, flour). Before Second World War, pop. 50% Jewish.

ubawa (lōōbä'vä), Ger. *Löbau* (lû'bou), town (pop. 4,679), Olsztyn prov., N Poland, 9 mi. NNW of Nowe Miasto; rail spur terminus; flour milling, sawmilling.

ubawka (lōōbäf'kä), Ger. *Liebau* (lē'bou), town (1939 pop. 5,702; 1946 pop. 6,280) in Lower Silesia, after 1945 in Wroclaw prov., SW Poland, at E foot of the Riesengebirge, on Bobrawa R. and 13 mi. WSW of Waldenburg (Walbrzych). Frontier station on Czechoslovak border; coal mining, cotton and linen milling; health and winter-sports resort.

übbecke (lü'bĕ"kŭ), town (pop. 7,670), in former Prussian prov. of Westphalia, NW Germany, after 1945 in North Rhine-Westphalia, on N slope of Wiehen Mts., 12 mi. W of Minden; grain.

übben (lü'bŭn), town (pop. 9,433), Brandenburg, E Germany, in Lower Lusatia, on several small isls. in the Spree, 23 mi. NW of Cottbus, in Spree Forest; knitting, woodworking, brewing, tile and cardboard mfg. Vegetable and flax market. Tourist resort. Has late-Gothic church, 16th-cent. palace. First mentioned 1007. In Middle Ages, chief town of Saxonian Lower Lusatia. Passed to Prussia 1815.

übbenau (lü'bŭnou), town (pop. 5,626), Brandenburg, E Germany, in Lower Lusatia, on several isls. in the Spree, 18 mi. WNW of Cottbus, in Spree Forest; vegetable-market center, noted for its pickled cucumbers and horse-radish. Tourist resort, in flax-growing region.

ubbock (lŭ'bŭk), county (□ 892; pop. 101,048), NW Texas; ⊙ Lubbock. Drained by intermittent Double Mtn. Fork of Brazos R.; alt. 3,000–3,500 ft. One of state's leading agr. counties; cotton, sweet and grain sorghums, wheat, forage, fruit, truck, sugar beets; dairying; poultry (especially turkeys); beef cattle, sheep, hogs. Has several parks. Hunting, fishing. Formed 1876.

ubbock, city (1950 pop. 71,747), ⊙ Lubbock co., NW Texas, c.110 mi. S of Amarillo and on intermittent Double Mtn. Fork of Brazos R.; alt. 3,241 ft. Industrial, shipping, trade, distribution center of South Plains of the Llano Estacado; an important cotton market; processes and ships cotton, grain, poultry, dairy products, cattle, oil; mfg. (printing, beverages, foundry products, mattresses, leather). Seat of Texas Technological Col., with West Texas Mus., and an agr. experiment station. Reese Air Force Base here. Founded 1891, inc. 1909.

Lübbow (lü'bō), village (pop. 599), in former Prussian prov. of Hanover, NW Germany, after 1945 in Lower Saxony, 4 mi. NNE of Salzwedel.

Lubcz, Belorussian SSR: see Lyubcha.

Lubec (lōō'bĕk), town (pop. 2,973), Washington co., E Maine, on the coast just S of Eastport; resort, fishing (sardine canning). West Quoddy Head, SE of Lubec village (1,536), is easternmost point of U.S. On Treat's Isl., in Cobscook Bay, is North Lubec village; isl. is terminus of dam for Passamaquoddy Bay project. Settled c.1780, inc. 1811.

Lübeck (lōō'bĕk, Ger. lü'bĕk), city (□ 78; 1939 pop. 154,819; 1946 pop. 223,059; 1950 pop. 237,860), in Schleswig-Holstein, NW Germany, 37 mi. NE of Hamburg, on Mecklenburg border; 53°52'N 10°40' E. Germany's leading Baltic port, at head of Trave R. estuary; the N terminus of Elbe-Trave Canal, it is 15 mi. SW of the Baltic, where its outer port is Travemünde. Imports wood, cattle, meat products, iron and copper ores; exports pig iron, coal, machinery, fertilizer, chemicals, salt, porcelain, and glass. Industrial center, with shipbuilding, foundries, and mfg. of machinery, oxygen and electrical instruments, enamelware, textiles, rugs, organs, wood products, canned fish, pottery. Long noted for its red wine trade and its marzipan. Has marine acad.; engineering col.; state music school where musical tradition of Buxtehude, who was organist in Lübeck, is carried on. Although heavily damaged in Second World War, inner city of Lübeck still retains its medieval character. City hall (13th–16th cent.) is one of Germany's largest. The Romanesque-Gothic cathedral (founded 1173 by Henry the Lion) and splendid 13th–14th-cent. church of St. Mary were damaged; many medieval residences and guildhalls were destroyed. Church of St. Jacob (13th–14th cent.) has large organ (1504); noted 13th-cent. Holy Ghost Hosp. became (1825) home for the aged. Medieval fortifications were razed in 19th cent.; 2 gates, the Holstentor (1466–78; now housing a mus. of city relics) and the Burgtor (1444) are extant. Lübeck is 1st mentioned in 11th cent.; Henry the Lion in 1158 acquired and chartered the town, and in 1160 transferred bishopric of Oldenburg to Lübeck. Created (1226) free imperial city. Ruled by an enterprising merchant aristocracy, Lübeck soon rose to great commercial prosperity. Was head of Hanseatic League and meeting place of its diets until 1630, when last Hanseatic diet was held. After decline of the League, the city, despite failure of its efforts to engage in Atlantic trade, continued to flourish as Baltic port. Lübeck's powerful fortifications spared it the ravages of the Thirty Years War. During Napoleonic Wars it was occupied by Fr. troops. Lübeck, governed by a senate, joined North German Confederation and later the German Empire as free Hanseatic city; retained that status until inc. 1937 into Schleswig-Holstein. Heinrich and Thomas Mann were b. here. Territory of former bishops of Lübeck, residing at Eutin, did not include city of Lübeck.

Lübeck Bay, N Germany, SW arm of Mecklenburg Bay of the Baltic; c.20 mi. long, c.10 mi. wide. Receives Trave R. at Travemünde.

Lubefu (lōōbĕ'fōō), village, Kasai prov., central Belgian Congo, on Lubefu R. (a headstream of the Sankuru), and 75 mi. ENE of Lusambo; cotton ginning. Has R.C. mission.

Lubelenge (lōōbĕlĕng'gä) or **Lubelengo** (–gō), village, Kivu prov., central Belgian Congo, on Lualaba R., on railroad, and 80 mi. NNW of Kasongo; sawmilling, palm-oil milling; coffee plantations.

Lüben, Poland: see Lubin.

Lubero (lōōbĕ'rō), village, Kivu prov., E Belgian Congo, 80 mi. N of Costermansville; alt. 6,330 ft. Center for cultivation of wheat, coffee, and pyrethrum; large flour mills. Strawberries, European vegetables, and flowers also grown here. Tourist center. Has R.C. mission, hospital for Europeans. Lubero was founded 1925.

Lubéron, Montagne du (mōtä'nyŭ dü lübārō'), narrow wooded ridge in Vaucluse dept., SE France, extending c.25 mi. E-W bet. Coulon R. (N) and Durance R. (S). Rises to 3,691 ft. Cavaillon is at its W foot.

Lubersac (lübĕrsäk'), village (pop. 1,138), Corrèze dept., S central France, 20 mi. NNW of Brive-la-Gaillarde; preserves and ships fruit and vegetables.

Lubiana, Yugoslavia: see Ljubljana.

Lubiaz, Poland: see Leubus.

Lubica (lyōō'bĭtsä), Slovak *L'ubica*, Hung. *Leibic* (lā'bĭts), town (pop. 3,335), N Slovakia, Czechoslovakia, in the High Tatra, 6 mi. NE of Poprad; lumbering; sulphurous springs.

Lubien (lōō'byĕnyŭ), Pol. *Lubień*. **1** or **Lubien Kujawski** (kōōyäf'skē) Pol. *Lubień Kujawski*, Rus. *Lyuben* or *Lyuben'* (both: lū'bĕnyŭ), town (pop. 1,676), Bydgoszcz prov., central Poland, 18 mi. SSE of Wloclawek; distilling, flour milling. **2** Town, Opole prov., Poland: see Lewin Brzeski.

Lubieszow, Ukrainian SSR: see Lyubeshov.

Lubilash River, Belgian Congo: see Sankuru River.

Lubin (lōō'bēn), Ger. *Lüben* (lü'bŭn), town (1939 pop. 10,809; 1946 pop. 1,769) in Lower Silesia, after 1945 in Wroclaw prov., SW Poland, 13 mi. N of Liegnitz (Legnica); mfg. of food products, furniture, pianos; woodworking. Suffered heavy damage in Second World War.

Lublin (lōō'blēn), Rus. *Lyublin* (lū'blyĭn), province [Pol. *województwo*] (□ 10,525; pop. 1,889,650), SE Poland; ⊙ Lublin. Borders E on Bug R. (USSR line), W on the Vistula. Surface is hilly in S, becoming low and level toward N. Principal crops are rye, potatoes, wheat, oats, barley, flax, hemp; livestock. Phosphate deposits near the Vistula; limestone quarries near Lublin. Principal industries are metalworking, mfg. of electrical appliances, food products, glass, agr. implements. Chief cities: Lublin, Siedlce, Chelm, Zamosc, Biala Podlaska. Boundaries of pre-Second World War prov. (□ 12,039; 1931 pop. 2,085,746) were changed by transfer of territory (N) to Warsaw prov. Includes greater part of former Lublin govt. of Rus. Poland. Area (□ 185) W of Sokal passed 1951 from Lublin prov. to Lvov oblast of Ukrainian SSR.

Lublin, city (1950 pop. estimate 111,000), ⊙ Lublin prov., E Poland, on Bystrzyca R. 105 mi. SE of Warsaw; 51°20'N 22°30'E. Rail junction; trade center (large grain elevator); mfg. of aircraft, agr. machinery, boilers, pumps, trucks, electrical goods, glass; food processing, sugar milling. Brick mfg., limestone quarrying in vicinity. Former Catholic univ. of Lublin (founded 1918) was reopened 1944 as Marie Curie-Sklodowska Univ. City has anc. gates with towers, a castle, 15th-cent. churches, R.C. cathedral (16th cent.), and monuments. Situated above marshy river valleys, which formed natural defense, and on important crossroads, Lublin was for centuries one of leading Pol. towns. Known since early-11th cent.; became ⊙ a prov. in 1474 and seat of a tribunal in 1578. Several diets held here (16th–18th cent.); diet of 1569 united Poland and Lithuania. Lublin passed to Austria in 1795; included in Rus. Poland in 1815 and was ⊙ Lyublin govt. Construction of local railroad (19th cent.) caused growth of industry (especially tanning) and greatest development of city. Seat of temporary Pol. Socialist govt. in 1918. Before Second World War, pop. 50% Jewish. Majdanek or Maidanek (mīdä'nĕk), just SE of city, was site of Ger. concentration and extermination camp; here c.1,500,000 people were killed in gas chambers and burned in furnaces. City taken by Soviet forces in 1944; provisional Pol. govt. formed here was broadened (Feb., 1945) by inclusion of members of London cabinet; govt. was recognized at Potsdam Conference (Aug., 1945) as sole Pol. authority.

Lublin (lŭb'lĭn), village (pop. 161), Taylor co., central Wis., 41 mi NE of Eau Claire, in lumbering and dairying region.

Lubliniec (lōōblē'nyĕts), Ger. *Lublinitz* (lōōblē'nĭts), town (pop. 11,470), Katowice prov., S Poland, 21 mi. WSW of Czestochowa; rail junction; mfg. of textiles, machines, cement goods; flour milling; ironworks. Passed from Germany to Poland, 1921. During Second World War, under Ger. rule called Loben.

Lubnaig, Loch (lŏkh lōōb'näg), lake (4 mi. long 146 ft. deep), SW Perthshire, Scotland, 3 mi. NW of Callander, at foot of Ben Ledi. Outlet: Leny R., flowing to Teith R.

Lubny (lōōbnē'), city (1926 pop. 21,302), N central Poltava oblast, Ukrainian SSR, on high right bank of Sula R. and 75 mi. WNW of Poltava; distilling, tobacco products, flour; woolen milling, furniture mfg.; chemicals, machinery.

Lubochna, Czechoslovakia: see Kralovany.

Lubok Antu (lōōbôk' än'tōō), town (pop. 302), S Sarawak, in W Borneo, near border of Indonesian Borneo, on Lupar R. and 110 mi. ESE of Kuching; agr. (rice, sago), fishing.

Lubok Buntar (bōōntär'), village (pop. 704), southernmost Kedah, Malaya, near Krian R. (Perak line), 26 mi. SE of George Town; rubber.

Lubombo (lōōbōm'bō), township (pop. 40), Southern Prov., Northern Rhodesia, on railroad and 10 mi. E of Mazabuka; tobacco, wheat, corn.

Lubomierz (lōōbôm'yĕsh), Ger. *Liebenthal* (lē'bŭntäl"), town (1939 pop. 1,664; 1946 pop. 1,695) in Lower Silesia, after 1945 in Wroclaw prov., SW Poland, 13 mi. NW of Hirschberg (Jelenia Gora); agr. market (grain, potatoes, livestock). Has church of Benedictine (later Ursuline) convent, founded 1278. After 1945, briefly called Milosna, Pol. *Mitosna*.

Luboml, Ukrainian SSR: see Lyuboml.

Lubovna, Czechoslovakia: see Stara Lubovna.

Lubraniec (lōōbrä'nyĕts), Rus. *Lyubranets* (lūbrä'nyĭts), town (pop. 2,188), Bydgoszcz prov., central Poland, 13 mi. SW of Wloclawek; flour milling.

Lubrín (lōōvrēn'), town (pop. 1,155), Almería prov., S Spain, 14 mi. SW of Huércal-Overa; olive-oil, cereals, almonds. Iron deposits.

Lubrza (lōōb'zhä), Ger. *Liebenau bei Schwiebus* (lē'bŭnou bī shvē'bōōs), town (1939 pop. 1,170;

1946 pop. 579) in Brandenburg, after 1945 in Zielona Gora prov., W Poland, 6 mi. NW of Swiebodzin; agr. market (grain, vegetables, potatoes, livestock).

Lubsko (lo͝op'skô), Ger. *Sommerfeld* (zô'mûrfĕlt"), town (1939 pop. 10,752; 1946 pop. 2,698) in Brandenburg, after 1945 in Zielona Gora prov., W Poland, 16 mi. SE of Guben, in Lower Lusatia; rail junction; woolen milling, stone quarrying. Chartered 1283. Has 13th-cent. church, 16th-cent. castle, remains of 15th-cent. town walls. After 1945, briefly called Zemsz.

Lübtheen (lübt'hān), town (pop. 5,707), Mecklenburg, N Germany, 25 mi. SW of Schwerin; agr. market (stock, grain, potatoes). Potash formerly mined here.

Lubuagan (lo͞obwä'gän), village (1939 pop. 2,722; 1948 municipality pop. 7,821), Kalinga sub-prov., Mountain Prov., N Luzon, Philippines, on small tributary of Chico R. and 40 mi. ESE of Bangued; lumbering, rice growing.

Lubudi (lo͞obo͞o'dē), town (1948 pop. 4,745), Katanga prov., SE Belgian Congo, on railroad and 90 mi. NW of Jadotville; industrial center. Tin smelting; mfg. of cement, cast-iron and bronze articles, calcium carbide. Has hydroelectric power plant. R.C. mission.

Lubumbashi (lo͞obo͞ombä'shē), village, Katanga prov., SE Belgian Congo, on railroad just SW of Elisabethville; large copper-smelting and -refining plants; also coke ovens.

Lubunda, Belgian Congo: see BRAINE-L'ALLEUD SAINT-JOSEPH.

Lubutu (lo͞obo͞o'to͞o), village, Eastern Prov., E Belgian Congo, 120 mi. SE of Stanleyville, in rice-producing area; trading center. Has R.C. and Protestant missions. Former Arab post. Emin Pasha was murdered here, 1892, by the Arabs.

Lubyany (lo͞obyä'nē), town (1939 pop. over 500), N Tatar Autonomous SSR, Russian SFSR, on Vyatka R. and 22 mi. N of Mamadysh; sawmilling center.

Lübz (lübts), town (pop. 6,662), Mecklenburg, N Germany, on the regulated Elde and 8 mi. ENE of Parchim; sugar refining, potato-flour milling, flax processing, brewing.

Luc, Le (lü lük'), town (pop. 2,265), Var dept., SE France, 13 mi. SW of Draguignan; bauxite mining, mfg. (cork, olive oil).

Luca, Malta: see LUQA.

Lucainena de las Torres (lo͞okīnā'nä dhä läs tô'rĕs), town (pop. 1,148), Almería prov., S Spain, 20 mi. NE of Almería; terminus of mining railroad from Mediterranean port of Agua Amarga. Iron-mining center with iron foundries. Olive oil, cereals, esparto.

Lucama (lo͞okā'mů), town (pop. 405), Wilson co., E central N.C., 7 mi. SW of Wilson.

Lucan (lo͞o'kůn), village (pop. 631), S Ont., 16 mi. NW of London; lumbering, fruitgrowing.

Lucan, Gaelic *Leamhcán*, town (pop. 736), Co. Dublin, Ireland, on the Liffey, 7 mi. W of Dublin; spa resort and hunting center; also has woolen mills.

Lucan, village (pop. 246), Redwood co., SW Minn., 17 mi. SW of Redwood Falls; corn, oats, barley, potatoes.

Lucanas, province, Peru: see PUQUIO.

Lucanchau (lo͝ok'än'chou'), town, Yenbay prov., N Vietnam, 30 mi. NNW of Yenbay.

Lucania, Italy: see BASILICATA.

Lucania, Mount (lo͞okā'nēů) (17,150 ft.), SW Yukon, near Alaska border, in St. Elias Mts., 190 mi. W of Whitehorse; 61°2'N 140°28'W.

Lucas. 1 County (□ 434; pop. 12,069), S Iowa; ⊙ Chariton. Prairie agr. area (hogs, cattle, poultry, corn, hay) drained by Chariton R. and Whitebreast Creek. Bituminous-coal deposits mined in E. Has state parks. Formed 1846. 2 County (□ 343; pop. 395,551), NW Ohio; ⊙ TOLEDO. Bounded N by Mich. line, SE by Maumee R., and NE by W end of L. Erie. Chief agr. products are corn, vegetables, soybeans, livestock, fruit, wheat. Includes Fallen Timbers State Park and site of old Fort Meigs. Formed 1835.

Lucas. 1 Town (pop. 420), Lucas co., S Iowa, on Whitebreast Creek and c.40 mi. SSE of Des Moines, in livestock and grain area. John L. Lewis b. here in 1880. 2 City (pop. 631), Russell co., central Kansas, 18 mi. NE of Russell; livestock, grain. 3 Village (pop. 573), Richland co., N central Ohio, 6 mi. SE of Mansfield.

Lucas González (lo͞o'käs gōnsä'lĕs), town (pop. estimate 3,000), S central Entre Ríos prov., Argentina, on railroad and 15 mi. E of Nogoyá; agr. (fruit, grain, livestock, poultry); dairy products; flour mills.

Lucasville, village (1940 pop. 1,234), Scioto co., S Ohio, 9 mi. N of Portsmouth; sawmilling, creosoting.

Lucban (lo͞okbän'), town (1939 pop. 9,306; 1948 municipality pop. 15,060), Quezon prov., S Luzon, Philippines, 16 mi. ENE of San Pablo, at foot of Mt. Banahao in agr. area (coconuts, rice).

Lucca (lo͝ok'kä), province (□ 684; pop. 352,205), Tuscany, central Italy; ⊙ Lucca. Borders on Ligurian Sea; mtn. terrain (E Apuane Alps, GARFAGNANA) rising from narrow coastal plain. Drained by Serchio R. and its tributaries. Agr. (grapes, olives, corn, fruit); stock raising (cattle, sheep); forestry. Marble quarries (Seravezza, Pietrasanta, Querceta) in Apuane Alps. Bathing resorts (Viareggio, Forte dei Marmi) along coast. Mfg. at Lucca and Viareggio. Area decreased 1927 to help form Pistoia prov.

Lucca, city (pop. 32,896), ⊙ Lucca prov., Tuscany, central Italy, near Serchio R., 10 mi. NE of Pisa; 43°51'N 10°29'E. Rail junction; agr. and industrial center, noted for its olive oil; tobacco factories, foundries, paper, jute, silk, and woolen mills; mfg. of furniture, hats, macaroni, fertilizer; wine making. Archbishopric. Has churches with fine marble façades, including cathedral of San Martino, San Frediano (1112–47), and San Michele (started 1143), 16th-cent. palaces, art gall., remains of Roman amphitheater. A Ligurian settlement; later a Roman town; became (6th cent.) capital of Lombard duchy. A republic, with short interruptions, from Middle Ages until 1805, when Napoleon I made it a principality. United with Tuscany in 1847; annexed 1860 to Kingdom of Sardinia. Slightly damaged by bombing (1944) in Second World War.

Lucca Sicula (lo͞ok'kä sē'ko͞olä), village (pop. 3,086), Agrigento prov., SW Sicily, 6 mi. NNE of Ribera.

Luccus River, Sp. Morocco: see LUCUS RIVER.

Luce, county (□ 914; pop. 8,147), NE Upper Peninsula, Mich.; ⊙ Newberry. Bounded N by L. Superior; drained by Tahquamenon R. and small Two Hearted R. Includes part of Manistique L., and North Manistique L. Tahquamenon Falls are in E. Forest and farm area (potatoes, celery, hay, oats; dairy products); timber; hunting, fishing. Some mfg. at Newberry. Formed and organized 1887.

Lucea (lo͞osē'), town (pop. 1,806), ⊙ Hanover parish, NW Jamaica, minor port 17 mi. W of Montego Bay, 95 mi. WNW of Kingston; 18°27'N 78°12'W. Has fine, almost landlocked, harbor. Exports bananas and yams. Has old churches. Phosphate deposits near by.

Luce Bay, inlet of Irish Sea, S Wigtown, Scotland; 19 mi. wide at mouth bet. Mull of Galloway and Burrow Head; 20 mi. long.

Lucedale, town (pop. 1,631), ⊙ George co., SE Miss., 36 mi. WNW of Mobile (Ala.), in agr. and timber area; canned foods, tung oil, lumber.

Lucélia (lo͞osĕ'lyů), city, W São Paulo, Brazil, 75 mi. WNW of Marília, in zone of recent pioneer settlement; future railhead of line from Baurú; coffee, cotton, grain, livestock.

Lucena (lo͞osä'nä), town (1939 pop. 11,674; 1948 municipality pop. 33,092), ⊙ QUEZON prov., S Luzon, Philippines, near Tayabas Bay, 22 mi. SE of San Pablo, on railroad; 13°56'N 121°36'E. Trade center for fishing and agr. area (rice, corn).

Lucena (lo͞o-thā'nä), city (pop. 22,659), Córdoba prov., S Spain, in Andalusia, 37 mi. SE of Córdoba; industrial and agr. center. Metalworking (especially church appointments); olive-oil processing and shipping. Other mfg. includes chemicals (carbon disulphide, vegetable fats and oils, soap, lime), pottery (large earthen jars), plaster, footwear, furniture, knit and cotton goods, cookies; flour milling, brandy distilling. Stock raising; fruitgrowing. Mineral springs. Has some notable churches. Scene of Christian victory (1483) over the Moors led by Boabdil, last king of Granada, who was captured.

Lucena del Cid (dhĕl thēdh'), town (pop. 1,227), Castellón de la Plana prov., E Spain, 17 mi. NW of Castellón de la Plana; meat processing, flour milling; livestock market; cereals, wine. Anthracite, iron, and lead mining; marble quarries. Has Roman remains and medieval castle.

Lucena del Puerto (pwĕr'tō), town (pop. 1,514), Huelva prov., SW Spain, on the Río Tinto and 8 mi. ENE of Huelva; cereals, olives, white wine, timber, livestock.

Lucenay-l'Évêque (lüsůnā'-lāvĕk'), village (pop. 403), Saône-et-Loire dept., E central France, in the Monts du Morvan, 10 mi. NNW of Autun; lumbering.

Luc-en-Diois (lük-ā-dēwä'), village (pop. 614), Drôme dept., SE France, on the Drôme and 11 mi. SSE of Die; lavender essence processing, sawmilling.

Lucendro, Lago di (lä'gô dē lo͞ochĕn'drô), small lake in Ticino canton, S Switzerland, near St. Gotthard Pass. Near by are Lucendro hydroelectric plant and Piz Lucendro, peak (9,734 ft.).

Lucenec (lo͝o'chĕnyĕts), Slovak *Lučenec*, Hung. *Losonc* (lô'shônts), town (pop. 12,801), S Slovakia, Czechoslovakia, 37 mi. SE of Banska Bystrica, in fertile agr. region (wheat, potatoes, sugar beet); rail junction; trade center (notably for fruit and raw wool); mfg. of woolen textiles, enamelware, house appliances; large woodworking industry. Magnesite mining, tobacco growing in vicinity. Hung. element dominates in pop. Held by Hungary, 1938–45.

Luceni (lo͞o-thā'nē), village (pop. 1,744), Saragossa prov., NE Spain, near Ebro R., 24 mi. NW of Saragossa; sugar and flour mills.

Lucentum, Spain: see ALICANTE, city.

Lucera (lo͞ochâ'rä), anc. *Luceria*, town (pop. 17,472), Foggia prov., Apulia, S Italy, 12 mi. WNW of Foggia; rail terminus; leather goods, woolen textiles, cement, ceramics, agr. tools, vegetable oils. Clay quarries near by. Bishopric. Has Gothic cathedral, well-preserved 13th-cent. castle (built by Frederick II; later rebuilt), once the chief fortress of Apulia.

Lucéram (lüsäräm'), village (pop. 495), Alpes Maritimes dept., SE France, 13 mi. NNE of Nice; arsenic mined near by. Tourist and popular winter sports resort of Peira-Cava (alt. c.5,000 ft.) is 4 mi. N in Maritime Alps.

Lucerne (lo͞osûrn', Fr. lüsĕrn'), Ger. *Luzern* (lo͞otsĕrn'), canton (□ 576; 1950 pop. 223,409), central Switzerland; ⊙ Lucerne. Agr. and pastoral, with large forested areas; orchards in N. Alpine hills in S covered mainly with pastures. Drained by Reuss and Kleine Emme rivers; contains the Baldeggersee and L. of Sempach; borders on lakes of Lucerne and Zug. The RIGI and NW shores of L. of Lucerne are noted tourist areas (⊙ is largest resort). Mfg. (metal products, textiles, foodstuffs). Pop. German speaking and largely Catholic. Lucerne was one of the Four Forest Cantons, joining the Swiss Confederation in 1332.

Lucerne, Ger. *Luzern*, city (1950 pop. 60,365), ⊙ Lucerne canton, central Switzerland, on both banks of Reuss R., on W shore of L. of Lucerne; alt. 1,440 ft. One of largest resorts (mainly summer) in Switzerland; noted for fine mtn. views. Mfg. of metal products (aluminumware, elevators, sewing machines, electrical apparatus), chemicals, beer; printing. Older parts of town are on right bank of the Reuss; medieval town walls are in N; has bridges (2 protected by roofs decorated with paintings). Points of interest: Lion of Lucerne monument, Glacier Garden, old town hall (1602–06) with historical mus., Art and Assembly House, cantonal bldgs., *Hofkirche* (church founded c.735), 17th-cent. Jesuit church (baroque). Lucerne grew around 8th-cent. monastery of St. Leodegar and became an important trade center on St. Gotthard route.

Lucerne (lo͞osûrn'). 1 Town (pop. 227), Putnam co., N Mo., 16 mi. W of Unionville. 2 Village (pop. 1,073), Indiana co., W central Pa., just S of Indiana.

Lucerne, Lake of, or Lake of the Four Forest Cantons, Ger. *Vierwaldstättersee* (fĭrvält'-shtĕtůrzā'), central Switzerland, bordering on the Four Forest Cantons of Unterwalden, Uri, Schwyz, and Lucerne; □ 44, alt. 1,424 ft., max. depth 702 ft. Irregular in shape, it branches off in 3 narrow arms to which other names are given: L. of Küssnacht, Ger. *Küssnachtersee* (N); L. of Alpnach, Ger. *Alpnachersee* (SW); and L. of Uri, Ger. *Urnersee* (SE). Reuss R. flows into L. of Uri, emerging at Lucerne. Other streams which flow into lake include the Muota, the Sarner Aa, and the Engelberger Aa. The lake, surrounded by mts., notably the Rigi (N) and the Pilatus (SW), is a popular resort area noted for its fine scenery. Main town on lake is Lucerne; resorts include Küssnacht, Weggis, Vitznau, Gersau, Brunnen, Morschach, Flüelen, Seelisberg, Beckenried, Bürgenstock, Stansstad-Fürigen, and Hergiswil.

Lucerne-in-Maine, Maine: see DEDHAM.

Lucerne Lake, S Calif., intermittently dry bed (c. mi. long), in Mojave Desert, 17 mi. E of Victorville.

Lucero, Lake, N.Mex.: see WHITE SANDS NATIONAL MONUMENT.

Lucette, La, France: see GENEST, LE.

Luceville (lo͞os'vĭl), village (pop. 701), SE Que., near the St. Lawrence, 11 mi. NE of Rimouski; dairying, pig raising.

Luchang, China: see LUSHUI.

Lucheng or **Lu-ch'eng** (lo͞o'chŭng'). 1 Town, Kwangsi prov., China: see TIENSI. 2 Town, ⊙ Lucheng co. (pop. 108,798), SE Shansi prov., China, on road and 16 mi. NE of Changchih; sericulture center; winegrowing; pottery mfg.

Luchente (lo͞ochĕn'tā), town (pop. 1,844), Valencia prov., E Spain, 9 mi. ESE of Játiva; olive-oil processing; wine, almonds, cereals.

Luchenza (lo͞ochĕn'zä), rail station, Southern Prov., Nyasaland, 24 mi. SE of Blantyre, in agr. area; cotton, tobacco, tung, tea.

Lu-ch'i, China: see LUKI.

Lu-chiang, town, China: see LUKIANG.

Lu Chiang, river, China: see SALWEEN RIVER.

Lu-chiang, Formosa: see LUKANG.

Lu-ch'i-k'ou, China: see LUKIKOW.

Luchon or **Bagnères-de-Luchon** (bänyâr'-dů-lüshō'), town (pop. 3,840), Haute-Garonne dept., S France, in Luchon Valley, near Sp. border, 40 mi. SE of Tarbes; leading resort of the central Pyrenees, at foot of the MALADETTA. Its warm springs have been known since Roman times. Together with SUPERBAGNÈRES it is also a winter-sports center.

Luchon Valley, in central Pyrenees, Haute Garonne dept., S France, extending 10 mi. N–S from Marignac to Luchon; drained by small tributary of Garonne R. Resort area. Hydroelectric and metallurgical plants.

Lüchow, Anhwei prov., China: see HOFEI.

Luchow, Szechwan prov., China: see LUHSIEN.

Lüchow (lü'khō), town (pop. 5,305), in former Prussian prov. of Hanover, NW Germany, after 1945 in Lower Saxony, 8 mi. N of Salzwedel (E Germany); wood products; distilling.

Lu-chu: see RYUKYU ISLANDS.

Lu-ch'uan, Kwangsi prov., China: see LUCHWAN.

Luchüan or **Lu-ch'üan** (both: lōō'chüăn'), town, ⊙ Luchüan co. (pop. 108,222), NE central Yunnan prov., China, 38 mi. NNW of Kunming, in mtn. region; timber, rice, wheat, millet, beans. Asbestos mining near by.

Luchwan or **Lu-ch'uan** (both: lōō'chwän'), town, ⊙ Luchwan co. (pop. 255,791), SE Kwangsi prov., China, 20 mi. SE of Watlam; paper-milling center; rice, wheat, sugar cane, litchi nuts. Tin mines near by.

Luciana (lōō-thyä'nä), town (pop. 850), Ciudad Real prov., S central Spain, on Guadiana R. at mouth of Bullaque R., and 20 mi. W of Ciudad Real; cereals, olives, livestock.

Lucien (lōōsēn'), village, Noble co., N Okla., 25 mi. ESE of Enid; butane- and propane-gas mfg.

Lucie River (lōōsē'ů), W central Du. Guiana, rises at N foot of Eilerts de Haan Mts., flows c.150 mi. W to Courantyne R. at Br. Guiana border. Many rapids.

Lucignano (lōōchēnyä'nô), village (pop. 794), Arezzo prov., Tuscany, central Italy, 15 mi. SSW of Arezzo. Has 13th-cent. church and palace with mus. containing pictures by Luca Signorelli.

Lucillos (lōō-thē'lyōs), village (pop. 1,051), Toledo prov., central Spain, 11 mi. E of Talavera de la Reina; cereals, grapes, olives, sheep.

Lucindale (lōō'sĭndāl), village (pop. 189), SE South Australia, 175 mi. SSE of Adelaide, on Naracoorte-Kingston RR; dairy products, livestock.

Lucinda Point (lōōsĭn'dů), village and small port (pop. 84), E Queensland, Australia, on headland forming N end of entrance to Halifax Bay, 60 mi. NW of Townsville; sugar port for Ingham, 13 mi. inland, with which it is connected by electric railroad. Sometimes called Dungeness (dŭnj'nĕs').

Lucio Vicente Lôpez (lōō'syō vēsĕn'tā lō'pĕs), village (pop. estimate 700), S Santa Fe prov., Argentina, on Carcarañá R. and 26 mi. NW of Rosario; hydroelectric station in agr. area (wheat, corn, flax, livestock, poultry); dairying.

Lucivna, Czechoslovakia: see STRBA.

Luck, Ukrainian SSR: see LUTSK.

Luck, village (pop. 803), Polk co., NW Wis., 37 mi. WNW of Rice Lake, in wooded lake area; produces butter, powdered milk, furniture.

Lucka (lŏŏ'kä), town (pop. 4,048), Thuringia, central Germany, 17 mi. S of Leipzig, in lignite-mining region; textile milling.

Luckau (lŏŏ'kou), town (pop. 6,145), Brandenburg, E Germany, in Lower Lusatia, near Spree Forest, 15 mi. N of Finsterwalde; agr. market (grain, potatoes, stock); spa. Has 16th-cent. church, many half-timbered houses.

Luckeesarai or **Lakhisarai** (both: lŭk"ĭsŭrī'), town (pop. 14,073), Monghyr dist., central Bihar, India, on tributary of the Ganges and 28 mi. WSW of Monghyr; rail and road junction; rice, corn, wheat, grain, barley. Extensive Buddhist ruins near by.

Luckenwalde (lŏŏ"kůnväl'dů), town (pop. 30,979), Brandenburg, E Germany, 30 mi. SSW of Berlin; woolen and paper milling, metalworking; mfg. of hats, machinery, plastics, furniture, pianos, shoes, fire extinguishers. Site of plant-research institute. Power station. Site of concentration camp under Hitler regime. Has 16th-cent. church, old fortified tower. Chartered 1808.

Luckey, village (pop. 764), Wood co., NW Ohio, 10 mi. ENE of Bowling Green; limestone quarries.

Lucknow (lŭk'nō), village (pop. 867), S Ont., 18 mi. NE of Goderich; aircraft and furniture plants, flax, lumber, and flour mills; dairying.

Lucknow (lŭk'nou), district (□ 976; pop. 949,728), central Uttar Pradesh, India; ⊙ Lucknow. On Ganges Plain; drained by the Gumti; irrigated by Sarda Canal system. Agr. (wheat, rice, gram, millet, oilseeds, barley, sugar cane, corn); mango, orange, and ber groves. Main centers: Lucknow (mfg.), Malihabad, Kakori, Amethi. Formerly also spelled Lakhnau.

Lucknow, city (□ 36; pop., including Charbagh, Alambagh, and cantonment, 387,177), ⊙ Lucknow dist., central Uttar Pradesh, India, on Gumti R. (bridges) and 260 mi. SE of New Delhi; 26°52'N 80°55'E. Major rail and road junction; trade (grain, oilseeds, sugar cane) and industrial center; mfg. of paper, shoes, chemicals, carpets, electric and pharmaceutical supplies, cigarettes, binoculars, microscopes, copper and brass utensils, silverware, brocades; cotton and oilseed milling, sugar processing; extensive railroad shops; cold-storage plant. Noted handicrafts include leather goods, embroidery, and clay figurines. Educational center, with Lucknow Univ. (founded 1921; includes Canning Col. and Medical Col.), La Martinière School, Natl. Acad. of Hindustan Music, School of Arts and Crafts, Central Drug Research Inst., Inst. of Paleobotany; building research station. In NE area is Provincial Mus. (built 1863), with archaeological exhibits including sculptures from Muttra, Brahmanic statues, antiquities from Set Mahet and Kasia, and a coin collection. Among 16th–19th cent. buildings of Nawabs of Oudh are the Great Imambarah of Asuf-ud-daula, Jami Masjid, Husainabad Imambarah, and tombs in Kaisar Bagh (garden). Many parks, including Wingfield Park (80 acres), Horticultural Gardens, and Victoria Park. Once part of Jaunpur kingdom, city became important in 16th cent. under Mogul rule. During Sepoy Rebellion (1857–58), British garrison and colony were beseiged (July-Nov., 1857) in entrenchments surrounding the Residency (built 1800; now partially ruined), in N central area, near the Gumti, and suffered heavy casualties before relief arrived; after abandoning city, British recaptured it in March, 1858, under Sir Colin Campbell. Modern city is largely the work of Nawabs of Oudh; was their ⊙ from 1775 to 1856, when Lucknow became ⊙ OUDH prov. until it merged (1877) with Agra presidency. Allahabad became ⊙ United Provs. of Agra and Oudh (since 1950 called Uttar Pradesh) and remains so, although Lucknow has many state legislative offices. Former Br. military cantonment (S). Formerly also spelled Lakhnau.

Lucky (lōōch'kĭ), Slovak *Lúčky*, Hung. *Lucski* (lōōch'kĭ), village (pop. 1,881), N Slovakia, Czechoslovakia, 6 mi. NE of Ruzomberok; health resort (alt. 2,164 ft.) with ferruginous thermal springs.

Lucky Hill, village, St. Mary parish, N Jamaica, just S of Gayle and 8 mi. SW of Port Maria. A community project. Principal crops: bananas, citrus fruit, corn, peas, cacao.

Lucky Lake, village (pop. 309), SW Sask., near Lucky L. (4 mi. long, 3 mi. wide), 55 mi. NE of Swift Current; magnesium-sulphate production; grain elevators, lumbering.

Lucky Shot, village (1939 pop. 10), S Alaska, 40 mi. NNE of Anchorage; gold mining. Airfield.

Lucma (lōōk'mä), town (pop. 139), Cuzco dept., S central Peru, on affluent of Urubamba R., in Cordillera Vilcabamba, and 22 mi. SW of Quillabamba; sugar cane, coca, cereals. Gold, silver, copper, kaolin, nickel, and mercury deposits near by.

Lucnam (lŏŏk'näm'), town, Bacgiang prov., N Vietnam, 14 mi. E of Phulangthuong and on the Song Lucnam (tributary of the song Cau).

Luçon (lüsō'), town (pop. 6,674), Vendée dept., W France, 17 mi. W of Fontenay-le-Comte; small port, connected by 9-mi. canal across Marais POITEVIN with Bay of Biscay; machine shops; printing; horticulture. Seat of a bishop. Has 13th-14th-cent. cathedral with 280-ft. spire; episcopal palace encloses a 15th-cent. cloister. Richelieu was bishop of Luçon (1607–24).

Luco ne' Marsi (lōō'kô nĕmär'sē), town (pop. 5,228), Aquila prov., Abruzzi e Molise, S central Italy, near reclaimed Lago Fucino area, 5 mi. SSE of Avezzano, in agr. (cereals, potatoes, grapes) region. Damaged by earthquake (1915).

Lucre (lōō'krā), town (pop. 1,417), Cuzco dept., S central Peru, 19 mi. ESE of Cuzco, in agr. region (grain, potatoes); woolen mill.

Lucrecia Cape (lōōkrā'syä), on Atlantic coast of E Cuba, Oriente prov., 45 mi. ENE of Holguín; 21°5'N 75°37'W.

Lucrino, Lago (lä'gô lōōkrē'nô), small coastal lake in Campania, S Italy, 2 mi. WNW of Pozzuoli; oyster culture; bathing. An anc. embankment, Via Herculea, can still be traced under the water.

Luc-sur-Mer (lük-sür-mâr'), town (pop. 2,535), Calvados dept., NW France, beach resort on the Channel, 9 mi. N of Caen. Has marine zoological laboratory. Flanked by Allied landing beaches of Normandy invasion (1944) in Second World War.

Lucus, territory, Sp. Morocco: see LARACHE.

Lucus Augusti, Spain: see LUGO, city.

Lucus River (lōō'kōōs), Fr. *Loukkos* (lōōkôs'), in W Sp. Morocco, rises on W slope of Rif Mts., flows W and NW, past Alcazarquivir, to the Atlantic at Larache; 85 mi. long. Forms border bet. Sp. and Fr. Morocco in upper course. Irrigated lower valley is Sp. Morocco's most fertile agr. region (vegetables, citrus fruit). Also spelled Luccus.

Ludajana River, Bulgaria: see LUDA YANA RIVER.

Luda Kamchiya River (lōō'dä käm'chēä), E Bulgaria, rises SW of Kotel in Kotel Mts., flows c.75 mi. E and ENE to Rakla, here joining Golyama Kamchiya R. to form Kamchiya R. Also called Luda Ticha R.

Luda Ticha River, Bulgaria: see LUDA KAMCHIYA RIVER.

Luda Yana River (lōō'dä yä'nä), W central Bulgaria, rises in central Sredna Gora 7 mi. S of Pirdop; flows 49 mi. generally S, past Panagyurishte, to Maritsa R. 3 mi. ESE of Pazardzhik. Has gold-carrying sand. Sometimes spelled Ludajana R.

Ludbreg (lōōd'brĕk) or **Ludbrijeg** (–brēyĕk), village (pop. 1,610), N Croatia, Yugoslavia, on railroad and 14 mi. E of Varazdin, in lignite area; flour milling, brick mfg.

Ludden, village (pop. 96), Dickey co., SE N.Dak., 9 mi. S of Oakes, near James R.

Luddenden Foot, former urban district (1931 pop. 2,881), West Riding, SW Yorkshire, England, 3 mi. W of Halifax; woolen milling. Inc. 1937 in Sowerby.

Lude, Le (lů lüd'), town (pop. 2,509), Sarthe dept., W France, on Loir R. and 11 mi. ESE of La Flèche; mfg. (furniture, business machines), paper milling. Noted for 15th-cent. Gothic and Renaissance castle in the shape of a quadrilateral with machicolated towers.

Lüdenscheid (lü'dün-shīt), city (1950 pop. 51,451), in former Prussian prov. of Westphalia, W Germany, after 1945 in North Rhine-Westphalia, 18 mi. ESE of Wuppertal; metalworking center (household articles, fixtures, wire, screws, buttons). Chartered 1278. Was member of Hanseatic League.

Lüderitz (lü'důrĭts), formerly **Angra Pequena** (ăng'-rä pĕkē'nů), town (pop. 3,451), SW South-West Africa, on Angra Pequena or Lüderitz Bay (5 mi. long, 25 mi. wide) of the Atlantic, 180 mi. W of Keetmanshoop; 26°39'S 15°9'E; chief seaport of S part of country; serves surrounding diamond-mining region. There are important crayfish fisheries and several canneries. Rail terminus; airfield. Bartholomew Diaz landed here 1486 and erected a cross. Site was acquired 1883 by F.A.E. Lüderitz, a German merchant, and was taken under German protection, April 24, 1884. Occupied by Union forces at outbreak of First World War.

Ludes (lüd), village (pop. 614), Marne dept., N France, on N slope of the Montagne de Reims, 7 mi. SSE of Rheims; winegrowing (champagne).

Ludgershall (lŭd'gür-shůl, lŭ'gür–), town and parish (pop. 1,259), E Wiltshire, England, 7 mi. NW of Andover; agr. market in dairying and sheep-raising region. Has remains of Norman castle. Church is Norman to 13th cent.

Ludgvan (lŭ'jůn), former urban district (1931 pop. 1,897), W Cornwall, England, 3 mi. NE of Penzance; tin and copper mining; agr. market in fruit- and vegetable-growing region. Has 15th-cent. church.

Ludhiana (lōōdyä'nů), district (□ 1,399; pop. 818,-615), central Punjab, India; ⊙ Ludhiana. Bounded N by Sutlej R., S by Patiala and East Punjab States Union, in which it has several enclaves. Irrigated by Sirhind Canal system; agr. (wheat, gram, corn, cotton, oilseeds); hand-loom weaving. Chief towns: Ludhiana, Jagraon, Khanna. Invaded by Ranjit Singh, 1806–09; under Br. control soon after.

Ludhiana, city (pop. 111,639), ⊙ Ludhiana dist., central Punjab, India, 33 mi. SSE of Jullundur; rail junction; important textile center; agr. market (wheat, gram, corn, cotton, oilseeds). Hosiery mfg. is chief industry; also cotton, silk, and woolen milling, food processing, flour and oilseed milling, mfg. of rolled steel, machinery, machine tools, agr. implements, plywood, matches, furniture, leather goods, soap, dairy products, ink, ice. Handicrafts include woolen weaving (notably pashmina shawls), ivory turning, embroidering, dyeing. Govt. hosiery institute, medical school, art and engineering cols. Hq. in India of Amer. Presbyterian Mission. Founded in 1480 by Lodi dynasty; residence (1816–38) of Shah Shuja, in exile from Afghanistan.

Lüdinghausen (lü"dĭng-hou'zůn), town (pop. 7,538), in former Prussian prov. of Westphalia, NW Germany, after 1945 in North Rhine-Westphalia, 15 mi. SW of Münster; dairying; grain, cattle.

Ludington (lŭd'–), city (pop. 9,506), ⊙ Mason co., W Mich., on harbor on L. Michigan at mouth of Pere Marquette R.; port for Great Lakes shipping; ferries to Wis. points. Mfg. (motor parts, furniture, wood products, watchcases, clothing, shoes); fisheries, coal mines. Resort; fishing in many near-by streams and lakes. Has monument on site of 1st burial place (1675) of Father Marquette. Inc. as city 1873.

Lüdingworth (lü'dĭng-vôrt), village (pop. 2,498), in former Prussian prov. of Hanover, NW Germany, after 1945 in Lower Saxony, 5 mi. SE of Cuxhaven; food processing (flour products, beer).

Luditz, Czechoslovakia: see ZLUTICE.

Ludlam Bay, SE N.J., inlet of the Atlantic (c.2.5 mi. long) NW of Sea Isle City; entered from ocean by Corsons Inlet (NE); crossed by Intracoastal Waterway. Bet. bay and ocean is **Ludlam Beach,** barrier isl. (c.7 mi. long) bet. Corsons Inlet (N) and Townsends Inlet (S); site of Sea Isle City (bridge to mainland here).

Ludlow (lŭd'lō), municipal borough (1931 pop. 5,642; 1951 census 6,455), S Shropshire, England, on Teme R. at mouth of Corve R., and 23 mi. S of Shrewsbury; agr. market; sand quarrying. Has ruins of 11th-cent. castle, one-time residence of Prince Arthur, elder brother of Henry VIII, and an important fortress on the Welsh border. There are several half-timbered houses, and one of the original 7 town gates, a 12th-cent. chapel, and large 13th-15th-cent. parish church. Milton's *Comus* was 1st performed in Ludlow (1634). Butler wrote *Hudibras* here.

Ludlow. 1 Village (pop. 475), Champaign co., E Ill., 19 mi. NNE of Champaign, in agr. area. **2** City (pop. 6,374), Kenton co., N Ky., on left bank (levee) of the Ohio just W of Covington, within Cincinnati metropolitan dist. Railroad center (repair shops); mfg. of furniture, machinery, metal products, electrical equipment, feed, candy. Settled c.1790; inc. as village 1864, as city 1925. **3** Agr. town (pop. 361), Aroostook co., E Maine, 10 mi. W of Houlton. **4** Town (pop. 8,660), Hampden co., S Mass., on Chicopee R. and 6 mi. NE of Springfield; jute and flax products, stationery. Settled c.1750, inc. 1774. **5** Town (pop. 260), Livingston co., N central Mo., near branch of Grand R., 12 mi. SW of Chillicothe. **6** Village (1940 pop. 1,011), McKean co., N Pa., 14 mi. SE of Warren; tannery. Noted Olmsted Gardens here. **7** Town (pop. 2,428), including Ludlow village (pop. 1,678), Windsor co., S central Vt., on Black R. and 20 mi. SE of Rutland, in Green Mts.; mfg. (woolens, chemicals, wood products); agr. (potatoes, apples, dairy products); winter sports. Okemo Mtn. State Forest Park is near by. Calvin Coolidge attended Black River Acad. here.

Ludlow Falls, village (pop. 277), Miami co., W Ohio, 12 mi. SSW of Piqua.

Ludowici (lo͞o″dōwĭ'sē), city (pop. 1,332), ⊙ Long co., SE Ga., c.45 mi. SW of Savannah, near Altamaha R.; mfg. (naval stores, lumber).

Ludres (lü'drů), village (pop. 687), Meurthe-et-Moselle dept., NE France, 5 mi. S of Nancy; iron mines.

Ludsen, Latvia: see LUDZA.

Ludus (lo͞o'do͝osh), Rum. *Luduş*, Hung. *Marosludus* (mŏ'rôsh-lo͞o″do͝osh), village (6,275), Mures prov., NW central Rumania, in Transylvania, on Mures R. and 15 mi. SE of Turda; rail junction, agr. market (notably for grain and livestock).

Ludvika (lüd'vē″kä), city (1950 pop. 10,306), Kopparberg co., Sweden, in Bergslag region, on 10-mi.-long L. Vasma, Swedish *Väsman* (vĕs'män″), 35 mi. SW of Falun; rail junction; a center of heavy electrical-equipment industry; copper smelting, metalworking, sawmilling, brick mfg. Inc. 1919 as city. Large ironworks, founded in 16th cent., were closed in early 20th cent. Grangesberg, with important iron mines, is 9 mi. SW.

Ludweiler-Warndt (lo͞ot'vī″lůr-värnt'), town (pop. 5,512), SW Saar, near Fr. border, in the Warndt, on Rossel R. near its mouth on Saar R., and 3 mi. SW of Völklingen; coal mining; metal- and woodworking. Until 1936, called Ludweiler.

Ludwig Canal, Ger. *Ludwigskanal* (lo͞ot'vĭkhs känäl″), Bavaria, flows parallel to Regnitz R. from Bamberg to Fürth, then SE, through Nuremberg, to the Altmühl at Dietfurt, connecting the Danube and the Rhine via the Main. Length c.110 mi. Built 1832, it is navigable for vessels up to 180 tons. Forms part of the projected Rhine-Main-Danube Canal (started 1921; interrupted by Second World War).

Ludwigsburg (–bo͝ork), city (1950 pop. 58,205), N Württemberg, Germany, after 1945 in Württemberg-Baden, near the Neckar, 7 mi. N of Stuttgart; 48°54'N 9°12'E. Rail junction; mfg. center (machine tools; iron, steel, and metal goods; spark plugs, textiles, organs, coffee substitutes). Hot mineral springs in NE suburb of Hoheneck. Site of large garrison until 1945. City developed in regular layout around castle (1704–23). In 18th cent. it was repeatedly used as residence by dukes of Württemberg.

Ludwigsfelde (lo͞ot″vĭkhsfĕl'dů), town (pop. 5,806), Brandenburg, E Germany, 16 mi. SSW of Berlin; mfg. (automobiles, Diesel engines).

Ludwigshafen or **Ludwigshafen am Rhein** (–hä'fůn äm rīn'), city (1939 pop. 144,425; 1946 pop. 106,-556; 1950 pop. 122,329), Rhenish Palatinate, W Germany, port on left bank of the Rhine (bridge), opposite Mannheim; 49°28'N 8°27'E. Important water and rail transshipment point; a center of Ger. chemical industry (dyestuffs, fertilizers, plastics, pharmaceuticals). Mfg. of machinery, agr. apparatus, auto bodies, fittings; brewing, lumber and flour milling. Founded as small fortress in 17th cent. to protect Rhine-crossing to Mannheim. Was named and developed by Bavarian king Louis I. Chartered in 1850s. Harbor opened 1897. Captured by U.S. troops in March, 1945. Second World War destruction c. 60%. Scene (Sept., 1948) of a disastrous explosion of several chemical plants.

Ludwigskanal, Germany: see LUDWIG CANAL.

Ludwigslust (–lo͞ost'), town (pop. 12,487), Mecklenburg, N Germany, on Ludwigslust canal (linking Elbe and Elde rivers) and 21 mi. S of Schwerin; rail junction; agr. center (stock, fruit, vegetables, grain, potatoes); meat processing. Has 18th-cent. former grand-ducal palace. Founded 1756; until 1837 residence of grand dukes of Mecklenburg-Schwerin. Chartered 1876.

Ludwigsort, Russian SFSR: see LADUSHKIN.

Ludwigsstadt (–shtät), village (pop. 2,572), Upper Franconia, N Bavaria, Germany, in Thuringian Forest, 17 mi. NNE of Kronach, 3 mi. S of PROBSTZELLA; mfg. of metal products, textiles, chemicals; brewing, lumber milling. Has early-Romanesque chapel. Chartered 1377.

Ludwikowo, Poland: see MOSINA.

Ludwipol, Ukrainian SSR: see SOSNOVOYE.

Ludza (lo͝od'zä), Ger. *Ludsen*, Rus. (until 1917) *Lyutsin*, city (pop. 5,546), E Latvia, in Latgale, 15 mi. E of Rezekne, on small Ludza L.; tanning, sawmilling (timber trade), flour milling; rye, flax. Castle ruins. In Vitebsk govt. until 1920.

Luebo (lwĕ'bō), town, ⊙ Kasai dist. (□ 45,663; 1948 pop. c.731,000), Kasai prov., S Belgian Congo, on left bank of Lulua R. and 140 mi. WSW of Lusambo, in fiber-growing area; terminus of steam navigation, trading center. Airfield. Has R.C. and Protestant missions, hosp. for Europeans. Noted diamond-mining region extends S and E.

Lueders (lo͞o'důrz), village (pop. 708), Jones co., W central Texas, 25 mi. N of Abilene, and on Clear Fork of the Brazos; rail point in cotton, cattle area; limestone deposits; oil refinery.

Lüehyang, China: see LIOYANG.

Luembe River (lwĕm'bā), left tributary of Kasai R., in NE Angola and S Belgian Congo, rises above Nova Chaves (Lunda dist.), flows c.350 mi. N to the Kasai 15 mi. above Tshikapa village. Receives (left) the Chiumbe.

Luena (lwĕ'nä), village, Katanga prov., SE Belgian Congo, on railroad and 100 mi. ESE of Kamina; center of coal-mining area supplying, notably, the copper works at Jadotville.

Luepa (lwā'pä), village, Bolívar state, SE Venezuela, in Guiana Highlands, 110 mi. S of El Callo; 5°44'N 61°30'W; diamond-bearing area. Airfield.

Luesia (lwā'syä), town (pop. 1,365), Saragossa prov., N Spain, 36 mi. NW of Huesca; tanning; cereals, wine, livestock, lumber.

Lueta (lwā'tä), Hung. *Lövéte* (lû'vātĕ), village (pop. 3,801), Stalin prov., central Rumania, 10 mi. ESE of Odorhei; iron mining; ironworking. In Hungary, 1940–45.

Lufeng (lo͞o'fŭng'). **1** Town, Kwangtung prov., China: see LUKFUNG. **2** Town (pop. 2,467), ⊙ Lufeng co. (pop. 39,750), N central Yunnan prov., China, on Burma Road and 35 mi. W of Kunming; alt. 5,418 ft.; iron smelting; rice, wheat, millet.

Lufira River (lo͞ofē'rä), SE Belgian Congo, rises on Katanga highlands near Northern Rhodesia border 70 mi. WNW of Elisabethville, flows c.300 mi. NE and NNW to join Lualaba R. in S end of L. Kisale, 70 mi. NE of Bukama. Many rapids throughout its course. A major water reservoir has been formed in its lower middle valley c.20 mi. E of Jadotville, and its noted Cornet Falls are the site of the largest hydroelectric plant in Belgian Congo.

Lufkin, city (pop. 15,135), ⊙ Angelina co., E Texas, c.115 mi. NNE of Houston; commercial, processing center in heart of E Texas pine woods; center for lumbering, newsprint mfg. (from pine), woodworking; also creosoted products, foundry products, oil-field equipment, other metal products, mattresses. Angelina Natl. Forest is E, Davy Crockett Natl. Forest is W. Founded 1882, inc. 1890.

Luga (lo͞o'gů), city (1926 pop. 14,698), SW Leningrad oblast, Russian SFSR, on Luga R. and 85 mi. SSW of Leningrad; production of abrasives; metalworks, sawmills, tanneries, brickworks. Chartered 1777; in Second World War, held (1941–44) by Germans.

Lugagnano Val d'Arda (lo͞ogänyä'nô väl där'dä), village (pop. 1,310), Piacenza prov., Emilia-Romagna, N central Italy, on Arda R. and 8 mi. SW of Fiorenzuola d'Arda. Ruins of anc. Villeia are 6 mi. SW.

Lugan, river, Ukrainian SSR: see VOROSHILOVGRAD.

Lugano (lo͞ogä'nō), Ger. *Lauis* (lou'ĭs), largest town (1950 pop. 17,718) in Ticino canton, S Switzerland, on L. of Lugano, at mouth of Cassarate R., and 14 mi. S of Bellinzona, on Ital. border; popular summer resort noted for lake and mtn. scenery. Metal- and woodworking, printing; leather goods, chocolate, flour, biscuits. The old town is Italian in character; town hall (1844) is at traffic center; a mus. has varied collections; a park is noted for its flora. Has 13th-cent. church of San Lorenzo, 15th-cent. church of Santa Maria degli Angioli. Convent church retains fine old frescoes. Suburbs include Paradiso (SW), with ascent to Monte San Salvatore (3,002 ft.; chapel); Cassarate (E), with ascent to Monte Brè (3,061 ft.); Castagnola (E).

Lugano, Lake of, Ital. *Lago di Lugano* (lä'gô dē lo͞ogä'nô) or *Lago Ceresio* (chārā'zyô), bet. Italy and Switzerland, and bet. Lago Maggiore and L. Como; narrow, very irregular in shape; c.20 mi. long, □ 19 (□ 7 Italian, □ 12 Swiss), alt. 789 ft.; max. depth 944 ft. Numerous mtn. streams fall into lake; drained by short Tresa R. into Lago Maggiore. Fine scenery on shores near Lugano; NE arm is bounded by steep, rocky mts. Bridge bet. Melide (W) and Bissone (E) connects 2 banks. Main town on lake, LUGANO.

Lugan River, Ukrainian SSR: see VOROSHILOVGRAD.

Lugansk, Ukrainian SSR: see VOROSHILOVGRAD.

Luganskoye (lo͞ogän'skŭyů), town (1926 pop. 6,575), E Stalino oblast, Ukrainian SSR, in the Donbas, 15 mi. N of Yenakiyevo; metalworks.

Lugar (lo͞o'gůr), village in Auchinleck parish, E Ayrshire, Scotland, on Lugar Water; coal mining.

Lugarama (lo͞ogärä'mä), village, NE Ruanda-Urundi, in Ruanda, 28 mi. ENE of Kigali; center of tin-mining area, notably at Bugarura (bo͞ogäro͞o'rä), sometimes spelled Bugalula, 6 mi. W.

Lugareño or **Central Lugareño** (sĕnträl' lo͞ogärā'-nyō), sugar-mill village (pop. 3,837), Camagüey prov., E Cuba, on railroad and 28 mi. ENE of Camagüey.

Lugari (lo͞ogä'rē), village, Rift Valley prov., W Kenya, on railroad and 30 mi. WNW of Eldoret; coffee, tea, wheat, sisal, corn.

Luga River (lo͞o'gů), NW European Russian SFSR, rises in marshes NW of Novgorod, flows 215 mi. S and NW, past Luga and Kingisepp, to Luga Bay of Gulf of Finland at Ust-Luga. Forms rapids; navigable (April-Dec.) for 85 mi. above mouth. Receives Oredezh R. (right).

Lugar Water (lo͞o'gůr), river, Ayrshire, Scotland, rises 3 mi. WSW of Muirkirk, flows 15 mi. SW, W, and NW, past Lugar, Cumnock and Holmhead, and Ochiltree, to Ayr R. just SSW of Mauchline.

Lugasi (lo͝ogä'sē), town, N Vindhya Pradesh, India, 8 mi. E of Nowgong. Was ⊙ former petty state of Lugasi (□ 45; pop. 7,752) of Central India agency; since 1948, state merged with Vindhya Pradesh.

Lugau (lo͞o'gou), town (pop. 11,159), Saxony, E central Germany, at N foot of the Erzgebirge, 11 mi. SW of Chemnitz; coal-mining center; hosiery knitting, woolen milling.

Lugazi (lo͞ogä'zē), town, Buganda prov., S Uganda, 26 mi. E of Kampala; sugar mill; cotton, coffee, sugar cane.

Lügde (lü'dů), town (pop. 4,514), in former Prussian prov. of Westphalia, NW Germany, after 1945 in North Rhine-Westphalia, 2 mi. S of Bad Pyrmont; forestry. Has 12th-cent. church.

Lugdunum, France: see LYONS.

Lugdunum Batavorum, Netherlands: see LEIDEN.

Lugela (lo͞ozhĕ'lä), village, Zambézia prov., central Mozambique, 95 mi. N of Quelimane; cotton, sisal.

Lugenda River (lo͞ozhĕn'dä), Niassa prov., N Mozambique, rises in L. Chiuta (Nyasaland border), flows 300 mi. NE to the Ruvuma (Tanganyika border) at 11°24'S 38°30'E. Not navigable. Also spelled Lujenda.

Lugert Dam, Okla.: see ALTUS DAM.

Lugg River, Wales and England, rises in Radnor 7 mi. W of Knighton, flows 40 mi. SE into Hereford, past Leominster, to the Wye 4 mi. ESE of Hereford. Receives Arrow R. just SSE of Leominster, and Frome R. 3 mi. E of Hereford.

Lugh Ferrandi (lo͞og' fĕrän'dē), town (pop. 5,000), in the Upper Juba, SW Ital. Somaliland, on Juba R. and 45 mi. ESE of Mandera (Kenya), 220 mi. NW of Mogadishu, in agr. region (corn, durra); trade center.

Luginy (lo͞o'gĭnē), town (1926 pop. 3,796), N Zhitomir oblast, Ukrainian SSR, 12 mi. NW of Korosten; paper milling. Formerly called Lugin or Lugino.

Lugnaquillia (lŭg″nůkĭl'yů), mountain (3,039 ft.), central Co. Wicklow, Ireland, 18 mi. W of Wicklow.

Lugnvik (lŭng″ůnvēk'). **1** Village (pop. 741), Jamtland co., N central Sweden, on E shore of Stor L., 2 mi. N of Ostersund; dairying, lumbering. **2** Village, Vasternorrland co., NE Sweden: see NORRLAND.

Lugny (lünyē'), village (pop. 381), Saône-et-Loire dept., E central France, in the Monts du Mâconnais, 11 mi. N of Mâcon; winegrowing.

Lugo (lo͞o'gô), town (pop. 12,966), Ravenna prov., Emilia-Romagna, N central Italy, near Senio R., 14 mi. W of Ravenna. Rail junction; wine-making and commercial center; mfg. (alcohol, citrus-fruit syrups, barrels, macaroni, shoes, soap, wax, explosives). Has anc. castle.

Lugo (lo͞o'gō), province (□ 3,815; pop. 512,735), NW Spain, in Galicia, on Bay of Biscay; ⊙ Lugo. Crossed by Galician Mts.; has indented, rocky coast line. Drained by Miño R. and its tributaries flowing S and by several short rivers (including Deva) flowing N to Bay of Biscay. Temperate climate with abundant rainfall near coast, cold with less rain in interior. Widely scattered pop., with few towns; poor communications. Of mineral deposits (iron, antimony, copper, coal), only iron mines near Villaodrid and Vivero are exploited. Chief resources: stock raising (cattle, horses, hogs) and lumbering; important fisheries along coast. Agr. products: potatoes, rye, corn, nuts, vegetables, and honey; vineyards in Miño valley. Chief cities: Lugo, Monforte, Vivero.

Lugo, anc. *Lucus Augusti*, city (pop. 21,115), ⊙ Lugo prov., NW Spain, in Galicia, on left bank of Miño R. and 270 mi. NW of Madrid, 50 mi. SE of La Coruña; 43°1'N 7°33'W. Agr. trade center on fertile plateau producing livestock (especially cattle), cereals, potatoes, and wine. Meat processing, tanning, flour milling; mfg. of glass, dairy products, chocolate. Episcopal see and an anc. ⊙ Galicia. Has Roman walls and towers (3d cent. A.D.), a 12th-cent. bridge across the Miño, a 14th-cent. church, and a Gothic cathedral (12th cent., with later additions). Built on site of sacred grove; flourished under Romans and Suevi (6th cent.); fell to Moors (713), but was soon reconquered (755) by Christian king of Asturias.

Lugoj (lo͞o'gôzh), Hung. *Lugos* (lo͞o'gôsh), city (1948 pop. 26,707), Timisoara prov., W Rumania, in Banat, on Timis R. and 230 mi. WNW of Bucharest, 33 mi. ESE of Timisoara; rail hub and commercial center (trade in grain, fruit, livestock). Produces textiles (notably silk), leather goods, spraying equipment, bricks, tiles, paper; flour milling, distilling. Experimental sericulture station; extensive vineyards in vicinity. Has several old churches, a baroque 18th-cent. Minorite church, remains of old monastery, mus. with Roman mementoes. Originally Roman fortress, it was a royal city in 14th cent.; chartered 1428; occupied by Turks (1658–95). Was the political and cultural center of Rumanians in Banat throughout 19th cent. Orthodox and Uniate bishoprics.

Lugones (lo͞ogō'nĕs), outer NE suburb (pop. 761) of Oviedo, Oviedo prov., NW Spain; copper and tin processing; chemical works.

Lugos, Rumania: see LUGOJ.

Lugovaya Proleika or **Lugovaya Proleyka** (lo͞ogŭvī'ů prŭlyā'kŭ), village (1939 pop. over 500), central Stalingrad oblast, Russian SFSR, on low left bank of Volga R. and 50 mi. NNE of Stalingrad; wheat, fruit. Proleika, village (1926 pop. 3,227) is across river; limestone quarries.

Lugovoi or **Lugovoy** (lōōgŭvoi'), town (1948 pop. over 2,000), SW Dzhambul oblast, Kazakh SSR, on Turksib RR and 70 mi. E of Dzhambul, in irrigated agr. area (wheat); metalworks. Junction of branch line to Frunze and to Rybachye on the Issyk-Kul.

Lugugnana (lōōgōōnyä'nä), village (pop. 364), Venezia prov., Veneto, N Italy, 6 mi. SE of Portogruaro; beet-sugar refinery.

Lugus Island (lōō'gōōs), (□ 14.8; 1939 pop. 12,187), in Tapul Group, Sulu prov., Philippines, in Sulu Archipelago.

Luguvallum, England: see CARLISLE.

Luhacovice (lōō'hächô"vĭtsĕ), Czech *Luhačovice*, Ger. *Luhatschowitz*, town (pop. 3,633), E Moravia, Czechoslovakia, in W foothills of the White Carpathians, 9 mi. SSE of Gottwaldov. Rail terminus; popular health resort with alkaline muriatic springs and sulphur and peat baths, among extensive forests. Known since 16th cent.; bathing facilities established in 1790.

Luhaiya or **Luhayyah,** Yemen: see LOHEIA.

Luhe (lōō'ů), village (pop. 944), Upper Palatinate, NE Bavaria, Germany, on the Nab and 6 mi. S of Weiden; grain, livestock. Chartered before 1331.

Luhit River (lōōhĭt'), Tibetan *Zayul*, in Tibet prov., China, and NE Assam, India, rises in China in E syntax of the Himalayas, flows S across China border, and WSW past Sadiya, joining Dibang R. to form delta mouth at bend of the Brahmaputra; 191 mi. long.

Luho. 1 or **Liuho** (both: lyō'hŭ'), town (pop. 22,334), ⊙ Luho co. (pop. 390,961), N Kiangsu prov., China, 18 mi. NNE of Nanking, across Yangtze R.; rice, wheat, beans. **2** (lōō'hŭ') Town, ⊙ Luho co. (pop. 6,054), N Sikang prov., China, 125 mi. NW of Kangting and on highway; gold mining. Lamasery. Until 1914 called Changku, Tibetan *Drango*. Placed 1950 in Tibetan Autonomous Dist.

Lu Ho, river, China: see TO RIVER.

Lu-hsi, China: see LUSI.

Luhsien (lōō'shyĕn'), town (pop. 50,241), ⊙ Luhsien co. (pop. 989,155), SW Szechwan prov., China, on left bank of Yangtze R., at mouth of To R. and 50 mi. ENE of Ipin, in rice region; tung-oil trading center; sugar milling, match mfg. Produces hog bristles, wheat, sweet potatoes, sugar cane, kaoliang, rapeseed. Coal and iron mining, kaolin quarrying. Until 1913 called Luchow.

Lu-i, China: see LUYI.

Luichart, Loch (lŏkh lōōkh'ärt), lake (5 mi. long, 1 mi. wide, 164 ft. deep), S Ross and Cromarty, Scotland, 17 mi. W of Dingwall; fed and drained by Conon R.

Luichow, town, China: see HOIHONG.

Luichow Peninsula (lû'ējou'), Mandarin *Lei-chou*, SW Kwangtung prov., China, on S.China Sea, bet. Kwangchow Bay (E) and Gulf of Tonkin (W); 90 mi. long, 30–45 mi. wide. Separated from Hainan isl. (S) by Hainan Strait. Subtropical vegetation. Principal towns: Chankiang, Hoihong, Süwen.

Luigi di Savoia (lwē'jē dē sävô'yä), village (pop. 1,920), E Cyrenaica, Libya, on highway and 8 mi. S of Apollonia, on the plateau Gebel el Akhdar. Agr. settlement (cereals, olives, grapes) founded 1933 by the Italians.

Luigi Razza (räd'dzä), Arabic *Messa*, village (pop. 860), W Cyrenaica, Libya, on road and 15 mi. WSW of Cyrene, on the plateau Gebel el Akhdar; agr. settlement established here 1933 by the Italians. Near by are ruins (sepulchers) of anc. Messa. Formerly also Razza.

Luik, Belgium: see LIÉGE.

Luilaka River, Belgian Congo: see MOMBOYO RIVER.

Luing (lōō'ĭng), island (pop. 312) of the Inner Hebrides, Argyll, Scotland, just S of Seil isl., 12 mi. SW of Oban; 6 mi. long, 2 mi. wide; rises to 306 ft. Just off W coast is islet with lighthouse (56°12'N 5°40'W).

Luino (lwē'nô), town (pop. 5,381), Varese prov., Lombardy, N Italy, port on E shore of Lago Maggiore, 13 mi. NNW of Varese. Resort; foundries, silk, rayon, and cotton mills, mfg. of sewing machines, shoes, pharmaceuticals. Fish hatchery. Formerly Luvino.

Luisa (lwēzä'), village, Kasai prov., S Belgian Congo, on Lulua R. and 150 mi. SW of Kabinda, near Angola border; cotton ginning, cottonseed-oil milling. Also called Kamai (kämī').

Luisant (lwēzä'), SW suburb (pop. 1,602) of Chartres, Eure-et-Loir dept., NW central France; sawmilling, dairying.

Luis Calvo, Bolivia: see VACA GUZMÁN.

Luís Correia (lwēs' kôrā'ů), city (pop. 916), northernmost Piauí, Brazil, on the Atlantic, 9 mi. ENE of Parnaíba; state's only seaport at N terminus of railroad to Parnaíba and Piripiri; limited modern dock facilities; hydroplane landing. Saltworks. Until 1939, called Amarração. Formerly also spelled Luiz Correia.

Luís Domingues (dōōmĕng'gĭs), town (pop. 692), N Maranhão, Brazil, near the Atlantic and near Pará border, 130 mi. NW of São Luís, in gold-mining area.

Luís Gomes (gō'mĭs), city (pop. 690), SW Rio Grande do Norte, NE Brazil, 35 mi. NNE of Cajazeiras (Paraíba); cotton, manioc, hides. Formerly spelled Luiz Gomes.

Luishia (lwēsh'yä), village, Katanga prov., SE Belgian Congo, on railroad and 20 mi. SE of Jadotville; copper and cobalt mining center. Also copper and cobalt mines at Kamvali (kämvä'lē), 10 mi. NNE; copper mines at Kansongwe (känsông'gwā), 5 mi. NNW, and Shandwe (shän'dwā), 6 mi. ENE.

Luisiana (lwēsyä'nä), town (1939 pop. 2,318; 1948 municipality pop. 6,883), Laguna prov., S Luzon, Philippines, 15 mi. NE of San Pablo; agr. center (rice, coconuts, sugar cane).

Luisiana, La (lä), town (pop. 2,673), Seville prov., SW Spain, on railroad and 40 mi. ENE of Seville; olives, cereals, livestock (hogs, goats, sheep); vegetable-oil extracting.

Luis Moya (lwēs moi'ä), town (pop. 1,267), Zacatecas, N central Mexico, 30 mi. SE of Zacatecas; maguey, grain, beans, stock. Formerly San Francisco de los Adame.

Luiswishi (lwēswē'shē), village, Katanga prov., SE Belgian Congo, on railroad and 10 mi. N of Elisabethville; copper and cobalt mining.

Luitpold Coast (lōō'ĭtpōld, lōō'ĭtpôlt), Antarctica, forms part of Coats Land, on Weddell Sea; extends bet. 29° and 37°W. Discovered 1912 by Wilhelm Filchner, Ger. explorer.

Luiz: for Brazilian names beginning thus, see under LUÍS.

Luján (lōōhän'). **1** City (pop. 19,001), ⊙ Luján dist. (□ 300; pop. 40,197), NE Buenos Aires prov., Argentina, on Luján R. and 40 mi. W of Buenos Aires; rail junction and agr. center (grain, livestock). Mfg. of ceramics, brushes, soap; food processing, dairying. A noted pilgrimage city, it has Gothic basilica of Our Lady of Luján, and mus. of colonial history, several libraries and higher schools (including agr. col.). Founded 1630. **2** or **Luján de Cuyo** (dā kōō'yō), town (pop. estimate 2,000), ⊙ Luján dept. (□ 1,965; 1947 census 13,242), N Mendoza prov., Argentina, on Mendoza R. (irrigation) and 11 mi. S of Mendoza; rail junction; agr. and mfg. center. Oil refineries, sawmills, vegetable-oil factories, wineries. Agr. products: wine, alfalfa, fruit, potatoes, grain. Irrigation dam and hydroelectric plant near by. **3** Town (pop. estimate 500), N San Luis prov., Argentina, at foot of Sierra de San Luis, on railroad, and 70 mi. NNE of San Luis; agr. center (grain, goats, cattle).

Luján de Cuyo, Argentina: see LUJÁN, Mendoza prov.

Luján River, NE Buenos Aires prov., Argentina, rises near Suipacha 15 mi. SW of Mercedes, flows c.75 mi. ENE, past Mercedes and Luján, to the Río de la Plata at Paraná delta at Tigre, 16 mi. NNW of Buenos Aires; navigable for small steamers.

Lujenda River, Mozambique: see LUGENDA RIVER.

Lujeni, Ukrainian SSR: see LUZHENY.

Lukachek (lōōkä'chĭk), town (1942 pop. over 500), E Amur oblast, Russian SFSR, near Selemdzha R., 10 mi. WNW of Ekimchan; gold mines. Developed during Second World War.

Lukala (lōōkä'lä), village, Leopoldville prov., W Belgian Congo, on railroad and 100 mi. ENE of Boma; cementworks.

Lukang (lōō'gäng') or **Lu-chiang** (–jyäng'), Jap. *Rokko* (rōk'kō), town (1935 pop. 24,861), W central Formosa, minor port on W coast, 7 mi. WSW of Changhwa; saltworks; incense mfg., sugar refining, fish processing. Airfield. Formerly one of leading ports of Formosa.

Lukaragata (lōōkärägä'tä), village, W Ruanda-Urundi, in Ruanda, 28 mi. WNW of Kigali; tin mining.

Lukashevka (lōōkŭshĕf'kŭ), village (1939 pop. over 500), W central Kursk oblast, Russian SFSR, 25 mi. W of Kursk; distilling.

Lukchun (lōōk'chōōn'), village, E central Sinkiang prov., China, in the TURFAN depression, 30 mi. ESE of Turfan; 42°44'N 89°42'E. The depression is sometimes called Lukchun.

Luke, town (pop. 820), Allegany co., W Md., on North Branch of the Potomac at mouth of Savage R., and 20 mi. SW of Cumberland; large pulp and paper mill.

Lukenie River, Belgian Congo: see FIMI RIVER.

Lukfung (lōōk'fōōng'), Mandarin *Lufeng* (lōō'fŭng'), town, ⊙ Lukfung co. (pop. 356,852), SE Kwangtung prov., China, on coast, 70 mi. WSW of Swatow; cotton, rice, wheat, sugar cane. Tin mines near by.

Lukh (lōōkh), village (1926 pop. 1,132), E central Ivanovo oblast, Russian SFSR, on Lukh R. (affluent of Klyazma R.) and 19 mi. SE of Vichuga; flax, wheat.

Lukhovitsy (lōō'khŭvētsē), town (1926 pop. 2,818), SE Moscow oblast, Russian SFSR, 15 mi. SE of Kolomna; rail junction; dairying; clay quarries.

Luki or **Lu-ch'i** (both: lōō'chē'). **1** Town, ⊙ Luki co. (pop. 113,100), NW Hunan prov., China, on Yüan R. and 60 mi. NE of Chihkiang; river crossing; rice, wheat, beans, cotton. Gold, iron, copper, and mercury found near by. **2** Town, Kiangsi prov., China: see TZEKI.

Lukiang or **Lu-chiang** (both: lōō'jyäng'), town, ⊙ Lukiang co. (pop. 512,910), N Anhwei prov., China, 45 mi. S of Hofei, SW of Chao L.; rice, cotton, wheat.

Lukikow or **Lu-ch'i-k'ou** (both: lōō'chē'kō'), village, SE Hupeh prov., China, on Yangtze R. and 55 mi. SW of Hankow; former treaty port of call.

Lukmanier Pass (lōōkmä'nĭr) (6,296 ft.), in the Lepontine Alps, SE central Switzerland, on border of Grisons and Ticino cantons, 12 mi. S of Disentis.

Luknovo (lōōknô'vů), town (1947 pop. over 500), NE Vladimir oblast, Russian SFSR, 7 mi. SSW of Vyazniki; linen milling.

Lukolela (lōōkōlē'lä), village, Equator Prov., W Belgian Congo, on left bank of Congo R. opposite Loukolela and 115 mi. SSW of Coquilhatville; trading and agr. center; steamboat landing; cacao and rubber plantations, hardwood lumbering. Has R.C. and Baptist missions. One of 1st trading posts in Central Africa, it was established 1883 by Stanley.

Lukonzolwa (lōōkōnzōl'wä), village, Katanga prov., SE Belgian Congo, on W bank of L. Mweru, and 210 mi. NNE of Elisabethville; cattle raising. R.C. mission.

Lukov, Poland: see LUKOW.

Lukov (lōō'kůf), town (1931 pop. 2,980), W central Volyn oblast, Ukrainian SSR, 16 mi. W of Kovel; chalk- and kaolin-quarrying center; tanning, distilling, flour milling, brick mfg. Has old monastery. Until 1946, Matseyevo, Pol. *Maciejów*.

Lukovit (lōō'kôvĕt), city (pop. 7,755), Pleven dist., N Bulgaria, on Panega R. (hydroelectric station) and 27 mi. SW of Pleven; agr. center; flour milling, tanning, dairying. Karstlike rock formations and grottoes near by.

Lukovnikovo (lōōkôv'nyĭkůvů), village (1926 pop. 651), SW Kalinin oblast, Russian SFSR, 28 mi. N of Rzhev; flax processings.

Lukow (wōō'kōōf), Pol. *Łuków*, Rus. *Lukov* (lōō'kůf), town (pop. 8,513), Lublin prov., E Poland, on Krzna R. and 17 mi. S of Siedlce; rail junction; mfg. of soap, vinegar; weaving, flour and oil milling, brewing, distilling; brickworks. Before Second World War, pop. over 50% Jewish.

Lukowkiao, China: see WANPING.

Lukoyanov (lōōkŭyä'nůf), city (1926 pop. 6,459), SE Gorki oblast, Russian SFSR, 90 mi. SSE of Gorki; agr. center (hemp, potatoes, wheat); metalworks. Chartered 1779.

Lukuga River (lōōkōō'gä), E Belgian Congo, issues from W shore of L. Tanganyika at Albertville, flows c.200 mi. W to Lualaba R. 25 mi. N of Kabalo. There are low-grade coal deposits along its tributaries, N of Albertville and at Greinerville. It is L. Tanganyika's only outlet.

Lukula (lōōkōō'lä), village, Leopoldville prov., W Belgian Congo, on railroad and 40 mi. NNW of Boma; sawmilling and agr. center; palm-oil milling, rubber, palm, and cacao plantations.

Lukuledi River (lōōkōōlĕ'dē), SE Tanganyika, rises WNW of Masasi, flows 100 mi. ENE to Indian Ocean at Lindi. Below Mkwaya course is to be made navigable for shipment of peanuts from Nachingwa to Lindi.

Lukuni (lōōkōō'nē), village, Katanga prov., SE Belgian Congo, on railroad and 12 mi. NNW of Elisabethville; copper mining.

Lukunor (lōō'kōōnôr), atoll (□ 1; pop. 788), Nomoi Isls., Truk dist., E Caroline Isls., W Pacific, c.6 mi. NE of Satawan; 5°31'N 153°46'E; 7 mi. long, 4 mi. wide; 18 low islets on triangular reef, largest isl. being Lukunor (c.2 mi. long).

Lula (lōō'lä), village, Eastern Prov., E Belgian Congo, on railroad and 3 mi. SSE of Stanleyville; has agr. research station with rubber and coffee plantations.

Lula (lōō'lů). **1** Town (pop. 378), Hall co., NE Ga., 10 mi. NE of Gainesville, near source of Oconee R. **2** Town (pop. 488), Coahoma co., NW Miss., near Mississippi R., 18 mi. NNE of Clarksdale; lumber milling. Moon L. (c.4 mi. long; resort) is near by.

Lulea (lü'lůō"), Swedish *Luleå*, industrial and shipping city (1950 pop. 22,514), ⊙ Norrbotten co., N Sweden, on NW coast of the Gulf of Bothnia at mouth of Lule R., 450 mi. NNE of Stockholm; 65°35'N 22°10'E. Seaport (ice-bound in winter), shipping Lapland iron (from Kiruna, Gallivare, and Malmberget), timber, tar, reindeer hides. Iron smelting and pulp milling are chief industries. Large railroad shops. Agr. station. Seat of Lutheran bishop. Has cathedral (1888–93), old town hall, biological mus. Chartered 1621, when it was located 4 mi. NW of present site, to which it was moved, 1648–49.

Luleburgaz (lülĕ'bōōrgäz"), Turkish *Lüleburgaz*, anc. *Bergulae*, town (1950 pop. 12,830), Kirklareli prov., Turkey in Europe, 23 mi. SSW of Kirklareli; agr. trade center (grain, sugar beets, beans, potatoes). Also spelled Lule Burgas.

Lulenga, Belgian Congo: see RUTSHURU.

Lule River, Swedish *Luleälv* (lü'lůĕlv'), Lapland, N Sweden, rises in N Norway near Swedish border SW of Narvik, flows 280 mi. SE, over the falls STORA SJOFALLET, through Stora Lule L., then over high falls at PORJUS and HARSPRANGET (major power stations), past Boden, to Gulf of Bothnia at Lulea. Logging route. Receives Lilla Lule R., Swedish *Lilla Luleälv* (lĭ'lä), 150 mi. long.

Lules (lōō lĕs), town (pop. estimate 2,000), central Tucumán prov., Argentina, on Lules R. and 13 mi.

SW of Tucumán; rail terminus; lumbering and agr. center (sugar cane, tomatoes, corn, rice, cotton, livestock); sugar refinery. Experimental farm. Hydroelectric station near by.

Lules River, W central Tucumán prov., Argentina, rises in N outliers of Cumbre de Potrerillo, flows 45 mi. ESE, past Lules, to the Salí R. 4 mi. NE of Bella Vista. Irrigates sugar-cane area; hydroelectric stations along its course.

Luliang (lo͞o'lyäng'), town (pop. 9,213), ⊙ Luliang co. (pop. 134,425), E Yunnan prov., China, 60 mi. E of Kunming; alt. 6,102 ft.; road junction; pears, rice, wheat, millet, beans. Coal mines near by.

Luliang Mountains, Chinese *Luliang Shan* (lo͞o'-lyäng' shän'), W Shansi prov., China, form divide bet. Fen and Yellow rivers; rise to c.9,000 ft. 35 mi. NE of Lishih.

Luling, China: see KIAN.

Luling (lo͞o'lĭng). **1** Village (1940 pop. 1,336), St. Charles parish, SE La., on W bank (levee) of the Mississippi and 16 mi. W of New Orleans; machine-shop products, lumber. Ferry to Destrehan. **2** City (pop. 4,297), Caldwell co., S central Texas, on San Marcos R. and c.40 mi. S of Austin; oil-field supply and shipping center; also dairy products processing, cotton ginning. Here is experimental Luling Foundation Farm. Founded 1874; long a cow town, it boomed after oil discovery, 1922.

Lulonga (lo͞olông'gä), village, Equator Prov., NW Belgian Congo, on left bank of Congo R. at mouth of Lulonga R. and 45 mi. N of Coquilhatville; steamboat landing and mission center (R.C. and Protestant), palm-oil milling, copal treating.

Lulonga River, W Belgian Congo, formed by union of the Lopori and the Maringa at Basankusu, flows c.130 mi. W and SW to Congo R. at Lulonga. Navigable for steamboats along entire course.

Luluabourg (lo͞olwäbo͝or'), town (1948 pop. 10,861), Kasai prov., S Belgian Congo, on left bank of Lulua R., on railroad and 70 mi. SE of Luebo; commercial and communications center, and one of main centers of Baluba tribes. Mfg. of pharmaceuticals, cotton and food processing. Airport. Has R.C. mission with schools for Europeans (including junior college), business school for natives. Large military camp for African troops. Luluabourg is also known as Kananga (känäng'gä). Lulua-gare, c.5 mi. NE, is its rail station. Luluabourg-Saint-Joseph, c.10 mi. S is seat of vicar apostolic of Upper Kasai, with R.C. missions and schools, hosp. for Europeans. A mutiny of Congo Free State native troops took place in Luluabourg in 1895.

Lulua River (lo͞ol'wä), right tributary of the Kasai, S Belgian Congo, rises at Angola border 25 mi. S of Malonga, flows 550 mi. in wide curves N and NW, past Sandoa, Luisa, Luluabourg, and Luebo, to Kasai R. 28 mi. N of Charlesville. Navigable for steamers for c.35 mi. in lower course (below Luebo).

Lulung (lo͞o'lo͝ong'), town, ⊙ Lulung co. (pop. 162,431), NE Hopeh prov., China, 40 mi. NE of Tangshan and on Lwan R.; pears, grain; iron mining. Until 1913 called Yungping.

Lulworth Cove, England: see WEST LULWORTH.

Lumaco (lo͞omä''kō), town (pop. 1,063), Malleco prov., S central Chile, on railroad and 28 mi. SSW of Angol; agr. (cereals, potatoes, fruit, cattle); lumbering, flour milling.

Lumajang, Lumadjang, or **Loemadjang** (all: lo͞omä-jäng'), town (pop. 18,383), E Java, Indonesia, near Indian Ocean, 70 mi. SE of Surabaya; trade center for agr. area (sugar, tobacco, coffee, rubber, tea, cinchona bark). Near by are sugar mills.

Lumaku, Mount (lo͞omä'ko͞o) (8,200 ft.), Br. North Borneo, near Sarawak border, 25 mi. S of Beaufort.

Lumarao (lo͞omärä'ō,–rou'), town (1939 pop. 1,332), Zamboanga prov., W Mindanao, Philippines, 65 mi. NE of Zamboanga across Sibuguey Bay; sawmill.

Lumban (lo͞ombän'), town (1939 pop. 4,996; 1948 municipality pop. 7,516), Laguna prov., S Luzon, Philippines, near Laguna de Bay, 18 mi. NNE of San Pablo; agr. center (rice, coconuts, sugar).

Lumber Bridge, town (pop. 154), Robeson co., S N.C., 16 mi. SW of Fayetteville.

Lumber City. 1 Town (pop. 1,232), Telfair co., S central Ga., 22 mi. WNW of Baxley, near junction of Ocmulgee and Little Ocmulgee rivers; shipping point for hardwood, pine lumber; naval-stores mfg. Inc. 1889. **2** Borough (pop. 262), Clearfield co., W central Pa., 4 mi. SW of Curwensville.

Lumberport, town (pop. 1,198), Harrison co., N W.Va., on West Fork (headstream of the Monongahela) and 6 mi. N of Clarksburg, in coal, lumber, oil, and farm region. Inc. 1901.

Lumber River, in N.C. and S.C., rises near Biscoe in central N.C., flows SE, past Lumberton, and SSW into S.C., to Little Pee Dee R. N of Nichols; c.125 mi. long.

Lumberton. 1 City (pop. 1,803), Lamar co., SE Miss., 24 mi. SSW of Hattiesburg, in agr. and pine-timber area; pecans, wood products. Large pecan nursery. Settled in 1880s. **2** Town (pop. 9,186), ⊙ Robeson co., S N.C., on Lumber R. and 31 mi. S of Fayetteville; tobacco-processing and -market center; textile and lumber mills. Inc. 1787.

Lumbier (lo͞ombyĕr'), town (pop. 1,696), Navarre prov., N Spain, 20 mi. SE of Pamplona; flour milling, mfg. of sandals and brandy; wine, sheep.

Lumbo (lo͞om'bō), town, Niassa prov., NE Mozambique, on Mozambique Channel of Indian Ocean opposite Mozambique isl. (2 mi. E); 15°1'S 40°40'E. Ocean terminus of railroad to Nampula (95 mi. W). Has Mozambique city's airport.

Lumbrales (lo͞ombrä'lĕs), town (pop. 3,396), Salamanca prov., W Spain, 26 mi. NNW of Ciudad Rodrigo; agr. trade center (cereals, vegetables, wine, olive oil); flour milling; stock raising. Lead mines near by.

Lumbrera, Sierra (syĕ'rä lo͞ombrā'rä), subandean mountain range in central Salta prov., Argentina, E of Lumbreras; extends c.40 mi. ENE-WSW; rises to c.3,500 ft.

Lumbreras (–räs), village (pop. estimate 500), S central Salta prov., Argentina, at W foot of Sierra Lumbrera, on Pasaje or Juramento R., on railroad and 45 mi. SE of Salta; lumbering and stock-raising center; sawmills. Oil wells near by.

Lumbreras, village (pop. 2,780), Murcia prov., SE Spain, 10 mi. SW of Lorca; almonds and other fruit, cereals, wine. Its rail station is 7 mi. SSE.

Lumbres (lũ'brù), town (pop. 2,429), Pas-de-Calais dept., N France, on the Aa and 7 mi. SW of Saint-Omer; paper milling, Portland cement mfg., brewing.

Lumbwa (lo͞om'bwä), town, Nyanza prov., W Kenya, on railroad and 20 mi. WSW of Londiani; alt. 6,339 ft.; dairy plant; corn, coffee, wheat. Junction for road to Kericho and Sotik tea-growing areas. One of Kenya's 1st non-native settlements.

Lumby, village (pop. estimate 750), S B.C., 14 mi. E of Vernon; fruit, vegetables.

Lumding (lo͞om'dĭng), town (pop. 3,864), Nowgong dist., central Assam, India, 50 mi. SSE of Nowgong; rail junction; rice, jute, rape and mustard, tea.

Lumezzane (lo͞omĕtsä'nĕ), commune (pop. 8,363), Brescia prov., Lombardy, N Italy, 8 mi. N of Brescia. Chief towns: San Sebastiano (pop. 1,652; commune seat), Sant'Apollonio (pop. 2,551), Pieve (pop. 412). Numerous foundries and factories (firearms, cutlery).

Lumière, Cape (lo͞omyâr'), in Northumberland Strait, E N.B., 40 mi. N of Moncton; 46°40'N 64°43'W.

Lummen (lû'mùn), village (pop. 5,208), Limburg prov., NE Belgium, 8 mi. WNW of Hasselt; agr., cattle raising.

Lumparland (lŭm'pärländ), fishing village (commune pop. 468), Aland co., SW Finland, on Lumparland isl. (□ 13.5), one of Aland group, 11 mi. E of Mariehamn.

Lumphanan (lŭmfă'nùn), agr. village and parish (pop. 830), S Aberdeen, Scotland, 7 mi. S of Alford. Just NW is Macbeth's Cairn, reputed to mark site where Macbeth was killed by Macduff.

Lumpiaque (lo͞ompyä'kä), town (pop. 1,976), Saragossa prov., NE Spain, near Jalón R., 27 mi. W of Saragossa; ships sugar beets and wine.

Lumpkin, county (□ 292; pop. 6,574), N Ga., ⊙ Dahlonega. Blue Ridge area drained by Chestatee and Etowah rivers. Farming (cotton, corn, hay, potatoes), lumbering, gold mining. Chattahoochee Natl. Forest occupies N half of co. Formed 1832.

Lumpkin, city (pop. 1,209), ⊙ Stewart co., SW Ga., 30 mi. SSE of Columbus, in badly-eroded farm area; sawmilling. Near by are Providence Caverns. Inc. 1831.

Lumpsey, England: see SKELTON AND BROTTON.

Lumsden (lŭmz'dùn), town (pop. 474), S Sask., on Qu'Appelle R. and 17 mi. NW of Regina; grain elevators, stock.

Lumsden, town (pop. 481), S S.Isl., New Zealand, 50 mi. N of Invercargill and on New R.; rail junction; sheep raising, dairying.

Lumut (lo͞omo͞ot'), town (pop. 2,525), W Perak, Malaya, port on Dindings R. off Strait of Malacca, 45 mi. SSW of Taiping; chief town of the Dindings; coastwise trade in rubber; fisheries.

Luna (lo͞o'nä), ancient Etruscan town, N Italy, on the Macra (Magra), at its mouth on Gulf of Genoa, and 4 mi. SE of Sarzana. Made a Roman colony 177 B.C. Famed for its wine and marble (from Carrara). Destroyed by Saracens 1016. Scanty ruins include amphitheater, tower, Christian church. Modern Ital. name, Luni.

Luna, town (1939 pop. 2,436; 1948 municipality pop. 17,258), La Union prov., N central Luzon, Philippines, on W coast, 16 mi. NNE of San Fernando; rice-growing center.

Luna, town (pop. 1,834), Saragossa prov., N Spain, 28 mi. W of Huesca; cereals, livestock.

Luna, county (□ 2,957; pop. 8,753), SW N.Mex.; ⊙ Deming. Livestock and grain area bordering on Mexico. Tres Hermanas and Florida Mts. in SE, part of Cooks Range in N. Formed 1901.

Luna, Isla de la, Bolivia: see COATI ISLAND.

Luna, Laguna de (lägo͞o'nä dā), lake (□ 75) in Esteros del Iberá (swamps), N Corrientes prov., Argentina, 3 mi. N of L. Iberá; 12 mi. long.

Lunacharskoye, Uzbek SSR: see ORDZHONIKIDZE, Tashkent oblast.

Lunahuaná (lo͞onäwänä'), town (pop. 757), Lima dept., W central Peru, in irrigated Cañete R. valley, on road, and 19 mi. ENE of Cañete; major viticultural center; fruit; distilling.

Luna Island, N.Y.: see NIAGARA FALLS, city.

Lunan (lo͞o'nän'), town (pop. 7,298), ⊙ Lunan co. (pop. 91,860), E Yunnan prov., China, 40 mi. ESE of Kunming; alt. 5,433 ft.; rice, wheat, millet, cabbage. Coal mines near by.

Lunan Water (lo͞o'nùn), river, Angus, Scotland, rises SE of Forfar, flows 14 mi. E, past Friockheim and Inverkeilor, to North Sea 4 mi. SSW of Montrose.

Lunas (lünä'), village (pop. 636), Hérault dept., S France, near Orb R., 7 mi. WSW of Lodève; sheep, cheese.

Lunas (lo͞o''näs'), village (pop. 1,274), S Kedah, Malaya, 13 mi. E of George Town, on Penang line; rubber plantations.

Lunavada (lo͞onùvä'dù), village, Panch Mahals dist., N Bombay, India, 25 mi. N of Godhra; rail spur terminus; trades in corn, rice, millet, timber; match mfg., rice husking; leather goods. Was ⊙ former princely state of Lunavada (□ 419; pop. 105,318) in Gujarat States, Bombay; state inc. 1949 into Panch Mahals dist. Sometimes spelled Lunawada.

Lunawa Ceylon: see MORATUWA.

Lunca-Corbului (lo͞ong'kä-kôr'bo͞olo͞o), village (pop. 1,036), Arges prov., S central Rumania, 11 mi. SSW of Pitesti.

Luncarty (lŭng'kùrtē), village in Redgorton parish, SE Perthshire, Scotland, on the Tay and 4 mi. N of Perth; textile bleaching; site of salmon hatchery.

Lund (lŭnd). **1** City (1950 pop. 33,954), Malmohus co., S Sweden, 10 mi. NE of Malmo; 55°42'N 13°12'E; cultural center with univ., founded (1666) by Charles XI; see of Lutheran bishop. Rail junction; industries include cotton, woolen, and paper mills, sugar refineries, iron, brick, machinery, furniture works; publishing. Has cathedral, begun 1080; folk, historical, and zoological mus., observatory, and 12th-cent. monastery church. First mentioned in 10th-cent. sagas as Lunda, Lund was ⊙ Denmark in early Middle Ages. Became (1060) seat of bishop and (1103) of archbishop. Reduced (1536) to bishopric, city's importance declined; it also suffered heavily in 16th- and 17th-cent. wars bet. Sweden and Denmark. Passed to Sweden in 1658. Tegnér lived here (1813–26) and taught at univ. **2** Village (pop. 1,095), Gavleborg co., E Sweden, on small lake, 5 mi. WSW of Hudiksvall; linen milling.

Lunda (lo͞on'dä), district (□ c.64,430; pop. 243,400), Malange prov., NE Angola; ⊙ Vila Henrique de Carvalho. Bounded N and E by Belgian Congo. Drained by Kasai R. (which forms E border) and its left tributaries (especially the Chicapa), along which diamonds are washed.

Lundale, village (pop. 1,115, with adjoining Craneco), Logan co., SW W.Va., 12 mi. ESE of Logan.

Lundazi (lo͞ondä'zē), town (pop. 264), Eastern Prov., E Northern Rhodesia, near Nyasaland border, on road 100 mi. NNE of Fort Jameson; tobacco, corn.

Lunde (lo͞on'dù), village and canton (pop. 3,031), Telemark co., S Norway, on railroad and 19 mi. WNW of Skien; sawmill, brickworks.

Lunde (lŭn'dù), village (pop. 1,373), Vasternorrland co., NE Sweden, on Angerman R. estuary, 16 mi. N of Harnosand; shipbuilding, woodworking. Inc. Stromnas (strûm'nĕs''), Swedish *Strömnäs*, village.

Lunden (lo͝on'dùn), village (pop. 3,295), in Schleswig-Holstein, NW Germany, near the Eider, 10 mi. NNW of Heide, in the N Dithmarschen; mfg. of tools. Cattle.

Lundenburg, Czechoslovakia: see BRECLAV.

Lunderskov (lo͝o'nùrskou), town (pop. 1,069), Ribe amt, E central Jutland, Denmark, 33 mi. E of Esbjerg; rail junction; soap, furniture.

Lundevatn, Norway: see LUND LAKE.

Lundi River (lo͞on'dē), SE Southern Rhodesia, rises in high veld just S of Gwelo flows 260 mi. SE to Sabi R. at Mozambique border.

Lund Lake (lo͞ond), Nor. *Lundevatn* (□ 10), Rogaland co., SW Norway, on Sira R., 4 mi. NW of Flekkefjord; 1,017 ft. deep.

Lundsbrunn (lùnts'brŭn''), village (pop. 452), Skaraborg co., SW Sweden, 6 mi. N of Skara; health resort, with mineral springs.

Lundu (lo͞on'do͞o), town (pop. 768), SW Sarawak, W Borneo, 35 mi. W of Kuching; rice growing, stock raising, fishing.

Lundy Island (lŭn'dē) (1,047 acres; pop. 21), off N Devon coast, England, at entrance to Bristol Channel, 12 mi. NNW of Hartland Point; 51°12'N 4°40'W. Rocky isl. (3 mi. long, 1 mi. wide) with granite quarries, medieval castle ruins, 2 lighthouses, dangerous reefs. Constable Rock rises 800 ft. in extreme N. Stronghold of pirates and smugglers until 17th cent. Site of naval signal station.

Lundy's Lane, locality, S Ont., just W of Niagara Falls; scene of action (July 25, 1814) bet. Americans under Winfield Scott and British forces. Both sides suffered heavy losses.

Lüneburg (lü'nùbo͝ork), city (1950 pop. 58,269), in former Prussian prov. of Hanover, NW Germany, after 1945 in Lower Saxony, port on the Ilmenau (head of navigation) and 25 mi. SE of Hamburg; 53°16'N 10°25'E. Rail junction; large saltworks; foundries, enameling plants; mfg. of chemicals (sulphur processing; lime fertilizer, Burow's solution, artificial fiber, glue, soap, bone meal), plywood, garments, ceramics, candles, knäckebröd.

Woodworking. Resort with salt and mud baths. Town is predominantly late-Gothic in character; has several noted churches (St. John's, St. Michael's, St. Nicolai's), mammoth 12th–18th-cent. town hall. Numerous gabled dwellings in typical N German architectural style. Developed in 10th cent. around abundant salt springs. Was long ⊙ dukes of Brunswick-Lüneburg. Chartered 1247. Was powerful member of Hanseatic League; decline began in 17th cent. Progressed industrially after 1900; also developed as spa and tourist center. Captured April, 1945, in Anglo-American drive toward the Elbe.

Lüneburger Heide (lü'nubōōr"gur hī'dù), large heath, NW Germany, SW of Lüneburg. Sandy region; sheep raising; buckwheat fields (apiculture).

Lunel (lünĕl'), town (pop. 7,074), Hérault dept., S France, near Vidourle R., 14 mi. ENE of Montpellier; winegrowing and shipping center; distilling, fruit preserving, fertilizer mfg.

Lünen (lü'nùn), city (1950 pop. 60,931), in former Prussian prov. of Westphalia, W Germany, after 1945 in North Rhine-Westphalia, in the Ruhr, port on Lippe Lateral Canal, adjoining (S) Dortmund; rail junction; coal-mining center; foundries, coal-powered aluminum plants, glassworks; copper refining. Has 12th-cent. castle, rebuilt in 18th cent.

Lunenburg (lōō'nùnbûrg), county (□ 1,169; pop. 32,942), SW N.S., on the Atlantic; ⊙ Lunenburg.

Lunenburg, town (pop. 2,856), ⊙ Lunenburg co., SW N.S., on Lunenburg Bay of the Atlantic, 40 mi. WSW of Halifax; fishing and fish-processing center; also shipyards, brass foundries, marine-engine works. Settled 1753 by Germans.

Lunenburg, county (□ 443; pop. 14,116), S Va.; ⊙ Lunenburg. Rolling agr. region; bounded S by Meherrin R., N by Nottoway R. Tobacco; also grain, cotton, cattle. Lumbering (pine, oak), lumber milling; industries at Victoria. Formed 1746.

Lunenburg. 1 Agr. town (pop. 3,906), Worcester co., N Mass., just E of Fitchburg. Settled 1721, inc. 1728. **2** Town (pop. 1,299), Essex co., NE Vt., on Connecticut R. and 16 mi. E of St. Johnsbury, in agr. and lumbering region. Includes paper-milling village of Gilman. Chartered 1763. **3** Village, ⊙ Lunenburg co., S Va., 3 mi. SW of Victoria, 60 mi. WSW of Petersburg.

Luneray (lünrā'), village (pop. 1,437), Seine-Inférieure dept., N France, 10 mi. SW of Dieppe; jute and linen weaving.

Lune River (lōōn), Westmorland and Lancashire, England, rises near Ravenstonedale, flows 45 mi. S and SW, past Kirkby Lonsdale, Tunstall, and Lancaster, to Morecambe Bay 6 mi. SW of Lancaster. Navigable below Lancaster.

Lunéville (lünāvēl'), town (pop. 19,065), Meurthe-et-Moselle dept., NE France, on the Meurthe at mouth of Vezouze R. and 16 mi. ESE of Nancy; known for its faïence. Mfg. (railroad rolling stock, toys, hosiery), cotton mills, embroidering, fruit preserving; alcohol, grain, and tobacco trade. Horticulture and truck-gardening in suburbs. Its 18th-cent. palace, residence of Stanislaus I, damaged in Second World War. Treaty of Lunéville (1801) signed here.

Lung, province, China: see KANSU.

Lung, river, China: see LUNG RIVER.

Lunga (lŭng'gù), island (pop. 5) of the Inner, Hebrides, Argyll, Scotland, just N of Scarba, from which it is separated by strait noted for violent current; 2½ mi. long, up to 1 mi. wide; rises to 323 ft.

Lunga, Isola, Yugoslavia: see DUGI OTOK.

Lungan (lōōng'än'). **1** Town, ⊙ Lungan co. (pop. 115,189), SW Kwangsi prov., China, 50 mi. WNW of Nanning and on right bank of Yü R.; matmaking; rice, beans, peanuts. **2** Town, Szechwan prov., China: see PINGWU.

Lunga Point, Solomon Isls.: see GUADALCANAL.

Lungara (lōōng-gä'rä), NW prong of Ceraunian Mts. of S Albania, slopes c.30 mi. from Mt. Çikë N to the lower Vijosë R.

Lungau (lōōng'ou), valley of upper Mur R., Salzburg, W central Austria, extending c.15 mi. W from Tamsweg; cattle, rye, oats.

Lungavilla (lōōng-gävēl'lä), village (pop. 1,320), Pavia prov., Lombardy, N Italy, 11 mi. SSW of Pavia; mfg. (fertilizer, insulators).

Lungchang or **Lung-ch'ang** (lōōng'chäng'), town (pop. 46,386), ⊙ Lungchang co. (pop. 329,628), SW Szechwan prov., China, on railroad to Chengtu and 80 mi. W of Chungking, in rice region; ramie-producing center; exports hog bristles; sugar milling. Sweet potatoes, wheat, kaoliang, beans. Coal mines near by.

Lungchen (lōōng'jŭn'), town, ⊙ Lungchen co. (pop. 15,826), central Heilungkiang prov., Manchuria, 50 mi. NNE of Pehan.

Lung-ch'i, China: see LUNGKI.

Lung Chiang, China: see LUNG RIVER.

Lungching. 1 or **Lungchingtsun,** or **Lung-ching-t'sun** (lōōng'jĭng'tsōōn'), town (1938 pop. 34,579), SE Kirin prov., Manchuria, China, 10 mi. SW of Yenki and on railroad; commercial center of CHIENTAO. **2** or **Lung-ching,** town, Kwangsi prov., China: see LUNGTSIN.

Lungchow. 1 Town, Kwangsi prov., China: see LUNGTSIN. **2** Town, Shensi prov., China: see LUNGHSIEN.

Lungchüan or **Lung-ch'üan** (lōōng'chüän'). **1** Town (pop. 12,297), ⊙ Lungchüan co. (pop. 125,022), SW Chekiang prov., China, near Fukien line, 55 mi. WSW of Lishui, and on headstream of Wu R., in tea-growing dist.; sword mfg. **2** Town, Kiangsi prov., China: see SUICHWAN.

Lungchün (lōōng'chün'), Mandarin *Lung-ch'uan* (lōōng'chwän'), town (pop. 12,362), ⊙ Lungchün co. (pop. 314,940), E central Kwangtung prov., China, on East R. and 65 mi. WSW of Meihsien; agr. trade. The commercial center Laolung is 5 mi. NE on East R.

Lungchwan or **Lung-ch'uan** (both: lōōng'chwän'), district (pop. 8,541) of westernmost Yunnan prov., China, on Burma border, near Shweli R. Its administrative seats of SHANMULUNG (winter and spring) and CHANGFENGKAI (summer and fall) are also known as Lungchwan.

Lungchwan River, China: see SHWELI RIVER.

Lungern (lōōn'gûrn), village (pop. 1,828), Obwalden half-canton, central Switzerland, on L. of Lungern, 8 mi. SSW of Sarnen, near Brünig Pass; resort (alt. 2,477 ft.); woodworking. Lungernsee hydroelectric station is N.

Lungern, Lake of, Ger. *Lungernsee* (lōōn'gûrnzā"), Obwalden half-canton, central Switzerland; □ 1; supplies Lungernsee hydroelectric plant (N).

Lunghai Railroad (lōōng'hī'), chief E-W railroad of central China, extending from Yellow Sea port of Lienyün, W past Sinhai, Süchow (crossing of Tientsin-Pukow RR), Chengchow (crossing of Peking-Canton RR), Sian, Tienshui, and Lanchow. Begun in 1910. The Tienshui-Lanchow section was under construction in 1951.

Lunghingchang, China: see WUYÜAN, Suiyuan prov.

Lung-hsi, China: see LUNGSI.

Lunghsien (lōōng'shyĕn'), town (pop. 10,090), ⊙ Lunghsien co. (pop. 110,434), SW Shensi prov., China, 30 mi. NW of Paoki and on road to Lanchow; wheat, kaoliang. Until 1913, Lungchow.

Lung-hua, China: see LUNGHWA.

Lung-hui, China: see LUNGHWEI.

Lunghwa or **Lung-hua** (both: lōōng'hwä'). **1** Town, ⊙ Lunghwa co. (pop. 82,451), SW Jehol prov., Manchuria, 27 mi. NW of Chengteh; gold mining, stock raising. Formerly called Hwangkutun. **2** Town, S Kiangsu prov., China, 5 mi. SSW of Shanghai and on Shanghai-Hangchow RR; site of Shanghai's chief civil airport.

Lunghwasze, China: see MUCHWAN.

Lunghwei or **Lung-hui** (both: lōōng'hwā'), town, ⊙ Lunghwei co. (pop. 212,835), central Hunan prov., China, 30 mi. WNW of Shaoyang.

Lungi (lōōng'gē), town (pop. 2,071), Northern Prov., W Sierra Leone, on Atlantic Coast, 10 mi. N of Freetown (across Sierra Leone R. mouth); fisheries. Sierra Leone's chief airport, formerly at Waterloo, is now 3 mi. SSE of Lungi (reached by launch and road from Freetown).

Lunging Island, N.H.: see ISLES OF SHOALS.

Lungki or **Lung-ch'i** (both: lōōng'chē'), town (pop. 62,399), ⊙ Lungki co. (pop. 280,548), S Fukien prov., China, on left bank of Lung R. and 25 mi. WNW of Amoy; commercial center; silk milling, printing; produces rice, sugar cane. Long a leading city on the Fukien coast, it declined (19th cent.) and was supplanted by Amoy. Had Portuguese settlement (1547–49). Called Changchow until 1913.

Lungkiang or **Lung-chiang** (both: lōōng'jyäng'), former province (□ 26,055; 1940 pop. 3,093,500) of N central Manchukuo; ⊙ Tsitsihar (Lungkiang). Formed 1934 out of old Heilungkiang prov., it lost (1937–43) E section to Pehan prov.; and after Second World War returned (1949) to the new Heilungkiang prov. (Manchuria).

Lungkiang, city and county, Manchuria: see TSITSIHAR.

Lung Kiang, river, China: see LUNG RIVER.

Lungkow or **Lung-k'ou** (both: lōōng'kō'), city, NE Shantung prov., China, port on N coast of Shantung peninsula, on Gulf of Chihli, 110 mi. N of Tsingtao; exports chiefly flour products (noodles, macaroni).

Lungkwan or **Lung-kuan** (both: lōōng'gwän'), town, ⊙ Lungkwan co. (pop. 79,827), E Chahar prov., China, 40 mi. E of Kalgan, near the Great Wall; iron-mining center. Mines are at Chaochwanpu, 30 mi. ESE of Kalgan, on rail spur. Called Lungmen until 1914. Until 1928 in Chihli (Hopeh).

Lungleh (lōōng'lā), village, Lushai Hills dist., S Assam, India, 58 mi. S of Aijal, in Lushai Hills (extensive bamboo tracts); rice, cotton.

Lungli (lōōng'lē'), town (pop. 5,082), ⊙ Lungli co. (pop. 68,642), S central Kweichow prov., China, on railroad and 18 mi. SE of Kweiyang; cotton-textile making; mfg. of paper, tobacco, pottery; rice, wheat, millet, beans. Coal, iron deposits near by.

Lungling (lōōng'lĭng'), town, ⊙ Lungling co. (pop. 73,641), W Yunnan prov., China, on Burma Road and 50 mi. SW of Paoshan; alt. 1,585 ft.; zinc mining; chemical industry. Rice, wheat, millet, beans, figs. Occupied 1942–44 by Japanese from Burma.

Lungmen. 1 Town, Chahar prov., China: see LUNGKWAN. **2** Town, Kwangtung prov., China: see LUNGMOON.

Lungmen (lōōng'mŭn'), caves in the Sung Mts., NW Honan prov., China, 12 mi. SW of Loyang. Contain large rock carvings of the Buddha and rock temples, dating from A.D. 500.

Lungming (lōōng'mĭng'), town, ⊙ Lungming co. (pop. 79,854), SW Kwangsi prov., China, 45 mi. NW of Tsungshan; cotton textiles; rice, wheat, timber, bamboo, medicinal herbs. Antimony deposits near by.

Lungmoon (lōōng'mōōn'), Mandarin *Lungmen* (lōōng'mŭn'), town (pop. 7,679), ⊙ Lungmoon co. (pop. 107,309), central Kwangtung prov., China, on the Tseng and 45 mi. SSW of Linping; rice, wheat, beans, sugar cane.

Lungnan (lōōng'nän'), town (pop. 8,189), ⊙ Lungnan co. (pop. 108,683), S Kiangsi prov., China, 80 mi. SSW of Kanchow, in Kiulien Mts., near Kwangtung line; tungsten mining.

Lungping, China: see LUNGYAO.

Lung River, Chinese *Lung Kiang* or *Lung Chiang* (both: lōōng'jyäng'), S Fukien prov., China, rises in several branches in the coastal ranges, flows 60 mi. SE, past Nantsing and Lungki, forming common estuary with Kiulung R. (left) on Amoy Bay of Formosa Strait.

Lungro (lōōng'grô), town (pop. 3,772), Cosenza prov., Calabria, S Italy, 7 mi. SW of Castrovillari; salt refining, cheese making; wine, olive oil. Bishopric. Chief rock salt mines of Italy near by.

Lungshan (lōōng'shän'). **1** Town, ⊙ Lungshan co. (pop. 235,973), northwesternmost Hunan prov., China, on Hupeh line, 85 mi. NW of Yüanling; tea, hemp, cotton. Lead and zinc mining near by. **2** Town, ⊙ Lungshan co. (pop. 133,981), W central Kwangsi prov., China, 70 mi. SW of Liuchow, near Hungshui R.; paper-milling center; rice, millet, beans, potatoes.

Lungsheng (lōōng'shŭng'). **1** Town, ⊙ Lungsheng co. (pop. 71,272), NE Kwangsi prov., China, 30 mi. NNW of Kweilin, near Hunan line; wheat, millet, beans; silver deposits. Occupied mostly by Miao and Yao tribes. **2** Town, ⊙ Lungsheng co., E Suiyuan prov., China, on railroad and 50 mi. E of Kweisui. Called Chotzeshan until 1949.

Lungshih, China: see NINGKANG.

Lungsi or **Lung-hsi** (both: lōōng'shē'), town, ⊙ Lungsi co. (pop. 91,907), SE Kansu prov., China, 90 mi. SE of Lanchow; grain, medicinal herbs, cotton; sheep raising. Important saltworks near by. Until 1913 called Kungchang.

Lungsinhü, China: see YUNGYÜN.

Lungtan or **Lung-t'an** (lōōng'tän'), Jap. *Ryutan* (ryōō'tän), village (1935 pop. 1,672), NW Formosa, 16 mi. ENE of Sinchu; tea-producing and -processing center; peanuts, tea oil.

Lungteh or **Lung-te** (lōōng'dŭ'), town, ⊙ Lungteh co. (pop. 64,658), SE Kansu prov., China, 35 mi. W of Pingliang; cotton weaving, tobacco processing; wheat, corn.

Lungtsin or **Lung-ching** (both: lōōng'chĭng'), town, ⊙ Lungtsin co. (pop. 64,854), SW Kwangsi prov., China, port on Li R. and 80 mi. WSW of Nanning, near Vietnam border; major transit center for trade with Vietnam; indigo, beans, sugar cane. Opened to foreign trade in 1887. Until 1937 called Lungchow.

Lungwan, Manchuria: see NUNGAN.

Lungwebungu River (lōōng-gwĕbōōng'gōō), Port. *Lungué-Bungo*, SW central Africa, right tributary of the Zambezi, rises in central plateau of Angola, flows c.400 mi. SE into Barotseland (Northern Rhodesia) and to the Zambezi 60 mi. N of Mongu.

Lungwu (lōōng'wōō'), village, ⊙ Lungwu dist., (pop. 23,427), S Yunnan prov., China, 35 mi. NW of Kienshui, in mtn. region; timber, rice, wheat, millet.

Lungwusze, China: see TUNGJEN, Tsinghai prov.

Lungyang, China: see HANSHOW.

Lungyao (lōōng'you'), town, ⊙ Lungping co. (pop. 196,988), SW Hopeh prov., China, 25 mi. NE of Singtai, near Peking-Hankow RR; wheat, millet, kaoliang. Called Lungping until 1949. A former co. seat, Yaoshan (until 1928, Tangshan), is 5 mi. W.

Lungyen (lōōng'yĕn'), town (pop. 21,608) ⊙ Lungyen co. (pop. 141,204), SW Fukien prov., China, 60 mi. SE of Changting; sugar and tobacco processing, cotton milling. Coal, iron mines near by. Exports tea, paper, timber, camphor, and orchids.

Lungyen, iron-mining district, China: see SÜANHWA.

Lungyu (lōōng'yō'), town (pop. 13,718), ⊙ Lungyu co. (pop. 176,664), SW Chekiang prov., China, on tributary of Tsientang R. and 28 mi. W of Kinhwa, and on railroad; lumbering center; tung-oil and vegetable-tallow processing; sugar cane.

Luni (lōō'nē), village, W central Rajasthan, India, 19 mi. S of Jodhpur, near Luni R.; rail junction; millet, wheat, oilseeds.

Lunigiana (lōōnējä'nä), mountain district (□ 375), in Massa e Carrara prov., Tuscany, central Italy, watered by upper and middle course of MAGRA RIVER. Has mild climate and abundant rainfall. Agr. (cereals, chestnuts, grapes, vegetables); stock raising (cattle, sheep). Chief center, Pontremoli. Colonized by Romans, who founded Luna (177 B.C.).

Luninets (lōōnyĕnyĕts'), Pol. *Łuniniec* (wōōnyē'-nyĕts), city (1931 pop. 8,715), central Pinsk oblast, Belorussian SSR, in Pripet Marshes, 32 mi ENE of Pinsk; rail junction; agr. center; tanning, flour milling. Passed (1793) from Poland to Russia; reverted (1921) to Poland; ceded to USSR in 1945.

Luning (lōō'nĭng'), village, ⊚ Luning dist., E Sikang prov., China, 50 mi. NW of Sichang and on Yalung R. bend; rice, wheat, kaoliang, corn. Called Luningying until 1946. Until 1938 in Szechwan.

Luniniec, Belorussian SSR: see LUNINETS.

Lunino (lōō'nyĭnŭ). **1** Village (1939 pop. 364), N Kaliningrad oblast, Russian SFSR, 13 mi. SE of Sovetsk; road junction. Until 1945, in East Prussia where it was called Lengwethen (lĕng'vātŭn) and, later (1938–45), Hohensalzburg (hō"ŭnzälts'bōōrk). **2** Town (1926 pop. 2,527), N Penza oblast, Russian SFSR, on Sura R. and 30 mi. NNE of Penza, in grain and hemp area; bast-fiber processing, metalworking.

Luni River, seasonal stream in Ajmer and SW Rajasthan, India, rises in Aravalli Range, in 2 main headstreams joining W of Ajmer city; flows WSW past Balotra, and SSW into NE end of Rann of Cutch; c.320 mi. long. Receives drainage from SW slopes of Aravalli Range.

Lunkaransar (lōōng'kŭrŭnsŭr), village, N Rajasthan, India, 45 mi. NE of Bikaner; exports salt (natural deposits just N). Selenite deposits near by; red sandstone quarried (S).

Lunlunta (lōōnlōōn'tä), village (pop. estimate 500), N Mendoza prov., Argentina, in Mendoza R. valley, on railroad and 10 mi. S of Mendoza; wine-growing, stock raising; oil wells.

Lunna (lōō'nŭ), Pol. *Łunna* (wōō'nä), town (1937 pop. 2,400), central Grodno oblast, Belorussian SSR, on Neman R. (landing) and 13 mi. W of Mosty; flour milling, brick mfg. Has old church.

Lunsar, Sierra Leone: see MARAMPA.

Luntai, China: see BUGUR.

Lunugala (lōōnōōgă'lŭ), town (pop. 449), Uva Prov., SE Ceylon, in E Ceylon Hill Country, 10 mi. ENE of Badulla; tea, rice, rubber, vegetables.

Lunugala Ridge, just W, is E outlier of Ceylon Hill Country; 16 mi. long N-S, up to 3 mi. wide. Highest point, Dorepotagala Peak (4,964 ft.), is 6 mi. SW of Bibile. Rubber plantations on lower, tea gardens on upper slopes.

Lunyevka or **Lun'yevka** (lōō'nyĭfkŭ), town (1939 pop. over 2,000), E central Molotov oblast, Russian SFSR, 5 mi. NNE of Kizel, on rail spur; mining center in Kizel bituminous-coal basin. Developed prior to First World War. Until c.1928, Lunyevskiye Kopi.

Lunz or **Lunz am See** (lōōnts' äm zā'), town (pop. 2,444), SW Lower Austria, on picturesque Lunzersee (small Alpine lake) and 20 mi. SE of Amstetten; mfg. (scythes, cutlery); summer resort (alt. 1,968 ft.).

Lunzenau (lōōn'tsŭnou), town (pop. 4,027), Saxony, E central Germany, on the Zwickauer Mulde and 12 mi. NW of Chemnitz; hosiery, glove knitting.

Luossavaara, Sweden: see KIRUNA.

Luozi (lwō'zē) village, Leopoldville prov., W Belgian Congo, on right bank of Congo R. and 90 mi. NE of Boma; palm-oil milling, fiber growing.

Lupa, Tanganyika: see CHUNYA.

Lupac (lōō'päk), Hung. *Lupák* (lōō'päk), village (pop. 898), Severin prov., SW Rumania, 5 mi. SW of Resita; coal mining.

Lupao (lōōpä'ō, lōōpou'), town (1939 pop. 1,724; 1948 municipality pop. 13,410), Neva Ecija prov., central Luzon, Philippines, 27 mi. NNW of Cabanatuan; rice, corn.

Lupar River (lōōpär'), S Sarawak, in W Borneo, rises in Kapuas Mts. on Indonesian border, flows SW to Lubok Antu, thence WNW past Simanggang to S.China Sea 40 mi. E of Kuching; 142 mi. long; navigable c.50 mi. by small craft.

Lupburg (lōōp'bōōrk), village (pop. 1,420), Upper Palatinate, central Bavaria, Germany, 18 mi. NW of Regensburg; grain, cattle.

Lupeh or **Lupei** (both: lōō'bā'), town, ⊙ Lupeh co. (pop. 14,766), S Inner Mongolian Autonomous Region, Manchuria, 135 mi. SW of Taonan; banner hq. in Jooda league. Founded 1924; in Jehol until 1949.

Lupeni (lōōpān'), Hung. *Lupény* (lōō'pānyŭ), village (pop. 12,595), Hunedoara prov., W central Rumania, on headstream of Jiu R. in the Transylvanian Alps, and 40 mi. SSE of Deva; rail terminus, coal-mining center; mfg. of cellulose, rayon, soap; coke ovens and flour mills.

Luperón (lōōpārōn'), town (1950 pop. 736), Puerto Plata prov., N Dominican Republic, on small inlet of the Atlantic, and 17 mi. WNW of Puerto Plata, in agr. region (coffee, cacao, tobacco, corn). Until 1927, called Blanco. The ruins of ISABELA are 9 mi. W.

Lupin, Manchuria: see MANCHOULI.

Lupkow Pass (wōōp'kōōf), Pol. *Przełęcz Łupkowska* (pshĕ'wĕch wōōpkôf'skä), pass (alt. 1,917 ft.) bet. E Beskids and Beshchady Mts., on Pol.-Czechoslovak border, 22 mi. SSW of Sanok, Poland; used by railroad.

Lupton City, village (1940 pop. 1,173), Hamilton co., SE Tenn., N suburb of Chattanooga, across the Tennessee.

Lupus (lōō'pŭs), town (pop. 97), Moniteau co., central Mo., on Missouri R. 10 mi. SW of Columbia.

Luputa (lōōpōō'tä), village, Kasai prov., S Belgian Congo, on railroad and 85 mi. SW of Kabinda; agr. center (manioc, yams, groundnuts, livestock), with veterinary laboratory.

Luqa or **Luca** (lōō'kä), town (pop. 4,318), E central Malta, 3 mi. SSW of Valletta, in agr. region (vegetables, livestock). Site of Malta's civil airport. Has limestone quarries. Leprosarium. Suffered severely in Second World War air raids. Its Nativity church was removed for military reasons.

Luque (lōō'kā), town (pop. estimate 2,000), central Córdoba prov., Argentina, 55 mi. ESE of Córdoba; grain, flax, fruit, stock.

Luque, city (dist. pop. 23,232), Central dept., S Paraguay, on railroad and 8 mi. E of Asunción; mfg. and agr. center (fruit, sugar cane, tobacco, cotton, livestock); soap factories, alcohol distilleries, brick- and tileworks, maté mills. Founded 1635; temporary capital during War of the Triple Alliance (1865-70).

Luque, town (pop. 6,577), Córdoba prov., S Spain, 5 mi. SE of Baena; olive-oil processing, flour milling, plaster mfg. Agr. trade (cereals, almonds, vegetables); lumber; stock raising. Marble, stone, and gypsum quarries.

Luquillo (lōōkē'yō), town (pop. 2,262), NE Puerto Rico, on the Atlantic, on railroad and 27 mi. ESE of San Juan; sugar-growing center and bathing resort, towered over by Sierra de Luquillo.

Luquillo, Sierra de (syĕ'rä dā), mountain range in NE Puerto Rico, 20 mi. SE of San Juan, in Caribbean Natl. Forest; extends c.15 mi. SW-NE, rising to c.3,500 ft. Its best-known peak is El Yunque (3,497 ft.). Largely forested; timber is used for charcoal. Resort area.

Luras (lōō'räs), village (pop. 2,515), Sassari prov., N Sardinia, 35 mi. ENE of Sassari.

Lurate Caccivio (lōōrä'tĕ kät-chē'vyô), commune (pop. 4,930), Como prov., Lombardy, N Italy, 5 mi. WSW of Como. Chief towns: Caccivio (pop. 3,030; commune seat), near-by Lurate (pop. 1,632); silk-milling centers.

Luray (lōō'rā). **1** City (pop. 351), Russell co., central Kansas, 16 mi. NNE of Russell; livestock, grain. **2** Town (pop. 184), Clark co., extreme NE Mo., near North Wyaconda R., 9 mi. WNW of Kahoka. **3** Town (pop. 102), Hampton co., SW S.C., 15 mi. SSE of Allendale; peanuts, strawberries. **4** Town (pop. 2,731), ⊙ Page co., N Va., in Shenandoah Valley, 22 mi. SSW of Front Royal. Tourist center for Luray Caverns (discovered 1878), a series of limestone caves noted for size and beauty of stalactite formations over small lakes. Trade center for agr. area; makes textiles, clothing, canned foods, feed; flour milling; poultry hatching. Hq. of Shenandoah Natl. Park (E, in the Blue Ridge). Inc. 1812.

Lurcy-Lévy (lürsē'-lāvē'), village (pop. 1,328), Allier dept., central France, 20 mi. E of Saint-Amand-Montrond; mfg. of woodworking machinery. Gypsum and kaolin quarries near by.

Lure (lür), town (pop. 5,486), Haute-Saône dept., E France, near the Ognon, 17 mi. WNW of Belfort; cotton-milling center; metalworks (weaving machines, winches). Leather, iron, and grain trade. A 7th-cent. abbey, rebuilt in 18th cent., now houses the sub-prefecture.

Lure, Lake, N.C.: see LAKE LURE town.

Lure, Montagne de (mõtä'nyŭ dŭ lür'), range of Provence Pre-Alps, in Basses-Alpes dept., SE France, extending c.20 mi. from the Durance valley below Sisteron (E) to Mont Ventoux (W). Rises to 5,994 ft.

Luretha, Ky.: see FERGUSON.

Lurgan (lûr'gŭn), municipal borough (1937 pop. 13,-766; 1951 census 16,181), Co. Armagh, Northern Ireland, near S shore of Lough Neagh, 19 mi. WSW of Belfast; linen milling, tobacco processing. Linen industry was introduced 1619. Has modern Lurgan Castle.

Luri (lürē'), village (pop. 310), N Corsica, on Cape Corse peninsula, 14 mi. N of Bastia; footwear mfg., antimony mining; citrus and winegrowing.

Luribay (lōōrĭbī'), town (pop. c.5,200), ⊙ Loayza (until 1930s, Loaiza) prov., La Paz dept., W Bolivia, on Luribay R. (branch of La Paz R.) and 55 mi. SE of La Paz; vineyards, orchards.

Luribay Valley, in La Paz dept., W Bolivia, bet. Serranía de Sicasica (SW) and Cordillera de Tres Cruces (NE); watered by Luribay R. and its affluent, the Caracato.

Lurín (lōōrēn'), town (pop. 2,141), Lima dept., W central Peru, on coastal plain, near the Pacific, on highway and railroad, and 13 mi. SE of Lima; rail terminus; sugar cane, cotton, vegetables.

Lúrio River (lōō'ryō), Niassa prov., N Mozambique, rises W of Namuli Mts. near Nyasaland border, flows 335 mi. NE to the Mozambique Channel 40 mi. S of Pôrto Amélia. Not navigable. Reached by railroad from Lumbo (opposite Mozambique city).

Luristan (lōōrĭstän') or **Lorestan** (lōrĕstän'), former province (□ 15,000; pop. 500,000) of SW Iran; main towns, Burujird and Khurramabad. Bounded S by Khuzistan, W by Kermanshah, N by Malayer and Arak, and E by Isfahan, it is situated in the Zagros mtn. country. Drained by the river Ab-i-Diz, which separates the Bakhtiari tribal region (E) from the Lur tribal country (W), and by upper Karkheh R. Sheep raising, dairying; figs, pomegranates. Merged (1938) with KHUZISTAN and Gulpaigan to form Iran's Sixth Prov.

Lurlei, Germany: see LORELEI.

Lury-sur-Arnon (lürē'-sür-ärnõ'), village (pop. 419), Cher dept., central France, on Arnon R. and 7 mi. S of Vierzon; agr.-machinery mfg.

Lusaka (lōōsä'kä), township (pop. 10,336), ⊙ Northern Rhodesia, near country's geographical center, on railroad and 230 mi. NE of Livingstone (former ⊙), 250 mi. NW of Salisbury, Southern Rhodesia (linked by road); alt. 4,191 ft.; 15°25'S 28°17'E. Administrative, agr., and livestock center; junction of Great North Road (to Tanganyika) and Great East Road (to Nyasaland). Wheat and corn milling; tobacco, potatoes, market gardening; dairy products, cattle, sheep, goats. Has modern airport, govt. and convent schools. Lusaka consists of old township along railroad line and modern govt. section (1.5 mi. E) with administrative offices. Became ⊙ Northern Rhodesia in 1935.

Lusaka-Saint-Jacques (lōōsäkä'-sē-zhäk'), village, Katanga prov., SE Belgian Congo, 85 mi. SSE of Albertville; cattle raising, vegetable farming. R.C. mission with small seminary and convent for natives.

Lusambo, province, Belgian Congo: see KASAI.

Lusambo (lōōsäm'bō, lōōzäbō'), town (1948 pop. 7,387), ⊙ Kasai prov. and Sankuru dist. (□ 44,794; 1948 pop. c.465,000), central Belgian Congo, on right bank of Sankuru R. and 550 mi. E of Leopoldville; 4°59'S 23°23'E. Commercial, cotton, and communications center. Sawmilling (notably railroad-sleeper mfg.), cotton ginning, cottonseed-oil milling, rice processing. Coffee, cacao, and rubber plantations in vicinity. Airport. Has R. C. and Protestant missions, various schools for natives, including business school for sons of chiefs, hospitals for Europeans and natives. Lusambo post was founded in 1889 and was the hq. of Congo Free State troops during the campaign against Arab slave traders (1892–94).

Lusatia (lōōsā'shŭ), Ger. *Lausitz* (lou'zĭts), Pol. *Łużyca* (wōō-zhĭ'tsĕ), region in E Germany and SW Poland, consists of Upper Lusatia, Ger. *Oberlausitz*, in NE Saxony, and Lower Lusatia, Ger. *Niederlausitz*, in S Brandenburg and Lower Silesia (after 1945, in Poland W of Bober R.); bounded by Lusatian Mts. (S) and the Oder (NE). Lusatian Neisse R. separates Pol. from Ger. part of region. Hilly and fertile in S, especially on slopes of Lusatian Mts.; N part of region is level, generally sandy and forested, and includes marshy Spree Forest. Drained by Bobrawa (Bober), Kwisa (Queis), Lusatian Neisse, Spree, and Black Elster rivers. Forestry, grain growing, stock raising. Important lignite fields in Lower Lusatia (Spremberg and Senftenberg regions). Woolen and linen mills; glass mfg. Zittau, Bautzen, Kamenz, Görlitz, Cottbus, Guben, and Forst in E Germany, and Sagan (Zagan), Szprotawa (Sprottau), and Luban (Lauban) in Poland are chief cities. Lusatians are descended from Slavic Wends; part of pop., particularly in Spree Forest, is Wendish-speaking and has preserved traditional dress and customs. Lusatia was colonized by Germans in late-10th cent. and was divided into 2 margraviates of Upper and Lower Lusatia. Upper Lusatia was under Pol. rule, 1002–31, then alternated bet. Ger. and Bohemian sovereignty; passed 1320 to Bohemia, 1467 to Hungary; returned 1490 to Bohemia. Lower Lusatia passed 1136 to Margraves of Meissen, 1303 to Brandenburg, and 1368 to Bohemia. Bautzen, Görlitz, Zittau, Kamenz, Löbau, and Luban formed (1346) Lusatian League and preserved considerable independence. Reformation was generally adopted in 16th cent. throughout the region. Under Treaty of Prague (1635) all of Lusatia passed to Saxony; Lower Lusatia and large part of Upper Lusatia came to Prussia in 1815.

Lusatian Mountains (lōōsā'shŭn), Czech *Lužické Hory* (lōō'zhĭtskā hō'rĭ), Ger. *Lausitzer Gebirge* (lou'zĭ"tsŭr gŭbĭr'gŭ), Pol. *Góry Łużyckie* (gōō'rĭ wōō-zhĭts'kyĕ), westernmost range of the Sudetes, in Upper Lusatia, along Czechoslovak-Ger. and Czechoslovak-Pol. border; extend c.60 mi. bet. the Elbe (W) and upper Lusatian Neisse R. (E). Highest peaks are Jested (3,314 ft.), 3 mi. SW of Liberec, and Kozakov (2,437 ft.), 5 mi. ENE of Turnov. Iron mined in W part of range; semiprecious stones (Bohemian garnets, agates, amethysts) quarried on SE slope (gem industry at Turnov).

Lusatian Neisse River, Czechoslovakia, Germany, and Poland: see NEISSE RIVER.

Lus Bela, W Pakistan: see LAS BELA; BELA.

Lusby (lŭz'bē), village, Calvert co., S Md., near Chesapeake Bay, 12 mi. SE of Prince Frederick. Near by is "Charlesgift," formerly called Preston-at-Patuxent (built 1650), one of oldest Md. houses; home of Richard Preston, whom Cromwell appointed a commissioner of Md. in 1652, it was seat (1652–56) of Puritan govt. of Md.

Luscar (lŭ'skŭr), village (pop. estimate 500), W Alta., in Rocky Mts. at foot of Luscar Mtn. (8,534 ft.), near E side of Jasper Natl. Park, 30 mi. ENE of Jasper; coal mining.

Lusci Palanka or **Lushtsi Palanka** (both: lo͞osh'tsē pä'län-kä), Serbo-Croatian *Lušci Palanka*, village (pop. 6,262), NW Bosnia, Yugoslavia, 12 mi. W of Sanski Most.

Luseland (lo͞os'lănd), village (pop. 394), W Sask., 65 mi. SW of North Battleford; wheat.

Lusengo (lo͞osĕng'gō), village, Equator Prov., NW Belgian Congo, on right bank of Congo R. and 20 mi. ENE of Nouvelle-Anvers; steamboat landing and trading post; palm groves.

Luserna San Giovanni (lo͞ozĕr'nä sän jôvän'nē), commune (pop. 7,137), Torino prov., Piedmont, NW Italy, in Monte Viso region of Cottian Alps. Includes Airali (pop. 1,448; commune seat), 6 mi. SW of Pinerolo, and adjacent villages of Luserna (pop. 1,183) and San Giovanni (pop. 453). Produces woolen textiles, chocolate. Has talc mines.

Lushai Hills (lo͞o'shī), southernmost autonomous district (□ 8,143; pop. 152,786) of Assam, India; ⊙ Aijal. Coextensive with Lushai Hills (S continuation of Manipur Hills), rising to over 5,500 ft. Bounded E by Burma, along Tyao and Boinu rivers (headstreams of Kaladan R.), W by E Pakistan. Drained by tributaries of Barak (Surma; N), Kaladan (S), and Karnaphuli (W) rivers. Agr. (rice, cotton, sesame, sugar cane, tobacco); orange groves (center at Sairang). Extensive bamboo tracts. Main villages: Aijal, Lungleh. Present dist., assigned to Assam in 1898, received special status (1950) in accordance with Indian Constitution. Pop. 96% tribal (Lushai), 1% Hindu.

Lushan (lo͞o'shän'). **1** Town, ⊙ Lushan co. (pop. 195,276), W Honan prov., China, on Sha R. and 50 mi. NNE of Nanyang, in coal- and iron-mining region; foundry; mfg. of farm wagons; silk weaving, papermaking, pottery mfg. **2** Town (pop. 2,556), ⊙ Lushan co. (pop. 92,530), E central Kweichow prov., China, 60 mi. E of Kweiyang and on main road to Hunan; alt. 2,821 ft.; cotton weaving; tobacco processing; embroideries. Rice, wheat, millet, beans. Until 1914 called Tsingping. **3** Town ⊙ Lushan co. (pop. 32,234), E Sikang prov., China, 55 mi. ENE of Kangting, at Szechwan border; tea, rice, wheat, corn. Until 1938 in Szechwan.

Lü Shan (lü' shän'), mountain in northernmost Kiangsi prov., China, S of Kiukiang and W of Hukow Canal; rises to 4,500 ft. Here are the hill resort of KULING and the WHITE DEER CAVE, where Chu Hsi lived and taught.

Lushih (lo͞o'shû'), town, ⊙ Lushih co. (pop. 107,137), NW Honan prov., China, on upper Lo R. and 100 mi. WSW of Loyang, in mtn. region; wheat, millet, beans. Lead mines near by.

Lushnje (lo͞osh'nyĕ) or **Lushnja** (lo͞osh'nyä), town (1945 pop. 5,495), W central Albania, on road and 21 mi. NW of Berat at N edge of Myzeqe plain; agr. center with agr. school and tree nursery.

Lushoto (lo͞oshō'tō), town (pop. c.1,000), NE Tanganyika, in Usambara Mts., 60 mi. WNW of Tanga; alt. 4,579 ft. Mtn. resort and sisal-growing center. Known as Wilhelmstal under Ger. rule.

Lushton, village (pop. 60), York co., SE Nebr., 12 mi. SW of York and on W.Fork of Big Blue R.

Lushtsi Palanka, Yugoslavia: see LUSCI PALANKA.

Lushui (lo͞o'shwā'), village (pop. 386), ⊙ Lushui dist. (pop. 17,306), NW Yunnan prov., China, 60 mi. NNW of Paoshan, and on right bank of Salween R., near Hpimaw (Burma border town); timber, rice, millet, beans. Until 1935 called Luchang.

Lüshun, Manchuria: see PORT ARTHUR.

Lusi or **Lu-hsi** (both: lo͞o'shē'). **1** Town, ⊙ Lusi co. (pop. 121,881), E Yunnan prov., China, 75 mi. SE of Kunming, in mtn. region; timber, rice, millet, beans. Coal mines near by. Until 1929 called Kwangsi. **2** Village, ⊙ Lusi dist. (pop. 31,014), westernmost Yunnan prov., China, 50 mi. S of Tengchung, near Burma Road and near Burma line; timber, rice, millet, beans. Until 1935 called Mengka.

Lusignan (lüzēnyä'), village (pop. 1,406), Vienne dept., W central France, 14 mi. SW of Poitiers; cattle and mule raising. Limekilns. Has ruins of a castle inhabited by the Lusignan family, rulers of Cyprus during Middle Ages.

Lusigny-sur-Barse (lüzēnyē'-sür'-bärs'), village (pop. 779), Aube dept., NE central France, 9 mi. ESE of Troyes; sawmilling.

Lusitania (lo͞osĭtā'nēŭ, -nyŭ), historic name for Portugal; stems from Roman prov. of Lusitania, which, constituted by Augustus about A.D. 5, included all of modern central Portugal and much of W Spain. It was inhabited by the Lusitani, who put up a fierce resistance against Roman domination.

Lusk (lŭsk), Gaelic *Lusca*, town (pop. 344), NE Co. Dublin, Ireland, 14 mi. NE of Dublin; agr. market.

Lusk, town (pop. 2,089), ⊙ Niobrara co., E Wyo., on Niobrara R. (flows intermittently here), near Nebr. line, and 100 mi. E of Casper; alt. 5,017 ft. Trading point in dry-farming, cattle and sheep region; oil refinery; leather goods, granite. Lance Creek oil field near by. Local mus. has pioneer relics. Settled in late 1880s, inc. 1898.

Lus-la-Croix-Haute (lüs-lä-krwä-ōt'), village (pop. 231), Drôme dept., SE France, resort in Dauphiné Pre-Alps, on the Buëch and 17 mi. ESE of Die; alt. 3,445 ft.; winter sports. Col de la Croix-Haute (alt. 3,822 ft.), a pass on Grenoble-Sisteron road, is 4 mi. NNW.

Luso (lo͞o'zo͞o), village (pop. 1,218), Aveiro dist., N central Portugal, on railroad and 13 mi. NNE of Coimbra; spa with alkaline springs.

Lussac (lüsäk'), village (pop. 317), Gironde dept. SW France, 8 mi. ENE of Libourne; winegrowing. Stone quarries.

Lussac-les-Châteaux (-lā-shätō'), village (pop. 1,493), Vienne dept., W central France, near Vienne R., 21 mi. SE of Poitiers; flour milling, mfg. (slaked lime, macaroons).

Lussan (lüsã'), agr. village (pop. 161), Gard dept., S France, in the Garrigues, 15 mi. E of Alès.

Lussanvira, Brazil: see PEREIRA BARRETO.

Lussingrande; Lussinpiccolo, Yugoslavia: see LOSINJ ISLAND.

Lussino, island, Yugoslavia: see LOSINJ ISLAND.

Lustenau (lo͞o'stünou), town (pop. 10,154), Vorarlberg, W. Austria, on the Rhine (Swiss border), 4 mi. W of Dornbirn; customs station; embroidery center, textiles, brewery.

Luster, canton, Norway: see SKJOLDEN.

Luster Fjord (lo͞ost'ür), N arm of Sogne Fjord, in Sogn og Fjordane co., W Norway; c.30 mi. long, 2 mi. wide; terminates at Skjolden, where glacier streams from the Jostedalsbre give fjord water a milky appearance. Sometimes spelled Lyster.

Lustin (lüstē'), village (pop. 1,404), Namur prov., S central Belgium, near Meuse R., 7 mi. S of Namur; chalk quarrying; limekilns; tourist resort. Has modern church with 13th-cent. font.

Lustleigh (lŭst'lē), agr. village and parish (pop. 439) S central Devon, England, 11 mi. SW of Exeter; moorland community with 14th-cent. church.

Lutcher (lŭ'chür), town (pop. 2,198), St. James parish, SE central La., on E bank (levee) of the Mississippi (ferry here) and 36 mi. W of New Orleans, in timber and agr. area (sugar cane, truck, rice, perique tobacco); lumber milling, tobacco processing, moss ginning. Founded c.1890.

Lutécia (lo͞otĕ'syŭ), city (pop. 753), W São Paulo, Brazil, 28 mi. WSW of Marília, in coffee- and cotton-growing region.

Lutesville, town (pop. 694), Bollinger co., SE Mo., 25 mi. W of Cape Girardeau.

Lutetia or **Lutetia Parisiorum,** France: see PARIS.

Luteva, France: see LODÈVE.

Lutfabad or **Lotfabad** (both: lōtf"äbäd'), village, Ninth Prov., in Khurasan, NE Iran, 55 mi. ENE of Quchan, near Trans-Caspian RR; frontier station on USSR line in Daragaz agr. dist.; grain, opium, cotton, raisins. In earthquake zone.

Lutgardita, Cuba: see GENERAL PERAZA.

Lütgendortmund (lüt'gündôrt'mo͞ont), district (since 1929) of Dortmund, W Germany, 5 mi. WSW of city center; coal mining.

Luther. 1 Town (pop. 131), Boone co., central Iowa, 8 mi. SSE of Boone, in agr. area. **2** Village (pop. 314), Lake co., W central Mich., 20 mi. SW of Cadillac, in farm area. **3** Town (pop. 409), Oklahoma co., central Okla., 22 mi. NE of Oklahoma City, and on the Deep Fork.

Luthersville, town (pop. 312), Meriwether co., W Ga., 19 mi. NE of La Grange.

Lutherville, suburban village (1940 pop. 1,253), Baltimore co., N Md., bet. Loch Raven Reservoir and L. Roland and 9 mi. N of downtown Baltimore. Seat of Md. Col. for Women (chartered 1853).

Lutien (lo͞o'dyĕn'), town, ⊙ Lutien co. (pop. 65,007), northeasternmost Yunnan prov., China, 14 mi. SW of Chaotung; iron smelting, tung-oil processing; rice, buckwheat, millet.

Luting (lo͞o'dĭng'), town, ⊙ Luting co. (pop. 24,037), E Sikang prov., China, on Tatu R. and 20 mi. SE of Kangting, and on highway; agr. products. Until 1913 called Lutingkiao. Placed 1950 in Tibetan Autonomous Dist.

Lütjenburg (lüt'yŭnbo͝ork), town (pop. 4,715), in Schleswig-Holstein, NW Germany, 18 mi. E of Kiel; dairying, meat processing, distilling (kümmel), metal- and woodworking. Has late-Romanesque church. Chartered 1275.

Luton (lo͞o'tŭn), municipal borough (1931 pop. 68,523; 1951 census 110,370), S Bedford, England, on the Lea at S base of Chiltern Hills, and 30 mi. NNW of London; industrial center with important automobile, ball-bearing, and vacuum-cleaner works. Also center of English hat and straw-plaiting industries, established in time of James I by weavers from Lorraine. Has 14th-cent. church, straw-plait market hall, and mus. containing Rodin bronzes. In municipal borough are industrial suburbs of Leagrave (NW) and Limbury (N).

Lutong (lo͞oto͝ong'), village (pop. 2,140), N Sarawak, in NW Borneo, 5 mi. N of Miri; port and oil-refining center serving oil fields at Seria (23 mi. ENE, in Sarawak) and Miri. Ships oil to Indonesia and Australia.

Lutro, Crete: see PHOENIX.

Lutry (lütrē'), residential town (pop. 2,540), Vaud canton, W Switzerland, on L. of Geneva, 3 mi. E of Lausanne. Church (13th–16th cent.); fine views of mts. (SE).

Lütschine River (lüt'shē'nŭ), S central Switzerland, rises in Bernese Alps in 2 headstreams, the White and the Black Lütschine, which join 4 mi. S of Interlaken; flows N to L. of Brienz; total length (including the White Lütschine), 17 mi.

Lutsk (lo͞otsk), Pol. *Łuck* (wo͞otsk), city (1931 pop. 35,700), ⊙ Volyn oblast, Ukrainian SSR, on Styr R. and 85 mi. NE of Lvov; 50°44'N 25°19'E. Agr.-processing (grain, hides, flax, hops) center; mfg. of agr. machinery, sawmilling. Has teachers col., technical schools, cathedral, ruins of 16th-cent. castle. Allegedly founded before 11th cent.; became ⊙ independent principality; dominated by Lithuanians and Poles; developed as commercial center. Severely damaged by 4 successive fires (1781–1803). Passed from Poland to Russia in 1795. Noted strategic point and scene of Rus. general Brusilov's breakthrough (1916) of Austrian front; reverted to Poland (1921); ceded to USSR in 1945. Pop. largely Jewish prior to Second World War.

Lutsun or **Lu-t'sun** (lo͞o'tso͞on'), salt pan in SW Shansi prov., China, 35 mi. E of Yüngtsi, along railroad; 18 mi. long, 3 mi. wide. Major salt-production source, with centers in towns of Chiehsien and Anyi.

Lutten (lŭ'tŭn), village (pop. 1,689), Overijssel prov., E Netherlands, 7 mi. WSW of Coevorden; potato-flour milling.

Luttenberg, Yugoslavia: see LJUTOMER.

Lutter or **Lutter am Barenberge** (lo͞o'tür äm bä'rŭnbĕr"gŭ), village (pop. 2,547), in Brunswick, NW Germany, after 1945 in Lower Saxony, 9 mi. NW of Goslar; leatherworking, flour milling. Scene (1626) of Tilly's victory over Christian IV of Denmark.

Lutterade (lŭ'türädŭ), town, Limburg prov., SE Netherlands, 11 mi. NNE of Maastricht; coal-mining center (site of Maurits mine, SW); brickworks, large coke plants, chemicals (nitrogen fixation); electric power station.

Lutterbach (lütĕrbäk', Ger. lo͞o'türbäkh), outer WNW suburb (pop. 2,062) of Mulhouse, Haut-Rhin dept., E France; mfg. (chemicals, soap, galvanized metal, beer).

Lutterworth (lŭ'türwûrth, -wŭrth), town and parish (pop. 2,395), S Leicester, England, 6 mi. NNE of Rugby; iron and steel foundries. Has 12th-cent. church at which Wyclif was rector in his last years.

Luttrell (lŭ'trŭl), village (1940 pop. 570), Union co., NE Tenn., 17 mi. NNE of Knoxville.

Lüttringhausen (lü"trĭng-hou'zŭn), outer district (since 1927) of REMSCHEID, W Germany, 2.5 mi. NE of city center; textile mfg.

Lutugino (lo͞oto͞o'gĭnŭ), town (1939 pop. over 2,000), S central Voroshilovgrad oblast, Ukrainian SSR, in the Donbas, 11 mi. SSW of Voroshilovgrad; machinery works.

Lutunguru (lo͞oto͝ong-go͞o'ro͞o), village, Kivu prov., E Belgian Congo, 70 mi. N of Costermansville; gold-mining center. Also gold mining at Bilati (bēlä'tē), 3 mi. SE, and Mohanga (mōhäng'gä), 11 mi. ENE. Vicinity of Lutunguru known for production of African staples (manioc, corn).

Lutynia, Poland: see LEUTHEN.

Lutzelbourg (lütsŭlbo͞or'), Ger. *Lützelburg* (lüt'sŭlbo͝ork), village (pop. 694), Moselle dept., NE France, on Zorn R. and Marne-Rhine Canal, 5 mi. W of Saverne, in Saverne Gap; woodworking machinery and leatherette mfg., glass milling. Resort.

Lützelflüh (lüt'sŭlflü"), town (pop. 3,766), Bern canton, NW central Switzerland, on Emme R. and 12 mi. ENE of Bern; textiles (linen, cotton), flour; woodworking.

Lutzelhouse (lütslo͞oz'), Ger. *Lützelhausen* (lüt'sŭlhou"zŭn), village (pop. 1,159), Bas-Rhin dept., E France, in the E Vosges, on Bruche R. and 10 mi. WSW of Molsheim; makes cotton fabrics.

Lützelstein, France: see PETITE-PIERRE, LA.

Lützen (lü'tsŭn), town (pop. 5,739), in former Prussian Saxony prov., central Germany, after 1945 in Saxony-Anhalt, 13 mi. WSW of Leipzig; sugar refining, fennel processing. Has 13th-cent. castle. In Thirty Years War, scene (Nov., 1632) of Swedish victory over imperial forces under Wallenstein; Gustavus Adolphus killed, Pappenheim mortally wounded here. Several monuments commemorate the battle. Action (1813) in which French defeated Prusso-Russian forces at Gross Görschen, 4 mi. SE, is sometimes called battle of Lützen.

Lützkendorf, Germany: see KRUMPA.

Lützow-Holm Bay (lüt'sôf-hōlm'), large bay (130 naut. mi. wide, 110 naut. mi. long), in Antarctica, on Indian Ocean, bordered by Prince Olav Coast, Prince Harald Coast, and Cook Peninsula at NE end of Ragnhild Coast, bet. 33°30' and 40°E. Discovered 1931 by Hjalmar Riiser-Larsen, Norwegian explorer.

Lützschena (lüchä'nä), village (pop. 3,736), Saxony, E central Germany, 7 mi. NW of Leipzig city center; machinery mfg.

Luverne. 1 (lo͞ovûrn') Town (pop. 2,221), ⊙ Crenshaw co., S Ala., on Patsaliga Creek and 45 mi. S of Montgomery; processing and shipping point in cotton, corn, and peanut area; clothing, peanuts, lumber. Inc. 1891. **2** (lo͞ovûrn') Town (pop. 553), on Humboldt-Kossuth co. line, N central Iowa, 29 mi. NNE of Fort Dodge; livestock, grain. **3** (lüvûrn') City (pop. 3,650), ⊙ Rock co., extreme SW Minn., on Rock R., near Iowa line, and 27 mi. ENE of Sioux Falls, S.Dak.; trading point in grain, livestock, and poultry area; dairy products. Granite quarries and state park near by. Settled 1867, platted 1870, inc. as village 1877, as city 1904. **4** (lo͝ovûrn') Village (pop. 154), Steele co., E N.Dak., 60 mi. WNW of Fargo, near Sheyenne R.

Luvino, Italy: see LUINO.

Luvironza River (lo͞ovērōn'zä), in Ruanda-Urundi, rises E of Usumbura (N tip of L. Tanganyika) at 3°48'S 29°42'E, flows 110 mi. NNE to the Ruvuvu, which in turn joins the Nyawarongo to form the Kagera. It is considered the remotest headstream of the Nile, its source being over 4,150 river mi. from the Mediterranean. Also spelled Luwironza.

Luvua River (lo͞ov'wä), SE Belgian Congo, issues from N end of L. Mweru, flows c.215 mi. NW, past Kiambi, to Lualaba R. opposite Ankoro. Navigable for shallow-draught boats for c.100 mi. in its lower course below Kiambi. Rapids in its middle course. Large hydroelectric plant at Piana-Mwanga. Luvua R. is sometimes considered to be a continuation of Luapula R. (which enters L. Mweru from the S), so that the whole Luvua-Mweru-Luapula-Bangweulu-Chambezi system represents an E headstream of the Congo.

Luvungi (lo͞ovo͞ong'gē), village, Kivu prov., E Belgian Congo, near Ruzizi R., on railroad and 28 mi. SSE of Costermansville; trading center in cotton-growing area; cotton ginning, palm-oil milling. Airfield. Lubarika (lo͞obärē'kä), 4 mi. WSW, is a center of agr. research, notably on cotton cultivation.

Luwingu (lo͞owĭng'go͞o), township (pop. 540), Northern Prov., N Northern Rhodesia, 80 mi. W of Kasama; corn, wheat; livestock.

Luwironza River, Ruanda-Urundi: LUVIRONZA RIVER.

Luxapalila Creek (lo͝ok"süpûlĭ'lü, lo͞o"sü–), W Ala. and E Miss., rises in SE Marion co., Ala., flows 60 mi. SSW, W, and SSW to Tombigbee R. 3 mi. below Columbus, Miss.

Luxembourg (lŭk'sŭmbûrg, Fr. lüksäbo͞or') or **Luxemburg** (lŭk'sŭmbûrg, Ger. lo͝ok'so͝obo͝ork), local dialect *Letzeburg* (lĕt'so͝obo͝orzh), grand duchy (□ 999; pop. 290,992), W Europe; ⊙ LUXEMBOURG. A constitutional monarchy. Borders W on Belgium, E on Germany (along Moselle, Sûre, and Our rivers), S on France (Lorraine). A little smaller in area than Rhode Island, it is of roughly triangular shape, c.55 mi. long (N-S), up to c.35 mi. wide, situated bet. 49°27'–50°11'N and 5°45'–6°30'E. Despite its size, it is of varied topography, the N, more rugged section (called *Oesling*) being crossed by the Ardennes (rising to 1,716 ft.), and the more fertile S being a pleasant, undulating country of broad valleys. Drained by tributaries of the Moselle, chiefly the Alzette and the Sauer. Mean annual temp. 50°F., average rainfall 32 inches. Luxembourg has extensive forests (oak, pine) and pasture lands. It is essentially a land of small farms; 60% of the total area is agricultural. Principal crops are potatoes, oats, wheat, barley, rye, beet root, and grapes, some of which are exported. Cattle and hog raising; dairying. However, it is for the SW mining section, part of the Luxembourg-Lorraine iron basin, that the country is of international importance. Its enormous output of iron and steel, centered at ESCH-SUR-ALZETTE, makes tiny Luxembourg a first-rate industrial power, ranking 6th among the steel-producing countries of Europe outside the USSR (after England, Germany, France, Belgium, and Czechoslovakia). Pig iron and steel are the major exports. Luxembourg steelworks are also active in foreign mining companies, especially in France. Connected with the heavy industry is the mfg. of metalware and appliances. Other industries include wine making (sparkling wine), brewing, tanning, charcoal burning, cement and textile milling (clothing); mfg. of chemicals, fertilizers, explosives, leather and tobacco goods. Most of these are in Luxembourg city and its suburbs. Among other industrial centers are DIFFERDANGE, DUDELANGE, PÉTANGE. There are some gypsum, lime, and slate deposits, as well as several thermal springs, e.g., spas of MONDORF-LES-BAINS and ECHTERNACH. The scenic countryside of rolling hills, medieval castles, and picturesque market towns attracts a great number of tourists. Luxembourg has relatively one of the densest railroad nets in the world; it possesses excellent highways. There is an airport 2 mi. outside Luxembourg city. Located on strategic crossroads, the region has been all through its history a battleground of Western Europe. Originally named *Lützelburg*, it emerged as a county in 10th cent., when it extended bet. the Meuse and the Moselle, including present Belgium Luxembourg prov. Among largest fiefs in Holy Roman Empire, it rose into prominence when its ruler was elected emperor as Henry VII in 1308. Raised to a duchy in 1354. Was seized (1443) by Philip the Good of Burgundy. Passed (1482) to the house of Hapsburg and shared for following 3 centuries the history of the S Netherlands; transferred from Sp. to Austrian rule in 1714. Temporarily occupied (1684–1697) by Louis XIV and during French Revolutionary Wars. Congress of Vienna (1814–15) made Luxembourg a grand duchy in personal union with the Netherlands; at the same time it became a member of the German Confederation, with a Prussian garrison at the capital. Rebelled (1830) with Belgians against Netherlands. It lost (1839) major part, the present Luxembourg prov., to Belgium. At London Conference (1867) the grand duchy was declared a neutral territory, Prussian troops were withdrawn, and the fortress was dismantled. In 1890 a collateral line of Netherlands kings, the dukes of Nassau, became ruling house, thus severing ties with Netherlands. Luxembourg neutrality was twice violated by Germany, in the First World War (occupied 1914–18) and in the Second World War (held May, 1940–Sept., 1944), when grand duchess and her cabinet fled abroad. Both times liberated by American troops. Luxembourg entered (1922) into a customs union with Belgium. It joined (1947) the United Nations, formed (in same year) a close alliance (Benelux bloc) with Belgium and Netherlands, and abolished (1948) by constitutional amendment its neutrality. Signed (1948) the Five Power Pact with England, France, Belgium, and the Netherlands and took part in the European Recovery Program and the North Atlantic Pact. The people are predominantly R.C. Education and military service (since 1944) are compulsory. French is the official, German the literary language, but a Low German dialect—with French and Dutch admixture—is widely spoken.

Luxembourg or **Luxemburg,** province (□ 1,706; pop. 213,917), SE Belgium, in the Ardennes; ⊙ Arlon. Bounded by grand duchy of Luxembourg (E), France (S), Namur prov. (W), Liége prov. (N). Wooded country with little arable soil; coniferous forests supply pit props and wood chemicals; subsoil consists of Devonian and Cambrian rock, quarried commercially. Drained by Ourthe, Semois, and Lesse rivers. Potato and tobacco growing (Neufchâteau and Dohan), extensive pig, cattle, and horse raising; beekeeping, bird raising; dairying and meat packing. Industry concentrated in SE, near frontiers of Luxembourg and France (steel center, Athus); villages in this area also supply labor for industrial centers of Longwy and Mont-Saint-Martin (France), Rodange and Pétange (Luxembourg). Extensive tourist industry. Chief towns: Neufchâteau, Virton, Marche, Bastogne, and Libramont. Mostly French-speaking, but there is a large German minority. Prov. was detached from grand duchy of Luxembourg in 1839. NE section suffered much destruction in Second World War, especially during Battle of the Bulge (1944–45).

Luxembourg or **Luxemburg,** local dialect *Letzeburg*, city (pop. 61,996), ⊙ grand duchy of Luxembourg, on heights above Alzette R. and 120 mi. SE of Brussels; 49°36'N 6°7'E. Rail center; mfg. of clothing, metal products, chemicals, machinery, tobacco, soap; food processing and canning, beer brewing. Its industries are concentrated in suburbs: Pfaffenthal or Paffenthal (refrigeration and air-conditioning machinery); Kockelscheuer, Fr. *La Chéchère* (explosives, gun powder); Pulvermühle (knitting mills); Septfontaines, Ger. *Siebenbrunnen* (ceramics, faïence); Merl (chalk quarrying). Has 16th-cent. cathedral, 19th-cent. town hall (contains Pescatore mus. of paintings), 16th-cent. grand-ducal palace (rebuilt in 19th cent), mus. of zoology and mineralogy, archaeological mus., ruins of 16th-cent. Mansfeld castle. Originally a small fort, Luxembourg was continuously strengthened until it became one of Europe's strongest fortresses; walled town grew around fortress in 10th cent. Once part of a duchy under Holy Roman Empire, the town came into Spanish hands (1477); captured (1684) by the French, who rebuilt fortifications. City went to Spain under Treaty of Ryswick (1697); Austrian possession 1714–94. Joined German Confederation in 1815; garrisoned by Prussia until demilitarized (and its fortifications razed) under Treaty of London (1867). Held by Germans in First and Second World War.

Luxemburg (lŭk'sŭmbûrg). **1** Town (pop. 120), Dubuque co., E Iowa, 21 mi. WNW of Dubuque. State park near by. **2** Village (pop. 519), Kewaunee co., E Wis., on Door Peninsula, 15 mi. E of Green Bay; dairying; flour and feed milling.

Luxeuil-les-Bains (lüksû'ē-lā-bē'), town (pop. 5,264), Haute-Saône dept., E France, at foot of the Vosges, 17 mi. NE of Vesoul; noted watering place with mineral springs (salt, iron, manganese). Also known for its fine lace. Wool and flour milling, furniture, hardware, and perfume mfg. Has 13th–14th-cent. abbatial church, 16th-cent. abbatial palace, and several remarkable 15th–16th-cent. lay bldgs. Known to Romans, it was destroyed (451) by Huns and grew up again around the Abbey of Luxeuil (founded 6th cent.). Devastated c.732 by Arabs, the abbey was restored by Charlemagne and became a center of learning. It was suppressed in French Revolution.

Luxhattipet, India: see LAKSHETTIPET.

Luxor (lŭk'sôr, lo͝ok'–), Arabic *El Uqsor* or *Al-Uqsur* (both: ĕl o͝ok'so͝or), town (pop. 24,118), Qena prov., Upper Egypt, on E bank of the Nile, on railroad, and 32 mi. SSW of Qena, 450 mi. S of Cairo; pottery making, sugar refining; cereals, sugar cane, dates. It is on part of site of anc. THEBES, and shares with KARNAK (adjoining NE), the celebrated Theban ruins. Chief of the Luxor ruins is the temple of Luxor, built by Amenhotep III, of the XVIII dynasty, on the site of an older sanctuary. One of the obelisks is now on the Place de la Concorde in Paris.

Luxora (lŭksô'rü), town (pop. 1,302), Mississippi co., NE Ark., 10 mi. S of Blytheville, near the Mississippi, in cotton-growing area. Founded 1882.

Luxulyan or **Luxulian** (both: lŭksŭl'yŭn, –sĭl'yŭn, –sŭl'yŭn), village and parish (pop. 1,010), central Cornwall, England, 6 mi. S of Bodmin; granite quarrying; paper milling. Treffry Viaduct (100 ft. high, 660 ft. long) spans the valley. Has 15th-cent. church.

Luya, province, Peru: see LAMUD.

Luya (lo͞o'yä), city (pop. 977), Amazonas dept., N Peru, on E Andean slopes, 5 mi. NNW of Chachapoyas; corn, potatoes, alfalfa, sugar cane; sulphur and coal deposits.

Luya Mountains, Chinese *Luya Shan* (lo͞o'yä'shän'), NW Shansi prov., China, rise to over 4,500 ft. 25 mi. SW of Ningwu.

Luyi or **Lu-i** (both: lo͞o'yē'), town, ⊙ Luyi co. (pop. 334,685), E Honan prov., China, 95 mi. SE of Kaifeng, on Anhwei line; cotton weaving; rice, wheat, sesame.

Luynes (lwēn), village (pop. 826), Indre-et-Loire dept., W central France, on Loire R. and 5 mi. W of Tours; winegrowing. Has troglodyte dwellings and feudal castle.

Luy River (lwē'), Basses-Pyrénées and Landes depts., SW France, formed by 2 headstreams (Luy de France and Luy de Béarn) below Amou, flows 20 mi. W to the Adour below Dax.

Luz (lo͞ozh), city (pop. 2,825), W central Minas Gerais, Brazil, near upper São Francisco R., 50 mi. NW of Divinópolis; dairying. Bishopric.

Luz or **Luz-Saint-Sauveur** (lüz-sē-sōvûr'), village (pop. 758), Hautes-Pyrénées dept., SW France, in central Pyrenees, on the Gave de Pau and 10 mi. SSE of Argelès-Gazost; resort; mfg. of woolen textiles. Hydroelectric plants. Has 12th–14th-cent. church. Near-by Saint-Sauveur-les-Bains has sulphur springs.

Luz or **Luz de Lagos** (lo͞ozh dĭ lä'go͞osh), village (pop. 539), Faro dist., S Portugal, on the Atlantic (S coast), 3 mi. WSW of Lagos; seaside resort.

Luz, La, Mexico: see LA LUZ.

Luz, La, Nicaragua: see SIUNA.

Luza (lo͞o'zŭ), city (1944 pop. over 2,000) NW Kirov oblast, Russian SFSR, on railroad, on Luza R. and 45 mi. SSE of Kotlas; sawmilling center; metalworks. Became city in 1944.

Luzarches (lüzärsh'), village (pop. 1,291), Seine-et-Oise dept., N central France, 18 mi. NNE of Paris; mfg. (agr. instruments, saws).

Luza River (lo͞o'zŭ), N central European USSR, rises SE of Oparino, Kirov oblast; flows NNE, past Obyachevo, and generally W, past Lalsk and Luza, to Yug R. S of Veliki Ustyug; c.225 mi. long. Navigable for 50 mi. above mouth, below Lalsk.

Luze (lo͞o'zhĕ), Czech *Luže*, village (pop. 1,275), E Bohemia, Czechoslovakia, 7 mi. SW of Vysoke Myto; summer resort noted for trout fishing. Ruins of 14th-cent Kosumberk castle are 7 mi. SW.

Luzech (lüzĕsh'), village (pop. 685), Lot dept., SW France, within bend of Lot R. 8 mi. W of Cahors; furniture factory; wine, fruit, tobacco growing. Has ruins of Gallic oppidum.

Luzenac (lüzünäk'), village (pop. 450), Ariège dept., S France, in the Pyrenees, on Ariège R. and 16 mi. SSE of Foix; talc quarrying and processing center.

Luzern, Switzerland: see LUCERNE.

Luzerne (lo͞ozûrn'), county (□ 891; pop. 392,241), E central Pa.; ⊙ Wilkes-Barre. Anthracite-mining and industrial region, drained by Susquehanna and Lehigh rivers; hilly, except for broad WYOMING VALLEY. First permanent settlements 1753 by people from Conn. Anthracite, sandstone; mfg. (textiles, clothing, food products, beverages, wire, tobacco products), printing; agr. (vegetables, fruit, grain, poultry, dairy products). Formed 1786.

Luzerne. **1** Town (pop. 186), Benton co., E central Iowa, 27 mi. WSW of Cedar Rapids, in agr. area. **2** Village, Warren co., N.Y.: see LAKE LUZERNE. **3** Borough (pop. 6,176), Luzerne co., NE central Pa., 3 mi. N of Wilkes-Barre; anthracite. Inc. 1882.

Luzheny (lo͞ozhĕ'nē), Rum. *Lujeni* (lo͞ozhĕn'), village (1941 pop. 2,923), N Chernovtsy oblast, Ukrainian SSR, in N Bukovina, on railroad and 8 mi. NW of Chernovtsy, near Prut R.; sugar milling.

Luziânia (lo͞ozyä'nyŭ), city (pop. 1,554), E Goiás, central Brazil, 65 mi. E of Anápolis; cheese mfg., fruit preserving, tobacco and coffee shipping. Nitrate and rock-crystal deposits in vicinity. Until 1944, called Santa Luzia.

Luzicka Nisa River, Czechoslovakia: see NEISSE RIVER.

Luzicke Hory, Czechoslovakia: see LUSATIAN MOUNTAINS.

Luzilândia (lo͞ozēlän'dyŭ), city (pop. 1,617), N Piauí, Brazil, on right bank of Parnaíba R. (Maranhão border) and 50 mi. SW of Parnaíba city; sugar cane, tobacco. Airfield. Until 1944, called Pôrto Alegre.

Luzinga (lo͞ozĭng'gä), Eastern Prov., SE Uganda, on railroad and 18 mi. N of Jinja; cotton, tobacco, coffee, bananas, millet.

Luz Island, Chile: see CHONOS ARCHIPELAGO.

Luznice River (lo͞oz'nyĭtsĕ), Czech *Lužnice*, Ger. *Lainsitz* (lĭn'zĭts), S Bohemia, Czechoslovakia, and N Austria, rises at Czechoslovak-Austrian border 12 mi. SE of Kaplice, flows c.16 mi. E and NNE in Austria, past Ceske Velenice (Bohemia), then NNW, through fish-pond area (around Trebon), past Sobeslav and Tabor, and SW to Vltava (Moldau) R. 1 mi. WNW of Tyn nad Vltavou; total length, 129 mi.

Luzon (lo͞ozŏn', Sp. lo͞osōn'), largest and most important island (□ 40,420; 1939 pop. 7,374,798) of the Philippines, at N end of the archipelago, separated from Formosa by Luzon Strait; 12°30'–18°40'N 119°45'–124°12'E. An irregular isl. (max. length 489 mi., max. width 138 mi.), with a long, deeply indented SE peninsula. Bordered E by Philippine Sea, W by S.China Sea, it is separated S from Mindoro by Verde Isl. Passage and from Samar by San Bernardino Strait. Of its great bays, the most important are MANILA BAY and LINGAYEN GULF. Several great ranges extend N-S, notably the Sierra Madre (NE), Cordillera Central (N), and Caraballo Mts. (S central); in S rise the active volcanoes Mt. MAYON and Mt. TAAL (on VOLCANO ISLAND). Of its many lakes, Laguna de BAY and L. Taal are the largest. CAGAYAN RIVER is longest in the Philippines; other streams are Agno, Pampanga, and the short but important Pasig. Off coast are numerous satellite isls., notably Babuyan and Batan isls. (N), Catanduanes (E), Marinduque (S), and Polillo (E). Luzon is a rich agr. area, and its great central Cagayan valley produces 40% of the total rice crop of the Philippines. Also grown are abacá (Manila hemp), sugar cane, tobacco, coconuts, coffee. There are mineral deposits (manganese, copper, gold, iron, and chromite), only partly developed; Baguio, the summer resort in the N central mts., is a gold-mining center. Isl. is inhabited mostly by Tagalogs (in S) and Ilokanos (in NW); there are also Negritos (in N hills) and others. The Hukbalahaps, a dissident group in central area, caused civil unrest, 1946–51. A rail line runs N from Manila to San Fernando (La Union prov.) and S to Legaspi. Besides its great metropolis MANILA, other notable cities include BAGUIO, QUEZON CITY, TARLAC, LEGASPI, BATANGAS, LAOAG, and SAN FERNANDO. See also the articles on each of the 24 provs. of Luzon: ABRA, ALBAY, BATAAN, BATANGAS, BULACAN, CAGAYAN, CAMARINES NORTE, CAMARINES SUR, CAVITE, ILOCOS NORTE, ILOCOS SUR, ISABELA, LAGUNA, LA UNION, MOUNTAIN PROVINCE, NUEVA ECIJA, NUEVA VIZCAYA, PAMPANGA, PANGASINAN, QUEZON, RIZAL, SORSOGON, TARLAC, ZAMBALES. In the Second World War, Luzon was the scene of the 1st Jap. attacks on the Philippines; in Dec., 1941, Manila and Cavite were bombed, and numerous Jap. landings (at Aparri, Vigan, Legaspi, and Lingayen Gulf) swiftly overran the isl., forcing the defenders into BATAAN PENINSULA in the S, where their gallant stand was made. In Jan., 1945, U. S. forces began the recapture of Luzon; the fighting was highlighted by the fierce battle which destroyed Manila and by the battle in the mts. before Baguio.

Luzon Strait, Philippines, channel connecting S. China Sea and Philippine Sea, bet. Formosa (N) and Luzon (S). Divided into 3 channels: Babuyan Channel (bäbo͞oyän') (bet. Babuyan Isls. and Luzon), Balintang Channel (bälĕntäng') (bet. Babuyan Isls. and Batan Isls.), and Bashi Channel (bä'shē) (bet. Batan Isls. and Formosa).

Luz-Saint-Sauveur, France: see LUZ.

Luzuriaga (lo͞oso͞o-ryä'gä), town (pop. estimate 1,000), N Mendoza prov., Argentina, in Mendoza R. valley (irrigation area), on railroad and 5 mi. SSE of Maipú; wine making.

Luzy (lüzē'), village (pop. 1,847), Nièvre dept., central France, in the S Morvan, 19 mi. SW of Autun; road junction and livestock market.

Luzyca, region, Poland: see LUSATIA.

Luzyckie, Gory, Poland: see LUSATIAN MOUNTAINS.

Luzy-sur-Marne (lüzē'-sür-märn'), village (pop. 298), Haute-Marne dept., NE France, on Marne R. and Marne-Saône Canal, and 5 mi. SSE of Chaumont; cutlery mfg.

Luzzara (lo͞otsä'rä), town (pop. 2,503), Reggio nell'Emilia prov., Emilia-Romagna, N central Italy, near Po R., 3 mi. NE of Guastalla; wine, sausage, straw hats. Scene of defeat (1702) of Imperialists under Prince Eugene by French and Spanish under Vendôme.

Luzzi (lo͞o'tsē), village (pop. 2,767), Cosenza prov., Calabria, S Italy, 11 mi. NNE of Cosenza; dried figs, wine, olive oil.

Lva Tolstogo or **L'va Tolstogo** (lyŭvä' tŭlstô'vô), village, central Kaluga oblast, Russian SFSR, 12 mi. NW of Kaluga, near Ugra R., in wooded area.

Lvov or **L'vov** (lyŭvôf'), oblast (□ 4,300; 1946 pop. estimate 1,500,000), W Ukrainian SSR; ⊙ Lvov. In highlands on Polish border (W and NW); includes SE Roztoche mts. and Gologory mts. Drained by upper Bug and Styr rivers and by tributaries of Dniester R. and San R.; dark prairie soils. Humid continental climate (short summers). Lignite mining near Zolochev, Zholkva, and Rava-Russkaya. Extensive agr. (rye, wheat, oats, livestock, truck); flour milling, distilling, brewing, meat and vegetable preserving. Lumbering, stone quarrying. Lvov is main industrial center; light mfg. at Zolochev, Zholkva, and Brody. Formed (1939) out of parts of Pol. Lwow and Tarnopol provs., following Soviet occupation of E Poland; held by Germany (1941–44); ceded to USSR in 1945.

Lvov or **L'vov,** Pol. *Lwów* (lŭvo͞of'), Ger. *Lemberg* (lĕm'bĕrk), city (1931 pop. 316,177), ⊙ Lvov oblast, Ukrainian SSR, bet. Roztoche and Gologory mts., on small left tributary of Bug R. and 250 mi. WSW of Kiev; 49°50'N 24°E. Major transportation (7 rail lines, airport) and mfg. center; metalworking (armatures, agr. machinery, railroad and printing equipment), mfg. of textiles, leather, radio and telegraph apparatus, electric bulbs, glass, chemicals; woodworking; food processing (sugar, cereals, meat, vegetables, hops). Petroleum refining (gasoline, benzine, lubricating oil, asphalt); auto assembling. Important commercial and cultural center; site of univ. (established 1658), polytechnical inst., technical schools, theaters, museums, and art galleries. Has 14th-cent. Roman and Armenian Catholic cathedrals, 16th-cent. palace, 18th-cent. Greek Catholic cathedral, town hall (1837), numerous old churches and monuments. Founded in 1250 by Galician prince Lev (Leo); became ⊙ Ruthenia. Ceded to Poland and chartered (1340) as Leopolis (its Latin name); later subjected to several Cossack, Turkish, Tatar, and Swedish assaults. Became ⊙ Austrian prov. of Galicia, following 1st partition of Poland (1772). Scene of battles during First World War; became ⊙ independent Ukrainian Republic (1918); reverted to Poland (1919); ceded to USSR in 1945. Jewish pop. (c.100,000) was largely exterminated during Second World War.

Lwan, China: see LWAN RIVER.

Lwancheng or **Luan-ch'eng** (both: lwän'chŭng'), town, ⊙ Lwancheng co. (pop. 93,997), SW Hopeh prov., China, 14 mi. SE of Shihkiachwang, near Peking-Hankow RR; cotton, wheat, millet. Also written Lancheng.

Lwan Ho, China: see LWAN RIVER.

Lwanhsien or **Luan-hsien** (both: lwän'shyĕn'), town, ⊙ Lwanhsien co. (pop. 735,948), NE Hopeh prov., China, on Lwan R. and 30 mi. ENE of Tangshan, and on Tientsin-Mukden RR; coal-mining center; medicinal herbs, nuts. Also written Lanhsien.

Lwanping or **Luan-p'ing** (both: lwän'pĭng'), town, ⊙ Lwanping co. (pop. 121,692), SW Jehol prov., Manchuria, on Lwan R. and 9 mi. W of Chengteh, and on railroad; gold, silver, and iron deposits; agr. (millet, kaoliang, medicinal herbs). Also written Lanping.

Lwan River, Luan River (lwän), or **Lan River** (län), Chinese *Lwan Ho, Luan Ho,* or *Lan Ho* (hŭ), N China, rises as Shangtu R. in NE Chahar prov., flows 500 mi. N, past Paoyüan and Shangtu, and SE through Jehol prov., past Lwanping, into Hopeh prov., past Sifengkow and Lwanhsien, to Gulf of Chihli. Unnavigable, it is obstructed by rapids in upper course.

Lwow, Ukrainian SSR: see LVOV, city.

Lwowek (lŭvo͞o'vĕk), Pol. *Lwówek*, Ger. *Neustadt bei Pinne* (noi'shtät bī pĭ'nŭ), town (1946 pop. 2,262), Poznan prov., W Poland, 32 mi. W of Poznan; rail spur terminus; machine mfg., sawmilling.

Lwowek Slaski (shlō'skē), Pol. *Lwówek Śląski*, Ger. *Löwenberg* (lû'vŭnbĕrk), town (1939 pop. 6,328; 1946 pop. 3,364) in Lower Silesia, after 1945 in Wroclaw prov., SW Poland, on Bobrawa R. and 25 mi. WSW of Liegnitz (Legnica); agr. market (grain, malt, potatoes, livestock); gypsum quarrying. Has 16th-cent. church, remains of medieval town walls. Chartered 1217. Had important woolen trade until Thirty Years War.

Lyady (lyä'dē). **1** Town (1926 pop. 3,625), SE Vitebsk oblast, Belorussian SSR, 31 mi. ENE of Orsha; linen milling. **2** Village (1939 pop. over 500), N Pskov oblast, Russian SFSR, on Plyussa R. and 40 mi. WSW of Luga dairying.

Lyailyak-Khana, Uzbek SSR: see ALTY-ARYK.

Lyakhi (lyä'khē), village (1926 pop. 2,584), SE Vladimir oblast, Russian SFSR, on Oka R. and 18 mi. SSW of Murom; potatoes.

Lyakhovichi (lyä'khŭvēchē), Pol. *Lachowicze* (läkhôvē'chĕ), city (1931 pop. 4,547), S central Baranovichi oblast, Belorussian SSR, 12 mi. SE of Baranovichi; agr. processing (flaxseed, grain), mfg. (haberdashery, soap). Has 17th-cent. castle. Old Pol. fortress, assaulted (1660) by Russians. Passed (1795) from Poland to Russia; reverted (1921) to Poland; ceded to USSR in 1945.

Lyakhov Islands (lyä'khŭf), S group (□ 2,660) of New Siberian Isls., bet. Laptev and E.Siberian seas; part of Yakut Autonomous SSR, Russian SFSR; 73°-74°15'N 133°-143°45'E. Separated from Anjou group of NEW SIBERIAN ISLANDS by Sannikov Strait, from mainland by Dmitri Laptev Strait. Includes Bolshoi Lyakhov, Maly Lyakhov, and Stolbovoi isls. Fossil mammoth ivory excavations. Discovered 1770 by Rus. trader, for whom they are named.

Lyakhovtsy, Ukrainian SSR: see BELOGORYE, Kamenets-Podolski oblast.

Lyaki (lyä'kē), town (1926 pop. 542), central Azerbaijan SSR, rail station 6 mi. S of Agdash; cotton ginning.

Lyallpur (lī'ălpo͝or), agr. district (□ 3,522; 1951 pop. 2,157,000), Punjab, W Pakistan; ⊙ Lyallpur. In S Rechna Doab area; bounded by Ravi R. (S, SE); extensively irrigated by Lower Chenab Canal system. Wheat is main crop; also millet, cotton, oilseeds, sugar cane; cotton ginning, hand-loom weaving. Chief towns: Lyallpur, Gojra, Kamalia.

Lyallpur, city (1951 pop. 180,000), ⊙ Lyallpur dist., Punjab, W Pakistan, 75 mi. WSW of Lahore. Rail junction (workshops); major agr. market; wheat and other grains collected here for export to Karachi; cotton ginning and milling, flour, oilseed, and sugar milling, tea packing, fruit canning, mfg. of ice, ghee, chemical dyes, agr. implements; engineering works; sulphuric-acid plant. Punjab Agr. Col.

Lyalya River (lyä'lyŭ), Sverdlovsk oblast, Russian SFSR, rises in the central Urals c.15 mi. WSW of Pavda, flows 110 mi. generally E, past Pavda, Staraya Lyalya, and Novaya Lyalya, to Sosva R. 12 mi. E of Sosva; lumber floating. Receives Lobva R. (left).

Lyambir or **Lyambir'** (lyŭmbēr'), village (1926 pop. 2,642), central Mordvinian Autonomous SSR, Russian SFSR, 7 mi. NNW of Saransk; truck, grain.

Lyamino (lyä'mēnŭ), town (1938 pop. over 500), E central Molotov oblast, Russian SFSR, near Chusovaya R., 5 mi. WSW (under jurisdiction) of Chusovoi, on railroad; mfg. of heat-insulating plates; woodworking, charcoal burning.

Lyangar (lyŭn-gär'). **1** Village (1939 pop. over 500), E Kashka-Darya oblast, Uzbek SSR, 25 mi. S of Shakhrizyabz; grain, livestock. **2** Town (1939 pop. over 500), NW Samarkand oblast, Uzbek SSR, in the Ak-Tau, 40 mi. NW of Katta-Kurgan; molybdenum and tungsten mining.

Lyangasovo (lyŭn-gä'sŭvŭ), town (1939 pop. over 2,000), central Kirov oblast, Russian SFSR, on railroad and 7 mi. WSW of Kirov.

Lyanozovo, Russian SFSR: see VAGONOREMONT.

Lyaskelya (lyä'skĭlyŭ), Finnish *Läskelä* (lăs'kĕlă), town (1948 pop. over 500), SW Karelo-Finnish SSR, on railroad and 12 mi. ENE of Sortavala; paper-milling center; mfg. of prefabricated houses. In Finland until 1940.

Lyaskovets (lyä'skôvĕts), city (pop. 5,560), Gorna Oryakhovitsa dist., N Bulgaria, adjoining Gorna Oryakhovitsa, on rail spur; market center in vegetable- and fruitgrowing dist.; wine making. Ruins of anc. monastery near by. Sometimes spelled Leskovec or Ljeskovec.

Lyasomin Island (lyä'sŭmēn), in Archangel oblast, Russian SFSR, in W section of Northern Dvina R. delta, 10 mi. NW of Archangel; forested and swampy.

Lybster (lĭb'stŭr), village, SE Caithness, Scotland, on Moray Firth, 12 mi. SW of Wick; herring-fishing center. Near by is Clyth Ness.

Lycaonia (lĭ"kāō'nēŭ), anc. country of S central Asia Minor, bordered S by Taurus Mts., bet. Galatia (N), Cappadocia (E), Cilicia (S), Pisidia (SW), and Phrygia (W). Passed successively to the Persians, Syrians, and Romans. Later divided bet. Galatia and Cappadocia. Chief city was Iconium (modern KONYA, Turkey).

Lychen (lü'khŭn), town (pop. 3,649), Brandenburg, E Germany, on small Lychen L. (connected by short canal with the Havel), 15 mi. SE of Neustrelitz; climatic health resort; forestry. Has early-Gothic church, remains of old town walls. Founded 1248.

Lychkovo (lĭchkô'vŭ), village (1948 pop. over 2,000), S central Novgorod oblast, Russian SFSR, 38 mi. E of Staraya Russa; flax.

Lycia (lĭ'shŭ), anc. country of SW Asia Minor, on the Mediterranean. Mountainous promontory, never politically important. In historic times, passed to Persians, Syrians, and finally (189 B.C.) Rome. Cities included Patara, Myra, and Xanthus. Caria was to NW, Phrygia, Pisidia, and Pamphilia to N.

Lyck, Poland: see ELK.

Lyckeby (lü'kŭbü"), village (pop. 2,169), Blekinge co., S Sweden, 3 mi. NNE of Karlskrona; grain, livestock.

Lyck River, Poland: see LEG RIVER, Bialystok prov.

Lycksele (lük'sā"lŭ), city (pop. 2,855), Vasterbotten co., N Sweden, on Ume R. and 70 mi. NW of Umea; Lapp trading center, with important fairs. Inc. as town 1929; as city 1946.

Lycoming (lĭkō'mĭng, -kō'-), county (□ 1,215; pop. 101,249), N central Pa.; ⊙ Williamsport. Hilly agr. and forested region; drained by West Branch of Susquehanna R. and by Loyalsock and Pine creeks. Metal, leather, and lumber products, food products, beverages, textiles; anthracite, limestone; dairying, agr. (grain, clover, poultry). Formed 1795.

Lycopolis, Egypt: see ASYUT, city.

Lycus, Iraq: see ZAB, GREAT.

Lycus River, in anc. times. **1** In N Asia Minor, a tributary of the Iris (modern Yesil Irmak): see KELKIT RIVER, Turkey. **2** In W Asia Minor, a tributary of the Maeander (modern Buyuk Menderes).

Lydd (lĭd), municipal borough (1931 pop. 2,778; 1951 census 2,774), S Kent, England, 3 mi. SSW of Romney; agr. market. It is a "member" of the Cinque Port of Romney. Has 15th-cent. church, damaged in Second World War, built by Cardinal Wolsey. The explosive Lyddite was 1st made here.

Lydda (lĭ'dŭ), Arabic *Ludd*, Hebrew *Lod* or *Lud*, town (1946 pop. estimate 18,250; 1949 pop. estimate 10,450), central Israel, in Judaean Plain, at foot of Judaean Hills, 11 mi. SE of Tel Aviv; rail junction. Just N is Israel's chief international airport (32°N 34°54'E). Town evacuated by Arab pop. prior to its capture (1948) by Israeli forces; by 1950 new Jewish immigrants had largely replaced the former Arab pop. New industries include mfg. of telephone equipment. Has remains of 13th-cent. Church of St. George, who was traditionally b. and buried here. Of anc. origin, Lydda is, in New Testament, scene of Peter's healing of the paralytic. Burned (A.D. 66) by Celestius Gallus and (A.D. 68) by Vespasian; rebuilt by Hadrian and named *Diospolis*. Episcopal see in 5th cent. Captured (1099) by Crusaders, who called it St. Jorge de Lidde; destroyed (1191) by Saladin. Rebuilt by Richard Coeur de Lion.

Lyden, N.Mex.: see VELARDE.

Lydenburg (lī'dŭnbûrg, Afrikaans lā'dŭnbûrkh"), town (pop. 3,846), E Transvaal, U. of So. Afr., on Dorps R. and 150 mi. ENE of Pretoria; alt. 4,820 ft.; platinum-mining and agr. center (cotton, wheat, tobacco, sheep). Founded 1839, it was ⊙ independent republic, inc. 1858 with Utrecht Republic.

Lydford (lĭd'fŭrd), town and parish (pop. 2,218), W Devon, England, 8 mi. SW of Okehampton; agr. market and tourist resort. Has Norman castle ruins. Lydford Cascade has a fall of 150 ft.

Lydia (lĭ'dēu), anc. country of W Asia Minor, on the Aegean and traversed by the Hermus (modern Gediz) and the Cayster (modern Kucuk Menderes). An anc. independent kingdom antedating 13th cent. B.C. Under its last dynasty, begun 687 B.C., it became an empire of great wealth, with its ⊙ at SARDIS. To Lydian rulers is ascribed 1st use of coined money. The Lydian empire for a time included some of the great Ionian cities, such as Erythrae and Colophon, and also Philadelphia and Magnesia. The last ruler was Croesus, who was defeated (before 540 B.C.) by Cyrus the Great of Persia. Mysia was on N, Phrygia on E, and Caria on S.

Lydia, Mount, Turkey: see MYCALE, MOUNT.

Lydia Mills, textile village (pop. 1,212), Laurens co., NW S.C., adjacent to Clinton; cotton milling.

Lydiate, residential village and parish (pop. 1,087), SW Lancashire, England, 9 mi. N of Liverpool.

Lydick, village (pop. 1,175), St. Joseph co., N Ind., 7 mi. WNW of South Bend.

Lydney, town and parish (pop. 4,158), W Gloucester, England, near Severn R., 19 mi. N of Bristol; tin-plate rolling mills, chemical works, paper mills. Church dates from 13th cent.; has 14th-cent. cross. Site of Roman settlement.

Lye and Wollescote (lī, wo͝olz'kŭt), former urban district (1931 pop. 12,237), N Worcester, England. Includes towns of Lye, on Stour R. and 10 mi. W of Birmingham, and (E) Wollescote, with sheet-metal industry. Inc. 1933 in Stourbridge.

Lyeksa, Lake, Karelo-Finnish SSR: see LEKSOZERO.

Lyell, Mount (11,495 ft.), on Alta.–B.C. border, in Rocky Mts., on W edge of Banff Natl. Park, 75 mi. SE of Jasper; 51°57'N 117°6'W.

Lyell, Mount (lī'ŭl), E Calif., peak (13,095 ft.) of the Sierra Nevada, on E boundary of Yosemite Natl. Park and c.20 mi. SSW of Mono L. Has large glacier.

Lyell Land (lüĕl'), Dan. *Lyells Land*, peninsula (35 mi. long, 15–28 mi. wide), E Greenland, on King Oscar Fjord; 72°35'N 25°30'W. Rises to 7,216 ft. near its base.

Lyemun Pass, Hong Kong: see LEIMUN PASS.

Lyerly (lī'ŭrlē), town (pop. 524), Chattooga co., NW Ga., 17 mi. NW of Rome and on Chattooga R.; sawmilling.

Lyford (lī'fŭrd), town (pop. 1,473), Willacy co., extreme S Texas, c.40 mi. NW of Brownsville; trade point in irrigated farm area.

Lygna River (lüng'nä), Nor. *Lygna, Lyngdalselv*, or *Lyngselv*, Vest-Agder co., S Norway, rises E of Knaben NE of Flekkefjord, flows c.40 mi. S to an inlet of North Sea at Lyngdal.

Lygoudista, Greece: see CHORA.

Lygudista, Greece: see CHORA.

Lykens (lī'kŭnz), borough (pop. 2,735), Dauphin co., E central Pa., 22 mi. NNE of Harrisburg; anthracite; clothing, paper boxes. Settled c.1740, laid out 1848, inc. 1872.

Lykodimos or **Likodhimos** (both: lĭkô'dhĭmôs), mountain in SW Peloponnesus, Greece, in Messenia Peninsula, rises to 3,146 ft. 16 mi. WSW of Kalamata. Also called Mathia.

Lyle, village (pop. 609), Mower co., SE Minn., on Iowa line, near Cedar R., and 11 mi. S of Austin, in grain, livestock, and poultry area; dairy products.

Lyman (lī'mŭn), county (□ 1,685; pop. 4,572), S central S.Dak.; ⊙ Kennebec. Agr. and cattle-raising region bounded S by White R., E by Missouri R.; Lower Brule Indian Reservation is in N. Livestock, dairy products, poultry, grain. Formed 1890.

Lyman. 1 Town (pop. 499), York co., SW Maine, 10 mi. WNW of Biddeford; includes village of Goodwin's Mills. **2** Village (pop. 666), Scotts Bluff co., W Nebr., 20 mi. W of Scottsbluff, near N.Platte R. and Wyo. line; beet sugar, livestock, grain, potatoes. **3** Town (pop. 241), Grafton co., NW N.H., 38 mi. SW of Berlin, in agr., recreational area. **4** Textile village (pop. 1,365), Spartanburg co., NW S.C., near Tyger R., 11 mi. W of Spartanburg. **5** Town (pop. 378), Skagit co., NW Wash., 15 mi. NE of Mt. Vernon and on Skagit R.; lumber, truck. **6** Town (pop. 483), Uinta co., SW Wyo., near Blacks Fork, 35 mi. E of Evanston; alt. 6,695 ft.; poultry center.

Lyme (līm). **1** Town (pop. 857), New London co., SE Conn., on the Connecticut and 12 mi. WNW of New London; agr., fishing, resorts. Includes Hadlyme village (furniture) and Hamburg, with yacht harbor at mouth of Eight Mile R.; 3 state parks. Formerly included EAST LYME and OLD LYME towns; Lyme village is in Old Lyme town. **2** Town (pop. 924), Grafton co., W N.H., on the Connecticut and 35 mi. NW of Franklin.

Lyme Regis (līm' rē'jĭs), municipal borough (1931 pop. 2,620; 1951 census 3,191), W Dorset, England, on Lyme Bay of the Channel and 22 mi. NW of Weymouth; seaside resort and port. Has 15th-cent. church. Landing place of Monmouth (1685) before battle of Sedgemoor. Blue Lias rock quarried near by, and archaeological finds have been made here.

Lyminge (lĭ'mĭnj, lī'–), town and parish (pop. 1,647), E Kent, England, 4 mi. N of Hythe; agr. market. The church was 1st built in 965.

Lymington (lĭ'–), municipal borough (1931 pop. 5,177; 1951 census 22,674), SW Hampshire, England, on Lymington R. near its mouth on The Solent, 11 mi. E of Christchurch; agr. market and coastal port, terminal of ferry to Yarmouth on the Isle of Wight. There are small dockyards (yacht building). Henry II landed here (1154) on way to his coronation. Just N are remains of Roman camp. It was site of anc. Br. saltworks.

Lymm (lĭm), urban district (1931 pop. 5,643; 1951 census 6,410), N Cheshire, England, on Bridgewater Canal and 5 mi. E of Warrington; stone quarrying, salt mfg., mfg. of tools.

Lympne, England: see HYTHE, Kent.

Lympstone, village and parish (pop. 1,042), S Devon, England, on Exe R. estuary and 7 mi. SE of Exeter; fishing port. Its 15th-cent. church contains personal relics of Sir Francis Drake.

Lynaes, Denmark: see HUNDESTED.

Lyna River (wĭ'nä), Pol. *Łyna*, Ger. *Alle* (ä'lŭ), in East Prussia, after 1945 in NE Poland and Kaliningrad oblast, Russian SFSR, rises in Poland in small lake S of Allenstein (Olsztyn), flows 137 mi. generally N, past Allenstein, Lidzbark Warminski, and Bartoszyce, into Russian SFSR, past Pravdinsk and Druzhba (head of navigation; junction with Masurian Canal), to Pregel R. at Znamensk.

Lynas, Point, Wales: see AMLWCH.

Lynbrook, residential village (pop. 17,314), Nassau co., SE N.Y., on SW Long Isl., 7 mi. ESE of Jamaica, in truck-farming area; mfg. (sportswear, machinery, metal products, lamps, buttons, pens and pencils, toys); nurseries. Settled before the Revolution; inc. 1911.

Lynch, Villa Lynch, or **Villa Linch** (vī'yä lēnch'), town (pop. estimate, 7,000) in W Greater Buenos Aires, Argentina, on federal dist. line. Industrial center: textiles (silk and wool), rubber goods, cement articles, chains, pistons, dairy products.

Lynch. 1 Mining village (pop. 7,952, with adjacent Benham), Harlan co., SE Ky., in the Cumberlands near Va. line, near Poor Fork of Cumberland R., 50 mi. ENE of Middlesboro; a company-owned bituminous-coal-mining center; airport. Big Black Mtn., highest peak in Ky., is just S. Founded 1917. **2** Village (pop. 440), Boyd co., N Nebr., 20 mi. ESE of Butte and on Ponca Creek; livestock, grain. Excavation of prehistoric settlements was begun near by in 1936.

Lynchburg. 1 Village (pop. 972), Highland co., SW Ohio, 14 mi. S of Wilmington and on East Fork of Little Miami R.; livestock, poultry, grain; limestone quarry. **2** Town (pop. 506), Lee co., NE central S.C., 18 mi. NE of Sumter; turpentine. **3** Town (pop. 401), ⊙ Moore co., S Tenn., 16 mi. SSE of Shelbyville, in timber and agr. area; makes whiskey. **4** City (pop. 47,727), in but independent of Campbell co., SW central Va., in Blue Ridge foothills, on James R. and 40 mi. ENE of Roanoke. Transportation (rail, highway), trade, and distribution center of W piedmont (tobacco, fruit, dairy products, grain); an important dark-tobacco market; a leading Va. mfg. center (shoes, textiles, clothing, paper, drugs, tanning extracts, fertilizer, farm equipment, wagons, foundry products, food products). Randolph-Macon Woman's Col., Va. Theological Seminary and Col., Lynchburg Col., and Va. Episcopal School for boys here. Sweet Briar Col. is 11 mi. N at Sweet Briar; APPOMATTOX is 17 mi. E; "Poplar Forest" (1806–9; restored), country home of Jefferson, is 8 mi. W. Settled 1757; founded 1786; inc. as town 1805, as city 1852. A Confederate supply base in Civil War; Union troops attacked unsuccessfully in June, 1864.

Lynches River, NE S.C., rises just over border in N.C., flows c.140 mi. SE to Pee Dee R. 5 mi. E of Johnsonville. Lee State Park is along river near Bishopville.

Lyndeboro or **Lyndeborough** (lĭnd'bŭrō), town (pop. 552), Hillsboro co., S N.H., 17 mi. SW of Manchester.

Lynden (lĭn'–), village (pop. estimate 500), S Ont., 16 mi. W of Hamilton; dairying, fruitgrowing.

Lynden (lĭn'dŭn), town (pop. 2,161), Whatcom co., NW Wash., 15 mi. N of Bellingham and on Nooksack R.; dairy products, fruit, poultry, flower bulbs. Port of entry. Settled c.1860; inc. 1891.

Lyndesnas, Norway: see LINDESNES.

Lyndhurst (lĭnd'–), village (pop. c.300), SE Ont., on Gananoque R. and 30 mi. NE of Kingston; dairying, mixed farming.

Lyndhurst (lĭnd'–), town and parish (pop. 2,594), SW Hampshire, England, in center of the New Forest, 8 mi. W of Southampton; agr. market and tourist resort. Site of 17th-cent. "King's House," residence of Deputy-Surveyor of the New Forest.

Lyndhurst. 1 Township (pop. 19,980), Bergen co., NE N.J., near Passaic R., 5 mi. NNW of Jersey City; mfg. (machinery, metal products, clothing, preserves, paints, asphalt, burlap). Inc. 1852. **2** City (pop. 7,359), Cuyahoga co., N Ohio, an E residential suburb of Cleveland. Inc. 1917.

Lyndon (lĭn'dŭn). **1** Village (pop. 594), Whiteside co., NW Ill., on Rock R. (bridged here) and 12 mi. WSW of Sterling, in agr. area. **2** City (pop. 729), ⊙ Osage co., E Kansas, on small affluent of Marais des Cygnes R. and 30 mi. S of Topeka; trade center in livestock and grain region; makes candy, brooms, rugs. **3** Suburban village (1940 pop. 681), Jefferson co., NW Ky., 9 mi. E of Louisville, within Louisville metropolitan dist. Seat of Ky. children's home and Kentucky Military Inst. Herr House here (built 1789) is one of earliest brick houses in Ky. **4** Town (pop. 3,360), Caledonia co., NE Vt., on Passumpsic R. and 7 mi. N of St. Johnsbury; wood and metal products. Includes villages of Lyndon Center (pop. 321), seat of teachers col., and LYNDONVILLE. Settled 1788.

Lyndon Station, village (pop. 377), Juneau co., S central Wis., near the Dells of the Wisconsin, 10 mi. SE of Mauston; lumber.

Lyndonville (lĭn'dŭnvĭl). **1** Village (pop. 777), Orleans co., W N.Y., 35 mi. NE of Buffalo, near L. Ontario; mfg. (chemicals, fruit products, beverages); agr. (fruit, truck, grain). Inc. 1903. **2** Village (pop. 1,506) in LYNDON town, Caledonia co., NE Vt.; veterinary medicines, wood, metal and dairy products, maple sugar.

Lyndora, village (pop. 5,410, with adjacent Highfield), Butler co., W Pa., just SW of Butler.

Lyneham (lī'nŭm), agr. village and parish (pop. 934), N Wiltshire, England, 9 mi. WSW of Swindon. Has medieval church. Important U.S. air base established here in Second World War maintained after the war.

Lyngdal (lüng'däl), village and canton (pop. 2,558), Vest-Agder co., S Norway, at head of Lyngdal Fjord (10-mi. inlet of the North Sea), at mouth of the Lygna, 18 mi. SE of Flekkefjord; lumber mills, cement factory. Lyngdal is also the name of the valley of the Lygna.

Lyngdalselv, Norway: see LYGNA RIVER.

Lyngen Fjord (lüng'ŭn), inlet (60 mi. long, 2–5 mi. wide) of Norwegian Sea, Troms co., N Norway, 30 mi. E of Tromso. Noted for spectacular scenery; mts. on W shore rise abruptly to c.4,700 ft. Further inland, 25 mi. E of Tromso, the Jegervasstind or Jaegervasstind (both: yä'gŭrväs-tĭn), surrounded by glaciers, rises to 6,283 ft. At its foot is large Lapp settlement. Villages on fjord include Skibotn (shē'bōtŭn) (pop. 121), 40 mi. ESE of Tromso; known as fur market in Middle Ages. Fjord formed N border of Norway under treaty of Novgorod (1252) with Russia.

Lyngor (lüng'ŭr), Nor. *Lyngør*, village (pop. 285) in DYPVAG canton, Aust-Agder co., S Norway, port on a tiny isl. in the Skagerrak, 18 mi. NE of Arendal; lighthouse. Scene of naval skirmish (1812) with the English.

Lyngselv, Norway: see LYGNA RIVER.

Lynhurst, town (pop. 160), Marion co., central Ind., just W of Indianapolis.

Lynkerdem (lĭngkär'dăm), village, Khasi and Jaintia Hills dist., W Assam, India, in Khasi Hills, 15 mi. S of Shillong; rice, cotton. Coal deposits near by.

Lynmouth (lĭn'mŭth). **1** Fishing village in Lynton urban dist., N Devon, England, on Bristol Channel and 13 mi. E of Ilfracombe; tourist resort. Shelley's cottage is here. Promontory of Foreland Point, 2 mi. NE, has lighthouse (51°15'N 3°47'W). **2** Town and parish (pop. 1,759), E Northumberland, England, on North Sea, 7 mi. NE of Morpeth; coal mining.

Lynn or **Lynn Regis,** England: see KING'S LYNN.

Lynn (lĭn), county (□ 915; pop. 11,030), NW Texas; ⊙ Tahoka. On the Llano Estacado; alt. c.3,000 ft. Agr. area, with large crops of grain sorghums; also legumes, cotton, wheat, watermelons, livestock (beef cattle, hogs, sheep, poultry), dairying. Sodium sulphate, magnesium sulphate mined and processed; silica, potash deposits. Includes Tahoka L., other intermittently dry lakes. Formed 1876.

Lynn. 1 Town (pop. 1,149), Randolph co., E Ind., 16 mi. N of Richmond; grain, poultry, livestock; mfg. of clothing. Just E is state's highest point (1,240 ft.). **2** Industrial city (pop. 99,738), Essex co., E Mass., on arm (Lynn Harbor) of Massachusetts Bay and 9 mi. NNE of Boston; important shoe-mfg. center (since 1636); electrical equipment, shoemakers' supplies, machinery, leather, clothing, paper boxes, patent medicines, bakery products. Settled 1629, inc. as town 1631, as city 1850.

Lynn Canal, SE Alaska, N arm (90 mi. long, 7–12 mi. wide) of Chatham Strait and Stephens Passage, extending to Skagway. Navigable throughout, it provides sea lane to Haines, Chilkoot, and Skagway (railroad to Yukon). Mts. and glaciers on both sides. SSE of Haines it divides into 2 arms: Chilkoot Inlet extends 20 mi. NNW to Chilkoot; Chilkat Inlet extends 15 mi. NW to mouth of Chilkat R. N of Haines, Taiya Inlet (arm of Chilkoot Inlet) extends 12 mi. NNE to Skagway.

Lynndyl (lĭn'dĭl″), town (pop. 241), Millard co., W Utah, on Sevier R., 32 mi. WSW of Nephi.

Lynnfield, town (pop. 3,927), Essex co., E Mass., just W of Lynn. Settled c.1640, set off from Lynn 1782.

Lynn Garden, village, Sullivan co., NE Tenn., just N of Kingsport.

Lynn Haven, city (pop. 1,787), Bay co., NW Fla., 5 mi. N of Panama City, on N arm of St. Andrew Bay, in lumbering area. Settled 1912, inc. 1915.

Lynnhaven, village, Princess Anne co., SE Va., 15 mi. E of Norfolk, on 2-branched Lynnhaven Bay, an arm (c.5 mi. long) of Chesapeake Bay, which it joins via narrow Lynnhaven Inlet (bridged); noted for oysters.

Lynn Lake, town, NW Man., 200 mi. N of The Pas; nickel- and copper-mining center; mfg. of ammonium sulphate fertilizer. Succeeded (early 1950s) exhausted copper property of Sherridon, 120 mi. S, from which railroad was extended to Lynn Lake.

Lynn Lake, W.Va.: see CHEAT RIVER.

Lynn Regis, England: see KING'S LYNN.

Lynnville. 1 Village (pop. 101), Morgan co., W central Ill., 7 mi. WSW of Jacksonville, in agr. area. **2** Town (pop. 404), Warrick co., SW Ind., 22 mi. NE of Evansville, in agr. and bituminous-coal area. **3** Town (pop. 406), Jasper co., central Iowa, on North Skunk R. and c.45 mi. E of Des Moines; livestock, grain. **4** Town (pop. 356), Giles co., S Tenn., 12 mi. N of Pulaski, in dairy, agr., livestock area.

Lynton (lĭn'tŭn), urban district (1931 pop. 2,011; 1951 census 2,123), N Devon, England, 13 mi. E of Ilfracombe, near Bristol Channel, on steep cliff 400 ft. above Lynmouth harbor; tourist resort and agr. market. Has 13th-cent. church.

Lynwood, residential city (pop. 25,823), Los Angeles co., S Calif., suburb 9 mi. S of downtown Los Angeles; some mfg. (metal products, signaling devices, chemicals). Oil refinery near by.

Lynxville, village (pop. 217), Crawford co., SW Wis., on the Mississippi and 14 mi. NNE of Prairie du Chien, in livestock and dairy region. A U.S. fish hatchery is here.

Lyon, France: see LYONS.

Lyon. 1 County (□ 588; pop. 14,697), extreme NW Iowa; ⊙ Rock Rapids. Prairie agr. area (hogs, cattle, poultry, corn, oats), drained by Rock and Little Rock rivers, and bounded N by Minn. and W by Big Sioux R. (forms S.Dak. line here). Has state park. Formed 1851. **2** County (□ 852; pop. 26,576), E central Kansas; ⊙ Emporia. Level to hilly area, drained by Neosho and Cottonwood rivers. Livestock, grain. Formed 1860. **3** County (□ 262; pop. 6,853), W Ky.; ⊙ Eddyville. Bounded SW by Kentucky Reservoir (Tennessee R.); crossed by Cumberland R. Gently rolling agr. area (livestock, burley tobacco, grain); limestone quarries, hardwood timber. Includes part of Kentucky Woodlands Wildlife Refuge. Formed 1854. **4** County (□ 713; pop. 22,253), SW Minn.; ⊙ Marshall. Agr. area drained by Yellow Medicine, Cottonwood, and Redwood rivers. Corn, oats, barley, livestock. Formed 1868. **5** County (□ 2,012; pop. 3,679), W Nev.; ⊙ Yerington. East and West Walker rivers form the Walker R. below Yerington. Lahontan Reservoir, on Carson R., supplies water for irrigation. Livestock, dairy products; silver, copper, gold. Formed 1861. Part of Mono Natl. Forest is in S, in Sierra Nevada.

Lyon, village (pop. 386), Coahoma co., NW Miss., just NE of Clarksdale, in agr. area (cotton, corn).

Lyon, Fort, Colo.: see LAS ANIMAS.

Lyon, Loch (lŏkh lī'ŭn), lake (2 mi. long; alt. 1,052 ft.; maximum depth 100 ft.), SW Perthshire, Scotland, 12 mi. WNW of Killin. Outlet: Lyon R.

Lyon Mountain, village (pop. 1,053), Clinton co., extreme NE N.Y., in the Adirondacks, 22 mi. W of Plattsburg; iron mining. Lyon Mtn. (3,810 ft.) is just SE.

Lyonnais (lī'ŭnā, lyônā'), region and former province, E central France, now forming RHÔNE and LOIRE depts. Bounded by the Saône-Rhone valley (E) and the Monts du Forez (W), it includes the Forez Plain, the Monts du Beaujolais, Monts du Lyonnais, and the industrial Lyons, Roanne, and Saint-Étienne areas. The prov. was composed of Lyonnais proper (region immediately surrounding Lyons) which Philip IV had incorporated into the royal domain in 1307, and of Forez and Beaujolais counties, added in 1531. In 1790 it became Rhône-et-Loire dept., which was split into 2 present depts. in 1793.

Lyonnais, Monts du (mõ dü lyônā'), mountain chain in E central France, forming part of E escarpment of the Massif Central, in Loire and Rhône depts. Bounded by the Forez Plain (SW), the Brévenne (N), the Rhone valley (E), and the JAREZ (S), it rises to c.3,000 ft. Cattle and sheep raising; silk handicrafts. Overlooks Lyons (NE) and Saint-Étienne (SSW).

Lyon River, Perthshire, Scotland, rises near SW border of co., 4 mi. NE of Tyndrum, flows 34 mi. E, through Glen Lyon, to the Tay 4 mi. W of Aberfeldy. On upper course of river is Loch Lyon.

Lyons (lī'ŭnz), Fr. *Lyon* (lēō'), anc. *Lugdunum*, city (1946 pop. 439,861; 1936 pop. 546,683), ⊙ Rhône dept., E central France, at confluence of Rhone and Saône rivers. Third-largest city of France, 240 mi. SSE of Paris and 170 mi. N of Marseilles; 45°46'N 4°50'E. For centuries a leading textile center, its silk industry has now been largely replaced by modern rayon and other artificial-fiber factories. City still specializes in mfg. of hosiery and various fine fabrics (including embroidered ones). Lyons also has important chemical works (dyes, superphosphates, ammonia, glycerine, pharmaceuticals, photographic material), electrical and metallurgical plants (foundries, copper and bronze smelters, machine shops, auto assembly). Other industries: gold and silver working for embroidery and religious articles, tanning, distilling, printing, mfg. of glass, tobacco, flour products, chocolate, paper, clocks. Lyons is a hub of communications (linking Paris with Switzerland, Italy, and the Mediterranean) and a river port (chiefly navigation on the Saône). It is also a financial (has head office of Crédit Lyonnais; oldest stock exchange in France, founded 1506) and cultural center (univ. founded 1808, fine museums including noted textile mus.), and seat of an archbishop. It is known for its excellent cuisine. The 2 rivers divide Lyons into a central town (on peninsula bet. their confluence), old town (on W bank of the Saône), and new town (E of Rhone R.). Central town consists, N-S, of the Croix-Rousse and Terreaux quarters (silk districts); the business dist. near the Bourse; Bellecour quarter (leading hotels, cafés, and shops); and Perrache dist. (reclaimed from rivers in 18th cent.; site of main railroad station). The old town, clinging to steep river slopes, is dominated by Fourvière hill (960 ft. high), crowned by a semi-oriental basilica (built 1872–96; panorama from observatory in one of its 4 lofty towers). New town has wealthy residential quarters (N), workers' districts (center), and univ. bldgs. (S), and merges (E) with sprawling industrial suburbs, chief of which is Villeurbanne. A handsome modern city with wide quays and 23 bridges, Lyons suffered some damage in Second World War. The 12th-14th-cent. primatial cathedral of St. Jean lost its stained-glass windows. Founded 43 B.C. as a Roman colony, it soon became chief city of Gaul. Here Christianity was first introduced into Gaul. Ruled by its archbishops until c.1307, when Philip IV incorporated city (which had passed to Kingdom of Arles after breakup of Carolingian empire) into Fr. crownland together with surrounding Lyonnais. Its citizens obtained self-rule in 1320. Lyons became a silk center in 15th cent., utilizing silkworms raised in S France. In recent times, increasingly dependent on raw material imports from Far East, the industry has declined and Lyons has begun to switch to artificial textile industry (a trend accelerated by Second World War). In 1793, Lyons was devastated by French Revolutionary troops after a counter-revolutionary insurrection. It recovered quickly, thanks to invention here (1802) of the Jacquard loom. The annual international fair held here has made Lyons a leading commercial center. Among famous men b. here were emperors Claudius and Caracalla, and St. Ambrose and Ampère.

Lyons. 1 Town (pop. 689), Boulder co., N Colo., at junction of headstreams of St. Vrain Creek, just E of Front Range, 15 mi. N of Boulder; alt. 5,375 ft. Mining and lumbering point. Rocky Mtn. Natl. Park near by. **2** City (pop. 2,799), ⊙ Toombs co., E central Ga., 5 mi. ESE of Vidalia, in farm and timber area; mfg. (clothing, lumber). Inc. 1897. **3** Residential village (pop. 6,120), Cook co., NE Ill., W suburb of Chicago. Inc. 1888. **4** Town (pop. 695), Greene co., SW Ind., 32 mi. NE of Vincennes, in agr. and bituminous-coal area. **5** City (pop. 4,545), ⊙ Rice co., central Kansas, 25 mi. NW of Hutchinson, in wheat area; flour and feed milling; salt mining. Oil fields. Laid out 1876 on Santa Fe Trail; inc. 1880. **6** Village (pop. 683), Ionia co., S central Mich., 6 mi. E of Ionia and on Grand R., in farm area; furniture mfg. **7** Village (pop. 1,011), Burt co., NE Nebr., 50 mi. NNW of Omaha and on Logan Creek, near Missouri R.; grain, livestock, dairy and poultry produce. Inc. 1869. **8** Village (pop. 4,217), ⊙ Wayne co., W N.Y., on the Barge Canal and Clyde R., and 32 mi. ESE of Rochester, in fruitgrowing region; mfg. (canned foods, chemicals, condiments, clothing, furniture, silk, brandy). Summer resort. Settled 1800, inc. 1831. **9** Village (pop. 511), Fulton co., NW Ohio, 27 mi. W of Toledo, near Mich. line. **10** or **Lyon Station,** borough (pop. 545), Berks co., E central Pa., 12 mi. NE of Reading.

Lyons Falls, village (pop. 864), Lewis co., N central N.Y., on Black R. (falls here) at influx of Moose R., and 14 mi. SSE of Lowville; paper milling.

Lyons-la-Forêt (lēõ'-lä-fôrĕ'), village (pop. 517), Eure dept., NW France, 11 mi. NNE of Les Andelys; resort surrounded by domanial forest of Lyons (□ 40).

Lyons River, Australia: see GASCOYNE RIVER.

Lyon Station, Pa.: see LYONS.

Lypiatt Park, England: see BISLEY WITH LYPIATT.

Lysa Hora (lĭ'sä hô'rä), Czech *Lysá Hora*, second-highest mountain (4,346 ft.) of the Beskids, E Silesia, Czechoslovakia, 5 mi. SE of Frydlant nad Ostravici; winter-sports area.

Lysaker (lü'säkûr), village (pop. 4,156) in Baerum canton (pop. 32,543), Akershus co., SE Norway, at head of Oslo Fjord, on railroad and 4 mi. W of Oslo city center; port, with paper, wood-pulp, and cellulose mills; also mfg. of chemicals, soap, cosmetics. Fridtjof Nansen died at his estate here.

Lysa nad Labem (lĭ'sä näd' läbĕm), Czech *Lysá nad Labem*, Ger. *Lissa* (lĭ'sä), village (pop. 6,500), central Bohemia, Czechoslovakia, near Elbe R., 20 mi. NW of Kolin; in sugar-beet and potato dist.; rail junction. Has picturesque castle.

Lysa Pass (lĭ'sä) (alt. 1,495 ft.), E Moravia, Czechoslovakia, 5 mi. NE of Valasske Klobouky, at NE edge of the White Carpathians; railroad corridor.

Lysaya Gora (lĭ'sĭŭ gŭrä'), village (1926 pop. 8,489), NW Nikolayev oblast, Ukrainian SSR, 14 mi. NE of Pervomaisk; wheat.

Lyse Fjord (lü'sŭ), long, narrow SE arm of Bokn Fjord, Rogaland co., SW Norway, extends 25 mi. NE from Hogs Fjord; popular tourist area.

Lysekil (lü'sŭchĕl″), city (pop. 5,443), Goteborg och Bohus co., SW Sweden, on the Skagerrak at mouth of Gullmarn (gŭl'märn″), 15-mi.-long fjord, 45 mi. NNW of Goteborg; fishing center (herring, anchovy), with shipyards, canneries, fish-meal and fish-oil plants; stone quarries. Resort. Inc. 1903.

Lysi (lē'sē), village (pop. 2,927), Famagusta dist., E Cyprus, 18 mi. ESE of Nicosia; wheat, barley, olives, wines; sheep, hogs.

Lysica, peak, Poland: see SWIETOKRZYSKIE, GORY.

Lysiec, Ukrainian SSR: see LISETS.

Lysimachia, Lake, or **Lake Lisimakhia** (both: lĭsĭmä'khēŭ) (□ 5.4), in Acarnania nome, W central Greece, on outlet of L. Trichonis, 10 mi. N of Missolonghi; 4 mi. long, 2 mi. wide; fisheries. Formerly called Angelokastron.

Lyskamm (lēs'käm″), W summit (14,888 ft.) of Monte Rosa group, on Swiss-Italian frontier. On E side is the Alpine crossing of Lysjoch or Lys Pass (13,934 ft.).

Lyskovo (lĭs'kŭvŭ), city (1939 pop. over 10,000), E central Gorki oblast, Russian SFSR, on Volga R. and 45 mi. ESE of Gorki; metalworking center; flour mills. Became city in 1922.

Lys-lez-Lannoy (lē-lā-länwä'), outer SE suburb (pop. 6,556) of Roubaix, Nord dept., N France, near Belg. border; cotton and wool blankets, rugs, building materials, chocolates. Truck gardening.

Lysoysundet (lüs'ûüsōōn″dŭ), Nor. *Lysøysundet*, village in Jossund (Nor. *Jøssund*) canton (pop. 1,928), Sor-Trondelag co., central Norway, on North Sea, 35 mi. NNW of Trondheim; fishing and canning center (herring).

Lys River (lēs), Flemish *Leie*, formerly *Leye* (both: lī'ŭ), N France and Belgium, rises in Artois hills near Fruges, flows NE, past Aire (head of navigation; junction with Flanders plain canals) and Merville, forms Franco-Belg. border bet. Armentières and Menin, continues into Belgium past Courtrai, to the Scheldt at Ghent; 135 mi. long. Receives the Deûle (right). Flax-growing, linen-spinning industry along its banks. Scene of one of last battles (Oct.–Nov., 1918) of First World War.

Lys River (lēs), Val d'Aosta region, NW Italy, rises in glaciers on S slope of Monte Rosa, flows 22 mi. S, through Gressoney valley, to Dora Baltea R. near Pont-St.-Martin. Descends over 6,000 ft. Used for hydroelectric power at several stations, including Gressoney-la-Trinité and Pont-St.-Martin.

Lyss (lēs), town (pop. 3,523), Bern canton, NW Switzerland, on Alte Aare R. and 11 mi. NNW of Bern; metal products, cement, tiles, foodstuffs, watches.

Lyster (lī'stûr), village (pop. 805), S Que., on Bécancour R. and 35 mi. SW of Quebec; lumbering, dairying, stock raising.

Lyster, canton, Norway: see SKJOLDEN.

Lyster Fjord, Norway: see LUSTER FJORD.

Lystra (lĭs'trŭ), anc. town of Lacaonia, S central Asia Minor, whose ruins are 20 mi. SW of Konya, Turkey; visited by St. Paul, who was stoned and left for dead, and by Barnabas.

Lysva or **Lys'va** (lĭs'vŭ), city (1939 pop. 51,192), E Molotov oblast, Russian SFSR, on Lysva R. (left tributary of the Chusovaya) and 50 mi. E of Molotov, on railroad. Major metallurgical center, producing quality steels and sheet metal (automobiles aircraft); mfg. (metal- and enamelware, furniture, clothing, tiles). Founded 1785 as ironworking plant; became city in 1926. Steel industry, largely developed prior to First World War, modernized after Bolshevik revolution.

Lysyanka or **Lisyanka** (lĭsyän'kŭ), town (1926 pop. 6,218), S Kiev oblast, Urainian SSR, 45 mi. NE of Uman; lignite mine.

Lysye Gory or **Lysyye Gory** (lĭ'sēŭ gô'rē), village (1929 pop. 1,145), S central Saratov oblast, Russian SFSR, on Medveditsa R. and 15 mi. E of Balanda; flour mill, metalworks; wheat, sunflowers. Quartz sand deposits.

Lytchett Minster (lĭ'chĭt) agr. village and parish (pop. 1,317), SE Dorset, England, on Lytchett Bay (extension of Poole Harbour) and 4 mi. WNW of Poole.

Lytham Saint Anne's (lĭ'dhŭm), municipal borough (1931 pop. 25,764; 1951 census 30,298), W Lancashire, England. Includes town of Lytham, on Ribble R. estuary and 11 mi. W of Preston; seaside resort; mfg. of pharmaceuticals. Has 18th-cent. mansion. On the Irish Sea (WNW) is town of Saint Anne's-on-the-Sea, seaside resort; mfg. of shoes.

Lytkarino (lĭtkä'rēnŭ), town (1939 pop. over 500), central Moscow oblast, Russian SFSR, on Moskva R. and 7 mi. S of Lyubertsy; quartz quarries.

Lytle (lī'tŭl), village (1940 pop. 576), Atascosa co., SW Texas, 23 mi. SW of San Antonio; rail, trade point in agr. area (cotton, corn, peanuts).

Lytle, Lake, W central Texas, impounded by dam in small Lytle Creek (a S tributary of Clear Fork of Brazos R.), just S of Abilene; c. 2 mi. long; capacity 6,500 acre-ft.

Lyttelton (lĭ'tŭltŭn), borough (pop. 3,407), port of Christchurch, E S.Isl., New Zealand, on Banks Peninsula; connected with Christchurch by tunnel (c.1.5 mi. long); on N shore of Lyttelton harbor (1.5 mi. wide across mouth, 8 mi. long). Exports frozen meat, hides, timber. Sometimes called Port Lyttelton.

Lytton, village (pop. estimate 500), S B.C., on Fraser R. at mouth of Thompson R., and 65 mi. SW of Kamloops; fruit and vegetable growing, gold mining, lumbering. Commercial apple growing in B.C. began in this area.

Lytton (lĭ'tŭn), town (pop. 373), on Calhoun-Sac co. line, central Iowa, 7 mi. E of Sac City, in agr. area.

Lyub-, in Yugoslav names: see LJUB-.

Lyubachovka River, Poland and Ukrainian SSR: see LUBACZOWKA RIVER.

Lyuban or **Lyuban'** (lyōō'bän'yŭ). **1** Town (1926 pop. 2,162), SW Bobruisk oblast, Belorussian SSR, 25 mi. SE of Slutsk; food and flax processing. **2** City (1926 pop. 4,286), S Leningrad oblast, Russian SFSR, 50 mi. SE of Leningrad; sawmills, brickworks. Chartered 1912.

Lyubar (lyōō'bŭr), town (1926 pop. 11,752), SW Zhitomir oblast, Ukrainian SSR, 37 mi. W of Berdichev; flour mill.

Lyubartov, Poland: see LUBARTOW.

Lyubashevka (lyōōbä'shĭfkŭ), village (1939 pop. over 500), central Odessa oblast, Ukrainian SSR, 30 mi. WSW of Pervomaisk; metalworks.

Lyubazh, Russian SFSR: see VERKHNI LYUBAZH.

Lyubcha (lyōōp'chŭ), Pol. *Lubcz* (lōōpch), village, N Baranovichi oblast, Belorussian SSR, on Neman R. and 15 mi. NE of Novogrudok; rail-spur terminus; lumbering; rye, oats, potatoes. Noted residence of Pol. gentry in 15th cent.; declined in 17th cent.

Lyubech (lyōō'byĭch), village (1926 pop. 4,074), W Chernigov oblast, Ukrainian SSR, on Dnieper R. and 30 mi. NW of Chernigov; grain, flax. Dates from 9th cent. Formerly also spelled Lyubyach and Lyubich.

Lyuben, Poland: see LUBIEN.

Lyubertsy (lyōōbyĕr'tsē), city (1939 pop. over 10,000), central Moscow oblast, Russian SFSR, 12 mi. ESE of Moscow; rail junction; machine-mfg. center; electrical goods, weights, glass, plastics; oil cracking, rug weaving. Agr.-machinery mfg. at adjoining Ukhtomskaya. One of Moscow's civil airports here. Became city in 1925.

Lyubeshov (lyōōbyĕ'shŭf), Pol. *Lubieszów* (lōōbyĕ'-shōōf), town (1939 pop. over 500), NE Volyn oblast, Ukrainian SSR, in Pripet Marshes, on Stokhod R. (head of navigation) and 25 mi. NE of Kamen-Kashirski; flax, potatoes, lumbering. Has 18th-cent. basilica. Founded in 1693; passed from Poland to Russia (1795); reverted to Poland (1921); ceded to USSR in 1945.

Lyubim (lyōō'bēm), city (1926 pop. 3,696), NE Yaroslavl oblast, Russian SFSR, 20 mi. NE of Danilov; flour- and sawmilling, flax processing. Chartered 1560.

Lyubimets (lyōōbē'mĕts), village (pop. 6,117), Khaskovo dist., SE Bulgaria, on Maritsa R. and 8 mi. NW of Svilengrad; sericulture center; cotton yarn; tobacco and winegrowing. Formerly Khebibchevo.

Lyubinski or **Lyubinskiy** (lyōō'bĭnskē), town (1939 pop. over 2,000), SW Omsk oblast, Russian SFSR, on Trans-Siberian RR and 30 mi. NW of Omsk; metalworks. Until 1947, Novo-Lyubino.

Lyublin, Poland: see LUBLIN, city.

Lyublino (lyōō'blyĭnŭ), city (1926 pop. 8,391; 1939 pop. 64,332), central Moscow oblast, Russian SFSR, on Moskva R., adjoining (SE of) Moscow on E bank of its S port; railway-car mfg. center; foundries. Includes Pererva, just S; site of Moskva R. locks and dam with hydroelectric plant. Became city in 1925.

Lyublinski or **Lyublinskiy** (lyōō'blyĭnskē), town (1946 pop. over 500), central Moscow oblast, Russian SFSR, on E bank of S port of Moscow (SE); waterworks.

Lyubokhna (lyōō'bŭkhnŭ), town (1926 pop. 2,291), NE Bryansk oblast, Russian SFSR, 7 mi. S of Dyatkovo; metalworking center.

Lyuboml or **Lyuboml'** (lyōōbô'mŭl), Pol. *Luboml* (loobô'mŭl), city (1931 pop. 4,111), W Volyn oblast, Ukrainian SSR, near Bug R. (Pol. border) 30 mi. W of Kovel; tanning, distilling, flour milling, sawmilling, crating, mfg. (cotton wad, blankets). Has medieval palace and church. Allegedly founded in 14th cent.; passed from Poland to Russia (1795); reverted to Poland (1921); ceded to USSR in 1945.

Lyubotin (lyōōbô'tyĭn), city (1939 pop. over 10,000), N central Kharkov oblast, Ukrainian SSR, 10 mi. W of Kharkov; rail junction; machine works, cotton mill, tobacco factory.

Lyubranets, Poland: see LUBRANIEC.

Lyubytino (lyōōbĭ'tyĭnŭ), village (1939 pop. over 500), central Novgorod oblast, Russian SFSR, on Msta R. and 35 mi. NW of Borovichi; refractory-clay quarries.

Lyudinovo (lyōōdyē'nŭvŭ), city (1939 pop. over 10,000), SW Kaluga oblast, Russian SFSR, 40 mi. N of Bryansk; produces railroad cars, steam tractors; iron foundry (radiators, heating equipment). Became city in 1938.

Lyudvipol, Ukrainian SSR: see SOSNOVOYE.

Lyuksemburg. 1 or **Lyuksemburgi,** Georgian SSR: see BOLNISI. **2** Ukrainian SSR: see ROZOVKA.

Lyuta (lyōō'tä), village (pop. 3,126), Vratsa dist., NW Bulgaria, on Ogosta R. and 12 mi. NE of Mikhailovgrad; grain, legumes, livestock.

Lyutsin, Latvia: see LUDZA.

M

Ma, Song (shông' mä'), river in N Vietnam, rises in high plateau near Dienbienphu, flows over 250 mi. SE, cutting wild, tortuous gorges through plateaus inhabited by the Muong, to the Thanhhoa plain and the Gulf of Tonkin near Thanhhoa.

Maabaroth, Israel: see MABAROT.

Ma'abda, El, or **Al-Ma'abidah** (both: ĕl mä-ä'bĭdŭ), village (pop. 13,258), Asyut prov., central Upper Egypt, on the Nile and 15 mi. NW of Asyut; cereals, dates, sugar cane.

Maajen-bel-Abbès, Tunisia: see MAJEN-BEL-ABBÈS.

Maala, Maalla, or **Ma'alla** (mŭä'lŭ), urban division (1946 pop., including KHORMAKSAR, 7,889) of Aden town, on N shore of Aden peninsula, 2 mi. NW of Crater; native-craft harbor on Aden Bay; coffee and other warehouses. Shipbuilding, sailmaking, mfg. of aluminum utensils. Includes Somali quarter known as Somalipura. Infectious Diseases Hosp. near by.

Maalaea Bay (mä'älä-ä'ŭ), on S coast of isthmus, Maui, T.H.

Maale hab Bashan, Ma'ale hab Bashan (mä-ălä' häbäshän'), or **Lehavoth Habashan** (lĕhävōt'), agr. settlement (pop. 150), Upper Galilee, NE Israel, near Syrian border, at W foot of Bashan hills, 15 mi. NE of Safad. Founded 1945; heavily shelled during Arab invasion, 1948. Also spelled Maale Habashan.

Maale ha Hamisha, Ma'ale ha Hamisha, or **Maale Hahamisha** (hähämēshä'), settlement (pop. 300), E Israel, in Judaean Hills, 7 mi. WNW of Jerusalem; fruit, vegetables; dairying, poultry. Summer resort. Founded 1938; shelled by Arabs, 1948. Formerly called Maale or Ma'ale.

Maaloula, Syria: see MA'LULA.

Maalov (mô'lŭv), Dan. *Maaløv*, town (pop. 860), Copenhagen amt, Zealand, Denmark, 11 mi. NW of Copenhagen; fruit canning, furniture mfg.

Maaloy, Norway: see VAGSOY.

Ma'ameltein (mă-ä'mĕltān) or **Mu'amaltayn** (mōō-ä'mĕltān), Fr. *Mouamaltein*, coastal village, central Lebanon, on Mediterranean Sea, 12 mi. NNE of Beirut; summer resort; bathing facilities.

Ma'an (mä-än'), town (pop. c.9,000), S Jordan, S terminus of used section of Hejaz RR, and 100 mi. S of Amman; alt. 3,497 ft.; road junction, airfield. Economic center of S Jordan. Tobacco mfg., home handicrafts. Grain (barley, wheat); camel, sheep, and goat raising. Lumbering (S).

Maanith, Israel: see NARBATA.

Ma-ao (mä″ou'), town (1939 pop. 24,065) in Bago municipality, Negros Occidental prov., W Negros isl., Philippines, 13 mi. SSE of Bacolod; trade center for agr. area (rice, sugar cane).

Maardu (mär'dōō), village, N Estonia, 10 mi. E of Tallinn; phosphorite deposits.

Maaret el Noman, Syria: see MA'ARRET EN NU'MAN.

Maarianhamina, Finland: see MARIEHAMN.

Ma'arra, El, or **Al-Ma'arrah** (both: ĕl mä-ăr'rŭ), village, Aleppo prov., NW Syria, 21 mi. SW of Aleppo; cotton, cereals.

Ma'arret en Nu'man, Ma'arret el Nu'man, or **Ma'arrat al-Nu'man** (all: mä-ăr'rĕt ĕn-nōō'măn), Fr. *Maaret el Noman*, town, Aleppo prov., NW Syria, 45 mi. SW of Aleppo; cotton, cereals. Birthplace of noted Arabic freethinking poet Abu-l-Ala al-Maarri or Abul 'Ala al-Ma'ari.

Maarssen or **Maarsen** (mär'sŭn), town (pop. 4,264), Utrecht prov., central Netherlands, on Vecht R. and 5 mi. NW of Utrecht, on Merwede Canal; machine shops; mfg. (chemicals, quinine, soap, shoes), preserves, fruit juices, feed cakes.

Maaseik (mä'zīk), town (pop. 7,397), Limburg prov., NE Belgium, on Meuse R. and 22 mi. NE of Hasselt, near Netherlands border; market center. Painters Hubert and Jan van Eyck b. here. Formerly spelled Maeseyck.

Maasin (mä-ä'sēn). **1** Town (1939 pop. 1,689; 1948 municipality pop. 16,384), Iloilo prov., S central Panay isl., Philippines, 16 mi. NW of Iloilo; rice-growing center. **2** Town (1939 pop. 4,861; 1948 municipality pop. 31,458), SW Leyte, Philippines, on Canigao Channel, 80 mi. SSW of Tacloban; agr. center (coconuts, rice, hemp).

Maasland (mäs'länt), village (pop. 1,335), South Holland prov., SW Netherlands, 7 mi. W of Rotterdam; cement mfg.; truck gardening, cattle raising.

Maas River, Belgium and Netherlands: see MEUSE RIVER.

Ma'asser el Shuf, Ma'asser esh Shuf, or **Ma'assir al-Shuf** (all: mä-äs'sĭr ĕsh-shōōf'), Fr. *Maasser el Chouf*, village (pop. 1,411), central Lebanon, 21 mi. SE of Beirut; known for its arrack. Summer resort.

Maassluis (mäs'lois'), town (pop. 10,252), South Holland prov., SW Netherlands, on the New Waterway and 10 mi. W of Rotterdam; hq. for tug and pilot service; bunker station; mfg. of ropes, packing crates.

Maastricht (mäs'trĭkht), old Flemish *Maestricht*, anc. *Trajectum Superius*, later *Trajectum ad Mosam*, city (pop. 74,449), ⊙ Limburg prov., SE Netherlands, on Maas R. and 15 mi. NNE of Liége (Belgium), on the Albert Canal system at junction of Juliana Canal, Liége-Maastricht Canal, and the Zuid-Willemsvaart; 50°47'N 5°41'E. Rail junction and industrial center; mfg. (textiles, ceramics, glass, crystal, chemicals, rubber, paper, tobacco products); vegetable and butter market. Sandstone quarries near by. An anc. place; has 6th-cent. Romanesque cathedral of St. Servatius (oldest church in the Netherlands), 11th-cent. Romanesque church of Onze Lieve Vrouw, 13th-cent. Old Maas Bridge. A Maas ford in Roman times; seat (382–721) of a bishopric transferred from Tongres by St. Servatius. Originally a possession of Frankish kings; later under joint rule of dukes of Brabant and prince-bishops of Liége. Frequently besieged; taken (1579) by Spaniards after a siege and (1632) by Prince Frederick Henry of Orange. In 17th and 18th cent., 3 times in Fr. hands.

Maas-Waal Canal (mäs'-väl'), central Netherlands, extends 9 mi. N-S, bet. Maas R. (1.5 mi. NW of Mook) and Waal R. (2.5 mi. WNW of Nijmegen). Completed 1927.

Maayan Tsvi, Ma'ayan Tsvi (Tsevi), or **Maayan Zvi** (all: mä-äyän' tsvē'), settlement (pop. 200), NW Israel, near Mediterranean, at N end of Plain of Sharon, just SW of Zikhron Yaa'qov, near railroad; mixed farming, fishing. Founded 1938. Formerly called Maayan or Ma'ayan.

Mabalacat (mäbälä'kät), town (1939 pop. 884; 1948 municipality pop. 25,281), Pampanga prov., central Luzon, Philippines, 15 mi. NW of San Fernando; sugar milling.

Mabama (mäbä'mä), village, Western Prov., W central Tanganyika, on railroad and 20 mi. WSW of Tabora; beeswax; millet, corn. Also called Useko.

Mabang (mäbäng'), village (pop. 330) South-Western Prov., W Sierra Leone, on railroad and 29 mi. ESE of Freetown; palm oil and kernels, piassava.

Mabank (mā'băngk), town (pop. 896), Kaufman co., NE Texas, c.50 mi. SE of Dallas; rail, trade point in agr., timber area; oil wells.

Ma'bar (mă'bär), town (pop. 1,200), Sana prov., S central Yemen, on central plateau, 40 mi. S of Sana; junction of motor roads from Hodeida and Yarim to Sana.

Mabarot, Ma'barot, or **Maabaroth** (mä-äbärōt'), settlement (pop. 600), W Israel, in Plain of Sharon, 4 mi. NE of Natanya; mixed farming. School serves surrounding region. Founded 1933.

Mabaruma (mäbŭrōō'mŭ), village (pop. 343), ⊙ North West Dist., Essequibo co., NW Br. Guiana, in hills S of Morawhanna, 10 mi. from the coast, 150 mi. NW of Georgetown, in fruitgrowing region (citrus, coconuts, bananas, cacao, etc.).
Mabel, village (pop. 788), Fillmore co., SE Minn., near Iowa line, 19 mi. SE of Preston, in grain, dairy area.
Mabel Lake (22 mi. long, 1-2 mi. wide), S B.C., 27 mi. SW of Revelstoke. Drained W by Shuswap R. into Shuswap L.
Maben (mā'bĭn), town (pop. 616), on Oktibbeha-Webster co. line, E Miss., 17 mi. WNW of Starkville; cheese, lumber.
Mabesi, Lake (mäbĕ'sē), SE Sierra Leone, near Atlantic coast, 10 mi. S of Pujehun; 6 mi. long, 3 mi. wide. Connected with Waanje R. (W). Sometimes spelled Mabessi.
Mabirou (mäbērōō'), agr. village, central Middle Congo territory, Fr. Equatorial Africa, on Alima R. and 130 mi. NNE of Djambala.
Mabla Mountains (mä'blä), basalt range of Fr. Somaliland, on N coast of Gulf of Tadjoura, 25 mi. NNW of Djibouti; rise to about 4,000 ft.
Mablethorpe and Sutton, urban district (1931 pop. 3,928; 1951 census 5,394), Parts of Lindsey, E Lincolnshire, England, on North Sea. Includes resorts of Mablethorpe (11 mi. E of Louth), Sutton (2 mi. SE of Mablethorpe), and Trusthorpe (just SE of Mablethorpe).
Mabole (mŭbō'lā), town (pop. 1,979), Western Prov., Ceylon, 6 mi. NNE of Colombo city center; coir-rope mfg.; vegetables, rice. Administered by urban council (pop. 12,419) jointly with Wattala (1.5 mi. SSW) and Peliyagoda (3 mi. S).
Mabonto (mäbōn'tō), town (pop. 903), Northern Prov., central Sierra Leone, 13 mi. NE of Magburaka; alluvial gold-mining center. Hq. Tonkolili dist.
Mabou (mă'bōō, mŭbōō'), village (pop. estimate 600), NE N.S., W Cape Breton Isl., on Mabou R., near its mouth on the Gulf of St. Lawrence, 12 mi. SSW of Inverness; coal mining.
Mabou River, NE N.S., on W Cape Breton Isl., rises in the Craignish Hills; formed 4 mi. SE of Mabou, flows 15 mi. WNW, past Mabou, to Gulf of St. Lawrence 5 mi. W of Mabou.
Mabrouk (mäbrōōk'), village, N Fr. Sudan, Fr. West Africa, in the Sahara, on desert trail and 210 mi. NE of Timbuktu.
Mabscott, mining town (pop. 1,665), Raleigh co., S W.Va., just SW of Beckley, in semibituminous-coal region. Inc. 1906.
Mabton, town (pop. 831), Yakima co., S Wash., on Yakima R. and 35 mi. SE of Yakima, near Yakima Indian Reservation.
Mabualau, Fiji: see MAMANUTHA.
Macá, Monte (mōn'tā mäkä'), Andean peak (9,510 ft.), Aysén prov., S Chile, on Moraleda Channel, 25 mi. NW of Puerto Aysén.
Macabebe (mäkäbā'bā), town (1939 pop. 2,851; 1948 municipality pop. 17,647), Pampanga prov., central Luzon, Philippines, 8 mi. S of San Fernando; agr. center (sugar cane, rice).
Macabí Island (mäkäbē'), small rocky island (pop. 391), 6 mi. off Pacific coast of Libertad dept., NW Peru, 36 mi. WNW of Trujillo; 7°49'S 79°29'W; lighthouse; guano deposits.
Macabu, Brazil: see CONCEIÇÃO DE MACABU.
Macaca, Sierra, Cuba: see MAESTRA, SIERRA.
Macachín (mäkächēn'), town (pop. estimate 1,500), ⊙ Atreucó dept. (pop. 8,081), E La Pampa prov., Argentina, on railroad and 50 mi. SE of Santa Rosa; wheat, oats, alfalfa, wine, livestock.
Macacu River (mŭkŭkōō'), central Rio de Janeiro state, Brazil, rises in the Serra do Mar S of Nova Friburgo, flows 60 mi. SW to Guanabara Bay 12 mi. NNE of Niterói.
McAdam, village (pop. estimate c.2,000), SW N.B., 40 mi. SW of Fredericton and 5 mi. ENE of Vanceboro, Maine; rail junction; lumbering, hunting, tourist center.
McAdenville (mŭkă'dŭnvĭl), town (pop. 1,060), Gaston co., S N.C., 13 mi. W of Charlotte; cotton and woolen mills.
McAdoo (mă'kŭdōō), borough (pop. 4,260), Schuylkill co., E central Pa., 3 mi. S of Hazleton; anthracite; paper boxes, textiles. Founded 1880, inc. 1896.
Macaé (mŭkăĕ'), city (pop. 9,534), E Rio de Janeiro, Brazil, port on the Atlantic, on railroad and 50 mi. SW of Campos (connected by ship canal); textile and paper milling, coffee and rice processing, brandy distilling, match mfg. Outport and bathing beach at Imbetiba (S). Formerly spelled Macahé.
Macael (mäkäĕl'), town (pop. 2,649), Almería prov., S Spain, near Almanzora R., 20 mi. WSW of Huércal-Overa; olive-oil processing, flour milling; marble quarrying.
Macagua or **Macagua Vieja** (mäkä'gwä vyā'hä), village (pop. 675), Matanzas prov., W Cuba, 60 mi. ESE of Matanzas, in sugar-cane region.
Macahé, Brazil: see MACAÉ.
Macahubas. 1 City, Bahia, Brazil: see MACAÚBAS. **2** Town, São Paulo, Brazil: see MACAUBAL.
Macaíba (mŭkăē'bŭ), city (pop. 3,604), E Rio Grande do Norte, NE Brazil, head of navigation on Jundiaí R. and 10 mi. WSW of Natal; cattle-raising center; ships cotton, sugar. Formerly spelled Macahyba.
Macajalar Bay (mäkähälär'), inlet (17 mi. long, 20 mi. wide at mouth) of Mindanao Sea in N Mindanao, Philippines. Receives Cagayan R.
McAlester (mŭkă'lĭstŭr), city (pop. 17,878), ⊙ Pittsburg co., SE Okla., c.60 mi. SSW of Muskogee; trade center for agr. area (cotton, corn, grain, livestock, peanuts; dairy products). Meat packing; cottonseed, soybean, and peanut processing; cotton ginning; mfg. of food products, and of petroleum, concrete, and aluminum products. Coal mines; oil and natural-gas wells; timber. State penitentiary is near by. Settled c.1870; inc. as city 1906 upon merger with South McAlester. Was ⊙ Choctaw Nation.
McAllen (măk″ă'lŭn), city (pop. 20,067), Hidalgo co., extreme S Texas, in the lower Rio Grande valley, c.45 mi. WNW of Brownsville; port of entry near Mex. border (c.8 mi. S); a shipping and processing center in rich irrigated truck, citrus, cotton area; canned, frozen, dehydrated foods, canvas products, chemicals, refined petroleum (oil fields near). Winter resort. Settled 1904, inc. as town 1910, as city 1927.
McAlpin, village (pop. 1,612, with near-by Stotesbury), Raleigh co., S W.Va., 8 mi. SW of Beckley.
Macaluba or **Maccaluba,** Sicily: see ARAGONA.
Macamic, Que.: see MAKAMIK.
McAndrews, mining village (1940 pop. 533), Pike co., E Ky., in the Cumberlands, 7 mi. S of Williamson, W.Va.; bituminous coal.
Macáo, Brazil: see MACAU.
Macao or **Macau** (mŭkou'), Portuguese colony (□ 6; pop. 374,737), S China, on the S.China Sea at the deltaic mouth of Canton R., 65 mi. S of Canton and 40 mi. W of Hong Kong across Canton (Pearl) R. estuary. The colony consists of the city (pop. 312,717) of **Macao,** Chinese *Aomenkow* (ou'mŭn'kō'), later *Aomen,* on the S tip of a large deltaic isl. (CHUNGSHAN isl.; sometimes called Macao Isl.), and 3 small offshore isls.—the 2 Taipa Isls. (□ 2; pop. 6,148) and Coloane Isl. (□ 2; pop. 2,764). The city, at 22°11'N 113°34'E, is situated on a hilly, 3-mi.-long peninsula linked with Chungshan isl. by 700-ft.-wide isthmus on which lies the customs frontier port of Portas do Cêrco. It is a leading trade and fishing center, exporting mainly fresh and salted fish. Most of its transit trade with China in tea, tobacco, oranges, wine, lacquer, and opium is via its shallow harbor on W side of the peninsula. A promenade, Praia Grande, extends along E sea wall. Macao has a cathedral, seminary and col., and statues to Vasco da Gama and Camões, who wrote part of *The Lusiads* here in 1558–59. Its healthful though humid climate (in the monsoon zone) makes it a popular resort. Leased 1557 from China for settlement by the Portuguese, Macao is the oldest, permanent European outpost in the Far East. It rapidly developed as a leading port for China's foreign trade and flourished through 18th cent. With the rise (19th cent.) of Hong Kong and the gradual silting up of the harbor, Macao lost its preeminent position and became identified to a large extent with smuggling and gambling interests. The Portuguese proclaimed its complete separation from China in 1848–49, and this was confirmed in 1887 by China.
Mação (mŭsā'ō), village (pop. 1,443), Santarém dist., central Portugal, 12 mi. NE of Abrantes; mfg. of oil-cloth and carpets.
Macapá (mŭkŭpä'). **1** City (1950 pop. 10,094), ⊙ Amapá territory, N Brazil, on northernmost branch of Amazon delta 200 mi. NW of Belém; 0°4'N 50°32'W. Airport. Ships rubber, gold, cattle, corn. Old fortified colonial settlement. **2** City, Maranhão, Brazil: see PERI MIRIM.
Macará (mäkärä'), town (1950 pop. 2,702), Loja prov., S Ecuador, on Andean slopes at Peru line, on Pan American Highway, 60 mi. WSW of Loja; trade center in stock-raising area. Customhouse.
Macaracas (mäkärä'käs), village (pop. 543), Los Santos prov., S central Panama, in Pacific lowland, 18 mi. WSW of Las Tablas; bananas, livestock.
Macarao (mäkärä'ō), town (pop. 250), Federal Dist., N Venezuela, 10 mi. SW of Caracas; coffee, corn, fruit.
Macará River (mäkärä'), Andean stream flowing c.75 mi. along Ecuador-Peru border and joining the Río Grande or Catamayo R. to form the Chira 20 mi. SW of Celica.
Macarena, Cordillera (kôrdĭyā'rä mäkärā'nä), E outlier of the Cordillera Oriental, Meta intendancy, S central Colombia; extends c.80 mi. N–S at 74°W; rises to over 7,000 ft.
Macareño or **Central Macareño** (sĕntrāl' mäkärā'nyō), town (pop. 1,192), Camagüey prov., E Cuba, 45 mi. S of Camagüey; sugar milling.
Macareo, Caño (kä'nyō mäkärā'ō), central arm of Orinoco R. delta, Delta Amacuro territory, NE Venezuela; branches off 4 mi. S of Coporito, flows c.100 mi. NNE to the Atlantic into Serpent's Mouth at 9°48'N 61°35'W. It is arm most frequently used for navigation, providing link with Trinidad.
Macarsca, Yugoslavia: see MAKARSKA.
MacArthur, formerly **Ormoc** (ôrmōk'), city (1939 pop. 7,446; 1948 metropolitan area pop. 72,733), W Leyte, Philippines, port at head of Ormoc Bay, 32 mi. SW of Tacloban; agr. center, exporting rice, sugar. Sugar milling. During Second World War, city was principal Jap. supply port on Leyte; taken Dec., 1944, by U.S. forces after a bitter struggle. Called Ormoc until 1950.
McArthur, village (pop. 1,466), ⊙ Vinton co., S Ohio, 27 mi. ESE of Chillicothe, in livestock and orchard area; chemicals, lumber, clay products. Coal mine, oil and gas wells, limestone quarries. Platted 1815, inc. 1851.
MacArthur, village (pop. 1,650), Raleigh co., S W.Va., 2 mi. SW of Beckley, in coal region.
MacArthur, Fort, Calif.: see SAN PEDRO.
McArthur, Mount. 1 Peak (9,892 ft.), SE B.C., near Alta. border, in Rocky Mts., in Yoho Natl. Park, 50 mi. NW of Banff; 51°32'N 116°36'W. **2** Peak (14,400 ft.), SW Yukon, near Alaska border, in St. Elias Mts., 180 mi. W of Whitehorse; 60°36'N 140°12'W.
McArthur, Port, harbor, NE Northern Territory, Australia, in Gulf of Carpentaria; formed by Sir Edward Pellew Isls. (N) and mainland (W, S); 25 mi. long, 10 mi. wide; receives McArthur R.
McArthur-Burney Falls State Park, Calif.: see BURNEY.
McArthur Falls, waterfalls in SE Man., on Winnipeg R., at N end of Lac du Bonnet, 65 mi. NE of Winnipeg; hydroelectric-power center.
McArthur River, NE Northern Territory, Australia, rises in N hills of Barkly Tableland, flows 125 mi. NE to Port McArthur of Gulf of Carpentaria; navigable 40 mi. by barges; flooded after summer rains.
Macas (mä'käs), town (1950 pop. 1,079), ⊙ Santiago-Zamora prov., SE Ecuador, on E slopes of the Andes, 60 mi. SE of Riobamba, 150 mi. S of Quito; 2°17'S 78°6'W; alt. 3,445 ft. Military base. Stock-raising, lumbering, and agr. center (yucca, bananas, papaya, coffee, cacao, curare drug). Airfield.
Macassar or **Makassar** (mŭkă'sŭr), largest town (pop. 84,855) of Celebes, Indonesia, on SW peninsula, on Macassar Strait, 480 mi. ENE of Surabaya; 5°8'S 119°25'E. Exports coffee, teak, vegetable oils, spices, corn, copra, rattan. Site of airport and terminus of submarine cables to Java and Borneo. First settled by Portuguese, town came under Du. control in 1668. After Second World War, it was (1946–50) ⊙ state of East Indonesia.
Macassar Strait, wide channel connecting Celebes Sea (N) with Java and Flores seas (S), bet. Borneo (W) and Celebes (E); 600 mi. long, 80–230 mi. wide. Balikpapan and Kotabaru are on W shore; Macassar on E shore. Contains numerous isls., largest being Pulu Laut and Sebuku off SE coast of Borneo. In Second World War, the Allies inflicted (Jan., 1942) heavy losses on Jap. fleet in battle here, but failed to prevent Jap. landing on Balikpapan.
Macatawa Lake, Mich.: see BLACK RIVER, SW Mich.
Macatuba (mŭkŭtōō'bŭ), city (pop. 570), central São Paulo, Brazil, 15 mi. SW of Jaú; distilling; coffee, rice, beans. Until 1944, Bocaiúva.
Macau (mŭkou'), city (pop. 6,584), N Rio Grande do Norte, NE Brazil, port on the Atlantic, at mouth of Piranhas (or Açu) R., and 45 mi. E of Mossoró; important saltworking and -shipping center; also exports cotton, carnauba wax. Manganese deposits in area. Formerly spelled Macáo.
Macau, China: see MACAO.
Macau (mäkō'), village (pop. 743), Gironde dept., SW France, on the Garonne, near its junction with Dordogne R., and 12 mi. N of Bordeaux; ordinary wines, artichokes.
Macaubal (mŭkoubäl'), town (pop. 1,735), NW São Paulo, Brazil, 50 mi. W of São José do Rio Prêto, near westernmost extension of coffee region; cotton, fruit, cattle. Until 1944, called Macaúbas (formerly spelled Macahubas).
Macaúbas (mŭkăōō'bŭs). **1** City (pop. 1,568), W central Bahia, Brazil, 35 mi. SE of Paratinga; deposits of semiprecious stones. Formerly spelled Macahubas. **2** Town, São Paulo, Brazil: see MACAUBAL.
Macaulay Island, New Zealand: see KERMADEC ISLANDS.
Maçayó, Brazil: see MACEIÓ.
McBain, city (pop. 506), Missaukee co., N central Mich., 10 mi. SE of Cadillac.
McBaine, town (pop. 75), Boone co., central Mo., near Missouri R., 7 mi. SW of Columbia.
McBee (măk'bē), town (pop. 420), Chesterfield co., NE S.C., 38 mi. NW of Florence, in fruit-growing area.
McBride, village (pop. 237), E B.C., on Fraser R. and 120 mi. ESE of Prince George; lumbering.
McBrides, village (pop. 223), Montcalm co., central Mich., 20 mi. W of Alma, in agr. area.
McCall, resort village (pop. 1,173), Valley co., W Idaho, on North Fork Payette R., at S end of Payette L., and 27 mi. N of Cascade in recreation area; alt. 5,025 ft.; lumber milling. Hq. Idaho Natl. Forest. Near-by deposits of monazite sand contain thorium, used in production of atomic energy.
McCallsburg, town (pop. 290), Story co., central Iowa, 15 mi. NE of Ames; livestock, grain.
Maccaluba or **Macaluba,** Sicily: see ARAGONA.

McCamey (mŭkā'mē), city (pop. 3,121), Upton co., W Texas, 60 mi. S of Midland, near Pecos R.; distributing center for oil and sheep-ranching region; oil refinery; mfg. of oil-field supplies. Founded 1925 after oil discovery; inc. 1926.

McCammon, village (pop. 578), Bannock co., SE Idaho, 20 mi. SE of Pocatello and on Portneuf R.; alt. 4,719 ft.; grain, hay, sugar beets.

McCarthy, village (1939 pop. 49), S Alaska, 120 mi. NE of Cordova, at foot of Wrangell Mts., 3 mi. S of Kennicott; copper mining; outfitting point for hunting expeditions. Airfield. Formerly terminus of Copper River and Northwestern RR, closed down 1938. Sometimes called Shushanna Junction.

MacCarthy Island, division (□ 959; pop. 53,841) of central Gambia; ⊙ Georgetown. Extends along 100-mi. section of Gambia R. Produces peanuts, palm kernels, rice. River fisheries. Main centers: Georgetown (on MacCarthy Isl.). Kuntaur, Bansang. Pop. is largely Mandingo.

MacCarthy Island, island (□ 3) in Gambia R., MacCarthy Isl. div., central Gambia, 120 mi. E of Bathurst; 3 mi. long, 1 mi. wide. Site of GEORGETOWN. Formerly called Lemain Isl. Acquired by Br. traders in 1785; ceded 1823 to the Crown and renamed MacCarthy Isl.; became settlement for liberated African slaves and hq. of Wesleyan mission. Part of Gambia colony land, it was placed (1896) under the protectorate for administration.

McCarty, Alaska: see BIG DELTA.

McCaskill (mŭkă'skŭl), town (pop. 122), Hempstead co., SW Ark., 18 mi. N of Hope.

McCauley Island (□ 108; 18 mi. long, 2–12 mi. wide), W B.C., in Hecate Strait W of Pitt Isl.

McCausland, town (pop. 150), Scott co., E Iowa, near Wapsipinicon R., 15 mi. NNE of Davenport.

McCaysville, city (pop. 2,067), Fannin co., N Ga., 35 mi. ENE of Dalton, near Tenn.-N.C. line, in copper-mining region.

McChesneytown, village, Westmoreland co., SW Pa., just E of Latrobe.

Macchiagodena (mäkyägō'dĕnä), village (pop. 951), Campobasso prov., Abruzzi e Molise, S central Italy, 13 mi. W of Campobasso; woolen mills.

Macchiareddu (mäk"kyärĕd'dōō), village (pop. 155), Cagliari prov., S Sardinia, near Stagno di Cagliari, 4 mi. W of Cagliari; extensive saltworks (yearly production, 150,000 tons) just S. Bromine is also extracted.

McChord Air Force Base, Wash.: see TACOMA.

Macchupicchu, Peru: see MACHUPICCHU.

McClain, county (□ 559; pop. 14,681), central Okla.; ⊙ Purcell. Bounded NE by Canadian R., and drained by small creeks. Agr. (cotton, alfalfa, oats, peaches, corn, broomcorn, livestock; dairy products). Some mfg. Oil and natural-gas wells. Formed 1907.

McCleary, town (pop. 1,175), Grays Harbor co., W Wash., 17 mi. W of Olympia.

McClellan, Fort, Ala.: see ANNISTON.

McClellan, Lake, Texas: see MCCLELLAN CREEK.

McClellan, Mount, Colo.: see FRONT RANGE.

McClellan Creek, extreme N Texas, rises in Carson co., flows c.40 mi. E and NE to North Fork of Red R. 10 mi. N of McLean. In upper course, dam impounds L. McClellan (capacity 5,000 acre-ft.); recreational area (fishing, bathing, camping) here.

McClelland, town (pop. 159), Pottawattamie co., SW Iowa, 10 mi. ENE of Council Bluffs.

McClellan Field, Calif.: see SACRAMENTO, city.

McClellanville, summer-resort town (pop. 417), Charleston co., SE S.C., on the coast, on Intracoastal Waterway, and 23 mi. SSW of Georgetown; oyster canning. Near by are Harrietta House and gardens.

Macclenny, town (pop. 1,177), ⊙ Baker co., N Fla., 28 mi. W of Jacksonville, in lumbering and truck-farming area.

Macclesfield (mă'kŭlz–), municipal borough (1931 pop. 34,905; 1951 census 35,981), E Cheshire, England, 15 mi. SSE of Manchester; England's silk-milling center (mfg. of silk, rayon, and milling machinery); also leather tanning, mfg. of light metal products, electrical equipment. Has church of St. Michael (founded 1278) and early-16th-cent. grammar school. Silk milling introduced here 1756. Just E is Macclesfield Forest, moorland rising to 1,600 ft.

Macclesfield, town (pop. 370), Edgecombe co., E central N.C., 13 mi. E of Wilson; lumber milling.

Macclesfield Bank, Chinese *Chungsha* [middle reef], group of low coral reefs, in S.China Sea, part of Kwangtung prov., China, bet. 15°25'–16°15'N and 113°40'–114°57'E, c.350 mi. SE of Hainan. Consists of more than 20 shoals scattered over an area 75 mi. long (NE-SW), 33 mi. wide (NW-SE). Outlying shoals are Scarborough Shoal (15°8'N 117°45'E; c.200 mi. ESE), Helen Shoal (19°12'N 113°53'E; c.220 mi. NNW), and Truro Shoal (16°19'N 116°41'E; c.100 mi. ENE).

Maccles Lake (□ 12), E N.F., 30 mi. SE of Gander; 8 mi. long, 5 mi. wide.

McClintock Channel, S Franklin Dist., Northwest Territories, arm (170 mi. long, 65–130 mi. wide) of the Arctic Ocean, bet. Victoria Isl. and Prince of Wales Isl.; 72°N 103°W. Opens N on Viscount Melville Sound.

MacClintock Island, in S Franz Josef Land, Russian SFSR, in Arctic Ocean, W of Hall Isl.; 20 mi. long, 15 mi. wide; 80°15'N 56°30'E. Rises to 1,624 ft.

McCloud, lumber-milling village (pop. 1,394), Siskiyou co., N Calif., near McCloud R., 17 mi. SE of Weed, at S base of Mt. Shasta.

McCloud River, N Calif., rises in S Siskiyou co., on slope of Mt. Shasta, flows c.50 mi. SW to Shasta L., 19 mi. S of Dunsmuir.

McCluer Gulf, inlet of Ceram Sea, NW New Guinea, bet. Vogelkop peninsula (N) and Bombarai peninsula (S); c.150 mi. E–W, c.15–50 mi. N–S. Also called Telok Berau.

McClure. **1** Village (pop. 508), Henry co., NW Ohio, 10 mi. E of Napoleon, near Maumee R. **2** Village (1940 pop. 742), Snyder co., central Pa., 15 mi. NE of Lewistown, in agr. area; hatcheries; clothing mfg.

McClure, Cape, N extremity of Banks Isl., W Franklin Dist., Northwest Territories, on McClure Strait; 74°28'N 120°41'W.

McClure Strait, W Franklin Dist., Northwest Territories, arm (170 mi. long, 60 mi. wide) of Beaufort Sea of the Arctic Ocean, extending W from Viscount Melville Sound, bet. Melville and Eglinton isls. (N) and Banks Isl. (S); 75°N 118°W.

McClusky, city (pop. 850), ⊙ Sheridan co., central N.Dak., 50 mi. NNE of Bismarck; dairy products, livestock, poultry.

McColl (mŭkôl'), town (pop. 2,688), Marlboro co., NE S.C., 8 mi. ENE of Bennettsville, at N.C. line; cotton milling; cannery.

McComas (mŭkŏ'mŭs), village (pop. 2,999), Mercer co., S W.Va., 9 mi. N of Bluefield; coal region.

McComb (mŭkōm'). **1** City (pop. 10,401), Pike co., SW Miss., 60 mi. ESE of Natchez, near La. line; trade and shipping center for cotton, truck, dairy, timber area; mfg. of clothing, cotton textiles, cottonseed products; lumber milling; railroad shops; flower growing. Founded c.1857. **2** Village (pop. 1,026), Hancock co., NW Ohio, 9 mi. WNW of Findlay; corn, wheat, oats; glass products, lumber. **3** Town, Pottawatomie co., Okla.: see MACOMB.

McComb Mountain (4,425 ft.), Essex co., NE N.Y., in the Adirondacks, 9 mi. SE of Mt. Marcy and c.20 mi. SE of Lake Placid village.

McConaughy, Lake, Nebr.: see KINGSLEY DAM.

McCone, county (□ 2,638; pop. 3,258), NE Mont.; ⊙ Circle. Agr. region bounded N by Missouri R.; drained by Redwater Creek. In W is Fort Peck Reservoir. Grain, livestock. Formed 1919.

McConnells, town (pop. 255), York co., N S.C., 12 mi. WSW of Rock Hill. Post office name formerly McConnellsville.

McConnellsburg, agr. borough (pop. 1,126), ⊙ Fulton co., S Pa., 22 mi. W of Chambersburg; flour and planing mills; mtn. resort. Site of birthplace of James Buchanan is in state forest monument, just SE. Settled c.1730, laid out 1786, inc. 1814.

McConnellsville, S.C.: see MCCONNELLS.

McConnelsville, village (pop. 1,941), ⊙ Morgan co., E central Ohio, on Muskingum R. and 20 mi. SSE of Zanesville; meat products, lumber, cigars; gas and oil wells. Platted 1817.

McCook, county (□ 577; pop. 8,828), SE S.Dak.; ⊙ Salem. Agr. area drained by branches of Vermillion R. Dairy and poultry products, livestock, corn, barley. Formed 1873.

McCook. **1** Village (pop. 361), Cook co., NE Ill., suburb SW of Chicago; aluminum milling; limestone quarrying. **2** City (pop. 7,678), ⊙ Red Willow co., S Nebr., 65 mi. S of North Platte and on Republican R., near Kansas line; trade center, railroad div. point in rich grain-raising region; railroad repair shops; beverages, meat and dairy products, grain, livestock. Junior col., co. fairgrounds here. Founded as Fairview 1881, named McCook 1882, inc. 1883.

McCool, town (pop. 305), Attala co., central Miss., 17 mi. NE of Kosciusko.

McCool Junction, village (pop. 297), York co., SE Nebr., 9 mi. S of York and on W.Fork of Big Blue R.

McCormick, county (□ 403; pop. 9,577), W S.C.; ⊙ McCormick. Bounded W by Savannah R.; includes part of Sumter Natl. Forest. Agr. area, with timber; textile milling. Formed 1916.

McCormick, rural town (pop. 1,744), ⊙ McCormick co., W S.C., 21 mi. SSW of Greenwood; lumber and textile mills.

McCoy, Camp, Wis.: see SPARTA.

McCracken, county (□ 251; pop. 49,137), SW Ky.; ⊙ PADUCAH. Bounded N by Ohio R. (Ill. line), NE by the Tennessee, here entering the Ohio; drained by Clarks R. and its forks and by Mayfield Creek. Gently rolling agr. area (dark tobacco, corn, dairy products, poultry, livestock, fruit). Clay, fluorspar, and coal mines; timber. Mfg. at Paducah. Formed 1824.

McCracken, city (pop. 553), Rush co., W central Kansas, 13 mi. WNW of La Crosse; wheat, cattle.

McCreary (mŭkrĕ'rē, mŭkrā'rē), county (□ 421; pop. 16,660), S Ky.; ⊙ Whitley City. In the Cumberlands; bounded S by Tenn., N and E by Cumberland R.; drained by South Fork Cumberland R. Bituminous coal-mining and timber region; oil wells, some farms (dairy products, poultry, livestock, apples, Irish and sweet potatoes, corn, lespedeza, tobacco). Some lumber milling. Includes a natural bridge, natural caves, and parts of Cumberland Natl. Forest and Cumberland Falls State Park. Formed 1912.

McCrory (mŭkrô'rē), town (pop. 1,115), Woodruff co., E central Ark., 28 mi. NW of Forrest City and on Cache R.; agr. (rice, cotton, peaches). Cotton ginning, grist-and sawmilling. Settled 1886.

McCulloch (mŭkŭ'lŭ), county (□ 1,066; pop. 11,701), central Texas; ⊙ Brady. Geographical center of state, on N Edwards Plateau, with Brady Mts. (c.2,000 ft.) crossing E-W; bounded N by Colorado R. and drained by San Saba R. and Brady Creek. Diversified agr. and livestock raising; oats, corn, grain sorghums, cotton, barley, wheat, fruit, pecans; sheep and goats (wool, mohair marketed), polo ponies, poultry (especially turkeys). Formed 1856.

McCune, city (pop. 532), Crawford co., extreme SE Kansas, 18 mi. WSW of Pittsburg, in diversified agr. area. Coal mines and oil wells near by.

McCurtain, county (□ 1,854; pop. 31,588), extreme SE Okla.; ⊙ Idabel. Bounded E by Ark. line, S by Red R., here forming Texas line; drained by Little R. and its Mountain Fork; part of Ouachita Mts. in N. Lumbering, agr. (truck, grain, fruit, cotton, corn, alfalfa, hay, livestock). Includes a state park (fishing) and a game refuge. Formed 1907.

McCurtain, town (pop. 705), Haskell co., E Okla., 35 mi. WSW of Fort Smith (Ark.), in agr. area.

McDade, village (pop. c.400), Bastrop co., S central Texas, 30 mi. E of Austin; pottery plant.

MacDavid, village (pop. c.400), Escambia co., NW Fla., near Escambia R., 32 mi. N of Pensacola; naval stores.

Macdhui, Ben, Scotland: see BEN MACDHUI.

MacDill Air Force Base, Fla.: see TAMPA.

McDonald, county (□ 540; pop. 14,144), extreme SW Mo., in Ozarks; ⊙ Pineville. Drained by Elk R. Fruit (strawberries, grapes, tomatoes), grain, dairying, poultry; lumber. Formed 1849.

McDonald. **1** City (pop. 426), Rawlins co., NW Kansas, 16 mi. W of Atwood, in grain region. **2** Village (pop. 1,858), Trumbull co., NE Ohio, just NW of Youngstown and on Mahoning R.; produces pig iron. **3** Borough (pop. 3,543), Washington and Allegheny counties, SW Pa., 14 mi. WSW of Pittsburgh; bituminous coal, oil; oil-well supplies; agr.

Macdonald, Lake, E Western Australia, 540 mi. S of Wyndham, near W border of Northern Territory; 20 mi. long, 12 mi. wide. Usually dry; surrounded by swamps.

McDonald, Lake, Mont.: see GLACIER NATIONAL PARK.

McDonald Islands, tiny subantarctic rocks in S Indian Ocean, c.20 mi. W of Heard Isl. and c.250 mi. SSE of the Kerguelen Isls., at approximately 53°S 72°25'E.

MacDonald Pass (alt. c.6,330 ft.), in Continental Divide, W central Mont., 14 mi. W of Helena. Named for Alexander MacDonald, who built and maintained 1st road (1870–75) through pass.

McDonald Peak, Mont.: see MISSION RANGE.

McDonalds (mŭkdŏ'nŭldz), town (pop. 78), Robeson co., S N.C., 10 mi. WSW of Lumberton.

Macdonnell Ranges, S Northern Territory, Australia, consist of 2 parallel ranges extending 200 mi. W from Arltunga; highest peak, Mt. Zeil (4,955 ft.); quartzite, eucalyptus. Site of towns of Alice Springs and Hermannsburg.

McDonough (mŭkdŏ'nŭ), county (□ 582; pop. 28,199), W Ill.; ⊙ Macomb. Agr. (livestock, corn, wheat, oats, soybeans, hay, poultry; dairy products). Bituminous-coal mining; clay pits. Macomb is trade and mfg. center, with diversified products. Drained by La Moine R. and branches. Formed 1826.

McDonough, city (pop. 1,635), ⊙ Henry co., N central Ga., 24 mi. SSE of Atlanta; mfg. (electrical equipment, hosiery, pajamas, plastic raincoats, furniture). Inc. 1823.

Macdougall, Lake (□ 265), NW Keewatin Dist., Northwest Territories, NE of L. Garry; 66°N 99°W; 37 mi. long, 1–10 mi. wide. Drained SE by Back R.

McDowell. **1** County (□ 442; pop. 25,720), W central N.C.; ⊙ Marion. In the Blue Ridge; drained by Catawba R. (forms L. James in E); N part in Pisgah Natl. Forest. Farming (corn, apples, soybeans, dairy products, poultry), livestock raising, lumbering. Resort area; textile mfg. at Marion. Formed 1842. **2** County (□ 533; pop. 98,887), S W.Va.; ⊙ Welch. On Allegheny Plateau; bounded W, S, and SE by Va.; drained by Tug and Dry forks (headstreams of the Big Sandy). Extensive semibituminous-coal mining (Pocahontas coal field); some natural gas, timber, agr. (livestock, tobacco, truck, fruit). Formed 1858.

McDowell. **1** Mining village (1940 pop. 1,014), Floyd co., E Ky., in the Cumberlands, 12 mi. W of Pikeville; bituminous coal. Timber, oil, gas in area. **2** Town (pop. 107), Highland co., NW Va., in the Allegheneis 25 mi. WNW of Staunton.

MacDowell Colony, N.H.: see PETERBORO.

McDowell Mountains, central Ariz., rise to 4,022 ft. in McDowell Peak, c.20 mi. NE of Phoenix.

Macduff, burgh (1931 pop. 3,276; 1951 census 3,322), NE Banffshire, Scotland, on Moray Firth, at mouth of Deveron R. (1779 bridge), just E of Banff; herring-fishing center, seaside resort.

McDuffie, county (□ 263; pop. 11,443), E Ga.; ⊙ Thomson. Bounded N by Little R. Intersected by the fall line. Farming (cotton, corn, grain, truck, fruit) and sawmilling area. Formed 1870.

Maceda (mä-thä'dhä), town (pop. 1,059), Orense prov., NW Spain, 11 mi. ESE of Orense; ceramics factory; trades in rye, potatoes, cattle.

Macedo de Cavaleiros (mŏosä'dōō dĭ kŭvŭlā'rōōsh), town (pop. 1,859), Bragança dist., N Portugal, on railroad and 21 mi. SSW of Bragança; rye, potatoes; olive-oil, wine.

Macedon (mă'sĭdŭn), town (pop. 551), S central Victoria, Australia, 35 mi. NW of Melbourne, in forest area; softwood.

Macedon, village (pop. 614), Wayne co., W N.Y., on the Barge Canal and 12 mi. SE of Rochester.

Macedonia (măsĭdō'nēŭ), Bulg. and Macedonian *Makedoniya*, Greek *Makedonia* or *Makedhonia*, Serbo-Croatian *Makedonija* or *Makedoniya*, region of SE Europe, in S Balkan Peninsula, on Aegean Sea, divided politically among Bulgaria, Greece, and Yugoslavia. It is bounded S by Thessaly along Olympus, Kamvounia, and Chasia mts., W by Epirus along the Pindus-Sar (Shar) mtn. system, N by Serbia, and NE and E by Thrace along Rila and Rhodope mts. and lower Mesta R. It includes the 3-pronged Chalcidice Peninsula and is drained by Mesta, Struma, Vardar, and Aliakmon (Bistritsa) rivers. Predominantly mountainous, it contains the massifs of the Baba (Varnous), rising to 8,530 ft. in the Perister; the Nidze (Voras), rising to 8,280 ft. in the Kajmakcalan; and the Belasica (Kerkine), rising to 6,660 ft. Parallel ranges of the Pindus system (W) enclose intermontane basins oriented N–S and occupied by L. Prespa, L. Kastoria, and the upper Aliakmon R. (W of the Baba massif) and by the Pelagonija, Eoraia (Ptolemais), and Kozane basins (E of the Baba massif). The extensive lowlands of Giannitsa and Salonika, formed by Aliakmon, Loudias, and Vardar rivers, occupy the S central portion. In the east, the Serrai and Drama lowlands are enclosed by outlying massifs of the Rhodope system. The economy is primarily pastoral and agricultural; the raising of crops is restricted to the intermontane basins, river valleys, and lowlands, where irrigation methods are used during hot, dry summers. The leading grains are wheat and corn in the plains, rye, millet, and barley in the hills. Tobacco is the leading export crop, followed by cotton, sesame, hemp, and the opium poppy. Fruit, mulberry trees (sericulture), and grapes are also grown. Stock raising, particularly of sheep and goats, is a mainstay of the economy. Forestry is important in the wet SW section, leading to considerable charcoal production. Macedonia's pop. is today predominantly Slav, speaking a language akin to Serbo-Croatian and Bulgarian. Other elements of pop. are Greeks, Turks, Bulgars, Albanians, and Walachians. In anc. times, Macedon was inhabited by Thraco-Illyrian tribes (including the Macedni), possibly related to the Dorians. Originally located in SW, they were brought (7th cent. B.C.) under common rule and expanded their holdings eastward to Salonika plain, with the capital at Aegae (Edessa), later at Pella. Macedonian development was first hampered by the Greek Ionian city states on the Aegean coast and (490–480 B.C.) by the Persian occupation. However, under Philip II (359–336 B.C.), the state annexed Thrace, Chalcidice, Thessaly, and, following the battle of Chaeronea (338 B.C.), extended its rule over Greece. As a result of the military conquests (336–323 B.C.) of Alexander the Great, Macedon became a leading world power, ruling an empire that extended through Egypt, Asia Minor, and Persia, to the Indus R. on the borders of India. The break-up of the empire, following the death of Alexander, was completed by the Roman victories of Cynoscephalae (197 B.C.) and Pydna (168 B.C.). Temporarily set up as 4 republics, Macedonia became a Roman prov. in 148 B.C., comprising Thessaly and N Epirus. Under Roman rule, it became the field of the missionary activity of St. Paul. On the partition (395) of the Roman Empire, Macedonia fell to the Byzantine domain. Devastation by the Visigoths and the Huns was followed by permanent settlement (6th cent.) by the Slavs, who rapidly absorbed the classical Macedonian pop. Continuing under intermittent Byzantine rule, Macedonia passed to Bulgarians (in 9th cent.) and to Serbs (in 14th cent.). By the middle 15th cent. it had been invested by the Turks, who held it until 1912, its allocation to Bulgaria by the Treaty of San Stefano (1878) having been nullified by the Congress of Berlin. After the middle 19th cent., strife among the various nationalities, independence movements, and claims by Greece, Serbia, and Bulgaria created the *Macedonian question*, the immediate cause of the Balkan Wars (1912–13). The Treaty of Bucharest (1913), which ended the Second Balkan War, divided Macedonia among Greece, Serbia (later Yugoslavia), and Bulgaria, with boundaries that have remained in effect since, except for minor adjustments (STRUMICA) since the Treaty of Neuilly (1919). Population exchanges after the First World War resulted in the replacement of most Bulg. and Turkish elements in Gr. Macedonia by Gr. refugees from Asia Minor. In Second World War most of Macedonia was briefly (1941–44) under Bulgaria, which had sided with the Axis against Yugoslavia and Greece, but the Bulg. armistice (1944), confirmed by the peace treaty of 1947, restored the pre-war boundaries. **Greek Macedonia** or **Aegean Macedonia,** a N division (□ 13,380; 1940 pop. 1,754,092) of Greece, with ⊙ Salonika, occupies greater (S) portion of Macedonia, extending from the Pindus E along Aegean Sea to lower Mesta R., where it borders on Thrace. It is bounded SW by Thessaly and Epirus and W by S Albania. It contains the larger Macedonian lowlands, Chalcidice peninsula, and lakes Prespa, Kastoria, Vegoritis, Koroneia, and Volve. The chief traits of the economy are stock raising and lumbering (charcoal) in W, agr. and industry in central lowlands, and tobacco growing in W (Serrai, Drama, Kavalla). Lignite, magnesite, and chromium are the chief mineral resources. The leading industrial centers are Salonika (rail hub), Edessa, and Veroia. As a result of the pop. exchanges after First World War, Gr. Macedonia has a nearly homogeneous Gr. pop., with Slav elements along N border and several small Walachian pockets. It is divided administratively into the nomes of KASTORIA, KOZANE, and PHLORINA (W), PELLA, HEMATHEIA, KILKIS, SALONIKA, CHALCIDICE with autonomous MOUNT ATHOS, and SERRAI (center), and DRAMA and KAVALLA (E). **Yugoslav Macedonia** or **Vardar Macedonia,** officially **Macedonian People's Republic,** southernmost constituent republic (□10,229; 1948 pop. 1,152,054) of Yugoslavia, with ⊙ Skoplje (Skopje), occupies NW portion of Macedonia and is nearly coextensive with upper Vardar drainage basin, bounded W by Albania and N by Serbia. Mostly mountainous, except for Bitolj (Pelagonija), Tetovo (Polog), Skoplje, and Strumica basins, where agr. is carried on. Tobacco, cotton, sesame, poppy are the chief crops besides grains. Sheep and goats constitute the main stock. Chromium is mined at Radusa and near Valandovo. The Belgrade-Salonika RR (along Vardar valley) is the chief line of communication, linking with its several branches the centers of Skoplje (industrial hub), Bitolj, Prilep, Kumanovo, Tetovo, Titov, Veles, Stip, Ochrid, and Strumica. Allocated 1913 to Serbia, Vardar Macedonia became part of Yugoslavia after First World War. It had a separate official status and was divided (1921–29) into oblasts, included (1929–41) in the Vardar banovina, and occupied (1941–44) by Bulgaria. After Second World War, it was constituted (1946) as one of the federal republics of Yugoslavia on the basis of the nearly homogeneous Macedonian pop. and with an official Macedonian language. Since 1949, the republic is divided into the oblasts of Skoplje, Bitolj, and Stip. **Bulgarian Macedonia** or **Pirin Macedonia** is coextensive with GORNA DZHUMAYA district, one of the dists. into which Bulgaria was divided in 1949; ⊙ Gorna Dzhumaya. It includes the Struma and Mesta valleys and the intervening Pirin Mts. Tobacco, cotton, and wine are the chief agr. products in the valleys; stock raising and lumbering are carried on in the mts. In addition to Gorna Dzhumaya, the leading urban centers are Nevrokop, Petrich, Sandanski, Razlog, and Bansko.

Macedonia. 1 Village (pop. 127), on Franklin-Hamilton co. line, S Ill., 21 mi. SSE of Mount Vernon, in agr. and coal area. **2** Town (pop. 298), Pottawattamie co., SW Iowa, on West Nishnabotna R. and 24 mi. ESE of Council Bluffs, in agr. region.

Maceió (mŏosĭyô'), city (1950 pop. 102,301), ⊙ Alagoas, NE Brazil, port on the Atlantic, 130 mi. SSW of Recife; 9°38'S 35°43'W. Chief exports: sugar and cotton. Growing industries include textile mills, sugar refineries, distilleries, cigarette and soap factories. Situated on level strip of land bet. ocean and a shallow lagoon (c.6 mi. long; seaplane port). Connected by canal with Marechal Deodoro (10 mi. SW on Manguaba Lagoon). Jaraguá harbor dist. is just E. City has two airports (5 mi. and 10 mi. NNW), is linked by rail with Recife (Pernambuco) and Palmeira dos Índios (in the interior). Chief bldgs. are govt. palace (Port.-colonial style), and a church with tile-decorated façade. Streets are lined with palm trees. Lighthouse on hill in city center is principal landmark. City has faculty of law (established 1931). Old spelling, Maçayó.

Macenta (mäsĕn'tä), town (pop. c.1,450), SE Fr. Guinea, Fr. West Africa, near Liberia border, 125 mi. S of Kankan; rice, coffee, palm kernels, kola nuts, manioc, millet. Bouro diamond mines near.

Macequece (mäsĕkĕ'sä), village, Manica and Sofala prov., W central Mozambique, near Southern Rhodesia border, 140 mi. WNW of Beira; customs station on Beira RR opposite Umtali; gold mines; copper and tin deposits.

Macerata (mächĕrä'tä), province (□ 1,071; pop. 290,057), The Marches, central Italy, bordering on the Adriatic; ⊙ Macerata. Crossed by the Apennines; watered by Chienti, Potenza, and Musone rivers. Agr. (cereals, grapes, raw silk, olives, fruit); stock raising (cattle, swine). Mfg. at Macerata, Porto Civitanova, Recanati, and Tolentino.

Macerata, town (pop. 14,460), ⊙ Macerata prov., The Marches, central Italy, on hill bet. Potenza and Chienti rivers, 22 mi. SSW of Ancona; 43°18'N 13°27'E. Agr. center; mfg. (agr. machinery, cutlery, harmoniums, cotton textiles, macaroni). Bishopric. Has medieval town walls, university (founded 1290), several palaces (16th-17th cent.), cathedral (1771–90). Damaged in Second World War by air bombing (1944).

Macerata Feltria (fĕl'trēä), village (pop. 848), Pesaro e Urbino, The Marches, central Italy, 11 mi. NW of Urbino; pharmaceuticals.

Maces Bay, fishing village, SW N.B., on Maces Bay or Mace Bay, inlet of the Bay of Fundy, 24 mi. SW of St. John.

Macestus River, Turkey: see SIMAV RIVER.

McEwen (mŭkyōō'ŭn), town (pop. 710), Humphreys co., central Tenn., 45 mi. W of Nashville, in timber and dairying region; cheese, lumber.

McEwensville, borough (pop. 297), Northumberland co., E central Pa., 14 mi. N of Sunbury.

McFadden, village (pop. c.250), Carbon co., SE Wyo., on Rock Creek, in foothills of Medicine Bow Mts., and 36 mi. NW of Laramie; alt. c.7,200 ft.; oil wells.

McFall, city (pop. 255), Gentry co., NW Mo., near Grand R., 40 mi. NE of St. Joseph.

McFarlan, town (pop. 136), Anson co., S N.C., 12 mi. SSE of Wadesboro, near S.C. line.

McFarland. 1 Village (pop. 2,183), Kern co., S central Calif., 5 mi. S of Delano; cotton-ginning center; also packs fruit, truck. **2** City (pop. 279), Wabaunsee co., NE central Kansas, 30 mi. W of Topeka, in cattle, poultry, and grain region. **3** Village (pop. 593), Dane co., S Wis., near Yahara R. and L. Waubesa, 7 mi. SE of Madison, in dairy and lake-resort region.

McGehee (mŭgē'), city (pop. 3,854), Desha co., SE Ark., 25 mi. NW of Greenville (Miss.), in stock-raising and agr. area (cotton, corn, rice, hay); meat packing, rice milling, cotton ginning; railroad shops. Inc. 1906.

McGill, village (pop. 2,297), White Pine co., E Nev., in Shell Creek Range, 12 mi. NNE of Ely; alt. c.6,400 ft.; copper smelting.

McGillivray Falls (mŭgĭ'lĭvrē), village, SW B.C., in Coast Mts., on Anderson L., 23 mi. WSW of Lillooet; gold mining.

Macgillycuddy's Reeks (mŭgĭ'lĭkŭdēz), mountain range, Co. Kerry, Ireland, extending 12 mi. W from the Lakes of Killarney; rise to 3,414 ft. in Carrantuohill, Carrauntuohil, or Carrantual (all: kă"rŭntōō'ŭl), highest peak in Ireland.

McGrann, village (pop. 1,418), Armstrong co., W Pa., on Allegheny R., just below Kittanning.

McGrath (mŭgrăth'), village (pop. 169), SW central Alaska, on upper Kuskokwim R. (head of navigation) and 220 mi. NW of Anchorage; 62°58'N 155°35'W; transshipment point for river freight to upper Kuskokwim R. region; sawmilling, gold mining, trapping. Has airfield and wharves; school. Established 1905.

McGrath, village (pop. 135), Aitkin co., E Minn., on Snake R., E of Mille Lacs L., and 30 mi. SE of Aitkin in grain area.

McGraw, village (pop. 1,197), Cortland co., central N.Y., 4 mi. E of Cortland; clothing, wood products. Inc. 1869.

MacGregor, village (pop. estimate 550), S Man., 22 mi. W of Portage la Prairie; grain elevators.

McGregor. 1 Town (pop. 1,138), Clayton co., NE Iowa, on Mississippi R. almost opposite mouth of Wisconsin R., and 3 mi. SW of Prairie du Chien (Wis.), in hilly "Little Switzerland" region; dairy products, pearl buttons, novelties, beverages, millwork products. Effigy Mounds Natl. Monument and state parks near by. The American School of Wild Life Protection holds annual (Aug.) sessions here. Settled 1836, inc. 1857. **2** Resort village (pop. 322), Aitkin co., E central Minn., on small lake, 20 mi. ENE of Aitkin; dairy products. State forest and wildlife refuge near by. **3** Town (pop. 2,669), McLennan co., E central Texas, 18 mi. SW of Waco, near branch of Bosque R.; cotton ginning; flour, feed milling. State park is SW. An ordnance plant was near in Second World War.

McGregor, Lake (23 mi. long, 1–3 mi. wide), S Alta., 60 mi. SE of Calgary. Drains N into Bow R. Irrigation dams at N and S extremities.

McGrew, village (pop. 105), Scotts Bluff co., W Nebr., 15 mi. SE of Scottsbluff and on N.Platte R.

McGuffey, village (pop. 639), Hardin co., W central Ohio, 9 mi. WNW of Kenton; onions, corn, peppermint, potatoes.

McGuire, Mount, Idaho: see YELLOWJACKET MOUNTAINS.

McGuire Air Force Base, N.J.: see WRIGHTSTOWN.

Mach (mŭch), town (pop. 2,220), ⊙ Bolan subdivision, NE central Baluchistan, W Pakistan, 27 mi. SSE of Quetta, in Bolan Pass; wheat. Near-by coal and limestone deposits worked. Sometimes spelled Machh.

Macha (mä'chä), town (pop. c.6,300), Potosí dept., W central Bolivia, 10 mi. SSW of Colquechaca; road center; corn, potatoes.

Machacamarca (mächäkämär′kä), town (pop. c.4,300), Oruro dept., W Bolivia, in the Altiplano. 17 mi. SSE of Oruro, and on Oruro-Uyuni RR; junction for branch to Uncía; alt. 12,145 ft. Tin-ore concentration plant.

Machachi (mächä′chē), town (1950 pop. 2,582), Pichincha prov., N central Ecuador, in high valley, on Pan American Highway and 20 mi. S of Quito; alt. 9,632 ft. Health resort (with Thesalia spa) and stock-raising center in fertile region, where also cereals and potatoes are grown. Mfg. of dairy products and woolen goods, bottling of mineral water. Because of its picturesque Alpine setting and cool climate, it is a favorite vacationing place for Quito residents.

Machado (mŏoshä′dōō), city (pop. 5,498), SW Minas Gerais, Brazil, terminus of rail spur, and 45 mi. ENE of Poços de Caldas; coffeegrowing center.

Machado River, Brazil: see Gi-Paraná River.

Machagay or **Machagai** (mächägī′), town (1947 pop. 4,748), S central Chaco natl. territory, Argentina, on railroad and 28 mi. ESE of Presidencia Roque Sáenz Peña; agr. (cotton, corn, livestock) and lumbering center; sawmills, cotton gins.

Machakos (mächä′kōs), town (pop. c.2,000), S central Kenya, 40 mi. SE of Nairobi; 1°38′S 37°12′E; agr. trade center; deciduous fruits, wheat, coffee, corn; dairy farming.

Machala (mächä′lä), town (1950 pop. 7,491), ⊙ El Oro prov., S Ecuador, in lowlands, 75 mi. S of Guayaquil, 235 mi. SSW of Quito; 3°16′S 79°57′W. Commercial center in agr. region, trading in cacao, coffee, hides. Its port, Puerto Bolívar, is 2 mi. SW.

Machalí (mächälē′), town (pop. 2,135), O'Higgins prov., central Chile, in Andean foothills, 5 mi. E of Rancagua. Picturesque colonial town in agr. area (alfalfa, grain, potatoes, fruit, wine, cattle).

Machalilla (mächälē′yä), village, Manabí prov., W Ecuador, small port on the Pacific, 18 mi. SW of Jipijapa, in agr. region (cacao, rice, sugar cane, tagua nuts).

Machanao (măchă′nou), municipality (pop. 684), NW Guam; farms, coconut plantations.

Machang or **Kampong Machang** (kämpŏŏng′ mŭchäng′), village (pop. 465), N Kelantan, Malaya, on road and 25 mi. S of Kota Bharu; rubber, rice.

Machang Sahatun, mine, Malaya: see Chukai.

Macharavialla (mächärävyä′lyä), town (pop. 161), Málaga prov., S Spain, 12 mi. E of Málaga; grapes, raisins, lemons, almonds. Has fine church.

Macharetí (mächärätē′), town, Chuquisaca dept., SE Bolivia, on E slopes of Serranía de Aguaragüe and 32 mi. NNE of Villa Montes; oil fields.

Machattie, Lake (mŭchă′tē) (□ 120), SW Queensland, Australia, 410 mi. WNW of Charleville; 17 mi. long, 10 mi. wide.

Machault (mäshō′), village (pop. 450), Ardennes dept., N France, 10 mi. WSW of Vouziers.

Machecoul (mäshkōōl′), village (pop. 1,664), Loire-Inférieure dept., W France, 20 mi. SW of Nantes; alcohol distilling, bicycle assembling. Has ruined 14th-cent. castle. Here began the Vendean insurrection in 1793.

Macheke (mächĕ′kä), township (pop. 234), Salisbury prov., E Southern Rhodesia, in Mashonaland, on Macheke R. (left affluent of Sabi R.), on railroad and 20 mi. ENE of Marandellas; alt. 5,042 ft. Tobacco, peanuts, citrus fruit, dairy products.

Machekha (mä′chĭkhŭ), village (1939 pop. over 500), NW Stalingrad oblast, Russian SFSR, on Buzuluk R. and 22 mi. SW of Yelan; metalworks; wheat, sunflowers. Until c.1938, Machikha.

Machelen (mä′khŭlŭn), residential town (pop. 6,410), Brabant prov., central Belgium, NE suburb of Brussels; adjoins industrial installations along Willebroek Canal (automobile assembly, metalworking, concrete mfg., textile dyeing). Melsbroek airport is E. Has 16th-cent. church; site of Beaulieu Castle, built 1653, hq. of William III of England in 1695.

Machen, England: see Bedwas and Machen.

Machena, Nigeria: see Matsena.

Macheng or **Ma-ch'eng** (mä′chŭng′), town (pop. 30,244), ⊙ Macheng co. (pop. 533,172), E Hupeh prov., China, 65 mi. NE of Hankow, near Honan line; cotton weaving; rice, ramie.

McHenry. 1 County (□ 611; pop. 50,656), NE Ill., on Wis. line (N); ⊙ Woodstock. Dairying area; also livestock, poultry, corn, wheat. Many lakes, with resorts; fishing, duck hunting. Industry at Woodstock. Drained by Fox and Kishwaukee rivers. Formed 1836. **2** County (□ 1,890; pop. 12,556), N central N.Dak.; ⊙ Towner. Agr. area with extensive lignite deposits; drained by Souris R. Livestock, dairy produce, poultry, wheat. Formed 1873.

McHenry. 1 City (pop. 2,080), McHenry co., NE Ill., on Fox R. (bridged here) and 22 mi. W of Waukegan; trade and processing center in dairying, agr., and lake-resort area; mfg. (boats, pickles, cigars); fishing, duck hunting. Settled 1836; inc. as village in 1855, as city in 1923. **2** Town (pop. 511), Ohio co., W Ky., 30 mi. SSE of Owensboro, in bituminous-coal and agr. area. **3** Summer resort, Garrett co., W Md., in the Alleghenies on Deep Creek L., 32 mi. W of Cumberland. State game refuge near. **4** Village (pop. 189), Foster co., E central N.Dak., 26 mi. ENE of Carrington.

McHenry, Fort, Md.: see Baltimore.

Macherio (mäkĕ′rēō), village (pop. 2,092), Milano prov., Lombardy, N Italy, adjacent to Sovico, 4 mi. N of Monza; cotton-milling center.

Macherla (mä′chĕrlŭ), village, Guntur dist., NE Madras, India, 70 mi. WNW of Guntur; rail spur terminus; steatite mines.

Machetá (mächätä′), village (pop. 981), Cundinamarca dept., central Colombia, 45 mi. NE of Bogotá; alt. 7,004 ft.; cereals, potatoes, fruit, cattle.

Machete or **Central Machete** (sĕnträl′ mächā′tā), locality, SE Puerto Rico, on railroad and 2½ mi. S of Guayama; sugar mill.

Machgara, Lebanon: see Meshghara.

Machh, W Pakistan: see Mach.

Machha Bhawan, Kashmir: see Bawan.

Machhlishahr (mŭch′lēshŭhŭr), town (pop. 8,488), Jaunpur dist., SE Uttar Pradesh, India, 18 mi. WSW of Jaunpur; barley, rice, corn, wheat, sugar cane. Anc. fort, extensive mosque ruins.

Ma-chiang, China: see Makiang.

Machias (mŭchī′ŭs). **1** Town (pop. 2,063), including Machias village (pop. 1,621), ⊙ Washington co., E Maine, 65 mi. ESE of Bangor, near mouth of the Machias. Lumbering center; seat of state normal school. English trading post here (1633) destroyed shortly thereafter by the French. Burnham Tavern (1770), historical mus., has mementos of early naval battle of Machiasport. Settled 1763, inc. 1784. **2** Village (pop. c.600), Cattaraugus co., W N.Y., 25 mi. N of Olean; resort, with small Lime L. near by. Dairy products, poultry, maple-sugar products, lumber.

Machias Bay, Washington co., E Maine, at mouths of Machias and East Machias rivers, 25 mi. SW of Eastport; 7 mi. long, 4 mi. wide.

Machias Lakes, Washington co., E Maine, 5 lakes (First to Fifth Machias lakes) in upper course of Machias R.; from 1 to 5 mi. long.

Machiasport, town (pop. 781), Washington co., E Maine, at head of Machias Bay, E of Machias. Lumber shipping, fish canning. Earthworks of Revolutionary War fort taken (1814) by British in state park. Off Machiasport in June, 1775, occurred "first naval battle of the Revolution," capture of Br. ship. Set off from Machias 1862.

Machias River. 1 River (c.65 mi. long) in E Maine, rises in W Washington co., forms Machias Lakes in its upper course, then flows c.40 mi. S and SE to Machias Bay at Machiasport. **2** River in N Maine, rises in Big Machias L. in Aroostook co., flows c.35 mi. SE and E to the Aroostook near Ashland.

Machias Seal Islands, group of islets (international status undetermined) off Maine and New Brunswick, 24 mi. SE of Machias, Maine; Canadian-operated lighthouse (44°39′N 67°06′W) on Machias Seal, the southernmost.

Machichaco, Cape (mächēchä′kō), on Bay of Biscay, Vizcaya prov., N Spain, 17 mi. NE of Bilbao; 43°28′N 2°47′W. Lighthouse.

Machico (mächē′kō), town (pop. 10,820), Madeira, on E coast of Madeira isl., 10 mi. NE of Funchal; 32°43′N 16°46′W. Fishing port, resort. Mineral springs. João Gonçalves Zarco landed here 1420.

Machida (mä″chē′dä) or **Machita** (–tä), town (pop. 19,282), Greater Tokyo, central Honshu, Japan, 13 mi. W of Kawasaki; collection center for raw silk; agr. (rice, wheat).

Machikha, Russian SFSR: see Machekha.

Machine, La (lä mäshēn′), town (pop. 5,390), Nièvre dept., central France, 16 mi. ESE of Nevers; iron and coal mines.

Machinery City, Ga.: see Fair Oaks.

Machino (mä″chē′nō), town (pop. 6,892), Ishikawa prefecture, central Honshu, Japan, 10 mi. ENE of Wajima; rice, wheat.

Machiques (mächē′käs), town (pop. 3,896), Zulia state, NW Venezuela, at E foot of Sierra de Perijá, 75 mi. SW of Maracaibo; cattle raising and dairying. Formerly Perijá.

Machita, Japan: see Machida.

Machkund River (mŭch′kōōnd), in NE Madras and SW Orissa, India, rises in Eastern Ghats in W Vizagapatam dist., NW of Madugula; flows NW and SSW, mainly along Madras-Orissa border, to Sabari R. opposite Konta, 60 mi. NNW of Rajahmundry; c.190 mi. long. Dam at Jalaput; hydroelectric plant planned to power industries in NE Madras and S Orissa. In lower course, called Sileru.

Machlata, Bulgaria: see Makhlata.

Machtum (mäkh′tōōm), village (pop. 322), SE Luxembourg, on Moselle R., just S of Grevenmacher, on Ger. border; vineyards, plum growing.

Machuca Rapids, Nicaragua–Costa Rica: see San Juan River.

Machupicchu or **Machu Picchu** (mä′chōō pēk′chōō), ruined pre-Incan city, Cuzco dept., S central Peru, on Vilcanota R., on railroad (built 1947) and 50 mi. NW of Cuzco. The well-preserved citadel city of impressive bulky structures stands on top of a mtn., c.6,750 ft. high. Though vaguely known for years, it was rediscovered (1911) by Dr. Hiram Bingham of Yale Univ. Recent expeditions (1940–41) have found near by other anc. fortress cities, such as Phuyu Pata Marka ("city above the clouds") and Sayaq Marka ("inaccessible city"), which are said to surpass Machupicchu in grandeur. At foot of the ruins, on Urubamba R., is a hydroelectric plant. Sometimes also spelled Macchupicchu or Macchu Picchu.

Machupo River (mächōō′pō), Beni dept., NE Bolivia, rises in marshy area near San Pedro, c.25 mi. N of Trinidad; flows 150 mi. N and NE, past San Ramón and San Joaquín, to the Itonamas just above its confluence with the Guaporé. Navigable for c.50 mi. below San Ramón. Called Cocharca R. in its upper course, below San Ramón.

Machva, county, Yugoslavia: see Macva.

Machynlleth (măkh-ŭn′thlĕth), urban district (1931 pop. 1,892; 1951 census 1,875), W Montgomery, Wales, on Dovey R. and 10 mi. E of Towyn; agr.

Macia (mä′syŏŏ), village, Sul do Save prov., S Mozambique, on road and 35 mi. W of Vila de João Belo; cotton, mafura, rice, beans.

Maciejow, Ukrainian SSR: see Lukov.

Maciel (mäsyĕl′), town (pop. estimate 2,000), S central Santa Fe prov., Argentina, 37 mi. NNW of Rosario; rail junction and agr. center (corn, wheat, flax, potatoes, livestock).

Maciel, town (dist. pop. 5,682), Caazapá dept., S Paraguay, on railroad and 95 mi. SE of Asunción, W of Caazapá; lumbering, orange-growing, cattle-raising center.

Macin (mŏochēn′), Rum. *Măcin*, town (1948 pop. 5,217), Galati prov., SE Rumania, in Dobruja, on the Dunarea Veche arm of the Danube and 9 mi. E of Braila; trade in fish, grain, wine. Stone and granite quarrying. Has old mosque.

Macina (mäsēnä′), depression along the middle Niger R. in Fr. Sudan, Fr. West Africa, a vast lacustrine region extending for c.300 mi. NE-SW (up to c.60 mi. wide) from Timbuktu to Ségou and covered by a network of lakes, swamps, and channels. Flooded during rainy period. One of Africa's most fertile regions, it has been utilized for irrigation (cotton, rice). A large dam built (completed 1946) at Sansanding supplies irrigation canals. Principal lakes are Débo (SW), Faguibine (NE).

McIntire (mă′kĭntīr), town (pop. 300), Mitchell co., N Iowa, near Minn. line, on Wapsipinicon R. and 15 mi. NE of Osage. Limestone quarries, sand pits near by.

McIntosh (mă′kĭntŏsh). **1** County (□ 431; pop. 6,008), SE Ga.; ⊙ Darien. Bounded SE by the Atlantic, SW by Altamaha R.; includes Sapelo Isl. Coastal plain dairying, truck-farming, fishing, and sawmilling area; seafood canning at Darien. Formed 1793. **2** County (□ 993; pop. 7,590), S N.Dak., on S.Dak. line; ⊙ Ashley. Rich prairie land watered by Beaver Creek. Dairy products, flour, grain, livestock, poultry. Formed 1883. **3** County (□ 715; pop. 17,829), E Okla.; ⊙ Eufaula. Bounded S by Canadian R.; intersected by North Canadian R. Agr. (cotton, potatoes, peanuts, corn, livestock, grain; dairy products). Farm-products processing, some mfg. Oil and natural-gas wells. Formed 1907.

McIntosh. 1 Town (pop. 247), Marion co., N central Fla., 15 mi. SSE of Gainesville, near Orange L.; ships citrus fruit and truck produce. **2** Village (pop. 881), Polk co., NW Minn., on Poplar R. and 35 mi. ESE of Crookston, in grain, livestock, poultry area; dairy products. **3** City (pop. 628), ⊙ Corson co., N S.Dak., 110 mi. NNW of Pierre; lignite mines; livestock, grain.

McIntosh, Fort, Texas: see Laredo.

McIntyre (mă′kĭntīr), town (pop. 194), Wilkinson co., central Ga., 26 mi. E of Macon; kaolin mining, sawmilling.

MacIntyre, Mount (5,112 ft.), Essex co., NE N.Y., 10 mi. S of Lake Placid village; highest peak of MacIntyre Mts., a short range of the Adirondacks. The peak faces Wallface Mtn. (W) across scenic Indian Pass.

McIntyre Mountain (1,030 ft.), SW Cape Breton Isl., E N.S., 12 mi. N of Port Hawkesbury; highest in Craignish Hills.

Macintyre River, NE New South Wales, Australia, rises in New England Range near Tingha; a headstream of Darling River.

Mack, village, Mesa co., W Colo., near Utah line and Colorado R., 20 mi. NW of Grand Junction, in livestock and agr. region producing grain, potatoes, sugar beets; alt. 5,540 ft. Near by are deposits of uintaite.

Macka (mächkä′), Turkish *Maçka*, village (pop. 458), Trebizond prov., NE Turkey, 12 mi. SSW of Trebizond; antimony. Formerly Cevizlik.

Mackay (mŭkī′), city and port (pop. 13,500), E Queensland, Australia, 175 mi. NW of Rockhampton, on coast; sugar-producing center; sugar mills; meat, dairy products, tobacco. Exports sugar, copper, gold. Copper, gold, silver, lead, and zinc mines near by.

Mackay, village (pop. 760), Custer co., S central Idaho, 25 mi. NW of Arco; alt. 5,897 ft.; gold, silver, copper; agr.

Mackay, Lake (mŭkī′), W central Australia, on Western Australia–Northern Territory border, 320 mi. WNW of Alice Springs; 65 mi. long, 40 mi. wide; usually dry.

McKay, Mount (mŭkī′, –kā′) (1,581 ft.), W Ont., overlooking entrance of Thunder Bay, 3 mi. S of Fort William.

McKay Creek, NE Oregon, formed by confluence of 2 forks in Umatilla co., flows 20 mi. W and N to Umatilla R. just W of Pendleton. McKay Dam (180 ft. high, 2,700 ft. long; completed 1927) is 5 mi. S of Pendleton. Used for irrigation.

McKay Lake (12 mi. long, 3 mi. wide), central Ont., 28 mi. E of Geraldton and 10 mi. E of Long Lake; alt. 1,052 ft. Drains S into L. Superior through Pic R.

McKean (mŭkēn'), county (□ 997; pop. 56,607), N Pa.; ⊙ Smethport. Plateau area, drained by Allegheny R.; bounded N by N.Y. Largest producer of Pennsylvania lubricating oils. Petroleum, natural gas; mfg. (gasoline, oil-well supplies, explosives, chemicals, glass, clay, and wood products); dairying. Formed 1804.

McKean, borough, Pa.: see MIDDLEBORO.

McKean Island or **M'Kean Island,** uninhabited coral islet (142 acres), Phoenix Isls., S Pacific, 75 mi. SW of Canton Isl. Discovered 1840 by Americans, included 1937 in Br. colony of Gilbert and Ellice Isls.

McKee, village (pop. c.200), ⊙ Jackson co., central Ky., in the Cumberlands 40 mi. SSE of Winchester, in Cumberland Natl. Forest; agr. (corn, hay, tobacco), coal mines, timber in region.

McKeesport, industrial city (pop. 51,502), Allegheny co., SW Pa., 10 mi. SE of Pittsburgh and on Monongahela R., at mouth of Youghiogheny R., in bituminous-coal area. Steel products, pipe, tin plate, heating equipment, machine parts, cargo barges, oxygen, beer, chocolate; meat packing. A center of Whisky Rebellion, 1794. Important armament center in Second World War. Settled 1755, laid out 1795, inc. as borough 1842, as city 1890.

McKees Rocks, industrial borough (pop. 16,241), Allegheny co., SW Pa., on Ohio R. just below Pittsburgh. Steel products, chemicals, chewing gum, paint; railroad shops, shipyards; bituminous coal; agr. On site of old Indian village. Settled c.1764, inc. 1892.

Mackeim, Poland: see MAKOW.

Mackenna or **Vicuña Mackenna** (vēkōō'nyä mäkĕn'ä), town (pop. 2,699), S Córdoba prov., Argentina, 55 mi. S of Río Cuarto; rail junction and agr. center (grain, flax, sunflowers, livestock); dairying. Airport.

McKenney, town (pop. 476), Dinwiddie co., SE central Va., 23 mi. SW of Petersburg, in agr. area; cooperage.

Mackenzie, village (pop. 1,770), Demerara co., N central Br. Guiana, port on right bank of Demerara R., just SE of Wismar, and 55 mi. S of Georgetown; shipping center for bauxite, mined on large scale in vicinity. Connected by rail with Ituni mine (S). Head of navigation for ocean-going vessels. Airport. Sometimes spelled McKenzie.

Mackenzie, district of Canada, a provisional administrative division (land area □ 493,225, total □ 527,490) of the Northwest Territories, comprising W mainland part of territory, bounded by Sask., Alta., and B.C. (S), by the Yukon (W), by several arms of the Arctic Ocean (Beaufort Sea, Amundsen Gulf, Coronation Gulf, Dease Strait, and Queen Maud Gulf) (N), and by Keewatin Dist. (E). In W part are Mackenzie Mts., N range of the Rocky Mts., here rising to 9,049 ft. on Mt. Sir James McBrien. E of this range extends the Mackenzie R. valley, widest part of which lies bet. Great Bear L. and Great Slave L. E of lakes is plateau, c.350 mi. wide (E–W), followed by plain E of line bet. Dubawnt L. and Bathurst Inlet. Dist. is drained by Mackenzie R. and its tributaries (Hay, Slave, Liard, Arctic Red, and Great Bear rivers), and by Coppermine, Anderson, and Thelon rivers. N coastline is irregular and indented by several large bays. Gold mining is centered on Yellowknife, largest town of the Northwest Territories, site of discovery of important deposits in 1934. Uranium and pitchblende are mined on E shore of Great Bear L.; operations centered on Port Radium. Oil is found near Norman Wells, site of oil refinery and, during Second World War, terminal of *Canol* project pipeline. Copper, found near Coppermine, is not exploited because of transportation difficulties. Fur trapping is chief occupation of native Eskimo and Indian population. Chief town is Fort Smith; other important trading posts are Aklavik, Fort Norman, Fort Simpson, Fort Providence, Fort Reliance, Hay River, Coppermine, Fort Liard, and Arctic Red River. There are extensive game preserves: Mackenzie Mts. Preserve, Yellowknife Preserve, Slave River Preserve, and the Reindeer Grazing Reserve. Thelon Game Sanctuary has largest herd of musk oxen on North American mainland. Transportation in dist. is by river and lake ships during summer navigation season (June–Oct.); almost all trading posts have land plane or seaplane landing facilities. Dist. was created 1895; present boundaries were defined 1918.

Mackenzie, New Zealand: see FAIRLIE.

McKenzie, county (□ 2,810; pop. 6,849), W N.Dak., on Mont. line; ⊙ Watford City. Agr. area watered by Missouri and Yellowstone rivers; rich in lignite, coal, and timber. Wheat, livestock, dairy products. Irrigation projects in NW along Missouri R. Formed 1883.

McKenzie. 1 Town (pop. 504), Butler co., S Ala., 20 mi. S of Greenville; strawberries, lumber. **2** City (pop. 3,774), on Carroll-Weakley co. line, NW Tenn., 10 mi. NNW of Huntingdon; rail junction; processing and shipping center in timber, clay, agr. area; cheese, flour, lumber. Has Bethel Col. Inc. 1923.

Mackenzie, town (pop. 247), St. Louis co., E Mo.

MacKenzie Bay (70 naut. mi. long, 100 naut. mi. wide), in Antarctica, on Indian Ocean, along Lars Christensen Coast, bet. Cape Darnley and W shore of Amery Shelf Ice, bet. 69°30' and 72°25'E. Discovered 1931 by Sir Douglas Mawson.

Mackenzie Bay, NW Mackenzie Dist., Northwest Territories, inlet (100 mi. long, 120 mi. wide at mouth) of Beaufort Sea of the Arctic Ocean, at mouth of Mackenzie R. delta; 68°40'–69°45'N 134°30'–139°W. On E side of bay are Richards, Ellice, and several smaller isls.; on W side is Herschel Isl.

Mackenzie Mountains, N range of Rocky Mtn. in E Yukon and SW Mackenzie Dist., Northwest Territories; extends c.500 mi. SE-NW bet. B.C. border to Peel R. valley, forming S part of Yukon–Northwest Territories border. Highest peak, Mt. Sir James McBrien (9,049 ft.); other peaks over 8,000 ft. are Mt. Hunt, Keele Peak, Dome Peak, Mt. Sidney Dobson, and Mt. Ida. In S part of range is Mackenzie Mts. Preserve, game reserve (□ 69,-440) established 1938.

Mackenzie River, E Queensland, Australia, formed by junction of Nogoa and Comet rivers; flows 170 mi. NE and SSE, joining Dawson R. to form Fitzroy R. Drains mining area (gold, copper).

Mackenzie River, W Mackenzie Dist., Northwest Territories, issues from W end of Great Slave L., flows generally WNW to Fort Simpson, where it receives Liard R., thence flows NW, past Wrigley, Fort Norman, Norman Wells (oil center), Fort Good Hope, and Arctic Red River, to Beaufort Sea of the Arctic Ocean through 70–80 mi. delta. W channel of delta flows NNW, past Aklavik; E channel flows N, past Reindeer Depot. Mackenzie R. proper is 1,120 mi. long and is navigable throughout from mid-June to mid-Oct.; steamer service is maintained by Hudson's Bay Co. Chief tributaries are Keele, Great Bear, Hare Indian, and Arctic Red rivers. Basin of the Mackenzie extends into B.C., Alta., and Sask.; its major headstreams include LIARD RIVER, PEACE RIVER, ATHABASKA RIVER, Slave, and Hay rivers. The Mackenzie-Slave-Peace-Finlay (the last its farthest headstream) forms a continuous stream 2,514 mi. long (2d longest in North America) and provides navigable waterway almost 2,000 mi. long, broken by one portage on Slave R. rapids. River is named after Sir Alexander Mackenzie, who explored it to its tidewater, 1789.

McKenzie River, W Oregon, formed in Cascade Range near the Three Sisters, flows 86 mi. W to Willamette R. N of Eugene.

Mackillop, Lake, Queensland, Australia: see YAMMA YAMMA, LAKE.

Mackinac (mă'kĭnô, mă'kĭnăk), historic region in N Mich., centering on Straits of Mackinac and MACKINAC ISLAND; the Michilimackinac of the Indians, whose gathering place it had been since anc. times. In 17th and 18th cent., a shifting settlement here (including Father Marquette's mission, French forts and, after 1780, British forts) included sites of present-day MACKINAW CITY and SAINT IGNACE. Name was sometimes applied to a vast region of the Old Northwest whose furs came to Mackinac trading posts. First visited (1634–35) by Jean Nicolet; Marquette established a mission in 1671 at St. Ignace, and French forts were established at St. Ignace and Old Mackinac (Mackinaw City). By end of 17th cent., this was chief fur-trading center of Old Northwest. British occupation (1761) was followed (1763) by Indian massacre of garrison at Old Mackinac; fort was removed (1780–81) to Mackinac Isl. After passing to U.S. under Treaty of Paris (1783), isl. was captured (1812) by British in War of 1812, returned to U.S. by Treaty of Ghent. After decline of fur trade at isl. after 1830s, region has principally been known to vacationers.

Mackinac, county (□ 1,014; pop. 9,287), SE Upper Peninsula, Mich.; ⊙ St. Ignace. Bounded S by lakes Michigan and Huron and by their connection, the Straits of Mackinac; drained by Carp and small Pine rivers. Part of historic MACKINAC region; includes Mackinac and Bois Blanc isls. Forest, resort, and agr. area (fruit, truck, potatoes; dairy products); commercial fishing. Part of Marquette Natl. Forest and several lakes (part of Manistique; and South Manistique, Brevoort, Milakokia, Millecoquins) are in co. Formed 1818.

Mackinac, city, Mich.: see MACKINAC ISLAND.

Mackinac, Straits of, N Mich., channel (c.4 mi. wide) separating Upper and Lower peninsulas and forming important waterway bet. lakes Huron (E) and Michigan (W); heart of historic MACKINAC region. To E and SE of St. Ignace (on N shore) are Mackinac, Round, and Bois Blanc isls. South Channel of straits lies bet. Bois Blanc Isl. and the Lower Peninsula.

Mackinac Island or **Mackinac,** resort city (pop. 572), Mackinac co., SE Upper Peninsula, Mich., 5 mi. E of St. Ignace, on S end of **Mackinac Island** (c.3 mi. long, 2 mi. wide; a state park since 1895), in the Straits of Mackinac. Summer and health resort, connected by ferry with Mackinaw City and St. Ignace. The Astor House (built c.1817 by American Fur Company), and the ruins of Fort Mackinac (established 1780), now housing a historical mus., are reminders of isl.'s role in history of MACKINAC region.

Mackinaw (mă'kĭnô), village (pop. 1,011), Tazewell co., central Ill., on Mackinaw R. (bridged here) and 16 mi. E of Pekin, in agr. and bituminous-coal area; sand, gravel pits; mfg. (dairy products, uniforms, raincoats).

Mackinaw City, village (pop. 970), on Cheboygan-Emmet co. line, N Mich., 15 mi. NW of Cheboygan, at N tip of the Lower Peninsula, on the Straits of Mackinac, opposite St. Ignace; ferries to Upper Peninsula and Mackinac Isl. Trade center for resort area. State park contains reconstruction of old Fort Michilimackinac. Settled c.1715, it was the Old Mackinac of the historic MACKINAC region.

Mackinaw River, central Ill., rises in W Ford co., flows c.130 mi. W, SW, and N, to Illinois R. below Pekin.

McKinley, county (□ 5,456; pop. 27,451), NW N.Mex.; ⊙ Gallup. Livestock-grazing area, watered by Rio Puerco; borders on Ariz. Wool, Indian artifacts. Coal mines near Gallup. Includes Zuni Mts. (S), Cibola Natl. Forest, and parts of Navajo (NW) and Zuni (SW) Indian reservations. Formed 1899.

McKinley. 1 Village (pop. 196), St. Louis co., NE Minn., on Mesabi iron range, 7 mi. E of Virginia. Iron mines near by. **2** Village, Montgomery co., Pa.: see ABINGTON.

McKinley, Fort, Philippines: see RIZAL, city.

McKinley, Mount (20,270 ft.), S central Alaska, in Alaska Range, 130 mi. NNW of Anchorage, in MOUNT MCKINLEY NATIONAL PARK; 63°4'N 151°W. Highest peak in North America. First climbed 1913 by Hudson Stuck. Indian name was Denali (dĭnä'lē, dĭ'nŭlē); the Russians called it Bolshaya (bŭlshī'ŭ) [great].

McKinley Park, village (pop. 59), central Alaska, 100 mi. SW of Fairbanks, on Alaska RR; tourist gateway to Mt. McKinley Natl. Park.

McKinley Sea, marginal sea of Arctic Ocean, off N Greenland, bet. 16° and 32°W at 84°N.

McKinney, city (pop. 10,560), ⊙ Collin co., N Texas, near East Fork of Trinity R., 30 mi. NNE of Dallas; a trade, processing center in rich blackland agr. region (cotton, grain, corn, pecans, truck, livestock, dairy products); textile, flour, cottonseed-oil milling, pecan shelling, mfg. of clothing, soap, mattresses. Founded 1842.

McKinney, Lake, Kearny co., SW Kansas, 18 mi. W of Garden City; 5 mi. long, 1 mi. wide. Used for irrigation; drains into Arkansas R.

Mackinnon Road (mŭkĭ'nŭn), town, Coast Prov., SE Kenya, on railroad and 50 mi. WNW of Mombasa; 3°42'S 39°3'E. Br. military base developed after Second World War. Airport.

McKittrick. 1 Village (pop. c.250), Kern co., S central Calif., at base of Temblor Range, 35 mi. W of Bakersfield; oil and natural-gas field. **2** Town (pop. 100), Montgomery co., E central Mo., on Missouri R., opposite Hermann.

Macklin, town (pop. 457), W Sask., on Alta. border, 75 mi. WSW of North Battleford; rail junction; grain elevators, stockyard; dairying.

Mackmyra (mäk"mü'rä), village (pop. 575), Gavleborg co., E Sweden, on Gavle R. and 6 mi. WSW of Gavle; lumber, pulp, and cellulose mills.

McKnight, Mo.: see LADUE, city.

Macksburg. 1 Town (pop. 220), Madison co., S central Iowa, 38 mi. SW of Des Moines, in agr. area. **2** Village (pop. 272), Washington co., SE Ohio, 14 mi. N of Marietta, in coal-mining area.

Macks Creek, town (pop. 108), Camden co., central Mo., in Ozarks, near L. of the Ozarks, 60 mi. SW of Jefferson City.

Macksville, town (pop. 1,388), E New South Wales, Australia, 170 mi. NNE of Newcastle; dairying center.

Macksville, city (pop. 624), Stafford co., S central Kansas, 11 mi. WSW of St. John, in wheat and livestock region; mfg. of lathes.

Mackworth Island, SW Maine, in Casco Bay, near Falmouth, to which a bridge leads; c.½ mi. in diameter.

McLaren Vale (mŭklă'rŭn), town (pop. 595), SE South Australia, 22 mi. S of Adelaide; vineyards.

McLaughlin (mĭglôf'lĭn), city (pop. 713), Corson co., N S.Dak., 100 mi. NNW of Pierre, near Oak Creek; trading point for ranching and farming area; lignite mines; dairy produce, livestock, poultry, grain.

Maclean (mŭklān'), municipality (pop. 1,665), NE New South Wales, Australia, on Clarence R. and 145 mi. S of Brisbane; dairying center; bananas, timber.

McLean. 1 County (□ 1,173; pop. 76,577), central Ill.; ⊙ Bloomington. Drained by Sangamon and Mackinaw rivers, and by Kickapoo, Salt, and small Money and Sugar creeks. Includes L. Bloomington (resort). Agr. (corn, oats, wheat, soybeans, livestock, poultry; dairy products). Bituminous-coal fields; limestone quarries. Mfg., shipping at Bloomington. Formed 1830. **2** County (□ 257; pop. 10,021), W Ky.; ⊙ Calhoun. Crossed by Green R.; bounded W by Green and Pond rivers; drained by Rough R. Agr. area (soybeans, corn, wheat, livestock, tobacco); timber; bituminous coal mines. Some mfg. at Livermore. Formed 1854. **3** County (□ 2,289; pop. 18,824), central N.Dak.; ⊙ Washburn. Agr. area bounded W by Fort Berthold Indian Reservation and W and S by Missouri R. Coal mines; livestock, dairy products, poultry, grain. Formed 1883.

McLean. 1 Village (pop. 667), McLean co., central Ill., 14 mi. SW of Bloomington, in rich agr. area. **2** Village (pop. 67), Pierce co., NE Nebr., 13 mi. N of Pierce. **3** Town (pop. 1,439), Gray co., extreme N Texas, in the Panhandle, 75 mi. E of Amarillo, in cattle, wheat, cotton region; cotton gins, gas and oil wells. Settled 1901, inc. 1909. **4** Village (pop. 1,094), Fairfax co., N Va., near the Potomac just N of Arlington co. line.

McLeansboro (mŭklānz'–), city (pop. 3,008), ⊙ Hamilton co., SE Ill., 25 mi. SE of Mount Vernon, in agr. area; mfg. (clothing, flour, wood products); corn, wheat, livestock, dairy products, poultry. Inc. 1840.

Maclean Strait, Northwest Territories: see PRINCE GUSTAV ADOLPH SEA.

Maclear, town (pop. 2,156), E Cape Prov., U. of So. Afr., near Transkeian Territories, at foot of Drakensberg range, on Mooi R. and 100 mi. ESE of Aliwal North; rail terminus; agr. center (stock, grain).

Maclear, Cape, central Nyasaland, on S shore of L. Nyasa, 40 mi. NNW of Fort Johnston; tourist resort (hotel); airfield; steamer landing.

Macleay River (mŭklā'), E New South Wales, Australia, rises in New England Range, flows 250 mi. generally ESE then ENE, past Kempsey, to the Pacific near Smoky Cape. Navigable 30 mi. below Kempsey by small craft.

McLemoresville (măklŭmôrz'vĭl), town (pop. 242), Carroll co., NW Tenn., 8 mi. W of Huntington.

McLennan, village (pop. 823), W Alta., on Kimiwan L. (7 mi. long, 4 mi. wide), 40 mi. SSE of Peace River, 40 mi. NW of Lesser Slave L.; lumbering, wheat, mixed farming.

McLennan, county (□ 1,035; pop. 130,194), E central Texas; ⊙ WACO, commercial, distribution, mfg. center for wide region. Co. drained by Brazos R. and branches of Bosque R.; includes L. Waco. Rich agr. area: oats, cotton, corn, grain sorghums, peanuts, pecans, fruit, truck; extensive dairying, poultry raising; beef cattle, hogs, sheep, horses, mules. Limestone, clay, cement rock. Fishing. Formed 1850.

Macleod (mŭkloud'), town (pop. 1,649), SW Alta., on Oldman R. and 25 mi. W of Lethbridge; coal mining, dairying, ranching. Near by was Fort Macleod (1874) of North West Mounted Police.

McLeod, county (□ 498; pop. 22,198), S central Minn.; ⊙ Glencoe. Agr. area watered by forks of Crow R. Dairy products, livestock, corn, oats, barley, potatoes. Formed 1856.

McLeod, Fort, Hudson's Bay Co. trading post, E central B.C., on McLeod L. (14 mi. long), 75 mi. N of Prince George. Established 1805 by Simon Fraser for the North West Co.; taken over 1821 by Hudson's Bay Co.

McLoud, town (pop. 718), Pottawatomie co., central Okla., 12 mi. NW of Shawnee, and on North Canadian R., in rich agr. area (cotton, corn, wheat; dairy products); cotton ginning.

McLoughlin, Mount (mŭglŏk'lĭn) (9,497 ft.), SW Oregon, in Cascade Range, W of Upper Klamath L., c.30 mi. NW of Klamath Falls.

McLouth, city (pop. 477), Jefferson co., NE Kansas, 27 mi. ENE of Topeka, in stock-raising, dairying, and general-farming region.

Mac-Mahon (Fr. mäk-mäō'), village (pop. 1,401), Constantine dept., NE Algeria, in the Aurès massif, on railroad and 20 mi. SW of Batna; cereals, sheep, esparto.

McMasterville, village (pop. 1,097), S Que., on Richelieu R., S suburb of Beloeil.

McMechen (mŭkmĕ'kŭn), residential city (pop 3,518), Marshall co., NW W.Va., in Northern Panhandle, on the Ohio and 8 mi. S of Wheeling, in industrial area. Inc. 1895.

Macmerry, village in Pencaitland parish, E East Lothian, Scotland, just E of Tranent; coal mining.

McMicken Heights, village (pop. 2,550), King co., W Wash.

McMillan, village (pop. c.300), Luce co., NE Upper Peninsula, Mich., 9 mi. W of Newberry, in lumbering and agr. area.

McMillan, Lake, N.Mex.: see PECOS RIVER.

Macmillan River, E Yukon, rises in Mackenzie Mts. near Northwest Territories border, flows c.200 mi. W to Pelly R. 45 mi. E of Fort Selkirk.

McMinn, county (□ 435; pop. 32,024), SE Tenn.; ⊙ Athens. In Great Appalachian Valley; Cherokee Natl. Forest lies along SE border; bounded SW by Hiwassee R. Agr. (corn, cotton, tobacco, hay), livestock raising, dairying. Timber (pine, hardwood). Formed 1819.

McMinnville. 1 City (pop. 6,635), ⊙ Yamhill co., NW Oregon, on South Yamhill R. and 35 mi. SW of Portland; trading point in livestock and wheat area; lumber, dairy products. Has own power system. Seat of Linfield Col. Laid out 1855, inc. as town 1876, as city 1882. **2** Town (pop. 7,577), ⊙ Warren co., central Tenn., on branch of Caney Fork and 50 mi. NW of Chattanooga, in timber and farm area; mfg. of wood products, shoes, hosiery, textiles. Marble and granite quarries, tree nurseries near by. Great Falls Dam is NE, Center Hill Reservoir N. Settled 1800; inc. 1808.

McMullen, county (□ 1,159; pop. 1,187), S Texas; ⊙ Tilden. Drained by Frio and Nueces rivers. Cattle ranching, agr. (grain sorghums, corn, peanuts, some cotton; hogs, poultry, dairy products). Oil, natural-gas wells. Formed 1858.

McMurdo Sound (mŭkmûr'dō), channel (80 naut. mi. long, 20–40 naut. mi. wide), Antarctica, bet. Ross Isl. and Victoria Land, in 77°30'S 165°E. Discovered 1841 by Sir James Clark Ross.

McMurray, Fort, Alta.: see FORT McMURRAY.

McNab, town (pop. 206), Hempstead co., SW Ark., 14 mi. W of Hope, near Red R.

McNair, village (pop. 1,313), Harris co., S Texas, 21 mi. E of downtown Houston.

McNairy (mŭknâ'rē), county (□ 569; pop. 20,390), SW Tenn.; ⊙ Selmer. Bounded S by Miss.; drained by tributaries of South Fork of Forked Deer, Hatchie, and Tennessee rivers. Cotton, corn, hay; timber. Formed 1823.

McNary. 1 Company town (pop. 1,902), Apache co., E Ariz., near White R., in Fort Apache Indian Reservation, 40 mi. SW of St. Johns; alt. 7,580 ft.; lumber milling; wood products. Natl. forests near by. Greens Peak is 16 mi. ENE in White Mts. **2** Village (pop. 267), Rapides parish, central La., 23 mi. SSW of Alexandria; agr. **3** Village (pop. c.200), Hudspeth co., extreme W Texas, c.50 mi. SE of El Paso, near the Rio Grande; shipping point in irrigated farm area. Ruins of old Fort Quitman are SE.

McNary Dam, in Wash. and Oregon, on Columbia R. (the state line) just above mouth of Umatilla R., Oregon; 158 ft. high, 8,725 ft. long over all (including 1,320-ft. spillway section); begun 1947 for navigation, hydroelectric power, and irrigation. Also called Umatilla (or Umatilla Rapids) Dam.

MacNean, Upper Lake (mŭknēn'), (5 mi. long, 1 mi. wide) on Ireland–Northern Ireland border, bet. cos. Leitrim (W), Cavan (S), and Fermanagh (N), 10 mi. WSW of Enniskillen. Lower Lake MacNean is just SE.

McNeil, town (pop. 597), Columbia co., SW Ark., 6 mi. NNE of Magnolia, in agr. area.

McNeil Island (c.3 mi. long), W central Wash., in Puget Sound WSW of Tacoma and just W of Steilacoom; site of a Federal penitentiary.

MacNutt, village (pop. 229), SE Sask., on Man. border, 40 mi. ESE of Yorkton; mixed farming.

McNutt Island (4 mi. long, 2 mi. wide), in the Atlantic at entrance to Shelburne Harbour, SW N.S., 7 mi. S of Shelburne; 43°38'N 65°47'W.

Macocha, Czechoslovakia: see MORAVIAN KARST.

Macolin, Switzerland: see BIEL.

Macomb (mŭkōōm', –kōm'), county (□ 481; pop. 184,961), SE Mich.; ⊙ Mt. Clemens. Bounded SE by L. St. Clair and Anchor Bay; drained by Clinton R. and its affluents. Farm area (truck, grain, poultry; dairy products). Mt. Clemens is health resort. Army air base and a state park are situated in co. Formed and organized 1818.

Macomb (mŭkōm'). **1** City (pop. 10,592), ⊙ McDonough co., W Ill., 37 mi. SSW of Galesburg; trade and industrial center in agr. and bituminous-coal-mining area; clay pits; corn, wheat, soybeans, livestock, poultry, dairy products. Mfg. (clay and steel products, porcelain insulators, pottery, electric fencing, furniture, stokers, sheet metal, thermos jugs, poultry incubators, beverage dispensers). Seat of Western Ill. State Col. Laid out 1831; inc. as village in 1841, as city in 1856. **2** or **McComb,** town (pop. 123), Pottawatomie co., central Okla., 13 mi. SSW of Shawnee, and on Little R.

Macomb, Fort, SE La., old U.S. fortification built c.1828 on bank of Chef Menteur Pass bet. L. Pontchartrain and L. Borgne, c.20 mi. ENE of New Orleans. Partly restored; surrounded by state park.

Macomer (mäkômĕr'), town (pop. 4,950), Nuoro prov., W central Sardinia, in Catena del Marghine, 29 mi. W of Nuoro; road and rail junction. Cheese center, woolen mill. Nuraghi near by.

Macomia (mäkōmē'ä), village, Niassa prov., N Mozambique, on road and 60 mi. NNW of Pôrto Amélia; cotton.

Mâcon (mäkõ'), anc. *Matisco*, town (pop. 18,221), ⊙ Saône-et-Loire dept., E central France, port on right bank of Saône R. and 38 mi. N of Lyons; commercial center known for strong red Burgundy wines grown in region. Produces winegrowing equipment, bicycle parts, hardware, rennet, shirts. Distilling, grape juice mfg. Mâcon was acquired by French crown in 13th-cent., became part of Burgundy in 1435, and was recovered by France in 1477. Huguenot stronghold in 16th-cent. Its bishopric was suppressed during Fr. Revolution. Lamartine b. here.

Macon (mā'kŭn, –kŏn). **1** County (□ 616; pop. 30,561), E Ala.; ⊙ Tuskegee. In the Black Belt; drained by Tallapoosa R. and its branches. Cotton, corn, peanuts, sweet potatoes; cattle, dairying. Formed 1832. **2** County (□ 399; pop. 14,213), central Ga.; ⊙ Oglethorpe. Coastal plain agr. area (peaches, cotton, corn, truck, peanuts, pecans) drained by Flint R. Formed 1837. **3** County (□ 577; pop. 98,853), central Ill.; ⊙ Decatur. Agr. (corn, wheat, soybeans, oats, livestock, poultry; dairy products). Diversified mfg.; Decatur is industrial and commercial center. Bituminous-coal mining. Drained by Sangamon R., dammed to form L. Decatur (recreation area). Includes Spitler Woods and Lincoln Homestead state parks. Formed 1829. **4** County (□ 814; pop. 18,332), N central Mo.; ⊙ Macon. Drained by Chariton R.; coal mining; agr. (corn, wheat, oats, hay), livestock. Formed c.1838. **5** County (□ 520; pop. 16,174), W N.C., on Ga. line; ⊙ Franklin. Partly (SE) in the Blue Ridge; crossed N-S by Nantahala Mts.; drained by Nantahala R. (dam, reservoir, and gorge here) and the Little Tennessee. Included in Nantahala Natl. Forest. Farming (vegetables, apples, corn), dairying, poultry raising, lumbering, mica mining; resort area. Formed 1828. **6** County (□ 304; pop. 13,599), N Tenn.; ⊙ Lafayette. Bounded N by Ky.; drained by affluents of Barren and Cumberland rivers. Timber, agr. (corn, tobacco), livestock raising; oil wells. Formed 1842.

Macon. 1 City (pop. 70,252), ⊙ Bibb co., central Ga., c.75 mi. SE of Atlanta, at head of navigation on Ocmulgee R., and on the fall line, near the geographical center of Ga.; 32°49'N 83°39'W. Industrial, rail, and shipping center for fertile agr., livestock, and clay-mining region. Manufactures clothing, yarn, tire fabric, paper products, boxes, lumber, furniture, prefabricated houses, venetian blinds, insulation, brick, tile, concrete products, canned and frozen foods, pecan and peanut products, cottonseed oil, candy, feed, fertilizer, chemicals, and farm implements. Has railroad shops and stockyards. Mercer Univ., Wesleyan Col., a state school for the blind, and the home of Sidney Lanier are here. Ocmulgee Natl. Monument near by. Robins Air Force Base is 12 mi. S. Settled as Fort Hawkins (1806) on E side of river, renamed Newton, 1821. Macon laid out on W bank 1823; annexed Newton 1829. **2** City (pop. 942), Macon co., central Ill., 8 mi. S of Decatur, in agr. and bituminous-coal area. **3** City (pop. 2,241), ⊙ Noxubee co., E Miss., 28 mi. SSW of Columbus, and on Noxubee R., in cotton, timber, and dairying area; processes cotton, cottonseed, milk, lumber. Inc. 1836. **4** City (pop. 4,152), ⊙ Macon co., N central Mo., 25 mi. S of Kirksville; ships agr. products, livestock; coal. Osteopathic sanatorium. Inc. 1859. **5** Town (pop. 238), Warren co., N N.C., 4 mi. NE of Warrenton.

Macon, Bayou (bī'ō mā'kŭn), in Ark. and La., rises in SE Ark., flows S into La., past Delhi, to Tensas R. 19 mi. SE of Winnsboro; c.145 mi. long; partly navigable. It was a rendezvous of the bandits Frank and Jesse James.

Mâconnais (mäkônā'), old district of E central France, formerly in Burgundy prov., now part of Saône-et-Loire dept. Historical ⊙ was Mâcon. Bounded by Saône R. (E) and Charolais region (W). Has noted vineyards.

Mâconnais, Monts du (mõ' dü), hill range in Rhône and Saône-et-Loire depts., E central France, forming section of E escarpment of the Massif Central. Parallels Saône R. valley bet. Beaujeu (S) and Sennecey-le-Grand (N). Average alt. 1,500 ft. On E slopes, near Mâcon, are noted vineyards.

Macoraba, Saudi Arabia: see MECCA.

Macôt (mäkō'), village (pop. 546), Savoie dept., SE France, in Alpine Tarentaise valley, 16 mi. SE of Albertville; anthracite and lead mining.

Macotera (mäkōtā'rä), town (pop. 3,613), Salamanca prov., W Spain, 22 mi. ESE of Salamanca; agr. trade center (cereals, vegetables, wine); cattle.

Macouba (mäkōōbä'), town (pop. 870), N Martinique, 18 mi. NNW of Fort-de-France; cacao growing, rum distilling.

Macoupin (mŭkōō'pĭn), county (□ 872; pop. 44,210), SW central Ill.; ⊙ Carlinville. Agr. (livestock, corn, wheat, oats, soybeans, poultry; dairy products). Bituminous-coal mining; timber; clay pits. Some mfg. (burial vaults and monuments, brick, gloves, tile). Drained by Macoupin, Cahokia, and small Otter creeks. Formed 1829.

Macoupin Creek, SW Ill., rises in NW Montgomery co., flows c.100 mi. SW and W to Illinois R. SE of Hardin.

Macouria (mäkōōrēä'), town (commune pop. 597), N Fr. Guiana, on coast at mouth of Cayenne R., 3 mi. SW of Cayenne; coffee, manioc, fruit.

McPhee, village (1940 pop. 716), Montezuma co., SW Colo., on Dolores R. and 11 mi. NNE of Cortez; alt. c.7,000 ft. Mesa Verde Natl. Park near by.

McPherson. 1 (mŭkfûr'sŭn) County (□ 895; pop. 23,670), central Kansas; ⊙ McPherson. Rolling plain, drained (NW) by Smoky Hill R. Wheat, livestock. Oil and gas fields. Formed 1870. **2** (mŭkfûr'sŭn) County (□ 855; pop. 825), W central Nebr.; ⊙ Tryon. Agr. area; livestock, grain. Formed 1887. **3** (mŭkfĕr'sŭn) County (□ 1,151; pop. 7,071), N S.Dak., on N.Dak. line; ⊙ Leola.

Agr. and cattle-raising region watered by intermittent streams in E and by small lakes. Feed crops, livestock, grain. Formed 1873.

McPherson (mŭkfûr'sŭn), city (pop. 8,689), ⊙ McPherson co., central Kansas, 26 mi. NNE of Hutchinson; trade and shipping center for oil and agr. region; oil refining, flour milling, mfg. of concrete products. Oil wells near by. Seat of McPherson Col. (Dunker; 1887). City was laid out 1872 on Santa Fe Trail; inc. 1874.

McPherson, Fort, Ga.: see ATLANTA.

McPherson Range, E Australia, E spur of Great Dividing Range, extends c.140 mi. W and SW from Point Danger on Pacific coast to Wallangarra; forms part of boundary bet. Queensland and New South Wales. Highest point, Mt. Barney (4,300 ft.). Sometimes spelled MacPherson.

Macquarie, Lake (mŭkwŏ'rē), lagoon (□ 45), E New South Wales, Australia, opening into the Pacific 8 mi. SW of Newcastle; 15 mi. long, 5 mi. wide; summer resorts.

Macquarie Harbour, inlet of Indian Ocean, on W coast of Tasmania; 19 mi. long, 8 mi. wide; c.½ mi. wide at mouth, near which is Cape Sorell. Numerous islets; Settlement Isl. (5 mi. long) was once penal colony. Strahan is on NW shore. Receives Gordon R.

Macquarie Island, uninhabited volcanic isl. (21 mi. long, 3 mi. wide) in S Pacific, 850 mi. SE of Tasmania, Australia, to which it belongs; 54°30'S 158°40'E. Rises to 1,421 ft.; rocky, with small glacial lakes. Meteorological station. With the 2 small uninhabited groups (Bishop and Clerk, and Judge and Clerk), the group is called Macquarie Isls.

Macquarie River, central New South Wales, Australia, rises in Blue Mts., flows 590 mi. NW, past Bathurst, Wellington, Dubbo, Narromine, and Warren, thence through swamps to Darling R. 35 mi. W of Walgett; drains sheep and agr. area.

Macquarie River, Tasmania: see SOUTH ESK RIVER.

McQueen, Mont.: see MEADERVILLE.

McQueeney, village (pop. c.300), Guadalupe co., S central Texas, 5 mi. WNW of Seguin, on L. McQueeney (c.1.5 mi. long) in Guadalupe R.; recreational area.

Macra, Italy: see MAGRA RIVER.

McRae (mŭkrā'). **1** Town (pop. 414), White co., central Ark., 37 mi. NE of Little Rock, in agr. area. **2** City (pop. 1,904), ⊙ Telfair co., S central Ga., 32 mi. S of Dublin, adjacent to Helena (W), and on Little Ocmulgee R.; mfg. (lumber, naval stores, fertilizer). State park near by. Settled by Scotch in mid 19th cent. Inc. 1874.

Mac-Robertson Coast, Antarctica, on Indian Ocean, extends from William Scoresby Bay to Cape Darnley, bet. 59°40' and 69°30'E. Discovered 1930 by Sir Douglas Mawson.

Macroom (mŭkrōōm'), Gaelic *Maghchromtha*, urban district (pop. 2,230), W Co. Cork, Ireland, on Sullane R., near its mouth on Lee R., and 21 mi. W of Cork; agr. market (dairying; potatoes, oats), with iron foundries. Castle reputedly dates from 12th cent.

McSherrystown, borough (pop. 2,510), Adams co., S Pa., 2 mi. W of Hanover. Inc. 1882.

Mactan Island (mäktän') (□ 24; 1948 pop. 44,396), Cebu prov., Philippines, in Bohol Strait, just off E coast of Cebu isl., opposite Cebu city; 7 mi. long, 4.5 mi. wide, with narrow NE peninsula. Generally low; coconut growing, fishing. On NE coast is monument dedicated to Magellan, who was killed here in 1521. Chief center is OPON.

Macuchi (mäkōō'chē), village, Cotopaxi prov., N central Ecuador, on W slopes of the Andes, 40 mi. W of Latacunga; silver, gold, copper deposits.

Macuelizo (mäkwälē'sō), town (pop. 879), Santa Bárbara dept., NW Honduras, in Sierra de la Grita, 10 mi. WNW of San Marcos; livestock, corn, beans.

Macuelizo, town (1950 pop. 119), Nueva Segovia dept., NW Nicaragua, 8 mi. W of Ocotal; sugar mill; sugar cane, livestock. Silver deposits.

Macugnaga (mäkōōnyä'gä), village (pop. 696), Novara prov., Piedmont, N Italy, near Monte Rosa, on Anza R. and 19 mi. SW of Domodossola, near Swiss frontier; resort. Gold mines at Pestarena, 2 mi. E.

Macumba River (mŭkŭm'bŭ) or **Treuer River,** N central South Australia; formed by junction of 2 streams; flows 145 mi. SE to L. Eyre; usually dry.

Macungie (măkŭn'jē), borough (pop. 983), Lehigh co., E Pa., 7 mi. SSW of Allentown.

Macuro (mäkōō'rō) or **Cristóbal Colón** (krēstō'bäl kōlōn'), town (pop. 521), Sucre state, NE Venezuela, minor port on Gulf of Paria, at E tip of Paria Peninsula, 25 mi. ENE of Güiria. Easternmost port of Venezuela, it is 29 mi. W of Port of Spain. Ships cacao, coffee, and corn to Trinidad. Customhouse. Gypsum deposits near by.

Macusani (mäkōōsä'nē), town (pop. 832), ⊙ Carabaya prov. (□ 2,617; pop. 26,543), Puno dept., SE Peru, in Cordillera Oriental of the Andes, 125 mi. NNW of Puno; alt. 14,225 ft. Alfalfa, livestock (sheep, alpacas, llamas).

Macuspana (mäkōōspä'nä), city (pop. 1,671), Tabasco, SE Mexico, on navigable affluent of Grijalva R. and 27 mi. SE of Villahermosa; corn growing.

Macuto (mäkōō'tō), town (pop. 2,517), Federal Dist., N Venezuela, on the Caribbean, at foot of coastal range, 2½ mi. E of La Guaira; seaside resort.

Macva or **Machva** (both: mäch'vä), Serbo-Croatian *Mačva*, county (pop. 60,283), W Serbia, Yugoslavia, NW of SABAC; ⊙ BOGATIC. Bounded partly by Sava (N) and Drina (W) rivers. Densely populated. Sugar beets, hogs. Marsh draining 1947–51.

McVeigh (mŭkvā'), village (pop. 1,292), Pike co., E Ky., in the Cumberlands, 9 mi. S of Williamson, W.Va., in bituminous-coal-mining area.

McVeytown (mŭkvā'toun), residential borough (pop. 546), Mifflin co., central Pa., 12 mi. SW of Lewistown and on Juniata R.

McVille, city (pop. 626), Nelson co., E central N.Dak., 21 mi. SSE of Lakota, near Sheyenne R.

Macwahoc (mŭkwŏ'hŏk), plantation (pop. 131), Aroostook co., E Maine, 23 mi. ESE of Millinocket; hunting, fishing.

McWatters, village (pop. estimate 400), W Que., 6 mi. ESE of Rouyn; gold mining.

Macy, town (pop. 288), Miami co., N central Ind., 15 mi. N of Peru, in agr. area.

Mad (mäd), Hung. *Mád*, town (pop. 3,528), Zemplen co., NE Hungary, in the Hegyalja, 23 mi. ENE of Miskolc; excellent wine. Szilvasfürdö, with mineral springs, is near by.

Madaba (mă'dăbă), town (pop. c.5,000), N central Jordan, 18 mi. SSW of Amman and 22 mi. WNW of Jericho, alt. 2,575 ft.; road junction; tumbak, wheat.

Madagali (mädägä'lē), town (pop. 215), N Br. Cameroons, administered as part of Adamawa prov. of Nigeria, 45 mi. S of Bama; peanuts, pepper, hemp, rice, cotton; cattle, skins.

Madagascar (mădŭgă'skŭr), also known to the French as *Grande-Île* or *Grande-Terre*, large island (□ 227,602; 1948 pop. 4,123,100; including Nossi-Bé and Sainte-Marie isls. □ 227,760, pop. 4,149,200) in Indian Ocean, c.250 mi. off E coast of Africa across Mozambique Channel. Together with its dependencies, it is a French overseas territory under authority of a high commissioner and with representation in the French Natl. Assembly. The 4th largest isl. in the world (after Greenland, New Guinea, and Borneo), it lies bet. 11°52'S and 25°40' S. Its length from Cape Ambre, its northernmost point, to Cape Sainte-Marie, its S extremity, is 975 mi.; its breadth averages 300 mi. Physiographically it consists of a central belt of eroded highlands extending NNE–SSW, which slope steeply eastward to a narrow strip of swampy, lagoon-filled coast, while in W they pass gradually to more extensive lowlands. The inland plateau of crystalline and volcanic rocks rises to 9,450 ft. in Tsaratanana Massif and 8,522 ft. in Ankaratra; its depressions contain Aloatra, Kinkony, and Itasy lakes Numerous islets and coral reefs fringe isl.'s W shores. Chief streams, Betsiboka, Ikopa, Tsiribihina, Mangoky, Onilahy, flow W; only river of importance in E is Mangoro. Climate is tropical, marked in the interior (savanna grasslands) by alternating warm, rainy (Oct.–April) and dry, cooler (May–Sept.) seasons. Intense heat and humidity (rainfall up to 110 inches) prevail through the year on E littoral; large tracts of primeval forests still exist here, particularly along Antongil Bay, and yield valuable hardwoods. Most of W, save for humid Sambirano region, receives much less rain. In S and SW, semidesert conditions (rainfall under 10–15 inches) reduce vegetation to xerophytic plants or scrubland. Madagascar's distinctive fauna includes many species of lemurs. Red, lateritic soils cover half of the isl., which, because of this mantle, is often called *Île Rouge* [red island]. Rice cultivation and cattle raising (zebu cattle) are the basic farming activities. Chief rice fields lie near Tananarive (Betsimitatra), Majunga (lower Betsiboka valley), and L. Alaotra. Also grown for native consumption are manioc, corn, sweet potatoes, pulse, peanuts, sorghum, arrowroot. Cash crops include coffee (mainly on E slopes of central uplands), sisal, vanilla (at Antalaha), cloves, essential oils (Nossi-Bé isl.), sugar cane, fibers, tobacco, cinchona (N). Temperate-zone fruit (peaches, apricots, apples), grapes, and silkworms are raised in Imerina. Agr. products are processed: beef canning, sugar milling, rice milling, essential oils and rum distilling, tanning, woodworking. Mfg. of construction materials, soap, edible oils, chocolate, shoes, straw hats, sacking, paper. Fishing, including gathering of tortoise shell, mother-of-pearl, and edible molluscs, is common off W coast. Mineral resources consist of graphite, coal (Sakoa basin), gold, mica, rock crystal, industrial beryl, semiprecious stones; uranium deposits have been reported. Natives spin, weave, make pottery and lace, work iron and stone. Tamatave, Diégo-Suarez (Fr. naval base), and Majunga are major seaports; Tuléar, Fort-Dauphin, Hellville, Morondava, Manakara, Morombe, Mananjary engage chiefly in cabotage trade. Four rail tracks (Tamatave-Tananarive, Tananarive-Antsirabe, Moramanga-L. Alaotra, Manakara-Fianarantsoa) connect inland centers with E seaboard; a 5th railroad was begun (early 1940s) bet. Soalara (W coast) and Sakoa basin. Several highways radiate from Tananarive. An important artery for freight is the Canal des Pangalanes (E). Administratively, Madagascar is divided into 5 provs.: TANANARIVE, TAMATAVE (including SAINTE-MARIE Island), MAJUNGA (including NOSSI-BE isl.), FIANARANTSOA, TULÉAR. The natives of Madagascar, the Malagasys (Fr. *Malgaches*), are a mixed strain with predominance of Malayo-Polynesian blood. Both numerically and culturally the Hova people are the principal tribe. [The name Hova is, in modern usage, a tribal or racial designation, but this meaning has gradually evolved from the meaning which *Hova* had before the French arrived on the scene—the middle class of the tribal society as opposed to *Andriana* (the aristocrats) and *Andrevo* (the slaves).] The Sakalavas are chiefly pastoralists, while the Betsileos, Baras, and Betsimirakas are farmers. The Negroid Makwas descend from African slaves imported in 18th and 19th cent. Christianity is widespread, especially Protestantism, although the cult of ancestorworship often assumes pagan forms. Nonnative pop. (including French and other Europeans) numbers c.60,000. Early Malagasy history, 1st recorded in Arabic script, reveals strong Arab influence, with Arab colonies established (9th-14th cent.) mainly along NW coast. Successive Polynesian invasions brought to power at first the Sakalavas (until 18th cent.), then came the Hovas, who gradually extended their rule from their stronghold of Imerina and unified (19th cent.) Madagascar under a monarchy just before the ultimate Fr. conquest. Portuguese explorers discovered the isl. in 1500 but their and Fr. attempts at permanent trading settlements (notably in 1642 at Fort Dauphin) met with failure. Soon Madagascar's shores became the haunt of Indian Ocean pirates and a field for territorial claims by various European adventurers. France and Great Britain waged, in 19th cent., a bitter struggle for influence at the Malagasy court, with Britain often having the upper hand. Radama I (1810–28) and Radama II (1861–63) sought to open the isl. to foreign ideas, while the queens Ranavalona I (1828–61), Rasoaherina (1863–68), Ranavalona II (1868–83) fiercely opposed modernization. In 1885, however, the colony known as *Etablissements Français de Diégo Suarez* was founded and a general Fr. protectorate was recognized by Ranavalona III and the powerful prime minister Rainilaiarivony. Repeated defiance by the queen of Imerina led the French to the occupation of Tananarive (1895) and formal abolition of royal power (1896). Pacification was completed by Gallieni (1896–1905) COMORO ISLANDS were placed under Madagascar's administration in 1908, and various scattered subantarctic isls. (see AUSTRALES, ÎLES) were attached to it as outlying dependencies in 1924. During Second World War England seized (1942) some points of Madagascar, then under Vichy govt., and then released them to the Free French. Madagascar was a colony until it became a Fr. overseas territory under the new Fr. constitution of 1946; the Comoros were granted an almost autonomous status.

Madagiz (mŭdŭgēs'), town (1947 pop. over 500), N Nagorno-Karabakh Autonomous oblast, Azerbaijan SSR, on Terter R. (hydroelectric station) and 7 mi. W of Mir-Bashir; cotton; sericulture.

Madain, Al, Iraq: see MAIDAN, AL.

Madakasira (mŭdŭkŭsē'rē), town (pop. 5,334), Anantapur dist., W Madras, India, 55 mi. SSW of Anantapur; betel and coconut palms. Corundum mines near by.

Madalena (mŭdŭlē'nŭ), town (pop. 2,001), Horta dist., central Azores, on W coast of PICO ISLAND, 5 mi. E of Horta (on Faial Isl.) across Faial Channel; 38°32'N 28°32'W. Alcohol distilling, dairying. Winegrowing on slopes of Pico volcano (just SE). Formerly spelled Magdalena.

Madame, Île (ēl mädäm'), small island in the Pertuis d'Antioche of Bay of Biscay, Charente-Maritime dept., W France, opposite mouth of Charente R., 7 mi. W of Rochefort. Fortified by Vauban in 17th cent. as part of Rochefort defenses.

Madame Island or **Isle Madame** (ēl mädäm') (12 mi. long, 9 mi. wide), in the Atlantic, E N.S., just S of Cape Breton Isl., 8 mi. N of Canso, near entrance of the Strait of Canso. On S coast is ARICHAT.

Madampe (mŭdŭm'pā). **1** Town, North Western Prov., Ceylon, on irrigation tank, 6.5 mi. SSE of Chilaw; acetic-acid mfg.; extensive coconut-palm groves. Coconut research institute. **2** Village (pop., including near-by villages, 2,910), Sabaragamuwa prov., S central Ceylon, in Sabaragamuwa Hill Country, 17 mi. SE of Ratnapura; rice, vegetables, tea, rubber.

Madan (mädän'), village (pop. 343), Plovdiv dist., S Bulgaria, in SE Rhodope Mts., 14 mi. ESE of Smolyan; lead, zinc mines.

Madan, Iran: see NISHAPUR.

Madanapalle (mŭ'dŭnŭpŭlē), town (pop. 11,898), Chittoor dist., W Madras, India, 45 mi. NW of Chittoor; road center; rice milling; sugar cane, millet. Tuberculosis sanatorium. Theosophical Col. Dyewood (red sanders) in near-by forested hills.

Madang (mŭdăng', mä'däng), town and harbor, Madang dist., NE New Guinea, on Astrolabe Bay and 300 mi. N of Port Moresby; landlocked harbor. Exports copra, gold. In Second World War, site of Jap. air base taken 1944 by Allied forces. Formerly Friedrich-Wilhemshafen.

Madanganj, India: see Kishangarh, city.

Madanganj or **Mudungunj** (both: mŭdŭn'gŭnj), village, Dacca dist., E central East Bengal, E Pakistan, on Dhaleswari R. and 12 mi. SE of Dacca; rice, jute, oilseeds; rice milling; jute press.

Madanpur, India: see Mahroni.

Madaoua (mädä'wä), town (pop. c.2,100), S Niger territory, Fr. West Africa, near Nigeria border, 80 mi. NE of Sokoto; peanuts, millet; livestock. Landing strip.

Madapollam, India: see Narasapur.

Madara (mä'därä), village (pop. 1,644), Kolarovgrad dist., E Bulgaria, on headstream of Provadiya R. and 9 mi. E of Kolarovgrad; grain, livestock. Has excavations of anc. fortresses, grottoes, 10th-cent. bas-relief commemorating Bulg. king Krum.

Madaras (mŏ'dŏrŏsh), town (pop. 6,477), Bacs-Bodrog co., S Hungary, 6 mi. SW of Bacsalmas; grain, paprika, cattle, hogs.

Madares, Mount, Crete: see Leuka, Mount.

Madari Hat (mä'därē hät'), village, Jalpaiguri dist., N West Bengal, India, 36 mi. ENE of Jalpaiguri; rail terminus; tea processing, rice milling; trades in rice, tea, mustard, tobacco.

Madaripur (mädä'rēpŏŏr), town (pop. 26,624), Faridpur dist., S central East Bengal, E Pakistan, on Arial Khan R. and 36 mi. SE of Faridpur; jute trade center; rice, oilseeds, sugar cane.

Madaus, Germany: see Radebeul.

Madawaska (mădŭwŏ'skŭ), county (□ 1,262; pop. 28,176), NW N.B., on Maine and Quebec borders; ⊙ Edmundston.

Madawaska, town (pop. 4,900), including Madawaska village (pop. 2,975), Aroostook co., N Maine, on St. John R. opposite Edmundston, N.B.; port of entry; paper mills. Includes Saint David, agr. village. Settled 1785 by Acadians, inc. 1869.

Madawaska River. 1 In SE Ont., rises in Algonquin Provincial Park, flows 250 mi. E, through several lakes, to Chats L. of Ottawa R. at Arnprior. **2** In SE Quebec and NW N.B., issues from SE end of L. Temiscouata, flows 30 mi. SE to St. John R. at Edmundston.

Madaya (mŭdŭyä'), village, Mandalay dist., Upper Burma, 15 mi. N of Mandalay (linked by railroad), in irrigated rice area.

Madbury, town (pop. 489), Strafford co., SE N.H., on Oyster R. and just SW of Dover; agr.

Maddagiri, India: see Madhugiri.

Maddalena (mäd-dälā'nä), village (pop. 1,968), W Cyrenaica, Libya, 7 mi. NE of Barce, on a plateau; agr. settlement (cereals, olives, grapes) founded 1936 by Italians.

Maddalena, La (lä mäd-dälā'nä), town (pop. 8,740), Sassari prov., port on Maddalena Island, just off NE Sardinia, 55 mi. NE of Sassari; lobster fisheries; granite quarries; sawmills. Formerly an important naval base. Bombed (1943) in Second World War.

Maddalena Island (□ 8; pop. 10,850), 1 mi. off NE Sardinia, Sassari prov., in Tyrrhenian Sea; 4 mi. long; rises to 515 ft. Lobster fisheries; granite quarries; corn, barley, vineyards. Chief port, La Maddalena. Causeway to Caprera Isl. (E).

Maddalena Pass or **Larche Pass** (lärsh), Ital. *Colle della Maddalena* or *Colle dell'Argentera*, Fr. *Col de Larche* or *Col de l'Argentière*, pass (alt. 6,548 ft.) bet. Maritime Alps (S) and Cottian Alps (N), on Fr.-Ital. border, 12 mi. ENE of Barcelonnette (France); crossed by road (completed 1870) bet. Cuneo (Italy) and Barcelonnette. Stura di Demonte R. rises just S. An army under Francis I crossed Alps here in 1515. Villages of Larche and Meyronnes (on Fr. slope) totally destroyed in Second World War.

Maddaloni (mäd-dälō'nē), town (pop. 19,558), Caserta prov., Campania, S Italy, 15 mi. NNE of Naples; agr. center (grapes, citrus fruit); sausage mfg., food canning.

Madden Dam, town, Balboa dist., E central Panama Canal Zone, on transisthmian highway and 19 mi. NNW of Panama city. Here concrete Madden Dam (3,674 ft. long, 223 ft. high), completed 1935, creates Madden Lake (□ c.22; c.12 mi. long) on Chagres R.; used for navigation, power, and flood control. Formerly called Alajuela.

Maddikera (mŭdĭ kā'rŭ), town (pop. 8,880), Kurnool dist., N Madras, India, 55 mi. SW of Kurnool; cotton ginning, oilseed (peanut) milling. Bamboo, dyewood in near-by forests.

Maddock, city (pop. 741), Benson co., central N.Dak., 32 mi. WSW of Devils Lake; dairy, grain, livestock, poultry.

Maddur (mŭ'dŏŏr), town (pop. 3,838), Mandya dist., SE Mysore, India, on Shimsha R. and 11 mi. ENE of Mysore; road center in sugar-cane and silk-growing area; hand-loom silk weaving.

Maddy, Loch, Scotland: see North Uist.

Madeba (mă'dŭbŭ), anc. *Medeba* (mĕ'dĭbŭ, mē'–), town, N central Jordan, c.20 mi. SW of Amman, 11 mi. E of N tip of Dead Sea. In early times it was in Moab and is so mentioned in the Bible. Later it was a holy place and became a bishop's see. One of the oldest of extant maps was found in a mosaic in a Byzantine church here.

Madeira (mŭdā'rŭ) [Port.,=wood], volcanic archipelago (□ c.305; 1950 pop. 269,179) in N Atlantic, over 600 mi. SW of Lisbon and c.400 mi. W of Fr. Morocco, forming an administrative dist. of Portugal named for the chief city and port, Funchal (32°38'N 16°54'W). Consists of 2 inhabited isls., Madeira and Porto Santo Island, and of 2 uninhabited isl. groups, Desertas and Selvagens, the latter but 120 mi. N of the Canary Isls. Madeira isl. (□ 286; 1950 pop. 266,245), 35 mi. long, up to 13 mi. wide, is by far the most important. It is an internationally known resort and a haven for tuberculosis patients. It has an unusually mild climate (marred only infrequently by the *leste*, a hot drying wind from the Sahara), with annual mean temp. at sea level of 65°F., yearly extremes of 49°F. and 85°F. respectively. Rainfall (Oct.–Dec.) averages under 30 in. Madeira's backbone is a serrated mtn. range rising to 6,106 ft. in the Pico Ruivo. Spurs reach the rugged coast in sheer basaltic cliffs, and short torrents have cut deep ravines into the mtn. slopes. Madeira's vegetation is of almost tropical exuberance. Besides pines and European deciduous trees at higher elevations, there are palms, araucarias, hickory, camphor, and eucalyptus trees. bamboos, ferns, dragon trees, and laurel. Cultivation on terraces reaches alt. of 2,000 ft. Agr. products include famed Madeira wine (especially in Câmara de Lôbos area), sugar cane (grown since 1452), sweet potatoes, early vegetables (especially onions), and cereals. Chief fruits grown are oranges, bananas, guavas, avocado pears, mangoes. Cattle raised for dairying. Machico and Câmara de Lôbos are chief fishing ports (tuna, mackerel). Isl.'s most widespread industries are embroidering and mfg. of wicker furniture and baskets. Scenic coastal roads link Funchal with villages on S and E shore. São Vicente, on N shore, is reached by only road across rugged interior. Chief mtn. resorts are Monte (overlooking Funchal), Santo António da Serra, and Camacha. Pop., though Portuguese in origin, includes Moorish, Italian, and Negro elements. Known to Romans as *Insulae Purpurariae*, isls. were rediscovered (1418–20) by João Gonçalves Zarco and Tristão Vaz Teixeira, under orders of Prince Henry the Navigator. Funchal was founded in 1421. Madeira was temporarily occupied by British in early 19th cent.

Madeira (mŭdĕr'ŭ), village (pop. 2,689), Hamilton co., extreme SW Ohio, a NE suburb of Cincinnati.

Madeira Beach, town (pop. 916), Pinellas co., W Fla., 10 mi. WNW of St. Petersburg, on the Gulf.

Madeira River (mŭdā'rŭ), NW Brazil, most important affluent of the Amazon, formed by Mamoré River and Beni River at Villa Bella (Bolivia), flows N c.60 mi. along Brazil-Bolivia border, then NE through Guaporé territory and Amazonas, past Pôrto Velho, Humaitá, and Borba, to the Amazon (right bank) 90 mi. E of Manaus. A minor distributary of Madeira R. enters Amazon R. 100 mi. NE, thus creating marshy Tupinambaranas isl. Length, including the Mamoré, c.2,100 mi. Navigable from Pôrto Velho, the N terminus of Madeira-Mamoré RR, which was built around 227 mi. of falls and rapids extending upstream to Guajará Mirim (Guaporé territory). Chief tributaries: Roosevelt and Canumã rivers (right).

Mädelegabel (mā'dŭlūgä"bŭl), highest peak (8,678 ft.) of Allgäu Alps, on Austro-Ger. border, 7 mi. S of Obersdorf.

Madeleine, Îles, Que.: see Magdalen Islands.

Madeleine, La (lä mädlĕn'). **1** Town, Dordogne dept., France: see Eyzies, Les. **2** N suburb (pop. 21,534) of Lille, Nord dept., N France; textiles (cotton, linen); metalworking (chains, auto chassis), sugar refining, mfg. of chemicals, mirrors, glass flasks, malt.

Madeleine, Montagnes de la (mōtā'nyŭ dŭ lä mädlĕn'), wooded upland of Massif Central, central France, on border of Allier and Loire depts., extends c.20 mi. bet. Saint-Juste-en-Chevalet (S) and Lapalisse (N). Forms N outlier of Monts du Forez, separating the valleys of the Allier (W) and the Loire (E) and bordering on the Sologne Bourbonnaise (N). Cheese making.

Madeley (măd'lē). **1** Town, Shropshire, England: see Wenlock. **2** Village and parish (pop. 2,829), NW Stafford, England, 7 mi. W of Stoke-on-Trent; tile- and pottery works; agr. market. Former site of Haleigh Castle, destroyed in Civil War. Has church with 14th-cent. tower.

Madelia (mŭdēl'yŭ), village (pop. 1,790), Watonwan co., S Minn., on Watonwan R. and 23 mi. WSW of Mankato, in agr. area; dairy products, cattle feed, truck. Settled 1855, platted 1857, inc. 1873

Madeline Island, Wis.: see Apostle Islands.

Maden (mädĕn'). **1** Village, Ankara prov., Turkey: see Keskin. **2** Village (pop. 4,377), Elazig prov., E central Turkey, on railroad and Tigris R., and 45 mi. NW of Diyarbakir; copper mines; also chrome; wheat. Formerly Erganimadeni.

Madera (mädā'rä), town (pop. 4,549), Chihuahua, N Mexico, in Sierra Madre Occidental, on railroad and 125 mi. WNW of Chihuahua; alt. 6,955 ft.; silver and gold mining; grain, stock.

Madera, volcano (4,495 ft.), SW Nicaragua, on S Ometepe Isl. in L. Nicaragua, 14 mi. SE of Alta Gracia.

Madera (mŭdâ'rŭ), county (□ 2,148; pop. 36,964), central Calif.; ⊙ Madera. From level San Joaquin Valley in W, co. stretches NE to crest of the Sierra Nevada; Mt. Ritter rises to 13,156 ft. Watered by San Joaquin, Chowchilla, and Fresno rivers and Madera Canal (a unit of Central Valley project). Includes part of Yosemite National Park (N), part of Sierra Natl. Forest (N and NE), and Devil Postpile Natl. Monument. Rich irrigated valley lands produce cotton, alfalfa, barley, potatoes, fruit (especially grapes), truck, dairy products, livestock, poultry. Lumbering (chiefly pine); mining of pumice, gold, copper, sand and gravel; natural-gas wells; granite quarries. Industries at Madera and Chowchilla. Formed 1893.

Madera. 1 (mŭdâ'rŭ) City (pop. 10,497), ⊙ Madera co., central Calif., in San Joaquin Valley, 20 mi. NW of Fresno; trade and processing center of diversified agr. area irrigated by Madera Canal, a unit of Central Valley project. Cotton gins; canned foods, wine, feed, lumber, packed meat. Laid out 1876, inc. 1907. **2** (mŭdĕr'ŭ) Village (1940 pop. 1,152), Clearfield co., central Pa., 22 mi. N of Altoona.

Madera Canal (mŭdâ'rŭ), S central Calif., an irrigation unit (completed 1945) of Central Valley project; conducts San Joaquin R. water (by gravity) 37 mi. NW from Friant Dam, to supply Madera co. farm lands.

Maderas, Las, Nicaragua: see Las Maderas.

Maderno (mädĕr'nô), village (pop. 1,875), Brescia prov., Lombardy, N Italy, port on W shore of Lago di Garda, 20 mi. NE of Brescia, in olive-, grape-, and citrus-fruitgrowing region; winter resort; mfg. (paper, artificial silk). Has 12th-cent. church (restored 1580), 17th-cent. palace.

Madero, Ciudad, Mexico: see Ciudad Madero.

Madero, Villa, Mexico: see Villa Madero.

Maderuelo (mä-dhĕrwā'lō), town (pop. 709), Segovia prov., central Spain, 16 mi. SE of Aranda de Duero; flour milling; stock traising; lumbering.

Madha (mä'dŭ), village, Sholapur dist., E Bombay, India, 37 mi. NW of Sholapur; agr. market (millet, cotton, oilseeds).

Madhavnagar, India: see Ujjain.

Madhavpur (mä'doupŏŏr), village, SW Saurashtra, India, on Arabian Sea, 37 mi. SW of Junagarh; coconuts, rice; fishing. Here, according to Hindu legend, Krishna was married.

Madher, El- (ĕl-mädär'), village (pop. 1,498), Constantine dept., NE Algeria, 12 mi. NE of Batna, in N outlier of the Aurès; sheep raising.

Madhoganj (mä'dōgŭnj), town (pop. 3,650), Hardoi dist., central Uttar Pradesh, India, on branch of Sarda Canal system and 19 mi. S of Hardoi; rail and road junction; trades in wheat, gram, barley, oilseeds, sugar cane.

Madhogarh (mä'dōgŭr), town (pop. 3 896), Jalaun dist., S Uttar Pradesh, India, 13 mi. NW of Jalaun, gram, wheat, oilseeds, jowar.

Madhopur (mä'dōpŏŏr), village, Gurdaspur dist., NW Punjab, India, on Ravi R. and 26 mi. NNE of Gurdaspur; headworks and repair shops of Upper Bari Doab Canal here.

Madhra (mŭd'rŭ), village (pop. 3,278), Warangal dist., SE Hyderabad state, India, 27 mi. SSE of Khammam; rice and oilseed milling; tobacco market. Also spelled Madira.

Madhubani (mŭd'ŏŏbŭnē), town (pop. 20,272), Darbhanga dist., N Bihar, India, on Ganges Plain, on rail spur and 18 mi. NE of Darbhanga; trades in rice, corn, wheat, barley, sugar cane; jute.

Madhugiri (mŭ'dŏŏgĭrē), town (pop. 1,460), Tumkur dist., E Mysore, India, 23 mi. NNE of Tumkur; rice, millet, oilseeds, tobacco; cattle raising, hand-loom weaving. Fortified in 17th cent., town and hill (S) were alternately held by Mysore sultans and Mahrattas during 18th cent. Granite and corundum quarrying in near-by hills (sandalwood, lac). Formerly spelled Maddagiri.

Madhukhali (mŭdŏŏkä'lē), village, Faridpur dist., S central East Bengal, E Pakistan, on distributary of Madhumati R. and 13 mi. WSW of Faridpur; rail junction, with spur to Kamarkhali Ghat, 5 mi. WSW.

Madhumati River (mŭ'dŏŏmŭtē), East Bengal, E Pakistan, a main distributary of Ganges Delta, leaves Padma R. 3 mi. N of Kushtia, flows 190 mi. SSE, past Kushtia, Kumarkhali, Gopalganj, and Pirojpur, through the Sundarbans, to Bay of Bengal. In upper course, called Garai; in Bakarganj and Khulna dists., called Baleswar; estuary mouth called Haringhata. Navigable for entire course by river steamers.

Madhupur (mŭd'ŏŏpŏŏr), town (pop. 11,577), Santal Parganas dist., E Bihar, India, 38 mi. W of Dumka; rail junction (spur to Giridih coal fields); health resort; rice, corn, barley, oilseeds, rape and mustard.

Madhupur Jungle (□ c.420), densely wooded area, S Mymensingh and N Dacca dists., East Bengal, E Pakistan; c.45 mi. long, 6–16 mi. wide; sal timber. Also called Garh Gazali.

Madhu Road (mŭd'ōō), village, Northern Prov., Ceylon, near the Aruvi Aru, 25 mi. SE of Mannar; rice. Ceylonese Christian pilgrimage center. Giant's Tank, one of largest (□ 8) irrigation tanks in Ceylon, is 8 mi. NW, on tributary of the Aruvi Aru; restored in late-19th cent.

Madhya Bharat (mŭ'dyŭ bä'rŭt) [Sanskrit,=central India], constituent state (in 1951: □ 46,710; pop. 7,941,642), in W central India; the winter ⊙ is Lashkar, summer ⊙ Indore. Bounded N and NW by Chambal R., S by Satpura Range; bordered by Rajasthan (W), Bombay (SW, S), Madhya Pradesh and Bhopal (E), and Uttar Pradesh (NE, N); surrounds enclaves of Rajasthan (N center) and of Vindhya Pradesh (NE). Vindhya Range crosses S section and forms S edge of MALWA plateau, on which central and S central portions of state lie. Drained by Narbada R. (S) and by Chambal, Kali Sindh, Parbati, and Sind rivers, which rise in the Vindhyas and flow N to Jumna R. Timber forests and jungles cover large areas, especially S. Annual rainfall, 30 to 50 in. Mainly agr. (millet, wheat, cotton, corn, oilseeds, poppy), with processing industries (cotton ginning and milling, handloom weaving, oilseed pressing). Indore, Ujjain, and Gwalior are cotton markets and commercial centers; sugar mills at Ratlam, Jaora, Mehidpur Road; pottery works at Gwalior; leather-goods and tent mfg. at Morar. Important historical sites at Gwalior, Mandu, Ujjain, Chanderi, Bhilsa, and Bagh. State created 1948 by merger of former princely state of GWALIOR and former CENTRAL INDIA princely states of INDORE, BHOPAL AGENCY (except Bhopal and Makrai), and MALWA AGENCY; in 1950, former princely state of Khaniadhana and former chief commissioner's prov. of Panth Piploda were inc.; small outlying enclaves were transferred (1950) to and from neighboring states of Rajasthan and Vindhya Pradesh. Comprises 16 dists.: Bhilsa, Bhind, Dewas, Dhar, Gird, Gwalior, Guna, Indore, Jhabua, Mandasor, Nimar, Rajgarh, Ratlam, Shajapur, Shivpuri, Tonwarghar (Morena), and Ujjain. Pop. 77% Hindu, 15% tribal, 6% Moslem. Main languages: Rajasthani, Western Hindi.

Madhya Pradesh (prŭdāsh'), constituent state (□ 130,323; 1951 census pop. 21,327,898), central India, mainly on N DECCAN PLATEAU; ⊙ Nagpur. Bordered N by Vindhya Pradesh (bet. 2 small sections, E and W, of Uttar Pradesh), NE by Bihar, E by Orissa, S by Madras and Hyderabad, W by Bombay and Madhya Bharat, NW by Bhopal. Crossed in N by SATPURA RANGE (W), S branch of VINDHYA RANGE, and CHOTA NAGPUR PLATEAU (E). Uplands descend steeply S to undulating plains which cover most of state and N to upper valleys of Narbada and Son rivers. The S plains are broken in SW by Ajanta Hills and in SE by rugged W outliers of N Eastern Ghats. Madhya Pradesh has monsoon climate; average annual rainfall, 48 in. In Wardha R. valley (SW) lies one of India's most productive black-soil cotton tracts; further E, in Wainganga and Mahanadi river basins (including CHHATTISGARH PLAIN) are extensive rice lands. The alluvial W Narbada valley is a rich wheat tract. Millet, oilseeds (flax, peanuts, sesame), mangoes, betel palms and vines are grown widely throughout plains. Teak, sal, and bamboo are found in most hill ranges, especially on Chota Nagpur Plateau (India's major lac-producing area); forests also yield sunn hemp (jute substitute), mahua, and myrobalam. W half of state is underlain by basaltic lava beds. State is principal producer of India's manganese, with mines concentrated in Balaghat, Bhandara, Chhindwara, and Nagpur dists. Coal mining is an important source of state's income; mines chiefly in dists. of Chhindwara (in Pench R. valley), Surguja, and Chanda. Extensive limestone deposits support large cement industries in Jubbulpore dist., which also has numerous major bauxite, steatite, pottery-clay, and ocher workings. There are numerous iron-ore (mainly hematite) mines and marble, sandstone, road metal, mica, and fuller's earth quarries; asbestos, corundum, and copper are also found. Main cotton-textile centers are Nagpur, Hinganghat, Akola, Raj-Nandgaon, and Burhanpur. Other industries include rice, flour, oilseed, and dal milling, cotton ginning, pottery mfg., sawmilling, ghee processing, sericulture (central experimental farm at Nagpur), cattle raising, mfg. of biris and sunn-hemp products (mats and cordage), and handicraft cotton and silk weaving. Construction begun 1949 on large newsprint plant at Chandni. Main Indian rail lines and highways meet at industrial center and distribution point of Nagpur (airport); Jubbulpore (airport) and Katni are also important rail junctions. Main educational institutions include Nagpur and Saugor universities and their affiliated colleges, and industrial schools, notably at Nagpur, Jubbulpore, Saugor, Khandwa, and Khamgaon. Pachmarhi (health resort) is summer hq. of state govt. SEVAGRAM, Mahatma Ghandi's residence during last years of his life, is now a natl. shrine. Main languages: Hindi, Marathi. State's pop. (over 80% rural) comprises Hindus (75%), hill tribes (20%; largest concentration of Gonds in India), and Moslems (4%). A rock edict of Asoka in Jubbulpore dist. testifies to extension of his empire over N part of area in 3d cent. B.C. From 1st cent. A.D., area was under successive Deccan dynasties (including the Andhras) and sultans of Delhi until, together with large N and E territory of GONDWARA under Gond chieftains, it passed to Mogul empire in early-17th cent. and to the Mahrattas in 18th cent. The British acquired separate sections of whole region during 19th cent., combining them in a single prov. in 1861; in 1903, BERAR was inc. as an administrative div. and the unit called Central Provs. and Berar. In 1937, it was constituted an autonomous prov. (in 1941: □ 98,575; pop. 16,813,584). Enlarged 1948 by inc. of Bhopal Agency and of following former Chhattisgarh States (total □ 31,478; total pop. 2,834,197): Chhuikhadan, Kawardha, Khairagarh, and Nandgaon into Drug dist.; Bastar and Kanker into new dist. of Bastar; Jashpur, Raigarh, Sakti, Sarangarh, and Udaipur into new dist. of Raigarh; Changbhakar, Korea, and Surguja into new dist. of Surguja; Makrai into Hoshangabad dist. Became a constituent state of republic of India in 1950 and name changed to Madhya Pradesh; enclaves exchanged with Madhya Bharat and Vindhya Pradesh. State comprises 22 dists.: Akola, Amraoti, Balaghat, Bastar, Betul, Bhandara, Bilaspur, Buldana, Chanda, Chhindwara, Drug, Hoshangabad, Jubbulpore, Mandla, Nagpur, Nimar, Raighar, Raipur, Saugor, Surguja, Wardha, Yeotmal.

Madhya Saurashtra (souräsh'trŭ) or **Central Saurashtra**, district, central Saurashtra, India; ⊙ Rajkot.

Madian (mă'dēŭn), **Midian**, or **Midyan** (mĭ'dēŭn), northernmost coastal district of Hejaz, Saudi Arabia, on Red Sea and its Gulf of Aqaba, at Jordan border. A wild mountainous dist. with narrow Tihama coastal plain (up to 15 mi. wide), it forms the uptilted and buckled W edge of the Arabian shelf. Its pre-Cambrian crystalline rocks, covered with Tertiary lava flows, rise to 8–9,000 ft. and are cut by deeply incised wadies. Bedouin pop. is sparse, with Dhaba and Muwailih the chief coastal settlements, and Tebuk the principal inland oasis.

Madidi River (mädē'dē), La Paz dept., NW Bolivia, rises on Peru border c.20 mi. NNE of San Fermín, flows c.180 mi. NE to Beni R. just W of Cavinas. Navigable for c.125 mi. Dense forests along its lower course; rubber and quinine bark found here. Until 1938 formed border bet. La Paz dept. and Colonias natl. territory.

Madill (mŭdĭl'), city (pop. 2,791), ⊙ Marshall co., S Okla., 21 mi. ESE of Ardmore, near L. Texoma, in oil-producing, agr., and stock-raising area; petroleum processing, pecan packing, cotton ginning; mfg. of feed, machinery, furniture; railroad shops. Timber. Settled c.1900, inc. 1905.

Madimba (mädĕm'bä), village, Leopoldville prov., W Belgian Congo, on railroad and 45 mi. S of Leopoldville; agr. center (manioc, plantains, yams, groundnuts, sweet potatoes), supplying Leopoldville.

Madina, Al, or **Al-Madinah** (äl mädē'nŭ), town, Basra prov., SE Iraq, on Euphrates R. and 45 mi. NW of Basra; dates, rice, corn, millet.

Madinat al 'Abid (mădē'nŭ ăl äbēd'), village, Sana prov., central Yemen, 50 mi. SSW of Sana and on motor road to Hodeida.

Madinat al-Fayyum, Egypt: see FAIYUM, city.

Madingo, Fr. Equatorial Africa: see KAYES.

Madingou (mädĭng-gōō'), agr. village, SE Middle Congo territory, Fr. Equatorial Africa, on railroad and 120 mi. W of Brazzaville. R. C. mission.

Madioen, Indonesia: see MADIUN.

Madira, India: see MADHRA.

Madirovalo (mädērōōvä'lōō), agr. village, Majunga prov., N central Madagascar, on Betsiboka R. and 10 mi. W of Ambato-Boéni; rice, cattle. Airfield.

Madison. **1** County (□ 803; pop. 72,903), N Ala.; ⊙ Huntsville. Bounded N by Tenn., drained in SW by Wheeler Reservoir (in Tennessee R.), crossed (N–S) by Flint R. Cotton, corn, tobacco, mules, cattle, hay; textiles. Formed 1808. **2** County (□ 832; pop. 11,734), NW Ark., in the Ozark region; ⊙ Huntsville. Drained by White and Kings rivers and small War Eagle Creek. Agr. (truck, hay, grain, livestock; dairy products); timber. Part of Ozark Natl. Forest is in S. Formed 1836. **3** County (□ 702; pop. 14,197), N Fla., on Ga. line (N); ⊙ Madison. Flatwoods area with swamps and many small lakes; bounded by Aucilla (W), Withlacoochee (NE), and Suwannee (SE) rivers. Agr. (corn, peanuts, cotton, tobacco, hogs, poultry) and some forestry (lumber, naval stores). Formed 1827. **4** County (□ 281; pop. 12,238), NE Ga.; ⊙ Danielsville. Piedmont agr. area (cotton, corn, sweet potatoes, hay) drained by Broad R. Formed 1811. **5** County (□ 473; pop. 9,156), E Idaho; ⊙ Rexburg. Irrigated agr. region in Snake River Plain. Teton R. and Henrys Fork R. join Snake R. near Rexburg. Sugar beets, seed peas, dry beans, potatoes, wheat, livestock. Formed 1913. **6** County (□ 713; pop. 182,307), SW Ill., bounded W by Mississippi R.; ⊙ Edwardsville. Industrial W portion is part of St. Louis metropolitan dist. Bituminous-coal mines, oil and natural-gas wells, agr. (corn, wheat; dairy products; poultry, livestock) in E. Drained by Cahokia and Silver creeks. Formed 1812. **7** County (□ 453; pop. 103,911), E central Ind.; ⊙ Anderson. Drained by West Fork of White R. and by small Pipe, Kilbuck, Fall, Duck, and Lick creeks. Rich agr. area (corn, hogs, cattle, tomatoes, soybeans, poultry). Diversified mfg.: includes processing of farm and dairy products, oil refining. Limestone quarrying. Formed 1823. **8** County (□ 565; pop. 13,131), S central Iowa; ⊙ Winterset. Prairie agr. area (hogs, cattle, corn, oats, soybeans, apples) drained by North and Middle rivers. Bituminous-coal deposits, limestone quarries. Includes state park. Formed 1846. **9** County (□ 446; pop. 31,179), central Ky.; ⊙ Richmond. Bounded NW, N, and NE by Kentucky R.; drained by several creeks. Rolling agr. area, partly in outer Bluegrass region; burley tobacco, livestock, corn, hay, poultry, dairy products. Bituminous coal mines; clay pits. Some mfg. at Berea and Richmond. Formed 1785. **10** Parish (□ 662; pop. 17,451), NE La.; ⊙ Tallulah. Bounded W by Bayou Macon, E by Mississippi R.; intersected by Tensas R. Fertile lowland agr. area (cotton, corn, oats, hay, soybeans). Cotton ginning, lumber milling; mfg. of cottonseed and soybean products. Fishing and waterfowl hunting on oxbow lakes formed by the Mississippi. Formed 1838. **11** County (□ 751; pop. 33,860), central Miss.; ⊙ Canton. Bounded SE by Pearl R., NW by Big Black R. Agr. (cotton, corn, hay, truck, fruit); lumbering. Formed 1828. **12** County (□ 496; pop. 10,380), SE Mo.; ⊙ Fredericktown. Partly in St. Francois Mts.; drained by St. Francis and Castor rivers. Farming (wheat, corn, hay, livestock) and mining (tungsten, manganese, lead, zinc, iron, cobalt, copper, antimony, nickel, granite. Part of Clark Natl. Forest is here. Formed 1818. **13** County (□ 3,530; pop. 5,998), SW Mont.; ⊙ Virginia City. Agr. and mining region, drained by Madison and Ruby rivers and Beaverhead R. in Jefferson R. system. Livestock; gold, silver, lead, copper. Sec. of Beaverhead Natl. Forest in S, Tobacco Root Mts. in N, Gravelly Mts. in S, part of Madison Range in SE. Formed 1865. **14** County (□ 572; pop. 24,338), NE central Nebr.; ⊙ Madison. Agr. area drained by Elkhorn R. Livestock, grain, dairy and poultry produce. Formed 1867. **15** County (□ 661; pop. 46,214), central N.Y.; ⊙ Wampsville. Drained by Chenango and Unadilla rivers and several creeks. Includes Cazenovia L., part of Oneida L., and many small lakes and reservoirs; resorts. Dairying, truck-farming (especially onions, cabbage); also grain, poultry. Mfg. at Oneida and Canastota. Formed 1806. **16** County (□ 456; pop. 20,522), W N.C.; ⊙ Marshall. Mtn. region, bounded N by Tenn.; Bald Mts. along N border; drained by French Broad R. Partly in Pisgah Natl. Forest. Farming (tobacco, corn), cattle raising, sawmilling; resort area. Formed 1851. **17** County (□ 464; pop. 22,300), central Ohio; ⊙ London. Drained by Deer, Paint, and Darby creeks. Agr. area (livestock, corn, wheat, soybeans, fruit); some mfg. at London and Mount Sterling. Formed 1810. **18** County (□ 561; pop. 60,128), W Tenn.; ⊙ JACKSON. Drained by Middle and South forks of Forked Deer R. Agr. area (truck, cotton, livestock); diversified mfg. at Jackson, a rail junction. Formed 1821. **19** County (□ 478; pop. 7,996), E central Texas; ⊙ Madisonville. Bounded W by Navasota R., E by Trinity R. Agr. (cotton, corn, legumes, potatoes, fruit, truck); livestock (cattle, poultry, hogs, sheep, horses); some dairying. Lumbering. Formed 1853. **20** County (□ 327; pop. 8,273), N Va.; ⊙ Madison. In N piedmont; rises in NW to the Blue Ridge; bounded SW and S by Rapidan R.; drained by short Robertson R. Includes part of Shenandoah Natl. Park. Agr. (grain, fruit, tobacco, hay), livestock, dairying. Timber; sawmilling. Trout fishing. Formed 1792.

Madison. **1** Town (pop. 530), Madison co., N Ala., 9 mi. WSW of Huntsville. **2** Town (pop. 718), St. Francis co., E Ark., 4 mi. E of Forrest City and on St. Francis R., in agr. area. **3** Resort town (pop. 3,078), including Madison village (pop. 1,225), New Haven co., S Conn., on Hammonasset R. and Long Isl. Sound and 17 mi. E of New Haven. Many fine 17th- and 18-cent. houses; once shipbuilding, shipping center. Includes East River village (on small East R.) and Hammonasset Beach State Park, at Hammonasset Point. Set off from Guilford 1826. **4** Town (pop. 3,150), ⊙ Madison co., N Fla., near Ga. line, c.50 mi. E of Tallahassee; trade center for farming region. Settled in 1830s. Cherry Lake Farms, U.S. resettlement development, is near by. **5** City (pop. 2,489), ⊙ Morgan co., N central Ga., 26 mi. SSW of Athens; farm trade center; mfg. (clothes, furniture, lumber, cottonseed oil). Has ante-bellum houses. Inc. 1809. **6** Industrial village (pop. 7,963), Madison co., SW Ill., on the Mississippi (bridged here to St. Louis) and 5 mi. N of East St. Louis, within St. Louis metropolitan area; mfg. of steel products, railroad cars, asphalt, wood products, burial vaults; meat packing; railroad yards. Inc. 1890; grew with establishment of steel industry in early 1890s. **7** City (pop. 7,506), ⊙ Jefferson co., SE Ind., on the

Ohio (bridged), opposite Milton (Ky.), and 40 mi. NNE of New Albany; tobacco market; some mfg. (textiles, furniture and other wood products, petroleum products, packed meat). Military proving ground near by. Has notable old houses. Clifty Falls State Park is just W. Settled c.1809. **8** City (pop. 1,212), Greenwood co., SE Kansas, on Verdigris R. and 18 mi. S of Emporia; mfg. point in oil-producing and agr. region; produces oil tanks, separators, gasoline. Oil wells near by. Laid out 1879, inc. 1885. **9** Town (pop. 3,639), including Madison village (pop. 2,554), Somerset co., central Maine, on the Kennebec, near Skowhegan. Its water power developed paper and textile mills. Inc. 1804. Lakewood resort is E of village. **10** Fishing village, Dorchester co., E Md., 9 mi. WSW of Cambridge, in truck-farm area; vegetable cannery. **11** City (pop. 2,303), ⊙ Lac qui Parle co., SW Minn., near S.Dak. line, 23 mi. WNW of Montevideo; agr. trade center for grain, livestock, and poultry area; dairy products, flour, beverages. Settled c.1875, platted 1884, inc. as city 1902. **12** Village (pop. 540), Madison co., central Miss., 13 mi. NNE of Jackson. **13** City (pop. 571), Monroe co., NE central Mo., 12 mi. ENE of Moberly; grain, saddle horses; coal. **14** City (pop. 1,663), ⊙ Madison co., NE central Nebr., 14 mi. S of Norfolk and on branch of Elkhorn R.; grain, dairy and poultry produce, watermelons. Settled 1868, inc. 1873. **15** Town (pop. 486), Carroll co., E N.H., on small Silver L. (site of Silver Lake village) just SW of Conway; wood products. **16** Residential borough (pop. 10,417), Morris co., N N.J., 4 mi. SE of Morristown; rose-growing center in agr. region (truck, dairy products); makes flavoring extract, cement blocks. Drew Univ. here. Sayre House (1745) was Anthony Wayne's Revolutionary hq. Settled 1685, called Bottle Hill to 1834, inc. 1889. **17** Village (pop. 335), Madison co., central N.Y., 20 mi. SW of Utica, in dairying area. **18** Town (pop. 1,789), Rockingham co., N N.C., on Dan R. and 25 mi. NNE of Winston-Salem; agr. market center; textile mfg. Laid out 1818. **19** Village (pop. 1,127), Lake co., NE Ohio, 15 mi. WSW of Ashtabula, near L. Erie; makes pipe, wine, mats, wood products; nurseries. Resort. **20** Borough (pop. 386), Westmoreland co., SW Pa., 8 mi. SSW of Greensburg. **21** City (pop. 5,153), ⊙ Lake co., SE S.Dak., 38 mi. NW of Sioux Falls, near L. Madison and L. Herman. Trade center for agr. region; resort; dairy products, livestock, poultry, grain, flour. State teachers col., 1st in S.Dak. (1881), is here; also hosp. and airport. Platted 1873. **22** Residential village (1940 pop. 2,992), Davidson co., N central Tenn., on Cumberland R. and 7 mi. NE of Nashville. Madison Col. is just SE. **23** Town (pop. 308), ⊙ Madison co., N Va., near E foot of the Blue Ridge, 26 mi. NNE of Charlottesville; clothing mfg. Rail station at Somerset, 12 mi. SSE. **24** Town (pop. 2,025), ⊙ Boone co., SW W.Va., on Little Coal R. (left tributary of Coal R.) and 23 mi. SSW of Charleston, in agr. (livestock, fruit, tobacco) and bituminous-coal region; timber; gas wells. Inc. 1906. **25** City (pop. 96,056), S Wis., ⊙ Wis. and Dane co., on isthmus bet. lakes Mendota and Monona in the Four Lakes group, on Yahara R. and 75 mi. W of Milwaukee; 43°5'N 89°22'W; alt. 859 ft. Second-largest city, cultural and administrative center of the state. Trade center for a rich dairying area, it also has diversified mfg. (machinery, electrical supplies, furniture, processed meat, chemicals). The wooded lake shores of the isthmus form a large part of the residential area and the campus of Univ. of Wisconsin. The univ. arboretum (1,200 acres) on shores of small L. Wingra contains Indian mounds. Edgewood Col. is in city. Madison's landmarks include the high-domed capitol, and the State Historical Society Mus. Among the many parks is Vilas Park, containing a zoo. The U.S. Forests Products Laboratory is here. A state hosp. for the insane and a sanatorium are near by. Founded 1836; inc. as a village in 1846, as a city in 1856.

Madison, Lake, Lake co., E S.Dak., SE of Madison; 4 mi. long, 1.5 mi. wide; popular resort.

Madison, Mount, N.H.: see PRESIDENTIAL RANGE.

Madison Heights, residential suburb (pop. 2,830), Amherst co., central Va., across James R. just NE of Lynchburg. State institution for feebleminded near.

Madison Lake, resort village (pop. 357), Blue Earth co., S Minn., on small lake 9 mi. ENE of Mankato, in grain and livestock area; dairy products.

Madison Range, in Rocky Mts. of SW Mont., rises SW of Bozeman, extends c.40 mi. S, bet. Gallatin and Madison rivers, to Hebgen L. Partly within Gallatin Natl. Forest. Highest points: Lone Mtn. (11,194 ft.), Koch Peak (11,293 ft.).

Madison River, in SW Mont. and NW Wyo., formed in NW corner of Yellowstone Natl. Park, Wyo., by confluence of short Gibbon and Firehole rivers; flows W, through Hebgen L. in SW Mont., thence N, bet. Madison Range and Tobacco Root Mts., to point just NE of Three Forks, where it joins Gallatin and Jefferson rivers to form Missouri R. Length, 183 mi. Hydroelectric project at Ennis L., an artificial widening of stream, 5 mi. N of Ennis.

Madisonville. 1 City (pop. 11,132), ⊙ Hopkins co., W Ky., 33 mi. N of Hopkinsville, in coal, oil, and agr. (burley tobacco, dairy products, livestock, poultry, corn, hay) area. Important loose-leaf tobacco market; shipping point for hardwood timber; mfg. of shirts, stationery, tiles, food products; lumber. Has airport. Indian artifacts have been found near by. Settled 1807. **2** Town (pop. 861), St. Tammany parish, SE La., 30 mi. N of New Orleans and on Tchefuncta R.; resort; lumber milling, boatbuilding. **3** Town (pop. 1,487), ⊙ Monroe co., SE Tenn., 40 mi. SW of Knoxville; agr., lumbering. Seat of Hiwassee Col. **4** City (pop. 2,393), ⊙ Madison co., E central Texas, c.85 mi. NNW of Houston; shipping, trade center in agr. area (cattle, poultry, cotton, corn); timber.

Madiun or **Madioen** (both: mädēōōn'), town (pop. 41,872), central Java, Indonesia, 90 mi. WSW of Surabaya; 7°37'S 111°30'E; trade center for agr. area (sugar, tobacco, cinchona bark, rice, coffee, cassava, corn); textile and lumber mills, railroad workshops.

Madjalengka, Indonesia: see MAJALENGKA.

Madoc (mā'dŏk), village (pop. 1,188), SE Ont., on Deer Creek and 24 mi. N of Belleville; woolen and lumber milling, dairying, mixed farming.

Madoera, Indonesia: see MADURA.

Madona (mä'dōnä), Ger. *Modohn*, city (pop. 2,357), E central Latvia, in Vidzeme, 80 mi. E of Riga; cement, dairy products, leather, foodstuffs; flax.

Madonie Mountains (mädô'nyĕ), N Sicily, range extending 30 mi. from Torto R. E to Nebrodi Mts.; rise to 6,480 ft. in Pizzo Antenna (center). Snow-covered 9 months of year. Source of Salso, Torto, Grande rivers.

Madraka, Ras, or **Ras Madrakah** (räs' mä'drŭkŭ), cape on SE Oman coast, at NE side of Sauqira Bay of Arabian Sea; 19°N 57°52'E; 450-ft.-high limestone cliff.

Madras (mŭdrăs', mŭdräs'), constituent state (□ 127,768; 1951 census pop. 56,952,332), S India; ⊙ Madras. Extends c.1,500 mi. along India's E coast on Bay of Bengal from Orissa (N) almost to Cape Comorin at S tip of India, and is skirted on W for most of its length by the Eastern Ghats (average alt. 2,000 ft.). In N central section, Madras extends westward beyond the Eastern Ghats onto Deccan Plateau bet. Hyderabad (N) and Mysore (S) and touches Bombay. In SW it almost encircles Mysore, extending westward once more, at S apex of Deccan Plateau, through Palghat Gap and Nilgiri Hills (average alt. 6,500 ft.) to Malabar Coast of Arabian Sea, where it has a coast line of over 250 mi. S of Palghat Gap, Madras is bordered W by S section (Anaimali Hills and Cardamom Hills) of Western Ghats, which forms boundary bet. Madras and Travancore-Cochin. The 4 settlements of FRENCH INDIA (Karikal, Pondicherry, and Yanam on E coast, and Mahé on W coast) are enclaves in Madras. The LACCADIVE ISLANDS, off W coast, are controlled by Madras. Off SE coast, across Palk Strait and Gulf of Mannar, is Ceylon. E coast from Point Calimere (on Palk Strait) to Kistna R. is called COROMANDEL COAST. Climate is mostly tropical except in Nilgiri Hills (mean temp. 60°F.; 8,640 ft. in Dodabetta peak) and other elevated areas; state is subject to rainfall of NE and SW monsoons, receiving its heaviest rainfall (reaching over 100 in. in June) on MALABAR COAST. Hill resorts include Coonoor and Ootacamund (in the Nilgiris) and Kodaikanal and Yercaud (in Palni Hills and Shevaroy Hills, respectively). The major rivers, the Godavari and the Kistna (entering NE coastal strip from Hyderabad) and the Cauvery (flowing from Mysore across broader S coastal plains) debouch into Bay of Bengal, forming wide, fertile deltas, the most intensively cultivated areas for state's important crops of rice and sugar cane. Madras is a leading producer of India's peanuts (largely in drier Deccan dists.) and other oilseeds (sesame, castor beans, cashew nuts) and of tobacco, mainly concentrated in Kistna R. delta. Cotton is extensively cultivated, especially in the S black-soil dists. Sunn hemp (jute substitute) is grown in NE dists. Malabar Coast is known for dense coconut groves (source of coir and copra) along its network of lagoons and for its upland spice gardens (pepper, ginger, cardamom). Millet, plantain, betel palms and vines, and mangoes are widely grown. Extensive silk growing (major concentration in N Coimbatore dist.). Forested areas (total over □ 18,700), yielding valuable timber and other woods, are mainly on SW ranges (state's main plantation area for tea, coffee, rubber). The Nilgiris are noted as center of cinchona and eucalyptus cultivation. Many varieties of bamboo cover lower hill slopes of most ranges. Casuarina and mangrove tracts along E coast. Pearl oyster and chank fishing in Gulf of Mannar; shark (yielding valuable liver oil) is fished off W coast; trout hatcheries in the Nilgiris. Varied industrial minerals include important resources of magnesite (in Chalk Hills), manganese (in Vizagapatam and Bellary dists.), and mica (in Nellore dist.); also magnetite and chromite (in Salem dist.), barite, steatite, and asbestos (mainly in Deccan dists.), fire clays (in South Kanara and Chingleput dists.), and lignite in South Arcot dist.); dispersed limestone and gypsum workings; extensive salt pans on E coast. While textile mfg. and agr. processing form basis of Madras industry, it also has a large number of tanneries and manufactures chemicals (fertilizers, dyes), matches, paper, cement, tiles, plywood, and soap. These and other varied industries are partly centered in environs of Madras city and surrounding dist. of Chingleput, but industrial centers elsewhere throughout the state include Bezwada, Coimbatore, Dindigul, Madura, Mangalore, Mettur, Negapatam, Rajahmundry, Salem, and Trichinopoly. Due to state's shortage of industrial fuel, growth of industry has depended largely on hydroelectric power generated in plants at METTUR, PAPANASAM, and PYKARA. In late 1940s construction was begun of additional works on the Godavari (N of Rajahmundry), the Machkund (on Madras-Orissa border), and the Tungabhadra (near Hospet), interconnection bet. existing and projected works being planned to increase and diversify industrialization and expand irrigation facilities. Small-scale processing of agr. products and hand-loom weaving and other handicrafts (biris, paper, pottery, metalware, jewelry, gold and silver thread) are the main activities of numerous small towns and villages. COCHIN (on Malabar Coast; linked by rail and highway via Palghat Gap with state's E trade centers) and VIZAGAPATAM (on Bay of Bengal; reached by rail from central India over Eastern Ghats) are shipbuilding centers and ports rivaling Madras, the state's leading harbor. Other ports are Tuticorin and Calicut. Rail net, radiating from Madras, connects main towns with Bombay via Hyderabad city and Bangalore (in Mysore); with Calcutta via Cuttack (in Orissa); and with New Delhi via Kazipet (in Hyderabad). Airports at Cochin, Coimbatore, Madras, Madura, Trichinopoly, Vizagapatam. Major educational institutions include Madras Univ. (at Madras), Andhra Univ. (in suburb of Vizagapatam), Annamalai Univ. (near Chidambaram), Madras Forest Col. (at Coimbatore); electroplating research institute at Karaikudi. Main languages: Tamil (mainly in Madras city and the S plains area called TAMILNAD), Telugu (in NE coastal strip, in ANDHRA region), Malayalam (on Malabar Coast, in KERALA region), and Kanarese (in KANARA region). State's pop. (c.70% rural) comprises Hindus (87%), Moslems (7%; mainly on Malabar Coast), Christians (4%), hill tribes (1%; mainly in Vizagapatam dist.). Madras is noted for its archaeological landmarks, including outstanding examples of Brahmanic Dravidian architecture at Chidambaram, Conjeeveram, Hampi, Madura, Mahabalipuram, Srirangam, and Tanjore, and Buddhist ruins at Amaravati. From 3d to 1st cent. B.C., N area came under the Buddhist Mauryas and Andhras; in the S, the Hindu Chera, Pallava, Pandya, and Chola dynasties succeeded each other, the Cholas gaining ascendency by end of 11th cent. A.D. In early 14th cent., Delhi sultanate spread over all but extreme S area, but Hindu Vijayanagar kingdom (⊙ was Hampi) rose in 1330s and by early-16th cent. united whole peninsula S of the Kistna, so that further Moslem expansion was checked until Vijayanagar power was overthrown at battle of Talikota (1565) by Deccan sultans (successors of the Delhi sultans). Local warring dynasties disintegrated during 17th cent. as armies of the Mahrattas and the Mogul empire turned the CARNATIC into arena of their struggle for power. In mid-18th cent., chief Indian powers in S India were the Nizams of Hyderabad, who asserted their independence from the declining Mogul empire in 1724, their quasi-dependent governors of the Carnatic (the nawabs of Arcot), the Mahrattas, and the Mysore sultans (Hyder Ali and Tippoo Sahib). Trading posts were established by the Portuguese (Calicut; 1511), the Dutch (Pulicat; 1609), the English (1st major settlement at Masulipatam in 1611; Madras was founded 1639 and named Fort St. George), the Danes (Tranquebar; 1620), and the French (Pondicherry; 1672). In 1653, the Br. territories controlled by Fort St. George were designated a presidency. Wars bet. the English and the French (1741–63; decisive battles at Arcot and Wandiwash) resulted in supremacy of the English. With the acquisition of the Northern CIRCARS and the territories of Tippoo Sahib, approximate present boundaries were established in 1801. In 1937, it was constituted an autonomous prov. (in 1941: □ 126,166; pop. 49,341,810). Enlarged 1948–49 by inc. of Banganapalle, Pudukkottai, and Sandur states (□ 1,602; pop. 498,754) of former MADRAS STATES into existing dists. Became a constituent state of republic of India in 1950; enclaves exchanged with Hyderabad, Mysore, and Travancore-Cochin. State comprises 25 dists.: Anantapur, Bellary, Chingleput, Chittoor, Coimbatore, Cuddapah, East Godavari, Guntur, Kistna, Kurnool, Madras, Madura, Malabar, Nellore, Nilgiri, North Arcot, Ramnad, Salem, South Arcot, South Kanara, Tanjore, Tinnevelly, Trichinopoly, Vizagapatam, West Godavari.

Madras, city (3d largest in India), coextensive with Madras district (□ 30; pop. 777,481), ⊙ Madras state, important port on Coromandel Coast of Bay of Bengal, 850 mi. SW of Calcutta, 640 mi. SE of Bombay; 13°5'N 80°15'E. Surrounded on its land side by Chingleput dist. Communications hub (major rail junction; Minambakkam airport near St. Thomas Mount); commercial and cultural center. Chief exports from its large artificial harbor are tanned leather, peanuts, cotton (raw and milled), hides and skins; other exports include mica, magnesite, tobacco, wool, sandalwood oil. A cotton-textile center with modern mills and a thriving hand-loom industry. Some of India's largest tanneries are located in outlying areas. Other industries include mfg. of military clothing and saddlery, biris, jewelry, pencils, matches; processing of aluminum, micanite, chemicals, and glass; cement and engineering (electrical and railway equipment) works. City lies along coast in rectangular form, intersected by meandering Cooum R.; bounded S by the Adyar; traversed (near coast) by Buckingham Canal. Its main thoroughfare, Mount Road, passes through the fashionable hotel and shopping area, continuing beyond city's SW limits, across the Adyar, to residential suburbs and Guindy Race Course. A beautiful shore drive, the Marina, runs (S to N) from R.C. cathedral of St. Thomé (traditional burial place of the apostle Thomas; early-16th-cent. Portuguese settlement, here, finally ceded to English in 1749 after occupation by Du., Fr., and Indian powers), past govt. bldgs. and principal cols. of Madras Univ. (founded 1857), and continues (as Beach Road) past Fort St. George (older govt. bldgs.; site of oldest English church in India) to the harbor. George Town (just W of harbor; called Black Town until 1906) is main commercial dist. (bazaars, banks). Industrial areas (including Perambur, Tondiarpet, Triplicane, Vepery) are mainly W and N. Residential areas (notably Mylapore) are mostly S; modern garden-city development of Thyagarayanagar is SW. Places of interest include Horticultural Gardens, St. George's Cathedral (consecrated 1816; became a diocesan cathedral 1835; united Protestant church of South India inaugurated here 1947), Central Mus., meteorological observatory, and recreation parks. Govt. School of Technology (formerly called Madras Trades School; includes courses in cinematography), School of Arts, textile and other technological schools, Central Leather Research Inst. Major fresh-water piscicultural research station is in area called Chetput. Madras dates from 17th cent. An English settlement was founded 1639 at village of Madraspatam or Madraspatnam (also called Chennappattanam) and as Fort St. George (fort was built 1645 on grant from representatives of declining Vijayanagar kingdom) soon became chief English trading station of E coast and was given rank of presidency in 1653; captured 1746 by French and held by them until 1749, when it was returned to English under terms of Treaty of Aix-la-Chapelle; unsuccessfully attacked again by French and by Hyder Ali during last half of 18th cent. City grew to its present size by gradual absorption (mostly late-17th and early-18th cent.) of scattered villages which have given their names to city's present sections. Main suburbs: SAIDAPET, SEMBIYAM, TIRUVOTTIYUR, SAINT THOMAS MOUNT, ADYAR, ENNUR.

Madras (mă'drŭs), town (pop. 1,258), ⊙ Jefferson co., N central Oregon, 40 mi. N of Bend in livestock and grain area.

Madras River, India: see COOUM RIVER.

Madras States (mŭdrăs'), former agency (□ 10,757; pop. 7,991,647), S India, comprising Banganapalle, Cochin, Pudukkottai, Sandur, and Travancore. In 1939, Banganapalle and Sandur were transferred from Madras States agency to political charge of Mysore. In 1948–49, Banganapalle, Pudukkottai, and Sandur were inc. into dists. of Madras, and Cochin and Travancore merged to form the union of Travancore-Cochin.

Madre, Laguna, Texas and Mexico: see LAGUNA MADRE.

Madre de Deus, Brazil: see BREJO DA MADRE DE DEUS.

Madre de Dios, Bolivia: see LAS PIEDRAS.

Madre de Dios (mäd'rā dā dyōs'), department (□ 58,842; enumerated pop. 5,212, plus estimated 20,000 Indians), SE Peru, bordering on Brazil (Acre R.) and Bolivia (Heath R.); ⊙ Puerto Maldonado. Almost entirely in Amazon basin, it is drained by Madre de Dios R. and its affluents. Has a humid, tropical climate. Largely covered by virgin forests; rubber is still its main source of income; also balata, chicle, tagua nuts, and timber. In the settled regions cotton, rice, sugar cane, coffee, cacao, yucca, and fruit are grown. There is some gold washing. Formerly part of Cuzco and Puno, the dept. was set up 1902.

Madre de Dios Archipelago, uninhabited island group off coast of S Chile, just SW of Wellington Isl. and separated from Chatham and Hanover isls. (SE) by Concepción Strait; bet. 50° and 51°S at 75°W. Main isls.: Madre de Dios (N) and Duke of York (S).

Madre de Dios River, in Amazon basin of Peru and Bolivia, rises in Cordillera de Carabaya near Paucartambo (Cuzco dept., S Peru), flows c.700 mi. N and NE, past Manú, Puerto Maldonado (Peru), and Puerto Heath (Peru-Bolivia border), to Beni R. at Riberalta (Bolivia). Receives: Manú, Inambari, Tambopata, and Sena rivers. Generally navigable for small craft on upper course; traffic is interrupted by rapids just below Puerto Heath. It serves as main communication line in NW Bolivia. Rubber is collected along its course.

Madrès, Pic de (pēk dü mädrĕs'), peak (8,107 ft.) in E Pyrenees, S France, on border of Aude and Pyrénées-Orientales depts., 10 mi. NNE of Mont-Louis.

Madre Vieja River (mä'drā vyā'hä), SW Guatemala, rises in highlands W of Tecpán, flows c.90 mi. SSW, past Patulul, to the Pacific at Tiquisate, 14 mi. ESE of Tahuesco. Forms Chimaltenango-Sololá dept. boundary in upper course.

Madrid (mädh-rēdh'), town (pop. 2,255), Cundinamarca dept., central Colombia, in Cordillera Oriental, on highway and railroad, and 15 mi. NW of Bogotá, in agr. region (cereals, potatoes, fruit, stock); alt. 8,481 ft. Natl. airfield.

Madrid (mŭdrĭd', Sp. mädh-rēdh', –rē'), province (□ 3,089; pop. 1,579,793), central Spain, in New Castile; ⊙ Madrid. Situated on the monotonous central plateau (Meseta), it is bounded NW by the rugged, frequently snow-capped Sierra de Guadarrama (crossed by several passes and rising in the Peñalara to 7,972 ft.), separating Madrid from Old Castile (Segovia and Ávila provs.). Bordered E by Guadalajara prov., SE by Cuenca prov., S by Toledo prov. Watered by Jarama, Henares, Tajuña, and Manzanares R., tributaries of the Tagus. The climate varies considerably with alt., but is generally of the rigorous continental type (long, cold winters, hot summers). Agr. is generally backward because of soil erosion and large landholdings, but fertile sections in S and SE grow wheat, rye, barley, olives, grapes, beans, hemp, fruit, forage. Livestock, mainly sheep, goats, and bulls for the ring, are grazed widely. Lime, gypsum, and stone quarries. Several medicinal springs (Loeches, El Molar). While industry is predominantly based on agr., it has made great strides in Madrid. Other leading towns include Alcalá de Henares, Getafe, Colmenar Viejo, Chamartín, Aranjuez. Aranjuez, ESCORIAL, and El Pardo are known for their fine royal palaces. Apart from the SW and W outskirts of the capital, most of the prov. remained in Loyalist hands until the end of Sp. civil war (1936–39), but some of the decisive battles were fought here.

Madrid, city (pop. 1,088,647), ⊙ Spain and Madrid prov., in New Castile, situated almost in geographic center of Spain, on the bleak central plateau (Meseta), on small Manzanares R. (canalized), 320 mi. WSW of Barcelona and at about the same distance ENE of Lisbon; 40°25'N 3°40'W; alt. c.2,130 ft. The newest of the great Sp. cities, lacking the traditions of the anc. Castilian and Andalusian towns, and little favored by nature. Originally without commerce, industry, or an agr. hinterland, it is, among the capitals of Europe a singularly artificial creation. Climatic conditions, of the rigorous continental type, are equally disadvantageous, with long, cold winters and excessively hot summers (mean temp. in Jan., 39°F.; in Aug., 73.5°F.); daily variations are sometimes as much as 40°F. The once extensive, surrounding forests have been entirely depleted. Madrid's rise to become the country's largest urban area thus has only been the more spectacular. Today Spain's leading communications center, served by natl. and international highways, railroads, and airlines. it is the administrative and cultural hub of the nation and major distributing point for the interior. An archiepiscopal see, seat of a famed univ. (transferred in 1836 from Alcalá de Henares), and hq. for chief govt. bodies, financial agencies, and foreign representatives. Its numerous expanding industries place Madrid next in rank to Barcelona. It produces all kinds of machinery—airplanes, motorcycles, optical instruments, electrical appliances, radio and telephone equipment, agr. implements, watches, etc.—as well as aluminum, light bulbs, jewelry, leather goods, textiles, clothing, shoes, furniture, pharmaceuticals, fertilizers, plastics, explosives, glassware, ceramics, cement products, paper. Processing works include wineries, breweries, flour mills, dairy plants. Madrid is also foremost as a printing, publishing, and motion-picture center. Besides the univ., many other institutions cater to the arts and sciences, among them excellent theaters, the Sp. Acad., Natl. Library, and schools of engineering, agr., arts, and industry. Its museums of archaeology, anthropology, technology, modern art, science, and naval history are led by the Prado (or Mus. of Painting and Sculpture), one of the outstanding art galleries in the world, which includes the best works of Velázquez and other great Sp. masters, such as El Greco, Zurbarán, Ribera, Murillo, Berruguete, etc., and equally fine examples of Flemish, Italian, and German painting. There are numerous smaller collections. The sumptuous Royal Palace, built on site of old alcazar, also houses great art treasures, and its impressive structure and dimensions make it equal to any edifice of its kind in Europe. Narrow, winding streets of the old quarters (W and SW) contrast with the well-planned newer sections, which are traversed by spacious promenades, such as Paseo del Prado and Paseo de Recoletos. The city's focal point is the Puerta del Sol, once an old gateway and now its principal square. Among the chief religious monuments are 17th-cent. San Isidro cathedral, San Francisco el Grande church and convent (founded in 15th cent.), and the outstanding bishop's palace. There are 2 bull rings; also zoological and botanical gardens. Of the old medieval walls, only 3 gates remain. Several fine bridges (e.g., Segovia, Toledo) cross the Manzanares. The new University City (*Ciudad Universitaria*), rebuilt after its destruction during civil war, is in NW outskirts. Madrid's modern sections spread into the countryside, especially towards NE. Several industrial suburbs adjoin (e.g., Chamartín, Carabanchel Alto and Carabanchel Bajo, Vallecas). Has subway system. Water is supplied by the c.40-mi.-long Isabel II or Lozoya Canal. Though Roman and prehistoric antiquities have been found, the town is first mentioned in 10th cent. as Moorish fortress *Madjrit*, guarding the passes of the Sierra de Guadarrama. Held shortly in 10th cent. by Ramiro II of Leon, it was finally captured in 1083 by Alfonso VI. The Cortes met here for the 1st time in 1329. While some Castilian kings visited it occasionally, in 1561 Philip II established his court (*única corte*) at Madrid permanently; apart from the capital's short residence (1601–06) at Valladolid, Madrid has served as the Sp. capital ever since. The town developed slowly, but it early became a center of the arts. Cervantes here completed his *Don Quixote* and died here; Lope de Vega and Calderón, both natives of Madrid, here wrote their plays; and in Madrid, Velázquez was the royal painter. Magnificent building programs were inaugurated by the Bourbons in early 18th cent., and the city expanded rapidly. From that period date the Royal Palace and the Prado. Occupied during Peninsular War (1808–14) by the French, Madrid was the scene of a popular uprising (May 2, 1808) which was brutally quelled by the invaders. The events of that day have been depicted in famous canvases by Goya. With the construction of railroads in 2d half of 19th cent., Madrid rose to its present dominant position. Besieged by the Nationalists during Sp. civil war (1936–39), the city held out heroically for 29 months. With its fall (May 29, 1939), hostilities came to an end. Since then the Nationalist govt. has energetically pushed industrialization, and rebuilt the greatly damaged western suburbs.

Madrid (mă'drĭd). **1** (also mŭdrĭd') Town (pop. 312), Houston co., SE Ala., 14 mi. S of Dothan, near Fla. line. **2** City (pop. 1,829), Boone co., central Iowa, near Des Moines R., 14 mi. SSE of Boone, in coal-mining and agr. area. Platted 1852, inc. 1883. **3** Town (pop. 162), Franklin co., W central Maine, on branch of Sandy R. and 21 mi. NW of Farmington. Settled c.1807, inc. 1836. **4** Village (pop. 379), Perkins co., SW central Nebr., 10 mi. E of Grant; grain. **5** Village (pop. c.1,000), Santa Fe co., N central N.Mex., 23 mi. SSW of Santa Fe; alt. c.6,000 ft.; coal mining. Several Pueblo Indian villages, ruins of Paako Pueblo near by. **6** Village (1940 pop. 504), St. Lawrence co., N N.Y., on Grass R. and 17 mi. ENE of Ogdensburg; summer resort; lumber.

Madridejos (mä-dhrē-dhā'hōs), town (pop. 8,082), Toledo prov., central Spain, in New Castile, communications center on small Amarguillo R., and 40 mi. S of Aranjuez. Exports and processes agr. produce of fertile region (olives, grapes, grain, potatoes, cereals, saffron); sheep raising. Alcohol and liquor distilling, wine making, olive-oil extracting, cheese processing; mfg. of tiles and plaster.

Madrigal de la Vera (mä-dhrēgäl' dhā lä vā'rä), village (pop. 2,223), Cáceres prov., W Spain, 31 mi. NW of Talavera de la Reina; olive oil, cherries, chestnuts, pepper.

Madrigalejo (mä-dhrēgälā'hō), village (pop. 4,170), Cáceres prov., W Spain, 30 mi. SSE of Trujillo; olive-oil processing, flour milling; cereals, vegetables, flax. Ferdinand V died here (1516).

Madrigueras (mä-dhrēgā'räs), town (pop. 4,030), Albacete prov., SE central Spain, 17 mi. NNE of Albacete; mfg. of scales and pruning shears; alcohol and brandy distilling, olive- and peanut-oil processing. Wine, saffron, cereals.

Mad River. **1** In N Calif., rises in SE Trinity co., flows c.95 mi. NW to the Pacific c.15 mi. N of Eureka. **2** In Grafton co., central N.H., rises in White Mts. E of Woodstock, and flows c.15 mi. SW to Pemigewasset R. near Campton. **3** In W Ohio, rises in Logan co., flows S and SW, past Springfield, to Great Miami R. at Dayton; c.60 mi. long. **4** In W central Vt., rises S of Warren, in Green Mts.; flows c.25 mi. NE to Winooski R. W of Montpelier. Winter-sports area (Mad R. Glen) near Waitsfield.

Madríz (mä-dhrēs'), department (□ 530; 1950 pop. 33,286), NW Nicaragua, on Honduras border; ⊙ Somoto. Drained by Coco, Estelí, and Yali rivers. Varied agr.: coffee on mtn. slopes (Telpaneca), grain and livestock (SW), tobacco, sugar cane, rice (S). Mfg. (hats, mats, hammocks). Exports dairy products. Served by Inter-American Highway. Main centers: Somoto, Telpaneca. Formed 1935 out of Nueva Segovia.

Madron (mă′drŭn), former urban district (1931 pop. 3,273), W Cornwall, England, 2 mi. NW of Penzance; agr. market. Church dates from 13th cent. Site of disused tin mine. Prehistoric monuments near by. Inc. 1934 in Penzance.

Madroñera (mä-dhrōnyā′rä), town (pop. 5,103), Cáceres prov., W Spain, 7 mi. ESE of Trujillo; tanning, meat and cheese processing, flour milling; agr. trade (olive oil, cereals, wine, livestock).

Madroño, El (ĕl mä-dhrō′nyō), town (pop. 442), Seville prov., SW Spain, near Huelva prov. border, 33 mi. NW of Seville; livestock, grain. Copper mining. Also iron and manganese deposits.

Madruga (mädrōō′gä), town (pop. 4,325), Havana prov., W Cuba, on Central Highway, on railroad and 34 mi. ESE of Havana; spa and agr. center (sugar cane, tobacco, coffee). The sugar central San Antonio is just NW.

Madrushkent, Tadzhik SSR: see MATCHA.

Madryn, Argentina: see PUERTO MADRYN.

Madugula (mä′dŏŏgōō′lŭ), town (pop. 6,667), Vizagapatam dist., NE Madras, India, 20 mi. NW of Anakapalle; oilseeds, rice, tobacco. Timber (sal, teak), myrobalan, lac, coffee in Eastern Ghats (W).

Madukarai, India: see COIMBATORE, city.

Madü Lake, Poland: see MIEDWIE LAKE.

Madumabisa (mädōōmābē′sä), village, Bulawayo prov., W Southern Rhodesia, in Matabeleland, on rail spur and 4 mi. W of Wankie, in Wankie coal area; coal mining.

Madura (măd′ŭrŭ), since 1949 officially **Mathurai** (mŭtŏŏrī′) or **Madurai** (mŭdŏŏrī′), district (□ 4,883; pop. 2,446,601), S Madras, India; ⊙ Madura. Bordered W by Western Ghats; mainly lowland (drained by Vaigai R.) except for Sirumalai Hills and spurs of Western Ghats (N) and Palni and Varushanad hills (W), which enclose KAMBAM VALLEY. Includes black-soil cotton tract (S) and alluvial soils along tributaries of Amaravati R. (N). Mainly agr. (cotton, grain, sesame); coffee, tea, cardamom, plantain in hills; rice, tobacco, coconut and date palms in river valleys; rice and sugar cane in SE area (irrigated by channels of PERIYAR LAKE project). Teak in the hills. Cotton milling (Madura), tobacco and cigar mfg. (Dindigul), silk-weaving and dyeing industries, tanning. Health resort and solar observatory at Kodaikanal. Architectural landmarks at Madura. Dindigul area passed from Mysore sultans to English in 1792, rest of dist. from nawabs of Arcot in 1801.

Madura, since 1949 officially **Mathurai** or **Madurai,** city (pop. 239,144), ⊙ Madura dist., S Madras, India, on Vaigai R. and 265 mi. SW of Madras; rail junction; airport; trade and cotton-textile center; silk weaving and dyeing industries; mfg. of agr. implements; exports rice, tobacco, cardamom. Pykara and Pallivasal (MUNNAR) hydroelectric systems linked here. American Col. and Madura Col. (both affiliated with Madras Univ.), women's col., industrial and trade schools. Temple-festival cattle fair. Has large Dravidian temple complex, built 14th–17th cent. Was ⊙ Pandyan kingdom (5th cent. B.C. to 14th cent. A.D.) and Nayak (Hindu) dynasty (mid-16th cent. to 1743); under rule of nawabs of Arcot from 1743 until it passed 1801 to English.

Madura or **Madoera** (both: mädōō′rŭ), island (□ 1,762; □ 2,112, including offshore isls.; pop. 1,858,183), Indonesia, in Java Sea, just off NE coast of Java, across Madura Strait (2–40 mi. wide); 6°52′–7°15′S 112°40′–114°7′E; 100 mi. long, 25 mi. wide. Generally level, with low hills rising to 1,545 ft. in center of isl. Rice, corn, cassava, peanuts, and tobacco are grown, but large areas are unfit for agr., because of chalky soil and inadequate rainfall. Salt panning, cattle raising, fishing. Chief centers: PAMEKASAN, SUMENEP, BANGKALAN, SAMPANG. From 11th to 18th cent. Madura was dominated by rulers of Java. In Second World War, part of battle of Java Sea was fought (Feb., 1942) in Madura Strait. The Du.-sponsored state of Madura (created 1948) became part of Indonesia in 1950.

Madurantakam (mŭdŏŏrän′tŭkŭm), town (pop. 9,720), Chingleput dist., E Madras, India, 40 mi. SW of Madras; agr. trade (rice, oilseeds, coconuts). Megalithic remains near by.

Madwar, El, or **Al-Madwar** (both: ĕl-măd′wär), village, N Jordan, 6 mi. E of Jerash; grain (wheat), fruit. Also spelled El Medwar and El Midwar.

Madzhalis (mŭjä′lyĭs), village (1926 pop. 1,021), SE Dagestan Autonomous SSR, Russian SFSR, 24 mi. WNW of Derbent; wheat, orchards. Dist. inhabited by Kaitaks, one of mtn. tribes of Dagestan.

Mae or **Me** [Thai,=river]: for Thailand names beginning thus and not found here, see under following part of the name.

Maeander River, Turkey: see BUYUK MENDERES RIVER.

Maebaru (mä-ä′bärōō), town (pop. 16,860), Fukuoka prefecture, N Kyushu, Japan, 11 mi. W of Fukuoka, in agr. area (rice, wheat, barley); charcoal.

Maebashi (mä-ä′bäshē), city (1940 pop. 86,997; 1947 pop. 90,432), ⊙ Gumma prefecture, central Honshu, Japan, 60 mi. NW of Tokyo; 36°23′N 139°5′E. Silk-textile center; aircraft mfg. during Second World War. Bombed 1945. Sometimes spelled Maebasi.

Mae Chan (mă′chän′), village (1937 pop. 3,701), Chiangrai prov., N Thailand, on Lampang-Kengtung (Burma) highway and 16 mi. NNE of Chiangrai; road junction; teak. Adjoining village of Ban Kasa was known as Chiang Saen in 1930s.

Maehongson (mă′hông′sôn′), town (1947 pop. 2,318), ⊙ Maehongson prov. (□ 5,906; 1947 pop. 66,280), northwesternmost Thailand, near Burma line, in Daen Lao Range, 80 mi. NW of Changmai; teak-lumbering center; airport. Lead and tungsten deposits. Sometimes spelled Meh Hongsuen.

Mae Klong, town, Thailand: see SAMUTSONGKHRAM.

Mae Klong River (mă′klŏng′), W central Thailand, rises near Burma line in Thanon Thong Chai Range at 16°N, flows 250 mi. S and SE in forested valley past Kanchanaburi (confluence with Khwae Noi R.) and Ratburi, to Gulf of Siam at Samutsongkhram. Navigable by shallow-draught vessels below Kanchanaburi. Linked by irrigation and navigation canals with Tha Chin and Chao Phraya rivers. Sometimes called Khwae Yai [Thai,=greater Khwae] above Kanchanaburi; also spelled Meklong.

Mael, Norway: see RJUKAN.

Maël-Carhaix (mäĕl′-kärĕ′), village (pop. 726), Côtes-du-Nord dept., W France, 23 mi. SSW of Guingamp; rye, barley.

Maella (mäĕ′lyä), town (pop. 2,935), Saragossa prov., NE Spain, 12 mi. SE of Caspe; olive-oil center; flour and sawmilling; cereals, wine, almonds.

Maello (mäĕ′lyō), town (pop. 1,156), Ávila prov., central Spain, near Segovia prov. border, 14 mi. NE of Ávila; cereals, grapes; potteries.

Maelstrom (māl′strŭm), Nor. *Malstrøm* (mäl′-strŭm), **Moskenstraum** (môsk′ŭnstroum), or **Moskenstrom** (–strŭm), Nor. *Moskenstrøm,* strait (c.3 mi. wide) of the North Sea, in Lofoten Isls., N Norway, bet. Moskenesoy (N) and Mosken islet (S), traversed by strong tidal currents which reverse frequently. It has become the epitome of the fatal whirlpool.

Mae Nam or **Menam** [Thai,=river], name commonly applied to CHAO PHRAYA RIVER, Thailand. For other Thai rivers beginning thus, see under following part of the name.

Maen Du, Wales: see DINAS MAWDDWY.

Maentwrog (mīntŏŏ′rôg), agr. village and parish (pop. 647), NW Merioneth, Wales, on Dwyryd R. and 4 mi. SW of Blaenau-Ffestiniog; site of hydroelectric station.

Maeotis, Palus: see AZOV, SEA OF.

Maere, Norway: see SPARBU.

Maes, Belgium: see MEUSE RIVER.

Mae Sai (mă′sī′), village (1937 pop. 4,027), Chiangrai prov., N Thailand, customs post on Burma border, 35 mi. N of Chiangrai, on Lampang-Kengtung highway.

Mae Sariang (mă′sŭryăng′), village (1937 pop. 7,469), Maehongson prov., NW Thailand, near Burma line, in valley E of Thanon Thong Chai Range, 85 mi. SW of Chiangmai; teak center; airport. Sometimes spelled Mae Sarieng.

Maescar, Wales: see DEVYNOCK.

Maeser (mā′zŭr), town (pop. 643), Uintah co., NE Utah, 10 mi. NW of Vernal, in foothills of Uinta Mts.

Maeseyck, Belgium: see MAASEIK.

Maeshowe (mās′hou), prehistoric artificial mound on Pomona isl., Orkneys, Scotland, just E of Stenness. Chamber within was apparently broken into by 12th-cent. Norse invaders. There are runic inscriptions on walls. Structure has circumference of c.300 ft. and is 36 ft. high.

Mae Sot (mă′sôt′), village (1937 pop. 10,166), Tak prov., W Thailand, on Thaungyin R. line opposite Myawaddy, 40 mi. WSW of Tak and 60 mi. ENE of Moulmein (Burma); rice. Airport. Sometimes spelled Meh Sot.

Maesteg (mīstăg′), urban district (1931 pop. 25,570; 1951 census 23,124), central Glamorgan, Wales, 6 mi. E of Port Talbot; coal-mining center. Urban dist. includes coal-mining towns of Maesteg, in Cwmdu (kŏŏmdē′), parish (pop. 12,976), Nantyffyllon (năntŭfŭ′thlŭn) (N; pop. 5,793), Caerau (kī′rī)(N; pop. 6,801), and Garth (SE).

Maestra, Sierra (syĕ′rä mī′strä), range, Oriente prov., E Cuba, most formidable of the isl., extending from Cape Cruz on the Gulf of Guacanayabo c.150 mi. E beyond Santiago de Cuba to depression around Guantánamo. Precipitous and heavily wooded, it rises abruptly at Caribbean coast (S), and is gently rolling in N and NE. Pico TURQUINO (6,560 ft.) is highest point of Cuba. The range yields hardwood (mahogany, cedar, ebony); coffee is grown on its slopes. Mineral deposits: copper (Cobre), iron (Caney); also manganese, silver, chromium, asphalt, marble. Its E section is called Sierra del COBRE. Sometimes the Sierra Maestra is considered to reach only as far as Santiago de Cuba, or to include the highlands near E tip of Cuba. An alternative name is Macaca, which also refers to central group around Pico Turquino.

Maestrazgo (mäĕsträth′gō), mountainous district of Castellón de la Plana and Teruel provs., E Spain, with forests and pastures (cattle raising) in higher W part and fertile valleys (cereals and wine) in lower E part. Was important in Middle Ages under lordship of military order of Montesa. Chief town, Morella.

Maestre de Campo Island (mäā′strā dā käm′pō) (1948 pop. 2,187), Romblon prov., Philippines, in Tablas Strait, just off E coast of Mindoro isl.; 3.5 mi. in diameter. Rice, coconuts.

Maestricht, Netherlands: see MAASTRICHT.

Maesycrugiau, Wales: see LLANFIHANGEL AR ARTH.

Maesycwmmer, England: see BEDWAS AND MACHEN.

Maevatanana (mäĕvätänä′nŭ), town (1946 pop. 6,660), Majunga prov., N central Madagascar, on highway, on Ikopa R. (main tributary of Betsiboka R.) and 90 mi. SE of Majunga; rice center. Gold mining, cattle raising. Hosp., meteorological station.

Maewo (mī′wō′), volcanic island (□ c.135; pop. 246), New Hebrides, SW Pacific, 65 mi. E of Espiritu Santo; c.30 mi. long, 5 mi. wide; central mtn. range. Formerly Aurora Isl.

Maeystown (māz′–), village (pop. 137), Monroe co., SW Ill., 26 mi. S of East St. Louis, in agr. area.

Maezawa (mī′zäwä), town (pop. 9,249), Iwate prefecture, N Honshu, Japan, on Kitakami R. and 7 mi. S of Mizusawa; rice, wheat, soybeans.

Mafafa (mäfä′fä), village (pop. 171) on S coast of San Miguel Isl., Panama, in Gulf of Panama of the Pacific, 14 mi. S of San Miguel. Fishing center; pearl beds. Pineapple plantations.

Mafamude (mŭfŭmōō′dĭ), town (pop. 7,641), Pôrto dist., N Portugal, S suburb of Oporto, on left bank of Douro R., adjoining Vila Nova de Gaia (W); textile milling (carpets, knitwear), shoe, soap mfg.

Mafate (mäfä′tä), village (pop. 1,997), N central Réunion isl., on the upper Rivière des Galets and 11 mi. SSE of La Possession, in Mafate cirque of central massif; thermal springs.

Mafaza or **El Mafaza** (ĕl mŭfă′zŭ), village, Kassala prov., NE Anglo-Egyptian Sudan, on Rahad R., on road, and 65 mi. SW of Gedaref; cotton, wheat, barley, corn, fruit; livestock.

Mafeking (mă′fŭkĭng), town (pop. 5,864), Bechuanaland dist., N Cape Prov., U. of So. Afr., near Bechuanaland Protectorate and Transvaal borders, on Molopo R. and 160 mi. W of Johannesburg; alt. 4,194 ft.; 25°52′S 25°39′E. It is the extraterritorial ⊙ Bechuanaland Protectorate; rail junction with repair shops; center of dairying, cattle-raising, ranching region. Cementworks near by. Seat of local native-affairs council established 1927, with jurisdiction over Mafeking dist. (□ 4,265; total pop. 48,539; native pop. 41,046). Founded 1885 to protect Baralong tribe (hq. in Mafeking Stad, S suburb), it became base of operations in Matabele war (1893) and Matabele rebellion (1896–97). Pitsani, 25 mi. N, in Bechuanaland Protectorate, was starting point (Dec. 30, 1895) of Jameson Raid. In South African War British garrison under Lord Baden-Powell was besieged here (Oct. 12, 1899–May 17, 1900) by Boer forces.

Mafeteng (mă′fŭtĕng), village, ⊙ Mafeteng dist. (pop. 68,536, with absent laborers 77,982), SW Basutoland, on main road and 40 mi. SSE of Maseru; alt. 6,450 ft.

Maffo (mä′fō), town (pop. 1,141), Oriente prov., E Cuba, at N slopes of the Sierra Maestra, 32 mi. WNW of Santiago de Cuba; fruit and sugar region.

Maffra (mă′frŭ), town (pop. 2,443), S Victoria, Australia, 110 mi. E of Melbourne; rail junction in livestock and agr. region; cheese, beet sugar.

Mafia Island (mäfē′ä) (□ 170), E Tanganyika, in Indian Ocean, off mouth of Rufiji R., 80 mi. S of Zanzibar; separated from mainland by 10-mi.-wide Mafia Channel; 30 mi. long, 10 mi. wide. Town of Kilindoni is on SW shore. Copra industry; deep-sea fishing. Limestone deposits. Transferred from Zanzibar protectorate in 1922. Pop. in 1948, c.12,000.

Máfil (mä′fēl), village (1930 pop. 355), Valdivia prov., S central Chile, on railroad and 20 mi. NE of Valdivia; coal-mining center.

Maflahi or **Muflahi** (both: mă′flŭhē), sectional Upper Yafa sheikdom of Western Aden Protectorate; ⊙ Al Jurba. Protectorate treaty was concluded in 1903.

Mafolie (măfō′lē), village, St. Thomas Isl., U.S. Virgin Isls., ¾ mi. N of Charlotte Amalie; has a celebrated panorama over the whole isl. Brazilian astronomers established here (1882) a station to observe transit of Venus.

Mafra (mä′frŭ), city (pop. 7,268), N Santa Catarina, Brazil, on the Rio Negro (Paraná border) opposite city of Rio Negro, and 65 mi. W of Joinvile; rail junction (spur to Curitiba); maté processing, flour milling, lumbering. Ships livestock (especially hogs).

Mafra, town (pop. 3,009), Lisboa dist., W central Portugal, near the Atlantic, 18 mi. NNW of Lisbon. Noted for its huge 18th-cent. white marble convent built by John V in imitation of Spain's Escorial. In the shape of a rectangle (820 ft. long, 720 ft. wide), it is surmounted by 2 towers (350 ft. high) and by a central dome. It contains a church, a fine library, and extensive royal quarters.

Mafraq, El, or **Al-Mafraq** (both: ĕl-măf′räk), town (pop. c.2,000), Jordan, on Hejaz RR and 30 mi. NE of Amman; alt. 2,280 ft.; road junction and major air base; wheat, barley. Oil pipe line passes just N.

Magacela (mägä-thä'lä), town (pop. 1,791), Badajoz prov., W Spain, 33 mi. E of Mérida; cereals, vegetables, sheep. Limekilns; pottery, tiles.

Magadan (mŭgŭdän'), city (1944 pop. 40,000), N Khabarovsk Territory, Russian SFSR, on Sea of Okhotsk, 1,000 mi. NNE of Khabarovsk; 59°35'N 150°50'E. Port of entry to Kolyma gold region; supply point; ship repair yards, auto repair shops; mfg. (electric lamps, glassware, ceramics), assembly of construction machinery. Founded 1932 near Nagayevo, its present port and SW suburb.

Magadha (mŭ'gŭdŭ), anc. kingdom in NE India, occupying roughly present central Bihar and extreme E Uttar Pradesh; early ⊙ was Rajagriha (modern RAJGIR); later ⊙ was Pataliputra (modern PATNA). During reign of Bimbisara (mid-6th cent. B.C.) Vardhamana Mahavira (historical founder of Jainism) and Gautama Buddha preached their doctrines here. Kingdom flourished under Mauryan emperors, especially Asoka (c.273–232 B.C.), and Buddhism spread to Ceylon and E Asia. Magadha was visited (A.D. c.405–411) by Chinese pilgrim Fa-hsien during renowned period (4th–5th cent.) of Gupta dynasty, when a revival of Brahmanism took place and Indian art and literature, culminating in works of poet-dramatist Kalidasa, reached a golden age.

Magadi (mä'gŭdē), town (pop. 7,134), Bangalore dist., S central Mysore, India, 25 mi. W of Bangalore; trades in millet, rice; handicraft lacquer- and brassware. Bamboo, sandalwood in near-by hills.

Magadi (mägä'dē), town, ⊙ Masai dist., S Kenya, in Great Rift Valley on E shore of L. Magadi, 50 mi. SW of Nairobi; alt. 1,978 ft.; 1°55'S 36°17'E; soda- and salt-mining center. Railhead, airport.

Magadi, Lake (□ 240), in Great Rift Valley, S Kenya, 50 mi. SW of Nairobi; 30 mi. long, 8 mi. wide. Contains large deposit of carbonate of soda exploited commercially. Town of Magadi on E shore.

Magaguadavic River (mă"gŭdā'vĭk), SW N.B., rises WSW of Fredericton, flows 80 mi. S, through L. Magaguadavic (□ 10.5), past St. George (hydroelectric station), to Passamaquoddy Bay 5 mi. W of St. George.

Magalakwin River (mägälä'kwĕn), N Transvaal, U. of So. Afr., rises W of Nylstroom, flows 250 mi. generally N, past Nylstroom, to Limpopo R. 70 mi. W of Beitbridge.

Magalang (mägä'läng), town (1939 pop. 3,614; 1948 municipality pop. 13,049), Pampanga prov., central Luzon, Philippines, 13 mi. NNW of San Fernando; terminus of spur of Manila–San Fernando RR; agr. center (sugar cane, rice).

Magalhães de Almeida (mŭgŭlyā'ĭs dĭ älmā'dŭ), town (pop. 1,074), NE Maranhão, Brazil, on left bank of Parnaíba R. (Piauí border), opposite Luzilândia, and 40 mi. SW of Parnaíba; rice and tobacco growing.

Magaliesberg (mäkhä'lēsbĕrkh"), Afrikaans *Magaliesberge*, mountain range, SW Transvaal, U. of So. Afr., extends c.100 mi. parallel to NE part of Witwatersrand; rises to 6,078 ft. on Nooitgedacht, 20 mi. NW of Krugersdorp.

Magaliesburg (–bûrkh"), village, SW Transvaal, U. of So. Afr., on W Witwatersrand, 30 mi. NW of Krugersdorp; alt. 4,682 ft.; rail junction; tobacco-growing and processing center.

Magallanes, Argentina: see SAN JULIÁN.

Magallanes (mägäyä'nĕs), province (□ 52,285; 1940 pop. 48,813; 1949 estimate 49,219), S Chile, extending from about 48°40'S to Cape Horn; ⊙ PUNTA ARENAS. Includes a narrow strip of mainland bet. Argentina and the Pacific, and most of the isls. of TIERRA DEL FUEGO (S of the Strait of Magellan), as well as, N of the strait, numerous archipelagoes and isls. (e.g., Wellington, Madre de Dios, Hanover, Adelaide, Riesco) of the partly submerged Andes, which form a labyrinth of channels and fjords. Among its numerous peninsulas are Brunswick and Muñoz Gamero. Largely covered by snow-capped mts. and glaciers, it is a bleak area and has a cold, foggy climate, with heavy rainfall (up to 200 inches annually) and frequent snowstorms. Inhabited largely by small Indian tribes, who engage mostly in sheep raising and lumbering. Some agr. (barley, oats, potatoes) on small scale; fishing. At Punta Arenas are meat packing, fish canning, tanning, sawmilling. Mineral resources, largely unexploited, include coal (on Brunswick Peninsula near Punta Arenas, and on Riesco Isl. near Elena), petroleum (at Springhill), gold (mostly in stream beds). Originally set up as a penal colony, the prov. was formed 1929.

Magallanes, city and department, Chile: see PUNTA ARENAS.

Magallanes (mägäyä'nĕs, –lyä'nĕs), town (1939 pop. 4,723; 1948 municipality pop. 17,982), Sorsogon prov., extreme SE Luzon, Philippines, at S side of entrance to Sorsogon Bay, opposite Bagatao Isl. (2.5 mi. long, 1 mi. wide), 15 mi. SW of Sorsogon; agr. center (abacá, coconuts, rice); fishing.

Magallanes, Estrecho de: see MAGELLAN, STRAIT OF.

Magallon (mägäyōn', –lyōn'), town (1939 pop. 13,689) in Isabela municipality, Negros Occidental prov., W central Negros isl., Philippines, 28 mi. SSE of Bacolod; agr. center (rice, sugar cane).

Magallón (mägälyōn'), town (pop. 2,104), Saragossa prov., NE Spain, 15 mi. ESE of Tarazona; olive-oil processing, mfg. of brandy and alcohol. Wine, cereals, sheep in area.

Magalloway (mŭgă'lŭwā), plantation (pop. 83), Oxford co., W Maine, c.30 mi. NW of Rumford, near Rangeley Lakes.

Magalloway Mountain, Coos co., N.H., peak (3,360 ft.) in wilderness area SE of First Connecticut L., near Maine line.

Magalloway River, NW Maine and NE N.H., rises in N Oxford co., Maine; flows S, through Parmachenee L., to Aziscohos L. (Formed by dam), thence c.15 mi. generally SW into N.H. where, with outlet of Umbagog L., it forms Androscoggin R.

Magalo (mä'gälō), town (pop. 2,000), Harar prov., S Ethiopia, near Web R., 20 mi. S of Ginir; trade center (hides, cereals, wax, honey).

Magán (mägän'), town (pop. 1,005), Toledo prov., central Spain, on canal of the Tagus, and 9 mi. NE of Toledo; cereals, grapes, olives; olive-oil pressing, cheese processing.

Magane (mä"gä'nā) or **Makane** (mä"kä'nā), town (pop. 2,562), Okayama prefecture, SW Honshu, Japan, 5 mi. W of Okayama; rice, wheat, raw silk, persimmons.

Magangué (mägäng-gā'), town (pop. 9,770), Bolívar dept., N Colombia, river port on the Brazo de Loba (a left arm of Magdalena R.) and 120 mi. S of Barranquilla. Outlet for agr. products of fertile Bolívar savannas; ships cattle; dairying and agr. center (corn, rice, fruit, livestock). Airport.

Maganik (mä'gänĭk), mountain in Dinaric Alps, central Montenegro, Yugoslavia, bet. Zeta and Moraca rivers; highest point, Medjedji Vrh (7,016 ft.), is 18 mi. ESE of Niksic.

Maganja da Costa (mŭgän'zhŭ dŭ kôsh'tŭ), village, Zambézia prov., central Mozambique, 60 mi. NE of Quelimane; sisal, rice, copra.

Maganwadi, India: see WARDHA, town.

Magaramkent (mŭgŭrŭmkyĕnt'), village (1939 pop. over 500), SE Dagestan Autonomous SSR, Russian SFSR, on Samur R. (irrigation) and 32 mi. S of Derbent; wheat, rice. Pop. largely Lezghian.

Magaria (mägä'ryä), village (pop. c.1,200), S Niger territory, Fr. West Africa, near Nigeria border, 55 mi. S of Zinder; peanuts, millet, corn; livestock.

Magar Pir, W Pakistan: see PIR MANGHO.

Magarwara, India: see UNAO, town.

Magas Tatra, mountains, Czechoslovakia and Poland: see TATRA MOUNTAINS.

Magat River (mägät'), N Luzon, Philippines, rises in mts. in Nueva Vizcaya prov. 30 mi. SE of Baguio, flows c.120 mi. generally NE, past Bayombong and Solano, to the Cagayan near Hagan.

Magazine, town (pop. 503), Logan co., W Ark., 37 mi. ESE of Fort Smith, in rich farmland of Petit Jean valley (corn, truck, cotton; dairy products). Magazine Mtn. is near by.

Magazine Mountain, W central Ark., one of 2 highest peaks (c.2,850 ft.) in state, c.45 mi. SE of Fort Smith, in Ouachita Mts. Land-utilization project devoted to forestry, game refuges, and recreational development is near by.

Magazzolo River (mägätsô'lô), SW Sicily, rises SE of Santo Stefano Quisquina, flows 22 mi. SW to Mediterranean Sea 3 mi. NW of Cape Bianco.

Magburaka (mägbŏŏrä'kä), town (pop. 2,115), Northern Prov., central Sierra Leone, on Rokel R. and 12 mi. SSE of Makeni, on railroad; road and trade center; palm oil and kernels, cacao, coffee. Has 2 mission schools. Formerly called Makump.

Magdagachi (mŭgdŭgä'chē), town (1926 pop. 2,206), SW Amur oblast, Russian SFSR, 80 mi. ESE of Skovorodino and on Trans-Siberian RR, in lumbering area; metalworks; agr. processing.

Magdala (mäg'dälä, măg'dŭlŭ), village, Wallo prov., NE Ethiopia, 23 mi. NW of Dessye. Capital of Ethiopia under Emperor Theodore, who committed suicide here after his defeat (1868) by Napier.

Magdala (mäk'dälä), town (pop. 1,174), Thuringia, central Germany, 6 mi. W of Jena; grain, sugar beets, livestock.

Magdala (măg'dŭlŭ, mäg'dälä), Biblical locality, Lower Galilee, NE Palestine, on E shore of Sea of Galilee, 3 mi. NNW of Tiberias; reputed birthplace of Mary Magdalen. In Roman times hq. of Josephus Flavius. Sometimes called Migdal; modern settlement of that name is just NW. In modern times site of village of Majdal (măj'dăl); abandoned by Arabs 1948.

Magdalena (mägdälā'nä), town (pop. 4,589), ⊙ Magdalena dist. (□ 1,288; pop. 19,103), NE Buenos Aires prov., Argentina, near the Río de la Plata, 26 mi. ESE of La Plata; cattle- and sheep-raising center; meat-salting industry. Founded 1730. Atalaya, on coast 3 mi. N, is popular beach resort.

Magdalena, Azores: see MADALENA.

Magdalena, town (pop. c.2,600), ⊙ Iténez prov., Beni dept., NE Bolivia, port on Itonamas R. and 105 mi. NNE of Trinidad; rubber-collecting center; cattle. Airport.

Magdalena, department (□ 20,819; 1938 pop. 342,322; 1950 estimate 458,770), N Colombia, on Caribbean Sea; ⊙ SANTA MARTA. Located bet. Magdalena R. (W) and Cordillera Oriental (E), the latter forming its border with Venezuela, it consists of marshy lowlands in W section (Magdalena basin), dominated N by great massif Sierra Nevada de Santa Marta (N), rising abruptly from the coast to highest peak (18,950 ft.) in Colombia, the Pico Cristóbal Colón. César and Ranchería rivers water its E part. Has generally dry, tropical climate, with rainy season (May–Sept.); temperate, alpine conditions in undeveloped high plateaus of Sierra Nevada. Mineral resources include petroleum (El Difícil), copper and alluvial gold in Valledupar region (E), gold, iron, and coal near Ríohacha, marble in Ciénaga vicinity. But its main product is its large crop of bananas grown in valley S of Santa Marta, and shipped from that port. Other agr. products are cotton, corn, rice, beans, henequen, and yucca; and coffee in uplands. The dense forests on coastal plains yield fine wood (mahogany, cedar, etc.), rubber, tagua nuts, balata, kapok, tolu balsam, medicinal plants. Ríohacha is a base for pearl fishing; deep-sea fishing and canning at Santa Marta and Ciénaga. Most of the pop. are mestizo and mulatto.

Magdalena or **Magdalena Milpas Altas** (mēl'päs äl'täs), town (1950 pop. 1,092), Sacatepéquez dept., S central Guatemala, 5 mi. SE of Antigua; alt. 6,158 ft.; corn, beans, fodder grasses.

Magdalena. **1** Officially Magdalena de Araceo, town (pop. 1,827), Guanajuato, central Mexico, 5 mi. S of Valle de Santiago; grain, sweet potatoes, vegetables, livestock. **2** Town (pop. 2,249), Jalisco, W Mexico, on L. Magdalena, on railroad, and 45 mi. WNW of Guadalajara; alt. 5,096 ft. Agr. center (grain, maguey, sugar cane, cotton, vegetables, fruit, livestock). **3** City (pop. 4,249), Sonora, NW Mexico, on Magdalena R. and 110 mi. N of Hermosillo, 50 mi. S of Nogales, on railroad; alt. 2,464 ft. Agr. center (wheat, fruit, chick-peas, vegetables, cotton) in rich silver- and copper-mining area. Yearly Indian festivals (Oct.) in honor of St. Francis Xavier draw many pilgrims. Known to Aztecs were gold placers near by. **4** Town, Tabasco, Mexico: see FRANCISCO LEÓN. **5** Town (pop. 123), Veracruz, E Mexico, in Sierra Madre Oriental, 7 mi. SSE of Orizaba; coffee.

Magdalena, town (pop. 516), Amazonas dept., N Peru, on Utcubamba R. and 9 mi. SSE of Chachapoyas; sugar cane, fruit.

Magdalena (măgdŭlē'nŭ), village (pop. 1,297), Socorro co., W central N.Mex., just NW of Magdalena Mts., 20 mi. WNW of Socorro; alt. 6,557 ft. Trade and shipping point in livestock area. Lead, zinc deposits near by. Parts of Cibola Natl. Forest N and S, South Baldy 9 mi. SSE. Founded 1884.

Magdalena, La, Mexico: see LA MAGDALENA.

Magdalena, Lake, Jalisco, W Mexico, 40 mi. NW of Guadalajara; 10 mi. long N–S, 5 mi. wide; alt. c.4,500 ft.

Magdalena Bay (mägdälā'nä), inlet of Pacific, in SW coast of Lower California, NW Mexico, sheltered by several isls., including Santa Margarita (S); 17 mi. long NW-SE, 12 mi. wide. Well known as good harbor and fishing ground.

Magdalena Bay, Nor. *Magdalenefjorden*, inlet (7 mi. long, 2–3 mi. wide) of the Arctic Ocean, NW West Spitsbergen, Spitsbergen group, 110 mi. NNW of Longyear City, at foot of extensive glacier region; 79°33'N 11°E. Noted for its magnificent scenery. Here are remains of 12th-cent. graves of whaling crews.

Magdalena Contreras, La, Mexico: see CONTRERAS.

Magdalena del Mar (dĕl mär'), SW residential section (pop. 16,057) of Lima, Lima dept., W central Peru; beach resort on the Pacific. Known for cool climate; sanatoriums. Inc. 1940 into Lima proper. Sometimes Magdalena Nueva.

Magdalena Island, off coast of Aysén prov., S Chile, across Moraleda Channel from Chonos Archipelago; circular, c.40 mi. in diameter. Mountainous, uninhabited area, rising to 5,450 ft.

Magdalena Milpas Altas, Guatemala: see MAGDALENA.

Magdalena Mountains (măgdŭlē'nŭ), W central N. Mex., in Socorro co., W of Socorro and the Rio Grande; largely within Cibola Natl. Forest. Prominent peaks: North Baldy (9,856 ft.); South Baldy (10,787 ft.), highest point. Zinc is mined.

Magdalena Nueva, Peru: see MAGDALENA DEL MAR.

Magdalena River (mägdälā'nä), most important river of Colombia, rises in the SW, near 2°N 76°30'W, in Cauca dept., at S foot of Páramo del Buey in Cordillera Central 35 mi. S of Popayán, and flows N c.1,000 mi. to the Caribbean near Barranquilla. In its upper course it flows bet. Cordillera Central and Cordillera Oriental, then enters alluvial lowlands, where it is joined by Cauca R. and reaches the Caribbean 9 mi. NW of Barranquilla in wide, irregular delta. Principal tributaries, besides the Cauca, are San Jorge, Bogotá, and Sogamoso. Navigable from Barranquilla, near the coast, to Honda, where the rapids have been circumvented by a railroad to Ambalema on the left bank, it was opened to the sea when its mouth, the Bocas de Ceniza, was dredged to Barranquilla. Later a rail line from La Dorada, below Honda, was constructed to Bogotá. Above Honda the river is navigable again to Neiva, only 150 mi. from its source. At Girardot rail and highway connect it with Bogotá and with Buenaventura on Pacific coast. Other landings are: Natagaima, Purificación, Puerto Berrío (linked by railroad with Medellín), Barrancabermeja, Puerto Wilches, El Banco, Mompós, Magangué, and Calamar. At Calamar a navigable arm of the Magdalena called Canal del Dique flows W to Cartagena. The river carries a large part of Colombia's trade. Its fertile valley has a tropical, humid climate, with a dry period Dec.–April, when navigation becomes more difficult. Along its upper and mid course sugar cane, tobacco, cacao, and cotton are grown; and coffee on slopes of the cordilleras. Around Barrancabermeja is Colombia's main petroleum-producing dist., connected by pipe line with Cartagena. The Magdalena was discovered (1501) by Bastidas and further explored (1536) by Jiménez de Quesada.

Magdalena River, Sonora, NW Mexico, rises SE of Nogales near U.S. border; flows c.200 mi. SW and W, past Imuris, Magdalena, Santa Ana, and Pitiquito, to Gulf of California 22 mi. NW of Cape Tepoca. Receives Altar R., whose name sometimes designates its lower course; middle course also called Asunción R., the section above its mouth Concepción R. Used for irrigation in an otherwise arid region; chick-peas, fruit, cereals, vegetables are produced.

Magdalena Tetela, Mexico: see LA MAGDALENA.

Magdalena Vieja (vyā'hä) or **Pueblo Libre** (pwĕ'blō lē'brā), SW residential section (pop. 5,859) of Lima, Lima dept., W central Peru, just N of Magdalena del Mar. Mus. of anthropology; natl. mus. of the republic. Here resided Bolívar and San Martín after their meeting at Guayaquil (1822). Inc. 1940 into Lima proper.

Magdalen Channel or **Magdalen Sound,** in Tierra del Fuego, Chile, S arm (25 mi. long) of Strait of Magellan, bet. Clarence Isl. and W coast of main isl. of Tierra del Fuego.

Magdalen Islands (măg'dulun) or **Îles Madeleine** (ēl mädlĕn'), group (□ 102; pop. 8,940) of 9 main isls. and numerous islets in the Gulf of St. Lawrence, E Que., 100 mi. W of Newfoundland, 50 mi. N of Prince Edward Isl.; 47°13'–47°49'N 61°23'–62°1'W. Chief isls. are Amherst, Grindstone, Alright, Grosse, Coffin, East, Brion, and Entry isls. Gypsum was quarried and exported in 19th cent., but fishing (cod, herring, mackerel, lobster) and sealing are now main occupations; some of the land is arable. Villages are Étang du Nord, House Harbour, and Havre Aubert. Discovered 1534 by Jacques Cartier, isls. became property of Sir Issac Coffin in 1787; in 1903 group was purchased by the Magdalen Island Company. Pop. is almost wholly of French origin.

Magdalinovka (mŭgdŭlyē'nŭfkŭ), village (1939 pop. over 500), N Dnepropetrovsk oblast, Ukrainian SSR, 30 mi. N of Dnepropetrovsk; wheat, sunflowers.

Magdeborn (mäk'dubôrn), village (pop. 3,939), Saxony, E central Germany, 8 mi. SSE of Leipzig, in lignite-mining region.

Magdeburg, former province, Germany: see SAXONY, province.

Magdeburg (măg'dubûrg, Ger. mäk'dubŏŏrk), city (1939 pop. 336,838; 1946 pop. 236,326), ⊙ former Prussian Saxony prov., E central Germany, after 1945 in Saxony-Anhalt, port on the Elbe, at E end of Weser-Elbe Canal, and 80 mi. WSW of Berlin; 52°8'N 11°38'E. Rail hub; industrial center; paper and textile milling, sugar refining, metalworking, zinc smelting; synthetic-oil plant. Mfg. also of steel products, machinery, automobiles, cranes and elevators, sewing machines, chemicals, glass, leather goods, margarine. Center of important sugar-beet-growing region; extensive grain, feed, potash, vegetable-seed trade. Potash and lignite mined near by. Lutheran bishopric. Heavily bombed in Second World War (destruction about 65%); entire old city destroyed; cathedral (1209–63) damaged. The composer Telemann, the physicist von Guericke, and Baron von Steuben were b. here. First mentioned 805 as Saxon outpost; became center for colonization of Slav territories under Otto I. Archbishopric established 968. Town received charter from archbishops which became model of numerous medieval town charters in Holy Roman Empire. Was a leading member of Hanseatic League. Accepted (1524) the Reformation; joined (1531) Schmalkaldic League and continued resistance against emperor until captured (1551) by Maurice of Saxony. The archbishops, members of house of Brandenburg, were converted to Protestantism, and the family consequently ruled archbishopric as administrators. In Thirty Years War, Magdeburg held off siege (1629) by Wallenstein, but was stormed and burned (May, 1631) by imperial forces under Tilly. Under Treaty of Westphalia (1648), secularized archbishopric passed to Brandenburg. Was fortress until 1912. In Second World War, captured (April 18, 1945) by U.S. troops; later occupied by Soviet forces. Chief suburbs include Rothensee (N), with ship elevator at E end of Weser-Elbe Canal, and power station; Friedrichstadt (E), site of airport; and Buckau (S).

Magdiel (mägdē-ĕl'), settlement (pop. 1,600), W Israel, in Plain of Sharon, 10 mi. NE of Tel Aviv; citriculture, mixed farming. Site of agr. school. Founded 1924. Attacked by Arab forces, 1948.

Magdiwang, Philippines: see SIBUYAN ISLAND.

Magé or **Majé** (both: mŭzhĕ'), city (pop. 5,168), S Rio de Janeiro state, Brazil, near N end of Guanabara Bay, 20 mi. NNE of Rio; rail junction (spur to Teresópolis); cotton mill (6 mi. NW), match factory, pottery works. Piedade (2 mi. SSW) is its port on the bay.

Magee (mŭgē'), town (pop. 1,738), Simpson co., S central Miss., c.40 mi. SE of Jackson, in agr. (cotton, truck, poultry) and timber area. A state tuberculosis sanatorium is near by.

Magee, Island (mŭgē'), peninsula on SE coast of Co. Antrim, Northern Ireland, on the North Channel, forming E side of Lough Larne, extending 8 mi. NNW from Black Head. It is notorious for massacre of its Catholic inhabitants in 1642.

Magelang (mŭgĕläng'), town (pop. 52,944), central Java, Indonesia, 25 mi. NNW of Jogjakarta, in highlands bet. Mt. Sumbing and Mt. Merapi; alt. 1,312 ft.; trade center for agr. area (sugar, rice, corn, tobacco, cassava); textile mills. Until 1949, important Du. military establishment was here. BOROBUDUR (famous monument) 8 mi. S.

Magellan, Strait of (mŭjĕl'ŭn), Sp. *Estrecho de Magallanes,* channel (350 mi. long, 2–20 mi. wide) bet. the Atlantic and Pacific oceans, separating mainland of South America from Tierra del Fuego. Entirely in Chilean territory except for E extremity touched by Argentina, it extends from the Atlantic bet. Cabo Vírgenes (52°20'S 68°21'W) and Cape Espíritu Santo, generally SW along Brunswick Peninsula to Froward Cape (N of 54°S), then NW to the Pacific at Cape Pillar (52°42'S 74°41'W) on Desolation Isl. Discovered 1520 by Magellan, it was important in days of sailing ships, especially before building of Panama Canal. PUNTA ARENAS is the major town on it. Along its majestic, fjordlike course are snow-capped peaks. It threads its way among numerous isls. and channels. Has cold and frequently foggy climate.

Magens Bay (mā'gŭnz), bay of N St. Thomas Isl., U.S. Virgin Isls., c.1½ mi. N of Charlotte Amalie; fine beach and public park; popular tourist site.

Magenta (mŭjĕn'tŭ, It. mäjĕn'tä), town (pop. 10,470), Milano prov., Lombardy, N Italy, 15 mi. W of Milan, in rice-growing region. Foundries, silk mill, alcohol distillery, furniture and match factories. Noted for victory of French and Sardinians over Austrians in 1859.

Magerov (mä'gyĭrŭf), Pol. *Magierów* (mägyĕ'rŏŏf), town (1931 pop. 2,470), NW Lvov oblast, Ukrainian SSR, 9 mi. SSE of Rava-Russkaya; agr. processing (grain, vegetables), sawmilling.

Mageroy (mä'gŭr-ûü), Nor. *Magerøy,* island (□ 106; pop. 3,501) in Barents Sea of the Arctic Ocean, Finnmark co., N Norway, 45 mi. ENE of Hammerfest, on W side of mouth of Porsang Fjord; 22 mi. long, 17 mi. wide; rises to 1,368 ft. (W). On N coast are KNIVSKJELLODDEN, northernmost point of Europe, and NORTH CAPE. HONNINGSVAG (SE) is chief village.

Magersfontein (mä'khŭrsfôntän"), locality, NE Cape Prov., U. of So. Afr., near Orange Free State border, 14 mi. SSW of Kimberley. Scene (Dec. 11, 1899) of battle in South African War; Boers here checked Lord Methuen's advance on Kimberley.

Magetan (mŭgĕtän'), town (pop. 15,152), central Java, Indonesia, 35 mi. E of Surakarta, at foot of Mt. Lawu; alt. 1,181 ft.; trade center for agr. area (corn, cassava, coffee); sugar mills.

Maggia River (mäd'jä), S Switzerland, rises SW of Airolo, flows 35 mi. SSE, through VALLEMAGGIA dist., Lago Maggiore at Locarno.

Maggiolo (mäzhō'lō), town (pop. estimate 3,000), SW Santa Fe prov., Argentina, 105 mi. SW of Rosario; agr. center (corn, wheat, flax, alfalfa, livestock); mfg. of agr. machinery.

Maggiorasca, Monte (môn'tĕ mäd-jôrä'skä), highest peak (5,915 ft.) in Ligurian Apennines, N Italy, 19 mi. NNE of Chiavari. Near by is Monte BUE.

Maggiore, Lago (lä'gô mäd-jô'rĕ), anc. *Verbanus Lacus,* second largest lake (□ 82) of Italy, lying largely (□ 65) in provs. of Novara (W) and Varese (E), partly (□ 17) in Swiss canton of Ticino (N); 40 mi. long, average width 2 mi., alt. 636 ft., max. depth 1,220 ft. Fishing (trout, perch, shad) and hatcheries. Contains famous BORROMEAN ISLANDS. Traversed by Ticino R. Receives water from L. of Orta via Toce R., L. of Lugano via short Tresa R., and L. of Varese. Other affluent, Maggia R. On its picturesque banks are towns of Locarno, Pallanza, Intra, Arona, Cannobio, Luino, and Laveno. Small steamers ply bet. them. Another Ital. name for lake is Lago Verbano.

Maggiore, Monte, Yugoslavia: see UCKA.

Maggotty (mă'gŭtē), town (pop. 1,350), St. Elizabeth parish, W Jamaica, on Black R., on Kingston–Montego Bay RR and 23 mi. SE of Montego Bay, in agr. region (corn, spices, livestock). Known for near-by Maggotty Falls.

Maghagha or **Maghaghah** (mă'găgŭ), town (pop. 21,171), Minya prov., Upper Egypt, on W bank of the Nile, on Ibrahimiya Canal, on railroad, and 38 mi. NNE of Minya; cotton ginning, woolen and sugar milling; cotton, cereals, sugar cane.

Maghama (mägä'mä), village, S Mauritania, Fr. West Africa, near Senegal R., 55 mi. SE of Kaédi; gum arabic, millet, livestock.

Maghar (mŭg'ŭr), village, Basti dist., NE Uttar Pradesh, India, 14 mi. W of Gorakhpur; handloom cotton-weaving center; rice, wheat, barley. Tomb of noted Moslem and Hindu saint, Kabir. Important military outpost of Oudh in 18th cent.

Maghera (măkhŭrä'), town (pop. 1,343), E Co. Londonderry, Northern Ireland, at foot of Sperrin Mts., 16 mi. W of Ballymena; agr. market (potatoes, flax, oats). Has ruins of old church.

Magherafelt (mă'rŭfĕlt'), town (pop. 1,956), SE Co. Londonderry, Northern Ireland, 15 mi. WSW of Ballymena; agr. market (flax, potatoes, oats); salmon fishing.

Magheramorne (mŏrŭmôrn'), village, E Co. Antrim, Northern Ireland, on Larne Lough, 3 mi. SE of Larne; limestone quarrying, cement mfg. Traditionally, St. Comgall b. here.

Maghreb, Maghrib, or **Moghreb** (all: mŭ'grĭb, mä'–) [Arabic,=the West], Arabic designation for N Africa from Egypt to the Atlantic Ocean, bet. the Mediterranean and the Sahara. Region therefore includes Libya, Tunisia, Algeria and Morocco. Spain (at time of Moslem domination) was also part of the Maghreb.

Maghull (mŭgŭl'), residential village and parish (pop. 2,601), SW Lancashire, England, on Leeds-Liverpool Canal and 8 mi. N of Liverpool; truck gardening.

Magic Dam, Idaho: see BIG WOOD RIVER.

Magierow, Ukrainian SSR: see MAGEROV.

Magil, Iraq: see MA'QIL.

Magione (mäjô'nĕ), village (pop. 1,362), Perugia prov., Umbria, central Italy, near lake Trasimeno, 9 mi. WNW of Perugia; mfg. (metal furniture, wire, nets).

Maglaj, Maglai, or **Maglay** (all: mä'glī), town (pop. 2,311), N central Bosnia, Yugoslavia, on Bosna R., on railroad and 50 mi. NNW of Sarajevo; center of prune- and cereal-growing area.

Magland (mäglã'), village (pop. 209), Haute-Savoie dept., SE France, in Arve R. gorge and 3 mi. SE of Cluses, at foot of Chaîne du Reposoir; precision metalworking.

Magliano Alpi (mälyä'nô äl'pē), village (pop. 2,249), Cuneo prov., Piedmont, NW Italy, 15 mi. NE of Cuneo.

Magliano de' Marsi (dĕmär'sē), village (pop. 2,324), Aquila prov., Abruzzi e Molise, S central Italy, 5 mi. NW of Avezzano; macaroni mfg.

Magliano in Toscana (ēn tôskä'nä), village (pop. 833), Grosseto prov., Tuscany, central Italy, 15 mi. SSE of Grosseto. Travertine quarries near by.

Magliano Sabina (säbē'nä), town (pop. 2,001), Rieti prov., Latium, central Italy, near the Tiber, 20 mi. W of Rieti; foundry; mfg. of agr. machinery.

Maglic or **Maglich** (both: mä'glĭch), Serbo-Croatian *Maglić,* peak (7,829 ft.) in Dinaric Alps, Yugoslavia, on Montenegro (SE) and Bosnia-Herzegovina (NW) border, W of Piva R., 15 mi. SSW of Foca.

Maglie (mä'lyĕ), town (pop. 10,305), Lecce prov., Apulia, S Italy, 17 mi. SSE of Lecce. Rail junction; agr. trade center (olive oil, wine, figs, cereals); mfg. (macaroni, furniture, lace).

Maglizh (mŭglēsh'), village (pop. 4,059), Stara Zagora dist., central Bulgaria, in Kazanlik Basin, 8 mi. E of Kazanlik; grain, horticulture (roses, mint); chestnut and mulberry groves.

Maglod (mŏg'lōd), Hung. *Maglód,* town (pop. 5,318), Pest-Pilis-Solt-Kiskun co., N central Hungary, 12 mi. E of Budapest; grain, dairy farming.

Magna, village (pop. 3,502), Salt Lake co., N Utah, 10 mi. W of Salt Lake City; alt. 4,278 ft. Copper, silver, gold, lead processed. Diversified farming (grain, fruit, sugar beets) in vicinity.

Magna Charta Island, England: see EGHAM.

Magnac-Laval (mänyäk'-läväl'), village (pop. 1,002), Haute-Vienne dept., W central France, 8 mi. NE of Bellac; sugar-beet distilling. Site of annual religious festival.

Magnac-sur-Touvre (-sür-tōō'vrŭ), village (pop. 1,532), Charente dept., W France, on the Touvre and 4 mi. ENE of Angoulême; paper milling.

Magnago (mänyä'gô), village (pop. 2,058), Milano prov., Lombardy, N Italy, 3 mi. SW of Busto Arsizio; cotton-milling center; mfg. of textile machinery.

Magna Graecia (măg'nŭ grē'shŭ) [Latin,=greater Greece], name for anc. Greek colonies in S Italy, founded in 8th cent. B.C. along E and W coasts and Gulf of Taranto. Included Tarentum (now Taranto), Heraclea, Sybaris, Crotona (now Crotone), Locris, Neapolis (now Naples), Paestum, Elea, etc. Flourishing cities were a center of pre-Socratic philosophy in 6th cent., but declined in 5th cent.

Magnavacca, Italy: see PORTO GARIBALDI.

Magnesia (măgnē'zhŭ,–shŭ). **1** or **Magnesia ad Maeander** (ăd mēăn'dŭr), anc. city of Lydia, W Asia Minor, on Buyuk Menderes R. (Maeander) and 10 mi. N of Soke, 45 mi. SSE of Smyrna, Turkey. Supposedly founded by Magnesians from Thessaly, destroyed by Cimmerians, recolonized by Ionians; ruins include temple of Artemis Leucophryne. **2** or **Magnesia ad Sipylum** (ăd sĭ'pĭlŭm), anc. city of Lydia, W Asia Minor, on Gediz R. (Hermus) and 20 mi. NE of Smyrna, where its ruins are at modern city of Manisa. Here Antiochus the Great was defeated (190 B.C.) by the Romans.

Magnesia or **Magnisia,** nome (□ 1,563; pop. 149,193), SE Thessaly, Greece; ⊙ Volos. Bounded SW by the Orthrys massif, it includes the Gulf of Volos, nearly closed off by hook-shaped Magnesia peninsula, which rises to the Pelion. Includes the Northern Sporades (except Skyros group of Euboea nome). Agr.: wheat, corn, tobacco, citrus fruit, almonds, olives. Livestock raising; fisheries. Volos is the economic center. In anc. times, Magnesia was the entire coastal dist. of Thessaly S of the Vale of Tempe.

Magness (măg'nĭs), town (pop. 229), Independence co., NE central Ark., 10 mi. ESE of Batesville.

Magnet, village (pop. 115), Cedar co., NE Nebr., 15 mi. SW of Hartington.

Magnetawan (măgnĕ'tùwän), village (pop. 213), SE central Ont., on Magnetawan R. and 30 mi. NE of Parry Sound; lumbering.

Magnetawan River, SE central Ont., rises in NW part of Algonquin Provincial Park, flows 100 mi. SW and W, past Magnetawan, to Georgian Bay of L. Huron, through the Byng Inlet, 40 mi. NW of Parry Sound.

Magnetic Island (□ 19), in Coral Sea just off E coast of Queensland, Australia, bet. Cleveland and Halifax bays; roughly triangular, 6 mi. long, 5 mi. wide; rises to 1,628 ft. Tourist resort. Papayas, pineapples.

Magnetic Springs, village (pop. 321), Union co., central Ohio, 17 mi. SSW of Marion.

Magnisia, Greece: see MAGNESIA.

Magnitka (mŭgnyĕt'kŭ), town (1948 pop. over 2,000), W Chelyabinsk oblast, Russian SFSR, in the S Urals, on left tributary of Ai R. and 9 mi. E of Kusa, on rail spur (Titan station); titanium-mining center; charcoal burning.

Magnitnaya (–nĭŭ), mountain (2,020 ft.) in S Urals, Russian SFSR, just W of upper Ural R.; 53°24'N. Site of extensive magnetite deposits, whose exploitation led to the founding of MAGNITOGORSK (at W foot).

Magnitogorsk (măgnē'tùgôrsk, Rus. mŭgnyĕtŭgôrsk'), city (□ 30; 1929 pop. estimate 30,000; 1939 pop. 145,870; 1946 pop. estimate 200,000), SW Chelyabinsk oblast, Russian SFSR, on SW slope of MAGNITNAYA mtn., on dammed upper Ural R. and 135 mi. SW of Chelyabinsk, on S.Siberian RR (formerly W terminus of rail spur from Kartaly). The leading metallurgical center of USSR, based on magnetite mined at Magnitnaya mtn., iron ore and alloys from the Urals, and coal from Karaganda and Kuzbas. Stalin Steel Works (city's industrial giant; constructed 1931) consisted (1948) of 8 blast furnaces, 26 open-hearth furnaces, 2 blooming mills, 8 rolling mills, and 10 coke batteries; mfg. (heavy and mining machinery, nitrate fertilizers, cement, clothing, shoes, foodstuffs). Has metallurgical and teachers colleges. Consists of several settlement nuclei established during construction period (1929) and merged into single urban center. Major industrial installations and temporary housing units are on left Ural R. bank. Construction of permanent residential section on right bank of Ural R. reservoir began during Second World War (pop. expected to reach 270,000 upon completion of this project). Preliminary planning of Magnitogorsk (1929) was assisted by American engineers. Was boom town and major objective of Soviet industrialization plans in 1930s.

Magnolia. 1 City (pop. 6,918), ⊙ Columbia co., SW Ark., 34 mi. W of El Dorado; center, since 1938, for important oil-producing area; also trade center for farm region (cotton, corn, hogs). Oil refining, cotton processing, lumber milling; textile mill. Seat of the Southern State Col. Settled 1852, inc. 1855. **2** Town (pop. 207), Kent co., E Del., 6 mi. SSE of Dover, in agr. region. **3** Town (pop. 285), Putnam co., N central Ill., 14 mi. S of Spring Valley, in agr. and bituminous-coal area. **4** Town (pop. 207), Harrison co., W Iowa, 30 mi. N of Council Bluffs, in agr. area. **5** Village, Essex co., Mass.: see GLOUCESTER. **6** Village (pop. 260), Rock co., extreme SW Minn., 7 mi. E of Luverne, near Iowa line, in grain and potato area. **7** City (pop. 1,984), ⊙ Pike co., SW Miss., 7 mi. S of McComb, in agr., dairying, and timber area; mfg. of textiles, cottonseed products; lumber milling. Near by is a state park. **8** Borough (pop. 1,883), Camden co., SW N.J., 8 mi. SE of Camden; farming. Inc. 1915. **9** Town (pop. 585), Duplin co., SE N.C., 34 mi. S of Goldsboro, in agr. area; crate mfg. **10** Village (pop. 901), on Stark-Carroll co. line, E Ohio, 11 mi. SSE of Canton; clay products; coal mining.

Magnolia Beach, resort village, Calhoun co., S Texas, on Lavaca Bay and 7 mi. SE of Port Lavaca.

Magnor (mäng'nōr), village (pop. 683) in Eidskog canton (pop. 7,111), Hedmark co., SE Norway, on railroad and 20 mi. SE of Kongsvinger; frontier station on Swedish border, 5 mi. NW of Charlottenberg, on Oslo-Stockholm main line. Has glassworks. On border line, monument commemorates peaceful separation (1905) of Norway and Sweden.

Magny-en-Vexin (mänyē'-ā-vĕksē'), village (pop. 1,850), Seine-et-Oise dept., N central France, 12 mi. NNE of Mantes-Gassicourt; furniture factory; cider distilling. Old houses.

Mago, Fiji: see MANGO.

Mago (mä'gù), village, SE Lower Amur oblast, Khabarovsk Territory, Russian SFSR, major fishing port on lower Amur R. and 20 mi. W of Nikolayevsk; fish-processing center; can mfg., barrel making.

Magoari, Cape, Brazil: see MAGUARI, CAPE.

Magocs (mä'gôch), Hung. *Mágocs,* town (pop. 3,703), Baranya co., S Hungary, 5 mi. E of Dombovar; nuts, grapes, hogs.

Magodes, Uganda: see MOLO.

Magoffin (mùgŏ'fĭn), county (□ 303; pop. 13,839), E Ky.; ⊙ Salyersville. In the Cumberlands; drained by Licking R. and by several creeks. Agr. area (livestock, fruit, tobacco, potatoes, corn). Bituminous-coal mines, oil wells, timber. Formed 1860.

Magog (mā'gŏg), town (pop. 9,034), S Que., at N end of L. Memphremagog, 16 mi. SW of Sherbrooke; textile-milling center; woodworking, dairying, mfg. of textile machinery; resort.

Magothy River (mă'gù-thē), central Md., irregular arm of Chesapeake Bay (c.12 mi. long), penetrating Anne Arundel co. just N of Sandy Point; yachting.

Magoye (mägō'yä), township (pop. 114), Southern, Prov., Northern Rhodesia, on railroad and 15 mi. SSW of Mazabuka; tobacco, wheat, corn.

Magra, India: see BANSBARIA.

Magra River (mä'grä), anc. *Macra,* N Italy, rises 4 mi. SE of La Cisa pass, flows 35 mi. S, through the Lunigiana, past Pontremoli, Aulla, and Vezzano Ligure, to Gulf of Genoa 2 mi. E of Gulf of Spezia. Chief affluents, Vara (right) and Aulella (left) rivers. Used for irrigation and hydroelectric power.

Magrath (mùgrăth'), town (pop. 1,295), S Alta., 19 mi. S of Lethbridge; coal mining; grain, stock, sugar beets. Mormon settlement, founded 1899.

Magrè Vicentino (mägrā' vēchĕntē'nô), village (pop. 2,431), Vicenza prov., Veneto, N Italy, adjacent to Schio; candy, marmalade, mustard.

Magruder Mountain, Nev.: see SILVER PEAK MOUNTAINS.

Magsingal (mägsĭng-gäl'), town (1939 pop. 3,560; 1948 municipality pop. 11,697), Ilocos Sur prov., N Luzon, Philippines, 8 mi. NNE of Vigan, near W coast; rice-growing center.

Magstadt (mäk'shtät), village (pop. 3,659), N Württemberg, Germany, after 1945 in Württemberg-Baden, 5 mi. NNW of Böblingen; cattle.

Magú (mägōō'), officially San Francisco Magú, town (pop. 1,727), Mexico state, central Mexico, 23 mi. NW of Mexico city; cereals, livestock. Airfield near by.

Maguari, city, Brazil: see CRUZ DO ESPÍRITO SANTO.

Maguari, Cape (mùgwùrē'), E Pará, Brazil, forms NE tip of Marajó isl. and marks mouth of Pará R. on the Atlantic; 0°17'S 48°24'W. Lighthouse. Formerly spelled Magoari and Maguary. Cape Maguarinho is 5 mi. NNW.

Maguarichic (mägwärēchēk'), mining settlement (pop. 3,387), Chihuahua, N Mexico, in Sierra Madre Occidental, on railroad and 130 mi. SW of Chihuahua; silver and gold mining.

Magude (mägōō'dä), village, Sul do Save prov., S Mozambique, on Incomati R., on railroad and 65 mi. N of Lourenço Marques; sugar, citrus, cotton, castor beans, corn; cattle raising.

Mâguez (mä'gĕth), village (pop. 1,104), Lanzarote, Canary Isls., just N of Haría, 13 mi. N of Arrecife; cereals, grapes, fruit, vegetables.

Maguilla (mägē'lyä), town (pop. 1,940), Badajoz prov., W Spain, 13 mi. NE of Llera; cereals, grapes, olives, vegetables, fruit, livestock.

Maguiresbridge (mùgwī'ùrzbrĭj'), agr. village (district pop. 663), E central Co. Fermanagh, Northern Ireland, 8 mi. ESE of Enniskillen; potatoes, cattle.

Maguntan-hama, Russian SFSR: see PUGACHEVO.

Magura (mä'gōōrŭ), village, Jessore dist., W East Bengal, E Pakistan, on distributary of the Madhumati and 26 mi. NNE of Jessore; rice, jute, oilseeds.

Maguse Lake (□ 540), SE Keewatin Dist., Northwest Territories, near Hudson Bay; 61°30'N 95°W; 45 mi. long, 1–7 mi. wide. Drained E into Hudson Bay by Maguse R. (35 mi. long); at mouth of river is trading post.

Magwe (mùgwā'), administrative division (□ 17,302; 1941 pop. 1,719,404) of Upper Burma; ⊙ Yenangyaung. Located astride Irrawaddy R., bet. Chin Hills and Arakan Yoma (W) and Pegu Yoma (E), it includes dists. of Pakokku, Minbu, Magwe, and Thayetmyo. In the dry zone (annual rainfall, 25-45 in.), it has irrigated agr.: rice, cotton, sesame, peanuts, catechu; extensive teak forests. Leading petroleum-producing region of Burma, with chief fields at Yenangyaung, Chauk, Yenangyat, and Lanywa. Served by Irrawaddy steamers and Pyinmana-Kyaukpadaung RR. Pop. is 90% Burmese, 5% Chin.

Magwe, district (□ 3,724; 1941 pop. 559,926); Magwe div., Upper Burma; ⊙ Yenangyaung. Bet. Irrawaddy R. and Pegu Yoma, in dry zone (annual rainfall, 31 in.). Agr.: sesame (chief producer), rice (in Taungdwingyi plain), corn, peanuts, beans. Oil fields at Yenangyaung and Chauk. Served by Irrawaddy steamers and Kyaukpadaung-Pyinmana RR. Pop. is 95% Burmese.

Magwe, town (pop. 8,209), Magwe dist., Upper Burma, on left bank of Irrawaddy R. (opposite Minbu) and 95 mi. N of Prome; 20°10'N 94°55'E; airfield. Until Second World War, ⊙ Magwe dist. and div.

Magyarbanhegyes (mŏ'dyŏrbän"hĕ-dyĕsh), Hung. *Magyarbánhegyes,* town (pop. 3,863), Csanad co., SE Hungary, 16 mi. SSW of Bekescsaba; grain, cattle, horses.

Magyarcseke, Rumania: see CEICA.

Magyarkanizsa, Yugoslavia: see KANJIZA.

Magyarkeszi (mŏ'dyŏrkĕsē), town (pop. 2,504), Tolna co., W central Hungary, 34 mi. NW of Szekszard; wine.

Magyarlapos, Rumania: see TARGU-LAPUS.

Magyarorszag, Europe: see HUNGARY.

Magyarovar, Hungary: see MOSONMAGYAROVAR.

Magyar Pass, Ukrainian SSR: see YABLONITSA PASS.

Maha, China: see MAKIANG.

Mahabad, Iran: see MEHABAD.

Mahabaleshwar (mŭhä"bŭlā'shvŭr), town (pop. 5,090), Satara North dist., W central Bombay, India, 27 mi. NW of Satara; fruit and vegetable gardening. Noted health resort (sanitarium) on scenic plateau of Western Ghats, rising to 4,719 ft. in peak 1 mi. E. Bauxite deposits near by. Annual rainfall averages 280 in. Source of Kistna R. is 4 mi. N. Other spellings: Mahabaleshvar, Mahableshwar; also called Malcompeth after its founder, Sir John Malcolm.

Mahabalipuram (mŭhä'bŭlĭpōōrŭm), village, Chingleput dist., E Madras, India, on Coromandel Coast of Bay of Bengal, 30 mi. S of Madras. Noted archaeological remains represent some of earliest-known examples of Dravidian architecture (A.D. 7th cent.) in India. Numerous monolithic temples, hewn out of rocks rising abruptly from sandy plain, are dedicated variously to Siva and Vishnu. Sculptures include bas-reliefs of mythological scenes (most noted known as Arjuna's Penance). Site is often called Seven Pagodas for the high pinnacles of 7 of the temples. Also called Mahabalipur or Mamallapuram.

Mahaban (mŭhä'bŭn), town (pop. 4,104), Muttra dist., W Uttar Pradesh, India, near the Jumna, 5 mi. SSE of Muttra; pilgrimage center. Has palace of Nanda (covered court consisting of 80 pillars; rebuilt by Moslems in 17th cent.). Sacked by Mahmud of Ghazni in 1018.

Mahabharat Lekh (mŭhäbä'rŭt läk'), mountain range, S Nepal; extends WNW-ESE across Nepal, bet. S foothills of Nepal Himalayas and Siwalik Range; 8–10 mi. wide. Highest point, 9,710 ft., is 18 mi. SE of Katmandu. Nepal Valley lies on N slope.

Mahableshwar, India: see MAHABALESHWAR.

Mahabo (mähä'bōō), town, Tuléar prov., W Madagascar, 220 mi. NNE of Tuléar; lima beans, corn, peanuts. Has agr. station.

Mahad (mŭhäd'), town (pop. 8,150), Kolaba dist., W Bombay, India, 70 mi. SE of Bombay; port (27 mi. inland) on short Savitri R.; trades in rice, onions, potatoes, jaggery; tanning; copper and brass products. Buddhist caves (1st cent. A.D.) 2 mi. NW.

Mahaddei Uen (mähäd'dā wĕn'), village (pop. 700), S Ital. Somaliland, on the Webi Shebeli and 15 mi. N of Villaggio; wood- and leather-working, rope making.

Mahad Dhahab, Saudi Arabia: see MAHD DHAHAB.

Mahadha, Mahadhah, or **Mahadah** (all: mä'hädhù), village and oasis (pop. 1,000), ⊙ Mahadha dist. of Independent OMAN, 75 mi. SE of Sharja and 22 mi. NE of Baraimi; date groves. Sometimes spelled Mahdha.

Mahaffey, borough (pop. 646), Clearfield co., W central Pa., 22 mi. WSW of Clearfield and on West Branch of Susquehanna R.

Mahagi (mähä'gē), village, Eastern Prov., NE Belgian Congo, on Uganda border, 95 mi. NE of Irumu; alt. 5,656 ft. Tourist center in L. Albert region. Mahagi Port (17 mi. ESE), on the lake, is a steamboat landing for navigation on Albert Nile and excursions to Murchison Falls (on Victoria Nile).

Mahaica (mùhī'kù), village (pop. 486), Demerara co., N Br. Guiana, near the Atlantic, on railroad 18 mi. ESE of Georgetown, in rice-growing area.

Mahaicony, village (pop. 1,179), Demerara co., N Br. Guiana, in fertile Atlantic lowland, on railroad and 28 mi. SE of Georgetown; rice and coconut growing; rice mill.

Mahajamba River (mähädzäm'bù), central and NW Madagascar, rises 45 mi. NE of Ankazobe, flows 200 mi. NW to Mahajamba Bay of Mozambique Channel, in a large delta. Navigable only in lower course, for c.50 mi. Rice growing in its valley. Formerly spelled Majamba.

Mahakam River (mùhùkäm'), **Kutai River,** or **Koetai River** (both: kōōtī'), Indonesian Borneo, rises in mts. in central part of isl., on Sarawak border c.200 mi. ENE of Sintang, flows c.450 mi. generally SE past Samarinda to Macassar Strait 30 mi. E of Samarinda; has wide delta.

Mahalapye (mähälä'pyā), town (pop. 2,453), Ngwato dist., E Bechuanaland Protectorate, in Bamangwato reserve, 200 mi. NNE of Mafeking and on railroad; 23°34'S 26°48'E. Airfield.

Mahalingpur (mŭhä'lĭngpŏŏr), town (pop. 6,990), Bijapur dist., S Bombay, India, 50 mi. SW of Bijapur; trade center for cotton, millet, peanuts, wheat; handicraft cloth weaving. Annual fair.

Mahalla el Kubra, El, or **Al-Mahallat al-Kubra** (both: ĕl măhăl'lĕl-kōōb'rä), city (pop. 115,509), Gharbiya prov., Lower Egypt, on railroad 4 mi. W of Damietta branch of the Nile, and 16 mi. NE of Tanta, 65 mi. N of Cairo. A major textile center of Egypt: cotton ginning, cotton and silk weaving; also cigarette mfg., rice milling. Agr.: cotton, cereals, rice, fruits. Sometimes spelled Mehallet el Kubra and Mehallet el Kebir. In Egypt, popularly called Mahalla.

Mahallat (mähälät'), town (1941 pop. 9,248), Second Prov., in Qum, N central Iran, 60 mi. SSW of Qum, in fertile region; grain, fruit; rugmaking. Hot spring. Home of Agha Khan family. Was ⊙ former Mahallat prov., inc. (1938) into Iran's Second Prov. (see TEHERAN).

Mahallet Damana or **Mahallat Damanah** (măhäl'lĕt dä'mănŭ), village (pop. 6,816), Daqahliya prov., Lower Egypt, on El Bahr el Saghir Canal opposite Minyet Mahallet Damana and 7 mi. ENE of Mansura; cotton, cereals.

Mahallet Marhum or **Mahallat Marhum** (both: märhōōm'), village (pop. 14,185), Gharbiya prov., Lower Egypt, 3 mi. WNW of Tanta; cotton.

Mahallet Minuf or **Mahallat Minuf** (both: mĭnōōf'), village (pop. 6,387), Gharbiya prov., Lower Egypt, 7 mi. NNW of Tanta; cotton.

Mahallet Zaiyad or **Mahallat Zayyad** (both: zī'yăd), village (pop. 9,326), Gharbiya prov., Lower Egypt, 5 mi. NE of El Mahallah el Kubra; cotton.

Maham (mŭhŭm'), town (pop. 11,145), Rohtak dist., SE Punjab, India, 17 mi. WNW of Rohtak; millet, gram, wheat, cotton. Sometimes spelled Meham and Mahm.

Mahamandir, India: see JODHPUR, city.

Mahameroe, Mount, Indonesia: see MAHAMERU, MOUNT.

Mahameru, Mount, or **Mount Mahameroe** (both: mähämĕ'rōō), highest peak (12,060 ft.) of Java, Indonesia, in Semeru Mts., 60 mi. S of Surabaya; volcanic.

Mahamuni (mähämōō'nē) or **Thayettabin** (thŭyĕt'-tŭbĭn"), village, Akyab dist., Lower Burma, in the Arakan, 5 mi. E of Kyauktaw, on arm of Kaladan R.; pilgrimage center with noted pagoda; head of navigation.

Mahan (mähän'), town, Eighth Prov., in Kerman, SE Iran, 20 mi. SE of Kerman and on road to Zahidan; grain, cotton, fruit; noted for its opium. Rugmaking (Kerman rugs). Has tomb of 15th-cent. religious leader of the Sufi sect; center of pilgrimage. Also spelled Mahun.

Mahanadi River (mŭhä'nŭdē) [Sanskrit,=great river], E India, rises in W spur of Eastern Ghats in E Madhya Pradesh, 30 mi. ESE of Kanker; flows WNW, then NNE and E through Chhattisgarh Plain into Orissa, then S past Sambalpur and Sonepur, and ESE through narrow gorge of Eastern Ghats, debouching on coastal plain just W of Cuttack and splitting into numerous branches, its main channel reaching Bay of Bengal near False Point; total length, c.560 mi. Discharges huge volume of water during rainy season, causing severe floods. Fertile valley yields good crops of rice, oilseeds, sugar cane. Supplies several irrigation canals (mainly near Cuttack); dam and hydroelectric plants planned near Sambalpur. Little used for navigation. Chief tributaries are Tel (right), Seonath, Hasdo, Mand, and Ib (left) rivers.

Mahananda River (–nŭndŭ), in West Bengal and Bihar (India) and East Bengal (E Pakistan), formed in SE Nepal Himalayas by headstreams joining NW of Kurseong; flows SSW past Siliguri, and SSE through rich agr. area (rice, jute, barley, corn, mustard), past Old Malda, English Bazar, and Nawabganj, to Padma R. at Godagari; length, c.225 mi.

Mahanayim (mähänä'yēm) or **Mahanaim** (mähä-nīm'), settlement (pop. 175), Upper Galilee, NE Israel, 4 mi. ENE of Safad; tile mfg., mixed farming. Founded 1939, after repeated attempts (since 1898) to settle region had failed.

Mahanoro (mähänōō'rōō), town, Tamatave prov., E Madagascar, small port on coast and Canal des Pangalanes, just N of mouth of Mangoro R., 125 mi. SSW of Tamatave; coffee-shipping center; also vanilla, cloves. R.C. and Protestant missions.

Mahanoy City (mähŭnoi'), borough (pop. 10,934), Schuylkill co., E central Pa., 10 mi. NNE of Pottsville, in hilly anthracite region; clothing, beer. Settled 1859, inc. 1863.

Mahanoy Creek, E central Pa., rises in NW Schuylkill co., flows c.60 mi. W, through coal-mining area, to Susquehanna R. 9 mi. S of Sunbury.

Mahantango Creek (măŭntăng'gō), E central Pa., rises in W Schuylkill co., flows c.35 mi. WSW to Susquehanna R. 5 mi. N of Millersburg.

Maha Nuwara, Ceylon: see KANDY, city.

Maha Oya (mŭ'hŭ ō'yŭ), village, Eastern Prov., Ceylon, 28 mi. SW of Batticaloa. Hot springs near by.

Maharajganj (mŭhäräj'gŭnj). **1** Village, Gorakhpur dist., E Uttar Pradesh, India, 30 mi. NNE of Gorakhpur; rice, wheat, barley. **2** Town (pop. 1,993), Rae Bareli dist., central Uttar Pradesh, India, 11 mi. NNE of Rae Bareli; rice, wheat, barley, gram. Sometimes spelled Maharajgunj.

Maharajnagar, India: see CHARKHARI, town.

Maharajpur (mŭhä'räjpŏŏr). **1** Village, Madhya Bharat, India: see LASHKAR. **2** Rail settlement, Madhya Pradesh, India: see MANDLA, town. **3** Town (pop. 5,195), N Vindhya Pradesh, India, 11 mi. NE of Chhatarpur; millet, gram, oilseeds; betel gardens.

Maharashtra (mŭhä'rŭshtrŭ), region of W peninsular India; traditional country of the Mahrattas and home of the Marathi-speaking community. Comprises all of the Konkan in Bombay from Karwar to Damão; in N, extends inland across Western Ghats and onto N Deccan Plateau as far as Nagpur in Madhya Pradesh; E boundary runs roughly SW through NW Hyderabad to Sholapur, Kolhapur, and Karwar in Bombay. Mahrattas—a Scytho-Dravidian race—have played important part in Indian history; asserted independence under Sivaji in 2d half of 17th cent., upon breakup of Mogul empire and Deccan sultanates. In late-18th cent., while under the peshwas, Mahrattas became dominant power in India but internal dissensions led to rapid downfall and eventual defeat by the English in 1818. Poona and Satara are principal centers of Maharashtra.

Mahares (mähärĕs'), town (pop. 5,347), Sfax dist., E Tunisia, fishing port on Gulf of Gabès, 20 mi. SW of Sfax; oil-processing and marketing center.

Mahasamund (mŭhä'sŭmōōnd), village, Raipur dist., E Madhya Pradesh, India, 32 mi. ESE of Raipur; rice milling. Sal, bamboo, myrobalan in near-by forests (sawmilling).

Mahasarakham (mŭhä'sä'rŭkäm'), town (1947 pop. 11,816), ⊙ Mahasarakham prov. (□ 3,463; 1947 pop. 390,294), E Thailand, in Korat Plateau, on Chi R. and 55 mi. ESE of Khonkaen; road center; cotton, rice, corn, tobacco; hog raising. Sometimes spelled Mahasaragam. N section of prov. was separated in 1940s to form KALASIN prov.

Mahaska (mŭhă'skŭ), county (□ 572; pop. 24,672), S central Iowa; ⊙ Oskaloosa. Rolling prairie agr. area (hogs, cattle, sheep, poultry, corn, oats, hay) drained by Des Moines, Skunk, and North Skunk rivers. Bituminous-coal deposits mined in SW; limestone quarries. Includes Lake Keomah State Park. Formed 1843.

Mahaska, city (pop. 179), Washington co., N Kansas, near Nebr. line, 33 mi. NNE of Concordia, in grain and livestock area.

Mahasu (mŭhä'sōō), district, Himachal Pradesh, India; ⊙ Kasumpti.

Mahates (mähä'tĕs), town (pop. 3,238), Bolívar dept., N Colombia, in Caribbean lowlands, near Canal del Dique, 28 mi. SE of Cartagena; sugar cane, corn, cattle.

Mahatsinjo (mähätsĕn'dzōō), village, Majunga prov., N central Madagascar, on highway and 60 mi. SSE of Maevatanana; communications point; rice, cattle.

Mahatwar, India: see SAHATWAR.

Mahavavy River (mähävä'vē). **1** In N Madagascar, rises in Tsaratanana Massif, flows N past Ambilobe and NW, forming a large estuary, to Mozambique Channel; c.100 mi. long. **2** In W central and NW Madagascar, rises 200 mi. WNW of Tananarive, flows N past Mitsinjo and Namakia to Mozambique Channel; c.200 mi. long.

Mahavinyaka (mŭhä'vĭnyŭkŭ), sacred hill (1,294 ft.) in Cuttack dist., E Orissa, India, 20 mi. NE of Cuttack; Hindu shrines.

Mahaweli Ganga (mŭhä'vĕlē gŭng'gŭ), longest (206 mi.) river of Ceylon, rises on Hatton Plateau just NW of Hatton; flows N through extensive tea and rubber plantations on Hatton and Kandy plateaus, past Nawalapitiya, Gampola, Kadugannawa, and Kandy, E past MINIPE, and N past Alutnuwara to Koddiyar Bay 7 mi. S of Trincomalee. Main tributary, the Amban Ganga (left). In middle course, forms Central Prov.–Uva Prov. boundary.

Mahbubabad (mäbōō'bäbäd), town (pop. 7,463), Warangal dist., SE Hyderabad state, India, 40 mi. SE of Warangal; rice and oilseed milling; matches. Sometimes spelled Mahboobabad.

Mahbubnagar (mäbōōb'nŭgŭr), district (□ 5,326; pop. 1,088,209), S Hyderabad state, India, on Deccan Plateau; ⊙ Mahbubnagar. Bounded S by Kistna R.; mainly lowland except for forested hills in SE (teak, ebony, gum arabic). Largely sandy red soil; millet, oilseeds (chiefly castor beans, peanuts), rice. Oilseed and rice milling, biri mfg., tanning; cattle raising. Main towns: Mahbubnagar, Narayanpet. Became part of Hyderabad during state's formation in 18th cent. Pop. 85% Hindu, 9% Moslem.

Mahbubnagar, town (pop. 16,462), ⊙ Mahbubnagar dist., S Hyderabad state, India, 55 mi. SW of Hyderabad; road center; millet, tobacco; oilseed and rice milling here and in surrounding villages.

Mahdara Maryam (mä'därä mär'yäm), village, Begemdir prov., NW Ethiopia, 13 mi. SW of Debra Tabor, in cereal-growing and stock-raising (horses, mules, sheep) region; trade center. Has church and monastery.

Mahd Dhahab (mä'hŭd dhähäb'), village, central Hejaz, Saudi Arabia, 100 mi. SE of Medina; gold mining center. Also spelled Mahad Dhahab.

Mahdha, Oman: see MAHADHA.

Mahdia, gold fields and airfield, Essequibo co., central Br. Guiana, along small river (affluent of the Potaro) of the same name, SW of Tumatumari.

Mahdia (mädē'ä), town (pop. 9,251), ⊙ Mahdia dist. (1946 pop. 77,709), E Tunisia, fishing port on the central Mediterranean, 32 mi. SE of Sousse; rail-spur terminus; sardine canning, fish salting and drying, olive-oil processing, soap mfg., textile spinning. Sponge fisheries, saltworks. Situated on a narrow promontory (1 mi. long) called Cape Africa, Mahdia preserves a *casbah* (16th cent.) and old fortifications. The port (S) was cut out of sheer rock. Founded A.D. 912 on site of a Phoenician and Roman settlement, it became capital of the Fatimite dynasty. A stronghold of Barbary pirates in 16th-17th cent., town was visited by several European punitive expeditions. Mahdia dist. was carved out of Sousse dist. in 1941. Also spelled Mahedia.

Mahé (mää'), town and settlement (after 1947 officially "free city"; □ 23; pop. 18,293) of Fr. India, within Malabar dist., SW Madras, India, on Arabian Sea, 35 mi. NW of Calicut; consists of town proper (on coast) and a detached rural section (just NE). Trades in coconuts, mangoes, areca nuts, and in pepper from forested hills of the Wynaad. The only Fr. possession on India's W coast; occupied c.1725 by French; taken twice (1761, 1779) by English; finally restored 1817 to French.

Mahébourg (mä-ābōōr'), town (pop. 6,020), SE Mauritius, port on the Grand Port (inlet of Indian Ocean), 20 mi. SE of Port Louis; railhead for rich sugar-growing region. Sugar milling and alcohol distilling at Beau Vallon (pop. 1,031), just S. Was ⊙ Mauritius in 18th cent. Developed as auxiliary naval base during Second World War, with airfield at Plaisance, 3 mi. SW.

Mahedia, Tunisia: see MAHDIA.

Mahee (mŭhē'), island (176 acres, 1½ mi. long) in Strangford Lough, NE Co. Down, Northern Ireland, 7 mi. SSE of Newtownards; site of remains of Nendrum Abbey, probably founded in 5th cent., restored 1922.

Mahé Group (mä-ā'), archipelago of the Seychelles off NE Mahé Isl. Includes St. Anne, Cerf, Moyenne, and Longue isls.

Mahé Island, second largest but most important island (□ 56; pop. 28,197) of the Seychelles, in Indian Ocean 1,100 mi. E of Mombasa (Kenya) and 700 mi. NE of N tip of Madascar; 4°40'S 55°30'E; 17 mi. long, 3–7 mi. wide. Consists of a rugged granitic upland and a narrow littoral. Highest point is Morne Seychellois (2,993 ft.). Grows coconuts, patchouli, vanilla, palmarosa. Cinnamon and Casuarina trees. Victoria, ⊙ Seychelles, is on NE coast.

Mahendraganj (mŭhän'drŭgŭnj), village, Garo Hills dist., W Assam, India, near Brahmaputra R., 27 mi. WSW of Tura; rice, cotton, mustard, jute.

Mahendragiri (–gĭ"rē). **1** Peak (4,923 ft.) of Eastern Ghats, in Ganjam dist., SE Orissa, India, 36 mi. SW of Berhampur; temples at summit include one built (11th cent.) by Chola dynasty. Sometimes written Mahendra Giri. **2** Peak (5,427 ft.) near S end of Western Ghats, S India, 45 mi. ESE of Trivandrum.

Mahenge (mähĕng'gā), town, Eastern Prov., Tanganyika, on road and 125 mi. S of Kilosa; rice, corn, cotton; cattle, sheep, goats.

Mahesh, India: see SERAMPORE.

Maheshpur, E Pakistan: see MAHESPUR.

Maheshwar (mŭhäsh'vŭr), town (pop. 6,946), SW Madhya Bharat, India, on Narbada R. and 40 mi. SSW of Indore; markets cotton, millet, oilseeds; handicraft cloth weaving and dyeing (saris, dhotis). An anc. site in Hindu legend; from c.1767 to 1818, was ⊙ Holkar family.

Mahespur (mŭhās'pŏŏr), town (pop. 3,785), Jessore dist., W East Bengal, E Pakistan, on river arm of Ganges Delta and 23 mi. NW of Jessore; rice, jute, oilseeds, tobacco. Also spelled Maheshpur.

Mahia Peninsula (mä'hyŭ), E N.Isl., New Zealand, 55 mi. across Hawke Bay from Napier; 15 mi. long, 5 mi. wide. Joined to mainland by narrow isthmus.

Mahidasht (mähēdäsht'), village, Fifth Prov., in Kermanshah, W Iran, 15 mi. WSW of Kermanshah and on road to Qasr-i-Shirin; grain, tobacco, opium; sheep raising (wool); rugmaking.

Mahidpur, India: see MEHIDPUR.

Mahim (mä'hēm). **1** Village (pop. 6,561), Thana dist., W Bombay, India, on Arabian Sea, 45 mi. N of Bombay; trades in sugar cane, plantains, rice; betel farming, fishing (pomfrets), bone-fertilizer mfg. Also called Kelve. **2** Section of Bombay, India: see BOMBAY, city.

Mahina (mähēnä'), railroad station for Bafoulabé, SW Fr. Sudan, Fr. West Africa, on Bafing R., on Dakar-Niger RR, and 3½ mi. S of Bafoulabé.

Mahi River (mŭ'hē), W India, rises in W Vindhya Range just S of Sardarpur, W Madhya Bharat;

flows N into S Rajasthan, and SW through N Bombay to head of Gulf of Cambay; c.360 mi. long.
Mahiyangana, Ceylon: see ALUTNUWARA.
Mahjaba (mä'jăbŭ), town, ⊙ Upper Yafa sultanate, Western Aden Protectorate, 70 mi. NNE of Aden; 13°49'N 45°13'E. Also spelled Majaba.
Mahlaing (mŭhlīn'), village, Meiktila dist., Upper Burma, on railroad and 20 mi. NW of Meiktila.
Mahlberg (mäl'bĕrk), village (pop. 1,062), S Baden, Germany, 4 mi. SSW of Lahr; tobacco industry. Has castle.
Mahlog, former princely state, India: see MAILOG.
Mahm, India: see MAHAM.
Mahmudabad (mämōō'däbäd), town (pop. 9,738), Sitapur dist., central Uttar Pradesh, India, 32 mi. SE of Sitapur; brassware mfg.; trades in wheat, rice, gram, barley, sugar cane.
Mahmudiya, Al, or **Al-Mahmudiyah** (äl mämōō-dē'yŭ), town, Baghdad prov., central Iraq, on railroad and 20 mi. S of Baghdad, bet. the Tigris and the Euphrates; dates, sesame, millet.
Mahmudiya, El, or **Al-Mahmudiyah** (both: ĕl–), town (pop. 13,610), Beheira prov., Lower Egypt, at E end of Mahmudiya Canal on Rosetta branch of the Nile and 10 mi. NNE of Damanhur; wool weaving; cotton.
Mahmudiya Canal or **Al-Mahmudiyah Canal,** navigable canal, Lower Egypt, extends 50 mi. from Rosetta branch of the Nile at El 'Atf, W through Beheira prov., to Mediterranean Sea at Alexandria; average width, 100 ft. Constructed 1819, it diverted most of the Nile trade to Alexandria.
Mahne Yehuda (mä'hŭnä yĕhōōdä'), residential settlement (pop. 800), W Israel, in Plain of Sharon, just SW of Petah Tiqva. Founded 1912.
Mahnomen (mônō'mŭn), county (□ 574; pop. 7,059), NW Minn.; ⊙ Mahnomen. Agr. area drained by Wild Rice R. Dairy products, livestock, grain. Lies within White Earth Indian Reservation. Co. formed 1906.
Mahnomen, village (pop. 1,464), ⊙ Mahnomen co., NW Minn., on Wild Rice R., in White Earth Indian Reservation, and c.50 mi. WSW of Bemidji; trading point for livestock, poultry, dairy cooperatives; also flour, lumber.
Maho (mŭhō'), village, North Western Prov., Ceylon, 24 mi. NNW of Kurunegala; rail junction; rice, vegetables, coconuts.
Mahoba (mŭhō'bŭ), town (pop. 17,224), Hamirpur dist., S Uttar Pradesh, India, on railroad and 80 mi. ESE of Jhansi; road junction; trade center (gram, jowar, oilseeds, wheat, pearl millet). Has 14th-cent. mosque. Founded A.D. c.800 by a noted Chandel Rajput; civil ⊙ Chandel Rajputs until moved (c.1182) to Kalinjar. Captured by Kutb-ud-din Aibak in 1202. Extensive Chandel Rajput, Jain, and Buddhist remains surround near-by artificial lakes, including 24 rock-hewn images dated 1149.
Maholi, India: see MUTTRA, city.
Mahomet (mŭhŏ'mĭt), village (pop. 1,017), Champaign co., E central Ill., on Sangamon R. and 9 mi. WNW of Champaign, in agr. area.
Mahón (mäōn'), anc. *Portus Magonis*, chief city (pop. 14,301) of Minorca, Balearic Isls., port on fine sheltered inlet (c.2½ mi. long, 600 yards wide) guarded by La Mola (or Isabel II) and San Felipe forts, 90 mi. ENE of Palma (Majorca) and 150 mi. SE of Barcelona; 39°53'N 4°16'E. Important air and naval base (torpedo boats, submarines). Ships barley, dried fruit, wine, cheese, honey, cattle, iron, shoes. Historic city was founded by Carthaginians and named for Hannibal's brother Mago. Passed to Romans and Moors, and later became tributary to kings of Aragon. It was taken (1535) and held by corsairs, until occupied (1708) by the British, who called it Port Mahon (mŭhōn'); for a short period the French held it; finally recovered (1782) by Spain.
Mahon, Lough (lŏkh mŭhōōn', mŭhōn'), NW reach (4 mi. long) of Cork Harbour, Co. Cork, Ireland; estuary of Lee R.
Mahonda (mähōn'dä), village, N Zanzibar, on road and 13 mi. NNE of Zanzibar town; cloves, copra, citrus fruit.
Mahone Bay (mŭhōn'), town (pop. 1,025), S N.S., on W shore of Mahone Bay, 40 mi. WSW of Halifax; shipbuilding, lumbering.
Mahone Bay, inlet (12 mi. long, 9 mi. wide at entrance) of the Atlantic, S N.S., 30 mi. WSW of Halifax. On bay are towns of Chester and Mahone Bay. There are numerous isls., including Oak Isl., reputed site of Captain Kidd's hidden treasure. Great Tancook Isl. (3 mi. long) is the largest.
Mahoning (mŭhō'nĭng), county (□ 419; pop. 257,629), E Ohio; ⊙ YOUNGSTOWN. Bounded E by Pa. line; intersected by Mahoning and Little Beaver rivers. Agr. (livestock, grain, poultry, fruit; dairy products); coal mining; limestone quarries. Includes Milton Reservoir and part of Berlin Reservoir. Formed 1846.
Mahoning Creek, W central Pa., rises in W Clearfield co., flows c.60 mi. generally W, past Punxsutawney, to Allegheny R. 9 mi. N of Kittanning. Flood-control dam (160 ft. high, 926 ft. long; completed 1943) is c.22 mi. above mouth.
Mahoning River, in Ohio and Pa., rises in region E of Canton, Ohio, flows NW to Alliance, then NE to Warren, whence it turns SE, flowing past Warren, Niles, and Youngstown, and into Pa., joining Shenango R. to form Beaver R. at New Castle; c.90 mi. long. Near Alliance, Berlin Dam (completed 1943; 5,750 ft. long, 95 ft. high) impounds Berlin Reservoir (capacity 91,200 acre-ft.) for flood control and industrial water supply. Just downstream is Milton Reservoir (c.5 mi. long), impounded in 1916.
Mahopac (mā'ōpăk, mā'hō–), resort and residential village (1940 pop. 1,109), Putnam co., SE N.Y., on E shore of L. Mahopac (c.1½ mi. in diameter), 12 mi. NE of Peekskill, in dairying and poultry-raising area.
Mahopac, Lake, N.Y.: see MAHOPAC.
Mahora, Kashmir: see MAHURA.
Mahora (mäō'rä), town (pop. 2,332), Albacete prov., SE central Spain, 17 mi. NE of Albacete; brandy distilling; stock raising, lumbering; wine, cereals, saffron, fruit.
Mahot or **Mahwat** (both: măhōt'), town of SE Oman, on Mahot isl. (1 mi. across) in the Ghubbah Hashish (an inlet of Arabian Sea); 20°32'N 58°10'E. Chief trade center of SE Oman coast.
Mahra, Aden: see MAHRI.
Mahrah, Aden: see MAHRI.
Mahras, El, or **Al-Mahras** (both: ĕl mä'räs), village (pop. 7,726), Asyut prov., central Upper Egypt, on Ibrahimiya Canal, on railroad, and 19 mi. S of Minya; cereals, dates, sugar cane.
Mahrauli or **Mehrauli** (mŭrou'lē), town (pop. 6,050), S Delhi, India, 8 mi. SSW of New Delhi city center; handicraft glass-bangle making, cotton weaving, pottery, and leather work. Just N, within ruined walls of a 12th-cent. Chauhan Rajput citadel, is Lal Kot (red fort; 1052). Here are several mosques and tombs (late-12th to late-14th cent.)—remarkable examples of synthesis of Islamic and earlier architectural styles. Most notable is the Kutb (or Qutb) Minar, a free-standing stone tower (erected 1225), rising 238 ft. from base diameter of 47 ft.; its lower 3 stories are of fluted red sandstone, upper 2 (rebuilt 1368) are faced with white marble. Near by stands the famous Iron Pillar—a shaft of purely wrought iron (c.24 ft. high; c.1 ft. in diameter; has early Gupta inscriptions). Believed forged at least as early as 5th cent. A.D., this remarkable example of anc. metallurgical skill has remained rustless through the centuries; brought here from an unknown site in 11th cent. Town also spelled Meherauli; sometimes called Qutb or Old Delhi (for the ruins of several cities in vicinity which figured in early history of DELHI state).
Mähren, Czechoslovakia: see MORAVIA.
Mahri, Mahra, or **Mahrah** (all: mä'rŭ), easternmost tribal area (pop. 20,000) of Eastern Aden Protectorate, forming mainland section of the Mahri sultanate of Qishn and SOCOTRA; ⊙ Qishn. Situated on Arabian Sea at entrance to Gulf of Aden, it extends from c.50°30'E to the cape Ras Dharbat 'Ali on Oman frontier. Area has fisheries and some trade in frankincense. Chief centers are Qishn, Seihut, and Hafat. Protectorate relations with Socotra date from 1886, but the Aden govt. exercises no control over the Mahri mainland. Pop. speaks South Arabic dialect, similar to that of Socotra and differing from the standard North Arabic language.
Mährisch-Altstadt, Czechoslovakia: see STARE MESTO.
Mährisch-Budwitz, Czechoslovakia: see MORAVSKE BUDEJOVICE.
Mährisch-Kromau, Czechoslovakia: see MORAVSKY KRUMLOV.
Mährisch-Neustadt, Czechoslovakia: see UNICOV.
Mährisch-Ostrau, Czechoslovakia: see OSTRAVA.
Mährisch-Schönberg, Czechoslovakia: see SUMPERK.
Mährisch-Trübau, Czechoslovakia: see MORAVSKA TREBOVA.
Mährisch-Weisskirchen: see HRANICE.
Mahroni (mŭrō'nē), town (pop. 3,232), Jhansi dist., S Uttar Pradesh, India, 21 mi. ESE of Lalitpur; jowar, oilseeds, wheat, gram. Sandstone quarry and extensive Chandel Rajput remains 23 mi. S, at village of Madanpur.
Mahtomedi (mä"tōmē'dī), village (pop. 1,375), Washington co., E Minn., on White Bear L. and 11 mi. NNE of St. Paul, in agr. area (grain, potatoes, livestock, poultry). Inc. 1931.
Mahun, Iran: see MAHAN.
Mahura (mŭhō'rŭ) or **Mahora** (mŭhō'rŭ), village, Muzaffarabad dist., W Kashmir, on Jhelum R. and 4 mi. NE of Uri; hydroelectric station completed 1907. Anc. Hindu temple ruins near by.
Mahuva (mŭ'hōōvŭ). **1** Town (pop. 2,093), Surat dist., N Bombay, India, on Purna R. and 22 mi. SE of Surat; cotton, millet, rice. **2** Town (pop. 22,058), SE Saurashtra, India, near Gulf of Cambay, 55 mi. SSW of Bhaunagar; market center (grain, cotton, oilseeds, timber, cloth fabrics); cotton, oilseed, and flour milling, hand-loom weaving, wood carving; sawmills. Coconuts, betel vine, mangoes grown near by. Several annual festival fairs celebrated here. Port is 2 mi. S; exports cotton and grain. Town formerly in Bhaunagar state.
Mahwah (mô'wô), village (pop. 2,471, with Cragmere), Bergen co., extreme N N.J., near Ramapo R. and N.Y. line, 12 mi. N of Paterson; railroad and automotive supplies.
Mahwat, Oman: see MAHOT.
Mahya Dag, Turkey: see MAYA DAG.
Mai, New Hebrides: see SHEPHERD ISLANDS.
Mai, El, or **Al-May** (both: ĕl mī'), village (pop. 8,335), Minufiya prov., Lower Egypt, 2 mi. SW of Shibin el Kom; cereals, cotton, flax.
Maia (mä'yŭ), town (pop. 711), Pôrto dist., N Portugal, 6 mi. N of Oporto; distilling.
Maiamai or **Meyamey** (both: määmä'), town (1933 pop. estimate 5,000), Second Prov., in Shahrud, NE Iran, 38 mi. E of Shahrud and on Meshed-Teheran road; wheat, cotton; rugmaking. Airfield. Sometimes spelled Mayamay and Meiomai.
Maiana (mī'ä'nä), island (□ 10.3; pop. 1,425), N Gilbert Isls., W central Pacific; 55'N 173°E; 9 mi. long; copra. Formerly Hall Isl.
Maiano (mäyä'nô), village (pop. 1,209), Udine prov., Friuli–Venezia Giulia, NE Italy, 11 mi. NW of Udine; shoe factory.
Maiao (mī'ou') or **Tubuai Manu** (tōō'bōōī'mä'-nōō), atoll (□ c.3; pop. 200), Windward group, Society Isls., Fr. Oceania, S Pacific, 60 mi. W of Tahiti, of which it is a dependency. Coconuts, large crabs. Sometimes called Tupuaemanu.
Maibang or **Maibong** (both: mī'bŭng), village, North Cachar Hills dist., central Assam, India, in NW foothills of Barail Range, 40 mi. NNE of Silchar; rice, cotton, sugar cane. Was ⊙ 16th-cent. Kachari kingdom. Rock carvings near by.
Maibara (mī'bärä), town (pop. 7,492), Shiga prefecture, S Honshu, Japan, on E shore of L. Biwa, 4 mi. NNE of Hikone; rail junction; commercial center in agr. area (rice, market produce); raw silk. Fishing. Site of trout farm of prefectural fisheries experiment station.
Maibong, India: see MAIBANG.
Maibud or **Meybod** (both: mābōd'), village, Tenth Prov., in Yezd, central Iran, 40 mi. NW of Yezd; cotton, pistachio nuts, grain, pomegranates. Handmade earthenware.
Maicanesti (mŭēkŭnĕsht'), Rum. *Măicăneşti*, village (pop. 34), Putna prov., E central Rumania, 22 mi. NE of Ramnicu-Sarat.
Mai Ceu, Ethiopia: see MAI CHIO.
Maîche (māsh), town (pop. 2,055), Doubs dept., E France, in the central Jura, 18 mi. S of Montbéliard; produces watches, lighters, pipes; cheese making, distilling.
Mai Chio (mī'chē'ō), Ital. *Mai Ceu*, village (pop. 500), Tigre prov., N Ethiopia, N of L. Ashangi, on road and 16 mi. N of Quoram, in cereal- and coffee-growing region; salt market. Bet. here and L. Ashangi (S) a decisive battle was won (1936) by Italians in Italo-Ethiopian War.
Maida (mī'dä), town (pop. 3,962), Catanzaro prov., Calabria, S Italy, 13 mi. WSW of Catanzaro; olive oil, wine.
Maida (mā'dŭ), village, Cavalier co., NE N.Dak., port of entry at Can. line, 15 mi. N of Langdon.
Maidan, Al, El Maidan, or **Al-Maydan** (äl mī'dän, ĕl) [Arabic,=the cities], name applied by the Arabs (A.D. c.641) to a group of cities in Mesopotamia (modern Iraq), including principally CTESIPHON and SELEUCIA. Also spelled Al Madain and Al Medain.
Maidane Ekbez, Syria: see MEIDAN EKBES.
Maidanek, Poland: see LUBLIN, city.
Maidan Kazenny, Russian SFSR: see KAZENNY MAIDAN.
Maidanpek, Yugoslavia: see MAJDAN PEK.
Maiden, town (pop. 1,952), Catawba co., W central N.C., 6 mi. S of Newton; textile mfg.
Maiden Castle, ancient fortress town, S Dorset, England, 2 mi. SW of Dorchester; finest earthwork in Great Britain; c.115 acres. Evidences of neolithic village dating from c.2000 B.C. were found during excavations, 1934–37. An Iron Age fortified village, established here c.300 B.C., is believed to have been taken later by Romans and occupied until about A.D. 70.
Maidenhead, residential municipal borough (1931 pop. 17,515; 1951 census 27,125), E Berkshire, England, on the Thames (bridged) and 27 mi. W of London; resort.
Maiden Rock, fishing village (pop. 269), Pierce co., W Wis., on L. Pepin, 11 mi. E of Red Wing (Minn.), surrounded by bluffs. Silicate-rock mine is near by.
Maidens, Scotland: see KIRKOSWALD.
Maidens, Va.: see GOOCHLAND, village.
Maidens, The, or **Hulin Rocks** (hū'lĭn), group of islets in the North Channel off E coast of Co. Antrim, Northern Ireland, 7 mi. NE of Larne; 54°56'N 5°44'W; has 2 lighthouses.
Maidi, Yemen: see MIDI.
Maidos, Turkey: see ECEABAT.
Maidstone, village (pop. 453), W Sask., 50 mi. WNW of North Battleford; grain elevators.
Maidstone (mād'stŭn), municipal borough (1931 pop. 42,280; 1951 census 54,026), ⊙ Kent, England, in center of co., on Medway R. and 30 mi. ESE of London; hop market and brewing center, with mfg. of paper, cement, agr. machinery, pharmaceuticals. The Elizabethan Chillington Manor contains mus. and library and is hq. of Kent Archaeological Society. Other features are grammar school (1549), All Saints Church (14th cent.), archbishops' palace (15th cent.), All Saints Col., and hosp. for Canterbury pilgrims, founded 1260

Penenden Heath is large recreation area. The town was a Roman station. Center of rebellions led by Tyler (1381), Cade (1450), and Sir Thomas Wyatt (1554). Disraeli fought his 1st successful election here. William Hazlitt b. here, and near by is Cobtree Manor, the "Dingley Dell" of Dickens's *Pickwick Papers.*

Maidstone (mād′stōn), town (pop. 81), Essex co., NE Vt., on the Connecticut, just above Guildhall. Maidstone L. (c.3 mi. long; fishing) is W.

Maiduguri (mīdōō′gŏorē), town (pop. 24,359), ⊙ Bornu prov., Northern Provinces, NE Nigeria, 320 mi. E of Kano; alt. 1,186 ft.; 11°49′N 13°9′E. Agr. trade center; peanuts, cotton, cassava, millet, durra, gum arabic; cattle raising, lumbering. Has hosp., leper colony, experimental farm. Airfield. Town consists of Maiduguri proper, Br. residency, and native town of Yerwa, (just N). Capital of Bornu moved here (1908) from Kukawa.

Maidum, Egypt: see MEDUM.

Maiella (mäyĕl′lä), second highest mountain group of the Apennines, S central Italy, SSE of Gran Sasso d'Italia; extends c.20 mi. N–S along Chieti-Aquila prov. border; rises to 9,170 ft. in Monte Amaro. Formerly also Majella.

Maienfeld (mī′ŭnfĕlt″), circle (pop. 3,607) and town (pop. 1,488), Grisons canton, E Switzerland. The town, on the Rhine and 11 mi. N of Chur, has a ruined castle.

Maifa, Aden: see MEIFA.

Maifa'a, Wadi, Aden: see MEIFA'A, WADI.

Maignelay (mĕnyŭlā′), village (pop. 684), Oise dept., N France, 7 mi. SSW of Montdidier; mfg. (pumps, flour products). Has Gothic 15th–16th-cent. church.

Maigualida, Cordillera (kôrdĭyā′rä mīgwälē′dä), range in S Venezuela, on Bolívar state–Amazonas territory border, spur of Guiana Highlands, 150 mi. E of Puerto Ayacucho; extends c.70 mi. N–S; rises over 5,000 ft.

Mai Gudo (mī′ gōō′dō), peak (c.11,120 ft.), SW Ethiopia, 30 mi. ESE of Jimma, in mts. bet. Omo, Gibbe, and Gojab rivers. Iron mined at village of Omo.

Maihar (mī′hŭr), town (pop. 8,495), S Vindhya Pradesh, India, 22 mi. S of Satna; trades in wheat, millet, gram; limestone works. Was ⊙ former princely state of Maihar (□ 412; pop. 79,558) of Central India agency; since 1948, state merged with Vindhya Pradesh.

Maihaugen, Norway: see LILLEHAMMER.

Maihingen (mī′ĭng-ŭn), village (pop. 735), Swabia, W Bavaria, Germany, 5 mi. N of Nördlingen. The former Franciscan monastery contains, since 1840, the large library of the princes of Öttingen-Wallerstein, including 1,500 incunabula, 1,500 manuscripts, 33,000 copper engravings, a collection of coins and of 11th–16th-cent. ivory carvings.

Maikain or **Maykain** (mīkŭēn′), town (1948 pop. over 2,000), SW Pavlodar oblast, Kazakh SSR, near S.Siberian RR, 75 mi. SW of Pavlodar; gold-mining center; copper deposits.

Maikaiti, China: see MERKET.

Maikammer (mī′kä″mŭr), village (pop. 3,691), Rhenish Palatinate, W Germany, on E slope of Hardt Mts., 3 mi. S of Neustadt; wine.

Maikapchakai, China: see CHIMUNAI.

Maikoor, Indonesia: see ARU ISLANDS.

Maikop or **Maykop** (mīkôp′), city (1939 pop. 67,302), ⊙ Adyge Autonomous Oblast, Krasnodar Territory, Russian SFSR, at N foot of the Greater Caucasus, on Belaya R. and 60 mi. SE of Krasnodar, on rail branch from Belorechenskaya. Industrial center; lumber and tobacco industry; furniture mfg., food processing (flour and dairy products, canned goods), distilling, tanning. Maikop oil fields (discovered 1900–01) are SW, with main centers at APSHERONSK, NEFTEGORSK, KHODYZHENSKI, and KUTAIS. City has regional mus., teachers col. Founded 1858 as Rus. fortress. During Second World War, held (1942–43) by Germans.

Maikor or **Maykor** (mīkôr′), town (1926 pop. 3,932), central Molotov oblast, Russian SFSR, on right tributary of Kama R. and 20 mi. NNW of Chermoz, on rail spur; metallurgical center (pig iron). Peat digging, charcoal burning near by. Formerly Maikorski Zavod.

Maikur, Indonesia: see ARU ISLANDS.

Mailisai or **Maylisay** (mīlyĭsī′), town (1947 pop. over 500), central Dzhalal-Abad oblast, Kirghiz SSR, on small Maili-Sai R. and 38 mi. NW of Dzhalal-Abad; oil wells; mining of vanadium and radioactive ores.

Maillane (mīän′), village (pop. 1,094), Bouches-du-Rhône dept., SE France, 12 mi. NNE of Arles; fruits, olives. Poet Mistral b. near by.

Maillén Island (mīyĕn′) (□ 6.6; pop. 1,118), Llanquihue prov., S central Chile, in Reloncaví Sound, 7 mi. S of Puerto Montt; stock raising, dairying.

Maillezais (mäyŭzā′), village (pop. 617), Vendée dept., W France, 7 mi. SSE of Fontenay-le-Comte; dairying, sawmilling. Has ruins of an abbey surrounded by 16th–17th-cent. fortifications.

Mailly-Champagne (mäyē′-shăpä′nyŭ), village (pop. 668), Marne dept., N France, on NE slope of the Montagne de Reims, 8 mi. SSE of Rheims; wine-growing (champagne).

Mailly-le-Camp (–lŭ-kā′), village (pop. 1,211), Aube dept., NE central France, 17 mi. WSW of Vitry-le-François. Large military camp near by.

Mailog or **Mahlog** (mī′lōg), former princely state (□ 49; pop. 8,631) of Punjab Hill States, India, SW of Simla; ⊙ was Patta. Since 1948, merged with Himachal Pradesh.

Mailpatti, India: see AMBUR.

Mailsi (mīl′sē), town (pop. 6,511), Multan dist., S Punjab, W Pakistan, 50 mi. SE of Multan, near Sutlej R.; local market for wheat, rice, millet; cotton ginning.

Maimachen or **Maimachin,** Mongolia: see ALTAN BULAK.

Maimana or **Maimanah** (mī′mŭnŭ, mī″mŭnŭ′), province (□ 15,000; pop. 400,000), N Afghanistan, in Afghan Turkestan; ⊙ Maimana. Bounded N by Turkmen SSR of USSR, it consists of desert lowland and irrigated oases (N) and mountainous outliers (Band-i-Turkestan) of the Hindu Kush (S). Main oasis centers are Maimana, Daulatabad, and Andkhui, all located on highway bet. Herat and Mazar-i-Sharif. Prov. is leading karakul-producing area of country. Oases, drained by Qaisar R., produce grain, oilseed (sesame), fruit, and wine. Karakul, hide, and wool trade, and rug weaving are important. Pop. is largely Turkmen and Uzbek. Long ruled by semi-independent Uzbek khanate, area in 1880s came under Afghan rule.

Maimana or **Maimanah,** town (pop. 25,000), ⊙ Maimana prov., N Afghanistan, in Afghan Turkestan, on Qaisar R. and 140 mi. WSW of Mazar-i-Sharif, on highway to Herat, at N foot of the Band-i-Turkestan; alt. 2,860 ft.; center of irrigation area (fruit, sesame, beans); karakul trade with nomads. Weaving of carpets, woolen and cotton cloth. Was ⊙ semi-independent Uzbek khanate until final subjection (1880s) by Afghanistan.

Maimansingh, E Pakistan: see MYMENSINGH, district.

Maimará (mīmärä′), town (pop. estimate 500), central Jujuy prov., Argentina, on railroad, on the Río Grande de Jujuy and 40 mi. NNW of Jujuy; corn, alfalfa, cotton, fruit, livestock; flour milling.

Mai Munene (mī′mōōnĕ′nā), village, Kasai prov., S Belgian Congo, landing on Kasai R. and 90 mi. SSW of Luebo. Has R.C. mission, agr. school.

Ma'in, Yemen: see JAUF.

Maina (mī′nŭ) or **Mani** (mä′nē), region in the S Taygetus, Laconia nome, S Peloponnesus, Greece. The Mainotes were known for their resistance against Turkish rule; played active role in Gr. war of independence.

Maina or **Mayna** (mī′nŭ), village (1948 pop. over 2,000), N Ulyanovsk oblast, Russian SFSR, 35 mi. SW of Ulyanovsk; coriander-oil extracting.

Main à Dieu (mănŭdōō′), village (pop. estimate 200), NE N.S., E Cape Breton Isl., on the Atlantic, 19 mi. SE of Sydney; cod fisheries.

Mainalon (mā′nŭlôn), Lat. *Maenalus,* mountains in central Peloponnesus, Greece; rise to 6,496 ft. 11 mi. NNW of Tripolis.

Mainau (mī′nou), small island (15 acres), S Baden, Germany, in the Überlinger See (a branch of L. of Constance), 3 mi. N of Constance; connected by bridge with mainland. Belonged (1272–1805) to Teutonic Knights. Castle (18th-cent.) is property of Swedish royal house.

Mainbernheim (mīn″bĕrn′hīm), town (pop. 1,977), Lower Franconia, W Bavaria, Germany, 14 mi. SE of Würzburg; mfg. of metal products, brewing. Wheat, barley, cattle; vineyards.

Mainburg (mīn′bŏork), village (pop. 4,928), Lower Bavaria, Germany, on small Abens R. and 18 mi. NW of Landshut; textile mfg., brewing, printing, woodworking.

Maindargi (mīn′dŭrgē), town (pop. 7,905), Sholapur dist., E Bombay, India, 28 mi. SE of Sholapur; agr. (millet, cotton, wheat); handicraft cloth weaving. Was ⊙ former Deccan state of Kurandvad Junior; state inc. (1949) into Sholapur and Belgaum dists.

Maindu, India: see MENDU.

Maine (mĕn), old province of W France, forming Mayenne, Sarthe, and part of Orne and Eure-et-Loir depts.; ⊙ Le Mans. Generally level region S of Normandy Hills and N of the middle Loire valley, drained by Mayenne, Sarthe and Loir rivers. Primarily agr. (with important stock raising in PERCHE). Chief towns are Le Mans (industrial and commercial center), Laval, and Mayenne. Made a county in 10th cent., it passed (1110) to Anjou, was held for long periods by England bet. 1156 and 1448, became a duchy (15th cent.), and was incorporated into royal domain in 1481. Later given in appanage to several Valois and Bourbon princes. In 1790, Maine was divided into present depts.

Maine (mān), state (land □ 31,040; with inland waters □ 33,215; 1950 pop. 913,774; 1940 pop. 847,226), extreme NE U.S., largest of the New England states, on the Atlantic; bordered NE and N by New Brunswick, N and W by Quebec, SW by New Hampshire; 38th in area, 35th in pop.; admitted 1820 as 23d state; ⊙ Augusta. It extends 315 mi. NNE–SSW and 205 mi. E–W, at its widest points. The "Pine Tree State" is generally hilly and forested, with intervening valleys and cultivated lowlands. Its 2,380-mi. shore line, bold and rugged, is deeply indented (elongated bays, rocky peninsulas) and fringed with over 1,000 isls., the largest of which is MOUNT DESERT ISLAND. The coastal lowland, varying considerably in width, is broken in places by hills, as around Penobscot Bay. In the W and central parts is a subdued mtn. mass of crystalline rocks (chiefly granite), including an extension of the White Mts. of N.H. Rising above the general surface are several resistant peaks, called monadnocks, chief of which is Mt. Katahdin (5,268 ft.), highest point in Maine. In the N and bet. the mts. and seaboard are upland sections with alternating level tracts and hilly regions. Many glacial features appear throughout the state—numerous lakes, kames and eskers, and diverted stream courses. Maine's longest rivers, flowing to the Atlantic, are the Penobscot, Androscoggin, Kennebec, Saco, and the St. John and St. Croix rivers, the last 2 forming parts of the N and E boundaries respectively. The humid continental climate has an annual rainfall of 35–45 in., short summers, and cold winters, with more temperate conditions along the coast. Portland (SW) has mean temp. of 22°F. in Jan., 70°F. in July, and 42 in. of annual rainfall. The growing season averages less than 100 days in the N and c.150 days along the coast. Maine still has some 16,500,000 acres of valuable forest land, of which c.875,000 acres are in natl. forest reserves. Important timber species include white pine, spruce (for wood pulp), balsam fir, white oak, hemlock, birch, beech, maple, and ash. Lumbering is a major industry, with numerous sawmills and pulp mills throughout the state. Maine's farmland, much of it in woodland and pasture, is restricted to the relatively level lowlands. Almost half the farms are of the subsistence type. Chief field crops are hay, potatoes, oats, corn, buckwheat, and barley. The state ranks 1st in potatoes, the fertile Aroostook valley being the chief center of production. Apples (E) and truck crops (S; beans, peas, and sweet corn for canning) are important, and 75% of the country's blueberries are grown in Maine, especially in Washington co. (E). Some dairying and poultry raising is carried on (S and SW). The large annual fish catch includes most of the U.S. herring sardines (Eastport is main canning center) and lobsters (Rockport and Rockland main ports), as well as cod, haddock, halibut, mackerel, hake, alewives, pollock, clams, and scallops. Portland is a major fishing port. Maine's mineral wealth is small, consisting primarily of granite, slate, limestone (in Penobscot Bay area, especially at Rockland, Thomaston), feldspar, and clay. There are also some precious stones (tourmaline, beryl), diatomaceous earth, and unworked deposits of mica, pyrite, and manganese ore. Principal manufactures are paper and pulp, wood products (from canoes and snowshoes to tooth picks), cotton and woolen textiles, shoes, canned fish, canned vegetables, machinery, and boats and ships. Most factories are located near the coast or at inland water-power sites. Largest cities (in order of size): Portland, Lewiston, Bangor, Auburn, South Portland, Augusta, Biddeford, Waterville, Westbrook, Sanford, Bath, and Saco. Maine is a great vacation area, and tourism a major source of revenue. Main recreational sites include the coastal resorts of Acadia Natl. Park and Bar Harbor (on Mt. Desert Isl.) and the string of beaches S of Portland, such as Old Orchard, Kennebunk, and Ogunquit; and the inland lakes Moosehead L., Rangeley Lakes, Belgrade Lakes, Sebago L.; there are many other seashore, lake, and woodland resorts, where fishing and hunting (deer, bear, grouse) are plentiful; winter sports are popular in the White Mts. area. Leading educational institutions: Univ. of Maine (at Orono), Colby Col. (at Waterville), Bowdoin Col. (at Brunswick), Bates Col. (at Lewiston). Maine's contributions to American literature include Henry Wadsworth Longfellow, Edwin Arlington Robinson, Sarah Orne Jewett, and Edna St. Vincent Millay. Artifacts of a paleolithic people, the Red Paint Indians, have been found in the state. In 16th and 17th cent. Indian tribes in Maine were of the Abnaki group, of which the present Penobscots and Passamaquoddies are the only survivors. It is probable that Norse navigators sailed off the coast of Maine in the early 11th cent. and that the Cabots reached these shores in 1497–99. A short-lived settlement was made (1604) on St. Croix Isl. by de Monts and Champlain. Much of the region was included in a grant to the Plymouth Co. and a colony was founded (1607) near present Phippsburg. French missionaries became active in the area, and around the same time English settlements were made at York and Saco in the prov. of Maine, bet. the Merrimack and Kennebec rivers, acquired (1622) by Gorges and Mason. In 1652 the Maine colonies came under the jurisdiction of Massachusetts; confirmed (1691) by royal charter. Fr. influence declined toward the close of the 17th cent., although Fr. attacks continued to harass the prov. Indian raids were a constant menace until peace was made in 1760. During the Revolution British ships inflicted great damage along the Maine coast. The Dist. of Maine—so designated by the Continental Congress in 1775—increased rapidly in pop.; lumbering shipbuilding, and foreign commerce were the leading occupations. In the War of 1812 the British occupied the region E of the Penobscot, but it reverted to Maine in 1814–15. Separated from Mass. in 1819, Maine was admitted to the Union the following year as part of the Missouri Compromise. The NE boundary dispute with Great Britain was finally settled by the Webster-Ashburton Treaty in 1842. The state was the 1st to adopt (1846) a prohibition law, which remained on the books until 1934. Republican control of state politics, dominated in the 2d half of the 19th cent. by such leaders as James G. Blaine and Thomas B. Reed, has continued almost uninterruptedly since the Civil War. Maine's efforts to develop local industries include a law prohibiting the sale of hydroelectricity outside the state. See also articles on the cities, towns, geographic features, and the 16 counties: ANDROSCOGGIN, AROOSTOOK, CUMBERLAND, FRANKLIN, HANCOCK, KENNEBEC, KNOX, LINCOLN, OXFORD, PENOBSCOT, PISCATAQUIS, SAGADAHOC, SOMERSET, WALDO, WASHINGTON, YORK.

Maine-et-Loire (mĕn-ā-lwär'), department (□ 2,787; pop. 496,068), in Anjou, W France; ⊙ Angers. Generally level region traversed by the Loire and drained by its tributaries, the Mayenne, the Sarthe, the Loir, and the Thouet. Very fertile area with noted vineyards, orchards, and diversified agr. Has important slate quarries (near Angers and Segré), some iron and coal deposits and textile industry. Chief towns are Angers (food processing), Saumur (known for its sparkling wines), and Cholet (textiles).

Maine River (mĕn). **1** In Maine-et-Loire dept., W France, formed by confluence of the Mayenne and the Sarthe above Angers; empties into Loire R. 5 mi. SSW of Angers; 7 mi. long; navigable. **2** In Vendée and Loire-Inférieure depts., W France, rises in Gâtine hills near Les Herbiers, flows 35 mi. NW, past Montaigu and Aigrefeuille-sur-Maine, to the Sèvre Nantaise 7 mi. SE of Nantes.

Maine River (mān), Ireland, rises on E border of Co. Kerry, flows 24 mi. W, past Castleisland and Castlemaine, to Castlemaine Harbour of Dingle Bay.

Mainero, Mexico: see VILLA MAINERO.

Maïné-Soroa (mī'nā-sōrō'ä), village (pop. c.800), S Niger territory, Fr. West Africa, on Nigeria border, 210 mi. E of Zinder. Meteorological station, dispensary, airstrip.

Maine Turnpike, part of Maine highway system extending NE from near Portsmouth, N.H., to Portland, Maine; toll road.

Maineville, village (pop. 312), Warren co., SW Ohio, 20 mi. NE of Cincinnati, in agr. area.

Mainfranken, Germany: see LOWER FRANCONIA.

Maing (mē), town (pop. 2,695), Nord dept., N France, on Escaut R. and 4 mi. SSW of Valenciennes; truck, sugar beets.

Maingay Island, Burma: see MAINGY ISLAND.

Maingkwan (mĭng"kwän'), village, Myitkyina dist., Kachin State, Upper Burma, in Hukawng Valley, on road and 80 mi. NW of Myitkyina; amber mines near by.

Maingy Island (mĭn'jē', Burmese mĭn'jē"), in Mergui Archipelago, Lower Burma, in Andaman Sea, 3 mi. W of King Isl.; 5 mi. long, 3 mi. wide; mountainous, surrounded by mangrove swamps. Large galena deposits. Also called Maingay Isl.

Mainit (mäē'nĭt), town (1939 pop. 7,651; 1948 municipality pop. 17,681), Surigao prov., Philippines, NE Mindanao, 17 mi. S of Surigao, and on N shore of L. Mainit (□ 67; c.20 mi. long); coconuts. Gold mining.

Mainland. 1 or **Pomona,** island, largest of the Orkneys, Scotland: see POMONA. **2** Island (□ 406.5; pop. 15,172), largest of the Shetlands, Scotland, 120 mi. NE of Wick, Caithness: 55 mi. long, 20 mi. wide; rises to 1,475 ft. on Ronas Hill (N), 28 mi. NNW of Lerwick. Isl. has irregular coastline; main inlets are Ronas Voe (NW), Sullom Voe (NW), site of seaplane base, Dury Voe (NE), Swarbacks Minn (NE), and the Deeps (W). Chief town, Lerwick, ⊙ Shetlands, on E coast of isl. On NW coast is St. Magnus Bay (10 mi. long, 12 mi. wide at mouth), containing Papa Stour isl. In S is long narrow promontory ending in Sumburgh Head, 22 mi. SSW of Lerwick, site of lighthouse (59°51'N 1°16'W). Near by is an airfield. N extremity of Mainland is the Point of Fethaland, 34 mi. NNW of Lerwick; 60°38'N 1°19'W. Mainland has been identified with *Ultima Thule.*

Mainleus (mīn'lois), village (pop. 2,136), Upper Franconia, N Bavaria, Germany, at confluence of the Red and White Main where they form Main R., 4 mi. W of Kulmbach; textile mfg., woodworking.

Mainpuri (mīn'pŏŏrē), district (□ 1,679; pop. 872,601), W Uttar Pradesh, India; ⊙ Mainpuri. On W Ganges Plain and Ganges-Jumna Doab; irrigated by Upper and Lower Ganges canals and their distributaries. Agr. (wheat, gram, pearl millet, corn, barley, jowar, oilseeds, cotton, rice, sugar cane); mango, sissoo, and dhak groves. Main towns: Mainpuri, Skikohabad, Bhongaon, Karhal.

Mainpuri, town (pop., including civil station, 21,221), ⊙ Mainpuri dist., W Uttar Pradesh, India, on tributary of the Ganges and 60 mi. E of Agra; road center; oilseed milling; trades in grains, cotton, sugar cane, hides.

Main River (män, Ger. mīn), W Germany, formed at Mainleus by RED MAIN and WHITE MAIN rivers; flows 307 mi. generally W—forming large bends at Bamberg, Schweinfurt, Würzburg, Gemünden, and Wertheim—past Aschaffenburg and Frankfurt, to the Rhine just opposite Mainz. Regulated from mouth of Regnitz R. (just NW of Bamberg). LUDWIG CANAL connects it with the Danube; a direct Main-Danube canal is planned. Excellent wine grown along picturesque middle course. Receives the Franconian Saale (left) and the Tauber (right).

Main River, Co. Antrim, Northern Ireland, rises SE of Ballymoney, flows 30 mi. S, past Randalstown, to Lough Neagh.

Main-Taunus, Germany: see FRANKFURT.

Maintenon (mētūnō'), village (pop. 1,793), Eure-et-Loir dept., NW central France, on the Eure and 10 mi. NNE of Chartres; agr. market; cider distilling. Has 16th-cent. castle (given in 1674 by Louis XIV to Françoise d'Aubigné, later Marquise de Maintenon), and ruins of 17th-cent. aqueduct (both damaged in Second World War) which was to supply Versailles with water from upper Eure R., but was never completed.

Maintirano (mäntērä'nōō), town, Tuléar prov., W Madagascar, port of Mozambique Channel, 370 mi. N of Tuléar; ships beans, raphia, canned beef. Airfield.

Main Topsail, mountain (1,822 ft.), W central N.F., 30 mi. E of NE end of Grand L.; 49°8'N 56°33'W.

Mainvault (mēvō'), agr. village (pop. 1,286), Hainaut prov., SW Belgium, 3 mi. WNW of Ath.

Mainvilliers (mēvēlyā'), W suburb (pop. 2,245), of Chartres, Eure-et-Loir dept., NW central France.

Mainz (mīnts) or **Mayence** (mīās', mīäns'), city (1939 pop. 158,533; 1946 pop., less right-bank suburbs, 75,020; 1950 pop. 87,046), ⊙ Rhenish Hesse, W Germany, after 1945 nominal ⊙ Rhineland-Palatinate (though Coblenz became the temporary ⊙), port on left bank of the Rhine, opposite mouth of Main R., and 20 mi. WSW of Frankfurt; 50°N 8°17'E. Rail junction. One of the great historical cities of Germany, it developed only recently as an industrial center. Mfg. of chemicals (sulphuric acid), vehicles, machinery, precision instruments, building materials, furniture, textiles, shoes. Leather-, metal-, and woodworking; printing. Food processing (meat and bakery products, wine, beer). Once-active river trade (wine, lumber, coal) declined because of loss (19th cent.) of duty rights and opening of Mannheim harbor. Suffered great destruction in Second World War (inner city 80% destroyed). Heavily damaged were: the cathedral (consecrated 1009; burned in 11th, 12th, and 18th cent;. finally restored in 19th cent.); Renaissance electoral palace, which housed picture gall. and mus. of antiquities; 18th-cent. church of St. Peter. Has univ. (founded 1477, discontinued 1816, reconstituted 1946 by Fr. occupation authorities); conservatory. Mainz developed around Roman camp, *Maguntiacum* or *Mogontiacum.* St. Boniface was made (745) 1st archbishop of Mainz. The archbishops, ruling over considerable territory, had the right to crown the Holy Roman Emperor and in 14th cent. became archchancellors and electors of the empire. City became autonomous in 12th cent., but in 1462 it again came under domination of the archbishops. Was flourishing trade and cultural center (birthplace and principal residence of Gutenberg) until French Revolutionary Wars, when electoral state of Mainz collapsed. Under Fr. rule, 1798–1814. Archbishopric secularized and see degraded to bishopric in 1803. Passed to Hesse-Darmstadt in 1816 and became ⊙ newly created Rhenish Hesse prov. Was fortress (1873–1918) of German Empire. Hq. of Fr. army of occupation (1918–30) in the S Rhineland. Following its capture (March, 1945) by U.S. troops, the city's right-bank suburbs (Bischofsheim, Ginsheim, Gustavsburg, Kastel, Kostheim) were transferred to Hesse; this accounts for its low post-war pop. figure.

Maio (mä'yōō), island (□ 104; 1940 pop. 2,251; 1950 pop. 1,872), one of Cape Verde Isls., easternmost of the Leeward group, in the Atlantic, bet. Boa Vista Isl. (50 mi. NNE) and São Tiago Isl. (15 mi. SW). Pôrto Inglês (15°8'N 23°13'W), its chief town, is on SW coast. Isl. is 14 mi. long, 9 mi. wide, with a hilly interior (Monte Penoso, 1,430 ft.) and a low, sandy N and W coast. Extensive salt pans. Some agr. (corn, beans, potatoes), horse raising. Occupied by British until end of 18th cent. Formerly spelled Mayo.

Maiolati or **Maiolati Spontini** (mäyôlä'tē spôntē'nē), village (pop. 495), Ancona prov., The Marches, central Italy, 7 mi. WSW of Iesi; silk mill.

Maiorga (mŭyôr'gŭ), village (pop. 1,164), Leiria dist., central Portugal, 14 mi. SSW of Leiria; wine, olives. Battlefield of Aljubarrota just E.

Maiori (mäyô'rē), town (pop. 3,375), Salerno prov., Campania, S Italy, port on Gulf of Salerno, 6 mi. WSW of Salerno; bathing resort; paper milling center; macaroni mfg.

Maipo, department, Chile: see BUIN.

Maipo (mī'pō), town (pop. 1,344), Santiago prov., central Chile, on Maipo R. and 22 mi. SSW of Santiago, just W of Buin; agr. center (grain, alfalfa, fruit, wine, tobacco, livestock). The town of MAIPÚ is 15 mi. N.

Maipo, battlefield, Chile: see MAIPÚ, battlefield.

Maipo Pass (11,230 ft.), in the Andes, on Argentina-Chile border, at S foot of Maipo Volcano, on road bet. San Rafael (Argentina) and El Volcán (Chile); 34°14'S 69°50'W.

Maipo River, Santiago prov., central Chile, rises in the Andes at foot of Maipo Volcano near Argentina border, flows c.155 mi. NW and W, past Queltehues (hydroelectric plant), San José de Maipo, Buin, Melipilla, and Llolleo, to the Pacific at La Boca 2 mi. S of San Antonio. It receives the Mapocho, and irrigates the fertile central valley S of Santiago. Just SW of Santiago and c.10 mi. from the river, was fought (1818) the decisive battle of MAIPÚ or Maipo in the war for Chilean independence. The river was formerly also spelled Maipú.

Maipo Volcano (17,355 ft.), in the Andes, on Argentina-Chile border, 65 mi. SE of Santiago (Chile); 34°10'S 69°52'W.

Maipú (mīpōō'). **1** Town (pop. 5,239), ⊙ Maipú dist. (□ 1,004; pop. 7,904), E Buenos Aires prov., Argentina, 80 mi. NNW of Mar del Plata; rail junction and agr. center (flax, oats, sunflowers, sheep, cattle). **2** or **Villa Maipú** (vē'yä), town (pop. estimate 3,000), ⊙ Maipú dept. (□ 260; 1947 pop. 49,949), N Mendoza prov., Argentina, in Mendoza R. valley (irrigation area), on railroad and 8 mi. SSE of Mendoza; agr. and mfg. center. Distilling, wine making, tanning, lumbering, plow mfg. Agr. products: wine, alfalfa, fruit, corn, potatoes.

Maipú, town (pop. 2,894), Santiago prov., central Chile, on railroad and 7 mi. SW of Santiago, c.10 mi. N of Maipo R.; agr. (cereals, fruit, livestock) and mfg. (shoes, tires). Near by was fought the battle of Maipú or Maipo.

Maipú (mīpōō') or **Maipo** (mī'pō), battlefield, Santiago prov., central Chile, 7 mi. SW of Santiago, near town of Maipú, c.10 mi. N of Maipo R. Here on April 5, 1818, San Martín crushingly defeated the Sp. royalist army and assured Chilean independence.

Maipures Rapids (mīpōō'rĕs), on Colombia-Venezuela border, obstacle to navigation on upper Orinoco R., c.35 mi. S of Atures Rapids; 5°15'N. The 2 sets of rapids are circumvented by a road.

Maiquetía (mīkātē'ä), town (pop. 15,911), Federal Dist., N Venezuela, on the Caribbean, at foot of coastal range, just W of La Guaira, 6 mi. N of Caracas (linked by railroad and highway). Resort. Glass factory, brewery, caustic-soda plant. Landing field for Pan American Airways.

Mairabari, India: see NOWGONG, town, Assam.

Mairana (mīrä'nä), town (pop. c.2,100), Santa Cruz dept., central Bolivia, in E foothills of Cordillera de Cochabamba, on Cochabamba-Santa Cruz road and 9 mi. NW of Samaipata; wheat, corn.

Maira River (mī'rä), NW Italy, rises in Cottian Alps 7 mi. NW of Acceglio, flows E, past Dronero, and NNE, past Savigliano and Racconigi, to the Po 3 mi. E of Pancalieri; 65 mi. long. Used for hydroelectric power at Acceglio.

Mairena del Alcor (mīrā'nä dhĕl älkōr'), town (pop. 7,779), Seville prov., SW Spain, on railroad and 13 mi. E of Seville; agr. center (cereals, olives, cotton, timber, livestock). Mus.

Mairena del Aljarafe (älhärä'fā), town (pop. 1,526), Seville prov., SW Spain, 5 mi. SW of Seville; olives, grapes.

Mairhofen, Austria: see MAYRHOFEN.

Mairinque (mīrēng'kĭ), town (pop. 1,675), S São Paulo, Brazil, 35 mi. W of São Paulo; important rail junction (new branch line to Santos); citrus groves, vineyards. Formerly Mayrink. Rodovalho (5 mi. W) has new aluminum plant.

Mairiporã (mīrēpōōrä'), city (pop. 727), SE São Paulo, Brazil, 15 mi. N of São Paulo; kaolin quarrying; thread mfg., distilling. Until 1948, called Juqueri.

Maisaka (mī'säkä), town (pop. 8,903), Shizuoka prefecture, central Honshu, Japan, on SE shore of L. Hamana, near its outlet, 7 mi. WSW of Hamamatsu; fishing center.

Maisí, Cape, or **Maisí Point** (mīsē'), easternmost headland of Cuba, Oriente prov., on Windward Passage, 110 mi. E of Santiago de Cuba, 50 mi. WNW of Cape St. Nicolas, Haiti; 20°15'N 74°8'W. Has lighthouse. Old spelling, Maysí.

Maiskhal Island (mīs-khäl'), island (16 mi. long, N-S; 6 mi. wide), just off coast of Chittagong dist., extreme SE East Bengal, E Pakistan, N of Cox's Bazar.

Maiski or **Mayskiy** (mī'skē). **1** Town (1939 pop. over 500), E Amur oblast, Russian SFSR, 160 mi. N of Blagoveshchensk, near Salemdzha R.; gold mines. **2** Town (1926 pop. 2,407), NE Kabardian Autonomous SSR, Russian SFSR, on railroad (Kotlyarevskaya station) and 25 mi. NE of Nalchik; rail junction (branch to Nalchik); bast-fiber processing (common and ambary hemp); metalworks. Kotlyarevskaya village (1939 pop. over 2,000), 4 mi. S, has poultry farm and meat-packing plant. **3** Settlement, Molotov oblast, Russian SFSR: see KRASNOKAMSK.

Maiskoye or **Mayskoye** (mī'skŭyŭ). **1** Village (1948 pop. over 2,000), S Pavlodar oblast, Kazakh SSR, on Irtish R. and 110 mi. SSE of Pavlodar; cattle, sheep. **2** Village (1939 pop. 780), E central Kaliningrad oblast, Russian SFSR, 9 mi. N of Gusev. Until 1945, in East Prussia where it was called Mallwischken (mäl'vĭsh"kŭn) and, later (1938–45), Mallwen (mäl'vŭn).

Maison-Blanche (māzõ'-blāsh'), village (pop. 407), Alger dept., N central Algeria, on railroad and 9 mi. SE of Algiers; vineyards. Site of Algiers airport.

Maison-Carrée (–kärā'), town (pop. 30,911), Alger dept., N central Algeria, in the Mitidja plain, 6 mi. SE of Algiers; important livestock market and site of Algeria's agr. inst., with extensive experimental farms; chemical and metalworks, distilleries; mfg. of building materials and flour products. Citrus groves, vineyards, tobacco fields surround town. Maison-Blanche airport is just E.

Maisonette Point (māzŭnĕt'), cape on Chaleur Bay, NE N.B., 35 mi. NE of Bathurst; 47°50'N 65°W; lighthouse.

Maisons-Alfort (māzõzälfôr'), town (pop. 35,578), Seine dept., N central France, a SE suburb of Paris, 5.5 mi. from Notre Dame Cathedral, on right bank of the Seine just above influx of the Marne; cement- and metalworks, mfg. (soap, hosiery, furniture, eye glasses, cartons), distilling, truck gardening. Has natl. veterinary school.

Maisons-Laffitte (māzõ'-läfēt'), town (pop. 13,074), Seine-et-Oise dept., N central France, a fine residential NW suburb of Paris, 11 mi. from Notre Dame Cathedral, on left bank of the Seine, at E edge of Saint-Germain forest; boat building, mfg. of electrical equipment. Has noted race track. Its 17th-cent. château, built by Mansart, contains mus. of paintings and tapestries. Formerly named Maisons-sur-Seine.

Maïssade (mäēsäd'), town (1950 census pop. 1,202), Artibonite dept., central Haiti, 40 mi. S of Cap-Haïtien, in coffee- and cotton-growing region. Lignite deposits near by.

Maisur, India: see MYSORE.

Maitén, Argentina: see EL MAITÉN.

Maitencillo (mītĕnsē'yō), village (1930 pop. 108), Coquimbo prov., N central Chile, 18 mi. SE of La Serena; high-grade iron-ore deposits.

Maitenes (mītā'nĕs), mining settlement (1930 pop. 115), Santiago prov., central Chile, in the Andes, 20 mi. NE of Santiago; hydroelectric station; copper mining.

Maitland. **1** Municipality (pop. 19,151), E New South Wales, Australia, 16 mi. NW of Newcastle and on Hunter R., which divides it into E. Maitland and W.Maitland; rail junction; mining and mfg. center. R.C. cathedral. **2** Town (pop. 700), S South Australia, on central Yorke Peninsula, 85 mi. SSW of Port Pirie; wheat; sheep, wool.

Maitland, village (pop. estimate 400), central N.S., on Chignecto Bay, at mouth of Shubenacadie R., 12 mi. WSW of Truro; dairying, mixed farming; former shipbuilding center.

Maitland, residential town, SW Cape Prov., U. of So. Afr., E suburb of Cape Town. Just E is Wingfield airport.

Maitland. **1** Town (pop. 889), Orange co., central Fla., 5 mi. N of Orlando. **2** City (pop. 456), Holt co., NW Mo., on Nodaway R. and 33 mi. NNW of St. Joseph; grain, stock, poultry; ships bluegrass seed. **3** Village (pop. 1,697, with adjacent Superior), McDowell co., S W.Va., just SE of Welch.

Maiwand (mī'wŭnd), village, Kandahar prov., S Afghanistan, 33 mi. W of Kandahar and 10 mi. NE of Kushk-i-Nakhud. Scene of severe defeat (1880) of British by Afghan faction.

Maiya (mī'yä), town (pop. 5,931), Miyagi prefecture, N Honshu, Japan, 4 mi. N of Tome; rice, silk cocoons, charcoal.

Maiya or **Mayya** (mī'ŭ), village (1948 pop. over 500), SE Yakut Autonomous SSR, Russian SFSR, 40 mi. SE of Yakutsk, in agr. area.

Maíz, Mexico: see CIUDAD DEL MAÍZ.

Maize, city (pop. 266), Sedgwick co., S Kansas, 10 mi. NW of Wichita, in wheat region.

Maíz Gordo, Sierra del (syĕ'rä dĕl mäēs' gōr'dō), subandean mountain range on Jujuy-Salta prov. border, NW Argentina, N of Piquete; extends c.50 mi. NW-SE; rises to c.6,500 ft. Covered with subtropical forests.

Maizières-lès-Metz (māzyâr-lā-mĕs'), town (pop. 1,649), Moselle dept., NE France, 7 mi. N of Metz; metalworks.

Maizuru (mī'zŏorŏo), city (1940 pop. 29,903; 1947 pop. 92,139), Kyoto prefecture, S Honshu, Japan, port on inlet of Wakasa Bay, 39 mi. NW of Kyoto. Rail junction; mfg. center; canneries, woodworking factories; charcoal, raw silk, lumber. Exports woodwork, lumber. Site of naval base in Second World War. Includes (since early 1940s) former city of Higashi-maizuru (1940 pop. 49,810).

Majaba, Aden: see MAHJABA.

Majaceite River (mähä-thā'tā), Cádiz prov., SW Spain, rises at Málaga prov. border, flows c.40 mi. W, through subtropical L. Guadalcacín, to the Guadalete 4 mi. SSW of Arcos de la Frontera. Used for irrigation.

Majadahonda (mähä"dhäōn'dä), village (pop. 931), Madrid prov., central Spain, 11 mi. W of Madrid; cereals, truck produce, fruit, grapes, stock.

Majadas, Las (läs mähä'dhäs), town (pop. 673), Cuenca prov., E central Spain, in the Serranía de Cuenca, 17 mi. NNE of Cuenca; cereals, goats, cattle; apiculture. Flour milling, lumbering. Unexploited coal, copper, lead deposits.

Majagua (mähä'gwä), town (pop. 2,394), Camagüey prov., E Cuba, on railroad and 15 mi. WNW of Ciego de Ávila; sugar cane, fruit, cattle.

Majagual (mähägwäl'), town (pop. 1,752), Bolívar dept., N Colombia, in savannas, 50 mi. S of Magangué; cattle, fruit.

Majalengka or **Madjalengka** (both: mŭjŭlĕng'kŭ), town (pop. 8,596), W central Java, Indonesia, 25 mi. WSW of Cheribon, at foot of Mt. Charemai; trade center for agr. area (rice, sugar, peanuts); textile mills.

Majdaha (măj'dăhŭ), **Maqdaha**, or **Maqdahah** (măk'dăhŭ), village, Wahidi sultanate of Bir Ali, Eastern Aden Protectorate, on the cape Ras Majdaha on Gulf of Aden, 10 mi. E of Bir Ali; airfield.

Majdal or **Al Majdal**, Israel: see MIGDAL GAD; MAGDALA.

Majdanek, Poland: see LUBLIN, city.

Majdan Pek, Majdanpek, Maidanpek, or **Maydanpek** (all: mī'dänpĕk"), village, E Serbia, Yugoslavia, 40 mi. ESE of Pozarevac. Iron pyrite mine, here, connected with Donji Milanovac (ENE) by 11-mi.-long aerial ropeway. Former copper mining. Gold mining near by.

Majé, Brazil: see MAGÉ.

Majen-bel-Abbès (mäzhĕn'-bĕl-äb-bĕs'), village, Kasserine dist., W Tunisia, on railroad and 26 mi. NNW of Gafsa; olives, esparto grass, sheep. Also spelled Maajen-bel-Abbès.

Majes River (mä'hĕs), Arequipa dept., S Peru, rises as Colca R. near Puno dept. border, flows c.250 mi. W and S to the Pacific 2 mi. W of Camaná. Used for irrigation.

Majestic, mining village (1940 pop. 528), Pike co., E Ky., in the Cumberlands near Tug Fork, 13 mi. SE of Williamson, W.Va.; bituminous coal.

Majestic Mountain (10,125 ft.), W Alta., near B.C. border, in Rocky Mts., in Jasper Natl. Park, 11 mi. SE of Jasper; 52°53'N 118°13'W.

Majevica or **Mayevitsa** (both: mī'yĕvētsä), mountain range in Dinaric Alps, NE Bosnia, Yugoslavia; extends c.30 mi. NW-SE; highest point (3,094 ft.) is 6 mi. E of Tuzla. Contains petroleum. Bituminous coal at Majevica mine, 6 mi. NE of Tuzla.

Maji (mä'jē), Ital. *Magi*, town (pop. 3,000), Kaffa prov., SW Ethiopia, on plateau, 85 mi. SW of Bonga; 6°10'N 35°34'E; alt. 7,970 ft. Trade center (hides, ivory). Until recently was market for slave trade which considerably depopulated the surrounding region.

Majicoshima, Ryukyu Isls.: see SAKISHIMA ISLANDS.

Maji Mazuri (mä'jē mäzŏo'rē), village, Rift Valley prov., W Kenya, on railroad and 8 mi. SSW of Eldama Ravine; hardwood industry.

Majitha (mŭjē'tŭ), town (pop. 9,004), Amritsar dist., W Punjab, India, 10 mi. NNE of Amritsar; wheat, cotton, gram, rice; hand-loom woolen weaving (carpets).

Maji-ya-Chumvi (mä'jē-yä-chŏŏm'vē), village, Coast Prov., SE Kenya, on railroad and 25 mi. NW of Mombasa; sugar cane, fruits, copra.

Majma'a or **Majma'ah** (măj'mä), town, N central Nejd, Saudi Arabia, in Sudair dist., 40 mi. SE of Zilfi; 25°55'N 45°25'E. Trading center; grain, dates, vegetables, fruit; stock raising.

Major, county (□ 945; pop. 10,279), NW Okla.; ⊙ Fairview. Drained by Cimarron R. Agr. (wheat, barley, broomcorn, oats, peanuts, livestock; dairy products). Milling, dairying at Fairview. Formed 1907.

Majorca (mŭjôr'kŭ), Sp. *Mallorca* (mälyôr'kä), anc. *Balearis Major* or *Majorica*, largest island (□ 1,405; pop. 327,102) of the Balearic Isls., Spain, in the W Mediterranean bet. Minorca (NE) and Iviza (SW); 39°16'–39°57'N 2°22'–3°29'E. PALMA or Palma de Mallorca, its ⊙ and chief port, is c.120 mi. SSE of Barcelona and 160 mi. E of Valencia. Isl. is up to 53 mi. long E-W, and up to 45 mi. wide N-S. Deeply indented coast possesses fine natural harbors. Along NW coast extends a ridge from Cape Formentor 20 mi. SW to a point opposite Dragonera Isl. and which rises in the Torrellas or Puig Mayor to 4,741 ft.; it protects the isl. from north winds. Majorca's mild year-round climate makes it a much-frequented resort. The undulating, picturesque landscape, blessed with a rich vegetation, has long been celebrated for its beauty. Intensive agr. is isl.'s mainstay. Principal crops are grapes, olives, almonds, carobs, cereals, capers, hemp, citrus fruit. Hogs and sheep are grazed widely. Among mineral resources are lignite, marble, lead, salt, gravel; medicinal springs. The isl. has important processing industries, such as tanning, flour milling, alcohol and liquor distilling, wine making, olive-oil distilling, meat packing, food canning, dairying; also mfg. of shoes, textile goods, embroidered articles, glassware, ceramics, jewelry, paper, cellulose, soap, cement. Extensive forests yield timber. Fishing along coast. Commerce and industry are centered at Palma, from which radiate railroads and highways. Other leading cities include Inca, Manacor, Pollensa, Sóller, La Puebla, Artá. Majorca is also known for its stalagmite caves and for its architectural treasures and prehistoric monuments. There are also Phoenician, Carthaginian, and Roman remains. The Romans conquered the isl. under the consul Metellus, who founded (276 B.C.) Palma and Pollensa. It underwent successively Vandal, East Roman (Belisarius), and Moorish (797) invasions, becoming eventually a hq. for Saracen pirates who attacked the Sp. coast. Majorca was conquered in 1229 by James I of Aragon, and under his successors it became, in 1276, a kingdom. It suffered from the decline of Mediterranean trade after discovery of America. In Sp. civil war (1936–39), Majorca early passed to Nationalist side, and was turned into an important air and naval base, chiefly operated by Italians.

Majorenhof, Latvia: see RIGAS JURMALA.

Majori, Latvia: see RIGAS JURMALA.

Major Isidoro (mŭzhôr' ēzēdô'rŏo), city (pop. 916), central Alagoas, NE Brazil, 25 mi. WSW of Palmeira dos Índios; cotton. Until 1944, called Sertãozinho.

Majszin, Rumania: see MOISEI.

Majuba Hill (mŭjŏo'bŭ), locality, NW Natal, near Transvaal border, U. of So. Afr., 9 mi. S of Volksrust, in Drakensberg range; scene (Feb. 27, 1881) of battle in Transvaal revolt; British under Sir George Colley (killed here) were routed by Boer force under Joubert.

Majuli (mä'jŏolē), village, Sibsagar dist., E central Assam, India, on Majuli Isl., 13 mi. NNW of Jorhat. Surrounding area grows calamus palms.

Majuli Island, Sibsagar dist., E central Assam, India, bet. Brahmaputra R. (S, E), Subansiri R. (W), and a branch of the Brahmaputra (N) flowing to the Subansiri; 48 mi. long NE-SW, 5–12 mi. wide; ferry service. Calamus palms grown extensively.

Majunga (mŭjŭng'gŭ), province (□ 59,000; 1948 pop. 682,900), NW Madagascar; ⊙ Majunga. Drained by the Betsiboka and the 2 Mahavavy rivers. E part is in central highlands of Madagascar, rising to 9,450 ft. in Tsaratanana Massif; coffee, cattle here. The swampy coast is studded with rice fields. Sugar, cassava products, fibers, waxes, mangrove bark, canned beef, hardwoods are exported. Some gold and copper deposits. Majunga and Diégo-Suarez are important ports. Offshore isl. of Nossi-Bé is part of prov.

Majunga, town (1948 pop. 27,181), ⊙ Majunga prov., NW Madagascar, on Bombetoka Bay of Mozambique Channel, at mouth of Betsiboka R., 225 mi. NNW of Tananarive; 15°40'S 46°20'E. Important commercial center and 3d largest seaport of Madagascar. Processes meat, bones, rice, fibers. Manufactures soap, edible oils, tallow, sugar, rum, sackcloth, jute bags. Machine shops, sawmills, paper mills, cement works. Its chief exports are coffee, cassava starch, raphia, sugar, hides, rice, vanilla, cloves, essential oils, waxes. Boanamary (bwänämär'), 12 mi. S, has large meat-processing and cold-storage plants. Near-by Amboanio (ämbwänē'ŏo) has cement and rice mills. Katsepe (kätsĕ'pā), 10 mi. W across the bay, is notable for its oysters. Majunga has a military camp, military hosp., airport, seaplane base, meteorological station, R.C. and Protestant missions. Seat of vicar apostolic. Founded (c.1700) by Arab traders, it served as a French base for conquest (1895) of the interior of Madagascar. Has large Indian pop.

Majuro (mäjŏo'rō), atoll (□ 4; pop. 1,537), RATAK CHAIN, Marshall Isls., W central Pacific, 300 mi. SE of Kwajalein; 7°10'N 171°13'E; ⊙ Majura dist.; 57 islets on reef 20 mi. long; copra. Site of radio beacon.

Makaba (mäkä'bä), village, Eastern Prov., NE Belgian Congo, 10 mi. E of Irumu; livestock farms here and at N'dele or Dele (dĕ'lä), 4 mi. NNE.

Makabe (mä"kä'bā), town (pop. 10,275), Ibaraki prefecture, central Honshu, Japan, 15 mi. NNW of Tsuchiura, in agr. area (rice, wheat, tobacco); mfg. (soy sauce, sake).

Makaha (mäkä'hä), village, Salisbury prov., NE Southern Rhodesia, in Mashonaland, 28 mi. ENE of Mtoko; cattle, sheep, goats; gold deposits.

Makahuena Point (mä'kähŏo-ā'nŭ), SE coast, Kauai, T.H.; 21°52'N 159°26'W.

Makala (mäkä'lä). **1** Village, Eastern Prov., E Belgian Congo, on Lindi R. and 165 mi. E of Stanleyville; noted as site of defeat of last of the Arab slave traders, marking end of the Arab campaign (1890–94). **2** Village, Katanga prov., Belgian Congo: see GREINERVILLE.

Makalakari, Bechuanaland: see MAKARIKARI.

Makale (mä'kälā), town, ⊙ Tigre prov., N Ethiopia, 60 mi. SE of Aduwa; 13°30'N 39°29'E; alt. c.6,700 ft. Trade center (salt, cereals, honey, beeswax, cotton goods).

Makalla, Aden: see MUKALLA.

Makallé (mäkäyā'), town (pop. estimate 1,500), SE Chaco natl. territory, Argentina, on railroad and 25 mi. NW of Resistencia; cotton center; lumbering, stock raising, citriculture.

Makalu (mŭ'kŭlŏo), peak (27,790 ft.) on undefined Nepal-Tibet border, in NE Nepal Himalayas, at 27°53'N 87°5'E. Up to 1950, unattempted by climbers. Also spelled Makalut.

Makamik or **Macamic** (mäkämēk'), village (pop. 645), W Que., on Macamic L., 35 mi. N of Rouyn; lumbering, dairying; mining region (gold, copper, molybdenum, zinc, lead).

Makanalua Peninsula (mä'känälōō'ŏŏ), N Molokai, T.H.; site of KALAUPAPA leper settlement.

Makanchi (mŭkünchē'), village (1948 pop. over 2,000), SE Semipalatinsk oblast, Kazakh SSR, near China border, 110 mi. SE of Ayaguz (joined by highway), in irrigated agr. area (wheat, opium, medicinal plants).

Makanda (mŭkŏn'dŭ), village (pop. 214), Jackson co., SW Ill., 16 mi. SW of Herrin, in agr. region. Giant City State Park near by.

Makane, Japan: see MAGANE.

Makania or **Makanya** (mäkä'nyä), village, Tanga prov., NE Tanganyika, at foot of Pare Mts., 20 mi. SSE of Same, on railroad; hardwood.

Makanpur, India: see BILHAUR.

Makanru Island or **Makanrushi Island** (mäkän'rōō, –shē), uninhabited island of N main Kurile Isls. group, Russian SFSR; separated from Onekotan Isl. (SE) by 5th Kurile Strait; 49°47'N 154°26'E; 6 mi. long, 4 mi. wide. Rises to 3,835 ft. in extinct volcano.

Makanya, Tanganyika: see MAKANIA.

Makapala (mä'kŭpä'lŭ), village (pop. 382), N Hawaii, T.H., on Kohala Peninsula; sugar-cane cultivation.

Makapuu Point (mä'käpōō'ōō), SE Oahu, T.H.; 21°18'N 157°39'W; site of lighthouse with one of most powerful lights (built 1909) in the world.

Makara, New Zealand: see WELLINGTON, city.

Makarakski or **Makarakskiy** (mŭkŭräk'skē), town (1943 pop. over 500), NE Kemerovo oblast, Russian SFSR, 45 mi. SSW of Tyazhin; gold mining.

Makarikari (mäkärēkä'rē), region (c.100 mi. long, 30–50 mi. wide), Ngwato dist., NE Bechuanaland Protectorate, 150 mi. WSW of Bulawayo; consists of sandy depression, formerly filled with salt water. Also called Makarikari Salt Lake or Makarikari Salt Pan; sometimes called Makalakari.

Makarov (mŭkä'rŭf). **1** City (1940 pop. 16,098), S Sakhalin, Russian SFSR, port on Terpeniye Gulf, on E coast railroad and 120 mi. N of Yuzhno-Sakhalinsk; coal mining, wood-pulp and paper milling; fisheries. Under Jap. rule (1905–45), called Shiritori or Shirutoru (shērē'tōrē, –rōō'tōrōō). **2** Agr. town (1926 pop. 2,738), W Kiev oblast, Ukrainian SSR, 30 mi. W of Kiev; grain, potatoes.

Makarovo (–rŭvŭ), village (1939 pop. over 2,000), NW Saratov oblast, Russian SFSR, on Khoper R. and 20 mi. W of Rtishchevo; wheat, fruit.

Makarpura (mŭk'ŭrpŏŏrŭ), village (pop. 1,583), Baroda dist., N Bombay, India, 4 mi. SSW of Baroda; cotton, millet, tobacco. Noted stepped well near by.

Makarska (mä'kärskä), Ital. *Macarsca* (mäkär'skä), village (pop. 3,101), S Croatia, Yugoslavia, small port on Adriatic Sea, 32 mi. ESE of Split, at W foot of Biokovo Mts., in Dalmatia. Seaside resort noted for its long beach; wine making (muscatel). Old churches and monastery (11th–16th cent.). First mentioned in 9th cent.

Makarwal Kheji (mŭk'ŭrväl kä'jē), village, Mianwali dist., NW Punjab, W Pakistan, on rail spur and 30 mi. NW of Mianwali; coal mining. Sometimes called Makerwal.

Makarye or **Makar'ye** (mŭkä'ryĭ), village (1948 pop. over 2,000), W Kirov oblast, Russian SFSR, 18 mi. NNW of Kotelnich; flax processing.

Makaryev or **Makar'yev** (mŭkä'ryĭf). **1** Village (1926 pop. 1,206), E central Gorki oblast, Russian SFSR, on left bank of Volga R. and 45 mi. ESE of Gorki; sawmilling. Has 14th-cent. monastery. Scene of large fairs, following their transfer (1524) from area of Kazan, until removal (1817) to Nizhni Novgorod. **2** City (1926 pop. 6,516), S Kostroma oblast, Russian SFSR, on Unzha R. and 70 mi. NE of Kineshma, in lumber region; metalworks, flax and potato processing. Chartered 1779.

Makasan, Thailand: see MAKKASAN.

Makassar, Indonesia: see MACASSAR.

Makasser, Indonesia: see MACASSAR.

Makat (mŭkät'), oil town (1939 pop. over 500), N Guryev oblast, Kazakh SSR, on railroad and 70 mi. NE of Guryev, in Emba oil field; junction of branch line to Koschagyl.

Makatea (mä'kätā'ä), island (pop. 1,826), dependency of Tahiti, Society Isls., Fr. Oceania, S Pacific, 130 mi. NE of Tahiti; 5 mi. long, 3 mi. wide; rises to 300 ft. Fringe of vegetation, with central mass of solid phosphate. Britain and France agreed (1908) to exploit phosphate cooperatively. Formerly Aurora.

Makati (mäkätē', mäkä'tē), town (1939 pop. 5,037; 1948 municipality pop. 41,335), Rizal prov., S Luzon, Philippines, just SE of Manila, on railroad; agr. center (rice, fruit). Near-by Nielson Field (important airport serving Manila) was formerly U.S. base. The Philippines acquired it by pact with U.S. signed 1947.

Makato (mäkä'tō), town (1939 pop. 1,502; 1948 municipality pop. 9,939), Capiz prov., NW Panay isl., Philippines, 33 mi. WNW of Capiz; agr. center (tobacco, rice).

Makawao (mä'käwä'ō), village (pop. 1,097), NE Maui, T.H., in center of sugar-cane area.

Makaweli (mä'käwä'lē), coast village (1940 pop. 1,010), S Kauai, T.H.; landing in sugar-cane area.

Makaz Pass (mŭkäz') (alt. 2,130 ft.), in SE Rhodope Mts., on Bulgaro-Greek border, on road bet. Momchilgrad (Bulgaria) and Komotine (Greece), 10 mi. N of Komotine.

Makedhonia, Makedonia, Makedonija, or **Makedoniya,** SE Europe: see MACEDONIA.

Makemo (mäkā'mō), atoll (pop. 215), central Tuamotu Isls., Fr. Oceania, S Pacific, 125 mi. E of Fakarava. Formerly Philips Isl.

Makena Bay (mäkā'nŭ), SW Maui, T.H., near Molokini isl.

Makengo, Belgian Congo: see BOMBOMA.

Makeni (mäkĕ'nē), town (pop. 7,500), ⊙ Northern Prov. (□ 13,875; pop. 712,212), central Sierra Leone, 85 mi. ENE of Freetown; rail terminus, trade center; palm oil and kernels, cacao, coffee. Has hosp., mission school, agr. station. Hq. Bombali dist. Govt. livestock farm at near-by Teko.

Makerere, Uganda: see KAMPALA.

Makeyevka (mŭkyā'ŭfkŭ), mfg. city (1926 pop. 79,421; 1939 pop. 240,145), central Stalino oblast, Ukrainian SSR, in the Donbas, 8 mi. NE of Stalino. Major coal-mining and metallurgical center; iron, steel, and pipe-rolling mills, coking plants. Formerly (1920s) also called Dmitriyevsk.

Makha, Yemen: see MOCHA.

Makhachkala (mŭkhäch"kŭlä'), city (1926 pop. 33,552; 1939 pop. 86,847), ⊙ Dagestan Autonomous SSR, Russian SFSR, port on Caspian Sea, at N end of narrow littoral belt, on railroad and 220 mi. NW of Baku, 90 mi. ESE of Grozny (linked by oil pipe lines). Major commercial and (with near-by KASPISK) industrial center; oil refining, shipbuilding, railroad repair shops; meat packing, fish and fruit processing, mfg. of chemicals, cotton milling, leather and woodworking (matches). Has Dagestan mus., agr., technical, medical, and viticultural schools, teachers col. An important Caspian port, shipping crude petroleum and refined products, fish, rice, grain, and cotton. Founded 1844 on site of reputed 18th-cent. camp of Peter the Great; named Petrovsk. Sharply contested (1917–20) during Rus. civil war; renamed Makhachkala and developed considerably under Soviet rule. Became ⊙ Dagestan in 1922. Formerly written Makhach-Kala.

Makhadar (mäkhä'där), town, Ibb prov., S Yemen, 12 mi. NNE of Ibb and on main route to Yarim. Also spelled Mekhadir.

Makhanpur, India: see SHIKOHABAD.

Makharadze (mŭkhŭrä'dzyĭ), city (1939 pop. over 10,000), SW Georgian SSR, on rail spur and 40 mi. SW of Kutaisi; chief town of Guria; industrial center; silk milling, tea growing, metalworking, sawmilling. Until 1936, Ozurgeti or Ozurgety.

Makhchesk (mŭkhchĕsk'), village (1939 pop. over 500), SW North Ossetian Autonomous SSR, Russian SFSR, in the central Greater Caucasus, on upper Urukh R. (left affluent of the Terek) and 24 mi. WSW of Alagir; hardy grain, livestock.

Makhdumi (mäkhdōō'mē), petty sheikdom of SUBEIHI tribal area, Western Aden Protectorate; ⊙ Marasa. Protectorate treaty concluded in 1897.

Makhir Coast (mäkhēr'), section of E Br. Somaliland coast on Gulf of Aden.

Makhlata (mäkhlä'tä), village (pop. 6,537), Pleven dist., N Bulgaria, 18 mi. W of Pleven; flour milling; livestock, truck. Sometimes spelled Machlata.

Makhmudzhug (mŭkhmŏŏjōōk'), SW suburb (1931 pop. estimate 1,555) of Artik, Armenian SSR; pumice quarries. Inc. c.1935 into Artik.

Makhmur (mäkhmōōr'), town, Erbil prov., N Iraq, in Kurdistan, 37 mi. SW of Erbil, 45 mi. SSE of Mosul; sesame, millet, corn, livestock.

Makhnevo (mŭkhnyĕ'vŭ), village (1932 pop. estimate 540), central Sverdlovsk oblast, Russian SFSR, on Tagil R. and 40 mi. N of Alapayevsk; wheat, rye, livestock.

Makhnovka, Ukrainian SSR: see KOMSOMOLSKOYE, Vinnitsa oblast.

Makhsusabad, India: see MURSHIDABAD, town.

Makhtal (mŭk'tŭl), town (pop. 5,862), Mahbubnagar dist., S Hyderabad state, India, 35 mi. WSW of Mahbubnagar; cotton and rice milling, biri mfg.

Maki (mä'kē), town (pop. 10,814), Niigata prefecture, central Honshu, Japan, 10 mi. NW of Sanjo; rice-growing center; sake, soy sauce.

Makian (mŭkēän'), volcanic island (□ 33; pop. 11,637), N Moluccas, Indonesia, in Molucca Sea, just W of Halmahera, 30 mi. S of Ternate; 0°19'N 127°23'E; roughly circular, 7 mi. in diameter. Mountainous, rising to 4,452 ft. (active volcanic peak). Agr. (tobacco, sago, coconuts), fishing. First Du. settlement 1608; Du. sovereignty established 1683. Sometimes spelled Makjan.

Makiang or **Ma-chiang** both: mä'jyäng'), town (pop. 1,430), ⊙ Makiang co. (pop. 95,244), SE central Kweichow prov., China, 55 mi. ESE of Kweiyang, near sources of Yüan R.; cotton textiles, embroidered goods; tobacco processing; wheat, millet, tea. Until 1930 called Maha.

Makiling, Mount, or **Mount Maquiling** (both: mäkē'lĭng) (3,750 ft.), Laguna prov., S Luzon, Philippines, 10 mi. WNW of San Pablo, near Laguna de Bay, in natl. forest. Mineral pigments are mined.

Makin (mä'kĭn, mŭ'gĭn), triangular atoll (□ 4.5; pop. 1,824), N Gilbert Isls., W central Pacific, in Br. colony of Gilbert and Ellice Isls.; 3°8'N 172°54'E. Butaritari on southernmost islet is port of entry and hq. of copra company. In Second World War, occupied Dec., 1941, by Japanese, regained Nov., 1943, by U.S. forces, who established air base and radio beacon. Atoll is officially called Butaritari. Formerly Pitt Isl.

Makindu (mäkēn'dōō), town, Central Prov., S central Kenya, on railroad and 100 mi. SE of Nairobi; alt. 3,277 ft.; 2°17'S 37°50'E; sisal and rubber center. Airfield. Game reserve.

Makin Meang, Gilbert Isls.: see LITTLE MAKIN.

Makinsk (mŭkēnsk'), city (1944 pop. over 2,000), N Akmolinsk oblast, Kazakh SSR, on railroad and 60 mi. SE of Kokchetav, in wooded area; mfg. of agr. machines. Until 1944, Makinka.

Makisono (mäkē'sōnō) or **Makizono** (–zōnō), town (pop. 15,074), Kagoshima prefecture, S Kyushu, Japan, 21 mi. NNE of Kagoshima; commercial center in livestock and agr. area. Sulphide hot springs in vicinity.

Makjan, Indonesia: see MAKIAN.

Makkah, Saudi Arabia: see MECCA.

Makkasan or **Makasan** (both: mäk'kŭsän'), E suburb of Bangkok, Thailand, 3 mi. from city center; extensive railroad workshops.

Mak Khaeng, Thailand: see UDON.

Makkhanpur, India: see SHIKOHABAD.

Makkovik (mŭkŏŏ'vĭk), village (pop. 74), E Labrador, on Makkovik Bay of the Atlantic; 55°5'N 59°6'W; fishing port.

Makkovik, Cape, on the Atlantic, E Labrador; 55°15'N 59°4'W.

Makkum (mä'kŭm), town (pop. 2,086), Friesland prov., N Netherlands, on the Ijsselmeer, 11 mi. W of Sneek; tiles, pottery.

Maknassy (mäknä'sē, Fr. mäknäsē'), village, Gafsa dist., S central Tunisia, on Sfax-Tozeur RR and 50 mi. ENE of Gafsa; esparto trade; olive trees. Phosphate mine at Meheri Zebbeus (4 mi. N; rail spur). Scene of heavy fighting during Tunisian campaign (1943).

Mako (mŏ'kō), Hung. *Makó*, city (pop. 35,705), ⊙ Csanad co., S Hungary, on Maros R. and 17 mi. E of Szeged; center of agr. area (large onion crop); sawmills, flour mills, brickworks; ducks, geese, vineyards; fishing. Large Slovak pop.

Mako, Pescadores: see MAKUNG.

Makogai, Fiji: see MAKONGAI.

Makokou (mäkōkōō'), village, NE Gabon, Fr. Equatorial Africa, on Ivindo R. and 75 mi. NE of Booué; customs station.

Makongai or **Makogai** (both: mä'kōng'ī), volcanic island (□ 5; pop. 743), Fiji, SW Pacific, c.40 mi. E of Viti Levu; 2.5 mi. long. Chief leper station in South Seas.

Makor, Indonesia: see ARU ISLANDS.

Makoti (mŭkō'tē), village (pop. 219), Ward co., NW central N.Dak., 30 mi. SW of Minot.

Makotsevo (mä'kôtsĕvô), village (pop. 785), Sofia dist., W Bulgaria, 25 mi. E of Sofia, on railroad; grain, livestock. Site of mineral springs.

Makoua (mäkwä'), village, central Middle Congo territory, Fr. Equatorial Africa, on Likouala R. and 40 mi. N of Fort-Rousset. Has R.C. mission and center for treatment of leprosy and trypanosomiasis.

Makow (mä'kōōf), Pol. *Maków*. **1** or **Makow Podhalanski** (pôd-hälä'nyŭskē), Pol. *Maków Podhalański*, town (pop. 3,886), Krakow prov., S Poland, on Skawa R. and 25 mi. SSW of Cracow; sawmilling; lumber trade. **2** or **Makow Mazowiecki** (mäzôvyĕts'kē), Pol. *Maków Mazowiecki*, Rus. *Makov* (mä'kŭf), town (pop. 2,642), Warszawa prov., E central Poland, on Orzyc R. and 45 mi. N of Warsaw; cement mfg., tanning, flour milling. During Second World War, under administration of East Prussia, called Mackeim.

Makrai (mŭkrī'), village, Hoshangabad dist., W Madhya Pradesh, India, 60 mi. SW of Hoshangabad; wheat, millet, oilseeds; surrounded by dense teak and sal forests. Was ⊙ former princely state of Makrai (□ 151; pop. 14,357), one of the Central India states; since 1948, state inc. into Hoshangabad dist.

Makran or **Mekran** (both: mŭkrän'), coastal region of BALUCHISTAN, in SE Iran and W Pakistan, on Arabian Sea. A desert plateau area with a few cultivated valleys (dates), mainly that of Dasht (Kej) R. It came in 643 under Arab control, and was visited in 1294 by Marco Polo, who called it Kes (Kej) Macoran. Its later history is that of Baluchistan. Since the boundary demarcation of 1895–96, Makran has been divided between Iran and India (after 1947, Pakistan). Iranian Makran (also Mokran or Mukran), since 1938 part of Eighth Prov. (see KERMAN), is served by the ports of Jask, Chahbahar, and Gwatar. Pakistani Makran consists of the princely state of Makran (see following article).

Makran (mŭkrän'), princely state (□ 23,196; 1951 pop. 143,000), Baluchistan, Pakistan; ⊙ Turbat. Bounded W by Iran, S by Arabian Sea, E by Kalat state; bordered N by Siahan Range; crossed by Central Makran Range and Makran Coast Range (S). Rainfall very scanty. Chief rivers: Dasht, Rakhshan. Consists of barren hills and hot, dry valleys. Its dates are famous; some wheat and barley grown; palm-mat weaving, fishing (off coast; chiefly catfish), leather working. Main towns: Pasni, Turbat, Panjgur. Formerly under suzerainty of Kalat; acceded independently in 1948 to Pakistan. Pop. 99% Moslem.

Makrana (mŭkrä'nŭ), town (pop. 11,404), central Rajasthan, India, 120 mi. NE of Jodhpur; trades in marble, salt, millet, hides. Noted marble quarries just W; material used in construction of Taj Mahal in Agra.

Makran Coast Range (mŭkrän'), Makran state, S Baluchistan, W Pakistan, extends c.250 mi. E-W, parallel to Arabian Sea, bet. Dasht R. (W) and W hills of Pab Range (E); 15–40 mi. wide. Several peaks over 4,000 ft.; rises to 5,185 ft. in E peak. Watered by tributaries of lower Hingol and Dasht rivers, with many narrow gorges. Generally dry and barren.

Makran Range, Central, Makran state, SW Baluchistan, W Pakistan, extends c.250 mi. NE–SW in arc, bet. Iran border (W) and E end of Siahan Range (NE); 15–40 mi. wide. Rises to 7,522 ft. in N peak. SW section watered by tributaries of Dasht R.

Makri, Turkey: see FETHIYE.

Makrikambos, Mount, Greece-Albania: see MAKRYKAMBOS, MOUNT.

Makronesos or **Makronisos** (both: mŭkrô'nĭsôs), anc. *Helena*, northwesternmost island (□ 6.4; pop. 36) of the Cyclades, in Aegean Sea, in Attica nome, Greece, 2 mi. off Attica peninsula, opposite Laurion; separated from Kea by Kea Channel; 8 mi. long, 1 mi. wide. Mountainous, rugged terrain; fisheries. Also called Makronesi or Makronisi, Helene or Eleni.

Makrykambos, Mount, or **Mount Makrikambos** (both: mäkrē'kämbôs) (5,485 ft.), on Albanian-Greek border, in Epirus, 14 mi. ESE of Argyrokastron; 40°N 20°23'E. Also Tsouka (tsōō'kä).

Makryplagi, Greece: see GERANEIA.

Maksatikha (mŭksŭtyē'khŭ), town (1948 pop. over 2,000), N central Kalinin oblast, Russian SFSR, on Mologa R. and 30 mi. W of Bezhetsk; sawmilling center; wood distillation.

Maksudabad, India: see MURSHIDABAD, town.

Maktar (mäktär'), town (pop. c.950), ⊙ Maktar dist. (□ 1,110; pop. 77,202), central Tunisia, 35 mi. SE of Le Kef; agr. settlement; livestock, olives, esparto grass. Remains of anc. civilization include a triumphal arch (A.D. 116), temples, a Christian chapel, and 12 arches of a Roman aqueduct. Excavations are continuing.

Maku (mäkōō'), town (1940 pop. 10,687), Fourth Prov., in Azerbaijan, northwesternmost Iran, 125 mi. NW of Tabriz, near Turkish border; grain, cotton; rug weaving.

Ma-kuan, China: see MAKWAN.

Makubetsu (mäkōō'bätsōō) or **Makumbetsu** (mäkōōm'–), town (pop. 17,382), S central Hokkaido, Japan, just S of Obihiro; agr. (rice, potatoes, sugar beets), dairying; flour and sawmilling.

Makuhari (mäkōō'-hä'rē) or **Makuwari** (–wä'rē), town (pop. 17,315), Chiba prefecture, central Honshu, Japan, at NW base of Chiba Peninsula, on Tokyo Bay, 5 mi. NW of Chiba, in agr. area (rice, sweet potatoes); summer resort. Flour milling, soy-sauce mfg.

Makumbi (mäkōōm'bē), village, Kasai prov., S Belgian Congo, on right bank of Kasai R. and 60 mi. SW of Luebo; regional transshipment point at head of railroad to Charlesville circumnavigating the rapids; cottonseed-oil milling, soap mfg., sawmilling.

Makump, Sierra Leone: see MAGBURAKA.

Makunduchi (mäkōōndōō'chē), town (pop. 6,000), near SE coast of Zanzibar, 30 mi. SE of Zanzibar town; tobacco- and pepper-growing center; matmaking, limeburning.

Makung (mä'gōōng'), Jap. *Mako* (mä'kō), formerly *Makyu* (mä'kyōō), officially *Penghu* (bŭng'hōō'), chief town (1935 pop. 7,854) of the Pescadores, on W shore of Penghu Isl.; 23°34'N 119°34'E. Major naval base and fishing port; fish processing, peanut-oil and sugar milling. Has tomb of French admiral Courbet, who occupied town during Franco-Chinese War (1884–85).

Makungu (mäkōōng'gōō), village, Kivu prov., E Belgian Congo, near W shore of L. Tanganyika, 55 mi. N of Albertville; gold-mining center.

Makurazaki (mäkōōrä'zäkē), town (pop. 32,717), Kagoshima prefecture, SW Kyushu, Japan, port on E.China Sea, on S Satsuma Peninsula, 26 mi. SW of Kagoshima; rail terminus; fishing port and mining center (gold, silver). Fisheries inst.

Makurdi (mäkōōr'dē), town (pop. 7,655), ⊙ Benue prov., Northern Provinces, central Nigeria, port on Benue R., on railroad (bridge) and 115 mi. NNE of Port Harcourt; 7°54'N 8°30'E. Agr. trade center; shea-nut processing; sesame, cassava, durra, yams. Has hosp.

Makurti, peak, India: see MUKURTI.

Makushin (mŭkōō'shĭn), native fishing village, N Unalaska Isl., Aleutian Isls., SW Alaska.

Makushino (mŭkōō'shĭnŭ), town (1939 pop. over 5,000), E Kurgan oblast, Russian SFSR, on Trans-Siberian RR and 75 mi. ESE of Kurgan; metalworks, flour mill.

Makushin Volcano (mŭkōō'shĭn) (6,680 ft.), NE Unalaska Isl., Aleutian Isls., SW Alaska, 15 mi. W of Dutch Harbor; 53°53'N 166°55'W; flat-topped, snow-covered, active volcano.

Makuwari, Japan: see MAKUHARI.

Makuyuni (mäkōōyōō'nē), village, Tanga prov., NE Tanganyika, on railroad and 15 mi. NW of Korogwe at foot of Usambara Mts.; sisal.

Makwan or **Ma-kuan** (both: mä'gwän'), town, ⊙ Makwan co. (pop. 104,191), SE Yunnan prov., China, 25 mi. S of Wenshan, near Vietnam border; rice, millet. Antimony and tungsten deposits near by. Until 1914 called Anping.

Makwar, dam, Anglo-Egyptian Sudan: see SENNAR.

Makwi, Sierra Leone: see KAMAKWI.

Makwiro (mäkwē'rō), village, Salisbury prov., central Southern Rhodesia, in Mashonaland, on railroad and 22 mi. NE of Hartley; alt. 4,307 ft. Chrome mining.

Makyu, Pescadores: see MAKUNG.

Mala (mä'lä), town (pop. 1,500), Lima dept., W central Peru, on coastal plain, on Mala R., on Lima-Cañete highway, and 34 mi. NNW of Cañete, in cotton-growing region.

Malabar (mă'lŭbär), district (□ 5,790; pop. 3,929,-425), SW Madras, India; ⊙ Calicut. Lies bet. Western Ghats (E) and Malabar Coast of Arabian Sea (W). Agr.: rice (mainly terrace farming), coconuts, areca nuts, jack, mangoes, cashew nuts (on coastal plain). Extensive tea, rubber, spice (pepper, ginger), and coffee plantations in the Ghats (mainly in the Wynaad; teak and blackwood forests). Dist. is main coconut-producing area of Madras; mfg. of copra, coir rope and mats. Main towns: Calicut, Palghat, Tellicherry, Cannanore, Cochin. S group of Laccadive Isls. (Laccadives proper) administered by dist.

Malabar Coast or **Malabar,** region of SW India extending c.450 mi. NNW from Cape Comorin to Madras-Bombay border and reaching inland (30–70 mi.) from Arabian Sea to the Western Ghats; comprises TRAVANCORE-COCHIN state, MALABAR and SOUTH KANARA dists. of Madras, and small Fr. possession of MAHÉ; sometimes considered to extend N to Goa. Its sandy shore line is broken by numerous inlets; these—especially towards the S—widen out into lagoons, which parallel the coast for many miles and with their interconnecting canals form a unique and picturesque system of inland waterways (navigable for native craft). Behind this narrow strip is fairly level, alluvial land, well watered by perennial streams, rising in densely forested Ghats to the E. Malabar has tropical monsoon climate, characterized by heavy annual rainfall (mostly June–Sept.) of 80–120 in., increasing to over 200 in. on mtn. slopes; mean annual temp. is 82°F. Rice and spices (pepper, cardamom) are chief crops, and coconut palms abound; coffee, rubber, and cinchona estates are found in the Ghats, which also have valuable bamboo, teak, ebony, and sandalwood forests. Fishing (sardines, mackerel, seerfish, pomfrets, catfish) and coir matting are major industries. Only important port is COCHIN, exporting coir products, copra, tea, rubber, and spices; other coastal cities include Mangalore, Cannanore, CALICUT, Quilon, and TRIVANDRUM. But for Palghat Gap and another railway route through Cardamom Hills (S), region is largely isolated from rest of India. Its c.13,000,000 inhabitants—predominantly of Dravidian stock—have their own distinctive cultural heritage and social customs. Malayalam is principal language, with Tulu and Kanarese spoken to the N. The Hindus of Malabar, who adhere to a matriarchic family system, have preserved (especially in Travancore) a noted classical school of dancing and other forms of Hindu art. The sizeable Christian community (c.2,575,000) here, allegedly founded A.D. c.52 by the Apostle Thomas, includes Malabar Jacobites and a Nestorian (Syrian) sect, dating back to earliest centuries of Christian era. Cochin has a small Jewish colony, centering at Mattancheri, where there are 3 c.6th-cent. A.D. synagogues. Over 2,000,000 Moslems live in the region, some of them, called Moplahs or Mappilas, descended from early Arab traders and known for their religious fanaticism, periodically demonstrated in outbreaks of violence. Much of the Malabar Coast was part of the anc. kingdom of KERALA. Its wealth in spices attracted the 1st Europeans to visit India, including Vasco da Gama (1498–1503) and other Portuguese, who established trading posts at Calicut, Cochin, Mangalore, and other coastal points. The Dutch appeared in 1656 and the French took Mahé in 1720s; the British won control of the area from the Mysore sultans in late-18th cent.

Malabar Hill, India: see BOMBAY, city.

Malabon (mäläbōn'), town (1939 pop. 3,125; 1948 municipality pop. 46,455), Rizal prov., S Luzon, Philippines, on Manila Bay, just NNW of Manila; agr. center (rice, sugar cane, fruit); sugar milling. Also called Tanong.

Malabrigo (mäläbrē'gō) or **Colonia Ella** (kōlō'nyä ĕ'yä), town (pop. estimate 1,500), N Santa Fe prov., Argentina, on railroad and 24 mi. SW of Reconquista, in agr. flax, corn, livestock, poultry and lumbering area; flour milling, sawmilling.

Malabrigo, Peru: see PUERTO CHICAMA.

Mal Abrigo (mäl'äbrē'gō), town (pop. 630), San José dept., S Uruguay, rail junction 19 mi. NW of San José, in stock-raising region.

Malabuyoc (mäläbōō'yōk, mäläbōōyōk'), town (1939 pop. 1,639; 1948 municipality pop. 14,096), S Cebu isl., Philippines, 15 mi. NE of Tanjay across Tañon Strait; agr. center (corn, coconuts).

Mala Bytca, Czechoslovakia: see BYTCA.

Malaca, Spain: see MÁLAGA, city.

Malacacheta (mŭ'lŭkŭshĕ'tŭ), city (pop. 1,580), NE Minas Gerais, Brazil, 40 mi. WSW of Teófilo Otoni; coffee.

Malacalzetta, Sardinia: see IGLESIAS.

Malacatán (mäläkätän'), town (1950 pop. 2,002), San Marcos dept., SW Guatemala, in Pacific piedmont, on Inter-American Highway, near Mex. border, and 17 mi. WSW of San Marcos; market center; coffee, sugar cane, grain; livestock.

Malacatancito (mäläkätänsē'tō), town (1950 pop. 527), Huehuetenango dept., W Guatemala, on headstream of Chixoy R. and 5 mi. SSW of Huehuetenango; alt. 5,203 ft.; corn, wheat, beans.

Malacatoya (mäläkätoi'ä), village, Granada dept., SW Nicaragua, 19 mi. NNE of Granada, near L. Nicaragua, and on small Malacatoya R.; lumbering; livestock.

Malacca (mŭlă'kŭ), Malay *Malaka*, city (pop. 54,507), ⊙ Settlement of Malacca, Malaya, port on Strait of Malacca, at mouth of small Malacca R. and 125 mi. NW of Singapore; 2°12'N 102°14'E. Port of call (off-shore anchorage) on spur (from Tampin junction) of W coast railroad; ships rubber, copra. Extending 3 mi. along coast, Malacca has a hill (once fortified by Portuguese), old Port. and Dutch churches and buildings. One of oldest towns on Malay Peninsula, it was settled c.1400 by Malays and became a rich trade center of SE Asia. Aided by friendship of China, the kings of Malacca extended their power (15th cent.) over Malay Peninsula as far as Kedah and Pattani and over near-by W coast of Sumatra. It was through Malacca that Islam was introduced to Malay world. Malacca's pre-eminence continued under Portuguese rule (after 1511) and the Dutch (after 1641), but declined with the rise of Penang in late 18th cent. and, later, of Singapore. During Napoleonic wars, Malacca was held (1795–1814) by the British, and was finally ceded 1824 by the Dutch to Great Britain. Pop. is 73% Chinese, 12% Malay.

Malacca, Settlement of, civil division (□ 633; pop. 239,356) of Malaya, on Strait of Malacca; ⊙ Malacca. Bounded N by Negri Sembilan and E by Johore, it is situated on S slopes of central Malayan hills. Agr.: rubber, coconuts, rice, tapioca, gambier, betel nuts. Chief towns, besides Malacca, are Alor Gajah and Jasin. Pop. is 48% Malay, 40% Chinese. One of the Straits Settlements after 1826, it joined the Federation of Malaya following Second World War.

Malacca, Strait of, sea arm bet. Malay Peninsula and Sumatra, connecting Andaman Sea of Indian Ocean and South China Sea of the Pacific; 500 mi. long, 30-200 mi. wide. One of world's leading shipping lanes on route bet. Europe and the Far East; main ports are George Town (Penang), Port Swettenham and Malacca in Malaya, and Belawan in Sumatra. Singapore is at its S extremity.

Malacky (mä'lätskĭ), Hung. *Malacka* (mŏ'lŏtskŏ), town (pop. 7,366), W Slovakia, Czechoslovakia, on railroad and 20 mi. NNW of Bratislava; petroleum field; iron mining (pyrite); artillery range.

Malacota (mäläkō'tä), officially San Lorenzo Malacota, town (pop. 1,995), Morelos, central Mexico, 25 mi. NW of Mexico city; cereals, maguey, fruit.

Mala Cvrstnica, mountain, Yugoslavia: see VELIKA CVRSTNICA.

Malad (mŭl'äd), town (pop. 12,212), Bombay Suburban dist., W Bombay, India, on Salsette Isl., 17 mi. N of Bombay city center; rice; motion-picture studios. Glass-bangle factory just N.

Malad City or **Malad** (mŭlăd', mŭlăd'), village (pop. 2,715), ⊙ Oneida co., SE Idaho, on Deep Creek, near Utah line, and 18 mi. WNW of Preston; alt. 4,700 ft. Shipping point for agr. area (sugar beets, wheat, potatoes); dairy products, flour. Settled by Mormons 1864.

Maladetta or **Maladeta** (mälädĕ'tä), highest massif of the Pyrenees (central range), in N Huesca and Lérida prov., NE Spain, near Fr. border. Bounded by Val d'Aran (NE) and Esera R. valley (W). Culminates in Pico de Aneto (11,168 ft.; highest in Pyrenees). Reaches 11,004 ft. in Pico del Medio (Fr. Pic du Milieu) and 10,866 ft. in Pico de la Maladeta. Sometimes called Montes Malditos (Sp.) and Monts Maudits (Fr.).

Malad River (mŭlăd', mŭlăd'), in SE Idaho and N Utah, formed by confluence of Little Malad R. with Deep Creek and Devil Creek in Oneida co., Idaho, flows S, into Box Elder co., Utah, entering Bear R. NW of Brigham; c.50 mi. long.

Mala Fatra, mountains, Czechoslovakia: see LESSER FATRA.

Málaga (mä'lägä), town (pop. 5,210), Santander dept., N central Colombia, in valley of Cordillera Oriental, on Cúcuta-Bogotá highway and 40 mi. SE of Bucaramanga; trading and agr. center (wheat, oats, peas, sugar cane, cattle, sheep); textile milling, liquor distilling. Resort.

Málaga (mă'lŭgŭ, Sp. mä'lägä), province (□ 2,813; pop. 677,474), S Spain, in Andalusia; ⊙ Málaga, a major port. On the Mediterranean, bounded by Granada prov. (E), Córdoba and Seville provs. (N), and Cádiz prov. (W). Crossed by spurs of the Cordillera Penibética, among them Sierra de Ronda (W) and Sierra de Yeguas (N). Narrow strip of lowland (*vega*) along coast. N section belongs to the interior Andalusian plain of the Guadalquivir. Drained by Guadalhorce R., Guadiaro R., and tributaries of the Guadalquivir. Climate is very mild in winter (especially near the coast), cooler in the uplands; summers are of semitropical, North African nature. The fertile intramontane basins and coastal lowlands produce mostly olives, grapes, almonds, figs, citrus fruit, cereals, truck produce, livestock. Olive oil, raisins, and wine (the renowned sweet Malaga) are its chief exports. Sugar cane was introduced in the 1870s. While agr. is its mainstay, mineral resources have some importance. Iron is mined near Marbella, nickel milled at Ojén and Carratraca; the Sierra de Ronda has deposits of iron, platinum, antimony, bismuth, gold, and coal. The main industries process agr. products. Besides important fisheries and fish-salting plants, there are also tanneries, textile mills, and foundries, chiefly centered at Málaga. Other cities are Antequera, Ronda, Vélez-Málaga, Coín, Álora, Estepona. Administratively, Melilla in Sp. North Africa belongs to Málaga prov.

Málaga, anc. *Malaca*, city (pop. 208,344), ⊙ Málaga prov., S Spain, in Andalusia; major Mediterranean port on Málaga Bay, on fertile coastal plain (*vega*), 260 mi. S of Madrid and 65 mi. NE of Gibraltar; 36°43′N 4°25′W. Its benign winter climate and luxuriant vegetation have made it one of Spain's leading resorts. As entrepôt of rich agr. region, it exports chiefly wine (the celebrated sweet Malaga), grapes, raisins, oranges, lemons, almonds, figs, olive oil, cork, fish; and lead and iron ore from near-by mines. Also an important industrial center, with sugar refineries, alcohol and liquor distilleries, wineries, breweries, olive-oil presses, fish canneries, foundries, machine shops, textile and cement mills, shipyards. Picturesquely situated in undulating valley, the city is divided by the Guadalmedina R. Above it tower (E) the ruins of the Gibralfaro and the Alcazaba (citadels), said to be of Phoenician and Roman origin, though embellished by the Moors. Largely modern in aspect, Málaga, nevertheless, has notable old religious bldgs. Foremost is the Renaissance cathedral (begun in 16th cent.) with a Greco-Roman doorway. Santiago parish church was founded (1490) by Ferdinand and Isabella, in whose reign the baroque church of Holy Martyrs was also begun. Other edifices include bishop's palace, natl. institute, seminary, school of business, customhouse. The seashore suburbs of La Caleta, Limonar, and El Palo, the latter with a noted Jesuit col., attract tourists. Málaga, founded by the Phoenicians, has successively been a Carthaginian, Greek, Roman, and Visigothic town. Taken in 711 by the Moors. Flourished from 13th cent. as ⊙ Moorish kingdom of Málaga, dependent on that of Granada, for which it served as a seaport until conquered in 1487 by Ferdinand and Isabella, after which it lost much of its importance. During 16th cent. it was scene of several Moorish rebellions, and in 19th cent. became a cradle of the liberal movement. Held during Sp. civil war by Loyalist forces until Feb., 1937. Pablo Picasso b. here (1881). The García Morata airport is SW.

Malaga (mălʹlūgŭ), village (pop. c.400), Gloucester co., S N.J., on Maurice R. and 12 mi. N of Millville, in fruit-growing area. Methodist camp-meeting ground here.

Malaga Lake (8 mi. long, 3 mi. wide), W N.S., 13 mi. W of Bridgewater. Fed and drained by Medway R.

Malagarasi River (mä″lägärä′sē), W Tanganyika, rises near L. Tanganyika on Ruanda-Urundi border NNE of Kigoma, flows 250 mi. NW, SSE, and W in circular course, past Uvinza, to L. Tanganyika 25 mi. SSE of Kigoma. Receives (left) swampy lower course of Ugalla R. (ōōgä′lä).

Malagash (mă′lŭgăsh, mălŭgăsh′), village (pop. estimate 150), N N.S., at head of Tatamagouche Bay, 40 mi. WNW of New Glasgow; salt-production center.

Malagón (mälägōn′), town (pop. 8,876), Ciudad Real prov., S central Spain, on railroad to Madrid and 13 mi. N of Ciudad Real; processing and agr. center (cereals, olives, truck produce, vegetables, fruit, grapes, stock); apiculture; tree nursery. Olive-oil pressing, flour milling, liquor distilling, wine making, lumbering, wool processing; mfg. of fertilizer. Taken from the Moors in 1212.

Malagueño (mälägā′nyō), town (pop. 2,099), W central Córdoba prov., Argentina, 10 mi. WSW of Córdoba; rail terminus; quarrying center with lime kilns, granite quarries. Agr.: olives, flax, corn, livestock.

Malahide (mă″lŭhīd′), Gaelic *Mullach Ide*, town (pop. 1,540), NE Co. Dublin, Ireland, on inlet of the Irish Sea, 10 mi. NNE of Dublin; fishing port and seaside resort. Malahide Castle has been seat of lords Talbot since time of Henry II and contains noted art collection. There are remains of 14th-cent. abbey.

Malahra (mŭlä′rŭ), town (pop. 5,232), N Vindhya Pradesh, India, 10 mi. NNE of Chhatarpur; local market for grain, cloth fabrics. Sometimes spelled Malehra.

Malaita (mälā′tä), volcanic island (□ 1,572; pop. c.40,000), most populous of Solomon Isls., SW Pacific, 30 mi. NE of Guadalcanal; 115 mi. long, 15 mi. wide. Auki, on NW coast, is chief town. Produces copra. Inhabited principally by Melanesians.

Malaiyandipattanam, India: see KOTTUR.

Malakal (mäläkäl′), town (pop. 11,250), ⊙ Upper Nile prov., S central Anglo-Egyptian Sudan, on right bank of the White Nile, on road and 430 mi. S of Khartoum; 9°3′N 31°39′E; commercial and stock-raising center (cattle, sheep, and goats); some agr. (cotton, peanuts, sesame, corn, durra). Veterinary laboratory. Airport on Cairo–Cape Town route.

Malakal (mä′läkäl), volcanic island, central Palau, W Caroline Isls., W Pacific; 7°20′N 134°27′E; c.¾ mi. in diameter; rises to 393 ft. Malakal Harbor is chief port of Palau.

Malakand (mŭl′ŭkŭnd), agency (1951 pop. 1,241,-000), North-West Frontier Prov., W Pakistan; hq. at Malakand. Comprises princely states of Dir, Swat, and Chitral, petty states of Amb and Phulra, and large tribal areas W of Hazara dist. Formed 1895.

Malakand, fort and village, Swat state, N central North-West Frontier Prov., W Pakistan, in hill pass, 44 mi. NNE of Peshawar; hq. of Malakand agency. Here Upper Swat Canal runs through hills via 2-mi.-long tunnel; hydroelectric plant (20,000 kw.) near by. Scene of fighting during tribal disturbances in 1895 and 1897.

Mala Kapela mountain range, Yugoslavia: see VELIKA KAPELA.

Malakastër or **Malakastra**, Albania: see MALLAKASTËR.

Malakhov (mŭlä′khŭf), hill [Rus. *kurgan*] overlooking Sevastopol, Crimea, Russian SFSR, just E of the city. A fortified height during Crimean War (1854–55), its capture by the French, after long siege, sealed fate of Sevastopol.

Malakoff (mäläkôf′), town (pop. 27,424), Seine dept., N central France, just SSW of Paris, 3 mi. from Notre Dame Cathedral, bet. Vanves (W) and Montrouge (E); mfg. (machine tools, electrical equipment, pharmaceuticals); wool spinning.

Malakoff (mă′lŭkôf), city (pop. 1,286), Henderson co., E Texas, 27 mi. ENE of Corsicana; rail point in agr. area; lignite mines; brick making. Inc. after 1940.

Mala Krsna (mä′lä kŭr′snä), village, E Serbia, Yugoslavia, 7 mi. SSE of Smederevo; rail junction.

Malakwal (mŭlŭkväl′), town (pop. 6,445), Gujrat dist., NE Punjab, W Pakistan, near Jhelum R., 50 mi. W of Gujrat; rail junction (workshop); market center (wheat, cotton, millet, oilseeds, cloth fabrics); cotton ginning, chemical mfg.

Malalbergo (mälälbĕr′gō), village (pop. 1,046), Bologna prov., Emilia-Romagna, N central Italy, near Reno R., 9 mi. SSE of Ferrara; marmalade, brooms.

Malali or **Mallali**, village (pop. 234), Demerara co., central Br. Guiana, landing on right bank of Demerara R. and 85 mi. SSW of Georgetown, in tropical forest region (timber, charcoal, balata). Head of navigation for small craft on Demerara R.

Mala Ljubisnja, mountain, Yugoslavia: see VELIKA LJUBISNJA.

Malambo (mäläm′bō), town (pop. 2,986), Atlántico dept., N Colombia, on Magdalena R., in Caribbean lowlands, and 8 mi. S of Barranquilla; cotton, sugar cane, corn, stock. Airfield.

Malamir, Iran: see IZEH.

Malamocco (mälämôk′kō), village (pop. 1,089), Venezia prov., Veneto, N Italy, on chief isl. (Lido or Lido di Venezia) of chain separating Lagoon of Venice from the Adriatic, 3 mi. S of Lido; resort.

Malampaka (mälämpä′kä), village, Lake Prov., NW Tanganyika, on railroad and 38 mi. N of Shinyanga; cotton, peanuts, corn; livestock.

Maland, Sweden: see NORRLAND.

Malang (mŭläng′), town (pop. 86,649), E Java, Indonesia, 50 mi. S of Surabaya, at foot of Semeru Mts.; 7°59′S 112°38′E; trade center for agr. area (coffee, corn, rice, sugar, tea, cinchona bark, peanuts, cassava). Has textile and lumber mills, railroad workshops, factories (cigars, cigarettes, soap). Until 1949, was important Du. military center.

Malangali (mäläng-gä′lē), village, Southern Highlands prov., S Tanganyika, on road and 75 mi. SSW of Iringa; wheat, peanuts, livestock.

Malangas (mäläng′gäs), town (1939 pop. 3,465) in Margosatubig municipality, Zamboanga prov., W Mindanao, Philippines, 31 mi. WSW of Pagadian, on Dumanquilas Bay; coal-mining center.

Malange or **Malanje** (mŭlăn′zhŭ), province (□ c.103,400; pop. 678,721), NE Angola; ⊙ Malange. Bounded N and E by Belgian Congo, it lies on N slopes of Angola's central plateau. Drained by the Kasai (which forms E frontier) and by its left tributaries (Chicapa, Kwilu, Kwango). Agr. (cotton, coffee, sisal, beans, manioc, corn) mostly in W section around town of Malange. Rubber and hardwoods shipped from interior. Important diamond washings along Chicapa R. Chief towns are Malange and Vila Henrique de Carvalho, capitals of Malange and Lunda dists. respectively.

Malange or **Malanje**, town (pop. 5,299), ⊙ Malange prov., N central Angola, on central plateau, 220 mi. ESE of Luanda; 9°33′S 16°21′E; alt. 3,800 ft. Inland terminus of railroad from Luanda. Agr. center (coffee, sugar, rice, beans, corn, manioc). Processing industries. Airfield.

Malangen (mä′läng-ŭn), fishing village and canton (pop. 2,296), Troms co., N Norway, on Malangen Fjord (30-mi.-long inlet of Norwegian Sea), 20 mi. SSW of Tromso.

Malangwa (mŭlŭng′gvŭ), town, SE Nepal, in the Terai, 60 mi. SSE of Katmandu, on road to Sitamarhi (India); rice, wheat, oilseeds, barley, millet.

Malanje, town and province, Angola: see MALANGE.

Malanville (mälänvēl′), village, N Dahomey, Fr. West Africa, on right bank of the Niger (Niger territory border) and 55 mi. NE of Kandi; cotton, kapok, corn, millet.

Malanzán (mälänsän′), village (pop. estimate 500), ⊙ Rivadavia dept. (□ 1,295; 1947 census pop. 3,685), S La Rioja prov., Argentina, in Sierra de Malanzán (a short pampean mtn. range), 100 mi. SSE of La Rioja; agr. center (corn, alfalfa, wine, goats, cattle). Dam near by.

Mala Panew River (mä′wä pä′nĕf), Pol. *Mala Panew*, Ger. *Malapane* (mäläpä′nŭ), in Upper Silesia, after 1945 in Opole prov., S Poland, rises N of Tarnowskie Gory, flows 75 mi. WNW to the Oder just below Oppeln (Opole). Irrigation dam at TURAWA.

Mala Plazenica, mountain, Yugoslavia: see VELIKA PLAZENICA.

Mala Point (mä′lä), SE extremity of Azuero Peninsula, Panama, on Gulf of Panama of the Pacific; 7°28′N 80°1′W.

Malapuram, India: see HOSPET.

Malaqa, El, or **Al-Malaqah** (both: ĕl mă′lăkŭ), village (1937 pop. 5,636), Daqahliya prov., Lower Egypt, bet. L. Manzala and Damietta branch of the Nile, 6 mi. NNE of Damietta; fisheries.

Malar, Lake, Swedish *Mälaren* (mĕ′lärŭn) (□ 440), E Sweden, extends W from Stockholm; 70 mi. long (E–W), 1–25 mi. wide; max. depth 210 ft. Drains E into the Baltic by narrow strait at Stockholm; short Sodertalje Canal provides further navigable outlet at Sodertalje (SE). Lake contains 1,260 isls. with total area of 189 sq. mi. Favorite residential and resort region; on shore are cities of Sigtuna, Vasteras, Strangnas, Mariefred, Sodertalje, and many W suburbs of Stockholm as well as W part of the city. Notable castles and ruins include Gripsholm, Drottningholm, and Skokloster. Lake receives Fyris, Arboga, Kolback, and many smaller rivers.

Malargüe (mälärgwā′), town (pop. estimate 1,000), W Mendoza prov., Argentina, 100 mi. SW of San Rafael; rail terminus; coal-mining and agr. center (alfalfa, potatoes, wheat, livestock). Oil was discovered here 1891.

Mala River (mä′lä), Lima dept., W central Peru, rises in Cordillera Occidental of the Andes 14 mi. ESE of Matucana, flows 70 mi. S and SW, past Huarochirí, San Lorenzo de Quinti, and Mala, to the Pacific 5 mi. WSW of Mala. Irrigation in lower course.

Malartic (mälärtĕk′), town (pop. 2,895), W Que., 40 mi. ESE of Rouyn; mining center (gold, copper, molybdenum, zinc, lead). Inc. 1939.

Malasiqui (mäläsēkē′, mäläsē′kē), town (1939 pop. 3,202; 1948 municipality pop. 40,786), Pangasinan prov., central Luzon, Philippines, 10 mi. SSE of Dagupan, near railroad; agr. center (rice, copra, corn).

Malaspina, Philippines: see CANLAON, MOUNT.

Malaspina Glacier (mălŭspē′nŭ), SE Alaska, W of Yakutat Bay, S of 60°N bet. 140° and 141°W; part of St. Elias Mts. glacier system.

Malaspina Strait (mălŭspē′nŭ), arm of Strait of Georgia in SW B.C., bet. Texada Isl. and mainland; 40 mi. long, 3–5 mi. wide. Jervis Inlet branches off (NE). Near NE entrance is Powell River.

Malato Dag, Turkey: see SASUN DAG.

Malatrask (mäl″ō″trĕsk′), Swedish *Malåträsk*, village (pop. 729), Vasterbotten co., N Sweden, on 6-mi.-long Mala L., Swedish *Malåträsk*, 40 mi. N of Lycksele; cattle; dairying.

Malatya or **Malatia** (mälä′tyä), province (□ 7,690; 1950 pop. 481,386), central Turkey; ⊙ Malatya. Bordered E and S by the Euphrates. Mountainous and unproductive; grain, goats.

Malatya or **Malatia**, anc. *Melitene*, city (1950 pop. 49,077), ⊙ Malatya prov., E central Turkey, in Armenia, at E foot of Taurus Mts., near the Euphrates, 100 mi. NE of Maras, 300 mi. ESE of Ankara; alt. c.2,600 ft.; 38°25′N 38°18′E. Rail junction; cotton milling and agr. trade center (opium, wheat, barley, vetch, onions; orchards, vineyards). An important town of Cappadocia under the Romans. Terrible massacre of Christians in 1895.

Malatya Mountains, S central Turkey, part of Taurus Mts., extend 65 mi. SW from the Euphrates, S of Malatya. In it are Buz Dag (9,091 ft.; also given as 11,850 ft.) and Nuruhak Dag (9,850 ft.)

Malaucène (mälōsĕn'), village (pop. 836), Vaucluse dept., SE France, at NW foot of Mont Ventoux, 9 mi. NNE of Carpentras; cigarette-paper mfg., winegrowing.

Malaunay (mälōnā'), town (pop. 2,540), Seine-Inférieure dept., N France, 6 mi. NNW of Rouen; rail junction; textile dyeing, margarine mfg.

Malavalli, India: see MALVALLI.

Malawi, Malavi, Tang-i-Malawi, or **Tang-e-Malavi** (both: tăng'ĕmälävē'), village, Sixth Prov., in Luristan, SW Iran, on Khurramabad-Dizful road and 35 mi. SW of Khurramabad, in gorge of Kashgan R. (left tributary of Karkheh R.).

Malaya (mùlā'ù), officially **Federation of Malaya**, federation (□ 50,600; pop. 4,908,086; including transients, 4,922,821) of the 9 British-protected Malay states and 2 settlements on southern MALAY PENINSULA; ⊙ Kuala Lumpur. Bounded N by Thailand (along the Kalakhiri Range), W by Strait of Malacca and E by South China Sea, the federation consists of the former Federated (PERAK, SELANGOR, NEGRI SEMBILAN, PAHANG) and Unfederated (PERLIS, KEDAH, KELANTAN, TRENGGANU, JOHORE) Malay States and the former Straits Settlements of PENANG (including PROVINCE WELLESLEY) and MALACCA. The central Malayan range, rising to 7,186 ft. in the Gunong Tahan, extends *en échelon* from N to S and gives rise to Perak (W) and Pahang (E) rivers. The Malayan rivers have a quick-flowing, precipitous upper course, but meander slowly across the coastal lowlands. Covered in four-fifths of its surface by dense tropical jungle, the country is generally cleared in N and along W coast in the great rice-producing areas of Perak (Krian dist.) Kedah, Perlis, and Kelantan. Off the W coast (mangroves, mudflats) are the isls. of Langkawi, Penang, and Pangkor, while Tionan is off the sandy, surf-beaten E coast. The Malayan climate is featured by copious rainfall (100 in. yearly in the plain, 200 in. in the hills), high humidity, and a uniform high temperature (average 71°–91°F.) with a small diurnal range; seasons are faintly marked by the NE and SW monsoons. Hill stations (Cameron Highlands, Fraser's Hill, and Maxwell's Hill at Taiping) afford climatic relief. Aside from deficient production of rice (only ⅓ of total consumption), agr. is largely devoted to export crops. Malaya is one of the great rubber producers of the world. About 65% of total area under cultivation is in large European rubber estates and Chinese and Malay small holdings, and an estimated third of Malaya's working pop. depend on rubber for a livelihood. Coconuts and related products (copra, oil), palm oil and kernels, canned pineapples, sago, and tapioca are other agr. exports. Next to rubber, tin is Malaya's leading product. Tin mines are scattered throughout the country, but the KINTA VALLEY of Perak has the greatest production, which is smelted at the 2 great works of Butterworth (Penang) and Pulau Brani (Singapore). Coal is mined at Batu Arang (Selangor) and lesser minerals are gold (Raub), iron ore (Trengganu, Johore), bauxite, manganese, tungsten, and kaolin. Although Singapore has been separated politically from Malaya, it continues to be the country's primary port and distribution center, as well as railhead of the Malayan W coast and E coast lines leading N to Thailand. The Federation's own seaports (all on W coast, except Kota Bharu) are George Town (Penang; with its mainland railhead of Prai), Port Swettenham, Malacca, and Port Dickson. The leading pop. centers are George Town and Kuala Lumpur, Ipoh (the chief tin-mining town), and Malacca. Pop. is 50% Malay, 38% Chinese (largely from S China), 11% Indian (mainly Tamil). Prior to Second World War, Malaya was organized politically into 3 subdivisions—the Straits Settlements, a Br. crown colony; the Federated Malay States, a federation of Br. protected states; and the Unfederated (or Non-Federated) Malay States, also under Br. protection. Following the surrender of Japan, the Malayan Union (under a Br. governor) was set up in April, 1946, with colony status, comprising all Malaya except Singapore, which became a separate Br. crown colony. In Feb., 1948, the Malayan Union was reorganized into the Federation of Malaya, under a Br. high commissioner. As a result of political unrest, a state of emergency was declared in 1948.

Malaya [Rus.,=LESSER, LITTLE], in Rus. names: see also MALO- [Rus. combining form], MALOYE, MALY, MALYE.

Malaya Danilovka (mä'lĭù dŭnyē'lùfkù), town (1939 pop. over 500), N Kharkov oblast, Ukrainian SSR, on railroad (Lozovenka station) and 3 mi. S of Dergachi, in Kharkov metropolitan area.

Malaya Devitsa (dyĭvē'tsù), village (1926 pop. 3,639), S Chernigov oblast, Ukrainian SSR, 12 mi. NW of Priluki; grain, sugar beets, tobacco.

Malayagiri (mŭlī'ùgĭrē), peak (3,896 ft.) in Dhenkanal dist., N Orissa, India, 75 mi. NNW of Cuttack, just SE of Pal Lahara.

Malaya Kandala (kŭndùlä'), village (1939 pop. over 500), NE Ulyanovsk oblast, Russian SFSR, 20 mi. NNW of Melekess; grain, sunflowers. Sawmilling at Bolshaya Kandala, 5 mi. NNW.

Malaya Kheta (khyĕ'tù), village, W Taymyr Natl. Okrug, Krasnoyarsk Territory, Russian SFSR, N of Arctic Circle, on Lesser [Rus. *Malaya*] Kheta R. and 45 mi. W of Dudinka; oil fields.

Malayan Union: see MALAYA.

Malaya Purga (pōōr'gù), village, S Udmurt Autonomous SSR, Russian SFSR, 20 mi. SSW of Izhevsk; grain, livestock.

Malay Archipelago (mā'lā, mùlā', mālā') or **Malaysia** (mùlā'zhù, -shù), island group (□ c.773,000; pop. c.100,000,000) off SE Asia, in Pacific and Indian oceans, bet. Malay Peninsula and Indochina (NW) and Australia and New Guinea (SE); 10°S–19°N 95°–130°E. Includes isls. of Republic of INDONESIA—Sumatra, Java, Borneo (in Borneo are also the British possessions of Sarawak, North Borneo, and Brunei), Celebes, Timor, Lesser Sunda Isls., Moluccas—and PHILIPPINE ISLANDS. New Guinea is sometimes included in the group. Group is crossed by the Equator. Also called East Indies.

Malaya Serdoba (mä'lĭù syĭrdô'bù), village (1926 pop. 8,979), S Penza oblast, Russian SFSR, on Serdoba R. (left branch of Khoper R.) and 22 mi. NW of Petrovsk; wheat, sunflowers.

Malaya Sopcha (sŭpchä'), town (1939 pop. over 500), central Murmansk oblast, Russian SFSR, 3 mi. SW of Monchegorsk; nickel and copper mines.

Malaya Vishera (vē'shĭrù), city (1939 pop. over 10,000), N Novgorod oblast, Russian SFSR, on left headstream of Vishera R. and 40 mi. NE of Novgorod; major glassworking center.

Malaya Viska (vē'skù), town (1926 pop. 5,937), W Kirovograd oblast, Ukrainian SSR, 30 mi. WNW of Kirovograd; sugar-refining center; distillery.

Malaybalay (mä"lībä'lī), town (1939 pop. 1,876; 1948 municipality pop. 16,458), ⊙ Bukidnon prov., Philippines, N central Mindanao, 85 mi. NNW of Davao, in abacá, coconut, and pineapple area.

Malayer (mäläyĕr'), town (1940 pop. 32,357), Fifth Prov., W Iran, 100 mi. E of Kermanshah and 40 mi. SSE of Hamadan; main town of former Malayer prov. Agr. center (grapes, tobacco, opium); sheep raising; rugmaking. Until 1930s called Daulatabad. The small prov. of Malayer became part (1938) of Iran's Fifth Prov. (see KERMANSHAH).

Malay Peninsula (mā'lā, mùlā', mālā'), anc. *Chersonesus Aurea* [=Golden Chersonese], southernmost appendix (□ 70,000) of Asiatic mainland, in SE Asia, bet. Andaman Sea of Indian Ocean and Strait of Malacca (W) and South China Sea and Gulf of Siam (E); 700 mi. long, up to 200 mi. wide. Extending from Isthmus of KRA (10°N) to the cape Tanjong Piai (1°16'N), southernmost point of Asia, just W of Singapore, it comprises politically the Federation of MALAYA (S) and, in N, the peninsular (SW) section of Thailand. The central tin-bearing Malayan mtn. range forms (frequently *en échelon*) the peninsular backbone, rising to 7,186 ft. in the Gunong Tahan and to 7,160 ft. in the Gunong Korbu. It divides the peninsula into 2 unequal sections, the W mangrove coast open to the SW monsoon and the E sandy beaches exposed to NE monsoon. Largely covered by jungle, the region is one of the richest tin and rubber producers of the world. The peninsula forms a physical and a cultural link bet. the Asiatic mainland and the isls. of Indonesia (often called Malay Archipelago). The Malays, historically the dominant historical group, probably came originally from S China, but their ethnic characteristics have been modified by fusion with other groups. They are Moslems, speak a Malayo-Polynesian (Austronesian) language and use the Arabic script. The Chinese (mainly Southerners) are now nearly as numerous as the Malays, while Indians (largely Tamils) and Thais form important minority groups. Small tribes of aboriginal Proto-Malays are found in the jungle lowlands (Semang) and in the hills (Sakai). The Malay Peninsula was visited c.1st cent. A.D. by Indian traders from the Coromandel Coast who laid the foundation of small Hinduized city-states, such as Langkasuka (in modern Kedah). In 8th cent., the peninsula fell under the domination of the Indo-Malay kingdom of Srivijaya, with its ⊙ at Palembang (Sumatra). In 14th cent., the forces of the Javanese Majapahit domain overran the S Malay Peninsula, while the young state of Thailand ruled the north. The 15th cent. saw the rise of a Malay state of Malacca, which extended its sway as far north as Pattani and introduced Islam to the peninsula. The first Europeans came in the 16th cent., when the Portuguese seized (1511) Malacca, whose last sultan founded the Riouw-JOHORE kingdom. The Dutch followed in 1641 and controlled the Malacca area until the Napoleonic wars, after which British dominance in Malaya became paramount with formal Du. cession of Malacca in 1824; Penang (1786) and Singapore (1819) had previously been founded by the British. In the 19th cent., the British gradually extended their protectorate over the Malay states in face of Thai rivalry, and in 1909 the boundary bet. Thailand and Br. Malaya was fixed by Br. annexation of Kedah, Perlis, Kelantan, and Trengganu. Until the Second World War, when the peninsula was overrun by the Japanese, Br. Malaya was organized as the STRAITS SETTLEMENTS, and the Federated and Unfederated Malay States (see Federation of MALAYA). Sometimes called Kra Peninsula.

Malay Settlement, village (pop. 4,119), E Singapore isl., 5 mi. NE of Singapore; rubber. Pop. is 50% Malay.

Malaysia, SE Asia: see MALAY ARCHIPELAGO.

Malay States, Federated and **Unfederated**: see MALAYA.

Malazgirt (mäläzgĭrt') or **Manzikert** (măn'zĭkûrt), village (pop. 1,516), Mus prov., E Turkey, 85 mi. SE of Erzurum, 25 mi. NW of L. Van; wheat. Important town (Manavazagerd) of anc. Armenia. Here the Seljuk Turks under Alp Arslan defeated the Byzantines (1071) and captured the emperor, Romanus IV Diogenes, thereby winning most of Asia Minor. Sometimes spelled Malazkirt and Melazgerd.

Malbaie, La (lä măl'bā, Fr. lämälbĕ'), or **Murray Bay**, village (pop. 2,324), E Que., on the St. Lawrence at mouth of Malbaie R., and 80 mi. NE of Quebec; lumbering, dairying; popular resort.

Malbaie River (măl'bā, Fr. mälbĕ') or **Murray River**, S Que., rises in E part of Laurentides Natl. Park, flows 100 mi. in an arc NE and then SSE to the St. Lawrence at La Malbaie.

Mal Bay, inlet (6 mi. long) of the Atlantic, W Co. Clare, Ireland. Miltown Malbay is on the bay, which contains Mutton Isl., noted shipping hazard.

Malbodium, France: see MAUBEUGE.

Malbon, village, W central Queensland, Australia, 30 mi. SSW of Cloncurry; rail junction; livestock.

Malborghetto (mälbôrgĕt'tô), Ger. *Malborgeth*, village (pop. 443), Udine prov., Friuli-Venezia Giulia, NE Italy, on Fella R. and 7 mi. W of Tarvisio.

Malbork, Poland: see MARIENBURG.

Malbrán (mälbrän'), town (pop. estimate 1,000), SE Santiago del Estero prov., Argentina, on railroad and 65 mi. SE of Añatuya, in agr. area (corn, alfalfa, oats, livestock).

Mal Branch, canal, India: see GANGES CANALS.

Malbuisson (mälbwēsô'), resort (pop. 220), Doubs dept., E France, on L. of SAINT-POINT, 7 mi. SSW of Pontarlier; Gruyère cheese mfg.

Malcantone (mälkäntô'nĕ), mountainous region in the Alps, Ticino canton, S Switzerland, W of Lugano, bet. W arm of L. of Lugano (E) and Ital. border (W).

Malchen (mäl'khùn), highest elevation (1,696 ft.) of the Bergstrasse, S Hesse, W Germany, 3 mi. NNE of Bensheim; excellent view of the Odenwald and Rhine plain from summit (tower erected 1772). Locally known as Melicobus, a name which seems to have been, in anc. times, the name for the Harz.

Malchevskaya or **Mal'chevskaya** (mäl'chĭfskĭù), village (1948 pop. over 2,000), NW Rostov oblast, Russian SFSR, 10 mi. NNW of Millerovo; flour mill, metalworks; wheat, sunflowers, livestock.

Malchin (mäl-khēn'), town (pop. 6,825), Mecklenburg, N Germany, on the canalized Peene and 25 mi. E of Güstrow, bet. Malchin and Kummerow lakes; sugar refining, sawmilling; mfg. of soap, window frames. Agr. market (grain, sugar beets, potatoes, stock). Has 14th-cent. church and 15th-cent. town gates. Founded in 13th cent.; was alternate meeting place (1621–1918) with Sternberg of annual parliament of Mecklenburg-Schwerin and Mecklenburg-Strelitz.

Malchin Lake, Ger. *Malchiner See* (mäl-khē'nùr zā"), lake (□ 6), Mecklenburg, N Germany, 4 mi. E of Malchin; 6 mi. long, c.1 mi. wide; greatest depth 52 ft., average depth 7 ft. Connected by canal with Kummerow L., 7 mi. NE.

Malchow (mäl'khō), town (pop. 8,049), Mecklenburg, N Germany, on the Elde and 25 mi. E of Parchim, in lake region; woolen- and sawmilling, brick mfg. Has bldgs. of Augustinian convent (founded in 13th cent.; secularized in 16th cent.). Town was 1st mentioned 1235.

Malcocinado (mälkō-thēnä'dhō), town (pop. 2,096), Badajoz prov., W Spain, in the Sierra Morena, 9 mi. S of Azuaga; olives, cereals, goats, sheep. Limekilns.

Malcolm (măl'kùm), village (pop. 93), Lancaster co., SE Nebr., 10 mi. NW of Lincoln.

Malcolm Island (□ 32), SW B.C., in Queen Charlotte Strait just off N Vancouver Isl., 3 mi. N of Alert Bay; 15 mi. long, 2–4 mi. wide; lumbering, farming; salmon fishing. Sointula is trade center.

Malcom, town (pop. 406), Poweshiek co., central Iowa, 9 mi. ESE of Grinnell, in agr. area.

Malcompeth, India: see MAHABALESHWAR.

Malda (mäl'dù), district (□ 1,391; pop. 844,315), N West Bengal, India; ⊙ English Bazar. On Ganges Plain (silk growing in low hill area, N); bounded W by the Ganges and Bihar, E by East Bengal (E Pakistan). Alluvial soil; rice, wheat, oilseeds, jute, barley, corn, tobacco; noted mango-growing area; major mulberry-growing dist. of West Bengal. Highly malarial swamps (S). Main towns: English Bazar, Old Malda. Archaeological landmarks include GAUR and PANDUA. Decisive victory, here, of the Mogul Aurangzeb over his brother in 1660. Formerly called Maldaha. Original dist. reduced 1947 by inc. of SE area (including Nawabganj town) into Rajshahi dist., East Bengal, E Pakistan, following creation of Pakistan.

Malda, town, India: see OLD MALDA.

Maldaha, India: see MALDA, district.

Maldegem (mäl'dù-khùm), town (pop. 12,554), East Flanders prov., NW Belgium, 16 mi. NW of

Ghent; market center for truck-gardening region; textile industry.

Malden, England: see THE MALDENS AND COOMBE.

Malden (môl'dŭn). **1** Village (pop. 217), Bureau co., N Ill., 6 mi. ENE of Princeton, in agr. and bituminous-coal area. **2** Residential city (pop. 59,804), Middlesex co., E Mass., on tributary of Mystic R. and 5 mi. N of Boston; mfg. (metal products, rubber footwear, fire hose, paint, shoes, confectionery, chemicals, knit goods, soap, radio equipment, canned foods), printing. Settled 1640, inc. as town 1649, as city 1881. **3** City (pop. 3,396), Dunklin co., extreme SE Mo., in Mississippi flood plain, 29 mi. SE of Poplar Bluff; cotton products; ships cotton, livestock. Platted 1877. **4** Town (pop. 332), Whitman co., SE Wash., 25 mi. N of Colfax, in agr. region.

Malden Island (môl'dŭn), uninhabited atoll (□ c.15), Line Isls., S Pacific, 373 mi. SE of Jarvis Isl.; 4°3'S 154°59'W; 5 mi. long. Discovered 1825 by the British; claimed by U.S. under Guano Act (1856). Leased 1922 by the British to Australian guano firm; now abandoned. Site of anc. Polynesian shrines. Formerly Independence Isl.

Maldive Islands (măl'dīv, môl'–), chain of coral islets (□ c.115; pop. 82,068) in Indian Ocean, extending 550 mi. N-S, bet. 7°7'N and 0°42'S, S of Laccadive Isls., SW of Ceylon. The isls., a "protected state" of the United Kingdom (whose agent is the high commissioner for Ceylon), are ruled by a sultan and (since 1932) an elected assembly; ⊙ Male Isl. The Maldives are grouped into several atolls, of which Tiladummati, Male, Suvadiva, Miladummadulu, Malosmadulu, and Addu are most populous. Islets nowhere exceed 20 ft. in elevation; mostly protected by coral reefs, formerly the cause of many shipwrecks. Coconut palms cover larger isls.; breadfruit, figs, millet, and edible nuts are also grown. Fishing and weaving are main occupations and there is an active trade among the isls. as well as with Ceylon and India's Malabar Coast; coconuts, coir, copra, palm mats, dried fish, cowries, and tortoise shells comprise bulk of exports. The islanders—predominantly Moslem—are noted sailors. After resisting Portuguese efforts to establish themselves on isls. and suffering frequent raids by Malabar pirates in 16th and 17th cent., Maldivians sought protection of Dutch rulers of Ceylon. In Second World War, Addu Atoll (S) served as Br. naval anchorage.

Mal di Ventre Island (mäl dē vĕn'trĕ), in Mediterranean Sea, 5 mi. SW of Cape Mannu, W Sardinia; 1.5 mi. long.

Maldon (môl'dŭn), village (pop. 1,098), central Victoria, Australia, 75 mi. NW of Melbourne, in gold-mining region; livestock, some wheat and oats.

Maldon, municipal borough (1931 pop. 6,559; 1951 census 9,721), E central Essex, England, on the Blackwater estuary at mouth of Chelmer R., 9 mi. E of Chelmsford; agr. market and oyster-fishing port, with iron foundries, saltworks, flour mills. Has 13th-cent. church with notable hexagonal spire, 15th-cent. town hall, and 16th-cent. grammar school. There are traces of prehistoric and Saxon or Danish occupation. Laurence Washington, great-great-grandfather of George Washington, is buried here. Near by is site of battle (991) in which Danish raiders defeated the East Saxons and killed their leader, Byrhtnoth. Battle was celebrated in one of last Anglo-Saxon heroic poems, "The Battle of Maldon" (author unknown). Also near by are remains of Beeleigh Abbey (1180).

Maldonado (măldōnä'dō), department (□ 1,587; pop. 67,015), S Uruguay, on the Atlantic at mouth of the Río de la Plata; ⊙ Maldonado. Smallest of the depts., except for Montevideo, it is known for its many beach resorts (e.g., Piriápolis, Punta del Este, and Solís), which make this hilly, partly wooded region, with its pleasant climate, a favorite playground for foreign tourists. Also important for its livestock (cattle, sheep) and agr. crops (grain, corn, wine, sugar beets, vegetables). Maldonado has deposits of lime, granite, marble, porphyry, and other building material. Flour milling, sugar refining (La Sierra), wine making, quarrying. Maldonado city is hq. for seal hunting on near-by Lobos Isl. Dept. was set up 1816 and formerly included Rocha.

Maldonado, city (pop. 8,000), ⊙ Maldonado dept., S Uruguay, near mouth of the Río de la Plata, 65 mi. E of Montevideo (connected by rail); 34°54'S 54°58'W. Its port is protected by Gorriti Isl. Principal industry is seal fishing at Lobos Isl., 10 mi. SSE. Also trade in grain and wool. Airfield. An old city (founded 1757), it still retains its colonial character. Remains of Sp. fortifications are near by.

Malé, Malét, or **Mallet** (all: mŭlĕ'), city (pop. 1,247), S Paraná, Brazil, on railroad and 105 mi. WSW of Curitiba; furniture mfg., linen milling, tanning, wine making. Mineral springs. Ships lumber, maté. Until 1930s, called São Pedro de Mallet.

Malé (mälā'), town (pop. 1,076), Trento prov., Trentino–Alto Adige, N Italy, on Noce R. and 24 mi. SW of Bolzano; alcohol distillery. Chief center of Val di Sole.

Malea, Cape (mŭlā'ŭ). **1** SE extremity of Lesbos isl., Greece, on Mytilene Channel: 39°1'N 26°36'E. Also called Zeitin and Agrelios. **2** SE Peloponnesus, Greece, on Aegean Sea, bet. gulfs of Laconia (W) and Argolis (E); 36°25'N 23°12'E. Also called Cape Maleas.

Male Atoll (mä'lā), central group (pop. 11,190) of Maldive Isls., in Indian Ocean, bet. 3°48'N and 4°42'N, 440 mi. WSW of Ceylon. Larger N section (including MALE ISLAND) is separated from S section by narrow channel; coconuts, breadfruit; fishing (bonito), palm-mat weaving.

Malegaon (mälā'goun), town (pop., including NW suburban area, 39,924), Nasik dist., central Bombay, India, on Girna R. and 60 mi. NE of Nasik; trade center for cloth fabrics (saris), millet, gur; cotton ginning and milling, handicraft cloth weaving, oilseed milling. Sugar and candy mfg. 7 mi. NW, at Ravalgaon.

Malehra, India: see MALAHRA.

Male Island (mä'lā), small island (pop. 8,431) of Male Atoll, ⊙ Maldive Isls., in Indian Ocean, 450 mi. WSW of Colombo (Ceylon); 4°10'N 73°30'E. Seaplane base, ship anchorage; center of interisland trade (coconuts, coir, palm mats, copra, cowries). Seat of Maldivian people's assembly and residence of sultan. Sometimes called Sultan's or King's Isl.

Male Karpaty, Czechoslovakia: see LITTLE CARPATHIAN MOUNTAINS.

Malekula (mäläkōō'lä), volcanic island (pop. c.5,000), 2d largest isl. of NEW HEBRIDES, SW Pacific, 20 mi. S of Espiritu Santo and across Bougainville Channel; 45 mi. long, 23 mi. wide. Fr. administrative hq. at Port Sandwich on SE coast, Br. hq. at Bushman's Bay on NE coast. Highest peak is Mt. Penot (2,925 ft.). Copra, coffee, *bêche-de-mer* (edible sea cucumbers); sandalwood. Also called Mallicolo.

Malela (mälĕ'lä). **1** Village, Kivu prov., central Belgian Congo, near left bank of the Lualaba, on railroad and 35 mi. WNW of Kasongo; agr. center (rice, cotton, coffee); palm-oil milling, rice processing, hardwood lumbering. Has R.C. mission with trade schools. **2** Village, Leopoldville prov., W Belgian Congo, on N shore of Congo R. estuary (Angola border) and 35 mi. WSW of Boma; palm-oil milling, hardwood lumbering. Hydrographic station.

Malema, Mozambique: see ENTRE RIOS.

Maleme (mä'lĭmē), air base in W Crete, on N coast, 12 mi. W of Canea; 35°31'N 23°48'E. German parachutists landed here (1941).

Malemort-sur-Corrèze (mälmôr'-sür-kôrĕz'), village (pop. 391), Corrèze dept., S central France, on Corrèze R. and 2 mi. ENE of Brive-la-Gaillarde; paper milling, fruit and vegetable canning.

Male Morze, Poland: see PUCK BAY.

Malente (mälĕn'tŭ) or **Malente-Gremsmühlen** (–grĕms'mü"lŭn), village (pop. 13,068), in Schleswig-Holstein, NW Germany, 3 mi. NW of Eutin, bet. 2 lakes; popular summer resort. Mfg. (chemicals, precison instruments, paper products, knitwear). Until 1937 in Oldenburg.

Maleo (mälā'ō), village (pop. 2,322), Milano prov., Lombardy, N Italy, near Adda R., 9 mi. WNW of Cremona; rice, flour, and silk mills, cheese factory.

Maler Kotla (mä'lăr kōt'lŭ), town (pop. 29,321), N central Patiala and East Punjab States Union, India, 33 mi. NW of Patiala; trades in wheat, millet, cotton, sugar, oilseeds; cotton ginning, hand-loom weaving, mfg. of coarse paper. Was ⊙ former princely state of Maler Kotla (□ 165; pop. 88,109) of Punjab States, India; since 1948, state merged with Patiala and East Punjab States Union. Sometimes written Malerkotla.

Malesherbes (mälzârb'), town (pop. 1,916), Loiret dept., N central France, on the Essonne and 11 mi. NE of Pithiviers; rail junction, agr. market. Furniture mfg. Has 13th-cent. Gothic church. The 18th-cent. castle was owned by Malesherbes.

Malesina (mälĭsē'nŭ), **Malessine,** or **Malessini** (both: mälĭsē'nē), village (pop. 2,572), Phthiotis nome, E central Greece, 47 mi. ESE of Lamia; livestock raising; fisheries along coast.

Males Mountains or **Malesh Mountains** (both: mä'lĕsh), Serbo-Croatian *Maleške Planine*, Bulg. *Maleshevska Planina*, extend c.35 mi. N-S, along Yugoslav-Bulgarian border, E of upper Bregalnica R., bet. Osogov Mts. (N) and the Ograzden (S); heavily forested. Highest peak (6,337 ft.) is the KADIJICA. Includes Vlakhina Mts. (N).

Malestroit (mälätrwä'), town (pop. 2,028), Morbihan dept., W France, on Oust R. (Brest-Nantes Canal), 8 mi. S of Ploërmel; road junction; woodworking, horse raising. Tanning extracts made at near-by Roc-Saint-André.

Malét, Brazil: see MALÉ.

Maletsunyane Falls (mä"lĕtsōōnyä'nä), Basutoland, on an affluent of Orange R. and c.75 mi. SE of Maseru; drops 630 ft.

Malevon, Greece: see PARNON.

Male Zernoseky, Czechoslovakia: see VELKE ZERNOSEKY.

Malfors (mäl"fôrs', –fōsh'), village (pop. 1,513), Ostergotland co., SE Sweden, on Motala R. (falls) and on Gota Canal, 7 mi. NW of Linkoping; large hydroelectric station; chocolate mfg.

Malgaon (mŭl'goun), town (pop. 7,496), Satara South dist., S central Bombay, India, 10 mi. E of Sangli; local trade center (millet, cotton, wheat); betel farming, handicraft cloth weaving.

Malgara, Turkey: see MALKARA.

Malgobek (mŭlgŭbyĕk'), city (1939 pop. over 10,000), N North Ossetian Autonomous SSR, Russian SFSR, in Terek Range, 50 mi. WNW of Grozny and on rail spur from Mozdok; petroleum-producing center; natural-gas wells. Oil is piped to Mozdok and Grozny, natural gas to Dzaudzhikau. Developed in late 1930s near village of Voznesenskaya (1926 pop. 2,111). Became city c.1940. During Second World War, briefly held (1942) by Germans in their nearest approach to Grozny.

Malgrat (mälgrät'), town (pop. 4,536), Barcelona prov., NE Spain, on the Mediterranean, 11 mi. NE of Arenys de Mar; knitwear and leather-goods mfg.; trades in hazelnuts, fruit, potatoes, livestock. Summer resort.

Malhão (mŭlyä'ō), highest peak (6,532 ft.) of Portugal, in Serra da Estrêla, just NW of Covilhã.

Malheur (mŭlōōr'), county (□ 9,870; pop. 23,223), SE Oregon; ⊙ Vale. Drained by Malheur and Owyhee rivers, which flow to Snake R.; borders on Nev. and Idaho. OWYHEE DAM, 20 mi. SW of Nyssa, creates Owyhee Reservoir in E. Dairying, agr. (sugar beets, fruit, truck, hay). Formed 1887.

Malheur Lake, receding body of fresh water in Harney co., SE central Oregon, SSE of Burns; 17 mi. long, 2 mi. wide. Drains into Harney L. (W); is fed by Silvies R. (N) and Donner und Blitzen R. (S). Part of U.S. migratory bird refuge here.

Malheur River, E Oregon, rises in Strawberry Mts., flows SE, N, and ENE to Snake R. at Ontario; c.165 mi. long; North Fork is tributary. Warm Springs Dam (106 ft. high, 469 ft. long; completed 1919), on main stream in upper course, forms Warm Springs Reservoir (8 mi. long, max. width 3 mi.; capacity 192,400 acre-ft.). Unit in Vale irrigation project.

Mali (mä'lē), village (pop. c.500), N Fr. Guinea, Fr. West Africa, in Fouta Djallon mts., on road and 50 mi. N of Labé; cattle raising. Meteorological station.

Malia or **Maliya** (mäl'yŭ), village, N Saurashtra, India, 55 mi. N of Rajkot; local trade in salt, millet, cotton. Was ⊙ former Western Kathiawar state of Malia or Maliya (□ 103; pop. 10,788) of Western India States agency, along SW edge of Little Rann of Cutch; state merged (1948) with Saurashtra.

Maliahs, The (mŭl'yärz), broken hill ranges in W Ganjam dist., S central Orissa, India, within Eastern Ghats; heights vary from 1,000 to 4,000 ft. Thickly forested (sal, bamboo); inhabited by primitive tribes (mainly Khonds). Administered as political agency.

Malian Gulf (mā'lēŭn) or **Gulf of Malis** (mā'lĭs), Gr. *Maliakos Kolpos*, Lat. *Maliacus Sinus*, Aegean inlet in E central Greece, sheltered by Euboea and connected SE with Gulf of Euboea and NE with Strait of Oreos; 15 mi. long, 5 mi. wide. On N shore is Stylis, port of Lamia. Receives Spercheios R. Also called Gulf of Lamia.

Maliaño (mälyä'nyō), village (pop. 2,433), Santander prov., N Spain, 4 mi. SW of Santander; metalworks; chemical-fertilizer mfg., brandy distilling cereals, cattle, lumber. Iron mines near by.

Malibu Beach (mă'lĭbōō), unincorporated beach community (pop. c.900), Los Angeles co., S Calif., on the Pacific, 11 mi. WNW of Santa Monica; many homes of Hollywood stars here.

Malibu Lake, Los Angeles co., S Calif., small lake (resort) in Santa Monica Mts., 16 mi. WNW of Santa Monica.

Malicorne-sur-Sarthe (mälēkôrn'-sür-särt'), village (pop. 1,262), Sarthe dept., W France, on Sarthe R. and 8 mi. N of La Flèche; hog market; mfg. (faïence, hosiery). Formerly called Malicorne.

Malignant Cove, village, E N.S., on Northumberland Strait, 12 mi. NNW of Antigonish; resort.

Maligne Lake (mŭlēn', mŭlĭn') (20 mi. long, 1 mi. wide), W Alta., in Rocky Mts., in Jasper Natl. Park, at foot of Mt. Unwin, 21 mi. SE of Jasper; alt. 5,490 ft. Drains NW into Athabaska R.

Maligne Mountains, W Alta., range of peaks in Rocky Mts., in Jasper Natl. Park, extends 20 mi. SE from Jasper; rises to 9,157 ft. Overlooks upper Athabaska R. valley.

Malihabad (mŭlē'häbäd), town (pop. 10,521), Lucknow dist., central Uttar Pradesh, India, on tributary of the Gumti and 13 mi. WNW of Lucknow; wheat, rice, gram, millet. Formerly a noted Pathan residence. Extensive mango and ber orchards near by.

Mali Hka, Burma: see MALI RIVER.

Mali Idjos, Yugoslavia: see KRIVAJA.

Mali Kvarner, gulf, Yugoslavia: see KVARNER.

Malilipot (mälēlēpōt'), town (1939 pop. 2,227; 1948 municipality pop. 9,971), Albay prov., SE Luzon, Philippines, on Tabaco Bay (small inlet of Lagonoy Gulf), 12 mi. N of Legaspi; agr. center (abacá, corn, coconuts).

Mali Losinj, Yugoslavia: see LOSINJ ISLAND.

Malim Nawar (mä"lĭm' nä"wär'), town (pop. 2,408), central Perak, Malaya, on railroad and 17 mi. S of Ipoh; tin mining.

Malin (mä'lēn), Czech *Malín*, village (pop. 1,018), central Bohemia, Czechoslovakia, 2 mi. NE of

Kutna Hora; horse-radish-growing center; wheat, sugar beets.

Malin (mŭlyĕn′), city (1939 pop. over 10,000), E Zhitomir oblast, Ukrainian SSR, 28 mi. ESE of Korosten; paper-milling center.

Malin (mŭlĭn′), town (pop. 592), Klamath co., S Oregon, near Calif. line, 25 mi. SE of Klamath Falls.

Malinalco (mälēnäl′kō), town (pop. 2,575), Mexico state, central Mexico, 25 mi. SSE of Toluca; sugar cane, cereals, fruit, livestock.

Malinaltepec (mälēnältāpĕk′), town (pop. 2,035), Guerrero, SW Mexico, in Sierra Madre del Sur, 55 mi. SE of Chilapa; cereals, sugar cane, fruit, livestock.

Malinao (mälē′nou), town (1939 pop. 1,376; 1948 municipality pop. 15,176), Albay prov., SE Luzon, Philippines, on small Tabaco Bay (inlet of Lagonoy Gulf), 13 mi. N of Legaspi; agr. (abacá, rice, coconuts).

Malinche, Malintzi, or **Malinzi** (mälĕn′chä, –tsē, –sē), dormant volcano (14,636 ft.), central Mexico, on Puebla–Tlaxcala border, 16 mi. NE of Puebla; has several extinct craters; snow-capped during winter. Aztec name is Matlalcueyatl.

Malindi (mälĕn′dē), town (pop. 3,292), Coast prov., SE Kenya, in coastal protectorate, port on Indian Ocean near mouth of Athi R., and 65 mi. NNE of Mombasa; 3°17′S 40°10′E. Cotton-ginning and sisal-processing center; copra, sugar cane. Fisheries. Airfield. Has an Arab-endowed school and native hosp. An early Arab center. Vasco da Gama landed here, 1497, and erected a fort (partly preserved).

Malines, Belgium: see MECHLIN.

Malin Head (mă′lĭn), cape on the Atlantic, NE Co. Donegal, northernmost point of Ireland, 17 mi. N of Buncrana; 55°23′N 7°24′W.

Malini (mŭ′lēn), Rum. *Mălini*, agr. village (pop. 1,088), Suceava prov., NE Rumania, on Moldava R. and 9 mi. W of Falticeni.

Malino (mŭlē′nōō), resort village, SW Celebes, Indonesia, 30 mi. ESE of Macassar, at foot of Mt. Lompobatang. Scene (July, 1946) of Dutch and Indonesian conference at which preliminary plans were made for foundation of federated Indonesian state.

Malino (–lyē′nŭ), village (1939 pop. over 500), S Moscow oblast, Russian SFSR, 22 mi. W of Kolomna; dairying.

Malinovka (mŭlyē′nŭfkŭ), town (1926 pop. 6,932), N central Kharkov oblast, Ukrainian SSR, 3 mi. S of Chuguyev (across the Northern Donets), in Kharkov metropolitan area.

Malinska (mä′lĭnskä), Ital. *Roveredo* (rôvĕrĕ′dō), village, NW Croatia, Yugoslavia, on Krk Isl., on Adriatic Sea, 7 mi. N of Krk; seaside resort. Monastery near by.

Malinta (mŭlĭn′tŭ), village (pop. 308), Henry co., NW Ohio, 7 mi. SE of Napoleon; machinery, clay, concrete, and plaster products.

Malintzi, Mexico: see MALINCHE.

Malinzi, Mexico: see MALINCHE.

Maliq (mä′lēk) or **Maliqi** (mä′lēkyē), village (1930 pop. 54), SE Albania, on SE shore of L. Maliq at efflux of Devoll R. and 7 mi. NW of Koritsa; sugar refinery. **Lake Maliq,** a residual lacustrine basin (□ c.30) with marshy shores, floods the surrounding Koritsa plain during spring high water of Devoll R. Scene of reclamation project.

Malir (mŭlĭr′), village, Karachi administration area, W Pakistan, 12 mi. E of Karachi; millet, barley, sugar cane; poultry farming; fertilizer (crushed bones). Cattle farm 3 mi. SW.

Mali River (mŭlē′), native *Mali Hka* (mŭlē′ kä), Chinese *Mai-li-k'ai* (mī′lē′kī′), right headstream of Irrawaddy R. in N Upper Burma, rises in high mts. on India line near Putao, flows 200 mi. S joining the Nmai R. 25 mi. N of Myitkyina to form Irrawaddy R.

Malis (mā′lĭs), anc. region of E central Greece, on S slopes of Othrys massif and on N shore of Malian Gulf. Its chief city was Lamia.

Malis, Gulf of, Greece: see MALIAN GULF.

Mali Stapar (mä′lē stä′pär), hamlet, Vojvodina, NW Serbia, Yugoslavia, on Danube-Tisa Canal and 11 mi. WSW of Sombor, in the Backa; terminus of 43-mi.-long branch canal to Novi Sad.

Malita (mŭlē′tŭ, Sp. mälē′tä), town (1939 pop. 8,681; 1948 municipality pop. 27,744), Davao prov., S Mindanao, Philippines, 45 mi. S of Davao, on Davao Gulf; abacá, coconuts.

Malitbog (mälēt′bōg), town (1939 pop. 1,752; 1948 municipality pop. 25,891), S Leyte, Philippines, on Sogod Bay, 75 mi. S of Tacloban; agr. center (coconuts, rice, hemp).

Maliya, India: see MALIA.

Malkanagiri (mŭl′kŭnŭgĭrē), village, Koraput dist., SW Orissa, India, 55 mi. SW of Jeypore; local rice and timber market. Also spelled Malkangiri.

Malkapur (mŭlkä′pōōr). **1** Town (pop. 2,840), Kolhapur dist., S Bombay, India, 25 mi. NW of Kolhapur, in Western Ghats; rice, timber (teak, sandalwood). **2** Town (pop. 20,598), Buldana dist., W Madhya Pradesh, India, 55 mi. WNW of Akola; millet, wheat; cotton ginning, oilseed milling.

Malkara (mäl′kärä), town (pop. 5,416), Tekirdag prov., Turkey in Europe, 32 mi. WSW of Tekirdag, in grain area. Lignite. Also spelled Malgara.

Malka River (mäl′kŭ), Kabardian Autonomous SSR, Russian SFSR, rises (at 10,700 ft.) in the central Greater Caucasus, on N slope of Mt. Elbrus; flows 135 mi. NE and E, past Sarmakovo and Kuba, to Terek R. W of Prokhladny. Iron mining in upper reaches.

Malki Iskar River (mäl′kē ē′skŭr), NW Bulgaria, rises in Yetropole Mts., flows generally N, past Yetropole, NW, and N to Iskar R. at Roman 13 mi. ESE of Lukovit. Length, 50 mi.

Malkinia (moukē′nyä), Pol. *Małkinia*, village, Warszawa prov., E central Poland, on right bank of Bug R. and 50 mi. NE of Warsaw; rail junction.

Malko Tirnovo (mäl′kô tŭr′nôvô), city (pop. 3,489), Burgas dist., SE Bulgaria, at NE foot of Strandzha Mts., 35 mi. S of Burgas, on Turkish border; agr. and livestock center; tanning, coopering. Wooden handicrafts and charcoal produced near by. Also Malko Trnovo; formerly called Tirnovo.

Mallacoota Inlet (mă″lŭkōō′tŭ), lagoon, SE Victoria, Australia, opening into Tasman Sea, near Cape Howe; 5 mi. long, 3 mi. wide; irregularly shaped. Timbered shoreline; contains mullet, whiting, sea trout.

Mallah, Syria: see MELLAH.

Mallaig (mă′läg, mŭläg′), village (pop. estimate 500), E Alta., 65 mi. NNW of Vermilion; mixed farming, lumbering.

Mallaig (mă′läg), town in W Inverness, Scotland, on the Sound of Sleat, at entrance to Loch Nevis, 30 mi. WNW of Fort William; fishing port and terminal of steamers to Skye and the Hebrides.

Mallakastër (mäläkä′stŭr) or **Mallakastra** (–kä′strä), hill range in S central Albania, NE of Valona, bet. Seman and Vijosë rivers. Also spelled Malakastër or Malakastra.

Mallali, Br. Guiana: see MALALI.

Malla-Malla, Cordillera de (kôrdēyä′rä dā mä′yä-mä′yä), Andean range in Bío-Bío prov., S central Chile, 60 mi. SE of Los Angeles, extends 12 mi. ENE from Callaqui Volcano to Copahué Volcano on Argentina line.

Mallankinar (mŭl′lŭngkĭnŭr), town (pop. 5,430), Ramnad dist., S Madras, India, 7 mi. NNW of Aruppukkottai, in cotton area. Also spelled Mallanginar and Mallanjinar.

Mallanwan (mŭl-län′vän) or **Mallawan** (mŭl-lä′vän), town (pop. 11,084), Hardoi dist., central Uttar Pradesh, India, on branch of Sarda Canal system and 14 mi. S of Hardoi; metalware mfg.; wheat, gram, barley, oilseeds, sugar cane.

Mallapuram, India: see HOSPET.

Mallard (mă′lŭrd), town (pop. 399), Palo Alto co., NW Iowa, 12 mi. S of Emmetsburg; livestock, grain.

Mallawan, India: see MALLANWAN.

Mallawi or **Mellawi** (both: mĕl′läwē), town (pop. 34,011; with suburbs, 38,126), Asyut prov., central Upper Egypt, on W bank of the Nile, on Ibrahimiya Canal, on railroad, and 43 mi. NNW of Asyut; cotton ginning, wool weaving and spinning, pottery making, wood and ivory carving; cereals, dates, sugar cane.

Malleco (mäyā′kō), province (□ 5,512; 1940 pop. 154,174; 1949 estimate 157,609), S central Chile; ⊙ Angol. In S part of the central valley bet. the Andes (E) and the Cordillera de Nahuelbuta (W), N of Cautín R.; drained by Bío-Bío and Malleco rivers. Includes the volcanoes Tolhuaca and Lonquimay. Has humid, temperate climate. A predominantly agr. area, it produces wheat, oats, barley, potatoes, peas, lentils, wine, apples; cattle and sheep raising on smaller scale. Rich in timber. Industries at Angol, Victoria, and Traiguén. Health resorts with thermal springs: Tolhuaca and Río Blanco. The landlocked prov., formerly a part of Arauco prov., was set up 1887.

Malleco, Lake, Andean lake (□ 4.5) in Malleco prov., S central Chile, formed by upper Malleco R. at NW foot of Tolhuaca Volcano near Tolhuaca.

Malleco River, Malleco prov., S central Chile, rises at NW foot of Tolhuaca Volcano, flows c.85 mi. WNW, past Collipulli, joining the lesser Rehue R. (left) near Angol to form the Vergara.

Mallemort (mälmôr′), village (pop. 1,094), Bouches-du-Rhône dept., SE France, on left bank of the Durance and 19 mi. NW of Aix-en-Provence; fruit and vegetable canning, winegrowing.

Mallén (mälyĕn′), town (pop. 2,899), Saragossa prov., NE Spain, 8 mi. NE of Borja; agr. trade center (sugar beets, alfalfa, olive oil).

Malles Venosta (mäl′lĕs vĕnō′stä), Ger. *Mals*, village (pop. 1,276), Bolzano prov., Trentino–Alto Adige, N Italy, in Val Venosta, 30 mi. W of Merano, on Passo di Resia road.

Malleswaram, India: see BANGALORE, city.

Mallet, Brazil: see MALÉ.

Mallicolo, New Hebrides: see MALEKULA.

Mallnitz (mäl′nĭts), village (pop. 1,290), Carinthia, W central Austria, in the Hohe Tauern, 21 mi. NW of Spittal; highest station (3,886 ft.) of Tauern RR, near S exit of Tauern Tunnel; health resort. Large hydroelectric plant near by powers Tauern RR.

Malloa (mäyō′ä), village (1930 pop. 863), O'Higgins prov., central Chile, on railroad and 23 mi. SSW of Rancagua, in agr. area (wheat, oats, beans, wine, potatoes, livestock).

Malloco (mäyō′kō), town (pop. 1,516), Santiago prov., central Chile, on railroad and 15 mi. SW of Santiago; resort in agr. area (grain, fruit, wine, livestock).

Mallorca, Balearic Isls.: see MAJORCA.

Mallorquinas (mälyôrkē′näs), village (pop. 1,102), Barcelona prov., NE Spain, 7 mi. NE of Barcelona; produces chemicals (ammonic, acetic, and sulphuric acid; copper sulphate), brandy.

Mallory, coal-mining village (pop. 1,286), Logan co., SW W.Va., near Guyandot R., 11 mi. SSE of Logan.

Mallow (mă′lō), Gaelic *Magh Ealla* [plain of the Allo, old name for the Blackwater], urban district (pop. 5,215), central Co. Cork, Ireland, on the Blackwater and 16 mi. NNW of Cork; rail center and agr. market (sugar beets, potatoes, oats; dairying), with sugar refinery, tanneries, and salmon fisheries; spa resort with mineral springs. It is site of racecourse. The modern Mallow Castle has adjoining fragments of anc. stronghold of the Desmonds.

Mallow, village (pop. 1,621, with near-by Fairlawn), Alleghany co., W Va., 2 mi. SW of Covington.

Mallwen; Mallwischken, Russian SFSR: see MAISKOYE, Kaliningrad oblast.

Mallwyd (mă′thōōĭd), village (1931 pop. 679), S Merioneth, Wales, on Dovey R. and 9 mi. ESE of Dolgelley; agr. market. Has 17th-cent. wooden church. Near by are slate quarries.

Malm, Finland: see MALMI.

Malm (mälm), village and canton (pop. 1,922), Nord-Trondelag co., central Norway, on an inlet of Trondheim Fjord, 10 mi. WNW of Steinkjer. Iron mine near by.

Malmaison, France: see RUEIL-MALMAISON.

Malmaison, Fort (fôr mälmāzō′), Aisne dept., N France, 8 mi. SSW of Laon. Its capture in Oct., 1917, gave Pétain possession of the CHEMIN DES DAMES.

Malmback (mälm′bĕk″), Swedish *Malmbäck*, village (pop. 919), Jonkoping co., S Sweden, 10 mi. WSW of Nassjo; sawmilling, woodworking.

Malmberget (mälm′bĕr″yŭt), village (pop. 4,007), Norrbotten co., N Sweden, 50 mi. SSE of Kiruna; iron-mining center, 2 mi. NW of Gallivare. Ore shipped by rail to Lulea or Narvik.

Malmédy (mälmādē′), town (pop. 5,569), Liége prov., E Belgium, in N Ardennes, on Warche R. and 25 mi. SE of Liége, near Ger. line; mfg. of tanning fluid; paper mills. Until 1815, part of independent territory of abbey of Stavelot; awarded to Prussia by Congress of Vienna; awarded (1919) to Belgium, after plebiscite under Treaty of Versailles.

Malmesbury (mämz′bŭrē), municipal borough (1931 pop. 2,334; 1951 census 2,509), N Wiltshire, England, on the Avon and 14 mi. W of Swindon; agr. market; silk mills, dairy plants. Famous for its magnificent abbey, founded (7th cent.) by Maildulphus; Aldhelm and William of Malmesbury worked and studied here; contains tomb of Æthelstan. Abbey church dates from 12th cent. Agr. village and parish (pop. 119) of Garsdon, where George Washington's ancestors are buried, is 2 mi. E. Thomas Hobbes b. near Malmesbury.

Malmesbury, town (pop. 5,752), SW Cape Prov., U. of So. Afr., on Diep R. and 35 mi. NNE of Cape Town; center of wheat, tobacco, wine region; resort with medicinal hot springs. Founded 1745. Jan Christiaan Smuts b. here.

Malmi (mäl′mē), Swedish *Malm* (mälm), village in Helsinki rural commune (pop. 13,678), Uusimaa co., S Finland, 7 mi. NNE of Helsinki; 60°16′N 25°3′E. Site of Helsinki airport. Machine shops.

Malmkoping (mälm′chû″pĭng), Swedish *Malmköping*, town (pop. 1,399), Sodermanland co., E Sweden, 17 mi. SSE of Eskilstuna; woodworking.

Malmo (măl′mō), Swedish *Malmö* (mäl′mû″), maritime industrial city (1950 pop. 192,498), ⊙ Malmohus co., S Sweden, on the Oresund opposite and 16 mi. ESE of Copenhagen; 55°35′N 13°E. Large seaport and naval base; transportation center (rail hub, terminus of train ferry to Copenhagen; airport at Bulltofta, E suburb). Third-largest city of Sweden, it is commercial and industrial center, with shipyards, sugar refineries, textile mills, machine shops; mfg. of chemicals, rubber and tobacco products; brewing. Has Malmohus Castle (begun 1434, completed 1542), scene of Bothwell's imprisonment; Church of St. Peter (1319); city hall (1546); and several 16th-cent. houses. Founded in 12th cent., its present charter dates from 1353. Major herring-fishing port during Hanseatic period; under Danish rule until annexed (1658) by Sweden as part of Skane. Successfully resisted (1677) Danish siege. Construction of modern port begun 1775.

Malmo (măl′mō), village (pop. 151), Saunders co., E Nebr., 30 mi. N of Lincoln and on branch of Platte R.

Malmohus (mäl′mûhüs″), Swedish *Malmöhus*, county [Swedish *län*] (□ 1,871; 1950 pop. 583,008), S Sweden; ⊙ Malmo. Part of SKANE prov., it is bounded by the Baltic (S), the Oresund (W), and the Kattegat (NW). Low, level surface is drained by Kavlinge and several smaller streams; fertile soil produces grain, sugar beets, potatoes; cattle raised. Fisheries. Industries include sugar refining, shipbuilding, coal mining and clay quarrying (in Halsingborg and Hoganas region), metalworking; mfg. of machinery, rubber products, bricks, pottery. Most densely populated county of Sweden; chief cities are Malmo (port), Lund (univ.), Halsingborg, Landskrona, Trelleborg, and Ystad. Malmo, Halsingborg, and Trelleborg are termini of train ferries to Denmark and the Continent. There are many old castles and manor houses.

Malmon (mälm'ûn″), Swedish *Malmön*, fishing village (pop. 733), Goteborg och Bohus co., SW Sweden, on isl. (□ 2) of same name in the Skagerrak, 6 mi. NW of Lysekil; granite quarries.

Malmsbury (mämz'bûrē), village (pop. 319), central Victoria, Australia, on Campaspe R. and 55 mi. NW of Melbourne, near Kyneton, in gold-mining area. Site of reservoir; irrigation center.

Malmslatt (mälm'slĕt″), Swedish *Malmslätt*, village (pop. 1,201), Ostergotland co., SE Sweden, 3 mi. W of Linkoping; 58°25'N 15°31'E. Air base. Metalworking.

Malmyzh (mäl'mĭsh). **1** Village (1948 pop. over 500), S Khabarovsk Territory, Russian SFSR, on Amur R. and 45 mi. S of Komsomolsk, fish cannery. **2** City (1926 pop. 5,664), SE Kirov oblast, Russian SFSR, on Vyatka R. and 80 mi. NE of Kazan (connected by road), in wheat area; distilling. Former ⊙ Cheremiss domain; chartered 1601.

Malnate (mälnä'tĕ), town (pop. 4,429), Varese prov., Lombardy, N Italy, on Olona R. and 3 mi. SE of Varese; rail junction; mfg. (machinery, silverware, jewelry).

Malo (mä'lô), town (pop. 3,471), Vicenza prov., Veneto, N Italy, 10 mi. NW of Vicenza; silk milling.

Malo (mä'lō) volcanic island (pop. 476), New Hebrides, SW Pacific, 3 mi. S of Espiritu Santo; 34 mi. in circumference; rises to 1,200 ft.; copra, cacao. Formerly St. Bartholomew Isl.

Malo- [Rus. combining form, =LESSER, LITTLE, SMALL], in Rus. names: see also MALAYA, MALOYE, MALY, MALYE.

Malo, Arroyo (äroi'ō mä'lō), river, Tacuarembó dept., N central Uruguay, rises in the Cuchilla de Haedo S of Tambores, flows 75 mi. SE, past Curtina, to the Río Negro 14 mi. NE of San Gregorio.

Maloarkhangelsk or **Maloarkhangel'sk** (mä″lŭŭrkhän'gĭlsk), city (1926 pop. 6,238), S Orel oblast, Russian SFSR, 40 mi. SSE of Orel; fruit and vegetable processing, poultry farming. Chartered 1778.

Maloelap (mä″lō'ĕläp'), atoll (□ 4; pop. 451), Ratak Chain, Majuro dist., Marshall Isls., W central Pacific, 220 mi. E of Kwajalein; 8°45'N 171°3'E; c.25 mi. long; 71 islets. Jap. air base in Second World War. Sometimes spelled Maloelab.

Malo-Ilinovka or **Malo-Il'inovka** (mä″lŭ-ĭlyē'nŭfkŭ), town (1926 pop. 995), NE Stalino oblast, Ukrainian SSR, in the Donbas, on railroad (Stupki station) and 3 mi. N of Artemovsk; metalworks; salt mines.

Maloja, Ital. *Maloia* (both: mälō'yä) or *Maloggia* (mälôd'jä), district (pop. 9,089), Grisons canton, SE Switzerland. Resort hamlet of Maloja (5,910–5,940 ft.) lies at SW end of L. of Sils, near source of Inn R. and 9 mi. SW of St. Moritz. **Maloja Pass,** at the hamlet, is crossed by Maloja Road, which crosses Rhaetian Alps from Upper Engadine to Val Bregaglia. It is lowest of passes to Italy.

Malo Konare (mä'lô kônä'rĕ), village (pop. 5,049), Plovdiv dist., W central Bulgaria, 5 mi. E of Pazardzhik; rice, vineyards, hemp. Formerly Doganovo-Konare.

Malokurilskoye or **Malokuril'skoye** (mä″lŭkōōrēl'skŭyŭ), fishing village on NW shore of Shikotan Isl., in lesser Kurile group, Russian SFSR; 43°52'N 146°49'E; fish canning; whale-oil factory. Under Jap. rule (until 1945), called Shakotan.

Malo-les-Bains (mälō'-lā-bē'), NNE suburb (pop. 8,630) of Dunkirk, Nord dept., N France, on North Sea coast; beach resort heavily damaged in Second World War.

Malolo (mälō'lō), volcanic island (□ 4; pop. 223), Western Dist., Fiji, SW Pacific, 5 mi. W of Viti Levu; c.3 mi. long; copra.

Malolos (mälō'lōs), town (1948 municipality pop. 38,779), ⊙ Bulacan prov., S central Luzon, Philippines, 20 mi. NW of Manila, near railroad; trade center for rice-growing area. Short-lived revolutionary capital was established here in 1898 under Emilio Aguinaldo.

Malomalsk or **Malomal'sk** (mŭlŭmälsk'), town (1939 pop. over 2,000), W Sverdlovsk oblast, Russian SFSR, in the central Urals, on Tura R. and 7 mi. SE of Is, on railroad; gold placers. Until 1933 called Glubokoye.

Malombe, Lake (mälōm'bā), S Nyasaland, 12 mi. S of L. Nyasa; 16 mi. long, 12 mi. wide; 6–8 ft. deep; marshy shores. Traversed by Shire R. Fall of level of L. Nyasa caused L. Malombe to dry up, c.1925. Sometimes called L. Pamalombe.

Malomir (mä'lômĕr), village (pop. 3,489), Yambol dist., SE Bulgaria, 12 mi. S of Yambol; grain, tobacco, rice. Formerly Karapcha.

Malón (mälōn'), town (pop. 1,218), Saragossa prov., NE Spain, 5 mi. NE of Tarazona; sugar beets, olive oil, wine, cereals.

Malone (mŭlōn'). **1** Town (pop. 521), Jackson co., NW Fla., near Ala. line, 14 mi. NNE of Marianna, in agr. area. **2** Village (pop. 9,501), ⊙ Franklin co., N N.Y., on Salmon R., near Que. line, and 30 mi. ESE of Massena, in agr. area (dairy products, truck, potatoes, grain); port of entry. Summer resort. Mfg. of aluminum and bronze powder, footwear, concrete blocks, paper, clothing, cheese, lumber, furniture, machinery; railroad shops. Was gathering point for the Fenians, who raided Canada in 1866. State school for the deaf here. Settled c.1800, inc. 1833. **3** Town (pop. 352), Hill co., central Texas, 15 mi. SE of Hillsboro; trade, shipping point in farm area.

Malonga (mälông'gä), village, Katanga prov., E Belgian Congo, on railroad and 220 mi. WNW of Jadotville; agr. trade (manioc, yams, beans).

Malonne (mälôn'), agr. village (pop. 3,547), Namur prov., S central Belgium, near Sambre R., 4 mi. SW of Namur.

Malonno (mälôn'nô), village (pop. 1,165), Brescia prov., Lombardy, N Italy, in Val Camonica, on Oglio R. and 22 mi. ESE of Sondrio; iron mining.

Malorad (mä'lôrät), village (pop. 4,508), Vratsa dist., NW Bulgaria, 13 mi. W of Byala Slatina; grain, legumes, livestock.

Malorita (mŭlŭrē'tŭ), Pol. *Maloryta* (mälôrĭ'tä), town (1948 pop. over 2,000), S Brest oblast, Belorussian SSR, 27 mi. SE of Brest; lumber-trading center; mfg. (tar products, bricks), flour milling, sawmilling.

Malo-Ryazantsevo (mä″lŭ-ryŭzän'tsyĭvŭ), town (1939 pop. over 500), W Voroshilovgrad oblast, Ukrainian SSR, in the Donbas, 3 mi. SW of Lisichansk; coal mining.

Maloryta, Belorussian SSR: see MALORITA.

Maloshuika or **Maloshuyka** (mŭlŭshōō'ēkŭ), town (1943 pop. over 500), NW Archangel oblast, Russian SFSR, on railroad, on inlet of Onega Bay and 25 mi. WSW of Onega; sawmilling. Developed in early 1940s.

Malosmadulu Atoll (mŭlōs″mŭdōō'lōō), N group (pop. 8,630) of Maldive Isls., in Indian Ocean, bet. 5°N and 6°N; coconuts.

Malo-Uchalinski or **Malo-Uchalinskiy** (mä″lŭ-ōōchŭlyēn'skē), town (1943 pop. over 500), E Bashkir Autonomous SSR, Russian SFSR, 4 mi. S of Uchaly, on small lake. Manganese mining near by.

Malouines, Îles: see FALKLAND ISLANDS.

Malovitsa or **Mal'ovitsa** (mälyôvē'tsä), peak (8,957 ft.) in NW Rila Mts., W Bulgaria, 14 mi. ESE of Marek. Sometimes spelled Malevitsa.

Maloy, Norway: see VAGSOY.

Maloy (mŭloi'), town (pop. 90), Ringgold co., S Iowa, on Little Platte R. and 26 mi. S of Creston.

Maloyaroslavets (mä″lŭyŭrŭslä'vyĭts), city (1939 pop. over 10,000), NE Kaluga oblast, Russian SFSR, near Protva R., 35 mi. NNE of Kaluga, in orchard (cherries) area; metalworking, machine mfg.; railroad shops, brickworks. Peat and gravel found near by. Chartered 1410. Scene of Russian victory (1812) over Napoleon's army. During Second World War, briefly held (1941–42) by Germans in their Moscow campaign.

Maloyaz (mŭlŭyäs'), village (1939 pop. over 500), NE Bashkir Autonomous SSR, Russian SFSR, on Yuryuzan R. and 60 mi. W of Zlatoust; lumbering; livestock.

Maloye [Rus., =LESSER, LITTLE, SMALL], in Rus. names: see also MALAYA, MALO- [Rus. combining form], MALY, MALYE.

Malo-Yekaterinovka (mä″lŭ-yĕkŭtyĭrē'nŭfkŭ),town (1939 pop. over 500), NW Zaporozhe oblast, Ukrainian SSR, on railroad and 10 mi. S of Zaporozhe; truck produce.

Maloye Kozino (mä'lŭyŭ kô'zĭnŭ), town (1939 pop. over 2,000), W Gorki oblast, Russian SFSR, on Volga R. and 4 mi. SE of Balakhna; truck produce.

Malozemelskaya Tundra or **Malozemel'skaya Tundra** (mŭlŭzĕ'mĭlskĭŭ) [Rus., =little land], in Nenets Natl. Okrug, Archangel oblast, Russian SFSR; extends along Barents Sea coast from Indiga 140 mi. NE to mouth of Pechora R.; reindeer raising.

Malpaís, Mexico: see SAN NICOLÁS DE BUENOS AIRES.

Malpartida de Cáceres (mälpärtē'dhä dhä kä'thĕrĕs), town (pop. 6,104), Cáceres prov., W Spain, 7 mi. WSW of Cáceres; wool trade; cereals, olive oil, sheep.

Malpartida de la Serena (lä sārā'nä), town (pop. 2,129), Badajoz prov., W Spain, 5 mi. WSW of Castuera; cereals, tubers, lentils, grapes, livestock.

Malpartida de Plasencia (pläsĕn'thyä), village (pop. 4,536), Cáceres prov., W Spain, 4 mi. SE of Plasencia; agr. trade center (cereals, livestock); olive-oil processing, flour- and sawmilling. Its rail station (4 mi. SW) is junction of lines from Salamanca and Madrid to Portugal.

Malpas. **1** (môl'pŭs, măl'–, mô'pŭs) Town and parish (pop. 1,101), SW Cheshire, England, 13 mi. SSE of Chester; agr. market for dairying region. Has church begun in 14th cent., completed in Tudor times. **2** (mō'pŭs) Village, SW Cornwall, England, just SE of Truro. **3** Residential town and parish (pop. 2,275), S Monmouth, England, just N of Newport.

Mal Paso, Alto de (äl'tō dhä mäl'pä'sō), highest elevation (4,330 ft.) of Hierro, Canary Isls., 8 mi. SW of Valverde. Sometimes spelled Malpaso.

Malpe, India: see UDIPI.

Malpelo Island (mälpā'lō), small islet in the Pacific, belonging to Colombia, 310 mi. W of Buenaventura; 4°N 90°30'W.

Malpeque Bay (môl'pĕk), inlet (12 mi. long, 10 mi. wide at entrance) of the Gulf of St. Lawrence, NW P.E.I., 4 mi. N of Summerside. Entrance of bay is protected by several islets. Oyster beds.

Malpica (mŭlpē'kŭ), town (pop. 2,443), Castelo Branco dist., central Portugal, near Sp. border, 12 mi. SSE of Castelo Branco; corn, wheat, olives, beans. Cork-oak woods.

Malpica (mälpē'kä). **1** Town (pop. 1,702), La Coruña prov., NW Spain, fishing port on the Atlantic, 21 mi. W of La Coruña. Also bathing resort. **2** Town (pop. 1,580), Toledo prov., central Spain, on the Tagus and 16 mi. ESE of Talavera de la Reina; olives, cereals, grapes, stock. Hunting (wild boar). Has old castle. Sometimes called Malpica de Tajo.

Malplaquet (mälpläkā'), hamlet, Nord dept., N France, near Belg. border, 5 mi. NW of Maubeuge. Here in 1709, Marlborough and Eugene of Savoy won costly victory over French under Villars.

Malpura (mäl'pōōrŭ), town (pop. 6,615), E central Rajasthan, India, 50 mi. SSW of Jaipur; local market for millet, wheat, gram, cotton; handicrafts (felts, woolen blankets, saddle cloths). Headworks of small canal irrigation system 6 mi. SSE.

Mals, Italy: see MALLES VENOSTA.

Malsch (mälsh), village (pop. 6,079), N Baden, Germany, after 1945 in Württemberg-Baden, 5 mi. SW of Ettlingen; paper milling.

Malse River (mäl'shĕ), Czech *Malše*, N Austria and S Bohemia, Czechoslovakia; rises in Austria 9 mi. SE of Horni Dvoriste, flows generally NW, along Czechoslovak–Austrian border, and N, past Kaplice, to Vltava R. at Budweis; 62 mi. long.

Malsiras (mäl'sĭrŭs), village, Sholapur dist., central Bombay, India, 70 mi. WNW of Sholapur; agr. market; sugar milling.

Malstatt-Burbach (mäl'shtät-bōōr'bäkh), NW section (since 1909) of Saarbrücken, S Saar, on Saar R.; coal mining; coal-shipping port; coke ovens.

Malstrom, Norway: see MAELSTROM.

Malta (môl'tŭ), anc. *Melita*, principal island (□ 94.87; pop. 278,311) of the British crown colony of Malta (or Maltese Isls.). The colony (□ 121.8; pop. 305,991), which also includes Gozo, COMINO, and a few adjacent islets, is a self-governing unit, apart from foreign affairs and defense; ⊙ VALLETTA. Malta, the great Br. bastion in the Mediterranean, is strategically situated about half way bet. Gibraltar and Suez, c.60 mi. S of Sicily and c.180 mi. E of Tunisia, North Africa. The isl. of Malta lies just S of 36°N latitude; it is oval shaped (17 mi. long, 9 mi. wide) and, except in SW, deeply indented along its steep, rocky coast. Among the numerous inlets are MARSAXLOKK or Marsa Scirocco Bay (SE), St. Paul's Bay (NE), and, particularly, the double bay (MARSAMUSCETTO HARBOUR and GRAND HARBOUR) formed by the projecting peninsula on which lies Valletta, a foremost Br. naval base and port of call, surrounded by a string of fortifications and subsidiary ports, such as the "Three Cities" of SENGLEA, COSPICUA, and VITTORIOSA. The former capital, MDINA, lies inland. The isl.'s relief is hilly, broken by low limestone ridges that rise near S coast to 817 ft. Though there are no rivers, subterranean basins occur widely, as in all karst formations. Equable climate, with annual mean temp. of 66°F. and annual rainfall of c.17 inches. Most rains fall in winter. During the summer, when the sirocco blows from the Sahara, the heat is sometimes oppressive. The isl. has no native trees, and the thin layer of calcareous soil has been turned productive only through great labor. While revenue is chiefly derived from the transit trade and the great many people employed in the naval dockyards, agr. remains the principal occupation. Leading crops are of the subsistence type (wheat, barley, potatoes, onions, beans, grapes, citrus fruit, forage, tomatoes, cotton). These have, however, to be supplemented by imports, though small quantities of potatoes, onions, vegetables, and cumin seed, as well as hides and skins, are exported. There is small-scale grazing (goats, sheep, cattle), fishing, and beekeeping. Among its industries are mfg. of lace, buttons, textiles, shoes, gloves, pipes, wine, beer, sausages, cigarettes, food preserves—of which minor quantities are shipped. The trade balance is very unfavorable, but substantial income is derived from tourist trade, reshipment of goods, and bunkering. Many Maltese emigrate to other Mediterranean countries, Britain, the U.S., and Australia. The educational level is high; there is a univ. at Valletta. The population is believed to be of Semitic origin. Their native language is akin to Arabic but has strong Italian elements. Both English and Maltese are official languages. Among the educated class, Italian is also widely spoken. The overwhelming majority (c.95%) are R.C. Many nations and civilizations have left their imprint on the archipelago. Megalithic remains abound, notably the enormous ruins at TARXIEN. Malta was successively held by Phoenicians (after c.1000 B.C.), Greeks, Carthaginians, and Romans. It was here that St. Paul was shipwrecked (perhaps at St. Paul's Bay). Upon division of the Roman

Empire (A.D. 395) it fell to the Byzantine emperor. Conquered 870 by the Arabs, from whom it was wrested (1090) by the Norman Sicilians. In 1530 Charles V gave Malta to the Knights Hospitalers (Knights of St. John of Jerusalem; also called, therefore, Knights of Malta), who had been driven from Rhodes by the Turks. The Knights turned the archipelago into a fortified stronghold of Christendom. To their great wealth and artistic taste testify a galaxy of fine structures—churches, monasteries, palaces, and forts, reaching their highest level in the baroque. A long siege (1565) by the Turks was successfully resisted. To commemorate the victory, grand master Jean Parisot de la Vallette founded the new capital, Valletta. Malta capitulated to Napoleon in 1798, but soon rose in rebellion and blockaded the Fr. garrisson, which surrendered (1800) to a Br. fleet. Great Britain formally annexed (1814) the isls. by Treaty of Paris. Malta became a key point in the Br. Empire's defense line. Responsible govt., established 1921, was suspended in 1930 and 1936. Some measure of self-government was granted in 1939, enlarged through 1947 constitution. Malta suffered severely during Second World War when it was mercilessly bombed (1940–43) by Axis airplanes. Many of its art treasures were damaged beyond repair. For their valor the entire population of Malta was awarded (1942) the George Cross.

Malta. **1** (mäl'tů) Town (pop. 510), De Kalb co., N Ill., 6 mi. W of De Kalb, in rich agr. area. **2** (môl'tů) City (pop. 2,095), ⊙ Phillips co., N Mont., on Milk R., near L. Bowdoin, and 85 mi. E of Havre; trading point in irrigated agr. area; livestock, dairy products, grain, sugar beets; gas wells; flour. Inc. 1909. **3** (môl'tů) Village (pop. 968), Morgan co., E central Ohio, on Muskingum R., opposite McConnelsville; agr. machinery, wood products.

Malta Bend (môl'tů), town (pop. 414), Saline co., central Mo., 10 mi. NW of Marshall.

Malta Channel, strait (c.60 mi. wide) in the Mediterranean bet. SE Sicily and the Maltese Isls.

Maltahohe, Ger. *Maltahöhe* (mäl'tähû"ů), trading town (pop. 706), S central South-West Africa, 140 mi. NNW of Keetmanshoop; sheep raising. Formerly noted horse-breeding center. Site of Duwisib Castle (1900).

Maltby, urban district (1931 pop. 10,010; 1951 census 12,485), West Riding, S Yorkshire, England, 6 mi. E of Rotherham; coal mining; agr. market.

Malte Brun Range (môlt' brŭn'), W central S.Isl., New Zealand, in Southern Alps; extends 7 mi. N–S, bet. Murchison and Tasman glaciers; highest peak, Mt. Malte Brun (10,421 ft.).

Maltepe, Turkey: see MANYAS.

Malterdingen (mäl'tůrdĭng"ůn), village (pop. 1,687), S Baden, Germany, on W slope of Black Forest, 4 mi. NW of Emmendingen; tobacco mfg.

Malters (mäl'tůrs), town (pop. 4,021), Lucerne canton, central Switzerland, near Kleine Emme R., 6 mi. W of Lucerne; flour.

Maltese Islands (môl"tēz'), archipelago (□ 121.8; pop. 305,991), British possession in the central Mediterranean, c.60 mi. S of Sicily and crossed by 36°N. Consists of the 2 major isls., MALTA (SE) and Gozo (NW), besides tiny COMINO, COMINOTTO, and FIFLA. Principal city is VALLETTA, an important naval base. Generally they are called simply Malta, the official name for the entire colony.

Malton (môl'tůn), village (pop. estimate 600) S Ont., 10 mi. W of Toronto; 43°42'N 79°39'W; Toronto airport.

Malton or **New Malton** (môl'tůn), urban district (1931 pop. 4,419; 1951 census 4,235), North Riding, E Yorkshire, England, on Derwent R. and 17 mi. NE of York; steel-rolling mills, leather tanneries, foundries, breweries. Old Malton, in urban dist. (NW), has Norman church and ruins of Gilbertine priory.

Maltot (mältō'), village (pop. 111), Calvados dept., NW France, near the Orne, 5 mi. SW of Caen. Captured (July, 1944) by British in Caen offensive of Second World War.

Maltrata (mälträ'tä), town (pop. 3,807), Veracruz, E Mexico, in valley at S foot of Pico de Orizaba, on railroad and 12 mi. WSW of Orizaba; alt. 5,544 ft.; coffee-growing center.

Maltsevskaya, Russian SFSR: see URITSKI.

Maluenda (mälwĕn'dä), village (pop. 1,731), Saragossa prov., NE Spain, on Jiloca R. and 5 mi. SSE of Calatayud; sugar beets, cereals, wine, fruit, cattle.

Malujowice, Poland: see MOLLWITZ.

Maluko (mälōō'kō), town (1939 pop. 903; 1948 municipality pop. 9,560), Bukidnon prov., N Mindanao, Philippines, 20 mi. E of Cagayan; coconuts, abacá.

Maluku, Indonesia: see MOLUCCAS.

Ma'lula (mälōō'lä), Fr. *Maaloula,* village (pop. c.2,000), Damascus prov., SW Syria, 26 mi. NNE of Damascus on E slope of the Anti-Lebanon mts.; alt. 5,650 ft. Summer resort; orchards, cereals. Has a Greek Catholic convent, with the cupola dating from Byzantine times. Pop. largely Greek Catholic.

Malung (mä'lōōng'), town, ⊙ Malung co. (pop. 46,006), E Yunnan prov., China, on railroad and 10 mi. WSW of Kütsing; alt. 6,857 ft.; rice, wheat, millet, beans, timber.

Malung (mä'lŭng"), village (pop. 977), Kopparberg co., central Sweden, on West Dal R. and 60 mi. W of Falun; tanning, shoe and leather-goods mfg., metalworking.

Malungsfors (mä"lŭngsfôrs', –fôsh'), village (pop. 919), Kopparberg co., central Sweden, on West Dal R. and 70 mi. W of Falun; tanning, stock raising, dairying.

Malur (mä'lōōr), town (pop. 5,185), Kolar dist., E Mysore, India, 15 mi. SW of Kolar; tobacco curing; handicrafts (pottery, biris, weaving). Kaolin deposits near by.

Maluti Mountains (mälōō'tē), W Basutoland, branch of Drakensberg; extend NE and SW; rise to 11,000 ft. at Machache Peak.

Malvalli or **Malavalli** (mŭl'vŭlē), town (pop. 9,055), Mandya dist., SE Mysore, India, 16 mi. SE of Mandya; road center in sugar-cane and silk-growing area; hand-loom silk weaving. Famous Cauvery Falls are 10 mi. SE.

Malvan (mäl'vŭn), town (pop., including suburban area, 25,677), Ratnagiri dist., S Bombay, India, port on Arabian Sea, 65 mi. S of Ratnagiri, in the Konkan; fish-curing center (mackerel, sardines, catfish); local market for rice, sugar cane, coconuts, mangoes; mfg. of pen nibs, coir products; cashewnut processing, shark-oil extracting. Iron-ore deposits near by. Lighthouse (S). A Mahratta stronghold in 18th cent.

Malvar (mäl'vär), town (1939 pop. 1,493; 1948 municipality pop. 7,787), Batangas prov., S Luzon, Philippines, 11 mi. W of San Pablo; rail junction; agr. center (rice, sugar cane, corn, coconuts).

Malvasia, Greece: see MONEMVASIA.

Malvatu Oya, river, Ceylon: see ARUVI ARU.

Malveira (mŭlvā'rů), village (pop. 1,561), Lisboa dist., central Portugal, on railroad and 15 mi. NNW of Lisbon; hardware mfg.; olives, honey.

Malvern (môl'vůrn, mô'–), municipality (pop. 49,114), S Victoria, Australia, 5 mi. SE of Melbourne, in metropolitan area; residential.

Malvern (môl'vůrn, mô–), urban district (1931 pop. 15,634; 1951 census 21,681), SW Worcester, England, on E slope of MALVERN HILLS. Includes: spa of Great Malvern, 7 mi. SW of Worcester, with leather industry; spa of Malvern Wells (SSW); Malvern Link (N), with automobile, chemical, asbestos, and asphalt works; and Little or West Malvern (S), a residential area. In urban dist. are Malvern Col., a public school founded 1863; ruins of 11th-cent. Benedictine priory church; and an 11th-cent. priory church, rebuilt in 14th–16th cent. Mineral springs, climate, and pleasant surroundings make the area a favorite watering place. The annual dramatic Malvern Festival was established 1928 as a tribute to George Bernard Shaw.

Malvern (môl'vůrn), town (pop. 1,080), St. Elizabeth parish, SW Jamaica, resort 9 mi. SE of Black River, town in agr. region (corn, tropical fruit and spices, stock).

Malvern, New Zealand: see SHEFFIELD.

Malvern. **1** Residential town (pop. 7,973), SE Natal, U. of So. Afr., 7 mi. WSW of Durban, in fruitgrowing region. **2** E suburb of Johannesburg, S Transvaal, U. of So. Afr.

Malvern (măl'vůrn, –vůrn). **1** Town (pop. 196), Geneva co., SE Ala., 10 mi. SW of Dothan. **2** City (pop. 8,072), ⊙ Hot Spring co., central Ark., 17 mi. SE of Hot Springs, near Ouachita R., in agr. area (sweet potatoes, corn, cotton). Mfg. of wood products, brick, tile, chemicals, shoes; cotton ginning, sawmilling; aluminum plant at near-by Jones Mill. L. Catherine and a state park are near by. Laid out 1873, inc. as city 1876. **3** Town (pop. 1,263), Mills co., SW Iowa, on Silver Creek and 23 mi. SSE of Council Bluffs, in hay, grain, livestock area; feed milling. Founded 1869 with coming of railroad; inc. 1870. **4** Village (pop. 1,277), Carroll co., E Ohio, 13 mi. ESE of Canton, and on small Sandy Creek, in dairying and fruitgrowing area; makes clay products, chocolate; coal mining. **5** Agr. borough (pop. 1,764), Chester co., SE Pa., 19 mi. WNW of Philadelphia; platinum works. Settled 1866, inc. 1889.

Malverne, residential village (pop. 8,086), Nassau co., SE N.Y., on SW Long Isl., 8 mi. ESE of Jamaica, in truck-farming area. Settled c.1790, inc. 1921.

Malvern Hill, battlefield, Henrico co., E central Va., near the James, 18 mi. SE of Richmond. Here (July 1, 1862) Confederates under Lee were repulsed by McClellan in the last of the Seven Days Battles.

Malvern Hills (môl'vůrn, mô'–), range (c.8 mi. long) on Worcester-Hereford border, England. Highest elevations are Worcestershire Beacon (1,395 ft.) and North Hill (1,307 ft.) in Worcester, and Herefordshire Beacon (1,114 ft.) in Hereford. On Herefordshire Beacon are remains of anc. Br. camp.

Malvik, Norway: see HOMMELVIK.

Malvinas, Islas: see FALKLAND ISLANDS.

Malwa (mäl'vů), plateau in W central India, comprising large part of Madhya Bharat, N Bhopal, and small section of SE Rajasthan; bounded S by W Vindhya Range, W by offshoot of Vindhyas which extends N toward Mandasor, E by another offshoot which extends N toward Guna, and N by irregular line of hills bet. Chitor and Guna; average height c.1,600 ft. Fertile area of black cotton soil, drained by Chambal, Sipra, Kali Sindh, and Parbati rivers; millet, wheat, gram, cotton, poppy are chief crops. Important trade centers are Indore, Ujjain, Ratlam, and Dewas. Name often applied to larger surrounding area; originally a tribal country, mentioned vaguely in early Hindu legends; in 6th cent. B.C. known as Avanti. Under Mauryan (3d cent. B.C.) and Magadhan (4th–5th cent. A.D.) dynasties. Moslems 1st appeared in 1235; from 1401 to 1531 Malwa was strong independent state with ⊙ at Mandu. Later (c.1560) fell to the Moguls and (in mid-18th cent.) to the Mahrattas.

Malwa Agency, subdivision (□ 7,427; pop. 1,091,274) of former CENTRAL INDIA agency; hq. were at Indore. Comprised former princely states of Alirajpur, Barwani, Dhar, Jaora, Jhabua, Jobat, Kathiwara, Mathwar, Piploda, Ratlam, Sailana, Sitamau, and several petty states. Created 1925.

Malwatu Oya, river, Ceylon: see ARUVI ARU.

Malxe River (mälk'sů), E Germany, rises in Lower Lusatia just S of Döbern, flows 50 mi. N and WNW, in a wide arc, through Spree Forest, to the Spree 1.5 mi. SSE of Lübben.

Maly or **Malyy** [Rus.,=LESSER, LITTLE, SMALL], in Rus. names: see also MALAYA, MALO- [Rus. combining form], MALOYE, MALYE.

Maly Dunaj, river, Czechoslovakia: see LITTLE DANUBE RIVER.

Malye or **Malyye** [Rus.,=LESSER, LITTLE, SMALL], in Rus. names: see also MALAYA, MALO- [Rus. combining form], MALOYE, MALY.

Malye Chapurniki, Russian SFSR: see BOLSHIYE CHAPURNIKI.

Malye Derbety or **Malyye Derbety** (mä'lēů dyĭrbyĕ'tē), village (1939 pop. over 500), SE Stalingrad oblast, Russian SFSR, in Sarpa Lakes valley, on Stalingrad–Stepnoi road and 55 mi. S of Stalingrad; wheat, mustard; cattle, sheep raising.

Malye Karmakuly or **Malyye Karmakuly** (kŭrmůkōō'lē), settlement on W coast of S isl. of Novaya Zemlya, Russian SFSR; 72°23'N 52°40'E. Govt. observation station.

Malygin Strait, Russian SFSR: see BELY ISLAND.

Maly Krivan (mä'lē krĭ'vänyů), Slovak *Malý Kriváň,* Hung. *Kriván* (krĭ'vän), highest mountain (5,612 ft.) of the Lesser Fatra, NW Slovakia, Czechoslovakia, 14 mi. NW of Ruzomberok.

Maly Lyakhov Island (mä'lē lyä'khŭf) [Rus.,=little Lyakhov], one of Lyakhov Isls., bet. Laptev and E. Siberian seas, off Yakut Autonomous SSR, Russian SFSR; separated from Kotelny Isl. by Sannikov Strait, from Bolshoi Lyakhov Isl. by Eterikan Strait.

Maly Ston, Yugoslavia: see STON.

Maly Taimyr Island or **Malyy Taymyr Island** (mä'lē tīmĭr') [Rus.,=little Taimyr], in Laptev Sea of Arctic Ocean, 25 mi. off SE Severnaya Zemlya archipelago, in Krasnoyarsk Territory, Russian SFSR; 78°10'N 107°E. Discovered 1913 by Vilkitski. Formerly Tsesarevich Aleksei Isl.

Maly Yenisei River, Russian SFSR: see YENISEI RIVER.

Malzéville (mälzāvēl'), N residential suburb (pop. 4,355) of Nancy, Meurthe-et-Moselle dept., NE France, on right bank of Meurthe R.; chemical works.

Malzieu-Ville, Le (lů mälzyû'-vēl'), village (pop. 697), Lozère dept., S France, on SW slope of Montagnes de la Margeride, on Truyère R. and 17 mi. SE of Saint-Flour; silk spinning.

Mama (mä'mä), town (pop. 1,577), Yucatan, SE Mexico, 15 mi. NE of Ticul; henequen, sugar cane, fruit.

Mama (mä'mů), town (1939 pop. over 2,000), NE Irkutsk oblast, Russian SFSR, on Vitim R., at mouth of Mama R., and 60 mi. NW of Bodaibo; center of mica-mining area.

Mamada (mä"mä'dä), town (pop. 9,893), Tochigi prefecture, central Honshu, Japan, 8 mi. S of Tochigi; rice, sweet potatoes, gourds.

Mamadysh (mŭmŭdĭsh'), city (1936 pop. estimate 7,200), N Tatar Autonomous SSR, Russian SFSR, on Vyatka R. (landing) and 25 mi. W of Yelabuga; distilling center; metal- and woodworking. Developed in 1740s as copper-smelting center; chartered 1781.

Mamahatun, Turkey: see TERCAN.

Mamahuasi (mämäwä'sē), town (pop. c.13,800), Chuquisaca dept., S central Bolivia, on left branch of upper Pilcomayo R. and 15 mi. NW of Sucre; wheat, barley, vegetables.

Mamaia (mämä'yä), beach resort on Black Sea, Constanta prov., SE Rumania, 5 mi. N of Constanta.

Mamakhel (mä'mŭkhāl), village, Eastern Prov., E Afghanistan, on N slopes of the Safed Koh, 26 mi. SW of Jalalabad, just off highway to Kabul; hill resort.

Mamallapuram, India: see MAHABALIPURAM.

Mamanguape (mŭmăng-gwä'pĭ), city (pop. 4,019), E Paraíba, NE Brazil, 25 mi. NW of João Pessoa; cotton, sugar, and manioc processing; fruit, rice, medicinal plants.

Mamanutha or **Mamanuca** (both: mämänōō'thä), volcanic group of islands in Fiji, SW Pacific, c.10 mi. W of Viti Levu; largest isl. is Tavua, 1 mi. long. Sometimes called Mabualau.

Mamara (mämä'rä), city (pop. 1,655), Apurímac dept., S central Peru, on affluent of Apurímac R. and 40 mi. SSE of Abancay; silver mining.

Mama River (mä'mŭ), N Buryat-Mongol Autonomous SSR and NE Irkutsk oblast, Russian SFSR, rises NE of L. Baikal, flows 200 mi. NE to Vitim R. at Mama. Large mica deposits along its course.

Mamaroneck (mŭmă'rŭnĕk), suburban residential village (pop. 15,016), Westchester co., SE N.Y., on Mamaroneck Harbor (□ c.1), on Long Isl. Sound, bet. Larchmont (SW) and Rye; mfg. (food products, wood and metal products, raincoats, chemicals, machinery, dental plates, asbestos packing, motorboats, aircraft equipment). Settled 1661, inc. 1895.

Mamatla (mämät'lä), town (pop. 1,576), Mexico state, central Mexico, 45 mi. SSW of Toluca; sugar cane, coffee, fruit.

Mamawi Lake (16 mi. long, 10 mi. wide), NE Alta., 8 mi. SW of Fort Chipewyan, in Wood Buffalo Natl. Park, bet. L. Claire and L. Athabaska; 58°35'N 111°30'W.

Mamba (mäm'bä), town (pop. 6,919), Gumma prefecture, central Honshu, Japan, 15 mi. SSW of Takasaki; charcoal, rice, raw silk.

Mambajao (mämbä'hou), town (1939 pop. 4,657; 1948 municipality pop. 25,193) on Camiguin Isl., Misamis Oriental prov., Philippines, on NE coast of isl.; agr. center (corn, coconuts). Just S of town is volcanic Mt. Mambajao (5,619 ft.); its eruption in 1948 caused temporary evacuation of isl.'s inhabitants.

Mambasa (mämbä'sä), village, Eastern Prov., NE Belgian Congo; trading center; rice processing. Gold-mining near by. Has Protestant mission. Members of Pygmy tribes still live in vicinity.

Mambau (mämbou'), village (pop. 215), W Negri Sembilan, Malaya, on railroad and 4 mi. SW of Seremban; tin mining; rubber.

Mamberamo River (mämbĕräm'ō) or **Rochussen River** (rôkh'ŭsŭn), largest river of Netherlands New Guinea, formed by junction (in marshy area N of Nassau Range) of Idenburg and Rouffaer rivers, flows generally NW to the Pacific near Cape D'Urville; length (with its headstream, the Idenburg) is c.500 mi. Sometimes called Tarikaikea R.

Mambone (mämbō'nä), village, Sul do Save prov., central Mozambique, on Mozambique Channel at mouth of Sabi R., 75 mi. S of Beira; agr. trade (corn, beans); fishing.

Mambulao, Philippines: see JOSE PAÑGANIBAN.

Mambunga (mämbōōng'gä), village, Eastern Prov., NE Belgian Congo, 25 mi. ESE of Paulis; cattle-raising center; cotton ginning.

Mambusao (mämbōō'sou), town (1939 pop. 1,325; 1948 municipality pop. 18,619), Capiz prov., N Panay isl., Philippines, 15 mi. SW of Capiz; rice-growing center.

Mameki, Turkey: see KALAN.

Mameli or **Mammelli** (mäm-mĕl'lē), village (pop. 1,370), W Cyrenaica, Libya, on the plateau Gebel el Akhdar, on road and 17 mi. SW of Cyrene; agr. settlement (cereals, olives, grapes, almonds) established by Italians 1938–39.

Mamelle Island or **Mamelles Island** (mämĕl'), one of the Seychelles, in Indian Ocean, 10 mi. NNE of Victoria; 4°29'S 55°32'E. Copra. Lighthouse.

Mamer (mä'mûr), village (pop. 1,347), SW Luxembourg, 5 mi. WNW of Luxembourg city; chalk quarrying; agr. (potatoes, wheat, oats).

Mamers (mämâr'), town (pop. 4,450), Sarthe dept., W France, 13 mi. ESE of Alençon; agr. trade center; lace, curtain, and fringe mfg.

Mamey, El, Mexico: see MINATITLÁN, Colima.

Mameyes (mämā'ĕs), village, NE Puerto Rico, on railroad and 23 mi. ESE of San Juan; road center in sugar-growing region. Cultivates the mammee tree, which yields preserves, medical gum, and construction timber.

Mamfe (mäm'fĕ), town (pop. 3,264), S Br. Cameroons, administered as part of Eastern Provinces of Nigeria, on Cross R. and 80 mi. NNW of Kumba; trade center; cacao, bananas, palm oil and kernels; hardwood, rubber. Has hosp. Airfield.

Mamihara (mämē'härä), town (pop. 3,250), Kumamoto prefecture, central Kyushu, Japan, on Gokase R. and 27 mi. ESE of Kumamoto; produces tea. Sometimes called Mamiwara.

Mamiña (mämē'nyä), village (pop. 525), Tarapacá prov., N Chile, on W slopes of the Andes (alt. 9,005 ft.), 60 mi. E of Iquique; hot sulphur springs with curative properties.

Mamison Pass (mŭmēsôn'), the central Greater Caucasus, 32 mi. SW of Alagir, at Russian SFSR–Georgian SSR line; crossed by Ossetian Military Road; alt. 9,550 ft. Links Ardon and Rion river valleys.

Mamiwara, Japan: see MAMIHARA.

Mamlyutka (mŭmlyōōt'kŭ), town (1948 pop. over 2,000), N North Kazakhstan oblast, Kazakh SSR, on Trans-Siberian RR and 25 mi. WNW of Petropavlovsk, in wheat area; metalworks.

Mammelli, Cyrenaica: see MAMELI.

Mammola (mäm'môlä), town (pop. 7,021), Reggio di Calabria prov., Calabria, S Italy, 7 mi. NNW of Siderno Marina, in agr. (olives, fruit) and livestock-raising region; rail terminus.

Mammoth, village, Pinal co., SE Ariz., on San Pedro R. and 39 mi. NNE of Tucson; molybdenum deposits. In 1880s was busy mining camp (gold, silver).

Mammoth Cave. 1 Cavern near San Andreas, Calaveras co., central Calif.; contains many chambers and a subterranean lake. **2** Cavern in Modoc co., N Calif., near Lava Beds Natl. Monument.

Mammoth Cave National Park (□ 79.2; established 1936), S Ky., on both banks of Green R. (which receives Nolin R. in NW corner of park), and 24 mi. NE of Bowling Green. Mammoth Cave, in E, is series of huge, subterranean chambers formed by dissolution of limestone, connected by passages (more than 150 mi. have been explored), and lying on 5 levels. Has stalactites and stalagmites and other fantastic and beautiful limestone formations, lofty domes, deep pits, underground lakes. Prevailing temp. is 54°F. Small Echo R. (360 ft. below surface; contains blind fish) flows through lowest level and drains into Green R. There are 2 principal entrances: the Old, or Historic (a natural opening), and Frozen Niagara (manmade), which is near enormous deposit of onyx in form of a waterfall. Long known to Indians, cave was discovered by white men in 1799; saltpeter was mined here during War of 1812. Surrounding area in park is hilly and forested, containing variety of plant, animal, and bird life. Park hq. within park; tourist accommodations, recreational facilities (swimming, boating, fishing, guided naturalist tours).

Mammoth Caves, Australia: see MARGARET RIVER.

Mammoth Hot Springs, Wyo.: see YELLOWSTONE NATIONAL PARK.

Mammoth Lakes, Mono co., E Calif., resort settlement and region of many small lakes, in the Sierra Nevada, c.35 mi. NW of Bishop; alt. c.8,900 ft.; fishing, boating, camping, hiking, horseback riding, winter sports. Devil Postpile Natl. Monument is just W. Scene of small-scale gold rush, 1879–80.

Mammoth Onyx Cave, Ky.: see MUNFORDVILLE.

Mammoth Spring, town (pop. 870), Fulton co., N Ark., c.65 mi. NW of Jonesboro, at Mo. line, in agr. area; lumber mill. Ships moss. Has U.S. fish hatchery. Named for spring (N end of town), one of largest in U.S., which feeds Spring R.; site of resort, power plant.

Mamoi (mä'moi'), Mandarin *Mawei* (mä'wā'). town, E Fukien prov., China, port on Min R. near its mouth on E.China Sea, 10 mi. SE of Foochow; naval base (shipyards); naval acad., arsenal.

Mamoiada (mämôyä'dä), village (pop. 2,834), Nuoro prov., E central Sardinia, 8 mi. SSW of Nuoro; agr. tools, cutlery. Muraghe near by.

Mamonal (mämōnäl'), petroleum port on the Caribbean just S of Cartagena, N Colombia, at end of pipe line from Barrancabermeja.

Mamonovo (mŭmō'nŭvŭ), city (1939 pop. 12,100), W Kaliningrad oblast, Russian SFSR, on railroad and 28 mi. SW of Kaliningrad, near Vistula Lagoon and Pol. line; mfg. of agr. implements, woodworking. Until 1945, in East Prussia and called Heiligenbeil (hī'lĭgŭnbīl").

Mamontovo (mä'mŭntŭvŭ), village (1926 pop. 2,871), central Altai Territory, Russian SFSR, 50 mi. WNW of Aleisk; metalworking, dairy farming.

Mamont Peninsula, Russian SFSR: see GYDA PENINSULA.

Mamora Forest, NW Fr. Morocco, bet. Salé (SW), Port-Lyautey (NW), and the Oued Beth (E). One of Morocco's largest cork-oak forests.

Mamoré, Bolivia: see SAN JOAQUÍN.

Mamoré River (mŭmōōrĕ'), N central Bolivia, formed by confluence of Chaparé and Ichilo rivers 80 mi. S of Trinidad, and joined 20 mi. further by the Río Grande (usually considered chief headstream); flows N to Brazil border, where it receives GUAPORÉ RIVER, then continues along Brazil–Bolivia line to Villa Bella, where it is joined by BENI RIVER to form MADEIRA RIVER. Length, including the Río Grande, c.1,200 mi. Navigable through Bolivian llanos and tropical forest to Guajará Mirim (Brazil), S terminus of Madeira–Mamoré RR.

Mamou (mämōō'), town (pop. c.6,500), W central Fr. Guinea, Fr. West Africa, on railroad and 125 mi. ENE of Conakry; trading, cattle-raising, and agr. center. Produces bananas, rice, peanuts, potatoes, orange essence, rubber, indigo, beeswax, honey. Meteorological station; experimental gardens; R.C. and Protestant missions; mosque. Gold deposits near by.

Mamou (mă'mōō), village (pop. 2,254), Evangeline parish, S central La., 55 mi. NE of Lake Charles city, in rice-producing area; cotton ginning; rice, feed, sugar, and lumber mills.

Mampochin, Korea: see MANPOJIN.

Mampong or **Mampong Ashanti** (mämpông' äshän'tē), town (pop. 3,967), Ashanti, S central Gold Coast, on road and 30 mi. NNE of Kumasi; road and trade center; cacao, kola nuts, hardwood, rubber. English church mission (convent and girls col.). Agr. experiment station. Trade training center (opened 1949). Just S is Mampong Scarp, section of main mtn. range of Gold Coast.

Mampong or **Mampong Akwapim** (äkwäpēm'), town, Eastern Prov., SE Gold Coast colony, in Akwapim Hills, 25 mi. NNE of Accra; road junction; cacao, palm oil and kernels, cassava.

Mamprusi, Gold Coast: see GAMBAGA.

Mamre, Palestine: see HEBRON.

Mamre (măm'rē), agr. village (pop. 1,552), SW Cape Prov., U. of So. Afr., near the Atlantic, 30 mi. N of Cape Town. Military post established here 1697; later site of Moravian mission.

Mamry, Lake (mäm'rĭ), Ger. *Mauer* (mou'ŭr), second-largest (□ 40) of Masurian Lakes, in East Prussia, after 1945 in NE Poland, bet. Gizycko (S) and Wegorezo (N), 35 mi. S of Chernyakhovsk, Kaliningrad oblast; irregular in shape; 12 mi. long N–S, up to 8 mi. wide. Drained (N) by Angerapp R. S terminus of Masurian Canal.

Mam Soul (măm soul') or **Mam Sodhail**, mountain (3,862 ft.) in SW Ross and Cromarty, Scotland, 15 mi. E of Dornie, at Inverness line.

Mamuil-Malal Pass (mämwēl'-mäläl') (4,100–4,500 ft.), in the Andes, on Argentina-Chile border, at NE foot of Lanín Volcano; 39°35'S 71°32'W.

Mamulique Pass (mämōōlē'kä) (2,280 ft.), in N outliers of Sierra Madre Oriental, Nuevo León, N Mexico, on Inter-American Highway and 40 mi. NNE of Monterrey.

Mamuret-el-Aziz, Turkey: see ELAZIG, province.

Mamykovo (mä'mĭkŭvŭ), village (1948 pop. over 2,000), S Tatar Autonomous SSR, Russian SFSR, 17 mi. NNW of Nurlat; wheat, livestock.

Man, canal and river, Burma: see MAN RIVER.

Man, town (pop. c.4,600), W Ivory Coast, Fr. West Africa, on road to Fr. Guinea and 290 mi. WNW of Abidjan; agr. center (coffee, rice, kola nuts, bananas, manioc, potatoes). Sawmilling, brickmaking. Plant research station (coffee, cinchona). R.C. and Protestant missions.

Man, trading town (pop. 1,632), Logan co., SW W.Va., 10 mi. SW of Logan, in bituminous-coal, agr. (livestock, fruit, tobacco) area. Inc. 1918.

Man, Isle of, anc. *Mona* or *Monapia*, island (□ 220.7; 1939 pop. 50,829; 1951 census 55,213) in the Irish Sea bet. Lancashire, England, and Northern Ireland; ⊙ Douglas. It is 33 mi. long, 12 mi. wide, and has rocky, indented coastline; Calf of Man is detached islet off SW coast. Hilly country, rising to 2,034 ft. in Snaefell. With striking and beautiful scenery and a mild climate (subtropical plants grown), the isle is a resort. More than half the isle is cultivated; crops include fruits, grain, flowers, vegetables. Dairying, fishing, and quarrying (granite, silica, quartz) carried on. Occupied c.600 by Vikings, isle was a dependency of Norway until 1266, when it was ceded to Scotland, but from 14th cent. to 1735 it belonged to the earls of Derby. Since 1827 it has been under the British crown. Has its own legislature consisting of Council (upper house) and House of Keys (lower house). Traces of occupants of the isle from neolithic times exist; there are anc. crosses and other stone monuments, a round tower at Peel, an old fort, and castles. Towns include Douglas, Peel, Ramsey, and Castletown. Sir Hall Caine lived on isl. and described Manx life in many novels. Manx language, of Celtic origin, is now spoken by very few people.

Mana (mänä'), town (commune pop. 1,443), NW Fr. Guiana, on Mana R. near its mouth on the Atlantic, and 110 mi. WNW of Cayenne; sugar cane, cattle. Founded 1830 as orphan asylum by Fr. nun. Has leprosarium.

Mana, river, Fr. Guiana: see MANA RIVER.

Mana (mô'nä), Nor. *Måna*, river in Telemark co., S Norway, flows from Mos L. 18 mi. E to Tinn L. On it are Rjukan Falls (983 ft.), which supply power for the industry of RJUKAN.

Manaar, Ceylon and India: see MANNAR.

Manabe, Japan: see TSUCHIURA.

Manabí (mänäbē'), province (□ 7,602; 1950 pop. 382,109), W Ecuador, on the Pacific, traversed by the equator; ⊙ Portoviejo. Apart from low Andean ridges (E), it consists of densely forested lowlands drained by Portoviejo and Chone rivers. Has tropical climate, with rains Dec.-June, when the climate is most trying. Its fertile soil yields coffee, cacao, rice, sugar cane, cotton, bananas, and forest products (*toquilla* straw, tagua nuts, balsa wood, and other fine cabinet woods). The prov. is the leading producer of Panama hats, which are exported to the U.S. Bahía de Caráquez and Manta are its seaports. Portoviejo, Jipijapa, Montecristi, and Chone are other centers.

Manabique, Cape, Guatemala: see TRES PUNTAS, CABO DE.

Manacapuru (mŭnŭ"kŭpōōrōō'), city (pop. 1,385), E central Amazonas, Brazil, on left bank of the Amazon and 40 mi. WSW of Manaus; rubber, Brazil nuts, hardwood.

Manacas (mänä'käs), town (pop. 1,428), Las Villas prov., central Cuba, on Central Highway, on railroad and 27 mi. NW of Santa Clara; sugar cane, tobacco, fruit, cattle.

Manachanalloor, India: see MANNACHCHANALLUR.

Manacle Point, England: see SAINT KEVERNE.

Manacor (mänäkôr'), city (pop. 13,585), Majorca, Balearic Isls., on railroad and 30 mi. E of Palma. Leading city of isl.'s central plain, in agr. region (cereals, grapes, almonds). Sawmilling, tanning, alcohol and liquor distilling, flour milling, dairying, meat packing; mfg. of celluloid, artificial pearls, jewelry, cement, tiles, apricot purée. Has notable secular and religious bldgs., among them the palace of kings of Majorca and fine parochial church. Near by at Porto Cristo (7 mi. E) are the Cuevas del Drach (Dragon's Cave), a favorite tourist site.

Manadhir, Saudi Arabia: see ABHA.

Manado, Indonesia: see MENADO.

Manage (mänäzh'), town (pop. 5,347), Hainault prov., S central Belgium, 12 mi. WNW of Charleroi; mfg. of railroad rolling stock; glass-blowing center.

Managua (mänä'gwä), town (pop. 823), Havana prov., W Cuba, at N foot of Managua hills, 15 mi. SSE of Havana; sugar cane, livestock.

Managua, department (□ 1,330; 1950 pop. 162,455), SW Nicaragua; ⊙ Managua. Includes coastal plain and E section of L. Managua basin, separated by coastal range rising to 3,000 ft. Agr.: coffee (in coastal hills), corn, beans, plantains, cotton. Forests in N highlands are largely denuded. Livestock raising in L. Managua basin. Mfg. at Managua city. Served by railroad and Inter-American Highway. Tipitapa (thermal baths) and Masachapa (on Pacific coast) are tourist resorts. Puerto Somoza is new Pacific port, developed in 1940s.

Managua, city (1950 pop. 107,444), ⊙ Nicaragua and ⊙ Managua dept., on SE shore of L. Managua, on railroad and Inter-American Highway, 45 mi. SE of León; 12°8'N 86°18'W. Administrative, commercial, and mfg. center; international and domestic airport. Its port on the Pacific is Puerto Somoza. Produces cement, soap, candles, textiles, perfumes, liquors, canned goods, pharmaceutical products; railroad workshops. Laid out in checkerboard fashion, Managua centers on the Parque Central (near lake shore) surrounded by public bldgs. (natl. palace, city hall, cathedral, Club Managua). Site of natl. mus., library, teachers institute, hospitals. Univ. moved to Natl. Univ. at León. Extending into hills S of city, Managua reaches SW to Las Piedrecitas (läs pyādrāsē'täs), residential suburb on L. Asososca, SE to Tiscapa Hill (site of presidential palace) on L. Tiscapa. A large Indian town at coming (16th cent.) of Spaniards, Managua was eclipsed in early colonial period by Granada and León. Remained loyal to the Crown in early independence movements (1811–12); became city in 1846, chosen ⊙ Nicaragua in 1855. Stricken repeatedly by disaster, Managua was ruined by flood (1876), earthquake (1885), arsenal explosion (1902), civil war (1912), and was almost entirely destroyed by earthquake and fire in 1931. The municipio of Managua was made a natl. dist. [Sp. *distrito nacional*] in 1932.

Managua, Lake, second largest lake (□ 390) of Nicaragua, in León and Managua depts., NW of L. Nicaragua; 38 mi. long, 16 mi. wide, 65 ft. deep, alt. 120 ft. Fisheries; alligator hunting; shallow-draught navigation. Managua is on SE shore. Other ports: Mateare, Momotombo, San Francisco del Carnicero, Tipitapa. Drains via Tipitapa R. (SE) into L. Nicaragua. Its Indian name is Xolotlán.

Manahawkin (mănŭhô'kĭn), village (1940 pop. 732), Ocean co., E N.J., near coast, 18 mi. S of Toms River village. **Manahawkin Bay** is E; link in N.J. sec. of Intracoastal Waterway, which enters from Barnegat Bay (N) and continues S into Little Egg Harbor. Bay is crossed SE of Manahawkin by highway bridge to Long Beach isl., barrier bet. bay and the Atlantic.

Manaia (mănī'ŭ), town (pop. 618), ⊙ Waimate West co. (□ 83; pop. 2,814), W N. Isl., New Zealand, on S. Taranaki Bight and 35 mi. S of New Plymouth; head of rail spur; dairy products.

Manakambahiny, Madagascar: see AMBATONDRAZAKA.

Manakara (mänäkä'rŭ), town (1948 pop. 3,345), Fianarantsoa prov., E Madagascar, 75 mi. SE of Fianarantsoa; cabotage port on Indian Ocean and Canal des Pangalanes; rail line to Fianarantsoa; ships coffee, cloves. Railroad shops. R.C. and Protestant missions.

Manakha or **Manakhah** (mănă'khŭ), town (pop. 3,000), Hodeida prov., W Yemen, in maritime range, 55 mi. ENE of Hodeida, and on mule track to Sana; alt. 7,500 ft. Center of coffeegrowing dist.; fruit and vegetables. Once situated on main Hodeida-Sana route, it declined when by-passed (1930s) by motor road (S). Also spelled Menakha or Menakhah.

Manakundur or **Manakondur** (both: mänŭkōōn'dōōr), town (pop. 5,500), Karimnagar dist., E central Hyderabad state, India, 4 mi. SE of Karimnagar; rice, millet, cotton.

Manalapan (mănŭlă'pŭn), resort town (pop. 54), Palm Beach co., SE Fla., 10 mi. S of Palm Beach.

Manali (mŭnä'lē), village, Kangra dist., NE Punjab, India, 50 mi. E of Dharmsala, in Kulu valley; wheat, barley, rice, fruit (apples, pears, apricots). Medicinal hot springs 2 mi. NE.

Manam (mänäm'), volcanic island (□ c.32; pop. c.3,000), Madang dist., Territory of New Guinea, SW Pacific, 9 mi. NE of New Guinea; 6 mi. long; active crater (4,265 ft.). Sometimes called Vulcan.

Manama or **Manamah** (mănă'mŭ), town (1950 pop. 39,648), ⊙ Bahrein, Persian Gulf port on NE point of main Bahrein isl., linked by 1.7-mi.-long road causeway with MUHARRAQ; commercial center; govt. offices, business houses, banks; power plant. Has sheik's residency, British political agency, and American mission hosp. Hq. of pearling and fishing fleet; dhow building.

Manamadurai (mänä'mŭdōōrī) or **Manamadura** (–dōōrŭ), town (pop. 7,189), Ramnad dist., S Madras, India, on Vaigai R. and 27 mi. SE of Madura; rail junction; tile mfg.

Mânamo, Caño (kä'nyō mä'nämō), westernmost arm of Orinoco R. delta, NE Venezuela; branches off S of Coporito, flows along Delta Amacuro territory–Monagas state border to Gulf of Paria at Pedernales; c.110 mi. long.

Mananara (mänänä'rŭ), town, Tamatave prov., NE Madagascar, on coast, 140 mi. NNE of Tamatave; trading center, customs station; coffee, vanilla, cloves. Hosp.

Mananjary (mänänjä'rē, –dzä'rē), town (1948 pop. 8,151), Fianarantsoa prov., E Madagascar, 85 mi. ENE of Fianarantsoa; cabotage port on Indian Ocean and Canal des Pangalanes at mouth of Mananjary R.; highway terminus and coffee center. Ships coffee, cacao, vanilla, cloves, rice, manioc, rum, tobacco. Has meteorological station, R.C. and Protestant missions.

Manantiales (mänäntyä'lĕs), town (pop. estimate 500), N Corrientes prov., Argentina, on railroad and 55 mi. SE of Corrientes; agr. (cotton, tobacco, sugar cane, peanuts); subtropical woods.

Manantoddy (mŭnŭtŏ'dē), village, Malabar dist., SW Madras, India, 40 mi. NNE of Calicut, in densely forested section of the Wynaad yielding valuable timber (teak, blackwood). Extensive tea, rubber, pepper, and coffee estates near by.

Manaoag (mänä'wäg), town (1939 pop. 3,071; 1948 municipality pop. 34,304), Pangasinan prov., central Luzon, Philippines, 10 mi. E of Dagupan, near Lingayen Gulf; agr. center (sugar cane, rice, copra, corn); sugar mill.

Manáos, Brazil: see MANAUS.

Manapad, India: see KULASEKHARAPATNAM.

Manaparai or **Manapparai** (mŭnŭpä'rī), town (pop. 5,327), Trichinopoly dist., S Madras, India, 22 mi. SW of Trichinopoly; cattle market; saltpeter extraction. Mica, gypsum, limestone deposits near.

Mana Pass (mänä') (alt. c.18,000 ft.), in S Zaskar Range of Kumaun Himalayas, SW Tibet, 23 mi. N of Badrinath (India), NNW of Kamet mtn., at 31°5'N 79°25'E. Source of left headstream of Alaknanda R.

Manapire River (mänäpē'rä), Guárico state, central Venezuela, rises NW of Valle de la Pascua, flows c.150 mi. S to Orinoco R. 5 mi. NE of Caicara.

Manapla (mänä'plä), town (1939 pop. 4,211; 1948 municipality pop. 35,218), Negros Occidental prov., NW Negros isl., Philippines, on Guimaras Strait, 23 mi. NNE of Bacolod; sugar milling.

Manapouri, Lake (mănŭpōōr'ē), deepest lake (1,458 ft.), in New Zealand, in Fiordland Natl. Park, SW S.Isl., 70 mi. NW of Invercargill; □ 56, 12 mi. long, 6 mi. wide. Source of Waiau R.

Manappadu, India: see KULASEKHARAPATNAM.

Manapparai, India: see MANAPARAI.

Manaqil or **El Manaqil** (ĕl mŭnä'kĭl), town, E central Anglo-Egyptian Sudan, in the Gezira, on road and 35 mi. WSW of Wad Medani; cotton, wheat, barley, corn, fruits, durra; livestock. Also spelled Menagil.

Manar, Ceylon and India: see MANNAR.

Manara (mänärä') or **Ramim** (rämēm'), settlement (pop. 200), Upper Galilee, NE Israel, in Hills of Naftali, on Lebanese border, 16 mi. N of Safad; alt. 3,018 ft.; dairying, fruitgrowing, sheep raising; machine shop. Founded 1943.

Mana River (mänä'), W Fr. Guiana, rises at S foot of the Chaîne Granitique, flows c.200 mi. N through tropical forests to the Atlantic 5 mi. below Mana. Navigable for small craft c.30 mi. upstream. Gold placers near its source.

Mana River (mä'nŭ), S Krasnoyarsk Territory, Russian SFSR, rises in Eastern Sayan Mts., flows 330 mi. NW, through wooded area, to Yenisei R. 15 mi. W of Krasnoyarsk.

Manas or **Manass** (mänäs'), Chinese *Suilai* (swä'lī'), town and oasis (pop. 21,783), central Sinkiang prov., China, on highway N of the Tien Shan, 70 mi. WNW of Urumchi, and on Manas R. (bridge; tributary of the Telli Nor); wheat, millet, melons, fruit. Oil wells near by.

Manasa (mŭnä'sŭ), town (pop. 5,515), NW Madhya Bharat, India, 28 mi. N of Mandasor; cotton, millet; sugar milling, handicraft blanket making.

Manasarowar Lake (mä"nŭsŭrō'ŭr), Chinese *Ma-na-sa-lo-wu Ch'ih* (mä'nä'sä'lô'wōō' chŭ'), Tibetan *Mapham Tso* (mä'päm tsō'), lake (□ 200) in W Himalayas, SW Tibet, bet. Kailas peak (N) and Gurla Mandhata peak (S); 12 mi. long, 14 mi. wide; alt. 14,950 ft. Linked with Rakas L. (W) by its N outlet, the river Ganga Chu (6 mi. long, 40–100 ft. wide; hot springs near banks). A Hindu pilgrimage center, lake is encircled by a path 54 mi. in circumference; traveled annually by large bands of pilgrims. In Hindu mythology, formed by Brahma's soul. Borax deposits near by.

Manasbal Lake (mŭnŭs'bŭl), in N Vale of Kashmir, W central Kashmir, 13 mi. NW of Srinagar; 3 mi. long, 1 mi. wide, c.50 ft. deep. Connected by channel with right bank of Jhelum R.; canal, which waters extensive terraces at E end, joins it with right tributary (Sind R.) of the Jhelum. Lake abounds in lotus; has anc. Hindu temple ruins (partially submerged); visited by houseboats. Limestone deposits near by.

Manaslu (mŭnäs'lōō) or **Kutang I** (kōōtäng'), peak (26,658 ft.) in central Nepal Himalayas, N Nepal, 38 mi. N of Gurkha, at 28°33'N 84°34'E. Up to 1950, unattempted by climbers.

Manasquan (mă'nŭskwän), resort borough (pop. 3,178), Monmouth co., E N.J., on coast, at mouth of Manasquan R., and 7 mi. S of Asbury Park; fishing, agr. (truck, fruit, poultry). Inc. 1887.

Manasquan River, E N.J., rises S of Freehold, flows c.30 mi. generally SE to the Atlantic at Manasquan. Manasquan Inlet, at mouth of river, is N entrance of N.J. sec. of Intracoastal Waterway, which continues S, through Bayhead-Manasquan Canal, to head of Barnegat Bay.

Manas River (mŭnäs'), in Tibet, Bhutan, and India, rises in SE Tibet (as the Nyamjang Chu), N of Tsona; flows S and SSW through Assam Himalayas and Bhutan (here called Dangme Chu), bifurcating just inside Assam (India); right stream (Manas proper) continues SSW to the Brahmaputra opposite Goalpara; total length, c.220 mi. Left stream (Mora Manas R.) flows S and W, rejoining the Manas 10 mi. NNE of Goalpara. Chief tributary, Tongsa R. (right).

Manassa (mŭnă'sŭ), town (pop. 832), Conejos co., S Colo., on Conejos R., just E of San Juan Mts., and 20 mi. S of Alamosa; alt. 7,700 ft. Trading point in San Luis Valley. Jack Dempsey b. here.

Manassas (mŭnă'sŭs). **1** City (pop. 128), Tattnall co., E central Ga., 7 mi. W of Claxton. **2** Town (pop. 1,804), ⊙ Prince William co., N Va., near the Bull Run, 25 mi. WSW of Washington, D.C.; rail junction; trade center for agr., dairying, livestock area. Has regional vocational school. L. Jackson (recreational area) is 4 mi. S. Near by are fields (included in Manassas Natl. Battlefield Park) of Civil War battles of BULL RUN (also known as 1st and 2d battles of Manassas). Town inc. 1873; rechartered 1938.

Manassas Gap, N Va., lowest pass (alt. c.950 ft.) in the Blue Ridge, 8 mi. E of Front Royal; followed by railroad, highway. Linden village, just W, in Warren co., was formerly called Manassas Gap.

Manatee (mănŭtē', mă'nŭtē), county (□ 701; pop. 34,704), SW Fla., on Gulf of Mexico and Tampa Bay; ⊙ Bradenton. Level and rolling terrain, drained by Manatee and Myakka rivers; has scattered lakes, part of Sarasota Bay, and small offshore isls., including Anna Maria Key. Truck-farming and citrus-fruitgrowing area, with dairying, poultry raising, some fishing and lumbering. Formed 1855.

Manatee, town (1940 pop. 3,595), Manatee co., SW Fla., fishing port on Manatee R. near its mouth on Tampa Bay, and just E of Bradenton; ships citrus fruit and vegetables. Founded 1842.

Manatee Bay (mă'nŭtē), small Caribbean inlet, St. Catherine parish, S Jamaica, at foot of low Healthshire Hills, 14 mi. SW of Kingston. Its shore line with adjacent area (□ c.12) was leased in 1940 to U.S. for a naval base.

Manatee River (mănŭtē', mă'nŭtē), SW Fla., rises in small lake in E Manatee co., flows c.50 mi. SW and W to Tampa Bay near Bradenton; lower course dredged.

Manatí (mänätē'), town (pop. 5,426), Atlántico dept., N Colombia, in Caribbean lowlands, 40 mi. SSW of Barranquilla; agr. center (cotton, corn, sugar cane, fruit, stock); gypsum quarries.

Manatí or **Central Manatí** (sĕnträl'), sugar-mill village (pop. 2,286), Oriente prov., E Cuba, near Puerto Manatí Bay (6 mi. long, 3 mi. wide) of the Atlantic, on railroad and 25 mi. N of Victoria de las Tunas.

Manatí, town (pop. 10,092), N Puerto Rico, on railroad and 24 mi. W of San Juan; agr. center (sugar cane, tobacco, coffee, citrus fruit, coconuts); sugar milling, tobacco stripping; mfg. of pearl buttons. Just W is the Montserrate sugar mill. The Tortuguero army camp is 4 mi. ENE.

Manatí River or **Río Grande de Manatí** (rē'ō grän'dā dā), central and N Puerto Rico, rises in Cordillera Central just N of Barranquitas, flows c.40 mi. NW, past Ciales, to the Atlantic 4 mi. NW of Manatí. Sugar plantations along it.

Manatuto (mŭnŭtōō'tō), town (pop. 400), ⊙ Manatuto dist. (□ 1,168; pop. 32,063), Portuguese Timor, in central Timor, on Wetar Strait, 30 mi. E of Dili, in rice-growing area; ceramics.

Manaure (mänou'rā), village, Guajira commissary, N Colombia, on SW Caribbean coast of Guajira peninsula, 19 mi. WNW of Uribia; saltworks.

Manaus (mŭnous'), city (1950 pop. 110,678), ⊙ Amazonas, NW Brazil, on left bank of the Rio Negro just above its influx into the Amazon, 925 river mi. above Belém, and 2,800 air mi. from Rio de Janeiro; 3°10'S 60°W. Economic, cultural, and educational center and chief inland port of Amazonia, reached by ocean-going steamers from the Atlantic; collecting and distributing center for areas along the Rio Negro, Rio Branco, and Madeira,

Purus, Juruá, and upper Amazon (Solimões) rivers. Ships Brazil nuts, rubber, guarana, tonka beans, cacao, hardwood, miscellaneous fibers, hides and skins. Industries (minor): brewing, soap mfg. Kaolin deposits near by. Port facilities (built after 1902) include floating wharves to allow for 33-ft. change in water level. Manaus is a city of clean, wide avenues, with modern electricity and water supply, and streetcar lines. Outstanding is the luxurious opera house (built in rubber boom, and now in disuse), surrounded by a square paved in mosaics. City also has fine cathedral (episcopal see since 1892), municipal bldgs., zoological and botanical garden, Salesian school for orphans, faculty of law (established 1909), mus., leprosarium, and agr. experiment station. Manaus is completely surrounded by tropical rain forest; there is no agr. in area. First settled 1660 and named São José do Rio Negro. Later known as Villa da Barra; was ⊙ Rio Negro prov. after 1825. Named Manáos in 1850, after creation of Amazonas prov. Rubber boom town in early 20th cent., it has declined since establishment of SE Asia rubber plantations. Spelled Manaus since 1939.

Manavadar (mänä'vŭdŭr), former Western Kathiawar state (□ 101; pop. 26,209) of Western India States agency; ⊙ was Bantva. Merged 1948 with Saurashtra. Sometimes spelled Manavdar.

Manavadar, town (pop. 8,064), SW Saurashtra, India, 20 mi. W of Junagarh; markets cotton, millet, ghee; hand-loom weaving.

Manavgat (mänävgät'), village (pop. 1,093), Antalya prov., SW Turkey, near Mediterranean Sea, 40 mi. E of Antalya; chromium; wheat, sesame.

Manawa (mŭnä'wŭ, mă'nŭwä), village (pop. 990), Waupaca co., central Wis., on Little Wolf R. (tributary of Wolf R.) and 32 mi. E of Stevens Point, in dairying and farming area; feed, cheese, pickles, cement blocks.

Manawar (mŭnŭvŭr'), town (pop. 5,502), SW Madhya Bharat, India, 28 mi. SSW of Dhar, on tributary of Narbada R.; cotton, corn, millet; cotton ginning.

Manawar, town (pop. 2,580), Mirpur dist., SW Kashmir, 22 mi. NNW of Sialkot; wheat, bajra, corn, pulse. Largely destroyed in 1947, during India-Pakistan struggle for control.

Manawatu, county, New Zealand: see SANSON.

Manawatu River (mănŭwŭtōō'), S N.Isl., New Zealand, rises in W Ruahine Range, flows 100 mi. SW, past Palmerston North, to Cook Strait 60 mi. NNE of Wellington; drains agr. area.

Manawoka, Indonesia: see GORAM ISLANDS.

Manay, Lake, Turkey: see SOGUT, LAKE.

Manazuru (mänä'zōōrōō), town (pop. 6,360), Kanagawa prefecture, central Honshu, Japan, on SW shore of Sagami Bay, 7 mi. S of Odawara; fishing port; summer resort; agr. (potatoes, wheat).

Manbhum (män'bōōm), district (□ 4,131; pop. 2,032,146), SE Bihar, India, in Chota Nagpur div.; ⊙ Purulia. Mainly in Damodar Valley; foothills of Chota Nagpur Plateau in W; bounded SW by Subarnarekha R.; drained by Damodar, Kasai, and Subarnarekha rivers and their tributaries. Major Indian coal fields at Jharia (main coal-mining center) and Nirsa; mining and fuel-research institute at Dhanbad; gold and ochre mining; fire-clay, phosphate, barite, and mica deposits. Agr. (rice, corn, oilseeds, bajra, sugar cane, cotton, tobacco); lac (near Chandil) and silk growing; sal timbering; bhabar, mahua in forest area (W). Mfg. of shellac, cutlery, firearms, fertilizer, cement; rice and oilseed milling, stone carving. Jain temple ruins near Purulia.

Manbij, Syria: see MEMBIJ.

Manby, village and parish (pop. 137), Parts of Lindsey, NE central Lincolnshire, England, 4 mi. E of Louth; air base.

Mancelona (mănsŭlō'nŭ), village (pop. 1,000), Antrim co., NW Mich., 29 mi. NE of Traverse City, adjoining Antrim, in dairy and agr. area (livestock, poultry, potatoes, beans, alfalfa); mfg. of auto parts, pig iron; sawmilling. Inc. 1889.

Mancenille, Baie de, Dominican Republic and Haiti: see MANZANILLO BAY.

Mancetter (măn'sŭtŭr), agr. village and parish (pop. 702), N Warwick, England, just SE of Atherstone; granite quarrying. Has church dating from 13th cent. Site of a Roman station.

Mancha, La (lä män'chä), historic region of central Spain, chiefly in New Castile, comprising Ciudad Real prov. (formerly called La Mancha), and part of Toledo, Albacete, and Cuenca provs. An immense, monotonous plain, it covers the SE section of the Meseta, the great central plateau; average alt. c.2,000 ft. The generally arid region has a rigorous climate of extreme temperatures, but has more inviting aspects towards Andalusia. Interspersed with little oases (in Campo de Calatrava, Campo de Montiel). Mainly grain growing and stock raising. Numerous windmills are a distinctive feature of the landscape, made familiar to the world as the scene of most of the adventures of Don Quixote de la Mancha in the novel by Cervantes. The upper La Mancha (La Mancha Alta) is in Cuenca prov.

Manchac, Bayou (bī'ō măn'shăk), SE La., waterway (c.19 mi. long) heading toward the Mississippi (with which it was formerly connected) S of Baton Rouge and entering Amite R. 9 mi. S of Denham Springs; partly navigable.

Manchac, Pass, navigable waterway in SE La., connects L. Pontchartrain and L. Maurepas, c.27 mi. NW of New Orleans; c.6 mi. long.

Manchao, Sierra de, Argentina: see AMBATO, SIERRA DE.

Mancha Real (män'chä rääl'), town (pop. 8,667), Jaén prov., S Spain, 10 mi. ENE of Jaén; mfg. of linen and woolen cloth, plaster; olive-oil processing, flour milling. Cereals, fruit, livestock in area.

Manchas, Las (läs män'chäs), village (pop. 758), Palma, Canary Isls., 8 mi. SW of Santa Cruz de la Palma; bananas, tomatoes, tobacco, fruit.

Manchaug, Mass.: see SUTTON.

Manchazh (mŭnchäsh'), village (1926 pop. 1,306), SW Sverdlovsk oblast, Russian SFSR, 17 mi. SE of Krasnoufimsk; metalworking.

Manche (mäsh), department (□ 2,295; pop. 435,-432), in Normandy, NW France; ⊙ Saint-Lô. Bordering (W, N, and NE) on the Channel, its N part consists of COTENTIN PENINSULA. S part traversed by W outliers of Normandy Hills. Drained by the Vire, Douve, Sienne, and Sélune (hydroelectric plants). Long coastline is rocky in N and has sandy approaches in W (especially Bay of Saint-Michel). Channel Isls. (Br.) and Chausey Isls. (Fr.) off W shore. Numerous hedgerows break up land into small fields and apple orchards. Small-scale agr. (early fruits and vegetables in N coast area, for export to England; also barley, flax). Dairying important, especially in Valognes-Carentan area. Horse and cattle raising. Chief industries: cider and apple-brandy (Calvados) mfg., metalworking (copper ware at Villedieu, cutlery at Sourdeval), textile milling (Saint-Hilaire-du-Harcouët), meat processing. Chief towns: CHERBOURG (transatlantic port), Saint-Lô, Avranches, Granville (port), and Coutances. Tourists visit MONT-SAINT-MICHEL and several bathing resorts on W coast (Carteret, Barneville, Granville, Carolles). American troops landed (June 6, 1944) on E coast, bet. Saint-Marcouf and Carentan, in Normandy invasion during Second World War.

Manche, La: see ENGLISH CHANNEL.

Mancheng or **Man-ch'eng** (män'chŭng'), town, ⊙ Mancheng co. (pop. 136,034), NW central Hopeh prov., China, 10 mi. NW of Paoting, near Peking-Hangkow RR; cotton, wheat, kaoliang, corn.

Manchester (măn'chĭstŭr), anc. *Mancunium*, county borough (1931 pop. 766,311; 1951 census 703,-175) and city, SE Lancashire, England, on Irwell R. and on small Medlock, Irk, and Tib rivers, 160 mi. NW of London; 53°28'N 2°14'W; center of most densely populated area of England and leading center of Br. textile industry. Commercial focus and distribution point for cotton mills of S Lancashire and center of other industries connected with textile milling (machinery and chemicals); also mfg. of iron and steel products and paper. Steam power was 1st applied (1789) to cotton spinning, and 1st English passenger railroad was built bet. Manchester and Liverpool in 1830 by George Stephenson. MANCHESTER SHIP CANAL gives city direct outlet to sea, and large seaport has developed here, importing chiefly raw cotton, exporting finished textiles. Since First World War artificial silk industry has grown and helped offset part of decline of cotton industry. Site of walled fort in Roman times; later site of Saxon settlement. It was mentioned in *Domesday Book* and received 1st charter in 1301; manorial rights bought by city in 1845. In 14th cent. woolen and linen industries were introduced from Flanders. During Civil War Manchester withstood royalist siege (1642). Growth of cotton industry, favored by moist climate and proximity to coal resources, dates from mid-18th cent. From early 19th cent. Manchester was in forefront of liberal reform movements; Manchester school of economics, of which Cobden and Bright were leading exponents, favored laissez faire. Free Trade Hall (destroyed in Second World War) was built 1856 on site of earlier building of Anti-Corn Law League on Peter's Field, scene of 1819 Peterloo massacre. *Manchester Guardian*, great liberal daily, was founded 1821. Among notable features of city are: Victoria Univ., founded 1846 by John Owens, independently chartered in 1903; Cooperative Col., founded 1919; 15th-cent. Chetham Hosp., now school, with library founded in 1653, reputedly 1st public library in Europe; John Rylands Library, containing Althorp collection; 2 art galleries; symphony orchestra founded 1857 by Sir Charles Hallé; and late-15th-cent. collegiate church, since 1847 a cathedral. David Lloyd George b. here. In literature Manchester figures largely in Dickens's *Hard Times*, and in Mrs. Gaskell's *Mary Barton* and *North and South.* In Second World War city suffered heavy damage and casualties from air raids (1940–41).

Manchester (măn'chĕ"stŭr, măn'chĭstŭr), parish (□ 339.79; pop. 92,745), Middlesex co., W central and S Jamaica; ⊙ Mandeville. A predominantly mountainous region of no rivers and scarce water supply. Its leading settlements, such as Mandeville, Christiana, and Williamsfield, are popular resorts. Tropical fruit and spices (grapefruit, oranges, annatto, ginger, pimento, etc.) are grown widely. Parish traversed by Kingston–Montego Bay RR.

Manchester (măn'chĕ"stŭr, măn'chĭstŭr). **1** Village (pop. c.500), Mendocino co., NW Calif., near the coast, 34 mi. S of Fort Bragg, in farming, dairying, and stock-raising region. **2** Town (pop. 34,116), Hartford co., central Conn., on Hockanum R. and 8 mi. E of Hartford; mfg. (textiles, paper products, machinery, tools, electrical appliances, soap, cleansers, cigars, sports equipment, clothing, leather and rubber products); dairy and nursery products. Textiles made here since late 18th cent. Includes industrial South Manchester village and residential Manchester Green. Settled c.1672, inc. 1823. **3** City (pop. 4,036), Meriwether and Talbot counties, W Ga., 33 mi. NE of Columbus, in farm and livestock area; textile, lumber milling. Franklin D. Roosevelt State Park near by. Settled 1905, inc. 1909. **4** Village (pop. 351), Scott co., W central Ill., 13 mi. SSW of Jacksonville, in agr. area. **5** City (pop. 3,987), ⊙ Delaware co., E Iowa, on Maquoketa R. and c.40 mi. W of Dubuque; agr. trade and processing center; canned tomatoes, dairy products; mfg. of boxes, gates. A U.S. fish hatchery is near by. Settled 1850, inc. 1886. **6** City (pop. 151), Dickinson co., N central Kansas, 23 mi. NE of Salina; wheat, cattle. **7** City (pop. 1,706), ⊙ Clay co., SE Ky., 39 mi. N of Middlesboro, in Cumberland foothills, in coal-mining, timber, and agr. (corn, tobacco, hay) area; lumber, stoves. Has airport. Settled c.1790; inc. 1932. **8** Town (pop. 664), Kennebec co., S Maine, just W of Hallowell and Augusta and on L. Cobbosseecontee. **9** Town (pop. 1,027), Carroll co., N Md., 29 mi. NW of Baltimore; makes clothing. Near by is site of Susquehannock Indian town. **10** Resort town (pop. 2,868), Essex co., NE Mass., on Massachusetts Bay and 8 mi. NE of Salem. Settled 1626, inc. 1645. Includes village of West Manchester. Offshore is Norman's Woe Rock. **11** Village (pop. 1,388), Washtenaw co., SE Mich., 18 mi. SW of Ann Arbor, in diversified agr. area; feed milling. Inc. 1867. **12** Village (pop. 113), Freeborn co., S Minn., 7 mi. NW of Albert Lea; dairying. **13** City (pop. 82,732), a ⊙ Hillsboro co., S N.H., on both sides of the Merrimack, below Concord; 42°59'N 71°28'W; alt. 220 ft. Largest city, industrial center of N.H.; textiles, shoes, mill machinery, electrical instruments, building materials, food products, clothing, luggage, metal and lumber products, cigars. Seat of St. Anselm's Col., Historic Assoc. Bldg. (art gall., mus.), art gall., inst. of arts and sciences, fine library. Amoskeag (ăm'ŭskĕg) textile mills (power from Amoskeag Falls on the Merrimack), developed (after 1832) from Benjamin Prichard's first plant (1805), grew to be country's largest cotton textile factory. Closed in 1935; bought (1936) by local group which leased its parts to numerous other industries. Grenier Air Force Base built 1941. Massabesic L. is just E. Settled 1722, granted 1735 as Tyngstown, inc. 1751 as Derryfield, renamed 1810. Amoskeag annexed 1853. **14** Village (pop. 1,262), Ontario co., W central N.Y., on Canandaigua Outlet and 23 mi. SE of Rochester; freight transfer point, shipping fruit and truck crops; canning. Agr. (truck, potatoes). Inc. 1892. **15** Village (pop. 2,281), Adams co., S Ohio, on the Ohio and 35 mi. W of Portsmouth; mfg. (clothing, buttons, bakery products). One of Ohio's earliest towns, founded 1791. **16** Town (pop. 190), Grant co., N Okla., c.40 mi. N of Enid, near Kansas line, in agr. area (grain, livestock; dairy products). **17** Borough (pop. 1,264), York co., S Pa., 6 mi. NNE of York. Laid out c.1815, inc. c.1869. **18** Town (pop. 2,341), ⊙ Coffee co., central Tenn., near Duck R., 55 mi. NW of Chattanooga; shipping center in timber and farm area; clothing, wood products, canned foods. Settled 1836; inc. 1905. **19** Resort town (pop. 2,425), including Manchester village (pop. 454), a ⊙ Bennington co., SW Vt., on Batten Kill and 20 mi. N of Bennington, bet. the Taconics (W) and Green Mts.; also includes Manchester Center and Manchester Depot villages. Seat of Burr and Burton Seminary (1829). Mfg. (fishing tackle, toys, printing); lumber, dairy products; marble. Summer, winter resort; skiing at near-by Bromley (or Big Bromley) Mtn. and Snow Valley. Mt. Equinox is just W. Vt. Council of Safety met here 1777. Settled c.1764, laid out 1784.

Manchester Ship Canal, S Lancashire and N Cheshire, England, extends 35½ mi. W from Manchester to the Mersey R. estuary at Eastham; serves Salford, Widnes, and Runcorn. Is crossed by Bridgewater Canal (on aqueduct) at Barton-upon-Irwell. Average bottom width 120 ft., average depth 30 ft. Main traffic carried to Manchester is in raw cotton and crude oil, westbound traffic carries mainly finished textiles. Several large petroleum refineries are located on the canal. Navigable for ships to 15,000 tons. Begun 1887, opened 1894. The canal revolutionized Lancashire's industrial life.

Manchhar Lake (mŭn'chŭr), in Dadu dist., W Sind, W Pakistan, 8 mi. W of Sehwan; c.10 mi. long, 2–6 mi. wide (considerably larger when flooded); formed by seasonal drainage at outliers (W,S) of Kirthar Range. Fish (chiefly carp) exported;

snipe, quail, partridge provide good hunting. Flood waters irrigate wheat and rice fields.

Manchinabad, W Pakistan: see MINCHINABAD.

Manchioneal (mănchŭnēl′), town (pop. 1,990), Portland parish, NE Jamaica, on Jamaica Channel, 14 mi. SE of Port Antonio; bananas, coconuts.

Manchita (mänchē′tä), town (pop. 810), Badajoz prov., W Spain, 19 mi. ESE of Mérida; wheat, olives, grapes.

Manchoukuo: see MANCHURIA.

Manchouli (män′jō′lē′) or **Manchuli** (män′jōō′lē′), Rus. *Manchuria, Manchzhuriya,* or *Man′chzhuriya* (all: mänjōō′rēŭ), city, ⊙ but independent of Lupin co. (pop. 3,044), NW Inner Mongolian Autonomous Region, Manchuria, in the Barga, 105 mi. WNW of Hailar, on USSR border; customs station on Chinese Eastern RR; flour milling, tanning, distilling. Developed after construction (1903) of railroad. Called Lupin (lōō′bĭn′) from 1913 until 1949, when it became an independent municipality.

Manchukuo: see MANCHURIA.

Manchuli, Manchuria: see MANCHOULI.

Manchuria (mănchŏŏ′rēŭ), Rus. *Manchzhuriya* or *Man′chzhuriya* (mänjōō′rēŭ), known to the Chinese simply as the Northeast [*Tung-pei*], major division (□ 585,000; pop. 44,000,000) of NE China; ⊙ Mukden. Bounded W by Mongolian People's Republic, N and E by USSR along Argun, Amur, and Ussuri rivers, SE by Korea along Tumen and Yalu rivers, and SW by the N China provs. of Hopeh (along Great Wall) and Chahar, Manchuria juts S into the Yellow Sea in the Liaotung peninsula, separating Korea Bay and the Gulf of Liaotung. Physiographically, the region consists of the great central Manchurian plain hemmed in by forested mts.: the Khingan at the edge of the Mongolian plateau (W), the Ilkuri and Lesser Khingan (N), and the complex E Manchurian highlands, rising to 9,003 ft. in Changpai mtn. on Korea line. The central plain is drained by Manchuria's chief rivers, except for the Amur on the N frontier. These are the Sungari (N; with its main left affluent, the Nonni) and the Liao (S). Although located in the latitudes (38°40′–53°50′N) of central Europe, Manchuria has an extreme continental climate governed by the monsoons. The winter monsoon, which brings dry, cold air from the Siberian high-pressure area, lowers the mean Jan. temp. to 23°F. in Dairen and –4°F. in Harbin. The summer monsoon, however, sends warm, humid air from the S Pacific, raising the mean July temp. to 82°F. in Dairen and 73°F. in Harbin. The total annual precipitation, with a pronounced summer max., is 20–24 in. As a result of the extreme winter temp., the rivers are generally frozen Nov.–April. The fertile black and chestnut steppe soils of the central plain were largely undeveloped until Chinese settlement in early 20th cent. Since then Manchuria has become a great pioneering region of expanding agr., where more virgin prairie is gradually being put under the plow. The chief crops are soybeans (the great cash crop of the region), kaoliang (S; the staple local food), millet, wheat (N), corn, and rice in the SE. These make up 90% of the total agr. production. Among the other industrial crops are cotton (near Liaoyang), hemp, flax, sugar beets, tobacco (near Kirin), and oilseeds (castor beans, perilla, sesame, peanuts). Vegetables are widely grown for local consumption. Livestock raising is the major occupation of the Mongol pop. (W), whose herds consist largely of sheep and goats; they also have horses, cattle, and camels. In the agr. central plain, animal husbandry (hogs and draft animals) is secondary. Here poultry farming and sericulture (wild silk produced by oak-feeding worms) are also common. Hunting of game and fur-bearing animals is the occupation of the Tungusic tribes of the undeveloped N mtn. areas. Lumbering is developed in the forested mtn. areas (covering 35% of the country), particularly in the E Manchurian highlands in the vicinity of Mutankiang, where Korean pine and larch are the principal woods for the production of wood pulp, paper, and matches. Manchuria is one of China's leading mining areas, where the most important minerals (coking coal, iron ore, magnesite, and oil shale) have laid the foundations of a great metallurgical industry. Coal of coking grade is mined at Penki, Pehpiao, Hingshan (Kaolikang), and in Tungpientao, though the greatest coal-mining centers (producing a noncoking, bituminous grade) are Fushun and Fusin. Fushun is also the main oil-shale site. Iron ore is mined at Anshan (with near-by Kungchuling) and Penki (with near-by Miaoerhkow) and in the Tungpientao. Magnesite is found in the Haicheng-Tashihkiao area (magnesium plant at Yingkow) and alunite at Niusintai, Yentai, and Fushun (which has also an aluminum plant). Steel alloy metals, such as molybdenum, vanadium, and tungsten, are present in small amounts. Placer gold is mined primarily in N Manchuria along tributaries of the Amur (chief center is Moho) and lode gold near Antung. On the basis of the iron and coal reserves, China's largest steel mills have developed at Anshan and Penki, with the Tungpientao a potential 3d producer. Metal-fabricating industries are located in Mukden, Harbin, and Dairen. Agr. processing industries, mainly the production of soybean oil and cake, flour, alcohol, sugar, canned goods, and tobacco, are found throughout Manchuria. Industry is powered by the great hydroelectric stations of Fengman (on the Sungari) and Supung (on the Yalu). The region is served by an extensive rail net, based on the T-shaped trunk system of the Chinese Eastern and South Manchuria railroads. Except for the navigable Sungari (below Kirin) and the once-important Liao R. route, the railroads handle the bulk of the traffic. The chief border-crossing points are Manchouli, Suifenho, and Aigun (on USSR line), Antung (on Korea border), and Shanhaikwan (at Great Wall). Dairen handles most of the maritime trade; other ports are Antung (with the outer harbor Tatungkow), Yingkow, Hulutao, and the naval base Port Arthur. The industrial development of Manchuria is evident in the region's high urbanization. Among its largest cities (15 with more than 100,000 in 1940) are Mukden, Harbin, Changchun, Dairen, Antung, and Kirin. Pop. is overwhelmingly Chinese (90%; speaking North Mandarin dialect). Among the minorities are Mongols (W; 4%), Koreans (SE; 2–3%), Russians (N), Manchus; in NW are Tungusic tribes, such as the Daur, Orochon, Solon, and Golds. Chinese colonization in the lower Liao valley, largely from Shantung and Hopeh, dates at least from 300 B.C. In the remaining territory, tribes of Mongol-Tungusic stock frequently formed states, which then conquered parts of China. The earliest Manchurian kingdom, the Pohai state founded by the Sushen tribe, was succeeded (937) by the Kitan or Khitan, whose Liao dynasty ruled N China until 1125. This group was displaced by the Nuchen or Juchen, who founded the Chin dynasty and extended their sway nearly to the Yangtze, until overwhelmed (1234) by the Mongols under Jenghiz Khan. In 1606, remnants of the Nuchen (now called Manchus) were united by their leader Nurhachu (b. 1559) who laid the foundations for the rising Manchu power that conquered all of China in the course of the 17th cent. and founded China's last imperial dynasty. Encroachments by the Russians, who had reached N Manchuria as a result of their sweep through Siberia in the 16th and 17th cent., were halted by the Manchus by the treaty of Nerchinsk (1689); but in 1858 and 1860 the left (N) bank of the Amur and the right (E) bank of the Ussuri passed to Russia. The modern development of Manchuria began c.1900 as a result of penetration and railroad construction by the Russians, who had obtained the KWANTUNG lease in 1898. Continued penetration by the Russians, particularly the occupation of N Manchuria after the Boxer rebellion, was a cause of the Russo-Japanese war (1904–05). Following the Rus. defeat, S Manchuria came into the Japanese sphere of influence. The industrialization and settlement (by Chinese) of this pioneer territory continued after the Chinese revolution (1911) under the rule of war lords such as Chang Tso-lin. In 1931, seizing upon an incident, Japanese troops occupied Manchuria and in 1932 formally created the nominally independent state of Manchukuo (or Manchoukuo) [Chinese,= country of the Manchus]. Under this regime the development of the region accelerated greatly with Japanese aid and constituted a major economic asset for the Japanese during the Second World War. In July, 1945, the USSR, having declared war on Japan, occupied all of Manchuria (until May, 1946) and the Chinese Nationalist govt. maintained a tenuous foothold in the region until 1949, when it was completely driven out by the Communists. In the course of these political transfers in the 1st half of the 20th cent., Manchuria underwent a series of complex administrative changes. Under China's Manchu dynasty, E and N Manchuria had been divided into the 3 original prov. of Heilungkiang, Kirin, and Shengking or Fengtien (after 1914, Liaoning), for which Manchuria was sometimes called the Three Northeast Provs. (Chinese, *Tung-pei San Sheng*). In 1914, part of eastern Inner Mongolia was inc. into the 3 original provs., and the area (□ 424,523; pop. c.25,000,000) of Manchuria remained unchanged until the founding (1932) of Manchukuo. The new regime made 3 important administrative changes: (1) separated the Inner Mongolian section as the semi-autonomous HSINGAN prov. (after 1934 divided into 4 subprovs.); (2) absorbed (1933) JEHOL into Manchukuo; and (3) subdivided (1934) the 3 original Manchurian provs. into 9 provs.—Kirin, Lungkiang, Heiho, Sankiang, Pinkiang, Chientao, Antung, Fengtien, and Chinchow; these 9 provs. were for a time, 1937–43, redistricted to form 13 provs., the additional 4 being Peian, Tungan, Mutankiang, and Tunghwa. Manchukuo in 1940 included □ 503,144, pop. 43,202,880. Following the dissolution of Manchukuo after the Second World War, the Chinese Nationalist govt. of China divided Manchuria (except Jehol) into the short-lived (1946–49) 9 provs. of Antung, Heilungkiang, Hsingan, Hokiang, Kirin, Liaoning, Liaopeh, Nunkiang, and Sungkiang. Under Communist rule, after 1949, Manchuria became one of the 6 major administrative regions of China and was divided into 6 provs. (HEILUNGKIANG, JEHOL, KIRIN, LIAOSI, LIAOTUNG, SUNGKIANG) and the INNER MONGOLIAN AUTONOMOUS REGION. The PORT ARTHUR naval base dist. forms a separate administrative unit.

Manchuria, city, Manchuria: see MANCHOULI.

Manciano (mänchä′nô), village (pop. 2,610), Grosseto prov., Tuscany, central Italy, 24 mi. SE of Grosseto, in grape- and olive-growing region. Has 14th-cent. citadel. Travertine quarries, deposits of antimony and mercury near by.

Mancieulles (mäsyûl′), town (pop. 2,163), Meurthe-et-Moselle dept., NE France, 3 mi. NNW of Briey; iron mining.

Máncora (mäng′kōrä), village (pop. 547), Piura dept., NW Peru, minor port on the Pacific, on Pan American Highway, on railroad from Lobitos, and 35 mi. NNE of Talara, N of CABO BLANCO–RESTÍN oil fields; fisheries.

Mancor del Valle (mäng-kōr′ dhĕl vä′lyä), town (pop. 1,032), Majorca, Balearic Isls., 17 mi. NE of Palma; olives, fruit, grapes, timber, livestock. Charcoal burning.

Mancos (mäng′kōs), town (pop. 1,464), Ancash dept., W central Peru, in the Callejón de Huaylas, on Santa R. and 3 mi. SE of Yungay (connected by road); corn, grain, livestock, eggs. Thermal springs.

Mancos (măng′kŭs, –kōs), town (pop. 785), Montezuma co., SW Colo., in La Plata Mts., 23 mi. W of Durango; alt. 7,035 ft. Livestock-shipping and outfitting point in grain region. Coal and silver mines in vicinity.

Mancos River, in Colo. and N.Mex., formed in La Plata Mts., SW Colo., by confluence of W.Mancos R. (18 mi. long) and E.Mancos R. (12 mi. long), flows intermittently c.60 mi. SW and WSW, through part of Consolidated Ute Indian Reservation, to San Juan R. just across N.Mex. line. Jackson Gulch Dam (181 ft. high, 1,900 ft. long; completed 1948), on W.Mancos R. and 4 mi. N of Mancos, forms small reservoir used for irrigation.

Mancunium, England: see MANCHESTER.

Manda (män′dä), town, Southern Highlands prov., S Tanganyika, port on L. Nyasa, opposite Deep Bay (Nyasaland), 80 mi. S of Njombe; rice, tea, cattle, sheep, goats. Coal deposits along Ruhuhu R. just E.

Mandagadippattu (mŭndŭgŭ′dĭpŭtōō), Fr. *Mannadipeth* (mänädēpĕt′), town (commune pop. 23,232), Pondicherry settlement, Fr. India, 12 mi. W of Pondicherry; rice, peanuts, millet. Tirubhuvane, Fr. *Tiroubouvané*, 1.5 mi. NE, was former commune seat.

Manda Island (män′dä), in Indian Ocean, off Kenya coast, just E of Lamu Isl., 40 mi. NE of Kipini; 5 mi. long; 5 mi. wide. Copra center; fisheries.

Mandaitivu (mŭndĭtē′vōō), island (pop. 2,461) in Northern Prov., Ceylon, bet. W Jaffna Lagoon (N) and Palk Strait (S), opposite Jaffna (ferry); 3 mi. long, 1 mi. wide. Rice, coconut-, and palmyra-palm plantations.

Mandal (mŭn′dŭl), town (pop. 5,806), Ahmadabad dist., N Bombay, India, 45 mi. WNW of Ahmadabad; agr. market (cotton, wheat, millet); handicraft cloth weaving, cotton ginning.

Mandal (män′däl), Russian agr. village, Selenga aimak, N Mongolian People's Republic, 55 mi. N of Ulan Bator and on the Khara Gol. Extensive fireproof clay deposits near by.

Mandal (män′däl), city (pop. 3,996), Vest-Agder co., S Norway, port on the Skagerrak, at mouth of Mandal R., 22 mi. WSW of Kristiansand; fishing and industrial center; manufactures lumber, cement, wood products, wire, cable, rope, carpets, textiles. Norway's southernmost city, it is built in part on a rocky isl. Has seamen's school. Inc. as city in 1921, when a royal residence was established here.

Mandalay (măndŭlā′), administrative division (□12,494; 1941 pop. 1,907,703) of Upper Burma; ⊙ Mandalay. Bet. middle Irrawaddy R. (W) and Shan plateau (E). Includes dists. of Yamethin, Myingyan, Meiktila, Kyaukse, Mandalay. Alluvial plain along Irrawaddy R.; plateau N of Pegu Yoma (with Mt. Popa); hilly region along border of Shan State (E). Main rivers: Irrawaddy, Myitnge, Samon, Zawgyi. In dry zone (yearly rainfall, 26–30 in.) irrigated by canals and tanks; mostly agr. (rice, sesame, cotton, sugar cane) in plain and plateau; teak forests in hills. Served by railroads and Irrawaddy steamers. Pop. is 90% Burmese, 6% Indian.

Mandalay, district (□ 2,113; 1941 pop. 408,926), Mandalay div., Upper Burma; ⊙ Mandalay. Hilly region, E of Irrawaddy R., consisting of S spurs of Mogok hills and plateau around Maymyo (highest point 4,753 ft.). In dry zone (annual rainfall 33 in.), it is irrigated by Myitnge R., Mandalay canal (42 mi. long), NE of Mandalay, and other canals. Rice, beans, fruit crops in plain; govt. forest reserve (bamboo) in hills. Served by railroads and Irrawaddy steamers. Pop. is 80% Burmese, 10% Indian.

Mandalay, town (□ 24.5; 1941 pop. 163,527), ⊙ Mandalay div. and dist., Upper Burma, on left bank of Irrawaddy R. and 350 mi. N of Rangoon; alt. 251 ft.; 21°59′N 96°5′E. Largest town, communications and trading center of Upper Burma, linked by rail with Rangoon, Lashio, and Myitkyina. Its industries include silk weaving, jade cutting, gold and silver working, wood carving, brewing and distilling, match mfg. Mandalay contains Fort Dufferin, the old Burmese walled and moated city (□ 6) containing royal palace (destroyed in Second World War) in its exact center, the Br. govt. house, and numerous temples and monasteries, including the "Seven Hundred and Thirty Pagodas." NE of the fort rises Mandalay Hill (744 ft.). In the extra-mural city near the main railroad station is the large Zegyo bazaar. The Arakan Pagoda, SW of the city, contains an image of Buddha said to have been brought from Mahamuni in the Arakan (1784). Founded 1857 by King Mindon, Mandalay was the last capital (1860–85) of the Burmese kingdom, having succeeded Amarapura. It was captured by Br. troops in Nov., 1885. During Second World War, when it fell 1942 to Japanese, it was 85% destroyed, Fort Dufferin suffering the heaviest damage during a 12-day siege before city was retaken (March, 1945) from Japanese by the Allies.

Mandal Gobi (män'däl gō'bē), town, ⊙ Middle Gobi aimak, central Mongolian People's Republic, 200 mi. SSW of Ulan Bator and on highway to Dalan Dzadagad; auto repair shops. Formerly called Sharangad.

Mandali (män'dälē), town, Diyala prov., E Iraq, near Iran line, 75 mi. ENE of Baghdad; fruit, livestock. Sometimes spelled Mendeli and Mendali.

Mandal River (män'däl), Nor. *Mandalselv*, Vest-Agder co., S Norway, rises in lake near Aseral, flows c.45 mi. S to the Skagerrak at Mandal; salmon fishing.

Mandaluyong (mändälōō'yông), town (1939 pop. 3,851; 1948 municipality pop. 26,309), Rizal prov., S Luzon, Philippines, just E of Manila; sugar refining, pulp and paper milling, match mfg.

Mandalya, Gulf of (mändäl'yä), inlet of Aegean Sea in SW Turkey, 45 mi. W of Mugla; 21 mi. wide, 23 mi. long.

Mandamados or **Mandamadhos** (both: mändůmä'-dhôs), town (pop. 2,889), on N Lesbos isl., Greece, 17 mi. NW of Mytilene; olive oil, wine, wheat.

Mandan (măn'dăn), city (pop. 7,298), ⊙ Morton co., central N.Dak., 5 mi. W of Bismarck and on Heart and Missouri rivers. Railroad division point; ships grain, dairy products; flour, beverages, tile, culverts, livestock, poultry. Near by are Fort Abraham Lincoln State Park, a U.S. agr. experiment station, and a state reformatory. Inc. 1881.

Mandapam (mŭn'dŭpŭm), village (pop. 4,886), Ramnad dist., S Madras, India, on Pamban Channel, 85 mi. SE of Madura; fishing center. Fisheries Research Inst.

Mandapeta (mŭn'dŭpĕtŭ), town (pop. 13,209), East Godavari dist., NE Madras, India, in Godavari R. delta, 21 mi. WSW of Cocanada; rice milling; metalware; sugar cane, tobacco, coconuts, oilseeds.

Mandara Mountains (mändä'rä), in Fr. Cameroons and along Br. Cameroons–Fr. Cameroons border, extend c.120 mi. from Benue R. (NW of Garoua) to N of Mokolo, rising to over 3,500 ft. Savanna vegetation.

Mandar Hill, India: see BHAGALPUR, city.

Mandas (män'däs), village (pop. 2,586), Cagliari prov., S central Sardinia, 30 mi. N of Cagliari.

Mandasa (mŭn'dŭsŭ), town (pop. 6,300), Vizagapatam dist., NE Madras, India, 85 mi. NE of Vizianagaram; trades in coir, copra, and in products (bamboo, tanning bark, lac) of forested hills (W); aerated-water mfg.

Mandasor (mŭndŭsōr'), town (pop. 21,972), ⊙ Mandasor dist., W Madhya Bharat, India, 105 mi. NNW of Indore; trade center (grain, cotton, opium, cloth fabrics); cotton ginning and milling, sugar milling, food processing, hand-loom weaving. Technical institute. Two monolithic pillars, 2 mi. SE, mark spot where Yasodharman, king of Malwa, defeated White Huns in 6th cent. A.D. Near by, Humayun won victory over Bahadur Shah of Gujarat in 1535. Treaty signed here in 1818 bet. British and Mahrattas. Town formerly in Gwalior state. Also spelled Mandsaur.

Mandaue (mändou'ā), town (1939 pop. 2,287; 1948 municipality pop. 19,068), central Cebu isl., Philippines, opposite Mactan Isl., 4 mi. NE of Cebu city; agr. center (corn, coconuts).

Mandawa (mŭndä'vŭ), town (pop. 7,895), NE Rajasthan, India, 16 mi. WSW of Jhunjhunu; market center for cattle, millet, hides.

Mandawar (–vŭr), town (pop. 7,677), Bijnor dist., N Uttar Pradesh, India, 8 mi. N of Bijnor; rice, wheat, gram, barley, sugar cane. Visited by Hsüan-Tsang in 7th cent. A.D. Captured by Tamerlane in 1399.

Mandayona (mändīō'nä), town (pop. 676), Guadalajara prov., central Spain, 32 mi. NE of Guadalajara; cereals, grapes, truck; paper milling.

Mandello del Lario (mändĕl'lō dĕl lä'rēō), town (pop. 2,505), Como prov., Lombardy, N Italy, port on E shore of L. of Lecco, 6 mi. NNW of Lecco; silk and paper mills; mfg. (motorcycles, bicycles, textile machinery).

Mandelo, Cape, Greece: see MANDILI, CAPE.

Mandera (mändĕ'rä), village, at NE point of Kenya, in Northern Frontier Prov., on Ethiopian and Ital. Somaliland borders, on road and 390 mi. NE of Isiolo; 3°57'N 41°52'E; stock raising. Airfield.

Manderson, town (pop. 107), Big Horn co., N Wyo., on Bighorn R., just W of Bighorn Mts., and 8 mi. SSE of Basin; alt. 3,872 ft.; agr. (sugar beets, beans, alfalfa).

Mandeure (mädûr'), anc. *Epomanduodurum*, village (pop. 1,356), Doubs dept., E France, on the Doubs and 4 mi. S of Montbéliard; paper milling, mfg. of auto accessories. Ruins of Roman theater.

Mandeville (măn'dĭvĭl), town (pop. 2,110), ⊙ Manchester parish, W central Jamaica, mountain resort (alt. c.2,060 ft.) 45 mi. W of Kingston; 18°2'N 77°30'W. Road and market center. Its railroad station, Williamsfield, on Kingston–Montego Bay RR, is 2½ mi. NE.

Mandeville, resort town (pop. 1,368), St. Tammany parish, SE La., on L. Pontchartrain, 23 mi. N of New Orleans. Founded c.1830, inc. 1840. State park near by.

Mandhata, India: see GODARPURA.

Mandhili, Cape, Greece: see MANDILI, CAPE.

Mandi (mŭn'dē), district, central Himachal Pradesh, India; ⊙ Mandi.

Mandi, town (pop. 9,033), ⊙ Mandi dist., N central Himachal Pradesh, India, on Beas R. and 45 mi. NNW of Simla; trades in grain, wool, salt, timber; hand-loom weaving; handicrafts (brassware, woodwork). Was ⊙ former princely state of Mandi (□ 1,139; pop. 232,593) of Punjab States, India; since 1948, state merged with Himachal Pradesh.

Mandi Bahauddin (bŭhoud'dēn), town (pop. 12,752), Gujrat dist., NE Punjab, W Pakistan, 34 mi. W of Gujrat; local market center (cloth fabrics, wheat, millet, cotton, rice); cotton ginning, flour milling; electric supply works. Sometimes called Bahauddin.

Mandi Burewala, W Pakistan: see BUREWALA.

Mandi Giddarbaha, India: see GIDDARBAHA.

Mandi Guru Har Sahae, India: see GURU HAR SAHAI.

Mandih (män'dē), town (1939 pop. 8,479) in Sindañgan municipality, Zamboanga prov., W Mindanao, Philippines, 40 mi. NW of Pagadian, on Sindañgan Bay; coconuts, corn, rice; fishing.

Mandili, Cape, or **Cape Mandhili** (both: mündhē'lē), S extremity of Euboea, Greece, on Aegean Sea at SW entrance to Kaphereus Channel; 37°56'N 24°30'E. Formerly called Cape Mandelo.

Mandinga (mändēng'gä), village (pop. 494), San Blas territory, E Panama, port on San Blas Bay of Caribbean Sea, 55 mi. ENE of Colón; coastal trade. Airfield.

Mandioré, Lake (mändyōrā'), on Bolivia-Brazil border, 55 mi. NNE of Puerto Suárez (Bolivia); 13 mi. long, 5 mi. wide. Connected with Paraguay R. by SE outlet.

Mandi Pattoki, W Pakistan: see PATTOKI.

Mandi Sadiqganj (mŭn'dē sŭdēk'gŭnj), town (pop. 4,360), Bahawalpur state, W Pakistan, 135 mi. NE of Bahawalpur; local trade in grain, cotton, pottery. Sometimes called Mandi Sadiq.

Mandji (mänjē'), village, W central Gabon, Fr. Equatorial Africa, on N'Gounié R. and 20 mi. NNW of Mouila.

Mandla (mŭnd'lŭ), district (□ 5,115; pop. 504,580), NE Madhya Pradesh, India, on Deccan Plateau; ⊙ Mandla. Bordered NE by Vindhya Pradesh; on hilly plateau of central Satpura Range; drained by Narbada R. and its numerous tributaries. Rice, wheat, oilseeds in river valleys. Hills are covered with dense sal (also bamboo, teak, myrobalan) forests; lac growing, game hunting. Sawmilling, betel farming, mfg. of sunn-hemp products (mats, cordage), mainly at Mandla; cattle raising in E hills. Pop. 60% tribal (mainly Gond), 38% Hindu, 1% Moslem.

Mandla, town (pop., including adjacent railway settlement of Maharajpur, 12,209), ⊙ Mandla dist., NE Madhya Pradesh, India, on Narbada R. and 45 mi. SE of Jubbulpore. Terminus of rail spur from junction of Nainpur (20 mi. SW); sawmilling, mfg. of sunn-hemp products (mats, cordage), betel farming; rice, wheat, oilseeds. Has ruins of 17th-cent. Gond fortress. Lac grown in near-by dense sal forests.

Mandodra (män'dōdrŭ), town (pop. 4,185), SW Saurashtra, India, 20 mi. WSW of Junagarh; cotton, millet.

Mandok (män'dôk), Hung. *Mándok*, town (pop. 5,188), Szabolcs co., NE Hungary, 33 mi. NE of Nyiregyhaza; distilleries, flour and lumber mills; wheat, rye, sheep, hogs.

Mandor (mŭndōr'), village, W central Rajasthan, India, 4 mi. N of Jodhpur. Now largely in ruins; was ⊙ Rathor Rajputs before they founded Jodhpur in 1459. Contains several cenotaphs of former rulers and a pantheon (Gallery of Heroes).

Mandoudhion, Greece: see MANTOUDION.

Mandra (män'drŭ), town (pop. 3,410), Attica nome, E central Greece, 14 mi. WNW of Athens, on road to Thebes; wheat, vegetables, olive oil, wine; cattle and sheep raising.

Mandrael (mŭndrīl'), town (pop. 3,083), E Rajasthan, India, 18 mi. SE of Karauli; wheat, millet, gram. Sometimes spelled Mandrail or Mandril.

Mandra Lake (män'drä), salt lake (□ 6.4) in E Bulgaria, just SW of Burgas; connected with Gulf of Burgas by 23-ft.-deep channel. Receives Mandra and Fakiya rivers.

Mandra River, SE Bulgaria, rises E of Yambol, flows 50 mi. E, past Sredets, to Mandra L. Also called Sredets R.

Mandritsara (mändrētsä'rŭ), town, Majunga prov., N central Madagascar, 170 mi. E of Majunga; rice cultivation. Has model farm, meteorological station, hosp., sanatorium, leprosarium, R.C. and Protestant missions. Airfield.

Mandsaur, India: see MANDASOR.

Mandu (män'dōō), historic fort in Vindhya Range (alt. c.2,000 ft.), SW Madhya Bharat, India, 17 mi. SSE of Dhar; c.4 mi. long, 3 mi. wide. In 14th and 15th cent., noted ⊙ sultans of Malwa. Has many remains of tanks, palaces, and mosques, including fine Jami Masjid (built 1454). While under Moguls (late-16th and 17th cent.), visited by Akbar and Jahangir; passed 1732 to Mahrattas.

Manduel (mădwĕl'), village (pop. 972), Gard dept., S France, 6 mi. E of Nîmes; winegrowing.

Mandur (mŭndōōr'), village (pop. 830), Eastern Prov., Ceylon, 16 mi. S of Batticaloa. Anc. temple ruins; Hindu pilgrimage center.

Mandurah (măn'dūrä), town (pop. 1,016), SW Western Australia, 40 mi. S of Perth and on Indian Ocean, at mouth of Murray R.; summer resort.

Manduria (mändōō'rēä), town (pop. 17,475), Ionio prov., Apulia, S Italy, 22 mi. ESE of Taranto; agr. center; wine, olive oil, macaroni, cheese; wool, livestock. Has remains of pre-Roman town walls.

Mandvi (mänd'vē). **1** Village (pop. 5,906), Surat dist., N Bombay, India, on Tapti R. and 30 mi. E of Surat; market center for rice, cotton, millet; handicraft cloth weaving. **2** Town (pop., including suburban area, 28,750), S Cutch, India, port on Gulf of Cutch, 35 mi. SSW of Bhuj; trades in wheat, barley, salt, cotton fabrics, gypsum; cotton ginning, oilseed milling, match mfg.; metalworks; handicraft silver products. Airport. Lighthouse 1 mi. W.

Mandya (mŭnd'yŭ), district (□ 1,915; pop. 635,588), SE Mysore, India; ⊙ Mandya. On Deccan Plateau (undulating tableland); drained mainly by Cauvery R., with Krishnaraja Sagara (reservoir) on SW border and Sivasamudram isl. (major hydroelectric works) on SE border. SE half of dist. (irrigated by Irwin Canal) is a major sugar-cane area; silk growing in SE section. Other crops: millet, rice, tobacco, cotton. Dispersed chromite, asbestos, and feldspar mining. Hand-loom weaving of silk, woolen, and cotton. Chief towns: Malvalli, Mandya, Seringapatam. Created 1939 out of NE portion of Mysore dist.

Mandya, town (pop. 11,374), ⊙ Mandya dist., S Mysore, India, 22 mi. NE of Mysore. Sugar-milling center; sirup, candy, alcohol; tobacco and vegetable-oil processing, hand-loom weaving, handicraft cloth dyeing. Asbestos works near by.

Manea (mā'nē), agr. village and parish (pop. 1,496), in Isle of Ely, N Cambridge, England, 7 mi. NW of Ely; flour mills.

Manendragarh (mŭnān'drŭgŭr), town (pop. 5,027), Surguja dist., E Madhya Pradesh, India, 65 mi. W of Ambikapur; coal mining. Lac grown in surrounding dense sal forests (bamboo, khair).

Manerbio (mänĕr'byō), town (pop. 6,356), Brescia prov., Lombardy, N Italy, on Mella R. and 13 mi. SSW of Brescia, in cereal-growing, stock-raising region; silk mills, cheese factories.

Manermiut (mänĕr'myōōt), fishing settlement (pop. 104), Egedesminde dist., W Greenland, at W end of Sarqardlit Isl. (säkhkär'lĭt) (27 mi. long, 2–7 mi. wide), on Davis Strait, on S side of mouth of Disko Bay, 10 mi. SW of Egedesminde; 68°35'N 53°6'W.

Manes, Armenian SSR: see ALAVERDI.

Manetin (mä'nyĕtyĕn), Czech *Manětín*, town (pop. 807), W Bohemia, Czechoslovakia, 18 mi. NNW of Pilsen; coal mining. Former Czech border bastion.

Manevichi (mŭnyĕ'vēchē), Pol. *Maniewicze* (mänyĕvē'chĕ), town (1939 pop. over 500), NE Volyn oblast, Ukrainian SSR, 36 mi. ENE of Kovel, in woodland; sawmilling, parquetry mfg.

Manfalut (măn'fălōōt), town (pop. 20,939), Asyut prov., central Upper Egypt, on W bank of the Nile, on railroad, and 18 mi. NW of Asyut; cotton ginning, wool spinning and weaving, pottery making, wood and ivory carving; cereals, dates, sugar cane.

Manfredonia (mänfrĕdô'nyä), town (pop. 18,787), Foggia prov., Apulia, S Italy, port on Gulf of Manfredonia, at S foot of Gargano promontory, 23 mi. NE of Foggia. Rail terminus; fishing; mfg. (leather goods, stearine, lye, cement). Archbishopric. Founded by King Manfred in 13th cent.; has medieval fortifications. Near by is site of anc. Sipontum (abandoned in 13th cent.); its cathedral (consecrated 1117) remains.

Manfredonia, Gulf of, inlet of Adriatic Sea, S Italy, S of Gargano promontory; extends c.30 mi. N-S; c.15 mi. wide. Receives Candelaro and Carapelle rivers. Chief port, Manfredonia.

Manga (măng'gŭ), city (pop. 1,198), N Minas Gerais, Brazil, on left bank of São Francisco R. (navigable), near Bahia border, and 60 mi. NNE of Januária; cotton, rice, brandy, hides.

Mangabeiras, Serra das (sĕ'rŭ däs măng-gŭbā'rŭs), mountain range of Brazil, in NE highlands, extending c.100 mi. along Maranhão-Goiás border, and forming Tocantins-Parnaíba watershed. Rises to c.2,800 ft.

Mangai (mäng-gī'), village, Leopoldville prov., central Belgian Congo, on left bank of Kasai R. and 90 mi. NNE of Kikwit; center of native trade, steamboat landing; palm-oil milling. Ipamu (ēpä'mōō), R.C. mission and residence of prefect apostolic, is 8 mi. SSW.

Mangaia (mäng-ī'ä), volcanic island (□ c.25; pop. 1,845), COOK ISLANDS, S Pacific, 110 mi. SE of Rarotonga; 21°55'S 157°55'W; c.6 mi. in diameter. A *makatea*, or cliff of coral limestone, surrounds low hills in center of isl. Exports fruits, copra.

Mangal (mäng'gŭl), former princely state (□ 14; pop. 1,325) of Punjab Hill States, India, NW of Simla. Since 1948, merged with Himachal Pradesh.

Mangalagiri (mŭng'gŭlŭgĭrē), town (pop. 13,317), Guntur dist., NE Madras, India, in Kistna R. delta, 12 mi. NE of Guntur; cement works (limestone quarries near by); rice and oilseed milling; tobacco. Annual Hindu temple fair on hill just N.

Mangaldai (mŭng'gŭldī), town (pop. 2,093), Darrang dist., NW Assam, India, in Brahmaputra valley, near the Brahmaputra, 49 mi. WSW of Tezpur; tea, rice, rape and mustard, sugar cane, jute; tea processing.

Mangaldan (mäng"gäldän'), town (1939 pop. 2,113; 1948 municipality pop. 26,102), Pangasinan prov., central Luzon, Philippines, near Lingayen Gulf, 5 mi. ENE of Dagupan; rice, copra, corn.

Mangalia (mäng-gä'lyä), anc. *Callatis* or *Kallatis*, town (1948 pop. 4,547), Constanta prov., SE Rumania, in Dobruja, on the Black Sea and 27 mi. S of Constanta; rail terminus and popular health resort, with beach, sanatorium, and sulphurous springs. Anc. Greek colony established 504 B.C., it was restored by the Romans (29 B.C.) and by Constantine the Great (4th cent. A.D.).

Mangalore (mŭng'gŭlôr), city (pop. 81,069), ⊙ South Kanara dist., W Madras, India, seaport (roadstead) on Malabar Coast of Arabian Sea, 450 mi. SSE of Bombay, at Netravati R. mouth. Rail terminus; major shipping center for India's coffee (mainly from Mysore and Coorg); also exports cashew nuts, pepper, tea, sandalwood. Tile-mfg. center (floor and roofing tiles, glazed pottery, mosaics); coffee curing, cashew-nut and sugar milling, hand-loom cotton weaving. Mfg. (hosiery, coir yarn, biris) in S commercial suburb of Ullal. Art and civil engineering cols. (affiliated with Madras Univ.). A center of trade with Persian Gulf in 14th cent.; Port. trading post established mid-16th cent.; became strategic shipbuilding base under Mysore sultans in 1763; besieged several times by English, until ceded to English in 1799.

Mangalvedha (mŭnggŭlvā'dŭ), town (pop. 9,611), Sholapur dist., E central Bombay, India, 32 mi. WSW of Sholapur; trades in agr. products (millet, wheat, cotton); handicraft cloth weaving. Sometimes spelled Manglawedhe.

Manganese, village (pop. 41), Crow Wing co., central Minn., near Mississippi R., 15 mi. NE of Brainerd in lake and forest area. Iron mines near by in Cuyuna iron range.

Manganeses de la Lampreana (mäng-gänā'sĕs dhā lä lämprāä'nä), town (pop. 1,805), Zamora prov., NW Spain, 17 mi. NNE of Zamora; soap mfg.; cereals, vegetables, wine.

Manganeses de la Polvorosa (pôlvōrō'sä), village (pop. 1,372), Zamora prov., NW Spain, 5 mi. NW of Benavente; lumbering, stock raising; cereals, wine, flax.

Mangaon (män'goun), village (pop. 276), Kolaba dist., W Bombay, India, 60 mi. SSE of Bombay; rice; copper and brass products. Soap mfg. 6 mi. S, at Goregaon.

Mangapwani (mäng-gäpwä'nē), town, on W coast of Zanzibar, 12 mi. N of Zanzibar town; copra, cloves.

Mangaratiba (mãng-gŭrŏŏtē'bŭ), city (pop. 1,226), SW Rio de Janeiro state, Brazil, fishing port on Sepetiba Bay of the Atlantic, on rocky peninsula, and 50 mi. W of Rio; rail terminus. Fish processing, banana growing. Surrounded by small fishing villages. Settled 16th cent. by Jesuits. Since 1948, coal for Volta Redonda steel mill unloaded here.

Mangareva: see GAMBIER ISLANDS.

Mangarin, Philippines: see SAN JOSE, Mindoro prov.

Mangart, Mount (mäng'gärt) (8,786 ft.), in Julian Alps, on Italo-Yugoslav border, 6 mi. SE of Tarvisio, Italy.

Mangar-tepe, Bulgaria: see POLEZHAN.

Mangatarem (mäng-gätä'rĕm), town (1939 pop. 3,373; 1948 municipality pop. 20,425), Pangasinan prov., central Luzon, Philippines, 17 mi. S of Dagupan; agr. center (rice, copra, corn).

Mangazeya (mŭn-gŭzyä'ŭ), former 17th-cent. fur-trading center in NW Siberia, on Taz Bay, at mouth of Taz R., near site of modern Khalmer-Sede, at c.80°E long. Named for a local Samoyed tribe and founded 1601 by Rus. fur traders; town reached greatest development in mid-17th cent. Opening of new routes further S and local extinction of fur animals caused transfer (c.1670) of trade to Turukhansk (originally called Novaya Mangazeya [Rus.,=new Mangazeya]) and decline of old Mangazeya.

Mangde Chu, river, Bhutan: see TONGSA RIVER.

Mange (mäng'gā), town (pop. 1,039), Northern Prov., W Sierra Leone, on Little Scarcies R. and 10 mi. NNW of Port Loko; trade center; palm oil and kernels, piassava, kola nuts. African Methodist Episcopal mission here.

Mangerton Mountain (măng'gŭrtŭn) (2,756 ft.), Co. Kerry, Ireland, 6 mi. S of Killarney. Near summit is the DEVIL'S PUNCH BOWL.

Mangham (măng'gŭm), village (pop. 554), Richland parish, NE La., 24 mi. SE of Monroe; cotton gins.

Mangin (mãzhē'), village (pop. 621), Oran dept., NW Algeria, 8 mi. SE of Oran; winegrowing; truck.

Mangit (mŭn-gēt'), village (1939 pop. over 2,000), N Khorezm oblast, Uzbek SSR, in Khiva oasis, on railroad and 50 mi. NNW of Urgench; cotton ginning. Formerly spelled Mangyt.

Mangla (mŭng'glŭ), village, Mirpur dist., SW Kashmir, on Jhelum R. and 9 mi. SW of Mirpur; rail spur terminus; headworks of Upper Jhelum Canal. Hydroelectric station (10,000 kw.) near by.

Manglaralto (mäng-glärăl'tō), village, Guayas prov., W Ecuador, on the Pacific, 65 mi. WNW of Guayaquil; minor port with good harbor facilities, in fertile agr. region (cacao, coffee, sugar cane, rice, tagua nuts, balsa wood). Fishing. Customhouse.

Manglaur (mŭng'glour), town (pop. 11,093), Saharanpur dist., N Uttar Pradesh, India, on Upper Ganges Canal and 23 mi. SE of Saharanpur; furniture mfg.; wheat, rice, rape and mustard, gram. Mosque built 1825 by Balban.

Manglawedhe, India: see MANGALVEDHA.

Mangles Islands (mäng'glĕs), group of keys off SW Cuba, in Gulf of Batabanó, 8 mi. N of Isle of Pines, just NW of Los Canarreos archipelago.

Mangles Point, Pacific headland on coast of Nariño dept., SW Colombia, at mouth of main arm of Mira R. delta, 26 mi. SW of Tumaco; 1°37'N 79°3'W. Westernmost point of Colombia.

Mangli, China: see KIANGCHENG.

Manglisi (mŭn-glyē'sē), town (1926 pop. 2,883), S Georgian SSR, on road and 20 mi. W of Tiflis; summer resort in wooded mtn. dist. Has cathedral (built 4th cent.; restored in 1850s). Until 1936, called Manglis.

Manglun (mĭng'lăn), SE state (sawbwaship) (□ 3,360; pop. 38,304), Northern Shan State, Upper Burma; ⊙ Pangyang, village, 35 mi. SE of Tangyan. Astride Salween R., which divides it into East Manglun (□ 2,482; pop. 19,649) and West Manglun (□ 878; pop. 18,655); bounded E by Chinese Yunnan prov. and (N) by Wa States. Agr.: hill rice, opium, cattle. Pop. has many Was.

Mangniuyingtze, Manchuria: see TSINGPING, Jehol prov.

Mango or **Mago** (both: mäng'ō), limestone island (□ 8; pop. 144), Lau group, Fiji, SW Pacific; 3 mi. long; copra.

Mango, Fr. Togoland: see SANSANNÉ-MANGO.

Mangoase or **Mangoasi** (mängwä'sē), town, Eastern Prov., S Gold Coast colony, on railroad and 10 mi. NNE of Nsawam; cacao, palm oil and kernels, cassava, corn.

Mangoche, Nyasaland: see NAMWERA.

Mangoky River (mäng-gō'kē), S central and W Madagascar, rises as the Matsiatra 30 mi. SE of Fianarantsoa, flows N and SW to Beroroha, and, thereafter known as Mangoky, flows W and NW to Mozambique Channel, forming a wide estuary. Total length, c.350 mi. Navigable c.160 mi. for shallow-draught boats below Beroroha.

Mangole or **Mangoli** (both: mäng-ō'lē), island (72 mi. long, 10 mi. wide; pop. 3,598), Sula Isls., N Moluccas, Indonesia, in Molucca Sea, just E of Taliabu; 1°55'S 125°50'E; mountainous. Agr. (coconuts, corn, sago), fishing.

Mangonia Park, town (pop. 348), Palm Beach co., SE Fla.

Mangonui, New Zealand: see KAITAIA.

Mangoro River (mäng-gōō'rōō), E Madagascar, rises S of L. Alaotra, 10 mi. SW of Ambatondrazaka, flows 130 mi. S and E to Indian Ocean just S of Mahanoro. Navigable for small vessels in lower course, for 65 mi.

Mangotsfield, urban district (1931 pop. 11,251; 1951 census 17,871), SW Gloucester, England. Includes towns of Mangotsfield (pop. 1,202), 5 mi. ENE of Bristol, with coal mines, Downend (W; pop. 5,023), and Soundwell (SW; pop. 5,026), with shoe mfg.

Mangrol (mäng'grōl). **1** Town (pop. 2,513), Surat dist., N Bombay, India, 27 mi. NE of Surat; local market for cotton and millet; cotton ginning. **2** Town (pop. 5,404), SE Rajasthan, India, 45 mi. ENE of Kotah; agr. market (millet, wheat, gram); hand-loom weaving. **3** Town (pop. 18,818), SW Saurashtra, India, near Arabian Sea, 36 mi. SSW of Junagarh; market center for millet, cotton, fish, coconuts, rice; handicrafts (cloth fabrics, ivory and sandalwood products, metalware). Betel vine and melons grown near by. Has fine 14th-cent. mosque. Harbor lies c.1 mi. SW; lighthouse. Captured 1531 by Portuguese.

Mangrove Bay, inlet of Somerset Isl., Bermuda.

Mangrove Cay (kā, kē), settlement (pop. 1,292), W Bahama Isls., on E Andros Isl., 60 mi. SSW of Nassau; sponge fishing.

Mangrullo, Rincón del (rēng-kōn' dĕl mäng-grōō'yō), marshy area in Cerro Largo dept., NE Uruguay, on Uruguay-Brazil boundary, formed by Yaguarón R. (NE), L. Mirim (E), and Tacuarí R. (S); 15 mi. wide, 20 mi. long.

Mangrul Pir or **Mangrulpir** (mŭng-grōōl'pēr), town (pop. 6,865), Akola dist., W Madhya Pradesh, India, in Ajanta Hills, 36 mi. SE of Akola; road center; millet, wheat; cotton ginning.

Manguaba, city, Brazil: see PILAR, Alagoas.

Manguaba Lagoon (mãng-gwä'bŭ), shallow salt lake (12 mi. long, 3 mi. wide) in Alagoas, NE Brazil, separated from the Atlantic by sandy coastal strip. Has canalized outlet to Maceió (8 mi. E). On its shore are Marechal Deodoro and Pilar amidst sugar-cane fields.

Mangualde (mãng-gwäl'dĭ), town (pop. 2,393), Viseu dist., N central Portugal, on railroad and 9 mi. SE of Viseu; flour milling, sawmilling, wool spinning and weaving. Surrounded by vineyards and orchards.

Mangueigne (mäng-gĕn'yŭ), village, SE Chad territory, Fr. Equatorial Africa, 85 mi. ESE of Am-Timan; livestock, millet.

Mangueira, Lagoa da (lŭgō'ŭ dä mãng-gā'rŭ), shallow lagoon in S Rio Grande do Sul, Brazil, bet. Mirim L. (W) and the open Atlantic (from which it is separated by a narrow sand bar) just E; 60 mi. long, 8 mi. wide. Has marshy, uninhabited shores.

Manguito (mäng-gē'tō), town (pop. 2,226), Matanzas prov., W Cuba, on railroad and 35 mi. SE of Cárdenas, in agr. region (sugar cane, fruit, poultry, cattle). Several refineries and sugar centrals near.

Mangum (măng'gŭm), city (pop. 4,271), ⊙ Greer co., SW Okla., on Salt Fork of Red R. and 20 mi. NNW of Altus; trade center for irrigated agr. area (wheat, cotton, corn, livestock); cotton ginning; mfg. of cottonseed products, brick, tile, flour, food products. Seat of Mangum Jr. Col. State park (recreation) and Altus Dam are near by. Laid out 1883, inc. 1900.

Manguredjipa, Belgian Congo: see MOTOKOLEA.

Mangush, Ukrainian SSR: see PERSHOTRAVNEVOYE.

Mangwato, Bechuanaland Protectorate: see SHUSHONG.

Mangwe (mäng'gwä), village, Bulawayo prov., SW Southern Rhodesia, in Matabeleland, 23 mi. SE of Plumtree; livestock. Police post.

Mangwendi (mäng-gwĕn'dē), village, Salisbury prov., E Southern Rhodesia, in Mashonaland, 20 mi. SW of Marandellas; tobacco, peanuts, dairy products.

Mangyshlak Peninsula (mŭn-gĭshläk'), on NE shore of Caspian Sea, in Guryev oblast, Kazakh SSR; dry steppe, salt lakes; coal, petroleum, manganese deposits (in the Kara-Tau); camel breeding. Fisheries along shore (at Fort Shevchenko).

Manhao (män'hou'), village, SE Yunnan prov., China, 22 mi. SSW of Mengtsz and on Red River (head of junk navigation); was trading center until opening (1910) of Kunming-Hanoi RR.

Manharpur, India: see MANOHARPUR, Bihar.

Manhasset (mănhă'sĭt), residential village (1940 pop. 5,099), Nassau co., SE N.Y., on N shore of W Long Isl., near head of Manhasset Bay, 4 mi. NNW of Mineola, in resort and estate area; wood products, insecticides.

Manhasset Bay, SE N.Y., inlet of Long Island Sound indenting N shore of W Long Isl., just E of Great Neck; 1 mi. wide at entrance, which lies bet. Barker Point on Manhasset Neck (E) and Hewlett Point (W); c.3½ mi. long. Yachting. On or near its shores are Port Washington, Plandome, Manhasset, Great Neck.

Manhasset Neck, SE N.Y., peninsula on N shore of W Long Isl., bet. Manhasset Bay (W) and Hempstead Harbor (E); c.5 mi. long, 1½–3 mi. wide. At its blunt tip are (SW to NE) Barker Point, Sands Point (lighthouse), Prospect Point. Residential area, with summer colonies.

Manhattan. 1 Village (pop. 728), Will co., NE Ill., 8 mi. SSE of Joliet, in agr. and bituminous-coal area. **2** City (pop. 19,056), ⊙ Riley co., NE Kansas, on Kansas R., near mouth of Big Blue R., and 50 mi. W of Topeka; shipping, trade, and processing center for grazing and agr. region; poultry packing, bottling, paint mfg.; machine work. Seat of Kansas State Col. of Agr. and Applied Science (opened 1863). Founded in 1854 as Boston, renamed Manhattan in 1855; inc. in 1857. Extensively damaged by great flood of July, 1951. **3** Town (pop. 716), Gallatin co., SW Mont., on Gallatin R. and 20 mi. NW of Bozeman; dairy products, livestock, grain; apiaries. **4** Ghost town, Nye co., central Nev., 65 mi. S of Austin in Toquema Range. Great gold producer (1906–15), still mildly active. **5** Borough (□ 22; 1950 pop. 1,960,101; 1940 pop. 1,889,924) of NEW YORK city, SE N.Y., coextensive with New York co.; mainly occupies Manhattan Isl. (12½ mi. long, 2½ mi. wide), which is bounded W by the Hudson (North) R. (boundary with N.J.), N and NE by Harlem R. and Spuyten Duyvil Creek (boundary with the Bronx), E by East R. (boundary with Queens and Brooklyn), and S by New York Bay; also includes Randalls, Wards, Welfare, Governors, Ellis, and Bedloe's isls. New York city's boundaries did not extend beyond Manhattan until 1874; today the borough is still the city's heart, and in common parlance "Manhattan" and "New York" are virtually synonymous. A web of bridges, rail, vehicular, and subway tunnels, and ferry lines links the isl. with the other boroughs and with N.J. It is the city's commercial, financial, and cultural center, and hence a world center. Its wharves and piers accommodate the world's largest passenger vessels, and in addition handle a large share of the enormous commerce of NEW YORK HARBOR. Through rail and truck freight terminals in Manhattan passes enormous transfer and distribution traffic, and market districts (mainly in S) handle most of city's wholesale trade in foodstuffs and many other consumer goods. Manhattan is laid out in a street pattern of longitudinal avenues (numbered or named) and numbered or named cross streets; Broadway, cutting diagonally across part of this grid, is the major departure from the street pattern, although older sections (such as Wall St. and Greenwich Village districts) have narrow, irregular streets, survivals of an earlier day. Broadway, one of world's longest streets, extends c.150 mi. N, eventually to Albany. The N tip (the Battery) of the isl. is site of small Battery Park, in which old Castle Clinton (built as fort c.1807; later an amusement center, then an immigration station, then a noted aquarium) has been designated a natl. monument. Adjacent is South Ferry plaza, terminus of ferry lines, and Manhattan entrance to Brooklyn-Battery vehicular tunnel. Express highways extend up W and E sides of isl. from the Battery. Just above the Battery are Whitehall dist., with consular and shipping offices, seamen's and maritime supply establishments, and tiny Bowling Green Park at the S end of Broadway. Also in downtown Manhattan (S of 14th St.) are Wall St. dist., with the New York Stock Exchange and the Curb Exchange, world's largest securities markets, and many skyscrapers housing banks and brokerage offices; U.S. Customs House (1907); N.Y. Produce Exchange; Fraunces Tavern (1719), where Washington bade farewell to his officers in 1783; Trinity Church (1846), seat of a parish chartered 1697; the Subtreasury Bldg. (1842), on site (now a natl. monument) of Federal Hall, 1st seat of Federal govt., where Washington took the Presidential oath in 1789; N.Y. Cotton Exchange (founded 1871; world's most important cotton market); a Federal Reserve Bank; N.Y. Chamber of Commerce (formed 1768); City Hall (1811); St. Paul's Chapel (1764), oldest in Manhattan; Woolworth Bldg. (60 stories; world's tallest until 1930); the Civic Center group lying E of City Hall; Chinatown; the BOWERY dist.; Washington Market (in W), and Fulton Fish Market (E); Park Row, the "Newspaper Row" of late 19th and early 20th cent.; the crowded Lower East Side, with its tenements and large nationality groups (Jewish, Italian, Russian, Greek, Spanish); GREENWICH VILLAGE, abutting on Sheridan Square (W), Washington Square (E); Henry St. Settlement (1893); Cooper Union (founded 1859); and other points of interest, including Brooklyn, Williamsburg, and Manhattan bridges across East R.; Holland Tunnel to N.J.; historic South St. waterfront; West St., along North R., with docks and terminals for freight trans-shipped from N.J. railroads. Beginning on S at Washington Square (with Washington Arch, 1895), 5th Ave., city's best-known thoroughfare, famed for its fashionable shops and apartment houses, divides the West Side from the East Side through most of Manhattan; N of 14th St. on the West Side are residential CHELSEA; HELL'S KITCHEN; Manhattan approach to Lincoln Tunnel; the Garment Center dist. (bet. 25th and 42d streets and bet. 6th and 9th avenues); the Pennsylvania Railroad station; Times Square, from which Broadway extends N as "the Great White Way" of motion picture houses, amusements, restaurants, huge advertising signs, and legitimate theaters (mostly on side streets just off Broadway); Metropolitan Opera House (1883); Madison Square Garden; and Columbus Circle, a large plaza at SW corner of Central Park. Riverside Park extends N along the Hudson from 72d St. The upper West Side includes part of HARLEM, the districts known as MORNINGSIDE HEIGHTS, MANHATTANVILLE, WASHINGTON HEIGHTS, and INWOOD (bordering Harlem R.); beyond river and surrounded by the Bronx is MARBLE HILL section. George Washington Bridge crosses Hudson R. to N.J. from the upper West Side. On 5th Ave. at 34th St. the Empire State Bldg. rises 1,250 ft., highest bldg. in the world. The Rockefeller Center group, farther uptown, has 14 skyscrapers; across from it is St. Patrick's Cathedral, dedicated 1879. In the Grand Army Plaza (popularly "the Plaza"), is Saint-Gaudens' statue of Sherman, at SE corner of Central Park. The huge Public Library is on 5th Ave., as are the Frick Collection (art gall.) and the enormous Metropolitan Mus. of Art, opened 1880. Central Park, 840 acres in heart of Manhattan bet. Central Park South (60th St.) and 110th St., is naturalistically landscaped. The E side of Manhattan N of 14th St. contains depressed fringes of tenement streets, industrial and warehouse areas, as well as some of city's most expensive hotels, apartments, restaurants, and shops. In SE part of the East Side is the old Gashouse Dist., once notorious as stronghold of hoodlums; not far away are sedate Stuyvesant Square and Gramercy Park sections, Union Square, traditional forum for open-air speakers; Madison Square dist. (once site of Madison Square Garden, now on West Side). The MURRAY HILL dist. is near Grand Central Terminal on 42d St., one of world's largest rail passenger terminals. E of Fifth Ave. in midtown area are Madison Ave., famed for its shops, and Park Ave., lined by large apartment bldgs., churches, and hotels. East 57th St. is known for its art galleries; on W. 57th St. are Carnegie Hall (home of N.Y. Philharmonic-Symphony) and the Art Students League. The United Nations' hq. is along the East R. N of 42d St., near the Beekman Place and Sutton Place residential sections. Queens-Midtown Tunnel and several bridges span East R. in this section. Upper East Side N of 72d St. contains YORKVILLE and the E part of HARLEM. Triborough Bridge at 125th St. links Manhattan to Queens and the Bronx. Other points of interest in Manhattan include Chrysler Bldg. (1,046 ft. high); Temple Emanu-El; the Bache Collection of art works; Whitney Mus.; the many hospitals and research institutions which have made New York a medical center; St. George's Church (1847); Grace Church (1846); Little Church Around the Corner; Church of Notre Dame de Lourdes; the Morgan Library; N.Y. Mus. of Science and Industry; Mus. of Modern Art (opened 1929); City Center of Music and Drama; Town Hall; American Mus. of Natural History and the adjacent Hayden Planetarium; the Cloisters, a branch (in Fort Tryon Park) of Metropolitan Mus., with fine medieval collections; Mus. of City of New York (opened 1923); Cathedral of St. John the Divine (Episcopalian; construction begun 1892), world's largest Gothic cathedral; Riverside Church; Broadway Temple; Gracie Mansion, the mayor's residence, in Carl Schurz Park; the museums and learned societies of Washington Heights, including the Mus. of the American Indian, the American Geographical Society, Hispanic Society of America, American Numismatic Society, and the American Acad. of Arts and Letters; the N.Y. Historical Society; International House for students, in Morningside Heights; Grant's Tomb (1891–7) in Riverside Park; the many "nationality neighborhoods" in which old-country customs, foods, and festivals have survived; the Polo Grounds, home of the N.Y. Giants baseball team; Jumel Mansion (c.1765); Dyckman House (1783). Randalls Isl. has been developed for recreational use; municipal institutions are on Wards and Welfare isls.; GOVERNORS ISLAND, off the Battery, is a military reservation; BEDLOE'S ISLAND is site of Statue of Liberty; and ELLIS ISLAND was long the gateway to America for hordes of immigrants. Educational institutions in Manhattan include Columbia Univ. (1754), City Col. (with Lewisohn Stadium), parts of Hunter Col. and of New York Univ., New School for Social Research, Manhattanville Col. of the Sacred Heart, Juilliard School of Music, General Theological Seminary, Union Theological Seminary, Jewish Theological Seminary of America, Cooper Union, Manhattan Col., Yeshiva Col., 4 medical colleges, and several jr. colleges, schools of fine and commercial art, and many music, technical, and professional schools. Manhattan was sold to the Dutch in 1626 by the Manhattan Indians; 1st known as New Amsterdam, in 1664 it became New York under the English. Its boundaries were those of New York city until 1874, when several Westchester communities were incorporated into city. In 1898, Manhattan became one of the 5 boroughs of greater New York.

Manhattan Beach. 1 Residential and resort city (pop. 17,330), Los Angeles co., S Calif., on the Pacific, 15 mi. SW of downtown Los Angeles; pottery making. Inc. 1912. **2** Village (pop. 72), Crow Wing co., central Minn., on Whitefish L. and 26 mi. N of Brainerd; grain. **3** Section of New York city, N.Y.: see CONEY ISLAND.

Manhattanville, SE N.Y., a residential district of the upper W side of Manhattan borough of New York city. Manhattanville Col. of the Sacred Heart is here.

Manheim (măn'hīm), borough (pop. 4,246), Lancaster co., SE Pa., 10 mi. NW of Lancaster; mfg. (asbestos, metal and rubber products, clothing); stone quarries. Settled 1716, laid out c.1760 by H. W. Stiegel, who here produced probably the first flint glass in America. Inc. 1848.

Manheulles (mänûl'), village (pop. 191), Meuse dept., NE France, 10 mi. ESE of Verdun; horse raising. Was N anchor of Ger. Saint-Mihiel salient in First World War.

Manhiça (mŭnyē'sŭ), village, Sul do Save prov., S Mozambique, on Incomati R. and 40 mi. N of Lourenço Marques; sugar-cane growing center; rice, almonds, beans; cattle raising.

Manhuassu (mŭ"nyōōŭsōō'), city (pop. 5,094), SE Minas Gerais, Brazil, on Manhuassu R. (right tributary of the Rio Doce) and 110 mi. W of Vitória (Espírito Santo); railroad terminus; coffee center. Beryl deposits. Here road from Vitória joins Rio de Janeiro–Bahia highway.

Manhumirim (mŭnyōōmērēn'), city (pop. 4,472), SE Minas Gerais, Brazil, at W foot of the Pico da Bandeira, on railroad and 100 mi. W of Vitória (Espírito Santo); rice, coffee, corn.

Mani, Greece: see MAINA.

Maní (mänē'), town (pop. 1,723), Yucatan, SE Mexico, 12 mi. E of Ticul; henequen, sugar cane, fruit. Maya ruins near by.

Maniago (mänyä'gô), town (pop. 3,700), Udine prov., Friuli-Venezia Giulia, NE Italy, 15 mi. NNE of Pordenone; mfg. (agr. machinery, refrigerators, artificial slate). Noted for its cutlery since medieval times. Has anc. loggia and cathedral reconstructed 1468.

Maniamba (mänyäm'bä), village, Niassa prov., N Mozambique, near L. Nyasa, on road and 40 mi. NNW of Vila Cabral; cotton, corn, beans.

Manianga, Belgian Congo: see MONIANGA.

Maniar (mŭn'yŭr), town (pop. 7,932), Ballia dist., E Uttar Pradesh, India, on the Gogra and 16 mi. N of Ballia; rice, gram, oilseeds, sugar cane.

Manica and Sofala (mŭnē'kŭ, sōōfä'lŭ), province (□ 88,274; 1950 pop. 1,048,550), central Mozambique; ⊙ BEIRA. Bounded N by Nyasaland, NW by Northern Rhodesia, W by Southern Rhodesia, S by Sabi R., E by Mozambique Channel (Indian Ocean), and NE by lower Shire and Zambezi rivers. A wide, and partially marshy coastal plain rising to interior plateau (2–4,000 ft.), which is bordered W and N by higher frontier ranges. The Zambezi, traversing the prov. from Zumbo (at Northern Rhodesia border) to its mouth near Chinde, is navigable except at Quebrabasa Rapids above Tete. Commercial agr. (especially sugar plantations) is found near river mouths. Chief products are sugar, cotton, sisal, corn, beans; stock raising. Coal is mined at Moatize (near Tete), and gold occurs in many streams along N frontier and near Macequece. New mineral deposits (uranium, asbestos) have been discovered in Tete dist. Prov. is served by Beira RR (to Southern Rhodesia) and Trans-Zambezia RR (to Nyasaland), both terminating at Beira. Territory, administered after 1891 by Mozambique Company under Port. govt. charter, reverted to Mozambique in 1942, and became prov. in 1943. It is subdivided into Beira and Tete dists.

Manicaland (mŭnē'kŭlănd"), territory in SE Africa along Southern Rhodesia–Mozambique border. Its E part is now in Manica and Sofala prov. (Mozambique), its W part in Umtali prov. (Southern Rhodesia). Rich gold deposits along Salisbury-Beira RR in Umtali-Macequece sector.

Manicani Island (mänēkä'nē) (□ 4; 1939 pop. 1,106), Samar prov., Philippines, in Leyte Gulf, just off narrow SE peninsula of Samar isl.; 2.5 mi. long, 2 mi. wide. Coconut growing.

Manicaragua (mänēkärä'gwä), town (pop. 4,261), Las Villas prov., central Cuba, on upper Arimao R. and 17 mi. S of Santa Clara; tobacco-growing and -processing center. Copper deposits near by.

Maniçobal, Brazil: see MANISSOBAL.

Manicoré (mŭnē"kōōrĕ'), city (pop. 1,533), S central Amazonas, Brazil, steamer and hydroplane landing on right bank of Madeira R., and 200 mi. SSW of Manaus; shipping center for tobacco, manioc, rubber, cacao, skins.

Manicouagan River or **Manikuagan River** (both: mănĭkwä'gŭn), E central Que., rises S of Opiskoteo L., near Labrador border, flows 310 mi. S, through Manicouagan L. (40 mi. long, 2 mi. wide), to the St. Lawrence just SSW of Baie Comeau.

Manicuare (mänēkwä'rā), town (pop. 1,149), Sucre state, NE Venezuela, on Araya Peninsula (SW), on Gulf of Cariaco, 7 mi. N of Cumaná; coconuts, goats. Saltworks near by.

Maniema, district, Belgian Congo: see KASONGO.

Maniewicze, Ukrainian SSR: see MANEVICHI.

Manihi, Tuamotu Isls.: see AHE.

Manihiki (mänēhē'kē) or **Humphrey Island,** atoll (□ c.2; pop. 435), S Pacific, c.655 mi. NNW of Rarotonga; 10°23'S 161°1'W; c.12 islets. Discovered 1822 by Americans, became British protectorate 1889, placed 1901 under N.Z. COOK ISLANDS administration. Produces copra, pearl shells. Polynesian natives. The name Manihiki is sometimes given to group of isls. (pop. 2,139) which includes Manihiki, PUKAPUKA, SUWARROW, RAKAHANGA, NASSAU, PENRHYN, PALMERSTON.

Manikganj (mä'nĭkgŭnj), village, Dacca dist., E central East Bengal, E Pakistan, near Dhaleswari R., 27 mi. WNW of Dacca; rice, jute, oilseeds.

Manikiala (mänĭkyä'lŭ), village, Rawalpindi dist., N Punjab, W Pakistan, 18 mi. SE of Rawalpindi; wheat, millet. Coins of Kushan period (c.1st-2d cent. A.D.) found in near-by noted Buddhist stupas. Sometimes spelled Mankiala and Manikyala.

Manikpur (mä'nĭkpōōr), town (pop. 4,807), Partabgarh dist., SE Uttar Pradesh, India, on the Ganges and 34 mi. WNW of Allahabad; rice, barley, wheat, gram, mustard. Mahrattas defeated here, 1761, by Rajputs.

Manikuagan River, Que.: see MANICOUAGAN RIVER.

Manikyala, W Pakistan: see MANIKIALA.

Manila (mŭnĭ'lŭ), city (□ 14; 1939 pop. 623,492; 1948 pop. 983,906), long the ⊙ Philippines (QUEZON CITY, on its E outskirts, was officially designated the ⊙ in 1948), in SW Luzon, surrounded on 3 sides by Rizal prov.; 14°35'N 120°59'E. A great port on

Manila Bay, and chief commercial and cultural center of the Philippines. Mean annual temp. 79.5°F. The city is divided into 2 sections by the short, navigable Pasig R. On S bank is Intramuros, the old walled city; on N bank is newer section including slum dists. of Binondo, San Nicolas, and Tondo. Before Second World War, Intramuros had fine examples of 17th-cent. Sp. architecture, but all notable bldgs. except San Agustin church were destroyed. The principal theater, shopping, and business dist. is the Escolta. Near Manila Bay is the Luneta, an oval-shaped park. Chief airports serving Manila are Nielson and Nichols fields in Rizal prov. The Philippines have few industries besides agr. processing plants, and these are mostly in Manila. Here are machine shops, coconut-oil plants, sugar refineries, cotton-textile mills, breweries. Also mfg. of rubber and leather goods, cigars and cigarettes, paint, nails. Among its several academic institutions are Univ. of Santo Tomas (1611), oldest univ. in Philippines; Univ. of Philippines (1908), and Philippine Women's Univ. The largest pop. element in Manila are the Tagalogs; there is also a sizable Chinese group. City was founded 1571 as fortified colony by López de Legaspi, and was developed chiefly by Sp. missionaries. Occupied briefly (1762–64) by the British. During Spanish-American War, city fell (1898) to U.S. In the Second World War, Manila was declared an open city, but the Japanese bombed it mercilessly and occupied it Jan. 2, 1942. In the battle for its recapture (Feb., 1945), the "Pearl of the Orient," long known for its beauty, was reduced to rubble. Almost all of Intramuros was destroyed, and much of the rest of the city leveled.

Manila. **1** Town (pop. 1,729), Mississippi co., NE Ark., 15 mi. WSW of Blytheville, near Big Lake (fishing). U.S. bird refuge near by. Founded 1852, inc. 1901. **2** Town (pop. 147), ⊙ Daggett co., NE Utah, 35 mi. NNW of Vernal, near Wyo. line and Uinta Mts.; alt. 6,376 ft.

Manila Bay, landlocked inlet of S.China Sea, in SW Luzon, Philippines, sheltered W by Bataan Peninsula; one of the world's great harbors, and finest in the Orient; c.35 mi. wide, extends inland c.30 mi. Its entrance (11 mi. wide) is divided into 2 channels by Corregidor isl. Manila and Cavite are on E shore. In Spanish-American War, Admiral George Dewey destroyed (1898) the Sp. fleet here.

Manilla, municipality (pop. 1,802), E central New South Wales, Australia, 160 mi. NNW of Newcastle; sheep and agr. center; chromite.

Manilla, town (pop. 1,035), Crawford co., W Iowa, on branch of West Nishnabotna R. and 10 mi. SSE of Denison; hydroelectric plant; metal and wood products. Inc. 1887.

Manilva (mänēl'vä), town (pop. 1,496), Málaga prov., S Spain, near the Mediterranean, 17 mi. NNE of Gibraltar; cereals, grapes, livestock; fish salting, flour milling.

Manin, Syria: see MENIN.

Maningory River, Madagascar: see ALAOTRA, LAKE.

Maniototo, New Zealand: see NASEBY.

Maniow (mä'nyōōf), Pol. *Maniów*, Ger. *Mohnau* (mō'nou), village, Wroclaw prov., SW Poland, 12 mi. NE of Schweidnitz (Swidnica). Storage reservoir on near-by Bystrzyca R.

Manipa (mŭnē'pä), island (□ c.30; pop. 1,691), S Moluccas, Indonesia, in strait bet. Ceram and Buru, 20 mi. W of Ceram; 3°19'S 127°34'E; 12 mi. long, 5 mi. wide. Wooded, hilly, rising to 2,165 ft.

Manipur (mŭn'ĭpōōr), chief commissioner's state (□ 8,620; pop. 512,069), NE India; ⊙ Imphal. Bordered E by Burma (Somra Tract, Kabaw Valley), S by Lushai and Chin hills, N by Barail Range and Naga Hills, W by Barak (Surma) R.; drained by Barak and Manipur rivers. Lies within Manipur Hills; central plateau region at c.2,500 ft. graduates S to large marsh lake. Agr. (rice, mustard, sugar cane, tobacco); bamboo tracts, teak, fruit orchards in forest area; silk growing. Road and trade center of Imphal (connected with Burma via Tamu and Tiddim), Bishenpur, Palel, and Ukhrul figured decisively in expulsion of Jap. forces from India in 1944. A former Assam state, inc. 1949 into India. Pop. 59% Hindu, 29% Animist tribes (including Nagas, Kukis), 5% Moslem.

Manipur Hills, name applied to hills in Manipur, on India-Burma border; continued S by Chin Hills and Lushai Hills, N by Naga Hills; consist of parallel ranges rising to 8,427 ft. in Siruhi Kashong or Sirohifara Peak, 38 mi. NE of Imphal. Extensive bamboo tracts; teak; silk growing. Inhabited mainly by Naga and Kuki tribes.

Manipur River, in Manipur, India, and N.Chin Hills dist., Upper Burma; rises in N Manipur Hills, flows 200 mi. S, past Imphal, through Chin Hills, past Falam, to Myittha R. 24 mi. E of Falam. Also called Imphal or Achauba.

Manipur Road, India: see DIMAPUR.

Manisa (mä'nĭsä), prov. (□ 5,537; 1950 pop. 519,-319), W Turkey; ⊙ Manisa. On N are Demirci Mts., on S Boz Mts.; drained by Gediz R. Merino sheep; valonia, tobacco, grapes, sesame, cotton, beans, raisins, olives. Scattered mineral deposits include mercury, zinc, antimony, manganese, magnesite, mica, emery, lignite. Sometimes spelled Manissa. Formerly Saruhan.

Manisa, city (1950 pop. 35,019), ⊙ Manisa prov., W Turkey, on railroad, on Gediz R., 20 mi. NE of Smyrna; agr. center, market for wheat, barley, beans, vetch, sesame, raisins, tobacco, olives; magnesite, zinc, and mercury deposits near by. Has old mosques, palace. Near by are ruins of anc. Magnesia ad Sipylum, where Antiochus the Great was defeated (190 B.C.) by the Romans. Sometimes spelled Manissa.

Manisa Dag (dä), Turkish *Manisa Dağ*, peak (4,-977 ft.), W Turkey, 6 mi. S of Manisa.

Manisees, R.I.: see BLOCK ISLAND.

Manises (mänē'sĕs), city (pop. 7,083), Valencia prov., E Spain, 5 mi. W of Valencia, and on Turia R.; center of ceramics and colored-tile industry. Other mfg.: water filters, toys, insecticides, candy, honey. Olive oil, wine, wheat, alfalfa in area. Military airport. Valencia's reservoir is near by.

Manissobal or **Maniçobal** (mŭnēsōōbäl'), city (pop. 1,181), W central Pernambuco, NE Brazil, near Ceará border, 35 mi. WNW of Serra Talhada; cotton, manioc, tobacco. Until 1944, called Belmonte.

Manistee (mănĭstē'), county (□ 558; pop. 18,524), NW Mich.; ⊙ MANISTEE. Bounded W by L. Michigan; drained by Manistee and Little Manistee rivers and small Bear Creek. Fruitgrowing and dairying; also livestock, truck, apples, berries, potatoes, cucumbers. Mfg. at Manistee. Salt mines, fisheries. Resorts. Includes part of Manistee Natl. Forest; also a state park. Portage, Bear, and Manistee lakes are in W. Organized 1855.

Manistee, city (pop. 8,642), ⊙ Manistee co., NW Mich., c.50 mi. SW of Traverse City; port on L. Michigan, at mouth of Manistee R. here draining Manistee L. (just E). Resort, shipping, and industrial center; salt mining and processing, mfg. of paper, furniture, wood products, boats, forgings, pumps, chemicals, hardware, shoes, clothing; fisheries. Agr. products (fruit, potatoes, dairy products). Annual forest festival held here. Inc. as city 1869.

Manistee Lake, Mich.: see MANISTEE RIVER.

Manistee River, NW Mich., rises in lakes in SW Otsego co., flows generally SW c.170 mi., past Mesick, and through Manistee Natl. Forest, to L. Michigan just W of Manistee. It widens into Manistee L. (c.5 mi. long, 1 mi. wide) just E of Manistee.

Manistique (mănĭstēk'), city (pop. 5,086), ⊙ Schoolcraft co., S Upper Peninsula, Mich., c.40 mi. NE of Escanaba, at mouth of Manistique R. on L. Michigan. Resort, industrial, and shipping center; lumber and paper milling, saltmaking, processing of hardwood products and dairy products. Limestone quarrying near by. Commercial fishing. Indian L., with 2 state parks (camping, bathing), is just NW. Inc. as village 1885, as city 1901.

Manistique Lake, SE Upper Peninsula, Mich., 13 mi. SW of Newberry; c.7 mi. long, 3 mi. wide; drained by Manistique R. Joined by streams to South Manistique L. (c.4½ mi. long, 2 mi. wide), just S, and to North Manistique L. (c.2 mi. long, 1½ mi. wide), just N.

Manistique River, S Upper Peninsula, Mich., rises in Manistique L., flows SW to L. Michigan just below Manistique. Receives many small tributaries from N and NW.

Manito (mănĭtō'), village (pop. 869), Mason co., central Ill., 20 mi. SSW of Peoria; corn, wheat, watermelons, truck.

Manitoba (mănĭtō'bŭ), province (land area □ 219,-723, total □ 246,512; 1946 pop. 726,923; 1948 estimate 757,000), central Canada, westernmost of the Prairie Provs.; ⊙ Winnipeg. Bounded by Ont. (E), Hudson Bay (NE), Keewatin Dist. (N), Sask. (W), N.Dak. and Minn. (S). Much of the area consists of lakes of glacial origin; largest are lakes Winnipeg, Manitoba, Winnipegosis, Southern Indian, Moose, Cedar, Island, Gods, Oxford, and Knee. Prov. is drained by Red, Assiniboine, Winnipeg, Saskatchewan, and Dauphin rivers flowing into L. Winnipeg, and by Nelson, Churchill, Hayes, and Gods rivers flowing into Hudson Bay. Principal elevations (all 2–3,000 ft.) are Riding Mtn. (natl. park), Pembina Mts., Porcupine Mtn., and Duck Mtn. Surface is generally undulating, rising toward W. S part of prov., the center of population, is prairie country; N part is forested. Mean annual rainfall is 16–21 inches; snowfall is light in S part of prov. Grain (wheat, barley, oats), hay, clover, potatoes are chief agr. products; Winnipeg is one of world's largest grain centers. Stock raising and dairying are carried on. Mining industry (copper, gold, lithium, silver, zinc, cadmium) is centered on Flin Flon, The Pas, and Sherridon, and has been developed since early 1920s; gypsum is quarried. There are extensive lake fisheries; lumbering (timber, pulpwood) and fur trapping are carried on in N. Major hydroelectric-power plants are on Winnipeg R. Besides Winnipeg, other cities are Brandon, Portage la Prairie, and St. Boniface. Towns include Dauphin, Selkirk, The Pas, Neepawa, Virden, Minnedosa, Carman, Souris, Beauséjour, and Morden. Churchill is major grain port on Hudson Bay. Region was 1st visited by Sir Thomas Button, who discovered mouth of Nelson R., 1612, and was followed by other British explorers. Hudson's Bay Co. charter (1670) included title to all land draining into Hudson Bay. La Vérendrye 1st visited Red R. area in 1738; French claims and trading posts were turned over to the British under Treaty of Paris, 1763. Settlement on the Red R.was begun by Lord Selkirk in 1812. The Dominion bought all land bet. Ont. and B.C. from the Hudson's Bay Co. in 1869. On July 15th, 1870, Man. became prov. of Canada but was, until Aug. of that year, under control of Louis Riel, leader of "Red River Insurrection." Canadian Pacific Railway reached Winnipeg in 1881, and era of development and prosperity began. Its area was greatly enlarged in 1881 and in 1912. Pop. was 25,228 in 1871; 62,260 in 1881; 152,506 in 1891; 255,211 in 1901; 461,394 in 1911; and 610,118 in 1921.

Manitoba, Lake (□ 1,817), SW Man., 15 mi. N of Portage la Prairie; 130 mi. long, 28 mi. wide; alt. 814 ft. Drained NE into L. Winnipeg by Dauphin R. Receives (NW) outlet of L. Winnipegosis. Has important fisheries. It was once part of glacial L. Agassiz.

Manito Lake (mă'nĭtōō) (□ 67), W Sask., near Alta. border, 55 mi. W of North Battleford; 12 mi. long, 7 mi. wide.

Manitou (mă'nĭtōō), village (pop. 636), S Man., in Pembina Mts., 50 mi. S of Portage la Prairie; alt. 1,590 ft.; grain elevators; dairying, mixed farming.

Manitou, town (pop. 293), Tillman co., SW Okla., 9 mi. NNE of Frederick, in cotton and grain area; cotton ginning, bootmaking.

Manitou, Lake, Ind.: see ROCHESTER.

Manitou Beach, village (pop. 186), S Sask., on Little Manitou L., 4 mi. N of Watrous; resort.

Manitou Beach, village (pop. 1,273, with adjacent Devils Lake), Lenawee co., SE Mich., on Devils L. and 19 mi. SSE of Jackson.

Manitou Falls, Wis.: see BLACK RIVER.

Manitou Island, off Upper Peninsula, Mich., in L. Superior 3 mi. E of Keweenaw Point; c.3 mi. long, 1 mi. wide. MANITOU ISLANDS are in L. Michigan.

Manitou Islands, NW Mich., two islands in L. Michigan, c.14 mi. W of Leelanau Peninsula; southernmost isls. of BEAVER ISLANDS archipelago. North Manitou Isl. is 8 mi. long, 4 mi. wide; South Manitou Isl. is c.4 mi. long, 3 mi. wide. Cherry orchards; farming, lumbering, fishing; resorts. MANITOU ISLAND is NW, in L. Superior.

Manitou Lake (□ 60), W Ont., 50 mi. E of Whitefish Bay (L. of the Woods); 27 mi. long, 5 mi. wide. Divided into Upper Manitou L. and Lower Manitou L. by narrow strait. Drains S into Rainy L.

Manitoulin (mănĭtōō'lĭn), district (□ 1,588; pop. 10,841), S central Ont.; comprises Manitoulin Isl., in L. Huron, and surrounding isls; ⊙ Gore Bay.

Manitoulin Island (□ 1,600), S central Ont., largest of the Manitoulin Isls., in L. Huron, 80 mi. NW of Owen Sound, separated from N shore of L. Huron by North Channel (16 mi. wide). Largest lake isl. in the world, it is 80 mi. long, 2–32 mi. wide, and rises to 1,120 ft. Coastline is deeply indented by several bays; there are a number of large lakes. Manitoulin Isls. consist of 3 large isls. (Manitoulin Isl. and COCKBURN ISLAND in Ont., and DRUMMOND ISLAND in Mich.) and a number of smaller isls., including Great Duck, Fitzwilliam, Barrie, Great Cloche, and Clapperton isls. Lumbering, dairying, fishing, mixed farming are carried on; isls. are popular resort. LITTLE CURRENT, on NE Manitoulin, is largest town and has railroad connection with mainland. GORE BAY village is also on Manitoulin.

Manitou Springs (mă'nĭtōō), town (pop. 2,580), El Paso co., central Colo., on Fountain Creek, at foot of PIKES PEAK, and 5 mi. W of Colorado Springs; alt. 6,336 ft. Tourist and health resort with mineral springs and sanitarium. Cog railroad to summit of peak. Near by are Pike Natl. Forest, Cave of the Winds, and GARDEN OF THE GODS. Founded 1872, inc. 1888.

Manitowaning, village (pop. estimate 750), S central Ont., on NE Manitoulin Isl., on Manitowaning Bay, 18 mi. SSE of Little Current; lumbering, dairying, mixed farming.

Manitowick Lake (mă"nĭtou'ĭk) (12 mi. long, 2 mi. wide), central Ont., 100 mi. N of Sault Ste. Marie. Drained S into L. Superior by Michipicoten R.

Manitowish River (mă"nĭtŭwĭsh'), N Wis., rises in lake region in Vilas co., flows W and SW through wooded lake area to Flambeau Reservoir; c.45 mi. long. Fishing.

Manitowoc (mă"nĭtŭwŏk'), county (□ 589; pop. 67,159), E Wis.; ⊙ Manitowoc. Bounded E by L. Michigan; partly on Door Peninsula; drained by Manitowoc R. Farming (oats, alfalfa), dairying, stock raising. Mfg. at Manitowoc, Two Rivers, and Kiel. Contains Point Beach State Forest. Formed 1836.

Manitowoc, city (pop. 27,598), ⊙ Manitowoc co., E Wis., at base of Door Peninsula, port of entry on L. Michigan at mouth of Manitowoc R., 34 mi. SE of Green Bay; industrial center (shipbuilding; mfg. of aluminum ware, machinery, furniture); cheese factories, canneries, breweries. The North West Company established a trading post here in 1795, but permanent settlement began in 1837. Inc. 1870.

Manitowoc River, E Wis., formed by several branches rising in Calumet and Fond du Lac counties near L. Winnebago, flows c.40 mi. generally E to L. Michigan at Manitowoc.

Maniwaki (mănĭwô'kē), village (pop. 2,320), ⊙ Gatineau co., SW Que., on Gatineau R., at mouth of Desert R., and 70 mi. NNW of Ottawa; lumbering, pulp milling, dairying.

Maniyachi (mŭnĭyä'chē), village (pop. 801), Tinnevelly dist., S Madras, India, 9 mi. WNW of Tuticorin; rail junction. Formerly spelled Maniyachchi.

Manizales (mänēsä'lĕs), city (pop. 51,025), ⊙ Caldas dept., W central Colombia, on W slopes of Cordillera Central, in Cauca valley, backed SE by snow-capped Nevado del Ruiz, 100 mi. WNW of Bogotá; 5°5'N 75°32'W; alt. 7,063 ft. Communication, trading, and processing center for a rich coffee dist. (also sericulture, cattle raising); textile milling, liquor distilling; mfg. of carpets, matches, cordage products, footwear, chocolate, pharmaceuticals. Airport. Silver, gold, and mercury mines near by. The city has a pleasant climate, though a heavy rainfall, and is connected by rail with Buenaventura; aerial tramways thread the mts., one of them crossing the Cordillera Central to Mariquita, on the Bogotá RR. A modern city with fine parks, cathedral, theaters, stadium. Founded c.1846.

Manja (män'dzŭ), town, Tuléar prov., W Madagascar, 135 mi. NNE of Tuléar; agr. center and cattle market. R.C. and Protestant missions.

Manjaca or **Manyacha** (both: mä'nyächä), Serbo-Croatian *Manjača*, mountain (3,982 ft.) in Dinaric Alps, NW Bosnia, Yugoslavia, along left bank of the Vrbas; highest point is 15 mi. SSW of Banja Luka.

Manjacaze (mänjäkä'zā), village, Sul do Save prov., S Mozambique, on railroad and 30 mi. NNE of Vila de João Belo; cashew nuts, mafura, corn.

Manjakandriana (mändzäkändrē'nŭ), town, Tananarive prov., central Madagascar, on railroad and 20 mi. E of Tananarive; mfg. of carbonated drinks; coffee plantations. R.C. and Protestant missions.

Manjeri (mŭnjä'rē), town (pop. 5,547), Malabar dist., SW Madras, India, 25 mi. ESE of Calicut; road center; rice, cassava, pepper.

Manjhand (män'jŭnd), town (pop. 3,025), Dadu dist., W Sind, W Pakistan, on Indus R. and 65 mi. SSE of Dadu; local market (rice, millet, fish, dates); handicraft cloth weaving, shoe mfg.

Manjhanpur (mŭn'jŭnpŏŏr), village, Allahabad dist., SE Uttar Pradesh, India, 29 mi. W of Allahabad; gram, rice, wheat, barley, jowar. Oilseed milling 8 mi. ENE, at Bharwari village.

Manjil (mänjēl'), village, First Prov., in Gilan, N Iran, in Elburz range, 40 mi. SSW of Resht and on Teheran-Resht road, and on the Sefid Rud (projected dam); olive-growing center. Coal, iron, copper deposits.

Manjimup (măn'jĭmŭp), town (pop. 1,227), SW Western Australia, 160 mi. S of Perth; sawmills; butter, dairy products, fruit, tobacco.

Manjira River, India: see MANJRA RIVER.

Manjlegaon (mŭnj'lägoun), town (pop. 5,234), Bir dist., NW Hyderabad state, India, on tributary of the Godavari and 32 mi. ENE of Bir; millet, cotton, wheat, oilseeds. Formerly Mazalgaon.

Manjra River (mänj'rŭ), N central Hyderabad state, India, rises in isolated W hills of Deccan Plateau SW of Bir, flows c.385 mi. ESE and N to Godavari R. 17 mi. NW of Nizamabad. Forms Nizam Sagar (reservoir) NW of Hyderabad. Sometimes spelled Manjira.

Manjuyod (mäng-hōō'yōdh), town (1939 pop. 1,908; 1948 municipality pop. 25,190), Negros Oriental prov., E Negros isl., Philippines, on Tañon Strait, 12 mi. N of Tanjay; agr. center (corn, coconuts, sugar cane).

Manka, Formosa: see TAIPEI.

Mankaiana (mängkäyä'nä), village, central Swaziland, 25 mi. SSW of Mbabane.

Mankato (măn-kā'tō). **1** City (pop. 1,462), ⊙ Jewell co., N Kansas, 33 mi. NW of Concordia; trading center for grain and livestock area; butter, feed. Founded 1872, inc. 1880. **2** City (pop. 18,809), ⊙ Blue Earth co., S Minn., on Minnesota R. at head of navigation, near mouth of Blue Earth R., and c.65 mi. SW of Minneapolis. Commercial and industrial center for grain, livestock, and poultry area; food processing (dairy products, flour, beverages, canned fish); mfg. (agr. equipment, cement, wood, and paper products); oil refining. Limestone quarries near by. Has state teachers col. and Bethany Lutheran Col. and Theological Seminary. Sibley Park occupies site on which 38 Sioux Indians were hanged after uprising of 1862. At confluence of Blue Earth and Minnesota rivers are 2 dams, units in flood-control project. Minneopa State Park is near by. Platted 1852, inc. as village 1865, as city 1868.

Mankayan (mängkä'yän), village (1939 pop. 1,352; 1948 municipality pop. 5,742), Bontoc sub-prov., Mountain Prov., N Luzon, Philippines, 35 mi. NNE of Baguio; copper and gold mining.

Mankera (mŭngkā'rŭ), village, Mianwali dist., W Punjab, W Pakistan, 85 mi. S of Mianwali, in Thal region; sheep and goat grazing. Was 17th-cent. Baluchi stronghold.

Mankia, Formosa: see TAIPEI.

Mankiala, W Pakistan: see MANIKIALA.

Mankono (mängkō'nō), town (pop. c.7,200), central Ivory Coast, Fr. West Africa, 75 mi. WNW of Bouaké; agr. center (coffee, cotton, palm kernels, rice, manioc, potatoes).

Mankota (mănkō'tŭ), village (pop. 233), SW Sask., 50 mi. WSW of Assiniboia; wheat. In coal-mining region.

Mankovka or **Man'kovka** (män'yŭkŭfkŭ), village (1926 pop. 6,577), SW Kiev oblast, Ukrainian SSR, 17 mi. NNE of Uman; sugar mill; distilling.

Mankoya (mängkō'yä), township (pop. 304), Barotse prov., W Northern Rhodesia, on Lusaka-Mongu road and 120 mi. ENE of Mongu; cattle, sheep, goats; corn, millet. Airfield.

Mankrong (mängkrông'), village, Eastern Prov., E central Gold Coast colony, on Afram R. (head of canoe traffic) and 28 mi. ENE of Mpraeso.

Mankulam (mŭng'kōōlŭm), town (pop. 77), Northern Prov., Ceylon, 46 mi. SE of Jaffna; timber center; trades in dried fish from Mullaitivu; rice plantations.

Manlio Fabio Altamirano (män'lēō fä'byō ältämērä'nō), village (pop. 1,322), Veracruz, E Mexico, 14 mi. SW of Veracruz; corn, fruit. Sometimes called, after its rail station, Purga or La Purga (lä pōōr'gä).

Manlius (măn'lēŭs). **1** Village (pop. 368), Bureau co., N Ill., 12 mi. WNW of Princeton, in agr. and bituminous-coal area. **2** Village (pop. 1,742), Onondaga co., central N.Y., 9 mi. ESE of Syracuse; mfg. (machinery, feed); sand and gravel; agr. (potatoes, cabbage, apples). Seat of Manlius School. Settled 1789 inc. 1842.

Manlleu (mänlyĕ'ōō), Catalan *Manllèu*, town (pop. 5,544), Barcelona prov., NE Spain, in Catalonia, on Ter R. and 5 mi. NNE of Vich; steel mill; cotton spinning and weaving, meat processing; mfg. of electrical equipment, knit goods, brandy, canned milk, flour products.

Manly. **1** Municipality (pop. 33,455), E New South Wales, Australia, on N shore of Port Jackson, 7 mi. NNE of Sydney; seaside resort; knitting mills, woodworking factories, confectioneries. Art gall. **2** Summer resort of Brisbane, SE Queensland, Australia, 10 mi. E of Brisbane and on Moreton Bay.

Manly. **1** Town (pop. 1,473), Worth co., N Iowa, 9 mi. N of Mason City; dairy and soybean products. Inc. 1898. **2** Town (pop. 280), Moore co., central N.C., just NE of Southern Pines.

Manmad (mŭn'mäd), town (pop., including suburban area, 16,838), Nasik dist., E Bombay, India, 45 mi. ENE of Nasik; rail junction (workshops); market center for cotton, peanuts, millet; handicraft cloth weaving.

Mannachchanallur or **Mannachchanellur** (mŭn-nä'-chŭnĕl-lōōr), town (pop. 6,560), Trichinopoly dist., S Madras, India, 5 mi. N of Trichinopoly; trades in agr. products (plantain, coconuts, millet) of Cauvery R. valley; rice milling, castor-oil extraction. Seasonal temple-festival cattle fair at village of Samayapuram, 3 mi. ENE. Also spelled Manachanalloor and Mannachenallur.

Mannadipeth, Fr. India: see MANDAGADIPPATTU.

Mannahill, village, E South Australia, 125 mi. ENE of Port Pirie, on Port Pirie–Broken Hill RR; wool. Sometimes spelled Manna Hill.

Mannar (mŭn-när'), town (pop. 5,190), ⊙ Mannar dist. (□ 943; pop., including estate pop., 31,471), Northern Prov., Ceylon, on SE shore of Mannar Isl., 50 mi. S of Jaffna; fishing port; rice and coconut-palm plantations. Fort Meteorological observatory. Also spelled Manaar and Manar.

Mannar, Gulf of, inlet of Indian Ocean, bet. S Madras (India) and Ceylon; bounded N by Rameswaram Isl., Adam's Bridge, and Mannar Isl.; 80–170 mi. wide (E–W), c.100 mi. long. Receives Tambraparni R. (India) and the Aruvi Aru (Ceylon). Tuticorin on W shore. Noted pearl banks off Ceylon. Also spelled Manaar and Manar.

Mannargudi (mŭn-när'gōōdē). **1** or **Kattumannarkoil** (kŭt"tōōmŭn-när'kōĭl), town (pop. 8,555), South Arcot dist., SE Madras, India, 35 mi. SSW of Cuddalore; rice, cassava, sesame; cotton and silk weaving. **2** City (pop. 23,288), Tanjore dist., SE Madras, India, on arm of Vennar R. delta and 23 mi. ESE of Tanjore; rail spur terminus (junction at Nidamangalam, 7 mi. NNW); rice milling, silk and cotton weaving; brass and copper vessels, silverware. Hindu temples.

Mannar Island (pop. 13,724), in Northern Prov., Ceylon, bet. Palk Strait (N), Gulf of Mannar (S), and Adam's Bridge (E); 16 mi. long, 4 mi. wide. Coconut- and palmyra-palm and rice plantations; extensive fishing. Main ports: Mannar, Talaimannar. Connected with Ceylon proper by road causeway and railroad, with India by ferry. Famous old pearl banks S, in Gulf of Mannar, 1st worked (1796) by British. Also spelled Manaar and Manar.

Männedorf (mĕ'nŭdôrf"), town (pop. 3,718), Zurich canton, N Switzerland, on L. of Zurich and 11 mi. SE of Zurich; woolen textiles, foodstuffs, organs.

Manners, N residential suburb (pop. 773) of Ndola, Western Prov., N Northern Rhodesia.

Mannersdorf or **Mannersdorf am Leithagebirge** (mä'nŭrsdôrf äm lī'tägŭbĭrgŭ), town (pop. 3,454), E Lower Austria, 20 mi. SE of Vienna. Limestone quarry near by.

Mannford (măn'fŭrd), town (pop. 426), Creek co., central Okla., 22 mi. W of Tulsa, in agr., oil-producing area. Near by is site of a flood-control reservoir in Cimarron R.

Mannheim (măn'hīm, Ger. män'hīm), city (1939 pop. 284,957; 1946 pop. 211,564; 1950 pop. 244,-000), N Baden, Germany, after 1945 in Württemberg-Baden, port on right bank of the Rhine (bridge, dike), at mouth of canalized Neckar R., opposite Ludwigshafen, and 44 mi. SSW of Frankfurt; 49°29'N 8°28'E. Major inland harbor and rail transshipment point; road center; airport (SE outskirts). Diversified-mfg. center, with heavy- (agr. and industrial machinery, vehicles, generators, transformers) and light-metal (precision instruments) industries; flour milling, vegetable-oil processing, and chemical mfg. (rubber, fertilizer, synthetic fiber, pharmaceuticals, cosmetics). Other products: textiles, shoes, glass, tobacco, pottery. Also paper milling, woodworking, brewing. Active trade (especially grain and coal) in harbor, begun 1834 on the Rhine, now extending also along the Neckar and canals connecting the 2 rivers. A small fishing village, Mannheim was fortified and chartered 1606–07. Residence of electors palatine (1720–78). Second World War damage (about 75%) of inner city (laid out in rectangular pattern with lettered and numbered streets and blocks; noteworthy bldgs. mostly baroque) included one of Germany's largest castles; Jesuit church; well-known National Theater, closely associated with Schiller; Kaufhaus, serving as city hall from 1910 until destruction; early 20th-cent. art gall., with noted picture collection (mostly preserved). Site of school of economics (founded 1907), engineering school, observatory. Frequent athletic festivals have made it a tourist center. Benz here invented 1st motor-driven vehicle.

Manning (män'nĭng'), Mandarin *Wanning* (wän'-nĭng'), town, ⊙ Manning co. (pop. 165,510), SE Hainan, Kwantung prov., China, 80 mi. S of Kiungshan, on S. China Sea; fisheries; poultry and cattle raising. Exports eggs, melon seeds, medicinal herbs. Sugar milling. Until 1912, Wanchow.

Manning (mă'nĭng). **1** Town (pop. 1,801), Carroll co., W central Iowa, on West Nishnabotna R. (hydroelectric plant) and 15 mi. SSW of Carroll; mfg. (dairy and wood products, feed, fertilizer). Inc. 1880. **2** Village, ⊙ Dunn co., W central N.Dak., 24 mi. N of Dickinson and on Knife R. **3** Town (pop. 2,775), ⊙ Clarendon co., E central S.C., 17 mi. SSE of Sumter; lumbering, dairying, canning; tobacco, cotton, sweet potatoes. Tourist trade.

Manningham, England: see BRADFORD.

Manning River, E New South Wales, Australia, rises in Great Dividing Range, flows 139 mi. E, past Wingham and Taree, to the Pacific SW of Crowdy Head. Navigable 27 mi. below Wingham by small craft carrying dairy products.

Mannington. **1** Mining village (pop. c.200), Christian co., SW Ky., 18 mi. N of Hopkinsville; bituminous coal. **2** City (pop. 3,241), Marion co., N W.Va., 12 mi. WNW of Fairmont. Processing center in oil, natural-gas, and bituminous-coal region; mfg. of farm equipment, pottery, glass; flour and lumber milling. Inc. 1871.

Manningtree, town and parish (pop. 790), NE Essex, England, on Stour R. estuary and 8 mi. ENE of Colchester; agr. market, with plastics works.

Männlifluh (mĕn'lēflōō"), cliff (8,713 ft.) in Bernese Alps, SW Switzerland, 6 mi. SW of Frutigen.

Manns Choice, borough (pop. 313), Bedford co., S Pa., 5 mi. WSW of Bedford and on Raystown Branch of Juniata R.

Manns Harbor, village, Dare co., NE N.C., on Croatan Sound (ferry) opposite Roanoke Isl.; fishing.

Mannsville. **1** Village (pop. 378), Jefferson co., N N.Y., 20 mi. SSW of Watertown. **2** Town (pop. 311), Johnston co., S Okla., 15 mi. E of Ardmore, near L. Texoma, in farm area.

Mannu, Cape (män'nōō), point on W coast of Sardinia, 15 mi. NW of Oristano; 40°2'N 8°22'E. Fisheries (tunny, lobster, coral).

Mannu d'Oschiri River (män'nōō dô'skērē), Sassari prov., N Sardinia, rises in Monti di Alà, flows S, cutting through Monti di Alà and Catena del Goceano, thence N to L. COGHINAS; c.32 mi. long.

Mannu D'Ozieri River (dôtsyä'rē), Sassari prov., N Sardinia, rises in several branches in Catena del Marghine, flows c.40 mi. NNE, past Chilivani, to L. COGHINAS.

Mannum (mă'nŭm), town (pop. 1,208), SE South Australia, 40 mi. E of Adelaide and on Murray R.; agr., dairying center; citrus, dried fruit.

Mannu River (män'nōō), Sassari prov., N Sardinia, rises near Thiesi, flows c.35 mi. NW to Gulf of Asinara at Porto Torres. Other Sardinian streams, including MANNU D'OSCHIRI RIVER and MANNU D'OZIERI RIVER, are sometimes called simply Mannu.

Mannville, village (pop. 472), E Alta., near Vermilion R., 14 mi. W of Vermilion; dairying, grain growing.

Mano (mä'nŭ), Dan. *Manø*, island (□ 2.3; pop. 172) of North Frisian group, Denmark, in North Sea, 4 mi. off SW Jutland; Mano By, town, is on W coast.

Mano (mä'nō), town (pop. 2,200), South-Western Prov., S central Sierra Leone, on Jong R. and 25 mi. ESE of Moyamba, on railroad; head of road to Taiama; trade center; palm oil and kernels, piassava, rice.

Manoa (mänō'ä), town, northernmost point of Bolivia, Pando dept., on Madeira R., at mouth of Abuná R., and 100 mi. NNE of Riberalta, on Brazil border; rubber. Abunã (Brazil), on Madeira-Mamoré RR, is 6 mi. ESE across the Madeira.

Manoa, Pa.: see HAVERFORD.

Man of War Bay, deep inlet of NW Tobago, B.W.I., 14 mi. NE of Scarborough; c.2 mi. long, 2 mi. wide. On it is Charlotteville. Sometimes spelled Man-of-War Bay.

Manoharpur (mŭnō'hŭrpŏŏr). **1** or **Manharpur** (mŭn'ŭrpŏŏr), town (pop. 4,397), Singhbhum dist., S Bihar, India, 70 mi. WSW of Jamshedpur; rice, oilseeds, corn. Major hematite mining in near-by hills; extensive sal lumbering; bhabur; limestone quarries. **2** Town (pop. 4,495), E Rajasthan, India, 25 mi. NNE of Jaipur; agr. (millet, gram).

Manoir Lake, Northwest Territories: see MAUNOIR, LAC.

Manokin River (mŭnō'kĭn), SE Md., rises in NE Somerset co., flows c.25 mi. SW, past Princess Anne (head of navigation), to Tangier Sound just S of Deal Isl.; its mouth is 5 mi. wide.

Manokotak (mänōkō'tăk), village (pop. 120), SW Alaska, on small Igushik R. and 22 mi. WSW of Dillingham; 58°59'N 159°3'W.

Manokwari (mänōkwä'rē), town (dist. pop. 4,650), Netherlands New Guinea, on E Vogelkop peninsula, port on NW side of entrance to Geelvink Bay; 2°29'S 134°36'E; trade center; exports copra, resin. Formerly ⊙ Netherlands New Guinea, supplanted by Hollandia.

Manomet, Mass.: see PLYMOUTH.

Manono (mänō'nō), village (1948 pop. 19,521), Katanga prov., SE Belgian Congo, 155 mi. SW of Albertville; center of major tin-mining area; terminus of railroad from Muyumba. Tin concentrating and smelting; also tantalite mining. Airport. Has R.C. and Protestant missions, hospitals for Europeans and natives, extensive recreation facilities for its African personnel.

Manono (mänō'nō), coral island (□ c.1; pop. 800), Western Samoa, S Pacific, under N.Z. mandate, in 10-mi. strait separating Upolu from Savaii; rises to c.230 ft.

Manoomukh, E Pakistan: see MANUMUKH.

Manoppello (mänôp-pĕl'lô), village (pop. 1,731), Pescara prov., Abruzzi e Molise, S central Italy, 9 mi. SSW of Chieti; asphalt factory.

Manor, village (pop. 234), SE Sask., at foot of Moose Mtn., 40 mi. SSW of Moosomin; mixed farming.

Manor. **1** Borough (pop. 1,230), Westmoreland co., SW Pa., 2 mi. W of Jeannette. Laid out 1873, inc. 1890. **2** Town (pop. 820), Travis co., S central Texas, 12 mi. ENE of Austin, in cotton, grain, truck area.

Manora, W Pakistan: see KARACHI, city.

Manorbier (mănûrbēr'), agr. village and parish (pop. 555), SE Pembroke, Wales, on Carmarthen Bay of Bristol Channel, 5 mi. ESE of Pembroke. Has remains of castle, built c.1100; Giraldus Cambrensis b. here. Church dates from 12th cent.

Manorhamilton (mă"nûrhă'mĭltûn), Gaelic *Cluain in Uí Ruairc*, town (pop. 841), N Co. Leitrim, Ireland, 12 mi. E of Sligo; agr. market (dairying; cattle, potatoes). Has ruins of 1641 mansion.

Manorhaven, village (pop. 1,819), Nassau co., SE N.Y., on N shore of W Long Isl., just NE of Port Washington, in summer-resort area. Inc. 1930.

Mano River (mä'nō), Liberia and Sierra Leone, rises near Vonjama (Liberia), on Fr. Guinea border; flows c.200 mi. SW and along Sierra Leone–Liberia border to the Atlantic at Mano Salija (Sierra Leone). Morro R., its right tributary, forms upper section of Liberia–Sierra Leone border.

Manor Park, England: see EAST HAM.

Manorville, borough (pop. 662), Armstrong co., W central Pa., 2 mi. S of Kittanning on Allegheny R.

Manos, Las, Nicaragua: see LAS MANOS.

Mano Salija (mä'nō sälē'jä), village, South-Western Prov., SE Sierra Leone, minor port on Atlantic Ocean, at mouth of Mano R. (Liberia border), and 32 mi. SE of Pujehun; exports palm oil and kernels, piassava, rice.

Manosque (mänôsk'), town (pop. 4,788), Basses-Alpes dept., SE France, in fertile alluvial Durance valley, 27 mi. NE of Aix-en-Provence; agr. trade center (olives, almonds, truffles, lavender, fruits, wine); flour milling. Lignite mines near by. Has 2 restored Romanesque churches and 2 14th-cent. fortified gates.

Manotick, village (pop. estimate 500), SE Ont., on Rideau R. and Rideau Canal, and 14 mi. S of Ottawa; dairying, mixed farming.

Manouba, La (lä mänōōbä'), W residential suburb of Tunis, N Tunisia; mfg. of explosives, tanning, flour milling, olive preserving; orange groves, vineyards.

Manpojin (män'pô'jĭn'), Jap. *Mampochin* (mäm'pô'chēn'), town, N.Pyongan prov., N Korea, on railroad and 115 mi. NNE of Sinanju, on Yalu R. (Manchuria line). opposite Tsian.

Manqabad (măn'käbăd), village (pop. 10,581), Asyut prov., central Upper Egypt, on W bank of the Nile, on railroad, and 5 mi. WNW of Asyut; pottery making, wood and ivory carving; cereals, dates, sugar.

Manra, Phoenix Isls.: see SYDNEY ISLAND.

Manresa (mänrā'sä), city (pop. 34,075), Barcelona prov., NE Spain, in Catalonia, on the Cardoner and 28 mi. NW of Barcelona; industrial and communications center. Produces textiles (cotton and silk fabrics, thread and braid, knitwear), tires, dyes, leather goods, textile machinery, auto accessories, cement, soap, liqueurs; sawmilling, olive-oil processing. Agr. trade (livestock, cereals, potatoes, fruit). Has Roman bridge and 14th-cent. collegiate church of Santa María de la Seo. Below Dominican convent is a grotto (retreat of St. Ignatius of Loyola), now a place of pilgrimage.

Manrique (mänrē'kä), town (pop. 552), Cojedes state, N Venezuela, 12 mi. NNE of San Carlos, cattle raising.

Man River (män), Burmese *Man Chaung* (män'-joun), in Minbu dist., Upper Burma, rises in Arakan Yoma, flows over 50 mi. NE, past Sagu, to Irrawaddy R. N of Minbu. Used for irrigation of S Minbu dist.; the left-bank Man Canal takes off at headworks 18 mi. W of Minbu.

Mans, Le (lù mä'), anc. *Cenomanum*, city (pop. 90,693), ⊙ Sarthe dept., W France, on Sarthe R. (canalized) and 115 mi. SW of Paris; important regional railroad, commercial and industrial center; metallurgy (motors, rolling stock, automobiles, agr. machinery, plumbing and heating equipment); large tobacco factory; paper and textile mills; food preserving, mfg. (shoes, sailcloth, chemicals, hosiery, biscuits, and candy). Hq. of several insurance companies. Its fine Romanesque and Gothic cathedral (11th-13th cent.), known for its daring system of flying buttresses, contains tomb of Berengaria. Of Celtic origin, developed by Romans, and christianized in 3d cent., Le Mans was the scene of many combats in the time of William the Conqueror and King John. Besieged 5 times during Hundred Years War, devastated by Huguenots in 1562, it witnessed defeat of the Vendée army in 1793 and a German victory in 1870. Damaged in Second World War. Henry II of England b. here.

Mansa (män'sŭ). **1** Town (pop. 9,543), Mehsana dist., N Bombay, India, 19 mi. SE of Mehsana; cotton, wheat, millet. Was ⊙ former princely state of Mansa (□ 25; pop. 18,681) of Western India States; state inc. 1949 into newly-created Mehsana dist. **2** Town (pop. 11,729), central Patiala and East Punjab States Union, India, 65 mi. WSW of Patiala; market (wheat, millet, cotton).

Mansafis (măn'săfēs), village (pop. 5,385), Minya prov., Upper Egypt, on railroad and 5 mi. NNW of Abu Qurqas; cotton, cereals, sugar cane.

Mansahra or **Mansehra** (both: män'sărŭ), town (pop. 10,217), Hazara dist., NE North-West Frontier prov., W Pakistan, 12 mi. N of Abbottabad; trades in maize, wheat, barley, rice, fruit, timber. Rock edict of Asoka (3d cent. B.C.) is NW.

Mansavillagra (mänsävĭlyä'grä), village, Florida dept., S central Uruguay, in the Cuchilla Grande Inferior, near the Arroyo Mansavillagra, on railroad and 25 mi. WSW of José Batlle y Ordóñez. Wheat, corn, linseed, livestock.

Mansavillagra, Arroyo, river, Florida dept., S central Uruguay, rises in the Cuchilla Grande Principal 10 mi. SSW of Illescas, flows 50 mi. NW to Yí R. 14 mi. WSW of Sarandí del Yí.

Mansei, Japan: see BANSEI.

Mansel Island (□ 1,317), E Keewatin Dist., Northwest Territories, in Hudson Bay, off N Ungava Peninsula; 62 mi. long, 4–30 mi. wide. Created reindeer reserve in 1920. On N coast is trading post (62°25'N 79°36'W).

Manseriche, Pongo de (pōng'gō dā mänsärē'chä), N Peru, gorge of Marañón R., on Amazonas-Loreto dept. border, near its junction with Santiago R. in Cerros de Campanquiz; 4°25'S 77°35'W. Marañón navigable for large boats to this point.

Mansfeld (mäns'fĕlt), town (pop. 3,294), in former Prussian Saxony prov., central Germany, after 1945 in Saxony-Anhalt, at E foot of the lower Harz, near the Wipper, 6 mi. NW of Eisleben; center (since 12th cent.) of major copper-slate mining region; copper smelting, furniture mfg. Molybdenum and silver also mined here. Has remains of 11th-cent. castle. Luther spent his childhood here. Mining became (1364) monopoly of counts of Mansfeld; declined in importance in 16th cent., revived after 1671 when monopoly rights were abolished.

Mansfield, town (pop. 1,068), central Victoria, Australia, 80 mi. NE of Melbourne; rail terminus in agr. area. Former gold-mining town.

Mansfield, municipal borough (1931 pop. 46,077; 1951 census 51,343), W Nottingham, England, on Maun R. and 14 mi. N of Nottingham, at W border of Sherwood Forest; shoe-mfg. center, with mfg. also of hosiery, chemicals; machinery and other metal products, concrete, cotton; coal mines. Has 13th-cent. church and grammar school founded 1561. Mansfield was site of Roman camp and residence of Mercian kings.

Mansfield. **1** Town (pop. 869), on Sebastian-Scot co. line, W Ark., 24 mi. SSE of Fort Smith, i farm area (cotton, truck, fruit); natural ga **2** Town (pop. 10,008), Tolland co., E central Conn on Willimantic R., just N of Willimantic; agr., mf (wood products, fiberboard, organ pipes, buttons Includes villages of STORRS (seat of Univ. Conn.), Eagleville, Merrow, and Gurleyville. Stat school, hosp. for epileptics and feeble-minded her Settled c.1692, inc. 1703. **3** Town (pop. 446), New ton co., N central Ga., 9 mi. SE of Covingto **4** Village (pop. 665), Piatt co., central Ill., 15 m WNW of Champaign, in grain-growing are **5** Town (pop. 4,440), ⊙ De Soto parish, NW La 33 mi. S of Shreveport; trading and shipping cent for fertile agr. area; oil wells; timber. Cotto ginning, lumber milling; mfg. of foundry product trailer bodies. The Civil War battle of Sabin Crossroads (April 8, 1864), a Confederate victory is commemorated by near-by park marking th site. Inc. 1847. **6** Town (pop. 7,184), includin Mansfield village (pop. 4,808), Bristol co., S Mass., 15 mi. NE of Providence, R.I.; machin parts, metal products, chocolate. Settled 165 set off from Norton 1770. **7** City (pop. 963 Wright co., S central Mo., in the Ozarks, 40 m ESE of Springfield; agr.; lead, zinc mines. **8** Cit (pop. 43,564), ⊙ Richland co., N central Ohi c.55 mi. WSW of Akron and on a fork of Mohica R.; electrical appliances, steel products, brass cas ings, machinery, furniture, rubber goods, plumbin fixtures. Seat of Ohio State Reformatory. Lai out 1808, inc. 1826. Annexed South Boulevard (pop. 321) in 1948. **9** Borough (pop. 2,657), Tiog co., N Pa., on Tioga R. and 24 mi. SW of Elmir N.Y.; agr.; toys; bituminous coal, natural ga State teachers col. Laid out 1824, inc. 185 **10** City (pop. 964), Tarrant co., N Texas, 16 m SE of Fort Worth, in agr. area (cotton, corn **11** Town (pop. 414), Douglas co., central Wash 45 mi. NE of Wenatchee, in Columbia basin ag region.

Mansfield, Mount (4,393 ft.), N central Vt., 20 m NE of Burlington, in resort and recreational are highest peak of Green Mts.; winter sports cente Summit has hotel built c.1860. Smugglers Notch gorge at base, is scenic feature.

Mansfield Dam, Texas: see MARSHALL FORD DAM

Mansfield Hollow Dam, Conn.: see NATCHAU RIVER.

Mansfield Woodhouse, residential urban distric (1931 pop. 13,721; 1951 census 17,819), V Nottingham, England, 2 mi. N of Mansfield; ston quarrying. Has 14th-cent. church.

Mansha'at, Egypt: see MINSHAT.

Manshah, El, El Minshah, El Menshah, or **Al-Manshah** (all: ĕl mĕn'shä), town (pop. 18,743), Girg prov., central Upper Egypt, on W bank of the Nil on railroad, and 11 mi. NW of Girga; cotton gin ning, pottery making, dairying; cotton, cereal dates, sugar cane. Site of a town built by Ptolem I Soter, 1st king of the Macedonian dynasty of an Egypt (c.300 B.C.).

Mansilla or **Gobernador Mansilla** (gōbĕrnädô mänsē'yä), town (pop. estimate 1,000), S centr Entre Ríos prov., Argentina, on railroad and 4 mi. N of Gualeguay; flax, wheat, oats, livestock a raised.

Mansilla de las Mulas (mänsē'lyä dhä läs mōō'läs) town (pop. 1,552), Leon prov., NW Spain, on Esl R. and 11 mi. SE of Leon; tanning, candy mfg. cereals, livestock, lumber. Has medieval castle.

Mansión, La, Costa Rica: see LA MANSIÓN.

Mansle (mäl), village (pop. 1,287), Charente dept W France, on the Charente R. and 15 mi. N o Angoulême; road junction; livestock market.

Manso, Rio, Brazil: see MORTES, RIO DAS.

Mansôa (mänzô'ŭ), village, W Port. Guinea, 23 m NE of Bissau; rice, almonds, coconuts, rubbe palm oil; hog and cattle raising.

Manson, town (pop. 1,622), Calhoun co., centr Iowa, 18 mi. W of Fort Dodge; rail junction; grai mills, creamery. Twin Lakes State Park near b Founded 1872, inc. 1877.

Mansonville, village (pop. estimate 750), S Que., o Missisquoi R., near Vt. border, 35 mi. SW o Sherbrooke; dairying.

Manston, village, Kent, England, 2 mi. WNW o Ramsgate; major air base.

Mansura (mănsōō'rŭ), **El Mansura**, or **Al-Mansurah** (both: ĕl), town (pop. 102,519), ⊙ Daqahliy prov., NE Lower Egypt, on Damietta branch of th Nile at mouth of El Bahr el Saghir (a delta canal and 36 mi. SW of Damietta; 31°3'N 31°23'E. Ra junction and important cotton trading center; co ton ginning, wool spinning, tanning, metal- an woodworking, dairying. Founded 1221 as sub stitute for Damietta, then occupied by the Crusa ders. Here in 1250 Louis IX and his forces we defeated by the Mamelukes.

Mansura (mănsōō'rŭ), town (pop. 1,439), Avoyelle parish, E central La., 29 mi. SE of Alexandria, i sugar-cane and cotton area; cotton and moss gin ning.

Mansurabad, Iran: see MEHRAN.

Mansuri (măn'sōōrē), petty sheikdom of SUBEIH tribal area, Western Aden Protectorate; ⊙ Al Masharij. Protectorate treaty concluded 1871.

Mansuriya, Al, or **Al-Mansuriyah** (äl mänsŏŏrē'yŭ), town, Diyala prov., central Iraq, on the Tigris and 30 mi. N of Baghdad; dates, fruits, livestock.

Mansuriya, El, or **Al-Mansuriyah** (both: ĕl–), village (pop. 10,729), Giza prov., Upper Egypt, 12 mi. NW of Cairo city center.

Manta (män'tä), town (1950 pop. 19,021), Manabí prov., W Ecuador, Pacific port on Manta Bay, 105 mi. NW of Guayaquil, 22 mi. WNW of Portoviejo (linked by railroad); 0°57'S 80°44'W. A center for mfg. and shipment of Panama hats, it also exports products of fertile timberland: coffee, cacao, tagua nuts, balsa wood, hides. Has sawmills, rice mills, tanneries. Airfield, customhouse.

Mantachie (măn'tŭ-chē), village (pop. 178), Itawamba co., NE Miss., 6 mi. NW of Fulton.

Mantador (măn'tŭdôr), village (pop. 138), Richland co., extreme SE N.Dak., 18 mi. WSW of Wahpeton.

Mantai (mŭn'tī), anc. *Mantota, Mahatittha*, village, Northern Prov., Ceylon, 6 mi. E of Mannar; coconut-palm plantations, vegetable gardens. Chief anc. landing place of Ceylon.

Mantalingajan, Mount (mäntälĭng-gä'hän), peak (6,839 ft.), S Palawan, Philippines, NW of Brooke's Point.

Mantare (mäntä'rā), town, Lake Prov., NW Tanganyika, on railroad and 25 mi. SE of Mwanza; cotton, peanuts, rice, corn. Diamond deposits at Misungwi, 10 mi. SW.

Mantaro River (mäntä'rō), central Peru, rises near Cerro de Pasco (Pasco dept.) in Cordillera Occidental, flows SE almost to Huanta, where it turns sharply NW and finally ENE to the Apurímac at Puerto Bolognesi (Apurímac R. is from here on called Ene R.); c.360 mi. long. On it are La Oroya, Jauja, and Huancayo. Mantaro R. is used for irrigation in Andean valleys; not navigable. Its upper course is linked through small affluent with L. Junín.

Mantasoa Reservoir, Madagascar: see Ikopa River.

Mante, Ciudad, Mexico: see Ciudad Mante.

Manteca (măntē'kŭ), city (pop. 3,804), San Joaquin co., central Calif., 10 mi. S of Stockton, in agr. region (grapes, olives, vegetables, sugar beets); ships dairy products. Founded 1870, inc. 1918.

Manteco, Venezuela: see El Manteco.

Mantee (măn'tē), village (pop. 189), Webster co., central Miss., 25 mi. WNW of West Point.

Manteigas (mäntā'gŭsh), town (pop. 3,257), Guarda dist., N central Portugal, in Serra da Estrêla, near headwaters of Zêzere R., 18 mi. SW of Guarda; butter-mfg. center; textile milling. Sulphur springs just S.

Mantel (mäntĕl'), village (pop. 1,949), Upper Palatinate, NE Bavaria, Germany, on small Heidenab R. and 5 mi. WSW of Weiden; metalworking, tanning. Chartered in early 16th cent.

Mantena, Brazil: see Barra de São Francisco.

Manteno (măntē'nō), village (pop. 1,789), Kankakee co., NE Ill., 9 mi. N of Kankakee, in agr. area. Inc. 1878.

Manteo (măn'tēō), resort and fishing town (pop. 635), ⊙ Dare co., NE N.C., on Roanoke Isl., 40 mi. SE of Elizabeth City. Fort Raleigh Natl. Historic Site near by.

Manter, city (pop. 200), Stanton co., SW Kansas, 27 mi. WSW of Ulysses, near Colo. line; grain.

Manternach (män'tŭrnäkh), town (pop. 262), SE Luxembourg, on Syre R. and 2 mi. NNW of Grevenmacher; pumps, presses, saws, agr. machinery, paper, farinaceous food products.

Mantero, Argentina: see Villa Mantero.

Mantes-Gassicourt (mãt-gäsēkōōr'), town (pop. 13,055), Seine-et-Oise dept., N central France, port on left bank of the Seine opposite Limay, and 30 mi. WNW of Paris; industrial and agr. trade center; metal foundries (railroad and electrical equipment, cast steel); mfg. (musical instruments, cigarette paper, cellophane, beer, hosiery). Has 12th-13th-cent. church (damaged 1939–45) and remains of old ramparts. Formerly called Mantes or Mantes-sur-Seine; present name results from absorption of Gassicourt, a NW suburb (heavily damaged 1944). At Rolleboise (6 mi. WNW) Allies established first bridgehead across the Seine (Aug., 1944) in Second World War.

Mantes-la-Ville (–lä-vēl'), S suburb (pop. 5,780) of Mantes-Gassicourt, Seine-et-Oise dept., N central France; mfg. (musical instruments, cellophane, cement, paints). Damaged in Second World War.

Manthani (mŭn'tŭnē), town (pop. 8,286), Karimnagar dist., NE Hyderabad state, India, on Godavari R. and 37 mi. ENE of Karimnagar; rice, mangoes, tamarind. Bamboo (used in paper mfg.) in near-by forests.

Manti (măn'tī), city (pop. 2,051), ⊙ Sanpete co., central Utah, in irrigated Sanpete Valley, 70 mi. S of Provo; alt. c.5,550 ft. Processing point in livestock, poultry, and dairying area; flour, cheese, canned vegetables. Oolite quarries near by. Mormon temple (built 1877–88) here. City founded by Mormons 1849. Wasatch Plateau is just E, in Manti Natl. Forest.

Mantin (män"tĭn'), town (pop. 1,073), W Negri Sembilan, Malaya, 7 mi. NNW of Seremban, near Selangor line; rubber; tin mining.

Mantinea (măn"tĭnē'ŭ), anc. city of Arcadia, central Peloponnesus, Greece, 8 mi. N of Tripolis. Has ruins of city walls, theater, and other bldgs. It was scene (418 B.C.) of victory of Spartans over Athenians, and of defeat of Spartans by Thebans under Epaminondas (killed here) in 362 B.C.

Mantiqueira, Serra da (sĕ'rŭ dä mäntēkā'rŭ), mountain range of SE Brazil, extends c.200 mi. parallel to the coast along Minas Gerais–São Paulo and Minas Gerais–Rio de Janeiro border, forming through most of its length the N limit of the Paraíba valley. Rises to 9,145 ft. in Itatiaia peak (also called Agulhas Negras). Traversed by railroads from Rio de Janeiro to interior of Minas Gerais. Contains several health resorts. Range merges in NE with the Serra do Espinhaço.

Manto (män'tō), town (pop. 1,075), Olancho dept., central Honduras, 21 mi. NNW of Juticalpa; sugar cane, rice, livestock. Airfield.

Mantoloking (măntŭlō'kĭng), resort borough (pop. 72), Ocean co., E N.J., on peninsula bet. Barnegat Bay (bridged here) and the Atlantic, 15 mi. S of Asbury Park; boat building; yachting center.

Manton, city (pop. 1,085), Wexford co., NW Mich., 11 mi. N of Cadillac; fruitgrowing; livestock, truck, potatoes, beans, corn; dairy products. Mfg. of lumber, chairs, food products. Settled 1871 as lumber town; inc. as village 1877, as city 1924.

Mantorville, village (pop. 477), ⊙ Dodge co., SE Minn., on branch of Zumbro R. and 15 mi. WNW of Rochester in grain, potato, and livestock area.

Mantoudion or **Mandoudhion** (both: mändōō'-dhēôn), town (pop. 2,210)NW Euboea, Greece, 25 mi. NNW of Chalcis; wheat, wines, stock raising (sheep, goats); magnesite deposits (S). Also called Mantoudi or Mantudi.

Mantova (män'tôvä), province (□ 903; pop. 407,977), Lombardy, N Italy; ⊙ Mantua. Consists of fertile, irrigated Po plain, S of Lago di Garda, with small area of glacial moraine hills in N; watered by Po, Mincio, Oglio, and Secchia rivers. Agr. (wheat, corn, sugar beets, raw silk, grapes) and stock raising (cattle, swine, horses) predominate. Produces 25% of Italy's cheese, including Parmesan. Peat digging.

Mantova, city, Italy: see Mantua.

Mänttä (mänt'tä), town (pop. 5,496), Häme co., S central Finland, in lake region, 45 mi. NE of Tampere; plup, cellulose, and paper mills.

Mantua (män'twä), town (pop. 1,073), Pinar del Río prov., W Cuba, on small Mantua R. and 40 mi. WSW of Pinar del Río; tobacco, fruit, cattle; lumbering.

Mantua (măn'tūŭ), Ital. *Mantova* (män'tôvä), city (pop. 36,489), ⊙ Mantova prov., Lombardy, N Italy, on lower Po plain, 22 mi. SSW of Verona, surrounded on 3 sides by lakes formed by Mincio R.; 45°9'N 10°48'E. Rail junction; agr. and commercial center; mfg. (macaroni, beet sugar, paper, fertilizer, pianos, furniture, dairy machinery, pottery, bricks). Bishopric. Among its chief bldgs. are ducal palace and fortress, churches of San Francesco (14th cent.; severely damaged 1945), San Sebastiano (begun 1460), and Sant'Andrea (begun 1472; designed by Alberti), cathedral, and Palazzo del Tè (1523–35; designed by Giulio Romano). Has Vergilian Acad. of Arts and Sciences, mus. of anc. sculpture, and technical institute. Famous in antiquity as home of Vergil, b. in near-by Pietole (anc. *Andes*). Achieved great splendor under Gonzaga family (1328–1708). Ruled by Austria from 1708 until 1797, when it was taken by Napoleon. Retaken by Austria in 1814 and held until 1866, when it passed to Italy. In Second World War, suffered air bombing.

Mantua. 1 (măn'chŭ) Village (1940 pop. 717), Gloucester co., SW N.J., on Mantua Creek and 10 mi. S of Camden, in farm area. **2** (măn'tŭwä) Village (pop. 1,059), Portage co., NE Ohio, 20 mi. NE of Akron, and on Cuyahoga R., in dairy, poultry, and truck area. **3** (măn'tŭwä) Town (pop. 271), Box Elder co., N Utah, 5 mi. NE of Brigham; alt. 5,175 ft.; agr.

Mantua Creek (măn'chŭ), Gloucester co., SW N.J., rises N of Glassboro, flows c.16 mi. generally NW, past Wenonah and Paulsboro, to Delaware R. opposite S Philadelphia. Navigable for c.9 mi. above mouth.

Mantua River (män'twä), Pinar del Río prov., W Cuba, rises in the Sierra de los Órganos, flows c.35 mi. SW, past Mantua, to the Ensenada de Guadiana.

Mantudi, Greece: see Mantoudion.

Manturovo (mŭntōō'rŭvŭ), **1** Town (1939 pop. over 2,000), S Kostroma oblast, Russian SFSR, on Unzha R. and 28 mi. W of Sharya, on railroad; sawmilling, veneering. Oil shale deposits. **2** Village (1939 pop. over 2,000), E central Kursk oblast, Russian SFSR, 32 mi. WNW of Stary Oskol; wheat, sunflowers.

Mäntyharju (män'tühär"yōō), village (commune pop. 10,002), Mikkeli co., S Finland, in lake region, 20 mi. SW of Mikkeli; granite and graphite quarries, graphite refinery.

Mäntyluoto (măn'tülōō"ōtō), outport of Pori, Turku-Pori co., SW Finland, on small isl. (bridge to mainland) in Gulf of Bothnia, 9 mi. NW of Pori city center; rail terminus.

Manú (mänōō'), town, ⊙ Manú prov. (□ 12,538; enumerated pop. 63, plus c.10,000 Indians), Madre de Dios dept., SE Peru, landing at junction of Madre de Dios and Manú rivers, 115 mi. WNW of Puerto Maldonado, in rubber region; 12°15'S 70°50'W.

Manua (mänōō'ä), district (pop. 2,597), American Samoa, S Pacific; comprises Tau, Ofu, and Olosega isls.; annexed 1899 by U.S. It is the cradle of their race, according to Samoan tradition.

Manuae (mänōōä'ĕ), atoll, Cook Islands, S Pacific, 124 mi. NE of Rarotonga; 2 islets (1,524 acres; pop. 28) joined by coral reef. W isl. (c.3 mi. in circumference) is named Manuae; E isl. (2 mi. long, 1 mi. wide) is Te-Au-o-Tu (tā'ou'ō'tōō), Copra plantation. Sometimes called Hervey Isl.

Manucan (mänōō'kän), town (1939 pop. 6,962) in Katipunan municipality, Zamboanga prov., NW Mindanao, Philippines, 50 mi. NW of Pagadian, on Sulu Sea; coconuts, rice, corn.

Manucho (mänōō'chō), town (pop. estimate 500), E central Santa Fe prov., Argentina, 26 mi. NNW of Santa Fe, in agr. area (flax, corn, wheat, livestock; apiculture); dairying.

Manuel (mänwĕl'), village (pop. 2,525), Valencia prov., E Spain, 5 mi. NNW of Játiva; rice- and sawmilling; cereals, oranges.

Manuel Alves Grande River (mŏŏnwĕl' äl'vĭs grän'dĭ), NE central Brazil, rises in the Serra das Mangabeiras, flows c.150 mi. NNW, forming Maranhão-Goiás border throughout its length, to the Tocantins above Carolina. Not navigable. Formerly spelled Manoel Alves Grande.

Manuel Benavides (mänwĕl' bänävē'dĕs), town (pop. 779), Chihuahua, N Mexico, near Rio Grande, 145 mi. ENE of Chihuahua; lead mining, cattle raising. Formerly San Carlos.

Manuel Derqui (dĕr'kē), town (pop. estimate 500), NW Corrientes prov., Argentina, on Paraná R., on railroad and 27 mi. S of Corrientes; agr. center (corn, peas, cotton, sugar cane, peanuts, oranges).

Manuel Doblado or **Ciudad Manuel Doblado** (syōōdädh', dōblä'dō), city (pop. 3,722), Guanajuato, central Mexico, on central plateau, 33 mi. SW of León; alt. 5,833 ft.; wheat-growing center; flour milling.

Manuel Florenco Mantilla (flōrĕng'kō mäntē'yä), village (pop. estimate 1,200), W Corrientes prov., Argentina, 45 mi. NW of Mercedes; rail junction and livestock center.

Manuel González (gōnsä'lĕs), officially Colonia Manuel González, town (pop. 519), Veracruz, E Mexico, 16 mi. NNE of Córdoba; fruit.

Manuel M. Diéguez (ā'mā dyā'gĕs), town (pop. 585), Jalisco, central Mexico, on central plateau, 55 mi. SE of Sayula; grain, beans, fruit, livestock.

Manuel Urbano (mŏŏnwĕl' ōōrbä'nōō), town (pop. 123), Acre territory, westernmost Brazil, on Purus R., near Amazonas line, and 45 mi. W of Sena Madureira. Until 1944, Castelo.

Manukau, county, New Zealand: see Auckland, city.

Manukau Harbour (mănŭkou'), N N.Isl., New Zealand, S harbor (15 mi. long, 10 mi. wide) of Auckland, 5 mi. S of Waitemata Harbour on E coast; connected with Tasman Sea by passage 2 mi. wide. Onehunga is on NE shore, Papakura on SE shore, Waiuku on small S arm of harbor.

Manuk Manka Island, Philippines: see Simunul Island.

Manumukh or **Manoomukh** (mŭn'ŏŏmŏŏk), village, Sylhet dist., E East Bengal, E Pakistan, near the Kusiyara, 23 mi. SSW of Sylhet; rice, tea, oilseeds; sawmilling.

Manurewa (mănŏŏrē'wŭ), borough (pop. 1,847), N N.Isl., New Zealand, 15 mi. SE of Auckland; agr. center.

Manuripi, Bolivia: see Puerto Rico.

Manuripi River (mänōōrē'pē), rises in Peru, flows c.250 mi. NE, crossing into Bolivia, past San Miguelito, joining Tahuamanu R. at Puerto Rico to form Orton River. Navigable in middle and lower course, c.90 mi. Rubber is exploited in tropical forests along its banks in Bolivia.

Manú River (mänōō'), Madre de Dios dept., SE Peru, rises in E Andean outliers at 12°15'S 71°25'W, flows c.120 mi. SE, through tropical lowlands, to Madre de Dios R. at Manú. Navigable for small craft. Linked through small affluent with a tributary of Urubamba R., traveled by rubber gatherers up to Iquitos (Loreto dept.).

Manus (mä'nŭs, mä'nōōs), volcanic island (□ 633), largest of Admiralty Isls., Manus dist., Bismarck Archipelago, Territory of New Guinea, SW Pacific, 230 mi. NW of New Britain; 2°4'S 147°E; 50 mi. long, 20 mi. wide; rises to 3,000 ft. Coconut plantations. In Second World War, site of large U.S. naval base established 1944. Sometimes called Admiralty Isl.

Manvel, village (pop. 278), Grand Forks co., E N.Dak., 12 mi. NNW of Grand Forks and on Turtle R.

Manvi (män'vē), town (pop. 7,312), Raichur dist., SW Hyderabad state, India, 26 mi. SW of Raichur; millet, oilseeds. Cotton ginning near by.

Manville. 1 Borough (pop. 8,597), Somerset co., N central N.J., 8 mi. NW of New Brunswick; mfg. (asbestos products, textiles, clothing, cement blocks); wood and fur processing; poultry, truck, dairy products. Laid out 1906, inc. 1929. Includes Finderne, mfg. village (electrical machinery, sewing machines). **2** Village (pop. 3,429) in Lincoln town, Providence co., NE R.I., on Blackstone R. and 11 mi. N of Providence; makes rayon and cotton goods, plushes. **3** Town (pop. 154), Niobrara co., E Wyo., 8 mi. W of Lusk; alt. c.5,250 ft. Trading point in ranching and wheat region.

Manwat or **Manwath** (both: män'vŭt), town (pop. 14,113), Parbhani dist., NW Hyderabad state, India, 18 mi. W of Parbhani; cotton ginning, rice and oilseed milling. Manwat Road, rail station, is 5 mi. NE.

Many (mä'nyŭ), Hung. *Mány*, town (pop. 2,625), Fejer co., N central Hungary, 18 mi. W of Budapest; grain, livestock.

Many (mĕ'nē), town (pop. 1,681), ⊙ Sabine parish, W La., c.70 mi. S of Shreveport; commercial center for lumber, oil, and agr. area (cotton, corn, potatoes); cotton gins, machine shops, lumber and grist mills. Old Fort Jesup (1882; now in a park) and site of Los Adais, old Sp. capital of region, are near by. Settled in early-19th cent.

Manyacha, mountain, Yugoslavia: see MANJACA.

Manyanga (mänyäng'gä), village, Leopoldville prov., W Belgian Congo, on both banks of Congo R., on Fr. Equatorial Africa border, and 105 mi. NE of Boma; center of native trade. Former trading post founded by Henry M. Stanley. Though this section of Congo R. is part of the noted Livingstone Falls, the river is navigable bet. here and Isangila.

Manyara, Lake (mänyä'rä), N Tanganyika, 60 mi. WSW of Arusha; 30 mi. long, 10 mi. wide. Has salt and soda deposits.

Manyas (mänyäs'), village (pop. 1,879), Balikesir prov., NW Turkey, near Koca R. and L. Manyas, 28 mi. N of Balikesir; cigarette factory. Also called Maltepe.

Manyas, Lake (□ 69), NW Turkey, 8 mi. S of Bandirma; 12 mi. long, 10 mi. wide. Koca R. enters and leaves it.

Manych (mä'nĭch), name of 2 rivers of the N Caucasus, Russian SFSR, in **Manych Depression**, a broad valleylike lowland extending c.350 mi. from lower Don R. SE to Caspian Sea. **Manych River** proper or **Western Manych River**, Rus. *Zapadnyy Manych*, a canalized stream, rises in area of Divnoye, flows c.200 mi. NW, through L. Manych-Gudilo, past Proletarskaya and Vesely (locks and reservoir), to Don R. SW of Bagayevskaya. Navigable below Proletarskaya. Receives Yegorlyk R. (left); forms part of Kuban-Yegorlyk irrigation scheme. **Eastern Manych River**, Rus. *Vostochnyy Manych*, rises in marshy central section of Arzgir, flows c.100 mi. E to system of salt lakes and marshes c.75 mi. from Caspian Sea, which it reaches only in rare spring floods. Western and Eastern Manych rivers link up in central section of Manych Depression during spring high-water stage. Projected **Manych Canal**, which is to link lower Don R. and Caspian Sea, will utilize the canalized Western Manych. Construction of E section (bet. Divnoye area and lower Kuma R.) interrupted by Second World War. Manych Depression is sometimes regarded as a natural boundary bet. Europe and Asia.

Manych-Gudilo, Lake (-gōōdĭlô'), or **Great Manych Lake**, Rus. *Ozero Bolshoi Manych*, in central section of Manych Depression, N Caucasus, Russian SFSR, NW of Divnoye; 35 mi. long, 5 mi. wide. Traversed by canalized Western Manych R.; to be used as central reservoir for projected Manych Canal.

Manyoni (mänyō'nē), town (pop. c.500), central Tanganyika, on railroad and 70 mi. WNW of Dodoma; agr. trade center: cotton, peanuts, gum arabic, beeswax; livestock; hides and skins.

Manzala (mĕnzä'lŭ, mĕn'zälŭ), **El Manzala, El Menzala**, or **Al-Manzalah** (both: ĕl), town (pop. 20,722), Daqahliya prov., NE Lower Egypt, on El Bahr el Saghir (a delta canal) and 34 mi. ENE of Mansura, near L. Manzala, 20 mi. SSE of Damietta; fisheries.

Manzala, Lake, or **Lake Manzalah**, salt lagoon (□ 660, not including marshes), Daqahliya prov., NE Lower Egypt, bet. Damietta branch of the Nile and Suez Canal; largest lake in Egypt, c.35 mi. long, 14 mi. wide. It covers former fertile lands once watered by several branches of the Nile, and is separated from the Mediterranean Sea by a narrow spit at E end of which is Port Said. The Navigable El Manzala Canal, 22 mi. long, crosses the lake connecting El Matariya and Damietta. The Suez Canal was dug through E area of Manzala basin. Important fisheries. It is the anc. L. Tanis. Sometimes spelled Menzala or Menzaleh.

Manzanar (măn'zŭnär), village, Inyo co., E Calif., in Owens Valley, bet. Lone Pine and Independence. Site during Second World War of a relocation camp for interned Pacific Coast residents of Japanese descent.

Manzanares (mänsänä'rĕs), town (pop. 3,088), Caldas dept., central Colombia, in Cordillera Central, 30 mi. ENE of Manizales; alt. 6,138 ft.; coffeegrowing; sericulture. Gold mines near by.

Manzanares (män-thänä'rĕs), city (pop. 18,182), Ciudad Real prov., S central Spain, in New Castile, rail and road junction on small Azuer R., and 30 mi. E of Ciudad Real. Agr. center (chiefly viticultural) on La Mancha plain (also grapes, olives, saffron, potatoes, vegetables, sheep). Industries include liquor and alcohol distilling, wine making, fruit canning, sawmilling, lime quarrying; mfg. of tartaric acid, sulphur, plaster, soap, firearms, knives, chocolate, jam, textile goods. Has old castle.

Manzanares el Real (ĕl rääl'), town (pop. 451), Madrid prov., central Spain, 21 mi. NNW of Madrid; lumbering, stone quarrying, stock raising, dairying. Near by is the Santillana dam and hydroelectric plant, adjoined by fine medieval castle.

Manzanares River, Madrid prov., central Spain, rises on E slopes of the Sierra de Guadarrama c.5 mi. N of Manzanares el Real, flows c.55 mi. SSE and E, past Colmenar Viejo, El Pardo, and Madrid (where canalized), to Jarama R. (a Tagus tributary) 11 mi. SE of Madrid. Used for water power and irrigation. On its upper course is Santillana reservoir.

Manzanares River (mänsänä'rĕs), Sucre state, NE Venezuela, rises at NW foot of Cerro Turumiquire, flows c.40 mi. NW, past Cumanacoa and Cumaná, to the Caribbean 1½ mi. NW of Cumaná.

Manzaneda, Cabeza de (kävä'thä dhä män-thänā'-dhä), highest peak (5,833 ft.) of Galician Mts., Orense prov., NW Spain, 30 mi. WSW of Orense.

Manzaneque (män-thänā'kā), town (pop. 898), Toledo prov., central Spain, on railroad and 20 mi. SE of Toledo; cereals, grapes, olives, sheep, goats.

Manzanera (män-thänā'rä), town (pop. 1,172), Teruel prov., E Spain, 23 mi. SE of Teruel; flour milling; cereals, potatoes, sheep.

Manzanilla (män-thänē'lyä), town (pop. 3,084), Huelva prov., SW Spain, 24 mi. W of Seville; viticulture; olive growing.

Manzanilla (mănzŭnĭ'lŭ), village, E Trinidad, B.W.I., 33 mi. ESE of Port of Spain, near fine Manzanilla Bay. Manzanilla Beach, lined by coconut palms, is a popular tourist site. Manzanilla Point is 3 mi. E.

Manzanilla, La, Mexico: see LA MANZANILLA.

Manzanillo, Colombia: see CARTAGENA.

Manzanillo (mänsänē'yō), village (dist. pop. 1,207), Puntarenas prov., W Costa Rica, port on Gulf of Nicoya of the Pacific, 16 mi. NW of Puntarenas. Exports gold from Abangares mines. Stock raising, lumbering. Also called Puerto Iglesias.

Manzanillo, city (pop. 36,295), Oriente prov., SE Cuba, port at head of shallow Gulf of Guacanayabo, 85 mi. WNW of Santiago de Cuba (linked by rail and highway); distributing and shipping center for fertile agr. region (sugar cane, molasses, tobacco, fruit, rice, beeswax, honey, cattle). Exports mainly sugar products, high-quality tobacco, and hardwood. Among its industries are sugar- and sawmills, cigar factories, tanneries, fish canneries. Has fine parks, church, airfield. Its semitropical climate is unhealthful because of surrounding swamps. Zinc and copper deposits near by. Founded 1784.

Manzanillo, city (pop. 6,831), Colima, W Mexico, Pacific port on Manzanillo Bay (8 mi. wide), 45 mi. WSW of Colima. Contains fine harbor; situated on railroad; serves as outlet and distribution point for W Mexico. Shipping, shark-fishing, and processing center; exports coffee, hides, shark products, limes, minerals, lumber, palm oil; industries: sawmilling, fish and fruit canning, vegetable-oil extracting, varnish and paint making. Iron deposits near by. Cuyutlán Lagoon is back of city.

Manzanillo Bay, Fr. *Baie de Mancenille* (bā dŭ māsnē'yŭ), inlet of Atlantic Ocean on N coast of Hispaniola, at border bet. Haiti and Dominican Republic; 19°45'N 71°45'E. Sheltered by Manzanillo Point (N). Port of Pepillo Salcedo is on S shore, at mouth of Massacre (Dajabón) R.

Manzanillo Bay, inlet (c.3 mi. long, 1 mi. wide) of Caribbean Sea, in Panama Canal Zone, E of Manzanillo Isl. (site of Colón city), which separates it from Limon Bay. On E shore are Fort Randolph, Coco Solo, and France Field.

Manzanillo Island, indented peninsula (c.1 mi. long, ¾ mi. wide) guarding Atlantic entrance to the Panama Canal, situated bet. Limon Bay (W) and Manzanillo Bay (E). On it is Colón city, which forms an enclave of Panama in the Canal Zone.

Manzanillo Keys, tiny coral reefs in the Gulf of Guacanayabo, Oriente prov., SE Cuba, just outside Manzanillo, the harbor of which they protect. Covered by mangroves. On Perla Key (W) is a lighthouse.

Manzanillo Point, northernmost point of Panama, on Caribbean Sea, 31 mi. NE of Colón; 9°38'N 79°33'W.

Manzanillo Point, on Caribbean coast of Falcón state, NW Venezuela, 29 mi. ENE of Coro; 11°32'N 69°16'W.

Manzanita (măn"zŭnē'tŭ), city (pop. 339), Tillamook co., NW Oregon, on the Pacific, 19 mi. N of Tillamook.

Manzano (mäntsä'nô), village (pop. 1,747), Udine prov., Friuli–Venezia Giulia, NE Italy, 9 mi. SE of Udine; toymaking.

Manzano Island, Chile: see GUAITECAS ISLANDS.

Manzanola (mănzŭnō'lŭ), city (pop. 543), Otero co., SE central Colo., on Arkansas R., near mouth of Apishapa R., and 40 mi. ESE of Pueblo; alt. 4,250 ft. Trading point in fruit, vegetable, sugar-beet region; canned goods.

Manzano Range (mănză'nō,–zä'nō), central N.Mex., E of Rio Grande; extends c.40 mi. N from Mountainair; largely within part of Cibola Natl. Forest. Prominent points: Mosca Peak (9,723 ft.), Manzano Peak (10,103 ft.).

Manzat (mäzä'), village (pop. 360), Puy-de-Dôme dept., central France, in Auvergne Mts., 10 mi. NW of Riom; cattle. Electrometallurgical factory (calcium carbide) at Les Ancizes-Saint-Georges, 5 mi. WSW.

Manzikert, Turkey: see MALAZGIRT.

Manzil, El, or **Al-Manzil** (both: ĕl-măn'zĭl), village, S central Jordan, on Hejaz RR and 19 mi. ESE of Kerak; barley, camel raising.

Manzovka (măn'zŭfkŭ), town (1944 pop. over 500), SW Maritime Territory, Russian SFSR, 38 mi. NNE of Voroshilov, on Trans-Siberian RR; rail junction for branches to Turi Rog (NW) and Varfolomeyevka (E).

Manzurka (mŭnzōō'r'kŭ), village (1926 pop. 2,215), SE Irkutsk oblast, Russian SFSR, on Irkutsk-Kachuga highway and 110 mi. NE of Irkutsk; agr., lumbering.

Mao (mou), town, W Chad territory, Fr. Equatorial Africa, 85 mi. WNW of Moussoro; native market for cotton, millet, camels, livestock; military outpost with fort; vegetable growing, date palms. Former ⊙ Kanem state.

Maobisse, Portuguese Timor: see MAUBISSE.

Maoemere, Indonesia: see FLORES.

Maoflang (mou'fläng), village, Khasi and Jaintia Hills dist., W Assam, India, on Shillong Plateau, on tributary of the Surma and 12 mi. SW of Shillong; rice, sesame. Coal deposits near by. Also spelled Mawphlang.

Maohsien, China: see MOWHSIEN.

Maoka, Russian SFSR: see KHOLMSK.

Maokhe (mou'khā'), town, Haiduong prov., N Vietnam, 4 mi. ESE of Dongtrieu; anthracite-mining center.

Maolang, India: see MAOLONG.

Maolong (mou'lông), village, Khasi and Jaintia Hills dist., W Assam, India, in Khasi Hills, 28 mi. SSW of Shillong; rice, cotton. Coal deposits near by. Also spelled Maolang.

Maoming, China: see MOWMING.

Maomu, China: see TINGSIN.

Maon Shan (mä'ôn' sän'), mountain of Hong Kong colony, in the New Territories; rises to 2,297 ft. 7 mi. NNE of Kowloon. Iron-ore mining.

Maopaisheng, China: see TATUNG, Tsinghai prov.

Maoz Haiyim, Ma'oz Haiyim, or **Maoz Haim** (all: mä-ōz' hī'yēm, hīm'), settlement (pop. 500), NE Israel, near the Jordan (border of kingdom of Jordan), 3 mi. E of Beisan; dairying, fish breeding; grain, vegetables. Founded 1937. Sometimes called Maoz.

Mapararí (mäpärärē'), town (pop. 1,466), Falcón state, NW Venezuela, 45 mi. SSE of Coro; coffee, cacao, corn, stock.

Mapastepec (mäpästāpĕk'), town (pop. 2,099), Chiapas, S Mexico, in Pacific lowland, on railroad and 55 mi. NW of Tapachula; cacao, tobacco, sugar cane, fruit, stock.

Mapavri, Turkey: see CAYBASI.

Mape, Lake (mä'pā), lagoon in SE Sierra Leone, on N side of Turner's Peninsula, 15 mi. SSW of Pujehun; 9 mi. long, 3 mi. wide. Formerly called L. Kasse.

Mapello (mäpĕl'lô), village (pop. 1,272), Bergamo prov., Lombardy, N Italy, 6 mi. W of Bergamo; silk mill. Sandstone quarries, near by.

Mapham Tso, Tibet: see MANASAROWAR LAKE.

Mapien (mä'byĕn'), town (pop. 7,768), ⊙ Mapien co. (pop. 36,040), SW Szechwan prov., China, near Sikang border, 65 mi. SW of Loshan; sweet potatoes, millet, beans, wheat.

Mapimí (mäpēmē'), town (pop. 2,204), Durango, N Mexico, at S edge of Bolsón de Mapimí, on railroad and 32 mi. NW of Torreón; alt. 4,485 ft.; silver, gold, lead mining.

Mapimí, Bolsón de (bōlsōn' dā), arid depression in plateau of N Mexico, in states of Chihuahua, Coahuila, and Durango, N of Mapimí (Durango). Desert region. Potentially fertile; has been irrigated in S, where cotton, wheat, alfalfa are grown. Average alt. c.3,000 ft.

Maping, China: see LIUCHOW.

Mapire (mäpē'rä), town (pop. 655), Anzoátegui state, E central Venezuela, landing on Orinoco R. (Bolívar state border) and 85 mi. WSW of Ciudad Bolívar; cattle grazing.

Mapiri (mäpē'rē), town, La Paz dept., W Bolivia, port on Mapiri R., on Sorata-Apolo road and 50 mi. NE of Sorata; tropical agr. center (cacao, sugar cane, rubber, quina).

Mapiri River, La Paz dept., W Bolivia, rises in 2 main branches (Consata and Camata rivers) in Cordillera de La Paz, flows c.40 mi. ESE past Mapiri and Guanay, joining Coroico R. at Puerto Ballivián to form KAKA RIVER. Receives Tipuani and Challana rivers near its mouth. Name sometimes applied also to Consata R. below Consata, and to Kaka R.

Maple, village (pop. estimate 400), S Ont., 15 mi. N of Toronto; dairying, truck gardening.

Maple Bluff, residential village (pop. 1,361), Dane co., S Wis., on L. Mendota, just N of Madison. Inc. 1930 as Lakewood Bluff; renamed 1931.

Maple Creek, town (pop. 1,280), SW Sask., on Maple Creek and 55 mi. ESE of Medicine Hat, at foot of the Cypress Hills; grain elevators, dairying, lumbering, stock raising.

Maplecrest, resort village, Greene co., SE N.Y., in the Catskills, 17 mi. WNW of Catskill.

Maple Grove, town (pop. 378), SW Que., on L. St. Louis, 2 mi. ENE of Beauharnois; resort.

Maple Heights, city (pop. 15,586), Cuyahoga co., N Ohio, residential suburb SE of Cleveland. Inc. as village in 1915.

Maple Hill, city (pop. 176), Wabaunsee co., NE Kansas, 18 mi. W of Topeka, in cattle, poultry, and grain area. Sometimes written Maplehill.

Maple Lake, resort village (pop. 780), Wright co., S central Minn., on small lake and c.40 mi. WNW of Minneapolis, in grain, livestock, poultry area; dairy products.

Maple Park, village (pop. 433), Kane co., NE Ill., c.45 mi. W of Chicago, in agr. area (dairy products; livestock).

Maple Plain, resort village (pop. 479), Hennepin co., E Minn., near L. Minnetonka, 20 mi. W of Minneapolis; dairying.

Maple Rapids, village (pop. 645), Clinton co., S central Mich., 27 mi. NNW of Lansing and on Maple R., in farm area.

Maple River. 1 In W Iowa, rises in Buena Vista co., flows S, past Ida Grove, and SW to Little Sioux R. 7 mi. ESE of Onawa; 90 mi. long. **2** In S central Mich., rises S of Corunna in Shiawassee co., flows NW, past Ovid and Elsie, then W and SW, past Maple Rapids, to Grand R. at Muir; c.65 mi. long. **3** In S Minn., rises in Blue Earth co., flows 40 mi. N, past Good Thunder, to Le Sueur R. 5 mi. S of Mankato. **4** In E N.Dak., largely in Cass co.; flows S to Enderlin, then NW to Sheyenne R.; 100 mi. long.

Maple Shade, village (1940 pop. 5,472), Burlington co., SW N.J., 5 mi. E of Camden; mfg. (clothing, bricks, radio parts, paper products); lumber and fur processing; truck, fruit, poultry, dairy products.

Maple Springs, resort village, Chautauqua co., extreme W N.Y., on Chautauqua L., 11 mi. NW of Jamestown.

Maplesville, town (pop. 806), Chilton co., central Ala., on Mulberry R. and 28 mi. NNE of Selma; lumber and veneer.

Mapleton. 1 Town (pop. 1,857), Monona co., W Iowa, on Maple R. and 40 mi. SE of Sioux City; rail junction; wood and dairy products. Inc. 1878. **2** City (pop. 213), Bourbon co., SE Kansas, 15 mi. NW of Fort Scott; dairying, general agr. **3** Town (pop. 1,367), Aroostook co., NE Maine, just W of Presque Isle.; mfg. (potato starch). Inc. 1880. **4** Village (pop. 1,083), Blue Earth co., S Minn., 17 mi. S of Mankato, in grain, livestock, poultry area; dairy products. Laid out and inc. 1878. **5** Town (1940 pop. 127), Hertford co., NE N.C., 4 mi. SE of Murfreesboro. **6** Village (pop. 169), Cass co., E N.Dak., 12 mi. W of Fargo and on Maple R. **7** or **Mapleton Depot,** borough (pop. 742), Huntingdon co., S central Pa., 3 mi. W of Mt. Union and on Juniata R.; glass sand. **8** Town (pop. 1,175), Utah co., central Utah, 8 mi. SE of Provo.

Mapleview, village (pop. 435), Mower co., SE Minn., on Cedar R., in grain area.

Mapleville, R.I.: see BURRILLVILLE.

Maplewood. 1 Village (pop. 2,671), Calcasieu parish, SW La., 5 mi. W of Lake Charles. **2** City (pop. 13,416), St. Louis co., E Mo., W of St. Louis. Settled c.1865, inc. 1908. **3** Village, Grafton co., N.H.: see BETHLEHEM. **4** Suburban township (pop. 25,201), Essex co., NE N.J., 6 mi. W of Newark; mfg. (metal products, golf clubs, buttons, celluloid); map publishing. Timothy Ball House (1743) visited frequently by Washington in the Revolution. Inc. 1922.

Mapocho River (mäpō'chō), Santiago prov., central Chile, rises in the Andes near Argentina border, flows 75 mi. W and S, past Las Condes, Santiago, Peñaflor, and Talagante, to Maipo R. 10 mi. E of Melipilla. Irrigates fertile central valley near Santiago. In its valley are copper and lead deposits. Its upper course (above Las Condes) is called Río del Cepo.

Mapou (mäpōō'), village (pop. 67), N Mauritius, on railroad and 6 mi. WNW of Rivière du Rempart. Administrative hq. of North Dist. Sugar milling at Labourdonnais (pop. 1,289), 1 mi. NE.

Mapperley. 1 Town and parish (pop. 435), SE Derby, England, 2 mi. W of Ilkeston; coal mining. **2** N suburb (pop. 29,767) of Nottingham, S Nottinghamshire, England; lace-mfg. center.

Mapuçá (mäpōōsä'), town (pop. 9,952), N Goa dist., Portuguese India, 6 mi. N of Pangim; trades in timber, fish, rice, copra, cashew nuts; cattle raising.

Mapulaca (mäpōōlä'kä), town (pop. 437), Lempira dept., W Honduras, near Lempa R. (Salvador border), 4 mi. SSW of Candelaria; corn, beans.

Maputo River, Mozambique: see PONGOLA RIVER.

Maqatin (măkätēn'), village, Fadhli sultanate, Western Aden Protectorate, on Gulf of Aden, 50 mi. E of Shuqra, at Lower Aulaqi border; fisheries.

Maqdaha or **Maqdahah,** Aden: see MAJDAHA.

Maqellarë (mäkyĕlä'rŭ) or **Maqellara** (mäkyĕlä'rä), village (1930 pop. 314), E central Albania, on Peshkopi-Debar road and 7 mi. SE of Peshkopi, near Gr. border; road junction.

Ma'qil (mä'kĭl), port for Basra, SE Iraq, at head of large-ship navigation on the Shatt al Arab just N of Basra, and 80 mi. from the Persian Gulf; here, too, is a rail station for Basra. Ma'qil, a modern port, was built up by the British after First World War. Sometimes spelled Magil.

Maquapit Lake (mă'kwŭpĭt") (□ 6.8; 5 mi. long, 2 mi. wide), S N.B., 20 mi. E of Fredericton and 2 mi. W of Grand L.

Maqueda Bay (mäkā'dhä), inlet (9 mi. long, 7 mi. wide) of Samar Sea, in W Samar isl., Philippines; Buad Isl. is near entrance. Wright is at head of bay, and Catbalogan near N side of entrance.

Maqueda Channel, strait in Philippines connecting Lagonoy Gulf with Philippine Sea, bet. Rungus Point of SE Luzon and Catanduanes isl.; c.5 mi. wide.

Maquela do Zombo (mŭkĕ'lŭ dōō zōm'bōō), town (pop. 1,103), ⊙ Congo dist. (pop. 203,995), Congo prov., NW Angola, near Belgian Congo border, 120 mi. S of Leopoldville; almonds, manioc, sesame; pottery mfg. Airfield.

Maqueripe Bay (mä'kŭrēp), bathing beach, NW Trinidad, B.W.I., 8 mi. NW of Port of Spain.

Maquiling, Mount, Philippines: see MAKILING, MOUNT.

Maquinchao (mäkēnchou'), village (pop. estimate 1,000), ⊙ Veinticinco (25) de Mayo dept., S Río Negro natl. territory, Argentina, 125 mi. E of San Carlos de Bariloche; sheep-raising and lead-mining center.

Maquiné, cave, Brazil: see CORDISBURGO.

Maquoit Bay (mŭkwoit'), SW Maine, 4-mi. indentation of Casco Bay, just SW of Brunswick and E of Freeport.

Maquoketa (mŭkō'kĭtŭ), city (pop. 4,307), ⊙ Jackson co., E Iowa, on Maquoketa R. near mouth of North Fork Maquoketa R., and 32 mi. S of Dubuque; mfg. (fishing tackle, loaders, saws). Ellis Mus. of Archaeology and Anthropology is here. Maquoketa Caves State Scientific Preserve is near by. Inc. 1853.

Maquoketa River, E Iowa, rises in SE Fayette co., flows c.130 mi. SE, past Manchester, Monticello, and Maquoketa, to Mississippi R. 7 mi. SE of Bellevue. Receives North Fork (c.75 mi. long) near Maquoketa.

Maquon (mŭkwän'), village (pop. 361), Knox co., W central Ill., on Spoon R. and 15 mi. SE of Galesburg, in agr. and bituminous-coal area.

Mar, Serra do (sĕ'rŭ dōō mär'), great coastal escarpment of S and SE Brazil, skirting the shoreline for over 800 mi. from Rio Grande do Sul (NE of Pôrto Alegre) to the Paraíba delta in NE Rio de Janeiro, and traversing E part of Santa Catarina, Paraná, and São Paulo states. It forms an effective barrier (average alt. 3,000 ft.) bet. the coastal strip and the interior plateau, all major streams draining westward toward the Paraná from the gentle back slope of the escarpment. It rises to 7,365 ft. (Pedra do Sino peak) in the Serra dos Orgãos, as one of its sections is called. Other components are the Serra da Estrêla, Serra do Cubatão, Serra Paranapiacaba. As a result of heavy precipitation (reaching 150 inches per year), the front range is clad with dense, subtropical vegetation. With the exception of several reentrants which surround the valleys of short coastal streams (Ribeira de Iguape, Itajaí Açu, Joinvile lowland) and a few deep inlets (Guanabara Bay, Paranaguá Bay), the escarpment closely parallels the coast and reappears offshore in the form of rocky isls.—Ilha Grande, São Sebastião, Santa Catarina. In NE, it effectively separates the Paraíba valley from the Atlantic. N of Rio, several well-known resorts—Petrópolis, Teresópolis, Nova Friburgo—have been established in the Serra do Mar because of its cooler summer temperatures. Using the sheer drop from the crest of the escarpment, Brazil's largest hydroelectric plant has been built at Cubatão, near Santos. Historically, the Serra do Mar has been a major impediment to the development of Brazil's huge interior. Most inland cities were frontier towns until railroads conquered the physical obstacle in mid-19th cent. through what often amounted to major feats of engineering, especially Santos-São Paulo RR.

Mara (mä'rä), village, Masai dist., S Kenya, on left bank of Mara R. and 55 mi. WSW of Narok; stock raising; peanuts, sesame, corn. Also called Mara Bridge. Lolgorien or Longorien goldfields (SW) were discovered 1920.

Mara (mä'rä), town (pop. 919), Apurímac dept., S central Peru, in the Andes, on affluent of Apurímac R. and 45 mi. SSW of Cuzco; cereals, sheep, cattle, horses.

Maraada, Cyrenaica: see MARADA.

Maraak, Norway: see GEIRANGER.

Marabá (mŭrŭbä'), city (pop. 2,894), SE Pará, Brazil, on left bank of Tocantins R., near Goiás and Maranhão border, and 270 mi. S of Belém; rubber, Brazil nuts. Diamonds found near by. Airfield.

Marabella (mărŭbĕ'lŭ), village (pop. 4,542, including adjoining Tarouba), W Trinidad, B.W.I., on the Gulf of Paria, on railroad and 2 mi. N of San Fernando; sugar cane, coconuts; manjak deposits. Thermal springs near by.

Marabios, Cordillera de los, or **Cordillera de los Marrabios** (kôrdĭyā'rä dā lōs märä'byōs), range of volcanic peaks in W Nicaragua; extends c.30 mi. NW from L. Managua, parallel to Pacific coast. Includes volcanoes of CHONCO, EL VIEJO, SANTA CLARA, TELICA, ROTA, CERRO NEGRO, LAS PILAS, and ASOSOSCA. Sometimes spelled Maribios.

Maracaçumé River (mŭrŭkŭsōōmĕ'), coastal stream in N Maranhão, NE Brazil, flows 100 mi. N to the Atlantic 30 mi. NNW of Turiaçu; gold washing. Large phosphorous bauxite deposits recently discovered on Trauíra isl. in river's mouth. Formerly spelled Maracassumé.

Maracaí (mŭrŭkäē'), city (pop. 1,138), W São Paulo, Brazil, 55 mi. ESE of Presidente Prudente; dairy products; lard processing, sawmilling. Formerly Maracahy.

Maracaibo (mărŭkī'bō, Sp. märäkī'bō), city (1941 pop. 112,519; 1950 census pop. 233,488), ⊙ Zulia state, NW Venezuela, port on narrows bet. L. Maracaibo and Gulf of Venezuela, 325 mi. W of Caracas; 10°38'N 71°37'W. Second largest city of Venezuela; hq. and export center for the great petroleum industry. Since sand bars block entrance to L. Maracaibo for ocean-going ships, oil is transferred here to lighters making for Willemstad (Curaçao) and Aruba in Dutch West Indies. Serves as outlet for W agr. region; ships coffee, cacao, sugar, hides, hardwood. Mfg. includes dairy products, sugar, chocolate, beer, pharmaceuticals, perfumes, soap, candles, bricks, cement, shoes, hats; sawmilling, tanning. Until development of oil industry after 1918, city was extremely unhealthful. With a mean annual temp. of 82.4°F. and excessive humidity, it is one of the hottest cities in South America. Foreign interests (British, Dutch, U.S.), in exploiting the vast petroleum resources, have made it a clean, thriving city. Airport. Has modern administrative bldgs. and fine residential sections (Bellavista, Paraíso, El Milagro) containing large foreign colonies connected with oil industry. Some old colonial edifices, a cathedral, and several churches remain, Univ. founded 1891, reopened 1946. First founded 1529 by Ger. adventurer Alfinger, but fell into decay; was refounded 1571 by Alonso Pacheco. During 17th cent. it was sacked several times, notably by English buccaneer Henry Morgan in 1669.

Maracaibo, Gulf of, Venezuela-Colombia: see VENEZUELA, GULF OF.

Maracaibo, Lake (□ c.5,000), NW Venezuela, almost entirely in Zulia state, S of Gulf of Venezuela (linked through narrows and Tablazo Bay); roughly 75 mi. wide and c.130 mi. long (S-N) from S shore to Zapara Isl. at head of Gulf of Venezuela, c.110 mi. long to Maracaibo in narrows; it is receding. Lies in extremely hot, disease-ridden lowlands of Maracaibo basin, a region which, almost enclosed by mts., is semiarid in N but has 50-in. annual rainfall in S. Although the fertile soil produces sugar cane, cacao, and a wealth of tropical hardwoods, absentee exploitation, unhealthful living, and scarce labor (drawn off by oil companies) have left the area undeveloped agriculturally. Some livestock is raised. By far the most vital activity is production of petroleum. Developed since 1918 by foreign concerns, the region is one of the greatest oil-producing localities in the world. Lake Maracaibo, with CATATUMBO RIVER, is a major artery of transportation for products of the adjacent region and those of Colombian-Venezuelan highlands. A 34-mi. channel, in places only 11 ft. deep, connecting lake with Gulf of Venezuela or Maracaibo, blocks ocean vessels, necessitating transshipment at Maracaibo. Among leading oil fields and production centers are Cabimas, San Lorenzo, Lagunillas, Bachaquero, La Rosa, Tía Juana, Campo Ambrosio. Discovered 1499 by Ojeda. Because the natives live in thatched huts on stilts above the water, the Sp. explorers, reminded of Venice, named the area Venezuela [Sp.,=little Venice].

Maracaju (mŭrŭkŭzhōō'), city (pop. 1,011), S Mato Grosso, Brazil, 85 mi. SSW of Campo Grande; cattle- and maté-shipping center at S terminus (as of 1948) of rail spur from Campo Grande projected to reach Ponta Porã. Was *de jure* ⊙ former Ponta Porã territory (1943–46).

Maracaju, Serra de (sĕ'rŭ dĭ), Sp. *Cordillera de Mbaracayú* (kôrdēyä'rä dĕmbäräkäyōō'), diabase range in Paraná and Mato Grosso, S Brazil, extending c.50 mi. E-W on either side of Guaíra Falls, where it is crossed by Paraná R. Its W part forms Brazil-Paraguay border and sends spurs into Paraguay. Continued (W) by Serra de Amambaí. Rises to c.1,500 ft.

Maracalagonis (mä"räkälägô'nēs), village (pop. 2,587), Cagliari prov., S Sardinia, 8 mi. NE of Cagliari.

Maracanã (mŏŏrŏŏkŏŏnä'), city (pop. 1,647), easternmost Pará, Brazil, near the Atlantic, 85 mi. NE of Belém; fishing, cattle raising, lumber shipping.
Maracanaú (mŏŏrŏŏkŏŏnä-ŏŏ'), town (pop. 1,187), N Ceará, Brazil, on Fortaleza-Crato RR (junction of spur to Maranguape) and 12 mi. SW of Fortaleza.
Maracanda, Uzbek SSR: see SAMARKAND, city, Samarkand oblast.
Maracás (mŏŏrŏŏkäs'), city (pop. 1,214), E central Bahia, Brazil, in the Serra do Sincorá, 40 mi. NW of Jiquié; coffeegrowing; kaolin deposits.
Maracas (mä'räkäs, mŏŏrä'kŏŏs), village (pop. 2,960), NW Trinidad, B.W.I., at S foot of El Tucuche mtn., 7 mi. E of Port of Spain. The Maracas Falls are 2 mi. N.
Maracas Bay, inlet of N Trinidad, B.W.I., towered over by the forest-clad El Tucuche mtn., 16 mi. NE of Port of Spain; resort.
Maracay (märäkī'), city (1941 pop. 32,992; 1950 census 65,761), ⊙ Aragua state, N Venezuela, near NE shore of L. Valencia, in basin of coastal range, on Pan American Highway, on railroad and 50 mi. WSW of Caracas; 10°15'N 67°36'W. Trading and industrial center in fertile country producing coffee, cacao, sugar cane, tobacco, cattle, timber. Textile and paper milling, meat canning; mfg. of dairy products, tobacco goods, soap, perfume. Has agr. school, military aviation school, large radio station. A natl. airport for hydroplanes is on adjoining lake. City was modernized by dictator Juan Vicente Gómez, who lived here.
Maracena (märäthä'nä), NW suburb (pop. 4,068) of Granada, Granada prov., S Spain, in fertile dist. yielding cereals, olive oil, sugar beets, tobacco. Large meat-processing plants.
Maracineni (mŏŏrŏŏchĕnān'), Rum. *Mărăcineni*, village (pop. 1,090), Buzau prov., SE central Rumania, on Buzau R. and 3 mi. NNW of Buzau.
Marackom, Bhutan: see MARICHONG.
Maracó, Argentina: see GENERAL PICO.
Marada (märä'dä), village, W Cyrenaica, Libya, on Tripolitania border, on road and 205 mi. SSW of Benghazi, in an oasis. Carnallite deposits discovered here in 1936. Also spelled Maraada.
Maradana (mŭrŭdä'nŭ), section (pop. 13,450) of Colombo, Western Prov., Ceylon, 2 mi. E of city center; rail junction; steel-rolling mill; shark-liver oil extraction.
Maradi (märädē'), town (pop. c.8,550), S Niger territory, Fr. West Africa, near Nigeria border, 125 mi. W of Zinder; trading, peanut-growing, and stock-raising center; also millet, manioc, corn; hides. Vegetable-oil extracting. Airfield.
Maragha, El, or **Al-Maraghah** (both: ĕl märä'gŭ), village (pop. 10,287), Girga prov., central Upper Egypt, on W bank of the Nile, on railroad, and 8 mi. SE of Tahta; cotton, cereals, dates, sugar.
Maragheh (märägĕ'), town (1940 pop. 33,335), Fourth Prov., in Azerbaijan, NW Iran, on railroad and 50 mi. S of Tabriz, and SE of L. Urmia; alt. 4,500 ft. Road and trade center on small Safi R. at SW foot of the Sahand; orchards, vineyards. Center of Azerbaijan under Arab rule; became (c.1260) residence of Hulagu, grandson of Jenghiz Khan and the 1st Ilkhan. Under his rule, Maragheh became a center of science, noted mainly because of the astronomer Nasir al-Din al-Tusi (1201–74). Remains of observatory and Hulagu's tomb are W of town. Sometimes spelled Maragha. Marble quarried at Dashkesan (20 mi. NW).
Maragogi (mŏŏrŏŏgŏŏzhē'), city (pop. 1,088), E Alagoas, NE Brazil, on the Atlantic, 55 mi. NE of Maceió; sugar, copra, fruit. Formerly spelled Maragogy.
Maragogipe (mŏŏrŏŏgŏŏzhē'pĭ), city (pop. 8,589), E Bahia, Brazil, on right bank of Paraguaçu R. at its influx into Todos os Santos Bay, and 32 mi. NW of Salvador; cigar-mfg. center. Also ships fruit, coffee. Fishing.
Maragua (märä'gwä), village, Central Prov., S central Kenya, on railroad and 7 mi. S of Fort Hall; coffee, wheat, corn.
Maraguaca, Cerro, Venezuela: see MARAHUACA, CERRO.
Marahra (mä'rŭrŭ), town (pop. 8,485), Etah dist., W Uttar Pradesh, India, 7 mi. SW of Kasganj; glass-bangle mfg.; wheat, pearl millet, barley, corn, jowar, oilseeds. Has 17th-cent. tombs, 18th-cent. mosque. Also spelled Marehra.
Marahú, Brazil: see MARAÚ.
Marahuaca, Cerro, or **Cerro Maraguaca** (both: sĕ'rō märäwä'kä), peak (8,461 ft.) in Amazonas territory, S Venezuela, just NE of Cerro Duida, 200 mi. SE of Puerto Ayacucho.
Marais (märĕ') [Fr.,=swamp], old quarter of Paris, France, on right bank of the Seine, now comprised in 3d and 4th *arrondissements*. Drained in 12th cent., it was an aristocratic residential section until 18th cent.
Marais Breton, France: see BRETON, MARAIS.
Maraisburg, U. of So. Afr.: see ROODEPOORT-MARAISBURG.
Marais des Cygnes River (mĕr' dŭ zēn, mĕ'rē dŭ sēn"), Kansas and Mo., rises NE of Emporia in Kansas, flows SE and E, past Ottawa and into Mo., joining Little Osage R. to form OSAGE RIVER SE of Rich Hill, Mo.; 140 mi. long.
Marais Poitevin, France: see POITEVIN, MARAIS.
Maraita (märī'tä), town (pop. 762), Francisco Morazán dept., S Honduras, 20 mi. SE of Tegucigalpa; corn, wheat, livestock.
Marajó (mŏŏrŭzhô'), island (□ 18,519; 1950 pop. 124,312), E Pará, Brazil, largest isl. in Amazon delta which it separates into 2 main distributaries, the Amazon proper (N), and the Pará (S); c.150 mi. long, 100 mi. wide. W part is low, swampy, intersected by numerous river channels, and has tropical rain-forest vegetation. Chief products: rubber, timber, medicinal plants. E part is somewhat higher, has healthful maritime climate and extensive grasslands where cattle and horses are raised. Chief settlements are Soure (health resort on E coast) and Arariúna. Formerly also called Joannes.
Marak, Norway: see GEIRANGER.
Marakei (märä'kā), atoll (□ 3.9; pop. 1,803), N Gilbert Isls., W central Pacific; 2°N 173°20'E; sponges.
Marakkanam, India: see MERKANAM.
Marakwet (mä'räkwĕt), town, Rift Valley prov., W Kenya, at W edge of Great Rift Valley, 38 mi. NNE of Eldoret; coffee, wheat, corn.
Marala (mŭrä'lŭ), village, Sialkot dist., E Punjab W Pakistan, near Chenab R., 12 mi. NNW of Sialkot; small market for wheat, corn, timber. Headworks of Upper Chenab Canal are just W. Sometimes spelled Merala.
Maralbashi (märälbäshē'), Chinese *Pachu* or *Pa-ch'u* (both: bä'chŏŏ'), town and oasis (pop. 86,605), SW Sinkiang prov., China, 120 mi. E of Kashgar, and on highway S of the Tien Shan; junction for road to Yarkand (S); carpet weaving; livestock, wheat. Salt and lead mines near by.
Marale (märä'lā), town (pop. 567), Francisco Morazán dept., central Honduras, 20 mi. N of Cedros; corn, wheat, coffee.
Maralik (mŭrŭlyēk'), village (1939 pop. over 500), NW Armenian SSR, at W foot of Mt. Aragats, 15 mi. S of Leninakan; wheat, livestock.
Maramarosszíget, Rumania: see SIGHET.
Marambaia Island (märămbī'ŭ), off coast of Rio de Janeiro state, Brazil, 8 mi. SSE of Mangaratiba; rises to over 2,000 ft. Fishing trade school. With the narrow, sandy tombolo (25 mi. long) linking it to mainland (25 mi. W of Rio), it encloses Sepetiba Bay.
Maramec (mâ'rŭmŭk, mă'rŭmăk), town (pop. 184), Pawnee co., N Okla., 9 mi. SE of Pawnee, in agr. area.
Maramjhiri, India: see BETUL, town.
Marampa (märäm'pä) or **Lunsar** (lŏŏnsär'), town (pop. 3,049), Northern Prov., W Sierra Leone, near Rokel R., 22 mi. ESE of Port Loko; trade center of Marampa chiefdom. Just W are important open-pit iron (hematite) mines, linked by private railroad with ocean-shipping point of Pepel (35 mi. WSW).
Maramures, region, Rumania: see CRISANA-MARAMURES.
Marana (mŭră'nŭ), village (1940 pop. 570), Pima co., S Ariz., near Santa Cruz R., 21 mi. NW of Tucson; trade center in cotton-growing area.
Maranacook, Lake (mŭrăn'ŭkŏŏk), resort lake, Kennebec co., S Maine, just N of Winthrop; 5.5 mi. long.
Maranboy, settlement (dist. pop. 47), NW central Northern Territory, Australia, 190 mi. SE of Darwin, on Darwin-Birdum RR; tin mines.
Maranchón (märänchōn'), town (pop. 1,168), Guadalajara prov., central Spain, 55 mi. NE of Guadalajara; grain growing, sheep raising; flour milling.
Marand (märänd'), town (1941 pop. 13,945), Third Prov., in Azerbaijan, NW Iran, on railroad and 35 mi. NW of Tabriz; road junction for Khoi; grain, cotton; dry fruit. Has many gardens and fruit orchards. Also spelled Merand and Merend.
Marandellas (mărŭndĕ'lŭs), town (pop. 1,205), Salisbury prov., E Southern Rhodesia, in Mashonaland, on railroad and 40 mi. SE of Salisbury; alt. 5,446 ft. Tobacco, peanuts, citrus fruit, dairy products. Police post for Marandellas dist.
Maranello (märänĕl'lô), village (pop. 829), Modena prov., Emilia-Romagna, N central Italy, 9 mi. SSW of Modena; agr. machinery. Has ruined castle.
Marang (märäng'), village (pop. 1,663), E central Trengganu, E Malaya, on South China Sea at mouth of small Marang R., 10 mi. SSE of Kuala Trengganu; coconuts; fisheries.
Maranganí (märäng-gänē'), town (pop. 595), Cuzco dept., S Peru, on Vilcanota R., on railroad and 8 mi. SSE of Sicuani; alt. 11,532 ft. Grain, potatoes; mfg. of woolen goods.
Maranguape (mŏŏrăng-gwä'pĭ), city (pop. 4,755), N Ceará, Brazil, on rail spur, and 15 mi. SW of Fortaleza; hill resort; ships coffee, sugar, cotton, and fruit to Fortaleza. Carnauba-wax mill.
Maranhão (mŏŏrŭnyä'ō), state (□ 129,270; 1940 pop. 1,235,169; 1950 census 1,600,396), NE Brazil; ⊙ São Luís. Bounded by the Atlantic (N), and the states of Pará (W), Goiás (SW), Piauí (E and SE). Situated on low coastal plain, it has monotonously high temperatures, heavy precipitation, and a tropical rain forest and savanna vegetation characterized by an abundance of babassu palms, which furnish an important source of income. In S, higher ground and outliers of Brazil's NE highlands have more salubrious climate, short-grass cover, and extensive cattle-grazing areas. Fertile valleys of the S-to-N-flowing streams (Pindaré, Grajaú, Mearim, Itapecuru, Parnaíba) support intensive agr. (cotton, sugar, rice, tobacco, grain). Alluvial gold deposits in Turiaçu and Gurupi river channels. Important phosphorous bauxite deposits recently discovered near mouth of Maracaçumé R. State is served by São Luís–Teresina RR, inadequate highway system, river navigation, and air transport. Pop. is concentrated in coastal area, especially on São Luís Isl. and along São Marcos and São José bays, and in river valleys (chiefly along Itapecuru R. section followed by railroad). Chief towns are São Luís (state's only good port; commercial and cotton-milling center), Caxias, Codó, and Coroatá (on railroad), and Carolina (on Tocantins R.). Chief industries are babassu processing (for export purposes), cotton and sugar milling, and distilling. São Luís Isl. was 1st occupied by the French, who founded (1612) city of São Luís, but were displaced by the Portuguese in 1615. In 1621, Maranhão, then embracing all known land N and W of Ceará, became one of two states (the other called Brazil) which constituted Port. holdings in South America. This colonial state was later (18th cent.) broken up into captaincies. Maranhão became a prov. (early 19th cent.) when Brazil assumed its independence, and, in 1889, one of the states of the federal republic. City of São Luís was formerly often called Maranhão.
Marano di Napoli (märä'nô dē nä'pôlē), town (pop. 10,001), Napoli prov., Campania, S Italy, 5 mi. NW of Naples, in wine- and fruitgrowing region.
Marañón, province, Peru: see HUACRACHUCO.
Marañón River (märänyōn'), one of the Amazon's main headstreams in Peru, rises in the Andes from a series of small lakes which have alternatively been called the source of the Amazon, among them L. Lauricocha, c.35 mi. WNW of Cerro de Pasco and 85 mi. E of the Pacific coast; flows NNW along high Andean ranges, almost reaching Ecuador border; turns NE to break through famous Pongo de Manseriche gorge into Amazon basin, flowing E, past Barranca and Nauta, to join the Ucayali in forming the Amazon 55 mi. SSW of Iquitos at 4°30'S 73°27'W. Its estimated length is c.1,000 mi. Main affluents are: left, Santiago, Morona, Pastaza, Tigre; right, Huallaga. Navigable for larger craft to Pongo de Manseriche. First of the Spaniards to descend the Marañón was Ursúa, in 1560. Sometimes the Marañón is considered to extend beyond the junction with the Ucayali to Iquitos, or to the mouth of the Napo just below Iquitos, before it becomes the Amazon.
Marano sul Panaro (märä'nô sŏŏl pänä'rô), village (pop. 844). Modena prov., Emilia-Romagna, N central Italy, on Panaro R. and 13 mi. S of Modena; lime- and cementworks.
Marano Vicentino (vēchĕntē'nô), village (pop. 2,390), Vicenza prov., Veneto, N Italy, 12 mi. NNW of Vicenza; foundries, machine shops, woolen mill.
Marans (märä'), town (pop. 2,522), Charente-Maritime dept., W France, in Marais Poitevin, port on the Sèvre Niortaise connected by canal with La Rochelle (12 mi. SW); grain and cattle market; mfg. (cement, fertilizer, artificial feed). Surrounding marshland (□ 150), reclaimed since 17th cent., now agr.
Maransart (märäsär'), village (pop. 407), Brabant prov., central Belgium, 5 mi. ESE of Braine-l'-Alleud; artificial silk.
Marão, Serro do (sĕ'rŭ dŏŏ mŭrā'ō), short range in N Portugal, N of Douro R. and just WSW of Vila Real; rises to 4,642 ft. Vineyards on S slope.
Marapanim (mŏŏrŭpä'nēn), city (pop. 1,645), easternmost Pará, Brazil, on the Atlantic and 80 mi. NE of Belém; fishing, lumbering.
Marapa River (märä'pä), S Tucumán prov., Argentina, rises in S outliers of Nevado del Aconquija, flows E 110 mi., past Graneros and La Madrid, and joins the Río Chico to form the Río Hondo, which enters the Salí (upper course of the Río Dulce). Irrigates sugar-cane area; dam at Escaba.
Marapi, Mount, or **Mount Merapi** (both: mŭrä'pē), volcanic peak (9,485 ft.), W central Sumatra, Indonesia, in Padang Highlands of Barisan Mts., 40 mi. NNE of Padang.
Mara River (mä'rä), N Tanganyika, rises in SW Kenya, in Mau Escarpment SE of Londiani, flows 160 mi. S and W to L. Victoria at Musoma.
Maras (mä'räs), town (pop. 2,464), Cuzco dept., S central Peru, 22 mi. NW of Cuzco, in agr. region (cereals, vegetables); salt, gypsum, marble deposits.
Maras (märäsh'), Turkish *Maraş*, prov. (□ 5,827; 1950 pop. 288,631), S central Turkey; ⊙ Maras. Bordered NW by Binboga Mts.; drained by Ceyhan R. Wheat, rice, legumes. Sometimes spelled Marash.
Maras, Turkish *Maraş*, city (1950 pop. 35,071), ⊙ Maras, S central Turkey, 100 mi. ENE of Adana, 80 mi. NNE of port of Iskenderun, in Taurus Mts. on a height overlooking Ceyhan R.; 37°34'N 36°55'E. Its rice factory mills local crop; agr. trade center (wheat, legumes, cotton). Inscriptions here indicate it may have been an anc. Hittite city;

held for several centuries by Turks, briefly (1097) by Crusaders, and (1832) by Egyptians. Large Armenian pop. Sometimes spelled Marash.

Marasa, Wadi Marasa, or **Wadi Marasah** (wă'dē mä'räsŭ), village, ⊙ Makhdumi sheikdom, Subeihi tribal area, Western Aden Protectorate, 26 mi. WNW of Lahej. Also called Dar Murshid.

Marasalcakmak, Turkey: see OVACIK.

Marasesti (mŭrŭshĕsht'), Rum. *Mărăşeşti,* town (1948 pop. 4,940), Putna prov., E Rumania, 12 mi. N of Focsani; important rail junction; chemical works (glue, gelatin, sulphuric and hydrochloric acids). Rumanian army here repulsed (1917) a great German offensive under Mackensen.

Marash, Turkey: see MARAS.

Maratea (märätā'ä), village (pop. 1,358), Potenza prov., Basilicata, S Italy, on Gulf of Policastro, 7 mi. SE of Sapri; bathing resort; olive oil, cheese, rope.

Marathokambos (märŭthô'kŭmbôs), town (pop. 3,-595), on W Samos isl., Greece, 20 mi. W of Limen Vatheos; wine, olive oil, tobacco.

Marathon (mă'rŭ-thŏn"), formerly **Peninsula,** town (pop. estimate 3,500), central Ont., on L. Superior, 130 mi. E of Port Arthur; gold mining. Airport, radio station.

Marathon, village (pop. 2,515), Attica nome, E central Greece, near Gulf of Marathon (inlet of Gulf of Petalion), 17 mi. NNE of Athens; wheat, wine, olive oil; sheep and goat raising. Just W is L. Marathon, chief water reservoir supplying Athens and Piraeus. In plain of Marathon (SE), Athenians under Miltiades defeated Persians under Darius I in 490 B.C. Ruins of tombs of Athenian warriors are in SW portion of plain. The Marathon race, an event in Olympic games since 1896, commemorates the feat of the runner who carried the news of victory to Athens.

Marathon, county (□ 1,592; pop. 80,337), central Wis.; ⊙ Wausau. Drained by Wisconsin R. and its tributaries (Eau Claire and Eau Pleine); contains Rib Mtn. (1,940 ft.) and Big Eau Pleine Reservoir. Primarily a dairying area, co. is a major producer of cheese; lumbering and stock raising are secondary industries. Diversified mfg. at Wausau. Rib Mountain State Park is popular center for winter sports. Formed 1850.

Marathon. 1 Village, Fla.: see FLORIDA KEYS. **2** Town (pop. 565), Buena Vista co., NW Iowa, near source of Raccoon R., 18 mi. NE of Storm Lake, in livestock and grain area. **3** Village (pop. 1,057), Cortland co., central N.Y., on Tioughnioga R. and 25 mi. NNW of Binghamton; mfg. (clothing, sporting goods, machinery, wood products). Agr. (dairy products; poultry, potatoes). **4** Village (1940 pop. 802), Brewster co., extreme W Texas, 28 mi. SE of Alpine; alt. c.4,000 ft. Trading center in ranch region (sheep, cattle, goats). Hq. for Big Bend Natl. Park (c.35 mi. S). **5** Village (pop. 853), Marathon co., central Wis., on Rib R. and 10 mi. W of Wausau, in dairying and lumbering area; cheese, evaporated milk, lumber, beer.

Marathonisi (märŭthônē'sē), islet in Gulf of Laconia, S Peloponnesus, Greece. Located in GYTHEION town, which for a time was also known as Marathonisi, it is the supposed Cranae of anc. Greece, where Paris brought Helen after her abduction.

Marathonisi, Gulf of, Greece: see LACONIA, GULF OF.

Marathovouno (märäthô'vōōnō), village (pop. 1,-788), Famagusta dist., E Cyprus, 15 mi. ENE of Nicosia; wheat, vetches, barley, oats; sheep, cattle.

Marathus, Syria: see AMRIT.

Marathwara (mŭrät'wŭrŭ), W division (□ 41,196; pop. 7,626,768) of Hyderabad state, India. Comprises dists. of Aurangabad, Bidar, Bir, Gulbarga, Nander, Osmanabad, Parbhani, and Raichur.

Maraú (mŭräōō'), city (pop. 868), E Bahia, Brazil, on the Atlantic, 50 mi. N of Ilhéus; oil-shale and asphalt deposits. Formerly spelled Marahú.

Maraua (märä'wä), town (pop. 1,000), W Cyrenaica, Libya, 30 mi. E of Barce, on the plateau Gebel el Akhdar; road junction. Scene of fighting (1942) bet. Germans and British in Second World War.

Maraussan (märōsã'), village (pop. 1,461), Hérault dept., S France, 3 mi. NW of Béziers; white wines.

Maraval (märŭväl'), N residential suburb (pop. 3,-291) of Port of Spain, N Trinidad, B.W.I.; resort.

Maravatío (märävätē'ō). **1** or **Santiago Maravatío** (säntyä'gō), town (pop. 2,226), Guanajuato, central Mexico, 29 mi. SSW of Celaya; alt. 5,715 ft.; grain, beans, alfalfa, livestock. **2** Town (pop. 4,147), Michoacán, central Mexico, on central plateau, 45 mi. ENE of Morelia; alt. 6,604 ft. Rail junction; processing and agr. center (cereals, fruit, vegetables, livestock); flour milling, tanning, lumbering; mfg. (shoes, textiles). Airfield.

Maravilla, Lake, Chile: see TORO, LAKE.

Maravillas (märävē'yäs), village, Pando dept., NW Bolivia, near Madre de Dios R., 50 mi. ESE of Puerto Rico; rubber. Also called Maravilla.

Mara Vista, Mass.: see FALMOUTH.

Marayes (märī'ĕs), village (pop. estimate 500), SE San Juan prov., Argentina, at S foot of Sierra de la Huerta, on railroad and 70 mi. ENE of San Juan; mining center (coal, lead, gold).

Marazion (mărŭzī'ŭn), village and parish (pop. 1,126), W Cornwall, England, on Mounts Bay of the Channel and 3 mi. E of Penzance; fishing port and tourist resort for SAINT MICHAEL'S MOUNT, near by.

Marazy (mŭrä'zē), village (1948 pop. over 2,000), E Azerbaijan SSR, at SE end of the Greater Caucasus, on road and 50 mi. W of Baku; livestock.

Marbach or **Marbach am Neckar** (mär'bäkh äm nĕ'kär), town (pop. 5,463), N Württemberg, Germany, after 1945 in Württemberg-Baden, on the Neckar and 4 mi. NE of Ludwigsburg; rail junction; wine. Has 15th-cent. church; small local mus. Schiller b. here.

Marbache (märbäsh'), village (pop. 1,360), Meurthe-et-Moselle dept., NE France, on left bank of the Moselle and 8 mi. NNW of Nancy; iron mining.

Marbacka (mōr'bä"kä), Swedish *Mårbacka,* village, Varmland co., W Sweden, on L. Fryk, 25 mi. NW of Karlstad. Here was residence of Selma Lagerlof.

Marbais (märbā'), village (pop. 2,063), Brabant prov., S central Belgium, 10 mi. ESE of Nivelles; fruit, cattle market.

Marbán, Bolivia: see LORETO.

Marbat, Oman: see MURBAT.

Marbehan (märbŭã'), town, Luxembourg prov., SE Belgium, in the Ardennes, 13 mi. WNW of Arlon; rail junction; mfg. of wood chemicals (acetates, creosote). Just E is commune center of Rulles (pop. 1,364).

Marbella (märvĕ'lyä), city (pop. 4,965), Málaga prov., S Spain, minor Mediterranean port, backed by a spur of the Cordillera Penibética, halfway bet. Gibraltar and Málaga, 30 mi. SW of Málaga, in fertile coastal strip. Exports sugar cane, grapes, wine, oranges, olive oil, cork, carob beans; also iron and lead ore (galena) from mines 2 mi. N (linked by narrow-gauge railroad). Has processing plants and fisheries. The San Pedro Alcántara sugar refinery is 6 mi. WSW.

Marbial Valley (märbyäl'), Ouest dept., S Haiti, rural region just N of Jacmel, chosen (1948) by UNESCO for campaign against illiteracy. Community center.

Marble. 1 Town (1940 pop. 240; 1950 pop. 8), Gunnison co., W central Colo., on Crystal R., in foothills of Elk Mts., and 40 mi. NNW of Gunnison; alt. 7,800 ft. Quarries produce high-grade marble. **2** Village (pop. 867), Itasca co., N central Minn., on Mesabi iron range, 14 mi. ENE of Grand Rapids. Open-pit iron mines near by. Swan L. 5 mi. E. **3** Town (1940 pop. 356), Cherokee co., extreme W N.C., 8 mi. NE of Murphy; marble quarrying; large dahlia farm near by.

Marble Arch, Libya: see MUGTAA, EL.

Marble Bar, town (pop. 224), N Western Australia, 90 mi. SE of Port Hedland; terminus of railroad from Port Hedland; mining center of Pilbara Goldfield; quartz, granite.

Marble City, town (pop. 285), Sequoyah co., E Okla., 33 mi. ESE of Muskogee, in agr. area. Crystal Caves are near by.

Marble Cliff, village (pop. 437), Franklin co., central Ohio, just W of Columbus; limestone quarry.

Marble Falls, town (pop. 2,044), Burnet co., central Texas, on Colorado R. (bridged) and 39 mi. NW of Austin; granite quarries. Settled 1887, inc. 1908.

Marble Gorge, canyon in Coconino co., N Ariz., extends c.60 mi. S along Colorado R. from mouth of Paria R., near Utah line, to mouth of Little Colorado R., at E end of Grand Canyon Natl. Park. Also known as Marble Canyon. Sometimes defined as upper part of Grand Canyon.

Marble Hall, town (pop. 1,790), central Transvaal, U. of So. Afr., 90 mi. NE of Pretoria; rail terminus; marble-quarrying center.

Marblehead. 1 Town (pop. 13,765), Essex co., NE Mass., on Massachusetts Bay and 15 mi. NE of Boston, on rocky peninsula with narrow, deep harbor sheltered by Marblehead Neck, rocky promontory c.1½ mi. long. Long an important fishing port; became a resort in 19th cent.; famous as a yachting center. Produces shoes, isinglass, paint; boatbuilding. Has many 18th-cent. buildings. Settled 1629, set off from Salem 1633. Includes village of Clifton (1940 pop. 2,920). **2** Village (pop. 867), Ottawa co., N Ohio, 6 mi. N of Sandusky, at tip of Marblehead Peninsula, which extends c.15 mi. E into L. Erie and shelters Sandusky Bay on N; resort, fishing center; has lighthouse. Limestone quarries; fruit orchards.

Marble Hill. 1 Town (pop. 454), ⊙ Bollinger co., SE Mo., 24 mi. W of Cape Girardeau; corn, wheat. **2** A residential district of Manhattan borough of New York city, SE N.Y., across Harlem R. from Manhattan Isl. and surrounded W, N, and E by the Bronx.

Marble Rock, town (pop. 470), Floyd co., N Iowa, on Shell Rock R. and 11 mi. WSW of Charles City, in livestock area; limestone quarries.

Marble Rocks, gorge of Narbada R., N Madhya Pradesh, India, WSW of Jubbulpore; c.2 mi. long; lies bet. magnesian limestone cliffs which rise to over 100 ft. (several inscriptions and sculptures date from 12th cent.). Near-by 12th-cent. Hindu temple is scene of annual pilgrimage. Steatite quarries in vicinity. Sometimes called Bheraghat.

Marbleton, town (pop. 20), Sublette co., W Wyo., near Green R., 24 mi. S of Pinedale; alt. 6,850 ft.

Marburg (mär'bûrg, Ger. mär'bŏŏrk) or **Marburg an der Lahn** (än dĕr län'), city (1950 pop. 39,256), in former Prussian prov. of Hesse-Nassau, W Germany, after 1945 in Hesse, picturesquely situated on the Lahn and 47 mi. N of Frankfurt; 50°48'N 8°46'E. Tourist center with noted Protestant univ. (founded 1527). Mfg. of basic and commercial chemicals, machinery, precision instruments, leather goods); pottery works. Gothic church of St. Elizabeth contains tomb of the saint and (since 1946) the remains of Frederick William I, Frederick the Great, and Hindenburg. Knights' Hall of 13th–15th-cent. castle was scene (1529) of religious disputation bet. Luther and Zwingli. Marburg developed in 12th cent. around a Thuringian border fortress. Was a residence of Hessian rulers from 13th to 17th cent. Part (1567–1604) of independent Hessen-Marburg, which was then divided bet. HESSE-DARMSTADT and HESSE-KASSEL. Captured by U.S. troops in spring, 1945.

Marburg, Yugoslavia: see MARIBOR.

Marbury (mär'bĕ"rē), village (1940 pop. 634), Charles co., S Md., near Mattawoman Creek, 24 mi. SSW of Washington, in agr. area. Near by is Doncaster State Forest.

Marca (mär'kä), city (pop. 716), Ancash dept., W central Peru, in Cordillera Negra of the Andes, 40 mi. S of Huarás; grain, alfalfa; sheep raising.

Marcaconga (märkäkōng'gä), town (pop. 1,377), Cuzco dept., S Peru, in the Andes, 40 mi. SE of Cuzco; grain, potatoes, fruit.

Marcala (märkä'lä), city (pop. 1,611), La Paz dept., SW Honduras, on continental divide, in Sierra de Guajiquiro, 50 mi. W of Tegucigalpa, 25 mi. ESE of La Esperanza (linked by road); alt. 4,167 ft. Commercial center; coffee, wheat.

Marcali (mŏr'tsŏlē), town (pop. 6,649), Somogy co., SW Hungary, 22 mi. NE of Nagykanizsa; market center; leather goods, bricks. Before 1918, Marczali.

Marcapata (märkäpä'tä), town (pop. 385), Cuzco dept., S central Peru, in Cordillera de Carabaya, 75 mi. E of Cuzco, in agr. region (potatoes, wheat, coca, coffee); gold washing; alt. 10,866 ft. Has thermal springs.

Marcaria (märkärē'ä), village (pop. 1,065), Mantova prov., Lombardy, N Italy, on Oglio R. and 13 mi. WSW of Mantua. Peat digging near by.

Marcelcave (märsĕlkäv'), village (pop. 880), Somme dept., N France, 13 mi. ESE of Amiens; hosiery mfg. Scene of fighting, 1918, in First World War.

Marcelin (märs'lĭn), village (pop. 254), central Sask., 45 mi. WSW of Prince Albert; mixed farming, dairying.

Marceline (märsŭlēn'), city (pop. 3,172), Linn co., N central Mo., 8 mi. SE of Brookfield; shipping center in grain, livestock (especially dairy), coal area. Platted 1887.

Marcelino Ramos (mŭrsēlē'nōō rä'mōōs), city (pop. 2,286), N Rio Grande do Sul, Brazil, on Uruguay R. (Santa Catarina border) at mouth of Peixe R., on railroad and 30 mi. NE of Erechim; growing industrial center (meat processing, lumbering).

Marcelino Ugarte, Argentina: see SALTO.

Marcellina, Mount (märsŭlē'nŭ,–lī'nŭ), peak (11,349 ft.) in Rocky Mts., Gunnison co., W Colo.

Marcellinara (märchĕl-lēnä'rä), village (pop. 1,707), Catanzaro prov., Calabria, S Italy, 6 mi. WNW of Catanzaro; cementworks. Gypsum quarries.

Marcellus. 1 Village (pop. 1,014), Cass co., SW Mich., 22 mi. SSW of Kalamazoo, in farm and lake-resort area. Inc. 1879. **2** Village (pop. 1,382), Onondaga co., central N.Y., 10 mi. WSW of Syracuse; mfg. (textiles, paper, confectionery, canned foods, feed). Agr. (dairy products; poultry, fruit). Inc. 1846.

Marcenat (märsŭnä'), village (pop. 1,195), Cantal dept., S central France, in Monts du Cézallier, 22 mi. NE of Saint-Flour; cattle market; linen trade.

March, urban district (1931 pop. 11,266; 1951 census 12,993), ⊙ Isle of Ely, N Cambridge, England, on Nene R. and 13 mi. NW of Ely; agr. market, with agr.-machinery works; railroad junction. Has 14th-cent. church of St. Wendreda.

March (märkh), village (pop. 1,340), Lower Bavaria, Germany, in Bohemian Forest, 8 mi. SW of Zwiesel; quartz quarries.

March (märkh), lowland on SE shore of L. of Zurich, NE central Switzerland; Siebnen and Lachen are on it.

March Air Force Base, Calif.: see RIVERSIDE, city.

Marchamalo (märchämä'lō), town (pop. 1,555), Guadalajara prov., central Spain, 3½ mi. NW of Guadalajara across the Henares; cereals, olives, vegetables, truck produce, livestock.

Marchand (märshã'), village, S Que., on St. Maurice R. and 10 mi. NW of Trois Rivières; ochre and iron-oxide mining.

Marchand, town (pop. 1,731), Rabat region, NW Fr. Morocco, 36 mi. SSE of Rabat; stock raising, lumbering, cork gathering.

Marchaux (märshō'), agr. village (pop. 217), Doubs dept., E France, 8 mi. NE of Besançon.

Marche or **Marche-en-Famenne** (märsh-ã-fämĕn'), town (pop. 4,208), Luxembourg prov., SE central Belgium, 20 mi. E of Dinant; agr. and pig market. Perpetual Edict bet. Holy Roman Empire and states of United Netherlands signed here (1577).

Marche (märsh), region and former province of central France, now comprised in Creuse and part of Haute-Vienne depts.; ⊙ Guéret. Crossed by W ranges of the Massif Central, with extensive tablelands where cattle and sheep are raised. Chief towns are Guéret and Aubusson (carpet mfg.). In 10th cent. Marche was a border dist. of duchy of Aquitaine. Later held by counts of Limousin; seized (14th cent.) by Philip IV of France. Given in appanage to various Valois and Bourbon princes; reunited with crown (1527) by Francis I. Broken up into present depts. in 1790.

Marche, Monts de la (mõ dů lä märsh′), highlands of the Massif Central, central France, extending c.50 mi. E–W across Creuse and Haute-Vienne depts. Average alt. 1,800 ft. Bounded by Monts du Limousin (S), Auvergne Mts. (SE), and Paris Basin (N). Crossed by Creuse and Cher river valleys. Extensive grazing.

Marchegg (märkh′ěk), village (pop. 2,206), E Lower Austria, on Czechoslovak border, on March R. and 28 mi. ENE of Vienna. Founded 13th cent., by Ottocar II of Bohemia, as border fortress.

Marche-les-Dames (märsh-lā-däm′), village (pop. 1,153), Namur prov., S central Belgium, on Meuse R. and 4 mi. E of Namur; chalk quarrying; limekilns. Ruins of 12th-cent. Cistercian nunnery, 14th-cent. church.

Marchena (märchā′nä), town (pop. 15,902), Seville prov., SW Spain, near the Guadalquivir, 31 mi. E of Seville; rail junction, processing and trading center in agr. region (cereals, olives, cotton, grapes, melons, livestock). Sawmilling, meat processing, olive-oil pressing, liquor distilling; clay and sand quarrying. Old historic town with remains of a wall; also has San Juan church, and palace belonging to dukes of Arcos. Mineral springs near by.

Marchena Island or **Bindloe Island** (bĭnd′lō) (□ 45), N Galapagos Isls., Ecuador, in the Pacific, 100 mi. NW of Puerto Baquerizo; 0°20′N 90°30′W.

Marchenoir (märshnwär′), village (pop. 503), Loir-et-Cher dept., N central France, 15 mi. E of Vendôme; sawmilling.

Marches, The, Ital. *Marche* (mär′kě), region (□ 3,744; pop. 1,278,071), central Italy; ⊙ Ancona. Bordered by Emilia-Romagna (N), Abruzzi e Molise (S), Adriatic Sea (E), and Umbria (W). Comprises 4 provs.: ANCONA, ASCOLI PICENO, MACERATA, PESARO E URBINO. Crossed by the Apennines; mtn. and hill terrain, with many valleys and a narrow coastal plain. Area c.15% forested. Watered by Chienti, Esino, Foglia, Metauro, Potenza, Tenna, and Tronto rivers, flowing from the Apennines to the Adriatic. Chiefly agr. (wheat, grapes, corn, fodder, olives, raw silk, fruit, vegetables). Stock raising (cattle, sheep, swine) widespread. Fishing (San Benedetto del Tronto); forestry; sulphur mining (Ancona and Pesaro e Urbino provs.). Chief industries include paper (Fabriano, Tolentino, Ascoli Piceno), shipbuilding (Ancona), furniture, railroad cars (Porto Civitanova), majolica (Pesaro, Urbino, Recanati), textiles (Iesi, Fossombrone), and hydroelectric power (Tronto R.). Conquered by Romans in 3rd cent. B.C.; later (6th cent.) N section ruled by Byzantines. Papal control, nominal in 8th cent., became firmly established in 16th cent. and continued until 1860, with exception of Fr. occupation (1797–1815).

Marchéville-en-Woëvre (märshāvēl′-ā-vōĕ′vrů), village (pop. 74), Meuse dept., NE France, 14 mi. ESE of Verdun; strongly defended Ger. position after retreat from Saint-Mihiel (1918) in First World War.

Marchfeld (märkh′fĕlt), plain in E Lower Austria, extending N of the Danube, bet. Vienna and Czechoslovak border. Scene of many battles.

Mar Chica (mär′chē′kä), coastal lagoon in E Sp. Morocco, separated by narrow sand bar from the open Mediterranean; 15 mi. long, 4 mi. wide, up to 25 ft. deep. Villa Nador is on W shore. Medilla's seaplane base is at N end.

Marchienne-au-Pont (märshyĕn-ō-pō′), town (pop. 22,275), Hainaut prov., S central Belgium, on Sambre R. and 3 mi. WSW of Charleroi; coal mines; coke ovens, blast furnaces; mfg. (ceramics, furniture).

Marchiennes (märshyĕn′), town (pop. 2,569), Nord dept., N France, port on the Scarpe and 9 mi. ENE of Douai; market for truck produce. Also called Marchiennes-Ville.

Marchigüe or **Marchihüe** (both: märchē′wā), village (1930 pop. 562), Colchagua prov., central Chile, on railroad and 35 mi. WNW of San Fernando, in agr. area (grain, potatoes, beans, tobacco, livestock).

Marchin (märshē′), town (pop. 4,612), Liége prov., E central Belgium, 4 mi. S of Huy; steel-rolling mills.

Mar Chiquita, district, Buenos Aires prov., Argentina: see CORONEL VIDAL.

Mar Chiquita (mär′ chēkē′tä). **1** Salt lake (□ 10) in N Buenos Aires prov., Argentina, on the upper Río Salado bet. Arenales and Junín; 10 mi. long, 2 mi. wide. **2** Lagoon (□ 18) in SE Buenos Aires prov., Argentina, 25 mi. NNE of Mar del Plata, connected with Atlantic Ocean; extends 15 mi. NE–SW. Resort area. **3** Salt lake (□ 580) in NE Córdoba prov., Argentina, in swampy region, 90 mi. NE of Córdoba; c.45 mi. long, 15 mi. wide. Receives the Río Primero (SW), Río Segundo (SE), and Río Dulce (N); has no outlet. Adjoining it (N) are the Porongos salt lakes. Contains sodium, calcium, and magnesium salts. Resort at Miramar, on S shore. Has group of islets, the largest El Médano.

March River, Czechoslovakia: see MORAVA RIVER.

Marchtrenk (märkh′trĕngk), town (pop. 2,866), E central Upper Austria, near Traun R., 4 mi. NE of Wels; artificial wool.

Marciac (märsyäk′), village (pop. 911), Gers dept., SW France, 12 mi. W of Mirande; cereals, wines.

Marciana (märchä′nä), village (pop. 362), on isl. of Elba, Livorno prov., central Italy, 8 mi. WSW of Portoferraio. Summer resort (alt. 1,230 ft.) amid fine chestnut woods. Has medieval fortifications. On the coast, 2 mi. NE, is port of Marciana Marina (pop. 1,274).

Marcianise (märchänē′zě), town (pop. 17,757), Caserta prov., Campania, S Italy, 3 mi. SSW of Caserta; agr. center (fruit, vegetables), wine.

Marcianopolis, Bulgaria: see REKA DEVNYA.

Marcigny (märsēnyē′), town (pop. 2,015), Saône-et-Loire dept., E central France, near Loire R., 16 mi. N of Roanne; important cattle market. Pottery.

Marcilla (märthē′lyä), town (pop. 1,708), Navarre prov., N Spain, near Aragon R., 20 mi. NNW of Tudela; sugar mills. Medieval castle near by.

Marcillac-Vallon (märsēyäk′-välō′), village (pop. 823), Aveyron dept., S France, 10 mi. NNW of Rodez; fruitgrowing.

Marcillat (märsēyä′), village (pop. 585), Allier dept., central France, in Combrailles, 12 mi. S of Montluçon; livestock market; limekilns.

Marcilly-le-Hayer (märsēyē′-lů-äyā′), agr. village (pop. 302), Aube dept., NE central France, 22 mi. WNW of Troyes.

Marcinelle (märsēnĕl′), town (pop. 23,887), Hainaut prov., S central Belgium, just S of Charleroi, near Sambre R.; coal mines; coke plants, blast furnaces.

Marcke, Belgium: see MARKE.

Marckolsheim (märkôlzĕm′), Ger. *Markolsheim* (mär′kôls-hīm), agr. village (pop. 1,520), Bas-Rhin dept., E France, in Alsatian lowland, on Rhone-Rhine Canal, 8 mi. SE of Sélestat; quarrying.

Marco (mär′kōō), town (pop. 1,653), N Ceará, Brazil, 12 mi. SW of Acaraú.

Marco, Fla.: see GOODLAND.

Marco de Canaveses (mär′kōō dĭ kůnůvā′zĭsh), town, Pôrto dist., N Portugal, on Tâmega R., on railroad and 23 mi. E of Oporto; watering place with mineral springs; paper milling.

Marcoing (märkwē′), village (pop. 1,585), Nord dept., N France, on the Escaut, on Saint-Quentin Canal, 4 mi. SSW of Cambrai, in sugar-beet dist.

Marco Island, Fla.: see GOODLAND.

Marcona (märkō′nä), iron-mining settlement, Ica dept., SW Peru, 15 mi. ENE of San Nicolás (on the Pacific); iron ore is shipped to Huachipato plant, San Vicente, Chile.

Marconi, Mount (märkō′nē) (10,190 ft.), SE B.C., near Alta. border, in Rocky Mts., 60 mi. N of Fernie; 50°23′N 115°7′W.

Marco Polo Bridge, China: see WANPING.

Marcos Juárez (mär′kōs hwä′rěs), town (pop. 9,447), ⊙ Marcos Juárez dept. (□ c.3,900; pop. 90,363), E Córdoba prov., Argentina, 70 mi. ESE of Villa María; agr. center (wheat, corn, flax, livestock) with tanneries, flour mills. Formerly Espinillos.

Marcos Paz (mär′kōs päs′), town (pop. 4,230), ⊙ Marcos Paz dist. (□ 168; pop. 8,109), NE Buenos Aires prov., Argentina, 27 mi. WSW of Buenos Aires; rail junction and agr. center (grain, alfalfa, livestock); dairying.

Marcourt (märkōōr′), village (pop. 657), Luxembourg prov., SE Belgium, on Ourthe R. and 8 mi. E of Marche; agr., lumbering.

Marcovia (märkō′vyä), town (pop. 565), Choluteca dept., S Honduras, on Choluteca R. and 7 mi. W of Choluteca; sawmilling, hardwood lumbering. Saltworks on near-by coast of Gulf of Fonseca.

Marcq-en-Baroeul (märk-ā-bärůl′), town (pop. 21,477), Nord dept., N France, 4 mi. NNE of Lille; textile-milling center in densely populated Lille-Roubaix-Tourcoing urban complex. Blast furnaces, forges.

Marcus. 1 Town (pop. 1,263), Cherokee co., NW Iowa, 14 mi. WNW of Cherokee; feed. Inc. 1892. **2** City (pop. 149), Stevens co., NE Wash., 11 mi. NW of Colville and on Roosevelt L., at mouth of Kettle R. City moved (1941) from site c.1.5 mi. S, now covered by reservoir.

Marcus Baker, Mount (13,250 ft.), S Alaska, in Chugach Mts. 55 mi. WNW of Valdez; 61°26′N 147°46′W.

Marcus Hook, borough (pop. 3,843), Delaware co., SE Pa., 2 mi. SW of Chester and on Delaware R.; oil refining, mfg. (textiles, rugs). Early 18th-cent. pirate rendezvous. Settled c.1640 by Swedes, laid out c.1701, inc. 1893.

Marcus Island, Jap. *Minami-tori-shima,* volcanic island (□ 1), W Pacific, 700 naut. mi. E of Bonin Isls.; 26°32′N 142°10′E; c.2 mi. long; rises to 204 ft. Phosphate deposits. Discovered 1896 by Japanese; annexed 1899 by Japan. In Second World War, site of Jap. naval and air bases; after Japan's defeat, placed under U.S. military govt.

Marcy, Mount (5,344 ft.), NE N.Y., highest peak of the Adirondacks and of N.Y. state, c.12 mi. SSE of Lake Placid village. Small L. Tear of the Clouds here is source of main headstream (Opalescent R.) of the Hudson. Mtn. 1st ascended in 1837.

Marczali, Hungary: see MARCALI.

Mardakert (můrdůkyĕrt′), village (1926 pop. 2,335), N Nagorno-Karabakh Autonomous oblast, Azerbaijan SSR, 27 mi. N of Stepanakert; wheat.

Mardakyany (můrdůkyä′nē), town (1939 pop. over 2,000) in Azizbekov dist. of Greater Baku, Azerbaijan SSR, on E Apsheron Peninsula, 18 mi. ENE of Baku, on electric railroad; seaside resort; vineyards. Oil fields offshore.

Mardan (můrdän′), district (□ 1,098; 1951 pop. 598,000), North-West Frontier Prov., W Pakistan; ⊙ Mardan. Bordered SE by Indus R., N by SW offshoots of Punjab Himalayas. Irrigated by Swat Canals; agr. (wheat, corn, barley, sugar cane); hand-loom weaving; some gold washing in the Indus. Part of Peshawar dist. until c.1936. Exercises political control over tribal area (pop. 35,000). Pop. 95% Moslem, 2% Hindu, 2% Sikh.

Mardan, town (1941 pop. 39,200; with cantonment area, 42,494), ⊙ Mardan dist., N central North-West Frontier Prov., W Pakistan, 28 mi. NE of Peshawar; market center (wheat, sugar cane); sugar milling, hand-loom weaving. Sometimes called Hoti Mardan (village of Hoti is just E; headgear mfg.). Asokan rock edict 7 mi. ENE, at Shahbazgarhi.

Mar da Palha, Portugal: see LISBON BAY.

Marda Pass (mär′dä) (alt. c.6,500 ft.), E central Ethiopia, on the plateau, 10 mi. W of Jijiga; crossed by Jijiga-Harar road. Taken (1941) by British in Second World War.

Mar de Espanha (mär dĭ ĭspä′nyů), city (pop. 2,546), S Minas Gerais, Brazil, 22 mi. SE of Juiz de Fora; rail-spur terminus. Noted for high-grade white-marble quarries. Formerly spelled Mar de Hespanha.

Mardela Springs (märdĕ′lů), town (pop. 428), Wicomico co., E Md., 11 mi. NW of Salisbury, in truck-farm area; makes clothing.

Mar del Plata (mär′ dĕl plä′tä), city (pop. 104,513), ⊙ General Pueyrredón dist. (□ 564; pop. 117,720), SE Buenos Aires prov., Argentina, port on Atlantic coast at Cape Corrientes, 230 mi. SSE of Buenos Aires; 38°S 57°28′W. Major seaside resort; commercial and industrial center. Flour milling, dairying, meat packing; mfg. of paper, cigarettes, shoes. Important fishing base with canneries (mackerel, anchovies, clams, shrimp). Its shore front (c.10 mi. long) extends from Parque Camet (a park 5 mi. N of city center), along fashionable beaches, to fishing port (S; submarine and seaplane base). Wide landscaped avenues cross at central Plaza Luro, site of city hall and Gothic San Pedro church (begun 1893). During summer season (Dec.–April), pop. swells to half a million. Founded 1874, the city rapidly developed as one of the foremost seaside resorts of South America.

Mar del Sur, Argentina: see MIRAMAR, Buenos Aires.

Marden (märdĕn), town and parish (pop. 2,342), central Kent, England, 7 mi. S of Maidstone. The courthouse and church date from 13th–14th cent.

Mardeuil (märdů′ē), W suburb (pop. 845) of Épernay, Marne dept., N France; winegrowing (champagne).

Mardin (märdĭn′), prov. (□ 4,476; 1950 pop. 269,080), SE Turkey; ⊙ Mardin. On N is Tigris R., on S Syria, on SE Iraq. Railroad parallels Syrian frontier W of Nusaybin. Lignite at Cizre. Lentils, chick-peas, onions, cereals, tobacco; mohair goats.

Mardin, town (1950 pop. 20,015), ⊙ Mardin prov., SE Turkey, 50 mi. SE of Diyarbakir, 14 mi. from Syrian border; rail terminus and agr. center; barley, wheat, onions, tobacco, mohair goats; makes vaccines. On near-by hill are ruins of once strongly fortified castle.

Mare (můrĕ′), volcanic island (2 mi. long; pop. 765), N Moluccas, Indonesia, in Molucca Sea, just W of Halmahera, 13 mi. S of Ternate; 0°34′N 127°24′E. Hilly, rising to 1,010 ft. Fishing. Sometimes spelled Mereh.

Maré (mä′rā), coral island (pop. 3,300), southernmost of Loyalty Isls., SW Pacific, 35 mi. S of Lifu; 21°32′S 168°E; c.22 mi. long, 18 mi. wide; rises to 300 ft.; copra, oranges.

Mare, island, Calif.: see VALLEJO.

Mare, Ilha da (ē′lyů dä mä′rĭ), islet in Todos os Santos Bay, E Bahia, Brazil, 15 mi. N of Salvador.

Mare aux Vacoas, Mauritius: see VACOAS.

Mareb, Yemen: see MARIB.

Mareb River, Eritrea: see GASH RIVER.

Marecchia River (märĕk′kyä), N central Italy, rises in Etruscan Apennines on Monte Fumaiolo, 9 mi. SE of Bagno di Romagna, flows 40 mi. NE to the Adriatic at Rimini.

Marechal Deodoro (můrĭshäl′ dēōdō′rōō), city (pop. 4,518), Alagoas, NE Brazil, at S tip of Manguaba Lagoon, 10 mi. SW of Maceió (canal connection) in intensive sugar-growing dist.; sugar mills. Until 1939, called Alagoas. Former state ⊙.

Marechal Floriano, Brazil: see PIRANHAS, Alagoas.

Mare d'Albert (mär′ dälbâr′), village (pop. 1,588), SE Mauritius, on railroad and 5 mi. WSW of Mahébourg; sugar milling.

Iaree, Loch (lŏkh mûrē′), lake (13 mi. long, up to 2½ mi. wide) in W Ross and Cromarty, Scotland, 5 mi. E of Gairloch, surrounded by mts. (rising to 3,217 ft. in the Slioch). Drains into Loch Ewe by the short Ewe R. Loch contains small Isle Maree, with ruins of 7th-cent. abbey.

Iareeba (mûrē′bù), town (pop. 2,504), NE Queensland, Australia, 22 mi. WSW of Cairns; rail junction; tobacco-growing center; sugar plantations.

Iarèges Dam, France: see ROCHE-LE-PEYROUX.

Iarehra, India: see MARAHRA.

Iare Island, Calif.: see VALLEJO.

Iarek (mä′rĕk), city (pop. 19,239), Sofia dist., W Bulgaria, at W foot of Rila Mts., on Dzherman R. and 32 mi. SSW of Sofia. Rail junction; market and agr. center (grain, vineyards, tobacco, poppies, fruit); wine making; tobacco warehouses. Has teachers col., technical school. Until 1949, Dupnitsa.

Iareka, peak (11,360 ft.) in the Drakensberg, in Basutoland, just W of Natal (U. of So. Afr.) line, c.70 mi. SSW of Ladysmith, N of Thabantshonyana; 29°14′S 29°17′E.

Iarele-Voevod-Mihai, Rumania: see FEBRUARIE 16, 1933.

Iaremma (märĕm′mä), district (□ c.1,930), in S Tuscany, central Italy, bordering on Tyrrhenian Sea. Mostly (90%) within Grosseto prov.; coastal area enclosed by Apennine hills. Watered by Ombrone and Cecina rivers. Flourished in Etruscan times, but was largely abandoned in Middle Ages because of malaria. Reclamation, begun by grand dukes of Tuscany, was continued on a large scale by Ital. government. Wide areas, formerly pestilential swamps, are now fertile agr. dists. devoted to cereals, grapes, olives, and fruit. Cattle and a noted breed of horses raised; good hunting grounds (foxes, wild boars). Fishing in lagoon of Orbetello and along coast. Rich in boric acid obtained from the *soffioni* of Larderello, Castelnuovo di Val di Cecina, and Serrazzano (Pisa prov.); many minerals, such as copper (Massa Marittima, Montieri), lignite (Ribolla, Roccastrada), manganiferous iron (Monte Argentario, Gavorrano), and mercury (Monte Amiata, Castell'Azzara, Manciano).

Iarene (märä′nĕ), village (pop. 1,007), Cuneo prov., Piedmont, NW Italy, 12 mi. E of Saluzzo.

Iarengo (märĕng′gō), town (pop. 6,991), Alger dept., N central Algeria, at W edge of the Mitidja plain, 23 mi. W of Blida; agr. trade center in wine-growing and truck-gardening region.

Iarengo (märĕng′gô), village, Alessandria prov., Piedmont, N Italy, 2 mi. SE of Alessandria, adjacent to Spinetta Marengo. Has mus. with Napoleonic collections. Famous for battle of June 14, 1800, when Napoleon turned apparent defeat into complete victory over Austrians, thereby completing his campaign in N Italy.

Iarengo (mûrĕng′gō), county (□ 978; pop. 29,494), W Ala.; ⊙ Linden. In the Black Belt; bounded W by Tombigbee R. Cotton, grain, cattle; lumber milling. Demopolis is in N. Formed 1818.

Iarengo. 1 (mûrĕng′gō) City (pop. 2,726), McHenry co., N Ill., on Kishwaukee R. and 24 mi. E of Rockford, in dairy and farm area; makes magnets, magnetic steel, mousetraps. Settled 1835; inc. as town in 1857, as city in 1893. **2** (märĕng′gō) Town (pop. 801), Crawford co., S Ind., on a fork of Blue R. and 30 mi. WNW of New Albany, in agr. area; tomato cannery; limestone quarries; timber. Marengo Cave here is tourist attraction. **3** (mûrĭng′gō) City (pop. 2,151), ⊙ Iowa co., E central Iowa, on Iowa R. and 24 mi. WSW of Cedar Rapids; canned corn, packed poultry. Inc. 1859. **4** (mûrĕng′gō) Village (pop. 275), Morrow co., central Ohio, 22 mi. SE of Marion.

Iarenisco (mârunĭ′skō), village (1940 pop. 886), Gogebic co., W Upper Peninsula, Mich., 24 mi. ESE of Ironwood and on Presque Isle R., in mining, lumbering, and agr. area. State park near by.

Iarennes (märĕn′), town (pop. 3,068), Charente-Maritime dept., W France, near mouth of Seudre R. on Bay of Biscay, opposite S end of Île d'Oléron, 10 mi. SW of Rochefort; has France's largest oyster and mussel beds; saltworks. Involved (1568–70) in Wars of Religion; damaged in Second World War.

Iareotis, Lake, Egypt: see MARYUT, LAKE.

Iares, Colombia: see BARRANCABERMEJA.

Iaresfield (mârz′fūl), town and parish (pop. 2,309) E central Sussex, England, 2 mi. N of Uckfield Has 13th-cent. church.

Iareshah (mârē′shù) or **Marisa** (mă′rĭsù, mûrĭ′sù), biblical locality, S Palestine, at W foot of Judaean Hills, at N edge of the Negev, 20 mi. WSW of Jerusalem, just SSE of Beit Jibrin. Repeatedly mentioned in the Bible; scene of important excavations (Hellenistic finds). Also spelled Marissa. Modern locality called Tell Sandahannah.

Iareth (mă′rĕth, Fr. märĕt′), village, Gabès dist., SE Tunisia, bet. Matmata Range (SW) and the Gulf of Gabès (NE), 19 mi. SSE of Gabès; olive and palm trees; sheep, camels. In Second World War it was N anchor point of a fortified defense line held by Germans after their retreat from Tripolitania, until outflanked and broken by British in March, 1943.

Ma Retraite (mä rùtrĕt′), village (pop. 321), Surinam dist., N Du. Guiana, 12 mi. ESE of Paramaribo; coffee plantations.

Marettimo (märĕt′tēmō), anc. *Hiera,* island (□ 4.5; pop. 1,103), one of Egadi Isls., in Mediterranean Sea off W Sicily, 28 mi. W of Trapani; 4.5 mi. long, 2 mi. wide; rises to 2,244 ft. Fisheries (tunny, coral). Chief port, Marettimo, on E coast. Also spelled Marittimo.

Mareuil (märû′ē). **1** or **Mareuil-sur-Belle** (–sür-bĕl′), village (pop. 778), Dordogne dept., SW France, 11 mi. WSW of Nontron; mfg. (hosiery footwear), flour milling. **2** or **Mareuil-sur-Lay** (–sür-lĕ′), village (pop. 957), Vendée dept., W France, on the Lay and 14 mi. SE of La Roche-sur-Yon; truck gardening, dairying.

Mareuil-sur-Ay (–sür-ā′), village (pop. 932), Marne dept., N France, on the Marne and its lateral canal, 4 mi. E of Épernay; winegrowing center (champagne).

Marevo (mä′ryĭvù), village (1939 pop. over 500), SW Novgorod oblast, Russian SFSR, 55 mi. SE of Staraya Russa; flax.

Marfa (mär′fù), (pop. 3,603), ⊙ Presidio co., extreme W Texas, c.175 mi. SE of El Paso, just S of Davis Mts.; alt. 4,688 ft. Market, shipping center for ranching (cattle, goats, sheep), silver-mining region; tourist trade. Old Fort D. A. Russell here was founded 1833. Hunting near by. Founded 1884, inc. 1887.

Marfa Peninsula (mär′fä), NW promontory of Malta; c.3 mi. long, 1 mi. wide. Crossed by low ridge. On its N coast is a landing, linked by ferry with Imjar on Gozo isl.

Marfino (mär′fēnŭ), village (1926 pop. 1,456), E Astrakhan oblast, Russian SFSR, port on Buzan arm of Volga R. delta mouth and 34 mi. ENE of Astrakhan; fisheries; cotton, fruit.

Marfrance, town (1940 pop. 875), Greenbrier co., SE W.Va., 23 mi. NNW of Lewisburg.

Marg, El (ĕl märg′), or **Al-Marj** (ĕl-märj′), village (pop. 8,190), Qalyubiya prov., Lower Egypt, 9 mi. NE of Cairo city center; cotton, flax, cereals, fruits. Site of some XVIII dynasty ruins.

Margam, town (pop. 18,247) in Port Talbot municipal borough, W central Glamorgan, Wales; coal mining. Has ruins of Cistercian abbey, founded 1147. There is also Norman abbey church and 13th-cent. chapter house. Mountain of Mynydd Margam (1,130 ft.) is 2 mi. NE.

Marganets (mär′gŭnyĭts) [Rus.,=manganese], city (1945 pop. over 10,000), S Dnepropetrovsk oblast, Ukrainian SSR, 12 mi. ENE of Nikopol; major manganese-mining center in Nikopol basin; railroad shops. Formerly called Gorodishche, and later (c.1926–40), Komintern.

Margão (märgä′ō), town (pop. 14,473), W Goa dist. Portuguese India, on railroad and 17 mi. SSE of Pangim; trade center (rice, copra, cashew nuts, mangoes, timber); sheep raising.

Margaree (märgùrē′), village (pop. estimate 300), NE N.S., on Cape Breton Isl., on Margaree R. and 15 mi. NW of Inverness; salmon-fishing center. At mouth of Margaree R., on the Gulf of St. Lawrence, 4 mi. NW, is fishing port of Margaree Harbour (pop. estimate 400).

Margaree River, NE N.S., on NE Cape Breton Isl., rises in 2 branches: Southwest Margaree R. issues from L. Ainslie, 8 mi. ESE of Inverness, flows 15 mi. N; Northeast Margaree R. rises 20 mi. SW of Ingonish, flows 40 mi. S and E; the branches unite 4 mi. S of Margaree, forming Margaree R., which flows 10 mi. NNW to the Gulf of St. Lawrence at Margaree Harbour.

Margaret, village (pop. 1,144), St. Clair co., N central Ala., 22 mi. NE of Birmingham; coal mining.

Margareten (märgärā′tùn), district (□ .8; pop. 68,508) of Vienna, Austria, 1.5 mi. SW of city center.

Margaret Island, Hung. *Margit Sziget,* in the Danube, N central Hungary; recreation area of Budapest, linked with both shores by a bridge. Thermal springs and baths; sanatorium. Ruins of convent where St. Margaret, daughter of Bela IV, lived.

Margaret River, village (pop. 452), SW Western Australia, 140 mi. SSW of Perth, N of Cape Leeuwin; dairy center; butter factory. Mammoth Caves (limestone caves containing bones of prehistoric animals) near by.

Margaretsville, town (pop. 113), Northampton co., NE N.C., 18 mi. ENE of Roanoke Rapids.

Margaretville, summer-resort village (pop. 905), Delaware co., S N.Y., in the Catskills, on East Branch of Delaware R. and 37 mi. NW of Kingston; railroad shops.

Margarita (märgärē′tä), town (pop. 2,046), Bolívar dept., N Colombia, on Margarita Isl., on the Brazo Seco de Mompós (a right arm of Magdalena R.) and 11 mi. SE of Mompós; tobacco, cattle.

Margarita, town (pop. 966), Cristobal dist., N Panama Canal Zone, 2½ mi. S of Colón; bananas, rubber, corn, rice; livestock.

Margarita Belén (bälĕn′), town (pop. estimate 1,500), SE Chaco natl. territory, Argentina, on railroad and 12 mi. N of Resistencia. Agr. (cotton, corn; citriculture); stock raising; cotton ginning.

Margarita Island, Bolívar dept., N Colombia; formed by arms of middle Magdalena R., the Brazo Seco de Mompós (E) and the Brazo de Loba (W); extends 60 mi. NW from El Banco, c.20 mi. wide. Marshy lowlands with savannas and tropical forests. Mompós is its largest town.

Margarita Island, Mexico: see SANTA MARGARITA ISLAND.

Margarita Island, in the Caribbean, 15 mi. off NE Venezuela, opposite Araya Peninsula, 165 mi. ENE of Caracas; constitutes most of state (□ 444; 1941 pop. 69,195; 1950 estimate 62,381) of Nueva Esparta (nwā′vä ĕspär′tä), which includes Coche Isl. and several smaller isls.; ⊙ La Asunción. Margarita, shaped roughly like a horseshoe, is really 2 isls. joined by narrow sand spit; 43 mi. long, 22 mi. wide; 10°52′–11°11′N 63°56′–64°25′W. W part, rising to c.4,800 ft., is mountainous goat-grazing area; E part, with warm, healthy climate, is popular resort area and fertile agr. region (sugar cane, cotton, tobacco, corn, yucca, coconuts, beans, divi-divi). Main sources of income, however, are the large magnesite deposits near Puerto Fermín (NE) and the pearl and deep-sea fisheries (sardines, tuna, herring, Sp. mackerel, sharks). Rural industries include corn and sugar milling, *aguardiente* distilling, coconut-oil extracting, mfg. hammocks, straw hats. La Asunción is in center of interior agr. region and contains some processing plants. Porlamar is the leading commercial center and hq. for pearl fishing, has several fish canneries. Pampatar is another important port on E coast. Discovered 1498 by Columbus on his 3d voyage, the isl. soon achieved prominence as a pearl-fishing base. The ill-famed adventurer Lope de Aguirre operated from here (1561). Because of Margarita's active part in struggle for independence, Nueva Esparta was set up as a separate state within Venezuelan federation.

Margaritas, Las, Mexico: see LAS MARGARITAS.

Margarition (märgûrē′tēôn), village (pop. 1,780), Thesprotia nome, S Epirus, Greece, 13 mi. SE of Egoumenitsa; olive oil; almonds, timber; livestock. Called Margalich under Turkish rule.

Margate (mär′gĭt), municipal borough (1931 pop. 31,341; 1951 census 42,487), NE Kent, England, on Isle of Thanet, at SE end of Thames estuary, 15 mi. NE of Canterbury; popular seaside resort (especially for Londoners), with port, fine beach, and piers (begun in 15th cent.). Has partly Norman church of St. John the Baptist, 18th-cent. Royal Seabathing Hosp., asylum for deaf and dumb, and Dane Park, with artificial grotto. Just E is residential dist. of Cliftonville (pop. 3,577).

Margate, village (pop. 486), SE Tasmania, 12 mi. SSW of Hobart and on North West Bay of D'Entrecasteaux Channel; sawmills.

Margate, town (pop. 2,284), SE Natal, U. of So. Afr., on Indian Ocean, 80 mi. SW of Durban; popular seaside resort.

Margate City (mär′gāt), resort city (pop. 4,715), Atlantic co., S N.J., on Absecon Beach, 3 mi. SW of Atlantic City. Inc. 1909.

Margaux (märgō′), village (pop. 932), Gironde dept., SW France, in Médoc, near the Gironde, 15 mi. NNW of Bordeaux; produces fine red wines, including the noted Château-Margaux.

Margecany, Czechoslovakia: see KROMPACHY.

Margelan (mûrgyĭlăn′), city (1926 pop. 44,327), E Fergana oblast, Uzbek SSR, in Fergana Valley, near railroad (Gorchakovo station), 5 mi. N of Fergana in cotton, silk, and orchard area. Large silk-milling center (complete production cycle); tobacco and food processing. Teachers col. Important since c.10th cent.; partly superseded by new Rus. city of Novy Margelan (founded 1876; now called FERGANA). Margelan was officially known (1876–1907) as Stary Margelan [Rus.,=old Margelan].

Margeride, Montagnes de la (mōtä′nyù dù lä märzhùrēd′), granitic range in Massif Central, S central France, bounded by Allier R. (E), upper Truyère R. (W), and Lot R. (S); extends c.35 mi. NNW–SSE along borders of Haute-Loire, Cantal and Lozère depts. Rises to 5,098 ft. Reforestation in progress.

Marggrabowa, Poland: see OLECKO.

Margherita (märgä′rĭtù), village, Lakhimpur dist., NE Assam, India, on Burhi Dihing R. and 50 mi. ESE of Dibrugarh; major Assam coal-mining center; trades in Burmese amber and rubber. It is ⊙ Tirap frontier tract.

Margherita (märgĕrē′tä), town, in the Benadir, S Ital. Somaliland, on Juba R. and 30 mi. NE of Kismayu; agr. center, livestock market.

Margherita, Lake, Ethiopia: see ABAYA, LAKE.

Margherita, Mount (mär″gärē′tä, märgĕrē′tä), highest summit (16,795 ft.) of the RUWENZORI, in E central Africa on Belgian Congo–Uganda border, 30 mi. ESE of Beni. First ascended by the duke of Abruzzi and his expedition in 1906, and named for Queen Margherita of Italy. Was thoroughly explored and mapped by a Belgian expedition in 1932. It is 3d highest peak in Africa, after Kilimanjaro and Kenya.

Margherita di Savoia (märgĕrē′tä dē sävô′yä), town (pop. 10,406), Foggia prov., Apulia, S Italy, on the Adriatic, near mouth of Ofanto R., 21 mi. SE of Manfredonia; bathing resort. Has extensive saltworks, including drained Salpi lagoon; most important on Ital. mainland.

Marghine, Catena del (kätä′nä dĕl märgē′nĕ), mountain range, W central Sardinia; extends 15 mi. SW from Catena del Goceano; rises to 3,936 ft. at Monte Palai.

Marghita (mär′gētä), Hung. *Margitta* (mŏr′gĕt-tŏ), village (pop. 6,608), Bihor prov., W Rumania, on Berettyo R., on railroad and 28 mi. NE of Oradea; white-wine production; pottery making. In Hungary, 1940–45.

Margiana, Turkmen SSR: see MARY, city.

Margina (mär′jēnä), Hung. *Marzsina* (mŏr′zhĕnŏ), village (pop. 797), Timisoara prov., W Rumania, on Bega R., on railroad and 22 mi. NE of Lugoj; wood cracking, charcoal mfg.

Marginea (märzhē′nyä), village (pop. 4,684), Suceava prov., N Rumania, 6 mi. SW of Radauti; agr. center with pottery mfg. Fortified 15–16th-cent. monastery of Sucevita (sōōchävē′tsä), Rum. *Sucevița*, is 7 mi. SW; it is famous for its 16th-cent. church covered with Byzantine frescoes, and for its valuable religious collections.

Margit Sziget, Hungary: see MARGARET ISLAND.

Margitta, Rumania: see MARGHITA.

Margny-lès-Compiègne (märnyē′-lā-kōpyĕ′nyů), NE suburb (pop. 4,563) of Compiègne, Oise dept., N France, on the Oise; iron and lead founding, furniture mfg.

Margona, town (pop. 306), St. Louis co., E Mo., W of St. Louis.

Margonin (märgô′nēn), town (pop. 1,829), Poznan prov., W Poland, on small lake, 40 mi. N of Poznan; flour milling.

Margos (mär′gōs), town (pop. 2,003), Huánuco dept., central Peru, in Cordillera Central, 17 mi. SW of Huánuco; barley, potatoes; sheep raising.

Margosatubig (mär″gōsätōō′bēg), town (1939 pop. 5,786; 1948 municipality pop. 28,587), Zamboanga prov., W Mindanao, Philippines, 25 mi. SW of Pagadian; corn, rice, coconuts. Sawmill.

Margraten (märkh-grä′tůn), village (pop. 1,540), Limburg prov., SE Netherlands, 6 mi. ESE of Maastricht. U.S. military cemetery here. Tufa quarry.

Margrethe, Lake (märgrēth′), Crawford co., N central Mich., 4 mi. SW of Grayling, in a state game refuge; c.3 mi. long, 1 mi. wide. Drained from W by a headstream of Manistee R.

Marguareis, Monte (môn′tě märgwärās′), highest peak (8,697 ft.) in Ligurian Alps, on Fr.-Ital. border, 6 mi. E of Tenda Pass. Until 1947, border passed 11 mi. SW. Also known as Cima Marguareis.

Marguerite Bay, inlet of Antarctica, on W coast of Palmer Peninsula, in the South Pacific, bet. Adelaide and Alexander I isls.; 68°30′S 68°30′W. Discovered 1909 by Jean B. Charcot, Fr. explorer. Most disputed area in Antarctic archipelago.

Marguerittes (märgůrēt′), village (pop. 1,306), Gard dept., S France, 4 mi. ENE of Nîmes; hosiery, chemicals.

Mari (mŭrē′), town (pop. 2,419), E Paraíba, NE Brazil, on railroad and 26 mi. W of João Pessoa; cotton, sugar, fruit. Until 1944, called Araçá.

Mari, W Pakistan: see KALABAGH.

Maria, village (pop. estimate 500), E Que., S Gaspé Peninsula, on Cascapedia Bay of Chaleur Bay, 20 mi. ENE of Dalhousie; fishing port; lumbering. Resort.

María (märē′ä), town (pop. 1,718), Almería prov., S Spain, 7 mi. NW of Vélez Rubio; chemical works (essential oils, resins). Lumbering, stock raising; cereals, esparto, aromatic plants.

María, Villa, Colombia: see VILLA MARÍA.

Mariabé (märyäbā′), village (pop. 422), Los Santos prov., S central Panama, in Pacific lowland, 6 mi. NW of Pedasí; sugar cane, livestock.

María Chiquita (märē′ä chēkē′tä), village (pop. 135), Colón prov., central Panama, minor port of Caribbean Sea, 11 mi. NE of Colón; bananas, cacao, abacá, livestock.

María Cleófas Island, Mexico: see TRES MARÍAS ISLANDS.

Maria Cristina Falls (mŭrē′ů krĭstē′nů), N Mindanao, Philippines, near Iligan Bay, 80 mi. SW of Cagayan; hydroelectric project.

María de la Salud (märē′ä dhā lä sälōōdh′), town (pop. 2,438), Majorca, Balearic Isls., 23 mi. ENE of Palma; almonds, cereals, figs, grapes, livestock; sawmilling.

María Elena (ālā′nä), mining settlement (1930 pop. 9,062), Antofagasta prov., N Chile, on railroad and 38 mi. SE of Tocopilla; nitrate and iodine center. Airport.

Maria Enzersdorf (märē′ä ĕnt′sůrsdôrf), town (pop. 3,729), after 1938 in Mödling dist. of Vienna, Austria, 10 mi. SW of city center; wine.

Mariager (märēyĕr′), city (pop. 1,383 and port, Randers amt, E Jutland, Denmark, on Mariager Fjord and 34 mi. NNW of Aarhus; cement mfg.

Mariager Fjord (c.25 mi. long), E Jutland, Denmark, inlet of the Kattegat. Mariager on S shore, Hobro at head. Inner part sometimes called Hobro Fjord.

María Grande (märē′ä grän′dā), town (pop. estimate 1,500), W Entre Ríos prov., Argentina, on railroad and 40 mi. ENE of Paraná, in grain and livestock area; poultry farming.

Mariahilf (märē′ä hĭlf″), district (□ .6; pop. 45,537) of Vienna, Austria, just W of city center.

Mariahu (mŭryä′hŭ), town (pop. 4,094), Jaunpur dist., SE Uttar Pradesh, India, 11 mi. SSW of Jaunpur; barley, rice, corn, wheat, sugar cane.

Maria Island (mŭrī′ů), in Tasman Sea, 3 mi. off E coast of Tasmania; 11 mi. long, 6 mi. wide. Consists of 2 mountainous parts joined by narrow isthmus; limestone. Largest town, Maria Island, on NW coast.

Maria Island (mŭrē′ů), uninhabited atoll of 4 islets, westernmost of Tubuai Isls., Fr. Oceania, S Pacific; 21°45′S 154°30′W. Sometimes called Hull Isl.

Mariakerke (mä′rēäkĕr″ků), town (pop. 4,752), East Flanders prov., NW Belgium, on Bruges-Ghent Canal and 2 mi. NW of Ghent; mfg. (rubber products).

María la Baja (märē′ä lä bä′hä), town (pop. 4,222), Bolívar dept., N Colombia, in Caribbean lowlands, 35 mi. SSE of Cartagena; sugar-cane center. Sugar refinery near by.

María Linda River, Guatemala: see MICHATOYA RIVER.

María Madre Island, Mexico: see TRES MARÍAS ISLANDS.

María Magdalena Island, Mexico: see TRES MARÍAS ISLANDS.

Mariampol, Lithuania: see MARIJAMPOLE.

Mariana (mŭrēä′nů), city (pop. 5,224), S central Minas Gerais, Brazil, in Serra do Espinhaço, on railroad and 6 mi. ENE of Ouro Prêto, 45 mi. SE of Belo Horizonte. Oldest city in state, 1st episcopal see, and archiepiscopal see since 1905. Has fine, early-18th-cent. cathedral, ornate churches, and city hall. Formerly known for its important gold mines (still worked). Tungsten and kaolin deposits. Formerly spelled Marianna.

Marianao (märēänou′), city (pop. 120,163), Havana prov., W Cuba, on Central Highway, on railroad and 5 mi. SW of Havana, of which it is a residential and industrial suburb. Mfg. of cement, tiles, bricks, tires, beer, fruit preserves. Has racetrack, casino. Adjoined (N) by military camp and fashionable Marianao Beach. The sugar central Toledo is just SE.

Marianas Islands (mă″rēă′nůz, märēä′näs), island group (□ 370; pop. c.29,700), W Pacific, 1,500 mi. E of Philippines; 13°25′–20°32′N 144°45′–144°54′E. N-S chain (extending 500 mi.) of volcanic isls.: GUAM (largest isl.), AGRIHAN, AGUIJAN, ALAMAGAN, ANATAHAN, ASUNCION, GUGUAN, MAUG, MEDINILLA, PAGAN, PAJAROS, ROTA, SAIPAN, SARIGAN, and TINIAN. N isls. are of volcanic rock, S isls. of madrepore limestone covering volcanic base. Mountainous, with highest peak (3,166 ft.) on Agrihan. Annual mean temp. 78°F., rainfall 83.5 in.; typhoons. Sugar cane, coffee, coconuts; fruit bats, lizards, some harmless snakes. Phosphate, sulphur, manganese ore. Ruins of anc. stone columns. Inhabitants are Micronesians, Chamorros, Japanese (most numerous). Discovered 1521 by Magellan, who called them Ladrone Isls. (Thieves Isls.); renamed Marianas Isls. by Sp. Jesuits arriving 1668; Sp. rule, 1668–1898. Guam became (1898) U.S. possession; other isls. were sold (1899) to Germany. Isls. belonging to Germany were occupied 1914 by Japan, placed 1922–35 under Jap. mandate, and became Jap. possession 1935. In Second World War, Jap. isls. (important bases) were taken 1944 by U.S. forces, who established naval and air bases on Saipan and Tinian. Group (exclusive of Guam) was included (1947) in U.S. Territory of the Pacific Islands under U.N. trusteeship. Sometimes spelled Marianne Isls. or Mariana Isls.

Marianas Trench, submarine depression in North Pacific Ocean, E of S Marianas Isls. The Nero Deep (31,614 ft.), discovered 1899 SE of Guam at 12°40′N 145°40′E, was considered the deepest point until the sounding (1930s) of a 32,197-ft. depth near by.

Mariânica, Cordillera, Spain: see SIERRA MORENA.

Marianna, Brazil: see MARIANA.

Marianna (mârēă′nů). **1** City (pop. 4,530), ⊙ Lee co., E Ark., c.50 mi. SW of Memphis (Tenn.), and on L'Anguille R.; agr. (cotton, corn, soybeans); timber; cotton ginning, sawmilling, mfg. of clothing. State univ. cotton experiment station near by. Inc. 1877. **2** City (pop. 5,845), ⊙ Jackson co., NW Fla., on Chipola R. and c.60 mi. WNW of Tallahassee; rail junction; lumber milling; mfg. of millwork articles, barrels, feed. Limestone quarrying. Has a jr. col. Near by are Florida Caverns State Park, the Blue Springs (with hydroelectric plant), and Florida Industrial School for Boys. Founded 1829. **3** Borough (pop. 1,269), Washington co., SW Pa., 13 mi. SE of Washington. Inc. 1901.

Marianne Islands: see MARIANAS ISLANDS.

Mariannelund (mä″rēä′nůlůnd″), town (pop. 1,528), Jonkoping co., S Sweden, 30 mi. E of Nassjo; wood- and metalworking. Near by is large tuberculosis sanitarium.

Mariano Comense (märēä′nô kômĕn′sě), town (pop. 6,708), Como prov., Lombardy, N Italy, 9 mi. SSE of Como. Furniture mfg. center; silk mills, aluminum industry; textile machinery, hardware.

Mariano del Friuli (dĕl frē′ōōlē), village (pop. 1,293), Gorizia prov., Friuli-Venezia Giulia, NE Italy, 8 mi. WSW of Gorizia; artisan chair mfg.

Mariano Escobedo (märyä′nō ĕskōbā′dō). **1** Town (pop. 1,763), Jalisco, central Mexico, 4 mi. ESE o Guadalajara; grain, alfalfa, beans, fruit, livestock Formerly San Andrés. **2** Town (pop. 391), Veracruz, E Mexico, in Sierra Madre Oriental, 10 mi WNW of Córdoba; coffee, fruit.

Mariano Moreno (mōrä′nō), town (pop. estimat 1,000), central Neuquén natl. territory, Argentina 10 mi. N of Zapala; stock-raising and oil-producin center. Formerly Covunco Centro.

Mariano Roque Alonso (rō′kā älōn′sō), town (dist pop. 5,113), Central dept., S Paraguay, on Paraguay R. and 10 mi. NE of Asunción, in agr. are (sugar cane, fruit, livestock).

Marianske Lazne, Czechoslovakia: see MARIENBAD

Maria Pereira, Ceará, Brazil: see MOMBAÇA.

María Pinto (märē′ä pēn′tō), village (1930 pop 178), Santiago prov., central Chile, 28 mi. WSW o Santiago, in agr. area (grain, fruit, alfalfa, livestock).

Mariaradna, Rumania: see RADNA.

Marías, Las, Puerto Rico: see LAS MARÍAS.

Maria Saal (märē′ä zäl′), town (pop. 2,512), Carinthia, S Austria, near Glan R., 4 mi. NNE of Klagenfurt. Gothic pilgrimage church. Remains c Roman city of Virunum near by.

Marias Pass (mŭrī′ůz) (alt. 5,216 ft.), in Lewi Range of Continental Divide, NW Mont., a Summit, on SE border of Glacier Natl. Park and 5 mi. SW of Cut Bank. Discovered 1889 by John F Stevens, the pass is now crossed by railroad an highway.

Marias River, NW Mont., rises in several branche in Continental Divide, flows 210 mi. E and S, pas Cut Bank, to Missouri R. 11 mi. NE of Fort Benton. Principal tributary, Teton R. Not navigabl

Maria Taferl (märē′ä tä′fůrl), village (pop. 781), V Lower Austria, near the Danube, 15 mi. ENE c Amstetten; well-known pilgrimage church.

Maria-Theresiopel, Yugoslavia: see SUBOTICA.

Mari Autonomous Soviet Socialist Republic (mä′rē) administrative division (□ 8,900; 1939 pop. 579,456) of central European Russian SFSR; ⊙ Ioshkar-Ola. In middle Volga R. valley, N of Chuvas Autonomous SSR; drained by left tributaries of th Volga (Vetluga, Greater Kokshaga, Ilet), used fo lumber floating. Humid continental climate (shor summers). Heavily forested (60% of area); pea deposits (SW). Agr., with wheat, rye, oats; fla (N), wheat (SW); livestock in treeless NE. Industries based on lumber (sawmilling, woodworkin mfg. of paper, cellulose, furniture, railroad sleeper prefabricated houses, musical instruments) an agr. (flax and food processing); glassworking (Leninski, Mariyets, Krasny Steklovar). Main cen ters: Ioshkar-Ola, Volzhsk, Kozmodemyansk. Po 51% Mari, 44% Russians, 4% Tatars. The Ma (formerly called Cheremiss) are a Finnic group c Rus. culture and Greek Orthodox religion. Firs mentioned (5 B.C.) by Herodotus, and known t Romans; dominated by Volga Bolgars (9th–12t cent.) and Golden Horde (13th cent.); conquere 1552 by Ivan the Terrible. Area ceded to Russia in 17th cent.; became autonomous oblast in 192 part of Gorki Territory (1929–36); gained preser status in 1936.

Maria Van Dieman, Cape (văn dē′mŭn), extreme N.Isl., New Zealand, 25 mi. W of N.Cape; 34°29′ 172°39′E; lighthouse.

Mariaville (mŭrī′ůvĭl), town (pop. 153), Hancoc co., S Maine, 18 mi. ESE of Bangor, in recreation area.

Maria Wörth (märē′ä vûrt′), village (pop. 1,460 Carinthia, S Austria, on S shore of the Wörthers and 7 mi. W of Klagenfurt; resort. Has 2 Roman esque churches; place of pilgrimage.

Mariazell (märē′ätsĕl′), town (pop. 2,330), Styri E central Austria, 29 mi. NNE of Leoben; winte summer mtn. resort (alt. 2,828 ft.). Place of pi grimage known for its 12th-cent. image of Virgi and Child; has 17th-cent. church with 14th-cen Gothic tower.

Marib or **Ma'rib** (mä′rĭb), outlying town, E Yeme 75 mi. E of Sana; alt. 3,900 ft. Site of anc. Sabaea (see SHEBA) capital (7th–2d cent. B.C.), note for irrigation works, whose final destruction (6t cent. A.D.) is alluded to in the Koran. Sometim spelled Mareb.

Maribios, Cordillera de los, Nicaragua: see MARABIOS, CORDILLERA DE LOS.

Maribo (mä′rēbō), amt (□ 693; 1950 pop. 135,337 Denmark, comprises Lolland, Falster, and sever smaller isls.; ⊙ Maribo. Chief cities: Nykobin Nakskov. Corn, wheat, fruit growing; meat can ning; dairying.

Maribo, city (1950 pop. 5,141), ⊙ Maribo amt, Denmark, on Lolland isl., on Maribo L.; 54°46′N 11° 31′E. Sugar refining, meat canning, machiner mfg. Has 15th-cent. church.

Maribojoc (mä″rēbōhōk′), town (1939 pop. 1,58 1948 municipality pop. 13,906), W Bohol isl., Philippines, 7 mi. NNW of Tagbilaran; agr. cent (rice, coconuts, hemp).

Maribondo Falls (mŭrēbōn′dōō), S central Brazi on the Rio Grande (São Paulo–Minas Gerais border), 35 mi. N of São José do Rio Prêto (São Paulo). Site of future hydroelectric plant. Sometimes spelled Marimbondo.

Maribor (mä'rēbôr), Ger. *Marburg* (mär'bōōrk), city (pop. 66,498), ⊙ Maribor oblast (formed 1949), Slovenia, Yugoslavia, on Drava R. (railroad bridge), on Zagreb-Vienna RR and 65 mi. NE of Ljubljana, bet. the Pohorje (W) and the Slovenske Gorice (N). Trade, transportation, and industrial center; rail junction (repair shops); automobile factory, textile mills; mfg. of leather, footwear, chemicals, asbestos products. Vineyards in vicinity. Seat (since 1857) of R.C. bishop. Consists of old section on left and new on right bank of the Drava. Has Gothic cathedral, palace of former prince-bishop, castle, fine 17th-cent. town hall, library, and mus. First mentioned in 1147. Until 1918, in Styria.

Maricá (mürēkä'), city (pop. 1,774), S Rio de Janeiro state, Brazil, on coastal lagoon of same name, 18 mi. E of Niterói; fish processing, rice milling; sugar, brandy, vegetables, poultry. Feldspar and quartz deposits.

Maricaban Island (mä"rēkäbän') (□ 12; 1939 pop. 4,795), Batangas prov., Philippines, in Verde Isl. Passage, off SW coast of Luzon, at entrance to Batangas Bay, 10 mi. SW of Batangas town; 8 mi. long, 2 mi. wide; rises to 1,469 ft. Fishing, rice growing. Chief town is Papaya (1939 pop. 1,189) on S coast. Isl. is part of Bauan municipality.

Maricao (märēkou'), town (pop. 1,360), W Puerto Rico, in W outliers of the Cordillera Central, 11 mi. E of Mayagüez; alt. 1,416 ft.; coffee-trading center; resort. Adjoining S is extensive reforestation project. Manganese deposits in vicinity.

Marica River, Bulgaria, Greece, Turkey: see MARITSA RIVER.

Marichchukkaddi (mŭrĭch'ōōkŭd"dē), village (pop. 685), Northern Prov., Ceylon, near Gulf of Mannar, 30 mi. N of Puttalam; rice and coconut-palm plantations. Center for pearl fishing in banks off coast; govt. opening of fishing season increases pop. to c.40,000. Has lowest recorded rainfall in Ceylon.

Marichong (mä'rēchông), village, SW Bhutan, on the Raidak and 40 mi. NNE of Cooch Behar (India), junction of routes to Paro and Punakha; market center (rice, oranges, corn, millet, potatoes, mustard). Formerly Murichom and Marackom.

Maricopa (mărĭkō'pŭ), county (□ 9,231; pop. 331,-770), SW central Ariz.; ⊙ Phoenix, the state capital. McDowell Mts. and part of Mazatzal Mts. are in NE. Irrigated agr. region extends along banks of Salt, Gila, Santa Cruz, Verde, and Agua Fria rivers. Co. includes Gila Bend, Salt River, and parts of Gila River and Papago Indian reservations. Mesa is a sports and cotton-ginning center. Long-staple cotton, citrus, truck, figs, alfalfa, lettuce; ranching; health resorts. Formed 1871.

Maricopa, city (pop. 800), Kern co., S central Calif., 6 mi. S of Taft, at S end of San Joaquin Valley; oil wells, refineries.

Maricopa Mountains, Maricopa co., SW central Ariz., E of Gila R. and Gila Bend; rise to c.3,000 ft.

Maricunga, Salar de (sälär' dā märēkōōng'gä), salt desert (alt. c.12,000 ft.) in S Atacama Desert, Atacama prov., N Chile, at 27°S; extends 13 mi. N-S (c.7 mi. wide) along SW foot of Cordillera Claudio Gay. Borax deposits.

Maridi, Anglo-Egyptian Sudan: see MERIDI.

Maridunum, Wales: see CARMARTHEN, municipal borough.

Marieberg, Sweden: see KOJA.

Marie Byrd Land, Antarctica, E of Ross Shelf Ice and Ross Sea, and S of Amundsen Sea. Discovered 1929 by R. E. Byrd.

Mariefred (märē"ūfrĕd'), city (pop. 1,490), Sodermanland co., E Sweden, on S shore of L. Malar, 30 mi. W of Stockholm; agr. market (grain, stock, dairy products). Has 17th-cent. church. Inc. 1605. Near by is Gripsholm Castle.

Marie-Galante (märē'-gälät'), island (□ 57.65; pop. 29,349), dependency of Guadeloupe, Fr. West Indies, 25 mi. E of Basse-Terre, Guadeloupe, and 20 mi. NE of Dominica; 15°52'–16°1'N 61°11'–61°20'W. Principal town, Grand-Bourg. Isl. is of low limestone formation, roughly circular in shape, c.10 mi. in diameter. Has occasional droughts. Almost entirely devoted to cultivation of sugar cane; rum distilling, sugar refining. Named by Columbus, who discovered it in 1493, for his ship *María Galanda*. Isl. was 1st settled by the French, though it was frequently occupied by the British.

Mariehamn (märē"ühä'mŭn), Finnish *Maarianhamina* (mä'rēänhä"mĭnä), city (pop. 3,506, ⊙ Aland co., SW Finland, on SW shore of Aland isl., on the Baltic, 170 mi. W of Helsinki, 90 mi. NE of Stockholm; 60°5'N 19°56'E. Seaport, with steamer lines to Turku and Stockholm; airfield (NW). Shipping and fishing center; seaside resort. Pop. is entirely Swedish-speaking. Founded 1861, Mariehamn was until recent times home port of major fleet of sailing vessels engaged in Australian grain trade.

Marieholm (märē"ühôlm'), village (pop. 1,004), Malmohus co., S Sweden, 18 mi. NNE of Malmo; woolen milling; grain, potatoes, stock.

Mariel (märyĕl'), town (pop. 3,954), Pinar del Río prov., W Cuba, on sheltered bay, 27 mi. WSW of Havana, in agr. region (sugar cane, tobacco, cattle). Mfg. of cement and cigars. Shark fishing. Near by are Cuba's principal asphalt reserves. There are also limestone and guano deposits; sulphurous springs. In the outskirts is the Cuban Naval Acad. The Central San Ramón is 3 mi. SW.

Marie Louise Island (pop. 31), in S Amirantes, outlying dependency of the Seychelles, 190 mi. SW of Mahé Isl., 6°11'S 53°9'E; 1 mi. long, ½ mi. wide; coral formation. Copra.

Mariembourg or **Marienbourg** (märēäbōōr'), town (pop. 1,528), Namur prov., S Belgium, 8 mi. S of Philippeville; agr., cattle raising. Founded 1542 as fortress against France; annexed to France 1659–1815. Half of village burned (1914) by Germans.

Mariemont (märēmō'), town, Hainaut prov., S central Belgium, 9 mi. WNW of Charleroi; coal mines; coke plants.

Mariemont (mŭrē'mŏnt), village (pop. 3,514), Hamilton co., extreme SW Ohio, an E suburb of Cincinnati; bakery products, electrical apparatus, beverages. Laid out 1922, inc. 1941.

Marienbad (märē'ŭnbät), Czech *Mariánské Lázně* (mä'rēänskä läz'nyĕ), town (pop. 6,027), W Bohemia, Czechoslovakia, 34 mi. WNW of Pilsen. Rail junction; mfg. of wood products; famous health resort in a valley (alt. 1,900 ft.), with c.40 mineral springs; known as spa since 16th cent. Antimony mining in vicinity.

Marienberg (märē'ŭnbĕrk). **1** Town (pop. 1,803), in former Prussian prov. of Hesse-Nassau, W Germany, after 1945 in Rhineland-Palatinate, in the Westerwald, 16 mi. S of Siegen; climatic health resort and winter-sports center (alt. 1,640 ft.). **2** Town (pop. 8,281), Saxony, E central Germany, in the Erzgebirge, 17 mi. SE of Chemnitz, near Czechoslovak border; textile milling (cotton, ribbon, lace), hosiery knitting, metal- and woodworking, button mfg. Marble and serpentine quarrying. Climatic health resort. Has 16th-cent. church and town hall. Founded c.1520 as silver-mining settlement, later became important staging point on Halle-Prague salt-trade route.

Marienborn (märē'ŭnbôrn), village (pop. 753), in former Prussian Saxony prov., central Germany, after 1945 in Saxony-Anhalt, 23 mi. W of Magdeburg, 5 mi. ESE of Helmstedt, in lignite-mining region. After 1945, rail and road traffic check point bet. East and West Germany.

Marienbourg, Belgium: see MARIEMBOURG.

Mariënburg (märē'ŭnbŭrkh), town (pop. 2,476), Commewijne dist., N Du. Guiana, on Commewijne R. and 7 mi. ENE of Paramaribo; sugar-milling center.

Marienburg (märē'ŭnbōōrk), village (pop. 439), in former Prussian prov. of Hanover, NW Germany, after 1945 in Lower Saxony, 3 mi. SSE of Hildesheim.

Marienburg, Latvia: see ALUKSNE.

Marienburg or **Malbork** (mäl'bôrk), town (1939 pop. 27,318; 1946 pop. 10,017) in East Prussia, after 1945 in Gdansk prov., N Poland, on Nogat R. and 25 mi. SE of Danzig, 18 mi. WSW of Elbing; rail junction; sugar refining, sawmilling; power station. Castle, founded 1274 by Teutonic Knights, became in 1309 seat of their Grand Master (moved here from Venice). Surrounding town chartered 1276. Castle (rebuilt 14th and 19th cent.) besieged (1410, 1454) by Poles; disgruntled mercenaries sold it to Poland in 1457, but it withstood siege until 1460. Town became (1466) ⊙ Pol. West Prussia; passed 1772 to Prussia; until 1919, in West Prussia prov. Retained by Germany in plebiscite of 1920. Until 1939, Ger. frontier station on border of Polish Corridor, 11 mi. ESE of Tczew. In Second World War, c.50% destroyed.

Marienburg, Rumania: see FELDIOARA.

Marienhausen, Latvia: see VILAKA.

Marienheide (märē"ŭnhī'dŭ), village (pop. 6,965), in former Prussian Rhine Prov., W Germany, after 1945 in North Rhine-Westphalia, 4 mi. N of Gummersbach; lead mining near by.

Marienhof, Russian SFSR: see NIKITOVKA, Kalinin-grad oblast.

Marienstein, Germany: see WAAKIRCHEN.

Mariental (märē'ŭntäl"), town (pop. 1,803), S central South-West Africa, 140 mi. N of Keetmanshoop; judicial and distributing center of Gibeon dist. (pop. 11,796), in sheep-raising region. Airfield. Large Iceland-spar deposits near by.

Mariental, Russian SFSR: see SOVETSKOYE, Saratov oblast.

Marienville (mâ'rēŭnvĭl), village (1940 pop. 844), Forest co., NW Pa., 28 mi. NE of Clarion; agr.; glass products.

Marienwerder (märē"ŭnvĕr'dŭr) or **Kwidzyn** (kvē'-jĭnyŭ), Pol. *Kwidzyń*, town (1939 pop. 20,484; 1946 pop. 7,986) in East Prussia, after 1945 in Gdansk prov., N Poland, near the Vistula, 45 mi. SSE of Danzig, 35 mi. SSW of Elbing; sawmilling; power station. In Second World War, c.50% destroyed; Gothic cathedral and 14th-cent. castle remain. Teutonic Knights founded castle (1233) on near-by isl. in the Vistula; later rebuilt on present site; town remained one of their centers until 1526. Became seat (1254) of bishops of Pomerania; bishopric dissolved 1526 when Reformation was introduced in region. Until 1919, was ⊙ West Prussia prov.

Maries (mâ'rēz), county (□ 526; pop. 7,423), central Mo.; ⊙ Vienna. In the Ozarks; drained by Gasconade R. Agr. region (wheat, corn, oats, especially livestock); fire clay, iron mines. Formed 1855.

Mariestad (märē"ŭstäd'), city (pop. 7,091), ⊙ Skaraborg co., S central Sweden, on E shore of L. Vaner, at mouth of Tida R., 90 mi. NE of Goteborg; 58°43'N 13°50'E. Lake port and rail junction; shipbuilding, paper milling, metalworking; mfg. of furniture, fibreboard. Has 17th-cent. church and castle. Chartered 1583, when it was called Tunaholm; renamed c.1600. Rebuilt (1895) after destructive fire.

Marietta (mâ"rēĕ'tŭ, mă"rē–). **1** City (pop. 20,687), ⊙ Cobb co., NW central Ga., 16 mi. NW of Atlanta, in Blue Ridge foothills; mfg. (hosiery, wood and aluminum furniture, prefabricated houses, marble products, castings, lumber, frozen foods, pottery); large aircraft plant built in Second World War. Air Force base here. Inc. 1834. Marietta Natl. Cemetery here. Kennesaw Mtn. Natl. Battlefield Park just W. **2** Village (pop. 178), Fulton co., W central Ill., 19 mi. WSW of Canton, in agr. and bituminous-coal area. **3** Village (pop. 380), Lac qui Parle co., SW Minn., near S.Dak. line, 11 mi. W of Madison, in grain, livestock, poultry area; dairy products. **4** Town (pop. 94), Robeson co., S N.C., 18 mi. SSW of Lumberton, near S.C. line. **5** City (pop. 16,006), ⊙ Washington co., SE Ohio, at confluence of the navigable Muskingum and Ohio rivers, 11 mi. NNE of Parkersburg, W.Va.; large ferroalloy plant; mfg. of metal products, chemicals, furniture, oil-well supplies, concrete vaults, pottery, rubber goods, food products, paints, dyes; petroleum refining. Truck and dairy farming. Seat of Marietta Col. In 1950 and 1951, annual Intercollegiate Regatta held here. Has bldgs. dating from 1st settlement. Mound Cemetery, enclosing a large Indian mound, contains graves of several noted officers of the American Revolution. The 1st planned permanent settlement in Ohio and in NORTHWEST TERRITORY, city was founded in 1778 by Ohio Company of Associates; inc. 1800. Shipping and shipbuilding were important in its growth. **6** City (pop. 1,875), ⊙ Love co., S Okla., 16 mi. S of Ardmore, in diversified agr. area (cotton, cattle, corn); cotton ginning; oil and gas wells. L. Murray (state park; recreation) is 7 mi. NE; L. Texoma is 8 mi. E. Founded c.1887. **7** Borough (pop. 2,442), Lancaster co., SE Pa., 3 mi. NW of Columbia and on Susquehanna R.; shoes, textiles, enamelware. Army depot here. Settled 1718, inc. 1812. **8** Village in Blue Ridge foothills, Greenville co., NW S.C., on North Saluda R. and 13 mi. NNW of Greenville; nurseries; textile mill.

Marieville (mä'rēvĭl), town (pop. 2,394), ⊙ Rouville co., S Que., near Richelieu R., 20 mi. ESE of Montreal; hat making, woodworking, dairying.

Marifu, Japan: see IWAKUNI.

Marigliano (märēlyä'nô), town (pop. 6,997), Napoli prov., Campania, S Italy, 11 mi. ENE of Naples, in grape- and vegetable-growing region. Has mineral waters.

Marignac (märēnyäk'), village (pop. 645), Haute-Garonne dept., S France, at N end of Luchon Valley, 9 mi. NNE of Luchon; electrochemical factory (fertilizer), metalworks.

Marignane (märēnyän'), agr. town (pop. 2,991), Bouches-du-Rhône dept., SE France, near E shore of Étang de Berre, 12 mi. NW of Marseilles, on Marseilles-Rhone Canal. Site of Marseilles airport.

Marignano, Italy: see MELEGNANO.

Marignier (märēnyā'), village (pop. 795), Haute-Savoie dept., SE France, on the Giffre near its influx into Arve R. and 5 mi. ENE of Bonneville, in Faucigny valley; hydroelectric plant and electrochemical works. Produces tools and parts for watch industry.

Marigny (märēnyē'), village (pop. 441), Manche dept., NW France, 7 mi. WSW of Saint-Lô; dairying. Here Americans broke through Ger. defenses in Saint-Lô offensive (July, 1944) of Second World War.

Marigny-le-Châtel (–lŭ-shätĕl'), village (pop. 1,040), Aube dept., NE central France, 8 mi. S of Romilly-sur-Seine; hosiery mills.

Marigot (märēgō'), village (pop. 810), NE Dominica, B.W.I., 18 mi. NNE of Roseau; coconuts, limes. At the Carib Reserve, 4 mi. S, live a few survivors of aboriginal inhabitants.

Marigot, agr. town (1950 census pop. 1,191), Ouest dept., S Haiti, on the Caribbean, 18 mi. E of Jacmel; banana growing.

Marigot, town (pop. 521), NE Martinique, on the Atlantic, 14 mi. N of Fort-de-France; sugar milling, rum distilling.

Marigot, village, St. Martin isl., Fr. West Indies, on W coast of isl., 160 mi. NW of Basse-Terre, Guadeloupe; 18°4'N 63°5'W. Principal settlement of the Fr. section of the isl., with a good harbor. Produces some sugar cane, tropical fruit, cotton, and cattle for local use.

Mariguana, Bahama Isls.: see MAYAGUANA.

Marigüitar (märēgwētär'), town (pop. 1,696), Sucre state, NE Venezuela, on Gulf of Cariaco, 18 mi. E of Cumaná; coconuts, cacao, sugar cane, vegetables.

Marihovo or **Marikhovo** (mä'rēhôvô, –khôvô), region in Macedonia, Yugoslavia, extending c.25 mi.

SW-NE, bet. the Crna Reka and Greek border. Chief village, ROZDEN. Also called Mariovo, Marijovo, or Mariyovo.

Mariinsk (mŭrē'ĭnsk), city (1936 pop. estimate 21,000), NE Kemerovo oblast, Russian SFSR, on Trans-Siberian RR, on Kiya R. and 85 mi. NE of Kemerovo; supply point for upper Kiya R. gold mines; distillery, flour mills, sawmills. Chartered 1856.

Mariinsk Canal, in NW Vologda oblast, Russian SFSR, links canalized Vytegra (NW) and Kovzha (SE) rivers; 5 mi. long; built 1808; reconstructed in 1940s. Formerly called Novo-Mariinsk Canal. Forms watershed section of Mariinsk canal system, which joins Volga R. and Rybinsk Reservoir (S) with Neva R. and Leningrad (NW). Entire waterway (N-S; repeatedly reconstructed and deepened) consists of Neva R., Ladoga Canals, Svir R., Onega Canal, Vytegra R., Mariinsk Canal, Kovzha R., Belozersk Canal, Sheksna R., and Rybinsk Reservoir. Lies on historic Baltic-Volga route, in use since 9th cent.

Mariinski or **Mariinskiy** (-skē), village, S Sverdlovsk oblast, Russian SFSR, on small left tributary of Chusovaya R. and 13 mi. S of Revda; lumbering; livestock. Site (until c.1930) of ironworks called Mariinski Zavod (1926 pop. 1,271).

Mariinski Posad or **Mariinskiy Posad** (pŭsät'), city (1936 pop. estimate 7,000), N Chuvash Autonomous SSR, Russian SFSR, port on right bank of the Volga, 17 mi. E of Cheboksary; shipbuilding, coopering; wine, sack-, mat-, and basketmaking. Forestry school. Chartered 1856.

Mariinskoye, Kazakh SSR: see MARYEVKA.

Marijampole or **Mariyampole** (märĭyämpô'lā), Lith. *Marijampolė*, Pol. *Mariampol*, city (pop. 15,768), S Lithuania, on the Sheshupe and 32 mi. SW of Kaunas; road center; major agr. market; sugar refining, flour milling, brewing, brickworking, sawmilling; mfg. of woolens, cotton goods, leather, furniture. Passed 1795 to Prussia, 1815 to Rus. Poland; in Suvalki govt. until 1920.

Marijovo, region, Yugoslavia: see MARIHOVO.

Marikhovo, region, Yugoslavia: see MARIHOVO.

Marikina (märēkē'nä), town (1939 pop. 2,700; 1948 municipality pop. 23,353), Rizal prov., S Luzon, Philippines, 8 mi. ENE of Manila; agr. center (rice, sugar cane, fruit); shoemaking.

Mariko, Japan: see MARUKO.

Marikuppam, India: see KOLAR GOLD FIELDS.

Marília (mŏrēl'yŭ), city (1950 pop. 36,306), W central São Paulo, Brazil, on railroad and 55 mi. W of Bauru; leading cotton-growing center in rich agr. dist. along watershed bet. Aguapeí and Peixe rivers, settled by pioneer farmers since 1920s. Cotton ginning, cottonseed-oil extracting, sawmilling, furniture mfg. City also trades in coffee, corn, rice, livestock (hogs and beef cattle), dairy products, and fruit, which are the result of efficient, diversified small-farm agr. Long a railhead, Marília has now become the supply center for new pioneer settlement further W in Tupã (present railhead) and Lucélia areas.

Marimba (mŏrēm'bŏ), town (pop. 983), Malange prov., N Angola, near Belgian Congo border, 100 mi. NNE of Malange; manioc, cotton.

Marimbondo Falls, Brazil: see MARIBONDO FALLS.

Marin (märē'), town (pop. 1,525), SE Martinique, minor port on bay, 16 mi. SE of Fort-de-France; trading and processing (alcohol, sugar), in agr. region (cacao, sugar cane). Sometimes called Le Marin.

Marín (märēn'), town (pop. 1,245), Nuevo León, N Mexico, 22 mi. NE of Monterrey; cereals, cactus fibers, livestock.

Marín, town (pop. 5,781), Pontevedra prov., NW Spain, Atlantic seaport on Pontevedra Bay, 4 mi. SW of Pontevedra; exports fish, lumber, salt. Fishing, shipbuilding; naval installations.

Marin (mŭrĭn'), county (□ 521; pop. 85,619), W Calif.; ⊙ San Rafael. Many residential suburbs of San Francisco (Golden Gate Bridge and ferry connections) on this wooded, hilly peninsula (Marin Peninsula) reaching S to the Golden Gate, and bet. San Pablo and San Francisco bays (E) and Pacific Ocean (W); Pacific coast is indented by Bodega, Tomales, Drakes, and Bolinas bays. Mt. TAMALPAIS and Muir Woods Natl. Monument are W of Mill Valley. Includes Angel Isl., largest in San Francisco Bay. State prison at San Quentin. Dairying, poultry and stock raising (cattle, sheep, hogs), farming (hay, truck, fruit); nurseries. Stone, sand, gravel, clay quarrying. Formed 1850.

Marín (märēn'), town (pop. 1,269), Yaracuy state, N Venezuela, 5 mi. NE of San Felipe; cacao, corn, sugar, fruit, stock.

Marina, La, Costa Rica: see LA MARINA.

Marina di Besca, Yugoslavia: see BASKA.

Marina di Carrara (märē'nä dē kär-rä'rä), town (pop. 5,518), Massa e Carrara prov., Tuscany, N Italy, port on Ligurian Sea, 4 mi. SW of Carrara; bathing resort. Exports marble.

Marina di Catanzaro (kätänzä'rô), town (pop. 3,924), Catanzaro prov., Calabria, S Italy, on Gulf of Squillace; port of Catanzaro (6 mi. N); rail junction; olive-oil refining.

Marina di Massa (mäs'sä), village (pop. 720), Massa e Carrara prov., Tuscany, central Italy, port on Ligurian Sea, 3 mi. SW of Massa; bathing resort. Exports marble.

Marina di Patti, Sicily: see PATTI.

Marina di Pietrasanta, Italy: see PIETRASANTA.

Marina di Pisa (pē'sä), town (pop. 3,053), Pisa prov., Tuscany, central Italy, port on Ligurian Sea, at mouth of the Arno, 7 mi. SW of Pisa. Bathing resort; airplane mfg.

Marina di Ravenna (rävĕn'nä), village (pop. 1,745), Ravenna prov., Emilia-Romagna, N central Italy, on the Adriatic, at mouth of Lamone R., 6 mi. NE of Ravenna, with which it is connected by canal. Bathing resort. Across the river is Porto Corsini, port of Ravenna, with sulphur refinery, cement and fertilizer plants.

Marina Falls (märē'nŭ), central Br. Guiana, on affluent of Potaro R., and 15 mi. NW of Kaieteur Falls; drop c.500 ft. in several leaps.

Marina Gorka or **Mar'ina Gorka** (mä'rēnŭ gôr'kŭ), town (1948 pop. over 2,000), central Minsk oblast, Belorussian SSR, near railroad (Pukhovichi station), 36 mi. SE of Minsk; paper, starch products. Pukhovichi village (pop. 2,161) lies 5 mi. NE.

Marinaleda (märēnälā'dhä), town (pop. 2,008), Seville prov., SW Spain, 12 mi. NE of Osuna; cereals, vegetables, olives, acorns, livestock.

Marincho, Arroyo (äroi'ō märēn'chō), river, Flores dept., SW Uruguay, rises in the Cuchilla Grande Inferior 7 mi. W of Trinidad, flows 37 mi. N to Yí R. 6 mi. above confluence with the Río Negro.

Marinduque (märēndōō'kā), island (□ 346; 1939 pop. 79,781), Philippines, bet. Bondoc Peninsula of S Luzon and Mindoro isl., near entrance to Tayabas Bay, and forming W shore of Mompog Pass; 13°24'N 121°58'E. Roughly circular, 24 mi. long, 22 mi. wide. Mountainous, rising to 2,894 ft.; watered by many small streams. Agr. (coconuts, rice, abacá); mining (iron, gold). Marinduque province (□ 355; 1948 pop. 85,828) comprises Marinduque isl. and several offshore isls.; ⊙ BOAC.

Marine. **1** Village (pop. 657), Madison co., SW Ill., 23 mi. ENE of East St. Louis, in agr. area (corn, wheat; dairy products; poultry, livestock). **2** Village (pop. 334), Washington co., E Minn., on St. Croix R. and 23 mi. NE of St. Paul; ice cream. Also known as Marine on St. Croix.

Marine City, city and port (pop. 4,270), St. Clair co., E Mich., 18 mi. S of Port Huron and on St. Clair R. at mouth of Belle R. Mfg. (boats, auto parts); grain elevator, lumber mill. Salt mines. Inc. as village 1865; named Marine City 1867; inc. as city 1887.

Marineland, town (pop. 9), Flagler co., E Fla., 18 mi. S of St. Augustine. Outdoor marine aquariums attract tourists.

Marinella (märēnĕl'lä), village (pop. 186), **Trapani** prov., W Sicily, port on Mediterranean Sea, 5 mi. SE of Campobello di Mazara; tunny fishing. Ruins of Selinunte, anc. *Selinus*, westernmost Greek settlement of isl. (founded 628 B.C.; destroyed by Carthaginians 409 B.C.) just W. Remains of 11 temples, several necropolises. Also called Marinella Selinunte.

Marineo (märēnā'ô), town (pop. 6,676), Palermo prov., N Sicily, 12 mi. SSE of Palermo, in citrus-fruit and corn region; summer resort.

Marine on Saint Croix, Minn.: see MARINE.

Mariners Harbor, SE N.Y., an industrial section of Richmond borough of New York city, on N Staten Isl., on the Kill van Kull; mfg. of clothing, chemicals, paints, lumber, machinery, metal products; shipbuilding; oil refining. Goethals and Bayonne bridges to N.J. are near by.

Marines (märēn'), village (pop. 1,309), Seine-et-Oise dept., N central France, 8 mi. NW of Pontoise; faïence mfg. Has 16th-cent. castle.

Marines, Los (lōs märē'nĕs), town (pop. 586), Huelva prov., SW Spain, in the Sierra Morena, 3 mi. WNW of Aracena; chestnuts, olives, cork, fruit, timber, hogs, goats.

Marinette (mărĭnĕt'), county (□ 1,388; pop. 35,748), NE Wis., bounded E by Menominee R. (here the Mich. line), SE by Green Bay; ⊙ Marinette. Wooded region, drained by Peshtigo R.; contains several resort lakes. Lumbering, dairying, potato growing; mfg. at Marinette. Formed 1879.

Marinette, city (pop. 14,178), ⊙ Marinette co., NE Wis., port of entry at mouth of Menominee R. on Green Bay, opposite Menominee, Mich.; mfg. (paper, chemicals, woolen goods, cutlery, wood products); commercial center for recreational area. Has fisheries and dairy plants. City grew as fur-trading post (established c.1795), and as lumbering center in late 1800s. Inc. 1887.

Maringa River (märĭng'gä), W Belgian Congo, rises 70 mi. SE of Djolu, flows c.325 mi. W and NW, past Befori, Mompono, Befale, and Waka, to join Lopori R. at Basankusu, forming the Lulonga. Navigable for 250 mi. below Befori.

Maringouin (mâ'rĭng-wĭn), village (pop. 898), Iberville parish, SE central La., 19 mi. W of Baton Rouge; wood products.

Maringues (märĕg'), village (pop. 1,368), Puy-de-Dôme dept., central France, in the Limagne, 10 mi. ENE of Riom; wheat and poultry market; flour milling.

Marinha Grande (mŭrē'nyŭ grän'dĭ), town (pop. 2,092), Leiria dist., W central Portugal, on railroad and 7 mi. W of Leiria, amidst pine forest; glass and crystal mfg. center known since mid-18th cent.

Marinilla (märēnē'yä), town (pop. 3,591), Antioquia dept., NW central Colombia, in Cordillera Central. 17 mi. ESE of Medellín; alt. 6,961 ft.; potatoes, coffee, livestock. Old colonial town. In Colombian folklore, the inhabitants of this town are known for their wit.

Marinka or **Mar'inka** (mä'rēnkŭ), village (1939 pop. over 2,000), central Stalino oblast, Ukrainian SSR, in the Donbas, 14 mi. WSW of Stalino.

Marino (märē'nô), town (pop. 8,062), Rome prov., Latium, central Italy, in Alban Hills, near L. Albano, 13 mi. SE of Rome. Noted as a health resort (alt. 1,165 ft.) and for its wine.

Marino (mŭrē'nō), seaside resort in Holywood urban dist., NE Co. Down, Northern Ireland, on S shore of Belfast Lough.

Marino or **Mar'ino** (mä'rēnŭ). **1** Village (1939 pop. over 500), central Kursk oblast, Russian SFSR, on railroad and 16 mi. E of Oboyan, at Rzhava rail junction; sugar beets. Rzhava village (1939 pop. over 500) lies 5 mi. N; sugar refinery. **2** Town, Mari Autonomous SSR, Russian SFSR: see LENINSKI.

Marins, Île aux (ēl ō märē'), tiny rocky islet (pop. 168) just outside Saint Pierre in SAINT PIERRE AND MIQUELON archipelago. Cod fishing.

Marinuka, Lake, Wis.: see GALESVILLE.

Marion (mă'rēun, mâ'–). **1** County (□ 743; pop. 27,264), NW Ala.; ⊙ Hamilton. Agr. area bordering on Miss., drained by Buttahatchee R., crossed (N–S) by fall line. Cotton, bees, poultry; coal mines. Formed 1818. **2** County (□ 628; pop. 8,609), N Ark., in the Ozark region; ⊙ Yellville. Bounded N by Mo. line; intersected by White R. (site of Bull Shoals Dam); drained by Buffalo R. and small Crooked Creek. Agr. (cotton, corn, truck, grain, livestock). Some mfg. at Yellville. Lead, zinc mines; timber. Buffalo R. State Park (fishing) in co. Formed 1835. **3** County (□ 1,617; pop. 38,187), N central Fla.; ⊙ Ocala. Flatwoods area with scattered lakes, including L. Weir and L. Kerr; drained by Oklawaha R. Ocala Natl. Forest occupies E part. Agr. (citrus fruit, vegetables, corn, peanuts), stock raising (cattle, hogs), forestry (lumber, naval stores), and quarrying (limestone, phosphate). Formed 1844. **4** County (□ 365; pop. 6,521), W Ga.; ⊙ Buena Vista. Coastal plain agr. (cotton, corn, peanuts, pecans, truck, fruit) and timber area drained by Kinchafoone R. Formed 1827. **5** County (□ 580; pop. 41,700), S central Ill.; ⊙ Salem. Agr., bituminous-coal, and oil-producing and -refining area; corn, wheat, fruit, livestock, poultry. Some mfg.: metal products, dairy and food products, shoes, clothing, lumber. Drained by Skillet Fork, Crooked Creek, and a small headstream of Kaskaskia R. Formed 1823. **6** County (□ 402; pop. 551,777), central Ind.; ⊙ INDIANAPOLIS. Transportation (rail, highway), commercial, market, and mfg. center at Indianapolis. Drained by West Fork of White R. and small Eagle Fall, and Buck creeks. Farming (wheat, corn, truck, soybeans), stock raising (cattle, hogs), dairying. Formed 1822. **7** County (□ 568; pop. 25,930), S central Iowa; ⊙ Knoxville. Rolling prairie agr. area (hogs, cattle, poultry, corn) drained by Skunk and Des Moines rivers and by Whitebreast Creek. Many bituminous-coal mines, some limestone quarries. Formed 1845. **8** County (□ 959; pop. 16,307), E central Kansas; ⊙ Marion. Gently rolling to hilly area, drained by Cottonwood R. Wheat, livestock. Oil fields (N and S). Formed 1860. **9** County (□ 343; pop. 17,212), central Ky.; ⊙ Lebanon. Drained by Rolling Fork and several creeks. Rolling upland agr. area, partly in outer Bluegrass region; burley tobacco, corn, hay. Timber; stone quarries. Some mfg. at Lebanon. Formed 1834. **10** County (□ 550; pop. 23,967), S Miss.; ⊙ Columbia. Partly bounded S by La. Drained by Pearl R. Agr. (cotton, corn, truck); lumbering. Formed 1811. **11** County (□ 440; pop. 29,765), NE Mo.; ⊙ Palmyra. Bounded E by Mississippi R.; drained by North R. and South Fabius R. Corn, wheat, oats, dairying; mfg. at Hannibal. Formed 1826. **12** County (□ 405; pop. 49,959), central Ohio; ⊙ MARION. Intersected by Scioto R.; also drained by Olentangy and Little Scioto rivers and small Tymochtee Creek. Agr. (livestock; dairy products; grain, fruit); mfg. at Marion; limestone quarries, sand and gravel pits. Formed 1823. **13** County (□ 1,173; pop. 101,401), NW Oregon; ⊙ Salem, the state capital. Agr. area bounded W by Willamette R., S by North Santiam R. Mfg. at Salem. Dairy products, poultry, fruit, truck, grain, seeds, hay. Includes part of Willamette Natl. Forest. Cascade Range is in E. Formed 1843. **14** County (□ 480; pop. 33,110), E S.C.; ⊙ Marion. Bounded W by Pee Dee, E by Little Pee Dee rivers. Agr. area (tobacco, cotton, truck), timber; some mfg. Formed 1798. **15** County (□ 507; pop. 20,520), SE Tenn.; ⊙ Jasper. Partly in the Cumberlands; bounded S by Ala. and Ga.; drained by Tennessee and Sequatchie rivers and small Little Sequatchie R. Includes Hales Bar Reservoir. Coal, iron-ore deposits; dairying, livestock raising, some agr. (corn, hay, soybeans, cotton, tobacco), especially in the Sequatchie valley. Formed 1817. **16** County

(□ 400; pop. 10,172), E Texas; ⊙ Jefferson. Bounded E by La. line; drained by Cypress Bayou; includes part of Caddo L. (hunting, fishing). Lumbering; oil, natural-gas wells; clay, iron deposits. Agr. (cotton, corn, sweet potatoes, peanuts, fruit, truck), cattle, poultry, hogs; dairying. Formed 1860. **17** County (□ 309; pop. 71,521), N W.Va.; ⊙ FAIRMONT. On Allegheny Plateau; drained by Monongahela and Tygart rivers. Coal mining; agr. (dairy products, truck, fruit); gas and oil fields. Mfg. at Fairmont, Mannington. Formed 1842.

Marion. 1 City (pop. 2,822), ⊙ Perry co., W central Ala., 23 mi. NW of Selma, near Cahaba R.; woodworking, cotton ginning. Judson Col. and military institute are here. Settled 1817. Talladega Natl. Forest is E. U.S. fish hatchery near by. **2** Town (pop. 883), ⊙ Crittenden co., E Ark., 12 mi. WNW of Memphis, Tenn., in cotton-growing area. **3** City (pop. 10,459), ⊙ Williamson co., S Ill., 11 mi. S of West Frankfort, in bituminous-coal-mining and agr. area (fruit, poultry, corn, wheat). Has state's oldest county fair (since 1856). Site of veterans' hosp. and home. A military ordnance plant is near by. Crab Orchard L. is just W. Robert Ingersoll and John A. Logan lived here. Inc. 1841. **4** City (pop. 30,081), ⊙ Grant co., E central Ind., on Mississinewa R. and 30 mi. NNW of Muncie; farm trade, railroad, and industrial center in agr. area, with gas and oil fields near by. Mfg.: motor trucks, electric-lighting equipment, glass, paper, oil-well machinery, radios, railroad equipment, shoes, furniture, brick, beer, food products. Seat of Marion Col. A U.S. veterans' hosp. is just S. Settled 1826; boomed with discovery of oil and gas, c.1880. **5** City (pop. 5,916), Linn co., E Iowa, just NE of Cedar Rapids; railroad division point with repair shops and freight yards; mfg. (feed, wood products, tools, dies). Settled 1839, inc. 1865. **6** City (pop. 2,050), ⊙ Marion co., E central Kansas, on Cottonwood R. and 45 mi. NNE of Wichita; shipping center for grain and livestock area; poultry and egg packing, grain milling. Co. fair takes place here annually in Oct. Settled 1860, laid out 1866, inc. 1875. Damaged by flood of July, 1951. **7** City (pop. 2,375), ⊙ Crittenden co., W Ky., 34 mi. ENE of Paducah, in oak-timber and agr. (corn, oats, wheat) area; ships fluorspar (mines near by). Limestone quarrying and crushing, lumber milling. Has airport. Inc. 1844. **8** Village (pop. 685), Union parish, N La., 29 mi. NNW of Monroe; agr., cotton ginning, lumbering. **9** Town (pop. 2,250), Plymouth co., SE Mass., on W shore of Buzzards Bay and 10 mi. NE of New Bedford; summer resort. Formerly shipbuilding. Settled 1679, set off from Rochester 1852. **10** Village (pop. 879), Osceola co., central Mich., 16 mi. SE of Cadillac, in farm area. **11** Village (1940 pop. 507), Lauderdale co., E Miss., 5 mi. NE of Meridian; ships strawberries. **12** Village (1940 pop. 771), Wayne co., W N.Y., 20 mi. E of Rochester, in fruitgrowing region; canning. **13** Town (pop. 2,740), ⊙ McDowell co., W N.C., 31 mi. ENE of Asheville, in the Blue Ridge, near Catawba R.; mfg. (textiles, yarn, hosiery, furniture). Linville Caverns are N. **14** Village (pop. 272), La Moure co., SE central N.Dak., 27 mi. SE of Jamestown. **15** City (pop. 33,817), ⊙ Marion co., central Ohio, c.45 mi. N of Columbus; rail, industrial, and agr.-trade center; makes steam shovels, farm and road-construction machinery, metal products, refrigerators, food products, wood products, auto parts. Limestone quarries. Home of Warren G. Harding is now a mus. U.S. ordnance plant and military engineers' depot here. Laid out 1820; inc. as village in 1830, as city in 1890. **16** Town (pop. 6,834), ⊙ Marion co., E S.C., 20 mi. E of Florence; trade center in agr. area; mfg. (lumber, lumber products, bricks, textiles, cottonseed oil). **17** City (pop. 794), Turner co., SE S.Dak., 7 mi. WNW of Parker; dairy products, poultry, grain. Hosp. and clinic for persons suffering with bone disorders are here. **18** Town (pop. 439), Guadalupe co., S central Texas, 24 mi. NE of San Antonio and on Guadalupe R.; rail point in agr. area (peanuts, poultry, cotton). **19** Town (pop. 6,982), ⊙ Smyth co., SW Va., on Middle Fork of Holston R. and 27 mi. ENE of Abingdon, bet. Walker Mtn. (N) and Iron Mts. (S). Mfg. of sports equipment, wood products, clothing, hosiery; lumber milling; limestone quarrying and processing. Jr. col., hosp. for the insane here. Hungry Mother State Park near by, White Top Mtn. and Mt. Rogers are S. Inc. 1832. **20** City (pop. 1,118), Waupaca co., E central Wis., on small Pigeon R. and c.40 mi. WNW of Green Bay, in timber, dairy, and grain area; dairy products, farm implements, excelsior, cheese boxes, steel cabinets. Settled 1878; inc. as village in 1898, as city in 1939.

Marion, Fort, Fla.: see SAINT AUGUSTINE.

Marion, Lake, S.C.: see SANTEE RIVER.

Marion, Mount (9,750 ft.), SE B.C., in Selkirk Mts., 55 mi. N of Nelson; 50°17′N 117°13′W.

Marion Center, borough (pop. 433), Indiana co., W central Pa., 11 mi. NNE of Indiana; grist mill, creamery.

Marion Heights, borough (pop. 1,551), Northumberland co., E central Pa., just N of Kulpmont.

Marion Island, subantarctic island (13 mi. long, 8 mi. wide) in S Indian Ocean, c.1,200 mi. SE of Cape Town, just SW of Prince Edward Isl., with which it forms the Prince Edward Isls. Located at 46°51′S 37°52′E. Rises to 4,200 ft. Formally annexed by U. of So. Afr. in Dec., 1947. Has meteorological station.

Marion Station, village (pop. c.500), Somerset co., SE Md., on the Eastern Shore near Big Annemessex R., 25 mi. SSW of Salisbury; strawberry, tomato market.

Marionville, city (pop. 1,167), Lawrence co., SW Mo., in the Ozarks, 24 mi. SW of Springfield; dairy, grain products. Laid out 1854.

Mariovo, region, Yugoslavia: see MARIHOVO.

Maripa (märēpä′), town, ⊙ Oyapock dist. (pop. 82), Inini territory, E Fr. Guiana, on Oyapock R. (Brazil border) and 45 mi. SW of St. Georges; customhouse.

Maripa (märē′pä), town (pop. 491), Bolívar state, SE Venezuela, on Caura R. and 125 mi. WSW of Ciudad Bolívar; rubber, balata gum.

Maripasoula (märēpäsōōlä′), town, ⊙ Maroni dist. (pop. 1,219), Inini territory, SW Fr. Guiana, on Aoua R. (Du. Guiana border); 3°39′N 54°5′W. Gold placers in vicinity.

Maripipi Island (mä″rēpēpē′) (□ 11; 1948 pop. 6,550), Leyte prov., Philippines, in Samar Sea, bet. Masbate and Leyte isls., 5 mi. NW of Biliran Isl.; 11°47′N 124°19′E; 4 mi. in diameter. Mountainous, rising to 3,020 ft. Coconut growing, fishing.

Mariposa (mărĭpō′zů), county (□ 1,455; pop. 5,145), central Calif.; ⊙ Mariposa. On W slope of the Sierra Nevada, at S end of Mother Lode gold country; has peaks over 10,000 ft. in NE. E portion is in YOSEMITE NATIONAL PARK. Also includes parts of Sierra and Stanislaus natl. forests. Drained by Merced R. (dammed here into Exchequer Reservoir), Tuolumne and Chowchilla rivers. Includes Merced and Mariposa groves of the big trees (*Sequoia gigantea*). Region famed for scenery and recreational resources (resorts; hunting, lake and stream fishing, camping, hiking, winter sports). A leading gold-mining co. (quartz mines) of Calif. Lumbering (pine, fir, spruce). Stock raising (cattle, sheep, hogs, poultry); little farming. Sand and gravel pits; silver mining. Mariposa, Hornitos, Coulterville, and ruins of old gold camps are reminders of gold rush. Formed 1850.

Mariposa, village (1940 pop. 628), ⊙ Mariposa co., central Calif., 32 mi. NE of Merced; gateway to Yosemite Natl. Park (NE). Airport near. An old gold rush town; its courthouse (1854) is said to be oldest in state.

Mariposa Grove, Calif.: see YOSEMITE NATIONAL PARK.

Mariposas (märēpō′säs), village (1930 pop. 1,298), Talca prov., central Chile, 20 mi. ESE of Talca; rail terminus in agr. area (wheat, barley, wine, livestock).

Mariquita (märēkē′tä), city (pop. 3,817), Tolima dept., W central Colombia, in Magdalena valley, on railroad and 10 mi. W of Honda. Terminus of aerial tramway from Manizales; communication and trading center in agr. region (sugar cane, yucca, corn, rice, coffee, bananas, fruit). Airport. Old colonial town, founded 1551, it was a former provincial capital. Gold mines near by.

Marisa, Palestine: see MARESHAH.

Mariscala or **La Mariscala** (lä märēskä′lä), town (pop. 1,500), Lavalleja dept., SE Uruguay, on highway, and 35 mi. NE of Minas; wheat, oats, corn, livestock.

Mariscal Cáceres, province, Peru: see JUANJUÍ.

Mariscal Canyon, Texas: see BIG BEND NATIONAL PARK.

Mariscal Estigarribia (märēskäl′ ĕstēgärē′byä), village (dist. pop. 8,760), ⊙ Boquerón dept., N Paraguay, in the Chaco, 300 mi. NW of Asunción; 22°1′S 60°38′W. Military post. Until 1945, López de Filippis.

Mariscal Nieto, province, Peru: see MOQUEGUA, city.

Marismas, Las (läs märē′zmäs), coastal plain in Andalusia, S Spain, along Guadalquivir estuary on the Atlantic c.10 mi. S of Seville. Sparsely inhabited alluvial marshland, used as pasture; some cotton and rice grown.

Marissa, Palestine: see MARESHAH.

Marissa (mûrĭ′sů), village (pop. 1,652), St. Clair co., SW Ill., 33 mi. SE of East St. Louis; stone and wood products; bituminous-coal mines; agr. (corn, wheat; dairy products; poultry, livestock). Inc. 1882.

Maristova (mä′rĭstôvä), tourist station in Borgund canton (pop. 605), Sogn og Fjordane co., W Norway, 34 mi. ESE of Sogndal; alt. 2,635 ft. A hospice has been here since 14th cent. Borgund stave church (12th cent.), 10 mi. WSW, is Norway's best-preserved wooden church.

Maris Town, village (pop. 1,796, with adjacent Mill Town), Madison co., central Miss.

Maritime Alps (mă′rūtĭm″), Fr. *Alpes Maritimes*, Ital. *Alpi Marittime*, S division of Western Alps along Fr.-Ital. border; extend in an arc 120 mi. from Ligurian Apennines at Cadibona Pass (ESE) to Cottian Alps at Maddalena Pass (WNW). Include LIGURIAN ALPS. Highest peaks; Punta Argentera (10,817 ft.), Cima dei Gelas (10,312 ft.), Mont Tinibras (9,944 ft.). Lower W spurs reaching out toward Rhone valley are Provence Alps.

Maritime Atlas, N Africa: see ATLAS MOUNTAINS.

Maritime Province, Russian SFSR: see MARITIME TERRITORY.

Maritime Provinces, the provinces of E Canada on the Atlantic seaboard; include NOVA SCOTIA, NEW BRUNSWICK, and PRINCE EDWARD ISLAND (total □ 50,400; pop. 1,130,410). Halifax and St. John are largest cities and chief ports; other important towns are Sydney, New Glasgow, Amherst, Annapolis Royal (N.S.), Charlottetown (P.E.I.), and Fredericton and Moncton (N.B.). In French phase of Canadian history, region was known as ACADIA.

Maritime Territory, Rus. *Primorski Krai* or *Primorskiy Kray*, administrative division (□ 64,900; 1946 pop. estimate 1,475,000) of SE Siberian Russian SFSR; ⊙ Vladivostok. In SE section of Soviet Far East, bet. Manchuria and Sea of Japan. Includes S part of densely wooded, coastal Sikhote-Alin Range, rich in minerals, and Ussuri R.–L. Khanka lowland along Manchurian border (W). Has continental climate, modified by Pacific monsoons (dry winters, rainy summers). Pop. (50% Russians, 25% Ukrainians; Koreans, Chinese, and, in NE, Ude) is densest in agr. KHANKA PLAIN (SW). Extensive coal and lignite mines in S (Suchan, Artem); lead, zinc, tin, molybdenum, and timber in Sikhote-Alin Range. Industry at Vladivostok (shipbuilding, fish processing), VOROSHILOV (food processing), Spassk-Dalni (cement works). Fishing along Sea of Japan coast. Trans-Siberian RR system passes through W and SW sections. Formed 1938 of Primorskaya and Ussuri oblasts (abolished 1939 and 1943, respectively) within former Far Eastern Territory. Also called Maritime Prov., Littoral Prov., or Littoral Territory.

Maritsa, Bulgaria: see SIMEONOVGRAD.

Maritsa River (mûrĭ′tsů), Gr. *Hevros, Evros*, or *Hebros* (all: ĕv′rôs), Turkish *Meriç* (mĕ′rĕch), Lat. *Hebrus*, SE Europe, rises in Bulgaria on Stalin Peak in Rila Mts., SSE of Sofia; flows 170 mi. E and ESE in Bulgaria, past Pazardzhik, Plovdiv, Dimitrovgrad, Simeonovgrad, and Svilengrad, forming Greco-Bulg. line for 10 mi. and then Greco-Turkish line for 115 mi., turning S at Adrianople (Edirne), and finally SW to the Aegean Sea, forming a delta on Gulf of Enos bet. Enos and Alexandroupolis; total length, 300 mi. Receives Vacha, Asenovitsa, and Arda rivers (right), Topolnitsa, Strema, Tundzha, and Ergene rivers (left). Several power plants and irrigation channels serve the valley, a fertile agr. dist. Not navigable, except for small boats in lower course. Sometimes spelled Maritza.

Marittimo, Sicily: see MARETTIMO.

Mari-Turek (mä″rē-tōōryĕk′), village (1932 pop. estimate 900), E Mari Autonomous SSR, Russian SFSR, 65 mi. E of Ioshkar-Ola; flax processing; grain.

Maritza River, Bulgaria, Greece, Turkey: see MARITSA RIVER.

Maritzburg, Natal, U. of So. Afr.: see PIETERMARITZBURG.

Mariupol, Ukrainian SSR: see ZHDANOV.

Mariusa, Caño (kä′nyō märū′sä), E central arm of Orinoco R. delta, Delta Amacuro territory, NE Venezuela; branches off from the Caño Araguaito, flows c.100 mi. NE and NW to the Atlantic.

Marivan (märēvän′), town, Fifth Prov., in Kurdistan, W Iran, 45 mi. WNW of Sanandaj, near Iraq border; grain; sheep raising; high-quality wool exported.

Mariveles (märēvä′lās), town (1939 pop. 2,235; 1948 municipality pop. 4,462), Bataan prov., S Luzon, Philippines, on S Bataan Peninsula, port on Mariveles Harbor (small inlet of S.China Sea), at N side of entrance to Manila Bay; ships sugar, rice.

Mariveles Mountains, S Bataan Peninsula, S Luzon, Philippines, near Mt. Bataan, just N of Mariveles; rise to 4,200 ft.

Mariyampole, Lithuania: see MARIJAMPOLE.

Mariyental, Russian SFSR: see SOVETSKOYE, Saratov oblast.

Mariyets (mä′rēĭts), town (1948 pop. over 2,000), E Mari Autonomous SSR, Russian SFSR, 55 mi. NNE of Kazan; glassworks.

Mariyovo, region, Yugoslavia: see MARIHOVO.

Marj, Al-, Egypt: see MARG, EL.

Marjamaa, Myaryama, or **Myar'yama,** Est. *Märjamaa* (all: măr′yămä), town (pop. 693), W Estonia, on railroad and 15 mi. WSW of Rapla; agr. market; barley, potatoes. Also spelled Maryama.

Marjan, Afghanistan: see WAZIKHA.

Märjelensee (mĕr′yĕlūnzā′), small lake in Bernese Alps, S central Switzerland, dammed by Aletsch Glacier; alt. 7,747 ft.

Marjioun, Lebanon: see MERJ 'UYUN.

Marj 'Uyun, Lebanon: see MERJ 'UYUN.

Mark (märk), former county of W Germany, astride middle Ruhr R. Passed 1614 (ratified 1666) to Brandenburg.

Mark, village (pop. 449), Putnam co., N central Ill., 5 mi. SSW of Spring Valley, in agr. and bituminous-coal area.

Markagunt Plateau (märkä′gōōnt), SW Utah, high tableland (rising to 11,315 ft. in BRIAN HEAD peak) chiefly in Iron co., bounded E of Cedar City; E by Paunsaugunt Plateau, S by Pink Cliffs. Extends through part of Dixie Natl. Forest; includes CEDAR BREAKS NATIONAL MONUMENT in S.

Marka-Kul or **Marka-Kul'** (mär"kŭ-kōōl'), lake (□ 165; alt. 5,710 ft.), East Kazakhstan oblast, Kazakh SSR, in Altai Mts., near China border, 85 mi. NNE of Zaisan; abounds in fish. Outlet: Kaldzhir R. (tributary of the Cherny-Irtysh); site of gold placers. Also spelled Marka-Kol.

Markala (märkälä'), village, S Fr. Sudan, Fr. West Africa, on right bank of the Niger opposite Sansanding and 25 mi. NE of Ségou; peanuts, shea nuts, cotton, kapok; livestock. A dam here serves Sahel and Macina irrigation canals. Sometimes Markala-Kirango.

Markandi, India: see GARHCHIROLI.

Markanum, India: see MERKANAM.

Markapur (mär'käpōōr), town (pop. 8,446), Kurnool dist., N Madras, India, in foothills of Eastern Ghats, on Gundlakamma R. and 55 mi. ENE of Nandyal; cotton ginning, hand-loom weaving, slate and lead mining, cattle grazing; peanuts, turmeric. Timber, bamboo, fibers in near-by forests.

Markaryd (mär'kärüd"), town (pop. 1,480), Kronoberg co., S Sweden, on Laga R. and 20 mi. N of Hassleholm; rail junction; woodworking, furniture mfg. Has folk mus.

Mark Canal, North Brabant prov., SW Netherlands, extends 4 mi. E–W, bet. MARK RIVER (3 mi. N of Breda) and WILHELMINA CANAL (1 mi. W of Oosterhout).

Markdale, village (pop. 870), S Ont., on Rocky Saugeen R. and 22 mi. SE of Owen Sound; dairying, woodworking, lumbering; grain elevators.

Markdorf (märk'dôrf), village (pop. 3,314), S Baden, Germany, 11 mi. ESE of Überlingen; winegrowing.

Marke (mär'kŭ), village (pop. 3,964), West Flanders prov., W Belgium, on Lys R. and 2 mi. SW of Courtrai; flax growing, linseed-oil pressing. Formerly spelled Marcke.

Marked Tree, city (pop. 2,878), Poinsett co., NE Ark., on St. Francis R. and 26 mi. SE of Jonesboro, in agr. area (cotton, corn, vegetables); cotton ginning and compressing, lumber milling. Settled c.1870.

Markelo (mär'kŭlō'), town (pop. 1,051), Overijssel prov., E Netherlands, 13 mi. W of Hengelo; biscuit mfg.; stone quarrying. Sometimes spelled Markeloo.

Marken (mär'kŭn), island (□ 1; pop. 1,471), North Holland prov., W central Netherlands, in the Ijsselmeer, 11 mi. NE of Amsterdam; 2 mi. long. Hay raising; tourist resort known for colorful local costumes. Ferries to Monnikendam and Volendam. Until 13th cent., linked with mainland. Fishing center until building of Ijsselmeer Dam.

Markesan (märkĭzăn'), village (pop. 1,010), Green Lake co., central Wis., on Grand R. and 28 mi. WSW of Fond du Lac, in farming, dairying, and stock-raising region; vegetable canneries, creamery. Silver-fox farm.

Market Bosworth (bŏz'-), town and parish (pop. 864), W Leicester, England, 12 mi. W of Leicester; agr. market. S 2 mi. is Bosworth Field, scene of battle (1485) in which Richard III was killed; the crown passed to his conqueror, the earl of Richmond (Henry VII).

Market Deeping, agr. village and parish (pop. 876), Parts of Kesteven, S Lincolnshire, England, on Welland R. and 7 mi. NNW of Peterborough. Has 13th–14th-cent. church.

Market Drayton, urban district (1931 pop. 4,749; 1951 census 5,638), NE Shropshire, England, on Tern R. and 17 mi. NE of Shrewsbury; agr. market and dairying center, with agr.-machinery works and flour mills. Has 12th-cent. church and grammar school (founded 1558) attended by Lord Clive.

Market Harborough, urban district (1931 pop. 9,312; 1951 census 10,401), S Leicester, England, on Welland R. and 17 mi. N of Northampton; mfg. of electrical equipment, machine tools, rubber goods, textiles, agr. machinery. Has church begun in 14th cent. and 17th-cent. grammar school. It is a fox-hunting center.

Markethill, town (pop. 808), central Co. Armagh, Northern Ireland, 6 mi. SE of Armagh; agr. market (cattle, potatoes). Site of Gosford Castle.

Marketine Lazne, Czechoslovakia: see PRACHATICE.

Market Lavington (lă'vĭngtŭn), agr. village and parish (pop. 1,013), central Wiltshire, England, 5 mi. S of Devizes. Has 14th-cent. church.

Market Rasen (rā'zŭn), urban district (1931 pop. 2,048; 1951 census 2,133), Parts of Lindsey, N central Lincolnshire, England, 14 mi. NE of Lincoln; agr. market; makes fertilizer, agr. machinery. Races are held here.

Market Warsop, England: see WARSOP.

Market Weighton and Arras (wē'tŭn, ă'rŭs), parish (pop. 1,735), East Riding, SE Yorkshire, England. Includes agr. market village of Market Weighton, 17 mi. ESE of York, with 12th–15th-cent. church; and, 3 mi. E, agr. village of Arras.

Mark Field, air base and commercial airport for Nome, NW Alaska, on S side of Seward Peninsula, on N shore of Norton Sound, just WNW of Nome; 64°31'N 165°26'W.

Markgräfler Land (märk'grā"flŭr länt'), region in S Baden, Germany, S of Freiburg, E of the Rhine, extending up to W slope of Black Forest; noted for its white wine. Chief town: Müllheim.

Markgröningen (märk'grû"nĭng-ŭn), town (pop. 4,602), N Württemberg, Germany, after 1945 in Württemberg-Baden, 5 mi. W of Ludwigsburg; wine. Has 16th-cent. church.

Markham, village (pop. 1,204), S Ont., on Rouge R. and 15 mi. NNE of Toronto; cereal and flour milling, dairying, lumbering, seed processing.

Markham (mär'käm), Chinese *Chiang-ch'ia* (jyäng'-chyä'), after 1913 *Ningtsing* or *Ning-ching* (both: nĭng'jĭng'), town [Tibetan *dzong*], E Tibet, in Kham prov., 125 mi. SE of Chamdo and 40 mi. SW of Paan; stock raising; tin and salt deposits.

Markham. 1 Village (pop. 2,753), Cook co., NE Ill., S suburb of Chicago. Inc. 1925. **2** Town (1940 pop. 7), Creek co., central Okla., 10 mi. NE of Cushing.

Markham, Mount (15,100 ft.), a triple-peaked mtn., Antarctica, S of Shackleton Inlet, at W edge of Ross Shelf Ice; 82°59'S 160°30'E. Discovered 1902 by R. F. Scott, Br. explorer.

Markhamat (mŭrkhŭmät'), 2 adjoining villages in S Andizhan oblast, Uzbek SSR, 12 mi. SSE of Leninsk, in cotton- and silkgrowing area. Uzbek village Markhamat I (1926 pop. 3,468) is at road junction just N of Rus. village of Markhamat II (1926 pop. 1,419; until 1936 called Russkoye Selo).

Markham Ferry Dam, Okla.: see NEOSHO RIVER.

Markham River, NE New Guinea, rises near Ramu R., flows 75 mi. SE to Huon Gulf; drains agr. land.

Markham Sound, strait of Arctic Ocean in central Franz Josef Land, Russian SFSR; separates S isls. (Champ, Luigi) of Zichy Land (N) and MacClintock and Hall isls. (S); 50 mi. long, 10 mi. wide.

Markhlevsk, Ukrainian SSR: see DOVBYSH.

Markinch (märk'ĭnch'), burgh (1931 pop. 1,989; 1951 census 2,306), central Fifeshire, Scotland, on Leven R. and 5 mi. W of Leven; coal mining, woolen and paper milling, textile bleaching. Church has Norman tower. Just SE is coal-mining village of Balgonie, where David Leslie, leader of the Covenanters, is buried. Site of remains of 12th-cent. Balgonie Castle. Just NW is Balbirnie, with paper mills.

Markirch, France: see SAINTE-MARIE-AUX-MINES.

Märkisch Buchholz (mĕr'kĭsh bōōkh'hôlts), town (pop. 1,027), Brandenburg, E Germany, on Dahme R. and 15 mi. SSE of Königs Wusterhausen; potatoes; forestry. Until 1937 called Wendisch Buchholz.

Märkisch Friedland, Poland: see MIROSLAWIEC.

Markkleeberg (märk"klā'bĕrk), town (pop. 20,517), Saxony, E central Germany, 4 mi. S of Leipzig city center; printing, woolen milling; mfg. of electrical equipment, chocolate, flour products. Just E is site of early-Stone Age excavations.

Markland, village (pop. 393), SE N.F., in central part of Avalon Peninsula, 40 mi. WSW of St. John's; scene of agr. resettlement scheme, begun 1934, for unemployed.

Markle, town (pop. 733), on Huntington-Wells co. line, NE central Ind., on the Wabash and 9 mi. SE of Huntington.

Markleeville (mär'klēvĭl), village (pop. c.125), ⊙ Alpine co., E Calif., in the Sierras, 32 mi. S of Carson City, Nev. Mineral springs (Grover's Hot Springs) near by. Hunting, fishing in region.

Marklesburg, borough (pop. 219), Huntingdon co., S central Pa., 11 mi. SW of Huntingdon. Post office is James Creek.

Markleville, town (pop. 314), Madison co., E central Ind., 32 mi. ENE of Indianapolis.

Markleysburg, borough (pop. 291), Fayette co., SW Pa., 18 mi. SE of Uniontown, near state line.

Marklissa, Poland: see LESNA.

Markneukirchen (märk"noi'kĭr"khŭn), town (pop. 8,903), Saxony, E central Germany, in the Erzgebirge, 16 mi. SE of Plauen; musical-instruments mfg. center.

Markoldendorf (märk"ôl'dŭndôrf), village (pop. 2,457), in former Prussian prov. of Hanover, W Germany, after 1945 in Lower Saxony, 4 mi. W of Einbeck; metalworking, sawmilling. Inc. (1939) neighboring Oldendorf (just S).

Markolsheim, France: see MARCKOLSHEIM.

Markopoulon (märkô'pōōlôn), town (pop. 4,668), Attica nome, E central Greece, on railroad and 13 mi. SE of Athens; wine center; wheat, olives, cattle, sheep raising.

Markovka (mär'kŭfkŭ), village (1926 pop. 8,632), NE Voroshilovgrad oblast, Ukrainian SSR, 35 mi. NE of Starobelsk; flour milling.

Markovo (mär'kŭvŭ). **1** Town (1940 pop. over 500), W central Ivanovo oblast, Russian SFSR, 18 mi. W of Ivanovo; peat center. Until 1940, Markovo-Sbornoye. **2** Village (1948 pop. over 500), S Chukchi Natl. Okrug, Kamchatka oblast, Khabarovsk Territory, Russian SFSR, on Anadyr R. and 215 mi. SW of Anadyr; air base; trading post.

Markranstädt (mär'krän-shtĕt), town (pop. 10,857), Saxony, E central Germany, 9 mi. W of Leipzig; machinery mfg., brewing, sugar refining.

Mark River, N Belgium and S Netherlands, rises 5 mi. N of Turnhout (Belgium); flows N, entering the Netherlands 6 mi. S of Breda, past Breda, thence W to the Volkerak 4 mi. SW of Willemstad; its lower course is called Dintel Mark R. Length, 50 mi. Receives Mark Canal 3 mi. N of Breda. Navigable below Breda.

Marks or **Marx** (märks), city (1926 pop. 12,461), central Saratov oblast, Russian SFSR, grain port on left bank of Volga R. and 30 mi. NE of Engels; industrial center; mfg. (power machinery, apparel, food products), sawmilling. Founded 1765 under Catherine II by Du. baron Beauregard. Called Baronsk or Yekaterinenshtadt [Ger. *Katharinenstadt*] until 1918 and later (in German Volga Autonomous SSR), Marksshtadt [Ger. *Marxstadt*] until 1941.

Marks, town (pop. 2,209), ⊙ Quitman co., NW Miss., 18 mi. ENE of Clarksdale and on Coldwater R.; trade center in rich agr. area (cotton, corn); lumber milling; cotton gins and compresses. Inc. 1906.

Marksville, town (pop. 3,635), ⊙ Avoyelles parish, E central La., 24 mi. SE of Alexandria, near Red R.; agr. (cotton, corn, sugar cane, sweet potatoes, rice); cotton ginning, rice milling, candy mfg., lumber milling. Fort De Russey, site of Civil War fighting, and Avoyel Indian park are near by. Settled in late-18th cent. by Acadians.

Marktbreit (märkt'brīt), town (pop. 2,998), Lower Franconia, W Bavaria, Germany, on the Main (canalized) and 13 mi. SE of Würzburg; mfg. of machinery, paint, vinegar; brewing, tanning, flour milling. Has Gothic church, and 16th-cent. castle. Portions of mid-16th-cent. wall still stand. Chartered 1558.

Markt Erlbach (märkt" ĕrl'bäkh), village (pop. 1,651), Middle Franconia, W Bavaria, Germany, 6 mi. SSE of Neustadt; brewing; carp hatching; rye, oats, hops, sheep.

Markt Grafing (märkt" grä'fĭng), village (pop. 4,418), Upper Bavaria, Germany, 20 mi. ESE of Munich; rail junction; metalworking, brewing, lumber milling, tanning. Has late-17th-cent. church. Chartered 1380.

Marktheidenfeld (märkt"hī'dŭnfĕlt), village (pop. 4,302), Lower Franconia, NW Bavaria, Germany, on the Main (canalized) and 15 mi. WNW of Würzburg; mfg. of precision instruments, paper milling, printing, brewing. Has early-17th-cent. church.

Marktleuthen (märkt'loi"tŭn), village (pop. 2,982), Upper Franconia, NE Bavaria, Germany, in the Fichtelgebirge, on the Eger and 7 mi. WSW of Selb; glassworks; brewing, tanning, lumber milling. Granite quarries in area.

Markt Oberdorf (märkt"ō'bŭrdôrf), village (pop. 4,333), Swabia, SW Bavaria, Germany, near the Wertach, 7 mi. S of Kaufbeuren; mfg. of flint glass, machinery, glass, textiles; dairying, woodworking. Has former 18th-cent. castle of prince-bishops of Augsburg; and Gothic church, renovated 1733.

Marktredwitz (märkt"rāt'vĭts), city (1950 pop. 15,820), Upper Franconia, NE Bavaria, Germany, in the Fichtelgebirge, 23 mi. ENE of Bayreuth; rail junction; mfg. of glass, porcelain, textiles, machine tools; woodworking, brewing. Has 14th- and 16th-cent. churches.

Markt Rettenbach (märkt"rĕ'tŭnbäkh), village (pop. 1,170), Swabia, SW Bavaria, Germany, 10 mi. ESE of Memmingen; brickworks; grain, cattle. Chartered 1790. Sometimes called Rettenbach.

Markt Sankt Florian (märkt'zängkt flō'rēän), town (pop. 4,456), E Upper Austria, 7 mi. SSE of Linz; pilgrimage church.

Markt-Schelkin, Rumania: see SEICA-MARE.

Marktschellenberg (märkt"shĕ'lŭnbĕrk) or **Schellenberg,** village (pop. 709), Upper Bavaria, Germany, on SE slope of the Untersberg, 2 mi. NW of Hallein, near Austrian border; lumber milling; resort (alt. 1,575 ft.).

Markt Schwaben (märkt" shvä'bŭn), village (pop. 4,259), Upper Bavaria, Germany, 15 mi. ENE of Munich; rail junction; mfg. of chemicals, brewing, woodworking. Chartered c.1340.

Marktsteft (märkt'shtĕft"), town (pop. 1,434), Lower Franconia, W Bavaria, Germany, on the Main (canalized) and 11 mi. SE of Würzburg; brewing. Has early-17th-cent. church.

Marktzeuln (märkt'tsoiln"), village (pop. 1,359), Upper Franconia, N Bavaria, Germany, on the Rodach near its junction with the Main, and 5 mi. E of Lichtenfels; basket weaving, brewing.

Markusovce, Czechoslovakia: see KOTERBACHY.

Marl, town (1950 pop. 51,246), in former Prussian prov. of Westphalia, W Germany, after 1945 in North Rhine-Westphalia, in the Ruhr, 5 mi. NW of Recklinghausen; mfg. of chemicals. Coal and iron-ore mining. Of anc. origin. Chartered 1936.

Marland, town (pop. 221), Noble co., N Okla., 10 mi. SSW of Ponca City, in oil-producing area.

Marland Heights, W.Va.: see WEIRTON.

Marlboro (märl'-), county (□ 482; pop. 31,766), NE S.C.; ⊙ Bennettsville. Bounded SW by Pee Dee R., N and NE by N.C. line. Mainly agr. (especially cotton; also corn, peaches, tobacco), some timber; mfg. at Bennettsville. Formed 1785.

Marlboro. 1 or **Marlborough,** town (pop. 901), Hartford co., central Conn., 15 mi. SE of Hartford, in agr. area. Has 18th-cent. tavern. **2** or **Marlborough,** city (pop. 15,756), Middlesex co., E central Mass., 15 mi. ENE of Worcester; lamps, shoes, paper and metal products. Inc. as town 1660, as city 1890. **3** or **Marlborough,** town (pop. 1,561), Cheshire co., SW N.H., just SE of Keene; mfg.

(wood products, textiles, toys). Inc. 1776. **4** Village (pop. c.300), Monmouth co., E N.J., 4 mi. N of Freehold, in agr. area. Marlboro State Hosp. near by. **5** or **Marlborough,** village (pop. 1,709), Ulster co., SE N.Y., on W bank of the Hudson and 7 mi. N of Newburgh; summer resort; mfg. (cement blocks, dairy and canned foods); agr. (truck, fruit). **6** Town (pop. 311), Windham co., SE Vt., 8 mi. W of Brattleboro; lumber. Seat of Marlboro Col.

Marlborough (môrl'bůrů), municipal borough (1931 pop. 3,492; 1951 census 4,556), E Wiltshire, England, on Kennet R. and 10 mi. SSE of Swindon; agr. market in dairying and sheep-raising region; bacon and ham curing, mfg. of agr. implements. Marlborough Col., public school founded 1843 on site of historic castle, is here. In school grounds is prehistoric mound, said to contain body of Merlin of Arthurian legend. Has 2 Norman churches and old St. Peter's church, where Wolsey preached. Marlborough was formerly important stage point on London-Bath road.

Marlborough, provincial district (□ 4,220; pop. 20,737), NE S.Isl., New Zealand; chief borough is Blenheim, with Picton as chief port. Largely mountainous; small plain near Cloudy Bay. Queen Charlotte and Pelorus sounds, in N, are inlets of Cook Strait. Produces grain, fruits. Area roughly corresponds to Marlborough land dist.

Marlborough, county, New Zealand: see Blenheim.

Marlborough, U.S.: see also Marlboro.

Marlborough, town (pop. 219), St. Louis co., E Mo.

Marle (märl'), town (pop. 2,337), Aisne dept., N France, on Serre R. and 14 mi. NNE of Laon; agr. trade center.

Marlengo (märlĕng'gô), Ger. *Marling,* village (pop. 912), Bolzano prov., Trentino–Alto Adige, N Italy, on Adige R. and 1 mi. SW of Merano; hydroelectric plant.

Marlenheim (märlůnĕm', Ger. mär'lůnhīm), village (pop. 1,352), Bas-Rhin dept., E France, at E foot of the Vosges, 5 mi. N of Molsheim; saw mfg., sawmilling; winegrowing.

Marles-les-Mines (märl-lā-mēn'), town (pop. 12,700), Pas-de-Calais dept., N France, 6 mi. WSW of Béthune, in coal-mining dist.

Marlette, village (pop. 1,489), Sanilac co., E Mich., c.40 mi. NW of Port Huron, in farm area (grain, sugar beets, livestock; dairy products; grain elevator, creamery. Inc. 1881.

Marlia (mär'lyä), village (pop. 307), Lucca prov., Tuscany, Italy, 4 mi. NE of Lucca; paper mill.

Marlin, city (pop. 7,099), ⊙ Falls co., E central Texas, near Brazos R., 23 mi. SE of Waco; health resort (mineral springs); trade center for agr. area; ships cotton, poultry, mineral crystals, dairy products; brick making. Has state institution for crippled children, many hospitals. Founded 1850.

Marling, Italy: see Marlengo.

Marlinton, town (pop. 1,645), ⊙ Pocahontas co., E W.Va., on Greenbrier R. and 50 mi. S of Elkins, in timber and agr. (livestock, poultry, grain, dairy products, fruit) region; tannery; lumber milling. Summer resort in hunting area. Settled 1749.

Marloie (märlwä'), village, Luxembourg prov., SE central Belgium, 2 mi. SW of Marche; rail junction. Just NE is commune center of Waha (wähä') (pop. 2,338).

Marlow (mär'lō) residential urban district (1931 pop. 5,086; 1951 census 6,480), S Buckingham, England, on the Thames (here crossed by 225-ft. suspension bridge) and 4 mi. S of High Wycombe; paper industry. Has church built by Pugin. Shelley lived in Marlow for some time. Just N is agr. parish (pop. 1,665) of Great Marlow.

Marlow, town (pop. 2,855), Mecklenburg, N Germany, 19 mi. ENE of Rostock; grain, sugar beets, potatoes, stock. First mentioned as fortified place in 12th cent.

Marlow. 1 Town (pop. 330), Cheshire co., SW N.H., on the Ashuelot and 14 mi. NNE of Keene; lumber mills. **2** City (pop. 3,399), Stephens co., S Okla., 10 mi. N of Duncan, in agr. area (corn, watermelons); cotton ginning, flour and feed milling, mattress mfg. Settled 1892.

Marlton, village (1940 pop. 511), Burlington co., W N.J., 11 mi. E of Camden; marl pits; makes knit goods. Has Baptist church (1805).

Marly (märlē'), E suburb (pop. 4,220) of Valenciennes, Nord dept., N France; copper smelting, mfg. (rolling stock for coal mines; corrugated iron; cement, bricks), textile printing.

Marly-le-Roi (märlē'-lů-rwä'), town (pop. 2,927), Seine-et-Oise dept., N central France, outer W suburb of Paris, 12 mi. from Notre Dame Cathedral, just S of Saint-Germain-en-Laye. The château, built here for Louis XIV by Mansart, was destroyed after French Revolution. Only its park remains. Near by a huge hydraulic engine (*machine de Marly*) was built in 1684 to supply fountains of Versailles (4 mi. SSE). In use until 1804, it has been replaced by modern pumping works.

Marma (mär'mä"), village (pop. 923), Gavleborg co., E Sweden, on Ljusna R. and 5 mi. WSW of Soderhamn; lumber and pulp mills.

Marmaduke (mär'mūdōōk), town (pop. 643), Greene co., NE Ark., 10 mi. NE of Paragould, near St. Francis R., in agr. area.

Marmagão, Portuguese India: see Mormugão.

Marmande (märmãd'), town (pop. 8,190), Lot-et-Garonne dept., SW France, on the Garonne and 30 mi. NW of Agen; agr. market and brandy-distilling center; canning (tomatoes, prunes, peas, meat, fruit preserves); mfg. of hosiery, butchers' equipment, furniture, cork stoppers. Has 13th–15th-cent. church.

Marmanhac (märmänäk'), village (pop. 245), Cantal dept., S central France, in the Massif du Cantal, 6 mi. N of Aurillac; mfg. of blue cheese and rattan furniture.

Marmara, Lake (mär'můrů) (□ 17), W Turkey, 28 mi. E of Manisa; 7 mi. long, 5 mi. wide.

Marmara, Sea of, or **Sea of Marmora** (both: mär'můrů), anc. *Propontis,* body of water (□ c.4,300) bet. Europe (N) and Asia (S), bet. European and Asiatic Turkey (which owns the entire shoreline). Connected E with Black Sea through the Bosporus, W with the Aegean Sea (part of the Mediterranean) by the Dardanelles (anc. Hellespont). Istanbul (Constantinople) is on NE shore, at entrance to the Bosporus. Its greatest length is c.170 mi. (from Gallipoli to head of Gulf of Izmit), greatest breadth nearly 50 mi. Greatest depth, in E section, c.4,500 ft. Marmara Isl. (from which it gets its modern name) is in W part, Princes Isls. in E, near Istanbul.

Marmara Eregli, Turkey: see Eregli.

Marmara Island or **Marmora Island,** anc. *Proconnesus,* island (□ 29; pop. 3,896), in Sea of Marmara, NW Turkey, 24 mi. S of Tekirdag; 12 mi. long, 5 mi. wide. Rises to 1,991 ft. in Ilyas Dag. Extensive marble quarries, from which its modern name is derived.

Marmaris or **Marmaras** (märmärĭs', –äs'), village (pop. 2,750), Mugla prov., SW Turkey, port on a sheltered bay 28 mi. N of Rhodes, 26 mi. SSW of Mugla; chromium mines; legumes, onions.

Marmarth, city (pop. 469), Slope co., SW N.Dak., 65 mi. SW of Dickinson, near Mont. line, on Little Missouri R.; ships livestock; wheat, hay.

Marmato (märmä'tō), village (pop. 787), Caldas dept., W central Colombia, in Cauca valley, 27 mi. NNW of Manizales; alt. 4,390 ft.; gold placer mines; coffeegrowing.

Marmaton River (mär'mǔtůn), Kansas and Mo., formed by confluence of forks in Bourbon co., SE Kansas, flows E and SE, past Fort Scott, Kansas, to Little Osage R. 7 mi. SSE of Rich Hill, Mo.; 73 mi. long, including longest fork.

Marmelade (märmůläd'), town (1950 pop. 868), Artibonite dept., N Haiti, in Massif du Nord, 20 mi. SSW of Cap-Haïtien; coffeegrowing.

Mar Menor (mär' mänôr'), salt-water lagoon (□ 63) on coast of Murcia prov., SE Spain, NE of Cartagena; separated from the Mediterranean by flat, sandy spit cut by few passages. Max. length 14 mi., width 1 mi., depth 20 ft. Some rocky islets. Fishing and bathing. Military airport on W shore.

Marmet (mär'mĭt), town (pop. 2,515), Kanawha co., W W.Va., on Kanawha R. and 9 mi. SSE of Charleston, in coal-mining region. Inc. 1921.

Marmion Lake (mär'mēůn) (14 mi. long, 6 mi. wide), W Ont., 30 mi. W of Lac des Milles Lacs, 110 mi. WNW of Port Arthur; alt. 1,363 ft. Drained S by Seine R.

Marmirolo (märmērô'lô), village (pop. 2,072), Mantova prov., Lombardy, N Italy, 5 mi. N of Mantua; trailer mfg.

Marmolada (märmôlä'dä), highest peak (10,964 ft.) in the Dolomites, N Italy, on Bolzano-Belluno prov. border, 25 mi. ESE of Bolzano. Has glaciers.

Marmolejo (märmōlā'hō), town (pop. 6,026), Jaén prov., S Spain, near Guadalquivir R., 7 mi. WNW of Andújar; olive-oil production center. Mfg. of willow articles, nougat candy, liqueurs; honey and wax processing. Cereals, wine, vegetables, livestock. Has mineral springs.

Marmolejo, Cerro (sĕ'rō), Andean peak (20,000 ft.) on Argentina-Chile border, 27 mi. SSW of Tupungato, 50 mi. SE of Santiago; 33°45'S.

Marmora (mär'můrů), village (pop. 1,106), SE Ont., 27 mi. NW of Belleville, in mining area (gold, iron, marble); stellite refining, woolen and lumber milling.

Marmora, Sea of, Turkey: see Marmara, Sea of.

Marmora Island, Turkey: see Marmara Island.

Marmorilik (märmô'rĭlĭk), settlement, Umanak dist., W Greenland, at head of E arm of Umanak Fjord, near edge of inland icecap, 35 mi. NE of Umanak; 71°8'N 51°17'W. Marble quarries; production suspended during Second World War.

Marmot Peak (mär'mŭt) (11,841 ft.), in Rocky Mts., bet. Chaffee and Park counties, central Colo.

Marmoutier (märmōōtyā'), Ger. *Maursmünster* (mours'münstůr), village (pop. 1,551), Bas-Rhin dept., E France, 4 mi. S of Saverne; footwear mfg., sandstone quarrying. Its Benedictine abbey (founded c.600) was abolished in French Revolution. Only abbatial church (with 11th-cent. façade) remains.

Marnay (märnā'), village (pop. 739), Haute-Saône dept., E France, on Ognon R. and 13 mi. WNW of Besançon; woodworking, dairying.

Marnaz (märnä'), village (pop. 896), Haute-Savoie dept., SE France, near Arve R., 3 mi. W of Cluses, in Faucigny valley; precision metalworking.

Marne (märn), department (□ 3,168; pop. 386,926), in old Champagne prov., N France; ⊙ Châlons-sur-Marne. Across it, E-W, are the Argonne, the humid Champagne, the barren Champagne badlands (*Champagne Pouilleuse*), and a wooded crest with wine-clad slopes. Drained by the Marne, its tributaries (Ornain, Saulx, Grand-Morin, Petit-Morin), the Aisne, and its tributaries (Suippe, Vesle). Here are the famous vineyards (Sillery, Verzy, Ay, Avize, Vertus) which supply the champagne industry of Rheims and Épernay; the extensive sheep ranges of the Champagne badlands furnish raw material for Rheims woolen manufactures. Other agr. products: wheat, oats, sugar beets, cherries. Lumbering in the Argonne and in recently planted pine forest of Champagne badlands. Chief towns are Rheims, Châlons-sur-Marne (commercial center), Épernay (champagne processing and storing), Vitry-le-François (transportation center). Most of dept. was battlefield of First World War.

Marne (mär'nů), town (pop. 7,025), in Schleswig-Holstein, NW Germany, 20 mi. W of Itzehoe, in the S Dithmarschen; food processing (sauerkraut, canned fish and crabs), brewing. Seed-selection station. Market center for surrounding reclaimed polder land (cattle, grain, vegetables). Chartered 1891.

Marne (märn), town (pop. 214), Cass co., SW Iowa, 6 mi. NW of Atlantic; concrete blocks, tile.

Marne, Haute-, France: see Haute-Marne.

Marne-Aisne Canal, France: see Aisne-Marne Canal.

Marne-Rhine Canal (märn"-rīn'), Fr. *Canal de la Marne au Rhin* (känäl dů lä märn' ōrē'), E France, connects the Marne (at Vitry-le-François) with the Rhine (at Strasbourg); 195 mi. long. Follows Ornain R. upstream, past Bar-le-Duc; crosses into Meuse R. valley in tunnel (3 mi. long); reaches the Meuse at Troussey (junction with Canal de l'Est); joins the Moselle at Toul, paralleling it to Frouard; thence it ascends the Meurthe valley, past Nancy; traverses Lorraine plateau N of Lunéville; crosses the N Vosges in Saverne Gap, entering Alsatian lowland E of Saverne. Ships iron ore, coal, building materials. Built 1841–52.

Marne River, anc. *Matrona,* NE and N central France, rises in Plateau of Langres just S of Langres, flows 325 mi. NW in a great arc, past Chaumont, Saint-Dizier, Vitry-le-François, Châlons-sur-Marne, Épernay, Château-Thierry, and Meaux, to the Seine at Charenton-le-Pont (just above Paris). Paralleled by Marne-Saône Canal from Langres to Vitry-le-François (W terminus of Marne-Rhine Canal). Thence river is either canalized or followed by a lateral canal. Near Épernay it traverses the Champagne winegrowing area. Receives the Blaise, Petit-Morin, Grand-Morin (left), the Saulx and Ourcq (right). Figured prominently in First World War. Two crucial battles (1914, 1918) have been named after it.

Marne-Saône Canal (märn-sōn'), E France, bet. Saône and Marne rivers. Begins at Pontailler-sur-Saône, runs N across Plateau of Langres (tunnel 3.5 mi. long), enters Marne R. valley near Langres and follows it past Chaumont and Saint-Dizier to Vitry-le-François, whence it is continued by lateral canal to the Marne, thus forming a link bet. Rhone-Saône R. valley and Paris. Total length, c.130 mi.

Marneuli (mŭrnyĭōō'lyē), village (1932 pop. estimate 2,860), S Georgian SSR, on railroad and 15 mi. S of Tiflis; tobacco; rug weaving. Until 1947, Borchalo.

Marnhull, agr. village and parish (pop. 1,175), N Dorset, England, 6 mi. WSW of Shaftesbury. Has 14th-cent. church, with Burne-Jones window.

Marnia (märnyä'), town (pop. 4,489), Oran dept., NW Algeria, near Fr. Morocco border, in fertile lowland irrigated by the Oued Tafna, on railroad and 24 mi. W of Tlemcen; agr. trade center (cereals, livestock, olive oil). Lead mine at Ghar Rouban (18 mi. S) in Tlemcen Mts. Formerly Lalla-Marnia.

Marnoch (mär'nŏkh, –nŏk), parish (pop. 2,087, including Aberchirder), NE Banffshire, Scotland. Includes Bridge-of-Marnoch.

Marnoz (märnō'), village (pop. 270), Jura dept., E France, 19 mi. SE of Dôle; carton and cheese mfg. Sparkling wines.

Maroa (můrō'ů), city (pop. 1,100), Macon co., central Ill., 12 mi. N of Decatur, in agr. area.

Maroa (märō'ä), town (pop. 392), Amazonas territory, S Venezuela, landing on Guainía R. (Colombia border) and 200 mi. S of Puerto Ayacucho, in tropical forest region (rubber, balata, vanilla); 2°44'N 67°33'W.

Maroantsetra (märwäntsĕ'trů), town (1948 pop. 4,412), Tamatave prov., NE Madagascar, small port in Antongil Bay, on coast, 190 mi. N of Tamatave; rice processing, sawmilling (notably rosewood), clove plantations. Has marine-trades school, school for Europeans, hosp.

Marochak, Afghanistan: see Maruchak.

Maroilles (märô'yů), village (pop. 557), Nord dept., N France, 8 mi. W of Avesnes; leather working.

Maroim, Brazil: see Maruim.

Marolles-les-Braults (märôl'-lā-brō'), village (pop. 948), Sarthe dept., W France, 17 mi. SE of Alençon; center of hemp-growing area; rope mfg., cider mill.

Maromandia (märōōmän'dyū), village, Majunga prov., NW Madagascar, near W coast, on highway and 40 mi. SSW of Ambanja; rice market; fiber growing.

Maromme (märôm'), town (pop. 4,404), Seine-Inférieure dept., N France, 4 mi. NW of Rouen; steel milling, textile dyeing, barrel making.

Marone (märô'nĕ), resort village (pop. 1,427), Brescia prov., Lombardy, N Italy, port on E shore of Lago d'Iseo, 15 mi. NNW of Brescia; felt mill; dolomite quarries.

Maroni, district, Fr. Guiana: see MARIPASOULA.

Maroni River (märônē', märō'nē) or **Marowyne River**, Du. *Marowijne* (both: märôvī'nū), in the Guianas, rises in Tumuc-Humac Mts. of Fr. Guiana near Brazil border, flows c.450 mi. N through tropical forest region for its greater part along Fr. Guiana–Du. Guiana border, past Albina and Saint-Laurent, to the Atlantic at Galibi Point. Navigable for smaller vessels c.60 mi. upstream. Interrupted by many waterfalls. Its upper course is called the Itany (in Fr. Guiana; ētänē') or Litani (in Du. Guiana; lē'tänē); its mid-course, to the mouth of the Tapanahoni, is called the Aoua (in Fr. Guiana; äwä') or Lawa (in Du. Guiana; lä'vä). Gold placers along the Aoua.

Maronne River (märôn'), Cantal and Corrèze depts., S central France, rises in Massif du Cantal E of Salers, flows c.50 mi. W to the Dordogne below Argentat.

Maroon Peak (14,126 ft.), W central Colo., in Elk Mts., 12 mi. SW of Aspen.

Maroon Town, town (pop. 900), St. James parish, NW Jamaica, in the Cockpit Country, 14 mi. SE of Montego Bay. Here rebellious maroons made their last stand (1795). Formerly Trelawny Town.

Marosberkes, Rumania: see BIRCHIS.

Marosheviz, Rumania: see TOPLITA.

Marosillye, Rumania: see ILIA.

Marosludus, Rumania: see LUDUS.

Maros River, Rumania and Hungary: see MURES RIVER.

Marostica (märô'stēkä), town (pop. 3,463), Vicenza prov., Veneto, N Italy, near Brenta R., 15 mi. NNE of Vicenza; straw-hat mfg.

Marosujvar, Rumania: see OCNA-MURESULUI.

Marosvasarhely, Rumania: see TARGU-MURES.

Marotiri, Fr. Oceania: see BASS ISLES.

Maroua or **Marua** (märōō'ä), town, ⊙ Nord-Cameroun region, N Fr. Cameroons, 500 mi. NNE of Yaoundé, 120 mi. SSW of Fort-Lamy (Fr. Equatorial Africa); 10°35'N 14°20'E. Stock-raising center, communications point; peanuts, cotton. Has hosp., agr. school, veterinary station. Protestant mission.

Marousi, Greece: see AMAROUSION.

Marovoay (märōōvwä'), town (1948 pop. 11,874), Majunga prov., NW Madagascar, on highway, at head of Betsiboka R. estuary, and 35 mi. SSE of Majunga; commercial and agr. center specializing in quality rice, cattle, peanuts; rice and leather (snake, cayman) processing, sawmilling; mfg. of pharmaceuticals, tapioca, cassava starch; boat building. The experiments of its agr. station bear mainly on rice, corn, fodder crops, kapok, mangoes, tobacco; there is also a model cattle-breeding farm.

Marowijne, district, Du. Guiana: see ALBINA.

Marowijne River or **Marowyne River**, Du. and Fr. Guiana: see MARONI RIVER.

Marpent (märpã'), town (pop. 2,714), Nord dept., N France, near Belg. border, on the Sambre and 5 mi. ENE of Maubeuge; mfg. of rolling stock, sandstone pipes. Marble quarries near by.

Marple, urban district (1931 pop. 7,389; 1951 census 13,068), NE Cheshire, England, 4 mi. E of Stockport; cotton milling.

Marquand (märkwänd'), town (pop. 369), Madison co., SE Mo., in the St. Francois Mts., on Castor R. and 11 mi. SE of Fredericktown.

Marquard (mär'kwärd, mär'kvärt), town (pop. 2,549), S Orange Free State, U. of So. Afr., 80 mi. ENE of Bloemfontein; alt. 4,977 ft.; rail terminus; grain, stock.

Marqués, Mexico: see EL MARQUÉS.

Marquesado (märkäsä'dō), town (pop. estimate 1,000), ⊙ Rivadavia dept. (□ c.260; 1947 pop. 14,759), S San Juan prov., Argentina, in San Juan R. valley (irrigation area), 5 mi. W of San Juan; railhead in wine- and fruitgrowing area; wine making.

Marquesas Islands (märkā'sŭz), Fr. *Îles Marquises*, volcanic group (□ 492; pop. 2,988), FRENCH ESTABLISHMENTS IN OCEANIA, S Pacific, c.740 mi. NE of Tahiti; 9°30'S 139°45'W. Consist of 11 isls. NUKU HIVA is largest isl.; ⊙ Atuona on HIVA OA, 2d largest isl. Fertile and mountainous; highest peak (c.4,130 ft.) on Hiva Oa. Taiohae Bay on Nuku Hiva and Bay of Traitors on Hiva Oa are excellent harbors. Two groups of isls.: S cluster (sometimes called Mendaña Isls.), including Hiva Oa, FATU HUKU, TAHUATA, MOTANE, and FATU HIVA, discovered 1595 by Mendaña; N cluster, including Nuku Hiva, HATUTU, EIAO, MOTU ITI, UA HUKA, and UA POU, discovered 1791 by American navigator Ingraham, who named group Washington Isls. Group was acquired 1842 by France, when natives numbered 20,000; of all Polynesian peoples, Marquesans suffered most from European diseases. Isls. have fruits, breadfruit and coconut trees; wild cattle and hogs. Exports copra, tobacco, vanilla.

Marquesas Keys (märkē'zŭz), coral atoll (c.5 mi. across) in Gulf of Mexico, off S Fla., 19 mi. W of Key West; natl. wildlife refuge.

Marquês de Valença (mŭrkās' dĭ vŭlĕn'sŭ), city (pop. 10,614), NW Rio de Janeiro state, Brazil, 55 mi. NW of Rio; rail junction; mfg. (textiles, lace, dairy products); agr. (coffee, tobacco, fruit). Until 1943, called Valença.

Marquette or **Marquette-lez-Lille** (märkĕt'-lā-lēl'), N suburb (pop. 4,928) of Lille, Nord dept., N France, on Deûle R. (canalized) and on canal to Roubaix (5 mi. ENE); starch-mfg. center; mfg. of paper, flour, mirrors, jute bags.

Marquette (märkĕt'). **1** County (□ 1,841; pop. 47,654), NW Upper Peninsula, Mich.; ⊙ Marquette. Bounded N by L. Superior; drained by Dead and Michigamme rivers, and by several branches of Escanaba R. Includes the Marquette Iron Range (extensive mining) and Huron Mts. Some marble quarrying, gold mining, lumbering. Mfg., iron-ore shipping at Marquette. Livestock, poultry, potatoes, and truck are produced. Resorts (fishing, hunting, camping). A natl. experimental forest, fish hatchery, state park, and several lakes are in co. Organized 1851. **2** County (□ 457; pop. 8,839), S central Wis.; ⊙ Montello. Stock-raising, dairying, and farming area (potatoes, vegetables); processing of dairy products. Granite quarries. Drained by Fox R. and its tributaries; includes Buffalo L. Formed 1836.

Marquette. 1 Town (pop. 641), Clayton co., NE Iowa, on Mississippi R. (bridged here), opposite Prairie du Chien, Wis.; railroad shops. **2** City (pop. 666), McPherson co., central Kansas, on Smoky Hill R. and 23 mi. SSW of Salina; grain milling. **3** City and port (pop. 17,202), ⊙ Marquette co., NW Upper Peninsula, Mich., c.60 mi. NNW of Escanaba, on L. Superior. Important iron-ore shipping point and rail center for a mining, lumbering, farming, and resort region. Mfg. (foundry and wood products, chemicals, machinery, railroad equipment, food products); railroad shops. Has a state teachers col. and a branch of state prison. Fish hatchery and state park are near by. Inc. as village 1859, as city 1871. **4** Village (pop. 218), Hamilton co., SE central Nebr., 20 mi. E of Grand Island, near Platte R.

Marquette Iron Range or **Marquette Range**, NW Upper Peninsula, Mich., low range in Marquette co., lying generally W of Marquette; rich iron-mining region. Ishpeming and Negaunee are mining centers; Marquette is ore-shipping port.

Marquette Island, Mich.: see LES CHENEAUX ISLANDS.

Marquette-lez-Lille, France: see MARQUETTE.

Marquette Range, Mich.: see MARQUETTE IRON RANGE.

Marquez (märkā'), town (pop. 287), Leon co., E central Texas, 40 mi. N of Bryan; rail point in agr. area.

Marquez River (märkĕs'), W Bolivia, rises on W slopes of Cordillera de los Frailes, 20 mi. E of Río Mulato; flows 70 mi. WNW to Poopó L. just E of Pampa Aullagas. Receives Mulato R. (left).

Marquina (märkē'nä), town (pop. 1,256), Vizcaya prov., N Spain, 21 mi. E of Bilbao; mfg. of arms, handballs; flour- and sawmilling. Mineral springs. Marble and stone quarries near by.

Marquion (märkyõ'), agr. village (pop. 772), Pas-de-Calais dept., N France, 7 mi. WNW of Cambrai. Scene of Canadian victory, Sept., 1918, in First World War.

Marquise (märkēz'), town (pop. 3,512), Pas-de-Calais dept., N France, 8 mi. NNE of Boulogne; copper and bronze smelting, marble quarrying.

Marrabios, Cordillera de los, Nicaragua: see MARABIOS, CORDILLERA DE LOS.

Marracuene, Mozambique: see VILA LUIZA.

Marradi (mär-rä'dē), village (pop. 1,830), Firenze prov., Tuscany, central Italy, on Lamone R. and 14 mi. NE of Borgo San Lorenzo; textile mills (silk, woolen). Heavily damaged by bombing in Second World War.

Marrakesh or **Marrakech** (mŭrä'kĕsh, Fr. märäkĕsh'), city (pop. 238,237), ⊙ Marrakesh region (□ 45,725; pop. 2,392,534), SW Fr. Morocco, at N foot of the High Atlas, 130 mi. S of Casablanca; 31°37'N 8°W. Morocco's traditional southern capital (Fez was northern capital; since establishment of Fr. protectorate, sultan resides at Rabat) and its 2d-largest city. S terminus of trunk railroad (electrified as far as Fez) extending across Algeria and into Tunisia; linked by rail spur with Safi, its chief port on the Atlantic (85 mi. NW). Also connected by road with Mogador (W), Agadir (SW; via Tizi n'Test pass), and S Morocco's Saharan oases (via Tizi n'Tichka pass). Airport (SW). A leading commercial center in the fertile irrigated Haouz plain (N'Fis Dam 25 mi. SSW), and former N terminus of trans-Saharan caravans. Fruit and vegetable preserving, wool spinning, flour milling, palm-fiber processing, mfg. of building materials. Principal handicraft manufactures are morocco-leather articles and carpets. There are lead, copper, and graphite mines in zone just N of Tensift R. (which flows E–W, 4 mi. N of city), and lead, zinc and molybdenum mines in the High Atlas c.30 mi S. The extensive date-palm groves (just N) and the oasis-like fertility of the Haouz lowland against a background of semi-arid steppe country give Marrakesh a Saharan touch. Yearly rainfall 9 inches, limited to winter months; extremely hot summers, mild winters; yearly average temp. 68°F The old city, with its labyrinth of crooked, dead end streets, presents an overcrowded, run-down appearance. Marrakesh's noted landmark is the 220-ft. tower of the Koutoubia mosque (completed end of 12th cent.); like the Giralda at Seville, it was built by Andalusians under the Almoravides S of the sultan's palace is the Aguedal, a beautiful park with many species of fruit trees. The modern city (begun 1913) has grown up to the W, along the road to Mogador. Overlooking city on S are the high, often snow-capped peaks of the High Atlas. Founded 1062 by Yusuf ibn Tashfin, Marrakesh was ⊙ of the Almoravide dynasty and (i 12th cent.) of the Almohades. Under the Saad rulers, it became a prosperous center trading with Timbuktu. Its modern growth dates from Fr occupation (1912). The city was formerly also called Morocco.

Marrak Point (mä'räk), small peninsula, SW Greenland, on Davis Strait, 55 mi. SSE of Godthaab 63°25'N 51°15'W; airfield.

Marra Mountains (mär'rū), highest section of Nile–L. Chad watershed, in Darfur prov., W Anglo Egyptian Sudan, W of El Fasher; c.100 mi. long 20 mi. wide; rise to c.10,100 ft. Of volcanic origin

Marrargiu, Cape (märär'jū), point on W coast of Sardinia, NW of Bosa; 40°20'N 8°22'E. Fisheries (tunny, lobster, coral).

Marratxí (märächē'), town (pop. 119; commun pop. 5,108), Majorca, Balearic Isls., on railroad and 5 mi. NE of Palma, in agr. region (cereals carobs, almonds, grapes); mfg. of perfume and pottery. Has Son Bonet airfield.

Marrawah, village (pop. 253), NW Tasmania, 13 mi. WNW of Launceston; agr. center; chees factory.

Marrazes (mŭrä'zĭsh), village (pop. 1,161), Leiri dist., W central Portugal, just N of Leiria; saw milling, furniture mfg.

Marree (mŭrē'), settlement (pop. 190), E centra South Australia, 230 mi. N of Port Pirie, on Por Pirie–Alice Springs RR; cattle.

Marrero (mŭrâ'rō), village (1940 pop. 4,094), Jeffer son parish, SE La., on the Mississippi, opposit New Orleans; mfg. (chemicals, molasses, petrol um, asbestos, sugar-cane fiber products, paper) truck farms.

Marri-Bugti Territory (mŭr'rē-bōōg'tē), tribal are (□ c.7,000) in Sibi dist., NE central Baluchistan W Pakistan, at junction of NE end of Centra Brahui and S Sulaiman ranges. Barren, hill region, with scanty rainfall; inhabited by Baluc tribes (Marris, Bugtis).

Marrickville, municipality (pop. 46,866), E New South Wales, Australia, 4 mi. SW of Sydney, i metropolitan area; mfg. center (woolen mills, sheet metal plants, aluminum ware, radio equipment asbestos products).

Marromeu (märōōmā'ōō), village, Manica an Sofala prov., central Mozambique, on right ban of lower Zambezi R. and 130 mi. NNE of Beira terminus of rail spur from Vila Fontes; sugar growing and processing center amidst larg plantations.

Marroquí, Point (märōkē'), southernmost cape o European mainland, in Cádiz prov., S Spain, o Strait of Gibraltar, just S of Tarifa; 36°N 5°36'W Lighthouse. Generally considered dividing poin bet. the Mediterranean and the Atlantic. Some times written Marroqui. Also called Tarifa Point

Marruás, Brazil: see PÔRTO.

Marrupa (märōō'pä), village, Niassa prov., N Mozambique, on road and 200 mi. W of Pôrt Amélia; corn, sorghum.

Mars, borough (pop. 1,385), Butler co., W Pa., 1 mi. N of Pittsburgh. Inc. 1882.

Marsa (mär'sä), town (pop. 11,560), E Malta, a head of Grand Harbour, 2 mi. SW of Valletta; shi repairing. Severely damaged during Second Worl War, but its monuments—except for 15th-cent church (now repaired)—suffered little.

Marsa, La (lä märsä'), town (pop. 6,122), N Tunisia on Gulf of Tunis, 10 mi. NE of Tunis; fashionabl summer and bathing resort; beylical and archiepis copal residences, summer palace of Fr. residen general. A convention held here in 1883, imple mented the treaty of Le Bardo (1881) establishin French Protectorate in Tunisia.

Marsabit (mär'säbĭt), village, Northern Frontie Prov., N Kenya, in volcanic Marsabit range (risin to 5,594 ft.), on road and 140 mi. N of Isiolo 2°21'N 37°59'E; nomadic livestock raising. Air field.

Marsafa (mär'säfä), village (pop. 7,206), Qalyubiya prov., Lower Egypt, 5 mi. SE of Benha; cotton flax, cereals, fruits.

Marsal (märsäl'), village (pop. 318), Moselle dept. NE France, on the Seille and 5 mi. SE of Château Salins. Its fortifications date back to Gallo-Roma times.

Marsala (märsä'lä), anc. *Lilybaeum,* town (pop. 24,650), Trapani prov., W Sicily, on Cape Boeo and 16 mi. SSW of Trapani; wine-shipping port (Marsala wine 1st produced here, 1773); mfg. (macaroni, bottles, bricks, wood products); tunny fishing. Site of cathedral, mus. (largely destroyed in Second World War). Garibaldi landed here, May 11, 1860, to begin successful expedition against Bourbons. Lilybaeum founded by Carthaginians 397–396 B.C.; it was their principal Sicilian fortress. Occupied by Romans in 241 B.C. after 9-year siege. Heavily bombed (1943) in Second World War.

Marsa Matruh, Egypt: see MATRUH.

Marsamuscetto Harbour (märsämōōshĕt'tō), Mediterranean inlet (c.1½ mi. long) of E Malta, on W shore of peninsula on which VALLETTA is built. Branches off into several creeks which enclose GZIRA isl. Lined by naval installations and dockyards. Its entrance is guarded by the old forts Tigné and St. Elmo. SLIEMA is NW, MSIDA SW.

Marsannay-la-Côte (märsänā'-lä-kōt'), village (pop. 874), Côte-d'Or dept., E central France, on E slopes of the Côte d'Or, 4 mi. SW of Dijon; Burgundy wines.

Marsanne (märsän'), village (pop. 267), Drôme dept., SE France, 9 mi. NE of Montélimar; tripoli quarrying.

Marsa Scala (mär'sä skä'lä), fishing port, SE Malta, 3½ mi. SE of Valletta. Has 18th-cent. church. Also called Wied il Ghain.

Marsa Scirocco, Malta: see MARSAXLOKK.

Marsassoum (märsäsōōm'), village, SW Senegal, Fr. West Africa, landing on right affluent of Casamance R. and 25 mi. NE of Ziguinchor; peanuts, timber.

Marsa Susa, Cyrenaica: see APOLLONIA.

Marsaxlokk (mär"säshlôk'), village (parish pop. 1,431), SE Malta, fishing port on Marsaxlokk Bay (c.2 mi. long, 1 mi. wide), 4½ mi. SSE of Valletta. Has 18th-cent. fortifications; 17th-cent. palaces and churches. Sometimes called Marsa Shlok or Marsa Scirocco.

Marschendorf, Czechoslovakia: see MARSOV.

Marsciano (märshä'nô), town (pop. 1,568), Perugia prov., Umbria, central Italy, 14 mi. SSW of Perugia; foundry, cotton dyeworks, mfg. of nails, agr. tools, tower clocks.

Marsden (märz'dŭn), former urban district (1931 pop. 5,723), West Riding, SW Yorkshire, England, on Colne R. and 7 mi. WSW of Huddersfield; woolen mills. Site of Huddersfield reservoirs. Inc. 1937 in Colne Valley.

Marsdiep (märz'dēp), strait (2 mi. wide) NW Netherlands, leading from North Sea to the Waddenzee; separates Texel isl. (N) from mainland of North Holland prov. Port of Helder on S shore. W part also known as Helsdeur.

Marseillan (märsēyā'), town (pop. 3,138), Hérault dept., S France, port on SW shore of the Étang de Thau, 9 mi. SW of Sète. Known for its white and rosé wines. Produces liqueurs.

Marseille, France: see MARSEILLES.

Marseille-en-Beauvaisis (märsā'-ā-bovĕzē'), village (pop. 766), Oise dept., N France, 11 mi. NNW of Beauvais; road junction. Dairying. Sawmilling at Achy (2 mi. SSE).

Marseilles (märsālz', -sā'), Fr. *Marseille* (märsā'-yü), Gr. *Massalia,* Latin *Massilia,* city (1946 pop. 551,640; 1936 pop. 794,914), ⊙ Bouches-du-Rhône dept., SE France, on Gulf of Lion, 400 mi. SSE of Paris; 43°18'N 5°24'E. Second largest city of France and its chief Mediterranean port, on a bay surrounded by barren limestone hills. Trades primarily with Fr. North Africa, Eastern Mediterranean countries, E coast of Africa, and the Far East. Chief exports: wines, liqueurs, olive oil, oil cake, soap, cement products, ocher, refined sugar, dried vegetables, glycerine, and finished metal goods. Chief imports: North African wines, olives and citrus fruit; tropical staple crops, spices, hides and skins, and miscellaneous oil seeds and nuts. Marseilles produces 90% of soap consumed in France, and mixes Fr. and Tunisian olive oil for re-export. Chemical industry includes mfg. of superphosphates, pharmaceuticals, and sulphur refining. Metallurgy is represented by iron, copper, and bauxite smelters, shipyards, and workshops mfg. marine engines and electrical apparatus. City also has petroleum and sugar refineries; brick-, tile-, and glassworks; tanneries, large flour mills, tobacco and match factories. Other mfg.: ready-to-wear clothing, tropical helmets, food preserves, playing cards. From picturesque *Vieux-Port* (old port) located at head of the Canebière (city's renowned main thoroughfare), the modern harbor extends 5 mi. northward to L'Estaque, where Rhone-Marseilles Canal enters ROVE Tunnel. It consists of adjacent, interconnected basins (Bassin de la Joliette, du Lazaret, d'Arenc, de la Gare Maritime, National, etc.) up to 40 ft. deep, with 15 mi. of quays and rail sidings. Offshore, just SSW of port, are islands of Ratonneau and Pomègues (connected by jetty) which serve as quarantine station. Bet. them and mainland is well-known If islet, site of Chateau d'If. Though France's oldest city, Marseilles preserves few relics of its past. Principal bldgs. are 19th-cent. cathedral of La Major, built of green and white stone (slightly damaged 1939–45); mus. of fine arts housed in 19th-cent. mansion; 13th-cent. church of St. Victor; and 19th-cent. neo-Byzantine basilica of Notre-Dame-de-la-Garde, which rises to 500 ft. atop an isolated hill just S of city center. The crowded waterfront dist., former meeting place of all races, just N of old port, was razed by Germans in Second World War. The huge cable freight conveyor across entrance to old harbor, formerly a landmark of Marseilles, was also destroyed. City has faculties of science and medicine of Aix-Marseilles Univ. Known for its teeming, almost Oriental, atmosphere, Marseilles has a citizenry who, with their individualism and manner of speech, have contributed a distinctive flavor to Fr. culture. Settled by Phocaean Greeks from Asia Minor c.600 B.C. Anc. Massilia became ally of Rome, which annexed it (49 B.C.) after it had supported Pompey against Caesar in civil war. It retained, however, its internal autonomy. Besieged by Visigoths, Burgundians, Saracens, and Normans, it was taken (1252) by Charles of Anjou, and thereafter shared history of Provence, passing definitively to France in 1486. During French Revolution, the Reign of Terror was particularly fierce here. Fr. conquest of Algeria and opening of Suez Canal gave a tremendous boost to the port of Marseilles, so that today it is rivalled only by Genoa (which has a more densely pop. hinterland) in the Mediterranean. During Second World War, city and harbor installations were damaged by German scorching and Allied naval bombarding prior to invasion (Aug., 1944) of S France. Thiers, Daumier, and Edmond Rostand b. here.

Marseilles (märsālz'). **1** City (pop. 4,514), La Salle co., N Ill., on Illinois R. (water power) and 35 mi. WSW of Joliet; bituminous-coal mines; mfg. (construction supplies, biscuits, sodium alkali). Marseilles Canal carries Illinois Waterway shipping around rapids in Illinois R. here. Illini State Park is near by. Inc. 1861. **2** Village (pop. 156), Wyandot co., N central Ohio, 12 mi. ENE of Kenton.

Marseilles-les-Aubigny (märsā-lāzōbēnyē'), village (pop. 410), Cher dept., central France, near left bank of the Loire, 9 mi. NW of Nevers; junction of Loire Lateral and Berry canals; cementworks.

Marseilleveyre, Massif de, France: see CROISETTE, CAPE.

Marsella (märsĕ'yä), town (pop. 3,380), Caldas dept., W central Colombia, in Cauca valley, 18 mi. SW of Manizales; coffeegrowing, sericulture.

Marsh, England: see HUDDERSFIELD.

Marshall or **Fortuna Ledge,** village (pop. 92), W Alaska, on Yukon R. and 75 mi. N of Bethel; placer gold mining. On Yukon R. steamship lines. Has Territorial school. Scene of gold rush, 1913.

Marshall, town, Marshall territory, S Liberia, port on Atlantic Ocean, at mouth of Farmington R. and 30 mi. ESE of Monrovia; until 1950, Liberia's chief rubber-shipping center. Sometimes called Junk; formerly called Little Bassa. Roberts Field airport N.

Marshall. 1 County (□ 571; pop. 45,090), NE Ala.; ⊙ Guntersville. Agr. area bounded on N by Paint Rock R.; Wheeler and Guntersville reservoirs are on Tennessee R. Cotton, bees; textiles. Formed 1836. **2** County (□ 395; pop. 13,025), N central Ill.; ⊙ Lacon. Agr. (corn, oats, wheat, soybeans, fruit, livestock, poultry; dairy products. Bituminous-coal mines; timber. Some mfg. (bunting goods, rocker grates, cigars, woolen goods, clothing, feed). Drained by Illinois R. and small Sandy Creek. Formed 1839. **3** County (□ 444; pop. 29,468), N Ind.; ⊙ Plymouth. Agr. area (livestock, grain, soybeans, poultry, fruit; dairy products), especially noted for truck and mint growing; processing especially of spearmint and peppermint oil. Resort lakes and recreation areas. Drained by Yellow and Tippecanoe rivers. Formed 1835. **4** County (□ 574; pop. 35,611), central Iowa; ⊙ Marshalltown. Prairie agr. area (cattle, hogs, poultry, corn, oats, wheat) drained by Iowa and North Skunk rivers. Bituminous-coal deposits (W), limestone quarries (E). Industry at Marshalltown. Formed 1846. **5** County (□ 911; pop. 17,926), NE Kansas; ⊙ Marysville. Gently rolling to hilly area, bordered N by Nebr.; drained by Big Blue and Little Blue rivers. Grain, livestock. Formed 1855. **6** County (□ 335; pop. 13,387), SW Ky.; ⊙ Benton. Bounded N by Tennessee R., E by its Kentucky Reservoir; drained by East and West forks of Clarks R. Includes Kentucky Dam State Park in NE. Agr. area (dairy products, poultry, livestock, corn, dark tobacco, strawberries, lespedeza); hardwood timber; clay pits. Formed 1842. **7** County (□ 1,800; pop. 16,125), NW Minn.; ⊙ Warren. Agr. area bounded W by N.Dak. and Red R., and drained by Snake, Thief, and Middle rivers. Wheat, small grains, livestock, dairy products, potatoes. Mud Lake Migratory Waterfowl Refuge is in marshy area in E. Co. formed 1879. **8** County (□ 710; pop. 25,106), N Miss., on Tenn. line (N) and bounded partly S by Tallahatchie R.; ⊙ Holly Springs. Drained by Coldwater R. Hilly agr. area (cotton, corn, hay); dairying; clay products; processing of farm products. Includes part of Holly Springs Natl. Forest. Formed 1836. **9** County (□ 414; pop. 8,177), S Okla.; ⊙ Madill. Bounded E and S by L. Texoma, formed by Denison Dam in Red R. Stock-raising and agr. area (cotton, corn, pecans, grain); dairying. Oil fields; gasoline plants. Timber. Formed 1907. **10** County (□ 875; pop. 7,835), NE S.Dak., on N.Dak. line; ⊙ Britton. Rich farming and livestock-raising region, with numerous lakes. Dairy produce, poultry, grain. Fort Sisseton, historic military outpost, and part of Sisseton Indian Reservation in E. Formed 1885. **11** County (□ 377; pop. 17,768), central Tenn.; ⊙ Lewisburg. Drained by Duck R. and its tributaries. Agr. (livestock, dairy products, grain, tobacco); timber; some mfg. Formed 1836. **12** County (□ 306; pop. 36,893), W.Va., southernmost co. of Northern Panhandle; ⊙ Moundsville. Bounded W by Ohio R. (Ohio line), E by Pa.; drained by small Wheeling, Fish, and Grave creeks. Industrial area; mfg. at Moundsville, Cameron, and Benwood is based on region's coal, natural gas, oil, glass sand, clay, and timber. Some agr. (livestock, dairy products, feed crops, tobacco, truck). Formed 1835.

Marshall. 1 City (pop. 1,189), ⊙ Searcy co., N Ark., 34 mi. SE of Harrison, in the Ozarks; vegetables, cotton; timber. **2** City (pop. 2,960), ⊙ Clark co., E Ill., 16 mi. WSW of Terre Haute (Ind.), in agr. area; cheese and paint factories, oil wells and refinery, rock-crushing plants. Inc. 1853. **3** Town (pop. 326), Parke co., W Ind., 30 mi. NNE of Terre Haute, in agr. and bituminous-coal area. **4** City (pop. 5,777), ⊙ Calhoun co., S Mich., 12 mi. SE of Battle Creek and on Kalamazoo R., in farm area (livestock, grain, onions). Mfg. (furnaces, auto parts, air-conditioning equipment, outboard motors, plumbing supplies, paint, drugs, meat products). Settled 1831; inc. as village 1836, as city 1859. **5** City (pop. 5,923), ⊙ Lyon co., SW Minn., on Redwood R. and c.90 mi. WNW of Mankato; trade and shipping center for grain, livestock, and poultry area; dairy products, beverages. Camden State Park is 8 mi. SW. Settled 1871, platted 1872, inc. 1901. **6** City (pop. 8,850), ⊙ Saline co., central Mo., bet. Missouri and Blackwater rivers, 28 mi. N of Sedalia; agr.; mfg. (shoes, flour, dairy products). Missouri Valley Col.; state school for defectives, homes for crippled children and aged women; 2 state parks and U.S. resettlement project near by. Settled c.1840. **7** Town (pop. 983), ⊙ Madison co., W N.C., 15 mi. NNW of Asheville and on French Broad R., in burley-tobacco region; cotton and lumber mills. Settled 1816; inc. 1852 **8** or **New Marshall,** town (pop. 386), Logan co., central Okla., 22 mi. NW of Guthrie, in oil-producing and agr. area. **9** City (pop. 22,327), ⊙ Harrison co., E Texas, 38 mi. W of Shreveport, La.; trade, shipping, industrial center for agr. (cotton, truck), oil, lumbering area; railroad shops, wheel foundry; flour, lumber, and cottonseed-oil milling, milk processing, mfg. of brick, carbon, clothing, steel products, crates. Seat of Wiley Col., Bishop Col., a Baptist jr. col. and a Catholic acad. Caddo L. (recreation) is 15 mi. NE. Settled 1838, inc. 1850. **10** Village (1940 pop. 515), Fauquier co., N Va., 10 mi. N of Warrenton; trade center in agr. area. Near by is "Oak Hill" (1773), home of John Marshall. **11** Village (pop. 541), Dane co., S Wis., on small Waterloo Creek and 17 mi. ENE of Madison, in farm area; dairy products; feed mill.

Marshall Air Force Base, Kansas: see JUNCTION CITY.

Marshall Ford Dam, S central Texas, in Colorado R. c.18 mi. NW of Austin; concrete dam 270 ft. high, 5,093 ft. long (including flanking earthfill wings); for flood control, power, and river regulation for irrigation; completed 1942. Sometimes called Mansfield Dam. Impounds L. Travis or Marshall Ford L. (□ 45; capacity 1,934,000 acre-ft.).

Marshall Hall, excursion resort, Charles co., S Md., on the Potomac c.16 mi. below Washington; has amusement park and old Marshall Hall (containing colonial relics).

Marshall Island, Maine: see SWANS ISLAND.

Marshall Islands, archipelago (□ 70; pop. 10,223), W central Pacific, 2,595 naut. mi. N of Auckland; 4°30'–14°45'N 160°50'–172°10'E. Comprise 34 atolls and coral isls. in 2 parallel NW–SE chains, 130 mi. apart. KWAJALEIN, in RALIK CHAIN, is largest atoll of Marshall Isls. and ⊙ Kwajalein dist.; Majuro, in RATAK CHAIN, is ⊙ Majuro dist. Former ⊙ group was JALUIT. Pandanus, coconut, breadfruit, papaya, arrowroot; hibiscus, orchids. Rats, lizards, coconut crabs; no snakes. Annual mean temp. 81°F.; rainfall 160 in. (S atolls), 80 in. (N atolls). Micronesian natives. Chief export, copra. Discovered 1526 by Spanish; visited 1788 by Capts. Gilbert and Marshall. German protectorate 1885–1914; Jap. military possession 1914; Jap. mandated territory 1922–35. Japan claimed (1935) sovereignty over group. In Second World War, isls. were captured 1944 by U.S. forces. Site (at BIKINI) of atom-bomb tests, 1946. Group wa included (1947) in U.S. Territory of the Paci Islands under U.N. trusteeship.

Marshall Pass, Colo.: see SAWATCH MOUNTAI

Marshallton. 1 Residential village (1940 pop. New Castle co., N Del., 5 mi. W of Wilr vulcanized-fiber plant. State tuberculosis sanatorium near by. 2 Village (pop. 3,390), Northumberland co., E central Pa.

Marshalltown, city (pop. 19,821), ⊙ Marshall co., central Iowa, on Iowa R. and c.50 mi. NE of Des Moines; industrial, trade, and rail center with gasket and valve factories, foundries, railroad shops, meat-packing and rendering plants, food cannery; also mfg. of furnaces, power lawn mowers, trowels, paint. Limestone quarries near by. Has state soldiers home and jr. col. Settled 1851, inc. 1863.

Marshallville. 1 Town (pop. 1,121), Macon co., W central Ga., 7 mi. SSW of Fort Valley, in a peach-growing section. 2 Village (pop. 458), Wayne co., N central Ohio, 13 mi. NE of Wooster, in agr. area; meat products.

Marshalsea (mär'shŭlsē), former prison in Southwark, London, England, closed 1842. Once attached to law court of king's marshal, it later became debtors' prison. It is setting of part of Dickens's *Little Dorrit*.

Marshbrook, village, Gwelo prov., E central Southern Rhodesia, in Mashonaland, 34 mi. NNE of Enkeldoorn; tobacco, wheat, citrus fruit, dairy products.

Marsh Chapel, agr. village and parish (pop. 507), Parts of Lindsey, NE Lincolnshire, England, 9 mi. SE of Grimsby; synthetic-fertilizer works. Has 16th-cent. church.

Marshfield, agr. village and parish (pop. 1,063), SW Gloucester, England, 12 mi. E of Bristol. Has 14th-cent. church, 17th-cent. almshouses, 17th-cent. inn.

Marsh-Field or **Base Station**, Coos co., N central N.H., valley station of 3-mi.-long Mt. Washington cog railway, completed 1869, 1st of its kind in the world.

Marshfield. 1 Town (pop. 221), Washington co., E Maine, on Machias R., just N of Machias. 2 Town (pop. 3,267), Plymouth co., E Mass., on coast, 25 mi. SE of Boston; summer resort; cranberries. Daniel Webster lived and is buried here. Resort villages include Humarock, Ocean Bluff, Brant Rock, Green Harbor, Sea View, and Marshfield Hills. Inc. 1642. 3 City (pop. 1,925), ⊙ Webster co., S central Mo., in the Ozarks, 22 mi. ENE of Springfield; ships farm products, especially tomatoes. Settled c.1830. 4 City, Oregon: see COOS BAY, city. 5 Town (pop. 830), including Marshfield village (pop. 274), Washington co., central Vt., on Winooski R., just E of Montpelier; wood products. Includes part of PLAINFIELD village. 6 City (pop. 12,394), Wood co., central Wis., 24 mi. NW of Wisconsin Rapids, in dairy belt; mfg. (dairy products, veneer, farm equipment, shoes, gloves, beer). Settled c.1868, inc. 1883. Rebuilt after devastating fire (1887).

Marshfield Hills, Mass.: see MARSHFIELD.

Marsh Harbour, town (pop. 289), N Bahama Isls., on E central shore of Great Abaco Isl., 5 mi. W of Hope Town; 26°33'N 77°4'W. Lumbering, fishing.

Mars Hill. 1 Agr. town (pop. 2,060), including Mars Hill village (pop. 1,239), Aroostook co., E Maine, 27 mi. N of Houlton and on Presquile R., near N.B. line; ships potatoes. Takes name from Mars Hill (1,660 ft.), 2 mi. E. 2 Town (pop. 1,404), Madison co., W N.C., 16 mi. N of Asheville, in farm area. Seat of Mars Hill Col.

Marsh Island, Iberia parish, S La., low marshy island (21 mi. long, 2–10 mi. wide) 25 mi. S of New Iberia, bet. Gulf of Mexico (S) and Vermilion and West Cote Blanche bays (NW and N).

Marsh Lake, enlargement of Minnesota R. bet. Lac qui Parle and Big Stone counties, W Minn., 13 mi. ESE of Ortonville; 7.5 mi. long, 2 mi. wide. Created by dam at SE end. Receives Pomme de Terre R.

Marsh Peak, Utah: see UINTA MOUNTAINS.

Marshville, town (pop. 1,258), Union co., S N.C., 10 mi. E of Monroe; sawmilling.

Marshyhope Creek (mär'shēhōp"), W central Del. and E Md., rises in swamps in S Kent co., Del., flows c.40 mi. generally SSW, past Federalsburg, Md. (head of navigation), and through Dorchester co., to the Nanticoke 2 mi. below Sharpstown. Formerly called Northwest Fork of Nanticoke R.

Marsico Nuovo (mär'sēkô nwô'vô), town (pop. 2,349), Potenza prov., Basilicata, S Italy, on upper Agri R. and 16 mi. SSW of Potenza; wine, olive oil. Bishopric. Marsico Vetere (pop. 1,053) is 6 mi. ESE.

Marsillargues (märsēyärg'), town (pop. 2,320), Hérault dept., S France, on the Vidourle and 15 mi. ENE of Montpellier; winegrowing, distilling.

Marsing, village (pop. 643), Owyhee co., SW Idaho, on Snake R. and 30 mi. W of Boise, near Deer Flat Reservoir; trading point in agr. area (potatoes, grain, livestock) served by Owyhee project.

Marsivan, Turkey: see MERZIFON.

Marske-by-the-Sea, resort town, North Riding, NE Yorkshire, England, on North Sea 2 mi. SE of Redcar.

Marsland (märz'lŭnd), village (pop. 84), Dawes co., NW Nebr., 30 mi. SSW of Chadron.

Mars-la-Tour (mär-lä-tōōr'), agr. village (pop. 728), Meurthe-et-Moselle dept., NE France, 13 mi. W of Metz. Has monument and mus. commemorating battle (1870) of Franco-Prussian War.

Marson (märsõ'), village (pop. 223), Marne dept., N France, 8 mi. ESE of Châlons-sur-Marne; sheep.

Marsov (mär'shôf), Czech *Maršov*, Ger. *Marschendorf* (mär'shŭndôrf), village (commune pop. 1,679), Bohemia, Czechoslovakia, in the Riesengebirge, at E foot of Cerna Hora, 34 mi. ESE of Liberec; paper mills; lumbering. Noted winter-sports center of Pec (pĕts) is 3 mi. NW.

Marssac-sur-Tarn (märsäk'-sür-tärn'), village (pop. 345), Tarn dept., S France, on the Tarn and 6 mi. W of Albi; slaked-lime and brickworks; distilling.

Marstal (märs'täl), town (pop. 1,965) and port, Svendborg amt, Denmark, on E shore of Aero isl.; shipbuilding.

Marstal Bay or **Vejsnaes Bay** (vīs'nĕs), Denmark, bet. S tips of Aero and Langeland isls.

Marston, city (pop. 610), New Madrid co., extreme SE Mo., near Mississippi R., 7 mi. SW of New Madrid.

Marston Moor (mär'stŭn), moorland area in West Riding, central Yorkshire, England, 7 mi. W of York. Site of Civil War battle (July 2, 1644) at which Parliamentarians under Cromwell, Fairfax, and the earls of Manchester and Leven defeated Royalists under Prince Rupert and duke of Newcastle. Just SE is agr. village and parish (pop. 254) of Long Marston.

Marston Moretaine or **Marston Moreteyne** (both: mär'sŭn môr'tŭn), agr. village and parish (pop. 1,064), W Bedford, England, 6 mi. SW of Bedford. Its anc. church (rebuilt in 15th cent.) has separate Norman tower.

Marstons Mills, Mass.: see BARNSTABLE, town.

Marstrand (mär'stränd"), city (pop. 1,274), Goteborg och Bohus co., SW Sweden, on isl. (□ 3) of same name in the Skagerrak, 18 mi. NW of Goteborg; fashionable seaside resort; herring-fishing port, with shipyards. Has 14th-cent. church and 17th-cent. fortress. Founded (c.1225) by a Norwegian king; became (14th cent.) trade center, disputed by Denmark, Norway, Sweden, and Hanseatic League. Passed (1658) to Sweden; then lost its trade to Goteborg.

Marsyaty (mŭrsyä'tē), town (1944 pop. over 500), N Sverdlovsk oblast, Russian SFSR, on Sosva R. and 30 mi. N of Serov, on rail spur; manganese-mining center, supplying Serov metallurgy.

Mart, town (pop. 2,269), McLennan co., E central Texas, 17 mi. E of Waco; trade center in cotton, corn, dairying area; cotton ginning; cottonseed-oil milling, food canning. Settled 1875, inc. 1903.

Marta (mär'tä), town (pop. 2,812), Viterbo prov., Latium, central Italy, on L. Bolsena near efflux of Marta R., 12 mi. NW of Viterbo; fishing. Has Farnese palace.

Martaban (mär"tŭbăn'), village, Thaton dist., Lower Burma, on mouth of Salween R., opposite Moulmein (ferry service); head of railroad to Pegu; trading center; pottery mfg.; rail workshops. Founded 6th cent. A.D.; was ⊙ independent kingdom (1281). Invested by Br. forces in 1st (1824) and 2d (1852) Anglo-Burmese Wars.

Martaban, Gulf of, triangular inlet of Andaman Sea, Lower Burma; main port, Moulmein. Receives Salween, Sittang, and Rangoon rivers.

Martand, Kashmir: see ANANTNAG, town.

Martanis, Turkey: see CATAK.

Martano (märtä'nô), town (pop. 6,267), Lecce prov., Apulia, S Italy, 13 mi. SSE of Lecce; wine, olive oil, cheese.

Marta River (mär'tä), outlet of L. Bolsena, central Italy; leaves lake near Marta, flows 30 mi. S and SSW to Tyrrhenian Sea 3 mi. SW of Tarquinia.

Martel (märtĕl'), village (pop. 865), Lot dept., SW France, in the Causse de Martel, near Dordogne R., 16 mi. SSE of Brive-la-Gaillarde; important truffle trade.

Martel, Causse de, France: see CAUSSES.

Martelange (märtŭlãzh'), village (pop. 1,625), Luxembourg prov., SE Belgium, on Sûre R. and 11 mi. NNW of Arlon, in the Ardennes, on grand duchy of Luxembourg border; stone quarrying.

Martelange, village (pop. 108), W Luxembourg, in the Ardennes, on Sûre R. and 7 mi. NW of Redange, on Belg. border; slate quarrying. Village of Rombach is contiguous.

Martell (märtĕl'), village (pop. c.175), Amador co., central Calif., just NW of Jackson; rail terminus; lumber milling.

Martelle (märtĕl'), town (pop. 228), Jones co., E Iowa, 16 mi. E of Cedar Rapids; soybean products.

Marten (mär'tĕn), village (pop. 2,762), Ruse dist., NE Bulgaria, on the Danube and 8 mi. NE of Ruse; sugar beets, sunflowers, vineyards.

Martensdale, town (pop. 161), Warren co., S central Iowa, 16 mi. SSW of Des Moines.

Martha, town (pop. 222), Jackson co., SW Okla., 7 mi. NNW of Altus, near the Salt Fork of Red R., in cotton and grain area.

Martha Brae River (brā), Trelawny parish, N Jamaica, rises in N Cockpit Country, flows c.20 mi. E and N to the Caribbean at Falmouth, for which it supplies water. The village of Martha Brae is 2 mi. S of Falmouth.

Marthasville, town (pop. 347), Warren co., E central Mo., near Missouri R., 45 mi. W of St. Louis; grain, livestock.

Martha's Vineyard (vĭn'yŭrd), island (20 mi. long, 10 mi. wide) in the Atlantic, 15 mi. off SE Mass., 5 mi. S of SW corner of Cape Cod across Vineyard Sound; part of Dukes co. Gosnold visited it in 1602; settlers came from Mass. in 1642. Divided into towns of EDGARTOWN, CHILMARK, GAY HEAD, OAK BLUFFS, TISBURY (including Vineyard Haven village), and WEST TISBURY. Harbors at Vineyard Haven, Oak Bluffs, and Edgartown. Whaling and fishing were important here; isl. now primarily a resort. Much of interior set aside as state forest. Isl. connected with mainland by steamers from New Bedford and Woods Hole and by airplane service.

Marthaville, town (pop. 121), Natchitoches parish, NW central La., 18 mi. W of Natchitoches; agr.; cotton gins, sawmills.

Martí (märtē'). 1 Town (pop. 652), Camagüey prov., E Cuba, on Central Highway and 33 mi. ESE of Camagüey; rail junction in sugar-cane region. 2 Town (pop. 2,640), Matanzas prov., W Cuba, on railroad and 19 mi. ESE of Cárdenas, in agr. region (sugar cane, oranges, sisal). Asphalt deposits and mineral springs in vicinity. Near by are the refineries and sugar centrals of Guipúzcoa (NW) and Santa Gertrudis (SE).

Martiago (märtyä'gō), village (pop. 1,211), Salamanca prov., W Spain, 10 mi. SSE of Ciudad Rodrigo; flour mills.

Martignacco (märtēnyäk'kô), village (pop. 1,979), Udine prov., Friuli–Venezia Giulia, NE Italy, 5 mi. WNW of Udine; biscuit mfg.

Martigné-Briand (märtēnyā'-brēä'), village (pop. 710), Maine-et-Loire dept., W France, 16 mi. W of Saumur; winegrowing center. Iron springs near by. Has ruins of castle built 1503.

Martigné-Ferchaud (fĕrshō'), village (pop. 1,353), Ille-et-Vilaine dept., W France, 8 mi. NNE of Châteaubriant; dairying, distilling.

Martigny-Bourg (märtēnyē-bōōr'), village (pop. 1,770), Valais canton, SW Switzerland, on Drance R., 1 mi. SSW of Martigny-Ville; hydroelectric plant; aluminum, chemicals, pastry.

Martigny-les-Bains (lā-bē'), resort (pop. 886), Vosges dept., E France, in the Monts Faucilles and 18 mi. SSE of Neufchâteau; mineral springs. Cheese mfg.

Martigny-Ville (–vēl'), town (pop. 3,221), Valais canton, SW Switzerland, on Drance R., 1 mi. S of the Rhone, and 16 mi. SW of Sion; aluminum, calcium carbide, flour, pastry; printing. Hydroelectric plant (S). An old town (Roman *Octodurum*), it has relics of Roman amphitheater (S), 13th-cent. castle tower (NW). Martigny-Bourg and Martigny-Combe are S of town. Road leads S to Great St. Bernard Pass, railroad to Chamonix.

Martigues (märtēg'), town (pop. 7,474), Bouches-du-Rhône dept., SE France, fishing port on Étang de Berre at its outlet (Caronte canal) to the Mediterranean, 18 mi. WNW of Marseilles; saltworks; vegetable-oil processing. Divided into 3 parts (right bank, left bank, isl. in channel) connected by revolving bridges. Town hall (17th cent.) and mus. on isl. Attracts painters. Suffered some damage in Second World War.

Martimprey or **Martimprey-du-Kiss** (märtĕmprā-dü-kēs'), town (pop. 5,102), Oujda region, northeasternmost Fr. Morocco, on Algerian border, 22 mi. NNW of Oujda, in barley- and winegrowing area; palm-fiber processing.

Martim Vaz (mŭrtĕn' väs'), rocky islet in South Atlantic Ocean, c.750 mi. E of Vitória (Espírito Santo), Brazil. Braz. possession; 28°51'W 20°31'S. Formerly spelled Martin Vaz. Trindade isl. is c.35 mi. W.

Martin. 1 County (□ 559; pop. 7,807), SE Fla., bet. L. Okeechobee (W) and the Atlantic (E), and partly sheltered E by Jupiter Isl. (barrier beach); ⊙ Stuart. Lowland area, with swamps and many small lakes in W; crossed by St. Lucie Canal. Truck-produce and citrus-fruit region, with some cattle raising and fishing. Formed 1925. 2 County (□ 345; pop. 10,678), SW Ind.; ⊙ Shoals. Drained by Lost R. and East Fork of White R. Agr. (chiefly grain; also corn, hay, livestock); bituminous coal, oil, natural gas, timber. Mfg. at Loogootee, Shoals. Formed 1820. 3 County (□ 231; pop. 11,677), E Ky.; ⊙ Inez. In the Cumberlands; bounded E by Tug Fork (W.Va. line); drained by several creeks. Mtn. agr. area (livestock, fruit, tobacco); bituminous-coal mines, oil wells. Formed 1870. 4 County (□ 707; pop. 25,655), S Minn.; ⊙ Fairmont. Agr. area bordering on Iowa. Watered by Tuttle L. and by Middle Chain of Lakes. Corn, oats, barley, potatoes, livestock. Formed 1857. 5 County (□ 481; pop. 27,938), E N.C.; ⊙ Williamston. Coastal plain; bounded N by Roanoke R. Agr. (peanuts, tobacco); timber (pine, gum). Sawmilling, fishing, tobacco and peanut processing. Formed 1774. 6 County (□ 911; pop. 5,541), W Texas; ⊙ Stanton. On S Llano Estacado, with E-facing Cap Rock escarpment in NW; alt. 2,600–3,000 ft. Cattle-ranching area; also hogs, sheep, dairying, agr. (cotton, grain sorghums, grain, fruit, truck, poultry). Some oil production; clay deposits. Formed 1876.

Martin. 1 Town (pop. 207), Stephens co., NE Ga., 9 mi. SE of Toccoa, near S.C. line. 2 Mining town (pop. 1,170), Floyd co., E Ky., in Cumberland foothills, 15 mi. WNW of Pikeville, in bituminous-coal area. **3** Village (pop. 407), Allegan co., SW Mich., 6 mi. ENE of Allegan. **4** Village (pop. 171), Sheridan co., central N.Dak., 25 mi. NW of Fessenden. **5** City (pop. 989), ⊙ Bennett co., S S.Dak., 100 mi. SE of Rapid City. Trading point for farm and livestock region; wheat, flax. Pine Ridge Indian Reservation and La Creek Teal and Migratory Fowl Refuge near by. Founded 1912, inc. 1926. **6** City (pop. 4,082), Weakley co., NW Tenn., 13 mi. ESE of Union City; trade center for timber and truck-farming area; makes cigars, shirts. Univ. of Tenn. Jr. Col. here. Founded 1873.

Martina Franca (märtē'nä fräng'kä), town (pop. 20,622), Ionio prov., Apulia, S Italy, 17 mi. NNE of Taranto. Rail junction; wine-making center; olive oil, cheese; hosiery.

Martinborough (mär'tŭnbŭrŭ), borough (pop. 899), ⊙ Featherston co. (□ 953; pop. 3,761), S N.Isl., New Zealand, 35 mi. E of Wellington; dairy plants.

Martín de la Jara (märtēn' dhā lä hä'rä), town (pop. 2,064), Seville prov., SW Spain, in the Sierra de Yeguas, near Málaga border, 12 mi. SE of Osuna; cereals, olives, livestock.

Martín de Yeltes (yĕl'tĕs), village (pop. 1,199), Salamanca prov., W Spain, 18 mi. NE of Ciudad Rodrigo; cereals, livestock.

Martinengo (märtēnĕng'gô), town (pop. 3,829), Bergamo prov., Lombardy, N Italy, near Serio R., 10 mi. SSE of Bergamo; silk mill.

Martinet, Le (lü märtēnā'), village (pop. 1,947), Gard dept., S France, in foothills of the Cévennes, 9 mi. N of Alès; coal mining.

Martínez (märtē'nĕs), city (pop. 24,937) in Greater Buenos Aires, Argentina, on the Río de la Plata and 12 mi. NW of Buenos Aires; mfg. of wire, ceramics, china, cement, varnish, footwear; poultry farming; flour milling. Moving-picture studios.

Martínez (märtē'nĕth), town (pop. 831), Ávila prov., central Spain, 28 mi. SE of Salamanca; cereals, forage; flour milling.

Martinez (märtē'nŭs), city (pop. 8,268), ⊙ Contra Costa co., W Calif., on Suisun Bay (here crossed by drawbridge), opposite Benicia and 16 mi. NNE of Oakland; oil refining, fishing, canning, copper smelting, wine making. Reservoir (completed 1947) is terminus of Contra Costa Canal of Central Valley project. Laid out 1849, inc. 1876.

Martínez de Hoz, Argentina: see PRESIDENCIA DE LA PLAZA.

Martínez de la Torre (märtē'nĕs dā lä tô'rā), town (pop. 1,962), Veracruz, E Mexico, in Gulf lowland, 33 mi. SE of Papantla; corn, sugar cane, coffee.

Martín García Island (märtēn' gärsē'ä), granite island (410 acres), Buenos Aires prov., Argentina, in Uruguay R. estuary, off coast of Colonia dept. (SW Uruguay), 30 mi. NNE of Buenos Aires. Military reservation (training center, marine hosp.). Rises to 160 ft.

Martinique (märtŭnēk', Fr. märtēnēk'), island constituting an overseas department (□ 427; pop. 261,595) of France, in the West Indies; ⊙Fort-de-France. It is in the Windward Isls., bet. Dominica (25 mi. N) and St. Lucia (20 mi. S), bet. 14°24'–14°53'N and 63°6'–63°32'W; 40 mi. long NW–SE, up to 16 mi. wide. Its climate is moist and tropical; mean temp. at Fort-de-France, 79°F.; rainfall averages 87 inches, considerably higher in mts. Frequently ravaged by hurricanes, earthquakes, tidal waves, and destructive eruptions. The rugged isl. is of volcanic origin, formed on a crystalline platform, and rising in Mont Pelée to 4,429 ft. There are few plains, steep mts. being intersected by narrow, fertile valleys with torrential streams. Its indented coastline provides good harbors. The N is largely covered by dense rain forests (little exploited), but most of its cultivable land (about 80%) is devoted to growing of sugar cane. This crop, and rum, account for the colony's chief exports. Among other products are coffee, cacao, pineapples, bananas, citrus fruit, mangoes, coconuts, tobacco, cotton, vanilla, cassava, sweet potatoes, cinnamon; livestock. Some fishing along the coast. Industrial activity is mainly sugar milling and rum distilling. Chief port and trading center is Fort-de-France, which replaced Saint-Pierre as the isl.'s leading city after 1902, when Mont PELÉE erupted and caused great destruction. Probably discovered 1502 by Columbus on his 4th voyage, though it had been sighted in 1493, Martinique was ignored by the Spanish. In 1635 the first Fr. colonization was undertaken. Wars with the Caribs, English, and Dutch followed, leading to the ruthless extermination of the native Indians. The English occupied the isl. at various times, but it has been continuously French since 1816. In Second World War, after the fall of France, its governor adhered to Vichy, but under Allied pressure an agreement was signed in 1943. The colony became an overseas dept. in 1946, and a prefect replaced the governor as chief executive officer. It is represented in the National Assembly by 3 deputies, elected through universal suffrage. The dept. is divided for administrative purposes into 2 *arrondissements* and 32 communes. French is the official language, and the predominantly Negro pop. speaks a Creole patois. Though largely rural, its density is over 600 people per sq. mi.

Martinique Passage, channel (c.25 mi. wide) in the Windward Isls., West Indies, bet. Dominica (N) and Martinique (S).

Martin Lake (□ 62.5), E Ala., chiefly in Tallapoosa co.; large, irregular lake (c.20 mi. long, average width 5 mi.) formed by Martin Dam (168 ft. high, 2,000 ft. long; completed 1927) on Tallapoosa R., 30 mi. NE of Montgomery. Dam is used for hydroelectric power and river control.

Martín Muñoz de las Posadas (märtēn' mōōnyōth' dhā läs pōsä'dhäs), town (pop. 1,251), Segovia prov., central Spain, 25 mi. W of Segovia; cereals, tubers, pepper, tomatoes, onions, vegetables, livestock. Lumbering; tile mfg.

Martinniemi (mär'tĭn-nē''ĕmē), village in Haukipudas commune (pop. 12,252), Oulu co., W Finland, on Gulf of Bothnia, 15 mi. NNW of Oulu; rail terminus; lumber and pulp milling.

Martinôpole (mŭrtēnô'pōōlĭ), town (pop. 1,256), N Ceará, Brazil, on railroad and 22 mi. SSE of Camocim; cotton.

Martinópolis (-pōōlēs), city (pop. 2,248), W São Paulo, Brazil, on railroad and 15 mi. E of Presidente Prudente, in coffee zone; mfg. (manioc flour, pottery, furniture, explosives).

Martin Point, NE Alaska, near Yukon border, cape on Beaufort Sea, 10 mi. E of Barter Isl.; 70°8'N 143°12'W. Eskimo settlement here.

Martin River, S Alaska, rises in Martin River Glacier at 60°29'N 144°19'W, flows 25 mi. SW to Gulf of Alaska E of Cordova.

Martins (mŭrtēns'), city (pop. 1,901), W Rio Grande do Norte, NE Brazil, in small hill range (alt. 2,500 ft.), 75 mi. SW of Mossoró; health resort with mineral springs; cotton, sugar, vegetables.

Martinsberg, Hungary: see GYÖRSZENTMARTON.

Martinsburg. **1** Town (pop. 219), Keokuk co., SE Iowa, 14 mi. NE of Ottumwa; livestock, grain. **2** Town, Ky.: see SANDY HOOK. **3** Town (pop. 296), Audrain co., NE central Mo., 13 mi. ESE of Mexico; grain, livestock, poultry; lumber, coal. **4** Village (pop. 79), Dixon co., NE Nebr., 20 mi. W of Sioux City, Iowa. **5** Village (pop. 264), Knox co., central Ohio, 11 mi. SE of Mount Vernon. **6** Borough (pop. 1,562), Blair co., S central Pa., 13 mi. SSE of Altoona; canned goods, flour; limestone; agr. Settled c.1793, laid out 1815, inc. 1832. **7** Industrial city (pop. 15,621), ⊙ Berkeley co., W.Va., in Eastern Panhandle, 17 mi. SSW of Hagerstown, Md. Mfg. of textiles, hosiery, furniture and wood products, bricks, tiles, cement, food products; ships limestone. Commercial, shipping center for apple-growing and agr. region (livestock, dairy products, grain). Belle Boyd, Confederate spy, lived here and was imprisoned in the old courthouse. Bunker Hill village (10 mi. SW; settled c.1729) is oldest recorded settlement in state. Martinsburg chartered 1778. First use of Federal troops for strikebreaking occurred here 1877 during railroad strike.

Martins Creek, village (1940 pop. 754), Northampton co., E Pa., on Delaware R. and 6 mi. N of Easton; cement mfg.

Martinsdale, village (pop. c.150), Meagher co., central Mont., on Musselshell R. and 30 mi. ESE of White Sulphur Springs, in sheep-raising region; wool.

Martins Ferry, city (pop. 13,220), Belmont co., E Ohio, on the Ohio (bridged), opposite Wheeling (W.Va.), in coal region; steel, galvanized-steel products, heaters, asphalt, boxes, gloves, stoves, beer. Coal mining. William Dean Howells was b. here. Settled 1785 as Norristown; platted 1795; inc. 1865.

Martin Siding, village, S Ont., in Muskoka lakes region, 35 mi. E of Parry Sound; diatomite mining.

Martins Pond, Mass.: see NORTH READING.

Martinsville. **1** City (pop. 1,440), Clark co., E Ill., 28 mi. ESE of Mattoon; agr. (corn, apples, poultry); oil wells; foundry, oil-storage and -pumping station. Platted 1833, inc. 1905. **2** City (pop. 5,991), ⊙ Morgan co., central Ind., on West Fork of White R. and 28 mi. SSW of Indianapolis, in grain-growing area; wood products, furniture, brick, flour, canned goods, dairy products; timber. Health resort, with artesian springs. Settled 1822. **3** Town (pop. 90), Harrison co., NW Mo., 8 mi. NW of Bethany. **4** Village (pop. 399), Clinton co., SW Ohio, 33 mi. ENE of Cincinnati. **5** Industrial city (pop. 17,251), in but independent of Henry co., S Va., in E foothills of the Blue Ridge, near Smith R., 28 mi. WNW of Danville, in timber and agr. (tobacco, corn, wheat) area; co. courthouse is here. Furniture-mfg. center; also makes nylon and cotton textiles, clothing, mirrors, fiberboard products. Fairy Stone State Park is 15 mi. WNW. Founded 1793; inc. as city 1929.

Martinswand, Austria: see ZIRL.

Martinton, village (pop. 292), Iroquois co., E Ill., 15 mi. SSE of Kankakee, in agr. area.

Mártires, Argentina: see LAS PLUMAS.

Martock, town and parish (pop. 2,049), S Somerset, England, near Parrett R., 6 mi. WNW of Yeovil; agr. market; mfg. (leather machinery, gloves, jute goods); dairying. Has 13th–15th-cent. church.

Marton, parish (pop. 4,476), W Lancashire, England. Includes residential village of Great Marton, just E of Blackpool, and dairy-farming village of Little Marton, 3 mi. ESE of Blackpool.

Marton, borough (pop. 2,915), ⊙ Rangitikei co. (□1,675; pop. 8,966), S N.Isl., New Zealand, 90 mi. NNE of Wellington; rail junction; dairy plant, sawmills.

Martonvasar (mŏr'tônvä-shär), Hung. *Martonvásár*, town (pop. 3,032), Fejer co., N central Hungary, 17 mi. SW of Budapest; distilleries. Large Ger. pop. near by; agr., cattle raising.

Martorell (märtôräl'), town (pop. 4,321), Barcelona prov., NE Spain, on Llobregat R. and 14 mi. NW of Barcelona. Cotton milling; mfg. of paper, soap, brandy, leather goods; produces table wines, olive oil, fruit. Just S is restored Roman bridge.

Martos (mär'tōs), city (pop. 17,206), Jaén prov., S Spain, 10 mi. WSW of Jaén; olive-oil production center. Cementworks; mfg. of soap, plaster, cotton textiles, pottery and tiles; flour milling. Cereals, vegetables, livestock in area. Mineral springs 3 mi. SSW. Was Roman colony; fell to Moors (8th cent.), freed (1225) by Ferdinand III.

Martre, Lac la (läk lä mär'trŭ), lake (□ 840), S central Mackenzie Dist., Northwest Territories, 100 mi. WNW of Yellowknife; 63°20'N 118°W; 50 mi. long, 12–28 mi. wide; drains SE into Great Slave L.

Martres-de-Veyre (mär'trŭ-dŭ-vĕ'rŭ), village (pop. 1,555), Puy-de-Dôme dept., central France, near the Allier, 8 mi. SE of Clermont-Ferrand; paint mfg., winegrowing.

Martres-Tolosane (-tôlōzän'), village (pop. 1,065), Haute-Garonne dept., S France, near the Garonne, 16 mi. ENE of Saint-Gaudens; faïence mfg. Roman relics were unearthed here.

Martuba (märtōō'bä), town (1950 pop. 3,155), E Cyrenaica, Libya, on coastal road and 15 mi. SE of Derna; sheep, goats; barley, fruit, vegetables. Scene of fighting (1942) bet. Axis and British in Second World War.

Martuk (mŭrtōōk'), village (1939 pop. over 500), NW Aktyubinsk oblast, Kazakh SSR, on Trans-Caspian RR, near Ilek R., and 40 mi. NNW of Aktyubinsk, in wheat and dairy-cattle area; metalworks.

Martuni (mŭrtōō'nyē) **1** Village (1932 pop. estimate 2,700), central Armenian SSR, on S shore of L. Sevan, 40 mi. E of Erivan; fisheries; wheat, potatoes. Formerly Nizhni Karanlug. **2** Village (1932 pop. estimate 900), SE Nagorno-Karabakh Autonomous Oblast, Azerbaijan SSR, 20 mi. E of Stepanakert; sericulture.

Martvili, Georgian SSR: see GEGECHKORI.

Martwa Wisla River, Poland: see VISTULA RIVER.

Martwick, village (1940 pop. 632), Muhlenberg co., W Ky., 26 mi. E of Madisonville, in bituminous-coal-mining and agr. area.

Martynovskoye, Russian SFSR: see BOLSHAYA MARTYNOVKA.

Marua, Fr. Cameroons: see MAROUA.

Maruchak, Marochak, or **Meruchak** (mŭrōōchäk'), village (pop. over 500), Herat prov., NW Afghanistan, 18 mi. NW of Bala Murghab, and on Murghab R. and USSR (Turkmen SSR) line; frontier post; transit trade.

Marudu Bay (mŭrōō'dōō), inlet (30 mi. long, 15 mi. wide) of S.China Sea, in extreme N Borneo. Kudat is on NW shore; Sampanmangio Point is at W side of entrance.

Maruf (märōōf'), town (pop. over 2,000), Kandahar prov., SE Afghanistan, 80 mi. E of Kandahar, and on Arghastan R., near Baluchistan line.

Marugame (märōō'gämä) or **Marukame** (-kämä), city and port (1940 pop. 26,928; 1947 pop. 36,339), Kagawa prefecture, N Shikoku, Japan, on Hiuchi Sea, 15 mi. WSW of Takamatsu; 34°17'N 133°48'E. Mfg. center (spinning mills, earthenware and umbrella factories). Exports rice, tobacco, cotton textiles, medicine, straw mats.

Maruggio (märōōd'jō), village (pop. 3,224), Ionio prov., Apulia, S Italy, near Gulf of Taranto, 7 mi. SSW of Manduria; wine, olive oil, cheese.

Maruim (mŭrōōēn'), city (pop. 4,769), E Sergipe, NE Brazil, on railroad and 12 mi. NNW of Aracaju, in sugar-growing area; sugar milling and distilling, cotton shipping. Formerly spelled Maroim.

Maruko (märōō'kō) or **Mariko** (märē'kō), town (pop. 11,844), Nagano prefecture, central Honshu, Japan, 5 mi. S of Ueda; spinning.

Marula (märōō'lä), village, Bulawayo prov., SW Southern Rhodesia, in Matabeleland, on railroad and 40 mi. SW of Bulawayo; alt. 4,765 ft. Cattle, sheep, goats.

Marull (märōōl'), town (pop. estimate 1,200), NE Córdoba prov., Argentina, 85 mi. ENE of Córdoba, near the Mar Chiquita; grain, flax, alfalfa, livestock.

Marum (mä'rŭm), village (pop. 4,475), Groningen prov., N Netherlands, 14 mi. WSW of Groningen; dairying; woodworking; agr.

Marumori (märōō'mōrē), town (pop. 7,799), Miyagi prefecture, N Honshu, Japan, on Abukuma R. and 4 mi. SSW of Kakuda; rice, charcoal, silk cocoons; horse breeding.

Marungu Mountains (märōōng'gōō), highlands (6,000–9,000 ft.) in Katanga, SE Belgian Congo, extending c.50 mi. inland from SW shore of L.

Tanganyika, just SE of Moba. The region is especially suitable for stock raising and temperate-climate agr.

Maruoka (mä̈rōō'ôkä), town (pop. 6,611), Fukui prefecture, central Honshu, Japan, 7 mi. NNE of Fukui; rayon textiles, soy sauce.

Marupatti, India: see MORUPPATTI.

Marutea (märōōtä'ä). **1** Atoll, Tuamotu Isls., Fr. Oceania, S Pacific; 17°S 143°11'W. Pearl-fishing lagoon. Formerly Furneaux Isl. **2** Atoll, Gambier Isls., Fr. Oceania, S Pacific; 21°30'S 135°40'W. Copra, pearls. Formerly Lord Hood Isl.

Maruter (mä'rōōtĕr) or **Maruteru** (–tĕrōō), town (pop. 6,107), West Godavari dist., NE Madras, India, in Godavari R. delta, 40 mi. E of Ellore, on irrigation canal; rice milling; oilseeds, tobacco, sugar cane, coconuts.

Maruyama, Japan: see SAPPORO.

Marvão, Brazil: see CASTELO DO PIAUÍ.

Marvão (mŭrvã'ō), town (pop. 276), Portalegre dist., central Portugal, 8 mi. NNE of Portalegre, near Sp. border; olive- and winegrowing. Old frontier fortress.

Marvdasht or **Mervdasht** (both: mĕrvdäsht'), irrigated plain, Seventh Prov., in Fars, S Iran, 25 mi. NE of Shiraz, along road to Isfahan; sugar-beet cultivation; sugar refinery. Ruins of PERSEPOLIS are here.

Marvejols (märvüzhôl'), town (pop. 3,252), Lozère dept., S France, on SE slope of Monts d'Aubrac, 11 mi. WNW of Mende; wool-spinning center; tanning, woodworking. Has gates of medieval fortifications.

Marvel, village (1940 pop. 838), Bibb co., central Ala., 30 mi. SSW of Birmingham.

Marvell (märvĕl'), town (pop. 1,121), Phillips co., E Ark., 18 mi. W of Helena, in agr. area.

Marvin, town (pop. 110), Grant co., NE S.Dak., 14 mi. W of Milbank.

Marvin, Lake, Hemphill co., extreme N Texas, impounded by dam in a small N tributary of Canadian R., 11 mi. E of Canadian; c.1 mi. long; fishing. Hunting in area.

Marvine, Mount (mär'vĭn), highest peak (11,600 ft.) in Fish Lake Plateau, S central Utah, 25 mi. ESE of Richfield.

Mar Vista (mär" vĭ'stŭ), SW residential section of LOS ANGELES city, Los Angeles co., S Calif., just W of Culver City.

Marwar, state, India: see JODHPUR, former princely state.

Marwar, rail junction, India: see PALI, Rajasthan.

Marwar Mundwa, India: see MUNDWA.

Marwayne, village (pop. estimate 250), E Alta., near Sask. border, near Vermilion R., 24 mi. NE of Vermilion; dairying, grain, stock.

Marx, Russian SFSR: see MARKS.

Marxstadt, Russian SFSR: see MARKS.

Mary (mŭrē'), oblast (□ 34,700; 1946 pop. estimate 350,000), SE Turkmen SSR; ⊙ Mary. Extends into Kara-Kum (N); borders on Afghanistan (S); watered by Murgab R. Intensive cotton cultivation along Murgab R. and on Murgab oasis; wheat, cattle, horses. Pistachio woods near Afghanistan border. Goat and karakul-sheep raising in desert. Cotton-ginning industry and cottonseed-oil extraction at Mary, Bairam-Ali, Iolotan. Trans-Caspian RR passes through Murgab oasis. Pop.: Turkmen, Russians. Formed 1939.

Mary, city (1939 pop. 37,100), ⊙ Mary oblast, Turkmen SSR, on Murgab oasis, on Murgab R. and 185 mi. ESE of Ashkhabad; 37°36'N 61°50'E. Junction of Trans-Caspian RR and branch to Kushka. Wool washing, cotton ginning; cotton milling, metalworking, food processing, carpet mfg. Teachers col. In 19th cent. this city developed as Merv, 18 mi. W of site of old city of Merv (anc. *Margiana*, modern BAIRAM-ALI), which was center of Islamic culture in Middle Ages. Conquered by Russians in 1884. In 1937 the new city was renamed Mary.

Mary, Lake, Douglas co., W Minn., 5 mi. SW of Alexandria; 4 mi. long, 1.5 mi. wide. Fishing resorts.

Maryama, Estonia: see MARJAMAA.

Maryanovka or **Mar'yanovka** (mŭryä'nŭfkŭ), village (1948 pop. over 2,000), SW Omsk oblast, Russian SFSR, on Trans-Siberian RR and 30 mi. W of Omsk; metalworks.

Maryanskaya or **Mar'yanskaya** (–yän'skīŭ), village (1926 pop. 13,375), W Krasnodar Territory, Russian SFSR, on right bank of Kuban R. and 17 mi. WNW of Krasnodar; flour mill, metalworks; wheat, sunflowers, tobacco, southern hemp, vineyards; dairying.

Maryborough. 1 City and port (pop. 14,395), SE Queensland, Australia, on Mary R., 23 mi. from its mouth, and 135 mi. NNW of Brisbane; commercial center; dairy plant, steel mill, shipyards. Exports sugar, fruit, coal, timber. School of Arts (1861). Coal mines near by. **2** Municipality (pop. 6,198), central Victoria, Australia, 85 mi. NW of Melbourne; rail and commercial center for agr. area; dairy plants, flour and knitting mills. Some gold mined in vicinity. Former gold-mining town.

Maryborough, Ireland: see PORT LAOIGHISE.

Maryburgh (mâ'rēbŭrŭ), agr. village in Fodderty parish, SE Ross and Cromarty, Scotland, at head of Cromarty Firth, at mouth of Conon R., 2 mi. S. of Dingwall.

Marychevka, Russian SFSR: see PAVLOVKA, Kuibyshev oblast.

Maryculter (mârēkōō'tŭr) agr. village and parish (pop. 925), NE Kincardine, Scotland, near the Dee, 7 mi. SW of Aberdeen. Has remains of anc. church of the Knights Templar.

Marydel, town (pop. 110), Caroline co., E Md., 12 mi. WSW of Dover, Del. Scene of duel (Jan. 3, 1877) bet. James Gordon Bennett of the New York *Herald* and Frederick May, explorer.

Mary Ellen, mining village, Harlan co., SE Ky., in the Cumberlands SE of Harlan, near Coalgood; bituminous coal.

Mary Esther, town (pop. 332), Okaloosa co., NW Fla., on the Gulf 32 mi. E of Pensacola.

Maryevka or **Mar'yevka** (mär'yĭfkŭ), village (1948 pop. over 2,000), SW North Kazakhstan oblast, Kazakh SSR, on Ishim R. and 100 mi. SW of Petropavlovsk; wheat, cattle. Until 1939, Mariinskoye.

Maryfield, agr. village (pop. 363), SE Sask., on Man. border, 22 mi. SSE of Moosomin; rail junction.

Mary Harmsworth, Cape, westernmost point of Franz Josef Land, Russian SFSR, in Arctic Ocean, on Alexandra Land; 80°37'N 42°10'E.

Maryhill, NW suburb (pop. 25,524) of Glasgow, Lanark, Scotland, on Kelvin R.; chemical works. Site of large military barracks.

Mary Island (4 mi. long, 2 mi. wide), SE Alaska, in Gravina Isls., in Revillagigedo Channel 25 mi. SE of Ketchikan; 55°5'N 131°12'W.

Mary Island, N.Y.: see WELLESLEY ISLAND.

Marykirk, agr. village and parish (pop. 1,163), S Kincardine, Scotland, 5 mi. SSW of Laurencekirk.

Maryknoll, locality, Westchester co., SE N.Y., near Ossining. Catholic Foreign Mission Society of America trains missionaries (the Maryknoll Fathers) here.

Maryland, county, SE Liberia, on Atlantic coast; ⊙ Harper. Bounded E by Cavalla R. (Fr. Ivory Coast border), W by Grand Cess R.; extends c.40 mi. inland. Agr. (rubber, palm oil and kernels, cacao, cassava, rice); cattle raising. Iron deposits. Main centers: Harper, Grand Cess.

Maryland, village, Salisbury prov., N Southern Rhodesia, in Mashonaland, 40 mi. WNW of Salisbury; rail junction; chrome-mining and -shipping point. Rail branch leads NE to Kildonan mine in Umvukwe Range.

Maryland, state (land □ 9,887; with inland waters □ 10,577; 1950 pop. 2,343,001; 1940 pop. 1,821,244), a Middle Atlantic seaboard state in E U.S., bordered N by Pa., E by Del. and the Atlantic, S and W by Va., Dist. of Columbia, and W.Va. along the Potomac and its North Branch, W by W.Va.; 41st in area, 24th in pop.; one of the original 13 states, the 7th to ratify (1788) the Constitution; ⊙ ANNAPOLIS, metropolis BALTIMORE. The "Old Line State" (or "Cockade State") extends c.195 mi. E-W on its straight N border (Mason-Dixon Line), and varies N-S from 3 or 4 mi. (in W) to c.125 mi. E portion of the state is in the Atlantic coastal plain. This is split by the great gash of Chesapeake Bay, which runs N almost to Pa. line, isolating the EASTERN SHORE (on Delmarva Peninsula) from Western Md. About ⅔ of the bay, from POTOMAC RIVER and Pocomoke Sound N, is in Md. Wide estuaries opening on W shore of the bay include (N-S) the Patapsco (approach to Baltimore), the Severn (approach to Annapolis), the Patuxent, and the Potomac (approach to Washington). The Potomac in its lower course carves out a large tidewater peninsula. Principal estuaries (N-S) of the Eastern Shore are Elk R. (W entrance to CHESAPEAKE AND DELAWARE CANAL), Chester, Choptank, Nanticoke, and Pocomoke rivers, which provide easy access to metropolitan markets from agr. and sea-food centers (Salisbury, Cambridge, Crisfield). KENT ISLAND is largest in the bay. On short Atlantic shore, barrier beach and isls. protect coastal lagoons from the ocean. Where the Susquehanna enters head of the bay, the Fall Line sweeps SW through Baltimore to Washington. Beyond it (NW), central Md. consists of rolling uplands (drained in W by Monocacy R.) of the piedmont (reddish sandy and clay loams) which extend W to CATOCTIN MOUNTAIN, E prong of the Blue Ridge of the Appalachians. Beyond Middletown Valley is South Mtn., W prong of the Blue Ridge; this is succeeded by CUMBERLAND VALLEY (locally Hagerstown Valley), which gives way to ridge and valley section of the Folded Appalachians. In westernmost part of the state (drained by Youghiogheny R.), on Backbone Mtn., a ridge of the Alleghenies, is highest point (3,340 ft.) in Md. The climate is moderate continental (mean annual summer temp. 75°F., winter 34°F.). Summers are usually hot and winters mild in S and E, while winters are severe and summers mild in W. Rainfall varies from 38 in. in the mts. to 46 in. on tidewater. In general, E Md. is distinguished for fish, fruit, and vegetables, central Md. for grains, and W Md. for coal and lumber. Although agr. is outranked today in cash value by mfg., the yield is still considerable. About ⅔ of Md. land is in farms. Growing season is 150–210 days. The Eastern Shore has numerous poultry (especially broilers), truck (particularly tomatoes for canning), and fruit (strawberries, peaches) farms. S Md. is still primarily a tobacco-producing region, as it has been for some 300 years. The piedmont produces corn, wheat, and oats, Md.'s chief crops, as well as dairy products, cattle, and thoroughbred horses. Diversified farming (grains, dairy products, truck, apples) in mtn. valleys. Chesapeake Bay provides the state with an enormous fishing industry, especially off the Eastern Shore. Oyster dredging comprises the largest part (almost ¾). There are also crabbing, clamming, and fin fishing (alewives, shad, striped bass). Rare diamondback terrapin is raised. Muskrat trapping in Eastern Shore marshes. For the state as a whole, food canning and processing industries (both of produce and sea food) rank 1st. At Baltimore, the great commercial and mfg. center of the state, 6th city of the nation, and an important world port, is the heaviest concentration of industry. It has large shipyards and, at SPARROWS POINT, nation's largest steel mill on tidewater. Also important are mfg. of transportation equipment, chemicals, fertilizer, textiles; oil and sugar refining. City contains almost ½ the pop. of Md. Cumberland (rayon), Hagerstown (pipe organs), and Frederick are other mfg. centers. Baltimore is a major seaboard transportation hub; Chesapeake Bay Bridge (1952) connects hitherto isolated Eastern Shore with W Shore bet. Kent Isl. and Sandy Point. Bituminous coal of W Md. (Cumberland is center) is Md.'s major mineral resource; sand and gravel, clays, granite, limestone, slate are quarried. Md. forests (c.⅓ of state area) are mostly mixed stands of hardwoods, but coastal area has pine as well as oak. Some northern conifers grow in mts., while lower Eastern Shore has some southern trees (e.g., loblolly pine, holly, bald cypress). Md. has numerous recreational facilities and resorts, including Ocean City (deep-sea fishing), Chesapeake Bay (fishing, water sports, duck hunting), and year-round mtn. resorts and hunting grounds in W Md. Horse racing (Pimlico track at Baltimore) and fox hunting are attractions in N and S Md. Historic sites are scattered throughout the state. Catoctin Recreational Demonstration Area (Federal) in Frederick co. contains the presidential retreat "Shangri-La." Some of the Natl. Capital Parks, including Chesapeake and Ohio Recreational Waterway, are in Md. around Washington. In and near the residential suburbs (e.g., Bethesda, Chevy Chase, Hyattsville, Silver Spring) of Washington are a number of U.S. govt. agencies. Aberdeen Proving Ground is near Havre de Grace. Institutions of higher learning in Md. include Johns Hopkins Univ. at Baltimore, Univ. of Md. at College Park and Baltimore, U.S. Naval Acad. and St. Johns Col. at Annapolis, Goucher Col. at Towson, and Peabody Inst. of Music at Baltimore. Md. was inhabited by Algonquin tribes when the Europeans arrived. Verrazano touched (probably 1524) the Atlantic shore of Md. Chesapeake Bay region was visited by Bartholomew Gilbert in 1603 and charted by Capt. John Smith in 1608. In 1631, Wm. Claiborne, under license from Charles I, set up a fur-trading post on Kent Isl., but in 1632 Charles I reissued to Cecelius Calvert, 2d baron Baltimore, a charter yielding him feudal rights to the region. The 1st Calvert colony, St. Marys, was set up (1634) in S Md. on a site vacated by friendly Indians. A struggle with Claiborne, who claimed the territory for Va., was settled by force in Md.'s favor in 1657. Of later boundary disputes, the one settled by running (1763–67) of the Mason-Dixon Line is perhaps best known. Though Calvert established Md. as a haven for his persecuted fellow Catholics, he guaranteed religious freedom; religious conflict grew, however, as the Puritans became more numerous in the colony. Act of Toelration, passed (1649) to save the Catholic settlers from persecution, was repealed when the Puritans seized and held control (near LUSBY) of the colony in the 1650s. After the Glorious Revolution of 1688, Md. became a royal prov. In 1694 Annapolis superseded SAINT MARYS CITY as ⊙ Md. The 18th cent. saw the emergence of Baltimore, which had a flourishing shipbuilding industry and coastal trade (flour) by 1800. During the American Revolution most Marylanders were patriots. A declaration of rights and state constitution were adopted 1776. In 1791 Md. gave money and all of the land now in the Dist. of Columbia. From then on, industry grew to support commerce, becoming its rival after the Civil War. In early 19th cent., when the Baltimore clipper was queen of the seas, Md. (especially Baltimore) promoted construction of routes to the W—National Road (1811) and Baltimore and Ohio RR (1829). War of 1812 was marked for Md. by the Br. attack of 1814 and defense of Ft. McHenry at Baltimore, immortalized in Francis Scott Key's *The Star-spangled Banner*. In the Civil War Md. was torn by conflicting interests and intense struggles of the true border state. Despite urgings for secession from Southern sympathizers, Md. remained in the Union. ANTIETAM campaign (1862) was only important action actually fought in Md. At close of the war many citizens were disenfranchised, but Reconstruction lasted only until a new constitution was adopted in 1867, and did not scar the state. Conflict bet. traditions of the North and South, somewhat mirrored in division bet. tidewater and upland, still persists. Eastern Shore farm and fisherfolk especially have preserved an older way of life. The First and Second World Wars and the post-war periods saw a further rise in the general economy of the state. See also articles on the cities, towns, geographic features, and the 23 counties (Baltimore city is an independent unit): ALLEGANY, ANNE ARUNDEL, BALTIMORE, CALVERT, CAROLINE, CARROLL, CECIL, CHARLES, DORCHESTER, FREDERICK, GARRETT, HARFORD, HOWARD, KENT, MONTGOMERY, PRINCE GEORGES, QUEEN ANNES, SAINT MARYS, SOMERSET, TALBOT, WASHINGTON, WICOMICO, WORCESTER.

Maryland Park, village (1940 pop. 931), Prince Georges co., central Md., E suburb of Washington.

Marylebone, Saint (sŭnt mâ'rēlubōn'), residential metropolitan borough (1931 pop. 97,627; 1951 census 75,764) of London, England, N of the Thames, 2 mi. NW of Charing Cross. Within borough are Regent's Park (NE) with zoological and botanical gardens and open-air theater; Oxford Street, one of London's shopping centers; Harley and Wimpole streets, centers of medical practice; the British Broadcasting Corporation's studios; Madame Tussaud's wax works; Marylebone railroad station (serving the Midlands); and district of SAINT JOHN'S WOOD. At Lord's Cricket Ground is hq. of Marylebone Cricket Club; in Regent's Park is Bedford Col. for Women of Univ. of London.

Marylhurst, Oregon: see PORTLAND.

Marymont (märĭ'mônt), residential suburb of Warsaw, Warszawa prov., E central Poland, on left bank of the Vistula and 3 mi. N of city center.

Maryport, urban district (1931 pop. 10,183; 1951 census 12,237) and port, W Cumberland, England, on Solway Firth, at mouth of Ellen R., 25 mi. WSW of Carlisle; coal mining, leather tanning, mfg. of chemicals, shoes, electrical goods; beer brewing. Imports chemicals, petroleum products, cement; exports coal, coke, creosote, tar. The town is of Roman origin and a number of Roman altars have been found here.

Mary Ridge, town (pop. 528), St. Louis co., E Mo.

Mary River, SE Queensland, Australia, rises in hills S of Gympie, flows N, past Gympie, and E at Maryborough, to Hervey Bay; 165 mi. long. Navigable 23 mi. below Maryborough by small steamers carrying sugar, fruit, coal, timber.

Mary's Harbour, settlement, SE Labrador, on inlet of the Atlantic, 10 mi. WNW of Battle Harbour; 52°19'N 55°51'W; fishing port and seaplane anchorage.

Marys Igloo, Alaska: see IGLOO.

Marys River, NE Nev., rises in N Elko co., flows c.45 mi. S to E fork of Humboldt R. 16 mi. W of Wells. Also written Mary's River.

Marysvale, city (pop. 520), Piute co., SW central Utah, on Sevier R. and 23 mi. SSW of Richfield; alt. 5,866 ft.; trading point for mining and agr. area (alfalfa, corn, potatoes). Gold, silver, potash, and alunite mines near by. Tushar Mts. are just W. Marysvale Peak (10,943 ft.) is 7 mi. ENE, in Sevier Plateau.

Marysville, village (pop. 776), S central Victoria, Australia, 45 mi. NE of Melbourne, near Healesville, in Great Dividing Range; mtn. resort.

Marysville (mâ'rēzvĭl"). **1** Village, SE B.C., on St. Mary R. and 4 mi. SE of Kimberley; silver, lead, zinc mining. **2** Town (pop. 1,651), S N.B., on Nashwaak R. and 3 mi. NE of Fredericton; cotton and lumber milling.

Marysville. 1 City (pop. 7,826), ⊙ Yuba co., N central Calif., opposite Yuba City, on Feather R. at influx of Yuba R., in Sacramento Valley, and 40 mi. N of Sacramento; trade and shipping center for fruitgrowing region. Gold dredging on Yuba R. Hydraulic mining raised Yuba R. bed above town, necessitating large levees (begun 1875). Seat of Yuba Col. U.S. Camp Beale near by was active in Second World War. Founded 1849, inc. 1851; city was supply point in gold rush, when it was head of Feather R. navigation. **2** Village (pop. 190), Fremont co., E Idaho, 15 mi. NE of St. Anthony; alt. 5,245 ft. **3** Town (pop. 165), Marion co., S central Iowa, near Cedar Creek, 13 mi. SSE of Knoxville, in bituminous-coal-mining and agr. area. **4** City (pop. 3,866), ⊙ Marshall co., NE Kansas, on Big Blue R. and 70 mi. NW of Topeka; railroad div. point in grain and stock region; dairying, poultry packing, flour milling, bottling. Former ferry crossing (1849) on Oregon Trail. Inc. 1861. **5** City (pop. 2,534), St. Clair co., E Mich., 5 mi. SSW of Port Huron and on St. Clair R.; mfg. (auto parts, boats, rubber products); salt mining. Inc. as village 1921, as city 1924. **6** Village (pop. c.150), Lewis and Clark co., W central Mont., 15 mi. NW of Helena. Near-by Drumlummon mine, once immensely rich in gold and silver, is still worked. **7** Village (pop. 4,256), ⊙ Union co., central Ohio, 27 mi. NW of Columbus; trade center for farming and stock-raising area; mfg. of heating equipment, dairy products, chairs, tile; lumber milling. Ohio State Reformatory for Women is here. Settled 1816, laid out 1820. **8** Borough (pop. 2,158), Perry co., S central Pa., 6 mi. NW of Harrisburg and on Susquehanna R. Laid out 1861, inc. 1866. **9** Town (pop. 2,259), Snohomish co., NW Wash., 5 mi. N of Everett and on Puget Sound, at mouth of Snohomish R. Timber, agr., fruit, poultry, dairy products. Tulalip Indian Reservation is near. Settled 1887, inc. 1890.

Marysville Buttes, Calif.: see SUTTER BUTTES.

Marytown, village (pop. 1,268), McDowell co., S W.Va., on Tug Fork and 6 mi. NW of Welch.

Maryut, Lake (mär'yōōt), or **Lake Mareotis** (mârēō'tĭs, mă–), salt lake (□ 96, with marshes □ c.200), Lower Egypt, in the Nile delta W of Rosetta branch, just S of Alexandria, which stands on a narrow strip of land separating the lake from the Mediterranean; 40 mi. long, 5–15 mi. wide; 8 ft. below sea level. Saltworks and fish-research station on NW shore at Mex. Salt marshes extend 80 mi. SW along Mediterranean coast. Level of lake is maintained by pumping works at Mex. Dry in Middle Ages, the lake was flooded (1801) during Br. siege operations. Sometimes spelled Mariut.

Maryville. 1 Village (pop. 539), Madison co., SW Ill., 12 mi. ENE of East St. Louis, in bituminous-coal and agr. area. **2** City (pop. 6,834), ⊙ Nodaway co., NW Mo., on One Hundred and Two R. and 40 mi. N of St. Joseph; hogs, poultry, dairy, corn, wheat; tools, cement blocks, milk products. State teachers col.; Benedictine convent near by. Settled c.1845. **3** City (pop. 7,742), ⊙ Blount co., E Tenn., 15 mi. S of Knoxville, in fruit- and wheat-growing region; lumbering; textiles, coffins, processed foods. Seat of Maryville Col. Settled around Fort Craig (built 1785); inc. as town 1907, as city 1927. Near by is log schoolhouse where Sam Houston taught.

Marzabotto (märtsäbôt'tô), village (pop. 350), Bologna prov., Emilia-Romagna, N central Italy, near Reno R., 13 mi. SE of Bologna; (hemp and paper mills), machinery mfg. Has ruins (temples, tombs) of Etruscan town (6th cent. B.C.; excavated 1871), mus.

Marzamemi (märtsämä'mē), village (pop. 453), Siracusa prov., SE Sicily, port on Ionian Sea, 2 mi. NE of Pachino. A major tunny fishery of Sicily.

Marzo, Cape (mär'sō), headland on Pacific coast of Chocó dept., W Colombia, 55 mi. SW of Ríosucio; 6°50'N 77°41'W.

Marzo, 1 de, Paraguay: see PRIMERO DE MARZO.

Marzo, 28 de, department, Argentina: see AÑATUYA.

Marzsina, Rumania: see MARGINA.

Masachapa (mäsächä'pä), village, Managua dept., SW Nicaragua, on the Pacific, 30 mi. SW of Managua (linked by road); seaside resort. PUERTO SOMOZA is just NW.

Masada or **Massada** (mŭsä'dŭ), anc. locality, SE Palestine, near W shore of Dead Sea, 20 mi. SE of Hebron. Herod fled here (42 B.C.) with Mariamne when Parthians captured Jerusalem; in A.D. 72–73 Jewish force held out against prolonged Roman siege. Remains of anc. Jewish fortress and of Roman positions extant.

Mâs Afuera Island, Chile: see JUAN FERNÁNDEZ ISLANDS.

Masagua (mäsä'gwä), town (1950 pop. 474), Escuintla dept., S Guatemala, in Pacific piedmont, on Guacalate R. and 6 mi. SSW of Escuintla, on railroad; grain, fruit; livestock; lumbering.

Masaguara (mäsägwä'rä), town (pop. 205), Intibucá dept., SW Honduras, on Río Grande de Otoro and 12 mi. ENE of La Esperanza; coffee, tobacco, sugar cane, livestock.

Masai (mäsī'), extra-provincial district (□ 15,232; pop. 72,421), S Kenya; ⊙ Magadi. A rolling hill region along Tanganyika border; semi-arid grasslands. Stock raising (cattle, sheep, goats); some agr. (coffee, wheat, flax). Chief food crops: peanuts, sesame, corn. Big-game hunting. Soda mining at Magadi in Great Rift Valley. Main centers are Magadi, Narok, and Ngong. Dist. inhabited by the Masai, a warlike Negro-Hamitic tribe, also found in Masai Steppe across Tanganyika border.

Masai Steppe, NE Tanganyika, plateau (4,000 ft.), extending c.200 mi. S from the Kilimanjaro and Mt. Meru, in semi-arid region. Nomadic livestock raising by over 30,000 Masai.

Masaka (mäsä'kä), town, Buganda prov., S Uganda, 75 mi. SW of Kampala; agr. trade center (cotton, coffee, bananas, corn, millet); coffee processing.

Masaki (mä"sä'kē), town (pop. 11,349), Ehime prefecture, NW Shikoku, Japan, on Iyo Sea, 5 mi. SW of Matsuyama; agr. center (rice, wheat); cotton textiles, raw silk.

Masalfasar (mäsälfäsär'), village (pop. 1,157), Valencia prov., E Spain, near the Mediterranean, 7 mi. NNE of Valencia; soap and glycerin mfg.; rice, truck produce.

Masally (mŭsä'lē), village (1932 pop. estimate 2,100), SE Azerbaijan SSR, on railroad and 20 mi. NNW of Lenkoran, in subtropical Lenkoran Lowland; rice, tea.

Masamagrell (mäsämägrāl'), town (pop. 3,661), Valencia prov., E Spain, in rich truck-farming area, 8 mi. NNE of Valencia; meat processing, flour and sawmilling; cereals, rice.

Masambolahun, Liberia: see BOLAHUN.

Masampo, Korea: see MASAN.

Masan (mä'sän'), city (1949 pop. 91,291), S.Kyongsang prov., S Korea, on Chinhae Bay, 28 mi. WNW of Pusan; fishing and commercial center. Its well-sheltered port is icefree. Sake brewing, soy-sauce making, metalworking, cotton weaving. Near by are hot springs and a bathing resort. Exports cotton, fish, salt. Formerly sometimes Masampo.

Masanasa (mäsänä'sä), outer S suburb (pop. 4,734) of Valencia, Valencia prov., E Spain, in rich truck-farming area; brandy and liqueur mfg.

Masandam, Cape, or **Cape Musandam** (mŭsăn'dŭm), northernmost point of Oman Promontory, on Strait of Hormuz, on small offshore Masandam Isl.; 26°23'N 56°31'E. The OMAN PROMONTORY is sometimes known as Masandam Peninsula.

Masanjor (mŭsän'jōr), village, Santal Parganas dist., E Bihar, India, on Mor R. and 11 mi. SE of Dumka. Site of 125-ft.-high dam and reservoir for MOR RIVER irrigation project. Also spelled Messanjore.

Masanki (mäsäng'kē), village, South-Western Prov., SW Sierra Leone, on railroad and 32 mi. SE of Freetown; oil-palm plantation; oil mill.

Masantol (mäsäntōl'), town (1939 pop. 3,165; 1948 municipality pop. 15,770), Pampanga prov., Luzon, Philippines, 9 mi. S of San Fernando, near Pampanga R.; agr. center (sugar cane, rice).

Ma'sara, El, or **Al-Ma'sarah** (both: ĕl mä'särŭ). **1** Village (pop. 13,864), Gharbiya prov., Lower Egypt, 13 mi. WNW of Shirbin; cotton. **2** Town (pop. 8,740), Giza prov., Upper Egypt, on E bank of the Nile and 10 mi. SSE of Cairo city center, near site of anc. MEMPHIS. Has important quarries, thought to have furnished part of the material for the pyramids. Consists of town proper (pop. 4,122) and river port (pop. 4,618).

Masardis (mŭsär'dĭs), agr. town (pop. 523), Aroostook co., NE Maine, on the Aroostook and 21 mi. SW of Presque Isle.

Masaryk, peak, Czechoslovakia: see STALIN PEAK.

Masasi (mäsä'sē), town, Southern Prov., SE Tanganyika, on road and 80 mi. SW of Lindi; agr. trade center; millet, beans, rice, corn, tobacco. Nachingwa peanut scheme 20 mi. N.

Masatepe (mäsätä'pä), town (1950 pop. 4,183), Masaya dept., SW Nicaragua, on railroad and 4 mi. SW of Masaya; health resort; agr. center; coffee and rice processing, tobacco. Has agr. school.

Más a Tierra Island, Chile: see JUAN FERNÁNDEZ ISLANDS.

Masaya (mäsī'ä), department (□ 230; 1950 pop. 69,152), SW Nicaragua; ⊙ Masaya. Smallest Nicaraguan dept., located in plateau sloping to NE; contains volcanoes Masaya and Santiago. Tipitapa R. forms N border. Agr. (coffee, rice on slopes, tobacco, manioc, corn, beans, sugar cane in lowlands); livestock (N; near Tisma). Industry (mainly Indian handicrafts) is concentrated at Masaya. Main centers (served by rail and road); Masaya, Masatepe. Cool summer climate makes dept. popular resort area.

Masaya, city (1950 pop. 16,765), ⊙ Masaya dept., SW Nicaragua, near L. Masaya, at E foot of volcano Masaya, 19 mi. SE of Managua; 11°66'N 85°55'W. Rail junction; center of Indian handicraft industry; fiber processing, mfg. (rope, hammocks, palm hats, reed matting, manioc starch, jams, clay trinkets). Large Indian pop. is concentrated in Monimbó section. Has modern rail depot, market, hosp., San Sebastian church.

Masaya, extinct volcano (c.2,000 ft.), SW Nicaragua, just W of Masaya. L. Masaya (3½ mi. long, 1½ mi. wide) occupies E crater above Masaya city.

Masazyr (mŭsŭzĭr'), town (1939 pop. over 2,000) in Kirov dist. of Greater Baku, Azerbaijan SSR, on W Apsheron Peninsula, on SW shore of Masazyr salt lake, 9 mi. NW of Baku; health resort; mud baths.

Masbate (mäsbä'tā), island (□ 1,262; 1939 pop. 145,065) of Visayan Isls., Philippines, in Sibuyan, Visayan, and Samar seas, separated from Ticao Isl. (NE) by Masbate Passage (7–14 mi. wide), and from Panay isl. by Jintotolo Channel; 11°43'–12°36'N 123°9'–124°4'E. Mountainous, rising to 2,285 ft.; S coast is deeply indented by Asid Gulf. The isl. is one of principal gold-bearing areas in Philippines. Gold (found mostly in W part) has been mined for centuries. Copper is also worked. Rice, coconuts, hemp, and corn are grown. Stock raising is important. Masbate province (□ 1,571; 1948 pop. 211,113) includes Masbate isl., and near-by TICAO ISLAND and BURIAS ISLAND.

Masbate, town (1939 pop. 5,336; 1948 municipality pop. 24,999), ⊙ Masbate prov., Philippines, on NE Masbate isl., port on Masbate Pass; 12°22'N 123°37'E. Exports copra, cattle. Airfield.

Mas-Cabardès (mäs-käbärdĕs'), village (pop. 448), Aude dept., S France, in the Montagne Noire, 11 mi. N of Carcassonne; gold and arsenic mining.

Mascali (mä'skälē), village (pop. 1,799), Catania prov., E Sicily, at E foot of Mt. Etna, 10 mi. N of Acireale.

Mascalucia (mäskälōō'chä), village (pop. 2,823), Catania prov., E Sicily, on S slope of Mt. Etna, 5 mi. N of Catania, in grape-growing region; mfg. of fireworks.

Mascara (măs'kŭrŭ, Fr. mäskärä'), city (pop. 26,086), Oran dept., NW Algeria, in the Tell, overlooking fertile Eghris lowland, on railroad and 50 mi. SE of Oran; alt. 1,900 ft. Commercial and wine-making center with trade in white wine, cereals, olives, truck, tobacco, and sheep. Mfg. of cement, footwear, agr. equipment, oriental rugs, flour milling, olive curing. Seat of western beys throughout 18th cent. Became (1832) hq. of Abdul-Kadir; burned (1835) by French in 1841.

Mascaraque (mäskärä'kä), town (pop. 916), Toledo prov., central Spain, on railroad and 15 mi. SE of Toledo; olives, cereals, livestock.

Mascardi, Lake (mäskär'dē) (□ 14; alt. 2,618 ft.), SW Río Negro natl. territory, Argentina, in Nahuel Huapí natl. park, 15 mi. SW of San Carlos de Bariloche; c.10 mi. long, c.2 mi. wide. Surrounded by dense forests. Fishing.

Mascareen Peninsula (măskurēn') (8 mi. long, 5 mi. wide), SW N.B., on E side of Passamaquoddy Bay, opposite St. Andrews.

Mascareignes, in Indian Ocean: see MASCARENE ISLANDS.

Mascarene Islands (măskurēn', măs'–), Fr. *Mascareignes* (mäskärĕn'yu), group of islands in Indian Ocean, comprising RÉUNION, MAURITIUS, RODRIGUES, Agalega, and Cargados Carajos Shoal. Named for Portuguese navigator Mascarenhas, who discovered them in 16th cent.

Mascat, Oman: see MUSCAT.

Maschito (mäskē'tô), village (pop. 3,467), Potenza prov., Basilicata, S Italy, 11 mi. SE of Melfi; wine, olive oil. Hot sulphur springs near by. Albanian refugees from Turks settled here in 15th-16th cent.

Mascoma Lake (măskō'mu), Grafton co., W N.H., resort lake 25 mi. WNW of Franklin; 4.5 mi. long. Receives from E and discharges W **Mascoma River** (c.30 mi. long), which rises to NE, flows W to the Connecticut at Lebanon (water power).

Mascot, municipality (pop. 17,984), E New South Wales, Australia, 5 mi. S of Sydney, in metropolitan area; mfg. center (shoes, furniture, bicycles, radios); aircraft plant. Horse racing.

Mascot, village (1940 pop. 987), Knox co., E Tenn., 13 mi. ENE of Knoxville; zinc mining and reducing.

Mascota (mäskō'tä), city (pop. 4,237), Jalisco, W Mexico, 48 mi. W of Ameca; agr. center (grain, sugar cane, cotton, tobacco, fruit, rice).

Mascotte, town (pop. 440), Lake co., central Fla., 16 mi. S of Leesburg, in citrus-fruit region.

Mascouche (măskōōsh'), village (pop. estimate 1,000), S Que., 18 mi. N of Montreal; dairying; pigs, poultry.

Mascoutah (muskōō'tu, mă–), city (pop. 3,009), St. Clair co., SW Ill., 20 mi. ESE of East St. Louis; mfg. (flour, feed, brick, beverages, hats); bituminous-coal mines; agr. (corn, wheat; dairy products; poultry, livestock). Inc. 1839.

Mas-d'Agenais, Le (lu mäs-däzhunä'), agr. village (pop. 685), Lot-et-Garonne dept., SW France, on the Garonne and Garonne Lateral Canal, and 7 mi. SSE of Marmande.

Mas-d'Azil, Le (lu mäs-däzēl'), village (pop. 932), Ariège dept., S France, in Plantaurel range, on Arize R. and 13 mi. WSW of Pamiers; wool spinning, sawmilling. A near-by grotto is traversed by the Arize and by a road. Has a predominantly Protestant pop.

Mas de Barberáns (mäs' dhā bärvärän s'), village (pop. 1,178), Tarragona prov., NE Spain, 10 mi. SW of Tortosa; olive-oil processing; sheep raising.

Mas de las Matas (läs mä'täs), town (pop. 1,961), Teruel prov., E Spain, 16 mi. SSW of Alcañiz; olive-oil processing, brandy mfg.; fruit, wine, alfalfa, livestock.

Mas-d'Orsières, Le (lu mäs'-dôrsyâr'), village (pop. 63), Lozère dept., S France, on N slope of Mont Lozère, 10 mi. ESE of Mende; lead mining.

Masein (mä'sän), village, Upper Chindwin dist., Upper Burma, on left bank of Chindwin R. and 12 mi. N of Kalewa.

Maselskaya or **Masel'skaya** (mä'syĭlskīŭ), Finnish *Maaselkä* (mä'sĕlkă), town (1939 pop. over 2,000), S central Karelo-Finnish SSR, on Murmansk RR and 20 mi. N of Medvezhyegorsk; wood- and metal-working; granite quarry. Formerly Maselgskaya. A short rail spur goes NW to talc quarry of Liste-Guba, Finnish *Liistepohja*, on lake Segozero.

Maserada sul Piave (mäzĕrä'dä sōōl pyä'vĕ), village (pop. 1,410), Treviso prov., Veneto, N Italy, near Piave R., 7 mi. NNE of Treviso; cotton and hemp mills.

Maseru (mă'zurōō), town (pop. c.3,500), ⊙ Basutoland and Maseru dist. (pop. 101,364, with absent laborers 114,024), W Basutoland, on Caledon R. and 80 mi. E of Bloemfontein, 1 mi. inside W border; 29°20'S 27°30'E; E terminus of rail spur from Marseilles. Alt. 4,942 ft. Distributing center; site of industrial school.

Masevaux (mäzvō'), Ger. *Masmünster* (mäs'mün-stur), town (pop. 2,592), Haut-Rhin dept., E France, on S slopes of the Vosges, 11 mi. NNE of Belfort; cotton milling, tanning. Formerly spelled Massevaux.

Mas-Grenier (mäs-grunyā'), village (pop. 470), Tarn-et-Garonne dept., SW France, on the Garonne and 12 mi. SW of Montauban; glue, wood-working machinery.

Mashaba (măshä'bä), township (pop. 171), Victoria prov., SE central Southern Rhodesia, in Mashonaland, on road and 22 mi. W of Fort Victoria; major asbestos-mining center, with near-by Gath and King mines; gold and chrome workings.

Masham (măs'um), former urban district (1931 pop. 1,994), North Riding, N central Yorkshire, England, on Ure R. and 8 mi. NW of Ripon; agr. market (cheese). Church dates mainly from 15th cent.

Mashapaug, Conn.: see UNION.

Masharij, Am, Am Misharij, or **Am Musharij** (all: ăm măshä'rĭj), village, ⊙ Mansuri sheikdom, Subeihi tribal area, Western Aden Protectorate, 26 mi. WNW of Lahej.

Masherbrum (mŭ'shurbrōōm), peak (25,660 ft.) in KAILAS-KARAKORAM RANGE of Karakoram mtn. system, Kashmir, 45 mi. NE of Skardu, at 35°39'N 76°18'E. English expedition in 1938 climbed to within 1,500 ft. of the top.

Mashevka (mä'shĭfkŭ), village (1926 pop. 936), E Poltava oblast, Ukrainian SSR, 17 mi. SE of Poltava; sugar beets.

Mashgharah, Lebanon: see MESHGHARA.

Mashhad, Iran: see MESHED.

Mashike (mä'shĭkä), town (pop. 13,997), W Hokkaido, Japan, on Sea of Japan, 45 mi. W of Asahigawa; fishing port; agr. (potatoes, soybeans, grain); hemp clothmaking.

Mashiko (mä'shĭkō), town (pop. 11,852), Tochigi prefecture, central Honshu, Japan, 8 mi. SE of Utsunomiya; mining (gold, silver, copper); pottery making.

Mashkel River (mäshkĕl'), in SE Iran and W Pakistan, rises in several branches in easternmost arid Zagros ranges E of Iranshahr, flows intermittently c.200 mi. E and N to the Hamun-i-Mashkel. Receives Rakhman R.

Mashobra, India: see SIMLA, town.

Mashonaland (mushō'nulănd"), region and former NE division (□ 80,344; pop. c.1,200,000) of Southern Rhodesia; chief city, Salisbury. Now subdivided into 23 dists. which form Salisbury, Victoria, Umtali, and part of Gwelo provs. Chiefly of historical and ethnological interest as the region inhabited by the Mashona, a Bantu-speaking tribe, dominated after 1837 by the warlike Matabele. Region was acquired 1889 by Cecil Rhodes for the Br. South Africa Company.

Mashpee (măsh'pē), town (pop. 438), Barnstable co., SE Mass., on W Cape Cod, 10 mi. WSW of Barnstable. Includes village of Succonesset (sŭkunĕ'sĭt).

Mashtagi (mŭshtugē'), district of Greater Baku, Azerbaijan SSR, on N shore of Apsheron Peninsula; oil fields; seaside resorts. Main centers: Mashtagi, Buzovny, Kyurdakhany.

Mashtagi, town (1948 pop. over 10,000) in Mashtagi dist. of Greater Baku, Azerbaijan SSR, on N Apsheron Peninsula, 14 mi. NE of Baku, on electric railroad; oil wells (developed in Second World War).

Mashuk (mŭshōōk'), laccolithic mountain (3,258 ft.) of the N Caucasus foothills, Russian SFSR, overlooking (NE) Pyatigorsk.

Mashur, Bandar, Iran: see BANDAR MASHUR.

Masi Manimba (mä'sē mänēm'bä), village, Leopoldville prov., SW Belgian Congo, 65 mi. WNW of Kikwit; palm-oil milling, rice processing.

Masimpur (mä'sēmpōōr), village, Cachar dist., S Assam, India, on Barak (Surma) R. and 4 mi. NW of Silchar; rice, tea, rape, and mustard. Oil wells near by.

Masindi (mäsēn'dē), town, ⊙ Western Prov. (□ 19,751, including 1,620 sq. mi. of lakes; pop. 1,156,246), Uganda, 110 mi. NW of Kampala, and on road from L. Kyoga to L. Albert; agr. trade center (cotton, tobacco, coffee, bananas, corn); tobacco factory. Has hosp., fine hotel, missions.

Masindi Port, town, Western Prov., W central Uganda, port on the Victoria Nile at its issuance from L. Kyoga, 26 mi. E of Masindi; steamer-road transfer point; cotton, tobacco, coffee, bananas, corn. Has cotton gin, sisal factory.

Masinloc (mäsēnlōk'), town (1939 pop. 1,547; 1948 municipality pop. 8,090), Zambales prov., central Luzon, Philippines, port on S.China Sea, 45 mi. W of Tarlac; mining and lumbering center. Near by are chrome-ore mines and sawmills.

Masira or **Masirah** (măsē'ru), island in Arabian Sea, off coast of Oman, 140 mi. SSW of Ras al Hadd; 20°30'N 58°45'E; 40 mi. long, 10 mi. wide. It is separated from mainland by 10-mi.-wide Masira Channel. Airfield on N tip. **Masira Bay** or **Bahr al Hadri** (bä'hur ăl hädrē'), is an inlet of Arabian Sea, extending from Masira isl. 100 mi. SW to the cape Ras Madraka.

Masisea (mäsēsā'ä), town (pop. 1,742), Loreto dept., E central Peru, landing on Ucayali R. and 23 mi. ESE of Pucallpa, in agr. region (sugar cane, yucca, bananas); liquor distilling. Airfield.

Masisi (mäsē'sē), village, Kivu prov., E Belgian Congo, 40 mi. NNW of Costermansville; center of native trade. Protestant mission. Coffee plantations in vicinity.

Masjed-e-Soleyman, Iran: see MASJID-I-SULAIMAN.

Masjid-i-Sulaiman or **Masjed-e-Soleyman** (both: măsjĕd'ĕsōlămän'), town, Sixth Prov., in Khuzistan, SW Iran, 20 mi. E of Shushtar and 125 mi. NE of Abadan (linked by pipe line); leading oil center of Iran; topping plant. Oil was struck here in 1908; pipe line built 1909–10.

Masjid Tanah (măsjĭd' tänä'), village (pop. 1,186), settlement of Malacca, SW Malaya, 15 mi. NW of Malacca; rice, coconuts.

Mask, Lough (lŏkh), lake (10 mi. long, 5 mi. wide), S Co. Mayo and NW Co. Galway, Ireland, 3 mi. N of N end of Lough Corrib, with which it is connected by partly subterranean stream. Contains several small isls. and receives Robe R.

Maskanah, Syria: see MESKENE.

Maskeliya (mŭskä'lĭyŭ), village (pop., including near-by villages, 1,602), Central Prov., Ceylon, on Hatton Plateau, 4.5 mi. SSW of Hatton; tea processing; extensive tea plantations.

Maskell (mă'skul), village (pop. 84), Dixon co., NE Nebr., 30 mi. WNW of Sioux City, Iowa, near Missouri R.

Maski (mŭs'kē), town (pop. 5,283), Raichur dist., SW Hyderabad state, India, 50 mi. WSW of Raichur; millet, rice, oilseeds; cotton ginning. Sometimes spelled Muski.

Maskinonge or **Maskinongé** (măskĕnōzhā'), county (□ 2,378; pop. 18,206), S Que., extending NW from the St. Lawrence; ⊙ Louiseville.

Maskinonge or **Maskinongé**, village (pop. 674), S Que., on Maskinonge R. near its mouth on the St. Lawrence, and 24 mi. WSW of Trois Rivières; dairying, pig raising.

Maskinonge River or **Maskinongé River**, S Que., issues from L. Maskinonge (4 mi. long), 25 mi. NNW of Sorel, flows 35 mi. SE and then S, past Maskinonge, to the St. Lawrence 10 mi. NNE of Sorel. Above its mouth it has fall of over 300 ft.

Maslovo (mä'sluvŭ). **1** Town (1943 pop. over 500), N Sverdlovsk oblast, Russian SFSR, on Sosva R. and 40 mi. S (under jurisdiction) of Ivdel, near railroad; limonite mining. **2** Village (1939 pop. under 500), W Yaroslavl oblast, Russian SFSR, 40 mi. WSW of Shcherbakov; flax.

Maslyanino (mä'slyŭnyēnŭ), town (1939 pop. over 2,000), SE Novosibirsk oblast, Russian SFSR, 35 mi. E of Cherepanovo; light mfg.

Masmünster, France: see MASEVAUX.

Masna'a, Aden: see 'AURA.

Masna'a or **Masna'ah** (măs'nä), town, Batina dist., N Oman, port on Gulf of Oman, 60 mi. WSW of Muscat; trade center for Rostaq.

Masnedo, Denmark: see SMAALANDSFARVAND.

Masnedsund, Denmark: see SMAALANDSFARVAND.

Masnières (mänyâr'), town (pop. 2,137), Nord dept., N France, on Escaut R., on Saint-Quentin Canal, and 4 mi. S of Cambrai; mfg. (paints, glass bottles, sugar).

Masnóu (mäsnō'), town (pop. 4,936), Barcelona prov., NE Spain, on the Mediterranean, and 10 mi. NE of Barcelona; wine-producing center; mfg. of cotton and silk fabrics, cordage, sails. Trades in hazelnuts and fruit. Bathing resort.

Masny (mänē'), residential town (pop. 2,716), Nord dept., N France, 6 mi. ESE of Douai, in coal-mining dist.

Masoala Peninsula (mäswä'lu), on NE coast of Madagascar; 40 mi. long, maximum width 30 mi. Terminates in Cape Masoala (15°55'S 50°10'E). Antongil Bay borders it (W).

Mason. **1** County (□ 541; pop. 15,326), central Ill.; ⊙ Havana. Bounded W by Illinois R. and S by Sangamon R. and Salt Creek. Bayou lakes along the Illinois. Includes Chautauqua Natl. Wildlife Refuge and Mason State Forest. Agr. (corn, wheat, truck, soybeans, livestock, poultry; dairy products; watermelons). Diversified mfg.; commercial fisheries; river, rail shipping. Formed 1841. **2** County (□ 239; pop. 18,486), NE Ky.; ⊙ Maysville. Bounded N by Ohio R. (Ohio line); drained by North Fork of Licking R. Gently rolling upland agr. area (burley tobacco, corn, wheat, apples, livestock, milk), in outer Bluegrass region. Mfg. at Maysville. Formed 1788. **3** County (□ 493; pop. 20,474), W Mich.; ⊙ Ludington. Bounded W by L. Michigan; drained by Pere Marquette, Big Sable and Little Manistee rivers and short Lincoln R. Agr. (livestock, poultry, fruit, truck, potatoes, beans; dairy products). Mfg. at Ludington. Fisheries; coal mines. Resorts. Hamlin L., Manistee Natl. Forest, and a state park are in co. Organized 1855. **4** County (□ 935; pop. 4,945), central Texas; ⊙ Mason. On Edwards Plateau; alt. c.1,200–2,300 ft.; drained by San Saba R., Llano R. and its tributaries. Ranching (beef cattle, sheep, goats); wool, mohair marketed; agr. (corn, grains, peanuts, fruit, truck, pecans); poultry raising. Hunting, fishing, scenery attract visitors. Fur trapping. Formed 1858. **5** County (□ 967; pop. 15,022), W Wash.; ⊙ Shelton. Mtn. area cut in E by Hood Canal; includes part of Olympic Natl. Forest, Squaxin and Skokomish Indian reservations, and L. Cushman. Lumber, wood products, shellfish. Formed 1854. **6** County (□ 432; pop. 23,537), W W.Va.; ⊙ Point Pleasant. Bounded N and W by Ohio R. (Ohio line); drained by Kanawha R. Bituminous-coal mines, some natural-gas wells; agr. (livestock, fruit, truck, corn, tobacco). Shipyards, mfg. at Point Pleasant. Formed 1804.

Mason. **1** Farming village (pop. 327), Effingham co., SE central Ill., 12 mi. SSW of Effingham. **2** City (pop. 3,514), ⊙ Ingham co., S central Mich., 12 mi. SSE of Lansing, in farm area (dairy products; beans, cabbage); mfg. of pharmaceuticals. State game farm near by. **3** Town (pop. 288), Hillsboro co., S N.H., 16 mi. W of Nashua, on Mass. line. **4** Village (pop. 1,196), Warren co., SW Ohio, 21 mi. NE of Cincinnati, in agr. area; canned foods, metal products. **5** Town (pop. 414), Tipton co., W Tenn., 34 mi. NE of Memphis, in cotton-growing area. **6** City (pop. 2,456), ⊙ Mason co., central Texas, on Edwards Plateau, 85 mi. SE of San Angelo and on Comanche Creek in Llano R. valley; shipping center for livestock, wool, mohair; resort (hunting, fishing near by). Settled by Germans before Civil War; inc. after 1940. **7** Trading town (pop. 924), Mason co., W W.Va., near the Ohio, 14 mi. NNE of Point Pleasant, in agr. and coal-mining area. **8** Village (pop. 140), Bayfield co., N Wis., 13 mi. SW of Ashland.

Mason, Fort, Calif.: see SAN FRANCISCO.

Mason and Dixon's Line, U.S.: see MASON-DIXON LINE.

Mason City. 1 City (pop. 2,004), Mason co., central Ill., 28 mi. N of Springfield, in agr., bituminous-coal, and clay area. Inc. 1869. **2** City (pop. 27,980), ⊙ Cerro Gordo co., N Iowa, on Lime Creek and c.65 mi. NW of Waterloo; industrial, transportation (rail, truck, bus), and trade center, noted for its production of tile, brick, and Portland cement. Also has packing plants (meat, poultry), beet-sugar refinery, creameries, bottling works, fertilizer factory, foundry, machine shop, refrigerator; lingerie and printing industries. Sand and gravel pits, clay deposits, limestone quarries near by. Has oldest public jr. col. (1918) in state. Clear L. resort area is 9 mi. W. Settled 1853 by Masons; platted 1854; inc. 1870. **3** Village (pop. 305), Custer co., central Nebr., 20 mi. SE of Broken Bow and on Mud Creek; grain. **4** Village (pop. 2,606), Okanogan co., central Wash., on the Columbia near Grand Coulee Dam and opposite Coulee Dam village.

Mason-Dixon Line or **Mason and Dixon's Line,** in U.S., boundary bet. Pa. and Md. (39°43′26.3″N) surveyed 1763–67 by Charles Mason and Jeremiah Dixon. It was completed to W limit of Md. in 1773, and in 1779 was extended to mark S boundary of Pa. with Va. (the section that is now W.Va.). Before the Civil War, the Line divided the slave states from free states, and is still used to distinguish the South from the North.

Masone (mäzô′nĕ), village (pop. 2,297), Genova prov., Liguria, N Italy, near Passo del Turchino, 13 mi. NW of Genoa; mfg. (textile machinery, nails).

Masongoleni (mäsông-gōlĕ′nē), village, Central Prov., S central Kenya, on railroad and 20 mi. SE of Makindu; sisal center.

Mason Hall, village (pop. 1,052), central Tobago, B.W.I., 3 mi. NW of Scarborough; cacao growing.

Masontown. 1 Borough (pop. 4,550), Fayette co., SW Pa., 40 mi. S of Pittsburgh; bituminous coal, gas, lumber; oil refining. Inc. 1876. **2** Town (pop. 941), Preston co., N W.Va., 9 mi. ESE of Morgantown; agr., coal-mining area.

Masonville, town (pop. 133), Delaware co., E Iowa, 7 mi. W of Manchester; limestone quarries near by.

Masovia (mŭsō′vēŭ), Pol. *Mazowsze* (ômäzf′shĕ), extensive historic region, central Poland, centered on Warsaw and Plock and bisected by the Vistula. Became (1138) one of 4 duchies under the 4 branches of the Piast dynasty; ⊙ was Plock. The Masowian Piasts became extinct in 1526. Name is retained as geographical term and as suffix to town names. Sometimes spelled Mazovia.

Masoy, Norway: see HAVOYSUND.

Maspalomas (mäspälō′mäs), village (pop. 710), Grand Canary, Canary Isls., on S shore, 25 mi. SSW of Las Palmas; resort with fine beach. Maspalomas Point (27°45′N 15°34′W) is 2 mi. S. Sometimes spelled Más Palomas.

Masparro River (mäspä′rō), Barinas state, W Venezuela, rises in Andean spur on Trujillo state border, flows c.100 mi. SE through llanos, past Libertad, to Apure R. 9 mi. W of Puerto Nutrias.

Maspeth (măs′pŭth), SE N.Y., a residential and industrial section of W Queens borough of New York city, at head of Newtown Creek; fur dressing; mfg. of pillows, candles, chemicals, cable and wire, food products; wood, glass, metal, and paper products; machinery, furniture. Several cemeteries here.

Masqat, Oman: see MUSCAT.

Masquefa (mäskā′fä), town (pop. 1,078), Barcelona prov., NE Spain, 20 mi. NW of Barcelona; wine-producing center; wheat, olive oil.

Masr, Arabic name of EGYPT.

Masr al-Qadimah, Egypt: see FUSTAT, EL.

Mas River, Indonesia: see KALI MAS RIVER.

Mass, village (1940 pop. 522), Ontonagon co., NW Upper Peninsula, Mich., 13 mi. SE of Ontonagon; cheese mfg.

Massa (mäs′sä), town (pop. 12,508), ⊙ Massa e Carrara prov., Tuscany, central Italy, near Ligurian Sea, 28 mi. NW of Pisa, at foot of Apuane Alps; 44°2′N 10°11′E. Important center of Ital. marble industry. Famous Carrara marble is extensively quarried and processed in its environs and widely exported. Bishopric. Upper old town is centered about 15th cent. Malaspina castle. In new section on a plain, are Cybo-Malaspina palace, 15th-cent. cathedral, marble fountain. From 15th to 19th cent., capital of independent principality, later duchy, of Massa and Carrara, ruled by Malaspina and Cybo-Malaspina families. Passed in 1829 to dukes of Modena. In Second World War, badly damaged by many air bombings (1944–45).

Massabesic Lake (măsŭbē′sĭk), SE N.H., irregularly shaped lake (4 mi. long) just E of Manchester, to which it supplies water; recreational center.

Massac (mă′sŭk, mă′săk), county (□ 246; pop. 13,594), extreme S Ill., bounded S by Ohio R. and NW by Cache R.; ⊙ Metropolis. Agr. area (corn, wheat, livestock, cotton, truck), with some mfg. (clothing, wood products), and lumbering. Includes part of Shawnee Natl. Forest; and Fort Massac State Park and Kincaid Indian Mounds. Formed 1843.

Massac, Fort, Ill.: see METROPOLIS.

Massachusetts (măsŭchōō′sĭts), state (land □ 7,907; with inland waters □ 8,257; 1950 pop. 4,690,514; 1940 pop. 4,316,721), NE U.S., in New England, on the Atlantic; bordered S by R.I. and Conn., W by N.Y., N by Vt. and N.H.; 44th in area, 9th in pop.; one of original 13 states, the 6th to ratify (1788) the Constitution; ⊙ Boston. The "Bay State" measures 145 mi. E-W, 47–90 mi. N-S; CAPE COD peninsula (SE) curves 65 mi. into the Atlantic. Chief Atlantic inlets are Mass. Bay (with its arms Cape Cod Bay and Boston Bay), Nantucket Sound, and Buzzards Bay. Cape Cod, along with Nantucket Isl., Martha's Vineyard, and Elizabeth Isls. to the S, is composed of glacial drift and forms the N extremity of the Atlantic coastal plain. The E seaboard section of Mass. proper contains several shallow depressions, largest of which are Narragansett and Boston basins, enclosed by higher areas of more resistant rocks; the Merrimack R. drains the NE part; there are good harbors. To the W, the major portion of Mass. lies in the New England upland, a dissected and glaciated surface, dominated by occasional residual hills (monadnocks), such as Wachusett Mtn. (c.2,000 ft.). This section is split by the N–S Connecticut R. valley, a lowland 2–20 mi. wide. The uplands W of the Connecticut R. merge with the BERKSHIRE HILLS and Hoosac Range, parts of the Appalachian system. Bet. the Berkshires and the Taconic Mts. (on N.Y. border) is the narrow Berkshire lowland, drained largely by the Housatonic R. Mt. Greylock (3,491 ft.), in NW corner, is highest point in state. Quabbin Reservoir (center) is the largest body of inland water. Mass. has a humid continental climate, with 40–45 in. of annual rainfall. Boston has mean temp. of 28° F. in Jan., 72°F. in July, and an annual rainfall of 40 in. The growing season varies from 190 days on Cape Cod to c.150 days in the inland areas. Some 3,300,000 acres are classified as forest land, the chief timber species being birch, beech, maple, oak, white pine, and hemlock. Agr. consists largely of general farming, with localized cash-crop production. Much farmland is in woodland and pasture; dairying (especially W) and hay, corn, potatoes, and oats are important. Vegetables and tobacco for cigar wrappers are grown in the Connecticut valley and Cape Cod is noted for its extensive cranberry bogs. There are many truck farms in Bristol co. (SE) and around Boston. Strawberries grow on the Cape, and apples are widely produced. Mass. leads the New England states in total annual fish catch, including cod, haddock, mackerel, halibut, sea and river herring, flounder, shad, bluefish, lobsters and other shellfish. Boston is the leading U.S. fishing port, and Gloucester is also an important center. The state's mineral resources are small, consisting of granite, marble (W), lime, sandstone, and traprock quarries, clay products, sand, and gravel. Mass.'s position as a leading mfg. state is based on its skilled labor supply and long tradition of industrial technique, good rail and coastwise shipping facilities, and the nearness of large urban markets. Water power—important to the early textile industry—is now utilized for hydroelectricity, but large quantities of Appalachian coal are imported. Principal manufactures are woolen, worsted, and cotton goods, boots and shoes, machinery, fabricated metal products, paper, chemicals, furniture, rubber products, and electrical equipment; also food processing, printing and publishing, and shipbuilding. The state's pop. is 84% urban; half the pop. is concentrated in a metropolitan region of 80-odd cities and towns of which Boston is the hub. A major seaport and rail terminus, Boston is the 3d largest wholesale market in the country and the principal distributing center for the New England area. Other important cities include Fall River, Lowell, and Lawrence (textiles), Lynn and Brockton (shoes), Worcester, Springfield, Cambridge, New Bedford, Somerville, Newton, Quincy, Medford, Malden, Holyoke (paper), Pittsfield, Chicopee, Waltham, Haverhill, Everett, and Salem. The 8-mi.-long Cape Cod Canal handles coastal craft bet. Cape Cod Bay and Buzzards Bay. Mass. is a popular summer vacation land, offering many fine beaches, deep-sea fishing, historical sites, and cultural attractions. The principal resorts are on Cape Cod, Martha's Vineyard, Nantucket Isl., Cape Ann, the North Shore above Boston, and in the Berkshire Hills (also skiing in winter); Marblehead is a noted yachting center. Leading educational institutions: Harvard Univ., Mass. Inst. of Technology, and Radcliffe Col. (all at Cambridge), Boston Univ. and Northeastern Univ. (at Boston), Boston Col. (at Chestnut Hill), Tufts Col. (at Medford), Smith Col. (at Northampton), Col. of the Holy Cross (at Worcester), Williams Col. (at Williamstown), Wellesley Col. (at Wellesley), Amherst Col. and Univ. of Mass. (at Amherst). The state boasts of a long list of distinguished native sons, among whom are Benjamin Franklin, the Adamses (Samuel, John, John Quincy, Henry), William Cullen Bryant, Ralph Waldo Emerson, Nathaniel Hawthorne, John Greenleaf Whittier, Henry David Thoreau, James Russell Lowell, Emily Dickinson, Oliver Wendell Holmes, Eli Whitney, and Samuel F. B. Morse. The Mass. coast was probably explored by Norsemen in the early 11th cent. and by John Cabot in 1497–98. In 16th–17th cent., Indian tribes in the area included the Massachusetts, Wampanoags, and Nausets. In 1602 Gosnold discovered and named Cape Cod. The Pilgrims, who landed at Plymouth in 1620, founded the first permanent white settlement in New England, and soon afterwards many other settlements—e.g., Salem (1626) and Boston (1630)—sprang up on Mass. Bay. These early Puritan communities were governed by their "town meetings," but church leadership was acknowledged. Harvard Col. was established in 1636, elementary and secondary schools in 1647. Mass. colony became a member of the New England Confederation in 1643, and joined in suppressing the Indians in King Philip's War (1675–76). A new charter, uniting Mass., Plymouth, and Maine as one royal colony, was granted in 1691. Because of the discriminatory Navigation Acts on trade with England, Mass. played a prominent part in the lucrative "triangular trade" with the West Indies and Africa. Later restrictive measures (e.g., Sugar Act, Stamp Act) were sorely felt in Mass.; feeling ran high after the "Boston Massacre" (1770) and the passage of the Tea Act (1773), which resulted in the "Boston Tea Party." The subsequent "Intolerable Acts" inflicted severe penalties on Mass., and the colony became the center of resistance to Br. colonial policy. The War of Independence broke out (1775) with skirmishes at Lexington and Concord; the siege of Boston, marked by battle of Bunker Hill, lasted until the British evacuated their troops in 1776. The constitution adopted in 1780 is still in use today. Although rural discontent, culminating in Shays' Rebellion (1786), appeared in W Mass., Yankee clipper ships out of Boston, Salem, and New Bedford plied a profitable trade with China. This commercial prosperity was interrupted by the Embargo Act of 1807 and the War of 1812, during which New England sectionalism and opposition to the war were expressed at the Hartford Convention. The dist. of Maine became a separate state in 1820. The development of mfg. was due largely to the decline of agr. and resulting labor supply, the availability of water power, the installation (1814) of America's 1st power loom in Waltham, which revolutionized the textile industry, and the beginning of rail transportation (1830–50). Throughout the 19th cent. the Boston area formed the cultural and intellectual center of the nation. The antislavery crusade, led by the abolitionist William Lloyd Garrison, was especially strong in the state. Numerous immigrants, particularly the Irish, arrived in the 1840s and 1850s, and industrialization and urbanization proceeded rapidly. The old shipping and whaling industries gradually faded. See also articles on cities, towns, geographic features, and the 14 counties: BARNSTABLE, BERKSHIRE, BRISTOL, DUKES, ESSEX, FRANKLIN, HAMPDEN, HAMPSHIRE, MIDDLESEX, NANTUCKET, NORFOLK, PLYMOUTH, SUFFOLK, WORCESTER.

Massachusetts Bay, inlet of the Atlantic formed by inward curve of Mass. coast, bet. Cape Ann (N) and Cape Cod (S); from NW to SE, c.65 mi. long. BOSTON BAY and CAPE COD BAY are its most important arms; others are the harbors of Gloucester and Salem, and Plymouth Bay.

Massaciuccoli, Lago di (lä′gô dē mäs-sächōōk′-kôlē), shallow coastal lake (□ 2.5) in Tuscany, central Italy, 8 mi. W of Lucca, bet. Apuane Alps and Ligurian Sea, into which it discharges. Used for irrigation of land reclaimed in vicinity. Rice grown in remaining marshes.

Massacre Bay, Alaska: see ATTU ISLAND.

Massacre Bay, New Zealand: see GOLDEN BAY.

Massacre River, flows c.35 mi. N along Dominican Republic–Haiti border, past Dajabón and Ouanaminthe, to the Atlantic W of Puerto Libertador.

Massada (mäsädä′). **1** Settlement (pop. 300), Lower Galilee, NE Israel, near Jordan and Syrian borders, near S shore of Sea of Galilee, bet. the Jordan (W) and the Yarmuk (SE), 8 mi. SSE of Tiberias; mixed farming, dairying, banana growing; fish ponds. Founded 1937. **2** Anc. locality in Palestine: see MASADA.

Massa e Carrara (mäs'sä ĕ kär-rä'rä), province (□ 446; pop. 196,716), Tuscany, central Italy; ⊙ Massa. On Ligurian Sea; mtn. terrain, including W Apuane Alps; watered by Magra R. and its affluents. Center of Ital. marble industry, with several hundred quarries in Apuane Alps. Carrara and Massa are chief producers. Agr. and livestock raising in the Lunigiana and along coast. Called Apuania c.1938–45.

Massa Fermana (mäs'sä fĕrmä'nä), village (pop. 302), Ascoli Piceno prov., The Marches, central Italy, 12 mi. W of Fermo; straw-hat mfg.

Massa Fiscaglia (mäs'sä fēskä'lyä), town (pop. 3,777), Ferrara prov., Emilia-Romagna, N central Italy, on Po R. delta mouth and 19 mi. E of Ferrara; agr. machinery factory.

Massafra (mäs-sä'frä), town (pop. 12,506), Ionio prov., Apulia, S Italy, 10 mi. NW of Taranto; agr. center (figs, vegetables, tobacco); olive oil, wine; has medieval castle.

Massakory (mäsäkōrē'), village, W Chad territory, Fr. Equatorial Africa, on the Bahr el Ghazal, in the drying marshes of L. Chad, 75 mi. NNE of Fort-Lamy; livestock, millet; mfg. of butter.

Massalia, France: see Marseilles.

Massa Lombarda (mäs'sä lômbär'dä), town (pop. 3,727), Ravenna prov., Emilia-Romagna, N central Italy, 4 mi. WNW of Lugo; wine, marmalade, beet sugar, paper, lumber.

Massalubrense (mäs-sälōōbrĕn'sĕ), village (pop. 1,752), Napoli prov., Campania, S Italy, port on Bay of Naples, 2 mi. SW of Sorrento; bathing resort.

Massa Marittima (mäs'sä märēt'tēmä), town (pop. 4,847), Grosseto prov., Tuscany, central Italy, 23 mi. NNW of Grosseto. Mining center (copper, iron, lead, borax); school of mining, mineralogical mus. Bishopric. Has 13th-cent. Pisan cathedral, communal palace with altarpiece by Ambrogio Lorenzetti.

Massa Martana (mäs'sä märtä'nä), village (pop. 419), Perugia prov., Umbria, central Italy, 6 mi. E of Todi.

Massambaba Beach, Brazil: see Araruama Lagoon.

Massana, La (lä mäsä'nä), village (pop. c.570), Andorra, on affluent of Valira R. and 1½ mi. N of Andorra la Vella, on road to Ordono.

Massandra (mŭsän'drŭ), town (1939 pop. over 500), S Crimea, Russian SFSR, Black Sea resort just E of Yalta; winegrowing center. Upper Massandra is site of former castle of Alexander III, now a sanatorium; has grotto formations (views). Lower Massandra has large park and tuberculosis institute with sanatorium.

Massanutten Mountain (măsŭnŭ'tŭn), N Va., ridge in center of N Shenandoah Valley, paralleling the Alleghenies (W) and Blue Ridge (E); from point E of Harrisonburg extends c.45 mi. NE to region W of Front Royal; rises to c.3000 ft. North and South forks of Shenandoah R. meet at N end. Massanutten Caverns (near S end, SE of Harrisonburg) and other caves attract tourists. Observation tower near N end, E of Woodstock.

Massapê (mŭsŭpā'), city (pop. 3,901), NW Ceara, Brazil, on Camocim-Crateús RR and 11 mi. N of Sobral; cotton, sugar, carnauba wax.

Massapequa (măsŭpē'kwŭ), village (1940 pop. 2,676), Nassau co., SE N.Y., near S shore of W Long Isl., 10 mi. SE of Mineola; mfg. (small arms, wood products).

Massapequa Park, village (pop. 2,334), Nassau co., SE N.Y., near S shore of W Long Isl., 10 mi. SE of Mineola. State park near by. Inc. 1931.

Massarossa (mäs-särôs'sä), village (pop. 1,353), Lucca prov., Tuscany, central Italy, 5 mi. E of Viareggio; shoe factory, woolen mill. Marble quarry near by.

Massa Superiore, Italy: see Castelmassa.

Massat (mäsä'), village (pop. 496), Ariège dept., S France, in central Pyrenees, 12 mi. SE of Saint-Girons; potatoes, rye, corn. Cattle raising.

Massawa (mäsä'wä, mŭsou'ŭ), administrative division, central and SE Eritrea, on the Red Sea; ⊙ Massawa. Consists of hot, arid coastal plain; E slope of central plateau (N); and Danakil desert in SE. Nomadic grazing (camels, goats). Agr. (cereals, sesame, agave, coffee) around chief settlements of Ghinda, Harkiko, and Zula. Fisheries (pearl, mother-of-pearl) in Dahlak Archipelago. Mineral deposits include iron and manganese (Mt. Ghedem), potash and sulphur (along Ethiopian border). Traversed (E–W) by railroad and highway; narrow-gauge line bet. Mersa Fatma and Ethiopian potash mines in Dallol region. Called Bassopiano Orientale [Ital.,=eastern lowland] under Italian administration (until 1941).

Massawa, Ital. *Massaua*, city (1947 pop. c.25,000) and chief port of Eritrea, on Red Sea opposite Dahlak Archipelago, 40 mi. NE of Asmara, in hot, arid coastal plain; railroad and highway terminus; 15°37'N 39°29'E. Commercial and industrial center situated on mainland and near-by islets of Massawa and Taulud (connected by causeway crossed by railroad and road). Chief Red Sea market for pearls and mother-of-pearl; exports hides, fish, coffee, dom nuts, oilseeds, gum arabic. Has fine sheltered harbor, shipyards, electric power plant, extensive saltworks, ironworks, cement, brick, and tobacco industries; fish drying, ice mfg., water distilling. Occupied by Italians in 1885; was ⊙ Eritrea until 1897. Largely rebuilt after 1921 earthquake. An Italian naval station (supply center for Ethiopian campaign, 1935–36), it was taken (1941) by British, who, after extensive clearing operations, turned it into an important Allied base. City is one of world's hottest places. Formerly also spelled Massowa.

Massawippi, Lake (mă"sŭwĭ'pē) (8 mi. long, 2 mi. wide), S Que., 10 mi. SSW of Sherbrooke; noted for scenic beauty. Drains N to St. Francis R.

Massegros, Le (lŭ mäsŭgrō'), village (pop. 213), Lozère dept., S France, 15 mi. NNE of Millau; dairying.

Masse Island, Marquesas Isls.: see Eiao.

Massen (mä'sŭn), village (pop. 6,626), in former Prussian prov. of Westphalia, W Germany, after 1945 in North Rhine-Westphalia, in the Ruhr, 2 mi. W of Unna.

Massena (mŭsē'nŭ). **1** Town (pop. 459), Cass co., SW Iowa, on West Nodaway R. and 16 mi. SE of Atlantic, in agr. area. **2** Village (pop. 13,137), St. Lawrence co., N N.Y., near the St. Lawrence, on Grass (N) and Raquette (S) rivers and 33 mi. NE of Ogdensburg, in dairying area; huge aluminum plant; also mfg. of mica and wood products, silk. Roosevelt International Bridge (1934) is 9 mi. NE. Settled 1790, inc. 1886.

Massénya (mäsän'yä, mäsĕnyä'), town, W Chad territory, Fr. Equatorial Africa, on arm of Shari R. and 90 mi. SE of Fort-Lamy; native trade center (livestock, cotton, millet) on old caravan route to Mecca. Former ⊙ Baguirmi state and famous slave market (notably for eunuchs). Heinrich Barth reached it in 1855, Gustav Nachtigal in 1872. Sometimes spelled Massénia.

Masseret (mäsrā'), village (pop. 371), Corrèze dept., S central France, in Monts du Limousin, 22 mi. NW of Tulle; hog and mule market.

Masset Inlet (20 mi. long, 2–8 mi. wide), W B.C., central Graham Isl., 20 mi. S of Massett, connected with Dixon Entrance by Masset Sound (25 mi. long); in lumbering and fishing area. Port Clements is on E shore; Massett village is at mouth of Masset Sound.

Massett, village (pop. estimate 400), W B.C., on N Graham Isl., on an inlet of Dixon Entrance, 80 mi. WSW of Prince Rupert across Hecate Strait; trade center and fishing port, inhabited largely by Haida Indians.

Masseube (mäsûb'), village (pop. 811), Gers dept., SW France, on the Gers and 10 mi. SE of Mirande; wine, cattle.

Massevaux, France: see Masevaux.

Massey, town (pop. 752), SE central Ont., on Spanish R. and 55 mi. WSW of Sudbury; nickel, copper, and gold mining; lumbering.

Massey, village, Kent co., E Md., 19 mi. NW of Dover, Del.; cannery.

Massiac (mäsyäk'), village (pop. 1,277), Cantal dept., S central France, on the Alagnon and 9 mi. WSW of Brioude; antimony processing, woodworking, cattle raising.

Massiaf, Syria: see Masyaf.

Massicault (mäsēkō'), village, Tunis dist., N Tunisia, 17 mi. WSW of Tunis; agr. settlement. Here German army made last stand before Tunis in May, 1943.

Massico, Monte (môn'tē mäs'sēkô), mountain (2,661 ft.) on coast of Gulf of Gaeta, central Italy, 18 mi. E of Gaeta; pierced by railroad tunnel. The wine from its vineyards was famous in Roman times.

Massif Central (mäsēf' sãträl') [Fr.,=central upland], great plateau region of central France, covering almost ⅙ (33,000 sq. mi.) of country's surface. Chief water divide of France (source of Loire R., of most of its left tributaries, and of right tributaries of the Garonne and of the Rhone); separates Paris Basin (N) from Rhone valley (E and SE) and from Aquitaine Basin (SW). Above a granitic core of terraced tablelands rise the volcanic Auvergne Mountains (culminating in Puy de Sancy, 6,187 ft.). The limestone Causses form a S abutment, and the crescent-shaped Cévennes constitute a steep E escarpment over the Rhone valley. The Monts du Limousin (a W outlier) reach out toward the Bay of Biscay. The southernmost ranges (Montagne Noire) meet the N foothills of the Pyrenees near Carcassonne. In N, the Morvan juts out into Paris Basin and links up with the Langres Plateau which continues the upland toward the Vosges. These mtn. masses are dissected by entrenched valleys and gorges (of Loire, Allier, Dordogne, Lot, Tarn, and Gard rivers), and by Tertiary lake bottoms (Limagne, Forez Plain) which form intermontane lowlands. There is little physiographic unity except for average elevation (c.2,600 ft.) common to most components of the Massif Central. Sheep grazing, cattle raising, dairying (Roquefort cheese), intensive agr. in valley bottoms and along SE slope (vineyards, olive and mulberry groves) are chief occupation of steadily decreasing population. Mineral deposits exploited on large scale are coal and kaolin. Hydroelectric power is harnessed especially in Dordogne R. valley. Metallurgy and textile milling are chief industries, centering at Saint-Étienne, Roanne, Le Creusot. Clermont-Ferrand is France's rubber capital, and Limoges is known for its porcelain. Chief spas and resorts are Vichy, Mont-Dore, La Bourboule, and Royat, all noted for their mineral springs. Sometimes called Plateau Central.

Massilia, France: see Marseilles.

Massillon (mă'sĭlŏn, -lŭn), city (pop. 29,594), Stark co., E central Ohio, 7 mi. W of Canton, and on Tuscarawas R., in coal and clay region; coal-shipping point and industrial center; steel products, bearings, machinery, aluminum products, furnaces, clothing, hardware, paper products, rubber goods. State hosp. for the insane is here. Settled 1812, laid out 1826.

Massing (mä'sĭng), village (pop. 1,252), Lower Bavaria, Germany, on Rott R. and 7 mi. W of Eggenfelden; beer; metalworking.

Massinga (mäsĭng'gä), village, Sul do Save prov., SE Mozambique, on road and 38 mi. N of Inhambane; cotton, mafura, cashew nuts.

Massis, Turkey: see Ararat, Mount.

Massive, Mount (14,418 ft.), central Colo., in Sawatch Mountains, 5 mi. NNW of Mt. Elbert, 10 mi. WSW of Leadville. Peak is 2d highest in Rocky Mts. of U.S., exceeded only by Mt. Elbert.

Masson (mä'sō), village (pop. 1,226), SW Que., on Lièvre R., just above its mouth on Ottawa R., and 16 mi. ENE of Ottawa; lumbering, dairying, stock raising.

Masson Island (mă'sŭn), off Antarctica, in Shackleton Shelf Ice, off Queen Mary Coast; 66°8'S 96°30'E; 15 naut. mi. long, 12 naut. mi. wide; alt. c.1,500 ft. Discovered 1912 by Sir Douglas Mawson.

Massow, Poland: see Maszewo.

Massowa, Eritrea: see Massawa.

Massy, Kirghiz SSR: see Lenindzhol.

Massyaf, Syria: see Masyaf.

Mastanli, Bulgaria: see Momchilgrad.

Masterton, borough (pop. 9,535), S N.Isl., New Zealand, 55 mi. NE of Wellington; agr. center; dairy plants, woolen mills, abattoirs. Masterton is ⊙ Masterton co. (□ 586; pop. 3,105) and ⊙ Mauriceville co. (□ 115; pop. 583), but it is an independent unit.

Mastgat (mäst'khät), channel on Zeeland coast, SW Netherlands; extends 10 mi. NE–SW bet. Duiveland isl. and Tholen isl.; joins the Krammer and the Eastern Scheldt. NE part is also called the Zijpe, SW part the Keeten.

Mastic, resort village, Suffolk co., SE N.Y., on an inlet of Moriches Bay, on S shore of Long Isl., 2 mi. W of Center Moriches.

Mastic Beach, village (pop. 1,079), Suffolk co., SE N.Y., 10 mi. E of Patchogue.

Mastuj (mŭstōōj'), village, Chitral state, N North-West Frontier Prov., W Pakistan, on headstream of Kunar R. and 165 mi. NNE of Peshawar.

Mastung (mŭstōōng'), town (pop. 3,140), administrative hq. of Kalat state, N Baluchistan, W Pakistan, 28 mi. SSW of Quetta; hq. of Sarawan div.; trade center for wheat, wool, ghee, tobacco, cattle; handicrafts (carpets, embroideries, palm mats).

Masua, Sardinia: see Iglesias.

Masuda (mä"sōō'dä). **1** Town (pop. 9,697), Akita prefecture, N Honshu, Japan, 8 mi. SSW of Yokote; rice, apples, sake. Gold, silver, copper, lead mined near by. **2** Town (pop. 6,236), Miyagi prefecture, N Honshu, Japan, 6 mi. S of Sendai; rice, wheat. **3** Town (pop 21,950), Shimane prefecture, SW Honshu, Japan, on Sea of Japan, 20 mi. SW of Hamada; commercial center in agr. and livestock area; mfg. (floor mats, sake, soy sauce, charcoal). Grave of Sesshu (celebrated 15th-cent artist) is near by. Includes (since early 1940s) former adjacent towns of Tokatsu and Yoshida. Sometimes called Iwami.

Masueco (mäswä'kō), village (pop. 1,113), Salamanca prov., W Spain, near Duero or Douro R., 52 mi. WNW of Salamanca; olive-oil processing; cereals, fruit, wine.

Masuleh (mäsōōlĕ'), village, First Prov., in Gilan, N Iran, 35 mi. WSW of Resht, in Elburz range; sheep raising; wool weaving. Ironworking (near-by deposits).

Masulipatam (mŭ'sōōlĭpŭtŭm) or **Bandar** (bŭn'dŭr), since 1949 officially **Masulipatnam** (-nŭm), city (pop. 59,146), ⊙ Kistna dist., NE Madras, India, port (roadstead) on Coromandel Coast of Bay of Bengal, 220 mi. NNE of Madras, at NE edge of Kistna R. delta. Rail spur terminus; exports peanuts, castor seed, oilcake; rice and oilseed milling; chemical works; hand-printed cotton goods. A main hq. of All-India Spinners' Assoc. Has Andhra Univ. Col. of Law, Noble Col. (affiliated with Madras Univ.). First major English trading station in India founded here in 1611; soon outgrew that at Pedapalle (now Nizampatam), which was founded earlier in same year. Contested by Dutch, French, and English until finally ceded to English in 1759 by French, who retained rights over small plot of land (*loge*) until they were renounced in 1947. Its once flourishing trade in handmade chintzes was crushed by English piece goods. Ruined fort just E.

Masuria (mŭzōō'rēŭ), Ger. *Masuren* (mäzōō'rŭn), Pol. *Mazury* (mäzōō'rĭ), lake-studded, forested region in East Prussia, after 1945 in Olsztyn and Bialystok provs., NE Poland, on USSR border. Hilly region, drained by many small rivers. Elk, Gizycko, and Wegorzewo are chief towns. Main occupations, fishing, forestry, agr. Original pop. was expelled by Teutonic Knights and replaced in 14th cent. with Pol. settlers; by 19th and early-20th cent. they were largely Germanized, but after 1945 they were replaced by an almost entirely German-speaking pop. Largest of **Masurian Lakes** are Sniardy (□ 47), Mamry (□ 40), and Niegocin (□ 10). In First World War, region was scene (Sept., 1914, and Feb., 1915) of heavy fighting, when Russians under Samsonov and Rennenkampf were defeated by Hindenburg and Mackensen. Region retained by Germany in 1920 plebiscite. After 1945, Olsztyn prov. was briefly called Mazury. Region sometimes called Masurenland (mäzōō'rŭnlänt") in German.

Masurian Canal (mŭzōō'rēŭn), Pol. *Kanał Mazurski* (kä'nou mäzōōr'skē), Rus. *Mazurski Kanal* or *Mazurskiy Kanal* (both: mŭzōōr'skyĭ kŭnäl'), in East Prussia, after 1945 in NE Poland and Kaliningrad oblast, Russian SFSR; from Lyna R. at Druzhba (Kaliningrad oblast) extends 32 mi. SSE to L. Mamry (northernmost of Masurian Lakes), W of Wegorzewo. Difference in water level of 364 ft. is overcome by 10 locks.

Masury (mă'zhŭrē), village (pop. 2,151), Trumbull co., NE Ohio, 11 mi. NE of Youngstown, at Pa. line; mfg. (freight cars, metal products).

Masyaf (mäsyăf'), Fr. *Massyaf* or *Massiaf*, town, Latakia prov., W Syria, 45 mi. SE of Latakia; cotton, sericulture, tobacco, cereals. Old fortress here, prominent in crusades.

Maszewo (mä-shĕ'vô), Ger. *Massow* (mä'sō), town (1939 pop. 3,828; 1946 pop. 1,219) in Pomerania, after 1945 in Szczecin prov., NW Poland, 11 mi. N of Stargard; yeast mfg.

Mat, river, Albania: see MAT RIVER.

Mat (mŭt), village, Muttra dist., W Uttar Pradesh, India, on the Jumna and 10 mi. N of Muttra; gram, jowar, wheat, barley, cotton.

Mata (mä'tä), town (pop. 1,184), Las Villas prov., central Cuba, on railroad and 15 mi. N of Santa Clara; sugar growing.

Mata, La (lä mä'tä), town (pop. 1,789), Toledo prov., central Spain, 22 mi. W of Toledo; cereals, chick-peas, olives, grapes, sheep. Olive-oil pressing, meat packing; tile mfg.

Mataana, El, Egypt: see ASFUN.

Matabeleland (mătŭbē'lĕlănd"), region and former SW division (□ 69,989; pop. c.800,000) of Southern Rhodesia; chief city, Bulawayo. Now subdivided into 13 dists. which form Bulawayo prov. and part of Gwelo prov. Chiefly of historic and ethnographic interest as the region inhabited by the Matabele, a Bantu-speaking tribe of Zulu origin. Driven out of Natal (1823) and Transvaal (1837), the Matabele occupied area N of Limpopo R. and absorbed surrounding tribes (especially the Mashona). From them Cecil Rhodes obtained permission (1890) to exploit gold deposits, but in 1893, Lobengula, the Matabele chief, attacked the settlers. The revolt was suppressed in 1897, and the Matabele subsequently became peaceful herdsmen and farmers.

Matabhanga or **Mathabhanga** (both: mätäbäng'gŭ), town (pop. 3,007), Cooch Behar dist., NE West Bengal, India, on the Jaldhaka and 15 mi. W of Cooch Behar; rice, jute, tobacco, oilseeds, sugar.

Matachel River (mätächĕl'), Badajoz prov., W Spain, rises in outliers of the Sierra Morena, flows c.80 mi. NW to the Guadiana 6 mi. SE of Mérida.

Matachic (mätächēk'), town (pop. 1,074), Chihuahua, N Mexico, on headstream of Yaqui R., in Sierra Madre Occidental, on railroad and 105 mi. W of Chihuahua; alt. 6,246 ft.; corn, wheat, beans, fruit, cattle.

Matacos, Argentina: see LA FLORENCIA.

Mata de Alcântara (mä'tä dhä älkän'tärä), town (pop. 1,522), Cáceres prov., W Spain, 29 mi. NW of Cáceres; cereals, wine, olive oil.

Mata de São João (mä'tŭ dĭ sã'õ zhwã'ō), city (pop. 3,523), E Bahia, Brazil, on railroad and 35 mi. NNE of Salvador; sugar, oranges, coconuts, manioc. Formerly spelled Matta de São João.

Matadi (mätä'dē, mätädē'), town (1948 pop. 22,-379), Leopoldville prov., W Belgian Congo, on left bank of Congo R. opposite Vivi, just below the last cataract of Livingstone Falls, near Angola border, and 25 mi. E of Boma; main port of Belgian Congo, c.100 mi. inland from the Atlantic coast, at the limit of navigation for ocean-going steamers; major commercial center and head of railroad to Leopoldville. Chief exports are coffee, cacao, palm products, rice, cotton, copal, and minerals. Mfg. of pharmaceuticals, printed matter. Matadi has large hospitals for Europeans and natives, R.C. and Protestant missions, and airport. Also seat of vicar apostolic. Matadi liquid-fuels port is at Ango Ango.

Matador (mă'tŭdôr), town (pop. 1,335), ⊙ Motley co., NW Texas, just below Cap Rock escarpment of Llano Estacado, 45 mi. SW of Childress, near huge Matador Ranch; trade point for cattle-ranching region, also producing cotton, wheat. Roaring Springs (7 mi. S) is its railroad point.

Matafao Peak (mätŭfou'), Tutuila, American Samoa, S Pacific; highest peak (2,141 ft.) on isl.

Matagalpa (mätägäl'pä), department (□ 3,380; 1950 pop. 135,475), central Nicaragua; ⊙ Matagalpa. Astride Cordillera Dariense; drained by navigable Tuma R. (N) and Río Grande (S). Gold mining (San Ramón). An important coffee region, with chief plantations in central portion; corn, beans, livestock raising (W), vegetables, potatoes, fruit, sugar cane (center), lumbering, rubber (E). Major export, coffee. Main centers (Matagalpa, Ciudad Darío, Sébaco) served by Inter-American Highway.

Matagalpa, city (1950 pop. 10,362), ⊙ Matagalpa dept., W central Nicaragua, 60 mi. NNE of Managua, on spur of Inter-American Highway; agr. and commercial center; coffee processing, flour milling, mfg. of turpentine, soap, bricks, shoes, clothing. Has cathedral dating from colonial period; bishopric.

Matagne-la-Grande (mätä"nyŭ-lä-grăd'), village (pop. 348), Namur prov., S Belgium, 6 mi. SSE of Philippeville; dynamite mfg.

Matagorda (mătŭgôr'dŭ), county (□ 1,141; pop. 21,559), S Texas; ⊙ Bay City. On Matagorda Bay, here sheltered from Gulf of Mexico by Matagorda Peninsula and traversed by Gulf Intracoastal Waterway; drained by Colorado R. A leading Texas cattle co.; also agr. (especially rice; also cotton, corn, grain, flax, truck, citrus, other fruits); dairying; horses, hogs, sheep, goats, poultry. Oil, natural gas, sulphur, salt. Fisheries. Beaches, fishing attract visitors. Formed 1836.

Matagorda, village (pop. c.1,250), Matagorda co., S Texas, on Matagorda Bay at mouth of Colorado R. and 20 mi. S of Bay City; fisheries; seafood, shell market. Christ Church here was built 1839. Settled 1825; served as port for Austin's colony.

Matagorda Bay, S Texas, inlet of Gulf of Mexico, from which it is sheltered by Matagorda Peninsula, a 50-mi. sandspit; c.50 mi. long SW–NE, 3–12 mi. wide. Its entrance is Pass Cavallo (kŭvä'lō), bet. tip of peninsula and NE end of Matagorda Isl. Traversed by Gulf Intracoastal Waterway. Receives Colorado R.; Lavaca Bay (14 mi. long, 4–8 mi. wide), its NW arm, receives Lavaca R. Bay was probably visited (1685) by La Salle's last expedition.

Matagorda Island, S Texas, low sandy isl. (36 mi. long, 1–4 mi. wide) lying bet. San Antonio and Espiritu Santo bays on the NW and the Gulf of Mexico (SE). Separated by channel from St. Joseph Isl. (SW) and by Pass Cavallo from tip of Matagorda Peninsula (NE). Air Force bombing and gunnery range.

Matagorda Peninsula, Texas: see MATAGORDA BAY.

Mata Grande (mä'tŭ grän'dĭ), city (pop. 1,833), W Alagoas, NE Brazil, 80 mi. WNW of Palmeira dos Índios; cotton, coffee, fruit. Until 1939, called Paulo Affonso.

Matahambre or **Minas de Matahambre** (mē'näs dä mätä-äm'brā), town (pop. 2,670), Pinar del Río prov., W Cuba, 20 mi. NW of Pinar del Río; copper-mining center. Linked by cableway with coast.

Matai or **Matay** (mătī'), village (pop. 5,984), Minya prov., Upper Egypt, on railroad and 9 mi. NE of Samalut; cotton ginning, sugar milling; cotton, cereals, sugar cane.

Matai or **Matay** (mŭtī'), town (1945 pop. over 500), N Taldy-Kurgan oblast, Kazakh SSR, on Turksib RR, on the Ak-Su (river) and 60 mi. N of Taldy-Kurgan, in desert area. Also spelled Motai.

Mataje River, Ecuador-Colombia: see SARDINAS, ANCÓN DE.

Matak, Indonesia: see ANAMBAS ISLANDS.

Matakaoa, New Zealand: see TE ARAROA.

Matala (mätä'lä), village, Central Prov., Northern Rhodesia, 65 mi. WNW of Lusaka; gold-mining center.

Matalaque (mätälä'kā), town (pop. 307), Moquegua dept., S Peru, at E foot of Nevado de Pichu Pichu, on Tambo R. and 50 mi. NNE of Moquegua; grain.

Matale (mŭt'ŭlä), town (pop. 14,046), ⊙ Matale dist. (□ 926; pop., including estate pop., 156,411), Central Prov., Ceylon, in Matale Valley, 12 mi. N of Kandy; rail spur terminus; trade (tea, rubber, cacao, rice, coconuts, vegetables) and cattle center. Limestone quarries near by. Buddhist rock temple of Aluwihare is 2 mi. N; here (1st cent. A.D.) Buddhist scriptures (Vinayapitakas) were 1st transcribed. Matale is main town in **Matale Valley**, in N Ceylon Hill Country, W of Knuckles Group; c.20 mi. long N-S, 5 mi. wide; extensive tea, rubber, and cacao plantations; limestone quarries. Average rainfall, 75–100 in.

Matallana de Torio (mätälyä'nä dhä tō'ryō), village (pop. 272), Leon prov., NW Spain, 19 mi. NNE of Leon, in coal-mining area.

Matam (mätäm'), town (pop. c.2,400), NE Senegal, Fr. West Africa, landing on Senegal R. (Mauritania border) and 215 mi. E of Saint-Louis. Produces millet, corn, cotton, livestock; fishing. Airfield. Phosphate deposits in vicinity.

Matamanó, Gulf of (mätämänō'), or **Ensenada de la Broa** (ĕnsänä'dä dä lä brō'ä), W Cuba, NE inlet (c.30 mi. long E-W, 15 mi. wide) of the Gulf of Batabanó, bounded SE by Zapata Peninsula.

Matamata, county, New Zealand: see TIRAU.

Matamata (mă'tŭmătŭ), borough (pop. 1,694), N N.Isl., New Zealand, 90 mi. SE of Auckland; dairy plants.

Matamoras (mătŭmô'rŭs), residential borough (pop. 1,761), Pike co., NE Pa., on Delaware R. opposite Port Jervis, N.Y.

Matamoros (mätämō'rōs). **1** City (pop. 7,961), Coahuila, N Mexico, in Laguna Dist., 12 mi. E of Torreón; rail junction; agr. center (cotton, corn, wheat, wine, vegetables). **2** or **Izúcar de Matamoros** (ēsōō'kär dā-), city (pop. 7,065), Puebla, central Mexico, on railroad, on Inter-American Highway and 35 mi. SW of Puebla; alt. 4,216 ft. Sugar-growing and -refining center; rice, fruit, livestock. Silver and copper mines near by. Site of battle in revolutionary war. **3** City (pop. 15,699), Tamaulipas, NE Mexico, near mouth of Rio Grande, opposite Brownsville (Texas), on railroad and 175 mi. E of Monterrey; mfg., trading, and agr. center (cotton, sugar cane, cattle); tanning, cotton ginning, vegetable-oil pressing, mescal distilling. Customhouse, point of entry for American tourists; exports hides, bones, hair, cotton. Radio stations. Founded 1824. Occupied (1846) by American forces under Zachary Taylor in Mexican War.

Mata'na, El, Egypt: see ASFUN.

Matana, Lake (mŭtä'nŭ) (20 mi. long, up to 5 mi. wide), central Celebes, Indonesia, 30 mi. S of Kolonodale. Also spelled Matano.

Matandu River (mätän'dōō), SE Tanganyika, rises NW of Liwale, flows 150 mi. NE to Indian Ocean just NW of Kilwa.

Matane (mŭtăn'), county (□ 1,631; pop. 25,488), E Que., on N shore of Gaspé Peninsula, on the St. Lawrence; ⊙ Matane.

Matane, town (pop. 4,633), ⊙ Matane co., E Que., on the St. Lawrence, at mouth of Matane R., on NW Gaspé Peninsula, 60 mi. ENE of Rimouski; lumbering center; woodworking, furniture mfg.; pulpwood port. Sometimes called St. Jérôme de Matane.

Matang (mätäng'), village (pop. 1,375), NW Perak, Malaya, near W coast, 5 mi. SW of Taiping; rice, rubber.

Matangatwani (mätäng-gätwä'nē), town N Pemba isl., Zanzibar protectorate, on road and 19 mi. NNW of Chake Chake; clove-growing center.

Matanilla Reef (mătŭnĭ'lŭ), northernmost part of the Bahama Isls., B.W.I., 50 mi. NNE of West End (Grand Bahama Isl.); 27°25'N 78°42'W.

Matano, Lake, Indonesia: see MATANA, LAKE.

Matanuska (mătŭnōō'skŭ), village (pop. 40), S Alaska, 30 mi. NE of Anchorage; Alaska RR junction for spur line to Matanuska Valley farming and coal-mining region.

Matanuska River, S Alaska, rises in Chugach Mts. near 61°47'N 147°40'W, flows 75 mi. SW past Moose Creek, Palmer, and Matanuska, to Knik Arm 30 mi. NE of Anchorage. Lower course flows through Matanuska Valley agr. region. Paralleled by Glenn Highway.

Matanuska Valley, region (□ c.1,000; pop. estimate c.3,500) of S Alaska, on lower Matanuska R., NE of Anchorage, extends c.40 mi. ENE from head of Knik Arm, bet. Talkeetna Mts. (NNW) and Chugach Mts. (SSE); c.9,000 acres are under cultivation, producing oats, barley, wheat, rye, buckwheat, vegetables, potatoes, berries, hogs, poultry, dairy produce. Region served by branch line of Alaska RR and by Glenn Highway. Large coal deposits (Jonesville) and timber stands are being worked. Market center is Palmer. Climate is temperate, with adequate rainfall. Valley became site of Federal experiment in rural resettlement, May, 1935, when 208 families from Middle Western drought areas were established here with aid of Federal loans. Matanuska Valley Farmers' Cooperating Association was established (1937) at Palmer. Control of project transferred (Sept., 1938) to Dept. of the Interior.

Matanza, Argentina: see SAN JUSTO, Greater Buenos Aires.

Matanza de Acentejo, La (lä mätän'thä dhä ä-thĕntä'hō), village (pop. 1,492), Tenerife, Canary Isls., 13 mi. W of Santa Cruz de Tenerife; winegrowing.

Matanzas (mŭtăn'zŭs, Sp. mätän'säs), province (□ 3,260; pop. 361,079), W Cuba; ⊙ Matanzas. Bet. Havana prov. (W) and Las Villas prov. (E), bordering S on Zapata Peninsula. Generally low and level, with extensive swamps (Ciénaga de Zapata) in S; hilly ranges (NW) rise in the Pan de Matanzas to 1,149 ft. N coast is indented by spacious bays, such as Matanzas and Cárdenas, with major ports. The prov. is chiefly agr., sugar cane being its mainstay; also sisal, rice, citrus fruit, bananas, tobacco, coffee, corn; cattle raising, apiculture. S section yields fine construction wood, and charcoal is made. There are numerous sugar refineries (centrals), distilleries, tanneries, and other processing plants, centered at Matanzas, Cárdenas, and Colón. Natural resources include copper, asphalt, iron, medicinal waters; saltworks on Hicacos Peninsula. Extensive fisheries along N shore. The prov. is popular with tourists because of its fine scenery (Yumurí Valley, Bellamar Caves) and beaches (Varadero).

Matanzas, city (pop. 54,844), ⊙ Matanzas prov., W Cuba, on N coast, port on Matanzas Bay, on Central Highway, on railroad and 50 mi. E of Havana; 23°3'N 81°35'W. Shipping, fishing, trading, and industrial center in rich agr. region (sugar cane, sisal, fruit, honey, livestock). Mfg. of shoes, bricks, rayon goods, hats; distilling, refining, tanning; foundries. In its spacious harbor is a free zone (set up 1934). The handsome city is traversed by 3 rivers, with new residential sections on surrounding slopes (Versalles, N; Pueblo Nuevo, S). Among main bldgs. are the Palace of Justice, 17th-cent. San Severino castle, cathedral, theater, polytechnic school, and large sugar warehouses. Matanzas ranks next to Havana as Cuba's principal tourist center; has fine beaches, promenades, and is near famous Yumurí Valley, Bellamar Caves, and the Monserrate Shrine. Copper deposits near by.

Matanzas, officially San José de Matanzas, town (1935 pop. 625), Samaná prov., N Dominican Republic, on Escocesa Bay, 15 mi. NW of Sánchez, in agr. region (rice, cacao, corn, coconuts, coffee, fruit). Damaged by 1946 earthquake and tidal waves.

Matanzas, Fort, Fla.: see Fort Matanzas National Monument.

Matanzas River, NE Buenos Aires prov., Argentina, formed near Cañuelas, flows c.25 mi. NE along SE border of the federal dist. (Buenos Aires proper)—where it is also called the Riachuelo (rēächwä'lō)—to the Río de la Plata 2 mi. NE of Avellaneda at Dock Sud; on its W bank is the oldest part of Buenos Aires and its port.

Matanzas River (mūtăn'zŭs), narrow lagoon in St. Johns co., NE Fla., sheltered from the Atlantic by Anastasia Isl.; extends c.17 mi. from St. Augustine (N end; ocean outlet) to Matanzas Inlet, which connects its S end with the ocean. Followed by Intracoastal Waterway.

Matão (mŏotā'ō), city (pop. 2,923), N central São Paulo, Brazil, on railroad and 45 mi. SW of Ribeirão Prêto; mfg. (agr. equipment, macaroni, furniture); cotton, rice, coffee. Formerly Mattão.

Mata Ortíz, Mexico: see Juan Mata Ortíz.

Mata Palacio (mä'tä pälä'syō), town (1935 pop. 5,504), Seibo prov., E Dominican Republic, 15 mi. N of San Pedro de Macorís, in agr. region (sugar cane, cacao, coffee, rice, fruit, cattle).

Matapalo, Cape (mätäpä'lō), SE extremity of Osa Peninsula, on the Pacific, S Costa Rica, at entrance to the Golfo Dulce.

Matapan, Cape (mă'tŭpăn"), or **Cape Tainaron** (tā'nŭrôn), Lat. *Taenarum* (tē'nŭrŭm), S extremity of Peloponnesus, Greece, on Ionian Sea, bet. gulfs of Messenia (W) and Laconia (E); 36°23'N 22°29'E. Except for Marroquí Point (Spain) it is the southernmost point of continental Europe. Once site of the Temple of Poseidon. It is the tip of **Matapan Peninsula** (28 mi. long), the middle of the 3 S peninsulas of Peloponnesus. In Second World War, the British won (1941) a naval victory over the Italians off the cape.

Matapeake, Md.: see Kent Island.

Matapedia or **Matapédia** (mătŭpē'dēŭ, –pā'dēŭ), county (□ 1,751; pop. 29,926), E Que., in central part of Gaspé Peninsula; ⊙ Amqui.

Matapedia or **Matapédia,** village (pop. estimate 500), E Que., SE Gaspé Peninsula, on Restigouche R., at mouth of Matapedia R., 12 mi. WSW of Campbellton; lumbering, dairying; railroad installations. Salmon-fishing center.

Matapedia, Lake, or **Lake Matapédia** (14 mi. long, 2 mi. wide), E Que., at base of Gaspé Peninsula, 20 mi. S of Matane. Drained S by Matapedia R., known for its salmon fishing.

Matapedia River or **Matapédia River,** E Que., at base of Gaspé Peninsula, issues from L. Matapedia, flows 50 mi. SE, past Amqui and Causapscal, to Restigouche R. at Matapedia. Noted salmon stream.

Mataporquera (mätäpôrkä'rä), village (pop. 1,149), Santander prov., N Spain, 33 mi. SSW of Torrelavega; cement mfg.; lumbering, stock raising; cereals.

Matapozuelos (mätäpōth-wā'lōs), town (pop. 1,614), Valladolid prov., N central Spain, 17 mi. SSW of Valladolid; flour mills; cereals, wine.

Mataquescuintla (mätäkĕskwēn'tlä), town (1950 pop. 2,130), Jalapa dept., E central Guatemala in highlands, at W foot of volcano Alzatate, 24 mi. ESE of Guatemala; alt. 5,300 ft. Road junction; corn, beans, coffee, livestock. Copper mine (SE). Until 1934–35, in Santa Rosa dept.

Mataquito, department, Chile: see Licantén.

Mataquito River (mätäkē'tō), central Chile, formed by union of Teno and Lontué rivers 5 mi. WNW of Curicó, flows c.65 mi. W, past Hualañé and Licantén, to the Pacific 25 mi. NNE of Constitución; forms border bet. Curicó and Talca provs. Length of Lontué-Mataquito, 140 mi.

Matar (mä'tŭr), town (pop. 4,144), Kaira dist., N Bombay, India, 4 mi. SSW of Kaira; local market for rice, millet.

Matará, dept., Argentina: see Suncho Corral.

Matará (mätärä'), town (pop. estimate 500), central Santiago del Estero prov., Argentina, on railroad and 32 mi. NW of Añatuya; agr., lumbering center; alfalfa, corn, livestock; sawmills.

Matara (mŭt'ŭrŭ) [Singhalese,=great ford], town (pop. 23,434), ⊙ Matara dist. (□ 502; pop., including estate pop., 352,260), Southern Prov., Ceylon, on SW coast, 24 mi. ESE of Galle; rail terminus; road junction; coastal trade (tea, rubber, rice, citronella grass, coconuts, cinnamon) center. Important under Portuguese (17th cent.) and Dutch (built Star fort, 1765). Sir Henry Lawrence b. here, 1806. Dist. has iron-ore, sapphire, and beryl deposits (notably about Morawaka); major citronella-grass area in Ceylon.

Mataram (mŭtŭräm'), former Moslem sultanate in Java. Founded 16th cent., it flourished in 17th cent., controlling most of Java. It fell to Dutch in mid-18th cent.

Mataram (mŭtŭräm'), chief town of Lombok, Indonesia, near W coast of isl.; trade center for agr. area. Its port is near-by Ampenan. Near Mataram are several palaces built by Balinese princes.

Matarani, Peru: see Mollendo.

Mataranka, settlement (dist. pop. 117), N central Northern Territory, Australia, 225 mi. SE of Darwin, on Darwin-Birdum RR; sheep.

Matarengi, Sweden: see Overtornea.

Matari, W Pakistan: see Matiari.

Mataripe (mŏotŏorē'pŏo), town (pop. 279), E Bahia, Brazil, on N shore of Todos os Santos Bay, c.25 mi. NNW of Salvador, near São Francisco do Conde; petroleum refinery (completed 1950). Called Socorro until 1944.

Matariya, El, or **Al-Matariyah** (both: ĕl mătärē'yŭ). **1** or **Matariah,** town (pop. 18,682), NE Egypt, 6 mi. NE of Cairo. It is on site of anc. Heliopolis. Residential suburb with fine gardens and important military airport. **2** Town (pop. 30,004), Daqahliya prov., Lower Egypt, on a peninsula shore of L. Manzala, 20 mi. SE of Damietta. Connected by canals with Port Said and Damietta; important fishing industry.

Mataró (mätärō'), anc. *Iluro,* city (pop. 27,573), Barcelona prov., NE Spain, in Catalonia, port on the Mediterranean, 18 mi. NE of Barcelona; a center of the knit-goods industry; also makes paper, dyes, textile machinery, lamps and bulbs, motors, soap, leather goods; shipbuilding, sawmilling, tanning. Trades in potatoes, wine, peas. Divided into upper, or old town, and lower, or modern one. First railroad in Spain was built from Barcelona to Mataró.

Matar Taris, Egypt: see Matir Taris.

Mataruge (mä'tärōōgĕ), village, central Serbia, Yugoslavia, on Ibar R., on railroad and 6 mi. WSW of Rankovicevo town. **Mataruska Banja** or **Matarushka Banya** (–rōōshkä bä'nyä), Serbo-Croatian *Mataruška Banja,* health resort, is just NE.

Matas, Las, Dominican Republic: see Las Matas.

Matathawa Levu, Fiji: see Yasawa.

Matatiele (mätätē'lŭ), town (pop. 2,708), East Griqualand dist., E Cape Prov., U. of So. Afr., near Basutoland border, at foot of Drakensberg range, 110 mi. SW of Pietermaritzburg; rail terminus in dairying, farming region. Airfield.

Mataúna, Brazil: see Palmeiras de Goiás.

Mataura (mătou'rŭ), borough (pop. 1,547), S S.Isl., New Zealand, 36 mi. NE of Invercargill and on Mataura R.; paper mill, dairy plant, coal mine.

Mataura River, S S.Isl., New Zealand, rises S of L. Wakatipu, flows 120 mi. SE, past Gore and Mataura, to Toetoes Bay of Foveaux Strait.

Matawan (mă'tŭwăn"), borough (pop. 3,739), Monmouth co., E N.J., 11 mi. N of Freehold, in truck-farming region; mfg. (tiles, metal goods, wood products, glue, rubber and plastic goods, concrete products). Has 18th-cent. buildings. Called New Aberdeen before 1715, inc. 1895.

Matay, Egypt: see Matai.

Matcha (mä'chŭ), village (1932 pop. estimate 690), SE Leninabad oblast, Tadzhik SSR, on Zeravshan R. and 45 mi. SE of Ura-Tyube; wheat, sheep; gold placers. Formerly called Madrushkent.

Matcha River, Tadzhik SSR: see Zeravshan River.

Mateare (mätäā'rā), town (1950 pop. 704), Managua dept., SW Nicaragua, port on L. Managua, on railroad and 12 mi. NW of Managua; agr.; fisheries; charcoal burning.

Mateba (mätĕ'bä), village, Leopoldville prov., W Belgian Congo, on S shore of Mateba Isl. in mouth of Congo R. (Angola border) and 15 mi. WSW of Boma; cattle-raising center.

Matecumbe Keys, Fla.: see Florida Keys.

Mateguá (mätägwä'), village (pop. c.300), Beni dept., NE Bolivia, on Guaporé R. and 95 mi. ENE of Magdalena, on Brazil border; rubber.

Matehuala (mätäwä'lä), city (pop. 16,548), San Luis Potosí, N central Mexico, on interior plateau, 105 mi. NNE of San Luis Potosí; alt. 5,955 ft. Rail terminus; mining center (gold, silver, lead, copper); large copper smelters; tanning; maguey processing (textile fibers, liquor). Airfield.

Matelica (mätā'lēkä), town (pop. 2,846), Macerata prov., The Marches, central Italy, on Esino R. and 7 mi. SE of Fabriano; tanneries, shoe factory, cement works, cutlery mfg. Bishopric.

Matelles, Les (lāmătĕl'), village (pop. 254), Hérault dept., S France, 10 mi. NNW of Montpellier; lumbering.

Matelot (mătŭlō'), village (pop. 559), N Trinidad, B.W.I., 18 mi. ENE of Port of Spain; bathing, fishing.

Matera (mätā'rä), province (□ 1,329; pop. 149,312), Basilicata, S Italy; ⊙ Matera. Borders on Gulf of Taranto; traversed by the Apennines, which descend gradually to coastal plain. Watered by Cavone and lower courses of Agri, Basento, Bradano, and Sinni rivers. Agr. (cereals, grapes, olives, fruit, cotton); stock raising (sheep, goats). Forestry. Formed 1927 from Potenza prov., to which it transferred (c.1947) □ 135 in NW.

Matera, town (pop. 21,762), ⊙ Matera prov., Basilicata, S Italy, in the Apennines, 35 mi. WNW of Taranto; 40°40'N 16°37'E. Agr. center (wine, olive oil, cereals, herbs); flour and woolen mills, macaroni factories, pottery works. Tufa quarries near by. Archbishopric. Has 13th-cent. cathedral and massive castle. Many cave dwellings still in use. Became prov. capital in 1927.

Matese, Lago di (lä'gô dē mätā'zĕ), narrow lake (c.3 mi. long) in the Apennines, Campania, S Italy, 24 mi. N of Caserta. Furnishes power to hydroelectric plant at Piedimonte d'Alife.

Mateszalka (mä'tāsŏlkŏ), Hung. *Mátészalka,* town (pop. 10,036), ⊙ Szatmar-Bereg co., NE Hungary, on Kraszna R. and 28 mi. E of Nyiregyhaza; rail junction; machine shops, vegetable-oil plants, flour mills, distilleries; tobacco, grain, cattle, hogs. Agr. acad. here.

Matetete, Belgian Congo: see Bayenga.

Matetsi (mätĕt'sē), village, Bulawayo prov., W Southern Rhodesia, in Matabeleland, on railroad and 25 mi. SSE of Victoria Falls; cattle, sheep, goats; corn.

Mateur (mätûr'), town (pop. 12,714), Bizerte dist., N Tunisia, 19 mi. SW of Bizerte; road and railroad center; heart of rich agr. region (wheat, barley, fruits, wine, cattle); flour milling, macaroni mfg. Unsuccessfully defended by Germans in final Allied attack on Tunis, May, 1943.

Matewan (mă'tŭwăn"), city (pop. 989), Mingo co., SW W.Va., on Tug Fork, at Ky. line, and 7 mi. SE of Williamson, in bituminous-coal region.

Matfield Green, city (pop. 119), Chase co., E central Kansas, on S fork of Cottonwood R. and 27 mi. SW of Emporia; livestock, grain.

Matfors (mät"fôrs', –fôsh'), village (pop. 1,645), Vasternorrland co., NE Sweden, on Ljunga R. (falls) and 8 mi. WSW of Sundsvall; pulp, paper, and woolen mills, chain works. Hydroelectric station.

Math (mŭt), village, Ratnagiri dist., S Bombay, India, in Western Ghats, 7 mi. NNE of Savantvadi; rice, mangoes; soap and sodium factories. Teak, blackwood in near-by forests.

Matha (mätä'), village (pop. 1,756), Charente-Maritime dept., W France, 11 mi. SE of Saint-Jean-d'Angély; brandy distilling, furniture mfg.

Mathabhanga, India: see Matabhanga.

Mathay (mätā'), village (pop. 554), Doubs dept., E France, on Doubs R. and 5 mi. S of Montbéliard; blast furnaces.

Mather (mă'dhŭr), village (pop. estimate 150), S Man., 60 mi. SE of Brandon; grain, stock.

Mather, village (pop. 1,395), Greene co., SW Pa., 7 mi. ENE of Waynesburg.

Mather, Mount (12,015 ft.), S central Alaska, in Alaska Range, in Mt. McKinley Natl. Park, 140 mi. N of Anchorage; 63°11'N 150°26'W.

Matheran (mă'tärăn), town (pop. 2,774), Kolaba dist., W Bombay, India, 28 mi. E of Bombay; health resort (sanatorium) on scenic outlier (alt. c.2,500 ft.) of Western Ghats; annual rainfall c.250 in.

Mather Field, Calif.: see Sacramento, city.

Mather Peak, Wyo.: see Bighorn Mountains.

Matherville (mă'dhŭrvĭl), village (pop. 590), Mercer co., NW Ill., on Edwards R. and 16 mi. S of Rock Island, in agr. and bituminous-coal area.

Matheson Point, E extremity of King William Isl., S Franklin Dist., Northwest Territories, on Rae Strait; 68°49'N 95°10'W.

Mathews, county (□ 87; pop. 7,148), E Va.; ⊙ Mathews. Tip of tidewater peninsula; bounded E by Chesapeake Bay, N (Piankatank R.) and S (Mobjack Bay) by inlets of bay. Truck and poultry farming, bulb growing; some tobacco, peanuts, grain. Fisheries are important. Summer-home area; waterfowl hunting. Formed 1791.

Mathews, village (pop. c.500), ⊙ Mathews co., E Va., near Chesapeake Bay, 28 mi. ESE of West Point, its rail station; bulb growing.

Mathews, Lake, S Calif., reservoir (c.5 mi. long) at W end of Colorado River Aqueduct, 9 mi. S of Riverside; formerly Cajalco Reservoir. Impounded by Mathews Dam (210 ft. high, 2,170 ft. long; completed 1938). From lake, gravity carries water to cities of Los Angeles metropolitan dist.

Mathews Bay, Ryukyu Isls.: see Buckner Bay.

Mathews Dam, Calif.: see Mathews, Lake.

Mathi, Italy: see Mati.

Mathia, Greece: see Lykodimos.

Mathias Barbosa, Brazil: see Matias Barbosa.

Mathinna (mŭthĭ'nŭ), village (pop. 276), NE Tasmania, 38 mi. E of Launceston, near S.Esk R.; cheese factory; gold.

Mathis (mă'thĭs), city (pop. 4,050), San Patricio co., S Texas, 34 mi. NW of Corpus Christi, near Nueces R.; rail, trade, shipping point in agr., oil-producing area. Just W is L. Corpus Christi (state park; recreation). Inc. 1937.

Mathiston (mă'thĭstŭn), town (pop. 584), on Webster-Choctaw co. line, central Miss., 60 mi. E of Greenwood, near Big Black R. Has jr. col.

Mathrake or **Mathraki** (both: mäthrä'kē), island (□ 2; pop. 366) in Ionian Sea, Greece, in Corfu nome, 5 mi. WNW of Corfu isl.; 39°48'N 19°29'E; 2 mi. long, 1 mi. wide; fisheries. Also called Samothrake or Samothraki.

Mathura, India: see MUTTRA.

Mathurai, India: see MADURA.

Mathwar (mŭtvär'), village, SW Madhya Bharat, India, 80 mi. WSW of Dhar. Was ⊙ former princely state of Mathwar (□ 138; pop. 3,889) of Central India agency, along right bank of Narbada R.; since 1948, state merged with Madhya Bharat.

Mati, river, Albania: see MAT RIVER.

Mati (mä'tē), village (pop. 2,315), Torino prov., Piedmont, NW Italy, 15 mi. N of Turin; textile and paper mills. Until c.1937 spelled Mathi.

Mati (mä'tē), town (1939 pop. 2,668; 1948 municipality pop. 11,562), Davao prov., SE Mindanao, Philippines, at head of Pujada Bay, 45 mi. ESE of Davao; iron mines. Abacá, coconuts.

Matiali (mätyä'lē), village, Jalpaiguri dist., N West Bengal, India, 29 mi. N of Jalpaiguri; rail spur terminus; tea processing; extensive tea gardens. Copper ore deposits near by.

Matiari (mŭtyä'rē), town (pop. 5,910), Hyderabad dist., central Sind, W Pakistan, 13 mi. NNE of Hyderabad; market center (grain, oilseeds, cotton, sugar, fruit); handicraft cloth weaving. Also spelled Matari.

Matias Barbosa (mùtē'ùs bùrbô'zù), city (pop. 1,931), S Minas Gerais, Brazil, in the Serra da Mantiqueira, on Paraibuna R., on railroad and 7 mi. S of Juiz de Fora; mfg. of pharmaceuticals, dairying. Formerly spelled Mathias Barbosa.

Matías Romero (mätē'äs rōmā'rō), town (pop. 4,495), Oaxaca, S Mexico, in foothills of Sierra Madre del Sur, on railroad and 22 mi. NNE of Ixtepec; processing, lumbering, and agr. center (cereals, sugar cane, fruit, livestock).

Matifou, Cape (mätēfōō'), headland, N central Algeria, on the Mediterranean, bounding Algiers Bay on E, 9 mi. ENE of Algiers city; 36°49'N 3°14'E. Lighthouse. Cap-Matifou village (pop. 234) has truck gardens and tobacco fields.

Matignon (mätēnyō'), village (pop. 758), Côtes-du-Nord dept., W France, 15 mi. NW of Dinan; produces early potatoes. Stone quarries near by.

Matiguás (mätēgwäs'), town (1950 pop. 681), Matagalpa dept., central Nicaragua, 37 mi. E of Matagalpa, on S slopes of Cordillera Dariense; sugar cane, potatoes; livestock.

Matilla de los Caños del Río (mätē'lyä dhā lōs kä'nyōs dhĕl rē'ō), town (pop. 1,333), Salamanca prov., W Spain, 18 mi. WSW of Salamanca; flour mills.

Matillas, Spain: see VILLASECA DE HENARES.

Matin, India: see KATGHORA.

Matina (mätē'nä), village (dist. pop. 4,694), Limón prov., E Costa Rica, on railroad and 19 mi. WNW of Limón, on Matina R. (a 50-mi. long Caribbean coastal stream); trading center: cacao, corn, bananas, rubber.

Matinecock (mùtĭ'nùkŏk), residential village (pop. 507), Nassau co., SE N.Y., on NW Long Isl., just E of Glen Cove, in resort area. Bird sanctuary near by.

Matinha (mùtē'nyù), town (pop. 1,590), N Maranhão, Brazil, 45 mi. SSW of São Luís; rice, cotton, babassu nuts.

Matinicock Point (mùtĭ'nùkŏk), SE N.Y., small peninsula extending N into Long Island Sound just N of Glen Cove, and marking E side of entrance to Hempstead Harbor.

Matinicus Isle (mùtĭn'ĭkùs), plantation (pop. 188), Knox co., S Maine, in the Atlantic, c.20 mi. SE of Rockland. Includes Matinicus Isl. (□ c.1), Ragged Isl. (with Criehaven village), Seal and Wooden Ball isls., and **Matinicus Rock** (lighthouse).

Matino (mätē'nô), town (pop. 7,914), Lecce prov., Apulia, S Italy, 9 mi. ESE of Gallipoli, in grape-, olive- and fig-growing region.

Mati River, Albania: see MAT RIVER.

Matir Taris (mă'tĭr tä'rĭs) or **Matar Taris** (mă'tär), village (pop. 9,774), Faiyum prov., Upper Egypt, 6 mi. NE of Faiyum; cotton, cereals, sugar, fruits.

Matisco, France: see MÂCON.

Matla, India: see PORT CANNING.

Matlalcueyatl, Mexico: see MALINCHE.

Matliary or **Tatranske Matliary** (tä'trănskā mät'lyärĭ), Slovak *Tatranské Matl'ary*, Hung. *Mátlarháza* (mät'lôrhä'zŏ), village, N Slovakia, Czechoslovakia, in the High Tatra, at SE foot of Lomnice Peak, 8 mi. N of Poprad; part of commune of Vysoke Tatry. Has several sanatoria (alt. 3,017 ft.).

Matlock or **The Matlocks,** urban district (1931 pop. 10,545; 1951 census 17,770), central Derby, England, on Derwent R. and 18 mi. S of Sheffield; includes towns of Matlock Green, Matlock Bath (SSW), and Matlock Bank (NNE). Popular resort with mineral springs and baths (since 1698). Also mfg. of woolens, hosiery, sewing cotton. Has church with 15th-cent. tower. Near by are lead mines and caves. In urban dist. (S) is cotton-milling and lead-smelting town of Cromford. The 1st cotton mill in Derby was installed here 1771 by Arkwright.

Matlock, town (pop. 104), Sioux co., NW Iowa, 6 mi. NW of Sheldon; livestock, grain.

Matmata (mätmätä'), village, Southern Territories, SE Tunisia, 25 mi. SSW of Gabès; olives, barley, dates, and figs are grown on crudely irrigated terraces; camels, sheep. Troglodyte dwellings. The **Matmata Range** (average alt. 2,000 ft.), extending c.70 mi. NW-SE from Matmata (N) beyond Foum-Tatahouine (S), is a barren upland inhabited by nomadic Berbers. During Second World War, it formed SW anchor of the Mareth Line.

Matnog (mätnōg'), town (1939 pop. 2,599; 1948 municipality pop. 12,036), Sorsogon prov., extreme SE Luzon, Philippines, on San Bernardino Strait, 27 mi. SSE of Sorsogon; fishing, agr. (abacá, coconuts, rice).

Mato, Formosa: see MATOW.

Matoaka (mùtō'kù), town (pop. 1,003), Mercer co., S W.Va., 9 mi. WNW of Princeton, in coal-mining and lumbering area.

Matobo, Southern Rhodesia: see FORT USHER.

Matochkin Shar (mä'tùchkĭn shär''), strait of Arctic Ocean, joining Barents and Kara seas at 73°15'N; separates N and S isls. of Novaya Zemlya; 60 mi. long, 1–2 mi. wide. Govt. observation stations at Cape Stolbovoi (W entrance), at Matochkin Shar (airfield), and at Cape Vykhodnoi (E entrance).

Matões, Brazil: see PARNARAMA.

Mato Grosso (mä'tōō grō'sōō), state (□ 487,479; 1940 pop. 420,835; 1950 census 528,451), central and W Brazil; ⊙ Cuiabá. Second largest state (after Amazonas) of Brazil. Bounded by Bolivia (W), Paraguay (SW and S), and Guaporé territory (NW), Amazonas and Pará (N); Araguaia R. forms E border with Goiás, and the Paraná (with its headstream, the Paranaíba) forms SE border with Minas Gerais, São Paulo, and Paraná. State lies on central Brazilian plateau, which extends ranges S to Paraguay border (Serra de Amambaí), and W toward Bolivia, the latter (Serra Azul, Serra dos Parecis) forming major drainage divide bet. the Amazon (N) and Paraguay (S) basins. In W and S, the plateau gives way to Paraguay R. flood plain (inundated Nov.–April). State is well drained by Amazon tributaries in N (Juruena, Arinos, São Manuel, Xingu, Araguaia), and by the Paraguay, Paraná, and their tributaries flowing southward. Mato Grosso is situated in tropical savanna climate zone which merges with the Amazon rain forest in N. Average temp., 77°F.; rainfall (60–70 inches; less in S) heaviest Nov.–April. Climate is salubrious on S plateau. Stock raising is chief occupation in S Mato Grosso and in Paraguay R. flood plain during dry season. Commercial agr. (sugar, rice, tobacco, beans) limited to vicinity of larger cities. Maté is gathered commercially in Ponta Porã region (extreme S), and quebracho in Pôrto Murtinho area. Rubber, medicinal plants, and lumber shipped from N regions. State has large, unexploited mineral resources. Gold and diamonds (found here in 17th cent.) still washed in Cuiabá, Cáceres, Diamantino, and Garças R. areas. Mining of important manganese deposits near Corumbá (Morro do Urucum) is in its initial state. S Mato Grosso is crossed E-W by São Paulo–Corumbá RR, which bridges the Paraguay at Pôrto Esperança and continues W into Bolivia. A spur under construction from Campo Grande to Ponta Porã city had reached (1948) Maracaju. Chief navigable streams are the Paraguay (ascended to Corumbá and Cáceres), the São Lourenço and Cuiabá (navigated to Cuiabá city), the Miranda, and several right tributaries of the Paraná used for maté shipments; the Paraná is navigable bet. Urubu-Pungá Falls and Guaíra Falls. Chief cities (Campo Grande, Cuiabá, Corumbá, Três Lagoas, Ponta Porã) are linked by airlines. First explored by prospectors from São Paulo and considered a part of São Paulo until formation (1748) of Mato Grosso captaincy. Capital was moved (1820) from Mato Grosso city (formerly Villa Bella) to Cuiabá. Mato Grosso became a prov. of Brazilian Empire in 1822, and a state of federal republic in 1889. It was invaded by Paraguayan army in 1860s. N part of state prospered during early 20th-cent. rubber boom after construction of Madeira-Mamoré RR. With agr. frontier moving westward from São Paulo into S Mato Grosso, latter state now has better prospects for development. In 1943, federal territory of Ponta Porã and part of Guaporé territory were carved out of S and NW Mato Grosso, respectively; Ponta Porã was dissolved and reincorporated into state in 1946. Its large Indian pop. (probably 400,000) is not enumerated in census. Formerly spelled Matto Grosso.

Mato Grosso, city (pop. 470), NW Mato Grosso state, Brazil, head of navigation on Guaporé R., near Bolivia border, and 250 mi. WNW of Cuiabá. Founded as Villa Bella in 17th cent., it was 1st ⊙ Mato Grosso captaincy, and was noted for its gold placers. It is now in ruins, its pop. having dwindled from c.20,000 in 18th cent. because of region's insalubrious climate.

Matola (mätō'lä), village, Sul do Save prov., S Mozambique, on Umbeluzi R. and 7 mi. W of Lourenço Marques; meat packing, cement mfg.

Matope (mätō'pā), center in native village area, Southern Prov., Nyasaland, on Shire R. and 20 mi. W of Zomba; corn rice. In 19th cent., end of Shire R. navigation from L. Nyasa.

Matopo Hills (mätō'pō), range in SW Southern Rhodesia, c.30 S of Bulawayo, at S edge of central Rhodesian plateau; 50 mi. long (E-W), 20 mi. wide; rise to 5,091 ft. At World's View (7 mi. SSE of Matopos), a scenic point, is tomb of Cecil Rhodes. Major part of hills forms game reserve.

Matopos (mùtō'pōz), village, Bulawayo prov., SW Southern Rhodesia, in Matabeleland, 20 mi. SSW of Bulawayo; peanuts, corn; livestock. Terminus of rail spur to MATOPO HILLS, popular tourist area. Matopos Dam (part of Bulawayo water supply) is 4 mi. NE.

Ma-t'ou, Formosa: see MATOW.

Matouba (mätōōbä'), thermal springs, S Basse-Terre isl., Guadeloupe, near Saint-Claude, 2 mi. NNE of Basse-Terre.

Matour (mätōōr'), agr. village (pop. 413), Saône-et-Loire dept., E central France, 17 mi. W of Mâcon.

Matoury (mätōōrē'), town (commune pop. 229), N Fr. Guiana, on Cayenne Isl., 5 mi. S of Cayenne; cacao, sugar, tropical fruit.

Matow or **Ma-t'ou** (both: mä'tō'), Jap. *Mato* (mä'tō), town (1935 pop. 14,108), W central Formosa, 13 mi. N of Tainan; sugar-milling center; soybeans, rice, sweet potatoes, vegetables.

Matozinhos (mŭtōōzē'nyōōsh), town (pop. 19,500), Pôrto dist., N Portugal, at mouth of small Leça R. on the Atlantic and 5 mi. NW of Oporto (linked by trolley); fishing port and bathing resort. With adjoining Leça da Palmeira (NW) it encloses artificial harbor of LEIXÕES; fish preserving, sugar refining, rope mfg.

Matpalli, India: see METPALLI.

Matra (mä'trä), village (pop. 173), E Corsica, 12 mi. E of Corte; arsenic mines.

Matrafüred (mät'rôfü''rĕd), Hung. *Mátrafüred*, town (pop. 440), Heves co., N Hungary, in Matra Mts., 4 mi. N of Gyöngyös; health resort; mineral springs, tuberculosis sanatorium.

Matrah (mä'trù), W suburb (pop. 8,500) of Muscat, Oman; chief commercial center of the sultanate and starting point for caravans to the interior; has trade in dates, pearls, dried limes, fresh fruit, and salted fish. Shipbuilding and repair. Pop. is Indian, Baluch, and Negro.

Matra Mountains (mä'trŏ), Hung. *Mátra*, N Hungary, S spur of the Carpathians; extend 25 mi. bet. Zagyva and Tarna rivers, rise to 3,330 ft. in Mt. Kekes. Forested slopes; lignite, limestone, basalt, trachyte deposits. Gyöngyös at S foot.

Matranovak (mät'rŏnōvăk), Hung. *Mátranovák*, town (pop. 2,703), Nograd-Hont co., N Hungary, 9 mi. SE of Salgotarjan; vineyards; wheat, cattle raising.

Matrei (mä'trī), town (pop. 3,048), East Tyrol, S Austria, near Isel R., 16 mi. NW of Lienz; cotton mills; cattle. Formerly called Windisch-Matrei.

Mat River (mät) or **Mati River** (mä'tē), N central Albania, rises SE of Klos, flows c.60 mi. NW and W, past Burrel, to Drin Gulf of the Adriatic 9 mi. SSW of Lesh. Receives Fan R. (right).

Matriz, La, Ecuador: see GUANO.

Matriz de Camaragibe (mùtrēs' dĭ kŭmùrùzhē'bĭ), town (pop. 2,444), E Alagoas, NE Brazil, 34 mi. NE of Maceió, in sugar-growing dist.

Matrona, France: see MARNE RIVER.

Matroosberg (mätrōōs'bĕrkh''), mountain (7,386 ft.), SW Cape Prov., U. of So. Afr., highest peak of Hex River Mts., 20 mi. E of Ceres; 33°25'S 19°38'E.

Matrosy (mŭtrô'sē), Finnish *Matrossa*, village, S Karelo-Finnish SSR, on Shuya R. and 18 mi. W of Petrozavodsk; wood cracking, lumbering.

Matru or **Mattru** (mä'trōō), town (pop. 1,385), South-Western Prov., SW Sierra Leone, on Jong R., on road, and 38 mi. SW of Bo; palm oil and kernels, piassava, rice.

Matruh, Mersa Matruh (mûr'sù mùtrōō'), or **Marsa Matruh** (mär'sù măt'rōō), Mediterranean port (pop. 3,047), ⊙ Western Desert frontier prov., Egypt, terminus of coastal railroad and 155 mi. W of Alexandria, bet. Alamein and Sidi Barrani. Has subterranean water supply. Airfield. Here the English, using airplanes, decisively checked (1915) the Senussi invasion of Egypt. In Second World War it was a strategic objective in the desert fighting of 1941–42 and, after falling (June, 1942) to the Germans, was recaptured by the British in Nov., after Rommel's rout at Alamein.

Matsang Tsangpo River, Tibet: see BRAHMAPUTRA RIVER.

Matsena or **Machena** (both: mächā'nä), town (pop. 4,346), Bornu prov., Northern Provinces, N Nigeria, near Fr. West Africa border, 35 mi. NW of Nguru; peanuts, cotton, millet; cattle, skins.

Matsesta (mŭtsyĕ'stù), town (1939 pop. over 2,000), S Krasnodar Territory, Russian SFSR, near Black Sea coast, 3 mi. SE of Sochi; subtropical health resort amid orchards and vineyards. Consists of 2 sections: Novaya [new] Matsesta, beach resort on coastal railroad, and Staraya [old] Matsesta, on rail spur 2 mi. inland, with warm sulphur springs.

Matsiatra River, Madagascar: see MANGOKY RIVER.

Matsova (mätsōvä') or **Matsuva** (–sōō–), settlement (pop. 300), Lower Galilee, NW Israel, near Mediterranean and near Lebanese border, 19 mi. NNW of Haifa; dairying; fruit, olives, bananas, mushrooms; poultry. Founded 1940. Also spelled Matzuba or Matzuva.

Matsqui (măt′skwē), village (pop. estimate 250), SW B.C., near Fraser R., 16 mi. WSW of Chilliwack; lumbering; fruit, hops, tobacco.
Matsuai (mätsōōī′), town (pop. 5,736), Kumamoto prefecture, W Kyushu, Japan, 13 mi. SSW of Kumamoto, on Yatsushiro Bay; rice, wheat.
Matsubara, Japan: see TAKAHAGI.
Matsubase (mä′tsōōbäsä), town (pop. 4,428), Kumamoto prefecture, W Kyushu, Japan, 11 mi. S of Kumamoto; rice-producing center. Plum orchards.
Matsuda (mätsōō′dä), town (pop. 7,912), Kanagawa prefecture, central Honshu, Japan, 7 mi. N of Odawara; wheat, sweet potatoes, soybeans.
Matsudo (mätsōō′dō), city (1940 pop. 24,446; 1947 pop. 54,513), Chiba prefecture, central Honshu, Japan, just N of Ichikawa, 11 mi. NE of Tokyo; agr. center (rice, wheat); poultry farms. Has agr. school. Includes several former villages since early 1940s.
Matsue (mätsōō′ā), city (1940 pop. 55,506; 1947 pop. 62,136), ⊙ Shimane prefecture, SW Honshu, Japan, port on isthmus bet. L. Shinji and lagoon Naka-no-umi, 80 mi. NNE of Hiroshima; distribution center; spinning mills. Ferry to Yonago. Mus. dedicated to Lafcadio Hearn has collection of his MSS. Hot springs near by. Formerly sometimes spelled Matsuye.
Matsuida (mätsōōē′dä), town (pop. 6,241), Gumma prefecture, central Honshu, Japan, 11 mi. W of Takasaki; rice, raw silk.
Matsu Island, Chinese **Matsu Shan** (mä′dzōō shän′), in E.China Sea, off Min R. estuary, Fukien prov., China, 45 mi. ENE of Foochow; 26°12′N 120°E. Remained a Nationalist-held outpost after Communist conquest (1949) of mainland.
Matsukawa (mätsōōkä′wä), town (pop. 4,779), Fukushima prefecture, N central Honshu, Japan, 6 mi. S of Fukushima; agr., mining (gold, silver).
Matsumae (mätsōōmä′ā), town (1947 pop. 6,759), extreme SW Hokkaido, Japan, on Tsugaru Strait, 40 mi. SW of Hakodate; fishing center; edible kelp. Seat of powerful Matsumae family in feudal times. First named Matsumae, later, until early 1940s, called Fukuyama (1940 pop. 8,388). Sometimes called Matsumai.
Matsumaru (mätsōōmä′rōō), town (pop. 6,324), Ehime prefecture, W Shikoku, Japan, 8 mi. E of Uwajima; rice, wheat, raw silk.
Matsumine (mätsōō′mĭnä), town (pop. 2,881), Yamagata prefecture, N Honshu, Japan, on Mogami R. and 8 mi. ESE of Sakata; rice, silk cocoons.
Matsumoto (mätsōōmō′tō), city (1940 pop. 72,795; 1947 pop. 84,258), Nagano prefecture, central Honshu, Japan, 110 mi. WNW of Tokyo; raw-silk center; mfg. (soy sauce, sake), woodworking.
Matsunaga (mätsōōnä′gä), town (pop. 7,440), Hiroshima prefecture, SW Honshu, Japan, 4 mi. NE of Onomichi, on inlet of Inland Sea; rice; salt-making; floor mats, soy sauce.
Matsuo (mätsōō′ō), town (pop. 5,567), Chiba prefecture, central Honshu, Japan, on N Chiba Peninsula, 7 mi. NE of Togane; rice-collection center.
Matsuoka (mä′tsōōōkä). **1** Town (pop. 6,067), Fukui prefecture, central Honshu, Japan, 5 mi. ENE of Fukui; silk textiles, sake. **2** Town (pop. 6,699), Ibaraki prefecture, central Honshu, Japan, on the Pacific, 10 mi. NNE of Hitachi; coal mining; agr. (rice, wheat, persimmons).
Matsusaka, Japan: see MATSUZAKA.
Matsushima (mätsōō′shĭmä), town (pop. 14,237), Miyagi prefecture, N Honshu, Japan, on Ishinomaki Bay, 12 mi. NE of Sendai; tourist center for hundreds of scenic pine-clad islets in the bay. Noted 9th-cent. Buddhist temple on one of the islets. Sometimes spelled Matusima.
Matsushiro (mätsōō′shĭrō), town (pop. 9,988), Nagano prefecture, central Honshu, Japan, 6 mi. S of Nagano; spinning.
Matsuto (mätsōōtō′), town (pop. 7,634), Ishikawa prefecture, central Honshu, Japan, 6 mi. WSW of Kanazawa; commercial center in rice-growing area.
Matsuwa-kaikyo, Russian SFSR: see GOLOVNIN STRAIT.
Matsuwa-to, Russian SFSR: see MATUA ISLAND.
Matsuyama, Formosa: see SUNGSHAN.
Matsuyama (mätsōōyä′mä). **1** City and port (1940 pop. 117,534; 1947 pop. 147,967), ⊙ Ehime prefecture, NW Shikoku, Japan, 43 mi. SSE of Hiroshima across Iyo Sea (SW section of Inland Sea); 33°50′N 132°46′E. On extensive coastal plain producing rice and wheat. Mfg. center; exports cotton textiles, paper products. Has agr. school. Includes (since early 1940s) former towns of Shinhama and Mitsuhama, both just NW of city, on Iyo Sea, and (since c.1947) former town of Dogoyuno-machi, just NE. Site of feudal castle containing mus. Bombed (1945) in Second World War. Sometimes spelled Matuyama. **2** Town (pop. 7,696), Miyagi prefecture, N Honshu, Japan, 7 mi. SE of Furukawa; rice, silk cocoons, charcoal; horse breeding. **3** Town, Nara prefecture, Japan: see OUDA. **4** Town (pop. 14,705), Saitama prefecture, central Honshu, Japan, 7 mi. S of Kumagaya; rice, wheat, raw silk; sake brewing.
Matsuye, Japan: see MATSUE.
Matsuzaka (mätsōōzä′kä) or **Matsusaka** (–sä′kä), city (1940 pop. 35,391; 1947 pop. 41,269), Mie prefecture, S Honshu, Japan, port on W shore of Ise Bay, 37 mi. SSW of Nagoya; mfg. center; textiles (cotton, silk, rayon), metalworking. Stockyards. Exports lumber, charcoal.
Matsuzaki (mätsōōzä′kē), town (pop. 5,468), Shizuoka prefecture, central Honshu, Japan, on W Izu Peninsula, on Suruga Bay, 27 mi. SE of Shizuoka; fishing port.
Matsya, India: see RAJASTHAN.
Mattabesset River (mătūbĕ′sĭt), central Conn., rises SE of New Britain, flows c.12 mi. generally SE to the Connecticut just above Middletown.
Matta de São João, Brazil: see MATA DE SÃO JOÃO.
Mattagami Lake (mŭtă′gūmē) (□ 88), W Que., 120 mi. N of Val d'Or; 26 mi. long, 10 mi. wide; alt. 765 ft. Drained NW by Nottaway R.
Mattagami River, NE Ont., rises SW of Timmins, flows 260 mi. N to confluence with Missinaibi R., 50 mi. SW of Moosonee, here forming Moose R., which flows to James Bay.
Matta Grande, Brazil: see MATA GRANDE.
Mattakuliya (mŭtŭk′ōōlyŭ), section of Colombo, Western Prov., Ceylon, 3.5 mi. NE of city center; leather mfg. Also spelled Mattakkuliya.
Mattamuskeet, Lake (mătūmŭ′skēt), E N.C., in S Hyde co., near Pamlico Sound; c.15 mi. long E–W, 5 mi. wide. Waterfowl and game-bird refuge.
Mattancheri (mŭtän′chĕrē), city (pop. 53,346), Cochin administrative div., N Travancore-Cochin, India, on Arabian Sea, just S of seaport of COCHIN; commercial center. Has large Jewish pop.; several anc. synagogues.
Mattão, Brazil: see MATÃO.
Mattapan, Mass.: see BOSTON.
Mattapoisett (mătūpoi′sĭt), town (pop. 2,265), Plymouth co., SE Mass., on W shore of Buzzards Bay, 6 mi. E of New Bedford; summer resort; good harbor. Formerly shipbuilding and whaling. Settled 1750, inc. 1857. Includes villages of Antassawamock Neck (ăntă″sūwŏ′mŭk) and East Mattapoisett.
Mattaponi River (mătūpūnī′), E Va., formed in Caroline co. by junction of short headstreams; flows 120 mi. SE, joining Pamunkey R. at West Point to form York R. Navigable for c.40 mi. above mouth; chief cargoes are wood products.
Mattawa (mä′tūwô, –wä), town (pop. 1,971), E Ont., on Ottawa R. at mouth of Mattawa R., and 36 mi. E of North Bay; lumbering, plywood mfg., mica mining.
Mattawamkeag (mătūwŏm′kĕg), town (pop. 803), Penobscot co., E central Maine, on the Penobscot, at mouth of the Mattawamkeag, and 45 mi. above Old Town; hunting, fishing.
Mattawamkeag Lake, Aroostook co., E central Maine, 18 mi. SW of Houlton, in lumbering, recreational area; 7 mi. long. A source of Mattawamkeag R.
Mattawamkeag River, E central Maine, rises in 2 branches in S Aroostook co., flows c.70 mi. generally S and SW to the Penobscot at Mattawamkeag.
Mattawa River, central Ont., issues from Trout L. (8 mi. long), 3 mi. E of North Bay, flows 45 mi. E to Ottawa R. at Mattawa.
Mattawin River (mă′tūwĭn), S Que., rises near Mont Tremblant, flows 100 mi. E, through L. Toro, to St. Maurice R. 25 mi. NNW of Grand′Mere. Several falls.
Mattawoman Creek (mă′tūwŏ″mŭn), S Md., rises just SE of Brandywine, flows c.35 mi. generally W through swampland, forming part of Charles-Prince Georges co. line, to the Potomac c.4 mi. below Indian Head.
Matteawan, N.Y.: see BEACON.
Matterhorn (mă′tūrhôrn, mä′tūrhôrn″), Fr. *Mont Cervin* (mõ sĕrvē′), Ital. *Monte Cervino* (môn′tĕ chĕrvē′nō), peak (14,701 ft.) in Pennine Alps, on Swiss-Ital. border, 6 mi. SW of Zermatt. First climbed 1865 by Edward Whymper; 4 of his party fell to their death on the descent. The near-by **Matterjoch** (mä′tūryôkh″) or **Théodule** (tāōdül′) pass (10,892 ft.) links Italy with Switzerland.
Mattersburg (mät′ūrsbōōrk), Hung. *Nagymarton* (nŏ′dymär′tôn), town (pop. 3,860), Burgenland, E Austria, 9 mi. SE of Wiener Neustadt; market center; strawberries raised in vicinity.
Matteseunk Lake (mă′tūsŭngk), Aroostook co., E Maine, 17 mi. ESE of Millinocket; 3 mi. long.
Matteson (măt′sūn), village (pop. 1,211), Cook co., NE Ill., S suburb of Chicago.
Matthews. **1** Town (pop. 100), Jefferson co., E Ga., 25 mi. SW of Augusta. **2** Town (pop. 501), Grant co., E central Ind., 14 mi. SSE of Marion, in agr. area; cannery. **3** Town (pop. 498), New Madrid co., extreme SE Mo., in Mississippi flood plain, 12 mi. NNW of New Madrid. **4** Town (pop. 589), Mecklenburg co., S N.C., 10 mi. SE of Charlotte.
Matthews Peak (9,403 ft.), NE Ariz., in Chuska Mts., near N.Mex. line, c.55 mi. SW of Farmington, N.Mex.
Matthew Town, minor port in S Bahama Isls., on W tip of Great Inagua Isl., 350 mi. SE of Nassau, 55 mi. NNE of Cape Maisí (E Cuba); 20°57′N 73°40′W. Produces salt.
Mattighofen (mä′tĭkh-hōfūn), town (pop. 3,679), Upper Austria, 13 mi. SSE of Braunau; breweries.
Mattituck (mă′tĭtŭk), resort village (pop. 1,089), Suffolk co., SE N.Y., on NE Long Isl., on inlet of Long Island Sound, 8 mi. NE of Riverhead; makes embroidery; agr. (potatoes, cauliflower).
Matto Grosso, Brazil: see MATO GROSSO.
Mattole River (mūtōl′), NW Calif., rises in NW Mendocino co., flows c.50 mi. NW to the Pacific c.35 mi. SW of Eureka.
Mattoon (măt′tōōn″, mă′–). **1** City (pop. 17,547), Coles co., E central Ill., 39 mi. SE of Decatur; trade and industrial center in rich agr. area (corn, soybeans, broomcorn); railroad shops; mfg. of shoes, brooms, furniture, Diesel engines, utilities equipment, roofing. Near by are a large fish hatchery, and Paradise L. (or L. Mattoon), impounded by dam in Little Wabash R. Inc. 1859. **2** Village (pop. 510), Shawano co., E central Wis., 29 mi. ENE of Wausau; lumbering.
Mattru, Sierra Leone: see MATRU.
Matty Island (20 mi. long, 15 mi. wide), S Franklin Dist., Northwest Territories, in James Ross Strait, bet. Boothia Peninsula (NE) and King William Isl. (SW); 69°30′N 95°30′W.
Matua Island (măt′wä), Jap. *Matsuwa-to* (mätsōōwä-tō′) (□ 20), one of central main Kurile Isls. group, Russian SFSR; separated from Raikoke Isl. (N) by Golovnin Strait, from Rasshua Isl. (S) by Nadezhda Strait; 48°5′N 153°13′E; 7 mi. long, 4 mi. wide. Rises to 4,872 ft. in active volcanic Sarychev Peak, Jap. *Fuyo-yama*. Settlement on SE coast; seal reserve; fisheries; farming.
Matua Strait, Indonesia: see OMBAI STRAIT.
Matucana (mätōōkä′nä), city (pop. 1,790), ⊙ Huarochirí prov. (□ 2,002; pop. 37,587), Lima dept., W central Peru, in Cordillera Occidental of the Andes, on Rímac R., on Lima–La Oroya RR and highway, and 45 mi. ENE of Lima; alt. 7,792 ft. Alfalfa, vegetables, livestock.
Matuku (mätōō′kōō), island (□ 11; pop. 873), Lau group, Fiji, SW Pacific; 4 mi. long; copra.
Matun (mūtōōn′), town (pop. 10,000), Southern Prov., E Afghanistan, 50 mi. ESE of Gardez, near Pakistan line; trade center in lumbering area (pine); stock raising. Also called Khost, for name of surrounding dist.
Matunga, India: see BOMBAY, city.
Matunuck, R.I.: see SOUTH KINGSTOWN.
Maturá, Brazil: see AMATAURÁ.
Maturei Vavao, Tuamotu Isls.: see ACTAEON ISLANDS.
Maturín (mätōōrēn′), city (1941 pop. 10,705; 1950 census 25,350), ⊙ Monagas state, NE Venezuela, in llanos, on Guarapiche R. and 85 mi. SE of Cumaná, 250 mi. ESE of Caracas; 9°45′N 63°11′W. Trading center in agr. region (cacao, cotton, tobacco, cereals, cattle); mfg. (starch, *aguardiente*). Petroleum fields near by (N and W). Airport. Founded 1710 by Capuchin missionaries. Birthplace of the brothers José Tadeo and José Gregorio Monagas, both of whom became presidents of Venezuela.
Matusima, Japan: see MATSUSHIMA.
Matuyama, Japan: see MATSUYAMA, Ehime prefecture.
Matveyev Island (mŭtvyā′ūf) (□ c.4), in SE Barents Sea, forms part of Archangel oblast, Russian SFSR, 45 mi. WSW of Khabarovo; 69°28′N 58°29′E.
Matveyevka (–kŭ), village (1926 pop. 4,090), NW Chkalov oblast, Russian SFSR, 40 mi. ESE of Buguruslan; wheat, sunflowers, livestock. Lignite deposits.
Matveyev-Kurgan (–kōōrgän′), village (1926 pop. 2,707), SW Rostov oblast, Russian SFSR, 25 mi. N of Taganrog and on Mius R.; metalworks; wheat, sunflowers, cattle.
Matyasföld (mä′tyäsh-fûld), Hung. *Mátyásföld*, town (pop. 4,573), Pest-Pilis-Solt-Kiskun co., N central Hungary, 5 mi. E of Budapest; automobile mfg. Budapest municipal airport, large commercial airport, near by.
Matzen (mät′sūn), village (pop. 1,384), E Lower Austria, 4 mi. N of Gänserndorf; oil well.
Matzuba or **Matzuva**, Israel: see MATSOVA.
Mau (mou). **1** or **Maunath Bhanjan** (mou′nät bŭn′jŭn), town (pop. 29,357), Azamgarh dist., E Uttar Pradesh, India, on Tons R. and 24 mi. SE of Azamgarh; rail and road junction; hand-loom cotton-weaving center; silk weaving, rice and flour milling. Has 17th-cent. serai. **2** Village, Banda dist., S Uttar Pradesh, India, on the Jumna and 31 mi. WSW of Allahabad; gram, jowar, wheat, oilseeds. Important glass sand deposits at Bargarh (10 mi. SSE) and Panhai (17 mi. SW) villages. **3** Town (pop. 13,105), Jhansi dist., S Uttar Pradesh, India, on tributary of the Dhasan and 37 mi. ESE of Jhansi; road center; brassware mfg.; trades in jowar, oilseeds, wheat, gram, barley, rice. Jain temple. Large annual cattle fair. Also called Mau-Ranipur. Projected irrigation dam near by on tributary of the Dhasan.
Mauá (mou-ä′), town (pop. 2,653), SE São Paulo, Brazil, outer SE suburb of São Paulo just SE of Santo André, on São Paulo–Santos RR.
Mau Aimma (mou′ ĭm′mŭ), town (pop. 5,722), Allahabad dist., SE Uttar Pradesh, India, 18 mi. NNE of Allahabad city center; hand-loom cotton-weaving center; trades in gram, rice, barley, wheat, sugar cane, cotton.

Mauban (mä″ōōbän′, moubän′), town (1939 pop. 4,976; 1948 municipality pop. 14,417), Quezon prov., S Luzon, Philippines, on Lopez Bay, 29 mi. ENE of San Pablo; fishing and agr. center (coconuts, rice).

Maubeuge (mōbûzh′), anc. *Malbodium*, town (pop. 20,310), Nord dept., N France, on the Sambre (canalized) and 47 mi. ESE of Lille, 9 mi. S of Mons (Belgium); industrial center with metalworks (railroad and heating equipment, machine tools, hardware), ceramic and mirror factories. Old ⊙ of Hainaut. Passed to France in 1678. Fortified by Vauban. Capitulated to Germans in Sept., 1914, after 2-week siege. Severely damaged in both world wars.

Maubin or **Ma-ubin** (both: mŭōō″bĭn′), district (□ 1,642; 1941 pop. 428,092), Irrawaddy div., Lower Burma, in Irrawaddy delta; ⊙ Maubin. Rice and fishing region. Largely swamps; the most malarial dist. in Lower Burma. Constituted 1903 from former Thongwa dist. Pop. is 65% Burmese, 30% Karen.

Maubin or **Ma-ubin**, town (pop. 8,897), ⊙ Maubin dist., Lower Burma, in Irrawaddy delta, 60 mi. E of Bassein; river port, center of rice area.

Maubisse (moubē′sē), town, Portuguese Timor, in central Timor, 19 mi. S of Dili; agr. (coffee, wheat, fruit), sheep raising. Also spelled Maobisse.

Maubourguet (mōbōōrgā′), town (pop. 2,234), Hautes-Pyrénées dept., SW France, on the Adour and 17 mi. N of Tarbes; iron foundry, wool-combing factory.

Mauch Chunk (môk′ chŭngk′, mô″ chŭngk′), borough (pop. 2,959), ⊙ Carbon co., E Pa., 23 mi. NW of Allentown and on Lehigh R., among steep hills; anthracite; clothing; agr. Some of the Molly Maguires were executed here. Settled 1815, inc. 1842.

Mauchline (mŏkh′lĭn), town and parish (pop. 2,484), central Ayrshire, Scotland, near Ayr R., 11 mi. ENE of Ayr; agr. market, noted for mfg. of wooden snuff boxes and other wooden articles. Burns lived here for some time and here married Jean Armour. Many local scenes (e.g., BALLOCHMYLE) and personalities are celebrated in Burns's poems. Just NW of Mauchline is Mossgiel (mŏsgĭl′), where Burns wrote 1st volume of poetry.

Mauckport (môk′pôrt), town (pop. 154), Harrison co., S Ind., on Ohio R. and 27 mi. SW of New Albany, in agr. area.

Maud. **1** City (pop. 1,389), Pottawatomie and Seminole cos., central Okla., 16 mi. SE of Shawnee, in agr. area (cotton, oats, wheat, livestock); oil wells; lumber milling, gasoline mfg. Inc. 1929. **2** Village (pop. 713), Bowie co., NE Texas, 18 mi. WSW of Texarkana, near Sulphur R.; shipping point in fruit, truck area; lumber milling.

Maudaha (mou′dŭhŭ), town (pop. 8,662), Hamirpur dist., S Uttar Pradesh, India, 30 mi. NNE of Mahoba; gram, jowar, sesame, wheat, pearl millet. Has 18th-cent. Moslem tomb.

Maudit, Mont (mõ mōdē′), peak (14,649 ft.) of Mont Blanc massif, on Fr.-Ital. border, just NE of Mont Blanc, at head of Brema glacier, which flows into Italy.

Maudits, Monts, Spain: see MALADETTA.

Mauer (mou′ŭr), town (pop. 6,754), after 1938 in Liesing dist. of Vienna, Austria, 6 mi. SW of city center; vineyards.

Mauer, village (pop. 1,698), N Baden, Germany, after 1945 in Württemberg-Baden, on the Elsenz and 6 mi. SE of Heidelberg; brickwork. Jawbone of Heidelberg man found near by in 1907.

Mauer, Poland: see PILCHOWICE.

Mauerbach (mou′ŭrbäkh), village (pop. 1,995), E Lower Austria, 8 mi. ENE of Vienna. Carthusian monastery (14th cent.).

Mauer Lake, Poland: see MAMRY, LAKE.

Maués (mou-ĕs′), city (pop. 1,374), E Amazonas, Brazil, head of navigation on the Maués-Guassú (right tributary of the Amazon) and 160 mi. E of Manaus; rubber, guarana.

Mau Escarpment (mou), section of W rim of Great Rift Valley in W Kenya, W and S of Nakuru; rises to 10,000 ft.

Maug (moug), uninhabited group of islands, Saipan dist., N Marianas Isls., W Pacific, c.50 mi. SSE of Pajaros; 20°1′N 145°13′E; 3 isls. (each c.1 mi. long) surround deep harbor. N isl. rises to 748 ft.

Maugansville (mô′gŭnzvĭl), village (1940 pop. 552), Washington co., W Md., 4 mi. NNW of Hagerstown.

Mauga Silisili (mou′gä sē′lēsē′lē), peak (6,094 ft.), Savaii, Western Samoa; highest in Samoan group.

Mauguio (mōgyō′), town (pop. 2,563), Hérault dept., S France, near a lagoon of the Gulf of Lion, 7 mi. E of Montpellier; winegrowing, fruit-juice canning.

Maui (mou′ē), county (□ 1,173; pop. 55,980), T.H., includes KAHOOLAWE, LANAI, MAUI, MOLOKAI isls.; ⊙ Wailuku, Maui. KALAWAO co. is officially a dist. of Maui co.

Maui, island (□ 728; pop. 47,982), T.H., 2d largest of Hawaiian Isls., c.70 mi. from Honolulu, separated from Hawaii by Alenuihaha Channel, from Molokai by Pailolo Channel; 20°47′N 156°22′W.; 25 mi. N-S, 38 mi. E-W. Two mtn. masses constitute E and W peninsulas, connected by isthmus; highest peak is HALEAKALA, in Hawaii Natl. Park. Important towns: WAILUKU, KAHULUI, LAHAINA (1st white settlement in Hawaiian Isls.). Produces livestock, sugar, pineapples. Fine tuberculosis sanitarium is on E peninsula.

Mauke (mou′kā′), low coral island (4,600 acres; pop. 804), most easterly of COOK ISLANDS, S Pacific, 150 mi. NE of Rarotonga; 2.5 mi. wide, 4 mi. long. Fertile soil; exports fruits, copra. Also known as Parry Isl.

Maulavi Bazar (mou′lŭvē bäzär′), town (pop. 5,855), Sylhet dist., E East Bengal, E Pakistan, in Surma Valley, on tributary of the Kusiyara and 29 mi. SSW of Sylhet; road center; trades in rice, tea, oilseeds. Mfg. of iron implements 6 mi. ENE, at Rajnagar. Also spelled Maulvibazar.

Maulbronn (moulbrôn′), town (pop. 2,311), N Württemberg, Germany, after 1945 in Württemberg-Baden, on the Saalbach near its source, and 13 mi. SE of Bruchsal; grain, cattle. Site of noted former Cistercian abbey (founded c.1150), now Protestant theological seminary.

Maulde (mōld), village (pop. 888), Hainaut prov., SW Belgium, 7 mi. E of Tournai; beet-sugar refining; agr.

Maulden (môl′dŭn), agr. village and parish (pop. 1,313), central Bedford, England, 7 mi. S of Bedford. Church has 15th-cent. tower.

Maule (mou′lā), province (□ 2,172; 1940 pop. 70,497, 1949 estimate 63,064), S central Chile; ⊙ Cauquenes. On the Pacific S of Maule R., in agr. area. Known for its wine; also produces wheat, corn, potatoes, lentils, peas. Sheep raised in its subandean ranges. Its high-quality construction timber is exported. Flour milling, lumbering; wineries at Cauquenes; shipyards at Constitución; cheese mfg. at Chanco. Major coast resorts: Constitución, Curanipe. Prov. was set up 1826.

Maule, village (1930 pop. 322), Talca prov., central Chile, on railroad, on Maule R. and 7 mi. S of Talca; wheat, barley, wine, livestock. Hydroelectric station.

Maule, Lake, Andean lake (□ 17) in SE Talca prov., central Chile, 75 mi. SE of Talca; c.6 mi. long, 2-4 mi. wide; alt. 7,200 ft. Maule R. rises here.

Mauléon-Barousse (mōlāõ′-bärōōs′), village (pop. 266), Hautes-Pyrénées dept., SW France, in central Pyrenees, 12 mi. N of Bagnères-de-Luchon; livestock raising, dairying. Has ruins of 15th-cent. castle.

Mauléon-Licharre (–lēshär′) or **Mauléon-Soule** (–sōōl′), town (pop. 4,033), Basses-Pyrénées dept., SW France, on Saison R. and 14 mi. W of Oloron-Sainte-Marie; footwear center (sandals, slippers); woodworking, flour milling.

Maule River (mou′lā), central Chile, rises in L. Maule in the Andes near Argentina border, flows c.175 mi. WNW to the Pacific at Constitución; forms border bet. Talca and Linares provs. Receives the Río Claro and Loncomilla R. Used for irrigation and hydroelectric power.

Maullín (mouyēn′), town (pop. 1,585), ⊙ Maullín dept. (□ 796; pop. 17,997), Llanquihue prov., S central Chile, on bay of the Pacific at mouth of Maullín R., 20 mi. NNE of Ancud; resort and agr. center (wheat, flax, potatoes, livestock); dairying, lumbering. Coal deposits near by.

Maullín River, Llanquihue prov., S central Chile, rises in L. Llanquihue, flows c.50 mi. SW, past Las Quemas and Maullín, to a wide estuary on Coronados Gulf of the Pacific; navigable c.25 mi. upstream.

Maulmain, Burma: see MOULMEIN.

Maumee (mômē′), city (pop. 5,548), Lucas co., NW Ohio, on Maumee R., just SW of Toledo; residential, with some mfg. (furniture, food colors, building materials, paper products); limestone quarries. Founded 1817; after 1680, site was occupied by French and British trading and military posts, the last being Fort Miami, surrendered by the British in War of 1812.

Maumee River, in Ind. and Ohio, formed at Fort Wayne, Ind., by junction of St. Joseph and St. Marys rivers, flows c.130 mi. NE, past Defiance and Toledo (Ohio), to Maumee Bay, an arm of L. Erie just NE of Toledo. For several mi. above its mouth, the Maumee serves as harbor of Toledo. Receives Auglaize R. at Defiance.

Maumere, Indonesia: see FLORES.

Maumusson, Pertuis de, (pĕrtwē′ dŭ mōmüsõ′), strait off Charente-Maritime dept., W France, bet. S end of Île d'Oléron and Pointe d'Arvert, connecting Bay of Biscay with the Pertuis d'Antioche; ½ mi. wide; used by shipping to estuary of Seudre R. (4 mi. E). Oyster beds.

Maun (moun), town, ⊙ Ngamiland dist., N Bechuanaland Protectorate, on SE edge of Okovanggo Basin, 220 mi. SW of Livingstone; hq. of Batawana tribe. Airfield; hosp.

Maunabo (mounä′bō), town (pop. 1,246), SE Puerto Rico, near coast, on small Maunabo R. and 14 mi. E of Guayama; sugar growing and milling. Its port is 1½ mi. SSE.

Mauna Kea (mou′nŭ kā′ŭ), mountain (13,825 ft.), central Hawaii, T.H., dormant volcano with numerous cinder cones; highest isl. mtn. in world. Snow-capped in winter.

Maunaloa (mou′nŭlō′ŭ), village (pop. 930), W Molokai, T.H.; pineapple plantation.

Mauna Loa (mou′nŭ lō′ŭ), mountain (13,675 ft.), S central Hawaii, T.H. It has numerous craters, notably KILAUEA (2d largest active crater in world, after Aniakchak; contains HALEMAUMAU, fiery pit), and on its summit MOKUAWEOWEO, one of largest active craters in world.

Maunalua Bay (mou′nŭlōō′ŭ), SE Oahu, T.H., bet. Diamond Head and Koko Head.

Maunath Bhanjan, India: see MAU, Azamgarh dist.

Maungdaw (moung′dô), village, Akyab dist., Lower Burma, in the Arakan, on Naaf R. (E Pakistan border) and 60 mi. NW of Akyab; rice port. Head of roads to Buthidaung and to Cox's Bazar (E Bengal) via Bawli Bazar.

Maunie (mô′nē″), village (pop. 412), White co., SE Ill., on Wabash R. and 35 mi. NE of Harrisburg, in agr. area.

Maunoir, Lac (läk mõnwär′), lake (30 mi. long, 1–15 mi. wide), NW Mackenzie Dist., Northwest Territories, NW of Great Bear L.; 67°30′N 125°W. Drains NE into Anderson R. Sometimes called Manoir L.

Maupin (mô′pŭn), town (pop. 312), Wasco co., N Oregon, 30 mi. S of The Dalles and on Deschutes R.; game fishing.

Maupiti (mou′pē′tē), volcanic island (pop. 561), Leeward group, SOCIETY ISLANDS, S Pacific, c.25 mi. W of Bora-Bora; circumference 6 mi.; rises to 800 ft. Known for deposits of jet-black basaltic rock. Sometimes called Maurua (mourōō′ä).

Maurage (mōräzh′), town (pop. 5,363), Hainaut prov., S Belgium, 7 mi. E of Mons; coal mines; coke plants.

Mau-Ranipur, India: see MAU, Jhansi dist.

Maurawan (mourä′vän), town (pop. 7,622), Unao dist., central Uttar Pradesh, India, 26 mi. ESE of Unao; wheat, barley, rice, gram, oilseeds.

Maure-de-Bretagne (mōr-dŭ-brŭtä′nyŭ), village (pop. 679), Ille-et-Vilaine dept., W France, 17 mi. NNE of Redon; dairying. Sometimes called Maure.

Mauren (mou′rŭn), village (pop. 1,027), N Liechtenstein, on railroad and 4.5 mi. NNE of Vaduz; corn, potatoes; cattle. Has prehistoric remains.

Maurepas, Lake (mă′rĭpô), SE La., c.28 mi. NW of New Orleans; c.13 mi. long. Receives navigable Tickfaw R. from N, navigable Amite R. from W; connected to L. Pontchartrain (E) by the Pass Manchac waterway.

Maures, Monts des (mõ dā mōr′) [Fr.,=mountains of the Moors], massif in Var dept., SE France, extending c.30 mi. along Mediterranean coast from lower Argens R. (NE) to Hyères (SW); c.15 mi. wide. Rises to 2,556 ft. at Notre-Dame-des-Anges. Heavily forested (cork oaks, pines). Its coastline, heavily indented (Gulf of Saint-Tropez, capes Camarat, Lardier, Bénat), forms W part of Fr. Riviera (resorts).

Mauretania (mô″rĭtā′nēŭ, –nyŭ), anc. country of N Africa, embracing roughly N part of modern Morocco and W part of Algeria, W of anc. Numidia. Named after the Mauri, a native Berber tribe, region was 1st under Carthaginian sway, but came under Roman influence in 1st cent. B.C., when Augustus made Juba II ruler of Mauretania (25 B.C.). Revolts (A.D. 41–42) were subdued by Claudius who divided region into 2 Roman provs. —Mauretania Caesariensis (E), ⊙ Caesarea (modern Cherchel), and Mauretania Tingitana (W), ⊙ Tingis (modern Tangier). Roman hold was later loosened, and region was invaded by Vandals in 5th cent. A.D. Anc. Mauretania is not to be confused with modern MAURITANIA, a territory of French West Africa.

Mauriac (mōrēäk′), town (pop. 2,820), Cantal dept., S central France, 20 mi. NNW of Aurillac; road junction and livestock market; cheese mfg., woodworking. Has fine 12th-cent. Romanesque basilica of Notre-Dame-des-Miracles.

Maurice, in Indian Ocean: see MAURITIUS.

Maurice. **1** (môr′ĭs) Town (pop. 256), Sioux co., NW Iowa, 12 mi. N of Le Mars, in livestock and grain area. **2** (môrēs′) Village (pop. 335), Vermilion parish, S La., 60 mi. SW of Baton Rouge; cotton, rice.

Maurice River (môrēs′), S N.J., rises near Glassboro, flows c.50 mi. S, past Millville (dam here forms 3-mi.-long Union L.), to Maurice River Cove on Delaware Bay, 2 mi. S of Port Norris. Navigable to Millville; carries chiefly sand and gravel; oystering, fishing docks at mouth.

Mauricetown (môrēs′toun), village (pop. c.300), Cumberland co., S N.J., on Maurice R. and 8 mi. SSE of Millville; oystering; sand and gravel pits.

Mauriceville, New Zealand: see MASTERTON.

Maurienne (mōrēĕn′), Alpine valley of Arc R., in Savoie dept., SE France, deeply intrenched bet. Savoy Alps (N) and Dauphiné Alps (S). Extends over 70 mi. in a great arc from Col de l'Iseran (E) to junction with Isère R. valley (NW). Followed by road and railroad to Italy via Mont Cenis Pass and tunnel. Its 18 hydroelectric plants power several large aluminum works (bet. Saint-Jean-de-Maurienne and Modane), a high-grade steel mill at Saint-Michel, and numerous electro-chemical plants. Chief town: Saint-Jean-de-Maurienne.

Mauripur (mou′rēpōōr), village, Karachi administration area, W Pakistan, on Karachi harbor, 5 mi.

W of city center; suburban settlement and airport. Extensive brine-salt deposits, here, form one of Pakistan's chief sources of supply. Also spelled Maurypur.

Mauri River, Bolivia: see Desaguadero River.

Mauritania (mô″rĭtā′nēŭ, -nyŭ), Fr. *Mauritanie*, French overseas territory (□ c.449,800; pop. 497,-000), NW Fr. West Africa, on the Atlantic. Borders NW on Sp. Sahara (Río de Oro and Saguia el Hamra), N on Algeria, E on Fr. Sudan, S on Senegal (along Senegal R.). Its extraterritorial ⊙, Saint-Louis, is in Senegal. A vast desert area of the W Sahara. Its long coast line, blocked by sand bars, has a good harbor only at Port-Étienne on Lévrier Bay. Beyond the coast it is hot and arid; the few winter rains are heavier and more regular in the S. The violent, scorching harmattan wind blows from the E. Several low, plateau-like ridges run generally NE–SW, among them the renowned Adrar, where a few large oases thrive. Main cultivated areas are along Senegal R. Economically the most important products are gum arabic, salt from the so-called sebkras (pans) in W, fish from the rich coastal waters, and livestock (camels, cattle, goats, sheep). Other exports include dates, ostrich feathers, native leather goods and jewelry. The territory has only short local railroads, but is crossed by important caravan trails to Algeria and Fr. Sudan. The great majority of the pop. are nomadic Moslems of Berber stock. Aboriginal Negroes have reentered from the S. First Europeans to explore the coast were the Portuguese, who penetrated towards the Adrar. After concluding (1900) a boundary treaty with Spain, the Fr. included (1904) Mauritania into the domain of Fr. West Africa. It became first a protectorate (1903), then a colony (1920), when it was finally pacified. As an overseas territory (since 1946), it is now represented by a deputy in the National Assembly of France. For the anc. region, see Mauretania.

Mauriti (mourētē′), city (pop. 1,761), SE Ceará, Brazil, near Paraíba border, 50 mi. ESE of Crato; cattle, carnauba. Formerly spelled Maurity.

Mauritius (mŭrĭsh′ŭs, -shēŭs, mô-), Fr. *Maurice* (mōrēs′), island (□ 720; pop. 419,185) of Mascarene group, in Indian Ocean, forming with its dependencies (Rodrigues and Agalega isls., Chagos Archipelago, Cargados Carajos Shoals) a Br. crown colony (inhabited □ 804½; pop. 432,648); ⊙ Port Louis. Located c.530 mi. E of Madagascar and 110 mi. NE of Réunion, Mauritius lies bet. 19°58′S and 20°32′S, 57°17′E and 57°46′E; 39 mi. long, 27 mi. wide. Reef-fringed coastal plain (widest in N) rises abruptly to central plateau, bordered by 3 mtn. ranges: Black River Range (2,711 ft.; SW); Grand Port Range (E), Moka Range (N, overlooking Port Louis). Of the many torrential streams, the longest (25 mi.) is Grand River South East; Black River (SW) cuts scenic gorges into the upland. Has a fairly equable climate, due to the SE tradewinds. Rainfall is 75–175 in. on windward coast and slopes; 40 in. on leeward side. Tropical cyclones often sweep across isl. (especially bet. Dec. and May). Almost 200 cyclones have been recorded in past 60 years. Depending largely on its one-crop sugar economy, Mauritius also produces tobacco, aloe hemp (for bag and rope mfg.), and tea. Distillery products include rum, industrial alcohol, vinegar, perfumes, and drugs. Secondary industries produce cigarettes, matches, wines, soap, building materials, furniture. Cane sugar represents 96% of all exports. Rail and road net serves sugar plantations and links ports of Port Louis and Mahébourg with residential towns in central plateau and towns on E and S coast. Pop. includes Hindi-speaking Indians (63%), Chinese (2½%), and the "general population," largely French- and Creole-speaking descendants of European immigrants and African slaves. Pop. density (one of highest in the world) ranges from 100 per sq. mi. in coastal plain to 1,500 in central plateau. Govt. is vested in a governor and executive council, assisted by a legislative council. Probably known to Arab and Malay traders in Middle Ages, Mauritius was 1st visited by Portuguese in early 16th cent. Named Mauritius by Dutch in 1598, it remained under intermittent Dutch occupation until 1710, during which time its great ebony forests were exploited and the dodo bird was exterminated. Claimed by France in 1715 and renamed Île de France, the isl. was occupied in 1721 and governed together with Réunion by Fr. East India Company (until 1767), and by Fr. crown until captured (1810) by British, in whose possession it was confirmed by Treaty of Paris (1814). After slavery was abolished (1834) in British Empire, large-scale immigration of laborers from India laid basis for present Indian majority. Mahé de La Bourdonnais, governor 1735–46, founded the isl.'s sugar economy.

Mauritius, Cape, Russian SFSR: see Zhelaniye, Cape.

Maurity, Brazil: see Mauriti.

Mauritzstad, Brazil: see Recife.

Maú River (mäōō′) or **Ireng River,** on Brazil–Br. Guiana border, NE South America, rises in the Serra Pacaraima, flows c.175 mi. S to Tacutú R. near 3°30′N 59°45′W. Diamond deposits.

Mauron (mōrõ′), village (pop. 1,085), Morbihan dept., W France, 11 mi. NNE of Ploërmel; dairying. Forest of Paimpont near by.

Maurosouli, Greece: see Polykastron.

Maurs (mōr), village (pop. 1,830), Cantal dept., S central France, 19 mi. SW of Aurillac; agr. market (wheat, cattle), fruit and meat preserving, tanning, mfg. of gallic acid and hardware.

Maursmünster, France: see Marmoutier.

Maurua, Society Isls.: see Maupiti.

Maurui (mourōō′ē), village, Tanga prov., NE Tanganyika, on Pangani R., on railroad, and 8 mi. W of Korogwe; sisal.

Maury (mōrē′), village (pop. 1,283), Pyrénées-Orientales dept., S France, 17 mi. NW of Perpignan; winegrowing.

Maury (mô′rē), county (□ 614; pop. 40,368), central Tenn.; ⊙ Columbia. Drained by Duck R. Livestock raising (especially mules), dairying, agr. (corn, tobacco, wheat). Phosphate rock deposits. Mfg. at Columbia and Mt. Pleasant. Formed 1807.

Maury, town (pop. 251), Greene co., E central N.C., 15 mi. N of Kinston, in agr. area.

Maury City, town (pop. 553), Crockett co., W Tenn., 26 mi. NW of Jackson, in diversified farm area.

Maury River, W Va., rises in SE Augusta co., flows c.30 mi. SSW, joining Calfpasture R. SE of Goshen to form North R.

Mausatta or **Mausata** (mou′sătŭ), sectional Upper Yafa sheikdom of Western Aden Protectorate; ⊙ Al Qudma. Protectorate treaty concluded in 1903.

Maussane (mōsän′), village (pop. 835), Bouches-du-Rhône dept., SE France, at S foot of the Alps, 10 mi. ENE of Arles; wool spinning, beekeeping, olive-oil mfg.

Mauston (mô′stŭn), city (pop. 3,171), ⊙ Juneau co., central Wis., on Lemonweir R. and 55 mi. E of La Crosse, in agr. area (grain, hay, potatoes); beverages, dairy products, tools, furniture, cigars. Settled c.1840, inc. 1883.

Mau Summit (mou), village, Nyanza prov., W Kenya, at edge of Mau Escarpment, on railroad and 5 mi. E of Londiani; alt. 8,322 ft.; coffee, tea, wheat, corn.

Mautern (mou′tŭrn). **1** Village (pop. 2,379), Styria, central Austria, 12 mi. W of Leoben; resort (alt. 2,340 ft.). **2** Town, Lower Austria: see Krems.

Mauthausen (mout′houzŭn), village (pop. 3,635), E Upper Austria, on left bank of the Danube, 3 mi. NE of Enns; rail junction; large granite quarries. Was site of notorious concentration camp under Hitler regime.

Mauvezin (mōvzẽ′), village (pop. 978), Gers dept., SW France, 16 mi. ENE of Auch; small grains, orchards; horse breeding. Stone quarries near by.

Mauzé-sur-le-Mignon (mōzā′-sür-lü-mēnyõ′), village (pop. 1,418), Deux-Sèvres dept., W France, 13 mi. SW of Niort; dairying, peat extracting. René Caillé b. here. Also called Mauzé.

Maveitural, Ceylon: see Delft, island.

Mavelikara (mä′vālĭkŭrŭ), city (pop. 16,022), W Travancore, India, 25 mi. N of Quilon; trades in coir rope and mats, rice, cassava, betel; cashew-nut processing, pottery mfg.

Maverick (mă′vŭrĭk), county (□ 1,279; pop. 12,292), SW Texas; ⊙ Eagle Pass. Bounded SW by the Rio Grande (Mex. border), bridged at Eagle Pass. Rich agr. area (part of Winter Garden region), irrigated by the Rio Grande, produces large part of state's spinach crop, other truck, also cotton, grain sorghums; uplands are ranching region (cattle, sheep, goats). Formed 1856.

Mavinga (mävĭng′gä), town (pop. 91), Bié prov., SE Angola, 190 mi. SE of Serpa Pinto.

Mavis Bank (mā′vĭs), village, St. Andrew parish, SE Jamaica, in interior mts. (alt. c.2,000 ft.), 11 mi. NE of Jamaica, in coffee dist. Noted scenery.

Maviya, Yemen: see Mawiya.

Mavli, India: see Nathdwara.

Mavrommati, Greece: see Messene.

Mavroneri River, Greece: see Cephisus River.

Mavropotamos River, Greece: see Acheron River.

Mavrosouli, Greece: see Polykastron.

Maw (mô), NW state (myosaship) (□ 741; pop. 6,775), Southern Shan State, Upper Burma, on edge of Shan Plateau; ⊙ Myogyi. Largely hilly and barren; drained by Zawgyi R.

Mawa (mä′wä), village, Eastern Prov., N Belgian Congo, on railroad and 120 mi. E of Buta; cotton ginning; coffee plantations. Also cotton gins at Mawa Geitu (gā′tōō), 12 mi. NNE.

Mawa Geitu, Belgian Congo: see Mawa.

Mawana (mŭvä′nŭ), town (pop. 12,194), Meerut dist., NW Uttar Pradesh, India, near distributory of Upper Ganges Canal, 15 mi. ENE of Meerut; wheat, millet, sugar cane, oilseeds.

Mawchi (môchē′), village, Karenni State, Upper Burma, on Loikaw-Toungoo road and 50 mi. E of Toungoo. Major tungsten and tin-mining center; producing 10% of world's tungsten.

Mawddach River (mou′dhäkh), Merioneth, Wales, rises 10 mi. NE of Dolgelley, flows 21 mi. S and W to Cardigan Bay of Irish Sea at Barmouth. Receives Wnion R. just NW of Dolgelley.

Mawei, China: see Mamoi.

Mawenzi, peak, Tanganyika: see Kilimanjaro.

Mawiya or **Mawiyah** (mă′wĭyŭ), town (pop. 1,000), Taiz prov., SW Yemen, on central plateau, 20 mi. E of Taiz; alt. 4,000 ft. Center of agr. area (coffee, millet, citrus fruit). Sometimes spelled Mawya and Maviya.

Mawkmai (môkmī′), S state (sawbwaship) (□ 2,803; pop. 38,796) of Southern Shan State, Upper Burma; ⊙ Mawkmai, village 55 mi. SE of Taunggyi. Astride Salween R., on Thailand border; central plain well irrigated (rice); hill ranges (teak); tobacco plantations.

Mawlaik (mô′lĭk′), town (pop. 2,278), ⊙ Upper Chindwin dist., Upper Burma; river port on right bank of Chindwin R.; 23°38′N 94°25′E; in mtn. and jungle country.

Mawphlang, India: see Maoflang.

Mawr (mour), agr. parish (pop. 1,721), W Glamorgan, Wales, 7 mi. N of Swansea.

Mawya, Yemen: see Mawiya.

Max, city (pop. 465), McLean co., central N.Dak., 30 mi. S of Minot.

Maxbass (măks′băs′), village (pop. 259), Bottineau co., N N.Dak., 32 mi. WSW of Bottineau.

Maxcanú (mäskänōō′), town (pop. 3,586), Yucatan, SE Mexico, on railroad and 36 mi. SW of Mérida; henequen-growing center. Oxcintok ruins (NE) and Calcehtoc grotto (E) near by.

Maxen (mäk′sŭn), village (pop. 897), Saxony, E central Germany, in Saxonian Switzerland, 10 mi. SSE of Dresden. Scene (1759) in Seven Years War of victory of the Austrians under Daun over the Prussians.

Maxéville (mäksāvēl′), NNW suburb (pop. 3,895) of Nancy, Meurthe-et-Moselle dept., NE France, on Marne-Rhine Canal; blast furnaces, breweries, glassworks, mfg. (soap, yeast). Iron mines, limestone quarries.

Maxeys (măk′sēz), town (pop. 204), Oglethorpe co., NE Ga., 19 mi. SE of Athens.

Maxfield, town (pop. 26), Penobscot co., S central Maine, 25 mi. ENE of Dover-Foxcroft; agr., lumbering.

Maxhütte (mäks′hü″tŭ), village (commune pop. 3,047), Upper Palatinate, E central Bavaria, Germany, 9 mi. S of Schwandorf; ironworks. Lignite mined at Ibenthann (pop. 172), 2 mi. SE.

Maxhütte, steelworks, Germany: see Unterwellenborn-Röblitz.

Maxilly-sur-Léman, France: see Évian-les-Bains.

Maximiliansau (măk″sēmēl′yänsou′), village (pop. 2,351), Rhenish Palatinate, W Germany, on the Rhine (rail bridge) and 5 mi. WSW of Karlsruhe; tobacco.

Máximo Gómez (mäk′sēmō gō′mĕs), town (pop. 3,770), Matanzas prov., W Cuba, 14 mi. SE of Cárdenas; rail junction in agr. region (sugar cane fruit, sisal, cattle).

Máximo River, Camagüey prov., E Cuba, rises at S foot of the Sierra de Cubitas, flows c.35 mi. ENE to N coast 15 mi. NW of Nuevitas.

Maxinkuckee, Lake (măk″sĭn-kŭ′kē), SW Marshall co., N Ind., at Culver; c.3 mi. long; resort.

Max Meadows, farming village (1940 pop. 649), Wythe co., SW Va., 7 mi. E of Wytheville, in rich agr. section.

Max Paredes (mäks′ pärā′dĕs), military post (Fortín Max Paredes), Santa Cruz dept., E Bolivia, in the Chaco, 115 mi. SSE of San José, on Paraguay border. Also Maximiliano Paredes or simply Paredes. Boundary marker established (1938) in Chaco Peace Conference.

Max Patch Mountains, N.C.-Tenn.: see Bald Mountains.

Maxton (măk′stŭn), town (pop. 1,974), Robeson co., S N.C., 6 mi. SE of Laurinburg; sawmilling. Seat of Presbyterian Jr. Col. for Men.

Maxula-Radès (mäksülä′-rädĕs′), town (pop. 11,-117), N Tunisia, on S shore of Gulf of Tunis at mouth of Miliane R., 6 mi. ESE of Tunis; artisan industries (carpets, furniture, baskets, footwear) in native village (Radès); bathing resort (Maxula) with sandy beach; orchards and truck farms.

Maxville, village (pop. 804), SE Ont., 19 mi. N of Cornwall; dairying, mixed farming.

Maxwell. 1 Village (1940 pop. 543), Colusa co., N central Calif., 10 mi. NW of Colusa; dairying. **2** Town (pop. 802), Story co., central Iowa, 23 mi. NNE of Des Moines; makes concrete blocks. **3** Village (pop. 347), Lincoln co., central Nebr., 13 mi. ESE of North Platte city, near Platte R.; hay-shipping point. **4** Village (pop. 404), Colfax co., NE N.Mex., on Canadian R., near Sangre de Cristo Mts., and 26 mi. S of Raton; alt. 5,909 ft. Shipping point in irrigated region; sheep, cattle, sugar beets.

Maxwell's Hill, Malaya: see Taiping.

Maxwelltown, Scotland: see Dumfries.

Maxwelton House, seat and 17th-cent. mansion in Glencairn parish, W Dumfries, Scotland, on the Cairn and 2 mi. ESE of Moniaive; Annie Laurie b. here. Just N is agr. village of Kirkland, site of early-17th-cent. Glencairn Castle. Annie Laurie is said to be buried in near-by Glencairn Church.

May. 1 Town (pop. 143), Harper co., NW Okla., 22 mi. WNW of Woodward, and on North Canadian R., in grain and livestock area. **2** Village (pop. c.500), Brown co., central Texas, 19 mi. N of Brownwood, in rich farm area.

May, Al-, Egypt: see Mai, El.

May, Cape, N.J.: see Cape May, county.

May, Isle of, island (1 mi. long) at mouth of Firth of Forth, off SE Fifeshire, Scotland, 6 mi. SE of Crail. Site of lighthouse (56°11'N 2°33'W). There are ruins of 13th-cent. priory of St. Adrian, killed here by Danes in 9th cent. It was formerly a place of pilgrimage, known as the Holy Wells.
Maya, La, Cuba: see LA MAYA.
Maya Dag or **Mahya Dag** (both: mäyä' dä), Turkish *Maya Dağ*, peak (3,340 ft.), Turkey in Europe, in Istranca Mts., near Bulgarian line, 18 mi. from Black Sea.
Mayadin, Sryia: see MEYADIN.
Mayafarkin, Turkey: see SILVAN.
Mayaguana (mäügwä'nü), island (27 mi. long, 2–6 mi. wide) and district (□ 96; pop. 591), SE Bahama Isls., bet. Acklins Isl. (W) and Caicos Isls. (E), 315 mi. SE of Nassau; 22°23'N 73°W. The isl. is low and wooded, with several ponds along the coast, where salt is raked. Main settlements are Abraham's Bay (S center) and Pirates' Well (NW). Was settled from the Turks Isls. Site for a naval base was ceded to U.S. in 1940. Formerly called Mariguana (mărĭgwä'nü), the original Indian name.
Mayaguana Passage, Atlantic channel, S Bahama Isls., c.25 mi. wide bet. Mayaguana isl. (E) and cays off E Acklins Isl. (W).
Mayagüez (mīägwĕs'), city (pop. 58,944), W Puerto Rico, port on Mona Passage, 70 mi. WSW of San Juan; 18°12'N 67°8'W. Third largest city of the isl.; shipping, processing, trading center in fertile agr. country (sugar, coffee, fruit, vegetables, tobacco, honey); rail and road hub. Here are concentrated well-known embroidery and needlework industries; sugar milling and refining; also mfg. of cigars, beer, alcohol, rum, candy, macaroni, furniture, tiles, soap, agr. implements. Seat of a senatorial dist. A port of entry with fine deep harbor. Of distinctly Sp. character, its fine bldgs. include a customhouse, church of Nuestra Señora de la Candelaria (rebuilt 1918), Col. of Arts and Mechanics, and agr. experiment station. City was founded 1760. Severely damaged by 1918 earthquake and tidal wave. Airport is 3½ mi. N. The extensive Las Mesas limonite deposits are near by.
Mayajigua (mīähē'gwä), town (pop. 1,583), Las Villas prov., central Cuba, on railroad and 33 mi. SE of Caibarién; resort with mineral springs.
Mayakonda (mä'yŭkŏndŭ), town (pop. 2,702), Chitaldrug dist., N Mysore, India, 22 mi. WNW of Chitaldrug; cotton ginning, hand-loom weaving.
Mayakovski or **Mayakovskiy** (mīŭkôf'skē), village (1939 pop. over 500), W Georgian SSR, 14 mi. SSE of Kutaisi; vineyards. Until 1940, Bagdadi or Bagdati.
Mayak-Salyn, Russian SFSR: see PRIMORSKOYE, Crimea.
Mayala (mäyä'lä), village, Leopoldville prov., SW Belgian Congo, on right bank of Kwango R. and 185 mi. SW of Inongo; hardwood lumbering.
Mayâls (mīäls'), town (pop. 1,988), Lérida prov., NE Spain, 18 mi. SSW of Lérida; olive-oil processing; sheep raising; cereals, almonds, honey.
Mayamay, Iran: see MAIAMAI.
Maya-Maya, Fr. Equatorial Africa, site of airport for BRAZZAVILLE.
Maya Mountains (mī'ä), mountain range in SW Br. Honduras, 50 mi. long (SW-NE); average alt. 2–3,000 ft. Rise to 3,681 ft. in Victoria Peak of the Cockscomb Mts., 30 mi. SW of Stann Creek. Timber.
Mayang (mä'yäng'), town, ⊙ Mayang co. (pop. 145,798), W Hunan prov., China, near Kweichow line, 15 mi. N of Chihkiang; tung oil, cotton, tea, rice. Lead and zinc mining near by.
Mayapán (mīäpän'), town (pop. 628), Yucatan, SE Mexico, 24 mi. SSE of Mérida, in henequen-growing area. Was capital of Maya empire; abandoned during great civil war of confederation. Many archaeological remains; central pyramid, idols, temple columns.
Mayarí (mīärē'), town (pop. 4,519), Oriente prov., E Cuba, on small Mayarí R., near Nipe Bay (Atlantic), and 40 mi. ESE of Holguín. Lumbering and agr. center (sugar cane, tobacco, fruit), in important mining region (chromium and iron refined at Felton, 8 mi. NE; nickel at Nicaro, 6 mi. E). The sugar central Preston is 7 mi. NNE.
Mayarí River, Oriente prov., E Cuba, rises NE of Alto Songo, flows 50 mi. N, past Mayarí, to Nipe Bay. Navigable for small boats below Mayarí.
Maya River (mī'ŭ), in central Khabarovsk Territory and SE Yakut Autonomous SSR, Russian SFSR, rises in N Dzhugdzhur Range, flows SSW, past Nelkan (head of navigation; 340 mi. from mouth), and NW to Aldan R. at Ust-Maya, 190 mi. ESE of Yakutsk; 660 mi. long. Ice-free May-Oct.
Mayaro (mīä'rō, mää'rō), county (□ 145.69; pop. 4,196), SE Trinidad, B.W.I., bordering on the Atlantic. Forms, together with St. David, St. Andrew, and Nariva, the administrative dist. of Eastern Counties.
Mayaro, village, E Trinidad, B.W.I., on N Mayaro Bay, 30 mi. E of San Fernando, in coconut-growing region. Fine beaches along the coast.
Mayaro Bay, along SE coast of Trinidad, B.W.I., ribbon of fine sand beaches, c.12 mi. long (N–S), lined by coconut palms.
Mayavaram (mä'yŭvŭrŭm), since 1949 officially **Mayuram** (mäyōō'rŭm), city (pop. 32,670), Tanjore dist., SE Madras, India, on arm of Cauvery R. delta and 40 mi. NE of Tanjore; rail junction; rice milling, cotton and silk weaving, pith carving of temple models; brass and copper vessels. Hindu pilgrimage center (Sivaite temple).
Maybee, village (pop. 428), Monroe co., extreme SE Mich., 9 mi. NW of Monroe, in farm area.
Maybeury (mā"bĕ'rē), coal-mining village (pop. 1,646, with adjoining Switchback), McDowell co., S W.Va., 13 mi. ESE of Welch.
Maybole (mābōl'), burgh (1931 pop. 4,212; 1951 census 4,766), SW central Ayrshire, Scotland, 8 mi. S of Ayr; agr. market, with mfg. of shoes and agr. machinery. It was once ⊙ of Carrick, domain of the Bruces. Red Lion Inn was scene of 3-day theological contest (1561) bet. John Knox and abbot of 13th-cent. Crossraguel Abbey (remains, 2 mi. SW of Maybole).
Maybrook, village (pop. 1,316), Orange co., SE N.Y., 10 mi. WSW of Newburgh; rail center; mfg. of clothing. Inc. 1925.
Maydan, Al, Iraq: see MAIDAN, AL.
Maydan Ikbis, Syria: see MEIDAN EKBES.
Maydanpek, Yugoslavia: see MAJDAN PEK.
Maydi, Yemen: see MIDI.
Maydos, Turkey: see ECEABAT.
Mayen (mī'ŭn), town (pop. 12,739), in former Prussian Rhine Prov., W Germany, after 1945 in Rhineland-Palatinate, in the Eifel, 16 mi. E of Coblenz; mfg. (textiles, leather goods, millstones). Basalt quarrying. Has Romanesque-Gothic church, 13th-cent. castle. Of Celtic origin, it became a Roman road station. Passed to electors of Trier in 13th cent.
Mayence, Germany: see MAINZ.
Mayenne (mäyĕn'), department (□ 2,012; pop. 256,317), in Maine, W France; ⊙ Laval. A generally level region, with hills in NE. Drained by Mayenne R. and its tributaries. Agr. (wheat, barley, sugar beet, apples, potatoes), dairying, flax and hemp growing. Chief towns: Laval, Mayenne, Château-Gontier.
Mayenne, town (pop. 6,514), Mayenne dept., W France, on both banks of Mayenne R. and 17 mi. NNE of Laval; agr. trade center; makes cotton goods (handkerchiefs), cider, and cheese. Has 13th-cent. feudal castle and 12th-cent. early Gothic church (damaged in Second World War).
Mayenne River, Mayenne and Maine-et-Loire depts., W France, rises on slopes of Mont des Avaloirs 3 mi. E of Pré-en-Pail, flows W, then S, past Couptrain, Mayenne (head of navigation), Laval, and Château-Gontier, joining the Sarthe above Angers to form the Maine; 125 mi. long. Receives Varenne and Oudon rivers (right).
Mayer (mī'ŭr), village (pop. 153), Carver co., S central Minn., on South Fork Crow R. and 32 mi. W of Minneapolis; dairy products.
Mayerling (mī'ŭrlĭng), village, E Lower Austria, 15 mi. SW of Vienna, 8 mi. WNW from Baden, and on Schwechat R. Here is hunting lodge (now a convent) where Crown Prince Rudolph met his mysterious death (1889).
Mayersville (mī'ŭrzvĭl), village (pop. c.150), ⊙ Issaquena co., W Miss., on the Mississippi and 34 mi. S of Greenville, in cotton-growing area.
Mayerthorpe (mā'ŭrthôrp"), village (pop. 303), central Alta., 70 mi. WNW of Edmonton; coal mining, lumbering, mixed farming.
Mayes, county (□ 680; pop. 19,743), NE Okla.; ⊙ Pryor. Intersected by Neosho R. (impounded here by Grand River Dam). Flat lands in W, rising to the Ozarks in E. Stock raising, agr. (corn, cotton, oats); some oil wells; timber. Formed 1907.
Mayesville, town (pop. 706), Sumter co., central S.C., 8 mi. ENE of Sumter, near Black R.
Mayet (mäyā'), village (pop. 1,784), Sarthe dept., W France, 17 mi. S of Le Mans; dairy and flour products; mushrooms; peat extracting.
Mayet-de-Montagne, Le (lŭ mäyā'-dŭ-mōtä'nyŭ), village (pop. 1,051), Allier dept., central France, on N slope of Bois Noirs, 12 mi. S of Lapalisse; livestock market; quarries of building material and granite for tombstones.
Mayetta, city (pop. 247), Jackson co., NE Kansas, 20 mi. N of Topeka; trading point in stock and grain area. Potawatomi Indian Reservation is W.
Mayevitsa, range, Yugoslavia: see MAJEVICA.
Mayfa'ah, Wadi, Aden: see MEIFA'A, WADI.
Mayfah, Aden: see MEIFA.
Mayfair, fashionable residential district of Westminster, London, England, N of the Thames, 1.5 mi. WNW of Charing Cross, bounded by Piccadilly (S), Bond St. (E), Oxford St. (N), and Park Lane and Hyde Park (W). Named for fair held here in May from 16th to 19th cent. District includes Grosvenor Square; most of Mayfair was taken over by U.S. armed forces hq. installations in Second World War.
Mayfair, W suburb of Johannesburg, S Transvaal, U. of So. Afr.
Mayfair Mine, township, Bulawayo prov., S Southern Rhodesia, in Matabeleland, 14 mi. NNW of Filabusi; former gold-mining center.
Mayfield. 1 Town, Derby, England: see ASHBOURNE. 2 Town and parish (pop. 3,080), NE Sussex, England, 8 mi. S of Tunbridge Wells; agr. market. Has 15th-cent. church and modern convent incorporating parts of 14th-cent. palace of archbishops of Canterbury.
Mayfield. 1 City (pop. 134), Sumner co., S Kansas, 8 mi. W of Wellington, in wheat area. 2 City (pop. 8,990), ⊙ Graves co., SW Ky., on Mayfield Creek and 22 mi. S of Paducah, near Kentucky Reservoir. Tobacco and mule market; industrial and trade center in agr. (wheat, corn, dark tobacco) area; mfg. of clothing, woolens, furniture, lamp bases, bricks, food products, snuff; lumber milling; poultry hatchery. Has airport. Local cemetery has curious Woolridge monuments (stone figures of Woolridge family, friends, and animal pets). Nearby site of Civil War Camp Beauregard is marked. City founded 1823. 3 Village (pop. 761), Fulton co., E central N.Y., on Sacandaga Reservoir, 6 mi. NE of Gloversville; makes leather gloves. 4 Village (pop. 1,926), Butler co., SW Ohio, near Middletown. 5 Village (pop. 805), Cuyahoga co., N Ohio, 13 mi. E of downtown Cleveland, and on Chagrin R., just S of Mayfield Heights. 6 Industrial borough (pop. 2,373), Lackawanna co., NE Pa., 11 mi. NE of Scranton; anthracite; mfg. (silk, clothing). Founded c.1840. 7 Town (pop. 390), Sanpete co., central Utah, 10 mi. SSW of Manti; alt. 5,500 ft.; wool, wheat, hay.
Mayfield Creek, SW Ky., rises in SW Calloway co., flows generally N, past Mayfield, and W to the Mississippi just S of Wickliffe; c.70 mi. long.
Mayfield Heights, residential city (pop. 5,807), Cuyahoga co., N Ohio, 13 mi. E of Cleveland. Inc. 1925.
Mayflower, town (pop. 293), Faulkner co., central Ark., 18 mi. NNW of Little Rock, near Arkansas R.
Mayhill, village, Otero co., S N.Mex., in E foothills of Sacramento Mts., 60 mi. W of Artesia, in Lincoln Natl. Forest; alt. c.6,800 ft. Lumber; sheep, fruit, truck.
Maykain, Kazakh SSR: see MAIKAIN.
Maykop, Russian SFSR: see MAIKOP.
Maykor, Russian SFSR: see MAIKOR.
Maylands, town (pop. 8,429), SW Western Australia, NE residential suburb of Perth.
Maylisay, Kazakh SSR: see MAILISAI.
Maymyo (māmyō'), town (pop. 16,586), Mandalay dist., Upper Burma, 25 mi. E of Mandalay and on railroad to Lashio; alt. c.3,500 ft. Center for trade with N Shan State and Yunnan (tea, tobacco, cotton goods, iron, foodstuffs); sericulture station; army cantonment. Summer seat of govt.
Mayna, Russian SFSR: see MAINA.
Maynard (mā'nŭrd). 1 Town (pop. 216), Randolph co., NE Ark., 12 mi. NNE of Pocahontas, near Mo. line. 2 Town (pop. 455), Fayette co., NE Iowa, 7 mi. NNE of Oelwein; dairying; limestone quarry. 3 Town (pop. 6,978), Middlesex co., NE central Mass., on Assabet R. and 21 mi. WNW of Boston; woolens, chemicals, beverages. Settled 1638, inc. 1871. 4 Village (pop. 507), Chippewa co., SW Minn., on small tributary of Minnesota R. and 13 mi. E of Montevideo, in grain, livestock, poultry area; dairy products.
Maynardville, village (pop. c.500), ⊙ Union co., NE Tenn., 20 mi. NNE of Knoxville, in fertile farm area.
Maynas, province, Peru: see IQUITOS.
Mayne Island (□ 9), SW B.C., Gulf Isls., in Strait of Georgia just off Vancouver Isl., bet. Galiano Isl. (NW) and Saturna Isl. (SE), 30 mi. S of Vancouver; 6 mi. long, 1–3 mi. wide; lumbering, farming. Village is at NW end.
Maynooth (mānōōth', mā'nōōth), Gaelic *Magh Nuadhad*, town (pop. 572), NE Co. Kildare, Ireland, on Royal Canal and 14 mi. W of Dublin; agr. market (cattle, potatoes). St. Patrick's Col., founded 1795, is principal R.C. theological col. of Ireland and constituent of Natl. Univ. of Ireland. It has bldgs. designed by Pugin. Remains of Maynooth Castle date from c.1176; in 1647 castle was dismantled. Near town is anc. round tower.
Mayo, Cape Verde Isls.: see MAIO.
Mayo (mā'ō), Gaelic *Mhuigheo*, county (□ 2,084.3; pop. 148,120), Connacht, NW Ireland; ⊙ Castlebar. Bounded by Co. Galway (S), the Atlantic (W and N), cos. Sligo (NE) and Roscommon (E). Drained by Moy R. and other streams. Co. borders S on Lough Corrib; loughs Mask, Conn, Cullin, and Carra are largest lakes. Surface is wild and mountainous in W, rises to 2,646 ft. in Nephin Beg Range, leveling toward fertile Moy R. valley (E). Coastline is bold and rugged, deeply indented by Clew, Blacksod, Broad Haven, and Killala bays. Largest isls. are Achill and Clare. Some marble and iron are worked. Sea fisheries and Moy R. salmon fishery are important, as is agr. (cattle, hogs, poultry; potatoes, oats). Industries include woolen milling, mfg. of shoes, hosiery, clothing, thread, furniture, toy mfg. Besides Castlebar, other towns are Westport, Ballina, Claremorris, Ballinrobe, Cong, Killala, Newport, Swinford, Louisburgh. There are several round towers, anc. castles, and monastic remains.
Mayo, Gaelic *Maigheo na Sacsan*, agr. village (district pop. 639), S central Co. Mayo, Ireland,

10 mi. SE of Castlebar; cattle, potatoes. Has slight remains of univ. founded in 7th cent. by St. Colman.

Mayo (mā'ō). **1** Town (pop. 679), ⊙ Lafayette co., N Fla., c.60 mi. WNW of Gainesville; lumbering, limestone quarrying. **2** Village, Spartanburg co., NW S.C., near Pacolet R., 10 mi. NNE of Spartanburg; yarn mill.

Mayo, 1 de, Argentina: see PRIMERO DE MAYO.

Mayo, 2 de, province, Peru: see LA UNIÓN, city, Huánuco dept.

Mayo, 25 de. **1** Department, Río Negro natl. territory, Argentina: see MAQUINCHAO. **2** Department, San Juan prov., Argentina: see VILLA SANTA ROSA.

Mayo, 25 de, city, Argentina: see VEINTICINCO DE MAYO.

Mayo, 25 de (vāntēsēng'kō dā mī'ō), town (pop. 2,000), Florida dept., S central Uruguay, near the Arroyo Santa Lucía Chico, 13 mi. SW of Florida; winegrowing, dairying; wheat, corn, cattle, sheep. Granite and limestone deposits near by. Its rail station is Isla Mala, 2 mi. ENE.

Mayodan (mā'ōdăn"), town (pop. 2,246), Rockingham co., N N.C., 27 mi. NNE of Winston-Salem; cotton milling. Settled 1894; inc. 1897.

Mayo-Darlé (mā'yō-därlā'), village, Adamaoua region, W Fr., Cameroons, 28 mi. SW of Banyo, near Br. Cameroons border; tin mining.

Mayo-Kebbi, region, Fr. Equatorial Africa: see BONGOR.

Mayo-Kebbi River (māyō-kĕbē'), in W Chad territory, Fr. Equatorial Africa, and N Fr. Cameroons, issues from Fianga and Tickem swamps near Fianga, flows c.150 mi. WSW, forming rapids and lakes, to the Benoué (Benue) 12 mi. ESE of Garoua. Through this watercourse, Logone R. is occasionally in communication in flood time with the Benoué. Sometimes spelled Mayo-Kabi; its upper course is also called Mayo-Pé (pā').

Mayo Landing, village (pop. estimate 250), central Yukon, on Stewart R. and 110 mi. ESE of Dawson; 63°36'N 135°53'W; center of silver- and lead-mining, fur-trapping region; airfield, radio and weather station, Royal Canadian Mounted Police post, hosp.

Mayombé, Africa: see MAYUMBE.

Mayon, Mount (māyōn'), active volcano (7,926 ft.), Albay prov., SE Luzon, Philippines, 10 mi. NNW of Legaspi; known for its perfect conical shape. Base of cone is 80 mi. in circumference. Last erupted 1947.

Mayo-Pé River, Fr. Equatorial Africa: see MAYO-KEBBI RIVER.

Mayor, Isla, Spain: see ISLA MAYOR.

Mayor Drummond, town (pop. estimate 500), N Mendoza prov., Argentina, in Mendoza R. valley, on railroad and 10 mi. S of Mendoza, adjoining Luján; wine-making center.

Mayorga (mīôr'gä), town (pop. 2,333), Valladolid prov., N central Spain, 24 mi. NNW of Medina de Ríoseco; flour milling; stock raising; cereals, wine, fruit.

Mayorga, Tonga: see VAVAU.

Mayori, Latvia: see RIGAS JURMALA.

Mayor Island, uninhabited volcanic island, New Zealand, in Bay of Plenty, N N.Isl., E of Coromandel peninsula, 22 mi. N of Tauranga; 3 mi. long, 2.5 mi. wide; deep-sea fishing.

Mayo River (mī'ō), in Patagonia, Comodoro Rivadavia military zone, Argentina, rises in the Andes at Chile border, flows c.100 mi. E to Senguerr R. 35 mi. WSW of Sarmiento.

Mayo River, NW Mexico, rises in Chihuahua NE of Ocampo, flows SW into Sonora, past Navojoa, and Etchojoa, to a lagoon inlet of Gulf of California, 5 mi. SW of Huatabampo; c.220 mi. long. Used for irrigation; along lower course chick-peas are produced on large scale for export to Spain.

Mayo River, San Martín dept., N central Peru, rises in E foothills of the Andes at 5°30'S, flows c.150 mi. SE to Huallaga R. at Shapaja, 9 mi. SE of Tarapoto.

Mayo River (mā'ō), Va. and N.C., rises in the piedmont in Patrick co., S Va.; flows SE past Stuart, Va., into N.C., and S to Dan R. just E of Madison; c 45 mi. long.

Mayotte Island (māyôt') (□ 137, including adjacent islets; pop. c.17,000), easternmost of the Comoro Isls., in Mozambique Channel of Indian Ocean, 280 mi. WSW of N tip of Madagascar; 25 mi. long, 10 mi. wide; rises to 2,165 ft. Well watered and fertile, it produces sugar, rum, sisal, vanilla, and essential oils (notably citronella and ilang-ilang). Main town and ⊙ Comoro Isls., Dzaoudzi, is part of adjacent Pamanzi islet, c.2 mi. off NE shore. Populated by Moslems of mixed African, Arab, and Malagasy stock. Moslems from Shiraz arrived here in 16th cent. Under sultan of Anjouan 1835, Fr. protectorate 1843 (while attached to Réunion); attached to Madagascar 1908.

Mayoumba, Fr. Equatorial Africa: see MAYUMBA.

Maypearl, town (pop. 373), Ellis co., N central Texas, 11 mi. SW of Waxahachie; rail point in agr. area.

May Pen (mā' pĕn"), town (pop. 6,038), ⊙ Clarendon parish, S Jamaica, on Minho R., on Kingston–Montego Bay RR and 30 mi. W of Kingston; 17°58'N 77°14'W. Rail junction, road and marketing center; citrus processing plant, canneries, rope factory.

Mayport, village (1940 pop. 954), Duval co., NE Fla., 14 mi. E of Jacksonville, on St. Johns R. near its mouth on the Atlantic; fishing.

Mayraira Point (mīrāē'rä), northernmost point of Luzon, Philippines, in Ilocos Norte prov., near entrance to Babuyan Channel in S.China Sea; 18°40'N 120°50'E.

Mayrán, Laguna de (lägōō'nä dā mīrän'), depression in LAGUNA DISTRICT of Coahuila, N Mexico, 45 mi. E of Torreón; 25 mi. long, c.15 mi. wide. Contains water only during rainy period, when Nazas R. flows to it.

Mayreau Island (mī'rō, mā'rō), islet (□ 1; pop. 154), S Grenadines, dependency of St. Vincent, B.W.I., 38 mi. SSW of Kingstown; 12°39'N 61°23'W. Sometimes called Mayaro or Mayero.

Mayrhofen or **Mairhofen** (both: mīr'hōfůn), town (pop. 2,504), Tyrol, W Austria, on Ziller R. and 22 mi. ESE of Innsbruck, bet. Zillertal and Tuxer Alps; rail terminus; processes magnesite mined in the vicinity. Mayrhofen is the main town of the ZILLERTAL.

Mayrink, Brazil: see MAIRINQUE.

Mayrouba, Lebanon: see MEIRUBA.

Mayrubah, Lebanon: see MEIRUBA.

Mayschoss (mī'shôs), village (pop. 975), in former Prussian Rhine Prov., W Germany, after 1945 in Rhineland-Palatinate, on the Ahr and 2.5 mi. WSW of Ahrweiler; known for its red wine.

Maysí, Cape, Cuba: see MAISÍ, CAPE.

Mayskiy, Russian SFSR: see MAISKI.

Mayskoye, Russian SFSR: see MAISKOYE.

Mays Landing, resort village (pop. 1,301), ⊙ Atlantic co., S N.J., on Great Egg Harbor R. (water power) and 16 mi. WNW of Atlantic City; bricks, boats; poultry, truck. Settled c.1710.

May-sur-Orne (mā-sür-ôrn'), village (pop. 329), Calvados dept., NW France, near the Orne, 5 mi. S of Caen; iron mining, cheese mfg.

Maysville. **1** Town (pop. 533), Banks and Jackson counties, NE Ga., 14 mi. E of Gainesville; textile mfg. **2** Town (pop. 70), Scott co., E Iowa, 10 mi. NW of Davenport, in agr. area. **3** City (pop. 8,632), ⊙ Mason co., NE Ky., on left bank (levee) of the Ohio (bridged here to Aberdeen, Ohio) and 50 mi. SE of Cincinnati, in outer Bluegrass agr. region. Trade and industrial center, with air, rail, and river connections; mfg. of power transmission equipment, tin cans, bicycles, motorcycles, evaporated milk, soft drinks, gasoline, bricks, cotton yarns, clothing, cigars; tobacco warehouses and curing plants, distilleries, nurseries. Daniel Boone and his wife ran a tavern here (c.1786–89). U. S. Grant attended a local school. Site of Kenton's station, a stockaded trading post, is near by. Settled c.1782 by Simon Kenton and others as Limestone; established 1787 by Va. legislature; inc. 1833. **4** City (pop. 973), ⊙ De Kalb co., NW Mo., 26 mi. ENE of St. Joseph; corn, wheat, poultry. Settled 1845. **5** Town (pop. 818), Jones co., E N.C., 18 mi. SW of New Bern; sawmilling. **6** Town (pop. 1,294), Garvin co., S central Okla., 12 mi. WNW of Pauls Valley, in cotton, wheat, and corn area; cotton ginning; grain elevators.

Maytown, village (1940 pop. 562), Lancaster co., SE Pa., near Susquehanna R., 15 mi. W of Lancaster, in agr. area.

Mayumba (māyōōmbä'), village, SW Gabon, Fr. Equatorial Africa, at mouth of M'Banio lagoon (inlet of the Atlantic), 50 mi. SSW of Tchibanga; small fishing port and customs station. French traders here in 17th–18th cent. Sometimes spelled Mayoumba.

Mayumbe (māyōōm'bů, māyōōmbā') or **Mayombé** (māyōbā'), region in W central Africa, extending roughly bet. the Atlantic coast and the Crystal Mts., N of mouth of Congo R. and S of Kouilou R. Its rich agr. and forest resources (coffee, cacao, palm products, bananas, rubber, hardwoods) are tapped in Belgian Congo by Boma-Tshela RR, with port of Boma as the outlet; some gold is also mined there. In Fr. Equatorial Africa lumber, copper, and lead are exported by Brazzaville–Pointe-Noire RR.

Mayum Chu, river, Tibet: see BRAHMAPUTRA RIVER.

Mayu Peninsula (mŭyōō'), on Arakan coast, Lower Burma, NW of Akyab, bet. Naaf (Pakistan line) and Mayu rivers; scene of fighting in Second World War. The **Mayu Range,** 70 mi. long, forms the peninsular backbone and rises to over 2,000 ft. The **Mayu River,** 70 mi. long, forms E side of the peninsula; it flows SSE, past Buthidaung (head of navigation) and Rathedaung to Bay of Bengal, NW of Akyab.

Mayuram, India: see MAYAVARAM.

Mayurbhanj (mŭyōōr'bŭnj), district (□ 4,034; pop. 990,977), NE Orissa, India; ⊙ Baripada. Bordered NE by West Bengal, N by Bihar; low alluvial tract (E); large hilly section (center), with extensive sal and bamboo forests. Rice is chief crop; corn, oilseeds also grown; lac, honey, beeswax from forests. Valuable iron-ore deposits worked (N); limestone, pottery clay. Formerly a princely state in Bengal States of Eastern States agency; acceded 1948 to India; inc. 1949 into Orissa as a dist.

Mayview, town (pop. 268), Lafayette co., W central Mo., 9 mi. S of Lexington.

Mayville, France: see GONFREVILLE-L'ORCHER.

Mayville. **1** Village (pop. 888), Tuscola co., E Mich., 3 mi. ESE of Saginaw, in agr. area; wood-products mfg.; creamery, hatchery. **2** Resort village (pop. 1,492), ⊙ Chautauqua co., extreme W N.Y., at NW end of Chautauqua L., 18 mi. SW of Dunkirk; mfg. of furniture, machinery, food products; printing. Inc. 1830. **3** City (pop. 1,790), Traill co., E N.Dak., 50 mi. NW of Fargo and on Goose R. Trade center; grain, livestock, dairy products. State teachers col. Settled 1881, inc. 1885. **4** City (pop. 3,010), Dodge co., S central Wis., on Rock R. and 15 mi. ENE of Beaver Dam, in farming, dairying, and resort area; mfg. (shoes, luggage, metal products, furniture, dairy products, canned foods); iron mines. Horicon Natl. Wildlife Refuge is near by. Settled c.1844, inc. 1885.

Maywood. **1** City (pop. 13,292), Los Angeles co., S Calif., suburb 6 mi. SSE of downtown Los Angeles, in industrial dist.; automobile-assembling, steel, and food-processing plants; residential. Founded 1920, inc. 1924. **2** Residential village (pop. 27,473), Cook co., NE Ill., W suburb of Chicago, on Des Plaines R., in industrial area; bottling works; mfg. of tin cans, water softener, branding irons, tubing. Chicago Lutheran Theological Seminary for men is here. Inc. 1881. **3** Village (pop. 409), Frontier co., S Nebr., 33 mi. S of North Platte; grain, livestock, poultry. **4** Residential borough (pop. 8,667), Bergen co., NE N.J., just NNW of Hackensack; chemicals, pharmaceuticals. Inc. 1894. **5** Suburban village (1940 pop. 1,226), Albany co., E N.Y., 8 mi. NW of downtown Albany.

Mayya, Russian SFSR: see MAIYA.

Maza (mä'sä), town (pop. estimate 1,000), W Buenos Aires prov., Argentina, near La Pampa line, 40 mi. NW of Carhué; wheat, corn, alfalfa, sheep, cattle.

Maza (mā'zů), village (pop. 82), Towner co., N N.Dak., 8 mi. S of Cando, in wheat and livestock area.

Mazabuka (mäzäbōō'kä), township (pop. 744; including suburbs, 1,212), Southern Prov., Northern Rhodesia, on railroad and 190 mi. NE of Livingstone; agr. and livestock center; cotton ginning; tobacco, corn, wheat, dairy products. Hq. of depts. of agr., veterinary services, and African education. Site of central agr. research station.

Mazaca, Turkey: see KAYSERI, city.

Mazagan (mäzägän'), city (pop. 40,318), Casablanca region, W Fr. Morocco, fishing port and bathing resort on the Atlantic, 55 mi. SW of Casablanca; 33°16'N 8°30'W. Ships early fruits and vegetables (grown in coastal area), cereals, eggs, and poultry from the Doukkala (Mazagan's fertile hinterland); also almonds, wool, and skins. Mfg. consists of fish canning and salting, palm-fiber processing, soap making. Situated on a bay sheltered by a natural breakwater, port has lost importance since development (after 1912) of Casablanca harbor. It is now used chiefly for coastal shipping. The mile-long beach is E of harbor. Founded 1502 and held by Portuguese until 1569, it was after 1541 their only stronghold on Moroccan coast. The walled Portuguese city is now surrounded by the newer town, built mostly since 1890.

Mazagão (mŭzŭgä'ō), city (pop. 162), S Amapá territory, N Brazil, near northernmost channel of the Amazon delta, 20 mi. SW of Macapá; rubber, cacao, Brazil nuts, sarsaparilla, timber. Formerly also called Mazaganópolis.

Mazagão Velho (vĕ'lyōō), town (pop. 231), S Amapá territory, N Brazil, near N channel of the Amazon delta, 30 mi. SW of Macapá; rubber, Brazil nuts, timber.

Mazagran (mäzägrän'), village (pop. 2,041), Oran dept., Algeria, near the Mediterranean, 3 mi. SSW of Mostaganem; winegrowing. Scene of fighting (1839–40) bet. Fr. garrison and Abd-el-Kader's raiders.

Mazaleón (mä-thälāōn'), town (pop. 1,189, Teruel prov., E Spain, 12 mi. E of Alcañiz; olive-oil processing; cereals, fruit.

Mazalgaon, India: see MANJLEGAON.

Mazama, Mount, Oregon: see CRATER LAKE NATIONAL PARK.

Mazamet (mäzämĕ'), town (pop. 12,058), Tarn dept., S France, on N slope of the Montagne Noire, 10 mi. SE of Castres, near Thoré R.; France's leading wool-cleaning and hide-processing center. Supplies French and foreign woolen and leather industries. Hosiery and fertilizer mfg.

Mazamitla (māsämēt'lä), town (pop. 1,855), Jalisco, central Mexico, 37 mi. E of Sayula; grain, beans, livestock.

Mazanderan or **Mazandaran** (both: mäzändĕrän'), former province of N Iran, on S shore of Caspian Sea, E of the lower Sefid Rud; main town, Babul. Bordered S by Elburz chain, it has a humid subtropical climate favoring some of Iran's richest commercial crops but also inducing malarial conditions. Rice, tea, citrus fruit, sugar cane, tobacco, silk, cotton, and jute are the chief products; lumbering and grazing on forested Elburz slopes. E section served by Trans-Iranian RR. The anc. *Tabaristan,* it long remained under Sassanian rule, and resisted Arab control in 8th cent. Mazanderan was among the Caspian provs. that were, during 1723–32, under Russian control. In 1938, the prov. was divided bet. Iran's First and Second provs.: the E section, including Babul (with its port Babulsar), Amul, Sari, Shahi, and Behshahr, passed to Second Prov. (see TEHERAN); and W section, including Shahsawar, Chalus, and Naushahr, to First Prov. (see GILAN).

Mazán River (mäsän'), Loreto dept., NE Peru, rises at about 2°40'S 74°55'W, flows c.150 mi. SE, through virgin forest region, to Napo R. (Amazon basin) 18 mi. N of Iquitos.

Mazapa (mäsä'pä), town (pop. 553), Chiapas, S Mexico, near Guatemala border, 4 mi. E of Motozintla; sugar cane.

Mazapil (mäsäpēl'), city (pop. 1,699), Zacatecas, N central Mexico, on interior plateau, near Coahuila border, 65 mi. SW of Saltillo; alt. 7,382 ft.; mining center (gold, silver, lead, copper, zinc, mercury).

Mazapiltepec de Juárez (mäsäpēltäpĕk' dā hwä'rĕs), town (pop. 728), Puebla, central Mexico, 35 mi. ENE of Puebla; cereals, maguey, fruit, livestock.

Mazar, El, or **Al-Mazar** (both: ĕl mӑzär'), village (pop. 343), Sinai prov., NE Egypt, near the coast, on Cairo-Haifa RR, 65 mi. ESE of Port Said.

Mazar, El, or **Al-Mazar,** village (pop. c.1,500), S central Jordan, 8 mi. S of Kerak; grain (wheat, barley), vegetables, fruit.

Mazara del Vallo (mätsä'rä dĕl väl'lō), town (pop. 24,276), Trapani prov., W Sicily, port on Mediterranean coast and 25 mi. S of Trapani; macaroni. Exports Marsala wine, vegetables, corn, olive oil. Fisheries (tunny, coral). Gypsum quarries near by. Bishopric. Has 11th-cent. cathedral (rebuilt in 17th and 20th cent.; damaged in Second World War) and ruined castle. Formerly Mazzara.

Mazarambroz (mä-thärämbrōth'), town (pop. 1,602), Toledo prov., central Spain, 11 mi. S of Toledo; cereals, olives, olive oil, potatoes, sheep.

Mazar-i-Sharif (mŭzär'-ĭ-shŭrēf') [Pashto,=tomb of the saint], province (□ 20,000; pop. 900,000), N Afghanistan, in Afghan Turkestan; ⊙ Mazar-i-Sharif. Situated on N slopes of the Hindu Kush system, it extends N to the Amu Darya, where it borders on the Tadzhik, Uzbek, and Turkmen republics of USSR. It is drained by the Khulm, Balkh, and Sar-i-Pul rivers, which irrigate the main agr. oases and then disappear into the desert before reaching the Amu Darya. Agr. specialization is in fruit, wine, and coriander along Khulm R. (Haibak and Tashkurghan oases); in grain (rice, wheat, barley), melons, vegetables, and opium along Balkh R. (Mazar-i-Sharif, Balkh, and Aqchah oases); and in melons, oilseed, and grain along Sar-i-Pul R. (Sar-i-Pul and Shibarghan oases). Pop. is largely Uzbek, with some Tadzhik (Tajik; NE) and Turkmen (NW) minorities. Prov. is linked by highways with towns of Maimana and Herat (W), Kataghan (E), and Kabul (SE). Main Amu Darya ferry crossing to USSR is at Pata Kesar–Termez.

Mazar-i-Sharif, city (pop. 50,000), ⊙ Mazar-i-Sharif prov., N Afghanistan, in Balkh R. oasis, 190 mi. NW of Kabul; 36°43'N 67°7'E. Largest center of Afghan Turkestan; mfg. of silk and cotton goods; cotton ginning, flour milling, brick mfg.; ordnance plant, power station, radio transmitter. Pop. is largely Uzbek and Tadzhik. Surrounding irrigated dist. produces grain (wheat, barley, millet), fruit, and cotton. Old town contains large bazaar and alleged 15th-cent. tomb of the caliph Ali, whose historical shrine is at Najaf (Iraq). New garden town surrounds the old section. Under Afghan rule since 1852, it became political center of Afghan Turkestan in 1869.

Mazarrón (mä-thärōn'), town (pop. 4,618), Murcia prov., SE Spain, near the Mediterranean, 20 mi. W of Cartagena; mining of silver-lead ore and iron in rich deposits near by. Part of ore is smelted here, part shipped directly from small seaport (pop. 1,463) 4 mi. SE; railroad. Also limestone and gypsum quarries.

Mazaruni-Potaro (mӑzŭrōō'nē pōtä'rō), district (□ 21,555; pop. 10,873), Essequibo co., W central Br. Guiana; ⊙ Bartica. Drained by Cuyuni, Mazaruni, and Potaro rivers.

Mazaruni River, N Br. Guiana, rises in the Guiana Highlands at 5°50'N 60°8'W, flows c.350 mi. in wide curve N and then E and NE, through tropical forests (greenheart), past Issano, to Essequibo R. at Bartica shortly after receiving the Cuyuni. Main source of alluvial diamonds. Because of frequent rapids, navigable only for short distances, mainly near its mouth.

Mazatán (mäsätän'). **1** Town (pop. 1,230), Chiapas, S Mexico, in Pacific lowland, 13 mi. WSW of Tapachula; coffee, sugar cane, cacao, mangoes, livestock. **2** Town (pop. 657), Sonora, NW Mexico, in valley 50 mi. E of Hermosillo; grain, beans, cattle.

Mazatecochco (mäsätäkōch'kō), officially San Cosme Mazatecochco, town (pop. 2,068), Tlaxcala, central Mexico, at W foot of Malinche volcano, 10 mi. N of Puebla; grain, stock.

Mazatenango (mäsätänäng'gō), city (1950 pop. 10,735), ⊙ Suchitepéquez dept., SW Guatemala, in Pacific piedmont, on railroad, on Sis R. (a Pacific coastal stream), and 21 mi. S of Quezaltenango; 14°31'N 91°30'W; alt. 1,250 ft. Commercial center in cotton, coffee, and sugar-cane dist., cotton ginning and milling, cottonseed-oil extraction; light mfg. Livestock raising near by.

Mazatepec (mäsätäpĕk'), city (pop. 1,454), Morelos, central Mexico, 16 mi. SW of Cuernavaca; sugar cane, rice, fruit, vegetables.

Mazatlán (mäsätlän'). **1** Town (pop. 1,731), Guerrero, SW Mexico, in Sierra Madre del Sur, 6 mi. S of Chilpancingo; alt. 4,269 ft.; cereals, sugar cane, fruit, forest products (resin, vanilla). **2** City (pop. 32,117), Sinaloa, NW Mexico, port on the Pacific, near entrance to Gulf of California, 130 mi. SE of Culiacán, 270 mi. NW of Guadalajara; 23°11'N 106°26'W. Rail terminus. Largest Mexican port on the Pacific. Industrial, commercial, and agr. center (sugar cane, tobacco, cotton, fruit, vegetables). Exports metals, hides, tobacco, bananas, chick-peas, istle, dyewood. Has sugar refinery, cotton gins, flour and textile mills, tequila distilleries, tobacco and cigarette factories, machine shops, brewery, leather industry, cold-storage plant, cement mill, foundries. Gold, silver, lead, copper mines near by. Airport. Resort; situated in luxuriant, semitropical setting overlooking picturesque islets surrounded by mangrove swamps. Has municipal palace, anc. Sp. fort, observatory. Known for spring carnival. Port developed in Sp. colonial times, traded with Philippines. Has wide but shallow harbor; ships anchor about a mile out.

Mazatzal Mountains (mӑzŭtsäl', mäsätsäl'), central Ariz., extend c.50 mi. S along Verde R. from East Verde R. to Salt. R., in Tonto Natl. Forest. **Mazatzal Peak** (7,888 ft.) is highest in range; FOUR PEAKS (7,691 ft.) and Mt. ORD (7,155 ft.) are other high points.

Mazé (mäzā'), village (pop. 696), Maine-et-Loire dept., W France, 13 mi. E of Angers; fruit growing, (chiefly melons), winegrowing.

Mazeikiai, Mazheikyai, or **Mazheykyay** (mä-zhā'-kyī), Lith. *Mažeikiai*, Rus. *Mozheiki* or *Mozheyki*, city (pop. 5,618), NW Lithuania, 45 mi. NW of Siauliai, near Latvian border; industrial center; mfg. (metalware, oils, fats, woolens, furniture, bricks, starches); flour milling, poultry raising. Cement mill 16 mi. ESE at Akmene [Lith. *Akmenė*] or Akmyany. Until 1920 Mazeikiai was in Rus. Kovno govt. and called Muravyevo.

Mazelspoort (mä'zŭlspōōrt), locality, W Orange Free State, U. of So. Afr., near Modder R., 15 mi. ENE of Bloemfontein; site of Boyden Station of Harvard Observatory; 29°12'S 26°29'15"E; alt. 4,575 ft., on small hill now called Harvard Kopje. Begun 1927, when it was transferred from Arequipa, Peru, observatory was completed 1929; 60-inch telescope completed 1933. Near by are Bloemfontein waterworks and reservoir.

Mazeppa (mŭzĕ'pŭ), village (pop. 523), Wabasha co., SE Minn., on branch of Zumbro R. and 18 mi. NNW of Rochester, in grain, livestock, poultry area; dairy products.

Mazeras (mäzĕ'räs), town, Coast Prov., SE Kenya, on railroad and 14 mi. WNW of Mombasa; copra, sugar cane, fruits. Lead deposits.

Mazères (mäzâr'). **1** Village (pop. 1,366), Ariège dept., S France, on Hers R. and 10 mi. NNE of Pamiers; sawmilling, poultry raising. Gaston de Foix b. here. **2** or **Mazères-sur-le-Salat** (–sür-lü-sälä'), village (pop. 647), Haute-Garonne dept., S France, on the Salat, near its mouth into the Garonne, and 13 mi. E of Saint-Gaudens; important cigarette-paper factory.

Mazgirt (mäzgĭrt'), village (pop. 908), Tunceli prov., E central Turkey, near Monzur R., 32 mi. NE of Elazig; wheat. Sometimes spelled Mazkirt.

Mazheikyai, Lithuania: see MAZEIKIAI.

Mazheykyay, Lithuania: see MAZEIKIAI.

Mazia Pata, Belgian Congo: see DIBAYA.

Mazidagi (mäzŭ'däŭ"), Turkish *Mazıdağı*, village (pop. 1,520), Mardin prov., SE Turkey, 18 mi. NW of Mardin; grain, chick-peas, lentils, mohair goats. Formerly Samrah.

Mazières-en-Gâtine (mäzyâr'-ā-gätēn'), village (pop. 280), Deux-Sèvres dept., W France, 8 mi. SSW of Parthenay; cattle breeding.

Mazinan (mäzēnän'), village, Ninth Prov., in Khurasan, NE Iran, just SW of Davarzan and 40 mi. W of Sabzawar; opium, cotton, grain.

Mazinde (mäzēn'dä), village, Tanga prov., NE Tanganyika, on railroad and 30 mi. NW of Korogwe; sisal.

Mazingarbe (mäzĕgärb'), town (pop. 5,768), Pas-de-Calais dept., N France, 5 mi. SE of Béthune in coal-mining dist.; coke ovens, breweries.

Mazkeret Batyah or **Mazkereth Batya,** Israel: see EQRON.

Mazo (mä'thō) or **El Pueblo** (ĕl pwĕ'blō), town (pop. 359), Palma, Canary Isls., 4 mi. S of Santa Cruz de la Palma; cereals, sweet potatoes, fruit, tobacco, wine, livestock; timber. Fishing.

Mazoe (mŭzō'ā), village, Salisbury prov., N Southern Rhodesia, on Mazoe R. and 23 mi. NNW of Salisbury; road center in citrus-fruit area; tobacco, corn, dairy products. Just SE is Mazoe Dam, used in irrigation of citrus dist.

Mazoe River, NE Southern Rhodesia, rises N of Salisbury, flows c.200 mi. ENE, past Mazoe and through Bindura-Shamva gold-mining dist., to the Zambezi in Mozambique, below Tete. Mazoe Dam on its upper course 20 mi. NNW of Salisbury irrigates citrus-growing area.

Mazomanie (mă"zōmā'nē), village (pop. 962), Dane co., S Wis., on tributary of Wisconsin R. and 22 mi. WNW of Madison; shipping point and trade center for agr. area.

Mazon (mŭzŏn'), village (pop. 586), Grundy co., NE Ill., 27 mi. SW of Joliet, in agr. and bituminous-coal area.

Mazorra (mäsô'rä), town (pop. 4,195), Havana prov., W Cuba, 17 mi. S of Havana, in agr. region (sugar, fruit, vegetables). Insane asylum.

Mazouna (mäzōōnä'), village, Oran dept., N Algeria, in the coastal Dahra range, 24 mi. W of Orléansville; handicraft weaving. Until 1701, seat of western Turkish beys.

Mazovetsk, Poland: see WYSOKIE.

Mazovia, region, Poland: see MASOVIA.

Mazowsze, region, Poland: see MASOVIA.

Mazra, El Mazra', or **Al-Mazra'** (all: mӑz'rä, ĕl), village (pop. c.5,000), central Jordan, on E shore of Dead Sea, at mouth of the Wadi Kerak, 13 mi. NW of Kerak; 981 ft. below sea level; vegetables. Salt and gypsum deposits.

Mazsalaca or **Mazsalatsa** (mäz'sälätsä), Ger. *Salisburg*, city (pop. 1,492), N Latvia, in Vidzeme, on the Salaca and 26 mi. NW of Valmiera; flax milling.

Maztkeret Batya, Israel: see EQRON.

Mazuecos (mä-thwā'kōs), town (pop. 1,032), Guadalajara prov., central Spain, near Tagus R., 37 mi. ESE of Madrid; grain, grapes, livestock; olive-oil pressing.

Mazulski or **Mazul'skiy** (mŭzōōl'skē), town (1942 pop. over 500), SW Krasnoyarsk Territory, Russian SFSR, 6 mi. SW (under jurisdiction) of Achinsk; manganese mining.

Mazunga (mäzōōng'gä), village, Bulawayo prov., S Southern Rhodesia, on road and 33 mi. NNW of Beitbridge; cattle-raising center.

Mazurski, Kanal, Poland and USSR: see MASURIAN CANAL.

Mazury, Poland: see MASURIA; OLSZTYN prov.

Mazy (mäzē'), village (pop. 940), Namur prov., S central Belgium, 10 mi. WNW of Namur; marble and chalk quarrying.

Mazza, El, or **Al-Mazzah** (both: ĕl mӑz'zŭ), Fr. *Mezzé*, town, Damascus prov., SW Syria, 3 mi. W of Damascus; olives, fruits.

Mazzara, Sicily: see MAZARA DEL VALLO.

Mazzarino (mätsärē'nō), town (pop. 16,926), Caltanissetta prov., S central Sicily, 15 mi. SE of Caltanissetta. Has anc. castle, palace.

Mba or **Ba** (both: ŭmbä'), town (pop. 1,315), NW Viti Levu, Western Dist., Fiji, SW Pacific, at mouth of Mba R.; sugar.

Mbabane (ŭmbäbä'nä), town, ⊙ SWAZILAND and Northern Dist., on main E-W road and 200 mi. E of Johannesburg, 100 mi. WSW of Lourenço Marques; 26°18'S 31°8'E; tin mines.

M'Backé or **M'Baké** (ŭmbä'kā), village, W Senegal, Fr. West Africa, on railroad and 22 mi. ENE of Diourbel; peanut growing.

M'Baïki (ŭmbīkē'), town, ⊙ Lobaye region (□ 8,900; 1950 pop. 77,100), S Ubangi-Shari, Fr. Equatorial Africa, near Lobaye R., 55 mi. SW of Bangui; market for rubber and palm products; sawmills. Gold is mined in vicinity. Has R.C. mission and agr. school.

M'Baké, Fr. Senegal, Fr. West Africa: see M'BACKÉ.

Mbale (ŭmbä'lā), town, Eastern Prov., Uganda, 80 mi. NE of Jinja, at W foot of Mt. Elgon; agr. trade center (cotton, corn, bananas, millet). Rail station is 2 mi. W.

M'Balmayo (ŭmbälmä'yō), town, Nyong et Sanaga region, S central Fr. Cameroons, on Nyong R. and 25 mi. S of Yaoundé; transshipment point, rail terminus, and trading center; brick mfg.; sawmilling. Nyong R. is navigable bet. here and Abong-M'Bang.

M'Bam (ŭmbäm'), administrative region (□ 12,548; 1950 pop. 102,800), W central Fr. Cameroons; ⊙ Bafia. Drained by M'Bam R. Transition zone bet. tropical rain forest and park-savanna. Rice growing, palm oil and kernels, manioc, yams.

Mbamba Bay (ŭmbäm'bä), village, Southern Prov., S Tanganyika, port on L. Nyasa, 75 mi. SW of Songea (linked by road), near Mozambique border; tobacco, coffee, wheat, oilseeds; livestock.

M'Bamou Island, Africa: see STANLEY POOL.

M'Bam River, in W and central Fr. Cameroons, formed by headstreams 40 mi. WSW of Tibati, flows c.175 mi. SW and S to Sanaga R. 25 mi. SE of Bafia.

M'Banga (ŭmbäng'gä), village, Mungo region, W Fr. Cameroons, on railroad and 40 mi. SW of N'Kongsamba, near Br. Cameroons border; banana-growing center; banana drying and processing for export. Also cacao and coffee.

Mbaracayú, Cordillera de, Paraguay and Brazil: see MARACAJU, SERRA DE.

Mbarara (ŭmbärä'rä), town, Western Prov., SW Uganda, 80 mi. WSW of Masaka; agr. trade center; coffee, corn, millet, bananas; cattle, sheep, goats. Hq. Ankole dist., inhabited by Iro and Hima tribes.

Mbatiki or **Batiki** (both: ŭmbä″tē′kē), volcanic island (□ 4; pop. 255), Fiji, SW Pacific, 35 mi. E of Viti Levu; 2.5 mi. long, rises to 750 ft.

Mbau or **Bau** (both: ŭmbou′), volcanic island (pop. 308), Fiji, SW Pacific; ½ mi. long; rises to c.100 ft. Coral causeway to Viti Levu. Old native ⊙ Fiji. Copra.

Mbengga or **Beqa** (both: ŭmbĕng′gä), volcanic island (□ 14; pop. 774), Fiji, SW Pacific, 6 mi. S of Viti Levu; 4 mi. long; rises to 1,450 ft. Wild lemons, bananas.

M'Béré River (ŭmbĕrā′), W headstream of Logone R. in E Fr. Cameroons and SW Chad territory, Fr. Equatorial Africa, rises 65 mi. SE of N'Gaoundéré, flows 275 mi. NE, past Baïbokoum and Moundou, to join Pendé R. (E branch of Logone) 28 mi. SSE of Laï. Also called Western Logone R.

Mbeya (ŭmbā′yä), town, Southern Highlands prov., S Tanganyika, on road, near Northern Rhodesia border, and 250 mi. SW of Dodoma; agr. trade center; tea, coffee, tobacco, pyrethrum; cattle, sheep, goats. Airfield. Has European school. Lupa goldfield 20 mi. N. Mbozi meteorite 40 mi. W.

M'Bigou (ŭmbēgōō′), village, S Gabon, Fr. Equatorial Africa, 60 mi. E of Mouila. R.C. mission.

Mbocayaty (bōkiätē′, –tŭ′), town (dist. pop. 10,019), Guairá dept., S Paraguay, 4 mi. NNE of Villarrica; agr. center (sugar cane, tobacco, maté, fruit, cotton, livestock).

M'Bomou, region, Fr. Equatorial Africa: see BANGASSOU.

M'Bomou River, Belgian Congo and Fr. Equatorial Africa: see BOMU RIVER.

M'bomu River, Belgian Congo: see BOMU RIVER.

M'Bour (ŭmbōōr′), town (pop. c.10,300), W Senegal, Fr. West Africa, minor port on the Atlantic, 37 mi. SE of Dakar. Ships peanuts. Fisheries. Food canning. Clinic for sleeping sickness. Mission.

M'Bout (ŭmbōōt′), village, S Mauritania, Fr. West Africa, 255 mi. E of Saint-Louis, Senegal; gum, millet, livestock.

M'Bridge River (ŭmbrĭj′), NW Angola, rises in central plateau SW of Maquela do Zombo, flows 220 mi. WSW to the Atlantic just N of Ambrizete. Not navigable.

Mbulamuti (ŭmbōōlämōō′tē), town, Eastern Prov., SE central Uganda, 30 mi. NNW of Jinja; rail junction (branch line to Namasagali); alt. 3,490 ft. Cotton, tobacco, coffee, bananas, corn.

Mbulu (ŭmbōō′lōō), town, Northern Prov., Tanganyika, on road and 90 mi. WSW of Arusha; coffee; livestock.

Mburucuyá (bōōrōōkōōyä′), town (pop. 2,590), ⊙ Mburucuyá dept. (□ c.350; pop. 12,209), N Corrientes prov., Argentina, 55 mi. SE of Corrientes; rail terminus; agr. center (oranges, cotton, tobacco, sugar cane, alfalfa, livestock).

Mbuyapey (bōōyäpā′, –pĕ′ŭ), town (dist. pop. 7,902), Paraguarí dept., S Paraguay, 85 mi. SE of Asunción; agr. center (fruit, livestock); lumbering. Trade in hides.

Mchangani (ŭmchäng-gä′nē), town, N central Zanzibar, on road and 13 mi. NE of Zanzibar town; clove-growing center.

M'Dilla or **Djebel-M'Dilla** (jĕ′bĕlmdēlä′), mining village, Gafsa dist., S central Tunisia, 10 mi. S of Gafsa, on rail spur; important phosphate mines; beneficiation plant.

Mdina (mŭdē′nä), Maltese *Città Notabile* (chēt-tä′ nōtä′bēlä) and *Città Vecchia* (vĕk′kyä), town (pop. 1,384), W central Malta, adjoining RABAT, 6 mi. W of Valletta, in agr. region (grapes, citrus fruit, potatoes, wheat). Has extensive Roman remains, also catacombs of various periods. The anc. ⊙ Malta until foundation (1565) of Valletta, it is a walled city of churches and palaces. Few of the monuments were damaged during Second World War air raids. Has cathedral of St. Paul (founded in 12th cent., rebuilt 1693 in baroque style), Carmelite church (1570), and numerous others built in 16th and 17th cent. There are also several palaces of Maltese nobles. Probably of Roman origin, town was named for Medina by the Saracens. Ta Qali airfield is NE. NW of Mdina are the Bingemma Hills.

Me, in Thai names: see MAE.

Mé, La (lä mā′), village, S Ivory Coast, Fr. West Africa, on small Mé R. near coastal lagoon, and 15 mi. NE of Abidjan; agr. experiment station (chiefly peanuts).

Mead. 1 Town (pop. 186), Weld co., N Colo., near S.Platte R., 35 mi. N of Denver, in sugar-beet region; alt. 5,280 ft. Reconstructed Fort Vasquez, once a fur-trading post, is near by. **2** Village (pop. 388), Saunders co., E Nebr., 25 mi. W of Omaha, near Platte R.

Mead, Lake, largely on state line bet. SE Nev. and NW Ariz., E of Las Vegas, Nev., formed by HOOVER DAM on Colorado R. at W end of Grand Canyon. One of world's largest artificial lakes (□ 246.5; capacity 10,000,000,000,000 gal.; 115 mi. long, 1–10 mi. wide). Receives Virgin R. in N arm (c.25 mi. long). Used by Natl. Park Service for recreational purposes.

Meade (mēd). **1** County (□ 976; pop. 5,710), SW Kansas; ⊙ Meade. Rolling prairie region, bordered S by Okla.; drained by Crooked Creek. Grain, livestock; volcanic ash deposits. Formed 1885. **2** County (□ 308; pop. 9,422), NW Ky.; ⊙ Brandenburg. Bounded N and NW by Ohio R. (Ind. line). Rolling agr. area (livestock, grain, burley tobacco); timber; limestone quarries. In E is Otter Creek Recreational Area (c.1,775 acres). Formed 1823. **3** County (□ 3,466; pop. 11,516), W central S.Dak.; ⊙ Sturgis. Ranching and agr. area rich in mineral resources; drained by Belle Fourche R. and bounded E by Cheyenne R. Gold, manganese, lignite, bentonite, fuller's earth; livestock, grain. Formed 1889.

Meade, city (pop. 1,763), ⊙ Meade co., SW Kansas, on Crooked Creek and 35 mi. SSW of Dodge City; shipping point for cattle and grain area; silica mining and refining. State park near by. Inc. 1885.

Meade, Fort George G., Md.: see ANNE ARUNDEL.

Meade River, N Alaska, S of Point Barrow, rises near 69°15′N 158°30′W, flows c.250 mi. N to Arctic Ocean at 70°50′N 155°46′W. Coal mining at Atkasuk, 60 mi. SSW of Barrow, for local consumption.

Meaderville (mē′dûrvĭl), NE suburb (pop. 1,704, with adjacent McQueen) of Butte, Silver Bow co., SW Mont.; copper mines. Precipitating plant recovers pure copper from water pumped out of mines.

Meadow. 1 Town (pop. 490), Terry co., NW Texas, on the Llano Estacado, 25 mi. SW of Lubbock; shipping point in agr. area. **2** Town (pop. 378), Millard co., W Utah, 8 mi. SW of Fillmore; alt. 5,000 ft.; livestock, grain, alfalfa.

Meadow Bridge, town (pop. 597), Fayette co., S central W.Va., 13 mi. N of Hinton, in coal-mining and agr. region.

Meadow Grove, village (pop. 461), Madison co., NE central Nebr., 15 mi. W of Norfolk and on Elkhorn R.; grain, livestock.

Meadow Lake, town (pop. 1,456), W Sask., on Meadow L. (6 mi. long, 3 mi. wide), 100 mi. N of North Battleford; grain elevators; woodworking, lumbering, fur trapping, fishing.

Meadowlands, village (pop. 134), St. Louis co., NE Minn., on Whiteface R. and c.40 mi. NW of Duluth; cheese.

Meadow Lands or **Meadowlands,** village (pop. 1,059), Washington co., SW Pa., just N of Washington.

Meadow Mountain, NW Md., ridge (c.3,000 ft.) of the Alleghenies, extends NE c.20 mi. from Deep Creek L. to state line just SE of Salisbury, Pa.; on it is part of Savage R. State Forest.

Meadow River, SW W.Va., rises on Keeney Knob in N Summers co., flows 53 mi. generally NW to Gauley R. 14 mi. E of Gauley Bridge.

Meadow Valley Wash, SE Nev., rises in mtn. region of Lincoln co., flows c.110 mi. S, past Caliente, to Muddy R. N of L. Mead.

Meadow View, town (pop. 722), Washington co., SW Va., 7 mi. NE of Abingdon.

Meadville. 1 Town (pop. 524), ⊙ Franklin co., SW Miss., 30 mi. ESE of Natchez; lumber milling. **2** City (pop. 446) Linn co., N central Mo., near Grand R., 12 mi. W of Brookfield. **3** Industrial city (pop. 18,972), ⊙ Crawford co., NW Pa., 33 mi. S of Erie and on French Creek; agr. trading center; slide fasteners, rayon, metal products. Allegheny Col. here. Settled c.1788, laid out 1793, inc. as borough 1823, as city 1866.

Meaford (mē′fûrd), town (pop. 2,662), S Ont., on Nottawasaga Bay, inlet of Georgian Bay, 18 mi. E of Owen Sound; port; woolen milling, fruit canning, woodworking, shipbuilding, dairying, flooring mfg.; apple-growing, trout-fishing region.

Meagher (mär), county (□ 2,354; pop. 2,079), central Mont.; ⊙ White Sulphur Springs. Mtn. region drained by Smith R. and branches of Musselshell R. Livestock. Part of Little Belt Mts. in NE, part of Lewis and Clark Natl. Forest in N. Formed 1866.

Meaghers Grant (märz, mē′gûrz), village (pop. estimate 150), S N.S., on Musquodoboit R. and 26 mi. NE of Halifax; lumbering; in gold-mining region. Settled 1692.

Meakerville, village (pop. 41), S Alaska, near Cordova.

Mealbank, England: see PATTON.

Mealfourvonie or **Mealfuarvonie** (both: mĕlfōōr-vō′nē), mountain (2,284 ft.) on W shore of Loch Ness, Inverness, Scotland.

Mealhada (mēūlyä′dŭ), town (pop. 986), Aveiro dist., N central Portugal, on railroad and 12 mi. N of Coimbra; winegrowing, olive-oil pressing, tar-pitch mfg.

Mealy Mountains, range, SE Labrador, extending c.120 mi. SW-NE along S shore of L. Melville; rises to 4,300 ft. There are several peaks over 3,000 ft. high; numerous small lakes.

Meámbar (māäm′bär), town (pop. 216), Comayagua dept., W central Honduras, 27 mi. NNW of Comayagua; sugar cane, coffee, tobacco, cacao, rubber.

Meana Sardo or **Meanasardo** (mĕä″näsär′dô), village (pop. 2,481), Nuoro prov., central Sardinia, 25 mi. E of Oristano. Nuraghe near by.

Meanguera Island (māäng-gā′rä), in Gulf of Fonseca, La Unión dept., E Salvador, 11 mi. SE of La Unión; 3 mi. long, 2 mi. wide; rises to 1,660 ft.; agr.; fisheries. Town of Meanguera del Golfo (pop. 554) on shore.

Meansville, town (pop. 224), Pike co., W central Ga., 16 mi. S of Griffin; food canning.

Meares, Cape, NW Oregon, promontory (c.700 ft. high) with lighthouse, 8 mi. NW of Tillamook.

Meares Island (□ 27; 10 mi. long, 2–7 mi. wide), SW B.C., in Clayoquot Sound off W Vancouver Isl., 45 mi. W of Port Alberni. Kakawis village (W); lumbering.

Mearim River (mēūrēn′), Maranhão, NE Brazil, rises in several branches above Barra do Corda, flows c.350 mi. N in a winding course throuth a lake dist. and cotton-growing region, past Pedreiras (head of navigation) and Vitória do Mearim, to São Marcos Bay of the Atlantic at Anajatuba. Receives Grajaú and Pindaré rivers (left).

Mearns (mârnz), agr. village and parish (pop. 4,635), S Renfrew, Scotland, 4 mi. SE of Barrhead. Parish includes BUSBY. Just N is Newton Mearns, with textile-bleaching works.

Mearns, The, Scotland: see KINCARDINE, county.

Mea Shearim (mā′ä shē-ārēm′), district in NNW part of Jerusalem, E Israel. Site of Abyssinian church; health center. Scene (1948) of heavy fighting.

Meath (mēdh, mēth), Gaelic *na Midhe,* county (□ 902.8; pop. 66,232), Leinster, E Ireland; ⊙ Trim. Bounded by cos. Kildare (S), Offaly (SW), Westmeath (W), Cavan (NW), Monaghan (N), Louth (NE), Dublin (SE), and the Irish Sea (E). Drained by Boyne and Blackwater rivers, and served by Royal Canal. Surface is level or undulating, with fertile soil; coastline is low and sandy; there are no harbors. Cattle and horse raising are important; potatoes are grown. Industries include woolen and paper milling, mfg. of clothing, furniture, tobacco processing. Besides Trim, other towns are An Uaimh (formerly Navan), Ceanannus Mór (formerly Kells), whence came the *Book of Kells*), Athboy, Dunboyne, Oldcastle, and Slane. Oldbridge was scene (1690) of the battle of the Boyne. Tara has remains of anc. seat of kings of Ireland. There are many anc. raths, round towers, and castle and abbey ruins. Noted are abbeys of Duleek, Bective, and Clonard.

Méaulte, France: see ALBERT.

Meauwataka (mēwŭtô′kŭ), resort village, Wexford co., NW Mich., 10 mi. NW of Cadillac, near small Meauwataka L.

Meaux (mō), town (pop. 13,030), Seine-et-Marne dept., N central France, on bend of the Marne and Ourcq Canal, and 25 mi. ENE of Paris; commercial and processing center of agr. BRIE region; flour and sugar milling, mfg. (starch, lubricants, agr. equipment, mustard, gingerbread, cheese). Supplies Paris with fresh fruit. Episcopal see since 4th cent. Has 12th-16th cent. cathedral which contains tomb of Bossuet, and 15th-cent. ramparts built on Gallo-Roman foundations. In Massacre of Meaux (1358) thousands of peasants who had participated in the Jacquerie were slain. Meaux was farthest point of Ger. advance in 1st battle of the Marne (1914).

Mebane (mĕ′bĭn, mā′–), town (pop. 2,068), Alamance and Orange counties, N central N.C., 9 mi. E of Burlington; tobacco market; mfg. of furniture, cotton yarn, hosiery; lumber milling. Founded 1854.

Mecapaca (mākäpä′kä), village (pop. c.3,180), La Paz dept., W Bolivia, on La Paz R. and 15 mi. SSE of La Paz; alt. 9,321 ft.; vineyards.

Mecapalapa (mäkäpälä′pä), town (pop. 1,707), Puebla, central Mexico, 28 mi. NNE of Huauchinango; coffee, sugar cane, tobacco, fruit.

Mecatina, Cape (mĕkŭtē′nŭ), on the Gulf of St. Lawrence, E Que.; 50°44′N 59°W; air base; lighthouse.

Mecatlán (mākätlän′), town (pop. 1,850), Veracruz, E Mexico, in Sierra Madre Oriental foothills, 28 mi. SW of Papantla; corn, coffee, tobacco, sugar cane.

Mecayapan (mākīä′pän), town (pop. 1,245), Veracruz, SE Mexico, 29 mi. W of Coatzacoalcos; tobacco, fruit.

Mecca (mĕ′kŭ), Arabic *Makkah* (măk′kŭ), city (pop. 90,000), ⊙ (with Riyadh) Saudi Arabia and ⊙ Hejaz, in coastal foothills of central Hejaz, 40 mi. E of Jidda, its Red Sea port, and 480 mi. SW of Riyadh; 21°25′N 39°49′E. Foremost sacred city of Islam, birthplace of Mohammed, and site of the Kaaba, the chief shrine of Moslem pilgrimage (hadj). Situated in a barren, rocky valley surrounded by hills, Mecca is a 2-mi.-long unwalled city of high stone houses. The longitudinal alignment of its streets, unusually wide for a Moslem city, is broken in the lowest part of the valley by the great mosque, which consists essentially of a vast courtyard enclosed by colonnades. In the center of the court stands the Kaaba, a small, nearly cubical stone bldg. of pre-Islamic origin and repeatedly rebuilt. The black stone, apparently of meteoric origin, embedded in the Kaaba's SE corner, is kissed by the pilgrims as part of the ceremonies of the hadj, which also involves the sevenfold circumambulation of the Kaaba itself. Within the courtyard is the sacred Zamzam (Zem-

zem) well, associated by Moslem tradition with the well Lahai-roi (Gen. 16.14) of Hagar and Ishmael. Near the great mosque is the broad Masah, Mecca's chief bazaar street, connecting the sacred hills Safa (SE) and Marwa (NW). Mecca owes its prosperity entirely to the pilgrims (100,000 yearly in normal times) and has few local industries (mfg. of religious ornaments). The climate is hot and dry and Mecca's surroundings are devoid of agr. settlement. An early hub of caravan routes, Mecca is Ptolemy's *Macoraba*. It was a pre-Islamic holy place, with the Kaaba used as repository of images of deities, and a flourishing commercial center. Here Mohammed was born (A.D. c.570), spent most of his life, and established the principle of Islam; however, the hostility of Mecca's pop. resulted in his hegira (622) to Medina. The northward shift of the center of Islam and subsequent Moslem expansion relegated Mecca to a minor role, especially after the defeat (692) of the local pretender to the caliphate, but it gained new prestige as Islam's chief sanctuary. It was sacked (930) by the Karmathians, a terrorist sect, who carried off the black stone (restored 951). Mecca was ruled by local emirs (later called sherifs) of the Hashemite family, 1st under Egyptian control and, after 1517, under the Turks. Turkish control became nominal by 18th cent. but was fully restored following the Wahabi revolt of early-19th cent. During First World War, however, the then sherif of Mecca, Husein ibn Ali of the Hashemite house, expelled the Turks and maintained himself as king of Hejaz until Mecca fell to Ibn Saud in 1924. Despite the ban against unbelievers, Mecca was visited in 19th cent. by Richard Burton and other non-Moslems in disguise.

Mecca, village (pop. c.550), Riverside co., S Calif., in Coachella Valley, near N end of Salton Sea, 32 mi. SE of Palm Springs; date gardens. Painted Canyon, a spectacular many-colored gorge, is E.

Mecejana, Brazil: see MESSEJANA.

Mecerreyes (mā-thĕrā'ĕs), town (pop. 1,016), Burgos prov., N Spain, 18 mi. SSE of Burgos; cereals, vegetables, sheep, hogs; charcoal mfg.

Mecham, Cape (mē'chŭm), S extremity of Prince Patrick Isl., W Franklin Dist., Northwest Territories, on Beaufort Sea of the Arctic Ocean, at entrance of McClure Strait; 75°44'N 121°23'W.

Mechanic Falls, town (pop. 2,067), Androscoggin co., SW Maine, on the Little Androscoggin and 8 mi. W of Auburn; paper mills. Set off from Minot and Poland 1893.

Mechanicsburg (mŭkă'nĭksbûrg"). **1** Village (pop. 464), Sangamon co., central Ill., 13 mi. E of Springfield, in agr. and coal area. **2** Village (pop. 1,920), Champaign co., W central Ohio, 18 mi. ENE of Springfield, in agr. area; drugs, metalworking tools, farm equipment. **3** Borough (pop. 6,786), Cumberland co., S central Pa., 8 mi. WSW of Harrisburg, in agr. area; mfg. (clothing, metal and food products). Large U.S. naval supply depot. Settled c.1790, inc. 1828.

Mechanicsville, suburb of Ottawa, SE Ont.

Mechanicsville. 1 Village, Windham co., Conn.: see THOMPSON. **2** Town (pop. 850), Cedar co., E Iowa, 22 mi. ESE of Cedar Rapids; feed mfg. **3** Village (pop. 1,294), Montour co., central Pa. **4** Borough (pop. 540), Schuylkill co., E central Pa., on Schuylkill R. just above Pottsville. **5** Hamlet, Hanover co., E central Va., on the Chickahominy just NE of Richmond. Near here, Lee's and McClellan's forces fought (June 26, 1862) the inconclusive battle of Mechanicsville (sometimes called battle of Beaver Dam Creek), 1 of Seven Days Battles.

Mechanicville, city (pop. 7,385), Saratoga co., E N.Y., on the canalized Hudson and 18 mi. N of Albany, in dairying area; mfg. of clothing, knit goods, food and paper products, brick; railroad shops. Settled before 1700; inc. as village in 1859, as city in 1915.

Mechant, Lake, (mĭ-shănt'), Terrebonne parish, SE La., 24 mi. SW of Houma, in marshy coastal region; c.5 mi. long, 3 mi. wide. Waterways connect it with Caillou L. and Gulf of Mexico (both S).

Mechelen, Antwerp prov., Belgium: see MECHLIN.

Mechelen-aan-de-Maas (măkh'ŭlŭn-ăn-dā-mäs'), village (pop. 3,677), Limburg prov., NE Belgium, on Meuse R., near the Zuid-Willemsvaart, and 8 mi. N of Maastricht, (Netherlands); agr., lumbering.

Mécheria (mäshĕryä'), town (pop. 5,121), Aïn-Sefra territory, NW central Algeria, in the High Plateaus, on Oran–Colomb-Béchar RR and 55 mi. N of Aïn-Sefra; livestock market.

Mechernich (mĕ'khŭrnĭkh), village (pop. 5,188), in former Prussian Rhine Prov., W Germany, after 1945 in North Rhine-Westphalia, 7 mi. SW of Euskirchen; foundries; lead mining.

Mechetinskaya (mĭchĕ'tyĭnskīŭ), village (1926 pop. 7,424), S Rostov oblast, Russian SFSR, on railroad and 50 mi. SE of Rostov; flour mill, metalworks; wheat, sunflowers, castor beans. Merino sheep farm near by.

Mechili, El, Cyrenaica: see MEKILI.

Mechita (măchē'tä), town (pop. 2,341), N central Buenos Aires prov., Argentina, 7 mi. NE of Bragado; cattle raising.

Mechlin (mĕk'lĭn), Fr. *Malines* (mälēn'), Flemish *Mechelen* (măkh'ŭlŭn), town (pop. 60,740), Antwerp prov., N central Belgium, on Dyle R. and 14 mi. NNE of Brussels; mfg. (furniture, machinery, wool, cotton, and linen textiles), leather tanning, printing, brewing, food canning; railroad repair shops. Formerly famous for its lace. Has 13th-cent. church of St-Rombaut with 319-ft. high tower and well-known carillon, and Van Dyck's famous *Crucifixion;* church of St. John with paintings by Rubens; 14th-cent. town hall, rebuilt 1715; 14th-cent. cloth hall; archbishop's palace. See of R.C. archbishop and primate of Belgium. Franz Hals b. here. Town came under sovereignty of counts of Flanders in 1333; transferred to dukes of Burgundy later in 14th cent. Became (1506) residence of Margaret of Austria, governor of the Netherlands. Made see of primate of Belgium (1559). The 1713 Treaty of Utrecht assigned Mechlin to Holy Roman Empire; taken by Fr. revolutionary armies in 1795; part of France until 1815.

Mechra bel Ksiri (mĕshrä' bĕl ksērē'), town (pop. 2,149), Rabat region, N Fr. Morocco, on Sebou R., on Fez-Tangier RR and 28 mi. NNW of Petitjean, in fertile Rharb lowland; agr. trade (cereals, livestock). U.S. air base.

Mechra Benabbou (bĕnäbōō'), village, Casablanca region, W Fr. Morocco, 60 mi. SE of Mazagan, at railroad bridge across the Oum er Rbia.

Mechtal, Poland: see MIECHOWICE.

Mechtras (mĕshträs'), village, Alger dept., N central Algeria, in Great Kabylia, 12 mi. S of Tizi-Ouzou; agr. school for arboriculture.

Mechuque Island, Chile: see CHAUQUES ISLANDS.

Mecidiye, Turkey: see ESKIPAZAR.

Mecina Bombarón (mā-thē'nä bōmbärōn'), town (pop. 1,639), Granada prov., S Spain, on S slope of the Sierra Nevada, 22 mi. S of Guadix; cereals, olive oil, wine, fruit. Stock raising, lumbering. Iron deposits.

Mecitozu (mĕjĭt'ûzü"), Turkish *Mecitözü*, village (pop. 3,653), Corum prov., N central Turkey, 18 mi. E of Corum; grain, mohair goats.

Meckenbeuren (mĕ"kŭnboi'rŭn), village (pop. 4,177), S Württemberg, Germany, after 1945 in Württemberg-Hohenzollern, on the Schussen and 5 mi. NE of Friedrichshafen; hops.

Meckenheim (mĕ'kŭnhīm). **1** Village (pop. 2,066), Rhenish Palatinate, W Germany, 6 mi. NE of Neustadt; wine. Roman remains excavated in area. **2** Town (pop. 2,069), in former Prussian Rhine Prov., W Germany, after 1945 in North Rhine-Westphalia, 8 mi. SSW of Bonn.

Meckesheim (mĕ'kŭs-hīm), village (pop. 2,246), N Baden, Germany, after 1945 in Württemberg-Baden, on the Elsenz and 8 mi. SE of Heidelberg; match mfg.

Mecklenburg (mĕ'klŭnbûrg, Ger. mā'klŭnbŏŏrk, mĕ'–), state (□ 8,856; pop. 2,139,640), N Germany; ⊙ Schwerin. Situated on the Baltic and occupying central portion of N German lowlands, it is bordered by Schleswig-Holstein (W), Lower Saxony (SW), Brandenburg (S), and Polish-administered Germany (E). Numerous lakes (Müritz, Schwerin, Plau, Kummerow); drained by Elde (affluent of the Elbe), Peene, Uecker, and Warnow (tributaries of the Baltic) rivers. Fertile region except in S; grain (rye), sugar beets, potatoes, stock. Rostock (with Warnemünde), Stralsund, and Wismar are important ports; fishing center at Sassnitz. Some industry (machinery and chemical mfg., processing of agr. produce); leading towns are Anklam, Greifswald, Neubrandenburg, Neustrelitz, and Schwerin. Universities at Greifswald and Rostock. Numerous resorts along Baltic coast and on Rügen isl. Occupied (6th cent. A.D.) by Slavic Wends, region was subdued (11th cent.) by Henry the Lion; Wendish prince Pribislaw became vassal of Holy Roman Empire. His dynasty acquired Stargard (1292) and Schwerin (1358); the princes were raised to dukes in 1348. In Thirty Years War, duchy belonged for short time (1628–32) to Wallenstein. Mecklenburg dynasty divided into several branches at various times; MECKLENBURG-SCHWERIN came into being in 1621, MECKLENBURG-STRELITZ in 1701. Both duchies were elevated to grand duchies at Congress of Vienna, sided with Prussia in Austro-Prussian War (1866), and joined (1871) the German Empire. Grand dukes were deposed in 1918; the 2 separate states of Mecklenburg-Schwerin and Mecklenburg-Strelitz were united 1934 into state of Mecklenburg (□6,070; 1939 pop. 900,400). Captured (May, 1945) by British and Soviet troops. Placed in Soviet occupation zone; inc. W POMERANIA (□ c.2,800); called for short time Mecklenburg-Vorpommern (–fôr'pô"mŭrn). Became (1949) one of the states of the German Democratic Republic (East Germany).

Mecklenburg. 1 County (□ 542; pop. 197,052), S N.C.; ⊙ CHARLOTTE. In piedmont region; bounded SW by S.C., W by Catawba R. (Catawba and Mountain Isl. lakes). Farming (cotton, corn, hay, dairy products, poultry); timber (pine, oak). Mfg. center at Charlotte; sawmilling. Formed 1762. **2** County (□ 665; pop. 33,497), S Va.; ⊙ Boydton. Bounded S by N.C., N by Meherrin R.; drained by Roanoke R., here joined by Dan R. A leading Va. tobacco-growing co.; also corn, cotton, hay, peanuts, livestock, poultry; some timber; lumber milling, woodworking. Chase City, South Hill, Clarksville are tobacco markets, with some mfg. Buffalo Springs is health resort. Formed 1765.

Mecklenburg Bay, N Germany, Baltic bight bet. Fehmarn isl. (W) and Darss peninsula (E); 55 mi. wide. Lübeck Bay forms SW arm, Wismar Bay S arm.

Mecklenburg-Schwerin (–shvārēn'), former state (□ 5,068; 1925 pop. 674,045), N Germany, after 1934 included in MECKLENBURG; ⊙ was Schwerin. Created as duchy in 1621; raised 1815 to grand duchy. Sided with Prussia in Austro-Prussian War of 1866 and joined (1871) the German Empire. Was free state from 1918 until 1934, when, with Mecklenburg-Strelitz, it was constituted state of Mecklenburg.

Mecklenburg-Strelitz (–shtrā'lĭts), former state (□ 1,131; 1925 pop. 110,269), N Germany, after 1934 included in MECKLENBURG; ⊙ was Neustrelitz. Consisted of 2 major portions, the lordship of Stargard (SE) and the territory of secularized bishopric of Ratzeburg (NW), separated by Mecklenburg-Schwerin; and of several small exclaves. Duchy of Mecklenburg-Strelitz was created 1701 (most recent division of Mecklenburg lands). Raised 1815 to grand duchy; sided with Prussia in Austro-Prussian War of 1866 and joined (1871) the German Empire. Was free state from 1918 until 1934, when, with Mecklenburg-Schwerin, it was constituted state of Mecklenburg.

Mecklenburg-Vorpommern, Germany: see MECKLENBURG.

Meckling, town (pop. 111), Clay co., SE S.Dak, 8 mi. NW of Vermillion; small trade center for farming region.

Meco (mā'kō), town (pop. 740), Madrid prov., central Spain, 20 mi. ENE of Madrid; grain growing, stock raising.

Meconta (mĕkōn'tä), village, Niassa prov., N Mozambique, on railroad and 40 mi. ENE of Nampula; cotton, sesame, castor beans.

Mecosta (mēkō'stŭ), county (□ 563; pop. 18,968), central Mich.; ⊙ Big Rapids. Drained by Muskegon, Little Muskegon, Chippewa, and Pine rivers. Agr.: livestock, poultry, grain, potatoes, fruit, corn; dairy products. Mfg. at Big Rapids. Oil and gas wells. Resorts. Fish hatchery. Manistee Natl. Forest is in W. Organized 1859.

Mecosta, village (pop. 305), Mecosta co., central Mich., 14 mi. SE of Big Rapids, in lake-resort and farm area.

Mecsekalja (mĕ'chĕkōlyŏ), town (pop. 2,895), Baranya co., S Hungary, on S slope of Mecsek Mts., 3 mi. W of Pecs; wine, lumber.

Mecsek Mountains (mĕ'chĕk), Baranya co., S Hungary, extend NE from Szentlörinc; consist of 2 ranges, E range rising to 2,237 ft. in Mt. Zengövar, W range to 2,007 ft. in Mt. Mecsektetö. Heavily forested slopes; coal mined in valley bet. ranges; orchards, vineyards on S slopes. PECS at foot of E range. Also called Baranya Mts.

Mecsekszabolcs (mĕ'chĕksŏ"bôlch), town (pop. 5,612), Baranya co., S Hungary, in Mecsek Mts., 3 mi. NE of Pecs; coal mines.

Mecúfi (mĕkōō'fē), village, Niassa prov., N Mozambique, on Mozambique Channel, 25 mi. S of Pôrto Amélia; salt-panning; copra, almonds.

Meda (mā'dä), town (pop. 9,045), Milano prov., Lombardy, N Italy, 14 mi. N of Milan; rail junction; furniture mfg. center; sausage factories.

Meda (mā'dŭ), town (pop. 2,191), Guarda dist., N central Portugal, 30 mi. N of Guarda; alcohol distilling.

Medain, Al, Iraq: see MAIDAN, AL.

Medak (mā'dŭk), district (□ 3,055; pop. 758,220), central Hyderabad state, India, on Deccan Plateau; ⊙ Sangareddipet. Mainly lowland, drained by Manjra R.; Nizam Sagar (reservoir) forms NW corner of dist. Largely sandy red soil; millet, oilseeds (chiefly peanuts, castor beans), rice, sugar cane. Oilseed and rice milling, cotton ginning. Main towns: Sangareddipet (experimental farm), Siddipet. Part of Hyderabad since beginning (early-18th cent.) of state's formation. Pop. 85% Hindu, 10% Moslem, 3% Christian.

Medak, town (pop. 7,565), Medak dist., central Hyderabad state, India, 45 mi. NNW of Hyderabad; rice, sugar cane.

Medan (mŭdän'), town (pop. 76,584), NE Sumatra, Indonesia, on Deli R. and 400 mi. WNW of Singapore, in Deli region; 3°35'N 98°40'E; rail junction; trade center for forested and agr. area (tobacco, rubber, tea, fibers, palm oil). Mfg.: machinery, bricks, tile. Has tobacco-research station, sultan's palace, and large mosque. BELAWAN, port of Medan, is 15 mi. N of town. Was briefly ⊙ state of East Sumatra after Second World War.

Medang, Indonesia: see RANGSANG.

Médano, El, Argentina: see EL MÉDANO.

Médano, El (ĕl mā'dhänō), village (pop. 225), Tenerife, Canary Isls., 33 mi. SW of Santa Cruz de Tenerife; cereals, tomatoes, potatoes, livestock. Airfield.

Médanos (mā'dhänōs), town (pop. 2,040), ⊙ Villarino dist. (□ 3,598; pop. 19,337), SW Buenos Aires prov., Argentina, 23 mi. WSW of Bahía Blanca, in agr. zone (wheat, sheep, cattle; vineyards). Salt mines of Salina Chica are near by (W). Irrigation on the lower Río Colorado (S).

Médanos, Isthmus of, Falcón state, NW Venezuela, links Paraguaná Peninsula with mainland, just N of Coro, separates Gulf of Coro (W) from the Caribbean (E); 15 mi. long, c.3 mi. wide. Salt deserts on W coast.

Medaryville (mŭdâ'rēvĭl), town (pop. 833), Pulaski co., NW Ind., on Big Monon Creek and 45 mi. N of Lafayette; agr.; makes tile, brick, cheese.

Medchal (mād'chŭl), village (pop. 3,322), Atraf-i-Balda dist., central Hyderabad state, India, 17 mi. N of Hyderabad; rice, oilseeds.

Meddybemps, town (pop. 109), Washington co., E Maine, 14 mi. SW of Calais and on **Meddybemps Lake** (6 mi. long), a resort.

Mede (mā'dĕ), town (pop. 4,254), Pavia prov., Lombardy, N Italy, 11 mi. S of Mortara; agr. center, in rice-growing area; mfg. of agr. machinery.

Médéa (mādāä'), anc. *Lambdia,* town (pop. 5,128), Alger dept., N central Algeria, on railroad and 15 mi. SSW of Blida, in the Tell Atlas; alt. 3,000 ft. Noted for its vineyards and orchards. High-quality wheat grown in intermontane basins. Mfg. of plastic and tenting equipment. Seat of a dey during Turkish occupation.

Medeba, Jordan: see MADEBA.

Medebach (mā'dŭbäkh), town (pop. 3,451), in former Prussian prov. of Westphalia, W Germany, after 1945 in North Rhine-Westphalia, 15 mi. SSE of Brilon; grain.

Mededsiz Dag, Turkey: see TOROS DAGI.

Medel, Piz, Switzerland: see PIZ MEDEL.

Medellín (mĕdŭlēn', mĕ'dŭlĭn, Sp. mā-dhĕyēn'), city (pop. 143,952), ⊙ Antioquia dept., NW central Colombia, in small valley of Cordillera Central, bounded by steep gorges along Porce R., 150 mi. NW of Bogotá; 6°15'N 75°33'W; alt. c.5,000 ft. Colombia's leading industrial city, linked by rail with Cali and Buenaventura, and by rail and river, via Puerto Berrío on Magdalena R., with Atlantic port Barranquilla. From it radiate several highways and air lines. Clean, modern city with healthy climate (dry and wet seasons alternate every 2 months). The center of the country's richest gold-mining and coffeegrowing region, it contains, too, the principal textile industries; mfg. also of wearing apparel, leather goods, tobacco products, china, enamel- and glassware, soap, pharmaceuticals, chemicals, electrical appliances, machinery, foodstuffs, beer, soft drinks, sugar, ice. There are also large new steelworks with electric furnaces and rolling mills, a cement plant, and sugar refineries. Has fine colonial and modern bldgs., parks, and cultural institutions, including a natl. mining acad. (founded 1887), the Univ. of Antioquia (founded 1871; 2d largest in the country), and the Univ. Bolivariana (R.C.). The Casa Moneda is Colombia's gold mint. Other noteworthy edifices include the new Villanueva Cathedral and the 17th cent. churches La Veracruz, San Benito, and San José. The city, founded 1675, was long isolated; it developed rapidly with the building of railroads in 19th cent. and with growth of coffee plantations after 1918.

Medellín, officially Medellín de Bravo, town (pop. 581), Veracruz, E Mexico, in Gulf lowland, on railroad and 11 mi. S of Veracruz; popular resort. Site of anc. Indian town with prehistoric Xicalanco ruins in forest near by. Cortés, who founded the new town, naming it after his native town in Estremadura, Spain, resided here briefly (1526).

Medellin, town (1939 pop. 1,504; 1948 municipality pop. 19,911), N Cebu isl., Philippines, on Visayan Sea, near entrance to Tañon Strait, 60 mi. N of Cebu city; agr. center (corn, tobacco); sugar mill.

Medellín (mā-dhĕlyēn'), town (pop. 1,743), Badajoz prov., W Spain, on Guadiana R. and 21 mi. E of Mérida; olives, cereals, grapes. Hernán Cortés b. here.

Medellín River, Colombia: see PORCE RIVER.

Medelpad (mā'dŭlpäd"), province [Swedish *landskap*] (□ 3,031; pop. 10,494), NE Sweden, on Gulf of Bothnia. In S part of Vasternorrland co.

Medemblik (mā'dŭmblĭk), town (pop. 4,423), North Holland prov., NW Netherlands, on the Ijsselmeer, at SE edge of Wieringermeer Polder, and 18 mi. NE of Alkmaar; market center. Has 13th-cent. Radboud Castle. Old ⊙ West Friesland, succeeded c.1400 by Hoorn.

Medenice, Ukrainian SSR: see MEDENITSA.

Médenine (mādnēn'), town (pop. 3,564), ⊙ Southern Territories (□ c.17,800; pop. 210,695), SE Tunisia, 40 mi. SSE of Gabès; 33°21'N 10°29'E; road and trading center; date-palms, olive trees, cereals, esparto. Its cave-like storehouses and habitations are known as *rhorfas.* Military post. Airfield.

Medenitsa (mĭdyĕ'nyĭtsŭ), Pol. *Medenice* (mĕdĕnyĕ'tsĕ), town (1939 pop. over 500), NE Drogobych oblast, Ukrainian SSR, 12 mi. NE of Drogobych; agr. market (grain, potatoes, livestock).

Meden-rudnik, Bulgaria: see BURGAS, city.

Mederdra (mĕdĕr'drä), village, SW Mauritania, Fr. West Africa, 80 mi. NE of Saint-Louis, Senegal; gum arabic, millet, livestock. Salt deposits near by.

Medesano (mĕdĕzä'nô), village (pop. 398), Parma prov., Emilia-Romagna, N central Italy, near Taro R., 9 mi. SW of Parma; canned tomatoes, sausage.

Medeshamstede, England: see PETERBOROUGH.

Medetsiz Dag, Turkey: see TOROS DAGI.

Medfield, residential town (pop. 4,549), including Medfield village (pop. 1,696), Norfolk co., E Mass., on Charles R. and 18 mi. SW of Boston. Settled and inc. 1650.

Medford. **1** City (pop. 66,113), Middlesex co., E Mass., on Mystic R. and 5 mi. NNW of Boston; paper boxes, machinery, beds, foundry products, floor polish, soap, chemicals; printing. Once famous for rum and ships. Has several 18th-cent. buildings. Tufts Col. here. Settled 1630, inc. as town 1684, as city 1892. **2** Village (pop. 409), Steele co., SE Minn., on Straight R. and 8 mi. S of Faribault; dairy products. Inc. 1936. **3** Village (pop. 1,462, with near-by Peacock), Burlington co., W central N.J., c.15 mi. E of Camden; concrete blocks, knit goods. Friends' meetinghouse here built 1814. **4** Village (1940 pop. 806), Suffolk co., SE N.Y., on central Long Isl., 4 mi. N of Patchogue, in dairying and truck-farming area; mfg. (machinery, aircraft parts). **5** Town (pop. 1,305), ⊙ Grant co., N Okla., 24 mi. W of Blackwell, in agr. area (mainly wheat; also alfalfa, oats); cotton ginning, flour milling; creamery, poultry hatchery. **6** City (pop. 17,305), ⊙ Jackson co., SW Oregon, on Bear Creek (small tributary of Rogue R.) and c.55 mi. W of Klamath Falls; resort; trade and shipping center for dairying, fruit, and truck-farming area; hq. Rogue River Natl. Forest; fruit canning, lumber milling. U.S. Air Force base. Rogue R. fishing and game area is near by. Crater Lake Natl. Park is 45 mi. NE; Oregon Caves Natl. Monument is 30 mi. SW. Founded 1883, inc. as town 1884, as city 1885. **7** City (pop. 2,799), ⊙ Taylor co., N central Wis., on Black R. and 37 mi. NW of Wausau, in lumbering, stock-raising, and dairying area; dairy and wood products, canned peas. Near by is a Mennonite colony. Inc. 1889.

Medford Lakes, borough (pop. 461), Burlington co., W central N.J., 9 mi. S of Mount Holly; small lakes here.

Medfra (mĕd'frŭ), village (pop. 25), S central Alaska, on upper Kuskokwim R. and 30 mi. ENE of McGrath; 63°6'N 154°43'W. Fur farming; placer gold mining.

Medgidia (mĕjē'dyä), town (1948 pop. 4,547), Constanta prov., SE Rumania, in Dobruja, on the Danube-Black Sea Canal and 18 mi. WNW of Constanta; rail junction and trading center; mfg. of agr. tools, ceramics, bricks, flour. Kaolin and limestone quarrying. Has 19th-cent mosque.

Medgyes, Rumania: see MEDIAS.

Medgyesbodzas (mĕd'dyĕsh-bôd"dzäsh), Hung. *Medgyesbodzás,* town (pop. 2,621), Csanad co., SE Hungary, 13 mi. SW of Bekescsaba; grain, onions, cattle, hogs.

Medha (mā'dŭ), village, Satara North dist., W central Bombay, India, 12 mi. NW of Satara, in Western Ghats; rice, millet.

Medi, Yemen: see MIDI.

Media (mē'dēŭ), anc. country of SW Asia, corresponding to NW Iranian plateau, bet. the Elburz and Zagros ranges, inhabited by the Medes. Originally a prov. of the Assyrian Empire, it rose c.700 B.C. as a powerful independent realm (⊙ Ecbatana) and, with the aid of the Persians of Parsis (modern Fars), overthrew the Assyrian Empire in late-7th cent. B.C. Media became a part of the Persian Empire after 550 B.C. and was conquered 330 B.C. by Alexander the Great. Under the Diadochi, the NW section—Media Minor or Media Atropatene (the modern AZERBAIJAN)—achieved autonomy, while the SW section—Media proper or Media Magna—remained under Seleucid rule. Media proper was known as Al-Jibal under the Arab caliphate, and later, under Seljuk rule, as IRAQ-i-Ajam.

Media. **1** (mŭdē'ŭ) Village (pop. 148), Henderson co., W Ill., 15 mi. ESE of Burlington (Iowa), in agr. area. **2** (mē'dēŭ) Borough (pop. 5,726), ⊙ Delaware co., SE Pa., 12 mi. W of Philadelphia; plastics, pork products; agr. Settled 1682, laid out c.1848, inc. 1850.

Media, Venezuela: see EL MENE.

Media Agua (mā'dhyä ä'gwä), town (pop. estimate 1,000), ⊙ Sarmiento dept. (□ c.3,000; 1947 pop. 8,086), S San Juan prov., Argentina, in San Juan R. valley (irrigation area), on railroad and 30 mi. SSE of San Juan. Wheat, alfalfa, wine, onions, livestock; flour milling.

Media Atropatene, Iran: see AZERBAIJAN.

Media Luna, Cayo (kī'ō mā'dyä lōō'nä), islet in the Gulf of Guacanayabo, E Cuba, 55 mi. S of Camagüey; 20°34'N 77°53'W. Fishing.

Mediano (mādhyä'nō), village (pop. 230), Huesca prov., NE Spain, on S slopes of the central Pyrenees, 33 mi. ENE of Huesca, near Cinca R. gorge. Irrigation reservoir, hydroelectric plant near by.

Mediapolis (mēdēă'pŭlĭs), town (pop. 834), Des Moines co., SE Iowa, 14 mi. N of Burlington; dairy products.

Medias (mĕdyäsh'), Rum. *Mediaş,* Hung. *Medgyes* (mĕd'dyĕsh), town (1948 pop. 23,247), Sibiu prov., central Rumania, in Transylvania, on railroad and 21 mi. WSW of Sighisoara, in a noted winegrowing region; wine and cattle trade, glass mfg.; methane production. Also produces textiles (cotton, rayon, wool), enamelware, hardware, leather goods, earthenware, salami; processes furs. Has military aviation school with airfield and agr. school. One of the first 7 towns established in 12th cent. by Ger. colonists, it still preserves 14th-cent. fortress and town walls. Has 17th-cent. Lutheran church. National assembly of Saxons of Transylvania voted here (1919) for union with Rumania. Germans and Magyars comprise 45% of pop.

Medical Lake, town (pop. 4,488), Spokane co., E Wash., 15 mi. SW of Spokane and on Medical L. State school and hosp. for mental deficients near here. Inc. 1889.

Medicina (mĕdēchē'nä), town (pop. 3,299), Bologna prov., Emilia-Romagna, N central Italy, 15 mi. E of Bologna; mfg. (agr. machinery, furniture).

Medicine Bow (bō), town (pop. 328), Carbon co., S Wyo., on Medicine Bow R., just N of Medicine Bow Mts., and 50 mi. NW of Laramie; alt. c.6,560 ft. Supply point in oil and livestock area. Oil well, deposits of magnesium sulphate and bentonite near by. Petrified forest in vicinity.

Medicine Bow Mountains, NW extension of Front Range in N Colo. and SE Wyo.; extend c.100 mi. NNW from Cameron Pass (just NW of Rocky Mtn. Natl. Park), Colo., to Medicine Bow town, Wyo. Prominent peaks in Wyo.: Elk Mtn. (11,162 ft.), Medicine Bow Peak (12,005 ft.). Much of Wyo. part of range lies within Medicine Bow Natl. Forest. Gold mined near Centennial, Wyo. Range is sometimes defined to include NEVER SUMMER MOUNTAINS of N Colo. Part of range in Albany and Carbon counties, just W of Centennial, Wyo., is known as Snowy Range.

Medicine Bow River, S Wyo., rises in N Medicine Bow Mts., flows 195 mi. N and W, past Medicine Bow, to Seminoe Reservoir.

Medicine Creek. **1** In S Iowa and N Mo., rises in S Iowa, flows c.100 mi. S to Grand R. 10 mi. SE of Chillicothe. **2** In SW central Nebr., rises in Lincoln co., flows 72 mi. SSE, past Curtis and Stockville, to Republican R. near Cambridge. Dam (building begun 1948) near Cambridge.

Medicine Hat, city (pop. 12,859), SE Alta., near Sask. border, at foot of Cypress Hills, on South Saskatchewan R. and 270 mi. SE of Edmonton; center of one of world's largest natural-gas fields; coal, shale, and clay mining, cattle and sheep ranching, and dryland farming are carried on in region. City is distributing center for SE Alta. and has important railroad shops and yards, foundries, feed and flour mills, potteries, machinery and farm-implement works. Site was chosen 1882 as North West Mounted Police post.

Medicine Lake. **1** Village (pop. 284), Hennepin co., E Minn., on small lake 7 mi. W of Minneapolis. **2** Town (pop. 454), Sheridan co., NE Mont., on Medicine L., near Big Muddy Creek, and 20 mi. S of Plentywood; wool, livestock, grain; coal mines.

Medicine Lake, NE Mont., in Sheridan co., 20 mi. S of Plentywood; 9 mi. long, 4 mi. wide; outlets into Big Muddy Creek. U.S. migratory waterfowl refuge here.

Medicine Lodge, city (pop. 2,288), ⊙ Barber co., S Kansas, on Medicine Lodge R. and 70 mi. WSW of Wichita; trade and refining point in wheat and livestock area; mfg. (gypsum cement, gasoline). Oil and gas wells, gypsum mines in vicinity. Founded 1873, inc. 1879. Quinquennial pageant (since 1927) commemorates signing of treaty (1867) near by with Plains Indians. Carry Nation started antisaloon crusade here in 1899.

Medicine Lodge River, in Kansas and Okla., rises in Kiowa co. in S Kansas, flows 101 mi. SE, past Medicine Lodge (Kansas), into Alfalfa co. in Okla., to Salt Fork of Arkansas R.

Medicine Park, Okla.: see LAWTONKA, LAKE.

Medina (mādē'nä), village (pop. estimate 1,000), S Tucumán prov., Argentina, 45 mi. SSW of Tucumán; rail terminus and agr. center (sugar, rice, livestock); sugar refining.

Medina, town (pop. 578), Cundinamarca dept., central Colombia, at E foot of Cordillera Oriental, 50 mi. E of Bogotá; coffee, corn.

Medina, Egypt: see FAIYUM, province.

Médina, Fr. Sudan: see MÉDINE.

Medina (mŭdē'nŭ), Arabic *Al-Madinah* (ăl mădē'-nŭ), city (pop. 12,000), N central Hejaz, Saudi Arabia, in basin of coastal plateau (alt. 2,200 ft.), 220 mi. N of Mecca, at head of the Wadi Hamdh; 24°35'N 39°53'E. One of the sacred cities of Islam, 2d only to Mecca, Medina was the later residence of Mohammed and the nucleus of the rapidly growing Islamic state. Primarily an agr. center, unlike the commercial Mecca, Medina is the center of a large date-growing oasis, producing also grapes and other fruit, grain and clover. It has an important pilgrimage trade and is served by the Red Sea port of Yenbo. Shaped like an irregular oval and 1 mi. long, it consists of the older walled town (NE) of small houses and tortuous streets and the larger modern town and garden suburbs dating from Turkish times. The Prophet's mosque in the old town has a spacious enclosed court, with a chamber supposed to contain the graves of Mohammed and Abu Bakr and Omar, the first 2 orthodox caliphs. The reputed tomb of Fatima is in a near-by smaller chamber. This mosque was enlarged in 8th cent. and burned twice (1256, 1481) before its final restoration. Originally called Yathrib (Ptolemy's *Lathrippa*), the city was an early Jewish colony. It was here that Mohammed came on the hegira (A.D. 622) from Mecca. Medina, later called formally *Medinat en Nabi* [city of the Prophet], *Medinat Rasul Allah* [city of the apostle of God], or *Medinat el Munawara* [greatly illuminated city], became the center of the Islamic state until the Omayyads established the caliphal residence at Damascus in 661. After its sack in 683 by the caliphs because of its rebellious attitude, Medina declined in importance under the rule of local emirs. It was controlled by the Mamelukes of Egypt, and after 1517 by the Turks. The rising Wahabis briefly held the city, 1804–12. In 1908, it was reached by the Hejaz railway (now in disuse) from Damascus; and it prospered until First World War through increased pilgrimage trade. During the war, it fell (1916) to Husein ibn Ali and (1924) to Ibn Saud. Largely depopulated during this period of unrest, Medina has rallied under Saudi Arabian rule but has not attained its prosperity of Hejaz railroad days.

Médina (mādē'nä), NW native quarter of Dakar, W Senegal, Fr. West Africa.

Medina. 1 (mŭdī'nŭ) County (□ 424; pop. 40,417), N Ohio; ⊙ Medina. Drained by Rocky and Black rivers and small Chippewa Creek. Includes Chippewa L. (resort). Agr. area (dairy products, grain, fruit, truck); mfg. at Wadsworth and Medina. Formed 1818. **2** (mŭdē'nŭ) County (□ 1,353; pop. 17,013), SW Texas; ⊙ Hondo. Crossed E–W by Balcones Escarpment, separating Edwards Plateau (in N) from plains of S. Drained by Medina R.; part of Medina L. (irrigation, recreation) is in NE. Ranching (cattle, sheep, goats); wool, mohair marketed; dairying, poultry raising, agr. (corn, grain sorghums, peanuts); irrigated truck farming. Some oil, natural gas; clay mining. Formed 1848.

Medina. 1 (mŭdī'nŭ) Industrial village (pop. 6,179), Orleans co., W N.Y., on the Barge Canal and Oak Orchard Creek, and 30 mi. NE of Buffalo; mfg. of textiles, canned foods, feed, furniture, machinery, pipes and fittings, vinegar, fruit products, pickles; iron foundries; sandstone quarries. Agr. (fruit, truck). Inc. 1832. **2** (mŭdē'nŭ, –dī'nŭ) City (pop. 564), Stutsman co., central N.Dak., 28 mi. W of Jamestown. **3** (mŭdī'nŭ) City (pop. 5,097), ⊙ Medina co., N Ohio, 18 mi. W of Akron, in agr. area (dairy products, poultry, fruit); apiary supplies, educational toys, candles, foundry products. Settled as Mecca; platted 1818. **4** (mŭdī'nŭ) Town (pop. 690), Gibson co., NW Tenn., 12 mi. N of Jackson; ships fruit, vegetables. **5** (mŭdē'nŭ) Village (pop. c.400), Bandera co., SW Texas, on Medina R. and c.50 mi. NW of San Antonio, in livestock-ranching area; tourist trade.

Medinaceli (mā-dhēnä-thä'lē), town (pop. 640), Soria prov., N central Spain, 40 mi. S of Soria; grain growing, sheep raising; flour milling. Has saltworks and hydroelectric plant near by. Anc. town, dating back to Romans. Once a Moorish stronghold, it was later seat of the dukes of Medinaceli, who built a Renaissance palace. Also has Roman arch and anc. grain exchange.

Medina Dam, Texas: see MEDINA RIVER.

Medina de las Torres (mā-dhē'nä dhä läs tô'rĕs), town (pop. 3,840), Badajoz prov., W Spain, on railroad and 40 mi. S of Mérida; agr. center (olives, cereals, grapes, livestock). Flour milling, olive-oil pressing; tile mfg.

Medina del Campo (dhĕl käm'pō), anc. *Methimna Campestris*, town (pop. 13,242), Valladolid prov., N central Spain, in Leon, communications center 25 mi. SW of Valladolid, on fertile plain covered with grainfields and vineyards; livestock and grain market. Flour milling; mfg. of chocolate, tiles, soap, leather goods, burlap, esparto cordage, flour products. Salt mines near by. Has Gothic parochial church (16th cent.) and 15th-cent. Castillo de la Mota, a favorite residence of Queen Isabella, who died here. City was partly burned down in 16th cent.

Medina de Pomar (dhä pōmär'), town (pop. 1,860), Burgos prov., N Spain, 40 mi. NNE of Burgos, on fertile plain (*La Losa*); cereals, truck produce, livestock; timber. Sawmilling, tanning, flour milling; mfg. of chocolate and meat products. Anc. historic city of Roman origin; has 14th-cent. castle, 13th-cent. church, convent, palace of the dukes of Frías.

Medina de Ríoseco (rē"ōsā'kō), city (pop. 4,633), Valladolid prov., N central Spain, in Leon, 24 mi. NW of Valladolid; agr. trade center (cereals, vegetables, wine) and terminus of one branch of Canal of Castile; cheese processing, flour milling; stock raising.

Medina Lake, Texas: see MEDINA RIVER.

Medina River (mĕdē'nŭ, mī–), Isle of Wight, Hampshire, England, rises 6 mi. S of Newport, flows 12 mi. N, past Newport, to The Solent at Cowes. Navigable below Newport.

Medina River (mŭdē'nŭ), S central Texas, rises on Edwards Plateau NW of Medina, flows c.100 mi. generally SE to San Antonio R. 14 mi. S of San Antonio. Medina Dam (completed 1913; 180 ft. high, 1,580 ft. long), 26 mi. WNW of San Antonio, impounds Medina L. (capacity 254,000 acre-ft.), 1st large Texas irrigation reservoir; fishing, recreation; state fish hatchery.

Medina-Sidonia (mä-dhē'nä-sē-dhō'nyä), city (pop. 8,361), Cádiz prov., SW Spain, in Andalusia, picturesquely located on a plateau, 21 mi. E of Cádiz; grain and livestock (cattle, horses) center. Has tanneries, potteries, flour mills. Notable Gothic cathedral. Probably of Phoenician origin. Seat of former Medina-Sidonia duchy. Near by are sulphur springs, and caves with prehistoric paintings.

Médine (mĕdē'nä), village, SW Fr. Sudan, Fr. West Africa, on the Senegal and 6 mi. SE of Kayes, linked by rail. Old fort. Captured (c.1855) by Faidherbe, who made it his base for further conquests of the Sudan. Sometimes Médina.

Medinet el Faiyum, Egypt: see FAIYUM, city.

Medinilla (mädēnē'yä) or **Farallon de Medinilla** (färäyōn' dä), uninhabited volcanic island, S Marianas Isls., W Pacific, 180 mi. NNE of Guam; 1.5 mi. long; phosphates.

Medinilla (mā-dhēnē'lyä), town (pop. 1,182), Ávila prov., central Spain, 36 mi. S of Salamanca; cereals, acorns, livestock; flour milling.

Medinipur, India: see MIDNAPORE.

Medio, Pico del, NE Spain: see MALADETTA.

Mediolanum, France: see ÉVREUX; SAINTES.

Mediolanum, Italy: see MILAN.

Mediomatrica, France: see METZ.

Medio River (mā'dyō), on Buenos Aires–Santa Fe prov. border, Argentina, rises 12 mi. NNE of Colón, flows c.70 mi. NE along border to the Paraná 5 mi. NW of San Nicolás.

Médiouna (mādyōōnä'), village, Casablanca region, NW Fr. Morocco, 12 mi. SSE of Casablanca; truck farming, palm-fiber processing.

Mediterranean Sea (mĕ"dĭtĕrā'nēŭn, –nyŭn), anc. *Mare Internum*, great inland sea (□ 965,000; including Black Sea, □ 1,145,000), an arm of the Atlantic Ocean, bet. Europe and Africa, extending from Strait of Gibraltar to coast of SW Asia; 2,400 mi. long; greatest width 1,000 mi.; mean depth, 4,500 ft.; greatest depth, 14,449 ft off Cape Matapan at 35°44'N 21°45'E. A ridge bet. Cape Bon (Tunisia) and Sicily, rising to within 1,300 ft. of the surface, separates the Mediterranean into W and E sections. These in turn fall into a series of basins—the Balearic and Tyrrhenian basins grouped as the West Mediterranean, and the Ionian and Levantine basins grouped as the East Mediterranean. The latter forms 2 shallow, isl.-strewn arms—the Adriatic and Aegean seas—and is connected with the Black Sea by the Turkish straits (Dardanelles, Sea of Marmara, Bosporus) and with the Red Sea by the Suez Canal. Very irregular in shape, it is penetrated by the Italian and Greek peninsulas and contains numerous isls.: the Balearic Isls., Corsica, Sardinia, Sicily (all W), and Malta, Crete, Cyprus, Rhodes, and the Dodecanese, Ionian, and Aegean isls. (all E). The Mediterranean is surrounded by warm, dry countries and receives several important rivers (Ebro, Rhone, Po, Nile). With evaporation exceeding precipitation and runoff, the Mediterranean has a water deficit, and a strong current of Atlantic water enters through the Strait of Gibraltar. Dense Mediterranean water, of relatively high temp. (55°F.) and high salinity (38 per mill), is returned to the Atlantic through the strait below the incoming flow. There is little variation in tides (about 1 ft.); fish, sponge, and coral are plentiful. Situated in latitudes (bet. 30° and 45°N) that are under the influence of subtropical highs in summer and the prevailing westerlies in winter, the Mediterranean has a distinctive type of climate, characterized by mild winters of moderate rainfall, warm, dry summers, abundant sunshine, natural vegetation of broad-leaved evergreens and drought-resistant trees, and such characteristic crops as citrus fruit and olives. The term "Mediterranean climate" has been given to similar climates throughout the world. The region of the Mediterranean Sea is further characterized by local winds, such as the dry, hot sirocco from Africa, the cold, dry mistral in the Rhone Valley, and the similar bora in the Adriatic. Used as a trade route by the Phoenicians, the Mediterranean and its shores were later disputed by Carthage, Greece, and Rome. Under the Roman Empire, it was virtually a Roman lake and was labeled *mare nostrum* [our sea]. In the Middle Ages, Genoa and Venice were the great Mediterranean powers, but with the opening (late-15th cent.) of the route to India around the Cape of Good Hope, the Mediterranean declined. Since the opening (1869) of the Suez Canal, it has resumed its importance as one of the world's busiest shipping lanes, linking Europe and Asia. In the European rivalry for control of this vital trade route, British supremacy (based on Gibraltar, Malta, and Cyprus) was unsuccessfully challenged in 1930s by Italy, which sought to revive the Roman *mare nostrum* concept. The chief modern ports are Barcelona, Marseilles, Genoa, Naples, Trieste, Piraeus, Smyrna, Haifa, Alexandria, Tunis, Algiers, and Oran.

Medium Lake (c.5 mi. long), Palo Alto co., NW Iowa; Emmetsburg is at S end.

Medjana (mĕjänä'), village (pop. 1,029), Constantine dept., NE Algeria, on SE slope of Biban range, 6 mi. NW of Bordj-bou-Arréridj; cereals, olives.

Medje (mĕ'jä), village, Eastern Prov., N Belgian Congo, 170 mi. ESE of Buta; native market and tourist center in Mangbettu territory; cotton gin.

Medjerda Mountains (mĕjĕrdä'), coastal range of the Atlas Mts. in NE Algeria and NW Tunisia, extending c.100 mi. WSW-ENE from Souk-Ahras to Béja bet. the Mediterranean (N) and the Medjerda valley (S). Average alt. 3,200 ft. Abundant rainfall. Cork-oak forests.

Medjerda River, anc. *Bagradas*, chief river of Tunisia, rises in the Medjerda Mts. of NE Algeria, WSW of Souk-Ahras, flows c.230 mi. ENE, past Ghardimaou (where it enters Tunisia), Souk-el-Arba, and Medjez-el-Bab, to the Gulf of Tunis 20 mi. N of Tunis. Receives the Mellègue and Siliana (right) and the Oued el Lil (left). It waters Tunisia's principal wheat-growing region, bet. Souk-el-Arba and Medjez-el-Bab, and provides chief route of access (road, railroad) to Tunis from the West. New irrigation dams projected for its Tunisian course. River formerly entered the Mediterranean through L. of Tunis. Sometimes Medjerdah.

Medjez-el-Bab (mĕ'jĕz-ĕl-bäb'), town (pop. 3,340), ⊙ Medjez-el-Bab dist. (□ 889; pop. 63,740), N central Tunisia, on Medjerda R. and 32 mi. WSW of Tunis; road center in Tunisia's great wheat-growing region. Damaged in heavy fighting (1942–43) during Second World War.

Medjumurje (mĕ'dyōōmōōr"yĕ), Serbo-Croatian *Međumurje*, Hung. *Muraköz* (mōō'rŏkûz), Ger. *Mittelmurgebiet* (mĭt'ŭlmōōrgŭbēt") or *Murinsel* (mōōr'ĭn"zŭl), agr. region, N Croatia and E Slovenia, Yugoslavia; bounded by Drava R. (S), Mur R. and Hung. frontier (NE). Petroleum region; turkey raising. Chief town, CAKOVEC. Until 1920, in Zala co., Hungary.

Medlar with Wesham (wĕ'sŭm), parish (pop. 2,308), W Lancashire, England. Includes village of Wesham, 7 mi. E of Blackpool; dairy farming, agr.

Medley, town (pop. 106), Dade co., S Fla.

Mednaya Shakhta (myĕd'nĭŭ shäkh'tŭ) [Rus.,= copper mine], rail junction in W Sverdlovsk oblast, Russian SFSR, 9 mi. E of Karpinsk.

Mednogorsk (myĕdnŭgôrsk'), city (1939 pop. over 10,000), E central Chkalov oblast, Russian SFSR, in S foothills of the S Urals, on left tributary of Sakmara R., on railroad (Medny station) and 45 mi. WNW of Orsk, in Orsk-Khalilovo industrial dist. Copper and sulphur-mining and -processing center; sawmilling, food processing. Within city limits is Blyava (6 mi. E of city center, on railroad; copper and pyrite mines). Developed (1938) as town of Medny; became city (1939) and renamed Mednogorsk.

Mednoye (myĕd'nŭyŭ), village (1926 pop. 720), S central Kalinin oblast, Russian SFSR, on Tvertsa R. and 16 mi. WNW of Kalinin; garment mfg.

Medny, town, Russian SFSR: see MEDNOGORSK.

Medny Island or **Mednyy Island** (myĕd'nē) [Rus.,=copper], in SW Bering Sea, 2d largest of KOMANDORSKI ISLANDS, Kamchatka oblast, Khabarovsk Territory, Russian SFSR, 29 mi. E of Bering Isl.; 34 mi. long, 4 mi. wide. Chief village, Preobrazhenskoye. Copper deposits; fur-seal preserve.

Médoc (mādôk'), region of Gironde dept., SW France, extending 50 mi. NNW from Blanquefort (near Bordeaux) to Pointe de Grave, bet. the Gironde (E) and Bay of Biscay (W). On the Gironde slopes are some of France's most famous vineyards (Château-Latour, Château-Lafite, Château-Margaux). Chief centers are Pauillac (port for Bordeaux), Saint-Estèphe, and Saint-Julien-Beychevelle. Along the Atlantic are dunes and pine forest marking N extremity of the LANDES.

Medo Island (mä'dōō), islet in São Marcos Bay, off Maranhão, NE Brazil, 7 mi. W of São Luís.

Medolla (mĕdôl'lä), village (pop. 519), Modena prov., Emilia-Romagna, N central Italy, 3 mi. S of Mirandola; foundry.

Medomak, village, Maine: see BREMEN.

Medomak River (mĭdŏ'mŭk), S Maine, rises in N Lincoln co., flows c.15 mi. S, widening below Waldoboro, to Muscongus Bay.

Medomsley (mĕ'dŭmzlē), town and parish (pop. 7,005), N Durham, England, 10 mi. SW of Newcastle-upon-Tyne; coal mining.

Medon (mē'dŭn), town (pop. 115), Madison co., W Tenn., 11 mi. S of Jackson.

Medora (mŭdô'rŭ). **1** Village (pop. 432), Macoupin co., SW Ill., 20 mi. N of Alton, in agr. and bituminous-coal area. **2** Town (pop. 627), Jackson co., S Ind., 18 mi. E of Bedford, in agr. area. **3** Village and township (pop. 241), ⊙ Billings co., W N.Dak., 35 mi. W of Dickinson; cattle raising, grain. Near by is site of Chimney Butte Ranch, where Theodore Roosevelt engaged in stock raising; it is a natl. park.

Médouneu (mādōōnû'), village, N Gabon, Fr. Equatorial Africa, 70 mi. SSW of Oyem, on Sp. Guinea border; customs station, cacao plantations.

Medpalli, India: see METPALLI.

Medrano (mädrä'nō), town (pop. estimate 1,000), N Mendoza prov., Argentina, on railroad, on Tunuyán R. and 22 mi. SE of Mendoza; agr. center (wine, corn, alfalfa, potatoes, fruit, livestock).

Medstead, village (pop. 183), W Sask., 40 mi. NNE of North Battleford; wheat, mixed farming.

Medum, Meidum, or **Maidum** (mā'dōōm), town (pop. 5,627), Beni Suef prov., Upper Egypt, on the Nile and 20 mi. ENE of Faiyum; site of pyramid of Snefru (c.2900 B.C.).

Medumurje, region, Yugoslavia: see MEDJUMURJE.

Meduncook River (mĭdŭn'kōōk), Knox co., S Maine, 5.5 mi. inlet of Muscongus Bay, bet. Friendship and Cushing.

Meduxnekeag River (mĭdŭks'nŭkĕg), in Maine and N.B.; N and S branches rise in SE Aroostook co., Maine; flow c.20 mi. to junction 8 mi. NE of Houlton (on S branch), in N.B., thence c.15 mi. SE to St. John R. at Woodstock, N.B.

Medvedevka (mĭdvĕ'dyĭfkŭ), village (1926 pop. 1,297), W Chelyabinsk oblast, Russian SFSR, on railroad (Baritnaya station) and 7 mi. SSE of Kusa; barite mining, mfg. of building materials. Formerly called Medvedevski.

Medvedevo (–dyĭvŭ), village (1939 pop. over 500), central Mari Autonomous SSR, Russian SFSR, 2 mi. W of Ioshkar-Ola; truck, wheat.

Medveditsa (–dyĭtsŭ) or **Medveditskoye** (–dyĭtskŭyŭ), village (1926 pop. 6,774), N Stalingrad oblast, Russian SFSR, near Medveditsa R., 39 mi. WSW of Krasnoarmeisk; canning, flour milling, metalworking; wheat, sunflowers. Until 1941 (in German Volga Autonomous SSR), Gussenbakh or Gussenbach.

Medveditsa River, S European Russian SFSR, rises W of Bazarny Karabulak, flows W, past Petrovsk (Saratov oblast), and generally SSW, past Atkarsk, Krasny Yar, and Mikhailovka (Stalingrad oblast), to Don R. opposite Serafimovich; 430 mi. long. Nonnavigable steppe river; frozen Dec.–Feb.

Medvedka, Russian SFSR: see GOFITSKOYE.

Medvednica (mĕd'vĕdnētsä), mountain, N Croatia, Yugoslavia, with central section (Zagreb Mtn., Serbo-Croatian *Zagrebačka Gora*) culminating in the Sleme or Sljeme (3,395 ft.), 6 mi. N of Zagreb. Winter sport center. Cement-rock deposits. Tunnel (3 mi. long; used by road and railroad) connects Zagreb (S) with mining regions (N).

Medvedok (mĭdvyĕ'dŭk), town (1926 pop. 477), S Kirov oblast, Russian SFSR, on Vyatka R. and 13 mi. SSE of Molotovsk; shipbuilding.

Medvenka (mĭdvyĕn'kŭ), village (1926 pop. 2,449), central Kursk Oblast, Russian SFSR, 20 mi. SSW of Kursk; sugar beets.

Medvezhi Ostrova, Russian SFSR: see BEAR ISLANDS.

Medvezhya Gora, Karelo-Finnish SSR: see MEDVEZHYEGORSK.

Medvezhye, Russian SFSR: see MOLOTOVSKOYE.

Medvezhyegorsk or **Medvezh'yegorsk** (mĭdvyĕzhĭgôrsk'), Finnish *Karhumäki* (kär'hōōmă"kē), city (1941 pop. 13,400), S central Karelo-Finnish SSR, on Povenets Gulf of L. Onega, on Murmansk RR and 75 mi. N of Petrozavodsk; lumber-milling center; mfg. (prefabricated houses, furniture), auto repair shops. Shipyards at Pindushi, 5 mi. E. Formerly called Medvezhya Gora.

Medvode (mĕd'vôdĕ), Ger. *Zwischenwässern* (tsvĭsh'ŭnvĕs"ŭrn), village, central Slovenia, Yugoslavia, on the Sava, at Sora R. mouth, on railroad and 7 mi. NNW of Ljubljana. Summer resort; mfg. (paper, cartons, chemicals) here and at near-by Vevce, Slovenian *Vevče*. In Carniola until 1918.

Medwar, El, Jordan: see MADWAR, EL.

Medway. 1 Town (pop. 725), Penobscot co., E central Maine, on the Penobscot and 10 mi. ESE of Millinocket, in lumbering area. **2** Town (pop. 3,744), including Medway village (pop. 1,276), Norfolk co., E Mass., on Charles R. and 22 mi. N of Providence, R.I.; woolens, shoes. Settled 1657, set off from Medfield 1713. Includes West Medway village (pop. 1,625).

Medway River, W N.S., rises ESE of Annapolis Royal, flows c.75 mi. SE, through Malaga and Ponhook lakes, to the Atlantic 8 mi. NE of Liverpool.

Medway River, England, rises in 2 headstreams (the N branch called Eden R.) in SE Surrey and NE Sussex, flows 70 mi. NE into Kent, past Maidstone, Rochester, Chatham, and Gillingham, to Thames estuary at Sheerness.

Medyka (mĕdĭ'kä), village, Rzeszow prov., SE Poland, frontier station on Ukrainian SSR border, 7 mi. E of Przemysl, 9 mi. W of Mostiska.

Medyka (myĕ'dĭkŭ), village (1939 pop. over 500), NW Drogobych oblast, Ukrainian SSR, custom rail station on Pol. border, 10 mi. W of Mostiska; grain, potatoes, livestock.

Medyn or **Medyn'** (myĭdĭn'yŭ), city (1948 pop. over 10,000), N Kaluga oblast, Russian SFSR, 35 mi. NNW of Kaluga; furniture factory; dairying, flax retting. Chartered 1389.

Medzhibozh (myĕjĕbôsh'), town (1926 pop. 11,609), E Kamenets-Podolski oblast, Ukrainian SSR, on the Southern Bug and 19 mi. E of Proskurov; fruit canning.

Medzilaborce (mĕd'zĭläbôrtsĕ), Hung. *Mezőlaborc* (mĕ'zûlŏbôrts), town (pop. 1,761), E Slovakia, Czechoslovakia, on Laborec R., on railroad and 35 mi. NE of Presov; lumbering, woodworking, petroleum refining. Site of heavy fighting bet. Austro-Hungarians and Russians in winter of 1915. Dukla Pass (alt. 1,647 ft.) is 13 mi. NW, Lupkow Pass (alt. 1,917 ft.) 8 mi. ESE.

Meekathara (mē"kŭthăr'ŭ), town (pop. 524), W central Western Australia, 280 mi. NE of Geraldton, on Geraldton-Wiluna RR; and mining center of Murchison Goldfield.

Meeker, county (□ 620; pop. 18,966), S central Minn.; ⊙ Litchfield. Agr. area drained by Crow R. Corn, oats, barley, potatoes, livestock, dairy products, poultry. Formed 1856.

Meeker. 1 Town (pop. 1,658), ⊙ Rio Blanco co., NW Colo., on White R. and 75 mi. NNE of Grand Junction; alt. 6,240 ft. Resort and trading point in grain and livestock area; flour, dairy and poultry products. Near by is Meeker Monument, at scene of "Meeker Massacre" (1879), in which Utes killed small group of whites including Nathan Meeker, Indian agent and co-founder of Greeley. Inc. 1885. **2** Town (pop. 672), Lincoln co., central Okla., 35 mi. E of Oklahoma City; trading point for agr. area; cotton ginning, feed milling.

Meeker, Mount, Colo.: see FRONT RANGE.

Meeks Field, Iceland: see KEFLAVIK.

Meelick, agr. village (district pop. 1,110), E central Co. Mayo, Ireland, on Moy R. and 12 mi. ENE of Castlebar; cattle, potatoes. There are remains of anc. round tower.

Meelpaeg Lake (mĕl'pŭĕg) (□ 37), central N.F., 40 mi. SSE of Buchans; 15 mi. long, 5 mi. wide. Contains numerous islets. Drained by Grey R.; connected SE with L. Ebbegunbaeg by 4-mi. stream.

Meenen, Belgium: see MENIN.

Meerane (märä'nŭ), town (pop. 26,804), Saxony, E central Germany, 9 mi. N of Zwickau; textile center (cotton, woolen, silk, rayon milling and knitting); machinery mfg. Textile industry introduced in 16th cent.

Meerbeke (mār'bākŭ), agr. village (pop. 4,553), East Flanders prov., W central Belgium, just SSE of Ninove.

Meerhout (mār'out), agr. village (pop. 7,219), Antwerp prov., N Belgium, on Grande Nèthe R. and 15 mi. SSE of Turnhout.

Meerle (mār'lŭ), agr. village (pop. 2,449), Antwerp prov., N Belgium, near Netherlands frontier, 8 mi. S of Breda (Netherlands).

Meersburg (mârs'bōōrk), town (pop. 2,347), S Baden, Germany, on the Überlinger See (a branch of L. of Constance), 7 mi. SE of Überlingen; steamer station; cotton mfg. Winegrowing. Has late-Gothic chapel; 16th-cent. granary, town hall, Old Castle; 18th-cent. New Castle was residence of bishops of Constance. Mesmer and poetess Droste-Hülshoff buried here.

Meerssen or **Meersen** (mār'sŭn), town (pop. 4,174), Limburg prov., SE Netherlands, 4 mi. NE of Maastricht; airport serving Maastricht. Mfg. (ceramics, china, paper, syrups); cattle raising, agr. Has 13th-cent. monastery church (*Kloosterkerk*). Residence (9th cent.) of Frankish kings. Here was signed (870) the treaty (Treaty of Mersen) bet. Charles the Bald and Louis the German, dividing the realm of Lothair.

Meerut (mē'rŭt), district (□ 2,323; pop. 1,896,582), NW Uttar Pradesh, India; ⊙ Meerut. On Ganges-Jumna Doab; irrigated by Eastern Jumna and Upper Ganges canals. Agr. (wheat, gram, jowar, sugar cane, oilseeds, cotton, corn, rice, barley); a leading sugar-processing dist. Main centers: Meerut, Harpur, Ghaziabad, Sardhana.

Meerut, city (pop., including cantonment, 169,290), ⊙ Meerut dist., NW Uttar Pradesh, India, 37 mi. NE of Delhi. Rail and road junction; trade center (wheat, millet, sugar cane, oilseeds, cotton, corn); sugar processing, flour and oilseed milling, mfg. of chemicals, soap, hosiery, leather goods, pottery, carpets; smelting and refining plant; handicrafts center (hand-loom cotton weaving, cutlery). Meerut Col. (founded 1892). Has mausoleum erected 1194 by Kutb-ud-din Aibak, 11th- and 17th-cent. mosques. Sacked (1199) by Tamerlane. Scene of one of 1st major outbreaks of Sepoy Rebellion of 1857.

Meerzorg (mār'zôrkh), village (pop. 3,563), Surinam dist., N Du. Guiana, on right bank of Surinam R. opposite Paramaribo; agr. center (rice, coffee, corn, tropical fruit).

Mées, Les (lāmā'), village (pop. 980), Basses-Alpes dept., SE France, near the Durance, 14 mi. WSW of Digne, in Provence Alps; olive- and winegrowing, fruit shipping.

Meesen, Belgium: see MESSINES.

Meeteetse (mĭtĕt'sē), town (pop. 404), Park co., NW Wyo., on Greybull R., in SE foothills of Absaroka Range, and 27 mi. SSE of Cody, in sheep-raising region; alt. 5,797.

Mega (mĕ'gä), town (pop. 2,000), Sidamo-Borana prov., S Ethiopia, near Kenya border, 100 mi. SSE of Burji, in agr. (corn, barley, potatoes, chick-peas) and stock-raising region; road junction; 4°2'N 38°18'E; commercial center. Salt extracting in near-by craters.

Mega, Japan: see SHIKAMA.

Megahatenna, Ceylon: see MIGAHATENNA.

Megale Delos, Greece: see RENEIA.

Megalo or **Megalo Petali** (mĕgä'lô pĕtŭlē') [Gr.,= great Petali], largest (□ 6.4; 1940 pop. 46) of Petalia Isls., in Gulf of Petalion, Greece, 2 mi. off Euboea; 4 mi. long, 3 mi. wide; fisheries. Also called Petali or Petalia.

Megalokastron, Crete: see CANDIA.

Megalopolis (mĕgŭlŏ'pŭlĭs), town (pop. 3,091), Arcadia nome, central Peloponnesus, Greece, on railroad, on branch of Alpheus R., and 15 mi. SW of Tripolis; trades in tobacco, wheat, wine, potatoes. Has archeological mus. Ruins of anc. city (just N) include large theater, temples and statues. Anc. Megalopolis was founded c.370 B.C. by Epaminondas as a fortress against Sparta and the center of the Arcadian League. It was the home of Philopoemen and Polybius. After repeated Spartan assaults, it finally fell to Cleomenus III and was razed. Modern town was formerly called Sinano.

Meganesi or **Meganisi** (mĕgŭnē'sē), island (□ 8.5; pop. 2,054) of Ionian group, Greece, off SE coast of Leukas (separated by narrow Meganesi Strait), in Leukas nome; 38°38'N 20°45'E; 4 mi. long, 2 mi. wide, with 5-mi.-long narrow peninsula (SW). Produces olive oil, wine, wheat. Sometimes called Taphos or Tafos. Main town (on NE shore) is Vathy or Vathi (pop. 1,198), formerly called Taphion or Tafion.

Megantic (mŭgăn'tĭk) or **Mégantic** (māgātĕk'), county (□ 780; pop. 40,357), S Que., on L. St. Francis; ⊙ Inverness.

Megantic, Mégantic, or **Lac Mégantic,** town (pop. 4,560), ⊙ Frontenac co., SE Que., on Chaudière R., at N end of L. Megantic, 50 mi. ENE of Sherbrooke, near Maine border; railroad center; pulp milling, lumbering, dairying; resort. Airport.

Megantic, Lake, or **Lake Mégantic** (9 mi. long, 2 mi. wide), S Que., extends S from Megantic, 50 mi. E of Sherbrooke; alt. 1,294 ft. Drained N by Chaudière R. into the St. Lawrence.

Megantic Mountain or **Mégantic Mountain** (3,625 ft.), S Que., 16 mi. SW of Megantic, near N.H. border.

Megara (mĕ'gŭrŭ), city (pop. 13,360), Attica nome, E central Greece, on railroad and 21 mi. W of Athens, on Megara peninsula, linking Attica and Peloponnesus; wine center, producing also flour and olive oil. Anc. Megara, a wealthy maritime city, flourished 8th–6th cent. B.C. and founded many colonies, including Chalcedon, Byzantium, and the Sicilian Megara Hyblaea (near modern Augusta). After the Persian Wars it was disputed by Corinth and Athens. The Megarian decree (432 B.C.), which excluded Megara from the Attic trade, was a contributory cause of the Peloponnesian War.

Megargel (mŭgär'gŭl), town (pop. 347), Archer co., N Texas, 40 mi. SW of Wichita Falls, in farm, ranch area.

Megaspelaion, Greece: see KALAVRYTA.

Megdova River or **Megdhova River** (both: mĕg'-dhôvŭ), in central Greece, rises in Pindus Mts. 15 mi. SW of Karditsa, flows 47 mi. SW to Achelous R. 15 mi. WSW of Karpenesion. Hydroelectric plants.

Megen (mā'khŭn), village (pop. 1,194), North Brabant prov., E central Netherlands, on Maas R. and 15 mi. NE of 's Hertogenbosch; cattle raising, agr.

Meget (mĭgyĕt'), town (1944 pop. over 500), S Irkutsk oblast, Russian SFSR, 14 mi. NW of Irkutsk and on Trans-Siberian RR; lumbering.

Mégève (mā-zhĕv'), village (pop. 1,252), Haute-Savoie dept., SE France, on upper Arly R., bet. the Chaîne du Reposoir (W) and Mont Blanc massif (E), 13 mi. SW of Chamonix; alt. 3,652 ft. A leading winter-sport and summer resort of Fr. Alps. Aerial tramways to Mont d'Arbois (E) and Mont Rochebrune.

Meggett, town (pop. 224), Charleston co., SE S.C., 18 mi. W of Charleston; shipping center for truck farms.

Meghna River (māg'nŭ), E Pakistan, formed in W Surma Valley just below union of numerous arms of the Surma (here called Kalni); flows 132 mi. SSW through rice- and jute-growing area, joining PADMA RIVER (the lower Ganges) NW of Chandpur and giving its name to the combined streams; continues c.90 mi. S to Bay of Bengal, entering it via 4 main mouths (W to E: Tetulia, Shahbazpur, and Hatia rivers, and Sandwip Channel); estuary mouth forms E boundary of Ganges Delta. During spring tides, sea rushes in forming single bore c.20 ft. high. Main tributaries: arm of old Brahmaputra and Dhaleswari (right), Gumti and Fenny (left) rivers.

Megiddo (mŭgĭ'dō), anc. city and road center, NW Palestine, at W edge of Plain of Jezreel, 18 mi. SSE of Haifa. In Biblical times ⊙ Canaanites. Anc. ruins and relics excavated here include citadel and stables ascribed to time of Solomon; other excavations date back as far as early Chalcolithic phase. Megiddo, believed also to be the biblical Armageddon, was scene of several important battles: Thothmas III defeated Syrians (1500 B.C.); Deborah and Barak defeated (13th cent. B.C.) Sisera at near-by Taanach; and Josiah was killed here by Pharaoh Necho II (608 B.C.). In modern times Napoleon here defeated Turks; in First World War

British under Allenby defeated (Sept., 1918) Turks. Jewish agr. settlement of Megiddo established 1949. Just SSE was site of Roman fortress and city of *Legio Maximianopolis*, junction of main roads to the sea.

Megra (myĕ'grŭ), village (1939 pop. over 500), NW Vologda oblast, Russian SFSR, near L. Onega, 20 mi. SW of Vytegra; grain, dairying. Formerly called Megorski Pogost.

Megreliya, Georgian SSR: see Mingrelia.

Megri (myĕ'grē), town (1926 pop. 1,161), S Armenian SSR, on Aras R. (Iran border), on railroad and 50 mi. ESE of Nakhichevan, in orchard dist.; dried fruit.

Mégrine (māgrēn'), SE suburb of Tunis, on L. of Tunis, N Tunisia; lead smelter, metalworks; olive-oil refinery and soap-mfg. plant. Silos. Truck gardening, salt working.

Megunticook, Mount, Maine: see Camden Hills.

Megunticook Lake (mŭgŭn'tĭko͝ok), S Maine, just NW of Camden, in recreational area; 3 mi. long, 1.5 mi. wide. Source of **Megunticook River** (c.4 mi. long), flowing SE to the Atlantic.

Megyaszo (mĕ'dyŏsō), Hung. *Megyaszó*, town (pop. 3,098), Zemplen co., NE Hungary, 13 mi. ENE of Miskolc; grain, beans, lentils, cattle.

Megyaungye, Burma: see Migyaungye.

Mehabad or **Mahabad** (both: mä"häbäd'), town (1940 pop. 12,858), Fourth Prov., in Azerbaijan, NW Iran, in the Kurd country, on road and 65 mi. SSE of Rizaiyeh and S of L. Urmia; alt. 4,800 ft. Grapes, tobacco; sheep raising. Was hq. of Kurdish uprising of 1946. Until 1930s called Saujbulagh or Savajbolagh.

Mehadia (mĕhä'dyä), anc. *Ad Mediam*, village (pop. 2,346), Severin prov., SW Rumania, at W extremity of the Transylvanian Alps, on railroad and 60 mi. SSE of Lugoj; lignite mining. Has picturesque Roman and 16th-cent. remains.

Mehallet, in Egyptian names: see Mahallat.

Meham, India: see Maham.

Mehamn (mä'hämŭn), fishing village (pop. 516) in Gamvik canton, Finnmark co., N Norway, on Barents Sea of Arctic Ocean, 80 mi. NW of Vardo, 5 mi. SE of Nordkyn cape.

Mehar (mā'hŭr), village, Dadu dist., W Sind, W Pakistan, 31 mi. N of Dadu; market center (rice, millet, wheat).

Mehdia (mĕdyä'), village, Rabat region, NW Fr. Morocco, on the Atlantic at mouth of the Sebou, 18 mi. NE of Rabat; rail-spur terminus; bathing beach; fish-processing plant. New outport for Port-Lyautey (10 mi. upstream) under construction here. An early Carthaginian settlement, it was coveted (16th cent.) by Portuguese and held (17th cent.) by Spaniards. In disuse as a port at time of Fr. occupation (1911), it was abandoned in favor of Kénitra (now Port-Lyautey). Two jetties (over 1 mi. long) flank river mouth to aid navigation. Lighthouse. Sometimes spelled Meheydia or Mehedya.

Mehekar, India: see Mehkar.

Mehelav, India: see Mehlav.

Meheri Zebbeus, Tunisia: see Maknassy.

Meherpur (mā'hŭrpo͝or), town (pop. 7,728), Kushtia dist., W East Bengal, E Pakistan, on distributary of Jalangi R. and 32 mi. WSW of Kushtia; trades in rice, jute, linseed, sugar cane, wheat; bell-metal mfg. Until 1947, in Nadia dist. of Br. Bengal prov. Formerly called Mihrpur.

Meherrin River (mŭhĕ'rĭn), in Va. and N.C., formed by headstreams joining in Lunenburg co., S Va.; flows ESE past Emporia, and SE into N.C., past Murfreesboro (head of navigation), to Chowan R. 8 mi. E of Murfreesboro; 126 mi. long.

Meheso, Ethiopia: see Miesso.

Mehetia (māhätē'ä), uninhabited volcanic island (□ c.1), Windward group, Society Isls., Fr. Oceania, S Pacific, 60 mi. E of Tahiti.

Meheydia, Fr. Morocco: see Mehdia.

Meh Hongsuen, Thailand: see Maehongson.

Mehidpur (mā'hĭdpo͝or), town (pop. 7,928), W central Madhya Bharat, India, on Sipra R. and 22 mi. NNW of Ujjain; market center (millet, cotton, wheat, opium); cotton ginning, hand-loom weaving; place of pilgrimage. In near-by battle, British defeated Mahrattas in 1817. Mehidpur Road, rail station (sugar milling, cotton ginning), is 11 mi. NW. Sometimes spelled Mahidpur.

Mehkar (mā'kŭr), town (pop. 8,257), Buldana dist., W Madhya Pradesh, in Ajanta Hills, on Penganga R. and 37 mi. SE of Buldana; cotton ginning. Sodium carbonate and salt extracted from lake 13 mi. S, near village of Lonar. Sometimes spelled Mehekar.

Mehkerek (mā'kĕrāk), Hung. *Méhkerék*, town (pop. 2,287), Bihar co., E Hungary, 4 mi. NE of Sarkad; corn, tobacco, hogs.

Mehlauken, Russian SFSR: see Zalesye.

Mehlav (mā'läv), town (pop. 5,002), Kaira dist., N Bombay, India, 14 mi. SSE of Kaira; local agr. market (millet, tobacco, cotton). Sometimes spelled Mehelav or Mehelao.

Mehlis, Germany: see Zella-Mehlis.

Mehmadabad (māhmŭdä'bäd), town (pop. 7,834), Kaira dist., N Bombay, India, 6 mi. NE of Kaira; rice, millet; cotton ginning, dairy farming. Sometimes spelled Mohammadabad.

Mehndawal (mān'dävŭl), town (pop. 11,000), Basti dist., NE Uttar Pradesh, India, 27 mi. NE of Basti; trades in rice, wheat, barley, oilseeds, sugar cane. Also spelled Mendhawal.

Mehomia, Bulgaria: see Razlog.

Mehrabad, Iran: see Teheran.

Mehran (mĕrän'), town, Fifth Prov., in the Pusht Kuh, on Iraq border, 100 mi. SSW of Kermanshah, and on road to Badra and Kut al Imara; customs post. Formerly called Mansurabad.

Mehrauli, India: see Mahrauli.

Mehrerau (mā'rŭrou), W suburb of Bregenz, Vorarlberg, W Austria, on L. of Constance; mineral springs. Benedictine monastery.

Mehrnbach (mārn'bäkh), town (pop. 2,171), W Upper Austria, 3 mi. W of Ried; potatoes, cattle.

Mehsana (māsä'nŭ), district, N Bombay, India; ⊙ Mehsana. Bounded W by Rann of Cutch, E by Sabarmati R. Agr. (millet, oilseeds, cotton, wheat); hand-loom weaving, tanning. Patan, Sidhpur, Kalol, and Kadi are cotton-milling centers. Dist. formed 1949 by merger of most of Mehsana div. of former Baroda state and parts of former Western India States, including Radhanpur and Idar.

Mehsana, town (pop. 16,986), ⊙ Mehsana dist., N Bombay, India, 40 mi. NNW of Ahmadabad, in Gujarat; major rail junction; trades in millet, wheat, oilseeds, cotton fabrics; handicraft cloth weaving, chemical mfg.

Meh Sot, Thailand: see Mae Sot.

Mehuín (māwēn'), village (1930 pop. 16), Valdivia prov., S central Chile, on Pacific coast, 26 mi. N of Valdivia; resort; salmon and trout fishing.

Mehun-sur-Yèvre (mŭŭ'-sür-yĕ'vrŭ), town (pop. 4,604), Cher dept., central France, on Yèvre R. and Berry Canal, and 9 mi. NW of Bourges; porcelain and optical glass factories; mfg. of plumbing equipment and shirts; dairying. In its 14th-cent. castle Charles VII was crowned (1422); here he also received (1429–30) Joan of Arc, and starved himself to death (1461).

Mei, China: see Mei River.

Mei Chiang, China: see Mei River.

Meidan Ekbes or **Maydan Ikbis** (both: mā'dăn ĕk'bĕs), Fr. *Maidane Ekbez*, town, Aleppo prov., NW Syria, on Turkish border, on railroad, and 45 mi. NNW of Aleppo; cereals, cotton.

Meiderich (mī'dŭrĭkh), industrial district (since 1905) of Duisburg, W Germany, N of Ruhr R., 2 mi. N of city center, on Rhine-Herne Canal (W), adjoining (E) Ruhrort; steel milling.

Meidling (mīd'lĭng), district (□ 3; pop. 80,998) of Vienna, Austria, 3 mi. SW of city center.

Meidum, Egypt: see Medum.

Meiel, Netherlands: see Meijel.

Meierhken, Manchuria: see Nunkiang.

Meifa, Maifa, or **Mayfah** (mā'fŭ), village, Quaiti state, Eastern Aden Protectorate, on Gulf of Aden, at mouth of the Wadi Hajr, 40 mi. SW of Mukalla; center of agr. area (grain, dates, citrus fruit).

Meifa'a, Wadi, Wadi Maifa'a, or **Wadi Mayfa'ah** (wă'dē mā'fä), intermittent coastal stream of Eastern Aden Protectorate, rises near Yeshbum, flows c.100 mi. through Wahidi sultanate of Balhaf, past Habban and Azzan, to Gulf of Aden 90 mi. WSW of Mukalla. Used for irrigation.

Meifod (mī'vôd), agr. village and parish (pop. 1,162), N central Montgomery, Wales, 6 mi. NW of Welshpool. Has Norman church.

Meiganga (māgäng'gä), village, Adamaona region, E Fr. Cameroons, near Fr. Equatorial Africa border, 80 mi. SE of N'Gaoundéré; stock raising, butter and cheese mfg.

Meighen Island (mē'ŭn) (□ 360), Sverdrup Isls., N Franklin Dist., Northwest Territories, in the Arctic Ocean, separated from Ellef Ringnes and Amund Ringnes isls. (S) by Peary Channel and from Axel Heiberg Isl. (E) by Sverdrup Channel; 80°N 99°W. Isl. is 30 mi. long, 8–15 mi. wide; central plateau rises to over 1,000 ft. Named 1921 by Stefansson after Arthur Meighen, Canadian prime minister.

Meigs (mĕgz). **1** County (□ 434; pop. 23,227), SE Ohio; ⊙ Pomeroy. Bounded SE by Ohio R., here forming W.Va. line; drained by small Shade R. and Leading Creek. Agr. (livestock; dairy products; fruit, grain, truck); mfg. at Pomeroy; coal and salt mines, limestone quarries. Formed 1819. **2** County (□ 213; pop. 6,080), SE Tenn.; ⊙ Decatur. In Great Appalachian Valley; bounded NW by the Tennessee; drained by Hiwassee R. Includes parts of Chickamauga and Watts Bar reservoirs. Livestock raising, agr. (fruit, tobacco); lumbering; saw- and planing mills. Formed 1836.

Meigs, town (pop. 1,125), Thomas and Mitchell counties, S Ga., 17 mi. NNW of Thomasville; mfg. (lumber, naval stores).

Meihsien (mā'shyĕn'). **1** Town (pop. 117,269), ⊙ Meihsien co. (pop. 466,165), E Kwangtung prov., China, on Mei R. and 70 mi. NNW of Swatow, in Hakka-inhabited area; coal-mining center; rice, wheat, tea, bamboo. Lead and tungsten mining, kaolin quarrying. Until 1912 called Kaying. **2** Town (pop. 1,801), ⊙ Meihsien co. (pop. 77,047), SW Shensi prov., China, on Wei R. and 70 mi. W of Sian, near Lunghai RR; cotton weaving; wheat, millet, beans. Graphite quarrying near by.

Meije (māzh), mountain of the Massif du Pelvoux, Dauphiné Alps, SE France, on Isère–Hautes-Alpes dept. border, 3 mi. S of La Grave, overlooking Oisans valley (N). Of its 3 serrate peaks the Grand-Pic de la Meije (13,081 ft.) is highest. Glaciers. First climbed 1877.

Meijel, Meiel, or **Meyel** (all: mī'ŭl), village (pop. 1,769), Limburg prov., SE Netherlands, 13 mi. W of Venlo; sand quarrying, peat digging.

Mei Kiang, China: see Mei River.

Meikle Bin, Scotland: see Lennox Hills.

Meikle Says Law, Scotland: see Lammermuir Hills.

Meiktila (mēk'tĭlŭ, Burmese māt"tēlä'), district (□ 2,232; 1941 pop. 344,025), Mandalay div., Upper Burma; ⊙ Meiktila. Astride Samon R.; consists largely of NE plateau (alt. c.800 ft.) of Pegu Yoma; in dry zone (annual rainfall 35 in.), mostly agr. (rice, sesame, cotton, peas); catechu and teak forests along Shan hills (E); small coal seams. Served by Rangoon-Mandalay RR and Thazi-Myingyan RR. Pop. is nearly all Burmese.

Meiktila, town (pop. 9,195), ⊙ Meiktila dist., Upper Burma, on Thazi-Myingyan RR and 80 mi. SSW of Mandalay, on NE plateau of the Pegu Yoma and on small Meiktila L. (□ 4), an anc. Burmese irrigation reservoir. Major road and rail hub of central Burma; cotton-trading center; ginning industry. Army cantonment; airfield. In Second World War, badly damaged (1945).

Meilen (mī'lŭn), town (pop. 5,014), Zurich canton, N Switzerland, on L. of Zurich and 8 mi. SSE of Zurich; coffee processing, printing.

Meilhan-sur-Garonne (mālä'-sür-gärôn'), village (pop. 412), Lot-et-Garonne dept., SW France, on the Garonne and Garonne Lateral Canal, and 6 mi. W of Marmande, in cattle-raising area; tobacco growing.

Meiling Mountains, China: see Tayü Mountains.

Meiling Pass (mā'lĭng'), in Tayü Mts., on Kwangtung-Kiangsi border, S China; alt. c.1,300 ft. On road bet. Tayü (N) and Namyung (S), it lies on one of chief Kwangtung-Kiangsi routes.

Meilu, China: see Muiluk.

Meimeh or **Meymeh** (both: māmĕ'), village, Second Prov., in Kashan, N Iran, 40 mi. SSW of Kashan and on Teheran-Isfahan road; center of Jushqan agr. area; wheat, barley, nuts (walnuts and almonds), dairy products; rugmaking. Exports wool. Has marble quarries.

Meina (mĕē'nä), village (pop. 1,301), Novara prov., Piedmont, N Italy, port on W shore of Lago Maggiore, 2 mi. N of Arona; resort; also has woolen mill.

Meinberg, Bad, Germany: see Bad Meinberg.

Meiners Oaks (mī'nŭrz), village (pop. 2,446), Ventura co., S Calif.

Meinerzhagen (mī"nŭrts-hä'gŭn), village (pop. 6,649), in former Prussian prov. of Westphalia, W Germany, after 1945 in North Rhine-Westphalia, 7 mi. S of Lüdenscheid; forestry.

Meiningen (mī'nĭng-ŭn), town (pop. 23,700), Thuringia, central Germany, on the Werra and 40 mi. SW of Erfurt; metalworking; lumbering; mfg. of machinery, textiles. Has former palace of dukes of Saxe-Meiningen (begun 1509, completed c.1700); memorials to Brahms and Jean Paul in the English Garden. First mentioned 982; chartered 1344. Was ⊙ duchy of Saxe-Meiningen, 1680–1918. Partly destroyed by fire in 1874. In 19th cent., noted for its dramatic acad. and stock-company theater; Hans von Bülow was conductor (1880–85) of the Meiningen Orchestra.

Meiomai, Iran: see Maiamai.

Meire Grove (mī'ŭr), village (pop. 128), Stearns co., central Minn., 35 mi. WNW of St. Cloud; grain, livestock, poultry.

Meiringen (mī'rĭng"ŭn), town (pop. 3,285), Bern canton, S central Switzerland, on Aar R. and 8 mi. ESE of Brienz; year-round resort; chief village of the Hasletal; alt. 1,968 ft. Near by are Gorge of the Aar and Reichenbach Falls.

Meirings Poort (mā'rĭngz po͝ort), rocky defile (c.5 mi. long; alt. 2,400 ft.), S Cape Prov., U. of So. Afr.; crosses Great Swartberg range 25 mi. NE of Oudtshoorn; noted for scenic beauty.

Mei River (mā), Chinese *Mei Kiang* or *Mei Chiang* (both: mā'jyäng'), E Kwangtung prov., China, rises on Kwangtung-Kiangsi border SW of Pingyün, flows 125 mi. S and NE, past Hingning and Meihsien, to Han R. SW of Taipu. Navigable below Meihsien.

Meir Shfeya or **Meir Shefeya,** Israel: see Shfeya.

Meiruba or **Mayrubah** (māro͞o'bŭ), Fr. *Mayrouba*, village (pop. 860), central Lebanon, 18 mi. ENE of Beirut; alt. 3,600 ft.; summer resort; apples, cotton, tobacco, lemons.

Meirun or **Meron** (both: mārōn'), village, Upper Galilee, N Israel, 3 mi. W of Safad, at foot of Mt. Jarmaq. Has remains of anc. synagogue, reputedly dating from time of destruction of Second Temple. Here is grave of the cabalist Simon ben Yohai; place of pilgrimage. Sometimes spelled Meiron.

Meisari, Aden: see Dathina.

Meisen, Korea: see Myongchon.

Meisenthal (mĕzätäl', Ger. mī'zŭntäl), village (pop. 731), Moselle dept., NE France, in the N Vosges, 16 mi. SE of Sarreguemines; glassworks.

Meishan (mā'shän'), town (pop. 17,763), ⊙ Meishan co. (pop. 372,876), W Szechwan prov., China, 35 mi. N of Loshan and on right bank of Min R.; silk spinning, tobacco processing, match mfg.; rice, wheat, sweet potatoes, beans. Thenardite deposits near by.

Meissen (mī'sůn), town (pop. 48,348), Saxony, E central Germany, on the Elbe and 14 mi. NW of Dresden; rail junction; porcelain-mfg. center, noted for its figurines (often called "Dresden china"); seat (since 1710) of Saxonian state porcelain works. Other mfg.: ceramics, machinery, electrical equipment, chemicals, pharmaceuticals, furniture, musical instruments; textile and paper milling, metal- and woodworking. Brickworks. Important kaolin deposits near by. Has 13th–14th-cent. cathedral; church of St. Afra (1295–1329); 15th-cent. Albrechtsburg castle, where china was made 1710–1864. Founded 929 by Henry the Fowler; became (965) seat of margraviate of Meissen, where Wettin dynasty of Saxony originated. Bishopric established 968, abolished 1581; recreated 1921 with seat at Bautzen. Chartered in 13th cent. Passed to Saxony in 1423. Sacked in Thirty Years War.

Meitan or **Mei-t'an** (both: mā'tän'), town (pop. 4,400), ⊙ Meitan co. (pop. 157,985), N Kweichow prov., China, 34 mi. E of Tsunyi; silk textiles; pottery making, lacquer processing; medicinal herbs, grain.

Meitene or **Meytene** (mā'tĕnā), railroad station, S Latvia, on Lith. border, 16 mi. S of Jelgava; junction of rail spur to Bauska; sugar beets.

Meitingen (mī'tĭng-ůn), village (pop. 1,917), Swabia, W Bavaria, Germany, on the Lech and 12 mi. N of Augsburg; hydroelectric plant; mfg. of electrotechnical machinery and equipment.

Meja (mā'jŭ), village, Allahabad dist., SE Uttar Pradesh, India, 27 mi. SE of Allahabad; gram, rice, wheat, barley.

Méjan, Causse, France: see CAUSSES.

Mejicana, Cumbre de la (kōōm'brā dā lä māhēkä'nä), Andean mountain (20,500 ft.) in Sierra de Famatina, N central La Rioja prov., Argentina, 23 mi. NW of Chilecito; copper and gold mines.

Mejicanos (māhēkä'nōs), residential town (pop. 8,159), San Salvador dept., S central Salvador, 2 mi. N of San Salvador; agr. market center; mfg. (baskets, pottery); grain, coffee, sugar cane.

Mejillones (māhĭyō'nĕs), town (pop. 1,056), Antofagasta prov., N Chile, Pacific port on a well-sheltered bay, 38 mi. N of Antofagasta, at terminus of rail line. Ships nitrates and Bolivian tin and other metals. Here in 1879, during the War of the Pacific, the capture of the Peruvian ironclad *Huáscar* gave Chile control of the sea; Mejillones was ceded 1882 to Chile. Formerly also called Mejillones del Sur to distinguish it from Mejillones del Norte, a now abandoned nitrate port c.25 mi. N of Iquique.

Mejit (mĕ'jĕt), coral island (pop. 302), Ratak Chain, Kwajalein dist., Marshall Isls., W central Pacific, 240 mi. ENE of Kwajalein; c.5 mi. long. Formerly Miadi.

Mejorada (māhōrä'dhä), town (pop. 1,602), Toledo prov., central Spain, 4 mi. NW of Talavera de la Reina; cereals, grapes, olives, livestock.

Mejorada del Campo (dhĕl käm'pō), town (pop. 1,783), Madrid prov., central Spain, near Jarama R., 10 mi. E of Madrid; cereals, olives, grapes, truck produce, livestock.

Mékambo (mĕkämbō'), village, NE Gabon, Fr. Equatorial Africa, 160 mi. NE of Booué; native rubber market. Has carpenters' and ironsmiths' school.

Mékerra, Oued (wĕd' mākĕrä'), stream in Oran dept., NW Algeria, rises in High Plateaus S of Bedeau, flows c.150 mi. NNE, past Sidi-bel-Abbès and Saint-Denis-du-Sig (below which it is called the Sig), to the coastal Sig lowland where its waters (dammed at Cheurfas Dam 12 mi. above Saint-Denis-du-Sig) are used for irrigation.

Mekhadir, Yemen: see MAKHADAR.

Mekhelta or **Mekhel'ta** (myĕkhĭltä'), village (1948 pop. over 2,000), W central Dagestan Autonomous SSR, Russian SFSR, on S slope of Andi Range, 32 mi. W of Buinaksk; grain, orchards, sheep.

Mekhliganj or **Mekliganj** (mā'klĭgŭnj), town (pop. 1,298), Cooch Behar dist., NE West Bengal, India, on the Tista and 33 mi. W of Cooch Behar; trades in rice, jute, tobacco, oilseeds, sugar cane.

Mekhomiya, Bulgaria: see RAZLOG.

Mekhonskoye (myĭkhôn'skŭyů), village (1948 pop. over 10,000), N Kurgan oblast, Russian SFSR, on Iset R., just below mouth of Miass R., and 35 mi. ENE of Shadrinsk; metalworks, flour mill.

Mekhtar (mākh'tŭr), village, Loralai dist., NE Baluchistan, W Pakistan, 45 mi. ENE of Loralai; market center for wheat, felts, mats.

Mekili or **El Mechili** (both: mĕkē'lē, ĕl), village, E Cyrenaica, Libya, 45 mi. SW of Derna, on Tobruk-Benghazi road; caravan center. Scene of fighting (1941–42) bet. Axis and British.

Mekkaw, Nigeria: see MEKO.

Mekliganj, India: see MEKHLIGANJ.

Meklong, town, Thailand: see SAMUTSONGKHRAM.

Meklong River, Thailand: see MAE KLONG RIVER.

Meknès (mĕknĕs'), city (pop. 159,811), ⊙ Meknès region (□ 35,901; pop. 873,399), N central Fr. Morocco, on a fertile plateau N of the Middle Atlas, 33 mi. WSW of Fez; alt. 1,740 ft.; 33°54'N 5°33'W. Commercial center for one of Morocco's richest agr. regions (olive and citrus groves, vineyards, truck gardens), and former residence of the sultan. Linked by rail with Rabat and Casablanca (W), Tangier (N), and Fez. A fine road leads to resort towns of Afrou and Ifrane (SE), high in the Middle Atlas. Airport is just E. Woolen milling, fruit and vegetable preserving and canning, palm-fiber and esparto processing; also metalworks and essential-oil distilleries; noted for its Moroccan carpets. Has Mediterranean subtropical climate (average yearly temp. 63°F.) with rainfall (24 inches) concentrated in winter months. Old city's principal tourist attraction is the huge market place, flanked by 2 imposing 17th–18th-cent. gateways. The sultan's palace and the remains of its Versailles-like grounds are just S. The military camp and the modern city (created after establishment of Fr. protectorate) are apart from Moslem city, E of the Oued bou Fekrane. The ruins of Roman *Volubilis* and the holy city of Moulay Idris (11 mi. N) are usually visited from Meknès. Founded in 11th cent. as an Almohade citadel, city rose to prominence when Sultan Ismail, a contemporary of Louis XIV, built his grandiose residence here in 1670s. After 1728, the capital once more reverted to Fez and Marrakesh, and Meknès declined. In 1947 city had only 23,619 European inhabitants, but was growing rapidly (1936 pop. 74,702). Formerly also spelled Mequinez.

Meko (mĕ'kō), town, Abeokuta prov., Western Provinces, SW Nigeria, 40 mi. NW of Abeokuta; customs depot on Dahomey border; cotton weaving, indigo dyeing; cacao, cotton. Also spelled Mekkaw.

Mekong River (mā'kông', mĕ'kông'), Chinese *Lantsang Chiang* (or *Kiang*) (län'dzäng'jyäng'), Thai *Mae Khong* (mă' kông') or *Mae Nam Khong* (näm'), Tibetan *Dza Chu* (dzä' chōō'), a great river of SE Asia; 2,600 mi. long. Rises at 33°N 94°E on N slopes of Tanglha Range in the Tibetan highlands of China's Tsinghai prov., flows S through E Tibet and W Yunnan prov., and in the Thai country forms the international line bet. Burma and Thailand (W) and Laos (E). In its lower course, the Mekong traverses Cambodia and in Cochin China (S Vietnam) forms a vast delta on South China Sea. In its upper reaches, the river flows through the NE Tibetan highlands in canyon-like gorges paralleling the Salween and the Yangtze. Local shallow-draught navigation begins at 21°N in area of Ban Houei Sai (Laos), and continues past Luang Prabang, Vientiane, Thakhek (opposite Nakhon Phanom, Thailand), Savannakhet (opposite Mukdahan, Thailand), Khemmarat (rapids), Pakse, Khone (falls on Cambodia line), and Stungtreng. In lower course at Kratie, 340 mi. from the sea, begins navigation for 15-ft.-draught vessels. At Pnompenh, in the QUATRE-BRAS confluence, the Mekong is linked with the lake TONLE SAP, its natural flood reservoir; and here also begins Bassac R., the Mekong's chief delta arm. The vast Mekong delta in Cochin China (S Vietnam) is one of the world's leading rice-surplus areas.

Mekoryok (mĕkōr'yŏk), village (pop. 155), SW Alaska, on N shore of Nunivak Isl.; 60°24'N 166°11'W.

Mekran, Iran and Pakistan: see MAKRAN.

Mel (mĕl), village (pop. 526), Belluno prov., Veneto, N Italy, on Piave R. and 8 mi. SW of Belluno. Has ruined castle.

Melada, island, Yugoslavia: see MULAT ISLAND.

Mélah, Syria: see MELLAH.

Melanesia (mĕlůnē'zhů, –shů) (□ c.60,000), one of 3 main divisions of Pacific isls., in W Pacific, S of equator; includes Fiji Isls., New Caledonia, Loyalty Isls., New Hebrides, Solomon and Santa Cruz isls., Admiralty Isls., Louisiade and Bismarck archipelagoes, D'Entrecasteaux Isls. The larger isls. are volcanic, the smaller coral. Rich mineral resources, precious and non-precious metals, coal. Inhabitants are largely of Negroid stock.

Melapalaiyam or **Melapalayam** (mālůpä'lůyům), town (pop. 31,505; 60% Moslem), Tinnevelly dist., S Madras, India, 3 mi. SE of Tinnevelly across Tambraparni R., in cotton- and palmyra-growing area; towel- and carpet-weaving center. Formerly also spelled Mel Palaiyam.

Melara (mĕlä'rä), village (pop. 1,360), Rovigo prov., Veneto, N Italy, on Po R. and 3 mi. E of Ostiglia.

Melazgerd, Turkey: see MALAZGIRT.

Melba, village (pop. 203), Canyon co., SW Idaho, 25 mi. SW of Boise; center of irrigated area.

Melbeta (mĕlbē'tů), village (pop. 138), Scotts Bluff co., W Nebr., 10 mi. ESE of Scottsbluff and on N. Platte R.

Melbo, Norway: see MELBU.

Melbourn (mĕl'bůrn), agr. village and parish (pop. 1,284), S Cambridge, England, 10 mi. SSW of Cambridge; fruitgrowing. Has Congregational chapel founded 1694 and 14th-cent. church.

Melbourne (mĕl'bůrn), municipality (pop. 99,863; metropolitan Melbourne 1,226,923), ⊙ Victoria, Australia, on N shore of Yarra R. and 5 mi. from its mouth on Hobson's Bay (N arm of Port Phillip Bay); 37°50'S 144°68'E. Second largest city of the Commonwealth, cultural and mfg. center of the state. The port of Melbourne, which includes wharves at city itself as well as at PORT MELBOURNE and WILLIAMSTOWN, is principal port of Victoria. Aircraft plant, engineering works, textile and knitting mills, fruit canneries, flour mills. Produces rubber goods, glass products, cigarettes, electrical appliances, automobiles. Exports wheat, flour, frozen meat, wool, fruits. Govt. buildings include Parliament House and Royal Mint. Seat of Univ. of Melbourne (1854), Conservatorium of Music (1910), Victorian Col. of Pharmacy (1880), Melbourne Technical Col. (1887), Natl. Art Gall. (1904), St. Paul's Cathedral (1880), St. Patrick's Cathedral (1840). Has large botanical gardens (103 acres). Mean annual temp., 59°F.; rainfall, 26 in. Site of Flemington Race Course, where Melbourne Cup is run annually. Seaside resorts near by. Principal suburbs are SOUTH MELBOURNE, BRIGHTON, CAMBERWELL, CAULFIELD, FOOTSCRAY, MALVERN, SAINT KILDA. Founded 1835 as Dootigala, renamed Melbourne in 1837 for Br. prime minister. It was 1st ⊙ (1901–27) of the Commonwealth, being succeeded by Canberra.

Melbourne, village (pop. estimate 350), S Que., on St. Francis R., opposite Richmond; dairying.

Melbourne, town and parish (pop. 3,714), S Derby, England, 7 mi. SSE of Derby; silk and rayon milling, shoe mfg., truck gardening. Has Norman church and Melbourne Hall, rebuilt in early 18th cent. Thomas Cook, pioneer of organized travel, b. here.

Melbourne. 1 Town (pop. 568), ⊙ Izard co., N Ark., 23 mi. NW of Batesville; stock raising, agr. (cotton, corn, hay); dairy products. **2** City (pop. 4,223), Brevard co., central Fla., 20 mi. S of Cocoa and on Indian R. lagoon; citrus-fruit shipping center and resort. Settled 1878, inc. 1888. Melbourne Beach, town (pop. 230), a bathing resort, is across the lagoon (E). **3** Town (pop. 510), Marshall co., central Iowa, 12 mi. SW of Marshalltown; packed poultry. **4** Town (pop. 102), Harrison co., NW Mo., 10 mi. WNW of Trenton.

Melbourne Island (18 mi. long, 10 mi. wide), S Franklin Dist., Northwest Territories, in Queen Maud Gulf, just E of base of Kent Peninsula, opposite SE Victoria Isl.; 68°30'N 104°15'W. On N coast is Eskimo winter camp.

Melbu (mĕl'bōō), village (pop. 1,018), in Hadsel canton (pop. 11,025), Nordland co., N Norway, on S shore of Hadseloy in the Vesteralen group, 18 mi. NNE of Svolvaer; cement casting, woolen milling, woodworking, oil-cloth mfg.; processing of guano, fish oil, oleomargarine. Formerly spelled Melbo. At Stokmarknes or Stokkmarknes village (pop. 1,099), 5 mi. NNE, is furniture mfg.

Melcher, town (pop. 898), Marion co., S central Iowa, near Whitebreast Creek, 33 mi. SE of Des Moines; coal mining; mfg. of wood products.

Melchora (mĕlchō'rä), village, dept., S Nicaragua, on San Juan R., at mouth of Melchora R. (a short left affluent), and 7 mi. E of San Carlos; lumbering.

Melchor Island, Chile: see CHONOS ARCHIPELAGO.

Melchor Múzquiz, Mexico: see MÚZQUIZ.

Melchor Ocampo (mĕlchōr' ōkäm'pō). **1** or **Ocampo**, town (pop. 2,584), Mexico state, central Mexico, 20 mi. N of Mexico city; cereals, livestock. **2** Village (pop. 810), Nuevo León, N Mexico, 55 mi. ENE of Monterrey; corn, cactus fibers. Formerly Charco Redondo. **3** Town (pop. 964), Zacatecas, N central Mexico, on Coahuila border, 55 mi. SW of Saltillo; alt. 6,886 ft. Rail terminus; mining center (silver, gold, lead, copper). Formerly San Pedro Ocampo.

Melcombe Regis, England: see WEYMOUTH AND MELCOMBE REGIS.

Meldal (mĕl'däl), village and canton (pop. 5,483), Sor-Trondelag co., central Norway, on Orkla R. and 34 mi. SW of Trondheim; mfg. of cement, roofing tiles. Lokken (Nor. *Løkken*) village (pop. 2,501), 5 mi. N, a pyrite-mining center since 1652, is terminus of electric railroad to Trondheim Fjord; has smelting works producing copper matte.

Melden (mĕl'důn), village (pop. 1,200), East Flanders prov., W central Belgium, on Scheldt R. and 3 mi. SW of Oudenaarde; agr., cattle raising.

Meldola (mĕl'dôlä), town (pop. 3,774), Forlì prov., Emilia-Romagna, N central Italy, on Ronco R. and 7 mi. SSE of Forlì; silk mills, alcohol distillery.

Meldorf (mĕl'dôrf), town (pop. 9,031), in Schleswig-Holstein, NW Germany, on small Miele R. near its mouth (harbor) on the North Sea, and 7 mi. S of Heide, in the S Dithmarschen; food canning and processing (dried vegetables, flour), fountain-pen mfg., woodworking. Market center (cattle, grain). Has 13th-cent. church on site of 9th-cent. bldg.; also Dithmarschen mus. Was main town of Dithmarschen (13th cent.-1447). Home of poet Boie. Residence (1778–1815) of explorer Karsten Niebuhr; his son Barthold Georg spent his youth here.

Mele, Cape (mā'lĕ), on Ligurian coast, NW Italy, 8 mi. NE of Imperia; 44°3'N 8°10'E; lighthouse.

Meleai or **Mileai** (both: mēlā'ĕ), town (pop. 1,983), Magnesia nome, SE Thessaly, Greece, at foot of the Pelion, 11 mi. ESE of Volos (linked by railroad); tobacco; olive oil.

Meleda, island, Yugoslavia: see MLJET ISLAND.
Melegnano (mĕlĕnyä'nô), town (pop. 8,757), Milano prov., Lombardy, N Italy, on Lambro R. and 10 mi. SE of Milan. Agr. center; cheese, sausage; mfg. (silk, linen, rope, furniture). Scene in 1515 of victory of Francis I and Venetians over Swiss under Cardinal Schinner, and in 1859 of battle bet. French and Austrians. Formerly Marignano.
Melekess (mĕlyĭkyĕs'), city (1937 pop. estimate 29,500), NE Ulyanovsk oblast, Russian SFSR, 50 mi. ESE of Ulyanovsk; agr.-processing center (grain, flax, meat, hops); sawmilling, metalworking. Teachers col. Peat digging near by. Became city in 1917.
Melen (mā'lŭn), town (pop. 1,763), Liége prov., E Belgium, 7 mi. E of Liége; coal mining.
Melena del Sur (mālā'nä dĕl sōōr'), town (pop. 3,485), Havana prov., W Cuba, on railroad and 26 mi. S of Havana; sugar-growing center, with the central Merceditas 1½ mi. N. Limekiln.
Melenci or **Melentsi** (both: mĕ'lĕntsē), Hung. *Melence* (mĕl'ĕntsĕ), village (pop. 8,125), Vojvodina, N Serbia, Yugoslavia, on railroad and 30 mi. NE of Novi Sad, in the Banat. Includes Banja Rusanda, health resort, on small Rusanda L.
Melendiz Dag (mĕlĕndĭz' dä), Turkish *Melendiz Dağ*, peak (9,630 ft.), central Turkey, 10 mi. NW of Nigde.
Melendugno (mĕlĕndōō'nyô), village (pop. 3,351), Lecce prov., Apulia, S Italy, 11 mi. SE of Lecce.
Melenki (mĕlyĭnkē'), city (1926 pop. 10,814), SE Vladimir oblast, Russian SFSR, 75 mi. SE of Vladimir; flax-milling center; food processing, peat working. Chartered 1778.
Melentyevskoye or **Melent'yevskoye** (mĕlyĭntyā'-ŭfskŭyŭ), town (1948 pop. over 2,000), W central Chelyabinsk oblast, Russian SFSR, on Miass R., on railroad and 6 mi. N (under jurisdiction) of Miass; gold mining.
Mêle-sur-Sarthe, Le (lù mĕl-sür-särt'), village (pop. 592), Orne dept., NW France, on the Sarthe and 9 mi. W of Mortagne; flour and sawmilling. Horse fair.
Melet, village, Turkey: see MESUDIYE.
Melet River (mĕlĕt'), N Turkey, rises in Giresun Mts. 20 mi. E of Mesudiye, flows 75 mi. W and N, past Mesudiye, to Black Sea near Ordu.
Meleuz (mĕlyăōōs'), town (1926 pop. 5,724), SW Bashkir Autonomous SSR, Russian SFSR, on Belaya R. and 45 mi. S of Sterlitamak, on rail spur; agr.-processing center; flour milling.
Melfi (mĕlfē'), village, central Chad territory, Fr. Equatorial Africa, 150 mi. W of Am-Timan; onion raising, experimental cotton station, apiculture.
Melfi (mĕl'fē), town (pop. 14,190), Potenza prov., Basilicata, S Italy, on N slope of extinct volcano (Monte Vulture), 26 mi. NNW of Potenza. Agr. trade center; wine, olive oil, cheese, cereals. Bishopric. Has medieval cathedral and Norman castle, both reconstructed. Flourished under Normans. Here Frederick II promulgated the Constitutions of Melfi or *Liber Augustalis*. Sacked by Lantrec in 1528. Suffered several earthquakes; rebuilt after that of 1851.
Melfort (mĕl'fŭrt), town (pop. 2,305), central Sask., on Melfort Creek and 55 mi. ESE of Prince Albert; stock-shipping center, oil-distributing point; flour and lumber milling, dairying; cold-storage plant.
Melfort, village, Salisbury prov., NE central Southern Rhodesia, in Mashonaland, on railroad and 20 mi. SE of Salisbury; alt. 4,957 ft. Tobacco, wheat, corn, citrus fruit, dairy products.
Melgaço (mĕlgä'sōō), northernmost town (pop. 866) of Portugal, in Viana do Castelo dist., near Minho R. (Sp. border), 42 mi. NE of Viana do Castelo; noted for its hams. Mineral springs. Founded 12th cent. as fortified frontier post by Alfonso I.
Melgar (mĕlgär'), town (pop. 1,259), Tolima dept., W central Colombia, in Magdalena valley, on Pan American Highway and 13 mi. SE of Girardot; coffeegrowing.
Melgar, Peru: see AYAVIRI.
Melgar de Fernamental (dhā fĕrnämĕntäl'), town (pop. 2,728), Burgos prov., N Spain, 28 mi. W of Burgos; cereals, vegetables, grapes, sheep, cattle, hogs. Lumbering, flour milling; mfg. of dairy and meat products, chocolate, tiles.
Melghir, Chott, Algeria: see MELRHIR, CHOTT.
Meliana (mälyä'nä), N suburb (pop. 3,398) of Valencia, Valencia prov., E Spain, in rich truck-farming area near the Mediterranean; tile and furniture mfg.
Melicobus, Germany: see MALCHEN.
Mélida (mā'lē-dhä), town (pop. 1,280), Navarre prov., N Spain, on Aragon R. and 21 mi. N of Tudela; sugar beets, cereals, alfalfa, sheep.
Meligala (mĕlēgŭlä'), town (pop. 2,482) Messenia nome, SW Peloponnesus, Greece, on railroad and 15 mi. NW of Kalamata, stock raising (sheep, goats); olive oil, cotton. Pyrolusite deposits near.
Melika (mälēkä'), walled Saharan village, Ghardaïa territory, central Algeria, one of the Mzab oases, just E of Ghardaïa, atop a rocky height.
Melilla (mälēl'yä), city (1940 pop. 77,192; 1948 estimated pop. 94,319), a Spanish possession on NW coast of Africa, an enclave in Sp. Morocco, port on the Mediterranean, 10 mi. S of Cape Tres Forcas and 130 mi. SE of Málaga (Spain), from which it is directly administered; 35°18'N 2°56'E. Chief export center for Sp. Morocco's iron and lead deposits; terminus of mining railroad from Beni bu Ifrur iron mine (11 mi. SW). Also important fishing and fish-processing port, and commercial center for Sp. Morocco's mountainous hinterland (Rif). Industries include mfg. of building materials, biscuits, and flour paste. There are boat-building and repair yards. Melilla has a radio transmitter, an airport (Tahuima, 11 mi. S, in Sp. Morocco), and a seaplane base (just SE on Mar Chica lagoon). Dominated (S) by the Gurugú range (alt. 2,900 ft.). Harbor is exposed to N winds. Pop. is predominantly Spanish. Old town (on a height) preserves 16th-cent. walls. New city presents modern European appearance. Founded by Phoenicians as *Rusaddir*, it later became a Carthaginian and a Roman settlement. Conquered by Spaniards in 1497, city was repeatedly subjected to sieges and blockades. Its hinterland (in Sp. Morocco) was pacified in 1909. Evacuated during Rif revolt led by Abd-el-Krim (1921–26), it was reoccupied by Spain in 1926. A revolt of army officers here (1936) was one of the signals for the outbreak of the Sp. civil war.
Melilli (mĕlēl'lē), village (pop. 5,890), Siracusa prov., E Sicily, 12 mi. NW of Syracuse; hemp, linen; honey. Saltworks on near-by coast. Numerous Siculian tombs in vicinity. Largely destroyed by earthquakes of 1542, 1693.
Melimoyu, Monte (mōn'tā mălēmoi'ōō), Andean peak (7,875 ft.), Aysén prov., S Chile, N of Magdalena Isl., 85 mi. N of Puerto Aysén.
Melincué, Argentina: see SAN URBANO.
Melinesti (mĕlĕnĕsht'), Rum. *Melineşti*, village (pop. 646), Gorj prov., S Rumania, 19 mi. NNW of Craiova; orchards.
Melinka, Chile: see GUAITECAS ISLANDS.
Melipilla (mālēpē'yä), town (pop. 9,316), ⊙ Melipilla dept. (□ 1,256; pop. 56,696), Santiago prov., central Chile, on Maipo R. and 35 mi. SW of Santiago; rail junction and fruitgrowing center (apples); alfalfa, wheat, potatoes, tobacco, stock.
Melisey (mŭlēzā'), village (pop. 650), Haute-Saône dept., E France, at foot of the Vosges, 6 mi. NE of Lure; cotton weaving, sawmilling.
Melissa (mĕlēs'sä), village (pop. 2,087), Catanzaro prov., Calabria, S Italy, 3 mi. NE of Strongoli; sulphur mining.
Melita (mŭlĭ'tŭ), town (pop. 659), SW Man., on Souris R. and 60 mi. SW of Brandon; dairying, mixed farming, stock raising.
Melita: see MALTA.
Melita, island, Yugoslavia: see MLJET ISLAND.
Melitene, Turkey: see MALATYA, city.
Melito di Napoli (mā'lētō dē nä'pôlē), town (pop. 5,184), Napoli prov., Campania, S Italy, 5 mi. NNW of Naples; sausage.
Melito di Porto Salvo (dē pôr'tô säl'vô), town (pop. 3,296), Reggio di Calabria prov., Calabria, S Italy, port on Ionian Sea, 15 mi. SE of Reggio di Calabria; alcohol distilling. At tip of "toe" of Italy; southernmost town (37°55'N) on Ital. mainland.
Melitopol or **Melitopol'** (mălyĕtô'pŭl), city (1926 pop. 25,289; 1939 pop. 75,735), SW Zaporozhe oblast, Ukrainian SSR, on Molochnaya R. and 65 mi. S of Zaporozhe, on railroad; road junction; machine (grain-elevator equipment, Diesel motors, pumps) and clothing mfg.; flour milling, meat packing, cottonseed-oil extraction. Teachers and agr. colleges. Developed in 19th cent. Held (1941–43) by Germans in Second World War.
Melk or **Mölk** (both: mĕlk), town (pop. 3,139), W Lower Austria, on the Danube and 13 mi. W of Sankt Pölten; was oldest residence of Austrian rulers. Benedictine abbey (founded 1089) has large library.
Melkote or **Melukote** (mĕlkō'tē), town (pop. 2,787), Mandya dist., S central Mysore, India, 24 mi. N of Mysore, on isolated, 3,500-ft.-high hill. Pilgrimage center, especially sacred to adherents of Vishnu as the abode of Ramanuja, 11th-cent. Vishnuite philosopher, during later years of his life. Priceless temple jewels are publicly displayed at large annual festival. Has col.
Melksham (mĕlk'sŭm), urban district (1931 pop. 3,881; 1951 census 6,727), W Wiltshire, England, on the Avon and 10 mi. E of Bath; agr. market and dairying center; engaged in canning milk, making rubber tires, and curing bacon and ham. Has 14th–15th-cent. church and anc. bridge.
Mellah or **Mallah** (both: mĕl-lä'), Fr. *Mêlah*, town, Jebel ed Druz prov., S Syria, in the mts. 20 mi. SE of Es Suweida; cereals.
Mellah, Oued (wĕd'), coastal stream in NW Fr. Morocco, entering the Atlantic at Fédala, after a NW course of 60 mi. Dam c.18 mi. above its mouth (built 1931; heightened 1940) irrigates truck farms in Casablanca area.
Mellaha, Tripolitania: see TRIPOLI.
Mellan Fryken, Sweden: see FRYK, LAKE.
Mella River (mĕl'lä), Lombardy, N Italy, rises in Alps 5 mi. ENE of Bovegno, flows 60 mi. S, through the Val TROMPIA, across Lombard plain, past Manerbio, to Oglio R. 12 mi. NE of Cremona. Chief tributary, Garza R. (left).
Mellawi, Egypt: see MALLAWI.
Melle (mĕ'lŭ), agr. village (pop. 7,590), East Flanders prov., NW Belgium, on Scheldt R. and 5 mi. SE of Ghent; tree nurseries.
Melle (mĕl), anc. *Metallum*, town (pop. 2,747), Deux-Sèvres dept., W France, 16 mi. SE of Niort; road center; cattle and mule market, alcohol distilling. Has 3 Romanesque churches. A Roman mint (which gave the town its name) has been excavated near by.
Melle (mĕ'lŭ), town (pop. 7,726), in former Prussian prov. of Hanover, NW Germany, after 1945 in Lower Saxony, at S foot of Wiehen Mts., 14 mi. NW of Bielefeld; mfg. of machine tools and synthetic chemicals. Resort with saline baths.
Mellègue River (mĕlĕg'), NW Tunisia, rises NW of Tebessa (E Algeria), flows 90 mi. NE to the Medjerda below Souk-el-Arba. Irrigation and flood-control dam under construction (1950) near Le Kef.
Mellen, city (pop. 1,306), Ashland co., N Wis., on Bad R. and 20 mi. SSE of Ashland, in wooded lake region, near Gogebic Range; commercial center for iron-mining and dairying area; woodworking. Copper Falls State Park is near by. Settled 1886, inc. 1907.
Mellerud (mĕ'lŭrüd"), town (pop. 1,727), Alvsborg co., SW Sweden, on SW shore of L. Vaner, 20 mi. NNE of Vanersborg; rail junction; textile mills, foundries, mechanical workshops.
Mellette (mŭlĕt'), county (□ 1,306; pop. 3,046), S S.Dak.; ⊙ White River. Farming and cattle-raising region bounded N by White R.; grain, livestock. Formed 1909.
Mellette, city (pop. 250), Spink co., NE central S.Dak., 20 mi. N of Redfield.
Mellid (mĕlyĕdh'), town (pop. 2,023), La Coruña prov., NW Spain, 26 mi. E of Santiago; agr. trade center (livestock, cereals, fruit); shoe mfg., tanning, flour milling. Summer resort.
Mellieha (mĕlyĕ'hä), Maltese *Mellieħa*, village (parish pop. 4,549), N Malta, near Mallieha Bay, 9 mi. NW of Valletta; marine salt raking, fishing. Has old troglodyte church, above which a new church was built during mid-19th cent. Near by are many coastal fortifications, including 17th-cent. Red and White Towers.
Mellita, Tunisia: see KERKENNAH.
Mello (mĕlō'), village (pop. 396), Oise dept., N France, on the Thérain and 11 mi. NW of Senlis; wool spinning.
Mellor, village and parish (pop. 1,206), central Lancashire, England, 3 mi. NW of Blackburn; cotton milling.
Mellott (mŭlŏt'), town (pop. 266), Fountain co., W Ind., 17 mi. NW of Crawfordsville; agr.
Mellrichstadt (mĕl'rĭkh-shtät), village (pop. 3,659), Lower Franconia, N Bavaria, Germany, on small Streu R. and 11 mi. SSW of Meiningen; rail junction; mfg. of metal products, brewing, malting. Surrounded by medieval wall; has Gothic church.
Melluzi, Latvia: see RIGAS JURMALA.
Melmerby (mĕl'mûrbē), village and parish (pop. 175), E Cumberland, England, 8 mi. NE of Penrith; sheep raising, agr. Mountain of **Melmerby Fell** (2,331 ft.) is 2 mi. ENE.
Melmoth (mĕl'môth), village (pop. 1,233), Zululand, E Natal, U. of So. Afr., 20 mi. N of Eshowe; wattle-bark industry. Site of tungsten, gold, tin deposits.
Melnik (mĕl'nĭk), city (pop. 469), Gorna Dzhumaya dist., SW Bulgaria, on W slope of Pirin Mts., 12 mi. NE of Petrich; winegrowing. Has ruins of anc. fortress. Once an important wine center, with pop. of c.5,000; pop. emigrated after Balkan Wars and an influx of phylloxera.
Melnik (myĕl'nyēk), Czech *Mělník*, town (pop. 11,251), N central Bohemia, Czechoslovakia, on Elbe R., opposite Vltava R. mouth, and 18 mi. N of Prague. Rail junction; fishing and trading port; noted for wine (Burgundy type) and sugar production. Hothouse vegetable growing, large orchards and vineyards in vicinity. Has 14th-cent. town hall with valuable 16th-cent. archives, Gothic castle with famous wine cellars. Regulating sluices and locks in harbor. Has gardening and viticulture school. During Second World War, oil pipe line laid by Germans from Bratislava to Melnik. Summer resort of Kokorin (kô'kŏrzhĕn), Czech *Kokořín*, with castle, is 6 mi. NNE.
Melnikovo or **Mel'nikovo** (myĕl'nyĭkŭvŭ), town (1948 pop. over 500), SE Tomsk oblast, Russian SFSR, 35 mi W of Tomsk, in flax-growing area. Shegarskoye is just E, on Ob R.
Melnitsa-Podolskaya or **Mel'nitsa-Podol'skaya** (myĕl'nyĭtsŭ-pŭdôl'skŭ), Pol. *Mielnica* (myĕlnyē'-tsä), village (1931 pop. 4,750), SE Ternopol oblast, Ukrainian SSR, in Dniester R. valley, 14 mi. SSE of Borshchev; rail terminus; flour milling, tanning, brickworking; vineyards. Has palace, church with medieval paintings.
Melo (mā'lō), city (pop. 23,000), ⊙ Cerro Largo dept., NE Uruguay, on the Arroyo Conventes (left affluent of Tacuarí R.), on railroad and highway, and 200 mi. NE of Montevideo; 32°22'S 54°10'W. Rail terminus and road junction; airport. Distributing center for surrounding region; wool, hides, agr. products (wheat, corn, oats), cattle. Bishopric. Has col., industrial school. Founded 1795.
Melocheville (mŭlôshvēl'), village (pop. estimate 800), SW Que., on L. St. Louis, near NE end of

Beauharnois Canal, 25 mi. SW of Montreal; quartz mining, dairying; resort. Formerly called Lac Saint Louis.

Melocotón (mälōkōtōn'), village (1930 pop. 474), Santiago prov., central Chile, on railroad, on upper Maipo R., in the Andes, and 27 mi. SE of Santiago; mtn. resort.

Melodunum, town, France: see MELUN.

Melón, Chile: see EL MELÓN.

Melones Dam, Calif.: see STANISLAUS RIVER.

Melor (mĕlôr'), village (pop. 496), N Kelantan, Malaya, on road and 12 mi. SSE of Kota Bharu; rice. Agr. station.

Meloria (mĕlô'rēä), islet, Italy, in Ligurian Sea, off coast of Tuscany, 4 mi. W of Leghorn. Near here, in 1284, Genoese overwhelmed Pisan fleet.

Melos, Milos (mē'lŏs, Gr. mē'lôs), or **Milo** (mē'lō), southwesternmost island (□ 61; pop. 6,045) of the Cyclades, Greece, in Aegean Sea, SW of Siphnos; 36°40'N 24°15'E; 12 mi. long, 6 mi. wide; deeply indented on N shore; rises to 2,465 ft. in the Prophet Elias. Of volcanic origin, Melos was known in anc. times for its monopoly of obsidian. Sulphur, gypsum, and argentiferous barite are exported. Wheat, barley, cotton, olive oil, wine, and citrus fruit are produced. Main town, Melos (pop. 1,682), formerly called Plaka, is on N shore. Settled by Dorians from Laconia, it sided with Sparta in Peloponnesian War and was destroyed (416 B.C.) by Athens. In Middle Ages, in Venetian duchy of Naxos. The Venus of Milo was discovered here, 1820.

Melouprey (mälōoprā'), town, Kompong Thom prov., N Cambodia, 50 mi. NW of Stungtreng, at foot of Dangrek Mts. In Thailand prior to 1904 and again in 1941–46.

Melovoye (myĕlŭvoi'ŭ), town (1926 pop. 3,262), NE Voroshilovgrad oblast, Ukrainian SSR, just SW of Chertkovo (Russian SFSR), 55 mi. E of Starobelsk; sunflower-oil press. Until c.1940, Melovoi.

Meloy (māl'ûü), Nor. *Meløy.* **1** Island (□ 8; pop. 320) in North Sea, Nordland co., N Norway, just offshore, 40 mi. NW of Mo; fishing, agr., cattle raising. Village of Meloy is on S shore. Canton (pop. 5,648) of Meloy includes part of the mainland, on which are villages of GLOMFJORD and HOLANDSFJORDEN. **2** Islet (pop. 129) in Norwegian Sea, N of Hinnoy, Troms co., N Norway, 18 mi. N of Harstad; iron mines.

Melozitna River (mĕlŭzĭt'nŭ), central Alaska, rises NW of Tanana, near 66°1'N 152°45'W, flows 180 mi. SW to Yukon R. opposite Ruby.

Mel Palaiyam, India: see MELAPALAIYAM.

Melpatti, India: see AMBUR.

Melrakkasletta (mĕl'räkäslyĕ"tä), Icelandic *Melrakkaslétta,* peninsula, NE Iceland, extends 25 mi. N into Greenland Sea bet. Axar Fjord (W) and Thistil Fjord (E); 66°20'N 16°10'W. N tip, Rifstangi cape, is N extremity of Iceland, near Arctic Circle. Raufarshofn, fishing port, on NE coast.

Melrhir, Chott (shôt' mĕlgēr'), shallow saline lake in Touggourt territory, E Algeria, the westernmost of a series of shotts reaching into the Sahara from the Gulf of Gabès. Its center is 50 mi. SE of Biskra. Surface is c.60 ft. below sea level. Length (E–W), c.80 mi., including lesser shotts near Tunisian border. The Chott Merouane is a SW inlet. Its marshy W edge is paralleled by Biskra-Touggourt RR. Receives intermittent waters of the Oued Djedi and of streams rising in the Aurès massif of the Saharan Atlas. Also spelled Melghir.

Melrose, village (pop. 249), S South Australia, 17 mi. NNE of Port Pirie; wheat, wool, dairy.

Melrose, burgh (1931 pop. 2,052; 1951 census 2,146), N Roxburgh, Scotland, on the Tweed and 6 mi. NE of Selkirk; agr. market. Site of remains of noted Melrose Abbey, founded 1136 by David I for Cistercian monks, destroyed and rebuilt several times. The heart of Robert Bruce is buried here. The ruins, now natl. property, are described in Scott's *The Lay of the Last Minstrel.* Melrose is the "Kennaquhair" of Scott's *The Abbot* and *The Monastery.* Near Melrose is ABBOTSFORD.

Melrose. 1 Village (1940 pop. 619), on Alachua-Putnam co. line, N Fla., on Santa Fe L., 17 mi. ENE of Gainesville, in citrus-fruit area; resort. **2** Town (pop. 310), Monroe co., S Iowa, on Cedar Creek and 14 mi. WSW of Albia, in bituminous-coal-mining and livestock area. **3** Residential city (pop. 26,988), Middlesex co., E Mass., 7 mi. N of Boston; laboratory equipment, mattresses, furniture, shades, screens, curtains, textile-mill supplies, chemicals. Settled c.1629, inc. as town 1850, as city 1899. **4** City (pop. 2,106), Stearns co., central Minn., on Sauk R. and 32 mi. WNW of St. Cloud; trade and shipping point in grain, livestock, and poultry area; dairy products, beverages. Settled 1857, platted 1871, inc. as city 1898. **5** Village (pop. c.300), Silver Bow co., SW Mont., on Big Hole R. and 30 mi. SSW of Butte, in livestock region. **6** Village (pop. 936), Curry co., E N.Mex., 20 mi. W of Clovis; stock-shipping point; grain, dairy products. **7** Village (pop. 237), Paulding co., NW Ohio, 13 mi. SSW of Defiance, near Auglaize R. **8** Village (pop. 497), Jackson co., W central Wis., 24 mi. NNE of La Crosse; creamery; limestone quarries.

Melrose Caverns, Va.: see HARRISONBURG.

Melrose Park. 1 Residential village (pop. 13,366), Cook co., NE Ill., W suburb of Chicago, just W of River Forest, in industrial area; makes plastics, railroad-car parts. Inc. 1893. **2** Village (pop. 1,803), Cayuga co., W central N.Y. **3** Village, Montgomery co., Pa.: see CHELTENHAM.

Mels (mĕls), village (pop. 577), Udine prov., Friuli-Venezia Giulia, NE Italy, 10 mi. NW of Udine; silk mill. Peat digging near by.

Mels (mĕls), town (pop. 5,118), St. Gall canton, E Switzerland, on Seez R. and 7 mi. SE of Wallenstadt; cotton textiles, foodstuffs, chemicals. Capuchin monastery (17th cent.), baroque church (18th cent.).

Melsbroek (mĕlz'brōōk), village (pop. 1,663), Brabant prov., central Belgium, 7 mi. NE of Brussels; airport for Brussels.

Melsele (mĕl'sälŭ), agr. village (pop. 5,284), East Flanders prov., N Belgium, 7 mi. W of Antwerp.

Melsetter, village (pop. 229), Umtali prov., E Southern Rhodesia, in Mashonaland, near Mozambique border, 60 mi. SSE of Umtali, in Chimanimani Mts.; tobacco, wheat, corn, citrus fruit; dairy products. Hq. of native commissioner for Melsetter dist. Police post.

Melstone, town (pop. 195), Musselshell co., central Mont., on Musselshell R. and 35 mi. ENE of Roundup; livestock-shipping point.

Melsungen (mĕl'zōong"ŭn), town (pop. 7,205), in former Prussian prov. of Hesse-Nassau, W Germany, after 1945 in Hesse, on the Fulda and 12 mi. S of Kassel; mfg. of surgical instruments. Has 16th-cent. castle.

Meltham (mĕl'thŭm), urban district (1931 pop. 5,051; 1951 census 5,107), West Riding, SW Yorkshire, England, 5 mi. SW of Huddersfield; woolen and cotton milling.

Melton, town and parish (pop. 2,197), E Suffolk, England, on Deben R. and just NE of Woodbridge; agr. market.

Melton Mowbray (mō'brā, –brē), urban district (1931 pop. 10,437; 1951 census 14,052), NE Leicester, England, on Wreak R. and 14 mi. NE of Leicester; produces leather and leather goods, Stilton cheese, pork pies. It is a fox-hunting center. Has church begun in 13th cent. Just W is Sysonby, with iron foundries.

Meltsany or **Mel'tsany** (mĕl'tsŭnē), village (1926 pop. 2,047), N central Mordvinian Autonomous SSR, Russian SFSR, 25 mi. NW of Saransk, in hemp area; distilling; legumes.

Melukote, India: see MELKOTE.

Melun (mŭlŭ'), anc. *Melodunum,* town (pop. 15,128), ⊙ Seine-et-Marne dept., N central France, on the Seine and 26 mi. SSE of Paris, at N edge of Forest of Fontainebleau; road center; produces pharmaceuticals, agr. machinery, thermometers; tanning, brewing, woodworking. Trade in Brie cheese, grain, poultry, fruits. Built around an isl. in the Seine, it preserves an 11th-cent. Romanesque church and vestiges of Roman and Capetian fortresses. Left bank dist. and 15th–16th-cent. church of Saint-Aspais heavily damaged in Second World War. Famous château of Vaux (or Vaux-le-Vicomte), built c.1660 by Le Vau for Fouquet, is 4 mi. NE.

Melur (mä'lōōr), town (pop. 9,592), Madura dist., S Madras, India, 16 mi. NE of Madura; road center in rich rice and sugar-cane area irrigated by PERIYAR LAKE project.

Melut (mĕlōōt'), village, Upper Nile prov., S central Anglo-Egyptian Sudan, on right bank of the White Nile and 75 mi. NNE of Malakal; cotton, corn, durra; livestock.

Melvern, city (pop. 389), Osage co., E Kansas, on Marais des Cygnes R. and 38 mi. S of Topeka; livestock, grain.

Melville (mĕl'vĭl), town (pop. 3,824), SE Sask., 25 mi. SW of Yorkton; grain elevators, flour mills, dairying.

Melville, Madagascar: see TAMATAVE, town.

Melville, NW suburb of Johannesburg, S Transvaal, U. of So. Afr.

Melville. 1 Town (pop. 1,901), St. Landry parish, S central La., 36 mi. NW of Baton Rouge and on Atchafalaya R.; mfg. of wood products, beverages; cotton gin. Settled c.1875, inc. 1911. Heavily damaged by floods in 1927. **2** Village, Sweet Grass co., S Mont., 19 mi. N of Big Timber; supply point in sheep region. Rodeo horses and other stock bred and trained here.

Melville, Cape, NE Queensland, Australia, in Coral Sea, near Princess Charlotte Bay; 14°10'S 144°31'E. Range of granite hills extends S.

Melville, Lake (120 mi. long, up to 25 mi. wide), SE Labrador; 53°19'–54°10'N 57°47'–60°25'W. Receives Hamilton R. in Goose Bay, SW arm of lake. Outlet to the Atlantic is Hamilton Inlet. At SW extremity of lake is Goose Bay air base. Receives Naskaupi R. 20 mi. NE of Goose Bay. On S shore of lake are Mealy Mts. Region is heavily wooded; lumbering.

Melville Bay, broad inlet of Baffin Bay, NW Greenland; 75°10'–76°10'N 58°5'–66°25'W. Cape York forms W extremity. Inland icecap reaches almost entire coast of bay; several large glaciers calve into its waters, but greater part of glacier front is stationary.

Melville Island (□ 2,400), in Timor Sea, 16 mi. off NW coast of Northern Territory, Australia, across Clarence Strait; forms W shore of Dundas Strait and NW shore of Van Diemen Gulf; 65 mi. long, 45 mi. wide. Separated from Bathurst Isl. (W) by Apsley Strait (45 mi. long, 1.3 mi. wide). Mangrove jungle, sandy soil; buffaloes. Aboriginal reservation. Site of 1st Br. settlement (1824–28) in Northern Territory.

Melville Island (□ 16,503), W Franklin Dist., Northwest Territories, in the Arctic Ocean; 74°24'–76°48'N 105°35'–117°45'W; largest of the Parry Isls., separated from Victoria Isl. (S) by Viscount Melville Sound, Banks Isl. (SW) by McClure Strait. Isl. is 200 mi. long, 30–130 mi. wide; coastline is deeply indented by Hecla and Griper Bay (N), Lyddon Gulf (SW), and Murray Inlet (SW). Generally hilly, rising to c.1,500 ft., with several ice-covered areas in interior. Large herds of musk oxen. Discovered (1818–20) by Sir William Parry.

Melville Island, Tuamotu Isls.: see HIKUERU.

Melville Peninsula (□ 24,156), just N of the Arctic Circle, in S Franklin Dist., Northwest Territories, N projection of Canadian mainland, at entrance of Hudson Bay, bet. Gulf of Boothia (W) and Foxe Basin. Fury and Hecla Strait (N) separates it from Baffin Isl. It is 250 mi. long, 70–135 mi. wide. In S part of peninsula are numerous connected lakes. N part is hilly, with coastal ranges (W and N) rising to c.1,000 ft. Near W coast is Hall L. (28 mi. long, 10 mi. wide). At base of peninsula is Repulse Bay trading post.

Melville Sound, Northwest Territories: see VISCOUNT MELVILLE SOUND.

Melville Water, Australia: see SWAN RIVER.

Melvin. 1 Village (pop. 535), Ford co., E central Ill., 30 mi. N of Champaign; agr. (grain, poultry, livestock); feed milling. **2** Town (pop. 325), Osceola co., NW Iowa, 14 mi. ENE of Sheldon, in livestock and grain area. **3** Village (pop. 204), Sanilac co., E Mich., 26 mi. NW of Port Huron, in farm area. **4** Town (pop. 696), McCulloch co., central Texas, on Brady Creek and 15 mi. WNW of Brady; trade, shipping point in cotton, livestock region.

Melvina (mĕlvī'nŭ), village (pop. 121), Monroe co., W Wis., 23 mi. E of La Crosse.

Melvindale, city (pop. 9,483), Wayne co., SE Mich., a SW residential suburb of Detroit. Settled 1870, inc. as city 1932.

Melvin Village, N.H.: see TUFTONBORO.

Melykut (mā'ĭkōōt), Hung. *Mélykút,* town (pop. 8,117), Bacs-Bodrog co., S Hungary, 6 mi. SSE of Janoshalma; wheat, corn, hogs.

Melzo (mĕl'tsô), town (pop. 6,739), Milano prov., Lombardy, N Italy, 12 mi. E of Milan; dairy and meat products, leather goods, textiles.

Memba (mĕm'bä), village, Niassa prov., N Mozambique, on Mozambique Channel, 80 mi. S of Pôrto Amélia; sisal, cotton, peanuts.

Membij or **Manbij** (both: mĕm'bĭj), Fr. *Membidj,* town, Aleppo prov., NW Syria, 50 mi. NE of Aleppo; pistachios, cereals.

Membrilla (mĕmbrē'lyä), town (pop. 6,472), Ciudad Real prov., S central Spain, in New Castile, 2 mi. SE of Manzanares; agr. center (grapes, potatoes, saffron, vegetables, corn, cereals, sheep, goats). Alcohol and liquor distilling, flour milling, plaster mfg.; dairying, lumbering. Has old, ornate sanctuary, and ruins of a castle. Was conquered from Moors by Alfonso VIII.

Membrío (mĕmbrē'ō), village (pop. 2,328), Cáceres prov., W Spain, 37 mi. WNW of Cáceres; lumbering, sheep raising; cereals, olive oil.

Memel (mĕ'mŭl, Ger. mā'mŭl), **Klaipeda,** or **Klaypeda** (both: klī'pĕdä), Lith. *Klaipėda,* city (1941 pop. 41,297), W Lithuania, ice-free Baltic port on Memel channel (outlet of Courland Lagoon), 75 mi. NNE of Kaliningrad and 125 mi. NW of Kaunas; 55°42'N 21°8'E. Industrial center; shipbuilding; paper and pulp milling, match and plywood mfg., amber processing, fish canning; mfg. of superphosphate, textiles, soap, bricks; brewing, flour milling. Has Rus. and Lith. theaters, noted city hall, exchange bldg., maritime acad., teachers col. Founded 1252 by Teutonic Knights as castle of Memelburg; briefly (1629–35) under Swedish occupation; last refuge (1807–08) of Prussian royal family. In 1920, it became ⊙ **Memel Territory,** Ger. *Memelland,* Lith. *Klaipėdos kraštas* (□ 1,026; 1941 pop. 134,034), the right Neman R. bank of former East Prussia which Germany was forced to cede according to Treaty of Versailles (1919). It was administered by Fr. troops under League of Nations. In 1923 Lithuanian troops occupied it and forced French garrison to withdraw. Council of ambassadors then drew up a new status for predominantly German Memel, accepted by Lithuania and ratified 1924. Territory was made an autonomous region within Lithuania. In March, 1939, a Ger. ultimatum demanded the return of the dist.; Lithuania complied. Occupied (1944) by Russian troops, and again inc. (Jan. 1945) into Lithuania.

Memel, river, Belorussian SSR and Lithuania: see NEMAN RIVER.

Memele River (mā'mĕlā), Lettish *Mēmele,* Lith. *Nemunėlis* (nĕ'mōōnālēs), right headstream of Lielupe R., in Lithuania and Latvia; rises N of

Rokiskis, Lithuania; flows 118 mi. generally WNW, partly along Latvian-Lithuanian border, joining Musa R. at Bauska, Latvia, to form Lielupe R.

Memel River, Belorussian SSR and Lithuania: see Neman River.

Memleben (mām′lā″bůn), village (pop. 925), in former Prussian Saxony prov., central Germany, after 1945 in Saxony-Anhalt, on the Unstrut and 10 mi. SW of Querfurt. Has remains of Benedictine monastery founded 975 by Emperor Otto II; traces of anc. imperial castle. Henry I and Otto I died here.

Memmingen (mĕ′mĭng-ůn), city (1950 pop. 25,250), Swabia, SW Bavaria, Germany, near the Iller, 43 mi. SW of Augsburg; 47°59′N 10°11′E. Important rail junction; metal industry (trailers, auto bodies, agr. and textile machinery, electrotechnical instruments, aluminum sheets, tools, wire); produces textiles (cloth, wool blankets, knitted articles), chemicals (fertilizer, disinfectants, glue, soap, oils and fats). Also tobacco mfg., cardboard and lumber milling, woodworking, brewing, dairying, meat preserving. Trades in hops, food and manufactured products. Partly surrounded by medieval walls with gates and towers. Has a Gothic and a late-Gothic church; also Fugger House (end of 16th cent.). Founded by the Guelphs; created free imperial city in 1286; passed to Bavaria in 1803.

Memo Nani, peak, Tibet: see Gurla Mandhata.

Memphis (mĕm′fĭs), anc. capital of the Old Kingdom of anc. Egypt (c.3400–c.2445 B.C.), above the apex of the Nile delta, 12 mi. S of Cairo. Reputedly founded by Menes, 1st king of united Egypt. The temples of Ptah, Isis, and Re, the Serapeum, 2 statues of Ramses II, and numerous dwellings have been brought to light. Along the Nile are the great pyramids, extending 20 mi. to Giza. Memphis remained important during the long dominance of Thebes and became seat of the Persian satraps (525 B.C.). Second only to Alexandria under the Ptolemies and under Rome, it finally decayed with the founding of near-by El Fustat by the Arabs, and its ruins were largely removed for building in the new city, later Cairo.

Memphis. 1 Village (pop. 800), on Macomb-St. Clair co. line, SE Mich., 18 mi. SW of Port Huron and on Belle R. **2** City (pop. 2,035), ⊙ Scotland co., NE Mo., on North Fabius R. and 28 mi. NE of Kirksville; ships livestock and grain. Settled 1838. **3** Village (pop. 92), Saunders co., E Nebr., 25 mi. WSW of Omaha near Platte R.; farm trade center in fertile valley. Near by are recreation grounds and artificial lake. **4** City (pop. 396,000), ⊙ Shelby co., extreme SW Tenn., on bluffs above the Mississippi (bridged), at Wolf R. mouth, and 235 mi. S of St. Louis; 35°8′N 90°4′W; alt. 2–300 ft. State's largest city; commercial and industrial center for wide region of Tenn., Miss., Ark., and Ala. A chief Mississippi R. port; port of entry; important railroad junction (repair shops). One of world's largest cotton and hardwood-lumber markets; also a market for livestock (especially mules), grain, other farm produce. Processes cottonseed, grain (flour, feed), lumber, meat, petroleum; mfg. of farm machinery, paper products, wire products, tires, tubes, and other rubber products, drugs, chemicals, electric-light bulbs, glass, furniture, textiles, dairy, bakery, and other food products. Army supply depot. Naval air station. Seat of Southwestern at Memphis (coeducational col.; 1875), Memphis State Col., Southern Col. of Optometry, medical divs. of Univ. of Tennessee, Le Moyne Col., Siena Col., Christian Brothers Col. Has Goodwyn Inst., mus. of natural history and industrial arts, art gall., several fine churches, Mid-South Fairgrounds, and a notable park system. Holds annual Cotton Carnival. Beale Street in city's Negro section has been made famous by W.C. Handy. City planned in 1819 on site of U.S. fort (built 1797); it has been claimed that De Soto crossed the Mississippi and that La Salle built (c.1682) Fort Prudhomme here. Inc. as town 1826, as city 1849; adopted commission govt. in 1909. In Civil War, a Federal naval force captured Memphis in 1862. Severe yellow-fever epidemic here in 1870s. **5** City (pop. 3,810), ⊙ Hall co., NW Texas, 28 mi. NW of Childress; trade, processing center for agr. area (cotton, grain, truck, fruit); mfg. (concrete blocks, cottonseed oil, wood products). Founded 1889, inc. 1906.

Memphremagog, Lake (mĕm″frůmā′gŏg), in S Que. and N Vt., lake (c.30 mi. long, up to 4 mi. wide) mainly in Que.; Newport, Vt., and Magog, Que., are trade centers and resorts. Drains through Magog R. and L. Magog into St. Francis R., Que.

Memramcook (mĕm′růmkŏk), village (pop. estimate c.400), SE N.B., on Memramcook R. and 13 mi. ESE of Moncton; lumbering; potatoes, grain. Near by is St. Joseph, site of univ.

Memramcook River, SE N.B., rises E of Moncton, flows 25 mi. ESE and S to Shepody Bay at Dorchester.

Memuro (māmōō′rō), town (pop. 15,338), S central Hokkaido, Japan, on Tokachi R. and 8 mi. W of Obihiro; agr. (rice, soybeans, sugar beets), stock.

Mena (myĕ′nů), town (1926 pop. 7,246), central Chernigov oblast, Ukrainian SSR, 39 mi. E of Chernigov; tobacco center.

Mena (mē′nů), city (pop. 4,445), ⊙ Polk co., W Ark., in Ouachita Mts., c.55 mi. S of Fort Smith, in rich farm area (cotton, corn, potatoes, poultry). Mfg. of wood products, brick, tile, dairy products, flour, feed; cotton ginning. Part of Ouachita Natl. Forest (recreation) is near by. Founded 1896.

Mena al Ahmadi or **Mina al-Ahmadi** (both: mē′nů ăl ämädē′), town in SE Kuwait, port on Persian Gulf, 22 mi. SSE of Kuwait town; loading terminal for Burgan oil field and Ahmadi tank farm (linked by pipe lines); small refinery. Developed after 1946 on site of Fahaihil village.

Menadir, Saudi Arabia: see Abha.

Menado (můnä′dōō), town (pop. 27,544), NE Celebes, Indonesia, on inlet of Celebes Sea, 600 mi. NE of Macassar, at foot of high mts.; 1°30′N 124°50′E. Chief port for N Celebes; trade center for agr. and lumbering area. Exports coffee, sugar cane, nutmeg, ebony. Has large Chinese pop. Town was free port 1854–94. Sometimes Manado.

Menafra (mänä′frä), town, Río Negro dept., W central Uruguay, in the Cuchilla de Haedo, on highway and railroad, and 60 mi. NE of Fray Bentos; cattle, sheep.

Menaggio (mĕnäd′jō), resort village (pop. 1,752), Como prov., Lombardy, N Italy, port on W shore of L. Como, 16 mi. NNE of Como; paper and silk mills, foundry; woodcarving industry.

Menagil, Anglo-Egyptian Sudan: see Manaqil.

Menahamiya or **Menahemia** (both: mĕnähůmē′ä), settlement (pop. 200), NE Israel, Lower Galilee, near right bank of the Jordan, 8 mi. S of Tiberias; mixed farming. Founded 1902.

Menahga (můnä′gů), village (pop. 849), Wadena co., W central Minn., 22 mi. N of Wadena; trade and shipping point in agr. area (grain, potatoes, livestock, poultry); dairy and wood products. State forest and small lakes near by.

Menai Bridge (mĕ′nī), urban district (1931 pop. 1,675; 1951 census 1,855), E Anglesey, Wales, on Menai Strait, 2 mi. W of Bangor; agr. market, with flour mills. Menai Strait here crossed by Telford's Menai Suspension Bridge (1826) for road traffic. Just E is Britannia Tubular Bridge, built 1850 by Stephenson, carrying railroad to Holyhead.

Menai Strait, narrow channel in Wales, separating Caernarvon from Anglesey isl.; 14 mi. long, 200–1,200 yards wide. Crossed by Menai Suspension Bridge (road) and Britannia Tubular Bridge (rail) near town of Menai Bridge.

Ménaka (mĕnä′kä), village (pop. c.400), E Fr. Sudan, Fr. West Africa, Saharan outpost, 160 mi. E of Gao; meteorological station.

Menakha or **Menakhah,** Yemen: see Manakha.

Menam, in Thai names: see Mae Nam.

Menan (mē′nůn), village (pop. 430), Jefferson co., SE Idaho, 5 mi. NW of Rigby; alt. 4,798 ft.; ships milled grain.

Menands (můnăndz′), village (pop. 2,453), Albany co., E N.Y., on the Hudson, just N of Albany; makes caskets. Inc. 1924.

Menard (můnärd′). **1** County (□ 312; pop. 9,639), central Ill.; ⊙ Petersburg. Agr. (corn, wheat, soybeans, livestock, poultry; dairy products). Bituminous-coal mining. Some mfg. (radiator guards, brick, tile, canned foods, beverages). Drained by Sangamon R. and Salt Creek (both partly forming N boundary of co.). Includes New Salem State Park, with reconstruction of town in which Lincoln lived during 1831–37. Formed 1839. **2** County (□ 914; pop. 4,175), W central Texas; ⊙ Menard. On Edwards Plateau; alt. 1,800–2,450 ft.; drained by San Saba R. Ranching (sheep, goats, cattle); wool, mohair marketed; some irrigated agr. (truck, grain, hay); poultry raising, dairying. Scenery, hunting, fishing attract tourists. Formed 1858.

Menard, town (pop. 2,685), ⊙ Menard co., W central Texas, on Edwards Plateau, c.55 mi. SE of San Angelo; market for wool, mohair, cattle of ranching region; irrigated agr. (truck, hay, grain); resort. Ruins of Sp. mission and a presidio (restored), both established 1757, are near.

Menarguéns (mänärgĕns′), town (pop. 1,234), Lérida prov., NE Spain, near Segre R., 10 mi. NE of Lérida; sugar milling; cereals, alfalfa.

Menasalbas (mänäsäl′väs), town (pop. 4,506), Toledo prov., central Spain, on N slopes of the Montes de Toledo, 20 mi. SW of Toledo; agr. center (cereals, chick-peas, carobs, olives, grapes, livestock). Cheese processing. Limekilns.

Menasha (můnă′shů), city (pop. 12,385), Winnebago co., E Wis., on L. Winnebago at its outlet through Fox R., opposite Neenah, 13 mi. NNE of Oshkosh; mfg. center (paper, paper products, woodwork, flour, machinery). Has hydroelectric plant. Region at lake outlet was visited by early French explorers. Settled before 1850, inc. 1874. On near-by Doty Isl. (partly in Neenah) is James Doty's log house, now a mus.

Menat (můnä′), village (pop. 265), Puy-de-Dôme dept., central France, in Combrailles, 18 mi. NW of Riom; extraction of mineral tars.

Mencheong (mŭn′chŭrng′), Mandarin *Wen-ch'ang* (wŭn′chäng′), town, ⊙ Mencheong co. (pop. 425,657), NE Hainan, Kwangtung prov., China, 30 mi. SE of Kiungshan; commercial center; sugar cane, coconuts; vegetable-oil extracting, cotton milling.

Mencué (mĕngkwā′), village (pop. estimate 100), W Río Negro natl. territory, Argentina, 110 mi. NE of San Carlos de Bariloche; sheep.

Menda (măn′dä), town (pop. 6,056), Kumamoto prefecture, S central Kyushu, Japan, 41 mi. SSE of Kumamoto; rice, wheat, sweet potatoes, millet, raw silk.

Mendali, Iraq: see Mandali.

Mendaña Islands: see Marquesas Islands.

Mendanau (mĕndůnou′), island (10 mi. long, 7 mi. wide), Indonesia, in Gaspar Strait (bet. S China and Java seas), just W of Billiton.

Mendavia (mĕndä′vyä), town (pop. 2,730), Navarre prov., N Spain, near the Ebro, 13 mi. E of Logroño; cereals, wine. Gypsum quarries near by.

Mende (mād), town (pop. 5,626), ⊙ Lozère dept., S France, at foot of the Causse de Mende, on Lot R. and 85 mi. SSE of Clermont-Ferrand; mfg. of woolens, tanning; cement works, breweries. Has 14th–16th-cent. cathedral. During Middle Ages it was ruled by powerful bishops. Sacked by Huguenots in 1580.

Mendeli, Greece: see Pentelikon.

Mendeli, Iraq: see Mandali.

Menden (mĕn′důn), town (pop. 19,573), in former Prussian prov. of Westphalia, W Germany, after 1945 in North Rhine-Westphalia, 5 mi. NE of Iserlohn; ironworks; mfg. of metal products and devotional articles. Has Gothic church. Chartered 1282.

Mendenhall (mĕn′důnhôl″), town (pop. 1,539), ⊙ Simpson co., S central Miss., 29 mi. SE of Jackson, near Strong R.; lumber, prefabricated bldgs. A state tuberculosis sanatorium is near by.

Mendenhall Glacier, SE Alaska, 25 mi. NW of Juneau; 58°26′N 134°33′W; 17 mi. long, 3 mi. wide. Accessible by highway from Juneau.

Menderes River (mĕndĕrĕs′), name of several rivers in Turkey, the most important being the Buyuk Menderes (anc. Maeander) and the Kucuk Menderes (anc. Scamander).

Mendes (mĕn′dĭs), town (pop. 4,511), W Rio de Janeiro state, Brazil, on railroad and 7 mi. SE of Barra do Piraí; paper milling, meat packing.

Méndez, Bolivia: see San Lorenzo, Tarija dept.

Méndez (mĕn′dĕs), town (1950 pop. 917), Santiago-Zamora prov., SE central Ecuador, on E slopes of the Andes, 30 mi. SSW of Macas, on road from Cuenca. Salesian mission among Jivaro Indians. Produces high-carat gold powder.

Méndez, town (pop. 550), Tamaulipas, NE Mexico, 85 mi. SW of Matamoros; cereals, sugar cane, stock.

Mendham (mĕn′dům), residential borough (pop. 1,724), Morris co., N central N.J., 6 mi. W of Morristown. Aeronautical-telephone laboratory established here (1930); has pre-Revolutionary tavern. Settled before 1750, inc. 1906.

Mendhar (män′dŭr), village, Punch jagir, W Kashmir, in W foothills of Pir Panjal Range, 11 mi. SSE of Punch; corn, wheat, rice, pulse.

Mendhawal, India: see Mehndawal.

Mendhi, Kashmir: see Rondu.

Mendi (mĕn′dē), town (pop. 3,000), Wallaga prov., W central Ethiopia, 35 mi. NW of Nejo; trade center (coffee, beeswax, hides, gold).

Mendieta, La, Argentina: see La Mendieta.

Mendigorría (mĕndēgôrē′ä), town (pop. 1,306), Navarre prov., N Spain, on Arga R. and 10 mi. ESE of Estella; olive-oil processing; wine, cereals.

Mendip Hills, ridge, N Somerset, England, extends 20 mi. ESE from Axbridge. Highest point, Black Down (1,068 ft.). At NW end is famous Cheddar Gorge and on SW edge is Wookey Hole. Lead mined here in Roman times.

Mendocino (mĕndůsē′nō), county (□ 3,510; pop. 40,854), NW Calif., on the coast; ⊙ Ukiah. Mtn. and valley region, traversed by several of the Coast Ranges; in E are summits over 6,000 ft. Partly in Mendocino Natl. Forest (E). Round Valley Indian Reservation is in NE. Drained by Eel, Russian, Big, Noyo, and Navarro rivers. Large stands of redwood near coast; inland are pine, fir, and oak. Extensive lumbering, sawmilling. Stock raising (sheep, cattle); farms in valleys produce fruit (apples, pears, prunes), nuts, grapes, hops, berries, hay, poultry, dairy products. Ocean fisheries. Hot springs (resorts); trout and steelhead fishing, deer hunting. Formed 1850.

Mendocino, coast village (1940 pop. 784), Mendocino co., NW Calif., at mouth of Big R., 9 mi. S of Fort Bragg; lumber milling (redwood, pine). State parks near by.

Mendocino, Cape, promontory, NW Calif., 27 mi. S of Eureka; westernmost point of Calif.; 40°26′N 124°24′W.

Mendol (mĕndôl′), island (12 mi. long, 10 mi. wide), Indonesia, in Strait of Malacca, just off E coast of Sumatra, 55 mi. SW of Singapore, opposite mouth of Kampar R. Low, swampy. Sometimes called Mendor, Pendjalai, or Penjalai.

Mendon. 1 Village (pop. 625), Adams co., W Ill., 11 mi. NNE of Quincy, in agr. area. **2** Agr. town (pop. 1,619), Worcester co., S Mass., 17 mi. SE of Worcester. Settled 1660, inc. 1667. **3** Village (pop. 844), St. Joseph co., SW Mich., 21 mi. SSE of Kalamazoo and on St. Joseph R., in rich farm area. **4** Town (pop. 349), Chariton co., N central Mo., 13 mi. S of Brookfield; dairying, stock raising. **5** Village (pop. 614), Mercer co., W Ohio, 9 mi. N of Celina, and on St. Marys R., in agr. area; cannery. **6** City (pop. 369), Cache co., N Utah, 8 mi. W of Logan, near Little Bear R.; alt. 4,495 ft.; agr. **7** Town (pop. 334), Rutland co., W central Vt., just NE of Rutland, partly in Green Mtn. Natl. Forest.

Mendong Gompa (mĕn'dông gôm'pä) or **Mendong Gomba,** (–bä), Chinese *Men-tung* (mŭn'dŏŏng'), lamasery, S central Tibet, in Aling Kangri range, 250 mi. NW of Shigatse; 31°9'N 85°14'E; alt. c.15,700 ft.

Mendota (mĕndō'tŭ). **1** City (pop. 1,516), Fresno co., central Calif., in San Joaquin Valley, 33 mi. W of Fresno; melons. Near here is terminus of Delta-Mendota Canal. Inc. 1942. **2** City (pop. 5,129), La Salle co., N Ill., 15 mi. N of La Salle; processing and shipping center in agr. area; mfg. (canned foods, beverages, woodworking machinery, farm tools, concrete products, cigars); corn, wheat, soybeans, livestock, poultry. Inc. 1859. **3** Village (pop. 243), Dakota co., SE Minn., at confluence of Minnesota and Mississippi rivers, just S of St. Paul. First permanent white settlement in Minn. Served as meeting place for traders and trappers before 1819 and known as St. Peter's. Settled 1834, name changed 1837. Homes of Henry Hastings Sibley, first governor of Minn., and of Jean Baptiste Faribault, early trader and fur trapper, are here. Reconstructed in 1930s, bldgs. date back, respectively, to 1835 and 1837. Near by is Mendota Bridge (4,119 ft. long, completed 1926) across Minnesota R. at its mouth on Mississippi R. **4** Town (pop. 173), Washington co., SW Va., on North Fork of Holston R. and 16 mi. ENE of Gate City.

Mendota, Lake, largest of the Four Lakes, Dane co., S Wis.; Madison is on SE shore; c.6 mi. long, c.4 mi. wide. A resort lake stocked with fish, it is fed by Yahara R.

Mendoza (mĕndō'sä), province (□ 58,239; pop. 588,231), W Argentina; ⊙ Mendoza. Bordered W by the Andes along Chile frontier; slopes gradually E to Desaguadero R. and the Río Salado. Watered by Mendoza, Atuel, and Tunuyán rivers. Its mountainous W border includes the highest peak, ACONCAGUA, in the Western Hemisphere. The Transandine RR (built 1887–1910) runs to Chile beneath USPALLATA PASS. In its inhabited lower valleys it has temperate, dry, Mediterranean climate. Among its abundant mineral resources are coal (Salagasta, Malargüe), petroleum (San Rafael, Las Barrancas, Perdriel, Tupungato), lime (Las Heras, Capdevila), lead, zinc (Sierra de los Paramillos, Uspallata), sulphur (El Sosneado), marble, onyx (San Rafael), serpentine, talc (Uspallata). Agr. activity in irrigated river valleys, producing mostly wine; also fruit, potatoes, olives, grain, vegetables. Stock raising (cattle, sheep, goats) of secondary importance. Fisheries in Huanacache lakes. Rural industries: mining, lumbering, wine making, alcohol distilling, flour milling, dairying, food canning. Petroleum refineries in Godoy Cruz and Tupungato, cement works at Capdevila and Panqueua. Fruit and wine industries concentrated in Mendoza and San Rafael. Has great number of hydroelectric power stations. Major resorts: El Sosneado, Los Molles, Potrerillos, and spas of Villavicencio and Cacheuta. Until 1776, the area was part of Chile.

Mendoza, city (pop. 92,243), ⊙ Mendoza prov. and Mendoza dept., W Argentina, in Mendoza R. valley (irrigation area), at SE foot of Sierra de los Paramillos, on Transandine RR and 600 mi. W of Buenos Aires, 118 mi. ENE of Santiago (Chile); 32°53'S 68°50'W; alt. 2,575 ft. Trading and processing center for a large, irrigated agr. area dealing principally in wine. Also fruit industries, lumbering, meat packing, food canning, flour milling; mfg. of cement, ceramics, machinery, rubber articles, textiles; lead foundries. The area developed rapidly upon completion (1883) of railroad to Buenos Aires and of Transandine RR (built 1887–1910), which runs to Chile beneath USPALLATA PASS and carries much of the Argentine trade with Chile. Influx of European immigrants, mostly Italian, in late 19th cent. An old colonial city, it has administrative bldgs., govt. palace, Jesuit church, San Francisco basilica, Cuyo Univ. (faculties of science and letters), art acad., natl. col., ethnological and agr. institutions, historical mus., theaters. On a peak (W) overlooking the city is monument to San Martín and his army of the Andes. The city was founded 1561 and belonged to Chile until 1776, when it was inc. into viceroyalty of Río de la Plata. Great part of city was destroyed by earthquake in 1861.

Mendoza or **Ciudad Mendoza** (syōōdädh'), city (pop. 10,970), Veracruz, E Mexico, in valley of Sierra Madre Oriental, at S foot of Pico de Orizaba, on railroad and 8 mi. WSW of Orizaba; textile-milling and agr. center (coffee, sugar cane, tobacco, fruit). Formerly Santa Rosa.

Mendoza or **San Nicolás** (sän nĕkōläs'), city (pop. 321), ⊙ Rodríguez de Mendoza prov. (□ 409; pop. 8,857), Amazonas dept., N Peru, in E Andean foothills, 30 mi. E of Chachapoyas; sugar cane, fruit.

Mendoza (mĕndō'sä), town (pop. 1,133), Trujillo state, W Venezuela, in Andean spur, 10 mi. SSW of Valera; alt. 3,970 ft.; wheat, corn, potatoes, coffee, fruit.

Mendoza River, N Mendoza prov., Argentina, rises on the Aconcagua massif near Chile line, flows generally E, past Uspallata, Potrerillos, and Luján, then N to the HUANACACHE lakes; c.200 mi. long. Used for hydroelectric power (Uspallata, Cacheuta) and irrigation (S of Mendoza). Transandine RR follows its valley.

Mendrisio (mĕndrē'zyô), town (pop. 4,265), Ticino canton, S Switzerland, 6 mi. NW of Como, Italy; metal products, hats, flour, pastry.

Mendu (mān'dōō), town (pop. 5,445), Aligarh dist., W Uttar Pradesh, India, 4 mi. ENE of Hathras; wheat, barley, pearl millet, gram, cotton, mustard. Also spelled Maindu.

Mene, El, Venezuela: see EL MENE.

Mene Grande (mā'nā grän'dā), town (pop. 869), Zulia state, NW Venezuela, in Maracaibo lowlands, 10 mi. E of San Lorenzo (connected by railroad and pipe line); major oil field, opened 1914.

Menemen (mĕnĕmĕn'), town (pop. 10,572), Smyrna prov., W Turkey, on railroad near Gediz R. and 13 mi. NNW of Smyrna; valonia, raisins, wheat, barley, sugar beets.

Menemsha, Mass.: see CHILMARK.

Menen, Belgium: see MENIN.

Menéndez, Lake (mānĕn'dĕs), (□ 25; alt. 1,690 ft.), in the Andes, W Chubut natl. territory, Argentina, N of the Cordón de las Pirámides; c.12 mi. long, 1-3 mi. wide; has several arms. L. Futalaufquén (SE) is connected with it by a river.

Menengai (mĕnĕng-gī'), village, Rift Valley prov., W Kenya, on railroad and 8 mi. WNW of Nakuru; pyrethrum, sisal, coffee, wheat, corn. Extinct Menengai volcano (7,440 ft.) rises just E.

Menera, Sierra (syĕ'rä mānā'rä), range of hills bet. Teruel and Guadalajara provs., E central Spain, a part of Iberian Mts. Rich iron mines at Ojos Negros, Almohaja, Setiles.

Ménerville (mānârvēl'), town (pop. 2,952), Alger dept., N central Algeria, on railroad and 28 mi. E of Algiers, in region producing citrus fruit, olives, truck produce and tobacco; alcohol and essential-oil distilling. Mfg. of explosives at Bellefontaine (3 mi. W).

Menes, Rumania: see MINIS.

Meneses (mānā'sĕs), town (pop. 1,569), Las Villas prov., central Cuba, in low Sierra de Meneses, 23 mi. SE of Caibarién; sugar cane, tobacco, cattle.

Menetou-Salon (mĕnùtōō'-sälō'), village (pop. 684), Cher dept., central France, 11 mi. NNE of Bourges; winegrowing, distilling.

Menevia, Wales: see SAINT DAVID'S.

Menfi (mĕn'fē), town (pop. 10,665), Agrigento prov., W Sicily, 11 mi. SE of Castelvetrano, in olive- and grape-growing region; cement. Limestone deposits near by.

Menfőcsanak (mān'fû-chŏnŏk), Hung. *Ménfőcsanak,* town (pop. 3,459), Győr-Moson co., NW Hungary, 4 mi. S of Győr; grain, peaches, horses.

Menfro, town (pop. 80), Perry co., E Mo., near Mississippi R., 9 mi. ENE of Perryville.

Mengabril (mĕng-gävrēl'), town (pop. 507), Badajoz prov., W Spain, 22 mi. E of Mérida; cereals, olives, grapes.

Mengcheng or **Meng-ch'eng** (mŭng'chŭng'), town, ⊙ Mengcheng co. (pop. 518,387), N Anhwei prov., China, 50 mi. ENE of Fowyang and on Kwo R.; wheat, beans, kaoliang, buckwheat, sweet potatoes, millet.

Meng-chiang, Mongolia: see Inner MONGOLIA.

Meng-ching, China: see MENGTSING.

Mengen (mĕng'ŭn), town (pop. 3,415), S Württemberg, Germany, after 1945 in Württemberg-Hohenzollern, near the Danube, 6 mi. SE of Sigmaringen; rail junction.

Mengene Dag (mĕngĕnĕ' dä), Turkish *Mengene Dağ,* peak (11,844 ft.), E Turkey, 40 mi. ESE of Van, near Iran line.

Mengeringhausen (mĕng"ŭrĭng-hou'zŭn), town (pop. 2,414), in former Prussian prov. of Hesse-Nassau, W Germany, after 1945 in Hesse, 8 mi. NE of Korbach; textiles. Until 1929 in former Waldeck principality.

Mengersgereuth-Hämmern (mĕng'ŭrsgŭroit"-hĕ'-mŭrn), village (pop. 4,182), Thuringia, central Germany, in Thuringian Forest, 3 mi. NW of Sonneberg; china mfg., woodworking; slate quarry.

Menggala (mĕng-gä'lŭ), town (pop. 14,174), S Sumatra, Indonesia, 110 mi. SSE of Palembang; 4°32'S 105°17'E; trade center for agr. and forested area (rubber, timber, coffee, pepper, fibers).

Menghai, China: see FOHAI.

Menghsien (mŭng'shyĕn'), town, ⊙ Menghsien co. (pop. 162,211), SW Pingyuan prov., China, 65 mi. SW of Sinsiang, and on Yellow R. (Honan line), opposite Mengtsing (road ferry); agr. center; rice, wheat, beans. Until 1949 in Honan prov.

Menghwa or **Meng-hua** (both: mŭng'hwä'), town (pop. 9,698), ⊙ Menghwa co. (pop. 120,512), NW Yunnan prov., China, 35 mi. SSE of Tali, in mtn. region; rice, wheat, millet, beans. Iron and arsenic mines near by.

Mengíbar (mĕng-gē'vär), town (pop. 5,145), Jaén prov., S Spain, near the Guadalquivir, 13 mi. SW of Linares; olive-oil processing, soap mfg., flour milling; lumbering. Agr. trade (cereals, truck produce, sugar beets, livestock).

Mengka, China: see LUSI, village, Yunnan prov.

Mengkarak (mĕngkä"räk'), village (pop. 446), S central Pahang, Malaya, on E coast railroad and 8 mi. S of Temerloh; rubber, rice.

Mengkiang, Manchuria: see TSINGYÜ.

Mengkiang, Mongolia: see Inner MONGOLIA.

Menglembu (mĕng-lĕm'bōō), town (pop. 9,751), central Perak, Malaya, 3 mi. SW of Ipoh, on slopes of Kledang Range; a tin-mining center of Kinta Valley.

Mengmao (mŭng'mou'), town, westernmost Yunnan prov., China, 65 mi. SW of Lungling, and on Shweli R. (Burma border), opposite Muse. Officially known as JUILI (rwā'lē') in winter and spring seasons, when Juili dist. seat, moved from LASA (28 mi. N), is situated here.

Mengo, Uganda: see KAMPALA.

Mengshan (mŭng'shän'), town, ⊙ Mengshan co. (pop. 102,644), E Kwangsi prov., China, 75 mi. ESE of Liuchow; ramie, indigo, medicinal herbs. Until 1914 called Yungan.

Mengtsing or **Meng-ching** (both: mŭng'jĭng'), town, ⊙ Mengtsing co. (pop. 125,876), N Honan prov., China, 15 mi. NE of Loyang and on Yellow R.; wheat, beans, kaoliang.

Mengtsz or **Meng-tzu** (both: mŭng'dzŭ'), town (pop. 9,093), ⊙ Mengtsz co. (pop. 88,762), SE Yunnan prov., China, on railroad and 130 mi. SSE of Kunming; alt. 4,655 ft.; center of tin-(KOKIU) and antimony-mining dist. Rice, tea, sugar cane, fruit; lumbering. Opened to foreign trade in 1887.

Mengwang, China: see NINGKIANG, Yunnan prov.

Mengyin (mŭng'yĭn'), town, ⊙ Mengyin co. (pop. 451,120), SE central Shantung prov., China, on road and 50 mi. NNW of Lini; beans, wheat, peanuts.

Menheniot (mĕnhĕn'yŭt), agr. village and parish (pop. 1,062), SE Cornwall, England, 3 mi. SE of Liskeard. Has 15th-cent. church.

Menidi or **Menidion,** Greece: see ACHARNAI.

Menifee (mĕ'nŭfē), county (□ 210; pop. 4,798), E central Ky.; ⊙ Frenchburg. Bounded NE by Licking R., S by Red R.; drained by several creeks. Rolling agr. area (livestock, grain, burley tobacco); oil and gas wells, timber; some sawmills. Includes part of Cumberland Natl. Forest. Formed 1869.

Ménigoute (mānēgōōt'), agr. village (pop. 462), Deux-Sèvres dept., W France, 14 mi. SE of Parthenay; dairying.

Menikion, Greece: see MENOIKION.

Menin (mŭnē'), Flemish *Menen* (formerly *Meenen*) (mā'nŭn), town (pop. 22,065), West Flanders prov., W Belgium, on Lys R. and 7 mi. WSW of Courtrai, on Fr. border opposite Halluin; textile industry (linen); market center for flax-growing region.

Menin or **Manin** (both: mĕnĕn'), Fr. *Mnine,* village (pop. c.2,500), Damascus prov., SW Syria, 9 mi. N of Damascus; alt. 4,000 ft.; summer resort; walnuts, orchards.

Menindee (mŭnĭn'dē), village (pop. 373), W New South Wales, Australia, on Darling R. and 65 mi. ESE of Broken Hill; sheep center.

Menindee, Lake (□ 60), W New South Wales, Australia, 55 mi. ESE of Broken Hill; 9 mi. long, 8 mi. wide; usually dry.

Meningie, village (pop. 376), SE South Australia, 70 mi. SE of Adelaide and on SE shore of L. Albert; dried and citrus fruits.

Meninx, Tunisia: see DJERBA.

Menlo. 1 Town (pop. 453), Chattooga co., NW Ga., 24 mi. NW of Rome, near Ala. line and Lookout Mtn., crate mfg. **2** Town (pop. 421), Guthrie co., W central Iowa, near source of North R., c.40 mi. W of Des Moines, in livestock and grain area. **3** City (pop. 113), Thomas co., NW Kansas, near source of South Fork Solomon R., 16 mi. E of Colby, in agr. and cattle region.

Menlo Park. 1 Residential city (pop. 13,587), San Mateo co., W Calif., c.25 mi. SSE of San Francisco, near Palo Alto. St. Patrick's Seminary and Menlo Col. are here. Inc. 1874. **2** Village (pop. c.300), Middlesex co., NE N.J., 7 mi. NE of New Brunswick. A 131-ft. memorial tower (1938) commemorates Edison, whose workshops were here, 1876–87.

Mennetou-sur-Cher (mĕntōō'-sür-shâr'), village (pop. 558), Loir-et-Cher dept., N central France, on Cher R. and 8 mi. SSE of Romorantin; dairying. Silica quarries near by. Has 13th-cent. ramparts with well-preserved gateways and towers.

Mennevret (mĕnùvrā'), village (pop. 838), Aisne dept., N France, 15 mi. NE of Saint-Quentin; iron-works.

Mennighüffen (mĕ"nĭkh-hü'fŭn), village (pop. 6,902), in former Prussian prov. of Westphalia, NW Germany, after 1945 in North Rhine-Westphalia, 7 mi. NNE of Herford; grain.

Menno (mĕ'nō), city (pop. 868), Hutchinson co., SE S.Dak., 40 mi. SE of Mitchell; cooperative creamery and grain elevator; cattle feed, dairy products.

Mennonite Colonies, Sp. *Colonia Mennonita* (kōlō'-nyä mānōnē'tä), settlements (pop. 5,076), Boquerón dept., N Paraguay, scattered colonies in the

Chaco, c.120 mi. W of Puerto Casado (connected by railroad). Cotton growing, cattle raising; also lumbering, grain growing, poultry farming; flour mills, sawmills. Founded 1926 by Russo-Ger. Mennonites from Canada on a Paraguayan concession (1921). Later enlarged by new settlers from Canada, Germany, and Russia. Altogether about 32 villages.

Meno (mē'nō), town (pop. 76), Major co., NW Okla., 17 mi. W of Enid, in grain and livestock area.

Menoikion or **Menikion** (both: mĕnē'kēôn), mountain massif in Macedonia, Greece, bet. Angites R. (Drama lowland) and Struma R. (Serrai lowland); rises to 6,437 ft. 11 mi. NE of Serrai. Also called Karagioz Giol and Smiginitsa or Smiginova (Smiyinitsa or Smiyinova).

Menominee (mŭnŏ'mŭnē), county (□ 1,032; pop. 25,299), SW Upper Peninsula, Mich.; ⊙ Menominee. Bounded SE by Green Bay and SW by Wis.; drained by Menominee, Cedar, and Little Cedar rivers. Agr. (livestock, poultry, potatoes, sugar beets; dairy products). Mfg. at Menominee. Commercial fishing, lumbering. Resorts. Has state park on Green Bay. Organized 1863.

Menominee. 1 Village (pop. 132), Jo Daviess co., extreme NW Ill., on short Little Menominee R. (bridged here) and 6 mi. ESE of Dubuque, Iowa. **2** City (pop. 11,151), ⊙ Menominee co., SW Upper Peninsula, Mich., on harbor on Green Bay at mouth of Menominee R. (bridged) opposite Marinette (Wis.). Fishing port and mfg. center (water power from river), producing wood and paper products, furniture, machinery, refrigerators, electric goods, chemicals, cheese, beet sugar; dairying. Resort (fishing, yacht and sailboat racing); state park. Settled c.1840, inc. as city 1883. In 1890s, was an important sawmilling and lumber-shipping center.

Menominee Iron Range or **Menominee Range**, mainly in Iron co., SW Upper Peninsula, Mich., along Mich.-Wis. line NW of Iron Mountain, Mich.; iron ore mining.

Menominee River. 1 In Mich. and Wis., formed by union of Brule and Michigamme rivers in SE Iron co. (Mich.), flows c.118 mi. SSE, through iron-ore region, into Green Bay at Menominee (Mich.). Forms part of Mich.-Wis. line; supplies hydroelectric power. Was important waterway in logging days. **2** In Wis.: see MENOMONEE RIVER.

Menomonee Falls, village (pop. 2,469), Waukesha co., SE Wis., at rapids of Menomonee R., 14 mi. NW of Milwaukee, in dairying and farming area; mfg. (machinery, iron castings, flour, dairy products). Settled c.1843, inc. 1892.

Menomonee River, SE Wis., rises in Washington co., flows c.25 mi. SE to Milwaukee R. at its mouth on L. Michigan at Milwaukee. Sometimes spelled Menominee.

Menomonie, city (pop. 8,245), ⊙ Dunn co., W Wis., on Red Cedar R. and 22 mi. WNW of Eau Claire; trade center for dairying area; mfg. of dairy products, aluminum ware, brick, cigars; flour milling, canning. Stout Inst. (a state col.) is here. Settled 1859, it grew as lumbering center, flourishing in 1870s. Inc. 1882.

Menongue, Angola: see SERPA PINTO.

Menorca, Balearic Isls.: see MINORCA.

Mens (mās), village (pop. 893), Isère dept., SE France, in Dauphiné Alps, 25 mi. S of Grenoble; alt. 2,543 ft. Health resort.

Mensabé or **Puerto Mensabé** (pwĕr'tō mĕnsäbä'), village (pop. 12), Los Santos prov., S central Panama, port (6 mi. ESE) for Las Tablas, on Gulf of Panama of the Pacific; sugar cane, coffee; stock raising.

Mensdorf (mĕns'dôrf), village (pop. 466), E Luxembourg, 8 mi. ENE of Luxembourg city; gravel quarrying; agr.

Menshah, El, Egypt: see MANSHAH, EL.

Menshikov, Cape, or **Cape Men'shikov** (myĕn'yŭshĭkŭf), SE extremity of S isl. of Novaya Zemlya, Russian SFSR; 70°43'N 57°37'E.

Menstrie, town, Clackmannan, Scotland, near Devon R., 2 mi. W of Alva; woolen-milling town in coal-mining region.

Mentakab (mĕntä"käb'), town (pop. 3,303), S central Pahang, Malaya, 6 mi. WNW of Temerloh; junction of highway and E coast railroad; rubber-growing center.

Mentana (mĕntä'nä), village (pop. 2,864), Roma prov., Latium, central Italy, 13 mi. NE of Rome. Here Garibaldi was defeated (1867) by Fr. and papal troops.

Mentasta (mĕntă'stŭ), village (1939 pop. 15), E Alaska, 40 mi. SW of Tanacross, on Tok Cut-off. Sometimes called Mentasta Lake.

Mentasta Mountains, E Alaska, SE extension of Alaska Range, bet. Tanana R. (NE) and Wrangell Mts. (SW); extend 50 mi. NW from upper Nabesna R. Rise to 8,300 ft. (62°35'N 142°50'W). Continued SE by Nutzotin Mts.

Mentawai Islands or **Mentawei Islands** (both: mĕntŭwä'), volcanic group (□ 2,354; pop. 18,149), Indonesia, off W coast of Sumatra, in Indian Ocean; 2°11'S 99°40'E. Comprises c.70 isls. Largest isl. is SIBERUT; other major isls. are North Pagi and South Pagi of PAGI ISLANDS, and SIPORA. Group is generally hilly and fertile. Agr. (sago, sugar, tobacco, coconuts), fishing. First visited c.1600 by the Dutch; became Du. possession in 1825.

Menteith, Lake of (mĕntēth'), lake (2 mi. long, 1 mi. wide) in SW Perthshire, Scotland, 12 mi. W of Dunblane. Contains 3 isls., most important of which is Inchmahome (ĭnch"mŭhōm'), with ruins of Augustinian priory founded 1238. Mary Queen of Scots was sent here as a child in 1547. Isl. of Inch Talla has remains of 13th-cent. castle of earls of Menteith.

Mentese, province and town, Turkey: see MUGLA.

Mentese Mountains (mĕntĕ-shĕ'), Turkish *Menteşe*, SW Turkey, extend over area 100 by 60 mi. with Buyuk Menderes R. on N, Aegean Sea on W, Mediterranean Sea on S; rise to 7,943 ft. in Bor Dag. Rich deposits include emery, chromium, and lignite in W; emery, manganese, and silver in center; chromium, manganese, and asbestos in E.

Menthon-Saint-Bernard (mätō'-sē-bĕrnär'), village (pop. 181), Haute-Savoie, SE France, on E shore of L. of Annecy, 5 mi. SE of Annecy; resort. St. Bernard of Menthon b. in near-by château. Village called Menthon until 1943.

Mentok, Indonesia: see MUNTOK.

Menton (mätō'), Ital. *Mentone* (mĕntô'nĕ), town (pop. 11,079), Alpes-Maritimes dept., SE France, on the Mediterranean and Ital. border, 13 mi. ENE of Nice and 5 mi. WSW of Ventimiglia; a leading winter and health resort of Fr. Riviera, charmingly situated amidst luxuriant subtropical vegetation (flowers, oranges, lemons, carobs) and backed by an amphitheater of mts. Mild winter climate. Its sheltered bay is bounded SW by Cap Martin. Prehistoric remains of Cro-Magnon man found in Grimaldi caverns just over Ital. border. A part of principality of Monaco until 1848, Menton was seized by Sardinia, then ceded to France, after a plebiscite, in 1860. Heavily damaged during Second World War by Ital. artillery in 1940 and by Allied bombardments in 1944.

Mentone. 1 (mĕn'tōn) Resort town (pop. 241), De Kalb co., NE Ala., on Lookout Mtn., 12 mi. NE of Fort Payne, near Ga. line. **2** (mĕn'tōn) Village (pop. c.600), San Bernardino co., S Calif., just E of Redlands; citrus fruit, poultry. **3** (mĕntōn') Town (pop. 798), Kosciusko co., N Ind., 37 mi. SSE of South Bend, in agr. area; lumber; ships eggs. **4** (mĕn'tŭn,–tōn) Village (pop. c.100), ⊙ Loving co., W Texas, 19 mi. NNW of Pecos and on Pecos R.; trading point in cattle-ranching region.

Mentor. 1 Village (pop. 321), Polk co., NW Minn., 23 mi. ESE of Crookston; dairy products. **2** Village (pop. 2,383), Lake co., NE Ohio, 22 mi. NE of Cleveland, near L. Erie; large nurseries; bookbinding; mfg. of machinery, knit goods. Founded 1799.

Mentor-on-the-Lake, village (pop. 1,413), Lake co., NE Ohio, on L. Erie, just NW of Mentor and 21 mi. NE of Cleveland.

Mentowkow or **Men-t'ou-kou** (both: mŭn'tō'gō'), town, NW Hopeh prov., China, 18 mi. W of Peking; coal-mining center.

Méntrida (mĕn'trē-dhä), town (pop. 1,773), Toledo prov., central Spain, 29 mi. WSW of Madrid; olive-oil pressing, wine making; truck, livestock.

Men-tung, Tibet: see MENDONG GOMPA.

Menucos, Los, Argentina: see LOS MENUCOS.

Menuf, Egypt: see MINUF.

Menufiya, Egypt: see MINUFIYA.

Menuma (mänōō'mä), town (pop. 6,632), Saitama prefecture, central Honshu, Japan, 5 mi. N of Kumagaya; rice, wheat.

Menzala, Egypt: see MANZALA.

Menzel-bou-Zelfa (mĕnzĕl'-bōō-zĕlfä'), town (pop. 5,517), Grombalia dist., NE Tunisia, on Cape Bon Peninsula, 24 mi. ESE of Tunis; cattle market and fruit-shipping center; oil-pressing plants; oranges.

Menzel-Djemil (–jēmēl'), SE suburb of Bizerte, Bizerte dist., N Tunisia, on N shore of L. of Bizerte; brick and tile works; olive groves.

Menzelinsk (myĕnzĭlyĕnsk'), city (1939 pop. estimate 10,900), E Tatar Autonomous SSR, Russian SFSR, on Menzelya R. (left tributary of Ik R.), near its mouth, and 150 mi. E of Kazan; agr.-trading center; metal- and woodworking. Founded 1645.

Menzel-Temime (mĕnzĕl'-tāmēm'), town (pop. 8,587), Grombalia dist., NE Tunisia, on E coast of Cape Bon Peninsula, 45 mi. E of Tunis; cereals, olives; fishing, handicraft mfg. Lignite mines near.

Menzies (mĕn'zēz), village (pop. 217), S central Western Australia, 350 mi. NE of Perth and on Perth-Laverton RR; gold mining. Formerly important mining center.

Menziken (mĕn'tsĭkŭn), town (pop. 3,008), Aargau canton, N Switzerland, 10 mi. SE of Aarau; aluminum, tobacco, clothes; metalware; printing.

Menzingen (mĕn'tsĭng-ŭn), residential town (pop. 2,922), Zug canton, N central Switzerland, 4 mi. E of Zug.

Menznau (mĕnts'nou), town (pop. 2,277), Lucerne canton, central Switzerland, 12 mi. WNW of Lucerne; farming.

Meolo (mä'ôlô), village (pop. 1,369), Venezia prov., Veneto, N Italy, 14 mi. NNE of Venice.

Meona or **Me'ona** (mŭ-ōnä'), village, NW Israel, near Lebanese border, 20 mi. NE of Haifa. Formerly called Tarshiha, it was abandoned (1948) by Arab inhabitants; now houses new immigrants.

Meopham (mĕ'pŭm), town and parish (pop. 1,491), NW Kent, England, 7 mi. W of Rochester; agr. market. Has 15th-cent. church.

Meoqui (māō'kē), town (pop. 3,780), Chihuahua, N Mexico, on affluent of Conchos R. and 45 mi. SE of Chihuahua; alt. 3,789 ft.; cotton center; cereals, beans, fruit, cattle.

Meota (mēō'tŭ), village (pop. 236), W Sask., on Jackfish L. (10 mi. long, 6 mi. wide), 20 mi. NNW of North Battleford; resort.

Meppel (mĕ'pŭl), town (pop. 14,418), Drenthe prov., N central Netherlands, at junction of the Meppelerdiep and the Smildervaart, 13 mi. N of Zwolle; rail junction; pharmaceuticals, soap, edible oils, tanning fluid, hides, shoes, bicycles, machinery, synthetic fertilizer, sails; meat packing. Has 15th-cent. church, 17th-cent. weighhouse.

Meppelerdiep (mĕ'pŭlŭrdēp"), channel, Drenthe and Overijssel provs., N Netherlands; extends 6.5 mi. SW–NE, bet. the Smildervaart at Meppel and the Zwartewater at Zwartsluis.

Meppen (mĕ'pŭn), town (pop. 10,114), in former Prussian prov. of Hanover, NW Germany, after 1945 in Lower Saxony, at junction of Ems R. and Dortmund-Ems Canal (here joined by Haase R.), 12 mi. N of Lingen, in oil region; rail junction. Has 15th-cent. town hall, 18th-cent. church.

Mequinenza (mäkēnĕn'thä), town (pop. 3,244), Saragossa prov., NE Spain, on the Ebro at influx of Segre R., and 20 mi. ENE of Caspe; olive-oil and meat processing, flour milling. Agr. trade (cereals, almonds, sheep). Coal and lignite mines near by.

Mequinez, Fr. Morocco: see MEKNÈS.

Mequon, Wis.: see THIENSVILLE.

Mer (mâr), town (pop. 2,513), Loir-et-Cher dept., N central France, near the Loire, 11 mi. NE of Blois; dairying, winegrowing; brick ovens.

Mera (mä'rä), village, Napo-Pastaza prov., E central Ecuador, in the Andes, on Pastaza R. and 38 mi. ESE of Ambato (connected by road). Petroleum wells and refinery near by.

Meraak, Norway: see GEIRANGER.

Merabello, Gulf of, Crete: see MIRABELLA, GULF OF.

Merak (mŭräk'), port in extreme NW Java, Indonesia, on Sunda Strait, 60 mi. W of Jakarta; 6°10'S 106°26'E; terminus of ferry to Panjang, Sumatra; westernmost rail terminus. Basalt quarries near by.

Meraker (mär'ôkŭr), Nor. *Meråker*, village and canton (pop. 2,980), Nord-Trondelag co., central Norway, on Stjordal R., on railroad and 40 mi. E of Trondheim; mining and industrial center (carbide, iron alloys, silicon). Carbide factory, smelting also at Koppera (kôp'pŭrô) (Nor. *Kopperå*) village (pop. 412), 5 mi. ESE. Hydroelectric station at waterfall (S) provides power.

Merala, W Pakistan: see MARALA.

Meramec River (mĕr'ŭmĕk) E Mo., rises in the Ozarks E of Salem, meanders 207 mi. N, NE, and SE to the Mississippi 20 mi. below St. Louis; fishing, recreation. Receives the Bourbeuse and the Big.

Merand, Iran: see MARAND.

Merangi (mä'rŭng-gē), town (pop. 6,357), Vizagapatam dist., NE Madras, India, 9 mi. ENE of Parvatipuram; rice, oilseeds, sugar cane. Graphite deposits near by. Also called Chinna-Merangi.

Merano (mĕrä'nô), Ger. *Meran* (mĕrän'), town (pop. 22,575), Bolzano prov., Trentino–Alto Adige, N Italy, near the Adige, 15 mi. NW of Bolzano. Tourist and industrial center; sulphur refinery, foundry, fruit cannery, pottery works; furniture, jewelry, sealing wax, soap, insecticides, sausage, beer, wine. Noted for its mild climate. Has Gothic church (1367–1495), 15th-cent. castle, and mus.

Merapi, Mount (mŭrä'pē). **1** Active volcanic peak (9,550 ft.), central Java, Indonesia, 20 mi. NNE of Jogjakarta. Eruption in 1867 severely damaged Jogjakarta. **2** Peak, W central Sumatra, Indonesia: see MARAPI, MOUNT.

Mera River (mä'rä), Switzerland and Italy, rises in Rhaetian Alps, 5 mi. W of Maloja Pass, Switzerland; flows W, through Val Bregaglia, into Italy, past Chiavenna, and S to N end of L. Como; 30 mi. long. Receives Liro R. near CHIAVENNA. Forms small lake, Lago di Mezzola (2 mi. long, 1 mi. wide), N of L. Como.

Merasheen Island (mērŭshēn') (□ 46; pop. 346), SE N.F., in Placentia Bay, 70 mi. W of St. John's; 21 mi. long, 5 mi. wide; 47°30'N 54°15'W. At S end is fishing settlement of Merasheen, site of govt. bait depot and of radio-direction finding station.

Merate (mĕrä'tĕ), village (pop. 3,034), Como prov., Lombardy, N Italy, near Adda R., 11 mi. S of Lecco; silk mill. Astronomical observatory near by.

Merauke (mŭrou'kŭ), town (pop. c.2,000), Netherlands New Guinea, on S coast of isl., port on Arafura Sea, at mouth of Merauke R. (c.220 mi. long), near border of Australian Territory of Papua; 8°27'S 140°22'E; exports copra. Has fort built in 1902.

Meraux (mŭrō'), village, St. Bernard parish, extreme SE La., on the Mississippi below New Orleans, bet. Chalmette and Violet; oil refining.

Merbabu, Mount, or **Mount Merbaboe** (both: mŭrbä'bōō), volcanic peak (10,308 ft.), central Java, Indonesia, 30 mi. WNW of Surakarta.

Merbein (mûrbēn′), town (pop. 2,710), NW Victoria, Australia, on Murray R. and 205 mi. ENE of Adelaide, near Mildura; fruitgrowing center; wineries. Agr. experiment station.

Merbes-le-Château (mârb-lů-shätō′), village (pop. 1,226), Hainaut prov., S Belgium, on Sambre R. and 6 mi. WSW of Thuin; chalk quarrying.

Merbok (mĕrbôk′), village (pop. 599), W Kedah, Malaya, 8 mi. NW of Sungei Patani; rice. The **Merbok River** (S) flows 25 mi. SW to Strait of Malacca at Tanjong Dawai.

Merca or **Merka** (mĕr′kä), town (pop. 12,000), in the Benadir, S Ital. Somaliland, port on Indian Ocean, 45 mi. SW of Mogadishu and 8 mi. SE of GENALE; 1°43′N 44°46′E. Banana exporting, oilseed pressing, mfg. of textiles, packing boxes, boats. Near by is livestock vaccinating station. Formerly belonged to Zanzibar; leased (1892), then sold (1905) to Italy.

Mercadal (mĕrkä-dhäl′), town (pop. 1,812), Minorca, Balearic Isls., 12 mi. NW of Mahón; grain growing, stock raising; flour milling; hunting.

Mercado, Cerro de, Mexico: see DURANGO, city.

Mercan Dagi (mĕrjän′ däŭ″), Turkish *Mercan Dağı*, peak (11,315 ft.), E central Turkey, 13 mi. SSE of Erzincan, in Mercan Mts., a range extending 40 mi. S of the Euphrates. Town of Pulumur on S slope.

Mercara (mārkä′rŭ), city (pop. 7,112), ⊙ Coorg, India, 65 mi. W of Mysore, on central plateau of state; trade center for products of surrounding coffee, tea, rubber, cardamom, and sandalwood plantations. Has 18th-cent. stone fort. K. M. Cariappa, 1st Indian commander in chief of Indian army, b. here (1900).

Mercatello (mĕrkätĕl′lô), village (pop. 790), Pesaro e Urbino prov., The Marches, central Italy, on Metauro R. and 16 mi. WSW of Urbino.

Mercato San Severino (mĕrkä′tô sän sĕvĕrē′nô), town (pop. 3,024), Salerno prov., Campania, S Italy, 8 mi. N of Salerno; rail junction; cotton milling, tomato canning, wine making. Formerly San Severino Rota.

Mercato Saraceno (säräch ä′nô), village (pop. 960), Forlì prov., Emilia-Romagna, N central Italy, on Savio R. and 18 mi. S of Cesena; sulphur mining.

Merced (mûrsĕd′), county (□ 1,983; pop. 69,780), central Calif.; ⊙ Merced. Extends across San Joaquin Valley from Diablo Range (W and SW) to foothills of the Sierra Nevada (E and NE). Fertile agr. area, irrigated by Merced, San Joaquin, and Chowchilla rivers. Grapes, figs, peaches, apricots, nuts, alfalfa, grain, sweet potatoes, tomatoes, melons, and other truck; dairying, stock and poultry raising. Mining of gold, platinum, sand and gravel, silver. Farm-products processing (fruit drying and canning, dairying, wine making, meat and poultry packing), lumber milling, cement mfg. Formed 1855.

Merced, city (pop. 15,278), ⊙ Merced co., central Calif., in San Joaquin Valley, 55 mi. NW of Fresno; shipping and processing center in irrigated farm and livestock area; cement plant, fruit-processing and -packing plants, potteries. Tourist center en route to Yosemite Natl. Park (45 mi. NE). Castle Air Force Base is 7 mi. NW. Founded 1870, inc. 1889.

Merced, La, Argentina: see LA MERCED.

Merced, La, Peru: see LA MERCED.

Mercedario, Cerro (sĕ′rō mĕrsädär′yō), Andean peak (21,885 ft.) in SW San Juan prov., Argentina, near Chile border, 60 mi. SW of Tamberías; 31°58′S.

Mercedes (mĕrsä′dĕs). **1** City (pop. 21,679), ⊙ Mercedes dist. (□ 405; pop. 38,044), N Buenos Aires prov., Argentina, on Luján R. and 60 mi. W of Buenos Aires; rail and industrial center. Lead foundry, metalworks; mfg. of lubricating oils, cement articles, footwear, clothing, furniture; dairying, flour milling, tanning. Has natl. col., Gothic church. Founded 1779. **2** Town (pop. 15,047), ⊙ Mercedes dept. (□ c.3,500; pop. 32,245), central Corrientes prov., Argentina, 160 mi. SSE of Corrientes; rail junction and agr. center (rice, olives, citrus fruit, livestock). Sandstone quarrying and lime mfg. Has natl. col. **3** or **Villa Mercedes** (vē′yä), city (pop. 25,417), ⊙ Pedernera dept. (□ 10,155; 1947 pop. 49,971), E central San Luis prov., Argentina, on the Río Quinto and 60 mi. SE of San Luis; rail junction; commercial and agr. center (wheat, corn, alfalfa, rye, sunflowers, livestock). Food industries; also mfg. of ceramics, cement articles, leather goods. Largest city of the prov., it has natl. col., theaters; military air base.

Mercedes (mûrsā′dēz), city (pop. 10,081), Hidalgo co., extreme S Texas, in the lower Rio Grande valley, 30 mi. WNW of Brownsville; a packing, canning, processing, shipping center in irrigated citrus, truck region; also packed meat, cheese, clay products, sheet-metal and machine-shop products. Pipeline (1,840 mi. long) to New York area from oil field here was begun 1949. Founded 1907, inc. 1909.

Mercedes (mĕrsä′dĕs), city (pop. 35,000), ⊙ Soriano dept., SW Uruguay, on the Río Negro, on railroad and 150 mi. NW of Montevideo; 33°17′S 58°5′W. Rail terminus, highway junction, and river port (reached from Uruguay R., 25 mi. WSW), it is an agr. and livestock center (sheep, cattle); wheat, corn, linseed, oats. Wool market. Paper mill. Airport. Popular health resort. Has parochial church, municipal bldg., public schools, col. Founded 1781.

Mercedes, Las, Argentina: see LAS MERCEDES.

Mercedes, Las, Venezuela: see LAS MERCEDES.

Merced Falls (mûrsĕd′), sawmilling village (1940 pop. 783), Merced co., central Calif., on Merced R., near Sierra Nevada foothills, and 17 mi. NE of Merced.

Mercedita or **Central Mercedita** (mĕrsädē′tä), large sugar mill in S Puerto Rico, on railroad and 3 mi. E of Ponce; refining and distilling plants. Has model settlement for employees and a private airport. Opened 1926.

Merced River (mûrsĕd′), central Calif., rises in the Sierra Nevada in YOSEMITE NATIONAL PARK (of which its valley is outstanding feature), flows generally SW c.150 mi., through Exchequer Reservoir (c.10 mi. long), to San Joaquin R. 19 mi. S of Modesto. Reservoir is impounded in W Mariposa co. by Exchequer Dam (943 ft. long, 326 ft. high; for power and irrigation; completed 1926).

Mercer. 1 County (□ 556; pop. 17,374), NW Ill.; ⊙ Aledo. Bounded W by Mississippi R.; drained by Edwards R. and Pope Creek. Agr. (livestock, corn, poultry, wheat, soybeans, hay, alfalfa; dairy products). Bituminous-coal mines. Some mfg. (brick, feed, pearl buttons). Formed 1825. **2** County (□ 256; pop. 14,643), central Ky.; ⊙ Harrodsburg. Bounded E by Kentucky R. and Herrington L. of Dix R. (impounded by Dix R. Dam); drained by Salt R. and Beech Fork. Includes Pioneer Memorial and High Bridge state parks. Rolling agr. area in Bluegrass region; livestock, poultry, grain, burley tobacco; calcite mines, limestone quarries. Formed 1785. **3** County (□ 456; pop. 7,235), N Mo.; ⊙ Princeton. Drained by Weldon R.; livestock, corn. Formed 1845. **4** County (□ 228; pop. 229,781), W N.J., bounded W by the Delaware; ⊙ TRENTON. Mfg. (wire and wire rope, pottery, electrical equipment, rubber products, incandescent lamps, steam turbines, hardware); agr. (truck, poultry, dairy products, fruit). Crossed by Delaware and Raritan Canal; drained by Millstone R. and Crosswicks Creek. Formed 1837. **5** County (□ 1,092; pop. 8,686), central N.Dak.; ⊙ Stanton. Agr. area drained by Knife R.; bounded N and E by Missouri R. Lignite mines; wheat, corn. Formed 1873. **6** County (□ 454; pop. 28,311), W Ohio; ⊙ Celina. Bounded W by Ind. line; drained by Wabash and St. Marys rivers; part of Grand L. is in E. Includes Fort Recovery State Park. Agr. area (livestock, grain, poultry). Mfg. at Celina, Coldwater, Fort Recovery. Limestone quarries; timber; oil wells; hunting, fishing. Formed 1824. **7** County (□ 681; pop. 111,954), NW Pa.; ⊙ Mercer. Mfg. area; drained by Shenango R. and tributaries of Allegheny R.; bounded W by Ohio. Settled by veterans of Revolution. Iron, steel, and tin products, electrical products, engines, railroad cars; dairy products, potatoes; bituminous coal, sandstone, limestone. Formed 1800. **8** County (□ 417; pop. 75,013), S W.Va.; ⊙ Princeton. On Allegheny Plateau; bounded S by Va.; drained by Bluestone R. BLUEFIELD, semibituminous-coal-mining center in Pocahontas coal field, is partly in Va. Includes a state forest and Pinnacle Rock State Park. Agr. (livestock, fruit, tobacco); limestone deposits. Industry at Bluefield, Princeton. Formed 1837.

Mercer. 1 Town (pop. 348), Somerset co., central Maine, on Sandy R. and 12 mi. SW of Skowhegan; farming, lumbering. **2** Town (pop. 377), Mercer co., N Mo., near Weldon R., 9 mi. N of Princeton. **3** Village (pop. 214), McLean co., central N.Dak., 21 mi. NE of Washburn. **4** Borough (pop. 2,397), ⊙ Mercer co., W Pa., 22 mi. ENE of Youngstown, Ohio; farm trading center; potatoes; bituminous coal; mfg. (stoves, textiles, brooms). Settled 1795, laid out 1803, inc. 1814. **5** Resort village, Iron co., N Wis., 20 mi. SSE of Hurley, in wooded lake region; fishing. Near by is a fish hatchery.

Mercer Island, Wash.: see WASHINGTON, LAKE.

Mercersburg, borough (pop. 1,613), Franklin co., S Pa., 15 mi. SW of Chambersburg; shirt factory, tannery, flour; timber. Goldfish hatcheries. Mercersburg Acad. here. Settled c.1729, laid out 1780, inc. 1831.

Mercês (mĕrsās′), city (pop. 2,332), S Minas Gerais, Brazil, 40 mi. N of Juiz de Fora; terminus of rail spur from Santos Dumont; coffee, dairy products. Mica mining.

Merchantville, residential borough (pop. 4,183), Camden co., SW N.J., just E of Camden; hosiery. Settled 1852, inc. 1874.

Merchtem (mĕrkh′tŭm), town (pop. 7,660), Brabant prov., central Belgium, 9 mi. NW of Brussels; market center for poultry region.

Merchweiler (mĕrkh′vī″lůr), town (pop. 6,015), central Saar, 6 mi. W of Neunkirchen; coal mining; iron smelting.

Mercia (mûr′shů), old Anglo-Saxon kingdom, one of the heptarchy, generally covering region of the Midlands, bordering N on Northumbria, E on East Anglia and Essex, S on Wessex, and W on Wales. First settled (c.500) by Angles, probably along Trent R. valley. Æthelbert of Kent was apparently accepted as its overking in late 6th cent. Penda of Mercia extended his power over Wessex (645) and East Anglia (650) to gain overlordship of England S of the Humber. After being converted to Christianity by a Northumbrian mission, a Greater Mercia was reestablished (after 658) bet. the Thames and the Humber under Wulfhere. In 8th cent., under Æthelbald, the kingdom covered all S England. It was further strengthened under Offa (757–92), who controlled East Anglia, Kent, Essex, and Sussex and maintained superiority of a sort over Northumbria and Wessex, and built the great Offa's Dyke to protect W Mercia from the Welsh. Victories (826 and 829) of Egbert of Wessex in Mercia established him briefly as overlord. In 874 Mercia succumbed to invading Danish armies; its E part became (886) part of the Danelaw, while W part was controlled by Alfred of Wessex.

Mercier-Lacombe (mĕrsyā-läkōb′), village (pop. 4,729), Oran dept., NW Algeria, in the Tell, on railroad and 22 mi. E of Sidi-bel-Abbès; cereal- and winegrowing.

Merckem, Belgium: see MERKEM.

Mercoal, village (pop. estimate 600), W Alta., in Rocky Mts., near E side of Jasper Natl. Park, 40 mi. SW of Edson; coal mining.

Mercœur (mĕrkûr′). **1** Agr. village (pop. 86), Corrèze dept., S central France, 19 mi. SSE of Tulle. **2** Village, Haute-Loire dept., France: see LAVOÛTE-CHILHAC.

Mercogliano (mĕrkôlyä′nô), village (pop. 1,856), Avellino prov., Campania, S Italy, 3 mi. W of Avellino; wine presses.

Mercur (mûr′kůr), city (1940 pop. 358; 1950 pop. 2), Tooele co., NW Utah, 20 mi. WSW of Lehi, in Oquirrh Mts.; alt. 6,700 ft. Deposits of gold and silver.

Mercurea (mĕrkōō′ryä), Hung. *Szerdahely* (sĕr′dŏhā), village (pop. 2,065), Sibiu prov., central Rumania, on railroad and 15 mi. NW of Sibiu; agr. center. Also spelled Miercurea and sometimes called Miercurea-Sibiu or Miercurea-Sibiului.

Mercurea-Ciuc or **Miercurea-Ciuc** (–chōōk′), Hung. *Csíkszereda* (chĕk′sĕrĕdŏ), town (1948 pop. 6,143), Stalin prov., E central Rumania, in Transylvania, in W foothills of the Moldavian Carpathians, on Olt R., on railroad and 130 mi. NNW of Bucharest; trading center for lumber; flour milling, sawmilling, mfg. of vinegar. Has old citadel restored in 18th cent. Over 90% pop. are Magyars. In Hungary, 1940–45. Pilgrimage center of Simuleu (shēmōōlĕ′ōō), Rum. *Şimuleu*, with 13th-cent. statue of the Virgin, an old Franciscan monastery, and 16th-cent. printing works, is 2 mi. NE.

Mercurea-Niraj or **Miercurea-Niraj** (–nē′räzh), Hung. *Nyárádszereda* (nyä′rätsĕ″rĕdŏ), village (pop. 2,840), Mures prov., central Rumania, 10 mi. E of Targu-Mures; methane production. In Hungary, 1940–45. Also called Mercurea-Nirajului or Miercurea-Nirajului.

Mercurey (mĕrkürā′), village (pop. 238), Saône-et-Loire dept., E central France, 8 mi. NW of Chalon-sur-Saône; noted Burgundy wines.

Mercury, village (pop. c.200), McCulloch co., central Texas, 22 mi. NE of Brady, near geographical center of Texas.

Mercury Bay, irregular inlet of Pacific Ocean, N N.Isl., New Zealand, on E coast of Coromandel peninsula, W of Bay of Plenty; 7 mi. wide (across mouth, N-S), 11 mi. long.

Mercury Islands, in S Pacific, off Coromandel peninsula of N.Isl., New Zealand, SE of Great Barrier Isl.; 36°35′S 175°45′E. Include Great Mercury Isl. (largest; 8 mi. long), Red Mercury Isl., several islets. Site of Capt. Cook's observation (1769) of transit of Mercury.

Mercus-Garrabet (mĕrküs′-gäräbā′), village (pop. 354), Ariège dept., S France, on Ariège R. and 6 mi. S of Foix; mfg. of abrasives.

Mercy, Cape, SE Baffin Isl., E Franklin Dist., Northwest Territories, on Davis Strait, on N side of entrance of Cumberland Sound; 64°56′N 63°39′W.

Mer de Glace (mâr dů gläs′) [Fr.,=sea of ice], glacier (□ 16; 3.5 mi. long) on NW slope of Mont Blanc, E France, formed by junction of Géant (or Tacul), Leschaux, and Talèfre glaciers, and descending to within ½ mi. of Les Tines in Chamonix valley. Gives rise to small Arveyron R., which enters the Arve above Chamonix. Glacier has deep crevasses and high *séracs* (ice needles), and attracts numerous tourists. It is easily reached from Montenvers terminus of rack-and-pinion railway.

Merdenik, Turkey: see GOLE.

Merdjayoune, Lebanon: see MERJ 'UJUN.

Merdrignac (mĕrdrēnyäk′), village (pop. 859), Côtes-du-Nord dept., W France, 25 mi. SW of Dinan; mixed grains.

Mere, town and parish (pop. 1,764), SW Wiltshire, England, 7 mi. NW of Shaftesbury; agr. market in dairying region; flour mills; limestone quarries. Has 13th-cent. church and 15th-cent. chantry.

Mere, The, England: see ELLESMERE.

Meredith (mĕ′rĭdĭth), resort town (pop. 2,222), including Meredith village (pop. 1,122), Belknap co., central N.H., on L. Winnipesaukee and L. Waukewan and 9 mi. N of Laconia; textiles, wood products, agr.; winter sports. Inc. 1768.

Meredosia (mĕrŭdō'sēŭ), village (pop. 940), Morgan co., W central Ill., on Meredosia L. (c.5 mi. long; a bayou lake of Illinois R.), 18 mi. WNW of Jacksonville, in agr. area; button factory. Fishing, hunting resort.

Mère et l'Enfant, La (lä mâr' ā läfä') [Fr.,=mother and child], spur of Annamese Cordillera, in central Vietnam extending NE c.20 mi. to Cape Varella; highest peak (6,729 ft. high) rises 33 mi. NW of Nhatrang.

Merefa (mĭrĕ'fŭ), city (1926 pop. 11,718), N central Kharkov oblast, Ukrainian SSR, 12 mi. SW of Kharkov; rail junction; ceramics; flour milling, woodworking.

Meregh (mĕrĕg'), town (pop. 300), in the Mudugh, central Ital. Somaliland, fishing port on Indian Ocean, 175 mi. NE of Mogadishu. Has fort and mosque.

Mereh, Indonesia: see MARE.

Merelbeke (mĕ'rŭlbĕkŭ), town (pop. 9,745), East Flanders prov., NW Belgium, S suburb of Ghent.

Merend, Iran: see MARAND.

Merendón, Sierra del (syĕ'rä dĕl mārĕndōn'), N spur of main Andean range in W Honduras; extends from San Jerónimo peak on continental divide 12 mi. NE to ERAPUCA peak (8,200 ft.), here joining Sierra del Gallinero. The name Merendón is sometimes applied to the entire great mtn. chain of W Honduras, including sierras del GALLINERO and ESPÍRITU SANTO, de la GRITA, and de OMOA.

Mere Point Neck, SW Maine, peninsula extending 4 mi. into Casco Bay, near Brunswick; site of summer colony.

Merevale, England: see ATHERSTONE.

Merevari River, Venezuela: see CAURA RIVER.

Méréville (mārāvēl'), agr. village (pop. 952), Seine-et-Oise dept., N central France, 9 mi. SSW of Étampes; cereals, poultry. Has romantic park laid out in 18th cent.

Merewether, SW suburb of Newcastle, New South Wales, Australia, on E coast; coal-mining center; bathing beach.

Mergen, Manchuria: see NUNKIANG.

Mergentheim or **Bad Mergentheim** (bät" mĕr'gŭnthīm), town (pop. 9,010), N Württemberg, Germany, after 1945 in Württemberg-Baden, on the Tauber and 21 mi. SSW of Würzburg; mfg. of clothing and parquet flooring; woodworking. Resort with mineral springs. Has two 14th-cent. churches, 16th-cent. town hall. An anc. settlement, it became property of Teutonic Knights in 13th cent. (residence of Grand Master, 1526–1809). Chartered 1340.

Merghen, Manchuria: see NUNKIANG.

Merghi, town, Burma: see MERGUI.

Mergozzo (mĕrgô'tsô), village (pop. 867), Novara prov., Piedmont, N Italy, on L. Mergozzo (1.5 mi. long; separated from Lago Maggiore by Toce R. delta), 6 mi. NW of Pallanza. Granite quarries at Monte Orfano, 1 mi. S. Marble quarries near by.

Mergui (mŭrgwē'), southernmost district (□ 11,325; 1941 pop. 180,827) of Tenasserim div., Lower Burma; ⊙ Mergui. Narrow strip of land (260 mi. long, 50 mi. wide) in Tenasserim Range bet. Andaman Sea and Thailand frontier, ending S at Victoria Point; drained by Tenasserim R. Mergui Archipelago is off irregular coast (mangrove swamps). Densely forested; tin, tungsten mining, especially in N; iron ore (unexploited); rubber plantations. Pop. is 60% Burmese, 13% Karen, 6% Thai.

Mergui, town (pop. 20,405), ⊙ Mergui dist., Lower Burma, in Tenasserim, port on Andaman Sea, on isl. at mouth of Tenasserim R. and 120 mi. S of Tavoy, sheltered by King Isl. Trade (rice, salt fish, tin, tungsten) with Burma and Malaya, pearl fisheries, birds' nests. Airport. Ancient ⊙ Thai prov.; occupied by Br. East India Company after massacre of European settlers (1695). Captured 1824 in 1st Anglo-Burmese War by Br. forces from Tavoy. Formerly spelled Merghi.

Mergui Archipelago, island group in Andaman Sea, off Tenasserim coast, Lower Burma, bet. 9° and 13°N lat. Summits of submerged mtn. ridges; consists of c.900 isls. ranging in size from rocks to King Isl.; includes Tavoy, Elphinstone, Ross, Sellore, Bentinck, Domel, Kisseraing, Sullivan, and St. Matthew's isls. Mountainous and jungle-covered (snakes, tigers, rhinoceroses); irregular coast, often set in mangrove swamps. Sparsely inhabited by Salons, related to the Malays. Produces birds' nests, *bêche-de-mer*, pearls; tin and tungsten mines; rubber plantations in some isls.; trade with mainland. Archipelago known for its beauty.

Merhavya or **Merhavia** (both: mĕrhä'vyä), settlement (pop. 850), N Israel, at NE edge of Plain of Jezreel, 2 mi. E of Afula; mixed farming; printing works. Founded 1910. School serves surrounding region.

Meribah, village (pop. 156), SE South Australia, 125 mi. E of Adelaide, near Victoria border; wheat, wool.

Meric (mĕrĭch'), Turkish *Meriç*, village (pop. 1,510), Adrianople prov., Turkey in Europe, 30 mi. S of Adrianople; grain, rice. Formerly called Büyükdoganca and Kavakli.

Merichleri (mĕrēchlĕ'rē), village (pop. 3,351), Stara Zagora dist., S central Bulgaria, 10 mi. ESE of Chirpan; watering place (mineral springs); vineyards, cotton, sesame.

Méricourt (mārēkōōr'), SE suburb (pop. 8,535) of Lens, Pas-de-Calais dept., N France; coal miners' residences.

Meric River, Turkey: see MARITSA RIVER.

Mérida (mä'rēdhä), city (pop. 96,852), ⊙ Yucatan, SE Mexico, on N Yucatan Peninsula, 23 mi. inland from Progreso (its port on Gulf of Mexico), 635 mi. E of Mexico city; 20°58'N 89°37'W; alt. 25 ft. Mexico's 4th largest city. It is a rail hub, and commercial and mfg. center which depends largely on sisal-hemp industry, founded on henequen production in the region. Market for agr. products (cereals, tropical fruit, tobacco, cotton, coffee, potatoes). Exports henequen, chicle, hides, sugar, indigo, dyewood, hardwood. Cordage mills (rope, twine, sacks), cement plant, flour mills, sugar refinery, alcohol distilleries; mfg. of soap, hammocks, cigars, leatherware, furniture, chocolate. Important airport. A clean, spacious city, it has a 16th-cent. cathedral and other colonial structures, bishop's palace, govt. house, theater, modern penitentiary, archaeological mus., univ. (established 1922). Since the region possesses no surface water supply, water is pumped up by rooftop windmills from underground wells and rivers. Founded 1542, upon order of Francisco de Montejo the Younger, on site of Maya city T'ho. Serves as tourist base for visits to Maya ruins of CHICHÉN ITZÁ (70 mi. ESE) and UXMAL (40 mi. S).

Merida, town (1939 pop. 2,000; 1948 municipality pop. 14,977), W Leyte, Philippines, on Ormoc Bay, 8 mi. SW of MacArthur (Ormoc); agr. center (coconuts, rice).

Mérida, anc. *Emerita Augusta*, city (pop. 22,440), Badajoz prov., W Spain, in Estremadura, on right bank of the Guadiana and 34 mi. E of Badajoz. Today an active rail hub, stock-raising and agr. center (olives, grain, grapes) with processing industries, it is famed as anc. ⊙ Lusitania, having some of the most remarkable ruins of the country, declared (1912) natl. monument. While it is of Iberian origin and also flourished under the Visigoths and Moors until the Christian reconquest (1230), the Roman remains are most notable. Among them are an arch of Trajan, a theater and amphitheater, a circus, aqueducts, a magnificent bridge across the Guadiana, Mars temple (now part of a church), and a Roman bldg. which was turned into an alcazar. Mérida was an archbishopric under the Visigoths. It suffered severely during the Peninsular War (1808–14).

Mérida, inland state (□ 4,360; 1941 pop. 192,994; 1950 census 209,811), W Venezuela; ⊙ Mérida. Mountainous state traversed SW–NE by great Andean spur SIERRA NEVADA DE MÉRIDA, rising in La Columna to highest elevation (16,411 ft.) in Venezuela. A narrow neck of state borders on L. Maracaibo. Bet. the high ranges flows Chama R., its course being followed by the transandine highway; in river's fertile upland valley are most of the important settlements. Mineral resources include petroleum (on L. Maracaibo), mica (near Timotes and Chachopo), gold (Mesa Bolívar, Zea), emeralds (San Rafael). Predominantly an agr. region; produces corn, coffee, sugar cane, cacao, tobacco, cotton, yucca, bananas; wheat, barley, potatoes, and cattle in higher altitudes; goats raised in desolate Andean *páramos*. State is known for dairy products. Exports coffee, fiber bags, tobacco, butter, hides. Mérida, a university city, is its commercial and mfg. center.

Mérida, city (1941 pop. 14,544; 1950 census pop. 24,994), ⊙ Mérida state, W Venezuela, on Chama R., on transandine highway, at N foot of Sierra Nevada de Mérida, and 300 mi. WSW of Caracas, 145 mi. SSE of Maracaibo; 8°36'N 71°9'W; alt. 5,384 ft. Cultural, processing, and trading center in fertile agr. valley (coffee, sugar cane, grain, cotton, fruit); mfg. of textiles (cotton, wool, silk) and cordage goods, tobacco products, sweets, vegetable oil, furniture. Archbishopric. Old colonial city, founded 1558. Contains Los Andes Univ., a Jesuit col., several convents, and a sericulture station. Known for flower gardens and yearly San Isidro fiesta. Frequently damaged by earthquakes, notably in 1812.

Mérida, Sierra Nevada de, Venezuela: see SIERRA NEVADA DE MÉRIDA.

Meriden (mĕ'rĭdŭn). **1** City (pop. 44,088), coextensive with Meriden town, New Haven co., S central Conn., on Quinnipiac R. and 17 mi. N of New Haven. Mfg. (silverware, telephone and electrical equipment, tools, ball bearings, machinery, automobile parts, china, glassware, wood, rubber and plastic products, bedding, cutlery), food packing; agr. Silver and pewter ware made here in 18th cent. State tuberculosis sanatorium, state school for delinquent boys here; Hanging Hills just NW. Settled 1661, town set off from Wallingford 1806, city inc. 1867, town and city consolidated 1922. **2** Town (pop. 164), Cherokee co., NW Iowa, 5 mi. WNW of Cherokee, in agr. area. **3** City (pop. 378), Jefferson co., NE Kansas, on branch of Delaware R. and 11 mi. NNE of Topeka; grain growing, dairying, general agr. **4** Village, Sullivan co., N.H.: see PLAINFIELD.

Meridi (mĕrē'dē) or **Maridi** (mä–), agr. village, Equatoria prov., S Anglo-Egyptian Sudan, near Belgian Congo border, on road and 150 mi. W of Juba; livestock.

Meridian (mŭrĭ'dēŭn). **1** Village (pop. c.400), Sutter co., N central Calif., on Sacramento R. and 16 mi. W of Yuba City; agr.; waterfowl hunting. **2** Village (pop. 1,810), Ada co., SW Idaho, 10 mi. W of Boise in agr. area (fruit, livestock, poultry, grain) served by Boise irrigation project; dairying, fruit packing. Founded 1891, inc. 1902. **3** City (pop. 41,893), ⊙ Lauderdale co., E Miss., 78 mi. E of Jackson, near Ala. line; 2d largest city (after Jackson) in Miss.; trade, railroad, highway, and industrial center for wide agr. and stock-raising region of E Miss. and W Ala. Railroad shops, cotton compresses, stockyards; mfg. of clothing, textiles, mattresses, hosiery, wallboard, lumber, cottonseed oil; creosoting and brick plants. Seat of a state mental hosp., and a jr. col. A U.S. agr. experiment station is near by. Founded c.1854, inc. 1860. Temporary ⊙ Miss. during 1863; destroyed 1864 by Gen. Sherman in Civil War. **4** Village (pop. 334), Cayuga co., W central N.Y., 17 mi. N of Auburn, in agr. area. **5** Town (pop. 187), Logan co., central Okla., 10 mi. ESE of Guthrie, in agr. area. **6** Village (pop. 1,317), Butler co., W Pa., 5 mi. WSW of Butler. **7** City (pop. 1,146), ⊙ Bosque co., central Texas, on Bosque R. and c.40 mi. NW of Waco; trade, shipping center for diversified agr. area; ships wool, mohair, poultry, eggs, pecans, cotton; feed milling; mfg. of tile. State park near. Settled 1854, inc. 1886.

Meridian Dam, Oregon: see MIDDLE FORK.

Meridian Hills, town (pop. 708), Marion co., central Ind.

Mérignac (mārēnyäk'), W suburb (pop. 19,550) of Bordeaux, Gironde dept., SW France; produces paints, varnishes, rubber, furniture; glassworks, vineyards; airport 2 mi. W.

Merigold, town (pop. 682), Bolivar co., NW Miss., 6 mi. N of Cleveland, in cotton-growing area.

Merigomish (mĕ"rĭgŭmĭsh'), village (pop. estimate 200), E N.S., on Northumberland Strait, 12 mi. ENE of New Glasgow; grindstone mfg.; lobster and salmon fishing.

Merigomish Island (5 mi. long, 2 mi. wide), NE N.S., in Northumberland Strait, sheltering small Merigomish Bay, 12 mi. E of Pictou; 45°40'N 62°25'W.

Merín, Laguna, Uruguay and Brazil: see MIRIM, LAKE.

Mering (mä'rĭng), village (pop. 4,910), Swabia, S central Bavaria, Germany, 8 mi. SSE of Augsburg; rail junction; textile and pottery mfg., brewing, tanning, woodworking.

Merino (mŭrē'nō), village (pop. 445), SW Victoria, Australia, 185 mi. W of Melbourne, near Casterton; sheep, cattle; dairy plant.

Merino, town (pop. 209), Logan co., NE Colo., on South Platte R. and 14 mi. SW of Sterling; alt. 4,042 ft. Shipping point in irrigated sugar-beet region.

Merino Jarpa Island (mārē'nō här'pä), off W coast of Aysén prov., S Chile, at mouth of Baker R., SE of Gulf of Peñas; 33 mi. long, 3–12 mi. wide. Rises to c.3,300 ft.

Merinos (mārē'nōs), town (pop. 1,200), Río Negro dept., W central Uruguay, in the Cuchilla de Haedo, on railroad and 70 mi. E of Paysandú; road junction; wheat, cattle, sheep.

Merino Village, Mass.: see DUDLEY.

Merion or **Merion Station** (mĕ'rēŭn), suburb (pop. 4,171), in LOWER MERION township, Montgomery co., SE Pa., just W of Philadelphia; residential; also mfg. (automobile parts, stone and clay products, textiles, clothing).

Merioneth or **Merionethshire** (mĕrēŏ'nŭth, –shĭr), county (□ 659.9; 1931 pop. 43,201; 1951 census 41,456), NW Wales, on Cardigan Bay; ⊙ Dolgelley. Bounded by Caernarvon and Denbigh (N), Montgomery (E and SE), Cardigan (SW). Drained by Dee, Dovey, Wnion, and Mawddach rivers. Mountainous terrain; chief elevations, Cader Idris (2,927 ft.) and Aran Mawddwy (2,970 ft.). There are numerous lakes; largest, Bala L. Main industries are slate and limestone quarrying (centered on Blaenau-Ffestiniog), manganese mining (Barmouth and Llanbedr), grazing and dairying. Other towns are Ffestiniog, Towyn, and Bala.

Merion Station, Pa.: see MERION.

Merir (mĕrĭr'), coral island (pop. 18), Palau dist., W Caroline Isls., W Pacific, c.29 mi. SE of Pulo Anna; 5°40'N 132°20'E; 1.3 mi. long, ¼ mi. wide; rises to 50 ft.

Merisani (mĕrēshän'), Rum. *Merişani*, village, Arges prov., S central Rumania, on railroad and 10 mi. NW of Pitesti.

Meriti, Brazil: see SÃO JOÃO DE MERITI.

Meriwether (mĕ'rĭwĕ"dhŭr), county (□ 499; pop. 21,055), W Ga.; ⊙ Greenville. Bounded E by Flint R. Piedmont peach-growing area; also produces pecans, melons, peppers, and cotton; livestock raising; textile mfg. at Manchester. Formed 1827.

Meriwether Lewis National Monument, Tenn.: see NATCHEZ TRACE.

Merizo (mĕrē'sō), town (pop. 511) and municipality (pop. 1,085), S Guam, on coast; rice farming, stock raising.

Merj 'Uyun (mĕrj' ōōyōōn') or **Marj 'Uyun** (märj), Fr. *Merdjayoune,* town (pop. c.5,000), S Lebanon, on a well-irrigated plain, 24 mi. ENE of Saida; alt. 2,500 ft.; sericulture, tobacco, cereals, oranges. Sometimes spelled Marjioun.

Merka, Ital. Somaliland: see MERCA.

Merkanam, Markanum, or **Marakkanam** (mŭrŭkä'-nŭm), village (pop. 3,513), South Arcot dist., E Madras, India, on lagoon on Coromandel Coast of Bay of Bengal, 21 mi. E of Tindivanam; S terminus of Buckingham Canal. Ships Casuarina and cashew plants. Saltworks.

Merke (myĭrkyĕ'), village (1926 pop. 5,488), SW Dzhambul oblast, Kazakh SSR, on branch of Turksib RR and 90 mi. E of Dzhambul, in irrigated agr. area (wheat, sugar beets). Sugar refinery at adjoining Oital.

Merkel (mûr'kŭl), city (pop. 2,338), Taylor co., W central Texas, 16 mi. W of Abilene; market, shipping point in agr. (cotton, wheat), cattle-ranching area. Settled c.1875, inc. 1906.

Merkem (mĕr'kŭm), agr. village (pop. 2,796), West Flanders prov., W Belgium, 8 mi. N of Ypres. Formerly spelled Merckem.

Merket or **Merket Bazar** (mĕrkĕt' bäzär'), Chinese *Maikaiti* or *Mai-kai-t'i* (both: mī'gī'tē'), town and oasis (pop. 53,409), SW Sinkiang prov., China, 30 mi. N of Yarkand and on Yarkand R.; cotton-growing center; livestock, agr. products.

Merksem (mĕrk'sŭm), town (pop. 29,406), Antwerp prov., N Belgian, on Scheldt-Meuse Junction Canal and 2 mi. NE of Antwerp; glass products; grain elevators; electric power station. Formerly spelled Merxem.

Merksplas (mĕrks'pläs), village (pop. 4,272), Antwerp prov., N Belgium, 5 mi. WNW of Turnhout; agr., lumbering. Site of work colony for tramps, prison school, 2 prison sanitaria. Formerly spelled Merxplas.

Merkstein (mĕrk'shtīn), village (pop. 8,998), in former Prussian Rhine Prov., W Germany, after 1945 in North Rhine-Westphalia, 7 mi. N of Aachen, near Dutch border; coal mining.

Merkwiller-Péchelbronn (mĕrkvēlär'-pāshĕlbrôn'), Ger. *Merkweiler-Pechelbronn* (mĕrk'vīlŭr-pĕkh'-ŭlbrôn), commune (pop. 693), Bas-Rhin dept., E France, 9 mi. N of Haguenau; oil wells.

Merl, Luxembourg: see LUXEMBOURG, city.

Merlara (mĕrlä'rä), village (pop. 803), Padova prov., Veneto, N Italy, 5 mi. SSW of Montagnana.

Merlebach (mĕrlbäk'), Ger. *Merlenbach* (mĕr'-lŭnbäkh), town (pop. 8,152), Moselle dept., NE France, on Saar border, 5 mi. SW of Forbach; coal-mining center. Large Slavic pop.

Merlera, Greece: see ERRIKOUSAI.

Merlerault, Le (lŭ mĕrlŭrō'), village (pop. 722), Orne dept., NW France, 15 mi. ESE of Argentan; cattle, horse center.

Merlimont (mĕrlēmō'), village (pop. 587), Pas-de-Calais dept., N France, 7 mi. W of Montreuil. Merlimont-Plage (2 mi. W) is small beach resort on English Channel, heavily damaged in Second World War.

Merlinau (mŭlēnou'), village (pop. 1,240), Settlement of Malacca, SW Malaya, on Strait of Malacca, 11 mi. ESE of Malacca; coconuts, rice.

Merlo (mĕr'lō). **1** Town (pop. 8,538), ⊙ Merlo dist. (□ 67; pop. 22,750), NE Buenos Aires prov., Argentina, 20 mi. W of Buenos Aires, in agr. region (corn, alfalfa, livestock); rail junction. **2** Town (pop. estimate 1,000), NE San Luis prov., Argentina, at W foot of Sierra de Comechingones, 100 mi. NE of San Luis; agr. center (corn, wine, fruit, livestock).

Mermentau (mûr'mŭntô), village (pop. 636), Acadia parish, S La., 13 mi. W of Crowley, and on navigable Mermentau R., in rice-growing area; rice mills, moss gins. Oil and natural-gas field near by.

Mermentau River, S La., formed just above Mermentau by junction of Nezpique and Cannes bayous, flows c.71 mi. SW to Gulf of Mexico 48 mi. E of Sabine Pass; navigable. Widens to form L. Arthur (c.7 mi. long) at Lake Arthur town, Grand L. (c.10 mi. long, 2–10 mi. wide) in central Cameron parish, and small Upper Mud and Lower Mud lakes in marshy coastal area above mouth. Crossed by Gulf Intracoastal Waterway just above Grand L., which is joined by navigation canals to White L. (SE) and thence to Vermilion Bay.

Merna, village (pop. 385), Custer co., central Nebr., 9 mi. NW of Broken Bow; grain, livestock, dairy and poultry produce. Near-by state park used for recreation.

Mernik, Czechoslovakia: see VRANOV.

Meroë (mĕr'ōē), anc. Egyptian city, on right bank of the Nile, in N Anglo-Egyptian Sudan, 4 mi. N of Kabushia and c.150 mi. NNE of Khartoum; 17°N. Succeeded NAPATA as ⊙ Ethiopian (Upper Nubian) kingdom c.300 B.C., and remained ⊙ of Meroitic kingdom until A.D. 350. Site includes extensive ruins (palaces, necropolis) and groups of pyramids (600 B.C.–A.D. 300) excavated 1909–14. Kingdom, comprising area (Isle of Meroë) bet. Main Nile, Blue Nile, and Atbara, was noted for its active caravan trade.

Merok, Norway: see GEIRANGER.

Merom (mŭ'rŭm, mē'–), town (pop. 374), Sullivan co., SW Ind., on the Wabash and 26 mi. N of Vincennes.

Merom, Waters of, Israel: see HULA, LAKE.

Meron, Israel: see MEIRUN.

Merope, Mount, Greece: see DOUSKON.

Merouane, Chott (shôt' mĕrwän'), shallow saline lake, in the Algerian Sahara, a SW arm of the Chott MELRHIR.

Merowe (mĕrōwĕ'), town, Northern Prov., Anglo-Egyptian Sudan, port on left bank of the Nile (in great bend), opposite KAREIMA railhead, and 150 mi. NW of Ed Damer; cotton center; also trade in wheat, barley, corn, fruits, livestock. Has small mus. of antiquities. A Nile dam is projected at 4th cataract (NE). Opposite Merowe, on right Nile bank, is site of anc. NAPATA.

Merredin (mĕ'rĭdŭn), town (pop. 1,855), SW central Western Australia, 145 mi. ENE of Perth; rail junction; wheat, oats.

Merriam, village (1940 pop. 1,238), Johnson co., E Kansas, 8 mi. S of Kansas City (Kansas), in grain and livestock area.

Merrick, mountain (2,784 ft.), NW Kirkcudbright, Scotland, 13 mi. N of Newton Stewart; highest elevation in S Scotland.

Merrick, county (□ 467; pop. 8,812), E central Nebr.; ⊙ Central City. Agr. region bounded S by Platte R., drained by its branches. Flour; livestock, grain. Formed 1858.

Merrick, residential village (1940 pop. 2,935), Nassau co., SE N.Y., on SW Long Isl., 13 mi. ESE of Jamaica; mfg. (clothing, signal flares and rockets, furniture, aircraft parts).

Merrickville, village (pop. 794), SE Ont., on Rideau R. and Rideau Canal, and 35 mi. SSW of Ottawa; woolen milling, mfg. of stoves, plows.

Merricourt, village (pop. 105), Dickey co., SE N.Dak., 18 mi. NW of Ellendale.

Merrill. 1 Town (pop. 605), Plymouth co., NW Iowa, on Floyd R. near confluence of West Branch Floyd R., and 6 mi. SW of Le Mars, in dairy, livestock, and grain area. Sand, gravel pits near by. **2** Town (pop. 383), Aroostook co., E Maine, 20 mi. WNW of Houlton, in agr., lumbering area. **3** Village (pop. 809), Saginaw co., E central Mich., 19 mi. W of Saginaw, in agr. area. **4** Resort village, Clinton co., extreme NE N.Y., on Upper Chateaugay L., 25 mi. WNW of Plattsburg. **5** Town (pop. 835), Klamath co., S Oregon, 15 mi. SE of Klamath Falls; alt. 4,064 ft.; entrance to Lava Beds Natl. Monument. **6** City (pop. 8,951), ⊙ Lincoln co., N central Wis., at confluence of Wisconsin R. and small Prairie R., 16 mi. N of Wausau, in dairying and farming area; mfg. (paper, furniture, woolen goods, beer). Near by are the Grandfather Falls of the Wisconsin and Council Grounds State Forest. Settled c.1847, Merrill grew as lumbering town; inc. 1883.

Merrillan (mĕr'ĭlăn", mĕr'ĭlŭn), village (pop. 579), Jackson co., W central Wis., 40 mi. SE of Eau Claire, in dairying region.

Merrill Peak, Ariz.: see PINALENO MOUNTAINS.

Merrillville, town (pop. 109), Thomas co., S Ga., 10 mi. NE of Thomasville.

Merrimac (mĕ'rĭmăk). **1** Rural town (pop. 2,804), including Merrimac village (pop. 1,618), Essex co., NE Mass., on Merrimack R., near N.H. line, and 13 mi. NE of Lawrence. Settled 1638, set off from Amesbury 1876. **2** Village (pop. 317), Sauk co., S central Wis., on Wisconsin R. at W end of L. Wisconsin, and 24 mi. NNW of Madison. Post office name formerly Merrimack.

Merrimack (mĕ'rĭmăk), county (□ 931; pop. 63,022), S central N.H.; ⊙ Concord, the state capital. Agr. (dairy products, poultry, truck, and fruit), mfg. (textiles, shoes, wood, leather and metal products, paper, machinery, electrical instruments), granite quarrying, mica mining and processing, flour milling. Resorts on lakes. Hilly region, drained by Merrimack, Contoocook, Suncook, Soucook, Blackwater, Mascoma, and Warner rivers, all furnishing water power. Formed 1823.

Merrimack. 1 or **Huntsville Park,** village (pop. 3,035), Madison co., N Ala., just S of Huntsville. **2** Town (pop. 1,908), Hillsboro co., S N.H., on Merrimack R., at mouth of the Souhegan; bet. Manchester and Nashua; mfg. (wood products, shoes). Inc. 1746. **3** Village, Sauk co., Wis.: see MERRIMAC.

Merrimack River, in N.H. and Mass., formed at Franklin, N.H., by junction of Pemigewasset and Winnipesaukee rivers; flows S through central N.H., past Concord, Manchester, and Nashua, then NE across corner of Mass., past Lowell, Lawrence, and Haverhill (head of navigation), to the Atlantic at Newbury. Furnishes abundant water power to mfg. cities along course of c.110 mi.

Merriman, village (pop. 260), Cherry co., N Nebr., 60 mi. W of Valentine and on branch of Niobrara R., near S.Dak. line.

Merriman Dam, N.Y.: see RONDOUT CREEK.

Merrionette Park, village (pop. 1,101), Cook co., NE Ill., SW suburb of Chicago. Inc. 1947.

Merriott, agr. village and parish (pop. 1,116), S Somerset, England, 2 mi. N of Crewkerne; sail cloth mfg. Has 13th-15th-cent. church.

Merritt, city (pop. 940), S B.C., on Nicola R. at mouth of Coldwater R., and 45 mi. SSW of Kamloops; coal, iron, copper mining; lumbering; fox farming; stock raising.

Merritt Island, Brevard co., E Fla., lying bet. Indian R. lagoon (W) and Banana R. lagoon (E) which separates isl. from Cape Canaveral (on barrier isl.); c.30 mi. long, up to 7 mi. wide; S part is thin sand bar c.15 mi. long. Causeway to mainland Orsino (N) and Merritt Island (S) are chief villages Orange groves, truck farms.

Merritton (mĕ'rĭtŭn), town (pop. 2,993), S Ont., on Welland Ship Canal, SE suburb of St. Catharines steel, paper, and pulp milling.

Merritt Parkway, in Conn., landscaped toll road part of state's express highway system; extends from N.Y. line E of White Plains, where it joins N.Y. parkway system, generally parallel to shore as far as New Haven, whence it is continued to NE, through Hartford, by Wilbur Cross Parkway System is planned to extend to Mass. line in NE Conn.

Merriwa, town (pop. 904), E central New South Wales, Australia, 95 mi. NW of Newcastle; terminus of railroad from Newcastle; sheep and agr center.

Mer Rouge (mûrōōzh'), village (pop. 784), Morehouse parish, NE La., 8 mi. E of Bastrop; farming cotton ginning, gravel processing.

Merrow, residential town and parish (pop. 1,690) central Surrey, England, 2 mi. ENE of Guildford

Merrow, Conn.: see MANSFIELD.

Merrygoen, village (pop. 170), E central New South Wales, Australia, on Castlereagh R. and 190 mi NW of Sydney; rail junction; sheep and agr center.

Merrymeeting Bay, Sagadahoc co., SW Maine tidal bay 5 mi. NE of Brunswick; formed by junction of Androscoggin and Kennebec rivers below Bowdoinham, it extends 16 mi. further S to the Atlantic. The surrounding marshes are noted for duck hunting.

Merrymeeting Lake, Strafford co., E central N.H. near New Durham, 27 mi. NE of Concord; 3 mi long. Drains through winding Merrymeeting R (c.10 mi. long) into L. Winnipesaukee to W.

Merrymount, Mass.: see QUINCY.

Merry Oaks, town (pop. 160), Chatham co., central N.C., 22 mi. SW of Raleigh; brick mfg.

Merryville, town (pop. 1,383), Beauregard parish W La., c.40 mi. NNW of Lake Charles city, near Sabine R.; wool market; lumber milling, cotton ginning. Oil field near by.

Mersa Fatma (mĕr'sä fät'mä), village, Massawa div., SE Eritrea, fishing port on Red Sea, 75 mi SE of Massawa. Exports potash mined at Dallol (Ethiopia) and transported here by narrow-gauge rail line and by road.

Mersa Matruh, Egypt: see MATRUH.

Mersch (mĕrsh), town (pop. 1,390), central Luxembourg, on Alzette R. and 10 mi. N of Luxembourg city; rubber products, chemicals (glues, polishes insecticides, chemicals for leather industry), inks metal products; market center for agr. (wheat barley, beets) region.

Merse (mûrs), lowland district of Berwick, Scotland, bet. Lammermuir Hills and the Tweed noted for its fertility.

Mersea Island (mûr'–, mär'–), E Essex, England bet. the Blackwater and Colne estuaries, 8 mi. SSE of Colchester, connected to mainland by causeway 5 mi. long, 2 mi. wide. At SW end is town of WEST MERSEA.

Merseburg (mĕr'zŭbōōrk), city (pop. 33,978) in former Prussian Saxony prov., central Germany after 1945 in Saxony-Anhalt, on the Saxonian Saale and 9 mi. S of Halle; 51°21'N 12°E. Rail junction; lignite-mining center; paper milling brewing; mfg. of steel products, machinery, synthetic rubber, cellulose, leather, cigars. Heavily bombed in Second World War (destruction about 45%). Noted bldgs. included cathedral (founded 1015; rebuilt in 13th and 16th cent.), 15th-cent. episcopal palace. First mentioned in 9th cent. Was site of important Carolingian fortress, a favorite residence of Henry I and Otto I. Seat (968–1561) of bishopric. Came to Saxony in 1561; in Thirty Years War captured (Sept., 1631) by Swedes. Was ⊙ duchy of Saxe-Merseburg (1656–1738). Passed to Prussia in 1815.

Mers-el-Kebir (mĕrs'-ĕl-kĕbēr'), fortified town (pop. 3,891), Oran dept., NW Algeria, on Oran Bay (Mediterranean Sea), 4 mi. NW of Oran; naval station in roadstead sheltered by a breakwater); fishing port with processing and canning plants; brickworks. As *Portus Divini,* it was leading anchorage along Algerian coast in Roman times. It was the port for Oran when French landed here in 1831. Superseded after 1860 by new harbor built at Oran proper. During the naval engagement of Oran Bay (July 3, 1940), most of Fr. fleet anchored here was destroyed by Br. warships. Construction of combined Mers-el-Kebir–Oran port was begun after Second World War. Sometimes spelled Mers-el-Kébir.

Mersey River (mûr'zē), W N.S., issues from Fishers L., flows S to L. Rossignol, thence to the Atlantic at Liverpool; 70 mi. long.

Mersey River, England, formed at Stockport by confluence of Tame R. and Goyt R., flows 70 mi. W, on Lancashire-Cheshire border, to Irish Sea 10 mi. NW of Liverpool, passing Ashton-upon-Mersey, Warrington, Widnes, Runcorn, Birkenhead, Liverpool, Wallasey, and Great Crosby. Its estuary is 16 mi. long and c.2 mi. wide, and is navigable for ocean-going liners. It receives the Irwell at Irlam, the Weaver 2 mi. SSW of Runcorn, and the Manchester Ship Canal at Eastham. The estuary's main navigational channel is called Crosby Channel. A great vehicular tunnel, 2 mi. long, under the Mersey connects (1934) Liverpool and Birkenhead.

Mersey River, N Tasmania, rises in small lakes N of L. St. Clair, flows 60 mi. generally N, past Latrobe, to Bass Strait at Devonport. Orchards on banks of estuary.

Mersin (mĕrsĭn'), city (1950 pop. 37,508), ⊙ Icel prov., S Turkey, port and rail terminus on Mediterranean Sea 40 mi. WSW of Adana, 16 mi. WSW of Tarsus; market for grain and legumes; oranges. Ships chrome, copper, agr. products. Formerly sometimes spelled Mersina; also called Icel, Turkish *Içel* (ĭchĕl').

Mersing (mĕrsĭng'), town (pop. 4,170), NE Johore, fishing port on South China Sea, 65 mi. N of Johore Bharu, in rubber-growing area.

Mersivan, Turkey: see MERZIFON.

Mers-les-Bains (mâr-lā-bē'), town (pop. 3,450), Somme dept., N France, 20 mi. WSW of Abbeville, bathing resort at mouth of Bresle R. on English Channel opposite Le Tréport; glassworks. Beach is dominated by high cliffs.

Merstham (mûr'stŭm, -stŭhăm), residential town and parish (pop. 4,495), E central Surrey, England, 3 mi. NE of Reigate; limestone quarrying. Has 13th-15th-cent. church.

Merta (mär'tŭ), town (pop. 4,776), central Rajasthan, India, 65 mi. ENE of Jodhpur; rail spur terminus; exports oilseeds, cotton, millet; cotton ginning, oilseed milling; handicrafts (palm fans, ivory goods, felts, pottery). Taken 1562 by Akbar. In battle near by, Mahrattas defeated joint forces of Jodhpur and Jaipur in 1790. Merta Road, rail junction, is 9 mi. NW.

Mertens, town (pop. 210), Hill co., N central Texas, 14 mi. E of Hillsboro; trade, shipping point in farm area.

Mertert (mĕr'tĕrt), village (pop. 806), E Luxembourg, on Moselle R., at mouth of Syre R., and 2 mi. NE of Grevenmacher, on Ger. border; sand and gravel quarrying; fruitgrowing.

Merthyr Tydfil (mûr'thûr tĭd'vĭl), county borough (1931 pop. 71,108; 1951 census 61,093), NE Glamorgan, Wales, on Taff R. and 20 mi. NNW of Cardiff, amid barren hills; coal-mining and steel-milling center, with chemical and various light industries. First steam locomotive built by Trevithick was tried (1804) on tramway bet. Merthyr Tydfil and Pontypridd. Near by is mansion of Cyfarthfa Castle, with mus. and art gall.

Merthyr Vale, town (pop. 7,129), in Merthyr Tydfil county borough, NE Glamorgan, Wales, on Taff R.; coal mining.

Mértola (mĕr'tōōlù), anc. *Myrtilis Julia*, town (pop. 1,121), Beja dist., S Portugal, head of navigation on the Guadiana and 28 mi. SSE of Beja; grain and livestock market; alcohol distilling. Overlooked by castle and keep (1292).

Merton, village (pop. 343), Waukesha co., SE Wis., on Bark R. and 20 mi. NW of Milwaukee, in dairying region; vegetable canning. Lakes near by.

Merton and Morden, residential urban district (1931 pop. 41,227; 1951 census 74,602), NE Surrey, England. Includes town of Merton, 7 mi. SSW of London, with remains of Augustinian priory (founded 1115), where met the 13th-cent. parliament that passed Statutes of Merton. Thomas à Becket and Walter de Merton received part of their education here. Has 12th-cent. church. Town of Morden has 17th-cent. church.

Mertzig (mĕrt'sĭkh), village (pop. 702), central Luxembourg, on Wark R. and 5 mi. WSW of Ettelbruck; building-stone quarrying; agr. (potatoes, wheat, oats).

Mertzon (mûr'tsŭn), town (pop. 768), ⊙ Irion co., W Texas, 25 mi. SW of San Angelo and on a tributary of Concho R.; retail, shipping point for sheep-ranching region; wool warehouses. Adjacent Sherwood village (just N) is former co. seat.

Mertzwiller (mĕrtsvēlâr'), Ger. *Merzweiler* (mĕrts'vīlûr), town (pop. 1,954), Bas-Rhin dept., E France, at W edge of Forest of Haguenau, 6 mi. NW of Haguenau; woodworking.

Méru (mārü'), town (pop. 4,662), Oise dept., N France, 14 mi. S of Beauvais; center of Fr. mother-of-pearl and bone industry (buttons, knitting needles, crochet hooks, chess sets, dice). Iron founding, paint mfg.

Meru (mā'rōō), town (pop. c.1,500), S central Kenya, on NE slope of Mt. Kenya, 110 mi. NNE of Nairobi; alt. 5,800 ft.; coffee, wheat, corn.

Meru, Mount, volcanic cone (14,979 ft.), N Tanganyika, 44 mi. WSW of Kilimanjaro. Its extinct crater can be easily reached from Arusha (at volcano's S base). Coffee plantations on densely populated S slopes. Rain forests at lower alt. Lion hunting.

Meruchak, Afghanistan: see MARUCHAK.

Merv, Turkmen SSR: see MARY, city.

Mervdasht, Iran: see MARVDASHT.

Merville (mĕrvēl'), town (pop. 4,470), Nord dept., N France, on the Lys and 8 mi. N of Béthune; market (peas, potatoes) in intensive agr. area. Metal-working, furniture mfg. Just W is Nieppe Forest, which figured prominently in battle of the Lys (1918) during First World War.

Merville-Franceville-Plage (-frãsvēl'-plăzh'), commune (pop. 603), Calvados dept., NW France, on the Channel just E of mouth of Orne R., 10 mi. NE of Caen. Bathing resort at Franceville-Plage (pine-planted dunes).

Mervino (myĕr'vēnŭ), village (1939 pop. over 2,000), NW Ryazan oblast, Russian SFSR, 4 mi. WNW of Ryazan; truck produce.

Merwede Canal (mĕr'vādù), W central Netherlands, extends 40 mi. N-S, bet. the Ij at Amsterdam and Waal R. at Gorinchem; 10 ft. deep, 65 ft. wide. Serves Breukelen, Maarssen, Utrecht, Vreeswijk, and Vianen. Crosses Lek R. bet. Vreeswijk (N) and Vianen (S). Entire length navigable by ships up to 2,000 tons.

Merwede River, SW Netherlands, formed as UPPER MERWEDE RIVER by junction of Maas and Waal rivers at Woudrichem; flows 5.5 mi. W, forking into LOWER MERWEDE RIVER (which flows 9 mi. W to form Old Maas R. and Noord R.) and NEW MERWEDE RIVER (which flows 10 mi. SW to form the Hollandschdiep).

Merwin, town (pop. 88), Bates co., W Mo., 17 mi. NW of Butler.

Merwin, Lake, Wash.: see LEWIS RIVER.

Merxem, Belgium: see MERKSEM.

Merxplas, Belgium: see MERKSPLAS.

Méry (mārē'), town, Liége prov., E central Belgium, on Ourthe R. and 6 mi. S of Liége; steel-rolling mills.

Méry-sur-Seine (mārē'-sür-sĕn'), village (pop. 953), Aube dept., NE central France, on right bank of Seine R. and 8 mi. E of Romilly-sur-Seine; hosiery mfg.; cattle.

Merzifon (mĕrzĭfôn'), town (1950 pop. 15,345), Amasya prov., N central Turkey, 25 mi. NW of Amasya; textiles; lignite; wheat. Sometimes spelled Marsivan and Mersivan.

Merzig (mĕr'tsĭkh), city (pop. 9,193), NW Saar, on Saar R. and 22 mi. NW of Saarbrücken; rail junction; mfg. of ceramics, glass, soap, chemicals, leather and tobacco products; metalworking, brewing. Has 12th-13th-cent. church, and town hall (1625).

Merzweiler, France: see MERTZWILLER.

Mesa (mā'sù), county (□ 3,313; pop. 38,974), W Colo.; ⊙ Grand Junction. Extensively irrigated farming area, bordering on Utah; drained by Colorado and Gunnison rivers. Fruit, beans, livestock, grain, sugar beets, potatoes. Includes COLORADO NATIONAL MONUMENT and GRAND VALLEY and parts of Grand Mesa, La Sal, and Uncompahgre natl. forests. Formed 1883.

Mesa, city (pop. 16,790), Maricopa co., S central Ariz., on Salt R. and 13 mi. E of Phoenix; agr. and cotton-ginning center; mfg. of helicopters; power and water from Roosevelt Dam; barite deposits near by. Seat of Mormon temple. Agr. experiment station of Univ. of Ariz. here. Founded 1878 by Mormons, inc. as town 1883, as city 1930.

Mesa, La, in Latin America: see LA MESA.

Mesaba (mùsä'bù), village (1940 pop. 10), St. Louis co., NE Minn., at E end of Mesabi iron range, 19 mi. ENE of Virginia.

Mesabi Range (mùsä'bē), long, narrow range of low hills (known as iron range) in Itasca and St. Louis counties, NE Minn., extending ENE from point near Grand Rapids to Babbitt. Leading iron-ore area that produces, in most years, more than 65% of total yield in U.S. Ore (c.51% iron) is found in horizontal strata and is mined largely by open-pit method and shipped from Duluth and Two Harbors. Iron was discovered (1887) by Merritt brothers. First shipment took place 1892. Merritts organized company to exploit their claims, but lost control of property to John D. Rockefeller during panic of 1893. Chief mining centers are Hibbing and Virginia. Much low-grade ore (taconite), averaging 20-30% iron, is now mined and beneficiated.

Mesa Bolívar (mā'sä bōlē'vär), town (pop. 533), Mérida state, W Venezuela, on slopes of Andean spur, 32 mi. WSW of Mérida; sugar cane, grain, fruit. Gold mines near by.

Mesagne (mĕzä'nyĕ), town (pop. 17,069), Brindisi prov., Apulia, S Italy, 9 mi. SW of Brindisi; agr. center (wine, olive oil, cheese, cereals, figs).

Mesão Frio (mĭzä'ō frē'ōō), town (pop. 1,013), Vila Real dist., N Portugal, on right bank of Douro R. and 12 mi. SW of Vila Real; vineyards (port wine); olives, figs, almonds, oranges also grown in area.

Mesara or **Messara** (both: mĕsürä'), agr. lowland, S Crete, on E coast of Gulf of Mesara. Its chief town is Tymbakion.

Mesara, Gulf of, or **Gulf of Messara,** inlet on S coast of central Crete; 15 mi. wide, 5 mi. long. Small port of Hagia Galene is on N shore.

Mesas, Las (läs mä'säs), town (pop. 2,816), Cuenca prov., E central Spain, 12 mi. S of Belmonte; cereals, grapes, livestock.

Mesa Verde National Park (mā'sù vûrd') (□ 79.7; established 1906), SW Colo., just S of Cortez, c.35 mi. W of Durango. Ruins of more than 300 pre-Columbian Pueblo Indian dwellings on top and in canyons of Mesa Verde, high tableland (15 mi. long, 8 mi. wide; alt. 8,752 ft. in N), which rises 2,000 ft. above base. Occupied for 1,200 years (until c.1300 when drought caused abandonment), the dwellings (pit houses, pueblos, and cliff houses) represent stages of progress from Basket Maker period (beginning c.1st cent. A.D.) to the Classic Pueblo period in which arts and crafts reached high development. Far View House on mesa top had 50 rooms, 5 kivas; well-preserved masonry Cliff Palace, in a huge cave, has more than 200 rooms, 23 kivas. Many houses have been excavated; mus. and library contain archaeological material. Southern Ute Indian Reservation adjoins park on E; Ute Mtn. Indian Reservation is on S and W.

Mescala River, Mexico: see BALSAS, RÍO DE LAS.

Mescalero (mĕskùlĕ'rō), village (pop. c.100), Otero co., S N.Mex., in Sacramento Mts., 21 mi. NNE of Alamogordo, in Mescalero Indian Reservation (pop. c.900); alt. 6,627 ft. Reservation hq. here. Lincoln Natl. Forest near by.

Meschede (mĕ'shùdù), town (pop. 7,530), in former Prussian prov. of Westphalia, W Germany, after 1945 in North Rhine-Westphalia, on the Ruhr and 10 mi. SE of Arnsberg; wool spinning. Henne dam and reservoir just SW.

Mescit Dag (mĕsjĭt'dä), Turkish *Mescit Dağ*, peak (10,680 ft.), NE Turkey, in Coruh Mts., 13 mi. SE of Ispir.

Mesegar (mäsägär'), town (pop. 783), Toledo prov., central Spain, 25 mi. W of Toledo; olives, fruit, grapes, esparto, stock.

Mesembria, Bulgaria: see NESEBAR.

Mesemvriya, Bulgaria: see NESEBAR.

Mesen, Belgium: see MESSINES.

Meseritz, Poland: see MIEDZYRZECZ.

Meservey (mùsûr'vē, -zûr'-), town (pop. 297), Cerro Gordo co., N Iowa, 22 mi. SW of Mason City.

Meseta (mäsä'tä) [Sp.,=tableland], geographic term for the entire interior of Spain, covering almost ¾ of the country and consisting of an immense plateau with Madrid at its center; average alt. c.2,000 ft. Partly broken, it is flanked N by the Cantabrian Mts. and S by the Sierra Morena, which separates it from Andalusia. The Sierra de Guadarrama and Sierra de Gredos form the horizontal divide bet. Old Castile and New Castile. The predominantly monotonous region has a rigorous continental climate with cold winters and hot summers. Generally 3 subbasins are distinguished: La RIOJA, drained by the upper Ebro; Old Castile, drained by the Duero (Douro); and New Castile, drained by the Tagus and Guadiana. La MANCHA forms the SE part of New Castile.

Meshanticut Park, R.I.: see CRANSTON.

Meshchera or **Meshchora** (myĭshchĕ'rŭ, -shchô'-), extensive wooded and swampy watershed in central European Russian SFSR, bet. Klyazma and Oka rivers; bounded by Shatura (NW), Ryazan (SW), and Kasimov (E). Has numerous lakes. Quartzite and peat deposits; lumbering, peat cutting, and glassworking are chief industries.

Meshchovsk (myĕ'shchùfsk), city (1926 pop. 2,724), central Kaluga oblast, Russian SFSR, 40 mi. WSW of Kaluga; fruit canning, dairying; printing. Chartered 1494. During Second World War, briefly held (1941-42) by Germans in Moscow campaign.

Meshed (mĕshĕd') or **Mashhad** (mäsh-häd') [Persian,=shrine], city (1940 pop. 167,471), ⊙ Ninth Prov., NE Iran, 440 mi. ENE of Teheran, just S of Kashaf R.; alt. 3,200 ft.; 36°16'N 59°36'E. Largest center of NE Iran and of Khurasan; head of railroad from Teheran; junction of highways to Teheran, Ashkhabad (USSR), Herat (Afghanistan), and Zahidan. Situated in fertile agr. dist. (fruit, opium, cotton, grain). Cotton ginning, wool milling, rug weaving, tanning, food processing (beet sugar, rice, flour, liquor, fruit); grain elevator. Exports wool, carpets, leather goods, cotton textiles. Has large hosp., medical col., radio station, and airfield (S). The golden-domed, 9th-cent. shrine of Imam Reza, the 8th Imam of the Shiites, for which Meshed is named, is one of the leading centers of Shiite pilgrimage. Near by is the noted Gauhar Shah mosque, built 1418 by wife of the Timurid Shah Rukh. Meshed is the successor of the anc. city of *Tus*, and developed after 14th cent. around Imam Reza's tomb. Repeatedly attacked (16th cent.) by the Uzbeks, it remained nevertheless under Persian control; it assumed great strategic importance after late-19th cent. because of proximity of USSR and Afghanistan frontiers. Held by Soviet troops during Second World War. Ruins of Tus, destroyed 1389, are 15 mi. NW and contain mausoleum of Firdausi, great Persian poet (11th cent.).

Meshed Ali, Iraq: see NAJAF.

Meshed-i-Sar, Iran: see BABULSAR.

Meshghara or **Mashgharah** (both: mĕsh'gärù), Fr. *Machgara*, village (pop. c.3,500), Bekaa prov., central Lebanon, 26 mi. SSE of Beirut; tanning; grapes, fruit, vegetables.

Meshkinshahr, Iran: see MISHKINSHAHR.

Meshkovskaya (myĭshkôf'skīŭ), village (1926 pop. 2,090), N Rostov oblast, Russian SFSR, on Tikhaya R. (small right affluent of the Don) and 40 mi. ENE of Chertkovo; flour mill, metalworks; wheat, sunflowers, livestock.

Meshoppen (mĭ-shŏ'pŭn), borough (pop. 574), Wyoming co., NE Pa., 25 mi. NW of Scranton and on Susquehanna R.; agr.; quarrying.

Meshra er Req (mĕsh'rŭ ĕr rĕk'), village, Bahr el Ghazal prov., S Anglo-Egyptian Sudan, on an isl. in L. Ambadi, at Head of navigation on the Bahr el Ghazal and 100 mi. NE of Wau; steamer landing.

Mesick (mē'sĭk), village (pop. 359), Wexford co., NW Mich., 19 mi. NW of Cadillac, and on Manistee R.

Mesilla (māsē'yŭ), village (pop. 1,264), Dona Ana co., S N.Mex., on Rio Grande, just S of Las Cruces, near Organ Mts. Central station on Overland mail route (c.1857); during Civil War was proclaimed capital of newly won Confederate territory. Billy the Kid mus. here. The whole Mesilla Valley became part of U.S. under the Gadsden Purchase (1853).

Mesilla Park, N.Mex.: see STATE COLLEGE.

Mesillas (māsē'yäs), town (pop. 1,065), Sinaloa, NW Mexico, in coastal lowland, 22 mi. SE of Mazatlán; cotton, chick-peas, tobacco, sugar cane, fruit, vegetables.

Mesilot, Israel: see MESSILOT.

Meskene, Meskena, or **Maskanah** (all: mĕs'kĕnŭ), village, Aleppo prov., N Syria, on the Euphrates and 60 mi. E of Aleppo. Just S are extensive ruins of anc. Barbalissus and medieval Balis.

Meskiana, La (lä mĕskyänä'), village (pop. 2,012), Constantine dept., NE Algeria, on railroad and 30 mi. NW of Tebessa; flour milling. Copper and lead mining.

Meslay-du-Maine (mĕlĕ'-dü-mĕn'), village (pop. 1,172), Mayenne dept., W France, 13 mi. SE of Laval; cheese making, sawmilling.

Mesnil-sur-Oger, Le (lŭ mānēl'-sür-ō-zhā'), village (pop. 1,341), Marne dept., N France, 8 mi. SSE of Épernay; winegrowing (champagne).

Mesocco (mĕzôk'kô), town (pop. 1,149), Grisons canton, SE Switzerland, on Moësa R., in Valle Mesolcina, and 17 mi. NE of Bellinzona, on road to San Bernardino Pass.

Mesola (mä'zôlä), village (pop. 800), Ferrara prov., Emilia-Romagna, N central Italy, on Po R. delta mouth and 12 mi. SE of Adria. Has 16th-cent. Este castle.

Mesolcina, Valle (māzôlchē'nä), Ger. *Misoxertal* (mēsôk'sŭrtäl), valley of Moësa R., in Lepontine Alps, Grisons canton, SE Switzerland; tourist area. Pop. Italian speaking and Catholic.

Mesolonghi, Greece: see MISSOLONGHI.

Mesopotamia (mĕ"sŭpŭtā'mēŭ) [Gr.,=between rivers], anc. country of Asia, the region about the lower Tigris and the lower Euphrates, included in the modern IRAQ. The region extends from the Persian Gulf N to the mts. of Armenia, from the Iranian plateau on the E to the Syrian Desert. From the mountainous country of the upper courses of the rivers, Mesopotamia slopes down through grassy steppes to the open central plain, which was once rendered exceedingly fertile by a network of canals. Now the region is generally barren and arid except for occasional oases. To the S the rivers unite in the Shatt al Arab, forming a delta which is a swampy wilderness of reeds. Deposits of silt have encroached on the Persian Gulf, so that sites of anc. towns, originally built on or near its shores, are now several miles inland. The S part of this region was, so far as is known, the cradle of civilization, a little older even than Egypt. Here appeared the cities of Eridu, Ur, Larsa, Lagash, Nippur, Akkad, and Babylon. Civilization was well settled in the 4th millennium B.C. The rise of kingdoms, notably that of Sargon, out of the rivalry of Sumerian and Semitic cities presaged the growth of the Babylonian might (see BABYLONIA), which gave rise to the Assyrian Empire (see ASSYRIA) and the Persian Empire (see PERSIA). The region, always threatened by Egypt and held by Egyptians for centuries in earlier times, began a slow decline under Persia. It still had prestige at the time of Alexander the Great, but became a more or less inconsiderable part of the Roman Empire. The Arabs took it from the Byzantine Empire, and it flourished again after Baghdad was made (A.D. 762) ⊙ the Abbasid caliphate of Mansur. This glory was destroyed when the Mongols under Hulagu Khan laid the area waste in 1298 and destroyed the anc. irrigation system. Mesopotamia did not recover from the ravaging and was not an important part of the Ottoman Empire. In the First World War, however, it gained new importance and was an important battlefield. The new kingdom of IRAQ, created in the territory, is of international importance because of its rich oil fields, but its status in the Moslem world is enhanced by the rich finds of archaeologists searching for remains of the incredibly distant past.

Mesopotamia (mĕ"sŭpŭtā'mēŭ, Sp. māsōpōtä'myä), region (□ 74,000) of NE Argentina, bet. Paraná (W) and Uruguay (E) rivers. Comprises ENTRE RÍOS and CORRIENTES provs. and MISIONES natl. territory.

Mesoraca (mĕzōrä'kä), village (pop. 4,473), Catanzaro prov., Calabria, S Italy, in S foothills of La Sila mts., 16 mi. NE of Catanzaro; meat, dairy, and wood products.

Mesquite (mŭskēt'), town (pop. 1,696), Dallas co., N Texas, 10 mi. E of Dallas; rail, processing point in cotton, truck area; rock quarries; cotton ginning, brick making. Inc. 1886.

Messa, Cyrenaica: see LUIGI RAZZA.

Messac (mĕsäk'), village (pop. 882), Ille-et-Vilaine dept., W France, on the Vilaine and 18 mi. NE of Redon; alcohol distilling, fertilizer mfg.

Messalonskee Lake, Maine: see BELGRADE LAKES.

Messamena (mĕsämĕ'nä), village, Haut-Nyong region, S central Fr. Cameroons, 30 mi. SW of Abong-M'Bang, in coffee-growing area.

Messana, Sicily: see MESSINA, city.

Messancy (mĕsäsē'), village (pop. 2,510), Luxembourg prov., SE Belgium, 6 mi. S of Arlon; residential area for near-by industrial Athus.

Messanjore, India: see MASANJOR.

Messaoria (mĕsäô'ryä) or **Messaria** (mĕsä'ryä), lowland in central and E Cyprus, occupying about ⅓ of the isl. Extends c.55 mi. from Morphou Bay (W) to Famagusta Bay (E), flanked N by the Kyrenia Mts. and S by the higher Troodos or Olympus Mts. Nicosia is in its center. Principal agr. region, producing wheat, barley, oats, wine, olive oil, almonds, citrus fruit. Has pleasant winter climate. Arid summers make irrigation necessary. It is traversed by Famagusta-Nicosia RR, now continued beyond Morphou. Sometimes spelled Mesaoria.

Messapion, Greece: see KTYPAS.

Messara, Crete: see MESARA.

Messaria, Cyprus: see MESSAORIA.

Messei (mĕsā'), village (pop. 440), Orne dept., NW France, 3 mi. SSE of Flers.

Messeix (mĕsĕks'), village (pop. 687), Puy-de-Dôme dept., central France, in Auvergne Mts., 12 mi. ENE of Ussel; coal mining.

Messejana (mĭsĭzhä'nŭ), town (pop. 2,190), N Ceará, Brazil, 5 mi. SE of Fortaleza; sugar, rice, cotton. Founded 1606. Formerly spelled Mecejana.

Messejana, town (pop. 1,782), Beja dist., S Portugal, 24 mi. SW of Beja; grain, sheep.

Messellemiya or **El Messellemiya** (ĕl mĕsĕl'lĕmĭyŭ), village, Blue Nile prov., central Anglo-Egyptian Sudan, in the Gezira, on the Blue Nile, on railroad, and 10 mi. N of Wad Medani; cotton, wheat, barley, corn, fruits, durra; livestock. Also spelled Mesellemiya or Messallemiya.

Messene or **Messini** (both: mĕsē'nē), town (pop. 7,323), Messenia nome, SW Peloponnesus, S Greece, on Pamisos R. and 5 mi. W of Kalamata; trade center (rice; also cotton, olives, figs, wheat), with rail connection to Kalamata. Formerly called Nision or Nisi, it was later renamed for anc. city of Messene, 10 mi. NNW, on W slope of Mt. Ithome, site of modern village of Maurommati, Mavrommati, or Mavromati (all: mävrōmä'tē) (pop. 755). Anc. Messene was founded 369 B.C. by Epaminondas as capital of Messinia. Ruins, partly unearthed, include theater, acropolis, and temple.

Messene, Gulf of, Greece: see MESSENIA, GULF OF.

Messenia or **Messinia** (both: mĕsē'nēŭ), nome (□ 1,127; pop. 240,355), SW Peloponnesus, Greece; ⊙ Kalamata. Bordered E by Taygetus Mts., W and S by Ionian Sea, with Lykodimos mts. SW. Messenia lowland (center) is drained by Pamisos R. Mainly agr.: subtropical fruits (citrus fruits, figs, raisins), wheat, olives, cotton, and silk; livestock (goats, hogs); fisheries along coast. Tourist trade. Industry centered at Kalamata, the main port. Originally settled by Dorians, the anc. region was subjugated by Sparta in 8th cent. B.C. in 1st Messenian War. As a result of subsequent unsuccessful revolts, the 2d (7th cent. B.C.) and 3d (5th cent. B.C.) Messenian Wars, the Messenian pop. emigrated to Messina (Italy) and Naupaktos, leaving the region to Sparta. It regained its independence (369 B.C.) with Messene as capital, joined the Achaean League, and fell 146 B.C. to Rome. Its anc. cities were MESSENE and PYLOS.

Messenia, Gulf of, inlet of Ionian Sea, in S Peloponnesus, Greece, bet. capes Akritas and Matapan; 30 mi. wide, 35 mi. long. Kalamata is on N shore. Also called Gulf of Messene, formerly Gulf of Korone and Gulf of Kalamata.

Messenia Peninsula, SW Peloponnesus, Greece, on Ionian Sea W of Gulf of Messenia; terminates S in Cape Akritas; 20 mi. long, 15 mi. wide. Pylos and Methone on W coast, Korone on E coast.

Messick, village (pop. 2,211, with near-by Jeffs), York co., SE Va., on tidewater near Chesapeake Bay, 7 mi. N of Hampton; crab and fish packing.

Messilot, Messiloth, or **Mesilot** (all: mĕsēlōt'), settlement (pop. 400), NE Israel, in Jordan valley, 2 mi. W of Beisan; mixed farming. Founded 1938.

Messina (mŭsē'nŭ, Ital. mĕs-sē'nä), province (□ 1,253; pop. 627,093), NE Sicily; ⊙ Messina. Traversed E-W by Nebrodi and Peloritani mts.; drained by mtn. streams; forests in SW. Agr. (olives, grapes, citrus fruit); livestock (goats, sheep); fisheries (tunny, lobster, swordfish). Mining (pumice, antimony). Industry concentrated at Messina. Antiquities at Taormina and Tyndaris.

Messina, anc. *Zancle,* later *Messana,* third largest city (pop. 121,605; metropolitan area pop. 192,051) of Sicily; ⊙ Messina prov.; port on Strait of Messina and 50 mi. NNE of Catania; 38°11'N 15°33'E. Transportation and industrial center; food processing (macaroni, citrus extracts), wine distilling, mfg. (cement, chemicals, soap, tobacco), printing; fishing industry; shipyards, foundries; power plant. Exports citrus fruit, wine, olive oil. Imports coal, cereals. Passenger port (service to mainland cities, Lipari Isls.); ferry across Strait of Messina to Villa San Giovanni. Archbishopric, with cathedral (badly hit in Second World War). Has univ. (founded 1548; suppressed 1680; later reestablished), Biological Marine Inst., mus. (founded 1806), botanical garden. Founded in 8th cent. B.C. by Greek colonists; seized by Anaxilas of Rhegium in 5th cent. B.C. Destroyed by Carthaginians in 396 B.C.; rebuilt shortly after by Dionysius I. Fell (288 B.C.) to the Mamertines, who allied themselves with Rome. Involved in war with Hiero of Syracuse and his Carthaginian allies, the Mamertines appealed to Rome, thereby bringing about First Punic War. Passed under Byzantines, Saracens (9th cent.), and Normans (11th cent.). Became an important city of kingdom of Sicily, until it declined under Spaniards in 16th cent. Last city of isl. liberated from the Bourbons by Garibaldi in 1860. Despite its long history, few of Messina's old buildings remain. Earthquake of 1783 did great damage and that of 1908 destroyed over 90% of its buildings, causing more than 30,000 deaths. In Second World War, severely damaged by heavy bombing and fighting (1943). With its fall (Aug. 17, 1943), the conquest of Sicily by the Allies was completed.

Messina, town (pop. 7,792), N Transvaal, U. of So. Afr., near Southern Rhodesia border, 115 mi. NNE of Pietersburg; copper-mining and refining center. Limpopo R. is crossed, 10 mi. NNW, by Beit Bridge to Southern Rhodesia border station of Beitbridge.

Messina, Strait of, anc. *Fretum Siculum,* channel separating Italy and Sicily, bet. Punta del Faro and rock of Scylla (N) and capes Alì and Pellaro (S); joins Ionian and Tyrrhenian seas; 20 mi. long, 2 to 10 mi. wide, c.300 ft. deep. Rich fisheries. Chief ports: Messina (Sicily), Reggio di Calabria (Italy). Its whirlpools, such as that of GAROFALO (N), and strong currents were feared by anc. sailors, resulting in legend of Scylla and Charybdis.

Messines (mĕsēn'), Flemish *Mesen* (formerly *Meesen*) (mā'zŭn), village (pop. 1,091), West Flanders prov., W Belgium, 6 mi. S of Ypres. Site of battle (1917) in First World War.

Messini, Greece: see MESSENE.

Messinia, Greece: see MESSENIA.

Messis, Turkey: see MISIS.

Messkirch (mĕs'kĭrkh"), town (pop. 2,754), S Baden, Germany, 14 mi. E of Tuttlingen; mfg. of clothing, precision instruments; woodworking, lumber milling. Has 17th-cent. castle. Sometimes spelled Mösskirch.

Messnerskreith (mĕs'nŭrskrīt"), village (commune pop. 1,446), Upper Palatinate, E central Bavaria, Germany, 10 mi. S of Schwandorf; metalworking and lignite mining at Haidhof (pop. 310), 1 mi. W.

Messoiuso (mĕs-sôyōō'zô), village (pop. 4,425), Palermo prov., N central Sicily, 18 mi. SSE of Palermo; an Albanian settlement.

Messolonghion, Greece: see MISSOLONGHI.

Mestanza (mĕstän'thä), town (pop. 2,406), Ciudad Real prov., S central Spain, on N slopes of the Sierra Morena, 29 mi. SSW of Ciudad Real; cereals, olives, livestock; timber; apiculture. Lead, silver, copper mining.

Mesta River (mĕ'stä), Gr. *Nestos* (nĕs'tôs), Turkish *Kara Su,* Lat. *Nestus,* SW Bulgaria and W Thrace, Greece, rises on Kolarov Peak of Rila Mts., flows 150 mi. generally SE bet. Pirin and Rhodope mts. to Aegean Sea in a delta opposite isl. of Thasos. Forms Thrace-Macedonia line in lower course.

Mestec Kralove (myĕ'stĕts krä'lôvä), Czech *Městec Králové,* Ger. *Königstadl* (kû'nĭkhshtädŭl), town (pop. 2,738), central Bohemia, Czechoslovakia, on railroad and 17 mi. N of Kutna Hora, in sugar-beet dist.

Mestia (myĕ'styĕŭ), village (1932 pop. estimate 530), NW Georgian SSR, in Svanetia, on S slope of the Greater Caucasus, near upper Ingur R., 55 mi. N of Kutaisi; livestock raising, lumbering. Airfield.

Mesto Libava, Czechoslovakia: see LIBAVA.

Mesto Litrbachy, Czechoslovakia: see KRASNO.

Mesto Tepla, Czechoslovakia: see TEPLA.

Mesto Touskov, Czechoslovakia: see TOUSKOV.

Mestre (mĕ'strĕ), town (pop. 23,887), Venezia prov., Veneto, N Italy, 5 mi. NW of Venice. Industrial center developed about adjacent PORTO MARGHERA; furniture, fertilizer, brooms.

Mestre Caetano (mā'strĭ kītä'nōō), town (pop. 311), S central Minas Gerais, Brazil, on railroad and 5 mi. E of Sabará; gold mining since 18th cent. Until 1944, called Cuiabá.

Mesudiye (mĕsōō'dĭyĕ"). **1** Village, Giresun prov., Turkey: see ALUCRA. **2** Village (pop. 1,662), Ordu prov., N Turkey, on Melet R. and 36 mi. S of Ordu; grain. Formerly Melet and Hamidiye.

Mesurado, county, Liberia: see MONTSERRADO.

Mesurado, Cape, Liberia: see MONTSERRADO, CAPE.

Mesvre (mĕ'vrŭ), agr. village (pop. 396), Saône-et-Loire dept., E central France, 7 mi. SSW of Autun.

Mesyagutovo (mĕsyŭgōō'tŭvŭ), village (1926 pop. 4,186), NE Bashkir Autonomous SSR, Russian SFSR, on Ai R. and 105 mi. NE of Ufa; rye, oats, stock.

Meta (mä'tä), intendancy (□ 32,903; 1938 pop. 51,674; 1950 estimate 52,230), central Colombia; ⊙ Villavicencio. Extends from Cordillera Oriental (E) to 71°5'W, bet. Meta R. (N) and Guaviare R. (S). Apart from Cordillera Oriental and its E spurs, it consists of llano grasslands and dense forests. It is undeveloped and sparsely populated, and has a hot, tropical climate. Mainly a cattle-grazing region. Coffee is grown in Andean foothills; also some subsistence crops and fruit. Forests yield timber, gums, vanilla, resins. Villavicencio is an important communication and trading center serving the entire Colombian Orinoco R. basin. Gold-placer mines are located at San Martín, saltworks at Restrepo and Cumaral.

Meta (mä'tä), town (pop. 5,005), Napoli prov., Campania, S Italy, on peninsula of Sorrento, 5 mi. SW of Castellammare di Stabia; mfg. of combustion motors.

Meta (mē'tŭ), town (pop. 353), Osage co., central Mo., near Osage R., 18 mi. S of Jefferson City; dairy, grain products; lead mines.

Metabetchouan, Métabetchouan (mē''tŭbĕch''wän'), or **Saint Jérôme** (sẽ zhārōm'), village (pop. 1,469), S central Que., on SE shore of L. St. John, 13 mi. SE of St. Joseph d'Alma; dairying, lumbering, pig raising.

Metabetchouan River or **Métabetchouan River**, S central Que., rises in N part of Laurentides Provincial Park, flows 50 mi. N to L. St. John at Desbiens.

Meta Gafersa, Ethiopia: see Araro.

Meta Incognita or **Kingait**, SE Baffin Isl., SE Franklin Dist., Northwest Territories, peninsula (170 mi. long, 30–80 mi. wide), extending SE into the Atlantic, bet. Frobisher Bay (NE) and Hudson Strait (SW); 61°52'–63°30'N 65°55'–70° W. Mountainous surface rises to c.2,500 ft. in center; on NE coast, near mouth of Frobisher Bay, are Grinnell Ice Cap (c.3,000 ft. high) and Southeast Ice Cap (c.2,800 ft. high), both extending tongues to Frobisher Bay.

Metairie (mĕ'trē), village (1940 pop. 2,892), Jefferson parish, SE La., a NW suburb of New Orleans.

Metalici, Muntii, Rumania: see Apuseni Mountains.

Metaline (mĕ'tŭlēn, mĕtŭlēn'), town (pop. 563), Pend Oreille co., NE Wash., on Clark Fork R. and 31 mi. NE of Colville.

Metaline Falls, town (pop. 547), Pend Oreille co., NE Wash., port of entry near B.C. line, 33 mi. NE of Colville, near Clark Fork R. Important lead, zinc mines; cementworks.

Metamma (mĕtä'mä), town (pop. 3,000), Begemdir prov., NW Ethiopia, on Anglo-Egyptian Sudan border opposite Gallabat, near Atbara R. Trade center (coffee, honey, butter, livestock). Flourished as a slave market. Here in 1889 Emperor John of Ethiopia was killed and his forces defeated in a battle with Mahdist troops from the Sudan. Also spelled Metemma.

Metamora. **1** (mĕ'tŭmôrŭ) Village (pop. 1,368), Woodford co., central Ill., 12 mi. ENE of Peoria, in agr. and bituminous-coal area; canned foods. Former ⊙ Woodford co. Old courthouse is now state memorial to Lincoln, who often argued cases here. Inc. 1845. **2** (mĕtŭmô'rŭ) Village (pop. 390), Lapeer co., E Mich., 7 mi. S of Lapeer, in farm area. **3** (mĕtŭmô'rŭ) Village (pop. 532), Fulton co., NW Ohio, 19 mi. W of Toledo, at Mich. line; agr. (sugar beets, tomatoes, corn); poultry hatcheries.

Metamorfosis or **Metamorphosis**, Greece: see Olympus.

Metán, Argentina: see San José de Metán.

Metangula (mĕtăng-gōō'lä), village, Niassa prov., NW Mozambique, only Portuguese port on L. Nyasa (Nyasaland border), 45 mi. NNW of Vila Cabral; 12°40'S 34°51'E; road terminus.

Metapa (mätä'pä), town (pop. 284), Chiapas, S Mexico, near Guatemala border, 6 mi. SE of Tapachula; coffee.

Metapa, Nicaragua: see Ciudad Darío.

Metapán (mätäpän'), city (pop. 2,000), Santa Ana dept., NW Salvador, just N of small L. Metapán, on railroad and 21 mi. N of Santa Ana, at S foot of the Sierra de Metapán; coffee, grain, livestock raising. Iron and copper mines and limestone quarries near by.

Metapán, Sierra de (syĕ'rä dā), S spur of main Andean divide, on Guatemala-Salvador-Honduras border, W of Lempa R.; 10 mi. long; rises to 7,920 ft. in Cerro Montecristo. Metapán (Salvador) is at S foot. Also called Sierra de Montepeque.

Meta Pond (mē'tŭ), lake (8 mi. long, 2 mi. wide), SE N.F.; 48°3'N 54°53'W.

Metapontum (mĕtŭpŏn'tŭm), anc. city of Magna Graecia, on Gulf of Taranto, S Italy, bet. mouths of Basento and Bradano rivers. Settled by Greeks from Achaea in 6th cent. B.C.; afforded refuge to Pythagoreans expelled from Crotona. Pythagoras taught and died here. Has remains of Doric temples (Tavole Paladine, Apollo Lyceus) and other ruins.

Meta River (mä'tä), central and E Colombia. Its headstreams (Guatiquía and Guayuriba) rise E and S of Bogotá in Cordillera Oriental; flows c.650 mi. NE and E through undeveloped llano lowlands, forms part of Venezuela-Colombia border, and enters Orinoco R. at Puerto Carreño. Navigable, but little used.

Metasville (mē'tŭzvĭl), town (pop. 82), Wilkes co., NE Ga., 8 mi. ENE of Washington.

Metauro River (mĕtäōō'rô), anc. *Metaurus*, The Marches, central Italy, rises in 2 headstreams (Meta, Auro) in Etruscan Apennines NE of Sansepolcro, flows 69 mi. ENE, past Sant'Angelo in Vado, Urbania, and Fossombrone, to the Adriatic 2 mi. SE of Fano. Here Romans defeated (207 B.C.) Carthaginians under Hasdrubal.

Metcalf. **1** Town (pop. 206), Thomas co., S Ga., 9 mi. S of Thomasville, near Fla. line. **2** Village (pop. 312), Edgar co., E Ill., 14 mi. NNW of Paris, in agr. area.

Metcalfe (mĕt'kăf''), county (□ 296; pop. 9,851), S Ky.; ⊙ Edmonton. Drained py several creeks. Rolling agr. area (livestock, corn, wheat, burley tobacco); timber. Formed 1860.

Metedeconk River (mŭtē'dŭkŏngk''), E N.J., rises SW of Freehold in North Branch (c.20 mi. long) and South Branch (c.15 mi. long), which flow SE to junction c.6 mi. above mouth on Barnegat Bay; navigable below the junction.

Meteghan (mĕtā'gŭn), village (pop. estimate 750), W N.S., on the Atlantic, at entrance of St. Mary Bay, 25 mi. N of Yarmouth; lobster and clam fishing and canning, woodworking.

Metemma or **El Metemma**, Anglo-Egyptian Sudan: see Shendi.

Metemma, Ethiopia: see Metamma.

Meteora (mĕtĕ'ôrŭ), group of monasteries, Trikkala nome, W Thessaly, Greece, on pillar-like racks just N of Kalambaka, 14 mi. NNW of Trikkala. Flourished 14th–16th cents., when they received special privileges under Turkish rule. Wall paintings, manuscripts are preserved. Of the original 23, five monasteries remain inhabited (1928 pop. 85).

Meteor Crater, SE Coconino co., central Ariz., 17 mi. W of Winslow; great pockmark (c.4,000 ft. in diameter, 600 ft. deep, with rim rising 120–160 ft. above surrounding plain) caused py meteor. Fragments of iron, containing some nickel, have been found. Sometimes Diablo Crater (dēä'blō).

Metepec (mätäpĕk'). **1** Town (pop. 743), Hidalgo, central Mexico, 27 mi. ENE of Pachuca; alt. 7,421 ft.; corn, maguey, livestock; mfg. of metal pipes. **2** Town (pop. 5,082), Mexico state, central Mexico, on railroad and 5 mi. SE of Toluca; agr. center (grain, fruit, livestock); dairying. **3** Town (pop. 4,347), Puebla, central Mexico, on central plateau, 19 mi. WSW of Puebla; yarn- and textile-mfg.

Methana (mĕ'thŭnŭ), town (pop. 1,243), Attica nome, Greece, in Peloponnesus, 30 mi. SSW of Piraeus, across Saronic Gulf, on SE shore of Methana Peninsula, a headland of the Argolis Peninsula.

Methil, Scotland: see Buckhaven and Methil.

Methimna Campestris, Spain: see Medina del Campo.

Methley, former urban district (1931 pop. 4,607), West Riding, S central Yorkshire, England, 7 mi. SE of Leeds; coal mining. Inc. 1937 in Rothwell.

Methlick, agr. village and parish (pop. 1,481), NE Aberdeen, Scotland, on Ythan R. and 7 mi. NNE of Old Meldrum. Just S is 18th-cent. Haddo House of marquis of Aberdeen, built by Robert Adam. Near by are remains of anc. Gight Castle or House of Gight.

Methone or **Methoni** (both: mĕthô'nē), town (pop. 2,087), Messenia nome, SW Peloponnesus, Greece, port on Ionian Sea opposite Oinousai Isls., 26 mi. SW of Kalamata; fisheries; livestock (goats, sheep). Site of anc. city, which became important Venetian port after 1206 and was then called Modon. Ruled by Turks after 1500, except for brief Venetian occupation (1699–1718).

Methora, India: see Muttra, city.

Méthouïa (mätōōyä'), village and oasis, Gabès dist., E Tunisia, 8 mi. NNW of Gabès; date-palms, sheep, camels.

Methow River (mĕt'hou), N Wash., rises in Cascade Range N of L. Chelan, flows c.80 mi. generally SE through irrigated agr. valley (apples) to Columbia R. at Pateros.

Methuen (mĭthōō'ŭn), town (pop. 24,477), Essex co., NE Mass., near N.H. line, just NW of Lawrence; worsteds, yarn, wooden heels, beverages, canvas goods, soap, chemicals. Settled c.1642, set off from Haverhill 1725, changed from city to town 1921.

Methven (mĕth'vŭn), township (pop. 1,026), E S.Isl., New Zealand, 50 mi. WSW of Christchurch; agr. railhead; linen mill.

Methven, agr. village and parish (pop. 1,670), SE Perthshire, Scotland, 6 mi. W of Perth. Has church dating from 15th cent. Near by is Trinity Col., public school founded 1841.

Methy Lake (mē'thē) (21 mi. long, 5 mi. wide), NW Sask., 20 mi. NW of Peter Pond L.; 56°25'N 109°30'W; alt. 1,460 ft. Main headstream of Churchill R. rises here.

Methymna or **Mithimna** (mĕthĭm'nŭ, Gr. mē'thĭmnŭ), town (pop. 2,276), on N shore of Lesbos isl., Greece, 26 mi. NW of Mytilene; trade in olive oil, wine, vegetables; fisheries. Its adjoining Aegean port is Molybdos or Molivdhos. Methymna was home of lyric poet Arion (7th cent. B.C.). It rivalled (5th–4th cent. B.C.) Mytilene for the leadership of the isl.

Metica River, Colombia: see Guayuriba River.

Meting (mä'tĭng), village, Tatta dist., SW Sind, W Pakistan, on railroad and 70 mi. ENE of Karachi; rice; handicraft cloth weaving. Coal deposits near by.

Metinic Island (mŭtĭ'nĭk), Knox co., S Maine, 6 mi. SE of Tenants Harbor; 2 mi. long, ¼ mi. wide.

Metis Beach (mĕ'tĭs) or **Métis sur Mer** (mātē' sür mâr'), village (pop. 332), E Que., on the St. Lawrence, 25 mi. WSW of Matane; popular resort.

Metkovets (mĕtkô'vĕts), village (pop. 4,998), Vidin dist., NW Bulgaria, 13 mi. SSW of Lom; grain, livestock, truck. Sometimes spelled Medkovets.

Metkovic (mĕt'kôvĭch), Serbo-Croatian *Metković*, village (pop. 3,166), S Croatia, Yugoslavia, Adriatic port (via Neretva Channel) on Neretva R., on railroad and 22 mi. S of Mostar, in Dalmatia, near Herzegovina border. Largely supplanted by new port of Kardeljevo. Roman ruins near by. Sometimes spelled Metkovich.

Metlakahtla or **Metlakatla** (mĕtlŭkăt'lŭ), village (pop. 816), SE Alaska, on W shore of Annette Isl., 17 mi. S of Ketchikan. A model cooperative village of the Tsimshian Indians. Fishing, logging; cooperative cannery and sawmill. Established 1887 by Rev. Wm. Duncan, missionary, and Indians emigrating from Fort Simpson, B.C.

Metlaltoyuca (mätlältoiōō'kä), town (pop. 1,351), Puebla, central Mexico, at foot of Sierra Madre Oriental, in Gulf plain, 33 mi. SW of Tuxpan; sugar cane, coffee, tobacco, fruit. Pre-Columbian ruins near by.

Metlaoui (mĕtläwē'), village, Gafsa dist., W central Tunisia, 22 mi. WSW of Gafsa; hq. of phosphate-mining region at junction of mining railroads. Mine 2 mi. N of station. Miners live in Philippe-Thomas, an adjoining "company" village.

Metlatonoc (mätlätōnōk'), town (pop. 1,216), Guerrero, SW Mexico, in Sierra Madre del Sur, near Oaxaca border, 25 mi. SE of Tlapa; cereals, fruit, stock.

Metlika (mĕt'lĭkä), Ger. *Möttling* (mŭt'lĭng), anc. *Metulum*, village, S Slovenia, Yugoslavia, on Kupa R., on railroad and 13 mi. SSE of Novo Mesto, on Croatia border; trade center (1st mentioned in 1300). Old castle. Until 1918, in Carniola.

Metlili (mĕtlēlē'), Saharan village, Ghardaïa territory, central Algeria, one of the Mzab oases, 15 mi. S of Ghardaïa.

Metnitz (mĕt'nĭts), village (pop. 2,211), Carinthia, S Austria, in Gurktal Alps, 25 mi. NNW of Klagenfurt; cattle, sheep.

Metohija or **Metokhiya** (mĕ'tôhēä, –khēä), fertile valley bet. North Albanian Alps and Sar Mts., SW Serbia, Yugoslavia, among forested mts., on Albania border; since 1946 part of Kosovo-Metohija oblast. Largely agr. (fruit, chestnuts, beans); winegrowing; meadows. Drained by the White Drin and its tributaries. Chief towns: Prizren, Pec, Djakovica. Under Turkish rule (until 1913), part of Kosovo vilayet. Sometimes spelled Metochia.

Metolius (mĭtō'lēŭs, –lŭs), town (pop. 157), Jefferson co., N central Oregon, 5 mi. SW of Madras.

Metolius River, N central Oregon, rises in Cascade Range in Deschutes Natl. Forest, flows c.60 mi. N and E through recreational area to Deschutes R. SW of Madras.

Metomkin Inlet, Va.: see Metomkin Island.

Metomkin Island (mĭtŏm'kĭn), E Va., barrier island (c.6 mi. long), 5 mi. E of Accomac; cut off by tidal channels from E shore of Accomack co.; Metomkin Inlet is at S, Gargathy Inlet at N end.

Metpalli or **Matpalli** (both: mŭtpŭl'lē), town (pop. 5,316), Karimnagar dist., NE central Hyderabad state, India, 19 mi. W of Jagtial; rice. Sometimes spelled Medpalli.

Metropolis (mĭtrŏ'pŭlĭs), port city (pop. 6,093), ⊙ Massac co., extreme S Ill., on Ohio R. and 28 mi. ENE of Cairo, in agr. and lumbering area; mfg. (wood products, furniture, clothing); shipping center for corn, wheat, livestock. Fort Massac State Park (c.450 acres), on site of French fort (1757), and Kincaid Indian Mounds are near by. Laid out 1839, inc. 1845.

Metsovon (mĕ'tsôvôn), town (pop. 2,907), Ioannina nome, S Epirus, Greece, in the Pindus, 19 mi. ENE of Ioannina, near source of Arachthos R.; stock raising; olive oil. Center of Walachian (Vlach) pop. of Greece.

Mettawee River (mĕ'tŭwē), in Vt. and N.Y., rises in Taconic Mts. near Dorset, Vt. flows c.50 mi. NW, past Pawlet, Vt., and Granville, N.Y., to L. Champlain near Whitehall, N.Y.

Mettelhorn (mĕt'tŭlhôrn), peak (11,184 ft.) in Pennine Alps, S Switzerland, 2 mi. N of Zermatt.

Metten (mĕ'tŭn), village (pop. 3,227), Lower Bavaria, Germany, at SW foot of the Bohemian Forest, near the Danube, 3 mi. WNW of Deggendorf; granite quarrying. Wheat, vegetables, livestock. Has Benedictine abbey founded in late 8th cent.

Metter, city (pop. 2,091), ⊙ Candler co., E central Ga., 17 mi. W of Statesboro, near Canoochee R.; tobacco market; peanut shelling, lumber milling.

Mettet (mĕtā'), village (pop. 2,905), Namur prov., S central Belgium, 13 mi. SW of Namur; marble quarrying.

Mettingen (mĕ'tĭng-ŭn), village (pop. 8,116), in former Prussian prov. of Westphalia, NW Germany, after 1945 in North Rhine-Westphalia, 11 mi. NW of Osnabrück; grain.

Mettlach (mĕt'läkh), town (pop. 3,649), NW Saar, on Saar R. and 23 mi. S of Trier, near Ger. border; glass mfg.; important hydroelectric power station. Former Benedictine abbey (founded c.700; rebuilt in mid-18th cent.) now houses ceramics works.

Mettmach (mĕt'mäkh), town (pop. 2,434), W Upper Austria, 8 mi. SW of Ried, in Hausruck Mts.; rye, dairy farming.

Mettmann (mĕt'män"), town (pop. 16,332), in former Prussian Rhine Prov., W Germany, after 1945 in North Rhine-Westphalia, 8 mi. ENE of Düsseldorf; mfg. of metal goods.

Mettray (mĕtrĕ'), village (pop. 144), Indre-et-Loire dept., W central France, 4 mi. NNW of Tours. Has agr. reformatory for juveniles, founded 1839.

Mettupalaiyam (mĕtōōpä'lĭyŭm), town (pop. 17,-764), Coimbatore dist., SW Madras, India, on rail spur (to Ootacamund) and 21 mi. N of Coimbatore; road center; cattle grazing; tannery; shellac mfg. Also spelled Mettuppalaiyam and Mettupalayam.

Mettupalayam, India. **1** Town, Coimbatore dist.: see METTUPALAIYAM. **2** Village, Trichinopoly dist.: see MORUPPATTI.

Mettuppalaiyam, India. **1** Town, Coimbatore dist.: see METTUPALAIYAM. **2** Village, Trichinopoly dist.: see MORUPPATTI.

Mettur (māt'tōōr), town (pop. 8,670), Salem dist., W Madras, India, on Cauvery R. and 26 mi. WNW of Salem; industrial center; textile and sugar mills, chemical plants (alkalies, soap, vegetable ghee, fertilizers), cement factory; fish processing. Cauvery-Mettur hydroelectric and irrigation system consists of Mettur Dam (5,300 ft. long, 176 ft. high; terminus of rail spur from Salem), across the Cauvery just N of Mettur, and power plant (in operation since 1937); dam impounds STANLEY RESERVOIR. The Mettur system (linked at Erode with Pykara transmission network) powers industries at Mettur and Salem and furthers industrial development in 12 dists. of S Madras; supplies and controls irrigation works (Grand Anicut and Vadavar canals) of the Cauvery delta and non-deltaic tracts of Tanjore dist. Sometimes spelled Metur.

Mettur Canal, India: see GRAND ANICUT CANAL.

Metuchen (mŭtŭ'chŭn), residential borough (pop. 9,879), Middlesex co., NE N.J., 5 mi. NE of New Brunswick; automobile assembly plant; mfg. (insulation products, chemicals, metal products, textiles, ceramics); truck, dairy products. Has several 18th-cent. buildings. Veterans' home, tuberculosis hosp., and U.S. Raritan Arsenal near by. Settled before 1700, inc. 1900.

Metulla (mĕtōō'lä), settlement (pop. 220), Upper Galilee, NE Israel, frontier point on Lebanese border, at S foot of the Lebanon range, 22 mi. NNE of Safad; alt. c.2,790 ft.; mixed farming. Summer resort. Founded 1896. In Second World War British base for operations (1941) against French Vichy govt. forces in Syria.

Metur, India: see METTUR.

Metz (mĕts, Fr. mĕs, Ger. mĕts), anc. *Divodurum* and *Mediomatrica*, city (pop. 65,472), ⊙ Moselle dept., NE France, on braided Moselle R. (canalized) at influx of the Seille, and 175 mi. ENE of Paris; 49°7'N 6°11'E. Strategic communications center and gateway to Paris Basin, in Lorraine iron-mining belt. Chief industries are tanning and shoe mfg., metalworking (machine tools, elevators, agr. equipment, household articles), printing, brewing, canning, and fruit preserving. Long known as a key fortress and garrison city. Old town, in triangle bet. right arm of Moselle and the Seille, contains 13th–16th cent. cathedral of St. Étienne; the Place Sainte-Croix (lined with 13th–15th-cent. houses); the fine arts mus.; and the Porte des Allemands, a fortified medieval gate built over the Seille. City has a perimeter of forts, begun by Vauban, strengthened by Napoleon III and by Germans (after 1871). Of pre-Roman origin, Metz became early episcopal see and, in 6th cent., ⊙ Austrasia. After division of Frankish empire, bishops of Metz grew powerful as princes of Holy Roman Empire. Metz became (12th cent.) a free imperial city. Here in 1356 Charles IV issued the Golden Bull. Annexed (with Toul and Verdun) to France by Henry II in 1552. Under leadership of François de Guise, city resisted long siege (1552–53) by Emperor Charles V. Peace of Westphalia (1648) confirmed it in Fr. possession. During Franco-Prussian War, Marshal Bazaine capitulated with 180,000 men after being defeated at Gravelotte and undergoing 2-month siege (1870). Incorporated into Germany (1871–1918) as part of Alsace-Lorraine; remained closely behind Ger. lines throughout First World War. During Second World War, Metz suffered under Ger. occupation, many of its French-speaking citizens being expelled or deported. Ger. garrison resisted (autumn, 1944) U.S. forces of General Patton. Metz and its fortified outskirts were damaged during the siege. Verlaine b. here.

Metz, town (pop. 178), Vernon co., W Mo., on Little Osage R. and 12 mi. NNW of Nevada; agr.

Metzeral (mĕzŭräl'), village (pop. 1,162), Haut-Rhin dept., E France, in the high Vosges, 14 mi. WSW of Colmar; rail terminus; cotton spinning, cheese mfg., granite quarrying. Virtually leveled (1915) in First World War fighting.

Metzervisse (mĕsĕrvēs'), Ger. *Metzerwiese* (mĕ'-tsŭrvēzŭ), village (pop. 757), Moselle dept., NE France, 6 mi. SE of Thionville; limekilns.

Metzingen (mĕ'tsĭng-ŭn), town (pop. 8,024), S Württemberg, Germany, after 1945 in Württemberg-Hohenzollern, at N foot of Swabian Jura, 4 mi. NE of Reutlingen; rail junction; mfg. of textiles (cotton, cloth; weaving), machinery, metal goods, leather gloves; tanning, paper milling. Vineyards. Has late-Gothic church. Chartered 1831.

Metzquititlán (mätskētētlän'), town (pop. 1,479), Hidalgo, central Mexico, 30 mi. NNE of Pachuca; alt. 4,675 ft.; corn, beans, maguey, fruit, stock.

Metztitlán (mätstētlän'), town (pop. 1,344), Hidalgo, central Mexico, on central plateau, near L. Metztitlán (6 mi. long), 33 mi. N of Pachuca; alt. 4,413 ft. Agr. center (corn, beans, oranges, melons, tomatoes, livestock).

Meu, river, France: see MEU RIVER.

Meudon (mûdō'), town (pop. 20,106), Seine-et-Oise dept., N central France, a SW suburb of Paris, 7 mi. from Notre Dame Cathedral, on a height above left bank of Seine R. opposite Boulogne-Billancourt; forges, munitions factory; woodworking, mfg. of electrical equipment. Has chemical laboratories. At S end of the wide terrace (laid out in 17th cent.) is the pavilion of a 17th-cent. château which houses the astrophysics observatory of Paris and commands a magnificent view of that city. Just SW is the forest of Meudon (□ 4½), a favorite excursion center. Rabelais was curate here.

Meugia Pass, Laos-Vietnam: see MUGIA PASS.

Meulaboh, Indonesia: see MULABO.

Meulan (mûlā'), town (pop. 2,965), Seine-et-Oise dept., N central France, on right bank of Seine R., opposite industrial Les Mureaux, 23 mi. WNW of Paris; agr. trade; boatbuilding. Old fortress town.

Meulebeke (mû'lŭbākŭ), town (pop. 10,222), West Flanders prov., W Belgium, 9 mi. N of Courtrai; cotton mfg.; agr. market.

Meulín Island (mĕōōlēn') (□ 4.5; pop. 1,177), off E coast of Chiloé Isl., S Chile, 25 mi. ENE of Castro; 3 mi. long, 1–3 mi. wide. Stock raising, lumbering, fishing.

Meung-sur-Loire (mŭ-sür-lwär'), town (pop. 2,984), Loiret dept., N central France, on right bank of the Loire and 11 mi. SW of Orléans; foundries, tanneries. Has early 13th-cent. church and partly medieval castle of bishops of Orléans.

Meurad (mûräd'), village (pop. 752), Alger dept., N central Algeria, at W edge of Mitidja plain, 22 mi. W of Blida; winegrowing, essential-oil processing.

Meu River (mû), Ille-et-Vilaine dept., W France, rises near Merdrignac, flows c.40 mi. ESE, past Montfort and Mordelles, to Vilaine R. 7 mi. SW of Rennes.

Meursault (mûrsō'), village (pop. 1,599), Côte-d'Or dept., E central France, on SE slope of the Côte d'Or, 4 mi. SW of Beaune; noted Burgundy wines.

Meurthe (mûrt'), former department of NE France, part of which was ceded to Germany in 1871, remainder inc. in MEURTHE-ET-MOSELLE dept. Upon its return to France in 1919, territory was included in MOSELLE dept.

Meurthe-et-Moselle (–ā-mōzĕl'), department (□ 2,039; pop. 528,805), in Lorraine, NE France; ⊙ Nancy. Abutting on the Vosges (SE), it is chiefly occupied by Lorraine tableland and Côtes de Moselle which extend along Moselle R. to Luxembourg and Belg. border. Agr. is of secondary importance; some vineyards along the Moselle (Pagny-sur-Moselle). Leading iron-mining region, with 3 of 4 iron basins of Lorraine concentrated around Briey, Longwy, and Nancy, where a metallurgical industry (pig-iron and steel mills) has developed. Supplies most of W Europe's steel industry (including the Ruhr) with iron ore. For its own production it receives coking coal from N France and the Saar. Other mfg. includes chemical works (based on salt mines bet. Nancy and Lunéville), glass works (Baccarat, Cirey), breweries (Saint-Nicolas-de-Port, Maxéville, Champigneulles) and textile mills. Dept. crossed S-W by Canal de l'Est, W-E by Marne-Rhine Canal. Chief cities: NANCY, Lunéville (faïence), Toul (fortress town), Longwy (metallurgical center). Dept. formed 1871 from parts of Meurthe and Moselle depts., which remained with France after Franco-Prussian War.

Meurthe River, Vosges and Meurthe-et-Moselle depts., NE France, rises in the Vosges above Fraize, flows 105 mi. NW, past Saint-Dié, Baccarat, Lunéville (head of navigation), and Nancy, to the Moselle at Frouard 5 mi. NNW of Nancy. Marne-Rhine Canal is near its course bet. Dombasle and Frouard. In lower course it traverses Nancy iron-mining and metallurgical dist. Receives Vezouze (right) and Mortagne (left) rivers.

Meuse (mûz, Fr. mûz), department (□ 2,410; pop. 188,786), in Lorraine, NE France; ⊙ Bar-le-Duc. Borders on Belgium (N). Traversed ESE-NNW by 2 ridge lines: the Argonne and the Côtes de Meuse. Drained by the Meuse and by tributaries of the Marne (Saulx, Ornain) and of the Aisne (Aire). Diversified agr. (cereals, fruits, textile plants, wine) in river valleys. Horse raising; lumbering. Numerous stone quarries. Chief industries: metallurgy (Commercy, Stenay, Cousances-aux-Forges), paper milling, woodworking, and food processing (cheese, beer, kirsch, biscuits). Principal towns are Verdun (First World War fortress), Bar-le-Duc, Commercy, and Saint-Mihiel. Dept. was scene of bitter fighting (1914–18), with active American participation in Saint-Mihiel and Meuse-Argonne offensives (1918).

Meuselwitz (moi'zŭlvĭts), town (pop. 10,688), Thuringia, central Germany, on Schnauder R. and 20 mi. S of Leipzig; lignite-mining center; cotton milling, metal- and woodworking; mfg. of machinery, chemicals, china.

Meuse River (mūz, Fr. mûz), Flemish (old spelling *Maes*) and Du. *Maas* (mäs), anc. *Mosa*, rises in NE France and flows generally N, through Belgium and Holland, to the North Sea, forming a common delta with the Rhine; c.560 mi. long. From its source in the Plateau of Langres, 6 mi. WNW of Bourbonne-les-Bains, it passes Neufchâteau (above which it flows underground for 3 mi.), continues NNW bet. the Argonne (W) and Côtes de Meuse (E), past Troussey (whence it is paralleled to Verdun by Canal de l'EST), Saint-Mihiel, Verdun (head of river navigation), Sedan, and Mézières-Charleville, entering Belgium below Givet in a meandering valley cut into the Ardennes. Passing Dinant, Namur, and Liége, it forms Du.-Belg. border for 31 mi. bet. Eijsden and Stevensweert, except at Maastricht where it is wholly in Netherlands. Swinging W beyond Roermond and Venlo, it joins WAAL RIVER (a distributary of the Rhine) at Woudrichem to form the UPPER MERWEDE. The combined Rhine-Meuse delta, beginning here, is formed by the Upper Merwede, which has 2 distributaries, the NEW MERWEDE (which enters the HOLLANDSCHDIEP), and the LOWER MERWEDE (which near Dordrecht breaks up into 2 distributaries, the OLD MAAS and the NOORD RIVER); the Noord links up with LEK RIVER at Krimpen aan den Lek to form NEW MAAS RIVER, which below Rotterdam reaches North Sea as the NEW WATERWAY. The BERGSCHE MAAS and DORTSCHE KIL are lesser delta distributaries. Chief tributaries are the Chiers, Semoy, Lesse, Ourthe, Roer (right) and the Bar and Sambre (left). River paralleled by LIÉGE-MAASTRICHT CANAL and by JULIANA CANAL, and linked to the Oise, Moselle, Marne, Rhine and Scheldt by canals. Main shipping lane from North Sea is through New Waterway, New Maas, Noord R., Lower and Upper Merwede. The Meuse has irregular volume, especially in upper course where it receives few tributaries. Its basin in France has been encroached upon by the Seine and the Moselle through river captures. Its upper valley, especially bet. Saint-Mihiel and Sedan, was scene of heavy fighting in First World War.

Mevagissey (mĕvŭgĭ'sĭ, –zĭ), town and parish (pop. 1,739), S central Cornwall, England, on the Channel 5 mi. S of St. Austell; fishing port, resort. Has medieval church.

Mewar, India: see UDAIPUR, former Rajputana state.

Mewar and Southern Rajputana States, India: see RAJPUTANA STATES.

Mewe, Poland: see GNIEW.

Mew Island, islet (32 acres) in the Irish Sea, at SE entrance to Belfast Lough, Co. Down, Northern Ireland, 4 mi. N of Donaghadee; lighthouse (54°42'N 5°30'W).

Mex (mĕks) or **Miks** (mĭks), W suburb of Alexandria, Egypt, on isthmus bet. L. Maryut and Mediterranean Sea. Near by are limestone quarries used since anc. times. Also has saltworks, fish-breeding ponds, and pumping works which maintain the level of water in L. Maryut.

Mexborough, urban district (1931 pop. 15,848; 1951 census 18,965), West Riding, S Yorkshire, England, on Don R. and 11 mi. NE of Sheffield; agr. market; flour milling, metalworking; pottery.

Mexcala River, Mexico: see BALSAS, RÍO DE LAS.

Mexia (mŭhā'ŭ, –hē'ŭ), city (pop. 6,627), Limestone co., E central Texas, 39 mi. ENE of Waco; commercial, processing center for agr. (cotton, grain, cattle), oil-producing area; oil refining, cotton ginning, textile and cottonseed-oil milling, mfg. of clay products, clothing. State park, with restored Fort Parker, is SW. Settled 1873; oil discovery (1920) led to boom.

Mexiana Island (mĭshä'nŭ) (□ c.600), NE Pará, Brazil, in Amazon delta, just N of Marajó isl. and E of Caviana Isl. Crossed by the equator, 120 mi. NW of Belém.

Mexicalcingo (māhēkälsĕng'gō), officially San Mateo Mexicalcingo, town (pop. 1,973), Mexico state, central Mexico, on railroad and 8 mi. SE of Toluca; cereals, stock, dairying. Sometimes Mexicaltzingo.

Mexicali (mĕksĭkă'lē, Sp. māhēkä'lē), town (pop. 18,775), ⊙ Northern Territory, Lower California, NW Mexico, on U.S. border adjoining Calexico (Calif.), in Imperial Valley irrigation area, on railroad and 100 mi. E of San Diego (Calif.), 1,400 mi. NW of Mexico city; 32°40'N 115°29'W; alt. is at sea level. Agr. (principally cotton; also alfalfa, wine, grapefruit, dates, vegetables), distributing, and processing center. Exports cotton, fruit, dried chili, hides, minerals. Cotton gins, cottonseed-oil mills, flour mills, brewery, soap and lard factory.

Mexicaltzingo, Mexico: see Mexicalcingo.

Mexico (mĕk'sĭkō), Sp. *México* or *Méjico* (both: mĕ'hēkō), republic (□ 760,373, including 1,822 sq. mi. of uninhabited islets; 1940 pop. 19,653,552; 1950 pop. 25,581,250), S North America, bet. the Pacific and the Gulf of Mexico and Caribbean. Administratively divided into 29 states, 1 territory, and the Federal Dist. (in which is the capital, Mexico or Mexico City). Third largest of the Latin American countries in area (about ¼ of the U.S.), it ranks third in pop. among the nations of the Americas. From its 2,013-mi.-long border with the U.S. (land borders with Calif., Ariz., and N.Mex.; a river border—Rio Grande—with Texas), it extends c.1,600 mi. SE to the Isthmus of Tehuantepec, where it narrows to c.125 mi. and then widens again, stretching another c.200 mi. towards its S boundary with Guatemala (Usumacinta River and Suchiate River); the Yucatan Peninsula juts NE, helping to separate the Caribbean from the Gulf of Mexico and bordering Br. Honduras. It is roughly bet. 14°30'–32°45'N and 86°45'–117°10'W. There are few adjacent or outlying isls., apart from the Revilla Gigedo group in the Pacific. In the extreme NW the 750-mi.-long Gulf of California separates the long narrow peninsula of Lower California almost completely from the Mexican mainland. By far the most important physical feature is the country's rugged mtn. backbone (c.¾ of entire surface) constituted by the great Sierra Madre, consisting of 2 distinct ranges, the Sierra Madre Oriental (separated by the Rio Grande from connecting ranges of S Rockies in Texas) along the Gulf of Mexico, and the more abrupt and dissected Sierra Madre Occidental along the Pacific. Both ranges are adjoined by narrow coastal strips (never exceeding 200 mi.) and enclose the all-important central plateau, a vast semi-arid expanse, comprising basins (*bolsons*), broken ranges, and deep valleys (*barrancas*). The plateau is drained by moderately large, unnavigable river systems, such as the Santiago-Lerma and L. Chapala, the Río de las Balsas, and the Pánuco River, which is artificially joined to Cuautitlán and Tula rivers by Tequixquiac tunnel. There are several interior drainage basins without outlet to the sea, such as Casas Grandes and the agriculturally important Laguna District (Nazas River). The intramontane highland rises gradually from c.4,000 ft. in N Coahuila and Chihuahua states to c.8,000 ft. in the country's interior, the densely populated Anáhuac region, which is flanked S by the transverse E-W range of volcanoes rising in the Pico de Orizaba or Citlaltépetl (18,700 ft.) to highest elevation of the country. Other famed peaks include the Popocatepetl, Ixtacihuatl, and the recently formed (1943) Paricutín. The volcanic belt is adjoined S of the Río de las Balsas in Guerrero and Oaxaca states by the large, tumbled massif of the Sierra Madre del Sur, sloping down to the Isthmus of Tehuantepec, beyond which it merges into the Chiapas highlands and the Sierra Madre of Guatemala. Though the Tropic of Cancer passes through the center of Mexico, altitude rather than geographic latitude is the decisive determinant of Mexico's diverse climate. As in all Andean countries of South America, vegetation follows a characteristic pattern of zoning (hot, temperate, and cool), in *tierra caliente, tierra templada*, and *tierra fría*. The rainy period lasts generally from June through Sept. all over Mexico. Rainfall is slight on the coasts of Lower Calif., Sonora, Sinaloa, and N Tamaulipas, whose crops depend on irrigation (like, e.g., Imperial Valley). It increases in the tropical belt farther S, particularly at Gulf coast, until, in the steaming jungles of Tabasco, it reaches 120 in. annually. All the coastal lowlands and the piedmont up to 3,000 ft. are hot and tropical, yielding coffee, cacao, sugar cane, cotton, coconuts, fruit, corn, rice. Tropical climate prevails in Yucatan, the world's largest source of henequen (c.50% of the total). Along with Campeche, Quintana Roo, and Chiapas, Yucatan also furnishes chicle (shipped to U.S.), hardwood, gums, and other forest products. The temperate zone, chiefly on central plateau, at about 3–6,000 ft. has the finest climate, and from it come subsistence crops, coffee, sugar cane, maguey, istle, tobacco, cereals, fruit, alfalfa, and cotton—grown in the basins or "valleys" of Mexico, Puebla, Toluca, Guanajuato, Jalisco, Aguascalientes, and Morelos. The irrigated Laguna Dist. (in Durango and Coahuila states) has been turned into the country's most productive cotton region, also noted for its communal farming system (*ejido*) introduced by Cárdenas. However, large tracts, though fertile, are, because of scant rains, only suitable for stock raising. A bare 5% of the land is under cultivation. Goats are predominantly grazed in the dry north, while cattle (hampered since 1947 by foot and mouth disease) and sheep raising becomes increasingly important in S central plateau. The environs of Mexico city are given to truck gardening (Xochimilco) and dairying. Extensive pine forests cover the slopes of the *tierra fría* (above c.6,000 ft.), producing valuable naval stores. Here, the days are warm, the nights cold. Many principal cities, including the capital, are in this zone. Mexico city has an annual mean temp. of 63°F. While the little-urbanized Mex. pop. is mostly engaged in agr., the country still has to import food. The immensely rich mining industry, employing comparatively few and being almost entirely foreign owned, furnishes about 70% of all exports; but the trade balance remains unfavorable. The region has yielded precious metals since pre-Columbian days. Mexico leads in the world production (c.40%) of silver, mined all over the central plateau, foremost at Pachuca. It is in the front rank for its lead, zinc, copper (Cananea, Santa Rosalía), antimony; also mined are coal (from Coahuila), gold, arsenic, manganese, cadmium, mercury, molybdenum, bismuth, tin, tungsten—found in almost all interior states. The peak Cerro de Mercado, in outskirts of Durango city, is almost pure iron. As a petroleum producer, Mexico is 2d only to Venezuela among the Latin American republics. The major petroleum fields are located in the E coastlands of Tamaulipas, Veracruz, and Isthmus of Tehuantepec, centered on Tampico (chief ore port), Tuxpan, and Coatzacoalcos (Puerto Mexico). Important fisheries (shrimp, sharks, sardines, bass, pike, abalons, red snappers) are operating on both coasts, and shark livers constitute a substantial export. While mining and petroleum drilling and refining are the principal industries, mfg., of which an estimated 40% is located in the Mexico city area, has made great strides. Monterrey is the nation's iron and steel center; Puebla is hq. of the country's extensive textile industry (mainly cotton goods), which also flourishes at Querétaro. Aguascalientes has largest railroad shops; the republic's 2d largest city, Guadalajara, is an agr.-processing, steel, and textile center; Mérida, in Yucatan, served by its port Progreso, makes cordage products. Other prominent metallurgical centers are Monclova, Aquiles Serdán, Hidalgo de Parral, Torreón, San Luis Potosí, Guanajuato, Zacatecas, Matehuala. Among the principal consumer goods, in which Mexico has achieved some measure of self sufficiency, are shoes and leather goods, lacquer, carved wood, wrought silver, jewelry, glassware, pottery, bricks, cement, soap, paper, furniture, electrical appliances, radios, chemicals, vegetable oil, cigars and cigarettes, beer, alcohol, refined sugar. An extensive railroad and highway system links the interior cities with its ports, of which the largest for passengers and foreign trade is Veracruz, while Tampico ships most of the petroleum. Other Gulf ports are Tuxpan, Coatzacoalcos, Carmen, and Campeche. Compared to those, the Pacific ports, such as Guaymas, Mazatlán, and Manzanillo, are only of secondary importance, though they have the finer harbors. Acapulco, once the base for Sp. expeditions to the Philippines, has become an international beach resort, visited mostly in winter. Salina Cruz in Oaxaca is the chief entrepôt for the S Isthmus of Tehuantepec, linked by railroad with Coatzacoalcos. Inland, along the boundary with the U.S., are several important border towns and customs stations immediately communicating with American towns across the line—Matamoros with Brownsville (Texas), Nuevo Laredo with Laredo (Texas), Ciudad Juárez with El Paso (Texas), Nogales with Nogales (Ariz.). Mexicali and especially Tiajuana have profited by the border traffic with S Calif., booming during prohibition. Some of the principal imports pass through these towns. Mexico received (in 1948) 86.7% of all her imported goods from the U.S. Transcontinental railroads, among them those from Laredo and El Paso, establish direct communication with Mexico city. There is also a railroad to Guatemala. A rail link to isolated Yucatan via Tenosique has been recently (1950) completed. Of major importance in carrying the great stream of American tourists which pour every year into Mexico is the Inter-American Highway, now extending beyond Oaxaca into Central America. The great metropolis Mexico city, picturesque upland cities like Taxco and Cuernavaca, the stupendous pyramids and archaeological remains of Teotihuacán, Chichén Itzá, Palenque, and Uxmal, are among the continent's most remarkable sites. Three of the hemisphere's great pre-Columbian cultures thrived in Mexico, the Toltecs and the Aztecs on the central plateau, and the fabulous Mayas, who had migrated from present-day Guatemala to Yucatan. First Spaniard to land on Mexican soil was Fernández de Córdoba, who discovered (1517) Yucatan, and Grijalva (1518). The land was called New Spain, and Hernán Cortés in 1519 was dispatched from Cuba to explore it. Landing near Veracruz he advanced to the interior Anáhuac region and conquered (1521) Tenochtitlán, the Aztec ⊙ since 1325, upon whose ruins he founded Mexico city. The viceroyalty of New Spain was set up in 1535 with Antonio de Mendoza, one of the ablest of all Sp. administrators, as viceroy. Mercantilist Spain, little interested in the economic development of the country and the welfare of the Indian natives, instituted the *economienda* system. Large estates were held by few landholders, while along with the exploited Indians an underprivileged mestizo class came into existence. The spread of revolutionary ideas, the example of the U.S., and the collapse of Spain before Napoleon, strengthened the country's independence movement. First leader of the revolution was the priest Miguel Hidalgo y Castilla, who issued (Sept. 16, 1810) his famous *El Grito de Dolores* [cry of Dolores]; he gained several victories over the royalists but was defeated at Calderón bridge and executed in 1811. Another priest, Morelos y Pavón, assembled (1813) a congress at Chilpancingo, but met (1815) the same fate. The revolution collapsed, except for sporadic outbursts, until Gen. Iturbide proclaimed (1821) the Mexican independence under the Plan of Iguala. Iturbide, as Agustín I, made himself emperor the following year, but was forced into exile by Santa Anna and Guadalupe Victoria. He was upon his return (1824) captured and shot. Personalism, the curse of Sp. American politics, tore the republic bet. revolution, civil warfare, and dictatorships. In spite of the loss of Texas (1836) and the disastrous Mexican War (1846–48), Santa Anna maintained his hold until the revolution of Ayutla (1855). Through the Treaty of Guadalupe Hidalgo, Mexico had ceded all her territory N of the Rio Grande, including Calif., Ariz., and N.Mex., to the U.S. The 1st truly republican president to emerge (1857) was Benito Juárez, a full-blooded Zapotec Indian. The liberal constitution, however, caused opposition from conservative elements and foreign powers, which combined in support of French intervention (1864–67). Ill-fated Maximilian became emperor; he was shot when outside aid was withdrawn. Juárez returned to the presidency, though unable to accomplish his program. Gen. Porfirio Díaz, an unsuccessful presidential candidate, virtually ruled Mexico as dictator from 1876 to 1911. During his autocratic regime, the material development of Mexico, under the stimulus of foreign capital, made rapid strides, but social maladjustment remained extreme. While the small, white landholding class enriched itself, more and more Indians succumbed to peonage. The liberal revolt was led by Francisco I. Madero, who was assassinated in 1913, leaving the country in anarchy, disputed bet. his reactionary successor Victoriano Huerta and the liberal revolutionaries Carranza, Obregón, Villa, and Zapata, who soon turned against each other. American troops dispatched (1914) to Veracruz, forced Huerta's resignation. Gen. Pershing led (1916) a campaign against Villa in the north, greatly embittering U.S.-Mex. relations. The 1917 constitution promulgated agrarian, educational, and labor reforms, and nationalization of minerals. With Calles ruling the country as strong man after 1924, little of this materialized. A new era began (1934) with the presidency of Lázaro Cárdenas who started a 6-year plan, particularly of long-needed social legislation, continued by his democratically elected successors Manuel Avila Camacho (1940) and Miguel Alemán (1946). Material progress began to be made. Communal lands were redistributed under the *ejido* system. The foreign oil wells were expropriated in 1938. Relations with the U.S. were close, and the country declared (1942) war on the Axis powers. Anticlerical excesses have subsided. An exemplary educational program was instituted, and the govt. sponsored public art works, notably murals executed by the great Mex. painters Rivera, Orozco, and Siqueiros. Great strides are being made in raising the living standards of the pop., which, according to recent estimates, is 29% Indian, 55% mestizo, 15% white, and 1% foreign. Backward Indian tribes and fierce Apaches survive in Lower Calif. and the NW. Though Spanish is the official, most widely used language, more than 30 different Indian language groups persist. A great many Mexicans have infiltrated into Calif. and the SW states of the U.S. For further information see separate articles on cities, regions, physical features, and the following territorial units: states of Aguascalientes, Campeche, Coahuila, Colima, Chiapas, Chihuahua, Durango, Guanajuato, Guerrero, Hidalgo, Jalisco, Lower California (became a state in 1951), Mexico, Michoacán, Morelos, Nayarit, Nuevo León, Oaxaca, Puebla, Querétaro, San Luis Potosí, Sinaloa, Sonora, Tabasco, Tamaulipas, Tlaxcala, Veracruz, Yucatán, and Zacatecas; and the territory of Quintana Roo.

Mexico, Sp. *México* or *Méjico*, state (□ 8,268; 1940 pop. 1,146,034; 1950 pop. 1,383,640), central Mexico; ⊙ Toluca. Bordered by Hidalgo (N), Puebla and Tlaxcala (E), Morelos and Guerrero (S), Michoacán (W), Querétaro (NW). Envelops most of the Federal Dist., including Mexico city. The heartland of the great central plateau, sometimes called Meseta de Anáhuac, it rises above 8,000 ft.; consists of part of the fertile, densely populated Valley of Mexico and Toluca Valley. Bounded SE by the volcanic peaks Ixtacihuatl and Popo-

Area in square miles is indicated by the symbol □, capital city or county seat by the symbol ⊙.

catepetl. Includes the Nevado de Toluca and a number of lake depressions (among them L. Texcoco and L. Zumpango), now almost dry. Drained by Lerma R. and affluents of the Río de las Balsas; artificially linked with Pánuco R. system through the Tequixquiac tunnel, joining Cuautitlán and Tula rivers. Climate varies from cool to subtropical on plateaus, tropical in SW near Guerrero border. Silver, gold, lead, copper, and zinc mines at El Oro, Zacualpan, Sultepec, Temascaltepec, and Toluca. Primarily an agr. region of intensive dairy farming, it produces corn, wheat, barley, beans, chick-peas, potatoes, fruit (in uplands); maguey (NE); coffee, sugar cane, tropical fruit (SW). The Valley of Toluca, noted for its bulls, supplies Mexico city rings. Rural industries: mining, lumbering, flour milling, dairying, pulque distilling, hand weaving and other native handicrafts. A number of larger settlements maintain textile mills, flour mills, metallurgical plants. Toluca is a processing center, and a popular tourist resort. The state has many archaeological remains of Aztec and pre-Aztec civilizations; most famous is the Pyramid of the Sun at Teotihuacán.

Mexico or **Mexico City,** Sp. *México, Méjico,* or *Ciudad de México* (syōōdädh' dā mĕ'hĕkō), city (1940 pop. 1,448,422), central Mexico, ⊙ and largest city of Mexico and ⊙ of the Federal District (□ 573; 1940 pop. 1,757,530; 1950 pop. 2,942,594), on small plain in SW part of the Valley of Mexico, near S end of the large central plateau (Anáhuac) of the Sierra Madre; alt. 7,800 ft.; 19°25'45"N 99°7'W. Has mild climate with little seasonal variation; average temp. is 42°–66° (Jan.), 55°–76 (June). High barren mts. nearly block the horizons of the city, and contain the majestic, snow-capped IXTACIHUATL and POPOCATEPETL (SE) and Ajusco (S) volcanoes. The city is on the Inter-American Highway and 200 mi. W of its Gulf port Veracruz, 190 mi. NNE of Pacific port of Acapulco. It is in a lake basin with no outlet, and from the time when the Aztec capital of Tenochtitlán stood on an isl. in L. Texcoco—now the heart of Mexico city—measures have been taken to provide for expansion by draining Texcoco and other lakes. The Spaniards in 17th cent. initiated important works. In 1900 a central canal with tunnel was completed to headwaters of Pánuco R. The Caracol [Sp.,=snail], 12-mi. spiral canal fed by longitudinal canals, begun in 1936, acts as evaporating basin, from which valuable minerals (salt, caustic soda, sodium bicarbonate, potash, sodium sulphate, and borax) are taken. The climate is generally cool, dry, and healthful, with rainy season late May-Sept. (annual rainfall 20–25 inches). One of the great cities of the continent, and one of the oldest metropolitan centers in North America, it is geographically in the heart of Mexico, the communication, political, industrial, economic, social, cultural, and educational center of the country. From it radiate numerous roads, railways, and airlines. Industries include textile mills (cotton, woolen, silk, and rayon goods), auto assembly plant, tire factory, gold and silver refineries, iron foundries (steel castings, bolts, nuts, springs, electrical appliances, machinery, etc.), glassworks, paper mills, cement plants, tanneries, breweries, electric power stations; also mfg. of glass and leather goods, tobacco products, building materials, clothing, soap, chemicals, petroleum by-products, pharmaceuticals, alcohol, processed food. The city, built in compact Sp. fashion with many parks, squares, and broad avenues, has both fine colonial baroque architecture and large modern office bldgs. and apartment houses. Center of the city is the Plaza de la Constitución or Plaza Mayor, generally called Zócalo, around which are grouped the imposing cathedral (begun 1573), Municipal Palace, and Natl. Palace (containing senate chamber, presidential residence, archives, observatory, and natl. mus.). Back of the Natl. Palace is the San Carlos art gall. W of the Plaza the business center extends on both sides of Avenida de Francisco I. Madero, which becomes Avenida Juárez, leading to the Palace of Fine Arts and spacious Alameda Park, containing Juárez Monument. On Plaza de Santo Domingo lies the old convent and church Santo Domingo, the natl. pawn shop, and the school of mining. Farther on is the Monument of the Revolution, with the Mexican Pantheon. Other important bldgs. include the Iturbide Palace (now a hotel), Chamber of Deputies, Palace of Justice, customhouse, natl. library, mint, a large bull ring, the Natl. Univ. (founded 1551), other institutions of higher learning (agriculture, commerce, fine arts, music, pharmacy, technology), and a number of fine churches (Loreto, El Sagrario Metropolitano, Santa Teresa, San Hipólito). Many official bldgs. are decorated by works of great modern muralists: Rivera, Orozco, Siqueiros. The city's main artery, the spacious Paseo de la Reforma, continues W for c.3 mi. from Avenida Juárez to CHAPULTEPEC; this boulevard is intersected by circular spaces, so-called *glorietas,* on which stand monuments to Charles II, Columbus, and Cuauhtémoc, last Aztec emperor. The finest residential sections, called *colonias,* are W and SW (TACUBAYA, TACUBA, CUAUHTÉMOC). Poorer sections, rendered unhealthy by dust from dry L. Texcoco, are E. Main industrial suburbs include MIXCOAC, GENERAL ANAYA, CHURUBUSCO. In the outskirts, belonging to Federal Dist., are VILLA OBREGÓN (SW), COYOACÁN, CONTRERAS, and TLALPAN (S), GUADALUPE HIDALGO and AZCAPOTZALCO (NE). The city serves as base for excursions to many matchless tourist spots near by; the "floating gardens" of XOCHIMILCO (13 mi. S) can be reached by La Viga canal. Probably the oldest city on the continent, Mexico city is sometimes believed to have been founded in 1176 as Tenochtitlán by the Aztecs, who made it their ⊙ in 1325; at the time it occupied several isls. of L. Texcoco (now almost dry). Cortés entered Tenochtitlán on Nov. 8, 1519, but was driven out on June 30, 1520; after a long siege the city fell again on Aug. 13, 1521, and with its fall ended the Aztec Empire. In preconquest days the city is said to have had a pop. of 300,000. Cortés leveled it entirely and constructed a colonial Sp. town. On the site of the main Aztec temple he built the first Christian church on Amer. soil (1525), later replaced by a cathedral. Mexico city became the metropolis of New Spain, administered by the Spanish for 3 centuries. On Sept. 27, 1821, Gen. Iturbide took it with an army of patriots. In the Mexican War it was occupied (1847) by Winfield Scott's U.S. forces, which had marched inland from Veracruz. A French army entered it in 1863, and Maximilian was proclaimed emperor. Until the city was recaptured by Benito Juárez 3 years later, Maximilian and Carlotta did much to beautify it in the current, florid style of the Second French Empire. During the 1910 revolution, when it was a hotbed of insurrection, it was temporarily occupied (1914–15) by Francisco Villa and Emiliano Zapata. With the presidency of Lázaro Cardenas (1934–40), Mexico city developed rapidly as an industrial center.

Mexico, town (1939 pop. 1,675; 1948 municipality pop. 18,678), Pampanga prov., central Luzon, Philippines, on railroad and 4 mi. NE of San Fernando; sugar cane, rice.

Mexico. 1 Residential town (pop. 4,762), including Mexico village (pop. 3,821), W Maine, on Androscoggin R. opposite industrial Rumford. Inc. 1818. **2** City (pop. 11,623), ⊙ Audrain co., NE central Mo., on South Fork of Salt R. and 28 mi. NE of Columbia; agr. (grain, soy beans), saddle horses; mfg. (fire-clay products, shoes); food-processing plants; railroad shops. Mo. Military Acad. Laid out 1836. **3** Village (pop. 1,398), Oswego co., N central N.Y., near L. Ontario, 13 mi. E of Oswego, in rich agr. area; mfg. (diabetic foods, flour, wood products, burial vaults). Inc. 1851.

Mexico, Gulf of, arm (□ 700,000) of Atlantic Ocean, on SE coast of North America; bounded N by U.S. (Fla., Ala., Miss., La., Tex.) and SW by Mexico, it communicates with the open Atlantic via the Straits of Florida bet. Florida and Cuba, and with the Caribbean Sea via Yucatan Channel bet. Cuba and Yucatan; 1,000 mi. long (E-W), 800 mi. wide; average depth, 4,700 ft.; greatest depth is Sigsbee Deep (12,480 ft.) off Mexican coast. A regularly shaped basin with wide continental shelves, the Gulf receives several important rivers, including the Rio Grande and the Mississippi. Because of generally low shores, lined with flat, sandy isls. and numerous lagoons, there are few good harbors. The principal ports are: Veracruz and Tampico in Mexico; Galveston, Houston, Port Arthur, Beaumont, New Orleans, Mobile, and Tampa in U.S.; and Havana in Cuba. A branch of the Equatorial Current enters the Gulf of Mexico through Yucatan Channel, flows out through the Straits of Florida, and joins the Antilles Current to form the Florida Current, the initial section of the Gulf Stream system.

Mexico, Valley of, oval basin (50 mi. by 40 mi.) in Federal Dist. and Mexico state, central Mexico; part of the large central plateau S of Pánuco R. system, to which its now almost dry lakes (Zumpango, Xaltocan, San Cristóbal, Texcoco), fed by Cuautitlán R., are linked by drainage tunnels. Average alt. c.7,500 ft. Has temperate to subtropical climate. Site of Mexico city, it is one of Mexico's most densely populated areas, with important agr. and industrial activities.

Meximieux (mäksĕmyû'), village (pop. 1,544), Ain dept., E France, near the Ain, 21 mi. NE of Lyons; hog commerce. Barbed-wire mfg.

Mexquitic (mĕskētĕk'), town (pop. 323), San Luis Potosí, N central Mexico, 12 mi. NW of San Luis Potosí; corn, beans, maguey. Sometimes Mezquitic.

Mexquititlán, Mexico: see SANTIAGO MEXQUITITLÁN.

Mexticacán (mĕstēkäkän'), town (pop. 2,253), Jalisco, central Mexico, 13 mi. SW of Teocaltiche; alt. 6,100 ft.; grain, vegetables, livestock.

Meyadin or **Mayadin** (both: mĕyă'dēn), Fr. *Meyadine,* town, Euphrates prov., E Syria, on right bank of Euphrates R. and 28 mi. SE of Deir ez ZOR.

Meyamey, Iran: see MAIAMAI.

Meyasir, Aden: see DATHINA.

Meybod, Iran: see MAIBUD.

Meycauayan (mākou-äyän'), town (1939 pop. 2,416; 1948 municipality pop. 21,695), Bulacan prov., S central Luzon, Philippines, on railroad and 9 mi. N of Manila; rice-growing center; cutlery mfg.

Meyel, Netherlands: see MEIJEL.

Meyenburg (mī'ünbŏŏrk), town (pop. 3,329), Brandenburg, E Germany, on Stepenitz R. and 25 mi. NE of Perleberg; grain, potatoes, sugar beets, stock.

Meyers Chuck, Alaska: see MYERS CHUCK.

Meyersdale, borough (pop. 3,137), Somerset co., SW Pa., 14 mi. SSE of Somerset and on Casselman R.; maple sugar, cement products, fertilizer, feed, clothing; agr. Laid out 1844, inc. 1871.

Meyers Lake, village (pop. 301), Stark co., E central Ohio, just NW of Canton, on small Meyers L.

Meyerton (mī'ùrtùn), town (pop. 4,825), S Transvaal, U. of So. Afr., 9 mi. NE of Vereeniging; alt. 4,889 ft.; coal mining.

Meylieu-Montrond, France: see MONTROND-LES-BAINS.

Meymac (mĕmäk'), town (pop. 1,959), Corrèze dept., S central France, in Plateau of Millevaches, 8 mi. W of Ussel; agr. trade center (wine, cattle, fruits). Bismuth deposits near by. Has 12th-cent. church and 15th-16th-cent. houses.

Meymeh, Iran: see MEIMEH.

Meyronne (mā'rŭn), village (pop. 243), SW Sask., on Pinto Creek and 40 mi. W of Assiniboia; mixed farming, stock.

Meyrueis (märüā'), village (pop. 758), Lozère dept., S France, bet. Causse Méjan (N) and Causse Noir (SW), on the Jonte and 13 mi. SW of Florac; agr., cheese making. Well-known caverns of Dargilan (2 mi. NW) and Aven Armand (5 mi. NW) attract tourists.

Meyssac (mĕsäk'), agr. village (pop. 692), Corrèze dept., S central France, in Brive Basin 10 mi. SE of Brive-la-Gaillarde; woodworking.

Meytene, Latvia: see MEITENE.

Meyzieux (māzyû'), village (pop. 1,480), Isère dept., SE France, 9 mi. E of Lyons; mfg. of corsets, footwear.

Meza, hamlet, Yugoslavia: see DRAVOGRAD.

Mezaligon (mĕzä-lēgōn'), village, Henzada dist., Lower Burma, on railroad and 20 mi. NW of Henzada.

Meza River (mĕ'zhä), Slovenian *Meža,* Ger. *Missbach* (mĭs'bäkh), N Slovenia, Yugoslavia, rises on Austrian border 5 mi. ESE of Eisenkappel, Austria; flows c.35 mi. ENE, past Crna, Mezica, Prevalje, and Gustanj, to Drava R. at Dravograd. Lower course followed by Klagenfurt-Maribor RR. Four hydroelectric plants.

Mezcala (mĕskä'lä), town (pop. 1,331), Jalisco, central Mexico, on N shore of L. Chapala and 32 mi. SE of Guadalajara; grain, fruit, livestock; fishing.

Mezcalapa River, Mexico: see GRIJALVA RIVER.

Mezcala River, Mexico: see BALSAS, RÍO DE LAS.

Mezdra (mĕzdrä'), village (pop. 2,967), Vratsa dist., NW Bulgaria, on Iskar R. and 8 mi. ESE of Vratsa; rail junction; clothmaking, liquor distilling.

Mèze (mĕz), town (pop. 3,894), Hérault dept., S France, port on NW shore of the Étang de Thau, 5 mi. WNW of Sète; winegrowing center. Distilling, barrel making. Oyster beds.

Mezek, Bulgaria: see SVILENGRAD.

Mézel (māzĕl'), village (pop. 325), Basses-Alpes dept., SE France, on the Asse and 7 mi. SSW of Digne, in Provence Alps; lavender.

Mezen or **Mezen'** (myĕ'zĭnyù), city (1926 pop. 2,952), N Archangel oblast, Russian SFSR, port on Mezen R., 18 mi. above its mouth, and 135 mi. NE of Archangel; sawmilling center; fish canning, dairying. Exports lumber, fish, furs. Chartered c.1600.

Mezen Bay or **Mezen' Bay,** inlet of White Sea, N Archangel oblast, Russian SFSR, W of Kanin Peninsula; 60 mi. wide, 55 mi. deep. Receives Mezen and Kuloi rivers.

Mézenc, Mont (mō māză'), volcanic peak (alt. 5,755 ft.) of the Monts du Vivarais, S central France, on Haute-Loire–Ardèche dept. border, 16 mi. SE of Le Puy; high-grade cattle raised on its slopes. The Lignon rises here.

Mezen River or **Mezen' River** (myĕ'zĭnyù), N European Russian SFSR, rises on W slope of Timan Ridge, flows 565 mi. S and NNW, past Koslan, Leshukonskoye, and Mezen, to Mezen Bay of White Sea; forms estuary. Upper course strewn with rapids; navigable (May-Nov.) below Leshukonskoye. Receives Vashka (left) and Peza (right) rivers.

Mezere, Turkey: see ELAZIG, city.

Mézériat (māzārēä'), village (pop. 1,298), Ain dept., E France, 9 mi. W of Bourg; meat processing.

Mezhdurechye or **Mezhdurech'ye** (myĕzhdŏŏryĕ'-chyĭ), village (1926 pop. 11,717), SE Grozny oblast, Russian SFSR, on right affluent of Sunzha R. and 16 mi. SE of Grozny; flour mill; wheat, corn. Until 1944, Shali.

Mezhevaya (myĕzhĭvī'ù), village, E Dnepropetrovsk oblast, Ukrainian SSR, 20 mi. W of Krasnoarmeiskoye; fire clays.

Mezhireche, Poland: see MIEDZYRZEC.

Mezhirichi (myĕzhĭrē'chē), Pol. *Międzyrzec* or *Międzyrzecz* (myĕ'dzĭzhĕch), village (1931 pop. 2,380), central Rovno oblast, Ukrainian SSR, 27 mi. E of Rovno; tanning, flour milling. Iron deposits near by.

Mezica (mĕ'zhĭtsä), Slovenian *Mežica*, Ger. *Missdorf* (mĭs'dôrf), village, N Slovenia, Yugoslavia, on Meza R. and 4 mi. SW of Prevalje, in the Karawanken, near Austrian border. Open-pit mining of lead ore (galena and wulfenite), zinc, smithsonite, pyrites, and marcasite dates from 15th cent.; ore-dressing plant, smelter (pig lead). Power supplied by hydroelectric, Diesel, and steam plants. Summer resort. Until 1918, in Carinthia.

Mézidon (māzēdõ'), town (pop. 2,135), Calvados dept., NW France, on the Dives and 15 mi. SE of Caen; rail junction; biscuit mfg. Damaged in Second World War.

Mézières (māzyâr'), town (pop. 7,898), ⊙ Ardennes dept., N France, in narrow isthmus of a Meuse R. meander and 50 mi. NE of Rheims, adjoining (S) CHARLEVILLE, its twin city; metalworks. Its 15th-16th-cent. Flamboyant church with Renaissance spire was severely damaged in Second World War. Anc. fortress (dismantled 1886). Successfully defended (1521) by Bayard against Emperor Charles V. Invested by Prussians in 1815 and again in 1870. Its recapture (1918) by Allies marked last major battle of First World War.

Mézières-en-Brenne (-ā-brĕn'), village (pop. 662), Indre dept., central France, on Claise R. and 15 mi. NNE of Le Blanc; woodworking, horse breeding. Has 14th-16th-cent. church.

Mézières-sur-Issoire (-sür-ēswär'), village (pop. 513), Haute-Vienne dept., W central France, 7 mi. W of Bellac; cattle, pottery.

Mezimosti nad Nezarkou (mĕ'zĭmôstyē nād' nĕ-zhärkō), Czech *Mezimostí nad Nežárkou*, town (pop. 2,348), S Bohemia, Czechoslovakia, on Luznice R. and 17 mi. NNE of Budweis; rail junction; part of urban area of Veseli nad Luznici.

Mézin (māzē'), village (pop. 1,478), Lot-et-Garonne dept., SW France, on the Gélise and 7 mi. SW of Nérac; mfg. of cork stoppers, Armagnac brandy. President Fallières b. here.

Mezinovski or **Mezinovskiy** (myĕzĭnôf'skē), town (1946 pop. over 500), SW Vladimir oblast, Russian SFSR, 13 mi. WNW of Gus-Khrustalny; peat works.

Mezöband, Rumania: see BAND.

Mezöbereny (mĕ'zûbĕ"rānyû), Hung. *Mezőberény*, town (pop. 14,578), Bekes co., SE Hungary, 10 mi. N of Bekescsaba; pottery, flax products, bricks. Grain, tobacco, flax, sheep near by.

Mezöcsat (mĕ'zû-chät), Hung. *Mezőcsát*, town (pop. 6,210), Borsod-Gömör co., NE Hungary, 20 mi. SSE of Miskolc; flour mills; grain, potatoes, vineyards; cattle, sheep.

Mezögyan (mĕ'zûdyän), Hung. *Mezőgyán*, town (pop. 2,407), Bihar co., E Hungary, 11 mi. NE of Sarkad; wheat, dairy farming.

Mezöhegyes (mĕ'zûhĕ"dyĕsh), Hung. *Mezőhegyes* town (pop. 8,159), Csanad co., SE Hungary, 17 mi. ENE of Mako; rail and market center; agr. experiment station; mfg. (hemp, agr. tools); sugar refineries, distilleries. Large stud near by.

Mezökeresztes (mĕ'zûkĕ"rĕstĕsh), Hung. *Mező-keresztes*, town (pop. 4,371), Borsod-Gömör co., NE Hungary, 20 mi. S of Miskolc; flour mills; grain, lentils, dairy farming. Turks defeated Hungarians here, 1596.

Mezökovacshaza (mĕ'zûkôväch-häzŏ), Hung. *Mező-kovácsháza*, town (pop. 5,985), Csanad co., SE Hungary, 28 mi. E of Hodmezövasarhely; market center; grain, cattle.

Mezökövesd (mĕ'zûkû"vĕzhd), Hung. *Mezőkövesd*, town (pop. 20,838), Borsod-Gömör co., NE Hungary, at S foot of Bükk Mts., 22 mi. SSW of Miskolc; tobacco warehouses, flour mills; exports embroidery. Has 14th-cent. church.

Mezölaborc, Czechoslovakia: see MEDZILABORCE.

Mezörücs, Rumania: see RACIU.

Mezöszilas (mĕ'zûsĭlŏsh), Hung. *Mezőszilas*, town (pop. 4,196), Veszprem co., W central Hungary, 26 mi. S of Szekesfehervar; corn, wheat, flax, cattle, hogs.

Mezötelegd, Rumania: see TILEAGD.

Mezötur (mĕ'zûtōōr), Hung. *Mezőtúr*, city (pop. 28,192), Jasz-Nagykun-Szolnok co., E central Hungary, on branch of Berettyo R. and 24 mi. SE of Szolnok; rail junction; flour mills, brickworks, pottery; grain, hemp, tobacco, cattle, horses.

Mezözombor (mĕ'zûzôm"bôr), Hung. *Mezőzombor*, town (pop. 2,471), Zemplen co., NE Hungary, 21 mi. E of Miskolc; wine.

Mezquital (mĕskētäl'), town (pop. 651), Durango, N Mexico, on Mezquital R. (upper San Pedro R.) and 45 mi. SE of Durango; alt. 4,657 ft.; grain, sugar cane, fruit, vegetables, tobacco.

Mezquital del Oro (dĕl ō'rō), town (pop. 2,046), Zacatecas, N central Mexico, 35 mi. S of Tlaltenango; grain, fruit, vegetables, livestock.

Mezquital River, Mexico: see SAN PEDRO RIVER.

Mezquitic (mĕskētēk'). **1** Town (pop. 1,632), Jalisco, W Mexico, on headstream of Bolaños R., near Zacatecas border, and 38 mi. NW of Colotlán; cereals, beans, chili, alfalfa, stock. **2** Town, San Luis Potosí, Mexico: see MEXQUITIC.

Mezre, Turkey: see ELAZIG, city.

Mezzano (mĕtsä'nô), village (pop. 1,745), Ravenna prov., Emilia-Romagna, N central Italy, on Lamone R. and 6 mi. NW of Ravenna; beet-sugar refinery.

Mezzaselva (mĕtsäsĕl'vä), village (pop. 227), Bolzano prov., Trentino-Alto Adige, N Italy, on Isarco R. 7 mi. NNW of Bressanone; paper mill.

Mezzé, Syria: see MAZZA, EL.

Mezzo, island, Yugoslavia: see LOPUD ISLAND.

Mezzocorona (mĕdzôkôrô'nä), town (pop. 3,312), Trento prov., Trentino-Alto Adige, N Italy, on Noce R. opposite Mezzolombardo and 10 mi. N of Trent; wine making. Has one of Italy's major hydroelectric plants.

Mezzola, Lago di, Italy: see MERA RIVER.

Mezzolombardo (mĕdzôlômbär'dô), town (pop. 4,309), Trento prov., Trentino-Alto Adige, N Italy, on right bank of Noce R. opposite Mezzocorona, 10 mi. N of Trent. Wine-making center; alcohol distillery, cotton mill.

Mezzouna (mĕzōōnä'), village, Sfax dist., E Tunisia, on Sfax-Tozeur RR and 50 mi. NNW of Gabès; esparto trade.

M'fumbiro or **Mfumbiro,** range, E central Africa: see VIRUNGA.

Mga (ŭmgä'), town (1939 pop. over 2,000), N Leningrad oblast, Russian SFSR, on Mga R. (left affluent of the Neva) and 29 mi. ESE of Leningrad; rail junction; lumber mills. During Second World War, held (1941–44) by Germans in siege of Leningrad.

Mgachi (ŭmgŭchē'), town (1948 pop. over 10,000), N Sakhalin, Russian SFSR, on Tatar Strait, 10 mi. N of Aleksandrovsk; coal mines.

Mglin (ŭmglyēn'), city (1926 pop. 6,519), W Bryansk oblast, Russian SFSR, 15 mi. NNE of Unecha; tannery, starch factory. Orchards near by. Chartered 1500.

M'Goun, Djebel (jĕ'bĕlmgōōn'), or **Ighil M'Goun** (ēgēl'), peak (13,353 ft.) of the High Atlas, in S central Fr. Morocco, 50 mi. NE of Ouarzazate. Seasonally snow-covered; 31°31'N 6°26'W.

Mhasva (mäs'vŭ), village, East Khandesh dist., NE Bombay, India, 2 mi. E of Parola; cotton and oilseeds. Noted for its ghee. Mhasva L., 1 mi. N, has dam which supplies 2 small irrigation canals.

Mhasvad (mŭs'väd), town (pop. 8,138), Satara North dist., central Bombay, India, 50 mi. E of Satara; market center for grain (millet, wheat), cattle, handicraft cloth fabrics. Large irrigation tank 3 mi. SE. Sometimes spelled Mhaswad.

Mhow (mŭhou'), town (pop. 34,823), SW central Madhya Bharat, India, 12 mi. SSW of Indore, on S Malwa plateau; important military station; airport; dairy farming. Founded by British in 1818; formerly in princely state of Indore.

Mi, Ban, Thailand: see BAN MI.

Miacatlán (myäkätlän'), town (pop. 2,439), Morelos, central Mexico, 12 mi. SW of Cuernavaca; alt. 3,458 ft.; sugar, rice, coffee, wheat, fruit, stock.

Miadi, Marshall Isls.: see MEJIT.

Miadziol, Belorussian SSR: see MYADEL.

Miagao (myägä'ō, -gou'), town (1939 pop. 4,511; 1948 municipality pop. 30,143), Iloilo prov., S Panay isl., Philippines, 23 mi. W of Iloilo, on Panay Gulf; agr. center (rice, sugar cane, hemp).

Miahuatlán (myäwätlän'). **1** Officially San Andrés Miahuatlán, city (pop. 3,968), Oaxaca, S Mexico, in Sierra Madre del Sur, 50 mi. S of Oaxaca; agr. center (cereals, sugar cane, coffee, livestock, timber). Airfield. **2** Town, Puebla, Mexico, SSE of Tehuacán: see SAN JOSÉ MIAHUATLÁN. **3** Town, Puebla, Mexico, NW of Tehuacán: see SANTIAGO MIAHUATLÁN. **4** Town (pop. 1,550), Veracruz, E Mexico, in Sierra Madre Oriental, 13 mi. N of Jalapa; corn, sugar cane, coffee, tobacco.

Miajadas (myähä'dhäs), town (pop. 8,302), Cáceres prov., W Spain, 22 mi. SSW of Trujillo; olive-oil and wine processing, tanning, flour milling. Agr. trade (cereals, fruit, vegetables, livestock). Phosphate deposits near by.

Miakka River, Fla.: see MYAKKA RIVER.

Miallet (myälā'), village (pop. 445), Dordogne dept., SW France, 12 mi. E of Nontron; woodwork.

Miami (mīă'mē), village (pop. estimate 350), S Man., 40 mi. S of Portage la Prairie, in Pembina Mts.; lumbering; grain elevators; clay and bentonite quarrying.

Miami, village, Salisbury prov., N Southern Rhodesia, in Mashonaland, 55 mi. NNW of Sinoia; mica-mining center; police station for Urungwe dist.

Miami (mīă'mē, -mŭ). **1** County (□ 380; pop. 28,201), N central Ind.; ⊙ Peru. Intersected by Wabash, Mississinewa, and Eel rivers, and by Deer Creek. Agr. (grain, fruit, livestock, poultry; dairy products). Mfg. at Peru. Formed 1832. **2** County (□ 592; pop. 19,698), E Kansas; ⊙ Paola. Rolling plain region, bordering E on Mo.; drained by Marais des Cygnes R. Livestock, grain. Oil and gas fields. Formed 1861. **3** County (□ 407; pop. 61,309), W Ohio; ⊙ Troy. Intersected by Great Miami and Stillwater rivers. Agr. area (livestock, corn, tobacco, wheat); mfg. at Piqua, Troy, Tipp City; sand and gravel pits, stone quarries; nurseries. Formed 1807.

Miami. 1 Town (pop. 4,329), Gila co., SE central Ariz., near Globe, just N of Pinal Mts., 70 mi. E of Phoenix; ore-refining center. Mines (copper, gold, silver, lead, asbestos, molybdenum, perlite) near by. Founded 1908. **2** City (pop. 249,276), ⊙ Dade co., S Fla., c.70 mi. S of West Palm Beach, on Biscayne Bay, at mouth of short Miami R. (connected by canal with L. Okeechobee, c.70 mi. NW); largest city in state, and one of the leading resorts (especially in winter) of the E U.S., with numerous recreational facilities; Jan. average temp. 68° F., July average 82°. Also a notable air transportation center containing a number of large airfields (private, governmental) and important connections with Latin America. Port of entry, handling coastal and foreign shipping. Mfg.: concrete; metal, wood, meat, and bakery products; novelties, clothing, beverages; also citrus-fruit and vegetable packing. Limestone quarrying. At Musa Isle there are a Seminole Indian village and an alligator farm. Greater Miami includes Miami, MIAMI BEACH, CORAL GABLES, and HIALEAH. City was settled in the 1870s near site of Fort Dallas, built during the Seminole War. In 1895, Henry M. Flagler became interested in the area, made it a railroad terminus in 1896, dredged the harbor, and thus initiated the development of the city as a recreation center. It received its greatest impetus during the Fla. land boom of the mid-1920s. Occasional hurricanes have damaged the city. **3** City (pop. 217), Saline co., central Mo., on Missouri R. and 14 mi. N of Marshall. **4** City (pop. 11,801), ⊙ Ottawa co., extreme NE Okla., on Neosho R. near head of L. of the Cherokees (impounded by Grand River Dam), and 25 mi. WSW of Joplin, Mo.; trade center for rich lead- and zinc-mining region, producing also cattle, grain. Meat packing, dairying (butter, cheese), flour milling; mfg. of tires, glass, wood and metal products, clothing, beverages, bedding; railroad shops. Seat of Northeastern Okla. Agr. and Mechanical Col. Platted 1891. **5** City (pop. 646), ⊙ Roberts co., extreme N Texas, in high plains of the Panhandle, 23 mi. NE of Pampa; market and shipping point for livestock, grain, cotton region.

Miami Beach, city (pop. 46,282), Dade co., S Fla., on isl. bet. Atlantic Ocean (E) and Biscayne Bay (W), part of Greater Miami, and connected with Miami, across the bay, by several causeways; noted resort, with numerous recreational facilities and palatial estates. Mfg. of dairy and concrete products, feed, fertilizer, furniture, millwork, clothing; vegetable packing, boat building. Inc. 1915, it developed rapidly during the Fla. land boom of the mid-1920s.

Miami River, Ohio: see GREAT MIAMI RIVER.

Miamisburg (mīă'mēzbûrg), city (pop. 6,329), Montgomery co., W Ohio, on Great Miami R. and 10 mi. SW of Dayton, within Dayton metropolitan dist., in state's leading tobacco-growing area; mfg. (wood and paper products, cordage, metal articles, tobacco products). MIAMISBURG MOUND is near by. Laid out 1818.

Miamisburg Mound, Montgomery co., W Ohio, just SSW of Miamisburg; largest prehistoric conical mound in Ohio; 68 ft. high and 1½ acres in extent. Picnic grounds here.

Miami Shores (mīă'mē,-mŭ), village (pop. 5,086), Dade co., S Fla., a N suburb of Miami, from which it was separated in 1932. NORTH MIAMI town was called Miami Shores, 1926–31.

Miami Springs, town (pop. 5,108), Dade co., S Fla., a NW suburb of Miami; mfg. of prefabricated bldgs.

Mianabad or **Miyanabad** (mēyän"äbäd'), village, Ninth Prov., in Khurasan, NE Iran, 30 mi. SSE of Bujnurd; center of Isfarain agr. dist.

Mian Channu (myän' chŭn-nōō') or **Mian Channun** (-nōōn'), town (pop. 7,503), Multan dist., S Punjab, W Pakistan, 55 mi. ENE of Multan; wheat, oilseeds, millet; cotton ginning, sheep grazing.

Miandoab or **Mianduab,** Iran: see MIYANDUAB.

Miandrivazo (myändrēvä'zōō), town, Tuléar prov., W Madagascar, on a headstream of Tsiribihina R., 225 mi. NNE of Tuléar; tobacco center. Gold mines in vicinity.

Miane (myä'nĕ), village (pop. 2,048), Treviso prov., Veneto, N Italy, 6 mi. NE of Valdobbiadene.

Mianeh (mēänĕ'), town (1940 pop. 14,758), Fourth Prov., in Azerbaijan, NW Iran, on headstream of the Sefid Rud and 95 mi. SE of Tabriz, and on railroad; grain, cotton, grapes. Was rail terminus, 1941–51. Formerly called Garmrud.

Miangas (myäng'ŭs) or **Palmas** (päl'mäs), island, Indonesia, off SE tip of Mindanao, Philippines; 5°33'N 126°35'E.

Miani (myä'nē). **1** Town (pop. 6,051), Hoshiarpur dist., N Punjab, India, near Beas R., 23 mi. NW of Hosiarpur; wheat, gram, cotton, rice. **2** Village, W Saurashtra, India, on inlet of Arabian Sea, 19 mi. NW of Porbandar; small fishing port.

Miani. 1 Village, Las Bela state, Baluchistan, W Pakistan: see SONMIANI. **2** Town (pop. 6,713), Shahpur dist., central Punjab, W Pakistan, 38 mi. NNE of Sargodha; millet, wheat, cotton; handloom weaving. **3** Battlefield, Hyderabad dist., Sind, W Pakistan: see HYDERABAD, city.

Mianus River (mīă'nŭs), N.Y. and Conn., rises NE of Armonk, N.Y.; flows NE then S, through Conn., to Long Isl. Sound at Cos Cob Harbor in Greenwich town; c.25 mi. long.

Mianwali (myän'välē), district (□ 5,401; 1951 pop. 550,000), W Punjab, W Pakistan; ⊙ Mianwali. Bounded W by Indus R., NE by W end of Salt

Range; lies mainly in Sind-Sagar Doab; includes large part of Thal region. Wheat, millet grown along fertile river bank; hand-loom weaving, cattle grazing. Rock salt, coal, alum, gypsum, and limestone on N hills. Hydroelectric project under construction on Indus R. Chief towns: Mianwali, Kalabagh. Constituted a dist. 1901.

Mianwali, town (pop. 22,825), ⊙ Mianwali dist., W Punjab, W Pakistan, 175 mi. WNW of Lahore; market center for wheat, millet, salt, wool, hides; hand-loom weaving.

Miaoerhkow, Manchuria: see PENKI.

Miao Islands, China: see CHANGSHAN ISLANDS.

Miaoli (myou'lē'), Jap. *Byoritsu* (byō'rētsōō), town (1935 pop. 7,635), NW Formosa, 20 mi. SSW of Sinchu and on railroad; center of Miaoli oil field, with chief production at Chukwangkeng, 7 mi. SE. Sugar milling. Area is noted for watermelons and persimmons (KUNGKWAN).

Miao Tao, China: see CHANGSHAN ISLANDS.

Miarinarivo (myärēnärē'vōō), town, Tananarive prov., central Madagascar, 40 mi. W of Tananarive; alt. 4,395 ft.; center of native trade, highway terminus. R.C. and Protestant missions.

Miass (mēäs'). **1** City (1926 pop. 19,378), W Chelyabinsk oblast, Russian SFSR, in the S Urals, on Miass R. and 50 mi. WSW of Chelyabinsk, near railroad (station at Miass town); center of major gold-mining dist.; automobile mfg., metalworking, wood distilling, flour milling, sawmilling. Marble and talc quarries near by. Founded 1777 as copper-smelting plant; developed as gold-mining and corn-trading town in 19th cent. Metallurgical center, called Miasski Zavod prior to First World War; became city in 1926. **2** Town (1938 pop. over 500), W Chelyabinsk oblast, Russian SFSR, just N (under jurisdiction) of Miass city, on railroad; gold mining. Peat and marble deposits near by.

Miasskoye (mēä'skŭyŭ), village (1939 pop. over 2,000), E Chelyabinsk oblast, Russian SFSR, on Miass R. and 15 mi. NE of Kopeisk, near railroad; dairying, truck gardening. Lignite deposits.

Miass River, SW Siberian Russian SFSR, rises on E slope of the S Urals, NNE of Iremel mtn.; flows N, through noted gold-mining dist., past Miass, Melentyevskoye, and Turgoyak, generally ENE, past Kuluyevo, Chelyabinsk, Dolgoderevenskoye, and Miasskoye, and NE, past Kirovo and Kargapolye, to Iset R. 4 mi. SSW of Mekhonskoye; 390 mi. long. Forms several small lakes in upper course.

Miasteczko (myästĕts'kô) [Pol.,=small town], Ger. *Georgenberg* (gäôr'gŭnbĕrk), town (pop. 2,686), Katowice prov., S Poland, 17 mi. NNW of Katowice.

Miasteczko Krainskie (krī'nyŭskyĕ), Pol. *Miasteczko Kraińskie*, Ger. *Friedheim* (frēt'hīm), town (pop. 1,083), Bydgoszcz prov., NW Poland, on railroad and 12 mi. ESE of Schneidemühl (Pila), near Notec R.

Miastko (myäst'kô), Ger. *Rummelsburg* (rōō'mŭls-bōōrk), town (1939 pop. 8,516; 1946 pop. 3,417) in Pomerania, after 1945 in Koszalin prov., NW Poland, 25 mi. NNE of Szczecinek; linen milling, dairying, mfg. of distilling equipment.

Miava, Czechoslovakia: see MYJAVA.

Mibu (mē'bōō). **1** Town (pop. 3,505), Hiroshima prefecture, SW Honshu, Japan, 20 mi. NNE of Hiroshima; ironworks; livestock, sake, charcoal, rice. **2** Town (pop. 11,668), Tochigi prefecture, central Honshu, Japan, 10 mi. SSW of Utsunomiya; commercial center for agr. area (rice, wheat, gourds).

Mica Mountain (mī'kŭ), SE Ariz., highest peak (8,800 ft.) in Rincon Mts., c.25 mi. E of Tucson.

Micanopy (mĭkŭnō'pē), town (pop. 612), Alachua co., N Fla., 23 mi. NNW of Ocala; citrus fruit.

Micaville (mī'kŭvĭl), village (pop. c.150), Yancey co., W N.C., 8 mi. W of Spruce Pine; mica and feldspar mining.

Miccosukee, Lake (mĭkŭsōō'kē), Jefferson co., NW Fla., 20 mi. ENE of Tallahassee; triangular-shaped, c.7 mi. long, 1–5 mi. wide.

Michaelston Higher, parish (pop. 1,499), W central Glamorgan, Wales, 4 mi. E of Neath; coal mining.

Michalany (mĭ'khälyänĭ), Slovak *Michal'any*, Hung. *Alsómihályi* (ŏl'shōmĭ'hī), village (pop. 1,141), SE Slovakia, Czechoslovakia, 37 mi. SSE of Presov; rail junction; customs station on Hung. border.

Michalkovice (mĭ'khälkô"vĭtsĕ), Czech *Michálkovice*, town (pop. 5,554), NE Silesia, Czechoslovakia, on railroad and 3 mi. E of Ostrava; coal mining and industrial community, part of Greater OSTRAVA.

Michalovce (mĭ'khälôftsĕ), Hung. *Nagymihály* (nŏ'dyŭmĭ'chī), town (pop. 10,399), E Slovakia, Czechoslovakia, on Laborec R., on railroad and 35 mi. SE of Presov, agr. trade center (corn, wheat, sugar beets, potatoes).

Michatoya River (mēchätoi'ä), S Guatemala, rises in L. Amatitlán at Amatitlán, flows c.55 mi. generally S, bet. volcanoes Agua and Pacaya, past Palin (falls and power station), to the Pacific at Iztapa. Navigable for 15 mi. below mouth of María Linda R. (left). Also called María Linda in lower course.

Micheh or **Michih** (both: mē'jû'), town, ⊙ Micheh co. (pop. 19,242), NE Shensi prov., China, 40 mi. SSE of Yülin, in mtn. region; rice, millet, beans.

Michel (mĭ'chŭl), village (pop. estimate 800), SE B.C., near Alta. border, in Rocky Mts., on Elk R. and 18 mi. NE of Fernie; alt. 3,861 ft.; coal mining, coke production.

Michel, Baraque, Belgium: see BARAQUE MICHEL.

Michelau (mĭ'khŭlou), village (pop. 4,021), Upper Franconia, N Bavaria, Germany, on the Main and 2 mi. NE of Lichtenfels; woodworking, basket weaving.

Michelbach (mĭ'khŭlbäkh), village (pop. 1,630), Lower Franconia, NW Bavaria, Germany, on small Kahl R. and 9 mi. N of Aschaffenburg; machine-repair shop; tobacco- and winegrowing.

Micheldorf (mĭ'khŭldôrf), town (pop. 3,781), S Upper Austria, on Krems R. and 16 mi. ESE of Gmunden; scythes.

Michelena (mĕchälā'nä), town (pop. 1,149), Táchira state, W Venezuela, in Andean spur, 13 mi. N of San Cristóbal; coffee, grain, cattle.

Michelet (mēshlā'), village (pop. 249), Alger dept., N central Algeria, in Great Kabylia (Djurdjura range), 18 mi. SE of Tizi-Ouzou; alt. 3,540 ft. Olive groves.

Michelson, Mount (mī'kŭlsŭn) (9,239 ft.), NE Alaska, in Romanzof Mts., NE Brooks Range; 69°19'N 144°15'W.

Michelstadt (mĭ'khŭl-shtät), town (pop. 5,541), S Hesse, W Germany, in former Starkenburg prov., on the Mümling and 16 mi. ENE of Heppenheim; chief town of the Odenwald; textile mfg., woodworking. Has 15th-cent. town hall. First mentioned 741.

Micheroux (mēshrōō'), town (pop. 1,176), Liége prov., E Belgium, 6 mi. E of Liége; coal mining; fruit-syrup mfg.

Miches (mē'chĕs), town (1950 pop. 1,554), Seibo prov., E Dominican Republic, on the coast at entrance of Samaná Bay, 17 mi. N of Seibo; agr. products (cacao, coffee, coconuts, rice, corn, fruit). Until 1936, Jovero or El Jovero.

Micheville, France: see VILLERUPT.

Michiana (mĭ"shēä'nŭ), village (pop. 102), Berrien co., extreme SW Mich., at Ind. line, 3 mi. SW of New Buffalo.

Michiana Shores, town (pop. 107), La Porte co., NW Ind., on L. Michigan, 5 mi. ENE of Michigan City.

Michie, Fort, N.Y.: see GULL ISLANDS.

Michielsgestel, Sint, Netherlands: see SINT MICHIELSGESTEL.

Michigamme, Lake (mĭ"shĭgă'mē), Marquette and Baraga counties, NW Upper Peninsula, Mich., c.26 mi. W of Ishpeming; c.6 mi. long, 1½ mi. wide; resort (camping, bathing). Michigamme village is on NW shore. Source of Michigamme R.

Michigamme River, SW Upper Peninsula, Mich., rises in L. Michigamme, flows c.60 mi. SSW, joining Brule R. in SE Iron co. to form Menominee R. Has 2 dams in lower course.

Michigan (mĭ'shĭgŭn), state (land □ 57,022, including offshore isls.; with inland waters, but without □ c.38,500 of Great Lakes, □ 58,216; 1950 pop. 6,371,766; 1940 pop. 5,256,106), N U.S.; 22d in area, 7th in pop.; admitted 1837 as 26th state; ⊙ Lansing. Michigan (the "Wolverine State" or the "Lake State") consists of 2 sections, separated by c.4-mi.-wide Straits of Mackinac: the S section, called Lower Peninsula, extends N from Ind. and Ohio and is bounded W by L. Michigan and E by lakes Huron, St. Clair, and Erie and by the St. Clair and Detroit rivers (forming part of Ont. line); the N section, called Upper Peninsula, extends NE and E from Wis. bet. L. Superior (N) and L. Michigan (S) to the Ont. line, here marked by St. Marys R. and Soo Canals. Lower Peninsula (land □ 40,484; pop. 6,069,508) measures 285 mi. (N-S) and 195 mi. (E-W) at its widest points, while Upper Peninsula (land □ 16,538; pop. 302,258) extends 320 mi. E-W and 125 mi. N-S. Largest lake isls. are Isle Royale (in L. Superior), Drummond (L. Huron), and Beaver (L. Michigan). The 2 parts are structurally and topographically different. The Lower Peninsula lies in the interior lowlands region of the U.S. and is of basin structure with sedimentary strata; averaging 850 ft. in elevation, the fairly level terrain exhibits all the features of continental glaciation. In the Upper Peninsula, the W half comprises part of the Laurentian Plateau or Upland (here sometimes called Superior Highlands), an area of Pre-Cambrian crystalline rocks, bordered on the E by early Paleozoic rock formations. In the W, several low hill ranges rise above the generally rugged surface: Huron Mts., Menominee Iron Range, GOGEBIC RANGE, Porcupine Mts. (rising to highest point, 2,023 ft., in state), and COPPER RANGE (extends into Keweenaw Peninsula). The low-lying, partly swampy tract to the E is crossed by the Niagara cuesta, a limestone escarpment running parallel to L. Michigan shore. Mich. is entirely within the Great Lakes drainage basin; its rivers (e.g., Grand, Muskegon, Manistee, Huron, Tahquamenon) are not large and, in the N, contain falls and rapids. The state's continental climate is considerably modified by the proximity of the Great Lakes. Annual rainfall varies from 30–35 in. in S Lower and W Upper peninsulas to 25–30 in. in N Lower and E Upper peninsulas. Growing season averages 90–170 days (N-S). Detroit (SE) has mean temp. of 25°F. in Jan., 73°F. in July, and annual rainfall of 31 in.; Sault Ste. Marie (N) has mean temp. of 12°F. in Jan., 63°F. in July, and 30 in. of rain. Some 18,392,000 acres is classified as farm and range land, of which 8,521,000 acres are in crops. Best farming sections are in the S half of Lower Peninsula; to the N much of the area is forested or cut-over land with poor, sandy soil. Chief field crops are hay, corn, oats, wheat, barley, potatoes. Beans and sugar beets are grown in Saginaw R. valley and the "Thumb" region (bet. Saginaw Bay and L. Huron). Truck crops (cucumbers, celery, onions, melons) and oil-bearing crops (soybeans, peppermint, spearmint) are important, especially in SW; Holland (Ottawa co.) is noted for its tulip industry. The counties bordering L. Michigan from Grand Traverse Bay to Ind. line comprise a major fruitgrowing area—apples, grapes, cherries, peaches, pears, plums, and strawberries. Much of the agr. produce supports a large livestock industry, primarily dairying (1,016,000 milch cows in 1950), but also raising of hogs (927,000), beef cattle, and sheep (c.425,000). Fresh-water fisheries are important, trout, herring, whitefish, chub, pike, and perch being the chief commercial species. There are about 19,000,000 acres of forest land, including valuable stands of maple, white pine, hemlock, oak, birch, elm, spruce, and basswood; natl. forest reserves comprise 5,189,000 acres. Most important of the state's minerals is the iron ore in W Upper Peninsula, mined in the Gogebic (around Ironwood), Menominee (around Iron Mountain), and Marquette (at Ishpeming and Negaunee) ranges and shipped from lake ports of Ashland (Wis.), Marquette, and Escanaba. High-grade copper (mines now very deep and costly to operate) is also mined in the Upper Peninsula, in Copper Range (at Calumet and Houghton) on Keweenaw Peninsula. Other mineral resources are in Lower Peninsula. Petroleum occurs mainly in the Saginaw–Mt. Pleasant sector, with refineries at Trenton, Detroit, Alma, Muskegon, and elsewhere. Salt is pumped and mined from porous rock strata in the E and SE, especially in Saginaw, Midland, St. Clair, and Wayne counties; it forms the basis of an important chemical industry (bromine, calcium chloride, iodine). Limestone is quarried near Alpena, Rogers City, and Petoskey in the N and gypsum is produced near Alabaster (NE) and Grand Rapids. Bituminous coal, of low quality, is worked on a small scale, chiefly in Saginaw Bay area. There is also natural gas, sand and gravel, magnesium, coke, and clay products. Mich. is largely an industrial state and is noted for its huge automotive industry, which produces c.60% of the country's motor vehicles. Other major products are steel, machinery, chemicals and drugs, metal products, cement, food, paper and pulp, furniture, machine tools, airplanes, household and office appliances; meat packing, shipbuilding, printing and publishing. Principal industrial area is DETROIT and its satellite towns of DEARBORN, HAMTRAMCK, HIGHLAND PARK, RIVER ROUGE, PLYMOUTH, and WYANDOTTE; their great mfg. output is dominated by the automobile industry, which is also important at FLINT, PONTIAC, and LANSING. Detroit, the nation's 5th largest city, is also a major commercial center, rail and air hub, and inland port. Other large mfg. centers are GRAND RAPIDS (furniture), SAGINAW, KALAMAZOO (paper), BAY CITY, JACKSON, BATTLE CREEK (cereal foods), ANN ARBOR, MUSKEGON, PORT HURON, YPSILANTI (with nearby WILLOW RUN), and TRAVERSE CITY. With over 3,000 mi. of shore line, Mich. occupies a commanding position in Great Lakes commerce. The annual freight traffic through the SAULT SAINTE MARIE CANALS (or Soo Canals) bet. lakes Superior and Huron is the greatest of any canal in the world; Detroit R. is also an important waterway. Hydroelectric power is developed on several rivers. Recreational facilities include lake and isl. resorts, fishing, hunting, ISLE ROYALE NATIONAL PARK, and many state parks. Leading educational institutions are Univ. of Mich. (at Ann Arbor), Wayne Univ. (at Detroit), Mich. State Col. of Agr. and Applied Science (at East Lansing), Univ. of Detroit, and Mich. Col. of Mining and Technology (at Houghton). Prehistoric remains in Mich. consist of early Indian burial mounds (S) and artifacts on Keweenaw Peninsula and Isle Royale. When the French adventurer Étienne Brulé landed at Sault Sainte Marie in 1618, the chief Indian tribes in the region were the Ojibwa, Ottawa, and Potawatami. Jean Nicolet explored the Straits of Mackinac in 1634, Father Marquette established a mission at St. Ignace in 1671, and in 1679 La Salle sailed to the area in the *Griffon*, the 1st sailing ship on the Great Lakes. As more Fr. posts were built, the MACKINAC region (called Michilimackinac by the Indians) became the center of a prosperous fur trade. Fort Pontchartrain was founded in 1701 on the site of present city of Detroit. At the end of the French and Indian War (1754–63) the area was ceded to the British, who at first incurred the Indian's hostility and had to suppress a widespread rebellion under Pontiac. Despite provisions in the Treaty of Paris

(1783), by which England relinquished its claims to the region, the British held on to their rich fur trade in Mich. until 1796. Included in the NORTHWEST TERRITORY in 1787 after Mass. and Conn. had withdrawn their claims, Mich. was divided (1800) bet. Ind. Territory (W) and Ohio Territory (E), then wholly inc. into Ind. Territory (1802), and in 1805 organized as a separate territory, comprising only the Lower Peninsula. In War of 1812 Mich. fell to the British until the victories (1813) of Perry on L. Erie and Harrison at the Thames R. Settlement increased under the energetic governorship of Lewis Cass, during which time much public land was sold in the state and the new Erie Canal (opened 1825) facilitated communication with the East; the new settlers were farmers and lumbermen as well as fur trappers. Statehood (1837) was accompanied by an adjustment of the S boundary with Ohio and the acquisition of the Upper Peninsula, where the discovery of iron and copper led to the building of the Soo ship canal in 1853–55. Anti-slavery sentiment was instrumental in the creation of the natl. Republican party in 1854 at Jackson. Later on, farmer discontent with high prices and railroad monopolies was expressed in the strong Granger movement. Automobile mfg., developed in the early 1900s by Henry Ford and others, was based on the old coach and carriage industry at Detroit, Flint, Pontiac, and elsewhere. Mass-production methods in industry speeded the unionization of labor. The Upper Peninsula (except its E end, Keweenaw Peninsula, and Isle Royale) lies in the Central Time Zone, while the Lower Peninsula is in the Eastern Time Zone. See also articles on cities, towns, geographic features, and the 83 counties: ALCONA, ALGER, ALLEGAN, ALPENA, ANTRIM, ARENAC, BARAGA, BARRY, BAY, BENZIE, BERRIEN, BRANCH, CALHOUN, CASS, CHARLEVOIX, CHEBOYGAN, CHIPPEWA, CLARE, CLINTON, CRAWFORD, DELTA, DICKINSON, EATON, EMMET, GENESEE, GLADWIN, GOGEBIC, GRAND TRAVERSE, GRATIOT, HILLSDALE, HOUGHTON, HURON, INGHAM, IONIA, IOSCO, IRON, ISABELLA, JACKSON, KALAMAZOO, KALKASKA, KENT, KEWEENAW, LAKE, LAPEER, LEELANAU, LENAWEE, LIVINGSTON, LUCE, MACKINAC, MACOMB, MANISTEE, MARQUETTE, MASON, MECOSTA, MENOMINEE, MIDLAND, MISSAUKEE, MONROE, MONTCALM, MONTMORENCY, MUSKEGON, NEWAYGO, OAKLAND, OCEANA, OGEMAW, ONTONAGON, OSCEOLA, OSCODA, OTSEGO, OTTAWA, PRESQUE ISLE, ROSCOMMON, SAGINAW, SAINT CLAIR, SAINT JOSEPH, SANILAC, SCHOOLCRAFT, SHIAWASSEE, TUSCOLA, VAN BUREN, WASHTENAW, WAYNE, WEXFORD.

Michigan, Lake, in U.S., 3d largest of the GREAT LAKES, and the only one entirely in U.S.; 307 mi. long, 118 mi. wide, 923 ft. deep, it lies c.580 ft. above sea level and covers □ 22,400. Bordered E and N by Mich., W by Ill. and Wis., S by Ind. GREEN BAY, a large W arm, indents Wis. shore. NE end of L. Michigan is connected with L. Huron by Straits of Mackinac. From Chicago, the Illinois Waterway system links lake with the Mississippi and the Gulf of Mexico. Ice closes its N ports for generally 4 months yearly and lake is subject to sudden dangerous storms; nevertheless it carries a vast amount of shipping, mainly handled at Michigan City and Gary, Ind.; Chicago, Evanston, and Waukegan, Ill.; Kenosha, Racine, Milwaukee, Manitowoc, Wis.; and Escanaba, Manistee, Ludington, Muskegon, Grand Haven, and Benton Harbor, Mich. Beaver Isls. are in N part of lake. Jean Nicolet discovered L. Michigan in 1634; Marquette and Jolliet were also among its early explorers.

Michigan Center, village (pop. 3,012), Jackson co., S Mich., 4 mi. SE of Jackson, on small Michigan Center L.

Michigan City. 1 City (pop. 28,395), La Porte co., NW Ind., on L. Michigan, 5 mi. ENE of Gary; summer resort, with harbor (yachting) in dunes area; fisheries; mfg. (furniture, Pullman cars, catalysts for oil refining, industrial and agr. machinery, wire, building materials, clothing, sports equipment). State prison here. Settled 1830, inc. 1836. **2** City (pop. 486), Nelson co., E central N.Dak., 11 mi. E of Lakota; livestock, poultry, dairy products, wheat.

Michigantown, town (pop. 443), Clinton co., central Ind., 8 mi. ENE of Frankfort.

Michih, China: see MICHEH.

Michikamau Lake (mĭ″chĭkä′mô) (65 mi. long, 30 mi. wide), SW Labrador, near Quebec border; 53°50′–54°30′N 63°22′-64°48′W; alt. 1,650 ft. It is largest body of water in region of numerous small lakes; drained by Hamilton R.

Michilimackinac, Mich.: see MACKINAC, region.

Michinmáhuida, Chile: see MINCHINMÁVIDA.

Michipicoten Harbour (mĭchĭpĭkō′tŭn), village (pop. estimate 200), central Ont., on Michipicoten Bay of L. Superior, at mouth of Michipicoten R., 110 mi. NNW of Sault Ste. Marie; iron and pulpshipping port; gold, iron mining.

Michipicoten Island (17 mi. long, 3–6 mi. wide), central Ont., in NE part of L. Superior, at entrance of Michipicoten Bay, 110 mi. NW of Sault Ste. Marie; rises to 1,598 ft. (W).

Michipicoten River, central Ont., issues from L. Wabatongushi, 120 mi. N of Sault Ste. Marie, flows 70 mi. generally SW, through Dog and Manitowick lakes, to Michipicoten Bay of L. Superior, 3 mi. SE of Michipicoten Harbour.

Michoacán (mēchwäkän′), state (□ 23,202; 1940 pop. 1,182,003; 1950 pop. 1,412,830), central and W Mexico; ⊙ Morelia. Bounded by the Pacific (W), Mexico state (E), Guanajuato (N), Jalisco and Colima (NW), Guerrero and Río de las Balsas (S). Contains narrow coastal strip; otherwise it is extremely mountainous, lying partly within great central plateau and traversed by Sierra Madre Occidental and E-W volcanic belt of central Mexico, including PARICUTÍN and JORULLO. Large lakes Pátzcuaro and Cuitzeo, and part of L. Chapala on Jalisco border, situated in state. Drained by Lerma R. (N border) and Río de las Balsas (S border). Climate cold in high sierras, temperate on N plateau, subtropical in SW valleys, hot and humid along coast. Rich mineral resources include silver, lead, copper at Angangueo and Tlapujahua, iron at Aguililla; and sulphur, tungsten, antimony, mercury, petroleum deposits. Wooded sierras supply fine cabinet and construction woods and dyewood. Primarily rich agr. area; produces cereals (N), and sugar cane, rice, fruit, coffee, vanilla, and tobacco in fertile lower valleys. Considerable sheep and cattle grazing. Low malarial Pacific coast almost uninhabited. Rural industries: mining, lumbering, fishing (in lakes), flour milling, distilling, native handicrafts. Morelia, Uruapan, Zamora, Pátzcuaro, La Piedad, Yurécuaro, Maravatío, Sahuayo are important processing centers. Pátzcuaro, in lake district, a popular resort. Michoacán is inhabited mainly by Tarascan Indians, whose pre-Columbian empire had its ⊙ at Tzintzuntzan.

Michoacanejo (mēchwäkänā′hō), town (pop. 1,208), Jalisco, central Mexico, near Zacatecas border, 33 mi. SW of Aguascalientes; grain, vegetables, stock.

Michurin, Bulgaria: see TSAREVO.

Michurinsk (mēchōō′rĭnsk), city (1939 pop. 70,202), W Tambov oblast, Russian SFSR, on right headstream of Voronezh R. and 40 mi. WNW of Tambov; rail junction; locomotive repair works; tractor parts, horsehair products (brushes); vegetable and fruit processing. Noted horticulture center (experimental institute founded by Rus. 19th-cent. scientist Michurin); teachers col., regional mus. Founded 1636 as fortified outpost; called Kozlov until early 1930s.

Mickle Fell, mountain (2,591 ft.) in the Pennines of NW Yorkshire, England, 16 mi. WNW of Barnard Castle; highest point in Yorkshire. On N slope are lead mines.

Mickleham (mĭk′lŭm), agr. village and parish (pop. 815), central Surrey, England, on Mole R., at foot of Box Hill, and 2 mi. N of Dorking. Has remains of priory founded 1228. Fanny Burney lived here for some time.

Mico, Sierra del (syĕ′rä dĕl mē′kō), range in Izabal dept., E Guatemala; E continuation of Sierra de las MINAS. Extends 50 mi. NE to Bay of Amatique, forming divide bet. L. Izabal (N) and Motagua R. (S); rises to over 1,500 ft. NE sec. (S of Río Dulce; known as San Gil Mts.) rises to over 6,000 ft.; coal deposits.

Mico Point (mē′kō), E headland of Nicaragua, on Caribbean Sea, 30 mi. S of Bluefields. Sometimes called Monkey Point, Sp. *Punta del Mono.*

Mico River, S Nicaragua, rises near La Libertad, flows c.100 mi. E, past San Pedro de Lóvago, Muelle de los Bueyes, and El Recreo, joining Siguia and Rama rivers at Rama to form Escondido R. Navigable for launches below El Recreo.

Micoud (mēkōō′), village (pop. 1,138), SE St. Lucia, B.W.I., minor port 14 mi. SE of Castries; growing of tropical fruit, fishing.

Micro (mī′krō), town (pop. 310), Johnston co., central N.C., 17 mi. NW of Goldsboro; lumber milling.

Micronesia (mīkrōnē′zhŭ, –shŭ) (□ c.1,300), one of 3 main divisions of Pacific isls., in W Pacific, N of equator; includes Caroline, Marshall, Marianas, and Gilbert isls. Except for Marianas Isls. and a few Caroline isls. which are volcanic, the isls. are coral atolls. Inhabitants are related to Malays, and stem from Negroid and Mongoloid stock.

Midagalola (mē′dägälō″lä), village, Harar prov., E central Ethiopia, 45 mi. S of Harar, in durra-growing region.

Midai (mēdī′), island (pop. 1,755; 4 mi. long, 3 mi. wide), Indonesia, in S.China Sea, 145 mi. WNW of Cape Datu (Borneo); 3°1′N 107°48′E; coconuts, trepang.

Midale, village (pop. 312), SE Sask., 27 mi. SE of Weyburn; mixed farming.

Mid Calder (kôl′dŭr), town and parish (pop. 2,793), W Midlothian, Scotland, 11 mi. WSW of Edinburgh, in shale-oil mining region; paper mills. Has 13th-cent. church.

Middelberg (mĭ′dŭlbûrg, –bĕrkh), mountain range, W Cape Prov., U. of So. Afr., at W edge of the Great Karroo, extends 50 mi. bet. Cold Bokkeveld range (S) and Clanwilliam (N); rises to 6,618 ft. on Sneeuwberg Pup mtn., 30 mi. SE of Clanwilliam.

Middelburg (mĭ′dŭlbûrkh), town (pop. 20,605), ⊙ Zeeland prov., SW Netherlands, on Walcheren isl. and 4 mi. NNE of Flushing; 51°29′N 3°37′E. Trade and mfg. center; railroad repair and machine shops; electrical industry; mfg. of pianos, furniture, wood products, brass products, synthetic fertilizer, candy, dairy products; fish canning, artificial-silk weaving. Has 15th-cent. town hall (destroyed in Second World War), 12th-cent. abbey (where in 1505 Knights of the Golden Fleece met). Center of attraction for artists. Flourishing medieval trade center; member of Hanseatic League. Captured (1574) from Spain by the Beggars of the Sea; temporarily occupied (1809) by British. Inundated in Second World War.

Middelburg (mĭ′dŭlbûrg, –bûrkh). **1** Town (pop. 5,807), E central Cape Prov., U. of So. Afr., on Klein Brak R. and 115 mi. WNW of Queenstown; rail junction; agr. center (stock, wheat, feed crops). Just NE is Grootfontein Agr. Col. **2** Town (pop. 8,099), S Transvaal, U. of So. Afr., on Little Olifants R. and 80 mi. E of Pretoria, in coal-mining, agr. region (wheat, tobacco, potatoes); alt. 4,971 ft. Grain elevator. Site of technical college. Copper, iron, cobalt deposits near by.

Middelfart (mĭ′dŭlfärt), city (pop. 8,089) and port, Odense amt, Denmark, on NW Fyn isl., on the Little Belt (here bridged) and 26 mi. WNW of Odense; fishing; pottery, hardware.

Middelharnis (mĭ′dŭlhärnĭs), town (pop. 4,812), South Holland prov., SW Netherlands, on Overflakkee isl. and 5 mi. SSE of Hellevoetsluis (ferry across the Haringvliet); mfg. (synthetic fertilizer, cement, furniture), chicory drying; fishing.

Middelkerke (mĭ′dŭlkĕrkŭ), town (pop. 4,161), West Flanders prov., W Belgium, 5 mi. SW of Ostend, near North Sea. Just NW, on North Sea, is seaside resort of Middelkerke-Bains.

Middelstum (mĭ′dŭlstŭm), village (pop. 1,634), Groningen prov., NE Netherlands, 5 mi. ENE of Winsum; stoneware, agr.

Middle, in Rus. names: see also SREDNE-, SREDNEYE, SREDNI, SREDNIYE, SREDNYAYA.

Middle America, a term sometimes used to designate the isthmian tract bet. the U.S. border and Colombia, marking transition from North America to South America; it differs from CENTRAL AMERICA in that it includes Mexico and, sometimes, the West Indies.

Middle Andaman Island: see ANDAMAN ISLANDS.

Middle Atlas, Fr. Morocco: see ATLAS MOUNTAINS.

Middleback Range, S South Australia, extends 40 mi. S from Iron Knob, parallel with E coast of Eyre Peninsula; rises to 500 ft. Includes iron-producing hills of Iron Knob, Iron Monarch, Iron Prince, Iron Baron; sandstone.

Middle Bass Island, Ohio: see BASS ISLANDS.

Middlebie (mĭ′dŭlbē), agr. village and parish (pop. 1,440), S Dumfries, Scotland, 6 mi. N of Annan.

Middleboro. 1 or **Middleborough,** town (pop. 10,164), including Middleboro village (pop. 5,889), Plymouth co., SE Mass., near Assawompsett Pond, 18 mi. N of New Bedford; mfg., principally shoes. Settled 1660, inc. 1669. **2** or **McKean,** borough (pop. 379), Erie co., NW Pa., 9 mi. SSW of Erie; dairying

Middlebourne (mĭ′dŭlbôrn), town (pop. 741), ⊙ Tyler co., NW W.Va., 37 mi. NE of Parkersburg, in agr., gas, oil region.

Middle Brewster Island, Mass.: see BREWSTER ISLANDS.

Middleburg. 1 Resort village (pop. 1,298), Schoharie co., E central N.Y., on Schoharie Creek and 30 mi. WSW of Albany; trade center for dairying and farming area. Settled 1712, inc. 1881. **2** Town (pop. 217), Vance co., N N.C., 6 mi. NE of Henderson. **3** Borough (pop. 1,283), ⊙ Snyder co., central Pa., 15 mi. WSW of Sunbury; tannery, silk mill; lumber, flour; dairying. Settled c.1760, laid out 1800, inc. 1856. **4** Town (pop. 663), Loudoun co., N Va., 35 mi. W of Washington, D.C.; center of country-estate area known for fox hunting, horse breeding.

Middleburgh Heights, village (pop. 2,299), Cuyahoga co., N Ohio, a SW suburb of Cleveland.

Middleburg Island, islet (1 mi. long), just off Vogelkop peninsula, Netherlands New Guinea, in the Pacific, 17 mi. W of Cape of Good Hope; 0°21′S 132°10′E.

Middlebury. 1 Town (pop. 3,318), New Haven co., SW Conn., just W of Waterbury, in summer resort area; agr., mfg. (watches, clocks). Quassapaug Pond just W. Settled in early 18th cent., inc. 1807. **2** Town (pop. 839), Elkhart co., N Ind., on small Little Elkhart R. and 14 mi. E of Elkhart, in agr. area; nursery stock; dairy products, metal products, clocks. **3** Town (pop. 4,778), including Middlebury village (pop. 3,614), ⊙ Addison co., W Vt., on Otter Creek and 32 mi. S of Burlington. Agr., resort area; poultry, fruit, dairy products; marble milling; winter sports. Seat of Middlebury Col., art mus. (1829). Partly in Green Mtn. Natl. Forest. Chartered 1761, 1st settled 1773, permanently settled 1783.

Middle Caicos or **Grand Caicos** (kī′kōs, kī′kŭs), island (□ 72.8; 25 mi. long, 12 mi. wide; pop. 717), Turks and Caicos Isls., dependency of Jamaica, largest isl. of the archipelago, just W of East Caicos; 21°50′N 71°45′W. Some cotton growing.

Middle Chain of Lakes, Martin co., S Minn. System of small lakes and connecting streams extending 15 mi. N, past Fairmont, from Iowa line.

Middle Congo, district, Belgian Congo: see LEOPOLDVILLE, city.

Middle Congo, Fr. *Moyen-Congo* (mwäyĕ-kōgō'), French overseas territory (□ 132,100; 1950 pop. 684,500), S Fr. Equatorial Africa; ⊙ POINTE-NOIRE, although BRAZZAVILLE, ⊙ Fr. Equatorial Africa, is in the territory. Bounded S and E by Belgian Congo (along Congo and Ubangi rivers), W by the Atlantic, N by Fr. Cameroons; adjacent to Gabon (NW) and Ubangi-Shari (NE). Drained by Sanga, Alima, and Kouilou rivers. Tracts of dense equatorial forests and swamps alternate with wooded savannas; humid, warm climate (mean annual temp. 77°F.; mean annual rainfall 80–100 inches). Chief products: palm oil and kernels, hardwoods, kola nuts, copal, rubber, tobacco, lead (at M'Fouati), and some gold. Also groundnuts, manioc, corn, bananas (plantains). Some stock raising and rice cultivation in S. Railroad (built 1921–34) bet. Pointe-Noire and Brazzaville stimulated domestic industries. Middle Congo coast was discovered by Portuguese in 15th cent. In 17th–19th cent. chartered Fr. companies set up factories in several bays, notably at Loango. De Brazza explored (1875–78) Alima R. and in 1880 reached right shore of Stanley Pool, which he claimed for France. Berlin Conference (1885) adjusted conflicting claims of France and Congo Free State in lower Congo, Kouilou-Niari, and Pool areas. Originally named French Congo, a name later (1891–1910) applied to all Fr. Equatorial Africa, the area became known as Middle Congo in 1903; acquired colony status in 1910, territory status in 1946 (with representation in Fr. Parliament), when some minor frontier adjustments with Gabon were effected.

Middle Creek, Ky.: see PRESTONSBURG.

Middle East, term whose content has greatly varied. It is in more current usage applied to the countries of SW Asia lying W of Pakistan and India, thus including Afghanistan, Iran, Iraq, Turkey, Syria, Lebanon, Israel, Jordan, and the Arabian Peninsula; Egypt and the Anglo-Egyptian Sudan in NE Africa, and Cyprus in the E Mediterranean are often included. Originally the concept Middle East was made to oppose the NEAR EAST, lying farther W, and the FAR EAST, lying farther E, but it soon came to overlap somewhat with both regions. Some writers use the term to mean the group of lands (now or until recently) predominantly Moslem in religion and Arab in background. The British in former times even referred to India, Burma, and Tibet (in S and central Asia) as the Middle East, and their current official publications add to the general concept Libya (with Tripolitania and Cyrenaica), Ethiopia, Eritrea, Malta, and the 3 Somalilands, but leave out Turkey. In America the term Near East is often used as a synonym for Middle East and is the term used by the U.S. Dept. of State.

Middle Fabius River, Mo.: see FABIUS RIVER.

Middlefield. 1 Industrial town (pop. 1,983), Middlesex co., S Conn., bet. Middletown and Meriden; mfg. (gun sights, brake linings, tools, bone and ivory products); agr. (apples, peaches). Includes Rockfall village. State park here. Dinosaur tracks found here now in Peabody Mus. of Yale Univ. Settled c.1700, set off from Middletown 1866. **2** Town (pop. 295), Hampshire co., W Mass., 14 mi. ESE of Pittsfield. **3** Village (pop. 1,141), Geauga co., NE Ohio, 30 mi. E of Cleveland, in agr. area; rubber, plastic and metal products, lumber, food products.

Middle Fork, W Oregon, formed by confluence of several small branches in Cascade Range, flows c.115 mi. NW, past Oakridge, joining Coast Fork near Eugene to form Willamette R. About 20 mi. SE of Eugene is Lookout Point Dam (250 ft. high, 3,106 ft. long; begun 1947), a unit of Willamette R. flood-control plan; also called Meridian Dam.

Middle Franconia (frăngkō'nēŭ), Ger. *Mittelfranken* (mĭ'tŭlfräng"kŭn), administrative division [Ger. *Regierungsbezirk*] (□ 2,941; 1946 pop. 1,209,844; 1950 pop. 1,279,240) of W Bavaria, Germany; ⊙ Ansbach. Bounded S by Swabia, SE by Upper Bavaria, E by Upper Palatinate, N by Upper and Lower Franconia, W by Württemberg-Baden. Hilly region in Franconian Jura; drained by Altmühl, Rednitz, and Pegnitz rivers. Wheat, barley, cattle, hogs; intensive hop growing in NE. Industries (machinery, vehicles, precision instruments) centered at Nuremberg (Bavaria's 2d-largest city) and Fürth; and Erlangen, site of Bavaria's only Protestant univ., has electromedical industry. Pop. is predominantly Protestant. Part of old historic region of FRANCONIA.

Middle Gobi (gō'bē), Mongolian *Dund Gobi* or *Dunda Gobi* (dōōn'dä), aimak (□ 31,000; pop. 45,000), S central Mongolian People's Republic; ⊙ Mandal Gobi. Steppe and semi-desert plateau.

Middle Granville, village (1940 pop. 869), Washington co., E N.Y., near Vt. line, 20 mi. ENE of Glens Falls, in slate-quarrying area.

Middle Grove, town (pop. 48), Monroe co., NE central Mo., 9 mi. E of Moberly.

Middle Haddam, Conn.: see EAST HAMPTON.

Middleham, agr. village and parish (pop. 651), North Riding, N Yorkshire, England, on Ure R. and 9 mi. SSW of Richmond. Has castle (built in late 12th cent.) which belonged to Warwick the Kingmaker.

Middle Island, S Ont., tiny isl. in L. Erie just S of Pelee Isl., near Ohio boundary; southernmost point of Canada, 41°41'N.

Middle Island, New Zealand: see SOUTH ISLAND.

Middle Island, village, W St. Kitts, B.W.I., 7 mi. NW of Basseterre. Has St. Thomas Church and tomb of Sir Thomas Warner, founder of the Br. colony, who died in 1648.

Middle Island Creek, NW W.Va., rises in Doddridge co. SW of Clarksburg, flows NW past West Union and Middlebourne, and SSW to Ohio R. just N of St. Marys; c.85 mi. long.

Middle Loup River, Nebr.: see LOUP RIVER.

Middle Nodaway River, Iowa: see NODAWAY RIVER.

Middle Palisade, Calif.: see KINGS CANYON NATIONAL PARK.

Middle Pease River, Texas: see PEASE RIVER.

Middlepoint, village (pop. 583), Van Wert co., W Ohio, 7 mi. E of Van Wert, and on Little Auglaize R., in agr. area.

Middleport. 1 Village (pop. 1,641), Niagara co., W N.Y., on the Barge Canal and 30 mi. NNE of Buffalo; mfg. (chemicals, canned foods, flour, machinery, baskets). Settled 1812, inc. 1859. Grew after completion of Erie Canal (1825). **2** Village (pop. 3,446), Meigs co., SE Ohio, on Ohio R. and 34 mi. SW of Parkersburg, W.Va.; coal mines, gas and oil wells; railroad shops; mfg. of food products, cement blocks. **3** Borough (pop. 942), Schuylkill co., E central Pa., 8 mi. ENE of Pottsville.

Middle Raccoon River, Iowa: see RACCOON RIVER.

Middle River. 1 Industrial suburb, Baltimore co., central Md., at head of Middle R. (5-mi. navigable inlet of Chesapeake Bay), 9 mi. ENE of downtown Baltimore; has one of world's largest aircraft plants (here since 1929) and a U.S. Army signal depot. **2** Village (pop. 356), Marshall co., NW Minn., on Middle R. and 22 mi. N. of Thief River Falls, in livestock and poultry area; dairy products.

Middle River. 1 In S central Iowa, rises in SW Guthrie co., flows 105 mi. SE and ENE to Des Moines R. 13 mi. SE of Des Moines. **2** Rises in marshy area of Marshall co., NW Minn., flows 70 mi. W, past Newfolden and Argyle, to Snake R. 12 mi. N of Alvarado. **3** In NW Va., formed by headstreams joining in Augusta co.; flows c.60 mi. E and NE, to North R. near Port Republic.

Middle Saranac Lake, N.Y.: see SARANAC LAKES.

Middlesboro or **Middlesborough,** city (pop. 14,482), Bell co., extreme SE Ky., in the Cumberlands near meeting-point of Ky., Tenn., and Va., 50 mi. NNE of Knoxville, Tenn., in area of bituminous coal, limestone, iron, and some farms (livestock, dairy products, tobacco). Resort (alt. 1,138 ft.); rail junction; trade and coal-mining center; mfg. of foundry and machine-shop products, wood products, leather, stone products, food products, mining equipment, elastic webbing, overalls, sports goods, coke. Has airport. Fishing resort, wild-game sanctuary at Fern L. (just S; 3 mi. long; dammed in fork of small Yellow Creek). Near-by points include: Cumberland Gap; Pinnacle Mtn.; Henderson Settlement School; ruins of Fort Lyon, a strategic point in Civil War; Cudjo's Cave (kŭ'jōz)—where Ky., Tenn., and Va. meet—a series of enormous rooms with colorful stone formations; Soldiers' Cave. City founded 1889 on old Wilderness Road.

Middlesbrough (–brŭ, –brŭf), county borough (1931 pop. 138,274; 1951 census 147,336), North Riding, NE Yorkshire, England, on S bank of the Tees and 3 mi. ENE of Stockton; iron and steel center, with blast furnaces, steel mills, and chemical works. Developed after opening of Darlington-Stockton RR and after discovery of iron in the Cleveland hills, near by. Has technical and metallurgical schools, libraries, and museums. There is a port, handling chiefly coal. Large breakwaters protect the city. Just E is the steel-milling suburb of Cargofleet.

Middlesex, county (□ 1,420; pop. 127,166), S Ont., on Thames R.; ⊙ London.

Middlesex, county (□ 232.3; 1931 pop. 1,638,728; 1951 census 2,268,776), S England. Bounded by Buckingham (W), Hertford (N), Essex and London (E), and Surrey (S). Drained by Thames, Colne, and Brent rivers. Concentrated residential dist., forming part of London's metropolitan area. Agr. is confined to market gardening. There are various industries, mostly of recent date. There is no administrative center, administrative functions being carried out at Middlesex guildhall, Westminster. Important towns are Tottenham, Hendon, Willesden, Heston and Isleworth, Ealing, Brentford and Chiswick, Edmonton, and Harrow (site of famous public school). Major airports of Northolt and Heath Row, serving London, are within county. Middlesex was a subkingdom of Essex and of Mercia and played important part in English history, especially in wars with Danes. There are many area. mains of early occupation.

Middlesex, county (□ 2,026.04; pop. 524,377), central Jamaica, B.W.I., bet. Cornwall co. (W) and Surrey co. (E); consists of St. Catherine, St. Mary, Clarendon, St. Ann, and Manchester parishes. Set up 1758; no longer has administrative functions.

Middlesex. 1 County (□ 374; pop. 67,332), S Conn. on Long Isl. Sound, bisected by Connecticut R.; ⊙ Middletown. Agr. (tobacco, potatoes, truck, dairy products, fruit, poultry), mfg. (tools, hardware, electrical equipment, boats, textiles, metal products, cosmetics, bells, thread, rubber and elastic goods, piano parts, paper and fiber products clothing, automobile parts, farm implements, chemicals, machinery, asbestos, cigars); fishing; sandstone and feldspar quarries; resorts on shore. Includes Pocotopaug L., several state parks and forests. Drained by Connecticut (E boundary) Hammonasset (W boundary), Salmon, and Mattabesset rivers. Constituted 1785. **2** County (□ 829; pop. 1,064,569), NE Mass., bordering N on N.H.; ⊙ Cambridge and Lowell. Intersected by Merrimack and Nashua rivers and drained by Charles, Concord, Sudbury, and Assabet rivers, which furnish water power. Industrial towns: Lowell, Cambridge, Somerville, Framingham, Everett, Waltham. Produces shoes, textiles, machinery and other metal products, watches, food products, wood products, rubber goods, and agr. produce. Formed 1643. **3** County (□ 312; pop. 264,872), E N.J., bounded E by Raritan Bay and Arthur Kill; ⊙ New Brunswick. Industrial, agr., residential area, with extensive clay deposits and allied industries; oil refineries, ore smelters and refineries, shipyards, drydocks on Raritan Bay; diversified mfg.; agr. (truck, poultry, dairy products, fruit) Drained by Raritan R. (navigable) and Millstone and South rivers. Formed 1675. **4** County (□ 132 pop. 6,715), E Va.; ⊙ Saluda. In tidewater region; bounded N by Rappahannock R., S by short Dragon Run and Piankatank R. Agr. (truck, tobacco corn, melons), livestock raising (cattle, hogs, poultry, sheep); lumbering (pine, oak); fishing, oystering. Summer-resort area. Formed 1673.

Middlesex. 1 Borough (pop. 5,943), Middlesex co., NE N.J., 2 mi. NE of Bound Brook; mfg. (paint, tiles, metal products, clothing, aircraft parts, optical goods); hothouse flowers. Inc. 1913. **2** Resort village, Yates co., W central N.Y., near Canandaigua L., 19 mi. SW of Geneva, in grape-growing region. **3** Town (pop. 446), Nash co., E central N.C., 25 mi. E of Raleigh. **4** Town (pop. 887), Washington co., central Vt., on Winooski R., just NW of Montpelier; lumber.

Middle Teton, Wyo.: see GRAND TETON NATIONAL PARK.

Middleton, town (pop. 1,172), W N.S., on Annapolis R. and 25 mi. ENE of Annapolis Royal; furniture mfg., lumbering; agr. market in fruitgrowing area.

Middleton. 1 Municipal borough (1931 pop. 29,188; 1951 census 32,602), SE Lancashire, England, 5 mi. NNE of Manchester; cotton and silk textile milling; engineering (textile machinery, boilers); aircraft construction. Has 15th-cent. church and 16th-cent. grammar school. **2** Town, Yorkshire, England: see HUNSLET CARR AND MIDDLETON.

Middleton, Ireland: see MIDLETON.

Middleton. 1 Town (pop. 144), Elbert co., NE Ga., 6 mi. ESE of Elberton, near Savannah R. **2** Village (pop. 496), Canyon co., SW Idaho, 5 mi. NE of Caldwell and on Boise R., in fruit and grain area. **3** Town (pop. 2,916), Essex co., NE Mass., on Ipswich R. and 8 mi. NW of Salem; resort; mfg. (chemicals). Settled 1659, organized 1728. **4** Town (pop. 255), Strafford co., SE N.H., 23 mi. NNW of Dover. **5** Town (pop. 362), Hardeman co., SW Tenn., 40 mi. S of Jackson, in cotton, corn, livestock area; rail junction. **6** Village (pop. 2,110), Dane co., S Wis., near L. Mendota, 7 mi. W of Madison, in farming and dairying area; mfg. (condensed milk, drapery rods, cleaning supplies). Inc. 1905.

Middleton-in-Teesdale, town and parish (pop. 1,657), W Durham, England, on Tees R. and 9 mi. NW of Barnard Castle; lead mining, flour milling; agr. market.

Middleton Island (5 mi. long), S Alaska, in Gulf of Alaska, 80 mi. SSW of Cordova; 59°26'N 146°20'W; fur farming under govt. lease. Radio beacon.

Middletown. 1 Village (pop. c.450), Lake co., NW Calif., 22 mi. N. of Santa Rosa, in a valley of the Coast Ranges; quicksilver mining; agr. Mineral springs (resorts) near by. **2** Industrial city (pop. 29,711), coextensive with Middletown town, ⊙ Middlesex co., central Conn., on the Connecticut and 14 mi. S of Hartford. Mfg. (textiles, elastic webbing, metal products, hardware, automobile parts, clothing, rubber goods, chemicals, machinery, cigars, asbestos); tobacco, apples, dairy products. Wesleyan Univ., state training school for girls, a state hosp. for insane here. Suspension bridge (1938; 3,420 ft. long) spans the Connecticut to Portland. Settled 1650, inc. as town 1651, inc. as city 1784. **3** Town (pop. 1,755), New Castle co., W Del., 25 mi. SSW of Wilmington, near Silver L., marketing and shipping center in agr. area; flour, canned foods, hosiery. Near by is pre-Revolutionary St. Anne's Episcopal Church. Inc. 1861. **4** Village (pop. 480), Logan co., central Ill., 20 mi. N of Springfield; bituminous-coal mines; timber; agr. (grain, soybeans, livestock). **5** Town (pop. 1,731), Henry co., E central Ind., on small Fall Creek and 8 mi. ESE of Anderson; livestock, grain, tomatoes; cannery. **6** Town (pop. 229), Des

Moines co., SE Iowa, 8 mi. W of Burlington, in agr. area. **7** Village (1940 pop. 1,003), Jefferson co., N Ky., 15 mi. E of downtown Louisville; makes feed, metal stampings. **8** Town (pop. 936), Frederick co., W Md., in Middletown Valley and 8 mi. WNW of Frederick; trade center in agr. area (grain, dairy products); makes shoes. Vicinity was scene of much Civil War activity. **9** Town (pop. 240), Montgomery co., E central Mo., near West Fork of Cuivre R., 11 mi. NNE of Montgomery City; agr. **10** Village, Monmouth co., E N.J., 4 mi. NW of Red Bank. Settled 1665; 1st Baptist church in N.J. (1668) built here. Marlpit Hall (c.1684) now a mus. **11** Industrial city (pop. 22,586), Orange co., SE N.Y., 21 mi. WSW of Newburgh; farm trade center; railroad shops, foundries. Mfg. of clothing, textiles, machinery; metal, stone, and paper products; cosmetics, chemicals, leather and fur goods. Seat of Middletown Collegiate Center. Inc. 1888. **12** City (pop. 33,695), Butler co., extreme SW Ohio, 28 mi. NNE of Cincinnati and on Great Miami R.; trade and industrial center in agr. area; steel-rolling mills, paper mills; mfg. of aircraft, industrial machinery, paper, tobacco products, metal products. Laid out 1802, inc. 1886. **13** Borough (pop. 9,184), Dauphin co., S Pa., on Susquehanna R. and 8 mi. SE of Harrisburg, at mouth of Swatara Creek; stoves, clothing, shoes. Olmsted Air Force Base. Laid out 1755, inc. 1828. **14** Resort town (pop. 7,382), Newport co., SE R.I., on Rhode Isl. just N of Newport; agr., nurseries. Set off from Newport and inc. 1743. "Whitehall," where Bishop Berkeley lived (1729–31), has been preserved. **15** Town (pop. 386), Frederick co., N Va., in Shenandoah Valley, 12 mi. SSW of Winchester; lime. Near by on Cedar Creek (small N tributary of North Fork of the Shenandoah), Gen. P. H. Sheridan defeated (Oct. 19, 1864) Confederates under Gen. J. G. Early.

Middletown Springs, town (pop. 496), Rutland co., W Vt., on Poultney R. and 11 mi. SW of Rutland.

Middletown Valley, Frederick co., NW Md., fertile agr. valley (c.15 mi. long, 6 mi. wide) drained by Catoctin Creek; extends N from the Potomac bet. prongs (Catoctin Mtn. on E, South Mtn. on W) of the Blue Ridge. In it are Middletown, Brunswick.

Middle Tunguska River, Russian SFSR: see STONY TUNGUSKA RIVER.

Middle Village, SE N.Y., a residential section of Queens borough of New York city; mfg. (clothing, machine parts).

Middleville. 1 Village (pop. 1,047), Barry co., SW Mich., 20 mi. SE of Grand Rapids and on Thornapple R., in farm area; flour mill, creamery, poultry hatchery. **2** Village (pop. 647), Herkimer co., central N.Y., on West Canada Creek and 13 mi. ENE of Utica, in dairying area; summer resort.

Middle Volga Territory, Rus. *Sredne-Volzhskiy Kray* (sryĕ"dnyĭ-vôlzh'skē krī'), former administrative division of central European Russian SFSR; ⊙ was Kuibyshev (Samara). Formed 1928 out of govts. of Orenburg, Penza, Samara, and Ulyanovsk, it was originally an oblast, converted into a territory in 1930, when Mordvinian Autonomous Oblast was formed; dissolved 1934 into Samara (after 1935, Kuibyshev) Territory and Orenburg (after 1938, Chkalov) oblast.

Middle West or **Midwest,** name given to N part of central U.S.; in general, region includes the N part of the Mississippi valley (N of the Ohio and the Missouri rivers), the Great Lakes region W of L. Erie, and the E edge of the Great Plains. In its widest application, embraces Ohio, Ind., Ill., Mich., Wis., Minn., Iowa, Mo., Kansas, Nebr., N.Dak., and S.Dak. One of world's richest farm regions, known especially for its corn and hogs, although W part has huge wheat acreages and the Great Lakes portion has great industrial centers.

Middlewich (-wĭch), urban district (1931 pop. 5,458; 1951 census 6,734), central Cheshire, England, on Dane R., on Trent and Mersey Canal, and 7 mi. N of Crewe; salt refining and processing, formerly an important industry; mfg. of pottery, agr. machinery. Has medieval church.

Middle Yuba River, Calif.: see YUBA RIVER.

Middridge, town and parish (pop. 447), central Durham, England, 3 mi. SE of Bishop Auckland; coal mining.

Midelt (mēdĕlt'), town (pop. 4,356), Meknès region, central Fr. Morocco, on N slope of the Djebel Ayachi (High Atlas), in upper Moulouya valley, 95 mi. SSE of Meknès; alt. 4,900 ft. Market center; footwear mfg. Lead mine at Aouli (14 mi. NE). Fr. military post since 1917.

Midhurst (mĭd'hûrst), town and parish (pop. 1,812), W Sussex, England, on Rother R. and 10 mi. N of Chichester; agr. market. Has grammar school and 15th-cent. church. Site of large tuberculosis sanitarium.

Midi (mē'dē), **Maidi,** or **Maydi** (mā'dē), town (pop. 2,500), Hodeida prov., NW Yemen, minor Red Sea port 105 mi. N of Hodeida, near Asir line. Considered part of Asir until Yemen–Saudi Arabia treaty (1934). Sometimes spelled Medi.

Midi, Aiguille du, France: see AIGUILLE DU MIDI.

Midi, Canal du (känäl' dü mēdē'), in Hérault, Aude, and Haute-Garonne depts., S France, extends 150 mi. from the Étang de THAU, near Sète, to Toulouse, whence it is continued by the Garonne Lateral Canal to Bordeaux. Traverses drainage divide at Col de NAUROUZE by means of numerous locks. Chief towns on it are Béziers, Carcassonne, and Castelnaudary. Although built to carry ocean shipping bet. the Mediterranean and the Atlantic, thus eliminating voyage through Straits of Gibraltar, its size has permitted barge traffic only.

Midi, Dent du, Switzerland: see DENT DU MIDI.

Midi, Pic du, France: see PIC DU MIDI DE BIGORRE and PIC DU MIDI D'OSSAU.

Midia, Cape (mē'dyä), SE Rumania, on the Black Sea coast, 10 mi. N of Constanta. Terminus of the Danube-Black Sea Canal. Major seaport in construction here.

Midia, Midiah, Turkey: see MIDYE.

Midian, Saudi Arabia: see MADIAN.

Midi de Bigorre, Pic du, France: see PIC DU MIDI DE BIGORRE.

Midi d'Ossau, Pic du, France: see PIC DU MIDI D'OSSAU.

Midilli or **Midillii,** Greece: see MYTILENE.

Midland, town (pop. 6,800), S Ont., on Georgian Bay of L. Huron, 80 mi. NNW of Toronto; port with govt. coal dock; silk and woolen milling; mfg. of machinery, underwear. Govt. radio station. Near by is shrine of Jesuit martyrs of Canada; place of pilgrimage.

Midland. 1 County (□ 520; pop. 35,662), E central Mich.; ⊙ MIDLAND. Drained by Tittabawassee, Pine, and Chippewa rivers. Agr. (livestock, poultry, grain, beans, sugar beets; dairy products). Oil and gas wells, salt deposits, coal mines. Midland city is chemical and metallurgical center. Co. has state game refuge. Organized 1855. **2** County (□ 938; pop. 25,785), W Texas; ⊙ Midland. On S Llano Estacado; alt. c.2,500–3,000 ft.; drained by tributaries of Colorado R. Important oil fields (development begun 1950–51); ranching (cattle, sheep), agr. (grain sorghums, cotton, corn); dairying. Midland city is hq. for many oil companies. Large potash deposits. Formed 1885.

Midland. 1 Town (pop. 356), Sebastian co., W Ark., 20 mi. S of Fort Smith, near Okla. line. **2** Village (1940 pop. 594), Riverside co., S Calif., 20 mi. NNW of Blythe, in N Palo Verde Valley; gypsum quarrying, processing. **3** Town (pop. 889), Allegany co., W Md., in the Alleghenies, 11 mi. WSW of Cumberland; bituminous coal mines. **4** City (pop. 14,285), ⊙ Midland co., E central Mich., 19 mi. W of Bay City, at confluence of Pine and Chippewa rivers with the Tittabawassee. Important metallurgical and chemical-mfg. center (magnesium alloys, silicone products, pharmaceuticals). Oil and gas wells, coal mines, salt deposits. Oil refining; mfg. of tools, toys, cement products, beer; seed processing, shipping. Game refuge near by. Inc. as village 1869, as city 1887. Chemical industry started here in 1890. **5** Village (pop. 338), Clinton co., SW Ohio, 35 mi. ENE of Cincinnati. **6** Borough (pop. 6,491), Beaver co., W Pa., 28 mi. NW of Pittsburgh and on Ohio R.; steel, machinery, coke; shipyard, railroad shops. Settled c.1820. **7** Village (pop. 1,158), Washington co., SW Pa., near Washington. **8** Town (pop. 387), Haakon co., central S.Dak., 25 mi. E of Philip and on Bad R.; livestock, grain. Artificial lake near by. **9** City (pop. 21,713), ⊙ Midland co., W Texas, on S Llano Estacado, c.100 mi. WNW of San Angelo; oil-field center (boomed 1950–51), in former ranching and agr. region; 1951 pop. was c.23,000. Has offices of many oil companies, oil refineries, carbon-black and natural-gasoline plants; mfg. of oil-field equipment. Cattle shipping, cotton ginning, cottonseed-oil milling. Airport (SW) handles transcontinental traffic. Settled 1885, inc. 1906.

Midland Acres, village (pop. 1,551), Clark co., SW Wash.

Midland Beach, SE N.Y., a section of Richmond borough of New York city, on E Staten Isl.; beach and amusement resort.

Midland City, town (pop. 784), Dale co., SE Ala., 8 mi. NW of Dothan.

Midland Junction, municipality (pop. 6,182), SW Western Australia, 8 mi. ENE of Perth; rail junction; fruit, wheat.

Midland Park, borough (pop. 5,164), Bergen co., NE N.J., 5 mi. N of Paterson; mfg. (textiles, towels, hosiery, embroideries, yarn); agr. (truck, dairy products). Inc. 1894.

Midlands, region of central England. Generally coextensive with the Anglo-Saxon Mercia, it is usually considered to include the present counties of Bedford, Buckingham, Derby, Leicester, Northampton, Nottingham, Rutland, and Warwick.

Midleton or **Middleton,** Gaelic *Mainistir na Coran,* urban district (pop. 2,792), SE Co. Cork, Ireland, near NE end of Cork Harbour, 13 mi. E of Cork; woolen milling, whisky distilling; agr. market (dairying; potatoes, oats).

Midlothian (-lō'dhēŭn), formerly **Edinburghshire,** county (□ 366.1; 1931 pop. 526,296; 1951 census 565,746), SE Scotland, on S shore of Firth of Forth; ⊙ EDINBURGH. Bounded by Peebles (S), Lanark (W), West Lothian (NW), and East Lothian and Berwick (E). Drained by the Water of Leith, Gala Water, Esk, Almond, and Tyne rivers. Surface is flat in N, rising S to the Pentland Hills and Moorfoot Hills. Soil is of noted fertility; truck gardening, fruitgrowing, stock raising, dairying, and fishing are important. Industries include coal and oil-shale mining and refining, ironstone and limestone quarrying, paper milling, whisky distilling, brewing, carpet weaving, metal-working; there are shipyards at Leith and Granton. Tolbooth prison in Edinburgh was popularly named the Heart of Midlothian. Other towns are Dalkeith, Musselburgh, Portobello, Lasswade, Bonnyrigg, Penicuik, Mid Calder. There are many traces of Roman occupation and ruins of anc. castles. In co. are sites of battles of Pinkie and Carberry Hill.

Midlothian (mĭdlō'thēŭn). **1** Village (pop. 3,216), Cook co., NE Ill., SW suburb of Chicago; mfg. of grease lubricators; truck, poultry farms; nursery. Inc. 1927. **2** City (pop. 1,177), Ellis co., N Texas, 25 mi. SSW of Dallas, in rich cotton, grain, cattle area; mfg. (foundry products, cottonseed oil, mattresses). Settled 1880, inc. 1898.

Midnapore (mĭd'nŭpôr), district (□ 5,274; pop. 3,190,647), SW West Bengal, India; ⊙ Midnapore. Bounded NW by Bihar, SW by Orissa, SE by Hooghly R., S by Bay of Bengal; drained by Subarnarekha, Kasai, and Rupnarayan rivers. Lateritic soil W, alluvial soil E. Agr. (rice, corn, pulse, wheat, mustard, jute, potatoes, peanuts, castor); sal, mahua, dhak in forested area (W); silk growing (E). Railroad workshops at Kharagpur; rice milling at Midnapore; regional cotton-cloth distributing center near Pingla; cotton weaving, metalware mfg., general engineering works. Rail Inst. at Kharagpur, col. at Contai. Former Buddhist temple now dedicated to Kali at Tamluk. Buddhist stronghold in 5th cent. B.C. Hijili was site of Job Charnock's victory (1687) over Mogul army; ceded to English in 1760. Formerly spelled Medinipur.

Midnapore, town (pop. 43,171), ⊙ Midnapore dist., SW West Bengal, India, on the Kasai and 65 mi. W of Calcutta; road and trade center (rice, pulse, corn, wheat, peanuts); rice milling, mfg. of chemicals, silk cloth. Has col. Formerly spelled Medinipur.

Midongy-du-Sud (mēdôn'gē-dü-süd'), town, Fianarantsoa prov., SE Madagascar, 150 mi. S of Fianarantsoa; stock raising. R.C. and Protestant missions, hosp. for natives.

Midoun (mēdōōn'), village, SE Tunisia, on Djerba isl., 9 mi. SE of Houmt-Souk, in rich fruitgrowing area (orchards, olive trees, date palms).

Midouze River (mēdōōz'), Landes dept., SW France, formed at Mont-de-Marsan by confluence of 2 small streams, the Douze (right) and the Midou (left), flows 27 mi. SW to the Adour 4 mi. below Tartas. Navigable; timber floating.

Midsayap (mĭdsäyäp'), town (1939 pop. 6,162; 1948 municipality pop. 42,473), Cotabato prov., central Mindanao, Philippines, 20 mi. E of Cotabato, at edge of a marshy area in lower Pulangi valley; rice, coconuts.

Midsomer Norton, England: see NORTON RADSTOCK.

Midvale. 1 Village (pop. 231), Washington co., W Idaho, 18 mi. NNE of Weiser and on Weiser R.; center of agr. area. **2** Village in Wanaque borough, Passaic co., NE N.J., on Wanaque Reservoir and 11 mi. NNW of Paterson; knit goods. **3** Village (pop. 632), Tuscarawas co., E Ohio, 5 mi. SE of New Philadelphia and at junction of Tuscarawas R. and Stillwater Creek; clay products. **4** Town, Pa.: see PLAINS. **5** City (pop. 3,996), Salt Lake co., N Utah, 10 mi. S of Salt Lake City and on Jordan R.; alt. 4,390 ft. In mining area (lead, zinc, copper, gold, silver); has large smelter. Produces flour and beet sugar. Settled 1859, known as Brigham Junction and East Jordan, named Midvale and inc. 1909.

Midville, agr. village (pop. 682), Burke co., E Ga., 23 mi. SSW of Waynesboro and on Ogeechee R.

Midwar, El, Jordan: see MADWAR, EL.

Midway, village (pop. estimate 250), S B.C., on Wash. border, on Kettle R., at mouth of Boundary Creek, and 14 mi. W of Grand Forks; fruit, vegetables.

Midway, islands (□ 2; pop. 437) consisting of an atoll and 2 islets (Sand and Eastern), halfway across N Pacific, c.1,150 mi. NW of Honolulu, T.H.; 28°15'N 177°20'W. An American discovery (1859), it was annexed 1867 and became an air-line base 1935. Site of cable station (opened 1903), lighthouse, air-line hotel, and U.S. naval air base (1941). Midway was the scene (June 3–6, 1942) of the battle of Midway, one of the decisive battles of the Second World War. The engagement, fought entirely between U.S. and Jap. aircraft, resulted in the destruction of a large Jap. battle fleet and crippled the Jap. navy.

Midway. 1 Town (pop. 544), Bullock co., SE Ala., 12 mi. SE of Union Springs. **2** Village (pop. 1,830, with adjacent Canaan), Seminole co., E central Fla., near Sanford. **3** Village (pop. 14,774, with adjacent Hardwick), Baldwin co., central Ga., near Milledgeville. **4** Town (pop. 228), Liberty co., SE Ga., 27 mi. SW of Savannah. **5** City (pop.

950), Woodford co., central Ky., near Elkhorn Creek, 12 mi. WNW of Lexington, in Bluegrass agr. region; makes whisky, headache powders. Has a jr. col. 6 Town, Ohio: see SEDALIA. 7 Village (pop. 1,271), Adams co., S Pa., just NW of Hanover. 8 Borough (pop. 993), Washington co., SW Pa., 15 mi. WSW of Pittsburgh. 9 Village (pop. c.500), Madison co., E central Texas, 26 mi. SW of Crockett; trade point in agr. area. 10 Town (pop. 711), Wasatch co., N central Utah, 5 mi. W of Heber and on Provo R.; alt. 5,567 ft.; dairying; limestone.

Midway City, village (pop. 1,421), Orange co., S Calif., 17 mi. W of Santa Ana.

Midway Park, village (pop. 3,703), Onslow co., E N.C., 6 mi. SE of Jacksonville.

Midway Village, Va.: see STEELES TAVERN.

Midwest, region in U.S.: see MIDDLE WEST.

Midwest, village (1940 pop. 806), Natrona co., central Wyo., on Salt Creek and 40 mi. N Casper; alt. 4,820 ft.; oil wells.

Midwest City, residential town (pop. 10,166), Oklahoma co., central Okla., a suburb ESE of Oklahoma City. Inc. 1941.

Midwolda or **Midwolde** (both: mĭt'vōldŭ), village (pop. 1,505), Groningen prov., NE Netherlands, 4 mi. NNW of Winschoten; clockmaking; agr.

Midyan, Saudi Arabia: see MADIAN.

Midyat (mĭdyät'), town (pop. 7,660), Mardin prov., SE Turkey, 36 mi. ENE of Mardin; wheat, barley, vetch, lentils.

Midye (mĭdyĕ'), anc. *Salmydessus*, village (pop. 1,318), Kirklareli prov., Turkey in Europe, port on Black Sea 60 mi. WNW of Istanbul; grain, timber. Also spelled Midia and Midiah.

Midzhur or **Midzhor** (mē'jŏŏr, –jôr), Serbo-Croatian *Midžor* (mē'jôr), highest peak (7,113 ft.) in Western Balkan Mts., on Bulg.-Yugoslav border, in Chiporov Mts., 18 mi. N of Pirot (Yugoslavia).

Mie (mē'ä), prefecture [Jap. *ken*] (□ 2,226; 1940 pop. 1,198,783; 1947 pop. 1,416,494), S Honshu, Japan; ⊙ TSU. Partly on Kii Peninsula; bounded E by Ise Bay and Kumano Sea (both inlets of Philippine Sea); MATSUZAKA is chief port. Generally mountainous terrain, drained in S by Kumano R. Hot springs in N; fertile plains on W coast of Ise Bay. Agr. (rice, wheat, tea, citrus fruit); extensive stock raising, sawmilling, fishing. Ago Bay is known for pearl culture. Mfg. (textiles, ceramic products) and woodworking at Tsu, Matsuzaka, YOKKAICHI, KUWANA, UENO. UJI-YAMADA is most important Shintoist center of Japan.

Mie, town (pop. 11,243), Oita prefecture, E Kyushu, Japan, 28 mi. N of Nobeoka; agr. center (rice, wheat).

Miechow (myĕ'khŏŏf), Pol. *Miechów*, town (pop. 6,878), Krakow prov., S Poland, 20 mi. N of Cracow; rail junction; mfg. of agr. machinery, tanning, flour milling.

Miechowice (myĕ-khôvē'tsĕ), Ger. *Mechtal* (mĕkh'-täl), commune (1939 pop. 16,919; 1946 pop. 12,672) in Upper Silesia, after 1945 in Katowice prov., S Poland, 3 mi. W of Beuthen (Bytom); coal, zinc, lead mining. Until 1936, called Miechowitz.

Miedwie Lake (myĕd'vyĕ), Ger. *Madü* (mä'dü) (□ 14), in Pomerania, after 1945 in NW Poland, 5 mi. W of Stargard; 9 mi. long, 2 mi. wide. Drained NW by Plona R.

Miedzyborz (myĕdzĭ'bŏŏzh), Pol. *Międzybórz*, Ger. *Neumittelwalde* (noi'mĭ'tŭlväl"dŭ), town (1939 pop. 1,649; 1946 pop. 586) in Lower Silesia, after 1945 in Wroclaw prov., SW Poland, 35 mi. NE of Breslau (Wroclaw); agr. market (grain, potatoes, livestock). Was (1919–39) Ger. frontier station on Pol. border.

Miedzychod (–khŏŏt), Pol. *Międzychód*, Ger. *Birnbaum* (bĭrn'boum), town (1946 pop. 4,632), Poznan prov., W Poland, on Warta R. and 45 mi. WNW of Poznan; rail junction; mfg. of machinery, bricks; canning, brewing.

Miedzylesie (myĕdzĭlĕ'syĕ), Pol. *Międzylesie*, Ger. *Mittelwalde* (mĭ'tŭlväl"dŭ), town (1939 pop. 2,586; 1946 pop. 4,746) in Lower Silesia, after 1945 in Wroclaw prov., SW Poland, at S foot of Habelschwerdt Mts., on the Glatzer Neisse and 20 mi. S of Glatz (Klodzko). Frontier station on Czechoslovak border; silk milling. Has 16th-cent. castle.

Miedzyrzec or **Miedzyrzec Podlaski** (myĕdzĭ'zhĕts pôdlä'skē), Pol. *Międzyrzec Podlaski*, Rus. *Mezhireche* or *Mezhirech'e* (both: myĭ-zhĕ'rĭchyĕ), town (pop. 8,696), Lublin prov., E Poland, on Krzna R., on railroad and 55 mi. N of Lublin. Trade center (grain, hides); mfg. of bristles, agr. implements, scales, soap, pen holders; tanning, flour milling, distilling. Before Second World War, pop. 75% Jewish.

Miedzyrzec, Ukrainian SSR: see MEZHIRICHI.

Miedzyrzecz (–zhĕch), Pol. *Międzyrzecz*, Ger. *Meseritz* (mā'zŭrĭts), town (1939 pop. 12,096; 1946 pop. 4,385) in Brandenburg, after 1945 in Zielona Gora prov., W Poland, on Obra R. and 25 mi. SE of Landsberg (Gorzow Wielkopolski); grain, livestock, and lumber market; distilling; oil and flour mills. Has 13th-cent. church, remains of medieval town walls. First mentioned as site of abbey in 1005; chartered 1485; destroyed 1476 by Hungarians. In Second World War, c.40% destroyed.

Miedzyzdroje (myĕdzĭzdrô'yĕ), Pol. *Międzyzdroje*, Ger. *Misdroy* (mĭs'droi), town (1939 pop. 4,145; 1946 pop. 1,949) in Pomerania, after 1945 in Szczecin prov., NW Poland, on N shore of Wolin isl., 10 mi. E of Swinemünde; seaside resort. Chartered after 1945.

Miejska Gorka (myā'skä gŏŏr'kä), Pol. *Miejska Górka* [=town hill], Ger. *Görchen* (gûr'khŭn), town (1946 pop. 2,635), Poznan prov., W Poland, 39 mi. N of Breslau (Wroclaw); rail junction; mfg. (bricks, cement, beet sugar). Has cloister.

Miélan (myālā'), village (pop. 726), Gers dept., SW France, 7 mi. SW of Mirande; hog market; wine-growing.

Mielau, Poland: see MLAWA.

Mielec (myĕ'lĕts), town (pop. 8,271), Rzeszow prov., SE Poland, on Wisloka R., on railroad and 31 mi. NW of Rzeszow; airport; mfg. of ceramics, perfume; lumbering, flour milling; tannery.

Mielle, La (lä myĕl'), E suburb (pop. 5,385) of Cherbourg, Manche dept., NW France; truck gardening.

Mielnica, Ukrainian SSR: see MELNITSA-PODOLSKAYA.

Miena, village, central Tasmania, 65 mi. NW of Hobart and on S shore of Great Lake; site of dam for Waddamana hydroelectric plant.

Mienchih or **Mien-ch'ih** (myĕn'chû'), town, ⊙ Mienchih co. (pop. 107,031), NW Honan prov., China, 40 mi. W of Loyang and on Lunghai RR, near Yellow R.; wheat, beans, millet, kaoliang.

Mienchu (myĕn'jŏŏ'), town (pop. 25,273), ⊙ Mienchu co. (pop. 286,494), NW Szechwan prov., China, 45 mi. NNE of Chengtu, near source of To R.; tobacco and tea processing; produces rice, millet, sweet potatoes, sugar cane, wheat.

Mienhsien (myĕn'shyĕn'), town (pop. 6,714), ⊙ Mienhsien co. (pop. 135,572), SW Shensi prov., China, 30 mi. WNW of Nancheng; grain. Iron deposits.

Mienning (myĕn'nĭng'). 1 Town, ⊙ Mienning co. (pop. 88,014), SE Sikang prov., China, 50 mi. N of Sichang and on highway; wheat, corn, kaoliang. Until 1938 in Szechwan. 2 Town (pop. 10,851), ⊙ Mienning co. (pop. 64,871), SW central Yunnan prov., China, 100 mi. SE of Paoshan; alt. 4,987 ft.; cotton textiles; rice, millet, beans.

Mienyang (myĕn'yäng'). 1 Town (pop. 27,606), ⊙ Mienyang co. (pop. 791,465), SE central Hupeh prov., China, 60 mi. WSW of Hankow, in lake region; silk and cotton weaving. 2 Town (pop. 30,789), ⊙ Mienyang co. (pop. 379,887), NW Szechwan prov., China, 30 mi. NNW of Santai and on right bank of Fow R.; paper milling; sweet potatoes, sugar cane, rice, wheat, rapeseed. Saltworks near by.

Mier (mēĕr'), city (pop. 1,866), Tamaulipas, N Mexico, on Rio Grande opposite Roma (Texas), and 90 mi. NE of Monterrey; agr. center (cotton, sugar cane, corn, stock).

Miera River (myā'rä), Santander prov., N Spain, rises in Cantabrian Mts., flows 27 mi. N to inlet of Bay of Biscay opposite Santander.

Miercurea, Rumania: see MERCUREA.

Miercurea-Ciuc, Rumania: see MERCUREA-CIUC.

Miercurea-Niraj, Rumania: see MERCUREA-NIRAJ.

Mieres (myā'rĕs), town (pop. 9,616), Oviedo prov., NW Spain, in Asturias, on Lena R. and 9 mi. SSE of Oviedo; industrial center of rich mining area (coal, iron, cinnabar, mercury); iron- and steelworks (rolling stock); coke industry. Has mining school.

Mieroszow (myĕrô'shŏŏf), Pol. *Mieroszów*, Ger. *Friedland* (frēt'länt), town (1939 pop. 4,386; 1946 pop. 5,135) in Lower Silesia, after 1945 in Wroclaw prov., SW Poland, at N foot of the Sudetes, 9 mi. SSW of Waldenburg (Walbrzych); cotton milling, furniture mfg. Frontier station on Czechoslovak border. After 1945, briefly called Frydland.

Miersdorf (mērs'dôrf), village (pop. 4,564), Brandenburg, E Germany, near Seddin L., 15 mi. SE of Berlin; market gardening.

Mier y Noriega (mēĕr' ē nōryā'gä), town (pop. 1,003), Nuevo León, N Mexico, in Sierra Madre Oriental 37 mi. ESE of Matehuala (Zacatecas); grain, livestock; lumbering.

Mies, town, Czechoslovakia: see STRIBRO.

Miesbach (mēs'bäkh), town (pop. 5,217), Upper Bavaria, Germany, in Bavarian Alps, 13 mi. WSW of Rosenheim; paper milling, printing, textile mfg., brewing. Summer resort (alt. 2,250 ft.).

Mies River, Czechoslovakia: see MZE RIVER.

Miesso (myĕ'sō), village (pop. 200), Harar prov., E central Ethiopia, in Great Rift Valley, on railroad and 80 mi. WSW of Diredawa; road junction. Formerly Meheso. Taken (1941) by British in Second World War.

Mieza (myā'thä), village (pop. 1,039), Salamanca prov., W Spain, near Duero or Douro R., 57 mi. WNW of Salamanca; olive-oil processing, flour milling; ships olives, wine, potatoes.

Mifengshantze, Manchuria: see MISHAN.

Mifflin county (□ 431; pop. 43,691), central Pa.; ⊙ Lewistown. Agr. region, bisected NE–SW by Jacks Mtn. in center of co.; area bet. Jacks Mtn. and Blacklog Mtn. (on SE border) drained by Juniata R. Grain, fruit; mfg. (textiles, metal products, bricks); limestone, sand. Formed 1789.

Mifflin. 1 Village (pop. 186), Ashland co., N central Ohio, 8 mi. E of Mansfield. Near by on Black Fork of Mohican R., is Charles Mill Reservoir (capacity 88,000 acre-ft.), for flood control. 2 Borough (pop. 835), Juniata co., central Pa., on Juniata R. opposite Mifflintown.

Mifflinburg, borough (pop. 2,259), Union co., central Pa., 9 mi. WSW of Lewisburg; truck and auto bodies, textiles, furniture, clothing; agr. Laid out 1792, inc. 1827.

Mifflintown, agr. borough (pop. 1,013), ⊙ Juniata co., central Pa., 35 mi. NW of Harrisburg and on Juniata R.; shirt mfg.; limestone and shale quarries. Laid out 1791, inc. 1833.

Mifune (mēfōō'nä), town (pop. 7,434), Kumamoto prefecture, W Kyushu, Japan, 8 mi. SE of Kumamoto; commercial center in agr. area (rice, wheat).

Migahatenna (mĭgŭhŭtĕn'nŭ), village (pop. 2,505), Western Prov., Ceylon, 18 mi. SE of Kalutara; graphite-mining center; vegetables, rubber, rice. Sometimes spelled Megahatenna.

Migdal (mēgdäl'). 1 Agr. settlement (pop. 250), Lower Galilee, NE Israel, near W shore of Sea of Galilee, 4 mi. NNW of Tiberias. Modern village founded 1909 on site of village of same name known at time of Second Temple. 2 Anc. locality, NW Palestine: see MAGDALA.

Migdal Gad (gäd), village (1946 pop. estimate 10,900), W Israel, in Judaean Plain, near Mediterranean, on railroad and 30 mi. SSW of Tel Aviv; tweed milling, concrete-pipe mfg. Captured by Israeli forces, Oct., 1948; until then called Majdal, Arabic *Al Majdal* (ĕl măj'dăl). Modern village on site of biblical locality of *Migdal-gad*. Near by is site of anc. city of ASCALON.

Migennes (mēzhĕn'), market town (pop. 5,502), Yonne dept., N central France, near junction of Yonne R. and Burgundy Canal, 13 mi. N of Auxerre; transshipment of wood, coal, and building materials. Important railroad station and yards at Laroche-Migennes (1 mi. SW).

Migir Tepe (mŭgŭr' tĕpĕ"), Turkish *Mıgır Tepe*, peak (7,418 ft.), in Amanos Mts., S Turkey, 10 mi. E of Dortyol.

Migiurtinia, Ital. Somaliland: see MIJIRTEIN.

Migliarino (mēlyärē'nō), village (pop. 1,380), Ferrara prov., Emilia-Romagna, N central Italy, on Po R. delta mouth and 16 mi. ESE of Ferrara; mfg. (bricks, tiles).

Miglionico (mēlyô'nēkô), village (pop. 3,711), Matera prov., Basilicata, S Italy, 9 mi. SW of Matera; wine, olive oil.

Mignano (mēnyä'nō), village (pop. 1,790), Caserta prov., Campania, S Italy, 10 mi. SE of Cassino; hemp mill. Damaged in Second World War.

Migné (mēnyā'), village (pop. 352), Vienne dept., W central France, 4 mi. N of Poitiers; stone quarries.

Mignon (mĭn'yŏn), village (pop. 3,053), Talladega co., E central Ala., 20 mi. SW of Talladega.

Miguel Alves (mēgĕl' äl'vĭs), city (pop. 1,857), N Piauí, Brazil, landing on right bank of Parnaíba R. (Maranhão border) and 60 mi. N of Teresina; cotton ginning, rice milling; ships babassu nuts, tobacco, manioc, cotton.

Miguel Azuza (äsōō'sä), town (pop. 4,753), Zacatecas, N central Mexico, on interior plateau, near Durango border, 35 mi. NW of Nieves; alt. 6,483 ft.; silver mining, stock raising. Formerly San Miguel de Mezquital.

Miguel Calmon (käl'mō), city (pop. 2,996), E central Bahia, Brazil, on railroad and 70 mi. SSW of Senhor do Bonfim; cattle, sugar, tobacco, coffee; manganese mines. City was called Djalma Dutra, 1939–44.

Miguel de la Borda, Panama: see DONOSO.

Miguel Esteban (ĕstā'vän), town (pop. 3,913), Toledo prov., central Spain, in upper La Mancha, 45 mi. SE of Aranjuez; cereals, grapes, potatoes, sheep; sawmilling, plaster mfg.

Miguel Pereira (pĭrā'rŭ), town, W central Rio de Janeiro state, Brazil, in the Serra do Mar (here called "Brazilian Switzerland"), 30 mi. NW of Rio; summer resort.

Migueltурra (mēgĕltōō'rä), town, (pop. 6,254), Ciudad Real prov., S central Spain, on railroad and 2 mi. E of Ciudad Real; processing and agr. center (potatoes, cereals, grapes, olives, livestock). Olive-oil pressing, alcohol and liquor distilling, tanning, textile milling, soapmaking. Resort with mineral springs.

Migues (mē'gĕs), town (pop. 2,500), Canelones dept., S Uruguay, 40 mi. NE of Montevideo; grain, stock. Railroad station is 3 mi. S. Sometimes spelled Miguez.

Migulinskaya (mēgōōlyĕn'skĭŭ), village (1948 pop. over 2,000), N Rostov oblast, Russian SFSR, on Don R. and 10 mi. SE of Kazanskaya; wheat, sunflowers, livestock. Pop. largely Cossack.

Migyaungye or **Megyaungye** (mē'jounjē"), village, Magwe dist., Upper Burma, on right bank of Irrawaddy R. and 20 mi. SSE of Magwe.

Mihaileni (mēhŭēlān'), Rum. *Mihăileni*, agr. town (1948 pop. 3,807), Botosani prov., NE Rumania, on USSR border, 14 mi. W of Dorohoi.

Mihailesti (mēhŭēlĕsht'), Rum. *Mihăileşti*, village (pop. 916), Buzau prov., SE central Rumania, 18 mi. SSW of Buzau.

Mihalic, Turkey: see KARACABEY.

Mihaliccik (mĭhă″lĭchĭk′), Turkish *Mihaliççik*, village (pop. 1,970), Eskisehir prov., W central Turkey, 50 mi. E of Eskisehir; rich deposits of potter's clay; grain, onions, tobacco.

Mihara (mēhä′rä), city (1940 pop. 39,072; 1947 pop. 48,513), Hiroshima prefecture, SW Honshu, Japan, port on inlet of Hiuchi Sea, just W of Onomichi, 36 mi. E of Hiroshima. Mfg. center; spinning mills, sake breweries. Chief exports: sake, floor mats. Has feudal castle. Includes (since 1936) former adjacent town and port of Itozaki.

Mihara, Mount, Jap. *Mihara-yama*, active volcanic cone (2,477 ft.) on central O-shima, of isl. group Izushichito, Greater Tokyo, Japan; surrounded by desert land. Known for numerous suicides committed here. In 1934, two Japanese made a 1,250-ft. descent into crater in steel cage.

Miharu (mēhä′rōō), town (pop. 10,306), Fukushima prefecture, central Honshu, Japan, 7 mi. NE of Koriyama, in agr. area (rice, tobacco); horse trade.

Mihijam, India: see CHITTARANJAN.

Mihintale (mĭhĭn′tŭlä), isolated peak (1,019 ft.) in North Central Prov., Ceylon, 7 mi. E of Anuradhapura. A Buddhist pilgrimage center; cradle of Buddhism in Ceylon and traditional site where, 3d cent. B.C., Buddhist apostle Mahinda converted Devanampiya Tissa, 1st Buddhist king of Ceylon. Buddhist remains include hundreds of stone steps leading to a large stupa built 1st cent. A.D., Ambasthala stupa (built 2d cent. B.C.; contains some ashes of Mahinda) with Mahinda's Bed (the center of pilgrimage) near by, Lion Bath, convocation hall, and Kaludiya Palace. Anc. park to be restored.

Mihonoseki (mē′hōnō′sākē), town (pop. 2,120), Shimane prefecture, SW Honshu, Japan, on Sea of Japan, 15 mi. ENE of Matsue, on narrow peninsula N of Naka-no-umi; summer resort; charcoal, rice, raw silk, soy sauce. Fishery.

Mihrpur, E Pakistan: see MEHERPUR.

Mihsien (mē′shyĕn′), town, ⊙ Mihsien co. (pop. 167,835), N Honan prov., China, 30 mi. SW of Chengchow; rice, wheat, millet, beans.

Mii, Japan: see KURUME.

Miike, Japan: see OMUTA.

Mijares (mēhä′rĕs), town (pop. 1,382), Ávila prov., central Spain, in Sierra de Gredos, 25 mi. SSW of Ávila; olives, vegetables; flour milling, olive-oil pressing. Hydroelectric plant.

Mijares River, Teruel and Castellón de la Plana provs., E Spain, rises 18 mi. W of Teruel, flows 65 mi. generally ESE to the Mediterranean 6 mi. SSE of Castellón de la Plana. Two dams and reservoirs feed several canals (Canal de Castellón) irrigating orange groves.

Mijas (mē′häs), town (pop. 1,619), Málaga prov., S Spain, at S slopes of the Sierra de Mijas, near the Mediterranean, 15 mi. SW of Málaga, in agr. region (olives, lemons, figs, raisins, aromatic plants, honey, livestock); timber. Marble and agate quarrying, lead-silver mining.

Mijdrecht (mī′drĕkht), village (pop. 1,887), Utrecht prov., W central Netherlands, 13 mi. NW of Utrecht; mfg. (biscuits, bicycle parts); agr., cattle raising, dairying; peat digging. Sometimes spelled Mydrecht.

Mijirtein (mējĕrtän′), Ital. *Migiurtinia*, region, N Ital. Somaliland. Occupies E African "horn"; bordered by Gulf of Aden (N), Indian Ocean (E), Br. Somaliland (W). Hot, arid region with high plateau (1,500–3,000 ft.) in W and low plateau (600 ft.) in E. Has narrow coastal plain lined with sand dunes. Capes Hafun and Guardafui are easternmost points of Africa. Fishing (tunny, mother of pearl) and pastoralism (sheep, cattle, camels). Frankincense and gum arabic are gathered in N. Extensive saltworks in Hafun bay. Chief towns: Bender Kassim, Alula, Hordio, Hafun, Gardo.

Mikage (mēkä′gā), town (pop. 12,044), Hyogo prefecture, S Honshu, Japan, on Osaka Bay, bet. Uozaki (W) and Ashiya (E); sake brewing, woodworking.

Mikame (mēkä′mā), town (pop. 8,014), Ehime prefecture, W Shikoku, Japan, on Hoyo Strait, 40 mi. SW of Matsuyama; agr. center (rice, wheat, oranges); fishing port. Spinning mill, sake brewery.

Mikasa (mēkä′sä), town (pop. 44,682), W central Hokkaido, Japan, 30 mi. NE of Sapporo; coal-mining center. Within town area are Horonai (or Poronai) and Ikushumbetsu coal mines. Until early 1940s, called Mikasayama.

Mikashevichi (mēkŭshĕ′vēchē), Pol. *Mikaszewicze* (mēkäshĕvē′chĕ), town (1939 pop. over 500), E Pinsk oblast, Belorussian SSR, in Pripet Marshes, 29 mi. E of Luninets, on former USSR-Pol. border; plywood mfg.

Mikawa (mēkä′wä), former province in central Honshu, Japan; now part of Aichi prefecture.

Mikawa, town (pop. 6,403), Ishikawa prefecture, central Honshu, Japan, on Sea of Japan, 6 mi. NNE of Komatsu; rice growing.

Mikazuki (mēkä′zōōkē), town (pop. 3,878), Hyogo prefecture, S Honshu, Japan, 17 mi. NW of Himeji, in agr. area (rice, wheat, fruit, flowers, poultry). Produces raw silk, processed tea, *konnyaku* (paste made from devil's tongue).

Mikeno, Mount (mēkĕ′nō), 2d-highest peak (c. 14,600 ft.) of the Virunga range, E Belgian Congo, near Ruanda-Urundi border, 20 mi. S of Rutshuru and 3 mi. NW of Mt. Karisimbi; extinct volcano in SE section of Albert Natl. Park.

Mikepercs (mĭ′kĕpärch), Hung. *Mikepércs*, town (pop. 2,696), Hajdu co., E Hungary, 6 mi. S of Debrecen; brickworks.

Mikese or **Mikesse** (mēkĕ′sā), village, Eastern Prov., Tanganyika, on railroad and 17 mi. E of Morogoro; mica deposits.

Mikhailo-Kotsyubinskoye or **Mikhaylo-Kotsyubinskoye** (mēkhī′lŭ-kŭtsyōōbēn′skŭyŭ), village (1926 pop. 3,974), W Chernigov oblast, Ukrainian SSR, 8 mi. W of Chernigov; grain. Until c.1935, Kozel.

Mikhailov or **Mikhaylov** (mēkhī′lŭf), city (1926 pop. 11,592), W Ryazan oblast, Russian SFSR, 38 mi. SW of Ryazan; metal goods, clothing (lace work); flour milling, peat working. Limestone quarries near by. Large cement works at OKTYABRSKI (W). Founded 1238 as Moscow fortress against steppe nomads. During Second World War, briefly held (1941) by Germans in Moscow campaign.

Mikhailovgrad or **Mikhaylovgrad** (mēkhī′lôvgrät), city (pop. 8,067), Vratsa dist., NW Bulgaria, on Ogosta R. and 22 mi. NW of Vratsa; agr. and cattle center. Has ruins of Roman town of Montanensia. Formerly called Golyama Kutlovitsa, later Ferdinand (1891–1945).

Mikhailovka or **Mikhaylovka** (mēkhī′lŭfkŭ). **1** Village (1948 pop. over 2,000), SW Dzhambul oblast, Kazakh SSR, 8 mi. NE of Dzhambul; cotton. **2** Village (1948 pop. over 2,000), N Pavlodar oblast, Kazakh SSR, 110 mi. N of Pavlodar; wheat. **3** Village (1926 pop. 3,519), SW Altai Territory, Russian SFSR, on railroad and 65 mi. WNW of Rubtsovsk; flour mill, dairy plant. **4** Village (1926 pop. 3,787), NW Kursk oblast, Russian SFSR, 14 mi. NE of Dmitriyev-Lgovski; woodworking. **5** Town, Moscow oblast, Russian SFSR: see KIMOVSK. **6** Village (1926 pop. 2,560), SW Maritime Territory, Russian SFSR, on Trans-Siberian RR (Dubininski station) and 10 mi. N of Voroshilov, in agr. area (grain, soybeans, sugar beets, rice); metalworks. **7** City (1926 pop. 12,944), central Stalingrad oblast, Russian SFSR, on railroad (Sebryakovo station), on Medveditsa R. and 105 mi. NW of Stalingrad; major flour-milling center; canning, meat packing, dairying; furniture mfg. Limestone quarrying; poultry farming. Became city in 1948. **8** Village (1926 pop. 11,339), E central Kamenets-Podolski oblast, Ukrainian SSR, 13 mi. SE of Proskurov; sugar beets, fruit. Until 1946, Mikhalpol. **9** Town (1939 pop. over 500), SW Voroshilovgrad oblast, Ukrainian SSR, in the Donbas, 4 mi. W of Voroshilovsk; coal mines. **10** Village (1926 pop. 17,519), W central Zaporozhe oblast, Ukrainian SSR, 35 mi. S of Zaporozhe; flour.

Mikhailovo or **Mikhaylovo** (mēkhī′lôvô), village (pop. 2,131), Stara Zagora dist., S central Bulgaria, 11 mi. ENE of Chirpan; rail junction; tobacco, cotton, vineyards. Formerly Gok-pala.

Mikhailovo, Georgian SSR: see KHASHURI.

Mikhailovsk, Turkmen SSR: see KRASNOVODSK.

Mikhailovskaya or **Mikhaylovskaya** (–lŭfskīŭ), village (1939 pop. over 500), NW Stalingrad oblast, Russian SFSR, on Khoper R. and 11 mi. NNW of Uryupinsk; fruit, wheat.

Mikhailovski or **Mikhaylovskiy** (–skē). **1** Town (1948 pop. over 2,000), SW Altai Territory, Russian SFSR, 10 mi. S of Mikhailovka; soda-extraction plant. **2** Town (1926 pop. 5,772), SW Sverdlovsk oblast, Russian SFSR, on small lake, near Ufa R., 75 mi. SSE of Nizhniye Sergi, on railroad; metallurgical center (steel); mfg. (aluminum sheet, paper), metalworking, charcoal burning, food processing. Developed prior to First World War. Until 1942, Mikhailovski Zavod.

Mikhailovski Khutor or **Mikhaylovskiy Khutor** (khōō′tŭr), town (1926 pop. 2,834), N Sumy oblast, Ukrainian SSR, 25 mi. N of Glukhov; rail junction; sugar refining.

Mikhailovskoye or **Mikhaylovskoye** (–skŭyŭ). **1** Village, Pskov oblast, Russian SFSR: see PUSHKINSKIYE GORY. **2** Village (1926 pop. 10,487), W Stavropol Territory, Russian SFSR, 5 mi. N of Stavropol; flour mill, metalworks.

Mikhalitch, Turkey: see KARACABEY.

Mikhalpol, Ukrainian SSR: see MIKHAILOVKA, Kamenets-Podolski oblast.

Mikhaltsi (mēkhäl′tsē), village (pop. 3,105), Gorna Oryakhovitsa dist., N Bulgaria, 4 mi. SE of Pavlikeni; grain, vineyards, truck.

Mikha Tskhakaya (mē′khŭ tsŭkhä′kīŭ), city (1939 pop. over 10,000), W Georgian SSR, in Mingrelia, on railroad and 32 mi. W of Kutaisi, in Colchis lowland; junction for rail spur to Poti; wine making, carpet mfg.; marlpits. Formerly Senaki or Akhal-Senaki.

Mikhayl-, in Rus. names: see MIKHAIL-.

Mikhaylovgrad, Bulgaria: see MIKHAILOVGRAD.

Mikhaylovo, Bulgaria: see MIKHAILOVO.

Mikhmoret or **Mikmoreth** (both: mēkhmōrĕt′), settlement (pop. 100), W Israel, in Plain of Sharon, on Mediterranean, 4 mi. SW of Hadera; fishing, fish breeding. Near by is agr. experimental station.

Mikhnevo (mēkhnyĕ′vŭ), village (1948 pop. over 2,000), S Moscow oblast, Russian SFSR, 22 mi. NNW of Kashira; rail junction; dairying.

Miki (mē′kē), town (pop. 14,585), Hyogo prefecture, S Honshu, Japan, 13 mi. NW of Kobe; rail terminus; agr. center (rice, wheat, fruit, flowers, poultry); woodworking, mfg. (soy sauce, paper products); sawmilling.

Mikindani (mēkēndä′nē), town (pop. c.4,000), SE Tanganyika, port on Mikindani Bay of Indian Ocean, 35 mi. SE of Lindi, near Mozambique border; 10°17′S 40°5′E. Ships sisal, millet, copra, mangrove bark. Construction of a new port on Mtwara lagoon just SE was begun c.1948 to serve peanut scheme at Nachingwa (100 mi. W); a rail link to Nachingwa was built at same time.

Mikir Hills (mē′kēr), isolated hills in Brahmaputra valley, central Assam, India, ENE of Shillong; c.65 mi. long, 40 mi. wide; rise to over 4,470 ft. Coal, hematite, and limestone deposits. Tea gardens (mostly N). Inhabited chiefly by tribal Mikirs. Area was constituted (1950), from parts of Nowgong and Sibsagar dists. having large Mikir elements, into an autonomous dist. (□ 4,174; pop. 128,531; ⊙ Diphu) of Assam.

Mikita (mēkē′tä), town (pop. 6,084), Tokushima prefecture, E Shikoku, Japan, on Philippine Sea, 20 mi. S of Tokushima; agr. center (rice, wheat, raw silk); fishing port.

Mikkabi (mēk′kä′bē), town (pop. 13,269), Shizuoka prefecture, central Honshu, Japan, on NW cove of L. Hamana, 10 mi. ENE of Toyohashi; agr. center (rice, citrus fruit).

Mikkaichi, Japan: see SAKURAI, Toyama prefecture.

Mikkeli (mĭk′kĕlē), Swedish *Sankt Michel* (sängkt″ mē′kŭl), county [Finnish *lääni*] (□ 6,748; including water area, □ 8,884; pop. 239,217), SE Finland; ⊙ Mikkeli. Almost ⅓ of area consists of lakes of the Saimaa and Päijänne systems. Surface is generally low and marshy. Fishing, grain growing, and stock raising are important. Industries include lumbering, timber processing, wood- and metalworking, machinery mfg. Minerals worked include granite, limestone, and graphite. Cities are Mikkeli, Savonlinna, and Heinola.

Mikkeli, Swedish *Sankt Michel*, city (pop. 16,475), ⊙ Mikkeli co., SE Finland, at head of W arm of L. Saimaa, 130 mi. NE of Helsinki; 61°40′N 27°15′E. Plywood mills, machine shops, granite quarries. Summer and winter-sports resort. Seat of Lutheran bishop. Has remains of 14th-cent. church (now mus.). Inc. 1838. Sometimes called Saint Michels or Saint Michael.

Mikmoreth, Israel: see MIKHMORET.

Mikolajki (mēkōwĭ′kē), Pol. *Mikołajki*, Ger. *Nikolaiken* (nē″kōlī′kŭn), town (1939 pop. 2,627; 1946 pop. 1,531) in East Prussia, after 1945 in Olsztyn prov., NE Poland, on L. Sniardwy, 50 mi. E of Allenstein (Olsztyn); lake fisheries; limestone quarrying.

Mikolajow, Ukrainian SSR: see NIKOLAYEV, Drogobych oblast.

Mikolongwe (mēkōlông′gwä), rail station, Southern Prov., Nyasaland, 10 mi. ESE of Limbe; tea, tobacco, cotton, corn, rice.

Mikolow (mēkô′wōōf), Pol. *Mikołów*, Ger. *Nikolai* (nē″kōlī′), town (pop. 12,824), Katowice prov., S Poland, 8 mi. SW of Katowice; brickworks, chemical factories, iron foundries, coal mines. During Second World War, under Ger. control, called Nikolei.

Mikomeseng (mēkōmä′sĕn), town (pop. 360), continental Sp. Guinea, near Fr. Cameroons border, 70 mi. NE of Bata; cacao, coffee. Also spelled Mikomesen.

Mikonos, Greece: see MYKONOS.

Mikoyan (mēkŭyän′), village (1926 pop. 1,580), central Armenian SSR, near the Eastern Arpa-Chai, 50 mi. ESE of Erivan; cotton, wheat. Until c.1935, Keshishkend.

Mikoyana, Imeni (ē′mĭnyē mēkŭyä′nŭ). **1** Town, Kirghiz SSR: see KARABALTY, town. **2** Town (1940 pop. over 500), Kamchatka oblast, Khabarovsk Territory, Russian SFSR, on Sea of Okhotsk, on S Kamchatka Peninsula, 20 mi. S of Ust-Bolsheretsk; fish cannery.

Mikoyanabad (mēkŭyä″nŭbät′), village (1948 pop. over 2,000), SW Stalinabad oblast, Tadzhik SSR, on Kafirnigan R. and 40 mi. SSW of Kurgan-Tyube; long-staple cotton; karakul sheep. Until c.1935, Kabadian.

Mikoyanovka (mēkŭyä′nŭfkŭ), town (1939 pop. over 500), S Kursk oblast, Russian SFSR, 14 mi. SW of Belgorod; sugar refinery.

Mikoyanovsk (mēkŭyä′nŭfsk), town (1949 pop. over 500), W Jewish Autonomous oblast, Khabarovsk Territory, Russian SFSR, 10 mi. SE of Obluchye, in Little Khingan Range; tin mining.

Mikoyan-Shakhar, Georgian SSR: see KLUKHORI.

Mikra Delos, Greece: see DELOS.

Mikropolis (mĭkrô′pôlĭs), town (pop. 3,169), Drama nome, Macedonia, Greece, 17 mi. WNW of Drama; tobacco, barley, cotton; wine. Formerly Karlikova.

Miks, Egypt: see MEX.

Mikstat (mēk′stät), Ger. *Mixstadt* (mĭk′shtät), town (1946 pop. 1,455), Poznan prov., W central Poland, 17 mi. SSW of Kalisz; trades in horses, cattle; flour milling.

Mikulasovice (mĭ′kōōlä″shôvĭtsĕ), Czech *Mikulášovice*, village (pop. 3,213), N Bohemia, Czechoslovakia, 26 mi. NNE of Usti nad Labem; rail junction; mfg. of cutlery, needles, buttons, carpeting.

Mikulczyce (mēkōōl-chĭ'tsĕ), Ger. *Klausberg* (klous'bĕrk), commune (1939 pop. 20,260; 1946 pop. 17,647) in Upper Silesia, after 1945 in Katowice prov., S Poland, 3 mi. N of Hindenburg (Zabrze); rail junction; coal mining. Until 1935, called Mikultschütz.

Mikulince, Ukrainian SSR: see MIKULINTSY.

Mikulintsy (mēkōō'lyĭntsē), Pol. *Mikulińce* (mēkōō-lyē'nyūtsĕ), town (1931 pop. 3,127), central Ternopol oblast, Ukrainian SSR, on Seret R. and 11 mi. S of Ternopol; agr.-trading center; food processing (pork, cheese, flour, honey), distilling (liquor, vinegar, beer), stone quarrying, brick mfg., lumbering. Has ruins of 16th-cent. castle. An old Pol. commercial town; assaulted by Turks in 17th cent. Passed to Austria (1772); reverted to Poland (1919); ceded to USSR in 1945.

Mikulov (mĭ'kōōlôf), Ger. *Nikolsburg* (nē'kôlsbōōrk), town (pop. 5,220), S Moravia, Czechoslovakia, on railroad and 18 mi. S of Brno, near Austrian border; textile mfg. Has old Jewish cemetery, picturesque castle. Extensive vineyards in vicinity. Peace treaty bet. Prussia and Austria signed here, 1866.

Mikultschütz, Poland: see MIKULCZYCE.

Mikun or **Mikun'** (mēkōōn'yù), town (1948 pop. over 500), W Komi Autonomous SSR, Russian SFSR, on Vychegda R., just SW of Aikino.

Mikuni (mēkōō'nē). **1** Town (pop. 10,599), Fukui prefecture, central Honshu, Japan, on Sea of Japan, 11 mi. NNW of Fukui; fishing port. Boatyards; mfg. (silk textiles, soy sauce), metalworking. **2** Town, Hokkaido, Japan: see BIKUNI.

Mikura-jima (mēkōōrä'jĭmä), island (□ 8; pop. 404) of isl. group Izu-shichito, Greater Tokyo, Japan, in Philippine Sea, 50 mi. NNW of Hachijo-jima; roughly circular, 3 mi. in diameter. Has central volcanic cone rising to 2,798 ft. Agr. (rice, wheat, sweet potatoes); raw silk.

Mikuriya (mēkōō'rēyä). **1** Town, Nagasaki prefecture, Japan: see SHIN-MIKURIYA. **2** Town (pop. 6,547), Tochigi prefecture, central Honshu, Japan, just S of Ashikaga; rice, silk textiles. **3** Town (pop. 2,776), Tottori prefecture, SW Honshu, Japan, on Sea of Japan, 11 mi. NE of Yonago; rice, wheat, raw silk. Produces sake, soy sauce, *konnyaku* (paste made from devil's tongue). Fishing.

Mikve Israel, Israel: see MIQVE YISRAEL.

Mila (mēlä'), anc. *Mileu*, village (pop. 4,747), Constantine dept., NE Algeria, 20 mi. WNW of Constantine, in cereal-growing region. Preserves walls built 6th cent. A.D. by Justinian.

Milaca (mĭlä'kù), village (pop. 1,917), Mille Lacs co., E Minn., on Rum R. and c.60 mi. NNW of Minneapolis; trading point in agr. area (grain, potatoes, livestock, poultry); dairy products, beverages. Settled 1888, inc. 1897.

Miladummadulu Atoll (mĭlŭdōōm'mŭdōō'lōō), N group (pop. 8,931) of Maldive Isls., in Indian Ocean, bet. 5°35'N and 6°30'N, just S of Tiladummati Atoll; coconuts.

Milagres (mēlä'grĭs), city (pop. 1,606), SE Ceará, Brazil, 40 mi. ESE of Crato; cheese mfg.; cotton, tobacco, livestock.

Milagro or **El Milagro** (ĕl mēlä'grō), town (pop. estimate 1,500), SE La Rioja prov., Argentina, on railroad and 45 mi. SW of Serrezuela (Córdoba prov.); stock raising (goats, cattle), lumbering.

Milagro, town (1950 pop. 16,081), Guayas prov., W central Ecuador, in tropical plain, on railroad to Quito, and 22 mi. ENE of Guayaquil; processing and trading center for fertile agr. center (sugar cane, rice, cacao, tropical fruit); sugar refining, rice milling. At its outskirts is the large San Carlos sugar refinery.

Milagro, town (pop. 2,700), Navarre prov., N Spain, on Aragon R. near its influx into the Ebro, and 15 mi. NW of Tudela; vegetable canning; cherries, sugar beets, alfalfa.

Milagros (mēlä'grōs), town (1939 pop. 1,248; 1948 municipality pop. 33,502), central Masbate isl., Philippines, at head of Asid Gulf, 13 mi. SW of Masbate town; agr. center (rice, coconuts). Near by are copper mines.

Milak (mĭl'ŭk), town (pop. 5,604), Rampur dist., N central Uttar Pradesh, India, 16 mi. SSE of Rampur; corn, wheat, rice, gram, millet, sugar cane.

Milakokia Lake (mĭlŭkō'kēù), Mackinac co., SE Upper Peninsula, Mich., 22 mi. NE of Manistique; c.3 mi. long, 1½ mi. wide.

Milam (mē'lŭm), village, Almora dist., N Uttar Pradesh, India, in E Kumaun Himalayas, on tributary of Kali (Sarda) R. and 65 mi. NNE of Almora; barley, buckwheat. Summer trade hq. of Tibetan Bhotiyas.

Milam (mī'lùm), county (□ 1,027; pop. 23,585), central Texas; ⊙ Cameron. Bounded E by Brazos R., drained by Little R. Diversified agr. (especially cotton; also corn, grain sorghums, truck); livestock (cattle, poultry, some sheep, goats); some dairying. Large lignite deposits planned (1951) to be used as power-producing fuel for aluminum plant. Oil wells; also peat, clay, mineral salts. Formed 1836.

Milan (mĭlăn'), Ital. *Milano* (mēlä'nô), anc. *Mediolanum*, city (pop. 1,068,079; metropolitan area pop. 1,115,548), N Italy, ⊙ Lombardy and Milano prov., on fertile, irrigated Po plain, bet. Adda and Ticino rivers, on Olona R. and 300 mi. NW of Rome; 45°28'N 9°11'E. Rail, highway, and canal center; 2d largest city of Italy and its chief center of industry, commerce, and banking. Leads in fields of textiles, printing and publishing, chemicals, photography, and metallurgy. Principal market for silk (in all Europe); also cereals, oilseeds, stock, fruit, and vegetables. Major products: airplanes, automobiles, motorcycles, locomotives, refrigerators, elevators, paper, rubber tires, machinery (textile, printing, mining, hydroelectric), precision instruments, explosives, pharmaceuticals, chemicals, paint, alcohol, soap, plastics, glass, silverware, furniture, leather goods, hats, food products. Archbishopric. Has white marble Gothic cathedral, one of largest and most famous in Europe (begun 1386; elaborately ornamented with over 100 pinnacles and thousands of statues). Chief medieval bldg. is Romanesque church of Saint Ambrose (founded 386; badly damaged in 1943). Several churches represent the work of Bramante. In one, Santa Maria delle Grazie (badly damaged) Leonardo da Vinci painted The Last Supper. The Brera palace (badly damaged) houses a picture gall., library, astronomical observatory, and inst. of fine arts. Other notable galleries and museums are located in the Borromeo (badly damaged), Poldi-Pezzoli palaces (largely destroyed), and Castello Sforzesco (badly damaged). The Ambrosian Library (damaged) is one of the richest and most famous in Europe. There are 2 universities. Hq. of Touring Club Italiano. Long a center of music and drama, it possesses an excellent conservatory (damaged) and the world-famous La Scala theater, rebuilt after being severely damaged by bombs. Of Celtic origin, Milan achieved importance under the Romans. From 374 to 379 Ambrose was its bishop; became religious center of N Italy. Destroyed by Huns (c.450) and Goths (539); conquered by Lombards in 569. Again destroyed in 1163 by Frederick Barbarossa. Later, as member of Lombard League, it helped defeat him (1176) near Legnano. Ruled by the Visconti from 1277 to 1447, and by their successors, the Sforza, until 1535. A period of Spanish and Austrian rule followed. Bonaparte made it capital of Cisalpine Republic (1797) and of kingdom of Italy (1805–14). Reverted to Austria and became a revolutionary center throughout the Risorgimento. United with kingdom of Sardinia in 1859; inc. into Italy in 1861. In Second World War severely damaged by air bombings, especially in 1943. Of its 930,000 residences, 360,000 were destroyed or gravely damaged.

Milan. **1** (mī'lùn) Town (pop. 750), Telfair and Dodge counties, S central Ga., 13 mi. SSE of Eastman. **2** (mī'lùn) Village (pop. 1,737), Rock Island co., NW Ill., on Rock R. (bridged), just S of Rock Island, in agr. and bituminous-coal-mining area. Black Hawk State Park is near by. Inc. 1893. **3** (mī'lùn, mĭlăn') Town (pop. 1,014), Ripley co., SE Ind., 42 mi. ESE of Shelbyville, in agr. area. **4** (mī'lùn) City (pop. 165), Sumner co., S Kansas, 15 mi. W of Wellington, near Chikaskia R.; wheat. **5** (mī'lùn) Village (pop. 2,768), on Washtenaw-Monroe co. line, SE Mich., 14 mi. SSE of Ann Arbor and on small Saline R., in farm area (beans, sugar beets). Mfg. (boilers, furnaces, auto parts, lumber, wood products). A Federal detention farm is near by. Inc. 1885. **6** (mĭlăn') Village (pop. 561), Chippewa co., SW Minn., near Lac qui Parle (in Minnesota R.), 14 mi. NW of Montevideo, in grain, livestock, and poultry area; dairy products. **7** (mī'lùn) City (pop. 1,972), ⊙ Sullivan co., N Mo., 28 mi. W of Kirksville; rail junction; truck, livestock. Laid out 1845. **8** (mī'lùn) Agr. town (pop. 743), Coos co., N N.H., on the Androscoggin just N of Berlin; stock farms. Includes West Milan, village on Upper Ammonoosuc R. **9** (mī'lùn) Village (pop. 846), Erie co., N Ohio, 12 mi. SSE of Sandusky, and on Huron R., in agr. area; clay and wood products, beer. Thomas A. Edison was b. here. Settled 1804 by Moravian missionaries. **10** (mī'lùn) Town (pop. 4,938), Gibson co., NW Tenn., 11 mi. ESE of Trenton; rail and road junction; shipping center in fruit, vegetable, cotton-growing region; mfg. of shirts, food cartons, rubber goods; cotton gins. U.S. arsenal here.

Milang, village (pop. 319), SE South Australia, 40 mi. SE of Adelaide and on W shore of L. Alexandrina; rail terminus; citrus and dried fruits.

Milange (mēläng'gā), village, Zambézia prov., central Mozambique, on Nyasaland border, on road to Blantyre (Nyasaland) and 140 mi. NW of Quelimane; tea-growing center.

Milano (mēlä'nô), province (□ 1,065; pop. 2,175,400), Lombardy, N Italy; ⊙ Milan. Comprises most of fertile Po plain lying bet. Adda and Ticino rivers; watered by Lambro and Olona rivers and by many irrigation canals. Most industrialized prov. of Italy, with textile, iron, metallurgical, printing and publishing, furniture, and chemical industries. Has many centers, including Milan, Monza, Sesto San Giovanni, Lodi, Legnano, Rho, and Abbiategrasso. Agr. (cereals, rice, raw silk, fruit, vegetables); large dairy industry. In 1927 area reduced to help form Varese prov.

Milano, city, Italy: see MILAN.

Milano (mùlă'nō), village (pop. c.500), Milam co., central Texas, 29 mi. W of Bryan; rail junction in cattle, cotton, corn area.

Milanovac or **Milanovats** (both: mēlä'nôväts). **1** or **Donji Milanovac** or **Donyi Milanovats** (dô'nyē), village (pop. 2,180), E Serbia, Yugoslavia, on the Danube (Rum. border) and 45 mi. ESE of Pozarevac; fishing. Connected with MAJDAN PEK (WSW) by aerial ropeway. **2** or **Gornji Milanovac** or **Gornyi Milanovats** (gôr'nyē), village (pop. 3,129), central Serbia, Yugoslavia, on railroad and 23 mi. W of Kragujevac.

Milas (mīlăs'), Turkish *Milâs*, anc. *Mylasa*, town (pop. 8,853), Mugla prov., SW Turkey, 32 mi. WNW of Mugla; tobacco, fruit, olives, cereals; rich emery deposits near by, with chromium and lignite. In anc. times a city of Caria noted for its buildings of white marble quarried near by.

Milatyn Nowy, Ukrainian SSR: see NOVY MILYATIN.

Milazzo (mēlät'tsô), anc. *Mylae*, town (pop. 10,378), Messina prov., NE Sicily, port on promontory extending into Gulf of Milazzo, 17 mi. WNW of Messina. Produces chemicals, soap, glass, wine, macaroni, flour. Tunny fishing. Exports citrus fruit, olive oil, wine. Steamer service to Lipari Isls. Has Norman castle (now a prison) built by Charles V. Founded 716 B.C. by colonists from Zancle (Messina). Harbor was scene of Roman naval victory over Carthaginians in 260 B.C. Garibaldi defeated Bourbons here in 1860. Bombed (1943) in Second World War.

Milazzo, Cape, NE Sicily, N headland of promontory separating gulfs of Milazzo and Patti; 38°16'N 15°14'E.

Milazzo, Gulf of, inlet of Tyrrhenian Sea in NE Sicily, bet. Cape Rasocolmo (E), and Cape Milazzo (W); 16 mi. long, 5 mi. wide; tunny fisheries. Chief port, Milazzo.

Milbank, city (pop. 2,982), ⊙ Grant co., NE S.Dak., 30 mi. NE of Watertown near Minn. line; shipping point for dairying region; cheese, butter, livestock, wheat, corn; granite quarries furnish material for gravestones and monuments.

Milborne Port, town and parish (pop. 1,655), SE Somerset, England, 3 mi. ENE of Sherborne; glove mfg.; dairying. Has 15th-cent. church.

Milbridge, town (pop. 1,199), Washington co., E Maine, 26 mi. E of Ellsworth, at mouth of the Narraguagus, and on Pleasant Bay; light mfg.; fishing, lumbering area. Inc. 1848. Formerly sometimes Millbridge.

Milburn (mĭl'bûrn), town (pop. 350), Johnston co., S Okla., on Blue R. and 20 mi. NNW of Durant.

Milcupaya (mēlkōōpī'ä), town (pop. c.6,900), Potosí dept., S central Bolivia, 9 mi. NE of Puna; truck, grain.

Milden, village (pop. 234), SW central Sask., 21 mi. E of Rosetown; wheat.

Mildenhall (mĭl'dùnhôl, mī'nôl), town and parish (pop. 3,235), NW Suffolk, England, on Lark R. and 8 mi. NE of Newmarket; agr. market; flour mills. Site of Royal Air Force station. Has 15th-cent. market cross. A Roman station was here.

Mildmay, village (pop. 771), S Ont., 7 mi. SSE of Walkerton; dairying, lumbering.

Mildred, city (pop. 79), Allen co., SE Kansas, 14 mi. NE of Iola; livestock, grain; dairying.

Mildura (mĭldū'rù), municipality (pop. 9,527), NW Victoria, Australia, on Murray R. (here dammed) and 210 mi. ENE of Adelaide, on New South Wales border; commercial, irrigation center for sheep-raising, agr. area. Flour mill, fruit and vegetable canneries, brickyards; wool, butter, dried fruit, wheat.

Mileai, Greece: see MELEAI.

Miles. **1** Town (pop. 344), Jackson co., E Iowa, 18 mi. E of Maquoketa; livestock, grain. **2** Town (pop. 739), Runnels co., W central Texas, 17 mi. NE of San Angelo, near Concho R.; market point in cattle, grain, cotton, dairying area.

Miles, Fort, Del.: see HENLOPEN, CAPE.

Milesburg, borough (pop. 733), Centre co., central Pa., 2 mi. N of Bellefonte and on Bald Eagle Creek.

Miles City, city (pop. 9,243), ⊙ Custer co., SE Mont., on Yellowstone R., at mouth of Tongue R., and 140 mi. ENE of Billings, in irrigated area; trade center, shipping point for wool, livestock; railroad shops; gas wells; saddles and other leather goods, flour, dairy and meat products; sugar beets, grain. Near-by Fort Keogh (built 1877) has been rebuilt and, with former military reservation, is used as livestock experiment station. Rodeo and fair take place annually. Inc. 1887.

Miles Glacier, in Chugach Mts., S Alaska, N of Martin River Glacier; 60°40'N 144°45'W; flows into Copper R. ENE of Cordova.

Miles Platting, NE suburb (pop. 24,564) of Manchester, SE Lancashire, England; textile milling, engineering, leather tanning, mfg. of chemicals, soap, paint, asbestos.

Miles River, E Md., irregular estuary (c.20 mi. long) entering Eastern Bay (arm of Chesapeake Bay) in Talbot co.; navigable for c.16 mi.

Milestone, town (pop. 395), S Sask., 32 mi. S of Regina, in the rich prairie region; grain elevators, lumbering.

Mileto (mēlä'tô), town (pop. 3,797), Catanzaro prov., Calabria, S Italy, 5 mi. SSW of Vibo Valentia; agr. trade center (cereals, olives, grapes, citrus fruit). Bishopric. Has cathedral (built 1928–29), seminary, meteorological and seismological observatory. Severely damaged by earthquake in 1905. Roger II b. here.

Miletus (mīlē'tùs), anc. seaport of W Asia Minor, in Caria, on the mainland SE of Samos, near mouth of the Maeander (modern Buyuk Menderes), in modern Turkey. Occupied by Greeks c.1000 B.C. and became one of principal cities of Ionia. From 8th cent. B.C. it led in colonization, especially on the Black Sea. In 499 B.C. the Milesians stirred up the revolt of Ionian Greeks against Persia, who sacked the city in 494 B.C. Although less flourishing, Miletus remained an important port until the harbor silted up early in Christian era. Thales, Anaximander, and Aspasia b. here.

Milevo Mountains (mē'lĕvô), in Krajiste highland, on Bulg.-Yugoslav border; extend c.35 mi. bet. Rui Mts. (N) and Osogov Mts. (S); rise to 5,686 ft. at Milevets peak (mē'lĕvĕts), 27 mi. W of Radomir, Bulgaria.

Milevsko (mĭ'lĕfskô), Ger. *Mühlhausen* (mül'houzùn), town (pop. 3,182), S Bohemia, Czechoslovakia, on railroad and 14 mi. WNW of Tabor, in rye and timber region. Has old abbey with Romanesque church.

Miley, Fort, Calif.: see SAN FRANCISCO.

Milford, town and parish (pop. 1,181), central Derby, England, on Derwent R. just S of Belper; cotton milling.

Milford or **Millford,** Gaelic *Baile na nGallóglach,* town (pop. 297), N Co. Donegal, Ireland, 9 mi. NNE of Letterkenny; agr. market (flax, oats, potatoes; cattle, sheep).

Milford. 1 Town (pop. 26,870), including Woodmont village (1940 pop. 748), New Haven co., SW Conn., on Long Isl. Sound, at mouth of the Housatonic, and 6 mi. E of Bridgeport. Woodmont and Devon (pop. 6,726) are resorts; yachting at Milford Harbor. Agr. (seeds, potatoes, truck, hay, dairy products), mfg. (metal products, hardware, tools, dies, elastic goods); oysters. Many old buildings extant. Settled 1639. **2** City (pop. 5,179), Kent and Sussex counties, E Del., 18 mi. SSE of Dover and at head of navigation on Mispillion R., which divides city into North and South Milford. Trade and shipping center in truck-farming area; boatbuilding, canning, mfg. (dental supplies, wood products). Has several 18th-cent. bldgs. Inc. 1867. **3** Village (pop. 1,648), Iroquois co., E Ill., 35 mi. N of Danville; trade and shipping center in agr. area (grain, soybeans, livestock, poultry; dairy products); canned foods. Settled c.1830, platted 1836, inc. 1874. **4** Town (pop. 175), Decatur co., SE central Ind., 7 mi. W of Greensburg. Post office name, Clifty. **5** Town (pop. 952), Kosciusko co., N Ind., near Wawasee L. (resort), 27 mi. SE of South Bend; makes furniture, leather. **6** Town (pop. 1,375), Dickinson co., NW Iowa, 13 mi. N of Spencer, near Okoboji lakes and Little Sioux R.; agr. trade center and summer resort; wood products. Founded 1869, inc. 1892. **7** City (pop. 284), Geary co., NE central Kansas, on Republican R. and 11 mi. NNW of Junction City; livestock, grain. **8** Town (pop. 1,435), Penobscot co., S central Maine, on the Penobscot opposite Old Town; light mfg., hunting, fishing. **9** Town (pop. 15,442), including Milford village (pop. 14,396), Worcester co., S Mass., 17 mi. SE of Worcester; shoes, metal products, rubberized fabric; granite; dairying, truck. Settled 1662, inc. 1780. **10** Village (pop. 1,924), Oakland co., SE Mich., 16 mi. WSW of Pontiac and on Huron R. Mfg. (auto parts, machinery). The General Motors proving ground is near by. Inc. 1869. **11** Village (pop. 951), Seward co., SE Nebr., 20 mi. W of Lincoln and on Big Blue R.; dairy and poultry produce, grain. Soldiers' and sailors' home, state industrial home for women here. **12** Town (pop. 4,159), including Milford village (pop. 3,269), Hillsboro co., S N.H., on the Souhegan and 10 mi. NW of Nashua; mfg. (textiles, lumber products) in agr. area; granite quarries. Set off 1794. **13** Borough (pop. 1,012), Hunterdon co., W N.J., on Delaware R. and 10 mi. SE of Phillipsburg; paper mill; agr. (poultry, truck, grain, dairy products). **14** Village (pop. 502), Otsego co., central N.Y., on the Susquehanna and 11 mi. NNE of Oneonta, in dairying area. **15** Village (pop. 2,448), on Clermont-Hamilton co. line, SW Ohio, 14 mi. E of downtown Cincinnati and on Little Miami R.; makes burial vaults, hosp. supplies, wood products, toys. **16** Agr. borough (pop. 1,111), ⊙ Pike co., NE Pa., on Delaware R. and 7 mi. SW of Port Jervis, N.Y.; summer resort. Settled 1733. **17** Town (pop. 690), Ellis co., N central Texas, c.45 mi. SSW of Dallas; rail point in cotton, grain, cattle area. **18** Town (pop. 1,673), Beaver co., SW Utah, on Beaver R. and 21 mi. WNW of Beaver; alt. 4,958 ft. Railroad div. point and trade center for dairying and irrigated agr. area (alfalfa, peas). Ships livestock. Lead, silver, gold, copper mines near by. Settled 1880, inc. 1903. **19** Village, Caroline co., Va.: see BOWLING GREEN.

Milford Center, village (pop. 753), Union co., central Ohio, 27 mi. WNW of Columbus, and on Darby Creek, in agr. area.

Milford Haven, urban district (1931 pop. 10,104; 1951 census 11,717), S Pembroke, Wales, on Milford Haven inlet of Atlantic, 6 mi. WNW of Pembroke; 51°43'N 5°1'W; fishing port. Of considerable maritime importance in Middle Ages, it was until 1814 site of a royal dockyard. In 1485 Henry VII landed here from France. Urban dist. includes Hakin (W; pop. 2,689).

Milford Haven, inlet of the Atlantic, S Pembroke, Wales, forming a fine harbor; extends 12 mi. E from St. Anne's Head; 1–2 mi. wide. The short Eastern and Western Cleddau rivers enter it. Chief ports: Milford Haven, Pembroke Dock, Neyland.

Milford-on-Sea, town and parish (pop. 2,374), SW Hampshire, England, on the Channel, 15 mi. SW of Southampton; seaside resort. Has Norman church. On The Solent, 2 mi. ESE, is 16th-cent. Hurst Castle (built by Henry VIII as coastal defense), where Charles I was imprisoned in 1648.

Milford Sound, inlet of Tasman Sea, Fiordland Natl. Park, SW S.Isl., New Zealand; 12 mi. long, 2 mi. wide; surrounded by mts.; Mitre Peak (5,560 ft.) and Pembroke Peak (6,710 ft.) are highest.

Milgravis (mēl'grävēs), Lettish *Milgrāvis,* Ger. *Mühlgraben* (mül'gräbùn), outer port of Riga, Latvia, on right bank of the Western Dvina, 3 mi. from Gulf of Riga, and 6 mi. N of Riga city center.

Milhau, France: see MILLAU.

Milhaud (mēlō'), village (pop. 1,038), Gard dept., S France, 4 mi. SW of Nîmes; winegrowing.

Mili (mē'lē), southernmost atoll (□ 6; pop. 272), Ratak Chain, Majuro dist., Marshall Isls., W central Pacific, 325 mi. SE of Kwajalein; 6°10'N 171°55'E; c.30 mi. long; 102 islets. Jap. air base in Second World War. Formerly Mulgrave Isls.

Milia, El- (ĕl-mēlyä'), village (pop. 797), Constantine dept., NE Algeria, on the Oued el Kebir and 34 mi. NW of Constantine; cork stripping; lead and zinc mining.

Miliana (mēlyänä'), town (pop. 5,717), Alger dept., NW Algeria, on S slope of the Djebel Zaccar, overlooking the Chéliff valley, 55 mi. SW of Algiers; situated at 2,400 ft. amidst fruit orchards and citrus groves, it is also noted for its table grapes and wines. Commercial importance lost to Affreville (4 mi. S) located in lowland along railroad. Iron mined on Djebel Zaccar. Founded probably in 10th cent. on site of Roman *Zucchabar.* Occupied by French in 1840, and besieged by Abd-el-Kader until 1842. Town is surrounded by walls pierced by 2 gates. Magnificent panorama from the esplanade. Teachers col.

Miliane River (mēlyän'), N central and N Tunisia, rises 8 mi. NE of Siliana, flows c.80 mi. NE, past Pont-du-Fahs, to the Gulf of Tunis at Maxula-Radès 6 mi. ESE of Tunis. Its waters are diverted for the irrigation of Mornag lowland.

Milicz (mē'lēch), Ger. *Militsch* (mē'lĭch), town (1939 pop. 5,390; 1946 pop. 2,929), in Lower Silesia, after 1945 in Wroclaw prov., SW Poland, on Barycz R. and 30 mi. NNE of Breslau (Wroclaw); linen milling. Has remains of old castle of prince-bishops of Breslau. First mentioned 1136; chartered c.1300. Considerably damaged in Second World War.

Milieu, Pic du, NE Spain: see MALADETTA.

Milig (mĭlēg') or **Milij** (mĭlēj'), village (pop. 11,465), Minufiya prov., Lower Egypt, on the Bahr Shibin and 4 mi. NE of Shibin el Kom; cereals, cotton, flax.

Milis (mē'lēs), village (pop. 1,357), Cagliari prov., W Sardinia, 10 mi. N of Oristano, in orchard (oranges, lemons, tangerines) area; dried herbs.

Mili Steppe, Azerbaijan SSR: see KURA LOWLAND.

Militari (mēlētä'ry), outer W suburb (pop. 15,492) of Bucharest, Bucharest prov., S Rumania, on right bank of Dambovita R.; dairying.

Militello in Val di Catania (mēlētĕl'lō ēn väl dē kätä'nyä) or **Militello,** town (pop. 11,138), Catania prov., E Sicily, 16 mi. ENE of Caltagirone, in cereal-growing region; olive oil. Rebuilt after earthquake of 1693.

Militsch, Poland: see MILICZ.

Miljacka River or **Milyatska River** (both: mē'lyätskä), river, S Bosnia, Yugoslavia, rises in 2 headstreams joining 4 mi. SE of Sarajevo, flows c.15 mi. W, past Sarajevo, to Bosna R. 3 mi. N of Ilidza.

Milje, Free Territory of Trieste: see MUGGIA.

Milkovitsa (mēlkôvē'tsä), village (pop. 3,576), Pleven dist., N Bulgaria, 4 mi. SSW of Somovit; grain, livestock, truck. Formerly Gavren or Gaurene.

Milkovo or **Mil'kovo** (mēl'kùvù), village (1947 pop. over 500), Kamchatka oblast, Khabarovsk Territory, Russian SFSR, on S central Kamchatka Peninsula, on Kamchatka R. (head of shallow-draught navigation), and 115 mi. N of Petropavlovsk, in agr. area.

Milk River, village (pop. 437), S Alta., near Mont. border, on Milk R. and 50 mi. SW of Lethbridge; coal mining, mixed farming, ranching.

Milk River, S Jamaica, rises N of Porus, flows c.20 mi. S, past village of Milk River (spa), to the Caribbean. Abounds in fish. Navigable for 2 mi. upstream.

Milk River, in Canada and Mont., rises in 2 branches E of St. Mary and Lower St. Mary lakes in NW Mont., near Continental Divide, joining in S Alta.; flows E, re-entering Mont. at long. 110°35'W, thence generally SE and E, past Havre, Malta, and Glasgow to Missouri R. near Fort Peck Dam. Milk R. irrigation project (established 1911) includes Fresno Dam (111 ft. high, 2,070 ft. long) near Havre, creating Fresno Reservoir, and another near Malta, creating Nelson Reservoir. These and future developments are part of Missouri R. Basin plan. Main stream is 625 mi. long; length including S.Fork, 729 mi. Not navigable.

Millaa Millaa, village (pop. 510), NE Queensland, Australia, 40 mi. S of Cairns; rail terminus; sugar.

Milladore, village (pop. 247), Wood co., central Wis., 14 mi. N of Wisconsin Rapids, in dairy belt; rail junction.

Millanes, Los, Venezuela: see LOS MILLANES.

Millard (mĭ'lùrd), county (□ 6,648; pop. 9,387), W Utah; ⊙ Fillmore. Agr. area bordering on Nev. and watered by Sevier R. and Sevier L. Irrigated lands around Delta produce alfalfa seed and wheat. Fishlake Natl. Forest and Pavant Mts. in E, semiarid region in W. Co. formed 1852.

Millard, village (pop. 391), Douglas co., E Nebr., 10 mi. W of Omaha; farm trade center in rich agr. region.

Millares (mīyä'rĕs), town (pop. c.1,100), Potosí dept., S central Bolivia, on Mataca R. (branch of the Pilcomayo) and 38 mi. ENE of Potosí; orchards. Until 1900s, Llanta Apacheta.

Millares (mēlyä'rĕs), town (pop. 1,346), Valencia prov., E Spain, on Turia R. and 20 mi. WNW of Alcira; olive oil, wine, sheep.

Millas (mēyäs'), village (pop. 1,941), Pyrénées-Orientales dept., S France, on the Têt and 10 mi. W of Perpignan; wine trade; alcohol distilling, olive-oil processing, fruit and vegetable shipping.

Millau (mēyō'), anc. *Aemilianum,* town (pop. 15,891), Aveyron dept., S France, bet. Causse Noir (NE) and Causse du Larzac (S), on Tarn R. at mouth of the Dourbie, and 30 mi. SE of Rodez; leading glove-mfg. center; tanneries, furniture and woolen-textile factories. Trade in Roquefort cheese. Has 14th–16th-cent. church and a Gothic belfry. A Huguenot stronghold (16th cent.), its walls were demolished by Louis XIII. Formerly Milhau.

Millbank, village (pop. estimate 450), S Ont., on tributary of Nith R. and 18 mi. WNW of Kitchener; dairying, mixed farming.

Millboro, village, Bath co., W Va., in the Alleghenies, 12 mi. E of Hot Springs, in resort area. Millboro Spring village (sawmilling) is 2 mi. NW and on Cowpasture R.

Millboro Spring, Va.: see MILLBORO.

Millbourne, borough (pop. 901), Delaware co., SE Pa., W suburb of Philadelphia.

Millbrae (mĭl'brā), city (pop. 8,972), San Mateo co., W Calif., on San Francisco Bay, 13 mi. S of San Francisco; residential; has large dairies, nurseries. Inc. 1948.

Millbridge, Maine: see MILBRIDGE.

Millbrook, village (pop. 751), S Ont., 15 mi. SW of Peterborough; lumbering, dairying, mixed farming.

Millbrook. 1 Town (pop. 2,546) in Stalybridge urban dist., NE Cheshire, England, near Tame R., cotton, woolen milling. **2** Fishing village and parish (pop. 1,840), SE Cornwall, England, on inlet of Tamar R. and 4 mi. WS of Plymouth. **3** Town and parish (pop. 2,299), S Hampshire, England, on Test R. estuary, 3 mi. W of Southampton.

Millbrook. 1 Village, Plymouth co., Mass.: see DUXBURY. **2** Residential and resort village (pop. 1,568), Dutchess co., SE N.Y., 12 mi. NE of Poughkeepsie, in dairying and poultry- and stock-raising area. An artists' colony. Bennett Jr. Col., and Millbrook School for boys are here. Inc. 1896.

Millburn, residential township (pop. 14,560), Essex co., NE N.J., on Rahway and Passaic rivers and 7 mi. W of Newark; mfg. (metal and wood products). Includes Short Hills, with wealthy estates. Settled c.1725, inc. 1857.

Millbury. 1 Town (pop. 8,347), Worcester co., S Mass., on Blackstone R. and 6 mi. SSE of Worcester; woolens, textile supplies, wire, tools, castings. Settled 1716, inc. 1813. Includes village of West Millbury. **2** Village (pop. 482), Wood co., NW Ohio, 9 mi. SE of Toledo.

Mill City, town (pop. 1,792), in Linn and Marion counties, W Oregon, on North Santiam R. and 30 mi. ESE of Salem in grain, fruit, and dairying area; lumber milling, wood products. Inc. 1947.

Mill Creek. 1 Village (pop. 127), Union co., S Ill., 24 mi. N of Cairo, in Ill. Ozarks. **2** Town (pop. 299), Johnston co., S Okla., 26 mi. SSW of Ada; cotton ginning; sand quarrying. **3** Residential borough (pop. 417), Huntingdon co., central Pa., 5 mi. SE of Huntingdon and on Juniata R. **4** Town (pop. 800), Randolph co., E W.Va., on Tygart R. and 15 mi. SSW of Elkins.

Mill Creek. 1 In N Calif., rises in Lassen Volcanic Natl. Park in Shasta co., flows c.50 mi. SW to Sacramento R. near Tehama. **2** In W central Ind., rises in W Hendricks co., flows c.50 mi. SW and NW to Eel R. in SW Putnam co.

Milldale, Conn.: see SOUTHINGTON.

Millecoquins Lake (mĭlùkō'kĭnz, –kĭn), Mackinac co., SE Upper Peninsula, Mich., c.40 mi. ENE of Manistique; c.2½ mi. long, 1½ mi. wide; resort.

Milledgeville (mĭl'lĭjvĭl). **1** City (pop. 8,835), ⊙ Baldwin co., central Ga., 29 mi. NE of Macon, at head of navigation on Oconee R.; trade and processing center for cotton and clay area; mfg. (tile, brick, clothing, candy, lumber). Ga. State Col. for Women, Ga. Military (jr.) col., Ina Dillard Russell Library (with Ga. History Mus.) and many fine ante-bellum houses are here. State institutions include a reform school, prison, and mental hosp. Laid out 1803 as site of the state capital and was seat of govt. 1804–67. Inc. 1836. **2** Village (pop. 1,044), Carroll co., NW Ill., 12 mi. NNW of Sterling, in rich agr. area; makes cheese. **3** Village (pop. 208), Fayette co., S central Ohio, 9 mi. WNW of Washington Court House.

Mille Îles River or **Milles Îles River** (mēl ēl'), S Que., branch of Ottawa R., flowing from L. of the Two Mountains NE along shore of Jesus Isl. to the St. Lawrence. Also Mille Isles.

Mille Lacs (mĭl" lăk', –lăks'), county (□ 568; pop. 15,165), E central Minn.; ⊙ Princeton. Resort and agr. area drained by Rum R. Dairy products, livestock, poultry, potatoes; peat. Large part of the lake Mille Lacs and Mille Lacs Lake Indian Reservation in N. Formed 1857.

Mille Lacs, Lac des (läk dā mēl läk'), lake (□ 102), NW Ont., 60 mi. WNW of Port Arthur; 18 mi. long, 12 mi. wide; alt. 1,496 ft. Drains SW into Rainy L.

Mille Lacs Lake (mĭl" lăk', –lăks') (□ 197), in Aitkin and Mille Lacs counties, E central Minn., E of Brainerd; 18 mi. long, 14 mi. wide. Mille Lacs Indian Reservation is on SW shore. Lake is tourist and vacation center with numerous boating, bathing, and fishing resorts. Drains into Rum R. and several small lakes. Was visited (1679) by Sieur Duluth. Villages of Wahkon and Isle are on SE shore.

Millen, city (pop. 3,449), ⊙ Jenkins co., E Ga., on Ogeechee R. and c.45 mi. S of Augusta; mfg. (lumber, veneer, fertilizer). Magnolia Spring state Park near by. Settled early 1830s, inc. 1881.

Miller. 1 County (□ 627; pop. 32,614), extreme SW Ark.; ⊙ TEXARKANA. Bounded W by Texas, S by La., E and N by Red R.; drained by Sulphur R. Agr. (cotton, oats, truck, livestock; dairy products). Timber; oil. Mfg. at Texarkana. Formed 1874. **2** County (□ 287; pop. 9,023), SW Ga.; ⊙ Colquitt. Coastal plain agr. (corn, peanuts, sugar, cane, truck, livestock) and forestry (lumber, naval stores) area drained by Spring Creek. Formed 1856. **3** County (□ 603; pop. 13,734), central Mo.; ⊙ Tuscumbia. In Ozark region; drained by Osage R. Tourist area; agr. (corn, wheat), livestock, especially dairy; barite mines. Formed 1837.

Miller. 1 Town (pop. 615), Lawrence co., SW Mo., in the Ozarks, near Spring R., 30 mi. W of Springfield; agr., flour mills. **2** Village (pop. 179), Buffalo co., S central Nebr., 23 mi. NW of Kearney and on Wood R. **3** City (pop. 1,916), ⊙ Hand co., central S.Dak., 70 mi. ENE of Pierre and on Turtle Creek; farm trade center; dairy products, livestock, grain. Settled 1882, inc. as city 1910.

Miller, Mount (11,000 ft.), S Alaska, in Chugach Mts. 30 mi. NNE of Cape Yakataga; 60°28'N 142°14'W.

Miller City, village (pop. 144), Putnam co., NW Ohio, 17 mi. SE of Defiance.

Miller Field, N.Y.: see STATEN ISLAND.

Mille Roches (mēl rôsh'), village (pop. estimate 750), SE Ont., on Cornwall Canal and 5 mi. W of Cornwall; dairying, mixed farming.

Millerovo (mē'lyĭrŭvŭ), city (1926 pop. 12,822), NW Rostov oblast, Russian SFSR, 120 mi. NNE of Rostov; rail junction (repair shops); agr. center; machine mfg., oilseed and flour milling. Became city in 1926. During Second World War, held (1942–43) by Germans.

Miller Peak (9,445 ft.), SE Ariz., highest in Huachuca Mts., near Mex. line, 11 mi. S of Fort Huachuca.

Millersburg. 1 Village, on Bond-Madison co. line, Ill.: see PIERRON. **2** Town (pop. 437), Elkhart co., N Ind., 17 mi. SE of Elkhart. **3** Town (pop. 200), Iowa co., E central Iowa, 37 mi. SW of Cedar Rapids, in agr. area. **4** Town (pop. 828), Bourbon co., N central Ky., 8 mi. NE of Paris, in Bluegrass region. Millersburg Military Inst. is here. **5** Village (pop. 281), Presque Isle co., NE Mich., 13 mi. SW of Rogers City and on short Ocqueoc R., in farm area. **6** Village (pop. 2,398), ⊙ Holmes co., central Ohio, 32 mi. SW of Canton, and on Killbuck Creek, in agr. area; dairy products, furniture, burial vaults. Coal mines, gravel pits, sandstone quarries. Settled 1816, laid out 1824. **7** Borough (pop. 2,861), Dauphin co., central Pa., 20 mi. NNW of Harrisburg and on Susquehanna R.; shoes, metal products, clothing; agr. Settled c.1790, laid out 1807, inc. 1850.

Miller's Dale, town in Wormhill parish (pop. 1,631), NW Derby, England, on Wye R. and 5 mi. E of Buxton; cotton milling and limestone quarrying. Just W is agr. village of Wormhill.

Millers Falls, village (pop. 1,134) in Erving and Montague towns, Franklin co., NW Mass., on Millers R. and 5 mi. E of Greenfield; tool mfg.

Millers Mills, resort village, Herkimer co., central N.Y., 15 mi. SSE of Utica, on Little Unadilla L.

Millersport, village (pop. 605), Fairfield co., central Ohio, 24 mi. E of Columbus, near Buckeye L. (resort), in agr. area.

Millers River, N Mass., rises in N Worcester co., flows c.60 mi. SW and W, furnishing water power to mfg. towns, to the Connecticut c.5 mi. E of Greenfield.

Millerstown. 1 Borough (pop. 1,172), Butler co., W Pa., 10 mi. NE of Butler; wood products; bituminous coal; agr. Post office is Chicora (chĭkô'rŭ). Inc. 1855. **2** Agr. borough (pop. 682), Perry co., central Pa., 25 mi. NW of Harrisburg and on Juniata R.

Millersville, borough (pop. 2,551), Lancaster co., SE Pa., 4 mi. SW of Lancaster. State teachers col. here. Inc. 1932.

Millerton, New Zealand: see WESTPORT.

Millerton. 1 Town (pop. 140), Wayne co., S Iowa, 12 mi. S of Chariton; livestock, grain. **2** Village (pop. 1,048), Dutchess co., SE N.Y., near Conn. line, 28 mi. NE of Poughkeepsie, in dairying and poultry area; mfg. (meat products, textiles, construction materials). **3** Village (pop. c.250), McCurtain co., SE Okla., 30 mi. E of Hugo. Seat of Wheelock Acad. (1832), a U.S. school for Indians.

Millerton Lake, Calif.: see FRIANT DAM.

Miller Valley, suburb (pop. 2,953) of Prescott, Yavapai co., central Ariz.

Millerville, village (pop. 173), Douglas co., W Minn., 16 mi NW of Alexandria, in lake region; grain, livestock. Inspiration Peak State Park is near by.

Milles Îles River, Que.: see MILLE ÎLES RIVER.

Millésimo (mēlāsēmō'), village (pop. 1,029), Constantine dept., NE Algeria, on railroad and 2 mi. E of Guelma; wine, truck, olives.

Millesimo (mēl-lā'zēmô), village (pop. 1,748), Savona prov., Liguria, NW Italy, on Bormida di Millesimo R. and 14 mi. WNW of Savona; limekilns. Noted for victory of Napoleon over Austrians in April, 1796.

Millet (mĭ'lĭt), village (pop. 348), central Alta., 30 mi. S of Edmonton; coal mining.

Millevaches, Plateau of (mēlvăsh'), tableland of Massif Central, central France, in Corrèze and Creuse depts., forming France's central watershed, dividing Loire and Garonne R. drainage. Rises to c.3,200 ft. at Mont Bessou.

Millfield, village (1940 pop. 681), Athens co., SE Ohio, 8 mi. N of Athens, in coal region. Mine disaster here (1930) killed 82 men.

Millford, Co. Donegal, Ireland: see MILFORD.

Mill Grove, town (1940 pop. 139), Mercer co., N Mo., on Weldon R. and 7 mi. S of Princeton.

Mill Hall, borough (pop. 1,677), Clinton co., N central Pa., 2 mi. SW of Lock Haven; electric fixtures. Laid out 1806, inc. 1850.

Millheim (mĭl'hīm), agr. borough (pop. 750), Centre co., central Pa., 16 mi. E of Bellefonte; hosiery, flour; timber.

Mill Hill, England: see HENDON.

Millhousen (mĭl'houzŭn), town (pop. 184), Decatur co., SE central Ind., 29 mi. SE of Shelbyville, in agr. area.

Millicent, town (pop. 1,654), SE South Australia, 210 mi. SSE of Adelaide, NW of Mt. Gambier; sheep, grain. Paper mill near by.

Milligan, village (pop. 367), Fillmore co., SE Nebr., 10 mi. E of Geneva and on branch of Big Blue R.; flour; grain.

Milligan College, town (pop. 213), Carter co., NE Tenn., 4 mi. ESE of Johnson City. Milligan Col. (1881) here.

Milliken (mĭ'lĭkŭn), town (pop. 510), Weld co., N Colo., near S.Platte R., 40 mi. N of Denver; alt. 4,760 ft.; beet sugar, beans.

Milliken Park, town in Kilbarchan parish, central Renfrew, Scotland, just N of Johnstone; paper milling.

Millington. 1 Village, Middlesex co., Conn.: see EAST HADDAM. **2** Village (pop. 270), on Kendall-La Salle co. line, NE Ill., on Fox R. (bridged here) and 20 mi. SW of Aurora, in rich agr. area. **3** Town (pop. 356), Kent and Queen Annes counties, E Md., 18 mi. WNW of Dover, Del., at head of navigation on Chester R., in truck-farm area. **4** Village (pop. 1,043), Tuscola co., E Mich., 23 mi. SE of Saginaw, in agr. area (potatoes, beans, wheat). **5** Village (1940 pop. 643), Morris co., N central N.J., on Passaic R. and 8 mi. SSW of Morristown; asbestos products, fireworks. **6** Town (pop. 4,696), Shelby co., SW Tenn., 15 mi. NE of Memphis, in cotton, dairying, livestock area.

Millinocket (mĭl"lĭnŏ'kĭt), town (pop. 5,890), Penobscot co., central Maine, on West Branch of Penobscot R. and c.55 mi. N of Bangor; developed around paper mills built here 1899–1900. Inc. 1901. Millinocket L. (c.6 mi. wide) and Mt. Katahdin are NW.

Millinocket Lake, Piscataquis co., N central Maine, 43 mi. NNW of Millinocket, in lumbering, recreational area; 3 mi. long. Winter-sports area here.

Millis, town (pop. 2,551), Norfolk co., E Mass., on Charles R. and 20 mi. SW of Boston; beverages, asphalt roofing, shoes. Settled 1657, inc. 1885.

Mill Island (c.10 naut. mi. long), off Antarctica, W of Bowman Isl., N of Queen Mary Coast; 65°9'S 101°15'E. Discovered 1936 by Br. expedition.

Mill Island (20 mi. long, 14 mi. wide), SE Franklin Dist., Northwest Territories, in Hudson Strait, at S end of Foxe Channel; 63°59'N 78°W.

Millmerran (mĭlmĕ'rŭn), village (pop. 761), SE Queensland, Australia, 110 mi. WSW of Brisbane rail terminus; wheat.

Mill Neck, residential village (pop. 505), Nassau co., SE N.Y., on N shore of Long Isl., on an inlet of Oyster Bay Harbor, 2 mi. NW of Oyster Bay village.

Millom (mĭ'lŭm), former urban district (1931 pop 7,405), S Cumberland, England, on Duddon R estuary and 7 mi. NNW of Barrow-in-Furness; iron mining and smelting, limestone quarrying, wool weaving. Has remains of 14th-cent. castle.

Millport, burgh (1931 pop. 2,083; 1951 census 2,012), Buteshire, Scotland, on S coast of Great Cumbrae, 4 mi. SW of Largs, Ayrshire; fishing port resort. Has 19th-cent. Cathedral of Argyll and the Isles. Site of marine biological station.

Millport. 1 Town (pop. 682), Lamar co., W Ala., 38 mi. NW of Tuscaloosa; lumber. **2** Village (pop 362), Chemung co., S N.Y., 12 mi. N of Elmira, in agr. area.

Mill River, village, Mass.: see NEW MARLBORO.

Mill River. 1 In SW Conn., rises W of Monroe, flows c.17 mi. S to Long Isl. Sound, forming harbor at Fairfield. **2** In W central Mass., rises in ponds in N Hampshire co., flows c.25 mi. SE to the Connecticut at Northampton.

Millry, town (pop. 607), Washington co., SW Ala, 11 mi. N of Chatom.

Mills. 1 County (□ 431; pop. 14,064), SW Iowa, on Nebr. line (W; formed here by Missouri R.); ⊙ Glenwood. Prairie agr. area (hogs, cattle, poultry corn, wheat, oats) drained by West Nishnabotna R. and by Keg and Silver creeks; bituminous-coal deposits. Formed 1851. **2** County (□ 734 pop. 5,999), central Texas; ⊙ Goldthwaite. Bounded SW by Colorado R.; drained by Pecan Bayou other tributaries. Diversified agr., ranching area sheep, goats, beef and dairy cattle, poultry, oats grain sorghums, barley, peanuts, cotton, fruit Formed 1887.

Mills. 1 Village (1940 pop. 136), Harding co., NE N.Mex., near Canadian R., 26 mi. NW of Mosquero. **2** Village (pop. 5,180, with adjacent East Rockingham), Richmond co., S N.C., near Rockingham. **3** Village (pop. 2,233), Grayson co., N Texas, near Denison. **4** Town (pop. 866), Natrona co., central Wyo., on N.Platte R. just W of Casper.

Millsboro. 1 Town (pop. 470), Sussex co., SE Del. 8 mi. SSE of Georgetown and on Indian R.; make crates, holly wreaths; poultry, truck. **2** Village (pop. 2,121, with adjacent Fredericktown), Washington co., SW Pa., on the Monongahela and 1[illegible] mi. SE of Washington.

Mill Shoals, village (pop. 417), White co., SE Ill. near Skillet Fork, 31 mi. ESE of Mount Vernon, in agr. area.

Mill Springs, village, Wayne co., S Ky., on Cumberland R. and 15 mi. SW of Somerset. In Civil War battle (Jan. 19, 1862) fought here, Union troops opened way for advance into E Tenn. Natl cemetery here. Prehistoric remains have been found in near-by caves.

Millstadt (mĭl'stŏt), village (pop. 1,566), St. Clair co., SW Ill., 11 mi. SSE of East St. Louis; clothing mfg., lumber and flour milling; bituminous-coal mines; agr. (corn, wheat; dairy products; poultry) Inc. 1878.

Millstatt (mĭl'shtät), village (pop. 1,521), Carinthia S Austria, on N shore of the Millstättersee and [illegible] mi. E of Spittal; resort.

Millstättersee (mĭl'shtĕtŭrzā"), lake (□ 5.14) in Carinthia, S Austria, just E of Spittal an der Drau 7 mi. long, 1 mi. wide, average depth 298 ft., alt 1,900 ft. Resorts of Millstatt and Seeboden on N shore.

Millstone. 1 Village, Conn.: see WATERFORD **2** Mining village (1940 pop. 706), Letcher co., SE Ky., in the Cumberlands, on North Fork Kentucky R. and 6 mi. W of Jenkins; bituminous coal **3** Borough (pop. 289), Somerset co., central N.J. on Millstone R. and 8 mi. W of New Brunswick.

Millstone River, central N.J., rises SW of Freehold flows c.40 mi. NW and N, past Hightstown Princeton (dam here forms L. Carnegie), and Millstone, to Raritan R. below Somerville.

Millstreet, Gaelic *Sráid na Mhuilinn*, town (pop 891), W Co. Cork, Ireland, on the Blackwater and 11 mi. SW of Kanturk; agr. market (dairying; potatoes, oats). Near by is modern Drinshane Castle with adjoining tower built 1436.

Milltown, town (pop. 1,876), SW N.B., on St. Croix R. (international bridge), opposite Milltown and Calais, Maine, and 60 mi. W of St. John; cotton milling, lumbering.

Milltown, Gaelic *Baile an Mhuilinn*. **1** SSE residential suburb of Dublin, Co. Dublin, Ireland. **2** Town Co. Kerry, Ireland: see MILTOWN.

Mill Town, village (pop. 1,796, with adjacent Mari Town), Madison co., central Miss.

Milltown. 1 Town (pop. 760), Crawford and Harrison counties, S Ind., on Blue R. and 25 mi. WNW of New Albany; limestone quarrying and processing; poultry hatcheries. **2** Village, Maine: see CALAIS. **3** Borough (pop. 3,786), Middlesex co.

E N.J., 3 mi. S of New Brunswick; mfg. (textiles, furniture polish, clothing, cables, paper products); sand, gravel, clay pits; agr. (poultry, fruit, dairy products). Settled before 1800, inc. 1889. **4** Village (pop. 580), Polk co., NW Wis., 45 mi. NE of St. Paul (Minn.), in dairying area; vegetable canning.

Milltown Malbay, Ireland: see MILTOWN MALBAY.

Milluachaqui (mīyōōächä'kē), village (pop. 546), Libertad dept., NW Peru, in Cordillera Occidental, near Salpo; gold and silver mining.

Milluni (mēyōō'nē), village (pop. 1,240), La Paz dept., W Bolivia, on S slope of the Huayna Potosí and 10 mi. NNW of La Paz; alt. 15,847 ft.; tin mining.

Millvale, industrial borough (pop. 7,287), Allegheny co., SW Pa., on Allegheny R. opposite N Pittsburgh; metal products, wooden boxes, meat packing; agr. Settled c.1844, inc. 1868.

Mill Valley, residential town (pop. 7,331), Marin co., W Calif., NW suburb across San Francisco Bay from San Francisco, at foot of Mt. Tamalpais. Inc. 1900. Muir Woods Natl. Monument is near by.

Mill Village. 1 Borough (pop. 324), Erie co., NW Pa., 17 mi. SSE of Erie and on French Creek; cheese. **2** Village (pop. 2,163), Marlboro co., NE S.C.

Millville. 1 Town (pop. 270), Sussex co., SE Del., 18 mi. SE of Georgetown, in truck and poultry area. **2** Residential town (pop. 1,692), Worcester co., S Mass., on Blackstone R. and 20 mi. SE of Worcester, at R.I. line. Settled 1662, set off from Blackstone 1916. **3** Village (pop. 168), Wabasha co., SE Minn., on Zumbro R. and 18 mi. NNE of Rochester; dairy products. **4** City (pop. 16,041), Cumberland co., S N.J., at head of navigation of Maurice R., 10 mi. E of Bridgeton; commercial center for agr. region (truck, poultry, fruit); river fisheries, mfg. (glass, textiles, cast iron, fertilizer, bricks, concrete products). Home for aged near by. Union L., formed by dam in Maurice R., is NW. Settled 1756, laid out 1801, inc. 1866. **5** Village (pop. 458), Butler co., extreme SW Ohio, 5 mi. W of Hamilton. **6** Borough (pop. 878), Columbia co., E central Pa., 10 mi. NNW of Bloomsburg; flour. **7** Town (pop. 401), Cache co., N Utah, 3 mi. S of Logan; alt. 4,542 ft.; agr.

Millwood, town (pop. 1,240), Spokane co., E Wash., 7 mi. E of Spokane and on Spokane R.; paper milling.

Millwood Reservoir, Ark.: see LITTLE RIVER.

Milly (mēyē'), town (pop. 2,397), Seine-et-Oise dept., N central France, 11 mi. W of Fontainebleau, resort at W edge of Forest of Fontainebleau; leading center of cultivation of medicinal plants. Has 15th-cent. church, market hall, and houses. Also called Milly-la-Forêt.

Milmarcos (mēlmär'kōs), town (pop. 759), Guadalajara prov., central Spain, 17 mi. N of Molina; grain growing, sheep raising; flour milling.

Milna, Yugoslavia: see BRAC ISLAND.

Milnathort (mĭlnŭ-thôrt'), town in Orwell parish (pop. 1,997), Kinross, Scotland, 2 mi. N of Kinross; agr. market; bacon and ham curing. Near by are ruins of 15th-cent. Burleigh Castle.

Milne Bay (mĭln), easternmost bay of New Guinea, c.225 mi. SE of Port Moresby; 10°20'S 150°27'E; 15 mi. wide, 30 mi. long. In Second World War, site of Allied air base.

Milne Land, Greenland: see SCORESBY SOUND.

Milner, town (pop. 345), Lamar co., W central Ga., 10 mi. SSE of Griffin.

Milner Pass, Colo.: see ROCKY MOUNTAIN NATIONAL PARK.

Milngavie (mĭlgī'), residential burgh (1931 pop. 5,057; 1951 census 7,883), SE Dumbarton, Scotland, 7 mi. NNW of Glasgow. Near by is 16th-cent. Bardowie Castle.

Milnor (mĭl'nŭr), city (pop. 674), Sargent co., SE N.Dak., 14 mi. NE of Forman.

Milnrow (mĭln'rō), urban district (1931 pop. 8,623; 1951 census 8,585), SE Lancashire, England, near Yorkshire boundary 2 mi. ESE of Rochdale; textile industry (cotton, rayon); coal mining.

Milnthorpe (mĭl'thôrp), village and parish (pop. 1,075), S Westmorland, England, 7 mi. S of Kendal; dairy farming.

Milo (mī'lō), village (pop. 108), S Alta., near N end of L. McGregor, 60 mi. N of Lethbridge; wheat.

Milo (mē'lŭ'), town, ⊙ Milo co. (pop. 78,218), E Yunnan prov., China, 60 mi. SE of Kunming; alt. 4,593 ft.; cotton textiles; timber, rice, wheat, millet, sugar cane. Coal mines near by.

Milo, Greece: see MELOS.

Milo (mī'lō). **1** Town (pop. 525), Warren co., S central Iowa, 23 mi. SSE of Des Moines, in agr. area. **2** Town (pop. 2,898), Piscataquis co., central Maine, at confluence of the Piscataquis and the Sebec, c.35 mi. NNW of Bangor. Agr. trade center, with mfg. (lumber products, yarn, thread). Center for Schoodic, Seboois, and Sebec lakes region. Railroad shops at Derby village. Settled 1803, inc. 1823. **3** Town (pop. 124), Vernon co., W Mo., 7 mi. SSE of Nevada.

Milo River (mē'lō), Fr. Guinea, Fr. West Africa, rises in S outliers of the Fouta Djallon mts. E of Macenta, flows c.200 mi. N, past Kankan, to the Niger 20 mi. S of Siguiri. Partly navigable.

Milos, Greece: see MELOS.

Milosevo or **Miloshevo** (both: mē'lôshĕvô), Serbo-Croatian *Miloševo*, village (pop. 9,325), Vojvodina, NE Serbia, Yugoslavia, 11 mi. SW of Kikinda, in the Banat. Formed (1947) by union of Dragutinovo, Hung. *Karlova*, and Beodra.

Miloslavskoye (mēlŭsläf'skŭyŭ), village (1926 pop. 519), W Ryazan oblast, Russian SFSR, 18 mi. SSW of Skopin; grain, hemp.

Miloslaw (mēwô'swäf), Pol. *Miłosław*, town (1946 pop. 2,311), Poznan prov., W central Poland, on railroad and 28 mi. ESE of Poznan; brewing, tanning.

Milosna, Poland: see LUBOMIERZ.

Milot (mē'lôt) or **Miloti** (mē'lôtē), village (1930 pop. 672), W central Albania, on Mat R. and 8 mi. SSE of Lesh, on Lesh-Durazzo road.

Milot (mēlō'), village (1950 census pop. 1,179), Nord dept., N Haiti, in foothills of the Massif du Nord, 9 mi. S of Cap-Haïtien, in agr. region (sugar cane, citrus fruit, tobacco). Base for visitors to near-by Sans Souci palace and Citadelle La Ferrière (a stupendous fortress), both built by Henri Christophe, king of Northern Haiti (1811–20).

Milovice (mĭ'lôvĭtsĕ), village (pop. 5,384), central Bohemia, Czechoslovakia, 20 mi. NW of Kolin; rail terminus; sugar-beet farming. Has military camp and shooting range.

Milpa Alta (mēl'pä äl'tä), town (pop. 4,084), Federal Dist., central Mexico, 18 mi. SSE of Mexico city; agr. center (cereals, fruit, vegetables, stock).

Milparinka (mĭl"pŭrĭng'kŭ), village, NW New South Wales, Australia, 155 mi. N of Broken Hill; sheep.

Milroy. 1 Village (pop. 268), Redwood co., SW Minn., 23 mi. WSW of Redwood Falls; dairy products. **2** Village (pop. 1,443), Mifflin co., central Pa., 9 mi. N of Lewistown.

Milspe, Germany: see ENNEPETAL.

Milstead, village (pop. 1,075), Rockdale co., N central Ga., just N of Conyers.

Miltenberg (mĭl'tŭnbĕrk), town (pop. 7,682), Lower Franconia, W Bavaria, Germany, on the Main (canalized) and 19 mi. SSE of Aschaffenburg; mfg. of precision instruments, and of wood, metal, and food products; brewing, lumber and flour milling. Chartered in 2d half of 13th cent. Has 14th-cent. church, renovated in 19th cent.; 15th-cent. gate tower and chapel; many 16th-cent. houses. Town mus. contains prehistoric and Roman relics. The 13th-cent. castle Miltenburg, surrounded by old-German double wall, towers above town.

Milton. 1 Village (pop. estimate 1,000), SW N.S., on Mersey R. and 3 mi. NW of Liverpool; lumbering center. **2** Town, Ont.: see MILTON WEST.

Milton, former urban district (1931 pop. 5,293), SW Hampshire, England, near Christchurch Bay of the Channel, 6 mi. E of Christchurch; agr. market, resort. Just NE is New Milton.

Milton, borough (pop. 1,472), ⊙ Bruce co. (□ 520; pop. 3,763), SE S.Isl., New Zealand, 35 mi. SW of Dunedin; rail junction; dairy plants, woolen mills.

Milton. 1 Village, Inverness, Scotland: see SOUTH UIST. **2** or **Milton of Campsie**, town in Campsie parish, S Stirling, Scotland, 2 mi. N of Kirkintilloch; textile printing.

Milton. 1 Town (pop. 1,321), Sussex co., SE Del., 10 mi. W of Lewes and on Broadkill R., in farm area; buttons, packed meat, flour, canned goods. **2** Town (pop. 2,040), ⊙ Santa Rosa co., NW Fla., on Blackwater R. and 18 mi. NE of Pensacola; lumber milling. Founded c.1825. **3** Village (pop. 8,232), Madison co., SW Ill. **4** Village (pop. 337), Pike co., W Ill., near Illinois R., 24 mi. WSW of Jacksonville, in agr. area. **5** Town (pop. 752), Wayne co., E Ind., on Whitewater R. and 14 mi. W of Richmond. **6** Town (pop. 719), Van Buren co., SE Iowa, near Mo. line, 27 mi. SSE of Ottumwa, in livestock and grain area. **7** Village (pop. c.350), Trimble co., N Ky., on the Ohio (toll bridge here to Madison, Ind.) and 40 mi. NNE of Louisville; strawberry preserves, flour, concrete blocks, lumber. **8** Residential town (pop. 22,395), Norfolk co., E Mass., on Neponset R. just S of Boston; mfg. (crackers, chocolate, metal products), engraving. Milton Acad., Blue Hill observatory here. Settled 1636, set off from Dorchester 1662. Includes village of East Milton. **9** Town (pop. 1,510), Strafford co., SE N.H., on Salmon Falls R. and just N of Rochester (from which set off 1802). Mfg. (fiberboard, blankets, shoes); woolen mills at Milton Mills village are over a century old. **10** Village (1940 pop. 1,144), Ulster co., SE N.Y., on W bank of the Hudson and 4 mi. S of Poughkeepsie; shipping point in fruitgrowing area. **11** Town (pop. 317), Caswell co., N N.C., 15 mi. NW of Roxboro and on Dan R., at Va. line. **12** Village (pop. 322), Cavalier co., NE N.Dak., 18 mi. SE of Langdon. **13** Town (pop. 2,362), Umatilla co., NE Oregon, adjoining Freewater, 10 mi. S of Walla Walla, Wash., in wheat, fruit, and vegetable area; lumber, wood products. Ships canned fruit and vegetables. Inc. 1886. **14** Borough (pop. 8,578), Northumberland co., E central Pa., 11 mi. NNW of Sunbury and on West Branch of Susquehanna R.; metal products, clothing, railroad tank cars, food products; railroad shops. Laid out 1792, inc. 1817. **15** Town (pop. 1,874), including Milton village (pop. 739), Chittenden co., NW Vt., on Lamoille R. and L. Champlain, and 12 mi. N of Burlington; lumber, dairy products. Includes state game preserve. Settled 1782, organized 1788. **16** Town (pop. 1,374), Pierce co., W central Wash., 6 mi. E of Tacoma. **17** Town (pop. 1,552), Cabell co., W W.Va., on Mud R. and 16 mi. E of Huntington, in agr. (grain, truck), coal, gas, and oil region; mfg. of glassware, stained glass, canned goods; flour and sawmills. Inc. 1876. **18** Village (pop. 1,549), Rock co., S Wis., near L. Koshkonong (resort), 8 mi. NE of Janesville, in farming and dairying area; mfg. of physiotherapy equipment. Seat of Milton Col. Inc. 1904.

Miltona, village (pop. 150), Douglas co., W Minn., near L. Miltona, 12 mi. NNE of Alexandria; dairy products.

Miltona, Lake (□ 8), Douglas co., W Minn., 10 mi. N of Alexandria; 5.5 mi. long, 2 mi. wide. Resorts.

Milton Abbas (ă'bŭs), agr. village and parish (pop. 486), central Dorset, England, 6 mi. SW of Blandford. Has 14th-cent. church. The abbey is on site of 10th-cent. abbey.

Milton Center, village (pop. 201), Wood co., NW Ohio, 10 mi. WSW of Bowling Green, in agr. area.

Milton Junction, resort village (pop. 1,104), Rock co., S Wis., bet. L. Koshkonong and Janesville, just W of Milton. Inc. 1949.

Milton Mills, N.H.: see MILTON.

Milton-next-Gravesend, England: see GRAVESEND.

Milton of Campsie, Scotland: see MILTON.

Milton Regis, England: see SITTINGBOURNE AND MILTON.

Milton Reservoir, Ohio: see MAHONING RIVER.

Miltonsburg, village (pop. 100), Monroe co., Ohio, 11 mi. S of Barnesville, in agr. area; limestone quarry.

Milton Siding, village, Rift Valley prov., W central Kenya, on railroad and 18 mi. N of Nakuru in Great Rift Valley; coffee, tea, wheat, corn. Also called Milton's Siding.

Miltonvale, city (pop. 911), Cloud co., N central Kansas, 19 mi. SE of Concordia, in wheat region.

Milton West, town (pop. 1,964), ⊙ Halton co., S Ont., 18 mi. N of Hamilton; mfg. of rails, hardware; yarn spinning, dairying, lumber and flour milling. Formerly Milton.

Miltown or **Milltown**, Gaelic *Baile an Mhuilinn*, town (pop. 297), central Co. Kerry, Ireland, on Maine R. and 8 mi. S of Tralee; agr. market (dairying, grain, potatoes). Near by are remains of anc. Kilcolman Abbey.

Miltown Malbay or **Milltown Malbay**, Gaelic *Sráid na Cathrach*, town (pop. 732), W Co. Clare, Ireland, on Mal Bay, 17 mi. W of Ennis; agr. market (dairying; potatoes, grain) and seaside resort; racecourse.

Milun, Formosa: see HWALIEN.

Milverton, village (pop. 1,015), S Ont., 15 mi. NNE of Stratford; mfg. of textiles, felt, furniture.

Milverton, town and parish (pop. 1,286), W Somerset, England, 4 mi. NNW of Wellington; agr. market. Has 16th-cent. church.

Milwaukee (mĭlwô'kē), county (□ 239; pop. 871,047), SE Wis.; ⊙ Milwaukee. Bounded E by L. Michigan; drained by Milwaukee, Menomonee, and Root rivers. Highly industrialized area, centered at Milwaukee. Dairying, stock raising, truck gardening, horticulture. Formed 1834.

Milwaukee. 1 Town (pop. 302), Northampton co., NE N.C., 24 mi. E of Roanoke Rapids. **2** Largest city (pop. 637,392) of Wis., ⊙ Milwaukee co., SE Wis., c.80 mi. N of Chicago, on crescent-shaped bay of L. Michigan, at mouths of Milwaukee, Menomonee, and small Kinnickinnic rivers; 43°3'N 87°57'W; alt. 581 ft. Railroad, commercial, and industrial center known for brewing and meat-packing industries; lake port, with fine harbor sheltered by breakwaters; port of entry. Intersecting the city are canals crossed by many bridges. An important grain market, with large grain elevators. Besides its vast breweries and meat-packing plants, Milwaukee has railroad shops and factories producing heavy construction, industrial, and agr. machinery, turbines, Diesel and gas engines, leather and leather goods (especially gloves and work shoes), knitwear, hosiery, automobile bodies and parts, motorcycles, outboard motors, electrical appliances, tin and enamel ware. Educational institutions include Marquette Univ., Milwaukee-Downer Col., a state teachers col., Mt. Mary Col., Milwaukee School of Engineering, Concordia Col., St. Francis Seminary, Alverno Col., Cardinal Stritch Col., and schools of art and music. Large veterans' institution here. Has mus. with collection of historical relics, art institute, art. gall., and a large auditorium. Among the numerous parks are Washington Park with a zoo, Mitchell Park containing botanical gardens, and Juneau and Estabrook parks. There is a scenic lake-shore drive. Industrial suburbs include CUDAHY, SOUTH MILWAUKEE, WAUWATOSA, WEST ALLIS; SHOREWOOD and WHITEFISH BAY are residential suburbs. The site was visited by French missionaries in late-17th cent., and a fur-trading post was established 1795 by North West Company. The site of what is now Milwaukee was bought (1835) by 3 men, among whom was Solomon Juneau, who had come in 1818. Inc. 1846. After 1848, influx of Germans, among them Carl Schurz, stimulated the city's economic, cultural, and political development. Victor L. Berger, 1st Socialist member of Congress, was influential here. The Socialist mayor, Daniel W. Hoan, made the city well known for its efficient administration.

Milwaukee Depth, Atlantic Ocean: see PUERTO RICO TRENCH.

Milwaukee River, SE Wis., rises in lake region of Fond du Lac co., flows S, past West Bend, turns E, then generally S, past Grafton, reaching L. Michigan at Milwaukee; c.75 mi. long.

Milwaukie, city (pop. 5,253), Clackamas co., NW Oregon, on Willamette R. just S of Portland; wood products. Cherry trees brought here (1847) from Iowa, began state's cherry-growing industry. Founded 1848, inc. 1903.

Milyatska River, Yugoslavia: see MILJACKA RIVER.

Milyutinskaya (mēlyōō'tyĭnskīŭ). **1** Village (1939 pop. over 500), E central Rostov oblast, Russian SFSR, 35 mi. NNW of Morozovsk; metalworks; wheat, sunflowers, livestock. **2** Village, Samarkand oblast, Uzbek SSR: see GALLYA-ARAL.

Mimasaka (mēmä'säkŭ), former province in SW Honshu, Japan; now part of Okayama prefecture.

Mimbres (mĭm'brŭs, –ĕs, –ĭs), village (pop. c.100), Grant co., SW N.Mex., 18 mi. ENE of Silver City; alt. c.6,000 ft. Resort with hot mineral springs. Gila Natl. Forest and Black Range near by.

Mimbres Mountains, SW N.Mex., extend N from Cooks Range to Black Range, in Grant and Sierra counties. Chief peaks: Pine Flat Mtn. (7,875 ft.), Thompson Cone (7,932 ft.), Seven Brothers Mtn. (8,547 ft.). Range is largely within part of Gila Natl. Forest.

Mimiapan (mēmyä'pän), officially San Miguel Mimiapan, town (pop. 2,103), Mexico state, central Mexico, 23 mi. W of Mexico city; cereals, livestock.

Mimico (mĭ'mĭkō), town (pop. 8,070), S Ont., on L. Ontario, SW suburb of Toronto; resort.

Mimitsu (mēmē'tsōō), town (pop. 4,553), Miyazaki prefecture, E Kyushu, Japan, on Hyuga Sea, 32 mi. NNE of Miyazaki; agr. (rice, wheat, melons) and fishing center; paper mill.

Mimizan (mēmēzã'), village (pop. 496), Landes dept., SW France, near the Bay of Biscay, 40 mi. WNW of Mont-de-Marsan; paper milling, woodworking, turpentine extracting. Mimizan-les-Bains (3 mi. W) is a small bathing resort.

Mimon (mĭ'mônyŭ), Czech *Mimoň*, Ger. *Niemes* (nē'mŭs), town (pop. 4,605), N Bohemia, Czechoslovakia, on railroad and 30 mi. E of Usti nad Labem; tanning trade center; lumbering, oat growing.

Mimongo (mēmông-gō'), village, S Gabon, Fr. Equatorial Africa, 60 mi. ENE of Mouila, in gold-mining area.

Mimoso do Sul (mēmō'zōō dōō sōōl'), city (pop. 3,558), S Espírito Santo, Brazil, on railroad and 20 mi. SW of Cachoeiro de Itapemirim; coffee and rice hulling, corn-meal mfg., leatherworking. Until 1944, called João Pessoa.

Mimot (mēmôt'), town, Kompong Cham prov., S Cambodia, 45 mi. S of Kompong Cham, on Vietnam line.

Min, province, China: see FUKIEN.

Min, river, China: see MIN RIVER.

Mina (mē'nä), town (pop. 918), Nuevo León, N Mexico, in foothills of Sierra Madre Oriental, near Salinas R., 27 mi. NW of Monterrey; cereals, cactus fibers, livestock.

Mina, Oued (wĕd' mēnä'), stream in Oran dept., N Algeria, rises in the High Plateaus 30 mi. S of Tiaret, flows c.150 mi. NW across the Tell Atlas, past Relizane, to the Chéliff 25 mi. E of Mostaganem. The Bakhada Dam (148 ft. high; W of Tiaret) stores water for irrigation in Relizane area.

Mina al-Ahmadi, Kuwait: see MENA AL AHMADI.

Minab (mēnäb'), town, Eighth Prov., in Kerman, SE Iran, 50 mi. E of Bandar Abbas and on Minab R. (small coastal stream); center of rich agr. area; date groves, fruit orchards (oranges, mangoes, bananas); tobacco, wheat, millet, vegetables. Near by, at mouth of Minab R., was anc. HORMUZ, Persian Gulf port.

Minabe (mēnä'bā), town (pop. 8,133), Wakayama prefecture, S Honshu, Japan, on Philippine Sea, on S Kii Peninsula, 4 mi. NW of Tanabe, in agr. area (citrus fruit, plums); fishing; weaving.

Mina Clavero (mē'nä klävā'rō), town (pop. estimate 1,500), W Córdoba prov., Argentina, popular mtn. resort on small Mina Clavero R., and 55 mi. SW of Córdoba.

Mina de São Domingos (mē'nŭ dĭ sã'ō dōōmēng'-gōōsh), village (pop. 3,859), Beja dist., S Portugal, near the Chanza (Sp. border), 30 mi. SE of Beja; major copper-mining center, connected by mining railroad with Pomarão on the Guadiana.

Minahassa (mĭnŭhä'sŭ), name sometimes given to NE part of N peninsula of Celebes, Indonesia. So called because area is largely inhabited by the Minahassa, a Malayan group converted to Christianity in 19th cent.

Minakuchi (mēnä'kōōchē), town (pop. 13,632), Shiga prefecture, S Honshu, Japan, 24 mi. E of Kyoto; agr. center (rice, tea, wheat); rattan products. Sometimes called Mizukuchi.

Mina La India, Nicaragua: see LA INDIA.

Minalin (mēnä'lēn), town (1939 pop. 2,125; 1948 municipality pop. 9,856), Pampanga prov., central Luzon, Philippines, 4 mi. SSW of San Fernando; agr. center (sugar cane, rice).

Minamata (mēnä'mätŭ), town (pop. 39,818), Kumamoto prefecture, W Kyushu, Japan, on Yatsushiro Bay, 44 mi. SSW of Kumamoto; rail junction; agr. center (rice, wheat, sweet potatoes); raw silk, lumber. Ironworks.

Minambakkam, India: see MADRAS, city.

Minami-arima (mēnä'mē-ä'rēmä), town (pop. 11,330), Nagasaki prefecture, W Kyushu, Japan, on SE coast of Shimabara Peninsula, 23 mi. ESE of Nagasaki, on Shimabara Bay, in rice-producing area.

Minami-ashigara (mĭnä'mē-ä'shĭgärŭ), town (pop. 6,874), Kanagawa prefecture, central Honshu, Japan, just NW of Odawara; wheat, soybeans, sweet potatoes.

Minami-daito-shima, Ryukyu Isls.: see DAITO-SHIMA.

Minami-gyotoku (mēnä'mē-gyō'tōkōō), town (pop. 6,124), Chiba prefecture, central Honshu, Japan, just N of Urayasu; rice growing, fishing.

Minami-hadano (mēnä'mē-hädä'nō), town (pop. 8,057), Kanagawa prefecture, central Honshu, Japan, just S of Hadano; tobacco, wheat, sweet potatoes, millet.

Minami-iwo-jima (mēnä'mē-ēwō'jĭmä) [Jap.,=south sulphur island], uninhabited island (□ 1.5), Volcano Isls., W Pacific, 38 mi. SSW of Iwo Jima; contains highest peak (3,181 ft.) of group.

Minami-nayoshi, Russian SFSR: see SHEBUNINO.

Minami-oagari-shima, Ryukyu Isls.: see DAITO-SHIMA.

Minami-oji, Japan: see YASAKA.

Minami-shitaura (mēnä'mē-shētä'ōōrä), town (pop. 8,351), Kanagawa prefecture, central Honshu, Japan, on S Miura Pensinsula, 8 mi. S of Yokosuka; potatoes, wheat, soybeans, millet.

Minami-tori-shima: see MARCUS ISLAND.

Minami-uruppu-suido, Russian SFSR: see URUP STRAIT.

Minano, Japan: see MINO, Saitama prefecture.

Mina Pirquitas (mē'nä pērkē'täs) or **Pirquitas,** town (1947 pop. 2,162), W Jujuy prov., Argentina, 70 mi. SW of La Quiaca; tin-mining center.

Mina Ragra (mē'nä räg'rä), village (pop. 434), Pasco dept., central Peru, in Cordillera Occidental of the Andes, 22 mi. WSW of Cerro de Pasco; vanadium-mining center.

Minarets, The, E Calif., odd formation of jagged summits (c.12,000 ft.) of the Sierra Nevada, in scenic region SE of Yosemite Natl. Park.

Minari (mēnä'rē), town (pop. 3,284), Shimane prefecture, SW Honshu, Japan, 20 mi. SSW of Matsue, in rice-growing area; raw silk, sake, soy sauce.

Minas. 1 Department, Córdoba prov., Argentina: see CIÉNAGA DEL CORO. **2** Department, Neuquén natl. territory, Argentina: see ANDACOLLO.

Minas (mē'näs), town (pop. 3,305), Camagüey prov., E Cuba, on railroad and 20 mi. ENE of Camagüey. Asphalt, iron, and copper mining.

Minas, department, Uruguay: see LAVALLEJA, department.

Minas (mē'näs), city (pop. 32,000), ⊙ Lavalleja dept., SE Uruguay, on railroad and highway, and 60 mi. NE of Montevideo. Rail terminus, airport. Granite crushing, quarrying; marble; wool, wheat, corn, oats; cattle and sheep raising. Lead deposits near by. Has public library, theater, public schools. Founded 1783.

Minas, Las, Mexico: see LAS MINAS.

Minas, Las. 1 Village, Colón prov., Panama: see PUERTO PILÓN. **2** Village, Herrera prov., Panama: see LAS MINAS.

Minas, Sierra de las (syĕ'rä dā läs), range along Alta Verapaz–Zacapa dept. border, E central Guatemala; extends c.60 mi. E–W bet. Polochic R. (N) and Motagua R. (S); rises to c.10,000 ft. Sierra del Mico adjoins (E).

Minas Basin (mī'nŭs, mē'nŭs), central N.S., central part of deep inlet of the Bay of Fundy, with which it is connected (W) by Minas Channel; 24 mi. long, up to 25 mi. wide. Continued E by Cobequid Bay. Narrows bet. Cape Sharp and Cape Split separate it from Minas Channel. On N coast is Parrsboro. Receives Cornwallis, Avon, and several smaller rivers.

Minas Channel, inlet (24 mi. long, 10–14 mi. wide), N central N.S., connects the Bay of Fundy (W) with the Minas Basin (E). Its mouth is bet. Cape Chignecto and Cape Sharp. N shore is indented by Advocate Bay (4 mi. long, 8 mi. wide) and Greville Bay (5 mi. long, 16 mi. wide). On S side, Cape Split extends 6 mi. into the channel. On N shore is Port Greville. High tides of Bay of Fundy extend into Minas Channel.

Minas da Panasqueira (mē'nŭzh dä pŭnŭshkā'rŭ), village (pop. 1,749), Castelo Branco dist., central Portugal, near Zêzere R., 14 mi. SW of Covilhã; tungsten mining.

Minas de Corrales, Uruguay: see CORRALES, Rivera dept.

Minas de la Reunión, Spain: see VILLANUEVA DE LAS MINAS.

Minas del Tauler, Spain: see TAULER.

Minas de Matahambre, Cuba: see MATAHAMBRE.

Minas de Oro (mē'näs dā ō'rō) [Sp.,=gold mines], town (pop. 1,407), Comayagua dept., W central Honduras, 40 mi. NNW of Tegucigalpa; footwear mfg.; tobacco, coffee. Airfield. Near-by gold deposits were formerly exploited.

Minas de Ríotinto, Spain: see RÍOTINTO.

Minas do Rio de Contas, Brazil: see RIO DE CONTAS.

Minas Gerais (mē'nŭs zhĭrīs') [Port.,=various mines], inland state (□ 224,701; 1940 pop. 6,736,-416; 1950 census 7,839,792) of E Brazil; ⊙ Belo Horizonte. Second most populous state (after São Paulo), with ⅙ of country's inhabitants. Bounded by Rio de Janeiro (SE), São Paulo (S and SW), Goiás (NW), Bahia (N), and Espírito Santo (E). Lies almost wholly within geologically ancient central plateau of Brazil; separated from coastal region by the Serra da Mantiqueira (S), Serra do Caparaó (SE), and Serra dos Aimorés (E). Traversed S–N by the Serra do Espinhaço, which forms watershed bet. São Francisco basin (W) and streams flowing directly E (Rio Doce, Mucuri, Jequitinhonha). W section is drained by 2 headstreams (Rio Grande, Paranaíba) of the Paraná, which enclose a triangle-shaped protuberance called the Triângulo Mineiro, noted for its livestock economy. Healthful, subtropical climate because of alt. of plateau (1,800–3,500 ft.). Although Minas Gerais is the second coffee state and grows quantities of cotton, tobacco, rice, corn, sugar, fruit, and small grains, it is particularly noted for its livestock and dairy industry, which supplies Rio and São Paulo markets. State is Brazil's mineral storehouse. Its high-grade iron deposits are world's largest known reserves, and are now mined at Itabira and Itabirito (in the Serra do Espinhaço) for natl. steel industry and for export (chiefly to U.S.). Large manganese deposits are exploited at Conselheiro Lafaiete and São João del Rei. Near Nova Lima, one of the deepest gold mines in existence has been worked since 1834. Gold is also panned in numerous streams. Diamonds mined near Diamantina are supplemented by extensive washings in Paranaíba R. area of the Triângulo Mineiro and in headstreams of the São Francisco. Additional mineral wealth includes semiprecious stones (in the Jequitinhonha valley); rock crystals, bauxite, and zirconium (near Poços de Caldas); iron pyrites (at Ouro Prêto); and rutile, graphite, and chromite. Iron and steel industry (based on local ores, fueled by charcoal) is concentrated E of Belo Horizonte along the Rio Doce valley RR; chief centers are Sabará, Barão de Cocais, Monlevade. Juiz de Fora (in S) is a leading textile town. Teófilo Otoni is known for cutting of semiprecious stones. Uberaba and Uberlândia are livestock centers. Several well-known mtn. resorts (with thermal springs) are located in S border ranges within easy reach of Rio and São Paulo. They are Araxá, Caxambu, Lambari, Poços de Caldas, São Lourenço. Communications are adequate in S, linking Belo Horizonte, mining centers, and resorts with coast. In E, the Rio Doce valley RR ships iron to port of Vitória (Espírito Santo) for export. Towns in N are served by river transport on the São Francisco and by air. Minas Gerais was 1st explored from the E in 1553. Gold was discovered at end of 17th cent. and brought influx of prospectors from São Paulo. Was independent captaincy after 1720. An uprising (1788) against Portuguese, led by the patriot Tiradentes, was put down by colonial govt. In 1824, Minas Gerais became a prov. of Brazilian empire and, in 1889, a state of federal republic. In 1897, state ⊙ was transferred from Ouro Prêto to planned city of Belo Horizonte. The region of Serra dos Aimorés (□ 3,914, along E border) is disputed bet. Minas Gerais and Espírito Santo, and final settlement by federal govt. is pending. Old spelling, Minas Geraes.

Minas Novas (mē'nŭs nô'vŭs), city (pop. 1,341), NE central Minas Gerais, Brazil, 80 mi. WNW of Teófilo Otoni; alt. 3,000 ft. Semiprecious stones found here. Known since 1727, when diamonds were discovered in near-by streams.

Minas Prietas (mē'näs prēā'täs), village (pop. 100), Sonora, NW Mexico, 32 mi. SE of Hermosillo; gold mines.

Minatare (mĭn'ŭtâr), village (pop. 890), Scotts Bluff co., W Nebr., 8 mi. ESE of Scottsbluff and on N. Platte R.; beet sugar, dairy and poultry produce, grain. Near by is L. Minatare, artificial lake created (1915) for irrigation.

Minatitlán (mēnätētlän'). **1** Town (pop. 797), Colima, W Mexico, 24 mi. WNW of Colima; rice, corn, beans, sugar cane, cotton, coffee, fruit, livestock. Iron deposits near by. Formerly El Mamey. **2** City (pop. 18,539), Veracruz, SE Mexico, port on navigable Coatzacoalcos R. (20 mi. from mouth), on Isthmus of Tehuantepec, 135 mi. SE of Veracruz. Rail terminus; major petroleum-drilling and -refining center (pipe line to Salina Cruz); lumber mills. Radio station, airfield. Agr. products: coffee, rice, corn, sugar cane, fruit, livestock.

Minato (mēnä'tō). **1** Town (pop, 5,197), Chiba prefecture, central Honshu, Japan, on W Chiba Peninsula, 12 mi. SSW of Kisarazu; rice, wheat, poultry. **2** Town (pop. 3,088), on W Awaji-shima, Hyogo prefecture, Japan, on Harima Sea, 10 mi. W of Sumoto; agr. center (rice, wheat, fruit, flowers, poultry); mfg. (soy sauce, tiles), woodworking.

Minaya (mĕnī'ä), town (pop. 3,321), Albacete prov., SE central Spain, 32 mi. NW of Albacete; esparto-rope mfg., brandy distilling, sawmilling; melons, saffron, wine, cereals.

Minbu (mĭm'bōō), district (□ 3,602; 1941 pop. 302,373), Magwe div., Upper Burma; ⊙ Minbu. Bet. Arakan Yoma and Irrawaddy R.; in dry zone (annual rainfall 25 in.) irrigated by Salin, Man, and Mon rivers. Agr.: rice, millet, sesame, beans, tobacco; fisheries, teak forests, oil fields. Served by Irrawaddy steamers. Pop. is 90% Burmese and 7% Chin.

Minbu, town (pop. 6,005), ⊙ Minbu dist., Upper Burma, river port on Irrawaddy R. (opposite Magwe) and 100 mi. NNW of Prome; head of road, through An Pass, over Arakan Yoma to An (Kyaukpyu dist.). Oil field, mud volcanoes near by.

Minburn, village (pop. 198), E Alta., 22 mi. W of Vermilion; dairying, grain, stock.

Minburn, town (pop. 353), Dallas co., central Iowa, 25 mi. WNW of Des Moines, in agr. area.

Minbya (mĭn'byä), village (pop. 2,244), Akyab dist., Lower Burma, in the Arakan, on Lemro R. and 30 mi. NE of Akyab.

Minch, The, or **North Minch** (mĭnch), strait (c.35 mi. wide) of the Atlantic, separating Lewis with Harris of the Outer Hebrides from mainland of Scotland. It is continued SW by the Little Minch (15–25 mi. wide), separating Skye from North Uist and Benbecula, and leading S into the Sea of the Hebrides.

Mincha (mĕn'chä), village (1930 pop. 452), Coquimbo prov., N central Chile, on Choapa R. and 15 mi. WNW of Illapel, in agr. area (grain, fruit, livestock).

Min Chiang, China: see MIN RIVER.

Min-ch'in, China: see MINTSIN.

Minchinabad (mĭn"chĭnäbäd'), town (pop. 3,558), Bahawalpur state, W Pakistan, 125 mi. NE of Bahawalpur; agr. market (wheat, cotton, millet, dates); pottery mfg. Sometimes Manchinabad.

Min-ch'ing, China: see MINTSING.

Minchinhampton, town and parish (pop. 3,735), central Gloucester, England, 11 mi. SSE of Gloucester; woolen milling; agr. market. Has 14th-cent. church.

Minchinmávida or **Michinmâhuida** (both: mĕnchĭn-mä'wĕdä), Andean volcanic peak (8,100 ft.), Chiloé prov., S Chile; 42°50'S. A massif with several peaks and glaciers.

Minchow, China: see MINHSIEN.

Minchüan or **Min-ch'üan** (mĭn'chüăn'), town, ⊙ Minchüan co. (pop. 145,292), NE Honan prov., China, 50 mi. ESE of Kaifeng and on Lunghai RR; agr. products.

Minchumina, Lake, Alaska: see LAKE MINCHUMINA.

Mincio River (mĕn'chō), anc. *Mincius,* N Italy, rises as Sarca R. in Adamello mtn. group W of La Presanella, 12 mi. E of Edolo; flows 47 mi. generally E and S, entering N end of Lago di Garda (32 mi. long) near Riva. Emerges as Mincio R. from SE end of lake, at Peschiera del Garda; flows 41 mi. SE, past Mantua, where it widens to form 3 lakes (□ 4), to Po R. 10 mi. SE of Mantua. The Sarca-Garda-Mincio line (120 mi. long) marks the natural boundary bet. Venetia and Lombardy and has been of strategic importance, especially in wars of the Risorgimento (1848–49).

Minco (mĭng'kō), town (pop. 978), Grady co., central Okla., 18 mi. N of Chickasha, in agr. area (cotton, corn, wheat, livestock); cotton ginning.

Mindanao (mĭndŭnä'ō, -nou', Sp. mēndänä'ō), second largest island (□ 36,537; 1939 pop. 1,828,071) of the Philippines (after Luzon), at S end of the archipelago, S of Visayan Isls., NE of Borneo; c.300 mi. long; 5°33'–9°49'N 121°54'–126°36'E. Bordered E by Philippine Sea, S by Celebes Sea, N by Mindanao Sea, W by Sulu Sea. Of irregular shape, with the long Zamboanga or Sibuguey peninsula in W, it is cut by numerous deep bays (e.g., Iligan Bay, Illana Bay, Moro Gulf, Davao Gulf). Its mts., heavily forested, rise to highest point in Philippines—Mt. Apo (9,690 ft.), an active volcano near W shore of Davao Gulf. In E and N are its 2 great rivers, the Agusan and the Pulangi or Rio Grande de Mindanao. Chief cities are Davao, Cagayan, Cotabato, Surigao, Ozamiz (formerly Misamis), and Zamboanga. Mostly agr. (abacá, coconuts, rice, corn); one of chief exports is copra. Important, too, is the export of canned pineapple grown and canned in N Mindanao. Gutta-percha is grown. There are iron, coal, gold, and copper deposits, and mining is being developed in N peninsula near Mainit. Moros inhabit central and W areas, Visayans the N. Off coast of Mindanao are numerous satellite isls., notably Siargao and Dinagat (NE), Camiguin (N), and Basilan (SW). See also articles on the 9 provs. which comprise Mindanao: AGUSAN, BUKIDNON, COTABATO, DAVAO, LANAO, MISAMIS OCCIDENTAL, MISAMIS ORIENTAL, SURIGAO, ZAMBOANGA. In Second World War, Japanese fought on around Davao in 1945 long after rest of Philippine Isls. had been liberated.

Mindanao, Rio Grande de, Philippines: see PULANGI RIVER.

Mindanao Deep: see MINDANAO TRENCH.

Mindanao Sea, S Philippines, bet. Mindanao (S), Leyte, Bohol, and Cebu (N), and Negros (W), opening E via Surigao Strait to Philippine Sea, W to Sulu Sea, and N to Visayan Sea via Tañon Strait, Bohol Strait, and Canigao Channel; c.170 mi. E–W.

Mindanao Trench or **Philippine Trench,** submarine depression in North Pacific Ocean, off NE Mindanao; the deepest (34,440 ft.) area on the surface of the globe. The trench was sounded in 1912 to 32,112 ft. by the ship *Planet* at 9°56'N 126°50'E. In 1927, the German cruiser *Emden* obtained a depth of 35,400 ft. at 9°41'N 126°50'E, a value long recognized internationally as the Mindanao Deep or Philippine Deep. However, subsequent soundings in the same area were shallower, and the *Emden* reading was regarded as erroneous. In 1945, the *U.S.S. Cape Johnson* sounded a depth of 34,440 ft. at 10°27'N 126°39'E, regarded as the greatest reliable sounding off Mindanao.

Minde, Norway: see BERGEN.

Minde (mĕn'dĭ), town (pop. 1,187), Santarém dist., central Portugal, 19 mi. N of Santarém; mfg. of woolens.

Mindelheim (mĭn'dŭlhīm), town (pop. 7,673), Swabia, SW Bavaria, Germany, on Mindel R. and 15 mi. ENE of Memmingen; textile mfg., brewing, dairying, printing, woodworking; summer resort. Has 17th-cent. church.

Mindêlo (mĕndā'lōō), city and main port of Cape Verde Isls., on NW shore of São Vicente Isl., c.500 mi. WNW of Dakar (Fr. West Africa); 16°53'N 25°W. Important coaling station on Pôrto Grande bay, the archipelago's best harbor. Coal mining, fishing. Submarine cable station. Radio transmitter. Often called Pôrto Grande for its harbor. Old spelling, Mindello.

Mindel River (mĭn'dŭl), Bavaria, Germany, rises 4 mi. W of Kaufbeuren, flows 52 mi. N to the Danube, 3 mi. S of Gundelfingen.

Minden (mĭn'dŭn), village (pop. estimate 600), ⊙ Haliburton co., S Ont., bet. Minden L. (N) and Gullfoot L. (S), 40 mi. N of Lindsay; dairying, mixed farming.

Minden (mĭn'dŭn), town (pop. 34,293), in former Prussian prov. of Westphalia, NW Germany, after 1945 in North Rhine-Westphalia, port on the Weser at junction of Ems-Weser and Weser-Elbe canals (here carried across the Weser by bridge), and 20 mi. NE of Bielefeld; rail junction; foundries; mfg. of furniture, chemicals, glass, cigars; distilling, sawmilling. Second World War destruction included 11th–13th-cent. cathedral, 13th–17th-cent. town hall. Bishopric founded here c.800 by Charlemagne. Constantly struggling for its independence from bishopric, town joined Hanseatic League in 13th cent. Accepted Reformation in 1530. Minden and secularized bishopric passed to Brandenburg by Treaty of Westphalia. Was garrison (1648–1945). In Seven Years War, English and Hanoverians here defeated the French (1759).

Minden. **1** Town (pop. 328), Pottawattamie co., SW Iowa, on Keg Creek and 20 mi. NE of Council Bluffs. **2** City (pop. 9,787), ⊙ Webster parish, NW La., 28 mi. ENE of Shreveport; trading and shipping center for agr. area (cotton, corn, potatoes); cotton gins and compress, cottonseed mills, sand and gravel plants, lumber mills, railroad shops; oil wells. Recreational areas on near-by lakes and streams. Inc. as a town in 1850, as a city in 1928. **3** City (pop. 2,120), ⊙ Kearney co., S Nebr., 30 mi. WSW of Hastings and on branch of Little Blue R.; grain, livestock, dairy and poultry produce. Old persons' home here. City founded 1876. **4** Village (pop. c.300), ⊙ Douglas co., W Nev., on East Carson R. and 15 mi. S of Carson City; alt. 4,700 ft.; alfalfa, cattle, grain, poultry, potatoes. Mono Natl. Forest near by. **5** Village (pop. 2,307, with adjacent Rock Lick), Fayette co., S central W.Va., near New R. 14 mi. N of Beckley, in coal-mining region.

Minden City, village (pop. 359), Sanilac co., E Mich., c.50 mi. NNW of Port Huron, in farm area.

Minden Lake (3 mi. long, 1 mi. wide), S Ont., 3 mi. N of Minden, 50 mi. NNW of Peterborough; drains S through Gull R. into Balsam L. and Trent Canal.

Mindenmines (mĭndŭnmīnz'), city (pop. 425), Barton co., SW Mo., 8 mi. NE of Pittsburg, Kansas, in a coal-mining area.

Mindigi (mĕndē'gē), village, Katanga prov., SE Belgian Congo, 50 mi. W of Jadotville; copper and cobalt mining. Also copper mining at near-by Mirungwe (mĕrōōng'gwä), 8 mi. SE, and at Tantara (täntä'rä), 25 mi. E.

Mindon (mĭn'dōn"), village, Thayetmyo dist., Upper Burma, 30 mi. W of Thayetmyo, at foot of the Arakan Yoma.

Mindoro (mĭndô'rō), island (□ 3,759; 1939 pop. 116,988) of the Philippines, bet. Mindoro Strait (W) and Tablas Strait (E), just SW of Luzon across Verde Isl. Passage; 12°12'–13°31'N 120°17'–121°33'E; c.90 mi. long, c.60 mi. wide. Has low coastal strips and mountainous interior rising to 8,484 ft. in Mt. Halcon. L. Naujan is in NE area. Primarily agr.; chief products are rice, copra, abacá. Coal is mined in S area. Inhabitants are mostly Tagalogs. Mindoro province (□ 3,891; 1948 pop. 167,705) includes Mindoro isl., LUBANG ISLANDS, ILIN ISLAND, AMBULONG ISLAND, and several other offshore isls.; ⊙ CALAPAN on N Mindoro isl. In Second World War, U.S. forces landed on Jap.-held Mindoro on Dec. 15, 1944.

Mindoro Strait, Philippines, separates Mindoro and Calamian Isls., leads from S.China Sea to Sulu Sea via the Cuyo passes; c.50 mi. wide. Apo Reef divides it into Apo West Pass and Apo East Pass.

Mindouli (mĕndōōlē'), village, S Middle Congo territory, Fr. Equatorial Africa, near Belgian Congo border, on railroad, and 100 mi. W of Brazzaville; copper-mining center. Zinc, silver, lead, and manganese also mined here. Stock raising. R.C. and Protestant missions. Mindouli copper deposits were worked by natives before European penetration of central Africa; deposits are nearly exhausted.

Mindszent (mĭnt'sĕnt), market town (pop. 9,630), Csongrad co., S Hungary, on Tisza R. and 10 mi. NW of Hodmezövasarhely; wheat, tobacco, cattle, sheep.

Mindyak (mĕndyäk'), town (1948 pop. over 2,000), E Bashkir Autonomous SSR, Russian SFSR, in the S Urals, 17 mi. ENE of Beloretsk; wheat, livestock.

Mine Centre, village (pop. estimate 100), W Ont., on Little Turtle L. (7 mi. long, 5 mi. wide), 40 mi. ENE of Fort Frances; gold, iron mining.

Minehead, urban district (1931 pop. 6,315; 1951 census 7,400), NW Somerset, England, on Bristol Channel and 21 mi. NW of Taunton; seaside resort; small fishing port; agr. market. Has 14th-15th-cent. church.

Mine Head, cape, S Co. Waterford, Ireland, 7 mi. SSE of Dungarvan; lighthouse (52°N 7°35'W).

Mine Hill, village (1940 pop. 998), Morris co., N central N.J., 3 mi. W of Dover; ships crushed stone, sand. Iron mine here opened 1858, reopened 1939.

Mineiros (mĕnā'rōōs). **1** City (pop. 1,851), SW Goiás, central Brazil, 110 mi. W of Rio Verde; sugar, tobacco, coffee. **2** City, São Paulo, Brazil: see MINEIROS DO TIETÊ.

Mineiros do Tietê (dōō tyĭtā'), city (pop. 1,372), central São Paulo, Brazil, on railroad and 10 mi. SSE of Jaú; produces beer, beverages, macaroni; coffee and rice processing, tanning. Until 1944, Mineiros.

Mine La Motte (mēn lä mŏt'), historic village, Madison co., SE Mo., in St. Francois Mts. 5 mi. N of Fredericktown. First lead mine in present-day Mo. was opened here in 1715 by Antoine de la Mothe Cadillac.

Mineo (mĕnā'ô), anc. *Menae,* town (pop. 8,568), Catania prov., SE central Sicily, 4 mi. S of L. Naftia, 10 mi. ENE of Caltagirone, in olive and almond region; soap mfg. Founded in 5th cent. B.C. Ruins of anc. fortifications.

Mineola (mĭnēō'lŭ). **1** Village (pop. 14,831), ⊙ Nassau co., SE N.Y., on W Long Isl., 8 mi. ENE of Jamaica; commercial and shipping center in potato- and truck-growing area; mfg. (clothing, fertilizers, radio parts, food products, wood and metal products, machinery, tools). Has repair, service shops for U.S. Mitchel Air Force Base (SE). Inc. 1906. **2** City (pop. 3,626), Wood co., NE Texas, near Sabine R., 24 mi. NNW of Tyler; commercial, shipping center (railroad junction, with shops), in agr. and truck-farming area; cotton ginning, lumber and cottonseed-oil milling, woodworking; mfg. of tile, cement blocks, mattresses. Settled 1872, inc. 1873.

Miner, county (□ 571; pop. 6,268), E central S.Dak.; ⊙ Howard. Agr. area watered by several streams and artificial lakes. Livestock, dairy produce, grain, poultry. Formed 1873.

Minera (mĭnĕ'rä), town and parish (pop. 1,191), E Denbigh, Wales, 4 mi. WNW of Wrexham; coal mining. Lead was formerly mined here.

Mineral. **1** County (□ 921; pop. 698), SW Colo.; ⊙ Creede. Mining and livestock-grazing region, drained by headwaters of Rio Grande. Silver, lead. Includes ranges of Rocky Mts. and parts of Rio Grande and San Juan natl. forests. Wheeler Natl. Monument is in NE. Formed 1893. **2** County (□ 1,223; pop. 2,081), W Mont.; ⊙ Superior. Agr. region bordering on Idaho; drained by the Clark Fork. Livestock, dairy products; small gold and silver mines. Has parts of Lolo and Cabinet Natl. Forests. Bitterroot Range in W. Formed 1914. **3** County (□ 3,734; pop. 5,560), W Nev.; ⊙ Hawthorne. Mtn. region bordering on Calif.; Walker L. and Wassuck Range in W. U.S. naval ammunition depot near Hawthorne; part of Walker River Indian Reservation in NW. Gold, silver, tungsten; ranching; tourist trade. Formed 1911. **4** County (□ 330; pop. 22,333), W.Va., in Eastern Panhandle; ⊙ Keyser. Bounded N and NW by North Branch of the Potomac; drained by short Patterson Creek; traversed by Allegheny Front (in W) and by Knobly and Patterson Creek Mts. and others. Timber, coal mines; agr. (livestock, dairy products, fruit). Some industry at Keyser. Formed 1866.

Mineral. **1** Resort village, Tehama co., N Calif., 35 mi. ENE of Red Bluff. Hq. for Lassen Volcanic Natl. Park (just NE). **2** Village (pop. 274), Bureau co., N Ill., 10 mi. NNE of Kewanee, in agr. and bituminous-coal area. **3** Town (pop. 414), Louisa co., central Va., 30 mi. E of Charlottesville; clothing mfg.

Mineral Bluff, town (pop. 209), Fannin co., N Ga., 4 mi. NE of Blue Ridge; sawmilling.
Mineral City, village (pop. 831), Tuscarawas co., E Ohio, 9 mi. NE of New Philadelphia, in coal-mining area; makes refractories.
Mineral de la Reforma (mēnäräl' dā lä räfôr'mä), town (pop. 2,139), Hidalgo, central Mexico, 5 mi. S of Pachuca; silver and gold mining.
Mineral del Chico (děl chē'kō) or **El Chico,** town (pop. 1,225), Hidalgo, central Mexico, 6 mi. N of Pachuca; silver and gold mining. Formerly Atotonilco. Resort in majestic mtn. setting near by.
Mineral del Monte (mōn'tā), city (pop. 13,536), Hidalgo, central Mexico, on central plateau, 4 mi. E of Pachuca; silver- and gold-mining center; foundries; mfg. of explosives. Sometimes Real del Monte.
Mineral Heights, town (pop. 552), Hunt co., NE Texas.
Mineral Hills, village (pop. 333), Iron co., SW Upper Peninsula, Mich., 2 mi. NNW of Iron River city.
Mineral Hot Springs, hamlet, Saguache co., S central Colo., on San Luis Creek, in S foothills of Sawatch Mts., and 13 mi. ENE of Saguache; alt. 7,767 ft.; resort. Ouray Peak is 19 mi. NW.
Mineral Mountains, in Beaver co., SW Utah, extend 25 mi. N from Minersville. Max. alt. 11,200 ft.
Mineralnye Vody or **Mineral'nyye Vody** (mĕnyĭrăl"-nēū vô'dē) [Rus.,=mineral waters], city (1926 pop. 17,576), S Stavropol Territory, Russian SFSR, on Kuma R., on Rostov-Baku RR and 12 mi. NNE of Pyatigorsk. Rail junction for Pyatigorsk resort dist. (S); freight yards, workshops; airport. Mfg. of mineral-water bottles; metalworks, flour mill; dairying, horticulture. During Second World War, held (1942–43) by Germans.
Mineral Point. 1 Town (pop. 304), Washington co., E central Mo., in the Ozarks, 13 mi. NW of Flat River. **2** City (pop. 2,284), Iowa co., S Wis., 43 mi. SW of Madison, in dairy and livestock area; dairy products, batteries, beer, foundry products. Inc. 1857. Has old Cornish miners' houses dating from lead-mining activity of mid-19th cent.
Mineral Ridge, village (1940 pop. 1,559), Trumbull co., NE Ohio, just NW of Youngstown; foundry products, canned foods.
Mineral Springs. 1 Town (pop. 751), Howard co., SW Ark., 6 mi. SW of Nashville. **2** Town (pop. 135), Union co., S N.C., 7 mi. SW of Monroe.
Mineral Wells, city (pop. 7,801), Palo Pinto co., N central Texas, 45 mi. W of Fort Worth; health resort with mineral wells; ships mineral crystals. Mfg. (hosiery, brick, feed, dairy products); sericulture recently begun. Just E is L. Mineral Wells (capacity 7,300 acre-ft.), a reservoir in Trinity R. system, formed by dam in small Rock Creek. Camp Wolters (just NE) was huge infantry training center in Second World War. City founded 1872.
Minerbe (mēnĕr'bĕ), village (pop. 1,688), Verona prov., Veneto, N Italy, 3 mi. NNE of Legnago.
Minerbio (mēnĕr'byô), town (pop. 1,445), Bologna prov., Emilia-Romagna, N central Italy, 11 mi. NE of Bologna; hemp mill, rope and macaroni factories.
Minersville. 1 Borough (pop. 7,783), Schuylkill co., E central Pa., 3 mi. NNW of Pottsville; anthracite; clothing. Settled c.1793, inc. 1831. **2** Town (pop. 593), Beaver co., SW Utah, on Beaver R. and 17 mi. WSW of Beaver, just SW of Mineral Mts., in irrigated agr. area (alfalfa, corn, fruit); alt. 5,625 ft.
Minerva. 1 Resort village, Essex co., NE N.Y., in the Adirondacks, 37 mi. NNW of Glens Falls. Hunting near by. **2** Village (pop. 3,280), on Stark-Carroll co. line, E Ohio, 15 mi. ESE of Canton, in agr. area; pottery, brick, tile, wax paper, electrical apparatus. Founded 1835.
Minerva Park, village (pop. 232), Franklin co., central Ohio, suburb N of Columbus.
Minervino Murge (mēnĕrvē'nô mōōr'jĕ), town (pop. 18,604), Bari prov., Apulia, S Italy, 15 mi. SW of Andria; wine, olive oil.
Minetto (mĭnĕ'tō), village (1940 pop. 600), Oswego co., N central N.Y., on Oswego R., just S of Oswego; wood products.
Mineville, village (1940 pop. 932), Essex co., NE N.Y., near L. Champlain, 18 mi. NNW of Ticonderoga, in iron-mining area.
Mineyama (mēnā'yämŏŏ), town (pop. 5,201), Kyoto prefecture, S Honshu, Japan, 20 mi. NW of Maizuru; textile center.
Mingaladon (mĭng'gŏŏlädōn'), town (pop. 3,910), Insein dist., Lower Burma, 10 mi. N of Rangoon; site of Rangoon civil and military airport; army cantonment.
Mingalay, Scotland: see MINGULAY.
Mingan (mĭng'gŭn), village, E Que., on Mingan Channel of the St. Lawrence and 120 mi. E of Clarke City, 400 mi. NE of Quebec; 50°18'N 64°2'W; radio station, airfield.
Mingan Islands, group of 15 small islands and numerous islets, E Que., in Mingan Passage of the St. Lawrence, extending along the coast bet. Mingan and Havre St. Pierre (N) and Anticosti Isl. (S). Discovered 1535 by Cartier, they were leased 1679 by Frontenac to Louis Jolliet; seigneury was sold (1836) to Hudson's Bay Co.
Mingan Passage, E Que., channel (30 mi. wide) of the St. Lawrence, bet. Mingan, on Que. mainland, and Anticosti Isl. Near N coast are Mingan Isls.
Mingaora (mĭng-gou'rŏŏ), village, Swat state, N North-West Frontier Prov., W Pakistan, 3 mi. N of Saidu, on Swat R. and 70 mi. NE of Peshawar; market center for wheat, fruit, barley, sugar cane, wool, ghee, honey.
Ming-ch'i, China: see MINGKI.
Ming-chiang, China: see MINGKIANG.
Mingchien, Formosa: see MINGKIEN.
Mingechaur (mēn-gyĭchŏŏŏr'), city (1948 pop. over 10,000), central Azerbaijan SSR, on Kura R. (dammed), at E end of Mingechaur Reservoir (40 mi. long, 10 mi. wide), 15 mi. NW of Yevlakh, on rail spur from 28 Aprelya; site of earth dam (250 ft. high) and hydroelectric station supplying Baku industrial dist. Developed after 1945.
Mingfeng, China: see NIYA.
Mingin (mĭng'-gĭn'), village, Upper Chindwin dist., Upper Burma, on right bank of Chindwin R. and 120 mi. NW of Mandalay; timber center.
Mingki or **Ming-ch'i** (both: mĭng'chē'), town (pop. 3,418), ⊙ Mingki co. (pop. 35,883), W Fukien prov., China, 65 mi. NE of Changting; rice, sweet potatoes, sugar cane. Until 1933, Kweihwa.
Mingkiang or **Ming-chiang** (both: mĭng'jyäng'), town, ⊙ Mingkiang co. (pop. 32,488), SW Kwangsi prov., China, on railroad and 70 mi. SW of Nanning; grain.
Mingkien or **Mingchien** (both: mĭng'jyĕn'), Jap. *Nama* (nä'mä), village (1935 pop. 3,401), W central Formosa, 20 mi. S of Taichung; bamboo articles; sugar cane, rice, fruit, tea, livestock.
Mingkwang or **Ming-kuang** (both: mĭng'gwäng'), town, NE Anhwei prov., China, 65 mi. NW of Nanking and on Tientsin-Pukow RR; commercial center.
Minglanilla (mĭng-glänē'lyä), town (pop. 3,114), Cuenca prov., E central Spain, road junction on Madrid-Valencia highway, and 45 mi. SE of Cuenca, in agr. region (saffron, grapes, sheep, goats); lumbering. Flour milling, vegetable canning, liquor distilling. Saltworks.
Mingo (mĭng'gō), county (□ 423; pop. 47,409), SW W.Va.; ⊙ Williamson. Bounded W by Tug Fork (Ky. line). Extensive bituminous-coal fields; natural-gas and oil wells, timber, agr. (livestock, fruit, tobacco). Formed 1895.
Mingo, town (pop. 227), Jasper co., central Iowa, 20 mi. ENE of Des Moines; livestock, grain.
Mingo Junction, city (pop. 4,464), Jefferson co., E Ohio, 4 mi. S of Steubenville and on Ohio R.; steel-milling center, with coal mines near by. Truck and fruit farming. Settled 1809, inc. 1882.
Mingorria (mĭng-gôr'yä), town (pop. 990), Ávila prov., central Spain, on Adaja R. and 6 mi. N of Ávila; cereals, melons, grapes. Stone quarrying; flour milling, dairying, chocolate mfg.
Mingoyo (mĭng-gō'yō), town, Southern Prov., SE Tanganyika, near Lukuledi R., 10 mi. SW of Lindi; cotton, copra, sisal. Salt deposits.
Mingrelia (mĭngrē'lēŭ), Rus. *Megreliya* (myĭgrĕ'-lyēŭ), region of W Georgian SSR, on Black Sea, bet. Ingur and Rion rivers. Tea, vineyards. Main town, Zugdidi. Includes part of Colchis lowland (S); sometimes identified with anc. Colchis. Passed 1803 to Russia.
Mingshan (mĭng'shän'), town (pop. 22,382), ⊙ Mingshan co. (pop. 121,156), W Szechwan prov., China, on Sikang border, just NE of Yaan; tea, millet, rice, wheat.
Mingshui (mĭng'shwā'). **1** Town, ⊙ Mingshui co. (pop. 148,979), S central Heilungkiang prov., Manchuria, 100 mi. E of Tsitsihar; kaoliang, corn, millet, soybeans. Until 1929 called Hinglungchen or Sanlisanchen. **2** Town, Shantung prov., China: see CHANGKIU.
Mingulay or **Mingalay** (both: mĭng'gŭlā), island (pop. 3) in S part of Outer Hebrides, Inverness, Scotland, bet. Pabbay (N) and Bernera (S), 10 mi. SW of Barra; 3 mi. by 1½ mi. Rises to 891 ft.
Mingus (mĭng'gŭs), city (pop. 310), Palo Pinto co., N central Texas, c.65 mi. WSW of Fort Worth; rail point in agr. area.
Mingus Mountain, peak (7,720 ft.) in Black Hills, central Ariz., 3 mi. S of Jerome. Copper is mined near by.
Minhang (mĭn'häng'), town, S Kiangsu prov., China, 17 mi. S of Shanghai, in cotton region.
Minhiung, Minsiung, or **Minhsiung** (all: mĭn'-shyŏŏng'), Jap. *Tamio* (tä'mēō), town (1935 pop. 4,481), W central Formosa, on railroad and 5 mi. N of Kiayi; mfg. of brick, bamboo paper; gold- and silverwork.
Minhla (mĭn-hlä'). **1** Village, Thayetmyo dist., Upper Burma, on right bank of Irrawaddy R. (landing) and 15 mi. SSE of Magwe; linked by pipe line with Yenanma oil field (SW). Site of old fort captured 1885 in 3d Anglo-Burmese War. **2** Town (pop. 4,413), Tharrawaddy dist., Lower Burma, on Rangoon-Prome RR and 65 mi. SSE of Prome.
Minhli (mĭng'lē'), village, Thainguyen prov., N Vietnam, port on the Song Cau and 7 mi. NW of Thainguyen; ships coal from Phanme and zinc from Langhit (linked by railroad).
Minho (mĭn'hŭ'), town, ⊙ Minho co. (pop. 100,443), NE Tsinghai prov., China, on Kansu border, on Sining R. at mouth of the Tatung, and 55 mi. ESE of Sining; agr. products; cattle raising; gold washing. Called Chwankow until 1933.
Minho (mē'nyŏŏ), province (□ 1,868; 1940 pop. 741,510), northernmost Portugal, formed 1936 from N part of old Entre Douro e Minho prov.; ⊙ Braga. It contains Braga and Viana do Castelo dists. Cities: Braga, Viana do Castelo, Guimarães.
Minho River or **Rio Minho** (rē'ō mĭ'nō), W central and S Jamaica, rises just E of Spaldings,' flows c.40 mi. SE and S through a fertile valley, past Frankfield, Chapleton, May Pen, and Alley, to the coast. Not navigable.
Minho River, Spain and Portugal: see MIÑO RIVER.
Minhow, China: see FOOCHOW.
Minhsien (mĭn'shyĕn'), town, ⊙ Minhsien co. (pop. 175,312), SE Kansu prov., China, on Tao R. and 90 mi. W of Tienshui; wheat, millet, corn. Gold deposits near by. Until 1913 called Minchow.
Minhsiung, Formosa: see MINHIUNG.
Minia, Egypt: see MINYA.
Minicoy Island (mĭ'nĭkoi), southernmost of Laccadive Isls., India, in Arabian Sea; 8°15'N 73°5'E. Separated from other isls. of the Laccadives proper (W) by Nine Degree Channel and from Maldive Isls. (S) by Eight Degree Channel; under administration of Malabar dist., Madras. Coconuts. Culturally akin to the Maldives, Minicoy was presented to a Moslem ruler of the Laccadives by a Maldive sultan in 16th cent. and has since shared the history of the Laccadives.
Minidoka (mĭnĭdō'kŭ), county (□ 750; pop. 9,785), S Idaho; ⊙ Rupert. Irrigated farm lands receive water from L. Walcott, formed by Minidoka Dam on Snake R. Potatoes, sugar beets, dry beans, alfalfa; livestock. Formed 1913.
Minidoka, village (pop. 113), Minidoka co., S Idaho, 15 mi. NE of Rupert; alt. 4,282 ft.; rail center in irrigated area. Minidoka Dam is 6 mi. S.
Minidoka Dam, S Idaho, on Snake R. and 18 mi. ENE of Burley. Earth-fill dam built as unit in Minidoka irrigation project. Storage was begun 1909, additional works completed 1913. Main unit is 86 ft. high, 650 ft. long. Power plant (13,400 kw). Forms L. Walcott (10 mi. long, 2 mi. wide; capacity 107,240 acre-ft.). Project area lies N and S of Snake R. and consists of 120,000 acres in vicinity of Minidoka and Burley and of 95,000 acres around Shoshone and Gooding. Other units are JACKSON LAKE DAM in Wyo., and AMERICAN FALLS DAM in Idaho. One of the system's canals extends 70 mi. NW from Snake R. W of Burley to Big Wood R. at Gooding.
Minieh, Egypt: see MINYA.
Minier (mĭnēr'), village (pop. 780), Tazewell co., central Ill., 17 mi. W of Bloomington, in agr. and bituminous-coal area.
Miniet el Heit (mĭn'yĕt ĕl hāt'), **Minya** (mĭn'yŭ), or **Minyat al-Hayt** (mĭn'yĕt ĕl hāt'), village (pop. 10,127), Faiyum prov., Upper Egypt, 3 mi. WSW of Itsa; cotton, cereals, sugar cane, fruits.
Mininco (mēnĕng'kō), village (1930 pop. 515), Malleco prov., S central Chile, on railroad and 13 mi. E of Angol, in agr. area (grain, apples, wine, cattle).
Miniota (mĭnēō'tŭ), village (pop. estimate 300), SW Man., on Assiniboine R. and 50 mi. WNW of Brandon; dairying; grain, stock.
Minipe (mĭn'ĭpä), village, Central Prov., Ceylon, on the Mahaweli Ganga and 22 mi. ESE of Kandy; rice. Irrigation project here, to reclaim □ 195.
Minis (mē'nĕsh), Rum. *Miniş*, Hung. *Ménes* (mā'nĕsh), village (pop. 1,047), Arad prov., W Rumania, near Mures R., just SE of Ghioroc; wine and fruit.
Minish, Ireland: see MWEENISH.
Minishant, village in Maybole parish, central Ayrshire, Scotland; woolen milling.
Minius, Spain and Portugal: see MIÑO RIVER.
Minkcreek or **Mink Creek,** village (pop. 124), Franklin co., SE Idaho, 11 mi. NE of Preston; poultry, dairy.
Min Kiang, China: see MIN RIVER.
Minkovtsy or **Min'kovtsy** (mē'nyŭkŭftsē), village (1926 pop. 1,922), SE Kamenets-Podolski oblast, Ukrainian SSR, 25 mi. ENE of Kamenets-Podolski; clothing industry.
Minlaton, village (pop. 617), S South Australia, on S central Yorke Peninsula, 55 mi. W of Adelaide across Gulf St. Vincent; wheat, wool.
Minlo (mĭn'lŭ'), town, ⊙ Minlo co. (pop. 39,278), central Kansu prov., China, near Tsinghai border, 38 mi. SE of Changyeh; alt. 7,874 ft.; grain. Gold deposits near by. Until 1933 called Hungshui.
Minna (mēnä'), town (pop. 2,590), ⊙ Niger prov., Northern Provinces, W central Nigeria, 200 mi. SSW of Kano; 9°37'N 6°32'E. Rail junction (branch to Baro); gold-mining center; shea-nut processing; cotton, ginger, cassava, durra, yams. Has hosp.
Minneapolis (mĭ"nēă'pŭlĭs). **1** City (pop. 1,801), ⊙ Ottawa co., N central Kansas, on Solomon R. and 20 mi. NNW of Salina; trade and shipping center for livestock, grain, and poultry region; grain milling and grain storage. State park is E. Rock City, area of strikingly eroded rock formations, is W. Laid out 1866, inc. 1871. **2** City (pop. 521,718), ⊙ Hennepin co., E Minn., on both banks of Mississippi R., near mouth of Minnesota R., adjacent to

St. Paul, and c.350 mi. NW of Chicago; 44°58′N 93°16′W; alt. 828 ft.; largest city in state. Minneapolis and St. Paul, the Twin Cities, are the financial, commercial, and industrial center of vast agr. area. Principal industries are flour milling and processing of dairy products. Important manufactures are farm and electrical equipment, structural steel, construction machinery, clothing, chemicals, bags, candy, beverages. City was settled c.1847 on W bank of Mississippi R. at head of navigation near Falls of St. Anthony (visited and named by Father Hennepin in 1680). Inc. as town 1856, as city 1867; annexed village of St. Anthony (settled c.1839 on E bank of river) in 1872. Falls were convenient source of water power and important factor in early development of city first as lumber center and later, with increase in wheat cultivation, as flour-milling center. City is now port of entry and transportation center served by several air lines (airport is Wold Chamberlain Field) and railroads; has Air Force base and a naval air station. Noted for wide streets and numerous lakes and parks; has many bridges across Mississippi. Univ. of Minn., Minneapolis Col. of Music, MacPhail Col. of Music, Minneapolis School of Art, Augsburg Col. and Theological Seminary (Lutheran), Dunwoody Institute (large trade school), and Minn. Bible Col. are here. City is also known for symphony orchestra (established 1903) and for Institute of Arts. Points of interest are Walker Art Galleries, Foshay Tower (highest building in city), Municipal Auditorium (with seating capacity of 15,000), Federal Reserve Bank Building (designed by Cass Gilbert), and Minnehaha Park, with MINNEHAHA FALLS and Stevens House (built 1849). Just SE is Fort Snelling, historic military outpost (completed 1823) that once included much of what is now Minneapolis and is now used as military training camp. L. Minnetonka is 12 mi. W of city.

Minnedosa (mĭnĭdō′sū), town (pop. 1,837), SW Man., on Minnedosa R. and 30 mi. N of Brandon; lumbering, mixed farming; resort.

Minnedosa River, SW Man., rises in Riding Mtn. Natl. Park, flows c.150 mi. in a winding course generally S, past Minnedosa, to Assiniboine R., 8 mi. W of Brandon.

Minnehaha (mĭ″nēhä′hä) [traditionally Indian, =laughing water], county (□ 815; pop. 70,910), E S.Dak., on Minn. line; ⊙ Sioux Falls. Highly productive agr. area drained by Big Sioux R. Mfg. at Sioux Falls; dairy produce, grain, livestock, poultry. Formed 1862.

Minnehaha Falls, E Minn., just W of Mississippi R. in Minnehaha Park, Minneapolis. Formed by Minnehaha Creek, which drops more than 50 ft. at this point and flows c.30 mi. from L. Minnetonka to Mississippi R. Name is immortalized in Longfellow's *Hiawatha.*

Minneiska (mĭ″nēĭ′skŭ), village (pop. 134), Wabasha co., SE Minn., on Mississippi R. and 15 mi. NW of Winona, in grain, potato, livestock area.

Minneola (mĭnēō′lŭ). **1** Town (pop. 399), Lake co., central Fla., 23 mi. W of Orlando, on small lake; ships citrus fruit. **2** City (pop. 660), Clark co., SW Kansas, 20 mi. S of Dodge City; shipping point in wheat and livestock region.

Minneota (mĭ″nēō′tŭ), village (pop. 1,274), Lyon co., SW Minn., on branch of Yellow Medicine R. and 12 mi. NW of Marshall, in grain, livestock, poultry area; dairy products. Settled 1868, inc. 1881.

Minneriya (mĭn-nä′rĭyŭ), town (pop. estimate c.5,000), North Central Prov., Ceylon, 40 mi. SE of Anuradhapura; agr. colony (irrigation project). Buddhist ruins. Just S is one of most extensive (□ 7) of anc. irrigation tanks of Ceylon, built A.D. 275 by King Maha Sena.

Minnesota (mĭ″nĭsō′tŭ), state (land □ 80,009; with inland waters, but without □ 2,212 of L. Superior, □ 84,068; 1950 pop. 2,982,483; 1940 pop. 2,792,300), N U.S., bordered N by Can. provs. of Ont. and Man., W by N.Dak. and S.Dak., S by Iowa, E by Wis.; 11th in area, 18th in pop.; admitted 1858 as 32d state; ⊙ St. Paul. The "Gopher State" is 405 mi. in its extreme length (N–S) and 180–350 mi. in width (E–W). It is bounded largely by natural features, including L. Superior (NE), Rainy L. and Rainy R. (N), Red R. of the North (NW), St. Croix R. (E), and Mississippi R. (SE). The Mississippi rises in the L. Itasca section (NW center) and winds southward through the state, receiving the Minnesota R. at the Twin Cities of Minneapolis and St. Paul. Despite its relatively low alt. (mostly 1,000–1,500 ft.), Minn. forms the watershed for 3 major river systems; the Hudson Bay (N and NW), Great Lakes-St. Lawrence (NE), and Mississippi-Missouri (center and S). In LAKE OF THE WOODS, on N border, is an isolated projection of land (known as the Northwest Angle), comprising the northernmost portion of continental U.S. Minn. has much level prairie (especially in the S), but the topography exhibits many features of continental glaciation, such as numerous lakes (e.g., RED LAKE, LEECH LAKE, Mille Lacs L., Winnibigoshish L.), and the boulder-strewn hills, the swamps, and fertile deposits; the Red R. valley shows the effect of prehistoric L. AGASSIZ. The Laurentian Plateau or Canadian Shield, consisting of Pre-Cambrian crystalline rocks, extends into the NE part of the state; here sometimes called the Superior Highlands, it includes the low Mesabi and Vermilion ranges and the Misquah Hills (2,230 ft.), the state's highest alt. Climate is continental, with severe winters and, sometimes, extremely hot summers. Annual rainfall is 20–30 in. over much of the state, increasing to c.35 in. in the SE. Days with snow cover range from 120 (N) to 60 (S). Minneapolis has mean temp. of 12°F. in Jan., 73°F. in July, and 27 in. of annual rainfall; Bemidji (N center) has mean temp. of 4°F. in Jan., 69°F. in July, and 23 in. of rain. The growing season varies from 160 days (S) to less than 100 days (N). Minn. has over 30,000,000 acres of farm and range land, of which the harvested crop acreage is c.19,000,000. The state is a leading producer of oats, corn, flaxseed, barley, rye, hay, hogs, cattle, poultry, and eggs, and also has large areas under wheat, potatoes, soybeans, and truck crops. Corn and oats, in the SW and S, where hog raising is basic, are grown primarily for feed. The fertile Red R. valley lies in the spring-wheat belt but is also a region of diversified farming—potatoes, flax, and rye, oats, and barley (forage crops). Apples (SE) and sugar beets (center) are also grown. Livestock is especially important, cattle totaling 3,275,000, hogs 3,500,000, and sheep 700,000. Large quantities of creamery butter (in which Minn. ranks 1st) and milk come from the SE dairying areas. The iron ore (hematite) mined in the MESABI RANGE and, in smaller amounts, the VERMILION RANGE and Cuyuna Range represents almost 70% of the U.S. output. Chief mining centers (mostly open-pit mines) are Hibbing, Ely, Chisholm, Virginia, and Crosby, which are linked by rail to the shipping points of DULUTH and Two Harbors on L. Superior. With the gradual depletion of the better deposits, much low-grade ore (taconite) is now being beneficiated in the Mesabi Range; manganiferous ore is worked in the Cuyuna Range. Other mineral deposits are granite (near St. Cloud), limestone, marl, sandstone, sand and gravel, and clay. Natl. forest reserves comprise c.5,000,000 acres; total commercial forest land amounts to 16,700,000 acres, which supports a declining lumber industry in the N and NE. At International Falls is a large paper mill. Minn.'s principal industries are meat packing (concentrated at South St. Paul), flour and other grain milling, and the mfg. of non-electrical machinery, farm implements, chemicals, dairy products, textiles, food and beverages, wood products, and leather goods; also printing and publishing. Minneapolis, the state's largest city, is a major flour-milling and grain center, communications hub, and distribution point; St. Paul is an important industrial center; and Duluth is a great inland port, shipping vast quantities of iron ore and grain. A steel plant is in the vicinity of Duluth. Other mfg. and commercial towns include Rochester (seat of famous Mayo Clinic), St. Cloud, Austin, Winona, Mankato, and Faribault. A wealth of picturesque lakes and forests makes Minn. a popular recreation area for boating, fishing (trout, bass, lake herring), and hunting, especially in the NE section, known as the "Arrowhead Country." PIPESTONE NATIONAL MONUMENT (Indian lore), Minnehaha Falls, L. Minnetonka, the North Shore of L. Superior, and several scenic state parks are other points of tourist interest. The Univ. of Minn. is at Minneapolis, Hamline Univ. at St. Paul, St. Olaf Col. at Northfield. Before the white man's arrival, the dominant Indian tribes in Minn. were the Sioux and Ojibwa. The 1st pioneers in the region were French fur trappers and missionaries, including Radisson and Groseilliers (1655–60), Duluth (1679–90), Father Hennepin, who discovered the Falls of St. Anthony in 1680, and Vérendrye (1730s–1740s). The French officially withdrew from the area c.1763 and the great British fur-trading companies moved in. The section E of the Mississippi was acquired by the U.S. in 1783, and later (1787) included in the NORTHWEST TERRITORY, and then in Ind. Territory (1800); the land W of the Mississippi came to the U.S. in the Louisiana Purchase of 1803. Development quickened after the War of 1812, as trappers of John Jacob Astor's American Fur Co. opened up the hinterland, American and European settlers arrived, Fort Snelling (on site of present Minneapolis) was founded c.1820, and steamboats began to ply the upper Mississippi. Lumber camps were established in the E, missionary activity continued, and land was purchased from the Indians for further white settlement. The explorers Joseph Nicollet and George Catlin contributed much to the knowledge of the country. Minn. became a territory in 1849, and as immigrants poured into the area and villages sprang up overnight there followed a short boom period of land speculations, which collapsed suddenly with the panic of 1857. Soon after statehood was achieved, the Sioux, resentful of the rapid advance of the white man's civilization and the consequent destruction of their own, took advantage of the departure of Civil War contingents (1862) and rose in rebellion. Hundreds of white settlers were killed before the Indians were suppressed and confined to reservations. In the '60s and '70s settlement was pushed by the Homestead Law (1862) and the extension of the railroads; large areas were planted in wheat, but lumbering was still the major industry—whose logging operations were immortalized in the stories of the legendary Paul Bunyan. The prosperity enjoyed by railroad barons (e.g., James J. Hill) and flour manufacturers (e.g., John S. Pillsbury) was not shared by most farmers, who suffered from excessive rail rates, blizzards, and grasshopper plagues; dissent in the late 19th cent. found political expression in the Farmers' Alliance and Granger and Populist parties; in the 1920s and '30s Minn. was the stronghold of the Farmer-Labor party. The 1st shipment of iron ore was dispatched via the Great Lakes in 1884. Minn. has a sizable Scandinavian community, which has been partly responsible for the wide use of agr. cooperatives throughout the state. The mfg. industry was greatly stimulated by the Second World War. See also articles on cities, towns, geographic features, and the 87 counties: AITKIN, ANOKA, BECKER, BELTRAMI, BENTON, BIG STONE, BLUE EARTH, BROWN, CARLTON, CARVER, CASS, CHIPPEWA, CHISAGO, CLAY, CLEARWATER, COOK, COTTONWOOD, CROW WING, DAKOTA, DODGE, DOUGLAS, FARIBAULT, FILLMORE, FREEBORN, GOODHUE, GRANT, HENNEPIN, HOUSTON, HUBBARD, ISANTI, ITASCA, JACKSON, KANABEC, KANDIYOHI, KITTSON, KOOCHICHING, LAC QUI PARLE, LAKE, LAKE OF THE WOODS, LE SUEUR, LINCOLN, LYON, MCLEOD, MAHNOMEN, MARSHALL, MARTIN, MEEKER, MILLE LACS, MORRISON, MOWER, MURRAY, NICOLLET, NOBLES, NORMAN, OLMSTED, OTTER TRAIL, PENNINGTON, PINE, PIPESTONE, POLK, POPE, RAMSEY, RED LAKE, REDWOOD, RENVILLE, RICE, ROCK, ROSEAU, SAINT LOUIS, SCOTT, SHERBURNE, SIBLEY, STEARNS, STEELE, STEVENS, SWIFT, TODD, TRAVERSE, WABASHA, WADENA, WASECA, WASHINGTON, WATONWAN, WILKIN, WINONA, WRIGHT, YELLOW MEDICINE.

Minnesota City, village (pop. 201), Winona co., SE Minn., on Mississippi R. just NW of Winona, in grain, potato, livestock raising area. State park is near by.

Minnesota Lake, village (pop. 609), Faribault co., S Minn., 27 mi. NW of Albert Lea, in grain, livestock, and poultry area; dairy products. Small, nearly dry lake is here.

Minnesota River, rises in Big Stone L., on Minn.-S.Dak. line, flows 224 mi. SE through SW Minn. to Mankato, where it turns sharply N and flows 108 mi. NE to Mississippi R. at Mendota, just S of St. Paul; total length 332 mi. Drains rich agr. area (corn, small grains, vegetables, dairy products, sugar beets). There are small dams at SE ends of Marsh L. and Lac qui Parle, along its course. Early known as the St. Peter, or St. Pierre, river was important route for explorers and fur traders. It follows valley of prehistoric River Warren, S outlet of L. Agassiz.

Minnetonka, Lake (mĭ″nĭtŏng′kŭ), largely in Hennepin co., E Minn., 12 mi. W of Minneapolis; □ 23; 10 mi. long, max. width 2.5 mi. Has deeply indented shore line (97 mi. long) and several small islands and peninsulas. Drains through Minnehaha Creek into Mississippi R. Lake is celebrated in songs by Thurlow Lieurance ("By the Waters of Minnetonka") and Charles W. Cadman ("From the Land of the Sky-Blue Water"). There are numerous resorts.

Minnetonka Beach, resort village (pop. 376), Hennepin co., E Minn., on small peninsula in L. Minnetonka, 17 mi. W of Minneapolis.

Minnewanka, Lake (mĭnĭwăng′kŭ) (12 mi. long, 1 mi. wide), SW Alta., near B.C. border, in Rocky Mts., in Banff Natl. Park, 6 mi. NE of Banff, at foot of Mts. Aylmer and Girouard; alt. 4,769 ft.

Minnewaska, Lake (mĭ″nĭwŏ′skŭ). **1** In Pope co., W Minn., at Glenwood; □ 19; 7.5 mi. long, 2 mi. wide. Resorts. Drains through small stream into L. Emily, 6 mi. SW. **2** In N.Y.: see LAKE MINNEWASKA.

Minnewaukan (mĭ″nĭwô′kŭn), city (pop. 443), ⊙ Benson co., central N.Dak., 18 mi. W of Devils Lake, in grain area.

Minnewawa, Lake (mĭ″nĭwä′wŭ), Aitkin co., NE central Minn., just SE of Sandy L., 22 mi. NE of Aitkin in state forest; 5 mi. long, max. width 2 mi. Resorts.

Minnigaff, agr. village and parish (pop. 1,144), W Kirkcudbright, Scotland, on Cree R. just N of Newton Stewart; woolen milling.

Minnipa, village (pop. 255), S South Australia, on W central Eyre Peninsula, 135 mi. NNW of Port Lincoln, on Port Lincoln–Penong RR.; wheat, wool.

Mino (mē′nō), former province in central Honshu, Japan; now part of Gifu prefecture.

Mino. 1 Town (pop. 11,249), Gifu prefecture, central Honshu, Japan, 12 mi. NE of Gifu; commercial center in rice-growing area; paper milling. **2** Town (pop. 17,738), Saitama prefecture, central Honshu, Japan, 5 mi. N of Chichibu; silk textiles; raw silk, wheat. Formed in early 1940s by combining former town of Minano (1940 pop. 3,751) and several villages. **3** Town (pop. 8,388), Tokushima prefecture, N central Shikoku, Japan, on Yoshino R. and 34 mi. W of Tokushima; agr. center (rice, wheat); raw silk.

Minoa (mĭnō'ŭ), village (pop. 1,008), Onondaga co., central N.Y., 8 mi. E of Syracuse, in dairying area.

Minobu (mēnō'bōō), town (pop, 5,310), Yamanashi prefecture, central Honshu, Japan, 22 mi. SSW of Kofu; rice, wheat.

Minocqua (mĭnŏ'kwŭ), resort village (1940 pop. 683), Oneida co., N Wis., 21 mi. NW of Rhinelander, in lake region; lumbering.

Minong (mĭ'nŏng), resort village (pop. 357), Washburn co., NW Wis., 20 mi. N of Spooner, in wooded lake region.

Minonk (mĭ'nŭngk), city (pop. 1,955), Woodford co., central Ill., 29 mi. N of Bloomington; bituminous-coal mines; agr. (dairy products; livestock, grain). Inc. 1867.

Minooka (mĭnōō'kŭ). **1** Village (pop. 369), Grundy co., NE Ill., 11 mi. WSW of Joliet, in agr. and bituminous-coal area. **2** Residential village (1940 pop. 2,828), Lackawanna co., NE Pa., on Lackawanna R. just SW of Scranton.

Minorca (mĭnôr'kŭ), Sp. *Menorca* (mānôr'kä), anc. *Balearis Minor* or *Minorca*, second largest island (□ 271; pop. 43,025) of the Balearic Isls., Spain, in the W Mediterranean, separated by 23-mi.-wide channel from Majorca (SW), 125 mi. SE of Barcelona. Chief city and port, MAHÓN. Isl. is roughly 30 mi. long NW-SE, c.10 mi. wide. Has indented coast line, particularly in arid N; fringed by numerous islets. Its low elevation (highest: El Toro, 1,107 ft.) exposes it to north winds. Less fertile than Majorca, it nevertheless grows cereals, wine, olives, hemp, tubers. Considerable stock raising. Fishing for local consumption. Some iron is mined. Chief industrial products for export are shoes and cheese. Also mfg. of metalware, business machines, textile goods, soap, sandals, wine, liquor, chocolate, sweets, meat products. Mahón, on fine sheltered bay, is an important naval and air base. Historic Ciudadela, fishing port on W shore, is a bishopric. Isl. is remarkable for its many Celtic and Druid megalithic monuments. Like the other isls. of the group, Minorca was successively held by Carthaginians, Romans, Vandals, and Moors. Later, it came under rule of kings of Aragon. Occupied (1708) by the English during War of Spanish Succession and later seized by the French, it was recovered by Spain in 1782, Sp. possession being confirmed by Peace of Amiens (1802). In the Sp. civil war (1936–39), remained in Loyalist hands until Feb., 1939, while Majorca early passed to Nationalists.

Minori (mēnō'rē), town (pop. 2,189), Salerno prov., Campania, S Italy, port on Gulf of Salerno, 7 mi. WSW of Salerno; paper milling.

Miño River (mē'nyō), Port. *Minho* (mē'nyōō), anc. *Minius*, in NW Spain and northernmost Portugal, rises in N Galicia S of Mondoñedo, flows S, past Lugo and Orense, then turns SW and forms Sp.-Port. border for a distance of 47 mi. above its mouth on the Atlantic at Caminha. Length, 210 mi. Navigable 28 mi. to Monção. Chief tributary, the Sil, flows entirely in Spain.

Minorski or **Minorskiy** (mēnôr'skē), town (1940 pop. over 500), SE Yakut Autonomous SSR, Russian SFSR, 45 mi. S of Allakh-Yun; gold mining.

Mino-seki, Japan: see SEKI, Gifu prefecture.

Minoshima (mēnō'shĭmä), town (pop. 17,146), Wakayama prefecture, S Honshu, Japan, on Kii Channel, on W Kii Peninsula, 10 mi. SSW of Wakayama; fishing port; agr. (citrus fruit, chrysanthemums for making insecticide).

Minot (mĭ'nŭt). **1** Town (pop. 750), Androscoggin co., SW Maine, on the Little Androscoggin just W of Auburn; mfg., food canning. **2** Village, Plymouth co., Mass.: see SCITUATE. **3** City (pop. 22,032), ⊙ Ward co., NW central N.Dak., 110 mi. NNW of Bismarck and on Souris R.; 48°14'N 101°17'W. Rail center; lignite mines; grain refining, shipping; processing of dairy produce, poultry; wheat, livestock, sausages, building materials. State teachers col. Dikes and dams have been built for flood control. Settled 1886, inc. 1887.

Minots Ledge (mĭnŭts), E Mass., reef in Massachusetts Bay, c.2.5 mi. off Cohasset. First lighthouse here (built 1850) destroyed by gale in 1851; present 114-ft. structure built 1860; 42°16'N 70°46'W.

Miño Volcano (mē'nyō), Andean peak (18,440 ft.), N Chile, near Bolivia border; 20°11'S. At its NE foot rises Loa R.

Minowa (mēnō'wä), town (pop. 6,266), Gumma prefecture, central Honshu, Japan, 6 mi. W of Maebashi; silk cocoons, rice.

Minquiers Islands (mēkyā'), group of small uninhabited isls., 13 mi. S of Jersey, part of Channel Isls. Used by fishermen of Channel Isls. and France under Anglo-French treaty of 1839 providing equal fishing rights.

Min River (mĭn), Chinese *Min Kiang* or *Min Chiang* (both: -jyăng'). **1** Chief river of Fukien prov., China, formed in area of Nanping by confluence of several headstreams, including Kien, Futun, and Sha rivers, flows generally SE, past Nanping and Shuikow (head of regular navigation), to E.China Sea below Foochow. Accessible for ocean-going vessels up to PAGODA, deepwater anchorage for Foochow. Total length, including Kien R., 350 mi. **2** River in W Szechwan prov., China, rises in the Min Shan on Kansu-Szechwan border, flows over 500 mi. S, past Sungpan, Mowhsien, and Kwanhsien, through the Chengtu plain, and past Pengshan and Loshan (head of junk navigation), to the Yangtze at Ipin. At Kwanhsien the river is diverted into numerous canals which irrigate the fertile Chengtu plain and are again united near Pengshan. Receives Tatu R. at Loshan.

Minsen, Germany: see HOOKSIEL.

Minshah, El, Egypt: see MANSHAH, EL.

Min Shan (mĭn' shän'), outlier of the Kunlun mtn. system, China, on Tsinghai-Kansu-Szechwan border, forming an extension of Amne Machin Mts. E of upper Yellow R.; average alt. 8,200 ft. Min R. of W Szechwan rises on S slopes.

Minshat el Bakkari or **Minshat al-Bakkari** (both: mĭn'shăt ĕl băk-kä'rē), village (pop. 7,309), Giza prov., Upper Egypt, 7 mi. WSW of Cairo's center.

Minshat Sabri (sä'brē) or **Mansha'at Sabri** (măn'-shă-ăt), village (pop. 8,224), Minufiya prov., Lower Egypt, 7 mi. E of Shibin el Kom; cereals, cotton, flax.

Minshat Sultan or **Mansha'at Sultan** (sōōl'tän), village (pop. 8,168), Minufiya prov., Lower Egypt, on railroad and 5 mi. N of Minuf; cereals, cotton, flax.

Minsiung, Formosa: see MINHIUNG.

Minsk (mĭnsk, Rus. mēnsk), oblast (□ 8,500; 1946 pop. estimate 1,000,000), central Belorussian SSR; ⊙ Minsk. In Lithuanian-Belorussian Upland; drained by Berezina, upper Ptich, and Svisloch rivers. Chiefly agr., with potatoes (E, NE), grain (SW, W; mainly rye, oats, barley, buckwheat); flax (NE). Truck gardens and orchards near Minsk and Borisov, principal industrial centers. Lumbering, peat cutting, woodworking, and distilling in rural areas. Formed 1938.

Minsk, city (1926 pop. 131,803; 1939 pop. 238,772), ⊙ Belorussian SSR and Minsk oblast, on Svisloch R. and 400 mi. WSW of Moscow; 53°53'N 27°34'E. Industrial and cultural center; mfg. (automobiles, tractors, bicycles, lathes, instruments, machine tools, radios, phonographs, fine linen cloth, cotton goods, shoes, porcelain ware, mirrors), woodworking (furniture, prefabricated houses), food processing (meat, poultry, pastry); railroad shops, cement works. Has Belorussian state univ., polytechnic, lumber trade, medical, and teachers colleges, Belorussian acad. of sciences, swamp research institute, large modern civic center, state mus., theater of opera and ballet, cathedral (1615), university and hospital "cities." First mentioned 1066; became ⊙ principality after 12th cent.; conquered 1326 by Lithuania, in 15th cent. by Poles; sacked 1505 by Tatars. Acquired 1793 by Russia. Virtually destroyed during Second World War, when it was held (1941–44) by Germans. Pop. 40% Jewish until 1941.

Minsk Mazowiecki (mē'nyŭsk mäzôvyĕts'kē), Pol. *Mińsk Mazowiecki*, Rus. *Novo Minsk* (nô'vô mēnsk'), town (pop. 10,023), Warszawa prov., E central Poland, 24 mi. E of Warsaw. Rail junction; mfg. (machinery, shingles, flour).

Minster, town and parish (pop. 3,198), NE Kent, England, on Isle of Thanet, 5 mi. W of Ramsgate; agr. market. Has Norman church and some remains of 8th-cent. Saxon abbey.

Minster, village (pop. 1,728), Auglaize co., W Ohio, 10 mi. S of St. Marys, near L. Loramie; mfg. (foundry products, machinery, beer, flour). Settled 1831, inc. 1833.

Minster-in-Sheppey, town and parish (pop. 3,782), N Kent, England, on Isle of Sheppey, on Thames estuary, 3 mi. ESE of Sheerness; agr. market and bathing resort. The 13th-cent. church incorporates remains of a nunnery established in 7th cent., later destroyed by Danes. Town figures in *Ingoldsby Legends*.

Minsterley, agr. village and parish (pop. 744), W Shropshire, England, 9 mi. SW of Shrewsbury; dairying, milk canning. Has 17th-cent. church. In parish, 2 mi. S, is barite-mining village of Snailbeach.

Minster Lovell (lŭ'vŭl), town and parish (pop. 445), W Oxfordshire, England, 3 mi. WNW of Witney; woolen milling. Has 15th-cent. church and remains of 12th-cent. monastery.

Minter, town (pop. 143), Laurens co., central Ga., 10 mi. ESE of Dublin.

Minthes or **Minthis** (both: mĭn'thĭs), mountains in W Peloponnesus, Greece, bet. Andritsaina and Gulf of Kyparissia; rise to 4,000 ft.

Minto, village (pop. 153), central Alaska, on Tanana R., and 40 mi. W of Fairbanks, outfitting base for gold-prospecting region. Has Indian mission.

Minto. 1 Village (pop. estimate 200), SW Man., 30 mi. S of Brandon; grain, stock. **2** Village (pop. estimate c.750), central N.B., near NW shore of Grand L., 60 mi. N of St. John; coal-mining center. Coal was 1st shipped to New England from here in 1643.

Minto, agr. village and parish (pop. 379), central Roxburgh, Scotland, on Teviot R. and 5 mi. NE of Hawick. Just N are craggy Minto Hills (905 ft.), site of remains of anc. Fatlips Castle. Here also is "Barnhill's Bed," described in Scott's *The Lay of the Last Minstrel*.

Minto, city (pop. 592), Walsh co., NE N.Dak., 10 mi. S of Grafton and on Forest R.

Minto, Lake (□ 485), N Que., at 57°25'N 74°30'W; 60 mi. long, 15 mi. wide; drained by Leaf R.

Minto Inlet, W Victoria Isl., SW Franklin Dist., Northwest Territories, arm (75 mi. long, 8–25 mi. wide) of Amundsen Gulf, at S end of Prince of Wales Strait; 71°15'N 117°W.

Minto Mine, village, SW B.C., in Coast Mts., on Bridge R. and 40 mi. WNW of Lillooet; gold and antimony mining.

Mintsin or **Min-ch'in** (both: mĭn'chĭn'), town, ⊙ Mintsin co. (pop. 116,682), central Kansu prov., China, at S edge of the Gobi, 60 mi. NNE of Wuwei, at the Great Wall; alt. 4,484 ft.; wheat, millet. Until 1928 called Chenfan.

Mintsing or **Min-ch'ing** (both: mĭn'chĭng'), town (pop. 28,997), ⊙ Mintsing co. (pop. 123,863), E Fukien prov., China, 30 mi. WNW of Foochow and on Min R.; rice, wheat, sweet potatoes, sugar cane; pottery. Kaolin quarrying near by.

Minturn (mĭn'tûrn). **1** Town (pop. 138), Lawrence co., NE Ark., 20 mi. WNW of Jonesboro. **2** Lumbering town (pop. 509), Eagle co., W central Colo., on Eagle R., just W of Gore Range, and 25 mi. NNW of Leadville; alt. 7,825 ft. Near by is mtn. experiment station of Colo. State Col. of Agr. and Mechanic Arts.

Minturno (mēntōōr'nô), town (pop. 3,720), Latina prov., Latium, S central Italy, on hill overlooking Gulf of Gaeta, 7 mi. E of Formia. Has castle and mid-12th-cent. church, both damaged in Second World War. In the plain below are ruins (aqueduct, temples) of anc. *Minturnae* and a Br. military cemetery with over 2,000 dead of the Ital. campaign.

Minudasht or **Minudesht** (both: mēnōōdĕsht'), town, Second Prov., in Gurgan, NE Iran, 10 mi. ESE of Gunbad-i-Qawus.

Minuf (mĭnōōf'), town (pop. 30,289), Minufiya prov., Lower Egypt, rail and canal junction 8 mi. SW of Shibin el Kom, in a rich agr. area, 35 mi. NW of Cairo; cotton ginning, linen mfg.; cereals, cotton, flax. Also spelled Menuf.

Minufiya or **Minufiyah** (mĭnōōfē'yŭ), province (□ 613; pop. 1,168,777), Lower Egypt, in Nile Delta; ⊙ SHIBIN EL KOM. Bounded N by Gharbiya prov., E and W by the Damietta and Rosetta branches of the Nile, and S by the Cairo Governorate. Rich agr. area: cotton, flax, cereals. Industries: cotton ginning, textile milling; mfg. of belts, handkerchiefs, straw mats. Main urban centers: Ashmun, Tala, Shibin el Kom, Sirs el Laiyana, Minuf. Served by railroads from Cairo. Irrigated mainly by the canals Raiyah el Minufiya and Bahr Shibin. Sometimes spelled Menufiya.

Minufiya, Raiyah, or **Rayah Minufiyah** (rä'yŭ, rī'yŭ), navigable canal of the Nile Delta, Lower Egypt, extends c.19 mi. from Delta Barrage to the Damietta branch of the Nile 6 mi. SW of Benha. Irrigation.

Minusinsk (mēnōōsēnsk'), city (1926 pop. 21,427), S Krasnoyarsk Territory, Russian SFSR, port on the Yenisei (opposite Abakan) and 150 mi. SSW of Krasnoyarsk. Center of Minusinsk-Khakass coal and industrial area; grain market; flour mills, sawmills; center for trade with Tuva Autonomous Oblast. Seat of regional Martyanov Mus.

Minusio (mēnōō'zyô), town (pop. 2,344), Ticino canton, S Switzerland, on Lago Maggiore; residential suburb E of Locarno; mineral spring.

Minuwangoda (mĭnōōvŭng-gō'dŭ), town (pop. 1,199), Western Prov., Ceylon, 16 mi. NNE of Colombo; road junction; trades in coconuts, rubber, rice.

Minvoul (mēnvōōl'), village, N Gabon, Fr. Equatorial Africa, on N'Fem R. and 55 mi. NE of Oyem, near Fr. Cameroons border; large cacao plantations are near by.

Minya (mĭn'yŭ), **El Minya,** or **Al-Minya** (both: ĕl mĭn'yă), province (□ 782; pop. 1,056,466), N Upper Egypt, in Nile valley; ⊙ Minya. Bounded S by Asyut prov., E by Arabian Desert, N by Beni Suef prov., W by Libyan Desert. Cotton ginning, woolen and sugar milling; agr. (cotton, cereals, sugar cane). Main urban centers, besides Minya, are Beni Mazar, Maghagha, El Fashn, Abu Qurqas, Samalut. Served by railway along W bank of Nile R. Important archaeological finds at BENI HASSAN and OXYRHYNCUS. Also spelled Minia.

Minya. 1 Village, Faiyum prov., Egypt: see MINIET EL HEIT. **2** or **El Minya** or **Al-Minya,** city (pop. 69,667), ⊙ Minya prov., N Upper Egypt, 140 mi. SSW of Cairo; 28°6'N 30°46'E. Important Nile port and trading center; cotton ginning, woolen and sugar milling, dairying; cotton, cereals, sugar cane. Also spelled Minia or Minieh.

Minya Konka (mĭnyä' kôngkä'), Chinese *Kungka Shan* (gōōng'gä' shän'), highest peak (24,900 ft.) of the Tahsüeh Mts., in Sikang prov., China, 25 mi. SSW of Kangting. Climbed 1932 by U.S. expedition. Sometimes spelled Minya Gongkar.

Minyar or **Min'yar** (mēnyär'), city (1937 pop. estimate 10,586), W Chelyabinsk oblast, Russian SFSR, in the S Urals, on Sim R., on railroad and 10 mi. ENE of Asha; metallurgical center (pig and sheet iron); metalworking, charcoal burning. Founded 1784; became city in 1943. Until c.1928, Minyarski Zavod.

Minyat al-Hayt, Egypt: see MINIET EL HEIT.

Minyet el Qamh or **Minyat al-Qamh** (both: mĭn'yăt ĕl käm'), town (pop. 13,829), Sharqiya prov., Lower Egypt, on the Bahr Muweis, on railroad, and 10 mi. SW of Zagazig; cotton ginning.

Minyet Mahallet Damana or **Minyat Mahallat Damanah** (măhăl'lăt dä'mănŭ), village (pop. 4,529), Daqahliya prov., Lower Egypt, on El Bahr el Saghir (a delta canal) opposite Mahallet Damana and 7 mi. ENE of Mansura; cotton, cereals.

Minyip (mĭn'yĭp), town (pop. 520), W central Victoria, Australia, 160 mi. WNW of Melbourne, in wheat-raising area.

Mio (mī'ō), village (pop. c.300), ⊙ Oscoda co., NE central Mich., c.45 mi. SW of Alpena and on Au Sable R., in Huron Natl. Forest.

Mionica or **Mionitsa** (mē'ônētsä), village, ⊙ Kolubara co., W Serbia, Yugoslavia, 10 mi. E of Valjevo.

Miory (mēô'rē), village (1939 pop. over 500), W central Polotsk oblast, Belorussian SSR, 45 mi. WNW of Polotsk, in poorly drained area; match mfg., lumbering.

Mios Lake, Norway: see Mos Lake.

Mios Num, Netherlands New Guinea: see Japen Islands.

Miquelon (mĭ'kŭlŏn, Fr. mēkŭlō'), island (□ 83; 1946 pop. 550) of Saint Pierre and Miquelon, Fr. territory (archipelago), NW of Saint Pierre and off S coast of Newfoundland. Consists of 2 sections, Grande Miquelon (N) and Petite Miquelon or Langlade (S), now joined by narrow sandbar, the Isthmus of Langlade (at 46°55'N 56°20'W). Sparsely populated and rocky isl., covered by evergreen scrub. Principal occupation is cod fishing. It has some slate and ocher deposits.

Miquihuana (mēkēwä'nä), town (pop. 1,847), Tamaulipas, NE Mexico, in Sierra Madre Oriental, 45 mi. WSW of Ciudad Victoria; alt. 6,207 ft.; cereals, livestock.

Miqve Yisrael (mēkvä' yēsrä-ĕl') or **Mikve Israel,** settlement (pop. 900), W Israel, in Plain of Sharon, 3 mi. SE of Tel Aviv; mixed farming. Has agr. research station, seed nurseries, botanical gardens. Founded 1870 as agr. school for Jews then living in Palestine. Sometimes spelled Mikveh Israel.

Mir (mēr), village (pop. 9,242), Asyut prov., central Upper Egypt, 10 mi. SW of Dairut; cereals, dates, sugar cane. About 3 mi. SW are the ruins of the Necropolis of Gosu.

Mir (mēr), town (1931 pop. 3,740), E central Baranovichi oblast, Belorussian SSR, 11 mi. W of Stolbtsy; parchment mfg., pitch processing, lumbering, flour milling, dairying (powdered milk). Has old Gothic palace, ruins of 16th-cent. castle. Noted horse-trading center until First World War.

Mira (mē'rä), town (pop. 4,684), Venezia prov., Veneto, N Italy, on Naviglio di Brenta, and 10 mi. W of Venice; mfg. (alcohol, lye, soap, candles, fertilizer, brushes, biscuits).

Mira (mē'rŭ), town (pop. 2,166), Coimbra dist., N central Portugal, near the Atlantic, 22 mi. NW of Coimbra; agr. and fishing. Has 17th-cent. church. Just W, along coast, are pine-covered dunes.

Mira (mē'rä), town (pop. 1,504), Cuenca prov., E central Spain, 45 mi. SE of Cuenca; cereals, grapes, saffron, truck, fruit, sheep, goats; flour milling.

Mira Bay (mī'rŭ), inlet of the Atlantic, NE N.S., on NE coast of Cape Breton Isl., 12 mi. SE of Sydney. Leads inland into Mira R.

Mirabeau (mēräbō'), village (pop. 1,753), Alger dept., N central Algeria, in Great Kabylia, near the Oued Sebaou, 5 mi. NNW of Tizi-Ouzou; olive-oil pressing, soap mfg., fig shipping.

Mirabel (mērävĕl'), town (pop. 1,522), Cáceres prov., W Spain, 14 mi. SW of Plasencia; olive-oil processing; fruit, wine, flax. Has some Roman remains, and medieval castle.

Mirabella, Gulf of, or **Gulf of Merabello** (both: mĭrŭbĕ'lŭ), Gr. *Kolpos Merabello,* inlet of Aegean Sea, on N coast of E Crete; 20 mi. wide, 15 mi. long. Named for village of Mirabella (Merabello; airport), N of port of Hagios Nikolaos.

Mirabella Eclano (mēräbĕl'lä ĕklä'nō), village (pop. 2,360), Avellino prov., Campania, S Italy, 14 mi. NE of Avellino; macaroni mfg.

Mirabella Imbaccari (ēmbäk'kärē), village (pop. 7,671), Catania prov., SE central Sicily, 7 mi. NNW of Caltagirone, in cereal- and grape-growing region.

Mirabello Monferrato (–lô mônfĕr-rä'tô), village (pop. 1,989), Alessandria prov., Piedmont, N Italy, 10 mi. NNW of Alessandria.

Miracatu (mērŭkŭtōō'), city (pop. 275), S São Paulo, Brazil, on railroad and 70 mi. WSW of Santos; fruit and rice processing, sawmilling. Until 1944, Prainha.

Miracema (mērŭsā'mŭ), city (pop. 6,242), NE Rio de Janeiro state, Brazil, near Minas Gerais border, 60 mi. WNW of Campos; rail terminus; textile milling, coffee and rice processing.

Miracema do Norte (dōō nôr'tĭ), city (pop. 738), N Goiás, N central Brazil, on left bank of Tocantins R. and 80 mi. N of Pôrto Nacional. Until 1944, called Miracema; and, 1944–48, Cherente (or Xerente).

Mira Daire (mē'rŭ dī'rĭ), village (pop. 1,841), Leiria dist., central Portugal, 15 mi. SSE of Leiria; textile milling. Also called Mira de Aire.

Mirador (mērŭdôr'), city (pop. 816), central Maranhão, Brazil, on upper Itapecuru R. and 120 mi. SW of Caxias; cotton, cattle, hides. Roads to Caxias, Loreto, and Nova Iorque.

Mirador Nacional (mērädôr' näsyōnäl'), mountain (1,644 ft.), Maldonado dept., S Uruguay, in the Sierra de las Ánimas, 45 mi. E of Montevideo; highest point in Uruguay.

Miradoux (mērädōō'), village (pop. 324), Gers dept., SW France, 16 mi. SSE of Agen; winegrowing, dairying.

Miraflores (mēräflō'rĕs), mining settlement (pop. c.4,500), Potosí dept., W central Bolivia, at E foot of Cordillera de Azanaques, adjoining Catavi; tin.

Miraflores. 1 Town (pop. 2,066), Boyacá dept., central Colombia, in valley of Cordillera Oriental, 25 mi. SE of Tunja; alt. 4,698 ft.; cacao, coffee, tobacco, rice, livestock. **2** Town, Tolima dept., Colombia: see Rovira.

Miraflores, town (pop. 452), Southern Territory, Lower California, NW Mexico, in valley 65 mi. SE of La Paz; produces sugar cane and fruit (coconuts, dates, figs, grapes).

Miraflores (mĭ"rŭflō'rĭs, Sp. mēräflō'rĕs), town (pop. 55), Balboa dist., S Panama Canal Zone, on small artificial Miraflores Lake of the Panama Canal, on transisthmian railroad and 5 mi. NW of Panama city.

Miraflores. 1 Town (pop. 16,146), Arequipa dept., S Peru, NE suburb of Arequipa; agr. center in irrigation area (wheat, barley, alfalfa, potatoes, vegetables). **2** Town (pop. 1,005), Huánuco dept., central Peru, on E slopes of Cordillera Blanca of the Andes, near Marañón R., 5 mi. N of Llata; barley, vegetables, potatoes; sheep raising. **3** S residential section (pop. 45,489) of Lima, Lima dept., W central Peru; beach resort on the Pacific just N of Barranco. Scene of battle (1881) in War of Pacific. Inc. 1940 into Lima proper.

Miraflores, Puerto Rico: see Isla Grande.

Miraflores de la Sierra (dhā lä syĕ'rä), town (pop. 1,666), Madrid prov., central Spain, resort on E slopes of the Sierra de Guadarrama, 28 mi. N of Madrid; stock raising, dairying; flour milling, charcoal burning; apiculture. Hydroelectric plant.

Miraflores Lake (mĭ"rŭflō'rĭs, Sp. mēräflō'rĕs), tiny artificial lake (c.1 mi. long; alt. 54 ft. above sea level) in S Panama Canal Zone, 5 mi. NW of Panama city; used as part of the canal route, linking Gaillard Cut (NW) with the Pacific section. Pedro Miguel Locks at NW end raise (to 85 ft.) and lower (to 54 ft.) vessels in 1 step. The Miraflores Locks (SE) overcome in 2 sets of locks the level bet. Pacific Ocean and the lake.

Miragoâne (mērägwän'), town (1950 census pop. 2,499), Sud dept., SW Haiti, minor port on N Tiburon Peninsula, 50 mi. W of Port-au-Prince; ships coffee, fruit, logwood. Good port facilities. Bauxite deposits in vicinity.

Miraí (mēräē'), city (pop. 2,817), SE Minas Gerais, Brazil, 15 mi. NNE of Cataguases; rail-spur terminus; coffee, tobacco. Formerly spelled Mirahy.

Miraj (mĭr'äj), town (pop. 32,455), Satara South dist., S central Bombay, India, 6 mi. ESE of Sangli; rail and road junction; trades in grain, cotton, sugar cane, oilseeds, cloth fabrics; cotton milling, hand-loom weaving, mfg. of chemicals, musical instruments. Was ⊙ former Deccan state of Miraj Senior and hq. of former Wadi Estate.

Miraj Junior, former princely state (□ 194; pop. 46,295) in Deccan States, Bombay, India; ⊙ was Budhgaon. Inc. 1949 into Satara South, Belgaum, Dharwar, and Sholapur dists., Bombay.

Miraj Senior, former princely state (□ 368; pop. 108,547) in Deccan States, Bombay, India; ⊙ was Miraj. Inc. 1949 into Satara South, Dharwar, Belgaum, and Sholapur dists., Bombay.

Miraki (mērăkē'), village, Kashka-Darya oblast, S Uzbek SSR, 15 mi. from Kitab.

Mira Loma (mĕr"ŭ lō'mŭ), village (pop. 1,555), Riverside co., S Calif., 10 mi. W of Riverside; vineyards. U.S. army supply depot here.

Miramar (mērämär'). **1** Town (pop. 3,496), ⊙ General Alvarado dist. (□ 463; pop. 14,528), SE Buenos Aires prov., Argentina, 24 mi. SW of Mar del Plata. Seaside resort and agr. center (grain, flax, livestock); dairying. Beach resort Mar del Sur is 10 mi. WSW. **2** Town (pop. 2,513), NE Córdoba prov., Argentina, beach resort on S shore of the Mar Chiquita, 100 mi. NE of Córdoba; hotels, sanitariums.

Miramar, town (1947 pop. 899), ⊙ Montes de Oro canton, Puntarenas prov., W Costa Rica, 10 mi. NW of Puntarenas; commercial center in gold-mining area; lumbering.

Miramar, resort, Tamaulipas, NE Mexico, on Gulf at mouth of Pánuco R., 6 mi. NE of Tampico.

Miramar, village (pop. 115), Colón prov., central Panama, on Caribbean Sea, 1 mi. E of Palenque, railhead in banana region; cacao, coconuts, corn, livestock.

Miramar (mĭ'rŭmär), Ital. *Miramare* (mērämä'rä), seaside resort, N Free Territory of Trieste, 4 mi. NW of Trieste, on Gulf of Trieste; site of park and former castle (built 1856) of Emperor Maximilian of Mexico. After 1945, hq. of U.S. troops in Trieste.

Miramas (mērämä'), town (pop. 5,932), Bouches-du-Rhône dept., SE France, at E edge of the Crau, near NW tip of Étang de Berre, 27 mi. NW of Marseilles; rail junction. Soap mfg., codfish drying.

Mirambeau (mēräbō'), village (pop. 805), Charente-Maritime dept., W France, 8 mi. SW of Jonzac; winegrowing.

Miramichi (mĭ"rŭmŭshē'), river system in N central N.B., consisting of several streams rising in N central highlands of prov. and flowing E to estuarial section, which begins at Newcastle and extends 15 mi. ENE, past Chatham, to Miramichi Bay, inlet (20 mi. long, 15 mi. wide at mouth) of the Gulf of St. Lawrence. Main river of Miramichi system, the Southwest Miramichi, is 135 mi. long. Miramichi Bay, visited by Cartier in 1534, contains several small isls.; on shore are Acadian fishing settlements.

Miramont (mērämō'), village (pop. 989), Haute-Garonne dept., S France, on the Garonne and 1 mi. SE of Saint-Gaudens; woolen milling.

Miramont-de-Guyenne (–dŭ-gēyĕn'), village (pop. 1,785), Lot-et-Garonne dept., SW France, 12 mi. NE of Marmande; agr. market (cattle, poultry, hogs); vegetable canning, mfg. of shoes.

Miram Shah (mĭrŭm' shä'), village, hq. of North Waziristan agency, SW North-West Frontier Prov., W Pakistan, 105 mi. SW of Peshawar; local trade in hides, mats, timber, grain; fruit and vegetable nurseries. Also spelled Miranshah.

Miranda (mērăn'dŭ), city (pop. 1,545), S Mato Grosso, Brazil, head of navigation on Miranda R. at edge of Paraguay R. flood plain, on São Paulo–Corumbá RR and 120 mi. SE of Corumbá; ships dried meat and maté. Marble quarries. Captured by Paraguayans in 1865. In Ponta Porã territory, 1943–46.

Miranda (mērän'dä), town (pop. 2,102), Cauca dept., SW Colombia, on Popayán–Manizales highway, on W slopes of Cordillera Central, 22 mi. SE of Cali; sugar cane, tobacco, coffee, cereals, fruit, livestock. Founded 1772.

Miranda or **Central Miranda** (sĕnträl'), sugar-mill village (pop. 1,038), Oriente prov., E Cuba, at S foot of Sierra de Nipe, 28 mi. N of Santiago de Cuba.

Miranda (mērän'dä), state (□ 3,070; 1941 pop. 227,604; 1950 census 277,761), N Venezuela, on the Caribbean; ⊙ Los Teques. Bounded N by Federal Dist.; here along border the coastal range rises to its highest elevation. Predominantly mountainous, apart from alluvial valley of lower Tuy R., it includes Tacarigua Lagoon along Caribbean coast. Climate is hot and tropical in E lowlands, with rains all year round; fertile higher sections are semitropical and dry, with rainy season June-Oct. An agr. region, it produces coffee, cacao, sugar cane, corn, rice, yuca, potatoes, bananas, coconuts. Some fishing and cattle raising. Sugar milling and sawmilling are its main industries. Its asbestos, marble, copper, iron, gold, coal, and asphalt deposits are thus far little exploited.

Miranda, town (pop. 3,089), Carabobo state, N Venezuela, 27 mi. W of Valencia; agr. center (coffee, sugar cane, corn, fruit, livestock).

Miranda, Lo, Chile: see Lo Miranda.

Miranda de Arga (dhā är'gä), town (pop. 1,382), Navarre prov., N Spain, on Arga R. and 15 mi. SE of Estella; wine, cereals, vegetables.

Miranda de Ebro (ā'vrō), city (pop. 13,639), Burgos prov., N Spain, on the Ebro (bridges), at Álava prov. border, and 45 mi. NE of Burgos. Rail and road junction; has important trade and industries. Mfg. of cellulose, rayon, textile fibers, paper, cement, chocolate, soap, tiles; sawmilling, beet-sugar milling. The region produces potatoes, sugar beets, cereals, grapes, timber, livestock. An anc. city, with remains of castle and walls.

Miranda del Castañar (dhĕl kästänyär'), town (pop. 2,012), Salamanca prov., W Spain, 15 mi. NW of Béjar; olive oil, fruit, wine.

Miranda do Corvo (mērăn'dŭ dōō kôr'vōō), town (pop. 707), Coimbra dist., N central Portugal, on railroad and 9 mi. SSE of Coimbra; mfg. (earthenware, doormats).

Miranda do Douro (dō'rōō), anc. *Sepontia,* city (pop. 742), Bragança dist., northeasternmost Portugal, above gorge of Douro R. (Sp. border), and 34 mi. SE of Bragança. Accessible only by poor road. Has Renaissance cathedral and ruins of 13th-cent. fort.

Miranda River (mērăn'dŭ), S Mato Grosso, Brazil, rises above Nioaque, flows c.200 mi. NW, past Miranda (head of navigation), through Paraguay flood plain, to Paraguay R. 35 mi. SE of Corumbá. Also called Mondego R.

Mirande (mērăd'), town (pop. 2,694), Gers dept., SW France, on Baïse R. and 13 mi. SW of Auch; agr. market (poultry, hogs, cattle, horses, wine); tanning, brick making. Has 15th-cent. church. Founded 1285.

Mirandela (mērăndĕ'lŭ), town (pop. 2,958), Bragança dist., N Portugal, on Tua R., on railroad and 30 mi. SW of Bragança; produces port wine; mfg. of ceramics; cork processing. Airfield.

Mirandilla (mērändē'lyä), town (pop. 2,359), Badajoz prov., W Spain, 6 mi. NNE of Mérida; olives, cereals, livestock; flour milling.

Mirando City (mŭrăn'dŭ), village (pop. c.1,200), Webb co., SW Texas, 30 mi. E of Laredo, in oil field.

Mirandola (mērän'dôlä), town (pop. 6,171), Modena prov., Emilia-Romagna, N central Italy, 18 mi. NNE of Modena. Rail terminus; mfg. (truck chassis, shoes, pumps), canned foods, macaroni, sausage, hemp products. Has cathedral, Jesuit church, old palace of dukes of Mirandola.

Mirandópolis (mērändô'pŏŏlēs), city (pop. 1,731), NW São Paulo, Brazil, on railroad and 40 mi. W of Araçatuba; coffee, rice, forest products. Until 1944, Comandante Arbues.

Mirano (mērä'nô), town (pop. 2,939), Venezia, N Italy, 11 mi. WNW of Venice; brooms, brushes, vinegar.

Miranpur (mē'ränpŏŏr), town (pop. 7,306), Muzaffarnagar dist., N Uttar Pradesh, India, 19 mi. SE of Muzaffarnagar; wheat, gram, sugar cane, oilseeds; hand-loom woolen weaving.

Miranpur Katra (kŭt'rŭ), town (pop. 7,355), Shahjahanpur dist., central Uttar Pradesh, India, 19 mi. NW of Shahjahanpur; trades in wheat, rice, gram, oilseeds, sugar cane. Rohilla defeated (1774) near by by combined forces of nawab of Oudh and British. Also called Katra.

Miran Sahib (mē'rän sä'hĭb), village, Jammu dist., SW Kashmir, 7 mi. SSW of Jammu; mfg. of rosin, turpentine, sports goods; indianite works.

Miranshah, W Pakistan: see MIRAM SHAH.

Mira Por Vos (mē'rä pôr vōs') [Sp.,=look out for yourself], islets and reefs, S central Bahama Isls., 15 mi. W of S tip of Acklins Isl., 270 mi. SE of Nassau; 22°10'N 74°32'W. Low, dangerous rocks.

Mira River (mī'rŭ), tidal inlet in E part of Cape Breton Isl., NE N.S., extending 30 mi. W and S from Mira Bay; 1–2 mi. wide.

Mira River (mē'rä), in Ecuador and Colombia, rises in the Andes SW of Ibarra (Ecuador), flows c.150 mi. NW to the Pacific in a large delta, its main arm reaching the ocean at Mangles Point (Colombia).

Mira River (mē'rŭ), in Beja dist., S Portugal, rises 4 mi. SW of Almodôvar, flows 80 mi. NW, past Odemira (head of navigation), to the Atlantic at Vila Nova de Milfontes.

Mirasaka (mērä'säkŏŏ), town (pop. 6,869), Hiroshima prefecture, SW Honshu, Japan, 26 mi. NNW of Mihara; spinning mills; raw silk, livestock, rice. Iron mine near by.

Mirassol (mērŭsŏl'), city (pop. 6,929), NW São Paulo, Brazil, on railroad and 7 mi. W of São José do Rio Prêto, in coffee- and cotton-growing zone; cotton ginning, coffee processing, livestock shipping. Formerly Mirasol.

Miravalles (mērävä'yĕs), active volcano (6,627 ft.) in the Cordillera de Guanacaste, NW Costa Rica, 16 mi. NNE of Bagaces; 10°45'N 85°10'W. Sulphur springs.

Miravalles (mērävä'lyĕs), town (pop. 1,449), Vizcaya prov., N Spain, 5 mi. SSE of Bilbao; metalworking. Cereals, peppers, *chacolí* wine, livestock in region.

Mir-Bashir (mēr-bŭshēr'), city (1932 pop. estimate 2,080), central Azerbaijan SSR, on Terter R., on railroad and 20 mi. SSW of Yevlakh, on border of Nagorno-Karabakh Autonomous oblast; cotton dist. Until 1949, called Terter.

Mircesti (mērchĕsht'), Rum. *Mirceşti*, village (pop. 1,027), Jassy prov., NE Rumania, on railroad, near Siret R., 11 mi. NNW of Roman.

Mirditë (mērdē'tŭ) or **Mirdita** (mērdē'tä), Ital. *Mirdizia* (mērdē'tsēä), tribal region (pop. c.20,000) of N Albania, c.25 mi. ESE of Scutari. Highland area drained by Fan R. Pastoral, R.C. pop. was long known for independent spirit. Main villages are Orosh and Blinisht.

Mirdjaveh, Iran: see MIRJAVEH.

Mirebalais (mērbälā'), town (1950 census pop. 1,858), Ouest dept., S central Haiti, on Artibonite R. and 25 mi. NE of Port-au-Prince; cotton, rice, construction wood.

Mirebeau (mērbō'). **1** or **Mirebeau-sur-Bèze** (–sür-bĕz'), village (pop. 806), Côte-d'Or dept., E central France, 14 mi. ENE of Dijon; hop growing. **2** Village (pop. 1,937), Vienne dept., W central France, 12 mi. W of Châtellerault; wine, fruit, vegetable growing.

Mirecourt (mērkŏŏr'), town (pop. 4,901), Vosges dept., E France, 17 mi. NW of Épinal; center for mfg. of stringed instruments. Cotton milling, lace-making. Has 16th-cent. Gothic church and 17th-cent. market halls.

Mirepoix (mērpwä'), town (pop. 2,246), Ariège dept., S France, on Hers R. and 14 mi. E of Pamiers; road center and agr. market; woodworking. Has 15th-16th-cent. cathedral of Saint-Maurice. Was episcopal see (1317–1789).

Mirfield, urban district (1931 pop. 12,114; 1951 census 11,885), West Riding, SW Yorkshire, England, on Calder R. and 4 mi. ENE of Huddersfield; railroad junction; woolen and cotton milling. In urban dist. (WSW) is cotton-milling suburb of Hopton (pop. 2,479).

Mirgorod (mēr'gŭrŭt), city (1926 pop. 14,422), central Poltava oblast, Ukrainian SSR, on Khorol R. and 50 mi. WNW of Poltava; flour-milling center; dairying, sugar refining; brickworks. Peat bogs near by. Health resort (salt and carbonic springs).

Mirhleft (mēglĕft'), Saharan military outpost, Agadir frontier region, SW Fr. Morocco, on the Atlantic, near N border of Ifni enclave (Spanish), 20 mi. SW of Tiznit; 29°35'N 10°2'W. Also spelled Mighleft, Mirleft.

Miri (mĭ'rē), town (pop. 8,809), N Sarawak, NW Borneo, port on S.China Sea, 75 mi. WSW of Brunei; 4°25'N 114°E; outlet for oil refined at near-by Lutong. Has important oil fields. Severely damaged during Second World War.

Miri, peak, W Pakistan: see KOH-I-SULTAN.

Miriakani (mērēäkä'nē), village, Coast prov., SE Kenya, on railroad and 20 mi. NW of Mombasa; sugar cane, fruits, copra.

Mirialguda, India: see MIRYALGUDA.

Miribel (mērēbĕl'), town (pop. 2,755), Ain dept., E France, on the Rhone and 8 mi. NE of Lyons; paper and carton mills, hosiery factory.

Mirigama (mĭrĭgä'mŭ), village (pop. 895), Western Prov., Ceylon, 30 mi. NE of Colombo; coconut processing; trades in coconut, rubber, pan, graphite, rice. Buddhist rock temple (1st cent. B.C.) near by.

Miri Hills (mērē'), extension of E Assam Himalayas in NE Balipara frontier tract, Assam, India, N of Dafla Hills. Inhabited by Miri tribe of Tibeto-Burman origin.

Mirik, Cape (mērĕk'), or **Cape Timiris** (tēmērēs'), headland on Atlantic coast of Mauritania, Fr. West Africa, 230 mi. N of Saint-Louis; 19°22'N 16°30'W.

Mirimire (mērēmē'rä), town (pop. 564), Falcón state, NW Venezuela, 38 mi. NW of Tucacas; corn, fruit.

Mirim Lake (mērēn'), Port. *Lagoa Mirim*, Sp. *Laguna Merín* (mārēn'), shallow tidewater lagoon (□ 1,145; 110 mi. long, up to 25 mi. wide) in southernmost Brazil and E Uruguay, separated from the Atlantic by low, marshy bar (10–35 mi. wide; dotted with smaller lagoons); it discharges (at N end) into the Lagoa dos PATOS, through São Gonçalo Canal. Navigable for small vessels. International boundary traverses lake's S half from mouth of Jaguarão R. to southernmost tip of lake W of Chuí. More than ¾ of lake is in Brazil (Rio Grande do Sul).

Miriñay River (mērēnyī'), SE Corrientes prov., Argentina, rises in swamps S of Esteros del Iberá, flows c.100 mi. S to Uruguay R., 5 mi. N of Monte Caseros, opposite mouth of Quaraí R. at Brazil–Uruguay border.

Miritiba, Brazil: see HUMBERTO DE CAMPOS.

Miriti Paraná River (mērē'tē päränä'), Amazonas commissary, SE Colombia, in densely forested lowlands; flows c.175 mi. SE to the Caquetá.

Mirjaveh or **Mirdjaveh** (mērjävĕ'), village, Eighth Prov., in Baluchistan, SE Iran, 50 mi. SE of Zahidan and on railroad to Quetta, on Pakistan line and on short intermittent Mirjaveh R. (frontier stream); customs station. Sometimes spelled Mirjawa.

Mirle (mĭr'lĕ), town (pop. 3,102), Mysore dist., SW Mysore, India, 28 mi. NW of Mysore; tobacco, rice, millet.

Mirna River (mēr'nä), Ital. *Quieto* (kwēĕt'ô), NW Croatia, Yugoslavia, in Istria; rises 6 mi. SE of Buzet, flows c.30 mi. W, past Buzet and Motovun, to Adriatic Sea near Cittanova d'Istria. In lower course, forms boundary bet. Yugoslavia and Free Territory of Trieste.

Mironovka (mērô'nŭfkŭ), town (1926 pop. 4,484), central Kiev oblast, Ukrainian SSR, 40 mi. ESE of Belaya Tserkov; rail junction; sugar refining, metalworking.

Miropolye or **Miropol'ye** (mērŭpô'lyĭ), town (1932 pop. estimate 4,790), E Sumy oblast, Ukrainian SSR, on Psel R. and 20 mi. ENE of Sumy; metalworks.

Miroslawiec (mērôswä'vyĕts), Pol. *Mirosławiec*, Ger. *Märkisch Friedland* (mĕr'kĭsh frēt'länt), town (1939 pop. 2,707; 1946 pop. 827) in Pomerania, after 1945 in Koszalin prov., NW Poland, 45 mi. E of Stargard; grain, sugar beets, potatoes, livestock. Until 1938, in former Prussian prov. of Grenzmark Posen–Westpreussen.

Mirosov (mĭ'rôshôf), Czech *Mirošov*, village (pop. 1,437), SW Bohemia, Czechoslovakia, on railroad and 13 mi. ESE of Pilsen; coal mining. Metalworks of Hradek (hrä'dĕk), Czech *Hrádek*, producing steel and bar iron, are 2 mi. NNW.

Mirov, Czechoslovakia: see MOHELNICE.

Mirovice (mĭ'rôvĭtsĕ), Ger. *Mirowitz*, town (pop. 1,096), S Bohemia, Czechoslovakia, 12 mi. SSE of Pribram; rye, potatoes.

Mirow (mē'rō), town (pop. 3,801), Mecklenburg, N Germany, on Mirow L. (8 mi. long), 12 mi. WSW of Neustrelitz; agr. market (grain, potatoes, stock). Has early-Gothic church; 18th-cent. former castle of grand dukes of Mecklenburg-Strelitz. Founded 1227 as monastery (secularized 1522).

Mirowitz, Czechoslovakia: see MIROVICE.

Mirpur (mēr'pŏŏr), district (□ 1,627; pop. 386,655), Jammu prov., SW Kashmir; ⊙ Mirpur. In S Punjab Himalayas; bounded W by Jhelum R. and W Pakistan; drained by Punch R. Agr. (wheat, bajra, corn, pulse, cotton, oilseeds); bentonite mines N of Bhimbar. Headworks of Upper Jhelum Canal at Mangla. Main towns: Mirpur, Manawar, Bhimbar, Kotli. Occupied 1948 by Pakistan, except for small area in SE. Pop. 80% Moslem, 19% Hindu. Prevailing mother tongue, Panjabi.

Mirpur, town (pop. 8,556), ⊙ Mirpur dist., SW Kashmir, 18 mi. NNE of Jhelum; cotton weaving; trades in wheat, bajra, corn, pulse. Occupied 1948 by Pakistan.

Mirpur Khas (khäs'), town (pop. 19,591), Thar Parkar dist., E central Sind, W Pakistan, 45 mi. WNW of Umarkot; rail junction; trade center (cotton, grain); cotton ginning, handicraft cloth weaving, embroidering. Agr. farm, fruit research station. Ruins of Buddhist stupa and monastery. Also written Mirpurkhas.

Mirpur Sakro (sŭk'rō), village, Tatta dist., SW Sind, W Pakistan, 45 mi. SE of Karachi; rice, millet.

Mirror, village (pop. 562), S central Alta., near Buffalo L., 32 mi. ENE of Red Deer; lumbering, dairying, mixed farming.

Mirror Lake, small alpine lake, SW Alta., near B.C. border, in Rocky Mts., in Banff Natl. Park, 4 mi. WSW of Lake Louise. Drains E into Bow R.

Mirror Lake, village, N.H.: see TUFTONBORO.

Mirror Lake. 1 Lake in N.J.: see BROWNS MILLS. **2** Lake in N.Y.: see LAKE PLACID. **3** Lake in Wis.: see DELL CREEK.

Mirror Landing, Alta.: see SMITH.

Mirs Bay (mûrz), Chinese *Taipang Wan* or *Ta-p'eng Wan* (both: dī'pŭng' wän'), inlet of S.China Sea, in northeasternmost Hong Kong colony; 14 mi. long, 7–15 mi. wide. Fisheries. Leased with New Territories to British in 1898.

Mirsk (mērsk), Ger. *Friedeberg* (frē'dŭbĕrk), town (1939 pop. 2,883; 1946 pop. 2,399) in Lower Silesia, after 1945 in Wroclaw prov., SW Poland, near Czechoslovak border, at N foot of the Isergebirge, on Kwisa R. and 16 mi. WNW of Hirschberg (Jelenia Gora); linen milling. Town hall with 16th-cent. tower. After 1945, briefly called Spokojna Gora, Pol. *Spokojna Góra*.

Mirtag, Turkey: see MUTKI.

Mirungwe, Belgian Congo: see MINDIGI.

Miryalguda or **Mirialguda** (both: mĭryŭl'gŏŏdŭ), town (pop. 5,628), Nalgonda dist., SE Hyderabad state, India, 19 mi. SE of Nalgonda; rice milling, cotton ginning, castor-oil extraction.

Miryang (mē'rĕăng'), Jap. *Mitsuyo*, town (1949 pop. 32,660), S.Kyongsang prov., S Korea, 30 mi. NW of Pusan; commercial center for fruitgrowing area (pears, persimmons, grapes, peaches).

Mirza-Aki (mērzä"-ŭkē'), village, NE Osh oblast, Kirghiz SSR, c.30 mi. SE of Karasu; wheat; livestock.

Mirzaani (mērzŭä'nyē), town (1926 pop. over 2,000), SE Georgian SSR, 60 mi. ESE of Tiflis, on Shiraki Steppe; rail terminus; center of petroleum region; oil-cracking plant.

Mirzachul or **Mirzachul'** (–chŏŏl'), town (1932 pop. estimate 4,600), SW Tashkent oblast, Uzbek SSR, on Trans-Caspian RR and 60 mi. SSW of Tashkent, in irrigation area; cotton ginning, fiber-plant processing. Formerly called Golodnaya Step.

Mirzapur (mĭr'zäpŏŏr), district (□ 4,322; pop. 899,929), SE Uttar Pradesh, India; ⊙ Mirzapur. Bounded N by the Ganges; drained by Son R. and RIHAND RIVER (hydroelectric project). Vindhya Range in S (lac cultivation in sal jungle). Agr. (rice, gram, barley, wheat, oilseeds, millet, sugar cane, corn). Sandstone quarries near Chunar. Main centers: Mirzapur, Ahraura, Chunar.

Mirzapur, city (pop., including W suburb of Bindhachal, 70,944), ⊙ Mirzapur dist., SE Uttar Pradesh, India, on the Ganges, on railroad and 35 mi. WSW of Benares; road junction; trade (grain, oilseeds, sugar cane) and mfg. (shellac, woolen carpets) center; cotton milling; brassware. Ghats and temples along river front. At Bindhachal (also spelled Bindhyachal) is a noted Kali temple (pilgrimage site); formerly a Thug rendezvous. Extensive anc. ruins near by.

Mirzoyan, Kazakh SSR: see DZHAMBUL, city.

Misahohé (mēsähō'hā), village, S Fr. Togoland, near Br. Togoland border, 4 mi. E of Klouto; cacao, palm oil and kernels, cotton. Customhouse.

Misaki (mēsä'kē), town (pop. 17,725), Kanagawa prefecture, central Honshu, Japan, at SW tip of Miura Peninsula, on SE shore of Sagami Bay, 9 mi. SSW of Yokosuka; fishing port.

Misakubo, Japan: see MIZUKUBO.

Misamis, city, Philippines: see OZAMIZ.

Misamis Occidental (mēsä'mēs ōksēdhäntäl'), province (□ 802; 1948 pop. 207,575), W Mindanao, Philippines, bounded N by Mindanao Sea, E by Iligan Bay; ⊙ OROQUIETA. Mountainous terrain, rising to 7,965 ft. Has fertile coastal strip producing corn and coconuts. OZAMIZ city is in, but independent of, the prov.

Misamis Oriental (ōryäntäl'), province (□ 1,512; 1948 pop. 369,671), N Mindanao, Philippines, bounded N by Mindanao Sea and its inlets (Macajalar and Gingoog bays), W by Iligan Bay; ⊙ CAGAYAN. Includes CAMIGUIN ISLAND. Mountainous terrain, drained by many small streams. Agr. (corn, coconuts), fishing. Chromite deposits.

Misano Adriatico (mēzä'nô ädrēä'tēkô), village (pop. 212), Ravenna prov., Emilia-Romagna, N central Italy, 3 mi. S of Riccione; canned foods. Formerly Misano in Villa Vittoria.

Misantla (mēsän'tlä), city (pop. 2,847), Veracruz, E Mexico, in Sierra Madre Oriental foothills, 29 mi.

N of Jalapa; agr. center (corn, sugar cane, coffee, tobacco). Anc. ruins near by.

Misasa (mēsä'sä), village (pop. 2,221), Tottori prefecture, S Honshu, Japan, 5 mi. ESE of Kurayoshi; health resort (radioactive hot springs); agr. (rice, wheat), raw silk, pottery. Anc. temple near by.

Misau or **Missau** (mēshou'), town (pop. 6,867), Bauchi prov., Northern Provinces, N Nigeria, 35 mi. SE of Azare; agr. trade center; cotton, peanuts, millet, durra.

Misawa (mēsä'wä"), town (pop. 11,871), Aomori prefecture, N Honshu, Japan, 14 mi. NNW of Hachinohe; air base.

Misaz, Turkey: see KOYULHISAR.

Misburg (mĭs'bo͝ork), village (pop. 8,828), in former Prussian prov. of Hanover, W Germany, after 1945 in Lower Saxony, on the Weser-Elbe Canal and 5 mi. E of Hanover city center; petroleum refining.

Mischabelhörner (mĭshä'bŭlhûr'nŭr) or **Mischabel** (mĭshä'bŭl), Fr. *les Mischabels* (lā mēshäbĕl'), group of peaks in Pennine Alps, S Switzerland, near Zermatt; highest peak is the DOM (14,923 ft.). Other peaks include Täschhorn (14,744 ft.; 1st ascended 1862), Nadelhorn (14,206 ft.), and Lenzspitze (14,098 ft.). Mischabel Hütte (10,933 ft.) is E of the Nadelhorn. **Mischabeljoch** (–yôkh"), a pass (12,644 ft.), is S of the Täschhorn.

Miscouche (mĭsko͞osh'), village (pop. estimate 200), W P.E.I., 5 mi. WNW of Summerside; mixed farming, dairying; potatoes.

Miscou Island (mĭ'sko͞o) (9 mi. long, 5 mi. wide), in Gulf of St. Lawrence, NE N.B., at entrance to Chaleur Bay just N of Shippigan Isl.; 47°55'N 64°30'W. Lobster, hake, herring, mackerel, cod fisheries; peat digging.

Misdroy, Poland: see MIEDZYZDROJE.

Miseno, Cape (mēzā'nô), S Italy, bet. Gulf of Gaeta and Bay of Naples, opposite Procida isl.; 40°47'N 14°5'E; lighthouse. Just N, at anc. Misenum, Augustus founded a naval station; destroyed (9th cent.) by Arabs. Ruins of Roman theater and reservoir near by.

Misere (mēzâr'), village on central Mahé Isl., Seychelles, on road and 3¼ mi. SSE of Victoria, in central range; copra, essential oils.

Miserey-Salines (mēzürā'-sälēn'), village (pop. 463), Doubs dept., E France, 5 mi. NW of Besançon; salt mines.

Misericórdia, Brazil: see ITAPORANGA, Paraíba.

Misery, Mount (3,711 ft.), NW St. Kitts, Leeward Isls., B.W.I., 7 mi. NW of Basseterre.

Misery Island, Mass.: see GREAT MISERY ISLAND.

Misery Point, N extremity of Belle Isle, N N.F., 40 mi. NE of Cape Norman; 52°1'N 55°17'W; lighthouse.

Misgar (mĭs'gŭr), village, Hunza state, Gilgit Agency, NW Kashmir, in NW Karakoram mtn. system, on right tributary of Hunza R. and 65 mi. NNE of Gilgit; alt. c.10,150 ft. On important trade route from Gilgit, via Kilik Pass, into China.

Mis-hal (mĭs-hăl'), village, Fadhli sultanate, Western Aden Protectorate, 22 mi. NE of Shuqra and on road to Lodar; agr. Airfield.

Mishan (mē'shän'), town (pop. 15,000), ⊙ Mishan co. (pop. 95,000), S Sungkiang prov., Manchuria, 140 mi. NE of Mutankiang, and on Muling R., near N shore of L. Khanka; coal-mining center; mica and gold deposits; honey production. Formerly called Mifengshantze; and when in Manchukuo, Tungan for the name of its railroad station. It was ⊙ Manchukuo's Tungan prov. (⊙ 15,980; 1940 pop. 512,240) during 1937–43.

Misharij, Am, Aden: see MASHARIJ, AM.

Mishawaka (mĭsh-ŭwô'kŭ), city (pop. 32,913), St. Joseph co., N Ind., on St. Joseph R. and just E of South Bend; mfg.: clothing, rubber and plastic goods, metal products, automobile transmission units, industrial machinery, woolen goods, bedding, furniture, trunks, food products. Settled c.1830, inc. 1899.

Mishelevka (mē'shĭlyĭfkŭ), town (1926 pop. 2,766), S Irkutsk oblast, Russian SFSR, on Belaya R. and 20 mi. S of Cheremkhovo; porcelain industry.

Misheronski or **Misheronskiy** (mēshĭrôn'skē), town (1926 pop. 1,388), E Moscow oblast, Russian SFSR, 13 mi. NNE of Shatura; glassworks.

Mishih, China: see NINGTUNG.

Mishima (mē'shĭmä), sometimes spelled Misima. **1** Town (pop. 22,089), Ehime prefecture, N Shikoku, Japan, on Hiuchi Sea, 45 mi. ENE of Matsuyama; paper-milling center in agr. area; spinning mills. **2** City (1940 pop. 32,992; 1947 pop. 46,180), Shizuoka prefecture, central Honshu, Japan, just ENE of Numazu, 32 mi. ENE of Shizuoka; collection center (citrus fruit, dairy products, charcoal); sake brewing. Has anc. Shinto shrine.

Mi-shima (mē'shĭmä), island (□3; pop. 2,759), Yamaguchi prefecture, Japan, in Sea of Japan, 27 mi. NNW of Hagi off SW Honshu; 3 mi. long, 1.5 mi. wide; hilly, fertile. Extensive stock raising; rice, raw silk.

Mishkino (mēsh'kĭnŭ). **1** Village (1939 pop. over 2,000), N Bashkir Autonomous SSR, Russian SFSR, 55 mi. N of Ufa; flour milling, lumbering. **2** Town (1939 pop. over 5,000), central Kurgan oblast, Russian SFSR, on Trans-Siberian RR and 55 mi. W of Kurgan; flour milling, dairying.

Mishkinshahr or **Meshkinshahr** (both: mĕshkēnshä'hûr), town (1941 pop. 4,218), Third Prov., in Azerbaijan, NW Iran, 32 mi. E of Ahar and 85 mi. ENE of Tabriz, at N foot of the Savalan; dried fruit; rugmaking. Sometimes called Khiav or Khiov.

Mishmar ha Emeq or **Mishmar Haemek** (both: mēshmär' hä-ĕ'mĕk), settlement (pop. 550), NW Israel, at foot of Hills of Ephraim, at W edge of Plain of Jezreel, 16 mi. SSE of Haifa; mixed farming. Founded 1926. Arab armies suffered decisive defeat here, April, 1948.

Mishmar han Negev or **Mishmar Hanegev** (both: hänĕ'gĕv), agr. settlement (pop. 100), S Israel, in N part of the Negev, 10 mi. NNW of Beersheba. Founded 1946.

Mishmar ha Sharon or **Mishmar Hasharon** (both: häshärōn'), settlement (pop. 400), W Israel, in Plain of Sharon, 4 mi. NE of Natanya; flower-growing center; mixed farming. Founded 1933.

Mishmar ha Yam or **Mishmar Hayam** (both: häyäm'), residential settlement (pop. 300), NW Israel, on Mediterranean, in Zebulun Valley, on railroad and 7 mi. NE of Haifa. Founded 1939.

Mishmar hay Yarden or **Mishmar Hayarden** (both: häyär'dĕn), settlement (pop. 150), Upper Galilee, NE Israel, on the Jordan (Syrian border) and 8 mi. ENE of Safad; mixed farming. Modern village founded 1890 on site of medieval Le Chastellet, fortified 1178 by Knights Templars, captured 1179 by Saladin. Ruins extant. During Arab invasion settlement was captured (June, 1948) by Syrians; became demilitarized zone under Israeli-Syrian armistice (July, 1949). Jacob's Ford, just N, is historically important gateway to Palestine.

Mishmarot or **Mishmaroth** (both: mēshmärōt'), settlement (pop. 300), W Israel, in Plain of Sharon, 5 mi. NE of Hadera; plywood mfg.; citriculture, banana growing; mixed farming. Founded 1933.

Mishmi Hills (mĭsh'mē), hill range in former Sadiya frontier tract, NE Assam, India, N and E of Sadiya; drained by Dibang R.; rise to c.15,000 ft.; limestone deposits. Constituted (1950) as Mishmi Hills tribal dist. (□ c.9,000; pop. c.70,000; ⊙ Sadiya), part of Assam's NE frontier tract. Inhabited by 4 Mishmi tribes. Also spelled Misimi.

Misho (mēshō'), town (pop. 7,543), Ehime prefecture, SW Shikoku, Japan, on Hoyo Strait, 18 mi. S of Uwajima; fishing port; agr. center (rice, sweet potatoes, wheat). Cattle ranches near by.

Mishongnovi (mŭshŏng'nŭvē), Hopi Indian pueblo, NE Ariz., in Hopi Indian Reservation c.55 mi. N of Winslow; alt. 6,230 ft. The Snake Dance is held here biennially.

Mishta (mĭsh'tä), village (pop. 8,536), Girga prov., central Upper Egypt, on railroad and 7 mi. NNW of Tahta; cotton, cereals, dates, sugar cane.

Misida, Malta: see MSIDA.

Misilmeri (mē"zēlmä'rē), town (pop. 11,665), Palermo prov., NW Sicily, 7 mi. SE of Palermo, in cereal, citrus-fruit region; wine, canned tomatoes.

Misima, Japan: see MISHIMA.

Misima (mēsē'mä), volcanic island (□ 100), Louisiade Archipelago, Territory of Papua, SW Pacific, 125 mi. SE of New Guinea; 10°41'S 152°42'E; c.25 mi. long. Most important gold-bearing isl. of group; site of chief town, Bwagaoia. In Second World War, battle of Coral Sea (1942) was fought near by.

Misimi Hills, India: see MISHMI HILLS.

Misión, Mexico: see LA MISIÓN.

Misiones (mēsyō'nĕs), national territory (□ 11,514; pop. 246,396), NE Argentina, in Mesopotamia, bet. the Uruguay (SE), Paraná (W), and Iguassú (N) rivers; ⊙ POSADAS. Subtropical, densely forested region, with low mtn. ranges. Some agr. (maté, tobacco, citrus fruit, rice, cotton, corn, tung trees, tea, sugar cane); small-scale stock raising. Lumbering. Processing of maté, tobacco, tung oil. Tourists are attracted to the great Iguassú Falls on the Brazilian line. Many of the farmers are from Paraguay, Brazil, and Europe. Jesuit missions founded here in 17th cent. were later dissolved.

Misiones, department (□ 2,985; pop. 49,483), S Paraguay, bet. Tebicuary R. (N) and Paraná R. (S); ⊙ San Juan Bautista. Forested lowlands (marshy), drained by numerous small rivers. Has subtropical, humid climate. Among its little-exploited mineral resources are iron and copper ores, talc, ocher. Predominantly a cattle-raising area; also agr. (maté, oranges, rice, corn, sugar cane, timber). Processing at San Juan Bautista, San Ignacio, Santa Rosa, and Santiago. Many Jesuit missions were founded here during 17th cent. and early 18th cent.

Misiones, Sierra de (syĕ'rä dā), low mountain range (c.1,500 ft.) in central Misiones natl. territory, Argentina, extends c.110 mi. SW from Bernardo de Irigoyen on Brazilian border, forming watershed bet. the Alto Paraná and Uruguay rivers.

Misir or **Missir** (both: mĭsēr'), village (pop. 7,396), Gharbiya prov., Lower Egypt, 5 mi. SE of Kafr el Sheikh; cotton.

Misis (mĭsĭs'), town (pop. 959), Seyhan prov., S Turkey, on Ceyhan R. and 20 mi. E of Adana. Ruins of anc. Mopsuestia, a free city of Cilicia under the Romans, are here. Formerly spelled Missis and Messis.

Misitra, Greece: see MISTRA.

Misivri, Bulgaria: see NESEBAR.

Miskin, town (pop. 5,976) in Mountain Ash urban dist., NE Glamorgan, Wales; coal mining.

Miskolc (mĭsh'kôlts), city (pop. 77,362), ⊙ but independent of Borsod-Gömör co., NE Hungary, on the Sajo, at E foot of Bükk Mts., and 90 mi. NW of Budapest; rail, air, mfg. center; 2d only to Budapest in industrial importance; large trade in wine and tobacco. Agr. chemical experiment station; steel and iron mills, machine shops (railroad cars, locomotives); mfg. (textiles, food products, furniture, shoes, paper, flour, lumber, soap, candles, bricks); tobacco warehouses, wine cellars. Town created an independent municipality in 15th cent. Law school; mus. with Scythian excavations from 6th cent. B.C. and Bronze Age; 13th-cent. church; music conservatory. State vineyards on near-by Mt. Avas. Extensive lignite mining in vicinity. Formerly spelled Miskolcz.

Mislata (mēslä'tä), W suburb (pop. 6,638) of Valencia, Valencia prov., E Spain, on Turia R.; tanning, flour milling, meat processing; mfg. of toys, plaster, burlap. Cereals, vegetables.

Mislovshtitsa, Bulgaria: see TRIN.

Misolonghi, Greece: see MISSOLONGHI.

Misool (mĭso͞ol'), island (pop. 2,018), Raja Ampat Isls., Netherlands New Guinea, in Ceram Sea, 40 mi. SW of Vogelkop peninsula (NW New Guinea); 1°55'S 130°E. Partly hilly, rises to c.3,250 ft. in central area. Sago growing; trepang fishing. Became 1667 Du. possession.

Misore Islands, Netherlands New Guinea: see SCHOUTEN ISLANDS.

Mispillion River (mĭspĭl'yŭn), E Del., rises in streams W of Milford, flows 15 mi. E and NE, past Milford (head of navigation) to Delaware Bay 16 mi. NW of Cape Henlopen.

Misquah Hills (mĭ'skwō), extreme NE Minn., bet. Can. border and L. Superior; small group of monadnock-type hills, rising to 2,230 ft. (highest point in state).

Misquamicut (mĭskwô'mĭkŭt), summer resort village in Westerly town, Washington co., SW R.I., on Block Isl. Sound and 4 mi. S of Westerly village. Renamed from Pleasant View 1928.

Misquihué (mēskēwā'), village (1930 pop. 1,206), Llanquihue prov., S central Chile, 28 mi. WSW of Puerto Montt; agr. center (wheat, potatoes, livestock); dairying, lumbering.

Misr, Arabic name of EGYPT.

Misrikh (mĭs'rĭk), town (pop. 2,686), Sitapur dist., central Uttar Pradesh, India, 13 mi. SW of Sitapur; wheat, rice, gram, barley.

Miss, Yugoslavia: see DRAVOGRAD.

Missão Velha (mēsä'ō vĕ'lyŭ), city (pop. 3,895), S Ceará, Brazil, on Fortaleza-Crato RR and 18 mi. E of Crato; cotton, sugar, livestock.

Missau, Nigeria: see MISAU.

Missaukee (mĭsô'kē), county (□ 565; pop. 7,458), N central Mich.; ⊙ Lake City. Drained by Muskegon R. and its affluents. Livestock, poultry, potatoes, grain, hay; dairy products. Resorts. Many small lakes (fishing). Part of Manistee Natl. Forest, a state forest, and state park are in co. Organized 1871.

Missaukee, Lake, Mich.: see LAKE CITY.

Missbach, river, Yugoslavia: see MEZA RIVER.

Missdorf, Yugoslavia: see MEZICA.

Misserghin (mēsĕrgēn'), village (pop. 2,145), Oran dept., NW Algeria, at N edge of the Oran Sebkha, on railroad and 8 mi. SW of Oran; tanning; truck gardening, olive and winegrowing.

Missinaibi River (mĭ"sĭnä'bē), in central and NE Ont., issues from Missinaibi L. (27 mi. long, 5 mi. wide), 65 mi. SW of Kapuskasing, flows 265 mi. N and NE to confluence with Mattagami R. 50 mi. SW of Moosonee, here forming Moose R., which flows to James Bay.

Missinipi River, Canada: see CHURCHILL RIVER.

Mission, village (pop. 1,957), SW B.C., on Fraser R. and 35 mi. E of Vancouver; fruit and vegetable canning, jam making, lumbering, dairying, fishing. Established c.1860 as mission station.

Mission, Northern Rhodesia: see CHISEKESI.

Mission. 1 City (1951 pop. c.1,850), Johnson co., E Kansas, a suburb of Kansas City. Inc. after 1950. **2** Town (pop. 388), Todd co., S S.Dak., 75 mi. S of Pierre and on Antelope Creek; trading point for Rosebud Indian Reservation; flour, cattle feed, livestock, dairy products. Hare Industrial School is here. **3** City (pop. 10,765), Hidalgo co., extreme S Texas, c.55 mi. WNW of Brownsville, in rich irrigated citrus area (also producing truck, cotton) of lower Rio Grande valley; packs, cans, ships fruits (especially grapefruit), vegetables; cotton ginning, mfg. of clay and concrete products. Has annual Citrus Fiesta. Founded 1908 on site near Sp. chapel (La Lomita mission, completed 1824); extant; inc. 1910.

Missionary Ridge (c.1,000 ft.), in Tenn. and Ga., in Great Appalachian Valley, E of Chattanooga; 10 mi. long N–S. A Civil War battleground (1863) where Union forces won a costly victory; partly included in Chickamauga and Chattanooga Natl. Military Park.

Mission Bay, S Calif., shallow lagoon (c.3 mi. long) within San Diego city limits; state park here, on peninsula bet. bay and the Pacific.

Mission Beach, Calif.: see SAN DIEGO, city.

Mission Hill, town (pop. 169), Yankton co., SE S.Dak., 7 mi. ENE of Yankton; trading point for farming region.

Mission Hills, Kansas: see MISSION.

Mission Range, in Rocky Mts. of NW Mont., rises bet. Flathead L. and Swan R., extends c.45 mi. S toward Missoula. Highest point, McDonald Peak (10,300 ft.).

Mission River, S Texas, coastal stream formed by branches NW of Refugio, flows c.25 mi. SE, through oil fields, to Copano Bay.

Mission San Jose (săn hůzā'), village (1940 pop. 849), Alameda co., W Calif., 14 mi. N of San Jose; site of San Jose Mission (Mission San Jose de Guadalupe), built 1797.

Mission Woods, city (pop. 205), Johnson co., E Kansas, a suburb of Kansas City.

Missir, Egypt: see MISIR.

Missis, Turkey: see MISIS.

Missisquoi (mĭsĭ'skwoi), county (□ 375; pop. 21,442), S Que., on Vt. border; ⊙ Bedford.

Missisquoi River (mĭsĭ'skwoi), N Vt. and S Que., rises near Lowell, Vt.; flows N, past Troy, into Que., thence W and SW, re-entering Vt. near Richford, thence generally W, through Green Mts., to L. Champlain N of Swanton; c.100 mi. long.

Mississagi River (mĭsĭsä'gē), central Ont., issues from Mississagi L. (6 mi. long) at 47°9'N 82°32'W, flows in a wide arc 170 mi. W, S, and SE, through several small lakes, to L. Huron 3 mi. W of Blind River. Several rapids: Aubrey Falls (108 ft. high), 50 mi. NNW of Blind River; Grand Falls (150 ft.), 30 mi. NW of Blind River; and Lake Falls (55 ft.), 20 mi. WNW of Blind River.

Mississinewa River (mĭ"sĭsĭ'nůwä), in Ohio and Ind., rises in Darke co., W Ohio, flows W into Ind., thence generally NW, past Marion, to the Wabash at Peru; c.100 mi. long.

Mississippi (mĭ"sůsĭ'pē), state (land □ 47,420; with inland waters □ 47,716; 1950 pop. 2,178,914; 1940 pop. 2,183,796), S U.S., bordered by Tenn. (N), Ala. (E), Gulf of Mexico (SE), La. and Ark. (W); 31st in area, 26th in pop.; admitted 1817 as 20th state; ⊙ Jackson. The "Magnolia State" or "Bayou State" is 330 mi. long, 180 mi. wide. In the extreme SE corner is a 90-mi.-wide panhandle where La. extends E beyond the Mississippi to Pearl R. Miss. is largely in the Gulf coastal plain, rising to 806 ft. in WOODALL MOUNTAIN (NE), but part of it is in the low Mississippi alluvial plain, bounded E by steep bluffs. The widest part of the Mississippi plain, N of Vicksburg, bet. the Mississippi and the Yazoo R. is called the Yazoo Basin or, locally, the Delta. The state drains SW to the Mississippi through the Yazoo R. system and the Big Black and Homochitto rivers; and S to the Gulf through the Pearl, Pascagoula, and Tombigbee river systems. Swamps are in the Mississippi flood plain and the river bottoms, and in coastal marshes. There are oxbow lakes along the Mississippi, and reservoirs (ARKABUTH, SARDIS, PICKWICK LANDING) formed by power dams in the N. The soils are generally red and yellow clays in the N and center, and sandy in the S. Notable exceptions are the fertile alluvial plain of the Mississippi and the loess-covered bluffs bordering it, and the BLACK BELT in the NE. Pine and hardwood forests, which cover c.55% of the area, make lumbering the chief industry in the state, while the prairies support cattle herds. Miss. is a leading U.S. hardwood producer and her pines, particularly the yellow pine covering most of the S part of the state, furnish large amounts of pulpwood and some turpentine. Centers include JACKSON, the largest city (pop. 62,107), MERIDIAN, LAUREL, and HATTIESBURG on or near the larger rivers of the S coastal plain; GULFPORT and BILOXI on the narrow coastal strip; VICKSBURG and NATCHEZ, where the Mississippi meets the bluffs; and GREENVILLE on the levees which border the Mississippi and guard against its recurrent floods. Farming is favored by the humid subtropical climate, characterized by long, hot summers and short, mild winters. The growing season is long, from c.200–260 days (N–S), and the rainfall plentiful, averaging c.55 in. Cotton and corn are still the most widely planted crops. Miss. ranks 2d (after Texas) as a U.S. cotton producer, while leading the nation as a grower of long-staple cotton. The Yazoo basin is the chief cotton-growing region, especially for the long-staple variety, with GREENWOOD a major market. Also widely planted are sweet potatoes, oats, and hay. In recent years, the serious soil depletion and erosion resulting from the dependence on cotton and corn, together with the inroads of the boll weevil in the 1920s and earlier, have promoted diversification. As a result, other crops (soybeans, hay, grain, truck, sugar cane, tung and pecan nuts) and livestock raising (beef and dairy cattle, hogs, poultry) have become much more important. Miss. leads the U.S. in the production of tung nuts. The TVA program in the NE, where the Tennessee forms part of the state line, has aided the state's efforts to balance agr. with industry. Some of the chief industries, in addition to lumbering, are food processing (meat, dairy and poultry products, grain), cotton milling (clothing), cottonseed processing, fertilizer mfg., and paper milling. Mineral production has also been expanded. Oil, discovered 1939 in Yazoo co., and natural gas are the chief minerals; the fields cross the central part of the state. Clay, sand, and gravel, and limestone are also important. In addition, there are fishing (especially for oysters and shrimp), canning, and resort industries along the coast. The 1st white settlement was made by the French on Biloxi Bay in 1699, and the region was part of La. until 1763 when France ceded its possessions E of the Mississippi to England. After the La. Purchase (1803), a land boom swept the territory, which until 1817 also included what is now Ala. The high prices for cotton and cheap land brought many settlers, especially from the southern piedmont. In 1832 the Indians yielded their remaining lands. Miss. fought with the Confederacy in the Civil War, and large-scale fighting in the state was ended by Grant's Vicksburg campaign (1863). A lasting result of the war was the shattering of the plantation system and the ascendancy of share cropping. The race problem, also aggravated by the war, has continued to plague the state. Negroes had for years constituted slightly more than 50% of the total pop. until 1940, when they numbered slightly less. During the Second World War, thousands of Negroes migrated to the North. Illiteracy, another major problem, with Miss. long having the highest rate in the U.S., has declined in recent years. The state's leading educational institution is the Univ. of Mississippi at Oxford. See also articles on cities, towns, geographic features, and the 82 counties: ADAMS, ALCORN, AMITE, ATTALA, BENTON, BOLIVAR, CALHOUN, CARROLL, CHICKASAW, CHOCTAW, CLAIBORNE, CLARKE, CLAY, COAHOMA, COPIAH, COVINGTON, DE SOTO, FORREST, FRANKLIN, GEORGE, GREENE, GRENADA, HANCOCK, HARRISON, HINDS, HOLMES, HUMPHREYS, ISSAQUENA, ITAWAMBA, JACKSON, JASPER, JEFFERSON, JEFFERSON DAVIS, JONES, KEMPER, LAFAYETTE, LAMAR, LAUDERDALE, LAWRENCE, LEAKE, LEE, LEFLORE, LINCOLN, LOWNDES, MADISON, MARION, MARSHALL, MONROE, MONTGOMERY, NESHOBA, NEWTON, NOXUBEE, OKTIBBEHA, PANOLA, PEARL RIVER, PERRY, PIKE, PONTOTOC, PRENTISS, QUITMAN, RANKIN, SCOTT, SHARKEY, SIMPSON, SMITH, STONE, SUNFLOWER, TALLAHATCHIE, TATE, TIPPAH, TISHOMINGO, TUNICA, UNION, WALTHALL, WARREN, WASHINGTON, WAYNE, WEBSTER, WILKINSON, WINSTON, YALOBUSHA, YAZOO.

Mississippi. 1 County (□ 919; pop. 82,375), NE Ark., ⊙ Blytheville and Osceola. Bounded N by Mo. line, E by Mississippi R.; drained by small Tyronza R. Agr. (cotton, soybeans, corn, alfalfa, vegetables); timber. Industries at Blytheville and Osceola. U.S. bird refuge on Big L. Formed 1833. **2** County (□ 411; pop. 22,551), extreme SE Mo.; ⊙ Charleston on Mississippi R. (levees), with drainage canals. Agr. region (corn, wheat, potatoes), livestock; cotton growing and processing; lumber. Formed 1845.

Mississippi City, village (pop. 3,400, with adjacent Handsboro), Harrison co., SE Miss., 9 mi. W of Biloxi, on Mississippi Sound, in shore-resort area.

Mississippi Palisades State Park, Ill.: see SAVANNA.

Mississippi River (mĭ"sůsĭ'pē), SE Ont., rises NNW of Kingston, flows 110 mi. NE, through Mississippi L. (11 mi. long), past Galetta, to Chats L. of Ottawa R. 30 mi. W of Ottawa, near Arnprior.

Mississippi River, great river (c.2,350 mi long) of central U.S., 2d in length only to the Missouri, its main affluent. However, the Missouri is often considered part of the main stream, and from the head of the Red Rock-Jefferson R. (longest Missouri R. headstream) to the mouth of the Mississippi delta the total length is 3,892 mi., the combined stream thus ranking (after the Nile) as the world's 2d longest river. The Mississippi proper rises in the small creeks draining into L. Itasca in N Minn. and flows generally S to the Gulf of Mexico in SE La., separating Minn., Iowa, Mo., Ark., and La. on the W from Wis., Ill., Ky., Tenn., and Miss. on the E. The huge Missouri-Mississippi drainage basin (□ 1,244,000; of which □ 13,000 are in Alta. and Sask., Canada) is the 3d largest in the world (after the Amazon and the Congo) and comprises ⅖ of the total U.S. area, covering all or parts of 31 states. It drains vast expanses of the interior lowlands, Great Plains, and central Gulf coastal plain and its farthest headstreams reach deep into the Appalachians and Rockies. The Mississippi itself is fed, from the W, by the Minnesota, Des Moines, Missouri (with the tributaries Yellowstone, Platte, Kansas), Arkansas (with tributary Canadian), and Red rivers and, from the E, by the Illinois and Ohio (with the tributaries Wabash, Cumberland, Tennessee) rivers. The Ohio R. system—in a region of 40–50 inches of annual rainfall—discharges the greatest amount of water into the parent stream. From its source in L. Itasca (alt. 1,463 ft.) the Mississippi follows a semicircular course through glacial lakes (e.g., Winnibigoshish L.) and moraines past Bemidji and the Mesabi Range, then flows S and SE past St. Cloud to the Twin Cities of Minneapolis and St. Paul, where it receives the Minnesota R. and becomes navigable. Though it averages a fall of 7–8 inches per mi. throughout its course, the river here descends 65 ft. in ¾ of a mi. at Falls of St. Anthony. It continues SE, widening into L. Pepin along Minn.–Wis. line, past La Crosse (Wis.) and Dubuque (Iowa). Farther S, the rapids near Rock Island (Ill.) and Keokuk (Iowa; hydroelectric power station) are circumvented by canals. Much of the Mississippi's upper course (1,170 mi. above Missouri confluence) is flanked by steep limestone bluffs. About 17 mi. above St. Louis (Mo.) it meets the Missouri R., while at Cairo, at the S tip of Ill., it receives the Ohio. From this point it trends SSW past Memphis (Tenn.), Greenville (Miss.), Vicksburg (Miss.), and Natchez (Miss.) to its confluence with the Red R. in La., whence it turns SE past Baton Rouge and New Orleans to the Gulf of Mexico. The river is c.3,500 ft. wide at St. Louis, c.4,500 ft. wide at Cairo, and c.2,500 ft. wide at New Orleans. The lower Mississippi (below Cairo) meanders freely in a 40–70-mi.-wide flood plain, its shifting course forming many cut-offs or abandoned loops (oxbow lakes) and leaving several small areas of Tenn., Ark., Miss., and La. on opposite sides of the river. Deposition of sediment is considerable, especially along the main stream, where natural levees make it possible for the river level in places to be higher than the surrounding country. At many points artificial levees have been constructed on the banks to cope with flood waters. The fertile flood plain, in which cotton, rice, and sugar cane are grown, is drained by a number of parallel tributary streams (e.g., Yazoo, St. Francis), which eventually find their way through the levees into the Mississippi. S of the Red R. mouth is the Mississippi delta, consisting of much salt marsh, wooded swampland, and low-lying alluvial tracts, dissected by numerous distributaries (bayous), including the ATCHAFALAYA RIVER and Bayou Lafourche. The main stream enters the Gulf some 100 mi. SE of New Orleans via several small channels (passes), chief of which are South Pass (14 mi. long), Southwest Pass, and Pass a Loutre. The Intracoastal Waterway crosses the delta and is connected with the Mississippi by locks. The river's total annual discharge averages 600,000 to 700,000 cu. ft. per second. Although traffic (mostly by barge) on the Mississippi is still considerable, navigation is not as important a problem as flood control. Normal flood waters (in the spring) rise to as much as 50–55 ft. above the lowest stage, but heavy floods from the Ohio and Missouri rivers have caused the Mississippi to burst its banks and inundate vast areas of the surrounding country, as was the case in the disastrous 1927 flood. Levees were built by the French at New Orleans in 1717, but the 1st comprehensive flood-control scheme was authorized by the Federal govt. in 1917. A larger program, begun in 1928, provided for channel improvements (dredging, cut-offs), diversion-floodway and levee construction, and storage reservoirs on the main tributaries. Important projects include the Birds Point–New Madrid floodway on W bank below Cairo; the Morganza and West Atchafalaya floodways along the Atchafalaya R. in La.; and the BONNET CARRE FLOODWAY draining into L. Pontchartrain above New Orleans. The MISSOURI RIVER flood-control projects are also of great importance to the lower Mississippi. Since the 1870s jetties have provided sediment-free navigation through South Pass, and a 35-ft. channel for ocean-going vessels is now maintained to Baton Rouge. In the N, the Mississippi is connected with the Great Lakes by the Illinois Waterway. The river was much used by the Indians. De Soto discovered it in 1541–42. In 1673 Marquette and Jolliet descended to the confluence of the Arkansas, and in 1682 La Salle claimed the whole Mississippi country for France. The French built New Orleans (1718) and a chain of fur-trading posts along the upper course and its tributaries. Control of the river was transferred to Spain in 1762. The problem of American rights to the use of the Mississippi was solved by the Louisiana Purchase of 1803. The great waterway played an important part in the opening of the West, and, as an outlet for frontier products, it linked the new West economically to the South. A prosperous traffic, by flatboat and, later, steamboat, was carried on in the 1st half of the 19th cent. In the Civil War the Mississippi Valley figured prominently as an invasion route for the North; New Orleans fell to Adm. Faragut in 1862 and Vicksburg was the scene (1863) of Grant's decisive victory. After the war the river declined as a commercial highway, as the railroads took over more and more freight traffic. However, the heyday of side-wheelers and river ports, as depicted by Mark Twain and others, has become a permanent part of American folklore.

Mississippi Sound, arm of Gulf of Mexico bordering La., Miss., and Ala.; it lies bet. coast (N) and series of narrow isls. (S), and bet. L. Borgne (La.; W) and Mobile Bay (Ala.; E), communicating with the latter through Grants Pass; c.80 mi. long, 7–15 mi. wide. Traversed by Gulf Intracoastal Waterway. On its shores are Bay St. Louis, Pass Christian, Gulfport, Biloxi, and Pascagoula (all in Miss.).

Missolonghi or **Mesolonghi** (mĭsůlông'gē), Gr. *Mesolongion* (mĕsôlông'gēôn), city (pop. 10,565), ⊙ Acarnania nome, W central Greece, on lagoon of

Gulf of Patras, 20 mi. NW of Patras and 130 mi. WNW of Athens; 38°21'N 21°17'E. Trade in fish, caviar, tobacco, livestock. Accessible only to shallow-draught vessels, it has a deep-water port at KRYONERI (linked by rail) and also has rail connection with Agrinion and Neochorion. Seat of Gr. metropolitan. On site of anc. Elaeus, it was a fishing village under Turkish rule and became a Gr. stronghold in Gr. war of independence. It was successfully defended (1822–23) against an initial Turkish siege by Marco Bozzaris, who fell here in a sortie (1823). The poet Byron, who had moved here from Cephalonia, died of a fever in 1824. It was finally taken (1826) by the Turks after a 1-year siege when the garrison failed in a suicidal attempt to break through the Turkish lines. Rebuilt after 1828, it developed into an important trade center. The siege is commemorated by the Heroon (a mass grave), the tomb of Bozzaris, and a statue to Byron (1881). Also spelled Messolonghion, Misolonghi.

Missoula (mĭzōō'lù), county (□ 2,629; pop. 35,493), W Mont.; ⊙ Missoula. Irrigated agr. region drained by the Clark Fork, Bitterroot, and Blackfoot rivers. Livestock, sugar beets, grain, lumber. Part of Lolo Natl. Forest in NW. Formed 1865.

Missoula, city (pop. 22,485), ⊙ Missoula co., W Mont. 95 mi. WNW of Helena and on the Clark Fork (known locally as Missoula R.), near mouth of Bitterroot R., just E of Bitterroot Range; 46°52'N 114°W; alt. c.3,200 ft. Educational center of Mont., commercial and industrial point in rich agr. and mining region. Has copper, lead, gold mines, railroad shops; tourist trade; deals in culverts, paint, glass, wood products, flour, beet sugar, beverages, meat and dairy products, timber, fruit. Mont. State Univ., R.C. church, acad., hosp. here. Nearby points of interest: Fort Missoula (army post and military reservation), Mt. Sentinel, Mt. Jumbo, Hell Gate Canyon, Mont. Power Park. Established at present site 1865, inc. 1889. Development stimulated by arrival of railroads and creation of state univ.

Missour (mēsōōr'), village, Fez region, E central Fr. Morocco, in semi-arid upper Moulauya valley, bet. the Middle Atlas (N) and the High Atlas (S), 50 mi. NE of Midelt; sheep, esparto. Trade in cotton goods.

Missouri (mĭzōō'rē, –zōō'–, –rù), state (land □ 69,-270; with inland waters □ 69,674; 1950 pop. 3,954,653; 1940 pop. 3,784,664), central U.S.; bordered N by Iowa, W by Nebr., Kansas, and Okla., S by Ark., E by Tenn., Ky., and Ill.; 18th in area, 11th in pop.; admitted 1821 as 24th state; ⊙ Jefferson City. At its widest points Mo. (the "Bullion State") extends 305 mi. E–W and 285 mi. N–S. It lies largely in the vast interior lowlands region of the U.S., which stretches across the N and W parts of the state; the OZARK MOUNTAINS cover most of the S half; and in the extreme SE is a portion of the Mississippi flood plain. Most important of its natural features are the Mississippi R., forming the E boundary, and the Missouri R., which flows SE along the W boundary to Kansas City then generally E across center of state to the Mississippi just N of St. Louis. The area N of the Missouri, drained by the Salt, Chariton, Grand, and Little Platte rivers, comprises a rich farming land of soils of glacial and loessial (NW) origin. Here the rolling prairies, slightly higher in the N and W than in the E, attain an alt. of 750–1,000 ft. S of the Missouri R., the central W section is also plains country, broken in places by low hills. To the E are the Ozarks, covering c.⅓ of the state's area and extending NE to the Missouri, E to the Mississippi, and S into Ark. Averaging 1,000–1,200 ft. in height, the Ozarks are an old, eroded plateau of limestone and dolomites, rising to 1,772 ft. on Taum Sauk Mtn. (highest point in Mo.) in the SAINT FRANCOIS MOUNTAINS, an exposed group of igneous rocks near the E edge. The Ozark region is dissected by the Osage, Gasconade, White, and Black rivers and is characterized by rugged, well-timbered tracts, steep valleys, underground streams, and numerous springs; its isolated nature, produced by the rough topography, has retarded social and economic progress in the area. In the SE corner, the Mississippi embayment—northernmost extension of the Gulf coastal plain—consists of a fertile, alluvial lowland, intersected by the N end of Crowley's Ridge; much swampland here has now been reclaimed. Most of the state has a humid continental climate, while in the SE humid subtropical conditions prevail. Annual rainfall varies from 30–40 in. in N half to 40–50 in. in S half; snowfall averages 15–22 in. (S–N). St. Louis has mean temp. of 32°F. in Jan., 80°F. in July, and 39 in. of annual rainfall. Native vegetation consisted of tall prairie grass (N and W), oak-hickory (Ozarks and river valleys), oak-pine (St. Francois Mts.), and cypress-tupelo-red gum (extreme SE). Total forest land amounts to c.19,000,000 acres, including 1,300,000 acres in natl. forest reserves. Soil erosion is serious in the NE. Farm and range land comprises about 35,000,000 acres. Nearly ⅓ of the c.13,000,000 acres of harvested cropland is in corn, which is raised extensively in the N (especially NW), W, and SE parts of the state, primarily for fodder. Other crops are winter wheat (W and center), oats (mainly along N border), hay, soybeans, cotton (in SE lowland), potatoes, and tobacco. Apples, strawberries, peaches, and grapes are grown in places, chiefly in the SW counties. Mo. is an important livestock region, with some 3,000,000 head of cattle, 4,400,000 hogs (in the corn belts), 1,200,000 sheep, 350,000 horses, and 80,000 mules. The cattle, distributed throughout the state, are raised principally for slaughter, although dairying is also carried on. Poultry farming is important. Mo. is the leading U.S. producer of lead, mined in the St. Francois Mts. and in the Tri-State region (Mo.-Kansas-Okla.) in the SW (around JOPLIN), where it is associated with large zinc deposits. Extensive coal fields cover the W and N sections. Other mineral resources include limestone, granite, marble (notably at Carthage), barite (Washington co.), fire clay, glass sand (large plate-glass factory at Crystal City), nickle-copper-cobalt (at Fredericktown), iron ore, and manganese. The St. Francois mtn. region, with a wide variety of deposits, is the state's major mining dist. Mo.'s geographical location makes it a center of transportation and commerce, with rail, road, river, and air routes converging on St. Louis and Kansas City, by far the state's largest cities and most important industrial centers, handling over 75% of the large-scale mfg. Chief industries are meat packing, mfg. of footwear, food and grain products, malt liquors, drugs and chemicals; printing and publishing; mfg. of clothing and textiles, cement, lumber products, and farm machinery. Mo. is also noted for its corn-cob pipes. St. Joseph, Springfield, Joplin, Independence, Jefferson City, Hannibal, Sedalia, and Cape Girardeau are other mfg. and trade centers. BAGNELL DAM, which impounds 110-mi.-long L. of the Ozarks on Osage R., and Forsyth Dam, impounding L. Taneycomo on White R., are hydroelectric power sites; Clearwater and Wappapello dams, in the SE, are flood-control projects. Leading educational institutions include Univ. of Mo. (at Columbia and Rolla), St. Louis Univ., Washington Univ. (at St. Louis), and Univ. of Kansas City. The first white exploration in the region was via the Mississippi by French missionaries and traders, led by Marquette and Jolliet in 1673 and La Salle in 1682. Although searches for silver proved fruitless, lead was discovered at Mine La Motte in 1715; Ste. Genevieve, on the Mississippi, became the 1st permanent settlement in Mo. (c.1735). To expedite the profitable trade in furs, St. Louis was founded in 1764 by Laclede and Chouteau, and French initiative in establishing trading posts continued even after the area had been ceded (1762) to Spain. The U.S. acquired Mo. in 1803 by the Louisiana Purchase, and in the next year Lewis and Clark set out to explore the Missouri R. hinterland. From 1808 to 1815, when treaties were concluded, several skirmishes took place with the Indians, particularly with the Osage tribe. Mo. became a territory in 1812, and as more settlers (including cotton planters in the SE) began to arrive a petition for statehood was sent to Congress, which passed the Missouri Compromise of 1820, admitting Mo. as a slave-holding state but prohibiting slavery in the West N of 36°30'N. With St. Louis and, later, Independence the major outfitting points, Mo. figured prominently in the development of the West, as steamboat traffic pushed up the Missouri and down the Mississippi and traders and pioneers headed westward over the Santa Fe and Calif. trails. Settlement of W Mo. quickened, and in 1836 the state's present boundaries were fixed; the Mormons, however, were driven into Ill. by 1839. In the 1850s proslavery elements in Mo. were very active in trying to win neighboring Kansas for the slave cause. During the Civil War, Mo. was the scene of much fighting; Southern sympathizers at first gained the ascendancy but Union forces soon secured control of the state, although guerrilla activity continued throughout the war (a hangover of which was the exploits of Jesse James in the '60s and '70s). The post-war period saw the extension of the railroads, which tied Mo. more closely to the East, and the gradual decline of steamboat and overland traffic, which had tied the state to the West and South. Immigration increased; mining, agr., and stock raising were extensively developed; and manufactures multiplied in the important centers of St. Louis and Kansas City. Mark Twain, whose stories of 19th-cent. life along the Mississippi have become part of Amer. folklore, was born in Mo. and spent his boyhood in Hannibal. See also articles on cities, towns, geographic features, and the 114 counties (St. Louis City constitutes the 115th): ADAIR, ANDREW, ATCHISON, AUDRAIN, BARRY, BARTON, BATES, BENTON, BOLLINGER, BOONE, BUCHANAN, BUTLER, CALDWELL, CALLAWAY, CAMDEN, CAPE GIRARDEAU, CARROLL, CARTER, CASS, CEDAR, CHARITON, CHRISTIAN, CLARK, CLAY, CLINTON, COLE, COOPER, CRAWFORD, DADE, DALLAS, DAVIESS, DE KALB, DENT, DOUGLAS, DUNKLIN, FRANKLIN, GASCONADE, GENTRY, GREENE, GRUNDY, HARRISON, HENRY, HICKORY, HOLT, HOWARD, HOWELL, IRON, JACKSON, JASPER, JEFFERSON, JOHNSON, KNOX, LACLEDE, LAFAYETTE, LAWRENCE, LEWIS, LINCOLN, LINN, LIVINGSTON, MCDONALD, MACON, MADISON, MARIES, MARION, MERCER, MILLER, MISSISSIPPI, MONITEAU, MONROE, MONTGOMERY, MORGAN, NEW MADRID, NEWTON, NODAWAY, OREGON, OSAGE, OZARK, PEMISCOT, PERRY, PETTIS, PHELPS, PIKE, PLATTE, POLK, PULASKI, PUTNAM, RALLS, RANDOLPH, RAY, REYNOLDS, RIPLEY, SAINT CHARLES, SAINT CLAIR, SAINT FRANCOIS, SAINT LOUIS, SAINTE GENEVIEVE, SALINE, SCHUYLER, SCOTLAND, SCOTT, SHANNON, SHELBY, STODDARD, STONE, SULLIVAN, TANEY, TEXAS, VERNON, WARREN, WASHINGTON, WAYNE, WEBSTER, WORTH, WRIGHT.

Missouri City, city (pop. 314), Clay co., W Mo., on Missouri R. and 20 mi. NE of Kansas City.

Missouri River, longest river (2,714 mi. long from its farthest headstream) of the U.S., and chief tributary of the Mississippi. The "Big Muddy" is formed at c.4,000 ft. alt. at Three Forks in W Mont., where the Red Rock-Jefferson (its main headstream) is joined by the Gallatin and the Madison, all rising in the Rockies; it flows N and NE near Helena, Mont., then E across N Mont., turning SE in NW N.Dak. and continuing past Bismarck, N.Dak., Pierre, S.Dak., Sioux City and Council Bluffs, Iowa, Omaha and Nebraska City, Nebr., Atchison, Leavenworth, and Kansas City, Kansas, and St. Joseph, Kansas City, Jefferson City, and St. Charles, Mo., to the Mississippi c.17 mi. above St. Louis. Tributaries include the Musselshell, Milk, Yellowstone, Grand (of S.Dak.), Cheyenne, White, Niobrara, James, Big Sioux, Little Sioux, Platte, Kansas (with its tributaries the Republican and the Smoky Hill), Grand (of Iowa and Mo.), Chariton, Osage, and Gasconade rivers. The Missouri River Basin Project authorized 1944 by Congress contemplates a coordinated control and development program for the river's basin, □ 529,350 of the Great Plains and Interior Plains, in Mont., Colo., Wyo., N.Dak., S.Dak., Nebr., Kansas, Mo., Iowa, and Minn.; its purposes are flood control (to eliminate annual losses averaging many millions of dollars), supply of irrigation water to c.5,500,000 additional acres on which agr. yields are now uncertain because of drought, improvement of navigation from Sioux City to river's mouth, municipal water supply, abatement of stream pollution, and conservation of wildlife. Chief executing agencies are the Bureau of Reclamation of the Dept. of the Interior, and the Corps of Engineers; coordinating body for project also includes representatives of the Dept. of Agr., Federal Power Commission, Dept. of Commerce, and the states affected. In addition to existing dams, reservoirs, and other structures on the Missouri and its tributaries, project contemplates more than 100 other major works, including c.20 power plants. Principal units of the project on the main stream are FORT PECK DAM, FORT RANDALL DAM, GARRISON DAM, Canyon Ferry Dam (begun 1948 E of Helena, to replace a small privately-owned dam; 172 ft. high, 1,000 ft. long, it will impound c.2,000,000 acre-ft.), OAHE DAM, and projected Big Bend Dam c.25 mi. above Chamberlain, S.Dak. First known explorations of the Missouri were made in the period after 1762, although the river had long been a route for trade and transport for the Indians and, probably, for early French traders. Lewis and Clark expedition (1804–6) opened the mtn. country of the river's headwaters to the world, and the overland Astoria expedition (1811) used the Missouri as a route across much of the continent. The "Mountain Men" of the 1820s and 1830s made the remote headwaters better known as the fur trade became well established. Steamboats were introduced on the river in 1819, and the American Fur Co. brought (1832) the 1st steamer to the mouth of the Yellowstone; Fort Benton, Mont., eventually became the head of navigation on the Missouri. In the 1840s and 1850s, the river (with its tributary the Platte) was the beginning of the route to Oregon and Calif., and the path for the Mormons bound for Utah. River traffic boomed before the Civil War and for a time after, despite the coming of the railroads; then river's use as a waterway became secondary to importance of its falls for power, and, later, to use (begun 1903) of system's waters for irrigation projects which have now been embraced in the over-all development plan for the great Missouri River Basin.

Missouri Valley, city (pop. 3,546), Harrison co., W Iowa, near Boyer R., 21 mi. N of Council Bluffs; rail junction, with repair shops; mfg. (feed, beverages, concrete blocks). Settled 1854, inc. 1871.

Mistassibi River (mĭstŭsĭ'bē), central Que., rises E of L. Mistassini, flows 200 mi. S to Mistassini R. at Dolbeau, near L. St. John.

Mistassini (mĭstŭsē'nē), village (pop. 1,294), S central Que., on Mistassibi R., near its mouth on Mistassini R., 3 mi. NE of Dolbeau; blueberry canning, dairying, pig raising.

Mistassini, Lake (□ 840), central Que.; 51°N 72°45'–74°4'W; alt. 1,243 ft.; 80 mi. long, 12 mi. wide. Bisected by a chain of isls. Drains into James Bay by headstream of Rupert R.

Mistassini River, central Que., rises E of L. Mistassini, flows 200 mi. S, past Dolbeau, where it receives Mistassibi R., to St. John. On upper course are numerous rapids.

Mistek (mē'stěk), Czech *Místek*, town (pop. 8,749), E Moravia, Czechoslovakia, on left bank of Ostravice R., opposite Frydek; part of commune of Frydek-Mistek, 11 mi. SSE of Ostrava; noted textile industry.

Mistelbach or **Mistelbach an der Zaya** (mĭs'tŭlbäkh, än děr tsä'yä), town (pop. 5,553), NE Lower Austria, 21 mi. NE of Stockerau; market center for corn and wine region.

Misterbianco (mē"stĕrbyäng'kô), town (pop. 10,679), Catania prov., E Sicily, 4 mi. W of Catania, in grape- and orange-growing region; wine, soap. Largely destroyed by eruption of Mt. Etna in 1669.

Misterton, town and parish (pop. 1,573), N Nottingham, England, 5 mi. NW of Gainsborough; chemical- and tileworks. Has 13th-cent. church, rebuilt in 19th cent.

Misti, El (ĕl mē'stē), volcano (19,166 ft.), Arequipa dept., S Peru, in Cordillera Occidental, flanked by the volcanoes Chachani (NW) and Pichu Pichu (SE), 10 mi. NE of Arequipa, for which its perfect snow-capped cone is a famous landmark. El Misti, apparently of religious significance to the Incas, has figured much in Peruvian legends and poetry. Sometimes called Arequipa. Near its summit is an observatory established by Harvard Univ.

Mistley, town and parish (pop. 1,881), NE Essex, England, on Stour R. estuary and 9 mi. ENE of Colchester; agr. market.

Mist Mountain (10,303 ft.), SW Alta., near B.C. border, in Misty Range of Rocky Mts., 50 mi. SW of Calgary; 50°33'N 114°55'W.

Mistra or **Misitra** (both: mēsträ'), medieval fortress in Laconia nome, S Peloponnesus, Greece, on Mistra Hill, a spur of Taygetus Mts., 3 mi. W of Sparta; founded 1248–49 by French crusaders. Site of extensive Greco-Byzantine ruins (palaces, tower, monasteries). Modern village of Mistras (pop. 1,988) is just ESE.

Mistretta (mēstrĕt'tä), anc. *Amestratus*, town (pop. 11,546), Messina prov., N Sicily, in Nebrodi Mts., 13 mi. N of Nicosia, in stock-raising region; olive oil, wine. Has govt. mule-breeding station.

Misumi (mēsōō'mē). **1** Town (pop. 8,920), Kumamoto prefecture, W Kyushu, Japan, port on Shimabara Bay, 19 mi. SW of Kumamoto, on W tip of small peninsula, opposite Oyano-shima; commercial center in agr. area; rice, oranges, pears, raw silk. Exports lumber, wheat flour. **2** Town (pop. 3,542), Shimane prefecture, SW Honshu, Japan, 6 mi. SW of Hamada, in agr. area (rice, wheat); floor mats, sake, charcoal, raw silk, tiles; paper milling. **3** Town (pop. 8,875), Yamaguchi prefecture, SW Honshu, Japan, 9 mi. WSW of Hagi; commercial center in rice-producing area; sake, soy sauce, charcoal, timber. Copper mining near by.

Misungwi, Tanganyika: see Mantare.

Misurata (mēzōōrä'tä), town (pop. 5,000), Tripolitania, Libya, on coastal highway and 120 mi. ESE of Tripoli, in an oasis (c.10 mi. long, 5 mi. wide) near W entrance to Gulf of Sidra. Commercial center (dates, figs, cereals, livestock) noted for its artisan carpet industry. Has modern European quarter and airport. Its port, Misurata Marina (tunny fishing), is 7 mi. E on Cape Misurata, at edge of extensive salt flat. Bombed (1941–42) in Second World War.

Mit Abu Ghalib (mēt' ă'bōō gä'lĭb), village (pop. 5,361), Gharbiya prov., Lower Egypt, on Damietta branch of the Nile, 11 mi. NE of Shirbin; cotton.

Mitaka (mētä'kä), residential town (pop. 50,699), Greater Tokyo, central Honshu, Japan, just W of Tokyo; agr. (rice, wheat).

Mitake (mētä'kā). **1** Town (pop. 3,640), Gifu prefecture, central Honshu, Japan, 7 mi. N of Tajimi; agr. center (rice, wheat, soybeans). Lignite mining. **2** Town, Miyagi prefecture, Japan: see Tsuya.

Mitan (mētän'), village (1939 pop. over 2,000), S Samarkand oblast, Uzbek SSR, on the Ak Darya (S arm of Zeravshan R.) and 33 mi. NW of Samarkand; cotton; metalworks.

Mita Point (mē'tä), cape on the Pacific, at NE entrance of Banderas Bay, W Mexico, 65 mi. SW of Tepic; 20°46'N 105°33'W.

Mitare (mētä'rä), town (pop. 311), Falcón state, NW Venezuela, in Gulf of Venezuela lowlands, 25 mi. WSW of Coro; saltworks.

Mitau, Latvia: see Jelgava.

Mitava, Latvia: see Jelgava.

Mit Badr Halawa or **Mit Badr Halawah** (mēt' bă'dûr hälä'wŭ), village (pop. 7,038), Gharbiya prov., Lower Egypt, 8 mi. S of Samannud; cotton.

Mit Bashshar (mēt' băsh'shär), village (pop. 6,281), Sharqiya prov., Lower Egypt, 7 mi. SW of Zagazig; cotton.

Mit Bera, Mit Bira, or **Mit Birah** (all: mēt' bĭ'rŭ), village (pop. 7,238), Minufiya prov., Lower Egypt, on railroad just N of Benha; cotton ginning; cereals, cotton, flax.

Mitcham. 1 Town (pop. 23,573), SE South Australia, 4 mi. S of Adelaide, in metropolitan area; agr. center. **2** E suburb of Melbourne, S Victoria, Australia, in fruitgrowing area.

Mitcham, residential municipal borough (1931 pop. 56,859; 1951 census 67,273), NE Surrey, England, 7 mi. S of London; also mfg. (leather, chemicals, soap, pharmaceuticals, paint, glass, food products). Once noted for its lavender. Has 480-acre common. The annual fair dates from Middle Ages. John Donne lived here for some time.

Mitchel Air Force Base, U.S. installation at Mitchel Field, Nassau co., SE N.Y., just E of Garden City. Air Defense Command hq. here until 1951.

Mitchell, town (pop. 1,193), S central Queensland, Australia, 110 mi. E of Charleville; sheep-raising center; wheat.

Mitchell, town (pop. 1,777), S Ont., on Thames R. and 12 mi. NW of Stratford; knitting, flax, flour, and lumber mills, milk canneries, grain elevators, cold-storage plants.

Mitchell. 1 County (□ 511; pop. 22,528), SW Ga.; ⊙ Camilla. Bounded NW by Flint R. Coastal plain agr. (cotton, corn, pecans, peanuts, livestock) and sawmilling area; mfg. at Camilla and Pelham. Formed 1857. **2** County (□ 467; pop. 13,945), N Iowa, on Minn. line; ⊙ Osage. Prairie agr. region (cattle, hogs, corn, hay) drained by Wapsipinicon, Cedar, and Little Cedar rivers. Has many limestone quarries, sand and gravel pits. Formed 1851. **3** County (□ 716; pop. 10,320), N Kansas; ⊙ Beloit. Plains region, drained by Solomon R. Wheat, livestock. Formed 1870. **4** County (□ 220; pop. 15,143), W N.C.; ⊙ Bakersville. Bounded N by Tenn., W by Nolichucky R.; Unaka Mts. in N, the Blue Ridge in S; largely in Pisgah Natl. Forest. Farming (tobacco, corn, potatoes, apples, clover, dairy products), livestock raising, mining (mica, feldspar, kaolin), sawmilling; resort area. Formed 1861. **5** County (□ 922; pop. 14,357), W Texas; ⊙ Colorado City. Rolling prairies, broken by Colorado R.; alt. 1,900–2,500 ft. Ranching (cattle, sheep), agr. region (cotton, grain sorghums, oats, wheat, alfalfa, peanuts); dairy products. Oil wells. Formed 1876.

Mitchell. 1 Town (pop. 240), Glascock co., E Ga., c.45 mi. WSW of Augusta, near Ogeechee R.; sawmilling. **2** City (pop. 3,245), Lawrence co., S Ind., 9 mi. S of Bedford; agr. (fruit, grain); mfg. (cement, dairy products, clothing, lime); limestone quarrying. Spring Mill State Park (recreation), with restored pioneer village, is near by. **3** Town (pop. 168), Mitchell co., N Iowa, 4 mi. NW of Osage; livestock, grain. **4** City (pop. 2,101), Scotts Bluff co., W Nebr., 8 mi. NW of Scottsbluff and on N.Platte R., in irrigated agr. region; beet sugar, honey, dairy products, potatoes. Co. fairgrounds here. **5** Town (pop. 415), Wheeler co., N central Oregon, 40 mi. NE of Prineville. **6** City (pop. 12,123), ⊙ Davison co., SE central S.Dak., 70 mi. WNW of Sioux Falls, near James R. and L. Mitchell; 43°43'N 98°W. Trade and shipping point for farming, dairying, cattle region; cement; grain, meat, dairy and poultry products. Agr. festival takes place annually in the Corn Palace. Dakota Wesleyan Univ. and a jr. col. are here. City platted 1879, chartered 1883.

Mitchell, Lake. 1 In Wexford co., NW Mich., 3 mi. W of Cadillac, in resort area; c.3 mi. long, 2 mi. wide. Joined to L. Cadillac (E) by short stream. **2** In SE central S.Dak., near Mitchell; 3 mi. long, 1 mi. wide; created by dam on Firesteel Creek; recreation.

Mitchell, Mount, Yancey co., W N.C., in Black Mts. (a range of the Appalachians), 20 mi. NE of Asheville. Highest point (6,684 ft.) E of the Mississippi; part of Mt. Mitchell State Park.

Mitchell Dam, central Ala., in Coosa R., 30 mi. NNW of Montgomery. Privately built power dam (106 ft. high, 1,264 ft. long) completed 1923; forms small reservoir (□ 9). Hydroelectric plant generates c.75,000 kw.

Mitchell Heights, residential town (pop. 185), Logan co., SW W.Va., 5 mi. W of Logan.

Mitchell Island, Ellice Isls.: see Nukulaelae.

Mitchell Lake (10 mi. long, 2 mi. wide), E B.C., in Cariboo Mts., 75 mi. E of Quesnel; alt. 3,170 ft. Drains SW into Quesnel L.

Mitchell Peak (7,947 ft.), E Ariz., in Blue Range, 10 mi. N of Morenci.

Mitchell River. 1 In N Queensland, Australia, rises in Great Dividing Range near Rumula, flows 350 mi. generally WNW to Gulf of Carpentaria 165 mi. N of Normanton. Palmer and Lynd rivers, main tributaries. **2** In SE Victoria, Australia, formed by 2 headstreams rising in Australian Alps S of Mt. Hotham; flows 60 mi. S and ESE, past Bairnsdale, to L. King on SE coast.

Mitchellville. 1 Town (pop. 906), Polk co., central Iowa, near Skunk R., 14 mi. ENE of Des Moines, in agr. and coal-mining area. Seat of state training school for girls. **2** Town (pop. 202), Sumner co., N Tenn., near Ky. line, 35 mi. NNE of Nashville.

Mitchelstown, Gaelic *Baile an Mhistéalaigh*, town (pop. 2,054), NE Co. Cork, Ireland, 15 mi. SSW of Tipperary, at foot of Galty Mts.; agr. market in dairying region, with dairy-processing plants. Near by are noted Mitchelstown limestone caves.

Mit el 'Amil or **Mit al-'Amil** (both: mēt' ĕl ä'mĭl), village (pop. 7,304), Daqahliya prov., NE Lower Egypt, 10 mi. S of Mansura; cotton, cereals.

Mit el Ghuraqa or **Mit al-Ghuraqa** (both: mēt ĕl gōō'räkä), village (pop. 6,234), Gharbiya prov., Lower Egypt, on Damietta branch of the Nile, on railroad, and 2 mi. WSW of Talkha; cotton.

Mit el Nasara, Mit en Nasara, or **Mit al-Nasara** (all: mēt' ĕn-nä'särŭ), village (pop. 7,650), Daqalhiya prov., NE Lower Egypt, 13 mi. ENE of Mansura; cotton, cereals.

Mit Ghamr (mēt' gă'mŭr), town (pop. 28,968), Daqahliya prov., Lower Egypt, on Damietta branch of the Nile, on railroad, and 15 mi. NW of Zagazig; cotton ginning, cottonseed-oil extraction.

Mithankot (mĭt'ŭnkōt), town (pop. 5,889), Dera Ghazi Khan dist., SW Punjab, W Pakistan, near Indus R., 75 mi. SSW of Dera Ghazi Khan; local market for wheat, rice, millet, dates.

Mithapur, India: see Okha.

Mitha Tiwana (mĭt'ŭ tĭvä'nŭ), town (pop. 6,567), Shahpur dist., W central Punjab, W Pakistan, 34 mi. WNW of Sargodha; cotton, oilseeds, wheat.

Mithimna, Greece: see Methymna.

Mitiaro (mētēä'rō), coral island (2,500 acres; pop. 229), Cook Islands, S Pacific, 142 mi. NE of Rarotonga; 4 mi. long, 1 mi. wide; exports copra, sandalwood.

Mitidja (mētējä'), fertile alluvial plain of N central Algeria, enclosed bet. northernmost range of the Tell Atlas and a hilly coastal strip (*sahel*), just inland from Algiers; c. 65 mi. long, 20 mi. wide. Because of its proximity to Algiers, it was 1st region intensively cultivated by Europeans after Fr. occupation of Algeria in 1830. It is today covered with vineyards, truck gardens, and citrus groves, and grows tobacco, perfume flowers, and cereals. E section is irrigated from Hamiz Dam. Chief towns are Blida and Boufarik. Formerly spelled Métidja.

Mitidja Atlas, coastal range of the Tell Atlas, in N central Algeria, overlooking the Mitidja lowland, S of Algiers. Rises to 5,344 ft. in Abd-el-Kader peak. City of Blida at NW foot. N slopes covered with vineyards and citrus groves. Also called Atlas of Blida.

Mitikas, Greece: see Olympus.

Mitilini, Greece: see Mytilene.

Mitilinoi, Greece: see Mytilenoi.

Mitiyagoda (mĭtĭyŭgō'dŭ), village (pop., including near-by villages, 1,749), Southern Prov., Ceylon, 4 mi. SE of Ambalangoda; major moonstone-mining center of Ceylon; vegetables, cinnamon, coconuts, rice, rubber.

Mit Khaqan (mēt' khă'kän), village (pop. 8,061), Minufiya prov., Lower Egypt, 2 mi. NE of Shibin el Kom; cereals, cotton, flax.

Mit Kinana or **Mit Kinanah** (mēt' kĭnă'nŭ), village (pop. 11,459), Qalyubiya prov., S Lower Egypt, 20 mi. N of Cairo; cotton, flax, cereals, fruits.

Mitkof Island (mĭt'kôf) (24 mi. long, 7–17 mi. wide), SE Alaska, in Alexander Archipelago, bet. Kupreanof Isl. (W) and mainland (E), 10 mi. NW of Wrangell; 56°40'N 132°47'W; rises to 3,960 ft. (SE). Fishing, fish processing, lumbering, and fur farming. Petersburg town, N.

Mitla (mēt'lä), officially San Pablo Villa de Mitla, town (pop. 2,676), Oaxaca, S Mexico, in Sierra Madre del Sur, 25 mi. ESE of Oaxaca; alt. 5,413 ft. Famed for its astonishing ruins, the best-preserved in Mexico, Mitla [=City of the Dead] was a great center of Zapotec civilization; massive bldgs. include temples, subterranean tombs, and impressive structure known as the "hall of monoliths"; bldgs. are decorated by chiseled, lace-like patterns, and have noted mosaics. Believed to have succeeded Monte Albán, nearer Oaxaca, as anc. Zapotec capital.

Mit Mihsin (mēt' mĭ'sĭn), village (pop. 5,306), Daqahliya prov., Lower Egypt, 2 mi. NE of Mit Ghamr; cotton, cereals. Also spelled Mit Mohsin.

Mito (mē'tō). **1** Town (pop. 10,461), Aichi prefecture, central Honshu, Japan, 5 mi. NW of Toyohashi; rice-growing center; raw silk. **2** City (1940 pop. 66,293; 1947 pop. 61,416), ⊙ Ibaraki prefecture, central Honshu, Japan, near E coast, 60 mi. NE of Tokyo and on Naka R. Rail junction; commercial center for tobacco-raising area; stock raising, fishing. Memorial hall has statue of Emperor Meiji. Seaside resorts in suburbs. Was 17th-cent. seat of important branch of Tokugawa family. Bombed (1945) in Second World War.

Mitoginski or **Mitoginskiy** (mētŭgēn'skē), town (1948 pop. over 500), Kamchatka oblast, Khabarovsk Territory, Russian SFSR, on SW Kamchatka Peninsula, on Sea of Okhotsk, 15 mi. N of Ust-Bolsheretsk; fish-processing plant.

Mitontic (mētōntēk'), town (pop. 241), Chiapas, S Mexico, in Sierra de Hueytepec, 10 mi. NNE of San Cristóbal de las Casas; alt. 7,285 ft.; wheat, fruit.

Mitoya (mētō'yä), town (pop. 5,909), Shimane prefecture, SW Honshu, Japan, 17 mi. SW of Matsue, in rice-growing area; raw silk, charcoal; poultry.

Mitre, Argentina: see Unión.

Mitre Peak, New Zealand: see Milford Sound.

Mit Riheina, Mit Rahineh, or **Mit Rihaynah** (all: mēt' rĭhā'nŭ), village (pop. 6,351), Giza prov., Upper Egypt, 20 mi. S of Cairo; corn, cotton. On part of site of anc. Memphis, it has 2 colossal statues of Ramses II.

Mitrofanovka (mētrŭfä'nŭfkŭ), village (1939 pop. over 500), S Voronezh oblast, Russian SFSR, 17 mi. SSE of Rossosh; flour mill, metalworks.

Mitrovica or **Mitrovitsa** (both: mē'trôvētsä). **1** or **Kosovska Mitrovica** or **Kosovska Mitrovitsa** (kô'-

sôfskä), town (pop. 13,947), S Serbia, Yugoslavia, on Ibar R., at Sitnica R. mouth, on railroad and 22 mi. NNW of Pristina, in the Kosovo; flour milling, stone working. Magnesite deposits. Mining, milling, and smelting of metal ores at near-by TREPCA and ZVECAN. Until 1913, under Turkish rule. Also called Mitrovica Kosovska or Mitrovitsa Kosovska. **2** or **Sremska Mitrovica** or **Sremska Mitrovitsa** (srĕm'skä), anc. *Sirmium*, town (pop. 13,671), Vojvodina, NW Serbia, Yugoslavia, port on Sava R. (head of passenger navigation), on railroad and 21 mi. SSW of Novi Sad, in the Srem; tannin mfg.; fishing.

Mit Salsil (mēt' săl'sēl), village (pop. 10,713), Daqahliya prov., Lower Egypt, on El Bahr el Saghir (a delta canal) and 8 mi. WNW of Manzala; cotton, cereals.

Mitsang or **Mi-ts'ang** (mē'tsäng'), town (pop. 1,225), ⊙ Mitsang co. (pop. 57,537), W Suiyuan prov., China, near Ningsia line, 25 mi. W of Linho, in Howtao oasis; cattle raising; grain. Until 1942 called Santaokiao.

Mitsikeli (mĭtsĭkä'lē), mountain outlier of central Pindus system, S Epirus, Greece, N of L. Ioannina; 15 mi. long; rises to 5,936 ft. 4 mi. NE of Ioannina.

Mitsinjo (mētsēn'dzōō), town, Majunga prov., NW Madagascar, on Mahavavy R., near W coast N of L. Kinkony, 35 mi. WSW of Majunga; cattle market; sugar mills.

Mitsu, Japan: see AKITSU.

Mitsuhama, Japan: see MATSUYAMA, Ehime prefecture.

Mitsuishi (mētsōō'ĭshē), town (pop. 5,133), Okayama prefecture, SW Honshu, Japan, 22 mi. ENE of Okayama, in agr. area (rice, wheat, persimmons); raw silk, charcoal. Alabaster quarrying. Sometimes spelled Mituisi.

Mitsuke (mē'tsōōkä). **1** Town (pop. 17,812), Niigata prefecture, central Honshu, Japan, 7 mi. NE of Nagaoka; commercial center for rice-growing area; textiles. Sometimes spelled Mituke. **2** Town, Shizuoka prefecture, Japan: see IWATA.

Mitsunosho (mē'tsōōnōshō), town (pop. 6,116) on Inno-shima, Hiroshima prefecture, Japan, on SE coast of isl.; agr. and livestock center; rice, raw silk, sake, charcoal.

Mitsuyo, Korea: see MIRYANG.

Mittaghorn (mĭ'täk-hôrn"), peak (12,796 ft.) in Bernese Alps, S central Switzerland, 13 mi. S of Interlaken.

Mittagong (mĭ'tŭgŏng), town (pop. 2,094), E New South Wales, Australia, 60 mi. SW of Sydney; iron-mining center; coal.

Mittagskogel (mĭt'äkskō"gŭl) or **Kepa** (kĕ'pä), peak (c.7,030 ft.) in the Karawanken, on Austro-Yugoslav border, 9 mi. SE of Villach, Austria.

Mitta Mitta River, NE Victoria, Australia, rises in Australian Alps SSW of Omeo, flows 125 mi. N and NNW, past Tallandoon, to Hume Reservoir near Tallangatta.

Mittelbach (mĭ'tŭlbäkh), village (pop. 2,643), Saxony, E central Germany, at N foot of the Erzgebirge, 6 mi. WSW of Chemnitz; synthetic-oil plant.

Mittelberg (–bĕrk), town (pop. 2,811), Vorarlberg, W Austria, 20 mi. ESE of Dornbirn; dairy farming.

Mittelbexbach (mĭ'tŭlbĕks'bäkh), town (1948 pop. 7,561), E Saar, near Ger. border, 5 mi. WNW of Homburg; coal mining, clay quarrying; brewing. Formed part of Höcherberg commune (1937–46).

Mittelfranken, Germany: see MIDDLE FRANCONIA.

Mittelhorn, peak (12,163 ft.) in Bernese Alps, S central Switzerland, 4 mi. E of Grindelwald.

Mittelland, Switzerland: see BERN, canton.

Mittelland Canal (mĭ'tŭl-lănt"), name applied in Germany to EMS-WESER CANAL and WESER-ELBE CANAL. Mittelland Canal system links the Rhine (W) and the Elbe (E) via Rhine-Herne and Dortmund-Ems canals and the Mittelland Canal proper; extends c.290 mi. bet. Duisburg (W) and Magdeburg. In its widest application, system includes Brandenburg network (Havel R.; Hohenzollern, Ihle, and Plaue canals), which links it with the Oder.

Mittelmurgebiet, region, Yugoslavia: see MEDJUMURJE.

Mittelwalde, Poland: see MIEDZYLESIE.

Mittenwald (mĭ'tŭnvält"), village (pop. 6,918), Upper Bavaria, Germany, bet. the Karwendelgebirge and the Wettersteingebirge, on the Isar and 8 mi. ESE of Garmisch-Partenkirchen; frontier station (Austrian border) on Innsbruck-Munich RR.; violins, zithers (home industry). Summer and winter resort (alt. 2,995 ft.). Has baroque church. Chartered 1307; was important trade center in 15th and 16th cent.

Mittenwalde (mĭ"tŭnväl'dŭ), town (pop. 3,432), Brandenburg, E Germany, 18 mi. SSE of Berlin; market gardening. Has remains of old town walls.

Mitterbach (mĭ'tŭrbäkh), village (pop. 723), S Lower Austria, 30 mi. SSW of Sankt Pölten, at Styria line; hydroelectric station is just S.

Mitterburg, Yugoslavia: see PAZIN.

Mittersill (mĭt'ŭrzĭl), town (pop. 3,175), Salzburg, W central Austria, on the Salzach and 12 mi. SSE of Kitzbühel; brewery. Old restored castle near by.

Mitterteich (mĭ'tŭrtīkh), town (pop. 5,978), Upper Palatinate, NE Bavaria, Germany, on S slope of the Fichtelgebirge, 4.5 mi. SW of Waldsassen; mfg. (optical glass, porcelain, precision instruments). Chartered 1501.

Mittweida (mĭtvī'dŭ), town (pop. 22,794), Saxony, E central Germany, on Zschopau R. and 11 mi. NNE of Chemnitz; paper and cotton milling, hosiery knitting, metalworking; mfg. of machinery, precision instruments, glass, clothing. Has 15th-cent. church.

Mitu (mē'dōō'), town, ⊙ Mitu co. (pop. 101,904), NW central Yunnan prov., China, 35 mi. SE of Tali, near Burma Road; silk textiles; rice, wheat, millet, beans. Coal mines near by.

Mitú (mētōō'), town (pop. 312), ⊙ Vaupés commissary, SE Colombia, on Vaupés R., in region of tropical forests, 14 mi. W of Brazil border, 375 mi. SE of Bogotá; 1°7'N 70°2'W; forest products (rubber, gums). Founded 1935.

Mitubiri (mētōōbē'rē), village, Central Prov., S central Kenya, on railroad and 30 mi. NE of Nairobi; coffee, wheat, corn; wattle growing.

Mituisi, Japan: see MITSUISHI.

Mituke, Japan: see MITSUKE, Niigata prefecture.

Mitungu (mētōōng'gōō), town, Central Prov., S central Kenya, on road and 15 mi. SSE of Meru, E of Mt. Kenya; 0°8'S 37°49'E; coffee, wheat, corn. Airfield. Also spelled Mitungugu.

Mitwaba (mētwä'bä), village, Katanga prov., SE Belgian Congo, 170 mi. NNE of Jadotville; tin-mining and trading center; tin concentrating. Has hydroelectric plant, airfield.

Mitwitz (mĭt'vĭts), village (pop. 1,703), Upper Franconia, N Bavaria, Germany, 5 mi. W of Kronach; lumber milling.

Mityana (mētyä'nä), town, Buganda prov., S Uganda, 38 mi. WNW of Kampala, on swampy L. Wamala; coffee and tea center; cotton, bananas, corn; dairy products.

Mitzic (mētsĕk'), village, N Gabon, Fr. Equatorial Africa, 60 mi. S of Oyem; cacao and coffee plantations. R.C. and Protestant missions.

Miura Peninsula (mēōō'rä), Jap. *Miura-hanto*, Kanagawa prefecture, central Honshu, Japan, E of Sagami Bay, W of Tokyo Bay and Uraga Strait; 14 mi. long, 2-5 mi. wide. Yokosuka (naval base) is on E coast.

Mius River (mēōōs'), in E Ukrainian SSR and Rostov oblast, Russian SFSR; rises in Donets Ridge near Gorlovka, flows c.100 mi. SSE, past Matveyev-Kurgan and Pokrovskoye, to Mius Liman (inlet of Sea of Azov) NW of Taganrog. A fortified Rus. border (1695–1711); during Second World War, a Soviet-Ger. battle line (1941-42, 1943).

Mivtahim (mēftähēm'), agr. settlement (pop. 60), SW Israel, in the Negev, 20 mi. S of Gaza. Founded 1947.

Miwa (mē'wä), town (pop. 4,699), Nara prefecture, S Honshu, Japan, 11 mi. S of Nara; sake, noodles, medicine.

Miwani (mēwä'nē), village, Nyanza prov., W Kenya, on railroad and 15 mi. E of Kisumu; sugar mill.

Mixco (mē'skō), town (1950 pop. 4,217), Guatemala dept., S central Guatemala, on Inter-American Highway and 4 mi. W of Guatemala; alt. 5,551 ft. Market center; pottery making; truck (fruit, vegetables), corn; cattle raising.

Mixcoac (mēskwäk'), SW section of Mexico city, central Mexico; mfg. suburb (cement plant, processing industries); nursery gardens. Villa Obregón adjoins (S).

Mixnitz (mĭks'nĭts), village, Styria, E central Austria, on Mur R. and 20 mi. N of Graz; hydroelectric station; summer resort.

Mixquiahuala (mēskyäwä'lä), town (pop. 3,802), Hidalgo, central Mexico, on Tula R. and 32 mi. WNW of Pachuca, on railroad; grain, beans, potatoes, fruit, stock.

Mixquic (mēskēk'), town (pop. 2,552), Federal Dist., central Mexico, 18 mi. SE of Mexico city; cereals, fruit, vegetables, livestock.

Mixstadt, Poland: see MIKSTAT.

Mixtecapán (mēstäkäpän'), plateau in Oaxaca, S Mexico, forms part of Sierra Madre del Sur, comprises most of uplands of state from Puebla border to Isthmus of Tehuantepec. Average alt. 5,000 ft. Situated on it are city of Oaxaca and great Zapotec ruins at Mitla.

Mixtepec or **San Juan Mixtepec** (sän whän' mēstāpĕk'), town (pop. 2,331), Oaxaca, S Mexico, in S Sierra Madre del Sur, 34 mi. SE of Ejutla; antimony mining.

Mixtla (mē'slä). **1** Officially San Francisco Mixtla, town (pop. 479), Puebla, central Mexico, 23 mi. ESE of Puebla; cereals, vegetables. **2** Officially Mixtla de Altamirano, town (pop. 1,400), Veracruz, E Mexico, in Sierra Madre Oriental, 21 mi. SSW of Córdoba; coffee, sugar cane, fruit.

Mixtlán (mēslän'), town (pop. 1,495), Jalisco, W Mexico, 23 mi. WSW of Ameca; corn, chick-peas, beans, sugar cane.

Miya (mē'yä), town (pop. 11,043), Aichi prefecture, central Honshu, Japan, on Atsumi Bay, 9 mi. WNW of Toyohashi; fishing port; summer resort. Marine experiment station.

Miyada, Japan: see MIYATA.

Miyagi (mēyä'gē), prefecture [Jap. *ken*] (□ 2,808; 1940 pop. 1,271,238; 1947 pop. 1,566,831), N Honshu, Japan; ⊙ SENDAI. Bounded E by the Pacific; generally mountainous and forested. Chief port, ISHINOMAKI. Kitakami R. drains fertile plains producing rice, wheat, tea, soybeans. Fishing, lumbering, horse breeding; raw-silk culture. Mining (lignite, gold, silver, copper). Mfg. (textiles, lacquer ware, pottery).

Miyaji (mēyä'jē), town (pop. 5,961), Kumamoto prefecture, central Kyushu, Japan, 25 mi. ENE of Kumamoto; rice, wheat, fish, lumber.

Miya-jima, Japan: see ITSUKU-SHIMA.

Miyajuku (mēyä'jōōkōō), town (pop. 7,419), Yamagata prefecture, N Honshu, Japan, 11 mi. WNW of Yamagata; rice, China grass.

Miyake-jima (mēyäkā'jĭmä), island (□ 19; pop. 6,553) of isl. group Izu-shichito, Greater Tokyo, Japan, in Philippine Sea, 38 mi. S of O-shima; roughly circular, 5 mi. in diameter. Has active volcano (2,668 ft. high). Agr., silkworm culture, livestock.

Miyako (mē'yä'kō). **1** City (1940 pop. 23,189; 1947 pop. 36,715), Iwate prefecture, N Honshu, Japan, fishing port on the Pacific, 45 mi. E of Morioka; lumbering center; boat yards. **2** City, Kyoto prefecture, Japan: see KYOTO, city.

Miyako-gunto (–gōōntō) or **Miyako-retto** (–rĕtō), island subgroup (□ 96; 1950 pop. 74,612) of Sakishima Isls., in the S Ryukyus. Includes Miyako-shima, Irabu-shima, and Tarama-shima.

Miyako-jima (mēyä'kō-jĭmä), volcanic island (□ 70; 1950 pop. 59,384, including offshore islets) of Sakishima Isls., in the Ryukyu Islands, bet. E.China Sea (W) and Philippine Sea (E), 60 mi. ENE of Ishigaki-shima; 13 mi. long, 12 mi. wide; roughly triangular. Hilly, fertile; surrounded by coral reef. Produces sugar cane, sweet potatoes, soybeans, some rice. Formerly called Taipinsan. Chief town is Hirara.

Miyakonojo (mēyä"kōnōjō'), city (1940 pop. 58,819; 1947 pop. 71,621), Miyazaki prefecture, S Kyushu, Japan, 24 mi. SW of Miyazaki; rail junction; commercial center in agr. area; spinning and textile mills. Ships rice, raw silk, lumber.

Miyanabad, Iran: see MIANABAD.

Miyanduab, **Mianduab**, or **Miandoab** (all: mēändōäb'), town, Fourth Prov., in Azerbaijan, NW Iran, in the Kurd country, 80 mi. S of Tabriz, and on Zarineh R., SE of L. Urmia; alt. 4,200 ft. Grain, fruit, sugar beets; sheep; beet-sugar refinery.

Miyang (mē'yäng'), town, ⊙ Miyang co. (pop. 273,834), S Honan prov., China, 60 mi. NW of Sinyang; cotton weaving; medicinal herbs, wheat, beans, kaoliang. Sometimes written Piyang.

Miyan Kaleh Peninsula (mēyän' kälĕ'), narrow sandspit, on SE Caspian Sea, in NE Iran; 35 mi. long, 2–3 mi. wide, nearly closing off Gurgan Lagoon. Ashuradeh Isls. are off E tip.

Miyanohara (mēyä'nōhärŭ), town (pop. 5,423), Kumamoto prefecture, W Kyushu, Japan, 17 mi. S of Kumamoto; agr. center (rice, wheat). Sometimes called Miyanoharu.

Miyanojo (mēyä"nōjō'), town (pop. 18,126), Kagoshma prefecture, S Kyushu, Japan, 23 mi. NNW of Kagoshima; livestock and agr. center (rice, wheat); raw silk. Hot springs.

Miyata (mēyä'tä) or **Miyada** (–yä'dä). **1** Town (pop. 6,152), Aichi prefecture, central Honshu, Japan, on Kiso R. and 4 mi. NE of Ichinomiya; truck gardening; mulberry fields. **2** Town (pop. 36,718), Fukuoka prefecture, N Kyushu, Japan, 18 mi. NE of Fukuoka; coal-mining center; rice, wheat, barley.

Miyauchi (mēyä'ōōchē), town (pop. 11,975), Yamagata prefecture, N Honshu, Japan, 11 mi. N of Yonezawa; rice, raw silk. Sericulture experiment station.

Miyazaki (mēyä'-zä'kē), prefecture [Jap. *ken*] (□ 2,998; 1940 pop. 840,357; 1947 pop. 1,025,689), E Kyushu, Japan; ⊙ Miyazaki. Bounded E by Hyuga Sea (N arm of Philippine Sea), S by Ariake Bay. Mountainous terrain; rises to 5,650 ft. at Ichibusa-yama. N area drained by Gokase R. Primarily agr. (rice, wheat, soybeans, sweet potatoes, millet). Extensive forested area, with pine and Japan cedar trees. INO, in interior, is horse-breeding center. Numerous small fisheries along coast. Products include rice, lumber, raw silk, charcoal. Many small ports export agr. produce and lumber. Chief centers: Miyazaki (E), NOBEOKA (NE), MIYAKONOJO (S).

Miyazaki, city (1940 pop. 66,497; 1947 pop. 92,144), ⊙ Miyazaki prefecture, SE Kyushu, Japan, on Hyuga Sea, 75 mi. SE of Kumamoto and on Oyobo R.; 38°37'N 141°46'E. Cultural center; produces chinaware, trays. Seat of great Shinto shrine Miyazaki-jingu (containing archaeological mus.), dedicated to Jimmu, 1st emperor of Japan. Site of feudal castle. Race tracks in suburbs. Includes (since early 1940s) former adjacent town of Akae (1940 pop. 10,630).

Miyazu (mēyä'zōō), town (pop. 15,229), Kyoto prefecture, S Honshu, Japan, port on inlet of Wakasa Bay, 10 mi. NW of Maizuru; summer resort; silk making. Exports fish, edible seaweed. Near by is Ama-no-hashidate (a sandbar, 2 mi. long), known as vantage point for scenic views.

Miyoshi (mēyō'shē), town (pop. 9,194), Hiroshima prefecture, SW Honshu, Japan, 37 mi. NE of Hiroshima; commercial center for agr. area; spinning mills; livestock, lumber, charcoal, raw silk.

Miyün (mē'yün'), town, ⊙ Miyün co. (pop. 146,100), N Hopeh prov., China, on Pai R. and 40 mi. NE of Peking, and on railroad; cotton, grain. Gold mines near by.

Mizata (mēsä'tä), village (pop. estimate 350), La Libertad dept., SW Salvador, minor Pacific port, 24 mi. WSW of Nueva San Salvador; coastal trade.

Mizda (mēz'dä), village (pop. 1,133), W Tripolitania, Libya, on road and 50 mi. S of Garian, in an oasis (dates, barley, cayenne pepper); carpets, tents, bags. Ruins (forts, walls) in region.

Mize (mīz), town (pop. 430), Smith co., S central Miss., 27 mi. WNW of Laurel.

Mizen Head (mī'zŭn). **1** anc. *Notium Promontorium*, Atlantic cape, SW Co. Cork, at SW extremity of Ireland, 25 mi. WSW of Skibbereen; 51°27'N 9°49'W. **2** Promontory on the Irish Sea, SE Co. Wicklow, Ireland, 9 mi. S of Wicklow; 52°41'N 6°3'W.

Mizil (mē'zēl), town (1948 pop. 6,528), Buzau prov., SE central Rumania, on railroad and 22 mi. SW of Buzau; oil refining, flour milling.

Mizoch (mē'zŭch), Pol. *Mizocz* (mē'zôch), town (1931 pop. 1,250), S Rovno oblast, Ukrainian SSR, 15 mi. SSW of Rovno, on rail spur; agr. processing (sugar beets, cereals, vegetable oils, hops), cloth-making, sawmilling.

Mizoguchi (mēzō'gōōchē), town (pop. 4,506), Tottori prefecture, S Honshu, Japan, 8 mi. SE of Yonago; rice, wheat, raw silk; livestock; timber.

Mizpah (mĭz'pŭ). **1** Village (pop. 166), Koochiching co., N Minn., 60 mi. SW of International Falls in forest area; grain, potatoes. **2** Village (1940 pop. 666), Atlantic co., S N.J., 15 mi. NE of Millville, in agr. area; makes toys.

Mizque (mē'skä), city (pop. c.4,100), ⊙ Mizque prov., Cochabamba dept., central Bolivia, on S outliers of Cordillera de Cochabamba, on Mizque R. and 70 mi. SE of Cochabamba; alt. 6,693 ft. On highway from Cochabamba to Sucre, with a branch to Santa Cruz; wheat, corn, potatoes; livestock. Flourishing center (pop. c.20,000) in colonial period, with 8 monasteries and prosperous plantations; later declined because of isolation and malaria.

Mizque River, Cochabamba dept., central Bolivia; rises in S outliers of Cordillera de Cochabamba near Villa Viscarra; flows 130 mi. E and SE, past Mizque, to Río Grande 18 mi. SW of Valle Grande. Forms Cochabamba–Santa Cruz dept. border in lower course.

Mizra (mēzrä'), settlement (pop. 500), N Israel, at N edge of Plain of Jezreel, 4 mi. S of Nazareth; viticulture, fruitgrowing; agr.-machinery and truck repair shops. Founded 1923.

Mizuhashi (mēzōō'-hä'shē), town (pop. 11,195), Toyama prefecture, central Honshu, Japan, on SE shore of Toyama Bay, 7 mi. NE of Toyama; patent medicines. Fishery. Formed in early 1940s by combining former towns of Nishi-mizuhashi and Higashi-mizuhashi.

Mizuho (mēzōō'hō), town (pop. 8,860), Greater Tokyo, central Honshu, Japan, just W of Hachioji; agr. (wheat, rice). Formed in early 1940s by combining several small villages.

Mizukaido (mēzōōkī'dō), town (pop. 11,118), Ibaraki prefecture, central Honshu, Japan, 12 mi. WSW of Tsuchiura; commercial center for agr. area (rice, soybeans); soy sauce, sake.

Mizukubo (mēzōō'kōō'bō) or **Misakubo** (mēsä'-kōō'bō), town (pop. 9,399), Shizuoka prefecture, central Honshu, Japan, on Tenryu R. and 25 mi. S of Iida; mining (gold, silver, copper, nickel); lumbering.

Mizukuchi, Japan: see MINAKUCHI.

Mizumaki (mēzōō'-mä'kē), town (pop. 28,268), Fukuoka prefecture, N Kyushu, Japan, 7 mi. W of Yawata; rice, wheat, barley, raw silk.

Mizunami (mēzōō'-nä'mē), town (pop. 7,808), Gifu prefecture, central Honshu, Japan, 8 mi. ENE of Tajimi; homespun cloth, pottery; raw silk, poultry. Lignite mining.

Mizur (mēzōōr'), town (1948 pop. over 2,000), S North Ossetian Autonomous SSR, Russian SFSR, in the central Greater Caucasus, on Ossetian Military Road, on upper Ardon R. and 31 mi. WSW of Dzaudzhikau; concentrating mill for SADON lead and zinc mine (linked by cableway).

Mizusawa (mēzōō'säwŭ), town (pop. 18,189), Iwate prefecture, N Honshu, Japan, on Kitakami R. and 39 mi. S of Morioka; commercial center for agr. area (rice, soybeans, wheat); makes fish nets. Internatl. Lat. Observatory is here, on 39°8' N.

Mizzen Topsail, mountain (1,761 ft.), W central N.F., 25 mi. E of NE end of Grand L.; 49°5'N 56°37'W.

Mjallom (myĕ'lôm"), Swedish *Mjällom*, fishing village (pop. 618), Vasternorrland co., NE Sweden, on small inlet of Gulf of Bothnia, 20 mi. SSW of Ornskoldsvik; fish curing, shoe mfg.

Mjanji (ŭmjän'jē), village, Eastern Prov., SE Uganda, minor port on L. Victoria, 31 mi. SSW of Tororo; potash deposits.

Mjolby (myûl'bü"), Swedish *Mjölby*, city (pop. 6,896), Ostergotland co., S Sweden, on Svart R. and 18 mi. WSW of Linkoping; railroad center on Malmo-Stockholm and Malmo-N Sweden main lines; hosiery knitting, metal- and woodworking; mfg. of shoes, bricks. Known since 13th cent., its importance dates from construction of railroad in 1870s. Inc. 1920.

Mjondalen (myûn'dälŭn), Nor. *Mjøndalen*, village (pop. 2,904), in Nedre Eiker canton (pop. 8,304), Buskerud co., SE Norway, on Drammen R. (falls), on railroad and 8 mi. W of Drammen; paper, cellulose, and textile mills; lime mfg., dairying, sawmilling. Hydroelectric plant.

Mjor, Lake, Swedish *Mjörn* (myûrn), expansion (8 mi. long, 1–3 mi. wide) of Save R., SW Sweden, 14 mi. NE of Goteborg. At NE end is Alingsas.

Mjosa, Lake (myû'sä), Nor. *Mjøsa*, largest lake (□ 141) in Norway, in Opland and Hedmark counties, SE Norway, in the Gudbrandsdal; 65 mi. long, 1–9 mi. wide, up to 1,453 ft. deep. On shore are Lillehammer (N), Gjovik (W), and Hamar (E) cities. Receives Lagen R. (N); drained S by 25-mi.-long Vorma R. into Glomma R. Contains small isl. of Helgoy, Nor. *Helgøy*.

Mjos Lake, Norway: see MOS LAKE.

Mkhoma (ŭmkō'mä), village, Central Prov., Nyasaland, 25 mi. E of Lilongwe; tobacco. Hq. of Du. Reformed Church mission.

Mkoani (ŭmkōä'nē), town (pop. 883), on W coast of Pemba isl., Zanzibar protectorate, 11 mi. SW of Chake Chake; cloves.

Mkokotoni (ŭmkōkōtō'nē), town, on NW coast of Zanzibar, opposite Tumbatu Isl., 20 mi. NNE of Zanzibar town; copra, cloves; fishing.

Mkomazi or **Mkomasi** (ŭmkōmä'zē), village, Tanga prov., NE Tanganyika, on railroad and 18 mi. NW of Lushoto, bet. Pare and Usambara mts.; hardwood lumbering.

Mkumbara (ŭmkōōmbä'rä), village, Tanga prov., NE Tanganyika, on railroad and 35 mi. NW of Korogwe; sisal. Connected by cable railroad with Shume (shōō'mä) (6 mi. N; alt. 4,700 ft.), hardwood-lumbering center.

Mkushi (ŭmkōō'shē), township (pop. 146), Central Prov., Northern Rhodesia, 65 mi. ENE of Broken Hill; tobacco, wheat, corn; livestock.

Mkwaya (ŭmkwä'yä), village, Southern Prov., SE Tanganyika, on Lukuledi R. and 12 mi. SW of Lindi. Rail-river transfer point for shipment of peanuts from Nachingwa to Lindi.

Mlada Boleslav (mlä'dä bô'lĕsläf), Czech *Mladá Boleslav*, Ger. *Jungbunzlau* (yōōngbōōnts'lou), city (pop. 19,573), N Bohemia, Czechoslovakia, on Jizera R. and 25 mi. SSW of Liberec; rail junction; noted for metallurgical works (automobiles, machines, electrical parts); various agr. industries, notably distilling and mfg. of soap, candles, and woolen textiles. Has 15th-cent. cathedral, 18th-cent. baroque church, old town hall, castle (now used as barracks), mus. Former seat of United Brethren assembly. Numerous castle remains in vicinity.

Mlada Vozice (vô'zhĭtsĕ), Czech *Mladá Vožice*, Ger. *Jungwoschitz* (yōōng'vôshĭts), town (pop. 1,572), S Bohemia, Czechoslovakia, 10 mi. NE of Tabor; oats, barley, potatoes; metal products.

Mladejov, Czechoslovakia: see MORAVSKA TREBOVA.

Mladenovac or **Mladenovats** (both: mlä'dĕnôvāts), village (pop. 5,159), N central Serbia, Yugoslavia, 27 mi. SSE of Belgrade, in the Sumadija; rail junction; mfg. of jute bags. Mineral waters.

Mlangeni (mläng-gĕ'nē), village, Central Prov., W Nyasaland, on Mozambique border, on road and 25 mi. SE of Dedza; tobacco, wheat, corn, peanuts.

Mlanje (mlän'jä), administrative center, Southern Prov., Nyasaland, on road to Quelimane (Mozambique) and 40 mi. SE of Blantye; tea-growing center; also tung, cotton, tobacco, corn, rice. Has tea experimental station.

Mlanje Mountains, syenite outcrop in SE Nyasaland, NE of Mlanje; rise abruptly from surrounding plateau; 12 mi. across. Highest point (in center) is Mt. Mlanje (9,843 ft.). Bauxite deposits.

Mlava, Poland: see MLAWA.

Mlava River (mlä'vä), E Serbia, Yugoslavia, rises in the Crni Vrh near Zagubica, flows c.60 mi. NNW, past Petrovac, to an arm of the Danube N of Kostolac.

Mlawa (mwä'vä), Pol. *Mława*, Rus. *Mlava* (mlä'vŭ), town (pop. 13,817), Warszawa prov., NE central Poland, 65 mi. NNW of Warsaw; rail junction; mfg. of cement, thread, candy; flour milling, tanning. During Second World War, under administration of East Prussia, called Mielau.

Mlazovice, Czechoslovakia: see LAZNE BELOHRAD.

Mlinov (mlyē'nŭf), Pol. *Młynów* (mwĭ'nōōf), village (1931 pop. 1,263), SW Rovno oblast, Ukrainian SSR, on Ikva R. and 7 mi. NNW of Dubno; agr. processing (cereals, vegetable oils), soap mfg.

Mljet Island (mlyĕt), Ital. *Meleda* (mĕlĕ'dä), anc. *Melita*, Dalmatian island (□ 38) in Adriatic Sea, S Croatia, Yugoslavia, 30 mi. W of Dubrovnik; 24 mi. long E-W; rises to 1,686 ft.; has 3 sweet-water lakes and 2 grottoes; emits sulphur fumes. Romans once exiled here; has Roman palace, Benedictine cloister. Chief village, Babino Polje. Mljet Channel, Serbo-Croatian *Mljetski Kanal*, separates isl. from the Peljesac (N).

Mlynany, Czechoslovakia: see ZLATE MORAVCE.

Mlynow, Ukrainian SSR: see MLINOV.

Mnichovo Hradiste (mnĭ'khôvô hrä'dyĭshtyĕ), Czech *Mnichovo Hradiště*, Ger. *Münchengrätz* (mün'khŭngrāts), town (pop. 3,733), N Bohemia, Czechoslovakia, on left bank of Jizera R., on railroad and 17 mi. SSW of Liberec; footwear mfg.; textile industry. Noted for Prussian victory (1866) over Austrians. Wallenstein buried here in castle chapel. On right bank, across Jizera R., are remains of old Cistercian abbey (notable 13th-cent. portal) at village of Klaster Hradiste (klä'shtĕr hrä'dyĭshtyĕ), Czech *Klášter Hradiště*.

Mnine, Syria: see MENIN.

Mnisek nad Hnilcom (mnyē'shĕk nät' hŭnyĭl"-tsôm), Slovak *Mníšek nad Hnilcom*, Hung. *Szepesremete* (sĕ'pĕshrĕ'mĕtĕ), village (pop. 1,652), E central Slovakia, Czechoslovakia, on railroad and 16 mi. NE of Roznava; iron mining.

Mnyusi (ŭmnyōō'sē), village, Tanga prov., NE Tanganyika, on railroad and 11 mi. SE of Korogwe; sisal, cotton.

Mo, canton, Telemark co., Norway: see BANDAKSLI.

Mo or **Mo i Rana** (mō' ē rä'nä), town (pop. 2,729), Nordland co., N central Norway, at head of Ran Fjord, at mouth of Ran R., on railroad and 70 mi. S of Bodo; steel-milling center, in mining (zinc, copper, pyrite, lead) region. Lumbering; furniture making.

Mo (mōō), village (pop. 616), Vasterbotten co., N Sweden, on islet in Gulf of Bothnia, 20 mi. SW of Umea; sawmills.

Moa (mōä'), largest island (□ 169; pop. 3,641) of LETI ISLANDS, S Moluccas, Indonesia, in Banda Sea, 40 mi. ENE of E tip of Timor; 8°20'S 127°57'E; 25 mi. long, 7 mi. wide. Fishing, coconut growing. Du. fort built here 1734.

Moa, Cayo Grande de, Cuba: see GRANDE DE MOA, CAYO.

Moa, Sierra de (syĕ'rä dā mō'ä), small range, Oriente prov., NE Cuba, NW of Baracoa, extends c.20 mi. NW along Atlantic coast; rises to above 2,000 ft. Yields timber; has iron deposits. Has 300-ft. cascade on small Moa R.

Moab (mō'ăb), nation inhabiting in anc. times the upland area E of Dead Sea, now part of Jordan. The Moabites were close kin to the Hebrews and the language of the Moabite stone is practically the same as biblical Hebrew. The stone, with a long inscription dating from 850 B.C., was erected by Mesha of Moab to commemorate a victory in his revolt against Israel. A large part of the stone was discovered at Dibon (Dhiban) in 1868.

Moab, town (pop. 1,274), ⊙ Grand co., E Utah, on Colorado R. (crossed here by bridge) and 100 mi. SE of Price; alt. 4,000 ft.; tourist point; trade center for livestock and irrigated agr. area (fruit, truck). Vanadium and uranium mines near by. La Sal Mts. are E, in section of La Sal Natl. Forest (hq. at Moab); Arches Natl. Monument is N. Grew as ranching point after 1876.

Moabit (mōäbēt'), workers' residential section of Wedding dist., N central Berlin, Germany. Site of large prison. After 1945 in French sector.

Moala (mōä'lä), limestone island (□ 24; pop. 1,027), Lau group, Fiji, SW Pacific; 7 mi. long; rises to 1,535 ft.; copra.

Moalboal (mōälbōäl'), town (1939 pop. 2,134; 1948 municipality pop. 15,019), S Cebu isl., Philippines, on Tañon Strait, 40 mi. SW of Cebu city; agr. center (corn, coconuts).

Moama (mōă'mŭ), municipality (pop. 662), S New South Wales, Australia, 120 mi. N of Melbourne and on Murray R., on Victoria border; sheep and agr. center.

Moamba (mwäm'bä), village, Sul do Save prov., S Mozambique, 35 mi. NW of Lourenço Marques; rail junction; cattle-raising center; beans, corn.

Moanda (mwän'dä), village, Leopoldville prov., W Belgian Congo, on Atlantic coast, 50 mi. W of Boma; tourist center with beach and baths; palm oil milling, cattle raising. Lighthouse. R.C. mission.

Moa River (mō'ä), in Fr. Guinea and Sierra Leone, rises W of Kissidougou, S Fr. Guinea, flows c.200 mi. SW, past Daru, to the Atlantic at Sulima. Sometimes called Sulima R. or Gallina R. (for Gallina tribe settled along lower course).

Moate (mōt), Gaelic *Móta*, town (pop. 1,340), SW Co. Westmeath, Ireland, 10 mi. ESE of Athlone; agr. market (dairying; cattle, potatoes). Near by is anc. rath.

Moatize (mwätē'zä), village, Manica and Sofala prov., NW Mozambique, 12 mi. ENE of Tete; coal mines (linked by short railroad with Benga on the Zambezi).

Moba (mō'bä), village, Katanga prov., SE Belgian Congo, on W shore of L. Tanganyika, 85 mi. SSE of Albertville; terminus of navigation on the Tanganyika, customs station.

Mobara (mōbä'rŭ) or **Mohara** (-hä'rŭ), town (pop. 15,172), Chiba prefecture, central Honshu, Japan, on E central Chiba Peninsula, 16 mi. SE of Chiba; spinning, glassmaking.

Mobarakeh, Iran: see MUBARAKEH.

Mobaye (mōbäyā'), village, S Ubangi-Shari, Fr. Equatorial Africa, on Ubangi R. opposite Banzyville (Belgian Congo), and 100 mi. SSE of Bambari; steamboat terminus and customs station; cotton ginning, fishing, elaeis-palm plantations.

Mobeetie (mōbē'tē), village (pop. c.500), Wheeler co., extreme N Texas, in the Panhandle 30 mi. E of

Pampa; shipping point in agr., cattle region. Near by is Old Mobeetie (pop. c.350), site of old Fort Elliot.

Mobeka, Belgian Congo: see GUMBA.

Mobendi, Belgian Congo: see BRABANTA.

Moberly (mō'bůrlē), city (pop. 13,115), Randolph co., N central Mo., 32 mi. N of Columbia. Agr.; mfg. (shoes, tools, hosiery, dairy products); railroad shops; coal, fire-clay deposits. Has jr. col. Laid out 1866.

Mobile (mōbēl'), county (□ 1,248; pop. 231,105), extreme SW Ala.; ⊙ Mobile. Coastal plain, bounded S by Mississippi Sound, E by Mobile Bay and Mobile R., W by Miss. Truck and dairy products, berries, subtropical fruits, seafood; naval stores. City of Mobile (mfg. center) is Alabama's only seaport. Formed 1812.

Mobile, city (pop. 129,009), ⊙ Mobile co., SW Ala., on Mobile Bay, at mouth of Mobile R., and c.200 mi. SSW of Birmingham; 30°41'N 88°4'W. Only seaport in state; important shipping center with extensive docking, loading, and storage facilities; port of entry. Imports bauxite, crude rubber, manganese, and iron ore, nitrates, bananas, coconuts, sulphur, sugar, newsprint; exports cotton and cotton goods, kraft paper, naval stores, lumber, cast-iron pipe, steel products, coal, corn, flour. Has large South American trade. Leading industries: ship, dry-dock, and barge construction, meat packing, maintenance of railroad rolling stock, woodworking; chief manufactures: paper, alumina, insulation materials, cement, clothing, foundry and bakery products, industrial chemicals. French settlement established near by in 1702, when Bienville moved his hq. from Iberville's settlement of Biloxi. City founded at present site 1710; ⊙ La. 1710–19. Ceded to Britain in 1763; taken (1780) by Gálvez for Spain, who held it until 1813, when Gen. James Wilkinson seized it for the U.S. Inc. as town 1814, as city 1819. Ships out of Mobile eluded Federal blockade during Civil War until Aug., 1864, when Admiral David Farragut won battle of Mobile Bay. City was surrendered to Gen. E. R. S. Canby and Gen. F. Steel in April, 1865. Developed after war as outlet for extensive agr. and timber regions; toward end of 19th cent. became shipping point for iron and steel from Birmingham. State docks and terminal completed 1929. In Sept., 1937, 2d free port in U.S. was established here. Bankhead Tunnel (vehicular) under river completed 1941. Seat of R.C. cathedral. Has many fine antebellum homes, U.S. marine hosp., and airport. Brookley Air Force Base is just S. Annual events are Mardi Gras (from 1704), Azalea Trail Festival (from 1929). Spring Hill Col. near by.

Mobile Bay, SW Ala., arm of Gulf of Mexico; c.35 mi. long, from outlet in Gulf (S) to mouth of Mobile R. at Mobile; 8–18 mi. wide. Includes Bon Secour Bay in SE. Crossed in S by INTRACOASTAL WATERWAY, which passes from Mississippi Sound (W) into Bon Secours Bay. Dredged channel (32 ft. deep, 300–500 ft. wide) extends S from Mobile R., intersecting waterway and entering Gulf bet. Dauphin Isl. and Mobile Point. Admiral David Farragut won battle of Mobile Bay (Aug., 1864) at S entrance. On **Mobile Point,** at tip of 15-mi.-long sandspit forming S boundary of Bon Secour Bay at entrance to Mobile Bay, is Fort Morgan, which served in War of 1812, when it was known as Fort Bowyer. **Mobile River,** formed by confluence of TOMBIGBEE RIVER and ALABAMA RIVER, enters bay at Mobile after a S course of 45 mi. through delta region; with its tributaries, drains □ 42,300. It carries heavy traffic in goods bet. Birmingham area and Montgomery.

Mobjack Bay, E Va., arm of Chesapeake Bay in Gloucester and Mathews counties, 25 mi. N of Newport News; c.5 mi. wide at SE entrance, up to 10 mi. long; numerous inlets.

Mobridge (mō'brĭj), city (pop. 3,753), Walworth co., N S.Dak., on Missouri River and 80 mi. N of Pierre. Trade and distribution point for agr. region; lignite coal; cement blocks, beverages, livestock, dairy produce. Lutheran academy is here. City founded 1906, inc. 1908.

Moca (mō'kä), city (1935 pop. 5,703; 1950 pop. 9,739), ⊙ Espaillat prov., N Dominican Republic, on S slope of Cordillera Setentrional, on railroad and highway, and 13 mi. ESE of Santiago; 19°25'N 70°30'W; coffeegrowing center; also cacao and tobacco. Founded 1780.

Moca, town (pop. 1,965), NW Puerto Rico, on railroad and 3 mi. SE of Aguadilla; coffeegrowing center.

Mocaboc Point (mōkābŏk'), easternmost point of Negros isl., Philippines, in Tañon Strait near its entrance; shelters small Escalante Bay; 10°50'N 123°33'E.

Mocache (mōkä'chā), village, Los Ríos prov., W central Ecuador, landing on Vinces R. (Guayas system) and 29 mi. NNE of Vinces, in fertile agr. region (cacao, rice, sugar cane, tropical fruit).

Mocajuba (mo͝okůzho͞o'bů), city (pop. 507), E Pará, Brazil, on right bank of Tocantins R. and 100 mi. SW of Belém; cacao, rubber, medicinal plants.

Mocal River (mōkäl'), W Honduras, rises in Sierra de Celaque 12 mi. NE of San Marcos (Ocotepeque dept.), flows c.50 SSE, through Lempira dept., to Lempa R. 7 mi. SW of Candelaria.

Moçambique, SE Africa: see MOZAMBIQUE.

Mocambo, Mexico: see BOCA DEL RÍO.

Moçâmedes, Angola: see MOSSÂMEDES.

Mocanaqua (mōkůnä'kwů), village (pop. 1,496), Luzerne co., E central Pa., on the Susquehanna and 15 mi. SW of Wilkes-Barre.

Mocanguê Island (mo͝okāng-gā'), in Guanabara Bay, SE Brazil, 3.5 mi. NE of center of Rio de Janeiro, near harbor of Niterói; dry docks.

Mocatán (mōkätän'), town (pop. 3,632), Caldas dept., W central Colombia, on E slopes of Cordillera Occidental, 28 mi. WNW of Manizales; agr. center (coffee, corn, rice, bananas, yucca, sugar cane, forest products).

Mocay (mô'kī'), village, Bentre prov., S Vietnam, in Mekong delta, 8 mi. SSW of Bentre; rice center.

Moccasin, village, Mohave co., NW Ariz., 18 mi. SW of Kanab, Utah; hq. for Kaibab Indian Reservation. Pipe Spring Natl. Monument is just S.

Mocejón (mō-thāhōn'), town (pop. 2,765), Toledo prov., central Spain, on canal of the Tagus, and 8 mi. NE of Toledo; potatoes, pepper, sugar beets, cereals, melons, sheep; furniture mfg.

Mocenok (mô'chĕnôk), Slovak *Močenok,* Hung. *Mocsonok* (mô'chônôk), village (pop. 5,163), SW Slovakia, Czechoslovakia, 9 mi. SW of Nitra; sugar beets, barley, wheat.

Mocha, Mokha, or **Mukha** (all: mō'khů), town (pop. 600), Taiz prov., SW Yemen, minor Red Sea port 45 mi. N of the strait Bab el Mandeb, 105 mi. S of Hodeida; 13°19'N 43°15'E. It was formerly chief port of Yemen, flourishing in Middle Ages as export center of the S Arabian coffee to which it gave its name. A Dutch trading post was established here in 1614, and the French bombarded and occupied the port in 1738. Its complete decline in 19th cent. is laid to the rise of Aden (S) and Hodeida (N). Sometimes spelled Makha.

Mocha Island (mō'chä) (pop. 482), in the Pacific, 20 mi. off coast of Arauco prov., S central Chile, 50 mi. SSW of Lebu; 8 mi. long, c.3 mi. wide; rises to 1,768 ft. Horse breeding.

Moche (mō'chā), town (pop. 2,148), Libertad dept., NW Peru, on coastal plain, on railroad and 4 mi. SSE of Trujillo, on Pan-American Highway; corn, coca, fruit.

Mo-chiang, China: see MOKIANG.

Mochigase (mōchē'-gä'sä), town (pop. 2,431), Tottori prefecture, S Honshu, Japan, 11 mi. S of Tottori; rice, wheat, raw silk, charcoal, sake.

Mochis, Mexico: see LOS MOCHIS.

Mochitlán (mōchētlän'), town (pop. 2,244), Guerrero, SW Mexico, in Sierra Madre del Sur, 9 mi. E of Chilpancingo; cereals, sugar cane, fruit, forest products (resin, vanilla).

Mochito, El, Honduras: see EL MOCHITO.

Mochrum (mŏkh'rům), parish (pop. 1,478), S Wigtown, Scotland. Includes agr. village of Kirk of Mochrum, 8 mi. SW of Wigtown. Near by is mansion of marquess of Bute, with two 15th-cent. towers.

Mo Chu, river, Bhutan: see SANKOSH RIVER.

Mochu, China: see SHWANGPO.

Mochudi (mōcho͞o'dē), town (pop. 11,767), ⊙ Bakgatla dist., SE Bechuanaland Protectorate, near U. of So. Afr. border, 110 mi. NNE of Mafeking; agr. center. Hq. of Bakgatla tribe; hosp.

Mochumí (mōcho͞omē'), town (pop. 1,797), Lambayeque dept., NW Peru, on coastal plain, on Pan American Highway and 10 mi. NNE of Lambayeque, in irrigated Leche R. valley (rice, corn, cotton); carob pastures; goat raising.

Mocímboa da Praia (mo͝osēm'bwä dů prī'ů), village, Niassa prov., northernmost Mozambique, on Mozambique Channel of Indian Ocean, 135 mi. N of Pôrto Amélia, 60 mi. S of Tanganyika border; ships copra, sisal, castor beans. Airfield.

Mociu (môch), Hung. *Mocs* (môch), village (pop. 3,017), Cluj prov., W central Rumania, on Somesul Mic R. and 20 mi. E of Cluj; flour milling.

Mockau (mô'kou), industrial N suburb of Leipzig, Saxony, E central Germany. Has Leipzig airport.

Mockel, Lake, Swedish *Möckeln* (mû'kůln). **1** Lake (9 mi. long, 1–4 mi. wide), S Sweden, extends N from Almhult. Drained W by Helge R. **2** Expansion (6 mi. long, 1–2 mi. wide) of Let R., S central Sweden, extends SW from Karlskoga and Bofors.

Möckern (mû'kůrn). **1** Town (pop. 2,846), in former Prussian Saxony prov., central Germany, after 1945 in Saxony-Anhalt, 10 mi. SE of Burg; sugar beets, grain, potatoes; brick mfg. Scene (April, 1813) of Prussian victory under Bülow and Yorck over French forces under Beauharnais. **2** Industrial NW suburb of Leipzig, Saxony, E central Germany. Scene (Oct., 1813) of major engagement during battle of Leipzig.

Mockingbird Valley, town (pop. 150), Jefferson co., N Ky., just NE of Louisville.

Möckmühl (mûk'mül"), town (pop. 2,389), N Württemberg, Germany, after 1945 in Württemberg-Baden, on the Jagst and 14 mi. NNE of Heilbronn; rail junction; paper milling.

Mocksville (mŏks'vĭl), town (pop. 1,909), ⊙ Davie co., central N.C., 22 mi. SW of Winston-Salem; mfg. of furniture, wooden boxes, hosiery; lumber and flour mills. Settled before 1750.

Moclín (mōklēn'), town (pop. 855), Granada prov., S Spain, on small Moclín R. and 15 mi. NW of Granada, in fertile agr. region (olives, cereals, tubers, sugar beets, beans, potatoes, livestock); olive-oil pressing, flour milling. Old town, once a Moorish stronghold.

Moclinejo (mōklēnā'hō), town (pop. 706), Málaga prov., S Spain, 9 mi. ENE of Málaga; exports raisins, lemons, olives. Goat raising.

Mocoa (mōkō'ä), town (pop. 1,446), ⊙ Putumayo commissary, SW Colombia, on affluent of Caqueta R., in Andean foothills, and 45 mi. E of Pasto (Nariño dept.), 300 mi. SW of Bogotá; 1°8'N 76°38'W. Trading post in tropical forest region yielding rubber, balsam, resins, fine wood. Some livestock and subsistence crops.

Mococa (mo͝okō'ků), city (pop. 7,681), E São Paulo, Brazil, near Minas Gerais border, on rail spur from São José do Rio Pardo, and 55 mi. ESE of Ribeirão Prêto; dairying center; coffee processing.

Mocochá (mōkōchä'), town (pop. 438), Yucatan, SE Mexico, 13 mi. NE of Mérida; henequen.

Mocomoco (mōkōmō'kō), town (pop. c.7,600), La Paz dept., W Bolivia, 21 mi. ENE of Puerto Acosta, in the Altiplano; alt. 10,193 ft.; barley, corn.

Mocorito (mōkōrē'tō), town (pop. 2,357), Sinaloa, NW Mexico, on small Mocorito R. and 55 mi. NW of Culiacán; agr. center (corn, sugar cane, tomatoes, chick-peas, fruit).

Moçoró, Brazil: see MOSSORÓ.

Mocs, Rumania: see MOCIU.

Mocsa (mô'chŏ), town (pop. 3,323), Komarom-Esztergom co., N Hungary, 25 mi. E of Györ; grain, potatoes, cattle, horses.

Moctezuma (mōktāso͞o'mä). **1** City (pop. 1,765), San Luis Potosí, N central Mexico, on interior plateau, 43 mi. N of San Luis Potosí; grain, beans, cotton, maguey. Railroad station 5 mi. E. Thermal springs near by. **2** Town (pop. 2,298), Sonora, NW Mexico, on Moctezuma R. and 90 mi. NE of Hermosillo; copper-mining, wheat-growing center.

Moctezuma River. **1** In N central and NE Mexico, rises in Sierra Madre Oriental SW of San Juan del Río, flows c.175 mi. NE along Querétaro–Hidalgo border, past Tamazunchale and Tanquián, in fertile La Huasteca plains in San Luis Potosí, to join Santa María (or Tamuin) R. in forming Pánuco R. on Veracruz border 50 mi. SW of Tampico. Used for irrigation. **2** In Sonora, NW Mexico, rises in W outliers of Sierra Madre Occidental, flows c.110 mi. S, past Cumpas and Moctezuma, to Yaqui R. near Suaqui.

Mocuba (mōko͞o'bä), village, Zambézia prov., central Mozambique, 70 mi. N of Quelimane (linked by rail); agr. center; ships sisal, cotton.

Mocupe (mōko͞o'pā), town (pop. 1,243), Lambayeque dept., NW Peru, on coastal plain, on irrigated Saña R. and 20 mi. SE of Chiclayo; rice, corn.

Modale (mō'dāl"), town (pop. 283), Harrison co., W Iowa, near mouth of Soldier R. on Missouri R., 26 mi. NNW of Council Bluffs, in agr. area.

Modane (môdän'), village (pop. 1,649), Savoie dept., SE France, in Alpine Maurienne valley, on the Arc and 17 mi. ESE of Saint-Jean-de-Maurienne; alt. 3,468 ft. International railroad station (customs) at N entrance of Mont Cenis (or Fréjus) tunnel through Cottian Alps, linking France and Italy. Paper and rice milling, mfg. of chemical fertilizer. Heavily damaged in Second World War. Mont Cenis pass is 12 mi. ENE.

Modasa (mōdä'sů), village (pop. 11,643), Sabar Kantha dist., N Bombay, India, 23 mi. ESE of Himatnagar; trade center for cotton, millet, wheat, peanuts; calico-cloth dyeing and printing, oilseed pressing. Gujarat fortress in 15th cent.

Modbury (mŏd'–), town and parish (pop. 1,110), S Devon, England, 11 mi. E of Plymouth; agr. market; agr.-implement works. Has 13th-cent. church.

Modderfontein (mô'důrfôntān"), town (pop. 5,900), S Transvaal, U. of So. Afr., on Witwatersrand, 8 mi. NNE of Johannesburg; chemical mfg. (explosives, nitrates, ammonia, insecticides).

Modder River (mŏ'důr), Afrikaans *Modderrivier* (mô"důr-rĭfēr'), village (pop. 500), NE Cape Prov., U. of So. Afr., on Orange Free State border, on Modder R. near its mouth on Reit R., 20 mi. SSW of Kimberley; resort. Scene (Nov. 28, 1899) of battle in South African War.

Modder River, Orange Free State and Cape Prov., U. of So. Afr., rises NW of Wepener, flows c.225 mi. in a wide arc NW and W, past Glen, Paardeberg, and Modder River town, to Riet R. 22 mi. SSW of Kimberley.

Modéliarpeth, Fr. India: see MUDALIARPET.

Model Town, W Pakistan: see LAHORE, city.

Modena (mŭdē'nů, It. mô'dĕnä), province (□ 1,038; pop. 467,355), Emilia-Romagna, N central Italy; ⊙ Modena. Extends from Etruscan Apennines N to the Po, with plain occupying c.50% of area. Drained by Secchia and Panaro rivers. Agr. (cereals, fodder, grapes, hemp, tomatoes); stock raising (cattle, pigs, sheep). Hydroelectric plant at Farneta. Sausage making extensively carried on. Mfg. at Modena, Mirandola, Sassuolo.

Modena, anc. *Mutina,* city (pop. 50,541), ⊙ Modena prov., Emilia-Romagna, N central Italy, on Aemilian Way, in fertile plain bet. Secchia and Panaro rivers, 23 mi. WNW of Bologna; 44°38'N 10°55'E. Transportation and agr. center; mfg. (agr. machinery, automobiles, sausage, macaroni, vegetable oils, fertilizer, liquor, alcohol, furniture, glass); foundries, steelworks. Archbishopric. Has Romanesque cathedral (begun 1099), large ducal palace (begun 1634; seat of military school), university (reopened 1774), observatory, and Palazzo dei Musei (1753–67; contains mus., picture gall., and Biblioteca Estense). Roman colony after 183 B.C.; ruled by house of Este from 1288 to 1796, when it passed to Hapsburg dynasty. Became part of Italy in 1860. Heavily bombed (1944) in Second World War.

Modena (mōdē'nů). **1** Town (pop. 95), Mercer co., N Mo., bet. Thompson and Weldon rivers, 8 mi. SW of Princeton. **2** Borough (pop. 824), Chester co., SE Pa., just S of Coatesville. Formerly Paperville.

Moder River (mōdâr', Ger. mō'dŭr), Bas-Rhin dept., E France, rises in the N Vosges 2 mi. N of La Petite-Pierre, flows c.35 mi. generally ESE, past Ingwiller, Haguenau, and Bischwiller, to the Rhine below Drusenheim. Receives the Zorn near its mouth.

Modesto (mōdĕ'stō). **1** City (pop. 17,389), ⊙ Stanislaus co., central Calif., in San Joaquin Valley, 25 mi. SE of Stockton, and on Tuolumne R.; trade, processing, and shipping center for irrigated farming and dairying area; dairy products, poultry, dried and canned fruit, clothing. Has a col. Don Pedro, Turlock, Modesto reservoirs are E. Founded 1870, inc. 1884. **2** Village (pop. 232), Macoupin co., SW central Ill., 26 mi. SW of Springfield, in agr. and bituminous-coal area.

Modesto Reservoir, Calif.: see TUOLUMNE RIVER.

Modica (mô'dēkä), anc. *Motyca,* town (pop. 27,928), Ragusa prov., SE Sicily, 4 mi. S of Ragusa; olive oil, wine; cheese, macaroni, candy. Annual livestock fairs. Anc. Siculian center. Cava d'Ispica (5 mi. E) is a noted limestone ravine with numerous grottoes containing prehistoric necropolises, cave dwellings, and early Christian tombs.

Modigliana (môdēlyä'nä), town (pop. 3,969), Forlì prov., Emilia-Romagna, N central Italy, 10 mi. SSW of Faenza. Bishopric.

Modjokerto, Indonesia: see MOJOKERTO.

Modlimb (mŏd'lĭmb), town (pop. 3,260), Sholapur dist., E central Bombay, India, 37 mi. NW of Sholapur; local trade center (millet, wheat, cotton). Also spelled Modnimb.

Modlin (môd'lēn), village, Warszawa prov., E central Poland, on the Vistula, at Narew R. mouth, and 20 mi. NW of Warsaw. In Rus. Poland (1815–1919), called Novogeorgievsk, it was site of strong fortress built (1807–12) by Napoleon; captured (1915, 1939) by Germans after heavy attacks.

Mödling (mûd'lĭng), outer S district (□ 77; pop. 48,185) of Vienna, Austria. Formed (1938) through incorporation of 21 towns, including Brunn am Gebirge, Gumpoldskirchen, Guntramsdorf, Laxenburg, Maria Enzersdorf, Wiener Neudorf, and Mödling (pop. 17,015), at entrance of picturesque Brühl valley, 9 mi. SSW of city center; ironworks; shoe mfg.; 15th-cent. Gothic church.

Modnimb, India: see MODLIMB.

Modoc (mō'dŏk), county (□ 4,094; pop. 9,678), NE Calif.; ⊙ Alturas. Bounded N by Oregon, E by Nev. line. On high, semiarid volcanic plateau (lowest elevation in co. is 4,000 ft.), with extensive lava beds; rises to Eagle Peak (9,934 ft.) in Warner Mts. (E). Drained by Pit R. Includes Clear Lake Reservoir (for irrigation), part of Goose L., and Surprise Valley (in E), which contains intermittently dry Alkali Lakes. Fort Bidwell Indian Reservation, part of Modoc Natl. Forest, and part of Klamath irrigation project (N) are in co. Stock raising (beef and dairy cattle, sheep, hogs, poultry), farming (barley, potatoes, hay), lumbering (mainly pine). Pumice, sand and gravel, and gold deposits are worked. Good waterfowl and deer hunting, fishing. Formed 1874.

Modoc. 1 Town (pop. 32), Emanuel co., E central Ga., 5 mi. N of Swainsboro. **2** Town (pop. 275), Randolph co., E Ind., 16 mi. SE of Muncie.

Modohn, Latvia: see MADONA.

Modon, Greece: see METHONE.

Modor, Czechoslovakia: see MODRA.

Modos, Yugoslavia: see JASA TOMIC.

Modoura, India: see MUTTRA, city.

Modra (mô'drä), Hung. *Modor* (mô'dôr), town (pop. 5,768), W Slovakia, Czechoslovakia, on railroad and 15 mi. NE of Bratislava; wine making. Has wine school.

Modrany (mô'dŭrzhänĭ), Czech *Modřany,* town (pop. 8,948), S central Bohemia, Czechoslovakia, on Vltava R. just below Berounka R. mouth, on railroad and 5 mi. S of Prague, in sugar-beet and wheat dist.; sugar mills; confectionery mfg.

Modrica or **Modricha** (both: mô'drĭchä), Serbo-Croatian *Modriča,* village (pop. 2,932), N Bosnia, Yugoslavia, on Bosna R., on railroad and 18 mi. NE of Doboj.

Modry Kamen (mô'drē kä'mĕnyů), Slovak *Modrý Kameň,* Hung. *Kékkő* (kāk'kû), town (pop. 1,836), S Slovakia, Czechoslovakia, 35 mi. SSE of Banska Bystrica; sugar beets, wheat.

Modugno (môdōō'nyō), town (pop. 11,047), Bari prov., Apulia, S Italy, 5 mi. SW of Bari; wine, olive oil.

Modum, Norway: see GEITHUS.

Moe (mō'ē), town (pop. 2,260), S Victoria, Australia, 75 mi. ESE of Melbourne; rail junction in forested region; sawmill.

Moearaenim, Indonesia: see MUARAENIM.

Moecherville (mō'kûrvĭl), village (pop. 2,922, with adjacent Scraper), Kane co., NE Ill.

Moel Famman, Wales: see CLWYDIAN HILLS.

Moelingen (mōō'lĭng-ŭn), Fr. *Mouland* (mōōlã'), village (pop. 699), Liége prov., E Belgium, on Meuse R. just NNE of Visé, in cherry-growing area.

Moel Sych, Wales: see BERWYN MOUNTAINS.

Moelv (mō'ĕlv), village (pop. 995) in Ringsaker canton, Hedmark co., SE Norway, on E shore of L. Mjosa, on railroad and 13 mi. SE of Lillehammer; metalworking; mfg. of agr. implements, leather soles, tools, farm vehicles; cellulose, lumber mills.

Moelwyn Mawr (moil'wĭn mour'), mountain (2,527 ft.), MW Merioneth, Wales, 3 mi. W of Blaenau-Ffestiniog; slate quarrying.

Moen (mōōn), town (pop. 2,352), West Flanders prov., W Belgium, 7 mi. SE of Courtrai; cotton weaving.

Moen, Caroline Isls.: see TRUK.

Moen (mûn), Dan. *Møen* or *Møn,* island (□ 84; pop. 14,156), Denmark, in Baltic Sea, separated from S Zealand by Ulvsund strait and from Falster isl. by Gronsund strait. On NW coast is Stege, its chief city, on Stege Bay. E part, known as Hoje Moen, ends on E coast with Moensklint, a limestone cliff; highest point, 469 ft. Beet-sugar refineries.

Moena, Indonesia: see MUNA.

Moena (môä'nä), village (pop. 1,405), Trento prov., Trentino–Alto Adige, N Italy, on Avisio R. and 17 mi. SE of Bolzano; mfg. (furniture, packing boxes).

Moengo (mōōng'ō), town (pop. 2,080), Commewijne dist., NE Du. Guiana, on upper Cottica R. and 55 mi. ESE of Paramaribo. Center of bauxite mining, with large crushing and drying plant and docking facilities for ocean vessels. Most of the ore is shipped to U.S.

Moensklint, Denmark: see MOEN.

Moerbeke (mōōr'bākŭ). **1** Town (pop. 5,612), East Flanders prov., N Belgium, 13 mi. NE of Ghent; beet-sugar refining. Has remains of anc. Benedictine monastery. **2** Village (pop. 2,037), East Flanders prov., NW Belgium, just SE of Grammont.

Moerbeke or **Moerbeke-Kwilu** (–kwē'lōō), village (1948 pop. 10,236), Leopoldville prov., W Belgian Congo, on railroad and 120 mi. ENE of Boma; sugar plantations, sugar mills.

Moerdijk (mōōr'dĭk), village (pop. 393), North Brabant prov., SW Netherlands, on the Hollandsch-diep and 11 mi. NNW of Breda, at S end of Moerdijk Bridge. Sometimes spelled Moerdyk.

Moerdijk Bridge, SW Netherlands, spans the Hollandschdiep bet. Moerdijk (S) and Willemsdorp (N). Railroad bridge (8,320 ft. long; completed 1871) and road bridge (slightly shorter; completed 1937) are on main routes bet. Amsterdam, The Hague, and Rotterdam (N) and North Brabant and Belgium (S). Both bridges destroyed (1944) in Second World War by retreating Germans; rebuilt 1946.

Moeris, Lake, Egypt: see BIRKET KARUN.

Moero, Lake, Belgian Congo and Northern Rhodesia: see MWERU, LAKE.

Moers (mûrs), town (pop. 30,828), in former Prussian Rhine prov., W Germany, after 1945 in North Rhine-Westphalia, in the Ruhr, 6 mi. WNW of Duisburg; coal-mining center. Has 14th–15th-cent. castle. Formerly also spelled Mörs.

Moerzeke (mōōr'zākŭ), village (pop. 4,675), East Flanders prov., N Belgium, on Scheldt R. and 3 mi. NE of Dendermonde; tobacco, early potatoes. Formerly spelled Moerseke.

Moesala, Indonesia: see SIBOLGA.

Moësa River (mōä'zä), SE Switzerland, rises near San Bernardino Pass, flows 27 mi. SSW, through Valle Mesolcina, to Ticino R. just N of Bellinzona.

Moesia (mē'shů), anc. region, SE Europe, S of the lower Danube. It was not penetrated by Grecian influences and was organized as a Roman prov. only in A.D. 44, when it included roughly what is now Serbia (Upper Moesia) and Bulgaria (Lower Moesia). Thrace and Macedonia were to S. Under the empire Roman colonies and agr. flourished in the Danube valley.

Moesi River, Indonesia: see MUSI RIVER.

Moeskroen, Belgium: see MOUSCRON.

Moetis, Mount, Indonesian Timor: see MUTIS, MOUNT.

Moffat (mŏ'fŭt), burgh (1931 pop. 2,006; 1951 census 2,114), N Dumfries, Scotland, on Annan R., at foot of Moffat Hills, and 20 mi. NNE of Dumfries; agr. market and spa resort, with medicinal springs discovered c.1630. Near-by Dumcrieff mansion was residence of John McAdam, who is buried in Moffat. Also near by is Burns's Cottage and Craigieburn House, birthplace of Jean Lorimer, Burns's "Chloris." Peak of Hart Fell is in Moffat Hills 5 mi. NNE.

Moffat, county (□ 4,754; pop. 5,946), extreme NW Colo.; ⊙ Craig. Livestock-grazing area; borders on Utah and Wyo.; drained by Yampa, Little Snake, and Green rivers. Includes natl.-forest area; part of Dinosaur Natl. Monument in W. Formed 1911.

Moffat, town (pop. 109), Saguache co., S Colo., on San Luis Creek and 14 mi. ESE of Saguache; alt. 7,564 ft. Shipping point in livestock region. Crestone Peak 18 mi. E.

Moffat Hills, range in Scotland, in Dumfries, Selkirk, and Peebles cos., extending 25 mi. NE–SW bet. Moffat and Peebles; 10 mi. wide. Chief peaks: Hart Fell (2,651 ft.) in Dumfries, 5 mi. NNE of Moffat; Broad Law (2,754 ft.) on Selkirk-Peebles border, 12 mi. NNE of Moffat; Dollar Law (2,680 ft.) in Peebles, 9 mi. SSW of Peebles; and Dun Law (2,650 ft.), on Selkirk-Peebles border, 10 mi. SSW of Peebles. On E slope is SAINT MARY'S LOCH. Clyde, Tweed, Yarrow, and Annan rivers rise in Moffat Hills.

Moffat Tunnel (6.4 mi. long; alt. c.9,000 ft.), N central Colo., passage through shoulder of James Peak in Front Range of the Rockies, 50 mi. WNW of Denver. Pioneer bore (8 ft. in diameter; built 1923–27) is used to transport water to Denver. Second bore (24 ft. high, 18 ft. wide; completed 1928) is used by railroad. With Dotsero cutoff (finished 1934; links 2 railroads in Eagle co.) tunnel shortens route from Denver to Salt Lake City, Utah, by 173 mi.

Moffet Inlet, Anglican mission station, N Baffin Isl., SE Franklin Dist., Northwest Territories, on E side of Admiralty Inlet, 65 mi. SSE of Arctic Bay trading post; 77°11'N 84°28'W.

Moffett, town (pop. 380), Sequoyah co., E Okla., on Arkansas R. (bridged), opposite Fort Smith, Ark.

Moffett Field, Calif.: see SUNNYVALE.

Moga (mō'gŭ), town (pop. 27,785), Ferozepore dist., W Punjab, India, 35 mi. ESE of Ferozepore; agr. market center (gram, wheat, cotton, oilseeds); hand-loom weaving, palm-mat making. Has col. Annual festival fair.

Mogadishu (mŏgŭdĭ'shōō), Ital. *Mogadiscio,* city (pop. 50,000), ⊙ and chief port of Ital. Somaliland, on Indian Ocean, along Benadir coast; 2°2'N 45°21'E. Commercial center connected by road with Bender Kassim on Gulf of Aden, and with Ethiopia and Kenya; oilseed pressing, sawmilling, ice mfg. Has modern Eur. section, cathedral (1925–28), 13th-cent. mosques, and native fort (restored 1933–34) with mus. of antiquity. Airfield. Taken (1871) by Sultan of Zanzibar, who leased it (1892), then sold it (1905) to Italy. Occupied (1941) by British in Second World War. Railroad (70 mi. long) to Villabruzzi was dismantled and removed to Kenya. Eur. pop. (1947) c.3,000. Formerly also spelled Magadoxo.

Mogador (mŏgädôr'), city (pop. 28,620), Marrakesh region, SW Fr. Morocco, port on the Atlantic, 10 mi. W of Marrakesh, bet. Safi (60 mi. NNE) and Agadir (75 mi. S); 31°31'N 9°47'W. Harbor, though sheltered by offshore islets and a rocky headland, is exposed to SW winds, and has therefore remained a cabotage port. Chief industries are fish processing and canning (lobster), sheep- and goatskin tanning, palm-fiber working, sugar refining, soap mfg. Local artisans make inlaid furniture, jewelry, copper articles. Trade in wool, olive oil, cereals. Because of its fine beach and equable climate, Mogador is growing as a bathing resort. Founded in 1760s by Sultan Mohammed XVI, it was laid out on a rectilinear plan and fortified in the style of Vauban. It has a sizable Jewish pop. (c.5,000 in 1947), concentrated in the N quarter (*mellah*). Its importance as a terminus of caravans from Fr. West Africa has decreased. Formerly often known as Souirah (also spelled Souira, Suira).

Mogadore (mŏ'gŭdôr), village (pop. 1,818), on Summit-Portage co. line, NE Ohio, just E of Akron; tools, clay products.

Mogadouro (mōōgŭdō'rōō), town (pop. 1,439), Bragança dist., N Portugal, in hill region, 32 mi. S of Bragança; agr. trade (vegetables, white wine, lumber). Lead deposits near by.

Mogale (mōgä'lā) or **Mogalo** (–lō), village, Equator Prov., NW Belgian Congo, on Lua R. and 180 mi. WNW of Lisala; terminus of navigation; cotton ginning. Yembongo trading post is on right bank.

Mogalturru, India: see NARASAPUR.

Mogami River (mōgä'mē), Jap. *Mogami-gawa,* Yamagata prefecture, N Honshu, Japan, formed by union of 2 headstreams S of Nagai; flows generally NNE, past Nagai, Yachi, and Oishida, and NW to Sea of Japan at Sakata; 134 mi. long. Drains large rice-growing area.

Mogán (mōgän'), village (pop. 242), Grand Canary, Canary Isls., 24 mi. SW of Las Palmas; resort with near-by beach and landing. Region produces grapes, cereals, bananas, tomatoes, cochineal, tobacco. Flour milling; fishing.

Mogarraz (mōgäräth'), town (pop. 1,038), Salamanca prov., W Spain, 13 mi. NW of Béjar; olive-oil processing; lumbering; wine, chestnuts.

Mogaung (mō'goung'), village, Myitkyina dist., Kachin State, Upper Burma, on railroad and 3[illegible] mi. W of Myitkyina, on Magaung R. (right affluent of the Irrawaddy); shipping point for jade mines o[illegible]

Lonkin and amber mines of Hukawng Valley; carving handicrafts. Was ⊙ of petty Shan State (13th cent.), rivaling Mohnyin; passed to Burma (18th cent.) under Alaungpaya. Scene of heavy fighting (1944) during Second World War.

Mogelnitsa, Poland: see MOGIELNICA.

Mogelsberg (mō'gŭlsbĕrk"), town (pop. 2,315), St. Gall canton, NE Switzerland, 12 mi. WSW of St. Gall; embroideries, metal products.

Mogente (mōhĕn'tä), town (pop. 2,874), Valencia prov., E Spain, 15 mi. SW of Játiva; olive-oil and meat processing, toy and plaster mfg.; lumbering; wine, cereals, fruit. Summer resort.

Moggio, Ethiopia: see MOJJO.

Moggio Udinese (môd'jô ōōdēnā'zē), village (pop. 1,211), Udine prov., Friuli-Venezia Giulia, NE Italy, 9 mi. E of Tolmezzo; mfg. (cutlery, agr. tools).

Moghalpura or **Mughalpura** (both: mōōgŭl'pōōrŭ), industrial E suburb of Lahore, Lahore dist., E Punjab, W Pakistan; large railroad workshops; general engineering, mfg. (locomotive and car parts, drugs, clothing); grain depot. Has col. of engineering.

Moghal-Sarai, India: see MUGHAL SARAI.

Moghreb, N Africa: see MAGHREB.

Mogi (mō'gē), town (pop. 12,696), Nagasaki prefecture, W Kyushu, Japan, port on Tachibana Bay, on E Nomo Peninsula, 3 mi. SE of Nagasaki; fishery. Exports loquats, fish.

Mogi das Cruzes (mōōzhē' däs krōō'zĭs), city (1950 pop. 31,782), SE São Paulo, Brazil, on Tietê R., on railroad and 28 mi. E of São Paulo; mfg. center (textiles, hats, chemicals, wine, brandy). Has new blast furnaces, and aluminum-rolling mill. Pegmatite mined in area. Founded 1611. Formerly spelled Mogy das Cruzes.

Mogielnica (môgyĕlnē'tsä), Rus. *Mogelnitse* or *Mogel'nitse* (both: môgĕ'lyŭnĭtsĕ), town (pop. 4,667), Warszawa prov., E central Poland, 40 mi. SSW of Warsaw; tanning, flour milling.

Mogi-Guaçu (mōōzhē'-gwŭsōō'), city (pop. 2,773), E São Paulo, Brazil, 4 mi. N of Mogi-Mirim, and on Mogi-Guaçu R.; rail junction (spur to Pinhal); dairying, pottery mfg., sawmilling; coffee, sugar, cattle. Formerly spelled Mogy-Guassú.

Mogi-Guaçu River, NE São Paulo, Brazil, rises in Minas Gerais near Ouro Fino, flows 220 mi. NW, past Mogi-Guaçu and Pôrto Ferreira (head of navigation), to the Rio Pardo 30 mi. NW of Ribeirão Prêto.

Mogila, Poland: see NOWA HUTA.

Mogilev (mō'gĭlĕv, Rus. mŭgĕlyôf'), oblast (□ 8,000; 1946 pop. estimate 1,000,000), E Belorussian SSR; ⊙ Mogilev. In Dnieper Lowland; drained by Dnieper and Sozh rivers. Forested and agr. region, with flax (N, E), potatoes (S), grain (rye, oats, barley); pig and dairy-cattle raising. Rural industries: flour milling, flax processing, lumber and paper milling, glassworking, peat cutting. Phosphorite deposits. Truck gardens, orchards near Mogilev, principal industrial center. Formed 1938.

Mogilev, city (1939 pop. 99,440), ⊙ Mogilev oblast, Belorussian SSR, on Dnieper R. and 110 mi. E of Minsk; 53°53'N 30°20'E. Industrial and transportation center; mfg. (steam-driven tractors, artificial fiber, apparel); tanning. Has auto repair plant, pipe foundry. Picturesque location on both banks of Dnieper R.; junction of 4 rail lines and 5 highways. Has cathedral, city mus., teachers col., experiment station for medicinal plants. Developed around castle dating from 1267; ruled for many years by Lithuania and Poland; acquired (1772) by Russia. Pop. 30% Jewish until Second World War, when city was held (1941–44) by Germans. Formerly also known as Mohilev.

Mogilev-Podolski or **Mogilev-Podol'skiy** (-pŭdôl'-skē), city (1926 pop. 22,993), SW Vinnitsa oblast, Ukrainian SSR, in Podolia, on Dniester R. (head of navigation), opposite Ataki, and 60 mi. SSW of Vinnitsa; machine repair shops; tanning, fruit canning, sawmilling, distilling, flour milling; limestone quarries. In Middle Ages, trading center on Ukraine-Moldavia frontier, with large Greek, Moldavian, and Armenian pop. Annexed to Russia in 1793. Pop. 40% Jewish until Second World War, when city was held (1941–43) by Germans.

Mogilno (môgēl'nô), town (pop. 5,193), Bydgoszcz prov., central Poland, 16 mi. SW of Inowroclaw; rail junction; machine mfg., distilling, flour milling.

Mogi-Mirim (mōōzhē'-mērēn'), city (pop. 8,295), E São Paulo, Brazil, 33 mi. N of Campinas; rail junction (spur to Minas Gerais); cotton ginning, meat packing, brewing, brandy distilling, mfg. of flour products; coffee, sugar, rice processing. Sericulture. Airfield. Founded in 18th cent. Formerly spelled Mogy-Mirim.

Mogincual (mōōzhĭngkwäl'), village, Niassa prov., E Mozambique, on Mozambique Channel, 40 mi. SSW of Mozambique city; cotton, sisal.

Moglia (mô'lyä), village (pop. 1,518), Mantova prov., Lombardy, N Italy, near Secchia R., 17 mi. SSE of Mantua; alcohol distillery.

Mogliano Veneto (môlä'nô vä'nĕtô), town (pop. 1,870), Treviso prov., Veneto, N Italy, 7 mi. S of Treviso, in peach-growing region; mfg. (shoes, agr. machinery, bicycles, wax, silk textiles). Agr. center noted for its aviculture.

Mogocha (mŭgŭchä'), town (1939 pop. over 10,000), NE Chita oblast, Russian SFSR, on Trans-Siberian RR and 170 mi. W of Skovorodino, in gold-mining area; metalworks.

Mogochin (-chēn'), town (1939 pop. over 2,000), SE central Tomsk oblast, Russian SFSR, on Ob R., near mouth of Chulym R., and 45 mi. SE of Kolpashevo; sawmilling center.

Mogoitui or **Mogoytuy** (mŭgoitōō'ē), village, NE Aga Buryat-Mongol Natl. Okrug, Chita oblast, Russian SFSR, on branch of Trans-Siberian RR and 75 mi. SE of Chita, in agr. area (livestock, grain).

Mogok (mō'gôk"), village, Katha dist., Upper Burma, in Shan Plateau, 70 mi. NNE of Mandalay and linked by road with Irrawaddy R. landing of Thabeikkyin; alt. 3,761 ft.; major gem-mining center; rubies, sapphires.

Mogollon (mŭgēōn', mŭgŭyōn'), village, Catron co., SW N.Mex., near San Francisco R., just NW of Mogollon Mts., 22 mi. S of Reserve; alt. c.7,000 ft. Silver mines in vicinity.

Mogollon Mountains, SW N.Mex., just E of San Francisco R., in Gila Natl. Forest, near Ariz. line. Prominent points: Granite Peak (8,699 ft.), Mogollon Mtn. (10,788 ft.), Whitewater Baldy (10,892 ft.). Silver is mined.

Mogollon Plateau (c.7–8,000 ft.), tableland in E central Ariz., S of Winslow; extends c.75 mi. E–W. Mogollon Rim, its rugged S escarpment, is sometimes called Mogollon Mts.; not directly linked to Mogollon Mts. of W N.Mex.

Mogol-Tau (mŭgôl"-tou'), section of Tien Shan mountain system, on Uzbek-Tadzhik SSR border, at W end of Fergana Valley; 25 mi. long (NE–SW); rises to c.5,000 ft. Rich iron (magnetite) deposits. The Syr Darya flows around S end of range; forms Begovat rapids.

Mogonori (mōgōnô'rē), village, Northern Territories, NE Gold Coast, 5 mi. NNW of Bawku, on Fr. West Africa border; border and cattle-quarantine station. Sometimes spelled Mogonawri.

Mogoro (mô'gôrô), village (pop. 3,996), Cagliari prov., W Sardinia, 18 mi. SSE of Oristano. Nuraghe just S.

Mogosoaia (môgôshwä'yä), Rum. *Mogoşoaia*, village (pop. 1,961), Bucharest prov., S Rumania, on Colentina R. and 8 mi. NW of Bucharest; poultry research farm. Has 18th-cent. palace (now a children's home), built by Constantine Brancovan.

Mogotes (mōgō'tĕs), town (pop. 1,810), Santander dept., N central Colombia, in Cordillera Oriental, 12 mi. ESE of San Gil; alt. 5,728 ft. Fique fiber, sugar cane, fruit, vegetables, stock. Mfg. of straw hats, guava preserves; tanning, sawmilling.

Mogoytuy, Russian SFSR: see MOGOITUI.

Mograt Island (mō'grät), long, narrow isl. in Nile R., Northern Prov., Anglo-Egyptian Sudan, bet. 4th and 5th cataracts, opposite Abu Hamed; 17 mi. long; 2 mi. wide.

Mogre, India: see ANDHERI.

Moguer (mōgĕr'), city (pop. 6,663), Huelva prov., SW Spain, in Andalusia, on left bank of the Río Tinto estuary, and 6 mi. E of Huelva; viticultural center. Alcohol, brandy, and vermouth distilling; flour milling; mfg. of tiles, pottery; lumbering. An old city noted for its fine bldgs., such as church with Mozarabic tower, and the Santa Clara convent in whose archives are documents pertaining to discovery of America.

Mogy das Cruzes, Brazil: see MOGI DAS CRUZES.

Mogy-Guassú, Brazil: see MOGI-GUAÇU.

Mogy-Mirim, Brazil: see MOGI-MIRIM.

Mogzon (mŭgzôn'), town (1939 pop. over 2,000), SW Chita oblast, Russian SFSR, on Trans-Siberian RR, on Khilok R. and 65 mi. WSW of Chita; metalworks.

Moha (mōä'), village (pop. 1,738), Liége prov., E Belgium, 3 mi. NW of Huy; chalk quarrying.

Mohacs (mô'häch), Hung. *Mohács*, city (pop. 18,355), Baranya co., S Hungary, on the Danube and 23 mi. ESE of Pecs; rail terminal, river port. Coal for Budapest and Vienna loaded here; hemp, silk, leather mfg.; brewery, sawmills, flour mills, brickworks. Heavy industry introduced c. 1950. Metallurgical center; foundries, coke batteries. Scene of decisive Turkish victory over Hungarians, 1526.

Mohacs Island, Hung. *Mohács*, S Hungary and NW Yugoslavia, in the Danube; c.35 mi. long, greatest width 11 mi.; swampy.

Mohales Hoek (mōhä'lĕs hōōk'), village, ⊙ Mohales Hoek dist. (pop. 65,932, with absent laborers 73,896), S Basutoland, on main N-S road and 60 mi. S of Maseru. Also spelled Mohaleshoek or Mohale's Hoek.

Mohall (mō'hôl), city (pop. 1,073), ⊙ Renville co., N N.Dak., 38 mi. N of Minot; dairy produce, livestock, poultry, wheat, flax.

Mohamadabad-Bidar, India: see BIDAR.

Mohamdi, India: see MUHAMDI.

Mohamédia, La, Tunisia: see MOHAMMÉDIA, LA.

Mohammadabad, India: see MEHMADABAD.

Mohammadbad, India: see MUHAMMADABAD, Ghazipur dist.

Mohammadpur, India: see ROORKEE.

Mohammareh or **Mohammerah,** Iran: see KHURRAMSHAHR.

Mohammedabad, Iran: see MUHAMMADABAD.

Mohammédia, La (lä mōämädyä'), village, Tunis dist., N Tunisia, 8 mi. S of Tunis; winegrowing. Has extensive remains of an abandoned 19th-cent. beylical palace. Also spelled La Mohamédia.

Mohanga, Belgian Congo: see LUTUNGURU.

Mohanganj, E Pakistan: see SHAMGANJ.

Mohanlalganj (mōhŭnläl'gŭnj), village, Lucknow dist., central Uttar Pradesh, India, 12 mi. SSE of Lucknow; road center; trades in wheat, rice, gram, millet.

Mohanpur (mō'hŭnpōōr), town (pop. 2,493), Etah dist., W Uttar Pradesh, India, 20 mi. ESE of Kasganj; wheat, pearl millet, barley, corn, jowar, oilseeds.

Mohapa, India: see MOHPA.

Mohara, Japan: see MOBARA.

Moharraq, Bahrein: see MUHARRAQ.

Mohattanagar (mō'hŭt-tŭnŭgŭr), village, Nawabshah dist., central Sind, W Pakistan, 17 mi. E of Nawabshah; wheat, millet; sugar milling, handicraft cloth weaving. Formerly called Pritamabad.

Mohave, for names beginning thus and not found here: see under MOJAVE.

Mohave (mōhä'vē), county (□ 13,260; pop. 8,510), NW Ariz.; ⊙ Kingman. Hualpai, Mohave, and Black mts. in SW. Colorado and Bill Williams rivers drain co. Parts of Grand Canyon Natl. Monument, Hoover Dam Recreational Area, and Hualpai and Kaibab Indian reservations are in co., as is Fort Mohave Indian Reservation. Hoover Dam forms L. Mead on Nev. line. Mining (lead, silver, zinc, gold, copper), cattle grazing. Formed 1864.

Mohave Mountains, in W Ariz. and SE Calif., on both sides of Colorado R., S of Kingman, Ariz., and Needles, Calif.; rise to 5,102 ft. in Ariz., to 3,688 ft. in Calif.

Mohawk (mō'hôk). **1** Village (pop. 1,131, including near-by Fulton), Keweenaw co., NW Upper Peninsula, Mich., 10 mi. NE of Houghton. **2** Village (pop. 3,196), Herkimer co., central N.Y., on Mohawk R. and the Barge Canal, and 13 mi. SE of Utica; mfg. (cheese, fishing reels, knit goods). Settled 1826, inc. 1844. **3** Village, Coshocton co., Ohio: see NELLIE.

Mohawk, Lake, NW N.J., formed by dam on upper Wallkill R., near Sparta, 7 mi. ESE of Newton, in recreational area; c.2.5 mi. long.

Mohawk Dam; Mohawk Reservoir, Ohio: see WALHONDING RIVER.

Mohawk River. **1** In Coos co., N N.H., rises N of Dixville Notch, flows 10 mi. SW and W to the Connecticut at Colebrook. **2** In central and E N.Y., largest tributary of the Hudson, rises in Oneida co., flows c.140 mi. S and SE, past Rome, Utica, Amsterdam, and Schenectady, to the Hudson at Cohoes (falls here). Drains 3,412 sq. mi. From Rome to its mouth, river is paralleled by N.Y. State Barge Canal joining Great Lakes and E coast ports via Hudson R. The beautiful and fertile Mohawk valley, as the E–W passage bet. the Adirondacks (N) and the Allegheny Plateau (S), was scene of many battles in the French and Indian War and in the Revolution, and was an important route for west-bound pioneers; the old Erie Canal followed the river.

Mohawk Trail. **1** Historic route in N.Y. state from the Hudson into Great Lakes region following Mohawk R. through the Appalachians. Traverses territory which was occupied by Iroquois Confederacy. Consisted of series of turnpikes from Schenectady to Rome, with trails further W in colonial days, when it served as major artery for settlers emigrating W. Importance diminished by Erie Canal (1825) and later railroads. **2** Highway extending (E–W) from Greenfield to North Adams across NW Mass. through scenic Hoosac Range and Berkshire Hills; follows trail blazed by Mohawk Indians.

Mohawk Valley, Calif.; see BLAIRSDEN.

Moheda (mōō"hä'dä), village (pop. 821), Kronoberg co., S Sweden, on Morrum R. and 12 mi. NW of Vaxjo; shoe mfg.

Mohedas (mōä'dhäs), village (pop. 1,038), Cáceres prov., W Spain, 18 mi. NNW of Plasencia; olive oil, wine, sheep.

Mohedas de la Jara (dhä lä hä'rä), village (pop. 1,353), Toledo prov., central Spain, 30 mi. SW of Talavera de la Reina; olives, cereals, fruit, livestock. Flour milling, olive-oil pressing.

Mohegan (mōhē'gŭn). **1** Community, New London co., Conn.: see MONTVILLE. **2** or **Mohegan Lake,** resort village, Westchester co., SE N.Y., on L. Mohegan (c.1 mi. long), 5 mi. NE of Peekskill.

Mohéli Island (mōhĕ'lē, môälē') (□ 112; pop. c.5,000), one of 4 main isls. of Comoro Isls. colony, in Mozambique Channel of Indian Ocean, W of Anjouan Isl. and SE of Grande Comore Isl., off NW Madagascar; 18 mi. long, 8 mi. wide; rises to c.2,000 ft. Very fertile; palms, vanilla, cacao, copra. Populated by Arabs, Makwas, and Malagasys. Main town, Fomboni, is on N shore. Part of domain of Sultan of Anjouan till 1827; ruled by a Malagasy dynasty thereafter. Placed under Fr. protectorate 1886.

Mohelnice (mô'hĕlnyĭtsĕ), Ger. *Müglitz* (mü'glĭts), town (pop. 3,109; commune pop. 3,825), NW central Moravia, Czechoslovakia, on railroad and 19 mi. NW of Olomouc; sugar beets, oats. Large state reformatory at Mirov (mĭ'rôf), 3 mi. NW.

Mohenjo-Daro (mōhĕn'jō dä'rō) [Sindhi, =mound of the dead], a famous site of Indus Valley Civilization, Larkana dist., NW Sind, W Pakistan, near right bank of the Indus, 17 mi. S of Larkana. Since its prehistoric nature was 1st realized in 1922, excavations have uncovered remains of 6 or 7 successive cities, generally considered to have existed bet. 4000 and 2000 B.C., in chalcolithic era. Ruins include brick dwellings, baths, drains, and streets; artifacts are engraved seals, implements, weapons, jewelry, sculpture, and pottery. Inhabitants apparently enjoyed a high degree of culture. In NW section is Buddhist stupa of a 2d-cent. A.D. Kushan king. Near by is archaeological camp and mus. with numerous antiquities.

Mohican, Cape (mōhē'kŭn), W Alaska, W extremity of Nunivak Isl., on Bering Sea; 60°12'N 167°24'W.

Mohican River, central Ohio, formed by junction of forks in region E of Mansfield, flows c.40 mi. S, joining Kokosing R. to form Walhonding R. 16 mi. NW of Coshocton. Among its headstreams and tributaries (some with flood-control works) are Black, Lake, Clear, and Jerome forks.

Mohicanville Reservoir, N central Ohio, flood-control reservoir (capacity 102,000 acre-ft.) impounded in a headstream of Mohican R., 7 mi. NE of Loudonville.

Mohilev, Belorussian SSR: see MOGILEV, city.

Mohill, Gaelic *Maothail*, town (pop. 877), S Co. Leitrim, Ireland, 9 mi. ESE of Carrick-on-Shannon; agr. market (dairying; cattle, potatoes).

Mohindargarh (mō'hĭndŭrgŭr), town (pop. 9,771), ⊙ Narnaul dist., S Patiala and East Punjab States Union, India, 29 mi. W of Rewari; local market for millet, gram; metal handicrafts. Formerly called Kanaud.

Mohinora, Cerro (sĕ'rō mōēnō'rä), peak (13,097 ft.) in Sierra Madre Occidental, Chihuahua, N Mexico, 80 mi. NNE of Culiacán, near 26°N 107°W.

Möhlin (mû'lĭn), town (pop. 3,229), Aargau canton, N Switzerland, just S of the Rhine and Ger. border, 12 mi. E of Basel; shoe mfg., salt mining. Ryburg-Schwörstadt hydroelectric plant is N.

Möhne River (mû'nù), W Germany, rises 2 mi. NW of Brilon, flows 40 mi. W to the Ruhr at Neheim-Hüsten. Dammed at GÜNNE.

Mohnton (mōn'tŭn), borough (pop. 2,004), Berks co., SE central Pa., 5 mi. SW of Reading. Founded 1850, inc. 1907.

Mohnyin (mōn-yĭn'), village, Myitkyina dist., Upper Burma, on railroad, 75 mi. SW of Myitkyina. Former ⊙ petty Shan kingdom rivaling Mogaung.

Moho (mô'hŭ'), town, ⊙ Moho co. (pop. 3,636), northernmost Heilungkiang prov., Manchuria, 320 mi. NW of Aigun and on Amur R. (USSR border); a leading gold-mining center of China.

Moho (mō'ō), village (pop. 800), Puno dept., SE Peru, port on NE shore of L. Titicaca and 19 mi. ESE of Huancané; alt. 12,595 ft.; fibers, barley, quinoa, livestock.

Mohol (mō'hōl), town (pop. 5,437), Sholapur dist., E Bombay, India, 20 mi. NW of Sholapur; millet, cotton; handicraft cloth weaving.

Mohol, Yugoslavia: see MOL.

Moholm (mōō"hôlm'), village (pop. 565), Skaraborg co., S Sweden, on Tida R. and 10 mi. SE of Mariestad; rail junction; pulp milling, woodworking.

Mohon (mōô'), SE industrial suburb (pop. 6,541) of Mézières, Ardennes dept., N France, on left bank of the Meuse (canalized); important tool- and hardware-mfg. center. Railroad shops.

Mohonk, Lake (mōhŏngk', -hŭngk'), Ulster co., SE N.Y., small lake in scenic resort area of the Shawangunk range, 4 mi. WNW of New Paltz. Mohonk Lake village is here.

Moho River (mō'ō), in Guatemala and Br. Honduras, rises in Maya Mts. 30 mi. W of Punta Gorda, flows 24 mi. E to Bay of Amatique of Caribbean Sea, 5 mi. SSW of Punta Gorda. Navigable for small craft; timber floating.

Mohoro (mōhō'rō), town, Eastern Prov., Tanganyika, near mouth of Rufiji R., 30 mi. ESE of Utete; cotton center; sisal, copra.

Mohotane, Marquesas Isls.: see MOTANE.

Mohoza, Bolivia: see LANZA.

Mohpa (mō'pŭ), town (pop. 5,471), Nagpur dist., central Madhya Pradesh, India, 20 mi. NW of Nagpur; cotton ginning; millet, wheat, oilseeds. Sometimes spelled Mohapa.

Mohpani, India: see GADARWARA.

Möhra (mû'rä), village (pop. 800), Thuringia, central Germany, at SW foot of Thuringian Forest, 9 mi. SSW of Eisenach. Home of Luther's family. Copper slate formerly mined here.

Mohrin, Poland: see MORYN.

Möhringen (mû'rĭng-ùn), S suburb of STUTTGART, Germany. Inc. 1942 into Stuttgart.

Mohrungen, Poland: see MORAG.

Moiale, Ethiopia: see MOYALE.

Moiano (môyä'nô), village (pop. 2,134), Benevento prov., Campania, S Italy, 11 mi. E of Caserta.

Moidart (moi'dŭrt), barren mtn. region in W Inverness, Scotland, extending N-S bet. the Sound of Arisaig (N) and Loch Shiel (S), rising to 2,852 ft. on Druim Fiaclach, 10 mi. SE of Arisaig. At SW extremity of region is Loch Moidart, sea inlet (6 mi. long) containing isl. of SHONA.

Moiese, Mont.: see DIXON.

Moikovats, Yugoslavia: see MOJKOVAC.

Moimenta da Beira (mwēmān'tù dä bā'rù), town (pop. 1,304), Viseu dist., N central Portugal; 13 mi. SE of Lamego; rye, potatoes, wheat, oil, wine.

Moinabad (mō"ēnäbäd'), town (pop. 9,705), Bidar dist., W central Hyderabad state, India, 25 mi. SW of Bidar; millet, cotton, rice, tobacco. Formerly called Chitgopa.

Moindou (mwēdōō'), village (dist. pop. 309), W New Caledonia, 65 mi. NW of Noumea; coffee, livestock; coal mining.

Moines, Île-aux- (ēl-ō-mwän'). **1** Islet in English Channel, off coast of N Brittany (Côtes-du Nord dept.), W France; largest of the SEPT-ÎLES. **2** Island (pop. 1,051) in Gulf of Morbihan (Bay of Biscay), off S Brittany (Morbihan dept.), W France, 5 mi. SSW of Vannes; 3.5 mi. long, 2 mi. wide; oyster beds, granite quarry. Megalithic monuments (cromlech, dolmen). Also spelled L'Isle-aux-Moines.

Moinesti (moinĕsht'), Rum. *Moineşti*, town (1948 pop. 5,868), Bacau prov., E central Rumania, in E foothills of the Moldavian Carpathians, 20 mi. SW of Bacau; rail terminus, oil and natural-gas center; oil refining, woodworking, tanning, mfg. of candles. Also a health resort.

Moineville (mwänvēl'), village (pop. 394), Meurthe-et-Moselle dept., NE France, on Orne R. and 3 mi. S of Briey; iron mining.

Mointy (mŭēn'tē), town (1942 pop. over 500), SE Karaganda oblast, Kazakh SSR, rail junction on Trans-Kazakhstan RR, 70 mi. NW of Balkhash (linked by rail branch); rail shops. Iron, lead-zinc, and arsenic deposits.

Moi Plateaus (moi), series of basaltic plateaus (average alt. 2,500 ft.), S central Vietnam, on land side of Annamese Cordillera, including (N-S) Kontum, Darlac, Langbiang, and Djiring plateaus. Abundant rainfall and red residual soils support luxuriant forest vegetation interrupted by grassy plains (big game) and favor tea, coffee, and rubber plantations introduced by European colonization. Indigenous pop. are the primitive Moi tribes, the original inhabitants of Indochina, expelled from the lowlands by the invading Annamese. Main centers are Dalat, Djiring, Banmethuot, Pleiku, and Kontum. Except in Dalat, European penetration began only in 1924, with introduction of plantation economy. Roads were built linking the plateaus with the coast and directly with Saigon. Owing to its individualized traits, the region was separated after 1946 from Annam and set up as the territory of the Hill Peoples of South Indochina [Fr. *Populations Montagnardes du Sud Indochinois;* abbr. *P.M.S.I.*] (□ 25,700; 1943 pop. 427,100; ⊙ Dalat), administered directly by Vietnam govt.

Moira, England: see ASHBY WOULDS.

Moira (moi'rù), agr. village (district pop. 1,430), NW Co. Down, Northern Ireland, near Lagan R., 4 mi. ENE of Lurgan. In 637 king Congal of Ulster was defeated here by Domhnall.

Mo i Rana, Norway: see Mo, town.

Moirans (mwärä'), town (pop. 2,183), Isère dept., SE France, near the Isère, 12 mi. NW of Grenoble; rail junction; paper mills, brickworks.

Moirans-en-Montagne (-ā-mōtä'nyù), village (pop. 1,378), Jura dept., E France, near Ain R., 7 mi. WNW of Saint-Claude; wood turning, mfg. of plastic objects.

Moira River (moi'rù), SE Ont., rises W of Sharbot L., flows 60 mi. SW to the Bay Quinte at Belleville. Course is rapid; supplies water power.

Moisakula, Myzakyula, or **Myyzakyula**, Est. *Mõisaküla* (mù'ēsäkülä), Ger. *Moisaküll*, city (pop. 2,222), SW Estonia, 33 mi. SE of Parnu, on Latvian border; rail junction (repair shops); flax-growing center; lumbering.

Moisalen, Norway: see MOYSALEN.

Moisdon-la-Rivière (mwädō'-lä-rēvyâr'), village (pop. 525), Loire-Inférieure dept., W France, on Don R. and 6 mi. S of Châteaubriant; horse and cattle raising.

Moisei (moisā'), Hung. *Majszin* (moi'sēn), village (pop. 5,615), Rodna prov., NW Rumania, on W slopes of the Carpathians, on railroad, and 35 mi. SE of Sighet; pilgrimage center with 18th-cent. monastery. In Hungary, 1940–45.

Moisés Bertoni, Paraguay: see DOCTOR MOISÉS S. BERTONI.

Moisés Ville (moisĕs' vē'yā), town (pop. estimate 1,500), central Santa Fe prov., Argentina, 31 mi. SSW of San Cristóbal; agr. center (alfalfa, corn, wheat, livestock).

Moisie (mwäzē'), village (pop. estimate 350), E Que., on the St. Lawrence, near mouth of Moisie R., 10 mi. E of Sept Îles; Hudson's Bay Co. post.

Moisie River, E Que., rises in E central Que. lake region, near Labrador border, flows 210 mi. SE to the St. Lawrence 14 mi. E of Sept Îles.

Moissac (mwäsäk'), town (pop. 4,562), Tarn-et-Garonne dept., SW France, on the Garonne Lateral Canal, on Tarn R. near its influx into the Garonne, and 5 mi. N of Castelsarrasin; fruit and vegetable shipping center (grapes, peaches, cherries, apricots, artichokes, asparagus); poultry and dairy market. Has noteworthy 12th-cent. church portal and a fine Romanesque cloister (c.12th cent.).

Moïssala (moisälä'), village, S Chad territory, Fr. Equatorial Africa, on the Bahr Sara and 75 mi. SW of Fort-Archambault; cotton ginning. Until 1946, in Ubangi-Shari colony.

Moisson (mwäsō'), village (pop. 257), Seine-et-Oise dept., N central France, on the Seine and 6 mi. N of Mantes-Gassicourt.

Moistrana, Yugoslavia: see MOJSTRANA.

Moita (mwē'tù), town (pop. 2,781), Setúbal dist., S central Portugal, near S bank of Tagus R. estuary, on railroad and 10 mi. SE of Lisbon; fruit- and vegetable-growing center; resin processing, pottery and cheese mfg.

Moitaco (moitä'kō), town (pop. 135), Bolívar state, SE Venezuela, landing on Orinoco R. and 55 mi. WSW of Ciudad Bolívar, in cattle-raising region.

Mojácar (mōhä'kär), city (pop. 1,568), Almería prov., S Spain, 18 mi. SSE of Huércal-Overa; almonds, cereals, potatoes; sheep raising. Tourist resort, visited for its typical medieval Moorish quality; has ruined castle.

Mojada, Sierra (syĕ'rä mōhä'dä), low NW spur (average alt. c.5,000 ft.) of Sierra Madre Oriental, on Coahuila–Chihuahua border, N Mexico, W of Esmeralda; c.30 mi. long NW-SE. Rich in minerals (silver, gold, lead, copper, zinc).

Mojados (mōhä'dhōs), town (pop. 1,529), Valladolid prov., N central Spain, 16 mi. SSE of Valladolid; flour milling; sheep, grain, wine.

Moján, El, Venezuela: see SAN RAFAEL, Zulia state.

Mojave (mōhä'vē), village (pop. 2,055), Kern co., S central Calif., in Mojave Desert, c.50 mi. ESE of Bakersfield; supply point for mines (tungsten, silver, borax, gold), cattle and wheat ranches.

Mojave Desert (□ c.15,000), S Calif., part of the Great Basin, lying S of the Sierra Nevada (and Owens and Death valleys, which flank mts. on E), and N and NE of ranges enclosing Los Angeles basin; meets Colorado Desert on SE. Region of flat basins (many occupied by playas) with interior drainage, separated by low, bare ranges. Receives little rain (2–5 inches annually) and supports agr. only where artesian water occurs, as in Lancaster and Palmdale dists. of Antelope Valley (□ c.2,500), which is desert's W part, lying N of Los Angeles. Mojave R., flowing mainly underground, is the only stream. Mining of silver, tungsten, gold, iron (Rand Mts. and other locations); granite quarrying; chemicals (borax, potash, salt) obtained from dry lakes. Cattle, dude ranches. Includes parts of San Bernardino, Los Angeles, Kern counties. Barstow, Victorville, Mojave are chief towns.

Mojave River, SE Calif., intermittent stream rising in San Bernardino Mts. near L. Arrowhead, flows c.100 mi. N and NE (mostly underground), through Mojave Desert, to Soda L. (60 mi. E of Barstow), an intermittently dry sink which river reaches aboveground only in floodtime.

Moji (mō'jē), city (1940 pop. 138,997; 1947 pop. 109,567), Fukuoka prefecture, N Kyushu, Japan, port on E shore of Shimonoseki Strait, opposite Shimonoseki, 40 mi. NE of Fukuoka, and adjacent to Kokura (SW). A major port of Kyushu; industrial and transportation center; steel mills; sugar refinery, breweries, rice mill. Tunnel (built 1942) under Shimonoseki Strait connects city with Shimonoseki on Honshu. Exports coal, cotton thread, refined sugar, cement, beer, flour. Opened 1887 to foreign trade. Heavily bombed (1945) in Second World War. Known in feudal times as Mojigaseki. Sometimes spelled Mozi.

Mojjo (mō'jō), Ital. *Moggio*, village, Shoa prov., central Ethiopia, on railroad and 40 mi. SE of Addis Ababa, in cereal-growing and cattle-raising region.

Mojkovac, Moikovats, or **Moykovats** (all: moi'-kôväts), village, E Montenegro, Yugoslavia, on Tara R., on Bijelo Polje–Kolasin road and 10 mi. NNE of Kolasin.

Mojo, Indonesia: see MOYO.

Mojocoya (mōhōkoi'ä), town (pop. c.5,780), Chuquisaca dept., S central Bolivia, 28 mi. NNE of Zudañez; vegetables, corn, potatoes, fruit.

Mojokerto or **Modjokerto** (both: mōjōkĕr'tō), town (pop. 23,600), E Java, Indonesia, on Brantas R. and 27 mi. SW of Surabaya; trade center in agr. area (sugar, rice, peanuts, corn); textile mills, railroad shops. Extensive irrigation works near by.

Mojones, Cerro (sĕ'rō mōhō'nĕs), Andean volcano (19,650 ft.) in N Catamarca prov., Argentina, 30 mi. N of Antofagasta.

Mojstrana, Ger. *Moistrana* (both: moi'stränä), village, NW Slovenia, Yugoslavia, on the Sava Dolinka, on railroad and 39 mi. NW of Ljubljana, bet. Julian Alps and the Karawanken; climatic resort; sports center; cementworks. Includes hamlet of Dovje, Ger. *Lengenfeld*.

Moju (mōōzhōō'), city (pop. 376), E Pará, Brazil, on Moju R. (navigable) and 40 mi. SSW of Belém; ships rubber, lumber. Road to Abaetetuba. Formerly spelled Mojú.

Moju River, E Pará, Brazil, rises near 3°30'S 49°20'W, flows c.200 mi. NNE, past Moju (where it is joined by a distributary of the Tocantins), to junction with Acará R. 15 mi. S of Belém. Navigable in lower course.

Moka (mō'kä), town (pop. 13,771), Tochigi prefecture, central Honshu, Japan, 11 mi. SE of Utsunomiya; commercial center for agr. area (rice, tobacco); spinning. Sometimes spelled Mooka.

Mokambo (mōkäm'bō), village, Katanga prov., SE Belgian Congo, on Northern Rhodesia border, on railroad and 85 mi. SE of Elisabethville; customs station.

Mokameh (mō'kŭmä), town (pop. 19,984), Patna dist., N central Bihar, India, in Ganges Plain, on Ganges R. (rail ferry) and 51 mi. ESE of Patna; trade center (rice, gram, wheat, barley, oilseeds, corn, sugar cane, millet). Site of projected steel plant. Formerly spelled Mukama.

Mokane (mōkān'), town (pop. 477), Callaway co., central Mo., on Missouri R. and 12 mi. S of Fulton; grain, livestock.

Mokan Shan (mŭ'gän' shän'), mountain (2,500 ft.) in N Chekiang prov., China, 30 mi. NW of Hangchow; noted summer resort.

Mokapu Point (mōkä'pōō), E Oahu, T.H.; 21°27'N 157°43'W. SE end of Koolau Range.

Moka Range (mō'kä), N central Mauritius, rises to 2,690 ft. in the Pieter Both, 4 mi. SE of Port Louis.

Mokau River (mōkou'), W N.Isl., New Zealand, rises S of Te Kuiti, flows 75 mi. SW to N.Taranaki Bight; navigable 24 mi. by small steamers, to site of Mokau coal mines.

Mokelumne Hill (mōkĕ'lŭmē, mōkŏ'–), village (pop. c.600), Calaveras co., central Calif., on Mokelumne R. and c.40 mi. NE of Stockton, in Mother Lode country. During gold rush, it was co. seat for a time and an important freighting point for the mines. Rail point is Valley Springs (10 mi. SW).

Mokelumne Peak (9,371 ft.), Amador co., E Calif., in the Sierra Nevada, 27 mi. S of L. Tahoe.

Mokelumne River, E central Calif., rises in the Sierra Nevada in S central Alpine co., flows 140 mi. SW, past Mokelumne Hill and Lodi, to San Joaquin R. 20 mi. NW of Stockton. Near Mokelumne Hill, Pardee Dam (358 ft. high, 1,337 ft. long; completed 1929) impounds Pardee Reservoir, which supplies water to cities on E shore of San Francisco Bay. On a headstream (North Fork), on Calaveras-Amador co. line, is Salt Springs Dam (328 ft. high, 1,260 ft. long; completed 1931; for power).

Mokena (mōkē'nŭ), village (pop. 903), Will co., NE Ill., 10 mi. E of Joliet, in agr. and bituminous-coal area; brewery.

Mokha, Yemen: see MOCHA.

Mokhotlong (mōkhō'tlông), village, ⊙ Mokhotlong dist. (pop. 36,765; with absent laborers 40,624), NE Basutoland, in mtn. region, 95 mi. E of Maseru.

Mokhovoye (mŭkhŭvoi'ŭ). **1** Village, Altai, Russian SFSR: see PARFENOVO. **2** Village (1939 pop. over 500), central Orel oblast, Russian SFSR, 19 mi. E of Orel; coarse grain.

Mokiang or **Mo-chiang** (both: mŭ'jyäng'), town, ⊙ Mokiang co. (pop. 45,415), S Yunnan prov., China, on road and 45 mi. NE of Ningerh; alt. 6,332 ft.; cotton textiles; timber, rice, millet, beans. Gold deposits. Until 1916, Talang.

Mokil (mō'kĕl'), atoll (pop. 449), Ponape dist., E Caroline Isls., W Pacific, 88 mi. E of Ponape; 2 mi. long, 1 mi. wide; 3 wooded islets. Formerly Duperry Isl.

Moknine (môknēn'), town (pop. 15,699), Sousse dist., E Tunisia, near Mediterranean coast, on railroad and 20 mi. SE of Sousse; olive-oil pressing, citrus-fruit growing; artisan industry (textiles, esparto products). Saltworks near by. Known until 19th cent. for its Byzantine-style jewelry.

Mokochung (mōkō'chōōng), village, Naga Hills dist., E Assam, India, 57 mi. NNE of Kohima; rice, cotton, oranges, potatoes.

Mokolo (mōkō'lō), village, Nord-Cameroun region, N Fr. Cameroons, near Br. Cameroons border, 40 mi. WNW of Maroua; stock raising; peanuts, millet. Has hosp., Protestant mission.

Mokotow (môkô'tōōf), Pol. *Mokotów*, residential suburb of Warsaw, Warszawa prov., E central Poland, 2 mi. S of city center. Site of airfield; before First World War, Rus. military training ground.

Mokpalin (mōk'pùlĭn), village, Thaton dist., Lower Burma, on left bank of Sittang R. estuary and 60 mi. NE of Rangoon, on Pegu-Martaban RR.

Mokpo (môk'pō'), Jap. *Moppo* (mōp'pō), city (1949 pop. 111,128), S.Cholla prov., SW Korea, port on Yellow Sea, 190 mi. SSW of Seoul; 34°47'N 126°23'E; commercial center for area producing rice and cotton. Rice refineries, cottonseed-oil and cotton-ginning factories, canneries, sake breweries, fish-processing plants. Exports rice, cotton, marine products, hides. Port was opened 1897 to foreign trade.

Mokra, peak, Yugoslavia: see JAKUPICA.

Mokran, Iran: see MAKRAN.

Mokra Planina (mô'krä plänē'nä), NE spur of North Albanian Alps, SW Yugoslavia, just N of Albanian line, bet. upper Ibar R. (N) and the Metohija (S). Lim R. flows at W foot. Highest peak, Zljeb or Zhlyeb, Serbo-Croatian *Žljeb* (7,813 ft.), is 6 mi. NNW of Pec, on Serbia-Montenegro border.

Mokraya Kaligorka (mô'krĭū kŭlyĕgôr'kŭ), village (1926 pop. 2,780), S Kiev oblast, Ukrainian SSR, 45 mi. ENE of Uman; metalworks.

Mokraya Olkhovka or **Mokraya Ol'khovka** (ŭlkhôf'kŭ), village (1926 pop. 4,295), N Stalingrad oblast, Russian SFSR, on railroad and 32 mi. NW of Kamyshin; wheat, sunflowers. Netkachi, village (1939 pop. over 500), 6 mi. N, has metalworks.

Mokrin (mô'krĭn), village (pop. 8,179), Vojvodina, NE Serbia, Yugoslavia, near Rum. border, 8 mi. NNW of Kikinda, in the Banat.

Mokronog (mô'krônôk), village, S Slovenia, Yugoslavia, on railroad and 10 mi. N of Novo Mesto. Until 1918, in Carniola.

Mokrous (mŭkrōōs'), village (1939 pop. over 500), S central Saratov oblast, Russian SFSR, on railroad and 32 mi. WSW of Yerskov; metalworks; wheat, cattle. Fedorovka, agr. village (1926 pop. 2,172), is 8 mi. N.

Mokrousovo (–ōō'sùvŭ), village (1939 pop. over 2,000), E Kurgan oblast, Russian SFSR, 37 mi. NNE of Lebyazhye; dairy plant, flour mill.

Mokrye Gory or **Mokryye Gory** (mô"krēŭ gô'rē) [Rus.,=wet mountains], highest central range of the Lesser Caucasus, athwart Georgian-Armenian SSR border; extends c.35 mi. S from upper Khram R. at Tsalka; rises to c.10,500 ft.

Mokshan (môk'shŭn), village (1926 pop. 9,858), N Penza oblast, Russian SFSR, on Moksha R. and 23 mi. NW of Penza; road center in grain and hemp area. Until c.1926, also called Mokshany.

Moksha River (môk'shŭ), E central European Russian SFSR, rises c.20 mi. WNW of Penza, flows WNW past Mokshan and Golitsino, N past Rybkino and Krasnoslobodsk, W past Purdoshki and Temnikov, SSW past Tengushevo and Kadom, and NNW to Oka R. 15 mi. W of Yermish; length, 430 mi. Seasonal (175 mi.) and regular (30 mi.) navigation in lower course (grain, lumber). Receives Tsna R. (left).

Mokuaweoweo (mōkōō'ùwä'ōwä'ō), volcanic crater, S central Hawaii, T.H., on summit of Mauna Loa; 2d largest active crater (□ 3.7, length 3.7 mi., width 1.7 mi.) in world; Kilauea is larger. Lava flow of 1880–81 was 50 mi. long.

Mol (môl), town (pop. 19,404), Antwerp prov., N Belgium, 12 mi. SE of Turnhout; electric-power station. Formerly spelled Moll.

Mol (môl), Hung. *Mohol* (mô'hôl), village (pop. 7,869), Vojvodina, N Serbia, Yugoslavia, on Tisa R. and 12 mi. S of Senta, in the Backa.

Mola, Cabo de la (kä'vō dhā lä mō'lä), headland, SW Majorca, Balearic Isls., 15 mi. W of Palma; 39°32'N 2°23'E.

Mola di Bari (mô'lä dē bä'rē), town (pop. 19,514), Bari prov., Apulia, S Italy, port on the Adriatic, 13 mi. ESE of Bari; tanneries, soap and button factories.

Mola di Gaeta, Italy: see FORMIA.

Molai, Greece: see MOLAOI.

Molakalmuru or **Molkalmuru** (mōlkäl'mōōrōō), town (pop. 3,746), Chitaldrug dist., N Mysore, India, 40 mi. NNE of Chitaldrug; hand-loom silk weaving, handicraft glass bangles. Asokan edicts of 3d cent. B.C. carved on rocks 7 mi. NNE, near village of Siddapura.

Molalla (mōlă'lù), city (pop. 1,497), Clackamas co., NW Oregon, 14 mi. S of Oregon City in fruit, grain, and dairying region; lumber milling.

Molango (mōläng'gō), town (pop. 1,539), Hidalgo, central Mexico, 45 mi. N of Pachuca; alt. 5,413 ft.; corn, wheat, beans, fruit, livestock.

Molaoi or **Molai** (both: môlä'ē), town (pop. 2,914), Laconia nome, SE Peloponnesus, Greece, 30 mi. SE of Sparta; livestock.

Molar, El (ĕl mōlär'), town (pop. 1,718), Madrid prov., central Spain, spa 22 mi. N of Madrid; grain- and winegrowing.

Molara Island (môlä'rä) (□ 1.5; pop. 12), off NE Sardinia, in Tyrrhenian Sea, in Sassari prov.; rises to 518 ft.

Molares, Los (lōs mōlä'rĕs), town (pop. 2,027), Seville prov., SW Spain, 21 mi. SE of Seville; olive industry. Anc. castle in vicinity.

Molassana (môläs-sä'nä), town (pop. 6,203), Genova prov., Liguria, N Italy, 4 mi. N of Genoa, within Greater Genoa.

Molat, Yugoslavia: see MULAT ISLAND.

Molcaxac (mōlkähäk'), town (pop. 773), Puebla, central Mexico, near Atoyac R., 29 mi. SW of Puebla; grain, maguey.

Molchanovo (mŭlchä'nùvŭ), village (1926 pop. 794), SE central Tomsk oblast, Russian SFSR, on Ob R., above Chulym R. mouth, and 90 mi. NW of Tomsk, in flax-growing area.

Mold, Welsh *Y Wyddgrug* (ù wŭdh'grĭg), urban district (1931 pop. 5,137; 1951 census 6,436), ⊙ Flintshire, Wales, on Alyn R. and 6 mi. S of Flint; coal mining. Has 15th-cent. church and remains of anc. castle, captured and reduced (1199) by Llewelyn ab Iorwerth. Just W is traditional battlefield of St. Germanus of Auxerre. Urban dist. includes coal-mining town of Broncoed (brŏnkoid') (pop. 907).

Moldau River, Czechoslovakia: see VLTAVA RIVER.

Moldautein, Czechoslovakia: see TYN NAD VLTAVOU

Moldava nad Bodvou (môl'dävä nädʹ bôdvō), Hung. *Szepsi* (sĕp'shē), town (pop. 2,241), S Slovakia, Czechoslovakia, on Bodva R. and 14 mi. SW of Kosice; rail junction.

Moldava River (mōldä'vù), Rum. *Moldova* (môldô'vä), Ger. *Moldau* (môl'dou), E Rumania, in Moldavia and Bukovina; rises on E slopes of the Moldavian Carpathians 45 mi. WSW of Radauti, flows E past Campulung and SE past Roman to Siret R. 14 mi. NW of Bacesti; c.110 mi. long.

Moldavia (mŏldā'vēŭ), Rum. *Moldova* (môldô'vä), historical province (□ 14,690; 1948 pop. 2,598,258), E Rumania, bounded E by Prut R. (Moldavian SSR border), separated in W from Transylvania by the Moldavian Carpathians. Borders N on Ukrainian SSR, S on Walachia. Its early ⊙ was Suceava (1388–1564); later it was Jassy. Drained by Seret R. and affluents. Continental climate. Fertile level plain and plateau make it the granary of Rumania. It produces 20% of grain crops, 50% of sugar beets, and 50% of sunflower seed used in edible-oil mfg. and as cattle feed. Orchards, vineyards, soya growing; stock raising (notably of wool-sheep). Extensively forested Moldavian Carpathians (Ceahlau rises to 6,245 ft.) contain some lignite, salt, and oil deposits. Lumbering for export, woodworking, and food processing are main industries; also a limited textile industry. Principal centers: Jassy, Galati, Bacau, Focsani. It was noted before Second World War for its large Jewish pop., still important in number of towns. Formerly part of the Roman prov. of Dacia, Moldavia was founded in 14th cent. as a principality which then included BUKOVINA and BESSARABIA. It reached its height under Stephen the Great, who temporarily routed the Turks at Rahovo (1475). Turkish domination began in 1504. A brief union (1594–1601) with Walachia and Transylvania was achieved under Michael the Brave. After unsuccessful attempts at liberation from Turkey through alliance with Russia, it fell under the domination of the Phanariots (1711) and was frequently occupied by Russia (18th–19th cent.). Bukovina was taken by Austria (1775) and Bessarabia annexed by Russia (1812). After Russo-Turkish War of 1828–29, Moldavia and Walachia were virtual protectorates of Russia, though politically still tied to Turkey. Emancipation of Moldavia and WALACHIA—the Danubian Principalities—by Congress of Paris (1856) led to final unification of Rumania (1861).

Moldavia or **Moldavian Soviet Socialist Republic** (mŏldā'vēŭ), Rus. *Moldaviya*, constituent republic (□ 13,000; 1947 pop. estimate 2,660,000) of SW European USSR; ⊙ KISHINEV. Occupies central portion of former Bessarabia; borders on Rumania along Prut R. (W), on the Ukraine (N, E, S). Mainly a fertile, black-earth lowland; includes treeless Beltsy Steppe (N; corn, wheat, sunflowers), wooded, podsolic Kodry hills (center; vineyards, orchards, Turkish tobacco), and dry, level Budzhak Steppe (S; grain, sheep raising). Clays, limestone, and building stone are chief mineral resources. Moderate continental climate; mean temp. 23°–26°F. (Jan.), 68°–72°F. (July); yearly precipitation, 18 in. (N), 12 in. (S). Pop. consists of Moldavians (65%; a Rum. language group), Russians, Ukrainians, Jews, Gypsies. Administratively, Moldavian SSR is divided (since 1947) into independent cities and *raions* (*rayons*). Industry (based largely on agr. production) includes canning (Tiraspol), wine making, distilling, flour milling, sugar refining, tobacco processing. Chief exports are grapes, wine, fruit, nuts, hides, wheat, canned goods. The main cities, Kishinev, Beltsy, Bendery, Tiraspol, are linked by railroads. The Dniester (E) is chief navigable river. History of the region before the formation (1940) of the republic is essentially that of BESSARABIA. When Rumania annexed all of Bessarabia in 1918, the USSR established (1924) Moldavian Autonomous SSR (□ 3,200; 1938 pop. estimate 600,000; ⊙ was Tiraspol after 1930) of the Ukraine out of Moldavian-minority dists. of Odessa and Podolia govts. on left bank of the Dniester. Following Soviet annexation (1940) of Bessarabia, Moldavian Autonomous SSR (except for predominantly Ukrainian dists., which remained in the Ukraine) joined central Bessarabia to form Moldavian SSR. During Second World War, held (1941–44) by Germans and Rumanians.

Moldavian Carpathians, Rumania: see CARPATHIAN MOUNTAINS.

Molde (môl'dù, môl'lù), city (pop. 3,774), More og Romsdal co., W Norway, on Molde Fjord (60-mi.-long inlet of North Sea), 30 mi. SW of Kristiansund; fishing port and rose-growing center. Has fish-curing and cold-storage plants; mfg. of marine engines, clothing. Tourist center with noted view over the Dovrefjell, near Romsdal Fjord. Founded in 15th cent.; rebuilt 1916 after destructive fire. In Second World War, it was briefly seat (April, 1940) of Norwegian govt.; heavily bombed by Germans.

Molde Fjord, inlet of North Sea, in More og Romsdal co., W Norway, extending c.10 mi. E from Molde, and branching into ROMSDAL FJORD (E), Fanne Fjord (NE; 16 mi. long), and Tres Fjord (S; 8 mi. long). Otteroy guards its mouth.

Moldes (môl'dĕs), town (pop. 4,079), S Córdoba prov., Argentina, 38 mi. SSW of Río Cuarto; cereals, flax, alfalfa; cattle raising, dairying. Sometimes called Coronel Moldes.

Moldgreen, England: see HUDDERSFIELD.

Moldova, province, Rumania: see MOLDAVIA.
Moldova, river, Rumania: see MOLDAVA RIVER.
Moldova-Noua (môldô'vä-nō'ŏŏ), Rum. *Moldova-Nouă*, Hung. *Újmoldova* (ōō'ēmôl'dôvŏ), village (pop. 3,412), Severin prov., SW Rumania, 22 mi. S of Oravita; noted wine production; flour milling, lumbering.
Moldova-Veche (–vä'kā), Hung. *Ómoldova* (ō'-môldôvŏ), village (pop. 2,012), Severin prov., SW Rumania, on the Danube (Yugoslav border) and 22 mi. S of Oravita; customs and shipping station; white-wine production, sericulture. Built on ruins of anc. Roman city.
Moldoveanu Peak or **Moldoveanul Peak**(môldô-vyä'nōō,–l), second highest peak (8,344 ft.) of Fagaras Mts., S central Rumania, 25 mi. NNW of Campulung.
Moldovita (môldô'vētsä), Rum. *Moldovița*, village (pop. 2,682), Suceava prov., N Rumania, in the Moldavian Carpathians, 9 mi. N of Campulung; rail terminus and lumbering center. Has 16th-cent. monastery with notable Byzantine frescoes, valuable religious collections.
Moldoy, Norway: see VAGSOY.
Molechunkamunk Lake, Maine: see RANGELEY LAKES.
Mole Creek, village (pop. 414), N central Tasmania, 40 mi. W of Launceston; dairying and agr. center; limestone caves.
Molegbwe (mōlĕg'bwā), village, Equator Prov., NW Belgian Congo, 15 mi. W of Banzyville, in cotton area; has Capuchin and Franciscan missions and mission schools, hosp. for Europeans. Seat of vicar apostolic of Congo-Ubangi dist.
Molena (mûlē'nů), city (pop. 307), Pike co., W central Ga., 13 mi. NW of Thomaston, near Flint R.; sawmilling.
Molenbeek-Saint-Jean (mō'lůnbāk-sē-zhã'), Flemish *Sint-Jans-Molenbeek* (sĭnt-yäns'-mō'lůbāk), W suburb (pop. 63,853) of Brussels, Brabant prov., central Belgium; mfg. (sugar, oleomargerine, leather, shoes, clothing, chemicals, tobacco, metal and wood products).
Molepolole (mōläpōlō'lä), town (pop. 14,805), ⊙ Kweneng dist., SE Bechuanaland Protectorate, 100 mi. N of Mafeking; road junction at edge of Kalahari Desert. Hq. of Bakwena tribe; hosp.
Môle River, England, rises in Sussex 3 mi. S of Horley, flows 30 mi. NW into Surrey, past Dorking, Leatherhead, Cobham, and Esher, to the Thames at East Molesey.
Môle-Saint-Nicolas (mōl-sē-nēkôlä'), coastal town (1950 census pop. 477), Nord-Ouest dept., NW Haiti, port on inlet of Windward Passage, 115 mi. NW of Port-au-Prince, near NW extremity of Hispaniola isl., where Columbus landed on Dec. 6, 1492. In agr. region (sisal, cotton, fruit). Has fine natural harbor. Iridium deposits near by.
Moléson (môlāzõ'), Alpine peak (6,581 ft.) in Fribourg canton, W Switzerland, 5 mi. SSW of Bulle.
Molfetta (môlfĕt'tä), city (pop. 48,898), Bari prov., Apulia, S Italy, port on the Adriatic, 15 mi. WNW of Bari. Mfg. center (macaroni, cement, soap, rope, pottery, electrical apparatus); shipbuilding, food canning. Exports wine, olive oil, almonds. Bishopric. Has Romanesque-Apulian cathedral (11th cent.).
Molholm (mûl'hôlm), Dan. *Mølholm*, town (pop. 1,404), Vejle amt, E Jutland, Denmark, 1 mi. S of Vejle.
Molière (môlyâr'), village, Alger dept., N central Algeria, in the Ouarsenis Massif, 25 mi. SE of Orléansville; zinc and lead mine; mineral springs.
Molières (môlyâr'), agr. village (pop. 442), Tarn-et-Garonne dept., SW France, 12 mi. N of Montauban; fruit.
Molières-sur-Cèze (–sür-sĕz'), village (pop. 1,897), Gard dept., S France, on the Cèze and 10 mi. NNE of Alès; coal mines, limekilns.
Molina (mōlē'nä), town (pop. 5,117), ⊙ Lontué dept. (□ 708; pop. 33,508), Talca prov., central Chile, on railroad and 31 mi. NE of Talca; agr. center (wine, wheat, flax). Tobacco factories. Lumbering. Known for its wines.
Molina. 1 or **Molina de Aragón** (dhā ärägōn'), city (pop. 2,634), Guadalajara prov., central Spain, in New Castile, at foot of a ridge, on affluent of the Tagus and 50 mi. NW of Teruel; alt. c.3,450 ft. Historic city surrounded by pine forests. It is considered coldest city in all Spain. Region produces wheat, potatoes, livestock; apiculture. Lumbering; flour milling, mfg. of woolen goods and plaster. Some silver is mined. Besides remains of an old castle, it has a superb alcazar, Aragon tower, and pantheon of Molina family. Has religious col. **2** or **Molina de Segura** (sāgōō'rä), town (pop. 7,-536), Murcia prov., SE Spain, on Segura R. and 6 mi. NW of Murcia; pepper processing and shipping, fruit and vegetable canning, flour- and sawmilling; mfg. of furniture, footwear, esparto rope, citrus-fruit extracts. Agr. trade (truck produce, saffron, olive oil, livestock); sericulture. Mineral springs. Limestone and gypsum quarries near by.
Molina, Parameras de (pärämä'räs dhā), high tableland of the Cordillera IBÉRICA, Guadalajara prov., central Spain, on E edge of central plateau (Meseta), just E of Molina. Extends c.30 mi. WNW from Teruel prov. border; rises to 4,980 ft.
Molina de Aragón, Spain: see MOLINA, Guadalajara prov.
Molina Pass (12,500 ft.), in the Andes, on Argentina-Chile border, 20 mi. SW of Maipo Volcano, on road bet. San Rafael (Argentina) and Rancagua (Chile); 34°24'S 70°3'W.
Molinara (mōlēnä'rä), village (pop. 2,152), Benevento prov., Campania, S Italy, 13 mi. NE of Benevento.
Moline (mōlēn'). **1** City (pop. 37,397), Rock Island co., NW Ill., on the Mississippi (bridged; power dam) at mouth of Rock R., adjacent to ROCK ISLAND and East Moline and opposite DAVENPORT (Iowa); the 4 cities form the closely knit Quad-Cities group, linked together by several bridges. Sometimes called the "Plow City," Moline has a huge farm-equipment and -machinery industry (shared with Rock Island), brought here in 1847 by John Deere. Large U.S. arsenal is near by, on Rock Isl. in the Mississippi. Rail, air, river, and highway transportation and trade center; railroad shops. Mfg. of wagons, furniture, air-conditioning equipment, clothing, paint; wood, metal, and rubber products; scales, machinery and tools, elevators, sporting goods, electric appliances. Seat of Moline Community Col. Black Hawk State Park is near by. Platted 1843; inc. as town in 1848, as city in 1872. First a river port and lumber-milling center, it grew into an equipment-mfg. center after the post-Civil War decline in steamboating and log-rafting on the Mississippi. **2** City (pop. 871), Elk co., SE Kansas, 38 mi. ENE of Winfield; shipping point in cattle and grain region; rock crushing; dairying.
Moline Acres, town (pop. 99), St. Louis co., E Mo.
Molinella (môlēnĕl'lä), town (pop. 2,129), Bologna prov., Emilia-Romagna, N central Italy, near Reno R., 15 mi. S of Ferrara; beet-sugar refinery.
Molinges (môlĕzh'), village (pop. 347), Jura dept., E France, on the Bienne and 5 mi. SW of Saint-Claude; sawmilling and wood turning, marble quarrying.
Molini, Cape (môlē'nē), point on E coast of Sicily, at N end of Gulf of Catania; 37°34'N 15°11'E.
Molino (mûlē'nō), village (pop. c.450), Escambia co., NW Fla., 22 mi. NNW of Pensacola; agr.-produce shipping point, with brickworks and clay pits.
Molino, El, Mexico: see VISTA HERMOSA DE NEGRETE.
Molino del Rey (mōlē'nō dĕl rā'), group of massive stone bldgs. SW of Mexico city, Mexico, just W of CHAPULTEPEC. Scene (Sept. 8, 1847) of battle in Mexican War in which U.S. forces were victorious.
Molinopampa (mōlēnōpäm'pä), town (pop. 410), Amazonas dept., N Peru, in E Andean foothills, on Chachapoyas-Moyobamba trail, and 16 mi. E of Chachapoyas; sugar growing; coal deposits.
Molinos (mōlē'nōs), town (pop. estimate 500), ⊙ Molinos dept. (□ 1,060; 1947 pop. 4,677), S Salta prov., Argentina, in Calchaquí valley, 70 mi. SW of Salta; alfalfa, wheat, wine, livestock.
Molinos, Los (lōs). **1** Town (pop. 754), Madrid prov., central Spain, summer resort in the Sierra de Guadarrama, 30 mi. NW of Madrid; cereals, potatoes, livestock. Stone quarries. **2** Town, Murcia prov., Spain: see PERAL.
Molíns de Rey (mōlēns' dhā rā'), town (pop. 6,395), Barcelona prov., NE Spain, in Catalonia, on Llobregat R. and 9 mi. WNW of Barcelona, in wine-growing area. Mfg. of cement, insecticides, tiles, flour products; sawmilling, canning. Truck farming. River spanned by 15-arch bridge.
Moliro (mōlē'rō), village, Katanga prov., SE Belgian Congo, on SW shore of L. Tanganyika, on Northern Rhodesia border, 185 mi. SE of Albertville; terminus of lake navigation; customs station.
Molise, Italy: see ABRUZZI E MOLISE.
Moliterno (môlētĕr'nô), town (pop. 4,609), Potenza prov., Basilicata, S Italy, 28 mi. S of Potenza; wine, cheese.
Mölk, Austria: see MELK.
Molkalmuru, India: see MOLAKALMURU.
Molkom (môl'kôm"), village (pop. 1,090), Varmland co., W Sweden, bet. 2 small lakes, 17 mi. NNE of Karstad; sawmilling, woodworking, concrete mfg.
Moll, Belgium: see MOL.
Molla-Kara, Turkmen SSR: see DZHEBEL.
Mollaro (môl-lä'rô), village (pop. 156), Trento prov., Trentino–Alto Adige, N Italy, near Noce R., 19 mi. SW of Bolzano. Produces chemical products (solvents, pharmaceuticals), asphalt, bitumen. Bituminous schist mine near by.
Molle (mû'lů), Swedish *Mölle*, fishing village (pop. 561), Malmohus co., SW Sweden, on W shore of Kullen peninsula, on the Kattegat, 18 mi. NNW of Halsingborg; seaside resort.
Mollendo (mōyĕn'dō), city (pop. 12,628), ⊙ Islay prov. (□ 2,432; pop. 25,691), Arequipa dept., S Peru, port on the Pacific, on Pan American Highway and 50 mi. SW of Arequipa; 17°2'S 72°1'W. Rail terminus; fishing, trading, and processing center, situated in irrigation area (rice, sugar, cotton, grain, fruit). Industries include textile and flour mills, bottling plant, shoe and furniture factories, fish canneries, liquor distilleries. Airport. Its main export is alpaca wool. Once the second port of the country and leading entrepôt for S Peru and Bolivia, it is now, because of its lack of natural protection (its artificial harbor, created 1871, is open to the sea), replaced by Matarani (mätärä'nē), 7 mi. NW, with installations completed 1941.
Mollepata (mōyäpä'tä), town (pop. 1,011), Cuzco dept., S central Peru, 40 mi. W of Cuzco; grain, sugar cane, potatoes.
Moller, Port (mō'lůr), bay (20 mi. long, 10 mi. wide at mouth), SW Alaska, on Alaska Peninsula, on Bristol Bay; 60°N 160°26'W. Port Moller village is on N shore.
Mollerusa (môlyärōō'sä), village (pop. 3,290), Lérida prov., NE Spain, 14 mi. E of Lérida; chief center of irrigated Urgel plain (cereals, wine, almonds, cherries); olive-oil processing; mfg. of soda water, soap.
Molles, Uruguay: see CARLOS REYLES.
Molles, Los, Argentina: see LOS MOLLES.
Mollet (môlyĕt'), town (pop. 5,982), Barcelona prov., NE Spain, 12 mi. NNE of Barcelona; cotton and silk milling and dyeing, brandy mfg. Wine, livestock, cereals, potatoes in area.
Molleturo (môyätōō'rō), village, Azuay prov., S central Ecuador, in the Andes, 31 mi. WNW of Cuenca; alt. 8,389 ft.; silver deposits; sheep grazing.
Molliens-Vidame (môlyē'-vēdäm'), agr. village (pop. 594), Somme dept., N France, 12 mi. W of Amiens.
Mollina (môlyē'nä), town (pop. 4,145), Málaga prov., S Spain, at S foot of the Sierra de Yeguas, 30 mi. NNW of Málaga; agr. center (olives, cereals, livestock). Olive-oil pressing, flour milling.
Mollis (mô'lĭs), town (pop. 2,074), Glarus canton, E central Switzerland, on Linth R., at upper end of Escher Canal, opposite Näfels; cotton textiles, knit goods.
Molln (môln), town (pop. 3,315), SE Upper Austria, 13 mi. SSW of Steyr, in the Sengsengebirge; knives, metal products.
Mölln (mûln), town (pop. 12,907), in Schleswig-Holstein, NW Germany, harbor on Elbe-Trave Canal, and 16 mi. S of Lübeck, situated bet. 2 small lakes; foundry; mfg. of chemicals, textiles, furniture, mattresses, chewing tobacco; food processing. Has 13th-cent. church, 14th-cent. town hall. First mentioned 1188. Chartered c.1220. According to legend, Till Eulenspiegel died here.
Mollosund (môl"ů"sůnd'), Swedish *Mollösund*, fishing village (pop. 516), Goteborg och Bohus co., SW Sweden, on SW coast of Orust isl., on the Skagerrak, 14 mi. S of Lysekil; fish-salting and canning plants.
Möll River (mûl), in Carinthia, S Austria, rises in PASTERZE glacier, flows 50 mi. S and E, past Heiligenblut and Obervellach (hydroelectric station), to the Drau 6 mi. W of Spittal.
Molltorp (mûl'tôrp"), Swedish *Mölltorp*, village (pop. 541), Skaraborg co., S Sweden, at S end of L. Bott, Swedish *Bottensjön* (bô'tůn-shûn") (5 mi. long, 2 mi. wide), on Gota Canal route, 20 mi. W of Motala; woodworking. Has medieval church.
Mollwitz (môl'vĭts) or **Malujowice** (mäwōōyôvē'tsĕ), Pol. *Małujowice*, village in Lower Silesia, after 1945 in Opole prov., SW Poland, 5 mi. W of Brieg (Brzeg). In War of the Austrian Succession, Austrians were defeated here (April, 1741) by Prussians under Frederick the Great. The battle was important in military history as it demonstrated the superiority of modern infantry over cavalry.
Molndal (mûln'däl"), Swedish *Mölndal*, city (1950 pop. 20,857), Goteborg och Bohus co., SW Sweden, 3 mi. SE of Goteborg; rail junction; textile, paper milling, metalworking, margarine mfg. Inc. 1922. Near by is Gunnebo, noted 18th-cent. manor house.
Molnlycke (mûln'lü"ků), Swedish *Mölnlycke*, village (pop. 1,889), Goteborg och Bohus co., SW Sweden, 6 mi. SE of Goteborg; cotton milling.
Molo (mō'lō), village, Rift Valley prov., W Kenya, in picturesque highlands forming W rim of Great Rift Valley, on railroad and 20 mi. W of Nakuru; alt. 8,064 ft.; coffee, tea, wheat, corn; dairying.
Molo (mō'lō), town, Eastern Prov., SE Uganda, near railroad, 10 mi. N of Tororo; cotton, corn, millet, sweet potatoes. Busumbu apatite is shipped by rail via Magodes station, 1 mi. W.
Molo, Gulf of, inlet of Ionian Sea in E Ithaca isl., Greece, penetrates deeply into isl., almost dividing it into 2 parts; 3 mi. long, 2 mi. wide; fisheries. Town of Ithaca on SE shore.
Moloacán (mōlwäkän'), town (pop. 742), Veracruz, SE Mexico, on Isthmus of Tehuantepec, 13 mi. E of Minatitlán; fruit. Petroleum wells near by.
Moloch, Mount (mō'lŏk) (10,195 ft.), SE B.C., in Selkirk Mts., near Glacier Natl. Park, 26 mi. NNW of Revelstoke; 51°20'N 117°56'W.
Molochansk (mŭlůchänsk'), city (1948 pop. over 10,000), central Zaporozhe oblast, Ukrainian SSR, on Molochnaya R. and 6 mi. SW of Bolshoi Tokmak; railroad shops; metalworks; flour milling, tanning. Developed in 1930s.
Molochnaya River (mŭlôch'nīů), Zaporozhe oblast, Ukrainian SSR, rises in Azov Upland, flows W past Bolshoi Tokmak and Molochansk, and S past Melitopol, to Molochny Liman, W inlet of Sea of Azov; c.80 mi. long.
Molochnoye (–nŭyů), town (1939 pop. over 500), S Vologda oblast, Russian SFSR, 10 mi. NW of Vologda, in dairy area; milk canning.

Molodechno (mŭlŭdyĕch'nŭ), oblast (□ 5,700; 1946 pop. estimate 700,000), NW Belorussian SSR; ⊙ Molodechno. In heavily forested upper Viliya R. valley. Humid continental climate (short summers). Agr. (flax, rye, oats, barley, potatoes), fruit gardens (Volozhin, Vileika); livestock. Extensive fisheries in Naroch, Svir, and Myadel lakes. Industries based on agr. (flour and linen milling, distilling, tanning, brewing) and timber (sawmilling, lumbering, wood distilling); concrete-block (Volozhin, Radoshkovichi) and brick mfg. Light industries and handicrafts in main centers (Molodechno, Oshmyany, Vileika, Volozhin, Smorgon). Formed 1939 out of Pol. Wilno and Nowogrodek provs., following Soviet occupation of E Poland. Held by Germany (1941–44); called Vileika oblast until 1944, when administrative seat was transferred from Vileika to Molodechno.

Molodechno, Pol. *Molodeczno* (môlôdĕch'nô), city (1931 pop. 5,964), ⊙ Molodechno oblast, W Belorussian SSR, 40 mi. NW of Minsk; 54°19'N 26°53'E. Rail junction; agr. center (grain, flax); flour milling, fruit preserving, mfg. of musical instruments. Has old palace. Passed (1793) from Poland to Russia; reverted (1921) to Poland; ceded to USSR in 1945.

Molo di Girgenti, Sicily: see PORTO EMPEDOCLE.

Molodoi Tud or **Molodoy Tud** (mŭlŭdoi' tōōt"), village (1926 pop. 541), SW Kalinin oblast, Russian SFSR, 28 mi. WNW of Rzhev; flax processing.

Mologa (mŭlô'gŭ), former city, Yaroslavl oblast, Russian SFSR, on Volga R., at mouth of the Mologa, and 17 mi. NW of Shcherbakov. Pop. evacuated (1940) and city flooded by filling of RYBINSK RESERVOIR.

Mologa River, W European Russian SFSR, rises in hills W of Bezhetsk, flows E, past Bezhetsk, W, N, past Pestovo (head of navigation), and generally W, past Ustyuzhna, to Rybinsk Reservoir N of Vesyegonsk; c.200 mi. long. Receives Chagodoshcha R. (left), a section of Tikhvin canal system.

Molokai (mō'lōkī'), island (□ 259; pop. 4,939), T.H., c.8 mi. W of Maui across Pailolo Channel, c.23 mi. E of Oahu across Kaiwi Channel; 21°8'N 157°W; 37 mi. long, 10 mi. wide. Mountainous, with Mt. Kamakou (4,958 ft.) highest peak. Kaunakakai is chief port; KALAUPAPA leper settlement (Kalawao co.) is on N coast. Landholding by native Hawaiians encouraged by Hawaiian Homestead Settlement. Cattle ranches, pineapple plantations here.

Molokini (mō'lōkē'nē), island, T.H., bet. Maui and Kahoolawe isls., in Alalakeiki Channel; barren, rocky; lighthouse.

Molokovo (mô'lŭkŭvŭ), village (1926 pop. 1,027), NE Kalinin oblast, Russian SFSR, near Mologa R., 28 mi. N of Bezhetsk; flax.

Molong (mō'lŏng), municipality (pop. 1,662), E central New South Wales, Australia, 145 mi. WNW of Sydney; rail junction; copper-mining center.

Molopo River (mōlō'pō), Cape Prov., U. of So. Afr., and Bechuanaland Protectorate, rises E of Mafeking, flows in a winding course generally W, past Mafeking, then forms border bet. Cape Prov. and Bechuanaland Protectorate, to Orange R. 70 mi. W of Upington; c.600 mi. long.

Molotov (mŏ'lŭtŏf, Rus. mô'lŭtŭf), oblast (□ 65,950; 1946 pop. estimate 2,250,000) in E European Russian SFSR; ⊙ Molotov. Includes Komi-Permyak Natl. Okrug (NW). In middle Kama R. valley and W foothills of the central and N Urals. Humid continental climate (short summers; severe winters in N part). Major mining region: potash (Solikamsk-Berezniki dist.; leading in USSR), bituminous coal (Kizel basin; leading in Urals), petroleum (Krasnokamsk, Verkhne-Chusovskiye Gorodki), magnesium and common salts (Solikamsk-Berezniki dist.), chromite (Sarany, Biser), gold (NE), iron, gypsum, limestone, and peat. Unexploited hematite, magnetite, titanium, and vanadium deposits in the N Urals (upper Vishera R. valley). Rye, oats, flax, potatoes (SW, S), wheat (S), clover (SE); livestock. Heavily forested (N, E). Industry based on steel and pig-iron production (Molotov, Chusovoi, Lysva, Nytva, Chermoz, Pashiya, Maikor, Dobryanka) and chemical processing (coke in Gubakha, fertilizers and aniline dyes in Berezniki, superphosphate in Molotov). Timber and pulpwood utilization: shipbuilding (Zaozerye, Borovsk), building materials (Molotov), paper and cellulose mfg. (Krasnovishersk, Krasnokamsk, Solikamsk, Severny Kommunar). Machine mfg. (Molotov, Yugo-Kamski, Ocher), oil cracking (Verkhne-Chusovskiye Gorodki, Krasnokamsk), leather mfg. (Kungur), agr. processing. Lumbering and hunting in N taiga. Main urban centers: Molotov, Berezniki, Solikamsk, Chusovoi. Served by navigable Kama, Chusovaya, and Vishera rivers, and by Kirov-Sverdlovsk and Solikamsk-Molotov RRs. Formed 1938 out of W Sverdlovsk oblast. Until 1940, called Perm oblast.

Molotov, city (1939 pop. 255,196; 1946 pop. estimate 450,000), ⊙ Molotov oblast, Russian SFSR, on left bank of Kama R. and 700 mi. ENE of Moscow; 58°N 56°17'E. Major transportation center; extensive waterfront with passenger and freight-loading accommodations; rail stations of Perm I (city center) and Perm II (junction 3 mi. WSW of Perm I) with locomotive and car repair shops; airport. Industrial center, based on local metallurgy (largely pig iron) and timber floated down Kama R.; machine mfg. (equipment for metal, coal, petroleum, lumber, and peat industries; harbor cranes, excavators, aircraft and tractor parts, telephone apparatus, milk separators, gramophones); mfg. of superphosphate, pyrite and sulphur chemicals, building materials; woodworking, agr. processing. State univ. (established 1916), medical, stomatological, pharmaceutical, teachers, and agr. colleges. Has art gall., museums, opera house, theaters, monuments, and old churches. City center (original site of former Perm) is bounded by small Yegoshikha and Danilikha rivers. Industrial establishments extend along left Kama R. bank, through former Molotovo (2 mi. NE of Perm I; until c.1930, Motovilikha) and Kislotny (6 mi. NE of Perm I; chemical works), to port of Levshino at Chusovaya R. mouth (N city limit, 9 mi. NNE of Perm I; mfg. of prefabricated houses, cardboard, metalware, foodstuffs). Within city limits, on right Kama R. bank, are former health resort of Zakamsk (8 mi. WNW of Perm I) and site of projected hydroelectric plant and dam with planned reservoir of □ c.600, at mouth of Gaiva R. (7 mi. NNE of Perm I). Known in 17th cent. as Rus. settlement of Yegoshikha; developed after building of copper works in 1724. Chartered and renamed Perm (⊙ Perm govt.) in 1781. Industrialization and commercialization in 19th cent. largely attributed to opening of Kama R. navigation (1856) and building of railroad (1878). Major development began after First World War. Perm (1926 pop. 84,815) merged with Molotovo (1933 pop. estimate 68,900) in 1938; renamed Molotov in 1940. During Second World War, Molotov absorbed Levshino (1939 pop. over 10,000) and Zakamsk (1939 pop. 18,000), and was placed (1943) under direct jurisdiction of Russian SFSR. The Permian geological period, reaching its greatest extent here, is named for Perm.

Molotov, SW district of Greater Baku, Azerbaijan SSR, at base of Apsheron Peninsula, SW of Baku, on Caspian Sea. Oil fields, developed in 1930s.

Molotov, Cape, northernmost point of Komsomolets Isl., Severnaya Zemlya archipelago, Krasnoyarsk Territory, Russian SFSR; 81°15'N 95°50'E. Govt. observation post.

Molotova, Imeni, Uzbek SSR: see MOLOTOVO, Fergana oblast.

Molotova, Imeni V. M. (ē'mĭnyē mô'lŭtŭvŭ), town (1939 pop. over 500), W Gorki oblast, Russian SFSR, on Volga R. and 6 mi. SE of Bor; shipyards.

Molotovabad (mŭ"lŭtŭvŭbät'). **1** Village (1939 pop. over 2,000), N Osh oblast, Kirghiz SSR, in Fergana Valley, 4 mi. SW of Kizyl-Kiya; cotton. Until 1938, Uch-Kurgan. **2** Village (1939 pop. under 500), S Stalinabad oblast, Tadzhik SSR, 35 mi. S of Kurgan-Tyube (linked by narrow-gauge railroad); long-staple cotton; karakul sheep. Developed in 1930s.

Molotovo (mô'lŭtŭvŭ). **1** Town (1946 pop. 3,000), S Georgian SSR, on Khram R. and 35 mi. WSW of Tiflis, just S of Tsalka; site of Khram hydroelectric station (*Khramges*). **2** Village, Molotov oblast, Russian SFSR: see MOLOTOV, city. **3** Village (1948 pop. over 2,000), SE Omsk oblast, Russian SFSR, on Irtysh R. and 50 mi. SE of Omsk, in agr. area. Formerly Izylbash. **4** Village (1926 pop. 4,166), NW Voronezh oblast, Russian SFSR, 20 mi. SSE of Lipetsk; metalworks; grain, tobacco Until 1948, called Dryazgi. **5** Village (1939 pop. over 500), NW Fergana oblast, Uzbek SSR, 4 mi. E of Kokand; cotton; sericulture. Formerly Uch-Kupryuk and later (1937–c.1940), Imeni Molotova.

Molotovsk (mô'lŭtŭfsk). **1** Town (1945 pop. over 500), W Frunze oblast, Kirghiz SSR, in Chu valley, on railroad (Kainda station), just N of Panfilovskoye and 45 mi. W of Frunze; beet-sugar refinery. Called Kainda until c.1945. **2** City (1939 pop. over 10,000), NW Archangel oblast, Russian SFSR, lumber port on Dvina Bay, 20 mi. W of Archangel (connected by rail spur); shipbuilding center; pulp mill. Became city in 1938; formerly called Sudostroi. **3** City (1926 pop. 5,517), S Kirov oblast, Russian SFSR, 70 mi. S of Kirov; felt-boot mfg. center. Chartered 1780; until 1940, Nolinsk.

Molotovskoye (môl'ŭtŭfskŭyŭ), village (1926 pop. 13,699), NW Stavropol Territory, Russian SFSR, on Yegorlyk R. and 60 mi. NNW of Stavropol, in agr. area (wheat, sunflowers, castor beans); distilling, dairying; flour mill, metalworks. Originally known as Medvezhye; later (1936–39) called Yevdokimovskoye.

Moloundou (mōlōōn'dōō), village, Lom et Kadéï region, SE Fr. Cameroons, on N'Goko R. (Fr. Equatorial Africa border) and 180 mi. SSE of Batouri; center of trade; head of navigation on the N'Goko. Occupied 1914. by Belg. colonial troops.

Mols (môls), peninsula, E Jutland, Denmark, extending SW from Djursland peninsula, bet. Kalvo (sometimes called Kalo) Bay (W) and Aebeltoft Bay (E); c.8 mi. long, 4 mi. wide. Mols (or Agri) Hills (highest point, 55 ft.) in center. Helgenaes (hĕl'gŭnĕs) peninsula (S extension; 5 mi. long) forms Begtrup Bay bet. it and S Mols.

Molsheim (môlzĕm', Ger. môls'hīm), town (pop. 3,513), Bas-Rhin dept., E France, near E foot of the Vosges, on the Bruche and 12 mi. WSW of Strasbourg, in winegrowing area; rail junction; automobile-mfg. center. Has remains of medieval fortifications.

Molson (mōl'sŭn), town (1940 pop. 81), Okanogan co., N Wash., near British Columbia line, 11 mi. ENE of Oroville.

Molson Lake (mōl'sŭn) (27 mi. long, 12 mi. wide), central Man., 50 mi. NE of L. Winnipeg; drains N into Hayes R.

Moltai Lake or **Moltay Lake** (mŭltī') (□ c.1), in central Sverdlovsk oblast, Russian SFSR, 16 mi. NNE of Rezh, near Rezh R.; health resort (mud baths) developed in late 1940s.

Molteno (mōltē'nō), town (pop. 3,303), E Cape Prov., U. of So. Afr., in Stormberg range, 45 mi. NW of Queenstown; rail junction; agr. center (stock, grain); sawmilling, coal mining (formerly major industry). Airfield.

Möltenort, Germany: see HEIKENDORF.

Molucca Passage (mōlŭ'kŭ), wide channel, in Indonesia, connecting Molucca Sea (SW) and Ceram Sea (SE) with the Pacific, bet. Celebes (W) and Halmahera (E); c.150 mi. wide. A large W arm (Gulf of Tomini) indents E coast of Celebes.

Moluccas (mōlŭ'kŭz), Indonesian *Maluku* (mŭlōō'kōō), Du. *Molukken* (môlōō'kŭn), large island group (□ 33,315; pop. 525,580) and province of INDONESIA, comprising E part of Malay Archipelago, bet. Celebes (W) and New Guinea (E), in Molucca, Banda, Ceram, and Arafura seas; 2°38'N–8°12'S 124°20'–134°50'E. Comprises 2 groups, North Moluccas and South Moluccas. Isls. of N group (extending N–S) are MOROTAI, HALMAHERA (largest of Moluccas), TERNATE, TIDORE, MAKIAN, BACHAN, OBI ISLANDS, and SULA ISLANDS; isls. of S group (roughly forming a semicircle) are BURU, CERAM, AMBOINA, BANDA ISLANDS, KAI ISLANDS, ARU ISLANDS, TANIMBAR ISLANDS, BABAR ISLANDS, KISAR, and WETAR. Larger isls. are volcanic and mountainous; others are of coral formation and generally low. Rainfall of area is influenced by monsoon winds. Agr. (sago, coconuts, spices), fishing, lumbering. Chief exports: copra, forest products, fish, spices. Natives in interior represent transitional types bet. Malayan and Papuan; in coastal areas are the Javanese and other Malayan groups. The 1st Moluccan state was formed in 12th cent. with emergence of kingdom of Ternate. In 15th cent. Islam was introduced and widely accepted; during this period Chinese and Arab traders arrived, giving impetus to spice trade. When the Portuguese came in early 16th cent., they found the Moluccas under the rule of the rival sultans of Ternate and Tidore. The Spaniards soon began to compete, but rivalry was ended in 1580 when the Sp. king became ruler of Portugal also. Portuguese influence (maintained largely by Catholic missionaries) in the area lasted for most of the 16th cent. Arriving in 1599, the Dutch established scattered settlements. The Spaniards withdrew from area in 1663. The Du. conquest of Moluccas was completed 1667 when sultan of Tidore recognized Du. sovereignty. With decline of spice trade in late 17th cent., the area lost much of its economic importance. Group was under Br. rule 1796–1802, 1810–17. In Second World War, the group was seized in 1942 by the Japanese. After the war, the Moluccas were included in the temporary autonomous state of East Indonesia. The South Moluccas, led by Amboina, revolted (1950) against Indonesia. Formerly Spice Islands.

Molucca Sea, part of the Pacific, in Indonesia, bet. Celebes (W) and Buru (E), merges with Ceram and Banda seas (E), Flores Sea (SW), and Molucca Passage (N). Contains Sula Isls.

Molunkus Lake (mŭlŭng'kŭs), Aroostook co., E central Maine, 20 mi. E of Millinocket; 3 mi. long. Drains into **Molunkus Stream,** which rises to NW, flows c.35 mi. SE to Mattawamkeag R.

Molvitino, Russian SFSR: see SUSANINO.

Molvízar (mōlvē'thär), town (pop. 2,212), Granada prov., S Spain, 6 mi. NW of Motril; olive oil, wine, raisins, almonds.

Molvotitsy (mŭlvô'tyĭtsē), village (1926 pop. 630), S Novgorod oblast, Russian SFSR, 55 mi. SE of Staraya Russa; flax processing.

Molybdos, Greece: see METHYMNA.

Molyneux River, New Zealand: see CLUTHA RIVER.

Moma (mō'mä), village, Equator Prov., central Belgian Congo, on Tshuapa R. and 230 mi. SE of Boende; terminus of steam navigation and trading post in copal-gathering region.

Moma, village, Niassa prov., E Mozambique, on Mozambique Channel, 150 mi. SW of Mozambique city; salt panning; ships sisal, copra, peanuts.

Momauguin, Conn.: see EAST HAVEN.

Momauk (mō-mouk'), village, Bhamo dist., Kachin State, Upper Burma, 8 mi. E of Bhamo.

Momax (mōmäks'), town (pop. 1,180), Zacatecas, N central Mexico, 12 mi. NNW of Tlaltenango; grain, chick-peas, tobacco, alfalfa, livestock.

Mombaça (mōmbä'sŭ), city (pop. 1,307), central Ceará, Brazil, 22 mi. SW of Senador Pompeu; cattle; cotton, sugar. Until 1944, called Maria Pereira.

Mombach (môm'bäkh), NW suburb of Mainz, W Germany, on left bank of the Rhine.

Mombacho (mōmbä'chō), extinct volcano (4,472 ft.), SW Nicaragua, 6 mi. S of Granada, near NW shore of L. Nicaragua. Coffee is grown on its slopes.

Mombaruzzo (mômbärōō'tsô), village (pop. 1,541), Asti prov., Piedmont, NW Italy, 13 mi. SW of Alessandria.

Mombasa (mŏmbă'sü, mōmbä'sä), seaport city (pop. 84,746), ⊙ Coast Prov., SE Kenya, in coastal protectorate, 280 mi. SE of Nairobi, and 150 mi. N of Zanzibar, on Mombasa Isl. and surrounding mainland; 4°2'S 39°35'E. Kenya's chief port, with one of Africa's best harbors (Kilindini Harbor) on Indian Ocean. Railhead to rich agr. and stock-raising region of Kenya, NE Tanganyika, and Uganda. Commercial, shipping, and distributing center, exporting coffee, cotton, tea, sisal, pyrethrum, wattle bark, tin (from Uganda), soda, hides and skins, and elephant ivory. Modern brewery. Mombasa Isl. (□ 7; 3 mi. long, 2 mi. wide) is separated from enveloping mainland by old Mombasa harbor (E; native coastal trade), deep-water Kilindini Harbor (W; modern docking facilities, coal and oil depots developed in 1920s). Port Reitz airport is on mainland (NW). Old town of Mombasa (occupying isl.'s E section) has a strong Oriental flavor. The 16th-cent. Portuguese fort (now a prison) overlooking old harbor is well-preserved. There are Anglican and R.C. cathedrals, mosques, European and native hosps., Indian and African bazaars, and a Moslem univ. Mombasa Isl. is connected with mainland (N) by Makupa causeway (rail and road), which replaced former Salisbury Bridge c.1930. Originally a prosperous Arab and Persian settlement, Mombasa was visited by Vasco da Gama on his 1st voyage (1497) to India. Held by Portuguese in 16th–17th cent., until recaptured by Arabs (1698) after a long siege. Another brief Portuguese occupation ended with their expulsion (1729) by Arabs from Oman. Under Zanzibar rule 1830s–1880s. Was ⊙ Br. East Africa Protectorate 1888–1907. During Second World War, Kilindini became a Br. naval station. Non-native pop. (41,893) chiefly Indian, Arab.

Mombeltrán (mōmbĕlträn'), town (pop. 2,006), Ávila prov., central Spain, in the Sierra de Gredos, 31 mi. SW of Ávila, in fertile region (olives, grapes, fruit, chestnuts, potatoes, beans, livestock). Flour mill, potteries. Hydroelectric plant. Castle of dukes of Albuquerque near by.

Mombetsu (mōmbā'tsōō), town (pop. 17,863), N Hokkaido, Japan, on Sea of Okhotsk, 50 mi. WNW of Abashiri; mining center (gold, silver); fishing, agr.

Mombo (mōm'bō), town, Tanga prov., NE Tanganyika, on railroad and 6 mi. S of Lushoto, at SW foot of Usambara Mts.; sisal, cotton, livestock.

Momboyo River or **Momboyo-Luilaka River** (mōmbō'yo-lwēlä'kä), in central and W Belgian Congo. Rises as the Luilaka 50 mi. SW of Lomela, flows c.270 mi. NW and NNW, past Ikali and Monkoto, to a point 8 mi. upstream from Waka-sur-Momboyo, where it becomes the Momboyo and flows NW to join Busira R. at Ingende, forming the Ruki; total length, 315 mi. Momboyo-Luilaka is navigable for 170 mi. below Ikali.

Momchilgrad (mômchĕl'grät), city (pop. 3,150), Khaskovo dist., S Bulgaria, in E Rhodope Mts., near right branch of Arda R., 8 mi. S of Kirdzhali; agr. center (cotton), wool; tobacco processing. Linked with Komotine (Greece) via Makaz Pass road. Until 1934, Mastanli. Rail spur terminus Podkova (pop. 380) is 11 mi. S.

Momeik, Burma: see MONGMIT.

Momence (mōmĕns'), city (pop. 2,644), Kankakee co., NE Ill., on Kankakee R. (bridged here) and 10 mi. E of Kankakee, in agr. area; limestone quarries; mfg. (brick, food products, textiles). Platted 1844, inc. 1874.

Momignies (mōmēnyē'), town (pop. 2,113), Hainaut prov., S Belgium, 7 mi. W of Chimay, near Fr. border; glass industry (since 16th cent.); agr.

Momil (mōmēl'), town (pop. 2,461), Bolívar dept., N Colombia, in Caribbean lowlands, 9 mi. E of Lorica; rice, corn, sugar cane, fruit, livestock.

Mominabad (mō"mĭnäbäd'), town (pop., including Amba, 16,250), Bir dist., NW Hyderabad state, India, 45 mi. ESE of Bir; trades in agr. products (cotton, millet, wheat, oilseeds). Site of former cavalry cantonment.

Momina-banya (mômē'nä-bä'nyä), **1** Village (pop. 1,298), Sofia dist., W central Bulgaria, on left tributary of the Maritsa and 9 mi. SSE of Ikhtiman; health resort with radioactive springs; livestock, truck, fruit. Formerly Sulu-dervent. **2** Village, Plovdiv dist, S central Bulgaria: see KHISAR MOMINABANYA.

Momin-brod, Bulgaria: see LOM.

Momino (mômē'nô), village (pop. 3,016), Stalin dist., E Bulgaria, in woodland bet. Black Sea and Provadiya R., 13 mi. WSW of Stalin; lumbering. Ruins of 15th-cent. fortress near by (N). Formerly Avren.

Mömling River, Germany: see MÜMLING RIVER.

Momoishi (mōmō'ēshē), town (pop. 8,108), Aomori prefecture, N Honshu, Japan, 6 mi. NNW of Hachinohe; agr. (rice, potatoes), horse breeding.

Momostenango (mōmōstānäng'gō), town (1950 pop. 7,956), Totonicapán dept., W central Guatemala, on headstream of Chixoy R. and 11 mi. N of Totonicapán; alt. 7,546 ft. Wool and market center; corn, wheat, beans; sheep raising.

Momotombito (mōmōtōmbē'tō), volcano (2,549 ft.) and island in L. Managua, W Nicaragua, 19 mi. NW of Managua.

Momotombo (mōmōtōm'bō), volcano (4,128 ft.), W Nicaragua, on NW shore of L. Managua, 23 mi. E of León. Its 1609 eruption destroyed original city of LEÓN, situated at its W foot, on lake shore, at site of modern village and minor port of Momotombo. Other eruptions occurred in 1764, 1849, 1885, and 1905.

Mompog Pass (mōmpōg'), channel in Philippines, connecting Tayabas Bay of S Luzon with Sibuyan Sea, bet. Marinduque isl. (W) and Bondoc Peninsula (E); c.40 mi. long, 11 mi. wide.

Mompono (mōmpō'nō), village, Equator Prov., W Belgian Congo, on Maringa R. and 230 mi. E of Coquilhatville; palm products. Has R.C. and Baptist missions.

Mompós (mōmpōs'), town (pop. 6,694), Bolívar dept., N Colombia, river port on Margarita Isl., on the right arm of Magdalena R. (Brazo Seco de Mompós) and 125 mi. S of Barranquilla. Cattle-raising and tobacco-growing center reached by river boats from Barranquilla and Cartagena. Market for rich forest products (tagua and corozo nuts, etc.). Old colonial town, founded 1537. Its Pinillos Col. is renowned throughout Colombia. Since Sp. times it has been the site of impressive religious ceremonies during Holy Week. During War of Independence the town resisted a siege by royalist forces. Formerly sometimes spelled Mompox.

Mompós, Brazo Seco de, Colombia: see BRAZO SECO DE MOMPÓS.

Momungan (mōmōōng'gän), town (1939 pop. 2,358) in Baloi municipality, Lanao prov., W central Mindanao, Philippines, 15 mi. NW of Dansalan; rice, corn. Also spelled Mumungan.

Mon, canal and river, Burma: see MON RIVER.

Mon, Denmark: see MOEN.

Mon (mōn). **1** Village, Alvsborg co., SW Sweden, 20 mi. E of Stromstad; frontier station on Norwegian border, opposite Kornsjo. **2** Village (pop. 858), Kopparberg co., central Sweden, on West Dal R. and 65 mi. W of Falun; tanning.

Mona (mō'nü), Roman name of island sometimes identified either with Isle of MAN, England, or with Anglesey isl., Wales.

Mona, village and reservoir, St. Andrew parish, SE Jamaica, on small Hope R. and 4 mi. NE of Kingston. Construction of the reservoir, fed by Hope R., was begun during Second World War and is said to be the largest engineering work ever undertaken in the isl.; 673 acres were set aside here for the Jamaica Univ. Col.

Mona, island, Puerto Rico: see MONA ISLAND.

Mona, town (pop. 328), Juab co., central Utah, 8 mi. N of Nephi; alt. 4,917 ft. Mona Reservoir (5 mi. long, 1 mi. wide) is just N, formed by dam on small tributary of Utah L. Mt. Nebo (11,871 ft.) is E, in Wasatch Range.

Mona, Wales: see ANGLESEY.

Monaca (mŏ'nükü), borough (pop. 7,415), Beaver co., W Pa., on Ohio R., opposite mouth of Beaver R., and 22 mi. NW of Pittsburgh; glass, metal products, enamelware. Settled 1813, inc. 1839.

Monachil (mōnächēl'), village (pop. 1,380), Granada prov., S Spain, 5 mi. SE of Granada; olive-oil processing, flour milling. Hydroelectric power plant near by.

Monach Isles, Scotland: see HEISKER.

Monaco (mŭnä'kō, mŏ'nükō, Fr. mônäkō'), independent principality (c.370 acres; 1946 pop. 19,242) on the Mediterranean, an enclave within Alpes-Maritimes dept., SE France, 9 mi. ENE of Nice, near Ital. border. Surrounding a sheltered natural harbor, it consists of 3 adjoining sections, S-N: Monaco, the old ⊙, atop a rocky promontory; La CONDAMINE, the business dist.; and MONTE CARLO, the winter resort famous for its gambling casino. The principality is governed by Prince Rainier III (who succeeded his father, Prince Louis II, in 1949), by a cabinet of 3, and by a National Council, in accordance with the Constitution of 1911. It has a customs union with France, interchangeable currency; it prints its own postage stamps, has a radio transmitter and a natl. flag. Of its total pop. less than 2,000 are citizens of Monaco (Monégasques); these are not admitted to the gambling tables. Universal suffrage has existed since 1945. There is no income tax, the principality's chief source of revenue being Monte Carlo's casino. After the Vatican, Monaco is world's smallest sovereign state. Probably of Phoenician origin; Romans called it *Portus Herculis Monoeci.* Genoese built a fort here in 1215. Ruled by Genoese Grimaldi family since end of 13th cent. Annexed to France 1793–1814. Under Sardinian protection, 1815–1861. In 1848, Roquebrune and Menton, until then in Monaco, became free cities and joined France in 1860. By treaty of 1918, succession to the throne must be approved by French govt. Since mid-19th cent. the principality has attained great prosperity as a favorite resort area on French Riviera. In the capital (pop. 1,854), on rocky headland (over 200 ft. high) projecting c.½ mi. into the Mediterranean S of Monte Carlo, is 15th-16th-cent. palace, 19th-cent. cathedral, and noted oceanographical mus. founded 1910 by Prince Albert I.

Monadhliath Mountains (mō'nülē'ü), range in S Inverness, Scotland, extending 30 mi. E-W bet. Loch Ness and upper Spey valley. Highest peak is Carn Mairg or Carn Ban (3,087 ft.), 8 mi. W of Kingussie.

Monadnock, Mount, or **Grand Monadock** (mŭnăd'nŏk), solitary peak (3,165 ft.) in Cheshire co., SW N.H., NW of Jaffrey. A typical example of a hill (monadnock) of resistant rock surmounting the surrounding surface.

Monadnock Mountain, isolated peak (3,140 ft.), NE Vt., near the Connecticut, in Lemington town, opposite Colebrook, N.H.

Monagas (mōnä'gäs), state (□ 11,160; 1941 pop. 122,901; 1950 census 175,502), NE Venezuela; ⊙ Maturín. Bounded by Orinoco R. (SE), the Caño Mánamo (E), San Juan R. and Gulf of Paria (NE). Apart from coastal range (N), it consists of llanos and low tablelands, with marshes in Orinoco R. delta area. Climate is tropical, with rains in some parts all year round. Mineral resources include petroleum (wells at Quiriquire, Jusepín, Santa Bárbara, and Temblador fields), coal (Santa Bárbara), zinc and cadmium (Chaguaramal), asphalt, sulphur, marble, and salt deposits. Predominantly a cattle-raising region. N uplands grow coffee, tobacco, sugar cane, cacao, cotton, yuca, corn. Its vast forests abound in a variety of hardwood and palm trees. Maturín is its trading center. Caripito has oil-refining plant.

Monaghan (mŏ'nügün), Gaelic *Mhuineachain,* county (□ 498.4; pop. 57,215), Ulster, Ireland; ⊙ Monaghan. Bounded by cos. Cavan (S), Fermanagh (NW), Tyrone (N), Armagh and Louth (E), and Meath (SE). Drained by Fane and Blackwater rivers and affluents of Erne R.; served by Ulster Canal. Surface is undulating or hilly, partly boggy. There are several lakes; Lough Muckno, largest. Limestone and sandstone are quarried. Growing of flax, oats, and potatoes important. Industries include linen milling, flax scutching, mfg. of shoes, potato alcohol, clothing. Besides Monaghan, other towns are Clones, Carrickmacross, Castleblayney, and Ballybay. There are anc. round towers, raths, Danish forts; 6th-cent. abbey at Clones.

Monaghan, Gaelic *Muineachán,* urban district (pop. 4,676), ⊙ Co. Monaghan, Ireland, in N part of co., on the Ulster Canal and 70 mi. NNW of Dublin; agr. market (flax, oats, potatoes); bacon and ham curing; mfg. of leather goods, shoes, furniture. Has R.C. cathedral.

Monagrillo (mōnägrē'yō), village (pop. 1,372), Herrera prov., S central Panama, in Pacific lowland, 1 mi. N of Chitré; corn, rice, beans, livestock.

Monahans (mŏ'nühănz), city (pop. 6,311), ⊙ Ward co., extreme W Texas, in the Pecos valley, 35 mi. WSW of Odessa; trade, shipping, processing center for oil fields; mfg. (gasoline, carbon black, cottonseed products, metal products); ranches near by; chemical plant (sodium sulphate) in vicinity. Inc. 1928.

Mona Island (mō'nä) (□ c.19.5; c.6 mi. long, 4 mi. wide), belonging to Puerto Rico, in Mona Passage, 40 mi. W of the main isl. and 45 mi. W of Mayagüez. Formerly an uninhabited isl. visited by migratory families and forest service staff, it has been developed as a vacation resort, with cabins. Some crops are grown. Has airfield. Discovered by Columbus, who ceded it in 1511 to his brother. It later became a refuge for pirates.

Monango (mŭnăng'gō), village (pop. 138), Dickey co., SE N.Dak., 12 mi. N of Ellendale.

Mona Passage (mō'nä), strait (c.75 mi. wide) bet. Puerto Rico and Dominican Republic, leading from the Atlantic to the Caribbean. Mona Isl. is in its center.

Monarch (mŏ'nürk). **1** Village, Chaffee co., central Colo., on branch of Arkansas R., in Sawatch Mts., and 16 mi. W of Salida; alt. c.10,000 ft.; limestone quarries. Monarch Pass is near by, Mt. Shavano 7 mi. NNE. **2** Village, S.C.: see MONARCH MILLS.

Monarch, The, mountain (9,528 ft.), SE B.C., near Alta. border, in Rocky Mts., on SE edge of Kootenay Natl. Park, 16 mi. SW of Banff.

Monarch Mills or **Monarch,** textile-mill village (pop. 2,158), Union co., N S.C., just E of Union.

Monarch Mountain (11,714 ft.), W B.C., in Coast Mts., 200 mi. NW of Vancouver; 51°56'N 125°56'W.

Monarch Pass (11,312 ft.), central Colo. in Sawatch Mts., bet. Chaffee and Gunnison counties. Crossed by highway. View from highest point on pass includes 12 peaks exceeding 14,000 ft.

Monashee Mountains (mŭnă'shē), range of Rocky Mts., SE B.C., W of Selkirk Mts., extending c.200 mi. N from Wash. line bet. Columbia R. and Arrow Lakes (E) and upper North Thompson R., Shuswap L., and Okanagan L. (W). Peaks include Hallam Peak (10,560 ft.) and Cranberry Mtn. (9,470 ft.). Bet. Revelstoke and Shuswap L., the range is crossed by Canadian Pacific RR. In S part is important mining (gold, silver, copper, lead, zinc) region.

Monaster (mŏ'nŭstŭr), village, central Co. Limerick, Ireland, 2 mi. E of Croom; site of ruins of Cistercian abbey of Monasteranenagh (mŏ"nŭstĕrŭnĕ'nŭ), founded c.1151 by Turlough O'Brien, king of Munster.

Monasterboice (mŏ"nŭstŭrbois'), agr. village (district pop. 521), S Co. Louth, Ireland, 5 mi. NNW of Drogheda; site of relics of community founded by St. Boethius, consisting of round tower, 2 churches, and anc. crosses.

Monasterevan or **Monasterevin** (both: mŏ"nŭstŭrĕ'vŭn), Gaelic *Mainistir Eimhin*, town (pop. 448), W Co. Kildare, Ireland, on Barrow R., on branch of Grand Canal, and 7 mi. W of Kildare; agr. market (cattle, horses; potatoes), with iron foundries. Near-by Moore Abbey is on site of 12th-cent. monastery.

Monasterio, Spain: see MONESTERIO.

Monasterolo di Savigliano (mônästĕrô'lô dē sävēlyä'nô), village (pop. 1,009), Cuneo prov., Piedmont, NW Italy, 7 mi. ENE of Saluzzo.

Monasterzyska, Ukrainian SSR: see MONASTYRISKA.

Monastier, Le (lŭ mōnästyā'), village (pop. 1,203), Haute-Loire dept., S central France, 9 mi. SE of Le Puy; cattle market; lacemaking, silk throwing.

Monastir (mônästēr'), village (pop. 2,016), Cagliari prov., S Sardinia, 12 mi. N of Cagliari; dried herbs. Prehistoric rock tombs here.

Monastir (mŏnŭstēr', Fr. mônästēr'), anc. *Ruspina*, town (pop. 8,651), Sousse dist., E Tunisia, port on the Gulf of Hammamet (central Mediterranean), 11 mi. ESE of Sousse; olive-oil pressing, distilling, soap mfg., tunny canning; handicraft textile industry. Saltworks. A Phoenician and Roman settlement. Its old cloister (founded A.D. 180) now forms the core of the impressive *casbah*.

Monastir, Yugoslavia: see BITOLJ.

Monastir Gap, Yugoslavia: see PELAGONIJA.

Monastyrishche (mŭ"nŭstĭrēsh'chĭ), town (1926 pop. 2,045), E Vinnitsa oblast, Ukrainian SSR, 25 mi. NW of Uman; sugar refining, distilling.

Monastyriska (–ēs'kŭ), Pol. *Monasterzyska* (mônästĕrzhĭs'kä), city (1931 pop. 7,238), SW Ternopol oblast, Ukrainian SSR, 10 mi. W of Buchach; tobacco-growing center; cigar mfg., flour milling, brickworking. Has ruins of old palace. Passed from Poland to Austria (1772); reverted to Poland (1919); ceded to USSR in 1945.

Monastyrshchina (mŭnŭstĭr'shchĭnŭ), village (1926 pop. 2,198), W Smolensk oblast, Russian SFSR, 32 mi. SSW of Smolensk; dairying, distilling.

Monastyrskoye, Russian SFSR: see TURUKHANSK.

Mona Vale, town (pop. 1,428), E New South Wales, Australia, 15 mi. NNE of Sydney; coal-mining center.

Monaville, village (pop. 1,833, with adjoining Rossmore), Logan co., SW W.Va., 2 mi. S of Logan.

Monbazillac (mōbäzēyäk'), village (pop. 73), Dordogne dept., SW France, 4 mi. S of Bergerac; grows wines for liqueur.

Moncada (mōng-kä'dä), town (1939 pop. 2,372; 1948 municipality pop. 17,807), Tarlac prov., central Luzon, Philippines, on railroad and 17 mi. N of Tarlac; agr. center (coconuts, rice, sugar cane).

Moncada (mōng-kä'dhä), city (pop. 5,654), Valencia prov., E Spain, in rich truck-farming area, 6 mi. NNW of Valencia; mfg. of silk textiles, burlap, candy; olive-oil processing.

Moncada y Reixach (ē rāshäk'), village (pop. 4,056), Barcelona prov., NE Spain, on Besós R. and 7 mi. NNE of Barcelona; iron smelting, meat processing; mfg. of cement, beer, soap, gloves; cotton spinning. Trades in cereals, hemp, strawberries. Stone quarries near by.

Moncalieri (môong-kälyä'rē), town (pop. 9,578), Torino prov., Piedmont, NW Italy, on Po R. and 4 mi. S of Turin; rail junction; industrial and commercial center; foundries, canneries. Has royal palace (built 1789; now a military acad.) and meteorological observatory.

Moncalvo (môong-käl'vô), village (pop. 1,955), Asti prov., Piedmont, NW Italy, 11 mi. NNE of Asti.

Monção (mōsä'ō), city (pop. 898), N central Maranhão, Brazil, on Pindaré R. and 90 mi. SW of São Luís; rice, cotton, carnauba wax.

Monção, town (pop. 2,052), Viana do Castelo dist., northernmost Portugal, on left bank of Minho R. (Sp. border), 35 mi. N of Braga; Port. railroad terminus; agr. trade. Cold sulphur springs. Resisted Sp. siege in 1658. Sometimes spelled Monsão.

Moncay (môn'kī'), town, ⊙ Haininh prov. (□ 1,300; 1943 pop. 109,200), N Vietnam, in Tonkin, on China frontier (opposite Tunghing), near Gulf of Tonkin coast, 145 mi. ENE of Hanoi; fisheries; antimony deposits.

Moncayo, Sierra del (syĕ'rä dhĕl mōng-kī'ō) range of the Cordillera Ibérica, N Spain, on Aragon-Old Castile border, 35 mi. W of Saragossa. Rises to c.7,590 ft. Forms watershed bet. Ebro and Duero (or Douro) basins.

Monceau-sur-Sambre (mōsō-sür-sã'brü), town (pop. 10,289), Hainaut prov., S central Belgium, on Sambre R. and 3 mi. W of Charleroi; metal industry; electric-power station.

Mönch (mûnkh) [Ger.,=monk], Alpine peak (13,468 ft.) in Bernese Alps, S central Switzerland, NE of the Jungfrau, 5 mi. E of Mürren; 2 passes, Ober-Mönchjoch (11,870 ft.) and Unter-Mönchjoch (11,680 ft.), are E.

Mönchberg (mûnkh'bĕrk), village (pop. 1,589), Lower Franconia, NW Bavaria, Germany, 14 mi. SSE of Aschaffenburg; potatoes, cattle.

Monchegorsk (mŭnchĭgôrsk'), city (1939 pop. c.30,000), central Murmansk oblast, Russian SFSR, on L. Imandra, on spur of Murmansk RR and 70 mi. S of Murmansk; nickel- and copper-mining center; smelters. Mines at Malaya Sopcha, just SW. Founded c.1935.

Mönchhof (mûnkh'hōf), village (pop. 2,096), Burgenland, E Austria, 21 mi. NE of Sopron, Hungary, across Neusiedler L.; vineyards.

Monchique (mōshē'kĭ), town (pop. 1,722), Faro dist., S Portugal, in the Serra de Monchique, 13 mi. N of Portimão; fruits, potatoes, vegetables; cork, ships chestnut furniture. Spa of Caldas de Monchique is 3 mi. S.

Monchique, Serra de (sĕ'rŭ dĭ), hill range in Faro dist., S Portugal, near SW extremity of Iberian Peninsula; rises to 2,960 ft. at La Foia. Pine, oak, chestnut trees.

Monción (mōnsyōn'), town (1950 pop. 978), Monte Cristi prov., NW Dominican Republic, in N outliers of the Cordillera Central, 32 mi. W of Santiago, in agr. region (tobacco, coffee, cacao, beeswax, hides). Titanium deposits near by. Sometimes Benito Monción; formerly Guaraguanó.

Moncks Corner, town (pop. 1,818), ⊙ Berkeley co., SE S.C., 28 mi. N of Charleston and on Cooper R.; agr., lumber. Hydroelectric plant of Santee-Cooper power and navigation development near by.

Monclar or **Monclar-d'Agenais** (mōklär'-däzhŭnā'), village (pop. 495), Lot-et-Garonne dept., SW France, 9 mi. WNW of Villeneuve-sur-Lot; cattle.

Monclar-d'Agenais, France: see MONCLAR.

Monclar-de-Quercy (–dŭ-kĕrsē'), village (pop. 533), Tarn-et-Garonne dept., SW France, 12 mi. ESE of Montauban; wheat, corn, lumber; horse breeding.

Monclova (mōng-klō'vä), city (pop. 7,181), Coahuila, N Mexico, in E outliers of Sierra Madre Oriental, 110 mi. NW of Monterrey; agr. (cereals, fibers, cattle) and mining (silver, lead, zinc, copper) center; railroad shops, steelworks, wine and liquor distilleries, flour mills; ceramics. Airport.

Moncófar (mōng-kō'fär), town (pop. 1,244), Castellón de la Plana prov., E Spain, 14 mi. SSW of Castellón de la Plana; ships oranges and onions.

Moncontour (mōkōtōōr'). **1** Village (pop. 908), Côtes-du-Nord dept., W France, on N slope of Landes du Méné, 12 mi. SSE of Saint-Brieuc; dairying; stone quarries near by. Has 16th-cent. church with stained-glass windows. Also called Moncontour-de-Bretagne. **2** Village (pop. 573), Vienne dept., W central France, 10 mi. SSW of Loudun; dairying, truck gardening. Has restored 12th-cent. fortifications, a Romanesque church, and medieval houses. Here Huguenots were defeated (1569) by Henri III, then duke of Anjou. Sometimes called Moncontour-du-Poitou.

Moncoutant (mōkōōtā'), village (pop. 1,172), Deux-Sèvres dept., W France, near Sèvre Nantaise R., 17 mi. WNW of Parthenay; mfg. of hosiery and building materials.

Moncreiffe Hill, Moncrieff Hill, or **Moncrieffe Hill** (all: mŏn-krēf'), elevation (725 ft.) in SE Perthshire, Scotland, 3 mi. SE of Perth.

Moncrieff Hill or **Moncrieffe Hill,** Scotland: see MONCREIFFE HILL.

Moncton (mŭngk'tŭn), city (pop. 22,763), SE N.B., on Petitcodiac R. and 85 mi. NE of St. John; rail and road center; railroad repair shops, woolen and cotton mills, woodworking plants, iron foundries; center of oil, natural-gas, fur-farming, and dairying region; small port. Old Free Meeting House (interdenominational) dates from 1827. Originally named The Bend, town was renamed Moncton (1855) in honor of General Robert Monckton. Settled by the French, followed (1763) by Germans from Pennsylvania. There is an airport, radio station, and racecourse. Just N is suburb of Sunny Brae.

Mond, river, Iran: see MUND RIVER.

Monda (mōn'dä), town (pop. 2,795), Málaga prov., S Spain, in outliers of the Cordillera Penibética, 24 mi. WSW of Málaga; olives, olive oil, cork, grapes, almonds; flour milling, liquor distilling.

Mondaino (môndī'nô), village (pop. 571), Forlì prov., Emilia-Romagna, N central Italy, 15 mi. SSW of Rimini; harmonicas.

Mondamin (mŏndā'mĭn), town (pop. 489), Harrison co., W Iowa, near Soldier R., 30 mi. N of Omaha (Neb.), in fruitgrowing area; rail junction.

Mondego, Cape (mōndā'gōō), rocky headland on the Atlantic, in Coimbra dist., N central Portugal, 4 mi. NW of Figueira da Foz (at mouth of Mondego R.); 40°11'N 8°54'W; lighthouse. Buarcos hills (just E) rise to 700 ft.

Mondego River, N central Portugal, rises in the Serra da Estrêla 10 mi. N of Covilhã, flows 137 mi. generally SW, through fertile Coimbra plain, to the Atlantic at Figueira da Foz. Navigable seasonally for barges to influx of Dão R. (above Coimbra). Subject to flash floods. Largest river flowing entirely in Portugal.

Mondéjar (mōndā'här), town (pop. 2,611), Guadalajara prov., central Spain, 30 mi. E of Madrid; agr. center (cereals, grapes, olives, honey, livestock). Tanning, flour milling, soap mfg.

Mondeville (mōdvēl'), E industrial suburb (pop. 4,982) of Caen, Calvados dept., NW France; forges and metalworks; chemical fertilizer factory. Damaged in Second World War.

Mondicourt (mōdēkōōr'), village (pop. 577), Pas-de-Calais dept., N France, 16 mi. SW of Arras; chocolate factory.

Mondim de Basto (mōn'dēn dĭ bäsh'tōō), town (pop. 1,315), Vila Real dist., N Portugal, on Tâmega R. and 13 mi. NW of Vila Real; livestock, agr.

Mondolfo (môndôl'fô), town (pop. 1,345), Pesaro e Urbino, The Marches, central Italy, 7 mi. SSE of Fano; mfg. (harmoniums, harmonicas).

Mondoñedo (mōndōnyā'dhō), city (pop. 2,901), Lugo prov., NW Spain, in Galicia, 30 mi. NNE of Lugo; agr. trade center (livestock, potatoes, wine; lumber); brewery. Mineral springs. Bishopric with 13th-cent. Gothic cathedral. Graphite quarries near by.

Mondorf-les-Bains (mōdôrf'-lā-bē'), town (pop. 1,087), SE Luxembourg, 10 mi. SE of Luxembourg city, on Fr. border; tourist resort with mineral springs; mfg. of bakery equipment, stained glass.

Mondoubleau (mōdōōblō'), village (pop. 1,285), Loir-et-Cher dept., N central France, 15 mi. NW of Vendôme; livestock market; tanning, basket making. Has 12th-cent. keep.

Mondovi (mōdôvē'), town (pop. 4,186), Constantine dept., NE Algeria, on the Oued Seybouse, on railroad and 15 mi. S of Bône, in fertile agr. region (wine, citrus fruit, cotton, olives). Tobacco cooperative.

Mondovì (môndôvē'), town (pop. 11,046), Cuneo prov., Piedmont, NW Italy, on Ellero R. and 14 mi. E of Cuneo; rail junction. Comprised of lower town, Breo (pop. 7,225; industrial section); upper town, Piazza (pop. 2,498); and, just NE, Carassone (pop. 1,323; ceramics). Has food, paper, wood, chemical, iron and steel industries. Quarries (marble, quartz) near by. Bishopric with cathedral (1763). Santuario di Vicoforte, large pilgrimage church built 1596–1731, is 3 mi. SE. Napoleon defeated Austro-Sardinian forces at Mondovì in 1796. In Second World War, bombed (1942–43).

Mondovi (mŏndō'vē), city (pop. 2,285), Buffalo co., W Wis., on Buffalo R. (hydroelectric plant) and 19 mi. SSW of Eau Claire, in dairy, livestock, and poultry area; dairy products, canned vegetables, pickles; limestone quarries; poultry hatcheries. Settled 1855, inc. 1889.

Mondragón (mōndrägōn'), town (pop. 5,036), Guipúzcoa prov., N Spain, in the Basque Provs., 20 mi. WSW of Tolosa; metalworking (kitchen ranges, hardware, electrical equipment). Agr. trade (cereals, cattle; lumber). Limestone quarries and iron deposits near by. Mineral springs 3 mi. WSW at Santa Agueda (pop. 1,887).

Mondragone (môndrägô'nĕ), town (pop. 11,061), Caserta prov., Campania, S Italy, bet. Monte Massico and Gulf of Gaeta, 17 mi. W of Capua; canned foods, wine. Hot mineral baths near by.

Mondrain Island, Australia: see RECHERCHE ARCHIPELAGO.

Mondrainville (mōdrēvēl'), village (pop. 33), Calvados dept., NW France, 8 mi. SW of Caen. Here British established bridgehead S of Odon R. in Normandy campaign of Second World War.

Mond River, Iran: see MUND RIVER.

Mondsee (mōnt'zā), town (pop. 2,675), SW Upper Austria, on N shore of the Mondsee and 15 mi. ENE of Salzburg; brewery; summer resort (alt. 1,580 ft.).

Mondsee, lake (□ 5.48), SW Upper Austria, in the Salzkammergut, surrounded by mts., 15 mi. E of Salzburg; c.5 mi. long, 1 mi. wide, max. depth 225 ft., alt. 1,575 ft. A short stream connects it (N) with small Zeller See or Irrsee. Remains of prehistoric lake dwellings.

Monduli (mōndōō'lē), village, Northern Prov., Tanganyika, 16 mi. WNW of Arusha; coffee, corn, vegetables; cattle, sheep, goats. Hq. Masai tribe.

Mondy (môn'dē), village, SW Buryat-Mongol Autonomous SSR, Russian SFSR, on Irkutsk-Uliassutai route and 150 mi. WSW of Irkutsk; transit point in E.Sayan Mts., near Mongolian border; alt. 4,300 ft.; asbestos deposits.

Moneague (mŭnēg'), village, St. Ann parish, central Jamaica, resort at N foot of Mt. Diablo, 30 mi. NW of Kingston.

Moneasa, Rumania: see SEBIS.

Monédières, Monts de (mō dŭ mōnādyâr'), in Massif Central, Corrèze dept., S central France, extend c.20 mi. N–S bet. upper valleys of the Corrèze and the Vézère, rising to over 3,000 ft.

Monee (mōnē'), village (pop. 554), Will co., NE Ill., 19 mi. ESE of Joliet, in agr. and bituminous-coal area.

Moneglia (mônā'lyä), village (pop. 1,158), Genova prov., Liguria, N Italy, port on Gulf of Genoa and 10 mi. SE of Chiavari; resort.

Monein (mōnē'), village (pop. 940), Basses-Pyrénées dept., SW France, 9 mi. N of Oloron-Sainte-Marie; extensive vineyards and orchards; stock raising.

Monemvasia (mô″nĕmvūsē′ŭ), Ital. *Malvasia* (mălvŭsē′ŭ), village (pop. 638), Laconia nome, SE Peloponnesus, Greece, on the coast, 45 mi. SE of Sparta. Founded by Laconians on rocky isl., joined to mainland by 600-ft. mole. Important medieval silk and wine center. Its wines became known as malvasia or malmsey. Sometimes spelled Monembasia. Near by are ruins of anc. Epidaurus Limera.

Moneron Island (mŭnyĭrôn′), Jap. *Kaiba-to* (kī′-bä-tō′), in Sea of Japan, 30 mi. off SW Sakhalin, Russian SFSR; 4 mi. long, 2 mi. wide. Under Jap. rule, 1905–45.

Monessen (mŭnĕ′sŭn), city (pop. 17,896), Westmoreland co., SW Pa., 20 mi. S of Pittsburgh and on Monongahela R.; steel and tin products, glass; bituminous coal; dairying. Laid out 1897, inc. 1898.

Monesterio (mōnĕstā′ryō) or **Monasterio** (mōnä–), town (pop. 6,699), Badajoz prov., W Spain, in Sierra Morena, 32 mi. SE of Jerez de los Caballeros; stock raising (sheep, goats), lumbering, and agr. center (grain, olives, grapes; apiculture). Mfg. of plaster; meat products.

Monestier-de-Clermont (mônüstyā′-dù-klĕrmō′), village (pop. 599), Isère dept., SE France, in Dauphiné Alps, 19 mi. SSW of Grenoble; alt. 2,730 ft. Footwear mfg. Winter sports.

Monestiés or **Monestiés-sur-Cérou** (mônĕstyā′-sür-särōō′), village (pop. 398), Tarn dept., S France, on small Cérou R. and 10 mi. NNW of Albi; flour milling, biscuit mfg. Also spelled Monestiès.

Moneta (mōnē′tù). **1** Town (pop. 89), O'Brien co., NW Iowa, 12 mi. W of Spencer, in agr. area. **2** Village (pop. c.25), Fremont co., central Wyo., on branch of Bighorn R. and 75 mi. WNW of Casper; alt. 5,428 ft. Castle Gardens, area of picturesque sandstone formations, near by.

Monêtier-les-Bains, Le (lù mônĕtyā′-lā-bē′), Alpine village (pop. 400), Hautes-Alpes dept., SE France, on the Guisane and 9 mi. NW of Briançon, at NE foot of Massif du Pelvoux; alt. 3,602 ft. Anthracite mines; mineral springs, winter sports.

Monetny or **Monetnyy** (mŭnyĕt′nē), town (1948 pop. over 10,000), S Sverdlovsk oblast, Russian SFSR, on railroad (Monetnaya station) and 18 mi. NE (under jurisdiction) of Berezovski; major peat-digging center; tungsten mining. Developed in 1930s.

Monett (mō′nĕt), city (pop. 4,771), Barry and Lawrence counties, SW Mo., in the Ozarks, 35 mi. ESE of Joplin. Ships berries, apples, tomatoes; mfg. (dairy products, cigars). Has jr. col. State hosp. for venereal diseases is here. Horticultural experiment station near by. Surveyed 1887.

Monetta (mŭnĕ′tù), town (1940 pop. 242), Aiken and Saluda counties, W S.C., 5 mi. SW of Batesburg.

Monette (mōnĕt′), town (pop. 1,114), Craighead co., NE Ark., 21 mi. E of Jonesboro, in agr. area (cotton, corn, potatoes, beans, livestock). Inc. 1900.

Money Island, China: see CRESCENT GROUP.

Moneymore (mŭ″nēmôr′), town (pop. 1,154), SE Co. Londonderry, Northern Ireland, 30 mi. S of Coleraine; agr. market (flax, potatoes, oats).

Monfalcone (mônfälkô′nĕ), town (pop. 17,388), Gorizia prov., Friuli-Venezia Giulia, NE Italy, near the Adriatic, 10 mi. SSW of Gorizia. Industrial center, mineral- and vegetable-oil refineries, chemical factories; shipyards. Reconstructed following heavy damage in First World War.

Monferrato, Italy: see MONTFERRAT.

Monfestino in Serra Mazzoni, Italy: see SERRAMAZZONI.

Monflanquin (mōflăkē′), village (pop. 943), Lot-et-Garonne dept., SW France, 9 mi. NNE of Villeneuve-sur-Lot; brickworks; felt mfg.; plums.

Monforte (mōnfôr′tĭ), town (pop. 1,913), Portalegre dist., central Portugal, 16 mi. S of Portalegre; cheese mfg.

Monforte (mōmfôr′tā), city (pop. 11,168), Lugo prov., NW Spain, in Galicia, railroad junction 22 mi. NE of Orense; agr. trade center (cereals, vegetables, potatoes, wine); meat processing, tanning, flour- and sawmilling, mfg. of dairy products. Stock raising and lumbering in area. Iron mines near by. Dominated by hill with remains of medieval castle. Has former Benedictine monastery (now a hosp.) and Jesuit col. and church.

Monforte da Beira (mōnfôr′tĭ dù bā′rù), town (pop. 2,348), Castelo Branco dist., central Portugal, 12 mi. SE of Castelo Branco; pottery mfg.; grain, olives, livestock. Oak woods.

Monforte del Cid (mōmfôr′tā dhĕl thēdh′), town (pop. 2,407), Alicante prov., E Spain, 8 mi. NNW of Elche; wine-production center; alcohol, brandy, and liqueur distilling. Olive oil, cereals.

Monfurado, Serra de (sĕ′rù dĭ mōnfōōrä′dōō), hills in S Portugal, SW of Évora, rising to 1,400 ft. Iron deposits.

Monga (môngʹgä), village, Eastern Prov., N Belgian Congo, on a headstream of Ubangi R. and 155 mi. NW of Buta; customs station near Fr. Equatorial Africa border; cotton ginning, palm-oil milling. Has R.C. and Baptist missions.

Mongala River (mông-gä′lä), NW Belgian Congo, formed by 3 headstreams at Businga, flows c.205 mi. S and SW, past Likimi and Binga, to Congo R. at Gumba-Mobeka. Navigable downstream from Businga. Was 1st explored in 1886.

Mongalla (mông-gäl′lä), village, Equatoria prov., S Anglo-Egyptian Sudan, on right bank of the Bahr el Jebel (White Nile), on road, and 25 mi. NNE of Juba; cotton center. Former ⊙ Mongalla prov. (now Equatoria prov.). Inhabited by Bari tribe.

Mongbwalu (môngbwä′lōō), village (1948 pop. 19,071), Eastern Prov., NE Belgian Congo, 38 mi. NNE of Irumu; gold mining and trading center; gold processing. Hosp. for Europeans.

Mongeri (mông-gĕ′rē), town (pop. 715), South-Western Prov., central Sierra Leone, on Teye R. (headstream of Jong R.) and 25 mi. N of Bo; palm oil and kernels, cacao, coffee.

Monggumpo, Korea: see CHANGYON.

Monghidoro (mông-gēdô′rō), village (pop. 570), Bologna prov., Emilia-Romagna, N central Italy, 19 mi. S of Bologna; straw-hat mfg.

Monghopung, Burma: see TAHKILEK.

Monghsu (mông′shōō′), NE state (myosaship) (□ 470; pop. 16,410), Southern Shan State, E Upper Burma, on the Nam Pang; ⊙ Monghsu, village 80 mi. SE of Lashio.

Monghyr (mŭng′-gēr), district (□ 3,975; pop. 2,564,544), NE central Bihar, India; ⊙ Monghyr. On Ganges Plain; foothills of Chota Nagpur Plateau in S; NW corner bounded by Ganges R.; drained by tributaries of the Ganges. Mainly alluvial soil; rice, corn, wheat, gram, barley, oilseeds; mango, palmyra, and bamboo in forested hills. Mica (near Jamui), slate (near Jamalpur) quarries; lime extracting. Railway workshops at Jamalpur; firearms and cigarette mfg. at Monghyr. Extensively damaged by earthquake of 1934.

Monghyr, city (pop. 63,150), ⊙ Monghyr dist., NE central Bihar, India, on Ganges Plain, on the Ganges (rail ferry) and 33 mi. WNW of Bhagalpur. Terminus of rail spur from Jamalpur; road and trade (rice, corn, wheat, barley, oilseeds) center; firearms and cigarette mfg., ebony work. Mogul fort, here, figured in struggle bet. a nawab of Bengal and the English. Thermal springs and Hindu pilgrimage center 6 mi. ESE, at Sitakund.

Mongibello, Sicily: see ETNA, MOUNT.

Monginevro, France: see MONTGENÈVRE PASS.

Mongkolborey (môngkôl′bōrā′), village (1941 pop. 3,504), Battambang prov., W Cambodia, 5 mi. SE of Sisophon, on Mongkolborey R. and Pnompenh-Bangkok RR (formerly terminus, extension built 1942); rice-growing and trading center; orchards. In Thailand, 1941–46.

Mongkung (mông′kōōng′), N state (sawbwaship) (□ 1,593; pop. 37,208), Southern Shan State, Upper Burma; ⊙ Mongkung, village 65 mi. NNE of Taunggyi. Forests and rice; pottery.

Mongmit (mông′mĭt′), Burmese *Momeik* (mō′măk), NW state (sawbwaship) (□ 3,733; pop. 59,865), Northern Shan State, Upper Burma; ⊙ Mongmit. Bounded N by Kachin State, astride Shweli R., and on edge of Shan Plateau, it consists (W) of flat, jungle-covered country. Rice, tea, timber. Small coal deposits. Served by Mogok-Bhamo road.

Mongmit, village, ⊙ Mongmit state, Northern Shan State, Upper Burma, 85 mi. NNE of Mandalay; head of road (N) to Bhamo and trade center. Founded 1279; destroyed by Kachins 1858.

Mongnai (mông′nī′), E central state (sawbwaship) (□ 3,100; pop. 55,791), Southern Shan State, Upper Burma; ⊙ Mongnai, village 60 mi. ESE of Taunggyi. Rice, tobacco; paper mfg.

Mongnawng (mông′nông′), NE state (myosaship) (□ 1,646; pop. 42,990), Southern Shan State, Upper Burma, on the Nam Pang; ⊙ Mongnawng, village 90 mi. NE of Taunggyi.

Mongo (mông-gō′), village, central Chad territory, Fr. Equatorial Africa, 75 mi. SSE of Ati; road junction.

Mongolia (mŏngō′lēŭ), Rus. *Mongoliya* (mŭngô′-lēŭ), Chinese *Meng-ku* (mŭng′gōō′), geographical region (□ 1,000,000; pop. 3,500,000) of E central Asia, inhabited by the Mongols. Traditionally divided by the Gobi desert into N (Outer) Mongolia and S (Inner) Mongolia, it is bounded N by Siberia, E by Manchuria, SE by China proper, and SW by China's Sinkiang prov. (Chinese Turkestan). It includes the Gobi desert and is fringed by the Altai Mts. (NW), the Sayans and mts. of Transbaikalia (N), the Khingan Mts. (E) and, in S, roughly by zone of Chinese settlement along the Great Wall, the Ordos bend of Yellow R., and the Silk Road. Essentially a desert (Gobi) and dry short-grass steppe plateau (alt. 3–4,000 ft.), Mongolia has traditionally been a land of pastoral nomadism with some oasis agr. along its margins. During the 1st millenium A.D., it was inhabited by various Turkic tribes (Huns, Avars, Uigurs) with their hq. on upper course of Orkhon R. During the 12th cent., the Mongols, originally settled in the headwaters of Amur R., conquered the country under the leadership of Jenghiz Khan. Under his rule, the Mongols adopted a written language and Lamaist Buddhism was introduced for the 1st time (it was reintroduced in late-16th cent.). By the time of the death (1227) of the great Mongol leader, Mongol expansion had extended from the Pacific to the Caspian Sea, creating one of the greatest, though short-lived, empires of all time, with its capital at Karakorum Jenghiz Khan had begun (1211) the conquest of the Chin dynasty of N China; subdued the Hsia dynasty of the Tanguts (1217), the Kara-Khitai state of E Turkestan (1218), the Khorezm state of W Turkestan (1219–21); and had initiated the 1st raids into the S Russian steppe (1223). Under his successors, the Mongol empire disintegrated into the Golden Horde on Russia's SE approaches, the Hulagid dynasty of Persia, the Jagatai of Turkestan, and the Yüan dynasty (1280–1368) of China, which included Mongolia proper. After the overthrow of the Mongol dynasty of China by the Mings, a cleavage developed bet. the N (Outer) Mongols and the S (Inner) Mongols, who had been more closely associated with Mongol rule in China. From this time dates the traditional separation of the country into Inner Mongolia and Outer Mongolia. **Inner Mongolia,** Chinese *Nei Meng-ku* (nā), was settled chiefly by the Tumet-Ordos and Chahar tribes, and by the E Mongols in W Manchuria. Supremacy over the Inner Mongols was held (1530–83) by Anda (Altan Khan) of the Tumets, who harried N China and besieged Peking. After his death, leadership passed (c.1603) to Likdan Khan of the Chahars. He was defeated (1635) by the rising Manchus, who thus annexed E Inner Mongolia to China. W Inner Mongolia, inhabited by the West Mongols (Oirats or Kalmucks), contested Manchu supremacy until the 18th cent. Under Manchu rule, the Mongols of Inner Mongolia were given fixed territorial boundaries and were divided into leagues and these, in turn, into banners. At the same time, Chinese agr. colonization gradually began to encroach on the Mongol pastoral economy. After the Chinese revolution (1911), Inner Mongolia was governed temporarily as special administrative areas. In 1928 it was apportioned (1928) among the Chinese provs. of NINGSIA, SUIYUAN, CHAHAR, JEHOL, and W MANCHURIA, and thereafter, the name Inner Mongolia generally referred to Ningsia, Suiyuan, and Chahar. Following the establishment (1932) of Manchukuo under Japanese auspices, the Mongols of W Manchuria and N Jehol were constituted into the autonomous prov. of Hsingan, later divided into 4 sections. Similarly, after the outbreak (1937) of the Sino-Japanese war, the Mongols of Suiyuan and Chahar (under Japanese control) were set up as the autonomous Mongolian govt. of Mengkiang (or Meng-chiang), with hq. at Kweihwa. After the Second World War, the pre-Japanese *status quo* was briefly reestablished by the Chinese Nationalists. But after the Chinese Communist conquest of Inner Mongolia, the E section was set up (1947–49) as the Inner Mongolian Autonomous Region, while the Mongols of Suiyuan and Ningsia remained under the jurisdiction of these 2 provs. **Inner Mongolian Autonomous Region,** Chinese *Nei Meng Tzu-chih Ch'ü* (nā′-mŭng′ dzŭ′jû″chü′) is an autonomous division (□ 230,000; pop. 2,000,000) of Manchuria; ⊙ Ulan Hoto (formerly Wangyehmiao). Bounded W by Mongolian People's Republic and the USSR (along Argun R.), N and E by Heilungkiang, SE by Liaosi, S by Jehol and Chahar, and SW by Suiyuan, the region lies largely on the Mongolian plateau, which rises in center in the forested Khingan Mts. Along its E margin, the region reaches the Nonni and upper Liao valleys. The plateau section consists of chestnut-soil steppe in the BARGA (N) becoming progressively drier toward the desert-steppe in the SW. The economy of the overwhelmingly Mongolian pop. is based on nomadic stock raising, mainly of sheep, goats, horses, and camels. Chinese agr. colonization has penetrated into the region along the Chinese Eastern RR in the Barga and the railroad to Tungliao (SE). The main agr. products are millet and kaoliang in the S, and spring grain (wheat, rye, buckwheat, oats) in the N. Livestock products (wool, hides, skins) are the chief exports. Coal is mined at Chalainor and soda extracted near Hulun Nor. The Mongols are organized into the 6 leagues: the Huna (N; formed 1949 out of the Barga and Buteha leagues), the Khingan (center), the Jerim (SE), the Jooda (S), and the Silingol and Chahar leagues (SE; until 1949 in Chahar prov.). In addition to the Chinese farming minority, there are Russians in the Barga and Tungusic hunting tribes (Orochon, Solon, Daur) in the Khingan Mts. The few towns—Hailar, Manchouli, Ulan Hoto, and Tungliao—are located along rail lines. **Outer Mongolia,** Chinese *Wai Meng-ku* (wī), was settled chiefly by the North (Khalkha) Mongols, except for the West Mongols in the Altai-Kobdo region. After the fall of the Yüan dynasty of China, the history was marked by a struggle for supremacy bet. the Khalkhas and the West Mongols. The latter, also known as Oirat or Kalmucks, were in control in the 15th cent. and raided N China, holding the emperor prisoner (1450–58). In the 16th cent., the Khalkhas rose to power. Having sought Manchu aid against renewed West Mongol onslaughts, the Khalkhas accepted Manchu rule (1691). Under the ensuing loose Chinese control, the Khalkhas were divided into 4 aimaks: Jasakto (or Dzasaktu) Khan, Sain Noyan, Tushetu Khan, and Tsetsen Khan. Oriented economically toward Siberia (N), Outer Mongolia was traversed after early-18th cent. by the Kyakhta-Urga-Kalgan-Peking trade route bet. Russia and China, and Russian trade increasingly rivaled that of China through the 19th cent. Following the Chinese revolution, Manchu rule was overthrown by an assembly of Mongol princes who proclaimed (1911) an autonomous Outer Mongolia under the rule of the Living Buddha of Urga. In 1919, Chinese forces occupied the country, ending the period of autonomy. They were joined (early 1921) by Russian counterrevolutionary forces. The resulting chaotic situation was ended in July, 1921, with the victory of Mongolian revolutionary forces aided by Red Army troops, who expelled the Chinese and their allies from Outer Mongolia. A constitutional monarchy, headed by the Living Buddha, was proclaimed and lasted until the latter's death in 1924. It was succeeded by the creation, under Soviet auspices, of the **Mongolian People's Republic,** Mongolian *Mongol Arad Ulas* (mŏng'gŏl ä'räd ōō'läs), independent country (□ 615,000; pop. 1,000,000) of NE central Asia; ⊙ Ulan Bator. Bounded N by the Siberian part of the Russian SFSR, E and SE by the Inner Mongolian Autonomous Region of Manchuria, S by Suiyuan and Ningsia provs., and SW by Sinkiang prov. of China, the country extends 1,480 mi. W–E bet. 87°50'E and 119°54'E and 780 mi. N–S bet. 41°32' and 52°16' N. Essentially a vast plateau (average alt.: 3–4,000 ft.), the republic comprises a mountainous NW section (including the Kentei, Khangai, and Mongolian Altai mts.) and a rolling plain (SE)—the Gobi desert. The highest point is the Tabun Bogdo (15,266 ft.) in the Altai Mts., near the meeting point of the USSR, Chinese, and Mongolian frontiers. The country lies astride the great Asian divide separating the Arctic and Pacific drainage basins from the closed interior basin of central Asia. Principal rivers are in the N: the Selenga (of the Arctic watershed) and the Kerulen (of the Pacific). Among the main rivers of the interior system are the Tes, Kobdo, and Dzabkhan rivers (NW), which flow into some of the country's largest interior lakes: Ubsa Nor, Khara Usu, Airik Nor, and Kirgis Nor. L. Khubsugul drains into Selenga R. The Mongolian streams are characterized by a more or less regular flow without extreme high-water stages; they are little used for navigation or logging. Forests are found only on the N slopes of the mtn. ranges (NW), and occupy about 8% of the total area. Above an alt. of 6,500 ft. (W) and up to 8,000 ft. (E), alpine meadows and tundra vegetation are found. Apart from this vertical zoning, the plain areas of the country fall into roughly latitudinal belts, varying from wooded steppe along the USSR border (N) through steppe and semi-desert to the true Gobi desert (S). The pop. is predominantly Khalkha (80%), with some West Mongol tribes in the Altai-Kobdo region (W), and East Mongols (Chahars) along SE frontier. Other minorities include Buryat Mongols (N), Kazakhs (in Bayan Ulegei aimak) and Tuvinians (W), Chinese and Russians. With the exception of the settled pop. (15%) of the few cities and other urban centers, the people of the republic lead a nomadic mode of life dictated by the needs of their pastoral economy. The Mongolian People's Republic leads the world in the number of livestock per capita of pop. (32.1 in 1944). The chief types of livestock are sheep (57%), goats (20%), cattle (10%), horses (9%), and camels (4%). The vast grazing lands (72% of total area) permit the year-round pasturing of livestock. A state-sponsored program of haymaking was begun, however, in 1937–38 as a precautionary measure against severe or prolonged winters. State aid also led to the establishment of a network of veterinary stations. Agr. is still poorly developed and is important only in the N wooded steppe. In 1947 only 75,000 acres were under cultivation. The crops are mainly grain (wheat, barley, millet). Hunting of fur-bearing animals is an important branch of the economy, with furs a leading export item. Mining is in the 1st stages of development. Of greatest economic importance are the coal mines of Nalaikha (near Ulan Bator); other mines have been developed at Choibalsan, Yugodzyr, and Undur Khan. Gold, lead-zinc, and copper are also found. Industry is largely restricted to the small-scale processing of livestock products (woolwashing, dairying, tanning). A large plant using modern processing methods exists in Ulan Bator, which also has other industries (meat packing, metal- and woodworking). Since the 1940s, railroads penetrate into the republic from the USSR, to Ulan Bator from Ulan-Ude (since 1949) and to Choibalsan from Borzya (since 1944). Choibalsan, in turn, is the center of a narrow-gauge net serving the E part of the country. Auto highways radiate from Ulan Bator to the chief centers: Choibalsan, Altan Bulak (on USSR line), Kobdo, Uliassutai, Undur Khan, and Tsetserlik. Air lines link Ulan Bator with Moscow, Ulan-Ude, and the republic's aimak centers. Trade with the USSR passes primarily through Altan Bulak–Kyakhta (highway crossing) and through Sukhe Bator–Naushki (rail crossing). Other links are the Choibalsan-Borzya RR, the road-steamer connection through L. Khubsugul, and the Chuya R. highway across the Altai Mts. Trade with China is channeled almost entirely along the Ulan Bator-Kalgan road. The leading export items are livestock, wool, hides, furs, and meat products. The establishment (1924) of the Communist-led regime was followed by a struggle to divest the old privileged classes (such as hereditary ruling princes, the Lamaist monasteries) of their capital (largely in form of livestock). With the support of the USSR, this campaign continued until the final expropriation of the aristocracy (1926) and of the monasteries (1930–31). In 1936, the USSR signed a mutual-aid pact with the republic, thus formalizing the existing close relations bet. the 2 countries. However, deviationist revolts and conspiracies continued through the middle 1930s, supported by the presence of the Japanese army on the Manchurian border, where incidents multiplied and culminated in the Khalkha R. battle of the summer of 1939. The adoption (1940) of a new constitution marked the consolidation of the regime and the completion of the 1st stage of the economic development of the country. During the Second World War, the Mongolian army joined the USSR in Manchuria in the last, brief stage of the war against Japan. Under terms of a Soviet-Chinese agreement, a plebiscite was held (1945) in the republic to determine its continued independence, which was then only recognized by the Nationalist govt. of China. The close Soviet contact was emphasized in 1946 with the introduction of a new Mongolian alphabet based on the Cyrillic. A Soviet-sponsored application for admission to the U.N. was rejected in 1947, but the republic's friendly foreign relations, previously restricted to the USSR, were extended also to the "people's democracies" of E Europe and in 1949 to the People's Republic of China. Since 1946, the country has been divided into 18 aimaks: Bayan Khongor, Bayan Ulegei, Bulgan, Central, Choibalsan, Dzabkhan, East Gobi, Gobi Altai, Kentei, Khubsugul, Kobdo, Middle Gobi, North Khangai, Selenga, South Gobi, South Khangai, Sukhe Bator, and Ubsa Nor.

Mongolian Altai, Mongolia: see ALTAI MOUNTAINS.

Mongolian People's Republic: see MONGOLIA.

Mongono or **Mongonu** (both: mŏngōō'nōō), town (pop. 6,115), Bornu prov., Northern Provinces, NE Nigeria, near L. Chad, 65 mi. NNW of Maiduguri; road center; cattle raising; gum arabic, cassava, millet, durra.

Mongoumba (mông-gōōmbä'), village, S Ubangi-Shari, Fr. Equatorial Africa, on Ubangi R. at mouth of Lobaye R., opposite Libenge (Belgian Congo) and 55 mi. S of Bangui; customs station and small river port, shipping hardwoods, coffee, palm products; sawmilling; coffee plantations.

Mongpai (mông'pī'), southernmost state (sawbwaship) (□ 730; pop. 21,637) of Southern Shan State, Upper Burma, on Karenni State line; ⊙ Mongpai, village on the Nam Pilu and 10 mi. NW of Loikaw.

Mongpan (mông'pän''), SE state (sawbwaship) (□ 2,988; pop. 20,712), Southern Shan State, Upper Burma; ⊙ Mongpan, village 90 mi. ESE of Taunggyi. On Salween R., at Thailand border.

Mongpawn (mông'pôn), central state (sawbwaship) (□ 502; pop. 23,185), Southern Shan State, Upper Burma; ⊙ Mongpawn, village on Thazi-Kengtung road and 25 mi. E of Taunggyi, on the Nam Pawn.

Mongu (mông'gōō), township (pop. 1,294), ⊙ Barotse prov., W Northern Rhodesia, near Zambezi R., 250 mi. NW of Livingstone; 15°13'S 23°8'E. Cattle, sheep, goats; corn, millet. Airfield. Village of Lealui, native ⊙ Barotseland, is 8 mi. W, on the Zambezi.

Monguelfo (mông-gwĕl'fô), Ger. *Welsberg*, village (pop. 971), Bolzano prov., Trentino–Alto Adige, N Italy, on Rienza R. and 8 mi. ESE of Brunico; summer resort (alt. 3,365 ft.). Has 12th-cent. castle.

Mongyai (mông'yī, Burmese mông'yĕ), village, ⊙ South Hsenwi state, Northern Shan State, Upper Burma, on Lashio-Loilem road and 40 mi. SSE of Lashio, near head of the Nam Pang; road junction.

Mongyang (mông'yäng), village, Kengtung state, Southern Shan State, Upper Burma, 40 mi. N of Kengtung, on route to Chinese Yunnan prov.

Monhegan (mŭnhē'gĭn), plantation (pop. 75), Lincoln co., S Maine, on **Monhegan Island** (□ 2.5), 11 mi. ESE of Pemaquid Point; fishing and resort community, with lighthouse station. *Enterprise-Boxer* naval battle fought offshore, 1813.

Monheim (môn'hīm), town (pop. 2,215), Swabia, W Bavaria, Germany, 9 mi. NNE of Donauwörth; brewing, lumber and paper milling. Chartered before 1350.

Moniaive (mŏnĭ-īv'), agr. village in Glencairn parish (pop. 1,352), W Dumfries, Scotland, on the Cairn and 15 mi. NW of Dumfries. Monument to James Renwick, last of the Covenanters. Near by is MAXWELTON HOUSE.

Monianga (mōnyäng'gä) or **Manianga** (mä–), village, Equator Prov., NW Belgian Congo, on left bank of Giri R. and 175 mi. W of Lisala; terminus of navigation.

Monida (mōnī'dŭ), village, Beaverhead co., extreme SW Mont., 50 mi. SSE of Dillon, at SE extremity of Bitterroot Range, on Idaho line. Near-by Monida Pass (alt. 6,823 ft.) crosses the Continental Divide.

Monie Bay, Md.: see TANGIER SOUND.

Monifieth (mŭnĭfēth'), burgh (1931 pop. 2,984; 1951 census 3,417), S Angus, Scotland, on the Firth of Tay, 6 mi. ENE of Dundee; iron foundries.

Monikie (mōnē'kē), agr. village and parish (pop. 1,059), S Angus, Scotland, 9 mi. NE of Dundee. Site of reservoirs supplying Dundee. Near by are ruins of anc. Affleck Castle.

Monino (mô'nyĭnŭ), town (1946 pop. over 500), E central Moscow oblast, Russian SFSR, 9 mi. W of Noginsk; rail terminus; woolen mill; sanatorium. Stakhanovets is near by.

Moniquirá (mōnēkērä'), town (pop. 2,419), Boyacá dept., central Colombia, in Cordillera Oriental, 29 mi. NW of Tunja; alt. 5,767 ft.; coffee, sugar cane, fruit. Rich copper deposits near by; also silver and emeralds.

Monistrol or **Monistrol de Montserrat** (mōnēstrōl' dhā mōnsĕrät'), town (pop. 2,365), Barcelona prov., NE Spain, on Llobregat R. and 7 mi. S of Manresa; cotton milling, olive-oil processing. Starting point for ascension of the Montserrat.

Monistrol-sur-Loire (mônēstrôl'-sür-lwär'), town (pop. 2,068), Haute-Loire dept., S central France, near the Loire, 14 mi. SW of Saint-Étienne; mfg. of bicycle parts, elastic fabrics. Paper mill and hydroelectric plant near by.

Moniteau (mŏ'nŭtō, –tô), county (□ 418; pop. 10,840), central Mo.; ⊙ California. Bounded NE by Missouri R. Agr. (wheat, corn, oats), cattle, poultry, mules, sheep, saddle horses; coal, barite, limestone; mfg. at California. Formed 1845.

Monitor Range, central Nev., largely in Nye co., E of Toquema Range. Lies in Toiyabe Natl. Forest. Highest peak is Monitor (10,856 ft.), c.60 mi. NE of Tonopah. Antelope Peak (10,207 ft.) and Summit Mtn. (10,466 ft.) are in N.

Monjas (mōn'häs), town (1950 pop. 1,914), Jalapa dept., E central Guatemala, in highlands, 12 mi. SE of Jalapa; corn, wheat, beans, livestock.

Monk Bretton, England: see BARNSLEY.

Monkchester or **Monk Chester,** England: see NEWCASTLE-UPON-TYNE.

Monkey Bay, village, Southern Prov., central Nyasaland, port on Monkey Bay, inlet of L. Nyasa, 33 mi. NW of Fort Johnston; tourist resort (hotel); road-steamer transfer point.

Monkey Point, Nicaragua: see MICO POINT.

Monkey Point, W Trinidad, B.W.I., on the Gulf of Paria, just W of village of California, 18 mi. S of Port of Spain; 10°25'N 61°30'W. Sugar-loading pier, served by railroad.

Monkey River, town (pop. 421), Toledo dist., S Br. Honduras, port on Gulf of Honduras, at mouth of Monkey R. (small coastal stream), 28 mi. NE of Punta Gorda. Banana plantations; coconuts.

Monkoto (mông-kō'tō), village, Equator Prov., NW Belgian Congo, on Luilaba R. and 100 mi. S of Boende; agr. and trading center with rubber and coffee plantations; also palm products.

Monkseaton, England: see WHITLEY BAY.

Monkstown, Ireland: see PASSAGE WEST.

Monkton (mŭngk'tŭn), town and parish (pop. 3,396), NE Durham, England, 3 mi. SW of Sunderland; coal mining.

Monkton, town (pop. 520), Addison co., W Vt., 17 mi. S of Burlington; dairying.

Monkton and Prestwick, parish (pop. 9,427), W Ayrshire, Scotland. Includes burgh of PRESTWICK, agr. village of Monkton, 2 mi. NNE of Prestwick.

Monkton Combe (kōōm'), agr. village and parish (pop. 1,711), NE Somerset, England, 2 mi. SE of Bath.

Monkwearmouth, England: see SUNDERLAND.

Monlevade or **João Monlevade** (zhwã'ō mōlĭvä'dĭ), town, SE central Minas Gerais, Brazil, on Piracicaba R., on railroad and 50 mi. E of Belo Horizonte; steel-milling center (blast and open-hearth furnaces; blooming, rolling, and wire mills) using ore from Itabira (18 mi. NNW) and manganese mined in region.

Monmouth or **Monmouthshire** (mŏn'mŭth, –shĭr), county (□ 546.2; 1931 pop. 434,958; 1951 census 424,647), SW England; ⊙ Monmouth. Bounded by Welsh cos. of Glamorgan (W) and Brecknock (NW), and by Hereford (N), Gloucester (E), and Severn estuary (S). Drained by Wye, Usk, Monnow, Ebbw, and Rhymney rivers. Hilly in N and W, leveling toward E and S. Fruitgrowing and sheep raising in rural areas; important coal-mining, steel-milling, and tinplate-mfg. industry, centered on Pontypool, Tredegar, Ebbw Vale, and Rhymney. Besides Monmouth, other important towns are port of Newport, and Abertillery, Abercarn, Abergavenny, Chepstow, and Rhymney. Until 1536 co. was part of Wales, with which it has close geographical and cultural ties. There are some anc. abbeys, notably Tintern Abbey, and numerous traces of Roman occupation.

Monmouth, municipal borough (1931 pop. 4,731; 1951 census 5,432), ⊙ Monmouthshire, England, in NE part of co., on the Wye, at mouth of the Monnow, and 20 mi. NE of Newport; agr. market.

Has remains of anc. town walls and of 12th-cent. castle, birthplace of Henry V. Fragments remain of anc. Benedictine monastery containing Geoffrey of Monmouth's study. Monnow R. is crossed by old bridge, with Norman gatehouse. School and almshouses date from 1614.

Monmouth, county (□ 477; pop. 225,327), E N.J., bounded E by the Atlantic, N by Raritan and Sandy Hook bays; ⊙ Freehold. Many coastal resorts, including Asbury Park and Long Branch. Agr. area inland produces large truck, potato, and fruit crops, poultry and dairy products; some mfg. (rugs, textiles, clothing, clay products, food products, chemicals, other goods). Drained by Metedeconk, Manasquan, and Shark rivers; Navesink R. and Shrewsbury R. estuaries, Navesink Highlands, and Sandy Hook are in NE. Formed 1675.

Monmouth. **1** City (pop. 10,193), ⊙ Warren co., W Ill., 14 mi. WSW of Galesburg; trade and shipping center; mfg. (farm machinery, pottery, sheet-metal products, furnaces). Livestock fattening, agr. (grain, soybeans), dairying, coal and clay mining in region. Seat of Monmouth Col. Laid out 1831, inc. 1852. **2** Town (pop. 198), Jackson co., E Iowa, 11 mi. W of Maquoketa; livestock, grain. **3** Town (pop. 1,683), Kennebec co., S Maine, bet. Augusta and Lewiston, near L. Cobbosseecontee. Orchard center, with Univ. of Maine agr. experiment station. Textile mfg. at North Monmouth village. Seat of Monmouth Acad. Settled 1775, inc. 1792. **4** Town (pop. 1,956), Polk co., NW Oregon, 11 mi. SW of Salem in Willamette R. Valley, lumbering, dairying. Oregon Col. of Education here. Laid out 1855.

Monmouth, Fort, N.J.: see RED BANK.

Monmouth, Mount (10,470 ft.), SW B.C., in Coast Mts., 120 mi. NNW of Vancouver; 51°N 123°45'W.

Monmouth Beach, resort borough (pop. 806), Monmouth co., E N.J., bet. the coast and Shrewsbury R. inlet, 2 mi. N of Long Branch.

Monmouthshire, England: see MONMOUTH, county.

Monnaie (mŭnā'), village (pop. 791), Indre-et-Loire dept., W central France, 8 mi. NNE of Tours; road junction; small grains.

Monnerie-le-Montel, La (lä mônrē'-lù-mōtĕl'), village (pop. 946), Puy-de-Dôme dept., central France, 3 mi. NE of Thiers; cutlery mfg.

Monnetier-Mornex (mônùtyā'-mòrnā'), commune (pop. 1,002), Haute-Savoie dept., SE France, on N slope of Mont Salève, near Swiss border, 4 mi. SE of Geneva; Monnetier (alt. 2,329 ft.; pop. 991) is a health and winter-sport resort.

Monnikendam (mô'nēkùndäm), village (pop. 2,536), North Holland prov., W Netherlands, on the Ijsselmeer and 8 mi. NE of Amsterdam; tourist center; agr.; declining fishing industry. Ferry to Marken isl. (E).

Monnow River, Hereford and Monmouth, England, rises on Black Mts., on Brecon-Hereford border; flows 25 mi. SE to the Wye at Monmouth.

Mono, Solomon Isls.: see TREASURY ISLANDS.

Mono (mō'nō), county (□ 3,045; pop. 2,115), E Calif.; ⊙ Bridgeport. Rugged Sierra Nevada country; crest of range (with peaks over 13,000 ft.) is crossed in W by scenic Tioga Pass. Bounded E by Nev. line; drained by Owens, East Walker, and West Walker rivers; hydroelectric plants. Sweetwater Mts. in NE, White Mts. in SE. Much of co. is in Mono and Inyo natl. forests. Recreational region (hiking, camping, hunting, fishing, winter sports); includes saline Mono L., Mammoth Lakes, June L., many other small lakes (fishing), part of John Muir Trail, and scenic wilderness preserves. Stock raising (cattle, sheep), mining (pumice, gold, lead, silver, andalusite). Timber stands (chiefly pine) have been little exploited. Formed 1861.

Monocacy River (mùnŏ'kùsē), N Md., formed S of Gettysburg, Pa., by junction of several small creeks; winds c.60 mi. SSW to the Potomac 6 mi. SE of Point of Rocks. Civil War battle of Monocacy was fought on its banks near FREDERICK, July 9, 1864.

Mono Craters (mō'nō), E Calif., range of about 20 geologically recent volcanic cones (max. alt. c.9,000 ft.), just S of Mono L.

Monok (mô'nôk), town (pop. 2,901), Zemplen co., NE Hungary, 17 mi. ENE of Miskolc. Louis Kossuth b. here.

Mono Lake (mō'nō) (□ 87), E Calif., saline lake c.50 mi. NW of Bishop, just E of Sierra Nevada crest; alt. c.6,425 ft. It has no outlet, and its waters, which contain many chemicals, support only brine shrimp. Has 2 small volcanic isls.

Monolith, village, Kern co., S central Calif., in Tehachapi Mts., just E of Tehachapi; large cement plant.

Monomonac, Lake (mònùmō'năk), on N.H.–Mass. line, near Rindge, N.H., 17 mi. NW of Fitchburg, Mass.; 2.5 mi. long.

Monomoy Island, Mass.: see CHATHAM.

Monon (mō'nŏn"), town (pop. 1,439), White co., NW central Ind., on small Little Monon Creek and 29 mi. WNW of Logansport, in agr. area (corn, oats, soybeans); dairy products, beverages, crushed stone; railroad shops; stone quarrying. Inc. 1879.

Monona (mùnō'nù), county (□ 689; pop. 16,303), W Iowa, on Nebr. line (W; formed here by Missouri R.); ⊙ Onawa. Prairie agr. area (corn, hogs, cattle, poultry) drained by Little Sioux, Maple, and Soldier rivers; contains lakes (Blue, Badger) in W. Bituminous-coal deposits (E, S), sand and gravel pits. State parks. Formed 1851; lost territory in 1943 to Burt co., Nebr.

Monona. **1** Town (pop. 1,346), Clayton co., NE Iowa, 14 mi. N of Elkader, in grain, dairy, and timber area; concrete blocks, lime; ships livestock. Inc. 1897. **2** Village (pop. 2,544), Dane co., S Wis., near L. Monona, 2 mi. ESE of Madison, in dairy region. Inc. 1938.

Monona Lake, one of the Four Lakes, Dane co., S Wis.; Madison is on W shore; roughly triangular, c.4 mi. long, c.3 mi. wide. Drained by Yahara R.

Monongah (mùnŏng'gù), town (pop. 1,622), Marion co., N W.Va., on the West Fork and 5 mi. WSW of Fairmont, in bituminous-coal-mining region. In 1907, a mine disaster here killed 361 men. Founded c.1768.

Monongahela (mùnŏng"gùhē'lù), city (pop. 8,922), Washington co., SW Pa., 17 mi. S of Pittsburgh and on Monongahela R.; mfg. (metal products, chemicals, clay products); bituminous coal, gas; agr. A center of Whisky Rebellion, 1794. Settled 1770, inc. as borough 1833, as city 1873.

Monongahela River, in NW W.Va. and SW Pa., formed by junction of Tygart R. and the West Fork just S of Fairmont, Marion co., W.Va.; flows 128 mi. NNE past Morgantown, W.Va., and N into Pa., past industrial towns of Brownsville and Charleroi, joining Allegheny R. at Pittsburgh to form Ohio R. Entirely navigable by means of locks, it is an important freight artery. Joined at McKeesport, Pa., by Youghiogheny R.

Monongalia (mŏnùn-gā'lēù), county (□ 365; pop. 60,797), N W.Va.; ⊙ MORGANTOWN. On Allegheny Plateau; bounded N by Pa.; drained by Monongahela and Cheat rivers. Coal mining; gas and oil fields, limestone quarries, sand pits. Mfg. at Morgantown. Formed 1776.

Mono Pass (mō'nō) (alt. c.10,600 ft.), E Calif., in the Sierra Nevada, c.10 mi. SW of Mono L.

Monopoli (mônô'pôlē), town (pop. 18,092), Bari prov., Apulia, S Italy, port on the Adriatic, 26 mi. ESE of Bari. Industrial and commercial center; textile and flour mills, foundries, food cannery; mfg. of macaroni, soap, lubricating oils. Exports olive oil, wine, cherries. Bishopric. Has 12th-cent. cathedral, 16th-cent. castle.

Monor (mô'nôr), town (pop. 13,103), Pest-Pilis-Solt-Kiskun co., N central Hungary, 20 mi. SE of Budapest; granaries, flour mills, brickworks; brush factory. Ger. pop. here raises wheat, rye, cattle.

Mono River (mō'nō), chiefly in Fr. Togoland, rises near Dahomey border NE of Sokodé, flows c.250 mi. S in meandering course to Slave Coast (Gulf of Guinea) just W of Grand-Popo in Dahomey's coastal panhandle, its mouth communicating through channel with L. Togo (coastal lagoon). Lower course forms Fr. Togoland-Dahomey border. Navigable for small vessels near its mouth.

Monos Island (mō'nōs) (□ 1.52; alt. 942 ft.), off NW Trinidad, B.W.I., in the Dragon's Mouth, 11 mi. W of Port of Spain; bathing and fishing resort. Its central section was leased to U.S. in 1941.

Monostorpalyi (mô'nôsh-tôrpīē), Hung. *Monostorpályi*, town (pop. 2,648), Bihar co., E Hungary, 11 mi. SE of Debrecen; dairy farming.

Monóvar (mōnō'vär), city (pop. 7,528), Alicante prov., E Spain, in Valencia, 20 mi. WNW of Alicante; wine-production center. Brandy distilling, flour- and sawmilling, vegetable-oil processing; mfg. of glycerin, wax, soap, toys, footwear. Mineral springs. Marble and stone quarries. Salt-water lagoon 4 mi. NNW. Dominated by hill crowned by old castle.

Monowi, village (pop. 67), Boyd co., N Nebr., 27 mi. ESE of Butte and on Ponca Creek, near Missouri R.

Monpazier (mõpäzyā'), village (pop. 684), Dordogne dept., SW France, on the Dropt and 23 mi. SE of Bergerac; woodworking. Preserves its ramparts built 1284 by Edward I.

Monquhitter, Scotland: see CUMINESTOWN.

Monreal del Campo (mōnrāäl' dhĕl käm'pō), town (pop. 3,340), Teruel prov., E Spain, on the Jiloca and 33 mi. NNW of Teruel; agr. trade center (sugar beets, wine, cereals, sheep); chocolate and brandy mfg., sawmilling.

Monreale (mônrĕä'lĕ), town (pop. 14,340), Palermo prov., NW Sicily, 4 mi. SW of Palermo, in citrus-fruit and olive region; macaroni. Archbishopric. Has notable Norman cathedral (built 1174–89) and cloisters of Benedictine monastery (founded 1174). Near by is former Benedictine monastery of San Martino, founded by Gregory the Great in 6th cent. (restored 1346; enlarged in 1770s).

Mon River (mōn), Burmese *Mon Chaung* (mōn' joun), Upper Burma, rises in S Chin Hills, flows 150 mi. SE and E, past Sidoktaya and Pwinbyu, to the Irrawaddy 12 mi. N of Minbu. Used for irrigation in lower course; the Mon canals (on left and right banks) taking off at headworks 28 mi. WNW of Minbu.

Monroe (mùnrō'). **1** County (□ 1,035; pop. 25,732), SW Ala.; ⊙ Monroeville. Coastal plain, bounded SW by Alabama R., S by the Little R. Cotton, peanuts, bees, timber. Formed 1815. **2** County (□ 617; pop. 19,540), E central Ark.; ⊙ Clarendon. Drained by White and Cache rivers. Agr. (cotton, rice, corn); timber. Mfg. at Brinkley and Clarendon. Commercial fishing. Has state game refuge. Formed 1829. **3** County (□ 994; pop. 29,957), S Fla., at tip of peninsula; ⊙ Key West (pop. 26,433). Consists of sparsely populated Everglades area (including CAPE SABLE, Whitewater Bay, and part of Everglades Natl. Park) and most of the FLORIDA KEYS, enclosing Florida Bay. Has large Seminole Indian Reservation in N. Fishing, dairying, and poultry raising; citrus-fruit growing (especially limes) on Florida Keys. Formed 1824. **4** County (□ 399; pop. 10,523), central Ga.; ⊙ Forsyth. Bounded E by Ocmulgee R. Piedmont agr. (corn, truck, pecans, fruit) and livestock area; textile mfg. at Forsyth. Formed 1821. **5** County (□ 380; pop. 13,282), SW Ill.; ⊙ Waterloo. Bounded W by Mississippi R.; drained by Kaskaskia R. In N, includes part of St. Louis metropolitan area. Agr. (corn, wheat, hay, fruit, livestock, poultry; dairy products); limestone quarries. Formed 1816. **6** County (□ 412; pop. 50,080), S central Ind.; ⊙ BLOOMINGTON. Drained by West Fork of White R., Salt Creek, and small Bean Blossom and Clear creeks. Farming (grain, corn, tobacco), stock raising, dairying; limestone quarrying; timber. Mfg. at Bloomington. Formed 1818. **7** County (□ 435; pop. 11,814), S Iowa; ⊙ Albia. Prairie agr. (hogs, cattle, poultry, corn, oats, hay) and coal-mining area. Formed 1843. **8** County (□ 334; pop. 13,770), S Ky.; ⊙ Tompkinsville. Bounded S by Tenn.; drained by Cumberland R. and several creeks. Includes Old Mulkey Meeting House State Park near Tompkinsville. Hilly agr. area (corn, wheat, hay, burley tobacco, livestock). Oil wells; timber; limestone quarries. Formed 1820. **9** County (□ 562; pop. 75,666), extreme SE Mich.; ⊙ Monroe. Bounded S by Ohio line, E by L. Erie, NE by Huron R.; drained by Raisin R. Stock raising, dairying, agr. (grain, truck, corn); nurseries. Mfg. at Monroe and Dundee. Limestone quarrying; salt beds. Formed 1817. **10** County (□ 769; pop. 36,543), E Miss.; ⊙ Aberdeen. Bordered E by Ala.; drained by Buttahatchie R. and East Fork of the Tombigbee. Agr. (cotton, corn), dairying; timber. Formed 1821. **11** County (□ 669; pop. 11,314), NE central Mo.; ⊙ Paris. Drained by Salt R. Agr. (corn, oats, wheat); livestock, notably poultry and saddle horses; coal; lumber. Formed 1831. **12** (also mŭn'rō) County (□ 673; pop. 487,632), W N.Y.; ⊙ ROCHESTER. Bounded N by L. Ontario (resorts); crossed by the Barge Canal; drained by Genesee R. and Honeoye and other creeks. Applegrowing area, producing also truck, dairy products, grain, potatoes; extensive mfg. Formed 1821. **13** County (□ 455; pop. 15,362), E Ohio; ⊙ Woodsfield. Bounded SE by Ohio R., here forming W.Va. line; also drained by small Sunfish Creek and by Little Muskingum R. Agr. (livestock; dairy products; grain); coal mines, limestone quarries. Formed 1815. **14** County (□ 611; pop. 33,773), E Pa.; ⊙ Stroudsburg. Resort region; bounded E by Delaware R. Pocono plateau is in W; series of long high ridges of Kittatinny Mtn. in E, separated by narrow valleys and cut by scenic Delaware Water Gap. First settlers (1725) worked copper mines. Machinery, metal products, textiles; crushed stone; recreation. Formed 1836. **15** County (□ 665; pop. 24,513), SE Tenn.; ⊙ Madisonville. Bounded SE and E by N.C., NE by Little Tennessee R.; drained by its tributaries; Unicoi Mts. lie along S border. Includes part of Cherokee Natl. Forest. Lumbering, livestock raising, agr. (fruit, tobacco, hay, corn), dairying. Barite mines. Formed 1819. **16** County (□ 473; pop. 13,123), SE W.Va.; ⊙ Union. Bounded E and S by Va.; drained by tributaries of New and Greenbrier rivers. Mountainous region, with Peters Mtn. along Va. line and summits of the Alleghenies (including Bickett Knob) to W. Agr. (livestock raising, dairying, fruitgrowing); limestone and iron-ore deposits; some natural gas. Formed 1799. **17** County (□ 915; pop. 31,378), W central Wis.; ⊙ Sparta. Dairying and farming area (tobacco, grain, livestock, poultry); timber. Processing of dairy products, lumber. Drained by Lemonweir, Black, La Crosse, and Kickapoo rivers. Formed 1854.

Monroe (mùnrō'). **1** Town (pop. 2,892), Fairfield co., SW Conn., on the Housatonic and 10 mi. N of Bridgeport. Includes villages of Stepney Depot and Stevenson (site of power dam on Housatonic R. forming L. Zoar). Settled c.1775, inc. 1823. **2** City (pop. 4,542), ⊙ Walton co., N central Ga., 37 mi. E of Atlanta; textile-mfg. center. Has some fine old houses in classic-revival style. Inc. 1821. **3** Town (pop. 428), Adams co., E Ind., 25 mi. SSE of Fort Wayne. There is also a Monroe in Tippecanoe co., 13 mi. SE of La Fayette. **4** Town (pop. 1,108), Jasper co., central Iowa, 27 mi. E of Des Moines, in agr. and bituminous-coal-mining area. Laid out 1851. **5** Industrial city (pop. 38,572), ⊙ Ouachita parish, NE central La., on Ouachita R. and 95 mi. E of Shreveport, bet. lowland cotton area (E) and upland cattle, fruit, and timber region (W). Large natural-gas fields near by. Fourth-largest city in La.; mfg. of carbon black, chemicals, lumber, paper, packed meat, cotton and cottonseed products, concrete and metal products, brick; machine shops, foundries. Seat of a state jr. col. and a training school for boys. Fort Miro founded here by 1st settlers in 1785; town was renamed in 1818, and inc. as city in 1900. Greatest growth came after discovery of natural gas near by in 1916. **6** Agr. and lumbering town (pop. 593), Waldo co., S Maine, 11 mi. N of Belfast. **7** Rural town (pop. 174), Franklin co., NW Mass., on Deerfield R. (power dam) and 9 mi. E of North Adams. Includes Monroe Bridge village; glassine mfg. **8** City (pop. 21,467), ⊙ Monroe co., extreme SE Mich., 34 mi. SW of Detroit and on Raisin R. near its mouth on L. Erie. Steel and paper milling; mfg. of food products, auto parts, heating apparatus, furniture, construction materials. Limestone quarries; fisheries; large nurseries. Shipping point for farm area. Seat of St. Mary's Convent and Acad. Monroe was the scene (Jan., 1813) of the Raisin R. massacre of Amer. troops by Indian allies of the British in War of 1812, and was also the center of the "Toledo War." Many Indian relics have been found here. Settled c.1780, inc. as city 1837. **9** Village (pop. 269), Platte co., E central Nebr., 12 mi. W of Columbus and on Loup R. Powerhouse here is part of power project on Loup R. **10** Town (pop. 410), Grafton co., NW N.H., on the Connecticut and 40 mi. SW of Berlin; hydroelectric plants. **11** (also mŭn'rō) Summer-resort village (pop. 1,753), Orange co., SE N.Y., 15 mi. SW of Newburgh; small lakes near by. Mfg. of iron and steel products. Inc. 1894. **12** City (pop. 10,140), ⊙ Union co., S N.C., 23 mi. SE of Charlotte, near S.C. line; trade and distribution center for agr. and timber area; cotton and lumber mills, brick-and tile-works. Settled 1751; inc. 1844. **13** Village (pop. 360), Butler co., extreme SW Ohio, 11 mi. ENE of Hamilton. **14** Town (pop. 362), Benton co., W Oregon, 20 mi. NNW of Eugene; farm trade center. **15** or **Monroeton**, borough (pop. 466), Bradford co., NE Pa., 4 mi. SSW of Towanda. There is also a village, Monroe, in Clarion co. **16** Town (pop. 160), Turner co., SE S.Dak., 7 mi. NNW of Parker; small trading point. **17** Town (1940 pop. 69), Overton co., N Tenn., 5 mi. NE of Livingston. **18** City (pop. 1,214), Sevier co., SW central Utah, in Sevier R. valley, 10 mi. S of Richfield; alt. 5,380 ft.; livestock, orchards. Settled 1863. Sevier Plateau is E. **19** Village (pop. c.500), Amherst co., central Va., 6 mi. N of Lynchburg; railroad division point. **20** Town (pop. 1,556), Snohomish co., NW Wash., 15 mi. SE of Everett and on Skykomish R.; lumber, truck, potatoes, dairy products; food processing. State reformatory is here. **21** City (pop. 7,037), ⊙ Green co., S Wis., 35 mi. SSW of Madison, in dairying region; one of state's leading cheese-producing centers; mfg. also of cheese-making equipment, wood products, beer. Inhabitants mostly of Swiss descent; annual cheese fair is held. Inc. as village c.1859, as city in 1882.

Monroe, Fort, Va.: see OLD POINT COMFORT.

Monroe, Lake (c.5 mi. long, 3 mi. wide), E central Fla., on Seminole-Volusia co. line; a shallow widening of St. Johns R. Sanford is on S shore.

Monroe, Mount, N.H.: see PRESIDENTIAL RANGE.

Monroe Bridge, Mass.: see MONROE.

Monroe City. 1 Town (pop. 453), Knox co., SW Ind., 10 mi. SE of Vincennes, in agr. and bituminous-coal area. **2** City (pop. 2,093), Monroe and Marion counties, NE central Mo., near Salt R., 20 mi. W of Hannibal; poultry-shipping center; dairy products, lumber. Mark Twain b. in near-by Florida. Inc. 1869.

Monroe Peak (11,226 ft.), in Sevier Plateau, SW central Utah, 7 mi. SSE of Monroe.

Monroeton, Pa.: see MONROE.

Monroeville. 1 Town (pop. 2,772), ⊙ Monroe co., SW Ala., 75 mi. NE of Mobile; trade center in agr. area (cotton, corn, potatoes); underwear mfg. meat curing, woodworking. Settled c.1815. **2** Town (pop. 1,150), Allen co., NE Ind., 16 mi. ESE of Fort Wayne, near Ohio line. **3** Village (pop. 1,275), Huron co., N Ohio, 14 mi. S of Sandusky and on West Branch of Huron R.; livestock; pottery, leather goods, ax handles.

Monrovia (mŭnrō'vēŭ) [for President James Monroe], city (estimated pop. 12,000), ⊙ Liberia and Montserrado co., major Atlantic port on Cape Montserrado, just S of St. Paul R. mouth, 225 mi. SSE of Freetown (Sierra Leone); 6°19'N 10°49'W. Chief port and commercial center of Liberia; brickworks, modern cold-storage plant, soft-drink bottling works. Exports palm oil and kernels, rubber, gold, cassava, forest products. Site of Col. of West Africa, Liberia Col. (opened 1863). Has govt. general hosp. and several church missions. Airport, developed during Second World War at Roberts Field, 30 mi. ESE of Monrovia. Road to N'zérékoré (Fr. Guinea) via Ganta. Modern harbor and submarine base developed during Second World War on Bushrod Isl. (across short Mesurado Creek; bridge); it was opened 1948 as a free port for vessels drawing 28 ft. Iron-loading facilities begun 1950, for export of ores from Bomi Hills mine (40 mi. N; new rail link). Monrovia was founded 1822 by the American Colonization Society as a haven for ex-slaves from the U.S. Descendants of those early settlers still dominate the town. Has hot rainy climate.

Monrovia, city (pop. 20,186), Los Angeles co., S Calif., 15 mi. ENE of downtown Los Angeles, at base of San Gabriel Mts.; packing and trade center for citrus-fruit area also producing avocados, poultry. Mfg. of water heaters, lumber, paint, soap, monuments. Laid out 1886, inc. 1887.

Monroy (mōnroi'), town (pop. 2,609), Cáceres prov., W Spain, 14 mi. NE of Cáceres; meat processing, flour milling; cereals, olive oil, sheep. Has 13th-cent. castle.

Monrupino (mônrōōpē'nō), village (pop. 390), N Free Territory of Trieste, in the Karst, 5 mi. N of Trieste, near Yugoslav line. Pop. is Slovenian. Also called Rupin Grande, Slovenian *Veliki Repen*. Placed 1947 under Anglo-American administration

Mons (mŏnz, Fr. mōs). **1** Flemish *Bergen* (bĕr'-khŭn), town (pop. 25,684), ⊙ Hainaut prov., SW Belgium, at junction of Condé-Mons Canal and Canal du Centre, 32 mi. SW of Brussels; 50°27'N 3°58'E. Rail junction, processing and shipping center for Borinage coal-mining area; major coal and sugar market; leather tanning. Has 12th-cent. castle chapel, 15th-cent. church of Sainte-Waudru, 15th-cent. town hall, and 17th-cent. belfry with large carillon. Known in 7th cent., it was made ⊙ counts of Hainaut by Charlemagne in 9th cent. In 16th, 17th, and 18th cent., repeatedly attacked and occupied by Dutch, Spanish, and French forces. In First World War, site of a major battle in 1914 when British and Germans met for 1st time in the war; another battle in 1918. Has annual pageant and festival of St. George and the dragon. **2** Town (pop. 4,128), Liége prov., E Belgium, 7 mi. W of Liége; coal mining. Has 18th-cent château.

Monsanto, Brazil: see MONTE SANTO DE MINAS.

Monsanto (mŏnsăn'tō), industrial village (pop. 357), St. Clair co., SW Ill., near the Mississippi, just S of East St. Louis and within St. Louis metropolitan area; zinc processing, chemical mfg.

Monsão, Portugal: see MONÇAO.

Monsarás, Ponta de (pōn'tŭ dĭ mōsŭräs'), headland of Espírito Santo, E Brazil, on the Atlantic at mouth of the Rio Doce, and 60 mi. NE of Vitória; 19°35'S 39°47'W.

Monsaraz (mōsŭrăsh'), agr. village (pop. 256), Évora dist., S central Portugal, near the Guadiana and Sp. border, 31 mi. ESE of Évora.

Monschau (mŏn'shou), town (pop. 2,420), in former Prussian Rhine Prov., W Germany, after 1945 in North Rhine-Westphalia, on the Rur and 14 mi. SSE of Aachen, near Belgian line; textiles. Until 1920s, called Montjoie.

Monsefú (mōnsäfōō'), city (pop. 8,144), Lambayeque dept., NW Peru, on coastal plain, on Eten R., on railroad and 7 mi. S of Chiclayo. Rice milling, mfg. of straw hats, weaving of native textiles; rice, sugar cane, fruit.

Monségur (mōsāgür'), village (pop. 933), Gironde dept., SW France, on Dropt R. and 11 mi. NNW of Marmande; tobacco, poultry.

Monselice (mônsä'lēchĕ), town (pop. 5,895), Padova prov., Veneto, N Italy, at SE foot of Euganean Hills, 13 mi. SSW of Padova. Rail junction; flour and jute mills, mfg. (shoes, agr. tools, marmalade, candy, liquor). Has cathedral (1256; restored 1931) and ruins of castle built by Frederick II. Trachyte quarries near by.

Mons-en-Baroeul (mōs-ā-bärûl'), outer NE suburb (pop. 8,545) of Lille, Nord dept., N France, on road to Roubaix; printing, brewing, dairying, mfg. (varnishes, biscuits).

Monseñor Nouel (mōnsānyōr' nōĕl'), town (1950 pop. 4,426), La Vega prov., central Dominican Republic, in fertile valley of the Cordillera Central, 22 mi. SSE of La Vega; resort and agr. center (coffee, cacao, fruit). Formerly called Bonao for a fort which Columbus built here.

Monserrat (mōnsĕrät'), village (pop. 2,020), Valencia prov., E Spain, 15 mi. SW of Valencia; olive-oil processing, plaster mfg.; wine, cereals, oranges, grapes. Gypsum quarries near by.

Monserrat, mountain, Spain: see MONTSERRAT.

Monserrato (mônsĕr-rä'tô), town (pop. 9,136), Cagliari prov., S Sardinia, 2 mi. NNE of Cagliari; distilleries (beer, wine, denatured alcohol).

Monsey (mŏn'sē), village (1940 pop. 867), Rockland co., SE N.Y., 5 mi. E of Suffern, in resort and agr. area; braille printing.

Monsols (mōsôl'), village (pop. 302), Rhône dept., E central France, in the Monts du Beaujolais, 16 mi. SW of Mâcon; livestock raising.

Monsón, Peru: see MONZÓN.

Monson (mŭn'sŭn). **1** Town (pop. 855), Piscataquis co., central Maine, on small Hebron Pond and 15 mi. NW of Dover-Foxcroft; known for its slate quarries. **2** Town (pop. 6,125), including Monson village (pop. 2,436), Hampden co., S Mass., 13 mi. E of Springfield; woolens; granite; dairying, poultry, truck. Settled 1715, inc. 1760.

Monster (mŏn'stŭr), village (pop. 4,836) South Holland prov., W Netherlands, 7 mi. SW of The Hague, near North Sea, in Westland agr. area; market center for grapes, peaches, and other fruit, early potatoes, flowers.

Monsteras (mûn"stûrōs'), Swedish *Mönsterås*, town (pop. 1,609), Kalmar co., SE Sweden, on small bay of Kalmar Sound of Baltic, 15 mi. S of Oskarshamn; port; match mfg., sawmilling.

Monsummano (mônsōōm-mä'nô), town (pop. 2,671), Pistoia prov., Tuscany, central Italy, 7 mi. SW of Pistoia; mfg. (shoes, fertilizer, brooms). Near by is Giusti grotto (natural vapor baths), named after G. Giusti who was b. here.

Montà (môntä'), village (pop. 2,086), Cuneo prov., Piedmont, NW Italy, 9 mi. NNE of Alba.

Montabaur (môn'täbou"ŭr), town (1946 pop. 4,655), in former Prussian prov. of Hesse-Nassau, W Germany, after 1945 in Rhineland-Palatinate, 11 mi. ENE of Coblenz; main town of lower Westerwald [Ger. *Unterwesterwald*] dist.; iron foundries. Has late-Gothic church, and former castle of electors of Trier. After 1945, four districts [Ger. *Landkreis*] of former Prussian prov. of Hesse-Nassau were amalgamated into the administrative division [Ger. *Regierungsbezirk*] (□ 685; 1946 pop. 220,005; 1950 pop. 239,254) of Montabaur in newly formed state of RHINELAND-PALATINATE in Fr. occupation zone.

Montaberner (mōntävĕrnĕr'), village (pop. 1,179), Valencia prov., E Spain, 8 mi. S of Játiva; alcohol, vermouth mfg.; cereals, wine, olive oil.

Montafon (mŏn'täfōn"), upper valley of Ill R., in Vorarlberg, W Austria; 15 mi. long; dairy farming. Tourist trade, with centers at Schruns and Gaschurn. Hydroelectric works at Parthenen and Rodund.

Mont-Agel, France: see TURBIE, LA.

Montagnac (mōtänyäk'), village (pop. 2,296), Oran dept., NW Algeria, on railroad and 14 mi. NNW of Tlemcen; olives, cereals.

Montagnac, town (pop. 2,790), Hérault dept., S France, near the Hérault, 12 mi. NW of Sète; winegrowing.

Montagnana (môntänyä'nä), town (pop. 4,290), Padova prov., Veneto, N Italy, 23 mi. SW of Padua, mfg. (textile machinery, beet sugar, sausage, macaroni). Has Gothic cathedral (1431–1502) and picturesque medieval walls (13th–14th cent.) with 24 towers.

Montagnareale (môntä"nyärĕä'lĕ), village (pop. 906), Messina prov., NE Sicily, 1 mi. SW of Patti. Antimony mines near by.

Montagne, La (lä mōtä'nyù), town (pop. 3,645), Loire-Inférieure dept., W France, on Loire R. and 6 mi. W of Nantes.

Montagne, La, village (pop. 2,521), N Réunion isl., hill resort 1 mi. W of Saint-Denis.

Montagne Blanche (blăsh'), village (pop. 2,391), E Mauritius, on railroad, 7 mi. SSW of Flacq; sugar.

Montagne Noire (nwär'), southernmost range of Massif Central, S France, on Tarn-Aude dept. border bet. Dourgne (W) and Saint-Amans-Soult (E). Rises to 3,970 ft. in Pic de Nore. Densely forested. Gold, silver, arsenic mining on S slopes. Textile mfg. dist. of Mazamet on N slopes.

Montagnes Noires (mōtä'nyù nwär'), low granitic mountains in Finistère dept., W France, part of eroded Armorican Massif. Extend 40 mi. WSW–ENE across dept. S of Aulne R., reaching out into Crozon Peninsula. Rise to 1,080 ft. Also spelled Montagne Noire.

Montagne Tremblante Park (mōtä'nyù trāblät'), provincial park in the Laurentians, S Que., c.70 mi. NW of Montreal; Mt. Tremblant (Trembling Mtn.) rises to 3,150 ft. Resort area, notably for skiing.

Montagrier (mōtägrēā'), village (pop. 118), Dordogne dept., SW France, near Dronne R., 13 mi. WNW of Périgueux; wheat, vegetables.

Montagu (mŏn'tùgū), village (pop. 141), NW Tasmania, 120 mi. WNW of Launceston; cheese.

Montagu, town (pop. 4,242), SW Cape Prov., U. of So. Afr., in the Langeberg range, 40 mi. E of Worcester; health resort with radioactive mineral springs; viticulture, fruit drying. Bushman paintings in near-by caves.

Montague (mŏn'tùgū), town (pop. 769), E P.E.I., on short Montague R., near its mouth on Cardigan Bay, 24 mi. ESE of Charlottetown; agr. market in dairying, cattle-raising, potato-growing region.

Montague (mŏn"tāg'), county (□ 1,090; pop. 17,070), N Texas; ⊙ Montague. Bounded N by Red R. (here the Okla. line); drained by tributaries of Red and Trinity rivers. Diversified agr. (peanuts, cotton, corn, grains, fruit, truck); large poultry, dairy industries; cattle ranching. Oil, natural-gas fields; timber. Mfg., processing at Bowie, Nocona. Formed 1857.

Montague. 1 (mŏn'tùgū) Town (pop. 579), Siskiyou co., N Calif., at W base of Cascade Range, 6 mi. E of Yreka, and on Shasta R.; dairying, stock raising. **2** (mŏn'tùgū) Town (pop. 7,812), Franklin co., NW Mass., on Connecticut R. just SE of Greenfield; machinery, dies, fishing tackle. Large hydroelectric plant. Villages include Montague City, Turners Falls (pop. 5,179) (site of 1st dam across the Connecticut), MILLERS FALLS, Lake Pleasant. Settled 1715, set off from Sunderland 1754. **3** (mŏn'tùgū) City (pop. 1,530), Muskegon co., SW Mich., 14 mi. NNW of Muskegon, at head of White L. Shipping point for agr. and dairying area; mfg. (foundry products, canned goods); commercial fisheries. Resort; winter ice fishing. Inc.

as village 1883, as city 1935. **4** (mŏn″tăg′) Village (pop. c.300), ⊙ Montague co., N Texas, c.50 mi. ESE of Wichita Falls; market point in agr. area.

Montague Island (mŏn′tūgū) (50 mi. long, 5–12 mi. wide), S Alaska, on W side of entrance of Prince William Sound, 60 mi. E of Seward; 60°5′N 147°23′W; rises to 3,050 ft.

Montague Island, in Tasman Sea, 4 mi. off SE coast of New South Wales, Australia; 2 mi. long, 1 mi. wide; rises to 250 ft.; largely composed of granite.

Montague Island (□ 18), Lower California, NW Mexico, at mouth of Colorado R., at head of Gulf of California, 75 mi. SE of Mexicali; 6 mi. long, 3 mi. wide; flat, alluvial, uninhabited.

Montague Sound, inlet of Timor Sea, NE Western Australia, bet. Cape Voltaire (E) and Bigge Isl. (W); 20 mi. long, 30 mi. wide.

Montague Strait, S Alaska, entrance from Gulf of Alaska (S) to Prince William Sound (N), bet. Montague Isl. (E) and Latouche Isl. (W); 60°8′N 147°38′W.

Montagu Pass (2,348 ft.), S Cape Prov., U. of So. Afr., crosses Outeniqua Mts. 5 mi. N of George. Railroad from George climbs c.1,600 ft. over distance of 17 mi.

Montaigu, Belgium: see SCHERPENHEUVEL.

Montaigu (mōtĕgü′), town (pop. 2,021), Vendée dept., W France, on Maine R. and 20 mi. SSE of Nantes; road center; metalworks; mfg. of pottery, footwear; sawmilling.

Montaigu-de-Quercy (-dü-kĕrsē′), village (pop. 444), Tarn-et-Garonne dept., SW France, 16 mi. ESE of Villeneuve-sur-Lot; wool spinning.

Montaigut or **Montaigut-en-Combrailles** (mōtĕgü′-ã-kōbrī′), village (pop. 1,106), Puy-de-Dôme dept., central France, in Combrailles, 15 mi. SE of Montluçon; vegetable growing, dairying.

Montaione (môn″täyô′nĕ), village (pop. 867), Firenze prov., Tuscany, central Italy, 7 mi. NE of Volterra; marble quarrying.

Montalban (mōntälbän′), town (1939 pop. 1,726; 1948 municipality pop. 5,257), Rizal prov., S Luzon, Philippines, on small Montalban R. and 14 mi. NE of Manila; rice, sugar cane, fruit. Reservoir near by.

Montalbán (mōntälvän′). **1** or **Montalbán de Córdoba** (dhä kôr′dhōvä), town (pop. 4,384), Córdoba prov., S Spain, agr. trade center 22 mi. S of Córdoba; olive-oil processing; cereals, vegetables, melons. **2** Town (pop. 1,718), Teruel prov., E Spain, 38 mi. NNE of Teruel; produces wine, fruit, cereals. Summer resort. Lignite mines in vicinity.

Montalbán, town (pop. 2,324), Carabobo state, N Venezuela, 23 mi. W of Valencia; agr. center (sugar cane, coffee, tobacco, corn, fruit).

Montalbanejo (mōntälvänā′hō), town (pop. 938), Cuenca prov., E central Spain, 30 mi. SW of Cuenca; cereals, saffron, grapes; sheep, goats; apiculture. Lumbering (pine).

Montalbano di Elicona (môntälbä′nô dē ĕlēkô′nä), village (pop. 3,843), Messina prov., NE Sicily, in Peloritani Mts., 8 mi. SSE of Patti; weaving (cloth, blankets).

Montalbano Ionico (yô′nēkô), village (pop. 4,471), Matera prov., Basilicata, S Italy, near Agri R., 7 mi. S of Pisticci, in agr. region (cereals, vegetables, citrus fruit).

Montalbo (mōntäl′vō), town (pop. 1,546), Cuenca prov., E central Spain, 32 mi. WSW of Cuenca; cereals, einkorn, grapes, saffron, potatoes, vegetables, olives, sheep.

Montalcino (môntälchē′nô), town (pop. 2,803), Siena prov., Tuscany, central Italy, 20 mi. SSE of Siena; macaroni, acids. Alabaster quarries near by. Bishopric. Has cathedral, palace (13th–14th cent.) with picture gall.

Montale (môntä′lĕ), village (pop. 167), Pistoia prov., Tuscany, central Italy, 5 mi. E of Pistoia; woolen textiles, straw hats.

Montalegre (mōntŏolā′grĭ), town (pop. 1,452), Vila Real dist., northernmost Portugal, on S slope of Serra do Larouco, 19 mi. WNW of Chaves, near Sp. border; olive- and winegrowing; livestock.

Montalieu-Vercieu (mōtälyû′-vĕrsyû′), village (pop. 1,247), Isère dept., SE France, near left bank of the Rhone, 17 mi. N of La Tour-du-Pin; stone quarries; mfg. of slaked lime and cement pipe.

Montallegro (môntäl-lā′grô), village (pop. 3,062), Agrigento prov., SW Sicily, 14 mi. NW of Agrigento.

Montalto (môntäl′tô), highest peak (6,417 ft.) in Calabria, S Italy, in the ASPROMONTE, 15 mi. ENE of Reggio di Calabria.

Mont Alto (mŏnt ăl′tō), borough (pop. 984), Franklin co., S Pa., 6 mi. N of Waynesboro. State school of forestry; tuberculosis sanatorium here.

Montalto delle Marche (dĕl-lĕ mär′kĕ), village (pop. 689), Ascoli Piceno prov., The Marches, central Italy, 9 mi. N of Ascoli Piceno. Bishopric.

Montalto Ligure (lē′gōōrĕ), village (pop. 656), Imperia prov., Liguria, NW Italy, in Taggia R. valley, 8 mi. NNE of San Remo, in olive-growing region.

Montalto Uffugo (ōōf-fōō′gô), town (pop. 2,983), Cosenza prov., Calabria, S Italy, 10 mi. NNW of Cosenza; olive oil, wine, raw silk.

Montalvão (mōntŏolvã′ŏ), agr. village (pop. 1,697), Portalegre dist., central Portugal, near Sp. border, 22 mi. NNW of Portalegre.

Montalvo (mōntäl′vō), village, Los Ríos prov., W central Ecuador, on affluent of Guayas R. and 7 mi. E of Babahoyo; cacao plantation; also sugar cane, rice, oranges, pineapples.

Montamarta (mōntämär′tä), village (pop. 1,468), Zamora prov., NW Spain, 10 mi. NNW of Zamora; stock raising, lumbering; cereals, wine.

Montaña (mōntä′nyä), NE and E Peru; originally a name for the E forested slopes of the Andes, it now also includes the tropical lowlands of the Peruvian Amazon basin.

Montana (mōntä′nä), village (pop. 1,279), Valais canton, S Switzerland, 2 mi. W of Sierre; with Vermala (vĕrmä′lä), it is a resort (alt. 4,920–5,512 ft.) with sanatoria.

Montana (mŏntă′nů), state (land □ 146,316; with inland waters □ 147,138; 1950 pop. 591,024; 1940 pop. 559,456), NW U.S., bordered N by Canadian provs. of B.C., Alta., and Sask., E by N.Dak. and S.Dak., S by Wyo. and Idaho, W by Idaho; 3d in area, 42d in pop.; admitted 1889 as 41st state; ⊙ Helena. The "Mountain State" or "Treasure State" is 460–560 mi. E–W, c.280 mi. N–S. The state lies in 2 physiographic regions: the N ROCKY MOUNTAINS in the W, occupying 40% of the total area, and the GREAT PLAINS in the E. The Rockies consist of several broken ranges of metamorphosed sediments, deeply eroded and glaciated, and running generally NW–SE, sometimes in parallel ridges. The main ranges are the LEWIS RANGE (rising to 9–10,000 ft.), in which lies the beautiful GLACIER NATIONAL PARK, the CABINET MOUNTAINS, the Big Belt Mts., and, along the Idaho line, the BITTERROOT RANGE (9–10,000 ft.); in the extreme S is the ABSAROKA RANGE, with Granite Peak (12,850 ft.), the highest point in the state. Detached outliers of the Rockies—notably the LITTLE BELT MOUNTAINS, Crazy Mts., and BIGHORN MOUNTAINS—appear throughout central Mont. from the Canadian to the Wyo. border. The Continental Divide follows (N–S) the watersheds of the Lewis, Anaconda, and S Bitterroot ranges. W of the Divide the state is drained by the Kootenai R. and the CLARK FORK and its tributaries, the Flathead and Bitterroot rivers. FLATHEAD LAKE, S of Kalispell, is the largest natural lake in the state. In SW Mont., E of the Divide, the Missouri R. rises in 3 headstreams, flows N past Helena and Great Falls, and then E across the plains to the N.Dak. border, just beyond which it receives the YELLOWSTONE RIVER from the SW. Other Missouri R. tributaries in Mont. are the Musselshell, Marias, Sun, and Milk rivers. The Great Plains of E Mont. comprise a rolling tableland of 2,500–5,000 ft. (E–W), broken by river valleys and isolated hills. The winters here are severe, with cold winds and snowstorms sweeping down from Canada, although warm chinook winds along the E slopes of the Rockies frequently modify the cold conditions; the summers are hot and dry. Miles City (SE) has a mean Jan. temp. of 17°F. and a mean July temp. of 74°F., with an annual rainfall of 13 in. In the sheltered mtn. valleys of the W the winters are more moderate, the summers cooler, and rainfall slightly heavier. Butte has a mean Jan. temp. of 23°F. and a mean July temp. of 65°F., with an annual rainfall of 15 in. Because of the harsh climate in the plains large-scale dry farming is practiced and hardy crops predominate. Total farm and range acreage is c.58,780,000. The state is a major producer of wheat (chiefly the hard spring type), barley, hay, corn, sugar beets, and flaxseed; other crops include dry beans, potatoes, rye, and oats. The dark soils of the N and E prairies yield the best wheat, while sugar beets, beans, and potatoes are cultivated mainly in the irrigated areas along the Yellowstone, Milk, and other rivers. Most of the corn, hay, oats, and barley are grown as fodder. In the W mtn. valleys there are many fruit orchards (cherries, apples), especially in the Bitterroot and Flathead regions. Among the many irrigation projects in Mont. the major works are FORT PECK DAM in the Missouri, Fresno Reservoir in the Milk R., Canyon Ferry Dam in the Missouri, and Gibson Dam in the Sun R. In most of the S counties, where rainfall is scanty, much land is devoted to extensive cattle and sheep raising; MILES CITY, BILLINGS, and Dillon are the chief livestock markets, and the state ranks high in wool production. Several fur farms (muskrat, chinchilla) are located in the W and S. The state has over 20,000,000 acres of total forest land, most of it in the W, where Douglas fir, ponderosa pine, western larch, lodgepole pine, Engelmann spruce, and western white pine are the principal species. Forest clearings on the E slopes of the Rockies are used for grazing. The lumbering industry is centered in the NW, with large sawmills at Bonner and Libby; 35% of the state's total land area is under Federal control. Mont. is noted for its mineral resources and the BUTTE area, in Silver Bow co., is one of the richest mining dists. in the world, with extensive deposits of gold, silver, copper, zinc, and lead. The copper ore is shipped from the Butte mines to ANACONDA, where it is smelted, and then sent to an electrolytic refinery at GREAT FALLS. At East Helena is a large lead smelter. Manganese, sapphires and phosphate rock are mined in the SW part of the state, and coal (chiefly lignite) of an inferior quality is found in numerous scattered places, principally near Colstrip (SE), Roundup (center), Sandcoulee (W center), and Red Lodge (S). Petroleum and natural-gas fields occur in Toole, Glacier, Petroleum, and Carbon counties, with oil refineries at Great Falls, Cut Bank, and Lewistown. Vermiculite, calcite, chromite, and pyrite deposits are also worked. Mont.'s mfg. industry is based primarily on its mineral resources. Besides the smelting and refining of ore, cement, bricks, metal castings and wire, arsenic, sulphuric acid, and phosphate fertilizer are produced in such centers as Butte (Mont.'s largest city), Anaconda, Great Falls, HELENA, and LEWISTOWN. Power for the metal industry is obtained from dams on the Missouri R. Other mfg. towns include Miles City (leather goods), Billings (beet sugar, flour milling, meat packing; railway workshops), and LIVINGSTON (agr. processing) along the Yellowstone R., and BOZEMAN (vegetable canning), MISSOULA (lumber, dairy, agr. products), and KALISPELL (agr., lumber processing) in the W mtn. valleys; Havre and Chinook are agr. markets on the Milk R. The Rocky Mts. section has numerous recreational facilities, particularly the magnificent Glacier Natl. Park, the Flathead L. region, and the many other resort areas which offer hunting, fishing, camping, dude ranching, and mtn. climbing. The principal educational institutions are Mont. State Univ. (at Missoula), Mont. State Col. (at Bozeman), and Mont. School of Mines (at Butte). The SE part of what is now Mont. may have been visited by a French expedition in 1743, but it was not until the region became U.S. territory by the La. Purchase (1803) and Lewis and Clark had explored (1805–6) the upper Missouri R. that white settlement began. First came the fur trappers, who set up trading posts in the river valleys, and then missionaries, including the Jesuit, Father De Smet. Mont.'s boundary with Canada, along the 49th parallel, was settled by treaties in 1818 and 1846. Gold was discovered in the 1850s and mining towns, such as Bannack and Virginia City, sprang up overnight as thousands of prospectors rushed to the rich strikes. Soon vigilante groups were formed to suppress lawlessness. NW Mont. was part of Wash. territory from 1853–63, while the rest of the area was included in Nebr. and Dak. territories; in 1863 all of Mont. formed part of Idaho territory, and in 1864 it was organized as a separate territory. The growth of white settlement led to several skirmishes with the Indians, notably at the LITTLE BIGHORN RIVER (1876), where a force under Gen. Custer was wiped out by the Sioux, and at a site now preserved in BIG HOLE BATTLEFIELD NATIONAL MONUMENT, where U.S. troops repulsed the Nez Percé tribe in 1877. By 1880, gold, silver, and copper mining in the W and sheep and cattle ranching in the E had been firmly established, and the arrival of the railroad soon afterwards served to further develop Mont.'s extensive resources. Statehood was achieved in 1889. In the late 19th cent. Butte was the scene of the struggle for wealth and power among the "copper barons," which ended in the triumph of the big Amalgamated (later Anaconda) Co. The wheat boom, which followed the arrival of the homesteaders, ended disastrously in 1920, and since then only large-scale dry farming has been practiced on the plains. Irrigation and electric power have always been important to Mont.'s economy, and the state is playing a major role in the development of the Missouri R. basin project. See also articles on cities, towns, geographic features, and the 56 counties: BEAVERHEAD, BIG HORN, BLAINE, BROADWATER, CARBON, CARTER, CASCADE, CHOUTEAU, CUSTER, DANIELS, DAWSON, DEER LODGE, FALLON, FERGUS, FLATHEAD, GALLATIN, GARFIELD, GLACIER, GOLDEN VALLEY, GRANITE, HILL, JEFFERSON, JUDITH BASIN, LAKE, LEWIS AND CLARK, LIBERTY, LINCOLN, MCCONE, MADISON, MEAGHER, MINERAL, MISSOULA, MUSSELSHELL, PARK, PETROLEUM, PHILLIPS, PONDERA, POWDER RIVER, POWELL, PRAIRIE, RAVALLI, RICHLAND, ROOSEVELT, ROSEBUD, SANDERS, SHERIDAN, SILVER BOW, STILLWATER, SWEET GRASS, TETON, TOOLE, TREASURE, VALLEY, WHEATLAND, WIBAUX, YELLOWSTONE.

Montaña Blanca (mōntä′nyä bläng′kä), village (pop. 238) and mountain, Lanzarote, Canary Isls., 3 mi. NW of Arrecife; fruit- and winegrowing.

Montaña Clara Island (mōntä′nyä klä′rä), tiny islet (c.275 acres), N Canary Isls., just N of Graciosa Isl., 150 mi. NE of Las Palmas. A pinnacle rising to c.790 ft.

Montaña de Fuego or **Montañas del Fuego** (mōntä′nyä,–äs, dhĕl fwā′gō), semiactive volcanoes in SW Lanzarote, Canary Isls., 12 mi. W of Arrecife. Rise above 1,600 ft. Visited by tourists.

Montañana (mōntänyä′nä), suburb (pop. 2,477) of Saragossa, Saragossa prov., NE Spain, 3 mi. NE of city center; canning, paper mfg.

Montanaro (môntänä′rô), town (pop. 3,441), Torino prov., Piedmont, NW Italy, 14 mi. NNE of Turin.

Montañas del Fuego, Canary Isls.: see MONTAÑA DE FUEGO.

Montánchez (mōntän'chĕth), town (pop. 5,056), Cáceres prov., W Spain, 22 mi. SE of Cáceres; agr. center noted for its cured hams and sausage; olive-oil and cheese processing. Wine, cereals, livestock, cork in area. Has ruined medieval castle.

Montaner (mōtänā'), village (pop. 352), Basses-Pyrénées dept., SW France, 9 mi. NNW of Tarbes; winegrowing, sawmilling.

Montara (mŏntâ'rŭ), resort village (pop. c.175), San Mateo co., W Calif., on the Pacific, 16 mi. SSW of downtown San Francisco; flower growing. Near-by Montara Point has lighthouse and radio-compass station.

Montargis (mōtär-zhē'), town (pop. 13,529), Loiret dept., N central France, 39 mi. ENE of Orléans and on Loing R. and Briare Canal near its junction with Orléans Canal; rail center and agr. market (sheep, veals, poultry, dairy produce). Mfg. (clothing, furniture, shoes, jewelry, rubber goods, fertilizer); tanneries. Montargis was ⊙ of old dist. of Gâtinais and a royal residence in Middle Ages. Has preserved medieval aspect. Figured prominently in Hundred Years War. Mirabeau b. near by.

Montasio, Jôf del (jôf dĕl môntä'zyô), second highest peak (9,035 ft.) in Julian Alps, NE Italy, 9 mi. SW of Tarvisio.

Montastruc-la-Conseillère (mōtästrük'-lä-kōsĕyâr'), agr. village (pop. 435), Haute-Garonne dept., S France, 11 mi. NE of Toulouse; sawmilling.

Montataire (mōtätâr'), town (pop. 7,367), Oise dept., N France, on the Thérain and 8 mi. NW of Senlis; metalworking center (blast furnaces, foundries). Hosiery and clothing factories.

Montauban (mōtōbā'), village (pop. 334), S central Que., on Batiscan R. and 27 mi. NE of Grand'-Mère; dairying; cattle, pig, poultry raising.

Montauban. 1 Village (pop. 891), Ille-et-Vilaine dept., W France, 18 mi. WNW of Rennes; dairying. Also called Montauban-de-Bretagne. **2** City (pop. 23,016), ⊙ Tarn-et-Garonne dept., SW France, on the Tarn and 30 mi. N of Toulouse; commercial and transportation center; food processing (goose liver, vegetables, fruits, biscuits), textile milling (silk, coarse cloth), hatmaking, woodworking. Site of mus. containing paintings by Ingres (b. here), and of a 14th-cent. bridge built of brick. One of France's oldest fortresses (founded 1144), it became the stronghold of the Albigenses (13th cent.) and of the Huguenots (16th cent.).

Montauban les Mines (lā mēn'), village (pop. estimate 350), S central Que., 23 mi. NE of Grand'-Mère; zinc, lead mining.

Montauk (mŏn'tôk"), resort village (pop. c.500), Suffolk co., SE N.Y., on E Long Isl. near tip of its S peninsula, 14 mi. ENE of East Hampton; E terminus of S-shore line of Long Isl. RR; commercial- and sport-fishing center. Just E is L. Montauk (c.2 mi. long), sheltered inlet of Long Island Sound; yacht harbor. Montauk Point State Park is 5 mi. E; Hither Hills State Park (camping) is 4 mi. WSW.

Montauk Point, SE N.Y., promontory at tip of S peninsula of Long Isl., c.115 mi. E of Manhattan; easternmost point of state; 41°4'N 71°53'W. Site of U.S. lighthouse since 1795. Area is included in Montauk Point State Park (158 acres); surf fishing, picnicking.

Mont-aux-Sources (mō'tō-sōōrs'), mountain (10,822 ft.), W Natal, U. of So. Afr., on Basutoland and Transvaal borders, 50 mi. SE of Bethlehem; 28°46'S 28°53'E. For a time thought to be highest peak of Drakensberg range and of U. of So. Afr., but in 1951 Thabantshonyana, to S. in Basutoland, was found to be higher.

Mön Tawang, India: see TOWANG.

Montazzoli (môntä'tsôlē), village (pop. 2,156), Chieti prov., Abruzzi e Molise, S central Italy, 19 mi. SW of Vasto.

Montbard (mōbär'), town (pop. 4,021), Côte-d'Or dept., E central France, on Brenne R. and Burgundy Canal, and 40 mi. NW of Dijon; large steel-pipe factory, tile works. Buffon (b. here) acquired in 1740 the 14th-cent. ruined castle of dukes of Burgundy. NE, 2 mi., is 12th-cent. Cistercian abbey of Fontenay.

Montbarrey (mōbärā'), village (pop. 269), Jura dept., E France, on Loue R. and 9 mi. SE of Dôle; lumbering in near-by Forest of Chaux.

Montbazens (mōbäzā'), village (pop. 600), Aveyron dept., S France, 13 mi. NE of Villefranche-de-Rouergue; quarries.

Montbazon (mōbäzō'), village (pop. 929), Indre-et-Loire dept., W central France, on Indre R. and 7 mi. SSE of Tours; flour milling. Has 10th-cent. keep built by counts of Anjou. Natl. powder plant just W.

Montbéliard (mōbālyär'), town (pop. 13,596), Doubs dept., E France, on the Rhone-Rhine Canal and 10 mi. SSW of Belfort, in the Belfort Gap; center of industrial dist. (including Audincourt, Valentigney, Sochaux, Seloncourt, Pont-de-Roide) noted for its automobile plants. Has forges, foundries, cotton mills, hardware and watch factories. Cattle, lumber, cheese, and wine trade. Medieval castle of counts of Montbéliard was rebuilt in 18th cent. With surrounding area, Montbéliard constituted, after 12th cent., a countship of Holy Roman Empire. Held, with interruptions, by dukes of Württemberg from 1397 until French Revolution, it accepted the Reformation. Captured (1793) by French, it was formally included in France by Treaty of Lunéville (1801). Due to industrial expansion, pop. doubled since 1890. Cuvier b. here.

Mont Belvieu or **Mont Belview** (both: mŏnt bĕl'vū), village (1940 pop. 1,500), Chambers co., SE Texas, 28 mi. E of Houston, in oil-producing and agr. area.

Montbenoît (mōbùnwä'), village (pop. 146), Doubs dept., E France, on the Doubs and 8 mi. NE of Pontarlier, in the Jura; dairying. Has 13th-16th-cent. abbey church.

Montbeton (mōbùtō'), village (pop. 277), Tarn-et-Garonne dept., SW France, 3 mi. W of Montauban; grapes, vegetables.

Mont Blanc (mō blā'), Ital. *Monte Bianco*, highest Alpine massif, on Fr.-Ital. and Fr.-Swiss border, culminating in the peak Mont Blanc (15,781 ft.), which is in France. A granitic core flanked by crystalline schists, it extends c.30 mi. N from the Little St. Bernard Pass to a point overlooking bend of Rhone R. valley at Martigny-Ville. Maximum width: 10 mi. Bounded by Graian Alps (S), Chamonix valley and Savoy Alps (W), valley of Courmayeur (E), and Pennine Alps (NE). Facing Italy, it presents an abrupt wall; on Fr. side are numerous glaciers (total □ 48), of which the MER DE GLACE, Bossons, and Argentière are best known. Principal summits are Mont Blanc, Mont Blanc du Tacul, Mont Maudit, Aiguille du Géant, Grandes Jorasses, Mont Dolent, Aiguille du Midi, and Aiguille Verte. Dotted with hotels and hostels, and made accessible by rack-and-pinion and aerial tramways, it is a popular tourist and mountain-climbing region centered on Chamonix. Mont Blanc, highest European peak after Mt. Elbrus (18,481 ft.) in the Caucasus, was 1st ascended in 1786 by Dr. Michel Paccard of Chamonix and, in 1787, by H. B. de Saussure of Geneva. Today it is easily climbed, with guides, from mountain terminus of Aiguille du Midi aerial tramway.

Mont Blanc de Seilon (mō blā dù sālō'), peak (12,700 ft.) in Pennine Alps, S Switzerland, 11 mi. SE of Bagnes.

Mont Blanc du Tacul (dù täkül'), peak (13,940 ft.) of Mont Blanc massif, Haute-Savoie dept., SE France, just N of Mont Maudit, at head of Tacul (or Géant) glacier, 5 mi. S of Chamonix.

Montblanch (mōntblänch'), town (pop. 3,676), Tarragona prov., NE Spain, in Catalonia, 19 mi. NNW of Tarragona; mfg. of cement, alcohol, liqueurs, chocolate; olive-oil processing. Agr. trade (wine, cereals, fruit, filberts; lumber). Has old walls, gates, and towers, and 14th-cent. church. Cistercian abbey of Poblet is 4 mi. W.

Montbozon (mōbōzō'), village (pop. 552), Haute-Saône dept., E France, on Ognon R. and 12 mi. SSE of Vesoul.

Montbrió de Tarragona (mōntbrē'ō dhä tärägō'nä), town (pop. 1,363), Tarragona prov., NE Spain, 6 mi. WSW of Reus; mfg. of cotton textiles, needles; olive-oil and wine processing. Wheat, almonds, filberts in area.

Montbrison (mōbrēzō'), town (pop. 7,080), Loire dept., E central France, in Forez Plain, 19 mi. NW of Saint-Étienne; road and market center; steel milling, mfg. of precision tools (especially drills) and toys (chiefly dolls). Has 13th-16th-cent. church of Notre-Dame-d'Espérance, the medieval Diana chapter house, which now contains a lapidary mus., and old houses surrounded by a belt of boulevards. After 1441, Montbrison was seat of the counts of Forez, and for a time (1801-56) ⊙ Loire dept.

Montbron (mōbrō'), village (pop. 1,370), Charente dept., W France, on the Tardoire and 17 mi. E of Angoulême; mfg. (felt for pulp, transmission belts). Has 12th-cent. Romanesque church.

Montcalm (mäntkäm', Fr. mōkälm'), county (□ 3,894; pop. 15,208), SW Que., N of the St. Lawrence, on Gatineau R.; ⊙ Ste. Julienne.

Montcalm (mŏntkäm'), county (□ 712; pop. 31,013), central Mich.; ⊙ Stanton. Drained by Flat and Pine rivers, Fish Creek, and short Tamarack R. Agr. (potatoes, grain, beans, sugar beets, livestock, poultry; dairy products). Mfg. at Greenville. Oil and gas wells, refineries. Lake resorts. Has state game area. Organized 1850.

Montcalm, Pic de (pēk dù mōkälm'), peak (alt. 10,105 ft.) in central Pyrenees, Ariège dept., S France, near Sp. border, 8 mi. SW of Vicdessos.

Montceau-les-Mines (mōsō'-lā-mēn'), town (pop. 7,658), Saône-et-Loire dept., E central France, on Bourbince R. and Canal du Centre, 9 mi. SSW of Le Creusot; coal-mining center of Le Creusot industrial dist. Hosiery mills.

Montcenis (mōsùnē'), SW suburb (pop. 881) of Le Creusot, Saône-et-Loire dept., E central France.

Mont Cenis (mō sùnē'), Ital. *Moncenisio* or *Monte Cenisio*, Alpine pass (alt. 6,831 ft.), in Savoie dept., SE France, bet. Cottian Alps (S) and Graian Alps (N), 5 mi. NW of Ital. border and 2 mi. SSE of Lanslebourg, on Lanslebourg-Susa road connecting Maurienne valley (France) with Dora Riparia R. valley (Italy). L. Mont Cenis (2 mi. SE), converted (1901-21) into reservoir (□ 1) furnishes hydroelectric power now shared by Italy and France. At E end of lake is historic Mont Cenis hospice. Long a famous invasion route; present road built (1803-10) by Napoleon I. Until 1947, crest of pass was on Fr.-Ital. border. Mont Cenis tunnel (or Fréjus tunnel), 8.5 mi. long, opened in 1871, penetrates Pointe de FRÉJUS (13 mi. SW).

Montchanin-les-Mines (mōshänē'-lā-mēn'), town (pop. 3,585), Saône-et-Loire dept., E central France, on the Canal du Centre and 4 mi. SSE of Le Creusot; railroad center; forges. Produces tiles and refractories.

Montclair (mŏntklâr'), residential town (pop. 43,927), Essex co., NE N.J., 6 mi. NNW of Newark; mfg. (chemicals, paints, metal products). State teachers col. (1908), art mus. here. Settled 1669, inc. 1868. Includes residential Upper Montclair.

Mont Clare, village (pop. 1,063), Montgomery co., SE Pa., on Schuylkill R. opposite Phoenixville.

Montcornet (mōkôrnā'), village (pop. 1,384), Aisne dept., N France, on Serre R. and 11 mi. SSE of Vervins; agr. market.

Montcuq (mōkük'), agr. village (pop. 605), Lot dept., SW France, 14 mi. SW of Cahors.

Mont-Dauphin (mō-dōfē'), village (pop. 98), Hautes-Alpes dept., SE France, in Dauphiné Alps at influx of Guil R. into the Durance, and 16 mi. S of Briançon. Built and fortified by Vauban in 1693.

Mont-de-Lans (mō-dù-lās'), village (pop. 92), Isère dept., SE France, near upper Romanche R., 5 mi. ESE of Le Bourg-d'Oisans; alt. 4,200 ft. Alpine winter-sport resort in Massif du Pelvoux. CHAMBON DAM is 1 mi. N.

Mont-de-Marsan (mō-dù-märsā'), town (pop. 11,929), ⊙ Landes dept., SW France, on Midouze R. and 70 mi. S of Bordeaux; road center and lumber market; mfg. of furniture and pit props, resin processing (turpentine, wax), meat preserving.

Montdidier (mōdēdyā'), town (pop. 4,097), Somme dept., N France, 21 mi. SE of Amiens; road and market center (cattle, poultry); tanning, footwear mfg. Has two 15th-16th-cent. churches. Captured by Germans and partially destroyed in struggle for Amiens (1918). Retaken by French in great counteroffensive. Damaged in Second World War.

Mont-Dol (mō dôl'), granite rock in Ille-et-Vilaine dept., W France, 1 mi. N of Dol-de-Bretagne, in the midst of a reclaimed coastal marsh (Marais de Dol). Originally a Druid center, Mont-Dol later gave asylum to St. Malo, St. Sampson, and other apostles of Brittany. It rises to 210 ft. and is topped by a modern chapel. Village of Mont-Dol, with 12th-15-cent. church, on S slope.

Mont-Dore (mō dôr'), town (pop. 2,165), Puy-de-Dôme dept., central France, in the Auvergne Mts., on Dordogne R. and 19 mi. SW of Clermont-Ferrand; alt. 3,445 ft. Noted thermal station frequented since Roman times for respiratory diseases. Dominated by the PUY DE SANCY (cable car) and Capucin peak (funicular railway), it has become an important winter-sports center. Also called Mont-Dore-les-Bains and Le Mont-Dore.

Mont-Dore, settlement (dist. pop. c.500), New Caledonia, on SW coast, 8 mi. E of Nouméa; agr.

Monte or **San Miguel del Monte** (sän' mēgĕl' dĕl mōn'tā), town (pop. 3,642), ⊙ Monte dist. (□ 671; pop. 9,967), E central Buenos Aires prov., Argentina, 65 mi. SSW of Buenos Aires; agr. center (grain, flax, livestock).

Monte (mōn'tĭ), village, Madeira, 2 mi. N of Funchal; resort (alt. 1,965 ft.; rack-and-pinion railway) overlooking Funchal Bay. Church, founded 1470, contains tomb of ex-emperor Karl of Austria.

Monte (mōn'tĭ), fishing village (pop. 2,018), Aveiro dist., N central Portugal, on Aveiro lagoon, 7 mi. N of Aveiro; saltworks.

Monte, El, Chile: see EL MONTE.

Monte, Laguna del (lägōō'nä dĕl mōn'tā), salt lake (□ 60) in W Buenos Aires prov., Argentina, 20 mi. NE of Carhué; 10 mi. long, 7 mi. wide. Guaminí is on S shore. Tourist resort.

Monte Abierto (mōn'tā äbyĕr'tō), village (pop. 1,092), Piura dept., NW Peru, in lower Chira valley, 13 mi. W of Sullana, in irrigated cotton area.

Monteagle (mŏntē'gŭl), village (1940 pop. 691), Marion co., S Tenn., 32 mi. NW of Chattanooga, in the Cumberlands; alt. c.1,900 ft.; summer resort.

Monteagudo (mōntā-ägōō'dhō), village (pop. estimate 200), ⊙ Guaraní dept. (1947 pop. 1,217), SE Misiones natl. territory, Argentina, on Uruguay R., opposite Alto Uruguai (Brazil), and 110 mi. E of Posadas. Tung plantation center.

Monteagudo, town (pop. c.3,260), ⊙ Azero prov., Chuquisaca dept., S Bolivia, 100 mi. ESE of Sucre, on Camiri-Tintín oil pipe line; corn, sugar cane, fruit. Formerly called Sauces.

Monteagudo. 1 Town (pop. 1,428), Navarre prov., N Spain, 8 mi. SW of Tudela; olive-oil processing; wine, hemp, cereals, fruit. **2** or **Monteagudo de las Vicarías** (dhä läs vēkärē'äs), town (pop. 874), Soria prov., N central Spain, near Saragossa prov. border, on railroad and 32 mi. SE of Soria; wheat, barley, alfalfa, sugar beets, grapes, potatoes, sheep. Flour milling, plaster mfg. Near by is irrigation reservoir.

Monte Aguila (mōn'tā ä'gēlä), village (1930 pop. 951), Concepción prov., S central Chile, 40 mi ESE of Concepcíon; rail junction; wheat, corn, wine, vegetables, livestock; flour milling.

Monte Albán (mōn′tā älbän′), ruins in Oaxaca, S Mexico, in Sierra Madre del Sur, 3 mi. SW of Oaxaca; alt. 6,391 ft. Once a sacred city of Zapotec culture; has fine archaeological remains, including temples, pyramids, elaborate mosaics, stonework, sculptures, inscriptions. MITLA is believed to have succeeded it as capital of the Zapotec.

Monte Alegre (mōn′tĭ ălā′grĭ). **1** City, Maranhão, Brazil: see TIMBIRAS. **2** City (pop. 2,172), W central Pará, Brazil, on height near left bank of the Amazon, 55 mi. NE of Santarém; ships rubber, fish, alcohol; grain and sugar-cane growing, cattle raising. Jasper deposits near by. **3** Locality, E central Paraná, Brazil, 15 mi. NNW of Tibagi, 110 mi. NW of Curitiba. Here is large wood-pulp and newsprint plant built in 1940s, using Paraná pine. Hydroelectric power generated at Mauá Falls on Tibagi R. (24 mi. NW).

Montealegre del Castillo (mōntā-ālĕ′grā dhĕl kästē′lyō), town (pop. 3,077), Albacete prov., SE central Spain, 13 mi. WSW of Almansa; flour milling, plaster mfg.; stock raising; cereals, wine. Fine hunting grounds in vicinity.

Monte Alto (mōn′tĭ äl′tōō), city (pop. 3,136), N central São Paulo, Brazil, on railroad and 45 mi. W of Ribeirão Prêto; mfg. of flour products; coffee, rice, and cotton processing.

Monte Aprazível (mōn′tĭ äprŏozē′vĕl), city (pop. 2,629), NW São Paulo, Brazil, 21 mi. W of São José do Rio Prêto; pottery mfg.; processing of brown sugar, corn meal, rice, and coffee; distilling.

Montearagón (mōn″tāärägōn′), village (pop. 886), Toledo prov., central Spain, near the Tagus, on railroad and 11 mi. E of Talavera de la Reina; cereals, livestock; apiculture.

Monte Arruit (mōn′tā ärwēt′), village (pop. 638), Kert territory, E Sp. Morocco, on railroad and 19 mi. S of Melilla; barley, sheep.

Monte Azul (mōn′tĭ äzōōl′). **1** City, (pop. 1,170), N Minas Gerais, Brazil, 110 mi. NE of Montes Claros; future terminus of railroad from Corinto; cotton growing. Until 1939, called Tremedal. **2** City, São Paulo, Brazil: see MONTE AZUL PAULISTA.

Monte Azul do Turvo, Brazil: see MONTE AZUL PAULISTA.

Monte Azul Paulista (poulē′stŏo), city (pop. 3,893), N São Paulo, Brazil, on railroad and 25 mi. S of Barretos; coffee, rice, tobacco. Until 1944, Monte Azul; and, 1944–48, Monte Azul do Turvo.

Montebello (mŏntĭbĕ′lō), village (pop. 1,266), SW Que., on Ottawa R. and 40 mi. ENE of Ottawa; farming, lumbering; resort.

Montebello (môn″tĕbĕl′lô), village (pop. 1,284), Pavia prov., Lombardy, N Italy, 5 mi. E of Voghera. Austrians defeated here by French in 1800, by French and Sardinians in 1859.

Montebello (mŏntĭbĕ′lō), city (pop. 21,735), Los Angeles co., S Calif., suburb 8 mi. E of downtown Los Angeles; oil wells; truck and flower farms, nurseries. Inc. 1920.

Monte Bello Islands (mŏn′tē bĕ′lō), coral group in Indian Ocean, 12 mi. off NW coast of Western Australia; comprise cluster of islets and rocks surrounded by coral reef. Barrow Isl. (12 mi. long, 5 mi. wide), largest. Mangrove forests.

Montebello Vicentino (môn″tĕbĕl′lô vēchĕntē′nô), village (pop. 1,818), Vicenza prov., Veneto, N Italy, near Chiampo R., 10 mi. SW of Vicenza; mfg. (machinery, lead shot, wine).

Montebelluna (môn″tĕbĕl-lōō′nä), town (pop. 3,192), Treviso prov., Veneto, N Italy, at SW foot of the Montello, 12 mi. NW of Treviso. Rail junction; cotton and hemp mills, mfg. of agr. tools, metal furniture, leather belts, hosiery.

Monte Bianco, France: see MONT BLANC.

Monte Blanco (mōn′tā bläng′kō), village, La Paz dept., W Bolivia, at SE end of Cordillera de Tres Cruces, 65 mi. SE of La Paz; alt. over 16,000 ft.; tin-mining center.

Montebourg (mōtbōōr′), village (pop. 1,099), Manche dept., NW France, near E coast of Cotentin Peninsula, 15 mi. SE of Cherbourg; livestock market; dairying, cement mfg. Here Germans attempted to stop American advance on Cherbourg during Normandy campaign (June, 1944) of Second World War.

Monte Buey (mōn′tā bwā′), town (pop. 2,984), E Córdoba prov., Argentina, 28 mi. SW of Marcos Juárez; wheat, corn, flax, cattle.

Montecalvo Irpino (môn″tĕkäl′vô ērpē′nô), town (pop. 3,229), Avellino prov., Campania, S Italy, 14 mi. ENE of Benevento.

Monte Carlo or **Puerto Monte Carlo** (pwĕr′tō mōn′tā kär′lō), town (pop. estimate 1,000), ⊙ San Pedro dept. (1947 pop., 8,488), central Misiones natl. territory, Argentina, river port on Paraná R. (Paraguay border) and 85 mi. NE of Posadas; agr. center (corn, tobacco, maté, tung); sawmills.

Monte Carlo (mŏn″tē kär′lō), Fr. *Monte-Carlo* mōtē-kärlō′), chief resort (pop. 7,967) of principality of MONACO, on the Riviera (*Côte-d'Azur*), 10 mi. ENE of Nice. Built in 19th cent. on an escarpment just N of Monaco harbor, it has become famous for its gambling casino (established c.1858, concession granted 1861). Its luxurious hotels are frequented primarily in winter season when numerous artistic and sports events take place here. Also a popular summer watering place. Just NW, in Alpes-Maritimes dept., is French resort of Beausoleil.

Monte Carmelo (mōn′tĭ kŭrmā′lōō), city (pop. 2,790), W Minas Gerais, Brazil, in the Triângulo Mineiro, on railroad and 50 mi. ENE of Uberlândia; diamond washings. Formerly spelled Monte Carmello.

Monte Carmelo (mōn′tā kärmā′lō), town (pop. 768), Trujillo state, W Venezuela, in Andean spur, 16 mi. SW of Valera; coffee, sugar cane, corn.

Montecarotto (môn″tĕkärôt′tô), village (pop. 1,028), Ancona prov., The Marches, central Italy, 9 mi. W of Iesi.

Monte Caseros (mōn′tā käsā′rōs), town (pop. 10,288), ⊙ Monte Caseros dept. (□ c.1,000; pop. 27,412), SE Corrientes prov., Argentina, port on Uruguay R., opposite Bella Unión (Uruguay) and 80 mi. SSE of Mercedes. Rail junction; commercial and agr. center, trading with Uruguay and Brazil. Railroad shops, tobacco factories, sawmills; rice, corn, and flour mills; sand quarries. Flax, corn, peanuts, fruit, livestock. Airport.

Montecassiano (môn″tĕkäs-syä′nô), village (pop. 811), Macerata prov., The Marches, central Italy, 5 mi. N of Macerata; mfg. of harmoniums and harmonicas.

Monte Cassino (môn′tĕ käs-sē′nô), most famous monastery of Italy, in Frosinone prov., Latium, on a hill (alt. 1,703 ft.) overlooking the town of CASSINO. Founded c.529 by St. Benedict of Nursia, who established the Benedictine Order. For many centuries one of the greatest centers of Christian learning and piety, it greatly influenced European civilization. Abbey bldgs. were destroyed 4 times: by Lombards (581) and Arabs (883); by earthquake (1349); and, after their 17th-cent. restoration, by a concentrated Allied air bombing in 1944. The Ger. garrison, which had used the abbey as a fortress, withstood the bombing in previously dug caves, but the bldgs. were demolished and most of their art treasures destroyed. However, a considerable part of the invaluable MSS, removed by the Germans or safely stored by the monks, survived. Reconstruction plans have been made.

Montecastrilli (môn″tĕkästrēl′lē), village (pop. 344), Terni prov., Umbria, central Italy, 11 mi. NW of Terni.

Montecatini (môn″tĕkätē′nē), village (pop. 842), Pisa prov., Tuscany, central Italy, 6 mi. W of Volterra; lignite mining.

Montecatini Terme (tĕr′mĕ), town (pop. 8,292), Pistoia prov., Tuscany, central Italy, at foot of Etruscan Apennines, 8 mi. WSW of Pistoia. Health resort, noted for thermal saline springs; mfg. (cotton textiles, cork products, hats, gloves, macaroni). Near-by copper mine (now closed) was beginning of one of Italy's great chemical concerns.

Montecchio Emilia (môntĕk′kyô ĕmē′lyä), town (pop. 3,102), Reggio nell'Emilia prov., Emilia-Romagna, N central Italy, near Enza R., 9 mi. W of Reggio nell'Emilia; rail terminus.

Montecchio Maggiore (mäd-jô′rĕ), town (pop. 5,301), Vicenza prov., Veneto, N Italy, 7 mi. SW of Vicenza; mfg. (electric motorcars, canned fruit, marmalade, celluloid, liquor). Has 2 castles. Lignite mine near by.

Montecelio (môn″tĕchā′lyô), village (pop. 3,932), Roma prov., Latium, central Italy, 5 mi. NW of Tivoli. Has medieval castle. Travertine quarries near by.

Montecerboli (môn″tĕchĕr′bôlē), village (pop. 634), Pisa prov., Tuscany, central Italy, 11 mi. S of Volterra, near Larderello. Has *soffioni* used to produce boric acid.

Montech (mōtĕsh′), village (pop. 1,416), Tarn-et-Garonne dept., SW France, on Garonne Lateral Canal, 7 mi. WSW of Montauban; paper milling.

Montechiaro d'Asti (môntĕkyä′rô dä′stē), village (pop. 1,488), Asti prov., Piedmont, NW Italy, 9 mi. NNW of Asti. Marl quarries near by.

Montechiarugolo (môn″tĕkyärōō′gôlô), village (pop. 366), Parma prov., Emilia-Romagna, N central Italy, on Enza R. and 9 mi. SE of Parma; canned foods. Has fine castle.

Montechino (môn″tĕkē′nô), village (pop. 175), Piacenza prov., Emilia-Romagna, N central Italy, 17 mi. S of Piacenza; oil wells.

Montecilfone (môn″tĕchēlfô′nĕ), town (pop. 3,257), Campobasso prov., Abruzzi e Molise, S central Italy, 11 mi. SW of Termoli; cement, wine, olive oil, cheese.

Montecillos, Sierra de (syĕ′rä dā mōntäsē′yōs), N spur on main Andean divide, W central Honduras; extends c.20 mi. NW-SE bet. Jesús de Otoro and La Paz; forms watershed bet. Río Grande de Otoro section of Ulúa R. (W) and Comayagua R. (E); rises to 7,001 ft. in San Juanillo peak.

Montecito (mŏntĭsē′tō), residential suburb (1940 pop. 1,740), Santa Barbara co., SW Calif., near coast and just E of Santa Barbara.

Monte Comán (mōn′tā kōmän′), town (pop. estimate 1,000), central Mendoza prov., Argentina, on Diamante R. (irrigation area) and 25 mi. E of San Rafael; rail junction and agr. center (wine, alfalfa, corn, fruit, tomatoes; apiculture).

Monte Compatri (môn′tĕ kôm′pätrē), village (pop. 4,211), Roma prov., Latium, central Italy, in Alban Hills, 3 mi. E of Frascati.

Montecosaro (môn″tĕkô′zärô), village (pop. 711), Macerata prov., The Marches, central Italy, 10 mi. ENE of Macerata; mfg. of electrothermal apparatus.

Monte Cristi or **Montecristi** (mōntākrē′stē), province (□ 1,150; 1935 pop. 59,213; 1950 pop. 79,310), NW Dominican Republic, on the coast, bordering W on Haiti; ⊙ Monte Cristi. Watered by the Yaque del Norte, the irrigated valley of which here forms W section of fertile Cibao region; adjoined by Cordillera Setentrional (N) and Cordillera Central (S). Lumbering, stock-raising, agr. region. Main products: rice, bananas, cocoa, corn, livestock, beeswax, honey, dairy products, hides, hardwood. Titanium deposit near Monción. Main center is Monte Cristi city, with near-by harbor. Port of Pepillo Salcedo, built 1945, ships bananas. Prov. was set up 1879; in 1938 Libertador prov. was separated from it.

Monte Cristi or **Montecristi,** officially San Fernando de Montecristi, city (1935 pop. 3,816; 1950 pop. 4,600), ⊙ Monte Cristi prov., NW Dominican Republic, near coast and near mouth of the Yaque del Norte, 65 mi. WNW of Santiago, 150 mi. NW of Ciudad Trujillo; 19°51′N 71°40′W. Trading and agr. center (rice, cotton, coffee, bananas, goats) in irrigated W section of the fertile Cibao region. Exports, through its fine harbor (1 mi. away), hides and skins. Airfield. Founded 1533 by Sp. peasants on a site explored and named by Columbus in 1493. Leveled 1606 by the Spanish because of illegal trade with pirates; rebuilt c.1750.

Montecristi, town (1950 pop. 1,872), Manabí prov., W Ecuador, on Manta-Portoviejo RR 15 mi. W of Portoviejo; famous for mfg. of Panama hats; copra-trading center.

Monte Cristo (môn″tĕ krē′stô), rocky island (□ 3.5; pop. 10) in Tuscan Archipelago, in Tyrrhenian Sea, Italy, in Livorno prov., bet. Corsica and Ital. coast, 25 mi. S of Elba; 2.5 mi. long; rises to 2,116 ft. in center. Ruins of 13th-cent. monastery. Achieved fame through novel by Dumas père, *The Count of Monte Cristo.*

Montecristo, Cerro (sĕ′rō mōntākrē′stō), peak (7,920 ft.) in Sierra de Metapán, on Guatemala-Salvador-Honduras border, 10 mi. W of Nueva Ocotepeque (Honduras); 14°26′N 89°21′W.

Montedinove (môn″tĕdēnô′vĕ), village (pop. 401), Ascoli Piceno prov., The Marches, central Italy, 8 mi. N of Ascoli Piceno; bell foundry.

Montedoro (môn″tĕdô′rô), village (pop. 3,434), Caltanissetta prov., central Sicily, 7 mi. NNW of Canicattì. Sulphur mine is S.

Monte Escobedo (mōn′tā ĕskōbā′dō), town (pop. 1,312), Zacatecas, N central Mexico, 45 mi. SW of García; grain, alfalfa, sugar cane, livestock.

Monte Estoril (mōn′tĭ ŭsh-tōōrĕl′), village (pop. 2,502), Lisboa dist., W central Portugal, on the Atlantic, 14 mi. W of Lisbon (electric railroad); fashionable year-round resort along Portugal's Riviera bet. Estoril (just E) and Cascais (SW).

Montefalcione (môn″tĕfälchô′nĕ), village (pop. 1,788), Avellino prov., Campania, S Italy, 5 mi. NE of Avellino; wine.

Montefalco (môn″tĕfäl′kô), town (pop. 1,085), Perugia prov., Umbria, central Italy, 12 mi. NNW of Spoleto. In former church of San Francesco (mid-14th cent.; now a mus.) are frescoes by B. Gozzoli and Perugino.

Montefalcone di Valfortore (môn″tĕfälkô′nĕ dē välfôrtô′rĕ), village (pop. 3,700), Benevento prov., Campania, S Italy, near left headstream of Fortore R. 13 mi. NNW of Ariano Irpino.

Montefalcone nel Sannio (nĕl sän′nyô), town (pop. 3,049), Campobasso prov., Abruzzi e Molise, S central Italy, 21 mi. N of Campobasso.

Montefano (môn″tĕfä′nô), village (pop. 1,134), Macerata prov., The Marches, central Italy, 8 mi. N of Macerata.

Montefiascone (môn″tĕfyäskô′nĕ), town (pop. 3,307), Viterbo prov., Latium, central Italy, near L. Bolsena, 9 mi. NNW of Viterbo; wine, olive oil. Bishopric. Has cathedral designed by Sanmicheli and ruins of castle. Near by is 11th-cent. church of San Flaviano (remodeled 1262).

Montefiorino (môn″tĕfyôrē′nô), village (pop. 265), Modena prov., Emilia-Romagna, N central Italy, 15 mi. SSW of Sassuolo.

Montefollonico (môn″tĕfôl-lô′nēkô), village (pop. 623), Siena prov., Tuscany, central Italy, 3 mi. NW of Montepulciano; lignite mining.

Monteforte d'Alpone (môn″tĕfôr′tĕ dälpô′nĕ), town (pop. 2,951), Verona prov., Veneto, N Italy, 14 mi. E of Verona; wine, silk textiles, tomato paste.

Monteforte Irpino (ērpē′nô), village (pop. 2,599), Avellino prov., Campania, S Italy, 5 mi. WSW of Avellino.

Montefrío (mōntāfrē′ō), town (pop. 4,807), Granada prov., S Spain, 14 mi. NE of Loja; olive-oil processing, flour milling; wheat, livestock.

Montegiordano (môn″tĕjôrdä′nô), village (pop. 2,357), Cosenza prov., Calabria, S Italy, 29 mi. NNE of Castrovillari; olive oil, dried fruit.

Montegiorgio (môn″tĕjôr′jô), town (pop. 1,285), Ascoli Piceno prov., The Marches, central Italy, 9 mi. WSW of Fermo; explosives mfg.

Montegnée (mōtŭnyā′), town (pop. 10,545), Liége prov., E Belgium, 3 mi. W of Liége; coal mining.

Montego Bay (mŭntē'gō), city (pop. 11,547), ⊙ St. James parish, NW Jamaica, ocean port 190 mi. SW of Santiago de Cuba, 85 mi. WNW of Kingston (linked by railroad); 18°29'N 77°56'W. The isl.'s 3d largest city, rail terminus, and tourist resort, ranking 2d only to Kingston as harbor and commercial center. Principal products: sugar cane, coffee, bananas, ginger, rum, hides, dyewood. Mfg. of ice, aerated water, wine cordials, shoes. Has St. James Church, Dome battlement tower, and near-by ruins of old Sp. monastery. Airport. Doctor's Cave bathing beach, claimed to be the best in the isl., is here. The site of the town, an anc. Indian village, was visited by Columbus in 1494. Traces of Arawak life have been found in vicinity. Small Bogue Isls., just offshore (W), are coral atolls with oyster beds and marine gardens. The Catherine Hall sugar mill is just E.

Monte Gordo (mōn'tĭ gôr'dōō), village (pop. 1,221), Faro dist., S Portugal, 2 mi. WSW of Vila Real de Santo António, on the Atlantic (S coast); seaside resort; fisheries.

Montegranaro (môn"tĕgränä'rô), village (pop. 1,660), Ascoli Piceno prov., The Marches, central Italy, 7 mi. NW of Fermo; shoe mfg.

Monte Grande (mōn'tā grän'dā), town (pop. 8,439), ⊙ Esteban Echeverría dist. (□ 151; pop. 19,995), NE Buenos Aires prov., Argentina, 16 mi. SSW of Buenos Aires; cattle-raising and meat-packing center; tree nurseries.

Monte Hermoso (mōn'tā ĕrmō'sō), village (pop. estimate 300), S Buenos Aires prov., Argentina, beach resort on Atlantic coast, 28 mi. S of Coronel Dorrego.

Montehermoso (mōn"tāĕrmō'sō), village (pop. 4,321), Cáceres prov., W Spain, near Alagón R., 15 mi. WNW of Plasencia; agr. trade center (cereals, olive oil, pepper, tomatoes). Lead mines near by.

Monteiasi (môn"tĕyä'zē), village (pop. 2,779), Ionio prov., Apulia, S Italy, 8 mi. ENE of Taranto.

Monteiro (mōntā'rōō), city (pop. 2,460), central Paraíba, NE Brazil, on Borborema Plateau, 60 mi. S of Patos; sugar, rice, fruit. Formerly called Alagoa do Monteiro.

Monteith (mŏntēth'), village (pop. 151), SE South Australia, 50 mi. ESE of Adelaide; citrus fruit, dairy products.

Montejaque (mōntāhä'kā), town (pop. 1,874), Málaga prov., S Spain, on W slope of the Sierra de Ronda, 5 mi. W of Ronda; wheat, barley, chick-peas, wine, fruit, livestock; mfg. of liquor, meat products. Cueva del Gato (cave) is 2 mi. E.

Montejícar (mōntāhē'kär), town (pop. 3,693), Granada prov., S Spain, 28 mi. NNE of Granada; brandy distilling; stock raising, lumbering; cereals, wine.

Montejunto, Serra de (sĕ'rŭ dĭ mōntĭzhōōn'tōō), mtn. range of Lisboa dist., W central Portugal, extending c.20 mi. NE from Tôrres Vedras. Rises to 2,178 ft.

Monteleone di Calabria, Italy: see VIBO VALENTIA.

Monteleone di Puglia (môn"tĕlĕô'nĕ dē pōō'lyä), town (pop. 4,777), Foggia prov., Apulia, S Italy, 7 mi. SSW of Bovino, in livestock and agr. (cereals, potatoes) region.

Montelepre (môntĕlä'prĕ), town (pop. 5,184), Palermo prov., NW Sicily, 11 mi. W of Palermo.

Montélimar (mōtālēmär'), medieval Latin *Montilium Adhemari*, town (pop. 10,610), Drôme dept., SE France, on the Roubion near its influx into the Rhone, and 27 mi. SSW of Valence; noted nougat-mfg. center. Silk spinning, sawmilling, mfg. of building materials. Trade in fruits, vegetables, wines, and candy.

Montelimar (mōntālēmär'), village, Managua dept., SW Nicaragua, near Pacific coast, 4 mi. SW of San Rafael del Sur; sugar milling, alcohol distilling. Estate of President Anastasio Somoza.

Monte Lirio (mōn'tē lĭ'rēō), village, Cristobal dist., N central Panama Canal Zone, on Juan Gallegos Isl. of Gatun L., on transisthmian railroad and 9 mi. SSE of Colón; bananas, livestock.

Montellano (mōntĕlyä'nō), town (pop. 10,363), Seville prov., SW Spain, in W spur of the Cordillera Penibética, 35 mi. SW of Seville; processing and trading center for agr. region (cereals, olives, livestock). Flour- and sawmilling, vegetable-oil distilling; mfg. of shoes, brooms, soap, cheese. Limekilns; marble and jasper quarries.

Montello (môntĕl'lô), ridge (□ 25) in Veneto, N Italy, 10 mi. NE of Treviso, W of Piave R.; extends 15 mi. E-W, 4 mi. wide; rises to 1,207 ft. Heavily fought (June, 1918) in First World War.

Montello (mŏntĕ'lō), city (pop. 1,069), ⊙ Marquette co., central Wis., at E end of Buffalo L., at confluence of Fox R. and small Montello R., 45 mi. W of Fond du Lac; resort; livestock, grain; granite quarries. Settled 1849, inc. 1938.

Montelupo Fiorentino (môn"tĕlōō'pô fyôrĕntē'nô), town (pop. 2,325), Firenze prov., Tuscany, central Italy, on Arno R., at mouth of Pesa R., and 12 mi. W of Florence; glass mfg. Damaged in Second World War.

Montemaggiore Belsito (môn"tĕmäd-jô'rĕ bĕlsē'tô), town (pop. 5,934), Palermo prov., N Sicily, in Madonie Mts., 10 mi. SSE of Termini Imerese, in cereal- and almond-growing region.

Montemagno (môn"tĕmä'nyô), village (pop. 1,741), Asti prov., Piedmont, NW Italy, 8 mi. NE of Asti.

Monte Maíz (mōn'tā mäēs'), town (pop. 2,581), SE Córdoba prov., Argentina, 70 mi. SE of Villa María; wheat, corn, flax, alfalfa, hogs, cattle.

Montemar, Chile: see VIÑA DEL MAR.

Montemarano (môn"tĕmärä'nô), village (pop. 1,548), Avellino prov., Campania, S Italy, 11 mi. E of Avellino; macaroni mfg.

Montemarciano (môn"tĕmärchä'nô), village (pop. 1,256), Ancona prov., The Marches, central Italy, 10 mi. WNW of Ancona.

Montemayor (mōntāmīôr'), town (pop. 4,052), Córdoba prov., S Spain, 17 mi. SSE of Córdoba; olive-oil processing, plaster mfg. Cereals, vegetables, livestock.

Montemayor de Pililla (dhā pēlē'lyä), town (pop. 1,546), Valladolid prov., N central Spain, 17 mi. SE of Valladolid; lumbering, sheep raising; sugar beets, cereals, wine, chicory.

Montemboeuf (mōtābûf'), agr. village (pop. 302), Charente dept., W France, 13 mi. WSW of Rochechouart.

Montemesola (môn"tĕmā'zôlä), village (pop. 3,013), Taranto prov., Apulia, S Italy, NE of Taranto.

Montemilone (môn"tĕmēlô'nĕ), village (pop. 4,031), Potenza prov., Basilicata, S Italy, 9 mi. NE of Venosa, in cereal-growing region.

Montemolín (mōntāmōlēn'), town (pop. 2,554), Badajoz prov., W Spain, 8 mi. SE of Fuente de Cantos; cereals, grapes, olives, livestock.

Monte-Mor (mōn'tĭ-môr'), city (pop. 1,357), E central São Paulo, Brazil, 17 mi. W of Campinas; rum distilling, agr. processing. Airfield.

Montemorelos (mōn"tāmōrā'lōs), city (pop. 5,579), Nuevo León, N Mexico, in E foothills of Sierra Madre Oriental, on railroad and 45 mi. SE of Monterrey; resort and agr. center (oranges, sugar cane, pecans, cactus fibers, livestock). Known for yearly fiesta in July.

Montemor-o-Novo (mōntĭmôr-ō-nō'vō), town (pop. 5,133), Évora dist., S central Portugal, on rail spur and 18 mi. WNW of Évora; cork-processing center. Has a Moorish castle.

Montemor-o-Velho (–vĕ'lyōō), town (pop. 1,457), Coimbra dist., N central Portugal, on lower Mondego R. and 14 mi. W of Coimbra, in poorly drained rice-growing region. Has 11th-cent. feudal castle.

Montemuro, Serra de (sĕ'rŭ dĭ mōntĭmōō'rōō), mtn. range in Viseu dist., N central Portugal, 10 mi. SW of Lamego; rises to 4,535 ft.

Montemurro (môn"tĕmōōr'rô), village (pop. 2,664), Potenza prov., Basilicata, S Italy, 26 mi. SSE of Potenza; wine, olive oil.

Montendre (mōtā'drù), village (pop. 1,587), Charente-Maritime dept., W France, 11 mi. S of Jonzac; metalworks; mfg. of plastics.

Montenegro (mōn"tĭnā'grōō). **1** City, Bahia, Brazil: see CAMASSARI. **2** City (pop. 7,055), E Rio Grande do Sul, Brazil, on Caí R. and 28 mi. NW of Pôrto Alegre; rail junction (spur to Caxias do Sul); modern industrial center (meat packing and by-products processing); winegrowing. Settled by Italian immigrants in mid-19th cent. Until 1930s called São João de Montenegro.

Montenegro (mōntānā'grō), town (pop. 4,003), Caldas dept., W central Colombia, on W slope of Cordillera Central, on railroad and 6 mi. WNW of Armenia; alt. 4,239 ft. Coffeegrowing center; also sugar cane, cereals, fruit, cattle.

Montenegro (mŏn"tĭnē'grō), Serbo-Croatian *Crna Gora* or *Tsrna Gora* (tsŭr'nä gô'rä) [both names mean "black mountain"], constituent republic (□ 5,343; pop. 376,573), S Yugoslavia; smallest and least populated in the country; ⊙ Titograd. Bounded by Adriatic Sea (SW), Bosnia and Herzegovina (NW), Serbia (NE), and Albania (SE); at S end of Dinaric Alps; entirely mountainous. Consists of 2 regions: barren, karstlike Montenegro proper (W), which culminates in the LOVCEN; separated by Zeta R. from the higher Brda (E), which culminates in the DURMITOR, KOMOVI, and NORTH ALBANIAN ALPS and is covered with forests and pastures. The republic touches on the Adriatic bet. Bojana R. (Albanian border) and the Gulf of Kotor. Drained chiefly into the Drina by Piva, Tara, Cotina, and Lim rivers, and into L. Scutari by Moraca and Zeta rivers). Chief plain is ZETA lowland. Stock raising, mostly sheep and goats, provides leading source of revenue. Cultivation is poorly developed; chief crops are grain (corn and wheat in plains; barley and rye in mountains); potatoes, tobacco, cotton (as an experiment), fruit (figs and olives on coast; plums, apples, pears in interior), and nuts also grown; vineyards. Forestry is well developed, notably in the Brda. Deposits of building stone, sea salt (Ulcinj), and bauxite (Bar). Home industry makes up for lack of mfg. Several motor roads, narrow-gauge railroads, and small seaports (HERCEG NOVI, KOTOR, TIVAT, BUDVA, BAR, ULCINJ) constitute a poorly-developed transportation system. Besides TITOGRAD, only towns are CETINJE, NIKSIC, and PLJEVLJA. Pop. is Serbian and of Orthodox Eastern faith. In Middle Ages, Montenegro formed the virtually independent prov. of Zeta within Serbian Empire. Following the Serbian defeat (1389) by the Turks at Kosovo, Montenegrins retained their independence. After 1516, Montenegro was ruled by prince-bishops (secularized 1852) cultivating the friendship of Russia, and frequently repulsing the Turks, who, although never able to reduce the country, thrice sacked Cetinje. Greatly expanded by Treaty of Berlin (1878), Montenegro became a kingdom in 1910. It fought against Turkey in Balkan Wars, (gaining part of the Sanjak in 1913) and against Austria-Hungary in First World War, after which it was included (1918) in Yugoslavia as Montenegro prov. Renamed Zeta oblast in 1921; became part of Zeta banovina in 1929. During Second World War, under Ital. control. In 1946, became a people's republic.

Montenero (môn"tĕnā'rô), peak (6,171 ft.) in La Sila mts., S Italy, 19 mi. ESE of Cosenza.

Montenero di Bisaccia (dē bēzät'chä), town (pop. 5,870), Campobasso prov., Abruzzi e Molise, S central Italy, 12 mi. WSW of Termoli; cement, woolen textiles, flour, macaroni.

Monte Nievas (mōn'tā nyā'väs), town (pop. estimate 1,000), NE La Pampa natl. territory, Argentina, on railroad and 28 mi. SW of General Pico; grain, livestock.

Montenotte (mōtnôt'), village (pop. 1,388), Alger dept., N central Algeria, on branch railroad and 4 mi. S of Ténès; olive-oil pressing.

Montenotte (môn"tĕnôt'tĕ), village, Savona prov., Liguria, NW Italy, in W Ligurian Apennines, 26 mi. W of Genoa. Here Napoleon had 1st victory over Austrians in April, 1796.

Montenvers, France: see CHAMONIX.

Monteodorisio (môn"tĕōdôrē'zyô), town (pop. 2,324), Chieti prov., Abruzzi e Molise, S central Italy, 3 mi. WSW of Vasto.

Monteparano (môn"tĕpärä'nô), village (pop. 2,160), Ionio prov., Apulio, S Italy, 10 mi. ESE of Taranto; wine, olive oil.

Monte Patria (mōn'tā pä'trēä), village (1930 pop. 453), Coquimbo prov., N central Chile, on railroad, 18 mi. ESE of Ovalle; wheat, corn, fruit, stock.

Montepeque, Sierra de, Central America: see METAPÁN, SIERRA DE.

Monte Plata (mōn'tā plä'tä), town (1950 pop. 1,474), Trujillo prov., S Dominican Republic, at S foot of Cordillera Central, 23 mi. NNE of Ciudad Trujillo; rice, cacao, coffee.

Monteponi (môntĕpô'nē), village (pop. 288), Cagliari prov., SW Sardinia, 2 mi. SW of Iglesias; lead-zinc-silver mining; smelter (electrolytic extraction of zinc and cadmium).

Monteprandone (môn"tĕprändô'nĕ), village (pop. 799), Ascoli Piceno prov., The Marches, central Italy, 14 mi. ENE of Ascoli Piceno, near the Adriatic; mfg. of agr. machinery.

Montepuez (mōntĭpwĕzh'), village, Niassa prov., N Mozambique, on road and 95 mi. W of Pôrto Amélia; cotton, kapok.

Montepulciano (môn"tĕpōōlchä'nô), town (pop. 2,960), Siena prov., Tuscany, central Italy, 28 mi. SE of Siena, W of Lake of Montepulciano (1.5 mi. long; connected with the Chiana); wine making, woodworking. Bishopric. Rich in Renaissance bldgs.; has several palaces and churches, including some designed by the elder A. da Sangallo. Cardinal Roberto Bellarmine b. here.

Monte Quemado (mōn'tā kāmä'dō), town (pop. estimate 1,000), ⊙ Copo dept. (□ 5,160; 1947 pop. 17,381), N Santiago del Estero prov., Argentina, on railroad and 85 mi. N of Tintina, near Chaco line; stock-raising center. Formerly called Kilómetro 1243.

Montereale (môn'tĕrĕä'lĕ), village (pop. 860), Aquila prov., Abruzzi e Molise, S central Italy, near Pescara R. (here called Aterno) and 14 mi. NW of Aquila.

Montereau or **Montereau-faut-Yonne** (mōtùrō'-fō-yôn'), town (pop. 8,726), Seine-et-Marne dept., N central France, port on the Seine at influx of Marne R. and 17 mi. SE of Melun; industrial center specializing in refractory products (bricks, tiles, faïenceware, pottery). Its metalworks make agr. machinery, cables, and electrical equipment. Sugar mills. Other mfg. (organic fertilizer, furniture, biscuits, brushes, hosiery). Bet. two 18th-cent. bridges spanning the Seine and the Yonne is equestrian statue of Napoleon I, commemorating his near-by victory (1814) over Allies. Damaged in Second World War.

Monterey (mŏntùrā'), county (□ 3,324; pop. 130,498), W Calif., on the Pacific and Monterey Bay; ⊙ Salinas. Bounded N by Pajaro R. valley (apple-growing); Salinas R. valley in its center is flanked E by Gabilan and Diablo ranges, W by Santa Lucia Range (rising here to 5,844 ft. at Junipero Serra Peak). Monterey Peninsula (site of historic Monterey and Carmel) is famed scenic resort region. Co. includes Big Sur (redwoods); old Soledad, Carmel, and San Antonio de Padua missions; U.S. Fort Ord and Hunter Liggett Military Reservation; part of Los Padres Natl. Forest (E). Salinas valley is rich agr. (especially lettuce) area; also other vegetables, sugar beets, beans, grain, fruit; dairying, stock and poultry raising. Most of co.'s many industries handle farm products. Fisheries, fish canning; salt and beet-sugar refining. Magnesite mining; sand, gravel, sandstone quarrying. Formed 1850.

Monterey. 1 (mŏntùrā') City (pop. 16,205), Monterey co., W Calif., on MONTEREY BAY, c.85 mi. S

Area in square miles is indicated by the symbol □, capital city or county seat by the symbol ⊙.

of San Francisco; historic old city, today a tourist resort, and home of artists and authors. Important fishing industries, especially catching and canning of sardines (pilchards); fruit, vegetable canning. Seat of Monterey Peninsula Col. U.S. Fort Ord is near by. In 1770, Gaspar de Portolá established a presidio here (now Presidio of Monterey, a U.S. army post), and Junípero Serra founded a Franciscan mission (later moved to CARMEL). City was ⊙ Alta California, 1775–1846. U.S. occupation (1846) was followed (1849) by a state constitutional convention. Extant old bldgs. include the presidio chapel, Calif.'s 1st theater (1844), and 1st brick bldg. (1847). Holds a yearly fiesta. Inc. 1850. **2** (mŏntûrā') Town (pop. 250), Pulaski co., NW Ind., on Tippecanoe R. and 38 mi. SSW of South Bend, in agr. area. **3** (mŏn'tûrā) Village (pop. c.200), Owen co., N Ky., on Kentucky R. and 16 mi. N of Frankfort; fishing, camping. **4** (mŏntûrā', mŏn'tûrā) Town (pop. 367), Berkshire co., SW Mass., in the Berkshires, 19 mi. S of Pittsfield. State forest. **5** (mŏntûrā') Village (pop. 315), Martin co., S Minn., in lake region, 15 mi. WNW of Fairmont, in grain area. **6** (mŏn'tûrā) Town (pop. 2,043), Putnam co., central Tenn., 14 mi. E of Cookeville, in timber and farm area; lumber, wood products; railroad shops. Small Monterey L. (resort) is near by. **7** (mŏntûrā') Town (pop. 262), ⊙ Highland co., NW Va., in the Alleghenies, 32 mi. NW of Staunton; agr., lumber milling. Vacationers attracted by scenery, fishing.

Monterey Bay (mŏntûrā'), W Calif., crescent-shaped inlet of the Pacific formed by break in Coast Ranges, c.65 mi. S of San Francisco; 26 mi. long. Santa Cruz Mts. (with Santa Cruz at their base) rise steeply to N, Santa Lucia Range (behind MONTEREY, on Monterey Peninsula) to S. Pajaro R. enters from E; fertile Salinas R. valley extends SE from bay. Fisheries; beaches. Sighted (1542) by Cabrillo; entered (1602) and named by Vizcaíno.

Monterey Park, residential city (pop. 20,395), Los Angeles co., S Calif. suburb 5 mi. E of downtown Los Angeles. Founded 1910, inc. 1916.

Monterey Peninsula, W Calif., rugged, almost square peninsula jutting 4 mi. NW into the Pacific bet. Monterey Bay (N) and Carmel Bay (S); site of Monterey, Pacific Grove, Del Monte, Pebble Beach, Carmel, Asilomar, other resorts. Seventeen-Mile Drive is scenic toll road around shore. Point Pinos (pē'nōs) (lighthouse) is N tip, Point Cypress its W extremity. State parks.

Montería (mōntārē'ä), town (pop. 12,804), Bolívar dept., N Colombia, inland port on Sinú R., in savannas, and 120 mi. SSW of Cartagena; communication, trading, lumbering, and stock-raising (cattle, horses) center; forest products (tagua nuts, quinine). Cattle research station, airfield. Gold placer mines and petroleum deposits near by.

Monteriggioni (mōn"tĕrēd-jô'nē), village (pop. 180), Siena prov., Tuscany, central Italy, 7 mi. NW of Siena; wine making, alcohol distilling. Has 13th-cent. walls.

Monte Rio (mŏn"tĭ rē'ō), resort village (pop. c.500), Sonoma co., W Calif., on Russian R. and 15 mi. W of Santa Rosa.

Montero (mōntā'rō), town (pop. c.7,200), ⊙ Santiesteban or Obispo Santiesteban prov., Santa Cruz dept., central Bolivia, 30 mi. N of Santa Cruz; agr. center (sugar cane, rice). Formerly Víbora.

Montero Hoyos, Ingeniero, Bolivia: see INGENIERO MONTERO HOYOS.

Monteroni d'Arbia (mōn"tĕrō'nē där'byä), village (pop. 726), Siena prov., Tuscany, central Italy, 8 mi. SE of Siena and on Arbia R. (right affluent of upper Ombrone R.)

Monteroni di Lecce (dē lĕt'chĕ), town (pop. 6,779), Lecce prov., Apulia, S Italy, 4 mi. WSW of Lecce; olive oil, wine. Has 16th-cent. ducal palace.

Monteros (mōntā'rōs), town (pop. estimate 4,000), ⊙ Monteros dept. (□ c.750; 1947 pop. 54,532), S central Tucumán prov., Argentina, on railroad and 30 mi. SW of Tucumán. Agr. and lumbering center; sugar refineries, flour mills, sawmills; sugar, citrus fruit, potatoes. Tobacco research station.

Monte Rosa (mōn'tĕ rô'zä), Fr. *Mont Rose*, highest mountain group of the Pennine Alps, on Italo-Swiss border, 28 mi. SSW of Brig. Has 10 summits, of which the Dufourspitze (15,203 ft.) is highest. Several glaciers on N slope (largest, the Gorner) converge upon head of Matter Visp R. valley near Zermatt.

Monterosso al Mare (mōn"tĕrôs'sô äl mä'rĕ), village (pop. 1,534), La Spezia prov., Liguria, N Italy, port on Gulf of Genoa, 9 mi. NW of Spezia; wine.

Monterosso Almo (äl'mô), village (pop. 4,700), Ragusa prov., SE Sicily, 12 mi. N of Ragusa.

Monterosso Calabro (kä'läbrô), village (pop. 2,979), Catanzaro prov., Calabria, S Italy, 11 mi. ENE of Vibo Valentia; olive oil, dried figs, silk.

Monterotondo (mōn"tĕrôtôn'dô). **1** Village (pop. 1,141), Grosseto prov., Tuscany, central Italy, 7 mi. N of Massa Marittima. Has *soffioni* used to produce boric acid. **2** Town (pop. 5,548), Roma prov., Latium, central Italy, near the Tiber, 11 mi. NW of Tivoli; bricks, tiles, pottery, wine. Here Garibaldi defeated papal forces in 1867.

Monterrey, Guatemala: see PANAJACHEL.

Monterrey (mŏntûrā', Sp. mōntĕrā'), city (pop. 186,092), ⊙ Nuevo León, N Mexico, at NE foot of Sierra Madre Oriental, in fertile Santa Catarina R. valley (affluent of Pesquería R.), on Inter-American Highway and 140 mi. SSW of Laredo (Texas), 440 mi. NNW of Mexico city; 25°40'N 100°18'W; alt. 1,765 ft. Third largest city of Mexico, it is a railroad hub and road junction, and the leading industrial center after Mexico city. Has largest iron- and steelworks of the republic; and blast furnaces, important lead smelters, and silver, gold, copper, bismuth, and antimony refineries; cement plant, brewery. Mfg. also of soap, chemicals, plastics, celluloid goods, tobacco products, cottonseed oil, glass, textiles, furniture, ceramics. Natural gas, brought by pipe line from Texas, has increased industrial production. Lead, silver, gold mines are near by. Lime is from local kilns; coal and petroleum come from neighboring states of Coahuila and Tamaulipas. The mild dry climate, the cool mts. and foothills, and hot springs (Topo Chico mineral springs are 4 mi. NW) make Monterrey also a popular resort. Airport. The city has fine modern and colonial architecture, govt. palace, and a cathedral (there is a R.C. bishop). Founded 1546, it attained city rank in 1596. During Mexican War captured (1846) by Zachary Taylor after heroic defense by Mexican forces.

Monterrubio de la Serena (mōntārōō'vyō dhā lä sārā'nä), town (pop. 5,114), Badajoz prov., W Spain, on La Serena plain, 9 mi. SE of Castuera; spa; agr. center (olives, cereals, grapes, stock).

Monterubbiano (mōn"tĕrōōb-byä'nô), village (pop. 1,049), Ascoli Piceno prov., The Marches, central Italy, 5 mi. S of Fermo.

Montes (mōn'tĕs), town (pop. 800), Canelones dept., S Uruguay, on railroad and 45 mi. ENE of Montevideo; grain, beetroots, stock.

Montesa (mōntā'sä), town (pop. 1,188), Valencia prov., E Spain, 9 mi. SW of Játiva; olive oil, wine, oranges. Dominated by hill topped by ruins of fortress which belonged (14th cent.) to military order of Montesa.

Monte San Giovanni Campano (mōn'tĕ sän jôvän'nē kämpä'nô), village (pop. 1,056), Frosinone prov., Latium, S central Italy, 8 mi. E of Frosinone; paper mill, tannery.

Monte San Giuliano, Sicily: see ERICE.

Monte San Giusto (mōn"tĕ sän jū'stô), village (pop. 1,274), Macerata prov., The Marches, central Italy, 8 mi. SE of Macerata; shoe mfg.

Montesano (mŏntĭsä'nō), city (pop. 2,328), ⊙ Grays Harbor co., W Wash., 10 mi. E of Aberdeen and on Chehalis R.; lumber, dairy products, canned peas. Inc. 1883.

Montesano sulla Marcellana (mōn"tĕsä'nô sōōl'lä märchĕl-lä'nä), town (pop. 2,231), Salerno prov., Campania, S Italy, 10 mi. SSE of Sala Consilina.

Monte San Savino (mōn'tĕ sän sävē'nô), town (pop. 1,663), Arezzo prov., Tuscany, central Italy, 12 mi. SW of Arezzo; broom mfg. Has municipal palace designed by the elder A. da Sangallo and Renaissance loggia. A. Sansovino b. here.

Monte Sant'Angelo (mōn'tĕ säntän'jĕlô), town (pop. 20,130), Foggia prov., Apulia, S Italy, on S slope of Gargano promontory, 27 mi. NE of Foggia; agr. center (cereals, wine, olive oil, livestock). Has anc. pilgrimage church of San Michele.

Monte Santo (mōn'tĭ sän'tōō), city (pop. 1,191), NE Bahia, Brazil, 60 mi. E of Senhor do Bonfim; tobacco, beans, cattle.

Monte Santo, Greece: see HAGION OROS.

Monte Santo, Cape (mōn'tĕ sän'tô), point on E coast of Sardinia, at S end of Gulf of Orosei; 40°6'N 9°43'E. Lobster fisheries. Sometimes called Monte Santu.

Monte Santo de Minas (mōn'tĭ sän'tōō dĭ mē'nùs), city (pop. 4,313), SW Minas Gerais, Brazil, near São Paulo border, on railroad and 50 mi. E of Ribeirão Prêto; coffeegrowing center. Called Monsanto, 1944–48.

Montesarchio (mōn"tĕsär'kyô), town (pop. 7,291), Benevento prov., Campania, S Italy, 9 mi. SW of Benevento, in cereal- and fruit-growing region; resort (alt. 984 ft.). Has castle.

Montescaglioso (mōn"tĕskälyô'zô), town (pop. 7,486), Matera prov., Basilicata, S Italy, 8 mi. SSE of Matera; agr. center; olive oil, wine, cheese, fruit, wool. Has anc. Benedictine monastery (now a public bldg.).

Montes Claros (mōn'tĭs klä'rōōs), city (1950 pop. 20,795), N Minas Gerais, Brazil, on NW slope of the Serra do Espinhaço, on railroad and 220 mi. N of Belo Horizonte; 16°42'S 43°43'W. Has rich rock-crystal deposits. Textile milling; sugar, rice, livestock shipping. Airfield.

Montes Claros (mōn'tĭsh klä'rōōsh), locality, Évora dist., S central Portugal, 9 mi. SE of Estremoz. Column commemorates final Portuguese victory over Spaniards (1665).

Montesclaros (mōntĕsklä'rōs), town (pop. 986), Toledo prov., central Spain, 12 mi. NW of Talavera de la Reina; cereals, acorns, forage, stock. Marble and lime quarries; limekilns.

Montescudaio (mōn"tĕskōōdä'yô), village (pop. 867), Pisa prov., Tuscany, central Italy, 6 mi. E of Cecina, in grape- and olive-growing region.

Montes de Oca (mōn'tĕs dā ō'kä), town (pop. estimate 1,500), S Santa Fe prov., Argentina, 70 mi. WNW of Rosario; agr. center (wheat, flax, corn, livestock); dairying.

Montes de Oca, San Pedro de, Costa Rica: see SAN PEDRO, San José prov.

Montes de Oro, Costa Rica: see MIRAMAR.

Montes de Toledo, Spain: see TOLEDO, MONTES DE.

Montesilvano (mōn"tĕsēlvä'nô), village (pop. 387), Pescara prov., Abruzzi e Molise, S central Italy, near the Adriatic, 4 mi. WNW of Pescara; tomato canning.

Montespertoli (mōn"tĕspĕr'tôlē), village (pop. 1,691), Firenze prov., Tuscany, central Italy, 9 mi. SE of Empoli.

Montesquieu-Volvestre (mōtùskyû'-vôlvĕ'strù), village (pop. 1,108), Haute-Garonne dept., S France, on the Arize and 20 mi. WNW of Pamiers; candle mfg., horse breeding.

Montesquiou (mōtùskyōō'), village (pop. 229), Gers dept., SW France, 6 mi. NW of Mirande; grains, cattle.

Monte Sullón (mōn'tā sōōyōn'), village (pop. 1,379), Piura dept., NW Peru, in lower Piura valley, 2 mi. SW of Catacaos, in irrigated cotton area.

Montet, Le (lù mōtā'), village (pop. 430), Allier dept., central France, 17 mi. SW of Moulins; furniture mfg., cattle raising. Coal deposits. Sometimes called Le Montet-aux-Moines.

Montets, Col des, France: see MONTROC-LE-PLANET.

Monteux (mōtû'), town (pop. 2,086), Vaucluse dept., SE France, 3 mi. SW of Carpentras; fruit and vegetable canning; mfg. of pyrotechnics. Has 14th-cent. walls.

Montevago (mōn"tĕvä'gô), village (pop. 2,866), Agrigento prov., W Sicily, near Belice R., 10 mi. ENE of Castelvetrano.

Montevallo (mŏntĭvă'lō). **1** Town (pop. 2,150), Shelby co., central Ala., 30 mi. S of Birmingham, in cotton and watermelon area; lumber milling, cotton ginning. Alabama Col. here. Talladega Natl. Forest is S. Settled c.1815, inc. 1848. **2** Town (pop. 53), Vernon co., W Mo., 16 mi. SE of Nevada.

Montevarchi (mōn"tĕvär'kē), town (pop. 7,306), Arezzo prov., Tuscany, central Italy, near the Arno, 16 mi. WNW of Arezzo; mfg. (machinery, shoes, soap, alcohol, pharmaceuticals, woolen textiles, hats, brooms). Has acad. with valuable fossil collection. Damaged in Second World War.

Montevecchio (mōn"tĕvĕk'kyô), village (pop. 1,196), Cagliari prov., SW Sardinia, 17 mi. N of Iglesias; rail line terminus; lead-zinc-silver mine.

Monteverde (mōn"tĕvĕr'dĕ), village (pop. 2,634), Avellino prov., Campania, S Italy, near Ofanto R., 7 mi. W of Melfi.

Montevideo (mŏntùvĭdā'ō,–vĭ'dēō, Sp. mōntāvēdā'ō), department (□ 256; 1942 pop. 541,042), S Uruguay, on N bank of the Río de la Plata; ⊙ Montevideo. The smallest dept. of the country, almost coextensive with Montevideo city. Its indented coastline, bounded by Santa Lucía R. mouth (W), has the well-protected bay of Montevideo port and a string of fine beaches (Ramírez, Pocitos, Carrasco), which owe their fame also to the temperate climate of the region. The dept. is, despite its size, important for cattle and sheep raising; agr. crops include grain, flax, all kinds of vegetables and grapes. Montevideo city, with its large meat-packing and other processing industries, is the undisputed center for all commercial, industrial, cultural, and political activities of the country.

Montevideo, city (pop. c.750,000), ⊙ Uruguay and Montevideo dept., S Uruguay, major port on N bank of the Río de la Plata, and 130 mi. E of Buenos Aires (linked by regular shipping service); 34°53'S 56°9'W. One of the great cities of South America, it dominates the commercial, industrial, political, and cultural life of the country, harboring c.⅓ of its entire pop. and handling about 90% of the foreign trade. Here converge local as well as international air, sea, rail, and road communications. It is the site of foreign and natl. banks, of warehouses, embassies, stock exchange, customhouse, and govt. agencies. Situated in agr. region, where cattle and sheep are raised on large scale. Principal products for export are livestock, hides, skins, wool, cereals, flax, building material. Montevideo is hq. for South Atlantic fishing fleets. As Uruguay's only important industrial center, it has meat-packing houses, tanneries, flour and paper mills, cement factories. Also mfg. of textile goods, shoes, tobacco products, soap, candles, pharmaceuticals, glass- and enamelware. Because of its benign, temperate climate (mean temp. c.60°F.) and beautiful beaches near by, it is one of the continent's leading playgrounds, visited by a great many Argentineans and Brazilians. The clean, modern city, stretching from a well-protected bay with extensive port facilities, is notable for its splendid avenues (main artery: 18 de Julio), river promenades, the beautiful parks (Rodó and Prado); for fine bldgs. such as a cathedral, univ., natl. library, Solís Theater, Salvo Palace; and for many hospitals, museums, schools, and institutions of higher learning testifying to Uruguay's social advancement. Montevideo was founded 1726 by Maurillo de Zabala, governor of Buenos Aires, after the Port. fort (built 1717) on nearby "Cerro" hill was captured by the Spaniards. During colonial period the city was frequently disputed by Portuguese and Spanish. It became capital of the independent republic in 1828. Because of the turbulent 19th-cent. civil wars and foreign interventions, Montevideo suffered much and withstood a siege from 1843 to 1857 by troops of the Argentinian dictator Juan Manuel Rosas. The city's industrial suburbs are Cerro (SW) and Unión (N). Along the ocean stretch eastward the renowned beaches and residential sections of Ramírez, Pocitos, and Carrasco; the latter is also Montevideo's airport. Within easy reach are the bathing resorts Piriápolis (50 mi. E) and Punta del Este (65 mi. E).

Montevideo (mŏntuvĭ'dēō), city (pop. 5,459), ⊙ Chippewa co., SW Minn., on Minnesota R. at mouth of Chippewa R. and 35 mi. SW of Willmar; agr. trade center for grain, livestock, and poultry area; dairy products, beverages, canned corn. Platted 1870, inc. as village 1879, as city 1908. Near by is Camp Release State Park with granite monument commemorating release (1862) of 269 white captives of Sioux Indians.

Monte Vista (mŏn"tē vĭ'stū). **1** City (pop. 3,272), Rio Grande co., S Colo., on Rio Grande, just E of San Juan Mts., in San Luis Valley, and 17 mi. NW of Alamosa; alt. 7,500 ft. Shipping point in potato area; flour, dairy products; mechanical appliances. Hq. of Rio Grande Natl. Forest here. Dude ranches, gold and silver mines in vicinity. Near by are state soldiers' and sailors' home, Rio Grande Natl. Forest, and Picture Rocks, with pictographs. Inc. 1886. **2** Town (1940 pop. 36), Lake co., central Fla., 30 mi. W of Orlando, in citrus-fruit region.

Montezuma (mŏntĭzōō'mū), county (□ 2,095; pop. 9,991), SW Colo.; ⊙ Cortez. Livestock-raising area, bordering on N.Mex. and Utah; bounded E by La Plata Mts.; drained by Dolores R. Mesa Verde Natl. Park, Yucca House Natl. Monument, part of Consolidated Ute Agency in S; Hovenweep Natl. Monument in W, on Utah-Colo. line; part of Montezuma Natl. Forest in NE. SW boundary is only point in U.S. common to 4 states (Utah, Ariz., N.Mex., Colo.). Formed 1889.

Montezuma. 1 Town (pop. 48), Summit co., central Colo., on branch of Blue R., in Front Range, and 5 mi. SW of Grays Peak, 12 mi. NE of Breckenridge; alt. 10,295 ft. **2** City (pop. 2,921), Macon co., central Ga., c.45 mi. SW of Macon and on Flint R. opposite Oglethorpe; processing, shipping, and trade center for farm area; mfg. (frozen fruits, clothing). Inc. 1854. **3** Town (pop. 1,220), Parke co., W Ind., on Wabash R. and 22 mi. N of Terre Haute, in agr. and bituminous-coal area; mfg. (clay products, canned goods); fisheries; gravel and clay pits; mineral springs. Settled c.1820, platted 1849, inc. 1851. **4** Town (pop. 1,460), ⊙ Poweshiek co., central Iowa, 21 mi. NNE of Oskaloosa, near source of South Fork English R.; wood products, gloves, chemicals, tankage. Inc. 1868. **5** City (pop. 509), Gray co., SW Kansas, 25 mi. WSW of Dodge City; wheat-shipping point. **6** Village (pop. 299), Mercer co., W Ohio, 4 mi. SSE of Celina and on Grand L.

Montezuma Castle National Monument (738.09 acres; established 1906), central Ariz., near Verde R., c.40 mi. SSW of Flagstaff. Ruins of pre-Columbian Pueblo Indian cliff dwellings; best preserved is Montezuma Castle (90% intact), a bldg. of 5 stories and 20 rooms, built in a cavern in a limestone cliff 50 ft. above its base.

Montfaucon (mōfōkō'). **1** Village (pop. 776), Haute-Loire dept., S central France, in Monts du Vivarais, 10 mi. ENE of Yssingeaux; lumber market; mfg. of silk goods. **2** Village (pop. 698), Maine-et-Loire dept., W France, 21 mi. ESE of Nantes; winegrowing. **3** Village (pop. 412), Meuse dept., NE France, 13 mi. NW of Verdun. Atop Montfaucon hill, and amidst ruins of old Montfaucon village (destroyed 1918) rises Meuse-Argonne American Memorial (180 ft. high), largest U.S. First World War memorial in Europe.

Montfermeil (mōfĕrmā'), town (pop. 5,619), Seine-et-Oise dept., N central France, an outer ENE suburb of Paris, 11 mi. from Notre Dame Cathedral; mfg. (water-repellent clothing, brushes).

Montferrand, France: see CLERMONT-FERRAND.

Montferrat (mŏntfŭrăt', Fr. mōfĕrä'), Ital. *Monferrato* (mōn"fĕr-rä'tō), wine-producing district, Piedmont, N Italy, largely in Alessandria and Asti provs. Dry, hilly terrain ranges in alt. from c.700 ft. (E) to 2,349 ft. (W), 2,772 ft. (S); extends from Tanaro (S) to Po (N) rivers. A historic region; became marquisate after 10th cent. Casale Monferrato became its capital in 1435; was strongly fortified. Passed to Mantua in 1533, to house of Savoy in 1713.

Montferrier (mōfĕryā'), village (pop. 350), Ariège dept., S France, 11 mi. ESE of Foix; talc quarrying and processing, wool spinning.

Montfoort (mônt'fōrt), town (pop. 2,329), Utrecht prov., W central Netherlands, on Hollandsche IJssel R. and 8 mi. WSW of Utrecht; wood products, stoneware; agr., cattle market. Has old castle, now used as jail for women.

Montfort (mōfôr'). **1** or **Montfort-sur-Meu** (–sür-mû'), village (pop. 1,515), Ille-et-Vilaine dept., W France, on the Meu and 13 mi. WNW of Rennes; market center; dairying, horse raising; saltworks. Severely damaged in Second World War. **2** or **Montfort-en-Chalosse** (–ā-shälōs'), village (pop. 388), Landes dept., SW France, 11 mi. E of Dax; cork and furniture mfg., hog and poultry raising. Has 12th–15th-cent. church.

Montfort (mŏnt'fŭrt), anc. locality, NW Palestine, near Lebanese border, 20 mi. NE of Haifa. Seigneurial castle built in early 13th cent. by French knights; acquired (1228) by Teutonic Knights and renamed Starkenburg. Captured (1271) by Baibars. Ruins extant.

Montfort, village (pop. 576), Grant co., SW Wis., 16 mi. NE of Lancaster, in agr. area (dairy, poultry, grain farms).

Montfort-en-Chalosse, France: see MONTFORT.

Montfort-l'Amaury (mōfôr'-lämōrē'), village (pop. 1,600), Seine-et-Oise dept., N central France, 10 mi. N of Rambouillet, resort at N edge of Forest of Rambouillet; sawmilling. Has 15th-cent. church with 16th-cent. stained-glass windows and ruins of 11th–15th-cent. church.

Montfort-le-Rotrou (–lū-rôtrōō'), agr. village (pop. 545), Sarthe dept., W France, near the Huisne, 10 mi. ENE of Le Mans; stud. Has castle rebuilt 1820 in Italian style.

Montfort-sur-Meu, France: see MONTFORT.

Montfort-sur-Risle (–sür-rēl'), agr. village (pop. 434), Eure dept., NW France, on the Risle and 15 mi. N of Bernay.

Montfrin (mōfrē'), village (pop. 1,537), Gard dept., S France, on the Gard, near its influx into the Rhone, and 11 mi. ENE of Nîmes; fruit, olives.

Montgarrie (mŏntgă'rē), village, central Aberdeen, Scotland, on Don R., just N of Alford; woolen mill.

Montgenèvre Pass (mōzhūnĕ'vrū), Ital. *Monginevro,* in Cottian Alps, Hautes-Alpes dept., SE France, 1 mi. W of Ital. border, 5 mi. ENE of Briançon; alt. 6,083 ft. Connects valleys of Dora Riparia (Italy) and Durance (France) rivers. Crossed by Susa-Briançon road built (1802–07) by Napoleon. Hospice founded 14th cent. One of easiest Alpine passes, it was frequently used by invading armies. Until 1947, it formed Fr.-Ital. border. Also spelled Mont-Genèvre. Village of Montgenèvre (pop. 46) just W.

Montgeron (mōzhūrō'), town (pop. 10,401), Seine-et-Oise dept., N central France, on the Yères, near its influx into the Seine just S of Villeneuve-Saint-Georges, and 11 mi. SSE of Paris; forges; mfg. (gloves, candy).

Montgiscard (mō-zhēskär'), agr. village (pop. 461), Haute-Garonne dept., S France, on the Canal du Midi and 12 mi. SSE of Toulouse; brick and soap mfg.; horse raising.

Montgolfier (mōgôlfyā'), village (pop. 2,506), Oran dept., N Algeria, on Ouarsenis Massif of the Tell Atlas, on railroad and 20 mi. NW of Tiaret; cereals, wine.

Montgomery (mŭntgŭ'mŭrē), dist. (□ 4,204; 1951 pop. 1,814,000), SE Punjab, W Pakistan; ⊙ Montgomery. In Bari Doab, bet. Ravi R. (N) and Sutlej R. (S); bordered by Indian Punjab (E); irrigated by Lower Bari Doab, Pakpattan, and Dipalpur canal systems. Main crops: wheat, cotton, millet, rice, sugar cane; hand-loom weaving, cotton ginning, camel breeding. Noted prehistoric site at Harappa. Chief towns: Okara, Montgomery, Pakpattan.

Montgomery, town (pop. 38,345), ⊙ Montgomery dist., SE Punjab, W Pakistan, 95 mi. SW of Lahore, on Lower Bari Doab Canal; trades in grain, cotton, cloth fabrics, fruit, sugar cane; cotton ginning and milling, ice mfg., hand-loom weaving. Has col. Very hot place.

Montgomery (mŏntgŭm'rē, –gŭ'mŭrē). **1** County (□ 790; pop. 138,965); SE central Ala.; ⊙ Montgomery, the state capital. In the Black Belt. Bounded NW by Alabama R., N by Tallapoosa R. Cotton, livestock, grain, bees. Mfg. at Montgomery. Formed 1816. **2** County (□ 801; pop. 6,680), W Ark.; ⊙ Mount Ida. Drained by Ouachita and Caddo rivers; in Ouachita Mts. region. Agr. (cotton, grain, livestock, poultry); dairy products; cotton ginning, sawmilling, food processing, stone quarrying. Part of Ouachita Natl. Forest is here. Formed 1842, organized 1844. **3** County (□ 235; pop. 7,901), E central Ga.; ⊙ Mount Vernon. Bounded W by Oconee R., S by Altamaha R. Coastal plain agr. (cotton, corn, tobacco, peanuts, livestock) and timber area. Formed 1793. **4** County (□ 706; pop. 32,460), S central Ill.; ⊙ Hillsboro. Agr. (corn, wheat, oats, soybeans, livestock, poultry; dairy products). Bituminous-coal mining. Some mfg. (paper boxes, glass jars, concrete blocks, shoes, radiators, metal products, beverages); zinc smelters. Drained by Shoal and Macoupin creeks. Formed 1821. **5** County (□ 507; pop. 29,122), W central Ind.; ⊙ Crawfordsville. Drained by Sugar and Raccoon creeks. Agr. (grain, truck, livestock, poultry; dairy products). Clay pits; timber. Commerce and mfg. at Crawfordsville. Formed 1822. **6** County (□ 422; pop. 15,685), SW Iowa; ⊙ Red Oak. Prairie agr. area (hogs, cattle, corn, wheat, oats) drained by East Nishnabotna, West Nodaway, and Tarkio rivers and by Walnut Creek; bituminous-coal deposits. Formed 1851. **7** County (□ 649; pop. 46,487), SE Kansas; ⊙ Independence. Level to hilly region, bordering S on Okla.; drained by Verdigris and Elk rivers. Livestock, grain, poultry; dairying. Numerous oil and gas fields. Formed 1869. **8** County (□ 204; pop. 13,025), NE central Ky.; ⊙ Mt. Sterling. Drained by several creeks. Rolling upland agr. area, mainly in outer Bluegrass region; dairy products, livestock, poultry, burley tobacco, corn, wheat. Some mfg. at Mt. Sterling. Formed 1796. **9** County (□ 494; pop. 164,401), central Md.; ⊙ Rockville. Bounded NE by Patuxent R., S by Dist. of Columbia, W and SW by Potomac R. (forms Va. line here); drained by Rock Creek. Rolling piedmont area, containing many residential suburbs (including Chevy Chase, Bethesda, Takoma Park) of Washington; agr. hinterland produces dairy products, truck, apples, corn, wheat, hay, cattle, poultry; some mfg. (especially scientific instruments, lumber). Govt. installations at Bethesda, Silver Spring, Cabin John, Glen Echo Heights, and Forest Glen. Includes some of Natl. Capital Parks (W), among them Great Falls Park. Formed 1776. **10** County (□ 403; pop. 14,470), central Miss.; ⊙ Winona. Drained by Big Black R. Agr. (cotton, corn), dairying, stock raising; timber. Some mfg. at Winona. Formed 1871. **11** County (□ 533; pop. 11,555), E central Mo.; ⊙ Montgomery City. On Missouri R. and drained by the Loutre. Agr. (corn, wheat, oats), cattle, poultry; limestone, fire-clay pits. Formed 1818. **12** County (□ 409; pop. 59,594), E central N.Y.; ⊙ Fonda. Lies in fertile Mohawk R. valley; traversed by the Barge Canal; also drained by Schoharie Creek. Dairying region, with mfg. centers: Amsterdam (carpets), Canajoharie (food packing), Fort Plain and St. Johnsville (textiles). Formed 1772. **13** County (□ 488; pop. 17,260), central N.C.; ⊙ Troy. Bounded W by Yadkin R. (here becoming the Pee Dee), in which Badin and Tillery lakes are backed up by hydroelectric dams; also drained by Uharie R. Forested piedmont region; farming (peaches, cotton, tobacco, corn), dairying, poultry raising, lumbering; textile mfg. Formed 1778. **14** County (□ 465; pop. 398,441), W Ohio; ⊙ DAYTON. Intersected by Great Miami, Stillwater, and Mad rivers, and by small Bear, Wolf, and Twin creeks. Miamisburg Mound, and Englewood Dam are here. Agr. area (livestock, grain, tobacco, dairy products, truck); extensive mfg., especially at Dayton. Sand and gravel pits; cement plants. Formed 1803. **15** County (□ 492; pop. 353,068), SE Pa.; ⊙ Norristown. Agr. and mfg. area, bounded SE by Philadelphia; drained by Schuylkill R. First settled by Swedes and Welsh; later by Germans. Mfg. (metal products, textiles, rubber products); limestone. Formed 1784. **16** County (□ 543; pop. 44,186), N Tenn.; ⊙ CLARKSVILLE. Bounded N by Ky.; drained by Cumberland and Red rivers. Agr. (especially dark tobacco), livestock raising. Diversified mfg. at Clarksville. Iron ore and limestone deposits. Formed 1796. **17** County (□ 1,090; pop. 24,504), E Texas; ⊙ Conroe. Drained by tributaries of San Jacinto R. Includes part of Sam Houston Natl. Forest. Lumbering (including pulpwood), lumber milling, oil, natural-gas production and processing (gasoline, carbon black) are important industries. Also livestock (cattle, hogs, poultry), dairying, agr. (peanuts, sweet potatoes, truck, fruit, some corn, cotton). Hunting, fishing. Formed 1837. **18** County (□ 395; pop. 29,780), SW Va.; ⊙ Christiansburg. Mainly in Great Appalachian Valley traversed by ridges; the Alleghenies are in N and NW, the Blue Ridge in S and SE; bounded W by New R.; drained by Little and Roanoke rivers and Craig Creek. Includes part of Jefferson Natl. Forest. RADFORD (in but independent of co.) is in W. Agr. (grain, hay, fruit), livestock raising, dairying; mfg. at Christiansburg; some bituminous-coal mining. Formed 1776.

Montgomery. 1 City (pop. 106,525), ⊙ Ala. and Montgomery co., SE central Ala., on left bank of Alabama R. (navigable here) and c.85 mi. SE of Birmingham, in Black Belt; 32°22'N 86°19'W; alt. c.200 ft. Railroad center, with car and locomotive shops, and market for cotton, livestock, and dairy products. Manufactures work clothes and cotton fabrics, food containers, fertilizer, cottonseed and lumber products, plumbing and heating supplies; food packing (meat, fruit, vegetables), peanut and pecan shelling, creosoting. City was settled 1817, inc. 1819. Voted state capital 1846; became 1st capital of Confederacy 1861; taken by Union troops 1865. Grew as cotton center with development of railroads. Seat of Huntingdon Col., State Teachers Col. (for Negroes), mus. of fine arts. Points of interest: capitol building, "First White House of the Confederacy" (temporary home of Jefferson Davis), and St. John's Episcopal Church. Near by are Maxwell Air Force Base (with advanced air training school), Gunter Air Force Base, state prison and reform school, site of historic Fort Toulouse, and municipal airport. **2** Village (pop. 773), Kane co., NE Ill., on Fox R., just SW of Aurora, and c.35 mi. WSW of Chicago, in agr. area (dairy products; livestock). **3** Town (pop. 538), Daviess co., SW Ind., 26 mi. E of Vincennes, in agr. and bituminous-coal area. **4** Resort village (pop. c.150), Dickinson co., NW Iowa, near West

Okoboji L., 21 mi. N of Spencer. **5** Town (pop. 695), Grant parish, central La., 36 mi. NW of Alexandria and on Red R.; agr. (especially watermelons); lumber. **6** Town (pop. 157), Hampden co., SW Mass., 14 mi. NW of Springfield. **7** Village (pop. 397), Hillsdale co., S Mich., 13 mi. SW of Hillsdale, near Ohio line, in farm area. **8** City (pop. 1,913), Le Sueur co., S Minn., c.40 mi. SSW of Minneapolis; agr. trade center for grain, livestock, and poultry area; dairy products, canned vegetables, clothing. Platted 1877, inc. 1902. **9** Village (pop. 1,063), Orange co., SE N.Y., on small Wallkill R. and 11 mi. W of Newburgh; mfg. (dresses, textiles). Summer resort. **10** Village (pop. 579), Hamilton co., extreme SW Ohio, a NE suburb of Cincinnati. **11** Borough (pop. 2,166), Lycoming co., N central Pa., 10 mi. ESE of Williamsport and on West Branch of Susquehanna R.; furniture, leather products. Settled 1778, inc. 1887. **12** Town (pop. 1,091), Franklin co., NW Vt., on small Trout R. and 23 mi. E of St. Albans; agr., dairying. Chartered 1789, settled 1793. **13** City (pop. 3,484), Kanawha and Fayette counties, W W.Va., on Kanawha R. and 22 mi. SE of Charleston; bituminous-coal mines, gas and oil wells. Seat of W.Va. Inst. of Technology. Inc. 1890.

Montgomery or **Montgomeryshire** (-shĭr), county (□ 797; 1931 pop. 48,473; 1951 census 45,989), central Wales; ⊙ Montgomery. Bounded by Merioneth (NW), Denbigh (N), Shropshire (E), Radnor (S), Cardigan (SW). Drained by Severn, Wye, and Dovey rivers. Mountainous terrain. Offa's Dyke runs along E border of co. Chief industries are woolen milling, slate quarrying, lead mining, agr. Besides Montgomery, towns are Llanidloes, Newtown, Llanfyllin, Welshpool, Machynlleth.

Montgomery, Welsh *Trefaldwyn* (trĭfäld'wĭn), municipal borough (1931 pop. 918; 1951 census 904), ⊙ Montgomeryshire, Wales, in SE part of co., near the Severn, 20 mi. SW of Shrewsbury; agr. market. Has ruins of 13th-cent. castle. OFFA'S DYKE is particularly well preserved here.

Montgomery City, city (pop. 1,679), ⊙ Montgomery co., E central Mo., 25 mi. ENE of Fulton; grain, dairy products, cattle, poultry. Laid out 1853.

Montgomery Pass (alt. 7,123 ft.), SW Nev., in N White Mts., near Boundary Peak; highway passage.

Montgomery Peak, Calif.: see WHITE MOUNTAINS.

Montgomeryshire, Wales: see MONTGOMERY, county.

Montguyon (mõgēyõ'), village (pop. 572), Charente-Maritime dept., W France, 17 mi. S of Barbezieux; dairying, distilling. Has ruins of 12th–15th-cent. castle.

Mont Hawa, Belgian Congo: see HAWA.

Monthelie (mõtülē'), village (pop. 201), Côte-d'Or dept., E central France, on SE slope of the Côte d'Or, 4 mi. SW of Beaune; Burgundy wines.

Monthermé (mõtĕrmā'), town (pop. 2,790), Ardennes dept., N France, in the Ardennes, 9 mi. N of Mézières, on the Meuse near mouth of the Semoy; iron and steel foundries. Tourist center for Meuse and Semoy valley excursions.

Monthey (mõtā'), town (pop. 4,927), Valais canton, SW Switzerland, near the Rhone, 20 mi. W of Sion; chemicals, metal and cement products, tobacco. Has 14th-cent. castle.

Monthléry (mõlārē'), town (pop. 2,102), Seine-et-Oise dept., N central France, 16 mi. SSW of Paris; pumpkins, potatoes. Has massive 13th–15th-cent. keep of former feudal castle once occupied by Edward III of England.

Monthois (mõtwä'), agr. village (pop. 446), Ardennes dept., N France, 6 mi. S of Vouziers.

Monthureux-sur-Saône (mõtürû'-sür-sōn'), village (pop. 845), Vosges dept., E France, on upper Saône R. and 24 mi. SW of Épinal; grindstones.

Monti (môn'tē), village (pop. 1,100), Sassari prov., NE Sardinia, 40 mi. E of Sassari.

Monticelli d'Ongina (môntēchĕl'lē dônjē'nä), town (pop. 1,657), Piacenza prov., Emilia-Romagna, N central Italy, near Po R., 5 mi. SW of Cremona; button factories.

Monticello (mŏntĭsĕ'lō). **1** City (pop. 4,501), ⊙ Drew co., SE Ark., c.45 mi. SSE of Pine Bluff; industrial center for area growing cotton, fruit, and truck; cotton processing, lumber milling, mfg. of textiles. Seat of Ark. Agr. and Mechanical Col. **2** Town (pop. 2,264), ⊙ Jefferson co., NW Fla., 27 mi. ENE of Tallahassee, near Ga. line and L. Miccosukee; farm trade center, plywood mfg. Settled in early-19th cent. **3** City (pop. 1,918), ⊙ Jasper co., central Ga., 32 mi. N of Macon; mfg. (clothing, lumber, bobbins); food canning. Inc. 1810. **4** City (pop. 2,612), ⊙ Piatt co., central Ill., on Sangamon R. (bridged here) and 24 mi. ENE of Decatur, in rich agr. area; mfg. (fiber tile, patent medicines, health foods); corn, oats, soybeans, wheat, livestock, dairy products, poultry. Inc. 1841. **5** Resort city (pop. 3,467), ⊙ White co., NW central Ind., on Tippecanoe R., bet. Shafer and Freeman lakes, and 21 mi. W of Logansport, in agr. area (corn, oats, soybeans); flour, packed meat, furniture. Settled 1831, laid out 1834, inc. 1853. **6** City (pop. 2,888), Jones co., E Iowa, on Maquoketa R. and 30 mi. NE of Cedar Rapids; farm equipment, feather dusters, canned corn, feed, concrete products. Limestone quarries near by. Settled 1836, inc. 1867. **7** Town (pop. 2,934), ⊙ Wayne co., S Ky., in Cumberland foothills, 23 mi. SW of Somerset, in area of agr. (corn, burley tobacco, wheat), coal mines, oil wells, rock quarries, timber. Oil refining, mfg. of wood products, tanks, trailers, log carts; flour and feed mills. Airport. Settled before 1800. **8** Town (pop. 1,284), Aroostook co., E Maine, on Meduxnekeag R. and 13 mi. N of Houlton; potatoes shipped. Settled 1830, inc. 1846. **9** Village (pop. 1,231), Wright co., E Minn., on Mississippi R. and 35 mi. NW of Minneapolis, in grain and livestock area; dairy products. Settled 1852, platted 1854, inc. 1856. **10** Town (pop. 1,382), ⊙ Lawrence co., S central Miss., 50 mi. S of Jackson, and on Pearl R., in agr. and timber area; lumber, clothing. Founded 1798. **11** Town (pop. 154), ⊙ Lewis co., NE Mo., on North Fabius R., near the Mississippi, and 20 mi. NW of Quincy, Ill. **12** Resort village (pop. 4,223), ⊙ Sullivan co., SE N.Y., 20 mi. NW of Middletown, in timber, dairying and lake area; mfg. (paint, perfumes, bedding, lumber, food and wood products, lighting equipment). Inc. 1830. **13** Town (pop. 1,172), ⊙ San Juan co., SE Utah, 50 mi. SSE of Moab; alt. 7,066 ft.; flour-milling point in livestock and grain area; processing of uranium and vanadium ores. Abajo Mts. are just W, in section of La Sal Natl. Forest. **14** Village (pop. 792), Green co., S Wis., 10 mi. N of Monroe, in agr. area; mfg. (textiles, feed, cheese).

Monticello (mŏntĭsĕ'lō, -chĕ'lō), estate, Albemarle co., central Va., just SE of Charlottesville; home for 56 years and burial place of Thomas Jefferson, its designer. Mansion begun 1770, occupied 1772; additional construction continued for many years. Famous as one of earliest examples of Amer. classic revival. After many years of deterioration under changing ownership, it was acquired (1923) by Thomas Jefferson Memorial Foundation and restored. "Ash Lawn," home of James Monroe, is near by.

Monticello Conte Otto (môntēchĕl'lô kôn'tĕ ôt'tô), village (pop. 218), Vicenza prov., Veneto, N Italy, 4 mi. NNE of Vicenza; foundry, agr. machinery factory.

Monticello Dam, Calif.: see PUTAH CREEK.

Montichiari (môn"tēkyä'rē), town (pop. 4,131), Brescia prov., Lombardy, N Italy, on Chiese R. and 12 mi. SE of Brescia; agr. and livestock market; mfg. (agr. tools, hardware, silk textiles).

Monticiano (môn"tēchä'nô), village (pop. 978), Siena prov., Tuscany, central Italy, 15 mi. SW of Siena.

Montiel (mōntyĕl'), town (pop. 2,639), Ciudad Real prov., S central Spain, 26 mi. E of Valdepeñas; cereals, grapes, olives, livestock. Lumbering; gypsum quarrying; flour milling, plaster mfg. Over the town towers ruined castle in which Peter the Cruel was held prisoner by his half brother. The surrounding region, a plain of La Mancha stretching into Albacete prov., is called Campo de Montiel.

Montiel, Selvas de (sĕl'väs dā), hilly forests in N Entre Ríos prov., Argentina, extend c.60 mi. SSW from Corrientes prov. border to area S of Villa Federal; subtropical woods.

Montier-en-Der (mõtyā'-ã-dâr'), village (pop. 1,079), Haute-Marne dept., NE France, 14 mi. SW of Saint-Dizier; agr.-machinery mfg. Stud farm. Its 10th–12th-cent. abbatial church damaged in Second World War.

Montieri (môntyā'rē), village (pop. 1,161), Grosseto prov., Tuscany, central Italy, 9 mi. NE of Massa Marittima, in mining region (copper, iron, lead).

Montiers-sur-Saulx (mõtyā'-sür-sō'), village (pop. 587), Meuse dept., NE France, on the Saulx and 17 mi. SSE of Bar-le-Duc; sawmilling.

Montignac (mõtēnyäk'), village (pop. 1,874), Dordogne dept., SW France, on the Vézère and 12 mi. N of Sarlat; woodworking center (gun stocks, furniture); canning, tanning, mfg. (agr. equipment, fertilizer).

Montignies-le-Tilleul (mõtēnyē-lü-tēyûl'), town (pop. 5,775), Hainaut prov., S central Belgium, 4 mi. WSW of Charleroi, near Sambre R.; coal mining; metallurgical industry.

Montignies-sur-Sambre (-sür-sã'brü) town (pop. 23,145), Hainaut prov., S central Belgium, on Sambre R. and 2 mi. ESE of Charleroi; coke plants, blast furnaces.

Montigny-en-Gohelle (mõtēnyē'-ã-gôĕl'), residential town (pop. 7,683), Pas-de-Calais dept., N France, 4 mi. E of Lens, in coal-mining dist.

Montigny-le-Roi (-lü-rwä'), village (pop. 839), Haute-Marne dept., NE France, 12 mi. NE of Langres; agr. market. Near by rises the Meuse.

Montigny-lès-Metz (-lā-mĕs'), SSW residential suburb (pop. 12,726) of Metz, Moselle dept., NE France, on Moselle's right bank; railroad yards.

Montigny-sur-Aube (-sür-ōb'), agr. village (pop. 500), Côte-d'Or dept., E central France, on Aube R. and 11 mi. NE of Châtillon-sur-Seine.

Montijo (mōntē'hō), village (pop. 742), Veraguas prov., W central Panama, in Pacific lowland, near Montijo Gulf, 8 mi. S of Santiago; gold-mining center; sawmilling. Mercury deposits.

Montijo (mōntē'zhŏŏ), town (pop. 9,920), Setúbal dist., S central Portugal, near Lisbon Bay, on rail spur, 10 mi. E of Lisbon; cork-processing center; other mfg.: pottery, chemical fertilizer, hardware; fruit preserving, distilling.

Montijo (mōntē'hō), town (pop. 10,857), Badajoz prov., W Spain, on railroad and 19 mi. E of Badajoz; processing and agr. center (olives, olive oil, grapes, liquor, vegetables, livestock). Mfg. of knives, tiles. Has palace of counts of Montijo.

Montijo Gulf, inlet of the Pacific in W central Panama, bet. Las Palmas and Azuero peninsulas; 15 mi. wide, 20 mi. long. Barred by Cébaco Isl., off its mouth, it receives San Pablo R. Its port is Puerto Mutis.

Montilla (mōntē'lyä), city (pop. 18,224), Córdoba prov., S Spain, in Andalusia, built on 2 hills 23 mi. SSE of Córdoba; noted for its pale sherry (amontillado), widely exported. Olive- and peanut-oil processing, tanning, brandy distilling, flour milling; mfg. of pottery, soap, plaster, raincoats, esparto baskets, oilcloth, chocolate. Stock raising. Limestone and gypsum quarries. Palace of dukes of Medinaceli near by. Gonzalo Fernández de Córdoba b. here.

Montillana (mōntēlyä'nä), town (pop. 1,653), Granada prov., S Spain, 28 mi. NNW of Granada; peat processing, flour milling; olive oil, vegetables.

Montisola, Italy: see ISEO, LAGO D'.

Montivilliers (mõtēvēyā'), town (pop. 6,696), Seine-Inférieure dept., N France, 5 mi. NE of Le Havre; textile and flour milling. Has 11th–15th-cent. church.

Montjean (mõzhã'), village (pop. 1,034), Maine-et-Loire dept., W France, on Loire R. and 15 mi. WSW of Angers; winegrowing. Damaged in Second World War.

Montjoie, Germany: see MONSCHAU.

Mont Joli (mõ zhôlē'), village (pop. 3,533), E Que., near the St. Lawrence, 18 mi. NE of Rimouski; railroad workshops, metal foundries; hydroelectric station. Dairying, pig-raising region. Airfield.

Montjoly (mõzhôlē'), settlement, part of Rémire, on Cayenne Isl., N Fr. Guiana, 5 mi. E of Cayenne; farm colony, begun 1933.

Montjuich (mõnt-hwēch'), isolated hill (575 ft.), Barcelona prov., NE Spain, on Mediterranean bet. S dist. of Barcelona city and Llobregat plain; crowned by citadel (18th cent.).

Mont Laurier (mõ lōrēā'), village (pop. 2,661), ⊙ Labelle co., SW Que., in the Laurentians, at foot of Mt. Sir Wilfrid, on Lièvre R., 80 mi. N of Ottawa; alt. 733 ft.; dairying, lumbering; oat, potato growing; skiing center. Hydroelectric station.

Montlebon (mõlübõ'), village (pop. 221), Doubs dept., E France, near the Doubs, 7 mi. WSW of Le Locle (Switzerland); cutlery mfg., dairying.

Montlieu (mõlyû'), village (pop. 393), Charente-Maritime dept., W France, 16 mi. SE of Jonzac; dairying, distilling.

Mont-Louis (mõ-lwē'), village (pop. 278), Pyrénées-Orientales dept., S France, in E Pyrenees, near head of CONFLENT and CAPCIR valleys, 2 mi. ENE of Col de la PERCHE, and 17 mi. WSW of Prades; alt. 5,282 ft. Winter sports. Has 17th-cent. ramparts.

Montlouis-sur-Loire (mõlwē'-sür-lwär'), village (pop. 792), Indre-et-Loire dept., W central France, on Loire R. and 6 mi. E of Tours. Noted for its wines. Troglodyte dwellings. Formerly Montlouis.

Montluçon (mõlüsõ'), city (pop. 45,535), Allier dept., central France, at S end of Berry Canal, on the Cher and 45 mi. NNW of Clermont-Ferrand; major metallurgical center; steel mills (iron and steel rails, armor plate, railroad equipment); mfg. of rubber tires, glass and mirrors, synthetic textiles, fertilizer, furniture, porcelain; tanneries, breweries. Old town, with many 15th–16th-cent. houses; dominated by castle (now barracks) of dukes of Bourbon. Industrial dist. of La Ville-Gozet is on left bank of the Cher. Montluçon owes its industrial rise to the discovery (early 19th cent.) of extensive coal deposits in Commentry area.

Montluel (mõlwĕl'), village (pop. 1,757), Ain dept., E France, 13 mi. NE of Lyons.

Montmagny (mōmänyē'), county (□ 630; pop. 22,049), SE Que., on the St. Lawrence and Maine border; ⊙ Montmagny.

Montmagny, town (pop. 4,585), ⊙ Montmagny co., SE Que., on the St. Lawrence and 35 mi. ENE of Quebec; silk and rayon milling, woodworking, dairying, mfg. of stoves, pumps, biscuits. Founded 1678, inc. 1845.

Montmagny (mõmänyē'), town (pop. 3,203), Seine-et-Oise dept., N central France, an outer N suburb of Paris, 8 mi. from Notre Dame Cathedral; foundries, chocolate factory.

Montmarault (mõmärō'), village (pop. 1,312), Allier dept., central France, in Combrailles, 16 mi. E of Montluçon; brewing, dairying, edge-tool mfg.

Montmartin-sur-Mer (mõmärtē'-sür-mâr'), village (pop. 675), Manche dept., NW France, near Channel coast, 5 mi. SW of Coutances; marble quarries.

Montmartre, village (pop. 346), SE Sask., near small Chapleau Lakes, 23 mi. SE of Indian Head; mixed farming.

Montmartre (mõmär'trü), a N district of Paris, France, occupying an eminence (*Butte de Montmartre*) which rises 330 ft. (highest point of Paris) above right bank of the Seine. It is topped by 19th-cent. basilica of Sacré-Coeur surmounted by a large dome of Byzantine style. Parts of old quarter on its slopes were long a favorite residence of artists. Montmartre is also noted for its night clubs, of which the Moulin Rouge is best known. The cemetery of Montmartre contains the tombs, of Stendhal, Berlioz, Renan, Heine, and Alfred de Vigny. From earliest times the summit was a place of worship first of the Druids, and later of the Romans who built temples to Mercury and to Mars. A Benedictine abbey and the church of St. Pierre de Montmartre were founded here in 12th cent.

Montmédy (mõmādē'), anc. *Mons Medius*, village (pop. 1,394), Meuse dept., NE France, on the Chiers and 25 mi. N of Verdun; agr. market. Upper town (atop rock 330 ft. high) was fortified by Vauban after its capture (1656) for Louis XIV by Turenne. Fell to Germans in 1870 and in 1914. Damaged in Second World War. Avioth (ävyōt'), with noted 14th–15th-cent. church (damaged 1940), is 4 mi. NNE.

Montmélian (mõmālyã'), village (pop. 734), Savoie dept., SE France, on the Isère and 8 mi. SE of Chambéry, at N end of Grésivaudan valley (red wines); rail junction; mfg. (electrical equipment, combs). Was stronghold of dukes of Savoy.

Montmerle or **Montmerle-sur-Saône** (mõmĕrl'-sür-sōn'), village (pop. 961), Ain dept., E France, on the Saône and 7 mi. N of Villefranche; wine shipping, distilling.

Montmirail (mõmērī'). **1** Village (pop. 1,871), Marne dept., N France, on the Petit-Morin and 14 mi. SSE of Château-Thierry; grain, lumber. Here Napoleon I defeated Allies in 1814. First battle of the Marne (1914) was fought in area. **2** Agr. village (pop. 282), Sarthe dept., W France, 15 mi. S of Nogent-le-Rotrou. Has medieval castle.

Montmirey-le-Château (mõmērā'-lü-shätō'), agr. village (pop. 164), Jura dept., E France, 9 mi. N of Dôle.

Montmoreau (mõmôrō'), village (pop. 708), Charente dept., W France, 17 mi. S of Angoulême; cattle market.

Montmorenci (mŏntmurĕn'sē), village (pop. c.200), Aiken co., W S.C., 5 mi. ESE of Aiken; asparagus center.

Montmorency (mõmôrãsē', mŏntmurĕn'sē), county (□ 2,198; pop. 18,602, including Île d'Orléans), S Que., on the St. Lawrence; ⊙ Château Richer.

Montmorency, village, Que.: see MONTMORENCY VILLAGE.

Montmorency (mõmôrãsē'), town (pop. 10,511), Seine-et-Oise dept., N central France, an outer N suburb of Paris, 9 mi. from Notre Dame Cathedral; mfg. (safes, electric furnaces, textile machinery); noted for its artichokes, cherries, and pears. Castle of Montmorency ducal family was razed 1814. Rousseau lived here (1757–62). **Forest of Montmorency** (5,000 acres) extends 7 mi. NW toward Oise R. Consisting mainly of chestnut trees, it is a favorite Parisian excursion center.

Montmorency (mŏntmurĕn'sē), county (□ 555; pop. 4,125), N Mich.; ⊙ Atlanta. Drained by Thunder Bay, Rainy, and Black rivers. Dairying and potato-raising area; also a hunting and fishing region, with state forest, game refuge, small lakes. Organized 1881.

Montmorency River, S Que., rises in Laurentides Park, flows 60 mi. S to the St. Lawrence at Montmorency Village. Near mouth are noted falls, 275 ft. high.

Montmorency Village or **Montmorency**, village (pop. 5,393), S Que., on the St. Lawrence at mouth of Montmorency R. (waterfalls), and 7 mi. NE of Quebec; textile milling. Hydroelectric plant.

Montmorillon (mõmôrēyõ'), town (pop. 4,116), Vienne dept., W central France, on Gartempe R. and 27 mi. ESE of Poitiers; road and agr. trade center; mfg. (building materials, macaroons, furniture, beer). Has a 2-storied 12th-cent. sepulchral chapel called the Octagon.

Montmorot (mõmôrō'), W suburb (pop. 1,652) of Lons-le-Saunier, Jura dept., E France; paper milling, cement and cheese mfg. Extensive salt mines.

Montmort (mõmôr'), agr. village (pop. 358), Marne dept., N France, 10 mi. SW of Épernay. Has 16th-cent. church and 12th–15th-cent. church (damaged in 1940).

Montodine (môntô'dēnĕ), village (pop. 2,145), Cremona prov., Lombardy, N Italy, on Serio R., near its confluence with the Adda, and 5 mi. S of Crema.

Montoir-de-Bretagne (mõtwär'-dù-brütä'nyù), village (pop. 1,132), Loire-Inférieure dept., W France, 5 mi. NNE of Saint-Nazaire. Has Saint-Nazaire airport.

Montoire-sur-le-Loir (–sür-lù-lwär'), town (pop. 2,433), Loir-et-Cher dept., N central France, on Loir R. and 10 mi. WSW of Vendôme; horse and cattle market; dairying, wheat growing. Has 11th-cent. chapel of Saint-Gilles and ruins of a feudal castle. Ronsard b. near by.

Montois-la-Montagne (mõtwä'-lä-mõtä'nyù), village (pop. 1,309), Moselle dept., NE France, near the Orne, 4 mi. SE of Briey; iron mines.

Montolieu (mõtôlyû'), village (pop. 622), Aude dept., S France, 10 mi. NW of Carcassonne; woolens. Gothic church.

Monton, N suburb of Eccles, SE Lancashire, England; cotton milling, metalworking.

Montona, Yugoslavia: see MOTOVUN.

Montone River (môntô'nĕ), N central Italy, rises in Etruscan Apennines 10 mi. SSE of Marradi, flows 53 mi. NNE, past Rocca San Casciano and Forlì, joining Ronco R. near Ravenna to form the Fiumi Uniti, which flows 6 mi. E to the Adriatic. Used for irrigation and in mfg. (Forlì). Chief tributary, Rabbi R.

Montopoli in Val d'Arno (môntô'pôlē ēn väl där'nô), village (pop. 1,144), Pisa prov., Tuscany, central Italy, 5 mi. W of San Miniato; macaroni, pottery.

Mont-Organisé (mõt-ôrgänēzā'), agr. town (1950 census pop. 571), Nord dept., NE Haiti, near Dominican Republic border, 17 mi. SSE of Fort Liberté; coffeegrowing.

Montorio al Vomano (môntô'rēō äl vômä'nô), town (pop. 2,643), Teramo prov., Abruzzi e Molise, S central Italy, on Vomano R. and 6 mi. SW of Teramo; wrought-iron products.

Montorio nei Frentani (nā frĕntä'nē), village (pop. 2,532), Campobasso prov., Abruzzi e Molise, S central Italy, 3 mi. SSE of Larino; cementworks.

Montoro (môntô'rô), village (pop. 383), Terni prov., Umbria, central Italy, near Nera R., 3 mi. SW of Narni; chemical industry (synthetic ammonia, ammonium sulphate). Hydroelectric plant near.

Montoro (mōntō'rō), city (pop. 9,541), Córdoba prov., S Spain, in Andalusia, on the Guadalquivir and 24 mi. ENE of Córdoba; olive-oil-production and -shipping center. Mfg. of esparto baskets, hemp cloth and rope, soap, tiles; flour- and sawmilling, distilling (brandy, sirups). Trades in cereals, vegetables, livestock, lumber. Has 16th-cent. bridge. Was important fortress under Moors. Copper, iron, and lead deposits near by.

Montour (mŏn"tōōr'), county (□ 130; pop. 16,001), central Pa.; ⊙ Danville. Agr. and industrial area; drained by Susquehanna R. Mfg. (metal products, clothing); limestone. Formed 1850.

Montour, town (pop. 380), Tama co., central Iowa, on Iowa R. and 11 mi. ESE of Marshalltown. Limestone quarries near by.

Montour Falls, village (pop. 1,457), Schuyler co., W central N.Y., in Finger Lakes region, just SE of Watkins Glen, and on small Catherine Creek; summer resort. Mfg. of cranes and hoists. Chequaga (or Shequaga) Falls (156 ft. high) here attract tourists.

Montoursville, residential borough (pop. 3,293), Lycoming co., N central Pa., on West Branch of Susquehanna R. just E of Williamsport, at mouth of Loyalsock Creek; silk mills, furniture mfg. Settled 1807, laid out 1820, inc. 1850.

Montowese, Conn.: see NORTH HAVEN.

Montoz (mõtō'), mountain (4,366 ft.) in the Jura, NW Switzerland, 5 mi. NNE of Biel. Sur Montoz is its W part.

Montparnasse (mõpärnäs'), quarter of Paris, France, on left bank of the Seine, centering on intersection of Boulevard de Montparnasse and Boulevard Raspail. Its famous cafés (the *Dôme*, *Rotonde*, *Coupole*, and others) are the meeting places of French artists and intellectuals. Here are the Montparnasse railroad station, the Pasteur Inst., the anc. catacombs, and the Montparnasse cemetery (laid out in 1824), with the tombs of Saint-Saëns, Baudelaire, César Franck, Maupassant, Leconte de Lisle, and other well-known Frenchmen.

Mont-Pélerin (mō pālùrē'), resort, Vaud canton, W Switzerland, 2 mi. N of Vevey, on Mont Pélerin (2,644 ft.).

Montpelier (mŏnt"pĕl'yùr), town (pop. 2,100), St. James parish, NW Jamaica, on Kingston–Montego Bay RR and 8 mi. S of Montego Bay, in fertile agr. region, growing principally bananas.

Montpelier (mŏntpĕl'yùr). **1** City (pop. 2,682), Bear Lake co., extreme SE Idaho, near Bear R., 70 mi. SE of Pocatello; alt. c.5,950 ft.; railroad div. point, trade and shipping center for agr. and grazing area; dairy products. Phosphate deposits near by. Founded 1864 by Mormons. Early names: Clover Creek, Belmont. Renamed (1865) by Brigham Young in honor of Vt. capital. Has Mormon tabernacle. **2** Town (pop. 1,826), Blackford co., E Ind., on Salamonie R. and 27 mi. NNE of Muncie, in agr. area (livestock; dairy products; soybeans, grain); mfg. (oil-well and chemical supplies, glass products, gloves); natural-gas and oil wells; stone quarries. Settled 1836, inc. 1937. **3** Village (pop. 105), Stutsman co., SE central N.Dak., 15 mi. SSE of Jamestown and on James R. **4** Village (pop. 3,867), Williams co., extreme NW Ohio, on St. Joseph R. and 8 mi. NNW of Bryan; store and office fixtures, metal stampings, truck bodies, wood products. Settled 1855, inc. 1875. **5** City (pop. 8,599), ⊙ Vt. and Washington co., central Vt., on Winooski R. and 5 mi. NW of Barre; 44°15'N 72°34'W; alt. c.500 ft. Produces granite, textiles, wood and concrete products, machinery; printing. Jr. col. is here. Became state ⊙, 1805. Points of interest: granite capitol (1836; rebuilt 1857 after fire; contains Larkin G. Mead's statue of Ethan Allen); supreme court, containing libraries and hist. collection; Wood Gall.; Kellogg-Hubbard library; Hubbard Park. Admiral George Dewey b. here. Granted 1780, settled 1787, inc. 1894. **6** Hamlet, Hanover co., E Va., 25 mi. NNW of Richmond. "Montpelier," home of James Madison, is near ORANGE town.

Montpellier (mŏntpĕl'yùr, Fr. mõpĕlyā'), city (pop. 80,673), ⊙ Hérault dept., S France, on the Lez, near the Gulf of Lion, and 80 mi. WNW of Marseilles; 43°36'N 3°53'E. Commercial and cultural center of the Languedoc, with important wine and alcohol trade. Though not primarily an industrial city, it produces chemicals (soap and fertilizer), winegrowing equipment, biscuits, candies, perfumes, and hosiery. There are distilleries, saltworks, metal-construction and printing plants. The old city has narrow, winding streets and handsome 17th–18th-cent. bldgs. Its principal sites are the Fabre mus. (painting) and an archaeological mus.; the botanical garden founded 1593 by Henry IV; the much restored 14th-cent. cathedral; and the Promenade du Peyrou (with triumphal arch and fountain-temple) overlooking city. Montpellier is known for its univ. (founded 1289). The famous faculty of medicine, which has been traced to the 10th-cent., now occupies a 14th-cent. bldg. (old episcopal palace). The city also has schools of pharmacy, engineering, and fine arts, a theological seminary, and several scientific laboratories. A fief under the counts of Toulouse, Montpellier passed (13th cent.) to the kings of Majorca, from whom it was purchased (1349) by Philip VI of France. A Huguenot center, it was besieged and taken by Louis XIII in 1622. It was the seat of the provincial estates of Languedoc.

Montpezat or **Montpezat-sous-Bauzon** (mõpùzä'-sōō-bōzõ'), village (pop. 564), Ardèche dept., S France, in the Monts du Vivarais, 11 mi. NW of Aubenas; silk throwing and spinning, sheep raising.

Montpezat-de-Quercy (mõpùzä'-dù-kĕrsē'), village (pop. 528), Tarn-et-Garonne dept., SW France, 14 mi. S of Cahors; wheat, corn.

Montpon-sur-l'Isle (mõpõ'-sür-lēl'), town (pop. 2,258), Dordogne dept., SW France, on the Isle and 19 mi. NW of Bergerac; road center; paper milling (filter and packing paper), mfg. of felt slippers; flour milling, cheese making. Before 1925 also called Monpont, Monpont-sur-l'Isle, Montpon, and Montpont.

Montpont (mõpõ'), agr. village (pop. 252), Saône-et-Loire dept., E central France, SSW of Louhans.

Montreal or **Montréal** (mŏn"trēôl', Fr. mõrāäl'), city (pop. 903,007; metropolitan area pop. 1,138,431), S Que., on Montreal Isl., on the St. Lawrence (bridges) and Lachine Rapids, 320 mi. NNW of New York; 45°30'N 73°35'W. Largest city of Canada, commercial and cultural center, major seaport with extensive dock installations, accessible to largest ocean liners during St. Lawrence navigation season; world's largest grain-shipping port, transshipment point for the Great Lakes. Insurance and banking center of Canada; industries include mfg. of steel products, railroad equipment, machinery, paper, pulp, leather, clothing, textiles, chemicals, glass, electrical equipment, furniture, shoes; copper refining, flour milling, tobacco processing, sugar refining; there are large grain elevators, cold-storage warehouses. City's average temp. ranges from 13°F. (Jan.) to 69°F. (July); average annual rainfall is 38.89 inches. Montreal is seat of R.C. archbishop. Laid out on slopes of Mount Royal (900 ft.), extinct volcano; on upper slope is Mount Royal Park (463 acres), largest of city's many parks. Among Montreal's notable features are McGill Univ., founded 1829; Univ. of Montreal (French), founded 1876 as branch of Laval Univ., established independently 1889; Cathedral of St. James (1870), replica of St. Peter's in Rome; churches of Notre Dame (1824; originally founded 1656), Notre Dame de Bonsecours (founded 1657), and St. Patricks (1841); Château Ramezay (1705), formerly French governors' residence, home of British governors 1724–1837, hq. of Continental Army and U.S. Commissioners 1775–76, and since 1895 a mus.; Seminary of St. Sulpice (1710); Hôtel Dieu hospital (founded 1644); and Grey Nunnery (1738). There are several museums and many modern business bldgs. Victoria Jubilee Bridge across the St. Lawrence was opened 1860, remodeled 1898; Jacques Cartier Harbour Bridge opened 1930. City's chief centers are Dominion Square and Place d'Armes. Site of Montreal, then Indian village of Hochelaga, was 1st visited (1535) by Cartier; Champlain visited the area 1603, built a fort here 1611. Maisonneuve here founded (1642) mission settlement of Ville Marie; fort and hospital (Hôtel Dieu) were built. Suffering frequent Indian attacks, settlement slowly developed into furtrading center; stone fortifications were added, 1725. Montreal surrendered (1760) to the British without resistance. It was occupied (1775–76) by the Continental Army under Montgomery. It was ⊙ Canada, 1844–49. British garrison was withdrawn 1870. Montreal's chief suburbs are Outremont, Westmount, Verdun, Lachine, Longueuil, Montreal South, Montreal West, Montreal North, Montreal East, Côte des Neiges, and Côte St. Michel. City's airports are at Dorval and Cartierville. Hydroelectric power is supplied by plants at Lachine, Cedars, Soulanges, and Chambly.

Mont Réal, hill, Que.: see MOUNT ROYAL.
Montréal (mõrāäl'). **1** Village (pop. 368), Ain dept., E France, in the Jura, 3 mi. NW of Nantua; wood turning and hornworking. **2** Village (pop. 1,055), Aude dept., S France, 11 mi. W of Carcassonne; mfg. of visor caps, lingerie; winegrowing. **3** or **Montréal-du-Gers** (–dü-zhâr'), village (pop. 618), Gers dept., SW France, 9 mi. W of Condom; winegrowing, Armagnac brandy distilling.
Montreal (mŏn"trēôl'), city (pop. 1,439), Iron co., N Wis., in Gogebic Range, 2 mi. W of Hurley; iron-mining. Inc. 1924.
Montreal East, town (pop. 2,355), S Que., on Montreal Isl., NE suburb of Montreal; copper-refining center.
Montreal Island. 1 Island (13 mi. long, 2–4 mi. wide), S Franklin Dist., Northwest Territories, in Chantrey Inlet, on E side of Adelaide Peninsula; 67°52'N 96°20'W. **2** Island (□ 201; pop. 1,116,800), S Que., bounded by L. St. Louis (S), the St. Lawrence (E), and R. des Prairies (NW), branch of Ottawa R.; 30 mi. long, up to 10 mi. wide. Isl. is coextensive with Montreal Isl. co., including former cos. of Hochelaga and Jacques Cartier. Great part of isl. is occupied by Montreal city and its suburbs.
Montreal Lake (□ 162), central Sask., 60 mi. N of Prince Albert; 32 mi. long, 7 mi. wide. Drains N into Churchill R. through Lac la Ronge.
Montreal North, town (pop. 6,152), S Que., on Montreal Isl., N suburb of Montreal.
Montreal River, central Ont., flows 90 mi. S and WSW to L. Superior 50 mi. NNW of Sault Ste. Marie; 10 mi. above its mouth are 150-ft. Montreal Falls; hydroelectric power.
Montreal River, in Wis. and Mich., rises in Iron co., N Wis., in small Pine L., flows N and NW c.40 mi., past Ironwood, Mich., and Hurley, Wis., to L. Superior; forms part of Mich.-Wis. line.
Montreal South, town (pop. 1,441), S Que., on the St. Lawrence (bridge), opposite Montreal.
Montreal West, town (pop. 3,474), S Que., on Montreal Isl., SW suburb of Montreal.
Montreat (mŏntrēt'), resort (pop. c.500), Buncombe co., W N.C., 14 mi. E of Asheville, in the Blue Ridge. Seat of Montreat Col.
Montredon-Labessonnié (mõtrůdõ'-läbĕsônyā') village (pop. 719), Tarn dept., S France, 9 mi. NNE of Castres; lumbering, livestock raising.
Montréjeau (mõtrāzhō'), town (pop. 2,574), Haute-Garonne dept., S France, on the Garonne, near mouth of the Neste, and 8 mi. W of Saint-Gaudens; hosiery mfg., tanning, fruit shipping; wool trade.
Montrésor (mõtrāzôr'), village (pop. 529), Indre-et-Loire dept., W central France, 29 mi. SE of Tours; woodworking; limekilns near by. Has 16th-cent. castle and church with stained-glass windows.
Montret (mõtrā'), agr. village (pop. 317), Saône-et-Loire dept., E central France, 7 mi. NW of Louhans; poultry.
Montretout (mõtrůtōō'), residential W suburb of Saint-Cloud, Seine-et-Oise dept., N central France, 6 mi. W of Notre Dame Cathedral in Paris. Its reservoir (served by aqueduct from Avre R.) supplies Paris.
Montreuil (mõtrû'ē). **1** or **Montreuil-sur-Mer** (–sür-mâr'), town (pop. 2,440), Pas-de-Calais dept., N France, on left bank of Canche R. and 19 mi. SSE of Boulogne; soap mfg., oil refining, flour milling, brewing. It once stood on the sea and preserves a citadel and 13th–17th-cent. ramparts. Was Br. general hq., 1916–18, in First World War. Neuville-sous-Montreuil (on opposite bank of Canche R.) has a Carthusian monastery (now a sanatorium). **2** or **Montreuil-sous-Bois** (–sōō-bwä'), city (pop. 69,698), Seine dept., N central France, E suburb of Paris, 4 mi. from Notre Dame Cathedral, just N of Vincennes; hide- and skin-processing center (especially rabbit- and sheepskins). Also noted for its peaches. Mfg.: biscuits, porcelain, metal containers, chemicals for tanning. Distilling.
Montreuil-Bellay (–bĕlā'), town (pop. 2,082), Maine-et-Loire dept., W France, on the Thouet and 9 mi. SSW of Saumur; road and railroad center; winegrowing, distilling, barrelmaking. Has fine 13th–15th-cent. feudal castle and 15th-cent. town walls.
Montreuil-sous-Bois, France: see MONTREUIL.
Montreuil-sur-Blaise (–sür-blăz'), village (pop. 137), Haute-Marne dept., NE France, on Blaise R. and 12 mi. S of Saint-Dizier; iron foundries.
Montreuil-sur-Mer, N France: see MONTREUIL.
Montreux (mõtrû'), large resort, Vaud canton, W Switzerland, on E shore of L. Geneva, 4 mi. SE of Vevey. Composed of 3 communities: Le Châtelard (1950 pop. 11,540), Les Planches (1950 pop. 5,189), Veytaux (1950 pop. 695). An unbroken line of villages and resorts, noted for its mild climate and the proximity of both the lakeside and Alpine peaks (the Rochers de Naye, 6,709 ft., is near by). Tourist center; wood- and metalworking, printing, mfg. (chocolate, clothes). Villages include CLARENS, Caux (kō), Les Avants (lāz ävä'), Glion (glēō'), and Territet (tĕrētā'). Castle of CHILLON is near by.
Montrevault (mõtrůvō'), village (pop. 825), Maine-et-Loire dept., W. France, 24 mi. E of Nantes; winegrowing, dairying. At near-by Saint-Pierre-Montlimart (1 mi. NE) some gold is mined.
Montrevel (mõrůvĕl'), village (pop. 795), Ain dept., E France, 10 mi. NNW of Bourg; poultry and dairy market.
Montrichard (mõtrēshär'), town (pop. 2,538), Loir-et-Cher dept., N central France, on the Cher and 18 mi. SSW of Blois; known for its white wines; metalworks. Has remains of medieval castle built by Fulk Nerra.
Montricher (mõrēshā'), village (pop. 95), Savoie dept., SE France, in Maurienne valley, near the Arc, 5 mi. SE of Saint-Jean-de-Maurienne; electrometallurgy. Slate quarries.
Montroc-le-Planet (mõrôk'-lů-plänā'), Alpine village of Haute-Savoie dept., SE France, resort in Chamonix valley, 6 mi. NNE of Chamonix; winter sports. Just N is railroad tunnel (1 mi. long) under Col des Montets (4,797 ft.).
Montroig (mōntroig', –rôch'), town (pop. 2,103), Tarragona prov., NE Spain, 10 mi. SW of Reus; alcohol mfg., olive-oil processing; sheep raising.
Montrond-les-Bains (mõtrõ'-lā-bē'), village (pop. 1,501), Loire dept., E central France, in the Forez Plain, on the Loire and 8 mi. ENE of Montbrison; road and railroad center; health resort with thermal springs. Until 1937, called Meylieu-Montrond.
Montrose (mŏntrōz'), burgh (1931 pop. 10,196; 1951 census 10,760), E Angus, Scotland, on North Sea, at mouth of South Esk R., 25 mi. NE of Dundee; agr. market, fishing port, and seaside resort, with linen milling, shipbuilding, grain distilling, fertilizer mfg. Has 18th-cent. town hall and church. Just W is Montrose Basin, lagoon (2 mi. long, 2 mi. wide) at mouth of South Esk R.; dry at low tide. In mouth of river is Inchbrayock (ĭnch"brā'ŏk) or Rossie Isl., connected with Montrose by suspension bridge. In 13th cent. Montrose was important seaport. In 1296 John de Baliol surrendered here to Edward I. In 1534 Erskine of Dun established 1st Scottish school teaching Greek here. Rebellion of 1715 ended with embarkation at Montrose of the Old Pretender. James Graham, 5th marquess of Montrose, and Andrew Melville b. here. Just SE of Montrose is promontory of Scurdie Ness, site of lighthouse (56°42'N 2°26'W).
Montrose (mŏn'trōz, mŏntrōz'), county (□ 2,239; pop. 15,220), W Colo., ⊙ Montrose. Agr. region bordering Utah; drained by Dolores, San Miguel, and Uncompahgre rivers. Fruit, beans, hay, livestock; mining of uranium, radium, coal, silver, copper. Includes parts of Uncompahgre, Gunnison, and La Sal natl. forests and, in NE, Black Canyon of the Gunnison Natl. Monument. Formed 1883.
Montrose. 1 Town (pop. 344), Ashley co., SE Ark., 12 mi. W of Lake Village. **2** Unincorporated residential town (1940 pop. 2,710), Los Angeles co., S Calif., in foothills of San Gabriel Mts., 11 mi. N of downtown Los Angeles. **3** City (pop. 4,964), ⊙ Montrose co., W Colo., on Uncompahgre R. and 55 mi. SE of Grand Junction; alt. 5,820 ft. Trade center in irrigated fruit, potato, sugar-beet region; meat and dairy products, flour. Carnotite deposits near by are source of radium and uranium. Black Canyon of the Gunnison Natl. Monument just NE. Near-by Gunnison Tunnel conducts water from Gunnison R. to Uncompahgre valley. Founded and inc. 1882. **4** Town (pop. 242), Laurens co., central Ga., 15 mi. W of Dublin. **5** Village (pop. 309), Effingham co., SE central Ill., 8 mi. ENE of Effingham, in agr. area. **6** Town (pop. 643), Lee co., extreme SE Iowa, on Mississippi R. and 9 mi. N of Keokuk, in livestock area. One of the 1st permanent white settlements in Iowa was made here in 1799, when Louis Tesson, a French Canadian, established a trading post. Town was laid out in 1837. **7** Village (pop. 937), Genesee co., SE central Mich., 15 mi. NW of Flint, in farm area. **8** Village (pop. 300), Wright co., S central Minn., 33 mi. W of Minneapolis; dairy products. **9** Town (pop. 222), Jasper co., E central Miss., 35 mi. WSW of Meridian, in agr. and timber area. **10** City (pop. 518), Henry co., W central Mo., 14 mi. SW of Clinton. **11** Borough (pop. 2,075), ⊙ Susquehanna co., NE Pa., 31 mi. NNW of Scranton; mtn. resort; mfg. (machinery, shoes); printing; agr. Settled 1799, inc. 1824. **12** City (pop. 448), McCook co., SE S.Dak., 10 mi. E of Salem; sausages, corn, barley. **13** Village (pop. 79), Randolph co., E W.Va., 11 mi. N of Elkins.
Montross (mŏntrôs'), town (pop. 331), ⊙ Westmoreland co., E Va., 38 mi. SE of Fredericksburg; canneries. George Washington Birthplace Natl. Monument and "Stratford Hall," home of the Lees, are near by.
Montrouge (mõrōōzh'), town (pop. 34,508), Seine dept., N central France, just S of Paris, 3 mi. from Notre Dame Cathedral, bet. Malakoff (W) and Gentilly (E); mfg. (radio and television sets, projectors, fire extinguishers, and clothing); chemical works, tanneries. Petit-Montrouge (N) inc. (1860) into 14th *arrondissement* of Paris.
Montroulez, France: see MORLAIX.
Montroy (mōntroi'), village (pop. 1,427), Valencia prov., E Spain, 16 mi. SW of Valencia; wine, cereals, olive oil.
Monts, Pointe des (pwĕt dā mõ'), cape on the Gulf of St. Lawrence, E Que., on N side of mouth of the St. Lawrence, opposite Gaspé Peninsula, 36 mi. ENE of Baie Comeau; 49°20'N 67°22'W; lighthouse, radio beacon.
Mont-Saint-Aignan (mõ-sĕtĕnyã'), N residential suburb (pop. 6,462) of Rouen, Seine-Inférieure dept., N France.
Mont-Saint-Amand, Belgium: see SINT-AMANDSBERG.
Mont-Saint-Aubert (mõ-sĕtōbâr'), agr. village (pop. 624), Hainaut prov., SW Belgium, 4 mi. N of Tournai, on small hill (489 ft.).
Mont-Saint-Éloi (mõ-sĕtālwä'), village (pop. 457) and ridge (400 ft.), Pas-de-Calais dept., N France, 6 mi. NW of Arras; figured prominently in Lens-Arras battlefield of First World War. Atop ridge are remains of Augustinian abbey founded by St. Eloi in 7th cent.
Mont-Saint-Guibert (mõ-sē-gēbâr'), town (pop. 1,718), Brabant prov., central Belgium, 6 mi. S of Wavre; paper mfg.
Mont-Saint-Jean (–zhã'), village, Brabant prov., central Belgium, 2 mi. S of Waterloo, just N of field where battle of Waterloo was fought.
Mont-Saint-Martin (–märtē'), town (pop. 3,793), Meurthe-et-Moselle dept., NE France, near Belg. border, 2 mi. NNE of Longwy; customs station; important steel-milling center. Iron mines.
Mont-Saint-Michel (–mēshĕl'), rocky islet (3 acres; pop. 149) in Bay of Saint-Michel of English Channel, 1 mi. off coast of NW France, in Manche dept., 8 mi. SW of Avranches, and accessible from Pontorson (6 mi. S) by causeway (1 mi. long; trolley). A cone-shaped rock (alt. 256 ft.), girt at its base by medieval walls and towers, above which rise, in three levels, the clustered bldgs. of the village, crowned by graceful abbey church. Six abbatial bldgs. facing sea form unit called La Merveille (Fr.,=the marvel), built in 13th cent., including almonry and cellar (first story); refectory and Hall of Knights where order of St. Michael was founded in 1469 (second story); and dormitory and cloister (third story), the whole representing a marvel of Gothic architecture. Celebrated abbey founded in 708 by Aubert, bishop of Avranches. Frequently assaulted by English in Hundred Years War, but never captured. Surviving Second World War undamaged, it remains one of France's leading tourist attractions.
Mont-Saint-Michel, Bay of, France: see SAINT-MICHEL, BAY OF.
Mont-Saint-Vincent (–vēsã'), agr. village (pop. 224), Saône-et-Loire dept., E central France, 12 mi. SSE of Le Creusot.
Montsalvy (mõsälvē'), village (pop. 608), Cantal dept., S central France, 15 mi. SSE of Aurillac; cattle raising, cheese mfg. Abbatial church with Romanesque nave. Hydroelectric plant near by.
Montsauche (mõsōsh'), village (pop. 134), Nièvre dept., central France, on Cure R. and 11 mi. NNE of Château-Chinon, in the Morvan; lumbering. Les Settons storage reservoir (□ 1.5), 3 mi. SE, is formed by dam (876 ft. long, 65 ft. high) across the Cure. Tourist area.
Montsec (mõsĕk'), village (pop. 112), Meuse dept., NE France, 8 mi. E of Saint-Mihiel. Atop Montsec hill (key Ger. position in Saint-Mihiel salient 1914–18) is Saint-Mihiel American Memorial.
Montsech (mōntsĕch'), foothills of the Pyrenees, in Lérida prov., NE Spain, between crest of the central Pyrenees and Urgel plain, c.16 mi. N of Balaguer; rise to 5,500 ft. Gorge in foothills traversed by Noguera Pallaresa R.
Montserrado (mŏntsůrä'dō), county, W Liberia, on Atlantic coast; ⊙ Monrovia. Bounded E by Farmington R., W by Lofa R.; drained by St. Paul R.; extends c.40 mi. inland. Rubber (extensive plantations on right bank of Farmington R.), palm oil and kernels, coffee, citrus fruit; fisheries. Main centers (served by roads): Monrovia, Careysburg. Formerly called Mesurado.
Montserrado, Cape, or **Cape Mesurado** (mĕ"sůrä'-dō), headland of W Liberia, on Atlantic Ocean; rises to 290 ft.; 6°19'N 10°49'W. Site of Monrovia.
Montserrat (mŏntsůrăt'), island (□ 37.5; pop. 14,333), a presidency of Leeward Isls. colony, B.W.I., 33 mi. NW of Guadeloupe, 23 mi. SW of Antigua; ⊙ Plymouth. Rugged, volcanic isl. (11 mi. long, up to 7 mi. wide), rising in the Soufrière to 2,999 ft. Healthful climate; annual temp. 78°F., rainfall 40–80 inches. Subject to frequent earth tremors, occasional hurricanes. There are numerous small streams. Thermal springs, gypsum and sulphur deposits near Plymouth. Sugar cane has been replaced by sea-island cotton as chief product and export; also exports tomatoes, onions, limes, lime oil, lime juice, cottonseed oil, vegetables, cattle, and dairy products. Montserrat was discovered 1493 by Columbus, who named it for Montserrat monastery in Spain. First colonized 1632 by Irish settlers under Sir Thomas Warner. Captured by the French in 1664 and 1782; restored to England in 1783.
Montserrat or **Monserrat** (both: mŏn"sůrăt', mŏnt"–, Sp. mōnsĕrät'), mountain (4,054 ft.) of Barcelona prov., NE Spain, in Catalonia, NW of Barcelona and 8 mi. S of Manresa, rising abruptly from Llobregat valley. On terrace (alt. c.2,400 ft.) high on its precipitous cliffs, reached by rack-and-pinion railroad and motor road, is a celebrated Benedic-

tine monastery, one of the greatest religious shrines of Spain. Only ruins are left of the old Montserrat monastery which was founded in 11th cent. (near by are ruins of an older monastery, dating from 9th cent.). The new monastery was built in 19th cent. The Renaissance church (16th cent.; largely restored in 19th and 20th cent.) contains the black wooden image of the Virgin, which, according to one tradition, was carved by St. Luke, brought to Spain by St. Peter, and hidden in a cave near here during the Moorish occupation. In the Middle Ages, the place, also called Monsalvat, was thought to have been the site of the castle of the Holy Grail. At Montserrat, St. Ignatius of Loyola devoted himself to his religious vocation before he founded the Society of Jesus.

Montserrat Hills (mŏntsŭrăt'), low range in W central Trinidad, B.W.I., 20 mi. SE of Port of Spain; rises to 918 ft.

Montsinéry (mõsēnārē'), town (commune pop. 185), N Fr. Guiana, on small Montsinéry R. near the Atlantic, and 13 mi. W of Cayenne; sugar cane, manioc, tropical fruit.

Montsoreau (mõsôrō'), village (pop. 406), Maine-et-Loire dept., W France, on Loire R. and 7 mi. ESE of Saumur; wine and mushroom growing. Has 15th-cent. castle on river bank.

Monts-sur-Guesnes (mõ-sür-gĕn'), agr. village (pop. 589), Vienne dept., W central France, 8 mi. SE of Loudun. Has remains of 15th-cent. castle.

Mont-sur-Marchienne (–märshyĕn'), town (pop. 11,227), Hainaut prov., S central Belgium, 2 mi. SW of Charleroi; coal mining.

Montsûrs (mõsür'), village (pop. 1,345), Mayenne dept., W France, 11 mi. ENE of Laval; cheese making, flour milling.

Mont Tremblant (mõ trãblã'), village (pop. estimate 300), SW Que., in the Laurentians, at foot of Mt. Tremblant, on small L. Mercier, 20 mi. NW of Ste. Agathe des Monts; dairying; skiing center.

Montuiri (mōntwē'rē), town (pop. 2,632), Majorca, Balearic Isls., on railroad and 18 mi. E of Palma; cereals, vegetables, almonds, figs, apricots, livestock; timber; meat products.

Monturque (mōntōōr'kā), town (pop. 2,136), Córdoba prov., S Spain, 7 mi. NW of Lucena; olive-oil processing, soap and plaster mfg.; cereals.

Montvale, borough (pop. 1,856), Bergen co., NE N.J., 10 mi. N of Hackensack; fruit farms; makes clothing. Inc. 1894.

Montverde (mŏnt"vûrd'), town (pop. 293), Lake co., central Fla., near L. Apopka, 19 mi. W of Orlando; grapes.

Mont Vernon, town (pop. 405), Hillsboro co., S N.H., 13 mi. SW of Manchester; summer colony.

Montville. 1 Town (pop. 4,766), New London co., SE Conn., on the Thames and 5 mi. N of New London; farming. Mfg. (textiles, paper goods and boxes) at villages of Uncasville and Oakdale. Includes Mohegan (mōhē'gŭn), an Indian community. State park. Settled 1670, inc. 1786. **2** Town (pop. 466), Waldo co., S Maine, 11 mi. W of Belfast; agr., recreational area. **3** Village, Berkshire co., Mass.: see SANDISFIELD. **4** Village (1940 pop. 837), Morris co., N N.J., 10 mi. W of Paterson, in fruit-growing region; mfg. (buttons, drugs, crushed stone).

Montzeron, France: see TOUTRY.

Monument. 1 Town (pop. 126), El Paso co., central Colo., on Monument Creek, in SE foothills of Front Range, and 45 mi. S of Denver; alt. 6,895 ft. Pike Natl. Forest near by. **2** Town (pop. 228), Grant co., NE central Oregon, 37 mi. S of Heppner and on North Fork of John Day R.

Monument Beach, Mass.: see BOURNE.

Monument Creek, central Colo., rises in Front Range in NW El Paso co., flows 34 mi. generally S, past Palmer Lake and Monument towns, to Fountain Creek at Colorado Springs.

Monument Mountain (1,710 ft.), peak of the Berkshires, SW Mass., in Monument Mtn. State Reservation (260 acres), 4 mi. N of Great Barrington.

Monument Peak, Idaho: see SEVEN DEVILS MOUNTAINS.

Monville (mõvēl'), town (pop. 2,383), Seine-Inférieure dept., N France, 7 mi. N of Rouen; market; celluloid mfg., horse raising.

Monviso, Italy: see VISO, MONTE.

Monywa (mōnyŭwä'), town (pop. 10,800), ⊙ Lower Chindwin dist., Upper Burma, on left bank of Chindwin R., 60 mi. W of Mandalay, on railroad to Yeu. Timber-clearing station; copper deposits near by. In Second World War, recaptured (Jan., 1945) from Japanese by Br. forces.

Monza (môn'tsä), city (pop. 58,503), Milano prov., Lombardy, N Italy, on Lambro R. and 9 mi. NNE of Milan. Rail junction; industrial center; mfg. (hats, carpets, cotton and linen textiles, machinery, glass, furniture, organs, plastics, paint); foundries. Has cathedral on site of church founded by Lombard Queen Theolinda in late 6th cent.; contains famous iron crown used for coronation of Charlemagne, Charles V, and Napoleon. Also has 13th-cent. town hall, 18th-cent. royal palace (now a school of arts and crafts), and expiatory chapel built after assassination here of Humbert I in 1900.

Monze (mōn'zä), township (pop. 616), Southern Prov., Northern Rhodesia, on railroad and 35 mi. SSW of Mazabuka; agr. center (tobacco, wheat, corn). Connected by road with Namwala.

Monze, Cape (mōn'zä) or **Ras Muari** (räs' mwä'rē), headland in Arabian Sea, Karachi administration area, W Pakistan, 22 mi. W of Karachi; 24°49'N 66°40'E; lighthouse. Mouth of Hab R. is just N.

Monzen (mōn'zān), town (pop. 3,993), Ishikawa prefecture, central Honshu, Japan, on NW Noto Peninsula, 20 mi. NW of Nanao; rice, raw silk.

Monzón or **Monsón** (both: mōnsōn'), town (pop. 514), Huánuco dept., central Peru, on E slopes of Cordillera Central, on Monzón R. (left affluent of the Huallaga) and 33 mi. NE of Llata, at edge of tropical forests; rubber, lumber, coca.

Monzón (mōn-thōn'), city (pop. 4,641), Huesca prov., NE Spain, near Cinca R., 34 mi. SE of Huesca; agr. center (olive oil, wine, sugar beets, livestock, cereals); sugar and flour mills; mfg. of soap, chocolate. Has Gothic church. On hill above town is 10th–11th-cent. fortified castle which belonged to the Knights Templars.

Monzur, Turkey: see MUNZUR.

Mooar (mōō'ŭr), village, Lee Co., extreme SE Iowa, 4 mi. NNW of Keokuk; explosives plant.

Moodus (mōō'dŭs), village in East Haddam town, Middlesex co., S Conn., near the Connecticut; mfg. (cotton thread, twine). "Moodus noises," subterranean rumblings about which Indians had legends, believed to be caused by minor earthquakes beneath hill here.

Moody, county (□ 523; pop. 9,252), E S.Dak., on Minn. line; ⊙ Flandreau. Rich farming and livestock-raising region drained by Big Sioux R. Corn, wheat, oats, barley, rye, hogs, beef cattle. Formed 1873.

Moody, town (pop. 1,084), McLennan co., E central Texas, 21 mi. SSW of Waco, in farm area. Inc. 1901.

Moody Air Force Base, Ga.: see VALDOSTA.

Mooers (môrz, mōōrz), village (pop. 496), Clinton co., extreme NE N.Y., on Great Chazy R. and 20 mi. NNW of Plattsburg, port of entry, near Que.

Mooi River (mōō'ē), Afrikaans *Mooirivier* (mōō"-ĭrĭfēr'), town (pop. 1,396), W Natal, U. of So. Afr., in Drakensberg range, on Mooi R. and 35 mi. NW of Pietermaritzburg; alt. 4,556 ft.; resort; dairying, bacon curing. In stock-raising region.

Mook (mōk), village (pop. 801), Limburg prov., E Netherlands, on Maas R., near junction with Maas-Waal Canal, and 7 mi. S of Nijmegen; building stone, bricks, tiles. Battle here (1574), in which Henry and Louis of Nassau, brothers of William the Silent, were defeated and killed by Spaniards.

Mooka, Japan: see MOKA.

Mooltan, W Pakistan: see MULTAN, district.

Moon, Estonia: see MUHU, island.

Moon, Island of the, Bolivia: see COATI ISLAND.

Moonachie (mōōnä'kē), borough (pop. 1,775), Bergen co., NE N.J., 3 mi. SE of Passaic; truck farms. Inc. 1910.

Moonah (mōō'nä), town (pop. 7,464), SE Tasmania, N suburb of Hobart; sawmills.

Moondyne Cave, Australia: see AUGUSTA.

Moon Lake, Miss.: see LULA.

Moon Lake Dam, Utah: see LAKE FORK.

Moon Run, village (pop. 1,143), Allegheny co., W Pa., 8 mi. W of Pittsburgh, in bituminous-coal and agr. area. Steel plants near by.

Moonta (mōōn'tŭ), town (pop. 1,221), S South Australia, on W Yorke Peninsula and 65 mi. SSW of Port Pirie, near Port Hughes inlet of Spencer Gulf; rail terminus; wheat, barley, sheep, wool. Formerly important copper-mining center.

Moorabbin (mōōră'bĭn), municipality (pop. 29,236), S Victoria, Australia, 10 mi. SSE of Melbourne, in metropolitan area; truck gardening.

Moorcroft, town (pop. 517), Crook co., NE Wyo., on Belle Fourche R. and 30 mi. WSW of Sundance; alt. c.4,200 ft. Trade and shipping center in livestock, timber region; oil refinery. Oil wells near by.

Moordrecht (mōr'drĕkht), town (pop. 2,311), South Holland prov., W Netherlands, on Hollandsche Ijssel R. and 3 mi. SW of Gouda; rope, paint, varnish, woven mats, flour, dairy products.

Moore. 1 County (□ 672; pop. 33,129), central N.C.; ⊙ Carthage. Forested sand hills and piedmont region; drained by Deep R. Farming (tobacco, peaches, corn, poultry), sawmilling, textile mfg. Formed 1784. **2** County (□ 122; pop. 3,948), S Tenn.; ⊙ Lynchburg. Bounded SE by Elk R. Livestock, grain, tobacco, timber. Formed 1871. **3** County (□ 912; pop. 13,349), extreme N Texas; ⊙ Dumas. In high plains of the Panhandle; drained in SE by Canadian R.; alt. 3,000–4,000 ft. One of richest areas in the huge Panhandle natural-gas and oil field; carbon black, gasoline, nitrate and helium plants; wheat farming, cattle ranching. Formed 1876.

Moore. 1 Town (pop. 256), Butte co., SE central Idaho, 7 mi. NNW of Arco. **2** Town (pop. 224), Fergus co., central Mont., 13 mi. WSW of Lewistown; grain. **3** Town (pop. 942), Cleveland co., central Okla., 9 mi. S of Oklahoma City, in oil-producing and agr. area (grain, cotton; dairy products); flour milling, cotton ginning. **4** Village (pop. c.350), Frio co., SW Texas, c.40 mi. SW of San Antonio; rail point in winter truck-farming, cattle area; natural-gas wells.

Moore, Lake (□ 449), W central Western Australia, 150 mi. NE of Perth; 60 mi. long; usually dry.

Moorea (mōrā'ä), volcanic island (□ c.50; pop. 2,838), 2d largest of Windward group, SOCIETY ISLANDS, Fr. Occania, S Pacific, 12 mi. NW of Tahiti, of which it is a dependency. Mountainous; highest peak Mt. Tohivea (3,975 ft.). Cook Bay and Papetoai Bay on N coast; chief town, Afareaitu, on E coast. Produces copra, coffee. Formerly Eimeo.

Moorefield, village (pop. estimate 400), S Ont., on Conestogo R. and 25 mi. NNW of Kitchener; dairying, mixed farming.

Moorefield. 1 Town (1940 pop. 79), Switzerland co., SE Ind., 13 mi. ENE of Madison, in agr. area. **2** Village (pop. 58), Frontier co., S Nebr., 5 mi. NE of Curtis. **3** Town (pop. 1,405), ⊙ Hardy co., W.Va., in Eastern Panhandle, on South Branch of the Potomac and 27 mi. S of Keyser, in hunting, fishing, and agr. area; lumber, flour, and feed mills, tannery, dairy. Settled 1777.

Moore Haven, city (pop. 636), ⊙ Glades co., S Fla., c.50 mi. ENE of Fort Myers, on W shore of L. Okeechobee near entrance (lock here) of Caloosahatchee Canal; truck farming, fishing.

Mooreland. 1 Town (pop. 497), Henry co., E Ind., 8 mi. NE of New Castle, in agr. area. **2** Town (pop. 867), Woodward co., NW Okla., 10 mi. E of Woodward, in grain-growing area; also corn, alfalfa, dairy products.

Mooresboro, town (1940 pop. 296), Cleveland co., SW N.C., 8 mi. W of Shelby.

Moores Creek National Military Park, N.C.: see CURRIE.

Moores Hill, town (pop. 445), Dearborn co., SE Ind., 12 mi. W of Aurora, in agr. area.

Moores Mills, lumbering village (pop. estimate c.150), SW N.B., 7 mi. N of St. Stephen.

Moorestown (mōōrz'toun), residential township (pop. 9,123), Burlington co., SW N.J., 7 mi. NE of Camden; mfg. (wood and metal products, fungicides, insecticides); fruit, truck, dairy products, poultry. Friends' school, several 18th-cent. buildings here. Laid out 1722.

Mooresville. 1 Town (pop. 101), Limestone co., N Ala., 5 mi. E of Decatur, across Tennessee R. **2** Town (pop. 2,264), Morgan co., central Ind., on Whitelick R. and 16 mi. SW of Indianapolis, in agr. area (grain, fruit; dairy products); mfg. (burial vaults, flour, engine bearings). Settled 1824. **3** Town (pop. 134), Livingston co., N central Mo., near Grand R., 9 mi. WSW of Chillicothe. **4** Town (pop. 7,121), Iredell co., W central N.C., 14 mi. SSE of Statesville; cotton and flour mills, ironworks. Founded 1868.

Mooreton, village (pop. 161), Richland co., SE N.Dak., 13 mi. W of Wahpeton.

Moore Town, town, Portland parish, E Jamaica, on the Rio Grande, 7 mi. SSE of Port Antonio. Site of anc. Maroon settlement.

Moorfoot Hills, mountain range in Peebles and Midlothian, Scotland, extends 12 mi. NE from Peebles. Highest point is Blackhope Scar (2,136 ft.), 7 mi. NE of Peebles.

Moorhead. 1 Town (pop. 392), Monona co., W Iowa, on Soldier R. and 14 mi. SE of Onawa, in livestock and grain area. State park near by. **2** City (pop. 14,870), ⊙ Clay co., W Minn., on Red River of the North opposite Fargo, N.Dak.; trade center and shipping point for grain and potatoes; dairy products, beverages; sheet-metal works. State teachers col. and Concordia Col. are here. Inc. 1881. Growth followed arrival of railroad in 1871. **3** Town (pop. 1,749), Sunflower co., W Miss., 20 mi. W of Greenwood, in rich cotton-growing area; cottonseed products. Seat of a dist. jr. col. Inc. 1899.

Mooringsport, town (pop. 709), Caddo parish, extreme NW La., on Caddo L., 17 mi. NW of Shreveport, in oil-producing and agr. area.

Morringsport Reservoir, La.: see CYPRESS BAYOU.

Moorland, town (pop. 248), Webster co., central Iowa, 7 mi. SW of Fort Dodge, in agr. area.

Mooroopna (mōōrōōp'nŭ), town (pop. 1,888), N Victoria, Australia, 11 mi. NNE of Melbourne; W suburb of Shepparton; fruit canneries, flour mill.

Moorpark, village (pop. 1,146), Ventura co., S Calif., 15 mi. ENE of Oxnard; tomato-shipping point; walnut, apricot, citrus-fruit orchards, and oil fields near by.

Moorreesburg (mōō'rēsbûrkh), town (pop. 2,922), SW Cape Prov., U. of So. Afr., 20 mi. N of Malmesbury; wheat-growing center; grain elevator.

Moorriem, Germany: see GROSSENMEER.

Moorseele, Belgium: see MOORSELE.

Moorsel (mōr'sŭl), village (pop. 4,527), East Flanders prov., N central Belgium, 3 mi. ENE of Alost; hops, flowers.

Moorsele (mōr'sälŭ), town (pop. 4,775), West Flanders prov., W Belgium, 5 mi. W of Courtrai; cotton industry; market for flax and tobacco. Formerly spelled Moorseele.

Moorslede (mōr'slādŭ), agr. village (pop. 6,593), West Flanders prov., W Belgium, 5 mi. SW of Roulers. Largely destroyed in First World War.

Moosburg (mōs'bōōrk), town (pop. 7,514), Upper Bavaria, Germany, on the Isar and 10 mi. ENE of Freising; mfg. of fertilizer, metal- and woodworking, brewing. Has late-12th- and mid-14th-cent. churches. Chartered 1311.

Moose, village, Teton co., NW Wyo., on Snake R. and 12 mi. N of Jackson; a gateway to Grand Teton Natl. Park (W and N).

Moose Creek, village, S Alaska, in Matanuska Valley, on Matanuska R. and 40 mi. NE of Anchorage; grain, vegetables, hogs, poultry; dairying. Coal mined near by.

Moose Creek, village (pop. estimate 600), SE Ont., 20 mi. NW of Cornwall; dairying, mixed farming.

Moose Factory, village (pop. estimate 300), NE Ont., on isl. in Moose R., near its mouth on James Bay, opposite Moosonee; 51°16′N 80°36′W. Hudson's Bay Co. trading post, established 1671; it was later demolished and re-established in 1730.

Moosehead Lake, W central Maine, 50 mi. N of Skowhegan; largest lake (□ 120; 35 mi. long, 2–10 mi. wide) in Maine, with several isls.; alt. c.1,000 ft. Center of resort region; steamer service connects shore points. Source of Kennebec R.

Mooseheart, Ill.: see Batavia.

Moose Island, Washington co., E Maine. **1** Isl. at mouth of Indian R., just NW of Jonesport; 2 mi. long, ¾ mi. wide. **2** Isl. in Passamaquoddy Bay; site of Eastport.

Moose Jaw, city (pop. 23,069), S Sask., on Moosejaw Creek and 40 mi. W of Regina; railroad center and distribution point for S Sask., site of important Dominion grain elevators, stockyards; oil refining, meat packing; flour, lumber, woolen milling; dairying, brick mfg. Airport. Settled 1882, inc. 1884.

Moose Lake. 1 Lake (8 mi. long, 1½ mi. wide), E B.C., near Alta. border, in Rocky Mts., in Mt. Robson Provincial Park, 30 mi. W of Jasper; alt. 3,386 ft. Drained NW by Fraser R. **2** Lake (□ 525), W Man., 32 mi. E of The Pas; 43 mi. long, 30 mi. wide. Drained S into L. Winnipeg by Saskatchewan R., through Cedar L.

Moose Lake, resort village (pop. 1,603), Carlton co., E Minn., on small lake and 38 mi. SW of Duluth; dairy and wood products. Founded as lumber town before 1875, rebuilt after destruction by forest fire, 1918.

Mooseleuk Lake (mōōs′lōōk), Piscataquis co., N central Maine, 45 mi. WSW of Presque Isle, in wilderness recreational area; 1.5 mi. long. Source of **Mooseleuk Stream,** which flows c.13 mi. SE to Aroostook R.

Mooselookmeguntic Lake, Maine: see Rangeley Lakes.

Moose Mountain, range, SE Sask., extends 30 mi. E-W near Man. border; rises to 2,725 ft. 50 mi. NNE of Estevan. Here is Moose Mtn. Provincial Park (□ 152), a region of woods, lakes, resorts.

Moose Pass, village (pop. 60), S Alaska, on E Kenai Peninsula, 25 mi. N of Steward, and on Alaska RR; gold mining.

Moose Pond, Maine. **1** Narrow lake (c.8 mi. long), in Oxford and Cumberland counties; drains S, past Denmark, into the Saco. **2** Lake in Somerset co., 12 mi. NE of Skowhegan; 5 mi. long. Source of Sebasticook R.

Moose River, NE Ont., formed by Mattagami and Missinaibi rivers 50 mi. SW of Moosonee, flows NE to confluence with Abitibi R., thence flows past Moosonee to James Bay.

Moose River, plantation (pop. 203), Somerset co., W Maine, just N of Jackman in lumbering, recreational area.

Moose River. 1 In W Maine, rises in N Franklin co., flows 62 mi. generally E to Moosehead L., near Rockwood. **2** In N central N.Y., rises in the W Adirondacks in North, Middle, and South branches, which join near Fulton Chain of Lakes (drained by Middle Branch); flows c.30 mi. SW and W to Black R. at Lyons Falls. **3** In NE Vt., rises near East Haven, flows c.30 mi. S and W, past Concord, to the Passumpsic at St. Johnsbury.

Moosic (mōō′sĭk), borough (pop. 3,965), Lackawanna co., NE Pa., 5 mi. SW of Scranton and on Lackawanna R.

Moosilauke, Mount (mōō′sulôk), in Grafton co., W N.H., peak (4,810 ft.) of White Mts., near Benton, S of Kinsman Notch.

Moosomin (mōō′sōmĭn, mōōsō′mĭn), town (pop. 1,134), SE Sask., near Man. border, 80 mi. WNW of Brandon; grain elevators, dairying, stock raising.

Moosonee (mōō′sunē), village (pop. estimate 300), NE Ont., on Moose R., near its mouth on James Bay; 51°17′N 80°39′W; railroad terminus; Hudson's Bay Co. trading post. Opposite, on isl. in river, is Moose Factory.

Moosup (mōō′sŭp), industrial village (pop. 2,909) in Plainfield town, Windham co., E Conn., on small Moosup R. (water power) and 16 mi. NE of Norwich; textiles, thread, metal and wood products, oil burners.

Moosup River, R.I. and Conn., rises in W R.I., flows c.25 mi. S and W, past Sterling and Moosup, Conn. (water power), to Quinebaug R. near Wauregan village.

Mopa (mōpä′), town (pop. 3,157), Kabba prov., Northern Provinces, W central Nigeria, 25 mi. NNW of Kabba; tin-mining center; shea-nut processing; cotton, cassava, durra, yams.

Mopán River, Guatemala: see Belize River.

Mopeia (mōpē′yä), village, Zambézia prov., central Mozambique, near left bank of Zambezi R., 80 mi. WSW of Quelimane; sugar, corn, cotton.

Mopelia, Society Islands: see Mopihaa.

Mopihaa (mō′pēhä′) or **Mopelia** (mōpālē′ů), uninhabited atoll, most westerly of Society Isls., Fr. Oceania, S Pacific; 16°55′S 153°55′W; owned by Fr. copra company.

Moppo, Korea: see Mokpo.

Mopsuestia, Asia Minor: see Misis.

Mopti (môp′tē), town (pop. c.8,550), central Fr. Sudan, Fr. West Africa, at confluence of Niger and Bani rivers, 280 mi. ENE of Bamako; commercial and agr. center (millet, rice, cotton, tobacco, manioc, shea-nut butter, peanuts; livestock; meat; hides). Limekiln, tannery. Meteorological station. Airfield. Protestant mission. Mosque. Town is built on 3 islets, linked by barrages; has picturesque market.

Moquegua (mōkā′gwä), department (□ 4,716; pop. 35,709), S Peru, bordering W on the Pacific; ⊙ Moquegua. Crossed by ridges of Cordillera Occidental, it includes several snow-capped volcanic peaks. Watered by Tambo and Moquegua rivers. Climate is dry, semitropical on coast, cooler in uplands. Among its little exploited mineral resources are borax, salt, coal, sulphur. Predominantly agr.: irrigated fertile W section grows wine and olives on large scale; also cotton, sugar cane, figs, corn; wheat, barley, potatoes, stock in uplands. Moquegua city and Pacific port of Ilo are processing centers (wine, liquor, olive oil, canned fruit, flour). Carumas and Omate have thermal springs. Dept. was set up 1875.

Moquegua, city (pop. 3,888), ⊙ Moquegua dept. and Mariscal Nieto prov. (□ 4,005; pop. 17,793), S Peru, in oasis on Moquegua R., at W slopes of Cordillera Occidental, on Pan-American Highway, and 37 mi. NE of its Pacific port Ilo (linked by railroad), 550 mi. SE of Lima; 17°12′S 71°2′W; alt. 4,715 ft. Processing and agr. center (olives, wine, cotton, fruit); cotton ginning, wine making, liquor distilling, olive-oil processing, flour milling, bottling; mfg. of soap, spaghetti. Exports wine, olive oil, cotton, copper, lead. Has an excellent, though dry, mild climate. Has Jesuit col., convent.

Moquega River, Moquega dept., S Peru, rises on W slopes of Cordillera Occidental SE of Carumas, flows c.80 mi. SSW, past Moquegua, to the Pacific at Ilo. Used for irrigation.

Mor (mōr), Hung. *Mór,* market town (pop. 10,123), Fejer co., N central Hungary, at SW foot of Vertes Mts., 15 mi. NW of Szekesfehervar; brickworks; wheat, corn, cattle. Large Ger. pop.

Mora (mō′rä), village, Nord-Cameroun region, N Fr. Cameroons, 30 mi. NNW of Maroua; customs station near Br. Cameroons border; cattle, peanuts, millet.

Mora, canton, Costa Rica: see Villa Colón.

Mora, India: see Uran.

Mora (mô′rů), town (pop. 1,472), Évora dist., S central Portugal, 30 mi. NNW of Évora; rail spur terminus; cheese and pottery mfg.

Mora (mō′rä), town (pop. 10,354), Toledo prov., central Spain, in New Castile, 18 mi. SE of Toledo; agr. center (grapes, olives, esparto, saffron, sheep, goats). Among its numerous industries are wine making, alcohol and cognac distilling, olive-oil pressing, cheese processing. Once famous for its swords, it still makes scissors and bells; also mfg. of woolen and esparto goods, bottle corks, shoes, agr. implements, ceramics, glycerin, marzipan, chocolate. Iron foundries. A ruined castle is E; an airfield, S.

Mora (mōō′rä″) or **Morastrand** (mōō′rästrănd″), town (pop. 1,724), Kopparberg co., central Sweden, at N end of L. Silja, at mouth of East Dal R., 45 mi. NW of Falun; rail junction; tourist resort. Metalworking, sawmilling. Has 13th-cent. church with 17th-cent. tower. Gustavus Vasa took refuge (c.1520) from Danes here.

Mora (mô′rů), county (□ 1,942; pop. 8,720), NE N.Mex.; ⊙ Mora. Livestock and agr. region, watered by Mora R.; bounded E by Canadian R. Grain, fruit. Sangre de Cristo Mts. in W, Santa Fe Natl. Forest in SW. Formed 1860.

Mora. 1 Village (pop. 2,018), ⊙ Kanabec co., E Minn., on Snake R. and c.60 mi. N of Minneapolis; trading point in grain, livestock, and poultry area; dairy products, poultry feed. Mus. of Izaak Walton League is here. Platted 1881. **2** Village (pop. c.1,400), ⊙ Mora co., N N.Mex., on Mora R., in Sangre de Cristo Mts., and 27 mi. N of Las Vegas, in irrigated fruit region; alt. c.7,200 ft.; farming; resort. Santa Fe Natl. Forest just W; dude ranch near by.

Moraca River or **Moracha River** (both: mô′rächä), Serbo-Croatian *Morača,* Montenegro, Yugoslavia, rises in headstreams in the Stozac, joining 11 mi. SE of Savnik; flows c.60 mi. S, past Titograd, to L. Scutari 3 mi. W of Plavnica. Receives Zeta R.

Moradabad (mōrä′däbäd), district (□ 2,288; pop. 1,473,151), Rohilkhand div., N central Uttar Pradesh, India; ⊙ Moradabad. On W Ganges Plain; bounded W by the Ganges; drained by the Ramganga. Agr. (wheat, rice, pearl millet, mustard, sugar cane, barley, gram, corn, cotton, jowar); cotton weaving, sugar milling. Main centers: Moradabad, Sambhal, Amroha, Chandausi.

Moradabad, city (pop. 142,414), ⊙ Moradabad dist., N central Uttar Pradesh, India, on the Ramganga and 95 mi. ENE of Delhi; rail and road junction; trade center (grains, mustard, sugar cane); cotton milling, carpet weaving; lacquered brassware, cutlery. Large 17th-cent. mosque. Founded 1625 by Rohilla leader. Rohilla stronghold, 1740–74, ruled by nawab of Oudh. Ceded with surrounding area, 1801, to British. Rohilla fort ruins just N.

Morada Nova (mōōrä′dů nô′vů), city (pop. 1,214), E Ceará, Brazil, on left tributary of Jaguaribe R. and 60 mi. SW of Aracati; dairying; ships carnauba wax, cotton, sugar. Airfield.

Mora de Ebro (mō′rä dhā ā′vrō), town (pop. 2,788), Tarragona prov., NE Spain, on right bank of the Ebro and 11 mi. ENE of Gandesa; agr. trade center (wine, cereals, almonds, fruit); cement, soap mfg.; olive-oil processing and shipping.

Mora de Rubielos (rōōvyā′lōs), town (pop. 1,039), Teruel prov., E Spain, 29 mi. ESE of Teruel; wool spinning, flour milling.

Morag (mô′rōk), Pol. *Morąg,* Ger. *Mohrungen* (mō′rōōng-ůn), town (1939 pop. 8,737; 1946 pop. 2,746) in East Prussia, after 1945 in Olsztyn prov., NE Poland, in lake region, 30 mi. SE of Elbing (Elblag); rail junction; grain and cattle market. Herder b. here.

Moraga (môrä′gů), village (pop. c.800), Contra Costa co., W Calif., in Berkeley Hills E of Oakland. St. Mary's Col. is near by.

Morakhi River, India: see Mor River.

Mora la Nueva (mō′rä lä nwā′vä), town (pop. 2,156), Tarragona prov., NE Spain, on left bank of the Ebro and 12 mi. ENE of Gandesa; olive-oil and wine processing; agr. trade (cereals, almonds, fruit).

Moral de Calatrava (mōräl′ dhā käläträ′vä), city (pop. 7,134), Ciudad Real prov., S central Spain, in New Castile, on railroad and 22 mi. SE of Ciudad Real; agr. center on La Mancha plain (olives, cereals, grapes, sheep). Alcohol and liquor distilling, olive-oil pressing, cheese processing, sawmilling, lace mfg.

Moraleda Channel (mōrälā′dhä), strait of the Pacific, on coast of Aysén prov., S Chile, separating Chonos Archipelago from mainland and Magdalena Isl.; c.80 mi. long; bet. 44° and 45° S.

Moraleja (mōrälā′hä), town (pop. 2,923), Cáceres prov., W Spain, 45 mi. NNW of Cáceres; meat processing, olive pressing, carbon-disulphide and soap mfg. Fruit, honey, livestock, cork.

Moraleja del Vino (dhĕl vē′nō), village (pop. 1,820), Zamora prov., NW Spain, 6 mi. SE of Zamora; brandy distilling; wine, cereals, livestock.

Morales (mōrä′lĕs), town (1950 pop. 1,031), Izabal dept., E Guatemala, on Motagua R., on railroad, and 22 mi. SW of Puerto Barrios, in banana area. Gold placers near by.

Morales, town (pop. 2,352), San Luis Potosí, N central Mexico, 3 mi. W of San Luis Potosí; rail terminus; cereals, cotton, beans, fruit, stock.

Morales del Vino (mōrä′lĕs dhĕl vē′nō), village (pop. 1,050), Zamora prov., NW Spain, 4 mi. S of Zamora; cereals, wine, fruit.

Morales de Rey (dhā rā′), village (pop. 1,050) Zamora prov., NW Spain, 8 mi. NW of Benavente; cereals, flax, sugar beets.

Morales de Toro (tō′rō), town (pop. 2,161) Zamora prov., NW Spain, 5 mi. E of Toro; brandy distilling; wine, cereals, cattle.

Morales Island, Bolívar dept., N Colombia, formed by arms of lower Magdalena R., 28 mi. W of Ocaña; 40 mi. long, up to 11 mi. wide.

Moralzarzal (mōräl″thär-thäl′), town (pop. 730), Madrid prov., central Spain, 24 mi. NW of Madrid; grain, livestock; apiculture. Mineral springs.

Moram (mō′rŭm), town (pop. 7,425), Osmanabad dist., W Hyderabad state, India, 38 mi. SE of Osmanabad; millet, wheat, cotton.

Mora Manas River, India: see Manas River.

Moramanga (mōōrämäng′gů), town (1948 pop. 3,750), E central Madagascar, 100 mi. SW of Tamatave; trading and agr. center, railroad junction for L. Alaotra; mfg. of tapioca and starch, gold and graphite mining, hardwood lumbering. Coffee, essential oils (notably from geraniums).

Moran (mûrăn′, mô′răn″). **1** City (pop. 616), Allen co., SE Kansas, 13 mi. E of Iola; livestock, grain; dairying. **2** City (pop. 610), Shackelford co., N Texas, 33 mi. E of Abilene; trade, shipping point in wheat, cattle, oil area. **3** Village, Teton co., NW Wyo., on Snake R., at its influx to Jackson L., and 28 mi. NNE of Jackson; alt. 6,742 ft. Tourist point. Jackson L. Dam, unit in Minidoka reclamation project, here. Grand Teton Natl. Park near by.

Moran, Mount, Wyo.: see Grand Teton National Park.

Moranhat, India: see Nazira.

Morano Calabro (môrä′nô kä′läbrô), anc. *Muranum,* town (pop. 5,155), Cosenza prov., Calabria, S Italy, near Coscile R., 4 mi. WNW of Castrovillari; woolen mills, tannery.

Mora-Noret (mōō′rä-nōō′rŭt), village (pop. 1,207), Kopparberg co., central Sweden, on N shore of L. Silja, just E of Mora, 45 mi. NW of Falun; rail junction; sawmilling. Tourist resort.

Morano sul Po (môrä′nô sōōl pô′), village (pop. 1,459), Alessandria prov., Piedmont, N Italy, near Po R., 5 mi. NW of Casale Monferrato.

Morant Bay (mŭrănt'), town (pop. 3,699), ⊙ St. Thomas parish, SE Jamaica, port with open roadstead, at mouth of small Morant R., 25 mi. ESE of Kingston (linked by highway); 17°53'N 76°25'W. Ships cacao, coffee, pimento, ginger, coconuts, copra, honey, rum. Sea resort. Scene of 1865 rebellion.

Morant Cays (mŭrănt" kāz'), group of 3 Caribbean islets, dependency of Jamaica, B.W.I., at S entrance of Jamaica Channel, 45 mi. SE of Morant Bay (SE Jamaica). Northeast Cay is at 17°25'N 75°58'W, Southwest Cay at 17°23'N 75°58'W. The uninhabited isls. are of little economic importance, though sea-bird eggs and guano are collected. They were occupied by the British in 1862 and annexed to Jamaica in 1882. Sometimes called, together with Pedro Cays (120 mi. WSW), Guano Isls.

Morant Point, cape at E extremity of Jamaica, on Jamaica Channel, and 40 mi. E of Kingston; 17°55'N 76°11'W. Lighthouse. Another headland, South East Point, is c.1 mi. S.

Mora Passage (mô'rŭ), channel (c.7 mi. long), NW Br. Guiana, links Barima R. just above Morawhanna with Waini R. mouth on the Atlantic.

Morar (mō'rär), town (pop., including cantonment and suburban areas, 25,658), NE Madhya Bharat, India, 4 mi. NE of Lashkar; trades in millet, wheat, gram, leather goods; tanning, tent mfg. Founded 1844; scene of major uprising in Sepoy Rebellion of 1857.

Morar (mô'rŭr), agr. village, W Inverness, Scotland, 3 mi. S of Mallaig, at W end of Loch Morar (12 mi. long, up to 2 mi. wide; 1,017 ft. deep), one of deepest known depressions of the European plateau. The Morar dist. extends 19 mi. bet. Loch Nevis (N) and the Sound of Arisaig (S).

Mora River, Czechoslovakia: see MORAVICE RIVER.

Mora River (mô'rŭ), N N.Mex., rises in several forks in Sangre de Cristo Mts., flows SE, past Mora and Watrous, and E to Canadian R. 25 mi. NNW of Conchas Dam; 75 mi. long. Sapello Creek is tributary.

Moras-en-Valloire (môrä'-ā-välwär'), village (pop. 272), Drome dept., SE France, 17 mi. SSE of Vienne; hosiery mfg.

Morastrand, Sweden: see MORA.

Morat (môrä'), Ger. *Murten* (mŏŏr'tŭn), town (pop. 2,405), Fribourg canton, W Switzerland, on L. of Morat, 16 mi. W of Bern; woodworking, dyeing, knit goods. Scene (SW of town) of Swiss victory (1476) over Charles the Bold of Burgundy. Well-preserved medieval architecture; 13th-cent. castle, 15th-cent. Fr. church, 18th-cent. Ger. church, mus. with historical collections.

Morat, Lake of, Ger. *Murtensee* (mŏŏr'tŭnzā"), Fr. *Lac de Morat* (läk dü môrä'), W Switzerland, bordering on cantons of Fribourg and Vaud; 5.5 mi. long, □ 9, alt. 1,391 ft., max depth 154 ft. Broye R. enters SW, leaves NW, flowing 4 mi. W to L. of Neuchâtel. Main town on lake, Morat.

Morata, Territory of Papua: see GOODENOUGH ISLAND.

Morata de Jalón (mōrä'tä dhā hälōn'), town (pop. 2,630), Saragossa prov., NE Spain, on Jalón R. and 12 mi. NE of Calatayud, in winegrowing area; mfg. (cement, alcohol, tartaric acid); olive oil, fruit, sugar beets.

Morata de Jiloca (hēlō'kä), village (pop. 1,122), Saragossa prov., NE Spain, on Jiloca R. and 8 mi. SSE of Calatayud; wine, sugar beets.

Morata de Tajuña (tähōō'nyä), town (pop. 3,617), Madrid prov., central Spain, on Tajuña R. (irrigation), on railroad and 18 mi. SE of Madrid; agr. center (wine, cattle, sheep). Olive-oil pressing, wine making, alcohol distilling, vegetable canning; stone and lime quarrying.

Moratalla (mōrätä'lyä), town (pop. 5,543), Murcia prov., SE Spain, 7 mi. NNW of Caravaca; agr. trade center (cereals, rice, wine, fruit). Olive-oil processing, flour milling, brandy distilling, fruit-conserve mfg.; lumbering, stock raising.

Morat Island (mōrät'), in Bay Islands dept., N Honduras, in Caribbean Sea, bet. Santa Elena (W) and Barbareta (E) isls.; ½ mi. long, c.300 yards wide.

Moratuwa (mō'rŭtōōvŭ), town (pop. 50,093), Western Prov., Ceylon, on W coast, 10 mi. S of Colombo city center; fishing center; wood carving, furniture mfg.; trades in coconuts, rice, cinnamon, vegetables. Prince of Wales' Col. in N area (called Lunawa). Mfg. of tires, rubber goods, batteries.

Morava (môrä'vä) or **Morova** (môrô'vä), mountain ridge in SE Albania, just E of Koritsa; rises to 5,925 ft.

Morava, province, Czechoslovakia: see MORAVIA.

Morava River (mô'rävä), Ger. *March* (märkh), Moravia, central and S Czechoslovakia, rises on S slope of Kralicky Sneznik, 4 mi. NW of Stare Mesto; flows SSE past Olomouc, Kromeriz, and Otrokovice, SSW forming wide and fertile valley, past Uherske Hradiste and Hodonin, and S forming Austrian border (below Dyje R. mouth), to the Danube at Devin; total length, 227 mi. Together with its tributaries (Hana, Dyje, and Becva rivers), it waters almost the whole of Moravia. Navigable for 78 mi. in lower course.

Morava River or **Great Morava River** (mô'rävä), Serbo-Croatian *Morava* or *Velika Morava* (vě'lĭkä), main river of Serbia, Yugoslavia; formed by junction of the Southern Morava and the Western Morava (which receives the Ibar) near Stalac; flows 134 mi. N, past Cuprija, through a wide, fertile, and densely populated valley (the POMORAVLJE), to the Danube 10 mi. ENE of Smederevo, forming delta mouth. Receives Resava R. (right). Includes in its basin nearly all Serbia, uniting mtn. valleys into a natural region of communications. Marsh draining, 1947–51. Most of its course is followed by Belgrade-Salonika RR.

Moraveh Tappeh (mōrävě' täpě'), town, Second Prov., in Gurgan, NE Iran, on Atrek R. and 60 mi. NE of Gunbad-i-Qawus, near USSR line.

Moravia (mŭrā'vēŭ), Czech *Morava* (mô'rävä), Ger. *Mähren* (mâ'rŭn), central region (in 1948: □ 8,219; pop. 2,293,773) of Czechoslovakia, bounded by Austria (S), and adjoining Bohemia (W), Silesia (N), and Slovakia (E). With Silesia and Bohemia it forms (since 1949) one of the 2 constituent states (Czech *Země*) of Czechoslovakia; Slovakia is the other. Until 1949 Moravia and Silesia were a single administrative prov. (□ 10,350; 1948 pop. 3,134,614). A continuation of the Bohemian plateau, Moravia slopes to S and is dissected by Morava R. and its tributaries; NE section belongs, however, to Oder basin. Hilly character is reinforced on W rim by the Bohemian-Moravian Heights (2,738 ft.), and by S flanks of the Jeseniky (4,920 ft.) in NW. In the E the Little and White Carpathians separate Moravia from Slovakia. The Moravian Gate provides a natural corridor bet. the Sudetes and the Carpathians. Rich crops of wheat, barley, sugar beets, hemp, fruit, wine, tobacco are raised in center and S, noted for relatively mild climate (mean annual temp. at Brno 48°F.). Hana region is famous for fine-quality malt and hops and for horse breeding. Hardier cultures (oats, rye, flax, potatoes) grow on higher ground. Forestry, sheep-raising, forage cultures are well developed. Important mineral resources of coal (S end of Silesian coal field, Rosice-Oslavany coal seams) and iron ore laid foundation for the iron and steel industry in Ostrava area, and the machinery and arm mfg. at Brno. SE corner of Moravia has been extensively surveyed for oil (producing wells at Hodonin). Lignite, asbestos, graphite are also exploited. Light industries include production of textiles (woolen, cotton, silk), leather and rubber goods (mammoth factories at Gottwaldov, formerly Zlin), clothing, hats, beer, alcohol, sugar, and furniture. Main cities: Brno, Ostrava, Olomouc, Gottwaldov, Prostejov. Moravian Karst and Radhost areas are noted tourist attractions. Evidence of human occupation as early as the Paleolithic age was brought out by extensive excavations at Predmost. Historical times began with advent of the Boii (Celts), followed by Marcomanni and Quadi (Teutons). Slavs settled in 6th cent., took the name of Moravians from Morava R., and were converted to Christianity by Cyril and Methodius (c.865); they were continually at war with the Germans. The Great Moravian Empire (9th cent.) succumbed to Magyars in 906. Emperor Otto I defeated (955) the Magyars, and Moravia became a march of the Holy Roman Empire. From 1029 on, Moravia was a part of the Bohemian kingdom, either as an integral part or as a fief (margraviate). In 1526, both passed under rule of Austria; later Moravia was made a separate crownland with capital at Brno (1849). The towns of Moravia had undergone a process of Germanization since early 13th cent., but the surrounding countryside was Czech-speaking. In 1918 Hapsburg rule was overthrown and Moravia joined the Czechoslovak republic as a prov.; combined (1927) with Silesia. Dismemberment of Czechoslovak state after Munich pact (1938) resulted in inc. of all Czech Silesia and of N and S sections of Moravia into Germany, and in 1939 Bohemia and the remaining Moravia became a Ger. "protectorate." Liberated by USSR troops in 1945, the territory resumed its pre-1938 status but the area bet. Ostravice and Oder rivers was ceded to sub-province of Silesia. Since the reorganization of 1949 Moravia is formed of Brno and Gottwaldov provs., E section of Jihlava prov., a section of Ostrava prov., and most of Olomouc prov.

Moravia. 1 Town (pop. 652), Appanoose co., S Iowa, 11 mi. NNE of Centerville, in bituminous-coal-mining area; mfg. of cement blocks. Limestone quarry near by. **2** Resort village (pop. 1,480), Cayuga co., W central N.Y., near S end of Owasco L., 26 mi. WSW of Syracuse; mfg. of clothing, lumber milling; timber. Agr. (cabbage, potatoes, hay). Fillmore Glen State Park is near by. Inc. 1837.

Moravia, San Vicente de, Costa Rica: see SAN VICENTE.

Moravian Falls, village, Wilkes co., NW N.C., 5 mi. S of North Wilkesboro.

Moravian Gate (mŭrā'vēŭn), Czech *Moravská Brána* (mô'räfskä brä'nä), N Moravia, Czechoslovakia, wide pass (alt. c.900 ft.) bet. E end of the Sudetes and W end of the Carpathians; natural communications channel and important Central European trade route since pre-Roman times. Drained by upper Oder R. (N) and Becva R. (S). Used by Danube-Oder Canal (begun 1950).

Moravian Karst (kärst), Czech *Moravský Kras* (mô'räfskē kräs"), picturesque region of limestone formations, W central Moravia, Czechoslovakia, just E of Blansko. Noted for stalactite caves, precipitous cliffs, underground streams, and prehistoric sites; famous Macocha chasm is 600 ft. deep. Main tourist centers, Ostrov (E) and Sloup (N) of Blansko.

Moravian Slovakia (slōvä'kēŭ, –vă'–), Czech *Moravské Slovácko* (mô'räfskā slô'vätskô), region of E Moravia, Czechoslovakia, extending roughly from Breclav NNE to Napajedla; noted for colorful national costumes, song and dance festivals, and folk fairs. Trade and cultural centers, Uherske Hradiste and Uhersky Brod.

Moravica River, Yugoslavia. **1** Headstream of WESTERN MORAVA RIVER. **2** Headstream of SOUTHERN MORAVA RIVER.

Moravice River (mô'rävĭtsě), Ger. *Mora* (mō'rä), N Moravia and central Silesia, Czechoslovakia, rises in the Jeseniky on SE slope of Praded mtn., flows SE, past Rymarov, and NE to Opava R. just E of Opava city; 63 mi. long.

Moravska Brana, Czechoslovakia: see MORAVIAN GATE.

Moravska Ostrava, Czechoslovakia: see OSTRAVA.

Moravska Trebova (mô'räfskä tŭrzhě'bôvä), Czech *Moravská Třebová*, Ger. *Mährisch-Trubau* (mâ'rĭsh-trōō'bou), town (pop. 5,844), W Moravia, Czechoslovakia, on railroad and 28 mi. NNW of Olomouc; textile mfg. (silk, cotton, woolen). Clay quarrying near by. Has picturesque castle, military school. Coal mines of Mladejov (mlä'dyĕyôf), Czech *Mladějov*, Ger. *Blosdorf* (blōs'dôrf), are NW.

Moravske Budejovice (–skā bŏŏ'dyĕyôvĭtsě), Czech *Moravské Budějovice*, Ger. *Mährisch-Budwitz* (mâ'rĭsh-bŏŏd'vĭts), town (pop. 4,348), S Moravia, Czechoslovakia, 25 mi. SSE of Jihlava; rail junction; agr. center (barley, oats); mfg. of agr. machinery. Has 16th-cent. church and castle.

Moravske Slovacko, Czechoslovakia: see MORAVIAN SLOVAKIA.

Moravsky Beroun (–skē bě'rōn), Czech *Moravský Beroun*, Ger. *Bärn* (bârn), town (pop. 1,957), N Moravia, Czechoslovakia, on railroad and 16 mi. NNE of Olomouc; mfg. (linen and cotton textiles, leatherette, knit goods), slate quarrying.

Moravsky Kras, Czechoslovakia: see MORAVIAN KARST.

Moravsky Krumlov (krōōm'lôf), Czech *Moravský Krumlov*, Ger. *Mährisch-Kromau* (mâ'rĭsh-krō'mou), town (pop. 2,897), S Moravia, Czechoslovakia, on railroad and 17 mi. SW of Brno; barley, oats. Built as a fortress; still retains old castle (now mus. of prehistoric remains) and remnants of fortifications.

Morawaka (mō'rŭväkŭ), village (pop. 1,047), Southern Prov., Ceylon, 24 mi. NE of Galle; precious and semi-precious stone-mining center (including alexandrite, aquamarine, ruby, sapphire); beryl deposits.

Morawhanna (mô"rŭhwä'nŭ), village (pop. 305), Essequibo co., NW Br. Guiana, near Venezuela border and the Atlantic, port at head of navigation (52 mi.) on Barima R., and 150 mi. NW of Georgetown. In adjoining hills, citrus fruit, cacao, coconuts, pineapples, bananas, corn are grown. Former administrative ⊙ North West Dist., replaced by Mabaruma. Gold placers in vicinity.

Moray or **Morayshire** (mûr'ē,–shĭr), formerly **Elgin** or **Elginshire,** county (□ 476.4; 1931 pop. 40,806; 1951 census 48,211), NE Scotland, on Moray Firth and the North Sea; ⊙ Elgin. Bounded by Inverness (S), Nairn (W), and Banff (E). Drained by the Spey, Lossie, and Findhorn rivers. Surface is hilly in S, leveling toward sandy, even coastline. Sea fisheries, salmon fishing (Spey and Findhorn rivers), farming, and cattle and sheep grazing are main occupations; other industries are granite, sandstone, and slate quarrying, whisky distilling, shipbuilding. Besides Elgin, other towns are Lossiemouth, Forres, Burghead, Grantown-on-Spey, and Rothes. There are several tourist resorts. Among antiquities are cathedral at Elgin and Sweno's Stone at Forres, site of Duncan's court. Anc. province of Moray was considerably larger than present co.

Moray Firth (mûr'ē fûrth'), inlet of the North Sea on NE coast of Scotland. It is usually considered to cover the inlet bet. Kinnairds Head, Aberdeenshire (S), and Duncansbay Head, Caithness (N), a distance of 78 mi. In its more restricted sense the firth covers the inlet bet. Lossiemouth (S) and Tarbat Ness (N), a distance of 21 mi. At its head the firth is continued W by Beauly Firth. It is noted for its fish; important riparian fishing ports are Banff, Buckie, Findhorn, Cromarty, Helmsdale, and Lybster. At head of firth is Inverness. Main inlets of firth are Dornoch and Cromarty firths.

Morayshire, Scotland: see MORAY.

Morazán (mōräsän'), town (1950 pop. 1,081), El Progreso dept., E central Guatemala, on short branch of upper Motagua R. and 7 mi. NW of El Progreso; corn, wheat, sugar cane; livestock.

Morazán, Nicaragua: see PUERTO MORAZÁN.

Morazán, department (□ 909; pop. 119,384), E Salvador, on Honduras border; ⊙ San Francisco.

Mainly mountainous; drained by Torola R. (N; left affluent of the Lempa) and Río Grande de San Miguel (S). Its henequen industry (rope, hammocks) and gold and silver mines (El Divisadero) are important. Agr. (grain, fruit, sugar cane). Main centers: San Francisco, Guatajiagua, Cacaopera. Formed 1875.

Morbegno (môrbä'nyô), town (pop. 4,277), Sondrio prov., Lombardy, N Italy, in the Valtellina, 15 mi. WSW of Sondrio; resort; base for Alpine excursions. Food cannery, cheese factory, lumber and silk mills, foundry; hydroelectric plant.

Morbier (môrbyā'), village (pop. 348), Jura dept., E France, on the Bienne and 12 mi. NE of Saint-Claude; makes clocks and eyeglasses.

Morbihan (môrbēä') [Breton,=little sea], department (□ 2,739; pop. 506,884), Brittany, W France; ⊙ Vannes. On Bay of Biscay, with much indented coastline (Gulf of Morbihan, Quiberon Peninsula) and several offshore isls. (Belle-Île, Groix, Houat, Hoedic). Drained by short streams (Blavet, Scorff, Oust) rising in Armorican Massif (N) and flowing generally S. Chief crops: rye, buckwheat, flax, oats, barley, cabbage, green peas; apple orchards, vineyards (on Rhuis Peninsula); beekeeping, livestock raising. Extensive fisheries (sardines, tunny) and oyster beds (in coastal inlets). Important kaolin (Lorient area, Guiscriff) and slate (Gourin, Ploërmel) quarries. Chief industries are fish canning, tanning, furniture and lace mfg., and metalworking (Hennebont, Ploërmel, Vannes). Tourist trade centers around megalithic monuments at Carnac and Locmariaquer, and shrine of Sainte-Anne-d'Auray. Chief towns: Vannes, Lorient (virtually destroyed in Second World War), Pontivy.

Morbihan, Gulf of, tidewater basin (□ 40) in Morbihan dept., W France, linked with Bay of Biscay by channel (1 mi. wide), and enclosed by Rhuis Peninsula. Contains numerous sandy isls., including Île aux Moines. Port of Vannes is on N shore. The gulf has given its name to the dept.

Mörbisch am See (mûr'bĭsh äm zā'), village (pop. 2,227), Burgenland, E Austria, near W shore of Neusiedler L., 9 mi. SE of Eisenstadt; vineyards, sugar beets.

Morbylanga (mûr"bülông'ä), Swedish *Mörbylånga*, town (pop. 604), Kalmar co., SE Sweden, SW Oland isl., on Kalmar Sound of Baltic, 9 mi. S of Kalmar; sugar refining, metalworking.

Morcenx (môrsĕs'), town (pop. 3,004), Landes dept., SW France, 23 mi. WNW of Mont-de-Marsan; rail junction, lumbering center; chemical factory; mfg. of resinous products.

Morchenstern, Czechoslovakia: see SMRZOVKA.

Mörchingen, France: MORHANGE.

Morciano di Romagna (môrchä'nô dē rômä'nyä), village (pop. 1,637), Forlì prov., Emilia-Romagna, N central Italy, 6 mi. SW of Cattolica; woolen mill, macaroni factory.

Morcone (môrkô'nĕ), village (pop. 2,511), Benevento prov., Campania, S Italy, 16 mi. NNW of Benevento.

Mordab Lagoon, Iran: see MURDAB LAGOON.

Mor Dag (môr'dä), Turkish *Mor Dağ*, peak (12,500 ft.), SE Turkey, in Hakari Mts., 13 mi. NNE of Yuksekova, near Iran line.

Mordelles (môrdĕl'), village (pop. 679), Ille-et-Vilaine dept., W France, on the Meu and 9 mi. WSW of Rennes; apple orchards.

Morden, town (pop. 1,690), S Man., at foot of Pembina Mts., 65 mi. SW of Winnipeg; grain elevators, lumbering, dairying; stock, fruit. Site of dominion experimental fruit farm.

Morden, England: see MERTON AND MORDEN.

Mordialloc (môr"dēă'lŭk), municipality (pop. 14,513), S Victoria, Australia, 15 mi. SSE of Melbourne and on E shore of Port Phillip Bay, in metropolitan area; residential; truck gardening.

Mordington, parish (pop. 319), SE Berwick, Scotland. Includes LAMBERTON.

Mordov-, in Rus. names: see also MORDV-.

Mordovo (môr'dŭvŭ), village (1926 pop. 9,430), SW Tambov oblast, Russian SFSR, on railroad (Oborona station) and 45 mi. SE of Gryazi; rail junction; metalworks.

Mordovshchikovo (mŭrdôf'shchĭkŭvŭ), town (1926 pop. 1,181), SW Gorki oblast, Russian SFSR, near Oka R., 7 mi. E of Murom; truck produce. Shipyards near Lipiya (S).

Mordovskaya Bokla (mŭrdôf'skīŭ bŭklä'), village (1926 pop. 2,067), NW Chkalov oblast, Russian SFSR, 17 mi. NE of Buguruslan; wheat, sunflowers, livestock. Sometimes called Bokla Mordovskaya.

Mordovski Kameshkir, Russian SFSR: see RUSSKI KAMESHKIR.

Mordves (mŭrdvyĕs'), village (1939 pop. over 500), NE Tula oblast, Russian SFSR, 18 mi. S of Kashira; distilling.

Mordvinian Autonomous Soviet Socialist Republic (môrdvĭ'nēŭn), administrative division (□ 10,080; 1939 pop. 1,188,598) of central European Russian SFSR; ⊙ Saransk. In Volga Hills; bordered SE by Sura R.; drained by Moksha and Insar rivers. Humid continental climate (short summers). Mineral resources: oil shale (NE), peat (NW), phosphorite, tripoli, marl, chalk, limestone. Extensive agr., with wheat (W), hemp (W and Moksha R. valley), legumes (central), rye, oats, potatoes, sunflowers (scattered), truck (lower Insar R. valley); hogs (Temnikov, Tengushevo), cattle, fodder crops. Coniferous and deciduous forests in E (25% of total area). Industry based on agr. (hemp, bast-fiber, and food processing, flour milling, distilling) and lumber (sawmilling, woodworking). Mfg. in main urban centers: electrical equipment, agr. machinery, consumers goods (Saransk), paper (Temnikov), matches (Ardatov); metalworking (Ruzayevka). Well-developed rail and road net. Pop. 55% Russians, 40% Mordvinians, 5% Tatars. Mordvinians, Rus. *Mordva*, are a Finnic group of Rus. culture and Greek Orthodox religion, colonized by Russians in 16th cent. Area became a separate okrug in 1928 within Middle Volga oblast; autonomous oblast in 1930 within Middle Volga Territory; gained present status in 1934 within Samara (Kuibyshev) Territory, from which it was separated in 1936.

Mordy (môr'dĭ), town (pop. 2,114), Lublin prov., E Poland, on railroad and 11 mi. ENE of Siedlce; brewing, flour milling, brick mfg.

More (mû'rù), Nor. *Møre*, mountainous coastal region, More og Romsdal co., W Norway, cut by numerous fjords. Its N part (Nor. *Nordmør*), bet. Trollheimen mts. (E) and North Sea (W), includes isls. of Smola, Tustna, Ertvagoy, Frei, and Averoy, and is separated by the Romsdal from SW part of region (Nor. *Sunnmør*, formerly *Søndmør*), which lies bet. the Dovrefjell and North Sea near Alesund. Off the coast are the Nordoyane and Soroyane isls.

Morea, Greece: see PELOPONNESUS.

Moreau River (mô'rō), formed by confluence of N and S forks in Perkins co., NW S.Dak., flows 289 mi. E to Missouri R. S of Mobridge. The site of Bixby Dam, unit in Bureau of Reclamation plan for development of Missouri R. basin, is in upper course, in Perkins co.

Moreauville (mô'rōvĭl), village (pop. 835), Avoyelles parish, E central La., 33 mi. SE of Alexandria, in cotton-growing area; cotton and moss ginning.

Morecambe and Heysham (môr'kŭm, hā'shŭm), municipal borough (1931 pop. 24,542; 1951 census 37,000), NW Lancashire, England, on Morecambe Bay. Includes seaside resort of Morecambe, 3 mi. NW of Lancaster, with mfg. of cement; and port of Heysham, 4 mi. W of Lancaster, terminal of Irish Sea mail ships to Belfast, Northern Ireland, and site of lighthouse, radio station, and sanitarium. Has ruins of 8th-cent. chapel. Excavations near by have yielded Stone Age, Saxon, Viking, and Norman relics.

Morecambe Bay, inlet of the Irish Sea, NW Lancashire, England, separating the main part of Lancashire from Furness peninsula; c.16 mi. long, 10 mi. wide. Chief ports: Fleetwood, Morecambe and Heysham. Receives Kent R., Leven R., and Lune R. Its S part is called Lancaster Bay.

Moreda (mōrā'dhä). **1** Town (pop. 1,480), Granada prov., S Spain, rail junction 15 mi. NW of Guadix; cereals, olive oil. **2** Village (pop. 1,850), Oviedo prov., NW Spain, in Aller valley, 15 mi. SE of Oviedo; steel mill; tin-plate mfg.; bituminous coal mines.

Moree (mōrē'), municipality (pop. 5,106), N New South Wales, Australia, on Gwydir R. and 265 mi. NNW of Newcastle; rail junction; wool, wheat. Hot springs.

Morée (mōrā'), village (pop. 523), Loir-et-Cher dept., N central France, near Loir R., 11 mi. NE of Vendôme; sawmilling. Has some 15th-cent. houses.

Moree (mōrā'), town, Western Prov., S Gold Coast colony, on Gulf of Guinea, 5 mi. ENE of Cape Coast; fishing; cassava, corn. First Du. station in Gold Coast, founded 1598; passed 1872 to British. Sometimes spelled Mouree or Mouri.

Moreh, Hill of (mō'rē, mōrā'), Hebrew *Givath Hamoreh*, elevation (1,690 ft.), N Palestine, at NE edge of Plain of Jezreel, 4 mi. E of Afula. In biblical history Gideon camped here before defeating the Midianites.

Morehead, town (pop. 3,102), ⊙ Rowan co., NE Ky., in Cumberland Natl. Forest, 45 mi. E of Paris, in timber, clay, and burley-tobacco area; mfg. of firebricks, clay pipe, concrete blocks, clothing, wood products, soft drinks; lumbering. Seat of Morehead State Col.

Morehead City, town (pop. 5,144), Carteret co., E N.C., 32 mi. SSE of New Bern, on W shore of Beaufort Harbor (here receiving Newport R.) and N shore of Bogue Sound, and just W of Beaufort. Ocean port (with shipping terminal built 1935–37), resort, fishing center; mfg. of fish oil and meal, clothing; woodworking; shipyards, canneries. Fort Macon State Park near by. Founded 1857; inc. 1860.

Morehouse, parish (□ 804; pop. 32,038), NE La.; ⊙ Bastrop. Bounded E by Boeuf R., W by Ouachita R., N by Ark. line; intersected by Bayou Bartholomew. Natural-gas field (with carbon-black mfg.). Agr. (cotton, corn, hay, fruit, truck, livestock). Some mfg., including processing of agr. products and timber. Includes Chemin-a-haut State Park (recreation). Formed 1844.

Morehouse, city (pop. 1,635), New Madrid co., extreme SE Mo., on Little R. and 6 mi. WSW of Sikeston, in cotton area; woodworking plant. Private drainage development near by. Settled 1880.

Mörel (mû'rŭl), village (pop. 384), Valais canton, S Switzerland, on the Rhone and 4 mi. NE of Brig; hydroelectric plant.

Moreland, town (pop. 306), Coweta co., W Ga., 6 mi. S of Newman; hosiery mfg.

Moreland Hills, village (pop. 1,040), Cuyahoga co., N Ohio, a SE suburb of Cleveland, on Chagrin R.

Morelganj, E Pakistan: see MORRELGANJ.

Morelia (mōrā'lyä), city (pop. 44,304), ⊙ Michoacán, central Mexico, in fertile valley of central plateau, on railroad and 130 mi. WNW of Mexico city; alt. 6,187 ft.; 19°43'N 101°7'W. Commercial, processing, and agr. center (corn, beans, sugar cane, fruit, cattle); flour milling, coffee processing, sugar refining, vegetable-oil extracting, tanning, sawmilling, printing; mfg. of shawls, hats, cotton goods, tobacco products, sweets, chocolate, beer, soap, chemicals, resins and other forest products. Radio stations, airfield. Old aqueduct (built 1789) is at city's gates. The cathedral, built 1640–1744, is one of the finest in the country. Other bldgs. of note are the govt. palace, state mus. (archaeological collection) and San Nicolás Col. (moved to Morelia 1580 from Pátzcuaro). A mission was established c.1531 in the vicinity, and the town was founded 1541 as Valladolid by Antonio de Mendoza, 1st viceroy of New Spain. It was renamed in 1828 in honor of Morelos y Pavón, hero of Mex. independence, who was b. here. Agustín de Iturbide was also b. here.

Morell (mōrĕl'), village (pop. estimate 200), NE P.E.I., on St. Peters Bay, 23 mi. ENE of Charlottetown; cod, lobster, hake fisheries.

Morell (mōräl'), town (pop. 1,491), Tarragona prov., NE Spain, 6 mi. NNW of Tarragona; woolen textiles; agr. trade (olive oil, wine, carob beans, hazelnuts, almonds).

Morella (mōrä'lyä), city (pop. 2,466), Castellón de la Plana prov., E Spain, 32 mi. WNW of Vinaroz; chief town of Maestrazgo dist.; textile center (cotton and wool). Tanning, flour milling; lumbering; cereals, almonds, livestock. Dominated by medieval castle; has Gothic church (14th cent.), tower of Saloquia, and anc. walls. Founded by Romans; in Middle Ages was fortress of kingdom of Valencia; belonged to military order of Montesa; was Carlist stronghold (1838–40) until it fell to Gen. Espartero.

Morelos (mōrā'lōs), state (□ 1,917; 1940 pop. 182,711; 1950 pop. 268,863), central Mexico; ⊙ Cuernavaca. Bordered by Federal Dist. (N), Mexico state (N and W), Puebla (E and SE), Guerrero (SW). Situated mainly on S slope of great central plateau, bounded NE by Popocatepetl, it descends S in many broad valleys, drained by affluents of the Río de las Balsas. Climate varies with alt.: from cool to semitropical, with humid winds from the Pacific and summer rains. Essentially an agr. state; produces corn, rice, wheat, sugar cane, coffee, wine, oranges, tropical fruit, vegetables. Considerable cattle raising. Mineral resources, which include silver, gold, and lead, are little exploited. Forests yield fine woods. Sugar refining and other processing industries are centered at Cuautla and Cuernavaca; the former has noted thermal springs, and both are well-known tourist resorts. The region was conquered by Cortés in early colonial days. State was set up in 1869, and named after Morelos y Pavón, hero of Mex. independence.

Morelos. **1** Town (pop. 172), Chihuahua, N Mexico, in valley of Sierra Madre Occidental, 120 mi. W of Hidalgo del Parral; corn, cattle, timber. Sometimes Real Morelos. **2** Town (pop. 2,371), Coahuila, N Mexico, on railroad and 27 mi. SW of Piedras Negras (Texas border); cattle raising; wheat, bran, istle fibers, candelilla wax. **3** Officially San Bartolo Morelos, town (pop. 2,506), Mexico state, central Mexico, 28 mi. NW of Mexico city; cereals, fruit, maguey, livestock. **4** or **Morelos Cañada** (känyä'dä), town (pop. 1,627), Puebla, central Mexico, on railroad and 18 mi. S of Serdán; wheat, corn, vegetables. Sometimes Cañada Morelos. **5** Town (pop. 2,671), Zacatecas, N central Mexico, 8 mi. N of Zacatecas; alt. 7,621 ft.; silver mining; agr. (cereals, maguey, livestock).

Morelos, Ciudad, Mexico: see CUAUTLA, Morelos.

Morelos, Villa, Mexico: see VILLA MORELOS.

Morelos Cañada, Mexico: see MORELOS, Puebla.

Morena (mō'rānŭ), town (pop. 12,527), ⊙ Tonwarghar (or Morena) dist., NE Madhya Bharat, India, 23 mi. NNW of Lashkar; agr. market (millet, gram, wheat, barley); oilseed milling, hand-loom cotton weaving. Sometimes called Pech Morena.

Morena, Sierra, Spain: see SIERRA MORENA.

Morena Dam, Calif.: see COTTONWOOD CREEK.

Morenci (mûrĕn'sē). **1** Village (pop. 6,541), Greenlee co., SE Ariz., at S tip of Blue Range, 110 mi. NE of Tucson; alt. 4,836 ft.; built on steep hillside. Rich copper mines here, discovered 1872. **2** City (pop. 1,983), Lenawee co., SE Mich., on Tiffin R. and 15 mi. SW of Adrian, near Ohio line, in diversified farm area (corn, grain, livestock). Mfg. (chemicals, machinery, electrical products, hardware); dairy and food products, feed; chick hatcheries. Inc. as city 1934.

Moreni (môrän'), town (1948 pop. 9,046), Prahova prov., S central Rumania, in Walachia, on Ialomita R. and 17 mi. WNW of Ploesti; rail terminus and petroleum center; oil production and refining; machine shops. Lignite mines and extensive vineyards in vicinity. Rail and oil pipe line to Baicoi.

Moreno, department, Argentina: see TINTINA.

Moreno (mōrā'nō), town (pop. 7,220), ⊙ Moreno dist. (□ 58; pop. 16,838), NE Buenos Aires prov., Argentina, 22 mi. W of Buenos Aires, in agr. area (alfalfa, corn, livestock).

Moreno (mōōrā'nōō), city (pop. 7,282), E Pernambuco, NE Brazil, on railroad and 17 mi. WSW of Recife, in sugar-growing region; sugar milling, coconut processing.

More og Romsdal (mû'rû ô rôms'däl, rōōms'däl), Nor. *Møre og Romsdal*, county [Nor. *fylke*] (□ 5,810; pop. 182,859), W Norway; ⊙ KRISTIANSUND. Lies bet. the Dovrefjell and Trollheimen mts. and the coast, which is deeply indented by the fjords Halse, Sunndals, Molde, Stor, Volds, and their branches; includes MORE region split by the ROMSDAL valley area. Sor and Nord isl. groups are offshore. Chief occupations: agr. (barley, oats, potatoes), cattle raising, fishing (cod). Industries at ALESUND, Andalsnes, Molde, Kristiansund, Orstavik. Fjords, valleys (notably the Norangdal), mts. attract tourist trade. Roads in N part connect with Trondheim and the Gudbrandsdal; railroad to Oslo terminates at Andalsnes. Co. (then called *amt*) was named Romsdal until 1918, when it was renamed More; became More og Romsdal 1935.

Morera, La (lä mōrā'rä), town (pop. 1,068), Badajoz prov., W Spain, 29 mi. SE of Badajoz; cereals olives, grapes, livestock.

Morés (mōrās'), town (pop. 1,051), Saragossa prov., NE Spain, on Jalón R. and 10 mi. NE of Calatayud; cereals, wine, olive oil, fruit.

Moresby, parish (pop. 1,301), W Cumberland, England. Includes coal-mining village of Moresby Parks, 2 mi. ENE of Whitehaven.

Moresby Island (□ 1,060), W B.C., Queen Charlotte Isls., in the Pacific, separated from mainland by Hecate Strait, and just S of Graham Isl., from which it is separated by Skidegate Inlet; 85 mi. long, 4–34 mi. wide. Queen Charlotte Mts. here rise to 3,810 ft. Lumbering, fishing; cattle. Chief villages are Sandspit (radio station) and Aliford Bay, both on NE coast. Inhabitants are mostly Haida Indians.

Moresby Parks, England: see MORESBY.

Moresnet (môrûnā'), town (pop. 1,307), Liége prov., E Belgium, 5 mi. SW of Aachen, near Ger. border; zinc mining. The former neutral territory (□ 1.2) just E of Moresnet, under joint Belgian and Prussian suzerainty, was awarded (1919) to Belgium under Treaty of Versailles.

Morestel (môrĕstĕl'), village (pop. 940), Isère dept., SE France, 8 mi. N of La Tour-du-Pin; aluminum smelting, furniture and footwear mfg.

Moreton, Cape, Australia: see MORETON ISLAND.

Moreton Bay (môr'tůn), inlet of Pacific Ocean, SE Queensland, Australia, bet. Cape Moreton of Moreton Isl. (NE) and Bribie Isl. (NW); bounded W by mainland, E by Moreton, N.Stradbroke, and S. Stradbroke isls.; 65 mi. (N–S), 20 mi. (E–W). Contains many islets; receives Brisbane R. (site of Brisbane, 14 mi. inland). Resort towns of Sandgate, Wynnum, Southport, and Redcliffe on W shore. Area around Redcliffe was site (1824–43) of 1st penal settlement of state.

Moreton Hampstead or **Moretonhampstead** (both: môr'tůn hăm'stĭd), town and parish (pop. 1,587), central Devon, England, 12 mi. WSW of Exeter; agr. market and tourist resort. Has 17th-cent. almshouses, 13th-cent. inn, and 15th-cent. church.

Moreton-in-Marsh, town and parish (pop. 1,382), NE Gloucester, England, 13 mi. ESE of Evesham; agr. market.

Moreton Island (□ 71; pop. 8,792), in Pacific Ocean 15 mi. off SE coast of Queensland, Australia; forms E shore of Moreton Bay; 25 mi. long (N–S), 5 mi. wide (E–W); rises to 910 ft.; sandy. Cape Moreton, its N point (27°2'S 153°28'E), forms E side of entrance to Moreton Bay. Fishing.

Moreton Say, agr. village and parish (pop. 726), NE Shropshire, England, 3 mi. W of Market Drayton. Lord Clive, b. here, is buried in the parish church.

Moretown, town (pop. 883), Washington co., central Vt., on Mad R., 11 mi. W of Montpelier; lumber.

Moret-sur-Loing (môrā'-sür-lwē'), town (pop. 2,560), Seine-et-Marne dept., N central France, on the Loing (canalized) near its mouth into the Seine, and 6 mi. SE of Fontainebleau; known for its barley sugar. Precision metalworks; mfg. (elastic corsets, ceramics, photo equipment), printing. Has 13th–14th-cent. church, old houses, and 14th-cent. gates and bridge.

Moretta (môrĕt'tä), village (pop. 2,195), Cuneo prov., Piedmont, NW Italy, near Po R., 22 mi. SSW of Turin; rail junction.

Moreuil (môrû'ē), town (pop. 2,607), Somme dept., N France, on the Avre and 12 mi. SE of Amiens; hosiery mfg., tanning. Destroyed in First World War. Rebuilt and damaged in Second World War.

Morey, Lake, E Vt., resort lake near the Connecticut, 24 mi. SE of Barre, in Fairlee town; c.2 mi. long.

Morey-Saint-Denis (môrā'-sē-dûnē'), village (pop. 505), Côte-d'Or dept., E central France, on E slope of the Côte d'Or, 9 mi. SSW of Dijon; noted Burgundy wines.

Morez (môrĕz'), town (pop. 4,481), Jura dept., E France, near Swiss border, in gorge of Bienne R. and 12 mi. NE of Saint-Claude, in the E Jura; alt. 2,303 ft. Leading center of optical industry. Also produces large clocks, enamelware, and plastic objects. Large quantity of Gruyère cheese made in area. Site of natl. optical school.

Morfa Harlech, Wales: see HARLECH.

Mörfelden (mûr'fĕl"dûn), village (pop. 6,337), S Hesse, W Germany, in former Starkenburg prov., 8 mi. NNW of Darmstadt; metal and wood working, food processing.

Morgan, village (pop. 434), SE South Australia, 85 mi. NE of Adelaide and on Murray R.; rail terminus; fruit, livestock.

Morgan. 1 County (□ 574; pop. 52,924), N Ala.; ⊙ Decatur. Agr. area drained in N by Wheeler Reservoir (in Tennessee R.). Cotton, hogs; textiles. Deposits of coal, sandstone, fuller's earth, asphalt. Formed 1818. **2** County (□ 1,282; pop. 18,074), NE Colo.; ⊙ Fort Morgan. Irrigated agr. region, drained by South Platte R. Sugar beets, beans, livestock. Formed 1889. **3** County (□ 356; pop. 11,899), N central Ga.; ⊙ Madison. Bounded NE by Apalachee R.; drained by Little R. Piedmont agr. (cotton, corn, sorghum, grain, peaches), livestock, and lumber area. Formed 1807. **4** County (□ 565; pop. 35,568), W central Ill.; ⊙ Jacksonville. Bounded W by Illinois R.; drained by small Apple, Sandy, and Indian creeks. Agr. (corn, wheat, oats, livestock, poultry; dairy products). Meat packing; mfg. of clothing, steel products, shoes, wire novelties, cigars, books. Includes part of L. Meredosia (resort). Formed 1823. **5** County (□ 406; pop. 23,726), central Ind.; ⊙ Martinsville. Agr. area (hogs, grain, fruit, poultry). Mfg., including dairy-products and food processing at Martinsville and Mooresville. Clay deposits; timber; artesian springs. Includes a state forest. Drained by West Fork of White R., Whitelick R., and small Camp Creek. Formed 1821. **6** County (□ 369; pop. 13,624), E Ky.; ⊙ West Liberty. Drained by Licking R. and several creeks; includes part of Cumberland Natl. Forest. Hilly agr. area in Cumberland foothills; corn, tobacco, poultry, livestock, fruit. Bituminous-coal mines; oil and gas wells; timber. Formed 1822. **7** County (□ 596; pop. 10,207), central Mo.; ⊙ Versailles. In the Ozarks, on L. of the Ozarks; drained by Lamine R. Agr. (wheat, corn, oats), poultry, dairying; coal, barite; timber; tourist region. Formed 1833. **8** County (□ 418; pop. 12,836), E central Ohio; ⊙ McConnelsville. Intersected by Muskingum R. and small Meigs and Wolf creeks. Agr. area (livestock, dairy products, corn, wheat, cabbages); mfg. at McConnelsville; limestone quarries, coal mines. Formed 1818. **9** County (□ 539; pop. 15,727), NE central Tenn.; ⊙ Wartburg. On Cumberland Plateau. Lumbering, agr. (corn, hay, tobacco, fruit, vegetables), livestock raising, dairying. Formed 1817. **10** County (□ 610; pop. 2,519), N Utah; ⊙ Morgan. Irrigated agr. area watered by Weber R. Livestock, hay, sugar beets, fruit, truck. Wasatch Range throughout. Formed 1862. **11** County (□ 233; pop. 8,276), W.Va., in Eastern Panhandle; ⊙ Berkeley Springs. Bounded N by Potomac R. (Md. line), partly S by Va.; drained by Cacapon R. Cacapon State Park is here. Includes Cacapon Mtn. Agr. (livestock, dairy products, fruit); glass-sand pits, timber. Mfg. at Berkeley Springs (health resort). Formed 1820.

Morgan. 1 City (pop. 304), ⊙ Calhoun co., SW Ga., 23 mi. W of Albany and on Ichawaynochaway Creek, in farm area. **2** Village (pop. 949), Redwood co., SW Minn., near Minnesota R., 24 mi. WNW of New Ulm, in grain, livestock, poultry area; dairy products, feed. **3** Town (pop. 55), Laclede co., S central Mo., in the Ozarks, near Osage Fork of Gasconade R., 12 mi. S of Lebanon. **4** Village, Phillips co., N Mont., port of entry at Sask. line, c.70 mi. N of Malta. **5** Village (pop. 1,854, with adjacent Treveskyn), Allegheny co., W Pa., 10 mi. SW of downtown Pittsburgh. **6** Village (pop. 424), Bosque co., central Texas, 7 mi. N of Meridian, in farm area. **7** or **Morgan City**, resort city (pop. 1,064), ⊙ Morgan co., N Utah, on Weber R., in Wasatch Range, and 22 mi. NNE of Salt Lake City; alt. 5,068 ft. Trade center for agr. region (sugar beets, potatoes, cabbage, peas); vegetable canning, dairy products. Settled 1860 by Mormons. Surrounding area served by irrigation works on Weber R. **8** Town (pop. 296), Orleans co., N Vt., on Seymour L. and 9 mi. E of Newport; resorts, lumber.

Morgan, Fort, Ala.: see MOBILE POINT.

Morgan, Mount (13,739 ft.), Inyo co., E Calif., in the Sierra Nevada, 19 mi. W of Bishop.

Morgan City. 1 City (pop. 9,759), St. Mary parish, S La., 70 mi. WSW of New Orleans; port on Berwick Bay (bridged to Berwick) of navigable Atchafalaya R., and S terminus of Plaquemine–Morgan City Waterway, joining Gulf Intracoastal Waterway here. Port handles petroleum, sulphur, chemicals, steel and iron products, oystershell, canned sea food, lumber. Shipyards. Agr. (truck, sugar cane), fishing, hunting, fur trapping near by. Settled in 1850, inc. in 1860 as Brashear City, renamed in 1876. **2** City, Utah: see MORGAN, city.

Morganfield, city (pop. 3,257), ⊙ Union co., W Ky., 21 mi. WSW of Henderson; railroad shipping point in bituminous-coal-mining and agr. (corn, wheat, hay, tobacco) area; makes metal novelties, furniture; seed-cleaning plant. St. Vincent's Acad. (1820; for girls) is near by. U.S. Camp Breckinridge (E) was active in Second World War.

Morgan Hill, town (pop. 1,627), Santa Clara co., W Calif., 20 mi. SE of San Jose, in Santa Clara Valley; wineries; ships fruit. Inc. 1906.

Morgans Point, city (pop. 656), Harris co., S Texas, on Galveston Bay and c.20 mi. ESE of downtown Houston; post office is La Porte.

Morganton. 1 Town (pop. 244), Fannin co., N Ga., 4 mi. E of Blue Ridge and on Blue Ridge L. **2** Town (pop. 8,311), ⊙ Burke co., W central N.C., 50 mi. ENE of Asheville, near Catawba R.; mfg. center (textiles, hosiery, clothing, furniture, leather goods, electrical equipment). State school for deaf, state hosp. for insane near by. Inc. 1784.

Morgantown. 1 Town (pop. 838), Morgan co., central Ind., near small Camp Creek, 28 mi. S of Indianapolis; makes furniture. **2** Town (pop. 850), ⊙ Butler co., W central Ky., on Green R. and 20 mi. NW of Bowling Green, in agr., coal-mining, timber area. **3** City (pop. 25,525), ⊙ Monongalia co., N W.Va., on Monongahela R. and 55 mi. S of Pittsburgh. Center of bituminous-coal-mining, limestone, and glass-sand region; U.S. ordnance works produce chemicals from coal and natural gas; several glass plants; ships coal. Seat of W.Va. Univ. Cooper's Rock State Forest, largest in state, is 10 mi. NE. Settled 1767.

Morganville, city (pop. 278), Clay co., N Kansas, on Republican R. and 8 mi. NNW of Clay Center; grain, livestock.

Morganza (môrgăn'zů), village (pop. 817), Pointe Coupee parish, SE central La., on the Mississippi and 32 mi. NW of Baton Rouge.

Morganza Floodway, La.: see ATCHAFALAYA RIVER.

Morgardshammar (mōōr"gôrts"hä'mär), Swedish *Morgårdshammar*, village (pop. 785), Kopparberg co., central Sweden, on small lake, 6 mi. E of Ludvika; metalworking; hydroelectric station.

Morgarten (môr'gär"tůn), mountain (4,084 ft.) on border of Schwyz and Zug cantons, N central Switzerland, 5 mi. N of Schwyz. Here a small Swiss force decisively defeated Austrians in 1315, paving the way to Swiss independence.

Morgat (môrgä'), seaside resort of Finistère dept., W France, on Crozon Peninsula, 11 mi. S of Brest; sardine fishing in Douarnenez Bay.

Morgaushi (mŭrgōō'shē), village (1939 pop. over 500), NW Chuvash Autonomous SSR, Russian SFSR, 22 mi. SW of Cheboksary; wheat, rye, oats.

Morgenberghorn (môr'gûnbĕrk"hôrn'), peak (7,385 ft.) in Bernese Alps, S central Switzerland, 5 mi. SW of Interlaken.

Morgenroth, Poland: see NOWY BYTOM.

Morges (môrzh), town (pop. 5,689), Vaud canton, W Switzerland, on L. of Geneva, at mouth of short Morges R., and 7 mi. W of Lausanne; metalworking, fats, biscuits. Medieval castle with mus., 17th-cent. town hall, art mus. Small harbor.

Morgex (môrzhā'), village (pop. 517), Val d'Aosta region, NW Italy, on Dora Baltea R. and 14 mi. WNW of Aosta. Processes coal mined at La Thuile. Also called Valdigna d'Aosta.

Morgins (môrzhē'), health resort (alt. 4,330 ft.), Valais canton, SW Switzerland, 4 mi. W of Monthey at Fr. line.

Morgongava (môr'gôn-gō"vä, mô'rôn-), Swedish *Morgongåva*, village (pop. 1,104), Vastmanland co., central Sweden, 13 mi. E of Sala; agr.-machinery works.

Morhange (môräzh'), Ger. *Mörchingen* (mûrkh'ĭng-ůn), town (pop. 1,914), Moselle dept., NE France, 25 mi. SE of Metz; market; mfg. of building materials. Here French were defeated by Germans in one of earliest battles (Aug., 1914) of First World War.

Mori (mô'rē), village (pop. 1,864), Trento prov., Trentino–Alto Adige, N Italy, in Val Lagarina, 4 mi. SW of Rovereto; silk mill, cement and aluminum works. Rebuilt since First World War.

Mori (mō'rē). **1** Town (pop. 23,168), SW Hokkaido, Japan, on SW shore of Uchiura Bay, 25 mi. NNW of Hakodate; fishing; mining (gold, silver, copper); agr. Hot springs near by. **2** Town (pop. 9,074), Oita prefecture, N central Kyushu, Japan, 26 mi. WNW of Oita; agr. center (rice, wheat, barley); lumber; sake, silk thread. **3** Town (pop. 10,367), Shizuoka prefecture, central Honshu, Japan, 15 mi. NE of Hamamatsu; tea, charcoal.

Moriah (mûrī'ů), village (pop. 2,133), central Tobago, B.W.I., 4½ mi. N of Scarborough; cacao.

Moriah, village (1940 pop. 755), Essex co., NE N.Y., near L. Champlain, 14 mi. NNW of Ticonderoga, in iron-mining area.

Moriah, Mount. 1 In Nev.: see SNAKE RANGE. **2** In N.H.: see CARTER-MORIAH RANGE.

Morialmé (môrēälmā'), village (pop. 1,345), Namur prov., S central Belgium, 9 mi. SSE of Charleroi; ceramics, glassware.

Moriarty (môrēär'tē), hamlet, Torrance co., central N.Mex., near Manzano Range, 15 mi. N of Estancia; alt. c.6,200 ft.; agr.; livestock.

Morib (mōrĭb'), village, SW Selangor, on Strait of Malacca, 20 mi. S of Klang; seaside resort.

Morice Lake (□ 40; 27 mi. long, 1–5 mi. wide), W central B.C., in Coast Mts., 50 mi. SSW of Smithers, near Tweedsmuir Park. Drains N into Bulkley R.

Morichal Largo River (mōrēchäl' lär'gō), Monagas state, NE Venezuela, rises in low tableland NNW of Ciudad Bolívar, flows c.150 mi. NE to the Caño Mánamo (arm of Orinoco R. delta) 38 mi. SSW of Pedernales.

Moriches (mûrĭ'chēz), village (pop. c.500), Suffolk co., SE N.Y., on SE Long Isl., on Moriches Bay, 9 mi. E of Patchogue, in resort, truck-farming, and duck-raising area.

Morida, Japan: see MORITA.

Moriguchi (mōrē'gōōchē), town (pop. 52,042), Osaka prefecture, S Honshu, Japan, just E of Osaka, in agr. area (rice, wheat, giant radishes); poultry.

Moriles (mōrē'lĕs), town (pop. 2,975), Córdoba prov., S Spain, 7 mi. WNW of Lucena; wine, olive oil, cereals, livestock.

Morinda, India: see MURINDA.

Moringen (mō'rĭng-ŭn), town (pop. 3,952), in former Prussian prov. of Hanover, W Germany, after 1945 in Lower Saxony, 6 mi. W of Northeim; mfg. of chemicals.

Morinj, Bay of, Yugoslavia: see KOTOR, GULF OF.

Morinville (mô'rĭnvĭl), town (pop. 735), central Alta., 18 mi. NNW of Edmonton; railroad junction; mixed farming, dairying.

Morioka (mōrē'ōkä), city (1940 pop. 79,478; 1947 pop. 107,096), ⊙ Iwate prefecture, N Honshu, Japan, on Kitakami R. and 100 mi. NNE of Sendai; 39°42'N 141°9'E. Horse-trading center; sake brewing, toy making.

Moris (mō'rēs), town (pop. 417), Chihuahua, N Mexico, 165 mi. ESE of Hermosillo; alt. 3,400 ft.; silver, gold, lead, copper mining.

Morisset (mŏ'rĭsĭt), town (pop. 2,008), E New South Wales, Australia, 18 mi. SW of Newcastle; coal-mining center.

Morita (mōrē'tä) or **Morida** (mōrē'dä), town (pop. 7,830), Fukui prefecture, central Honshu, Japan, 3 mi. N of Fukui; textile mills (rayon, silk); fishing, poultry raising.

Moritzberg (mō'rĭtsbĕrk), W suburb of HILDESHEIM, NW Germany.

Moritzburg (mō'rĭtsbōōrk), village (pop. 2,533), Saxony, E central Germany, 8 mi. NNW of Dresden; market gardening. Site of 16th-cent. Moritzburg palace, former royal hunting lodge, and since 1947 Baroque Mus., containing salvaged remains of Dresden art collections.

Moriya (mōrē'yä), town (pop. 4,646), Ibaraki prefecture, central Honshu, Japan, 11 mi. WNW of Ryugasaki; rice, barley.

Moriyama (mōrē'yämŏ). **1** Town (pop. 29,375), Aichi prefecture, central Honshu, Japan, just NE of Nagoya; agr. center (rice, market produce). **2** Town (pop. 7,491), Fukushima prefecture, central Honshu, Japan, 4 mi. SSE of Koriyama; rice, silk cocoons, tobacco. **3** Town (pop. 8,896), Shiga prefecture, S Honshu, Japan, 14 mi. E of Kyoto, across L. Biwa, in agr. area (rice, wheat, tea, market produce); raw silk. Fishing.

Morki (môr'kē), village (1932 pop. estimate 780), SE Mari Autonomous SSR, Russian SFSR, near Ilet R., 45 mi. ESE of Ioshkar-Ola; wheat, rye, oats.

Morkovice (môr'kôvĭtsĕ), Ger. *Morkowitz*, village (pop. 1,961), central Moravia, Czechoslovakia, 9 mi. SW of Kromeriz; rail terminus; mfg. of basketwork, brushes, brooms.

Morkvashi, Russian SFSR: see ZHIGULEVSK.

Morlaàs (môrläs'), village (pop. 909), Basses-Pyrénées dept., SW France, 6 mi. NE of Pau; horse, cattle, poultry market. Has church (founded 1089) with fine Romanesque portal.

Morlacca, Canale della, Yugoslavia: see VELEBIT MOUNTAINS.

Morlaix (môrlĕ'), Breton *Montroulez*, town (pop. 12,176), Finistère dept., W France, seaport on inlet of English Channel, 33 mi. ENE of Brest; exports pit props and dairy products, imports British coal; mfg. (carved woodwork, paper, tobacco products), flour milling, butter making. Trades in leather, honey, linen, and horses. Attracts tourists. Has 15th- and 16th-cent. wooden houses. Railroad viaduct spans valley just above port.

Morland, city (pop. 287), Graham co., NW Kansas, on South Fork Solomon R. and 13 mi. W of Hill City; trade and shipping center for grain region.

Morlanwelz (môrläwā'), town (pop. 8,992), Hainaut prov., S central Belgium, 9 mi. WNW of Charleroi; coal mining; mfg. (steel tubing, chains, Portland cement). Has ruins of 13th-cent. abbey.

Morla Vicuña, Chile: see QUIDICO.

Morley, municipal borough (1931 pop. 23,396; 1951 census 39,783), West Riding, S central Yorkshire, England, 4 mi. SW of Leeds; coal mining, stone quarrying, woolen milling, leather tanning; also produces glass, pharmaceuticals, textile machinery. Scene of Royalist siege in Civil War.

Morley (môrlā'), village (pop. 305), Meuse dept., NE France, on the Saulx and 15 mi. ESE of Saint-Dizier; agr. equipment. Stone quarries near by.

Morley. 1 Village (pop. c.350), Las Animas co., S Colo., in E foothills of Sangre de Cristo Mts., 10 mi. S of Trinidad, near N.Mex. line; alt. c.7,000 ft.; coal-mining point. **2** Town (pop. 157), Jones co., E Iowa, 22 mi. E of Cedar Rapids; livestock, grain. **3** Village (pop. 413), Mecosta co., central Mich., 15 mi. S of Big Rapids and on Little Muskegon R. **4** Town (pop. 494), Scott co., SE Mo., in Mississippi flood plain, 4 mi. SE of Oran.

Morlunda (mûr'lŭn"dä), Swedish *Mörlunda*, village (pop. 743), Kalmar co., SE Sweden, near Em R., 20 mi. W of Oskarshamn; furniture mfg.

Mormanno (môrmän'nô), town (pop. 4,379), Cosenza prov., Calabria, S Italy, 13 mi. WNW of Castrovillari; tannery.

Mormant (môrmã'), village (pop. 1,177), Seine-et-Marne dept., N central France, 12 mi. NE of Melun; mfg. (agr. machinery, pharmaceuticals).

Mormoiron (môrmwärō'), village (pop. 530), Vaucluse dept., SE France, near Mont Ventoux, 7 mi. E of Carpentras; fruit, olives, wine; ocher quarries.

Mormon Flat Dam, S central Ariz., on Salt R. and c.35 mi. ENE of Phoenix. Unit in Salt R. irrigation project; concrete arch dam (224 ft. high, 505 ft. long), completed 1925. Used for irrigation and power. Forms reservoir with capacity of 57,900 acre-ft.

Mormon Lake (□ 12), central Ariz., 20 mi. SE of Flagstaff; 4 mi. long, 3 mi. wide; summer resorts. Mt. Mormon (8,440 ft.) is near W shore.

Mormugão (môrmōōgã'ō), town (pop. 11,200), W Goa dist., Portuguese India, port on Arabian Sea, 7 mi. SSW of Pangim; rail terminus; outlet for products of interior and of S Bombay state; exports rice, cotton, betel and cashew nuts, fish, salt, copra, manganese, timber; fish curing, fruit canning, wood carving; coir work. Consists of 2 sections, harbor and industrial area (pop. 2,092) and the modern commercial and residential development of Vasco da Gama (pop. 9,108; airport near by). Also spelled Marmagão.

Mornaghia, La (lä mômägyä'), village, Tunis dist., N Tunisia, 9 mi. WSW of Tunis; agr. settlement (wheat, barley, wine).

Mornant (môrnã'), village (pop. 969), Rhône dept., E central France, in the Monts du Lyonnais, 12 mi. SW of Lyons; woodworking.

Morne-à-l'Eau (môrn-ä-lō'), town (commune pop. 13,418), W Grande-Terre, Guadeloupe, on the Grand Cul de Sac, 7 mi. N of Pointe-à-Pitre; rum distilling, sugar milling.

Morne Diablotin, Dominica, B.W.I.: see DIABLOTIN, MORNE.

Morne-Rouge (môrn-rōōzh'), town (pop. 693), N Martinique, at S foot of Mont Pelée, 12 mi. NNW of Fort-de-France, in sugar-growing region; rum distilling. Destroyed (1902) by eruption of Pelée.

Morne Seychellois, Seychelles; see SEYCHELLOIS, MORNE.

Mornimont (môrnēmō'), town (pop. 806), Namur prov., S central Belgium, on Sambre R. and 7 mi. W of Namur; chemicals.

Morningdale, Mass.: see BOYLSTON.

Morningside, S suburb (pop. 21,548) of Edinburgh, Scotland.

Morningside, N residential suburb of Durban, E Natal, U. of So. Afr.

Morning Side, village (pop. 1,745), Delaware co., E central Ind., near Muncie.

Morningside. 1 Town (pop. 1,520), Prince Georges co., central Md., suburb SE of Washington. Andrews Air Force Base is near. Inc. 1949. **2** Village (pop. 1,699) and SW suburb of Minneapolis, Hennepin co., E Minn.

Morningside Heights, SE N.Y., a section of the West Side of Manhattan borough of New York city, lying bet. Riverside Park along the Hudson (W) and Morningside Park (E), N of 110th St.; Manhattanville section adjoins on N. Site of Columbia Univ., Cathedral of St. John the Divine, Riverside Church, Juilliard School of Music, Union Theological Seminary, Jewish Theological Seminary of America.

Morning Sun, town (pop. 939), Louisa co., SE Iowa, 25 mi. SSW of Muscatine; rail junction; creamery, rendering works. Limestone quarries near by.

Mornington, resort town (pop. 2,656), S Victoria, Australia, on SE shore of Port Phillip Bay and 30 mi. S of Melbourne.

Mornington, rural suburb (pop. 98), of Gatooma, Salisbury prov., central Southern Rhodesia.

Mornington Island, off coast of S Chile, on Trinidad Gulf just W of Wellington Isl.; 49°45'S 75°25'W; 28 mi. long, c.8 mi. wide; uninhabited.

Mornington Island, northernmost and largest of Wellesley Isls., in Gulf of Carpentaria, 15 mi. off NW coast of Queensland, Australia; 40 mi. long, 15 mi. wide; rises to 300 ft. Rocky, wooded; uninhabited.

Mornos River (môr'nôs), in W central Greece, rises in Oeta massif, flows 38 mi. SW to Gulf of Corinth just SE of Naupaktos. Hydroelectric plants.

Mörnsheim (mûrns'hīm), village (pop. 1,097), Middle Franconia, W central Bavaria, Germany, 15 mi. NE of Donauwörth; hops, cattle, hogs. Calcareous-slate quarries in area.

Moro, Japan: see MOROYAMA.

Moro (mō'rō), village, Nawabshah dist., central Sind, W Pakistan, 38 mi. NW of Nawabshah: wheat, millet, rice.

Moro (mô'rō). **1** Town (pop. 189), Lee co., E Ark., 19 mi. SW of Forrest City. **2** Plantation (pop. 84), Aroostook co., E Maine, on Rockabema L. and 26 mi. WNW of Houlton, in hunting, fishing area. **3** City (pop. 359), ⊙ Sherman co., N Oregon, 23 mi. ESE of The Dalles; wheat.

Morobe (mōrō'bā), district of Territory of New Guinea, in NE New Guinea; ⊙ Lae. Morobe gold fields near Wau and Bulolo are largest in New Guinea. Its former ⊙, Morobe, on coast, 80 mi. SE of Lae, was replaced in 1930s by Salamaua and after Second World War by Lae.

Morocco (mŭrŏ'kō), Arabic *El Maghreb el Aqsa* [the extreme west], Fr. *Maroc*, Sp. *Marruecos*, sultanate (□ c.160,000; pop. c.9,850,000) of NW Africa, along the Atlantic and Mediterranean coasts, bordered SW by Sp. West Africa and E and S by Algeria (the long SE boundary in the Sahara is mostly undefined); the traditional northern capital was FEZ, the southern MARRAKESH. Although the name Sherifian Empire [sherif is the title of ruling Alaouite or Alawite dynasty] is given to entire territory under the sultan's nominal rule, Morocco is politically divided into French Morocco (□ c.151,000; 1936 pop. 6,245,222; 1947 pop. 8,617,387; ⊙ Rabat), a protectorate and, since 1946, an associated state of the Fr. Union; Spanish Morocco (□ c.7,600; 1945 pop. 1,082,009; ⊙ Tetuán), a Sp. protectorate over the N coastal zone; and the International Zone of TANGIER (□ 147; 1947 pop. c.151,000), near N tip of Morocco, facing Spain across the Strait of Gibraltar. Several coastal enclaves are under direct sovereignty of Spain and outside of sultan's jurisdiction; these are the cities of CEUTA and MELILLA, and IFNI territory (an enclave on Morocco's SW coast). Several offshore islets in the Mediterranean are also part of metropolitan Spain. The Oued DRA has traditionally been Morocco's SW limit, but Morocco is sometimes considered to include the small, politically amorphous region S of the Dra and N of Cape Juby. This area, called, vaguely, SOUTHERN PROTECTORATE OF MOROCCO, is administratively a part of Sp. West Africa; with it, the area of Morocco is c.175,000 sq. mi. Physiographically, Morocco falls into 3 main natural regions: the RIF, the Atlas, and the Atlantic coastal plains and plateaus. The Sahara occupies its S and SE fringe. The Rif area, roughly coextensive with Sp. Morocco, is geologically a continuation of S Spain's Cordillera Penibética; it is separated from the Atlas ranges (S) by the Taza corridor (chief route from Algeria to W Morocco). The ATLAS MOUNTAINS, forming 3 parallel SW–NE ranges (High Atlas, Middle Atlas, Anti-Atlas), extend across the Fr. protectorate from the Atlantic S of Mogador to Algerian border; the High Atlas rises to 13,665 ft. in the Djebel Toubkal, highest in N Africa. The Atlantic coastal region is dissected by many short Atlas-fed streams. Of these the Oum er Rbia is the longest but the Sebou (crossing the Rharb plain) waters the richer agr. land. Other Atlantic streams are the Lucus (forming border bet. Fr. and Sp. Morocco in upper course), Bou Regreg, Tensift, and Sous. The Moulouya (also a border stream in lower course) drains semi-arid E Morocco to the Mediterranean. All streams which rise on SE Atlas slopes (except the Oued Dra) lose themselves in the Sahara after watering a string of oases, of which the TAFILALET is the largest. Morocco N of the Atlas has a Mediterranean subtropical climate modified by Atlantic influences. The coastal cities have equable climate, interior cities are excessively hot in summer. Rain, which always falls in winter, varies in amount from year to year and ranges from 35 inches in the W Rif and Middle Atlas to less than 10 inches in the lee of the Atlas (E and SE) and in areas near coast S of Marrakesh. Cork oaks, dwarf palms, jujube trees are native to the Atlantic coastal region, thuya and juniper trees to the Mediterranean; argan trees, unique in Morocco, grow in SW plains (especially in the Sous). Green oaks and cedars cover the Atlas slopes, and esparto grass is widespread in the steppe region of E Morocco, N of the Sahara. Morocco's pop. is predominantly Berber (Islamized) with an admixture of Arabs. Jews numbering just over 200,000 in 1940s, are concentrated in large cities. The native Moslem pop. is rapidly increasing. Moorish Arabic and numerous Berber dialects are spoken. French and Spanish are used for official purposes in the respective protectorates. Region was 1st visited by Phoenicians after 12th cent. B.C. Later the Roman prov. of Western Mauretania (*Mauretania Tingitana*) was established, A.D. 42; roughly coextensive with N and W Morocco, it contained 2 important cities Tingis (now Tangier) and VOLUBILIS (now in ruins). Ravaged by Vandals (5th cent.), region was conquered (end of 7th cent.) by Arabs, who imposed Islam on native Berber tribes. In 788, 1st independent state was established by Idris I, enlarged by Idris II (founder of Fez). Its power was increased under the Almoravides and the Almohades (11th–13th cent.), great Berber dynasties which invaded the Iberian Peninsula, but declined under the Merinides (13th–15th cent.). European encroachments began 1415 with Port. capture of Ceuta, followed by occupation of all principal ports (except Melilla and Larache, which later went to Spain). Defeated (1578) by the Moors at the battle of Alcazarquivir, the Portuguese abandoned their last Moroccan stronghold in 1769. Meanwhile, under the threat of Christian invasions, power had passed to native religious leaders, who in 1549 established the Saadian, or 1st Sherifian dynasty. Their successors, the Alaouites (2d Sherifian dynasty) are still the ruling house of Morocco. Bet. 17th and 19th cent., coastal cities were pirate strongholds. Renewed European interest in Morocco dates from c.1850, when Tangier (Morocco's gateway) became a center of diplomatic activity. Interference by European powers (with the French in the forefront) was temporarily halted by the Convention of Madrid (1880), which guaranteed Morocco's territorial integrity but soon led to political and economic rivalries (the "Morocco question"); these, early in 20th cent. repeatedly threatened world peace. Climaxing events were the provocative debarkation of German emperor William II at Tangier (1905), U.S. intervention and the Algeciras conference (1906), and the Agadir incident (1911). French and Spanish protectorates over Morocco were established in 1912. Tangier was internationalized in 1923. **French Morocco,** occupying about 9/10 of sultanate's area, has long Atlantic coast line but a Mediterranean frontage of only 9 mi. squeezed bet. Sp. Morocco and Algeria. Except for Oujda region (E), economically tributary to W Algeria (its port is Nemours in Oran dept.), majority of protectorate's pop. lives in Atlantic coastal plains and plateaus where most of Morocco's arable land (10% of total land area) is found. The economy is based on agr. and mining. Chief crops are hard and soft wheat, barley (occupying largest acreage), and corn. Orchards produce olives, almonds, figs, citrus fruit, dates. Wine and vegetables are grown near coastal cities (especially bet. Casablanca and Mazagan), and in Meknès, Marrakesh, and Oujda areas. Tobacco, hemp, cotton, still in experimental stage, are dependent on irrigation. River-harnessing projects are in full development along OUM ER RBIA RIVER, its tributaries, and the Oued Beth (tributary of Sebou R.). Sheep and goats are grazed in the semi-arid pastures of E and S Morocco. Cattle raising is growing in coastal plains. Forests (occupying 10% of land area) yield cork (only the Iberian Peninsula and Algeria have larger stands), cabinetwood, building material, and pit props for mines. Sardines are canned chiefly at Safi and Agadir. Fr. Morocco has extensive and variegated mineral reserves. Phosphates, mined at Khouribga and Louis Gentil, are a state monopoly and Morocco's chief export item. They are shipped by rail to special loading docks at Casablanca and Safi. Fr. Morocco also has N Africa's leading hard-coal deposits (Djérada). Other minerals mined are iron (Aït Amar), manganese (Bou Arfa and Ouarzazate area), lead (Bou Beker and upper Moulouya valley near Midelt), molybdenum (Azegour), and cobalt (Bou Azzer); there are also scattered but important copper, zinc, and tin deposits. Petroleum has been found in Rharb lowland near Petitjean. Although industry (aside from handicraft mfg. of rugs, leather goods, native apparel, and headgear) dates only from establishment of Fr. protectorate, it is becoming important here. In Casablanca-Fédala area are modern factories producing building materials, superphosphates, textiles, and footwear; here, too, are most of the food-processing plants. The Atlantic coast has no natural harbors, but the French have built extensive port facilities, especially at CASABLANCA (which handles ¾ of foreign trade and all passenger traffic), FÉDALA, and SAFI; existing harbors have been improved at MAZAGAN, MOGADOR, and AGADIR. PORT-LYAUTEY is a river port on the lower Sebou. RABAT, the seat of the sultan of Morocco and of Fr. resident general, is no longer used as a seaport. Principal cities of the interior are Fez and Marrakesh, the traditional capitals of the sultanate, MEKNÈS (also the onetime residence of sultans), strategic TAZA, and OUJDA. Ouezzane and Moulay Idris are Moslem pilgrimage centers. A railroad links chief cities (from Marrakesh in S to Oujda and beyond to Algeria); rail spurs lead from mines to shipping ports. The Tangier-Fez RR meets this rail net at Petitjean. There are good roads, some of which cross the Atlas ranges to the edge of the Sahara. Fr. Morocco exports mineral and agr. produce (especially France) and imports fuel, staples, and machinery. The French resident general promulgates and executes a large body of laws issued in the form of edicts (*dahirs*) by the sultan. For administrative purposes, Fr. Morocco is divided into 7 regions named after their chief cities: Casablanca, Fez, Marrakesh, Meknès, Oujda, Rabat, and Agadir. Marshal Lyautey, 1st resident general (1912–25), began the economic development and was largely responsible for the pacification (completed 1934) of the fiercely independent Berber pop. During Second World War, Allied troops landed (Nov. 8, 1942) along the Atlantic coast, encountering brief resistance only at Casablanca. After the war, a nationalist movement supported by the sultan won (1947) an increased measure of self-govt. for Moroccans and the promise of accelerated economic reforms. In 1947, 266,133 Fr. citizens (including Algerians) resided in the protectorate. **Spanish Morocco,** a mountainous coastal strip (c.200 mi. long, 40 mi. wide) N of Fr. Morocco and extending from Lucus R. (W) to mouth of Moulouya R. (E), occupies a strategic position on S shore of the Strait of Gibraltar, and has a frontage of 270 mi. on the W Mediterranean and 60 mi. on the Atlantic. The border with Fr. Morocco along S slopes of the Rif Mts. dates from 1912 and is partially undefined (an earlier Sp. claim in 1902 that the area extended S to the Sebou was gradually whittled down). Agr., limited to a few coastal valleys in W, is insufficient for native pop. Chief crops are wheat, barley, sorghum, corn; wine, figs, almonds, and citrus fruit are also produced. Mineral deposits include iron, lead, antimony, graphite, and bentonite, but only iron is mined in commercial quantities (in Beni bu Ifrur area) and exported via Melilla. A hydroelectric plant is in Uad Lau valley. Only industries are fish processing and canning. Chief towns are TETUÁN (seat of Sp. high commissioner and of the khalifa representing sultan of Morocco), Larache, Alcazarquivir, Villa Nador, Arcila, and Villa Sanjurjo. Xauen is a Moslem holy city. Chief ports are Ceuta and Melilla (coastal enclaves directly under Sp. sovereignty). Tunny, sardines, canary seed, eggs, cattle, and skins are only non-mineral exports. A railroad links Ceuta with Tetuán and its port of Río Martín; a mining railway connects Segangan with Melilla; and the Tangier-Fez RR traverses W Sp. Morocco, touching Arcila and Alcazarquivir (spur to Larache). A road connects main towns (Tangier to Melilla), but the interior of the Rif remains largely inaccessible. In 1921, the Berbers of the Rif Mts. (Riffians) revolted under the leadership of Abd-el-Krim and dislodged Spaniards from most of Sp. Morocco. They were finally subdued 1926 by a joint Franco-Spanish expedition. Sp. Morocco was also the scene of a revolt of army officers against the Sp. republican govt. at beginning of Sp. civil war (1936). The international zone of Tangier was incorporated 1940 into Sp. Morocco, but returned 1945 to its pre-war status.

Morocco, town (pop. 1,141), Newton co., NW Ind., near Ill. line, 48 mi. S of Hammond, in agr. area; dairy products, grain. Settled 1833, laid out 1850, inc. 1890.

Morochata (mōrōchä'tä), town (pop. c.3,400), Cochabamba dept., W central Bolivia, 23 mi. WNW of Cochabamba, in Cordillera de Cochabamba, on road; alt. 10,151 ft.; barley, potatoes.

Morochno (mŭrôch'nŭ), Pol. *Moroczno* (môrôch'-nô), village (1939 pop. over 500), NW Rovno oblast, Ukrainian SSR, in Pripet Marshes, 20 mi. SSW of Pinsk; potatoes, flax; lumbering.

Morococala (mōrōkōkä'lä), village (pop. c.4,700), Oruro dept., W Bolivia, at S foot of Morococala peak (17,060 ft.; highest point of Cordillera de Azanaques), 29 mi. ESE of Oruro; alt. 14,760 ft. Tin-mining center.

Morococha (mōrōkō'chä), town (pop. 1,522), Junín dept., central Peru, in Cordillera Occidental, on spur of Lima–La Oroya RR and 16 mi. WSW of La Oroya; alt. c.15,000 ft. Copper-mining center, shipping ore to LA OROYA smelter.

Moro Creek (mô'rō), S Ark., rises in Dallas co. NW of Fordyce, flows c.65 mi. S to Ouachita R. 19 mi. NE of El Dorado.

Moroczno, Ukrainian SSR: see MOROCHNO.

Moroeni (môroi'nē), village, Prahova prov., S central Rumania, 20 mi. N of Targoviste and on Ialomita R. (hydroelectric station).

Morogoro (mōrōgō'rō), town (pop. c.8,000), Tanganyika, on railroad and 115 mi. W of Dar es Salaam; alt. 1,708 ft. Agr. center: sisal, cotton. Has experimental station for animal husbandry. Mica mines in Uluguru Mts. (S and E); graphite, uranium deposits; gold placers.

Moro Gulf (mō'rō), large inlet of Celebes Sea, Philippines, in S coast of W Mindanao; Sibuguey Bay opens W along Zamboanga Peninsula. Sulu Archipelago stretches to SW.

Moroleón (mōrōlāōn'), city (pop. 10,418), Guanajuato, central Mexico, on central plateau, 36 mi. SW of Celaya; alt. 5,932 ft. Agr. center (grain, sugar cane, fruit, livestock); mfg. (shoes, scarves, shawls).

Morolica (mōrōlē'kä), town (pop. 678), Choluteca dept., S Honduras, on Choluteca R. and 26 mi. NE of Choluteca; ceramics (bricks, tiles, pottery); dairying.

Morombe (mōōrōōm'bā), town, Tuléar prov., W Madagascar, on Mozambique Channel, 110 mi. NNW of Tuléar; cabotage port shipping corn, beans, rice, hides.

Moromoro (mōrōmō'rō). **1** Town, Potosí dept., Bolivia: see RAVELO. **2** Town (pop. c.6,100), Santa Cruz dept., central Bolivia, near Mizque R., 15 mi. NW of Valle Grande; corn, potatoes, barley.

Morón (mōrōn') or **Seis de Septiembre** (sās' dā sĕptyĕm'brā), city (pop. estimate 25,000), ⊙ Morón or Seis de Septiembre dist. (□ 50; pop. 110,968), in Greater Buenos Aires, Argentina, 14 mi. WSW of Buenos Aires; industrial center; meat packing, dairying, food canning, tanning; chocolate, chemicals, ceramics, leather goods; airplane factory. Horticulture; grain, alfalfa, livestock. Airport.

Morón, city (pop. 13,954), Camagüey prov., E Cuba, near N coast (Leche Lagoon), 65 mi. NW of Camagüey; rail junction, trading and processing center in rich agr. region (sugar cane, tobacco, cacao, coffee, fruit, cattle). Lumbering; mfg. of meat products. Airfield. Has several sugar mills in outskirts. Asphalt and chromium deposits near by.

Moron (môrō'), town (1950 pop. 1,139), Sud dept., SW Haiti, on W Tiburon Peninsula, 12 mi. SW of Jérémie; cacao, coffee.

Mörön, Mongolia: see MUREN, town.

Moron (mōrōn'), town (1939 pop. 1,593; 1948 municipality pop. 3,336), Bataan prov., S Luzon, Philippines, on S.China Sea, on W Bataan Peninsula, 50 mi. W of Manila; sugar cane, rice.

Morón or **Morón de la Frontera** (mōrōn', dhā lä frōntā'rä), city (pop. 19,177), Seville prov., S Spain, in Andalusia, in NW outliers of the Cordillera Penibética, near Guadaira R., 35 mi. ESE of Seville (linked by rail). Trading center for rich agr. region (olives, cereals, wine, livestock). Its leading industries are the mfg. of cement and ceramics based on large lime and gypsum quarries. Also produces liquor, olive oil, plaster, soap, esparto and woolen goods, shoes, furniture. The anc. city has ruins of a large Moorish castle destroyed (1811) by the French.

Moron (môrō'), mountain (4,395 ft.) in the Jura, NW Switzerland, 8 mi. N of Biel.

Morón (mōrōn'), town (pop. 1,049), Carabobo state, N Venezuela, near Caribbean coast, 14 mi. W of Puerto Cabello; coconuts, divi-divi.

Morona River (mōrō'nä), Ecuador and Peru, rises in E Andean foothills of Ecuador NE of Macas, flows c.260 mi. S to Marañón R. 25 mi. WNW of Barranca. Navigable for almost its whole course, it is communication line bet. Ecuador and Peru.

Morondava (mōōrōōndä'vŭ, mō–), town (1948 pop. 4,525), Tuléar prov., W Madagascar, on Mozambique Channel at mouth of Morondava R., 215 mi. N of Tuléar; seaport and commercial center. Exports beans, raphia, corn, rice. Rice milling, sawmilling. Has R.C. and Protestant missions, school for Europeans, meteorological station.

Morón de Almazán (mōrōn' dhā älmä-thän'), town (pop. 999), Soria prov., N central Spain, on railroad and 24 mi. S of Soria; cereals, chick-peas, live-stock, wool, timber; flour milling.

Morón de la Frontera, Spain: see MORÓN.

Morong (mō'rông), town (1939 pop. 1,771; 1948 municipality pop. 10,035), Rizal prov., S Luzon, Philippines, on Laguna de Bay, 18 mi. ESE of Manila; rice, sugar, fruit. Also called San Juan.

Moroni (mōrō'nē), main town (pop. c.6,000) of Grande Comore Isl., in Comoro Isls.; 11°42'S 43°23'E. Trading center and steamboat landing. Vanilla, cacao, coffee. Has numerous mosques, including "Chiounda," a pilgrimage center.

Moroni (mŭrō'nē), city (pop. 1,076), Sanpete co., central Utah, on San Pitch R., in irrigated Sanpete Valley, and 20 mi. N of Manti; alt. 5,520 ft. Turkey-raising center. Settled 1859 by Mormons, inc. 1866. Wasatch Range is E.

Moronvilliers Massif (môrõvēlyā' mäsēf'), in Marne dept., N France, 13 mi. E of and dominating Rheims; rises to 744 ft. Scene of heavy fighting (1917) in First World War.

Mororan, Japan: see MURORAN.

Moros (mō'rōs), village (pop. 1,307), Saragossa prov., NE Spain, 11 mi. NW of Calatayud; cereals, wine, fruit, livestock (horses, sheep).

Morosaglia (môrôzä'lyä), village (pop. 1,018), N central Corsica, 12 mi. NNE of Corte; Paoli b. and buried here. Rail junction of Ponte-Leccia, 5 mi. WNW on Golo R., produces tanning extracts.

Morotai (môrōtī'), island (□ c.700; pop. 7,833), N Moluccas, Indonesia, 15 mi. NE of Halmahera across Morotai Strait; 1°58'–2°40'N 128°15'–128°45'E; 50 mi. long, 25 mi. wide. Generally wooded and mountainous, rising to 3,575 ft.; low, swampy area in SW. Chief products: timber, resin, sago. Chief anchorage is Wayabula or Wajaboela (both: wīäbōō'lŭ) on W coast. Airfield is at Pitu or Pitoe (both: pĭ'tōō) on S coast; leper colony at Bidoho on E coast. In Second World War, isl. was Jap. air base taken (Sept., 1944) by Allied troops who met little resistance. Formerly sometimes Morty.

Moroto (mōrō'tō), town, Northern Prov., E Uganda, 120 mi. ENE of Lira, near Kenya border; agr. trade center (millet, beans, corn; cattle). Hq. Karamoja dist., inhabited by Hamitic Negro tribes. Mt. Moroto, just E, rises to 10,000 ft. Limestone and mica deposits near by.

Morova, Albania: see MORAVA.

Morovis (mōrō'vēs), town (pop. 2,433), N central Puerto Rico, 21 mi. WSW of San Juan, in sugar- and fruitgrowing region; alcohol distilling, tobacco stripping, mfg. of cigars. There are many caves with fossil remains in vicinity.

Moroyama (mōrō'yämŭ), town (pop. 7,396), Saitama prefecture, central Honshu, Japan, 10 mi. W of

Kawagoe; rice, wheat, raw silk. Formed in early 1940s by combining former villages of Moro and Yamane.

Morozaki (mōrō'zäkē), town (pop. 7,276), Aichi prefecture, central Honshu, Japan, on SE tip of Chita Peninsula, on Ise Bay, 14 mi. SSE of Handa; seaside resort; fishing. Offshore are several pine-clad islets.

Morozova, Imeni (ē'mĭnyē mŭrô'zŭvŭ), town (1939 pop. over 2,000), N Leningrad oblast, Russian SFSR, on Neva R. and 2 mi. SW of Petrokrepost; cotton milling, dyeing.

Morozovsk (mŭrô'zŭfsk), city (1926 pop. 12,418), E Rostov oblast, Russian SFSR, on railroad and 75 mi. E of Kamensk; industrial center; mfg. (agr. machinery, pistons, cylinders), flour milling. Became city in 1941.

Morpeth (môr'pŭth), town and river port, E New South Wales, Australia, on Hunter R. and 13 mi. NNW of Newcastle; coal-mining center.

Morpeth, municipal borough (1931 pop. 7,391; 1951 census 10,797), E central Northumberland, England, on Wansbeck R. and 14 mi. N of Newcastle-upon-Tyne; woolen mills, iron foundries; agr. market. Of its anc. castle, only a 14th-cent. gatehouse remains. Has 14th-cent. church; town hall (1714) built by Vanbrugh. In municipal borough (ENE) is town of Pegswood, with coal mines and brick- and tileworks.

Morphou (môr'fōō), town (pop. 5,460), Nicosia dist., NW Cyprus, 20 mi. W of Nicosia, linked by rail; agr. center in fertile Messaoria plain; wheat, barley, oats, citrus fruit, olive oil; sheep, hogs. Has an experimental farm. Near by (W) on Morphou Bay is a crushing and concentrating plant for pyrites, which are shipped from there. Has teachers training col. and agr. school.

Morral (mŏ'rŭl), village (pop. 461), Marion co., central Ohio, 8 mi. NW of Marion; foundry products, food products.

Morrelganj (mô'rŭlgŭnj), village, Khulna dist., SW East Bengal, E Pakistan, in the Sundarbans, on distributary of lower Madhumati (Baleswar) R. and 31 mi. SE of Khulna; trades in rice, jute, oilseeds, sugar cane. Also spelled Morelganj and Morrellganj.

Morretes (mōōrā'tĭs), city (pop. 2,015), SE Paraná, Brazil, 27 mi. E of Curitiba; rail junction (spur to Antonina); paper mfg., distilling; rice, bananas. Iron deposits.

Morrice (mô'rĭs, mŏ'–), village (pop. 501), Shiawassee co., S central Mich., 21 mi. NE of Lansing, in agr. area.

Morrill (mŏ'rŭl), county (□ 1,403; pop. 8,263), W Nebr.; ⊙ Bridgeport. Irrigated farm area drained by N.Platte R. and its branches. Sugar beets, beans, livestock, grain. Formed 1909.

Morrill. 1 City (pop. 362), Brown co., NE Kansas, 10 mi. NW of Hiawatha, near Nebr. line, in grain and livestock region (corn belt). **2** Town (pop. 306), Waldo co., S Maine, just W of Belfast, in agr., recreational area. **3** Village (pop. 849), Scotts Bluff co., W Nebr., 15 mi. WNW of Scottsbluff and on N.Platte R.; dairy produce, livestock, grain, sugar beets, potatoes.

Morrilton (mŏ'rŭltŭn), city (pop. 5,483), ⊙ Conway co., central Ark., 40 mi. NW of Little Rock, and on Arkansas R. (here bridged), in stock-raising and cotton-growing area; cotton mill; sawmilling, dairying, cottonseed-oil milling, meat packing. Petit Jean State Park is near by, on Petit Jean Mtn. Founded in 1870s.

Morrin, village (pop. 177), S Alta., 14 mi. N of Drumheller; wheat.

Morrinhos (mōōrē'nyōōs), city (pop. 3,163), S Goiás, central Brazil, 75 mi. S of Goiânia; cattle, tobacco, rice, coffee. Rutile deposits.

Morrinsville, borough (pop. 2,175), N N.Isl., New Zealand, 70 mi. SSE of Auckland; corn, sheep, dairy products.

Morris (Fr. mōrēs'), village (pop. 1,666), Constantine dept., NE Algeria, in coastal lowland, 12 mi. SE of Bône; cereals, olives.

Morris, town (pop. 920), S Man., on Red R., at mouth of small Morris R., and 40 mi. SSW of Winnipeg; grain elevators; stock raising, dairying; oil-distributing point.

Morris. 1 County (□ 707; pop. 8,485), E central Kansas; ⊙ Council Grove. Rolling plain region, watered by Neosho R. Livestock, grain. Formed 1859. **2** County (□ 468; pop. 164,371), N N.J., bounded SE and E by Passaic R.; ⊙ Morristown. Hilly estate and resort area, with many lakes and mtn. ridges. Dairying, agr. (fruit, truck), nurseries; mfg. (electrical, electronic, and radar equipment, metal products, machinery, explosives, chemicals, rubber goods, clothing, wood products); iron mines. Drained by Pequannock, Rockaway, Whippany, and Musconetcong rivers, and branches of Raritan R.; includes Morristown Natl. Historical Park and part of L. Hopatcong. Formed 1739. **3** County (□ 263; pop. 9,433), NE Texas; ⊙ Daingerfield. Bounded N by Sulphur R., S by Cypress Bayou. Diversified agr., livestock; cotton, corn, peanuts, fruit, vegetables, cattle, hogs, dairy products. Iron deposits; pig-iron production. Lumbering (mainly pine). Formed 1875.

Morris. 1 Resort town (pop. 799), Litchfield co., W Conn., on Bantam L. and 10 mi. SW of Torrington; dairying. Includes Lakeside (resort village), part of state park, game sanctuary. **2** City (pop. 6,926), ⊙ Grundy co., NE Ill., on Illinois R. and 21 mi. SW of Joliet; shipping and industrial center in agr., bituminous-coal, and clay area; mfg. (paper, food products, beverages, leather and limestone products, egg cartons, vending machines). Platted 1842, inc. 1853. Near by is Gebhard Woods State Park (30 acres) along old Illinois and Michigan Canal Parkway. **3** City (pop. 3,811), ⊙ Stevens co., W Minn., on Pomme de Terre R. and c.50 mi. NW of Willmar; dairy products, flour, beverages. School of agr. and experiment station are here. State park near by. Platted 1869, inc. as village 1878, as city 1903. **4** Village (pop. 641), Otsego co., central N.Y., 13 mi. NW of Oneonta, in dairying and poultry-raising area; mfg. (chemicals, furniture, farm machinery). Gilbert Lake State Park is c.5 mi. NE. **5** City (pop. 1,122), Okmulgee co., E central Okla., 6 mi. E of Okmulgee, in oil-producing and coal-mining area; cotton ginning, flour and feed milling.

Morrisania (mŏrĭsā'nyŭ), SE N.Y., a residential section of S Bronx borough of New York city.

Morrisburg, village (pop. 1,575), SE Ont., on the St. Lawrence (rapids, by-passed by Rapide Plat Canal) and 24 mi. WSW of Cornwall; mfg. of stoves, sheet-metal products, brushes, agr. implements; dairying; resort. Ferry to Waddington, N.Y.

Morris Canal, N.J., abandoned canal (c.100 mi. long) joining Delaware R. at Phillipsburg and Newark Bay at Newark. Chartered 1824 as outlet for Pa. coal regions; opened 1831; extended to Jersey City, 1836; declined after peak traffic in 1860s; finally abandoned 1923. Bed at Newark utilized for subway (1935).

Morrisdale, village (1940 pop. 960), Clearfield co., central Pa., 12 mi. SE of Clearfield, in bituminous-coal area.

Morris Dam, Calif.: see SAN GABRIEL RIVER.

Morris Island, Charleston co., S S.C., an island (c.3.5 mi. long) of Sea Isls. at S side of entrance to Charleston Harbor; Charleston lighthouse on S tip (32°41'N 79°53'W).

Morris Jesup or **Morris K. Jesup, Cape,** world's northernmost point of land, at N extremity of Greenland, in Peary Land region, on Arctic Ocean, 440 mi. from North Pole; 83°39'N 34°12'W. Charted by Peary, 1892.

Morrison, town (pop. 2,505), E central Córdoba prov., Argentina, 28 mi. SE of Villa María; wheat, flax, corn, alfalfa, livestock.

Morrison, county (□ 1,136; pop. 25,832), central Minn.; ⊙ Little Falls. Agr. area drained by Mississippi R. Dairy products, livestock, grain; deposits of marl and peat. L. Alexander in NW. Co. formed 1855.

Morrison. 1 Town (pop. 306), Jefferson co., N central Colo., on branch of S.Platte R., just E of Front Range, and 10 mi. SW of Denver; alt. 5,669 ft. Resort; entrance to Denver mtn. park system. State industrial school for girls near by. Formerly Mt. Morrison. **2** City (pop. 3,531), ⊙ Whiteside co., NW Ill., on Rock Creek (bridged here) and 12 mi. E of Clinton (Iowa), in farming and dairying area; limestone quarries; mfg. (dairy products, refrigerators). Founded 1855, inc. 1867. **3** Town (pop. 169), Grundy co., central Iowa, 20 mi. WSW of Waterloo, in agr. area. **4** Town (pop. 291), Gasconade co., E central Mo., on Missouri R., at mouth of Gasconade R., and 7 mi. W of Hermann. **5** Town (pop. 297), Noble co., N Okla., 12 mi. NNE of Stillwater, in agr. area (grain, cotton, livestock; dairy products); cotton ginning. **6** Town (pop. 301), Warren co., central Tenn., 10 mi. SW of McMinnville. **7** Village (pop. 2,357), Warwick co., SE Va., 5 mi. NW of Newport News.

Morrison, Mount, Chinese *Sinkao Shan* or *Hsin-Kao Shan* (both: shĭn'gou' shän'), Jap. *Niitaka-yama* (nē'täkä-yä'mä), highest peak (13–14,000 ft.) of Formosa, in central range, 33 mi. E of Kiayi. First ascended in 1896 by Japanese. Until 1903 its Chinese name was *Yü Shan*, its Japanese name *Gyoku-zan*.

Morrison Cave State Park, SW Mont., recreational area in canyon of Jefferson R., 34 mi. ESE of Butte; includes large cave consisting of underground passages and chambers fretted with stalactites and stalagmites. Formerly known as Lewis and Clark Cavern Natl. Monument.

Morrison City, village, Sullivan co., NE Tenn., just N of Kingsport.

Morrisonville. 1 Village (pop. 1,182), Christian co., central Ill., 26 mi. SSE of Springfield; agr. (grain, livestock); soybean products. Inc. 1872. **2** Village (1940 pop. 725), Clinton co., extreme NE N.Y., on Saranac R. and 5 mi. W of Plattsburg.

Morris Plains, residential borough (pop. 2,707), Morris co., N N.J., just N of Morristown; coffee processing; crushed stone. State mental hosp. (1871) near by. Inc. 1926.

Morris Run, village (1940 pop. 846), Tioga co., N Pa., 31 mi. N of Williamsport, in bituminous-coal area.

Morriston, Wales: see SWANSEA.

Morristown. 1 Town (pop. 679), Shelby co., central Ind., on Big Blue R. and 26 mi. ESE of Indianapolis, in agr. area; toys, canned goods. **2** Village (pop. 533), Rice co., S Minn., on Cannon R. and 10 mi. WSW of Faribault, in grain, livestock, poultry area; dairy products, feed. **3** Residential town (pop. 17,124), ⊙ Morris co., N N.J., on Whippany R. and 17 mi. WNW of Newark, in hilly region; mfg. (electrical products, clothing, paving materials, umbrellas, metal products); greenhouses, stone quarries. Settled c.1710, inc. 1865; produced iron during American Revolution. Washington made his winter hq. here, 1776–77 and 1779–80. Morristown Natl. Historical Park (958.4 acres; established 1933) includes Ford house (completed 1774; Washington's hq. 1779–80; partially restored), reconstructed Fort Nonsense (built 1777), camp buildings used by Continental Army, and other historic sites. Historical mus. (opened 1938) contains relics of period. Other points of interest: Jabez Campfield house (now owned by D.A.R.), where Hamilton courted Elizabeth Schuyler; courthouse (1826); municipal building, built 1918 as home and mus. of Theodore N. Vail. Seeing Eye establishment for training guide dogs for the blind is near by. S. F. B. Morse, Alfred Vail, Thomas Nast, Bret Harte, Frank R. Stockton lived here. **4** Village (pop. 546), St. Lawrence co., N N.Y., on the St. Lawrence, opposite Brockville, Ont. (ferry), and 12 mi. SW of Ogdensburg; summer resort (fishing); port of entry. **5** Village (pop. 404), Belmont co., E Ohio, 28 mi. E of Cambridge, in coal-mining area. **6** Town (pop. 190), Corson co., N S.Dak., 18 mi. W of McIntosh and on N.Dak. line; supply point for ranching region; dairy produce, livestock, grain. **7** City (pop. 13,019), ⊙ Hamblen co., NE Tenn., 40 mi. ENE of Knoxville. An important tobacco, poultry, and dairy center; mfg. of wood products, hosiery, textiles, dairy products, canned vegetables; seat of Morristown Normal and Industrial Col. Cherokee Reservoir (Holston R.) is N; state fish hatchery near by. Settled 1783, inc. 1855. **8** Town (pop. 3,225), Lamoille co., N central Vt., on Lamoille R. and 20 mi. N of Montpelier, in agr., lumbering region. Includes MORRISVILLE village. Chartered 1781.

Morrisville. 1 Town (pop. 296), Polk co., central Mo., in the Ozarks, near Little Sac R., 20 mi. N of Springfield. **2** Village (pop. 1,250), Madison co., central N.Y., 28 mi. ESE of Syracuse, in dairying area. A state agr. and technical institute is here. **3** Town (pop. 221), Wake co., central N.C., 10 mi. W of Raleigh. **4** Borough (pop. 6,787), Bucks co., SE Pa., on Delaware R. opposite Trenton, N.J. Construction of one of largest U.S. steel plants was begun here 1951; plant includes blast and open-hearth furnaces, rolling, tinning, and pipe mills, coke plants, and ore docks on the Delaware. Near by is Pennsbury, William Penn's manor (reconstructed). Inc. 1804. **5** Village (pop. 1,995) in MORRISTOWN town, Lamoille co., N central Vt.; wood and metal products, machinery; lumber, dairy products; granite. Winter sports.

Morrito or **El Morrito** (ĕl mōrē'tō), town (1950 pop. 387), Río San Juan dept., S Nicaragua, port on E shore of L. Nicaragua, 40 mi. SE of Juigalpa; lumbering; livestock.

Mor River (mōr), in Bihar and West Bengal, India, rises in NE Chota Nagpur Plateau foothills, in headstreams joining 5 mi. NNW of Dumka; flows SE, past Dumka, Masanjor, and Sainthia, and E to Dwarka R. (tributary of the Bhagirathi) 7 mi. E of Kandi; length, c.100 mi. Also called Morakhi. Irrigation project consists of dam at Masanjor (impounding reservoir bet. Masanjor and Dumka) and barrage near Suri to supply canal system of c.630 mi. Project mainly benefits Birbhum and Murshidabad dists.

Morro (mô'rō), village, Guayas prov., SW Ecuador, in lowlands near Gulf of Guayaquil, 40 mi. SW of Guayaquil; has beaches near by and serves as fishing base.

Morro, El, Argentina: see EL MORRO.

Morro, El, Venezuela: see EL MORRO.

Morro Agudo (mô'rōō ägōō'dōō), city (pop. 1,756), N São Paulo, Brazil, 35 mi. NNW of Ribeirão Prêto; rail-spur terminus; pottery mfg., rice processing; coffee, corn, rice.

Morro Bay (mô'rō, mŏ'–), resort village (pop. 1,659), San Luis Obispo co., SW Calif., 12 mi. NW of San Luis Obispo, on landlocked Morro Bay (an inlet of Estero Bay), guarded by Morro Rock (576 ft.). State park.

Morro Castle (mô'rō, mŏ'–). **1** Fort at entrance to Havana Harbor, W Cuba; built in late 16th cent. as protection against buccaneers. Captured 1762 by the British under Pocock. **2** Fort at Santiago de Cuba, E Cuba; built shortly after the fort at Havana; taken 1898 by U.S. forces in Spanish-American War.

Morro Castle, fort at harbor of San Juan, Puerto Rico.

Morro Channel (mô'rō), off coast of Guayas prov., SW Ecuador, W of Puná Isl., linking Gulf of Guayaquil with Guayas R. estuary; c.25 mi. long.

Morro Chico (mô'rō chē'kō), village (1930 pop. 28), Magallanes prov., S Chile, on Patagonian mainland, 85 mi. NNW of Punta Arenas; resort.

Morro da Mina, Brazil: see CONSELHEIRO LAFAIETE.

Morro do Chapéu (mô'rōō dōō shŭpĕ'ōō), city

(pop. 1,187), central Bahia, Brazil, on the Chapada Diamantina, 50 mi. SW of Jacobina; diamond mining; nitrate deposits. Has noteworthy church. Formerly spelled Morro do Chapéo.

Morro do Urucum, Brazil: see CORUMBÁ, Mato Grosso.

Morro Grande, Brazil: see BARÃO DE COCAIS.

Morrone del Sannio (môr-rō'nĕ dĕl sän'nyô), village (pop. 3,055), Campobasso prov., Abruzzi e Molise, S central Italy, 12 mi. NE of Campobasso.

Mórrope (mô'rōpā), town (pop. 1,058), Lambayeque dept., NW Peru, on coastal plain, on S edge of Mórrope Desert, on Mórrope R. and 13 mi. NW of Lambayeque; salt mining, agr. products (corn, alfalfa).

Mórrope Desert, Lambayeque dept., NW Peru, on coastal plain, just NW of Leche River and the town of Mórrope; 40 mi. long, 35 mi. wide. It is continued by SECHURA DESERT (NW) and OLMOS DESERT (NE). Salt mining.

Mórrope River, Peru: see LECHE RIVER.

Morropón, province, Peru: see CHULUCANAS.

Morropón (môrōpōn'), town (pop. 3,909), Piura dept., NW Peru, in irrigated Piura R. valley, 15 mi. ESE of Chulucanas; trade center in rice region; cattle raising.

Morro River, Sierra Leone and Liberia: see MANO RIVER.

Morros (mô'rōōs), city (pop. 1,498), N Maranhão, Brazil, head of navigation on Monim R. and 38 mi. SE of São Luís; cotton, sugar, rice.

Morros Point (mô'rōs), headland on coast of Campeche, SE Mexico, on W Yucatan Peninsula, 15 mi. SW of Campeche; 19°41'N 90°42'W.

Morrosquillo, Gulf of (môrōskē'yō), inlet of Caribbean Sea in Bolívar dept., N Colombia; 20 mi. long from San Bernardo Point to mouth of Sinú R., c.8 mi. wide. Ports: Tolú and Coveñas.

Morro Velho, gold mine, Brazil: see NOVA LIMA.

Morrow. 1 County (□ 404; pop. 17,168), central Ohio; ⊙ Mount Gilead. Drained by Kokosing R. and small Whetstone and Big Walnut creeks. Agr. area (livestock, dairy products, grain, fruit, soybeans); mfg. at Mount Gilead and Cardington. Formed 1848. **2** County (□ 2,059; pop. 4,783), N Oregon; ⊙ Heppner. Bounded N by Columbia R. and Wash.; Blue Mts. in S. Grain, livestock. Formed 1885. Part of Umatilla Nat. Forest in SE.

Morrow. 1 Town (pop. 326), Clayton co., NW central Ga., 12 mi. S of Atlanta. **2** Village (pop. 1,137), Warren co., SW Ohio, 27 mi. NE of Cincinnati and on Little Miami R.; makes furniture. Rock quarries; timber.

Morrowville, city (pop. 229), Washington co., N Kansas, 7 mi. WNW of Washington; grain, livestock.

Morrum (mû'rŭm"), Swedish *Mörrum*, village (pop. 1,125), Blekinge co., S Sweden, on Morrum R. and 5 mi. W of Karlshamn; salmon fishing, canning.

Morrumbala (mōrōōmbä'lä), village, Zambézia prov., central Mozambique, 95 mi. WNW of Quelimane; cotton, rice.

Morrumbene (mōrōōmbĕ'nā), village, Sul do Save prov., SE Mozambique, small port on Mozambique Channel, 15 mi. N of Inhambane; copra; fishing.

Morrum River, Swedish *Mörrumsån* (mû'rŭms-ōn"), S Sweden, rises E of Varnamo, flows 80 mi. S, past Alvesta and Ryd, to the Baltic 4 mi. W of Karlshamn. Salmon fishing.

Mors (môrs), island (□ 140; pop. 26,988), largest in Lim Fjord, NW Jutland, Denmark; c.10 mi. wide, 23 mi. long; highest point, 289 ft. Fertile soil (agr.); oyster fisheries. Nykobing is chief city.

Mörs, Germany: see MOERS.

Morsang-sur-Orge (môrsā'-sür-ôrzh'), town (pop. 3,533), Seine-et-Oise dept., N central France, 13 mi. S of Paris.

Morsbach (môrs'bäkh), village (pop. 6,773), in former Prussian Rhine Prov., W Germany, after 1945 in North Rhine-Westphalia, 13 mi. W of Siegen; forestry.

Morsbronn-les-Bains (môrzbrôn'-lā-bē'), village (pop. 493), Bas-Rhin dept., E France, 6 mi. NNW of Haguenau; mineral springs. Scene of fighting (1870) in Franco-Prussian War.

Mörsch (mûrsh), village (pop. 4,151), N Baden, Germany, after 1945 in Württemberg-Baden, 5 mi. SW of Karlsruhe; asparagus, strawberries.

Morschach (môr'shäkh), village (pop. 591), Schwyz canton, central Switzerland, near L. of Uri, 3 mi. SW of Schwyz; health resort (alt. 2,116 ft.).

Morschwiller-le-Bas (môrshvēlâr'-lŭ-bä'), Ger. *Niedermorschweiler* (nē'dûrmôrsh'vīlûr), outer WSW suburb (pop. 1,637) of Mulhouse, Haut-Rhin dept., E France; chemical plant (utilizing local potash).

Morse, town (pop. 351), S Sask., 35 mi. ENE of Swift Current; grain elevators, lumbering.

Morse, village (pop. 679), Acadia parish, S La., 10 mi. SW of Crowley, in agr. area; sawmill.

Morse Bluff, village (pop. 142), Saunders co., E Nebr., 45 mi. WNW of Omaha and on Platte R.

Morshansk (mŭrshänsk'), city (1926 pop. 27,779), NE Tambov oblast, Russian SFSR, on Tsna R. (landing) and 50 mi. NNE of Tambov; woolen milling (coarse cloths), lumber milling (rosin production), tobacco processing, glass- and metal-working. Teachers col. City chartered 1779.

Morshin (môr'shĭn), Pol. *Morszyn* (môr'shĭn), town (1931 pop. 400), E Drogobych oblast, Ukrainian SSR, 7 mi. S of Stry, in coniferous woodland; health resort with mineral springs. Potassium deposits near by.

Morsi (mōr'sē), town (pop. 10,580), Amraoti dist., W Madhya Pradesh, India, 32 mi. NNE of Amraoti; trades in cotton, millet, wheat, oilseeds.

Morsil (mûr'sĭl"), Swedish *Mörsil*, village (pop. 838), Jamtland co., NW Sweden, on Jarp R., Swedish *Järpström* (yĕrp'strûm") (falls), tributary of Indal R., 30 mi. WNW of Ostersund; health resort, with sanitarium. Pulp mills, hydroelectric station. Includes Aggfors (ĕg"fôrs',-fôsh'), Swedish *Äggfors*.

Morsum (môr'zōōm), village (pop. 936), in Schleswig-Holstein, NW Germany, on Sylt isl., 6 mi. SE of Westerland, near W end of Hindenburgdamm.

Morszyn, Ukrainian SSR: see MORSHIN.

Mortagne (môrtä'nyŭ). **1** or **Mortagne-au-Perche** (-ō-pârsh'), town (pop. 3,042), Orne dept., NW France, in the Perche hills, 22 mi. ENE of Alençon; market for Percheron horses bred in area. Has restored 15th-16th-cent. church with 18th-cent. woodwork. **2** or **Mortagne-sur-Sèvre** (-sür-sĕ'vrŭ), village (pop. 1,868), Vendée dept., W France, on Sèvre Nantaise R. and 5 mi. SSW of Cholet; rail junction; textile milling, footwear mfg. Mineral springs.

Mortagne-au-Perche, Orne dept., France: see MORTAGNE.

Mortagne-du-Nord (-dü-nôr'), village (pop. 1,313), Nord dept., N France, frontier station on Belg. border 8 mi. SSE of Tournai, on the Escaut at mouth of the Scarpe; boatbuilding, mfg. of refractories.

Mortagne River, Vosges and Meurthe-et-Moselle depts., NE France, rises above Brouvelieures, flows c.30 mi. NW, past Rambervillers and Gerbéviller, to the Meurthe 4 mi. below Lunéville.

Mortagne-sur-Gironde (-sür-zhērōd'), village (pop. 686), Charente-Maritime dept., W France, near the Gironde, 17 mi. W of Jonzac; flour milling. Has small port and naval station (1 mi. SW).

Mortagne-sur-Sèvre, France: see MORTAGNE.

Mortágua (mōōrtä'gwŭ), town (pop. 593), Viseu dist., N central Portugal, on railroad and 18 mi. NE of Coimbra; wool milling, pottery mfg.

Mortain (môrtē'), village (pop. 904), Manche dept., NW France, in Normandy Hills, 19 mi. E of Avranches; iron mines. The 11th–13th-cent. Abbaye Blanche (now housing seminary) is 1 mi. N near a waterfall. Severely damaged in Second World War.

Mortara (môrtä'rä), town (pop. 8,913), Pavia prov., Lombardy, N Italy, 21 mi. WNW of Pavia; rail junction; agr. center. Chief town of the LOMELLINA; dairy products; mfg. (rice mill machinery, textiles, hats, buttons). Has church built 1375–80. Near by is 5th-cent. abbey (rebuilt 8th and 16th cent.).

Morteau (môrtō'), town (pop. 4,086), Doubs dept., E France, on the Doubs and 15 mi. NE of Pontarlier, near Swiss border; industrial center and resort in the E Jura; custom station; produces watches, cutlery, bicycle parts, sewing machines. Brewing, sawmilling, chocolate mfg. The falls of the Doubs (Saut du Doubs) are 6 mi. ENE.

Morteaux-Couliboeuf (môrtō'-kōōlēbûf'), commune (pop. 654), Calvados dept., NW France, on the Dives and 6 mi. NE of Falaise; cheese mfg.

Mortegliano (môrtēlyä'nô), town (pop. 3,267), Udine prov., Friuli–Venezia Giulia, NE Italy, 8 mi. SSW of Udine; wax industry.

Mortehoe (môrt'hō), fishing village and parish (pop. 1,164), N Devon, England, on Bristol Channel, and 5 mi. WSW of Ilfracombe. Has 15th-cent. church. Morte Point, 800-ft.-high promontory, is near by.

Morter (môrtĕr'), village (pop. 520), Bolzano prov., Trentino–Alto Adige, N Italy, in Val Venosta, 17 mi. WSW of Merano; marble quarries.

Morter, island, Yugoslavia: see MURTER ISLAND.

Morteratsch, Piz (pēts môr'tûräch), Alpine peak (12,315 ft.) in Upper Engadine, SE Switzerland, 8 mi. SSE of St. Moritz. **Morteratsch Glacier** descends N from Ital. line E of Piz Bernina and Piz Morteratsch to Bernina R.; one of Switzerland's largest glaciers.

Morteros (môrtā'rōs), town (pop. 6,027), NE Córdoba prov., Argentina, 50 mi. N of San Francisco; agr. and industrial center; mfg. of agr. machinery, shoes, dairy products; alfalfa, grain, livestock.

Mortes, Rio das (rē'ōō däs môr'tĭs), river in central Mato Grosso, Brazil, rises E of Cuiabá, flows 450 mi. ENE and NNE to the Araguaia (Goiás border) near 12°S. Diamond washings. Also called Rio Manso.

Mort-Homme, Le, France: see CUMIÈRES-LE-MORT-HOMME.

Mortier (môrtyā'), agr. village (pop. 701), Liége prov., E Belgium, 8 mi. ENE of Liége.

Mortimer, town (pop. 13), Caldwell co., W central N.C., 14 mi. WNW of Lenoir.

Mortlach (môrt'lăk), town (pop. 255), S Sask., 23 mi. W of Moose Jaw; wheat.

Mortlach (môrtlăkh'), agr. village and parish, central Banffshire, Scotland, just S of Dufftown. Has 12th-cent. church (rebuilt). Formerly a bishopric.

Mortlake (môrt'lāk), town (pop. 976), S Victoria, Australia, 115 mi. WSW of Melbourne; rail terminus; sheep.

Mortlake, parish in BARNES municipal borough, N Surrey, England, on the Thames and 7 mi. WSW of London. Terminus of Oxford-Cambridge boat races, which begin at Putney. Tapestry industry for which Mortlake was once famous established by James I. Has 15th-cent. church.

Mortlock Island, Solomon Isls.: see TAKU.

Mortlock Islands, Caroline Isls.: see NOMOI ISLANDS.

Morton. 1 Town and parish (pop. 1,388), E central Derby, England, 7 mi. S of Chesterfield; coal mining. **2** Residential town and parish (pop. 975), Parts of Lindsey, NW Lincolnshire, England, on Trent R. and 2 mi. NNW of Gainsborough; pharmaceuticals.

Morton, Scotland: see THORNHILL.

Morton. 1 County (□ 725; pop. 2,610), extreme SW Kansas; ⊙ Richfield. Rolling plain, bordered W by Colo. and S by Okla.; drained by Cimarron R. Wheat and grain sorghums. Gas field in E. Formed 1886. **2** County (□ 1,933; pop. 19,295), central N.Dak.; ⊙ Mandan. Agr. area drained by Muddy Creek and Heart R.; bounded E by Missouri R. Mfg., diversified farming, livestock, poultry, grain. Formed 1873.

Morton. 1 Village (pop. 3,693), Tazewell co., central Ill., 10 mi. SE of Peoria, in agr. and bituminous-coal area; corn, wheat, soybeans, livestock, poultry; mfg. (dairy and food products, washing machines, fencing, pottery). Inc. 1877. **2** Village (pop. 794), Renville co., SW Minn., on Minnesota R. and 7 mi. E of Redwood Falls, in grain and potato area. Near by are Sioux Indian reservation and Birch Coulee State Park, set aside in commemoration of battle with Sioux Indians during uprising of 1862. **3** Town (pop. 1,664), Scott co., central Miss., 32 mi. E of Jackson, in Bienville Natl. Forest; lumber milling. Roosevelt State Park is near by. **4** Borough (pop. 1,352), Delaware co., SE Pa., 9 mi. SW of Philadelphia; metal products. Inc. 1898. **5** Town (pop. 2,274), ⊙ Cochran co., NW Texas, on the Llano Estacado, c.55 mi. W of Lubbock; shipping, storage, trade center for agr. and cattle-ranching area (cotton, grain, poultry). Oil refinery. Inc. 1934. **6** Lumbering town (pop. 1,140), Lewis co., SW Wash., 34 mi. E of Chehalis; agr., dairying.

Morton, Cape, Greenland: see WASHINGTON LAND.

Morton Grove, village (pop. 3,926), Cook co., NE Ill., N suburb of Chicago, 5 mi. W of Evanston. Inc. 1895.

Mortons Gap, town (pop. 1,081), Hopkins co., W Ky., 7 mi. S of Madisonville, in coal-mining, agr., and timber area; sawmill.

Mortrée (môrtrā'), village (pop. 426), Orne dept., NW France, 9 mi. SE of Argentan; horse raising.

Mortsel (môrt'sŭl), town (pop. 17,052), Antwerp prov., N Belgium, 3 mi. SE of Antwerp; mfg. of photography products.

Morty (môr'tē), village (1939 pop. over 2,000), N Tatar Autonomous SSR, Russian SFSR, 13 mi. W of Yelabuga; grain, livestock.

Moru, district, Anglo-Egyptian Sudan: see AMADI.

Moruga (mōrōō'gŭ), village, S Trinidad, B.W.I., 18 mi. SE of San Fernando, in cacao- and coconut-growing region; beach.

Moruppatti or **Morupatti** (mō'rōōpŭt-tē), town (pop., including Mettuppalaiyam or Mettupalayam, 6,005), Trichinopoly dist., S Madras, India, 30 mi. NW of Trichinopoly; cotton weaving; sheep grazing. Magnetite deposits in Pachaimalai Hills (N). Sometimes spelled Marupatti.

Moruya (mŭrōō'yŭ), town (pop. 736), SE New South Wales, Australia, 70 mi. SE of Canberra; dairying and agr. center. Arsenic ore and gold are mined near by.

Morvan (môrvā'), northernmost spur of the Massif Central, E central France, in Nièvre. Saône-et-Loire, Yonne, and Côte-d'Or depts., reaching to S edge of Paris Basin. Anc. crystalline massif with rounded summits rising to 2,959 ft. at the Bois-du-Roi, and to 2,657 ft. at Mont BEUVRAY. Heavily forested area with infertile soil. Cattle raising, lumbering, charcoal mfg. Sparsely populated, with chief towns (Autun, Saulieu, Avallon, Clamecy, Château-Chinon) on perimeter. Yonne, Serein, and Cure rivers rise here.

Morvant (môr'vănt"), village (pop. 3,211), NW Trinidad, B.W.I., 1½ mi. E of Port of Spain, in coconut and citrus-fruit region; sawmilling. Has new housing development.

Morven (môr'vŭn). **1** Mountain (2,862 ft.) of the Grampians, SW Aberdeen, Scotland, 5 mi. N of Ballater. **2** Mountain (2,313 ft.) in SW Caithness, Scotland, 9 mi. N of Gelmsdale; highest elevation of co. It is celebrated in poems by Ossian.

Morven, mountainous district and peninsula, NW Argyll, Scotland, bounded by the Sound of Mull (SW), Loch Sunart (N), and Loch Linnhe (SE); c.25 mi. long, 14 mi. wide.

Morven. 1 Town (pop. 474), Brooks co., S Ga., 16 mi. WNW of Valdosta, in agr. area. **2** Town (pop. 601), Anson co., S N.C., 8 mi. SSE of Wadesboro.

Morvi (mōr′vē), town (pop. 37,048), N Saurashtra, India, on Kathiawar peninsula, 35 mi. N of Rajkot; trade center (cotton, millet, salt, ghee, wool); cotton ginning and milling, mfg. of pottery, matches, shoes, paint, bone fertilizer; glass- and metalworks; airport. Technical institute. Was ⊙ former princely state of Morvi (□ 822; pop. 141,761) of Western India States agency; state merged 1948 with Saurashtra.

Morvillars (môrvēyär′), village (pop. 630), Territory of Belfort, E France, near Rhone-Rhine Canal, 7 mi. SSE of Belfort; forges.

Morwell, town (pop. 2,951), S Victoria, Australia, 85 mi. ESE of Melbourne; rail junction; coal-mining center.

Morwenstow (môr′wŭntstō), village and parish (pop. 584), NE Cornwall, England, on the Atlantic and 6 mi. N of Bude. Has Norman church.

Moryakovski Zaton or **Moryakovskiy Zaton** (mŭryä′kŭfskē zŭtôn′), town (1948 pop. over 2,000), SE Tomsk oblast, Russian SFSR, on Tom R. and 18 mi. NNW of Tomsk; ship repair yards; sawmilling.

Moryn (mô′rĭnyŭ), Pol. *Moryń*, Ger. *Mohrin* (mō′rĭn), town (1939 pop. 1,227; 1946 pop. 440) in Brandenburg, after 1945 in Szczecin prov., NW Poland, 20 mi. NNW of Küstrin (Kostrzyn); grain, potatoes, vegetables, stock. Ruins of old town walls.

Morzhovoi (môr-shō′vē), village (1939 pop. 17), SW Alaska, on SW Alaska Peninsula, on narrow strait bet. the Pacific and Bering Sea, opposite Unimak Isl.; 54°55′N 163°18′W. Native pop. works in near-by canneries during summer.

Morzine (môrzēn′), village (pop. 224), Haute-Savoie dept., SE France, on Dranse R. and 17 mi. SE of Thonon-les-Bains, in the Chablais; alt. 3,150 ft. Winter-sport resort.

Mosa, France, Belgium, Netherlands: see MEUSE RIVER.

Mosaboni or **Musabani** (both: mōsä′bŭnē), town (pop. 8,270), Singhbhum dist., SE Bihar, India, near Subarnarekha R., 25 mi. SE of Jamshedpur; copper-mining center; major copper-smelting plant. Also spelled Mushabani. Cyanite mining 5 mi. NNE, near Ghatsila.

Mosalsk or **Mosal'sk** (mŭsälsk′), city (1926 pop. 2,306), W Kaluga oblast, Russian SFSR, 50 mi. W of Kaluga, in orchard region; fruit canning (jams). Chartered 1231; passed (16th cent.) to Moscow.

Mosan, Korea: see MUSAN.

Mosbach (mōs′bäkh), town (pop. 8,384), N Baden, Germany, after 1945 in Württemberg-Baden, 21 mi. ESE of Heidelberg; mfg. of small locomotives. Has 16th-cent. town hall; old frame houses.

Mosbas or **Mosbass,** Russian SFSR: see MOSCOW BASIN.

Mosby (mōs′bü), village (pop. 653), in Oddernes canton (pop. 6,513), Vest-Agder co., S Norway, on the Otra, on railroad and 6 mi. NNW of Kristiansand; mfg. of cotton and rayon textiles. Has forestry school. Includes villages of Ovre Mosby (ûv′rŭ), Nor. *Øvre Mosby* (pop. 420), and Ytre Mosby (ü′trŭ) (pop. 233).

Mosby (mŏs′bē), town (pop. 213), Clay co., W Mo., 20 mi. NE of Kansas City.

Mosca (mō′skä), town (pop. 1,002), Huánuco dept., central Peru, in Cordillera Central, 22 mi. SW of Ambo; potatoes, barley; sheep raising.

Mosca (mŏ′skŭ), hamlet, Alamosa co., S Colo., 12 mi. N of Alamosa. Great Sand Dunes Natl. Monument is E.

Mosca Pass (9,713 ft.), S Colo., in Sangre de Cristo Mts., bet. Huerfano and Saguache counties. Crossed by road and trail.

Mosca Peak, N.Mex.: see MANZANO RANGE.

Moscari (mōskä′rē), town (pop. c.3,300), Potosí dept., W central Bolivia, 7 mi. SSW of San Pedro; wheat, potatoes, *oca.*

Moschin, Poland: see MOSINA.

Mosciano Sant'Angelo (môshä′nô säntän′jĕlō), town (pop. 1,533), Teramo prov., Abruzzi e Molise, S central Italy, 12 mi. ENE of Teramo.

Moscice (môsh-chē′chĕ), Pol. *Mościce*, village (commune pop. 3,819), Krakow prov., SE Poland, just W of Tarnow; mfg. of nitrogen fertilizers.

Mosciska, Ukrainian SSR: see MOSTISKA.

Moscopolis, Albania: see VOSKOPOJË.

Moscow (mŏ′skou, –skō), Rus. *Moskva* (mŭskvä′), oblast (□ 18,500; 1946 pop. estimate 9,450,000) in W central European Russian SFSR; ⊙ Moscow. Occupies most populated and urbanized section of Volga-Oka watershed, with narrow strip reaching S to Stalinogorsk; drained by Klyazma, Moskva, and Protva rivers of Oka R. basin. Hilly plain, with Klin-Dmitrov Ridge (N of Moscow) cut by Moscow CANAL; mixed forest vegetation. Mineral resources include lignite (in Moscow BASIN), peat (E of Moscow), phosphorites (in Yegoryevsk-Voskresensk area), brick clays. Principal industrial and mfg. region of USSR, producing one-fifth of country's industrial output: steel milling at Moscow and Electrostal; mfg. (automobiles, locomotives; tram, subway, and railway cars; agr. implements, oil-cracking equipment) at Moscow, Mytishchi, Kolomna, Lyubertsy, Podolsk. There are important textile mills (cotton, woolen, silk), clothing and knitting mills (Moscow, Orekhovo-Zuyevo, Noginsk, Shchelkovo, Yegoryevsk, Serpukhov), chemical plants (phosphates at Voskresensk; nitrates at Stalinogorsk), and food industries (chiefly at Moscow). Widespread rural handicraft work (toys, haberdashery, clothing). Electric-power plants at Kaganovich and Stalinogorsk (lignite), Shatura, Orekhovo-Zuyevo, and Elektrogorsk (peat), Moscow (Donbas coal). Agr. plays secondary role, supplying truck (vegetables, potatoes) and dairy products to urban centers. Pop. (95% Russian) lives chiefly in cities and towns; only one-fifth is rural. Dense rail and highway network. Originally, Central Industrial Oblast; formed 1929 out of govts. of Moscow, Ryazan, Tver, and Tula.

Moscow, Rus. *Moskva*, city (□ 125; 1926 pop. 2,029,425; 1939 pop. 4,137,018; 1950 pop. estimate 5,100,000), ⊙ USSR, Russian SFSR, and Moscow oblast, on Moskva R., just E of its junction with Moscow Canal, and 400 mi. SE of Leningrad, 700 mi. ENE of Warsaw; 55°45′N 37°34′E. Leading political, cultural, industrial, and publishing center of the Soviet Union; transportation hub of rail and air lines, highways, and waterways. Mfg. ($^1/_7$ of industrial output of the USSR) includes quality steels, heavy and precision machinery, machine tools, automobiles, aircraft, electric locomotives and motors, chemicals, wood and paper products, ceramics, textiles, leather and rubber goods, cosmetics, cigarettes. Seat of govt. and Communist party organizations, Acad. of Sciences of the USSR (since 1934), higher educational institutions headed by univ. (founded 1755) and Timiryazev agr. acad., scientific research institutes, Moscow Art, Bolshoi, and Maly theaters, Tretyakov art gall., and numerous museums, notably those devoted to Lenin, literature, and graphic arts. City is on a hilly site (Lenin Hills rise to 655 ft. in SW) on both sides of the meandering Moskva R., at mouth of small Yauza R. Nucleus about which Moscow has developed concentrically is the noted Kremlin, which rises on a hill on the left bank of the Moskva. Principal thoroughfares fanning out from the Kremlin are joined by successive circular boulevards marking progressive historical limits. The Kremlin, a triangular citadel, is bounded by 1.5-mi.-long crenelated wall (dating from end of 15th cent.), topped on each side by 7 towers of varying architecture (completed 17th cent.). Within the Kremlin, the vast 19th-cent. Great Palace [Rus. *Bolshoi Dvorets*], built in old Rus. style and housing Supreme Soviets of the USSR and Russian SFSR, is connected with the *terems* (low-ceilinged 17th-cent. living quarters of Rus. rulers), with the 15th-cent. Granovitaya Palata [facetted-stone palace] with its old throne and banquet hall, and with Oruzheinaya Palata [hall of arms], a treasure chamber containing immense collections of crowns, scepters, thrones, costumes, and armor. Adjoining (NE of) the Great Palace is Cathedral Square, around which cluster Uspenski (Assumption) cathedral (end of 15th cent.) where Rus. tsars were crowned, Blagoveshchenski (Annunciation) cathedral, surmounted by 9 cupolas, and Arkhangelski (Archangel) cathedral, which contains tombs of 14th–17th cent. tsars. Other points of interest are the 300-ft.-high bell-tower of Ivan the Great with the near-by broken 200-ton Tsar Bell (cast 1735) on stone pedestal and the 40-ton Tsar Cannon (cast 1586). In N section of the Kremlin are former arsenal and 18th-cent. bldg. of the Presidium of the Supreme Soviet of the USSR (former Moscow senate or palace of justice). Adjoining the Kremlin (E) is vast Red Square, traditional center of political life and parade grounds, bounded W by the Kremlin walls, along which are Lenin Mausoleum and tombs of other noted Soviet leaders (Sverdlov, Dzerzhinski, Kalinin, Kirov, Ordzhonikidze, Kuibyshev, Gorki), and E by the Kitai-gorod, oldest section of Moscow outside of the Kremlin, once its commercial and banking section and, under the Soviets, the natl. govt. quarter. At N side of Red Square is 19th-cent. historical mus. and (S) 16th-cent. St. Basil church (now a mus.) of fantastic architecture. W of the Kremlin are Alexander Gardens and beyond, Moscow Univ. and Lenin Library (largest in USSR). N of the Kremlin, near large Sverdlov Square with Bolshoi (opera and ballet) and Maly (drama) theaters, begins wide Gorki Street lined with Council of Ministers bldg. and central telegraph office, and continued (NW) by Leningrad highway, past Dynamo sports stadium, central airport, and Khimki canal port. The S (right-bank) side of Moscow [Rus. *Zamoskvorechye*], a former merchants' suburb, is primarily a residential and industrial section, with educational institutions clustering (W) around USSR Acad. of Sciences. Industry is centered in old factory dists. such as Krasnaya Presnya (W; textile) and Zastava Ilicha (E; special steels) and in new industrial sections such as Leninskaya Sloboda (SE; automobiles, ball bearings, boilers, electrical goods). Among the large parks are Gorki Central Park (SW; on right bank), Izmailovo Park (on E outskirts), Sokolniki Park (NE), and Dzerzhinski (Ostankino) Park (N; botanical gardens). City is served by street transportation (streetcars, trolley and motor buses) and by 40 mi. of subways (1st opened 1935). Its 11 rail trunk lines fanning out from 10 passenger termini are linked by an inner belt line (at city limits) and an outer ring (completed 1942; 20–60 mi. from city). Water traffic is served by 3 inland ports: S port, an artificial basin (□ 4) on Moskva R. at SE city limits; W (Fili) landing on Moskva R.; and N (Khimki) port on Moscow Canal, at NW city limits. In addition to a central airport, Moscow air traffic passes through airports at Vnukovo, Bykovo, Lyubertsy, and Shcherbinka. Administratively, Moscow is an independent unit subordinated directly to the govt. of Russian SFSR. It is headed by a city soviet (council) and is divided into 25 *raions* (*rayons*). First mentioned (1147) as the estate of Yuri Dolgoruki, prince of Rostov and Suzdal, Moscow became (end of 13th cent.) capital of a separate (after 1359, grand) principality, including (by 1300) Ruza and Zvenigorod. Having superseded (1328) Vladimir as the chief seat of sovereignty, Moscow expanded through 14th and 15th cent. and by the end (1505) of the rule of Ivan III, the Muscovite realm became synonymous with a new Rus. natl. state, although the title of tsar was adopted only in 1547 by Ivan IV. Moscow remained ⊙ Russia until its transfer (1713) to St. Petersburg, the new residence of Peter the Great. It was entered (1812) by Napoleon and burned by the Russians, but was rebuilt in following years. During 19th cent., Moscow developed as foremost rail hub and industrial center (chiefly textiles) of Russia and became (1918) ⊙ Soviet govt. Limited to the area of the present Kremlin until end of 15th cent., Moscow acquired Kitai-gorod in mid-16th cent. The 1st boulevard ring (Ring A) marks the limits (end of 16th cent.) of Bely Gorod [white city], and 2d (Sadovaya) boulevard ring the earthen wall (mid-17th cent.) of Zemlyanoi Gorod [earthen city]. During 18th cent. it reached the zone of the modern railroad termini, and by 20th cent. extended beyond the belt railway. An urban plan (begun in 1930s) of reconstruction and expansion calls for the incorporation into the city of the cities of Kuntsevo (SW), Lenino (S), Lyublino and Perovo (E). During Second World War, Moscow was goal of Ger. army, which was, however, stopped (Dec., 1941) 20–25 mi. from the Kremlin. Moscow was not seriously damaged by bombing.

Moscow. 1 (mŏ′skō) City (pop. 10,593), ⊙ Latah co., NW Idaho, at Wash. line, 21 mi. N of Lewiston; trade and shipping center for agr. area (peas, wheat); food processing (peas, dairy products, flour), mfg. (agr. machinery, bricks, clay products), lumbering. University of Idaho (established 1889) and large experimental station of School of Forestry are here. City founded 1871. **2** (mŏ′skō) City (pop. 222), Stevens co., SW Kansas, 12 mi. NE of Hugoton, in agr. area. **3** (mŏ′skou) Town (pop. 482), Somerset co., W central Maine, on the Kennebec and c.20 mi. above Madison. **4** (mŏ′skou) Village (pop. 336), Clermont co., SW Ohio, 23 mi. SE of Cincinnati and on Ohio R. (here forming Ky. line). Grant Memorial Bridge is near by. **5** (mŏ′skou) Borough (pop. 1,050), Lackawanna co., NE Pa., 9 mi. SE of Scranton; lumber, maple syrup. Settled 1830. **6** (mŏ′skou,–skō) Town (pop. 394), Fayette co., SW Tenn., on Wolf R. and 34 mi. E of Memphis; lumber, boxes.

Moscow Basin, abbr. **Mosbas** (mŏs′băs), Rus. *Podmoskovnyy Basseyn*, abbr. *Mosbass*, lignite basin in central European USSR, extending over 600 mi. in arc from Borovichi (Leningrad oblast) W and S of Moscow, to area of Skopin (Ryazan oblast). Reserves (12 billion tons) include mainly brown coal and volatile Boghead coal. Chief mining centers: near Skopin (Pobedinski, Oktyabrski) in Ryazan oblast, Donskoi in Moscow oblast, Kaganovich, Bogoroditsk, Bolokhovo, Shchekino (Tula oblast), Nelidovo (Velikiye Luki oblast), near Selizharovo (Kalinin oblast), and near Borovichi (Novgorod oblast). Coal provides fuel for power plants in Moscow, Stalinogorsk, and Kaganovich (near Kashira); basis of nitrate chemical industry at Stalinogorsk.

Moscow Canal (mŏ′skou, –skō), Rus. *Kanal Imeni Moskvy*, waterway in Moscow oblast, Russian SFSR, linking VOLGA RIVER and MOSKVA RIVER; 80 mi. long. Leaves Volga R. at Ivankovo, at E end of Volga Reservoir; extends generally S, past Dmitrov and Yakhroma, then climbs by means of locks onto Klin-Dmitrov Ridge, here forming a series of reservoirs (Iksha, Pestovo, Pyalovo, Ucha, Klyazma), using courses of Ucha and Klyazma rivers. From Khimki Reservoir (N port of Moscow, on NW city limits; 5 mi. long, 1 mi. wide), the canal descends 100 ft., via 2 locks, to Moskva R. just W of Moscow. Completed 1937; called Moscow-Volga Canal, Rus. *Kanal Moskva-Volga*, until 1947.

Moscow Mills (mŏ′skou,–skō), town (pop. 350), Lincoln co., E Mo., on Cuivre R. and 4 mi. SE of Troy; agr.

Moscow Sea, Russian SFSR: see VOLGA RESERVOIR.

Moscow-Volga Canal, Russian SFSR: see MOSCOW CANAL.

Moscufo (môskōō′fô), village (pop. 946), Pescara prov., Abruzzi e Molise, S central Italy, 8 mi. NW of Chieti; tomato canning, olive-oil refining.

Mosel, river, France and Germany: see MOSELLE RIVER.

Moseley and King's Heath, S industrial suburb (pop. 39,728) of Birmingham, NW Warwick, England.

Moselle (mōzĕl'), department (□ 2,405; pop. 622,145), in Lorraine, NE France; ⊙ Metz. Borders on the Saar (NE) and Luxembourg (N). Bounded E by the N Vosges. Drained by the Moselle and the Saar. Center occupied by Lorraine plateau, of limited fertility, and dotted with shallow ponds (drained periodically for cultivation). Chief crops: barley, oats, rye, potatoes, hops, tobacco, fruits. Winegrowing along left bank of the Moselle. Mineral deposits are very important: iron is mined in Thionville basin (at Hayange, Knutange) and in Orne R. valley; coal mines (S extension of Saar basin) in Forbach-Saint-Avold dist.; saltworks in Château-Salins–Dieuze area. Principal industry is metallurgy, concentrated in Metz-Thionville region. Glassworks in the N Vosges, near Sarrebourg. Other industries: tanning and shoe mfg. (Metz), porcelain mfg. (Sarreguemines), woodworking, brewing, fruit and vegetable preserving. Chief cities are Metz and Thionville, with numerous smaller agglomerations in mining districts. Dept. was twice annexed to Germany (1871–1918; 1940–44). Has large German-speaking pop.

Moselle, town (pop. 130), Franklin co., E central Mo., on Meramec R. and 8 mi. SE of Union.

Moselle, Côtes de (kōt dü), ridge line in NE France, extending from Meuse R. above Neufchâteau (Vosges dept.) NNE to Nancy, thence N, principally along left bank of the Moselle, into Luxembourg. Of great strategic importance as an obstacle to invasions from E. Important strongholds and transport centers (Nancy, Metz, Thionville) have arisen where gaps provide access to Paris Basin. Some wine grown near Toul and Pagny-sur-Moselle. Important iron mines near Nancy, Briey, and Thionville.

Moselle River (mōzĕl', mü–), Ger. *Mosel* (mō'zül), in NE France and W Germany, rises in the central Vosges near Bussang Pass, flows 320 mi. generally N and NE, past Épinal, Toul, Metz, and Thionville, forming Luxembourg-Saar border bet. Sierck and Remich, thence Luxembourg-German border to Mertert, where it enters Germany and flows past Trier to the Rhine at Coblenz. Receives Meurthe and Saar rivers (right), Sûre R. (left). Paralleled (in France) for short stretches by Canal de l'EST and MARNE-RHINE CANAL; navigable for small craft from Frouard. Noted Moselle white wine grown on slopes of its lower valley in Germany. Extensive regulation planned bet. Trier and Coblenz, where it meanders through Rhenish Slate Mts.

Moselotte River (mōzülôt'), in Vosges dept., E France, rises in the central Vosges E of Gérardmer, flows c.25 mi. W to the Moselle just above Remiremont. Cotton weaving in valley.

Moserboden, Austria: see KAPRUN.

Moses Lake, town (pop. 2,679), Grant co., E central Wash., 18 mi. SE of Ephrata, in Columbia basin; agr. trade center on E shore of Moses L. (16 mi. long). Pop. greatly increased during Second World War because of near-by Larson Air Force Base.

Moses Point, locality, W Alaska, on SE Seward Peninsula, on Norton Sound, at mouth of Norton Bay, 100 mi. E of Nome; 64°45'N 161°46'W; air field.

Mosetenes, Serranía de (sĕrănē'ä dā mōsātā'nĕs), N outlier of Cordillera de Cochabamba, in Cochabamba dept., W central Bolivia; extends c.120 mi. NW from area N of Sacaba to area W of Huachi, parallel to Cordillera Real. Rises to 8,200 ft.; forms watershed bet. Beni and Mamoré river basins.

Mosgiel (mŏz'gēl, mŏsgĭl'), borough (pop. 2,349), ⊙ Taieri co. (□ 903; pop. 5,316), SE S.Isl., New Zealand, 10 mi. W of Dunedin; woolen mills, coal mines. Taieri airport near by.

Moshassuck River (mŏs-hă'sŭk), N R.I., rises SE of Woonsocket, flows c.10 mi. generally SSE, past Saylesville and Central Falls, through Providence, joining Woonasquatucket R. just before entering Providence R.

Moshenskoye (mŭshĕn'skŭyŭ), village (1939 pop. over 500), E Novgorod oblast, Russian SFSR, 25 mi. ENE of Borovichi; dairying.

Moshi (mō'shē), town (pop. 8,048), Northern Prov., NE Tanganyika, on railroad (from Tanga) and 45 mi. E of Arusha, at S foot of the Kilimanjaro; alt. 2,657 ft. Major coffee center; sisal, sugar, papain. Linked by rail and road with Mombasa, Kenya; airport.

Moshkovo (mô'shkŭvŭ), village (1939 pop. over 2,000), E Novosibirsk oblast, Russian SFSR, on Trans-Siberian RR and 30 mi. NE of Novosibirsk, in agr. area.

Mosier (mō'zhŭr), city (pop. 259), Wasco co., N Oregon, 12 mi. NW of The Dalles and on Columbia R.; apples.

Mosigkau (mō'zĭkou), village (pop. 3,854), in former Anhalt state, central Germany, after 1945 in Saxony-Anhalt, 5 mi. WSW of Dessau. Has former palace (1752), after 1780 secular convent, with noted art collection.

Mosina (mō-shē'nä), Ger. *Moschin* (mō-shēn'), town (1946 pop. 5,192), Poznan prov., W Poland, near Warta R., on railroad and 11 mi. S of Poznan; tanning, sawmilling. Ludwikowo, Ger. *Ludwigsberg*, 2 mi. W, is rail spur terminus, health resort.

Mosinee (mōzĭnē'), city (pop. 1,453), Marathon co., central Wis., on Wisconsin R. and 12 mi. SSW of Wausau, in lumbering and dairying area; paper and sawmilling, cheese making. Big Eau Pleine Reservoir is near by. Inc. 1931.

Mosjoen (mō'shûŭn), Nor. *Mosjøen*, town (pop. 3,139), Nordland co., N central Norway, on Vefsn Fjord (inlet of North Sea), at mouth of Vefsna R., on railroad and 100 mi. NNE of Namsos; shipbuilding, lumber milling, cement casting; mfg. of barrels, margarine. Cold-storage plant. Steatite (used for Trondheim cathedral) quarried near by. Inc. 1875.

Moskalenki (mŭskä'lyĭn-kē), village (1939 pop. over 2,000), SW Omsk oblast, Russian SFSR, near Trans-Siberian RR, 65 mi. WSW of Omsk; agr.

Moskalvo or **Moskal'vo** (–skäl'vŭ), village (1947 pop. over 500), N Sakhalin, Russian SFSR, major oil port on sheltered inlet of Sakhalin Gulf, 18 mi. W (under jurisdiction) of Okha. Has pipe line and rail connection (since 1932) with petroleum wells and Okha. Special oil-loading installations built here (1933–34).

Moskenaesoy, Norway: see MOSKENESOY.

Moskenes, canton, Norway: see SORVAGEN.

Moskenesoy (môsk'ŭnās-ûü), Nor. *Moskenesøy*, island (□ 72; pop. 2,395) in North Sea, Nordland co., N Norway, one of the Lofoten Isls., 30 mi. WSW of Svolvaer; 22 mi. long, 6 mi. wide; rises to 3,392 ft. Has fishing villages. Formerly spelled Moskenaesoy, Nor. *Moskenaesøy*. The Maelstrom or Moskenstraum current passes just S.

Moskenstraum, Norway: see MAELSTROM.

Moskenstrom, Norway: see MAELSTROM.

Moskushamn (môs'kōōs-häm"ŭn), coal-mining settlement, central West Spitsbergen, Spitsbergen group, on E shore of Advent Bay (small S arm of Is Fjord), 3 mi. NE of Longyear City; 78°15'N 15°45'E. Formerly called Hiorthamn.

Moskva, Russian SFSR: see MOSCOW, oblast, city.

Moskva River (mŭskvä'), Moscow oblast, Russian SFSR, rises W of Uvarovka in Smolensk-Moscow Upland, flows NW, E past Mozhaisk and Zvenigorod, and SE past Moscow, Bronnitsy, and Kolomna, to Oka R. opposite Shchurovo; 315 mi. long. Receives Kolocha (site of battle of BORODINO) and Pakhra (right), Ruza and Istra (left) rivers. Linked with Volga R. (N) by Moscow CANAL. Below mouth of Moscow Canal (just W of Moscow), the Moskva is canalized (lock system); forms Pererva Reservoir (S port of Moscow; 2.5 mi. long, 1 mi. wide) at Lyublino, on SE Moscow city limits. Navigable (April–Nov.) below Moscow Canal.

Mos Lake (môs), Dan. *Mossø*, largest (6 mi. long, 1.5 mi. wide) in Jutland, Denmark, 15 mi. SW of Aarhus; surrounded by farm land; forests on SW.

Mos Lake (mŭs), Nor. *Møsvatn*, mostly in Rauland canton, Telemark co., S Norway, W of Rjukan; □ 23; c.25 mi. long, 1–3 mi. wide, with several branches; 148 ft. deep. Fisheries. Outlet: Mana river. Dam built 1904–06, with later improvements. Formerly spelled Mios and Mjos.

Moslavina (mô'slävēnä), mountain, N Croatia, Yugoslavia, in Slavonia, 7 mi. ENE of Popovac; rises to 1,604 ft.

Mosman (mŏs'mŭn), municipality (pop. 27,562), E New South Wales, Australia, 4 mi. NNE of Sydney across Port Jackson, in metropolitan area; confectioneries, leather-goods factory.

Mosnang (mōs'näng), town (pop. 2,609), St. Gall canton, NE Switzerland, 17 mi. WSW of St. Gall; farming.

Mosolovo (mŭsô'lŭvŭ), village (1926 pop. 1,985), central Ryazan oblast, Russian SFSR, 40 mi. SE of Ryazan; woodworking.

Moson (mô'shôn), former co. of NE Hungary. Major portion ceded (1920) to Czechoslovakia; rest inc. with Györ co. to form GYÖR-MOSON co.

Mosonmagyarovar (mô'shônmŏ"dyŏrōvär), Hung. *Mosonmagyaróvár*, city (pop. 17,073), Györ-Moson co., NW Hungary, on arm of the Danube (here bridged), at mouth of Lajta R., and 21 mi. NW of Györ; industrial, agr., market center. Mfg. (agr. machinery and tools, munitions, chemicals, fertilizer, silk, starch); aluminum plants, breweries, distilleries, flour mills, brickworks. Summer resort; agr. experiment station and acad. Grain, honey, cattle, horses, ducks, geese in area. Formed 1939 by union of Moson, Ger. *Wieselburg*, and Magyarovar, Ger. *Ungarisch-Altenburg*.

Mosonszentjanos (mô'shônsĕntyä"nôsh), Hung. *Mosonszentjános*, town (pop. 4,482), Györ-Moson co., NW Hungary, 24 mi. WNW of Györ; vegetable canneries; mfg. of coffee substitute; distilleries, flour mills, brickworks.

Mosonszolnok (mô'shônsôl"nôk), town (pop. 3,171), Györ-Moson co., NW Hungary, 24 mi. NW of Györ; grain, sugar beets, cattle, horses. Bronze Age artifacts found near by.

Mosor (mô'sôr), mountain in Dinaric Alps, S Croatia, Yugoslavia, near Adriatic Sea, in Dalmatia. Highest points, 10 mi. E of Split: Ljuto Kame (4,395 ft.), Mosor (4,362 ft.).

Mosovce (mô'shôftsĕ), Slovak *Mošovce*, Hung. *Mosóc* (mô'shōts), village (pop. 1,434), W Slovakia, Czechoslovakia, 23 mi. SSE of Zilina. Poet Jan Kollar b. here.

Mospino (mô'spēnŭ), city (1939 pop. over 10,000), central Stalino oblast, Ukrainian SSR, in the Donbas, 11 mi. SE of Makeyevka; coal-mining center.

Mosqueiro (mōōskā'rōō), town (pop. 2,516), E Pará, Brazil, on isl. in Pará R. (Amazon delta), 20 mi. N of Belém (steamer connection); resort.

Mosquera (mōskā'rä), town (pop. 1,486), Cundinamarca dept., central Colombia, on railroad and highway, and 13 mi. NW of Bogotá; alt. 8,986 ft.; wheat, potatoes, fruit, stock.

Mosquero (mōskā'rō), village (pop. 583), Harding and San Miguel counties, ⊙ Harding co., NE N.Mex., 45 mi. NNW of Tucumcari.

Mosquito (mŭskē'tō, Sp. mōskē'tō), village on NW Vieques Isl., E Puerto Rico, on railroad and 5 mi. WSW of Isabela Segunda, in sugar region; fishing.

Mosquito Coast or **Mosquitia** (mŭskē'tēŭ, môskĭ'-shēŭ, Sp. mōskē'tyä), vast, undeveloped, sparsely settled region of Central America, on Caribbean coast bet. 11° and 16°N; shared by Honduras (COLÓN dept.) and Nicaragua (ZELAYA dept.). Bounded N by Aguán R. and S by San Juan R., it is a tropical, forested lowland with marshy lagoon shore. Inhabited chiefly by Mosquito (or Miskitto) Indians, lumber workers, and prospectors engaged in hardwood exploitation (mahogany, cedar), stock raising, and agr. (coconuts, bananas, manioc). A Br. protectorate (1655–1860), it was ceded to Honduras and Nicaragua; Nicaragua established the autonomous Indian reserve (sometimes called the Mosquito Kingdom), which was forcibly incorporated into Nicaragua in 1894 as Zelaya dept. Although the Mosquito Coast is divided bet. Nicaragua and Honduras by an undemarcated *de facto* frontier extending from TEOTECACINTE peak and along COLÓN MOUNTAINS and CRUTA RIVER to the Pacific, Nicaragua claims the entire Mosquito Coast, while Honduras claims the section S of Colón Mts. to the Poteca and Coco rivers.

Mosquito Creek. 1 In SW Iowa, rises in Shelby co., flows c.60 mi. SW, to Missouri R. 5 mi. S of Council Bluffs. **2** In NE Ohio, rises in Ashtabula co., flows c.30 mi. S, past Cortland, to Mahoning R. at Niles. About 9 mi. above mouth, a flood-control dam (5,650 ft. long, 47 ft. high) impounds Mosquito Creek Reservoir (capacity 104,100 acre-ft.).

Mosquito Gulf, bight of Caribbean Sea in W central Panama, E of Valiente Peninsula; 80 mi. wide, 10 mi. long. Contains Escudo de Veraguas isl.

Mosquito Lagoon (c.17 mi. long, 2 mi. wide), in Volusia and Brevard counties, NE Fla., separated from the Atlantic by narrow barrier beach; communicates with Hillsborough R. lagoon (N), Indian R. lagoon (S). Contains many small isls. Followed by Intracoastal Waterway.

Mosquito Peak; Mosquito Range, Colo.: see PARK RANGE.

Mosquitos, Uruguay: see SOCA.

Moss (môs), city (pop. 17,415), ⊙ Ostfold co., SE Norway, port on E shore of Oslo Fjord, on railroad and 35 mi. S of Oslo; 59°26'N 10°41'E. Has shipyards, and paper, aluminum, and cotton mills; mfg. of waterproof clothes, locks, cement, shoes, electrical equipment, asphalt, tar, yeast, tobacco and cork products; metalworking, brewing. City founded in 16th cent.; iron formerly mined in region. Under Convention of Moss (Aug., 1814), Norway and Sweden were united. Port is protected by Jeloy (yĕl'ûü), Nor. *Jeløy*, isl. (□ 7; pop. 5,417) in Oslo Fjord just W of Moss (bridge); seaside resort.

Moss, town in Gwersyllt (gwĕr'sĭlt) parish (pop. 5,657), E Denbigh, Wales, 3 mi. NW of Wrexham; coal mining.

Mossaka (mōsäkä'), village, central Middle Congo territory, Fr. Equatorial Africa, on Congo R. (Belgian Congo border) at confluence of Likouala R. and Sanga R., and 80 mi. SE of Fort-Rousset; ships hardwoods; palm-oil milling, elaeis-palm plantations. Customs station.

Mossâmedes or **Moçâmedes** (mōōsä'mĭdĭsh), town (pop. 4,926), ⊙ Mossâmedes dist. (□ 22,440; pop. 34,723), Huíla prov., SW Angola, fishing port on the Atlantic, 200 mi. SSW of Benguela; 15°12'S 12°9'E. Terminus of railroad to Sá da Bandeira, tapping fertile agr. upland c.100 mi. E. Ships dried and salted fish, hides, skins, cotton. Tobacco processing. Airfield.

Mossbank, village (pop. 552), S Sask., near Johnstone L., 35 mi. SW of Moose Jaw; coal mines, grain elevators.

Mossbank, village on NE coast of Mainland isl., Shetlands, Scotland, 21 mi. N of Lerwick; fishing.

Moss Beach, coast village (pop. c.425), San Mateo co., W Calif., c.20 mi. SSW of downtown San Francisco; fishing. Submarine gardens offshore.

Mossel Bay (mô'sŭl), Afrikaans *Mosselbaai* (–bī'), town (pop. 8,078), S Cape Prov., U. of So. Afr., seaport on Mossel Bay (20 mi. wide) of the Indian Ocean, 210 mi. W of Port Elizabeth, 40 mi. S of Oudtshoorn; 34°12'S 22°8'E. Serves agr. and wool-producing region; fishing center, with important oyster and mussel beds; seaside resort. Airport.

Yellow ochre and quartzite mined near by; platinum, iridium, osmiridium deposits discovered (1934) in vicinity. Just W is Cape St. Blaize, lighthouse; just N, in Mossel Bay, is Seal Isl., with large seal herds. Bay was visited (1487) by Bartholomew Diaz and (1497) by Vasco da Gama; Portuguese hermitage founded here 1501. Formerly called Aliwal South.

Mossendjo (mōsĕngō'), village, S Middle Congo territory, Fr. Equatorial Africa, 130 mi. NNE of Pointe-Noire; trading center; rice growing. R.C. and Protestant missions.

Mosses, Col des (kôl dā mōs'), pass (4,750 ft.) in the Alps, W Switzerland; road leads S from Château-d'Oex.

Mosset (môsā'), village (pop. 386), Pyrénées-Orientales dept., S France, 5 mi. NW of Prades; talc quarrying.

Mossgiel, Scotland: see MAUCHLINE.

Mossi (mō'sē), densely populated region of W Sudan, central Upper Volta, Fr. West Africa, named for Negro tribe. Principal settlement, Ouagadou-gou.

Mössingen (mû'sĭng-ùn), village (pop. 4,468), S Württemberg, Germany, after 1945 in Württemberg-Hohenzollern, on N slope of Swabian Jura, 7.5 mi. S of Tübingen; knitwear.

Mösskirch, Germany: see MESSKIRCH.

Moss Landing, village (pop. c.200), Monterey co., W Calif., on Monterey Bay, 15 mi. N of Monterey; fishing docks; oil-loading pipeline.

Mossley, municipal borough (1931 pop. 12,042; 1951 census 10,415), SE Lancashire, England, on Tame R., near Yorkshire and Cheshire boundaries, and 9 mi. ENE of Manchester; cotton and woolen milling, metal-working.

Mossman, town (pop. 1,022), NE Queensland, Australia, 35 mi. NNW of Cairns; sugar-producing center.

Mossoró (mōōsōōrô'), city (1950 pop. 20,576), Rio Grande do Norte, NE Brazil, head of navigation on Apodi (or Mossoró) R. and 150 mi. WNW of Natal; railroads S to Pôrto Franco opposite seaport of Areia Branca (N) and to the interior (completed 1949 to Almino Afonso). Saltworking and -shipping center; important livestock, cotton, and carnauba market. Gypsum and marble quarries. Manganese deposits near by. Airport. Also spelled Moçoró.

Mossoró River, Brazil: see APODI RIVER.

Moss Point, city (pop. 3,782), Jackson co., extreme SE Miss., 4 mi. N of Pascagoula and on Escatawpa R.; pine-pulp paper, lumber, fish meal and oil.

Moss Side, S suburb of Manchester, SE Lancashire, England; has cotton, engineering, and chemical industries.

Moss Town, town (pop. 216), central Bahama Isls., on central Great Exuma Isl., 5 mi. WNW of George Town; 23°30'N 75°51'W. Stock raising (sheep, goats, hogs).

Mossuril (mōōsōōrēl'), town Niassa prov., NE Mozambique, small port on Mozambique Channel, 7 mi. NW of Mozambique city. European residences.

Moss Vale, town (pop. 3,096), E New South Wales, Australia, 65 mi. SW of Sydney, dairy, agr. center; granite quarries.

Mossyrock, town (pop. 356), Lewis co., SW Wash., on Cowlitz R. and 25 mi. SE of Chehalis.

Most (môst), Ger. *Brüx* (brüks), city (pop. 23,077; including suburbs 35,330), NW Bohemia, Czechoslovakia, 11 mi. SW of Teplice; important rail junction; mining and industrial center with metallurgical and chemical works; mfg. of ceramics and earthenware. Starting point of gas pipe line to Prague. Most coal field is chief source of lignite output of Czechoslovakia. Because of synthetic-fuel plant at near-by ZALUZI, Most was repeatedly bombed by Allies in Second World War. Has 14th-, 15th-, and 18th-cent. churches, castle remains, mus. Quartzite quarrying near by.

Mosta (mō'stä) or **Musta** (mōō'stä), village (parish pop. 7,186), N central Malta, 5 mi. W of Valletta; olive oil, vegetables, honey; sheep, goats. Its parish church was destroyed in Second World War air raid. There are some Roman remains. Just S is the Ta Qali airport.

Mosta (mô'stŭ), town (1946 pop. over 500), SE Ivanovo oblast, Russian SFSR, 6 mi. SE of Yuzha; peat works.

Mostaganem (môstägänĕm'), city (pop. 50,403), Oran dept., NW Algeria, port on E shore of the Gulf of Arzew (Mediterranean Sea), 45 mi. ENE of Oran; 35°56'N 0°5'E. Exports wine, vegetables, and cereals grown in surrounding lowland, and sheep, wool, esparto shipped here from the Tell Atlas and from the High Plateaus (S). Distilling, mfg. (tobacco products, electrical equipment, furniture, cordage, cement, flour products); metal founding. Silver-bearing lead mined at Karouba (3 mi. N). Founded in 11th cent., city reached height of prosperity in 16th cent. under Turks, then declined. Its pop. was 3,000 when French arrived in 1833. Rapid growth since 1900 resulted from port development, still under way.

Mostar (mô'stär), city (pop. 23,239), ⊙ Mostar oblast (formed 1949), central Herzegovina, Yugoslavia, on Neretva R., on railroad and 50 mi. SW of Sarajevo. Chief city of Herzegovina; center of wine- and cherry-growing region; bauxite at SIROKI BRIJEG and KNEZPOLJE. Has brown-coal mine (330 ft. deep), aluminum plant (begun 1947), tobacco and cigarette factory. Orthodox Eastern bishopric (1777). Has Roman bridge (probably built 1556 on site of Roman structure), former Roman guardhouses and fortifications, and Turkish mosques. Became trade center and seat of Turkish governor in early-15th cent.

Mostar Lake or **Mostar Plain,** region (8 mi. long, 2 mi. wide) in W Herzegovina, Yugoslavia, c.5 mi. W of Mostar. Flooded bet. Nov. and June.

Moste (mô'stĕ), village, central Slovenia, Yugoslavia, 10 mi. NNE of Ljubljana; alumina plant. Until 1918, in Carniola.

Mosterhamn (môst'ùrhäm"ùn), village in Moster canton (pop. 1,710), Hordaland co., SW Norway, port at SE tip of Bomlo, 20 mi. N of Haugesund; limestone quarries. Olaf I Tryggvason landed here (995) from Dublin to claim crown of Norway. Sometimes spelled Mosterhavn.

Mostiska (mŭstyē'skŭ), Pol. *Mościska* (môshchē'skä), city (1931 pop. 4,770), N Drogobych oblast, Ukrainian SSR, on Vishnya R. and 35 mi. NNW of Drogobych; cement and brick mfg., distilling. Passed from Poland to Austria (1772); reverted to Poland (1919); ceded to USSR in 1945.

Mostki (mŭstkē'), village (1926 pop. 6,668), NW Voroshilovgrad oblast, Ukrainian SSR, 18 mi. WNW of Starobelsk; wheat.

Móstoles (mō'stōlĕs), town (pop. 1,773), Madrid prov., central Spain, on railroad and 11 mi. SW of Madrid, in agr. region (cereals, grapes, vegetables, truck produce, olives, sheep). Meat packing, vinegar distilling. Celebrated for its declaration of war on Napoleon, made by its mayor Andrés Torrejón.

Moston (mŏ'stŭn), NE suburb (pop. 23,133) of Manchester, SE Lancashire, England; coal mining; mfg. of radio receivers, electrical appliances, textile machinery.

Mostovoye (mŭstŭvoi'ù). **1** Village, Krasnodar Territory, Russian SFSR: see MOSTOVSKOYE. **2** Village (1926 pop. 2,300), E Odessa oblast, Ukrainian SSR, 15 mi. NNE of Berezovka; metalworks.

Mostovskoye (mŭstŭfskoi'ù), **1** Village (1939 pop. over 2,000), SE Krasnodar Territory, Russian SFSR, on Laba R. and 17 mi. S of Labinsk; gypsum quarries. In late 1930s, also called Mostovoye. **2** Village (1939 pop. over 500), NE Kurgan oblast, Russian SFSR, 35 mi. NNW of Lebyazhye; dairy farming.

Mosty (mŭstē'), town (1937 pop. 2,150), E Grodno oblast, Belorussian SSR, on Neman R. and 20 mi. NNE of Volkovysk; rail junction; plywood mfg.

Mostyn (mŏ'stĭn), town in Whitford parish (pop. 3,453), Flint, Wales, on the Dee estuary and 6 mi. ESE of Prestatyn; small port, with iron foundries. Mostyn Hall, dating from 15th cent., contains collection of Welsh antiquities and MSS.

Mosty Wielkie, Ukrainian SSR: see VELIKIYE MOSTY.

Mosul (mō'sŭl, mōsōōl'), province (□ 19,490; pop. 601,589), N Iraq, bordered N by Turkey, W by Syria, E by the Great Zab, and drained by the Tigris; ⊙ Mosul. Agr. (wheat, barley, oranges, apples). There are also petroleum deposits. In this area developed the beginnings of the Assyrian Empire, and the sites of the great capitals (ASHUR, CALAH, and NINEVEH) have yielded important archaeological finds.

Mosul, second largest city (pop. 203,273) of Iraq, ⊙ Mosul prov., N Iraq, on right bank of the Tigris (here crossed on a floating bridge), on railroad, and 220 mi. NNW of Baghdad; 36°20'N 43°8'E. On rail line leading S to Baghdad and Basra and NW to Syria and Turkey, it is an important trade and market center in a rich agr. area (barley, wheat, sesame, millet, apples, oranges; livestock). There are also rich oil fields in the area. The city was once known for its fine cotton goods, from which came the name muslin. Across the Tigris are the ruins of the great Assyrian capital NINEVEH, and 16 mi. NE is the great mound of archaeological finds TEPE GAWRA. Mosul became (c.750) the chief city of N Mesopotamia and was seat of independent dynasties in 10th and 11th cent. Its walls resisted sieges by Saladin and Nadir. Hulagu Khan sacked it, but Tamerlane spared it and repaired the picturesque pontoon bridge. It later was the object of Turkish-Persian struggle. The Mosul area was not an original part of the country of Iraq separated in 1920–21 from Turkey and was not relinquished by Turkey until 1925–26. The city is inhabited chiefly by Arabs, and the surrounding region is peopled by Kurds. Mosul has numerous mosques and several churches of the Assyrians (Nestorian Christians).

Mosulpo, Korea: see TAEJONG.

Mosün (mō'shün'), Mandarin *Wu-hsüan* (wōō'-shüän'), town, ⊙ Mosün co. (pop. 138,641), SE central Kwangsi prov., China, 55 mi. SE of Liuchow and on Hungshui R.; manganese-mining center; grain, tobacco, peanuts. Antimony deposits near by.

Moswansicut River (mŏswŏn'sĭkùt), N central R.I., short stream entering N arm of SCITUATE RESERVOIR; formerly joined Ponaganset R. to form North Branch of Pawtuxet R. in area now flooded by reservoir.

Mota (mō'tä), village, Gojjam prov., NW Ethiopia, on N slope of Choke Mts., near Blue Nile R., 55 mi. SSW of Debra Tabor; trade center.

Mota, New Hebrides: see BANKS ISLANDS.

Mota del Cuervo (mō'tä dhĕl kwĕr'vō), town (pop. 4,307), Cuenca prov., central Spain, in New Castile, 55 mi. SW of Cuenca; agr. center surrounded by fine pastures and vineyards. Olive-oil pressing, pottery mfg.

Mota del Marqués (märkās'), town (pop. 1,371), Valladolid prov., N central Spain, 24 mi. W of Valladolid; tanning, flour milling; cereals, wine. Has medieval mansion.

Motagua River (mōtä'gwä), longest (250 mi.) of Guatemala, rises in central highlands S of Quiché, flows E and ENE, past La Canoa, Rancho, Gualán, Los Amates, and Morales, to Gulf of Honduras on Honduras border, 25 mi. E of Puerto Barrios. In upper course it is known as the Río Grande. Navigable for c.125 mi.; carries bananas, coffee, fruit, hides. Chiquimula R. (right), main tributary. Gold placers along its course.

Motai, Kazakh SSR: see MATAI.

Motajica or **Motayitsa** (both: môtä'yĭtsä), mountain (2,139 ft.) in Dinaric Alps, N Bosnia, Yugoslavia along right bank of Sava R., 20 mi. E of Gradiska

Motala (mōō'tä"lä), city (1950 pop. 24,723), Ostergotland co., S Sweden, on NE shore of L. Vatter, at efflux of Motala R., 20 mi. WNW of Linkoping; terminu of E section of Gota Canal; rail junction. Mfg of locomotives, railroad cars, machinery, radios refrigerators, clothing. Site of Sweden's larges radio transmitter; hydroelectric station. Inc. 1881

Motala River, Swedish *Motala ström* (strûm') SE Sweden, issues from L. Vatter at Motala, flows E, through small L. Bor, to L. Rox, then flows N to L. Gla and E to Norrkoping, where it turns N and flows to Bra Bay, Swedish *Bråviken* (brō'vē"kùn) 30-mi.-long inlet of the Baltic, 3 mi. N of Norrkoping. Length, 60 mi. Bet. lakes Vatter and Ro course parallels Gota Canal.

Motalava, New Hebrides: see BANKS ISLANDS.

Motane (mōtä'nä), uninhabited volcanic island Marquesas Isls., Fr. Oceania, S Pacific, 11 mi. S of Hiva Oa; 5 mi. long, 2 mi. wide; rises to 1,640 ft Sometimes spelled Mohotane.

Motatán (mōtätän'), town (pop. 1,888), Trujill state, W Venezuela, on Motatán R. and 6 mi. N o Valera, in agr. region (sugar cane, corn, tobacco coffee); terminus of railroad from La Ceiba on L Maracaibo.

Motatán River, W Venezuela, rises in Andean spu at N foot of Mucuchíes Pass (Mérida state), flow c.100 mi. N and NW through Trujillo state, pas Valera and Motatán, to L. Maracaibo 2½ mi. S of San Lorenzo (Zulia state).

Motayitsa, mountain, Yugoslavia: see MOTAJICA.

Motegi (mōtä'gē), town (pop. 11,788), Tochigi pre fecture, central Honshu, Japan, 17 mi. E of Utsu nomiya; agr. (rice, wheat, tobacco), lumbering, to bacco processing.

Motembo (mōtĕm'bō), village (pop. 291), Matanza prov., W Cuba, 26 mi. ESE of Cárdenas; petroleun wells.

Moth (mōt), town (pop. 3,129), Jhansi dist., Uttar Pradesh, India, 30 mi. NE of Jhansi; jowa oilseeds, wheat, gram.

Mothe-Achard, La (lä môt'-äshär'), village (po 635), Vendée dept., W France, 11 mi. WSW of L Roche-sur-Yon; cereals.

Mother Lode, central Calif., belt of gold-bearin quartz, extends along W foothills of the Sierr Nevada from vicinity of Mariposa (S) to Neva da City region (N), through Mariposa, Tuolumn Calaveras, Amador, El Dorado, and Nevada cou ties. Sometimes limited to strip c.70 mi. long, 6½ mi. wide, running NW from Mariposa. Di covery of placer gold on South Fork of America R. led to 1848 gold rush; development of quar mines (some still producing) came later. Man famous tales of Bret Harte and Mark Twain hav their setting here.

Motherwell and Wishaw (mŭ'dhùrwùl, –wĕl, wĭ shô), burgh (1931 pop. 64,710; 1950 cens 68,137), N Lanark, Scotland. Includes Mothe well, near the Clyde, 11 mi. ESE of Glasgow; stee milling and coal-mining center, with mfg. of boiler electrical equipment, light metals, hosiery. W shaw, 3 mi. ESE of Motherwell, near the Clyd has steel mills, coal mines, mfg. of railroad equi ment, hosiery, cement, chocolate. Motherwell an Wishaw were united into one burgh in 1920.

Mothe-Saint-Héray, La (lä môt'-sē-ārā'), villag (pop. 1,544), Deux-Sèvres dept., W France, on th Sèvre Niortaise, 17 mi. E of Niort; dairying, mu raising. Megalithic monuments near by.

Moti or **Motir** (mōtē', –tĭr'), volcanic island (4 m wide; pop. 1,371), N Moluccas, Indonesia, i Molucca Sea, just W of Halmahera, 20 mi. S Ternate; 0°28'N 127°24'E; mountainous, rising t 3,117 ft.

Môtiers (mōtyā'), town (pop. 861), Neuchâtel ca ton, W Switzerland, 16 mi. WSW of Neuchât and on Areuse R., in Val de Travers; mfg. watches; wine growing.

Motihari (mōtĭhä'rē), town (pop. 20,717), ⊙ Champaran dist., NW Bihar, India, on Ganges Plain, 46 mi. NW of Muzaffarpur; road center; oilseed and sugar milling, cotton weaving.

Motilla del Palancar (mōtē'lyä dhĕl päläng-kär'), town (pop. 3,796), Cuenca prov., E central Spain, 37 mi. SSE of Cuenca; agr. center (grapes, saffron, cereals, fruit, sheep); sawmilling.

Motilones, Serranía de los (sĕränē'ä dā lōs mōtēlō'nĕs), Andean range on Colombia-Venezuela border. A N part of Cordillera Oriental, it forms together with Serranía de Valledupar and Montes de Oca, further N, the Sierra de Perijá; c.80 mi. long, bet. 9° and 10°15'N; rises to 12,300 ft.

Motir, Indonesia: see MOTI.

Motiti Island (mōtē'tē), uninhabited volcanic island, New Zealand, in Bay of Plenty, N N.Isl., 11 mi. ENE of Tauranga; 3.5 mi. long, 1 mi. wide. Deep-sea fishing.

Motley, county (□ 1,011; pop. 3,963), NW Texas; ⊙ Matador. In broken plains just below Cap Rock escarpment of Llano Estacado; drained by North, South, and Middle Pease rivers. Chiefly cattle-ranching region, producing also cotton, grain sorghums, wheat, some fruit, truck, hogs, sheep, horses, dairy cattle, poultry. Some production of clays, lignite, sand, gravel, caliche. Formed 1876.

Motley, village (pop. 435), Morrison co., central Minn., on Crow Wing R. and 22 mi. W of Brainerd; dairy products.

Moto (mō'tō), village, Eastern Prov., NE Belgian Congo, 16 mi. WSW of Watsa; gold-mining center; rice processing.

Motobu (mōtō'bōō), town (1950 pop. 20,254), on Okinawa, in Ryukyu Islands, on W peninsula, 25 mi. NNE of Naha; agr. center (sugar cane, sweet potatoes). Airfield.

Motodomari, Russian SFSR: see VOSTOCHNY.

Motokolea (mōtōkōkä'ä), village, Kivu prov., E Belgian Congo, 100 mi. N of Costermansville; gold-mining center. Also gold mining at Mangure-djipa (mäng-gōōrĕjē'pä), 15 mi. NW.

Motol or **Motol'** (mŭtôl'), town (1931 pop. 4,390), W Pinsk oblast, Belorussian SSR, port on Yaselda R. (head of navigation) and 25 mi. NW of Pinsk; tanning, flour milling.

Motomiya (mōtō'mēä), town (pop. 10,685), Fukushima prefecture, central Honshu, Japan, on Abukuma R. and 17 mi. SSW of Fukushima; rice-producing center; spinning.

Motomura (mōtō'mōōrä), village (pop. 3,870), on O-shima, of isl. group Izu-shichito, Greater Tokyo, Japan, on W coast of isl.; camellia oil, livestock.

Mototomari, Russian SFSR: see VOSTOCHNY.

Motovilikha, Russian SFSR: see MOLOTOV, city.

Motovka Gulf (mŭtôf'kŭ), Rus. *Motovskiy Zaliv*, inlet of Barents Sea bet. Rybachi and Kola peninsulas, Russian SFSR; 35 mi. long, 4–8 mi. wide; fisheries. Receives Titovka and Zapadnaya Litsa rivers.

Motovun (mô'tôvōōn), Ital. *Montona* (mōntô'nä), village (1936 pop. 1,781), NW Croatia, Yugoslavia, on Mirna R. and 22 mi. S of Trieste, in Istria. Has cathedral (1614) with Romanesque campanile.

Motoyama (mōtō'yämū), town (pop. 6,724), Kochi prefecture, central Shikoku, Japan, on Yoshino R. and 14 mi. N of Kochi; agr. center (rice, wheat); raw silk, lumber, cattle.

Motozintla (mōtōsēn'tlä), officially Villa de Motozintla de Mendoza, town (pop. 2,469), Chiapas, S Mexico, in Sierra Madre, near Guatemala border, 33 mi. N of Tapachula; alt. 4,462 ft. Sugar cane, coffee, fruit.

Motrico (mōtrē'kō), town (pop. 2,240), Guipúzcoa prov., N Spain, fishing port on Bay of Biscay, 21 mi. W of San Sebastián; fish processing, boatbuilding; makes fine jewelry. Limestone and gypsum quarries in vicinity.

Motril (mōtrēl'), city (pop. 15,961), Granada prov., S Spain, in Andalusia, near the Mediterranean, 30 mi. SSE of Granada; terminus of aerial tramway from Dúrcal. Picturesquely situated in amphitheater facing the sea and backed by mts. Sugar mills, alcohol and brandy distilleries; also makes esparto mats, sandals, cotton cloth, burlap. Sericulture and flower growing. Irrigated surrounding area yields sugar cane, olive oil, wine, raisins, oranges, almonds, tomatoes. Zinc mines near by. Small port El Verdadero (pop. 1,094) is on the Mediterranean 1.5 mi. S.

Motsa or **Motza** (both: mōtsä'), settlement (pop. 50), E Israel, in Judaean Hills, 4 mi. W of Jerusalem; brick and tile mfg. Founded 1894; destroyed (1929) in Arab riots, then rebuilt. Key Israeli position (1948) during battle for Jerusalem road. Sometimes spelled Motsah or Motzah.

Mott, city (pop. 1,583), ⊙ Hettinger co., SW N.Dak., 41 mi. SE of Dickinson and on Cannonball R. Rail junction; coal mines; flour, dairy products, wheat, flax. Inc. 1928.

Motta di Livenza (môt'lä dē lēvĕn'tsä), town (pop. 2,122), Treviso prov., Veneto, N Italy, on Livenza R. and 20 mi. ENE of Treviso; rail junction; mfg. (soap, lye, silk textiles). Has cathedral, completed 1650.

Mottarone, Monte (môn'tĕ môt-tärō'nĕ), mountain (alt. 4,890 ft.), Italy, bet. lakes Maggiore and Orta, 4 mi. W of Stresa; winter sports. Summit (ascended by light railway from Stresa) commands superb view of the Alps, from Tenda Pass (SW) to the Ortles (NE). Agogna R. rises here.

Motta San Giovanni (môt'tä sän jôvän'nē), village (pop. 1,759), Reggio di Calabria prov., Calabria, S Italy, 8 mi. SSE of Reggio di Calabria.

Motta Santa Lucia (sän'tä lōōchē'ä), village (pop. 1,212), Catanzaro prov., Calabria, S Italy, 8 mi. NNW of Nicastro; meat products, silk.

Motta Sant'Anastasia (säntänästä'syä), village (pop. 4,949), Catania prov., E Sicily, 6 mi. W of Catania.

Motta Visconti (vēskôn'tē), village (pop. 3,526), Milano prov., Lombardy, N Italy, near Ticino R., 15 mi. SW of Milan; silk mill.

Motte, La (lä môt'), village (pop. estimate 400), W Que., on L. La Motte, 16 mi. S of Amos; lithium, bismuth mining.

Motte, La (lä môt'). **1** or **La Motte-du-Caire** (–dü-kâr'), village (pop. 297), Basses-Alpes dept., SE France, in Provence Alps, 15 mi. S of Gap; orchards. **2** Agr. village (pop. 415), Var dept., SE France, 5 mi. SE of Draguignan. Captured by Allied airborne troops, Aug. 15, 1944.

Motte, Lac La (läk lä môt'), lake (8 mi. long, 6 mi. wide), W Que., 16 mi. NW of Val d'Or, in gold-mining region. Drained N by Harricanaw R.

Motte-Chalençon, La (–shäläsō'), village (pop. 458), Drôme dept., SE France, in Dauphiné Pre-Alps, 19 mi. S of Die; lavender-essence processing.

Motte-d'Aveillans, La (–dävĕyä'), town (pop. 1,938), Isère dept., SE France, in Dauphiné Alps, 16 mi. S of Grenoble; anthracite mines.

Motte-du-Caire, La, Basses-Alpes dept., France: see MOTTE, LA.

Motte-Servolex, La (–sĕrvôlĕks'), agr. village (pop. 481), Savoie dept., SE France, in Chambéry trough, 3 mi. NW of Chambéry; cheese mfg.

Mott Haven, SE N.Y., an industrial section of SW Bronx borough of New York city, along Harlem R. (bridges to Manhattan); mfg. of machinery, metal products; railroad yards. Site of Bronx Terminal Market, Yankee Stadium, and Bronx County Bldg.

Mottingham, residential town and parish (pop. 2,120), NW Kent, England, 2 mi. N of Bromley.

Mott Island, Mich.: see ISLE ROYALE NATIONAL PARK.

Möttling, Yugoslavia: see METLIKA.

Mottola (môt'tôlä), town (pop. 9,551), Ionio prov., Apulia, S Italy, 15 mi. NW of Taranto, in agr. region (cereals, grapes, olives, almonds). Has 15th-cent. cathedral.

Mottram in Longdendale (mŏ'trŭm), former urban district (1931 pop. 1,222), NE Cheshire, England, 7 mi. ENE of Stockport; cotton milling. Has 16th-cent. church. Inc. 1936 in Longdendale. Includes (S) cotton-milling town of Broadbottom.

Motueka (mōtōōē'kŭ), borough (pop. 1,909), N S.Isl., New Zealand, on W shore of Tasman Bay and 20 mi. NW of Nelson; fruit, tobacco.

Motuhora (mōtōōhō'rŭ), township (pop. 121), E N.Isl., New Zealand, 40 mi. NW of Gisborne; rail terminus for agr. area; sawmills, building stone.

Motu Iti (mō'tōō-ē'tē). **1** Uninhabited atoll, Leeward group, Society Isls., Fr. Oceania, S Pacific, 8 mi. NW of Bora-Bora; 5 mi. long; owned by Fr. copra company. Also called Tubai and Tupai. **2** Rock islet, Marquesas Isls., Fr. Oceania, S Pacific, c.25 mi. NE of Nuku Hiva; rises to 720 ft.

Motul (mōtōōl'), officially Motul de Felipe Carrillo Puerto, town (pop. 5,384), Yucatan, SE Mexico, on railroad and 23 mi. ENE of Mérida; henequen-growing center. Archaeological remains near by.

Motu One, Society Isls.: see BELLINGSHAUSEN ISLAND.

Motupe (mōtōō'pā), town (pop. 4,396), Lambayeque dept., NW Peru, in W foothills of Cordillera Occidental, on Pan American Highway and 40 mi. NNE of Lambayeque, on Motupe R. (an affluent of the Leche); agr. products (corn, fruit, tobacco, alfalfa); cattle raising.

Motutapu Island (mōtōōtä'pōō), volcanic island, off N N.Isl., New Zealand, in Hauraki Gulf, 6 mi. E of entrance to Waitemata Harbour of Auckland; 3 mi. long, 2 mi. wide; coral causeway to Rangitoto Isl. Summer resort.

Motya or **Motye**, Sicily: see STAGNONE ISLANDS.

Motza, Israel: see MOTSA.

Mou-, for Chinese names beginning thus and not found here: see under Mow-.

Mouamaltein, Lebanon: see MA'AMELTEIN.

Moucha Islands (mōō'shä), coral group in Gulf of Tadjoura, Fr. Somaliland, 9 mi. NNE of Djibouti; week-end resort; fishing; bathing beach.

Mouchard (mōōshär'), village (pop. 938), Jura dept., E France, 16 mi. SE of Dôle; rail junction. Woodworking school.

Mouchoir Bank (mōō'shwär, mōōshwär'), shoal with reefs, in the West Indies, 60 mi. N of Hispaniola, separated from Turk Isls. (W) by Mouchoir Passage (c.60 mi. long); Silver Bank is 25 mi. E, beyond Silver Bank Passage.

Moudhros, Greece: see MOUDROS.

Moudjéria (mōōjĕ'ryä), village, S central Mauritania, Fr. West Africa, oasis in low Tagant massif of the Sahara, 300 mi. ENE of Saint-Louis, Senegal; dates, millet, livestock. Meteorological station.

Moudon (mōōdō'), Ger. *Milden* (mĭl'dŭn), town (pop. 2,338), Vaud canton, W Switzerland, on Broye R. and 13 mi. NNE of Lausanne; watches, foodstuffs, cotton textiles. An old town (anc. *Minnodunum* or *Minidunum*), it has a Gothic church (13th cent.) and 2 castles (16th and 17th cent.).

Moudros or **Moudhros** (both: mōō'dhrôs), town (pop. 1,720), on Lemnos isl., Greece, port on E shore of Gulf of Mudros (of naval base value); trade in olive oil, wine; fisheries. Allied base (1915) in Gallipoli campaign. The Allied-Turkish armistice was signed here, 1918. Formerly spelled Mudros.

Mouguerre (mōōgâr'), village (pop. 278), Basses-Pyrénées dept., SW France, 4 mi. ESE of Bayonne; saltworks, soda and fertilizer factory. Basque pop.

Mouila (mwēlä'), town, ⊙ N'Gounié region (formed 1949; pop. 82,800), S Gabon, Fr. Equatorial Africa, on N'Gounié R. and 190 mi. SSE of Libreville; trading center in gold-mining region. R.C. and Protestant missions; military camp.

Moukhtara, Lebanon: see MUKHTARA, EL.

Mouland, Belgium: see MOELINGEN.

Moulara, island, Greece: see AMMOULIANE.

Moularès (mōōlärĕs'), mining settlement, Gafsa dist., W Tunisia, on railroad, 28 mi. W of Gafsa; important phosphate mines and beneficiation plant. Also called Aïn-Moularès.

Moulay Idris or **Moulay Idriss** (mōōlä' ēdrēs'), town (pop. 9,901), Meknès region, N central Fr. Morocco, picturesquely situated in a ravine of the Zerhoun massif, 11 mi. N of Meknès; holy Moslem city containing the shrine of Idris I (founder of 1st Arab dynasty in Morocco; father of Idris II, the founder of Fez). Ruins of Roman VOLUBILIS are 2 mi. NW.

Moulay Yacoub (yäkōōb'), spa, Fez region, N central Fr. Morocco, 10 mi. WNW of Fez; hot sulphur springs. Moslem pilgrimage center.

Mould Bay, U.S.-Canadian Arctic weather station, SE Prince Patrick Isl., W Franklin Dist., Northwest Territories; 76°5'N 119°45'W.

Moule (mōōl), town (commune pop. 15,920), E Grande-Terre, Guadeloupe, minor port 14 mi. ENE of Pointe-à-Pitre, in sugar-growing region; trading (sugar cane, rum, fruit, lumber); distilling. Sometimes LeMoule.

Moule à Chique, Cape (mōōl' ä shēk'), headland on S St. Lucia, B.W.I., 20 mi. S of Castries; 13°43'N 60°57'W. Forms a narrow neck of land running into the sea for 3 mi.

Moulescoomb, England: see BRIGHTON.

Moulin (mōō'lĭn), agr. village and parish (pop. 2,775), N Perthshire, Scotland, on Tummel R. just NW of Pitlochry. Just SE are ruins of Castle Dhu.

Moulins (mōōlē'), town (pop. 20,832), ⊙ Allier dept., central France, on right bank of the Allier and 55 mi. SE of Bourges; commercial and rail center with ironworks and tanneries; mfg. (machine tools, hosiery, furs, shoes, furniture, perfumes). Episcopal see. Its cathedral contains a remarkable 15th-cent. triptych. Former convent of Order of Visitation (now a school), founded 1616 by St. Jane Frances de Chantal (who died here), has sculptured tomb of Henri de Montmorency. Other historical bldgs. are ruined castle of dukes of Bourbon and Renaissance pavillion of Anne de Beaujeu. Old ⊙ duchy of Bourbonnais. In 1566, an assembly held here by Charles IX adopted important legal and administrative reforms proposed by Michel de l'Hôpital.

Moulins-Engilbert (–ăzhēlbâr'), village (pop. 1,198), Nièvre dept., central France, 8 mi. SW of Château-Chinon; livestock, pottery.

Moulins-la-Marche (–lä-märsh'), village (pop. 784), Orne dept., NW France, in the Perche hills, 10 mi. NNW of Mortagne; horse raising.

Moulis (mōōlē'). **1** Village (pop. 275), Ariège dept., S France, on the Lez (small tributary of the Salat) and 3 mi. SW of Saint-Girons; marble quarries. **2** Village, Gironde dept., France: see MOULIS-EN-MÉDOC.

Moulis-en-Médoc (–ā-mādŏk'), village (pop. 198), Gironde dept., SW France, 18 mi. NW of Bordeaux; noted red wines. Until 1937, Moulis.

Moulmein (mōōlmān', mōl–,–mīn'), Burmese *Mawlamyaing* (môlŭmyĭn'), town (pop. 65,506), ⊙ Tenasserim div. and Amherst dist., Lower Burma, Andaman Sea port on Gulf of Martaban, 100 mi. ESE of Rangoon, on Salween R. mouth (opposite Martaban; ferry service) at confluence of Gyaing and Ataran rivers; 16°29'N 97°38'E. A major communications center, head of railroad to Ye; airport. Port (sheltered by Bilagyun Isl.) exports rice and teak. Shipbuilding, rice- and sawmilling, brewing, distilling, gold- and silverworking. Pagodas; limestone caves near by. Was chief town of Br. Burma from Treaty of Yandabo (1826) to annexation of Pegu (1852). Sometimes spelled Maulmain.

Moulmeingyun (mōōl'mĕnjŭn, Burmese mōlŭmyĭnjōōn'), town (pop. 7,747), Myaungmya dist., Lower Burma, on right bank of Irrawaddy R. (ferry) and 45 mi. SE of Bassein.

Moulouya River (mōōlōōyä'), Sp. *Muluya* (mōōlōō'yä), in NE Fr. Morocco, rises in the High Atlas SW of Midelt, flows 320 mi. NNE, through a semi-arid valley past Guercif (where it is crossed by Fez-Oujda RR), to the Mediterranean 35 mi. SE of Melilla. In its lower course it forms border bet. Fr. and Sp. Morocco. Very irregular volume. Not navigable.

Moulton (mōl'tŭn). **1** Town (pop. 1,384), ⊙ Lawrence co., NW Ala., 20 mi. SW of Decatur; cotton ginning, lumber milling. **2** Town (pop. 985), Appanoose co., S Iowa, near Mo. line and source of North Fabius R., 11 mi. ESE of Centerville, in bituminous-coal-mining area; rail junction; mfg. of metal products. Settled 1867. **3** Town (pop. 692), Lavaca co., S Texas, 20 mi. N of Yoakum; rail point in dairying, poultry-raising, truck-farming area; cottonseed-oil mill; ships garlic.

Moultonboro or **Moultonborough** (mōl'tŭn-), resort town (pop. 880), Carroll co., E central N.H., on N side of L. Winnipesaukee. Includes Long Isl., bridged to mainland; lake's largest isl.

Moultrie (mōl'trē), county (□ 345; pop. 13,171), central Ill.; ⊙ Sullivan. Agr. (corn, wheat, soybeans, broomcorn, livestock, poultry). Mfg. (shoes, concrete products, cheese and other dairy products). Drained by Kaskaskia R. Formed 1843.

Moultrie, city (pop. 11,639), ⊙ Colquitt co., S Ga., 35 mi. SE of Albany and on Ochlockonee R.; tobacco market and commercial center for farm area; mfg. (clothing, sheeting, fertilizer, cottonseed oil, mattresses, lumber); meat packing, food canning, peanut milling. Inc. 1859.

Moultrie, Fort (mōōl'trē), old fortification on Sullivans Isl., at entrance to Charleston Harbor, S.C. Br. attack repulsed here in 1776; fell to the Confederates in 1861. It was used as a govt. post until 1947.

Moultrie, Lake, S.C.: see SANTEE RIVER.

Moultrieville, S.C.: see SULLIVANS ISLAND.

Mound. 1 Village (pop. 105), Madison parish, NE La., near the Mississippi, 8 mi. W of Vicksburg, Miss.; agr. **2** Resort village (pop. 2,061), Hennepin co., E Minn., on L. Minnetonka and 20 mi. W of Minneapolis, in dairying, potato, poultry area. Settled 1854, inc. 1912.

Mound Bayou (bī'ō), town (pop. 1,328), Bolivar co., NW Miss., 25 mi. SSW of Clarksdale, in rich agr. area; an all-Negro self-governing community. Founded 1887, inc. 1898.

Mound City. 1 City (pop. 2,167), ⊙ Pulaski co., extreme S Ill., on Ohio R. and 5 mi. N of Cairo; shipbuilding (since Civil War); mfg. of wood products, canned foods, flour; agr. (fruit, cotton, truck). Important Union naval base in Civil War. Natl. cemetery is near by. City severely damaged in 1937 flood. Inc. 1857. **2** City (pop. 707), ⊙ Linn co., E Kansas, 22 mi. NNW of Fort Scott, in livestock and fruit region. Oil and gas wells, coal mines near by. Annual co. fair is held here. **3** City (pop. 1,412), Holt co., NW Mo., 32 mi. NW of St. Joseph; ships fruit, grain, livestock. State park, U.S. wildlife refuge near. Laid out 1857. **4** Town (pop. 177), ⊙ Campbell co., N S.Dak., 80 mi. WNW of Aberdeen; dairy products, wheat.

Mound City Group National Monument (57 acres; established 1923), S Ohio, on Scioto R. and 4 mi. N of Chillicothe. Pre-Columbian conical burial mounds here have yielded copper ornaments, stone utensils, and other remains of Hopewell culture. First explored 1846.

Moundou (mōōndōō'), town, ⊙ Logone region (□ 20,100; 1950 pop. 420,600), SW Chad territory, Fr. Equatorial Africa, on M'Béré R. and 260 mi. SSE of Fort-Lamy; cotton center; fishing. Protestant mission. Until 1946, in Ubangi-Shari colony.

Moundridge, city (pop. 942), McPherson co., central Kansas, 14 mi. SSE of McPherson; flour, feed, butter. Oil and gas wells near by.

Mounds. 1 City (pop. 2,001), Pulaski co., extreme S Ill., 8 mi. N of Cairo, in agr. area (corn, fruit). Inc. 1908. **2** Town (pop. 560), Creek co., central Okla., 20 mi. S of Tulsa, in oil-producing and agr. area; cotton ginning.

Mound Station or **Timewell,** town (pop. 184), Brown co., W Ill., 27 mi. ENE of Quincy, in agr. and bituminous-coal area.

Moundsville, city (pop. 14,772), ⊙ Marshall co., NW W.Va., in Northern Panhandle, on the Ohio and 11 mi. S of Wheeling. Coal-mining and mfg. center; glass making (especially tableware), zinc smelting and refining, mfg. of enamelware, clothing, tobacco products. Seat of state penitentiary. City takes its name from large conical Indian mound (Grave Creek Mound) here. Organized 1865.

Mound Valley, city (pop. 566), Labette co., SE Kansas, 11 mi. SW of Parsons, in grain and diversified-farming area. Oil and gas wells near by.

Moundville. 1 Town (pop. 901), Hale co., W Ala., on Black Warrior R. and 15 mi. S of Tuscaloosa; trade and shipping point in cotton, corn, and truck area; cotton ginning, lumber milling; feed. Near-by state monument includes group of large Indian mounds and mus. (dedicated 1939). **2** Town (pop. 168), Vernon co., W Mo., near Marmaton R., 7 mi. SW of Nevada.

Moung (mwŭng), town, Battambang prov., W Cambodia, on Pnompenh-Bangkok RR and 25 mi. SE of Battambang; rice-growing center.

Moungo River, Br. and Fr. Cameroons: see MUNGO RIVER.

Mounier, Mont (mō mōōnyā'), summit (9,245 ft.) of Maritime Alps, in Alpes-Maritimes dept., SE France, 8 mi. NE of Guillaumes.

Mount, Cape, headland of SW Liberia, on Atlantic Ocean; rises to 1,068 ft.; 6°45'N 11°23'W. Site of Robertsport.

Mount Abu, town, India: see ABU.

Mount Aetna Caverns, Md.: see BEAVER CREEK, village.

Mountain, city (pop. 219), Pembina co., NE N.Dak., 11 mi. SW of Cavalier; fuller's earth deposit near by.

Mountainair, village (pop. 1,418), Torrance co., central N.Mex., 45 mi. SE of Albuquerque, bet. Manzano Range (NW) and Chupadero Mesa (S); alt. c.6,550 ft. Shipping point for pinto beans. Near by are Abo Pueblo Ruins and Quarai Ruins.

Mountain Ash, urban district (1931 pop. 38,386; 1951 census 31,528), NE Glamorgan, Wales, on Taff R. and 6 mi. NNW of Pontypridd; coal-mining center. Site of large Eisteddfod Hall, scene of annual Three Valleys Musical Festival.

Mountain Autonomous Soviet Socialist Republic, Rus. *Gorskaya ASSR,* former administrative division of S European Russian SFSR, in the Greater Caucasus; ⊙ was Vladikavkaz. Formed 1921 out of non-Russian (Karachai, Kabardian, Balkar, Ossetian, Chechen, and Ingush) ethnic areas of the Caucasus; dissolved 1924.

Mountain Badakhshan, Tadzhik SSR: see GORNO-BADAKHSHAN.

Mountain Brook, town (pop. 8,359), Jefferson co., N central Ala., a S suburb of Birmingham.

Mountainburg, resort town (pop. 405), Crawford co., NW Ark., 21 mi. NE of Fort Smith, at S edge of the Ozarks.

Mountain City. 1 Resort town (pop. 524), Rabun co., extreme NE Ga., 3 mi. N of Clayton, in the Blue Ridge. **2** Village (pop. 134), Elko co., NE Nev., on East Fork Owyhee R. and 70 mi. N of Elko; alt. c.5,600 ft.; trading point. Rio Tinto (just S) is company-owned, copper-mining town. **3** Town (pop. 1,405), ⊙ Johnson co., extreme NE Tenn., 33 mi. ENE of Johnson City, bet. Stone Mts. (E) and Iron Mts. (W); farm-trade center in summer-resort region; lumbering; toys.

Mountain Creek Lake, Dallas co., N Texas, reservoir (capacity c.40,000 acre-ft.) impounded 10 mi. WSW of Dallas by dam in small Mountain Creek, a S tributary of West Fork of Trinity R.

Mountain Dale, resort village (pop. c.400), Sullivan co., SE N.Y., in the Catskills, 8 mi. ENE of Monticello.

Mountain Fork, Ark. and Okla.: see LITTLE RIVER.

Mountain Grove, city (pop. 3,106), Wright co., S central Mo., in the Ozarks, 55 mi. E of Springfield, in agr., timber area. Trade center; mfg. (dairy products, shoes, lumber). State fruit experiment station near by. Settled 1851, inc. 1882.

Mountain Home. 1 Resort and agr. town (pop. 2,217), ⊙ Baxter co., N Ark., c.40 mi. ENE of Harrison, in the Ozarks, bet. White R. and the North Fork. **2** Village (pop. 1,887), ⊙ Elmore co., SW Idaho, near Snake R., 40 mi. SE of Boise; wool-shipping point in irrigated agr. area (sheep, cattle, fruit, hay). U.S. Air Force base near. Plans for further land reclamation in vicinity have been made. Copper, silver, gold mines near by. Inc. 1896.

Mountain Iron, village (pop. 1,377), St. Louis Co., NE Minn., on Mesabi iron range just W of Virginia. Superior Natl. Forest just N. Settled 1890, inc. 1892. Grew with exploitation of iron deposits. Experimental beneficiation plant for low-grade ore (taconite) built 1951.

Mountain Island Lake, N.C.: see CATAWBA RIVER.

Mountain Karabakh, Azerbaijan SSR: see NAGORNO-KARABAKH AUTONOMOUS OBLAST.

Mountain Lake. 1 Village (pop. 1,733), Cottonwood co., SW Minn., on small lake 10 mi. ENE of Windom, in livestock and grain area; dairy products. Laid out 1872, settled by Mennonites. Music festival takes place annually. **2** Summer resort, Greenville co., NW S.C., in the Blue Ridge, on South Saluda R. and 19 mi. NNW of Greenville. Sometimes called Venus. **3** Resort village, Giles co., SW Va., in the Alleghenies, on Mountain L. (1 mi. long, ½ mi. wide), 33 mi. WNW of Roanoke; alt. c.3,850 ft.

Mountain Lake, in chain of lakes on Can. line bet. Cook co., NE Minn., and W Ont.; 7 mi. long, 1 mi. wide. Source of Pigeon R.

Mountain Lake Park, town (pop. 891), Garrett co., W Md., in the Alleghenies just SE of Oakland; vegetable cannery.

Mountain Lakes, residential borough (pop. 2,806), Morris co., N N.J., 6 mi. E of Dover. Has several artificial lakes. Settled 1915 as real-estate development, inc. 1924.

Mountain Park, village (pop. estimate 400), W Alta., in Rocky Mts., near Jasper Natl. Park, 35 mi. E of Jasper; alt. 5,815 ft.; coal mining.

Mountain Park. 1 City (pop. 15), Fulton co., NW central Ga., 12 mi. NE of Marietta. **2** Town (pop. 418), Kiowa co., SW Okla., 25 mi. SSE of Hobart, in agr. area; granite, marble quarries.

Mountain Pine, village (pop. 1,155), Garland co., central Ark., 8 mi. NW of Hot Springs and on Ouachita R.

Mountain Point, village (pop. 100), SE Alaska, on S shore of Revillagigedo Isl., SE of Ketchikan; 55°18'N 131°32'W.

Mountain Province, province (□ 5,458; 1948 pop. 278,120), N Luzon, Philippines, partly bounded E by Magat R.; ⊙ BONTOC. Comprises 5 sub-provs.: Apayao (äpä'you) in N; Kalinga (kälĕng'gä), Bontoc (bŏntŏk'), and Ifugao (ēfōōgou') in central area; and Benguet (bĕng-gĕt') in S. Almost wholly mountainous; highest peak in prov. is Mt. Cauitan (8,427 ft.). The Agno drains S section. The chief mining area of the Philippines, the prov. has major gold and copper mines. Lumbering is important. Extensive rice growing, especially in Ifugao sub-prov., where mtn. slopes are carved into rice terraces rising to c.4,000 ft. The prov. is inhabited by pagan tribes of Malay origin: Igorots, Ifugao, and Kalingas. BAGUIO, the resort in Benguet sub-prov., is administratively independent of Mountain Prov.

Mountain Rest, summer resort, Oconee co., NW S.C., in the Blue Ridge, 45 mi. W of Greenville.

Mountainside, residential borough (pop. 2,046), Union co., NE N.J., 11 mi. SW of Newark. Park and bird sanctuary here. Inc. 1895.

Mountains of the Moon, central Africa: see RUWENZORI.

Mountaintop, village, Luzerne co., NE Pa., 5 mi. S of Wilkes-Barre; alt. 1,680 ft. Railroad yards. Founded 1788.

Mountain View, village (pop. 2,880), S Alaska, just E of Anchorage.

Mountain View, village (pop. estimate 250), S Alta., near Mont. border, 50 mi. SW of Lethbridge; gateway to Waterton Lakes Natl. Park; dairying.

Mountain View, village (pop. 746), SE Hawaii, T.H., 13 mi. NE of Kilauea crater; part of Olaa sugar plantation.

Mountain View. 1 or **Mountainview,** town (pop. 1,043), ⊙ Stone co., N Ark., 27 mi. WNW of Batesville, in the Ozarks; agr., woodworking, cotton ginning. Summer resort. **2** City (pop. 6,563), Santa Clara co., W Calif., just SE of Palo Alto; printing and publishing; fruit canning and packing. Inc. 1902. **3** W suburb (pop. 878) of Denver, Jefferson co., N central Colo.; alt. 5,370 ft. **4** Town (pop. 892), Howell co., S Mo., in the Ozarks, near Eleven Point R., 20 mi. NNE of West Plains; grain, lumber products. **5** Resort village (1940 pop. 2,008), Passaic co., NE N.J., on Pompton R. and 5 mi. W of Paterson, in agr. region (truck, fruit, poultry, dairy products); nurseries. **6** Town (pop. 1,009), Kiowa co., SW Okla., 20 mi. ENE of Hobart, and on Washita R. N of Wichita Mts., in wheat, cotton, dairying area; cotton ginning, cheese mfg.; hatchery.

Mountain Village, village (pop. 220), W Alaska, on Yukon R. and 110 mi. NW of Bethel; 62°5'N 163°43'W; supply center for trappers and prospectors. Served by Yukon R. steamship lines. Has Bureau of Indian Affairs hosp. and school; R.C. mission.

Mountainville. 1 Village, Hunterdon co., W N.J., 18 mi. WSW of Morristown, in summer-home area. **2** Resort village, Orange co., SE N.Y., 12 mi. SSW of Newburgh, in Hudson highlands.

Mountain Zebra National Park (3,545 acres), SE Cape Prov., U. of So. Afr., 15 mi. WNW of Cradock; reserve established 1937.

Mount Airy (â'rē). **1** Town (pop. 416), Habersham co., NE Ga., 11 mi. WSW of Toccoa. **2** Town (pop. 1,061), Carroll and Frederick counties, N Md., 30 mi. W of Baltimore, in agr. area; makes clothing. **3** Town (pop. 7,192), Surry co., NW N.C., 34 mi. NW of Winston-Salem, in Blue Ridge foothills; trade and mfg. (furniture, veneer, hosiery, clothing, buttons, bricks, metal products) center; pickle canning, granite quarrying. Inc. 1885.

Mount Albert, village (pop. estimate 600), S Ont., 32 mi. N of Toronto; dairying, mixed farming.

Mount Albert, borough (pop. 24,416), N N.Isl., New Zealand; residential suburb of Auckland.

Mount Angel, city (pop. 1,315), Marion co., NW Oregon, 13 mi. NE of Salem in valley of Willamette R.; trade center for fruit, grain, and dairying area; canned fruit, dairy products. Mt. Angel Women's Col. near by. Inc. 1905.

Mount Arlington, borough (pop. 639), Morris co., N N.J., on L. Hopatcong and 5 mi. NW of Dover; makes boats.

Mount Athos (ă'thŏs, ā'thŏs), Gr. officially *Hagion Oros* or *Ayion Oros* (both: ā'yôn ô'rôs) [=holy mountain], autonomous monastic district (□ 131; pop. 4,746) of Greek Macedonia, in Chalcidice nome; coextensive with AKTE prong of Chalcidice peninsula. Pop. consists entirely of Basilian monks, living in 20 monasteries and the administrative center of KARYAI, and administered by a representative committee under direct rule of Greek patriarch of Constantinople. Subsistence agr.: grain, olives, vineyards; goat and sheep raising. Formed in 10th cent., the community has enjoyed autonomy under Byzantine emperors, Ottoman sultans, and the modern Greek government. A great medieval center of Greek theology, it has preserved and furnished to Europe a great wealth of Byzantine manuscripts.

Mount Auburn (ô'bûrn). 1 Village (pop. 414), Christian co., central Ill., near Sangamon R., 21 mi. E of Springfield; grain, dairy products, livestock, poultry. 2 Town (pop. 164), Wayne co., E Ind., 16 mi. W of Richmond. There is also a Mt. Auburn in Shelby co., 4 mi. NE of Edinburg. 3 Town (pop. 216), Benton co., E central Iowa, near Cedar R., 29 mi. NW of Cedar Rapids, in agr. area. 4 Village, Middlesex co., Mass.: see CAMBRIDGE.

Mount Ayr (âr). 1 Town (pop. 222), Newton co., NW Ind., 7 mi. W of Rensselaer, in agr. area. 2 Town (pop. 1,793), ⊙ Ringgold co., S Iowa, 24 mi. SSE of Creston, in livestock and grain area. Founded c.1855, inc. 1875.

Mount Barker. 1 Town (pop. 1,609), SE South Australia, 18 mi. ESE of Adelaide; poultry, dairy products. 2 Town (pop. 796), SW Western Australia, 210 mi. SSE of Perth, at base of Mt. Barker (829 ft.); apple center.

Mount Bischoff, Tasmania: see WARATAH.

Mount Blanchard (blăn'chûrd), village (pop. 444), Hancock co., NW Ohio, 10 mi. SSE of Findlay and on Blanchard R.

Mount Braddock, village (1940 pop. 733), Fayette co., SW Pa., 6 mi. NE of Uniontown city; explosives, bricks, coke.

Mount Brydges, village (pop. estimate 600), S Ont., 15 mi. WSW of London; dairying, farming.

Mount Calm, town (pop. 456), Hill co., central Texas, 20 mi. NE of Waco; trade, shipping point in cotton area.

Mount Calvary, village (pop. c.500), Fond du Lac co., E Wis., near Sheboygan R., 10 mi. ENE of Fond du Lac, in dairying region. St. Lawrence Jr. Col. here.

Mount Carbon, borough (pop. 302), Schuylkill co., E central Pa., on Schuylkill R. just below Pottsville.

Mount Carmel (kär'mŭl). 1 Village, New Haven co., Conn.: see HAMDEN. 2 City (pop. 8,732), ⊙ Wabash co., SE Ill., on the Wabash and 24 mi. SSW of Vincennes, Ind.; center of rich agr. area (corn, wheat, soybeans); mfg. of electronic and sports equipment, clothing, flour, paper products; railroad shops. Bituminous coal, oil obtained near by. Mussel-shell industry flourished here after 1900. Indian mounds near by have yielded artifacts. Laid out 1818, inc. 1825. 3 Town (pop. 134), Franklin co., SE Ind., 30 mi. S of Richmond, in agr. area. 4. Borough (pop. 14,222), Northumberland co., E central Pa., 20 mi. ESE of Sunbury; anthracite; clothing, chemicals. Laid out 1835, inc. 1864. 5 Town (pop. 84), McCormick co., W S.C., 23 mi. SW of Greenwood. 6 Village (pop. c.100), Kane co., SW Utah, on East Fork Virgin R. and 15 mi. NNW of Kanab; alt. c.5,200 ft.; agr., livestock. Highway extends 25 mi. W to Zion Canyon, in Zion Natl. Park.

Mount Carroll, city (pop. 1,950), ⊙ Carroll co., NW Ill., 22 mi. SW of Freeport, in rich agr. area; dairy products, grain, livestock, poultry. Seat of Frances Shimer Col. for women. Founded 1843, inc. 1867.

Mountcharles, Gaelic *Montséarlas*, town (pop. 288), S Co. Donegal, Ireland, on N shore of Donegal Bay, 4 mi. W of Donegal; granite quarrying.

Mount Chase, plantation (pop. 250), Penobscot co., N central Maine, 31 mi. NNE of Millinocket, in hunting, fishing area.

Mount Clare. 1 Village (pop. 260), Macoupin co., SW central Ill., 12 mi. SSE of Carlinville, in agr. and bituminous-coal area. 2 Village (pop. 1,236), Harrison co., N W.Va., 5 mi. S of Clarksburg.

Mount Clemens (klĕ'mŭnz), city (pop. 17,027), ⊙ Macomb co., SE Mich., 20 mi. NNE of Detroit and on Clinton R. near its mouth on L. St. Clair; health resort, with mineral springs. Mfg. (auto parts, pottery, steel springs, farm implements, trailers, boats, food products); ships mineral water; truck farming. A U.S. military air base, Selfridge Field, is here. Settled c.1798; platted 1818; inc. as village 1837, as city 1879.

Mount Coolon (kōō'lŏn), town (pop. 63), E Queensland, Australia, 150 mi. SSE of Townsville; gold mines.

Mount Cory, village (pop. 302), Hancock co., NW Ohio, 11 mi. SW of Findlay, in agr. area.

Mount Crawford, town (pop. 303), Rockingham co., NW Va., in Shenandoah Valley, on North R. and 16 mi. NNE of Staunton.

Mount Croghan (krŏ'gĭn), town (pop. 209), Chesterfield co., N S.C., 20 mi. WNW of Cheraw, near N.C. line.

Mount Darwin, rural township (pop. 180), Salisbury prov., NE Southern Rhodesia, in Mashonaland, 40 mi. NNE of Bindura; tobacco, peanuts; cattle, sheep, goats. Police post for Darwin dist. Gold and asbestos mining near by.

Mount Desert (dĭzûrt', dĕ'zûrt), resort town (pop. 1,776), Hancock co., S Maine, on Mt. Desert Isl.; includes villages of Seal Harbor, Northeast Harbor, and Asticou. Settled 1762; formerly called Somesville; inc. 1789.

Mount Desert Island, Hancock co., S Maine, mountainous, wooded resort isl. (bridged to mainland) in Frenchman Bay of Atlantic Ocean, 40 mi. SE of Bangor; □ c.100. Somes Sound, narrow fjord 6 mi. long, divides S half of isl. into E and W segments, each c.10 mi. long, 5 mi. wide. Good harbors are found at BAR HARBOR, Northeast Harbor, and other resort villages. Cadillac Mtn. (1,532 ft.) is highest elevation on E seaboard. Lakes include Great Pond (4 mi. long), Eagle L. (2 mi. long), and several smaller ponds. Isl. named by Champlain, who visited it in 1604. Jesuit mission established 1613; 1st settlement made 1762. Resort development began in mid-19th cent. Large part of isl. in ACADIA NATIONAL PARK. Forests extensively damaged in fire (1947) that destroyed much of Bar Harbor.

Mount Dora. 1 Town (pop. 3,028), Lake co., central Fla., 23 mi. NW of Orlando, on L. Dora; yachting resort; citrus-fruit shipping center with packing houses, cannery, box and fertilizer factories. Settled 1874, inc. 1912. 2 Village (pop. c.250), Union co., NE N.Mex., near Texas and Okla. lines, 18 mi. WNW of Clayton; alt. c.5,400 ft. Shipping point for livestock and grain.

Mount Eagle, mountain (1,696 ft.), W Co. Kerry, Ireland, 2 mi. NE of Slea Head.

Mount Eaton, village (pop. 203), Wayne co., N central Ohio, 14 mi. ESE of Wooster, in agr. area.

Mount Eba, settlement, central South Australia, 100 mi. NW of Woomera and 200 mi. NW of Port Augusta, in arid dist.; 39°11'S 135°41'E; site of some installations of WOOMERA rocket-launching range.

Mount Eden, borough (pop. 20,167), N N.Isl., New Zealand; residential suburb of Auckland, at base of Mt. Eden (644 ft.).

Mount Eden, village (pop. c.500), Alameda co., W Calif., just SW of Hayward, in rich agr. area; salt refining. Near by is San Mateo Toll Bridge across San Francisco Bay.

Mount Edgecumbe, village (pop. 547), SE Alaska, on S Kruzof Isl., at foot of Mt. Edgecumbe.

Mount Enterprise, town (pop. 504), Rusk co., E Texas, 16 mi. SSE of Henderson; trade point in pine lumber, cotton, cattle, truck area.

Mount Ephraim (ē'frēŭm), borough (pop. 4,449), Camden co., SW N.J., 5 mi. S of Camden, in fruit-growing region. Settled before 1800, inc. 1926.

Mount Erie, village (pop. 149), Wayne co., SE Ill., 38 mi. ENE of Mount Vernon, in agr. area.

Mount Etna, town (pop. 171), Huntington co., NE central Ind., on Salamonie R. and 10 mi. SSW of Huntington, in agr. area.

Mount Forest, town (pop. 1,892), S Ont., on branch of Saugeen R. and 40 mi. NNW of Kitchener; woolen mills, agr.-machinery works; dairying, woodworking.

Mount Gambier (găm'bēr), town (pop. 6,771), extreme SE South Australia, 235 mi. SE of Adelaide, near Victoria line; rail junction; sheep and agr. center; acacia bark. Near by is Mt. Gambier, extinct volcano with collapsed craters (highest, 650 ft.). Limestone quarries near by.

Mount Garnet, village (pop. 414), NE Queensland, Australia, 70 mi. SW of Cairns; terminus of spur of Cairns-Charleston RR; tin mines; hot springs.

Mount Gay, village (pop. 4,201, with adjacent Cora), Logan co., SW W.Va., just W of Logan. Also called Gay.

Mount Gilead (gĭ'lēŭd). 1 Town (pop. 1,201), Montgomery co., S central N.C., 14 mi. SE of Albemarle; mfg. of hosiery, undergarments, bricks; lumber. Power dam on Pee Dee R. (W) forms L. Tillery. 2 Village (pop. 2,351), ⊙ Morrow co., central Ohio, 16 mi. ESE of Marion; produces hydraulic presses, electrical apparatus, pottery, chemicals; seed growing. Founded c.1824; renamed Mount Gilead in 1832.

Mount Gretna, borough (pop. 83), Lebanon co., SE central Pa., 6 mi. SSW of Lebanon.

Mount Hamilton Range, Calif.: see DIABLO RANGE.

Mount Harris, village (1940 pop. 891), Routt co., NW Colo., on Yampa R., near Park Range, and 12 mi. W of Steamboat Springs, in natl.-forest area; alt. 6,350 ft.; coal-mining point.

Mount Healthy, city (pop. 5,533), Hamilton co., extreme SW Ohio, a N suburb of Cincinnati; makes clothing, tools, brick, flour. Founded 1817.

Mount Herbert, county, New Zealand: see GOVERNOR'S BAY.

Mount Hermon. 1 Resort village, Santa Cruz co., W Calif., in Santa Cruz Mts., 5 mi. N of Santa Cruz. Redwood groves near by. 2 Village, Franklin co., Mass.: see NORTHFIELD.

Mount Holly. 1 Unincorporated village (pop. 8,206), ⊙ Burlington co., W N.J., on Rancocas Creek and 18 mi. E of Camden; mfg. (clothing, textiles, dyes, leather goods); trade center for agr. region. Settled by Friends c.1680; occupied by British in Revolution. Friends' meetinghouse (1775), courthouse (1796), John Woolman memorial building (1771), and other 18th-cent. buildings survive. 2 Town (pop. 2,241), Gaston co., S N.C., 10 mi. WNW of Charlotte, on Catawba L.; textile center with cotton, woolen, and hosiery mills. Hydroelectric plant near by. Inc. 1879. 3 Town (pop. 567), Rutland co., S central Vt., 13 mi. SE of Rutland, in agr. area; dairy products. Partly in Green Mtn. Natl. Forest.

Mount Holly Springs, borough (pop. 1,701), Cumberland co., S Pa., 6 mi. S of Carlisle; clothing, paper; clay. Laid out 1815.

Mount Hope, village (pop. 129), central New South Wales, Australia, 320 mi. WNW of Sydney; copper-mining center.

Mount Hope, town (pop. 73), Cristobal dist., N Panama Canal Zone, on transisthmian railroad and 1½ mi. S of Colón (Panama), adjoining (S) Cristobal, on mouth of old Fr. canal. Has rail yards, repair wharves, and drydocks; cold-storage plants.

Mount Hope. 1 City (pop. 473), Sedgwick co., S central Kansas, 22 mi. NW of Wichita, in wheat, livestock, and poultry area. Oil wells near by. 2 Mining village, Morris co., N central N.J., 3 mi. N of Dover, in lake and hill region. Iron mined here since 1772. 3 City (pop. 2,588), Fayette co., S central W.Va., 8 mi. N of Beckley; trade center for bituminous-coal fields. Inc. 1897. 4 Village (pop. 232), Grant co., extreme SW Wis., 16 mi. ESE of Prairie du Chien, in livestock and dairy region.

Mount Hope Bay, R.I. and Mass., NE arm of Narragansett Bay, just W of Fall River, Mass.; c.6 mi. long, 3 mi. wide. Opens S into Sakonnet R., SW into Narragansett Bay at N end of Rhode Isl., where it is crossed by Mt. Hope Bridge (1929), one of largest in New England.

Mount Horeb (hôr'ĕb), village (pop. 1,716), Dane co., S Wis., 19 mi. WSW of Madison, in dairying and farming area; processes dairy products, feed. Settled 1860 by Norwegians and Swiss; inc. 1899.

Mount Ida, town (pop. 566), ⊙ Montgomery co., W Ark., 32 mi. W of Hot Springs; ships livestock; dairying, sawmilling.

Mount Irvine Bay (ûr'vĭn) or **Little Courland Bay** (kōōr'lŭnd), SW Tobago, B.W.I.; popular bathing resort, 7 mi. W of Scarborough.

Mount Isa (ī'zŭ), town (pop. 3,504), W Queensland, Australia, 65 mi. W of Cloncurry; rail terminus, coke smelting. Silver, copper, lead, and zinc mines are near by.

Mount Jackson, town (pop. 732), Shenandoah co., NW Va., on North Fork of Shenandoah R. and 24 mi. NNE of Harrisonburg; mfg. of clothing, apple products, cinder blocks, fertilizer. Shenandoah Caverns (just S) attract tourists.

Mount Jewett, borough (pop. 1,415), McKean co., N Pa., 16 mi. S of Bradford; tannery, clay products; oil wells; hemlock timber. Settled c.1838, inc. 1893.

Mount Joy, borough (pop. 3,006), Lancaster co., SE Pa., 12 mi. NW of Lancaster; shoes, textiles, iron castings, chocolate. Settled 1768, laid out 1812, inc. 1851.

Mount Kisco (kĭ'skō), residential village (pop. 5,907), Westchester co., SE N.Y., 13 mi. N of White Plains; mfg. of furniture, wood products, machinery; radium extracting. Has a summer theater. Inc. 1874.

Mount Lavinia, town (pop. 9,346), Western Prov., Ceylon, on W coast, 7 mi. S of Colombo city center; resort and residential area for Colombo; coconuts, rice, cinnamon, vegetables. Col. Urban council (pop. 56,503) includes Dehiwala.

Mount Lebanon (lĕ'bŭnŭn). 1 Settlement, Columbia co., SE N.Y., 7 mi. W of Pittsfield, Mass. Here are a few members and bldgs. of once-flourishing Shaker community established in 1785. 2 Urban township (pop. 26,604), Allegheny co., SW Pa., just SW of Pittsburgh; residential.

Mount Lehman (lē'mŭn), village, SW B.C., 4 mi. WSW of Mission across Fraser R.; dairying; stock, vegetables, fruit.

Mount Leonard (lĕ'nûrd), town (pop. 142), Saline co., central Mo., near Missouri R., 10 mi. W of Marshall.

Mount Lofty, village (pop. 355), SE South Australia, 9 mi. SE of Adelaide, in Mt. Lofty Ranges; dairying center.

Mount Lofty Ranges, SE South Australia, extend 200 mi. S from Peterborough to Cape Jervis; rise to 3,063 ft. (Mt. Bryan). Fertile valleys (olive plantations, vineyards). Phosphate rock, marble, barite. Source of Torrens R. Mt. Lofty (2,384 ft.) is near Adelaide.

Mount Lyell, Tasmania: see QUEENSTOWN.

Mount McKinley National Park (□ 3,030.1), S central Alaska, in Alaska Range, 120 mi. SW of Fairbanks; center near 63°30'N 150°5'W; 110 mi. long, 30–40 mi. wide. In it is Mt. McKinley (20,270 ft.), highest point in North America, Mt. Foraker (17,280 ft.), Mt. Hunter (14,960 ft.), and several other peaks over 10,000 ft. high, with extensive glaciers. Spectacular mtn. scenery and rare wild life attract many tourists. McKinley Park village, on Alaska RR, is gateway to park. Established 1917, park was enlarged 1922 and 1932.

Mount Magnet, town (pop. 631), W central Western Australia, 200 mi. ENE of Geraldton and on Geraldton-Wiluna RR; mining center in Murchison Goldfield.

Mount Margaret, village, S central Western Australia, 440 mi. NE of Perth and on Perth-Laverton RR; mining center for Mt. Margaret Goldfield (□ 42,154).

Mount Marion, village, Ulster co., SE N.Y., near Esopus Creek and the Hudson, 3 mi. SSW of Saugerties, in resort and agr. area.

Mount Melleray (mĕlûrā'), locality in W Co. Waterford, Ireland, at foot of the Knockmealdown Mts., 5 mi. NE of Lismore; site of famous Trappist monastery, founded 1830, after expulsion of foreign Trappists from France.

Mountmellick (mountmĕ'lĭk), Gaelic *Móinteach Mílic*, town (pop. 2,737), N Co. Laoighis, Ireland, on branch of the Grand Canal and 6 mi. NNW of Port Laoighise; agr. market (wheat, barley, potatoes, beets); formerly important mfg. town.

Mount Morgan, town (pop. 3,942), E Queensland, Australia, 22 mi. SSW of Rockhampton; gold and copper mines.

Mount Moriah (mŭrī'ŭ), town (pop. 260), Harrison co., NW Mo., 13 mi. NE of Bethany.

Mount Morris. 1 Village (pop. 2,709), Ogle co., N Ill., 23 mi. SW of Rockford, in rich agr. area; large printing plant. Settled 1838, inc. 1857. **2** City (pop. 2,890), Genesee co., SE central Mich., 7 mi. N of Flint, in farm area (grain, potatoes; dairy products). Settled 1842; inc. as village 1867, as city 1930. **3** Village (pop. 3,450), Livingston co., W central N.Y., on Genesee R. and 34 mi. SSW of Rochester; mfg. (canned foods, condiments, machinery, electrical appliances). A tuberculosis hosp. is here. Letchworth State Park is near by. Mount Morris Dam (550 ft. long, 216 ft. high; for flood control) is on the Genesee here. **4** Borough (1940 pop. 432), Greene co., SW Pa., 13 mi. SE of Waynesburg.

Mount Morrison, Colo: see MORRISON.

Mount Mulligan, village (pop. 308), NE Queensland, Australia, 60 mi. W of Cairns; terminus of spur of Cairns-Charleston RR; coal mines.

Mount Olive. 1 City (pop. 2,401), Macoupin co., SW central Ill., 27 mi. ENE of Alton, in agr. and bituminous-coal-mining area; mfg. (brick, monuments, tile). Inc. 1917. Has graves of "Mother" Jones and "General" Alexander Bradley, pioneers in miners' union movement. **2** Town (pop. 827), Covington co., S central Miss., 36 mi. NNW of Hattiesburg. **3** Town (pop. 3,732), Wayne co., E central N.C., 13 mi. SSW of Goldsboro; bean market; trade center for truck, tobacco, and cotton area; crate and lumber mills, pickle cannery. Founded 1839–40.

Mount Oliver, borough (pop. 6,646), Allegheny co., SW Pa., within S part of Pittsburgh. Inc. 1892.

Mount Olivet (ŏ'lĭvĕt), town (pop. 455), ⊙ Robertson co., N Ky., 17 mi. WSW of Maysville, in Bluegrass agr. region.

Mount Olympus National Monument, Wash.: see OLYMPIC NATIONAL PARK.

Mount Orab (ô'rŭb), village (pop. 758), Brown co., SW Ohio, 11 mi. N of Georgetown, in tobacco and grain area.

Mount Penn, residential borough (pop. 3,635), Berks co., SE central Pa., just SE of Reading; hosiery. Laid out 1884, inc. 1902.

Mount Perry, village (pop. 295), SE Queensland, Australia, 180 mi. NNW of Brisbane; rail terminus; copper mine.

Mount Pleasant, village (pop. 356), SE South Australia, 28 mi. ENE of Adelaide; rail terminus; dairy products, livestock.

Mount Pleasant. 1 Village (pop. c.200), New Castle co., W Del., 17 mi. SSW of Wilmington; waterfowl hunting. **2** City (pop. 5,843), ⊙ Henry co., SE Iowa, 25 mi. WNW of Burlington; fountain-pen factory. Has Iowa Wesleyan Col. A soldiers' and sailors' hosp. and state hosp. for the insane (1861) are here. State park, limestone quarries near by. Founded 1839, inc. 1842. **3** City (pop. 11,393), ⊙ Isabella co., central Mich., c.45 mi. WNW of Saginaw and on Chippewa R., in oil and agr. (dairy products; grain, sugar beets, corn, beans) area; mfg. (plumbing fixtures, auto parts, food products); oil and sugar refineries. Seat of a state teachers col., and a state vocational school for feeble-minded children. Settled before 1860; inc. as village 1875, as city 1889. **4** Town (pop. 1,019), Cabarrus co., S central N.C., 8 mi. E of Concord; cotton and hosiery mills. **5** Village (pop. 760), Jefferson co., E Ohio, 6 mi. NW of Martins Ferry. **6** Borough (pop. 5,883), Westmoreland co., SW Pa., 30 mi. SE of Pittsburgh; bituminous coal; glass, coke, metal products, cigars, cement products; timber; agr. Laid out c.1897, inc. 1828. **7** Village, Providence co., R.I.: see BURRILLVILLE. **8** Summer-resort town (pop. 1,857), Charleston co., SE S.C., 4 mi. E of Charleston, across Charleston Harbor (here bridged); canning, boat repairs. **9** Town (pop. 2,931), Maury co., central Tenn., 11 mi. SW of Columbia, in phosphate-mining, lumbering, agr. area; makes fertilizer, chemicals, clothing; tobacco warehouses. Meriwether Lewis Natl. Monument is 14 mi. W. **10** City (pop. 6,342), ⊙ Titus co., NE Texas, c.50 mi. SE of Paris; trade, shipping center for agr., oil, lumbering region; cottonseed-oil milling, woodworking, oil refining, milk processing, pottery mfg. Settled before mid-19th cent., inc. 1900; formerly a lumbering center. **11** City (pop. 2,030), Sanpete co., central Utah, 22 mi. NNE of Manti, near San Pitch R., in irrigated Sanpete Valley; alt. c.5,850 ft. Shipping point for livestock and agr. area (alfalfa, wheat, oats); flour, cheese. Settled 1852 by Mormons, inc. 1868. Wasatch Range is E.

Mount Pocono (pō'kŭnō), resort borough (pop. 619), Monroe co., E Pa., 12 mi. NW of Stroudsburg in Pocono mts.; alt. 1,658 ft.

Mount Prospect, village (pop. 4,009), Cook co., NE Ill., NW suburb of Chicago, 12 mi. W of Evanston; mfg. of stapling machines; dairy, truck, grain farms. Inc. 1917.

Mount Pulaski (pŭlă'skē), city (pop. 1,526), Logan co., central Ill., 25 mi. NE of Springfield, in agr. and bituminous-coal area. Was ⊙ Logan co., 1847–53; inc. 1893. The old courthouse (1847) was made a state monument in 1936.

Mountrail, county (□ 1,900; pop. 9,418), NW central N.Dak.; ⊙ Stanley. Rich agr. area on Missouri R. and drained by White Earth R. Coal mines; livestock, dairy produce, grain, flax, vegetables. Verendrye Natl. Monument in S. Formed 1908.

Mount Rainier (rā'nûr), town (pop. 10,989), Prince Georges co., central Md., suburb NE of Washington.

Mount Rainier National Park (rŭnēr', rā–, rā'nēr) (□ 377.4; established 1899), W central Wash., in Cascade Range, c.40 mi. SE of Tacoma. Scenic wilderness area centering in Mt. Rainier (14,408 ft.), towering volcanic peak that occupies c.¼ of park area and has largest single-peak glacier system (□ c.40) in U.S. Best known of 26 glaciers are Emmons (5 mi. long) and Nisqually (nĭskwô'lē) (c.4 mi. long). Many streams are fed by glaciers, which are slowly receding. Heavily forested lower slopes (part of Mt. Rainier Natl. Forest) have dense stands of coniferous trees, beautiful alpine meadows and many lakes, supporting an abundance of wildlife and a notable variety of wildflowers. Facilities for camping, riding, hiking, and winter sports; lodges at Yakima Park (yă'kŭmô, –mŭ) in N and Paradise Valley and Longmire (park hq.) in S. Peak was discovered and named by Captain Vancouver in 1792 and 1st climbed in 1870. Mtn. sometimes called Mt. Tacoma.

Mountrath (mŏntrăth'), Gaelic *Móin Rátha*, town (pop. 1,086), central Co. Laoighis, Ireland, 8 mi. WSW of Port Laoighise; agr. market (wheat, barley, potatoes, beets); furniture mfg. Formerly an important trade center.

Mount Revelstoke National Park (rĕ'vŭlstōk), (□ 100), SE B.C., in Selkirk Mts., extends NE from Revelstoke, E of Columbia R. valley. Alpine plateau, rising to c.7,000 ft. on Mt. Revelstoke. Popular winter-sports resort. Established 1914.

Mount Robson (rŏb'sŭn), village, E B.C., near Alta. border, in Rocky Mts., 50 mi. W of Jasper; alt. 3,150 ft.; tourist center, gateway to Mt. Robson Provincial Park (NE).

Mount Robson Provincial Park (65 mi. long, 10–20 mi. wide), E B.C., on Alta. border, in Rocky Mts., adjoining Jasper Natl. Park (E) and Hamber Provincial Park (SW). A region of picturesque scenery, high peaks, and glaciers, its highest elevation is Mt. Robson (12,972 ft.). At foot of Mt. Robson is small Berg L., resort. Park is crossed by Canadian Natl. Railway, which crosses Rocky Mts. over Yellowhead Pass, on E boundary of park.

Mount Royal, town (pop. 4,888), S Que., on Montreal Isl., W suburb of Montreal.

Mount Royal or **Mont Réal** (mõrāäl') (900 ft.), S Que., in N part of Montreal city. On its upper slopes is Mount Royal Park (463 acres); on S slope is McGill Univ., on N slope Montreal Univ. Residential district.

Mount Rushmore National Memorial (1,220.3 acres; established 1929), W S.Dak., in the Black Hills near Harney Peak, 17 mi. SW of Rapid City. Gigantic sculptures carved out of granite side of Mt. Rushmore are visible for 60 mi.; representing faces of Washington, Jefferson, Lincoln, and Theodore Roosevelt, each measures 60 ft. from chin to top of head. Work was begun 1927 under direction of Gutzon Borglum; details incompleted at time of his death (1941) were finished by his son, Lincoln.

Mount Saint George, village (pop. 1,077), E Tobago, B.W.I., 4 mi. ENE of Scarborough; coconuts, sugar cane. Formerly called Georgetown.

Mount Saint Joseph, Ohio: see CINCINNATI.

Mount Savage, village (pop. 2,094), Allegany co., W Md., in the Alleghenies near Pa. line, 7 mi. WNW of Cumberland; bituminous coal and clay mining; firebrick plant, railroad shops. Big Savage Mtn. is just W.

Mounts Bay, inlet of the Channel, SW Cornwall, England, bet. Land's End and Lizard Head; 21 mi. long, 10 mi. wide. Penzance and Marazion are on it. Pilchard fisheries. SAINT MICHAEL'S MOUNT isl. is in it.

Mount Shasta (shă'stŭ) or **Mount Shasta City,** town (pop. 1,909), Siskiyou co., N Calif., tourist center at SW foot of Mt. SHASTA. Lumber mills, fish hatchery near by. Hq. of Shasta Natl. Forest. Settled in 1850s, inc. 1905. Known as Sisson until 1925.

Mount Silinda (sēlēn'dä), village, Umtali prov., E Southern Rhodesia, in Mashonaland, near Mozambique border, 15 mi. SSE of Chipinga, in tropical forest; hardwood.

Mountsorrel, town and parish (pop. 2,622), N Leicester, England, on Soar R. and 7 mi. N of Leicester; shoe industry. Granite quarries near by.

Mount Sterling. 1 City (pop. 2,246), ⊙ Brown co., W Ill., 33 mi. E of Quincy, in agr. and bituminous-coal area; corn, wheat, oats, livestock, poultry; mfg. (cheese, butter, brick). Settled 1830, inc. 1837. **2** Town (pop. 144), Van Buren co., SE Iowa, near Mo. line, on Fox R. and 37 mi. SE of Ottumwa; livestock, grain. **3** City (pop. 5,294), ⊙ Montgomery co., NE central Ky., 31 mi. E of Lexington. Trade center in outer Bluegrass agr. area (dairy products, livestock, poultry, burley tobacco, corn, wheat) area; mfg. of clothing, cotton fabrics, butter, candy, packed meat, soft drinks, concrete products, crushed lime; flour, feed, and lumber mills. Platted 1793. Captured and sacked (1863) by Confederate Gen. John Hunt Morgan in Civil War. **4** Village (pop. 1,172), Madison co., central Ohio, 22 mi. SW of Columbus, and on Deer Creek, in agr. area; makes artificial limbs, food products, rubber goods. Founded 1828. **5** Village (pop. 205), Crawford co., SW Wis., 21 mi. NNE of Prairie du Chien, in hog-raising and dairying area.

Mount Stewart, village (pop. estimate 350), N P.E.I., on Hillsborough R. and 16 mi. NE of Charlottetown; mixed farming, dairying; potatoes.

Mount Summit, town (pop. 295), Henry co., E Ind., 13 mi. S of Muncie, in agr. area.

Mount Tabor (tā'bŭr), town (pop. 186), Rutland co., S central Vt., in hunting, fishing area of Green Mtn. Natl. Forest, 16 mi. S of Rutland; ships florists' ferns.

Mount Tom, Mass.: see EASTHAMPTON.

Mount Tremper, resort village, Ulster co., SE N.Y., in the Catskills, on Esopus Creek and 16 mi. WNW of Kingston.

Mount Union. 1 Town (pop. 167), Henry co., SE Iowa, 22 mi. NW of Burlington, in livestock area. **2** Borough (pop. 4,690), Huntingdon co., S central Pa., 29 mi. ESE of Altoona and on Juniata R.; brickworks; ganister; timber; agr. Laid out 1849, inc. 1867.

Mount Vernon (vûr'nŭn). **1** Village (1940 pop. 1,331), Mobile co., SW Ala., near Mobile R., 27 mi. N of Mobile; lumber, flooring. Ala. insane asylum for Negroes here. **2** City (pop. 990), ⊙ Montgomery co., E central Ga., 9 mi. W of Vidalia, near Oconee R., in agr. and timber area. **3** City (pop. 15,600), ⊙ Jefferson co., S Ill., 19 mi. SE of Centralia; trade, shipping, and processing center for oil and agr. area; clothing, railroad cars, shoes, stoves, food products. Inc. 1837. **4** City (pop. 6,150), ⊙ Posey co., extreme SW Ind., 18 mi. W of Evansville, and on Ohio R. near influx of the Wabash; trade center for agr. area; oil refining; mfg. of threshing machines, stoves, handles, flour, corn products, canned foods, cheese, cigars. Settled 1816, inc. 1865. **5** Town (pop. 2,320), Linn co., E Iowa, 13 mi. ESE of Cedar Rapids; mfg. (feed, solders, soap). Cornell Col. (Methodist; coeducational; 1853) is here. State park near by. Inc. 1869. **6** Town (pop. 1,106), ⊙ Rockcastle co., central Ky., 32 mi. SE of Danville, on old Wilderness Road, in coal-mining, agr. (corn, burley tobacco, livestock) area; limestone and sandstone quarries, oil wells, coal mines, timber. Langford House here (built 1790) served as fort against Indians. Near by are Great Saltpeter Caves, mined extensively during Civil War, and Cumberland Natl. Forest. Hunting in vicinity. Settled 1810; inc. 1818. **7** Town (pop. 653), Kennebec co., S Maine, 17 mi. NW of Augusta, in lake dist.; agr., resorts, lumbering. **8** City (pop. 2,057), ⊙ Lawrence co., SW Mo., in the Ozarks, near Spring R., 30 mi. W of Springfield; agr., milk processing. State tuberculosis sanatorium. Laid out 1845. **9** Industrial and residential city (pop. 71,899), Westchester co., SE N.Y., in New York city metropolitan area, just N of the Bronx; mfg. of dies, machinery, silverware; radio, electrical, and X-ray equipment; truck bodies, firebrick, chemicals, rubber goods, vitamin and food products, decalcomania. Oil-distribution center; printing and publishing. Settled 1664, inc. 1892. St. Paul's Church (c.1761; Georgian Colonial) was occupied by Hessian troops during the Revolution; made natl. historic site (6.1 acres) in 1943. **10** City (pop. 12,185), ⊙ Knox co., central Ohio, 40 mi. NE of Columbus and on Kokosing R.; industrial and trade center for farming and stock-raising area. Mfg.: gasoline, Diesel, and steam engines; paperboard products, machine tools, glass products. Laid out 1805. **11** City (pop. 451), Grant co., NE central Oregon, on John Day R. and 8 mi. W of Canyon City; alt. 2,871 ft. Trading point in agr., stock area. Strawberry Mts. SE. **12** City (pop. 387), Davison co., SE central S.Dak., 10 mi. W of Mitchell; corn, wheat, and livestock. **13** Town (pop. 1,433), ⊙ Franklin co., NE Texas, 70 mi. WSW of Texarkana, and near White Oak Bayou; trade, processing center in agr., oil, timber area; cotton ginning, lumber milling, poultry hatching. Inc. 1910. **14** City (pop. 5,230), ⊙ Skagit co., NW Wash., 25 mi. SSE of Bellingham and on Skagit R.; seeds, peas, poultry, dairy products; food processing. Jr. col. is here. Settled c.1877.

Mount Vernon, national shrine, N Va., beautifully situated above the Potomac near Alexandria, S of Washington, D.C., with which it is connected by Mt. Vernon Memorial Highway. Estate and home (from 1747 until his death) of George Washington; the Georgian-style mansion, built 1743 and later improved, and the gardens and outbuildings have been restored after Washington's notes; family relics and much of the original furniture are here. A tomb (built 1831–37) on the grounds is burial place of George and Martha Washington and other members of the family. Estate is in custody of Mt. Vernon Ladies' Assn. (organized 1856), which purchased it in 1860.

Mount Vernon Memorial Parkway, Md. and Va.: see NATIONAL CAPITAL PARKS.

Mount Victory, village (pop. 609), Hardin co., W central Ohio, 9 mi. SSE of Kenton, in agr. area; food canning.

Mountville. **1** Town (pop. 142), Troup co., W Ga., 8 mi. E of La Grange, in agr. area. **2** Borough (pop. 1,064), Lancaster co., SE Pa., 6 mi. W of Lancaster; tobacco products. Laid out 1814. **3** Town (1940 pop. 139), Laurens co., NW S.C., 9 mi. SSE of Laurens.

Mount Washington. **1** Section of BALTIMORE, Md. **2** Resort town (pop. 34), Berkshire co., SW Mass., in the Berkshires, near N.Y. line, 25 mi. SSW of Pittsfield. Includes Union Church village and Mt. Everett.

Mount Wolf, borough (pop. 1,164), York co., S Pa., 6 mi. NNE of York.

Mountzinos (mōōn'tsēnôs), mountain massif in Macedonia, Greece, W of Mesta R.; rises to c.4,250 ft. 15 mi. NNE of Kavalla. Also called Tsali.

Mount Zion. **1** Town (pop. 141), Carroll co., W Ga., 7 mi. NW of Carrollton, near Ala. line. **2** Village (pop. 438), Macon co., central Ill., 6 mi. SE of Decatur, in agr. and bituminous-coal area. State park near by.

Moura (mō'rŏŏ), town (pop. 370), N central Amazonas, Brazil, steamer landing on right bank of the Rio Negro below influx of the Rio Branco, and 160 mi. NW ofManaus; rubber. Airport.

Moura, town (pop. 7,977), Beja dist., S Portugal, 24 mi. ENE of Beja; rail spur terminus; produces olive oil and cheese; trade in grain, sheep, figs. Has a Manueline church and a Moorish castle (rebuilt 1920).

Mourão (mōrā'ō), town (pop. 2,706), Évora dist., S central Portugal, bet. the Guadiana and Sp. border, 35 mi. ESE of Évora; grain, cork, sheep.

Mourcourt (mōōrkōōr'), agr. village (pop. 1,027), Hainaut prov., SW Belgium, 5 mi. NE of Tournai.

Mourdiah (mōōr'dyä), village, W Fr. Sudan, Fr. West Africa, on Saharan desert road and 130 mi. N of Bamako; peanuts, kapok, gum arabic; livestock.

Mouree, Gold Coast: see MOREE.

Mourgana, Mount, Greece-Albania: see TSAMANTA, MOUNT.

Mouri, Gold Coast: see MOREE.

Mouriès (mōōrēs'), village (pop. 1,046), Bouches-du-Rhône dept., SE France, at S foot of the Alpines, 12 mi. E of Arles; olive growing, beekeeping.

Mouriki (mōōrē'kē), mountain in Greek Macedonia, rises to 5,587 ft. 12 mi. ESE of Kastoria. Formerly called Vlatse (or Vlatsi) for former name of Vlaste village at SE foot.

Mourilyan, town (pop. 480), NE Queensland, Australia, 55 mi. SSE of Cairns, on coast; sugar port.

Mourmelon-le-Grand (mōōrmlō'-lŭ-grā'), town (pop. 2,468), Marne dept., N France, 13 mi. N of Châlons-sur-Marne. Military camp and aeronautical research station (SE).

Mourne Mountains (môrn), range in S Co. Down, Northern Ireland, extending 15 mi. NE-SW bet. Carlingford Lough and Dundrum Bay of the Irish Sea, rising to 2,796 ft. in Slieve Donard, 2 mi. SW of Newcastle.

Mourzouk, Fezzan: see MURZUK.

Mousam Lake (mou'sŭm), SW Maine, W York co.; c.6.5 mi. long; drains SE into Mousam R.

Mousam River, SW Maine, rises in Mousam L. (5 mi. long), W York co., flows 23 mi. SE to the Atlantic 4 mi. below Kennebunk, where it furnishes water power.

Mouscron (mōōskrō'), Flemish *Moeskroen* (mōō'-skrōōn), town (pop. 36,839), West Flanders prov., W Belgium, 6 mi. SSW of Courtrai; frontier station near Fr. border; cotton weaving, carpet mfg.

Mousehold, England: see NORWICH.

Mousehole (mous'hōl, mou'zŭl), fishing port (pop. 1,278), SW Cornwall, England, on Mounts Bay of the Channel and 3 mi. S of Penzance; pilchard-fishing center and seaside resort. Offshore is St. Clement's Isle, with ruins of anc. chapel.

Moussey (mōōsā'), village (pop. 197), Moselle dept., NE France, on Marne-Rhine Canal and 14 mi. ENE of Lunéville. Shoe factory at Hello-court (2 mi. NNE).

Moussoro (mōōsōrō'), town, ⊙ Kanem region, W Chad territory, Fr. Equatorial Africa, 140 mi. NE of Fort-Lamy; native trading center, military outpost; livestock, millet. Airfield.

Moustafouli, Greece: see PANAITOLION.

Moustier, Le, France: see EYZIES, LES.

Moustiers-Sainte-Marie (mōōstyā'-sēt-märē'), village (pop. 325), Basses-Alpes dept., SE France, in Provence Alps, 17 mi. S of Digne, in a precipitous ravine. Mus. of faïence ware. Canyon of Verdon R. 3 mi. S.

Moustier-sur-Sambre (mōōstyā-sür-sä'brŭ), town (pop. 2,507), Namur prov., S central Belgium, on Sambre R. and 8 mi. W of Namur; mfg. (mirrors, machinery), foundries.

Moutfort (mōōtfôr'), village (pop. 398), SE Luxembourg, 6 mi. ESE of Luxembourg; gypsum quarrying; fruitgrowing.

Mouthe (mōōt), village (pop. 709), Doubs dept., E France, on the Doubs, 15 mi. SW of Pontarlier; Gruyère cheese, beer.

Mouthiers-sur-Boëme (mōōtyā'-sür-bōĕm'), village (pop. 392), Charente dept., W France, 7 mi. S of Angoulême; paper milling.

Mouthoumet (mōōtōōmā'), village (pop. 155), Aude dept., S France, in the Corbières, 17 mi. ESE of Limoux; sheep.

Moutier (mōōtyā'), Ger. *Münster* (mün'stŭr), town (pop. 5,165), Bern canton, NW Switzerland, on Birs R. and 9 mi. NW of Solothurn; watches, metal products, glassware. Largest town of Moutier dist. (pop. 24,852).

Moutiers (mōōtyā'). **1** SE suburb (pop. 2,123) of Briey, Meurthe-et-Moselle dept., NE France; iron mining. **2** Town (pop. 2,822), Savoie dept., SE France, in Alpine Tarentaise valley 15 mi. SSE of Albertville, on the Isère at influx of Doron de Bozel R.; tourist center and old ⊙ Tarentaise. Electro-metallurgy. Electrochemical works at near-by Saint-Marcel and Notre-Dame-de-Briançon. Episcopal see with 15th-cent. cathedral. Sometimes spelled Moûtiers and called Moûtiers-Tarentaise.

Moûtiers-les-Mauxfaits, Les (lā mōōtyā'-lā-mōfĕ'), village (pop. 732), Vendée dept., W France, 12 mi. S of La Roche-sur-Yon; cereals. Has a Romanesque church.

Mouvaux (mōōvō'), W residential suburb (pop. 8,927) of Roubaix, Nord dept., N France; (biscuits, hosiery, wax; tanning.

Mouy (mwē), town (pop. 2,872), Oise dept., N France, on the Thérain and 13 mi. SE of Beauvais; mfg. (uniforms, elastic fabrics, rugs, shoes, brushes, optical glass).

Mouyondzi (mōōyōndzē'), village, S Middle Congo territory, Fr. Equatorial Africa, 90 mi. WNW of Brazzaville; palm products. R.C. and Protestant missions. Also spelled Muyondzi and Mouyoundzi.

Mouzaïa-les-Mines, Algeria: see LODI.

Mouzaïaville (mōōzäyävēl'), village (pop. 3,361), Alger dept., N central Algeria, in the Mitidja plain, 8 mi. W of Blida; distilling of alcohol and essential oils (geraniums); olive-oil pressing; winegrowing.

Mouzon (mōōzō'), village (pop. 1,384), Ardennes dept., N France, on island formed by Meuse R., 9 mi. SE of Sedan; brewery. Its former abbatial church (13th cent.) was heavily damaged in Second World War.

Movila, Rumania: see CARMEN-SYLVA.

Movilla, Northern Ireland: see NEWTOWNARDS.

Moville, Gaelic *Bun an Phobail*, town (pop. 1,008), NE Co. Donegal, Ireland, on W shore of Lough Foyle, 18 mi. NE of Londonderry; 55°11'N 7°2'W; resort, small port; furniture mfg.

Moville, town (pop. 964), Woodbury co., W Iowa, on West Fork Little Sioux R. and 17 mi. E of Sioux City, in agr. area.

Mowai, Al, Saudi Arabia: see MUWAIH.

Mowar (mō'vär), town (pop. 5,432), Nagpur dist., central Madhya Pradesh, India, 45 mi. NW of Nagpur; cotton, millet, wheat, oilseeds; mango groves.

Mowchow, China: see MOWHSIEN.

Moweaqua (mōwē'kwŭ), village (pop. 1,475), Shelby co., central Ill., 14 mi. S of Decatur; bituminous-coal mines; agr. (corn, wheat, soybeans; dairy products; livestock, poultry). Inc. 1877.

Mower (mou'ŭr), county (□ 703; pop. 42,277), SE Minn.; ⊙ Austin. Agr. area bordering on Iowa and drained by headwaters of Cedar R. Livestock, corn, oats, barley, dairy products, poultry. Food processing at Austin. Formed 1855.

Mowhsien or **Maohsien** (both: mou'shyĕn'), town (pop. 7,046), ⊙ Mowhsien co. (pop. 37,337), NW Szechwan prov., China, on left bank of Min R. and 70 mi. N of Chengtu, in mtn. region; medicinal plants, millet, potatoes, wheat, rapeseed. Gold placers near by. Until 1913 called Mowchow.

Mowkung or **Mou-kung** (both: mou'gōōng'), town (pop. 4,378), ⊙ Mowkung co. (pop. 21,804), W Szechwan prov., China, on Sikang border, 70 mi. NNE of Kangting, in mtn. region; medicinal plants, millet, potatoes. Gold mining near by.

Mowming (mou'mĭng'), Mandarin *Maoming*, town (pop. 13,566), ⊙ Mowming co. (pop. 596,492), SW Kwangtung prov., China, on Foshan R. and 50 mi. NE of Chankiang; cotton milling, furniture mfg.; pineapples, medicinal herbs. Gold and asbestos mined near by. Until 1912 called Kochow or Kaochow.

Mowping or **Mou-p'ing** (both: mō'pĭng'), town, ⊙ Mowping co. (pop. 653,178), NE Shantung prov., China, on road and 15 mi. SE of Chefoo, near Yellow Sea; gold-mining center; silk weaving; fruit, grain; fisheries. Until 1914, Ninghai.

Mowrystown (mou'rēztoun''), village (pop. 394), Highland co., SW Ohio, 40 mi. E of Cincinnati.

Mowting or **Mou-ting** (both: mou'dĭng'), town, ⊙ Mowting co. (pop. 90,434), N central Yunnan prov., China, 18 mi. N of Tsuyung; alt. 6,299 ft.; rice, wheat, millet, sugar cane. Iron and coal mines, saltworks near by. Until 1914, Tingyüan.

Moxee City (mŏk'sē, mŏksē'), town (pop. 543), Yakima co., S Wash., 8 mi. SE of Yakima; hops.

Moxico, Angola: see VILA LUSO.

Moxie Mountain (mŏk'sē) (2,925 ft.), Somerset co., W central Maine, 10 mi. N of Bingham.

Moxie Pond, Somerset co., W central Maine, lake (7 mi. long) 15 mi. NNE of Bingham in recreational area.

Moxley, town in Wednesbury urban district, S Stafford, England; blast furnaces, rolling mills, coal mines.

Moxos, Bolivia: see SAN IGNACIO, Beni dept.

Moxotó River (mōōshōōtô'), NE Brazil, left tributary of São Francisco R., which it enters just above Paulo Afonso Falls, after forming Pernambuco-Alagoas border. Length, c.120 mi. Intermittent-flowing stream.

Moy, town (pop. 1,218), SE Co. Tyrone, Northern Ireland, on Blackwater R. and 7 mi. N of Armagh; potatoes, flax, oats; cattle. Founded in 18th cent. by earl of Charlemont.

Moy, agr. village in Moy and Dalarossie parish (pop. 566), NE Inverness, Scotland, 9 mi. SE of Inverness, on Loch Moy, a small lake 1½ mi. long, ½ mi. wide. Near-by Moy Hall is seat of the Mackintosh.

Moya (moi'ä), town (pop. 841), Grand Canary, Canary Isls., 10 mi. W of Las Palmas; bananas, cereals, corn, cochineal, potatoes, livestock. Lumbering; flour milling. Medicinal springs. Prehistoric caves near by.

Moyá (moiä'), town (pop. 1,668), Barcelona prov., NE Spain, 15 mi. NE of Manresa; textiles (cotton, wool, hemp).

Moyahua (moiä'wä), town (pop. 1,566), Zacatecas, N central Mexico, on Juchipila R. and 35 mi. SSE of Tlaltenango; alt. 3,947 ft.; grain, sugar cane, fruit, vegetables, stock.

Moyale (mō'yälā mōyä'lā), Ital. *Moiale*, village, Sidamo-Borana prov., S Ethiopia, on border opposite Moyale (Kenya), 60 mi. SE of Mega, on plateau. Caravan center and customs station.

Moyale, village, Northern Frontier Prov., N Kenya, on border opposite Moyale (Ethiopia), on road and 245 mi. NNE of Isiolo; 3°30'N 39°08'E; customs station; stock raising. Airfield.

Moyamba (mōyäm'bä), town (pop. 2,500), South-Western Prov., SW Sierra Leone, on railroad and 60 mi. ESE of Freetown; palm oil and kernels, piassava, rice. Has United Methodist and United Brethren in Christ missions, hosp., school. Hq. Moyamba dist.

Moyar River (mōyär'), in Nilgiri and Coimbatore dists., SW Madras, India, rises in Nilgiri Hills on Mukurti peak, flows N past Pykara (falls and hydroelectric works 8 mi. NNW), and E to Bhavani R. 10 mi. WSW of Satyamangalam (160-ft. dam near confluence; built 1949); c.90 mi. long. Construction of regulating dam and headworks 8 mi. below falls (10 mi. NE of Pykara) begun 1946 to develop power from tail water of PYKARA power station. Called Pykara R. above Pykara falls.

Moÿ-de-l'Aisne (mōē'-dŭ-lĕn'), village (pop. 963), Aisne dept., N France, on Oise R. and Oise-Sambre Canal, and 7 mi. SSE of Saint-Quentin; rayon factory.

Moyen-Chari, Fr. Equatorial Africa: see FORT-ARCHAMBAULT.

Moyen-Congo, territory, Fr. Equatorial Africa: see MIDDLE CONGO.

Moyenmoutier (mwäyĕmōōtyā'), town (pop. 2,108), Vosges dept., E France, near the Meurthe, 7 mi. N of Saint-Dié, in the NW Vosges; textile weaving and bleaching. Has 18th-cent. abbatial church.

Moyenne Island (mwäyĕn'), one of the Seychelles, in the Mahé group, off NE coast of Mahé Isl., 4 mi. E of Victoria; 4°37'S 55°31'E; ¼ mi. long, ¼ mi. wide; separated from St. Anne Isl. (N) by St. Anne Channel.

Moyenne-Mana, district, Fr. Guiana: see P.I.

Moyenneville (mwäyĕnvēl'), agr. village (pop. 330), Somme dept., N France, 4 mi. SW of Abbeville.

Moyenvic (mwäyävēk'), village (pop. 249), Moselle dept., NE France, on the Seille and 4 mi. SE of Château-Salins; road junction. Saltworks in area.

Moyero River, Russian SFSR: see KHATANGA RIVER.

Moyeuvre-Grande (mwäyû'vrŭ-gräd'), Ger. *Gross-moyeuvre*, town (pop. 8,422), Moselle dept., NE France, on the Orne and 11 mi. NNW of Metz; iron-mining center; blast furnaces and forges. Building stone quarried near by.

Moyie (moi'ē), village (pop. estimate 200), SE B.C., at foot of Rocky Mts., on Moyie L. (8 mi. long), 16 mi. S of Cranbrook; silver, lead, zinc mining.

Moyie Springs, town (pop. 109), Boundary co., N Idaho, 8 mi. E of Bonners Ferry.

Moyingyi Reservoir, Burma: see PYINBONGYI.

Moykovats, Yugoslavia: see MOJKOVAC.

Moyne, Gaelic *Maighean*, agr. village, S Co. Wicklow, Ireland, 4 mi. E of Hacketstown; dairying; cattle, sheep; potatoes.

Moyo or **Mojo** (both: mō'yō), island (20 mi. long, 9 mi. wide), Indonesia, just off N coast of Sumbawa, at entrance of Sale Bay (inlet of Flores Sea); 8°14'S 117°34'E.

Moyo (mō'yō), town, Northern Prov., NW Uganda, near Anglo-Egyptian Sudan border, 25 mi. W of Nimule; cotton, peanuts, sesame.

Moyobamba (moiōbäm'bä), city (pop. 7,497), ⊙ San Martín dept. and Moyobamba prov. (□ 2,093; enumerated pop. 12,836, plus estimated 2,000 Indians), N central Peru, near Mayo R. (Amazon basin), in E outliers of the Andes, on road from Cajamarca, and 390 mi. N of Lima; 6°3'S 76°58'W; alt. 2,800 ft. Has a humid tropical climate. It is situated in a fertile agr. region (cotton, sugar cane, tobacco, cacao, rice, coca, coffee, grapes). Produces excellent wines; alcohol and liquor distilling; mfg. of straw hats. Airport. Hot springs, gold placers, and petroleum seepages in vicinity. Though dating back to an anc. Indian settlement under Inca influence, it is the 2d town in Peru to be founded (1539) E of the Andes by the Spanish.

Moyogalpa (moiōgäl'pä), town (1950 pop. 934), Rivas dept., SW Nicaragua, on W Ometepe Isl. and 6 mi. SW of Alta Gracia, at W foot of volcano Concepción; boatbuilding; coffee, tobacco, cotton, corn. Radio station.

Moyotzingo (moiōtsēng'gō), officially Santa María Moyotzingo, town (pop. 2,737), Puebla, central Mexico, on railroad and 19 mi. NW of Puebla; corn, wheat, maguey, stock.

Moy River, Ireland, rises in Slieve Gamph mts., Co. Sligo, flows SW into Co. Mayo, then N, past Foxford and Ballina, to Killala Bay; 40 mi. long. Navigable below Ballina. Salmon fisheries.

Moys, Poland: see ZGORZELEC.

Moysalen (mû'üsälûn), Nor. *Møysalen*, or **Moisalen** (moi'sälûn), Nor. *Møisalen*, highest peak (4,153) on Hinnoy of the Vesteralen group, Nordland co., N Norway, 30 mi. NE of Svolvaer; 68°32'N 15°24'E. Permanently snow-clad.

Moyü, China: see KARA KASH.

Moyuta (moi-ōō'tä), town (1950 pop. 1,408), Jutiapa dept., SE Guatemala, in Pacific piedmont, at E foot of volcano Moyuta (5,525 ft.), 20 mi. SW of Jutiapa; alt. 4,675 ft. Corn, beans, coffee, sugar cane, livestock.

Mozac (môzäk'), village (pop. 1,029), Puy-de-Dôme dept., central France, 1.5 mi. W of Riom; lava quarries. Has 12th-cent. church of St. Peter, with remarkable enameled shrine (1261).

Mozambique (mōzămbēk'), Port. *Moçambique* (mōōsămbē'kĭ), or **Portuguese East Africa,** Port. colony (□ 297,731; 1950 pop. 5,732,767) on SE coast of Africa, facing Madagascar across Mozambique Channel; ⊙ Lourenço Marques. Bounded N by Tanganyika (frontier along Ruvuma R.), NW by Nyasaland (which drives a deep wedge into Mozambique) and Northern Rhodesia, W by Southern Rhodesia, SW and S by U. of So. Afr. (Transvaal, Natal) and Swaziland. Extends from 10°30'S to 27°S; has 1,700-mi.-long coast line; width ranges from 120 to 400 mi. Major part of territory is a flat lowland (one of Africa's rare coastal plains) merging gradually in W with an undulating plateau 800–2,000 ft. high. Higher elevations are limited to NW frontier and in N to the rim of the Great Rift Valley (here occupied by L. Nyasa). Several isolated mtn. groups (Namuli Mts., 7,936 ft.) rise abruptly from N central lowland. Mozambique is drained by lower courses of several rivers rising in adjacent territories (Zambezi, Sabi, Limpopo, Komati) and by many short coastal streams. The coastal plain has a tropical savanna climate dominated (in N half) by monsoon system of Indian Ocean. In N and center mean yearly temp. is 77°F., with seasonal variation of 10°F.; rainfall (40–60 in.) occurs Dec.-April. In S, a somewhat cooler and drier climate prevails. Commercial agr. is limited to plantations found primarily in alluvial river valleys and deltas and along N coast; chief crops are sugar cane, sisal, coconuts, tea, citrus fruit, tobacco, peanuts. Cotton, rice, corn, beans, and millet are widely grown by natives, who also collect such uncultivated products as cashew nuts, castor beans, mafura, mangrove bark, and beeswax. Animal husbandry and forestry remain largely undeveloped. Diversified mineral deposits have been discovered (especially in TETE vicinity), but exploitation is limited to coal mining (near Tete), gold dredging (along NW frontier and near Macequece), and mica mining. Bauxite and corundum are also shipped in small quantities. Colony's major industries are sugar milling, cotton ginning, oil pressing, mfg. of tobacco products, cement, soap, and leather articles. Mozambique's railway system consists of several unconnected lines running E–W from principal ports. Thus Beira is an outlet for Nyasaland (Trans-Zambezia RR) and Northern Rhodesia (Beira RR), while Lourenço Marques is linked with Johannesburg (U. of So. Afr.). From Mozambique city a line taps the interior of Niassa prov.; Quelimane, Inhambane, and Vila de João Belo send short rail spurs to the immediate hinterland. Because of their rail connections and sheltered harbors, LOURENÇO MARQUES and BEIRA have become leading transshipping centers for S Africa's mineral and agr. exports. Cotton, copra, sugar, cashew nuts, and sisal are colony's own principal export items. Aside from Tete (head of navigation on lower Zambezi R.), there are no important urban centers in the interior. Mozambique (with airfields all along the coast) has air service to Southern Rhodesia, U. of So. Africa, and Portugal (via Angola). Portuguese founded settlements along Mozambique coast in early 16th cent. When Dutch occupied Angola (1640–48), Port. slave traders transferred to Mozambique, carrying on until abolition of slavery in 1878. In 1875, Delagoa Bay area (disputed bet. British and Portuguese) was awarded to Portugal. Boundaries with adjacent territories adjusted 1886–94. In 1891, Mozambique Company received charter from Portugal to administer area of present Manica and Sofala prov., including port of Beira; its charter expired 1942 and territory reverted to Port. control. Similarly, the Nyassa Company administered (1893–1929) area of present Niassa prov. N of Lúrio R. In 1907, Lourenço Marques officially succeeded Mozambique city as colony's ⊙. A governor-general rules Mozambique with assistance of elected councillors. Since administrative reform of 1946, colony is divided into 4 provinces (NIASSA, ZAMBÉZIA, MANICA AND SOFALA, SUL DO SAVE) and Lourenço Marques autonomous dist. Mozambique has dense native pop. of Bantu stock. By agreement with Transvaal almost 100,000 natives are supplied under labor contracts to Witwatersrand mines. Non-native pop. (Europeans, Indians, other Asiatics) totaled 55,451 in 1940.

Mozambique, Port. *Moçambique*, city (1950 pop. 12,510), Niassa prov., NE Mozambique, seaport on small coral isl. (Mozambique Isl.) in Mozambique Channel of Indian Ocean, 3 mi. from mainland and 525 mi. NE of Beira; 15°3'S 40°43'E. Exports cotton, corn, sisal, peanuts, mica, castor oil, timber. Oil-seed and tobacco processing, soap mfg. Harbor, bet. isl. and mainland, is sheltered and accommodates ships drawing 28 ft. The crowded city, occupying entire isl. (c.1½ mi. long, ¼ mi. wide), is dominated by 3 forts (especially Fort St. Sebastian, built 1508–11). It preserves its 16th-cent. appearance. Chief buildings are former governor's palace, 3 churches, and customhouse. Lumbo, on mainland opposite city, has airport and is ocean terminus of railroad to the interior. Mossuril, on mainland 7 mi. NW of city, is European residential town. Mozambique was 1st visited by Vasco da Gama in 1498; it became a Port. stronghold in 1508. Was ⊙ Port. East Africa until 1907 and ⊙ Niassa prov. until 1930s. Pop., predominantly Mohammedan, is of mixed Arab, Indian, and Bantu stock.

Mozambique Channel, strait in Indian Ocean bet. Madagascar and SE Africa mainland (Mozambique); over 1,000 mi. long, c.600 mi. wide in widest part (20°S lat.); 250 mi. wide in narrowest part (16°S lat.), bet. Mozambique city and Cape St. André. Comoro Isls. are at N entrance, small Bassas da India and Europa islets in S. Receives Zambezi R. Important shipping lane for E African navigation. Chief ports are Mozambique, Beira, and Lourenço Marques on mainland, Majunga and Tuléar on Madagascar's W coast.

Mozambique Current, warm current flowing SW from Indian Ocean, through Mozambique Channel, along coast of SE and S Africa; off Cape Agulhas (S tip of Africa) it is deflected southeastward. S part also called Agulhas Current.

Mozdok (mŭzdôk'), city (1926 pop. 14,034), N North Ossetian Autonomous SSR, Russian SFSR, on railroad, on left bank of Terek R. and 50 mi. N of Dzaudzhikau; agr. center in cotton area; distilling, wine making, food processing, brickworking. Horticulture, vineyards near by. Pumping station on oil pipe lines from Malgobek and Grozny. During Second World War, briefly held (1942) by Germans. City passed (1944) from Stavropol Territory to North Ossetian Autonomous SSR.

Mozema (mōzä'mŭ), village, Naga Hills dist., E Assam, India, in Naga Hills, 6 mi. W of Kohima; rice, cotton, oranges. Former stronghold of Naga tribes.

Mozet (mōzā'), agr. village (pop. 535), Namur prov., S central Belgium, 5 mi. ESE of Namur. Has 12th-cent. Romanesque chapel.

Mozhaisk or **Mozhaysk** (mŭzhīsk'), city (1939 pop. over 10,000), W Moscow oblast, Russian SFSR, on Moskva R. and 65 mi. WSW of Moscow; highway junction; metal- and brickworks; dairy plant. Has ruins of city wall, 15th-cent. church with stone ornaments. Chartered 1231; formerly an important fortress. During Second World War, held (1941–42) by Germans.

Mozhary (mŭzhä'rē), village (1939 pop. over 2,000), S Ryazan oblast, Russian SFSR, 40 mi. ENE of Ryazhsk; wheat, hemp.

Mozheiki Muravyevo, Lithuania: see MAZEIKIAI.

Mozhga (mŭzhgä'), city (1939 pop. over 10,000), SW Udmurt Autonomous SSR, Russian SFSR, on railroad (Syuginskaya station) and 45 mi. SW of Izhevsk; wood cracking, sawmilling, glassworking, food processing (meat, butter). Originally called Syuginski; renamed (c.1920) Krasny. In 1926, absorbed adjacent Syuginski Zavod (1926 pop. 1,406), became city, and renamed Mozhga.

Mozi, Japan: see MOJI.

Mozirje (mô'zĭryĕ), Ger. *Prassberg* (präs'bĕrk), village (pop. 1,544), N Slovenia, Yugoslavia, on Savinja R. and 16 mi. WNW of Celje; local trade center; summer resort. Hydroelectric plant. Has old monastery. Formerly called Prihova. Until 1918, in Styria.

Mozoncillo (mō-thōn-thē'lyō), town (pop. 1,597), Segovia prov., central Spain, 12 mi. NNW of Segovia; cereals, grapes, chicory; flour milling; lumbering. Naval stores.

Mozonte (mōsōn'tā), town (1950 pop. 285), Nueva Segovia dept., NW Nicaragua, 2 mi. ENE of Ocotal; coffee, sugar cane, livestock.

Mozyr or **Mozyr'** (mô'zĭr), city (1939 pop. over 10,000), ⊙ Polesye oblast, Belorussian SSR, on Pripet R. and 145 mi. SE of Minsk; 52°3'N 29°15'E. Lumber milling and transportation center; veneering, mfg. (prefabricated houses, furniture); fisheries. Teachers col.

Mozzate (môtsä'tĕ), village (pop. 2,053), Como prov., Lombardy, N Italy, 11 mi. SW of Como; textile mfg.

M'Pal (ŭmpäl'), village, NW Senegal, Fr. West Africa, on Dakar–Saint-Louis RR and 16 mi. ESE of Saint-Louis, in peanut-growing region; stock raising, cheese mfg.

M'pala (ŭmpä'lä) or **Pala** (pä'lä), village, Katanga prov., SE Belgian Congo, on W shore of L. Tanganyika, 55 mi. SSE of Albertville; cattle, vegetables. R.C. mission with school of marine trades for natives. Founded 1882.

Mpanda (ŭmpän'dä), village, Western Prov., SW Tanganyika, on rail spur (built after 1948) and 155 mi. SW of Tabora; copper-, lead-, silver-, and gold-mining center. Pilot plant for lead refining.

Mpemba, Nyasaland: see BLANTYRE.

M'Pésoba (ŭmpĕsō'bä), village, S Fr. Sudan, Fr. West Africa, 150 mi. E of Bamako; cotton research station; agr. school.

Mpigi (ŭmpē'gē), town, Buganda prov., S Uganda, 15 mi. NW of Entebbe; road junction; cotton, coffee, sugar cane, bananas, millet.

Mpika (ŭmpē'kä), township (pop. 117), Northern Prov., NE central Northern Rhodesia, in Muchinga Mts., 120 mi. SSE of Kasama; road junction; corn, livestock. Airfield.

M'Poko River (ŭmpōkō'), SW Ubangi-Shari, Fr. Equatorial Africa, rises 30 mi. S of Bossangoa, flows 160 mi. generally SSW to Ubangi R. 10 mi. SW of Bangui.

Mpologoma River, Uganda: see KYOGA, LAKE.

Mporokoso (ŭmpōrōkō'sō), township (pop. 26), Northern Prov., N Northern Rhodesia, 100 mi. NW of Kasama; road junction; corn, coffee.

M'Pouia (ŭmpōōyä'), village, central Middle Congo, Fr. Equatorial Africa, steamboat landing on Congo R. (Belgian Congo border) and 125 mi. NE of Brazzaville. Has trypanosomiasis and leprosy treating station.

Mpraeso (ŭmprī'sō), town (pop. 3,340), Eastern Prov., Gold Coast colony, near Nkawkaw rail station, 45 mi. NW of Koforidua; bauxite mining. Mines on near-by Mt. Ejuanema (ĕjwänĕ'mä) were developed during Second World War.

Mpulungu (ŭmpōōlōōng'gōō), township (pop. 29), Northern Prov., NE Northern Rhodesia, port at S tip of L. Tanganyika, 20 mi. WNW of Abercorn; holiday resort; fishing base; coffee.

Mpwapwa (ŭmpwä'pwä), town, Central Prov., E central Tanganyika, 10 mi. NNE of Gulwe (linked by road) and 50 mi. ESE of Dodoma; cotton, gum arabic; livestock. Govt. veterinary laboratory and breeding station. Limestone and phosphate deposits in area.

Mracaj, Yugoslavia: see GORNJI VAKUF.

Mragowo (mrōgô'vô), Pol. *Mrągowo*, Ger. *Sensburg* (zĕns'bŏŏrk), town (1939 pop. 9,877; 1946 pop. 3,254) in East Prussia, after 1945 in Olsztyn prov., NE Poland, in Masurian Lakes region, 35 mi. ENE of Allenstein (Olsztyn); sawmilling. Founded 1348 by Teutonic Knights. In Second World War, c.85% destroyed.

M'Raïer (mŭräyâr'), village and Saharan oasis, Touggourt territory, E Algeria, near W edge of the Chott Merouane, on Biskra-Touggourt RR and 65 mi. SSE of Biskra; date palms.

Mraijat, Lebanon: see MUREIJAT.

Mrakotin, Czechoslovakia: see TELC.

Mrakovo (mrä'kŭvŭ), village (1939 pop. over 2,000), SW Bashkir Autonomous SSR, Russian SFSR, on Greater Ik R. and 60 mi. SSE of Sterlitamak; flour mill.

Mramorski or **Mramorskiy** (mrä'mŭrskē), village (1926 pop. 910), SW Sverdlovsk oblast, Russian SFSR, on railroad and 10 mi. NE (under jurisdiction) of Polevskoi; marble and talc quarrying, lumbering. Formerly called Mramorski Zavod.

Mras-Su, Russian SFSR: see TOM RIVER.

Mrcajevci or **Mrchayevtsi** (mŭr'chäyĕftsē), Serbo-Croatian *Mrčajevci*, village (pop. 5,070), W central Serbia, Yugoslavia, 9 mi. ESE of Cacak.

Mreidjatt, Lebanon: see MUREIJAT.

Mrewa (ŭmrā'wŭ), township (pop. 290), Salisbury prov., NE Southern Rhodesia, in Mashonaland, 55 mi. ENE of Salisbury (linked by road); tobacco, corn, dairy products; cattle, sheep, goats. Mica, tin, gold deposits in dist.

Mreznica River (mŭrĕzh'nĭtsä), Serbo-Croatian *Mrežnica*, NW Croatia, Yugoslavia, rises 5 mi. WSW of Slunj, flows c.40 mi. N, past Duga Resa, to Korana R. 2 mi. S of Karlovac; hydroelectric plant.

Mrirasandu, Uganda: see MWIRASANDU.
Mrkonjic Grad or **Mrkonyich Grad** (both: mŭr'-kônyich grät"), Serbo-Croatian *Mrkonjić Grad,* village (pop. 2,209), W central Bosnia, Yugoslavia, on Vrbas R. and 20 mi. S of Banja Luka; copper mining. Until 1930s, called Varcar Vakuf.
Mrocza (mrô'chä), Ger. *Mrotschen* (mrô'chŭn), town (pop. 2,236), Bydgoszcz prov., NW Poland, 18 mi. WNW of Bydgoszcz; flour and sawmilling.
Msagali, Tanganyika: see HOGORO.
M'Saken (mŭsäkĕn'), town (pop. 21,804), Sousse dist., E Tunisia, in the coastal strip (*Sahel*), 7 mi. SSW of Sousse; rail junction; olive-processing center; oil pressing, flour milling, artisan mfg. (textiles sandals, furniture). Horse raising. Also spelled Msaken.
Msasani (ŭmsäsä'nē), N suburb of Dar es Salaam, E Tanganyika, on Indian Ocean. Modern meat-packing plant.
Msene (ŭmshĕ'nä), Czech *Mšené,* Ger. *Mscheno,* village (pop. 886), N central Bohemia, Czechoslovakia, on railroad and 23 mi. NNW of Prague; health resort with peat baths.
Mshchonov, Poland: see MSZCZONOW.
Msida or **Misida** (mĭsē'dä), town (pop. 6,064), E central Malta, at head of Mediterranean inlet, 1½ mi. W of Valletta. Boat repairing, fishing. Its monuments escaped severe damage during Second World War; among them are old troglodyte church, 17th-cent. church, arcaded 18th-cent. public bath.
M'Sila (mŭsēlä'), town (pop. 8,102), Constantine dept., NE Algeria, in the Hodna depression, 60 mi SW of Sétif, 40 mi. NNE of Bou-Saâda; horse and sheep market; leatherworking. Also spelled Msila. Agr. area (cereals) just S irrigated from Oued Ksob Dam (105 ft. high; 10 mi. N) at S edge of Hodna Mts.
Msonneddi (ŭmsōnĕ'dē), village, Salisbury prov., NE Southern Rhodesia, in Mashonaland, 33 mi. WNW of Bindura; tobacco, corn; cattle, sheep, goats.
Msoro (ŭmsō'rō), village (pop. c.30), Eastern Prov., E Northern Rhodesia, 55 mi. W of Fort Jameson; tobacco, corn, wheat. Mission.
Msta River (ŭmstä'), W European Russian SFSR, rises in small lake NW of Vyshni Volochek, flows NNW, past Borovichi, and generally W to L. Ilmen, forming delta mouth 7 mi. S of Novgorod; 275 mi. long. Forms part of VYSHNEVOLOTSK canal system; connected in upper course with TVERTSA RIVER via Vyshnevolotsk Canal. In lower course, near L. Ilmen, it is joined to VOLKHOV RIVER by 2 cut-off canals E of Novgorod: Siversov Canal (S; 6 mi. long) and Vishera Canal (N; 10 mi. long). Formerly an important navigation route; now only of local importance.
Mstera (ŭmstyĕ'rŭ), town (1926 pop. 4,047), NE Vladimir oblast, Russian SFSR, near Klyazma R., 13 mi. NW of Vyazniki; noted handicraft center (gold-leaf working, painting, stitching, jewelry making). Religious art mus.
Mstislavl or **Mstislavl'** (ŭmstyēslä'vŭl), city (1948 pop. over 10,000), E Mogilev oblast, Belorussian SSR, 60 mi. ENE of Mogilev; food processing, flax processing.
Mszczonow (mŭsh-chô'nōōf), Pol. *Mszczonów,* Rus. *Mshchonov* (mŭsh-chô'nŭf), town (pop. 3,161), Warszawa prov., E central Poland, 28 mi. SW of Warsaw; mfg. of matches, brewing, flour milling; grain trade.
Mtepatepa (ŭmtĕpätĕ'pä) or **Mtepetepa** (ŭmtĕpĕtĕ'-pä), village, Salisbury prov., NE Southern Rhodesia, in Mashonaland, 25 mi. N of Bindura; tobacco, peanuts, cotton; cattle, sheep, goats.
Mtito Andei (ŭmtē'tō ändā'), village, Central Prov., S central Kenya, on railroad and 140 mi. SE of Nairobi; magnesite mining; sapphire and corundum deposits.
Mtoko (ŭmtō'kō), township (pop. 237), Salisbury prov., NE Southern Rhodesia, in Mashonaland, on road and 85 mi. ENE of Salisbury; livestock center (cattle, sheep, goats). Hq. of native commissioner for Mtoko dist. Police post. Customs station serving Mozambique border (E).
Mtsensk (ŭmtsyĕnsk'), city (1926 pop. 10,142), N Orel oblast, Russian SFSR, 30 mi. NE of Orel; fruit (mainly berries) and vegetable canning; brickworks, stockyards. Chartered 1147.
Mtskheta (ŭmtskhyĕ'tŭ) or **Mtskhet** (ŭmtsŭkhyĕt'), town (1939 pop. over 2,000), E central Georgian SSR, on Kura R., at mouth of Aragva R., on Georgian Military Road and 7 mi. NW of Tiflis, on railroad; sawmilling, woodworking; Glauber's salt deposits. An anc. city; has 15th-cent. cathedral (with tombs of Georgia rulers) built on site of older building destroyed by Tamerlane, convent, and 12th-cent. church (medieval Georgian baroque; restored 1903). Was ⊙ Georgia until its transfer (5th cent.) to Tiflis. In 1936, its Rus. name (Mtskhet) was officially replaced by its Georgian (Mtskheta).
Mtwara, Tanganyika: see MIKINDANI.
Mu, canal and river, Burma: see MU RIVER.
Muai (mwī'), town (pop. 287), SW Szechwan prov., China, 45 mi. S of Ipin, near Yunnan line; tea, tobacco.
Muai, Mae, Burma-Thailand: see THAUNGYIN RIVER.
Mu'amaltayn, Lebanon: see MA'AMELTEIN.
Muaná (mwŭnä'), city (pop. 472), E Pará, Brazil, near S shore of Marajó isl. in Amazon delta, 45 mi. W of Belém; cattle and horse raising.
Muang [Thai, =town]: for names in Thailand beginning thus, see under following part of the name.
Muangsen (mwŭng'shĕn'), town, Nghean prov., N central Vietnam, on Vinh-Luang Prabang highway and 105 mi. NW of Vinh.
Muar, town, Malaya: see BANDAR MAHARANI.
Muara (mwä'rŭ), town, in W section of Brunei, NW Borneo, 13 mi. ENE of Brunei town, on Brunei Bay; agr. (rice, cassava, sago), stock raising, fishing. Coal was mined here until 1925. Completely destroyed during Second World War. Also called Brooketon.
Muaraenim or **Moearaenim** (both: mwärŭnĭm'), town (dist. pop. 3,546), SW Sumatra, Indonesia, on tributary of Musi R. and 80 mi. SW of Palembang; on spur of Palembang-Telukbetung RR; trade center for oil-producing and coal-mining region.
Muar River (mwär'), S Malaya, rises in S outliers of central Malayan range E of Seremban, flows 140 mi. E, past Kuala Pilah, and in an arc S through NW Johore rubber-growing dist. to Strait of Malacca at Bandar Maharani; navigable in lower course.
Mubarakeh or **Mobarakeh** (mōbäräkĕ'), village, Tenth Prov., in Isfahan, W central Iran, 27 mi. SSW of Isfahan and on Zaindeh R.; rice, opium, cotton.
Mubarakpur (mōōbä'rŭkpōōr), town (pop. 11,580), Azamgarh dist., E Uttar Pradesh, India, 7 mi. ENE of Azamgarh; hand-loom cotton-weaving center; silk weaving, sugar milling.
Mubarakpur, town (pop. 1,243), Bahawalpur state, W Pakistan, 20 mi. SW of Bahawalpur.
Mubarraz, Saudi Arabia: see HOFUF.
Mubende (mōōbĕn'dä), town, Buganda prov., W central Uganda, 85 mi. WNW of Kampala; agr. trade center (cotton, coffee, bananas, corn). Tungsten, beryl, tantalite deposits.
Mubi (mōōm'bē), town, N Br. Cameroons, administered as part of Adamawa prov. of Nigeria, 90 mi. NE of Yola; peanuts, pepper, hemp, rice, cotton, cattle, skins.
Mubo, New Guinea: see NASSAU BAY.
Much (mōōkh), village (pop. 7,653), in former Prussian Rhine Prov., W Germany, after 1945 in North Rhine-Westphalia, 20 mi. E of Cologne.
Muchachos, Picos de los (pē'kōs dhä lōs mōōchä'-chōs), small volcanic range in N Palma, Canary Isls., rising to 7,730 ft.
Muchalat Inlet (mōōchă'lĭt), SW B.C., in W Vancouver Isl., W arm (24 mi. long) of Nootka Sound, 50 mi. W of Courtenay.
Muchamiel (mōōchämyĕl'), town (pop. 1,874), Alicante prov., E Spain, near the Mediterranean, 6 mi. NE of Alicante, in irrigated area yielding truck produce, olive oil, wine, cereals.
Muchanes (mōōchä'nĕs), village, La Paz dept., W Bolivia, port on Beni R. and c.85 mi. NNW of Chulumani.
Muchawiec River, Belorussian SSR: see MUKHAVETS RIVER.
Mücheln (mü'khŭln), town (pop. 12,844), in former Prussian Saxony prov., central Germany, after 1945 in Saxony-Anhalt, 10 mi. WSW of Merseburg; lignite mined; chemicals. Has 16th-cent. town hall.
Much Hadham (hă'dŭm), town and parish (pop. 1,668), E Hertford, England, 4 mi. WSW of Bishop's Stortford; agr. market. Has 13th-cent. church.
Muchinga Mountains (mōōchĭng'gä), section of great African escarpment in NE Northern Rhodesia, along a spur of Great Rift Valley. Extend 300 mi. NNE-SSW, bet. Isoka and Serenje; form right watershed of Luangwa R.; rise over 6,000 ft.
Muchkap (mōōchkäp'), village (1926 pop. 10,420), SE Tambov oblast, Russian SFSR, on Vorona R. and 70 mi. SE of Tambov; flour milling, meat packing.
Muchwan or **Mu-ch'uan** (mōō'chwän'), town (pop. 12,941), ⊙ Muchwan co. (pop. 107,166), SW Szechwan prov., China, 33 mi. W of Ipin, in mtn. area; wheat, millet, potatoes. Until 1930, Lunghwasze.
Much Wenlock, England: see WENLOCK.
Much Woolton or **Woolton,** SE residential suburb (pop. 5,200) of Liverpool, SW Lancashire, England; hosiery mills.
Mucientes (mōō-thyĕn'tĕs), town (pop. 1,291), Valladolid prov., N central Spain, 7 mi. NNW of Valladolid; cheese processing, plaster mfg.
Muck, island (pop. 48), Inner Hebrides, Inverness, Scotland, 3 mi. SW of Eigg; 2½ mi. long, 1½ mi. wide; rises to 451 ft.
Muckalee Creek, SW central Ga., rises SE of Buena Vista, flows c.65 mi. SSE, past Americus, to Kinchafoonee R. just N of Albany.
Mückenberg (mü'kŭnbĕrk), village (pop. 6,001), in former Prussian Saxony prov., central Germany, after 1945 in Saxony-Anhalt, on the Black Elster and 12 mi. WSW of Senftenberg; lignite mining; chemical mfg. Has 18th-cent. castle.
Muckish (mŭ'kĭsh), mountain (2,197 ft.) of Derryveach Mts., N Co. Donegal, Ireland, 6 mi. SSW of Dunfanaghy.
Muckle Flugga (mŭ'kŭl flŭ'gŭ), islet (pop. 3), northernmost of the Shetlands, Scotland, just N of Unst isl.; site of North Unst Light (60°51'N 0°53'W). Isl. is most northerly habitation of Great Britain.
Muckle Roe (rō'), island (pop. 154) of the Shetlands, Scotland, in St. Magnus Bay, just off NW coast of Mainland isl., 16 mi. NW of Lerwick; circular, 3 mi. in diameter; rises to 557 ft. Many lakes.
Muckno, Lough (lŏkh mŭk'nō), lake (c.600 acres, 3 mi. long, 1 mi. wide), E Co. Monaghan, Ireland, extending S from Castleblayney; fed and drained by Fane R.
Muckross Lake, Ireland: see KILLARNEY, LAKES OF.
Mucuchíes (mōōkōōchē'ĕs), town (pop. 610), Mérida state, W Venezuela, on upper Chama R., at W foot of Pico Mucuñuque, on transandine highway and 19 mi. NE of Mérida; alt. 9,767 ft. Wheat, pomegranates, vegetables. Known for dog breeding.
Mucuchíes Pass or **Timotes Pass** (tēmō'tĕs), Mérida state, W Venezuela, on transandine highway, N of Pico Mucuñuque, and 27 mi. NE of Mérida; alt. c.13,500 ft. Often snowbound during wet season.
Mucugê (mōōkōōzhā'), city (pop. 2,865), central Bahia, Brazil, in the Serra do Sincorá, on upper Paraguaçu R. and 14 mi. S of Andaraí; diamond-mining center.
Mucuñuque, Pico (pē'kō mōōkōōnyōō'kä), peak (15,328 ft.) in Andean spur, Mérida state, W Venezuela, 28 mi. NE of Mérida; highest elevation of Sierra de Santo Domingo.
Mucur (mōōjōōr'), village (pop. 3,906), Kirsehir prov., central Turkey, 13 mi. ESE of Kirsehir; wheat, linseed, mohair goats.
Mucurapo (mōōkōōrä'pō), NW suburb of Port of Spain, NW Trinidad, B.W.I., adjoining wharves.
Mucuri River (mōōkōōrē'), in E Minas Gerais and southeasternmost Bahia, Brazil, rises in the Serra do Chifre, flows c.150 mi. ESE to the Atlantic 30 mi. SW of Caravelas; interrupted by rapids; navigable in Bahia. Cacao growing in lower valley. Formerly spelled Mucury.
Mudaliarpet (mōōdŭl'yŭrpĕt) or **Mudaliyarpettai** (-pĕtī), Fr. *Modéliarpeth* (môdālyärpĕt'), town (commune pop. 22,396), Pondicherry settlement, Fr. India; industrial suburb of Pondicherry, 1.5 mi. SW of city center; cotton, rice, and oilseed milling, mfg. of copra; dyeworks; pottery.
Mudanya or **Mudania** (mōōdä'nyä), town (pop. 5,624), Bursa prov., NW Turkey, port on S shore of Gulf of Gemlik of Sea of Marmara, 16 mi. NW of Bursa; rail terminus; copper, olives, Merinos.
Mudanya Mountains, NW Turkey, extend 100 mi. E of Bandirma along S shore of Sea of Marmara, Gulf of Gemlik, and L. Iznik; rise to 4,220 ft. Town of Mudanya on N slope. Iron and copper in W; iron, chromium, and mercury in E.
Muda River (mōō'dä), Kedah, NW Malaya, rises in Kalakhiri Mts. on Thailand border, flows 100 mi. S and W, past Kuala Ketil, to Strait of Malacca at Kuala Muda, forming Kedah–Prov. Wellesley border in lower course.
Mudawara or **Mudawarah** (mōōdärä'rŭ), village, S Jordan, 60 mi. ESE of Aqaba; last Jordan station on disused part of Hejaz RR; airfield. Sometimes spelled Mudauwara or Mudawwara.
Mudaybi, Oman: see MUDHAIBI.
Mudbidri, India: see KARKAL.
Mud Creek. 1 In central Nebr., rises in Custer co. near Broken Bow, flows 77 mi. SE to S.Loup R. near Ravenna. **2** In S Okla., rises SE of Duncan in Stephens co., flows c.65 mi. SE, through Jefferson co., to Red R. in Love co.
Muddebihal (mōōd-dä'bĭhäl), village, Bijapur dist., S Bombay, India, 45 mi. SE of Bijapur; cotton, millet, peanuts, wheat. Limestone deposits near.
Muddo Gashi (mōō'dō gä'shē), village, Northern Frontier Prov., E central Kenya, on road and 120 mi. ENE of Isiolo, near Lorian swamps; 0°45'N 39°9'E; stock raising. Airfield.
Muddus, Lake, Finnish *Muddusjärvi* (mōōt'tōōs-yăr"vē) (10 mi. long, 1–6 mi. wide), Lapland, N Finland, W of L. Inari, 4 mi. NW of Inari village; 69°N 27°E. Site of arctic experimental station of Helsinki univ.
Muddy Boggy Creek, SE Okla., rises E of Ada, flows c.110 mi. SE, past Atoka, to junction with Clear Boggy Creek in Choctaw co., c.18 mi. WNW of Hugo.
Muddy Creek or **Muddy River,** S central Utah, rises in Wasatch Plateau, flows 60 mi. SE, joining Fremont R. in Wayne co., N of Henry Mts., to form Dirty Devil R.
Muddy Creek Falls, Md.: see SWALLOW FALLS.
Muddy River, SE Nev., rises in Sheep Range, flows c.60 mi. SE to N arm of L. Mead just S of Overton. Sometimes called Muddy Creek. Grand Meadow Wash is tributary.
Mudersbach (mōō'dŭrsbäkh), village (pop. 4,433), in former Prussian Rhine Prov., W Germany, after 1945 in Rhineland-Palatinate, on the Sieg and 4 mi. SW of Siegen.
Mudfork, W.Va.: see VERDUNVILLE.
Mudgal (mōōd'gŭl), town (pop. 6,226), Raichur dist., SW Hyderabad state, India, 60 mi. WSW of Raichur; millet, cotton, oilseeds.

Mudgee (mŭ'jē), municipality (pop. 4,178), E central New South Wales, Australia, 130 mi. NW of Sydney; gold-mining center; wool.

Mudhaibi or **Mudaybi** (mōōdhī'bē), town (pop. 3,500), Sharqiya dist. of interior Oman, 30 mi. W of Ibra, at foot of Eastern Hajar hills; date groves.

Mudhnib or **Al Mudhnib** (ăl mōōdh' nĭb), town and oasis, Qasim prov. of Nejd, Saudi Arabia, 20 mi. SE of Anaiza; trading center; grain (wheat, sorghum), dates, vegetables, fruit; stock raising.

Mudhol (mōōd'ōl). **1** Town (pop. 8,179), Bijapur dist., S Bombay, India, on Ghatprabha R. and 45 mi. SW of Bijapur; market center for cotton, millet, peanuts, wheat; cotton ginning, hand-loom weaving, oilseed pressing. Was ⊙ former princely state of Mudhol (□ 350; pop. 72,447) in Deccan States, Bombay; state inc. (1949) into Bijapur dist. **2** Town (pop. 8,613), Nander dist., N Hyderabad state, India, 30 mi. ESE of Nander; extensive cotton ginning here and in near-by villages; millet, wheat, rice. Also spelled Mudhole.

Mudia (mōō'dēŭ) or **'Amudiyah** (ämōōdē'yŭ), broad plain in Dathina tribal dist. of Western Aden Protectorate, at S foot of the Kaur al Audhilla, inhabited by Hasani (Hasanah) and Meisari (Meyasir) tribes of Oleh confederation. Aden administration was set up here in 1944–45.

Mudigere (mōō'dĭgĕrē), town (pop. 1,961), Kadur dist., W Mysore, India, 15 mi. SW of Chikmagalur; rice milling, beekeeping. Coffee, tea, and cardamom estates in near-by hills.

Mud Junction, W.Va.: see VERDUNVILLE.

Mudkhed (mōōdkād'), town (pop. 5,140), Nander dist., N Hyderabad state, India, 12 mi. E of Nander; cotton ginning; millet, wheat.

Mudki (mōōd'kē), village, Ferozepur dist., W Punjab, India, 21 mi. SE of Ferozepore. Near by, British defeated Sikh forces, 1845, in 1st Sikh War.

Mud Lake. **1** In NW Nev., intermittent body of water in Washoe co., NNE of Pyramid L.; c.20 mi. long, 6 mi. wide. Sometimes known as Mud Flat. **2** In Jefferson co., N N.Y., 6 mi. SE of Alexandria Bay; c.2½ mi. long, ½ mi. wide. Resort; fishing.

Mud Mountain Dam, Wash.: see WHITE RIVER.

Mudon (mōō'dôn), village, Amherst dist., Lower Burma, in Tenasserim, on Moulmein-Ye RR and 15 mi. SSE of Moulmein. Canal to Salween R. mouth.

Mud River. **1** In S Ky., rises in Logan co. N of Russellville, flows c.70 mi. generally N to Green R. just NW of Rochester. **2** In SW W.Va., rises in Boone co. W of Madison, flows NNW and W past Milton to Guyandot R. at Barboursville; 72 mi. long.

Mudros, Greece: see MOUDROS.

Mudugh (mōōdōōg'), region, central Ital. Somaliland, bordering on Br. Somaliland (N), Indian Ocean (E), Ethiopia (W). Hot, arid plain with sand dunes along coast; rises to 600 ft. (N). Watered by the Webi Shebeli in extreme W. Pastoralism (cattle, sheep, camels); agr. (durra) along the Webi Shebeli. Chief centers: Bulo Burti, Belet Uen, Obbia.

Mudukulattur (mōōd"ōōkōōlŭt-tōōr'), village, Ramnad dist., S Madras, India, 15 mi. SSW of Paramagudi, in cotton, palmyra, grain area.

Mudungunj, E Pakistan: see MADANGANJ.

Mudurnu (mōōdōōrnōō'), village (pop. 3,038), Bolu prov., NW Turkey, 28 mi. SW of Bolu; grain, flax.

Mudyuga or **Mud'yuga** (mōōtyōō'gŭ), town (1943 pop. over 500), NW Archangel oblast, Russian SFSR, on railroad, on branch of Onega R. and 35 mi. E of Onega; sawmilling. Developed in early 1940s.

Mudzi Maria, Belgian Congo: see BUNIA.

Muecate (mwĕkä'tä), village, Niassa prov., N Mozambique, 33 mi. NE of Nampula; cotton.

Muêda (mwā'dŭ), village, Niassa prov., N Mozambique, near Tanganyika border, 120 mi. NW of Pôrto Amélia; cotton, peanuts. Handicraft industry.

Muel (mwĕl), town (pop. 1,528), Saragossa prov., NE Spain, 18 mi. SW of Saragossa; wine, cereals, sugar beets. In monastery near by are paintings by Goya.

Muela, Bolivia: see VILLA RIVERO.

Muelle de los Bueyes (mwĕ'yä dā lōs bwā'ĕs), village, Zelaya dept., E Nicaragua, on Mico R. and 19 mi. WSW of Rama, on road; sugar cane, livestock; lumbering.

Muelle de San Carlos (sän' kär'lōs), village, Alajuela prov., N Costa Rica, on San Carlos R. and 14 mi. NNW of Villa Quesada; stock raising, lumbering.

Muelle de Sarapiquí, Costa Rica: see SARAPIQUÍ.

Mueller Glacier (mōō'lŭr), W central S.Isl., New Zealand, in Tasman Natl. Park Southern Alps; rises near Ben Ohau Range, flows 8 mi. NW and NE to Tasman R.

Muenster (mŭn'stŭr, mĭn'–), town (pop. 896), Cooke co., N Texas, 14 mi. W of Gainesville; cheese, flour; oil refining.

Muermos, Los, Chile: see LOS MUERMOS.

Muerto, Cerro El (sĕ'rō ĕl mwĕr'tō), Andean mountain (21,450 ft.) on Argentina-Chile border, near the Nevados Tres Cruces, 30 mi. WSW of Cerro Incahuasi; 27°3'S.

Muerto, Mar (mär), lagoon of Gulf of Tehuantepec, on coast of Oaxaca and Chiapas, S Mexico, 60 mi. ESE of Juchitán; 45 mi. long, 2–7 mi. wide.

Muerto Island, Ecuador: see SANTA CLARA ISLAND.

Muertos Island or **Caja de Muertos** (kä'hä dā mwĕr'tōs), small island (c.1½ mi. long, ½ mi. wide), off S coast of Puerto Rico, 10 mi. SE of Ponce.

Muff, Gaelic *Magh*, town (pop. 154), NE Co. Donegal, Ireland, at head of Lough Foyle, 6 mi. NNE of Londonderry; shirt mfg.

Muflahi, Aden: see MAFLAHI.

Mufow Mountains, Chinese *Mu-fou Shan* (mōō'fō' shän'), on Kiangsi-Hupeh line, China, rise to 4,856 ft. 125 mi. WNW of Nanchang, in northeasternmost Hunan prov. Sometimes called Kiukung Mts.—for a lower peak, 90 mi. NW of Nanchang.

Mufulira (mōōfōōlē'rä), township (pop. 1,993), Western Prov., N Northern Rhodesia, near Belgian Congo border, on rail spur and 40 mi. NW of Ndola; commercial center for adjacent (E) Mufulira mining township (pop. 12,395), a major copper-mining center; smelter. Has govt. and convent schools, European and native hospitals.

Mufumbiro, range, E central Africa: see VIRUNGA.

Mugan Steppe, Azerbaijan SSR: see KURA LOWLAND.

Mugardos (mōōgär'dhōs), town (pop. 3,078), La Coruña prov., NW Spain, in Galicia, on S shore of Ferrol Bay, opposite (1 mi. SW of) El Ferrol; fishing, boatbuilding, lumbering, agr. Granite and graphite quarries near by.

Muge (mōō'zhĭ), village (pop. 1,402), Santarém dist., central Portugal, near left bank of the Tagus, 10 mi. S of Santarém; rice, corn, wheat; pine forest.

Mugello (mōōjĕl'lô), upper valley (□ c.230) of Sieve R., in Firenze prov., Tuscany, central Italy; agr. (cereals, grapes), livestock raising, forestry. Chief town, Borgo San Lorenzo.

Mügeln (mü'gŭln), town (pop. 4,638), Saxony, E central Germany, 12 mi. SW of Riesa; mfg. (chemicals, ceramics).

Mugera (mōōgĕ'rä), village, central Ruanda-Urundi, in Urundi, near Ruvuvu R., 7 mi. N of Kitega; coffee and palm products. Has R.C. mission with small seminary, convent for native nuns and schools. Seat of vicar apostolic of Urundi.

Müggel Lake, Ger. *Müggelsee* (mü'gŭlzā"), lake (□ 3), Brandenburg, E Germany, 10 mi. ESE of Berlin city center; 3 mi. long, 1–2 mi. wide; greatest depth 26 ft., average depth 20 ft. Traversed by the Spree. Popular excursion resort.

Muggendorf (mōō'gŭndôrf), noted summer resort (pop. 908), Upper Franconia, N Bavaria, Germany, in the Franconian Switzerland, on the Wiesent and 17 mi. SW of Bayreuth; metalworking. Stalactite caves in area.

Muggensturm (mōō'gŭnstōōrm), village (pop. 2,955), S Baden, Germany, 3 mi. NE of Rastatt; food processing, paper milling.

Muggia, Ethiopia: see MUJA.

Muggia (mōōj'jä), Slovenian *Milje* (mē'lyä), town (pop. 3,028), N Free Territory of Trieste, on S shore of Muggia Bay (Adriatic inlet of the Gulf of Trieste) opposite Trieste; shipyards. Has 15th-cent. church. Placed 1947 under Anglo-American administration.

Muggiano (mōōd-jä'nô), village (pop. 665), La Spezia prov., Liguria, N Italy, port on Gulf of Spezia and 3 mi. SE of Spezia; shipyards. First lead-extraction industry in Italy established here 1880. Formerly called Pertusola.

Muggiò (mōōd-jô'), town (pop. 4,073), Milano prov., Lombardy, N Italy, 2 mi. W of Monza; mfg. (furniture, machinery, hardware, shoes).

Mughalbhin, W Pakistan: see JATI.

Mughalpura, W Pakistan: see MOGHALPURA.

Mughal Sarai (mōōg'ŭl sŭrī'), town (pop. 5,567), Benares dist., SE Uttar Pradesh, India, 7 mi. ESE of Benares city center; rail junction (workshops); rice, barley, gram, wheat, sugar cane. Also spelled Moghal-Sarai.

Mugi (mōō'gē), town (pop. 9,936), Tokushima prefecture, E Shikoku, Japan, on Philippine Sea, 29 mi. SSW of Tokushima; fishing port.

Mugía (mōōhē'ä), town (pop. 1,048), La Coruña prov., NW Spain, near the Atlantic, 37 mi. NW of Santiago; lace mfg.; fishing, lumbering, stock raising.

Mugia Pass (mōō'zhä') (1,371 ft.), in Annamese Cordillera, on Laos-Vietnam line, 55 mi. WNW of Donghoi; used by Tanap-Thakhek road, paralleled on Vietnam slope by cable railway. Also spelled Meugia.

Mugla (mōōlä'), Turk. *Muğla*, prov. (□ 4,917; 1950 pop. 240,704), SW Turkey; ⊙ Mugla. Bordered W by Aegean Sea, S by Mediterranean Sea, E by Elmali Mts. Drained by Ak, Dalaman, and Koca rivers. Rich in forests and in minerals, including chromium, manganese, antimony, and silver, as well as emery, asbestos, salt, and lignite. Agr. products are sesame, millet, tobacco, olives, wheat. Formerly Mentese (Menteshe).

Mugla, Turkish *Muğla*, town (1950 pop. 10,477), ⊙ Mugla prov., SW Turkey, 100 mi. SSE of Smyrna; millet, wheat, tobacco, olives, onions; emery, chromium. Formerly, under the name of Mentese (Menteshe), capital of an independent duchy whose pirates dominated the Aegean in 13th cent.

Muglad (mōōg'läd), village, Kordofan prov., central Anglo-Egyptian Sudan, on road and 120 mi. SSW of Nahud.

Müglitz, Czechoslovakia: see MOHELNICE.

Mugnano del Cardinale (mōōnyä'nô dĕl kärdēnä'lĕ), village (pop. 3,463), Avellino prov., Campania, S Italy, 9 mi. WNW of Avellino.

Mugnano di Napoli (dē nä'pôlē), town (pop. 7,406), Napoli prov., Campania, S Italy, 4 mi. S of Aversa, in agr. region (grapes, fruit, vegetables).

Mugodzhar Hills (mōōgŭjär'), southernmost extension of the Urals, in Aktyubinsk oblast, Kazakh SSR; extend from source of Irgiz R. 250 mi. S to Ust-Urt plateau. Composed of 2 parallel ranges (rising to 2,145 ft. at Ber-Chogur) forming divide bet. Caspian and Aral sea basins. Coal, iron, nickel, and chrome deposits.

Mugreyevski or **Mugreyevskiy** (mōōgryā'ĭfskē), town (1942 pop. over 500), SE Ivanovo oblast, Russian SFSR, 8 mi. ENE of Yuzha; peat.

Mugron (mügrō'), village (pop. 656), Landes dept., SW France, near Adour R., 15 mi. E of Dax; footwear mfg. Quarries near by. Renaissance castle of Poyanne is 3 mi. W.

Mugtaa, El (ĕl mōōgtä'), village, E Tripolitania, Libya, on Cyrenaica border, 150 mi. ESE of Sirte, near Gulf of Sidra. The Marble Arch (c.100 ft. high; built 1937), 20 mi. WNW, spans the midway point on the Libyan coastal highway and commemorates its construction; scene of heavy fighting (1942) in Second World War.

Mugu, Point (mŭgōō'), S Calif., low foreland just SE of Port Hueneme and 7 mi. SSE of Oxnard; U.S. naval air-missile test center.

Mugur-Aksy (mōōgōōr"-ŭksē'), village, extreme SW Tuva Autonomous Oblast, Russian SFSR, 195 mi. SW of Kyzyl, in agr. area.

Muguru (mōō'gōōrōō), town (pop. 4,023), Mysore dist., S Mysore, India, 23 mi. SE of Mysore, in silk-growing area; hand-loom silk and cotton weaving; sugar cane. Also spelled Mugur.

Muhamdi (mōōhŭm'dē), town (pop. 7,618), Kheri dist., N Uttar Pradesh, India, 35 mi. W of Lakhimpur; sugar milling; trades in rice, wheat, gram, corn, oilseeds. Has 17th-cent. Moslem fort ruins. Sometimes spelled Mohamdi.

Muhammadabad (mōōhŭm'mŭdäbäd"). **1** Town (pop. 5,212), Azamgarh dist., E Uttar Pradesh, India, on Tons R. and 12.5 mi. E of Azamgarh; hand-loom cotton weaving, sugar milling; rice, barley, wheat. **2** Town (pop. 7,885), Ghazipur dist., E Uttar Pradesh, India, 11 mi. E of Ghazipur; trades in rice, barley, gram, oilseeds. Also spelled Mohammadbad.

Muhammadabad or **Mohammedabad** (both: mōhämĕd"äbäd'), town, Ninth Prov., in Khurasan, NE Iran, 45 mi. NE of Quchan; main town of Daragaz agr. dist.; grain, fruit, opium, cotton, raisins. In earthquake zone. Sometimes called Daragaz.

Muhammadgarh (mōōhŭm'mŭdgŭr), former princely state (□ 45; pop. 2,888) of Central India agency, E of Bhilsa. Since 1948, merged with Madhya Bharat.

Muhammad Ghul (mōōhäm'mĕd gōōl') or **Muhammad Qol** (kōl'), village, Kassala prov., NE Anglo-Egyptian Sudan, minor port on Red Sea and 90 mi. N of Port Sudan; exports gold from Gebeit mines.

Muhammadpur, India: see ROORKEE.

Muhammad Qol, Anglo-Egyptian Sudan: see MUHAMMAD GHUL.

Muhammed, Ras, or **Ra's Muhammad** (räs' mōōhäm'măd), southernmost tip of Sinai Peninsula, NE Egypt, on Red Sea; 27°45'N 34°15'E.

Muhammerah, Iran: see KHURRAMSHAHR.

Muharraq (mōōhä'răk), island of Bahrein archipelago, in Persian Gulf, separated by 1½-mi.-wide channel from NE shore of main Bahrein isl.; 4 mi. long, 1 mi. wide. Site of main airport and seaplane base of Bahrein. On SW point is Muharraq town (1950 pop., with near-by Hadd, 25,577), formerly chief residence of the sheik, linked by road causeway with Manama. Fishing and pearling are the chief industries. Sometimes spelled Moharraq.

Muheza or **Muhesa** (mōōhĕ'zä), town, Tanga prov., NE Tanganyika, on railroad and 25 mi. WSW of Tanga, in orange-growing area; sisal, cotton. Malaria research station.

Muhinga (mōōhĭng'gä), village, E Ruanda-Urundi, in Urundi, near Tanganyika border, 45 mi. NE of Kitega; customs station, center of native trade; cattle raising. Has veterinary laboratory.

Mühlacker (mül'ä"kŭr), town (pop. 8,194), Württemberg, Germany, after 1945 in Württemberg-Baden, on the Enz and 7 mi. NE of Pforzheim; rail junction; foundries. Mfg. of machine tools, tools, jewelry, ceramics; metalworking. Brickworks. Has ruined castle.

Mühlau (mü'lou), village (pop. 3,411), Saxony, E central Germany, 9 mi. NW of Chemnitz; hosiery, glove, and underwear knitting.

Mühlbach, Rumania: see SEBES.

Mühlberg or **Mühlberg an der Elbe** (mül'bĕrk än dĕr ĕl'bŭ), town (pop. 4,466), in former Prussian Saxony prov., central Germany, after 1945 in Saxony-Anhalt, on the Elbe and 9 mi. NNW of

Riesa; furniture mfg., basket weaving. Has 13th-cent. church of former Cistercian monastery of Güldenstern; and old moated castle, rebuilt 1545. On adjacent Lochauer Heide (heath), Emperor Charles V defeated (1547) the Elector John Frederick of Saxony, leader of Protestant forces in Schmalkaldic War.

Mühlburg (mül″bŏŏrk), W suburb of Karlsruhe, Germany.

Mühldorf (mül′dôrf), village (pop. 1,057), Carinthia, S Austria, on Möll R. and 8 mi. NW of Spittal; steelworks; textile mfg.; summer resort. Near by are excavations of Celtic-Roman city of Teurnia, with ruins of basilica.

Mühldorf (mül′dôrf), town (pop. 8,687), Upper Bavaria, Germany, on the Inn and 27 mi. NNW of Traunstein; rail junction; hydroelectric plant; mfg. of basic chemicals and textiles, brewing, printing, woodworking, lumber milling. Was important river crossing in Roman times. Chartered c.954. Bet. here and Ampfing took place, in 1322, one of the most important battles of the Middle Ages, in which Emperor Louis the Bavarian defeated his rival, Frederick of Austria.

Mühleberg (mü′lübĕrk″), town (pop. 2,138), Bern canton, W Switzerland, 9 mi. W of Bern; hydroelectric plant on near-by Wohlensee; farming.

Muhlenberg (mū′lùnbûrg), county (□ 482; pop. 32,501), W Ky.; ⊙ Greenville. Bounded NE by Green R., E by Mud R., W by Pond R. Important bituminous-coal-mining area; some farms (dairy products, poultry, livestock, soybeans, burley tobacco, grain, hay, truck); oil wells, clay pits; timber. Formed 1798.

Mühlfeld (mül′fĕlt″), village (pop. 449), Lower Franconia, N Bavaria, Germany, 2 mi. ENE of Mellrichstadt, 4 mi. E of Rentwertshausen; grain, cattle.

Mühlgraben, Latvia: see MILGRAVIS.

Mühlhausen, Czechoslovakia: see MILEVSKO.

Mühlhausen or **Mühlhausen in Thüringen** (mülhou′zùn ĭn tü′rĭng-ùn), city (pop. 48,013), in former Prussian Saxony prov., central Germany, after 1945 in Thuringia, on the Unstrut and 30 mi. NW of Erfurt, in barite-mining region; locomotive repair shops; metalworking, cotton and paper milling, dyeing, tanning, printing. Also mfg. of electrical equipment, shoes, sewing machines, bicycles, furniture. Has 13th- and 14th-cent. churches; town hall (1605); many 16th–18th-cent. houses. Fortified (remains of walls) by Henry I in 10th cent. Was a center of Teutonic Order in 13th cent. Created free imperial city in 1251; became member of Hanseatic League. Anabaptist center after Reformation. During Peasants' War, it was hq. of Thomas Münzer (executed here in 1525); subsequently it was deprived of privileges as free city. Passed to Prussia in 1815.

Mühlheim (mül′hīm). **1** or **Mühlheim am Main** (äm mīn′), town (pop. 11,912), S Hesse, W Germany, in former Starkenburg prov., on left bank of the canalized Main and 3 mi. ENE of Offenbach; mfg. of chemicals, metal pipes; leatherworking, paper milling. **2** or **Mühlheim an der Donau** (än dĕr dō′nou), town (pop. 1,210), S Württemberg, Germany, after 1945 in Württemberg-Hohenzollern, in Swabian Jura, on the Danube and 5 mi. NE of Tuttlingen; cattle.

Mühl River, Austria and Germany: see GROSSE MÜHL RIVER.

Mühltroff (mül′trôf), town (pop. 2,367), Saxony, E central Germany, 10 mi. WNW of Plauen; cotton milling.

Muho, Formosa: see WUFENG.

Muhoroni (mŏŏhōrō′nē), village, Nyanza prov., W Kenya, on railroad and 30 mi. ESE of Kisumu; hardwood and rubber center; coffee, corn. Limestone quarry and kilns near by.

Muhu (mōō′hōō) or **Mukhu** (mōō′khōō), Ger. *Moon*, third-largest island (□ 79) of Estonia, in Baltic Sea, bet. Saare isl. and mainland; 13 mi. long, 10 mi. wide. Consists of Silurian limestone with thin top layer of marine sediments; agr., fishing. Connected by 3-mi. causeway with Saare Isl. (SW). Main centers are Muhu village (center) and Kuivastu (ferry station on SE coast). Also called Muhumaa or Mukhuma.

Muhulu, Belgian Congo: see MUTIKO.

Muhu Sound, Est. *Muhu Vain*, arm of Baltic Sea, bet. Estonian mainland (E) and Muhu and Hiiumaa isls. (W); 4–15 mi. wide.

Muich-Dhui, Ben, Scotland: see BEN MACDHUI.

Muiden (moi′dùn), town (pop. 1,993), North Holland prov., W central Netherlands, on the Ijsselmeer, near mouth of Vecht R., and 8 mi. ESE of Amsterdam; mfg. (explosives, railroad supplies); shipbuilding; cattle raising. Has 13th-cent. castle.

Muika (mōōē′kä), town (pop. 10,267), Niigata prefecture, central Honshu, Japan, 27 mi. S of Nagaoka; textiles (silk, hemp), charcoal.

Muilrea or **Mweelrea** (both: mwēlrā′), mountain range, SW Co. Mayo, Ireland, extending 8 mi. NW-SE along Killary Harbour; rises to 2,688 ft.

Muiluk (mōō′ēlōōk′), Mandarin *Meilu* (mā′lōō′), town, SW Kwangtung prov., China, port on Foshan R. and 28 mi. ENE of Chankiang; commercial center; oranges, pears, bananas.

Muinak or **Muynak** (mōōēnäk′), town (1939 pop. over 2,000), N Kara-Kalpak Autonomous SSR, Uzbek SSR, port on Tokmak-Aty Isl. in Aral Sea, off the Amu Darya mouth, 95 mi. NNW of Nukus; fisheries. Shipping route to Aralsk.

Muine (mwē′nā′), village, Phanthiet prov., S central Vietnam, on South China Sea coast, 11 mi. E of Phanthiet; fishing and fish curing.

Muine Bheag, Muine Beag, or **Bagenalstown,** town (pop. 1,927), W Co. Carlow, Ireland, on Barrow R. and 8 mi. ENE of Kilkenny; agr. market (wheat, potatoes, beets; sheep), with sandstone and granite quarries.

Muir (myŏŏr), village (pop. 466), Ionia co., S central Mich., 7 mi. E of Ionia and on Grand R. at mouth of Maple R., in farm area.

Muir, Mount (14,025 ft.), E central Calif., in the Sierra Nevada, just S of Mt. Whitney and on Inyo-Tulare co. line.

Muiravonside (myŏŏră′vùn-), parish (pop. 5,561), SE Stirling, Scotland. Includes AVONBRIDGE.

Muir Glacier (myŏŏr) (□ c.350) SE Alaska, in St. Elias Mts., on SE slope of Mt. Leland, in Glacier Bay Natl. Monument, 40 mi. SW of Skagway; 59°1′N 136°8′W; 20 mi. long, 15 mi. wide. Flows SE into Glacier Bay. Explored (1880) by John Muir; its configuration was severely affected by earthquake, Sept., 1899.

Muirhead (myŏŏr′hĕd), town' in Cadder parish, N Lanark, Scotland, 7 mi. NE of Glasgow; coal.

Muirkirk (-kûrk), town and parish (pop. 4,358), E Ayrshire, Scotland, on Ayr R. and 9 mi. NE of Cumnock; coal mining, ironstone and limestone quarrying; ironworks. Parish includes agr. village of Kaimes (kā′mĭs), just S.

Muirkirk (myŏŏr′kûrk), village, Prince Georges co., central Md., 18 mi. NE of Washington; makes dry pigments. Near by are Ammendale Normal Inst. (R.C.) and U.S. Dept. of Agr. research center.

Muir-of-Ord (myŏŏr, ôrd), town, Urray parish, SE Ross and Cromarty, Scotland, 6 mi. S of Dingwall, near head of Beauly Firth; agr. market. Important livestock fairs were formerly held here. It is center of a crofting district. Near by are ruins of 17th-cent. Fairburn Tower.

Muir Woods National Monument (myŏŏr) (424.56 acres; established 1908), W Calif., near Pacific Ocean, 15 mi. NW of San Francisco, at foot of Mt. Tamalpais. Stand of virgin coast redwoods; tallest in monument area is 246 ft. high, 17 ft. in diameter, and c.2,000 yrs. old.

Muizen (moi′zùn), town (pop. 3,922), Brabant prov., N central Belgium, on Dyle R. and 2 mi. SE of Mechlin; metal industry; vegetable market. Formerly spelled Muysen.

Muizenberg (moi′zùnbûrg, Afrik. moi′zùbĕrkh), residential town, SW Cape Prov., U. of So. Afr., on False Bay, 12 mi. S of Cape Town; popular seaside resort. Scene (1795) of defeat of Dutch forces resisting British landing. Cecil Rhodes died here (1902); his cottage is now natl. historic memorial.

Muja (mōō′jä), Ital. *Muggia*, town (pop. 2,000), Wallo prov., NE Ethiopia, near source of Takkaze R., 27 mi. E of Lalibala; 12°3′N 39°38′E. Trade center (cattle, horses, salt, cereals).

Mujeres Island, Mexico: see ISLA MUJERES.

Mujib, Wadi el, or **Wadi al-Mujib** (both: wă′dē ĕl-mōō′jĭb), river in central Jordan, formed 4 mi. E of Kerak by union of 2 branches, flows 35 mi. N and W to Dead Sea 21 mi. NNW of Kerak. Bitumen deposits near mouth. It is the anc. Arnon.

Mukachevo (mōō′kŭchĭvù), Czech *Mukačevo* (mŏŏ′-kächĕvô), Hung. *Munkács* (mŏŏng′käch), city (1941 pop. 31,602), W Transcarpathian Oblast, Ukrainian SSR, on Latoritsa R., on railroad and 23 mi. SE of Uzhgorod; trading center (lumber, cattle, grain); mfg. (clothing, furniture, shoes), tobacco processing, imported crude-petroleum refining. Iron pyrite and alum crystals mined in vicinity. Founded in 14th cent. Has Ital. Renaissance church, agr. school. Was historical ⊙ Subcarpathian Ruthenia; former bishop's see. Until Second World War, an important center of Talmudic learning (rabbinical school); pop. was 50% Jewish. Hung. painter Munkacsy (1844–1900) b. here. On high rock c.2 mi. SW is 14th-cent. fortress, once prison of Alexander Ypsilanti, later converted into military barracks. Podgoryany breweries are 2 mi. NE. Mukachevo was a town of Austria-Hungary which passed 1920 to Czechoslovakia, 1938 to Hungary, and 1945 to USSR.

Mukachevo Pass, Ukrainian SSR: see VERETSKI PASS.

Mukah (mōōkä′), town (pop. 4,701), Sarawak, in W Borneo, on S.China Sea, 45 mi. NNE of Sibu; agr. (sago, pineapples), stock raising, fishing.

Mukaihara (mōōkī′härù), town (pop. 7,470), Hiroshima prefecture, SW Honshu, Japan, 22 mi. NE of Hiroshima; commercial center for agr. area (rice, fruit); sake, livestock, charcoal.

Mukai-shima (mōōkī′shĭmä), island (□ 9; pop. 24,371), Hiroshima prefecture, Japan, in Hiuchi Sea, nearly connected with city of Onomichi on SW Honshu; 4 mi. long, 3 mi. wide. Mountainous; fertile (fruit, rice, raw silk). Mfg. (sailcloth, canned food, floor mats).

Mukalla (mōōkă′lù), town (1946 pop. 20,000), ⊙ Quaiti state and its Mukalla prov., Eastern Aden Protectorate, port on Mukalla Bay of Gulf of Aden, 300 mi. ENE of Aden; 14°32′N 49°7′E. Principal port of entry of the Hadhramaut, and market for the interior; fishing center (curing, drying); dhow building, lime burning, tanning; sesame oil and oil cake. A miniature Zanzibar, the town is characterized by tall houses and narrow streets, some not 6 ft. wide. It is residence of Quaiti sultan; and of British resident adviser to the Hadhramaut states, who is also British agent for Eastern Aden Protectorate. Next to Aden, Mukalla is the chief port on the S coast of the Arabian Peninsula; during SW monsoon, vessels use sheltered BURUM anchorage. Exports fish products, tobacco (from Gheil Ba Wazir), and honey (from the Wadi Duan). Riyan airport is 15 mi. ENE. Sometimes spelled Makalla.

Mukama, India: see MOKAMEH.

Mukandwara Pass (mōōkŭndvä′rù), in range of low hills, SE Rajasthan, India, 27 mi. SSE of Kotah; used by road and railroad. Scene of many battles in Rajput history; on route of Br. retreat before Jaswant Rao Holkar in 1804.

Mukar, Afghanistan: see MUKUR.

Mukayyar, Iraq: see UR.

Mukdahan (mōōk′dä′hän′), village (1937 pop. 6,847), Nakhon Phanom prov., E Thailand, on right bank of Mekong R. (Laos line), opposite Savannakhet, and 60 mi. S of Nakhon Phanom; airport. Sometimes spelled Mukdahar or Mukdaharn.

Mukden (mōōk′dĕn), village, Pando dept., NW Bolivia, 23 mi. WSW of Cobija; rice, bananas.

Mukden (mōōk′dùn, mōōk′-), Chinese *Shenyang* (shŭn′yäng′), formerly *Fengtien* or *Feng-t'ien* (fŭng′tyĕn′), city (1947 pop. 1,120,918) ⊙ Manchuria, in, but independent of, Liaotung prov., 220 mi. NNE of Dairen, 380 mi. ENE of Peking, and on Hun (or Shen) R. (tributary of the Liao); 41°18′N 113°26′E. Political and economic center of Manchuria; rail and road hub in Manchuria's chief industrial and agr. dist., on South Manchuria RR. Agr.-processing industry (soybeans, flour, tobacco); cotton and silk milling, match and paper mfg. A major metal-fabricating center, it has aircraft and ordnance plants, and produces automobiles, rolling stock, machinery, and chemicals. Mukden's industry is supplied with raw materials by its satellite industrial centers of Fushun (coal), Anshan and Penki (steel). The sprawling metropolis consists of the old Chinese city, adjoined by the arsenal dist. (E); and of the new city (W), and the W Mukden industrial area. The Chinese city, bounded by a 10-mi.-long earthwall, contains the brick-walled inner city—the old Manchu residence—with former imperial palace and present administrative offices. The arsenal dist. (E) is the old Chinese industrial area with ordnance plant and airport. W of the Chinese city and extending to the railroad station is the new Mukden of broad, rectilinear avenues, which developed after 1905 out of the Japanese railway concession zone. Beyond the railroad is the W Mukden section (Chinese *T'ien-hsi*, Jap. *Tetsunishi*), a vast industrial and residential section developed under Manchukuo rule and housing most of the city's heavy and metal-fabricating industries. Mukden has a univ. The Peiling tombs of early Manchu emperors are in N outskirts. The name Shen (in Shenyang) dates from the Liao (Kitan) dynasty of 12th cent. City remained a Chinese center of colonization in S Manchuria until captured by the rising Manchus in 16th cent. The Manchus, who had their capital here (1625–44) prior to the transfer to Peking, named the city Mukden, later giving it the Chinese name Fengtien and the title Shengking [abundant capital]. City became ⊙ Fengtien or Shengking (later LIAONING) prov. Mukden's modern development was begun c.1900 by the Russians in connection with the building of the Manchurian railroads. After Russo-Japanese War, during which a decisive battle was won here (1905) by the Japanese, Russian interests passed to the Japanese. Following the Chinese revolution, the city regained its anc. name, Shenyang, and was the seat of the Manchurian war lords, notably Chang Tso-lin. At Peitaying (3 mi. NE) took place the Sino-Japanese incident of Sept., 1931, that led to the founding of Manchukuo. While in Manchukuo, Mukden regained the Manchu Chinese name of Fengtien as ⊙ Fengtien prov. (□ 28,900; 1940 pop. 7,565,599) during 1934–46. City underwent a spectacular economic development, with its pop. rising from 421,000 in 1931 to 1,890,600 in 1945. After the war, it was again renamed Shenyang, was made an independent municipality directly under the central govt., and in 1949 became ⊙ Manchurian regional govt.

Mukha, Yemen: see MOCHA.

Mukhairas, Aden: see MUKHEIRAS.

Mukhanovo (mōōkhä′nùvù). **1** Rail station, Kuibyshev oblast, Russian SFSR: see KROTOVKA. **2** Town (1943 pop. over 500), N Moscow oblast, Russian SFSR, 20 mi. from Zagorsk.

Mukhavets River (mōōkhŭvyĕts′), Pol. *Muchawiec* (mōōkhä′vyĕts), in Pripet Marshes, W Belorussian SSR, rises N of Pruzhany, flows S, past Pruzhany, and WSW, past Kobrin, to Bug R. at Brest; 75 mi. long. Navigable for c.50 mi. in lower course, up to

Dnieper-Bug Canal; forms W part of Dnieper-Bug waterway.

Mukhayras, Aden: see MUKHEIRAS.

Mukheiras, Mukhairas, or **Mukhayras** (all: mŏŏkhä-räs'), town, Audhali sultanate, Western Aden Protectorate, on plateau (7,000 ft.) at N foot of the Kaur al Audhilla, 45 mi. N of Shuqra and 100 mi. NE of Aden, at Yemen "Status Quo Line"; center of major agr. dist., supplying Aden market with fresh fruit and vegetables by air; airfield. Also spelled Mukheras.

Mukher (mŏŏkär'), town (pop. 6,825), Nander dist., N central Hyderabad state, India, 31 mi. S of Nander; millet, cotton, wheat. Also spelled Mukhed.

Mukheras, Aden: see MUKHEIRAS.

Mukhino (mŏŏ'khēnŭ), village, E Kirov oblast, Russian SFSR, 17 mi. SSW of Zuyevka; grain, flax.

Mukhor-Shibir or **Mukhor-Shibir'** (mŏŏkhôr"-shēbĕr'), village (1939 pop. over 2,000), SE Buryat-Mongol Autonomous SSR, Russian SFSR, 55 mi. S of Ulan-Ude, in agr. and livestock-raising area.

Mukhtara, El, or **Al-Mukhtarah** (both: ĕl mŏŏkh-tä'rŭ), Fr. *Moukhtara*, village, central Lebanon, 16 mi. SSE of Beirut; alt. 2,800 ft.; sericulture, cotton, cereals, oranges.

Mukhtolovo (mŏŏkhtŭlô'vŭ), town (1946 pop. over 500), SW Gorki oblast, Russian SFSR, 21 mi. W of Arzamas; sawmilling.

Mukhtuya (mŏŏkhtŏŏ'yŭ), village (1948 pop. over 2,000), SW Yakut Autonomous SSR, Russian SFSR, on Lena R. and 185 mi. W of Olekminsk, in agr. area; river port.

Mukhu, Estonia: see MUHU, island.

Mukilteo (mŭ"kŭltē'ō), town (pop. 826), Snohomish co., W Wash., on Puget Sound and 5 mi. SW of Everett; ferry to Whidbey Isl. (W).

Muko (mŏŏkō'), town (pop. 9,177), Kyoto prefecture, S Honshu, Japan; W residential suburb of Kyoto.

Muko-jima, Bonin Isls.: see PARRY ISLANDS.

Muko-jima-retto, Bonin Isls.: see PARRY ISLANDS.

Mukono (mŏŏkō'nō), town, Buganda prov., S Uganda, 12 mi. ENE of Kampala, near railroad; cotton, coffee, sugar, bananas, corn, millet; livestock.

Mukran, Iran: see MAKRAN.

Mukry (mŏŏk'rē), town (1939 pop. over 500), SE Chardzhou oblast, Turkmen SSR, on the Amu Darya, on railroad and 25 mi. SE of Kerki; cotton. Mukry station, 12 mi. SE of town, is junction of rail spur to Gaurdak (NNE).

Muk-Su (mŏŏk-sŏŏ'), river, N Tadzhik SSR, rises in FEDCHENKO GLACIER, flows 54 mi. W, through gold-mining area, joining the Kyzyl-Su 28 mi. ENE of Khait to form SURKHAB RIVER. Receives the Sauk-Sai.

Mukteswar, India: see NAINI TAL, town.

Muktinath (mŏŏk'tĭnät), Tibetan *Chumik Gyatsa*, village, N Nepal, 40 mi. N of Pokhara. One of most sacred of Nepalese shrines; Hindu and Buddhist pilgrimage center; has 108 sacred springs.

Muktsar (mŏŏk'tsŭr), town (pop. 20,651), Ferozepore dist., W Punjab, India, 34 mi. S of Ferozepore; trades in grain, cotton, oilseeds, cloth fabrics; cotton ginning, hand-loom weaving, ice mfg., oilseed milling. Annual Sikh festival.

Mukumari (mŏŏkŏŏmä'rē), village, Kasai prov., central Belgian Congo, 160 mi. NNW of Lusambo; agr. research station and rubber plantations.

Mukur (mŏŏkŏŏr'), town (pop. 12,000), Kabul prov., E Afghanistan, 65 mi. SW of Ghazni and on highway to Kandahar; irrigated agr. Sometimes spelled Mukar.

Mukurti (mŏŏkŏŏr'tē) or **Makurti** (mŭ–), peak (8,380 ft.) in Nilgiri Hills, SW Madras, India, 13 mi. WSW of Ootacamund; gives rise (E) to Moyar R. The name Mukurti also applies to a dam of PYKARA hydroelectric system. Also spelled Murkurti.

Mukwonago (mŭ"kwŭnä'gō), resort village (pop. 1,207), Waukesha co., SE Wis., on small Phantom L., 24 mi. SW of Milwaukee, in dairying, stock-raising, and farming region.

Mula (mōō'lä), city (pop. 9,632), Murcia prov., SE Spain, 21 mi. W of Murcia; agr. center in fertile garden region producing citrus and other fruit, olives, wine, cereals, rice. Flour milling, olive-oil processing, fruit-conserve mfg., brandy distilling; lumbering, stock raising. Has ruins of anc. castle; 2 Renaissance churches. Mineral springs 3 mi. W. Irrigation reservoir near by.

Mulabo or **Meulaboh** (mōōlä'bō, mŭ–), town (pop. 2,575), NW Sumatra, port on Indian Ocean, 115 mi. SE of Kutaraja; 4°8'N 96°8'E; ships timber, resin, copra, pepper, gold.

Mulag, India: see MULUG.

Mulainagiri, peak, India: see BABA BUDAN RANGE.

Mulaku Atoll (mōō'lŭkōō), small central group (pop. 1,560) of Maldive Isls., in Indian Ocean, bet. 2°45'N and 3°10'N.

Mulaly (mōōlŭlē'), town (1949 pop. over 500), Taldy-Kurgan oblast, Russian SFSR, on railroad and 25 mi. N of Taldy-Kurgan.

Mulan (mōō'län'), town, ⊙ Mulan co. (pop. 85,882), W Sungkiang prov., Manchuria, on left bank of Sungari R. and 75 mi. E of Harbin.

Mulanay (mōōlänī'), town (1939 pop. 1,038; 1948 municipality pop. 5,149), Quezon prov., S Luzon, Philippines, on W Bondoc Peninsula, on Mompog Pass, 60 mi. ESE of Lucena; fishing.

Mula Pass (mōō'lŭ), at S end of Central Brahui Range, central Baluchistan, W Pakistan, SE of Kalat town; highest alt. c.6,000 ft. Lies on trade route, formerly of some importance, bet. highlands of Kalat and plains (E). Name also applied to course of **Mula River,** which rises c.10 mi. SE of Kalat town and flows c.180 mi. SSE and NE into Kachhi plain near Gandava.

Mula River, Poona district, Bombay, India: see MUTHA MULA RIVER.

Mulatas Islands (mōōlä'täs) or **San Blas Islands** (sän bläs'), archipelago off NE (Caribbean) coast of Panama, in San Blas territory, E of San Blas Bay. Its coral isls. (over 300) are inhabited by almost pure-blooded aborigines of Carib origin. Coconuts; fisheries.

Mulatière, La (lä mülätyâr'), S suburb (pop. 3,609) of Lyons, Rhône dept., E central France, on right bank of Rhone R., at mouth of the Saône; produces scales, electric cables, plastic toys. Railroad yards.

Mulat Island (mōō'lät), Ital. *Melada* (mĕlä'dä), Dalmatian island in Adriatic Sea, W Croatia, Yugoslavia, 18 mi. NW of Zadar; 6 mi. long. Molat village on SE shore.

Mulatos (mōōlä'tōs), town (pop. 609), Sonora, NW Mexico, on W slopes of Sierra Madre Occidental, 140 mi. ESE of Hermosillo; corn, livestock.

Mulbagal (mōōlbä'gŭl), town (pop. 6,785), Kolar dist., E Mysore, India, 17 mi. E of Kolar; tobacco curing, sheep grazing.

Mulbekh (mōōlbăk'), village, Ladakh dist., central Kashmir, in Zaskar Range, on right tributary of Suru R. and 19 mi. SE of Kargil. Has Buddhist monastery, Dard castle ruins, rock inscriptions, and huge (c.8th cent. A.D.) Buddhist rock sculpture.

Mulberry. 1 Town (pop. 952), Crawford co., NW Ark., 22 mi. ENE of Fort Smith and on Mulberry R.; trade center for agr. area (fruit, vegetables, dairy products). **2** Village (pop. 2,545), Butte co., N central Calif., near Chico. **3** City (pop. 2,024), Polk co., central Fla., 10 mi. S of Lakeland; processes phosphate (from near-by mines); also mfg. of fertilizer, steel. **4** Village (pop. 950), Clinton co., central Ind., 10 mi. NW of Frankfort. **5** City (pop. 779), Crawford co., SE Kansas, at Mo. line, 11 mi. NNE of Pittsburg, in livestock, poultry, and grain area. Coal mines near by.

Mulberry Fork, river in N Ala., rises in NE Cullman co., flows c.100 mi. SW, past Cordova, to join Locust Fork c.20 mi. W of Birmingham, forming Black Warrior R.

Mulberry Gap (3,100 ft.), NW N.C., pass through the Blue Ridge, 15 mi. N of Wilkesboro.

Mulberry Grove, village (pop. 712), Bond co., S central Ill., 9 mi. WSW of Vandalia, in agr. area (corn, wheat, poultry, livestock; dairy products); ships sand.

Mulberry River. 1 In central Ala., rises in Chilton co., W of Clanton, flows c.35 mi. S to Alabama R. 9 mi. E of Selma. **2** In NW Ark., rises N of Clarksville in the Ozarks, flows c.70 mi. SW to Arkansas R. just S of Mulberry.

Mulchatna River, Alaska: see NUSHAGAK RIVER.

Mulchén (mōōlchĕn'), town (pop. 6,829), ⊙ Mulchén dept. (□ 1,237; pop. 24,379), Bío-Bío prov., S central Chile, in S part of the central valley, 19 mi. SSE of Los Angeles; rail terminus; wheat and cattle center; flour milling, lumbering.

Muldenberg (mōōl'dŭnbĕrk), village (pop. 486), Saxony, E central Germany, in the Erzgebirge, on upper Zwickauer Mulde R. (dam) and 5 mi. SSE of Falkenstein, near Czechoslovak border; hydroelectric power station.

Muldenhütten, Germany: see HILBERSDORF.

Mulde River (mōōl'dŭ), central Germany, formed 2 mi. N of Colditz by the FREIBERGER MULDE and the ZWICKAUER MULDE, flows c.80 mi. NNW, past Grimma and Wurzen, to the Elbe at Dessau.

Muldoon, village (pop. c.300), Fayette co., S central Texas, near Colorado R., 14 mi. SE of Smithville; fuller's earth.

Muldrow (mŭl'drō), town (pop. 828), Sequoyah co., E Okla., 10 mi. W of Fort Smith (Ark.), in agr. area; cotton ginning.

Mulegé (mōōlāgā'), town (pop. 846), Southern Territory, Lower California, NW Mexico, near Gulf of California, 35 mi. SE of Santa Rosalía; manganese-mining and agr. center (sugar cane, coconuts, dates, figs, grapes).

Muleiho (mōō'lä'hŭ'), town and oasis (pop. 13,302), E Sinkiang prov., China, 125 mi. E of Urumchi, and on highway N of the Bogdo Ola; wheat, kaoliang, millet, cattle.

Mule Mountains, Cochise co., SE Ariz., near Mex. line; rise to 7,500 ft. in Mt. BALLARD. Copper, gold, and silver are mined near Bisbee and Warren, in S part of range.

Muleng, Manchuria: see MULING.

Muleros, Mexico: see VILLA VICENTE GUERRERO.

Muleshoe (mŭl'shōō), town (pop. 2,477), ⊙ Bailey co., NW Texas, on the Llano Estacado, c.65 mi. NW of Lubbock; trade, processing center for cattle-ranching and irrigated agr. region; cotton gins, grain elevators; mfg. of canned foods, dairy products, feed. Lakes, with migratory waterfowl refuge, are S. Settled 1913, inc. 1926.

Muley-Hacén, Spain: see MULHACÉN.

Mulga, town (pop. 532), Jefferson co., N central Ala.

Mulgrave (mŭl'grāv), town (pop. 1,057), E N.S., on W shore of Strait of Canso, 30 mi. E of Antigonish; fishing port; ships lumber, pulpwood. Rail ferry to Point Tupper, Cape Breton Isl.

Mulgrave Island (□ 35), in Torres Strait 40 mi. N of Cape York Peninsula, N Queensland, Australia, just W of Banks Isl.; 7.5 mi. long, 6 mi. wide; rises to 686 ft. Wooded, rocky; pearl shell.

Mulgrave Islands, Marshall Isls.: see MILI.

Mulhacén (mōōlä-thĕn') or **Muley-Hacén** (mōōlā'-ä-thĕn'), highest peak (11,411 ft.) of continental Spain, in the Sierra Nevada, Granada prov., S Spain, 20 mi. SE of Granada; 37°3'N 3°17'W. Snow line at c.10,000 ft. Commands beautiful view of Andalusia, and N Africa can be seen. Copper deposits.

Mulhall, town (pop. 320), Logan co., central Okla., 13 mi. N of Guthrie, in farming area.

Mülhausen, France: see MULHOUSE.

Mülheim (mül'hīm). **1** or **Mülheim an der Ruhr** (än dĕr rōōr'), city (□ 34; 1950 pop. 148,606), in former Prussian Rhine Prov., W Germany, after 1945 in North Rhine-Westphalia, on Ruhr R., adjoining Essen (E), Oberhausen (N), and Duisburg (W); 51°25'N 6°50'E. Industrial center; railroad repair shops; mfg. of electrical machines and apparatus, motors, machine parts, textiles, shoes. Food processing (meat products, sweets, beer, liqueur); tanning. Cement works. Coal mining. Site of institute for coal research. First mentioned in 11th cent. Belonging to duchy of Berg, it shared its history. Chartered 1808. Bet. 1878 and 1929 it inc. numerous surrounding towns, including Broich, Heissen, Speldorf, and Styrum. **2** Village (1946 pop. 4,949), in former Prussian Rhine Prov., W Germany, after 1945 in Rhineland-Palatinate, 4 mi. W of Coblenz; grain. **3** or **Mülheim am Rhein** (äm rīn'), right-bank industrial suburb of Cologne, in former Prussian Rhine Prov., W Germany, after 1945 in North Rhine-Westphalia, on the Rhine (harbor); rail junction; mfg. (machinery, cables, textiles). Inc. 1913 into Cologne.

Mulhouse (mülōōz'), Ger. *Mülhausen* (mül'houzŭn), city (pop. 85,956), Haut-Rhin dept., E France, on the Ill, on Rhone-Rhine Canal, and 245 mi. ESE of Paris and 18 mi. NW of Basel, in Alsatian lowland; 47°46'N 7°19'E. A leading mfg. center with a diversified textile industry (sewing thread, calicoes, muslins, silk and rayon fabrics) known for its fine cotton prints; numerous chemical plants (utilizing France's largest potash deposits just N of Mulhouse for explosives, textile dyes, etc.); glass- and metalworks (textile and chemical machinery, rolling stock, boilers). Paper milling (at near-by Île Napoléon), printing, tanning, flour milling, brewing, kirsch distilling. Regularly laid out with extensive workers' residential districts. Has textile and chemical institutes. Only important old building is 16th-cent. town hall. Became (13th cent.) a free imperial city. Bet. 1515 and 1798 was an allied member (but not a canton) of Swiss Confederation. Thoroughly French in character, it voted its union with France in 1798. Held (1871–1918) by Germans, together with rest of Alsace. An important communications center, it was frequently bombed in Second World War.

Muli (mōōl'ē), town (pop. 5,602), NE Saurashtra, India, 15 mi. WSW of Wadhwan; cotton, millet; hand-loom weaving. Was ⊙ former Eastern Kathiawar state of Muli (□ 133; pop. 16,977) of Western India States agency; state merged (1948) with Saurashtra.

Muling (mōō'lĭng') or **Muleng** (–lŭng'), town, ⊙ Muling co. (pop. 88,052), S Sungkiang prov., Manchuria, 32 mi. E of Mutankiang and on railroad; timber; rye, beans. The name Muling was applied until c.1940 to Pamientung, 28 mi. NNE. Present Muling was then called Mulingchan [Muling station]. Coal-mining centers of Lishuchen and Lishukow are 45 mi. NNE, on railroad.

Muling River or **Muleng River,** E Manchuria, rises in highlands S of Muling, flows over 250 mi. N and NE, through coal-mining region, past Muling, Tsining, and Mishan, to Ussuri R. (USSR line) S of Hulin. Sometimes called Muren R.

Mulki (mōōl'kē), town (pop. 6,284), South Kanara dist., W Madras, India, on Malabar Coast of Arabian Sea, 16 mi. N of Mangalore; fish curing; coconuts, mangoes.

Mull (mŭl), island (□ 351.2, including surrounding small isls.; pop. 2,903) of the Inner Hebrides, Argyll, Scotland, separated from mainland by Sound of Mull (1–2 mi. wide) and 6-mi.-wide Firth of Lorne; 27 mi. long N-S, up to 30 mi. wide (ENE-WSW) at S end. Mountainous, rising to 3,169 ft. on BEN MORE. Coast is deeply indented and has picturesque sea cliffs; main inlets are Loch Tuath (NW), 8 mi. long and 2 mi. wide, and Loch Scridain (SW), 10 mi. long and 2 mi. wide. There are several lakes and wooded glens. The Ross of Mull (SW) is 15-mi.-long peninsula (up to 5 mi. wide), site of red-granite quarries. Chief town, TOBERMORY (NE). Other villages: Salen (E), 9 mi. SE of Tobermory, with ruins of anc. Aros Castle, stronghold of the Lords of the Isles, and Lochbuie (S), 20 mi. SSE of Tobermory. A beacon in Duart Point (56°25′N 5°38′W) commemorates the novelist William Black who wrote about the region. Industries: sheep and cattle grazing, fishing, granite quarrying; isl. also has good hunting.

Mullaghmore (mŭ″lumôr′), promontory on Donegal Bay, NE Co. Sligo, Ireland, 14 mi. N of Sligo; 54°28′N 10°28′W. On E side of promontory is fishing village of Mullaghmore.

Mullaitivu, district, Ceylon: see VAVUNIYA.

Mullaitivu (mōōl′lĭtē″vōō), town (pop. 1,800), Northern Prov., Ceylon, on E coast, 60 mi. SE of Jaffna; fishing port; trades in straw, vegetables; rice and tobacco plantations. Has 18th-cent. Du. fort; lighthouse.

Mullan, mining village (pop. 2,036), Shoshone co., N Idaho, 6 mi. E of Wallace in Coeur d'Alene Mts., near Mont. line; alt. 3,245 ft.; lead, silver, zinc mines. Founded 1884 at time of lead-silver strike. Inc. 1904.

Mullen, village (pop. 652), ⊙ Hooker co., central Nebr., 65 mi. NNW of North Platte, near Middle Loup R.; dairy and poultry produce, livestock, grain.

Müllendorf (mü′lundôrf), Hung. *Szárazvám* (sä′rŏzväm), village (pop. 1,019), Burgenland, E Austria, 3 mi. W of Eisenstadt; pencil mfg.

Müllendorf, Luxembourg: see STEINSEL.

Mullens, city (pop. 3,470), Wyoming co., S W.Va., near Guyandot R., 23 mi. NNW of Bluefield; trade and rail point in bituminous- and semi-bituminous-coal region; lumber milling; railroad shops.

Mullet Peninsula or **The Mullet**, NW Co. Mayo, Ireland, extending 17 mi. S bet. Blacksod Bay (E) and the Atlantic; connected with mainland by narrow isthmus at Belmullet. Broad Haven bay is N.

Mullett Lake, Cheboygan co., N Mich., 5 mi. S of Cheboygan; c.11 mi. long, 3 mi. wide. Mullett Lake, resort village (fishing), is on NW shore. State Park on E shore. Source of Cheboygan R.

Mullewa (mŭ′luwŭ), town (pop. 627), W Western Australia, 60 mi. ENE of Geraldton; rail junction; wheat, livestock.

Müllheim (mül′hĭm), town (pop. 4,247), S Baden, Germany, at W foot of Black Forest, 16 mi. SW of Freiburg; rail junction; wine-trade center of Markgräfler Land wine region; woodworking.

Mullhyttan (mŭl′hü″tän), village (pop. 559), Orebro co., S central Sweden, on Svart R. and 19 mi. WSW of Orebro; metal- and woodworking, peat digging. Adjoining is village of Mullhyttemo (mŭl″hü″tümōō′).

Mulliangiri, peak, India: see BABA BUDAN RANGE.

Mullica Hill (mŭ′lĭkŭ), village (1940 pop. 680), Gloucester co., SW N.J., on Raccoon Creek and 15 mi. SSW of Camden, in rich fruit and truck region

Mullica River, SE N.J., rises near Berlin, flows c.55 mi. generally SE, forming part of Burlington-Atlantic co. line, to Great Bay SW of Tuckerton. Receives Batsto, Wading, and Bass rivers. Navigable for c.23 mi. above mouth.

Mulliken, village (pop. 411), Eaton co., S central Mich., 17 mi. W of Lansing, in farm area.

Mullin, town (pop. 326), Mills co., central Texas, 21 mi. SE of Brownwood, in grain, livestock area.

Mullinavat (mŭ″lĭnuvăt′), Gaelic *Muileann an Bhata*, town (pop. 189), S Co. Kilkenny, Ireland, 10 mi. WSW of New Ross; agr. market (cattle; barley, potatoes).

Mullingar (mŭ″lĭn-gär′), Gaelic *Muileann Cearr*, town (pop. 5,445), ⊙ Co. Westmeath, Ireland, in central part of co., on Brosna R., on the Royal Canal, and 50 mi. WNW of Dublin; agr. market in dairying, cattle-raising, potato-growing region; furniture mfg. Has important annual horse fair. Seat of R.C. bishop of Meath and was formerly site of 13th-cent. Augustinian and Dominican abbeys. Near by are loughs Owel and Ennell, frequented by anglers.

Mullins, town (pop. 4,916), Marion co., E S.C., 28 mi. E of Florence, near Little Pee Dee R.; important tobacco market; lumber; cotton, timber, diversified farming.

Mullins River, village (pop. 302), Stann Creek dist., central Br. Honduras, on Caribbean coast at mouth of Mullins R. (20 mi. long), 12 mi. NNW of Stann Creek. Bananas, coconuts, citrus fruit; fisheries.

Mullinville, city (pop. 410), Kiowa co., S Kansas, 10 mi. W of Greensburg; grain, livestock.

Mull of Galloway, Scotland: see GALLOWAY.

Mull of Kintyre (mŭl, kĭntīr′), headland at SW extremity of Kintyre peninsula, S Argyll, Scotland, on the North Channel, 11 mi. SW of Campbeltown; lighthouse (55°17′N 5°47′W). The cape is nearest British point to Ireland, 13 mi. SW.

Mull of Oa (ō), headland (55°35′N 6°19′W) at S tip of ISLAY, Hebrides, Scotland.

Mullovka (mōōlôf′kŭ), town (1926 pop. 3,266), NE Ulyanovsk oblast, Russian SFSR, 10 mi. W of Melekess; woolen-milling center; distilling.

Müllrose (mül′rō″zŭ), town (pop. 2,917), Brandenburg, E Germany, on Oder-Spree Canal and on small Müllrose L., and 9 mi. SW of Frankfurt; mfg. (chemicals, food products).

Mullsjo (mŭl′shû″), Swedish *Mullsjö*, village (pop. 1,019), Skaraborg co., S Sweden, on Strak L., Swedish *Stråken* (strō′kun) (10-mi.-long expansion of upper Tida R.), 14 mi. NW of Jonkoping; metalworking, hosiery knitting.

Mullumbimby (mŭ″lŭmbĭm′bē), municipality (pop. 1,609), NE New South Wales, Australia, 80 mi. SSE of Brisbane; dairying center; banana plantations.

Mulobezi (mōōlōbĕ′zē), village (pop. 1,584), Southern Prov., SW Northern Rhodesia, 85 mi. NW of Livingstone (linked by lumber railroad); major teak-felling center.

Mulroy Bay (mŭlroi′), narrow inlet of the Atlantic, N Co. Donegal, Ireland, bet. Lough Swilly and Sheep Haven; 12 mi. long.

Mülsen Sankt Jakob (mül′zun zängkt″ yä′kôp), village (pop. 4,439), Saxony, E central Germany, 4 mi. E of Zwickau; cotton and woolen milling and knitting.

Multai (mōōltī′), town (pop. 5,196), Betul dist., W Madhya Pradesh, India, 25 mi. ESE of Betul; trades in wheat, millet, oilseeds. Lac cultivation in near-by forested hills (teak, sal, myrobalan). Source of Tapti R. (just W) is place of Hindu pilgrimage.

Multan (mōōltän′), district (□ 5,653; 1951 pop. 2,105,000), S Punjab, W Pakistan; ⊙ Multan. In Bari Doab; bounded S by Sutlej R., W by Chenab R., N by Ravi R. A hot, dry tract, largely of alluvial soil and widely irrigated (Sidhnai Canal; N). Agr. (wheat, millet, cotton, oilseeds, rice, dates); cotton ginning, hand-loom weaving, cattle grazing. Chief towns: Multan, Khanewal. Formerly also spelled Mooltan.

Multan, city (1950 pop., with cantonment area, 190,000), ⊙ Multan dist., S Punjab, W Pakistan, near left bank of Chenab R., on railroad and 195 mi. SW of Lahore. Important agr. supply center; trades in wheat, cotton, silk, sugar, wool, indigo, fruit; cotton ginning and milling, oilseed milling, mfg. of steel furniture, surgical instruments, hosiery, tongas, flour, biscuits; metalworks. Handicrafts include cotton and silk fabrics, carpets, glazed tiles and pottery, enamel work, leather goods, ivory bangles, silver ornaments. Has col.; 14th-cent. tombs of 2 Moslem saints. Site dates back to time of Alexander the Great; visited by Hsüan-tsang in A.D. 641; captured by Mahmud of Ghazni in 1005, by Tamerlane in 1398. Under Afghans when seized by Ranjit Singh in 1818. Sikh revolt (1848) against Br. control touched off Second Sikh War; city fell to British in 1849. Noted for extreme summer heat.

Multnomah (mŭltnō′mŭ), county (□ 424; pop. 471,537), NW Oregon; ⊙ Portland. Drained by Columbia and Willamette rivers; borders on Wash. Mfg. and shipping at Portland. Dairy products, poultry, fruit, truck, grain. Formed 1854.

Multnomah Falls, NW Oregon, beautiful waterfall c.850 ft. high (including upper and lower falls), in short stream rising on Larch Mtn. (4,100 ft.) and plunging into Columbia R. gorge 9 mi. WSW of Bonneville, near Columbia R. Highway.

Mulu, Mount (mōō′lōō), highest peak (7,798 ft.) of Sarawak, N central Borneo, 65 mi. ESE of Miri.

Muluá or **Santa Cruz Muluá** (sän′tä krōōs′ mōō-lwä′), town (1950 pop. 200), Retalhuleu dept., SW Guatemala, in Pacific piedmont, 3 mi. ENE of Retalhuleu, on railroad; coffee, sugar cane, grain; livestock. Junction for rail branch to San Felipe.

Mulug (mōōlōōg′) or **Mulag** (mōōlŭg′), village (pop. 2,486), Warangal dist., E Hyderabad state, India, 27 mi. NE of Warangal; rice, oilseeds. Noted 13th-cent. temples 5 mi. N, at Palampet.

Mulund (mōō′lōōnd), town (pop. 6,917), Bombay suburban dist., W Bombay, India, on Salsette Isl., 2 mi. SW of Thana; match mfg., salt drying; cement- and metalworks.

Mulungu, Belgian Congo: see TSHIBINDA.

Mulungu (mōōlōōng-gōō′), town (pop. 1,892), E Paraíba, NE Brazil, 37 mi. WNW of João Pessoa; junction (spur to Alagoa Grande) on Natal–João Pessoa RR. Called Camarazal, 1944–48.

Mulungushi Dam, Northern Rhodesia: see BROKEN HILL.

Muluya River, Sp. and Fr. Morocco: see MOULOUYA RIVER.

Mulvane (mŭlvān′), city (pop. 1,387), on Sedgwick-Sumner co. line, S Kansas, on Arkansas R. and 16 mi. SSE of Wichita, in diversified-farming area. Sand and gravel plant here. Laid out 1879, inc. 1883.

Mumbles, The, Wales: see SWANSEA.

Mumbles Head, promontory on Swansea Bay, SW Glamorgan, Wales, 5 mi. SSW of Swansea; 51°34′N 3°58′W. Lighthouse.

Mumbwa (mōōm′bwä), township (pop. 547), Central Prov., Northern Rhodesia, 90 mi. WNW of Lusaka; center of peanut-development scheme. In near-by Mumbwa Caves quantities of artifacts and fossils of middle and late Stone Age have been found.

Mumford (mŭm′furd), town, Western Prov., S Gold Coast colony, on Gulf of Guinea, 10 mi. WSW of Winneba; fishing.

Mumford, village (1940 pop. 530), Monroe, co., W N.Y., 17 mi. SSW of Rochester, in agr. area (fruit, poultry, dairy products).

Mumias (mōō′mēäs), village, Nyanza prov., W Kenya, on Nzoia R., on road, and 38 mi. NNW of Kisumu; cotton, peanuts, sesame, corn.

Muminabad (mōōmēnŭbät′), village (1932 pop. estimate 980), E Kulyab oblast, Tadzhik SSR, 18 mi. NE of Kulyab; wheat.

Mümling River (müm′lĭng), W Germany, rises in the Odenwald 7 mi. N of Eberbach, flows 30 mi. generally NNE to the canalized Main, 1 mi. S of Obernburg. Sometimes called Mömling R.

Mümliswil-Ramiswil (müm′lĭsvēl-rä′mĭsvēl),′ 2 villages (total pop. 2,515), Solothurn canton, N Switzerland, 2 mi. N and NNW of Balsthal; combs, metalworking.

Mummery, Mount (10,918 ft.), SE B.C., near Alta. border, in Rocky Mts., in Hamber Provincial Park, 65 mi. NW of Banff; 51°40′N 116°51′W.

Mummidivaram (mōōmĭdĭvŭ′rŭm), town (pop. 9,967), East Godavari dist., NE Madras, India, in Godavari R. delta, 23 mi. SSW of Cocanada; rice milling; sugar cane, tobacco, coconuts.

Mummy Mountain, Colo.: see MUMMY RANGE.

Mummy Range, spur of Front Range in NE corner of Rocky Mtn. Natl. Park, N. Colo. Prominent peaks: Mt. Dunraven (12,548 ft.), Mt. Chiquita (13,052 ft.), Mt. Chapin (13,059 ft.), Mummy Mtn. (13,413 ft.), Mt. Fairchild (13,502 ft.), Ypsilon Mtn. (13,507 ft.), Hague's Peak (13,562 ft.). Rowe Glacier is in NE tip of range.

Mumra (mōōm′rŭ), town (1948 pop. over 2,000), E Astrakhan oblast, Russian SFSR, on Volga R. delta mouth, at mouth of Bakhtemir arm, and 40 mi. SSW of Astrakhan; fish-processing center; metalworking.

Mumtrak, village (pop. 100), SW Alaska, near N shore of Goodnews Bay, 13 mi. NE of Platinum, in mining area, 59°8′N 161°31′W.

Mumungan, Philippines: see MOMUNGAN.

Muna or **Moena** (both: mōō′nŭ), island (□ 659; pop. 108,719), Indonesia, bet. Molucca and Flores seas, just off SE extremity of Celebes and just W of Buton; 4°36′–5°27′S 122°16′–122°46′E; 60 mi. long, 30 mi. wide; generally level. Chief products: teak, rice, sago, trepang. Principal town and port is Raha.

Muna (mōō′nä), town (pop. 3,798), Yucatan, SE Mexico, on railroad and 35 mi. SSW of Mérida; agr. center (henequen, sugar cane, corn, fruit, timber).

Munamagi or **Munamyagi**, Est. *Munamägi* (all: mōō′nämăgē), highest point (1,040 ft.) in Estonia and in the Baltic States, 9 mi. SSE of Voru.

Muñano (mōōnyä′nō) or **Kilómetro 1308**, village, W Salta prov., Argentina, 12 mi. SE of San Antonio de los Cobres; alt. 12,950 ft.; rail station.

Muncaster, England: see RAVENGLASS.

Munchar (münshär′), village, Béja dist., N Tunisia, 7 mi. E of Béja, in wheat-growing area.

Münchberg (münkh′bĕrk), town (pop. 9,689), Upper Franconia, NE Bavaria, Germany, at N foot of the Fichtelgebirge, 10 mi. SW of Hof; rail junction; metal- and woodworking, weaving, printing, tanning, brewing. Granite quarries in area.

Müncheberg (mün′khubĕrk), town (pop. 4,084), Brandenburg, E Germany, 20 mi. NW of Frankfurt, 30 mi. E of Berlin, in lignite-mining region; market gardening; distilling, starch mfg. Has early-Gothic church, anc. town walls. Site of plant-research institute.

München, Germany: see MUNICH.

Münchenbernsdorf (mün″khunbĕrns′dôrf), town (pop. 4,396), Thuringia, central Germany, 8 mi. SW of Gera; woolen and rayon milling, carpet mfg. Has 16th-cent. moated castle.

Münchenbuchsee (–bōōkh″zā′), residential town (pop. 2,248), Bern canton, NW Switzerland, 5 mi. N of Bern; former commandery of Knights of Malta. Has early-Gothic church.

München Gladbach (glät′bäkh), city (□ 38; 1939 pop. 128,306; 1946 pop. 110,444; 1950 pop. 122,388), in former Prussian Rhine Prov., W Germany, after 1945 in North Rhine-Westphalia, 15 mi. W of Düsseldorf; twin city (just N) of Rheydt; 51°12′N 6°25′E. Rail junction; center of Rhenish cotton industry; mfg. of metal building materials, machines for textile industry, steam engines, heating apparatus, air-conditioning systems, armatures, cloth, blankets, clothing. Woodworking. Has 13th-cent. church with 10th-cent. crypt; 14th–18th-cent. town hall, formerly a Benedictine abbey (founded 972), around which town developed. United (1929–33) with Rheydt and Odenkirchen to form Gladbach-Rheydt. Captured by U.S. troops in March, 1945.

Münchengrätz, Czechoslovakia: see MNICHOVO HRADISTE.

Münchenstein (–shtīn), town (pop. 5,189), Basel-Land half-canton, N Switzerland, on Birs R. and 3 mi. SSE of Basel; aluminum, chemicals, foodstuffs.

Munchon (mōōn′chŭn′), Jap. *Bunsen*, township (1944 pop. 12,005), S.Hamgyong prov., N Korea, 12 mi. NW of Wonsan; coal mining.

Muncie, (mŭn′sē). **1** Village (pop. 197), Vermilion co., E Ill., 10 mi. W of Danville, in agr. and bituminous-coal area. **2** City (pop. 58,479), ⊙ Delaware co., E Ind., on West Fork of White R. and 50 mi. NE of Indianapolis; railroad, industrial, and trade center in a rich agr. area; glass products, automobile parts, electrical equipment, castings, steel and wire products, cutlery, silver-plate ware, home-canning equipment, furniture, bedding, sporting goods; dairying, meat packing. Seat of Ball State Teachers Col. Platted 1827; inc. as town in 1847, as city in 1885. Muncie is the original of "Middletown" in sociological studies by Robert S. Lynd and Helen H. Lynd, published as *Middletown* (1929) and *Middletown in Transition* (1937).

Muncy (mŭn'sē), borough (pop. 2,756), Lycoming co., N central Pa., 14 mi. E of Williamsport and on West Branch of Susquehanna R.; machinery, textiles, wire rope, furniture. Laid out 1797, inc. 1826.

Muncy Creek, E central Pa., rises in central Sullivan co., flows c.40 mi. SW to West Branch of Susquehanna R. just NW of Muncy.

Mund, river, Iran: see MUND RIVER.

Munda, Solomon Isls.: see NEW GEORGIA.

Munda (mōōn'dä), anc. town in Andalusia, S Spain, known for Caesar's victory (45 B.C.) over Pompeian forces. Its location is disputed; believed to have been either in vicinity of Ronda (Málaga prov.) or Montilla (Córdoba prov.).

Mundaca (mōōndä'kä), fishing village (pop. 1,326), Vizcaya prov., N Spain, on Bay of Biscay, and 14 mi. NE of Bilbao; boatbuilding. Vegetables, *chacolí* wine, livestock in area.

Mundakayam (mōōndŭkä'yŭm), town (pop. 5,967), central Travancore, India, 25 mi. ESE of Kottayam, in foothills of Western Ghats; rubber and tea processing, sawmilling.

Mundalla (mŭndŭ'lŭ), village (pop. 143), SE South Australia, 155 mi. SE of Adelaide, near Bordertown; wheat.

Mundame (mōōndä'mä), village (pop. 950), S Br. Cameroons, administered as part of Eastern Provinces of Nigeria, on Mungo R. (Fr. Cameroons border) and 8 mi. SE of Kumba; customs station; cacao, bananas.

Mundare, village (pop. 727), central Alta., 14 mi. NW of Vegreville; mixed farming, dairying.

Mundaring (mŭndä'rĭng), residential town (pop. 150), SW Western Australia, 19 mi. E of Perth, in Darling Range. Near-by **Mundaring Weir** (built 1903) on Helena R. (tributary of Swan R.) supplies water for gold fields 350 mi. E.

Mundawa, India: see MUNDWA.

Munday (mŭn'dā), town (pop. 2,280), Knox co., N Texas, c.70 mi. WSW of Wichita Falls; trade, processing, rail center in cattle-ranching and agr. area (cotton, grain, dairy products, poultry). Inc. 1906.

Munday, Mount (11,000 ft.), W B.C., in Coast Mts., 170 mi. NW of Vancouver, just SE of Mt. Waddington; 51°21'N 125°14'W.

Mundelein (mŭn'dŭlīn), village (pop. 3,189), Lake co., NE Ill., 10 mi. SW of Waukegan, in dairy and farm area; shoes mfg. Small Diamond L. is resort. St. Mary of the Lake Seminary here was scene of a eucharistic congress (1925). Inc. 1909 as Area; renamed 1925.

Münden or **Hannoversch-Münden** (hänō'vŭrsh-mün'dŭn), town (pop. 19,193), in former Prussian prov. of Hanover, W Germany, after 1945 in Lower Saxony, head of navigation on the Weser (formed here by confluence of Fulda and Werra rivers), 10 mi. NE of Kassel; rail junction; mfg. of machinery, tools, abrasives, chemicals, rubber and leather goods, tobacco; food processing (flour products, canned goods, beer, spirits). Has castle, renovated after 1560; stone bridge across Werra R. (1397-1402); 15th–16th-cent. church; Renaissance town hall. First mentioned 860. Received customs right in 1246; was member of Hanseatic League.

Munden, city (pop. 169), Republic co., N Kansas, 8 mi. NE of Belleville, in corn and wheat region.

Münder am Deister, Bad, Germany: see BAD MÜNDER.

Munderfing (mōōn'dŭrfĭng), village (pop. 2,134), W Upper Austria, 15 mi. SSE of Braunau, in Hausruck Mts.; rye, hogs.

Munderkingen (mōōn"dŭrkĭng'ŭn), town (pop. 2,037), S Württemberg, Germany, after 1945 in Württemberg-Hohenzollern, on the Danube and 5 mi. SW of Ehingen.

Munderwa, India: see BASTI, town.

Mundesley, village and parish (pop. 990), NE Norfolk, England, on North Sea, 7 mi. SE of Cromer; seaside resort and small fishing port.

Mundgod (mōōnd'gōd), village (pop. 1,454), Kanara dist., S Bombay, India, 60 mi. ENE of Karwar; markets rice, millet.

Mundia (mōōn'dēŭ), town (pop. 2,609), Budaun dist., N central Uttar Pradesh, India, 4 mi. NW of Bisauli; wheat, pearl millet, mustard, barley, gram, jowar.

Mundo Novo (mōōn'dōō nō'vōō). **1** City (pop. 2,363), E central Bahia, Brazil, on railroad and 100 mi. SSW of Senhor do Bonfim; coffee, tobacco, copaiba oil; amethysts found here. **2** City, São Paulo, Brazil: see URUPÊS.

Mundo Nuevo (mōōn'dō nwā'vō), town (pop. 683), Anzoátegui state, NE Venezuela, 45 mi. ESE of Barcelona; cotton, coffee, sugar cane.

Mundo River (mōōn'dō), Albacete prov., SE central Spain, rises 8 mi. NW of Yeste, flows 75 mi. E and S to the Segura 6 mi. NNE of Calasparra. Used for irrigation and power.

Mundra (mōōn'drŭ), town (pop. 9,356), S Cutch, India, near Gulf of Cutch, 29 mi. S of Bhuj; exports wheat, barley, cloth fabrics; cotton ginning. Port facilities 3 mi. S.

Mund River or **Mond River** (mōnd), coastal stream of S Iran, rises in several branches in the Zagros ranges W of Shiraz, flows 300 mi. SE, S, and W, to Persian Gulf 60 mi. SSE of Bushire.

Mundwa (mōōn'dvŭ), town (pop. 5,779), central Rajasthan, India, 75 mi. NE of Jodhpur; local market. Sometimes called Mundawa or Marwar Mundwa.

Mundybash (mōōndĭbäsh'), town (1948 pop. over 10,000), S Kemerovo oblast, Russian SFSR, on railroad and 40 mi. S of Stalinsk; iron-ore concentrating plant, serving Temir-Tau, Telbes, and Odrabash mines.

Munébrega (mōōnā'vrāgä), village (pop. 1,215), Saragossa prov., NE Spain, 8 mi. SSW of Calatayud; wine, cereals, livestock.

Muñecas (mōōnyā'käs), town (pop. estimate 500), central Tucumán prov., Argentina, on railroad and 3 mi. NW of Tucumán, in agr. area (corn, alfalfa, sugar cane). Hydroelectric station near by.

Muñecas, Bolivia: see CHUMA.

Munera (mōōnā'rä), town (pop. 4,667), Albacete prov., SE central Spain, agr. center 18 mi. SSE of Villarrobledo; olive-oil and cheese processing, flour- and sawmilling, sandal mfg.; wine, saffron, truck produce, esparto; livestock.

Munford. 1 Village (1940 pop. 549), Talladega co., E Ala., 11 mi. NE of Talladega. Civil War battle here (1865). **2** Town (pop. 976), Tipton co., W Tenn., 24 mi. NNE of Memphis, in cotton-growing area.

Munfordville, town (pop. 894), ⊙ Hart co., central Ky., on Green R. and 35 mi. ENE of Bowling Green, in limestone cave region; agr. (poultry, dairy products, burley tobacco, corn); flour milling. Indian relics found in vicinity. Mammoth Onyx Cave, containing onyx formations resembling trees, flowers, human figures, and porticos, is near by. In Civil War, Confederate Gen. Braxton Bragg captured Union fort and garrison here in Sept., 1863.

Mungana (mŭng-gä'nŭ), village, NE Queensland, Australia, 90 mi. WSW of Cairns; terminus of spur of Cairns-Charleston RR; cattle.

Mungaoli (mōōng-gou'lē), town (pop. 5,108), E Madhya Bharat, India, 50 mi. ESE of Guna; markets wheat, millet, gram.

Mungbere (mōōngbĕ'rä), village, Eastern Prov., NE Belgian Congo, 120 mi. NW of Irumu; rail terminus and trading post in cotton and coffee area.

Mungeli (mōōng-gā'lē), village, Bilaspur dist., E central Madhya Pradesh, India, 30 mi. W of Bilaspur; agr. market (rice, wheat, oilseeds, corn).

Mungindi, village (pop. 915), N New South Wales, Australia, on Queensland border, 320 mi. NW of Newcastle and on Macintyre R.; rail terminus; sheep center.

Mungo (mōōng'gō), administrative region (□ 3,825; 1950 pop. 129,300), W Fr. Cameroons; ⊙ N'Kongsamba. Drained by Wouri R. In tropical rain-forest zone. Highlands in W have numerous European plantations (bananas, palms, cacao, coffee), the produce of which is shipped by rail to Douala.

Mungo River (mōōng'gō), Fr. *Moungo*, on Br. Cameroons–Fr. Cameroons border, rises in Br. Cameroons 20 mi. NE of Kumbai, flows c.100 mi. S to Gulf of Guinea 7 mi. E of Tiko, forming the Cameroon R. with Wouri R. Navigable in lower course for shallow-draught boats for 60 mi.

Mungra-Badshahpur (mōōng'grŭ bäd'shäpōōr), town (pop. 6,055), Jaunpur dist., SE Uttar Pradesh, India, 25 mi. NE of Allahabad; trades in sugar cane, cotton, barley, rice, corn. Also called Badshahpur.

Mungret, Gaelic *Mungairit*, agr. village, N Co. Limerick, Ireland, 3 mi. SW of Limerick; grain, potatoes; dairying. Has remains of monastery founded by St. Patrick.

Munguía (mōōng-gē'ä), village (pop. 1,323), Vizcaya prov., N Spain, on railroad and 7 mi. NNE of Bilbao; corn, wheat, hogs, cattle. Lumbering; flour milling; potteries.

Munhall (mŭn'hôl), industrial borough (pop. 16,437), Allegheny co., SW Pa., just ESE of Pittsburgh and on Monongahela R. Huge steel works here (at that time included in adjacent HOMESTEAD borough) were scene of famous Homestead strike, 1892. Inc. 1900.

Munhongo (mōōnyông'gō), village, Bié prov., central Angola, on Benguela RR and 125 mi. ENE of Silva Pôrto; road junction.

Muni, Río (rē'ō mōō'nē), estuarine inlet of the Gulf of Guinea, forming border bet. Sp. Guinea (N) and Gabon, Fr. Equatorial Africa (S); c.15 mi. long, up to 4 mi. wide. Navigable. Fed by many coastal streams, of which the Utamboni is longest. Kogo (Sp.) and Cocobeach (Fr.) are small ports on it. In Corisco Bay, at its mouth, are Sp. isls. of Corisco and Elobey. The name Río Muni is commonly applied to continental SPANISH GUINEA.

Munich (mū'nĭk), Ger. *München* (mün'khŭn), city (1939 pop. 840,586; 1946 pop. 751,967; 1950 pop. 831,017), ⊙ Bavaria and Upper Bavaria, Germany, on the Isar and 310 mi. SSW of Berlin; 48°9'N 11°36'E. Cultural, communications, industrial, and commercial center. Long known for its beer and artistic handicrafts. Has foundries and metalworks, producing agr. and office machinery, gasoline motors, machine tools, auto bodies, locomotives, and railroad cars; chemical works producing rubber goods, pharmaceuticals, fertilizer; and food-processing plants producing cooking fats, bakery goods, processed meal. It is also an important printing and publishing city (books, periodicals, newspapers). All types of precision and optical instruments are produced. Other mfg.: building materials, textiles, leather products, paper, paint, varnish, soap, flour, alcohol. Trade in fruit and vegetables. Site of Bavarian univ. (founded 1472 at Ingolstadt, transferred 1800 to Landshut and 1826 to Munich), now called Ludwig Maximilian Univ.; also of institute of technology, acad. of fine arts, state conservatory of music, Bavarian acad. of arts and sciences. The city, beautifully laid out and reflecting the attention given to it by its art-loving rulers of the 19th cent., suffered considerable damage (about 40%) in Second World War. The Old and New Pinakothek, noted art museums, were completely destroyed, but most of valuable collections were preserved. Of the chief landmark of Munich, the 15th-cent. Liebfrauenkirche [church of Our Lady], only the 2 belfries were relatively unharmed. Heavily damaged were: the Gothic cathedral, containing tomb of Emperor Louis the Bavarian; St. Michael's, S Germany's outstanding Renaissance church, with tombs of 25 Wittelsbach rulers; the Glyptothek (its Egyptian, Greek, and Roman collections were, however, intact); old city hall (c.1470). Other bldgs. damaged include the neo-Gothic new city hall, and the German Mus., built (1908–25) on an isl. in the Isar. The Hofbräuhaus, scene (1923) of Hitler's *Putsch*, was preserved. Munich (anc. *Monacium*), a monastic village under Carolingians, was chartered 1158. Became (1255) residence of Wittelsbach family, and since then has always been ⊙ Bavaria. Suffered disastrous fire in 1327. It was occupied 1632 by Gustavus Adolphus, and in 1705 and 1742 by Austrian orces. Developed into a center of Ger. culture in .9th cent., tripling its pop. bet. 1870 and 1900. In 20th cent. it became the birthplace and capital of the National Socialist movement, and was scene (1938) of Munich Pact. Captured in Second World War by U.S. troops (April, 1945). R.C. archbishop of Munich is also archbishop of Freising; Munich is also seat of Protestant bishop.

Munich, village (pop. 248), Cavalier co., N N.Dak., 22 mi. WSW of Langdon.

Muniesa (mōōnyā'sä), village (pop. 1,588), Teruel prov., E Spain, 35 mi. W of Alcañiz; brandy mfg.; produces wine, cereals, saffron.

Munilla (mōōnē'lyä), town (pop. 1,189), Logroño prov., N Spain, 20 mi. SE of Logroño; woolen mills; mfg. of shoes and chocolate; cereals, sheep.

Muniong Range (mŭ'nēōng), SE New South Wales, Australia, near Victoria line; part of Australian Alps extending c.60 mi. S from Kiandra to Murray R. on Victoria border. Mt. Kosciusko (7,305 ft.), here, is highest peak of Australia. Winter sports (May–Sept.). Sometimes called Snowy Range.

Munising (mū'nĭsĭng), city (pop. 4,339), ⊙ Alger co., N Upper Peninsula, Mich., 36 mi. ESE of Marquette on small Munising Bay of L. Superior, and facing Grand Isl. Resort; lumbering and agr. in area. Mfg. (wooden utensils, veneer, paper); fisheries. Hiawatha Natl. Forest is near by. Inc. as village 1897, as city 1916.

Muniz Freire (mōōnēs' frā'rĭ), city (pop. 876), S Espírito Santo, Brazil, 35 mi. NW of Cachoeiro de Itapemirim; coffee, bananas, rice.

Munkacs, Ukrainian SSR: see MUKACHEVO.

Munka-Ljungby (mŭng'kä"-yŭng'bü"), village (pop. 1,187), Kristianstad co., SW Sweden, 4 mi. E of Angelholm; furniture mfg. Has 13th-cent. church.

Munkedal (mŭng'kŭdäl"), village (pop. 2,693), Goteborg och Bohus co., SW Sweden, 13 mi. NW of Uddevalla; rail junction; paper mills, sulphite works.

Munkfors (mŭngk"fôrs', –fôsh'), village (pop. 4,159), Varmland co., W Sweden, on Klar R. and 20 mi. WNW of Filipstad; large ironworks; lumber mills; spring-mfg. works.

Munkholmen (mōōnk'hôlmŭn), tiny island in TRONDHEIM harbor, Sor-Trondelag co., central Norway, 1 mi. from the mainland. Has ruins of Nidarholm Benedictine abbey (12th cent.), fortress (1660). Used for political prisoners in 18th cent.

Munksund (mŭngk'sŭnd"), village (pop. 1,787), Norrbotten co., N Sweden, on Pite R., just above its mouth on Gulf of Bothnia, 2 mi. SE of Pitea; lumber and pulp milling, woodworking. Includes villages of Skuthamn (sküt"hä'mŭn) and Pitholm (pēt"hôlm').

Munku-Sardyk (mōōn-kōō"-sŭrdĭk'), highest peak (11,453 ft.) in Eastern Sayan Mts., on USSR-Mongolian border, N of L. Khubsugul, W of Mondy; small glaciers.

Munlochy (mŭnlŏkh'ē), agr. village in Knockbain parish, SE Ross and Cromarty, Scotland, on Munlochy Bay (inlet of Moray Firth), 6 mi. N of Inverness.

Munn, Cape, N extremity of Southampton Isl., E Keewatin Dist., Northwest Territories, on Roes Welcome Sound; 65°55'N 85°28'W.

Munnar (mōō'nŭr) or **Pallivasal** (pŭ'lĭvŭsŭl), village, NE Travancore, India, on right tributary of Periyar R. and 60 mi. NE of Kottayam, in tea-plantation area in Western Ghats. Hydroelectric power plant (opened 1940) utilizes near-by falls; auxiliary power provided since 1946 by link with hydroelectric works at Papanasam village, Madras. Transmission network serves industrial centers throughout Travancore-Cochin.

Munn Bay, Northwest Territories: see CORAL HARBOUR.

Munnsville, village (pop. 412), Madison co., central N.Y., on Oneida Creek and 19 mi. SW of Utica; crushed stone.

Muno (münō'), village (pop. 1,149), Luxembourg prov., SE Belgium, near Fr. border, on S slope of the Ardennes, 14 mi. SW of Neufchâteau; agr., lumbering.

Muñoz (mōōnyōs'), town (1939 pop. 4,149; 1948 municipality pop. 21,748), Nueva Ecija prov., central Luzon, Philippines, on railroad and 16 mi. NNW of Cabanatuan; rice-growing center.

Muñoz Gamero Peninsula (gämä'rō), mountainous area of Chilean Patagonia, SW of Puerto Natales, bordering on Strait of Magellan (SW). Adelaide Isls. are just off W coast. Rugged in outline, with many smaller peninsulas, it is 80 mi. long (N–S) and c.30 mi. wide. The uninhabited, snow-capped area rises to 5,740 ft. in Mt. Burney (NW).

Mun River (mōōn), E Thailand, rises in SW extremity of San Kamphaeng Range at alt. of c.1,500 ft., flows 300 mi. E through Korat Plateau, past Nakhon Ratchasima and Ubon, to Mekong R. NW of Pakse; main tributary, Chi R. Navigable below Tha Chang, 10 mi. E of Nakhon Ratchasima; used for irrigation.

Munro (mōōn'rō), town (pop. estimate 6,000) in Greater Buenos Aires, Argentina, adjoining Florida, 10 mi. NW of Buenos Aires; mfg. center: cement articles, rubberized textiles, metal fibers; food industries, sawmills.

Munroe Falls, village (pop. 933), Summit co., NE Ohio, 6 mi. NE of Akron and on Cuyahoga R.; paper products.

Munsey Park (mŭn'sē), residential village (pop. 2,048), Nassau co., SE N.Y., on NW Long Isl., bet. Manhasset (W) and Roslyn, in shore-resort area.

Munshiganj (mōōn'shĭgŭnj), anc. *Idrakpur,* town (pop. 7,186), Dacca dist., E central East Bengal, E Pakistan, on Dhaleswari R. and 13 mi. SSE of Dacca; trades in rice, jute, bananas, oilseeds, fish; ice mfg. Large annual fair near by.

Münsingen (mün'zĭng-ŭn), town (pop. 2,493), S Württemberg, Germany, after 1945 in Württemberg-Hohenzollern, in Swabian Jura, 7 mi. SE of Urach; cement works.

Münsingen, town (pop. 4,523), Bern canton, W central Switzerland, 7 mi. SE of Bern; printing; woolen textiles, clothes, flour, pastry, tobacco.

Munson, agr. village (pop. 93), S central Alta., near Red Deer R., 7 mi. N of Drumheller.

Munson, residential village (1940 pop. 1,373), Nassau co., SE N.Y., on W Long Isl., W of Hempstead.

Munson Lake, N.H.: see NELSON.

Munster (müstâr'), Ger. *Münster* (mün'stŭr), town (pop. 4,701), Haut-Rhin dept., E France, on the Fecht and 10 mi. WSW of Colmar, in the high Vosges; center of Munster valley, a noted cheese-mfg. region. Textile milling. Excursion center for Col de la Schlucht and Hohneck. Heavily damaged in First World War.

Munster (mōōn'stŭr), village (pop. 6,483), in former Prussian prov. of Hanover, NW Germany, after 1945 in Lower Saxony, 11 mi. E of Soltau; metalworking, flour- and sawmilling.

Münster (mün'stŭr). **1** Village (1946 pop. 4,266), S Hesse, W Germany, in former Starkenburg prov., on the Gersprenz and 9 mi. ENE of Darmstadt; grain. **2** or **Münster in Westfalen** (ĭn vĕst"fä'lŭn), city (1939 pop. 141,059; 1946 pop. 86,366; 1950 pop. 119,788), ⊙ former Prussian prov. of Westphalia, NW Germany, after 1945 in North Rhine-Westphalia, port on Dortmund-Ems Canal and 32 mi. NNE of Dortmund; 51°58'N 7°37'E. Cultural center. Rail hub; airport (SE outskirts); mfg. of agr. and mining machinery, hardware, cement goods, furniture, porcelain, cardboard; brewing, distilling, flour milling. Trade (grain, lumber, food products). Prior to its virtual destruction (about 60%) in Second World War, Münster was noted for its medieval appearance, with gabled houses and irregular streets. Heavily damaged were noted Gothic town hall; 12th–13th-cent. cathedral and numerous other churches, including Gothic St. Lambert and Church of Our Lady; univ. (founded 1773); Westphalian Mus. (collection was saved). Founded and created bishopric c.800. Powerful prince-bishops ruled large territory until secularization in 1803. City was important member of Hanseatic League. Scene (1534–35) of Anabaptist revolt. Part of Treaty of Westphalia signed here in 1648. Passed to Prussia in 1814. Captured by Br. troops in April, 1945. Recently developed coal fields in vicinity (SW).

Munster (mŭn'stŭr), largest province (□ 9,316.5; pop. 917,306) of Ireland, in S part of country, including cos. Clare, Cork, Kerry, Limerick, Tipperary, and Waterford. In anc. times it was one of the kingdoms of Ireland.

Münster, Bern canton, Switzerland: see MOUTIER.

Munster, town (pop. 4,753), Lake co., extreme NW Ind., on Ill. line, 4 mi. S of Hammond; ships garden produce; nursery stock.

Münster am Stein, Bad, Germany: see BAD MÜNSTER AM STEIN.

Münsterberg, Poland: see ZIEBICE.

Münstereifel (mün"stŭrī'fŭl), town (pop. 3,418), in former Prussian Rhine Prov., W Germany, after 1945 in North Rhine-Westphalia, on the Erft and 7 mi. S of Euskirchen; woodworking. Surrounded by 14th-cent. towers and gates; has 12th-cent. church, 13th-cent. ruined castle.

Münster in Westfalen, Germany: see MÜNSTER, Westphalia.

Münstertal (mün'stŭrtäl), Romansh *Val Müstair* (väl müsh-tĕr'), valley and district (pop. 1,770), Grisons canton, E Switzerland, SE of Ofen Pass; watered by Rombach R. Münster and Sta. Maria im Münstertal are main towns.

Munsungan Lake (mŭnsŭng'gŭn), Piscataquis co., N central Maine, 50 mi. NNW of Millinocket, in wilderness recreational area; 7.5 mi. long, 2 mi. wide.

Muntafiq (mōōn'täfĭk), province (□ 5,463; pop. 369,806), SE Iraq, astride the lower Euphrates and bordered S by the kingdoms of Kuwait and Saudi Arabia; ⊙ NASIRIYA. Rich agr. area, except for its desert region in the S (the desert is not included in the prov. area). Dates, sesame, wheat, barley. The Basra-Baghdad RR follows the river. The area is exceptionally rich in sites of famous anc. cities: LARSA, UR, ERECH, ERIDU, LAGASH.

Munte (mŭn'tŭ), agr. village (pop. 818), East Flanders prov., NW Belgium, 8 mi. S of Ghent.

Muntele-Mic, Rumania: see TARCU MOUNTAINS.

Muntenia (mōōntä'nyä) or **Greater Walachia** (wälā'kēŭ, wŭ-), the E part (□ 20,270; 1948 pop. 4,991,982) of WALACHIA, Rumania.

Muntervary, Ireland: see SHEEP HEAD.

Muntinlupa (mōōntēnlōō'pä), town (1939 pop. 2,654; 1948 municipality pop. 18,444), Rizal prov., S Luzon, Philippines, on Laguna de Bay, on railroad and 15 mi. SSE of Manila; agr. center (rice, sugar cane, fruit). Also spelled Muntinglupa.

Muntok or **Mentok** (mŭntôk'), chief port (pop. 6,929) of Bangka, Indonesia, on Bangka Strait, 65 mi. W of Pangkalpinang; exports tin. Has airfield.

Munuscong Lake (mĭnĕ'skŏng, mŭ'nŭskông), in S central Ont. and E Upper Peninsula, Mich., a widening of St. Marys R., 23 mi. SSE of Sault Ste. Marie and W of St. Joseph Isl.; c.15 mi. long, 5 mi. wide. Mich.-Ont. line passes through lake. Receives Munuscong R. (c.15 mi. long) from SW.

Münzkirchen (münts'kĭrkhŭn), town (pop. 2,387), NW Upper Austria, 7 mi. ENE of Schärding; vineyards.

Munzur Dag (mōōnzōōr' dä), Turkish *Munzur Dağ,* peak (10,460 ft.), E central Turkey, 13 mi. E of Kemaliye, in Munzur Mts., a range which extends 55 mi. S and E of the Euphrates. Silver deposits at Kemah. Sometimes spelled Monzur.

Munzur River, E central Turkey, rises in Munzur Dag 19 mi. E of Kemaliye, flows 90 mi. E and SE, past Ovacik, to Murat R. 10 mi. SE of Pertek. Receives Peri R. (left). Sometimes spelled Monzur.

Muong Hou, Laos: see PHONGSALY.

Muong Hou Neua (mŭ'ông hōō nŭ'ä), town, Phongsaly prov., N Laos, on the Nam Nou and 40 mi. NNW of Phongsaly.

Muonghung (mwŭng'hōōng'), town, Sonla prov., N Vietnam, 26 mi. S of Sonla.

Muongkhuong (mwŭng'khwŭng'), town, Laokay prov., N Vietnam, near China frontier, 21 mi. NNE of Laokay; rice.

Muong Lane (mŭ'ông län'), town, Xiengkhouang prov., N Laos, on the Song Ca and 50 mi. NE of Xiengkhouang.

Muong May (mä'), town, Champassac prov., S Laos, on the Se Khong and 65 mi. ESE of Pakse.

Muong Sing (sĭng'), town, Haut Mekong prov., NW Laos, 260 mi. NNW of Vientiane, near junction of Laos, China, and Burma borders, at alt. 2,608 ft.; rice, poultry, cattle trading. Agr.: castor beans, cotton, opium, sugar, rubber; lac.

Muong Soui (swē'), town, Xiengkhouang prov., N Laos, on Tranninh Plateau, 50 mi. SE of Luang Prabang, on highway to Vinh. Important monastery. Also called Ban Khai.

Muonio (mōō'ônēō), village (commune pop. 2,558), Lapi co., NW Finland, on Muonio R. (Swedish border) and 110 mi. NW of Rovaniemi; lumbering.

Muonio River, Finland and Sweden: see TORNE RIVER.

Muotathal (mōō-ō'tätäl"), town (pop. 2,349), Schwyz canton, central Switzerland, on Muota R. and 6 mi. SE of Schwyz; silk textiles, farming. Old nunnery, 18th-cent. church. Hölloch grottoes are E of town.

Muping, China: see PAOHING.

Muqaiyir, Tall al, Iraq: see UR.

Muqdadiyah (mōōkdädē'yŭ), town, Diyala prov. E Iraq, on the Tigris near Iran line, and 55 mi. NNE of Baghdad. Formerly Shahraban.

Muqui (mōōkē'), city (pop. 3,287), S Espírito Santo, Brazil, on railroad and 7 mi. SW of Cachoeiro de Itapemirim, in coffeegrowing area; sawmilling. Bauxite deposits near by. Until 1944, called São João do Muqui (formerly spelled Muquy).

Muquiyauyo (mōōkēyou'yō), city (pop. 1,932), Junín dept., central Peru, on Mantaro R. and 5 mi. SE of Jauja; hydroelectric plant (connected with Jauja); potatoes, grain.

Mûr or **Mûr-de-Bretagne** (mür-dŭ-brŭtä'nyŭ), village (pop. 1,079), Côtes-du-Nord dept., W France, 24 mi. SSW of Saint-Brieuc; cattle raising; slate quarries near by. Guerlédan dam and hydroelectric plant 5 mi. S on Blavet R.

Mur, river, Austria, Hungary, and Yugoslavia: see MUR RIVER.

Mur (mōōr), town (pop. 3,000), Hodeida prov., NW Yemen, on Tihama coastal plain, 20 mi. ESE of Loheia; sheepskin tanning; shoe, saddle and harness mfg.

Muradiye (mōōrä'dĭyĕ), village (pop. 1,348), Van prov., SE Turkey, near NE shore of L. Van, 40 mi. NNE of Van; wheat, naphtha. Formerly called Bargiri.

Muradnagar (mōōräd'nŭgŭr), town (pop. 5,529), Meerut dist., NW Uttar Pradesh, India, on Upper Ganges Canal and 18 mi. SW of Meerut; wheat, gram, jowar, sugar cane, oilseeds.

Murad River, Turkey: see MURAT RIVER.

Murakami (mōōrä'kä'mē), town (pop. 15,811), Niigata prefecture, N Honshu, Japan, on Sea of Japan, 32 mi. NE of Niigata; mfg. of lacquer ware, processed tea.

Murakeresztur (mōō'rŏkĕrĕstōōr), Hung. *Murakeresztúr,* town (pop. 2,235), Zala co., W Hungary, on Mura R. and 8 mi. SW of Nagykanizsa, on Yugoslav line; rail center for agr. (wheat, rye, corn), dairy area.

Muraköz, region, Yugoslavia: see MEDJUMURJE.

Muralto (mōōräl'tō), town (pop. 2,312), Ticino canton, S Switzerland, on Lago Maggiore; residential suburb E of Locarno; jewelry. Romanesque church.

Muramatsu (mōōrä'-mä'tsōō), town (pop. 10,066), Niigata prefecture, central Honshu, Japan, 18 mi. SSE of Niigata; agr. (rice, mulberry, tea); cotton textiles.

Muramvia (mōōräm'vyä), village, S Ruanda-Urundi, in Urundi, 50 mi. SW of Kitega; center of native trade and residence of *mwami* (sultan) of Urundi; dairying. Cinchona plantations near by.

Muran, Czechoslovakia: see TISOVEC.

Murano (mōōrä'nō), town (pop. 6,368), Venezia prov., Veneto, N Italy, on 5 islets in Lagoon of Venice, 1 mi. N of Venice. A famous center of Venetian glass industry since 13th cent. Has Venetian-Byzantine church of SS. Maria e Donata (7th-12th cent.), church of St. Peter the Martyr (rebuilt 1509) with paintings by Bellini and Veronese, and mus. (1861) with anc. and modern Venetian glass.

Muraoka (mōōrä'ōkä), town (pop. 4,050), Hyogo prefecture, S. Honshu, Japan, 21 mi. ESE of Tottori, in agr. area (rice, wheat, truck); livestock; mfg. (tiles, cutlery).

Murarai, India: see NALHATI.

Mura River, Austria, Yugoslavia, Hungary: see MUR RIVER.

Murashi (mōōrŭshē'), city (1948 pop. over 10,000), N Kirov oblast, Russian SFSR, on railroad and 60 mi. NNW of Kirov, on highway to Syktyvkar (N); sawmilling, wood distillation. Became city in 1944.

Muraszombat, Yugoslavia: see MURSKA SOBOTA.

Murat (mürä'), town (pop. 2,159), Cantal dept., S central France, on E slope of Massif du Cantal, on Alagnon R. and 12 mi. WNW of Saint-Flour; road junction; cheese and cattle shipping center. Kieselguhr quarries near by.

Murata (mōōrä'tä), town (pop. 10,215), Miyagi prefecture, N Honshu, Japan, 13 mi. SW of Sendai; rice, silk cocoons, charcoal; horse breeding.

Murat Dag (mōōrät' dä), Turkish *Murat Dağ.* **1** Peak (11,545 ft.), E Turkey, 27 mi. SE of Karakose. **2** Peak (7,585 ft.), W Turkey, 19 mi. SE of Gediz.

Murato (mōōrä'tō), village (pop. 1,027), N Corsica, 10 mi. SW of Bastia; winegrowing.

Murat River (mōōrät'), E central Turkey, a principal headstream of the Euphrates, rises c.40 mi. SW of Mt. Ararat, c.15 mi. S of Diyadin, and flows 380 mi. W, past Karakose, Tutak, Malazgirt, Genc, and Palu, to join the W headstream of the Euphrates (here sometimes called Kara Su), or Euphrates proper, 5 mi. NE of Keban, WNW of Elazig. From the source of the Murat to the Syrian line is 685 mi. Receives Hinis and Munzur rivers (right). Sometimes spelled Murad.

Murat-sur-Vèbre (mürä'-sür-vĕ'brŭ), village (pop. 325), Tarn dept., S France, in the Monts de Lacaune, 24 mi. W of Lodève; sheep raising.

Murau (mōō'rou), town (pop. 2,853), Styria, central Austria, on Mur R. and 23 mi. W of Judenburg; summer and winter resort (alt. 2,654 ft.).

Muravera (mōōrävā'rä), village (pop. 2,632), Cagliari prov., SE Sardinia, near mouth of Flumendosa R., 28 mi. NE of Cagliari; fruit canning; dried herbs. Lead-zinc-silver mine 1 mi. S.

Muravlyanka (mōōrŭvlyän'kŭ), village (1939 pop. over 500), SE Ryazan oblast, Russian SFSR, 45 mi. E of Ryazhsk; wheat, tobacco.

Muravyev-Amurski, suburb, Russian SFSR: see LAZO.

Muravyev-Amurski Peninsula or **Murav'yev-Amurskiy Peninsula** (mo͞orŭvyôf'-ŭmo͞or'skē), S Maritime Territory, Russian SFSR, in Vladivostok city limits; extends 25 mi. SSW into Peter the Great Bay, separating its 2 inlets, Amur (W) and Ussuri (E) bays. Across the Eastern Bosphorus (at S end) lie Russian, Popova, and Reineke isls. Amur Bay shore is lined with summer resorts. Vladivostok proper is on SW tip of the peninsula, on GOLDEN HORN BAY. Named for 19th-cent. governor-general of Eastern Siberia.

Murayjat, Lebanon: see MUREIJAT.

Murbach, France: see GUEBWILLER.

Murbad (mo͝or'bäd), village (pop. 2,683), Thana dist., W Bombay, India, 28 mi. E of Thana; local market for rice, timber.

Murbat or **Marbat** (both: mo͝orbät'), village, Dhofar dist., S Oman, on Arabian Sea, 40 mi. E of Salala, on the cape Ras Murbat, at foot of the Jabal Samhan; sheltered anchorage and chief port of Dhofar; airfield.

Murça (mo͞or'sŭ), town (pop. 1,540), Vila Real dist., N Portugal, 18 mi. NE of Vila Real; winegrowing; olives, figs, almonds, oranges.

Murchante (mo͞orchän'tā), village (pop. 2,213), Navarre prov., N Spain, 4 mi. SW of Tudela; olive oil, wine, sugar beets.

Murcheh Khurt or **Murcheh Khort** (mo͞orchĕ'khōrt'), village, Tenth Prov., in Isfahan, W central Iran, 32 mi. NNW of Isfahan and on Isfahan-Teheran road; cotton, barley, tobacco, madder root, melons. Nadir Shah defeated the Afghans here in 1729.

Murchison, village (pop. 595), N central Victoria, Australia, on Goulburn R. and 85 mi. N of Melbourne; rail junction; livestock, oats, barley.

Murchison, township (pop. 509), ⊙ Murchison co. (□ 1,412; pop. 1,270), S.Isl., New Zealand, 75 mi. NE of Greymouth and on Buller R.; center of sheep-raising area; dairy plant, sawmills.

Murchison, Cape, NE Ellesmere Isl., NE Franklin Dist., Northwest Territories, on Hall Basin, at S end of Robeson Channel, near N entrance of Lady Franklin Bay; 81°42'N 64°5'W.

Murchison, Mount (10,659 ft.), SW Alta., near B.C. border, in Rocky Mts., in Banff Natl. Park, 70 mi. NW of Banff; 51°55'N 116°38'W.

Murchison Falls, NW Uganda, rapids on the lower Victoria Nile, 22 mi. E of L. Albert. Here the river (only 19 ft. wide) flows through precipitously cleft rocks, dropping 400 ft. in a series of 3 cascades to level of L. Albert. Accessible by steamer from Butiaba on L. Albert.

Murchison Glacier, W central S.Isl., New Zealand, in Tasman Natl. Park Southern Alps; rises in Elie de Beaumont mtn., flows 11 mi. S to Murchison R.

Murchison Goldfield (□ 21,000), W central Western Australia; mining center is Meekathara. Gold discovered here 1891; area placed that year under govt. control and leased to mining interests.

Murchison Promontory, N extremity of Boothia Peninsula, S Franklin Dist., Northwest Territories, on Bellot Strait; 71°58'N 94°28'W. Rises steeply to c.2,500 ft.

Murchison Rapids, Nyasaland: see SHIRE RIVER.

Murchison River, W Western Australia, rises in SE Robinson Ranges, flows 440 mi. generally SW to Indian Ocean 80 mi. N of Geraldton; intermittent. Roderick and Sanford rivers, main tributaries.

Murcia (mo͞or'syä), town (1939 pop. 4,352; 1948 municipality pop. 28,243), Negros Occidental prov., W Negros isl., Philippines, 8 mi. SE of Bacolod; agr. center (rice, sugar cane).

Murcia (mûr'shŭ, mo͞or'–, Sp. mo͞or'thyä), region (□ 10,108; pop. 1,094,173) and former kingdom, S Spain, comprising provs. of Murcia (S) and ALBACETE (N); chief towns, Murcia and CARTAGENA. Bounded by the Mediterranean (S), and by Andalusia (W), New Castile (W and N), and Valencia (E), it reaches (N) into Spain's central plateau. Mostly mountainous, except for alluvial coastal plain; has low, sandy coast, with salt-water lagoon (Mar Menor) and fine Cartagena harbor (naval base). Drained by the Segura and the Júcar. One of hottest and driest regions of Spain, it resembles Africa in climate and vegetation. Crops vary, depending upon amount of rainfall, except for fertile garden regions irrigated since Moorish times. Mainly agr. Mineral deposits (especially silver-bearing lead, and iron) of Cartagena-Mazarrón dist., exploited by Carthaginians, Romans, and Moors, are now partly exhausted. Sericulture has lost much of former importance. Poor communications; chief exports: minerals, fruit, olive oil, esparto. Rose to importance under Carthaginians, who built main military base at *Carthago Nova* (now Cartagena). Belonged to Romans and Visigoths; fell to Moors (8th cent.), who created (11th cent.) independent kingdom of Murcia, which later included parts of Alicante and Almería. It became in 1243 a vassal state of Castile, which in 1266 annexed it outright.

Murcia, province (□ 4,639; pop. 719,701), SE Spain, on the Mediterranean; ⊙ Murcia. Generally mountainous, crossed by low, barren ranges interrupted by some fertile valleys. Drained by the Segura. Alluvial plain along coast (Mar Menor lagoon in SE) has only one usable harbor (CARTAGENA naval base). Dry, hot climate, with scarce but sudden rains which cause occasional floods. Has wide, deserted areas, and fertile garden regions irrigated since Moorish times (reservoirs). Hydroelectric plants along the Segura. Exports lead-silver ore, iron, zinc (La Unión, Mazarrón), sulphur (Lorca) from mines exploited since anc. times by Carthaginians, Romans, and Moors, but now partly exhausted. Saltworks. Marble, gypsum, clay, and limestone quarries; mineral springs. Essentially agr.: truck produce, cereals, olive oil, wine, pepper, some rice; esparto and hemp widely exported. Sericulture, a traditional occupation, has declined. Stock raising (mainly sheep), fishing. Agr. processing, brandy distilling; metalworking in mining dist. Other mfg.: explosives, footwear, pottery, furniture, textiles, candy. Chief cities: Murcia, Cartagena, Lorca, Cieza, Yecla.

Murcia, city (pop. 60,113), ⊙ Murcia prov. and region, SE Spain, on Segura R. and 220 mi. SE of Madrid, 30 mi. NNW of Cartagena; 37°59'N 1°8'W. Communications and agr. trade center in one of finest garden regions of Spain, yielding truck produce, almonds, cereals, olive oil, pepper. Sericulture is traditional industry. Fruit and vegetable canning, silk and cotton spinning, tanning, brandy and liqueur distilling, flour- and sawmilling; also mfg. of explosives, chemicals, essential oils, aluminum articles, furniture, soap, tiles, hats. See of bishop of Cartagena-Murcia. Seat of univ. (since 1915). Has narrow, crooked streets and some modern suburbs; fine promenades line river banks. Suffered heavily in civil war of 1936–39, when Gothic cathedral (14th cent.; rebuilt in 18th cent.; has fine baroque façade and 310-ft.-high tower) and church of Ermita de Jesús (containing series of sculptured processional figures) were sacked. Notable also are church of San Nicolás, episcopal palace, and modern town hall. Rose to prominence under Moors, who made it twice (in 11th and 13th cent.) the ⊙ independent kingdom of Murcia; liberated (1243) by Christians. Figured in War of Spanish Succession (18th cent.) and in Peninsular and Carlist wars (19th cent.). Climate subject to great variations, with scorching heat in summer. Suffered from frequent devastating floods.

Murdab Lagoon or **Mordab Lagoon** (mōrdäb'), Caspian inlet of N Iran, in Gilan, NW of Resht; 25 mi. long, 5 mi. wide, closed off by sandspit cut by shallow access channel. Ports of Pahlevi and Ghazian are opposite each other at entrance.

Mur-de-Barrez (mür-dŭ-bärĕz'), village (pop. 817), Aveyron dept., S France, on S slope of Massif du Cantal, 12 mi. ESE of Aurillac; cheese making, sawmilling. Hydroelectric works at BROMMAT.

Mûr-de-Bretagne, France: see MÛR.

Murderkill River, central Del., rises in W Kent co., flows 19 mi. E and NE, past Frederica (head of navigation), to Delaware Bay at Bowers.

Mur-de-Sologne (mür-dŭ-sôlô'nyŭ), village (pop. 375), Loir-et-Cher dept., N central France, in the Sologne and 7 mi. NW of Romorantin; asparagus growing, poultry and pig raising.

Murdo (mûr'dō), city (pop. 739), ⊙ Jones co., S central S.Dak., 40 mi. SSW of Pierre; livestock, poultry, grain; govt.-constructed dam 10 mi. S, on White R.

Murdock. 1 Village (pop. 393), Swift co., SW Minn., 19 mi. WNW of Willmar, in diversified-farming area; dairy products. **2** Village (pop. 225), Cass co., SE Nebr., 23 mi. ENE of Lincoln, near Platte R.

Mure, La, or **La Mure-d'Isère** (lä mür'-dēzâr'), town (pop. 4,762), Isère dept., SE France, near the Drac, 20 mi. S of Grenoble, in the Dauphiné Alps; shipping center of small anthracite basin; glove and footwear mfg. Just N is fertile Matésine (or Mateysine) plateau with 3 lakes.

Mureaux, Les (lā mürō'), town (pop. 5,319), Seine-et-Oise dept., N central France, on left bank of Seine R., opposite Meulan, and 22 mi. WNW of Paris; aircraft factory; mfg. (paints, paper, insulation, buckles).

Mureck (mo͞o'rĕk), village (pop. 2,224), Styria, SE Austria, on Mur R. and 11 mi. NNE of Maribor, Yugoslavia; summer resort, baths. Vineyards near by.

Mure-d'Isère, La, France: see MURE, LA.

Mureijat or **Murayjat** (mo͞orā'jăt), Fr. *Mraijat* or *Mreidjatt*, village (pop. 1,077), Bekaa prov., central Lebanon, 18 mi. SE of Beirut; alt. 3,800 ft.; grapes, tobacco, cereals, fruit. Summer resort.

Mureji (mo͞orājē'), town (pop. 750), Niger prov., Northern Provinces, W central Nigeria, on Niger R. opposite Pategi, at mouth of the Kaduna, and 35 mi. W of Katcha; river landing; shea-nut processing, twine, sackmaking.

Muren or **Mörön** (mŭ'rŭn) [Mongolian, =river], town, ⊙ Khubsugul aimak, NW Mongolian People's Republic, 330 mi. WNW of Ulan Bator and on the river Muren; 49°33'N 100°8'E. Site of former monastery.

Muren, Delger Muren, or **Delger Mörön** (dĕl'gĕr), left headstream of Selenga R., in NW Mongolian People's Republic; rises in mts. W of L. Khubsugul, flows 275 mi. SE, past Muren town, joining Ider R. to form the Selenga 35 mi. SE of Muren town.

Muren River, Manchuria: see MULING RIVER.

Mures, province, Rumania: see TARGU-MURES.

Mures River (mo͞o'rĕsh), Rum. *Mureş*, Hung. *Maros* (mŏ'rôsh), anc. *Marisus*, in central and W Rumania and E Hungary, rises in the Moldavian Carpathians 6 mi. SE of Gheorghieni, flows 550 mi. NW, SW, and W, past Reghin, Targu-Mures, Alba-Iulia, Deva, and Arad, to Tisa R. at Szeged. Navigable for c.200 mi. (below Deva) for small craft. Upper and middle course used for logging.

Muret (mürĕ'), town (pop. 2,632), Haute-Garonne dept., S France, on the Garonne and 11 mi. SSW of Toulouse; iron foundry, brick and tileworks; mfg. of surgical instruments, distilling, flour milling. Has powerful Toulouse radio transmitter.

Murfreesboro (mûr'frēzbŭ"rō). **1** Town (pop. 1,079) ⊙ Pike co., SW Ark., c.45 mi. SW of Hot Springs, in agr. area; mercury mines. Country's only diamond mine, now closed, is near by. **2** (also mûr'fēz–) Town (pop. 2,140), Hertford co., NE N.C., on Meherrin R. (head of navigation) and 31 mi. E of Roanoke Rapids; lumber, boxes. **3** City (pop. 13,052), ⊙ Rutherford co., central Tenn., on West Fork of Stones R. and 29 mi. SE of Nashville; shipping, processing, trading center in rolling livestock, cotton, and dairy region; mfg. of textile machinery, hosiery, rayon goods, dairy products, furniture, cedar woodenware; flour milling. Seat of Middle Tenn. State Col. Was (1819–25) state ⊙. Civil War battle of Murfreesboro (or Stones River) was fought here; near by is STONES RIVER NATIONAL MILITARY PARK. Inc. 1817.

Murgab (mo͞orgäp'), village (1948 pop. over 2,000), SE Gorno-Badakhshan Autonomous Oblast, Tadzhik SSR, in the Pamir, on Osh-Khorog highway, on Murgab R. and 140 mi. ENE of Khorog, in grazing area; 38°11'N 74°4'E; alt. 11,940 ft. Meteorological station. Until c.1929, called Pamirski Post.

Murgab River, Pashto *Murghab* (mo͞orgäb'), in NW Afghanistan and SE Turkmen SSR (USSR), rises in W outliers of the Hindu Kush bet. the Paropamisus Mts. and the Band-i-Turkestan, flows 530 mi. W and NW, past Bala Murghab, entering USSR at Maruchak, and flowing N through the Kara-Kum desert, past Tashkepristroi, to Mary (Murgab) oasis of Turkmen SSR, beyond which it disappears into the desert. Irrigation dams at Tashkepristroi (where it receives Kushka R.) and at Iolotan.

Murgab River, Tadzhik SSR, formed by junction of the Ak-Su and Ak-Baital headstreams at Murgab, flows c.60 mi. W to SAREZ LAKE.

Murgana, Mount, Albania-Greece: see TSAMANTA, MOUNT.

Murgash Mountains (mo͞or'gäsh), part of W Balkan Mts., N central Bulgaria; extend c.20 mi. bet. Iskar R. gorge (W) and Botevgrad Pass (E). Rise to 5,534 ft. at Murgash peak, 7 mi. SW of Botevgrad. Anthracite mining at Rebrovo.

Murgasu (mo͞orgäsh'), Rum. *Murgaşu*, village (pop. 986), Valcea prov., S Rumania, 15 mi. NNE of Craiova.

Murgeni (mo͞orgän'), village (pop. 1,664), Barlad prov., E Rumania, on railroad and 18 mi. ESE of Barlad; flour milling; mfg. of edible oils.

Murgenthal (mo͞or'gŭntäl"), town (pop. 2,484), Aargau canton, N Switzerland, on Aar R. and 8 mi. SSW of Olten; metal products, knit goods, cotton textiles; woodworking.

Murghab River, Afghanistan and USSR: see MURGAB RIVER.

Murgon (mûr'gŭn), town (pop. 1,463), SE Queensland, Australia, 105 mi. NW of Brisbane; rail junction in agr. area (corn, sugar, bananas).

Murg River (mo͝ork), S Germany, rises in the Black Forest 4 mi. ESE of Ottenhöfen, flows 45 mi. generally N, past Rastatt, to the Rhine 2 mi. N of Plittersdorf. Large hydroelectric station at Forbach.

Murgud (mo͞or'go͝od), town (pop. 4,524), Kolhapur dist., S Bombay, India, 22 mi. S of Kolhapur; agr. market (tobacco, sugar cane, chili).

Muri, India: see RANCHI, city.

Muri (mo͞o'rē), town (pop. 1,310), Adamawa prov., Northern Provinces, E Nigeria, near Benue R., 100 mi. W of Yola; agr. trade; cassava, durra, yams; cattle. Formerly called Hamarua.

Muri (mo͞o'rē), town (pop. 3,339), Aargau canton, N Switzerland, on Bünz R. and 11 mi. SW of Zurich; metal products, chemicals. Remains of abbey (founded 1027), abbey church (13th cent.; remodeled 17th cent.).

Muriaé (mo͞oryä-ĕ'), city (pop. 9,171), SE Minas Gerais, Brazil, terminus of rail spur from Patrocínio do Muriaé, and 75 mi. NW of Campos (Rio de Janeiro), and on Rio de Janeiro–Bahia highway; agr. trade center (sugar, coffee, cereals, dairy products) with processing plants and distilleries. White-marble quarries. Formerly spelled Muriahé.

Muriaé River, in SE Minas Gerais and NE Rio de Janeiro, Brazil, rises above Muriaé city, flows 90 mi. SE, past Itaperuna, to the Paraíba just above Campos. Navigable in lower course. Formerly spelled Muriahé.

Murias de Paredes (mo͞o'ryäs dhā pärā'dhĕs), town (pop. 381), Leon prov., N central Spain, on Órbigo R. and 35 mi. NW of Leon; livestock, lumber, cereals, flax. Antimony mining near by.

Muribeca (mo͞orēbĕ'kŭ), city (pop. 1,054), NE Sergipe, NE Brazil, on railroad and 17 mi. S of Propriá; sugar.

Muri bei Bern (mōō'rē bī bĕrn'), town (pop. 4,927), Bern canton, W central Switzerland, SE of Bern.

Murichom, Bhutan: see MARICHONG.

Murici (mōōrēsē'), city (pop. 3,796), E Alagoas, NE Brazil, on railroad and 27 mi. NW of Maceió, in sugar- and cotton-growing region; sugar mills. Formerly spelled Muricy.

Muriedas (mōōryā'dhäs), village (pop. 1,774), Santander prov., N Spain, 3 mi. SW of Santander; metalworking.

Murillo, Bolivia: see PALCA.

Murillo (mūrĭ'lō), village (pop. estimate 300), W Ont., 12 mi. W of Port Arthur; dairying; grain.

Murillo de Río Leza (mōōrē'lyō dhā rē'ō lā'thä), town (pop. 1,924), Logroño prov., N Spain, 8 mi. SE of Logroño; olive-oil processing, distilling (alcohol, brandy); wine, fruit, livestock, lumber.

Murillo el Fruto (ĕl frōō'tō), town (pop. 1,251), Navarre prov., N Spain, on Aragon R. and 16 mi. SE of Tafalla; olive-oil processing; sugar beets, wine, cereals, sheep.

Murilo (mōōrē'lō), atoll (pop. 279), Hall Isls., Truk dist., E Caroline Isls., W Pacific, 5 mi. ENE of Nomwin; 8°41'N 152°15'E; c.20 mi. long, 10 mi. wide; 11 low islets.

Murinda or **Morinda** (mōrĭn'dŭ), town (pop. 5,837), Ambala dist., E Punjab, India, 33 mi. NW of Ambala; wheat, gram, cotton.

Murinsel, region, Yugoslavia: see MEDJUMURJE.

Muritiba (mōōrētē'bŭ), city (pop. 7,095), E Bahia, Brazil, on right bank of Paraguaçu R. 2 mi. above Cachoeira, in tobacco-growing region; cigar mfg. Formerly spelled Murityba.

Müritz, Bad, Germany: see GRAAL-MÜRITZ.

Müritz Lake (mü'rĭts), largest lake (□ 45) entirely in Germany, 13 mi. E of Neustrelitz, Mecklenburg; 17 mi. long, 1–8 mi. wide; greatest depth 108 ft., average depth 21 ft.; alt. 203 ft. Waren at N tip.

Mu River (mōō), Upper Burma, rises N of Pinlebu, flows 300 mi. S, past Pinlebu, Kyunhla, and Yeu, to the Irrawaddy just E of Myinmu. Extensively used for irrigation; the Shwebo and Yeu irrigation canals branch off at Kabo headworks. The old left-bank Mu canal (dating from 18th cent.) is abandoned.

Murka Hill, Kenya: see TAVETA.

Murkurti, peak, India: see MUKURTI.

Murlo (mōōr'lô), village (pop. 113), Siena prov., Tuscany, central Italy, 12 mi. SSE of Siena; cement mfg.; lignite mining.

Murman Coast (mōōr'mŭn), Rus. *Murmanskiy Bereg*, ice-free N shore of Kola Peninsula, Russian SFSR, on Barents Sea; c.200 mi. long. Deeply indented (W) by fjordlike inlets: Kola Gulf (site of Murmansk), Ura, Titovka, and Zapadnaya Litsa bays. Sometimes called Norman Coast, of which Murman is a corrupt form.

Murmansk (mōōrmănsk', Rus. mōōr'mŭnsk), oblast (□ 57,760; 1946 pop. estimate 450,000), in NW European Russian SFSR; ⊙ Murmansk. Includes KOLA PENINSULA and mainland section along Finnish border; tundra (N), forests (S). Gulf Stream action tempers climate along ice-free Barents Sea (N) coast; Rus. fishing pop. along coasts, Lapp reindeer-raising pop. (c.2,000) in interior. Mainly fishing (trawling along N coast; canneries at Murmansk, Port Vladimir, Saida-Guba, Teriberka) and mining (apatite and nephelite at Kirovsk, nickel and copper at Monchegorsk, nickel at Nikel). Other industries based on lumbering (sawmills and woodworking plants at Murmansk, Kandalaksha, Lesnoi, and Lesozavodski) and minerals (aluminum and superphosphate works at Kandalaksha). Shipbuilding (Murmansk), net making. Agr. (truck and dairy farming) along Murmansk RR. Power supplied by hydroelectric stations along Tuloma and Niva rivers. Originally part of Archangel govt.; formed separate govt. (1921–27), and, later, an okrug within Leningrad oblast. Constituted as oblast in 1938; acquired former Finnish territories of W coast of Rybachi Peninsula in 1940 and Pechenga (Petsamo) dist. in 1944.

Murmansk, city (1926 pop. 8,777; 1939 pop. 117,054), ⊙ Murmansk oblast, Russian SFSR, ice-free port on E shore of Kola Gulf of Barents Sea, on NW Kola Peninsula, 625 mi. N of Leningrad; 68°59'N 33°E. World's largest city N of Arctic Circle; fishing and shipbuilding center; N terminus of Murmansk RR. Fish canning, metal- and woodworking; net and barrel factories, refrigerating plants. Exports fish, lumber, apatite; imports coal (from Spitsbergen) and machinery. Coastal shipping carries salt, food, manufactured goods. Site of polar research station. Naval base of Polyarny is N, Tuloma hydroelectric station SW. Founded 1915 as Romanov-na-Murmane, later named Murmansk; became rail terminus (1916); occupied by Allies (1918–20). Developed rapidly in 1930s.

Murmashi (mōōrmŭshē'), town (1939 pop. over 2,000), NW Murmansk oblast, Russian SFSR, on Tuloma R. and 12 mi. SW of Murmansk; site of Tuloma hydroelectric station.

Murmino (mōōr'mēnŭ), town (1926 pop. 2,954), NW Ryazan oblast, Russian SFSR, in Oka R. valley, 13 mi. E of Ryazan; woolen milling center.

Murnau (mōōr'nou), village (pop. 5,673), Upper Bavaria, Germany, at N foot of the Bavarian Alps, at SE tip of the Staffelsee, 11 mi. S of Weilheim; rail junction; textile mfg., metal- and woodworking, lumber and paper milling. Summer resort and winter-sports center (alt. 2,257 ft.). Has early-18th-cent. church. Chartered 1322.

Muro (mōō'rō), town (pop. 5,673), Majorca, Balearic Isls., 24 mi. ENE of Palma; winegrowing and stock-raising center. Rice processing; lime quarrying.

Muro, Capo di (kä'pô dē mōō'rô), headland of SW Corsica, on the Mediterranean, 13 mi. SSW of Ajaccio, bet. Gulf of Ajaccio (N) and Gulf of Valinco (S); 41°45'N 8°39'E.

Muroc (myōō'rŏk), former village, Kern co., S central Calif., c.65 mi. N of Los Angeles, in Mojave Desert at edge of Muroc Dry Lake (c.12 mi. long; sometimes called Rogers L.), a desert playa. Site taken over by Edwards Air Force Base.

Muroda, Japan: see MUROTA.

Muro de Alcoy (mōō'rō dhā älkoi'), town (pop. 2,993), Alicante prov., E Spain, 6 mi. NNE of Alcoy; cement and soap mfg., cottonseed- and olive-oil processing; honey, wine, cereals, flax, truck produce.

Muro Lucano (mōō'rô lōōkä'nô), town (pop. 8,516), Potenza prov., Basilicata, S Italy, 19 mi. WNW of Potenza, in agr. region (cereals, fruit). Bishopric. Has castle partly destroyed (1694, 1783) by earthquakes. Hydroelectric plant near by.

Murom (mōō'rŭm), city (1926 pop. 22,607), SE Vladimir oblast, Russian SFSR, on left bank of Oka R. and 75 mi. SE of Vladimir; rail junction; industrial center; mfg. (locomotives, machine tools), linen milling, veneering, food processing. Has cathedral and monasteries dating from 16th cent., regional mus., Oka R. biological station, teachers col. One of oldest cities of USSR; founded 864. Early center for Volga-Kama river trade; destroyed 1232 by Tatars; remained nearly deserted until 1393, when it was inc. into Muscovite state.

Muromtsevo (-tsyĭvŭ), village (1939 pop. over 2,000), E Omsk oblast, Russian SFSR, on Tara R. and 80 mi. NNW of Tatarsk; dairy farming.

Murongo (mōōrông'gō), village, Lake Prov., NW Tanganyika, on Kagera R. (Uganda border) opposite Kikagati and 80 mi. WNW of Bukoba; 1°4'S 30°40'E. Center of tin-mining dist. extending into Uganda and Ruanda-Urundi. Site of hydroelectric power station.

Muroran (mōōrō'rän), city (1940 pop. 107,628; 1947 pop. 96,722), SW Hokkaido, Japan, 55 mi. SSW of Sapporo, at SE entrance to Uchiura Bay; coal-loading port; industrial center (iron- and steel-works). Exports coal, lumber, paper. Seaweed Research Laboratory of Hokkaido Imperial Univ. here. Bombed (1945) in Second World War. Formerly sometimes spelled Mororan.

Muros (mōō'rōs), town (pop. 2,045), La Coruña prov., NW Spain, fishing port on inlet of the Atlantic, 27 mi. WSW of Santiago; fish processing, boatbuilding, lace mfg.; lumber, livestock.

Muros de Nalón (dhā nälōn'), town (pop. 1,898), Oviedo prov., NW Spain, near Nalón R. estuary 22 mi. W of Gijón; flour milling, meat processing. Agr. trade (corn, potatoes, cattle; lumber). Iron and copper mines in vicinity.

Murota (mōōrō'tä) or **Muroda** (mōōrō'dä), town (pop. 9,137), Gumma prefecture, central Honshu, Japan, 8 mi. NW of Takasaki; raw silk, rice, wheat.

Muroto (mōōrō'tō), town (pop. 9,418), Kochi prefecture, S Shikoku, Japan, on Tosa Bay, 40 mi. ESE of Kochi, near Muroto Point; fishing port; cattle-raising center. Produces ornamental coral. Sometimes called Murotsu.

Muroto Point, Jap. *Muroto-zaki*, cape in Kochi prefecture, S Shikoku, Japan, at E side of Tosa Bay; 33°14'N 134°11'E; lighthouse.

Murotozaki (mōōrō'-tō'zäkē), town (pop. 6,789), Kochi prefecture, S Shikoku, Japan, on Tosa Bay, 42 mi. ESE of Kochi, bet. Muroto Point and Muroto; summer resort, with beaches warmed by Japan Current. Produces rice, raw silk. Fishing. Called Tsuro until 1929.

Murotsu, Japan: see MUROTO.

Murovanye Kurilovtsy or **Murovanyye Kurilovtsy** (mōōrŭvä'nēŭ kōōrē'lŭftsē), town (1926 pop. 4,464), W Vinnitsa oblast, Ukrainian SSR, 22 mi. NW of Mogilev-Podolski; sugar beets, wheat, fruit. Also called Murovano-Kurilovtsy.

Murowana Goslina (mōōrôvä'nä gôsh-lē'nä), Pol. *Murowana Goślina*, Ger. *Murowana Goslin* (mōōrōvä'nä gôslēn'), town (1946 pop. 2,398), Poznan prov., W Poland, 12 mi. NNE of Poznan; flour milling, sawmilling.

Murozumi, Japan: see HIKARI.

Murphy. **1** Village, ⊙ Owyhee co., SW Idaho, 25 mi. S of Caldwell. **2** Resort town (pop. 2,433), ⊙ Cherokee co., extreme W N.C., on Hiwassee R. and 90 mi. WSW of Asheville, in Nantahala Natl. Forest, near Ga. line; mfg. of furniture, veneer, boxes, hosiery, clothing. Hiwassee and Apalachia reservoirs are near. Founded c.1830.

Murphy Island, St. Lawrence co., N N.Y., in the St. Lawrence, at Ont. line, c.2 mi. NE of Waddington; c.¾ mi. long, ½ mi. wide. Also called Allison Isl.

Murphysboro (mûr'fēzbŭ"rŭ), city (pop. 9,241), ⊙ Jackson co., SW Ill., on Big Muddy R. and c.50 mi. N of Cairo; trade and shipping center for dairying region; mfg. (clothing, beverages, dairy products, flour, metal products); silica and bituminous-coal mining. Has memorial to John Alexander Logan, b. here. Founded 1843, inc. 1867.

Murra (mōō'rä), town (1950 pop. 211), Nueva Segovia dept., NW Nicaragua, 36 mi. ENE of Ocotal; gold and silver mining. Sometimes called San Juan de Murra.

Murray. **1** County (□ 342; pop. 10,676), NW Ga.; ⊙ Chatsworth. Bounded N by Tenn. line, W by Conasauga R. Agr. area (corn, cotton, hay, fruit, livestock); textile mfg., sawmilling, talc mining. Part of Chattahoochee Natl. Forest (E). Formed 1832. **2** County (□ 708; pop. 14,801), SW Minn.; ⊙ Slayton. Agr. area drained by headwaters of Des Moines R.; L. Shetek in N. Corn, oats, barley, livestock. Formed 1857. **3** County (□ 428; pop. 10,775), S Okla.; ⊙ Sulphur. Intersected by Washita R. Includes part of Arbuckle Mts. (recreation area), and PLATT NATIONAL PARK. Stock raising, agr. (corn, cotton, wheat, poultry, fruit), dairying. Mining (asphalt, glass sand, gravel); oil wells. Sulphur is resort, with mineral springs. Formed 1907.

Murray. **1** Town (pop. 767), Clarke co., S Iowa, 9 mi. W of Osceola, in livestock and grain area. **2** City (pop. 6,035), ⊙ Calloway co., SW Ky., on East Fork Clarks R., near Kentucky Reservoir, and 37 mi. SSE of Paducah, in agr. (dark tobacco, corn, clover, livestock) area. Mfg. of gas ranges, hosiery, tobacco and dairy products, harness, pottery, monuments, concrete products; flour, feed, and lumber mills; airport. Seat of Murray State Col. (1922). **3** Village (pop. 244), Cass co., SE Nebr., 23 mi. S of Omaha, near Missouri R. **4** City (pop. 9,006), Salt Lake co., N Utah, on Jordan R., just S of Salt Lake City, near Wasatch Range; alt. 4,300 ft. Smelting center for near-by lead mines and trading point for irrigated agr. area (sugar beets, alfalfa, potatoes); canned foods, flour, lumber, textiles. Inc. 1902.

Murray, Lake. **1** In Love and Carter counties, S Okla., resort lake (c.8 mi. long) in Lake Murray State Park (c.21,000 acres), S of Ardmore; fishing, camping. **2** In central S.C., lake (30 mi. long) formed by Saluda Dam on Saluda R., 10 mi. W of Columbia. Used for hydroelectric power. Summer resort.

Murray Bay, Que.: see MALBAIE, LA.

Murray Bridge, town and river port (pop. 3,689), SE South Australia, on Murray R. and 40 mi. ESE of Adelaide; rail junction; agr. and dairying center; citrus and dried fruits, dairy products; building stone.

Murray Canal, SE Ont., connects Bay of Quinte with L. Ontario, cutting across narrow isthmus that connects peninsula of Prince Edward co. with mainland. Completed 1889.

Murray City, village (pop. 752), Hocking co., S central Ohio, 13 mi. E of Logan, in coal-mining area.

Murray Harbour, village (pop. estimate 400), SE P.E.I., on Murray Harbour of the Gulf of St. Lawrence, at mouth of Murray R., 33 mi. ESE of Charlottetown; lobster, oyster, salmon fisheries.

Murray Hill, SE N.Y., business and residential district of S central Manhattan borough of New York city, lying on the East Side S of 42d St.

Murray Island, Jefferson co., N N.Y., one of the Thousand Isls., in the St. Lawrence, bet. Wellesley and Grindstone isls., 7 mi. SW of Alexandria Bay; c.1 mi. long.

Murray River. **1** Principal river of Australia, rises in Australian Alps near Mt. Kosciusko, in New South Wales, flows generally W and WNW, past Albury, Echuca, Swan Hill, Mildura, and Renmark, thence S, past Murray Bridge, through L. Alexandrina, to Indian Ocean at Encounter Bay, on SE coast of South Australia; length, 1,600 mi. Forms 1,200 mi. of boundary bet. New South Wales and Victoria; 400 mi. above its mouth it receives its main tributary, Darling R. (the Darling-Murray watercourse is 2,310 mi.). On it are hydroelectric plants and reservoirs; Hume Reservoir (near Albury), largest. River development scheme financed and shared by New South Wales, Victoria, and South Australia. Important primarily for irrigation; navigation limited to excursion boats. Other tributaries: Murrumbidgee R. (N); Mitta Mitta, Goulburn, Campaspe, and Loddon rivers (S). **2** In SW Western Australia, rises in hills NE of Narrogin, flows 70 mi. generally W, past Pinjarra, to Indian Ocean at Mandurah; orchards.

Murray River, village (pop. estimate 400), SE P.E.I., on small Murray R. and 30 mi. ESE of Charlottetown; mixed farming, dairying; potatoes.

Murray River, stream, Que.: see MALBAIE RIVER.

Murraysburg, town (pop. 1,673), S central Cape Prov., U. of So. Afr., on Buffalo R. and 50 mi. WNW of Graaff Reinet, on the Great Karroo; wool-producing center; stock, feed crops.

Murrayville, village (pop. 405), Morgan co., W central Ill., 10 mi. S of Jacksonville, in agr. area.

Murree (mŭr'rē), town (pop., including cantonment areas, 2,422), Rawalpindi dist., N Punjab, W Pakistan, on W spur of Punjab Himalayas, 27 mi. NE of Rawalpindi; picturesque hill resort (sanitarium) and military station; brewery, bakery; sericulture. Near by are several forest-clad peaks (over 7,000 ft.) and vegetable- and fruitgrowing fields. At Upper Topa (E) is forest col., opened 1948.

Murrels Inlet, summer resort, Georgetown co., E S.C., on the coast, 18 mi. NE of Georgetown; fishing, boatbuilding. Brookgreen Gardens near by.

Mürren (mü'rŭn), health and winter sports resort (alt. 5,415 ft.), Bern canton, S central Switzerland, in Bernese Alps, near White Lütschine R., 9 mi. S of Interlaken, opposite the Jungfrau. Commands a magnificent panorama.

Murrhardt (mo͝or'härt), town (pop. 6,533), N Württemberg, Germany, after 1945 in Württemberg-Baden, 7 mi. ENE of Backnang; mfg. of tanning materials; metal- and woodworking, tanning. Has Romanesque–late-Gothic church. Was Roman castrum.

Murrieta (mŭrēē'tŭ), village (pop. c.150), Riverside co., S Calif., 30 mi. S of Riverside; resort, with thermal springs.

Mur River (mo͝or), Hung. and Serbo-Croatian *Mura*, in Austria, Hungary, and Yugoslavia; rises in Austria on the Ankogel of the Hohe Tauern, at Salzburg-Carinthia border; flows E, past Judenburg, Knittelfeld, and Leoben, then S at Bruck, past Graz, to Austro-Yugoslav border, which it forms for c.20 mi. before entering Yugoslavia below Radkersburg; thence SE, forming part of Yugoslav-Hung. border, to the Drau (Drava) at Legrad. Navigable below Graz. Hydroelectric stations at Mixnitz and Peggau; hydroelectric works at Graz. Length, 300 mi. The PREKMURJE and the MEDJUMURJE are Yugoslav regions along its lower course.

Murro di Porco, Cape (mo͝or'rô dē pôr'kô), point on SE coast of Sicily, 4 mi. SE of Syracuse; 37°N 15°20'E.

Murroes (mûr'ōz), agr. village and parish (pop. 919), S Angus, Scotland, 3 mi. NW of Monifieth.

Murrumbidgee River (mûr"ŭmbĭ'jē), S New South Wales, Australia, rises in Great Dividing Range near Cooma, flows N, through Australian Capital Territory, thence W, past Burrinjuck (dam, hydroelectric plant), Gundagai, Wagga Wagga, Narrandera, Hay, and Balranald, to Murray R. on Victoria border; 1,050 mi. long. Important primarily for irrigation. Lachlan R., main tributary. Explored by Charles Sturt.

Murrumburrah (mûr"ŭmbŭr'ŭ), municipality (pop. 2,595), S central New South Wales, Australia, 65 mi. NW of Canberra; rail junction; dairying center; wheat, sheep.

Murrurundi (mûr"ŭrŭn'dē), municipality (pop. 1,039), E New South Wales, Australia, 90 mi. NW of Newcastle; agr. and sheep center; wheat.

Mursa Major, Yugoslavia: see OSIJEK.

Mursan (mo͞orsän'), town (pop. 3,909), Aligarh dist., W Uttar Pradesh, India, 7 mi. W of Hathras; wheat, barley, pearl millet, gram, corn. Formerly principal Jat estate in Uttar Pradesh. Cutlery mfg. at Naya or Nayaganj Hathras, 8 mi. W.

Murshidabad (mo͝or"shĭdäbäd'), district (□ 2,063; pop. 1,640,530), central West Bengal, India; ⊙ Berhampore. Bounded NE by the Padma (Ganges) and East Bengal (E Pakistan); drained by Bhagirathi and Jalangi rivers; MOR RIVER irrigation project in W. Undulating plain interspersed with marshes. Area E of the Bhagirathi, in Ganges Delta, is major agr. region of dist. (rice, gram, oilseeds, jute, barley, mangoes, wheat); extensive mulberry cultivation (silk growing) in W area. Main industrial towns, BERHAMPORE and BELDANGA (silk weaving, rice, sugar, and oilseed milling, match mfg.). Silk-weaving center at Murshidabad; cotton weaving (Jangipur, Dhulian), metalware (Kandi), shellac (Nimtita). Bengal Silk Technological Inst., Krishnanath Col. at Berhampore (scene of 1st overt act of Sepoy Rebellion in 1857). Cossimbazar was major English trade center of Bengal in 17th cent. Dist. became (1197) part of Gaur kingdom; invaded 18th cent. by Mahrattas; in 1751, nawab of Bengal ceded Orissa to the Mahrattas.

Murshidabad, town (pop. 11,498), Murshidabad dist., E West Bengal, India, on the Bhagirathi and 5 mi. N of Berhampore; silk-weaving center; trades in rice, gram, oilseed, jute, wheat, barley. Has palace of titular nawab of Bengal; burial place of old nawabs of Bengal. Reputedly founded by Akbar. In 1704 became ⊙ Bengal following its removal from Dacca; continued to be ⊙ Bengal under English until 1790. Once famous for carved ivory and embroideries. Formerly called Maksudabad, Makhsusabad, or Muxadabad; sometimes Lalbagh.

Murska Sobota (mo͝or'skä sôbôtä), Hung. *Muraszombat* (mo͝o'rŏsômbät), village (pop. 4,902), NE Slovenia, Yugoslavia, on Lendava R., on railroad and 25 mi. ENE of Maribor. Chief village of the Prekmurje; trade center for cereal-growing region; poultry raising, meat packing.

Murtaugh (mûr'tô), village (pop. 239), Twin Falls co., S Idaho, 15 mi. ESE of Twin Falls and on Snake R.; alt. 4,630 ft.; agr. Inc. 1937.

Murtazapur (mo͞ortŭzä'po͝or), town (pop. 12,636), Akola dist., W Madhya Pradesh, India, 25 mi. E of Akola, in major cotton-growing area; rail junction; cotton ginning, oilseed milling. Also spelled Murtizapur.

Murten, Switzerland: see MORAT.

Murtensee, Switzerland: see MORAT, LAKE OF.

Murter Island (mo͞or'tĕr), Ital. *Morter* (môr'tĕr), anc. *Colentum*, Dalmatian island in Adriatic Sea, W Croatia, Yugoslavia, 13 mi. WNW of Sibenik; up to 7 mi. long, up to 2 mi. wide; bridged to mainland. Chief village, Tijesno, Ital. *Stretto*, on E coast; Murter, Ital. *Morter*, is on N coast, 3 mi. NW of Tijesno.

Murtizapur, India: see MURTAZAPUR.

Murtle Lake (17 mi. long, 1–6 mi. wide), E B.C., in Cariboo Mts., in Wells Gray Provincial Park, 100 mi. NNE of Kamloops; alt. 3,650 ft. Drains W into North Thompson R.

Murtoa (mûrtō'ŭ), town (pop. 1,197), W central Victoria, Australia, 160 mi. WNW of Melbourne; rail junction; wheat-growing center; flour mill.

Murtosa (mo͞ortō'zŭ), town (pop. 2,677), Aveiro dist., N central Portugal, on Aveiro lagoon, 6 mi. N of Aveiro; sardine fisheries, saltworks.

Murud (mo͝or'o͞od), town (pop. 8,436), Kolaba dist., W Bombay, India, on Arabian Sea, at mouth of wide creek, 45 mi. SSE of Bombay; fish-supplying center (mackerel, pomfrets); rice, coconuts; coir-rope and furniture mfg.; bakery. Teak forests N. Was ⊙ former Deccan state of Janjira.

Murupu (mo͞oro͞opo͞o'), town, Rio Branco territory, northernmost Brazil, 30 mi. N of Boa Vista, and on the Uraricoera.

Mururata (mo͞oro͞orä'tä), peak (18,965 ft.) in Cordillera de La Paz, W Bolivia, 19 mi. ESE of La Paz; tin-tungsten deposits on E slopes.

Murviedro, Spain: see SAGUNTO.

Murviel or **Murviel-les-Béziers** (mürvyĕl'-lā-bāzyā'), village (pop. 1,967), Hérault dept., S France, 8 mi. NW of Béziers; distilling, winegrowing.

Murwara, India: see KATNI.

Mürwick (mür'vĭk), N suburb of FLENSBURG, NW Germany.

Murwillumbah (mŭrwĭ'lŭmbŭ), municipality (pop. 4,954), NE New South Wales, Australia, near Queensland border, on Tweed R. and 65 mi. SSE of Brisbane; rail terminus; dairying center; banana plantations.

Murygino (mo͞orĭ'gĭnŭ), town (1948 pop. over 2,000), N central Kirov oblast, Russian SFSR, on Vyatka R. and 15 mi. NW of Kirov; paper milling.

Mürz River (mürts), E central Austria, rises in the Schneealpe in S Lower Austria, flows SE to Mürzzuschlag, thence SW, past Kapfenberg, to the Mur at Bruck. Length, 80 mi. Cattle raised along upper valley.

Murzuk (mo͞o'zo͝ok, mo͞orzo͞ok'), Arabic *Murzuq*, Ital. *Murzuch*, Fr. *Mourzouk*, town (pop. 2,129), central Fezzan, Libya, 85 mi. SW of Sebha, in an oasis; 25°55'N 13°53'E. Road terminus; trade center (cereals, natron, wood, vases, baskets). Has ruined fort (c.1310) and mosque. Founded early 14th cent., it was traditional capital of Fezzan for many centuries until recent times. Formerly chief market of Sahara for slaves and arms. Extensive ruins of the larger former town remain.

Mürzzuschlag (mürts"tso͞o'shläk), city (pop. 11,181), Styria, E central Austria, on Mürz R. and 24 mi. NE of Bruck, in scenic Semmering; rail junction; iron- and steelworks. Summer and winter resort (alt. 2,204 ft.).

Mus, Nicobar Isls.: see CAR NICOBAR ISLAND.

Mus (mo͞osh), Turk. *Muş*, prov. (□ 2,946; 1950 pop. 107,306), E Turkey; ⊙ Mus. Drained by Murat R.; mountainous and unproductive. Pop. largely Kurd. Also spelled Mush.

Mus, Turkish *Muş*, town (1950 pop. 7,057), ⊙ Mus prov., Turkey, near Murat R., 85 mi. S of Erzurum; wheat. Old Armenian town. Also spelled Mush.

Musa, Latvia and Lithuania: see MUSA RIVER.

Musa, Gebel (gĕ'bĕl mo͞o'sä, mo͞o'sŭ), **Jebel Musa,** or **Jabal Musa** (both: jĕ'bĕl) [Arabic,=mount of Moses], peak (c.7,400 ft.), S Sinai Peninsula, Egypt, 2 mi. N of Gebel Katherina; sometimes identified with Mt. Sinai. On its N slope is the famous monastery of St. Catherine, where the Codex Sinaiticus was found (see SINAI).

Musa, Jebel (jĕ'bĕl), mountain (2,790 ft.) in N Sp. Morocco, on the Strait of Gibraltar overlooking Ceuta (just E). Northernmost extremity of the Rif Mts., opposite Spain's Cordillera Penibética (of which it is the geological extension). Often identified with one of antiquity's Pillars of Hercules (the other being Gibraltar). Also called Jebel Sidi Musa.

Musabani, India: see MOSABONI.

Musacchia, Albania: see MYZEQE.

Musa Dag or **Musa Dagh** (mo͞o'sŭ däg', mū'sŭ däg'), Turkish *Musa Dağ* (mo͞osä' dä), peak (4,445 ft.), S Turkey, in Amanos Mts., rising from the Mediterranean coast 12 mi. W of Antioch. In First World War the Armenians here heroically resisted the Turks.

Musafirkhana (mo͞osä'fĭrkhä"nŭ), village, Sultanpur dist., E central Uttar Pradesh, India, 18 mi. WNW of Sultanpur; rice, wheat, gram, barley. Also written Musafir Khana.

Musaia (mo͞osä'yä), village, Northern Prov., N Sierra Leone, near Fr. Guinea border, 70 mi. NNE of Makeni; livestock station.

Musaiyib, Al, or **Al-Musayab** (äl mo͞osī'yäb), village, Hilla prov., central Iraq, on the Euphrates, on railroad, and 20 mi. NNW of Hilla, 5 mi. N of the point where the Euphrates divides into the Shatt Hilla and Shatt Hindiya; dates.

Musa Khel Bazar (mo͞o'sŭ kāl bäzär'), village, Loralai dist., NE Baluchistan, W Pakistan, 80 mi. NE of Loralai; wheat. Olives grown in Sulaiman Range (SE). Sometimes called Musakhel.

Musala, peak, Bulgaria: see STALIN PEAK.

Musala, Indonesia: see SIBOLGA.

Mus-Allah, peak, Bulgaria: see STALIN PEAK.

Musan (mo͞o'sän'), Jap. *Mosan*, town (1944 pop. 20,717), N.Hamgyong prov., N Korea, on Tumen R. (Manchuria line) and 60 mi. NW of Chongjin, in iron-mining area.

Musandam, Cape, Oman: see MASANDAM, CAPE.

Musa Qala (mo͞o'sŭ kŭ'lŭ), town (pop. over 2,000), Kandahar prov., S central Afghanistan, 40 mi. NNE of Girishk, and on right tributary of Helmand R., in outliers of the Hindu Kush.

Musa River or **Musha River,** Lettish *Mūša*, Lith. *Muša* (all: mo͞o'shä), left headstream of Lielupe R., in Lithuania and Latvia; rises W of Ioniskis, Lithuania; flows 112 mi. E and NNW, joining Memele R. at Bauska, Latvia, to form Lielupe R.

Musashi (mo͞osä'shē), former province in central Honshu, Japan; now Saitama prefecture and part of Kanagawa prefecture.

Musashi, town (pop. 4,696), Oita prefecture, NE Kyushu, Japan, on E Kunisaki Peninsula, 18 mi. NNE of Oita, on Iyo Sea; agr. and fishing center; sake.

Musashino (mo͞osä'shĭnō), residential town (pop. 63,479), Greater Tokyo, central Honshu, Japan, adjacent to Tokyo (E); agr. (wheat, sweet potatoes); raw silk.

Musawarat, ruins, Anglo-Egyptian Sudan: see WAD BAN NAGA.

Musayab, Al-, Iraq: see MUSAIYIB, AL.

Musaymir, Aden: see MUSEIMIR.

Muscat, Mascat, or **Masqat** (all: mŭs'kăt, măskăt'), town (pop. 4,200), ⊙ Oman sultanate, port on small Muscat Bay of Gulf of Oman, 110 mi. NW of Ras al Hadd (E cape of Arabian Peninsula) 23° 37'N 58° 35'E. Administrative center of Oman residence of sultan and British consul; British post and telegraph office; port of call of Persian Gul coastal navigation. Airfield at Bait al Falaj (SW) Isolated from interior by rugged hills, Muscat ha been eclipsed in commercial importance by it more accessible W suburb of MATRAH, which ha become the center of caravan routes. Pop. i largely Indian, Baluch, and Negro. Muscat be came important in early-16th cent., when it fel in 1508 to the Portuguese, and remained a nava station and trading post until mid-17th cent After the Portuguese loss (1622) of Hormuz Muscat was the last major Portuguese possessio on the Arabian coast. It was occupied by Persian in 1648 and by present ruling dynasty in 1741.

Muscat and Oman, sultanate: see OMAN.

Muscatatuck River (mŭskă'tŭtŭk"), S Ind., forme in W Jefferson co. by junction of small Grahar and Big creeks, flows c.50 mi. SW and W to Eas Fork of White R. 3 mi. S of Medora.

Muscatine (mŭskŭtēn'), county (□ 439; pop 32,148), SE Iowa, bounded SE by Mississippi R (forms Ill. line here); ⊙ Muscatine. Prairie ag area (hogs, cattle, poultry, grain, truck produce drained by Cedar R. Limestone; sand and grave pits; bituminous-coal deposits. Has state park Industry at Muscatine. Formed 1836.

Muscatine, city (pop. 19,041), ⊙ Muscatine co., S Iowa, on Mississippi R. (bridged here) and 25 m WSW of Davenport; mfg. and rail center noted fo its pearl-button industry (begun 1891), supplie by mussel shells from the river. Also produce button machinery, steel pulleys, pumps, casting metal cabinets, millwork, alcohol and fusel oi canned foods, meat and poultry. Has a jr. co Near by are Muscatine Isl. (bet. Mississippi I and one of its arms), noted for its fine melon and vegetables; and a fish hatchery (at Fairport and a state park. City was an early center of rive traffic and sawmilling. Settled as trading post i 1833; inc. 1839, reincorporated 1851.

Muscle Shoals, town (pop. 1,937), Colbert co., N Ala., on left bank of TENNESSEE RIVER opposi Florence. TVA industrial development (ou growth of U.S. nitrate plant built during Fir World War) is here; includes fertilizer-researc laboratories and chemical works producing pho phorus, phosphate ash, potash, ammonia, an monium nitrate, calcium carbide, lime, synthet rubber. Power is received from Wilson Da (just NE). Rapids (Muscle Shoals) in Tenness R. once extended 37 mi. upstream from Florenc had total fall of 134 ft., and were long an obstac to navigation; canalized in 1830s (unsuccessfully by state of Ala. and in 1890 by U.S. Army E gineers; submerged by reservoirs formed aft the construction of WILSON DAM and WHEELE DAM on the Tennessee.

Muscoda (mŭ'skŏdā), village (pop. 1,046), Gra co., SW Wis., on Wisconsin R. and 27 mi. NNE Lancaster, in livestock and dairy region; lumbe furniture, cheese.

Muscogee (mŭskō'gē), county (□ 220; pop. 118,028), W Ga.; ⊙ Columbus. Bounded W by Ala. line; drained by Chattahoochee R. Intersected by the fall line. Mfg. at Columbus; dairying, stock raising, truck farming. Fort Benning military reservation (S). Formed 1826.

Musconetcong, Lake (mŭs"kŭnĕt'kŏng), Sussex co., N N.J., small resort lake in hilly region, 7 mi. WNW of Dover; joined by Musconetcong R. to L. Hopatcong (just NW); state park here. SW is **Musconetcong Mountain** (alt. c.800–900 ft.), ridge of Appalachians; extends NE from Delaware R. near Riegelsville, paralleling on SE the fertile valley of **Musconetcong River,** which drains L. Musconetcong and L. Hopatcong in SE Sussex co. The river flows c.45 mi. SW to the Delaware at Riegelsville.

Muscongus Bay (mŭskŏng'gŭs), S Maine, bet. Pemaquid Point and Port Clyde; c.15 mi. across, 8 mi. deep.

Muscongus Island, Maine: see LOUDS ISLAND.

Muscotah (mŭ"skō'tŭ), city (pop. 248), Atchison co., NE Kansas, on Delaware R. and 21 mi. W of Atchison; diversified farming.

Muse (mōō'sē'), village, North Hsenwi state, Northern Shan State, Upper Burma, on Shweli R. (Chinese Yunnan prov. line) and 45 mi. N of Hsenwi, 9 mi. from Burma Road, on branch to Bhamo.

Muse (mūz), village (pop. 1,377), Washington co., SW Pa., 10 mi. NNE of Washington.

Museimir, Musemir, or **Musaymir** (all: mōōsā'mĭr), town, ⊙ Haushabi tribal area, Western Aden Protectorate, on road and 55 mi. NW of Aden, near Yemen border, on the Wadi Tiban; caravan center; agr. Sultan's residence. Airfield.

Muselim Remma (mōōsŭlĭm' rĕ'mŭ), arm of Aegean Sea bet. Lesbos isl. and Turkey; 10 mi. long, 6 mi. wide. Mythemna on SW shore. Connects E with Gulf of Edremit, SE with Mytilene Channel.

Musemir, Aden: see MUSEIMIR.

Museros (mōōsā'rōs), village (pop. 2,237), Valencia prov., E Spain, 8 mi. N of Valencia, in truck-farming area; vegetable canning.

Musgrave Ranges (mŭz'grāv), NW South Australia, extend 50 mi. E-W, parallel with Northern Territory border; rise to 4,970 ft. (Mt. Woodroffe; highest peak in state); granite. Aboriginal reservation in W part.

Mush, Turkey: see MUS.

Musha (mōō'shā), village (pop. 11,643), Asyut prov., central Upper Egypt, 7 mi. NW of Abu Tig; cereals, dates, sugar cane.

Mushabani, India: see MOSABONI.

Musharij, Am, Aden: see MASHARIJ, AM.

Musha River, Lithuania and Latvia: see MUSA RIVER.

Mushie (mōōsh'yā), village (1946 pop. c.3,200), Leopoldville prov., W Belgian Congo, on right bank of the Kwa, at mouth of Fimi R. and 130 mi. SW of Inongo; steamboat landing and trading center in sesame-growing region; rubber plantations in vicinity. R.C. mission.

Mushirouchi, Japan: see KOGA, Fukuoka.

Mushiru-kaikyo, Russian SFSR: see KRUZENSHTERN STRAIT.

Mushiru-retsugan, Russian SFSR: see LOVUSHKI ISLANDS.

Mushozu (mōōshō'zōō), town (pop. 6,077), on Ikishima, Nagasaki prefecture, Japan, on SW coast; chief town of isl.; agr. center.

Mushtuhur or **Mushtahir** (mōōsh'tähĭr), village (pop. 8,021), Qalyubiya prov., Lower Egypt, 20 mi. N of Cairo; cotton, flax, cereals, fruits.

Music Mountain, peak (6,761 ft.), Mohave co., NW Ariz., rises from tableland (c.6,000 ft.) at S end of Grand Wash Cliffs, 30 mi. NE of Kingman.

Musikot (mōōs'ĭkōt), village, S Nepal, near tributary of the Kali Gandaki, 35 mi. NNW of Butwal. Copper, bismuth, antimony, cobalt, sapphire, and ruby deposits near by.

Musinia Peak (mōōzĭ'nēŭ) (10,986 ft.), in Wasatch Plateau, central Utah, 16 mi. SSE of Manti.

Musiri (mōōs'ĭrĭ), town (pop. 9,167), Trichinopoly dist., S Madras, India, on Cauvery R. opposite Kulittalai (ferry) and 20 mi. WNW of Trichinopoly; rice, plantain, coconut palms; cotton textiles, wicker coracles.

Musi River (mōō'sē), in SE Hyderabad state, India, rises in isolated S hills of Deccan Plateau, near Vikarabad; flows E past Vikarabad and Hyderabad and S to Kistna R. 37 mi. SSE of Nalgonda; 180 mi. long; numerous irrigation canals.

Musi River or **Moesi River** (both: mōō'sē), S Sumatra, Indonesia, rises on Mt. Dempo in Barisan Mts., flows NNE, past Tebingtinggi, turns E to Palembang, thence N through extensive delta to Bangka Strait, 50 mi. N of Palembang; 325 mi. long. Navigable for ocean-going vessels below Palembang, and for river steamers for 180 mi. above its mouth.

Muskau or **Bad Muskau** (bät" mōō'skou), town (pop. 5,122) in former Prussian Lower Silesia prov., E Germany, after 1945 in Saxony, in Upper Lusatia, on the Lusatian Neisse and 15 mi. SSE of Forst; lignite mining; mfg. of glass, china, switch gear. Health resort. Has noted park. Captured (April, 1945) by Soviet forces.

Muskeget Channel (mŭs"kē'gĭt), SE Mass., separates Nantucket and its adjacent isls. from Martha's Vineyard; opens N on Nantucket Sound; c.7 mi. wide. Muskeget Isl. (c.1.5 mi. long) is just off NW tip of Tuckernuck Isl.

Muskego (mŭskē'gō) or **Muskego Center,** village (pop. 1,968), Waukesha co., SE Wis., 14 mi. SW of Milwaukee.

Muskegon (mŭskē'gŭn), county (□ 504; pop. 121,545), SW Mich.; ⊙ Muskegon. Bounded W by L. Michigan; drained by Muskegon and White rivers, and by small Crockery Creek. Agr. (livestock, poultry, fruit, beans, grain, truck; dairy products). Mfg. at Muskegon. Oil wells, refineries; commercial fisheries. Resorts. Has state park. Part of Manistee Natl. Forest is in N. Formed and organized 1859.

Muskegon, city (pop. 48,429), ⊙ Muskegon co., SW Mich., on L. Michigan and 35 mi. NW of Grand Rapids, at mouth of Muskegon R. (here forming L. Muskegon). Port of entry; important industrial and shipping center. Mfg. (castings, auto parts, aircraft, tools, wire, furniture, sporting equipment, paper and leather products, radios, phonographs); oil wells and refineries. Resort. Several parks, a jr. col., art gall. and Indian burial ground are here. Settled c.1810; inc. as village 1861, as city 1869. Was early center for fur trading, later (1837–c.1890) an important lumbering center.

Muskegon Heights, city (pop. 18,828), Muskegon co., SW Mich., suburb just S of Muskegon; machinery mfg. Inc. as village 1891, as city 1903.

Muskegon Lake, Mich.: see MUSKEGON RIVER.

Muskegon River, Mich., rises in Houghton L. in Roscommon co., flows 227 mi. SW, past Big Rapids and Newaygo, to Muskegon, widening to form Muskegon L. (c.5½ mi. long, 2½ mi. wide) just above its mouth on L. Michigan. Hardy Dam (earth fill; 120 ft. high above stream bed, 2,800 ft. long; completed 1932), a power dam, impounds Hardy Reservoir c.9 mi. SE of White Cloud.

Muski, India: see MASKI.

Muskingum (mŭskĭng'gŭm, mŭskĭng'ŭm), county (□ 667; pop. 74,535), central Ohio; ⊙ ZANESVILLE. Intersected by Muskingum and Licking rivers and small Salt and Jonathan creeks. Agr. (livestock; dairy products; fruit, grain); mfg. at Zanesville, Roseville. Coal mines, limestone quarries; sand, gravel, and clay pits. Formed 1804.

Muskingum River, central and SE Ohio, formed by junction of Walhonding and Tuscarawas rivers at Coshocton, flows c.112 mi. S, past Dresden (head of navigation), Zanesville, and McConnelsville, to the Ohio at Marietta. Receives Licking R. at Zanesville. Eleven locks and dams on river and 4 short lateral canals afford navigation; 14 dams for flood control on the Muskingum were built (1935–41) on tributaries.

Muskogee (mŭskō'gē), county (□ 822; pop. 65,573), E Okla.; ⊙ MUSKOGEE. Bounded N by Arkansas R., S by Canadian R. Agr. (cotton, corn, livestock, potatoes, grain; dairy products). Mfg., processing at Muskogee. Oil and natural-gas fields. Includes Fort Gibson Natl. Cemetery and Fort Gibson Dam. Formed 1907.

Muskogee, city (pop. 37,289), ⊙ Muskogee co., E Okla., 45 mi. SE of Tulsa, near Arkansas R.; 3d largest city in state, and railroad and trade center for area producing potatoes, livestock, cotton, grain, and oil. Oil refining, meat packing, flour milling. Also mfg. of oil-well supplies, feed, glass, iron, brick, leather, canvas goods; truck, wagon, and trailer bodies; clothing, furniture, brooms, mattresses, monuments. Railroad shops. Here are a U.S. veterans' hosp. and memorial park, agency hq. for the Five Civilized Tribes, a state school for the blind, and Muskogee Jr. Col. Near by are Bacone Jr. Col (at Bacone) and Fort Gibson Natl. Cemetery. Settled 1872, inc. 1898; made a Federal Indian agency in 1874. Adopted city-manager govt., 1920.

Muskoka (mŭskō'kŭ), district (□ 1,585; pop. 21,835), S Ont., on Georgian Bay of L. Huron; ⊙ Bracebridge.

Muskoka, Lake (15 mi. long, 5 mi. wide), S Ont., 30 mi. SE of Parry Sound. Drained W by Muskoka R. into Georgian Bay. It is one of the Muskoka Lakes (which also include Rosseau L., L. Joseph, and L. of Bays) in a popular resort region of forests, ponds, and rivers, drained by Muskoka R. into Georgian Bay (W).

Muskoka River, S Ont., rises in Algonquin Provincial Park in 2 branches which unite at Bracebridge (waterfalls near by), thence flows W through L. Muskoka to Georgian Bay 25 mi. S of Parry Sound; 120 mi. long. Drains Muskoka lake region.

Muskwa (mŭ'skwŭ), village, NE B.C., on Muskwa R. at mouth of Prophet R., on Alaska Highway, and 5 mi. W of Fort Nelson; lumbering.

Muskwa River, NE B.C., rises in Stikine Mts. near 57°45'N 124°50'W, flows 160 mi. generally NE to confluence with Sikanni Chief R. at Fort Nelson, forming Fort Nelson R.

Muslyumovo (mōōslyōō'mŭvŭ), village (1939 pop. over 2,000), E Tatar Autonomous SSR, Russian SFSR, on Ik R. and 28 mi. SSE of Menzelinsk; grain, legumes, livestock.

Musmar (mōōsmär'), village, Kassala prov., NE Anglo-Egyptian Sudan, on railroad and 120 mi. ENE of Atbara.

Musoma (mōōsō'mä), town, Lake Prov., N Tanganyika, port on SE shore of L. Victoria, at mouth of Mara R., 95 mi. NE of Mwanza; center of gold-mining dist. Cotton, peanuts, coffee, sisal; livestock; fisheries. Airfield. Prison.

Musone River (mōōzô'nĕ), The Marches, central Italy, rises in the Apennines 4 mi. E of Matelica, flows 45 mi. ENE to the Adriatic 3 mi. NE of Loreto.

Musonoi (mōōsōnoi'), village, Katanga prov., SE Belgian Congo, on railroad and 3 mi. W of Kolwezi; copper-mining center; also palladium, platinum, and cobalt mining; cattle raising.

Musquacook Lakes (mŭskwô'kŏŏk), Piscataquis and Aroostook counties, N Maine, 13-mi. chain of 5 lakes (First to Fifth Musquacook lakes), c.58 mi. W of Presque Isle; drain N, through **Musquacook Stream,** into Allagash R.

Musquash Lake (mŭs'kwŏsh), Washington co., E Maine, 29 mi. NW of Calais, in hunting, fishing area; 2.5 mi. long. West Musquash L. (3.5 mi. long) is 4 mi. SW.

Musquodoboit Harbour (mŭ"skōdŏ'bĭt), village (pop. estimate 500), S N.S., at head of an inlet of the Atlantic, at mouth of Musquodoboit R., 25 mi. ENE of Halifax; lumbering, salmon and trout fishing.

Musquodoboit River, central N.S., rises in Cobequid Mts. NW of Sheet Harbour, flows 60 mi. SW and S to the Atlantic 22 mi. E of Halifax.

Mussa Ali (mōō'sä ä'lē), volcanic mtn. (6,768 ft.) at S extremity of Danakil mts., near junction of Eritrea, Ethiopia, and Fr. Somaliland borders, 55 mi. SW of Assab. Also written Mussaali.

Mussau (mōōsou') or **Saint Matthias Islands** (mŭthī'ŭs), island group (pop. c.1,700), New Ireland dist., Bismarck Archipelago, Territory of New Guinea, SW Pacific, 100 mi. NW of New Ireland; 1°24'S 149°38'E. There are 2 volcanic isls., Mussau (□ c.160) and Emirau (□ 20); several coral islets. Coconut plantations; canoe building, handicraft.

Mussbach (mōōs'bäkh), village (pop. 3,062), Rhenish Palatinate, W Germany, at E foot of Hardt Mts., 2 mi. NE of Neustadt; aluminum works; wine making.

Musselburgh (mŭ'sŭlbŭrŭ), burgh (1931 pop. 17,007; 1951 census 17,012), NE Midlothian, Scotland, on Firth of Forth at mouth of Esk R., 6 mi. E of Edinburgh; seaside resort with golf links and race course; also paper milling, brewing, and net making. Has 16th-cent. tolbooth prison, anc. market cross and bridge, Loretto School (public school on site of 16th-cent. shrine), and Pinkie House, noted Jacobean mansion. There is monument to D. M. Moir. Burgh includes fishing district of Fisherrow (W) and DUDDINGSTON.

Musselshell, county (□ 1,886; pop. 5,408), central Mont.; ⊙ Roundup. Agr. region drained by Musselshell R. Livestock, grain, coal. Formed 1911.

Musselshell River, central Mont., rises in several branches in Crazy Mts., flows 292 mi. E and N, past Harlowton and Roundup, to Fort Peck Reservoir in Missouri R.; not navigable.

Mussidan (mŭsēdā'), town (pop. 2,750), Dordogne dept., SW France, on the Isle and 14 mi. NNW of Bergerac; road and rail center; mfg. (window blinds, shutters, locks, footwear, candles, cement); cotton weaving.

Mussolinia di Sardegna, Sardinia: see ARBOREA.

Mussomeli (mōōs"sômä'lē), town (pop. 13,861), Caltanissetta prov., central Sicily, 19 mi. WNW of Caltanissetta. Sulphur and rock salt mines are W. Restored 14th-cent. castle near by.

Musson (mŭsõ'), town (pop. 1,845), Luxembourg prov., SE Belgium, in the Ardennes, 10 mi. SSW of Arlon; blast furnaces.

Mussoorie (mŭs'ōōrē), town (pop. 5,966), Dehra Dun dist., N Uttar Pradesh, India, in W Kumaun Himalaya foothills, 9 mi. N of Dehra; noted hill resort; breweries.

Mussy-sur-Seine (mŭsē"-sŭr-sĕn'), village (pop. 1,252), Aube dept., NE central France, on Seine R. and 9 mi. NNW of Châtillon-sur-Seine; lumbering. Has 13th–15th-cent. church.

Musta, Malta: see MOSTA.

Mustadfors (mŭ"städfôrs', -fôsh'), village (pop. 1,051), Alvsborg co., SW Sweden, on Dalsland Canal (locks), 16 mi. SW of Amal; pulp and paper milling, shoe mfg., metalworking. Hydroelectric station.

Mustafa Kemalpasa (mōōstäfä' kĕmäl'pä-shä"), Turk. *Mustafa Kemalpaşa,* town (1950 pop. 15,273), Bursa prov., NW Turkey, on Kirmasti R. and 35 mi. WSW of Bursa; grain; lignite deposits. Formerly Kirmasti.

Mustafa Kemalpasa River, Turkey: see KIRMASTI RIVER.

Mustafa-Pasha, Bulgaria: see SVILENGRAD.

Mustahil (mōōs'tähĭl), village (pop. 700), Harar prov., SE Ethiopia, on the Webi Shebeli, on road, and 45 mi. SE of Callafo, in camel- and sheep-raising region.

Mustang, town (pop. 210), Canadian co., central Okla., 13 mi. WSW of Oklahoma City.

Mustang Creek, N.Mex. and Texas: see RITA BLANCA CREEK.

Mustang Island, S Texas, barrier isl. (c.15 mi. long, 1–4 mi. wide) across entrance to Corpus Christi Bay, 17 mi. E of Corpus Christi. Port Aransas is on Aransas Pass, at NE end; narrow channel separates isl. from Padre Isl. (S).

Mustang Mountain (10,316 ft.), SW Nev., in N White Mts., near Calif. line, 60 mi. WNW of Goldfield.

Mustasaari, Finland: see KORSHOLM.

Mustayevo (mōōstī'ūvŭ), village (1939 pop. over 500), SW Chkalov oblast, Russian SFSR, on right tributary of Ural R. and 19 mi. N of Ilek; wheat, livestock. Until c.1940, Mustayevka.

Mustèr, Switzerland: see DISENTIS.

Musters, Lake, large fresh-water lake (□ 167.5; alt. 890 ft.) in Patagonian highlands, central Comodoro Rivadavia military zone, Argentina, just NW of Sarmiento, 6 mi. W of L. Colhué Huapí (linked by short stream); 26 mi. long, 3–8 mi. wide. Receives Senguerr R.

Mustiala (mōōs'tēä"lä), locality, Häme co., SW Finland, in lake region, 5 mi. E of Forssa; site of agr. school.

Mustinka River, rises near Fergus Falls, W Minn., flows 80 mi. S and W, through several small lakes, to NE end of L. Traverse, on S.Dak. line, 8 mi. SW of Wheaton.

Mustique Island (mŭstēk', mū–), islet (□ 2; pop. 110 including, just N, Baliceaux and Battowia isls.), N Grenadines, dependency of St. Vincent, B.W.I., 20 mi. S of Kingstown; 12°53'N 61°11'W. Sea-island cotton growing.

Mustla (mōōst'lä), Ger. *Tarvast*, city (pop. 943), S Estonia, near W shore of L. Vortsjarv, 13 mi. SE of Viljandi; agr. market; flax, orchards, sheep, poultry.

Mustoh (mōōs'tō), village, Khasi and Jaintia Hills dist., W Assam, India, in Khasi Hills, 29 mi. SW of Shillong; rice, cotton. Coal deposits near by.

Mustvee (mōōst'vā), city (pop. 2,841), E Estonia, port on NW shore of L. Peipus, 40 mi. SE of Rakvere, in flax area; rail terminus; sawmilling.

Musún (mōōsōōn'), highest peak (5,600 ft.) of Cordillera Dariense, central Nicaragua, 30 mi. ENE of Matiguás.

Muswellbrook (mŭs'wŭlbrōōk), municipality (pop. 3,939), E New South Wales, Australia, on Hunter R. and 65 mi. NW of Newcastle; rail junction; coal-mining center.

Muswell Hill, England: see HORNSEY.

Muszyna (mōō-shĭ'nä), town (pop. 2,367), Krakow prov., S Poland, in the Carpathians, on Poprad R. and 5 mi. SSW of Krynica, near Czechoslovak border; rail junction; health resort. Large linden forest near by.

Mut (mōōt), village (pop. 2,529) in Dakhla oasis, S central Egypt, in Southern Desert prov., 16 mi. SSE of El Qasr; dates, oranges, wheat, barley.

Mut (mōōt), village (pop. 2,694), Icel prov., S Turkey, near Goksu R., 65 mi. W of Mersin; wheat, barley, sesame, beans, onions. Some anc. ruins.

Mutagacha (mōōtŭgä'chŭ), town (pop. 7,887), Mymensingh dist., central East Bengal, E Pakistan, 9 mi. W of Mymensingh; rice, jute, oilseeds.

Mutambara (mōōtämbä'rä), village, Umtali prov., E Southern Rhodesia, in Mashonaland, in Chimanimani Mts., on road and 23 mi. NW of Melsetter, near Mozambique border; corn, wheat, tobacco, livestock.

Mutankiang or **Mu-tan-chiang** (both: mōō'dän'-jyäng'), city (1946 pop. 200,319), S Sungkiang prov., Manchuria, on Chinese Eastern RR and 170 mi. ESE of Harbin; industrial and rail center, in rich lumbering region; sawmilling, pulp and paper mfg., machinery mfg., flour milling, soybean pressing. Formerly a small village, it owes its original development to the construction (1903) of the Chinese Eastern RR; it reached a pop. of 35,000 in 1931. While in Manchukuo, it boomed again through further rail construction and economic development; became an independent municipality in 1937 and was ⊙ Mutankiang prov. (□ 12,730; 1940 pop. 688,424) during 1937–43. After Second World War, it was briefly (1946–49) ⊙ Sungkiang prov. under the Nationalists.

Mutan River, Chinese *Mutan Kiang* or *Mutan Chiang* (both mōō'dän' jyäng'), Manchu *Hurka*, E Manchuria, rises in highlands 30 mi. SW of Tunhwa, flows 415 mi. NNE, past Tunhwa, through Kingpo L. (hydroelectric station), past Ningan (Ninguta) and Mutankiang, to Sungari R. at Ilan (Sansing). Unnavigable because of swift current and rapids; frozen Nov.–April.

Mutarara (mōōtärä'rä), village, Manica and Sofala prov., central Mozambique, on the Zambezi (left bank) and 170 mi. N of Beira. Bet. here and Sena (on right bank), the Trans-Zambezia RR (serving Nyasaland) crosses Zambezi R. on a steel bridge (12,064 ft. long; opened 1935). Airfield.

Mutha Mula River (mōō'tŭ mōō'lŭ), central Bombay, India, rises in Western Ghats in 2 headstreams joining at Poona, flows c.80 mi. E to Bhima R. 17 mi. NW of Dhond. Dam on N headstream (Mula R.) supplies Bhira hydroelectric plant. Dam on S headstream (Mutha R.) supplies canal irrigation system, with headworks 7 mi. SW of Poona; left (N) canal extends 18 mi. NE, right (S) canal 70 mi. E to point 8 mi. WNW of Dhond.

Muthill (mū'thĭl), agr. village and parish (pop. 1,212), S Perthshire, Scotland, near Earn R., 3 mi. S of Crieff. Has 15th-cent. church. Near by are remains of Drummond Castle (1491) with famous gardens.

Muthupet, India: see MUTTUPET.

Muti'a, El, or **Al-Muti'ah** (both: ĕl mōō'tēū), village (pop. 10,530), Asyut prov., central Upper Egypt, on W bank of the Nile and 6 mi. N of Abu Tig; cereals, dates, sugar cane.

Mutiko (mōōtē'kō), village, Kivu prov., E Belgian Congo, 42 mi. NW of Costermansville; tin-mining center; tantalite and wolfram mining in vicinity. Tin mines of Muhulu (mōōhōō'lōō) 30 mi. NW.

Mutina, Italy: see MODENA, city.

Mutis or **Ciudad Mutis** (syōōdädh' mōō'tēs), village, Chocó dept., W Colombia, on inlet of the Pacific (Solano Bay), 60 mi. NW of Quibdó; corn, fruit. Agr. settlement founded by the state in 1935.

Mutis, Mount, or **Mount Moetis** (both: mōōtĭs'), highest peak (7,759 ft.) of Indonesian Timor, in W part of isl., 60 mi. NE of Kupang. Also Mutus.

Mutki (mōōtkē'), village (pop. 500), Bitlis prov., SE Turkey, 10 mi. WNW of Bitlis; millet. Also called Hur and Mirtag.

Mutsamudu (mōōtsämōō'dōō), chief town and outlet of Anjouan Isl., in Comoro Isls., on wide bay on NW coast; 12°12'S 45°23'E. Coffee and vanilla plantations. Of curious Arab architecture, it has a 17th-cent. mosque and has been seat of sultans of Anjouan since early 19th cent.

Mutsu (mōō'tsōō), former province in N Honshu, Japan; now Aomori prefecture.

Mutsu Bay, Jap. *Mutsu-wan*, inlet of Tsugaru Strait, Aomori prefecture, N Honshu, Japan; merges W with Aomori Bay; 25 mi. long.

Mutsuji, Japan: see URAWA.

Muttenz (mōō'tĕnts), town (pop. 5,929), Basel-Land half-canton, N Switzerland, 3 mi. SSE of Basel; chemicals, pastry; woodworking. Medieval church.

Mutterstadt (mōō'tūr-shtät), village (pop. 6,115), Rhenish Palatinate, W Germany, 5 mi. SW of Ludwigshafen; wine; grain, tobacco, sugar beets.

Muttler (mōōt'lūr), peak (10,820 ft.) in Rhaetian Alps, E Switzerland, 5 mi. NW of Swiss-Austrian-Italian border.

Mutton Bird Islands, volcanic group in Tasman Sea, 1.5 mi. off SW coast of Stewart Isl., New Zealand. Comprise 7 isls., with Long Isl. (3 mi. long, 1.5 mi. wide) largest; many scattered islets. Mountainous; numerous petrels. Isls. owned by Maori families. Sometimes called Titi Isls.

Mutton Island. 1 Islet (185 acres; 1½ mi. long) in Mal Bay, W Co. Clare, Ireland, 3 mi. SW of Spanish Point. According to legend isl. was severed from mainland c.800 by a storm. Ruins of oratory of St. Senan. **2** Islet in Galway Bay, Co. Galway, Ireland, just S of Galway; lighthouse (53°15'N 9°4'W).

Muttontown, village (pop. 382), Nassau co., SE N.Y., on NW Long Isl., just SE of Glen Cove, in summer-resort area.

Muttra (mōōt'trŭ), since 1948 officially **Mathura** (mŭ'tōōrŭ), district (□ 1,447; pop. 806,897), W Uttar Pradesh (Agra), India; ⊙ Muttra. On Ganges-Jumna Doab (E); irrigated by Agra and Upper Ganges canals. Agr.: gram, jowar, wheat, barley, cotton, mustard, pearl millet, sesame, sugar cane, corn. Main centers: Muttra, Brindaban, Kosi, Chhata, and pilgrimage centers of Mahaban, Gokul, Baldeo, and Gopbardhan. Numerous places here connected with Krishna legend.

Muttra, since 1948 officially **Mathura,** city (pop., including cantonment, 80,532), ⊙ Muttra dist., W Uttar Pradesh, India, on the Jumna and 30 mi. NW of Agra. Rail and road junction; trade center (gram, jowar, wheat, cotton, oilseeds, sugar cane); mfg. (chemicals, noted calico prints), saltpeter processing. Regarded as one of 7 most sacred Hindu centers in India. Has col. and Curyon Mus. of Archaeology (opened 1933) with noted collection of anc. sculptures of Muttra school and inscriptions found here. First representation of Buddha as a human figure discovered here. Several mosques, including Jami Masjid (built 1661) and one built by Aurangzeb over a noted Hindu temple (in turn erected over a Buddhist monastery) were destroyed by Aurangzeb (17th cent.) during his demolition of chief Hindu temples for which city was famed. Traditionally celebrated as birthplace of Krishna. In Kushan times (2d cent. A.D.) a Buddhist and Jain stronghold. Visited (5th cent. A.D.) by Fa Hian, while still a Buddhist center, and (A.D. 634) by Hsüan-tsang. Plundered by Mahmud of Ghazni (1018) and by Silandar Lodi (1500), great harm being done to the temples. Called Modoura by Ptolemy, Methora by Arrian and Pliny. Vegetable-ghee processing at village of Maholi, 3 mi. SW of city center.

Muttupet or **Mutupet** (both: mōōt'ōōpāt), town (pop. 7,798), Tanjore dist., SE Madras, India, port (6 mi. inland; served by distributary of Vennar R.) of Palk Strait, 35 mi. SE of Tanjore, 8 mi. NE of Adirampatnam; exports rice. Also Muthupet.

Mutual. 1 Village (pop. 178), Champaign co., W central Ohio, 6 mi. ESE of Urbana. **2** Town (pop. 130), Woodward co., NW Okla., 19 mi. SE of Woodward, in livestock and grain area.

Mutubis (mōōtōō'bĭs), town (pop. 6,732; with suburbs, 7,917), Gharbiya prov., Lower Egypt, on Rosetta branch of the Nile, on railroad, and 7 mi. NNW of Fuwa; cotton.

Mutum or **Mutún** (both: mōōtōōn'), military post, Santa Cruz dept., E Bolivia, near Brazil border, 15 mi. SSW of Puerto Suárez.

Mutum (mōōtōōn'), city (pop. 2,053), E Minas Gerais, Brazil, near Espírito Santo border, 30 mi. SW of Aimorés; tobacco, coffee, cattle. Until 1939, São Manuel do Mutum.

Mutupet, India: see MUTTUPET.

Mutus, Mount, Timor: see MUTIS, MOUNT.

Mutwal (mōōtväl'), section (pop. 13,440) of Colombo, Western Prov., Ceylon, 2.5 mi. NE of city center; fishing center.

Mutwanga (mōōtwäng'gä), village, Kivu prov., E Belgian Congo, at W foot of the Ruwenzori, near Uganda border, 25 mi. ESE of Beni; tourist center in Semliki section of Albert Natl. Park and point of departure for ascents of the Ruwenzori.

Mutzig (müzĕg', Ger. mōōt'sĭkh), town (pop. 2,460), Bas-Rhin dept., E France, on the Bruche and 2 mi. W of Molsheim; industrial center mfg. machines, hardware, textiles, beer.

Mutzschen (mōō'chŭn), town (pop. 1,927), Saxony, E central Germany, 8 mi. E of Grimma, in lignite-mining region; ceramics mfg.

Muvattupula (mōō'vŭtōōpōōlŭ), town (pop. 9,079), N Travancore, India, 27 mi. N of Kottayam; trades in rice, cassava, coir rope and mats. Also spelled Muvatupuzha.

Muveran, Grand (grã müvùrä'), peak (10,043 ft.) in Bernese Alps, SW Switzerland, 11 mi. W of Sion. The Petit Muveran (9,250 ft.) is SSE.

Muwaih or **Muwayh** (mōōwā'), village, W Nejd, Saudi Arabia, 150 mi. NE of Mecca and on main highway to Riyadh. Also spelled Al Mowai.

Muwailih or **Al Muwailih** (ăl mōōwā'lē), village, N Hejaz, Saudi Arabia, minor port on Madian coast of Red Sea, 100 mi. SSE of Aqaba; 27°40'N 35°30'E. Bedouin trade center. Also spelled Muwaila.

Muwayh, Saudi Arabia: see MUWAIH.

Muxadabad, India: see MURSHIDABAD, town.

Muxima (mōōshē'mä), village (pop. 143), Congo prov., NW Angola, on left bank of Cuanza R. and 70 mi. SE of Luanda; oil palms.

Muxupip (mōō-shōōpēp'), town (pop. 805), Yucatan, SE Mexico, 20 mi. ENE of Mérida; henequen.

Muy, Le (lù mwē'), town (pop. 2,017), Var dept., SE France, on the Argens and 7 mi. SE of Draguignan; cork processing, fruit shipping; sericulture. Captured by Allied airborne troops (Aug., 1944) in Second World War.

Muya (mōō'yä), city and port (1940 pop. 17,228; 1947 pop. 43,020), Tokushima prefecture, NE Shikoku, Japan, on Naruto Strait, 6 mi. NNE of Tokushima; salt-producing center; fish, clams. Exports sake, magnesium, *tabi*. Kite festival held here annually since 17th cent. Since 1947, includes former towns of Naruto (pop. 6,713), Seto (pop. 7,222), and Satoura (pop. 4,817).

Muy Muy (mwē mwē'), town (1950 pop. 789), Matagalpa dept., central Nicaragua, 30 mi. ESE of Matagalpa; coffee, livestock.

Muynak, Uzbek SSR: see MUINAK.

Muyondzi, Fr. Equatorial Africa: see MOUYONDZI.

Muysen, Belgium: see MUIZEN.

Muyumba (mōōyōōm'bä), village, Katanga prov., SE Belgian Congo, on Lualaba R. and 175 mi. SW of Albertville; transshipment point (steamer-rail) for MANONO tin-mining area. Site of Protestant mission.

Muyuni (mōōyōō'nē), village, S Zanzibar, on road and 23 mi. SE of Zanzibar town; rice growing.

Muyun-Kum (mōōyōōn"-kōōm'), sandy desert, Dzhambul oblast, Kazakh SSR; extends S of Chu R. and E of the Kara-Tau; average alt. 1,000 ft.; sheep, camels.

Muyupampa, Bolivia: see VACA GUZMÁN.

Muzaffarabad (mōōzŭf'fŭrābäd"), district (□ 2,408; pop. 264,671), Kashmir prov., W Kashmir; ⊙ Muzaffarabad. In W Punjab Himalayas; bounded W by North-West Frontier Prov., W Pakistan; drained by Jhelum and Kishanganga rivers. Agr. (corn, rice, wheat, barley, oilseeds, pulse); ochre and lead deposits near Uri, limestone deposits near Rampur. Main towns: Muzaffarabad, Uri. Largely occupied by Pakistan, except for small E area. Prevailing mother tongues, Pahari and Panjabi. Pop. 92% Moslem, 7% Hindu.

Muzaffarabad, town (pop. 4,571), ⊙ Muzaffarabad dist., W Kashmir, in W Punjab Himalayas, on Jhelum R., at Kishanganga R. mouth, and 21 mi. NNE of Abbottabad; trades in grain, oilseeds. Damaged in fighting (1947), during India-Pakistan struggle for control.

Muzaffargarh (–gŭr), district (□ 5,605; 1951 pop. 761,000), SW Punjab, W Pakistan; ⊙ Muzaffargarh. In S Sind-Sagar Doab, bet. Indus R. (W), Chenab R. (E), and Panjnad R. (S). S section is alluvial tract (wheat, millet, rice, sugar cane) subject to periodic floods; N section consists mostly of low sand hills (S Thal region). Dates, mangoes widely cultivated; hand-loom weaving, camel and sheep grazing. Chief towns: Leiah, Muzaffargarh, Kot Adu.

Muzaffargarh, town (pop. 8,265), ⊙ Muzaffargarh dist., SW Punjab, W Pakistan, near Chenab R., 15 mi. SW of Multan; trades in grain, mangoes, dates, timber, ghee, indigo; cotton ginning, rice husking, hand-loom, palm-mat, basket weaving; sawmills.

Muzaffarnagar (–nŭg″ŭr), district (□ 1,682; pop. 1,056,759), N Uttar Pradesh, India; ⊙ Muzaffarnagar. On Ganges-Jumna Doab; irrigated by Eastern Jumna and Upper Ganges canals; dhak jungle in NW. Agr. (wheat, gram, sugar cane, oilseeds, corn, rice, barley, cotton); a leading sugar-processing dist. of India. Main towns: Muzaffarnagar, Kairana, Kandhla, Shamli.

Muzaffarnagar, town (pop. 46,758), ⊙ Muzaffarnagar dist., N Uttar Pradesh, India, on railroad and 60 mi. NE of Delhi; road junction; trade center (wheat, gram, sugar cane, oilseeds); sugar processing, cotton ginning, blanket mfg. Founded c.1633. Hydroelectric station (4,000 kw.) 11 mi. ENE, at village of Nirgajni.

Muzaffarpur (–po͝or), district (□ 3,025; pop. 3,244,651), N Bihar, India, in Tirhut div.; ⊙ Muzaffarpur. On Ganges Plain; bounded N by Nepal, W by Gandak R., S by the Ganges; drained by tributaries of the Ganges. Alluvial soil; rice, wheat, barley, corn, tobacco, sugar cane, cotton, oilseeds. Rice and sugar milling, cattle raising; hides. Main trade centers: Muzaffarpur, Hajipur. Buddhist pilgrimage center near Lalganj.

Muzaffarpur, city (pop., including cantonment, 54,139), ⊙ Tirhut div. and Muzaffarpur dist., N Bihar, India, on Ganges Plain, on Burhi Gandak R. and 39 mi. NNE of Patna; rail and road junction; river trade; rice, wheat, barley, corn, tobacco, sugar cane, oilseeds; rice and sugar milling, cutlery mfg. Has col.

Muzambinho (mo͞ozämbē'nyo͞o), city (pop. 4,561), SW Minas Gerais, Brazil, near São Paulo border, on railroad and 14 mi. ESE of Guaxupé; alt. 3,500 ft. Coffeegrowing, cattle raising.

Muzart (mo͞ozärt'), village, NW Sinkiang prov., China, in the Tien Shan, near USSR border, 90 mi. SSW of Kuldja, near Tenges R. (headstream of the Ili). Just S is **Muzart Pass** (11,480 ft.), in the central Tien Shan, on whose S slopes rises the Muzart R., a left affluent of the Tarim.

Muzhi (mo͞o'zhē), village (1939 pop. under 500), W Yamal-Nenets Natl. Okrug, Tyumen oblast, Russian SFSR, on left arm of Ob R. and 90 mi. SSW of Salekhard; reindeer raising.

Muzhichi, Russian SFSR: see Pervomaiskoye, Grozny oblast.

Muzillac (müzēyäk'), village (pop. 1,245), Morbihan dept., W France, near mouth of Vilaine R., 14 mi. ESE of Vannes; paper milling, woodworking.

Muzo (mo͞o'sō), village (pop. 362), Boyacá dept., central Colombia, in W foothills of Cordillera Oriental, 20 mi. WSW of Chiquinquirá; alt. 4,068 ft. Famed for emerald mines. Coffee, cattle.

Muzoka (mo͞ozō'kä), township (pop. 38), Southern Prov., Northern Rhodesia, on railroad and 23 mi. NE of Choma; tobacco, wheat, corn.

Muzon, Cape (mo͞o'zŏn), SE Alaska, S tip of Dall Isl., Alexander Archipelago, in Dixon Entrance, 60 mi. SW of Ketchikan; 54°40'N 132°41'W; southernmost point of Alaska Territory.

Múzquiz, Ciudad Melchor Múzquiz, or **Melchor Múzquiz** (syo͞odädh' mělchôr' mo͞o'skēs), city (pop. 7,040), Coahuila, N Mexico, 170 mi. NW of Monterrey; rail terminus; mining (coal, silver, gold, lead, zinc) and agr. center (grain, cattle).

Muztagh (mo͞oztäg', mo͞ostä'), peak (23,890 ft.) in the Kunlun mts., S Sinkiang prov., China, near Kashmir border; 35°56'N 80°14'E. Formerly called K^5, it was regarded as highest peak of Kunlun mts. until discovery of the Ulugh Muztagh.

Muztagh Ata Range (ätä'), westernmost Sinkiang prov., China, extends 200 mi. NNW-SSE parallel to E edge of the Pamir; rises to 25,146 ft. in the Kungur Massif, 70 mi. SW of Kashgar. The peak Muztagh Ata (24,388 ft.) is 95 mi. SW of Kashgar. Sometimes called Kashgar Range and Bolor Tagh.

Muztagh-Karakoram, range, Kashmir: see Karakoram.

Muztor (mo͞ostôr'), town (1945 pop. over 2,000), N Dzhalal-Abad oblast, Kirghiz SSR, near Naryn R., 60 mi. N of Dzhalal-Abad; economic center of Ketmen-Tyube valley, in cotton area; cotton ginning; cottonseed-oil press. Originally called Akchi-Karasu; named Toktogul (1940–44).

M'Vouti (ŭmvo͞otē'), village, S Middle Congo territory, Fr. Equatorial Africa, on railroad and 60 mi. NE of Pointe-Noire; hardwood lumbering center.

Mwadingusha or **Mwadingusha-Lipushi** (mwädĭng-go͞o'shä-lĭpo͞o'shē), village (1948 pop. 8.005), Katanga prov., SE Belgian Congo, on Lufira R. and 35 mi. NE of Jadotville. Site of leading hydroelectric power station of Belgian Congo, with reservoir (□ c.25) and dam. Mwadingusha plant is the oldest of the colony and supplies most of energy needs of copper industry of Katanga. It is also known as Cornet Falls, Fr. *Chutes-Cornet*. Additional hydroelectric installations are being built at Koni, 5 mi. N.

Mwadui (mwädo͞o'ē), village, Lake Prov., NW Tanganyika, 15 mi. NE of Shinyanga (rail spur); noted Williamson diamond mine discovered here, 1940.

Mwakete (mwäkĕ'tä), village, Southern Highlands prov., S Tanganyika, in Kipengere Range, 35 mi. W of Njombe; wheat, tea, coffee.

Mwanza (mwän'zä), village, Katanga prov., SE Belgian Congo, near Lualaba R., 125 mi. NE of Kamina. Protestant mission.

Mwanza, center in native village area, Southern Prov., Nyasaland, near Mozambique border, on road and 35 mi. WNW of Blantyre; police and customs station; cotton, tobacco.

Mwanza, town (pop. 11,296), ⊙ Lake Prov., NW Tanganyika, on S shore of L. Victoria and 175 mi. N of Tabora, with which it is linked by rail; rail-steamer transfer point for shipment of cotton, peanuts, rice to lake ports in Uganda and Kenya. Medical training center. Gold mining in Geita area (50 mi. SW) and in Musoma dist. (80 mi. NE). Diamond mines at Misungwi (25 mi. SSE) and in Shinyanga dist. (90 mi. SSE).

Mwatati (mwätä'tē), village, Coast prov., SE Kenya, on railroad and 18 mi. WSW of Voi; sisal, coffee, tea, corn. Also spelled Mwatate.

Mwaya (mwä'yä), village, Southern Highlands prov., S Tanganyika, small port at N tip of L. Nyasa, 30 mi. SE of Tukuyu; ships tea, coffee, rice.

Mweelrea, Ireland: see Muilrea.

Mweenish or **Minish,** island (613 acres; 2 mi. long) in Galway Bay, at entrance to Kilkieran Bay, SW Co. Galway, Ireland, 14 mi. SW of Clifden.

Mweka (mwĕ'kä), village, Kasai prov., central Belgian Congo, on railroad and 40 mi. NNE of Luebo; trading center for Bakuba tribe; also cotton center. Rubber plantations near by.

Mwene Ditu (mwĕ'nä dē'to͞o), village, Kasai prov., central Belgian Congo, on railroad and 90 mi. SW of Kabinda; sawmilling, cotton ginning.

Mwenga (mwĕng'gä), village, Kivu prov., E Belgian Congo, 45 mi. SW of Costermansville, in tin-mining area.

Mwera (mwĕ'rä), town, central Zanzibar, on road and 7 mi. E of Zanzibar town; cloves, copra.

Mweru, Lake (mwĕ'ro͞o), Fr. *Moero* (mwĕ'rō), lake (□ 173), central Africa, on Northern Rhodesia–Belgian Congo border; c.70 mi. long, 30 mi. wide, 30–50 ft. deep; alt. 3,025 ft. Receives Luapula R. (S). Luvua R. issues from its N end. Extensive swamps adjoin E and S. Navigated by small steamboats and barges. Large fisheries. Main ports: Kilwa and Pweto (Belgian Congo). L. Mweru is sometimes considered an expansion of Luvua-Luapula river system, which represents E headstream of the Congo. Region explored by Livingstone.

Mweru-Luapula, former prov., Northern Rhodesia: see Fort Rosebery.

Mwinilunga (mwēnēlo͝ong'gä), township (pop. 145), Western Prov., NW Northern Rhodesia, 150 mi. NW of Kasempa; beeswax; corn, millet; hardwood. Transferred 1946 from Kaonde-Lunda prov.

Mwirasandu (mwērasän'do͞o), village, Western Prov., SW Uganda, 30 mi. SE of Mbarara; tin-mining center. Sometimes spelled Mrirasandu.

Mwomboshi (mwōmbō'shē), township (pop. c.350), Central Prov., Northern Rhodesia, on railroad and 30 mi. S of Broken Hill; tobacco, wheat, corn; cattle, sheep, goats.

Myadel or **Myadel'** (myŭdyĕl'), Pol. *Miadzioł* or *Miadzioł Nowy* (myädzyô'o͞o nô'vē), village (1939 pop. over 500), N Molodechno oblast, Belorussian SSR, on small lake just E of L. Naroch, 27 mi. N of Vileika; fisheries, lumbering.

Myadel, Lake, or **Lake Myadel',** Pol. *Miadzioł* (□ 5), N Molodechno oblast, Belorussian SSR, 5 mi. NW of Myadel village. Noted summer resort, surrounded by forest. Has small isl. with ruins of castle.

Myaing (myĭng), village, Pakokku dist., Upper Burma, 25 mi. NW of Pakokku; road hub.

Myakka River (mīă'kŭ), SW Fla., rises in E Manatee co., flows SW, through swamps of Sarasota co., then SE, into Charlotte Harbor c.7 mi. W of Punta Gorda; c.50 mi. long; last 10 mi. an estuary. Formerly Miakka R.

Myaksa (myäk'sŭ), village (1932 pop. estimate 600), S Vologda oblast, Russian SFSR, on NE shore of Rybinsk Reservoir (landing) and 18 mi. SSE of Cherepovets; flax processing, dairying.

Myanaung (myä'noun), town (pop. 9,072), Henzada dist., Lower Burma, on right bank of Irrawaddy R. and 40 mi. S of Prome, on Henzada-Kyangin RR. Former ⊙ Henzada dist.

Myange (myäng'gä), village, Nyanza prov., W Kenya, near Uganda boundary, on railroad and 20 mi. SE of Tororo, Uganda; cotton, peanuts, sesame.

Myaryama, Estonia: see Marjamaa.

Myatlevo (myät'lyĭvŭ), agr. town (1926 pop. 1,286), N Kaluga oblast, Russian SFSR, 35 mi. NW of Kaluga; road-rail junction.

Myaung (myoung), village, Sagaing dist., Upper Burma, landing on right bank of Irrawaddy R. and 45 mi. WSW of Mandalay.

Myaungbwe (myoung'bwĕ), village, Akyab dist., Lower Burma, in the Arakan, on Lemro R. (head of navigation) and 35 mi. NE of Akyab.

Myaungmya (myoung'myä'), district (□ 2,835; 1941 pop. 488,031), Irrawaddy div., Lower Burma; ⊙ Myaungmya. Bet. Bassein R. (W) and Irrawaddy R. (E), embracing part of Irrawaddy delta on Andaman Sea; important rice production. Pop. is 65% Burmese, 25% Karen.

Myaungmya, town (pop. 7,773), ⊙ Myaungmya dist., Lower Burma, in Irrawaddy delta, 20 mi. SE of Bassein; rice-cultivation center. Steamer landing.

Myawaddy (myä'wŭdē″), village, Amherst dist., Lower Burma, in Tenasserim, on Thaungyin R. (Thailand line) opposite Mae Sot, 60 mi. ENE of Moulmein. Here Jap. forces invaded Burma from Thailand in Second World War. Sometimes spelled Myawadi.

Mycale, Mount (mĭ'kŭlē), Turkish *Samsun Dağ* (sämso͞on' dä), anc. *Lydia*, peak (3,832 ft.), SW Turkey, 16 mi. WSW of Soke, rising from the shore opposite Samos isl. Off Mycale Greeks won a great naval battle over Persians in 479 B.C.

Mycenae (mīsē'nē), anc. city of Argolis and Corinthia nome, NE Peloponnesus, Greece, 6 mi. NNE of Argos. Excavations (begun 1876) by Schliemann and others uncovered a wealth of remains, including an acropolis, palace, city walls, and many tombs. Reputedly the residence of Agamemnon and a major city of Bronze Age Greece, Mycenae flourished c.2,000 B.C. as the center of Mycenean civilization. Just SW of the ruins is modern village of Mykenai or Mikinai (pop. 626), formerly called Charvati.

Myckelbyn, Sweden: see Grimsaker.

Mydlovary (mĭd'lôvärĭ), village (pop. 469), S Bohemia, Czechoslovakia, 10 mi. NW of Budweis; lignite mined near by feeds large power station supplying electrical energy to most of S Bohemia.

Mydrecht, Netherlands: see Mijdrecht.

Mydzk, Ukrainian SSR: see Stepan.

Myebon (myābōn'), village, Kyaukpyu dist., Lower Burma, on Arakan coast, at mouth of Lemro R. and 30 mi. E of Akyab.

Myennes (myĕn'), village (pop. 510), Nièvre dept., central France, on right bank of Loire R. and 3 mi. N of Cosne; pottery.

Myer, Fort, Va.: see Arlington, county.

Myers Chuck, village (pop. 26), SE Alaska, on W side of Cleveland Peninsula, on Clarence Strait 37 mi. NW of Ketchikan; trading center; fishing. Also spelled Meyers Chuck.

Myerstown, borough (pop. 3,050), Lebanon co., SE Pa., 8 mi. NE of Lebanon; textiles, food products, chemicals. Laid out 1768, inc. c.1910.

Myersville, town (pop. 1,200), St. Elizabeth parish, SW Jamaica, 26 mi. W of May Pen; corn, spices, livestock.

Myersville, town (pop. 250), Frederick co., W Md., on Catoctin Creek, bet. Catoctin and South mts., and 11 mi. NW of Frederick.

Myggenaes (mü'gĭnĕs), Faeroese *Mykines*, island (□ 4; pop. 121) of the W Faeroe Isls., separated from W Vaago by Myggenaes Fjord. On W is a bridge to Myggenaes Holm (□ c.¼), a small isl. Terrain mountainous and rocky, less than 1% cultivated; highest point is 1,837 ft. Fishing, sheep raising.

Myingyan (myĭn'jăn'), district (□ 2,707; 1941 pop. 539,057), Mandalay div., Upper Burma; ⊙ Myingyan. On left bank of Irrawaddy R. and N plateau of Pegu Yoma; Mt. Popa most prominent feature. In dry zone (annual rainfall 26 in.) and poorly irrigated; produces rice, sesame, cotton, beans, peanuts. Oil fields at Singu; lacquer ware; small iron-ore smelting from local deposits.

Myingyan, town (pop. 25,457), ⊙ Myingyan dist., Upper Burma, on left bank of Irrawaddy R. and 55 mi. SW of Mandalay; river port, head of railroads to Thazi and Mandalay; cotton-trading center; cotton spinning mill. In Second World War, recaptured (March, 1945) from Japanese by Br. forces.

Myinmu (myĭn'mo͞o), town (pop. 5,072), Sagaing dist., Upper Burma, landing on right bank of Irrawaddy R. and 35 mi. W of Mandalay, on railroad to Yeu.

Myitche (myĭt'chĕ), village, Pakokku dist., Upper Burma, on right bank of Irrawaddy R. and 16 mi. SW of Pakokku. Sometimes spelled Myitchay.

Myitkyina (myĭt-chē″nä'), northern district (□ 29,723; 1941 pop. 298,323) of Kachin State, Upper Burma, on the Assam (India) and Yunnan (China) frontiers; ⊙ Myitkyina. Drained by Mali and Nmai headstreams of the Irrawaddy and upper course of Chindwin R. (Hukawng Valley), it is bounded by a horseshoe of high ranges (to nearly 20,000 ft.), and includes the Kumon Range and The Triangle. Agr.: rice, tobacco, vegetables, sugar cane (mill at Sawmaw); jade mining (Lonkin, Tawmaw), amber (on S edge of Hukawng Valley). Served by Mandalay-Myitkyina RR, Ledo (Stilwell) Road, and by Irrawaddy steamers during low-water season. Pop. is 35% Thai, 25% Kachin, and 22% Burmese.

Myitkyina, town (pop. 7,328), ⊙ Kachin State and Myitkyina dist., Upper Burma, on right bank of Irrawaddy R. (head of low-water navigation), head of railroad to Mandalay, near China line; 25°23'N 97° 24'E. Trading center, on Ledo (Stilwell) Road and at head of road to Tengchung (Yunnan prov.) via Sadon. In Second World War, a key point in the struggle for Burma, the town fell (Aug., 1944) to the Allies after 2½-month siege.

Myitmaka River (myĭtmŭkä'), Lower Burma, rises in marshy lake, 15 mi. SSE of Prome, flows over

100 mi. parallel to Irrawaddy R., past Tantabin and Insein, to Rangoon, where it joins the Pegu R. to form Rangoon R. Called Hlaing R. (hŭlĭng) in lower course.

Myitnge (myĭ'tŭng-ĕ'), town (pop. 5,682), Mandalay dist., Upper Burma, on Myitnge R. (rail and road bridges) and 8 mi. S of Mandalay, on Rangoon-Mandalay RR; rail workshops.

Myitnge River, Upper Burma, rises in Shan plateau E of Lashio, flows over 250 mi. SW, past Namtu, Hsipaw and Myitnge, to the Irrawaddy opposite Sagaing. Called Nam Tu in upper course.

Myittha (myĭt-thä'), village, Kyaukse dist., Upper Burma, on railroad and 38 mi. S of Mandalay.

Myittha River, in Upper Burma, rises in S Chin Hills W of Tilin, flows over 150 mi. N, past Gangaw and Kalemyo, to Chindwin R. at Kalewa. Receives Manipur R. (left). Lower valley is sometimes considered part of Kabaw Valley.

Myjava (mĭ'yävä), Hung. *Miava* (mē'ŏvŏ), town (pop. 9,662), W Slovakia, Czechoslovakia, in SE foothills of the White Carpathians, on railroad and 31 mi. E of Breclav. Refractory-clay deposits in vicinity.

Mykonos or **Mikonos** (both: mē'kônôs), Aegean island (□ 32.5; pop. 4,464) in the Cyclades, Greece, SE of Tenos isl.; 37°30'N 25°25'E; 9 mi. long, 6 mi. wide; rises to 1,195 ft. (NW). Mostly mountainous and rocky; produces wine, honey, cheese, olive oil, barley. Fisheries. Town of Mykonos (pop. 3,346) is on W shore. Mus. has archaeological finds of Delos and Reneia. The isl. is starting point for visit to Delos.

Mylae, Sicily: see MILAZZO.

Mylapore, India: see MADRAS, city.

Mylasa, Turkey: see MILAS.

Mylau (mē'lou), town (pop. 7,562), Saxony, E central Germany, on Göltzsch R. and 10 mi. NE of Plauen; woolen-milling center; metalworking. In center of town rises anc. castle (1st mentioned 1214), which became (1367) property of Emperor Charles IV; it is now a mus.

Mylliem (mĭl'lēăm), village, Khasi and Jaintia Hills dist., W Assam, India, on Shillong Plateau, 5 mi. SSW of Shillong; rice, sesame, cotton.

Myllykoski (mül'lükōs"kē), village in Anjala commune (pop. 5,004), Kymi co., SE Finland, on Kymi R. and 6 mi. SSE of Kouvola; pulp and paper mills, hydroelectric station.

Mylo (mī'lō), village (pop. 110), Rolette co., N N.Dak., 16 mi. SSE of Rolla.

Mylor (mī'lŭr), town and parish (pop. 2,037), Cornwall, England, on Mylor Creek (an inlet of Carrick Roads) and 2 mi. NNE of Falmouth; Mylor Pool (N) is anchorage for small vessels. Formerly site of royal dockyard. Has 15th-cent. church.

Mymensingh (mī'mŭnsĭng), district (□ 6,156; 1951 pop. 5,804,000), E central East Bengal, E Pakistan; ⊙ Mymensingh. Bounded N by Assam (India), SE by Meghna R., W by Jamuna R. (main course of the Brahmaputra); drained by Jamuna, old Brahmaputra, and Meghna rivers. Alluvial soil; rice, jute (major jute dist. of East Bengal), oilseeds, sugar cane, tobacco, cotton; red cotton trees, bamboo; sal timber in Madhupur Jungle. Jute pressing at Mymensingh and Sarishabari, rice and oilseed milling at Gouripur, sugar milling at Kishorganj; cotton weaving (Tangail, Bajitpur), metalware mfg. (Islampur, Tangail). Colleges at Mymensingh and Tangail. Part of 14th-cent. independent kingdom of Bengal under Moslem ruler; passed 1765 to English. Present dist. formed 1787; part of former Br. Bengal prov. until transferred 1947 to E Pakistan. Also spelled Maimansingh.

Mymensingh, city (pop. 52,950) ⊙ Mymensingh dist., E central East Bengal, E Pakistan, on the old Brahmaputra and 75 mi. N of Dacca; trades in rice, jute, oilseeds, sugar cane, tobacco; jute pressing, mfg. of electrical supplies; general-engineering factory. Has col. Formerly known as Nasirabad.

Mynachlogddu (mŭnäkh-lôg'dhē), village and parish (pop. 354), E Pembroke, Wales, 9 mi. NNE of Narberth; woolen milling.

Mynydd Eppynt (mŭ'nĭdh ĕ'pĭnt), mountain range, N central Brecknock, Wales, extends 15 mi. E–W bet. Carmarthen and Radnor; highest point is Drum Ddu (drĭm dhē') (1,554 ft.), 11 mi. NNW of Brecknock.

Mynyddislwyn (mŭ"nĭdh-ĭs'lōōĭn), urban district (1931 pop. 16,204; 1951 census 14,418), SW Monmouth, England, near Sirhowy R., 8 mi. SW of Pontypool; coal mines, iron foundries, stone quarries. In urban dist. are coal-mining towns of Pontllanfraith (pôntlänvrĭth') (pop. 4,596), with electrical-equipment works, and Fleur-de-Lis (flûr-dŭ-lēs') (pop. 1,126).

Mynydd Margam, Wales: see MARGAM.

Mynydd Moel, Wales: see CADER IDRIS.

Mynydd Prescelly (mŭ'nĭdh prĕsĕ'lē), mountain range, NE Pembroke, Wales, extends 5 mi. W from Carmarthen border; highest point is Foel Cwmcerwyn (voil kōōmkĕr'wĭn) (1,760 ft.), 10 mi. SW of Cardigan.

Myogi (myō'gē), town (pop. 3,635), Gumma prefecture, central Honshu, Japan, 8 mi. WNW of Tomioka; rice, wheat.

Myogyi (myōjē'), village, ⊙ Maw state, Southern Shan State, Upper Burma, on Zawgyi R. and 40 mi. SSE of Mandalay.

Myohaung (myō'-houng), village, Akyab dist., Lower Burma, in the Arakan, bet. Lemro and Kaladan rivers, 40 mi. NE of Akyab. Former ⊙ (15th–18th cents.) old Arakan kingdom and, later, of Burmese Arakan prov. until supplanted (1826), because of its unhealthy climate, by Akyab. Ruins of fortifications and palace.

Myohyang, Mount (myô'hyäng'), Korean *Myohyang-san*, Jap. *Myoko-san*, collective name for 6 peaks in N.Pyongan prov., N Korea, c.50 mi. NE of Sinanju. Highest peak is Mt. Piro (6,263 ft.).

Myoji (myō'jē), town (pop. 7,002), Wakayama prefecture, S Honshu, Japan, on N central Kii Peninsula, 21 mi. ENE of Wakayama; agr. center (citrus fruit, rice), poultry; spinning mill.

Myoko-san, Korea: see MYOHYANG, MOUNT.

Myongchon (myŭng'chŭn'), Jap. *Meisen*, town, N.Hamgyong prov., N Korea, 43 mi. SSW of Chongjin, in coal-mining area.

Myothit (myō'dhĭt'). **1** Village, Bhamo dist., Kachin State, Upper Burma, on Taping R. and 15 mi. NE of Bhamo on road to Myitkyina. **2** Village, Magwe dist., Upper Burma, on Pyinmana-Kyaukpadaung RR and 34 mi. E of Magwe.

Mypolonga, village (pop. 481), SE South Australia, 45 mi. ESE of Adelaide and on Murray R., near Murray Bridge; dairy products, livestock, fruit.

Myra (mī'rŭ), anc. town of Lycia, S Asia Minor, port on Mediterranean Sea 5 mi. W of Finike, Turkey; visited by St. Paul. Ruins.

Myra (mē'rä), Icelandic *Mýra*, county [Icelandic *sýsla*] (pop. 1,784), SW Iceland, on E shore of Faxa Bay; ⊙ Borgarnes. Has rocky coast line; marshy lowlands in interior. Sheep and cattle raising, fishing.

Myrdalsjokull (mĕr'däls"yû"kütŭl), Icelandic *Mýrdalsjökull*, extensive glacier, S Iceland, near the coast; 63°39'N 19°10'W. It is 30 mi. long (E–W), 10–20 mi. wide. W extension, called Eyjafjallajokull (ā'äfyät"läyû"kütŭl), Icelandic *Eyjafjallajökull*, rises to 5,466 ft. at 63°37'N 19°36'W. At S edge of glacier is Katla (kät'lä), active volcano (2,382 ft.) whose eruption in 1918 caused great floods.

Myriandrus (mĭrēăn'drŭs), anc. town in S Asia Minor, on Gulf of Iskenderun, 15 mi. SW of Iskenderun; northernmost Phoenician colony. Ruins.

Myrnam (mûr'nŭm), village (pop. 308), E Alta., near North Saskatchewan R., 26 mi. NW of Vermilion; mixed farming, grain, stock.

Myrtilis Julia, Portugal: see MÉRTOLA.

Myrtle. 1 Village (pop. 136), Freeborn co., S Minn., near Iowa line, 12 mi. SE of Albert Lea; dairy products. **2** Town (pop. 331), Union co., N Miss., 8 mi. NW of New Albany, in agr., lumbering, and dairying area.

Myrtle Beach, town (pop. 3,345), Horry co., E S.C., on the coast, 14 mi. SE of Conway; year-round beach resort; largest seashore resort in state. Socastee yacht basin, on Intracoastal Waterway, is near by. Inc. 1938.

Myrtle Creek, town (pop. 1,781), Douglas co., SW Oregon, 13 mi. S of Roseburg and on Umpqua R.; lumber.

Myrtleford, town (pop. 1,111), NE central Victoria, Australia, on Ovens R. and 130 mi. NE of Melbourne, in livestock area; dairy plant. Agr. experiment station.

Myrtle Point, town (pop. 2,033), Coos co., SW Oregon, on South Fork of Coquille R. and 9 mi. S of Coquille; trade center for dairying and livestock area; dairy and wood products. Siskiyou Natl. Forest near by. Settled 1858, inc. 1903.

Myrtoan Sea, Greece: see AEGEAN SEA.

Mysen (mü'sŭn), village and canton (pop. 2,460), Ostfold co., SE Norway, on railroad and 20 mi. NNE of Sarpsborg; vulcanizing plant, automobile workshops; mfg. of steel, copper, and lead wool. Site of agr. and domestic-industry schools, music col., mus., race track.

Myshega (mĭ'shĭgŭ), town (1939 pop. over 2,000), NW Tula oblast, Russian SFSR, 3 mi. W of Aleksin, across Oka R.; iron foundry, metalworks (metalware); limestone quarrying.

Myshkino (mĭsh'kēnŭ), town (1926 pop. 2,499), W Yaroslavl oblast, Russian SFSR, on Volga R. (landing) and 22 mi. SSW of Shcherbakov; metalworks. Also called Myshkin on Volga.

Mysia (mĭ'shēŭ), anc. region of NW Asia Minor, with Aegean Sea on W and Sea of Marmara on N. It passed successively to Lydia, Persia, Macedon, Syria, Pergamum, and Rome. Cities included Adramyttium, Cyzicus, and Lampsacus. Bithynia was on NE, Phrygia on E, Lydia on S.

Myski (mĭskē), town (1948 pop. over 500), S central Kemerovo oblast, Russian SFSR, in Kuznetsk Basin, 28 mi. E of Stalinsk, in agr. area.

Myslenice (mĭsh-lĕnē'tsĕ), Pol. *Myślenice*, town (pop. 6,520), Krakow prov., S Poland, on Raba R. and 15 mi. S of Krakow; mfg. of hats; brewing, tanning, flour milling; stone quarrying. Hydroelectric plant.

Mysliborz (mĭsh-lē'bōōzh), Pol. *Myślibórz*, Ger. *Soldin* (zôldēn'), town (1939 pop. 6,124); 1946 pop. 3,887) in Brandenburg, after 1945 in Szczecin prov., NW Poland, on small lake, 25 mi. NNE of Küstrin (Kostrzyn); dairy center; sawmilling. Has 13th-cent. basilica of former Dominican monastery (founded 1275) and remains of medieval town gates.

Myslowice (mĭswôvē'tsĕ), Pol. *Mysłowice*, Ger. *Myslowitz* (mĭs'lōvĭts), city (pop. 23,786), Katowice prov., S Poland, on the Czarna Przemsza, near its confluence with the Biala Przemsza, and 5 mi. E of Katowice, in dense rail network. Metal industry, brickworks, coal mines, chemical factory. In Germany (on Rus. Poland and Austrian border) until First World War.

Mysore (mĭsôr', –sōr') or **Maisur** (mīsōōr'), constituent state (□ 29,458; 1941 pop. 7,329,140; 1951 census pop. 9,071,678), S India, on S DECCAN PLATEAU; dynastic ⊙ Mysore; administrative ⊙ BANGALORE. Almost surrounded by Madras except for Bombay (NW) and COORG (on Mysore's SW border with Madras), state is landlocked but reaches to within 10 mi. of Arabian Sea near Bhatkal (Bombay). Framed in S by junction of Eastern and Western Ghats, Mysore consists of broken tableland (average alt. 2,500 ft.), rising to over 4,000 ft. on crest of Western Ghats and to 6,310 ft. in Mulliangiri peak in BABA BUDAN RANGE. Drainage is mainly E, via Tungabhadra R. and its tributaries (in N), Penner and Palar rivers (in E), and the Cauvery and its tributaries (in S); the Sharavati hurls itself NW (via GERSOPPA FALLS) down the Western Ghats to Arabian Sea. Mysore has equable tropical climate (average min. temp., 60°F. in Dec.; average max. temp., 90°F. in May); receives heaviest rainfall (over 60 in.) in tract (20–50 mi. wide) in Western Ghats during SW monsoon. Known for its extensive coffee, tea, rubber, cardamom, and pepper plantations, mainly in Western Ghats, Mysore also grows millet, rice, sugar cane, oilseeds, cotton, and tobacco; Mysore mangoes are known for their succulence. Important silk farms are mainly in E and S dists. State's famous sandalwood is found chiefly in isolated ridges in S central areas; valuable timber and bamboo in Western Ghats (chief natural habitat of Mysore's well-known elephants). Extensive sheep raising. Gold mines of KOLAR GOLD FIELDS produce over 95% of India's gold. Mysore's other mineral wealth includes manganese (major workings in Shimoga dist.), iron ore (in Baba Budan Range), asbestos, corundum, mica, limestone, and kaolin. Mysore is a major Indian textile (silk, cotton, wool) center; plants at BANGALORE, Davangere, Harihar, MYSORE, Nanjangud. Other industries (mainly powered by pivotal SIVASAMUDRAM hydroelectric works) include iron and steel milling (at BHADRAVATI), aircraft mfg. (at Bangalore), rice, sugar, tobacco, coffee, and rubber processing, mfg. of sandalwood soap and perfume, matches, plywood, and paper milling. Other industrial towns are Channapatna, Hassan, Mandya, and Shimoga. Handicrafts include silk and cotton weaving, goldsmithing, making of glass bangles, pottery, biris, wickerwork. State's rail net, radiating from Bangalore (airport), provides links with major cities of India. Main languages are Kanarese, Telugu, Hindi. Although literacy is low (13%), it has increased over 30% since 1901. Pop. comprises Hindus (91%), Moslems (6%), Christians (1%), Jains (1%). Mysore is rich in archaeological landmarks, notably Belur, Somnathpur, Sravana Belgola. Mysore dynasty asserted its independence (1610) from declining Vijayanagar kingdom and established itself in S area of present state. In 1761, Hyder Ali, general of the raja's army, usurped throne; although continually beset by the aggressive Mahrattas, he had (by time of his death in 1782) expanded state's area to over 3 times its present size. After Br. defeat of Hyder's son, Tippoo Sahib, at SERINGAPATAM in 1799, scion of original dynasty was restored and present boundaries settled. The British took over state's administration, 1831–81. Having acceded (1947) to dominion of India, Mysore became in 1950 a constituent state of republic of India; enclaves were exchanged with Madras. State comprises 9 dists.: Bangalore, Chitaldrug, Hassan, Kadur, Kolar, Mandya, Mysore, Shimoga, Tumkur.

Mysore, district (□ 3,542; pop. 1,059,542), S Mysore, India; ⊙ Mysore. On Deccan Plateau; bounded W by Coorg, S and E by Madras; undulating tableland, rising in forested hills (S; teak, bamboo, sandalwood; big-game hunting) toward Nilgiri Hills and the Wynaad (across border); drained mainly by upper Cauvery R. (Krishnaraja Sagara, reservoir, is on N border) and its tributaries, Kabbani and Lakshmantirtha rivers. Agr. (millet, rice, tobacco, cotton, sugar cane); silk growing (E); widespread mango gardening. Dispersed chromite mining. Cattle and sheep breeding; silk, tobacco, and coffee processing; hand-loom weaving. Diversified industries centered in and around Mysore city. Other chief towns: Chamarajanagar, Hunsur, Nanjangud. Noted archaeological remains at Talakad. Original dist. reduced in 1939, when Mandya dist. was formed out of its NE portion.

Mysore or **Maisur,** city (□ 13; pop. 150,540), ⊙ Mysore dist. and dynastic ⊙ Mysore state, S India,

250 mi. WSW of Madras, 530 mi. SSE of Bombay; 12°17′N 76°40′E. Industrial, commercial, and cultural center; airport. Well-known for its mfg. of fine silks, sandalwood perfumes, and handicraft art work in ivory, metal, and wood, Mysore also produces cotton textiles, paints and varnishes, bricks and tiles, plastics, neon signs, and road tar; rice and vegetable-oil milling, milk pasteurizing, railway car repairing. Mfg. of chrome dyes and chemical fertilizer at NW suburb of Belagola or Belagula. Industries are powered by hydroelectric works near Sivasamudram isl. (35 mi. E). Mysore has mild climate (alt. c.2,500 ft.); mean temp. ranges from 89°F. in May to 69°F. in Dec. Its wide streets and many parks have given it the reputation of the "garden city" of India. Mysore has one of the 2 centers of Univ. of Mysore (founded 1916; other center in Bangalore), Maharani's Women's Col., noted Oriental Library, and several institutions devoted to the advancement of Kanarese culture. In city's center, within an anc. fort (rebuilt on European lines in 18th cent.), is the maharajah's palace (1897; Indo-Saracenic architecture with Chalukyan decorative details); the throne in the great durbar hall has elaborate carvings of silver and gold mythological figures and is considered to rival in ornateness the Peacock Throne of Delhi. During annual Dashahara festival (Sept.–Oct.), the palace, entirely outlined at night with myriad electric lights, is focus of great processions. Founded 16th cent., Mysore has been state's dynastic ⊙ since siege of SERINGAPATAM in 1799; BANGALORE has been administrative ⊙ since 1831. Chamundi hill (just SE; c.3,490 ft.), with its monolithic statue of Nandi (sacred bull of Siva), is a place of pilgrimage and affords fine view of Mysore and of NILGIRI HILLS (S). Badanaval, near NANJANGUD (S), is noted handicraft center. KRISHNARAJASAGARA (NW), with its famed Brindavan Gardens, is a popular tourist resort.

Mysovka (mĭ'sŭfkŭ), village (1939 pop. 885), N Kaliningrad oblast, Russian SFSR, on E shore of Courland Lagoon, in Neman R. delta, 26 mi. WNW of Sovetsk (linked by narrow-gauge railroad); seaside resort amid pinewoods. Until 1945, in East Prussia and called Karkeln (kär'kŭln).

Mysovsk, Russian SFSR: see BABUSHKIN, Buryat-Mongol Autonomous SSR.

Mystic (mĭ'stĭk). **1** Resort village (pop. 2,266) in Stonington town, New London co., SE Conn., at mouth of Mystic R., opposite West Mystic; mfg. (cutlery, thread, marine engines, boats, soap, textiles, machinery, paper products). Formerly active shipbuilding and whaling port; marine mus. here. **2** Town (pop. 281), Irwin co., S central Ga., 9 mi. SW of Fitzgerald. **3** City (pop. 1,233), Appanoose co., S Iowa, 4 mi. NW of Centerville; coal-mining center. Inc. 1899.

Mystic Lakes, Middlesex co., E Mass., connected lakes (total length c.2 mi.), just W of Medford; recreational. Drained by Mystic R.

Mystic River. **1** Small stream in SE Conn., rises SE of Norwich, flows c.10 mi. S, past Old Mystic and Mystic villages, to Mystic Harbor (Long Isl. Sound) 6 mi. E of Groton. **2** Small stream in E Mass., rises in Mystic Lakes just NW of Medford, flows 7 mi. SE, past Medford (head of navigation), to NW side of Boston Harbor.

Mythen, Great, and **Little Mythen**, Switzerland: see SCHWYZ, town.

Mytho (mē'tô'), town (1936 pop. 12,500), ⊙ Mytho prov. (□ 890; 1943 pop. 430,800), S Vietnam, in Cochin China, on left bank of Mekong delta arm and 35 mi. SW of Saigon (linked by railroad), in fertile and highly irrigated area (canals); large rice-growing and trading center; coconuts (oil extraction; soap mfg.), fruit, sugar cane. Former Khmer dist.; colonized late-17th cent. by Annamese.

Mytholmroyd (mīdh-ŭmroid'), former urban district (1931 pop. 4,468), West Riding, SW Yorkshire, England, on Calder R., on Rochdale Canal, and 5 mi. W of Halifax; woolen and cotton milling. Inc. 1937 in Hebden Royd.

Mytikas, Greece: see OLYMPUS.

Mytilene or **Mitilini** (both: mĭtĭlē'nē), city (1951 pop. 27,125), ⊙ Aegean Isls. div. and Lesbos nome, Greece, port on SE shore of LESBOS isl. (also called Mytilene), on Mytilene Channel; trade in olive oil, citrus fruit, grain, hides. Soap mfg.; sponge fisheries. Airport. Seat of Gr. metropolitan. Originally on offshore isl. (site of Genoese fortress; 1373), it was connected by causeway and expanded to main isl. Under Turkish rule (until 1913), it was ⊙ Turkish Aegean Isls. and called Midilli or Midillii by the Turks. Formerly called Kastro or Kastron; sometimes spelled Mytilini.

Mytilene Channel, arm of Aegean Sea, bet. Lesbos isl. and Turkey; 30 mi. long, 10 mi. wide. Its ports are Mytilene (on Lesbos) and Ayvlik and Dikili (Turkey).

Mytilenoi or **Mitilinoi** (both: mĭtĭlĭnē'), town (pop. 5,286), on Samos isl., Greece, 4 mi. WSW of Limen Vatheos; olive oil, tobacco, wine.

Mytishchi (mĭtyē'shchē), city (1926 pop. 17,054; 1939 pop. 60,111), central Moscow oblast, Russian SFSR, 13 mi. NNE of Moscow; car-building center (tramway and subway cars); woolen mill. Became city in 1925.

Myton (mī'tŭn), town (pop. 435), Duchesne co., NE Utah, 18 mi. E of Duchesne and on Duchesne R.; alt. 5,085 ft.; stock raising; uintaite deposits.

Myvatn (mē'vä"tŭn), Icelandic *Mývatn*, lake (□ 10), NE Iceland, 30 mi. E of Akureyri; 60 mi. long, 1–4 mi. wide; max. depth 23 ft. Drains N into Greenland Sea. Lake is depression in volcanic basalt rock, surrounded by small craters and lava formations.

Myyzakyula, Estonia: see MOISAKULA.

Myzeqe (mü'zĕ'kyā) or **Myzeqeja** (müzĕk'yĕyä), Ital. *Musacchia* (mōōzäk'kēä), fertile agr. plain of S central Albania, traversed by Seman R.; produces mainly grain. Chief towns are Lushnje (N), Fier (S). Important agr. dist. in Roman times.

Mzab (mŭzäb'), group of Saharan oases in Ghardaïa territory, central Algeria, c.100 mi. SSE of Laghouat; ⊙ Ghardaïa. Principal oases: El-Ateuf, Melika, Béni-Isguen, Berrian, Guerrara, Metlili. Dates, grown exclusively on well water, are chief export product. The Mzabites, a heretic Moslem sect expelled from the coastal Tell region in 11th cent., have remained a closely-knit religious group. Although a large number are found as small shopkeepers in Algiers, they must return to their oases at regular intervals. Town sites, notably Ghardaïa, are tourist attractions. Also spelled M'zab.

M'Zaïta, Djebel, Algeria: see TOCQUEVILLE.

Mze River (ŭmzhĕ'), Czech *Mže*, Ger. *Mies* (mēs), W Bohemia, Czechoslovakia, rises in Bohemian Forest 13 mi. SW of Marienbad, flows c.45 mi. generally W, past Tachov [and Stribro, joining Radbuza R. at Pilsen to form Berounka R.

Mzi, Djebel, Algeria: see KSOUR MOUNTAINS.

Mzimba (ŭmzĕm'bä), town, ⊙ Northern Prov. (□ 10,670; pop. 290,859), Nyasaland, 145 mi. N. of Lilongwe; 11°53′S 33°37′E. Corn, cassava. Has African hosp. Mica deposits.

Mzymta River (ŭmzĭm'tŭ), S Krasnodar Territory, Russian SFSR, rises on S slope of the W Greater Caucasus at 9,780 ft., flows 51 mi. W and SW, past Krasnaya Polyana, to Black Sea at Adler.

N

Naab River, Germany: see NAB RIVER.

Naafkopf (näf'kôpf"), alpine peak (c.8,440 ft.) on Liechtenstein-Austrian-Swiss border, in the Rhätikon, 7 mi. SE of Vaduz.

Naaf River or **Naf River** (näf), tidal inlet of Bay of Bengal, on Burma-Pakistan border; 30 mi. long. Extends from Taungbro past Teknaf and Maungdaw to the sea; served by steamer route.

Naaldwijk (nält'vīk), town (pop. 7,268), South Holland prov., W Netherlands, 7 mi. SW of The Hague; center of Westland agr. area; market for grapes, peaches, plums, berries, potatoes.

Naalehu (nä'ŭlā'hōō), village (pop. 1,005), S Hawaii, T.H.; sisal grown here.

Naan or **Na'an** (both: nä'än), settlement (pop. 850), W Israel, in Judaean Plain, 3 mi. ESE of Rehovot; sprinkler mfg., metalworking; mixed farming. Founded 1930.

Naantali (nän'tä"lē), Swedish *Nådendal* (nō'dŭndäl"), city (pop. 1,918), Turku-Pori co., SW Finland, on inlet of Gulf of Bothnia, 8 mi. W of Turku; rail terminus; plywood mills. Seaside resort. Founded 1445, it was formerly site of monastery. Near by is Finnish president's summer residence of *Kultaranta* (kōōl'tärän"tä).

Naarden (när'dŭn), town (commune pop. 11,694), North Holland prov., W central Netherlands, on the Ijsselmeer, 1 mi. N of Bussum; light mfg.; tree nurseries. Has 14th-cent. church, 17th-cent. town hall. Sacked (1572) by Spaniards. A fortress until 1926.

Naarn (närn), town (pop. 2,367), NE Upper Austria, near left bank of the Danube, 14 mi. ESE of Linz. Ruins of castle Hartschlössl near by.

Naas (näs), Gaelic *Nás na Riogh*, urban district (pop. 3,774), E Co. Kildare, Ireland, on branch of Grand Canal and 19 mi. WSW of Dublin; cotton milling, shoe mfg. In anc. times it was ⊙ kings of Leinster, and site of castle and monastic establishments. There are remains of anc. rath, meeting place of the States of Leinster province.

Naast (näst), agr. village (pop. 2,011), Hainaut prov., SW central Belgium, 10 mi. NE of Mons.

Naauwpoort (nō'pōōrt"), town (pop. 1,449), E central Cape Prov., U. of So. Afr., 65 mi. SE of De Aar; rail junction; sheep, wool, wheat, feed crops, fruit. Region was scene (1899–1900) of cavalry operations in South African War.

Naba (nŭbä'), village, Katha dist., Upper Burma, 110 mi. SW of Myitkyina; junction of Mandalay-Myitkyina RR and branch line to Katha.

Naba, Japan: see O-o.

Nabadwip (nŭbŭdvēp'), town (pop. 30,583), Nadia dist., E West Bengal, India, at confluence of Bhagirathi and Jalangi rivers, 8 mi. W of Krishnagar; metalware and pottery mfg.; trades in rice, jute, linseed, sugar cane. Noted Sanskrit schools. Pilgrimage center. Birthplace (1485) of Chaitanya, famous Vaishnava saint. Was ⊙ Sen kingdom following its transfer (12th cent.) from Gaur. Formerly called Nadia.

Naband Bay (näbänd'), inlet of Persian Gulf in S Iran, 155 mi. SE of Bushire; sheltered S by Cape Naband (27°23′N 52°35′E). A good natural harbor; site of projected port development at Asalu village on N shore.

Nabari (näbä'rē), town (pop. 16,919), Mie prefecture, S Honshu, Japan, 25 mi. WSW of Tsu; agr. center (rice, wheat, tea); raw silk, poultry.

Nabaroh or **Nabaruh** (both: nă'bärōō), village (pop. 12,335), Gharbiya prov., Lower Egypt, on Bahr Shibin and 5 mi. NW of Talkha; cotton.

Nabatiye, En, El Nabatiye, or **Al-Nabatiyah** (all: ĕn-năbătē'ŭ), Fr. *Nabatié*, village (pop. 928), S Lebanon, 14 mi. SE of Saida; tobacco, cereals, sericulture.

Nabburg (nä'bōōrk), town (pop. 4,105), Upper Palatinate, E Bavaria, Germany, on the Nab and 9 mi. NNE of Schwandorf; woodworking, lumber and flour milling. Surrounded by 15th-cent. walls; has Romanesque and Gothic churches. Chartered 1296.

Naberezhnye Chelny or **Naberezhnyye Chelny** (nŭbĭryĕzh'nēŭ chĭlnē'), city (1932 pop. estimate 5,130), NE Tatar Autonomous SSR, Russian SFSR, port on left bank of Kama R. and 10 mi. ESE of Yelabuga; grain-trading center (elevators); flour milling, sawmilling, metalworking, mfg. (sleepers, bricks); wine making. Called Chelny until 1930, when it became a city.

Nabesna (nŭbĕz'nŭ), village (pop. 26), E Alaska, near Yukon border, on Nabesna R. and 70 mi. S of Tanacross, on N slope of Wrangell Mts.; supply point for trappers and prospectors. Airfield. Another Nabesna (pop. 84) is c.50 mi. downstream on Nabesna R. opposite Northway.

Nabesna Glacier (20 mi. long, 3 mi. wide), E Alaska, extends N from Wrangell Mts., near 62°5′N 142°55′W. Flows into Nabesna R.

Nabesna River, E Alaska, rises in Nabesna Glacier, in the Wrangell Mts., near 62°14′N 142°55′W; flows 70 mi. NNE, past Nabesna, to Tanana R. at 63°2′N 141°53′W. Flows through gold-mining region.

Nabesna Village, Indian village (pop. 84), E Alaska, near Yukon border, on Nabesna R. and 50 mi. SE of Tanacross, near Alaska Highway.

Nabeul (näbŭl'), anc. *Neapolis*, town (pop. 11,029), Grombalia dist., NE Tunisia, on Gulf of Hammamet, 38 mi. SE of Tunis; center of well-known handicraft pottery industry; perfume factories. Distilling, macaroni mfg., stone cutting. Chalk quarries near by. Extensive citrus plantations and perfume-flower gardens in area. Phoenician Neapolis was destroyed by Romans in 146 B.C. Later rebuilt as a Roman colony.

Nabha (nä'bŭ), town (pop. 22,625), central Patiala and East Punjab States Union, India, 14 mi. WNW of Patiala; trades in millet, wheat, gram, cloth fabrics, sugar; cotton ginning, wool carding, hand-loom weaving, embroidering. Has col. Was ⊙ former princely state of Nabha (□ 947; pop. 340,044) of Punjab States, India; comprised several small, scattered areas. State formed 1763 by Sikhs during breakup of Mogul empire; since 1948, merged with Patiala and East Punjab States Union.

Nabisar Road (nŭbē'sŭr), village, Thar Parkar dist., S Sind, W Pakistan, on railroad and 26 mi. SSW of Umarkot; cotton, millet; cotton ginning.

Nabk, Al-, Syria: see NEBK, EN.

Nablus (näblōōs', nă'blōōs), chief town (1946 pop. estimate 24,660) of Samaria, in Palestine, after 1948 in W Jordan, bet. Mt. Ebal (NE) and Mt. Gerizim (SE), on railroad and 30 mi. N of Jerusalem; soap mfg. Its Great Mosque was originally basilica of Justinian which was rebuilt (1167) as church of Crusaders. Hebrew town of *Shechem* was rebuilt by Hadrian and called *Neapolis;* under Crusaders it became royal city. Just SE are traditional sites of Jacob's well and Joseph's tomb.

Nabón (näbōn'), village, Azuay prov., S Ecuador, on Pan American Highway and 32 mi. S of Cuenca; alt. 8,865 ft.; cereals, potatoes, livestock.

Naboomspruit (nä'bōōmsproit"), village (pop. 1,695), N central Transvaal, U. of So. Afr., on Magalakwin R. and 60 mi. SW of Pietersburg; rail junction; agr. center (wheat, tobacco, peanuts).

Nabotas, Philippines: see NAVOTAS.

Nabresina, Free Territory of Trieste: see AURISINA.

Nabrezina, Free Territory of Trieste: see AURISINA.

Nab River or **Naab River** (both: näp), Bavaria, Germany, rises as the Waldnab (or Waldnaab) 2 mi. S of Bärnau, flows c.100 mi. generally S, past Weiden and Schwandorf, to the Danube 3 mi. W of Regensburg. Receives the Fichtelnab (or Fichtelnaab) and the Vils (right).

Nabua (nä'bwä), town (1939 pop. 3,704; 1948 municipality pop. 42,946), Camarines Sur prov., SE Luzon, Philippines, 19 mi. SE of Naga; agr. center (rice, corn, abacá); gypsum.

Nacajuca (näkähōō'kä), town (pop. 2,433), Tabasco, SE Mexico, on arm of Grijalva R. and 13 mi. NNW of Villahermosa; corn, rice, beans, tobacco, fruit, livestock.

Nacala (näkä'lä), village, Niassa prov., NE Mozambique, on Mozambique Channel of Indian Ocean, 35 mi. N of Mozambique city; rail-spur terminus; port (outlet for Niassa prov.) under construction; ships sisal, copra.

Nacaome (näkou'mä), city (pop. 2,630), ⊙ Valle dept., S Honduras, on Inter-American Highway, on Nacaome R. and 45 mi. SSW of Tegucigalpa; 13°31'N 87°29'W. Commercial center; mfg. (beverages, bricks), tanning. Has colonial church (rebuilt 1867). Dates from 16th cent.; became city in 1845. Gold and silver mining at El Tránsito, 7 mi. W.

Nacaome River, S Honduras, rises in Sierra de Lepaterique, flows c.50 mi. S, past Reitoca, Pespire, and Nacaome, to Gulf of Fonesca. Called Reitoca R. in upper course, Pespire R. in middle course. Navigable below Nacaome in rainy summer season.

Nacascolo, Nicaragua: see PUERTO MORAZÁN.

Nacebe (näsä'bä), village, Pando dept., N Bolivia, on Orton R. and 25 mi. S of Santa Rosa; rubber.

Nacfa, Eritrea: see NAGFA.

Nacham (nä'chäm'), town, Langson prov., N Vietnam, on the Song Kikong (headstream of Li R.; head of navigation) 90 mi. NE of Hanoi (linked by railroad); rail terminus; river-rail transfer point.

Naches (nă'chēz"), town (pop. 633), Yakima co., S Wash., 12 mi. NW of Yakima and on Naches R.; fruit, lumber, dairy products.

Naches Pass (alt. c.5,000 ft.), central Wash., gateway through Cascade Range used by pioneers, c.50 mi. E of Tacoma.

Naches River, central Wash., rises in Cascade Range near Naches Pass, flows c.75 mi. SE to Yakima R. above Yakima.

Nachi or **Na-ch'i** (nä'chē'), town (pop. 6,708), ⊙ Nachi co. (pop. 82,825), S Szechwan prov., China, 7 mi. SW of Luhsien, across Yangtze R., at mouth of small Süyung R.; rice, wheat, sugar cane, beans, rapeseed.

Nachi (nä'chē), town (pop. 5,844), Wakayama prefecture, S Honshu, Japan, on SE Kii Peninsula, 8 mi. SW of Shingu, in agr. area (rice, wheat, citrus fruit). Waterfall (430 ft. high) on small Nachi R. is highest in Japan. Site of 6th-cent. Buddhist temple.

Nachingwa (nächĭng'gwä), village, Southern Prov., SE Tanganyika, 70 mi. SW of Lindi; terminus (1949) of railroad from Mkwaya (transfer point for Lukuledi R. navigation to Lindi) in area designated for peanut scheme. Airfield. Rail line to be continued to Noli (35 mi. WNW), also in peanut area; peanuts scheduled to be shipped to new MIKINDANI port for export. Also spelled Nachingwea.

Nachlat Yehuda, Israel: see NAHALAT YEHUDA.

Nachlat Yitzhak, Israel: see NAHALAT YITS-HAQ.

Nachod (nä'khôt), Czech *Náchod,* town (pop. 13,953), NE Bohemia, Czechoslovakia, in NNW foothills of the Adlergebirge, on railroad and 22 mi. NE of Hradec Kralove, near Pol. border; mfg. of textiles (notably linen and cotton) and tires. Has historic castle with paintings and Gobelin tapestries, 14th-cent. cathedral. Prussians defeated Austrians here, in 1866. Health resort of Beloves (byĕ'lôvĕs), Czech *Běloves,* with peat baths and acidulous springs, is just ENE.

Nachrodt-Wiblingwerde (näkh'rōt"-vĭ"blĭng-vâr'dü), village (pop. 5,445), in former Prussian prov. of Westphalia, W Germany, after 1945 in North Rhine-Westphalia, on the Lenne and 4 mi. SW of Iserlohn; tin-plate mfg.

Nachterstedt (näkh'tŭr-shtĕt), village (pop. 3,015), in former Prussian Saxony prov., central Germany, after 1945 in Saxony-Anhalt, at NE foot of the lower Harz, 6 mi. NW of Aschersleben; lignite mining; power station.

Nachtigal, Cape, Br. Cameroons: see BIMBIA RIVER.

Nachvak Fiord (năch'văk), inlet (30 mi. long, 3 mi. wide) of the Atlantic, NE Labrador, at foot of Cirque Mtn.; 59°3'N 63°40'W.

Nacimiento (näsēmyĕn'tō), town (pop. 2,815), ⊙ Nacimiento dept. (□ 464; pop. 24,379), Bío-Bío prov., S central Chile, in S part of the central valley, on Bío-Bío R. at mouth of the Vergara and 18 mi. WSW of Los Angeles. Rail terminus and agr. center (wheat, rye, peas, wine); lumbering.

Nacimiento (nä-thēmyĕn'tō), village (pop. 1,298), Almería prov., S Spain, 21 mi. NNW of Almería; olive-oil processing, flour milling. Ships grapes.

Nacimiento, Cerro del (sĕ'rō dĕl näsēmyĕn'tō), Andean peak (21,300 ft.), W Catamarca prov., Argentina, near Chile border, 23 mi. SW of Cerro Incahuasi; 27°15'S.

Nacimiento Mountains (nă"sĭmyĕn'tō), range in NW N.Mex., just E of Rio Puerco; extend c.30 mi. S from Cuba. Prominent points: Pajarito Peak (pä"härē'tō) (9,042 ft.); San Miguel Mtn. (săn mēgĕl') (9,457 ft.); Nacimiento Peak (9,791 ft.). Range is partly in Santa Fe Natl. Forest.

Nacka (nä'kä), city (1950 pop. 15,521), Stockholm co., E Sweden, SE suburb of Stockholm, 3 mi. from city center; mfg. of machinery (steam turbines, Diesel motors, pneumatic drills); flour milling. Inc. 1950 as city.

Nackara, village, E South Australia, 75 mi. ENE of Port Pirie, on Port Pirie–Broken Hill RR; wool, some wheat.

Nackenheim (nä'kŭnhīm), village (pop. 2,544), Rhenish Hesse, W Germany, on left bank of the Rhine and 7 mi. SE of Mainz; wine.

Nacmine (năk'mīn), village (pop. eltimate 500), S Alta., on Red Deer R. and 4 mi. W of Drumheller; coal mining.

Naco (nä'kō), town (pop. 1,474), Sonora, NW Mexico, in NW spurs of Sierra Madre Occidental, on U.S. border adjoining Naco, (Ariz.), on railroad and 60 mi. E of Nogales; alt. 4,605 ft. In rich copper belt; cattle. Customhouse. Bull ring.

Naco (nă'kō), village (pop. c.500), Cochise co., SE Ariz., on Mex. line, 24 mi. W of Douglas; alt. 4,680 ft. U.S. customs and Mex. consulate are here. Mex. town of Naco is adjacent. Mule Mts. are N.

Nacogdoches (nă"kŭdō'chĭs), county (□ 963; pop. 30,326), E Texas; ⊙ Nacogdoches. Rolling, wooded area; chief industry is lumbering). Bounded W and S by Angelina R., partly E by Attoyac Bayou; includes part of Angelina Natl. Forest. Dairying. agr. (cotton, corn, hay, legumes, sugar cane, fruit, truck), livestock (cattle, hogs, poultry). Some oil, natural gas; clay, lignite mining. Lumber milling, some mfg. Formed 1836.

Nacogdoches, city (pop. 12,327), ⊙ Nacogdoches co., E Texas, near Angelina R., c.19 mi. NNE of Lufkin; rail, industrial center for rich pine-timber, truck, and cotton area; many sawmills; mfg. of cottonseed oil, canned foods, petroleum products, clay products, cigars, clothing, furniture, metal products. Seat of Stephen F. Austin State Teachers Col., whose campus has Old Stone Fort (replica of Sp. presidio). One of oldest Texas cities; Sp. mission founded here 1716; settled 1779 as Sp. colony; heavily garrisoned after La. Purchase, it was nevertheless twice seized (1812, 1819) by filibustering expeditions from U.S. Active on rebels' side in Texas Revolution (1835–36); grew to be cotton-plantation center, ruined by slump following Civil War. Became lumbering center after coming of railroad (1882).

Nácori Chico (nä'kōrē chē'kō), town (pop. 684), Sonora, NW Mexico, on affluent of Yaqui R., in W outliers of Sierra Madre Occidental, and 135 mi. ENE of Hermosillo; stock-raising and mining center (silver, gold).

Nacozari de García (näkōsä'rē dā gärsē'ä), town (pop. 4,502), Sonora, NW Mexico, in broad valley of W outliers of Sierra Madre Occidental, on railroad and 70 mi. S of Douglas, Ariz.; alt. 3,550 ft. Cattle-raising and copper-mining center; silver, gold, lead, zinc mines.

Ñacunday (nyäkōōndī'), town (dist. pop. 703), Alto Paraná dept., SE Paraguay, on upper Paraná R. and 45 mi. S of Hernandarias; maté, lumber.

Nadabula, Czechoslovakia: see ROZNAVA.

Nadachi (nä"dä'chē), town (pop. 2,613), Niigata prefecture, central Honshu, Japan, on Toyama Bay, 9 mi. WNW of Takada; agr., fishing.

Nadadores (nädädō'rĕs), town (pop. 2,158), Coahuila, N Mexico, 15 mi. NW of Monclova; cereals, wine, livestock.

Nadbai (näd'bī), village, E Rajasthan, India, 17 mi. W of Bharatpur; local market for millet, gram, oilseeds.

Nadelhorn, Switzerland: see MISCHABELHÖRNER.

Nadendal, Finland: see NAANTALI.

Naden Harbour (nā'dŭn), inlet (8 mi. long, 1–3 mi. wide) in N Graham Isl., W B.C., 17 mi. W of Massett; crabbing, crab canning; whaling station.

Nadezhda (nädyĕzh'dä), village (pop. 15,209), Sofia dist., W Bulgaria, N suburb of Sofia; light mfg.; poultry raising, dairying, truck gardening.

Nadezhda Strait (nŭdyĕzh'dŭ), Jap. *Rashowa-kaikyo* (räshō'ä-kīkyō'), in central main Kurile Isls. group, Russian SFSR, bet. Matua (N) and Rasshua (S) isls.; 17 mi. wide.

Nadezhdinsk, Russian SFSR: see SEROV.

Nadezhdinskaya (nŭdyĕzh'dyĭnskīŭ), village, S Maritime Territory, Russian SFSR, on Trans-Siberian RR and 18 mi. N of Vladivostok; grain, soybeans; lumbering. Junction of rail spur to Tavrichanka lignite mines.

Nadi, Fiji: see NANDI.

Nadia (nŭd'yŭ), district (□ c.1,600; pop. c.870,000), E West Bengal, India; ⊙ Krishnagar. In Ganges Delta; bounded E by East Bengal (E Pakistan), W by Bhagirathi R.; drained by the Jalangi. Alluvial plain; bamboo, Moringa, and areca palm groves; rice, jute, linseed, sugar cane, wheat, tobacco, chili, turmeric. Dispersed swamps, largely responsible for dist's. high malarial mortality. Sugar-cane processing is important industry (main center, Krishnagar); hand-loom cotton weaving (Santipur); clay-figure mfg. (Krishnagar). Noted Sanskrit schools at NABADWIP. Part of Sen kingdom, defeated (13th cent.) by a Delhi sultan. Robert Clive's decisive victory over nawab of Bengal (1757) at Plassey resulted in English acquisition of Bengal. Original dist. (□2,879; 1941 pop. 1,759,846) reduced 1947, when E area was separated to form new dist. of Kushtia, East Bengal, following creation of Pakistan.

Nadia, town, India: see NABADWIP.

Nadiad (nŭd'ēäd), town (pop. 46,510), Kaira dist., N Bombay, India, 12 mi. ESE of Kaira; rail junction; trade center (cotton, grain, tobacco, ghee, fruit, timber); cotton and sugar milling, food canning, mfg. of bobbins, handicraft cloth, leather goods; brass foundry; model experimental farm, creamery. Arts and science col. Near-by village was birthplace (1875) of Sardar Vallabhbhai Patel, Deputy Prime Minister of India (1947–50).

Nadlac (nŭdläk'), Rum. *Nădlac,* Hung. *Nagylak* (nŏ'dyŭlŏk), village (pop. 12,284), Arad prov., W Rumania, on Mures R. and 27 mi. W of Arad, on Hung. border; agr. center; hemp processing.

Nador, Sp. Morocco: see VILLA NADOR.

Nadrag (nŭdräg'), Rum. *Nădrag,* Hung. *Nadrág* (nŏ'dräk), village (pop. 1,427), Severin prov., W Rumania, 14 mi. E of Lugoj; iron foundries and rolling mills, producing sheet iron, steel tubes, saws, and nickelware.

Nadterechnaya (nŭdtyĕ'rĭchnĭŭ), village (1926 pop. 4,533), S Grozny oblast, Russian SFSR, on right bank of Terek R., opposite Naurskaya, and 28 mi. NW of Grozny; cotton, livestock. Until 1944, Nizhni Naur.

Nadudvar (nä'dōōdvŏr), Hung. *Nádudvar,* town (pop. 10,491), Hajdu co., E Hungary, on Kösely R. and 23 mi. WSW of Debrecen; rail terminal; flour mills; market for wheat, corn, cattle area.

Nadur (nädōōr'), town (pop. 3,465), SE Gozo, Maltese Isls., 3 mi. E of Victoria; fruit, vegetables; sheep, goats.

Nadushita (nŭdōōshē'tŭ), Rum. *Nădușita* (nŭdōōshē'tä), village (1941 pop. 3,056), N Moldavian SSR, 19 mi. SW of Soroki; wheat, sunflowers. Served by Drokiya (Rum. *Drochia*) rail station (1941 pop. 950), 4 mi. W.

Naduvattam (nŭdōōvŭ'tŭm), village, Nilgiri dist., SW Madras, India, 12 mi. WNW of Ootacamund, in tea- and cinchona-estate area; mfg. of quinine. Also spelled Naduvatam.

Nadvoitsy or **Nadvoytsy** (nŭdvoi'tsē), town (1939 pop. over 500), E Karelo-Finnish SSR, port on White Sea–Baltic Canal, at N end of lake Vygozero, 45 mi. SSW of Belomorsk; furniture mfg.

Nadvornaya (nŭdvôr'nīŭ), Pol. *Nadwórna* (nŭdvōōr'nä), city (1931 pop. 8,716), central Stanislav oblast, Ukrainian SSR, on Bystritsa Nadvornyanskaya R. and 22 mi. SSW of Stanislav, in petroleum dist.; mfg. center; petroleum refining, lumbering, flour milling. Has ruins of old castle. Passed from Poland to Austria (1772); scene of Russo-German battles in 1915; reverted to Poland (1919); ceded to USSR in 1945.

Nadym River (nŭdĭm'), Yamal-Nenets Natl. Okrug, Tyumen oblast, Russian SFSR, rises in Num-to (lake) at 63°45'N 72°E, flows 155 mi. N to Ob Bay, forming Nadym Bay (c.90 mi. long E–W) W of Nyda.

Naegi (nä-ā'gē), town (pop. 5,041), Gifu prefecture, central Honshu, Japan, 2 mi. NW of Nakatsu; mining center (quartz crystal, topaz, sapphire).

Naenwa (nīn'vŭ), town (pop. 4,847), E Rajasthan, India, 26 mi. NNE of Bundi; millet, oilseeds. Also spelled Nainwa.

Naeroy, canton, Norway: see ABELVAER.

Naeroy Fjord (năr'ûü), Nor. *Nærøyfjord,* S arm of Aurlands Fjord, Sogn og Fjordane co., W Norway; c.12 mi. long, less than 1 mi. wide. Entrance cuts through 5,600-ft. mts. On its W shore lies village of Bakka (băk'kä), formerly Bakke, 24 mi. SSW of Sogndal; at head of fjord, 2 mi. SSW, lies Gudvangen (gōōd'väng-ŭn) village, over which 6,000-ft. mts. tower vertically. Near by is scenic Kilofoss, a waterfall (500 ft.). Naerodal, the valley, continues as a canyon c.8 mi. SW to Stalheim (stäl'hām) village in Hordaland co., a tourist and skiing center on road leading to Voss. Formerly called Naerheims Fjord or Naerö Fjord.

Naerum (nâ'rōōm), town (pop. 1,742), Copenhagen amt, Zealand, Denmark, 9 mi. N of Copenhagen.

Naes, Norway: see NES, village, Aust-Agder co.

Naesby (nĕs'bü), town (pop. 1,550), Odense amt, Denmark, on Fyn isl., 2 mi. NNW of Odense; oil refinery.

Naesflaten, Norway: see NESFLATEN.

Naestved (nĕst'vĕdh), city (1950 pop. 17,557), Praesto amt, Zealand, Denmark, on Sus R. and 43 mi. SW of Copenhagen; industrial center, rail junction. Paper, glass, pottery, agr. machinery, meat canning; fishing. Dates from 12th cent.

Nafa, Ryukyu Isls.: see NAHA.

Nafada (näfä'dä), town (pop. 11,898), Bauchi prov., Northern Provinces, E central Nigeria, on Gongola R. and 50 mi. NNE of Gombe; cassava, millet, durra.

Nafadié (näfä'dyä), village, SW Fr. Sudan, Fr. West Africa, on Dakar-Niger RR and 55 mi. WNW of Bamako; peanuts, shea nuts; livestock.

Näfels (nä'fŭls), town (pop. 3,140), Glarus canton, E central Switzerland, on old bed of Linth R. and

4 mi. N of Glarus; metalworking; brushes, corks, sapsago, flour. Capuchin monastery, baroque church (1778–81), Freuler Palace (1645–47) with local antiquities. Scene of Swiss victory (1388) over Austrians.

Nafplion, Greece: see NAUPLIA.

Naf River, Burma-India: see NAAF RIVER.

Naftalan (nŭftŭlän'), town (1946 pop. over 500), central Azerbaijan SSR, 27 mi. ESE of Kirovabad, in oil-bearing dist. Health resort with petroleum baths.

Naftali, Hills of (näftälē'), small range of hills, S outcrop of the Lebanon mts., extending c.15 mi. N-S along border bet. NE Israel and SW Lebanon, W of headwaters of the Jordan; rise to c.2,900 ft.

Naftia, Lake, Sicily: see PALAGONIA.

Naft-i-Shah or **Naft-e-Shah** (both: näft'ĕshä'), oil town, Fifth Prov., in Kermanshah, W Iran, 95 mi. WSW of Kermanshah, on Iraq border; oil field, adjoining Iraqi Naft Khaneh field (W), is linked by pipe line with Kermanshah refinery.

Naft Kaneh or **Naft Kanah** (näft' kä'nŭ), oil-mining town, Diyala prov., E Iraq, at Iran border opposite Naft-i-Shah, 75 mi. NE of Baghdad.

Naftlug (nŭftlo͝ok'), Georgian *Naftlugi* (nŭftlo͝o'gē), SE suburb and rail hub of Tiflis, Georgian SSR. Junction of lines from Baku (SE), Erivan (S), Batum and Sukhumi (W), and Kakhetian wine dist. (E). Airport.

Naft Safid, Iran: see WHITE OIL SPRINGS.

Nafud, Nefud, or **Nufud** (all: nĕfo͞od'), desert area of Arabian Peninsula, consisting of continuous area of loose white to reddish sand, blown into high dunes, ridges, and mounds. Pasture is offered during winter and spring. It reaches its greatest extent in the Great Nafud or Northern Nafud, bet. the Syrian Desert (N) and Jebel Shammar (S); 180 mi. long (E-W), 140 mi. wide (N-S).

Naga, ruins, Anglo-Egyptian Sudan: see WAD BAN NAGA.

Naga (nä'gä). **1** City (1939 pop. 4,554; 1948 metropolitan area pop. 56,238), ⊙ CAMARINES SUR prov., SE Luzon, Philippines, on Bicol R., on railroad and 50 mi. NW of Legaspi; 13°37'N 123°11'E. Trade center for agr. area (rice, abacá, corn). Cementworks. Formerly Nueva Caceres. **2** Town (1939 pop. 2,935; 1948 municipality pop. 24,911), central Cebu isl., Philippines, on Bohol Strait, on railroad and 12 mi. SW of Cebu city; agr. center (corn, coconuts). Has cement factory.

Nagaa, ruins, Anglo-Egyptian Sudan: see WAD BAN NAGA.

Nagahama (nägä'hämŭ). **1** Town (pop. 7,375), Ehime prefecture, W Shikoku, Japan, port on Iyo Sea, 23 mi. SW of Matsuyama; fishing and lumber-collection center; woodworking factory, sake brewery. Exports lumber, raw silk, charcoal, livestock, fish, paper. Sometimes called Iyo-nagahama. **2** Town, Kochi prefecture, Japan: see KOCHI, city. **3** City (1940 pop. 16,409; 1947 pop. 45,991), Shiga prefecture, S Honshu, Japan, on NE shore of L. Biwa, 40 mi. WNW of Nagoya; mfg. of silk crepe. Includes (since early 1940s) former villages of Kamiteru (1940 pop. 7,338), Rokusho (1940 pop. 4,534), and several smaller villages.

Nagahama, Russian SFSR: see OZERSKI.

Naga Hills (nä'gŭ; Burmese nŭgä'), hill ranges on India-Burma border, bet. Brahmaputra and upper Chindwin rivers, N of Manipur Hills; culminate along frontier in PATKAI RANGE. Wild, undeveloped region; inhabited by Nagas, an Animist Tibeto-Burman group, related to Chins and Kachins, that still practices head hunting and human sacrifice; shifting hillside agr. (rice, corn, vegetables). Nagas are organized into: **Naga Hills** dist. (□ 13,245; 1941 pop. 83,690) of Sagaing div., Upper Burma, ⊙ Singkaling; and autonomous **Naga Hills** dist. (□ 4,289; 1941 pop. 189,641) of E Assam, India, ⊙ Kohima. These 2 dists. are separated by **Naga Tribal Area** (□ c.1,000; pop. c.60,000 ⊙ Tuensang), the most inaccessible Naga tract, extending along Indian side of Patkai Range.

Nagai (nägī'). **1** Town, Kanagawa prefecture, Japan: see YOKOSUKA. **2** Town (pop. 13,934), Yamagata prefecture, N Honshu, Japan, on Mogami R. and 19 mi. WSW of Yamagata; cotton textiles. Iron mining.

Nagai Island (nŭgī'), (32 mi. long, 1–11 mi. wide), Shumagin Isls., SW Alaska, off SW Alaska Peninsula; 55°6'N 160°W; rises to 1,970 ft. (NE); fishing.

Nagakubo-furu (nägä'ko͞obō-fo͞o"ro͞o), town (pop. 3,412), Nagano prefecture, central Honshu, Japan, 9 mi. S of Ueda; rice, wheat, raw silk.

Nagakubo-shin (nägä'ko͞obō-shēn), town (pop. 1,803), Nagano prefecture, central Honshu, Japan, 10 mi. S of Ueda; rice, raw silk, wheat.

Nagalama (nägälä'mä), town, Buganda prov., S Uganda, 19 mi. NNE of Kampala; cotton, coffee, sugar cane; cattle, sheep, goats. R.C. mission.

Nagamangala (nägŭmŭng'gŭlŭ), town (pop. 4,258), Mandya dist., S central Mysore, India, 21 mi. NNW of Mandya; training center for hand-loom weaving; handicraft brassware; millet, rice.

Nagambie (nŭgăm'bē), village (pop. 738), central Victoria, Australia, on Goulburn R. and 70 mi. N of Melbourne; livestock.

Nagamori (nägä'mōrē), town (pop. 5,452), Fukushima prefecture, central Honshu, Japan, 3 mi. SSW of Koriyama; rice, soybeans, tobacco.

Naga-Naga (nä"gä-nä'gä), town (1939 pop. 5,212) in Margosatubig municipality, Zamboanga prov., W Mindanao, Philippines, small port on small Maligay Bay, 40 mi. SW of Pagadian; sawmill; rice, corn, coconuts.

Nagano (nägä'nō), prefecture [Jap. *ken*] (□ 5,261; 1940 pop. 1,710,729; 1947 pop. 2,060,010), central Honshu, Japan; ⊙ Nagano. Mtn. range along W border, rising to 10,527 ft. at Mt. Hotaka; drained by Tenryu R. Hot springs in L. Suwa area. Chief industry is sericulture. Extensive rice growing, lumbering. Mfg. (textiles, sake), woodworking. Main centers: Nagano, MATSUMOTO, UEDA, IIDA, OKAYA, SUWA.

Nagano. **1** Town (pop. 6,576), Akita prefecture, N Honshu, Japan, 6 mi. NE of Omagari; rice growing. **2** City (1940 pop. 76,861; 1947 pop. 94,993), ⊙ Nagano prefecture, central Honshu, Japan, 110 mi. NW of Tokyo and on branch of Shinano R.; 36°39'N 138°11'E. Religious center (site of Zenkoji, a 7th-cent. Buddhist temple). Mfg. (candies, earthenware), woodworking, raw-silk collection. Formerly Zenkoji. **3** Town (pop. 16,536), Osaka prefecture, S Honshu, Japan, 15 mi. SSE of Osaka; rail junction; agr. (rice, oranges, pears; chrysanthemums for making insecticide).

Naganohara (nägä'nōhärŭ), town (pop. 7,789), Gumma prefecture, central Honshu, Japan, 26 mi. NW of Takasaki; agr., stock raising. Hot springs.

Naganuma (nägä'no͞omä), town (pop. 4,840), Fukushima prefecture, central Honshu, Japan, 12 mi. SW of Koriyama; rice, soybeans, silk cocoons; pottery.

Nagao (nä"gä'ō). **1** Town (pop. 8,121), Kagawa prefecture, NE Shikoku, Japan, 9 mi. SE of Takamatsu; agr. center (rice, wheat); lumber, bamboo products. Has artisan fan industry. **2** Town (pop. 4,737), Okayama prefecture, SW Honshu, Japan, 5 mi. WSW of Kurashiki, in agr. area (rice, wheat, peppermint, grapes); yarn, raw silk, sake.

Nagaoka (nägä'ōka), city (1940 pop. 66,987; 1947 pop. 54,958), Niigata prefecture, central Honshu, Japan, on Shinano R. and 35 mi. SSW of Niigata, in agr. area; industrial center (oil refining, chemical plants, engineering works, textile mills).

Nagar (nŭgŭr'). **1** Village, Shimoga dist., NW Mysore, India, 7 mi. S of Hosanagara. As ⊙ a 17th-cent. kingdom, known as Bednur or Bidaruhalli; in 1763, Hyder Ali made it an important arsenal and renamed it Haidarnagar (or Hydernagar). Called Nagar since 1789. Declined after 1893, when Hosanagara replaced it as a subdivisional administrative hq. of dist. **2** Village, Kangra dist., NE Punjab, India, 50 mi. ESE of Dharmsala, in Kulu valley; trades in fruit (apples, pears) and tea. Trout hatchery in Beas R., just W. Site of Urusvati Himalayan Research Inst. of Roerich Mus. Sometimes spelled Naggar. **3** Village, West Bengal, India: see RAJNAGAR.

Nagar or **Nagir** (both: nŭgŭr'), feudatory state (□ 1,600; pop. 14,874) in Gilgit Agency, NW Kashmir; ⊙ Nagar. In NW Karakoram mtn. system; bounded N by Hunza R., which separates Nagar and Hunza states. History parallels that of HUNZA. Prevailing mother tongue, Burushaski.

Nagar or **Nagir,** village, ⊙ Nagar state, Gilgit Agency, NW Kashmir, on left bank of Hunza R. and 35 mi. NE of Gilgit. Fort.

Nagara River, Japan: see KISO RIVER.

Nagar Aveli, Portuguese India: see DAMÃO, district.

Nagarcoil, India: see NAGERCOIL.

Nagar Devla (dāv'lŭ), town (pop. 7,022), East Khandesh dist., E Bombay, India, 14 mi. NE of Chalisgaon; cotton, millet, peanuts. Sometimes written Nagardevla.

Nagareyama (nägärā'yämŭ), town (pop. 7,779), Chiba prefecture, central Honshu, Japan, 5 mi. N of Matsudo; commercial center for rice-growing area; sake brewing.

Nagarjunakonda, hill, India: see GURUZALA.

Nagar Karnul or **Nagarkurnool** (both: nŭgŭr'kŭrno͞ol'), village (pop. 3,952), Mahbubnagar dist., S Hyderabad state, India, 28 mi. SE of Mahbubnagar; millet, rice, oilseeds. Sometimes spelled Nagerkurnool.

Nagarkot, India: see KANGRA, village.

Nagarote (nägärō'tā), town (1950 pop. 3,205), León dept., W Nicaragua, near L. Managua, on railroad and 21 mi. WNW of Managua; agr. (corn, sesame, rice, beans), livestock; lumbering.

Nagar Parkar (nŭgŭr' pär'kŭr), village, Thar Parkar dist., SE Sind, W Pakistan, 95 mi. SE of Umarkot, in small hilly area extending into NE Rann of Cutch; local market center (millet, wheat, salt).

Nagartse (nä'gärtsē) or **Nangkartse** (näng'kärtsē), Chinese *Lang-k'a* or *Lang-k'a-tzu* (läng'kä'dzŭ'), town (Tibetan *dzong*), S Tibet, near lake Yamdrok Tso, on main India-Lhasa trade route and 65 mi. SW of Lhasa. Noted lamasery of Samding, 4 mi. E, headed by abbess was, briefly, residence of 13th Dalai Lama after his return in 1912 from India.

Nagasaki (nä"gŭsä'kē, nägä'-sä'kē), prefecture [Jap. *ken*] (□ 1,574; 1940 pop. 1,370,063; 1947 pop. 1,531,674), NW Kyushu, Japan; chief port and ⊙ NAGASAKI. Bounded NW by Korea Strait, W by E. China Sea, S by Amakusa Sea, E by the Ariakeno-umi and Shimabara Bay. Includes TSUSHIMA, IKI-SHIMA, O-SHIMA (2 isls. with the same name), IKITSUKI-SHIMA, HIRADO-SHIMA, GOTO-RETTO, and numerous scattered islets. Comprises part of hilly Hizen Peninsula, which rises to 4,460 ft. at Mt. Unzen in hot-springs dist. on Shimabara Peninsula. Numerous streams drain many fertile valleys. Deeply indented coast provides numerous natural harbors. Coal fields near Sasebo and on Taka-shima. Primarily agr. (rice, sweet potatoes, grain, soybeans). Widespread production of raw silk. Whaling and fishing on Goto-retto, Tsushima, and other isls. Heavy industry concentrated at Nagasaki; fine porcelain ware produced on Hirado-shima. Sasebo (W) is important naval base.

Nagasaki. **1** City and port (1940 pop. 252,630; 1947 pop. 198,642), ⊙Nagasaki prefecture, W Kyushu, Japan, on S Hizen Peninsula, bet. Sonogi and Nomo peninsulas, on Nagasaki Harbor (2½ mi. long, ¾ mi. wide), in valleys of Urakami and Nakashima rivers, 600 mi. WSW of Tokyo; 32°44'N 129°53'E. DE-SHIMA, an artificial islet, forms a dist. of city. Shipbuilding. Exports coal, cotton yarn, cement, dried fish, rice. First Jap. port to receive Western trade. Visited by Portuguese c.1545; opened 1560 to Dutch, 1854 to U.S., and 1858 to other Western countries. In Second World War, city was the target (Aug. 9, 1945) of 2d atomic bomb, which killed or wounded c.75,000 people and devastated over ⅓ of city. Largest R.C. cathedral (built 1914) in Japan was also destroyed. **2** Town (pop. 7,958), Yamagata prefecture, N Honshu, Japan, 6 mi. NNW of Yamagata; rice, silk cocoons, textiles.

Nagashima (nägä'shĭmä), town (pop. 6,823), Mie prefecture, S Honshu, Japan, port on Kumano Sea, 29 mi. SW of Uji-yamada; exports lumber, woodwork, charcoal, fish, citrus fruit.

Naga-shima (nägä'shĭmä). **1** Island (□ c.35; pop. c.15,000, including offshore islets) of Amakusa Isls., in E.China Sea, Japan, in Kagoshima prefecture, off W coast of Kyushu just SE of Shimo-jima; 9.5 mi. long, 5.5 mi. wide; irregular coastline; mountainous, fertile. Chief products: grain, fish. **2** Island (□ 11; pop. 9,751, including offshore islets), Yamaguchi prefecture, Japan, in Iyo Sea, nearly connected with peninsula S of Yanai (on SW Honshu); 5 mi. long, 3 mi. wide; mountainous, fertile. Produces sweet potatoes, plums, oranges. Mfg. (shell buttons, insect powder, soy sauce) at Kaminoseki on NE coast. Near-by islets: Yashima (SSE), 2½ mi. long, ½ mi. wide; Iwai-shima (W), 2 mi. long, 1½ mi. wide.

Nagasu (nägä'so͞o). **1** Town (pop. 8,360), Kumamoto prefecture, W Kyushu, Japan, on the Ariakeno-umi, 18 mi. NW of Kumamoto; fishing. Makes fish nets. **2** Town (pop. 11,257), Oita prefecture, N Kyushu, Japan, on Suo Sea, 26 mi. NNW of Oita; agr. center (rice, wheat, barley). Fishing.

Nagate Point (nä"gä'tā), Jap. *Nagate-saki*, Ishikawa prefecture, central Honshu, Japan, at NE tip of Noto Peninsula, at NW entrance to Toyama Bay; forms easternmost point of peninsula; 37°27'N 137°22'E. Suzu Point is 4.5 mi. NNW, Rokugo Point is 6 mi. NNW, of Nagate Point.

Nagato (nä"gä'tō), former province in SW Honshu Japan; now Yamaguchi prefecture.

Naga Tribal Area: see NAGA HILLS.

Nagaur (nŭgour'), town (pop. 14,714), ⊙ Nagaur dist., central Rajasthan, India, 75 mi. NNE of Jodhpur; trade center for bullocks, wool, hides, cotton; hand-loom weaving, mfg. of camel fittings, metal utensils, ivory goods. Cattle raising near by.

Nagavali River (nŭ'gŭvŭlē), in S Orissa and NE Madras, India, rises in Eastern Ghats, S of Bhawanipatna (Orissa); flows c.150 mi. SSE, past Palkonda, to Bay of Bengal 5 mi. SSE of Chicacole. Formerly also called Langulya.

Nagayevo, Russian SFSR: see MAGADAN.

Nagbhir, India: see BRAMHAPURI.

Nagcarlan (näg"kärlän'), town (1939 pop. 4,254; 1948 municipality pop. 15,335), Laguna prov., S Luzon, Philippines, 8 mi. NE of San Pablo; agr. center (rice, coconuts, sugar cane).

Nagchu, Nagchhu (näg'cho͞o), or **Nagchuka** (–kä), Chinese *Na-ko-ch'u-tsung* (nä'gŭ'cho͞o'dzo͞ong'), town [Tibetan *dzong*], E Tibet, near headstream of Salween R., on main Lhasa-Jyekundo-Sining trade route and 135 mi. NNE of Lhasa; alt. 14,580 ft. Hot spring just S. Also spelled Nakchukha.

Nagem (nä'khŭm), village (pop. 218), W Luxembourg, 2 mi. NW of Redange; mfg. of agr. machinery; potato and wheat growing.

Nagercoil or **Nagarcoil** (nä'gŭrkoil), city (pop. 51,657), S Travancore, India, 40 mi. SE of Trivandrum; mfg. (coir rope and mats, copra, electrical supplies, palmyra-sugar), distilling, processing of monazite and ilmenite. Technical institute (weaving). Ruins of 9th-cent. Jain temple.

Nagerkurnool, India: see NAGAR KARNUL.

Nagfa (näg'fä), Ital. *Nacfa*, village (pop. 300), Keren div., N Eritrea, on road and 62 mi. N of Keren, in cattle-raising region; trade center. Hot springs near by.

Naggar, India: see NAGAR, Punjab.

Nag Hammadi, Nag Hamadi (năg' hämă'dē), or **Naj' Hamadi** (năj'), town (pop. 8,022), Qena prov.,

Upper Egypt, on W bank of the Nile, on railroad, and 30 mi. WSW of Qena; sugar refining, wool weaving; cereals, sugar cane, dates. Upper Egypt railway here crosses the Nile. Just NW are junction for Western Oasis RR to Kharga oasis and Nag Hammadi barrage on the Nile.

Nagichot, Anglo-Egyptian Sudan: see NAGISHOT.

Nagina (nŭgē'nŭ), town (pop. 26,077), Bijnor dist., N Uttar Pradesh, India, 13 mi. SSE of Najibabad; trade center (rice, wheat, gram, barley, sugar cane, oilseeds); noted carved-ebony work; glass mfg. Sacked 1805 by Pindaris.

Naginimara, India: see NAZIRA.

Nagir, Kashmir: see NAGAR.

Nagishot (nä'gēshōt), agr. village, Equatoria prov., S Anglo-Egyptian Sudan, in hilly region, near Uganda border, 145 mi. ESE of Juba. Formerly spelled Nagichot.

Nagles Mountains, range extending 10 mi. E–W in NE Co. Cork, Ireland; rises to 1,406 ft. 7 mi. WSW of Fermoy.

Nago (nä'gō). **1** Town (1950 pop. 14,842) on Okinawa island, in the Ryukyus, fishing port on W coast of isl., 20 mi. NE of Naha, on inlet of E.China Sea. Agr. center (rice, sweet potatoes, sugar cane); lumber, charcoal. Agr. experiment station. Locally called Nagu. **2** Town (1947 pop. 5,281), Yamaguchi prefecture, SW Honshu, Japan, on Sea of Japan, 7 mi. NE of Hagi; agr. and fishing center; rice, raw silk, lumber.

Nagod (nä'gōd), town (pop. 4,546), central Vindhya Pradesh, India, 16 mi. W of Satna; market center for millet, gram, wheat, building stone. Was ⊙ former princely state of Nagod (□ 532; pop. 87,911) of Central India agency; since 1948, state merged with Vindhya Pradesh.

Nagold (nä'gôlt), town (pop. 5,264), S Württemberg, Germany, after 1945 in Württemberg-Hohenzollern, in Black Forest, on the Nagold and 15 mi. WNW of Tübingen; rail junction; mfg. of textiles, clothing, machinery; woodworking. Summer resort. Has ruins of 12th-cent. castle.

Nagold River, S Germany, rises in Black Forest 7 mi. W of Berneck, flows E to Nagold, then N to the Enz at Pforzheim; 57 mi. long.

Nagolno-Tarasovka or **Nagol'no-Tarasovka** (nŭgôl'-nŭ-tŭrä'sŭfkŭ), town (1939 pop. over 500), S Voroshilovgrad oblast, Ukrainian SSR, in the Donbas, 8 mi. SE of Rovenki; coal mines.

Nagongera (nägông-gĕ'rä), town, Eastern Prov., SE Uganda, on railroad and 12 mi. WNW of Tororo; cotton, corn, millet, sweet potatoes, bananas.

Nagor, in Thai names: see NAKHON.

Nagore (nägôr'), town in NEGAPATAM municipality, Tanjore dist., SE Madras, India, port on Coromandel Coast of Bay of Bengal, 4 mi. N of twin port of Negapatam, at mouth of arm of Cauvery R., at S border of Fr. settlement of Karikal. Rail terminus. Moslem place of pilgrimage; Arabic schools.

Nagorn, in Thai names: see NAKHON.

Nagorno-Karabakh Autonomous Oblast (nŭgôr'nŭ-kŭrŭbäkh') [Rus.,=mountain Karabakh], administrative division (□ 1,700; 1946 pop. estimate 130,000) of SW Azerbaijan SSR; ⊙ Stepanakert. Mtn. region on E slopes of the Lesser Caucasus; bounded W by Karabakh Range; drained by Terter R. (N; hydroelectric station at Madagiz); 30% forested (mainly in W). Livestock raising (cattle, sheep, mules), butter and cheese production, leather working; cotton, orchards, vineyards, guayule; sericulture. Silk spinning and weaving, wine making, furniture mfg. Chief towns: Shusha, Stepanakert. Pop. 90% Armenian. Formed 1923. Formerly also spelled Karabagh.

Nagornoye (nŭgôr'nŭyŭ), town (1939 pop. over 2,000), central Leningrad oblast, Russian SFSR, just SE of Krasnoye Selo, in picturesque hilly location. Site of palace (built 1829). Until 1944, called Dudergof, Ger. *Duderhof*.

Nagornski or **Nagornskiy** (nŭgôrn'skē), town (1941 pop. over 500), E central Molotov oblast, Russian SFSR, on railroad (Nagornaya station) and 5 mi. S (under jurisdiction) of Gubakha; coal-mining center in Kizel bituminous-coal basin. Developed during Second World War.

Nagorny or **Nagornyy** (-gôr'nē), town (1948 pop. over 2,000), SE Yakut Autonomous SSR, Russian SFSR, in Stanovoi Range, on Yakutsk-Never highway and 180 mi. S of Aldan; mica and gold mines.

Nagorskoye (-skŭyŭ), village (1939 pop. over 500), N Kirov oblast, Russian SFSR, on Vyatka R. and 65 mi. NE of Kirov; coarse grain, flax.

Nagor Sridhamaraj, Thailand: see NAKHON SITHAMMARAT.

Nagorye or **Nagor'ye** (-yĭ), village (1926 pop. 1,018), SW Yaroslavl oblast, Russian SFSR, 26 mi. SE of Kalyazin; flax.

Nagoya (nä"gō'yä), city (1940 pop. 1,328,084; 1947 pop. 853,085), ⊙ Aichi prefecture, central Honshu, Japan, port on NE shore of Ise Bay, 90 mi. ENE of Osaka and on small Shonai R.; 35°10'N 136°55' E. Major industrial and transportation center; textile mills; wood-processing, dyeing, and chemical plants, engineering works, metalworking factories. Produces fine porcelain, cloisonné. Its port is at former town of Atsuta (now part of Nagoya). Exports cotton textiles, porcelain, pottery, looms, flour, sake. Site of Nagoya Imperial Univ., castle (built 1612 by Ieyasu, founder of Tokugawa shogunate), and important Buddhist temples of Higashi and Nishi Honganji. Atsuta-jingu (Shinto shrine; founded in 2d cent.) contains imperial treasures. Includes (since 1937) former towns of Shimo-no-isshiki and Shonai. Bombed (1944–45) in Second World War.

Nagpur (näg'pŏŏr), district (□ 3,836; pop. 1,059,989), central Madhya Pradesh, India, on Deccan Plateau; ⊙ Nagpur. At S base of central Satpura Range; partly bordered NW by Wardha, SE by Wainganga rivers; drained by Kanhan and Pench rivers. Mainly undulating plain; major cotton-growing tract in W, wheat area in E; famous Nagpur oranges, mango groves, betel farms, mahua, and tamarind in fertile central river valleys; millet, oilseeds (chiefly flax). Sal and satinwood in dispersed forest areas (notably around Umrer). An important source of India's manganese; extensive mining area in vicinity of Ramtek and bet. Khapa and Saoner. Sandstone and marble quarries near Kamptee (trade center). Nagpur (⊙ Madhya Pradesh) is a major communications hub and cotton-textile center. Cotton ginning, oilseed milling, handicraft glass making and silk weaving. Part of a Gond dynasty in early-18th cent.; in 1743, became part of Mahratta kingdom of Nagpur. In 1817, as a result of Br. victory over Mahrattas at fortified hill of Sitabaldi (in Nagpur city), area passed to British and, with SE portion of prov., was indirectly administered by govt. of India until formation 1861 of Central Provs. Pop. 86% Hindu, 7% Moslem, 6% tribal (mainly Gond).

Nagpur, city (pop. 301,957) ⊙ Madhya Pradesh and Nagpur dist., central Madhya Pradesh, India, on Deccan Plateau, on tributary of Kanhan R. and 420 mi. ENE of Bombay; 21°9'N 79°5'E; alt. 1,000 ft. Major communications hub (junction of main Indian railroads and highways; airport); a leading trade and industrial center; outlet for dist.'s extensive manganese deposits. An important cotton-textile center; sawmilling and paper industries; mfg. of dyes, hosiery, textile machinery, matches, explosives, ice, furniture; rubber processing, oilseed milling; pottery works, iron foundries. Railway workshops near Itawari (E station). Famous Nagpur oranges are a major export item. Industries mainly in E part of city; in W area are govt. bldgs. and Nagpur Univ. (founded 1923; has arts, law, science, technological, agr., and teachers training colleges); medical, engineering, and handicraft schools. Horticultural gardens are site of research in area's famous orange and other fruit trees. Experimental farm, 20 mi. ENE, at village of Tharsa, supplies mulberry and other seeds to state's silk-growing centers. City was seat of a Gond dynasty in early-18th cent.; in 1743, became ⊙ Mahratta kingdom of Nagpur. In 1817, fortified hill of Sitabaldi (in center of city) was scene of battle which led to final Br. overthrow of Mahratta power. Became ⊙ Central Provs. following prov. formation in 1861.

Nags Head, resort town (1940 pop. 45), Dare co., E N.C., 4 mi. NNE of Manteo, on barrier beach bet. Roanoke Sound and the Atlantic; bathing, game hunting; commercial fishing.

Nagu, Ryukyu Isls.: see NAGO, Okinawa.

Naguabo (nägwä'bō), town (pop. 4,442), E Puerto Rico, near the coast, 6 mi. ENE of Humacao; sugar-growing center. Sugar is loaded at its port Playa de Naguabo 2 mi. SE. Marble deposits near by.

Naguanagua (nägwänä'gwä), town (pop. 858), Carabobo state, N Venezuela, 5 mi. N of Valencia; coffee, sugar cane, cotton, corn, fruit.

Naguilian (nägēlē'än). **1** Town (1939 pop. 3,460; 1948 municipality pop. 7,359), Isabela prov., N Luzon, Philippines, on Cagayan R. near its junction with the Magat, and 8 mi. SSW of Ilagan; agr. center (rice, corn). **2** Town (1939 pop. 2,015; 1948 municipality pop. 15,227), La Union prov., N central Luzon, Philippines, near W coast, 8 mi. SE of San Fernando; rice-growing center.

Nagutskoye (nŭgŏŏt'skŭyŭ), village (1926 pop. 6,933), S Stavropol Plateau, 21 mi. NW of Mineralnya Vody; flour mill; wheat, sunflowers, castor beans; livestock.

Nagyag, Rumania: see SACARAMBU.

Nagyatad (nŏ'dyŏtäd), Hung. *Nagyatád*, town (pop. 7,047), Somogy co., SW Hungary, on Rinya R. and 22 mi. SW of Kaposvar; silk, thread, paint, bricks; tobacco market.

Nagybajom (nŏ'dyŭboi"ôm), town (pop. 5,467), Somogy co., SW Hungary, 14 mi. W of Kaposvar; wheat, cattle.

Nagybanhegyes (nŏ'dyŭbänhĕ"dyĕsh), Hung. *Nagybánhegyes*, town (pop. 3,743), Csanad co., SE Hungary, 18 mi. SSW of Bekescsaba; grain, onions, cattle, hogs.

Nagybanya, Rumania: see BAIA-MARE.

Nagybaracska (nŏ'dyŭbŏ"rŏch-kŏ), town (pop. 3,349), Bacs-Bodrog co., S Hungary, on arm of the Danube and 10 mi. SSW of Baja; grain, hogs, cattle; fishing.

Nagybatony (nŏ'dyŭbä"tônyŭ), Hung. *Nagybátony*, town (pop. 2,977), Heves co., N Hungary, 9 mi. S of Salgotarjan; lignite mines in vicinity.

Nagybecskerek, Yugoslavia: see ZRENJANIN.

Nagyberezna, Ukrainian SSR: see VELIKI BEREZNY.

Nagybocsko, Ukrainian SSR: see VELIKI BOCHKOV.

Nagycenk (nŏ'dyŭ-tsĕngk), town (pop. 1,886), Sopron co., W Hungary, on Ikva R. and 7 mi. SE of Sopron; beet-sugar refinery.

Nagyderzsida, Rumania: see BOBOTA.

Nagydisznod, Rumania: see CISNADIE.

Nagydorog (nŏ'dyŭdŏrôg), town (pop. 3,638), Tolna co., W central Hungary, 19 mi. N of Szekszard; wheat, barley, dairy farming.

Nagyecsed (nŏ'dyĕ-chĕd), town (pop. 7,534), Szatmar-Bereg co., NE Hungary, on Kraszna R. and 32 mi. ESE of Nyiregyhaza; hemp, clover, horses.

Nagyenyed, Rumania: see AIUD.

Nagy Fatra, mountains, Czechoslovakia: see GREATER FATRA.

Nagyhalasz (nŏ'dyŭhŏläs), Hung. *Nagyhalász*, town (pop. 7,909), Szabolcs co., NE Hungary, 12 mi. N of Nyiregyhaza; hemp, flour; wheat, tobacco, hogs, cattle.

Nagyhalmagy, Rumania: see HALMAGIU.

Nagyigmand (nŏ'dyĭgmänd), Hung. *Nagyigmánd*, town (pop. 2,438), Komarom-Esztergom co., N Hungary, 20 mi. E of Győr; grain, tobacco, horses.

Nagyilonda, Rumania: see ILEANDA.

Nagykallo (nŏ'dyŭkäl-lō), Hung. *Nagykálló*, town (pop. 9,863), Szabolcs co., NE Hungary, 8 mi. SE of Nyiregyhaza; tobacco warehouses; wheat, tobacco, corn; cattle, hogs. Agr. high school.

Nagykalota, Rumania: see CALATA.

Nagykamaras (nŏ'dyŭkŏmŏräsh"), Hung. *Nagykamarás*, town (pop. 4,437), Csanad co., SE Hungary, 15 mi. S of Bekescsaba; onions, corn, wheat, cattle.

Nagykanizsa (nŏ'dyŭkŏnĭ-zhŏ), city (pop. 30,791), Zala co., SW Hungary, 65 mi. WNW of Pecs; rail, market center; mfg. (machines, shoes, cognac, coffee substitute); distilleries, breweries, flour mills, brickworks. Truck farming, grain, livestock raising in area.

Nagykapos, Czechoslovakia: see VELKE KAPUSANY.

Nagykaroly, Rumania: see CAREI.

Nagykarolyfalva, Yugoslavia: see RANKOVICEVO, Vojvodina, Serbia.

Nagykata (nŏ'dyŭkätŏ), Hung. *Nagykáta*, town (pop. 10,764), Pest-Pilis-Solt-Kiskun co., N central Hungary, 31 mi. ESE of Budapest; flour mills, bricks, tiles. Castle.

Nagykikinda, Yugoslavia: see KIKINDA.

Nagykörös (nŏ'dyŭkŭ"rŭsh), Hung. *Nagykőrös*, city (pop. 29,899), Pest-Pilis-Solt-Kiskun co., central Hungary, 10 mi. NNE of Kecskemet; agr. market, wine center; distilleries, flour mills, canned goods, bricks. Exports apricots, cherries, mahalebs. Grain, melons, onions, beans, cattle, horses.

Nagykörü (nŏ'dyŭkŭrŭ), Hung. *Nagykörű*, town (pop. 3,599), Jasz-Nagykun-Szolnok co., E central Hungary, on Tisza R. and 14 mi. NNE of Szolnok; fishing.

Nagykovacsi (nŏ'dyŭkôvä-chē), Hung. *Nagykovácsi*, town (pop. 2,883), Pest-Pilis-Solt-Kiskun co., N central Hungary, in Buda Mts., 11 mi. NW of Budapest; quicklime mfg. Lignite mine, limestone quarry in vicinity.

Nagylajosfalva, Yugoslavia: see PADINA.

Nagylak, Rumania: see NADLAC.

Nagyleta (nŏ'dyŭlätō), Hung. *Nagyléta*, town (pop 6,586), Bihar co., E Hungary, 15 mi. SE of Debrecen; market, tobacco-shipping center; brick works.

Nagyloc (nŏ'dyŭlōts), Hung. *Nagylóc*, town (pop 2,305), Nograd-Hont co., N Hungary, 13 mi. ESE of Balassagyarmat; rye, potatoes, honey, sheep.

Nagymagocs (nŏ'dyŭmägôch), Hung. *Nagymágocs* town (pop. 4,476), Csongrad co., S Hungary, 1 mi. SE of Szentes; market center (grain, paprika poultry); distilleries.

Nagymaros (nŏ'dyŭmŏrôsh), town (pop. 4,470) Nograd-Hont co., N Hungary, on the Danube and 22 mi. NNW of Budapest; river port, summer resort; paper mills, brickworks, champagne mfg. Large Ger. pop. near by; truck farming (wine honey, poultry).

Nagymarton, Austria: see MATTERSBURG.

Nagymegyer, Czechoslovakia: see CALOVO.

Nagymihaly, Czechoslovakia: see MICHALOVCE.

Nagynyarad (nŏ'dyŭ-nyäräd), Hung. *Nagynyárád* town (pop. 2,120), Baranya co., S Hungary, 6 mi. WSW of Mohacs; grain, potatoes, livestock.

Nagyompoly, Rumania: see VALEA-DOSULUI.

Nagyoroszi (nŏ'dyôrôsē), town (pop. 2,199), Nograd-Hont co., N Hungary, 11 mi. WSW of Balassagyarmat; rye, potatoes, sheep.

Nagyrabe (nŏ'dyŭräbā), Hung. *Nagyrábé*, town (pop. 3,575), Bihar co., E Hungary, 20 mi. ESE of Karcag; wheat, tobacco, cattle.

Nagyrakoc, Ukrainian SSR: see VELIKO-RAKOVETSKAYA.

Nagyröce, Czechoslovakia: see REVUCA.

Nagysajo, Rumania: see SIEU.

Nagysarmas, Rumania: see SARMAS.

Nagyselyk, Rumania: see SEICA-MARE.

Nagysink, Rumania: see CINCUL.

Nagysomkut, Rumania: see SOMCUTA-MARE.

Nagyszalonta, Rumania: see SALONTA.

Nagyszeben, Rumania: see SIBIU, city.

Nagyszenas (nŏ'dyŭsănăsh), Hung. *Nagyszénás*, town (pop. 7,211), Bekes co., SE Hungary, 20 mi. W of Bekescsaba; brickworks, pottery; grain, sheep, cattle.
Nagyszöllös, Ukrainian SSR: see VINOGRADOV.
Nagyszombat, Czechoslovakia: see TRNAVA.
Nagytapolcsany, Czechoslovakia: see TOPOLCANY.
Nagyteteny (nŏ'dyŭtā"tānyü), Hung. *Nagytétény*, town (pop. 9,836), Pest-Pilis-Solt-Kiskun co., N central Hungary, on the Danube and 10 mi. SSW of Budapest; mfg. (chemicals, soap, metal and rubber goods); cement works, flour mills; handicraft woodworking. Hogs raised near by.
Nagyturany, Czechoslovakia: see TURANY.
Nagyvarad, Rumania: see ORADEA.
Naha (nä'hä), largest city (1950 pop. 44,779) on Okinawa island, in the Ryukyus, port on SW coast of isl., on inlet of E.China Sea. Mfg. center; textiles, Panama hats, pottery, lacquer ware. Exports sugar, dried fish, hats, textiles. Was ⊙ Okinawa prefecture until Aug., 1945, when it became hq. of U.S. military governor of the Ryukyus. Former names: Nawa, Nafa.
Nahalal (nähäläl'), settlement (pop. 1,000), N Israel, at N edge of Plain of Jezreel, 6 mi. W of Nazareth; dairying and agr. center. Site of girls' training farm. First smallholders' cooperative settlement in Palestine; modern village, founded 1921 on reclaimed land, is on site of biblical locality.
Nahalat Yehuda (nähälät' yĕhōōdä') or **Nachlat Yehuda** (näkhlät'), settlement (pop. 800), W Israel, in Judaean Plain, just N of Rishon le Zion; brick mfg.; mixed farming. Founded 1914. Also spelled Nahlat Yehuda.
Nahalat Yits-haq or **Nachlat Yitzhak** (both: yĕts-häk'), E industrial suburb of Tel Aviv, W Israel, in Plain of Sharon. Has works processing stone, marble, fruit products, chemicals, olive oil, cosmetics, soap.
Nahan (nä'hŭn), town (pop. 7,136), ⊙ Sirmur dist., S Himachal Pradesh, India, in Siwalik Range, 38 mi. SSE of Simla; local market center for wheat, corn, rice, potatoes, spices, timber; ironworks (sugar-cane crushers), rosin factory; hand-loom weaving, wood carving. Was ⊙ former Punjab Hill state of Sirmur. Cantonment of Shamsherpur (pop. 803) lies 1 mi. W.
Nahant (nŭhănt', nŭhänt'), resort town (pop. 2,679), Essex co., E Mass., on rocky peninsula jutting S of Lynn into Massachusetts Bay. Settled 1630, inc. 1853.
Nahar (nä'hŭr), village, Rohtak dist., SE Punjab, India, 35 mi. SSW of Rohtak; local trade in millet, gram, salt, cotton.
Naharayim or **Naharaim** (both: nähäräyēm'), village, N Jordan, on left bank of the Jordan (Israeli border), at mouth of the Yarmuk, 11 mi. S of Tiberias; site of Rutenberg Works, hydroelectric power station, completed 1932.
Nahari, Japan: see NAWARI.
Nahariya or **Naharia** (both: nähärē'ä), settlement (1949 pop. 2,900), Lower Galilee, NW Israel, on Mediterranean, near Lebanese border, on railroad and 15 mi. NNE of Haifa; seaside resort; poultry-raising center; fruit and vegetable canning, dairying. Founded 1934. Suffered repeated attacks during Arab riots, 1936–39.
Nahar Ouassel, Oued, Algeria: see CHÉLIFF RIVER.
Nahavand, Iran: see NEHAVEND.
Nahe River (nä'ŭ), W Germany, rises near Saar border, flows 60 mi. generally NE, past Bad Kreuznach, to the Rhine at Bingen. Receives the Glan (right).
Nahiya, Egypt: see NAHYA.
Nahlat Yehuda, Israel: see NAHALAT YEHUDA.
Nahma (nä'mŭ), village (1940 pop. 592), Delta co., S Upper Peninsula, Mich., 20 mi. ENE of Escanaba, on Big Bay De Noc; lumber milling. Indian settlement near by.
Nahmakants Lake, Piscataquis co., central Maine, 20 mi. WNW of Millinocket, in lumbering, recreational area; 4 mi. long. Joined by stream to Pemadumcook L.
Nahrin, Afghanistan: see NARIN.
Nahr-i-Siraj (nŭr'-ĭ-sĭräj'), irrigated district in S Afghanistan, on left bank of Helmand R. and 20 mi. NE of Girishk.
Nahr 'Umar or **Nahr Umr** (nä'hŭr ōō'mŭr), town, Basra prov., SE Iraq, on the Tigris, on E shore of the Hor al Hammar, and 20 mi. NNW of Basra. Oil well begun here 1947 began producing 1949.
Nahualá (näwälä'), town (1950 pop. 1,028), Sololá dept., SW central Guatemala, 10 mi. NW of Sololá, near head of Nahualate R. (here called the Nahualá); alt. 8,199 ft. Produces woolen blankets, corn-grinding stones; corn, black beans.
Nahualate River (näwälä'tä), SW Guatemala, rises in W highlands near Nahualá, flows c.100 mi. S past Santa Catarina, through coffee and sugar-cane region, to the Pacific 7 mi. SE of Tahuesco.
Nahuatzén (näwätsĕn'), town (pop. 3,046), Michoacán, central Mexico, 17 mi. NNE of Uruapan; sugar cane, fruit, tobacco, corn, livestock.
Nahud (nŭhōōd'), **El Nahud**, or **En Nahud** (both: ĕn nŭhōōd'), town (pop. 20,950), Kordofan prov., central Anglo-Egyptian Sudan, on road and 130 mi. WSW of El Obeid; agr. and trade center (gum arabic, sesame, peanuts).
Nahuelbuta, Cordillera de (kôrdĭyä'rä dä näwĕl-bōō'tä), pre-Andean forested range in S central Chile, extends c.90 mi. N-S in Arauco, Bío-Bío, and Malleco provs.; rises to 4,725 ft.
Nahuel Huapí (näwĕl' wäpē'), village (pop. estimate 400), ⊙ Los Lagos dept., SW Neuquén natl. territory, Argentina, on E end of L. Nahuel Huapí, at outlet of Limay R., in Nahuel Huapí natl. park; resort; stock-raising center. Coal deposits near by.
Nahuel Huapí, Lake (□ 210; alt. 2,516 ft.), in the Andes, in Neuquén and Río Negro natl. territories, Argentina, in the lake dist.; extends c.45 mi. NW-SE (1–5 mi. wide) along Sierra de Cuyin Manzano (NE), at foot of Monte Tronador and other peaks on Argentina-Chile border. Outlet: Limay R. With its many arms, peninsulas, and isls., surrounded by forests and snow-covered mts. and in a temperate climate, it is the favorite resort area of the Argentinian Andes. The region is a natl. park, established 1934. Among its resorts are Nahuel Huapí, Villa La Angostura, and San Carlos de Bariloche. Of considerable depth (up to 1,436 ft.), it is navigable for large steamers and is a noted fishing ground (salmon, trout). Its largest isl. is Victoria Isl., in its center, with forestry research station. Some coal deposits near by.
Nahuizalco (näwēsäl'kō), town (pop. 6,452), Sonsonate dept., W Salvador, on Río Grande and 4 mi. NNW of Sonsonate; mat and basket weaving, pottery making; grain, coffee, manioc. Pop. largely Indian.
Nahunta, city (pop. 739), ⊙ Brantley co., SE Ga., 22 mi. E of Waycross; sawmilling.
Nahya or **Nahiya** (nă'hĭyă), village (pop. 10,005), Giza prov., N Upper Egypt, 7 mi. W of Cairo; flax industry.
Naiak (nī'äk), town, Kabul prov., central Afghanistan, 25 mi. N of Panjao, in the Hazarajat; hq. of Yakaolang (Yakkaolang) dist., for which the town is sometimes named.
Naibandan or **Neybandan** (both: näbändän'), town, Tenth Prov., in Khurasan, E Iran, 100 mi. WSW of Birjand, bet. the deserts Dasht-i-Kavir (NW) and Dasht-i-Lut (SE). Also spelled Nehbandan.
Naiba River or **Nayba River** (nībä'), S Sakhalin, Russian SFSR, rises in W range at 47°35'N, flows SE, past Bykov, and N to Sea of Okhotsk near Starodubskoye; c.75 mi. long. Under Jap. rule (1905–45), called Naibuchi (nī'bōōchē).
Naibo, Russian SFSR: see DOBROYE, Sakhalin oblast.
Naibuchi, Russian SFSR: see BYKOV.
Naibuchi River, Russian SFSR: see NAIBA RIVER.
Naic (nä'ēk, nīk), town (1939 pop. 4,402; 1948 municipality pop. 15,222), Cavite prov., S Luzon, Philippines, near Manila Bay, 24 mi. SW of Manila; fishing and agr. center.
Naica (nī'kä), mining settlement (pop. 1,247), Chihuahua, N Mexico, in E outliers of Sierra Madre Occidental, 70 mi. SE of Chihuahua; alt. 4,429 ft. Rail terminus; silver, lead, gold mining.
Naicam (nā'kŭm), village (pop. 266), central Sask., 30 mi. ENE of Humboldt; grain elevators.
Nai Dab Wali, India: see DABWALI.
Naigawan Rebai (nī'gŭvän rä'bī), former petty state (□ 12; pop. 2,888) of Central India agency, N of Nowgong. In 1948, merged with Vindhya Pradesh.
Naiguatá (nīgwätä'), town (pop. 1,193), Federal Dist., N Venezuela, minor port on the Caribbean, at foot of coastal range, 13 mi. E of La Guaira; fishing.
Naiguatá, peak (9,070 ft.) in N Caribbean coastal range of Venezuela, 10 mi. ENE of Caracas.
Naihati (nīhä'tē), town (pop. 42,200), 24-Parganas dist., SE West Bengal, India, on Hooghly R. and 22 mi. N of Calcutta city center; jute, rice, oilseed, and paper milling, paint mfg. Gouripur is N suburb; large power station.
Naihoro, Russian SFSR: see GORNOZAVODSK.
Naiko, Formosa: see NEIHU.
Naila (nī'lä), town (pop. 6,549), Upper Franconia, NE Bavaria, Germany, in Franconian Forest, on small Selbitz R. and 9 mi. W of Hof; mfg. (shoes, rugs, cotton). Chartered 1454.
Naila, India: see JANJGIR.
Nailloux (näyōō'), agr. village (pop. 389), Haute-Garonne dept., S France, 19 mi. SSE of Toulouse; livestock raising.
Nailsea, agr. village and parish (pop. 2,142), N Somerset, England, 8 mi. WSW of Bristol. Has 15th-cent. church.
Nailsworth, urban district (1951 census pop. 3,523), central Gloucester, England, 11 mi. S of Gloucester; metal casting; bacon and ham curing.
Naimisharanya, India: see NIMKHAR.
Nain (nān), village (pop. 285), NE Labrador, on inlet of the Atlantic; 56°33'N 61°41'W; fishing port.
Nain or **Na'in** (näēn'), town (1940 pop. 6,790), Tenth Prov., in Yezd, central Iran, near railroad, 80 mi. ENE of Isfahan and on road to Yezd; grain, nuts, opium. Wool and carpet weaving.
Nain (nā'ĭn), biblical locality, N Palestine, at N foot of Hill of Moreh, 4 mi. ENE of Afula. Jesus here revived the widow's son. Modern village of Nein (nān, nĕn) was evacuated (1948) by Arab pop.
Naini, India: see ALLAHABAD, city.
Naini Tal (nī'nē täl) [*tal*=lake], district (□ 2,627; pop. 291,861), Kumaun div., N Uttar Pradesh, India; ⊙ Naini Tal. Crossed N by central Siwalik Range; bounded E by Sarda R. (Nepal border). Bhabar tract, a submontane area of gravel and shingle, in S; dense sal jungle; growing of oilseeds. Agr. (rice, wheat, gram, corn, barley, sugar cane); a major Indian sugar-processing dist. Main towns: Naini Tal, Kashipur, Haldwani.
Naini Tal, town (pop., including cantonment, 9,539), ⊙ Kumaun div. and Naini Tal dist., N Uttar Pradesh, India, 145 mi. ENE of Delhi, in outer Kumaun Himalayas; alt. 6,346 ft. Popular hill resort; summer hq. of Uttar Pradesh govt. St. Joseph's Col. Town founded 1841. Derives name from picturesque lake (4,703 ft. long, 1,518 ft. wide); yacht club; sulphur springs near S end. Suffered 1880 from severe landslide. China peak (8,565 ft.) is 1 mi. NW; highest point in dist. At Mukteswar, 13 mi. NE of town, is Imperial Veterinary Research Inst., founded 1890 at Poona and removed 1893 to present site.
Nainpur, India: see MANDLA, town.
Nainwa, India: see NAENWA.
Naipalganj Road, India: see NANPARA.
Naira, Indonesia: see BANDANAIRA.
Nairai (nī'rī), island (□ 9; pop. 508), Fiji, SW Pacific, c.50 mi. E of Viti Levu; 5 mi. long; copra, bananas. Once known for mats, baskets.
Nairn or **Nairnshire** (nârn', –shĭr), county (□ 162.9; 1931 pop. 8,294; 1951 census 8,719), NE Scotland, on S shore of Moray Firth; ⊙ Nairn. Bounded by Inverness (S and W) and Moray (E). Drained by Nairn and Findhorn rivers. Surface is mountainous in S (rising to 2,162 ft.), level along sandy coastline. Farming, cattle and sheep grazing, and fishing are main occupations; granite is quarried. Nairn is only burgh.
Nairn, burgh (1931 pop. 4,201; 1951 census 4,700), ⊙ Nairnshire, Scotland, in N part of co., on Moray Firth, at mouth of Nairn R., 16 mi. NE of Inverness; fishing center and seaside resort with good harbor. Has whisky distilleries. Near by is 15th-cent. Rait Castle. Nairn was created a burgh by William the Lion.
Nairne (nârn), village (pop. 454), SE South Australia, 20 mi. ESE of Adelaide; dairy products, livestock.
Nairn River (nârn), Inverness and Nairn, Scotland, rises 15 mi. E of Fort Augustus, flows 38 mi. NE, past Daviot, to Moray Firth at Nairn.
Nairnshire, Scotland: see NAIRN, county.
Nairo, Russian SFSR: see GASTELLO.
Nairobi (nīrō'bē), city (pop. 118,976), ⊙ Kenya, in E African highlands, on Kenya-Uganda RR and 280 mi. NW of Mombasa, its port on the Indian Ocean; 1°16'S 36°52'E; alt. 5,450–5,500 ft. In area of extensive European colonization, it is Br. East Africa's largest city. Administrative center; seat of governor of Kenya colony and protectorate and (since 1948) hq. of East Africa High Commission. Nairobi is also ⊙ Central Prov. (□ 33,916; pop. 2,096,108), Kenya's densely populated upland region noted for its temperate zone crops, livestock, and dairy farms. City's chief industries are meat packing and canning, fruit preserving, flour milling, mfg. of pottery, soap, chemicals, soft drinks, ice cream, furniture, leather goods, paper and sisal products. Principal exports are coffee, tea, pyrethrum, sisal. Nairobi has European and native hosps., govt. and missionary schools, modern hotels, racecourse, Coryndon memorial mus. (natural hist.), and McMillan Library. Hq. Church Missionary Society and R.C. missions. Eastleigh airport is 3 mi. E. Near-by Nairobi Natl. Park (□ 40, established 1946), is a game reserve (lions, hippopotamuses, giraffes, antelopes). Nairobi has healthy upland climate (mean yearly temp. 67°F.; average rainfall 34 in.; cool days and nights March-Nov.). It is an outfitting center for African safaris and a base for excursions (by rail and road) to Mt. Kenya (80 mi. NNE). Founded 1900 as a railhead camp on Mombasa-Uganda line, it was rebuilt (c.1920) on a modern town plan and the swampy plateau (now commercial section) was drained. It was raised to status of city in March, 1950.
Naissaar or **Nayssar** (nī'sär), Ger. *Nargen*, Estonian island (□ 7) in Gulf of Finland, 6 mi. NW of Tallinn; 5 mi. long, 2 mi. wide; lighthouse.
Naitamba or **Naitaba** (both: nītäm'bä), volcanic island (□ 3; pop. 48), Lau group, Fiji, SW Pacific; 2 mi. long; copra.
Naivasha (nīvä'shä), town, Rift Valley prov., W central Kenya, on NE shore of L. Naivasha, on railroad, and 50 mi. NNW of Nairobi; alt. 6,231 ft.; popular resort; wheat-growing, cattle-raising, horse-breeding, and dairying center. European settlements in dist.
Naivasha, Lake (□ 108), W central Kenya, in Great Rift Valley, 35 mi. SSE of Nakuru; 12 mi. long; 9 mi. wide; 60 ft. deep; alt. 6,200 ft. No outlet; water slightly alkaline. In it are hippopotamuses. Stocked with black bass. Flying-boat landing. Town of Naivasha on NE shore. In the lake is volcanic Crescent Isl.
Naix-aux-Forges (nā-ō-fôrzh'), village (pop. 186), Meuse dept., NE France, on Ornain R. and Marne-Rhine Canal, and 13 mi. SSE of Bar-le-Duc; iron foundry.

Najac (näzhäk'), village (pop. 504), Aveyron dept., S France, on height above Aveyron R., 9 mi. SSW of Villefranche-de-Rouergue; hogs, cattle, vegetables. Ruins of 12th-13th-cent. castle.

Najaf (nä'jăf), **An Najaf, Al Najaf** (both: ăn-), or **Nejef** (nĕ'jĕf), town, Karbala prov., central Iraq, on the shore of a small lake near the Euphrates, 50 mi. SSE of Karbala, c.100 mi. S of Baghdad. Founded 8th cent. A.D. by the caliph Harun-al-Rashid or Harun ar-Rashid, who believed this to be the site of the bones of Ali, son-in-law of Mohammed. Ali's tomb has become one of the greatest pilgrimage shrines of the Moslem Shiite sect. A horse-drawn tram leads to KUFA, 7 mi. N. Najaf is sometimes called Meshed Ali.

Najafabad, Iran: see NEJAFABAD.

Najafgarh (nŭ'jŭfgŭr), town (pop. 5,774), W Delhi, India, 15 mi. WSW of Delhi; model rural health center. Sometimes called Najafgarli.

Najasa River (nähä'sä), Camagüey prov., E Cuba, rises SE of Camagüey, flows c.50 mi. SW and S to the Caribbean 4 mi. E of Santa Cruz del Sur. Sometimes called San Juan de Najasa R. Small Sierra Najasa lies along its upper (left) course.

Najd, Saudi Arabia: see NEJD.

Nájera (nä'hārä), city (pop. 2,994), Logroño prov., N Spain, 14 mi. WSW of Logroño, at foot of hill crowned by ruins of anc. castle. Mfg. of furniture, hemp and jute cloth, chocolate, cement; flour milling, tanning, meat processing. Cereals and wine in area. Romanesque monastery of Santa María la Real (founded in 11th cent.) has church (rebuilt 15th cent.) with tombs of Navarrese and Castilian kings, and fine 16th-cent. cloisters. Was frequently residence of kings of Navarre in 11th cent. Near here Peter IV defeated (1367) Henry of Trastamara.

Najerilla River (nähärē'lyä), Logroño prov., N Spain, rises on outer N edge of central plateau, flows c.40 mi. NNE, past Nájera, to the Ebro 18 mi. W of Logroño.

Naj' Hamadi, Egypt: see NAG HAMMADI.

Najibabad (nŭjē'bäbäd), town (pop. 26,898), Bijnor dist., N Uttar Pradesh, India, 60 mi. NNW of Moradabad; trade center (rice, wheat, gram, barley, sugar cane, oilseeds, cotton, timber); sugar processing, blanket mfg. Has ruins of Afghan fort, built 1775 by town's founder, Najib-ud-daula, and his tomb. Glass mfg. 14 mi. W, at Balawali village.

Najimi (nä"jē'mē), village (pop. 2,950), Ishikawa prefecture, central Honshu, Japan, on N Noto Peninsula, on Sea of Japan, 8 mi. ENE of Wajima; rice growing, fishing. Includes Nanatsu-jima (group of 7 islets), in Sea of Japan, 14 mi. NW of village proper. Largest isl. is O-shima, c.½ mi. long; chief product is edible seaweed.

Najin (nä'jĕn'), Jap. *Rashin* or *Rasin* (both: rä'-shēn), city (1944 pop. 34,338), N.Hamgyong prov., N Korea, 40 mi. NE of Chongjin, on Sea of Japan; naval base. The commercial fishing port (ice-free) is connected by 10-mi. tunnel with near-by port of Unggi. In Second World War Najin was chief Jap. naval base in Korea; captured Aug. 13, 1945, by the Russians.

Najran or **Nejran** (both: nĕjrän'), town and oasis in Asir hinterland, Saudi Arabia, at Yemen border; 17°25'N 44°15'E. Agr.: dates, alfalfa, wheat, millet; stock raising. Corresponds to Yam tribal area. Reached (24 B.C.) by a Roman expedition from Egypt; seat of important Christian colony (500–635); visited (1869–70) by the French orientalist Joseph Halévy.

Naju (nä'jōō'), Jap. *Rashu*, town (1949 pop. 20,199), S.Cholla prov., S Korea, 25 mi. NE of Mokpo; commercial center for fruitgrowing area (pears, peaches); makes bamboo ware.

Naka (nä'kä). **1** Town (pop. 18,219), Fukuoka prefecture, N Kyushu, Japan, 3 mi. SE of Fukuoka; agr. center (rice, wheat, barley). **2** Town (pop. 16,138), Gifu prefecture, central Honshu, Japan, 4 mi. E of Gifu; agr. center (rice, raw silk, wheat, sweet potatoes). **3** Town (pop. 10,404), Hyogo prefecture, S Honshu, Japan, 20 mi. NE of Himeji; agr. center (rice, wheat); poultry. Produces tea, woodwork, tiles, soy sauce, floor mats.

Nakada, Egypt: see NAQADA.

Nakada (nä"kä'dä) or **Nakata** (-kä'tä), town (pop. 3,173), Toyama prefecture, central Honshu, Japan, 4 mi. S of Takaoka; patent medicine, tissue paper, textiles, sake, vegetable oil.

Naka-dake, Japan: see ASO-SAN.

Nakadori, Japan: see NAKADORI-SHIMA.

Nakadori-shima (näkä'dōrē-shĭmä), second largest island (□ 67; pop. 42,448, including offshore islets) of isl. group Goto-retto, Nagasaki prefecture, Japan, 25 mi. W of Kyushu; 24 mi. long (with long, narrow N and S peninsulas), 10 mi. wide; deeply indented coastline. Whaling, fishing. Sometimes called Nakadori. Chief town, Arikawa.

Nakagome (näkä'gōmā), town (pop. 6,970), Nagano prefecture, central Honshu, Japan, 17 mi. SE of Ueda; spinning.

Nakagusuku Bay, Ryukyu Isls.: see BUCKNER BAY.

Nakahagi (näkä'-hä'gē), town (pop. 10,538), Ehime prefecture, N Shikoku, Japan, 2 mi. S of Niihama; commercial center for rice-growing region; sake; sawmills.

Nakaizumi, Japan: see IWATA.

Nakajo (nä"kä'jō), town (pop. 12,705), Niigata prefecture, N Honshu, Japan, 21 mi. ENE of Niigata; commercial center for rice-growing area.

Nakama (nä"kä'mä), town (pop. 31,890), Fukuoka prefecture, N Kyushu, Japan, 5 mi. SW of Yawata; rail junction; agr. center (rice, wheat, barley). Coal mines in vicinity.

Nakaminato (näkä'-mē'nätō), town (pop. 18,538), Ibaraki prefecture, central Honshu, Japan, on the Pacific, 6 mi. ESE of Mito; fishing port; mfg. (textiles, soybean paste).

Nakamti (näkäm'tē) or **Lakamti** (lä-), Ital. *Lechemti*, town, ⊙ Wallaga prov., W central Ethiopia, on road and 145 mi. W of Addis Ababa; 9°5'N 36°30'E; alt. c.6,880 ft. Trade center (coffee, hides, beeswax, honey, cereals, gold). Also spelled Nekemti or Lekemti.

Nakamura (näkä'mōōrä). **1** Town (pop. 20,771), Fukushima prefecture, N Honshu, Japan, on the Pacific, 25 mi. E of Fukushima, in agr. area; spinning, pottery making. **2** Town (pop. 9,370), Kochi prefecture, SW Shikoku, Japan, on Shimando R. and 27 mi. SE of Uwajima; mfg. center in agr. area; sake, soy sauce, cotton thread.

Nakaniida (näkänē'dä), town (pop. 8,767), Miyagi prefecture, N Honshu, Japan, 22 mi. N of Sendai; rice, wheat, silk cocoons.

Nakano (näkä'nō). **1** Town (pop. 4,651), Kanagawa prefecture, central Honshu, Japan, 7 mi. SW of Hachioji; potatoes, wheat, millet; raw silk. **2** Town (pop. 13,124), Nagano prefecture, central Honshu, Japan, 12 mi. NE of Nagano; horse-breeding and agr. center. Hot springs.

Nakanojo (näkä"nōjō'), town (pop. 9,106), Gumma prefecture, central Honshu, Japan, 19 mi. NW of Maebashi; rice, raw silk.

Nakano-shima. 1 Island, Fukuoka prefecture, Japan: see HAKATA BAY. **2** Island, Ryukyu Isls.: see TOKARA-GUNTO.

Naka-no-shima (näkä'-nō-shĭmä), island (□ 13; pop. 6,705) of Dozen group of the Oki-gunto, Shimane prefecture, Japan, in Sea of Japan, 7 mi. SW of Dogo, just E of Nishi-no-shima; 6 mi. long, 4 mi. wide. Mountainous; cattle raising, fishing; raw silk.

Naka-no-umi (näkä'nō-ōō'mē), lagoon (□ 39) in Shimane prefecture, SW Honshu, Japan, connected with L. Shinji (W) and inlet of Sea of Japan (E); 10 mi. long, 7 mi. wide. Contains several islets; largest, Daikon-shima. Matsue is on W shore, Yonago on SE shore.

Naka-shima (näkä'shĭmä), island (□9; pop. 10,273), Ehime prefecture, Japan, in Iyo Sea, 7 mi. off NW coast of Shikoku, near Matsuyama; 5 mi. long, 2 mi. wide. Hilly; fertile (citrus fruit, sweet potatoes, ginger). Fishing.

Naka-shiretoko-misaki, Russian SFSR: see ANIVA, CAPE.

Nakata, Japan: see NAKADA.

Naka-tane (nä'kä-tä'nä), town (pop. 16,355) on Tanega-shima, Kagoshima prefecture, Japan, in central part of isl., on E.China Sea; fishing and agr. center; sugar cane, livestock, charcoal.

Nakatsu (näkä'tsōō). **1** Town (pop. 21,425), Gifu prefecture, central Honshu, Japan, 42 mi. NE of Nagoya; paper milling; matches, raw silk, yarn. **2** City (1940 pop. 29,414; 1947 pop. 51,976), Oita prefecture, Japan, port on Suo Sea, 29 mi. SE of Yawata; mfg. center; textile and steel mills; sake breweries, food canneries. Exports lumber, silk, sake.

Nakawn, in Thai names: see NAKHON.

Nakayama (näkä'yämŭ), town (pop. 8,028), Ehime prefecture, W Shikoku, Japan, 14 mi. SSW of Matsuyama; raw silk, rice, lumber, charcoal.

Nakayamaga (näkä'yä'mägŭ), town (pop. 4,142), Oita prefecture, NE Kyushu, Japan, on W Kunisaki Peninsula, 15 mi. NNW of Oita; agr. center (rice, wheat, barley); poultry.

Nakazato (näkä'-zä'tō), town (pop. 5,200), Aomori prefecture, N Honshu, Japan, 19 mi. NW of Aomori; rice, bamboo ware.

Nakchukha, Tibet: see NAGCHU.

Nakel, Poland: see NAKLO.

Nakhabino (nŭkhä'bēnŭ), town (1939 pop. over 500), central Moscow oblast, Russian SFSR, 17 mi. WNW of Moscow; summer resort; furniture.

Nakhichevan or **Nakhichevan' Autonomous Soviet Socialist Republic** (nŭkhēchĭvän'yŭ) (□ 2,100; 1946 pop. estimate 130,000), Azerbaijan SSR; ⊙ Nakhichevan. On Iran border; separated from Azerbaijan proper by a narrow strip of Armenian SSR; on SW slopes of Zangezur Range; drained by Aras R. (Iran frontier). Irrigated agr. (cotton, tobacco, rice, wheat) in lowlands, vineyards and sericulture in foothills. Salt and arsenic mining; cotton ginning, silk spinning, fruit canning. Chief cities: Nakhichevan, Ordubad. Pop. 80% Azerbaijani Turks, 15% Armenians. Formed 1924.

Nakhichevan or **Nakhichevan'. 1** anc. *Naxuana*, city (1926 pop. 10,296), ⊙ Nakhichevan Autonomous SSR, Azerbaijan SSR, near Aras R., on railroad and 80 mi. SE of Erivan; mfg. (furniture, clothing, building materials, metalware), food processing, wine making, cotton ginning. Salt mines at Nakhsol, 10 mi. NNW. Teachers col. Has well-preserved 12th-cent. ruins of towers, mausoleum, and khan's palace. An anc. city (relics from Gr. and Roman periods) ruled by Armenians, Persians, Arabs, Turks, and Mongols until it became a flourishing Armenian trade center in 15th cent. Passed from Persia to Russia in 1828. **2** City, Rostov oblast, Russian SFSR: see ROSTOV, city.

Nakhl (nä'khŭl), village (pop. 137), Sinai prov., NE Egypt, in the center of the plateau of El Tih, 60 mi. WNW of Aqaba. Has airfield.

Nakhodka (nŭkhôt'kŭ), town (1940 pop. over 500), S Maritime Territory, Russian SFSR, port on Sea of Japan, 55 mi. ESE of Vladivostok; rail terminus; shipyards, fish canneries.

Nakhon Chai Si (näkôn' chī' sē'), village (1937 pop. 2,818), Nakhon Pathom prov., S Thailand, on Tha Chin R., on railroad, and 20 mi. W of Bangkok; rice and sugar milling; sugar-cane plantation; fruit gardens.

Nakhon Nayok (nä'yôk'), town (1947 pop. 6,121), ⊙ Nakhon Nayok prov. (□ 834; 1947 pop. 117,547), S Thailand, on Nakhon Nayok R. and 55 mi. NE of Bangkok; rice center.

Nakhon Nayok River, S Thailand, rises in San Kamphaeng Range at alt. of c.3,000 ft., flows 40 mi. S, past Nakhon Nayok, to Bang Pakong R. Linked to Pa Sak R. canal system.

Nakhon Pathom (pätôm'), town (1947 pop. 16,348), ⊙ Nakhon Pathom prov. (□ 861; 1947 pop. 268,958), S Thailand, on railroad and 30 mi. W of Bangkok; head of canal to Tha Chin R. (E); rice, sugar cane, sesame; hog raising; rice milling. Has largest stupa (Phra Pathom) of Thailand, built in 1850s on site of original structure dating from 6th–8th cent. Sometimes called Phra Pathom.

Nakhon Phanom (pänôm'), town (1947 pop. 8,526), ⊙ Nakhon Phanom prov. (□ 3,747; 1947 pop. 307,172), E Thailand, on right bank of Mekong R. (Laos line), opposite Thakhek, and 130 mi. E of Udon (linked by road; projected railway); rice, hog and poultry raising; timber trade. Sometimes spelled Nagor (or Nakhon) Pnom. Religious center of That Phanom is S.

Nakhon Range, Thailand: see SITHAMMARAT RANGE.

Nakhon Ratchasima (rät'chŭsē'mä'), town (1947 pop. 21,774), ⊙ Nakhon Ratchasima prov. (□ 7,871; 1947 pop. 723,393), E Thailand, in SW Korat (Khorat) Plateau, on Mun R., on railroad, and 135 mi. NE of Bangkok; leading trade and communications center of E Thailand; junction of railroads to Udon (N) and Ubon (E); rice, corn, tobacco; sericulture; livestock (cattle, hogs). Founded 17th cent. in region that was part of Cambodia until 14th cent.; developed greatly after railroad construction (1890) from Bangkok. Formerly called Khorat or Korat; also variously spelled Nagor (or Nakon) Rajasima (or Rajsima).

Nakhon Sawan (sŭwän'), town (1947 pop. 12,499), ⊙ Nakhon Sawan prov. (□ 3,778; 1947 pop. 371,898), central Thailand, on right bank of Chao Phraya R. just below confluence of Ping and Nan rivers, 140 mi. NNW of Bangkok and on Bangkok-Chiangmai RR (Paknampho station on left bank); river-navigation hub and a leading teak-collecting center of Thailand; sawmilling, paper mfg.; rice, corn, cotton, hog raising; fisheries. Also called Paknampho or Paknampo; sometimes spelled Nagor Svarga.

Nakhon Sithammarat (sē'tämmŭrät'), town (1947 pop. 15,344), ⊙ Nakhon Sithammarat prov. (□ 3,952; 1947 pop. 494,261), S Thailand, near E coast of Malay Peninsula, on rail spur and 370 mi. S of Bangkok; its port on Gulf of Siam is PAK PHANANG. Agr. center; rice, fruit, coconuts and rubber plantations; handicrafts (weaving). Tin mining at Ronphibun and Cha Mai; iron and lead deposits (NW). An anc. walled town, it was until 13th cent. ⊙ of a state controlling middle Malay Peninsula. Sometimes spelled Nagor (or Nakon) Sridhamaraj (Srithamrat or Srithamarat).

Nakhrachi (nŭkhrä'chē), village, SW Khanty-Mansi Natl. Okrug, Tyumen oblast, Russian SFSR, on Konda R. and 50 mi. SW of Khanty-Mansisk.

Nakhtarana (nŭktŭrä'nŭ), village, W central Cutch, India, 26 mi. WNW of Bhuj.

Nakina (nŭkē'nŭ), village (pop. estimate 500), N central Ont., near Upper Twin L. (10 mi. long), 150 mi. NE of Port Arthur; alt. 1,052 ft.; gold mining, fur trapping. Airfield, radio station.

Nakiri (näkē'rē), town (pop. 6,677), Mie prefecture, S Honshu, Japan, port near entrance to Ise Bay (lighthouse, W) 18 mi. SE of Uji-yamada, in agr. area (rice, wheat, tea); livestock raising, sawmilling. Exports lumber.

Nakkila (näk'kĭlä), village (commune pop. 6,799), Turku-Pori co., SW Finland, on Kokemäki R. and 10 mi. SE of Pori; tanneries.

Naklerov (nä'klārôf), Czech *Naklérov*, Ger. *Nollendorf* (nô'lŭndôrf), village (pop. 54), NW Bohemia, Czechoslovakia, 5 mi. NW of Usti nad Labem. Prussians defeated French here, 1813. Naklerov Pass (alt. 2,204 ft.) marks NE end of the Erzgebirge.

Naklo or **Naklo nad Notecia** (nä'kwō näd nôtĕ'chō), Pol. *Nakło nad Notecią*, Ger. *Nakel* (nä'kŭl), town (pop. 9,649), Bydgoszcz prov., N central Poland, port on Notec R., at W end of Bydgoszcz Canal, and 17 mi. W of Bydgoszcz. Rail junction; mfg.

of tools, fertilizers, roofing materials; brewing, flour and beet-sugar milling, sawmilling, tanning, distilling, woodworking.

Naknek (năk'nĕk), village (pop. 164), S Alaska, near head of Alaska Peninsula, on Kvichak Bay of Bristol Bay at mouth of Naknek R.; 58°40'N 157°1'W; fishing, fish processing. Formerly known as Libbyville, Pawik, Suwarof, or Suworof.

Naknek Lake (40 mi. long, 3–8 mi. wide), S Alaska, near base of Alaska Peninsula; 58°40'N 156°12'W. Game-trout fishing. E part is in Katmai Natl. Monument. Drains W into Kvichak Bay of Bristol Bay by Naknek R. (35 mi. long).

Nako, Japan: see TATEYAMA.

Na-ko-ch'u-tsung, Tibet: see NAGCHU.

Nakodar (nŭkō'dŭr), town (pop. 10,981), Jullundur dist., central Punjab, India, 15 mi. SSW of Jullundur; rail junction; trade center (wheat, gram, corn, cotton); handicrafts (hookah tubes, iron jars, cotton cloth).

Nakon, in Thai names: see NAKHON.

Nakoso (nä"kō'sō), town (pop. 15,706), Fukushima prefecture, central Honshu, Japan, on the Pacific, 13 mi. SW of Taira; coal mines.

Nakskov (näk'skou), city (1950 pop. 16,074), Maribo amt, Denmark, on Lolland isl., on Nakskov Fjord and 15 mi. WNW of Maribo. Sugar-refining center; dairy plant, iron foundry, meat cannery, shipbuilding yards. Important commercial center since 17th cent.

Naktong River (näk'tông'), Jap. *Rakuto-ko*, largest river of Korea proper, in S Korea, rises in mts. just SW of Samchok, flows S, then W and generally SE past Samnangjin to Korea Strait near Pusan; 326 mi. long; navigable 214 mi. by motorboat. Lower course drains large agr. area. Was major Allied defense line in Korean war (1950).

Nakur (nŭkōōr'), town (pop. 6,036), Saharanpur dist., N Uttar Pradesh, India, 15 mi. WSW of Saharanpur; wheat, rice, rape, mustard, gram. Jain temple.

Nakuru (näkōō'rōō), town (pop. 17,625), ⊙ Rift Valley prov., W central Kenya, in Great Rift Valley on N shore of L. Nakuru, on railroad and 90 mi. NNW of Nairobi; alt. 6,071 ft.; 0°18'S 36°9'E. Center of important European farming dist. growing pyrethrum, wheat, corn, sisal, coffee; dairying, blanket mfg., pyrethrum processing. Farmers' cooperative, hosps., racecourse. Airport. Saline L. Nakuru, the feeding ground of flamingos, is drying up rapidly. Surrounding countryside is studded with extinct volcanic craters. Nakuru rail junction (lines to Kisumu and Uganda) 3 mi. NW.

Nakusp (nŭkŭsp'), village (pop. estimate 750), SE B.C., on Upper Arrow L. (Columbia R.) and 55 mi. SSE of Revelstoke; fruit, mixed farming.

Nal (näl), village, Kalat state, central Baluchistan, W Pakistan, on Hingol (Nal) R. and 95 mi. SSW of Kalat, in Jhalawan div. Excavations here have uncovered pottery of prehistoric Indus Valley Civilization.

Nala, Belgian Congo: see PAULIS.

Nalagarh (nä'lăgŭr), town (pop. 3,615), E Patiala and East Punjab States Union, India, 50 mi. NNE of Patiala; local market for wheat, corn, barley. Was ⊙ former princely state of Nalagarh (□ 276; pop. 52,780) of Punjab Hill States, India; since 1948, state (also called Hindur) merged with Patiala and East Punjab States Union.

Nalaikha, Nalaykha, or **Nalayha** (all: nä'līkhä), town, Central Aimak, central Mongolian People's Republic, on railroad and 20 mi. SE of Ulan Bator; leading coal-mining center of Mongolia. Mining, begun in 1915, was on a primitive basis until 1932, when machinery was introduced. Production increased greatly following completion of narrow-gauge railroad (1938–39).

Nalanda (nŭlän'dŭ), village (pop., including near-by villages, 775), Central Prov., Ceylon, in Matale Valley, 25 mi. N of Kandy; rubber processing; rice, coconut palms, vegetables. Has Hindu temple (7th cent. A.D.); residence (12th cent.) of Singhalese king, Parakrama Bahu, who built fortress here.

Nalanda, India: see BARAGAON.

Nalaykha, Mongolia: see NALAIKHA.

Nalbach (näl'bäkh), town (pop. 2,702), W central Saar, on Prims R. and 5 mi. NNE of Saarlouis; metalworking, flour milling.

Nalbari (nŭlbä'rē), town (pop. 3,578), Kamrup dist., W Assam, India, on tributary of the Brahmaputra and 27 mi. NW of Gauhati; road center; trades in rice, mustard, jute, cotton; silk-weaving factory.

Nalchik or **Nal'chik** (näl'chĭk), city (1939 pop. 47,993), ⊙ Kabardian Autonomous SSR, Russian SFSR, on plateau (alt. c.1,500 ft.) in outlier of the central Greater Caucasus, on small Nalchik R. (baths) and 320 mi. SE of Rostov, 880 mi. SSE of Moscow; 43°29'N 43°35'E. Industrial center; machine mfg. (hydroelectric turbines), wood distilling, food processing (meat, bakery products, fruit, dairy goods, flour). Limestone, volcanic tuff, and pumice quarries near by supply construction and cement industries. Health and summer resort since 1905; a tourist center for excursions to Elbrus, Dykh-Tau, Koshtan-Tau, and other high Caucasus peaks (S). Has agr., teachers, and medical colleges. Founded 1817 as Rus. stronghold. During Second World War, held (1942–43) by Germans.

Nalchiti (nŭl'chĭtē), town (pop. 1,953), Bakarganj dist., S East Bengal, E Pakistan, on Bishkhali R. (distributary of Arial Khan R.) and 8 mi. SW of Barisal; trades in rice, oilseeds, sugar cane, jute, betel nuts; rice and oilseed milling.

Nalda (näl'dä), town (pop. 1,112), Logroño prov., N Spain, 10 mi. SSW of Logroño; fruit, olive-oil, vegetables.

Nalden (nĕl'dŭn), Swedish *Nälden*, village (pop. 551), Jamtland co., NW Sweden, on S shore of Nald L., Swedish *Näldsjön* (nĕld'shûn") (10 mi. long, 1–3 mi. wide), 16 mi. NW of Ostersund; wood- and metalworking, woolen milling.

Naldrug (nŭl'drōōg), town (pop. 5,417), Osmanabad dist., W Hyderabad state, India, 29 mi. SE of Osmanabad; millet, wheat, cotton. Has 14th-cent. fort (remodeled in 16th cent.). Was ⊙ dist. until 1853. Also spelled Naldurg.

Nalemutu (nä'lŭmōō'tōō'), Rus. *Dragotsenka* (drägôt'sĭn-kŭ), village (pop. c.700), N Inner Mongolian Autonomous Region, Manchuria, 90 mi. NNE of Hailar; center of the Russian agr. Trekhrechye dist. and hq. of Orochon tribe.

Nalerigu (nälĕrē'gōō), town, Northern Territories, NE Gold Coast, 5 mi. E of Gambaga.

Nalgonda (nŭlgōn'dŭ), district (□ 6,049; pop. 1,275,352), S Hyderabad state, India, on Deccan Plateau; ⊙ Nalgonda. Bordered S by Kistna R.; mainly lowland, drained by Musi R. Largely sandy red soil, with alluvial soil along rivers; millet, oilseeds (chiefly peanuts, castor beans), rice. Rice and oilseed milling, cotton ginning, mfg. of brass and copper vessels. Trade centers: Bhongir, Nalgonda, Suriapet (experimental farm). Became part of Hyderabad during state's formation in 18th cent. Pop. 85% Hindu, 6% Moslem, 1% Christian.

Nalgonda, town (pop. 12,674), ⊙ Nalgonda dist., S Hyderabad state, India, 55 mi. ESE of Hyderabad; road center in agr. area; rice and oilseed milling.

Nalhati (nŭlhä'tē), village, Birbhum dist., W West Bengal, India, 35 mi. NNE of Suri; rail junction; rice milling, cotton weaving, metalware mfg.; rice, pulse, wheat, sugar cane. Rice milling and cotton weaving 10 mi. NNE, at Murarai. Silk growing near by.

Naliboki (nŭlyĭbô'kē), village, NE Baranovichi oblast, Belorussian SSR, 29 mi. NE of Novogrudok, in Naliboki forest (□ 160), noted for old coniferous and deciduous species. Has old wooden church.

Nalinnes (nälĕn'), village (pop. 2,637), Hainaut prov., S central Belgium, 7 mi. E of Thuin; agr., lumbering.

Naliya (nŭl'yŭ), town (pop. 4,512), SW Cutch, India, 55 mi. W of Bhuj; market center for wheat, barley, salt; embroidering.

Nalkhera (nŭlkā'rŭ), town (pop. 3,581), central Madhya Bharat, India, 27 mi. N of Shajapur; cotton, millet, wheat; cotton ginning.

Nalles (näl'lĕs), Ger. *Nals*, village (pop. 703), Bolzano prov., Trentino–Alto Adige, N Italy, near the Adige, 7 mi. NW of Bolzano; wine making.

Nallihan (nälŭhän'), Turkish *Nallıhan*, village (pop. 1,450), Ankara prov., central Turkey, 50 mi. NE of Eskisehir; grain, opium, mohair goats.

Nalón River (nälōn'), Oviedo prov., NW Spain, rises in Cantabrian Mts. 30 mi. ENE of Pajares Pass, flows 80 mi. NW, across rich coal- and iron-mining region, to Bay of Biscay 5 mi. NNE of Pravia.

Nal River, W Pakistan: see HINGOL RIVER.

Nals, Italy: see NALLES.

Naltagua (nältä'gwä), mining settlement (1930 pop. 851), Santiago prov., central Chile, on Maipo R. and 26 mi. SW of Santiago; copper-mining and -smelting center.

Nalut (nälōōt'), town (pop. 4,733), W Tripolitania, Libya, near Tunisian border and W edge of the plateau Gebel Nefusa, 100 mi. SW of Zuara; alt. c.2,000 ft. Road junction; barracans, camel hide tents. Has forts (Berber, Turkish) and troglodyte dwellings.

Nalwadi, India: see SEVAGRAM.

Nalwar, India: see YADGIR.

Nam [Thai,=river]: for Thai names beginning thus, see under following part of the name.

Nama, Burma: see NAMMA.

Nama (nä'mä), coral island (pop. 503), Truk dist., E Caroline Isls., W Pacific, 39 mi. SE of Truk; c.½ mi. in diameter; rises to 20 ft.

Nama (nä'mä'), town, ⊙ Nama co. (pop. 72,593), SW central Kwangsi prov., China, near Hungshui R., 55 mi. N of Nanning; paper-milling center; rice, wheat, millet.

Nama, Formosa: see MINGKIEN.

Namacurra (nämăkōō'rä), village, Zambézia prov., central Mozambique, on railroad and 25 mi. NNE of Quelimane.

Namados, river, India: see NARBADA RIVER.

Namakagon River, Wis.: see NAMEKAGON RIVER.

Namakan Lake (nă'mŭkăn"), NE Minn. and W Ont., in chain of lakes on Can. line; lies partly in St. Louis co., Minn., 35 mi. ESE of International Falls; 12 mi. long, 3 mi. wide. It is continuous with Rainy L., just NW, and with Kabetogama L., just W.

Namakia (nämäkē'ŭ), village, Majunga prov., NW Madagascar, on left arm of Mahavavy R. estuary, 5 mi. NNW of Mitsinjo; sugar milling, mfg. of rum and alcohol.

Namakkal (nä'mŭk-kŭl), town (pop. 12,515), Salem dist., S central Madras, India, 30 mi. S of Salem; road center in cotton area; saltpeter extraction. Magnetite, steatite, and limestone mining, chromite deposits near by.

Namak Lake (nămäk'), Persian *Daryacheh-i-Namak* (däryăchĕ'ĕnămäk'), great salt lake of N central Iran, S of Teheran and E of Qum; 40 mi. across. Salt marshes and deposits along shore. Receives the Qara Chai (W) and Shur R. (N).

Namakwaland, U. of So. Afr.: see NAMAQUALAND.

Namaland, U. of So. Afr. and South-West Africa: see NAMAQUALAND.

Namaliga (nämälē'gä), town, Buganda prov., S Uganda, 18 mi. N of Kampala; cotton, coffee, sugar; livestock. Just W is Bombo, Br. military camp.

Naman (näm'än'), Mandarin *Nanan* (nän'än'),town (pop. 15,377), ⊙ Naman co. (pop. 508,841), SE Fukien prov., China, 5 mi. NW of Tsinkiang; rice, wheat, sweet potatoes, peanuts.

Namanakula, peak, Ceylon: see UVA BASIN.

Namangan (nŭmŭn-gän'), oblast (□ 2,400; 1946 pop. estimate 600,000), E Uzbek SSR; ⊙ Namangan. In N Fergana Valley; drained by Naryn R. (E); bounded S by the Syr Darya. Extensive irrigation, especially in E; cotton growing, sericulture; wheat on mtn. slopes; cattle and horses; sheep breeding in non-irrigated areas. Extensive cotton ginning, some silk milling. Antimony mine at Kassansai. Kokand-Namangan-Andizhan RR passes through S section. Pop. chiefly Uzbek. Formed 1941.

Namangan, city (1939 pop. 77,351), ⊙ Namangan oblast, Uzbek SSR, in N Fergana Valley, on railroad and 125 mi. E of Tashkent; 41°N 71°40'E. Cotton-ginning center; cotton and silk milling, cottonseed-oil extracting, wine making, food processing. Teachers col. Destructive earthquake (1927).

Namangoza River, Ecuador: see PAUTE RIVER.

Namao (näm'ō'), Mandarin *Nanao* (nän'ou'), island (□ 50; pop. 26,032) in S.China Sea, off China coast, 20 mi. E of Swatow; 13 mi. long, 1–6 mi. wide; rises to 1,900 ft. With near-by rocky islets (SE), it forms a co. of Kwangtung prov. On NE shore lies Namao, co. seat and fishing port. Often mistakenly spelled Namoa.

Namapa (nämä'pä), village, Niassa prov., N Mozambique, on road and 110 mi. NNE of Nampula; cotton, sisal.

Namaqualand (nŭmä'kŭlănd) or **Namaland** (nä'-mŭlănd), Afrikaans *Namakwaland* (nämä'kwälänt"), coastal region of SW Africa. S part, called Little Namaqualand, is in NW Cape Prov., U. of So. Afr., and consists of administrative dist. of Namaqualand (□ 17,556; pop. 30,127); ⊙ Springbok; extends S from Orange R. at South-West Africa border to near 30°45'S. Site of copper deposits, since 1919 of diminished importance; important diamond finds made 1929 at mouth of Orange R.; tungsten mining since 1946. N part of region, called Great Namaqualand or Great Namaland, is in S South-West Africa and extends from Orange R. to vicinity of Windhoek; Keetmanshoop is chief town. Entire Namaqualand region is inhabited by Namaquas or Nama, a Hottentot tribe, now numbering c.25,000. Contact with Europeans was established when Governor Van der Stel entered territory (1685) in search of copper. In South-West African portion of region Namaquas were dominant power 1830–1864 when, led by Jager Afrikaner and his son, Jonker Afrikaner, they subdued the Hereros. They rebelled in 1903 and were subsequently decimated.

Namarrói or **Nhamarrói** (nämäroi'), village, Zambézia prov., central Mozambique, 130 mi. N of Quelimane; manioc, corn, beans.

Namasagali (nämäsägä'lē), town, Eastern Prov., Uganda, on the Victoria Nile and 13 mi. NNW of Mbulamuti; alt. 3,417 ft. Rail terminus and head of Nile navigation from Masindi Port on L. Kyoga. Has river-boat repair dock.

Namatanai (nämŭtünī'), town, on E coast of New Ireland, Territory of New Guinea; 3°40'S 152°30'E.

Nambe (nämbā'), pueblo (□ 29.4), Santa Fe co., N central N.Mex. Nambe village (1948 pop. 151) is 13 mi. N of Santa Fe, bet. Sangre de Cristo Mts. and the Rio Grande; alt. 6,100 ft. Inhabitants are Mexicans and Pueblo Indians; languages spoken are Spanish, English, and Tewa. Chief activity is agr. (grain, chili, fruit).

Namborn (näm'bôrn), village (pop. 1,372), NE Saar, 6 mi. NNW of St. Wendel; stock, grain.

Nambour (năm'bōōr), town (pop. 3,262), SE Queensland, Australia, 55 mi. N of Brisbane; rail junction; sugar mill. Agr. center (sugar cane, coffee, citrus fruit).

Nambroca (nämbrō'kä), town (pop. 1,031), Toledo prov., central Spain, 6 mi. SE of Toledo; olives, cereals, sheep; olive-oil pressing, dairying.

Namcha Barwa (nŭm'chŭ bŭr'vŭ), highest peak (25,445 ft.) in E Assam Himalayas, in E Tibet prov. (China), in bend of the Brahmaputra; 29°38'N 95°3'E.

Namchi (näm'chē), town, SW Sikkim, India, 19 mi. SW of Gangtok, in SE foothills of Nepal Himalayas; corn, rice, pulse. Noted Buddhist monasteries of Sangachelling (or Sangnga Chöling) and Pemiongchi (or Pamiongchi, Pemayangtse) are 17 mi. NW, that of Tashiding (Tassiding) 4 mi. W.

Namdal (näm'däl), valley of Nams R. in Nord-Trondelag co., central Norway. Chief occupations: cattle raising, lumbering, fishing (salmon), centered at Namsos and Grong.

Namdinh (näm'dĭng'), city (1936 pop. 30,000), ⊙ Namdinh prov. (□ 600; 1943 pop. 1,233,400), N Vietnam, in Tonkin, on canal linking the Song Dai and Red River, on railroad and 50 mi. SE of Hanoi; major silk and cotton center; spinning, weaving; jute mill, distillery; salt extraction. Traditional Annamese scholastic center.

Namêche (nämĕsh'), town (pop. 1,520), Namur prov., S central Belgium, on Meuse R. and 6 mi. E of Namur; steel foundries.

Namekagon River (nä"mukä'gŭn), NW Wis., rises in Bayfield co., flows SW, past Hayward, then NW, to St. Croix R. 45 mi. S of Superior; c.95 mi. long. Trout fishing. Formerly spelled Namakagon.

Namekawa (nämä'käwŏ), town (pop. 3,093), Chiba prefecture, central Honshu, Japan, 6 mi. NNE of Narita; rice, raw silk.

Namen, Belgium: see NAMUR.

Nameoki (nă'mēō"kē), village (1940 pop. 2,701), Madison co., SW Ill., 7 mi. N of East St. Louis, within St. Louis metropolitan area; steel, metal products.

Namerikawa (nämärē'käwŏ), town (pop. 13,251), Toyama prefecture, central Honshu, Japan, port on SE shore of Toyama Bay, 9 mi. NE of Toyama; fishing center; mfg. (patent medicines, sake, soy sauce). Exports rice, medicine.

Namest nad Oslavou (nä'myĕshtyŭ näd' ô"slävō), Czech *Náměšť nad Oslavou*, Ger. *Namiest an der Oslau*, town (pop. 2,300), W Moravia, Czechoslovakia, on railroad, on Oslava R. (affluent of Jihlava R.) and 21 mi. W of Brno; grain. Castle here is summer residence of Czechoslovak president.

Namestovo (nä'mĕstôvô), Slovak *Námestovo*, Hung. *Námesztó* (nä'mĕstō"), town (pop. 1,364), N Slovakia, Czechoslovakia, on S slope of the Beskids, on Biela Orava R. (headstream of Orava R.) and 24 mi. NNE of Ruzomberok. Peat marshes and lignite deposits near by. Large reservoir bet. here and confluence of Biela Orava and Cierna Orava rivers.

Nametil (nŏŏmĭtĕl'), village, Niassa prov., NE Mozambique, 40 mi. S of Nampula; cotton, peanuts.

Nam Falls, Swedish *Nämforsen* (nĕm"fôr'sŭn, –fô' shŭn), waterfalls on Angerman R., Vasternorrland co., NE Sweden, 20 mi. NW of Solleftea; major hydroelectric station (1947). Near by are rock carvings dating from c.2000 B.C.

Namhae Island (näm'hă'), Korean *Namhae-do*, Jap. *Nankai-to* (□ 115; 1946 pop. 11,513), S.Kyongsang prov., Korea, in Cheju Strait and nearly connected to S coast of Korean mainland, 20 mi. S of Chinju; 15 mi. long, it is nearly divided in two, with 3 wide peninsulas. Generally low and fertile. Agr. (rice, cotton, hemp), fishing, cattle raising, raw silk.

Namhkam (näm'käm), village, North Hsenwi state, Northern Shan State, Upper Burma, 40 mi. SE of Bhamo, on branch of Burma Road; trade center near Chinese border.

Namhoi (näm'hoi'), Mandarin *Nanhai* (nän'hī'), city (pop. 95,529), ⊙ Namhoi co. (pop. 638,777), S Kwangtung prov., China, in Canton R. delta, on railroad and 10 mi. SW of Canton; trade and industrial center in silk-raising area; iron- and steelworks, textile (silk, cotton, hemp) mills, lumber mills (paper, matches). Produces embroidery, matting, chinaware, firecrackers. Coal mines near by. City was called Fatshan, Mandarin *Foshan*, until 1912, when it was renamed Namhoi after the old Chinese name (Nanhai) once borne by the city of Canton.

Namhsan (näm'sän), village, ⊙ Tawngpeng state, Northern Shan State, Upper Burma, 35 mi. W of Lashio.

Namib Desert (nä'mĭb), arid coastal plain extending along entire Atlantic coast of South-West Africa; c.800 mi. long, 30–100 mi. wide. In wide S part the inland plateau rises to c.2,500 ft. on E edge of desert; in narrow N part there is an abrupt rise to c.5,000 ft.

Namie (nämĕ'ā), town (pop. 8,047), Fukushima prefecture, N central Honshu, Japan, 31 mi. NNE of Taira; rice, wheat, pottery.

Namiest an der Oslau, Czechoslovakia: see NAMEST NAD OSLAVOU.

Namin (nämēn'), town, Third Prov., in Azerbaijan, NW Iran, on road and 15 mi. NE of Ardebil, near USSR border.

Namioka (nämē'ôkä), town (pop. 5,512), Aomori prefecture, N Honshu, Japan, 11 mi. SW of Aomori; apples, rice.

Namiquipa (nämēkē'pä), town (pop. 607), Chihuahua, N Mexico, in Sierra Madre Occidental, on Santa María R. and 90 mi. WNW of Chihuahua; alt. 5,997 ft.; corn, beans, fruit, cattle.

Namirembe (nämĕrĕm'bä), town, Buganda prov., S Uganda, just W of Kampala. Has Protestant cathedral.

Namkom, India: see RANCHI, city.

Namkum, India: see RANCHI, city.

Namlea (nämlā'ŏ), chief town (dist. pop. 707) of Buru isl., Indonesia, on NE coast of isl., on Kajeli Bay (small inlet of Banda Sea), 80 mi. WNW of Amboina; 3°16'S 127°6'E; port and trade center; ships cajuput oil, resin, skins, rattan, timber; imports rice and dried fish.

Namling (näm'lĭng), Chinese *Na-mu-ling-hsün* (nä'mōō'lĭng'shün'), town [Tibetan *dzong*], SE Tibet, on left tributary of the Brahmaputra and 120 mi. W of Lhasa; alt. 12,220 ft.

Namma or **Nama** (nä'mä), village, Myitkyina dist., Kachin State, Upper Burma, on railroad and 70 mi. SW of Myitkyina.

Nam Mae [Thai,=river]: for Thai names beginning thus, see under following part of the name.

Nammekon (näm'mĕkōn"), village, Karenni State, Upper Burma, 5 mi. W of Loikaw. Former ⊙ Nammekon state, inc. into Kantarawadi.

Namoa, China: see NAMAO.

Namoi River (nă'moi), N central New South Wales, Australia, rises as Peel R. in Liverpool Range, flows 526 mi. generally NW, past Tamworth, Gunnedah, and Narrabri, to Barwon or Darling R. at Walgett.

Namoluk (nä'mōlŏŏk), atoll (pop. 226), Truk dist., E Caroline Isls., W Pacific, 140 mi. SE of Truk; c.3 mi. long, 2 mi. wide; 6 wooded islets on triangular reef. Formerly Hashmys Isl.

Namonuito (nä'mōnwē'tō), atoll (pop. 248), Truk dist., E Caroline Isls., W Pacific, 95 mi. NW of Truk; 45 mi. long, 24 mi. wide; Ulul (3 mi. long) is largest islet. Formerly Los Jardines.

Namorik (nä'mōrĕk), atoll (□ 1; pop. 429), Ralik Chain, Majuro dist., Marshall Isls., W central Pacific, 210 mi. S of Kwajalein; 5 mi. long; 2 islets.

Nampa (năm'pŭ), city (pop. 16,185), Canyon co., SW Idaho, 20 mi. W of Boise, near Boise R.; processing, shipping center for agr. and dairying area in Boise irrigation project; dairy products, flour, feed, beet sugar, beverages. Northwest Nazarene Col. here. Seat of state institution for feeble-minded. Townsite established 1885, inc. 1890.

Nampicuan (nämpēkōō'än), town (1939 pop. 2,319; 1948 municipality pop. 5,377), Nueva Ecija prov., central Luzon, Philippines, on railroad and 17 mi. NNE of Tarlac; rice-growing center.

Nampo, Korea: see CHINNAMPO.

Nampula (nämpōō'lä), town (1940 pop. 3,416), ⊙ Niassa prov., NE Mozambique, on railroad from Lumbo and 95 mi. W of Mozambique city; 15°12'S 39°20'E. Agr. trade center (cotton, peanuts, beans, corn). Also ⊙ Nampula dist. (□ 30,803; 1950 pop. 1,318,018).

Namsen, Norway: see NAMS RIVER.

Nams Fjord (näms), inlet of the North Sea, in Nord-Trondelag co., central Norway; extends inland (SE and E) 22 mi.; c.2 mi. wide. At its head (at mouth of Nams R.) lies Namsos. Sometimes called Namsen Fjord.

Namslau, Poland: see NAMYSLOW.

Namsos (näm'sōs), town (pop. 4,047), Nord-Trondelag co., central Norway, port on Nams Fjord at mouth of Nams R., 80 mi. NNE of Trondheim; terminus of railroad to Grong; lumber-milling center; mfg. of cement, wood products, plywood, wool, leather, fish oil, canned fish. Founded 1845; almost destroyed by fire in 1872 and 1897; center destroyed by Ger. bombing in 1940; site of Allied landing in 1940 campaign.

Nams River (näms), Nor. *Namsen*, Nord-Trondelag co., central Norway, issues from a lake of same name 10 mi. NNE of Gjersvika, flows SW and W to Nams Fjord at Namsos; 120 mi. long; waterfall Fiskemfoss is near Grong. Nordland railway follows its valley.

Namsskogan (näms'skōgän), village and canton (pop. 1,160), Nord-Trondelag co., central Norway, on Nams R., on railroad and 25 mi. NE of Grong; lumbering, hunting. Pyrite mining near by.

Namti (näm'tē), village, Myitkyina dist., Kachin State, Upper Burma, on railroad and 25 mi. W of Myitkyina.

Namtow (näm'tou'), Mandarin *Nan-t'ou* (nän'-tou'), town, S Kwangtung prov., China, on E shore of Canton R. estuary, near Hong Kong border, port for Poon (just NE), 22 mi. NW of Kowloon; commercial center; fisheries.

Nam Tso or **Nam Tsho Chhimo** (näm' tsō' chē'mō), Mongolian *Tengri Nor* (tĕng'grē nōr) or *Tengeriin Nuur* (tĕng'gĕrēn nōōr'), Chinese *Na-mu Hu* (nä'mōō' hōō') or *T'eng-ko-li Hu* (tŭng'gō'lē'), salt lake (□ 950), E Tibet, just N of Nyenchen Tanglha range, 70 mi. NNW of Lhasa; alt. 15,180 ft. Largest lake of Tibet.

Namtsy (näm'tsē), village, central Yakut Autonomous SSR, Russian SFSR, on Lena R. and 45 mi. N of Yakutsk, in agr. area.

Namtu (nămtōō', Burmese näm'tōō), town (pop. 12,780), Tawngpeng state, Northern Shan State, Upper Burma, on Myitnge R. (here called Nam Tu) and 25 mi. NW of Lashio; smelting center for Bawdwin mines (6 mi. W). Pop. largely Indian and Chinese.

Namu (nä'mōō), atoll (□ 2; pop. 341), Ralik Chain, Marshall Isls., W central Pacific, 40 mi. SSE of Kwajalein; 35 mi. long; 51 islets.

Namuli Mountains (nämōō'lē), group of high peaks (alt. 7,936 ft.) in N central Mozambique, rising above plateau of NW Zambézia prov., c.180 mi. N of Quelimane.

Na-mu-ling-hsün, Tibet: see NAMLING.

Namunukula, peak, Ceylon: see UVA BASIN.

Namur (nämür'), Flemish *Namen* (nä'mŭn), province (□ 1,413; pop. 357,774), SE Belgium; ⊙ Namur. Bounded by Luxembourg prov. (E), France (S), Liége prov. (NE), Brabant prov. (N), Hainaut prov. (W). Wooded, hilly country; drained by Meuse, Sambre, and Lesse rivers. Fruitgrowing, dairying (in S), lumbering. Major quarrying center (marble, chalk, building and paving stone); some coal and iron mining; glass and cutlery mfg. Important towns: Namur, Dinant, Andenne, Philippeville. Prov. is mainly French-speaking.

Namur, Flemish *Namen*, city (pop. 31,637), ⊙ Namur prov., S central Belgium, at confluence of Sambre and Meuse rivers, 35 mi. SE of Brussels; 50°28'N 4°52'E. Rail and highway junction, at head of roads into France. Leather tanneries, flour mills; cutlery, machine mfg. It is an episcopal see. Has 18th-cent. cathedral of St-Aubain, convent of Notre-Dame (destroyed in Second World War), archaeological mus., forestry mus. Ruled by counts of Namur from 908 until sold to house of Burgundy in 1421. Captured by Louis XIV (1692); retaken by William of Orange (1695). Captured by Fr. revolutionary forces (1792); ⊙ Fr. dept. of Sambre-et-Meuse until 1814. Old fortifications razed (1862–65); new ring of forts (built in 1887) played major part in 1st stages of First World War, although they were reduced in 1914 by Germans. Heavily damaged in Second World War.

Namur, Marshall Isls.: see KWAJALEIN.

Namwala (nämwä'lä), township (pop. 360), Southern Prov., Northern Rhodesia, on Kafue R. and 150 mi. NNE of Livingstone; corn, tobacco.

Namwendwa (nämwĕn'dwä), town, Eastern Prov., SE central Uganda, on railroad and 33 mi. N of Jinja; cotton, tobacco, coffee, bananas, corn.

Namwera (nämwä'rä), village, Southern Prov., E Nyasaland, on road and 20 mi. ENE of Fort Johnston, in tobacco-growing area; cotton, corn, rice. Sometimes called Mangoche. Fort Mangoche (abandoned c.1930) is 6 mi. SSW.

Namwon (näm'wŭn'), Jap. *Nangen*, town (1949 pop. 24,736), N.Cholla prov., S Korea, 30 mi. SSE of Chonju; agr. center (rice, cotton, persimmons, silk cocoons).

Namyslow (nämĭ'swōōf), Pol. *Namysłów*, Ger. *Namslau* (näm'slou), town (1939 pop. 8,194; 1946 pop. 4,095) in Lower Silesia, after 1945 in Opole prov., SW Poland, 30 mi. E of Breslau (Wroclaw); rail junction; agr. market (grain, sugar beets, potatoes, livestock); brewing, sawmilling. Has castle built 1360 by Emperor Charles IV.

Namyung (Cantonese läm'hōōng'), Mandarin *Nanhsiung* (nän'shyōōng'), town (pop. 23,612), ⊙ Namyung co. (pop. 199,669), N Kwangtung prov., China, at S foot of Tayü Mts., on Cheng R. and 55 mi. NE of Kükong, near Meiling Pass; trade center for tung oil, hogs, wine, tobacco.

Nan (nän), town (1947 pop. 10,041), ⊙ Nan prov. (□ 5,730; 1947 pop. 204,599), N Thailand, in Phi Pan Nam Mts., on Nan R. and 115 mi. E of Chiangmai, on road from rail station of Den Chai; rice, cotton, tobacco, lac. Trade in teak, forest products, hides, horns. Salt mining at Bo Klua (NE). Pop. is largely Lao.

Nan, river, Thailand: see NAN RIVER.

Nanacamilpa or **San José Nanacamilpa** (sän hōsā' nänäkämēl'pä), town (pop. 3,588), Tlaxcala, central Mexico, 22 mi. NW of Tlaxcala; maguey, cereals, stock.

Nanaimo (nŭnī'mō), city (pop. 6,635), SW B.C., on SE Vancouver Isl., on the Strait of Georgia, 55 mi. NNW of Victoria, 40 mi. W of Vancouver; 49°10'N 123°55'W; coal-shipping port, serving Extension, Wellington, South Wellington, East Wellington, and Cassidy mining dist. Base of herring-fishing fleet, and center of lumbering, fruitgrowing, dairying, mixed farming region.

Nana Kru (nä'nä krōō"), town, Sinoe co., SE Liberia, minor port on Atlantic Ocean, at mouth of Nana Kru R. (70. mi. long; rises in Niete Mts.), and 25 mi. ESE of Greenville; copra, cassava, rice; fishing. Mission station. Graphite deposits near by.

Nanakuli (nä'näkōō'lē), village (pop. 2,006), Oahu, T.H., on W coast; beach park; sugar cane.

Nanam (nä'näm'), Jap. *Ranan*, town (1937 pop. 20,936), N.Hamgyong prov., N Korea, 8 mi. SW of Chongjin, in fruitgrowing area: makes cider, sake. Site of army base established 1915. Became provincial ⊙ in 1920, supplanting Kyongsong; became part of CHONGJIN in 1943

Nanan. 1 Town, Fukien prov., China: see NAMAN. **2** Town, Kiangsi prov., China: see TAYÜ. **3** Town, Yunnan prov., China: see SHWANGPO.

Nanango (nŭnăng'gō), town (pop. 138), SE Queensland, Australia, 85 mi. NW of Brisbane; agr. center (corn, alfalfa).

Nanao, China: see NAMAO.

Nanao (nänä'ō), city (1940 pop. 29,987; 1947 pop. 39,471), Ishikawa prefecture, central Honshu, Japan, on E Noto Peninsula, port on W inlet of Toyama Bay, opposite Noto-shima, 37 mi. NNE of Kanazawa. Fishing and lumbering center; sake, cement. Exports lumber.

Nanatsu-jima, Japan: see NAJIMI.

Nanatsuka (nänä'tsōōkä), town (pop. 9,255), Ishikawa prefecture, central Honshu, Japan, on Sea of Japan, 13 mi. NNE of Kanazawa; fishing center; silk textiles.

Nanauta (nŭnou'tŭ), town (pop. 4,639), Saharanpur dist., N Uttar Pradesh, India, 19 mi. SSW of Saharanpur; wheat, rice, rape and mustard, gram, sugar cane, corn.

Nanay River (nänī'), Loreto dept., NE Peru, in Amazon basin, rises near 2°45'S 75°W, flows c.200 mi. SE, E, and NE to the Amazon at Iquitos. Navigable for small craft. Near its mouth below Iquitos are large sawmills (mahogany, cedar).

Nancagua (nängkä'gwä), town (pop. 1,464), Colchagua prov., central Chile, on railroad and 13 mi. SW of San Fernando. Agr. center (grain, potatoes, peas, fruit, wine, tobacco, cattle, sheep); flour milling, dairying.

Nance, county (□ 438; pop. 6,512), E central Nebr.; ⊙ Fullerton. Agr. region drained by Loup R. Grain, livestock, dairy produce. Formed 1879.

Nanchang. 1 (nän'jäng') Town (pop. 19,030), ⊙ Nanchang co. (pop. 354,051), NW Hupeh prov., China, 25 mi. SW of Siangyang; silk weaving; mushrooms, medicinal herbs. Asbestos deposits near by. 2 or **Nan-ch'ang** (nän'chäng), city (1948 pop. 266,651), ⊙ Kiangsi prov., China, port on right bank of Kan R. at head of its delta on Poyang L., and 160 mi. SE of Hankow, on fertile alluvial plain; 28°40'N 115°53'E. Major commercial center; rail-road junction, and air hub (airport outside E wall); cotton-milling industry; ramie weaving, electroplating; mfg. of glass, pottery, matches, soap. Trades in porcelain, tea, rice, hemp, tobacco, paper. Has univ. and medical col. An old walled city, it contains a lake (E) with flower gardens. City dates from Sung dynasty (12th cent.) and received present name in Ming dynasty. During Sino-Japanese War, it was held (1939–45) by Japanese. In 1935, when the city became an independent municipality, the seat of Nanchang co. (1948 pop. 301,412) was transferred to the town of Siehfow (1948 pop. 7,213), 5 mi. SE, thereafter also known as Nanchang.

Nanchao (nän'jou'), town, ⊙ Nanchao co. (pop. 161,193), W Honan prov., China, in Funiu Mts., 40 mi. NNW of Nanyang; wheat, beans, kaoliang. Coal mines near by. Until c.1947 called Litsingtien. The old Nanchao is 15 mi. ESE.

Nancheng. 1 or **Nan-ch'eng** (nän'chŭng'), town (pop. 18,474), ⊙ Nancheng co. (pop. 111,144), E central Kiangsi prov., China, 90 mi. SE of Nanchang; rice; mfg. of bamboo paper. Until 1912 called Kienchang. 2 (nän'jŭng') Town (pop. 59,496), ⊙ Nancheng co. (pop. 281,760), SW Shensi prov., China, near Szechwan line, 135 mi. SW of Sian, and on Han R.; major agr. and commercial center; cotton weaving, match mfg., lacquer and tung-oil processing. Airport. Until 1913 called Hanchung.

Nan-ch'i, China: see NANKI.

Nan Chia, Formosa: see OLWANPI, CAPE.

Nan-chiang, China: see NANKIANG.

Nan-chiao, China: see NANKIAO.

Nan-ching. 1 Town, Fukien prov., China: see NANTSING. 2 City, Kiangsu prov., China: see NANKING.

Nanchow, China: see NANHSIEN.

Nan-ch'uan, China: see NANCHWAN.

Nanchuang, Formosa: see NANCHWANG.

Nanchung or **Nan-ch'ung** (nän'chōōng'), town (pop. 60,381), ⊙ Nanchung co. (pop. 772,916), central Szechwan prov., China, 55 mi. NNW of Hochwan and on right bank of Kialing R.; important agr. trade center (rice, tung oil, sweet potatoes); cotton spinning and weaving; hog bristles, beans, millet, wheat, tobacco. Until 1913, Shunking.

Nanchwan or **Nan-ch'uan** (both: nän'chwän'), town (pop. 7,395), ⊙ Nanchwan co. (pop. 320,155), SE Szechwan prov., China, 50 mi. SE of Chungking; rice, sweet potatoes, wheat, millet. Large coal deposits, iron and sulphur deposits near by.

Nanchwang or **Nanchuang** (nän'jwäng'), Jap. *Nansho* (nän'shō), village (1935 pop. 1,692), NW Formosa, 14 mi. S of Sinchu; coal mining; tea, rice, sweet potatoes, vegetables. A Buddhist retreat is near by.

Nancinta or **Santo Domingo Nancinta** (sän'tō dōmēng'gō nänsēn'tä), town (pop. 269), Santa Rosa dept., S Guatemala, in Pacific coastal plain, near Esclavos R., 6 mi. SE of Chiquimulilla; sugar cane; livestock.

Nancito or **El Nancito** (ĕl nänsē'tō), village (pop. 300), Chiriquí prov., W Panama, in Pacific lowland, 9 mi. ENE of Remedios; stock raising, lumbering.

Ñancorainza (nyängkōrīn'sä), village, Chuquisaca dept., SE Bolivia, in Serranía de Aguaragüe, 40 mi. N of Villa Montes, on road; petroleum center. Oil fields of Buena Vista 2 mi. W. Formerly Yancorainza.

Nancowry Island (năn̄kou'rē), one of Nicobar Isls., in Bay of Bengal, 50 mi. NNW of Great Nicobar Isl.; 6 mi. long N–S. **Nancowry Harbour**, a land-locked anchorage, lies bet. Nancowry Isl. (S) and Camorta and another isl. (N); center of inter-island trade in coconuts, canoes, pottery. In Second World War, was (1942–45) Jap. naval station. Sometimes spelled Nankauri.

Nancy (năn'sē, Fr. nāsē'), city (pop. 108,131), ⊙ Meurthe-et-Moselle dept., NE France, on Meurthe R. and Marne-Rhine Canal, and 175 mi. E of Paris; 48°41'N 6°11'E. Cultural and commercial ⊙ of LORRAINE; center of Nancy iron-mining and metallurgical dist. Specializes in mfg. of men's wear and leather articles (shoes, transmission belts). Also produces modern furniture, electrical equipment, metal bldg. materials, glassware. Large rail yards and repair shops. Breweries, pig-iron and steel mills, and chemical factories in suburbs and in Meurthe R. valley bet. Lunéville and Frouard. Nancy is a model of urban planning and of fine 18th-cent. architecture. Outstanding are Place Stanislas (square surrounded by public bldgs.; closed off by wrought-iron screens, with triumphal arch at one end and statue of Stanislaus I in center), oblong Place de la Carrière, 18th-cent. cathedral, and 16th-cent. ducal palace. Has univ. (founded 1854), schools of forestry and mining, acad. of fine arts, and noteworthy museums (historical, fine arts). Growing around castle of dukes of Lorraine, Nancy became their ⊙ in 12th cent. In 1477, Charles the Bold of Burgundy was defeated and killed here by the Swiss and René II of Lorraine. Under rule (1736–1766) of Stanislaus I, ex-king of Poland, Nancy underwent its architectural and cultural growth. After 1871, it received many refugees from territories ceded to Germany. Industrial and commercial growth was aided by return of Alsace-Lorraine to France after First World War, during which Nancy had remained in Allied hands. Only slightly damaged in Second World War; easily recaptured by U.S. Third Army (Sept., 1944).

Nanda Devi (nŭn'dŭ dā'vē), mountain in SE Kumaun Himalayas, in Garhwal dist., N Uttar Pradesh, India, 33 mi. E of Chamoli. Consists of twin peaks (official height of highest, 25,645 ft.) surrounded by mtn. walls 70 mi. in circumference and 1st penetrated in 1934. First climbed (1936) by Anglo-American expedition; was highest mtn. climbed until ascent (1950) of Annapurna I.

Nandaime (nändī'mā), town (1950 pop. 3,565), Granada dept., SW Nicaragua, 14 mi. SSW of Granada and on Inter-American Highway; agr. center (coffee, sugar cane, cacao), livestock. Sugar mill near by.

Nandalur (nŭndŭlōōr'), town (pop. 6,000), Cuddapah dist., central Madras, India, 25 mi. SE of Cuddapah; rice, sugar cane, turmeric.

Nandasmo (nändäz'mō), town (1950 pop. 1,692), Masaya dept., SW Nicaragua, on road and 3 mi. SW of Masaya; rice, coffee.

Nander (nän'dār), district (□ 3,771; pop. 803,115), N Hyderabad state, India, on Deccan Plateau; ⊙ Nander. Bordered N by Penganga R., SE by Manjra R.; mainly lowland except for S spurs (in N) of Ajanta Hills; drained by the Godavari. Largely in black-soil area; millet, cotton, wheat, oilseeds (chiefly peanuts, flax), rice. Nander is cotton-milling and trade center; a Sikh place of pilgrimage. Agr. markets at Umri and Bhainsa. Became part of Hyderabad during state's formation in 18th cent. Pop. 85% Hindu, 12% Moslem. Sometimes spelled Nanded.

Nander, town (pop. 36,689), ⊙ Nander dist., N Hyderabad state, India, on Godavari R. and 140 mi. NNW of Hyderabad; road and cotton-milling center; agr. market (chiefly millet, wheat, oilseeds, rice); cotton ginning. Experimental farm. Industrial school. Sikh temple contains tomb of Guru Govind Singh; Sikh place of pilgrimage. Sometimes spelled Nanded.

Nandgaon (nänd'goun), former princely state (□ 872; pop. 202,973) of Chhattisgarh States, India; ⊙ was Raj-Nandgaon. Since 1948, inc. into Drug dist. of Madhya Pradesh.

Nandgaon, town (pop., including suburban area, 10,586), Nasik dist., E Bombay, India, on railroad (workshop), and 60 mi. ENE of Nasik; agr. market (peanuts, cotton, wheat); cotton ginning, oilseed pressing, tanning.

Nandi or **Nadi** (both: nän'dē), town (pop. 865), W Viti Levu, Fiji, SW Pacific, 70 mi. WNW of Suva; sugar cane, cotton. Airport.

Nandi, India: see CHIK BALLAPUR.

Nandi, Kenya: see KAPSABET.

Nandidrug. 1 Mining area, Mysore, India: see KOLAR GOLD FIELDS. 2 Health resort, Mysore, India: see CHIK BALLAPUR.

Nandigama (nŭn'dĭgămŭ), village, Kistna dist., NE Madras, India, on tributary of Kistna R. and 27 mi. NW of Bezwada; rice, peanuts, cotton.

Nandikotkur (nŭndĭkōt'kōōr), town (pop. 7,409), Kurnool dist., N Madras, India, 14 mi. E of Kurnool; cotton ginning; peanuts, rice, turmeric.

Nandlstadt (nän'dŭl-shtät), village (pop. 1,432), Upper Bavaria, Germany, 16 mi. W of Landshut; grain, livestock.

Nandod, India: see RAJPIPLA, town.

Nandura (nändōō'rŭ), town (pop. 13,292), Buldana dist., W Madhya Pradesh, India, 36 mi. WNW of Akola; millet, cotton, wheat grown in the region; oilseed milling.

Nandurbar (nŭn'dōōrbär), town (pop. 22,139), West Khandesh dist., N Bombay, India, at extreme N end of Western Ghats, 45 mi. NW of Dhulia; road and trade center (cotton, wheat, linseed, timber); cotton ginning, oilseed milling, tanning, hand-loom weaving, palmarosa-oil extracting; sawmills. Prosperous town in mid-17th cent., noted for its grapes and melons.

Nandyal (nŭndyäl'), city (pop. 25,886), Kurnool dist., Madras, India, 37 mi. SE of Kurnool; road and agr. trade center; cotton ginning, oilseed milling. Experimental farm (cotton, peanuts, sugar cane). Handmade paper at Gazulapalle village, 10 mi. ESE; big-game hunting in Eastern Ghats (E).

Nandydroog, mining area, India: see KOLAR GOLD FIELDS.

Nanfeng (nän'fŭng'), town (pop. 13,661), ⊙ Nanfeng co. (pop. 89,070), E Kiangsi prov., China, 28 mi. SSW of Nancheng and on Fu R.; rice, oranges. Iron mines (SE).

Nanga-Eboko (näng'gä-ĕbō'kä), village, Nyong et Sanaga region, S central Fr. Cameroons, on Sanaga R. and 80 mi. NE of Yaoundé; rice processing. Protestant mission. Airfield.

Nangal (nŭng'gŭl), village, W Bilaspur state, India, 22 mi. WNW of Bilaspur, 4 mi. SW of Bhakra, in outer W Himalayas. Weir under construction on Sutlej R. (just W) to supply projected irrigation canal and hydroelectric plants.

Nanga Parbat (nŭng'gŭ pŭr'bŭt) [Kashmiri,=naked mountain], seventh-highest mountain (26,660 ft.) in the world, in W Punjab Himalayas, W Kashmir, 17 mi. WSW of Astor. Here the noted climber A. F. Mummery disappeared in 1895. Other attempts include Ger.-American expedition of 1932 led by Willy Merkl, disastrous Ger. expeditions of 1934 (climbed to c.800 ft. from summit; 9 died, including Merkl) and 1937 (led by Dr. Karl Wien; of 17 climbers, 16 were killed), and 1938 Ger. expedition led by Paul Bauer. Up to 1951, unscaled. Locally called Diamir.

Nanga Parbat, Mount (10,780 ft.), on W Alta.-B.C. border, in Rocky Mts., at W edge of Banff Natl. Park, 65 mi. NW of Banff; 51°43'N 116°52'W.

Nang-ch'ien, China: see NANGTSIEN.

Nangen, Korea: see NAMWON.

Nangis (nāzhē'), town (pop. 2,966), Seine-et-Marne dept., N central France, 16 mi. E of Melun; metalworks (agr. machinery, auto jacks); sugar milling, distilling, corset mfg. Here Napoleon defeated Austrians in 1814. Rampillon (3 mi. ESE) has 13th-cent. Gothic church with fine portal.

Nangkartse, Tibet: see NAGARTSE.

Nango (näng'gō), town (pop. 12,487), Miyazaki prefecture, SE Kyushu, Japan, on Philippine Sea, 26 mi. SSW of Miyazaki; includes offshore islet of O-shima (2 mi. long, c.½ mi. wide); agr. (rice, oranges) and fishing center.

Nangpa La (nängpä' lä'), pass (alt. 19,050 ft.) in E Nepal Himalayas, on undefined Nepal-Tibet border, 34 mi. S of Tingri (Tibet) on a Nepal-Tibet trade route.

Nangtsien or **Nang-ch'ien** (both: näng'chyĕn'), town, ⊙ Nangtsien co. (pop. 30,000), southernmost Tsinghai prov., China, 70 mi. SW of Jyekundo, on Sikang border and on trade route to Chamdo; trades in wool, furs, tea, cotton cloth. Until 1933 called Seluma.

Nanguneri (näng"gōōnā'rē), town (pop. 9,024), Tinnevelly dist., S Madras, India, 17 mi. S of Tinnevelly, in large palmyra tract in grain-growing area; jaggery, palmyra mats. Coffee grown at Tirukurungudi, 7 mi. SW.

Nanhai, China: see NAMHOI.

Nan Hai: see SOUTH CHINA SEA.

Nanhaitze, China: see PAOTOW.

Nanho (nän'hŭ'), town, ⊙ Nanho co. (pop. 107,066), SW Hopeh prov., China, 10 mi. ESE of Singtai, near Peking-Hankow RR; cotton, wheat, kaoliang, beans.

Nan-hsiang, China: see NANSIANG.

Nanhsien (nän'shyĕn'), town (pop. 283,734), N Hunan prov., China, on N shore of Tungting L., 45 mi. ENE of Changteh; rice-growing center. Until 1913 called Nanchow.

Nan-hsiung, China: see NAMYUNG.

Nanhwei or **Nan-hui** (both: nän'hwā'), town, ⊙ Nanhwei co. (pop. 527,940), S Kiangsu prov., China, 20 mi. SE of Shanghai, near Pootung Point on E.China Sea; match mfg.; rice, wheat, beans, cotton, rapeseed.

Nanisana, Madagascar: see TANANARIVE.

Naniwa, Japan: see OSAKA, city.

Nanjangud (nŭn'jŭngōōd), town (pop. 10,725), Mysore dist., S Mysore, India, on Kabbani R. and 13 mi. S of Mysore city center, on rail spur; cotton and paper milling; mango gardens. Large temple, here, has annual car festival. Near-by Badanaval (or Badanval, Badanwala) village is major training center for revival of Mysore's village handicrafts; handspinning and weaving (khaddar, wool); handmade paper; beekeeping.

Nankai-to, Korea: see NAMHAE ISLAND.

Nankan (näng'kä), town (pop. 5,978), Kumamoto prefecture, W Kyushu, Japan, 18 mi. SE of Saga; rail terminus; rice, sweet potatoes, raw silk.

Nankana Sahib (nŭngkä'nŭ sä'hĭb), town (pop. 12,981), Sheikhupura dist., E central Punjab, W Pakistan, 24 mi. SW of Sheikhupura; local trade in cotton, wheat, millet; cotton ginning. Guru Nanak, founder of Sikh religion, b. here (1469).

Nankang or **Nan-k'ang** (both: nän'käng'). **1** Town (pop. 11,645), ⊙ Nankang co. (pop. 317,159), SW Kiangsi prov., China, 17 mi. SW of Kanchow; rice, beans, peanuts, sugar cane. Gold, tungsten, and tin mines. **2** Town, Kiangsi prov., China: see SINGTZE.

Nankauri, Nicobar Isls.: see NANCOWRY.

Nanki or **Nan-ch'i** (both: nän'chē'), town (pop. 15,049), ⊙ Nanki co. (pop. 290,345), SW Szechwan prov., China, 25 mi. W of Luhsien and on left bank of Yangtze R.; rice, sugar cane, sweet potatoes, wheat.

Nankiang or **Nan-chiang** (both: nän'jyäng'), town (pop. 14,234), ⊙ Nankiang co. (pop. 15,899), N Szechwan prov., China, on the Nan Kiang (headstream of Chü R.) and 35 mi. N of Pachung, in mtn. region; indigo and rice center; mushrooms, sweet potatoes, tobacco, millet, wheat. Graphite quarrying, iron deposits near by.

Nankiao. 1 or **Nan-ch'iao** (nän'chyou'), town, Kiangsu prov., China: see FENGSIEN. **2** or **Nan-chiao** (nän'jyou'), town, ⊙ Nankiao co. (pop. 25,459), S Yunnan prov., China, near Burma border, 85 mi. SW of Ningerh, in mtn. region; cotton textiles; rice, millet, beans. Until 1934 called Wufu.

Nanking or **Nan-ching** (both: năn'kĭng', nän'jĭng') [Chinese,=southern capital], city (1947 pop. 1,084,995) in, but independent of, S Kiangsu prov., China, on right bank of Yangtze R. and 170 mi. WNW of Shanghai (linked by railroad); 32°3'N 118°48'E. Former ⊙ China and its traditional literary center. Mfg.: silk goods, satin, cotton, cloth (nankeen was originally produced here), paper flowers and fans, India ink. Seat of Nanking and Chengchih universities, Ginling col., col. of law and commerce, and several scientific research institutions. Situated in a lake and hill dist., Nanking is surrounded by remains of a circuitous 26-mi.-long wall that enclosed not only the built-up section (3 mi. from the Yangtze) but also adjacent rural areas. The wall extends to Nanking's river port of Siakwan—the railhead, shipping and commercial suburb—linked by rail ferry with PUKOW across the Yangtze. In hills (NE), just outside the wall, are the tombs of the early Ming emperors and the Sun Yat-sen memorial. Although the present city dates from 1368, its site had been occupied since the Han dynasty (2d cent. B.C.) by cities variously known as Tanyang, Kienkang, Shengchow, and Kiangning. It was renamed Yingtien by the 1st Ming emperors, who made it (1368) their S capital prior to the transfer (1421) to the N capital (Peking means N capital). In 1842, at the end of the Opium War, there was signed here the Treaty of Nanking, which opened China to foreign trade. During the Taiping Rebellion, the city was held (1853–64) by the rebels, who destroyed the wall and the famous 15th-cent. octagonal porcelain tower, the city's most conspicuous bldg. Nanking itself was opened to foreign trade in 1899. During the Chinese revolution, Nanking was captured (1911) by the insurgents and served briefly (1912) as seat of Sun Yat-sen's provisional presidency. In 1927, the city fell to the Nationalist unification forces, and in 1928 became ⊙ Nationalist govt. of China, supplanting Peking. In the Sino-Japanese War, the ⊙ was moved (1937) to Chungking just before the city fell to the Japanese. The ensuing looting and atrocities—the "rape of Nanking"— shocked the world. Here the Japanese surrender in China was signed Sept., 1945, and the Nationalist ⊙ was returned here from Chungking in 1946. City was captured 1949 by the Chinese Communists, who moved Chinese ⊙ once more to Peking. The former ⊙ Kiangsu prov., Nanking became an independent municipality in 1927.

Nankow or **Nan-k'ou** (both: nän'kō'), village, N Hopeh prov., China, on railroad and 25 mi. NW of Peking, at east end of Nankow Pass (alt. 1,900 ft.) through hills and gate of Great Wall. Near by (E) are tombs of 13 Ming emperors.

Nankung (nän'gŏŏng'), town, ⊙ Nankung co. (pop. 283,556), SW Hopeh prov., China, 50 mi. W of Tehchow; cotton, wheat, millet, kaoliang, peanuts.

Nanliao, Formosa: see HWOSHAO ISLAND.

Nanling (nän'lĭng'), town, ⊙ Nanling co. (pop. 252,152), S Anhwei prov., China, 30 mi. SSW of Wuhu; rice, wheat, rapeseed.

Nan Ling or **Nan Shan** (shän'), main mountain system of S China, on border bet. Kwangtung prov. (S) and Hunan and Kiangsi provs. (N), separating the drainage basins of Yangtze and West rivers; rises to nearly 6,000 ft. It includes Kiulien and Tayü mts., and is crossed by Cheling and Meiling passes, China's traditional N–S routes. The Nan Ling forms main dividing line bet. Cantonese and North Chinese civilizations and linguistic areas. Its central section is also called Wu Ling.

Nanlo (nän'lô'), town, ⊙ Nanlo co. (pop. 215,372), N Pingyuan prov., China, near Hopeh line, 45 mi. E of Anyang; wheat, cotton, millet, beans. Until 1949 in Hopeh prov.

Nanlung, China: see ANLUNG.

Nannilam (nŭn'nĭlŭm), village (pop. 3,103), Tanjore dist., SE Madras, India, in Cauvery R. delta, 17 mi. WNW of Negapatam; rice milling.

Nannine, village, W central Western Australia, 265 mi. NE of Geraldton, on Geraldton-Wiluna RR; gold mining.

Nanning (nän'nĭng'), city (1946 pop. 202,720), ⊙ but independent of Yungning co. (1946 pop. 409,613), SW Kwangsi prov., China, on left bank of Yü R., on railroad and 115 mi. SW of Liuchow; road hub and major commercial center, on routes to Yunnan prov. and N Vietnam. Cotton- and silk-textile mfg., tung-oil processing, sugar milling, rice hulling, printing. Exports rice, hides, butter, tobacco, vegetable oil. Coal and gold mines near by. Opened 1907 to foreign trade. Was ⊙ Kwangsi prov., 1913–36. Briefly held (1944–45) by Japanese in Second World War. Called Yungning from 1913 until c.1945, when it became an independent city.

Nanomana, Ellice Isls.: see NANUMANGA.

Nanomea, Ellice Isls.: see NANUMEA.

Nanoose Bay (nănōōs'), village, SW B.C., on SE Vancouver Isl., on Strait of Georgia, 13 mi. WNW of Nanaimo; lumber-shipping port.

Nanortalik (nanôkh'tälĭk), fishing settlement (pop. 406), ⊙ Nanortalik dist. (pop. 1,000), S Greenland, on Atlantic, at mouth of Tasermiut inlet, 50 mi. SE of Julianehaab; 60°7'N 45°14'W. Radio station.

Nanos, peak, Yugoslavia: see HRUSICA.

Nanouki, Gilbert Isls.: see ARANUKA.

Nanpara (nänpä'rŭ), town (pop. 13,048), Bahraich dist., N Uttar Pradesh, India, 21 mi. NNW of Bahraich. Rail junction, with spur to Nepalganj (or Naipalganj) Road, 11 mi. NNE, on Nepal border; trades in rice, wheat, corn, gram, oilseeds, and in grains, hides, and ghee from Nepal.

Nanpi or **Nan-p'i** (nän'pē'), town, ⊙ Nanpi co. (pop. 195,240), NW Shantung prov., China, 45 mi. NNE of Tehchow, near Tientsin-Pukow RR; cotton, wheat, kaoliang. Until 1949 in Hopeh prov.

Nanping or **Nan-p'ing** (nän'pĭng'), town (pop. 29,177), ⊙ Nanping co. (pop. 162,389), N central Fukien prov., China, 85 mi. WNW of Foochow and on Min R. (formed here by its chief tributaries); industrial center; mfg. (machinery, chemicals); exports tea, bamboo, paper, timber, charcoal. Coal and copper mining near by. Until 1913 called Yenping.

Nanpu (nän'bōō'), town (pop. 34,150), ⊙ Nanpu co. (pop. 698,613), N central Szechwan prov., China, 37 mi. N of Nanchung and on right bank of Kialing R.; sweet-potato-producing center; match mfg.; rice, millet, wheat, kaoliang, cotton. Gold washing, saltworks near by.

Nan River (nän), one of the headstreams of the Chao Phraya (Menam), N Thailand, rises on Laos border in N Luang Prabang Range at 19°35'N 101°10'E, flows 500 mi. S, past Nan, Uttaradit (head of navigation), and Phitsanulok, forming (in lower course) a common flood plain with Yom R. The combined stream joins the Ping R. just above Nakhon Sawan to form the Chao Phraya.

Nanryo, Formosa: see HWOSHAO ISLAND.

Nansei-shoto, islands: see RYUKYU ISLANDS.

Nansemond (năn'sĭmŭnd), county (□ 402; pop. 25,238), SE Va.; co. courthouse is at SUFFOLK, in but independent of co. Bounded NE by Hampton Roads, S by N.C.; part of DISMAL SWAMP in E; drained by Nansemond R. Important peanut-growing area; a great peanut market and processing center at Suffolk. Also produces corn, cotton, truck, livestock, timber (pine, cypress, juniper, gum). Fishing, waterfowl hunting. Formed 1637 as Upper Norfolk co.; renamed 1642.

Nansemond River, SE Va., rises in Nansemond co., flows c.25 mi. N, past Suffolk (head of navigation) to James R. estuary near Hampton Roads.

Nansen, Cape, SE point of Alexandra Land, Franz Josef Land, Russian SFSR, in Arctic Ocean; 80°26'N 46°10'E. Formerly called Cape Fridtjof Nansen.

Nansen Island, in Franz Josef Land, Russian SFSR, in Arctic Ocean; 12 mi. long, 6 mi. wide; 80°30'N 54°E. Formerly Fridtjof Nansen Isl.

Nansen Sound or **Fridtjof Nansen Sound,** NE Franklin Dist., Northwest Territories, arm (90 mi. long, 10–35 mi. wide) of the Arctic Ocean, bet. Axel Heiberg Isl. (W) and NW Ellesmere Isl. (E); 81°N 90°W. Connects Eureka Sound and Greely Fjord (SE) with Arctic Ocean (NW). In N entrance are Lands Lokk and Fjeldhdmen isls.

Nansha Islands (nän'shä') [Chinese,=southern reefs], name applied by Chinese to China's southernmost territory of islands, cays, and reefs in S. China Sea, part of Kwangtung prov., extending from 12° to 4°N and 110° to 118°E. Includes Tizard Bank with Itu Aba Isl. and Spratly Isl. Held by France (1933-39) and Japan (1940–45); passed to China after Second World War.

Nan Shan (nän' shän') [Chinese,=south mountain]. **1** System of parallel ranges on Tsinghai-Kansu border, China, representing an E continuation of the Altyn Tagh of Sinkiang. Situated S of the Silk Road through the neck of Kansu prov., the system includes the Humboldt, Richthofen, and Tatung mts.; rises over 20,000 ft. **2** Mountain system, on Kwangtung-Hunan-Kiangsi prov. border, China: see NAN LING.

Nansho, Formosa: see NANCHWANG.

Nansiang or **Nan-hsiang** (both: nän'shyäng'), town, S Kiangsu prov., China, 12 mi. WNW of Shanghai and on Shanghai-Nanking RR; commercial center.

Nant (nä), village (pop. 693), Aveyron dept., S France, on Dourbie R. and 12 mi. ESE of Millau; coal and lignite mines.

Nantaches, Lake (năn'tăsh), Grant parish, central La., 8 mi. NW of Colfax; c.2 mi. long; drains S through outlet to Red R.

Nantahala Mountains (năntûhā'lû), mostly in W N.C. and partly in NE Ga., transverse range of the Appalachians bet. Great Smoky Mts. (N) and the Blue Ridge (S); from confluence of Nantahala and Little Tennessee rivers in N.C. extend c.50 mi. S to Tallulah Falls, Ga. Highest points are Wine Spring Bald Mtn. (5,500 ft.), 13 mi. SW of Franklin, N.C., and Wayah Bald Mtn. (wī'û) (5,400 ft.), 11 mi. W of Franklin. Partly in Nantahala (N.C.) and Chattahoochee (Ga.) natl. forests.

Nantahala River, W N.C., rises in Nantahala Mts. SW of Asheville, flows 40 mi. NNW and N, through Nantahala Natl. Forest, to Fontana Reservoir (Little Tennessee R.) SW of Bryson City. In lower course, traverses scenic, 8-mi.-long Nantahala Gorge, with steep sides up to 2,000 ft. high. Nantahala Dam (250 ft. high, 1,042 ft. long; completed 1942), privately-built power dam in middle course, is c.20 mi. SW of Bryson City; forms Nantahala Reservoir (5 mi. long, 1 mi. wide), sometimes known as Aquone L. (ā'kwōn).

Nantai, China: see FOOCHOW.

Nantan (nän'dän'), town, ⊙ Nantan co. (pop. 73,988), NW Kwangsi prov., China, near Kweichow line, 70 mi. WNW of Ishan and on railroad; cotton-textile mfg., tung-oil processing; rice, wheat, beans, potatoes. Tin mines near by.

Nantasket Beach (năntă'skĭt), resort village (pop. 1,092) of HULL town, Plymouth co., E Mass., 3 mi. NNE of Hingham, on narrow Nantasket Peninsula (5 mi. long), which extends NW into Massachusetts Bay to Point Allerton, then bends W to end at Windmill Point.

Nanterre (nätâr'), city (pop. 39,565), Seine dept., N central France, a WNW suburb of Paris, 7 mi. from Notre Dame Cathedral, near left bank of the Seine, just NE of Rueil-Malmaison; auto construction; precision foundries; mfg. (electrical equipment, hosiery, perfumes, toys, paints, fountain pens). Ravaged by English in 1346 and 1411. Scene of fighting bet. French and Allies in 1815.

Nantes (nănts, Fr. nät), Breton *Naoned*, anc. *Condivicnum*, city (pop. 187,259), ⊙ Loire-Inférieure dept. and largest city of W France, port on the Loire, just above its estuary, at influx of Erdre R. (right) and Sèvre Nantaise R. (left), and 215 mi. SW of Paris; 47°13'N 1°32'W. Industrial and commercial center of S Brittany and of lower Loire valley, with important foreign trade; chief industries are food processing (meat, vegetable, and fish preserving, rice milling, cane-sugar refining, flour milling, and mfg. of chocolates, macaroni, biscuits, soft drinks and beer); metallurgy (shipbuilding, lead and copper refining, mfg. of railroad, electrical, and heating equipment); tanning and leatherworking, and processing of imported raw materials (superphosphate and soap mfg.). Nantes also produces textiles, paper, umbrellas, office equipment, tobacco products. Active trade in imported hardwoods, tropical oils and fibers. City exports machinery, slate, pit props, flour, sardines. Harbor (on both sides of France's longest river, 35 mi. from the Atlantic), recently remodeled, is accessible to ocean-going vessels at high tide. Shipbuilding and oil refining concentrated along the Loire bet. Nantes and SAINT-NAZAIRE. Nantes has a feudal castle (founded 10th cent., rebuilt 15th cent.) of dukes of Brittany; 15th-cent. cathedral (unfinished until 19th cent., damaged in Second World War); museums of fine arts, natural history, archaeology. City noted for its spacious squares, fine monuments, and boulevards. Seat of anc. Namnetes before Roman conquest of Gaul. Unsuccessfully besieged by Huns; ravaged and occupied (843–936) by Normans. Fell to dukes of Brittany in 10th cent. Passed to France after marriage of Anne of Brittany to Louis XII. Here famous Edict of Nantes was issued by Henry IV in 1598. During French Revolution, Nantes was nearly stormed by royalist Vendéans and was scene (1793) of massacres (Noyades) by revolutionists. Supply base for American army in First World War. Heavily damaged (1943–44) during Second World War when it was a center of underground resistance movement. Extensive rebuilding of city and port began in 1946.

Nantes-Brest Canal, France: see BREST-NANTES CANAL.

Nanteuil-le-Haudouin (nätû'ē-lû-ōdwē'), village (pop. 1,421), Oise dept., N France, 11 mi. ESE of Senlis; road junction; agr. equipment mfg. A pivot point of Allied offensive in first battle of the Marne

(1914). Its 13th-cent. church was heavily damaged in Second World War.

antiat (nätyä'), village (pop. 565), Haute-Vienne dept., W central France, 13 mi. NNW of Limoges: rabbit skins.

anticoke (năn'tĭkōk). **1** Fishing village (1940 pop. 637), Wicomico co., SE Md., on the Eastern Shore, 18 mi. WSW of Salisbury and on estuary of Nanticoke R.; tomato cannery; ships seafood. Muskrat-trapping, truck farming in region. **2** City (pop. 20,160), Luzerne co., NE central Pa., 7 mi. WSW of Wilkes-Barre and on Susquehanna R.; anthracite center. Rayon and nylon yarn, cigars, mine supplies. Inc. as borough 1874, as city 1926.

anticoke River, S Del. and E Md., rises in several small branches in N Sussex co., Del., flows c.50 mi. SW, past Seaford, Del. (head of navigation and tides), Sharptown, Md., and Vienna, to N end of Tangier Sound near Nanticoke; marsh-bordered estuary is 3 mi. wide at mouth. Main tributary is Marshyhope Creek, formerly called Northwest Fork of Nanticoke R.

antien, China: see SANMEN.

antitien, China: see ICHWAN, Honan prov.

antmel (nănt'mĕl), agr. village and parish (pop. 02), W Radnor, Wales, 4 mi. NNW of Llandrinod Wells.

anto, Formosa: see NANTOW.

anton, town (pop. 873), S Alta., 50 mi. SSE of Calgary; flour and cereal-foods milling, dairying, ranching; wheat, stock.

an-t'ou, China: see NAMTOW.

antow or **Nan-t'ou** (both: nän'tō'), Jap. *Nanto* (nän'tō), town (1935 pop. 6,626), W central Formosa, 16 mi. S of Taichung and on railroad; agr. center (oranges, bananas); sugar milling, pineapple canning; porcelain and pottery goods.

antsing or **Nan-ching** (both: nän'jĭng'), town (pop. 5,698), ⊙ Nantsing co. (pop. 115,337), S Fukien prov., China, 45 mi. W of Amoy and on tributary of Lung R.; rice, wheat, sweet potatoes, sugar cane. Iron mines near by. Formerly called Shancheng. Until c.1945, the name Nantsing was applied to a town 15 mi. NE, now called Tsingchengchen.

antua (nätwä'), town (pop. 2,159), Ain dept., E France, in the Jura, 19 mi. ESE of Bourg, at SE end of L. of Nantua (1½ mi. long, ½ mi. wide); resort; mfg. (agr. and woodworking machines, furniture, eyeglasses, plastics).

antucket Island (năntŭ'kĭt) (14 mi. long), in the Atlantic, c.25 mi. S of Cape Cod, Mass., across Nantucket Sound; Muskeget Channel separates it from Martha's Vineyard (W). Nantucket and small adjacent Muskeget and Tuckernuck isls. comprise Nantucket co. (□ 46; pop. 3,484), coextensive with Nantucket town, its co. seat. Isl. is low-lying and sandy, largely of glacial drift, with sparse vegetation and good beaches. Visited by Gosnold 1602; settled after 1659; town inc. 1687; co. formed 1695. Nantucket was one of the chief whaling towns until mid-19th cent.; later developed as summer resort and artists' colony. Has whaling mus. in old sperm-candle factory. Village of Nantucket (pop. 2,901), trade center, with good harbor on N coast, has fine old houses; steamer connection with Woods Hole. State forest is just SE. Siasconset or 'Sconset (both: skŏn'sĭt) is summer resort on Atlantic coast (E); other resorts are Wauwinet (wôwĭ'nĭt), Quidnet, and Squam Head. Nantucket, or Great Point, Lighthouse is on Great Point, at N tip of long beach extending NNW into Nantucket Sound, forming Nantucket Harbor. Sankaty Head Lighthouse (săng'kútē) (1850) is on bluff on E coast. First U.S. lightship station (1856) is c.50 mi. offshore, outside Nantucket Shoals, which extend c.27 mi. E and c.45 mi. SE of isl.

ntucket Sound, channel of the Atlantic bet. S shore of Cape Cod, Mass., and Nantucket Isl. and Martha's Vineyard; c.30 mi. long, c.25 mi. wide.

ntung or **Nan-t'ung** (nän'tōōng'), town (1935 pop. 133,326), ⊙ Nantung co. (1946 pop. 1,749,737), Kiangsu prov., China, 65 mi. NW of Shanghai, across Yangtze R.; major cotton-growing and spinning center; food processing, cottonseed-oil pressing, lime burning. Saltworks and fisheries along near-by coast. Most industries are located in the industrial suburb of Tangkiachia (NW). City is served by Yangtze R. port of Tienshengkang, 7 mi. W. Nantung was called Tungchow until 1912.

ntu River, Chinese *Nantu Ho* (nän'dōō' hŭ'), N Hainan, Kwangtung prov., China, rises in mts. of Paksha, flows c.170 mi. NE, past Tsingmai and Tingan, to Hoihow Bay of Hainan Strait.

ntwich (nănt'wĭch), urban district (1931 pop. 33; 1951 census 8,840), S Cheshire, England, on Weaver R. and 4 mi. SW of Crewe; leather tanning, shoe mfg.; clothing industry; cheese market. Has brine baths and saltworks and was formerly an important center of salt industry. Its grammar school (opened 1611) and church dating from 13th and 15th cent.

ntyffyllon, Wales: see MAESTEG.

nty Glo (năn'tē glō'), borough (pop. 5,425), Cambria co., SW central Pa., 10 mi NNE of Johnstown; bituminous coal. Founded 1888.

ntyglo and Blaina (năn'tēglō', blī'nú), urban district (1931 pop. 13,189; 1951 census 11,427), W Monmouth, England, 4 mi. E of Tredegar; steel milling, coal mining. In urban dist. (S, on branch of Ebbw R.) is town of Blaina.

Nantymoel (năntúmoil'), town (pop. 5,276) in Ogmore and Garw urban district, central Glamorgan, Wales, on Ogwr R. and 8 mi. NNE of Bridgend; coal mining. Just S, on Ogwr R., are coal-mining towns of Price Town and Ogmore Vale.

Nanuet (nănūĕt'), village (1940 pop. 2,057), Rockland co., SE N.Y., 5 mi. W of Nyack; mfg. of bedding, lumber milling. International Shrine of St. Anthony is here.

Nanumanga (nä'nōōmäng'ä) or **Nanomana** (nä'nōmäng'ä), atoll (□ 1; pop. 524), N Ellice Isls., SW Pacific; 6°18'S 176°20'E; copra. Formerly called Hudson Isl.

Nanumea (nänōōmä'ä) or **Nanomea** (-nō-), atoll (□ 1.4; pop. 746), northernmost of Ellice Isls., SW Pacific; 9°39'S 176°8'E; included 1915 in Br. colony of Gilbert and Ellice Isls.; 6 mi. long. In Second World War, occupied 1943 by U.S. Formerly St. Augustine Isl.

Nanu Oya (nŭn'ōō ō'yŭ), village (pop., including near-by villages, 2,518), Central Prov., Ceylon, on Hatton Plateau, on small stream and 3 mi. SW of Nuwara Eliya; alt. 5,291 ft. Rail junction; tea, rubber, vegetables. Also written Nanuoya.

Nanvarnarluk (nänvärnär'lŏŏk), village (pop. 116), SW Alaska, near Bethel.

Nan Wan (nän' wän') [Chinese,=south bay], inlet at southern tip of Formosa, W of Cape Olwanpi. Small port of Tapanlieh is on N shore.

Nanwei Island, China: see SPRATLY ISLAND.

Nanyang (nän'yäng'), town (1942 pop. estimate 50,000), ⊙ Nanyang co. (1937 pop. 619,162), SW Honan prov., China, 160 mi. SW of Kaifeng and on Pai R. (head of navigation); road hub and leading agr. center of SW Honan; silk weaving, embroidering, jade carving; wheat, corn, beans, kaoliang. The Nanyang agr. area is oriented toward Kwanghwa (Laohokow) and Fancheng in Han R. valley of Hupeh.

Nanyuki (nänyōō'kōō), town (pop. 4,090), Central Prov., S central Kenya, at NW foot of Mt. Kenya, 90 mi. NNE of Nairobi; alt. 9,000 ft.; 0°03'N 37°02'E. Terminus of rail spur from Nairobi; resort and agr. center (coffee, sisal, wheat, corn); dairy farming. Airfield.

Nao, Cape (nä'ō), on the Mediterranean, in Alicante prov., E Spain, 50 mi. NE of Alicante; 38°43'N 0°15'E.

Naoetsu (nä"ō-ā'tsōō), town (pop. 18,807), Niigata prefecture, central Honshu, Japan, port on Sea of Japan, 4 mi. N of Takada; rail junction; collection center for agr. area; exports oil.

Naogaon, India: see NOWGONG, town, Assam.

Naogaon (nou'goun), town (pop. 10,066), Rajshahi dist., W East Bengal, E Pakistan, on Jamuna R. (tributary of the Atrai) and 36 mi. NNE of Rajshahi; ganja-growing center; silk-weaving factory; trades in rice, jute, oilseeds. Also spelled Naugaon.

Naolinco (noulĕng'kō), officially Naolinco de Victoria, city (pop. 3,453), Veracruz, E Mexico, in Sierra Madre Oriental, 9 mi. NNE of Jalapa; agr. center (coffee, corn, sugar cane, fruit).

Naoli River (nou'lē'), NE Manchuria, rises in hills N of Tsining, flows 250 mi. NE to Ussuri R. 100 mi. SSW of Khabarovsk.

Naomi (näō'mē), village (pop. 2,531), Oita prefecture, E Kyushu, Japan, 26 mi. SSE of Oita; tourist center; rice, wheat, barley. Limestone caves near.

Naomi Peak, Utah: see RICHMOND.

Naoned, France: see NANTES.

Naoshera (noushä'rŭ) or **Naushahra** (nou'shŭrŭ), cantonment town (pop. 612), Mirpur dist., SW Kashmir, on right tributary of the Chenab and 15 mi. SSW of Rajaori; wheat, bajra, corn, pulse. Also spelled Nowshera.

Naos Island (nä'ōs), islet in Panama Bay of Panama Canal Zone guarding Pacific entrance of the canal, 3 mi. S of Panama city. Mole to mainland.

Naos Point, Canary Isls.: see RESTINGA POINT.

Naoua, Syria: see NAWA.

Naours (nōōr), village (pop. 657), Somme dept., N France, 10 mi. N of Amiens; cheese mfg. Subterranean dwellings here have been traced back to Norman invasions.

Naousa or **Naoussa** (both: nou'sŭ), Macedonian *Negush*, city (pop. 13,217), Hematheia nome, Macedonia, Greece, near railroad (station, 3 mi. E) and 10 mi. NW of Veroia; textile-milling center (silk, wool, cotton fabrics); trades in wheat and wine. Hydroelectric plant (NE). Located on site of anc. Citium, it was formerly called Niaousta or Niausta.

Napa (nă'pŭ), county (□ 790; pop. 46,603), W Calif.; ⊙ Napa. Bounded S by San Pablo Bay, it is a mountainous area, in Coast Ranges; Napa R. valley (winegrowing) extends SE from base of Mt. St. Helena. Petrified redwood forest, hot springs (resorts) near Calistoga. Prunes, wine grapes, poultry, dairy products, livestock (beef cattle, lambs, hogs), nuts, pears, apples, grain, hay. Wine making (since 1850s) is principal industry; also fruit processing, some mfg. (at Napa). Mining and quarrying (quicksilver, pumice, sand and gravel). Formed 1850.

Napa, city (pop. 13,579), ⊙ Napa co., W Calif., at head of navigation (barges) on Napa R., 35 mi. N of Oakland; processing, mfg. center (canned and dried fruit, leather, clothing, gloves, dairy products); a shipping point for Napa valley (fruit, wine, dairy products, poultry, livestock, stone). Has a jr. col. State mental hosp. near by. Settled 1840, inc. 1872.

Napa, Cerro (sĕ'rō nä'pä), Andean peak (18,880 ft.) on Chile-Bolivia border; 20°32'S.

Napaimiut (nŭpī'mŭt), native village (pop. 45), W Alaska, on Kuskokwim R. and 60 mi. SE of Holy Cross; 61°32'N 158°48'W; river port; trapping, fishing. Airfield. Sometimes called Napai, Napamute, or Napamiute.

Napaiskak (nŭpī'skăk), Eskimo village (pop. 121), W Alaska, near mouth of Kuskokwim R., 9 mi. SW of Bethel; trapping, fishing. Sometimes spelled Napaskiak (nŭpă'skēăk).

Napajedla (nä'päyĕdlä), Ger. *Napajedl*, town (pop. 4,767), SE Moravia, Czechoslovakia, on Morava R., on railroad and 8 mi. WSW of Gottwaldov; mfg. of agr. machinery and leather goods. Has well-known stud farm for thoroughbreds.

Napakiak (nŭpă'kēăk), village (pop. 139), W Alaska, on Kuskokwim R. and 13 mi. SW of Bethel; fur trading post; outfitting base for trappers.

Napalpí, department, Argentina: see PRESIDENCIA ROQUE SÁENZ PEÑA.

Napalpí (näpälpē'), town (pop. estimate 1,000), S central Chaco natl. territory, Argentina, 18 mi. SE of Presidencia Roque Sáenz Peña; cotton, corn, livestock.

Napamute, Alaska: see NAPAIMIUT.

Napanee (nă'pŭnē", năpŭnē'), town (pop. 3,405), ⊙ Lennox and Addington co., SE Ont., on Napanee R., near its mouth on the Bay of Quinte, and 23 mi. W of Kingston; lumber and grist milling, food canning, dairying, brick and tile mfg.

Napanoch (nă'pŭnŏk"), resort village (pop. 1,094), Ulster co., SE N.Y., on Rondout Creek, just W of the Shawangunk range, and 2 mi. NE of Ellenville. Near by is a state institution for male delinquents.

Napareuli (nŭpŭrāōō'lyĕ), village, E Georgian SSR, in Kakhetia, 9 mi. NNE of Telavi; wine-making center.

Napa River (nă'pŭ), W Calif., rises in Napa co. near Mt. St. Helena, flows c.50 mi. S through a valley in the Coast Ranges, past St. Helena and Napa (head of navigation and of tidewater), to San Pablo Bay. Valley is known for its wines (St. Helena dist.), fruit, nuts.

Napas (nŭpäs'), village, N Tomsk oblast, Russian SFSR, on Tym R. and 70 mi. N of Narym; lumbering.

Napasar (nŭpä'sŭr), town (pop. 4,388), N Rajasthan, India, 15 mi. ESE of Bikaner; hand-loom woolen weaving.

Napassok or **Napassoq** (both: nä'pāshôk), fishing and seal-hunting settlement (pop. 133), Sukkertoppen dist., SW Greenland, on islet in Davis Strait, 30 mi. SE of Sukkertoppen; 65°3'N 52°21' W.

Napata (nŭpā'tŭ, nŭpä'tŭ, nă'pŭtŭ), anc. Egyptian city, on right bank of the Nile, at foot of the hill Jebel Barkal (302 ft.) just S of Kareima, opposite Merowe, N Anglo-Egyptian Sudan. Marking S limit of Egypt under New Empire (after 1500 B.C.), it flourished as a trade depot with Sudan. Was ⊙ (750–300 B.C.) of Ethiopian (Upper Nubian) kingdom. Remained religious center of kingdom after transfer of capital to Meroë. Sacked (23 B.C.) by Romans. Extant ruins include pyramids and temples of god Amon.

Napatree Point, R.I.: see WATCH HILL.

Napavine (nă'pŭvīn), town (pop. 242), Lewis co., SW Wash., 8 mi. S of Chehalis, in agr., dairying area.

Nape (näp), town, Khammouane prov., central Laos, in Annamese Cordillera at alt. of 1,935 ft., on road and 45 mi. SW of Vinh, on Vietnam line; cattle raising. Pagoda and monastery.

Naper (nā'pŭr), village (pop. 188), Boyd co., N Nebr., 13 mi. WNW of Butte bet. S.Dak. line and Keya Paha R.

Naperville (nā'pŭrvĭl), city (pop. 7,013), Du Page co., NE Ill., on West Branch of Du Page R. (bridged here) and WSW of Chicago, 8 mi. E of Aurora, in agr. and dairying area; mfg. (cheese, cotton and burlap bags, furniture, boilers). North Central Col. and Evangelical Theological Seminary are here. Several old bldgs. remain. Settled 1831–32, inc. 1857.

Napier (nā'pyŭr), borough (pop. 17,243; metropolitan Napier 20,297), ⊙ Hawke's Bay co. (□ 1,673; pop. 14,707), E N.Isl., New Zealand, 170 mi. NE of Wellington and on SW shore of Hawke Bay; center of grazing district; winter resort; tobacco factory, woolen mills. Port Ahuriri (its port) exports wool, leather, meat. Airport. Anglican cathedral. Napier is in, but independent of, Hawke's Bay co.

Napier, town (pop. 1,449), SW Cape Prov., U. of So. Afr., 9 mi. NW of Bredasdorp; agr. market (sheep, wool, grain).

Napier Peninsula (năp'yŭr), N Northern Territory, Australia, point of NE Arnhem Land just SE of Elcho Isl. across Cadell Strait; forms NW shore of Buckingham Bay; 20 mi. long, 6 mi. wide.

Napierville (nä′pyŭrvĭl), county (□ 149; pop. 8,329), S Que., bet. the St. Lawrence and N.Y. border; ⊙ Napierville.

Napierville, village (pop. 990), ⊙ Napierville co., SW Que., on Little Montreal R. and 24 mi. SSE of Montreal; dairying; vegetables.

Napinka (nŭpĭng′kŭ), village (pop. 240), SW Man., on Souris R. and 55 mi. SW of Brandon; grain elevators.

Napkor (nŏp′kôr), town (pop. 3,584), Szabolcs co., NE Hungary, 7 mi. E of Nyiregyhaza; rye, potatoes, hogs.

Naplate (nä′plāt), village (pop. 783), La Salle co., N Ill., just W of Ottawa.

Naples (nā′pŭlz), Ital. *Napoli* (nä′pôlē), city (pop. 739,349; including suburbs 865,913), ⊙ Campania and Napoli prov., S Italy, 120 mi. SE of Rome; 40°50′N 14°16′E. Second largest seaport and third largest city of Italy; built at the base and on the slopes of a ridge of hills rising from the Bay of NAPLES, considered one of the most beautiful sites of Europe. Has extensive passenger service; exports gloves, macaroni, textiles, olive oil, cheese, canned goods. A major industrial and commercial center; large food industry (macaroni, canned tomatoes), railroad shops, shipyards, aeronautical factories, iron- and steelworks (machinery), cotton, rayon, and hemp mills, tanneries, shoe factories, petroleum refinery; mfg. of gloves (75% of Italy's output), pharmaceuticals, chemicals, rubber articles, refrigerators. Famous for its songs and festivals, Naples is a crowded, noisy city. Most of its worst slums have been replaced by new bldgs.; the old Santa Lucia quarter remains the most characteristic. Archbishopric. Has many churches, mostly restored in 17th- and 18th-cent. baroque style. Many heavily damaged in Second World War; Santa Chiara, containing tombs of Angevin kings, and Monteoliveto, rich in Renaissance sculpture, suffered most severely. Cathedral of St. Januarius (also damaged) has chapel containing two vials of the saint's blood, said to liquefy miraculously twice a year. There are several medieval castles, including Castel dell'Ovo, Castel Sant'Elmo, and Castel Nuovo (damaged). The imposing royal palace (17th and 19th cent.) was badly damaged and despoiled. A cultural and artistic center, Naples is particularly famous for its Natl. Mus. (with Farnese collection and most of objects excavated at Pompeii and Herculaneum) and the San Carlo Opera, opened in 1737. City reached its greatest musical brilliance in 17th and 18th cent., with such representatives as Alessandro and Domenico Scarlatti, Porpora, Pergolesi, Paisiello, and Cimarosa. Naples has a conservatory, several art acads., and university (founded 1224). The institute of marine zoology, with its magnificent aquarium, is one of the best in Europe. An anc. Greek colony known as Parthenope, Palaeopolis, and Neapolis, Naples was conquered by the Romans in 4th cent. B.C. Vergil, who often stayed here, is buried near by. City was under Byzantine rule in 6th cent.; in 8th cent. an independent duchy; added (1139) to kingdom of Sicily by Roger II. After the Sicilian Vespers (1282) Sicily proper passed to the house of Aragon, and the Ital. peninsula S of the Papal States became known as the kingdom of Naples, with Naples as its capital. The kingdom was the constant center of both internal and external strife, and in 1495 the seizure of Naples by Charles VIII of France started the Italian Wars. The treaties of Blois (1504–5) gave Naples and Sicily to Spain for the next 2 centuries, but in the War of the Spanish Succession it passed (1707) to Austria (confirmed 1713 by Peace of Utrecht), and then to Spain (confirmed 1738 by treaty of Vienna) and to France (1799). In 1815, Ferdinand IV, restored to the throne he lost to the French in 1806, merged (1816) Sicily and Naples in the Kingdom of the Two Sicilies. Fell to Garibaldi in 1860 and in 1861 was inc. with Italy. In Second World War city suffered tremendous damage from Allied air bombing and particularly from destruction by retreating Germans in 1943. Its harbor section was demolished, entire blocks were reduced to rubble, and part of its rich archives and libraries were burned.

Naples. 1 Town (pop. 1,465), Collier co., S Fla., 35 mi. S of Fort Myers, on Gulf coast; fishing port, resort, and terminus of Tamiami Trail. Inc. 1927. **2** Town (pop. 141), Scott co., W central Ill., on Illinois R. and 19 mi. W of Jacksonville, in agr. area. **3** Resort town (pop. 747), Cumberland co., SW Maine, on Sebago and Long lakes, c.22 mi. SW of Auburn. Includes part of Sebago L. State Park. **4** Village (pop. 1,141), Ontario co., W central N.Y., in Finger Lakes region, near S end of Canandaigua L., 20 mi. SSW of Canandaigua, in grape-growing area; mfg. (wine, grape juice); timber; potatoes. Inc. 1894. **5** Town (pop. 62), Clark co. E central S.Dak., 13 mi. SE of Clark; trade center for farming region. **6** Town (pop. 1,346), Morris co., NE Texas, 40 mi. WSW of Texarkana; trade, shipping point in agr. area (cotton, corn, watermelons). Inc. 1909.

Naples, Bay of, S Italy, a semicircular inlet of Tyrrhenian Sea, bet. gulfs of Gaeta (N) and Salerno (S), bet. Cape Miseno (NW) and Punta della Campanella (SE); c.20 mi. long, 10 mi. wide. On its scenic shores are Naples, Pozzuoli, Portici, Torre del Greco, Torre Annunziata, Castellammare di Stabia, Vico Equense, and Sorrento. Vesuvius rises in E, with ruins of Pompeii and Herculaneum near by; in SE is Monte Sant'Angelo, highest point (4,734 ft.) near the bay. At its entrance are isls. of Ischia and Procida (NW) and Capri (SE). Its NW inlet is the Gulf of Pozzuoli.

Napo or **Puerto Napo** (pwĕr′tō nä′pō), village, Napo-Pastaza prov., E central Ecuador, landing on Napo R., on E slopes of the Andes, and 4 mi. S of Tena; stock raising.

Napoklu (nŭpōk′lōō), village (pop. 1,029), S Coorg, India, on Cauvery R. and 8 mi. SSW of Mercara; rice (terrace farming), cardamom, oranges. Evergreen forest (W).

Napoleon. 1 Town (pop. 143), Lafayette co., W central Mo., on Missouri R. and 29 mi. E of Kansas City. **2** City (pop. 1,070), ⊙ Logan co., S N.Dak., 52 mi. ESE of Bismarck; livestock, grain, dairy products. **3** City (pop. 5,335), ⊙ Henry co., NW Ohio, on Maumee R. and 14 mi. ENE of Defiance; market center for agr. area; farm machinery, food and dairy products, metal products, brick, tile.

Napoléon-Vendée, France: see ROCHE-SUR-YON, LA.

Napoléonville, France: see PONTIVY.

Napoleonville (nŭpō′lēŭnvĭl), town (pop. 1,260), ⊙ Assumption parish, SE La., 56 mi. W of New Orleans, at head of navigation on Bayou Lafourche, in agr. area (sugar cane, corn, rice); sugar milling, moss ginning, vegetable canning; machine shops. Founded c.1818, inc. 1878. Has fine old church, ante-bellum houses.

Napoli (nä′pôlē), province (□ 452; pop. 1,734,848), Campania, S Italy; ⊙ Naples. Extends around Bay of NAPLES; includes isls. of Ischia, Capri, Procida, and Ventotene. Agr. (grapes, olives, fruit, vegetables, hemp, tobacco). Fishing. Pozzuolana extracting (Pozzuoli, Bacoli) and lava quarrying (Torre del Greco). Has many ports which carry on extensive trade. Chief industries: macaroni mfg. (Naples, Torre Annunziata, Castellammare di Stabia, Gragnano), tomato canning, cotton milling. Its resorts (Capri, Ischia, Sorrento), historic ruins (Pompeii, Herculaneum, Cumae) and famous sights (Vesuvius, Phlegraean Fields) attract thousands of tourists annually. From 1927–45 it included Caserta prov.; prior to reconstitution of Caserta prov., it had an area of 1,206 sq. mi. and pop. of 2,192,245.

Napoli, city, Italy: see NAPLES.

Naponee (nă′pŭnē″), village (pop. 391), Franklin co., S Nebr., 10 mi. W of Franklin and on Republican R.

Napo-Pastaza (nä′pō-pästä′sä), province (□ 33,291; 1950 enumerated pop. 14,325, plus Indians probably numbering over 100,000), NE and E Ecuador, on the equator; ⊙ Tena. Bordering Colombia (N) and Peru (E); traversed by the Andes, with the Cayambe, Antisana, Cotopaxi, and Hermoso volcanoes along its W border. It consists largely of jungle lowlands intersected by a great number of tributaries (mostly navigable) of the Amazon system, among them the San Miguel or Sucumbíos, Putumayo, Napo, Curaray, Pastaza rivers. Has hot, humid climate. A vast undeveloped region, inhabited by semicivilized Indians, its virgin forests have rubber, balata, chicle, vanilla, a great variety of fine timber. Along the rivers some cattle are raised. In the W uplands agr. products include cereals, fruit, vegetables, coffee. Most of the settlements are maintained by missionaries. Mera (SW) has petroleum wells. Napo-Pastaza prov., along with Santiago-Zamora prov., was formed 1925 from the prov. of Oriente. The international boundary with Peru was settled (1942) at Rio de Janeiro.

Napo River (nä′pō), in NE Ecuador and NE Peru, rises in the Andes near the Cotopaxi volcano, flows more than 550 mi. SE, past Napo, Coca, and Nueva Rocafuerte, through tropical forests to the upper Amazon at 3°25′S 72°43′W, 40 mi. NE of Iquitos. Main affluents are Coca, Aguarico, and Curaray rivers. It has good navigability. Some cattle raising along its shores. The adjoining virgin forests yield rubber, balata, chicle, fine timber, furs. It was first explored (1540) by Orellana and later (1638) by Teixeira.

Napostá Grande, Arroyo (äroi′ō näpōstä′ grän′dā), river in SW Buenos Aires prov., Argentina, rises in Sierra de la Ventana SE of Tornquist at alt. of 1,600 ft., flows c.50 mi. S to Bahía Blanca (bay) below Bahía Blanca city.

Napoule, Golfe de la (gôlf dŭ lä näpōōl′), bay of the Mediterranean, off Alpes-Maritimes dept., SE France, along Fr. Riviera; 6 mi. wide, 2 mi. long. Cannes is on its NE shore. Sheltered from land by Estérel range (W), from sea by Îles de Lérins.

Nappanee (nă′pŭnē, năpŭnē′), city (pop. 3,393), Elkhart co., N Ind., 21 mi. SE of South Bend, in agr. area (mint, onions, grain); mfg. of furniture, canned goods, flour; lumber milling. Platted 1874, inc. 1926.

Napton-on-the-Hill, town and parish (pop. 816), E Warwick, England, 9 mi. SSW of Rugby; tile- and brickworks. Has church dating from 13th cent.

Napue, Finland: see ISOKYRÖ.

Napuka, Tuamotu Isls.: see DISAPPOINTMENT ISLANDS.

Naqada or **Naqadah** (năkă′dŭ), town (pop. 13,141 largely Coptic), Qena prov., Upper Egypt, across the Nile from and 3 mi. WSW of Qus; silk weaving pottery making, sugar refining; cereals, sugar cane, dates. Has Coptic and R.C. churches. Also spelled Nakada.

Naqb Ashtar (nä′kŭb ăsh′tär), village, S Jordan, in hills 30 mi. SW of Ma'an and on main Ma'an Aqaba road; trade center; camel, sheep, and goat raising. Reached by rail spur from Ma'an.

Nar (nŭr′), town (pop. 7,358), Kaira dist., N Bombay, India, 6 mi. W of Petlad; agr. market (tobacco, millet, cotton).

Nara (nä′rä), village (pop. c.2,200), W Fr. Sudan Fr. West Africa, 180 mi. N of Bamako; animal husbandry.

Nara (nä′rä), prefecture [Jap. *ken*] (□ 1,425; 194 pop. 620,509; 1947 pop. 779,935), S Honshu, Japan, partly on Kii Peninsula; ⊙ Nara. Largely mountainous, particularly in S area which is drained by Kumano R. Most of pop. is in vicinit of city of Nara, a religious center. Part of Yo shino-kumano Natl. Park is in prefecture; touris trade is important. Extensive cultivation of ric and fruit (oranges, persimmons, watermelons) Lumber and charcoal produced in S area. Hom industries (raw silk, sake, medicine, textiles Some copper mined at Shimoichi, mercury a Uda.

Nara, city (1940 pop. 57,273; 1947 pop. 82,399), ⊙ Nara prefecture, S Honshu, Japan, 18 mi. E of Osaka; rail center. An anc. city, Nara is a cultura and religious center. Artisan industries (woode dolls, writing brushes, India ink, lacquer war fans, hemp cloth). Site of many anc. Buddhi temples and Shinto shrines. The temple Todai has 8th-cent. bronze image (53 ft. high) of Budhh Near by is HORYUJI, site of oldest Buddhist temp of Japan. Near-by Mt. Kasuga (1,640 ft.) is sacred area. Imperial Mus. (1895) has art colle tion of Nara Period (7th-8th cent.). Nara Pa (□ c.2) is known for its tame deer. City was 1 permanent ⊙ (710–784), preceding Nagaoka.

Naracoorte (nă′rŭkōōrt), town (pop. 2,202), S South Australia, 190 mi. SSE of Adelaide, ne Victoria line; rail junction; agr., and sheep cente Limestone quarries, agr. experiment station nea

Narada Falls (nŭră′dŭ), W central Wash., waterfa 168 ft. high, in S Mount Rainier Natl. Park.

Naradhivas, Thailand: see NARATHIWAT.

Naraguta (närägōō′tä), town (pop. 1,710), Plate Prov., Northern Provinces, central Nigeria, Bauchi Plateau, 4 mi. N of Jos; tin-mining cent

Narail, E Pakistan: see NARAL.

Naraina (nŭrī′nŭ), town (pop. 4,055), E cent Rajasthan, India, 8 mi. S of Sambhar; mill gram. Hq. of small Hindu sect of reformers (call Dadupanthis), founded late-16th cent. by Dad

Naraini (nŭrī′nē), town (pop. 2,442), Banda dist. Uttar Pradesh, India, 22 mi. SSE of Banda; gra jowar, wheat, oilseeds. Pilgrimage site and exte sive Hindu shrines 23 mi. ENE, at village Chitrakut.

Naral (nŭräl′) or **Narail** (nŭrīl′), village, Jesso dist., SW East Bengal, E Pakistan, on river a of Ganges Delta and 19 mi. E of Jessore; trades rice, jute, linseed, tobacco. Has col.

Naramata (nărŭmă′tŭ), village (pop. estimate 45 S B.C., on Okanagan L., 7 mi. N of Pentict fruit, vegetables.

Nara Nag, Kashmir: see SRINAGAR.

Narang (nä′rŭng), village, Sheikhupura dist., Punjab, W Pakistan, on railroad and 34 mi. of Sheikhupura; agr. market; rice milling.

Naranjal (näränhäl′), village, Guayas prov., Ecuador, minor river port at foot of the And 38 mi. SSE of Guayaquil, in agr. region (cac rice, tropical fruit).

Naranjal, town (pop. 937), Veracruz, E Mexico mi. S of Córdoba; coffee, fruit.

Naranjal River, S and S central Ecuador, rises SW foot of Cerro Ayapunga, flows c.85 mi. W inlet of the Gulf of Guayaquil near mouth Guayas R. Its mid-course is called Cañar.

Naranjito (näränhē′tō), town (pop. 3,207), Sa Bárbara dept., W Honduras, near Jicatuyo R., mi. WNW of Santa Bárbara; commercial cer in coffee and tobacco area.

Naranjito, town (pop. 2,364), N central Puerto R 14 mi. SW of San Juan; tobacco-growing cen mfg. of artificial flowers. A hydroelectric pl with artificial lake is near by on the La Plata.

Naranjo (närän′hō), city (1950 pop. 2,108), Alaju prov., W central Costa Rica, on central plate on Inter-American Highway and 14 mi. NW Alajuela. Important coffee center; tapioca n ing; tobacco, corn, beans, rice, sugar cane, p tains.

Naranjo, Puerto (pwĕr′tō), small sheltered inlet mi. long, 1 mi. wide) on NE coast of Cuba Oriente prov., 10 mi. E of Gibara.

Naranjo River, SW Guatemala, rises just N of Marcos, flows c.60 mi. S, W, and S, past San Pe and Coatepeque, to the Pacific at Ocós.

Naranjos Agrios (närän′hōs ä′grēōs), village, G nacaste prov., NW Costa Rica, near E shore o

Arenal, 5 mi. N or Tilarán; coffee, beans, corn, sugar cane, livestock.

Naraq (närăk'), village, Second Prov., in Mahallat, N central Iran, 40 mi. S of Qum; grain, fruit; rug-making.

Narasannapeta (nŭrŭsŭ'nŭpĕtŭ), town (pop. 7,962), Vizagapatam dist., NE Madras, India, 45 mi. NE of Vizianagaram; rice, oilseeds, sugar cane, coconuts. Sometimes spelled Narsannapet.

Narasapatnam, India: see NARSIPATNAM.

Narasapur (nŭr'sŭpŏŏr), town (pop. 16,044), West Godavari dist., NE Madras, India, near mouth of Vasishta Godavari R., in Godavari delta, 45 mi. ESE of Ellore; rail spur terminus; rice milling; tobacco, sugar cane, coconuts. Former N suburb of Madapollam (now destroyed by river erosion) was site of early-17th-cent. Du. trading station; occupied 1677 by English, 1756 by French; finally ceded to English in 1759. Casuarina plantations near by. Saltworks 6 mi. WSW, at village of Mogalturru. Also spelled Narsapur.

Narasaraopet (nŭrŭsŭrou'pĕt), city (pop. 17,644), Guntur dist., NE Madras, India, 26 mi. W of Guntur; road and agr. trade center; rice and oilseed milling, cotton ginning. Experimental farm (cotton research). Also spelled Narasaravupet.

Narasimharajapura (nŭrŭsĭmhŭrä'jŭpŏŏrŭ), town (pop. 2,589), Kadur dist., W Mysore, India, 26 mi. NW of Chikmagalur; terminus of rail spur from Tarikere junction, 20 mi. ENE; serves iron mines and coffee, cardamom, and pepper estates in Baba Budan Range (SE).

Narastan, Kashmir: see AWANTIPUR.

Narathiwat (nŭrä'tēwät'), town (1947 pop. 11,352), ⊙ Narathiwat prov. (□ 1,613; 1947 pop. 166,527), S Thailand, port on E coast of Malay Peninsula, on South China Sea, 100 mi. SE of Songkhla, near Malaya line, on road from rail station of Ra Ngae; large coconut plantations; rice fields. Locally known as Bang Nara; also called Naradhivas.

Naraura, India: see DIBAI.

Narawa, Japan: see HANDA, Aichi prefecture.

Narayanganj (närä'yŭngŭnj), city (pop. 56,007), Dacca dist., E central East Bengal, E Pakistan, on tributary of the Dhaleswari and 8 mi. SE of Dacca. Rail terminus; river port for Dacca; trade (jute, rice, fish, oilseeds) and cotton-milling center; jute pressing, mfg. of hosiery, glass, ice; shipbuilding, rice and sugar milling, leather tanning; ironworks, general-engineering factories. Noted 16th-cent. mosque. Cotton ginning, leather and shoe mfg. near by.

Narayangarh (nä'räyŭngŭr), village, NW Madhya Bharat, India, 14 mi. N of Mandasor; gur mfg., hand-loom weaving.

Narayani River, Nepal: see GANDAK RIVER.

Narayanpet (nä'räyŭnpāt), town (pop. 16,396), Mahbubnagar dist., S Hyderabad state, India, 33 mi. W of Mahbubnagar; millet, oilseeds, rice; noted hand-woven silk textiles, leather goods. Rail station of Narayanpet Road is 10 mi. SW.

Narayanpur, India: see DUMDUM.

Narazim (nŭrŭzēm'), village, central Chardzhou oblast, Turkmen SSR, on isl. in the Amu Darya, 33 mi. SE of Chardzhou; cotton.

Narbada River (nŭrbŭ'dŭ), anc. *Namados*, central India, rises near village of Amarkantak on plateau at E junction of Vindhya and Satpura ranges, near Madhya Pradesh–Vindhya Pradesh border; through trough bet. the Vindhyas and Satpuras flows generally W past Mandla and Jubbulpore, then WSW along Madhya Pradesh–Bhopal line, past Hoshangabad, across S Madhya Bharat and N Bombay, to just below Broach, where it forms broad estuary and enters Gulf of Cambay; c.775 mi. long. Sacred stream to Hindus, with many pilgrimage sites and bathing ghats, including Suklatirtha, MARBLE ROCKS (noted gorge), Nemawar, and Amarkantak. Because of its several falls, steep banks, and the uneven adjacent terrain, river is not tapped for irrigation; navigable for c.60 mi. in lower course during rainy season. Considered traditional boundary bet. Hindustan (N) and Deccan region (S). Formerly also spelled Nerbudda.

Narbata (närbätä'), settlement (pop. 300), W Israel, near Jordan border, in Plain of Sharon, 7 mi. ENE of Hadera; mixed farming; glucose plant. Founded 1942; formerly called Maanith. Withstood heavy Arab attacks, 1948.

Narberth (när'bûrth), residential borough (pop. 5,407), Montgomery co., SE Pa., 6 mi. NW of Philadelphia. Settled 1860, inc. 1895.

Narberth, urban district (1931 pop. 1,046; 1951 census 1,053), SE Pembroke, Wales, 9 mi. N of Tenby; agr. market. Has remains of 13th-cent. castle, built on site of Danish and Norman castles.

Narbonne (närbôn'), anc. *Narbo Martius*, town (pop. 26,301), Aude dept., S France, near the Gulf of Lion, 34 mi. N of Perpignan; commercial center for important winegrowing region; distilling, sulphur refining, flour milling, barrel making, pottery mfg., and beekeeping. Connects by canal with La Nouvelle on the Gulf of Lion and with the Canal du Midi. Has unfinished 13th-15th-cent. basilica of St. Just and former archiepiscopal palace (13th-14th-cent.), now the town hall. Site of 1st Roman colony established (118 B.C.) in Gaul, it became ⊙ Gallia Narbonensis. Taken by Arabs (719), by Franks (759); later was seat of viscounts of Narbonne. Its port, once a source of great wealth, silted up in 14th cent. The town further suffered from ravages of the Black Death (1310). Archiepiscopal see (4th cent. to 1790).

Narborough, residential town and parish (pop. 2,245), central Leicester, England, on Soar R. and 6 mi. SW of Leicester; paper, concrete.

Narborough Island, Galápagos: see FERNANDINA ISLAND.

Narcao (närkä'ô), village (pop. 910), Cagliari prov., SW Sardinia, 12 mi. SE of Iglesias; barite, lead-zinc-silver, lignite, and trachyte mines.

Narcea River (när-thā'ä), Oviedo prov. (Asturias), N Spain, rises near Leon border, flows c.60 mi. NNE, past Cangas del Narcea, to Nalón R. just S of Pravia.

Narcondam Island (närkŏndäm'), small extinct volcano in Andaman Sea, 80 mi. E of N Andaman Isls.; 13°25'N 94°17'E; rises to 2,330 ft.

Narda, Greece: see ARTA.

Nardin (när'dŭn), town (pop. 184), Kay co., N Okla., 22 mi. WNW of Ponca City, in agr. area.

Nardò (närdô'), town (pop. 17,655), Lecce prov., Apulia, S Italy, 14 mi. SW of Lecce; agr. trade center (wine, olive oil, wheat, tobacco); ink mfg. Has 13th-cent. cathedral (restored 19th cent.).

Nare (nä'rā), village (pop. 816), Antioquia dept., N central Colombia, at mouth of Nare R., 25 mi. SSW of Puerto Berrío; cement plant.

Narechenski-bani, Bulgaria: see CHEPELARE.

Narela (nŭrä'lŭ), town (pop. 8,050), N Delhi, India, 8 mi. NNE of Delhi city center; handicraft pottery and glass bangles.

Narenta, Canale della, Yugoslavia: see NERETVA CHANNEL.

Narenta River, Yugoslavia: see NERETVA RIVER.

Nare River (nä'rā), Antioquia dept., N central Colombia, rises in Cordillera Central S of Medellín, flows c.100 mi. E to Magdalena R. 25 mi. SW of Puerto Berrío.

Nares, Cape, N Ellesmere Isl., NE Franklin Dist., Northwest Territories, on the Arctic Ocean; 83°6'N 71°45'W.

Nares Land, region in W part of Peary Land, N Greenland, on E coast of Victoria Fjord; 82°10'N 45°W.

Naresto (nä'rŭstû), Nor. *Narestø*, village in Flosta canton (pop. 1,316), Aust-Agder co., S Norway, on Flosteroy (Nor. *Flosterøy*), a small isl. (□ 3; 5 mi. long) 6 mi. NE of Arendal. On isl. there is feldspar quarrying, fishing, boatbuilding.

Narew River (nä'rĕf), Rus. *Narev* (nŭryĭf'), in W Belorussian SSR and NE Poland, rises 15 mi. NW of Pruzhany, flows generally WNW into Poland, past Lapy and Lomza, SSW past Ostroleka, Pultusk, and Serock, and WSW to Vistula R. just W of Nowy Dwor; c.275 mi. long. Navigable in lower course, below Biebrza R. mouth. Main tributaries: Western Bug (left), Wkra, Orzyc, Omulew, Biebrza, and Suprasl (right) rivers.

Nargen, Estonia: see NAISSAAR.

Nargund (nŭr'gŏŏnd), town (pop. 8,954), Dharwar dist., S Bombay, India, 31 mi. NE of Dharwar; market center for cotton, wheat, millet, sugar cane; cotton ginning.

Naria (nŭr'yŭ), village, Faridpur dist., S central East Bengal, E Pakistan, near the Padma, 16 mi. NE of Madaripur; road terminus; rice, jute, oilseeds, sugar cane.

Naricual (närēkwäl'), town (pop. 358), Anzoátegui state, NE Venezuela, 6 mi. SE of Barcelona (connected by railroad); govt.-owned coal mines; briquetting plant. Capiricual (käpērēkwäl') coal mines are near by.

Nariha (närē'hä), town (pop. 6,972), Okayama prefecture, SW Honshu, Japan, 23 mi. WNW of Okayama; agr. (rice, wheat, persimmons, peppermint), and livestock center; sake brewing.

Narihualá (närēwälä'), village (pop. 1,062), Piura dept., NW Peru, on coastal plain, near Piura R., 7 mi. SSW of Piura, in irrigated cotton area.

Nariman (nŭrēmän'), village (1939 pop. over 500), NE Osh oblast, Kirghiz SSR, near Osh; cotton.

Narimanova, Imeni, Azerbaijan SSR: see BANK.

Narimatsu (närē'-mätsoo), town (pop. 4,840), Hyogo prefecture, S Honshu, Japan, 10 mi. SSW of Fukuchiyama, in agr. area (rice, wheat, poultry); cutlery, yarn, straw products, tiles; tea processing.

Narin or **Nahrin** (nŭrēn'), town, Kataghan prov., NE Afghanistan, in Afghan Turkestan, 23 mi. SE of Baghlan; coal mining.

Nariño (närē'nyō), department (□ 11,548; 1938 pop. 465,868; 1950 estimate 563,620), SW Colombia, on the Pacific, bordering Ecuador; ⊙ Pasto. Its indented coastal lowland rises E to volcanic Andean peaks. Near Ecuador border, the main range of the Andes splits into the Cordillera Occidental and Cordillera Central, separated by the torrential Patía R. which, in N, cuts W through Cordillera Occidental to the Pacific. Climate ranges from hot and humid in lowlands to glacial conditions on Andean peaks; rain is heavy along coast throughout the year. There are many gold mines (Barbacoas, Samaniego, Túquerres). The abundant forests yield rubber, quinine, tagua nuts, balsam, resins, chicle, Pasto varnish, and fine tropical wood. Considerable cattle grazing on plateaus and in upper Patía R. valley. Agr. crops include corn, wheat, rice, coffee, cacao, sugar cane, bananas, tobacco, cotton, yucca, henequen. Pasto and Ipiales are trading, textile-milling, and processing centers; Tumaco, a Pacific port, is a major outlet.

Nari River (nä'rē), in E Baluchistan, W Pakistan, rises in Central Brahui Range 14 mi. N of Ziarat, flows E as Loralai R., S as Anambar R., WSW as Beji R., and finally S as the Nari, through center of Kachhi plain, past Bhag, to North Western Canal of Sukkur Barrage system 9 mi. W of Usta Muhammad; c.320 mi. long. Seasonal, but its flood waters irrigate small fields (S) of wheat, millet, and cotton.

Narita (närē'tä), town (pop. 13,550), Chiba prefecture, central Honshu, Japan, 16 mi. NE of Chiba; commercial center for agr. and poultry area. Has 18th-cent. Buddhist temple.

Nariva (nŭrē'vŭ), county (□ 206.30; pop. 11,815), E Trinidad, B.W.I., bordering on the Atlantic. Forms, together with St. David, St. Andrew, and Mayaro, the administrative dist. of the Eastern Counties.

Nariva Swamp, E Trinidad, B.W.I., c.35 mi. SE of Port of Spain, a low area stretching from palm-lined Cocos Bay on E coast c.5 mi. inland. Duck shooting.

Nariya or **Nariyah** (närē'yŭ), settlement in Hasa, Saudi Arabia, 130 mi. NW of Dhahran; 27°30'N 28°20'E. Oil-pumping station on pipe line from Abqaiq to Saida.

Narka, city (pop. 220), Republic co., N central Kansas, 14 mi. NE of Belleville, near Nebr. line, in grain region.

Narkanda (när'kŭndŭ), village, central Himachal Pradesh, India, 21 mi. NE of Simla, in NW Kumaun Himalayas; scenic hill resort (alt. c.9,460 ft.).

Narkatiaganj (nŭr"kŭtyä'gŭnj), village, Champaran dist., NW Bihar, India, 21 mi. N of Bettiah; rail junction, with spur to Bhikhna Thori station (town is just across Nepal border).

Narke (nĕr'kŭ), Swedish *Närke*, province [Swedish *landskap*] (□ 1,712; pop. 142,645), S central Sweden. Included in S part of Orebro co.

Narkher (nŭrkār'), town (pop. 8,775), Nagpur dist., central Madhya Pradesh, India, 40 mi. NW of Nagpur; cotton ginning; millet, wheat, oilseeds; cattle market. Sometimes spelled Narkhed.

Narmashir, Iran: see RIGAN.

Narnaul (när'noul), district, S Patiala and East Punjab States Union, India; ⊙ Mohindargarh.

Narnaul, town (pop. 23,063), Narnaul dist., S Patiala and East Punjab States Union, India, 155 mi. SSW of Patiala; trade center for cotton, grain, ghee, salt, oilseeds; hand-loom weaving, cart mfg.

Narni (när'nē), anc. *Nequinum* and *Narnia*, town (pop. 4,306), Terni prov., Umbria, central Italy, on hill above Nera R., 7 mi. WSW of Terni; mfg. (electric furnaces, electrodes, linoleum, woolen textiles). Bishopric. Has Romanesque cathedral (consecrated 1145), old castle (1360–70; now a prison), and 13th-cent. palace with picture gall. Roman emperor Nerva b. here.

Naro (nä'rô), town (pop. 14,401), Agrigento prov., S Sicily, 12 mi. E of Agrigento; rail junction; fertilizer, olive oil, jewelry. Site of anc. castle, 14th-cent. cathedral. Sulphur mines near by. Necropolis (E).

Naro, Tunisia: see HAMMAM-LIF.

Naroch, Lake, or **Lake Naroch'** (nŭrôch'), Pol. *Narocz* (nä'rôch) (□ 32), N Molodechno oblast, Belorussian SSR, 18 mi. S of Postavy; noted summer resort; fisheries.

Naroda (nä'rŭdŭ) or **Narodnaya** (–nīŭ), highest peak (6,184 ft.) of the Urals, Russian SFSR, in N section of the range; 65°N. Discovered in 1930s.

Narodichi (nŭrô'dyĭchē), agr. town (1926 pop. 6,124), NE Zhitomir oblast, Ukrainian SSR, on Uzh R. and 25 mi. NE of Korosten; flax, buckwheat, potatoes.

Narodnaya, Russian SSR: see NARODA.

Narodnoye (nŭrôd'nŭyŭ), village (1939 pop. over 500), E Voronezh oblast, Russian SFSR, 18 mi. NNW of Borisoglebsk; flour mill.

Naro-Fominsk (nä"rŭ-fŭmēnsk'), city (1937 pop. 29,750), S Moscow oblast, Russian SFSR, 40 mi. SW of Moscow; cotton-milling center; paper mill (S). Near by is former countryseat of Prince Shcherbatov, with English gardens. Became city in 1926; during Second World War, briefly held (1941) by Germans in Moscow campaign.

Narok (nä'rŏk), town, Masai dist., S Kenya, on road from Kijabe and 65 mi. NW of Magadi; 1°6'S 35°53'E; stock; tea, coffee, flax, corn. Airfield.

Naro Moru (nä'rō mō'rōō), town, Central Prov., S central Kenya, on W slopes of Mt. Kenya, on railroad and 20 mi. NNE of Nyeri; alt. 6,631 ft. Coffee, sisal, wheat, corn.

Narora, India: see DIBAI.

Narova River, Russian SFSR and Estonia: see NARVA RIVER.

Narovchat (nŭrŭfchät'), village (1926 pop. 5,646), N Penza oblast, Russian SFSR, in Moksha R. valley, 25 mi. N of Nizhni Lomov, in grain and hemp area. Marl deposits near by.

Narovlya (nŭrôv'lyŭ), town (1926 pop. 2,515), S Polesye oblast, Belorussian SSR, on Pripet R. and 21 mi. SSE of Mozyr; food products. Also called Narovl.

Narowal (nä'rōväl), town (pop. 12,021), Sialkot dist., E Punjab, W Pakistan, 33 mi. SE of Sialkot; rail junction; market center (wheat, rice, sugar cane); metalware, leather goods.
Narrabeen (nă'rŭbēn'), town (pop. 2,607), E New South Wales, Australia, 12 mi. NNE of Sydney, on coast, in metropolitan area; summer resort.
Narrabri (nă'rŭbrī), municipality (pop. 3,329), N New South Wales, Australia, on Namoi R. and 215 mi. NW of Newcastle; rail junction; sheep and agr. center.
Narracan, village (pop. 128), S Victoria, Australia, 80 mi. ESE of Melbourne, S of Moe; bauxite mines.
Narragansett (nărŭgăn'sĭt), town (pop. 2,288), Washington co., S R.I., along W shore of Narragansett Bay, N of Point Judith, 27 mi. S of Providence; resorts, fishing, agr. Includes resort village Narragansett Pier (pop. 1,247), and a state reservation with Scarborough Beach. Settled in mid-17th cent., set off from South Kingstown 1888, inc. 1901. The 1938 hurricane did great damage.
Narragansett Bay, R.I., inlet of the Atlantic, 30 mi. long, 3–12 mi. wide, almost dividing the state. Its many inlets and isls. provided active colonial shipping centers; now devoted mainly to resorts and fishing, with shipping mainly at Providence, on Providence R. at head of bay. Newport and Portsmouth are on RHODE ISLAND, at entrance; other isls. include Prudence and Conanicut isls. MOUNT HOPE BAY is NE arm; SAKONNET RIVER arm is E of Rhode Isl. The 1938 hurricane did great damage in bay area.
Narragansett Pier, R.I.: see NARRAGANSETT.
Narraguagus River (nărugā'gŭs), SE Maine, rises in Hancock and Washington counties, flows c.30 mi. SE to Pleasant Bay.
Narrandera (nŭrăn'drŭ), municipality (pop. 4,186), S New South Wales, Australia, on Murrumbidgee R. and 150 mi. WNW of Canberra; rail junction; sheep, agr. Airport.
Narran Lake, Australia: see TEREWAH, LAKE.
Narrogin (nă'rŭjĭn), municipality (pop. 2,558), SW Western Australia, 105 mi. SE of Perth; rail junction; wheat center; butter factory, flour mill. Govt. agr. school near by.
Narromine (nă'rŭmīn'), municipality (pop. 1,825), central New South Wales, Australia, on Macquarie R. and 205 mi. NW of Sydney; rail junction; agr. center (fruit, wheat).
Narrows, town (pop. 2,520), Giles co., SW Va., in the Alleghenies near W.Va. line, on New R. and 24 mi. E of Bluefield, in timber, coal-mining, and agr. (grain, apples) area; mfg. of synthetic fiber. Garrisoned by Confederates in Civil War. Inc. 1904.
Narrows, The, Caribbean strait (c.2 mi. wide), Leeward Isls., bet. St. Kitts (NW) and Nevis (SE) at about 17°13'N 62°37'W.
Narrows, the, N.Y.: see NEW YORK BAY.
Narrows, The, narrow passage (c.½ mi. wide) in the Virgin Isls., bet. St. John Isl. (S) and Great Thatch and Tortola isls. (N), 12 mi. E of Charlotte Amalie.
Narrows Arm, NE arm (10 mi. long, ½ mi. wide) of Seechelt Inlet, SW B.C., 45 mi. NW of Vancouver, in lumbering area.
Narrowsburg, resort village (pop. c.400), Sullivan co., SE N.Y., on Delaware R. (here forming Pa. line) and 20 mi. WSW of Monticello.
Narrows Dam, Ark.: see LITTLE MISSOURI RIVER.
Narrows Park and **The Narrows**, two villages (combined pop. 2,022), Allegany co., W Md., in the Alleghenies 6 mi. NW of Cumberland, in bituminous coal- and clay-mining area.
Narrung, village (pop. 210), SE South Australia, on S shore of L. Alexandrina and 55 mi. SE of Adelaide; citrus and dried fruits.
Narsak, Greenland: see NARSSAK.
Narsampet (nŭr'sŭmpăt), village (pop. 3,622), Warangal dist., E Hyderabad state, India, 22 mi. ESE of Warangal; rice, oilseeds.
Narsannapet, India: see NARASANNAPETA.
Narsapatnam, India: see NARSIPATNAM.
Narsapur, India: see NARASAPUR.
Narsarssuak (nākhsākh'shwăk), locality, SW Greenland, at head of Tunugdliarfik Fjord, 40 mi. NE of Julianehaab; 61°9'N 45°24'W. Site of Bluie West 1 air base, established by U.S. in Second World War.
Narsinghgarh (nŭr'sĭng-gŭr), town (pop. 111,036), central Madhya Bharat, India, 37 mi. NW of Bhopal; market center for millet, cotton, wheat; handicraft cloth weaving. Was ⊙ former princely state of Narsinghgarh (□ 731; pop. 125,178) of Central India agency; since 1948, state merged with Madhya Bharat. Sometimes Narsingarh.
Narsinghpur (–pŏŏr). **1** Town (pop. 12,908), Hoshangabad dist., NW Madhya Pradesh, India, in fertile Narbada valley, 95 mi. E of Hoshangabad; trades in wheat, millet, cotton, oilseeds; sawmilling. Was ⊙ former Narsinghpur dist. (□ 1,978; 1931 pop. 321,481) until merged in early 1930s with Hoshangabad dist. Marble quarries near by. Formerly spelled Nursingpur. **2** Village, Cuttack dist., E Orissa, India, 50 mi. W of Cuttack; trades in rice, oilseeds, bamboo. Was ⊙ former princely state of Narsinghpur (□ 204; pop. 48,448) in Orissa States, along left bank of Mahanadi R.; state inc. 1949 into Cuttack dist.
Narsipatnam or **Narsapatnam** (nŭr'sŭpŭtnŭm), town (pop. 16,644), Vizagapatam dist., NE Madras, India, 45 mi. W of Vizagapatam; road and trade center in agr. area (oilseeds, sugar cane, rice); shipping center for timber (sal, teak), myrobalan, lac, and coffee from Eastern Ghats (W). Graphite deposits near by. Silk-growing farm 22 mi. NW, at village of Chintapalle. Also spelled Narasapatnam or Narasapatam. Narsipatnam (also spelled Narasapatnam) Road, 17 mi. SSE, is rail station.
Narsoba Vadi (nŭrsō'bŭ vä'dē), town (pop. 2,686), Kolhapur dist., S Bombay, India, 25 mi. E of Kolhapur; sugar cane, millet. Large annual festival fair. Also spelled Narsobavadi, Narsubachi Vadi, or Narsobas Wadi.
Narssak or **Narssaq** (both: näkh'shäk). **1** Settlement (pop. 104), Godthaab dist., SW Greenland, on Davis Strait, 14 mi. SSE of Godthaab; 63°59'N 51°36'W. Radio station. **2** Settlement (pop. 399), Julianehaab dist., SW Greenland, on Tunugdliarfik Fjord, 14 mi. N of Julianehaab; 60°54'N 46°W; fishing port. Meteorological and radio station. Sometimes spelled Narsak.
Narssalik (näkh'shälĭk), fishing settlement (pop. 106), Frederikshaab dist., SW Greenland, on islet in the Atlantic, 25 mi. SSE of Frederikshaab; 61°8'N 49°22'W.
Nartan (nŭrtän'), village (1926 pop. 3,818), central Kabardian Autonomous SSR, Russian SFSR, 3 mi. ENE of Nalchik; truck.
Narthakion (närthä'kēôn), hill range on Thessaly-Phthiotis line, central Greece, just NW of the Othrys; rises to 3,317 ft. in the Kassidiares (Kassidiaris), 5 mi. S of Pharsala.
Narthang, Tibet: see SHIGATSE.
Nartovskoye (när'tŭfskŭyŭ), village (1926 pop. 3,611), central North Ossetian Autonomous SSR, Russian SFSR, on right branch of Terek R. and 7 mi. ENE of Beslan; corn, wheat, hemp. Until 1944 (in Chechen-Ingush Autonomous SSR), Kantyshevo.
Naru, Japan: see NARU-SHIMA.
Narugo (närōō'gō), town (pop. 6,144), Miyagi prefecture, N Honshu, Japan, 17 mi. NW of Furukawa; hot-springs resort.
Naruja (närōō'zhä), village (pop. 265), Putna prov., E Rumania, 22 mi. NW of Focsani.
Naruksovo (nŭrŏŏk'sŭvŭ), village (1926 pop. 4,814), S Gorki oblast, Russian SFSR, 28 mi. S of Lukoyanov; hemp, potatoes.
Narumi (närōō'mē), town (pop. 20,778), Aichi prefecture, central Honshu, Japan, just SE of Nagoya; agr. center (rice, wheat, herbs); poultry.
Naru-shima (närōō'shĭmä), island (□ 10; pop. 7,353, including offshore islets) of isl. group Gotoretto, Nagasaki prefecture, Japan, in E.China Sea, 40 mi. W of Kyushu; 5.5 mi. long, 5 mi. wide; fishing. Sometimes called Naru.
Naruto (närōōtō'). **1** Town (pop. 5,842), Chiba prefecture, central Honshu, Japan, on N central Chiba Peninsula, 4 mi. NE of Togane; rice, vegetable oil, raw silk. **2** Town, Tokushima prefecture, Japan: see MUYA.
Naruto Strait, Jap. *Awa-no-Naruto*, channel connecting Harima Sea (E section of Inland Sea) with Kii Channel, bet. Shikoku (W) and Awaji-shima (E); c.10 mi. long, c.1–5 mi. wide. Contains Ogeshima and Shimada-shima; Muya is on W shore. Known for whirlpools.
Narva, Ger. *Narwa* (both: när'vä), city (pop. 23,512), NE Estonia, on left bank of Narva R. (Russian SFSR border), 8 mi. from its mouth and 120 mi. E of Tallinn; 59°23'N 28°12'E. Industrial and commercial center; mfg. of cotton and linen textiles at large Kreenholm [Ger. *Krähnholm*, Rus. *Krengolm*] mills (S; powered by Narva R. falls); also machinery, foundry products, soap, leather goods; sawmilling. City is dominated by Hermann fortress (built 13th cent. by Danes) on left bank and, on right bank, by IVANGOROD castle fortress (built 1492 by Russians); has 14th-cent. Greek Orthodox cathedral (originally R.C.), 17th-cent. town hall and exchange bldg. Founded 1223 by Danes, Narva served as E border bastion under Livonian Knights (after 1346) and Swedes (after 1561). Peter the Great was defeated here (1700) by Charles XII of Sweden, but captured city in 1704. Developed as textile-milling center in mid-19th cent.
Narvacan (närväkän'), town (1939 pop. 2,465; 1948 municipality pop. 22,237), Ilocos Sur prov., N Luzon, Philippines, 13 mi. SE of Vigan, near W coast; rice-growing center.
Narva-Joesuu or **Narva-Yyyesu**, Est. *Narva-Jõesuu* (all: när'vä-yŭ'ĕsōō), Ger. *Hungerburg* (hŏŏng'ŭrbŏŏrk), town (pop. 1,635), NE Estonia, outer port of Narva, on Narva Bay (inlet of Gulf of Finland), at mouth of Narva R. (Russian SFSR border), 8 mi. NW of Narva; summer resort; sawmill.
Narva River (när'vä) or **Narova River** (närô'vä), outlet of L. Peipus, on Estonian-Russian SFSR border, leaves L. Peipus at Vasknarva, flows 48 mi. generally NNE, past Narva, (where its falls power Kreenholm textile mills), to Narva Bay of Gulf of Finland at Narva-Joesuu. Forming historical Estonian-Russian border, river was (1920–45) entirely within Estonia and Rus. line passed 5–8 mi. E; the territory E of the Narva was ceded to the Russian SFSR in 1945.
Narva-Yyyesu, Estonia: see NARVA-JOESUU.
Narvik (när'vĭk, när'vēk), city (pop. 10,281), Nordland co., N Norway, on Ofot Fjord, 110 mi. NE of Bodo; 68°26'N 17°24'E. Port, ice-free the year round; terminus of electric railroad from N Sweden and Stockholm, it is transshipment center for iron from Kiruna and Gallivare, Sweden. Port site chosen 1887 and called Victoriahavn; named Narvik in 1898. Port opened 1902; developed rapidly; inc. 1907. In Second World War, Narvik fell to the Germans when they invaded Norway on April 9, 1940. To prevent the Germans from using Narvik as a shipping base for Kiruna ore, a British and French expeditionary force recaptured the port on May 28, 1940, after heavy fighting, but it was abandoned on June 9.
Narwa, Estonia: see NARVA, city.
Narwana (nŭrvä'nŭ), town (pop. 7,066), S central Patiala and East Punjab States Union, India, 55 mi. SSW of Patiala; rail junction; agr. market (cotton, millet, gram, wheat); cotton ginning, handloom weaving.
Narwar (nŭr'vŭr), town (pop. 3,607), N central Madhya Bharat, India, 22 mi. NE of Shivpuri, near Sind R.; millet, gram, wheat. Has many ruins. Hill fort (W) held by Rajputs in 11th and 12th cent.
Naryan-Mar or **Nar'yan-Mar** (nŭryän'-mär"), city (1948 pop. over 10,000), ⊙ Nenets Natl. Okrug, Archangel oblast, Russian SFSR, port on E arm of Pechora R. delta mouth, 40 mi. inland from Pechora Bay and 400 mi. NE of Archangel; sawmilling (lumber export), tanning, brickworking. Reindeer experimental station; airport. Until 1935 (when it became a city), called Imeni Dzerzhinskogo.
Narym, okrug, Russian SFSR: see TOMSK, oblast.
Narym (nŭrĭm'), village (1926 pop. 1,000), central Tomsk oblast, Russian SFSR, on Ob R., near mouth of Ket R., and 210 mi. NNW of Tomsk; river port; fisheries, sawmilling. Founded 1595 on early Siberian colonization route; important 19th-cent. trading town; declined following construction of Trans-Siberian RR. Stalin (1912), Kuibyshev, and Sverdlov were exiled here.
Narym Range, branch of SW Altai Mts., East Kazakhstan oblast, Kazakh SSR; extends 90 mi. along Narym R. W to Irtysh R.; rises to 11,270 ft. (E); forms divide bet. Bukhtarma and Kurchum rivers.
Narym River, East Kazakhstan oblast, Kazakh SSR, rises in Narym Range, flows c.60 mi. W, past Bolshoye Narymskoye, to upper Irtysh R.
Naryn (nŭrĭn'). **1** City (1939 pop. 4,552), ⊙ Tyan-Shan oblast, Kirghiz SSR, on Naryn R., on highway and 120 mi. SE of Frunze; 41°27'N 76°E; alt. 6,610 ft. Center of high-mtn. valley agr. (wheat) and livestock (sheep) grazing; tanning industry, sawmilling, brickworking. **2** Town (1945 pop. over 500), SE Tuva Autonomous Oblast, Russian SFSR, 65 mi. ESE of Saryg-Bulun. **3** Village (1926 pop. 2,029), SE Namangan oblast, Uzbek SSR, on railroad (Khakulabad station) and 22 mi. ESE of Namangan; cotton ginning. Until c.1935, called Khakulabad.
Narynkol or **Narynkol'** (nŭrĭnkôl'), village, SE Alma-Ata oblast, Kazakh SSR, in N Tien-Shan foothills, on China frontier, 165 mi. E of Alma-Ata (linked by road); irrigated agr. (wheat).
Naryn River, a headstream of the Syr Darya in Kirghiz and Uzbek SSR; 449 mi. long; rises in several branches in central Tien Shan mtn. system (main branch, Yaak-Tash, rises in Petrov Glacier); flows W (as the Greater Naryn, until it receives the Lesser Naryn 20 mi. E of Naryn), through fertile wheat valley, then N, W, through Ketmen-Tyube valley (cotton), past Toktogul, and SW, past Tashkumyr and Uch-Kurgan, into Fergana Valley and Uzbek SSR, joining the Kara Darya near Balykchi to form the SYR DARYA. Tributaries: Son-Kul (outlet of lake Son-Kul); Kokomeren R. Lower course used for irrigation.
Naryn-Tau (–tou'), range in Tien Shan mountain system, Kirghiz SSR; extends c.80 mi. E-W, S of Naryn R. and E of Naryn; rises to 13,000 ft.
Naryshevo, Russian SFSR: see OKTYABRSKI, Bashkir Autonomous SSR.
Naryshkino (nŭrĭsh'kēnŭ), town (1948 pop. over 2,000), W Orel oblast, Russian SFSR, 13 mi. W of Orel; machine mfg.
Narzole (närtsô'lĕ), village (pop. 1,245), Cuneo prov., Piedmont, NW Italy, near Tanaro R., 3 mi. S of Bra.
Nasarawa (näsä'rä'wä), town (pop. 2,560), Benue prov., Northern Provinces, central Nigeria, 80 mi. NW of Makurdi; major tin-mining center; sheanut processing. An important native commercial center until end of 19th cent. Sometimes spelled Nassarawa.
Nasarpur (nŭsŭr'pŏŏr). **1** Village, Peshawar dist., North-West Frontier Prov., W Pakistan, 5 mi. E of Peshawar; fruit canning. **2** Town (pop. 3,610), Hyderabad dist., S central Sind, W Pakistan, 17 mi. NE of Hyderabad; market center (millet, rice, cotton); handicraft cloth weaving, dyeing. Also spelled Nasirpur.
Nasaud (nŭsŭōōd'), Rum. *Năsăud*, Hung. *Naszód* (nŏ'sōt), town (1948 pop. 3,716), Rodna prov., N central Rumania, in Transylvania, in S foothills

of the Rodna Mts., on Great Somes R., on railroad and 12 mi. NNW of Bistrita; trading center (lumber, livestock), with brewing industry. Dating from 13th cent., it was given as fief to Janos Hunyadi by Ladislaus V (15th cent.). In Hungary, 1940–45.

Nasavrky (nä'sävůrkĭ), Ger. *Nassaberg* (nä'säbĕrk), town (pop. 898), E Bohemia, Czechoslovakia, 8 mi. S of Chrudim, in cotton-spinning dist.; sugar beets, potatoes.

Nasbinals (näbēnäl'), village (pop. 550), Lozère dept., S France, in Monts d'Aubrac, 24 mi. WNW of Mende; cattle.

Nasby (nĕs'bü"), Swedish *Näsby*, residential village (pop. 1,015), Stockholm co., E Sweden, near inlet of Baltic, 7 mi. N of Stockholm city center. Site of naval col., housed in 17th-cent. castle.

Nasca, Peru: see NAZCA.

Naschel (näs-chĕl'), town (pop. estimate 500), NE San Luis prov., Argentina, on railroad and 60 mi. ENE of San Luis; corn, alfalfa, wheat, flax, livestock; granite and marble quarrying.

Nasea, Fiji: see LAMBASA.

Naseby (nāz'bē), agr. village and parish (pop. 399), N central Northampton, England, 12 mi. NNW of Northampton. Site of decisive defeat (1645) of Royalists (under Charles I and Prince Rupert) by Parliamentarians (under Cromwell and Fairfax); commemorated by an obelisk. Church dates from 14th cent.

Naseby, borough (pop. 153), ⊙ Maniototo co. (□ 1,340; pop. 2,720), E central S.Isl., New Zealand, 60 mi. NNW of Dunedin; gold mines, sheep farms. Sanatorium near by.

Naseri, Iran: see AHWAZ.

Nash (năsh), county (□ 552; pop. 59,919), E central N.C.; ⊙ Nashville. In coastal plain area; bounded NE by Fishing Creek; crossed by Tar R. Agr. (tobacco, cotton, corn); pine timber. Formed 1777.

Nash or **Nashville,** town (pop. 290), Grant co., N Okla., 21 mi. NNW of Enid, near Salt Fork of Arkansas R., in grain-growing and dairying area; oil wells.

Nashar, Malta: see NAXXAR.

Nashawena Island, Mass.: see ELIZABETH ISLANDS.

Nash Harbor, village (pop. 49), W Alaska, on N shore of Ninivak Isl.; 60°15'N 166°44'W.

Nash Island, Washington co., E Maine, small lighthouse isl. just E of entrance to Pleasant Bay.

Nashoba (năshō'bů), former community, Shelby co., SW Tenn., on Wolf R. just E of Memphis. Founded 1827 by Frances Wright as a colony in which slaves were to be educated for freedom, Nashoba failed as a social experiment and by 1830 had been dissolved.

Nasholim (näshōlēm') or **Nashonim** (–nēm'), agr. settlement, NW Israel, on Mediterranean, 15 mi. SSW of Haifa, near railroad. Established 1948 on site of former Arab village of Tantura. Modern village on site of anc. Canaanite city-state of Dor, seat of one of Solomon's "twelve officers over Israel."

Nashotah (nůshō'tů), village (pop. c.150), Waukesha co., SE Wis., 24 mi. W of Milwaukee, in farm and lake region. Seat of Nashotah House, an Episcopal seminary.

Nashua (nă'shōōů, năsh'wů). **1** Town (pop. 1,609), Chickasaw co., NE Iowa, on Cedar R. at mouth of Little Cedar R., and 11 mi. SE of Charles City; mfg. (manure spreaders, metal and wood products). Limestone quarries, sand pit near by. Inc. 1857. **2** Village (pop. 181), Wilkin co., W Minn., 21 mi. SE of Breckenridge; dairy products. **3** Town (pop. 691), Valley co., NE Mont., 13 mi. ESE of Glasgow and on Milk R., near Fort Peck Reservoir and Dam. Growth stimulated by construction of dam. **4** City (pop. 34,669), a ⊙ Hillsboro co., S N.H., on the Merrimack, at mouth of Nashua R. (water power), near Mass. line; 2nd largest city in N.H. Trade center, mfg. (shoes, textiles, paper and wood products, tools, hardware, machinery). Seat of Rivier Col. Settled c.1655, inc. as Dunstable 1673, named Nashua 1836, chartered as city 1853. Developed as textile-mill town in 1st half of 19th cent. A threatened closing in 1948 of the largest mill resulted in sale of mill to group of citizens who arranged for its partial operation immediately and planned for use of rest of the plant in other ways. Municipal airport.

Nashua River, Mass. and N.H., formed in E Worcester co., Mass., by junction of its N and S branches near Lancaster; flows c.30 mi. NNE to the Merrimack R. at Nashua, N.H.; water power. N branch rises W of Fitchburg, Mass., flows c.30 mi. generally SE, past Fitchburg (water power), joining S branch c.5 mi. below its issuance from WACHUSETT RESERVOIR.

Nashville. 1 City (pop. 3,548), ⊙ Howard co., SW Ark., 38 mi. NNE of Texarkana; shipping point for agr. area (peaches, cotton, corn, alfalfa, truck, livestock); mfg. of cement and wood products. **2** City (pop. 3,414), ⊙ Berrien co., S Ga., 26 mi. N of Valdosta; tobacco market; food canning; mfg. (sprayers, lumber). Inc. 1892. **3** City (pop. 2,432), ⊙ Washington co., SW Ill., 18 mi. SW of Centralia; mfg. (machinery, flour, beverages); agr. (corn, wheat, livestock, fruit, seed, poultry); bituminous-coal mines. Inc. 1853. **4** Town (pop. 526), ⊙ Brown co., S central Ind., 40 mi. S of Indianapolis, in agr. area; timber. Beautiful scenery here attracts tourists; town has an art gall. and several resident painters. **5** City (pop. 159), Kingman co., S Kansas, 21 mi. SW of Kingman, in wheat area. **6** Village (pop. 1,374), Barry co., SW Mich., 28 mi. SW of Lansing and on Thornapple R., in agr. area; mfg. (furniture, dairy products). Platted 1865, inc. 1869. **7** Town (pop. 1,302), ⊙ Nash co., E central N.C., 10 mi. W of Rocky Mount, in agr. and timber area; sawmilling. **8** Village (pop. 234), Holmes co., central Ohio, 24 mi. ESE of Mansfield. **9** Town, Grant co., Okla.: see NASH. **10** City (pop. 174,307), ⊙ Tenn. and Davidson co., central Tenn., on Cumberland R. and 195 mi. NE of Memphis, in NW part of fertile bluegrass region called the Nashville Basin (c.120 mi. long, 50–60 mi. wide); 36°10'N 86°46'W; alt. 380–750 ft. State's 2d-largest city (after Memphis); commercial, transportation, industrial, and educational center of middle Tenn.; port of entry; rail junction (with large repair shops); processing point for rich limestone-soil livestock and agr. region. Large rayon, shoe, aircraft, hosiery plants, printing and publishing houses; also mfg. of cellophane, tobacco products, clothing, stoves, yarn, fertilizers, farm implements, bricks, tiles, cement, furniture, bedding; meat packing, flour and feed milling, woodworking, stone working, oil refining. Seat of Vanderbilt Univ., Meharry Medical Col., Fisk Univ., George Peabody Col. for Teachers, Scarritt Col. for Christian Workers, Trevecca Nazarene Col., Tenn. Agr. and Industrial State Col., Andrew Jackson Univ., David Lipscomb Col., Ward-Belmont School, Nashville School of Social Work, state school for the blind. Points of interest: the Capitol (Greek Revival; built 1855) on city's highest hill, with tomb of James K. Polk in its grounds; First World War memorial bldg. with museums; replica (built 1930) of Fort Nashborough, built on same site in 1780; replica of the Parthenon, in Centennial Park; several old churches; fine ante-bellum houses. Near by is the HERMITAGE, home of Andrew Jackson; Madison Col. is NE, near Madison. Stones River Natl. Military Park is c.30 mi. SE. City founded 1780 by James Robertson; inc. as city 1806; made ⊙ Tenn. in 1843. As N terminus of NATCHEZ TRACE, grew as cotton center and river port; later became a railroad center. In Civil War, Confederates abandoned city to Union troops after fall (1862) of Fort Donelson (70 mi. NW; now in FORT DONELSON NATIONAL MILITARY PARK); city became Union base throughout rest of war; here Gen. G. H. Thomas won victory (battle of Nashville; Dec., 1864) over Confederates under J. B. Hood. Post-Civil War depression was succeeded in 1870s by beginning of city's modern commercial and industrial importance.

Nashville Dam, Calif.: see COSUMNES RIVER.

Nashwaak River (năsh'wôk), central N.B., issues from the small Nashwaak L., 30 mi. NE of Woodstock, flows 70 mi. SE and S, past Marysville, to St. John R. opposite Fredericton.

Nashwaaksis (năsh'wôksĭs"), lumbering village (pop. estimate c.250), S central N.B., on St. John R. at mouth of Nashwaak R., just NW of Fredericton.

Nashwauk (năsh'wôk), village (pop. 2,029), Itasca co., NE Minn., on Mesabi iron range, near Swan L., 13 mi. WSW of Hibbing; ice cream. Iron mining and dairying in vicinity. Growth followed discovery of iron near by in early 1900s.

Nasi, Indonesia: see PUNASU.

Näsi, Lake, Finnish *Näsijärvi* (nă'sēyăr"vē) (20 mi. long, 2–8 mi. wide), SW Finland, extends N from Tampere. Drained S into L. Pyhä by Tammer Rapids.

Nasice (nä'shĭtsĕ), Serbo-Croatian *Našice,* village (pop. 3,084), N Croatia, Yugoslavia, 24 mi. N of Slavonski Brod, at N foot of Krndija Planina, in Slavonia; rail junction; woodworking, tannin mfg.; fishing. Castle.

Nasielsk (nä'syĕlsk), Rus. *Nasyelsk* or *Nasyel'sk* (both: näsyĕ'lyůsk), town (pop. 4,028), Warszawa prov., E central Poland, 26 mi. NNW of Warsaw; rail junction; mfg. (buttons, cement, flour). Before Second World War, pop. 75% Jewish.

Nasigatoka, Fiji: see NASINGATOKA.

Nasik (nä'sĭk), district (□ 6,053; pop. 1,132,193), central Bombay, India; ⊙ Nasik. W section crossed N–S by Western Ghats, with spurs extending E; drained by Godavari and Girna rivers. Has small enclaves in Aurangabad dist. of Hyderabad state (E). Agr. (millet, wheat, oilseeds, rice, cotton); fruit, vegetables grown in S; teak and blackwood in W forests. Handicraft cloth weaving, oilseed pressing. In late-18th cent., under Mahratta control (several dispersed hill forts). Original dist. (□ 5,922; pop. 1,113,901) enlarged by inc. (1949) of former Gujarat state of Surgana. Pop. 77% Hindu, 15% tribal, 6% Moslem.

Nasik, city (pop., including suburban area, 55,524), ⊙ Nasik dist., central Bombay, India, on upper Godavari R. and 90 mi. NE of Bombay; road junction; trade center; cotton ginning, rice and oilseed milling, liquor distilling; handicraft cloth weaving, mfg. of brass lamps, soap, biris, snuff, chewing tobacco; copper, brass, and silver products. Fruit- (grapes, guavas) and vegetable growing. Has col. Boy's Town (in suburbs; founded 1949) is governed by its 200 young citizens; sponsored by Bombay govt. Soil testing laboratory near by. Connected with legend of Rama, Nasik is a very holy place of Hindu pilgrimage (Kumbh Mela held every 12th year), with many Vishnuite temples and shrines. Noted Buddhist caves of c.2d cent. A.D. are 5 mi. SW. Was ⊙ Andhra dynasty (c.230 B.C.–A.D. 225); in 18th cent. a Mahratta stronghold. At Nasik Road, rail station just SE, stamps and currency are printed.

Nasingatoka or **Nasigatoka** (both: näsĭng"ätō'kä), town (pop. 964), SW Viti Levu, Fiji, SW Pacific, 60 mi. W of Suva; sugar cane, copra.

Nasipit (näsēpĕt'), town (1939 pop. 1,884; 1948 municipality pop. 12,502), Agusan prov., N Mindanao, Philippines, on Butuan Bay of Mindanao Sea, 12 mi. W of Butuan; copra.

Nasir (nä'sĭr), town, Upper Nile prov., S central Anglo-Egyptian Sudan, on Sobat R. near Ethiopian border, 120 mi. ESE of Malakal; peanuts, sesame, corn, durra; livestock. Sudan United Mission.

Nasirabad (nŭsē'räbäd). **1** Town (pop., including cantonment area, 17,804), central Ajmer state, India, 11 mi. SSE of Ajmer; market center for millet, corn, wheat; mfg. (condiments, handicraft cloth); exports mica. **2** Town (pop. 14,392), East Khandesh dist., NE Bombay, India, 5 mi. E of Jalgaon; trades in cotton, millet, wheat; cotton ginning, glass-bangle mfg.

Nasirabad, Iran: see ZABUL.

Nasirabad, E Pakistan: see MYMENSINGH, city.

Nasiri, Iran: see AHWAZ.

Nasiriya (näsĭrē'ů), **An Nasiriya, Al Nasiriya,** or **Al-Nasiriyah** (all: änäsĭrē'ů), city (pop. 44,527), ⊙ Muntafiq prov., SE Iraq, on the Euphrates, on railroad, and 100 mi. WNW of Basra, in a date-growing area. SW 11 mi. are ruins of anc. city of UR. Nasiriya was captured (July 25, 1915) from Turkey by the British in the Mesopotamia campaign of First World War.

Nasirpur, W Pakistan: see NASARPUR.

Naskaupi River (năskō'pē), Labrador, issues from small lake 30 mi. E of Michikamau L. at 54°8'N 63°5'W, flows 180 mi. E and SE, through Grand L. (30 mi. long, 2 mi. wide), to W end of L. Melville, 20 mi. NE of Goose Bay air base. On its upper course are water falls.

Naskeag Point (năs'kĕg), Hancock co., S Maine, 3-mi. peninsula in Blue Hill Bay, S of Brooklin; Br. raid repulsed here, 1778. Naskeag village is in Brooklin town.

Naso (nä'zô), village (pop. 2,246), Messina prov., N Sicily, 10 mi. W of Patti, in sericulture region.

Nason (nā'sůn), city (pop. 199), Jefferson co., S Ill., 10 mi. SSW of Mount Vernon, in agr. area.

Nasonville, R.I.: see BURRILLVILLE.

Nasosny or **Nasosnyy** (nŭsôs'nē), town (1939 pop. over 500) in Sumgait dist. of Greater Baku, Azerbaijan SSR, on Caspian Sea, on railroad and 23 mi. NW of Baku.

Nasratabad, Iran: see ZABUL.

Nasretdin-Bek (näsrĕtēn'bĕk"), village (1939 pop. over 500), E Andizhan oblast, Uzbek SSR, in E Fergana Valley.

Nasriganj (näs'rĭgŭnj), town (pop. 7,817), Shahabad dist., W Bihar, India, bet. Son R. and Arrah Canal (branch of Son Canals system), 40 mi. SSW of Arrah; rice, gram, barley; oilseed, flour, and sugar milling.

Nasrullaganj (nŭsrōōl'lŭgŭnj), town (pop. 2,087), S Bhopal state, India, 40 mi. SSW of Bhopal; wheat, cotton, oilseeds.

Nassaberg, Czechoslovakia: see NASAVRKY.

Nassandres (näsä'drů), village (pop. 373), Eure dept., NW France, on the Risle and 7 mi. NE of Bernay; sugar refinery; pharmaceuticals.

Nassarawa, Nigeria: see NASARAWA.

Nassau (nă'sô), city, ⊙ BAHAMA ISLANDS, port on NE NEW PROVIDENCE ISLAND (pop. 29,391, sometimes considered coextensive with the city), 180 mi. ESE of Miami, Fla., and 335 mi. ENE of Havana, Cuba; 25°5'N 77°20'W. Major pleasure resort famed for its fine beaches and gentle climate (average temp. 70°F.), with slight rainfall and cool breezes. Its harbor, sheltered by Hog Isl., accommodates vessels of 24 ft. draught. Ships sponge, sisal, tomatoes, citrus fruit. Has an international airport (at Oakes Field, E), seaplane anchorage, and international cable station. Among the noteworthy bldgs. are Christ Church Cathedral, Govt. House, law courts, public library, and several forts overlooking the city, such as Fort Montagu (built 1742) and Fort Fincastle (1793). At E end of the harbor are the submarine "Sea Gardens." Hog Isl., just across the harbor, has a popular beach. While the city proper is a small area (pop. 1,347), Nassau is commonly considered to comprise an urban belt of much greater extent (pop. c.20,000). A S suburb, Grant's Town, has a fruit and vegetable market. Nassau was founded on the village of Charles Towne, but while the name Nassau was decreed in 1695, the city was not laid out until 1729. The Spanish and French made frequent incursions during 18th cent. and the city had to be fortified. An Amer. naval expedition landed here in 1776. During the Civil War, Nassau supplied blockade runners from the South.

Nassau (nă'sô, Ger. nä'sou), former duchy of W Germany, now included in HESSE; ⊙ was WIESBADEN. Duchy took its name from small town of Nassau, on the Lahn, where ancestral castle of Nassau family was built in 12th cent. by a count of Lauenburg. His descendants assumed the title counts of Nassau. Dynasty split (1255) into 2 main lines. Ottonian line acquired (15th cent.) lordship of Breda, settled in the Netherlands, and eventually became founders of Dutch ruling house of Orange. Walramian line (for Count Walram II) became ruling line of Nassau, which was raised to duchy in 1806. In 1816, territories belonging to various branches of Walramian line were united by Duke William. Having sided with Austria in Austro-Prussian War (1866), Nassau was annexed to Prussia and became the administrative division [Ger. *Regierungsbezirk*] (□ 2,301; 1939 pop. 1,461,425) of Wiesbaden in newly created prov. of HESSE-NASSAU. Was constituted briefly (1944–45) as separate Prussian prov. of Kurhessen (□ 2,845; pop. 1,651,379). After capture (spring, 1945) by Americans, it was inc. (with exception of MONTABAUR) into new state of Hesse in U.S. occupation zone. It is a fertile agr. and forested dist. and is famous for its Rhine wines, notably those of the Rüdesheim and Johannisberg regions. Besides Wiesbaden, there are many mineral spas, notably Bad Homburg, Bad Schwalbach, and Schlangenbad in the beautiful Taunus hills and Bad Ems on the Lahn R.

Nassau, town (pop. 2,164), in former Prussian prov. of Hesse-Nassau, W Germany, after 1945 in Rhineland-Palatinate, on the Lahn and 9 mi. ESE of Coblenz. Has ruined ancestral castle of Nassau family. First mentioned 790; chartered 1348. Baron Stein b. here.

Nassau (nă'sô), coral island (300 acres), MANIHIKI group, S Pacific, c.675 mi. NW of Rarotonga; copra; coconut groves. Placed 1901 under N.Z. COOK ISLANDS administration.

Nassau. 1 County (□ 650; pop. 12,811), extreme NE Fla., on Atlantic Ocean (E) and Ga. line (N; formed here by St. Marys R.); ⊙ Fernandina. Lowland area, with Amelia barrier isl. (E). Agr. (poultry, dairy products, corn), forestry (naval stores, lumber; paper), and fishing. Formed 1824. **2** County (□ 300; pop. 672,765), SE N.Y.; ⊙ Mineola. On W Long Isl.; bounded W by Queens borough of New York city, E by Suffolk co., S by the Atlantic, N by Long Island Sound. Part of New York city metropolitan area; chiefly residential, with many suburban trade centers. Deeply indented N shore has country-estate communities and summer colonies; yachting, fishing. The S shore has resorts; its bays, with many marshy isls., are sheltered from the Atlantic by fine barrier beaches (bathing, surf fishing) which are linked to Long Isl. by causeways; Jones Beach State Park is here. Co. is traversed by landscaped state parkways and by several highways; served by several lines of Long Isl. RR. Includes military airfield (Mitchel Air Force Base), several state parks (notably Bethpage, Jones Beach), several race tracks (notably Belmont Park, in W). Potatoes, truck, flowers are grown; also some dairying, poultry raising; important fisheries (especially shellfish). Diversified mfg., especially of aircraft. Separated in 1898 from old Queens co.

Nassau. 1 Village (pop. 205), Lac qui Parle co., SW Minn., on S.Dak. line, 13 mi. WNW of Madison, in grain area. **2** Village (pop. 952), Rensselaer co., E N.Y., 15 mi. SSE of Troy; mfg. (clothing, cider and vinegar, fountain pens, pencils). Co. fairgrounds are here.

Nassau Bay, NE New Guinea, opens on Huon Gulf, 10 mi. S of Salamaua. In Second World War, Allies landed here 1943 and captured Jap. base at near-by Mubo.

Nassau Gulf, Tierra del Fuego, bet. Navarino Isl. and Wollaston Isls.; c.60 mi. long, 15 mi. wide.

Nassau Range, W central New Guinea, adjacent to Orange Range and forming W part of Snow Mts.; extends c.200 mi. E from isthmus SE of Vogelkop peninsula to Orange Range. Contains Mt. Carstensz (c.16,400 ft., highest peak of isl.) and Mt. Idenburg (c.15,750 ft.).

Nassau River, NE Fla., rises in central Nassau co., meanders c.40 mi. E to Nassau Sound, a small inlet of the Atlantic bet. Amelia (N) and Talbot (S) isls.; lower course an estuary.

Nassen (nāsěn'), village, Tunis dist., N Tunisia, near Miliane R., on railroad, 7 mi. S of Tunis; vineyards, truck farms.

Nassereith (nä'sŭrīt), village (pop. 1,444), Tyrol, W Austria, 27 mi. W of Innsbruck at foot of Fern Pass (N); cotton milling. Lead and zinc mined near by.

Nass Head, Scotland: see WICK.

Nassjo (ně'shŭ"), Swedish *Nässjö*, city (1951 pop. 15,675), Jonkoping co., S Sweden, 20 mi. ESE of Jonkoping; railroad center on Stockholm-Malmo and Goteborg-Kalmar main lines; metal- and woodworking, paper and woolen milling; mfg. of clothing. Has medieval church. Chartered 1914.

Nassogne (näsôn'yů), village (pop. 902), Luxembourg prov., SE central Belgium, 7 mi. S of Marche, on NW slope of the Ardennes; lumbering.

Nass River, W B.C., rises in the Coast Mts. at about 56°50'N 130°W, flows in an arc S and SW to Portland Inlet of the Pacific; 200 mi. long; navigable for 25 mi. above its mouth. Valuable fisheries.

Nastätten (nä'shtě"tŭn), town (pop. 2,104), in former Prussian prov. of Hesse-Nassau, W Germany, after 1945 in Rhineland-Palatinate, 18 mi. NW of Wiesbaden.

Nasugbu (näsōōgbōō'), town (1939 pop. 5,254; 1948 municipality pop. 23,668), Batangas prov., S Luzon, Philippines, on S.China Sea, 45 mi. SW of Manila; agr. center (rice, sugar cane, corn, coconuts); sugar milling.

Nasvad (näs'vät), village (pop. 5,856), S Slovakia, Czechoslovakia, on Nitra R. and 11 mi. N of Komarno; wheat, corn, sugar beets.

Nasviken (něs'vē"kŭn), Swedish *Näsviken*, village (pop. 1,042), Gavleborg co., E Sweden, on South Dell L., Swedish *Södra Dellen* (sû'drä dě'lŭn) (9 mi. long, 1–4 mi. wide), 7 mi. WNW of Hudiksvall; lumber, pulp, and paper mills.

Nasworthy, Lake, Texas: see CONCHO RIVER.

Nasyelsk, Poland: see NASIELSK.

Naszod, Rumania: see NASAUD, town.

Nata, China: see NODOA.

Natá (nätä'), village (pop. 1,189), Coclé prov., central Panama, in Pacific lowland, 16 mi. SW of Penonomé, on Inter-American Highway; corn, rice, beans, sugar cane; stock raising; condensed milk factory. Formerly ⊙ Coclé prov.

Natagaima (nätägī'mä), town (pop. 4,066), Tolima dept., W central Colombia, landing on Magdalena R., on railroad and 50 mi. NNE of Neiva; copper-mining and agr. center (bananas, yucca, coffee, sugar cane, corn, rice). Gold mines near by.

Natal (nŭtăl'), city (1950 pop. 97,736), ⊙ Rio Grande do Norte, NE Brazil, 2 mi. above mouth of Potengi R., 160 mi. N of Recife; 5°47'S 35°9'W. Seaport and strategic air center at tip of Brazilian bulge nearest to Africa. Has transatlantic airport of Parnamirim (8 mi. SSW), enlarged by U.S. in Second World War, when it was used to ferry planes to Freetown (1,800 mi. NE) and Dakar (1,900 mi. NE) in Africa. Its port, used by coastwise shipping, handles cotton, sugar, salt, and hides. Industries: cotton milling, salt refining. Terminus of railroad to the interior and of coastal rail line to João Pessoa (Paraíba) and Recife (Pernambuco). Has naval depot, maritime-service and civil-aviation schools, seaplane base. City consists of upper (residential and administrative) and lower (commercial) town. Founded 1599 near site of Tres Reis Magos fort. Occupied briefly by Dutch in 17th cent.

Natal (nŭtăl'), village (pop. estimate 700), SE B.C., near Alta. border, in Rocky Mts., on Elk R. and 19 mi. NE of Fernie; alt. 3,782 ft.; coal mining, dairying.

Natal (nŭtăl'), province (□ 35,284; pop. 2,202,392), E U. of So. Afr., on the Indian Ocean, bounded by Cape Prov. (S), Basutoland (SW), Transvaal (NW), Swaziland and Mozambique (N); ⊙ Pietermaritzburg. Prov. includes ZULULAND (□ 10,427; pop. 398,460). Rises from coastal plain to Drakensberg range on Basutoland border. Drained by Tugela, Buffalo and Pongola rivers. Sugar is grown extensively; other crops include cotton, tea, tobacco, mealies, corn, vegetables. Stock raising is important. There are major coal deposits, supplying industrial Witwatersrand region in Transvaal. Other minerals mined include gold, chrome, tungsten, tin. Mfg. industries at Durban and Pietermaritzburg. DURBAN is largest city and chief port of E part of U. of So. Afr. Other towns include Ladysmith, Vryheid, Newcastle, Dundee, Eshowe, Utrecht, and Weenen. In Drakensberg range is Natal Natl. Park (□ c.15); along coast are numerous tourist resorts. Natal coast was 1st sighted Christmas Day, 1497, by Vasco da Gama, who named it *Terra Natalis*. Permanent European settlement established 1824 by British at Durban. Advance party of Boers arrived 1837 on their trek from the Cape. The Zulu chief Dingaan offered armed resistance until Andries Pretorius defeated him at Blood River (Dec. 16, 1838) and founded republic of Natal. Zulus subsequently became Boer vassals. British annexed Natal 1843; it became prov. of Cape Colony 1844 and was made separate crown colony 1856. Zulu War (1879) saw major engagements at Iswandhlwana, Rorkesdrift, and, finally, Ulundi. During Transvaal revolt (1880–81) battles were fought at Majuba Hill and Laing's Nek. During South African War Boers besieged Ladysmith, in course of which engagements were fought at Spion Kop and Colenso. Zululand became part of Natal 1897. Utrecht was annexed 1903, Vryheid 1902. Natal became prov. of U. of So. Afr., 1910. Restrictive measures, dating from 1896, against large Indian community of prov. have resulted in recurrent unrest and disturbances, especially since First World War.

Natalbany River (nŭtôl'bŭnē), SE La., rises in E St. Helena parish near Miss. line, flows c.45 mi. S to Tickfaw R. 2 mi. above its mouth on L. Maurepas; partly navigable.

Natal Bay (5 mi. long, 2 mi. wide), Natal, U. of So. Afr., inlet of Indian Ocean. Durban city is on it. Narrow entrance protected by breakwaters.

Natales, Chile: see PUERTO NATALES.

Natalia (nŭtăl'yŭ), village (1940 pop. 678), Medina co., SW Texas, 25 mi. SW of San Antonio, in irrigated farm area; canned foods; brick.

Natalicio Talavera (nätälē'syō tälävä'rä), town (dist. pop. 3,167), Guairá dept., S Paraguay, 9 mi. NNE of Villarrica; lumbering, agr. (maté, sugar cane, fruit, livestock). Founded 1918.

Natalinsk or **Natal'insk** (nŭtŭlyēnsk'), town (1943 pop. over 500), SW Sverdlovsk oblast, Russian SFSR, near Ufa R., 11 mi. SE of Krasnoufimsk; glassworking.

Natal National Park (□ c.15), W Natal, U. of So. Afr., on Basutoland and Transvaal borders, in Drakensberg range, 55 mi. WSW of Ladysmith. On W border of park is Mont-aux-Sources mtn. (10,750 ft.). Park is crossed by Tugela R., which here drops c.2,800 ft. in a series of high falls and flows through deep gorge.

Natang, Tibet: see SHIGATSE.

Natanya or **Nathanya** (both: nätä'nyä), town (pop. 9,000; 1950 pop. estimate 20,000), W Israel, in Plain of Sharon, on Mediterranean, 18 mi. NNE of Tel Aviv; seaside resort and industrial center; diamond polishing, radio mfg., textile milling; mfg. of chemicals, food, paper products; champagne bottling; commercial center for surrounding region. Has gardens overlooking sea. Founded 1929.

Natanz (nätänz'), town, Second Prov., in Kashan, N central Iran, on road and 45 mi. SE of Kashan; grain, tobacco, opium, fruit (celebrated for its pears). Woodworking, pottery mfg.; sericulture. Coal and copper deposits near by.

Natashquan River or **Natashkwan River** (both: nŭtăsh'kwŭn, nă"tăshkwŏn'), E Que., rises in S Labrador, flows 200 mi. S to the Gulf of St. Lawrence opposite E end of Anticosti Isl. At mouth are iron-sand deposits. Trout, salmon; noted hunting region.

Natazhat, Mount (13,480 ft.), S Alaska, in St. Elias Mts., 150 mi. NNW of Yakutat; 61°31'N 141°9'W.

Natchaug River (nă'chôg"), NE Conn., rises near Mass. line, flows c.25 mi. SW, joining Willimantic R. to form Shetucket R. at Willimantic. Mansfield Hollow Dam (for flood control) is just above Willimantic.

Natchez (nă'chĭz), city (pop. 22,740), ⊙ Adams co., SW Miss., on bluffs above the Mississippi (bridged to La.), 60 mi. SSW of Vicksburg; trade and shipping center for cotton and livestock region. Mfg. of rubber tires, rayon pulp, wallboard, boxes, lumber, clothing; meat packing, food canning. Noted for its fine colonial and ante-bellum houses, some dating from 18th cent.; during annual festival period (spring), visitors are guided through many of them. Founded 1716 with Bienville's establishment here of Fort Rosalie, whose garrison was annihilated by Indians in 1729; passed to England (1763), to Spain (1779), and finally to the U.S. (1798). Was ⊙ Territory of Mississippi, 1798–1802; inc. 1803. The NATCHEZ TRACE and city's location on the Mississippi early brought about cotton-based prosperity and the city's development as an important river port, 1st for flatboats, later for steamers. Had 1st newspaper (1800) in Miss. It lost political importance after movement (1802) of territorial capital to Washington, Miss., but continued to reign as a commercial, social, and cultural center of the South until its fall in 1863 to Federal forces in Civil War.

Natchez Trace, S U.S., old road which extended NE from Natchez, Miss., across NW corner of Ala., to Nashville, Tenn. Grew through linking of Indian footpaths and acquired great commercial, military, and political importance from the 1780s to 1830s. First traveled only northward by homebound frontiersmen who had floated down the Mississippi, it became a 2-way route with U.S. expansion into the Old Southwest. After becoming a post road in 1800, it was improved by the army. Andrew Jackson marched over it to New Orleans in War of 1812. Coming of steamboat transportation in mid-19th cent. ended its importance. Natchez Trace Parkway (established 1934), including 450 mi. of highway, generally following old route, memorializes the trace and near-by historic sites. Meriwether Lewis Natl. Monument (300 acres; established 1925) adjoins the old trace in S Tenn., 25 mi. WSW of Columbia; it includes explorer's grave and a mus. containing exhibits illustrating his career.

Natchitoches (nă'kĭtŏsh), parish (□ 1,297; pop. 38,144), NW central La.; ⊙ Natchitoches. Intersected by Red and Cane rivers; includes Saline and Black lakes and part of Kisatchie Natl. Forest. Agr. (mainly cotton; also corn, hay, peanuts); timber. Some mfg., including processing of timber and farm products. Formed 1805.

Natchitoches, city (pop. 9,914), ⊙ Natchitoches parish, NW central La., on Cane R., near Red R., and c.65 mi. SE of Shreveport; commercial, processing, and shipping center for a cotton region; cotton and cottonseed products, lumber, brick, tile. Here are state teachers col., U.S. fish hatchery. Has many old homes. Oldest city in La., founded 1714 as French military and trading post; inc. 1819, reincorporated 1872.

Nate (nä'tā), town (pop. 3,096), Wakayama prefecture, S Honshu, Japan, on W Kii Peninsula, 16 mi. ENE of Wakayama, in agr. area (rice, citrus fruit); raw silk.
Naters (nätā'), town (pop. 3,033), Valais canton, S Switzerland, on the Rhone, opposite Brig; woodworking, woolen textiles. Baroque church, medieval castle.
Natewa Bay (nätā'wä), E Vanua Levu, Fiji; 35 mi. long, 10 mi. wide; separates E peninsula from rest of isl.
Nathanya, Israel: see NATANYA.
Nathdwara (nätdvä'rŭ), town (pop. 9,704), S central Rajasthan, India, 25 mi. NNE of Udaipur, near Banas R.; markets corn, millet, barley; handicraft jewelry. A walled town; place of Hindu pilgrimage; has noted 17th-cent. Vishnuite shrine. Mavli, rail junction, is 14 mi. SE.
Nathia Gali (nŭ'tyŭ gŭ'lē), village, Hazara dist., NE North-West Frontier Prov., W Pakistan, 12 mi. ESE of Abbottabad, in extreme W Punjab Himalayas; hill resort; summer hq. of provincial govt. Also written Nathiagali.
Nathorst, Cape, S extremity of Ellef Ringnes Island, N Franklin Dist., Northwest Territories; 77°44'N 100°5'W.
Nathula, Fiji: see YASAWA.
Nathu La, pass, India and Tibet: see NATU LA.
Natick (nā'tĭk). **1** Town (pop. 19,838), Middlesex co., E Mass., 16 mi. WSW of Boston; mfg. (shoes, paper boxes, mince meat, metal products); truck, apples, peaches. Settled mid-17th cent., inc. 1781. South Natick village (1940 pop. 931) has marker on site of Indian meetinghouse established in 1651 by John Eliot. **2** Village, R.I.: see WEST WARWICK.
Natimuk, village (pop. 595), W central Victoria, Australia, 175 mi. WNW of Melbourne; rail junction; wheat, sheep.
National Capital Parks, E U.S., system (c.750 units; total □ 45.3) of natl. memorials, govt.-owned properties, and recreational areas in Washington, D.C., and in near-by areas of Va. and Md.; established 1790, became part of Natl. Park Service in 1933. In Washington, system includes the White House and President's Park, Washington Monument, Lincoln Memorial, Jefferson Memorial, 3 large parks (Rock Creek, East Potomac, West Potomac), and many statues, memorials, and small parks; in D.C. and Md., part of old Chesapeake and Ohio Canal; in Md., old Fort WASHINGTON, Catoctin Recreational Demonstration Area (just W of Thurmont), and most of Great Falls Park, at GREAT FALLS OF THE POTOMAC. In Va. are Lee Mansion Natl. Memorial (in ARLINGTON), Prince William Forest Park (near Quantico). Along shores of Potomac R. is George Washington Memorial Parkway (57 mi. long), planned to include landmarks in life of George Washington; 15-mi. section from Arlington Bridge (bet. Arlington and Washington) and Mt. Vernon (Va.) is known as Mt. Vernon Memorial Parkway.
National City. **1** City (pop. 21,199), San Diego co., S Calif., S suburb of San Diego, on San Diego Bay; residential, industrial (oil refining; mfg. of citrus-fruit by-products, wood products); lemon groves, truck farms. Inc. 1887. **2** or **National Stockyards**, village (pop. 207), St. Clair co., SW Ill., adjoining East St. Louis (S); large stockyards, meat-packing plants. **3** Village, Iosco co., NE Mich., c.45 mi. NNE of Bay City; gypsum quarrying and processing.
National Park, borough (pop. 2,419), Gloucester co., SW N.J., on Delaware R. and 7 mi. SW of Camden. Inc. 1902. Monument here commemorates Revolutionary battle of Red Bank (1777), named for former locality here.
National Road, historic U.S. highway extending (E–W) across the Alleghenies from Cumberland, Md., to St. Louis. Authorized 1806 by Congress and begun 1815, it was 1st Federal road and most ambitious road-building project of its day. Became the great highway of Western migration. First section reached Wheeling, W.Va., in 1818. Followed Indian trail traveled by George Washington and Gen. Edward Braddock. Continued (1825–33), through Henry Clay's efforts, across Ohio, using part of Ebenezer Zane's road. Final portions were later completed to Vandalia, Ill., and St. Louis. Bet. 1831 and 1856 control passed to the states, which levied tolls for maintenance. Old route, also known as the Cumberland Road, is closely followed today by U.S. Highway 40. Copies of the *Madonna of the Trail* statue erected at points along the road honor pioneer women.
National Stockyards, Ill.: see NATIONAL CITY.
Natitingou (nätēting'gōō), town (pop. 1,850), NW Dahomey, Fr. West Africa, 110 mi. NW of Parakou; shea nuts, peanuts, kapok, millet, corn. Iron and chromium deposits in dist.
Native States, India: see INDIAN STATES.
Natividade (nŏotēvēdä'dĭ). **1** City (pop. 804), central Goiás, central Brazil, on a tributary of the Tocantins and 80 mi. SE of Pôrto Nacional; cattle raising, dairying; sugar, corn. Nitrate deposits. **2** City, Rio de Janeiro, Brazil: see NATIVIDADE DO CARANGOLA. **3** City, São Paulo, Brazil: see NATIVIDADE DA SERRA.
Natividade da Serra (dä sĕ'rŭ), city (pop. 695), SE São Paulo, Brazil, in the Serra do Mar, 25 mi. S of Taubaté; brandy distilling; sugar cane, grain, tobacco. Until 1944, Natividade.
Natividade do Carangola (dōō kŏorāng-gô'lŭ), city (pop. 3,000), NE Rio de Janeiro state, Brazil, near Minas Gerais border, on railroad and 12 mi. NNW of Itaperuna; coffeegrowing center. Until 1944, called Natividade.
Natividad Island (nätēvēdädh'), islet (□ 3.3) off Pacific coast of Lower California, NW Mexico, at SW edge of Sebastián Vizcaíno Bay; 3¾ mi. long, ½–1½ mi. wide. Rises to 491 ft.; barren; rocky.
Natívitas (nätē'vētäs). **1** Town (pop. 1,421), Federal Dist., central Mexico, 14 mi. S of Mexico city, adjoining Xochimilco; cereals, fruit, livestock. **2** Officially Santa María Natívitas, town (pop. 618), Tlaxcala, central Mexico, 8 mi. SW of Tlaxcala; cereals, livestock.
Natmauk (nät'-mouk), village, Magwe dist., Upper Burma, on Pyinmana-Kyaukpadaung RR and 34 mi. ENE of Magwe, in rice area; salt extraction.
Natoena Islands, Indonesia: see NATUNA ISLANDS.
Natogyi (nătōjē'), village, Myingyan dist., Upper Burma, on Myingyan-Mandalay RR and 17 mi. E of Myingyan; trade center in cotton-growing area.
Natoma (nŭtō'mŭ), city (pop. 775), Osborne co., N central Kansas, on small affluent of Saline R. and 24 mi. SW of Osborne; grain, livestock.
Nator (nŭtōr'), town (pop. 10,632), Rajshahi dist., W East Bengal, E Pakistan, on distributary of the Atrai and 24 mi. E of Rajshahi; silk-weaving factory; rice, jute, oilseeds, wheat. Large palace of Nator rajas. Former ⊙ dist. Large sugar-processing factory 14 mi. S, at Gopalpur.
Natron, Lake (nā'trŭn), N Tanganyika, on Kenya border, in Great Rift Valley, 70 mi. NW of Arusha; 35 mi. long, 15 mi. wide. Has salt, soda, and magnesite deposits. Gelai volcano (9,653 ft.) at SE edge.
Natrona (nŭtrō'nŭ), county (□ 5,342; pop. 31,437), central Wyo.; ⊙ Casper. Livestock and mining region; watered by N.Platte R., Sweetwater R., headstreams of Powder R., and part of Pathfinder Reservoir. Oil, coal. Formed 1888.
Natrona, village (1940 pop. 6,890) in HARRISON township, Allegheny co., W central Pa., 19 mi. NE of Pittsburgh and on Allegheny R.; chemicals. Saltworks founded here 1853.
Natron Lakes, Egypt: see NATRUN, WADI EL.
Natrun, Wadi el, Wadi en Natrun, or **Wadi al-Natrun** (all: wä'dē ĕn-nät'rōōn), valley (pop. 4,765), Western Desert prov., N Egypt, c.60 mi. SSE of Alexandria, 65 mi. WNW of Cairo. An area c.30 mi. long and c.4 mi. wide, it has several lakes, sometimes called the Natron Lakes (nā'trŭn), as much as 25 ft. below sea level, which are rich in soda deposits exploited since anc. times.
Nattalin (nătŭlĭn'), town (pop. 5,633), Prome dist., Lower Burma, 35 mi. SSE of Prome, on railroad to Rangoon.
Nattam (nŭt'tŭm), town (pop. 8,754), Madura dist., S Madras, India, 22 mi. NNE of Madura; road center in millet- and sesame-growing area.
Nattam Hills, India: see SIRUMALAI HILLS.
Nattandiya (nŭt'tŭndĭyŭ), village (pop., including near-by villages, 1,935), North Western Prov., Ceylon, 12 mi. SSE of Chilaw; glass mfg.; coconuts, rice.
Nattarasankottai or **Nattarasankotai** (nä"tŭrŭsŭng-kō'tĭ), town (pop. 5,498), Ramnad dist., S Madras, India, 30 mi. E of Madura, in cotton area; peanut-oil extraction.
Natternbach (nä'tŭrnbäkh), village (pop. 1,764), NW Upper Austria, 25 mi. WNW of Linz; rye, potatoes, cattle.
Natu La (nä'tōō lä'), a much-traveled pass (alt. c.14,000 ft.) in SW Assam Himalayas, on Sikkim-Tibet border, 15 mi. ENE of Gangtok, India; road leads from Sikkim into Chumbi Valley, Tibet, and connects with main India-Tibet trade route. Also spelled Nathu La.
Natuna Islands or **Natoena Islands** (both: nŭtōō'-nŭ), group (pop. 10,272), Indonesia, in S.China Sea, bet. Borneo (E) and Malay Peninsula (W); 2°56'–4°42'N 102°51'–108°E; comprises 1 large isl. (GREAT NATUNA), in center of group, and 2 small groups: NORTH NATUNA ISLANDS and SOUTH NATUNA ISLANDS. Generally low and wooded. Chief products: timber, coconuts.
Natupe, Tuamotu Isls.: see REAO.
Natural Bridge. **1** Village, Jefferson co., N N.Y., 8 mi. NE of Carthage. Indian R. has cut through limestone here to form a bridge and caverns. Tourist resort. **2** Village, Rockbridge co., W Va., near James R., 27 mi. NW of Lynchburg, at entrance to Jefferson Natl. Forest. Just W is **Natural Bridge** over Cedar Creek, a limestone arch 215 ft. high, with span of 90 ft.; highway passes over it. Thomas Jefferson once owned the bridge.
Natural Bridges National Monument (□ 4.1; established 1908), SE Utah, c.30 mi. W of Blanding. Includes 3 natural sandstone bridges across canyons in high plateau (alt. c.6,000 ft.); largest is Sipapu Bridge (sĭ'pŭpōō), 222 ft. high, with 261-ft. span.
Natural Bridge State Park (1,127 acres), Powell and Wolfe counties, E central Ky., just SE of Slade (gateway to park). Wooded, hilly area, with recreational facilities; chief attraction is Kentucky Natural Bridge, a span of Paleozoic rock; largest natural bridge in Ky.; arch has c.90 ft. clearance, is c.75 ft. wide.
Naturaliste, Cape (nă'chŭrŭlĭst), SW Western Australia, in Indian Ocean; W headland of Geographe Bay; 33°32'S 115°1'E; lighthouse.
Naturaliste Channel, small strait of Indian Ocean, W Western Australia, bet. Dorre and Dirk Hartogs isls.; forms W entrance to Shark Bay; 15 mi. wide.
Natural Tunnel, SW Va., natural passageway (75–100 ft. high, c.900 ft. long) through Powell Mtn., 10 mi. WNW of Gate City; small stream and railroad pass through it.
Naturita (năchŭrē'tŭ), village (pop. c.600), Montrose co., SW Colo., on San Miguel R. and 40 mi. SW of Montrose; alt. 5,427 ft. Uranium and vanadium processed here.
Naturno (nätōōr'nô), Ger. *Naturns*, village (pop. 546), Bolzano prov., Trentino–Alto Adige, N Italy, on Adige R. and 7 mi. W of Merano; organ mfg.
Nau (nou), town (1926 pop. 2,314), central Leninabad oblast, Tadzhik SSR, on railroad (Pridonovo station) and 16 mi. SW of Leninabad; cotton, sericulture; cotton ginning. Fell to Russians (1866).
Naubinway (nô'bĭnŭwā"), village (pop. c.200), Mackinac co., SE Upper Peninsula, Mich., 39 mi. NW of St. Ignace, on L. Michigan; resort; commercial fishing.
Naucalpan or **San Bartolo Naucalpan** (sän bärtō'lō noukäl'pän), officially Naucalpan de Juárez, town (pop. 1,796), Mexico state, central Mexico, 7 mi. W of Mexico city; maguey growing, flour milling. A church in W outskirts is pilgrimage shrine; yearly fiesta, commemorating miracles, in September. Sometimes Naucalpam.
Naucampatépetl, Mexico: see PEROTE, COFRE DE.
Naucelle (nōsĕl'), village (pop. 910), Aveyron dept., S France, on Ségala Plateau, 15 mi. SW of Rodez; breweries; cereals.
Naucratis (nô'krŭtĭs), Greek city of anc. Egypt; site is in Beheira prov., Lower Egypt, 4 mi. W of Teh el Barud. Situated on Canopic branch of the Nile, it flourished during the reign of Amasis II (570–520 B.C.) and was for some time the only Greek trading center in Egypt. Discovered by Petrie (1884), it has since yielded several temples and pottery. Also spelled Naukratis.
Nauders (nou'dŭrs), village (pop. 1,114), Tyrol, W Austria, bet. Reschenscheideck and Finstermünz passes, 20 mi. S of Landeck, near Swiss and Ital. borders; road junction; resort (alt. 4,478 ft.).
Nauen (nou'ŭn), town (pop. 13,106), Brandenburg, E Germany, 25 mi. WNW of Berlin; mfg. of machinery, copper articles, soap, food products; sugar refining. Formerly site of major radio station, dismantled 1945–47. Has Gothic church. First mentioned 981; chartered 1292.
Naugaon, E Pakistan: see NAOGAON.
Naugaon Sadat (nou'goun sŭdŭt'), town (pop. 4,809), Moradabad dist., N central Uttar Pradesh, India, 8 mi. NNW of Amroha; wheat, rice, pearl millet, mustard, sugar cane. Also spelled Naugawan Sadat, Naugaon Saadat.
Naugard, Poland: see NOWOGARD.
Naugatuck (nô'gŭtŭk"), industrial town (pop. 17,-455), coextensive with Naugatuck borough, New Haven co., SW Conn., below Waterbury, bisected by Naugatuck R. Rubber center; metal and plastic products, wire goods, chemicals, jute and cotton fiber products, machinery, tools, candy. Includes Union City (mfg.). Part of state forest. Charles Goodyear established rubber factory here, 1843. Settled 1702, town inc. 1844, borough inc. 1893.
Naugatuck River, W Conn., rises in NW Conn., flows c.65 mi. S, past mfg. centers of Torrington, Thomaston, Watertown, Waterbury, Naugatuck, and Ansonia, to Housatonic R. at Derby.
Naugawan Sadat, India: see NAUGAON SADAT.
Nauhcampatépetl, Mexico: see PEROTE, COFRE DE.
Nauheim, Bad, Germany: see BAD NEUHEIM.
Naujan (nouhän'), town (1939 pop. 1,998; 1948 municipality pop. 22,382), near NE coast of Mindoro isl., Philippines, 10 mi. SE of Calapan; agr. center (copra, abacá, rice).
Naujan, Lake (□ 30), NE Mindoro isl., Philippines, 6 mi. SSE of Naujan; 8.5 mi. long, 4 mi. wide.
Nauja Vilnia, Nauya Vilnya, or **Nauya Vil'nya** (nou'yä vēl'nyä), Pol. *Nowa Wilejka* (nô'vä vēlā'kä), E industrial suburb (1931 pop. 6,958) of Vilna, SE Lithuania, on right bank of the Vilnia (small left tributary of the Viliya) and 6 mi. ENE of Vilna city center; rail junction (repair shops); mfg. (machine tools, agr. implements, cement, liquors, paper, prefabricated houses), meat packing. In Rus. Vilna govt. until it passed in 1921 to Poland, in 1939 to Lithuania. Inc. 1947 into Vilna city. Sometimes called Novo-Vilnya.
Naukratis, Egypt: see NAUCRATIS.
Naumburg (noum'bŏŏrk). **1** or **Naumburg in Hessen** (ĭn hĕ'sŭn), town (pop. 2,470), in former Prussian prov. of Hesse-Nassau, W Germany, after 1945 in Hesse, 14 mi. WSW of Kassel; grain. **2** or **Naumburg an der Saale** (än dĕr zä'lŭ), city (pop. 41,379), in former Prussian Saxony prov., central Germany, after 1945 in Saxony-Anhalt, on the Saxon-

ian Saale (head of navigation) at mouth of the Unstrut, and 25 mi. SSW of Halle; 51°9'N 11°49'E. Rail junction; center of winegrowing region; mfg. of machine tools, leather goods, combs, toys, soap, food products; metalworking. Has noted 13th–14th-cent. cathedral with fine Gothic sculptures and remains of medieval walls. Founded in 11th cent. by margraves of Meissen; seat (1028–c.1300) of bishopric transferred here from Zeitz. Was member of Hanseatic League. Passed to Saxony in 1564, to Prussia in 1815.

Naumburg am Queis, Poland: see NOWOGRODZIEC.

Naumiestis or **Naumiyestis** (nou'myĕstēs), Pol. *Władysławów*, Rus. *Vladislavov*, city (pop. 3,573), SW Lithuania, on the Sheshupe, opposite Kutuzovo (Kaliningrad oblast), and 43 mi. WSW of Kaunas; oilseed pressing, flour milling; goose raising. Passed 1795 to Prussia, 1815 to Rus. Poland; in Suvalki govt. until 1920.

Naungpale (noung'pŭlā'), village, Karenni State, Upper Burma, on Toungoo-Loikaw road and 10 mi. SSW of Loikaw. Former ⊙ Naungpale state, inc. into Kantarawadi.

Naunhof (noun'hōf), residential town (pop. 5,868), Saxony, E central Germany, on Parthe R. and 10 mi. ESE of Leipzig, in lignite-mining region; summer resort. Site of Leipzig waterworks.

Naupactus, Greece: see NAUPAKTOS.

Naupada, India: see TEKKALI.

Naupaktos or **Navpaktos** (nôpăk'tŭs, Gr. năf'păktôs), Lat. *Naupactus*, Ital. *Lepanto* (lĭpăn'tō, Ital. lāpän'tō), town (pop. 5,494), Acarnania nome, W central Greece, port on N shore of Gulf of Corinth, near strait leading to Gulf of Patras, 22 mi. E of Missolonghi; fisheries, stock raising; olive oil, grapes. The anc. Naupactus was the leading port of W (Ozolian) Locris and is identified with the legendary crossing of the Dorians to the Peloponnesus. Captured by Athens in 456 B.C. and assigned to the exiled Messenians following the 3d Messenian War, it became the chief Athenian naval base on Gulf of Corinth. After the Peloponnesian War, it was returned (404 B.C.) to Locris, and passed (399) to Achaea and (338) to Aetolia. Under Byzantine rule it was known as Epaktos or Epakhtos. Still a strategic station in Middle Ages, it was held (1407–99) by Venice before passing to the Turks. Venice recaptured it briefly, 1687–99. In independent Greece since 1832. The naval battle of Lepanto (1571), in which the fleet of a Holy League commanded by Don John of Austria defeated the Turks, was fought at mouth of Gulf of Patras.

Naupan (nou'pän), town (pop. 763), Puebla, central Mexico, in Sierra Madre Oriental, 5 mi. NW of Huauchinango; alt. 6,306 ft.; corn, coffee, sugar.

Nauplia (nô'plēŭ), Gr. *Nauplion* or *Navplion* (both: năf'plēôn), city (pop. 7,960), ⊙ Argolis and Corinthia nome, E Peloponnesus, Greece, port on Gulf of Argolis, on railroad, and 60 mi. WSW of Athens. Trading center for vegetables, tobacco, citrus fruits, livestock; fisheries. Has vegetable canneries and tobacco-processing plants. Ruins of fortifications. Anc. Nauplia was chief port of Argos and its allied states. After decline in later antiquity, it regained its importance as a trading center and regional capital under Byzantine and French rule. Venetian and Turkish occupants built fortress of Palamidi, overlooking city (SE). Following Gr. war of independence, it became (1830) 1st ⊙ Greece, until transfer (1834) to Athens. Also spelled Nafplion.

Nauplia, Gulf of, Greece: see ARGOLIS, GULF OF.

Nauplion, Greece: see NAUPLIA.

Nauplion, Gulf of, Greece: see ARGOLIS, GULF OF.

Nauporto, Yugoslavia: see VRHNIKA.

Na'ur (nă-ōōr'), village (pop. c.5,000), N central Jordan, 8 mi. SW of Amman; barley, wheat.

Naurouze, Col de (kôl dù nōrōōz'), divide (alt. 620 ft.) on Aude–Haute-Garonne dept. border, S France, separating Atlantic and Mediterranean drainage basins, bet. Massif Central (N) and outliers of the Pyrenees (S). It is on Bordeaux-Marseilles road and RR, and on Canal du Midi. An invasion route since Roman times. Also called Col de Lauragais.

Nauroy (nōrwä'), village (pop. 590), Aisne dept., N France, 8 mi. N of Saint-Quentin; cotton milling. Here Americans fought in Sept., 1918.

Naurskaya (nŭōōr'skŭ), village (1926 pop. 4,653), S Grozny oblast, Russian SFSR, on railroad, on left bank of Terek R. and 30 mi. NW of Grozny; cotton, livestock. Cotton gins near by.

Nauru (näōō'rōō), atoll (□ 8; pop. 2,855), SW Pacific, 1,300 mi. NE of Australia; 0°31'S 165°56'E; 12 mi. in circumference; 3.5 mi. long. Central plateau has large phosphate deposits. Native industries: canoe building, fishing, mat making. Discovered 1798 by British, annexed 1888 by Germany, occupied 1919 by Australian forces. Placed 1920 under League of Nations mandate, and 1947 under U.N. trusteeship held jointly by Great Britain, Australia, New Zealand and administered by Australia. Occupied throughout Second World War by Jap. forces. Formerly Pleasant Isl.

Nauset Harbor (nô'sĭt), Mass., sheltered inlet of the Atlantic, on E coast of Cape Cod, bet. Eastham and Orleans; lighthouse and coast guard station.

Naushahr or **Nowshahr** (nōshä'hûr), town, First Prov., in W Mazanderan, N Iran, port on Caspian Sea, 37 mi. ESE of Shahsawar. Developed after 1935; held by USSR during Second World War.

Naushahra, Kashmir: see NAOSHERA.

Naushahra, W Pakistan: see NOWSHERA.

Naushahro (nou'shärō), village, Nawabshah dist., central Sind, W Pakistan, 44 mi. NNW of Nawabshah; local agr. market (wheat, millet, cotton, rice). Also called Naushahro Firoz or Naushaharo Feroze.

Naushki (nŭōōsh'kē), village (1948 pop. over 500), S Buryat-Mongol Autonomous SSR, Russian SFSR, on Selenga R. and 15 mi. W of Kyakhta, at Mongolian border; Ulan-Ude rail spur terminus.

Naushon Island, Mass.: see ELIZABETH ISLANDS.

Nausori (nousō'rē), town (pop. 1,121), SE Viti Levu, Fiji, SW Pacific; on Rewa R.; agr. center; sugar mill.

Nauste (nou'stŭ), village (pop. 193) in Eresfjord og Vistdal canton (pop. 1,548), More og Romsdal co., W Norway, at head of Eres Fjord (5-mi. SW arm of Lang Fjord) and at mouth of Aura (Eira) R., 30 mi. E of Molde; cattle raising, river fishing; tourist center. The fjord is sometimes called Eiris or Eris.

Nauta (nou'tä), town (pop. 689), ⊙ Loreto prov. (formed 1943), Loreto dept., NE Peru, landing on Marañón R. near its confluence with Ucayali R., and 65 mi. SW of Iquitos; 4°37'S 73°34'W. Sugar cane, fruit; liquor distilling. Iron deposits. Founded 1830, it was former seat of dept. govt.

Nautanwa (nou'tŭnvŭ), town (pop. 5,806), Gorakhpur dist., E Uttar Pradesh, India, 45 mi. N of Gorakhpur, on Nepal border; rail spur terminus; rice, wheat, barley, oilseeds. Sometimes called Nautanwan.

Nautla (nout'lä), town (pop. 1,418), Veracruz, E Mexico, at mouth of small Nautla R., in Gulf lowland, 40 mi. SE of Papantla; minor port; tobacco growing.

Nauvoo. 1 (nôvōō') Town (pop. 416), Walker co., NW Ala., 16 mi. NW of Jasper; lumber. **2** (nävōō', nô–) City (pop. 1,242), Hancock co., W Ill., on heights overlooking the Mississippi, 9 mi. N of Keokuk (Iowa), in agr. area (fruit, grain); mfg. (dairy and grape products). Settled as Commerce shortly after 1830; occupied and renamed by Mormons under Joseph Smith in 1839; inc. 1841. Pop. reached c.20,000 under the Mormons; after Smith and his brother were killed (1844) by a mob in near-by Carthage, the group left Illinois for Utah (1846). The Icarians, a colony of French communists under Étienne Cabet, occupied the city during 1849–56. Smith's house, part of an old hotel, and other old bldgs. are still standing.

Nauya Vilnya, Lithuania: see NAUJA VILNIA.

Nauzad or **Nawzad** (nouzäd'), town (pop. over 2,000), Kandahar prov., S central Afghanistan, 40 mi. N of Girishk, in outliers of the Hindu Kush.

Nauzontla (nousōn'tlä), town (pop. 1,476), Puebla, central Mexico, 18 mi. NW of Teziutlán; corn, fruit, vegetables, coffee.

Nava (nä'vä), town (pop. 2,101), Coahuila, N Mexico, on railroad and 25 mi. SW of Piedras Negras; wheat, corn, cattle; istle fibers, candelilla wax.

Nava, La (lä). **1** or **La Nava de Santiago** (dhā säntyä'gō), town (pop. 1,498), Badajoz prov., W Spain, 13 mi. NW of Mérida; cereals, olives, vegetables, livestock. **2** Town (pop. 541), Huelva prov., SW Spain, in the Sierra Morena, 11 mi. WNW of Aracena; olives, cork, acorns, walnuts, figs, pears, apricots.

Navacchio (näväk'kyô), village (pop. 363), Pisa prov., Tuscany, central Italy, 5 mi. ESE of Pisa; cotton mill, stearine factory.

Navacerrada (nä"vä-thĕrä'dhä), town (pop. 362), Madrid prov., central Spain, on E slopes of the Sierra de Guadarrama, 28 mi. NW of Madrid; mtn. resort; stock raising, potato growing, lumbering. Sanatorium. The Navacerrada Pass is 4 mi. N.

Navacerrada Pass (c.5,905 ft.), in the Sierra de Guadarrama, central Spain, on Madrid-Segovia prov. border, at S foot of the Peñalara, on old Madrid-Segovia road. In vicinity is the royal Guadarrama hosp. Ski resort.

Navaconcejo (nä"väkōnthā'hō), town (pop. 1,984), Cáceres prov., W Spain, 18 mi. NE of Plasencia; flour mills; olive oil, wine, fruit, pepper.

Nava de la Asunción (nä'vä dhā lä äsōōnsyōn'), town (pop. 2,367), Segovia prov., central Spain, in Old Castile, on Medina del Campo–Madrid RR and 24 mi. NW of Segovia; lumbering and agr. center (cereals, carobs, chick-peas, beans, fruit, chicory, sugar beets, grapes, livestock). Flour milling, turpentine mfg.

Nava del Rey (dhĕl rā'), city (pop. 4,724), Valladolid prov., N central Spain, 30 mi. SW of Valladolid; wine-production center; cheese processing, alcohol distilling, flour milling. Agr. trade (cereals, vegetables, sheep; lumber). Aluminum silicate mines near by. Parochial church has fine 17th-cent. sculptures.

Nava de Recomalillo, La (lä nä'vä dhā rē"kōmälē'lyō), village (pop. 1,451), Toledo prov., central Spain, 23 mi. SSW of Talavera de la Reina; olive-oil pressing, flour milling; grapes, livestock.

Navahermosa (nä"väĕrmō'sä), town (pop. 4,632), Toledo prov., central Spain, on slopes of Montes de Toledo (at foot of Navahermosa Pass), 28 mi. SW of Toledo; agr. center (olives, cereals, grapes, goats). Olive-oil extracting, flour milling, tanning, bottle-cork mfg.; limekilns, iron foundry.

Navajo (nä'vŭhō), county (□ 9,911; pop. 29,446), E Ariz.; ⊙ Holbrook. Mtn. area bordering on Utah, crossed in S by Little Colorado R. Black Mesa and parts of Navajo and Hopi Indian reservations (including ORAIBI village and pueblo) are in N; parts of Mogollon Plateau and Fort Apache Indian Reservation in S. Navajo Natl. Monument is in N, near Utah line. Sheep, alfalfa; Indian handicraft, tourist trade. Formed 1895.

Navajo Lake, SW Utah, in Markagunt Plateau and Dixie National Forest, 20 mi. SE of Cedar City; alt. c.9,900 ft.; 3 mi. long, .5 mi. wide; fishing, camping. Sometimes called Duck L. Cedar Breaks Natl. Monument 5 mi. NW.

Navajo Mountain (10,416 ft.), S Utah, near Ariz. line, 11 mi. S of junction of San Juan and Colorado rivers, 5 mi. SE of Rainbow Bridge Natl. Monument.

Navajo National Monument (360 acres; established 1909), NE Ariz., in Navajo Indian Reservation, 120 mi. NE of Flagstaff. Ruins of 3 large Pueblo Indian cliff dwellings: Betatakin (restored), built in 13th cent. in large cave of canyon wall, contained 150 rooms; Keet Seel (700 yrs. old; partly excavated); and Inscription House (with inscription believed to be of Sp. origin, dating from 1660s). High-quality pottery has been found at Betatakin.

Naval, Philippines: see BILIRAN ISLAND.

Naval (näväl'), town (pop. 677), Huesca prov., NE Spain, 28 mi. E of Huesca; saltworks; lumbering; cereals, olives, sheep, goats.

Navalacruz (näväläkrōōth'), town (pop. 1,144), Ávila prov., central Spain, 18 mi. SW of Ávila; rye, vegetables, nuts; flour milling.

Navalcán (nävälkän'), town (pop. 3,697), Toledo prov., central Spain, in S spur of the Sierra de Gredos, 15 mi. WNW of Talavera de la Reina; grain, stock-raising center; apiculture; dairying.

Navalcarnero (nävälkärnä'rō), town (pop. 4,719), Madrid prov., central Spain, in New Castile, 20 mi. SW of Madrid, in fertile area (cereals, chick-peas, hemp, olives, carobs, grapes, stock). Known for its wines. Also brewing and mfg. of soap, resins, glycerin, sulphates.

Navalgund (nŭv'ŭlgōōnd), town (pop. 7,082), Dharwar dist., S Bombay, India, 24 mi. ENE of Dharwar; cotton, wheat, millet; carpet mfg. Cattle raising near by. Sometimes spelled Nawalgund.

Naval Hill, locality, W Orange Free State, U. of So. Afr., 2 mi. N of Bloemfontein; site of Lamont-Hussey Observatory of Univ. of Michigan; 29°5'45"S 26°14'15"E; alt. 4,888 ft. Begun 1927, completed 1928. Fossils of prehistoric giant reptiles found here 1934.

Navalmanzano (nävälmän-thä'nō), town (pop. 1,628), Segovia prov., central Spain, 20 mi. NNW of Segovia; cereals, carobs, chick-peas, vegetables, sugar beets, grapes, livestock; flour milling; lumber, resins.

Navalmoral (nävälmōräl'), town (pop. 1,369), Ávila prov., central Spain, 13 mi. S of Ávila; cereals, nuts, vegetables, fruit, grapes, livestock. Liquor distilling, flour milling.

Navalmoral de la Mata (dhā lä mä'tä), town (pop. 6,462), Cáceres prov., W Spain, 31 mi. ESE of Plasencia; agr. trade center (wine, olive oil, cereals, pepper, tobacco); meat and butter processing; stock raising.

Navalmorales, Los (lōs nävälmōrä'lĕs), town (pop. 4,774), Toledo prov., central Spain, on N slopes of the Montes de Toledo, 20 mi. SE of Talavera de la Reina; lumbering, stock raising (sheep, hogs, goats), agr. (olives, cereals, grapes). Olive-oil extracting, flour milling, mfg. of woolen goods and hats; stone quarrying. Mineral springs.

Navalonguilla (nävälōng-gē'lyä), town (pop. 829), Ávila prov., central Spain, in W Sierra de Gredos, 50 mi. SSE of Salamanca; truck produce, livestock; flour milling. Fishing on affluent of Tormes R.

Navalosa (nävälō'sä), town (pop. 1,088), Ávila prov., central Spain, 20 mi. SW of Ávila; forage, cereals; flour milling.

Navalperal de Pinares (näválpäräl' dhā pēnä'rĕs), town (pop. 883), Ávila prov., central Spain, on railroad to Madrid and 15 mi. ESE of Ávila. Resort with medicinal springs. Also produces cereals, grapes, vegetables, livestock. Stone quarrying; fertilizer mfg.

Navalpino (nävälpē'nō), village (pop. 945), Ciudad Real prov., S central Spain, 40 mi. WNW of Ciudad Real; cereals, olives, livestock.

Navalucillos, Los (lōs näválōō-thē'lyōs), village (pop. 4,937), Toledo prov., central Spain, in N Montes de Toledo, 23 mi. SSE of Talavera de la Reina; agr. center (olives, wheat, grapes, cork, livestock). Lumbering, olive-oil extracting, cheese processing, tanning. Lead mines.

Navaluenga (nävälwĕng'gä), town (pop. 2,351), Ávila prov., central Spain, on the Alberche, at S foot of Sierra de Gredos (crossed by Navaluenga Pass, 5,144 ft.), and 17 mi. S of Ávila; cereals, vegetables, grapes, fruit, livestock. Alcohol distilling, flour milling. At near-by falls are flour mills and hydroelectric plant.

Navalvillar de Pela (nävälvēlyär' dhā pä'lä), town (pop. 5,347), Badajoz prov., W Spain, 19 mi. ENE of Villanueva de la Serena; olive-oil pressing, flour milling, tile mfg. Stock raising.

Navamorcuende (nä"vämôrkwĕn'dā), town (pop. 2,001), Toledo prov., central Spain, 12 mi. N of Talavera de la Reina; olives, grapes, timber, wool; dairying.

Navan, Ireland: see AN UAIMH.

Navanagar (nŭvä'nŭgŭr), former princely state (□ 3,791; pop. 504,006) of Western India States agency, on Kathiawar peninsula; ⊙ was Jamnagar (also called Navanagar). Ruled by Rajputs of Jadeja clan. Merged 1948 with Saurashtra. Sometimes spelled Nawanagar.

Navanagar, city, India: see JAMNAGAR.

Navan Fort (nă'vŭn), anc. earthwork in NW Co. Armagh, Northern Ireland, just W of Armagh. The large elliptical mound was site of Emania, ⊙ and seat of legendary palace of kings of Ulster for several centuries.

Navapur (nŭvä'po͝or), town (pop. 6,731), West Khandesh dist., N Bombay, India, 65 mi. WNW of Dhulia; local market for wheat, rice, millet, timber; sawmills; cotton ginning. Sometimes spelled Nawapur.

Navarcles (nävär'klĕs), village (pop. 1,881), Barcelona prov., NE Spain, 9 mi. NE of Manresa; cotton spinning and weaving, sawmilling. Wine, wheat, vegetables in area.

Navarin, Cape (nŭvŭrēn'), NE Siberia, Russian SFSR, on Bering Sea; 62°15'N 179°8'E. Govt. arctic station.

Navarino, Greece: see PYLOS.

Navarino Island (nävärē'nō) (□ 955; pop. 200), Tierra del Fuego, Chile, just S of main isl. of Tierra del Fuego across Beagle Channel, SE of Ushuaia; 50 mi. long, 25 mi. wide. Mts. in center rise to 3,905 ft. Sheep raising.

Navarre (nŭvär'), Sp. *Navarra* (nävä'rä), region and former kingdom of N Spain and SW France, on both slopes of the W Pyrenees. Founded in 9th cent.; ruled from 13th cent. by several Fr. dynasties until Ferdinand the Catholic seized (1512) Sp. Navarre (the larger section in S; now the Sp. prov.) and united it (1515) with Spain. Lower Navarre or Fr. Navarre (in Basses-Pyrénées dept. since 1790) passed (1589) to Fr. crown when Henry, king of Navarre, became Henry IV of France.

Navarre, Sp. *Navarra,* province (□ 4,024; pop. 369,618), N Spain, one of the Basque Provs.; ⊙ Pamplona. Mostly mountainous, bounded N by crest of the W Pyrenees (Fr. border) and S by Ebro R. Drained by Ebro, Aragon, Arga, and Ega rivers. Has forests, pastures, and fertile valleys, and some barren tracts in S. Marble and gypsum quarries, and mineral springs. Essentially agr.: sugar beets, cereals, wine, vegetables, fruit, licorice, livestock; lumber. Agr. processing (canning, sugar and flour milling, meat packing). Other mfg.: chemical fertilizers, alcohol, cement, shoes, paper, mostly centered in Pamplona. Chief cities: Pamplona, Tudela, Estella, Tafalla. Approximately coextensive with Sp. part of former kingdom of Navarre. Basque language still spoken in some Pyrenean valleys.

Navarre, village (pop. 1,763), Stark co., E central Ohio, 9 mi. SW of Canton and on Tuscarawas R.; agr. trade center; makes bakery products, sewer pipe. Fort Laurens State Park is near by.

Navarredonda de la Sierra (nävärädōn'dä dhä lä syĕ'rä), town (pop. 581), Ávila prov., central Spain, resort near source of Tormes R., on N slopes of the Sierra de Gredos, 31 mi. SW of Ávila. Point of ascension for the mts.

Navarredondilla (nävärädōndē'lyä), town (pop. 996), Ávila prov., central Spain, 14 mi. SSW of Ávila; carobs, rye, nuts, potatoes, livestock.

Navarrenx (nävärā'), village (pop. 627), Basses-Pyrénées dept., SW France, on the Gave d'Oloron and 11 mi. S of Orthez; horse and poultry raising, dairying. Has 16th–17th-cent. fortifications built by Vauban.

Navarrés (nävärās'), town (pop. 2,780), Valencia prov., E Spain, 13 mi. NW of Játiva; olive-oil processing, mfg. of toys and soap; wine, truck produce.

Navarrete (nävärā'tā), town (pop. 1,672), Logroño prov., N Spain, 6 mi. WSW of Logroño; mfg. of earthen jars; flour mills; produces wine, olive oil, cereals. Dam and reservoir near by.

Navarrevisca (nävärāvēs'kä), town (pop. 1,082), Ávila prov., central Spain, near Alberche R. (trout fishing), 21 mi. SW of Ávila; cereals, vegetables, fruit, livestock. Lumbering; flour milling.

Navarro (nävä'rō), town (pop. 4,303), ⊙ Navarro dist. (□ 624; pop. 14,452), NE Buenos Aires prov., Argentina, 55 mi. SW of Buenos Aires; rail junction; grain, cattle; dairying.

Navarro (nŭvă'rō), county (□ 1,084; pop. 39,916), E central Texas; ⊙ Corsicana. Mainly rich blackland prairies; bounded NE by Trinity R. Diversified agr. (cotton, corn, grains, fruit, truck, pecans), livestock (beef and dairy cattle, poultry, some hogs, horses, mules). Oil, natural-gas wells; clay mining. Mfg., processing of farm products and petroleum at Corsicana. Formed 1846.

Navarro River, NW Calif., rises in SE Mendocino co., flows c.40 mi. NW to the Pacific 18 mi. S of Fort Bragg.

Navás (näväs'), village (pop. 1,990), Barcelona prov., NE Spain, on the Llobregat and 13 mi. NNE of Manresa; cotton spinning and weaving; lumbering. Wine, cereals in area.

Navas de Estena (nä'väs dhā ĕstā'nä), town (pop. 694), Ciudad Real prov., S central Spain, on S slopes of the Montes de Toledo, 45 mi. NW of Ciudad Real; lumber, cork, sheep. Flour milling, charcoal burning.

Navas de la Concepción, Las (läs, lä kōn-thĕpthyōn'), town (pop. 4,555), Seville prov., SW Spain, in the Sierra Morena, near Córdoba prov. border, 16 mi. E of Cazalla de la Sierra; cereals, flour, olives, olive oil, livestock; timber. Mfg. of soap and meat products.

Navas del Madroño (dhĕl mädhrō'nyō), town (pop. 3,197), Cáceres prov., W Spain, 18 mi. NW of Cáceres; olive-oil processing; wheat, potatoes, wine, livestock.

Navas del Marqués, Las (läs, märkās'), town (pop. 2,902), Ávila prov., central Spain, summer resort in SW Sierra de Guadarrama, 19 mi. E of Ávila; surrounded by pine forests yielding timber and naval stores. Also produces beans, cereals, livestock. Dairying, flour milling. Mineral springs.

Navas del Ray (rā'), town (pop. 824), Madrid prov., central Spain, 30 mi. W of Madrid; grapes, cereals, olives, livestock; wine making; tiles, pottery.

Navas de Oro (dhā ō'rō), town (pop. 1,913), Segovia prov., central Spain, 25 mi. NW of Segovia; grains, grapes, livestock. Forest industry (lumber, resins).

Navas de San Antonio (sän' äntō'nyō), town (pop. 802), Segovia prov., central Spain, 17 mi. SW of Segovia; grain growing, stock raising; flour milling; hunting.

Navas de San Juan, Las (läs, sän' hwän'), town (pop. 7,120), Jaén prov., S Spain, 12 mi. NNE of Ubeda; olive-oil processing, soap mfg.; ships olives. Cereals, beans, livestock in area. Granite quarries, lead and copper mines near by.

Navas de Tolosa (tōlō'sä), village (pop. 1,134), Jaén prov., S Spain, 2 mi. ENE of La Carolina; scene of decisive victory (1212) of the Christian armies under Alfonso VIII over the Moors.

Navasfrías (nävăsfrē'äs), town (pop. 1,627), Salamanca prov., W Spain, near Port. border, 25 mi. SW of Ciudad Rodrigo; flour milling; livestock, potatoes, rye.

Navasota (nă'vŭsō'tŭ), city (pop. 5,188), Grimes co., E central Texas, on Navasota R. near its confluence with the Brazos, and c.60 mi. NW of Houston; commercial, shipping center for cotton, cattle, lumber region; cotton ginning, cottonseed-oil milling; concrete blocks, creosoted lumber. Statue of La Salle commemorates tradition that he was killed near by. Active in Texas Revolution; laid out 1858.

Navasota River, E central Texas, rises in Limestone co., flows c.130 mi. SE and S to the Brazos 5 mi. SW of Navasota.

Navassa Island (nävăsä'), Fr. *La Navase* (lä näväs'), Caribbean islet (□ c.1) belonging to U.S., bet. Haiti and Jamaica, 35 mi. W of Cape Irois (Haiti); lighthouse (18°25'N 75°2'W). Formerly yielded guano. Isl. is also claimed by Haiti.

Navatalgordo (nävätäl"gôr'dō), town (pop. 616), Ávila prov., central Spain, near Alberche R., 18 mi. SW of Ávila; cereals, fruit, livestock.

Nave (nä'vĕ), village (pop. 727), Brescia prov., Lombardy, N Italy, 4 mi. NNE of Brescia; paper-milling center.

Navekvarn (nĕ'vŭkvärn"), Swedish *Nävekvarn,* village (pop. 739), Sodermanland co., E Sweden, on N shore of Bra Bay, Swedish *Bråviken* (brō'vē"kŭn), 30-mi.-long inlet of Baltic, 12 mi. SW of Nykoping; ironworks (founded in 17th cent.).

Naver, Loch (lŏkh nă'vŭr), lake, N central Sutherland, Scotland, 13 mi. S of Tongue; 6 mi. long; 108 ft. deep. Drained by Naver R., which issues from E end of loch, flows 19 mi. N to the Atlantic 7 mi. ENE of Tongue.

Navesink (nă'vŭsĭngk), village (pop. 1,085), Monmouth co., E N.J., on Navesink R. and 4 mi. NE of Red Bank.

Navesink Highlands or **Highlands of Navesink,** Monmouth co., E N.J., coastal ridge (alt. c.276 ft.) bet. Sandy Hook Bay (N) and Navesink R. estuary (S). One of highest points on U.S. Atlantic coast; site of one of most powerful U.S. lighthouses (40°24'N 73°59'W). Often called Atlantic Highlands.

Navesink River, Monmouth co., E N.J., estuary (c.8 mi. long) extending ENE from Red Bank (head of navigation) to junction with Shrewsbury R. estuary at entrance to passage to Sandy Hook Bay near Highlands. Navesink Highlands are N, on mainland.

Navia (nä'vyä), town (pop. 1,406), Oviedo prov., NW Spain, on Navia R. near its mouth on Bay of Biscay, and 16 mi. E of Ribadeo; fishing and fish processing; cereals, potatoes, lumber, cattle.

Navia River, in Oviedo and Lugo provs., NW Spain, rises in Cantabrian Mts. 20 mi. SE of Lugo, flows 65 mi. NNE to Bay of Biscay at Navia. Salmon fisheries.

Navibandar (nŭvĭbŭn'dŭr), village, W Saurashtra, India, on Arabian Sea, at mouth of Bhadar R., 18 mi. SE of Porbandar; small coastal trade (ghee, cotton, salt); fishing. Lighthouse.

Navidad (nävēdädh'), village (1930 pop. 668), Colchagua prov., central Chile, on the coast, near mouth of Rapel R., 65 mi. NW of San Fernando; grain, livestock.

Navidad River (nă'vŭdăd), S Texas, rises in headstreams in Fayette co., flows c.100 mi. generally SSE and parallel to Lavaca R., joining it 11 mi. above its mouth on Lavaca Bay.

Navigators' Islands: see SAMOA.

Navina (nŭvī'nŭ), town (pop. 15), Logan co., central Okla., 9 mi. WSW of Guthrie, in agr. area.

Navíos, Boca de, Venezuela: see GRANDE, BOCA.

Naviti, Fiji: see YASAWA.

Naviti Levu, Fiji: see VITI LEVU.

Navlakhi (nou'lŭkē), village, N Saurashtra, India, port at head of Gulf of Cutch, 25 mi. WNW of Morvi; rail terminus; exports cotton, vegetable oil, wool, grain.

Navlya (näv'lyŭ), town (1948 pop. over 2,000), E Bryansk oblast, Russian SFSR, 30 mi. S of Bryansk; rail junction; sawmilling, woodworking, wood cracking.

Navodari (nŭvôdä'rē), Rum. *Năvodari,* village (pop. 1,531), Constanta prov., SE Rumania, on L. Tasaul and 10 mi. N of Constanta; stone quarrying. Terminus of Danube–Black Sea Canal is just SE. Former Turkish Caracoium.

Navojoa (nävōhō'ä), city (pop. 11,009), Sonora, NW Mexico, on lower Mayo R., in coastal plain, on Gulf of California, and 100 mi. SE of Guaymas; rail junction; agr. center (wheat, corn, chick-peas, fruit, cattle); flour milling; native handicrafts, textiles.

Navolato (nävōlä'tō), town (pop. 5,151), Sinaloa, NW Mexico, on Culiacán R. and 20 mi. WSW of Culiacán, on railroad; agr. center (sugar cane, chick-peas, corn, vegetables, fruit); lumbering.

Navoloki (nŭvŭlô'kē), city (1939 pop. over 10,000), N Ivanovo oblast, Russian SFSR, on Volga R. and 7 mi. WNW of Kineshma; cotton textiles, flour. Became city in 1938.

Navotas (nävō'täs), town (1939 pop. 2,765; 1948 municipality pop. 28,889), Rizal prov., S Luzon, Philippines, just NW of Manila; agr. center (rice, fruit). Also spelled Nabotas.

Navpaktos, Greece: see NAUPAKTOS.

Navplion, Greece: see NAUPLIA.

Navrongo (nävrông'gō), town, Northern Territories, N Gold Coast, near Fr. West Africa border, 105 mi. NNW of Tamale; road junction; shea nuts, millet, durra, yams; cattle, skins. Airfield.

Navsar, Turkey: see SEMDINLI.

Navsari (nŭv'särē), town (pop. 35,445), Surat dist., N Bombay, India, on Purna R. and 17 mi. SSE of Surat; trades in cotton, millet, timber; cotton and silk milling, hand-loom weaving, cottonseed milling, wood carving; mfg. of copper and brass products, glass, leather goods, oil engines, textile bobbins, soap, perfume; metalworks. Has col. Hq. of Parsi community in India. Formerly in Navsari div. of Baroda state; div. inc. 1949 into Surat dist.

Navua (nävo͞o'ä), town (pop. 691), S Viti Levu, Fiji, SW Pacific, 18 mi. WSW of Suva; copra.

Navua River, S Viti Levu, Fiji, SW Pacific; rises in S mtn. range, flows 40 mi. SE to Rovondrau Bay. Its delta area produces dairy foods.

Navy Board Inlet, N Baffin Isl., SE Franklin Dist., Northwest Territories, arm (70 mi. long, 6-18 mi. wide) of Lancaster Sound, bet. Borden Peninsula of Baffin Isl. (W) and Bylot Isl. (E); 73°N 80°50'W.

Navy Yard City, village (pop. 3,030), Kitsap co., W Wash., near Bremerton.

Nawa (nä'vŭ), town (pop. 5,738), E central Rajasthan, India, 130 mi. ENE of Jodhpur, near Sambhar L.; salt mfg., hand-loom woolen weaving.

Nawa, Ryukyu Isls.: see NAHA.

Nawa (năwä'), Fr. *Naoua,* town, Hauran prov., SW Syria, 19 mi. N of Der'a; cereals, wheat.

Nawabashah, W Pakistan: see NAWABSHAH, town.

Nawabganj (nŭväb'gŭnj). **1** Town (pop. 18,207), Bara Banki dist., central Uttar Pradesh, India, 18 mi ENE of Lucknow; hand-loom cotton-weaving center; sugar processing; trades in rice, wheat, gram, oilseeds, barley. Founded by Shuja-ud-daula, a nawab of Oudh, in late–18th cent. Bara Banki town is just SW. **2** Town (pop. 4,577), Bareilly dist., N central Uttar Pradesh, India, 18 mi. NE of Bareilly; wheat, rice, gram, sugar cane, oilseeds. **3** Suburb, Cawnpore dist., Uttar Pradesh, India: see CAWNPORE, city. **4** Town (pop. 5,662), Gonda dist., NE Uttar Pradesh, India, near the Gogra, 5 mi. N of Fyzabad; sugar processing; trades in rice, wheat, corn, gram, oilseeds. Founded 18th cent. by a nawab of Oudh.

Nawabganj, town (pop. 23,164), Rajshahi dist., W East Bengal, E Pakistan, on the Mahananda and 25 mi. NW of Rajshahi; rail spur terminus; trades in rice, wheat, oilseed, jute, silk. Also Chapai Nawabganj; formerly Baragharia Nawabganj.

Nawabshah (nŭväb'shä), dist. (□ 3,908; 1951 pop. 688,000), central Sind, W Pakistan; ⊙ Nawabshah. Bounded E by Thar Desert, W by Indus R.; irrigated by Rohri Canal and its branches. Flat alluvial plain (wheat, millet, cotton, rice); sugar cane grown around Mohattanagar (milling); hand-loom weaving; fishing in the Indus. Market centers at Nawabshah and Tando Adam. Sometimes written Nawab Shah.

Nawabshah, town (pop. 17,509), ⊙ Nawabshah dist., central Sind, W Pakistan, 130 mi. NE of Karachi; rail junction; market center (millet, wheat, cotton, rice, dates); cotton ginning, handicraft carpet mfg.; perfume factory, engineering works. Sometimes spelled Nawabashah.

Nawada (nŭvä′dŭ), town (pop. 8,885), Gaya dist., central Bihar, India, on tributary of the Ganges and 35 mi. ENE of Gaya; road junction; trade center (rice, gram, wheat, barley, oilseeds, corn). Mica mining near by. Vishnuite sculpture and Hindu ruins 15 mi. NNE, at Afsar.

Nawadih, India: see JAMUI.

Nawai (nŭvī′), town (pop. 5,586), E Rajasthan, India, 39 mi. S of Jaipur; agr. market. Sometimes spelled Niwai.

Nawakot (nä′vŭkōt), town, N central Nepal, near the Trisuli, 17 mi. NW of Katmandu; fruitgrowing (mango and orange orchards); rice, vegetables. Nepalese military post. Home of Thakur dynasty, ruling Katmandu from late-11th to early-14th cent. Captured 1765 by Gurkha leader Prithwi Narayan; treaty signed here (1792) bet. Chinese and Gurkhas ended China-Nepal War. Winter residence of Gurkha kings until 1813. Formerly spelled Nayakot.

Nawalapitiya (nŭvŭlŭpĭt′ĭyŭ), town (pop. 7,700), Central Prov., Ceylon, in Ceylon Hill Country, on the Mahaweli Ganga, on railroad and 18 mi. SSW of Kandy; railroad workshops; trades in tea, rubber, rice, vegetables.

Nawalgarh (nŭvŭl′gŭr), town (pop. 20,620), NE Rajasthan, India, 18 mi. NNE of Sikar; trades in grain, wool, cattle, cotton; hand-loom weaving; enamel work. Commercial col.

Nawalgund, India: see NAVALGUND.

Nawanagar, India: see NAVANAGAR, former princely state.

Nawanshahr, India: see NAWASHAHR.

Nawanshahr (nŭvän′shŭhŭr) or **Ranbirsinghpura** (rŭnbēr″sĭng′po͝orŭ), town (pop. 2,150), Jammu dist., SW Kashmir, 12 mi. SW of Jammu; sugar mill, alcohol distillery; wheat, rice, bajra, corn. Also called Sri Ranbirsinghpura; also written Ranbir Singhpura.

Nawanshehr, W Pakistan: see NAWASHAHR.

Nawapara (nŭvä′pärŭ), village, Kalahandi dist., W Orissa, India, 75 mi. NW of Bhawanipatna; local market for rice, oilseeds, timber.

Nawapur, India: see NAVAPUR.

Nawargaon (nŭvŭr′goun), town (pop. 5,730), Chanda dist., S Madhya Pradesh, India, 35 mi. NNE of Chanda; rice, flax, millet. Hematite deposits near by. Sawmilling (teak) in forest (E). Sometimes spelled Nawergaon; sometimes called Nawargaon Buzurg.

Nawari (nä″wä′rē) or **Nahari** (nä″hä′rē), town (pop. 7,347), Kochi prefecture, S Shikoku, Japan, on Tosa Bay, 30 mi. ESE of Kochi; fishing port; rice, raw silk.

Nawashahr (nŭvä′shŭhŭr), town (pop. 10,275), Jullundur dist., central Punjab, India, 35 mi. SE of Jullundur; rail junction; agr. market (wheat, corn, cotton); hand-loom weaving. Sometimes spelled Nawanshahr.

Nawashahr, town (pop. 6,414), Hazara dist., NE North-West Frontier Prov., W Pakistan, 2 mi. ENE of Abbottabad; corn, wheat; handicraft cloth weaving. Sometimes spelled Nawanshehr.

Nawiliwili Harbor (näwē′lēwē′lē), SE Kauai, T.H., principal port of isl., near Lihue; exports sugar, rice, pineapples.

Nawzad, Afghanistan: see NAUZAD.

Naxos (năk′sŏs, -sŭs, Gr. näk′sôs), largest island (□ 169; pop. 20,132) of the Cyclades, Greece, in Aegean Sea, E of Paros; 37°N 25°35′E; 20 mi. long, 12 mi. wide; rises to 3,284 ft. in Mt. Dryos or Drios. Produces almonds, citrus fruit, olive oil, figs, wheat, barley, and a well-known white wine; sheep, goats; cheese. Emery is a major export item; there are marble and granite quarries. The chief town, Naxos (pop. 2,455), is on NW shore. In Gr. mythology Theseus abandoned Ariadne here. Known in antiquity for its wine and the worship of Dionysus, it was colonized by the Ionians and flourished in late 6th cent. B.C. as mistress of the Cyclades. It was sacked 490 B.C. by the Persians, joined the Delian League, and was subjected to Athens after a revolt (c.450 B.C.). In Middle Ages, it was seat (1207–1566) of Venetian Aegean duchy and passed 1579 to Turks and 1832 to Greece. Formerly also Naxia.

Naxos, earliest Greek colony of Sicily, on Cape Schisò, S of Taormina; founded 735 B.C. from Chalcis. Its inhabitants founded Catania and Lentini a few years later. Destroyed 403 B.C. by Dionysius. Site now occupied by lemon plantation.

Naxuana: see NAKHICHEVAN, city, Azerbaijan SSR.

Naxxar or **Nashar** (both: näshär′), village (parish pop. 4,389), central Malta, 4 mi. WNW of Valletta, in agr. region (wheat, potatoes, wine, cotton; goats, sheep). Limestone quarrying. Has fine baroque houses, parish church. Megalithic temples near by.

Nay (nā), town (pop. 2,854), Basses-Pyrénées dept., SW France, on the Gave de Pau and 10 mi. SE of Pau; textile and furniture center; produces berets, linen goods, lampshades.

Naya, India: see MURSAN.

Naya Dumka, India: see DUMKA.

Nayaganj Hathras, India: see MURSAN.

Nayagarh (nŭyä′gŭr), village, Puri dist., E Orissa, India, 55 mi. WNW of Puri; rice, sugar cane, oilseeds. Was ⊙ former princely state of Nayagarh (□ 562; pop. 161,409) in Orissa States; state inc. 1949 into Puri dist.

Nayakanhatti (nä′yŭkŭnhŭtē), town (pop. 1,772), Chitaldrug dist., N Mysore, India, 19 mi. NNE of Chitaldrug; rice, chili, millet. Annual temple-festival fair. Also spelled Nayakanahatti.

Nayakhan (nīŭkhän′), village (1948 pop. over 500), N Khabarovsk Territory, Russian SFSR, on Gizhiga Bay of Sea of Okhotsk, 320 mi. NNE of Magadan; trading point.

Nayakot, Nepal: see NAWAKOT.

Nayanagar, India: see BEAWAR.

Nayarit (nīärēt′), state (□ 10,547; 1940 pop. 216,698; 1950 pop. 292,343), W Mexico, on the Pacific; ⊙ Tepic. Bounded by Sinaloa (N), Durango (NE), Jalisco (SE and S). Traversed by broken outliers of the Sierra Madre Occidental which are, together with narrow coastal lowlands, intersected by many rivers, including Acaponeta R., San Pedro (or Tuxpan) R., and, principally, Santiago R. (lower course of the Lerma). Coastal marshes and lagoons, connected with the ocean, are well-known wild bird refuges. Subtropical climate: hot summers and abundant rainfall; dry, mild winters. The area is rich in minerals, mainly silver, gold, lead, and copper; mining centered at Huajicori, Acaponeta, Compostela, and Ixtlán. Nayarit's fertile plains and plateaus produce sugar cane, corn, cotton, tobacco, coffee, beans, rice, tomatoes, bananas; cattle raising. Largely covered by forests rich in dyewood, rubber, etc., thus far little exploited. Processing industries concentrated at Tepic. In early colonial days, the area was part of Nueva Galicia, with Compostela as ⊙. Later it became a dependency of Jalisco. Declared (1884) a federal territory, called Tepic. In May, 1917, it was set up as a separate state.

Nayar River (näyär′), Garhwal dist., N Uttar Pradesh, India, formed by junction of 2 headstreams in Kumaun Himalayas, 22 mi. ENE of Lansdowne; flows SW and WNW to Ganges R. 6 mi. S of Devaprayag; length, including E headstream, c.55 mi. Projected Nayar Dam (650 ft. high), with hydroelectric plant, is planned 10 mi. NNW of Lansdowne, with 2d hydroelectric plant at river mouth; will irrigate c.238,000 acres and greatly enlarge agr. area (food grain, sugar cane, cotton).

Nayba River, Russian SFSR: see NAIBA RIVER.

Naye, Rochers de (rôshā′ dŭ nā′), rocky peak (6,709 ft.) in the Alps, SW Switzerland, just E of Montreux; vicinity noted for sports, the Alpine Garden, and an ice cavern.

Nayland with Wissington, agr. village (pop. 1,268), S Suffolk, England. Village of Nayland, on Stour R. and 6 mi. N of Colchester, has 15th-cent. church. Wissington, just W, has beet-sugar refinery; Norman church.

Naylor. 1 Town (pop. 290), Lowndes co., S Ga., 13 mi. ENE of Valdosta, near Alapaha R. **2** City (pop. 520), Ripley co., S Mo., in Ozark region, 13 mi. E of Doniphan.

Nayoro (näyō′rō), town (pop. 21,476), N central Hokkaido, Japan, on Teshio R. and 40 mi. N of Asahigawa; rail junction; agr. center (rice, potatoes, soybeans, hemp), livestock; lumbering.

Nayoshi, Russian SFSR: see LESOGORSK.

Nayssar, Estonia: see NAISSAAR.

Nayudupeta (nä′yo͝odo͝opētŭ), town (pop. 7,595), Nellore dist., E Madras, India, 36 mi. S of Nellore; road center; oilseed milling; rice, millet, cashew. Also spelled Nayudupet.

Nayung (nä′yo͝ong′), town (pop. 6,509), ⊙ Nayung co. (pop. 114,051), W Kweichow prov., China, 30 mi. S of Pichieh; cotton weaving; wheat, beans, millet. Copper deposits near by. Until 1932 called Tatuchang.

Naz'a, El, En Naz'a, or **Al-Naz'ah** (all: ĕn-nă′zŭ), Fr. *Ennazé*, town, Latakia prov., W Syria, 28 mi. SSE of Latakia; sericulture, cotton, tobacco, cereals.

Nazacara (näsäkä′rä), town (pop. c. 3,100), La Paz dept., W Bolivia, in the Altiplano, on Desaguadero R. and 25 mi. NW of Corocoro; alpaca and sheep raising; barley, potatoes.

Nazan, Alaska: see ATKA.

Nazaré (nŭzŭrĕ′). **1** City (pop. 13,382), E Bahia, Brazil, on railroad and 32 mi. W of Salvador; ships manioc flour, coffee, sugar, rapeseed, hides; mfg. of tobacco products, distilling, leatherworking, vegetable-oil processing. Manganese mine at Onha (5 mi. W). Formerly spelled Nazareth. **2** City, Pernambuco, Brazil: see NAZARÉ DA MATA.

Nazaré, town (pop. 5,701), Leiria dist., W central Portugal, on the Atlantic, 17 mi. SW of Leiria; popular bathing resort and fishing port. Watch mfg. On a height (360 ft.; funicular) overlooking town is a noted pilgrimage chapel. Also called Praia de Nazaré.

Nazaré da Mata (dä mä′tŭ), city (pop. 5,418), E Pernambuco, NE Brazil, on railroad and 35 mi. NW of Recife; market center in sugar- and coffee-growing region. Until 1944, called Nazaré. Formerly spelled Nazareth.

Nazareno (näsärā′nō), town (pop. c.1,900), Potosí dept., SW Bolivia, on San Juan R. and 15 mi. SE of Tupiza, on Villazón-Uyuni RR; major lead-mining center; orchards, corn.

Nazaré Paulista (nŭzŭrĕ′ poulē′stŭ), city (pop. 466), E São Paulo, Brazil, 30 mi. NNE of São Paulo; distilling; grain, coffee, poultry. Formerly Nazaré (old spelling, Nazareth).

Nazaret (nă′zŭrĭth, Sp. näsärĕt′), village, Guajira commissary, N Colombia, near Caribbean coast, 80 mi. NE of Uribia; cotton plantations maintained by Capuchin missions.

Nazareth (nä′zärĕt), agr. village (pop. 4,583), East Flanders prov., NW Belgium, 8 mi. SW of Ghent.

Nazareth, Brazil: see NAZARÉ, Bahia.

Nazareth, (nă′zŭrĭth), town (pop. 3,648; 80% Christian), Tinnevelly dist., S Madras, India, 22 mi. SE of Tinnevelly; rice, palmyra. Seat of a Christian mission.

Nazareth (nă′zŭrĭth), town (1946 pop. estimate 15,540; 1949 pop. estimate 20,067), Lower Galilee, N Israel, in hilly region, 20 mi. ESE of Haifa. One of Christianity's holy places, closely associated with life of Jesus, it is great center of pilgrimage. Has 18th-cent. church (replacing 12th-cent. Crusaders' church) built on traditional scene of the Annunciation. Other notable features are Latin chapel containing large stone slab, reputed to be the *Mensa Christi;* chapel marking traditional site of synagogue in which Jesus preached, Mary's Well, and Joseph's workshop. Town has large Arab pop.; it is seat of Moslem religious court and of Greek Orthodox archimandrite. Of little importance in early times, Nazareth was captured (1099) by Crusaders, who established archbishopric. Several times captured by Moslems, it was finally sacked by Baibars, 1263. In First World War occupied by British, Sept., 1918. Captured July, 1948 by Israeli forces. In near-by cave (S) skeletons of prehistoric man have been found.

Nazareth (näsärĕt′). **1** Landing on upper Marañón R., Amazonas dept., N Peru, 85 mi. NNW of Chachapoyas; 5°6′S 78°19′W. **2** Village, Loreto dept., Peru: see AMELIA.

Nazareth (nă′zŭrĭth). **1** Village, Nelson co., Ky.: see BARDSTOWN. **2** Borough (pop. 5,830), Northampton co., E Pa., 6 mi. NW of Easton; clothing, cement. Settled c.1740, inc. 1863.

Nazarovka (nŭzä′rŭfkŭ), town (1944 pop. over 500), E central Ryazan oblast, Russian SFSR, 24 mi. W of Sasovo; agr. implements.

Nazarovo (-rŭvŭ), town (1948 pop. over 2,000), SW Krasnoyarsk Territory, Russian SFSR, on Chulym R., on Achinsk-Abakan RR (Adadym station) and 15 mi. S of Achinsk; lignite-mining center (developed in mid-1940s); dairying.

Nazas (nä′säs), city (1,688), Durango, N Mexico, on Nazas R. and 55 mi. SW of Torreón; agr. center (corn, wheat, cotton, sugar, vegetables, fruit).

Nazas River (nä′säs), N Mexico, formed in Durango by Río del Oro (or Sestín R.) and Ramos R. near El Palmito, flows c.180 mi. E, past Rodeo, Nazas, Lerdo, Gómez Palacio, and Torreón, to Laguna Dist., where, in rainy period, it reaches Laguna de Mayrán. Often referred to as "Mexican Nile," it is extensively used for irrigation.

Nazca or **Nasca** (both: nä′skä), city (pop. 2,175), ⊙ Nazca prov. (pop. 12,083), Ica dept., SW Peru, on Nazca R. (affluent of Río Grande), on highway, and 84 mi. ESE of Ica. Cotton, alfalfa, livestock. Gold placers near by. Ruins of pre-Incan civilization; tourist center. Nazca prov. was formed 1941 from part of Ica prov.

Naze (nä′zā), principal city (1950 pop. 29,009) on Amami-O-shima of isl. group Amami-gunto, in Ryukyu Isls., Japan, port on N coast of isl. Mfg. center; textile and sugar mills, sake brewery. Exports silk textiles, sugar, dried tuna.

Naze, The, promontory on North Sea, E extremity of Essex, England, 5 mi. S of Harwich; 51°52′N 1°17′E.

Naze, The, Norway: see LINDESNES.

Nazeing (nā′zĭng), residential town and parish (pop. 1,580), W Essex, England, 4 mi. NE of Epping.

Nazilli (näzĭlē′), town (1950 pop. 25,372), Aydin, W Turkey, on railroad near Buyuk Menderes R. and 28 mi. E of Aydin; manufactures cotton goods from local crop; olives, valonia, barley; antimony, emery, lignite.

Nazimiye (näzĭ′mĭyĕ), village (pop. 751), Tunceli prov., E central Turkey, 40 mi. SSE of Erzincan; wheat.

Nazimovo (nŭzē′mŭvŭ), town (1948 pop. over 2,000), on small Putyatin Isl. in Sea of Japan, S Maritime Territory, Russian SFSR, 30 mi. ESE of Vladivostok; fish canneries. Until c.1947, Putyatin.

Nazira (nä′zĭrŭ), anc. *Gargaon* or *Garhgaon*, town (pop. 3,436), Sibsagar dist., E central Assam, India, in Brahmaputra valley, on tributary of the Brahmaputra and 34 mi. ENE of Jorhat; tea-trade center; rice, rape and mustard, sugar cane, jute; weaving, printing, and dyeing factory. Coal mining near by. Rail junction 2 mi. E, at Simaluguri, with S spur to Naginimara in Naga Hills dist. and N spur to Moranhat, serving tea-garden area. As Gargaon, was ⊙ Ahom (Shan) kingdom from mid-16th to late-17th cent.

Nazirhat, E Pakistan: see SHOLASHAHAR.

Naziya (nä'zēŭ), town (1939 pop. over 2,000), N Leningrad oblast, Russian SFSR, on L. Ladoga, 13 mi. NE of Mga; lumber. Peatworks.
Nazlet el Qadi or **Nazlit al-Qadi** (both: năz'lĭt ĕl kä'dē), village (pop. 5,452), Girga prov., central Upper Egypt, 3 mi. S of Tahta; cotton, cereals, dates, sugar cane. Has Coptic monastery.
Nazran, Russian SFSR: see KOSTA-KHETAGUROVO.
Nazukawa, Japan: see KIBI.
Nazwa, Oman: see NIZWA.
Nchanga or **Nchanga Mine** (ŭnchäng'gä), mining township (pop. 5,305), Western Prov., N Northern Rhodesia, near Belgian Congo border, just N of Chingola and 60 mi. NW of Ndola; copper-mining center. Concentrates are smelted at Nkana.
Ncheu (ŭnchā'ōō), town, Central Prov., Nyasaland, near Mozambique border, 55 mi. NW of Zomba; tobacco processing; wheat, corn, peanuts, potatoes.
Ndagaa (ŭndägä'), town, N central Zanzibar, on road and 11 mi. NE of Zanzibar town; clove-growing center. Has govt. agr. experiment station.
N'Dande (ŭndän'dā), village, W Senegal, Fr. West Africa, on railroad and 75 mi. NE of Dakar; peanut growing. Sometimes spelled Ndandé.
Ndanga (ŭndăng'gä), village, Victoria prov., SE Southern Rhodesia, in Mashonaland, 33 mi. ESE of Fort Victoria; livestock center (cattle, sheep, goats); corn.
N'dele, Belgian Congo: see MAKABA.
N'Délé (ŭndĕlā'), town, ⊙ N'Délé autonomous dist. (□ 23,950; 1950 pop. 20,700), N Ubangi-Shari, Fr. Equatorial Africa, 310 mi. NE of Bangui; center of native trade, caravan terminus. Repeatedly devastated by Senussite raids in 19th and early 20th cent.
N'Dendé (ŭndĕndā'), village, S Gabon, Fr. Equatorial Africa, 40 mi. SE of Mouila.
Ndeni (ŭndā'nē) or **Santa Cruz,** volcanic island, Santa Cruz Isls., Solomon Isls., SW Pacific, 300 naut. mi. E of Guadalcanal; 10°45'S 165°55'E; 35 mi. long, 15 mi. wide; kauri pine. Graciosa Bay in NW.
Ndi (ŭndē'), village, Coast prov., SE Kenya, on railroad and 12 mi. N of Voi; coffee, tea, corn.
Ndian (ŭndēän'), village (pop. 4,645), S Br. Cameroons, administered as part of Eastern Provinces of Nigeria, on Ndian R. (tributary of Rio del Rey) and 45 mi. WNW of Kumba. Has large plantation for palm oil and kernels, rice, potatoes.
Ndibi Beach (ŭndē'bē), town, Ogoja prov., Eastern Provinces, SE Nigeria, port on Cross R. and 5 mi. S of Afikpo; palm oil and kernels, cacao, Kola nuts.
N'Dikinimeki (ŭndē"kēnēmĕ'kē), village, M'Bam region, W central Fr. Cameroons, 30 mi. W of Bafia. R.C. and Protestant missions.
N'Djolé (ŭnjōlā'), village, W central Gabon, Fr. Equatorial Africa, on Ogooué R. and 140 mi. ENE of Port-Gentil; gold-mining and trading center, terminus of navigation on the Ogooué. R.C. and Protestant missions. Sometimes spelled N'Jolé.
N'Dogo, lagoon, Fr. Equatorial Africa: see SETTÉ-CAMA.
Ndola (ŭndō'lä), municipality (pop. 7,398), ⊙ Western Prov. (□ 87,000; pop. 200,000), N Northern Rhodesia, on Lusaka-Elisabethville RR, near Belgian Congo border, 170 mi. N of Lusaka; 12° 59'S 28°38'E. Rail, commercial, and industrial center of the copper belt, with rail spurs to mining centers of Roan Antelope, Nkana, Mufulira, and Nchanga. Chemical works (acetylene, oxygen, hydrogen, nitrous oxide); sawmilling, woodworking, mfg. of soap and allied products, ferro-concrete pipes, mineral water, ice; lime burning, brickmaking, tire vulcanizing. Has govt. and convent schools, European and native hospitals, modern abattoir. Historically a crossroads of central African commerce routes, and a slave-trading post until end of 19th cent. An administrative center since 1904; made a municipality 1932.
N'dolo, Belgian Congo: see LEOPOLDVILLE, city.
N'Doulo (ŭndōō'lō), village, W Senegal, Fr. West Africa, on railroad to Niger and 11 mi. E of Dakar; trading post in peanut-growing region.
N'Douo River, Fr. Equatorial Africa: see KOUILOU RIVER.
Ndreketi River or **Dreketi River** (both: ŭndrĕkā'tē), largest river on Vanua Levu, Fiji, SW Pacific; rises in central mtn. range, flows 40 mi. W through central agr. lowlands to small bay on N coast.
Nea, Norway: see NID RIVER.
Nea Anchialos or **Nea Ankhialos** (both: nā'ŭ ŭnkhē'ŭlôs), town (pop. 2,759), Magnesia nome, SE Thessaly, Greece, 9 mi. SW of Volos, on Gulf of Volos; tobacco, wheat, olives.
Nea Artake or **Nea Artaki** (both: nā'ŭ ärtä'kē), town (pop. 3,093), W Euboea, Greece, port on N Gulf of Euboea, 4 mi. NNE of Chalcis; wheat, wine; fisheries. Formerly called Vatonta or Vatonda.
Nea Epidauros, Greece: see EPIDAURUS.
Nea Filippias, Greece: see NEA PHILIPPIAS.
Neagari (nää'gärē), town (pop. 8,595), Ishikawa prefecture, central Honshu, Japan, on Sea of Japan, just NW of Komatsu, in rice-growing area; silk textiles.
Neagh, Lough (lŏkh nā'), lake (□ 153; 18 mi. long, 11 mi. wide; maximum depth 102 ft.) in central Northern Ireland, bordering on counties Armagh (S), Tyrone (W), Londonderry (NW), and Antrim (N and E); largest fresh-water body in British Isles. It is fed by Upper Bann, Blackwater, and other rivers, drained (N) by Lower Bann R. Lough is noted for pollan, trout, eel fisheries. Its banks are low and marshy; there are a few small isls., including Ram's Isl. (26 acres; 1 mi. long), at E end of the lake, with remains of anc. round tower. According to legend, quoted by Giraldus Cambrensis and in Moore's *Irish Melodies*, lake occupies site of town whose fountains overflowed and whose bldgs. may sometimes be seen through the water.
Neah Bay (nē'ŭ), fishing village (1940 pop. 857), Clallam co., NW Wash., on Neah Bay of Juan de Fuca Strait and 60 mi. NW of Port Angeles; hq. of Makah Indian Reservation. State's 1st settlement made here by Spaniards in 1791.
Nea Ionia (nā'ŭ yônē'ŭ), suburb (1951 pop. 33,645), Athens, Greece, 4 mi. from city center; cotton textile mfg. Formerly called Podarades.
Nea Kokkinia (kôkĭnēä'), officially **Nikaia** (nē'käŭ), SW suburb (1951 pop. 71,934) of Athens, Greece, 5 mi. from city center.
Neales River, N central South Australia, rises in hills N of Stuarts Range, flows 200 mi. SE, past Oodnadatta, to L. Eyre; usually dry. Sometimes spelled Neale's R.
Nealtican (nääl tē'kän), officially San Buenaventura Nealtican, town (pop. 2,025), Puebla, central Mexico, 16 mi. W of Puebla; agr. center (cereals, sugar cane, fruit, maguey).
Nea Mechaniona or **Nea Mikhaniona** (both: nā'ŭ mĭkhänēô'nŭ), village (pop. 2,767), Salonika nome, Macedonia, Greece, 12 mi. SSW of Salonika, on Gulf of Salonika. Also spelled Nea Michaniona.
Neamt, monastery, Rumania: see TARGU-NEAMT.
Nean, Norway and Sweden: see NID RIVER.
Neanderthal (nēăn'dûrtäl", Ger. nāän'dûrtäl), small gorge, W Germany, 2 mi. SSW of Mettmann, 7 mi. E of Düsseldorf. Skeletal remains of Neanderthal man were discovered here in 1856. Also Neandertal.
Nea Orestias, Greece: see ORESTIAS.
Nea Philippias or **Nea Filippias** (both: nā'ŭ fĭlĭpēäs'), town (pop. 2,115), Preveza nome, S Epirus, Greece, on Louros R. and 19 mi. NNE of Preveza; trade center in barley, olive oil, almonds, citrus fruits. Sometimes called Philippias or Filippias.
Neapolis (nää'pôlĭs), town (pop. 3,634), Lasethi nome, E Crete, 9 mi. NW of Hagios Nikolaos; carobs, raisins, olives; olive oil.
Neapolis. 1 City, Macedonia, Greece: see KAVALLA, city. **2** Town (pop. 2,060), Laconia nome, SE Peloponnesus, Greece, port on small Vatika Bay, NW of Cape Malea and 50 mi. SE of Sparta; fisheries. Formerly Vatika.
Neapolis, Italy: see NAPLES.
Neapolis, Palestine: see NABLUS.
Neapolis, Tunisia: see NABEUL.
Nea Psara, Greece: see ERETRIA.
Near East, a term referring to the countries of SW Asia, NE Africa, and occasionally the Balkan States (according to British usage the Near East proper). In former times considered to be roughly coextensive with the Ottoman Empire, the concept is now largely supplanted by that of the MIDDLE EAST.
Near Islands, westernmost group of the Aleutian Isls., SW Alaska, c.1,500 mi. W of tip of Alaska Peninsula; 52°36'N 173°24'E. Largest isls. are: Agattu and ATTU. Except for Attu, they are uninhabited. Mountainous, uneven, and barren. Strategically important in Aleutian campaign of Second World War.
Nea Sfayia, Greece: see NEA SPHAGEIA.
Nea Smyrne or **Nea Smirni** (both: nā'ŭ smĭr'nē), S suburb (pop. 15,114) of Athens, Greece, 3 mi. from city center; developed following settlement (1922) of refugees from Smyrna (Turkey).
Nea Sphageia or **Nea Sfayia** (both: nā'ŭ sfŭyē'ŭ), SW suburb (pop. 12,157) of Athens, Greece, 2 mi. from city center; meat-packing industry. Also called Tauron or Tavron.
Neath, municipal borough (1931 pop. 33,340; 1951 census 32,305), W Glamorgan, Wales, on Neath R. and 7 mi. NE of Swansea; mfg. (tinplate, iron, copper, chemicals, coal by-products, metal cans). Site of ruins of Neath Abbey (founded 1130) and of anc. castle burned 1231. Municipal borough includes port of BRITON FERRY.
Neath Higher, parish (pop. 4,943), N Glamorgan, Wales, on Neath R. and 8 mi. NE of Neath; coal mining.
Neath River, Welsh *Cwm Nedd* (kōōm nĕdh'), Brecknock and Glamorgan, Wales, rises on Black Mtn. 9 mi. SW of Brecknock, flows 25 mi. SW, past Resolven and Neath, to Bristol Channel at Briton Ferry.
Neauphle-le-Château (nō'flŭ-lŭ-shätō'), village (pop. 958), Seine-et-Oise dept., N central France, 11 mi. W of Versailles; liqueur distilling. Just S is 17th-cent. castle of Pontchartrain, built by Mansart.
Nea Vysse or **Nea Vissi** (both: nā'ŭ vĭ'sē), town (pop. 3,873), Hevros nome, W Thrace, Greece, on railroad and 5 mi. S of Adrianople (Edirne), near Turkish border and Maritsa R. Formerly called Achyrochorion, Akhirokhorion, or Akhyrokhorion.
Nea Zichna or **Nea Zikhna** (both nā'ŭ zĭkhnŭ), town (pop. 3,993), Serrai nome, Macedonia, Greece, on road and 15 mi. ESE of Serrai; cotton, tobacco, beans, potatoes. Also spelled Nea Zichni. Formerly Zeliachova or Ziliakhova.
Neba, Jebel, or **Jabal Naba** (both: jĕ'bĕl nĕbä'), peak (2,644 ft.), N central Jordan, E of N end of Dead Sea, 5 mi. NW of Madaba. It is sometimes identified with the biblical Mt. Nebo (nē'bō), the summit of Mt. Pisgah (pĭz'gŭ), but the biblical peaks are also sometimes identified with Ras Siyagha, a peak a few mi. W.
Nebaj (nābäkh'), town (1950 pop. 4,256), Quiché dept., W central Guatemala, at E end of Cuchumatanes Mts., 8 mi. NW of Sacapulas; alt. 6,660 ft.; corn, beans.
Nebbons Hill, village (pop. 1,570, with adjacent Plateau Heights), Crawford co., NW Pa.
Nébeck, Syria: see NEBK, EN.
Nebel (nā'bŭl), village (pop. 1,145), in Schleswig-Holstein, NW Germany, on Amrum isl.; North Sea resort.
Nebeur (nŭbûr'), anc. *Castellum*, village, Le Kef dist., NW Tunisia, 7 mi. N of Le Kef; rail terminus; important iron mines; zinc and lead deposits.
Nebida, Sardinia: see IGLESIAS.
Nebit-Dag (nyĭbēt"-däk'), city (1945 pop. over 10,000), W Ashkhabad oblast, Turkmen SSR, on Trans-Caspian RR, at foot of Greater Balkhan Range, and 80 mi. ESE of Krasnovodsk; petroleum center; refining. Rail spur to oil field at Vyshka. Developed in 1930s; became city in 1946. Formerly called Neftedag.
Nebk, En, El Nebk, or **Al-Nabk** (all: ĕn-nĕ'bŭk), Fr. *Nébeck*, town (pop. c.2,500), Damascus prov., SW Syria, on Damascus-Homs RR, and 22 mi. NE of Damascus; alt. 4,690 ft., summer resort; potatoes, fruits.
Nebo (nē'bō). **1** Village (pop. 413), Pike co., W Ill., 35 mi. WSW of Jacksonville; grain, fruit, livestock, timber. **2** Town (pop. 282), Hopkins co., W Ky., 9 mi. WNW of Madisonville, in coal-mining and agr. area. **3** Town (1940 pop. 235), McDowell co., W central N.C., 5 mi. ENE of Marion, near L. James.
Nebo, Mount, Jordan: see NEBA, JEBEL.
Nebo, Mount, Utah: see MONA.
Nebolchi (nyĕ'bŭlchē), town (1948 pop. over 2,000), N Novgorod oblast, Russian SFSR, 35 mi. S of Tikhvin; rail junction; dairying.
Nebra (nā'brä), town (pop. 3,192), in former Prussian Saxony prov., central Germany, after 1945 in Saxony-Anhalt, on the Unstrut and 14 mi. NW of Naumburg; potash mining, sandstone quarrying. Has remains of anc. castle.
Nebraska (nŭbră'skŭ), state (land only □ 76,653; with inland waters □ 77,237; 1950 pop. 1,325,510; 1940 pop. 1,315,834), central U.S., bounded N by S.Dak., W by Wyo. and Colo., S by Kansas, E by Mo. and Iowa; 14th in area, 33d in pop.; admitted 1867 as 37th state; ⊙ Lincoln. The "Cornhusker State" is roughly rectangular in shape (c.210 mi. N–S, c.420 mi. E–W), except where Colo. cuts into SW corner. Lies in Great Plains, its surface sloping from W to SE; highest (5,340 ft.) in Banner co. (W) and lowest (840 ft.) in Richardson co. (SE). W part of state is dissected plain, rising to broken tableland in W and including small section of badlands in NW; E part is undissected plain, with drift hills in SE. Sand hills (more or less stabilized by growth of prairie grass) extend through N central and NW central parts of state. Strata of gravel in S central Nebr. store ground water and serve as medium for seepage from valley of Platte R. into SE Nebr. State is bordered on E and NE by Missouri R. and drained by 3 of its right tributaries: Niobrara R. (N), Platte R. (extending E–W across state to North Platte, where it branches into North Platte R. and South Platte R.), and Nemaha R. (SE). Republican R. flows through S Nebr.; central and E Nebr. are watered by right tributaries of Platte R. Climate is continental, characterized by hot summers (extreme of 114°F.) and cold winters (extreme of −32°F.); diurnal temperature range great; winters in NW moderated by the chinook, blowing down E slope of the Rockies. Rainfall is much greater in SE and E than in W, which is semiarid; average for state, 28 in. Nebr. is primarily agr., ranking high in production of corn, wheat (main cash crop), rye, and hay. Corn, wheat, alfalfa, apples, and vegetables are grown in loess-plain and drift-hills area in SE. Corn and livestock are raised in lowlands area in E along Missouri R.; corn, oats, rye, wheat, and livestock in loess-hills region in E central and NE Nebr. Stock raising predominates in sand-hills area. Livestock and some wheat and seed potatoes are raised in W tablelands, and sugar beets, potatoes, and beans are raised in irrigated sections of Dawes, Scotts Bluff, and Morrill counties. Subhumid S Nebr. is farmed in wheat, corn, and alfalfa. Most of state is in farms, 39% in harvested cropland, 47% in pasture. Principal industry is processing of agr. products (meat, flour, dairy products, beet sugar, vegetables). Other industries are mfg. (farm implements, bricks and tiles, cement), cattle feeding, and building construction. Mineral resources are limestone, gravel, and clay. OMAHA is largest city in state and distribution and processing center, with stockyards, meat-packing plants, and grain elevators. Other cities are Lin-

coln, Grand Island, Hastings, North Platte, Scottsbluff, Fremont, Beatrice, Norfolk. Rest of pop. is predominantly rural. Institutions of education at Lincoln are Univ. of Nebr., Union Col., and Nebr. Wesleyan Univ.; at Omaha, Univ. of Nebr. Col. of Medicine, Creighton Univ., Col. of St. Mary, Duchesne Col., and Municipal Univ. of Omaha. Others are Dana Col. (Blair), Doane Col. (Crete), Hastings Col. (Hastings), Midland Col. (Fremont), and York Col. (York). There are 5 state teachers colleges (at Seward, Chadron, Kearney, Peru, and Wayne). Nebr. Natl. Forest (2 sections) is in N and central Nebr. Santee and Ponca Indian reservations are in NE, at Niobrara; Winnebago and Omaha Indian reservations also in NE, at Winnebago. Homestead Natl. Monument of America is in SE, near Beatrice; Scotts Bluff Natl. Monument is in W, near Scottsbluff city. Earliest European explorers of what is now Nebr. were probably Coronado and his men, who visited region in 1541. French fur traders were active on the Missouri in 18th cent., and Lewis and Clark used the river (1804 and 1806). Later explorers were Zebulon M. Pike (1806) and Stephen H. Long (1819). First permanent settlement (c.1823) was Bellevue, which grew up around trading post. Steamboat traffic on the Missouri in 19th cent. provided commerce for river ports of Brownville, Nebraska City, and Omaha, and military outposts were established (1819–74) in basin of Platte R. for protection of migration over Oregon and Calif. trails. After passage (1854) of Kansas-Nebr. Act, Nebr. was organized as territory (⊙ Omaha, 1855–67). Settlement was stimulated by Homestead Act (1862), but statehood was delayed until 1867 by clause in provisional state constitution limiting vote to white men. In that year Nebr. became a state, having agreed to extend vote to Negroes, and Lincoln became ⊙. With completion (1867) of Union Pacific RR across Nebr., land boom took place, pop. increasing from 30,000 in 1860 to 122,000 in 1870. After cessation (c.1880) of Indian wars, farmers extended claims into open range and largely occupied it. During hard times of 1870s many of them supported Granger movement; in 1890s, rebelling against practices of the railroads and financiers, they organized farm and marketing cooperatives and joined Populist party. Initiative and referendum were adopted in 1897. Additional reforms took place in 20th cent., including establishment (1934) of unicameral legislature. The depression of late 1920s and early 1930s hit Nebr. hard, and drought added to state's troubles. Land and water conservation program was begun by state and Federal governments in middle 1930s, culminating in construction (1941) of Kingsley Dam for power and irrigation. W Nebr. is on Mountain Time, E Nebr. on Central Time. See also articles on cities, towns, geographic features, and the 93 counties: ADAMS, ANTELOPE, ARTHUR, BANNER, BLAINE, BOONE, BOX BUTTE, BOYD, BROWN, BUFFALO, BURT, BUTLER, CASS, CEDAR, CHASE, CHERRY, CHEYENNE, CLAY, COLFAX, CUMING, CUSTER, DAKOTA, DAWES, DAWSON, DEUEL, DIXON, DODGE, DOUGLAS, DUNDY, FILLMORE, FRANKLIN, FRONTIER, FURNAS, GAGE, GARDEN, GARFIELD, GOSPER, GRANT, GREELEY, HALL, HAMILTON, HARLAN, HAYES, HITCHCOCK, HOLT, HOOKER, HOWARD, JEFFERSON, JOHNSON, KEARNEY, KEITH, KEYA PAHA, KIMBALL, KNOX, LANCASTER, LINCOLN, LOGAN, LOUP, MCPHERSON, MADISON, MERRICK, MORRILL, NANCE, NEMAHA, NUCKOLLS, OTOE, PAWNEE, PERKINS, PHELPS, PIERCE, PLATTE, POLK, RED WILLOW, RICHARDSON, ROCK, SALINE, SARPY, SAUNDERS, SCOTTS BLUFF, SEWARD, SHERIDAN, SHERMAN, SIOUX, STANTON, THAYER, THOMAS, THURSTON, VALLEY, WASHINGTON, WAYNE, WEBSTER, WHEELER, YORK.

Nebraska City, city (pop. 6,872), ⊙ Otoe co., SE Nebr., 40 mi. S of Omaha and on Missouri R.; commercial, processing center for cattle-raising, agr. region; cigars, clothing, concrete products, bricks, canned goods; dairy and truck produce, livestock, grain, fruit. State school for blind, Arbor Lodge State Park here. Founded 1854, inc. 1855. Grew as river port.

Nebrodi Mountains (nĕ'brôdē), N Sicily, range extending 45 mi. NE from Madonie Mts. to Peloritani Mts.; rise to 6,060 ft. in Mt. Sori. Chestnut, oak, beech forests. Source of Simeto and Alcantara rivers. Also called Monti Caronie.

Nebula (nĕbōō'lä), village, Eastern Prov., N Belgian Congo, 95 mi. ESE of Buta; gold mining.

Nebyloye (nyĕbĭloi'ŭ), village (1926 pop. 1,236), N Vladimir oblast, Russian SFSR, 23 mi. NW of Vladimir; wheat, tobacco, rubber-bearing plants.

Necaxa, town, Mexico: see NUEVO NECAXA.

Necaxa River (nākä'hä), in Puebla and Veracruz, Mexico, rises NW of Zacatlán, flows c.125 mi. NE, past Huauchinango, to the Gulf of Mexico at Tecolutla. Used extensively for irrigation and hydroelectric power. Its lower course in Veracruz is called Tecolutla. The large Necaxa Falls are NW of Huauchinango, near Veracruz border.

Necedah (nĭsē'dŭ), village (pop. 862), Juneau co., central Wis., on Yellow R. and 60 mi. E of La Crosse; wood products, dairy products. Necedah Natl. Wildlife Refuge near by.

Necessity, Fort, Pa.: see FORT NECESSITY NATIONAL BATTLEFIELD SITE.

Nechako River (nĭchă'kō), central B.C., rises in Ootsa and Tetachuk lakes, flows NE and E, past Vanderhoof, to Fraser R. at Prince George; c.250 mi. long.

Nechanice (nĕ'khänyĭtsĕ), Ger. *Nechanitz* (nĕ'khänĭts), town (pop. 1,335), NE Bohemia, Czechoslovakia, 8 mi. WNW of Hradec Kralove, in sugar-beet dist.

Nechayevka (nyĭchī'ŭfkŭ), village (1948 pop. over 2,000), central Penza oblast, Russian SFSR, on railroad (Simanshchina station) and 22 mi. WNW of Penza, in grain area; flour milling.

Neche (nĭ'chē), city (pop. 615), Pembina co., NE N.Dak., port of entry 14 mi. NNE of Cavalier and on Pembina R.

Neches River (nĕ'chĭs), E Texas, rises in Van Zandt co., flows 416 mi. generally SE, past Beaumont, to head of Sabine L. Has deepwater channel (an arm of SABINE-NECHES WATERWAY) from Beaumont (port) to Sabine L. Plans were developed in 1947 for Rockland Dam and reservoir (for flood control, power, navigation) in N Tyler co.

Nechí River (nächē'), Antioquia dept., N central Colombia, rises in Cordillera Central SW of Yarumal, flows c.150 mi. NE and N, past Zaragoza, to Cauca R. near Bolívar dept. border. Main affluent, Porce R. Navigable for small craft during rainy season. Along its course are rich gold placer mines.

Neck or **Neck City,** city (pop. 117), Jasper co., SW Mo., on Spring R. and 12 mi. N of Joplin.

Neckarau (nĕ'kärou"), S suburb of Mannheim, Germany.

Neckarbischofsheim (nĕ"kärbĭ'shōfs-hīm"), town (pop. 2,436), N Baden, Germany, after 1945 in Württemberg-Baden, 11.5 mi. E of Wiesloch; chicory, sugar beets, tobacco.

Neckarelz (nĕ"kärĕlts'), village (pop. 2,909), N Baden, Germany, after 1945 in Württemberg-Baden, on canalized Neckar and 2 mi. WSW of Mosbach; rail junction; mfg. (machinery, cement, cigars, cigarettes). Church with 12th-cent. choir.

Neckargemünd (nĕ"kärgümünt'), town (pop. 6,114), N Baden, Germany, after 1945 in Württemberg-Baden, on canalized Neckar R., at mouth of the Elsenz, and 5 mi. E of Heidelberg; rail junction; dam and hydroelectric station. Leatherworking; red-sandstone quarrying. Has ruined castle.

Neckarhausen (–hou'zŭn), village (pop. 3,033), N Baden, Germany, after 1945 in Württemberg-Baden, on the canalized Neckar and 6 mi. ESE of Mannheim; tobacco, fruit.

Neckar River (nĕ'kär), S Germany, rises in the Black Forest just SW of Schwenningen, flows NE, past Rottweil, Rottenburg, and Tübingen, turns NNW at Plochingen, continues past Esslingen, Bad Cannstatt (head of navigation), and Heilbronn, to Eberbach, where it turns W to flow past Heidelberg to the Rhine at Mannheim. Whole course of 228 mi. is noted for its scenic beauty. Receives Jagst, Kocher, Fils, and Rems rivers (right), Enz and Elsenz rivers (left). It ships wood and salt down river, coal and other raw materials necessary for industries along its banks up river. Canalization, completed up to HEILBRONN, is projected to Plochingen; from there a canal is to be built across the Swabian Jura to Ulm, thus connecting the Rhine and the Danube.

Neckar-Steinach (nĕ"kär-shtī'nākh), town (pop. 2,618), S Hesse, W Germany, in former Starkenburg prov., at S foot of the Odenwald, on the Neckar and 6 mi. E of Heidelberg; woodworking. Has 4 castles. Sometimes spelled Neckarsteinach.

Neckarsulm (–zōōlm'), town (pop. 7,965), N Württemberg, Germany, after 1945 in Württemberg-Baden, on the canalized Neckar and 3 mi. N of Heilbronn; mfg. of bicycles, motorcycles, pistons; aluminum smelting, flax and hemp weaving. Damaged in Second World War; the Gothic-Renaissance castle was destroyed.

Necker Island, in N Pacific, c.400 mi. NW of Honolulu; 23°34'N 164°42'W; under jurisdiction of Territory of Hawaii.

Necochea (nākōchā'ä), city (pop. 17,816), ⊙ Necochea dist. (□ 2,612; pop. 51,426), S Buenos Aires prov., Argentina, port on the Atlantic at mouth of Quequén Grande R. (opposite Quequén), 75 mi. SW of Mar del Plata. Seaside resort; cattle raising, dairying, flour milling; mussel fishing. Has natl. col.

Neda (nä'dhä), town (pop. 1,000), La Coruña prov., NW Spain, at head of Ferrol Bay, 4 mi. ENE of El Ferrol. Lumber, livestock, cereals in area.

Nedan (nĕ'dän), village (pop. 3,156), Gorno Oryakhovitsa dist., N Bulgaria, 21 mi. NNE of Sevliyevo; horticulture, grain, livestock.

Neddick, Cape, SW Maine, promontory, with offshore lighthouse, 3 mi. NNE of York Harbor.

Neded (nyĕ'dyĕt), Hung. *Negyed* (nĕ'dyĕd), village (pop. 4,553), S Slovakia, Czechoslovakia, on Vah R. and 29 mi. SSW of Nitra; rail terminus; agr. center (sugar beets, barley, wheat).

Nedelcu P. Chercea (nĕdĕl'kōō pä kĕr'chä), N suburb (1941 pop. 11,621) of Braila, Galati prov., SE Rumania.

Nedelino (nĕdĕ'lĭnô), village (pop. 3,149), Khaskovo dist., S Bulgaria, in SE Rhodope Mts., 6 mi. N of Zlatograd; tobacco, stock. Formerly Uzundere.

Nedenes (nā'dŭnās), coastal lowland in Aust-Agder co., S Norway, bet. the Skagerrak and the interior highlands. Nedenes was the name of AUST-AGDER co. until 1919.

Nederbrakel (nā'dŭrbrä'kŭl), agr. village (pop. 5,930), East Flanders prov., W central Belgium, 7 mi. ESE of Oudenaarde; mineral springs.

Nederhasselt (nā'dŭrhä"sŭlt), agr. village (pop. 1,251), East Flanders prov., W central Belgium, 2 mi. WNW of Ninove.

Nederland. 1 (nĕ'dŭrlŭnd) Town (pop. 266), Boulder co., N central Colo., on headstream of Boulder Creek, in Front Range, and 30 mi. WNW of Denver; alt. 8,200 ft. Resort; tungsten mill and mines. Near-by dam serves hydroelectric plant. **2** (nē'dŭrlŭnd) City (pop. 3,805), Jefferson co., SE Texas, near Neches R., 10 mi. SE of Beaumont; rail point in oil-producing area; large oil refinery; dairying, truck farming. Inc. after 1940.

Neder Rijn, Netherlands: see LOWER RHINE RIVER.

Nederweert or **Nederweerd** (both: nā'dŭrvārt), village (pop. 1,403), Limburg prov., SE Netherlands, 3.5 mi. NE of Weert, near junction of Wessem-Nederweert Canal and the Zuid-Willemsvaart; agr.

Nedon River or **Nedhon River** (both: nē'dhôn), in SW Peloponnesus, Greece, rises in Taygetus Mts., flows 14 mi. SW to Gulf of Messenia at Kalamata; not navigable.

Nédouncadu, Fr. India: see NEDUNGADU.

Nedre Eiker, Norway: see MJONDALEN.

Nedre Fryken, Sweden: see FRYK, LAKE.

Nedrigailov or **Nedrigaylov** (nyĕdrĕgī'lŭf), village (1926 pop. 6,542), S central Sumy oblast, Ukrainian SSR, on Sula R. and 18 mi. ENE of Romny; fruit canning. Dates from 17th cent.

Nedroma (nĕdrômä'), town (pop. 7,855), Oran dept., NW Algeria, in coastal range (Trara) of the Tell Atlas, 26 mi. NW of Tlemcen; agr. trade (olives, cereals, early vegetables); palm-fiber processing; handicraft industries (pottery, wood carving, embroidering). First mentioned in 11th cent., town preserves old walls. The minaret of its chief mosque dates from 14th cent.

Nedrow (nĕ'drō), village (1940 pop. 1,704), Onondaga co., central N.Y., just S of Syracuse; sand and gravel. Onondaga Indian Reservation is near by.

Nedsttun, Norway: see NESTTUN.

Nedungadu (nā'dōōng-gŭdōō), Fr. *Nédouncadu* (nādōōnkädōō'), town (commune pop. 7,001), Karikal settlement, Fr. India, 5 mi. NW of Karikal.

Neduntivu Island, Ceylon: see DELFT ISLAND.

Nedvedice (nĕ'dvĕdyĭtsĕ), village (pop. 1,115), N Moravia, Czechoslovakia, on Svratka R., on railroad and 22 mi. NW of Brno; marble quarrying.

Neebish Island, E Upper Peninsula, Mich., in St. Marys R., just W of St. Joseph Isl. (Ont.) and 15 mi. SSE of Sault Ste. Marie; c.8 mi. long, 4 mi. wide. Resort; some agr.

Needham (nē'dŭm), residential town (pop. 16,313), Norfolk co., E Mass., on Charles R. and 10 mi. WSW of Boston; knit goods, rubber thread, elastic goods, surgical and dental instruments. Settled 1680, set off from Dedham 1711.

Needham Market (nē'dŭm), town and parish (pop. 1,366), central Suffolk, England, on Gipping R. and 9 mi. NW of Ipswich; agr. market; bacon and ham curing. Has 15th-cent. church and anc. grammar school.

Needle Mountain, Wyo.: see ABSAROKA RANGE.

Needles, city (pop. 4,051), San Bernardino co., SE Calif., on Colorado R. (Ariz. line), near Hoover Dam; railroad division point; trade center for mines, irrigated farms, and Fort Mojave Indian Reservation. Fishing; waterfowl hunting in river marshes. Temperatures here are extremely high (often in the 100s, F.), with wide daily range and low humidity. Founded 1883, inc. 1913.

Needles, The, 3 isolated chalk cliffs, c.100 ft. high, off W tip of Isle of Wight, Hampshire, England, at W end of rocky Alum Bay, on the Channel at entrance to The Solent, and 18 mi. SSW of Southampton. Site of lighthouse (50°40'N 1°35'W).

Needmore, Va.: see NORTH PULASKI.

Needville, town (pop. 609), Fort Bend co., S Texas, 11 mi. S of Rosenberg.

Needwood Forest, former royal forest (□ c.16), E Stafford, England, extending along Trent R. and Derbyshire boundary, near Burton-on-Trent.

Neelyville, town (pop. 457), Butler co., SE Mo., in Ozark region, near Black R., 15 mi. SSW of Poplar Bluff; cotton, rice.

Ñeembucú (nyāĕmbōōkōō'), department (□ 5,354; pop. 60,234), S Paraguay; ⊙ Pilar. A triangle formed by Paraguay and Paraná rivers, bordered W and S by Argentina, NE by L. Ypoá; marshy lowlands of dept. are intersected by Tebicuary R. Has subtropical, humid climate. Lumbering and agr. area (oranges, sugar cane, cotton, corn, and especially cattle). Processing concentrated at Pilar.

Neemuch, India: see NIMACH.

Neenah (nē'nŭ), city (pop. 12,437), Winnebago co., E Wis., on L. Winnebago at its outlet through Fox R., opposite Menasha, 11 mi. NNE of Oshkosh; mfg. center (paper, paper and wood products, machinery, metal products, textiles, flour). Settled 1835, inc. 1873. On near-by Doty Isl. (partly in Menasha) is James Doty's log house, now a mus.

Neepawa (nē'pŏŏwä,–wô), town (pop. 2,468), SW Man., on Whitemud R. and 35 mi. NE of Brandon; woodworking, marble processing; grain, stock.

Neer (nār), agr. village (pop. 1,235), Limburg prov., SE Netherlands, 5 mi. N of Roermond.

Neerheylissem (nār″hī'lĭsŭm), agr. village (pop. 1,961), Brabant prov., central Belgium, 4 mi. SSE of Tirlemont. Has 13th-cent. church.

Neerlinter (nār'lĭn″tŭr), agr. village (pop. 1,417), Brabant prov., central Belgium, 4 mi. ENE of Tirlemont.

Neeroeteren (nārōō'tŭrŭn), agr. village (pop. 4,421), Limburg prov., NE Belgium, 4 mi. W of Maaseik. Has 15th-cent. Gothic church.

Neerpelt, Belgium: see OVERPELT.

Neerwinden (nār'wĭndŭn), village (pop. 890), Liége prov., E central Belgium, 2 mi. NW of Landen. English forces under William III were defeated here (1693) by French under Marshal Luxembourg; French forces under Dumouriez defeated (1793) by Austrians.

Neeses (nē'sĭz), town (pop. 328), Orangeburg co., W central S.C., 15 mi. W of Orangeburg.

Nee Soon (nē sōōn'), village (pop. 2,963), N central Singapore isl., 8 mi. N of Singapore; rubber. Pop. is Chinese.

Nefasit (nĕfäsĕt'), town (pop. 1,890), Asmara div., central Eritrea, on railroad and 10 mi. E of Asmara; road junction; alt. c.5,400 ft.; coffee, bananas.

Neffs, village (pop. 1,024), Belmont co., E Ohio, just W of Bellaire, in coal-mining area.

Nefta (nĕftä'), town and oasis (pop. 14,167), Tozeur dist., SW Tunisia, in the Bled-el-Djerid, at NW edge of Chott Djerid, 15 mi. WSW of Tozeur; 33°53'N 7°53'E. Date-growing center. Artisan industries. Wool and camel hair trade. Trans-Saharan caravans equipped here. One of N Africa's most picturesque oases.

Nefteabad (nyĕftyĭŭbät'), town (1939 pop. over 500), NE Leninabad oblast, Tadzhik SSR, on railroad and 10 mi. SE of Kanibadam; oil field (producing since 1935).

Neftechala (nyĕf″tyĭchŭlä'), town (1939 pop. over 500), SE Azerbaijan SSR, near Kura R. mouth, 80 mi. SSW of Baku; rail terminus; oil fields; chemical plant (iodine production). Developed 1931.

Neftegorsk (nyĕftĭgôrsk'), town (1944 pop. over 10,000), S Krasnodar Territory, Russian SFSR, on rail spur and 25 mi. SW of Maikop, at N foot of the Greater Caucasus; petroleum center. Developed in 1930s.

Nefud, Arabia: see NAFUD.

Nefusa, Gebel (jĕ'bĕl nĕfōō'zä), hilly desert plateau (alt. 1,500–3,000 ft.) in W Tripolitania, Libya, bet. the GEFARA (N) and the HAMMADA EL HAMRA (S); extends from Nalut (W), near Tunisian border, to Cussabat (NE), near the Mediterranean. Rainfall ranges from 2 in. (W) to 16 in. (center and NE) and occurs mostly in winter. Chief products: cereals, esparto grass, olives, figs, livestock (sheep, goats). Tobacco growing at Tigrinna. Has quartz deposits. Contains towns of Garian, Tarhuna, Jefren, and Giado. Road runs almost entire length and connects with Tripoli-Mizda (N–S) road.

Nefzaoua (nĕfzäwä'), group of oases in Southern Territories, S Tunisia, near E edge of the Chott Djerid. Chief center: Kébili. Date palms.

Nega-Nega (nĕ'gä-nĕ'gä), township (pop. 43), Southern Prov., Northern Rhodesia, on railroad and 20 mi. E of Mazabuka; tobacco, wheat, corn.

Negapatam (nä'gŭpŭtŭm), since 1949 officially **Negapattinam** (nä″gŭpŭt'tĭnŭm), city (pop. of municipality, including NAGORE, 52,937), Tanjore dist., SE Madras, India, port (roadstead with wharves) on Coromandel Coast of Bay of Bengal, 160 mi. S of Madras, in Cauvery R. delta. Exports peanuts, cotton and silk goods, livestock, tobacco; timber landing and storing on extensive foreshore. Metallurgical center (electric furnaces, steel-rolling mills); industries powered by Mettur and Pykara hydroelectric systems; steel-trunk mfg., textile dyeing and printing; salt factory. Known to Ptolemy as Nigamos. Twin port of Nagore is 4 mi. N; rail terminus. Port of Velanganni is 6 mi. S; seat of R.C. missions. City is one of earliest Portuguese settlements in India (founded 1612); captured by Dutch in 1660, by English in 1781.

Negaunee (nĭgô'nē), city (pop. 6,472), Marquette co., NW Upper Peninsula, Mich., 10 mi. SW of Marquette, in Marquette Iron Range. Iron mining, lumbering, dairy and poultry farming. Resort. Iron was discovered here in 1844. Settled 1846; inc. as village 1862, as city 1873.

Negba (nĕgbä'), settlement (pop. 375), W Israel, in Judaean Plain, 18 mi. SSW of Rehovot; mixed farming. Founded 1939. Commanding main road to Negev, it resisted prolonged heavy Egyptian attacks, 1948.

Negeb, Israel: see NEGEV.

Negelli (nĕgĕ'lē), Ital. *Neghelli,* village, Sidamo-Borana prov., S Ethiopia, on plateau bet. Dawa and Ganale Dorya rivers, 125 mi. NE of Mega; road junction.

Negev (nĕ'gĕv) or **Negeb** (nĕ'gĕb), undulating semi-desert region (□ c.4,700), S Israel; triangular in outline, it extends bet. Mediterranean and Beersheba region (N) and Gulf of Aqaba (S); 120 mi. long (N–S), 5–60 mi. wide. Borders on Egypt (W) and on Jordan (E). Increasingly hilly on its W side; rises to 3,395 ft. 50 mi. SSW of Beersheba, near Egyptian border; slopes N toward Mediterranean and E toward Araba depression. In recent times efforts were made to establish Jewish settlements in N part of the Negev, and major irrigation schemes were begun; water pipe line now supplies most settlements in Beersheba region. Port of Elath established (1948) on Gulf of Aqaba. Beersheba is region's economic center. The Negev was scene (1948) of bitter fighting bet. Israelis and Egyptians; Egyptian forces were driven out of interior of region and under armistice agreement (1949) retain control of Rafa-Gaza coastal sector; El 'Auja region (W) was created neutral zone. In anc. times the Negev was fertile and well populated.

Neggio, Ethiopia: see NEJO.

Neghelli, Ethiopia: see NEGELLI.

Negoi Peak or **Negoiul Peak** (nĕgoi', nĕgoi'ōōl) highest peak (8,361 ft.) of the Transylvanian Alps, in the Fagaras Mts., S central Rumania, 30 mi. NW of Campulung.

Negombo (nägōm'bō), town (pop. 32,632), Western Prov., Ceylon, on W coast, at N mouth of Negombo Lagoon, 19 mi. N of Colombo; fishing center; mfg. of ceramics and brassware; trades in coconuts, rice, cinnamon. Has 17th-cent. Du. buildings. Was ⊙ former Negombo dist. (□ 247; inc. c.1946 into Colombo dist.). **Negombo Lagoon,** enclosed (W) by narrow peninsula, extends 8 mi. S; 2.5 mi. wide; fisheries (prawns, crabs).

Negoreloye (nyĕgŭryĕ'lŭyŭ), town (1939 pop. over 500) SW Minsk oblast, Belorussian SSR, 28 mi. SW of Minsk. Former Soviet border station (1921–39) on main Moscow-Warsaw RR.

Negotin (nĕ'gôtĭn). **1** or **Negotin Krajinski** or **Negotin Krayinski** (both: krī'ĭnskē), town (pop. 6,633), E Serbia, Yugoslavia, on railroad and 110 mi. ESE of Belgrade, near the Danube where Yugoslavia, Rumania, and Bulgaria meet; gardening, winegrowing. **2** or **Negotino** (–tēnô), village, Macedonia, Yugoslavia, on Vardar R., on railroad and 50 mi. SSE of Skoplje; trade center for winegrowing region.

Negra, Cordillera (kôrdĭyä'rä näg'rä), W section of Cordillera Occidental of the Andes, Ancash dept., W central Peru, bet. coastal plain and Callejón de Huaylas; extends 110 mi. SSE from Santa R. to area of Chiquián. Rises to 14,764 ft. Contains lead-, copper-, and silver-mining region of Ticapampa, and coal deposits at Aija.

Negra, Cuchilla (kōōchē'yä), Port. *Coxilha Negra* (kōōshē'lyŭ nĕ'grŭ), hill range along Brazil-Uruguay border, extending c.30 mi. SW from Livramento (Brazil) and Rivera (Uruguay); rises to 1,000 ft.

Negra, Laguna (lägōō'nä), Andean lake (□ 7), Santiago prov., central Chile, near Argentina border, 33 mi. SE of Santiago; c.3 mi. long.

Negra, Laguna, or **Laguna de los Difuntos** (dā lōs dĕfōōn'tōs), fresh-water lagoon (□ c.70), Rocha dept., SE Uruguay, near the Atlantic, 14 mi. NE of Castillos. Linked by short river with L. Mirim (N). Surrounded by marshes.

Negrais, Cape (nĕgrā'ĭs), SW headland of Lower Burma, on Bay of Bengal; 16°2'N 94°11'E. **Negrais Island,** Burmese *Hainggyi,* 10 mi. E, in mouth of Bassein R., was site (1753–59) of early Br. settlement in Burma.

Nègre, Cap (käp nĕg'rŭ), headland on the Mediterranean, in Var dept., SE France, at foot of Monts des Maures, 16 mi. E of Hyères. Here 1st Fr. units landed in Allied invasion of S France (Aug., 1944) during Second World War.

Negreiros (nāgrā'rōs), village (pop. 22), Tarapacá prov., N Chile, on railroad and 30 mi. SE of Pisagua. Former nitrate-mining center; flourished c.1900.

Nègrepelisse (nĕgrŭpŭlēs'), village (pop. 698), Tarn-et-Garonne dept., SW France, on the Aveyron and 9 mi. ENE of Montauban; hosiery mfg. Poultry shipping.

Negresti (nĕgrĕsht'), Rum. *Negreşti.* **1** Hung. *Felsőfalu* (fĕl'shŭfŏ″lōō), village (pop. 4,802), Baia-Mare prov., NW Rumania, on railroad and 26 mi. E of Satu-Mare in district noted for colorful original folklore; lumbering, andesite-trachyte mining. Health resort of Bicsad, Hung. *Bikszéd,* with saline springs, is 5 mi. NNW. Both in Hungary, 1940–45. **2** Agr. village (pop. 2,376), Jassy prov., E Rumania, on Barlad R. and 19 mi. NW of Vaslui.

Negrete (nāgrā'tā), town (pop. 1,558), Bío-Bío prov., S central Chile, on railroad and 13 mi. SW of Los Angeles; agr. center (wheat, rye, wine, peas, cattle); lumbering.

Negril (nĭgrĭl', nĕ–), minor port, Westmoreland parish, W Jamaica, just N of South Negril Point. Ships logwood.

Négrine (nāgrēn'), village and small oasis, Constantine dept., NE Algeria, on S slope of the Saharan Atlas, 70 mi. SSW of Tebessa; date palms. Ruins of Roman military camp.

Negri Sembilan (nŭgrē' sŭmbĕlän') [Malay,=nine states], state (□ 2,550; pop. 267,668; including transients, 269,304), SW Malaya, on Strait of Malacca; ⊙ Seremban. Bounded W by Selangor, N by Pahang, E by Johore, and S by Malacca; crossed NW–SE by S outliers of central Malayan range, it is drained by Linggi R. (W) and Muar R. (E). Agr.: rubber, rice, coconuts. Some tin mining. Served by W coast and E coast railroads (forking at Gemas) and Port Dickson on Strait of Malacca. Pop. is 43% Chinese, 38% Malay (descended from Sumatran immigrants) and ruled by a so-called Yang di-Pertuan Besar (sultan). Originally a group of 9 states, including Klang (present Selangor), Jelebu, Rembau, and Johol, Negri Sembilan was ruled by Malacca and, after 1511, by Johore. A loose confederation was formed (1773), accepted Br. protection (1874–89), and, having joined in a closer federation, became (1895) one of the Federated Malay States. After the Second World War, state joined Federation of Malaya.

Negrito, El, Honduras: see EL NEGRITO.

Negritos (nāgrē'tōs), town (pop. 7,078), Piura dept., NW Peru, minor port on the Pacific, 5 mi. SSW of Talara; major petroleum production center. Airport. Petroleum is shipped via pipe line through TALARA.

Négro, Cape (nāgrō'), headland on the Mediterranean, in Bizerte dist., N Tunisia, 16 mi. NE of Tabarka; 37°7'N 8°59'E.

Negro, Cerro (sĕ'rō nā'grō), active volcano (3,240 ft.) in Cordillera de los Marabios, W Nicaragua, 13 mi. ENE of León. Erupted last in 1947.

Negro, Río (rē'ō nā'grō). **1** River, E Chaco natl. territory, Argentina, rises in swamps 40 mi. WNW of El Zapallar, flows c.120 mi. SE, past Puerto Tirol, to Paraná R. at Corrientes. **2** Patagonian river in Río Negro natl. territory, S central Argentina, formed by junction of NEUQUÉN RIVER and LIMAY RIVER at Neuquén, flows 400 mi. E and SE (paralleling the Río Colorado), past Allen, Fuerte General Roca, Choele-Choel, and Viedma, to the Atlantic 20 mi. SE of Viedma. Navigable for 250 mi. upstream. In its irrigated valley are grown grain, fruit, wine. Used for hydroelectric power. Length of the Neuquén-Negro, c.700 mi.

Negro, Río, river in Santa Cruz and Beni depts., NE Bolivia; rises near Concepción, Santa Cruz dept.; flows c.220 mi. NNW to Río Blanco NNW of Baures.

Negro, Rio (rē'ōō nā'grōō). **1** Sp. *Río Negro* (rē'ō nā'grō), important left tributary of the Amazon in N Brazil, and known as the Guainía from its source in Vaupés commissary (Colombia) to its junction with the CASIQUIARE on Colombia-Venezuela line; enters Brazil at Cucuí, flows generally SE through Amazonas, past Uaupés, Tapuruquá (head of navigation), Barcelos, and Moura, to the Amazon 11 mi. below Manaus. Length, c.1,400 mi., although estimates range up to 1,860 mi. Chief tributaries: the Rio Branco (left), and Içana and Uaupés rivers (right). The Rio Negro communicates with Orinoco river system via Casiquiare Canal. It traverses tropical rain-forest area. Containing numerous isls., it is up to 20 mi. wide above Manaus, but only 1.5 mi. wide at its deep mouth. **2** River in SE Brazil, rises in the Serra do Mar on Paraná–Santa Catarina border SE of Curitiba, flows c.200 mi. W along the border, past Rio Negro and Mafra, to Iguassú R. S of São Mateus do Sul. Navigable in small sections.

Negro, Río, Guatemala: see CHIXOY RIVER.

Negro, Río, E Honduras: see SICO RIVER.

Negro, Río, in Nicaragua and Honduras, rises 5 mi. S of San Marcos de Colón (Honduras), flows c.70 mi. SW in an arc, through Chinandega dept. of Nicaragua, and, reentering Honduras, W to Gulf of Fonseca 18 mi. SSW of Choluteca.

Negro, Río, river, Uruguay, rises just over the line in Brazil just E of Bagé (Rio Grande do Sul), flows 500 mi. WSW through the center of Uruguay, past San Gregorio, Paso de los Toros, and Mercedes, to the Uruguay at Soriano. Receives Tacuarembó R. and the Arroyo Salsipuedes Grande (right), Yí R. and the Arroyo Grande (left). Forms dept. border bet. Rivera, Tacuarembó, Río Negro depts. (N) and Cerro Largo, Durazno, and Soriano depts. (S). Navigable for c.45 mi. above its mouth. Spreads out at its confluence with the Uruguay into 3 arms. Along its mid-course (above Paso de los Toros) the great Río Negro project has been completed, including a hydroelectric station at Rincón del Bonete and a vast reservoir along Tacuarembó-Durazno dept. border.

Negro Bay (nĕ'grō), inlet (30 mi. long, 5 mi. wide) of Indian Ocean, N Ital. Somaliland, at mouth of Nogal Valley; 8°N 49°52'E. Chief town, Eil.

Negro Island (nē'grō), Knox co., S Maine, small lighthouse isl. S of harbor of Camden.

Negro Mountain, NW Md. and SW Pa., a ridge of the Alleghenies, rising to 3,213 ft. in Mt. DAVIS, highest point in Pa.; extends c.35 mi. NNE from Deep Creek L. just SE of McHenry, Md., to a point just S of Somerset, Pa. Section of Savage R. State Forest is on its slopes in Md.

Negro Muerto, Cerro (sĕ'rō nā'grō mwĕr'tō), Andean volcano (19,190 ft.) in N Catamarca prov., Argentina, at S end of Sierra de Calalaste, 60 mi. SW of Antofagasta.

Negro Pabellón (nā'grō päbĕyōn'), mining settlement (pop. c.1,200), Oruro dept., W. Bolivia, in Cordillera de Azanaques, on road and 18 mi. SE of Oruro; tin mines.

Negropont, Greece: see EUBOEA; CHALCIS.

Negros (nā′grōs), island (□ 4,905; 1939 pop. 1,218,710), in Visayan Isls., 4th largest of the Philippines, bet. Panay and Cebu isls., bounded N by Visayan Sea, S by Sulu Sea, E by Tañon Strait, W by Guimaras Strait and Panay Gulf, and situated c.30 mi. N of Mindanao isl. across Mindanao Sea; 9°2′–11°N 122°22′-123°33′E. The isl. is c.135 mi. long, c.25–50 mi. wide. Largely mountainous, rising to 8,088 ft. at volcanic Mt. Canlaon in N central area. Large quantities of sugar cane and rice are produced on the wide coastal strips. Negros is densely populated. Negritos inhabit the forested interior; Visayans are in the coastal areas. The isl. comprises the provs. of NEGROS OCCIDENTAL and NEGROS ORIENTAL. Chief center is BACOLOD. Formerly called Buglas Isl.

Negros Occidental (ōksēdhäntäl′), province (□2,989; 1948 pop. 1,038,758), N and W Negros isl., Philippines; ⊙ BACOLOD. Mountainous terrain, drained by many small streams; highest peak is Mt. Canlaon (8,088 ft.). Major agr. area, producing sugar cane and rice. Chief centers are Bacolod, BINALBAGAN, MA-AO.

Negros Oriental (ōryäntäl′), province (□ 2,053; 1948 pop. 443,461), E Negros isl., Philippines, bounded E by Tañon Strait, S and SW by Sulu Sea; ⊙ DUMAGUETE. Includes SIQUIJOR isl. Largely mountainous terrain, drained by numerous small streams. Much of SW interior is unexplored territory. Principal agr. products: corn, coconuts, sugar cane, tobacco. Chief centers are Dumaguete, TANJAY, CALAMBA.

Negru-Voda (nā′grōō-vô′dŭ), Rum. *Negru-Vodă*, village (pop. 3,154), Constanta prov., SE Rumania, 32 mi. SW of Constanta; agr. center; mfg. of bricks and tiles. Sometimes called Cara-Omer.

Negus Mine, Northwest Territories: see YELLOWKNIFE.

Negyed, Czechoslovakia: see NEDED.

Nehalem (nĭhā′lŭm), town (pop. 270), Tillamook co., NW Oregon, 35 mi. S of Astoria and on Nehalem R., near mouth of North Fork.

Nehalem River, NW Oregon, rises in Columbia co., flows c.100 mi. generally SW to the Pacific near Nehalem.

Nehavend or **Nahavand** (nähävänd′), town (1933 pop. estimate 17,000), Fifth Prov., in Malayer, W central Iran, 75 mi. ESE of Kermanshah; agr. center; grain, fruit, gums. Site of battle (A.D. 642) bet. Arab and Persian armies, resulting in overthrow of Sassanian dynasty and beginning of Arab rule in Iran. Here, also, Abbas the Great defeated the Turks in 1602. Sometimes spelled Nihavand.

Nehawka (nēhô′kŭ), village (pop. 272), Cass co., SE Nebr., 28 mi. S of Omaha and on Weeping Water Creek, near Missouri R. Traces of prehistoric man discovered near here.

Nehbandan, Iran: see NAIBANDAN.

Neheim-Hüsten (nā′hīm-hü′stŭn), town (pop. 26,520), in former Prussian prov. of Westphalia, W Germany, after 1945 in North Rhine-Westphalia, on the Ruhr, at mouth of Möhne R., and 12 mi. NE of Iserlohn; iron foundries; mfg. of electrical household and kitchen implements, cables, nails, light bulbs, furniture, varnish. Neheim (chartered 1358) and Hüsten (chartered 1360) were united 1941.

Nehoiasu (nĕkoi-äsh′), Rum. *Nehoiaşu*, village (pop. 311), Buzau prov., SE central Rumania, on Buzau R. and 33 mi. NW of Buzau; rail terminus, lumbering center.

Nehoiu (nĕkhoi′ōō), village (pop. 781), Buzau prov., SE central Rumania, on Buzau R., on railroad and 32 mi. NW of Buzau; summer resort and lumbering center; foundries.

Nehuentué (nāwĕntwā′), village (1930 pop. 273), Cautín prov., S central Chile, on Imperial R. near its mouth on the Pacific, opposite Puerto Saavedra, and 45 mi. W of Temuco, in agr. area (cereals, vegetables, livestock). Tourist site.

Neiba (nā′bä), city (1935 pop. 1,246; 1950 pop. 2,131), ⊙ Bahoruco prov., SW Dominican Republic, near E shore of L. Enriquillo, 100 mi. W of Ciudad Trujillo; 18°28′N 71°23′W. Produces sugar cane and fine construction wood. Airfield. Since 1943, ⊙ prov. Rock-salt deposits near by.

Neiba, Sierra de (syĕ′rä dā), range in W Dominican Republic, S of the Cordillera Central, bet. San Juan Valley (N) and L. Enriquillo (S), extending c.60 mi. E from Haiti border to the Yaque del Sur; rises to 5,545 ft.

Neiba Bay, small inlet (c.6 mi. long, 6 mi. wide) of the Caribbean, SW Dominican Republic. Into it falls the Yaque del Sur. Barahona city on SW coast.

Nei-chiang, China: see NEIKIANG.

Nei-ch'iu, China: see NEIKIU.

Neiden (nā′dŭn), village in Sor-Varanger canton, Finnmark co., NE Norway, on arm of Varanger Fjord, 15 mi. W of Kirkenes. Near by is Lapp settlement with Greek Orthodox church.

Neidenburg, Poland: see NIDZICA.

Neide River, Poland: see WKRA RIVER.

Neietsu, Korea: see YONGWOL.

Neiges, Piton des (pētō′ dā nĕzh′), highest peak (10,069 ft.) of Réunion isl., 14 mi. S of Saint-Denis, at center of three-lobed volcanic massif.

Neihart (nī′härt), town (pop. 289), Cascade co., central Mont., 50 mi. SE of Great Falls and on small branch of Missouri R., in Little Belt Mts.; alt. c.5,700 ft.; trading point. Silver, gold, lead, zinc mines near by.

Nei-hsiang, China: see NEISIANG.

Neihu (nā′hōō′), Jap. *Naiko* (nī′kō), village (1935 pop. 3,072), N Formosa, 8 mi. ENE of Taipei; coal mining; mfg. (bricks and tiles, earthenware, drainage pipes, bamboo products).

Neihwang or **Nei-huang** (both: nā′hwäng′), town, ⊙ Neihwang co. (pop. 173,338), N Pingyuan prov., China, on Hopeh line, 32 mi. ESE of Anyang; wheat, rice, millet, fruit. Until 1949 in Honan prov.

Neikban (nāk′bän), village, Henzada dist., Lower Burma, on Bassein-Henzada RR and 12 mi. SW of Henzada.

Neikiang or **Nei-chiang** (both: nā′jyäng′), town (pop. 32,495), ⊙ Neikiang co. (pop. 569,667), SW Szechwan prov., China, on Chungking-Chengtu RR and 50 mi. NNW of Luhsien, on To R.; sugar-milling and weaving center; match mfg.; rice, beans, sweet potatoes, wheat, oranges. Projected rail junction on line to Kunming.

Neikiu or **Nei-ch'iu** (both: nā′chyō′), town, ⊙ Neikiu co. (pop. 113,980), SW Hopeh prov., China, 50 mi. S of Shihkiachwang and on Peking-Hankow RR; cotton, wheat, kaoliang, millet.

Neilgherry, India: see NILGIRI, Madras.

Neillsville (nēlz′vĭl), city (pop. 2,663), ⊙ Clark co., central Wis., on Black R. and 47 mi. ESE of Eau Claire, in hilly region; commercial center for dairying, stock-raising, and farming area; cheese, butter, beverages, canned vegetables. Has hydroelectric plant. Winnebago Indian Mission School is here. Settled c.1844, inc. 1882.

Neilston (nēl′stŭn), town and parish (pop. 15,305, including part of Barrhead burgh), S central Renfrew, Scotland, 5 mi. S of Paisley; textile industry.

Nein, Israel: see NAIN.

Neira (nā′rä), town (pop. 4,349), Caldas dept., W central Colombia, in W Cordillera Central, on Manizales Aranzazu aerial tramway, and 7 mi. N of Manizales; alt. 6,644 ft.; coffeegrowing center; sericulture.

Neira, Indonesia: see BANDANAIRA.

Neiriz, Iran: see NIRIZ.

Neisiang or **Nei-hsiang** (both: nā′shyäng′), town, ⊙ Neisiang co. (pop. 270,860), SW Honan prov., China, 40 mi. W of Nanyang, on Shensi-Hupeh trade route; wheat, beans, kaoliang. Asbestos quarrying near by.

Neisse (nī′sŭ) or **Nysa** (nĭ′sä), town (1939 pop. 37,859; 1946 pop. 11,559) in Upper Silesia, after 1945 in Opole prov., SW Poland, near Czechoslovak border, on the Glatzer Neisse and 45 mi. SSE of Breslau (Wroclaw); rail junction; mfg. of chemicals, machinery; cotton and linen milling, metalworking; power station. Was (1198–1810) ⊙ principality held by prince-bishops of Breslau. Captured 1741 by Frederick the Great; subsequently fortified; withstood (1758) Austrian siege. Occupied 1807–8 by French; fortifications razed 1862. Heavily damaged in Second World War. After 1945, briefly spelled Nisa.

Neisse River (nī′sŭ), Czech *Nisa* (nĭ′sä), Pol. *Nysa* (nē′sä). **1** or **Lusatian Neisse River** (lōōsā′shŭn), Czech *Lužická Nisa* (lōō′zhĭtskä), Ger. *Lausitzer Neisse* (lou′zĭ″tsŭr), Pol. *Nysa Łużycka* (wōōzhĭts′kä), in Czechoslovakia, E Germany, and Poland, rises in N Bohemia, Czechoslovakia, in the Isergebirge, 5 mi. NE of Liberec; flows S, WNW past Liberec and Hradek nad Nisou, into Germany, and N (after 1945 forming from Czech border to its mouth the boundary bet. E Germany and Poland) past Görlitz, Forst, and Guben (head of navigation) to the Oder 9 mi. N of Guben; 140 mi. long. Also called Görlitzer Neisse. **2** or **Glatzer Neisse River** (glä′tsŭr), Pol. *Nysa Klodzka* (kwôts′kä), in Lower Silesia, after 1945 in SW Poland, rises in the Sudetes on Czechoslovak border NE of Miedzylesie; flows SSW and N past Bystrzyca Klodzka and Glatz (Klodzko), generally E past Paczkow, Otmuchow (dam and irrigation reservoir), and Neisse (Nysa), and NNE past Lewin Brzeski (head of navigation), to Oder R. 10 mi. ESE of Brieg (Brzeg); 121 mi. long.

Neisu (nā′sōō), village, Eastern Prov., NE Belgian Congo, on railroad and 165 mi. E of Buta; palm-oil milling, soap mfg.

Neiva (nā′vä), city (pop. 15,096), ⊙ Huila dept., S central Colombia, landing on right bank of upper Magdalena R. and 150 mi. SW of Bogotá, reached by train from Girardot and by highway and air from Bogotá; 2°56′N 75°18′W. Trading and processing center in agr. region (rice, corn, cacao, coffee, tobacco, fique, cattle, horses, mules); mfg. of panama hats, fiber hammocks, cotton goods. Old colonial city with park, govt. and natl. palaces. Founded 1539, rebuilt 1612 after having been destroyed by Indians. Gold placer mines near by.

Nei-Valter, Russian SFSR: see SVERDLOVO.

Neiva River or **Neyva River** (nyä′vŭ), Sverdlovsk oblast, Russian SFSR, rises in the central Urals 10 mi. NNE of Verkh-Neivinski, flows N, past Nevyansk, E, past Petrokamenskoye and Neivo-Shaitanski, and generally NE, past Zyryanovski and Alapayevsk, joining Rezh R. 20 mi. ENE of Alapayevsk to form Nitsa R.; 202 mi. long. Has several dams holding industrial water supply.

Neivo-Rudyanka or **Neyvo-Rudyanka** (nyä″vŭ-rōōdyän′kŭ), town (1932 pop. estimate 3,700), SW central Sverdlovsk oblast, Russian SFSR, 5 mi. SSE (under jurisdiction) of Kirovgrad; rail junction; wood-cracking center; charcoal burning. Gold placers near by. Until 1928, Neivo-Rudyanski Zavod.

Neivo-Shaitanski or **Neyvo-Shaytanskiy** (–shītän′skē), town (1935 pop. estimate 6,500), S central Sverdlovsk oblast, Russian SFSR, on Neiva R. and 18 mi. SW (under jurisdiction) of Alapayevsk, on rail spur; metallurgical center (steel, pig iron); precious-stone mining and polishing. Developed prior to First World War.

Nejafabad or **Najafabad** (both: näjäf″äbäd′), town (1940 pop. 26,779), Tenth Prov., in Isfahan, W central Iran, 20 mi. W of Isfahan; grain, grapes, almonds, walnuts; noted for its pomegranates. Handmade cotton slippers.

Nejapa (nähä′pä), town (pop. 2,384), San Salvador dept., W central Salvador, on railroad and 7 mi. NNW of San Salvador; grain. Town originally located at NW foot of volcano San Salvador, 4 mi. SW of Quezaltepeque. Following its destruction in 1659 eruption, which created the large, picturesque lava field of El Playón, Nejapa was rebuilt on present site.

Nejapa, Lake, small crater lake, SW Nicaragua, 3 mi. SW of Managua; waters have medicinal value.

Nejd (nĕjd) or **Najd** (năjd), province (pop. 1,000,-000) of Saudi Arabia, forming with its dependencies a viceroyalty (□ 450,000; pop. 4,000,000) of Saudi Arabia; ⊙ Riyadh. The dependencies of Nejd are Jebel SHAMMAR (N), HASA (E), and ASIR (SW). Nejd proper occupies the center of the Arabian Peninsula, an anc. land block uptilted on the W and sloping gradually toward E, with a mean alt. of 2,500 ft. Pop. is largely settled in a crescent-shaped series of oasis dists., extending along the escarpment region of the Jabal Tuwaiq and the Arma Plateau. Oasis dists. are (from N to S): Qasim (bet. 26° and 27°N), Sudair, Washm, Aridh (the heart of Nejd with the capital, Riyadh), Kharj (site of major agr. development project), Hariq, Hauta, Aflaj, and Wadi Dawasir (at 20°30′N). Nomadic Bedouin tribes roam the steppe margins of these settled dists., where some precipitation permits oasis cultivation. Dates are the staple crop, with barley, wheat, millet, alfalfa, and fruit (figs, apricots, grapes) also produced. Nejd became (mid-18th cent.) the center of the Wahabi movement, which by 1811 had conquered most of the Arabian Peninsula. An Egyptian punitive expedition drove the Wahabis back into Nejd and destroyed their capital, Deraya, in 1818. The sect rose again after 1821, now being centered at Riyadh, and for a decade controlled the Hasa coast of the Persian Gulf. The domain thereafter weakened under pressure by the Turks and the Rashid dynasty of Hail, which contested the supremacy of the Saudi tribe of Riyadh. In late-19th cent., Rashid rule was paramount. Ibn Saud, however, rewon Riyadh in 1902, defeated the Rashids in 1905, and became the dominant force in Nejd. Expanding his holdings, Ibn Saud won Hasa in 1913–14, Jebel Shammar in 1921, and Asir in 1920–26. Following Ibn Saud's conquest of Hejaz in 1925, the union of Hejaz and Nejd led (1932) to the formation of Saudi Arabia. Pending the formulation of a single constitution for the whole nation, Nejd continues to be administered as a separate kingdom under a viceroy.

Nejdek (nā′dĕk), Ger. *Neudek* (noi′dĕk), town (pop. 5,748), W Bohemia, Czechoslovakia, in the Erzgebirge, on railroad and 10 mi. NW of Carlsbad; mfg. (lace, paper), spinning, dyeing; iron foundry and rolling mill.

Nejef, Iraq: see NAJAF.

Nejime, Japan: see NESHIME.

Nejo (nĕ′jō), Ital. *Neggio*, town (pop. 3,000), Wallaga prov., W central Ethiopia, 34 mi. NW of Gimbi; 9°29′N 35°28′E. Trade center (coffee, beeswax, hides, gold). Gold placers near by.

Nejran, Saudi Arabia: see NAJRAN.

Nekemti, Ethiopia: see NAKAMTI.

Nekhayevskaya (nyĭkhī′ŭfskīŭ), village (1932 pop. estimate 2,790), NW Stalingrad oblast, Russian SFSR, near Khoper R., 27 mi. SSW of Uryupinsk; metalworks; wheat, fruit, sunflowers.

Nekheb, Egypt: see KAB, EL.

Nekhela, Egypt: see NIKHEILA.

Nekhvoroshcha (nyĕkhvŭrô′shchŭ), town (1926 pop. 9,344), SE Poltava oblast, Ukrainian SSR, on Orel R. and 30 mi. SSE of Poltava; clothing mfg.

Neklyudovo (nyĭklyōō′dŭvŭ), town (1947 pop. over 500), W Gorki oblast, Russian SFSR, 5 mi. N of Gorki, across Volga R.; junction (Tolokontsevo station) of rail spur to Bor; woolen milling (for felt boots).

Nekmard, E Pakistan: see THAKURGAON.

Nekoma, village (pop. 140), Cavalier co., NE N.Dak., 12 mi. S of Langdon.

Nekoosa (nĭkōō′sŭ), city (pop. 2,352), Wood co., central Wis., on Wisconsin R. and 7 mi. SSW of Wisconsin Rapids, in dairy area; paper, foundry products. Settled 1892, inc. 1926.

Nekouz (nyĕkŭōōs'), village (1926 pop. 1,027), W Yaroslavl oblast, Russian SFSR, 30 mi. WSW of Shcherbakov; flax processing.

Nekrasovskoye (nyĭkrä'sŭfskŭyŭ), town (1940 pop. over 500), E Yaroslavl oblast, Russian SFSR, near Volga R., 19 mi. E of Yaroslavl; metalworking, food processing, clothing mfg. Until 1930s, called Bolshiye Soli.

Nekselo, Denmark: see SEJERO BAY.

Nekso (nĕk'sû), Dan. *Neksø*, city (pop. 3,074) and port, Bornholm amt, Denmark, on SE Bornholm isl.; fisheries; sandstone quarry, egg-packing plant, shipbuilding. Sometimes spelled Nexo.

Nelaag, Norway: see NELAUG.

Nelagoney (nŭlō'gŭnē), town (pop. 138), Osage co., N Okla., 6 mi. ESE of Pawhuska.

Nelamangala (nälŭmŭng'gŭlŭ), town (pop. 4,119), Bangalore dist., central Mysore, India, 15 mi. NW of Bangalore; trades in millet, rice, tobacco.

Nela Park, Ohio: see EAST CLEVELAND.

Nelas (nä'lŭsh), town (pop. 2,046), Viseu dist., N central Portugal, on railroad and 9 mi. SSE of Viseu; sawmilling and woodworking center; resin and pitch extracting. Pine, oak, and chestnut forests. Uranium deposits near by.

Nelaug (nä'loug), village in Amli canton, Aust-Agder co., S Norway, on Nelaug L. and on Nid R., and 15 mi. N of Arendal; rail junction. Sometimes spelled Nelaag.

Nelchina Glacier (nĕlchē'nŭ), S Alaska, rises in Chugach Mts. near 61°30'N 146°50'W, flows 22 mi. NW, drains into Tazlina L.

Nelidovo (nyĭlyē'dŭvŭ), city (1948 pop. over 2,000), E Velikiye Luki oblast, Russian SFSR, 55 mi. W of Rzhev; lignite-mining center; sawmilling, veneering. Mining developed after Second World War to fill Leningrad coal needs. Became city in 1949.

Neligh (nē'lē), city (pop. 1,822), ⊙ Antelope co., NE central Nebr., 30 mi. WNW of Norfolk and on Elkhorn R.; flour, beverages; grain. Inc. 1873.

Nelkan or **Nel'kan** (nyĭlkän'), village (1948 pop. over 10,000), central Lower Amur oblast, Khabarovsk Territory, Russian SFSR, on Maya R. (head of navigation) and 110 mi. WNW of Ayan, on Ayan-Yakutsk highway.

Nellie, village (pop. 165), Coshocton co., central Ohio, 12 mi. WNW of Coshocton and on Walhonding R. Also called Mohawk. Mohawk Dam is near by.

Nellie Juan, Port (nĕ"lē wän'), bay (30 mi. long, 3 mi. wide), S Alaska, on E side of Kenai Peninsula 50 mi. NE of Seward; opens into Prince William Sound at 60°32'N 148°17'W; fishing, fish processing, logging.

Nellikuppam (näl"lĭkōōp'pŭm), town (pop. 13,263), South Arcot dist., SE Madras, India, bet. Ponnaiyar and Gadilam rivers, 7 mi. WNW of Cuddalore; sugar-processing center; distillery; betel farms. Sometimes spelled Nellikkuppam.

Nellingen or **Nellingen auf den Fildern** (nĕ'lĭng-ŭn ouf dĕn fĭl'dŭrn), village (pop. 3,837), N Württemberg, Germany, after 1945 in Württemberg-Baden, 2 mi. S of Esslingen; wine.

Nellis Air Force Base, Nev.: see LAS VEGAS.

Nelliston, village (pop. 693), Montgomery co., E central N.Y., on Mohawk R. (bridged), opposite Fort Plain, and 22 mi. W of Amsterdam.

Nellore (nĕlōr'), district (□ 7,942; pop. 1,617,026), E Madras, India; ⊙ Nellore. On Coromandel Coast of Bay of Bengal; bordered W by Eastern Ghats; Pulicat L. (salt pans) on S coast; drained by Penner R. Agr. (millet, rice, oilseeds); extensive cashew and Casuarina growing (mainly on coast). An important mica-producing area; quarries (notably near Gudur and Atmakur) also yield ceramic clays and feldspar. Main towns: Nellore, Venkatagiri, Gudur.

Nellore, city (pop. 56,315), ⊙ Nellore dist., E Madras, India, near Coromandel Coast of Bay of Bengal (saltworks), on Penner R. and 95 mi. N of Madras; road and trade center; mica processing, rice and oilseed milling; cashew and Casuarina plantations. Col. (affiliated with Andhra Univ.).

Nelly Mine, village, Bulawayo prov., central Rhodesia, in Matabeleland, 8 mi. SE of Fort Rixon; tobacco, corn; livestock. Formerly a gold-mining center.

Nelma or **Nel'ma** (nyĕl'mŭ), town (1948 pop. over 10,000), SE Khabarovsk Territory, Russian SFSR, on Sea of Japan, 100 mi. S of Sovetskaya Gavan; fish canning.

Nelson, city (pop. 5,912), SE B.C., near Wash. border, on Kootenay R., at end of West Arm of Kootenay L., and 130 mi. N of Spokane; alt. 1,766 ft.; railroad divisional point, with railroad shops; center of extensive mining (gold, silver, copper, lead, zinc) region; mfg. of woodworking machinery; apple growing, dairying. Hydroelectric power.

Nelson, municipal borough (1931 pop. 38,304; 1951 census 34,368), E Lancashire, England, 4 mi. NNE of Burnley; cotton and rayon milling, electrical engineering.

Nelson, provincial district (□ 10,870; pop. 57,201), NW S.Isl., New Zealand; chief city is Nelson. Largely mountainous; highest range, Spenser Mts. Quartz, iron, coal, silver mines. Grain, tobacco, fruit grown on Waimea plain. Large iron deposits. Area roughly corresponds to Nelson land dist.

Nelson, city (pop. 13,030; metropolitan Nelson 16,577) and port, ⊙ Waimea co. (□ 1,539; pop. 11,497), N S.Isl., New Zealand, at SE end of Tasman Bay, 160 mi. N of Christchurch; canneries, sawmills, confectioneries. Exports tobacco, fruit, timber. Airport near by. Seat of Cawthron Institute for scientific research. Nelson is in, but independent of, Waimea co.

Nelson. 1 County (□ 437; pop. 19,521), central Ky.; ⊙ Bardstown. Bounded SW by Rolling Fork, E by Beech Fork. Rolling agr. area, partly in outer Bluegrass region; livestock, dairy products, grain, burley tobacco; hardwood timber. Some mfg. at Bardstown. Formed 1784. 2 County (□ 997; pop. 8,090), E central N.Dak.; ⊙ Lakota. Agr. area watered by Sheyenne R., Goose R., and Stump L.; dairy products, livestock, grain. Formed 1883. 3 County (□ 468; pop. 14,042), central Va.; ⊙ Lovingston. Rolling piedmont region, with the Blue Ridge in W and NW; bounded SE by James R.; drained by Rockfish R. Includes parts of Blue Ridge Parkway, Appalachian Trail, and George Washington Natl. Forest. Agr. (fruit, especially apples; tobacco, corn), livestock. Mining (titanium ores, apatite), soapstone quarrying. Formed 1807.

Nelson. 1 Town (pop. 645), Pickens and Cherokee counties, N Ga., 32 mi. W of Gainesville. 2 Village (pop. 289), Lee co., N Ill., on Rock R. and 6 mi. WSW of Dixon, in rich agr. area. 3 Village (1940 pop. 510), Muhlenberg co., W Ky., 25 mi. E of Madisonville, in bituminous-coal-mining and agr. area. 4 Village (pop. 160), Douglas co., W Minn., 5 mi. E of Alexandria, in lake region; dairy products. 5 City (pop. 297), Saline co., central Mo., on Blackwater R., near the Missouri, and 12 mi. SE of Marshall. 6 City (pop. 806), ⊙ Nuckolls co., S Nebr., 30 mi. SE of Hastings and on branch of Little Blue R.; grain. 7 Town (pop. 231), Cheshire co., SW N.H., 9 mi. NE of Keene; wood products. Summer colony on Munson L. (1.5 mi. long; alt. 1,276 ft.). 8 Village (pop. c.275), Buffalo co., W Wis., near the Mississippi (bridged near by), 37 mi. SW of Eau Claire, in coulee region.

Nelson, town (pop. 3,102) in Caerphilly urban district, E Glamorgan, Wales; coal mining.

Nelson, Cape, SW Victoria, Australia, in Indian Ocean, at S tip of peninsula forming W shore of Portland Bay; 38°26'S 141°33'E; lighthouse.

Nelson Forks, Hudson's Bay Co. trading post, NE B.C., near Yukon border, on Liard R. at mouth of Fort Nelson R., and 70 mi. NW of Fort Nelson; 59°30'N 124°W.

Nelson Island (42 mi. long, 20–35 mi. wide; 1939 pop. 254), W Alaska, separated from mainland (E) by narrow channel, from Nunivak Isl. (SW) by Etolin Strait; 60°37'N 164°22'W. Rises to 1,500 ft. (W). Tanunak village in W.

Nelson Island (10 naut. mi. long, 7 naut. mi. wide), South Shetland Isls., off Palmer Peninsula, Antarctica; 62°17'S 59°5'W.

Nelson Peak (10,772 ft.), SE B.C., in Selkirk Mts., 60 mi. SW of Banff; 50°28'N 116°21'W.

Nelson Reservoir, NE Mont., in Phillips co., 15 mi. NE of Malta; 10 mi. long, 2 mi. max. width; formed by dam on small branch of Milk R. Unit in Milk R. irrigation system.

Nelson River, N Man., issues from N end of L. Winnipeg, flows 400 mi. NE, through lakes Playgreen, Cross, and Split, to Hudson Bay at Port Nelson, 12 mi. W of York Factory. Its mouth was discovered (1612) by Sir Thomas Button. River was long a thoroughfare of fur traders, and the trade was long dominated by the Hudson's Bay Co. post, YORK FACTORY. Since the Saskatchewan R. (1,205 mi. long to its farthest headstream, the Bow) enters L. Winnipeg in NW, a continuous Watercourse (Saskatchewan–L. Winnipeg–Nelson) is formed (c.1,660 mi. long) and is sometimes given the name Nelson R.

Nelson Strait, inlet of the Pacific on coast of S Chile, N of entrance to Strait of Magellan, bet. Cambridge Isl. and the Adelaide Isls.

Nelsonville. 1 Village (pop. 522), Putnam co., SE N.Y., 9 mi. N of Peekskill, in dairying area. 2 Village (pop. 4,845), Athens co., SE Ohio, 35 mi. SSW of Zanesville, and on Hocking R., in coal- and clay-producing, dairying, and truck-farming area; makes footwear, brick, tile, machinery, pick handles. Laid out 1818. 3 Village (pop. 188), Portage co., central Wis., 12 mi. E of Stevens Point, in dairying area.

Nelspruit (nĕl'sproit), town (pop. 6,131), SE Transvaal, U. of So. Afr., on Crocodile R. and 110 mi. WNW of Lourenço Marques; rail junction; agr. center (fruit, tobacco, vegetables); tobacco processing, sawmilling. Site of govt. agr. research station; hydroelectric power.

Néma (nĕ'mä), town (pop. c.3,000), SE Mauritania, Fr. West Africa, in the Sahara, 290 mi. N of Bamako, Fr. Sudan; stock raising (camels, cattle, sheep, goats). Airstrip, meteorological station.

Nema (nyĕ'mŭ), village (1926 pop. 551), SE Kirov oblast, Russian SFSR, 20 mi. E of Molotovsk; flax processing.

Nemacolin (nĕmŭkō'lĭn), village (pop. 1,930), Greene co., SW Pa., 14 mi. E of Waynesburg.

Nemadji River (nĭmă'jē), in E Minn. and extreme NW Wis., rises in Carlton co., Minn., flows c.25 mi. NE to L. Superior at Superior.

Nemaha (nē'mŭhä, –hô, nē'–). 1 County (□ 709; pop. 14,341), NE Kansas; ⊙ Seneca. Gently sloping terrain, bordered N by Nebr.; watered by South Fork Nemaha R. Livestock, grain. Formed 1855. 2 County (□ 399; pop. 10,973), SE Nebr.; ⊙ Auburn. Farming area bounded E by Missouri R. and Mo.; drained by Little Nemaha R. Fruit, grain, livestock, dairy and poultry produce. Formed 1854.

Nemaha. 1 Town (pop. 184), Sac co., W Iowa, near Raccoon R., 8 mi. NNW of Sac City. 2 Village (pop. 288), Nemaha co., SE Nebr., 10 mi. ESE of Auburn and on Missouri R.

Nemaha River, SE Nebr., formed by confluence of North Fork and South Fork near Falls City, flows 40 mi. E to Missouri R. near Rulo. North Fork rises 15 mi. S of Lincoln, flows 95 mi. SE, past Tecumseh and Humboldt; South Fork rises in NE Kansas, near Seneca, flows 68 mi. N and E.

Neman (nĕ'mŭn, Rus. nyĕ'mŭn), city (1939 pop. 10,094), N Kaliningrad oblast, Russian SFSR, on Neman R. (Lith. line) and 6 mi. SE of Sovetsk; lumber milling; brickworks. Has 15th-cent. castle (once stronghold of Teutonic Knights). Chartered 1722. Until 1945, in East Prussia and called Ragnit (räg'nĭt).

Neman River (nĕ'mŭn), Ger. *Memel* (mā'mŭl), Lith. *Nemunas* (nă'mōōnäs), Pol. *Niemen* (nyā'mĕn), in Belorussian SSR and Lithuania, rises in Belorussia 30 mi. SSW of Minsk, flows generally W, past Stolbtsy (head of navigation), Mosty, and Grodno, then N into Lithuania, past Alytus, and W past Kaunas and Jurbarkas, forming border bet. Lithuania and Kaliningrad oblast, past Neman and Sovetsk, to Courland Lagoon, forming small delta mouth; total length, 597 mi. Receives Viliya, Nevezys, and Dubysa (right) and Shchara (linked by Oginski Canal with Pripet R.) and Sheshupe (left) rivers. Important for timber floating. Lithuanian resorts of Druskininkai and Birstonas are on its banks.

Nemausus, France: see NÎMES.

Nemawar (nămä'vŭr), village, S Madhya Bharat, India, on Narbada R. and 19 mi. SE of Kannod; annual festival fair.

Nembe or **Nimbi** (nĕm'bē), town, Owerri prov., Eastern Provinces, S Nigeria, port in Niger R. delta, 20 mi. NE of Brass; palm oil and kernels, hardwood, rubber.

Nembro (nĕm'brô), town (pop. 4,604), Bergamo prov., Lombardy, N Italy, on Serio R. and 5 mi. NE of Bergamo; whetstone factories, foundry, paper mill. Alabaster quarries near by.

Nemby (nyĕmbē') or **San Lorenzo de la Frontera** (sän lōrĕn'sō dā lä frōntä'rä), town (dist. pop. 5,938), Central dept., S Paraguay, 11 mi. SE of Asunción; processing and agr. center (bananas, oranges, cotton, sugar cane); sugar refining, alcohol and liquor distilling.

Nemea (nē'mēŭ, nĭmē'ŭ), town (pop. 4,249), Argolis and Corinthia nome, NE Peloponnesus, Greece, 13 mi. NNW of Argos; tobacco, wheat, vegetables; livestock. Formerly called Hagios Georgios. E 3 mi., in Nemea valley, are ruins of anc. Nemea with temple of Zeus, theater, and stadium (site of Nemean games). Nemea was the scene in Gr. mythology of strangling of Nemean lion by Hercules. At battle of Nemea (394 B.C.), Spartans scored decisive victory over Corinthians and Argives.

Nemecke Jablonne, Czechoslovakia: see JABLONNE V PODJESTEDI.

Nemecky Brod, Czechoslovakia: see HAVLICKUV BROD.

Nemencha Mountains (nŭmĕn'shŭ, Fr. nĕmĕnshä'), semi-arid range of the Saharan Atlas, in Constantine dept., NE Algeria, a SE extension of the Aurès massif, reaching out to the Tunisian border NW of Gafsa. Rises to 4,800 ft. Important phosphate deposits, especially at the Djebel Onk.

Nemërçka or **Nemërçkë,** Albania and Greece: see DOUSKON.

Nemetacum, France: see ARRAS.

Nemetboly (nā'mĕdbōl), Hung. *Németbóly*, town (pop. 3,085), Baranya co., S Hungary, 8 mi. W of Mohacs; wool, flour mills.

Nemetkeresztur, Austria: see DEUTSCHKREUTZ.

Nemetujvar, Austria: see GÜSSING.

Nemi, Lake (nā'mē), anc. *Nemorensis Lacus*, picturesque crater lake (c.1 mi. long), Latium, central Italy, in Alban Hills, 17 mi. SE of Rome. Here are the sacred woods and celebrated ruins of temple of Diana. In 1930–31 two pleasure ships of the Roman emperor Caligula were raised from the lake, after its level had been lowered c.70 ft.; they were burned (1944) by the retreating Germans. Village of Nemi (pop. 1,204) is on a height overlooking the lake; has old castle.

Nemirov (nyĭmē'rŭf). 1 Pol. *Niemirów* (nyĕmē'rōōf), town (1931 pop. 3,016), W Lvov oblast, Ukrainian SSR, on Lyubachovka R. and 11 mi. SW of Rava-Russkaya, near Pol. border; health resort; lumbering, flour milling. 2 Town (1926 pop. 7,300), central Vinnitsa oblast, Ukrainian SSR, 25 mi. SE of Vinnitsa; road junction; fruit canning, distilling.

Nemmara (nĕ'mŭrŭ), town (pop. 6,291), E Cochin, India, 26 mi. E of Trichur; trades in timber from Anaimalai Hills (S); sawmilling, match mfg.

Nemocón (nāmōkōn'), town (pop. 1,420), Cundinamarca dept., central Colombia, on railroad and 36 mi. NNE of Bogotá; alt. 8,543 ft.; salt mining. Its deposits have been used since pre-Spanish days.

Nemours (nŭmōōr'), anc. *Ad Fratres*, town (pop. 4,220), Oran dept., northwesternmost Algeria, growing port on the Mediterranean, near Fr. Morocco border, 80 mi. SW of Oran; 35°5'N 1°51'W. N terminus of Mediterranean-Niger RR, completed (1941) to Colomb-Béchar–Kenadsa area. Ships coal (from Colomb-Béchar), manganese (from Bou Arfa, Morocco), sheep, cereals, dried vegetables, and esparto. Fishing and canning (sardines). Modern town established 1844, as base for Fr. expedition against Morocco.

Nemours, town (pop. 5,336), Seine-et-Marne dept., N central France, on the Loing (canalized) and 10 mi. S of Fontainebleau; popular resort of Parisians; at S edge of Forest of Fontainebleau. Mfg. (agr. and woodworking machinery, furniture, corsets, locks), brewing, glassmilling (silica quarried near by). Has 12th-cent. castle (restored 15th–17th-cent.) containing 15th–16th-cent. tapestries. Was ⊙ medieval duchy, title to which was later born by branch of house of Savoy and several members of Bourbon-Orléans line. Here, in 1585, Henry III revoked concessions made to Protestants. Dupont family of Delaware originated here.

Nemrut Dag (nĕmrōōt' dä), Turkish *Nemrut Dağ*, peak (10,010 ft.), E Turkey, 20 mi. NNE of Bitlis, 10 mi. W of L. Van.

Nemunas River, USSR: see NEMAN RIVER.

Nemunelis River, Lithuania: see MEMELE RIVER.

Nemuro (nämōō'rō), town (pop. 17,342), E Hokkaido, Japan, port on the Pacific, on narrow peninsula, 65 mi. ENE of Kushiro; major fishing center (edible kelp, trout); fish canning; fox farming. Exports edible kelp, metalwork.

Nemuro Strait, Jap. *Nemuro-kaikyo* (nämōō'rō-kīkyō'), channel bet. E Hokkaido, Japan, and Kunashir Isl. of Kurile Isls., Russian SFSR; connects Sea of Okhotsk (N) with the Pacific (S); 10–30 mi. wide, 60 mi. long. Cape Shiretoko is at NW, Cape Noshappu at SW side of entrance. Frozen Dec.-March.

Nen, Manchuria: see NONNI RIVER.

Nen, river, England: see NENE RIVER.

Nenagh (nē'nä-nŭkh), Gaelic *Aonach Urmhumhan*, urban district (pop. 4,516), NW Co. Tipperary, Ireland, on Nenagh R. and 23 mi. NE of Limerick; agr. market (dairying; potatoes, beets); woolen milling, mfg. of aluminum ware, wicker goods. Of 12th-cent. castle, dismantled in 18th cent., the round keep remains.

Nenaka (nänä'kä), town (pop. 7,711), Toyama prefecture, central Honshu, Japan, just SW of Toyama; agr. (rice, watermelons). Formed in early 1940s by combining former towns of Uzaka (1940 pop. 1,670), and Hayahoshi (1940 pop. 2,868). Sometimes called Fuchu.

Nenana (nēnă'nŭ), village (pop. 239), central Alaska, on Tanana R. (700-ft. railroad bridge) at mouth of Nenana R., and 45 mi. WSW of Fairbanks; distributing and transshipment center from railroad to Yukon R. steamers, in placer gold-mining, trapping region. Scene of annual Nenana ice sweepstakes. Just N is Nenana Native Village, site of Indian mission. Nenana was established 1916 as base for construction of Alaska RR; at S end of bridge President Harding opened railroad, July, 1923.

Nenana River, central Alaska, S tributary of Tanana R., rises in central Alaska Range, near 63°19'N 147°46'W; flows 150 mi. NNW to Tanana R. at Nenana. Paralleled by Alaska RR for c.100 mi.

Nen-chiang, Manchuria: see NUNKIANG.

Nendaz (nĕndä'), town (pop. 3,427), Valais canton, SW Switzerland, S of the Rhone, 4 mi. SW of Sion; farming; skiing. Consists of Basse-Nendaz (alt. 3,324 ft.) and Haute-Nendaz (alt. 4,495 ft.).

Nendeln (nĕn'dŭln), village, Liechtenstein, on railroad and 4 mi. NNE of Vaduz. Mfg. of pottery.

Nene River or **Nen River** (nĕn, nĕn), Northampton, Cambridge, and Lincolnshire, England, rises just SSW of Daventry, flows 90 mi. NE, past Northampton, Wellingborough, Oundle, Peterborough, and Wisbech, to The Wash 3 mi. N of Sutton Bridge. Receives Ise R. at Wellingborough. Made navigable to Peterborough.

Nenets National Okrug (nyĕ'nyĭts), administrative division (□ 67,300; 1946 pop. estimate 30,000) of NE Archangel oblast, European Russian SFSR; ⊙ Naryan-Mar. Extends along tundra coast of Barents Sea From Kanin Peninsula E to Kara Sea; includes Malozemelskaya Tundra, Bolshezemelskaya Tundra, and mtn. range Pai-Khoi. Vaigach Isl. is attached administratively. Pop. (mainly Nentsy; formerly known as Samoyeds) engaged in reindeer raising, fishing, seal hunting, some dairy and truck farming. Fluorspar mined at Amderma, lumber milled at Naryan-Mar. Okrug includes N section of Pechora coal basin, N of Vorkuta, with mines at Khalmer-Yu and along Silova R. (left affluent of the Kara). Formed 1929 within Northern Territory; passed 1937 to Archangel oblast.

Nenkiang, Manchuria: see NUNKIANG.

Nenndorf, Bad, Germany: see BAD NENNDORF.

Neno (nĕ'nō), center in native village area, Southern Prov., Nyasaland, 38 mi. NW of Blantyre, near Mozambique border; tobacco, cotton, wheat, rice.

Nenoksa (nyĭnôk'sŭ), village (1926 pop. 1,545), N Archangel oblast, Russian SFSR, fishing port on Dvina Gulf of White Sea, 40 mi. W of Archangel; saltworks.

Nen River, England: see NENE RIVER.

Nensjo (nĕn'shû"), Swedish *Nensjö*, village (pop. 820), Vasternorrland co., NE Sweden, on Angerman R. estuary, 15 mi. N of Harnosand; lumber and pulp mills.

Nentón (nĕntōn'), town (1950 pop. 571), Huehuetenango dept., W Guatemala, on W slopes of Cuchumatanes Mts., 38 mi. NNW of Huehuetenango; alt. 2,671 ft. Sugar cane, bananas, tropical fruit; livestock.

Nenzel (nĕn'zŭl), village (pop. 24), Cherry co., N Nebr., 28 mi. W of Valentine, near S.Dak. line and Niobrara R.; small trading post. Near by is part of Nebr. Natl. Forest.

Nenzing (nĕn'tsĭng), town (pop. 2,977), Vorarlberg, W Austria, near Ill R., 6 mi. SE of Feldkirch; cotton mill, embroidery; potatoes, corn.

Neocaesarea, Turkey: see NIKSAR.

Neochorion or **Neokhorion** (both: nāôkhô'rēôn), village (pop. 2,623), Acarnania nome, W central Greece, on lower Achelous R. and 9 mi. WNW of Missolonghi; rail terminus; wheat, oats, wine.

Neodesha (nēō"dŭshā'), city (pop. 3,723), Wilson co., SE Kansas, on Verdigris R., near mouth of Fall R., and 27 mi. N of Coffeyville; refining center in agr. (grain, livestock, poultry) and oil area; mfg. of gasoline, bricks, dairy products. Site of Neodesha Reservoir (for flood control on the Verdigris) is near. Laid out 1869, inc. 1871.

Neoga (nēō'gŭ), city (pop. 1,125), Cumberland co., SE central Ill., 12 mi. SSW of Mattoon, in broom-corn-growing area; apples, peaches, hay, beans; mfg. (flour, cheese and other dairy products, gloves, brooms). Inc. 1930.

Neokastron, Greece: see PYLOS.

Neokhorion, Greece: see NEOCHORION.

Neola (nēō'lŭ), town (pop. 839), Pottawattamie co., SW Iowa, on Mosquito Creek and 18 mi. NE of Council Bluffs, in corn, wheat, livestock area.

Neon, mining town (pop. 1,055), Letcher co., SE Ky., in the Cumberlands, on North Fork Kentucky R. and 4 mi. W of Jenkins; bituminous coal; bottling works.

Neon Faliron, Greece: see NEON PHALERON.

Neon Karlovasi (nä'ôn kärlô'vŭsē), town (pop. 5,024), on N shore of Samos isl., Greece, 15 mi. WNW of Limen Vatheos; tanning industry; olive oil, wine, tobacco, carobs; fisheries.

Neon Petritsi (pĕtrē'tsē), town (pop. 5,422), Serrai nome, Macedonia, Greece, on Struma R. and 18 mi. NW of Serrai, on railroad, near Bulg. line; barley, beans, tobacco. Also called Neon Petritsion; formerly Vetrina.

Neon Phaleron or **Neon Faliron** (both: fä'lĭrôn) [=new Phaleron], S suburb (pop. 5,168) of Athens, Greece, in metropolitan area, just NE of Piraeus, on Phaleron Bay; silk milling; popular Athenian evening resort.

Neopit (nēō'pĭt), village (pop. 1,257), Shawano co., NE Wis., 18 mi. NNW of Shawano, in Menominee Indian Reservation; sawmilling.

Neópolis (nēô'pŏŏlēs), city (pop. 4,774), NE Sergipe, NE Brazil, on right bank of lower São Francisco R. (navigable here), diagonally opposite Penedo (Alagoas), and 20 mi. SE of Propriá; textile mill; rice and sugar growing. Formerly called Vila Nova.

Neoria Husainpur (nāōr'yŭ hŏŏsīn'pŏŏr), town (pop. 5,508), Pilibhit dist., N Uttar Pradesh, India, 9 mi. NE of Pilibhit; trades in rice, wheat, gram, sugar cane. Also called Neoria or Neoriya.

Neosho (nēō'shō), county (□ 587; pop. 20,348), SE Kansas; ⊙ Erie. Sloping to gently rolling area, drained by Neosho R. Grain, poultry; dairying. Oil, gas, coal. Formed 1864.

Neosho. 1 City (pop. 5,790), ⊙ Newton co., SW Mo., in the Ozarks, 16 mi. SE of Joplin; agr. (strawberries, raspberries), dairy products, especially condensed milk. U.S. fish hatchery and Camp Crowder near by. Inc. 1855. Pro-Confederate convention passed an ineffective ordinance of secession here, 1862. **2** Village (pop. 287), Dodge co., S central Wis., on small Rubicon R. and 19 mi. SE of Beaver Dam, in dairying region.

Neosho Falls, city (pop. 355), Woodson co., SE Kansas, on Neosho R. and 10 mi. NW of Iola; livestock, grain. Small oil fields near by.

Neosho Rapids, city (pop. 204), Lyon co., E central Kansas, on Neosho R. and 10 mi. ESE of Emporia; cattle, grain.

Neosho River, in Kansas and Okla., rises in Morris co. in E central Kansas, flows SE, past Iola and Chanute, into NE Okla. (where it is generally known as Grand R.), then S, past Miami, joining Arkansas R. just NE of Muskogee. Length c.460 mi. Units (all in Okla.) of flood-control and hydroelectric power plan for river include GRAND RIVER DAM near Disney, Markham Ferry Dam 8 mi. SE of Pryor, and FORT GIBSON DAM N of Fort Gibson.

Neos Skopos (nā'ôs skôpôs'), town (pop. 2,717), Serrai nome, Macedonia, Greece, on railroad and 5 mi. SE of Serrai, near Struma R. Formerly called Kisiklik and Toumbista.

Neot Mordekhai or **Neot Mordechai** (both: nĕ-ōt' môrdĕkhī'), settlement (pop. 200), Upper Galilee, NE Israel, in Hula swamp region, 14 mi. NNE of Safad; shoe mfg.; mixed farming. Founded 1946 on reclaimed soil.

Nepal (nŭpôl', nā'päl), independent kingdom (□ c.56,000; 1941 pop. 6,283,649), S central Asia, in Nepal Himalayas; ⊙ KATMANDU. Roughly rectangular in shape, oriented WNW-ESE; c.520 mi. long, c.90-150 mi. wide; bet. 26°20'–30°15'N and 80°5'–88°13'E. Bounded S and W by India, N by Tibet, E by Sikkim and India; drained (E–W) by Sarda, Gogra, Gandak, and Kosi rivers. Main range of Nepal Himalayas extends along N area, with spurs running generally NNE-SSW, some traversing greater part of Nepal; rises on or near Tibet border in a series of great peaks, including Mt. EVEREST. Foothills comprise MAKABHARAT LEKH and SIWALIK RANGE (in Nepal called Churia Range). At foot of Siwalik Range lies the Terai, an unhealthy, partly swampy area with thick jungles (mostly sal intermixed with sissoo, cotton trees, and, further N, chir) harboring extensive wild game (elephants, tigers, rhinoceros, leopards, hogs, buffalo), grassy tracts (extensive sabai grass), and cultivated open country. Agr. is confined to lower slopes of hills, valleys, and the Terai. Principal exports: rice, jute, timber, oilseeds, ghee, oranges, potatoes, hides and skins, cattle, sabai grass, lac, spices, borax, medicinal herbs. Nepal is gradually expanding industrially: jute, sugar, cotton milling at Biratnagar; mfg. of matches, plywood, bobbins, chemicals, soap, ceramics, rice and oilseed milling, sawmilling; gunpowder mfg. near Balaju; hand-loom cloth weaving. Mining operations include coal mines in Siwalik Range, mica mines near Kusma, copper mines (Pokhara, Wapsa Khani, Jantra Khani), salt mines at Panu Khani, graphite mines. Minerals include bismuth, antimony, cobalt, sapphire, and ruby deposits near Musikot, corundum near Kusma, iron-ore, bauxite, and sulphur. Divided administratively into dists. Has 3 cities (Katmandu, PATAN, BHADGAON) in NEPAL VALLEY; main towns are Butwal, Pokhara, Palpa, Doti, Jumla, Nawakot, GURKHA, and Biratnagar. Airfield (seasonal service) at Katmandu. Main access routes are from India; most important route is by rail from Raxaul to Amlekhganj terminus and thence by road, path, and freight aerial ropeway to Katmandu; others include roads from Indian rail termini of Nantanwa, Bhikhna Thori, Nepalganj Road, and Jogbani, and from Darjeeling to Ilam. Tibet-Nepal trade routes include 1 through Nangpa La pass. Archaeological exploration has so far been restricted mainly to the Terai, most notable discovery being that of Lumbini Garden (Gautama Buddha's birthplace) at PADERIA in 1895; other archaeological landmarks include Asokan pillar near Nigliva and 5 Asokan stupas at Patan. Major Hindu pilgrimage centers are Pashupati, Gosainkund, Riri Bazar, and Muktinath; major Buddhist pilgrimage centers are Swayambhunath and Boddhnath. Nepal is a military oligarchy ruled by a hereditary maharajdhiraja (king) of the Sah family; actual power was invested (1867–1950) in hereditary maharaja (prime minister) of the Rana family. Most of Nepal's history is concerned with Nepal Valley (the only area to which the name Nepal was originally applied), inhabited by Newars, a people of Mongoloid origin probably intermixed (9th cent. A.D.) with Nair invaders from S India. Newars of Malla dynasty held valley until their overthrow (1768–69) by Prithwi Narayan, leader of the Gurkhas, a people of mixed Mongol-Rajput extraction originally from the Gurkha kingdom, who have remained the dominant power to the present. Nepal was involved in war with China (1792), with Great Britain (1814; ended by treaty of Sagauli, 1816), and Tibet (1854–56). Nepal's complete independence was recognized (1923) by Great Britain. Diplomatic relations with U.S. since 1947. After a short-lived popular uprising in 1950, Nepal govt. announced that a constituent assembly would be set up by 1952 to frame Nepal's 1st democratic constitution. Nepal has a large standing army; traditionally, Nepalese recruits have formed an important element in the Indian army. Major tribes (other than Gurkha and Newar) are Chetri (or Khas), Gurung, Mangar, Limbu, Rai, Kiranti, Tharu, Murmi, and Sherpa. Dominant religion is Hinduism; adherents of Buddhism are diminishing. Main language is Nepali (Khas-kura).

Nepalganj (nä'pälgŭnj), town, SW Nepal, in the Terai, 15 mi. NNE of Nanpara (India); trade center (rice, wheat, corn, millet, ghee, oilseeds, hides). Nepalese military barracks. Sometimes called Banke for adjoining village. Rail terminus is 3 mi. SSW, at Nepalganj Road, just inside India.

Nepalganj Road, India: see NANPARA.

Nepal Himalayas (hĭmä'lŭyŭz, hĭmŭlā'yŭz), central subdivision of the HIMALAYAS, S central Asia, roughly coextensive with Nepal, N of Ganges

Plain; extend from Kali (Sarda) R. on Nepal-India border (W) to Tista R. in Sikkim, India (E). Paralleled (S) by foot ranges (SIWALIK RANGE and MAHABHARAT LEKH) running W-E. Singalila Range (on Nepal-Sikkim border; E) is principal N-S spur. Watershed lies 50–60 mi. N of main range, in Tibet. Contain some of highest peaks of the world, including Mt. EVEREST (29,002 ft.; highest), KANCHENJUNGA (28,146 ft.; 3d-highest), E[1] (27,890 ft.), Makalu (27,790 ft.), Cho Oyu (26,867 ft.), Dhaulagiri (26,810 ft.), Manaslu (26,658 ft.), and ANNAPURNA I (26,502 ft.). Divided (W–E) by Gogra, Gandak, and Kosi river systems into 3 distinct sections. Main range bifurcates near Dhaulagiri peak. Main town, exclusive of Katmandu, is noted Indian hill station of Darjeeling.

Nepal Valley, undulating plain (□ c.250; 1946 pop. 401,704) in central Nepal Himalayas, central Nepal; formed by bifurcation of ridge running S from Gosainthan peak; surrounded on all sides by mts.; bounded S by Mahabharat Lekh range; c.20 mi. long, 12–14 mi. wide; alt. c.4,700 ft. Drained by the Baghmati. Very fertile; main crops are rice, wheat, oilseeds, barley, vegetables, fruit. Contains the 3 cities of Nepal—Katmandu, Patan, and Bhadgaon. Main access route is across Chandragiri Pass (W) on major route from India. Historically the most important area of Nepal and center of Nepalese civilization under Newars; overcome in 18th cent. by Gurkhas. Pop. mainly Newar.

Nepaug Reservoir, Conn.: see FARMINGTON RIVER.

Nepean Bay (nĭpē'ŭn), inlet of Investigator Strait of Indian Ocean, on NE Kangaroo Isl., South Australia; 10 mi. long, 7 mi. wide. Kingscote on NW shore.

Nephi (nē'fī), city (pop. 2,990), ⊙ Juab co., central Utah, 38 mi. SSW of Provo, in mtn. region; alt. 5,100 ft. Livestock- and grain-shipping center; flour, plaster, rubber products. U.S. agr. experiment station near by. Gypsum mined in area. Settled 1851 by Mormons.

Nephin (nĕ'fĭn), mountain (2,646 ft.), W Co. Mayo, Ireland, 11 mi. NNW of Castlebar; highest in Nephin Beg Range (20 mi. long).

Nepi (nā'pē), anc. *Nepete* and *Nepet*, town (pop. 3,224), Viterbo prov., Latium, central Italy, 18 mi. SE of Viterbo, in agr. region (cereals, grapes, olives). Bishopric. Has anc. walls (Etruscan, Roman), cathedral, town hall designed by Vignola, and ruins of 15th-cent. castle. Mineral baths near by.

Nepomuceno (nĭpŏŏmōōsā'nŏŏ), city (pop. 3,102), S Minas Gerais, Brazil, near the Rio Grande, 25 mi. S of Campo Belo; coffee, sugar, cereals. Asbestos deposits.

Nepomuk (nĕ'pômŏŏk), town (pop. 1,646), SW Bohemia, Czechoslovakia, on Uslava R. and 14 mi. NE of Klatovy; rail junction; ironworks. St. John of Nepomuk, Bohemia's patron saint, b. here.

Neponset (nĭpŏn'sĭt). **1** Village (pop. 501), Bureau co., N Ill., 8 mi. NE of Kewanee, in agr. and bituminous-coal area. **2** Section of BOSTON, Mass.

Neponset River, E Mass., rises in SW Norfolk co., flows c.25 mi. NE, past Milton (head of navigation), to SW side of Boston Harbor, bet. Boston and Quincy.

Neponsit (nĭpŏn'sĭt), SE N.Y., a section of S Queens borough of New York city, on Rockaway Peninsula; residential; beach resort.

Neptune, Nicaragua: see BONANZA.

Neptune, township (pop. 13,613), Monmouth co., E N.J., on the coast and W and S of Asbury Park; mfg. (leather belting, structural steel), ironworks. Includes OCEAN GROVE (resort). Inc. 1879.

Neptune Beach, resort town (pop. 1,767), Duval co., NE Fla., 15 mi. E of Jacksonville, on the Atlantic. Inc. 1931.

Neptune City, resort borough (pop. 3,073), Monmouth co., E N.J., near the coast, 2 mi. SW of Asbury Park. Inc. 1881.

Neptune Islands, in Indian Ocean, near entrance to Spencer Gulf, 15 mi. SSE of Eyre Peninsula, South Australia. Comprise 2 small groups, North and South Neptunes. Largest isl. 3 mi. in circumference, 1.5 mi. long. Granite cliffs.

Nequasset, Maine: see WOOLWICH.

Nequinum, Italy: see NARNI.

Nérac (nāräk'), town (pop. 3,681), Lot-et-Garonne dept., SW France, on the Baïse and 15 mi. WSW of Agen; cork, wine, and brandy trade; brewery, metalworks; food processing, footwear mfg. Has ruins of 16th-cent. castle of Henry IV. Petit-Nérac, a suburb on right bank of Baïse R., preserves 15th-cent. aspect. Stronghold of princes of Béarn, who gave refuge to Calvin during Wars of Religion.

Nera River (nā'rä), anc. *Nar*, central Italy, rises in Monti Sibillini 4 mi. NE of Norcia, flows 80 mi. SSW, past Terni, to Tiber R. 8 mi. SW of Narni. Used for hydroelectric power (Montoro). Receives Velino R. (left).

Neratovice (nĕ'rätôvĭtsĕ), village (pop. 3,059), central Bohemia, Czechoslovakia, on Elbe R. and 7 mi. SSE of Melnik; important rail junction; truck gardening (early potatoes, cucumbers, onions); food processing.

Néravy, Fr. India: see NIRAVI.

Nerbudda River, India: see NARBADA RIVER.

Nerchau (nĕr'khou), town (pop. 3,510), Saxony, E central Germany, on the Mulde and 4 mi. NE of Grimma, in lignite-mining region; mfg. (chemicals, paint, ceramics).

Nerchinsk (nyĕr'chĭnsk, nyĭrchĕnsk'), city (1937 pop. estimate 15,300), central Chita oblast, Russian SFSR, on Trans-Siberian RR, and 130 mi. E of Chita; on Nercha R., near its confluence with Shilka R., distilling, sawmilling. Founded 1654; Russo-Chinese frontier treaty signed here, 1689; former exile center of silver-mining region.

Nerchinski Zavod or **Nerchinskiy Zavod** (nyĕrchĕn'skē zŭvôt'), village (1926 pop. 3,186), SE Chita oblast, Russian SFSR, 270 mi. E of Chita, near Argun R.; lead and zinc mining. Founded 1704 as silver-mining center.

Nerchinsk Range, SE Chita oblast, Russian SFSR, extends from Mongolian frontier 125 mi. NE to Argun R.; rises to 4,300 ft. Abounds in silver, lead, zinc. Mining centers: Nerchinski Zavod, Gazimurski Zavod, Aleksandrovski Zavod.

Nerdva (nyĭrdvä'), village (1926 pop. 842), W central Molotov oblast, Russian SFSR, 26 mi. SSE of Kudymkar; rye, oats, flax, livestock.

Nerekhta (nyĕ'ryĭkhtŭ), city (1939 pop. over 10,000), SW Kostroma oblast, Russian SFSR, 25 mi. SSW of Kostroma; rail junction; linen-milling center; flour milling, metal and woodworking. Peat and gravel near by. Dates from 1425.

Neresheim (nā'rŭs-hīm), town (pop. 1,798), N Württemberg, Germany, after 1945 in Württemberg-Baden, 13 mi. SE of Aalen; grain. Has Benedictine abbey (founded in 11th cent.) with splendid baroque church.

Neresi, Yugoslavia: see BRAC ISLAND.

Neresnica or **Neresnitsa** (both: nĕrĕs'nĭtsä), village, E Serbia, Yugoslavia, 28 mi. ESE of Pozarevac; gold-placer mining.

Nereto (nĕrā'tô), town (pop. 2,132), Teramo prov., Abruzzi e Molise, S central Italy, 13 mi. NE of Teramo; cotton mill.

Neretva Channel (nĕ'rĕtvä), Serbo-Croatian *Neretvanski Kanal* (nĕ'rĕtvänskĕ känäl'), Ital. *Canale della Narenta* (känä'lĕ dĕl-lä närĕn'tä), inlet of Adriatic Sea, S Croatia, Yugoslavia, bet. Peljesac peninsula (SW) and mainland (NE). Provides Herzegovina with an outlet to the Adriatic via Neretva R.

Neretva River, anc. *Naro*, Ital. *Narenta*, in Dinaric Alps, Herzegovina and Dalmatia, Yugoslavia; rises 7 mi. N of Gacko, flows NNW past Konjic, and SSW past Jablanica, Mostar, and Metkovic, to Adriatic Sea at Kardeljevo; 135 mi. long. Navigable for 65 mi. Receives Rama and Bregava rivers. Followed bet. Konjic and Gabela by Sarajevo-Dubrovnik RR. Cotton grown on plain along lower Neretva R. A hydroelectric plant is on the Rama.

Nerezisce, Yugoslavia: see BRAC ISLAND.

Néris-les-Bains (nārē'-lā-bē'), anc. *Neri* or *Neriomagus*, town (pop. 2,166), Allier dept., central France, 5 mi. SE of Montluçon; health resort with hot springs (125°F.). Roman thermae (built under Augustus) have been excavated.

Neris River, W Belorussian SSR and Lithuania: see VILIYA RIVER.

Nerja (nĕr'hä), town (pop. 5,441), Málaga prov., S Spain, minor port on the Mediterranean, 30 mi. E of Málaga; sugar industry; also fishing, stock raising, fruitgrowing; mfg. of soap, liquor.

Nerl or **Nerl'** (nyĕrl). **1** Town (1926 pop. 1,052), central Ivanovo Oblast, Russian SFSR, 14 mi. SSW of Teikovo; cotton milling. **2** Village (1939 pop. over 500), SE Kalinin oblast, Russian SFSR, on Nerl R. and 13 mi. SSE of Kalyazin; shoe mfg.

Nerl River or **Nerl' River. 1** In W central European Russian SFSR, rises in Pleshcheyevo L., flows 50 mi. NW, past Nerl (Kalinin oblast), to Volga R. SW of Kalyazin. **2** In central European Russian SFSR, rises N of Pereslavl-Zalesski in Uglich Upland, flows c.120 mi. E and SE, past Petrovski, to Klyazma R. at Orgtrud.

Nero, peak, Yugoslavia: see KRN.

Nero, Lake (nē'rō, Rus. nyĕ'rŭ), one of largest (□ 15) glacial lakes in USSR, in SE Yaroslavl oblast, Russian SFSR; 8 mi. long, 4 mi. wide; orchards. Rostov lies on NW shore. Truck produce grown near by.

Nero Deep, Pacific Ocean: see MARIANAS TRENCH.

Neroi or **Neroy** (nyĭroi'), town (1948 pop. c.2,000), SW Irkutsk oblast, Russian SFSR, 60 mi. SW of Nizhneudinsk.

Néronde (nārōd'), village (pop. 419), Loire dept., SE central France, in Monts du Beaujolais, 16 mi. SSE of Roanne; artisan weaving industry. Textile trade school.

Nérondes (nārōd'), agr. village (pop. 1,121), Cher dept., central France, 16 mi. W of Nevers; poultry shipping.

Nerone, Monte (môn'tĕ nĕrô'nĕ), peak (5,006 ft.) in Umbrian Apennines, N central Italy, 13 mi. SW of Urbino.

Nerópolis (nĭrô'pŏŏlĕs), city (pop. 1,226), S Goiás, central Brazil, 40 mi. NNE of Goiânia; extension of railroad from Anápolis under construction here.

Neroy, Russian SFSR: see NEROI.

Ner River (nĕr), central Poland, rises 6 mi. ESE of Lodz, flows c.70 mi. generally NW, past S suburbs of Lodz, Konstantynow Lodzki, and Dabie, to Warta R. 5 mi. S of Kolo.

Nersac (nĕrsäk'), village (pop. 495), Charente dept., W France, on Charente R. and 5 mi. WSW of Angoulême; felt processing (for pulp).

Nerstrand (nûr'strănd), village (pop. 228), Rice co., SE Minn., 11 mi. ENE of Faribault; dairy products.

Nerva (nĕr'vä), town (pop. 14,290), Huelva prov., SW Spain, in Andalusia, 35 mi. NW of Seville; copper and pyrite (copper-iron) mining center; also manganese deposits. Nerva is the old Ríotinto, a name now given to the mining town 3 mi. WNW.

Nervesa della Battaglia (nĕrvā'zä dĕl-lä bät-tä'lyä), village (pop. 960), Treviso prov., Veneto, N Italy, on Piave R. and 11 mi. N of Treviso; lime- and cementworks.

Nervi (nĕr'vē), town (pop. 4,002), Genova prov., Liguria, N Italy, port on Riviera di Levante, 6 mi. E of Genoa; cotton mills, macaroni factories, distilleries (olive oil, perfume); fisheries; active trade in citrus fruit. Much-frequented winter resort. Forms E boundary of Greater Genoa.

Nerviano (nĕrvyä'nô), town (pop. 5,178), Milano prov., Lombardy, N Italy, on Olona R. and 12 mi. NW of Milan; textile mfg. center; machinery, furniture, starch.

Nervión River (nĕrvyōn'), Vizcaya prov., N Spain, rises in E spurs of the Cantabrian Mts., flows 45 mi. N, past Bilbao (8 mi. upstream), to Bay of Biscay bet. Portugalete and Las Arenas; forms wide estuary (Bilbao Bay). From Bilbao to its mouth, its banks are lined with industrial towns (Baracaldo, Sestao, Alzaga) where Sp. metallurgical industries are concentrated. Navigable to Bilbao (inner harbor) for freighters up to 4,000 tons; outer harbor at head of estuary.

Nes, Netherlands: see NES OP AMELAND.

Nes. 1 Canton, Buskerud co., S Norway: see NESBYEN. **2** Canton, Vest-Agder co., S Norway: see LOGA.

Nes (nās). **1** Village in Holt canton (pop. 3,424), Aust-Agder co., S Norway, 12 mi. NNE of Arendal; production of crucible steel. Noted ironworks since 17th cent. Formerly spelled Naes. At Songe (sông'ŭ), village (pop. 209), 7 mi. ENE, there is lumber and wood-pulp mfg. **2** Village, More og Romsdal co., Norway: see ANDALSNES.

Nesbyen (nās'büün), village (pop. 621) in Nes canton (pop. 2,728), Buskerud co., S Norway, in the Hallingdal, on railroad and 50 mi. NW of Honefoss; communications and cultural center of the Hallingdal. Has folk mus. and old church.

Nescopeck (nĕ'skŭpĕk), borough (pop. 1,907), Luzerne co., E central Pa., 23 mi. SW of Wilkes-Barre and on Susquehanna R., at mouth of Nescopeck Creek. Settled 1786, inc. 1896.

Nescopeck Creek, E central Pa., rises in E Luzerne co., flows c.45 mi. SW and NW to Susquehanna R. at Nescopeck.

Nesebar (nĕ'sĕbŭr), anc. *Mesembria*, city (pop. 2,289), Burgas dist., E Bulgaria, port on rocky peninsula in Black Sea, 17 mi. NE of Burgas; fisheries; vineyards. Connected with a seaside resort on mainland by isthmus 50–75 ft. wide. Has ruins of 6th-9th-cent. episcopal basilicas and numerous medieval churches with interesting frescoes and incrustations. Founded over 2,000 years ago; rich commercial town under Byzantine rule. Called Misivri or Missivri under Turkish rule (15th-19th cent.). Until 1934, Mesemvriya or Mesembria.

Nesflaten (nās'flätŭn), village in Suldal canton, Rogaland co., SW Norway, at NE end of Suldal L. and at S end of the Brattlandsdal, 55 mi. ENE of Haugesund; tourist center. Formerly spelled Naesflaten.

Neshaminy Creek (nĕ'shŭmĭ"nē), SE Pa., rises in central Bucks co., flows c.50 mi. generally SE to Delaware R. 3 mi. SW of Bristol.

Neshava, Poland: see NIESZAWA.

Nesher (nĕ'shĕr), settlement (pop. 1,500), NW Israel, in Kishon R. valley, at E foot of Mt. Carmel, 5 mi. SE of Haifa; cement-mfg. center. Founded 1926. Just S is small settlement of Yajur.

Neshime (nāshē'mā) or **Nejime** (nājē'mā), town (pop. 12,878), Kagoshima prefecture, S Kyushu, Japan, on S Osumi Peninsula, on SE shore of Kagoshima Bay 34 mi. SSE of Kagoshima; commercial center for agr. area (rice, wheat, barley); raw silk. Site of an old feudal castle. Until 1943, called Koneshime.

Neshkoro (nĕshkô'rŭ), village (pop. 361), Marquette co., central Wis., on small White R. and 33 mi. W of Oshkosh, in livestock and dairy area.

Neshoba (nĭ-shō'bŭ), county (□ 568; pop. 25,730), E central Miss.; ⊙ Philadelphia. Drained by Pearl R. and tributaries. Includes Choctaw Indian reservation. Agr. (cotton, corn, fruit); lumbering. Formed 1833.

Neskaupstadur or **Neskaupstadhur** (nĕs'kŭüpstä"-dhŭr), Icelandic *Neskaupstaður*, city (pop. 1,320) in but independent of Sudur-Mula co., E Iceland, on Nord Fjord, Icelandic *Norðfjörður* (7-mi.-long inlet of Atlantic); 65°9'N 13°41'W; fishing center, with fish freezing, curing, and canning plants.

Nesle (nāl), village (pop. 1,868), Somme dept., N France, 12 mi. S of Péronne; agr. market; distilling, metalworking.

Nesna (nās'nä), village (pop. 532; canton pop. 3,459), Nordland co., N central Norway, on N shore of Ran Fjord, 30 mi. WSW of Mo; herring fishing and canning, fish-oil and peat processing; cattle raising, agr.

Nes op Ameland (nĕs' ôp ä'mülänt) or **Nes,** village (pop. 782), Friesland prov., N Netherlands, on Ameland isl. and 13 mi. NW of Dokkum; seaside resort; dairying. Ferry to Holwerd.

Nesowadnehunk Lake (nĕsüwäd'nĭhŭngk), Piscataquis co., central Maine, 32 mi. NNW of Millinocket, near W boundary of Baxter State Park; 3 mi. long, 1 mi. wide. Source of **Nesowadnehunk Stream,** which flows S to West Branch of Penobscot R. Formerly known as Sourdnahunk L.

Nespelem (nĕspē'lŭm), town (pop. 425), Okanogan co., N Wash., in Colville Indian Reservation, 30 mi. SE of Okanogan; Indian Agency hq. for Colville and Spokane reservations.

Nesquehoning (nĕskwŭhō'nĭng), village (pop. 4,186, with adjacent New Columbus), E Pa., 3 mi. W of Mauch Chunk; anthracite.

Ness, England: see NESTON.

Ness, county (□ 1,081; pop. 6,322), W central Kansas; ⊙ Ness City. Rolling prairie region, watered by Walnut Creek. Grain, livestock. Formed 1880.

Ness, Loch (lŏkh nĕs'), long, narrow lake in central and N Inverness, Scotland, part of the Caledonian Canal and extending 24 mi. NE-SW along the Great Glen of Scotland bet. Fort Augustus (SW) and Lochend (NE), 6 mi. SW of Inverness. Outlet: Ness R., flowing 7 mi. NNE to Moray Firth. Inlets: Oich R. at Fort Augustus, Enrick R. at Strone, and small Foyers R. at Foyers. Average width of loch is 1 mi., maximum depth 754 ft.; it is remarkably ice-free. Its shore is lined by mts., notably Mealfourvonie (2,284 ft.). In 1933 and later there were press accounts of a "monster," 40–50 ft. long, which was said to have been seen in the loch.

Ness City, city (pop. 1,612), ⊙ Ness co., W central Kansas, on headstream of Walnut Creek and c.60 mi. W of Great Bend, in agr. area (grain, poultry, truck); dairying. Oil fields (developed in 1930s) near by. Founded 1878, inc. 1886.

Nesseldorf, Czechoslovakia: see KOPRIVNICE.

Nesselrode, Mount (nĕ'sülrōd) (8,105 ft.), in Coast Range, on boundary bet. SE Alaska and Canada, 50 mi. N of Juneau; 58°58'N 134°19'W.

Nesselwang (nĕ'sülväng), village (pop. 3,227), Swabia, SW Bavaria, Germany, at E foot of Allgäu Alps, 5 mi. NW of Füssen; skiing center (alt. 2,844 ft.); mfg. of drawing and mathematical instruments, brewing, dairying. Chartered 1429.

Nesset, Norway: see RAUSAND.

Nessmersiel (nĕs'mĕrzēl), village (pop. 723), in former Prussian prov. of Hanover, NW Germany, after 1945 in Lower Saxony, in East Friesland, on North Sea, 8 mi. NE of Norden. Ferry to Baltrum.

Nessonvaux (nĕsōvō'), town (pop. 1,042), Liége prov., E Belgium, on Vesdre R. and 8 mi. SE of Liége; wool spinning and weaving.

Ness Point, England: see ROBIN HOOD'S BAY.

Ness Ziona, Israel: see NES TSIYONA.

Nestane or **Nestani** (both: nĕstä'nē), town (pop. 2,487), Arcadia nome, central Peloponnesus, Greece, 9 mi. NNE of Tripolis; livestock (goats, sheep), tobacco, wheat. Formerly called Tsipiana.

Nestemice (nĕsh'tyĕmĭtsĕ), Czech *Neštěmice,* village (pop. 2,705), N Bohemia, Czechoslovakia, on Elbe R., on railroad and 3 mi. ENE of Usti nad Labem; sugar refining; mfg. of soda chemicals and photographic equipment.

Neste River (nĕst), Hautes-Pyrénées dept., SW France, formed by several headstreams near Vielle-Aure, flows 40 mi. through the AURE VALLEY, past Arreau and Saint-Laurent, to the Garonne above Montréjean. A canal (17 mi. long) connects with headwaters of Baïse, Gers and Gimone rivers, irrigating the Lannemezan Plateau.

Nesterov (nyĕ'styĭrŭf), city (1939 pop. 6,608), E Kaliningrad oblast, Russian SFSR, on railroad and 15 mi. E of Gusev; mfg. of agr. implements, dairying, flour milling. Until 1945, in East Prussia where it was called Stallupönen (shtä'lōōpŭnŭn) and, later (1938–45), Ebenrode (ā'bŭnrōdŭ).

Nesterville or **Nestorville,** town (pop. 209), central Ont., on L. Huron, 3 mi. NW of Thessalon; dairying, mixed farming, lumbering.

Nesthorn (nĕst'hôrn), peak (12,533 ft.) in Bernese Alps, S Switzerland, 7 mi. NNW of Brig.

Neston, urban district (1931 pop. 5,676; 1951 census 9,727), on Wirral peninsula, NW Cheshire, England. Includes resort village of Neston, near Dee R. 8 mi. SSW of Birkenhead, and, just NW, resort village of Parkgate. Neston is birthplace of Lady Hamilton, Parkgate that of Sir Wilfred Grenfell. Renamed (1932) from Neston and Parkgate. Just SE of Neston village is market village and parish (pop. 523) of Ness.

Neston and Parkgate, England: see NESTON.

Nestorion (nĕstôr'ēōn), town (pop. 3,197), Kastoria nome, Macedonia, Greece, on upper Aliakmon R. and 13 mi. SW of Kastoria; charcoal burning; wheat, beans, skins. Formerly called Nestramion.

Nestorville, Ont.: see NESTERVILLE.

Nestos River, Bulgaria and Greece: see MESTA RIVER.

Nestramion, Greece: see NESTORION.

Nes Tsiyona or **Ness Ziona** (both: nĕs' tsēyōnä'), settlement (1949 pop. 5,000), W Israel, in Judaean Plain, 10 mi. SSE of Tel Aviv; textile milling; citriculture. Founded 1883. Sometimes spelled Nes Ziona.

Nesttun (nĕst'tōōn), village (pop. 8,692) in Fana canton, Hordaland co., SW Norway, 5 mi. S of Bergen; junction of Oslo-Bergen RR with narrow-gauge spur to Os; woolen-milling center. Formerly spelled Nedsttun.

Nestus River, Bulgaria and Greece: see MESTA RIVER.

Nesvetevich, Ukrainian SSR: see PROLETARSK, Voroshilovgrad oblast.

Nesvizh (nyĕsvēsh'), Pol. *Nieświeź* (nyĕsh'vyĕsh), city (1948 pop. over 10,000), E Baranovichi oblast, Belorussian SSR, 28 mi. ENE of Baranovichi; cement mfg., agr. processing (flaxseed, grain, potatoes, hops, powdered milk), hatmaking. Has 16th-cent. castle and several old churches. Developed as ⊙ independent Pol. duchy (13th–14th cent.); chartered 1586; suffered from Swedish assaults (1654, 1706). Passed (1793) from Poland to Russia; reverted (1921) to Poland; ceded to USSR in 1945.

Nes Ziona, Israel: see NES TSIYONA.

Netaim or **Neta'im** (both: nĕtä-ēm'), settlement (pop. 175), W Israel, in Judaean Plain, 2 mi. SW of Rishon le Zion; mixed farming, citriculture. Has children's home. Founded 1932.

Netawaka (nĕtüwä'kŭ), city (pop. 213), Jackson co., NE Kansas, 35 mi. N of Topeka; cattle, grain.

Netcong (nĕt'kŏng), borough (pop. 2,284), Morris co., N N.J., near L. Musconetcong, in resort area; mfg. (machinery, clothing), railroad repair shops; stone quarries; agr. (poultry, fruit, truck, dairy products). Transoceanic radio-telephone station here; state park near by. Inc. 1894; grew as residence for iron miners and ironworkers.

Nete River, Belgium: see NÈTHE RIVER.

Nethem or **Nethen** (nā'tŭm, -ŭn), agr. village (pop. 1,343), Brabant prov., central Belgium, 7 mi. S of Louvain.

Netherbury, agr. village and parish (pop. 1,065), W Dorset, England, on Brit R. just SSW of Beaminster. Has 14th- and 15th-cent. churches.

Nether Denton, parish (pop. 312), NE Cumberland, England. Includes coal-mining village of Low Ros, 13 mi. ENE of Carlisle.

Netherfield, England: see CARLTON.

Nether Haddon, England: see HADDON HALL.

Nèthe River (nĕt), Flemish *Nete* (nā'tŭ), NE Belgium; formed at Lierre by confluencee of GRANDE NÈTHE RIVER and PETITE NÈTHE RIVER; flows 11 mi. SW and W, past Duffel, joining Dyle R. at Rumpst to form RUPEL RIVER.

Netherland Island, Ellice Isls.: see NUI.

Netherlands (nĕ'dhŭrlŭndz), Du. *Nederland* (nā'dŭrlänt) or *Nederlanden* (-ländŭn), popularly **Holland,** kingdom (land area alone □ 12,868; with minor inland waters □ 13,025; with the Ijsselmeer and other coastal inlets □ 15,765; pop. 9,625,499), NW Europe; constitutional ⊙ AMSTERDAM, though de facto ⊙ is The HAGUE, where are the royal residence, seat of govt., and parliament. A constitutional monarchy divided into 11 provs., it is largest of the Low Countries. Borders W and N on the North Sea (from which a great part of its land has been wrested), S on Belgium, and E on Germany, bet. 50°45'–53°32'N and 3°20'–7°12'E. Greatest length N-S c.190 mi., E-W c.120 mi. England lies c.110 mi. W across the sea. The Netherlands forms the lowest section of the great N European plain, which reaches into Russia. The country extends bet. the Scheldt (SW) and Ems (NE) estuaries, virtually consisting of the delta of the Rhine and Meuse with their numerous arms, e.g., Ijssel, Lek, Waal, Lower Rhine. Apart from the more elevated SE section in Limburg prov. (rising to c.1,000 ft.), the country is the result of deposition of glacial and alluvial matter. In a certain sense it is also man-made, since about ¼ of the land—the so-called *polders*—lies below sea level (up to 21 ft. below) and has to be protected from incursions of the sea by an ingenious system of dikes, windmills, pumping stations, sluices, and ditches, without which approximately 40% of the entire surface would be flooded. In recent times large areas have been added through drainage. The greatest draining and reclamation has taken place in the Zuider Zee (now reduced to the freshwater body called *Ijsselmeer*). A long dam, the *Afsluitdijk* (c.20 mi. long, 300 ft. wide), now cuts across the entrance to the old Zuider Zee, joining the prov. of North Holland with Friesland. Newly settled is the reclaimed WIERINGERMEER POLDER below Wieringen isl., just S of the dam. The N tidal lands (*Wadden*) are fringed by the West FRISIAN ISLANDS. There are numerous isls. in the delta of Zeeland prov. (SW), notably the fertile WALCHEREN, which, like other vital sections, was inundated during Second World War and has since been again reclaimed. The country is traversed by an intricate network of canals (4,817 mi.), handling much of the inland trade, feeding the harbors through elaborate systems in the cities, and interconnecting with the canals and rivers of Germany and Belgium. Through the navigable Rhine delta, the country shares Europe's major waterway, at whose head (on NEW WATERWAY canal) is ROTTERDAM, one of the largest ports of Europe, with an enormous volume in transit trade. Almost as important as a port is Amsterdam (now linked directly by NORTH SEA CANAL with the ocean), where passenger and cargo ships call. The climate of the Netherlands is typically maritime, influenced by the Gulf Stream, though somewhat colder than England at same latitudes. Heavy fogs and violent winds occur frequently. Average annual temp. is about 50°F. While humidity often exceeds 80%, rainfall amounts only to 28 in. Physiographically, and hence agriculturally and demographically, there are 3 regions: an elevated strip of sand dunes along W coast (c.30–100 ft. and more high), largely occupied by a string of cities; the adjoining low, intensively cultivated *polders* reaching into the interior; and the eastern section, once a sandy heath land with peat bogs, now rendered productive by the use of fertilizer. The hilly Limburg prov. (SE) possesses older soil and is the source of Holland's only major mineral resources, coal and coke, which suffice for home consumption. Some crude petroleum is extracted at OUD SCHOONEBEEK (Drenthe prov.); salt from BOEKELO and HENGELO (Overijssel prov.). The Netherlands has evolved as an emporium for the continent, and, despite popular conceptions, the country's income depends rather on trade and industry than on agr. However, farming plays an important part in the well-balanced economic structure of the overpopulated (723 per sq. mi.) nation; 41% of the land is given to pasture, 28% to agr., and another 3% to intensive horticulture; 8% are forests. Few of the farms exceed 50 acres. High productivity of Dutch agr. is maintained by importation of fertilizers and fodder. The large agr. exports include potatoes, cheese, butter, canned and powdered milk, about 50% of its vegetables, and c.90% of its flower bulbs. Among other crops are rye, oats, barley, sugar beets, turnips, carrots, peas, flax. Wheat is grown chiefly in the provs. of Groningen (NE) and Zeeland (SW). Horticulture (tulips, hyacinths, narcissus; seeds, shrubs; nurseries) is centered on BOSKOOP and AALSMEER near HAARLEM. The WESTLAND region bet. The Hague and Rotterdam has extensive hothouses, where, irrespective of climate, grapes, fruit, vegetables, and flowers thrive. Dairying and cattle raising are, however, the most important primary industry; specially famed is the Dutch cheese traded at colorful markets of GOUDA, ALKMAAR, and EDAM. Most of the commercial and industrial activity is carried on in the W maritime provs. Approximately 30% of income is derived from industry, which employs 39% of the available labor. Holland's heavy industries make it an important producer of steel. It exports c.200,000 tons of iron annually. There are blast furnaces at IJMUIDEN at ocean entrance of North Sea Canal, rolling mills at adjoining (E) VELSEN. UTRECHT—seat of a fair dating back to 12th cent.—turns out steel and aluminum and has major railroad shops. Shipbuilding, one of the leading industries (the nation has the world's 4th largest merchant fleet), is concentrated at Amsterdam, Rotterdam, SCHIEDAM, VLAARDINGEN, DORTRECHT. ZAANDAM, with its lumberworks and shipwrights, is renowned for the residence there of Peter the Great. All the big W cities have textile, chemical, and engineering works. Amsterdam, one of the world's banking centers, is also a leading diamond-cutting center. DELFT is famous for its chinaware. HILVERSUM (hq. of radio stations) has mfg. of radio and electrical appliances. Textile and leather industries are located in the interior cities of S and E Netherlands: TILBURG, s'HERTOGENBOSCH, NIJMEGEN (imperial city of Charlemagne), ARNHEM (scene of Second World War airborne invasion), EINDHOVEN (noted for electronic industry), BREDA (historic ⊙ North Brabant). MAASTRICHT (an old fortress) and HEERLEN are the chief towns of coal-mining S Limburg. GRONINGEN (⊙ Groningen prov.) and LEEUWARDEN (⊙ Friesland prov.) are trading centers of dairying NE section. The Netherlands owns modern fishing fleets, catching principally herring and operating from Vlaardingen, Ijmuiden, SCHEVENINGEN, and other coastal towns. Scheveningen is also a popular beach resort just outside The Hague. Other popular seaside places are NOORDWIJK near Leiden and ZANDVOORT near Haarlem. The zeal and neatness of the homogeneous Dutch people has turned the flat, inherently monotonous country into an attractive landscape of green pastures, canals, drawbridges, and windmills, interspersed by teeming cities, which are unsurpassed in their architectural (both medieval and modern) charm. The famous art collections of Amsterdam, Haarlem, and The Hague treasure some of the world's great paintings, chiefly by Dutch masters, such as Rembrandt, Hals, Vermeer, Van Gogh, and a host of others. There are 4 public universities—at Amsterdam, Groningen, LEIDEN (founded 1575), Utrecht; a Calvinist univ. at Amsterdam; and a

R.C. univ. at Nijmegen. WAGENINGEN has an agr. acad., Tilburg and Rotterdam schools of economics. Illiteracy is almost unknown. Religion, which plays an important part in the people's life, is divided among Protestants (47%), Catholics (31%), and 20 other sects and denominations. The Netherlands had no unified political history before the 16th cent. The region left of the Rhine formed part of the Roman prov. of Lower Germany and was inhabited by the Batavi; on the right bank were the Germanic Frisians. Became part of Charlemagne's empire (768–814) and passed by Treaty of Verdun (843) to Lotharingia, and thus to Holy Roman Empire. After 10th cent. the region was ruled by powerful counts of Holland. In 15th cent. Holland, Zeeland, Gelderland, and Brabant passed to dukes of Burgundy. The rising cities and ports enjoyed autonomous privileges. The region was acquired through marriage by the Hapsburgs. Charles V made the prosperous provs. over (1555) to his son Philip II of Spain. Reformation had begun in 1517. Philip's attempt to introduce the Inquisition encountered determined opposition. Struggle for independence of Low Countries, which broke out in 1568, was fought mainly in Flanders and Brabant, while the northern provs. (i.e., present Netherlands), under William the Silent, prince of Orange, succeeded early in expelling the Sp. garrisons. The southern provs. were reconquered. The 7 northern provs.—Holland, Zeeland, Utrecht, Gelderland, Overijssel, Friesland, Groningen—drew together (1579) in the Union of Utrecht and declared (1581) their independence, recognized (1648) after Thirty Years War, when Spain ceded North Brabant with Breda and part of Limburg with Maastricht. While struggling for their independence, Dutch laid foundation for commercial and colonial empire. Dutch East India Co. was founded in 1602, the Dutch West India Co. in 1621. New Amsterdam, later New York, was settled in 1612, Batavia in 1619. Du. vessels captured major share of world's carrying trade. The country opened its doors to religious refugees, who contributed to its 17th-cent. prosperity. In same century Du. art reached its peak, but wars with England (1552–54; 1664–67) and France raged almost continuously. There was also civil strife bet. monarchist (favoring hereditary *stadholders* of Orange) and republican factions, the latter brilliantly led by De Witt. In 1689 William III of Orange became king of England. In French Revolutionary Wars the Netherlands was overrun (1794–95) by the French, who set up the Batavian Republic. Napoleon made (1806) his brother Louis Bonaparte king of Holland, but deposed him in 1810, when country was annexed to France. At Congress of Vienna (1814–15) former United Provs. and former Austrian Netherlands were united as kingdom under William I. In 1830 Belgium rebelled and declared its independence. Final agreement was made in 1839. The Netherlands was neutral in First World War, but it was invaded (May, 1940) by Germany during Second World War, when a vicious air attack wantonly destroyed Rotterdam, which had been declared an open city. Queen Wilhelmina and her govt. fled abroad. Indonesia was lost (1942) to Japan. German collapse (May, 1945) was followed by speedy recovery of the Netherlands. One of the original United Nations, the Netherlands joined (1947) in close alliance (the Benelux bloc) with Belgium and Luxembourg. The 3 neighboring countries concluded (1948) Five Power Pact with England and France, and participated in European Recovery Program and North Atlantic Pact. A major post-war problem was the uprising of INDONESIA, where a republic was proclaimed (1945), though nominally remaining a partner in Netherlands-Indonesia Union under Du. sovereign. Integral part of the Union of the Netherlands are the territories in the Western Hemisphere: Dutch GUIANA or Surinam, and the Dutch or Netherlands Antilles (called CURAÇAO territory until 1949), which include the isls. of Curaçao, ARUBA, BONAIRE, SABA, SAINT EUSTATIUS, and S half of SAINT MARTIN. For further information, see individual articles on cities, towns, physical features, and the 11 provs.: NORTH BRABANT, DRENTHE, FRIESLAND, GELDERLAND, GRONINGEN, NORTH HOLLAND, SOUTH HOLLAND, LIMBURG, UTRECHT, OVERIJSSEL, ZEELAND.

Netherlands Antilles, West Indies: see CURAÇAO.

Netherlands East Indies: see INDONESIA.

Netherlands Guiana: see GUIANA, DUTCH.

Netherlands New Guinea: see NEW GUINEA, NETHERLANDS.

Netherlands West Indies: see CURAÇAO; WEST INDIES.

Nether Stowey, agr. village and parish (pop. 564), W central Somerset, England, 7 mi. WNW of Bridgwater. Has 15th-cent. manor house. Here Coleridge lived for some time and wrote *The Ancient Mariner*.

Netherthong, England: see HOLMFIRTH.

Netherton. **1** Village and parish (pop. 535), SW Lancashire, England, on Leeds-Liverpool Canal and 6 mi. N of Liverpool; mfg. of chemicals, soap; truck gardening. **2** Town, Northumberland, England: see BEDLINGTONSHIRE. **3** Town, Worcestershire, England: see DUDLEY. **4** Town in Shitlingthorpe parish (pop. 3,410), West Riding, S Yorkshire, England, near Calder R. 4 mi. SW of Wakefield; coal mining. **5** Village in SOUTH CROSLAND urban dist., West Riding, SW Yorkshire, England, 3 mi. SW of Huddersfield; woolen milling.

Netherwitton, village and parish (pop. 139), central Northumberland, England, 7 mi. WNW of Morpeth; woolen milling.

Néthou, Pic de, NE Spain: see ANETO, PICO DE.

Nethy Bridge, agr. village, E Inverness, Scotland, on small Nethy R., a tributary of the Spey, and 5 mi. SSW of Grantown-on-Spey. Near by are ruins of anc. Castle Roy, a former stronghold of the Comyns.

Netkachi, Russian SFSR: see MOKRAYA OLKHOVKA.

Netley, village, S Hampshire, England, on Southampton Water, 3 mi. SE of Southampton. Has ruins of Cistercian abbey, established c.1240 by Henry III. Royal Victoria Hosp., here, one of the chief military hospitals in England, was built after Crimean War.

Netley Marsh, agr. village and parish (pop. 2,074), S Hampshire, England, 6 mi. W of Southampton.

Netolice (nĕ'tôlĭtsĕ), Ger. *Nettolitz* or *Netolitz*, town (pop. 2,066), S Bohemia, Czechoslovakia, 14 mi. WNW of Budweis, in moor and lake region; rail terminus; dray-horse breeding. Graphite and strontianite mining near by.

Neto River (nä'tô), in Calabria, S Italy, rises in La Sila mts. on Botte Donato, flows 52 mi. E, SE, and E to Gulf of Taranto 9 mi. N of Crotone. The Neto and its tributaries, the ARVO and AMPOLLINO, are major hydroelectric power sources (plants near SAN GIOVANNI IN FIORE and COTRONEI).

Netrakona (nātrŭkō'nŭ), town (pop. 14,180), Mymensingh dist., E central East Bengal, E Pakistan, 21 mi. ENE of Mymensingh; rice, jute, oilseeds.

Netravati River (nāträ'vŭtē), South Kanara dist., W Madras, India, rises in Western Ghats near W Mysore border, flows S and W past Bantval to Malabar Coast of Arabian Sea at Mangalore; 60 mi. long. Navigable for c.40 mi. above mouth.

Netstal (nĕts'täl), town (pop. 2,250), Glarus canton, E central Switzerland, at junction of the Löntschbach with the Linth R., 2 mi. N of Glarus; cotton textiles, paper; metalworking, cement works. Löntsch hydroelectric plant is here.

Nettapakkam (nĕ'tŭpŭkŭm), Fr. *Nettapacom* (nĕtäpäkôm'), town (commune pop. 14,423), Pondicherry settlement, Fr. India, 13 mi. SW of Pondicherry; rice, plantain, sugar cane.

Nettilling Lake (70 mi. long, 65 mi. wide), SW Baffin Isl., SE Franklin Dist., Northwest Territories; 66°30'N 71°W. Borders W on the Great Plain of the Koukdjuak. Drained W into Foxe Basin.

Nett Lake (□ 11), in Koochiching and St. Louis counties, N Minn., in Nett Lake Indian Reservation, 35 mi. SSE of International Falls; 6 mi. long, 4 mi. wide. Drains through small stream into Little Fork R. Nett Lake village is small Indian community on E shore of lake.

Nettlebed, agr. village and parish (pop. 519), SE Oxfordshire, England, 9 mi. N of Reading; farm implements.

Nettleton. **1** Town (pop. 1,382), Craighead co., NE Ark., 2 mi. ESE of Jonesboro; ships farm produce. Founded 1881. **2** Town (pop. 1,204), on Lee-Monroe co. line, E Miss., 13 mi. SSE of Tupelo; clothing mfg.

Nettolitz, Czechoslovakia: see NETOLICE.

Nettuno (nĕt-tōō'nô), town (pop. 8,598), Roma prov., Latium, S central Italy, on Tyrrhenian Sea, 2 mi. NE of Anzio. Bathing resort; fishing; alcohol distilling. Severely damaged in Second World War. Near by is chief American military cemetery in Italy, with c.7,400 dead of the ANZIO-Nettuno battle.

Netze River, Poland: see NOTEC RIVER.

Netzschkau (nĕch'kou), town (pop. 8,138), Saxony, E central Germany, 9 mi. NE of Plauen; textile (wool, cotton, silk, rayon) and paper milling, machinery mfg. Has 15th-cent. castle.

Neu (nä'ōō), town (pop. 3,834), Tottori prefecture, S Honshu, Japan, 15 mi. SSE of Yonago, in agr. area (rice, wheat, tobacco), livestock; charcoal, raw silk.

Neualbenreuth (noi"äl'bûnroit), village (pop. 1,581), Upper Palatinate, NE Bavaria, Germany, in Bohemian Forest, 6 mi. ESE of Waldsassen, on Czechoslovak border; grain, livestock.

Neubabelsberg, Germany: see BABELSBERG.

Neubau (noi'bou), district (□ .6; pop. 53,392) of Vienna, Austria, just W of city center.

Neubeckum (noi"bĕ'kōōm), village (pop. 6,421), in former Prussian prov. of Westphalia, NW Germany, after 1945 in North Rhine-Westphalia, 3 mi. NNW of Beckum; rail junction; cement works.

Neu Bentschen, Poland: see ZBASZYNEK.

Neuberg (noi'bĕrk), town (pop. 2,429), Styria, E Austria, at S foot of the Schneealpe, on Mürz R. and 6 mi. NNW of Mürzzuschlag; rail terminus; iron- and steelworks; summer resort. Magnesite mined near by.

Neu Bidschow, Czechoslovakia: see NOVY BYDZOV.

Neubistritz, Czechoslovakia: see NOVA BYSTRICE.

Neubourg, Le (lû nûbōōr'), town (pop. 2,096), Eure dept., NW France, 14 mi. NW of Évreux; market; mfg. of agr. machinery and furniture. Its 16th-cent. church damaged in 1940.

Neubrandenburg (noi"brän'dûnbōōrk), town (pop. 20,446), Mecklenburg, N Germany, on Tollense R. and 50 mi. S of Stralsund, 70 mi. N of Berlin, near N tip of Tollense L.; rail center; metalworking, paper milling; mfg. of machinery, chemicals, leather, construction materials. Heavily bombed in Second World War (destruction about 30%). Has 14th-cent. church, 14th-cent. town walls and gates, 18th-cent. palace and town hall. Founded 1248 as fortified outpost by margraves of Brandenburg; passed to Mecklenburg in 1292. Was ⊙ (1359–1471) duchy of Mecklenburg-Stargard.

Neubreisach, France: see NEUF-BRISACH.

Neubrunn (noi'brōōn), village (pop. 1,753), Lower Franconia, NW Bavaria, Germany, 12 mi. WSW of Würzburg; vegetables.

Neubukow (noi"bōō'kō), town (pop. 4,102), Mecklenburg, N Germany, near Mecklenburg Bay of the Baltic, 13 mi. NE of Wismar; agr. market (grain, sugar beets, potatoes, stock). Archaeologist Schliemann b. here.

Neubulach (noi"bōō'läkh), town (pop. 689), S Württemberg, Germany, after 1945 in Württemberg-Hohenzollern, in Black Forest, 4 mi. SSW of Calw; summer resort (alt. 1,916 ft.).

Neuburg (noi'bōōrk). **1** or **Neuburg an der Donau** (än dĕr dō'nou), city (1950 pop. 14,583), Swabia, central Bavaria, Germany, on the Danube and 11 mi. W of Ingolstadt; textile mfg., metalworking, printing; silica quarrying. Has castle and baroque city hall. It was ⊙ former principality of Neuburg (1507–1685). **2** or **Neuburg am Rhein** (äm rīn'), village (1946 pop. 1,827), Rhenish Palatinate, W Germany, on the Rhine, at mouth of the Lauter, and 6 mi. WSW of Karlsruhe, near French border; grain, tobacco.

Neuchâtel (nûshätĕl'), Ger. *Neuenburg* (noi'ûnbōōrk"), canton (□ 309; 1950 pop. 127,205), W Switzerland, in the Jura; ⊙ Neuchâtel. Forests, meadows, with some pastures (cattle) and cultivated fields, producing cheese and cotton goods; vineyards on shores of L. of Neuchâtel. Rich asphalt deposits in Valde Travers. Mfg. (chiefly watches and cutlery), notably at Le Locle and La Chaux-de-Fonds. Neuchâtel remained on autonomous principality until 1848, although in 1815 it joined Swiss Confederation, with which it had been allied since 15th cent. Pop. largely French speaking and Protestant.

Neuchâtel, Ger. *Neuenburg*, town (1950 pop. 27,573), ⊙ Neuchâtel, W Switzerland, on N shore of L. of Neuchâtel, at mouth of short Seyon R., on slopes (alt. 1,444 ft.) of the Jura. A Burgundian town by the 11th cent., Neuchâtel was later governed by counts under the Holy Roman Empire; a sovereign principality from 1648 to 1707; then under nominal Prussian rule. In 1815 became the capital of the newly admitted canton. Produces chocolate, tobacco, watches, paper; metal- and woodworking, printing. Noted for its univ. (originally founded 1838), Collège Latin (with mus. and town library), and a school of commerce. Important bldgs.: castle (12th-17th cent.) with governmental offices, church (12th-13th cent.) with Romanesque cloisters, mus. of fine arts, town hall; numerous statues, fountains, and old structures. Cable railways lead to the Crêt du Plan (1,833 ft.) and the Chaumont (3,862 ft.), noted for fine views. Cantonal observatory is NE of town.

Neuchâtel, Lake of, Ger. *Neuenburgersee* (noi'ûnbōōrgûrzā"), anc. *Lacus Eburodunensis*, W Switzerland, bordering on cantons of Neuchâtel, Bern, Fribourg, and Vaud; 24 mi. long, 4-5 mi. wide, alt. 1,407 ft., max. depth 502 ft.; extends SW–NE. The Jura rise on W and N shores; fine views of the Alps (E and S). Thièle or Zihl R. traverses lake from SW to NE and flows, as Thièle or Zihl Canal, to L. Biel. Broye R. enters lake (NE), connecting it with L. of Morat. Several steamer lines. Main towns on lake, NEUCHÂTEL and YVERDON.

Neudamm, Poland: see DEBNO.

Neudeck (noi'dĕk), Pol. *Podzamek* (pôdzä'mĕk), estate in East Prussia, after 1945 in Gdansk prov., N Poland, 19 mi. ESE of Marienwerder. Formerly country estate of Hindenburg family; Paul von Hindenburg d. here. Until 1919, it was in West Prussia.

Neudek, Czechoslovakia: see NEJDEK.

Neudenau (noi'dûnou), town (pop. 1,845), N Baden, Germany, after 1945 in Württemberg-Baden, on the Jagst and 7 mi. SE of Mosbach; cucumbers, sugar beets.

Neudorf (nū'dôrf), village (pop. 385), SE Sask., 17 mi. SW of Melville; mixed farming, stock.

Neudorf, Czechoslovakia: see SPISSKA NOVA VES.

Neudorf, France: see VILLAGE-NEUF.

Neudörfl (noi'dûrfûl), town (pop. 2,240), Burgenland, E Austria, 2 mi. E of Wiener Neustadt; cotton mills.

Neue Elde River, Germany: see ELDE RIVER.

Neueibau, Germany: see EIBAU.

Neuenahr, Bad, Germany: see BAD NEUENAHR.

Neuenberg an der Elbe, Czechoslovakia: see NYMBURK.

Neuenburg (noi'ŭnbŏŏrk), village (pop. 1,548), S Baden, Germany, on the Rhine (Fr. border; rail bridge) and 18 mi. SW of Freiburg; customs station; lumber milling. In Second World War, village was badly destroyed.
Neuenbürg (–bürk), town (pop. 3,067), S Württemberg, Germany, after 1945 in Württemberg-Hohenzollern, on N slope of Black Forest, on the Enz and 6 mi. SW of Pforzheim; summer resort. Has 16th-cent. castle; ruins of 12th–13th-cent. castle.
Neuenburg, Poland: see NOWE.
Neuenburg, Switzerland: see NEUCHÂTEL.
Neuenburgersee, Switzerland: see NEUCHÂTEL, LAKE OF.
Neuende, Germany: see RÜSTRINGEN.
Neuenegg (noi'ŭnĕk″), town (pop. 2,587), Bern canton, W Switzerland, on Sense R. and 8 mi. WSW of Bern; flour.
Neuengamme, Germany: see VIERLANDE.
Neuenhagen (–hä″gŭn), village (pop. 11,656), Brandenburg, E Germany, 12 mi. E of Berlin; market gardening; horse breeding.
Neuenhaus (–hous″), town (pop. 2,412), in former Prussian prov. of Hanover, NW Germany, after 1945 in Lower Saxony, near the Vechte, 6 mi. NW of Nordhorn, near Dutch border; textile mfg.
Neuenkirch (–kĭrkh″), town (pop. 2,615), Lucerne canton, central Switzerland, 6 mi. NW of Lucerne.
Neuenkirchen (–kĭr″khŭn), village (pop. 7,486), in former Prussian prov. of Westphalia, NW Germany, after 1945 in North Rhine-Westphalia, 4 mi. SW of Rheine; dairying.
Neuenrade (–rä'dŭ), town (pop. 4,152), in former Prussian prov. of Westphalia, W Germany, after 1945 in North Rhine-Westphalia, 4.5 mi. ESE of Altena; metalworking.
Neuenstadt or **Neuenstadt am Kocher** (noi'ŭn-shtät äm kô'khŭr), town (pop. 1,349), N Württemberg, Germany, after 1945 in Württemberg-Baden, on the Kocher and 8 mi. NE of Heilbronn; food processing. Has 16th-cent. castle.
Neuenstadt, Switzerland: see NEUVEVILLE.
Neuenstein (–shtīn), town (pop. 2,080), N Württemberg, Germany, after 1945 in Württemberg-Baden, 16 mi. ENE of Heilbronn; wine. Has Renaissance castle.
Neuerburg (noi'ŭrbŏŏrk), town (pop. 1,480), in former Prussian Rhine Prov., W Germany, after 1945 in Rhineland-Palatinate, in the Eifel, 24 mi. NW of Trier, 6 mi. W of Luxembourg border. Has ruined 13th-cent. castle.
Neuern, Czechoslovakia: see NYRSKO.
Neufahrwasser, Poland: see NOWY PORT.
Neuf-Brisach (nûbrēzäk'), Ger. *Neubreisach* (noi-brī'zäkh), village (pop. 1,138), Haut-Rhin dept., E France, on Rhone-Rhine Canal, near the Rhine, and 9 mi. SE of Colmar; custom station near Ger. border opposite Breisach; vegetable and snail canning. Built (17th cent.) by Vauban as a frontier fortress. Here last Ger. resistance W of the Rhine collapsed in Feb., 1945, during Second World War.
Neufchâteau (nûf-shätō'), town (pop. 2,598), Luxembourg prov., SE Belgium, in the Ardennes, 20 mi. NW of Arlon; market center for potato-growing area; cattle and horse market.
Neufchâteau (nûshätō'), town (pop. 3,895), Vosges dept., E France, on Meuse R. and 32 mi. SW of Nancy; road center and agr. market. Produces carved furniture and toys. Has 2 medieval churches and a 16th-cent. town hall. Just above town the Meuse reappears on surface after 2.5-mi. underground flow.
Neufchâtel (nûshätĕl'). **1** Village (pop. 1,772), Pas-de-Calais dept., N France, 8 mi. S of Boulogne; Portland cement works. Damaged in Second World War. **2** or **Neufchâtel-en-Bray** (—ã-brā'), town (pop. 3,335), Seine-Inférieure dept., N France, on the Béthune and 25 mi. NE of Rouen; market center for Bray agr. dist., known for its cheeses. Condensed milk, footwear mfg. Its 12th–16th-cent. church and 16th-cent. wooden houses damaged in Second World War.
Neufchâtel-en-Bray, Seine-Inférieure dept., France: see NEUFCHÂTEL.
Neufchâtel-sur-Aisne (—sür-ān'), agr. village (pop. 443), Aisne dept., N France, on the Aisne and its lateral canal, and 13 mi. N of Rheims.
Neufeld an der Leitha (noi'fĕlt än dĕr lī'tä), town (pop. 2,351), Burgenland, E Austria, 7 mi. W of Eisenstadt; cotton mills.
Neufelden (noi'fĕldŭn), village (pop. 1,123), N Upper Austria, on Grosse Mühl R. (here dammed), 18 mi. NW of Linz, N of the Danube; brewery.
Neuffen (noi'fŭn), town (pop. 3,083), N Württemberg, Germany, after 1945 in Württemberg-Baden, 5 mi. S of Nürtingen; cattle. Has 14th-cent. church; also ruined castle.
Neuffossé Canal (nûfôsā'), Pas-de-Calais dept., N France, bet. Aire and Saint-Omer, a connecting link in Flanders plain canal network; 11 mi. long. Ships agr. produce, coal.
Neufvilles (nûvēl'), village (pop. 2,416), Hainaut prov., SW central Belgium, 3 mi. W of Soignes; granite quarrying.
Neugedein, Czechoslovakia: see KDYNE.
Neugersdorf (noi'gŭrsdôrf), town (pop. 12,526), Saxony, E central Germany, in Upper Lusatia, in Lusatian Mts., 11 mi. NW of Zittau; frontier station on Czechoslovak border, opposite Jirikov; linen- and cotton-milling center; glass and furniture mfg. Spree R. rises just N.
Neuhaldensleben, Germany: see HALDENSLEBEN.
Neu Hannover, Bismarck Archipelago: see LAVONGAI.
Neuhaus, Czechoslovakia: see JINDRICHUV HRADEC.
Neuhaus (noi'hous). **1** Village (pop. 861), Upper Palatinate, NE Bavaria, Germany, on the Fichtelnab (a branch of the Nab) and 9 mi. N of Weiden; grain, livestock. Chartered 1415. **2** or **Neuhaus an der Pegnitz** (än dĕr päg'nĭts), village (pop. 1,812), Upper Palatinate, NE Bavaria, Germany, on the Pegnitz and 20 mi. NW of Amberg; brewing, flour milling; summer resort. Has rococo church. **3** or **Neuhaus an der Oste** (än dĕr ô'stŭ), in former Prussian prov. of Hanover, NW Germany, after 1945 in Lower Saxony, on the Oste and 14 mi. ESE of Cuxhaven; metalworking, distilling. **4** or **Neuhaus am Rennweg** (äm rĕn'väk), town (pop. 4,608), Thuringia, central Germany, in Thuringian Forest, 5 mi. SE of Sonneberg; mfg. of industrial ceramics and glass laboratory equipment. Climatic health resort. Physicist Geissler b. here. **5** Village (pop. 7,887), in former Prussian prov. of Westphalia, NW Germany, after 1945 in North Rhine-Westphalia, 2 mi. NW of Paderborn; pumpernickel. Has 17th-cent. castle.
Neuhaus, Yugoslavia: see DOBRNA.
Neuhäusel, Czechoslovakia: see NOVE ZAMKY.
Neuhausen or **Neuhausen auf den Fildern** (noi'-hou″zŭn ouf dĕn fĭl'dŭrn), village (pop. 3,908), N Württemberg, Germany, after 1945 in Württemberg-Baden, 4 mi. SSW of Esslingen (linked by tramway); grain.
Neuhausen, Russian SFSR: see GURYEVSK, Kaliningrad oblast.
Neuhausen am Rheinfall (äm rīn'fäl), town (pop. 7,402), Schaffhausen canton, N Switzerland, near Ger. border on right (N) bank of the Rhine at the Rheinfall (hydroelectric plants), just SW of Schaffhausen; railway cars, aluminum products, cotton goods (mainly bandages), chemicals (mainly cosmetics). Schloss Laufen (16th cent.) and Schlosschen Wörth, castles on the Rhine, are near by.
Neuhofen (noi'hō″fŭn), village (pop. 3,216), Rhenish Palatinate, W Germany, 4 mi. S of Ludwigshafen; grain, tobacco, sugar beets.
Neuhofen an der Krems (än dĕr krĕms'), town (pop. 3,004), E central Upper Austria, 9 mi. E of Wels; wheat, cattle.
Neuillé-Pont-Pierre (nûyā'-pō-pyâr'), village (pop. 769), Indre-et-Loire dept., W central France, 12 mi. NNW of Tours; rail junction.
Neuilly-en-Thelle (nûyē'-ā-tĕl'), village (pop. 1,499), Oise dept., N France, 13 mi. W of Senlis; rayon mfg.
Neuilly-le-Réal (–lŭ-rāäl'), village (pop. 553), Allier dept., central France, in the Sologne Bourbonnaise, 8 mi. SSE of Moulins; horse raising, sawmilling.
Neuilly-l'Évêque (–lāvĕk'), village (pop. 703), Haute-Marne dept., NE France, in Plateau of Langres, 6 mi. NE of Langres; surgical instruments, vegetable oil.
Neuilly-Plaisance (–plăzăs'), town (pop. 10,162), Seine-et-Oise dept., N central France, an outer E suburb of Paris, 7 mi. from Notre Dame Cathedral; mfg. (candy, brushes, plaster), metalworking.
Neuilly-Saint-Front (–sē-frō'), village (pop. 1,217), Aisne dept., N France, near the Ourcq, 11 mi. NW of Château-Thierry; sugar milling.
Neuilly-sur-Marne (–sür-märn'), town (pop. 6,792), Seine-et-Oise dept., N central France, an outer E suburb of Paris, 8 mi. from Notre Dame Cathedral, on right bank of the Marne; mfg. (rubber, bricks, electric wire, furniture). Insane asylum.
Neuilly-sur-Seine (–sür-sĕn'), city (pop. 58,658), Seine dept., N central France, a fine residential suburb just WNW of Paris, 4 mi. from Notre Dame Cathedral, on right bank of the Seine, bet. Levallois-Perret (NE) and Bois de Boulogne (SSW); auto construction; mfg. (machine tools, rubber, gloves, toys, perfumes). Here peace treaty bet. Allies and Bulgaria was signed in 1919.
Neu-Isenburg (noi″-ē'zŭnbŏŏrk), town (pop. 14,653), S Hesse, W Germany, in former Starkenburg prov., 4 mi. S of Frankfurt; leatherworking, paper milling. Just S is large Rhine-Main airport.
Neukalen (noi″kä'lŭn), town (pop. 4,121), Mecklenburg, N Germany, on the canalized Peene, near Kummerow L., and 6 mi. N of Malchin; agr. market (grain, sugar beets, potatoes, stock).
Neukirch (noi'kĭrkh″), village (pop. 7,563), Saxony, E central Germany, in Upper Lusatia, 11 mi. SW of Bautzen, near Czechoslovak border; cotton milling, woodworking, distilling; mfg. of leather articles, ceramics, biscuits.
Neukirch, Russian SFSR: see TIMIRYAZEVO.
Neukirchen (noi'kĭr″khŭn). **1** or **Neukirchen bei Heiligen Blut** (bī hī″lĭgŭn blōōt'), village (pop. 2,633), Lower Bavaria, Germany, in Bohemian Forest, at NE foot of the Hoher Bogen, 32 mi. NE of Straubing; rye, potatoes, cattle. Has Franciscan monastery (founded 1659), and early-18th-cent. pilgrimage church. **2** Town (pop. 2,671), in former Prussian prov. of Hesse-Nassau, W Germany, after 1945 in Hesse, 2 mi. E of Treysa; lumber milling. Has Gothic church. **3** Village (pop. 12,797), in former Prussian Rhine Prov., W Germany, after 1945 in North Rhine-Westphalia, in the Ruhr, 2 mi. W of Moers, in coal-mining region. Formed 1935 through incorporation of 3 neighboring villages. **4** Village (pop. 8,595), Saxony, E central Germany, 5 mi. SW of Chemnitz; hosiery knitting. **5** Village (pop. 1,056), Saxony, E central Germany, 3.5 mi. SSE of Borna; lignite mining. **6** or **Neukirchen an der Pleisse** (än dĕr plī'sŭ), village (pop. 3,858), Saxony, E central Germany, on the Pleisse and 2 mi. SSW of Crimmitschau; cotton, woolen milling.
Neukirchen an der Vöckla (än dĕr fû'klä), town (pop. 2,488), SW central Upper Austria, 6 mi. WNW of Vöcklabruck; wheat, rye, cattle.
Neukirchen-Balbini (–bälbē'nē), village (pop. 1,290), Upper Palatinate, E Bavaria, Germany, in Bohemian Forest, 15 mi. ESE of Schwandorf; flax, rye, oats, cattle.
Neukirchen bei Heiligen Blut, Germany: see NEUKIRCHEN, Bavaria.
Neukloster (noi'klō″stŭr), town (pop. 4,774), Mecklenburg, N Germany, 9 mi. E of Wismar; agr. market (grain, sugar beets, potatoes, stock); tourist resort. Has 13th-cent. church of former Cistercian convent (founded near by; moved here in 1219; secularized in 16th cent.).
Neukölln (noi″kŭln'), workers' residential district (1939 pop. 303,170; 1946 pop. 274,560), S Berlin, Germany, on Teltow Canal and 5 mi. SSE of city center. Mfg. (machinery, chemicals, clothing). After 1945 in U.S. sector. Formerly Rixdorf.
Neukuhren, Russian SFSR: see PIONERSKI.
Neu-Langenburg, Tanganyika: see TUKUYU.
Neu Lauenburg, Bismarck Archipelago: see DUKE OF YORK ISLANDS.
Neulengbach (noi″lĕng'bäkh), village (pop. 2,304), central Lower Austria, 12 mi. E of Sankt Pölten; wheat, rye, cattle.
Neulise (nûlēz'), village (pop. 672), Loire dept., SE central France, 11 mi. SSE of Roanne; mfg. of silk fabrics.
Neulussheim (noi″lŏŏs'hīm), village (pop. 3,472), N Baden, Germany, after 1945 in Württemberg-Baden, near the Rhine, 4 mi. ESE of Speyer; tobacco, sugar beets, strawberries.
Neum (nĕ'ōōm), hamlet, W Herzegovina, Yugoslavia, on Neretva Channel of Adriatic Sea, 9 mi. S of Metkovic, in narrow corridor providing Herzegovina with outlet to the sea.
Neumark (noi'märk), town (pop. 733), Thuringia, central Germany, 8 mi. NNW of Weimar; grain, sugar beets, livestock.
Neumark, Poland: see NOWE MIASTO, Olsztyn prov.
Neumarkt (noi'märkt), village (pop. 1,982), Styria, S central Austria, at N end of Neumarkt Pass leading into Carinthia, 12 mi. SW of Judenburg; resort (alt. 2,764 ft.).
Neumarkt or **Neumarkt in der Oberpfalz** (ĭn dĕr ō'bŭrpfälts), town (1950 pop. 12,145), Upper Palatinate, central Bavaria, Germany, on Ludwig Canal and 22 mi. SW of Amberg; rail junction; mfg. of chemicals, metal- and woodworking, brewing, lumber and paper milling. Has late-Gothic church, 14th-cent. town hall, 16th-cent. castle. Chartered 1305 as free imperial **city.** Mineral springs near by.
Neumarkt, Italy: see EGNA.
Neumarkt. 1 Town, Krakow prov., Poland: see NOWY TARG. **2** Town, Wroclaw prov., Poland: see SRODA SLASKA.
Neumarkt, Rumania: see TARGU-MURES.
Neumarkt im Mühlkreise (ĭm mül'krīzŭ), town (pop. 2,414), NE Upper Austria, 6 mi. S of Freistadt, N of the Danube; rye, potatoes.
Neumarkt-Köstendorf (–kû'stŭndôrf), town (pop. 3,801), Salzburg, W central Austria, 13 mi. NE of Salzburg; breweries, tanneries.
Neumarktl, Yugoslavia: see TRZIC.
Neumayer Escarpment (noi'mī″ŭr), Antarctica, extends from 74°S 1°15'E to c.73°25'S 0°25'E; constitutes E side of polar plateau of New Schwabenland; highest alt. 12,000 ft. Discovered 1939 by German expedition.
Neu Mecklenburg, Bismarck Archipelago: see NEW IRELAND.
Neumittelwalde, Poland: see MIEDZYBORZ.
Neumühlen-Dietrichsdorf (noi'mü″lŭn-dē'trĭkhs-dôrf″), NE industrial district of Kiel, NW Germany, on E bank of Kiel Firth; mfg. of ship machinery, fishing boats; milling. Heavily damaged in Second World War.
Neumünster (noi'mün″stŭr), city (1950 pop. 73,254), in Schleswig-Holstein, NW Germany, 18 mi. SSW of Kiel; rail center; railroad repair shops; active textile (cloth, knitwear, garments) and leather industries; mfg. of machinery, metalware, chemicals; paper milling. First mentioned 1163. Chartered 1870. Second World War destruction c.35%.
Neunburg or **Neunburg vorm Wald** (noin'bŏŏrk fôrm vält'), town (pop. 4,381), Upper Palatinate, E Bavaria, Germany, in Bohemian Forest, 12 mi. E of Schwandorf; glass grinding, brewing, lumber and flour milling. Has 11th-cent. Romanesque church, 14th–15th-cent. castle. Chartered 1354.
Neundorf (noin'dôrf), village (pop. 4,539), in former Anhalt state, central Germany, after 1945 in

Saxony-Anhalt, 3 mi. S of Stassfurt; potash mining; tarred-paper mfg.

Neung-sur-Beuvron (nŭ-sür-bûvrō'), village (pop. 626), Loir-et-Cher dept., N central France, in the Sologne on Beuvron R. and 12 mi. NNE of Romorantin; woodworking, game hunting.

Neunkirchen (noin'kĭr"khŭn), town (pop. 10,056), SE Lower Austria, on Schwarza R. and 10 mi. SW of Wiener Neustadt; rail junction; textile mills, ironworks, paper mills.

Neunkirchen or **Neunkirchen am Brand** (äm bränt'), village (pop. 1,610), Upper Franconia, N central Bavaria, Germany, 5 mi. E of Erlangen; brewing. Hops, horse-radish. Has 16th-cent. church and town gates.

Neunkirchen, city (pop. 37,250), E Saar, 13 mi. NE of Saarbrücken; rail junction; coal-mining center; iron- and steelworks, coke ovens, breweries; woodworking, shoe mfg. Iron industry here dates from mid-18th cent.

Neunkirch-lès-Sarreguemines (nŭkĕrsh'-lā-särgŭmēn'), Ger. *Neunkirchen* (noin'kĭrkh-ŭn), E suburb (pop. 1,699) of Sarreguemines, Moselle dept., NE France; mfg. of furniture and woodworking machinery.

Neuoderberg, Czechoslovakia: see Novy Bohumin.

Neuoelsburg (noi"ûls'bŏŏrk), village (pop. 2,148), in former Prussian prov. of Hanover, NW Germany, after 1945 in Lower Saxony, 3 mi. S of Peine, in oil dist. In Brunswick exclave until 1941.

Neu-Orsova, Rumania: see Ada-Kaleh.

Neuötting (noi"û'tĭng), town (pop. 5,251), Upper Bavaria, Germany, on the Inn, just NE of Altötting; mfg. of chemicals, brewing, lumber milling, printing. Has late-Gothic church. Chartered in 12th cent.

Neupaka, Czechoslovakia: see Nova Paka.

Neu-Pest, Hungary: see Ujpest.

Neu Petershain (noi" pā'tŭrs-hīn), village (pop. 3,657), Brandenburg, E Germany, in Lower Lusatia, 12 mi. SW of Cottbus; lignite mining; glass mfg.

Neupokoyev, Cape (nyĕŏŏpŭkoi'ŭf), southernmost point of Bolshevik Isl., Severnaya Zemlya archipelago, Krasnoyarsk Territory, Russian SFSR; 77°50'N 99°30'E. Govt. observation post.

Neu Pommern, Bismarck Archipelago: see New Britain.

Neuquén (nĕŏŏkĕn'), national territory (□ 36,429; pop. 86,836), W central Argentina; ⊙ Neuquén. Andean mountainous area bordering Chile, with Limay R. on S and the Río Colorado and Barrancas R. on N; intersected by Neuquén R. In W are numerous volcanoes (e.g., Copahue, Lanín), in SW is the Argentine lake dist. resort area (including lakes Nahuel Huapí and Traful), much of it in a natl. park. Climate, depending on alt., is temperate and dry in populated areas. Mineral resources include gold (Cordillera del Viento, Andacollo, Chos Malal), coal (Sierra de Huantraicó, Nahuel Huapí area), asphalt (Chos Malal), petroleum (Plaza Huincul, Challaco); also lead, copper, and sulphur. Extensive pine forests in Andean foothills; also oak, cypress. Agr. restricted to subandean valleys and semiarid E plains: alfalfa, wheat, corn; in irrigated valleys near Neuquén are fruitgrowing and viticulture. Stock raising (sheep, goats, cattle) in valleys and foothills. Mining, sawmilling, flour milling, wine making, dairying; paper mills (Aluminé), petroleum refineries (Plaza Huincul, Challaco). Established 1884 as natl. territory.

Neuquén, town (1947 pop. 7,236), ⊙ Neuquén natl. territory and Confluencia dept., S central Argentina, at confluence of Neuquén and Limay rivers (forming the Río Negro), on railroad and 600 mi. SW of Buenos Aires; 38°57'S 68°5'W. Inland river port and agr. center for irrigated area (Río Negro dam near by). Produces fruit, wine, alfalfa. Has administrative bldgs., theater. Bridge across Neuquén R.

Neuquén River, Neuquén natl. territory, Argentina, rises in the Andes at Chile border near 36°30'S, flows c.320 mi. S and SE, past Andacollo, Chos Malal, and Añelo, to Neuquén, where it joins the Limay to form the Río Negro. Lower course is used for irrigation (fruitgrowing). Receives the Río Agrio.

Neureut (noi'roit), village (pop. 6,006), N Baden, Germany, after 1945 in Württemberg-Baden, 3 mi. N of Karlsruhe; asparagus, strawberries.

Neurode, Poland: see Nowa Ruda.

Neuruppin (noi"rŏŏpēn'), town (pop. 26,040), Brandenburg, E Germany, on W shore of Ruppin L., 40 mi. NW of Berlin; lithographing and printing; mfg. of dyes, starch, brushes, flags, fire extinguishers. Climatic health resort. Racecourse. Has 13th-cent. church, high school (founded 1356), and old town walls. Chartered 1256; was ⊙ Ruppin county until 1524, then passed to Brandenburg. Frederick the Great, as crown prince, lived here (1732–36). Largely destroyed by fire in 1787. Dramatist Fontane and architect Schinkel b. here. Sometimes spelled Neu Ruppin.

Neusalz, Poland: see Nowa Sol.

Neusalza-Spremberg (noi"zäl'tsä-shprĕm'bĕrk) town (pop. 4,436), Saxony, E central Germany, in Upper Lusatia, at N foot of Lusatian Mts., on the Spree and 11 mi. SSE of Bautzen, near Czechoslovak border; cotton and linen milling; stone quarrying. Plastics mfg. Formed 1920 by joining of Neusalza town and Spremberg commune.

Neu Sandec, Poland: see Nowy Sacz.

Neusatz, Yugoslavia: see Novi Sad.

Neuschmecks, Czechoslovakia: see Novy Smokovec.

Neuschwanstein, Germany: see Schwangau.

Neuse River (nūs, nōōs), E N.C., formed 8 mi. NE of Durham by junction of small Flat, Eno, and Little rivers; flows generally SE past Kinston (head of navigation) to New Bern, at head of estuary (c.5 mi. wide) extending c.40 mi. SE and E to Pamlico Sound; total length, including estuary and Flat R. (c.25 mi. long), c.300 mi.

Neuses or **Neuses bei Coburg** (noi'zŭs bī kō'bŏŏrk), NW suburb of Coburg, Upper Franconia, NE Bavaria, Germany; home of poet Rückert.

Neusiedl am See (noi'zēdŭl äm zā'), town (pop. 3,577), Burgenland, E Austria, on N shore of Neusiedler L., 18 mi. SW of Bratislava, Czechoslovakia; oil refining; grain market; vineyards.

Neusiedl an der Zaya (än dĕr tsä'yä), village (pop. 2,100), NE Lower Austria, 10 mi. ENE of Mistelbach.

Neusiedler Lake (noi'zēdlŭr), Ger. *Neusiedlersee* (-zā"), Hung. *Fertő tó* (fĕr"tŭ tō'), E Austria and NW Hungary, indenting Burgenland, 25 mi. SE of Vienna; □ c.130, varying with seasons; c.20 mi. long, 4–8 mi. wide, average depth 5 ft., alt. 370 ft.; slight salt content. A canal (built 1873–95) to a tributary of the Repce, receives or discharges water, depending on the seasons. A heavy growth of reed reaches deep into lake, supplying Austrian cellulose industry with one of its principal raw materials. Remains of prehistoric lake dwellers on shore. Wild fowl, some fish. Region around lake is one of best winegrowing areas in Austria. Sopron is near its SW shore.

Neusohl, Czechoslovakia: see Banska Bystrica.

Neuss (nois), city (1950 pop. 62,926), in former Prussian Rhine Prov., W Germany, after 1945 in North Rhine-Westphalia, port near left bank of the Rhine, opposite Düsseldorf; 51°12'N 6°42'E. Rail junction; grain market and food-processing center (vegetable oil, margarine, pickled cabbage, ersatz coffee, rice starch, flour, chocolate). Bridge construction; mfg.: agr. machinery, tractors, heating apparatus, metal and wooden screws, rivets, chemicals, concrete goods, artificial fiber, cord, ceramics, cardboard. Lumber and paper mills; candle- and brickworks. Harbor (E) is connected with Rhine R. by Erft canal; accessible to small ocean-going craft. Second World War damage included 13th-cent. Quirinus church and 17th-cent. town hall. Neuss (anc. *Novesium*) was founded as Roman camp by Drusus. Chartered 1187–90. Besieged unsuccessfully (1474–75) by Charles the Bold. Burned 1586. Passed to Prussia in 1816.

Neussargues-Moissac (nûsärg'-mwäsäk'), village (pop. 995), Cantal dept., S central France, on the Alagnon and 9 mi. NW of Saint-Flour; rail center; woodworking.

Neustadl, Czechoslovakia: see Nove Mesto na Morave.

Neustadt (nū'stăt), village (pop. 419), S Ont., on South Saugeen R. and 35 mi. S of Owen Sound; dairying, mixed farming.

Neustadt (noi'shtät). **1** Town (1946 pop. 5,131), S Baden, Germany, in Black Forest, on the Gutach and 18 mi. ESE of Freiburg; rail junction; watch industry; mfg. of cellulose, paper, machinery; woodworking, lumber milling. Climatic health resort and winter-sports center (alt. 2,710 ft.). **2** or **Neustadt an der Donau** (än dĕr dō'nou), town (1946 pop. 3,315), Lower Bavaria, Germany, near the Danube, 9 mi. SW of Kelheim; tanning, metal- and woodworking. Chartered c.1273. **3** or **Neustadt an der Aisch** (än dĕr īsh'), town (1946 pop. 8,123), Middle Franconia, W Bavaria, Germany, on the Aisch and 18 mi. W of Erlangen; rail junction; hops market. Aluminum works; mfg. of drawing instruments, soap, wool, toys; woodworking, printing, brewing. Has late-16th-cent. castle, 17th-cent. Renaissance town hall. Chartered in early 14th cent. **4** or **Neustadt bei Coburg** (bī kō'bŏŏrk), city (1950 pop. 12,779), Upper Franconia, N Bavaria, Germany, 8 mi. NE of Coburg, 3 mi. SW of Sonneberg; toy-mfg. center; machinery and machine tools; lumber mills. **5** or **Neustadt an der Waldnaab** (än dĕr vält'näp), town (1946 pop. 5,587), Upper Palatinate, NE Bavaria, Germany, on the Waldnab (or Waldnaab) and 3.5 mi. N of Weiden; rail junction; cut-glass mfg. Grain, livestock. Has late-17th-cent. church. Chartered in early 14th cent. **6** or **Neustadt an der Dosse** (än dĕr dô'sŭ), town (1946 pop. 2,152), Brandenburg, E Germany, on Dosse R. and 17 mi. WSW of Neuruppin; site of stud farm, established 1786. Dairying; mfg. of agr. implements, mirrors. **7** or **Neustadt am Rübenberge** (äm rü'bŭnbĕr"gŭ), town (1946 pop. 6,622), in former Prussian prov. of Hanover, W Germany, after 1945 in Lower Saxony, on the Leine and 14 mi. NW of Hanover; mfg. of machinery. Has 13th-cent. church. **8** Town (1946 pop. 3,442), in former Prussian prov. of Hesse-Nassau, W Germany, after 1945 in Hesse, 16 mi. ENE of Marburg; grain. **9** Village, North Rhine-Westphalia, W Germany: see Bergneustadt. **10** or **Neustadt an der Weinstrasse** (än dĕr vīn'shträsŭ), city (1950 pop. 26,674), ⊙ Rhenish Palatinate, W Germany, on E slope of Hardt Mts., 16 mi. SW of Ludwigshafen; 49°21'N 8°8'E. Rail junction; wine center of Rhenish Palatinate. Metal (machinery, agr. and viticultural implements; steel, aluminum, and tin products) and textile (cloth, knitwear) industries. Other mfg.: paper, concrete goods, processed food. Wine trade. Has Gothic church. Casimirianum (16th cent.) housed (1579–85) Heidelberg univ. Site of noted horticultural institute. Chartered 1275. Capital of Rhenish Palatinate was moved here (1945) from Speyer. Until 1936, and during 1945–50, called Neustadt an der Hardt (Haardt). **11** or **Neustadt in Sachsen** (ĭn zăk'sŭn), town (1946 pop. 6,094), Saxony, E central Germany, in Saxonian Switzerland, 22 mi. E of Dresden, near Czechoslovak border; mfg. of agr. machinery, artificial flowers, enamelware, surgical instruments; woodworking. **12** or **Neustadt in Holstein** (ĭn hôl'shtīn), town (1946 pop. 13,391), in Schleswig-Holstein, NW Germany, port on Lübeck Bay, 18 mi. NNE of Lübeck; mfg. of metalware, concrete and leather goods, musical instruments; woodworking, food processing (condensed milk). Trade (grain, wood). Baltic seaside resort. Has 13th-cent. church. Chartered 1242. **13** or **Neustadt an der Orla** (än dĕr ôr'lä), town (1946 pop. 10,484), Thuringia, central Germany, on Orla R. and 15 mi. SE of Jena; woolen milling, metal- and woodworking; mfg. of machine tools, chemicals, pianos, glass, furniture, matches, bricks, leather and tobacco products. Has 16th-cent. church and 15th-cent. town hall.

Neustadt. 1 Town in Upper Silesia, now in Opole prov., Poland: see Prudnik. **2** Town, Poznan prov., Poland: see Lwowek. **3** Town, Gdansk prov., Poland: see Wejherowo.

Neustadt, Bad, Germany: see Bad Neustadt.

Neustadt an der Mettau, Czechoslovakia: see Nove Mesto nad Metuji.

Neustadt an der Saale, Bad, Germany: see Bad Neustadt.

Neustadt an der Tafelfichte, Czechoslovakia: see Nove Mesto pod Smrkem.

Neustadt-Eberswalde, Germany: see Eberswalde.

Neustädtel (noi'shtĕ"tŭl), industrial SSW suburb (1933 pop. 5,057) of Schneeberg, Saxony, E central Germany, in the Erzgebirge. Inc. 1939 into Schneeberg.

Neustädtel, Poland: see Nowe Miasteczko.

Neustadt-Glewe (noi'shtät-glā'vŭ), town (pop. 6,069), Mecklenburg, N Germany, on regulated Elde R. and 18 mi. SSE of Schwerin; mfg. of machinery, electric equipment, chemicals, leather products; woodworking. Hydroelectric power station. Has 17th-cent. palace; remains of old fort, town walls, and gates. Founded in 13th cent.

Neustadt in Holstein, Germany: see Neustadt, Schleswig-Holstein.

Neustadt in Sachsen, Germany: see Neustadt, Saxony.

Neustädtl, Yugoslavia: see Novo Mesto.

Neustettin, Poland: see Szczecinek.

Neustraschnitz, Czechoslovakia: see Nove Straseci.

Neustrelitz (noi"shtrā'lĭts), residential town (pop. 24,692), Mecklenburg, N Germany, on 2 small lakes, 60 mi. NNW of Berlin, 60 mi. SE of Rostock; rail junction; metal- and woodworking, machinery mfg. Heavily bombed in Second World War (destruction about 50%). Has 18th-cent. former palace (later mus.) of grand dukes of Mecklenburg-Strelitz, who founded and chartered (1733) town and here established ⊙ grand duchy of Mecklenburg-Strelitz after earlier residence at Strelitz (3 mi. SE) had been burned (1712).

Neustria (nūs'trēŭ), W portion of Merovingian kingdom of the Franks in 6th, 7th, and 8th cent., comprising parts of present-day France—the Seine and Loire country and the region to N. Principal city Soissons. It was formed by 511 partition among sons of Clovis I. Later temporarily reunited with Austrasia.

Neuteich, Poland: see Nowy Staw.

Neutitschein, Czechoslovakia: see Novy Jicin.

Neutla (nĕŏŏt'lä), town (pop. 1,854), Guanajuato, central Mexico, 16 mi. N of Celaya; cereals, sugar, fruit, stock.

Neutomischel, Poland: see Nowy Tomysl.

Neutra, Czechoslovakia: see Nitra.

Neutra River, Czechoslovakia: see Nitra River.

Neu-Ulm (noi"ŏŏlm'), city (1950 pop. 16,269), Swabia, W Bavaria, Germany, on right bank of the Danube (2 bridges), at mouth of the Iller, opposite Ulm; rail junction; textile mfg.; leather-, metal-, and woodworking; brewing. Founded 1810 on territory taken from Ulm.

Neuvecelle, France: see Évian-les-Bains.

Neuve-Chapelle (nûv-shäpĕl'), village (pop. 419), Pas-de-Calais dept., N France, 7 mi. NE of Béthune. Scene of severe fighting in First World War. Many Br. and Indian military cemeteries in area.

Neuves-Maisons (nûv-măzō'), town (pop. 5,241), Meurthe-et-Moselle dept., NE France, on the Moselle and Canal de l'Est, and 7 mi. SSW of Nancy; blast furnaces, forges. Iron mines.

Neuveville (nûv-vēl'), Ger. *Neuenstadt* (noi'ŭnshtät"), town (pop. 2,441), Bern canton, W Switzerland, at SW end of L. Biel and 9 mi. SW of Biel; watches, metal products.

Neuvic (nûvĕk'). **1** Village (pop. 1,500), Corrèze dept., S central France, 11 mi. S of Ussel; cattle market. Hydroelectric plant 4.5 mi. ESE on Dordogne R. Also called Neuvic-d'Ussel. **2** or **Neuvic-sur-l'Isle** (–sür-lēl'), village (pop. 481), Dordogne dept., SW France, on the Isle and 14 mi. SW of Périgueux; footwear mfg. Has 16th-cent. Renaissance château.

Neuville (nûvēl'), village (pop. 523), Namur prov., S Belgium, 2 mi. SW of Philippeville; marble quarrying.

Neuville, village (pop. 616), S Que., on the St. Lawrence and 20 mi. WSW of Quebec; dairying; fruit, vegetables.

Neuville or **Neuville-du-Poitou** (–dü-pwätōō'), village (pop. 1,598), Vienne dept., W central France, 8 mi. NW of Poitiers; wine, potatoes, vegetables.

Neuville-aux-Bois (–ō-bwä'), village (pop. 1,134), Loiret dept., N central France, at N edge of Forest of Orléans, 13 mi. NE of Orléans; cereals, cattle.

Neuville-du-Poitou, France: see NEUVILLE.

Neuville-en-Condroz (–ĕ-kōdrō'), village (pop. 609), Liége prov., E Belgium, 9 mi. SW of Liége. Site of U.S. military cemetery (Second World War).

Neuville-lès-Dieppe (–lā-dyĕp'), residential E suburb (pop. 4,568) of Dieppe, Seine-Inférieure dept., N France.

Neuville-Saint-Vaast (–sĕ-väst'), village (pop. 874), Pas-de-Calais dept., N France, 5 mi. N of Arras, just S of Vimy Ridge. Completely rebuilt after First World War. Near by are large Br., Fr., and Ger. military cemeteries, and allied memorials of battle of Arras (1917).

Neuville-sous-Montreuil, France: see MONTREUIL.

Neuville-sur-l'Escaut (–sür-lĕskō'), town (pop. 2,228), Nord dept., N France, on Escaut R. (canalized) and 3 mi. SW of Denain; Portland cement.

Neuville-sur-Saône (–sür-sōn'), town (pop. 3,294), Rhône dept., E central France, on left bank of Saône R. and 9 mi. N of Lyons; silk, rayon milling and dyeing, furniture mfg.

Neuvy-le-Roi (nûvē'-lù-rwä'), village (pop. 582), Indre-et-Loire dept., W central France, 15 mi. NNW of Tours; horse breeding.

Neuvy-Saint-Sépulchre (–sĕ-säpül'krù), village (pop. 1,149), Indre dept., central France, 9 mi. W of La Châtre; lingerie mfg., cattle raising. Has 11th–12th-cent. circular church patterned on Holy Sepulcher in Jerusalem.

Neuvy-sur-Loire (–sür-lwär'), village (pop. 714), Nièvre dept., central France, on Loire R., and 8 mi. NNW of Cosne; mfg. of bicycle tires, other rubber goods, and cartons.

Neu-Walter, Russian SFSR: see SVERDLOVO.

Neuwarp, Poland: see NOWE WARPNO.

Neuwedell, Poland: see DRAWNO.

Neuweier (noi'vī"ùr), village (pop. 1,530), S Baden, Germany, on W slope of Black Forest, 3 mi. NE of Bühl; noted for its wine (Mauerwein).

Neuwerk (noi'vĕrk"), North Sea island (□ 1.3) of East Frisian group, NW Germany, 8 mi. NW of Cuxhaven. Ship-salvage station; 14th-cent. light tower.

Neuwied (noi'vēt"), town (pop. 20,670), in former Prussian Rhine Prov., W Germany, after 1945 in Rhineland-Palatinate, on right bank of the Rhine (landing) and 7 mi. NW of Coblenz; rail junction; mfg. of machinery, chemicals; cement works. Has 18th-cent. castle of princes of Wied, where Queen Elizabeth of Rumania (Carmen Sylva) was born. Founded 1653.

Neuwürschnitz (noi"vür'shnĭts), village (pop. 5,456), Saxony, E central Germany, at N foot of the Erzgebirge, just S of Lugau; coal mining.

Neuzen, Netherlands: see TERNEUZEN.

Nevada (nùvă'dù, nùvä'dù), state (land □ 109,802; with inland waters □ 110,540; 1950 pop. 160,083; 1940 pop. 110,247), in W U.S., bordered W and SW by Calif., SE by Ariz., E by Utah, N by Idaho and Oregon; 6th in area, 48th in pop.; admitted 1864 as 36th state; ⊙ Carson City. The "Silver State" is 485 mi. long N–S; from its greatest width (320 mi.), at the middle, it tapers to a point in the S. Practically all of Nev. lies within the vast, arid GREAT BASIN, characteristic of which are the state's many broken mtn. ranges running N–S and the intervening flat, alluvial basins. Of the block mtn. type, but greatly eroded, these ranges average 50–75 mi. in length, 6–15 mi. in width, and 7–10,000 ft. in height. Highest point in the state is Boundary Peak (13,145 ft.), in the White Mts. near Calif. line; lowest point (c.470 ft.) is along Colorado R., which forms part of SE boundary. Wheeler Peak (13,058 ft.), in Snake Range (E), is 2d highest point. A spur (Carson Range) of the Sierra Nevada, overlooking picturesque L. TAHOE, projects into the extreme W part near the state line. Lying to the lee of the higher Calif. mts., which rob the prevailing westerlies of their moisture, Nev. has a very dry continental climate, marked by much sunshine, low humidity, and an annual rainfall of 5–10 in. Winters are generally mild (although in N mts. it becomes very cold and snowfall is heavy), and summers hot; diurnal temp. range is large. Winnemucca (N) has mean temp. of 28°F. in Jan. and 72°F. in July; Las Vegas (SE) averages 45°F. in Jan. and 86°F. in July. Except for a few streams in the NE and SE, flowing into the Snake and Colorado rivers respectively, the state's rivers have no sea outlet. Most of them are small, flow only during rainy months, and eventually disappear into the sands of some intermontane basin or empty into sinks or lakes, such as PYRAMID LAKE, Walker L., CARSON SINK, and Winnemucca L., remnants of prehistoric L. LAHONTAN. The HUMBOLDT RIVER, which cuts through the ranges of N central Nev., is by far the longest. Vegetation is largely xerophytic, with sagebrush (N) and creosote bush (S) predominating; cacti and yuccas are also common in the S, while on the higher mtn. slopes pine forests occur; 87% of the land is in federal ownership, including c.5,000,000 acres of natl. forest reserves (used mainly for cattle and sheep pasturing), the highest percentage in any state. Because of the arid conditions which render most of Nev. suitable only for grazing, livestock raising is important, the state having some 545,000 head of cattle and 470,000 sheep; dairy farming is carried on in W counties. Severe soil erosion has claimed almost ⅓ of the total land surface. Farms comprise over 6,000,000 acres, but agr. is not highly developed and depends heavily on irrigation, as along the Humboldt, Truckee, Carson, and Walker rivers. Principal crops—raised primarily as cattle fodder—are hay, alfalfa, barley, wheat, oats, potatoes, and sugar beets. Truck farms are found near the populated sections of the W and extreme SE, but most of the state's foodstuffs are imported. Some figs, almonds, and grapes are grown in the semi-tropical SE parts. Commercial forests are small. Nev.'s mineral wealth, a major factor in the state's development, consists of extensive deposits of gold, silver, copper, lead, zinc, tungsten, mercury, and lesser amounts of manganese, antimony, salt, gypsum, vanadium, and molybdenum. During Second World War large magnesite reserves in the S were worked; magnesium plant at Henderson. Because it lacks fuel, Nev. ships the bulk of its ore outside the state for processing; there are, however, smelters at McGill and Winnemucca. Chief mining centers are Ely (copper), Pioche (zinc, lead), Tonopah (silver), Goldfield (gold), and Lovelock, but hundreds of other mining dists. are scattered throughout the state. Few mfg. industries (flour mills, bricks, dairy products, meat-packing plants) exist. An atomic-weapons testing ground and U.S. Air Force bombing range is situated in Frenchman Flat, c.65 mi. NW of Las Vegas. Nev.'s pop. is 57.2% urban, though only 2 places—RENO (state's largest city) and LAS VEGAS—have more than 10,000 persons; other towns are Sparks, Elko, Boulder City, Ely, Carson City, Fallon, and Winnemucca. Places of tourist attraction include the gambling and divorce centers of Reno and Las Vegas, the resorts on L. Tahoe and L. MEAD (formed by huge HOOVER DAM in Colorado R., which supplies hydroelectric power to SE Nev.), and Lehman Caves Natl. Monument. A major source of revenue is a state tax on legalized gambling. Univ. of Nev. is at Reno. Among the Indian tribes (present pop. less than 5,000) inhabiting Nev. before the white man's arrival were Paiutes, Washoes, and Shoshoneans. The drab country failed to attract explorers—even the gold-seeking Spaniards avoided the area—until after 1825 when fur trappers and traders penetrated the Humboldt R. valley. In 1843–45 John C. Frémont explored the Great Basin region and his enthusiastic reports interested many in the East, including the persecuted Mormons, who migrated to Great Salt Lake (Utah) in 1847 and later (c.1849) founded a trading station at GENOA, the 1st permanent settlement in Nev. Until 1848 the area was part of Mexico; after cession to U.S. it was included (1850) in Utah territory and known as Western Utah. With the opening of the fabulous COMSTOCK LODE (silver and gold) in 1859 thousands of prospectors poured into Nev. and, almost overnight, small mining camps grew into boisterous boom towns, such as VIRGINIA CITY. During a short period of Indian trouble the section W of the 116th meridian was made (1861) a separate territory; present boundaries were established by 1866, after Nev. had been rushed to statehood in order to obtain 2 more senatorial votes for the 13th Amendment. Although diversification through stock raising and irrigated agr. was achieved, Nev.'s economy has been dominated by its mining industry. Rich strikes of silver, gold, and copper were made at the turn of the century and the 2 world wars brought about mining booms, but fluctuations in gold and silver production occasioned by national and international monetary policies have also resulted in severe depressions. The "free-silver" advocates have always had strong support in Nev. See also articles on the cities, towns, geographic features, and the 17 counties: CHURCHILL, CLARK, DOUGLAS, ELKO, ESMERALDA, EUREKA, HUMBOLDT, LANDER, LINCOLN, LYON, MINERAL, NYE, ORMSBY, PERSHING, STOREY, WASHOE, WHITE PINE.

Nevada. 1 (nùvă'dù, –vă'dù) County (□ 616; pop. 14,781), SW Ark.; ⊙ Prescott. Bounded N by Little Missouri R. and drained by Bayou Dorcheat. Agr. (fruit, cotton, corn); cotton ginning, lumber milling. Formed 1871. **2** (nùvă'dù, nùvä'dù) County (□ 979; pop. 19,888), E Calif.; ⊙ Nevada City. Narrow strip extending E across foothills to crest of Sierra Nevada, here crossed by Donner Pass; highest point is Mt. Lola (9,160 ft.). Rugged, wooded mtn. country, with many beautiful lakes (e.g., Donner L.). Popular recreational region (winter sports in Donner Pass area; camping, hiking, hunting, fishing). Partly in Tahoe Natl. Forest. Drained by Bear R. and forks of the Yuba. At N end of Mother Lode, it is a leading Calif. co. in gold production; also mining of silver, quarrying of sand and gravel. Lumbering (pine, fir, cedar); stock raising (cattle, sheep, poultry), dairying; some fruitgrowing in lower foothills. Grass Valley is largest city. Formed 1851.

Nevada. 1 (nùvā'dù) City (pop. 3,763), ⊙ Story co., central Iowa, 30 mi. NNE of Des Moines; livestock shipping; mfg. (feed, brooms, flower pots). Founded c.1853, inc. 1869. **2** (nùvā'dù) City (pop. 8,009), ⊙ Vernon co., W Mo., near Marmaton R., 52 mi. W of Joplin. Ships grain, livestock; mfg. (dairy products, bricks, tile); asphalt and coal mines, oil wells. Seat of Cottey Col. State mental hosp. near by. Founded 1855. **3** (nùvā'dù) Village (pop. 824), Wyandot co., N central Ohio, 8 mi. W of Bucyrus; meat products, building materials.

Nevada, Sierra: see SIERRA NEVADA.

Nevada City (nùvă'dù, nùvä'dù), city (pop. 2,505), ⊙ Nevada co., E central Calif., 55 mi. NE of Sacramento, on W slope of the Sierra Nevada; alt. c.2,500 ft. Center of rich placer- and hydraulic-mining area after 1850; lode gold is still produced. Hq. of Tahoe Natl. Forest. Recreational region. Laid out 1849, inc. 1851.

Nevada Fall, Calif.: see YOSEMITE NATIONAL PARK.

Nevadaville (nùvă'dùvĭl), town (pop. 6), Gilpin co., N central Colo., in Front Range, 35 mi. W of Denver; alt. c.9,150 ft. Former gold-mining camp, now ghost town. Near by is Glory Hole, huge mining pit still worked for ore.

Nevado, Cerro (sĕ'rō nāvä'dō), pre-Andean peak (12,500 ft.), S central Mendoza prov., Argentina, E of L. Llancanelo, 70 mi. S of San Rafael.

Nevado, Cerro el (ĕl), Andean peak (14,960 ft.), Meta intendancy, central Colombia, in Cordillera Oriental, 33 mi. WSW of Villavicencio.

Nevado, Cordón (kōrdōn'), Andean mountain range on Argentina-Chile border, N of 42°S; extends c.35 mi. along the frontier; rises to c.7,500 ft.

Neva River, Italy: see ARROSCIA RIVER.

Neva River (nē'vù, Rus. nyĭvä'), Leningrad oblast, Russian SFSR, issues from L. Ladoga at Petrokrepost, flows 46 mi. W to Gulf of Finland, forming delta mouth at LENINGRAD. Width varies bet. 1,600 and 4,000 ft.; canalized channel is navigable April-Nov. Receives Mga, Tosna, and Izhora rivers (left). Connected with Volga R. by means of Mariinsk, Tikhvin, and Vyshnevolotsk canal systems, and with White Sea by means of WHITE SEA–BALTIC CANAL.

Nevasa (nā'väsù), village (pop. 6,321), Ahmadnagar dist., E Bombay, India, on Pravara R. and 33 mi. NNE of Ahmadnagar; sugar cane, millet; gur mfg. Sometimes spelled Newasa.

Nevatim (nĕvätēm'), agr. settlement (pop. 40), S Israel, in the Negev, 7 mi. WSW of Beersheba. Founded 1946.

Neve Eitan or **Neve Etan** (both: nĕvä' ĕ'tän), settlement (pop. 225), NE Israel, in Jordan valley, 2 mi. ESE of Beisan; mixed farming, fish breeding. Founded 1938.

Neve Ilan (nĕvä' ēlän'), agr. settlement (pop. 100), E Israel, in Judaean Hills, 9 mi. W of Jerusalem. Founded 1946.

Neveklov (nĕ'vĕklôf), town (pop. 793), S Bohemia, Czechoslovakia, 7 mi. SW of Benesov; rye.

Nevel or **Nevel'** (nyĕ'vĭl), city (1926 pop. 12,923), S Velikiye Luki oblast, Russian SFSR, 32 mi. SW of Velikiye Luki; rail and road junction; food processing (dairy and bakery products); brush factory. Passed 1772 to Russia; chartered 1777. During Second World War, held (1941–43) by Germans.

Nevele (nā'vùlù), agr. village (pop. 2,588), East Flanders prov., NW Belgium, 8 mi. W of Ghent.

Nevelsk or **Nevel'sk** (nyĕ'vĭlsk), city (1940 pop. 11,180), S Sakhalin, Russian SFSR, port on Sea of Japan, on W coast railroad and 45 mi. WSW of Yuzhno-Sakhalinsk, in agr. area (potatoes, grain); fish canneries, cold-storage plant, shipyards. Coal mining at Gornozavodsk (S). Under Jap. rule (1905–45), called Honto (hōn'tō').

Nevelskoi, Mount, or **Mount Nevel'skoy** (nyĕvĭl-skoi'), highest point (6,604 ft.) in Sakhalin, Russian SFSR, in E range, 55 mi. SE of Aleksandrovsk.

Never (nyĭvyĕr'), town (1939 pop. over 2,000), SW Amur oblast, Russian SFSR, 10 mi. E of Skovorodino and on Trans-Siberian RR (Bolshoi Never station), on highway to Aldan gold fields and Yakutsk; road-rail transfer point. Formerly Larinski.

Neverí River (nävärē'), NE Venezuela, rises in coastal range of Sucre state SW of Cumanacoa, flows c.55 mi. W, past Barcelona, to the Caribbean 3 mi. NW of Barcelona, up to which it is navigable for small craft.

Neverkino (nyĭvyĕr'kēnŭ), village (1939 pop. over 500), SE Penza oblast, Russian SFSR, 25 mi. SSE of Kuznetsk; wheat, sunflowers, legumes.

Nevers (nůvâr'), anc. *Noviodunum*, town (pop. 32,246), ⊙ Nièvre dept., central France, on right bank of the Loire at mouth of Nièvre R. and 36 mi. ESE of Bourges; commercial center with important pottery and china manufactures. Foundries (agr. and dairying equipment, woodworking machines, machine tools), boat yards. Meat processing, jute weaving, pharmaceutical and furniture mfg. Has 13th–16th-cent. cathedral (damaged in Second World War); 11th-cent. Romanesque church of Saint-Étienne; 15th–16th-cent. ducal palace (now the courthouse); and convent of Saint-Gildard (containing remains of St. Bernadette, who lived here 1860–79). Old ⊙ of Nivernais prov.

Neversink River (nĕ'vůrsĭngk), SE N.Y., rises in the Catskills W of Ashokan Reservoir, flows c.65 mi. SW and S, paralleling W base of the Shawangunk range in lower course, to the Delaware at Port Jervis. In upper course (called Neversink Creek) is earth-fill Neversink Dam (2,800 ft. long, 200 ft. high; begun 1941), impounding Neversink Reservoir. A 5-mi. water tunnel extends to Rondout Reservoir, which connects with DELAWARE AQUEDUCT.

Never Summer Mountains, range of Rocky Mts. in N Colo.; extend c.20 mi. N–S along Continental Divide; form part of W boundary of Rocky Mtn. Natl. Park. Prominent peaks in park and range: Mt. Cumulus (12,724 ft.), Mt. Nimbus (12,730 ft.), Mt. Cirrus (12,804 ft.), Howard Mtn. (12,814 ft.), Mt. Richthofen (12,953 ft.). Range sometimes included within MEDICINE BOW MOUNTAINS of Wyo. and Colo.

Neves (nĕ'vĭs). **1** N suburb (1950 pop. 53,052) of Niterói, Rio de Janeiro, Brazil, on Guanabara Bay, opposite Rio; terminus of railroad to Cabo Frio city; industrial center (metalworks, shipbuilding yards). **2** City, São Paulo, Brazil: see NEVES PAULISTA.

Neve Shaanan (nĕvā' shä-änän'), SE residential suburb of Haifa, NW Israel, on NE slope of Mt. Carmel.

Nevesinje or **Nevesinye** (both: nĕvĕ'sĭnyĕ), town (pop. 1,658), central Herzegovina, Yugoslavia, 16 mi. ESE of Mostar, on crossroad; local trade center. Numerous mineral springs near by. First mentioned in 12th cent. Site of anti-Turkish uprising in 1875.

Neves Paulista (nĕ'vĭs poulē'stů), city (pop. 2,513), NW São Paulo, Brazil, 15 mi. W of São José do Rio Prêto; coffee, beans, rice. Until 1944, Neves; and, 1944–48, Iboti.

Nevezys River or **Nevezhis River** (nĕvā'zhēs), Lith. *Nevėžys*, in central Lithuania, rises W of Anyksciai, flows NW, past Panevezys, and S, past Kedainiai, to Neman R. just W of Kaunas; length, 132 mi. Navigable for 18 mi. above mouth.

Neviano (nĕvyä'nô), village (pop. 4,758), Lecce prov., Apulia, S Italy, 7 mi. SE of Nardò; wine, olive oil.

Neviano degli Arduini (dĕlyärdwē'nē), village (pop. 169), Parma prov., Emilia-Romagna, N central Italy, 15 mi. S of Parma; agr. tools.

Neviges (nā'vēgůs), town (pop. 13,804), in former Prussian Rhine Prov., W Germany, after 1945 in North Rhine-Westphalia, 2 mi. SE of Velbert; mfg. of machinery and textiles. Has pilgrimage church. Until 1935, called Hardenberg (här'dûnbĕrk).

Neville (nĕ'vĭl), village (pop. 127), Clermont co., SW Ohio, 26 mi. SE of Cincinnati and on Ohio R. (here forming Ky. line).

Neville's Cross (nĕ'vůlz), residential town and parish (pop. 939), central Durham, England, just W of Durham. Site of defeat of Scots and capture of King David Bruce by English in 1346.

Nevin, town and parish (pop. 1,781), on Lleyn Peninsula, SW Caernarvon, Wales, on Caernarvon Bay of Irish Sea, 5 mi. NW of Pwllheli; fishing port and seaside resort. Scene of famous tournament held here 1284 by Edward I to celebrate his Welsh victories. NE, 5 mi., is peak of Eifel (1,849 ft.), highest point of Yr Eifel range (ĕr ī'vůl) and of Lleyn Peninsula.

Nevinnomyssk (nyĭvēnŭmĭsk'), city (1926 pop. 16,322), W Stavropol Territory, Russian SFSR, on Kuban R., at mouth of Great Zelenchuk R., and 28 mi. S of Stavropol, at head of Nevinnomyssk Canal. Rail center (branch line S to Cherkessk) on Rostov-Baku RR; extensive freight yards, workshops; fuel depot; wool processing; flour mill, brick- and tile-works. During Second World War, held (1942–43) by Germans.

Nevinnomyssk Canal, irrigation waterway (32 mi. long) in W Stavropol Territory, Russian SFSR. Extends from Kuban R. at Nevinnomyssk NW, through Nedremannaya mtn. (3-mi. tunnel), to Yegorlyk R. 15 mi. WSW of Stavropol. Canal supplies spring and summer flood water from Kuban R. to parched Yegorlyk agr. basin. Svistukha hydroelectric station is on canal, SW of Stavropol. Construction (begun 1935) was interrupted by Second World War and completed 1948.

Nevis (nē'vĭs), island (□ 50; pop. 11,388), St. Kitts-Nevis presidency, Leeward Isls., B.W.I.; ⊙ Charlestown. Separated from St. Kitts (NW) by 2-mi.-wide strait (The Narrows); situated c.210 mi. ESE of Puerto Rico. Nearly circular isl. (8 mi. long, 6 mi. wide), rising symmetrically towards center (17°9'N 62°35'W) in Nevis Peak (3,596 ft.). Average temp. 79°F., annual rainfall c.55 inches. Sea-island cotton has replaced sugar as chief agr. product; also grows yams, sweet potatoes, corn. Charlestown is its leading port and sugar-milling center. Because of its thermal baths, the isl. was noted in 18th cent. as health resort. Discovered 1493 by Columbus, it was settled 1628 by the English from St. Kitts. Several incursions were made by the Spanish and French, but the isl. was finally restored (1783) to Great Britain. Alexander Hamilton was b. in Charlestown.

Nevis (nē'vĭs), village (pop. 332), Hubbard co., central Minn., 11 mi. ENE of Park Rapids, in lake region; dairying.

Nevis, Ben, Scotland: see BEN NEVIS.

Nevis, Loch (lŏkh nĕ'vĭs, nē'vĭs), sea inlet in W Inverness, Scotland, extending 15 mi. E from the Sound of Sleat at Mallaig.

Nevoso, Monte, Yugoslavia: see SNEZNIK.

Nevrokop (nĕvrôkôp'), after 1950 called **Delchev** (dĕl'chĕf), city (pop. 11,061), Gorna Dzhumaya dist., SW Bulgaria, in Macedonia, near Mesta R., E of Pirin Mts., 45 mi. SE of Gorna Dzhumaya, on road to Drama (Greece); major tobacco center; tobacco warehouses. Mineral baths. Ruins of anc. Roman town Nicopolis ad Nestos near by.

Nevsehir (nĕv-shĕhĭr'), Turkish *Nevşehir*, town (pop. 15,563), Nigde prov., central Turkey, 45 mi. N of Nigde; rye, vetch, legumes, potatoes, onions. Excavated ruins near by. Formerly sometimes Nev-Shehr.

Nevskoye (nyĕf'skŭyů), village (1939 pop. 791), SE Kaliningrad oblast, Russian SFSR, 9 mi. SSE of Nesterov, near Lith. border. Until 1945, in East Prussia where it was called Pillupönen (pĭ'lōōpûnůn) and, later (1938–45), Schlossbach (shlôs'bäkh).

Nevyansk or **Nev'yansk** (nyĭvyänsk'), city (1935 pop. estimate 24,300), SW central Sverdlovsk oblast, Russian SFSR, in E foothills of the central Urals, on Neiva R. and 50 mi. NNW of Sverdlovsk, on railroad; mfg. center (mining equipment, perforators, automobile parts, cement); metallurgy. Gold and platinum deposits near by. Founded 1689 as gun-mfg. plant; developed as metallurgical center; became city in 1917.

New Aberdeen, coal-mining suburb of Glace Bay, NE N.S., on Cape Breton Isl.

New Aberdour (ăbûrdour'), agr. village in Aberdour parish (pop. 1,180), N Aberdeen, Scotland, near North Sea, 13 mi. E of Banff. Near by, on the coast, are remains of Dundarg Castle.

Newagen, Cape (nůwă'gůn), Lincoln co., SW Maine, cape with summer colony at S tip of Southport town.

Newala (nĕwä'lä), town, Southern Prov., SE Tanganyika, 75 mi. SW of Lindi, near Mozambique border; tobacco, rice, corn, potatoes.

New Albany (ôl'bůnē). **1** Industrial city (pop. 29,346), ⊙ Floyd co., S Ind., on the Ohio (bridged here), opposite Louisville (Ky.), of whose metropolitan area it is a part; veneers and plywood, auto parts and equipment, furniture, clothing, leather goods, heating equipment, fertilizer, glue, prefabricated houses. Timber, sand and gravel. Home of William Vaughn Moody is here. A natl. cemetery is near by. Settled c.1800, inc. 1813. Was shipping and shipbuilding center in steamboat era. **2** City (pop. 152), Wilson co., SE Kansas, on Fall R. and 7 mi. WNW of Fredonia; stock raising, farming. **3** City (pop. 3,680), ⊙ Union co., N Miss., 23 mi. NW of Tupelo; trade center for agr. and dairying area; mfg. of clothing, furniture, lumber, cheese; cotton gins, gristmills. Settled c.1840. **4** Village (pop. 268), Franklin co., central Ohio, 13 mi. NE of Columbus, in agr. area. **5** Borough (pop. 365), Bradford co., NE Pa., 12 mi. S of Towanda.

New Albin (ăl'–), town (pop. 568), Allamakee co., extreme NE Iowa, on Minn. line, 18 mi. NNE of Waukon, near Mississippi and Upper Iowa rivers; mfg. (railroad ties, boxes, concrete blocks). Limestone quarries and Indian mounds near by.

New Alexandria. 1 Village (pop. 383), Jefferson co., E Ohio, 6 mi. SW of Steubenville, in coal-mining area. **2** Agr. borough (pop. 523), Westmoreland co., SW central Pa., 9 mi. NE of Greensburg; coal, timber.

Newalla (nūô'lů), village, Oklahoma co., central Okla., 21 mi. ESE of Oklahoma City, in oil-producing area.

New Almaden, Calif.: see ALMADEN.

New Alresford or **Alresford** (ôls'fůrd), town and parish (pop. 1,624), central Hampshire, England, on Itchen R. and 7 mi. ENE of Winchester; agr. market. Mary Mitford b. here. Just N is Old Alresford (pop. 524).

New Amsterdam, town (pop. 9,567), ⊙ Berbice co. and dist., NE Br. Guiana, port at mouth of Berbice R. (here joined by Canje R.), on the Atlantic, 55 mi. SE of Georgetown; 6°16'N 57°32'W. Trading center for fertile coastal region (sugar, rice, cattle). Reached by ships of 14-ft. draught. Rosignol, terminus of rail line from Georgetown, is across the river, reached by ferry. Town of Dutch character, intersected by canals. Has Anglican church. Built 1740 by the Dutch as Fort St. Andries. In 1790, seat of govt. was moved here from Fort Nassau (55 mi. SSW on the Berbice). Became British in 1803.

New Amsterdam, early name for NEW YORK city, SE N.Y.

New Amsterdam, town (pop. 76), Harrison co., S Ind., on Ohio R. and 28 mi. WSW of New Albany, in agr. area.

New Amsterdam Island, Indian Ocean: see AMSTERDAM ISLAND.

New Archangel, Alaska: see SITKA.

Newark, Ont.: see NIAGARA-ON-THE-LAKE.

Newark or **Newark-upon-Trent** (nū'ůrk), municipal borough (1931 pop. 18,060; 1951 census 22,909), E Nottingham, England, on a short branch of the Trent and 16 mi. NE of Nottingham: mfg. of plaster, brick, malt, boilers, agr. machinery and other metal products. Near by are gypsum and limestone quarries. Has ruins of castle partly built by Bishop Alexander in 12th cent., where King John died (1216); 13th-cent. church; 15th-cent. Beaumont market cross; grammar school founded 1529. Town besieged 3 times in Civil War. Site was occupied by anc. Britons and Romans.

Newark. 1 (nōō'ärk") Town (pop. 913), Independence co., NE central Ark., 12 mi. ESE of Batesville, in agr. and timber area. **2** (nōō'ůrk, nū'–) Village (pop. 1,532), Alameda co., W Calif., 23 mi. SSE of Oakland; dairying, salt refining, mfg. of chemicals. Dumbarton Bridge here crosses San Francisco Bay to Palo Alto (W). **3** (nōō'ärk", nū'–) City (pop. 6,731), New Castle co., N Del., 13 mi. WSW of Wilmington, in agr. area; mfg. (vulcanized fiber, paper, concrete products), food packing. Seat of Univ. of Del. Inc. 1852. Near-by Cooch's Bridge was scene (1777) of only Revolutionary battle fought in state. **4** (nōō'ärk", nū'–) Village (pop. 457), Kendall co., NE Ill., 20 mi. SW of Aurora, in rich agr. area. **5** (nōō'ärk", nū'–) Village, Worcester co., SE Md., 19 mi. ESE of Salisbury, in truck-farm and timber area; canneries. Railroad name is Queponco (kĕpŏng'kō). **6** (nōō'ärk, nū'ůrk) Town (pop. 156), Knox co., NE Mo., on South Fabius R. and 16 mi. SE of Edina. **7** (nōō'ůrk, nū'–, nōōrk) City (pop. 438,776), ⊙ Essex co., NE N.J., on Passaic R. and Newark Bay, and 9 mi. W of lower Manhattan; 40°44'N 74°10'W. Largest city in N.J.; known for its many industrial and commercial establishments; port of entry, and a major center for transshipment of rail, truck, and water freight; deepwater terminal (Port Newark), developed in First World War, and Newark Airport (opened 1929) are units of Port of N.Y. Produces electrical equipment, machinery, wire and metal products, fountain pens, cutlery, leather goods, celluloid, chemicals, pigments, paints, paper products, beverages, food products, jewelry; meat packing, fur dyeing; important insurance center. Port's chief incoming cargo is lumber. Settled from Conn. (1666) by Robert Treat and others, inc. 1836, adopted commission govt. 1917. Grew slowly until after Revolution (skirmishes fought here); tanning and shoemaking were once important; jewelry making began 1801; 1st insurance company came in 1810. In 19th cent. industrial growth was rapid, especially after improved rail and water transportation made city metropolis of a wide area. Celluloid (1872) and photographic film (1887) 1st made here. Newark colleges of Rutgers Univ., Newark Acad. for boys (1774), state teachers col., jr. col., and Newark Col. of Engineering (state and city supported; a development of Newark Technical School) here. Points of interest: Plume House (c.1710; probably city's oldest house); Trinity Cathedral (1810) in Military Park, with spire of church built 1743; Sacred Heart Cathedral (begun 1898); First Presbyterian Church (1791); public library, one of best in country, founded 1888 and developed by John Cotton Dana, who founded Newark Mus. (1909); co. courthouse (1906; designed by Cass Gilbert). Gutzon Borglum's statue of Lincoln stands in front of courthouse and his group *Wars of America* (1926) in Military Park. Playground, memorial to Stephen Crane, is on site of his birthplace. Has fine municipal park system. Newark Airport was leading Eastern terminal until opening of New York's La Guardia Field (1939). Notable Newark residents included Mary Mapes Dodge, Marion Harland, E. C. Stedman. Aaron Burr, whose father was later president of Col. of N.J., b. here. **8** (nōō'ůrk, nū'–) Village (pop. 10,295), Wayne co., W N.Y., on the Barge Canal and 29 mi. ESE of Rochester, in agr. area; large rose nurseries; mfg. (paper, chemicals, metal products, furniture, wood and leather products, canned foods). Site of a state school for mental defectives. Inc. 1839. **9** (nōō'ůrk, nū'–) City (pop. 34,275), ⊙ Licking co., central Ohio, 13 mi. E of Columbus and on Licking R.; industrial, rail, and trade center for diversified agr. area. Mfg. of wire and cables, electrical equipment, fiber glass, petroleum products, sporting goods, boxes; railroad shops; aluminum processing. Has a number of Indian mounds: Octagon Mound (50 acres), Circle Mound (20 acres), and a circular mound enclosing a huge eagle effigy. Platted 1801; inc. as city in 1860. **10** (nōō'ůrk) Town (pop. 80), Marshall co., NE S.Dak., 10 mi. N of Britton, on N.Dak. line; agr. trading point. **11** (nōō'ůrk, nū'–) Town (pop. 192), Caledonia co., NE Vt., 20 mi. N of St. Johnsbury.

Newark Bay (nōō'ûrk, nū'–, nŏŏrk), NE N.J., estuary (6 mi. long, 1 mi. wide) at confluence of Passaic and Hackensack rivers, bet. shores of Newark and Elizabeth (W), Jersey City and Bayonne (E), and Staten Isl. (S); linked to Upper New York Bay by Kill Van Kull, to Lower New York Bay by Arthur Kill. Port Newark is deepwater terminal on W shore, connected with dredged channel in bay.

Newark-upon-Trent, England: see NEWARK.

Newark Valley (nōō'ûrk, nū'–), village (pop. 1,027), Tioga co., S N.Y., on Owego Creek and 17 mi. NW of Binghamton; feed, wood products, dairy products, poultry.

Newasa, India: see NEVASA.

New Ashford, agr. town (pop. 118), Berkshire co., NW Mass., 11 mi. N of Pittsfield.

New Athens. 1 (ā'thĭnz) Village (pop. 1,518), St. Clair co., SW Ill., on Kaskaskia R. and 24 mi. SSE of East St. Louis; mfg. (stoves, enamelware, beverages, flour, feed); bituminous-coal mines; corn, wheat, dairy products, fruit, livestock, timber. Inc. 1869. **2** (ă'thĭnz, ā'–) Village (pop. 509), Harrison co., E Ohio, 6 mi. S of Cadiz, in coal-mining area.

New Auburn (ô'bûrn). **1** Village (pop. 290), Sibley co., S Minn., on small lake, 8 mi. N of Gaylord; dairy products. **2** Village (pop. 371), Chippewa co., W central Wis., 26 mi. N of Eau Claire; dairying, stock raising.

New Augusta, village (1940 pop. 502), ⊙ Perry co., SE Miss., 17 mi. ESE of Hattiesburg; lumber milling.

Newaygo (nēwā'gō), county (□ 857; pop. 21,567), W central Mich.; ⊙ White Cloud. Drained by Muskegon, Pere Marquette, and White rivers and short Tamarack and Rogue rivers. Stock and poultry raising, dairying, agr. (potatoes, beans, truck, fruit). Some mfg. at Newaygo. Sawmilling. Resorts (hunting, fishing). Manistee Natl. Forest, a state park, and Hardy Dam are here. Organized 1851.

Newaygo, village (pop. 1,385), Newaygo co., W central Mich., 27 mi. NE of Muskegon and on Muskegon R., in farm area (fruit, potatoes, beans); dairy products; mfg. (auto parts, cement, fishing tackle); hunting, fishing. Settled 1836, inc. as village 1867.

New Baden (bā'dŭn), village (pop. 1,428), on Clinton-St. Clair co. line, SW Ill., 15 mi. E of Belleville, in agr. and bituminous-coal-mining area; corn, wheat, poultry, dairy products. Inc. 1867.

New Baltimore. 1 City (pop. 2,043), on Macomb-St. Clair co. line, E Mich., 10 mi. NE of Mt. Clemens, on Anchor Bay of L. St. Clair. Resort; truck, dairy, and poultry farming; mfg. of trailer bodies, brooms, fishing rods. Inc. as village 1867, as city 1931. **2** Village, Greene co., SE N.Y., on W bank of the Hudson and 15 mi. S of Albany, in summer-resort region. **3** Borough (pop. 221), Somerset co., S Pa., 16 mi. E of Somerset.

New Barnet, England: see EAST BARNET VALLEY.

Newbattle, town and parish (pop. 7,455), NE Midlothian, Scotland, just S of Dalkeith; coal mining. Near by is Newbattle Abbey, seat of marquis of Lothian; includes remains of Cistercian abbey founded 1140 by David I and burned down 1544 by earl of Hertford. Present bldgs. date mostly from 18th–19th cent. and were donated (1937) by late marquis of Lothian to the Scottish universities as a col. for adult education.

New Bavaria (bŭvâ'rēŭ), village (pop. 132), Henry co., NW Ohio, 11 mi. ESE of Defiance.

New Bedford, city (pop. 109,189), a ⊙ Bristol co., SE Mass., on Buzzards Bay, at mouth of the Acushnet, and 12 mi. ESE of Fall River. Resort, with good harbor; mfg. (textiles, electrical equipment, tools, rubber goods, glass, clothing, machinery, hardware); fishing, boatbuilding. Port of entry. Port ships textiles, lubricating oils, rope; receives hemp, lumber, manufactured goods. Seat of a textile institute. First whaler fitted out here in 1755; New Bedford became world's greatest whaling port. As whaling waned in mid-19th cent., cotton mfg. grew. Settled 1640, inc. as town 1787, as city 1847.

New Bedford Inlet (10 naut. mi. long, 10 naut. mi. wide), Antarctica, on Weddell Sea, in Richard Black Coast; 73°58'S 59°30'W; fed by series of glaciers. Discovered 1940 by U.S. expedition.

Newberg, city (pop. 3,946), Yamhill co., NW Oregon, 20 mi. SW of Portland, in fruit- and nut-growing area of Willamette R. valley; lumber, flour, and pulp milling, fruit and nut packing. Seat of Pacific Col. Founded by Quakers; named 1869, inc. 1893.

New Berlin (bûr'lĭn). **1** Village (pop. 622), Sangamon co., central Ill., 15 mi. WSW of Springfield; bituminous-coal mining; agr. (corn, wheat, soybeans). **2** Village (pop. 1,178), Chenango co., central N.Y., on Unadilla R. and 36 mi. S of Utica, in dairying and farming area; feed, lumber. Inc. 1819. **3** Borough (pop. 589), Union co., central Pa., 11 mi. SW of Lewisburg; cheese.

New Bern (nū'bûrn), city (pop. 15,812), ⊙ Craven co., E N.C., on navigable Neuse R. (bridged) at Trent R. mouth, and 32 mi. ESE of Kinston; fishing, shipping, and mfg. (veneer, clothing, fertilizer, metal and dairy products) center; boatbuilding. An early colonial ⊙, settled 1710; in 1774, seat of 1st provincial convention. Old buildings include Tryon Palace (1767–70), capitol, and governor's mansion. An important Confederate seaport until captured (1862) by Union forces. New Bern Natl. Cemetery here. Inc. 1723.

Newbern. 1 Town (pop. 367), Hale co., W central Ala., 10 mi. SE of Greensboro. **2** Town (pop. 1,734), Dyer co., NW Tenn., 9 mi. NE of Dyersburg; trade and shipping point for agr. area (cotton, fruit, vegetables, livestock, wheat); mfg. of gloves, feed, canned foods; flour and lumber milling.

Newberry, county (□ 630; pop. 31,771), NW central S.C.; ⊙ Newberry. Bounded E by Broad R., S by Saluda R., N by Enoree R.; part of L. Murray in SE. Includes part of Sumter Natl. Forest. Mainly agr. (dairying, poultry, truck, grain, cotton); timber, granite. Mfg. at Newberry. Formed 1785.

Newberry. 1 Town (pop. 873), Alachua co., N Fla., 17 mi. W of Gainesville, in truck-farming area. Phosphate quarries near by. **2** Town (pop. 340), Greene co., SW Ind., on West Fork of White R. and 32 mi. ENE of Vincennes, in agr. and bituminous-coal area. **3** Village (pop. 2,802), ⊙ Luce co., NE Upper Peninsula, Mich., c.55 mi. WSW of Sault Ste. Marie, near Tahquamenon R. Lumber-milling center; trade point for farm area (potatoes, celery, hay, oats); mfg. of chemicals, cedar products. Starting point for hunters, fishermen, and visitors to Tahquamenon Falls (NE). Has a state hosp. for the insane. Settled 1882, inc. 1886. **4** Industrial town (pop. 7,546), ⊙ Newberry co., NW central S.C., 45 mi. WNW of Columbia, in dairying, agr. area; textiles, printing, mattresses, lumber, cottonseed oil, flour and feed; granite quarries. Seat of Newberry Col.

New Bethlehem (bĕth'lēŭm), borough (pop. 1,604), Clarion co., W central Pa., on Redbank Creek and 16 mi. NE of Kittanning; farm trading center; brick, tile, lumber, flour; bituminous coal, oil, gas. Settled 1785, laid out 1840, inc. 1853.

Newbiggin (nu"bĭ'gĭn). **1** Agr. village and parish (pop. 110), N Westmorland, England, 6 mi. NW of Appleby. **2** or **Newbiggin-on-Lune,** agr. village, central Westmorland, England, on Lune R. and 9 mi. S of Appleby. Has Norman church, rebuilt in 14th cent.

Newbiggin-by-the-Sea, urban district (1931 pop. 6,904; 1951 census 9,727), E Northumberland, England, on North Sea, 15 mi. N of Newcastle-upon-Tyne; coal mining; fishing port. Cable to Arendal, Norway. In urban dist. (W) is coal-mining town of Woodhorn Demesne (dĭmān').

Newbiggin-on-Lune, England: see NEWBIGGIN.

Newbliss, Gaelic *Lios Darach,* town (pop. 202), W Co. Monaghan, Ireland, 4 mi. ESE of Clones; agr. market (flax, oats, potatoes).

New Bloomfield, Pa.: see BLOOMFIELD.

New Bloomington, village (pop. 288), Marion co., central Ohio, 10 mi. W of Marion, in agr. area.

Newbold, England: see CHESTERFIELD.

Newborn, town (pop. 298), Newton co., N central Ga., 11 mi. ESE of Covington.

Newboro (nū'bûrō), village (pop. 332), SE Ont., on Newboro L. (8 mi. long, 3 mi. wide), 30 mi. NNE of Kingston; dairying, mixed farming.

New Boston. 1 City (pop. 767), Mercer co., NW Ill., on the Mississippi (ferry here) and 25 mi. NNE of Burlington (Iowa), in agr. area. **2** Village, Berkshire co., Mass.: see SANDISFIELD. **3** Village (1940 pop. 591), Wayne co., SE Mich., 21 mi. SW of Detroit and on Huron R. **4** Agr. town (pop. 865), Hillsboro co., S N.H., on South Branch of Piscataquog R. and 12 mi. W of Manchester. **5** Village (pop. 4,754), Scioto co., S Ohio, on the Ohio and surrounded on W, N, and E by Portsmouth; steel, wire, nails, brick. Founded 1891. **6** Village (1940 pop. 589), Schuylkill co., E central Pa., just S of Mahanoy City, in anthracite region. **7** Town (pop. 2,688), Bowie co., NE Texas, 22 mi. W of Texarkana; trade center in timber, agr. area; lumber milling, cotton ginning. In area settled in 1820s; town inc. 1910.

Newbottle, town and parish (pop. 6,811), NE Durham, England, 5 mi. SW of Sunderland; coal mining.

New Braintree, town (pop. 478), Worcester co., central Mass., 16 mi. WNW of Worcester, in agr. and dairying area.

New Brancepeth, England: see BRANDON AND BYSHOTTLES.

New Braunfels (broun'fŭlz), city (pop. 12,210), ⊙ Comal co., S central Texas, on Guadalupe R. and 29 mi. NE of San Antonio. Comal Springs here feed beautiful Comal R. (c.4 mi. long), which enters Guadalupe R. within city. Power plants supply San Antonio, other cities, and local plants processing wool and mfg. clothing, textiles, furniture, flour, feed, leather, lime, foundry products, cedar oil, rock wool. Limestone quarrying. Landa Park is near. Settled 1845 by Germans, inc. 1847, it retains much of the atmosphere brought by founders.

New Bremen (brē'mŭn), village (pop. 1,546), Auglaize co., W Ohio, 7 mi. S of St. Marys; dairy products, rubber goods, machinery, fabrics, brooms, brushes, tile. Settled 1832, inc. 1833.

Newbridge or **Droichead Nua,** town (pop. 3,151), central Co. Kildare, Ireland, on the Liffey and 5 mi. ENE of Kildare; agr. market (cattle, horses; potatoes); rope mfg. Town grew around barracks built here 1816.

New Brighton, England: see WALLASEY.

New Brighton, residential town, S Cape Prov., U. of So. Afr., on Algoa Bay of the Indian Ocean; N suburb of Port Elizabeth; resort.

New Brighton. 1 Village (pop. 2,218), Ramsey co., E Minn., near Mississippi R., 9 mi. N of St. Paul, in lake region; corn, oats, barley, potatoes, livestock, poultry. **2** A section of Richmond borough of New York city, SE N.Y., on N Staten Isl. at junction of Kill Van Kull and Upper New York Bay; residential, industrial. Mfg. of clothing, electrical equipment, furniture, leather goods, machinery, steel chains, artificial fruit, fire extinguishers, paints, textile products, chemicals; shipbuilding. Sailors' Snug Harbor, a home for retired seamen, is near by. **3** Borough (pop. 9,535), Beaver co., W Pa., 26 mi. NW of Pittsburgh and on Beaver R.; metal and clay products, machinery, lumber. State armory. Blockhouse erected here 1789. Settled c.1801, inc. 1838.

New Britain, volcanic island (□ 14,600; pop. c.80,000), largest of Bismarck Archipelago, Territory of New Guinea, SW Pacific, 55 mi. NE of New Guinea; 5°38'S 148°25'E; c.300 mi. long, 50 mi. wide. Mountainous; highest peak Ulawan (7,546 ft.). Volcanoes, hot springs. Gazelle Peninsula, in extreme NE, is site of Rabaul, former ⊙ Territory of New Guinea. Willaumez Peninsula is on N coast. Produces copper, gold, some iron and coal; coffee is grown. In Second World War, Rabaul was key Jap. naval base (1942–44); other bases at Cape Gloucester (W) and Gasmata (S). Formerly New Pommern, later New Pomerania.

New Britain. 1 Industrial city (pop. 73,726), coextensive with New Britain town, Hartford co., central Conn., 8 mi. SW of Hartford. Known as the Hardware City, mfg. also household appliances, tools, machinery, bearings, electrical equipment, clothing, wood and paper products. Metalworking began here in 18th cent. Has state teachers col. (1850; 1st in state), art mus. Settled 1686–90; inc. as town 1850, inc. as city 1870. **2** Borough (pop. 581), Bucks co., SE Pa., 3 mi. WSW of Doylestown.

New Brockton, town (pop. 1,055), Coffee co., SE Ala., 33 mi. WNW of Dothan; woodworking.

New Brookland, S.C.: see WEST COLUMBIA.

Newbrough (nū'brŭf), town and parish (pop. 656), S central Northumberland, England, 4 mi. NW of Hexham; coal mining, stone quarrying. In parish (E) is paper-milling village of Fourstones.

New Brunswick, province (land area □ 27,473, total □ 27,985; 1941 pop. 457,401; 1948 estimate 503,000), of E Canada, one of the Maritime Provinces; ⊙ Fredericton. Bounded by Maine (W), Quebec (NE and N), Chaleur Bay (N), the Gulf of St. Lawrence and Northumberland Strait (E), Nova Scotia (SE), and the Bay of Fundy (S); 45°2'–48°4'N 63°46'–69°3'W. Main rivers are the St. John, Petitcodiac, Richibucto, Miramichi, Nipisiguit, Restigouche, Madawaska, and Tobique, providing important inland transportation routes. Surface is generally low and level, rising to highland region in NW, an extension of the Appalachian system. Here are many ridges over 2,000 ft. high; Mount Carleton (2,690 ft.) is highest point. There are numerous lakes, specially in SW part of prov.; Grand Lake (□ 67.2) is the largest. Rainfall is heavy, averaging 42 in. annually; winter climate is severe, especially inland, with heavy snowfall in N part of prov. Bay of Fundy tides keep St. John an ice-free port the year round. S coast is rocky and deeply indented by Passamaquoddy and Chignecto bays; E coast is flat and marshy, with extensive tracts of reclaimed land. There are several large game reserves; moose, caribou, deer, and game birds abound and attract many sportsmen. Fur-bearing animals include fox, lynx, marten. Salmon and trout are found in most rivers. New Brunswick's timber resources are extensive: black spruce, birch, beech, cedar, hemlock, ash, oak. Forests are mainly crown property. Lumbering, pulp milling, and allied industries are leading activities of prov. Soil is fertile in central and S part of prov.: cattle, sheep, hogs, horses, poultry; grain, feed crops, potatoes, apples, small fruits. There is an extensive dairying industry. Coal is mined in Grand Lake region; oil, oil shale, natural gas are exploited near Moncton. Gypsum, zinc, lead, copper, albertite, sandstone are also worked. There is an abundance of hydroelectric power. Sea fisheries (cod, herring, sardines, haddock, lobster, oysters, smelt) are important, and there are several fish curing, freezing, and canning plants. Industries include cotton milling, shipbuilding, woodworking, mfg. of furniture, shingles, doors, window sashes, and leather goods. St. John is largest city and chief port, with major dock installations and important trade with the West Indies and South America. Other important towns are Fredericton, Moncton, Chatham, Dalhousie, St. Stephen, Newcastle, Bathurst, Woodstock, Sussex, Sackville, and Shediac. Prov. includes Campobello, Deer, and Grand Manan isls. in the Bay of Fundy, and Shippigan and Miscou isls. in the Gulf of St. Lawrence. Coast of New Brunswick was 1st visited (1497) by John and Sebastian Cabot; Cartier explored Chaleur Bay, 1534. In 1604 de Monts and Champlain established 1st settlement in S of prov.

The region was granted (1621) to Sir William Alexander by James I, but French continued to claim it and to establish trade and military posts here. In 1633 French peasants were brought here to establish ACADIA. Treaty of Utrecht (1713) assigned the region to Great Britain; in 1755 Acadians were expelled from their settlements on the coast and driven inland, and an influx of English and Scottish settlers ensued, followed, after the American Revolution, by arrival of United Empire Loyalists, chiefly from New York and New Jersey. In 1784 New Brunswick, until then part of Nova Scotia, became separate prov.; in 1785 ⊙ was established at Fredericton. In 1867 prov. helped to form the confederation that became the dominion of Canada.

New Brunswick, city (pop. 38,811), ⊙ Middlesex co., E N.J., at head of navigation of Raritan R., at terminus of old Delaware and Raritan Canal, 22 mi. SE of Newark; mfg. (machinery, motor vehicles and parts, hosp. supplies, chemicals, pharmaceuticals; metal, wood, concrete, cork, and felt products; clothing, leather goods, dairy products). Rutgers Univ., affiliated N.J. Col. for Women, theological seminary, state agr. col., U.S. atomic laboratory here. Near by is Camp Kilmer, an important troop center in Second World War. Settled 1681, inc. 1730. Privateering port, occupied by British and Americans, in Revolution. Grew as a shipping center; industry (rubber, chemicals, textiles) began in 19th cent.; Johnson and Johnson medical and surgical supply factory opened 1886. Joyce Kilmer's birthplace and pre-Revolutionary houses are preserved.

New Buffalo. 1 Village (pop. 1,565), Berrien co., extreme SW Mich., 34 mi. NE of Gary (Ind.), on L. Michigan, in orchard and farm area; summer camps, resorts. Settled 1835, inc. 1836. **2** Borough (pop. 155), Perry co., central Pa., 14 mi. NNW of Harrisburg and on Susquehanna R.

New Bullards Bar Dam, Calif.: see YUBA RIVER.

Newburg (nōō'bûrg, nū'-). **1** Town, Maine: see NEWBURGH. **2** City (pop. 949), Phelps co., central Mo., in the Ozarks, near Gasconade R., 8 mi. W of Rolla; in tourist and agr. region; railroad shops. Fort Leonard Wood (c.20 mi. SW) was active in Second World War. Settled 1823. **3** Village (pop. 105), Bottineau co., N N.Dak., 22 mi. WSW of Bottineau. **4** Village, Ohio: see NEWBURGH HEIGHTS. **5** Borough (pop. 182), Clearfield co., W central Pa., 22 mi. SW of Clearfield. Post office name is La Jose. **6** Borough (pop. 289), Cumberland co., S Pa., 6 mi. NNW of Shippensburg. **7** Town (pop. 657), Preston co., N W.Va., 9 mi. ENE of Grafton, in agr. and coal-mining area.

Newburgh (nū'bûrg), village (pop. 471), SE Ont., on Napanee R. and 7 mi. NE of Napanee; paper milling.

Newburgh (nū'bûrŭ). **1** Fishing village in Foveran parish (pop. 1,521), E Aberdeen, Scotland, on Ythan R., near its mouth on the North Sea, 13 mi. NNE of Aberdeen. Just SW is agr. village of Foveran. **2** Burgh (1931 pop. 2,152; 1951 census 2,367), NW Fifeshire, Scotland, on the Firth of Tay, 8 mi. ESE of Perth; fishing port. Just E are remains of Lindores Abbey, founded 1178 by David, earl of Huntingdon; David, duke of Rothesay, buried here 1402. There are remains of anc. Macduff's Cross, destroyed by a mob in 1559.

Newburgh (nōō'bûrg, nū'-). **1** Town (pop. 1,324), Warrick co., SW Ind., on Ohio R. and 9 mi. E of Evansville; agr. (grain, tobacco); bituminous-coal mines; mfg. (concrete blocks, tobacco, flour). Settled 1817. **2** or **Newburg,** agr. town (pop. 599), Penobscot co., S Maine, 13 mi. WSW of Bangor. **3** City (pop. 31,956), Orange co., SE N.Y., on W bank of the Hudson (ferry), opposite Beacon; deepwater port; mfg. of clothing, textiles, sportswear, rugs, aluminum products, machinery, tile, medicines; shipbuilding (barges, tugs). Stewart Air Force Base is near by. Points of interest include Hasbrouck House (now a state mus.), which was Washington's hq. from April, 1782, to Aug., 1783; Knox's Revolutionary hq.; and Temple Hill. Continental army was disbanded in Newburgh. Settled 1709 by Palatines; resettled 1752 by English and Scotch; inc. 1865. Formerly a whaling port.

Newburgh Heights (nōō'bûrg, nū'-), village (pop. 3,689), Cuyahoga co., N Ohio, a S suburb of Cleveland; ceramic plants. Post office name, Newburg.

Newburn, urban district (1931 pop. 19,542; 1951 census 21,940), SE Northumberland, England, on the Tyne and 5 mi. W of Newcastle-upon-Tyne; coal-mining center, with pharmaceutical works. In urban dist. are coal-mining towns of Denton (E); Lemington (E) with glassworks; Throckley (NW); and Wallbottle (N).

New Burnside, village (pop. 244), Johnson co., S Ill., 17 mi. SW of Harrisburg, in rich fruitgrowing region of Ill. Ozarks.

Newbury, village (pop. 285), S Ont., 28 mi. NE of Chatham; fruitgrowing.

Newbury, municipal borough (1931 pop. 13,340; 1951 census 17,772), SW Berkshire, England, on Kennet R. and 15 mi. WSW of Reading; agr. market, with mfg. of aircraft, brick, tile, malt products, pharmaceuticals. Has 15th-cent. church, 16th-cent. Cloth Hall (now mus.), and 13th-cent. St. Bartholomew's Hosp. It was formerly center of cloth industry. Site of 2 Civil War battles (1643 and 1644). In district of Speenhamland, now part of Newbury, originated 1st English poor-relief system (1795). Just N are ruins of 14th-cent. Donnington Castle.

Newbury. 1 Town (pop. 1,994), Essex co., NE Mass., on coast, at mouth of Merrimack R., just S of Newburyport; summer resort; boatbuilding. Settled and inc. 1635. Includes village of Byfield. **2** Town (pop. 320), Merrimack co., S central N.H., on L. Sunapee and 27 mi. NW of Concord. **3** Town (pop. 1,667), including Newbury village (1940 pop. 391), Orange co., E Vt., on the Connecticut and 24 mi. SE of Barre. Settled 1762 on site of Indian village. Site of Revolutionary fort and E terminus of military road built 1776. Includes industrial village of WELLS RIVER.

Newburyport, city (pop. 14,111), a ⊙ Essex co., NE Mass., on Merrimack R., just above its mouth, and 16 mi. ENE of Lawrence; mfg. (shoes, silverware, electrical apparatus, tools, machine-shop products), distilling. Former shipping, whaling, and shipbuilding center. Has fine old houses. Settled 1635, set off from Newbury 1764, inc. as city 1851.

New Butler, Wis.: see BUTLER.

New Byth (bīth'), agr. village, N Aberdeen, Scotland, 7 mi. ENE of Turriff.

New Calabar River (kă'lŭbär), arm of Niger R. delta, in Eastern Provinces, S Nigeria, entering Gulf of Guinea W of Bonny.

New Caledonia (kă"lūdō'nyŭ), Fr. *Nouvelle Calédonie* (nōōvĕl' kälādônē'), volcanic island (□ 8,548; pop. 48,000), in SW Pacific, forming with isl. dependencies an overseas territory (□ 9,401; pop. c.60,000) of the French Union, 750 mi. E of Australia; 21°10'S 165°30'E; ⊙ Nouméa. Isl. is 248 mi. long, 31 mi. wide. Steamship service to Sydney; air base (established 1939) on Calif.–N.Z. route. Mountainous; highest peak, Mt. Panié (5,412 ft.); interior plateaus, coastal plains. Temp. ranges from 86°F. (Jan.–Feb.) to 75°F. (July–Aug.); mean annual rainfall 43 in.; tropical hurricanes. No malaria. Extensive mineral resources include major nickel mines, and also chrome, cobalt, iron, manganese, antimony, mercury, cinnabar, silver, gold, lead, and copper deposits. Nickel smelters at Yaté and Doniambo (near Koné). Large livestock industry. Coffee is chief crop. Exports nickel, chrome, coffee. Kauri pine, tree ferns, coconuts. Kagu (*Rhinochetos jubatus*) are ground birds found nowhere else. Natives are blend of Melanesian and Polynesian; Javanese and Tonkinese indentured laborers. Discovered 1774 by Capt. Cook, claimed 1853 by France, used 1864–94 as penal colony. In Second World War colony was Free French; occupied 1942 and air base established at Nouméa by U.S. forces to prevent possible Jap. invasion. Became overseas territory in 1946. Dependencies are LOYALTY ISLANDS, Isle of PINES, HUON ISLANDS, CHESTERFIELD ISLANDS, WALPOLE ISLAND, BELEP ISLANDS. Wallis and Futuna Isls., a separate protectorate, are also dependency of New Caledonia.

New Cambria. 1 (kām'brēŭ) City (pop. 160), Saline co., central Kansas, on Saline R. near its mouth on Smoky Hill R., and 6 mi. ENE of Salina; wheat, livestock. **2** (kăm'brēŭ) Town (pop. 295), Macon co., N central Mo., near Chariton R., 15 mi. W of Macon; agr.

New Canaan (kā'nŭn), residential town (pop. 8,001), Fairfield co., SW Conn., 7 mi. NE of Stamford; nurseries; dairy products, wood products. Settled c.1700, inc. 1801.

New Canada, plantation (pop. 444), Aroostook co., NE Maine, on Fish R. and 42 mi. NW of Presque Isle; hunting, fishing.

New Canton, town (pop. 449), Pike co., W Ill., near the Mississippi, 24 mi. SE of Quincy, in agr. area.

New Carlisle, village (pop. estimate 1,000), ⊙ Bonaventure co., E Que., on SE Gaspé Peninsula, on N side of entrance of Chaleur Bay, 50 mi. E of Dalhousie; market center in lumbering, dairying region; resort.

New Carlisle (kärlīl'). **1** Town (pop. 983), St. Joseph co., N Ind., 12 mi. W of South Bend, in agr. area. **2** Village (pop. 1,640), Clark co., W central Ohio, 12 mi. W of Springfield, and on small Honey Creek, in agr. area; sporting goods, neon signs, food products, pottery. Founded 1810.

New Castile, Spain: see CASTILE.

Newcastle (nū'kă"sŭl), municipality (pop. 127,188), 2d largest city of New South Wales, Australia, a port 75 mi. NNE of Sydney, on S shore of Port Hunter (see HUNTER, PORT); 32°56'S 151°47'E. Center of largest coal-mining area of Australia. Industrial center; iron- and steelworks, abattoirs, govt.-owned shipyards, floating docks. Exports coal, wheat, wool. Anglican cathedral. Founded 1797.

Newcastle. 1 Town (pop. 3,781), ⊙ Northumberland co., NE N.B., on Miramichi R. estuary (bridge) and 75 mi. NNW of Moncton; 47°N 65°35'W; port of entry, with coastal trade, shipping lumber and iron; shipyards, pulp mills, mfg. of creosote, bldg. materials. Large radio station here was Br. govt.'s receiving station in First World War. **2** Village (pop. 742), S Ont., on L. Ontario, 15 mi. E of Oshawa; dairying, farming.

Newcastle or **Newcastle West,** Gaelic *Caisleán Nua*, town (pop. 2,792), W Co. Limerick, Ireland, near Deel R., 23 mi. SW of Limerick; agr. market (grain, potatoes; dairying). Has 12th-cent. castle of the Knights Templars.

Newcastle, town, St. Andrew parish, E Jamaica, in Blue Mts., 9 mi. NE of Kingston; alt. c.3,700 ft.; mtn. resort; military barracks.

Newcastle, urban district (1937 pop. 2,428; 1951 census 3,076), SE Co. Down, Northern Ireland, on Dundrum Bay of the Irish Sea, 28 mi. S of Belfast, at foot of the Mourne Mts.; fishing port and seaside resort. Castle, of which there are some remains, was built 1588 on site of earlier structure.

Newcastle, town (pop. 10,001), NW Natal, U. of So. Afr., on Incandu R. and 160 mi. NNW of Durban, 160 mi. SE of Johannesburg, at foot of Drakensberg range; steel center; coal mining; mfg. of stoves, bricks, tiles, dairy products; wool and grain market. Base of British military operations in Transvaal revolt (1880–81); peace treaty signed here 1881.

New Castle, county (□ 437; pop. 218,879), N Del.; ⊙ WILMINGTON, state's largest city and commercial and industrial center. Bounded N by Pa. line, W by Md. line, S by Smyrna R., E by Delaware R. Agr. (dairy products, poultry, corn, wheat, livestock); shipping at Wilmington. Crossed by Chesapeake and Delaware Canal; drained by Christina R. and Brandywine, Red Clay, and White Clay creeks. Formed 1672.

New Castle. 1 Town (pop. 483), Garfield co., W Colo., on Colorado R. and 11 mi. W of Glenwood Springs, in irrigated agr. region; alt. 5,552 ft. Coal deposits. **2** City (pop. 5,396), New Castle co., N Del., 5 mi. S of Wilmington and on Delaware R., here spanned to N.J. by Delaware Memorial Bridge; mfg. (rayon, steel, aircraft, shoes, paint, drugs). Seat of King's Col. Peter Stuyvesant built fort near here in 1651; settlement held successively by Swedes, Dutch, and English; William Penn took possession (1682). Was ⊙ of Three Lower Counties-on-the-Delaware from 1704 to 1777. Inc. 1875. Many historic sites extant. **3** City (pop. 18,271), ⊙ Henry co., E Ind., on Big Blue R. and 18 mi. S of Muncie; trade and distribution center in agr. area (livestock, grain, poultry). Mfg.: automobile parts, machinery, steel products, furniture, clothing, caskets. Greenhouses. Seat of state colony for epileptics. Has a monument to Wilbur Wright, b. near here. Founded c.1820, laid out 1836. Prehistoric remains have been discovered in this area. **4** Town (pop. 631), ⊙ Henry co., N Ky., 23 mi. NW of Frankfort, in Bluegrass agr. area. **5** Town (pop. 583), Rockingham co., SE N.H., on small isl. (□ .75) in Portsmouth harbor; bridged to mainland. Settlement here, chartered 1693, was pre-Revolutionary governors' seat; here are ruins of Fort Constitution (then Castle William and Mary), seized by colonists in 1774. **6** City (pop. 48,834), ⊙ Lawrence co., W Pa., 43 mi. NNW of Pittsburgh, at confluence of Shenango and Mahoning rivers to form Beaver R., in bituminous-coal and limestone area. Tin plate and metal products, pottery, bricks, cement, chemicals, heating equipment, machinery, explosives, automobile parts, clothing, beer. Early Indian trading center; growth stimulated by completion 1833 of Erie Extension canal. Settled 1798, laid out 1802, inc. as borough 1825, as city c.1869.

Newcastle. 1 Village (pop. c.750), Placer co., central Calif., in Sacramento Valley, just SW of Auburn; ships fruit. **2** Town (pop. 1,021), Lincoln co., S Maine, on Damariscotta R. inlet (bridged to Damariscotta) and 6 mi. NE of Wiscasset; wood products, machine parts. **3** Village (pop. 426), Dixon co., NE Nebr., 25 mi. WNW of Sioux City, Iowa, near Missouri R., in fertile agr. region; livestock, poultry produce, grain. **4** City (pop. 743), Young co., N Texas, near Brazos R., c.50 mi. SSW of Wichita Falls; oil fields near; tile mfg., some coal mining. Old Fort Belknap (1851; partly restored) is just S. Formerly coal-mining center. **5** Town (pop. 239), ⊙ Craig co., W Va., in the Alleghenies, on Craig Creek and 17 mi. NNW of Roanoke. **6** City (pop. 3,395), ⊙ Weston co., NE Wyo., just SW of Black Hills, near S.Dak. line, 50 mi. WSW of Rapid City, S.Dak.; alt. 4,334 ft. Shipping point for livestock, lumber, oil products, bentonite; food processing (dairy products, flour). Pioneer relics in 2 local museums. Scenic region of caves, canyons, lakes and streams in near-by Black Hills. Founded 1889.

Newcastle, town in Newcastle Higher parish (pop. 3,935), S Glamorgan, Wales, on Ogwr R., just W of Bridgend; agr.

Newcastle Bay, inlet of Torres Strait, N Cape York Peninsula, N Queensland, Australia, just S of Cape York; 11 mi. long, 10 mi. wide; shallow.

Newcastle Emlyn, urban district (1931 pop. 763; 1951 census 763), NW Carmarthen, Wales, on Teifi R. and 9 mi. ESE of Cardigan; agr. market, with woolen mills. Remains of 15th-cent. castle.

Newcastle Harbour, Australia: see HUNTER, PORT.

Newcastleton, agr. village in Castleton parish (pop. 1,794), S Roxburgh, Scotland, on Liddel Water and 8 mi. ENE of Langholm. Hermitage Castle (built c.1224, restored in 19th cent.) is 5 mi. N.

Newcastle-under-Lyme (līm), municipal borough (1931 pop. 23,246; 1951 census 70,028), N Stafford, England, in the Potteries area, 2 mi. W of Stoke-on-Trent; has coal mines; pottery, clothing, paper, steelworking, machinery, and tile industries. Has 13th-cent. church, rebuilt in 19th cent. City has absorbed near-by areas, notably Wolstanton United in 1932.

Newcastle-upon-Tyne or **Newcastle-on-Tyne** (tīn), county borough (1931 pop. 283,156; 1951 census 291,723) and city, ⊙ Northumberland, England, in SE part of co., on N bank of the Tyne (bridged) 8 mi. from the sea and 260 mi. NNW of London; 54°58'N 1°37'W; major industrial center. On site of Roman station of *Pons Aelii*, on Hadrian's Wall, it later became a settlement of the Angles, called Monkchester or Monk Chester, site of several monastic settlements. In 1080 Robert of Normandy built a castle here, from which town took its present name. Existing castle remains date from 1177. Newcastle has remains of 13th-cent. town walls, 14th-cent. cathedral, a grammar school founded 1525, guildhall (1658), and Trinity Almshouse (1492). Site of Col. of Medicine and Armstrong Col. of Science, affiliated with Univ. of Durham. An important shipbuilding and flour-milling center; other industries include machinery building, ironworking, leather tanning, mfg. of soap products and chemicals. Monument commemorates George and Robert Stephenson, who built one of the Tyne R. bridges (1849). In Second World War Newcastle was frequently bombed (1940–41). Chief industrial dists. are Elswick (W), Benwell (W), Fenham (W), Jesmond (N), Heaton (NE), and Walker (E).

Newcastle Waters, settlement (dist. pop. 174), N central Northern Territory, Australia, 375 mi. SSE of Darwin; airport; sheep.

Newcastle West, Co. Limerick, Ireland: see NEWCASTLE.

New Centerville, borough (pop. 145), Somerset co., SW Pa., 8 mi. SW of Somerset.

New Chicago, town (pop. 921), Lake co., extreme NW Ind., just SE of Gary, in industrial area.

Newchwang, Niuchwang, or **Niu-chuang** (all: nyō'-jwäng'), town, SW Liaotung prov., Manchuria, 25 mi. NE of Yingkow and on arm of lower Liao R. The oldest port for the Liao valley, Newchwang flourished throughout 18th cent. Changes in the lower Liao course and subsequent silting caused its gradual decline (19th cent.) and the outer port's transfer to TIENCHWANGTAI (c.1800) and to YINGKOW (1836).

New City, residential village (1940 pop. 992), ⊙ Rockland co., SE N.Y., 5 mi. NW of Nyack.

New Cold Harbor, Va.: see COLD HARBOR.

New Columbia, village (pop. c.400), Union co., E central Pa., 2 mi. NW of Milton, across West Branch of Susquehanna R.

New Columbus. 1 Village (pop. 4,186, with adjacent Nesquehoning), Carbon co., E Pa., 30 mi. NE of Pottsville. **2** Borough (pop. 152), Luzerne co., NE central Pa., 22 mi. WSW of Wilkes-Barre.

Newcomb (nōō'kům, nū'–), mining village, Essex co., NE N.Y., in the Adirondacks, 38 mi. WNW of Ticonderoga; ilmenite, magnetite.

Newcomerstown (nōō'kůmůrztoun), village (pop. 4,514), Tuscarawas co., E Ohio, 17 mi. SSW of New Philadelphia and on Tuscarawas R.; tools, hardware, iron pipe, clay products. Settled 1815 on site of Delaware Indians' capital; inc. 1838.

New Concord (kŏng'kůrd), village (pop. 1,797), Muskingum co., central Ohio, 15 mi. ENE of Zanesville, in agr. area. Seat of Muskingum Col. William Rainey Harper b. here. Founded c.1827.

New Corinth, Greece: see CORINTH.

New Coylton, Scotland: see COYLTON.

New Craighall (krāg'hôl), town in Inveresk parish, NE Midlothian, Scotland, 2 mi. WSW of Musselburgh; coal mining.

New Cristóbal (krēstō'bäl), NE residential section of Colón, Colón prov., central Panama.

New Cross, workers' residential and industrial district of Deptford, London, England, S of the Thames, 4.5 mi. ESE of Charing Cross.

New Croton Dam, N.Y.: see CROTON RIVER.

New Cumberland. 1 Borough (pop. 6,204), Cumberland co., S central Pa., on Susquehanna R. opposite Harrisburg; textiles, hosiery, tobacco products. Army depot and disciplinary barracks. Laid out c.1810, inc. 1831. **2** Town (pop. 2,119), ⊙ Hancock co., W.Va., in industrial Northern Panhandle, on the Ohio and 30 mi. W of Pittsburgh; mfg. of pottery, metal alloys, bricks; coal mines, clay pits. Fruit farms in region. Tomlinson Run State Park is near by. Platted 1839.

New Cumnock (kům'nůk), town and parish (pop. 6,420), SE Ayrshire, Scotland, on Nith R. at mouth of Afton R., 5 mi. E of Cumnock; coal-mining center.

New Dailly, Scotland: see DAILLY.

Newdale, village (pop. 312), Fremont co., E Idaho, 8 mi. SE of St. Anthony; alt. 5,068 ft.; livestock, potatoes.

New Deer, agr. village and parish (pop. 3,666), N Aberdeen, Scotland, 15 mi. W of Peterhead.

New Delhi (dě'lē), city (pop. 93,733; including cantonment area, 116,874), ⊙ India, in DELHI state, on right (W) bank of Jumna R. and 740 mi. NNE of Bombay, 800 mi. NW of Calcutta, and 660 mi. ENE of Karachi (⊙ Pakistan); 28°37'N 77°13'E. Predominantly an administrative center, constructed 1912–29 (inaugurated 1931) on previously unoccupied site (c.650 ft. high) just SSW of DELHI city to replace Calcutta as ⊙ India. Its broad, symmetrically aligned streets provide vistas of vicinity's historic monuments. Bet. the main govt. bldgs. (Palladian classic with Indian details) and official residences, a broad boulevard, flanked by lawns and pools, leads E–W from a massive war memorial arch (1921) through a great court (1,100 ft. by 400 ft.; the Raisina) to the resplendent red sandstone and marble Govt. House (formerly Viceroy's palace; now residence of India's president); 1 mile NE of Govt. House, Connaught Place (shopping center) sends out radial roads; on one of these is the hq. of All-India Radio (of contemporary modern architecture) and Jantar Mantar, the ruined early-18th-cent. observatory built by a Rajput astronomer. The estate of G. D. Birla, Indian industrialist, in S section of city, was the scene of Mahatma Gandhi's assassination on Jan. 30, 1948, as he was about to conduct a prayer meeting. In W area are Balmiki Temple, in a sweepers' colony, where Gandhi often stayed on visits to New Delhi, and Lakshminarayan Temple (built by R. B. Birla and opened 1939 by Gandhi as place of worship for all Hindus, including *harijans*—formerly outcastes). At Natl. Sports Stadium (holds over 30,000 spectators), SE of war memorial arch, 1st Asian Olympic meet was held in 1951. In city's vicinity are several institutes conducted by central India govt., including Indian Agr. Research Inst., Malaria Inst. of India, Tuberculosis Inst., Natl. Physical Laboratory (applied physics; 1950), Road Research Inst. (1950), and Central Inst. of Education (1947). Univ. of Delhi is in Delhi city. Intercontinental airport at Palam (10 mi. WSW of city center); Safdar Jang (formerly Willingdon) domestic airport is just S of city. During summer (Delhi temp. often exceeds 110°F. in May) most govt. business is carried on in SIMLA, in the Himalayas.

New Denver, village (pop. 310), SE B.C., 35 mi. N of Nelson; silver, lead, zinc mining.

New Dongola, Anglo-Egyptian Sudan: see DONGOLA.

New Dorp (nōō' dôrp", nū'), SE N.Y., a section of Richmond borough of New York city, on E central Staten Isl.; residential; some mfg. (clothing, electronic equipment, machinery). Bathing beaches near by.

New Douglas, village (pop. 359), Madison co., SW Ill., 20 mi. NE of Edwardsville, in agr. area (corn, wheat; dairy products; poultry, livestock).

New Dundee (důndē'), village (pop. estimate 400), S Ont., 8 mi. SSW of Kitchener; dairying, mixed farming.

New Durham (dů'rům), town (pop. 463), Strafford co., SE N.H., near Merrymeeting L., 23 mi. NW of Dover.

New Eagle, borough (pop. 2,316), Washington co., SW Pa., just below Monongahela on Monongahela R., S of Pittsburgh. Inc. 1912.

New Echota Marker National Memorial, Ga.: see CALHOUN, city, Ga.

New Effington, town (pop. 367), Roberts co., NE S.Dak., 25 mi. NNE of Sisseton; dairy products, livestock, corn, wheat.

New Egypt, village (pop. 1,294), Ocean co., central N.J., on Crosswicks Creek and 17 mi. SE of Trenton; agr., mfg. (clothing, canned cranberries).

Newell (nū'ůl). **1** Town (pop. 884), Buena Vista co., NW Iowa, 10 mi. ESE of Storm Lake; concrete and dairy products, feed. **2** Village (1940 pop. 980), Fayette co., SW Pa., on Monongahela R. and 25 mi. S of Pittsburgh; railroad shops, chemical plant. **3** City (pop. 784), Butte co., W S.Dak., 22 mi. E of Belle Fourche, in heart of irrigated area; diversified farming; sugar beets, grain, dairy products, honey. Near by is a substation of state experiment farm. **4** Village (pop. 2,101), Hancock co., W.Va., in Northern Panhandle, 2 mi. SW of East Liverpool, Ohio, across Ohio R.; large china factory.

New Ellenton, village, Aiken co., W S.C., 5 mi. S of Aiken; grew after establishment near by of Atomic Energy Commission's Savannah River plant (S).

Newellton (nū'ůltůn), village (pop. 1,280), Tensas parish, NE La., 29 mi. SW of Vicksburg (Miss.), on L. St. Joseph; agr.; cotton gins, sawmills.

New England, region (□ 63,206; pop. 9,314,453) of NE U.S., on the Atlantic; includes 6 states—MAINE, NEW HAMPSHIRE, VERMONT, MASSACHUSETTS, RHODE ISLAND, CONNECTICUT. Bordered N by Canada, S by Long Island Sound, W by N.Y. state line (L. Champlain in N). Land rises sharply from thin coastal strip to granitic New England upland of the Appalachian system. Chief ranges are Green Mts. (Vt.), White Mts. (N.H.), Berkshire Hills (Mass. and Conn.), Taconic Mts. (on N.Y.-Mass. border). Cliffs intermittently line the jagged coast, which offers numerous fine harbors. Only long river is the Connecticut (flows S from Canadian border to Long Island Sound), but there are many short, swift streams. Region is dotted with glacial lakes. Climate is humid continental, with cool summers and sometimes very severe winters (c.–50°F.). Growing season is 90 (N) to 150 days. Only specialty farming is profitable on rocky New England soils: dairying and sheep raising (in the hills), truck and tobacco farming (especially in Connecticut R. valley), potatoes (NE Maine). The land offered few natural resources but the fine coastal inlets led to early development of fishing industry from well-stocked ocean waters. Boston, Gloucester, and Portsmouth are leading fishing ports today; finfish (e.g., mackerel, herring) and Maine lobsters are taken from coastal waters; offshore and to NE are famous Newfoundland GRAND BANKS (cod). New England, specializing in skilled mfg., is heavily industrialized, with c.¾ of its pop. in cities. Products include textiles, shoes, light mfg., pulp, paper, ships, machinery. BOSTON (pop. 801,444) is the largest city, transportation hub, financial and commercial center of New England. Variety and beauty of natural features, plus a wealth of historic landmarks, provide New England with lucrative year-round tourist industry. Chief minerals are granite, marble, slate (Vt. and N.H.). Scene of second area of permanent English settlement in America (begun 1620 at PLYMOUTH, Mass.). Council of New England (1620–35), though granted all the territory of present New England, and much beyond, was ineffectual in governing the New England colonies, especially that of Mass. Bay. New England Confederation, 1st experiment in federation in America, a union for safety against Indians and for general welfare, formed by colonies of Mass. Bay, Plymouth, Conn., and New Haven, existed 1643–84. With the Dominion of New England (1686–89), the British govt. made the colonies of N.H., Mass., R.I., and Conn., plus N.Y. and N.J., into a short-lived single prov. In colonial days farmers eked out a meager living by raising grain (declined after 1825 because of Erie Canal). Shipping and shipbuilding flourished in 18th and 19th cent. The English Navigation Acts were particularly onerous to New England, which became chief center of events leading to the Revolution and scene of opening engagements. The early days of the Republic, when American clippers plied all the seas, saw much trade directed toward the American NW and China, as well as advent of great whaling industry (to 1850s). U.S. Embargo Act of 1807 and War of 1812 created such great opposition that New England threatened secession. The postwar period saw the growth of mfg., utilizing the abundant water power. There was also much migration to the Old Northwest. The geographic and early political conditions developed a New England type of British stock, generally referred to as Yankee; according to tradition, he has a genius for self-government, thrift, generosity to a cause considered worthy, and general resourcefulness. Notably in the period before the Civil War, the section furnished leaders for social and humanitarian movements, and it still ranks as a leading literary and educational center. The post-Civil-War period, with high industrial wages, brought tremendous immigrant influx, especially of Irish and French Canadians. The depression of the 1930s hit New England hard, and its industry suffered also from the development of the great textile industry of the South. But during the Second World War, the skilled New England factory worker again was in demand and industry boomed; post-war efforts were increased to maintain the skilled industries.

New England, city (pop. 1,117), Hettinger co., SW N.Dak., 23 mi. S of Dickinson and on Cannonball R.; wheat center; coal mines, grain elevators, dairy products, poultry, flax.

New England Range, NE New South Wales, Australia, part of Great Dividing Range; extends c.120 mi. S from Tenterfield to Uralla. Rises to 5,100 ft. at Ben Lomond, ENE of Emmaville. Sometimes called New England Plateau.

Newenham, Cape (nōō'ůnhăm), SW Alaska, on Bering Sea, bet. Kuskokwim Bay (N) and Bristol Bay (S), 130 mi. W of Dillingham; 58°39'N 162°2' W; extremity of small peninsula formed by rugged mts.

Newent, town and parish (pop. 2,299), NW Gloucester, England, 9 mi. NW of Gloucester; agr. market. Has 16th-cent. church and market house.

New Era (ēr'ů), village (pop. 247), Oceana co., W Mich., 9 mi. S of Hart.

New Fairfield, town (pop. 1,236), Fairfield co., SW Conn., bet. N.Y. line and L. Candlewood, just N of Danbury. State park, state forest here; resorts. Inc. 1740.

Newfane (nōō'fān"). **1** Village (pop. 1,578), Niagara co., W N.Y., near L. Ontario, 25 mi. NNE of Buffalo, in fruitgrowing area; mfg. (canned foods, felt, paper); nurseries. **2** Town (pop. 708), including Newfane village (pop. 156), ⊙ Windham co., SE Vt., on West R. and 10 mi. NW of Brattleboro; resort.

New Ferry, village (pop. 2,982) in Bebington and Bromborough urban dist., NW Cheshire, England, on Mersey R. and 2 mi. SSE of Birkenhead; mfg. of chemicals.

Newfield, town and parish (pop. 998), central Durham, England, 2 mi. N of Bishop Auckland; coal mining.

Newfield. 1 Town (pop. 355), York co., SW Maine, 32 mi. W of Portland. Severely damaged (1947) by forest fire. **2** Borough (pop. 1,010), Gloucester co., S N.J., 10 mi. N of Millville; glass products.

Newfields, town (pop. 469), Rockingham co., SE N.H., on Squamscott R. and 8 mi. WSW of Portsmouth.

New Fletton. 1 Town, Huntingdon, England: see OLD FLETTON. **2** Town, Northampton, England: see PETERBOROUGH.

New Florence. 1 Town (pop. 522), Montgomery co., E central Mo., 5 mi. SSE of Montgomery City; agr. (grain, livestock); brickworks; limestone quarries. **2** Borough (pop. 924), Westmoreland co., SW central Pa., 10 mi. WNW of Johnstown and on Conemaugh R.

Newfolden, village (pop. 367), Marshall co., NW Minn., on Middle R. and 18 mi. NNW of Thief River Falls; dairying.

New Forest, partly wooded area (□ 144.4), an anc. royal hunting ground, in SW Hampshire, England; 14 mi. long (N–S), 16 mi. wide (E–W), bounded by Avon R., The Solent, and Southampton Water. One quarter is under cultivation; the remainder is open wood, moor, or heathland. Pigs, cattle, and half-wild ponies are bred here. Named in 1079 and afforested under William I. It is administered as natl. park by Court of Verderers. Chief towns are Lyndhurst and Ringwood.

New Fort Hamilton, village (1939 pop. 15), W Alaska, on arm of Yukon R. delta, 80 mi. SW of St. Michael; supply point. Sometimes called New Hamilton. Hamilton village 10 mi. N.

Newfound Gap (alt. 5,048 ft.), on Tenn.–N.C. line, pass through Great Smoky Mts., 8 mi. SSE of Gatlinburg, Tenn. Crossed by highway bet. Gatlinburg and Cherokee, N.C., through Great Smoky Mts. Natl. Park.

Newfound Lake, Grafton co., central N.H., resort lake in hilly region 12 mi. NNW of Franklin; 6 mi. long, 2.5 mi. wide. Drains S through Newfound R. (2.5 mi. long), past Bristol (water power), to the Pemigewasset.

Newfoundland (nū″fŭndlănd′, nū′fŭndlŭnd), island (land area □ 37,392, total □ 42,734; 1945 pop. 314,573) and easternmost province (□ 152,734; pop. 320,101; including Labrador with area of □ c.110,000 and pop. of 5,528) of Canada; ⊙ St. John's. It is in the Atlantic, separated from the mainland by Cabot Strait (SW), the Gulf of St. Lawrence (W), the Strait of Belle Isle (NW). Extremities are Cape Pine (S), 46°37′N 53°32′W; Cape Anguille (W), 47°54′N 59°27′W; Cape Norman (N), 51°38′N 55°54′W; and Cape Spear (E), 47°32′N 57°38′W. Roughly triangular in shape (greatest length c.300 mi.), isl. has deeply indented coastline. Larger bays are Placentia, Fortune, Hermitage, d'Espoir, St. George's, Port au Port, Bonne, St. John, Hare, White, Notre Dame, Bonavista, Trinity, Conception, St. Mary's bays, and the Bay of Islands. Newfoundland is surrounded by numerous isls.; Fogo and Random are the largest; off N extremity is Belle Isle. Coast is mostly steep, rocky, and barren, indented by small fjordlike inlets. Of the many peninsulas, Great Northern (NW), Burin (S), and Avalon (SE) are important; Avalon peninsula is center of Newfoundland population. Surface of isl. consists generally of an undulating plateau, with low hills; highest elevations are in the Long Range Mts. (NW), which rise to 2,666 ft. on Gros Morne. In W and S parts of isl. are numerous lakes; largest are Grand (□ 129), Red Indian (□ 70), Sandy (□ 49), and Gander (□ 46.5) lakes. Isl. is drained by Humber, Lloyds, Victoria, Exploits, Gander, and Terra Nova rivers. These and numerous smaller streams also supply important hydroelectric power to the large newsprint mills at Corner Brook and Grand Falls; lead, copper, zinc, silver, gold mines at Buchans; fluorspar mines at Great St. Lawrence; and numerous lumber mills. Fauna include caribou, wolves, bears, hares, otters, lynxes, foxes. Game birds and fresh-water fish (salmon, trout) abound. Mink and fox are raised on fur farms. Marine climate of Newfoundland is modified by cold Labrador Current; average Jan. temp. ranges from 14°F. (N) to 25°F. (S); July temp. from 53.5°F. (N) to 57°F. (S). Annual rainfall ranges from 30 inches (N) to 60 inches (S); central part of isl. has annual snowfall of over 120 inches. Fishing (cod, salmon, herring, lobster) and fish processing are most important occupations; there are numerous fish canneries and filleting, freezing, cold-storage plants. Cod-liver oil is important product. Apart from shore fisheries, chief fishing grounds are the Grand Banks and Labrador coast. Seals are taken for their skins and oils. Whaling industry has declined in importance in recent years. Sale of bait is in hands of govt., which operates a number of large depots. Subsistence agr. is carried on near most larger settlements; sheep are raised extensively. Cattle raising, dairying, farming are centered on fertile Codroy and Humber R. valleys. Mfg. industries are concentrated on Avalon peninsula and are mainly connected with fishing (marine engines, shipbuilding, fishing equipment) and lumbering (woodworking, furniture making). Bell Island, in Conception Bay, is ironmining center; ore is shipped to Sydney (N.S.) steel plants. Other minerals worked include gypsum, limestone. Besides St. John's, other towns are Corner Brook, West Corner Brook, Grand Bank, Harbour Grace, St. Anthony, Wesleyville, Channel–Port aux Basques (terminus of steamers from North Sydney, N.S.), and Placentia. In Second World War, U.S. naval and military base was established at Argentia, and air bases were built at Gander and Stephenville. Gander subsequently became major transatlantic airport. Heart's Content (Trinity Bay) is transatlantic cable terminal; 1st transatlantic cable was laid bet. here and Valentia, Ireland, in 1858. Newfoundland is considered oldest colony of Great Britain, who claimed it after its discovery (1497) by John Cabot. It was formally claimed (1583) by Sir Humphrey Gilbert, and its fisheries were developed by the English, French, Portuguese, and Spaniards, with the English gaining leading position. Lord Baltimore established ⊙ at Ferryland in 1616; in 1637 Sir David Kirke received isl. as county-palatinate. Concurrently French developed S part of isl., with ⊙ at Placentia. Treaty of Utrecht (1713) assigned Newfoundland to England, allowing France fishing monopoly on W and NE coasts, the so-called French Shore. French fishing rights were revised by treaties of 1763 and 1783, and finally purchased by Great Britain in 1904. United States fishing rights were adjusted by the Hague Court of International Justice in 1910. In 1713 Newfoundland was given jurisdiction over Labrador coastal strip, and in 1927 larger area of the region was awarded it over claims of Quebec. Early laws prohibiting settlement in Newfoundland were finally revoked 1820; isl. was granted representative govt. in 1832, and responsible govt. in 1855. Because of its desperate financial condition, it ceased to be a dominion in 1933, when govt. by a royal commission was instituted; in 1949 Newfoundland voted for union with Canada, of which it became a province. The Atlantic Conference bet. President Roosevelt and Winston Churchill took place in Placentia Bay, off Argentia, in Aug., 1941.

Newfoundland Canal, W central N.F., extends 10 mi. WSW–ESE bet. NE end of Deer L. and NE end of Grand L.

Newfoundland Mountains, NW Utah, in Great Salt Lake Desert, W of Great Salt L. Desert Peak (6,985 ft.) is highest point.

New Franklin, city (pop. 1,060), Howard co., central Mo., just N of Boonville across the Missouri; grain, fruit, livestock; railroad shops near by. Laid out 1828.

New Freedom, borough (pop. 1,271), York co., S Pa., 16 mi. S of York, on Md. border. Inc. 1879.

New Galilee (gă′lĭlē), borough (pop. 507), Beaver co., W Pa., 6 mi. WSW of Ellwood City.

New Galloway (gă′lōwā, –lŭwā), burgh (1931 pop. 307; 1951 census 305), central Kirkcudbright, Scotland, on Ken Water and 17 mi. N of Kirkcudbright; agr. market. Just S, on the Ken, is Loch Ken (lake 5 mi. long) with ruins of 15th–17th-cent. Kenmure Castle. Near S end of lake is hamlet of Little Duchrae (dŭ′krā); Samuel Crockett b. here.

Newgate (nū′gĭt, –gāt), former prison in London, England, now site of the Central Criminal Court or Old Bailey.

New Georgia, volcanic island group, (□ c.2,000; pop. c.7,300), Solomon Isls., SW Pacific, 90 naut. mi. NW of Guadalcanal. Largest isl., also called New Georgia, is 50 mi. long, c.20 mi. wide; chief town is Hobu Hobu. Produces copra. In Second World War, isl. was occupied 1942 by the Japanese; Munda in SW (site of Jap. air base) was taken 1943 by U.S. forces. Roviana Lagoon in S, Marovo Lagoon in N. Other isls. of group are KOLOMBANGARA, VANGUNU, RENDOVA, GIZO, Tetipari, Gatukai, and several smaller isls.

New Georgia Sound, SW Pacific, in Solomon Isls., bounded N by Choiseul and Santa Isabel, S by the New Georgia isl. group; extends c.310 mi. SE from Shortland Isls. (off Bougainville) to Florida and Savo (both near Guadalcanal). During Second World War, the Japanese used (1942) the passage as supply route for reinforcement of Guadalcanal. Amer. nickname: The Slot.

New Germany, village (pop. estimate 1,000), W N.S., on Lahave R. and 15 mi. N of Bridgewater.

New Germany. 1 Village, Garrett co., W Md., in the Alleghenies 18 mi. W of Cumberland; hq. for surrounding Savage R. State Forest. **2** Village (pop. 286), Carver co., S central Minn., 35 mi. W of Minneapolis in grain, livestock, and poultry area.

New Glarus (glă′rŭs), village (pop. 1,224), Green co., S Wis., on branch of Sugar R. and 23 mi. SW of Madison, in dairying region; cheese center; makes Swiss embroidery. Annual Swiss festival held here. New Glarus Woods state park is S. Founded by Swiss in 1845; inc. 1901.

New Glasgow (glăs′gō, glăz′–, glăs′kō), town (pop. 9,210), N N.S., port on East R. near its mouth on Pictou Harbour, and 80 mi. NE of Halifax, in coal-mining region; mfg. of steel products, boilers, bricks, tiles. Inc. 1875.

New Gloucester (glŏs′tŭr), rural town (pop. 2,628), Cumberland co., SW Maine, 9 mi. S of Auburn; shoe factory. Settled c.1743, inc. 1794. In it is Sabbathday Lake village, Shaker community settled 1793 near Sabbathday L., and Pownal State School.

New Goa, Portuguese India: see PANGIM.

New Granada, South America: see COLOMBIA.

New Grand Chain, village (pop. 330), Pulaski co., extreme S Ill., near Ohio R., 19 mi. NNE of Cairo, in agr. area. Also called Grand Chain.

New Grove, village (pop. 2,328), SE Mauritius, on railroad and 6 mi. WSW of Mahébourg; sugar cane.

New Guinea (gĭ′nē) or **Papua** (pă′pūŭ), Indonesian *Irian*, island (□ c.304,200; pop. c.1,750,000), next to Greenland the largest island in the world, separated from N Australia by Torres Strait and Arafura Sea; 0°21′–10°41′S 130°56′–150°53′E; c.1,500 mi. long, c.400 mi. wide at the center (where isl. is broadest). Extremely irregular in shape, isl. consists of broad central mass from which project a W peninsula (Vogelkop) and a SE peninsula tapering to a point. Prominent coastal features are Gulf of Papua in SE and Geelvink Bay in NW. Largely tropical jungle, isl. has extensive unexplored areas in mountainous interior. A series of high mtn. ranges run the length of isl. In W are Nassau Range containing Mt. Carstensz (16,400 ft., highest isl. peak in the world) and Orange Range; in E are Bismarck Mts. and Owen Stanley Range. Lower courses of the large and navigable rivers (Fly, Sepik, Mamberamo, Purari) are generally swampy, with some grassy areas. Climate is humid and unhealthful in low-lying coastal areas but comfortable and cool in highlands. Port Moresby area (SE) is relatively dry, with temp. range of 72°–95°F. The SE trade winds prevail March–Oct., followed by NW monsoon period. Rainfall is abundant in most areas. There is dense tropical vegetation, with orchids and ferns thriving in the rain forests. Alpine flora found in mountainous interior. Among many varieties of trees are sago, coconut, nipa palm, sandalwood, ebony, rubber, casuarina, cedar, breadfruit, and mangrove. Generally similar to that of Australia, fauna consists largely of marsupials and monotremes; among reptiles are venomous snakes and crocodiles. There are many species of butterflies and large variety of tropical birds including birds of paradise and cassowaries. Chief commercial product is copra; other products are rubber, coffee, sisal hemp, kapok. Gold is mined in E area, with chief gold field in Morobe dist. Some oil is produced in W area, where natural resources are still virtually unexploited. Pearl-shell and tortoise fisheries are found along the coast. Natives comprise Melanesians, Negritos, and Papuans; headhunting is still practised in interior regions. Principal center is Port Moresby on SE coast. New Guinea is divided politically into 3 sections: Netherlands New Guinea (see NEW GUINEA, NETHERLANDS), W of the meridian of longitude 141°E; Territory of New Guinea (see NEW GUINEA, TERRITORY OF) occupying NE part, and Territory of Papua (see PAPUA, TERRITORY OF) the SE section. The 2 E sections are divided by a line running SE from Du. boundary at 5°S to a point 6°S 144°E, thence to a point 8°S 147°E, thence by the parallel of 8°S to the sea. Probably 1st sighted 1511 by the Portuguese Antonio d'Abreu, isl. was visited a few years later by Sp. and Port. explorers, who were followed in next 2 centuries by the Dutch, English, and Germans. In Second World War, Jap. invasion (1942) in N was followed by gallant defense by small Allied force based at Port Moresby; failure of Jap. push overland, and Allied reconquest (1943 to early 1944) by air, sea, and jungle fighting.

New Guinea, Netherlands, or **Dutch New Guinea,** territory (□ 159,375; pop. 345,687) comprising W half of NEW GUINEA (W of longitude 141°E) and offshore isls. (principally SCHOUTEN ISLANDS, JAPEN ISLANDS, RAJA AMPAT ISLANDS, SALAWATI); ⊙ HOLLANDIA. The Dutch visited 1606 W coast of isl. Br. East India Co. briefly maintained in 1793 a settlement on isl. in Geelvink Bay. In 1828 the Dutch claimed possession of coast W of 141st meridian, and in 1848 over N coast W of Humboldt Bay. The Du. claim to W half of isl. was recognized 1885 by Great Britain and Germany. Netherlands New Guinea, long administered by the Dutch as part of the Netherlands East Indies, was not included in the territory of the Indonesian Republic formed after the Second World War. This proved a source of friction bet. Indonesia (who claimed the area on geographic grounds) and the Netherlands (who held that the largely primitive native Negroes of New Guinea had no ties to the Malay isls. of Indonesia).

New Guinea, Territory of (□ 93,000; pop. 1,080,000), SW Pacific, includes NE New Guinea, BISMARCK ARCHIPELAGO, northernmost Solomon isls. (BUKA, BOUGAINVILLE), governed by Australia under U.N. trusteeship; ⊙ PORT MORESBY, which is also ⊙ Territory of PAPUA (SE New Guinea). Before Second World War, ⊙ Territory was Rabaul on New Britain. Territory is divided into Madang, Morobe, Sepik, Central Highlands dists. in NE New Guinea, BOUGAINVILLE dist. (with Buka), Manus dist. (ADMIRALTY ISLANDS), NEW BRITAIN, and NEW IRELAND dists. Territory was formerly German New Guinea (1884–1914); NE New Guinea constituted a separate unit called Kaiser-Wilhelmsland, which was governed along with Bismarck Archipelago and N Solomons. Occupied 1914 by Australian forces, mandated 1920 to Australia, which received (1947) U.N. trusteeship. See NEW GUINEA.

Newgulf, village (pop. 1,803), Wharton co., S Texas, c.45 mi. SW of Houston; center of sulphur-mining area; oil wells.

Newhalen, Alaska: see ILIAMNA.

Newhall, England: see SWADLINCOTE DISTRICT.

Newhall. 1 Town (pop. 2,527), Los Angeles co., S Calif., 27 mi. NW of downtown Los Angeles, in mtn. ranching region; oil refining. Oil, gas wells near by. Near by is Newhall Pass, leading S into San Fernando Valley bet. W end of San Gabriel Mts. and E end of Santa Susana Mts. **2** Town (pop. 366), Benton co., E central Iowa, 15 mi. W of Cedar Rapids; mfg. (feed, wood and metal products). **3** Village, Maine: see WINDHAM. **4** Village, W.Va.: see BERWIND.

New Halls, Scotland: see DALMENY.

New Hamburg (hăm'bûrg), village (pop. 1,402), S Ont., on Nith R. and 12 mi. WSW of Kitchener; mfg. of felt shoes, leather, furniture, brassware.

New Hamburg, town (pop. 156), Scott co., SE Mo., near Mississippi R., 6 mi. SE of Chaffee; agr.

New Hamilton, Alaska: see NEW FORT HAMILTON.

New Hampshire, state (land □ 9,024; with inland waters □ 9,304; 1950 pop. 533,242; 1940 pop. 491,524), NE U.S., in New England, bordered N by Canadian prov. of Quebec, E by Maine, SE by the Atlantic, S by Mass., W by Vermont, from which it is separated by Connecticut R.; 43d in area, 44th in pop.; one of the original 13 states, the 9th to ratify (1788) the Constitution; ⊙ Concord. The state extends 180 mi. N–S, 15–90 mi. E–W. Except for the rolling seaboard lowland in the SE, the topography is generally hilly, well wooded, and dotted with numerous lakes. The SW, W central, and S central sections are part of the New England upland, a dissected and glaciated region of complex crystalline rocks, surmounted by residual hills, such as Mt. Monadnock (3,165 ft.) and Mt. Kearsarge (2,937 ft.). L. Winnipesaukee, the largest in the state, is in S center. To the N, forming part of the Appalachian system, are the WHITE MOUNTAINS, a rugged, picturesque mtn. mass, cut by deep valleys and "notches" (e.g., Franconia Notch, Crawford Notch). Chief peaks here are mounts Adams (5,798 ft.), Jefferson (5,715 ft.), and Washington (6,288 ft.; highest point in state) in the Presidential Range and Mt. Lafayette (5,249 ft.) in the Franconia Mts. Extending N to the Canadian line are subdued glaciated mts., with several peaks over 3,000 ft. The state's drainage is S and SE to the Atlantic via the Connecticut, Merrimack, Androscoggin, Saco, and Salmon Falls rivers. N.H. has a continental climate, marked by short summers and rather severe winters (especially in N). Annual rainfall ranges from 50 in. in White Mts. to c.35 in. in the lower areas; snowfall amounts to 50 in. along the coast and 150 in. on the higher mtn. slopes. Concord (S) has mean temp. of 22°F. in Jan., 70°F. in July, and 36 in. of annual rainfall; Berlin (N) has mean temp. of 14°F. in Jan., 66°F. in July, and 39 in. of rain. The growing season varies from c.100 to 160 days. Native vegetation was predominately coniferous forest (N) and hardwood forest (S). Although little virgin forest remains, the lumber industry is of some importance, especially in Coos co. Commercial forests comprise c.4,700,000 acres, natl. forest reserves 806,000 acres; chief timber species are spruce, fir, white pine, birch, beech, maple, hemlock, and oak. Maple syrup and sugar are other forest produce. The rough terrain, poor soil, and short growing season restrict agr. to the relatively favored lower areas, such as the Connecticut and Merrimack valleys. Subsistence farming is characteristic, dairying being important. Chief field crop is hay, and there are much smaller acreages of corn, oats, and potatoes. Also grown are apples, peaches, berries, and truck crops. Fish resources include lobsters, sea and river herring, and mackerel. Though termed the "Granite State," N.H.'s mineral output, including granite, is relatively minor. Feldspar, mica, sand and gravel, abrasive garnets, and beryl are also worked. Mfg. is largely concentrated in the S part of the state (notably Hillsboro co.), where water power is developed on the Merrimack and other rivers. Principal products are boots and shoes, cotton fabrics, woolens and worsteds, paper and pulp, machinery, wood products, and fabricated metal goods; also food processing, printing and publishing; submarine building (at Portsmouth Naval Base). Chief industrial and commercial centers: Manchester (state's largest city), Nashua, Concord, Portsmouth, Berlin, Dover, Keene, Laconia, Rochester, and Claremont. N.H.'s picturesque natural setting and salubrious summer climate attract numerous visitors to the White Mts., to lakes Winnipesaukee, Squam, Sunapee, Ossipee, and Newfound, and to the seaside resorts in the SE. Winter sports are popular, especially skiing in the White Mts. Dartmouth Col. (at Hanover) and Univ. of N.H. (at Durham) are the leading educational institutions. At the time of the white man's coming N.H. was inhabited by tribes of the Algonquian Abnaki group. The coastal area was explored by Pring (1603), Champlain (1605), and Capt. John Smith (1614). In 1622 Gorges and Mason obtained a grant bet. the Merrimack and Kennebec rivers, and in 1629 Mason received sole rights to the land bet. the Piscataqua and Merrimack, which he named New Hampshire. The 1st English settlement was made (1623) at Odiorne's Point, but the 1st permanent colony was probably at Dover a short time later; Portsmouth, Exeter, and Hampton were founded soon afterwards. These 4 towns came under Mass. jurisdiction in 1641. N.H. became a separate royal prov. in 1679, although Mass. continued to press land claims until 1739–41, when boundaries were settled. Periodic Indian attacks harassed the colonists and settlement in the interior proceeded slowly. Lumbering and shipbuilding were important and gristmills sprang up at river falls. During the Revolution N.H. regiments were active in many campaigns, but no fighting took place on the state's soil. Claims to the Vermont territory were relinquished in 1782. In the War of 1812 Portsmouth was a base for Amer. privateers, but the port was closely blockaded (1814) by the Br. fleet. Economic activity expanded with the development of farming, textile and shoe factories, and the coming of the railroads. The N boundary with Canada and the "INDIAN STREAM REPUBLIC" issue were settled by the Webster-Ashburton Treaty of 1842. Franklin Pierce, a native son, was elected 14th president of U.S. in 1852. Increased industrialization brought many foreign-born workers into the state at the turn of the century. In 1905, the Russo-Japanese War was terminated by the Treaty of Portsmouth. A U.N. monetary conference, establishing the Internatl. Bank and Internatl. Monetary Fund, was held at Bretton Woods in 1944. See also articles on the cities, towns, geographic features, and the 10 counties: BELKNAP, CARROLL, CHESHIRE, COOS, GRAFTON, HILLSBORO, MERRIMACK, ROCKINGHAM, STRAFFORD, SULLIVAN.

New Hampton. 1 City (pop. 3,323), ⊙ Chickasaw co., NE Iowa, 18 mi. E of Charles City; mfg. (dairy products, feed, beverages, overalls). Inc. 1873. **2** City (pop. 375), Harrison co., NW Mo., 8 mi. W of Bethany. **3** Town (pop. 723), Belknap co., central N.H., on Pemigewasset R. and 11 mi. NW of Laconia. Site of state's oldest fish hatchery (1920). Winter sports.

New Hanover, Bismarck Archipelago: see LAVONGAI.

New Hanover (hă'nōvûr), county (□ 194; pop. 63,272), SE N.C., on the Atlantic; ⊙ Wilmington. Bounded E by Onslow Bay, W by Cape Fear R., N by Northeast Cape Fear R. Forested tidewater area; truck farming, dairying, poultry and stock raising; mfg. and shipping at WILMINGTON; resorts along coast. Formed 1729.

New Harbor, village, Maine: see BRISTOL.

New Harmony. 1 Residential town (pop. 1,360), Posey co., SW Ind., on the Wabash and 22 mi. WNW of Evansville; oil wells, sand and gravel pits; makes tanks. Founded 1815, it was settled by the Harmony Society under George Rapp; in 1825, the Harmonists sold their holdings to Robert Owen, who established here a noted communistic colony which existed until 1828. Many old Rappite buildings remain. **2** Town (pop. 126), Washington co., SW Utah, 18 mi. SW of Cedar City; alt. 5,250 ft. Settled 1852.

New Hartford. 1 Resort town (pop. 2,395), Litchfield co., NW Conn., on Farmington R., just SE of Winsted; mfg. (typewriters, metal products), agr. Includes Pine Meadow village, state forest, part of Nepaug Reservoir. Flooded (1936) when near-by Greenwood Dam broke. Settled 1733, inc. 1738. **2** Town (pop. 584), Butler co., N central Iowa, 15 mi. WNW of Waterloo. **3** Village (pop. 1,947), Oneida co., central N.Y., just SW of Utica; mfg. (temperature controls, metal products, fishing tackle, textiles). Settled c.1787, inc. 1870.

New Hartley, England: see SEATON DELAVAL.

Newhaven (nūhā'vŭn), urban district (1931 pop. 6,789; 1951 census 7,785), S Sussex, England, on the Channel at mouth of Ouse R., 7 mi. S of Lewes; 50°47'N 0°3'E; seaside resort and seaport; terminal of cross-Channel steamers to Dieppe. Church dates from 12th cent. Louis Philippe lived here in exile for some time. In urban dist. (ENE) is residential dist. of Denton (pop. 385).

Newhaven, fishing village in Edinburgh, S cotland, just N on the Firth of Forth.

New Haven, county (□ 609; pop. 545,784), S Conn., on Long Isl. Sound; ⊙ New Haven and Waterbury. Mfg., agr., resort region, with industrial Waterbury, Wallingford, Naugatuck, New Haven, Ansonia, Derby, and Meriden, producing wide variety of goods, especially brass and other metal products, hardware, firearms, rubber goods, silverware, clocks, electrical equipment and appliances, bricks, textiles; oil refining; agr. (truck, dairy products, poultry, fruit); seed growing; fisheries; shore resorts. Drained by Housatonic (W boundary), Naugatuck, Quinnipiac, and Hammonasset (E boundary) rivers. Constituted 1666.

New Haven. 1 City (pop. 164,443), coextensive with New Haven town, a ⊙ New Haven co., S Conn., on Long Isl. Sound and 70 mi. ENE of New York, 35 mi. SSW of Hartford; 41°19'N 72°56'W; second-largest city in state. Industrial center on New Haven Harbor, at mouth of small Quinnipiac, Mill, and West rivers; mfg. (firearms, ammunition, hardware, tools, elevators, electrical appliances, toys, clocks, sewing machines, rubber goods, textiles, wire and metal goods, paper boxes, clothing, lamps); meat packing; railroad shops; traprock quarries; market center for truck. Port of entry. Seat of Yale Univ. and affiliated institutions (e.g., New Haven Hosp. and the Institute of Human Relations); state teachers col., Univ. of Conn. col. of pharmacy, Berkeley Divinity School Albertus Magnus Col., Arnold Col., Larson Col., a jr. col., school of physical therapy. Laid out 1637–38 as Quinnipiac by Puritans under Theophilus Eaton and John Davenport, renamed 1640, inc. 1784 as New Haven Colony. Adopted constitution (1639) emphasizing religion; near-by settlements were admitted to the Colony, which retained independence until becoming part of Colony of Conn. in 1664. Joint capital with Hartford, 1701–1875. Raided by British in Revolution; blockaded in War of 1812. Was important commercial and sealing port in late 18th and early 19th cent.; Eli Whitney began firearms industry 1798; hardware mfg. began in mid-19th cent. Points of interest: the old Green, with 3 graceful early 19th-cent. churches; many historic buildings, including Pierpont House (1767); Yale Univ. campus; Tory Tavern; Noah Webster's home; library and mus. of New Haven Colony Historical Society; East and West Rock parks (latter with Judges' Cave, in which 2 regicides hid); state agr. experiment station; old Grove Street cemetery with graves of Samuel F. B. Morse, Roger Sherman, Theophilus Eaton, Noah Webster, Timothy Dwight, Eli Whitney, Lyman Beecher, Charles Goodyear. **2** Village (pop. 819), Gallatin co., SE Ill., on Wabash R. and 25 mi. ENE of Harrisburg, in agr. area. **3** Residential town (pop. 2,336), Allen co., NE Ind., on Maumee R. and 6 mi. E of Fort Wayne; trading center in agr. area; cement vaults, showcases, wood products. Military supply depot here. **4** Town (pop. 563), Nelson co., central Ky., on Rolling Fork and 15 mi. E of Elizabethtown; makes whisky. Near by is Abbey of Our Lady of Gethsemani (a Trappist monastery). Site of Knob Creek Farm, which was (1813–17) the Lincoln family home, also near, has a reproduction of Lincoln's birthplace. **5** Village (pop. 1,082), Macomb co., SE Mich., 10 mi. NNE of Mt. Clemens, in farm area. Inc. 1869. **6** City (pop. 1,009), Franklin co., E central Mo., on Missouri R. and 12 mi. W of Washington; grain products, hat factory. Laid out 1856. **7** Town (pop. 932), Addison co., W Vt., on New Haven R. and 25 mi. S of Burlington; lime; dairy products. **8** Town (pop. 969), Mason co., W W.Va., near the Ohio, 14 mi. NE of Point Pleasant, in agr. and coal-mining area.

New Haven River, W Vt., rises in Green Mts. E of Middlebury, flows c.25 mi. NW and SW to Otter Creek at Weybridge.

New Hebrides (hĕ'brĭdēz), Fr. *Nouvelles Hébrides,* island group (□ c.5,700; pop. 44,750), SW Pacific, 1,100 mi. E of Australia; 15°15'–20°12'S 166°55'–169°46'E. A 400-mi. chain of volcanic isls.; most important are ESPIRITU SANTO (largest), EFATE (seat of Vila, ⊙ condominium), MAEWO, EPI, MALO, MALEKULA, PENTECOST, TANNA, AOBA, AMBRYM, ERROMANGA, ANEITYUM, BANKS ISLANDS, TORRES ISLANDS; some coral isls. Mountainous; highest peak (6,195 ft.) on Espiritu Santo. Pandanus, coconut palms, orchids, some sandalwood; sheep, wild pigs. Malarial area; annual mean temp. 70.3° F., rainfall 95 in. Melanesian natives. Chief products: copra, coffee, cocoa, mother-of-pearl. Imported Tonkinese laborers. Discovered 1606 by Queiros, placed 1887 under Anglo-Fr. naval commission, Anglo-Fr. condominium established 1906. In Second World War, group supported Free French and became a military base.

Newhebron or **New Hebron** (nū"hē'brŭn), village (pop. 303), Lawrence co., S central Miss., 40 mi. SSE of Jackson.

Newhey or **New Hey,** town in Rochdale borough, SE Lancashire, England; cotton milling, wool finishing. Site of Oldham reservoirs.

Newhills, Scotland: see BUCKSBURN.

New Hogan Reservoir: see CALAVERAS RIVER.

New Holland. 1 Village (pop. 1,618), Hall co., NE Ga., 3 mi. NE of Gainesville; textile mfg. **2** Village (pop. 343), Logan co., central Ill., 25 mi. N of Springfield, in agr. and bituminous-coal area. **3** Village (pop. 799), on Pickaway-Fayette co. line, S central Ohio, 16 mi. WSW of Circleville, in livestock, poultry, and general agr. area. **4** Borough (pop. 2,602), Lancaster co., SE Pa., 12 mi. ENE of Lancaster; textiles, metal products. Settled 1728, inc. 1895.

New Holstein (hōl'stēn), city (pop. 1,831), Calumet co., E Wis., 23 mi. NW of Sheboygan, in dairying and grain-growing area; mfg. of farm machinery, shoes; vegetable canning. Settled 1849, inc. 1926.

New Hope. 1 Village (pop. c.350), Madison co., N Ala., near Paint Rock R., 17 mi. SE of Huntsville; lumber milling, cotton ginning. **2** Borough (pop. 1,066), Bucks co., SE Pa., 16 mi. NW of Trenton, N.J., and on Delaware R. (bridged here); paper bags; agr. Artist colony. Settled c.1712, inc. 1837.

New Hudson, village (pop. c.300), Oakland co., SE Mich., 18 mi. SW of Pontiac, in farm area; mfg. of trailers.

New Hunstanton (hŭnstăn'tŭn, hŭn'stŭn), urban district (1931 pop. 3,132; 1951 census 3,414), NW Norfolk, England, on The Wash inlet of the North Sea, 14 mi. N of King's Lynn; watering resort, sheltered by high cliffs. Near by is Hunstanton Hall, seat of the Lestrange family since 12th cent. Just N is village of Hunstanton, with Royal Navy radio station.

New Hyde Park, residential village (pop. 7,349), Nassau co., SE N.Y., on W Long Isl., 2 mi. W of Mineola, in truck-farming area; mfg. (hosiery, children's furniture, metal products, candy); nurseries. Inc. 1927.

Newi, Nigeria: see NNEWI.

New Iberia (ībēr'ēŭ), city (pop. 16,467), ⊙ Iberia parish, S La., c.50 mi. SW of Baton Rouge and on navigable Bayou Teche; commercial and processing center for rich area producing sugar cane, rice, cotton, vegetables, dairy products, sea food. Mfg. (machine-shop products, bricks, paper, wood products, wagons). Oil wells, salt mines near by. Has St. Peter's Col. Fine plantation house here. Probably settled in 1779 by the Spanish; inc. in 1839 as Iberia, renamed in 1868. Avery Isl. is c.9 mi. SW.

Newington. 1 Town (pop. 9,110), Hartford co., central Conn., just SW of Hartford; concrete products, tools. Home for crippled children, state tuberculosis sanatorium, veterans' hosp. here. Settled in late 17th cent., inc. 1871. **2** Town (pop. 429), Screven co., E Ga., 16 mi. SE of Sylvania, near S.C. line. **3** Agr. town (pop. 494), Rockingham co., SE N.H., on Great Bay and Piscataqua R. and just above Portsmouth.

New Inlet, E N.C., a channel through the Outer Banks, connecting Pamlico Sound with the Atlantic c.30 mi. N of Cape Hatteras.

New Ipswich, town (pop. 1,147), Hillsboro co., S N.H., 20 mi. W of Nashua, near Mass. line. State's 1st cotton mill built here (1803), 1st woolen mill (1801). Inc. 1762.

New Ireland, volcanic island (□ 3,340; pop. c.19,000), 2d largest of Bismarck Archipelago, Territory of New Guinea, SW Pacific; c.230 mi. long. Schleinitz Mts. (2–4,000 ft.) in center; plateau in E. Coconut plantations. Kavieng (N) is chief town and port. Formerly Neu Mecklenburg, later New Mecklenburg.

New Jersey, state (land □ 7,522; with inland waters □ 7,836; 1950 pop. 4,835,329; 1940 pop. 4,160,165), NE U.S., in Middle Atlantic region; fronting E on the Atlantic, it is bordered N and NE by N.Y., S by Delaware Bay, W by Del. and Pa.; 45th in area, 8th in pop.; one of original 13 states, the 3d to ratify (1787) the Constitution; ⊙ Trenton. Delaware R. marks W boundary with Pa. and Del., while in NE the Hudson R., Upper New York Bay, Kill Van Kull, and Arthur Kill separate the state from SE N.Y. (including Manhattan, Brooklyn, Staten Isl.). It is 167 mi. N–S, 35–75 mi. E–W. The major portion (center, S) of N.J. lies in the Atlantic coastal plain, a low-lying tract of sands and clays, with extensive areas of marshland; it rises, in the N, to c.275 ft. in the Navesink (or Atlantic) Highlands. The coast line is marked by barrier beaches (e.g., Long Beach), sand spits (e.g., Sandy Hook, Island Beach) and dunes, backed by lagoons (e.g., Barnegat Bay) and marshes; there are several shallow inlets but no good harbors. Running roughly NE–SW through Perth Amboy, Princeton, and Trenton is the fall line, where the coastal plain meets the piedmont, here represented by the Triassic Lowland. This 20–30-mi.-wide belt extends from the Delaware R. to the N.Y. border and is characterized by red soils of underlying sandstones and shales, with outcropping trap ridges (350–500 ft. high), such as the PALISADES, overlooking the Hudson, and the Watchung Mts. The section is drained by New Jersey's 3 main rivers, the Raritan, Passaic, and Hackensack. To the W are the N.J. Highlands, a series of NE–SW ranges (800–1,200 ft. high), including the Ramapo Mts., Schooleys Mtn., and Musconetcong Mtn. In the NW corner, beyond fertile Kittatinny valley (part of Great Appalachian Valley), is Kittatinny Mtn., a ridge of the Appalachians rising to 1,801 ft. at High Point, highest point in the state; it is pierced by the Delaware Water Gap on the Pa. line. N N.J. was covered by continental glaciation and there are terminal moraines and outwash plains. The state has a humid continental climate, with an annual rainfall of 40–50 in. Trenton has mean temp. of 32°F. in Jan., 75°F. in July, and 43 in. of rainfall. The growing season averages 150 days (N) to 200 days (S). Some 2,300,000 acres of hardwood forest remain, in which oak, pine, maple, cedar, beech, birch, hemlock, and yellow poplar are chief timber species. Broad areas of scrub oak and stunted pine in the S half of the state comprise the "Pine Barrens." Situated bet. the great metropolitan dists. of New York and Philadelphia, N.J. is noted for its large-scale truck farming and is aptly called the "Garden State." The lighter, sandy loams of the center and S parts produce considerable quantities of white and sweet potatoes, tomatoes, asparagus, peppers, eggplant, beans, sweet corn, lettuce, spinach, and other market crops. Food processing is a major industry. In the S, too, is extensive fruit cultivation, including apples, peaches, grapes, strawberries, blueberries; much marshland is utilized for cranberry bogs. In the N, especially in NW, general farming and dairying prevail; hay, corn, wheat, and oats are the chief crops. Poultry raising is important (N, center) and specialized horticulture (e.g., orchids) is carried on. The state has a large annual fish catch, consisting of oysters (mostly from Delaware Bay), clams, shad, mackerel, bluefish, sea trout, and cod. Glass sand, moulding sand, and green sand (for water softening) deposits are worked, and clay is used for pottery and sanitary ware mfg. The rich zinc reserves in the Franklin dist. are now almost depleted. Sandstone and traprock are quarried; some iron ore (magnetite) is mined. Although its own mineral resources are fairly small, the state ranks high in copper smelting and refining (at Perth Amboy) and petroleum refining (at Bayonne), its most valuable single industries. Easy access to fuel and raw materials by land and sea and proximity to large urban markets have made N.J. a leading mfg. state. Principal items among a wide variety of products are textiles, chemicals, machinery, transportation equipment, paints and varnishes, machine tools, electrical apparatus, rubber and leather goods, tobacco products, plastics, furniture, radios, and jewelry. Dyeing, shipbuilding and repairing, meat packing, printing and publishing are also important. The main industrial zone is in NE, forming part of the huge New York metropolitan area and containing most of the state's largest cities—NEWARK, JERSEY CITY, PATERSON (silk weaving), ELIZABETH, East Orange, Bayonne, Clifton, Irvington, Passaic, Union City, and Hoboken. TRENTON and CAMDEN, on the Delaware, are also large mfg. centers. Newark (has large airport), Jersey City, Hoboken (major rail terminus), Perth Amboy, and Camden handle ocean shipping. The state has a fine road network, including the N.J. Turnpike and Pulaski Skyway; it connects with New York city via George Washington Bridge and Lincoln and Holland tunnels, with Staten Isl. via Bayonne and Goethals bridges and Outerbridge Crossing, and with Del. via Del. Memorial Bridge. Within commuting distance of New York and Philadelphia are numerous suburban communities. The Jersey shore comprises one of the East's most popular summer vacation lands; notable seaside resorts are Atlantic City, Cape May, Ocean City, Asbury Park, Long Branch, Spring Lake, and Wildwood; some mtn. lakes (e.g., L. Hopatcong) also have tourist facilities. Leading educational institutions are Princeton Univ. and The Inst. for Advanced Study (at Princeton), Rutgers Univ. (at New Brunswick), Stevens Inst. of Technology (at Hoboken), Seton Hall Col. (at South Orange), and Rider Col. (at Trenton). Fort Dix, U.S. Army camp, is in central part of state. The region was 1st settled by the Dutch (c.1620) along the Hudson and by the Swedes (c.1640) along the Delaware. The New Sweden colonies were seized by the Dutch in 1655. Included in the area granted to the duke of York, N.J. was taken from the Dutch by the English in 1664 and given in proprietorship to Berkeley and Carteret. A territorial division in 1676 placed the N and E parts in East Jersey, the S and W parts in West Jersey (later purchased by William Penn), where, at Salem, the Quakers had founded (1675) a colony. In those days, just as today, the NE area was oriented economically and culturally toward New York, while the SW had close ties with Philadelphia. However, in 1702, the two colonies were merged into the royal prov. of N.J., with alternating capitals at Perth Amboy and Burlington. During the Revolution the state was the scene of important battles of Trenton, Princeton, and Monmouth, and Washington twice established his winter hq. at Morristown. At the Constitutional Convention (1787), N.J. sponsored the cause of the smaller states. Early industries were leather at Newark, pottery at Trenton, and textiles at Paterson; iron mining was important. The 1st railroad (Camden to South Amboy) was completed in 1834. Although commercial truck farming grew steadily, the state began to change from an agr. to an industrial commonwealth. European immigration in the late 19th cent. helped meet the expanding labor market. The reform movement during Woodrow Wilson's governorship (1910–12) checked the power of railroad monopolies and business trusts, which had been encouraged by easy incorporation laws in the '70s and '80s. Increased industrialization and suburbanization has given N.J.'s pop. a predominantly urban character (87% in 1950). See also articles on the cities, towns, geographic features, and the 21 counties: ATLANTIC, BERGEN, BURLINGTON, CAMDEN, CAPE MAY, CUMBERLAND, ESSEX, GLOUCESTER, HUDSON, HUNTERDON, MERCER, MIDDLESEX, MONMOUTH, MORRIS, OCEAN, PASSAIC, SALEM, SOMERSET, SUSSEX, UNION, WARREN.

New Jersey Turnpike, part of N.J. highway system extending NE from Deepwater on Delaware R. at Delaware Memorial Bridge to Ridgefield Park, near the Hudson; landscaped toll road.

New Kensington, city (pop. 25,146), Westmoreland co., W central Pa., on Allegheny R. and 14 mi. NE of Pittsburgh. One of largest producers of aluminum products in world; also makes magnesium sheets, glass, electrical and metal products; shale. Laid out 1891, inc. as borough 1892, as city 1933. Parnassus consolidated 1931 with New Kensington.

New Kent, county (□ 212; pop. 3,995), E Va.; ⊙ New Kent. In tidewater region, on peninsula bet. Chickahominy, Pamunkey (N), and York (NE) rivers. Agr. (truck, sweet and white potatoes), livestock and poultry raising; lumbering, lumber milling. Formed 1654.

New Kent, village (pop. c.50), ⊙ New Kent co. (since 1691), E Va., 25 mi. E of Richmond.

New Kilmainham (kĭlmā'nŭm), Gaelic *Cill Mhaighneann*, W suburb of Dublin, Co. Dublin, Ireland.

New Kilpatrick or **East Kilpatrick,** parish (pop. 11,568, including Milngavie burgh), SE Dumbarton, Scotland, 5 mi. NW of Glasgow. Includes BEARSDEN.

New Kingston, resort village, Delaware co., S N.Y., in the Catskills, c.40 mi. NW of Kingston.

Newkirk (nōō'kûrk), city (pop. 2,201), ⊙ Kay co., N Okla., 13 mi. N of Ponca City; poultry hatcheries, grain elevators; oil and gas wells; mfg. (wood products, brooms). Chilocco School for Indians is 7 mi. N, at Chilocco. Settled c.1893.

New Knock Hock, village (pop. 120), W Alaska, S of Yukon R. delta.

New Knoxville, village (pop. 662), Auglaize co., W Ohio, 5 mi. SE of St. Marys; lumber, clay products.

New Lambton, W suburb of Newcastle, New South Wales, Australia; coal-mining center.

New Lanark, Scotland: see LANARK.

Newland, England: see REDBROOK.

Newland (nū'lŭnd), resort town (pop. 425), ⊙ Avery co., NW N.C., 27 mi. NNW of Morganton, in the Blue Ridge.

Newlands, residential town, SW Cape Prov., U. of So. Afr., SSE suburb of Cape Town; site of Kirstenbosch Natl. Botanical Gardens (400 acres), established 1913.

New Leaksville, N.C.: see LEAKSVILLE.

New Lebanon (lĕ'bŭnŭn). **1** Village, Columbia co., SE N.Y., near Mass. line, 8 mi. W of Pittsfield, Mass. Samuel Tilden was b. here. Site of R.C. Shrine of Our Lady of Lourdes. **2** Village, Miami co., Ohio: see POTSDAM. **3** Village (pop. 696), Montgomery co., W Ohio, 10 mi. W of Dayton, in agr. area. **4** Borough (pop. 179), Mercer co., NW Pa., 16 mi. SSE of Meadville.

New Leipzig (nū lĭp'sĭk), village (pop. 447), Grant co., S N.Dak., 60 mi. WSW of Bismarck, near Cannonball R.; grain, dairy products, poultry, hogs.

New Lenox (lĕ'nŭks). **1** Village (pop. 1,235), Will co., NE Ill., 5 mi. E of Joliet. Inc. 1946. **2** Village, Mass.: see LENOX.

New Lexington, village (pop. 4,233), ⊙ Perry co., central Ohio, 19 mi. SSW of Zanesville; trade center and distribution point for coal, sand, and oil-producing area; makes tile, rock wool, machine tools. Laid out 1817.

New Liberty, town (pop. 126), Scott co., E Iowa, 20 mi. NW of Davenport, in agr. area.

New Limerick (lĭm'ŭrĭk), town (pop. 543), Aroostook co., E Maine, just W of Houlton; agr.

Newlin, village (pop. c.200), Hall co., NW Texas, 17 mi. NW of Childress and on Prairie Dog Town Fork of Red R.; cotton, truck, cattle.

New Lisbon (lĭz'bŭn), city (pop. 1,482), Juneau co., central Wis., on Lemonweir R. and c.55 mi. E of La Crosse, in dairying and farming region; butter, cement blocks, beer, feed. Inc. 1889.

New Liskeard (lĭ'skŭrd), town (pop. 3,019), E Ont., at N end of L. Timiskaming, 5 mi. NNW of Haileybury; pulp and lumber milling, food canning, dairying; resort. Market center for surrounding mining region.

Newllano (nūlă'nō), village (pop. 277), Vernon parish, W La., just S of Leesville. Llano Cooperative Colony was established here in 1917.

New London, county (□ 672; pop. 144,821), SE Conn., on Long Isl. Sound and R.I. line, bounded W by the Connecticut; ⊙ New London and Norwich. New London is coast guard and submarine center; co. has diversified mfg. (textiles, metal products, hospital supplies, machinery, printing presses, paper products, chemicals, clothing, thermos bottles, bedding, thread, silverware, boats, leather products); agr. (dairy products, poultry, fruit, truck). Resorts on coast. Drained by Yantic, Shetucket, Thames, Mystic, Quinebaug, Pawcatuck (E boundary), and Niantic rivers. Constituted 1666.

New London. 1 City (pop. 30,551), coextensive with New London town, a ⊙ New London co., SE Conn., on Long Isl. Sound and 45 mi. E of New Haven, at mouth of the Thames (bridged to Groton), here forming deepwater harbor. Port of entry and maritime center, with U.S. Coast Guard Acad. (1932), coast guard base, and maritime schools; navy submarine base is at Groton, across the Thames. Mfg. (metal products, printing presses, machinery, tools, chemicals, thread, bedding, clothing, wood and paper products, toys, clocks); summer resort. Has a jr. col. Laid out 1646 by John Winthrop, renamed from Pequot 1658, inc. 1784. Privateering port in Revolution, partially burned (1781) by Benedict Arnold; blockaded in War of 1812. Flourished as shipping, shipbuilding, and whaling port to end of 19th cent. Here are old Fort Trumbull (1849; on site of Revolutionary fort), New London Lighthouse (1760), whaling mus., many old buildings. Seat of Connecticut Col. for Women. Annual Yale-Harvard boat races held on the Thames here. **2** Town (pop. 1,510), Henry co., SE Iowa, 16 mi. WNW of Burlington, in livestock and grain area. Founded as Dover; inc. 1860. **3** Resort village (pop. 726), Kandiyohi co., S central Minn., near Green L., 14 mi. NNE of Willmar; dairy and cement products. State park near by. **4** City (pop. 858), ⊙ Ralls co., NE Mo., on Salt R., near the Mississippi, and 8 mi. S of Hannibal; agr. trade center. Fine courthouse (1857–58). **5** Town (pop. 1,484), Merrimack co., S central N.H., 27 mi. NW of Concord, in hilly country near L. Sunapee; alt. 1,326 ft. Seat of Colby Jr. Col. Winter sports. **6** Town (pop. 285), Stanly co., S central N.C., 21 mi. SE of Salisbury. **7** Village (pop. 2,023), Huron co., N Ohio, 16 mi. NNW of Ashland; trade and shipping point; makes uniforms, caps and gowns, vestments, clay and cement products. Settled 1816. **8** Village (1940 pop. 1,816), Rusk co., E Texas, 21 mi. ESE of Tyler; oil town in East Texas field. A school explosion here (March 18, 1937) took the lives of hundreds of pupils and teachers. **9** City (pop. 4,922), on Waupaca-Outagamie co. line, E central Wis., at confluence of Wolf and Embarrass rivers, 27 mi. NNW of Oshkosh, in agr. area (cabbage, poultry); mfg. of dairy products, wood products, brick, beer, canned foods; lumber milling; baby chicks. Has Carr Mus., with natural-history and historical exhibits. Founded c.1853, inc. 1877.

New Lothrop (lō'thrŭp), village (pop. 459), Shiawassee co., S central Mich., 16 mi. NW of Flint.

Newlyn (nū'lĭn), town (pop. 3,544), SW Cornwall, England, on Mounts Bay of the Channel, just SW of Penzance; leading fishing center of Cornwall (pilchard, mackerel, lobster). It is an artists' resort which has given name to an open-air school of painting; there is an art gallery. Church has modern murals.

New Lynn, borough (pop. 4,277), N N.Isl., New Zealand, SW suburb of Auckland; mfg. of brick, tile, pottery.

New Maas River, Du. *Nieuwe Maas* (nē'vŭ mäs'), SW Netherlands, formed by junction of LEK RIVER and NOORD RIVER just W of Krimpen aan den Lek; flows 13 mi. W, past Ijsselmonde, Rotterdam, Pernis, and Vlaardingen, joining Old Maas R. 7 mi. WSW of Rotterdam to form the SCHEUR and BRIELSCHE MAAS RIVER (sometimes also called New Maas R.). Receives Hollandsche Ijssel R. 2 mi. E of Rotterdam; forms N boundary of Ijsselmonde isl. W of Rotterdam it forms part of Rotterdam–North Sea waterway. Navigable by ocean-going ships.

New Machar (măkh'är), town and parish (pop. 2,113), E Aberdeen, Scotland, 9 mi. NNW of Aberdeen; agr. market.

New Madison, village (pop. 757), Darke co., W Ohio, 11 mi. SSW of Greenville; canned foods, grain.

New Madrid (măd'rĭd), county (□ 679; pop. 39,444), extreme SE Mo.; ⊙ New Madrid on the Mississippi (levees); crossed by Little R. and drainage canals. Cotton region; corn, wheat, lumber. Settled c.1788.

New Madrid, city (pop. 2,726), ⊙ New Madrid co., extreme SE Mo., on Mississippi R. (levees) and 35 mi. SW of Cairo, Ill.; port; cotton gins, wood products. U.S. farm rehabilitation project near by. Laid out 1789. In Civil War, Federal troops captured city before taking (1862) near-by Island No. 10 in the Mississippi; isl., then Tenn. territory, has since vanished.

New Malden, England: see THE MALDENS AND COOMBE.

New Malton, England: see MALTON.

Newman. 1 City (pop. 1,815), Stanislaus co., central Calif., in San Joaquin Valley, 22 mi. S of Modesto; dairying, farming (alfalfa, grain, truck). Laid out 1887, inc. 1908. **2** City (pop. 1,140), Douglas co., E Ill., 29 mi. SW of Danville; canned foods, cheese; ships grain. Founded 1857, inc. 1895.

Newman Grove, city (pop. 1,004), Madison co., E central Nebr., 30 mi. NW of Columbus and on Shell Creek of Platte R., in prairie region; dairy produce, grain.

Newmans Lake (c.5 mi. long), Alachua co., N Fla., 5 mi. E of Gainesville.

Newmanstown, village (pop. 1,314, with adjacent Sheridan), Lebanon co., SE central Pa., 12 mi. E of Lebanon.

New Margelan, Uzbek SSR: see FERGANA, city.

Newmarket, town (pop. 4,026), S Ont., on Holland R. and 27 mi. N of Toronto; tanning, dairying; mfg. of furniture, pencils, clothing, candy.

Newmarket, urban district (1931 pop. 9,752; 1951 census 10,184), W Suffolk, England, 12 mi. ENE of Cambridge, on Cambridgeshire border; agr. market. Racing center since 17th cent.; scene of several major racing events, including the Two Thousand Guineas, the Cambridgeshire, and the Cesarewitch. Courses on Newmarket Heath are c.4 mi. long, crossed by Devil's Dyke, an anc. earthwork. Numerous horses trained here. There are 13th-cent. church, parts of palace of Charles II, and houses of Nell Gwynne and of duke of Queensberry.

Newmarket, Gaelic *Áth Trasna*, town (pop. 792), NW Co. Cork, Ireland, 4 mi. NW of Kanturk; agr. market (dairying, potatoes, oats). John Philpot Curran b. here.

Newmarket, borough (pop. 2,980), N N.Isl., New Zealand; residential suburb of Auckland.

New Market. 1 Town (pop. 370), Montgomery co., W central Ind., 6 mi. S of Crawfordsville, in agr. area. **2** Town (pop. 573), Taylor co., SW Iowa, 7 mi. E of Clarinda, in coal-mining, agr. area. **3** Town (pop. 301), Frederick co., N Md., 8 mi. ESE of Frederick; trade point in agr. area. **4** Village (pop. 193), Scott co., S Minn., 28 mi. S of Minneapolis, in grain, livestock, and poultry area. **5** Town (1940 pop. 75), Platte co., W Mo., 18 mi. S of St. Joseph. **6** Village (1940 pop. 4,512), Middlesex co., NE N.J., 4 mi. N of New Brunswick; structural steel plant; nursery products, truck. Settled early in 18th cent.; a Revolutionary camp site. Has house built (1814) by Duncan Phyfe. **7** Village (1940 pop. 675), Jefferson co., E Tenn., 23 mi. ENE of Knoxville, in agr., zinc-mining area. **8** Town (pop. 701), Shenandoah co., NW Va., in Shenandoah Valley, 16 mi. NE of Harrisonburg. Endless Caverns (S), Shenandoah Caverns (N) attract tourists. In Civil War, Confederate troops under Gen. J. C. Breckinridge defeated Union forces under Gen. Franz Sigel here, May 15, 1864.

Newmarket, town (pop. 2,709), including Newmarket village (pop. 2,172), Rockingham co., SE N.H., W of Portsmouth and on Great Bay, at mouth of Lamprey R. (falls, water power); textiles, shoes, lumber. Set off from Exeter 1727.

Newmarket-on-Fergus, Gaelic *Cora Chaitlín*, town (pop. 417), S Co. Clare, Ireland, 13 mi. WNW of Limerick; agr. market (cattle; potatoes). Near by is Dromond Castle, birthplace of William Smith O'Brien.

New Marlboro or **New Marlborough,** town (pop. 989), Berkshire co., SW Mass., in the Berkshires, 23 mi. S of Pittsfield; dairy products. Mill River village is seat of town; also includes Hartsville and Southfield villages.

New Marshall, Okla.: see MARSHALL, town.

New Martinsville, town (pop. 4,084), ⊙ Wetzel co., NW W.Va., on the Ohio 30 mi. SSW of Wheeling, in area of oil and natural-gas wells, sandpits, agr. (livestock, grain, vegetables, tobacco); mfg. of glassware, tiles and other clay products, chemicals, metal products. Platted 1838.

New Matamoras (mĕtŭmō'rŭs, mătŭ–), village (pop. 781), Washington co., SE Ohio, on the Ohio (W.Va. line) and 21 mi. ENE of Marietta, in agr. area.

New Meadows, village (pop. 621), Adams co., W Idaho, 18 mi. NNE of Council, in cattle-grazing area.

New Meadows River, SW Maine, inlet of Casco Bay extending from S tip of Sebascodegan Isl. c.12 mi. inland, bet. Brunswick and Bath.

New Melones Dam, Calif.: see STANISLAUS RIVER.

New Merwede River, Du. *Nieuwe Merwede* (nē'vŭ mĕr'vādŭ), SW Netherlands, outlet of Maas and Waal rivers, formed by forking of UPPER MERWEDE RIVER into New Merwede R. and Lower Merwede R. 4.5 mi. W of Gorinchem; flows 10 mi. SW, joining Bergsche Maas R. 6 mi. SSE of Dordrecht to form the HOLLANDSCHDIEP. Forms N and NW boundary of the Biesbosch. Entire length navigable.

New Mexico, state (land □ 121,511; with inland waters □ 121,666; 1950 pop. 681,187; 1940 pop. 531,818), SW U.S., bordered W by Ariz., S by Mexico and Texas, E by Texas and Okla. Panhandle, N by Colo.; 4th in area, 39th in pop.; admitted 1912 as 47th state; ⊙ Santa Fe. The "Sunshine State" is roughly rectangular, measuring 395 mi. N–S and 355 mi. E–W. Comprising parts of 4 physiographic provs., the state presents many features of mountains, plateau, plains, and desert. It is crossed in W by the Continental Divide, W of which rise 3 major Colorado R. affluents, the San Juan, Little Colorado, and Gila rivers. E of the Divide, flowing roughly N–S, is the important RIO GRANDE, in whose valley Santa Fe and Albuquerque, the state's largest cities, are situated. The PECOS RIVER, a tributary of the Rio Grande, drains a wide lowland in the E. In the NE is the upper CANADIAN RIVER, which flows E to the Arkansas R. in the Mississippi basin. The southern Rocky Mtn. ranges Sangre de Cristo Mts. (E of Rio Grande) and San Juan Mts. and Valle Grande Mts. (W of Rio Grande) extend into the N central part of the state. Wheeler Peak (13,151 ft.), in the Sangre de Cristo Mts., is the highest point in N.Mex. The NW section lies on the COLORADO PLATEAU, here marked by lava flows, volcanic cones (e.g., Mt. Taylor, 11,389 ft.), colorful buttes and mesas, the domed Zuni Mts., and San Juan R. valley. The SW and S—including the Rio Grande valley up to Santa Fe—is basin and range country, characterized by eroded block mts. (e.g., Mimbres, San Andres, Sacramento, and Guadalupe mts.) and desert plains such as the Plains of San Augustin, Jornada del Muerto, and Tularosa Basin (containing WHITE SANDS NATIONAL MONUMENT). E N.Mex. falls within the Great Plains, considerably dissected in the N (canyons, mesas), where the Canadian R. has cut its course. Farther S is the broad Pecos valley, bordered on the E by an escarpment marking the W limit of the extremely level LLANO ESTACADO or Staked Plains. The state has an average alt. of c.5,700 ft., which, together with its low humidity and abundant sunshine, makes the climate generally healthful. Rainfall varies from 6 in. in the S desert and NW corner to 25 in. in the Sangre de Cristo Mts.; the E plains receive 10–20 in. (S–N). The N mts. have a winter snowfall. Santa Fe (N center) has mean temp. of 29°F. in Jan., 69°F. in July; Roswell (SE) averages 40°F. in Jan., 78°F. in July. Native vegetation consists of creosote bush, yuccas, cottonwood, cactus, and short grass in the S, scrub oak in the SE, piñon-juniper woodland at 5,000–7,500 ft., and the commercially valuable coniferous forests (ponderosa pine, Douglas fir, spruce) above 7,500 ft., mostly in the N and W mts. Of the large land area (44%) in Federal ownership, natl. forests comprise some 10,250,000 acres. Widespread soil erosion constitutes a major problem. Vast areas of arid or semi-arid land, suitable only for grazing, make stock raising an important industry in N.Mex. Cattle total c.1,165,000 head, and sheep, raised in large flocks in the N and SW, number c.1,400,000. Principal livestock centers are HOBBS, LAS VEGAS, TUCUMCARI, Santa Rosa, and Carrizozo. The percentage of harvested cropland is relatively small. Dry farming is practiced on the E plains and there are irrigated areas in the Rio Grande (ELEPHANT BUTTE DAM, Caballo Dam), Pecos (Carlsbad project), Canadian (CONCHAS DAM), and San Juan river valleys; artesian wells are used in the SE. Chief crops are alfalfa, hay, and grain sorghums (raised throughout state for fodder), wheat and corn (E), cotton (in irrigated dists. of S Pecos and Rio Grande valleys), beans or frijoles (NE and center), potatoes, and apples (San Juan valley); some oats, barley, chilies, and vegetables are also grown. The growing season varies from under 100 days in some mtn. valleys to 200 days in the S. N.Mex.'s mineral wealth consists of copper, potash, zinc, coal, lead, molybdenum, petroleum, natural gas and gasoline, gold, silver, gypsum, and small amounts of manganese, fluorspar, iron ore, and turquoise. The major mining centers are in the SE, where petroleum (refineries at Hobbs and Artesia) and natural gas fields and, near CARLSBAD, large potash deposits (c.80% of natl. output) occur, in the NW and RATON areas (bituminous coal), in San Juan R. dist. (oil, natural gas), and at Santa Rita (copper ore—smelted at El Paso, Texas—and molybdenum), Central, and Questa. Mfg., chiefly wood products and food, is comparatively unimportant. Main towns are ALBUQUERQUE, SANTA FE, Roswell, Hobbs, Clovis, Las Vegas, Las Cruces, and Gallup. At Los Alamos (NW of Santa Fe) is an atomic-energy laboratory, where the 1st atomic bomb—tested (July, 1945) in S desert region NW of Alamogordo—was made. The Univ. of N.Mex. is at Albuquerque, N.Mex. Col. of Agr. and Mechanic Arts at State College (near Las Cruces), N.Mex. School of Mines at Socorro. With its generally high alt., salubrious climate, mineral springs, Indian communities, and anc. Indian ruins, N.Mex. has become popular with winter tourists, health seekers, artists, and archaeologists. Points of interest include CARLSBAD CAVERNS NATIONAL PARK, Aztec Ruins, Chaco Canyon, Gila Cliff Dwellings, and White Sands natl. monuments, ACOMA pueblo, Elephant Butte Reservoir, and the resorts of Santa Fe, Albuquerque, TAOS, and Las Vegas. Part of the huge Navajo Indian reservation is in NW; in other reservations dwell Apaches, Zunis, and Hopis. Among the early Indian civilizations in N.Mex. were the Basket Maker and, later, the Pueblo, which the Spaniards found through the expeditions of the Franciscan priest Marcos de Niza in 1539, the explorer Francisco Coronado in 1540–42, and subsequent missionaries. The 1st permanent Sp. settlement in the area was at SAN JUAN pueblo (1598), and Santa Fe was founded c.1609. Colonization was mostly confined to missionary activity during the 17th cent., a period marked by several Indian uprisings, culminating in the Pueblo Revolt of 1680, which led to a temporary withdrawal of Sp. rule. American trappers began to make their way into N.Mex. soon after it became part of the independent republic of Mexico (1821). The country was ceded to U.S. after Mexican War of 1846–48, during which Santa Fe was occupied by American troops under Gen. Kearny. N.Mex., comprising most of the Southwest region, was made a territory in 1850. After addition of Gadsden Purchase in 1853, the area was reduced in size by the separation of Colo. (1861) and Ariz. (1863). During Civil War it was held for a short time (1861–62) by Confederate forces. The coming of the transcontinental railroads (1878) was followed by cattle and mining booms, and when artesian water was discovered in Pecos valley agr. was developed. In 1879 and 1885 the Apaches, under chiefs Victorio and Geronimo, left their govt.-assigned reservations and went on the warpath, but they were soon suppressed. As a border state N.Mex. has had to cope with problems such as smuggling and illegal immigration. A large percentage of the pop. is of Spanish-Mexican descent and the Spanish language is widely spoken. See also articles on the cities, towns, geographic features, and the 32 counties: BERNALILLO, CATRON, CHAVES, COLFAX, CURRY, DE BACA, DONA ANA, EDDY, GRANT, GUADALUPE, HARDING, HIDALGO, LEA, LINCOLN, LOS ALAMOS, LUNA, MCKINLEY, MORA, OTERO, QUAY, RIO ARRIBA, ROOSEVELT, SANDOVAL, SAN JUAN, SAN MIGUEL, SANTA FE, SIERRA, SOCORRO, TAOS, TORRANCE, UNION, VALENCIA.

New Miami (mīă'mē), village (pop. 1,860), Butler co., extreme SW Ohio, 4 mi. NNE of Hamilton and on Great Miami R.

New Middletown. **1** Town (pop. 153), Harrison co., S Ind., 15 mi. SW of New Albany, in agr. area. **2** Village (pop. 264), Mahoning co., E Ohio, 10 mi. SSE of Youngstown, near Pa. line.

New Milford. **1** Town (pop. 5,799), including New Milford village (pop. 2,673), a ⊙ Litchfield co., W Conn., on the Housatonic and 12 mi. N of Danbury; mfg. (metal products, electrical products, textiles, silverware, clothing, furniture, lumber, hatters' fur), agr. (dairy products, tobacco, poultry). Includes Gaylordsville village and part of L. Candlewood (resorts). Roger Sherman worked here, 1734–61. Settled 1707, inc. 1712. **2** Residential borough (pop. 6,006), Bergen co., NE N.J., on Hackensack R. and 4 mi. N of Hackensack; makes sweaters. Inc. 1922. **3** Borough (pop. 880), Susquehanna co., NE Pa., 9 mi. ENE of Montrose; lumber products.

New Mill, former urban district (1931 pop. 4,538), West Riding, SW Yorkshire, England, 5 mi. S of Huddersfield; woolen milling. Here are woolen-milling towns of Hepworth (S), Scholes (SSW), and Fulstone (NE). Inc. 1938 in Holmfirth.

Newmill, Scotland: see KEITH.

New Mills, urban district (1931 pop. 8,551; 1951 census 8,473), NW Derby, England, on Goyt R. and 8 mi. NNW of Buxton; cotton milling.

Newmilns and Greenholm (nū'mĭlz, grēn'hōm), burgh (1931 pop. 3,979; 1951 census 4,043), NE Ayrshire, Scotland, on Irvine R. and 7 mi. E of Kilmarnock; muslin and lace mfg. center.

New Minden (mĭn'dŭn), village (pop. 160), Washington co., SW Ill., 14 mi. WSW of Centralia, in agr. and bituminous-coal area.

Newminster, town and parish (pop. 1,124), E central Northumberland, England, on Wansbeck R. just W of Morpeth; woolen milling. Has remains of 12th-cent. abbey.

New Monkland, parish (pop. 38,499), N Lanark, Scotland; includes AIRDRIE.

New Munich (mū'nĭk), village (pop. 277), Stearns co., central Minn., on Sauk R. and 28 mi. W of St. Cloud; dairy products.

Newnan, city (pop. 8,218), ⊙ Coweta co., W Ga., 35 mi. SW of Atlanta. Mfg. (yarns, blankets, clothing, steel tanks, lumber) and trade center for fruit and farm region; meat packing. Has livestock market. Many old houses and gardens. Inc. 1828.

Newnes (nūnz), village, E New South Wales, Australia, 75 mi. NW of Sydney; rail terminus; hardwood timber.

Newnham (nū'nŭm), former urban district (1931 pop. 1,035), W Gloucester, England, on Severn R. and 10 mi. WSW of Gloucester.

New Norcia (nôr'shŭ), village (pop. 258), W Western Australia, 70 mi. NNE of Perth; wool, wheat, wine. Benedictine monastery.

New Norfolk, town (pop. 2,934), SE Tasmania, 14 mi. NW of Hobart and on Derwent R.; agr. center; hops, fruit, oats; sheep. Settled 1808 by *Bounty* mutineers from Norfolk Isl.

New Norway, village (pop. 179), S central Alta., 12 mi. SSW of Camrose; wheat, dairying.

New Orleans (ôr'lēŭnz), city (□ 363.5; pop. 570,445), coextensive with Orleans parish (□ 199), SE La., on E bank (levee) of the Mississippi c.107 mi. above its mouth, and extending N and NE to shores of L. Pontchartrain; 30°N 90°5'W; alt. from 4 ft. below sea level to c.15 ft. It is the largest city in La., the commercial metropolis of the South, and a major U.S. river- and seaport and port of entry; has foreign trade zone (free port), opened 1947. S terminus of river navigation on the Mississippi; and a center for coastwise traffic on the Gulf Intracoastal Waterway, crossing the Mississippi levees through locks at near-by Harvey and Algiers. Industrial Canal (Inner Harbor Navigation Canal), c.6 mi. long, connects L. Pontchartrain and the Mississippi; it is partly followed by Intracoastal Waterway. New Orleans exports petroleum, cotton, lumber, machinery, iron and steel, food products; imports coffee, sugar, bananas, bauxite. A leading U.S. cotton market. Served by 9 railroads, several domestic and international airlines. Has important sugar-milling, petroleum-refining, cottonseed-processing, shipbuilding, and textile industries; also produces food products, chemicals (especially industrial alcohol), cordage, wood products, furniture, building materials; city's extensive fisheries (especially shrimp) supply canneries. Built on lowlands within a bend of the Mississippi (hence its nickname "the Crescent City"), New Orleans is protected from the river by levees and the BONNET CARRE FLOODWAY, which diverts flood waters into L. Pontchartrain. Huey P. Long Bridge (1935) spans the river near by; several ferries ply bet. city and industrial communities (Gretna, Harvey, Marrero), and Algiers (a section of New Orleans), which are on opposite bank. City's many attractions for tourists stem from its historic past and its reputation for good living. Notable is the picturesque French quarter (*Vieux Carré*) of the old city below Canal Street; there on Jackson Square, the former *Place d'Armes*, are the Cabildo (formerly the govt. bldg.; now a mus.), and St. Louis Cathedral; quarter is famed for narrow streets, old houses with grillwork balconies, and subtropical courtyard gardens. Many of city's world-famous restaurants specialize in sea food. The annual pre-Lenten Mardi Gras is the best-known festival in the U.S. Other points of interest include the city's many parks, its levee water front, museums (including Delgado Art Mus.), historic churches and houses, and its educational institutions (Tulane, Loyola, Dillard, and Xavier universities). Camp Leroy Johnson is here. Bathing and amusement resorts are on the Pontchartrain lake front. Platted in 1718 by the sieur de Bienville, the settlement soon became important as a port; it was made ⊙ French colony of Louisiana in 1722. The Treaty of Paris (1763) gave the territory to Spain, under whose rule it remained (despite revolt in 1768) until 1803, when it was retransferred to France, thence immediately to the U.S. with the Louisiana Purchase. It was inc. in 1805. Commercial growth under American rule was rapid, but city's social life was dominated by Creole culture until late-19th cent. Was ⊙ La. from state's admission to the Union (1812) until 1849. Battle of New Orleans, fought against British (Jan. 8, 1815) after close of War of 1812, ended in victory for hastily organized U.S. defenders under Andrew Jackson. New Orleans flourished as the "Queen City of the Mississippi," a great port and market for slaves and cotton, until city's fall (1862) to Admiral Farragut in the Civil War. Its occupation by Union troops under Benjamin F. Butler and the turbulence of Reconstruction days were succeeded by events, notably the deepening (in 1870s) of channel at the Mississippi's mouth and the coming of railroads, which are the basis of the city's modern commercial and industrial importance. Latin American trade has increased greatly since 1930s, as result of U.S. Good Neighbor policy.

New Oxford, borough (pop. 1,366), Adams co., S Pa., 10 mi. ENE of Gettysburg; cannery; shoes, clothing, bricks. Laid out 1792, inc. 1874.

New Palestine (pă'lŭstīn), town (pop. 504), Hancock co., central Ind., on Sugar Creek and 15 mi. ESE of Indianapolis, in agr. area.

New Paltz (nōō' pôlts, nū'–), resort village (pop. 2,285), Ulster co., SE N.Y., on small Wallkill R. and 13 mi. SSW of Kingston, in agr. area (dairy products, poultry, potatoes, fruit). Seat of a state teachers col. Settled by Huguenots in 1677; inc. 1887.

New Paphos, Cyprus: see PAPHOS.

New Paris. **1** Village (pop. 1,046), Preble co., W Ohio, on East Fork of Whitewater R., at Ind. line, and 5 mi. ENE of Richmond, Ind.; tools, lumber. **2** Borough (pop. 202), Bedford co., S Pa., 10 mi. NW of Bedford.

Newpark, village in Mid Calder parish, W Midlothian, Scotland, 2 mi. ENE of West Calder; shale-oil mining.

New Patna, India: see PATNA, city.

New Pekin (pē'kĭn), town (pop. 543), Washington co., S Ind., 18 mi. NNW of New Albany, in agr. area.

New Perlican (pûr'lĭkŭn), village (pop. 516), SE N.F., on E side of Trinity Bay, 13 mi. NNW of Carbonear; fishing port, with cod and lobster canneries; lumbering.

New Philadelphia. **1** City (pop. 12,948), ⊙ Tuscarawas co., E Ohio, 22 mi. S of Canton, and on Tuscarawas R., in coal-mining and clay-producing area; machinery, clay products, metal and enamelware products, electrical goods, dairy products, cigars, brooms. Founded 1804, inc. 1833. **2** Borough (pop. 2,200), Schuylkill co., E central Pa., on Schuylkill R. and 5 mi. NE of Pottsville; anthracite; clothing. Laid out c.1828, inc. 1868. Post office name formerly Silver Creek.

New Pitsligo (pĭtslī'gō), town in Tyrie parish, NE Aberdeen, Scotland, 10 mi. SW of Fraserburgh; agr. market. It was once center of illicit whisky distilling.

New Plymouth, Bahama Isls.: see GREEN TURTLE CAY.

New Plymouth, borough (pop. 18,558; metropolitan New Plymouth 20,642), ⊙ Taranaki co. (□ 229; pop. 6,661), W N.Isl., New Zealand, on N.Taranaki Bight and 160 mi. NNW of Wellington, at base of Mt. Egmont; dairy plants, iron foundry, soap factory. Oil field at near-by Moturoa. New Plymouth is in, but independent of, Taranaki co.

New Plymouth, village (pop. 942), Payette co., SW Idaho, 10 mi. SE of Payette and on Payette R.; apples, peaches, cherries.

New Point, town (pop. 322), Decatur co., SE central Ind., 29 mi. ESE of Shelbyville, in agr. area.

New Point Comfort, E Va., low promontory at S tip of Mathews co., bet. Chesapeake Bay (E) and Mobjack Bay (W); lighthouse. Hunting, fishing.

New Pomerania, Bismarck Archipelago: see NEW BRITAIN.

New Port, town, S Curaçao, Du. West Indies, minor port 7 mi. SE of Willemstad. Ships phosphate, which is carried by cableway from Santa Barbara, 2½ mi. N. Sometimes written Newport.

Newport. **1** Municipal borough (1931 pop. 11,322; 1951 census 20,426), ⊙ Isle of Wight, Hampshire, England, near center of isl., on Medina R. and 11 mi. SW of Portsmouth; resort and agr. market. Grammar school, built 1612, was site of negotiations (1648) bet. Charles I and Parliamentarians. Newport's Latin name is *Novus Burgus;* possibly site of Roman station. Just N is village of Parkhurst, with large prison and barracks. **2** County borough (1931 pop. 89,203; 1951 census 105,285), S Monmouth, England, on the Usk (bridged), 4 mi. N of its influx into the Severn, and 20 mi. NW of Bristol; 51°35'N 2°59'W. Port with extensive docks; one of chief Br. coal- and steel-products exporting points. There are important iron, steel, copper, aircraft, boiler, leather, rubber, and asbestos works. On Stow Hill, above town, is partly-Norman church of St. Woollos, procathedral of Monmouth diocese since 1921. Remains of castle, founded before 1171, rebuilt later. Newport was scene (1839) of Chartist riots. **3** Urban district (1931 pop. 3,437; 1951 census 3,744), E Shropshire, England, 12 mi. WSW of Stafford; agr. market, with farm-equipment works. Has 14th-cent. church.

Newport. **1** Gaelic *Baile Uí bhFiacháin*, town (pop. 356), W Co. Mayo, Ireland, at head of Clew Bay, 6 mi. NNW of Westport; seaport, shipping coal, oatmeal, potatoes; iron foundries. **2** Gaelic *Tulach Sheasta*, town (pop. 507), W Co. Tipperary, Ireland, 10 mi. ENE of Limerick; agr. market (dairying, cattle raising; potatoes, beets).

Newport, burgh (1931 pop. 3,276; 1951 census 3,273), NE Fifeshire, Scotland, on the Firth of Tay, opposite and 2 mi. SE of Dundee; seaside resort and port, with ferry to Dundee. Village of Wormit is 2 mi. SW, at S end of the Tay Bridge.

Newport, county (□ 115; pop. 61,539), SE R.I., on Mass. line and the Atlantic, and including Block, Conanicut, Prudence, and Rhode isls. in Narragansett Bay; ⊙ NEWPORT. Resort, agr. area, with mfg. (textiles, rubber and metal products, electrical equipment, precision instruments, medical supplies, furniture, jewelry, canned seafood), fisheries, boat building. Inc. 1703.

Newport. **1** City (pop. 6,254), ⊙ Jackson co., NE Ark., 37 mi. WSW of Jonesboro and on White R.; rail and commercial center for farm area (cotton, rice, pecans, livestock). Mfg. of button blanks, wood products; cotton processing, lumber milling. Fishing (artificial lake) near by. Settled c.1873. **2** Town (pop. 1,171), New Castle co., N Del., on Christina R. and 2 mi. SW of Wilmington; pigments, chemicals. **3** Town (pop. 660), ⊙ Vermillion co., W Ind., on Little Vermilion R. near its mouth on Wabash R., and 30 mi. N of Terre Haute; clay products. U.S. ordnance works. **4** City (pop. 31,044), a ⊙ Campbell co., N Ky., on left bank (levee) of the Ohio (bridges here to Cincinnati), at mouth of Licking R. opposite Covington (W). Residential, commercial, industrial city, within Cincinnati metropolitan dist.; mfg. of metal products (especially steel), clothing, concrete and food products, stationery, sheet music, beverages, compacts, cigarette cases; millwork. Co. courthouse here. In 1936, new World War Veterans Memorial Bridge across Licking R. to Covington was opened. Military post here (1806–84) was moved to near-by Fort Thomas after Ohio R. flood in 1884. Laid out 1791; inc. as village 1795, as city 1835. Annexed Clifton (SW; 1930 pop. 3,080) in 1935. **5** Town (pop. 2,190), including Newport village (pop. 1,296), Penobscot co., S central Maine, 25 mi. W of Bangor and on Sebasticook L. Fishing resort; mfg. (textiles, wood products); highway center. Settled 1808, inc. 1814. **6** Village (pop. 1,672), Washington co., SE Minn., on Mississippi R. and 7 mi. SSE of St. Paul, in grain, livestock, and poultry area. **7** Village (pop. 207), Rock co., N Nebr., 10 mi. E of Bassett; hay-shipping point. **8** Town (pop. 5,131), including Newport village (pop. 3,062), ⊙ Sullivan co., SW N.H., on Sugar R. and 8 mi. E of Claremont, near L. Sunapee. Trade center, mfg. (woolens, shoes, tools, soap), fruit, poultry, truck. Includes Guild, mill village. Inc. 1761. **9** Village (1940 pop. 802), Cumberland co., SW N.J., on short Nantuxent Creek and 9 mi. SSE of Bridgeton; sand pits. **10** Village (pop. 752), Herkimer co., central N.Y., 13 mi. NE of Utica; makes footwear. **11** Town (pop. 676), Carteret co., E N.C., 13 mi. WNW of Beaufort, in Croatan Natl. Forest. **12** City (pop. 3,241), Lincoln co., W Oregon, on Yaquina Bay of the Pacific, at mouth of Yaquina R., and 40 mi. W of Corvallis; resort, port of entry, lumber-shipping point; salmon fisheries. Settled c.1855, inc. 1891. **13** Borough (pop. 1,893), Perry co., central Pa., 20 mi. NW of Harrisburg and on Juniata R.; metal products, hosiery, clothing; limestone. Settled 1789, laid out 1814, inc. 1840. **14** City (pop. 37,564), ⊙ Newport co., SE R.I., 25 mi. SSE of Providence, on peninsula at SW end of Rhode Isl., with harbor on Narragansett Bay (W), and the Atlantic on S and E; one of wealthiest U.S. summer resorts, with many elaborate homes. Seat of U.S. naval training station and naval war college, torpedo station, U.S. Fort Adams, and coast guard station. Port of entry. Some mfg. (precision instruments, rubber goods, medical supplies, electrical equipment, furniture, jewelry, dairy products); boat building; fisheries. Seat of Salve Regina Col. Settled 1639 by William Coddington and others; united with Portsmouth in 1640; entered permanent federation with Providence and Warwick in 1654; chartered as city 1784, returned to town status 1787, reinc. 1853; until 1900, was joint ⊙ R.I. with Providence. Shipbuilding (after 1646) and foreign shipping brought early prosperity ended temporarily by the Revolution, in which many buildings were destroyed; occupied by British, 1776–79. Early Newport harbored refugees of various groups: Friends and Jews came in the 1650s, and Seventh-Day Baptists organized a church here in 1671. The Jewish community contributed greatly to pre-Revolutionary prosperity; built Touro Synagogue in 1763 (oldest in U.S.; and since 1946 a natl. historic site). Other notable buildings: Trinity Church (1726; Episcopal), Sabbatarian Church (1729), Redwood Library (founded 1747), brick market house or city hall (1760), old state house (1739). The Old Stone Mill in Touro Park is believed by some to have been a gristmill owned by Benedict Arnold, 17th-cent. governor, and by others to be a Norse relic. Colony's 1st newspaper, the *Rhode Island Gazette*, issued here in 1732 by James Franklin. Development as fashionable resort of wealthy began in 19th cent.; polo, tennis, boating, and other meets held here. Severe damage done here by 1938 hurricane. **15** Town (pop. 3,892), ⊙ Cocke co., E Tenn., on Pigeon R. and 40 mi. E of Knoxville, at W foot of the Great Smokies; canning, tanning, lumbering, mfg. of hosiery, wood extracts, shirts. John Sevier fish and game preserve (125,000 acres), and Great Smoky Mts. Natl. Park are near by. **16** City (pop. 5,217), ⊙ Orleans co., N Vt., on L. Memphremagog and 50 mi. NNE of Montpelier, near Que. line. Resort, trade center, port of entry; wood products, clothing; lumber, truck, dairy products; granite. Settled 1793, chartered 1803, inc. 1917. Just W is Newport town (pop. 966), including Newport Center village (lumber). **17** Town (pop. 1,385), ⊙ Pend Oreille co., NE Wash., near Idaho line, 40 mi. NE of Spokane and on Clark Fork R.; lumber, potatoes, hay. Settled c.1885, inc. 1903.

Newport, fishing port and parish (pop. 1,188), N Pembroke, Wales, on Newport Bay of Irish Sea, 7 mi. ENE of Fishguard. Has remains of 13th-cent. castle.

Newport Bay, Orange co., S Calif., dredged harbor (yachting, sport and commercial fishing) 10 mi. S of Santa Ana. Sheltered from the Pacific by peninsula on which are Newport Beach and Balboa (resorts); Corona del Mar is on SE shore.

Newport Beach, resort city (pop. 12,120), Orange co., S Calif., 18 mi. SE of Long Beach, on peninsula bet. Newport Bay and the Pacific; yacht harbor; fisheries; boat yards. Causeway to Lido Isle in bay (residential; resort). Inc. 1906.

Newport Center, Vt.: see NEWPORT.

New Portland, town (pop. 733), Somerset co., W central Maine, on the Carrabassett and 13 mi. NW of Madison; wood products.

Newport News (nū″pûrt nūz′), city (pop. 42,358), in but independent of Warwick co., SE Va.; great port on James R. (bridged) at its estuary on HAMPTON ROADS opposite Norfolk (ferry); Hampton city is just NE. Has one of largest drydocks and one of largest shipbuilding plants in world. Tidewater terminus (since 1880) of Chesapeake and Ohio RR; transships coal, grain, tobacco, petroleum, ore (chrome, manganese), machinery, lumber, pulpwood, general cargoes; airport. Railroad shops; mfg. of pulp and paper, machinery (especially hydraulic turbines), foundry products, paint; fisheries; seafood packing. Seat of state school for deaf and blind Negro children. Mariners' Mus. (1930) is at suburban Hilton Village. Settled 1611 and 1621 by Irish colonists; inc. 1896. Became rail terminus in 1880; shipbuilding industry begun 1886.

Newport Pagnell (păg′nŭl), urban district (1931 pop. 3,956; 1951 census 4,366), N Buckingham, England, on Ouse R. at mouth of Ouzel R., 12 mi. N of Leighton Buzzard; agr. market, with agr.-machinery works. Has 14th-cent. church; 17th-cent. hosp. established by Anne of Denmark, wife of James I. Town formerly noted for its lace.

New Port Richey, resort city (pop. 1,512), Pasco co., W central Fla., 25 mi. NW of Tampa, near the Gulf; citrus fruit; concrete products.

New Prague (prāg), city (pop. 1,915), Le Sueur and Scott counties, S Minn., 33 mi. SSW of Minneapolis, in grain and livestock area; dairy products, flour, poultry, beverages. Inc. as village 1877, as city 1891.

New Preston, Conn.: see WASHINGTON.

New Providence. 1 Town (pop. 426), Clark co., SE Ind., 15 mi. NNW of New Albany, in agr. area. **2** Town (pop. 212), Hardin co., central Iowa, 7 mi. SW of Eldora, in agr. area. **3** Borough (pop. 3,380), Union co., NE N.J., on Passaic R. and 13 mi. WSW of Newark; horticultural center. Settled c.1720, inc. 1899. **4** Village (pop. 1,825), Montgomery co., central Tenn., on the Cumberland just NW of Clarksville. Old stone blockhouse (1788) here.

New Providence Island, island (20 mi. long, up to 6 mi. wide) and district (□ 58; pop. 29,391), N central Bahama Isls., on the Great Bahama Bank, bet. Andros Isl. (W) and Eleuthera Isl. (E), 170 mi. ESE of Miami, Fla.; on it is NASSAU, ⊙ Bahamas, at 25°5′N 77°20′W. Though not the largest, it is by far the most important isl. of the Bahamas, having about ¼ of the colony's pop. Mostly flat, with few low ridges, it is largely covered by pine "barrens" and includes swamps and several shallow lakes (L. of Killarney, L. Cunningham). It produces tomatoes, bananas, coconuts, citrus fruit, sisal; fishing (sponge, deep-sea fish) along its coast. Because of the fine beaches and climate (average temp. 70°F.), it has developed into a world-famous winter resort, centering on Nassau, which also has a good harbor, protected by small Hog Isl. The isl. was largely settled in last third of 17th cent., when the British built several forts; Fort Nassau was completed 1697. Nassau was laid out in 1729. During 18th cent. the Spanish and French made several incursions. Amer. loyalists took refuge here after the Revolution. The British maintained an air base here during Second World War.

Newquay (nū′kē), urban district (1931 pop. 5,959; 1951 census 9,928), central Cornwall, England, on the Atlantic and 11 mi. N of Truro; port and tourist resort; textile milling, fishing. Exports kaolin and building stone.

New Quay, urban district (1931 pop. 1,112; 1951 census 1,093), W Cardigan, Wales, on Cardigan Bay of Irish Sea, 16 mi. NE of Cardigan; resort.

New Quebec, Que.: see UNGAVA.

New Radnor (răd′nûr, –nōr), agr. village and parish (pop. 367), central Radnor, Wales, 10 mi. E of Llandrindod Wells, at edge of Radnor Forest. An anc. borough, with remains of Norman castle (destroyed 1401 by Owen Glendower). Has Norman church. ESE, 3 mi., is village of Old Radnor, in Old Radnor and Burlingjobb parish (pop. 352), with remains of Norman fortification.

New Raymer, Colo.: see RAYMER.

New Richland, village (pop. 908), Waseca co., S Minn., 12 mi. S of Waseca, in grain, livestock, and poultry area; dairy products; poultry packing.

New Richmond, village (pop. estimate 1,000), E Que., on S Gaspé Peninsula, on Chaleur Bay, at mouth of Little Cascapedia R., 26 mi. ENE of Dalhousie; fishing port, in zinc- and lead-mining region.

New Richmond. 1 Town (pop. 391), Montgomery co., W central Ind., 18 mi. SSW of Lafayette, in agr. area. **2** Village (pop. 1,960), Clermont co., SW Ohio, 17 mi. SE of Cincinnati, and on Ohio R., in agr. area; woolens, foundry products, paper specialties. Birthplace of Ulysses S. Grant is near by. Founded 1816. **3** City (pop. 2,886), St. Croix co., W Wis., on small Willow R. and 28 mi. ENE of St. Paul, Minn.; flour milling, vegetable canning, cheese processing.

New Riegel (rē′gŭl), village (pop. 317), Seneca co., N Ohio, 8 mi. WSW of Tiffin.

New Ringgold, borough (pop. 302), Schuylkill co., E central Pa., 8 mi. S of Tamaqua.

New River, S Br. Guiana, rises in the Serra Acaraí near Brazil border, flows c.200 mi. N, through dense forests, to the Courantyne at Du. Guiana line at 3°25′N 57°35′W.

New River, the outlet of New River Lagoon (15 mi. long, 2 mi. wide), N Br. Honduras, flows 60 mi. NNE, past Orange Walk, to Chetumal Bay of Caribbean Sea, 3 mi. S of Corozal. Navigable for small craft. Sugar cane, corn; lumbering.

New River, S S.Isl., New Zealand, rises S of L. Wakatipu, flows 105 mi. SE, past Lumsden, to Foveaux Strait on S coast, 3 mi. S of Invercargill. Sometimes called Oreti R.

New River, village (1940 pop. 506), Pulaski co., SW Va., on New R. and 2 mi. W of Radford. Coal mining near by.

New River. 1 In SE N.C., rises in NW Onslow co., flows SSE past Jacksonville (where it widens into estuary c.2 mi. wide), to Onslow Bay via New River Inlet; c.50 mi. long. **2** In S S.C., rises in N Jasper co., flows c.40 mi. S to the Atlantic S of Daufuskie Isl., near mouth of Savannah R.; partly navigable. **3** In N.C., Va., and W.Va., rises (as South Fork) in Watauga co., NW N.C.; flows NNE into SW Va., past Radford, and generally NNW through gorge in the Alleghenies, into W.Va., past Hinton, joining Gauley R. at Gauley Bridge (hydroelectric works) to form Kanawha R.; c.320 mi. long. Dammed (1939) above Radford to form Claytor L. (hydroelectric works); BLUESTONE DAM near Hinton impounds large flood-control reservoir. Receives short North Fork in N.C., near Va. line, and, in W.Va., Greenbrier and Bluestone rivers.

New Rives (rēvz), town (1940 pop. 79), Dunklin co., extreme SE Mo., in Mississippi flood plain, 10 mi. S of Kennett. Adjacent is town of Rives (1950 pop. 166), inc. 1947.

New Roads, town (pop. 2,818), ⊙ Pointe Coupee parish, SE central La., 24 mi. NW of Baton Rouge and on False R. (c.13 mi. long; an oxbow lake of the Mississippi); pecans, corn, sugar cane, cotton; cotton and moss ginning, sawmilling, food and cottonseed processing; fishing.

New Rochelle (rōshĕl′), city (pop. 59,725), Westchester co., SE N.Y., on harbor (yachting, fishing) on Long Island Sound, E of Mount Vernon, within New York city metropolitan area; residential, industrial. Mfg.: plumbing and heating equipment, surgical dressings, clothing, medicines, athletic equipment, wood and metal products. Seat of Col. of New Rochelle and Iona Col. Thomas Paine's house is occupied by Huguenot and Historical Association; Paine Memorial House (1925) contains some of his effects. Hudson Park, Glen Isl. amusement park are recreational centers. U.S. Fort Slocum is on David's Isl. (c.½ mi. long) offshore in the sound. Settled by Huguenots in 1688; inc. as village in 1858, as city in 1899.

New Rockford, city (pop. 2,185), ⊙ Eddy co., E central N.Dak., 60 mi. NNW of Jamestown and on James R.; dairy products, wheat, poultry, livestock. Inc. 1912.

New Rocky Comfort or **Foreman,** town (pop. 907), Little River co., extreme SW Ark., 27 mi. NW of Texarkana, in agr. area (cotton, corn, hay, livestock; dairy products); cotton ginning, sawmilling.

New Rome, village (pop. 75), Franklin co., central Ohio, 7 mi. W of downtown Columbus.

New Romney, England: see ROMNEY.

New Ross or **Ross,** Gaelic *Baile Nua*, urban district (pop. 4,894), W Co. Wexford, Ireland, on Barrow R. 2 mi. below mouth of the Nore, and 12 mi. NE of Waterford; tanning, woolen milling, iron founding, brewing. There are remains of anc. fortification and of 13th-cent. Franciscan friary. Traditionally, town was founded in 12th cent. by Strongbow's daughter. Here Cromwell crossed (1649) Barrow R. on pontoon bridge. In 1798 United Irishmen's attack on town was repulsed. On W shore of Barrow R., in Co. Kilkenny, is suburb of Rosbercon, once site of important abbey (no remains).

New Ross, town (pop. 336), Montgomery co., W central Ind., near Raccoon Creek, 12 mi. ESE of Crawfordsville, in agr. area.

Newry (nū′rē), urban district (1937 pop. 12,746; 1951 census 13,264), SW Co. Down, Northern Ireland, on Newry R. and on Newry Canal (linking town with Carlingford Lough, Bann R., and Lough Neagh), 33 mi. SSW of Belfast; 54°11′N 6°20′W; seaport, with mfg. of agr. implements, rope, fish nets, cattle feed; linen milling, tobacco processing. Part of town extends into Co. Armagh. Town grew around abbey founded here in 12th cent. by Maurice McLoughlin, king of Ireland; in 1543 abbey became collegiate church and was later dissolved. Anc. castle was destroyed in 14th cent. by Edward Bruce and again (1566) by Shane O'Neill. In 1689 duke of Berwick partly burned town on his retreat before Schomberg. St. Patrick's Church (16th cent.) is reputedly oldest Protestant church in Ireland. Newry is seat of R.C. bishop of Dromore. Near town is Crown Mount, a rath 600 ft. in diameter.

Newry. 1 Town (pop. 188), Oxford co., W Maine, on Bear R. and c.14 mi. WSW of Rumford, in agr., recreational area. Feldspar mined at North Newry village. **2** Borough (pop. 412), Blair co., S central Pa., 8 mi. S of Altoona. **3** Mill village (1940 pop. 864), Oconee co., NW S.C., near Keowee R., 30 mi. WSW of Greenville; textiles.

New Salem (sā′lŭm). **1** Town (pop. 184), Pike co., W Ill., 33 mi. ESE of Quincy, in agr. area. **2** Restored historic village (now a state park), Sangamon co., central Ill., on Sangamon R. and 16 mi. NW of Springfield. Here was home of Abraham Lincoln, 1831–37; bldgs. which were standing in Lincoln's day (including the Rutledge Tavern, Danton Offut's store, and the Lincoln-Berry store) have been restored. A small mus. houses pioneer relics. Settled 1828; decline and abandonment came after 1839. **3** Agr. town (pop. 392), Franklin co., central Mass., 19 mi. NE of Northampton, near Quabbin Reservoir; fruit. **4** City (pop. 942), Morton co., central N.Dak., 25 mi. W of Mandan; coal mines; dairy produce, livestock. **5** Village (pop. 2,131, with adjacent Buffington), Fayette co., SW Pa., 6 mi. W of Uniontown. **6** or **Delmont,** borough (pop. 695), Westmoreland co., SW central Pa., 22 mi. E of Pittsburgh. **7** Borough (pop. 333), York co., S Pa., 5 mi. SW of York.

New Sarum, England: see SALISBURY.

New Schwabenland (shwä'bŭnlănd), Antarctica, in Queen Maud Land, consists of edge of continental plateau back of Princess Astrid Coast and Princess Martha Coast, bet. 12°W and 20°30'E. Surveyed 1939 from air by German expedition.

New Scone, Scotland: see SCONE.

Newsham, England: see BLYTH.

New Sharlston, town in Sharlston parish (pop. 2,854), West Riding, S Yorkshire, 3 mi. E of Wakefield; coal mining.

New Sharon (shâ'rŭn, shă'–). **1** Town (pop. 1,089), Mahaska co., S central Iowa, near Skunk R., 12 mi. N of Oskaloosa; makes work clothes. Settled by Quakers. **2** Town (pop. 755), Franklin co., W central Maine, on Sandy R. and 7 mi. ESE of Farmington; agr.; wood products, canned vegetables.

New Shildon, England: see SHILDON.

New Shoreham, R.I.: see BLOCK ISLAND.

New Siberian Islands, Rus. *Novo-Sibirskiye Ostrova,* archipelago (□ 11,000) bet. Laptev and E.Siberian seas of Arctic Ocean, in Yakut Autonomous SSR, Russian SFSR, 30–355 mi. off mainland; 73°–77°N 133°–158°30'E. Central group, also called New Siberian Isls. (□ 8,200) or Anjou Isls., Rus. *Ostrova Anzhu,* includes KOTELNY ISLAND, FADDEI ISLAND, NOVAYA SIBIR ISLAND, and smaller Belkovski, Figurin, and Zheleznyakov isls. Settlement is sparse, tundra is scarce; mammoth fossils found here. Isls. discovered 1773 by Rus. merchant Lyakhov. Separated from LYAKHOV ISLANDS by Sannikov Strait. Lyakhov Isls. (S) and DE LONG ISLANDS (NE) are also considered part of New Siberian archipelago.

New Silksworth, England: see SILKSWORTH.

New Smyrna Beach (smûr'nŭ), resort city (pop. 5,775), Volusia co., NE Fla., 13 mi. SSE of Daytona Beach, on the Atlantic and on both shores of Hillsborough R. lagoon (bridged here); fishing, shrimping; citrus-fruit packing; railroad shops. Has remains of old fort. Spanish Franciscan mission established here in 1696; ruins are extant. Town recolonized 1767, abandoned 1776, and resettled c.1803. Called New Smyrna until 1937.

Newsome Park, suburb (pop. 14,960, with adjacent Hilton Park) of Newport News, Warwick co., SE Va.

Newsoms, town (pop. 392), Southampton co., SE Va., 12 mi. SW of Franklin.

New South Wales, state (□ 309,433; pop. 2,985,838) of Commonwealth of Australia, SE Australia; bounded by Queensland, Macintyre and Dumaresq rivers, and McPherson Range (N), Victoria and Murray R. (S), South Australia (W), S Pacific (E), Tasman Sea (SE); E of meridian of 141°E long., S of parallel of 29°S lat.; 680 mi. long (from Point Danger to Cape Howe), 780 mi. wide; chief port and ⊙ is SYDNEY. Includes Lord Howe Isl. in S Pacific. Most populous state of commonwealth. GREAT DIVIDING RANGE extends parallel with E seaboard, separating fertile coastal strip from W plains; its principal sections are: New England and Liverpool ranges (NE), Blue Mts. (W of Sydney), Muniong Range (SE) of Australian Alps, with Mt. Kosciusko (7,305 ft.; highest peak of Australia). Principal rivers are the Darling and Murrumbidgee; the Murray (principal river of Australia) forms greater part of S border, flowing W into South Australia. Lakes are generally small and shallow; lagoons on coast. State is in temperate zone. Temp. ranges from 30°F. (coastal area) to 69°F. (W plains). Subtropical NE corner has rainfall of 80 in.; W plains, 10 in. Snow (May-Sept.) in Mt. Kosciusko area. Abundant flora and fauna. Illawarra flame tree (*Brachychiton acerifolium*), kurrajong (*Brachychiton populneum*), banksias (evergreen shrubs), eucalyptus, acacias. Marsupials include kangaroos, koala bears, flying opossums. Monotremes include platypuses, spiny anteaters (echidna). Many varieties of birds: bowerbirds, lyrebirds, kookaburra or laughing jackass (kingfisher), brolga or native companion (crane), and emu (related to ostriches). Rich natural resources: coal, gold, iron, copper, silver, lead, zinc, opals. Primarily sheep-raising and agr. state, producing wheat, oats, fruit. Tropical fruits (bananas, pineapples) and sugar cane grown in NE coastal area. Hardwood timber in forest reserves. Principal centers are Sydney on Port Jackson, Newcastle on Port Hunter (coal-loading port), Lismore, Wollongong, and Broken Hill (chief silver-lead mining center). Exports wool, meat, hides, wheat, coal, steel, timber. Visited 1770 by Capt. Cook, who proclaimed Br. sovereignty over E coast of Australia; 1st settlement of Australia founded 1788 at Sydney as penal colony. Original colony of New South Wales included Tasmania, South Australia, Victoria, Queensland, Northern Territory, and New Zealand. These territories were separated (1825–1863) from New South Wales, becoming separate colonies. New South Wales and other colonies federated (1901) as states of Commonwealth of Australia. Australian Capital Territory (site of CANBERRA, federal⊙) ceded 1911, territory at Jervis Bay area ceded 1915, to the Commonwealth.

New Spain: see MEXICO, republic.

New Springville, SE N.Y., a section of Richmond borough of New York city, on central Staten Isl., 6 mi. SW of St. George.

Newstead (nū'stĭd), town and parish (pop. 1,933), W Nottingham, England, 9 mi. NNW of Nottingham; coal mining. Site of Newstead Abbey, founded 1170 by Henry II in atonement for murder of Thomas à Becket. Granted to Sir John Byron by Henry VIII, it became property of the poet Byron in 1798, who sold the property in 1816. His rooms are preserved as a mus. and are owned by the city of Nottingham.

New Straitsville, village (pop. 1,122), Perry co., central Ohio, 27 mi. SSW of Zanesville, in coal-mining area. Founded 1870.

New Stuyahok (stōō'yăhŏk), village (pop. 88), SW Alaska, near Dillingham.

New Suffolk (sŭ'fŭk), resort village (pop. c.300), Suffolk co., SE N.Y., on N peninsula of E Long Isl., on Great Peconic Bay, 11 mi. ENE of Riverhead; mfg. (aircraft parts, machinery).

New Sweden, Swedish colony (1638–55), on Delaware R. below Trenton (N.J.), including parts of present Pa., N.J., and DELAWARE. Colonists for the New Sweden Co. (organized 1637) under Peter Minuit founded Ft. Cristina (or Christina), where WILMINGTON now stands. TINICUM ISLAND was made ⊙ in 1643. Since Finland was then part of Sweden, half the colonists were Finns. Peter Stuyvesant, director general of New Amsterdam, with more Dutch soldiers than the entire pop. of New Sweden (c.300), took the little colony (1655).

New Sweden, agr. town (pop. 827), Aroostook co., NE Maine, 20 mi. NNW of Presque Isle. Settled 1870 by Swedish immigrants.

New Territories, leased section (□ 359; 1949 pop. estimate 200,000) of Hong Kong colony. Comprises greater part of colony's mainland, N of Kowloon peninsula, traversed by the railroad to Canton; most of the colony's isls., including Lan Tao and Lamma; and Mirs and Deep bays. Parts of the mainland and isls. are intensively cultivated, producing rice, vegetables, peanuts, fruit, and sugar cane. Hogs and poultry are raised. Administered in 3 dists. and headed by a dist. commissioner, the New Territories were leased by Britain from China in 1898 for 99 years.

Newton. 1 Agr. village and parish (pop. 672), S Cambridge, England, 5 mi. S of Cambridge; fruit-growing. Church dates from 13th–15th cent. **2** Town (pop. 10,986) in Hyde municipal borough, NE Cheshire, England; mfg. (chemicals, leather, light metals); cotton milling. **3** Parish, Lancashire, England: see HARDHORN WITH NEWTON.

Newton. 1 Town in Cambuslang parish, N Lanark, Scotland, near the Clyde; steel-milling center. **2** Village in Abercorn parish, N West Lothian, Scotland, 3 mi. W of Queensferry; shale-oil mining.

Newton, village (1931 pop. 336), Sierra Leone colony, on Sierra Leone Peninsula, on railroad and 3 mi. E of Waterloo; hog and poultry raising, truck gardens.

Newton. 1 County (□ 822; pop. 8,685), NW Ark.; ⊙ Jasper. Drained by Buffalo R. and its tributaries; situated in Ozark region. Agr. (livestock, poultry, fruit, truck; dairy products). Lead and zinc mining; lumber milling. Part of Ozark Natl. Forest is in S. Formed 1842. **2** County (□ 273; pop. 20,185), N central Ga.; ⊙ Covington. Drained by Alcovy and Yellow rivers; includes part of Lloyd Shoals Reservoir. Piedmont agr. (cotton, corn, truck, fruit), livestock, and lumber area; textile mfg. (Porterdale, Covington). Formed 1821. **3** County (□ 413; pop. 11,006), NW Ind.; ⊙ Kentland. Bounded W by Ill. line, N by Kankakee R.; also drained by Iroquois R. Farming and dairying area; poultry, grain, livestock. Some mfg. (feed, cheese, cosmetics); ships seeds, grain. Limestone quarrying. Formed 1835. **4** County (□ 580; pop. 22,681), E central Miss.; ⊙ Decatur. Drained by small Chunky and Tuscolameta creeks. Agr. (cotton, corn), dairying; lumbering. Formed 1836. **5** County (□ 629; pop. 28,240), SW Mo.; ⊙ Neosho. In the Ozarks; agr. (berries, hay, corn, wheat), dairying; mining (zinc, lead, tripoli); oak timber. Formed 1854. **6** County (□ 941; pop. 10,832), E Texas; ⊙ Newton. Bounded E by Sabine R. (here the La. line); drained by its tributaries. In pine-forest belt; lumbering is chief industry. Also agr. (cotton, corn, hay, fruit, truck), livestock (hogs, cattle). Formed 1846.

Newton. 1 Town (pop. 745), Dale co., SE Ala., on the Choctawhatchee and 15 mi. NW of Dothan, in truck and pecan area. **2** City (pop. 503), ⊙ Baker co., SW Ga., 22 mi. SSW of Albany and on Flint R. **3** City (pop. 2,780), ⊙ Jasper co., SE central Ill., on Embarrass R. and 22 mi. SE of Effingham, in agr. area; mfg. (wood products, brooms, beverages); livestock, corn, wheat, dairy products. Settled 1828, inc. 1831. **4** City (pop. 11,723), ⊙ Jasper co., central Iowa, 30 mi. ENE of Des Moines; rail junction; mfg. center: washing machines, construction machinery, farm power apparatus, foundry products, advertising specialties. Settled 1846, inc. 1857. **5** City (pop. 11,590), ⊙ Harvey co., S central Kansas, 24 mi. N of Wichita; trade and shipping center, and railroad-div. point with railroad repair shops; flour and alfalfa milling, dairying. Oil wells near by. Founded 1871, inc. 1872. Boomed (1871–73) as cattle town and railhead at end of Chisholm Trail. In early 1870s, German Mennonites from Russia introduced variety of hard winter wheat (Turkey red) that has since become chief crop of state. Bethel Col. (Mennonite; coeducational; 1887) is just N, in North Newton. **6** City (pop. 81,994), Middlesex co., E Mass., on Charles R., just W of Boston and Brookline; chiefly residential, with some mfg. (knit goods, radio and signal apparatus, yarn, fastening devices, machinery, rubber and paper goods, tractors, precision instruments). It is an aggregate of 14 villages: 7 "Newtons" (Newton Centre, Newton Corner, Newton Highlands, Newton Upper Falls, Newton Lower Falls, West Newton, Newtonville), plus Auburndale, CHESTNUT HILL (Boston Col.), Eliot, Nonantum (nōnăn'tŭm), Oak Hill, Riverside, and Waban (wô'bŭn). Andover Newton Theological School is at Newton Centre, Newton Jr. Col. at Newtonville. Horace Mann, Nathaniel Hawthorne, Mary Baker Eddy, and Samuel Francis Smith lived in city. Settled before 1640, inc. as town 1688, as city 1873. **7** Town (pop. 2,912), Newton co., E central Miss., 27 mi. W of Meridian; hardwood timber; clothing, cottonseed products, milk products. Seat of Clarke Memorial Col. Near by are a U.S. school for Indians and a dist. jr. col. **8** Town (pop. 1,173), Rockingham co., SE N.H., 7 mi. N of Haverhill, Mass. **9** Town (pop. 5,781), ⊙ Sussex co., NW N.J., 21 mi. NW of Morristown; dairying center; mfg. (clothing, textiles, farm implements); fur processing; poultry, fruit. Don Bosco Col. here. Little Flower Monastery (Benedictine) near by. Settled c.1760, inc. 1864. **10** Town (pop. 6,039), ⊙ Catawba co., W central N.C., 8 mi. SE of Hickory; mfg. center; hosiery, cotton, and rayon mills, furniture factories. Settled mid-18th cent. **11** Village (pop. 1,462), Hamilton co., extreme SW Ohio, suburb E of Cincinnati, across Little Miami R.; concrete products, plastics, machinery. Laid out 1801. **12** Town (pop. 929), ⊙ Newton co., E Texas, near Sabine R., c.55 mi. NNE of Beaumont, in agr., timber region; lumber milling, cotton ginning. **13** Town (pop. 497), Cache co., N Utah, on Clarkston Creek near its mouth in Bear R. and 12 mi. NW of Logan in irrigated agr. area; alt. 4,525 ft. Newton Dam is 3 mi. N.

Newton, Mount, Nor. *Newtontoppen,* highest peak (5,633 ft.) of West Spitsbergen, Spitsbergen group, in NE part of isl., near head of Wijde Fjord, near 79°N 16°30'E.

Newton Abbot, urban district (1931 pop. 15,010; 1951 census 16,393), S Devon, England, on Teign R. estuary, at mouth of Lemon R., and 14 mi. SSW of Exeter; rail junction; agr. market; tanneries, mfg. (leather goods, textiles). At Forde House William III was proclaimed king (1688). Church dates from 14th cent.

Newton and Chilwell, Australia: see GEELONG.

Newton Brook, village (pop. estimate 950), S Ont., 8 mi. N of Toronto; dairying, truck gardening.

Newton Centre, Mass.: see NEWTON.

Newton Dam, Utah: see CLARKSTON CREEK.

Newton Falls. 1 Village (1940 pop. 657), St. Lawrence co., N N.Y., near Cranberry L., on Oswegatchie R. (dam near by) and 32 mi. S of Potsdam; paper products. **2** Village (pop. 4,451), Trumbull co., NE Ohio, 18 mi. WNW of Youngstown and on Mahoning R.; mfg. of structural steel and tubing; also motor vehicles, machinery, tools.

Newtongrange (nū"tŭn-grānj'), village in Newbattle parish, NE Midlothian, Scotland, on South Esk R. and 2 mi. S of Dalkeith; coal mining.

Newton Grove, town (pop. 374), Sampson co., S central N.C., 22 mi. SW of Goldsboro, in farm area.

Newton Hamilton, borough (pop. 397), Mifflin co., central Pa., 2 mi. E of Mount Union and on Juniata R.

Newton Heath, NE part (pop. 20,867) of Manchester, SE Lancashire, England; cotton milling, railroad rolling stock and aircraft construction; mfg. of chemicals, dyes, shoes.

Newton Highlands, Mass.: see NEWTON.

Newtonia, city (pop. 190), Newton co., SW Mo., in the Ozarks, 10 mi. E of Neosho.

Newton-in-Makerfield, England: see NEWTON-LE-WILLOWS.

Newton-le-Willows (nū'tŭn-lŭ-wĭ'lōz), urban district (1931 pop. 20,152; 1951 census 21,862), S Lancashire, England, 5 mi. E of St. Helens; locomotive works; mfg. of paper, glassware, explosives. Formerly Newton-in-Makerfield. Just W is town of Earlestown; metalworking; sugar refining.

Newton Lower Falls, Mass.: see NEWTON.

Newton Mearns, Scotland: see MEARNS.

Newtonmore (nū'tŭnmôr'), agr. village, E central Inverness, Scotland, on the Spey and 3 mi. WSW of Kingussie; tourist resort.

Newton-on-Ayr, Scotland: see AYR.

Newton Saint Faith, England: see HORSHAM SAINT FAITH.

Newton Stewart, burgh (1931 pop. 1,914; 1951 census 2,000), E Wigtown, Scotland, on Cree R. and 7 mi. NNW of Wigtown; agr. market, with agr. implement works.

Newtonsville, village (pop. 182), Clermont co., SW Ohio, 23 mi. ENE of Cincinnati.

Newton Upper Falls, Mass.: see NEWTON.

Newtonville, Mass.: see NEWTON.

New Toronto (tŭrŏn'tō), town (pop. 9,504), S Ont., on L. Ontario, WSW suburb of Toronto; rubber and tire mfg.

Newtown, municipality (pop. 24,933), E New South Wales, Australia, 4 mi. SW of Sydney, in metropolitan area; mfg. (textiles, hosiery, shoes), brass foundry.

New Town, N residential suburb of Hobart, Tasmania, within city limits.

Newtown. 1 Town (pop. 7,448), including Newtown borough (pop. 782), Fairfield co., SW Conn., near the Housatonic, 17 mi. N of Bridgeport; mfg. (rubber, plastic, paper, plaster, and wire products), poultry, fruit, dairy products. Fairfield State Hosp. here. Includes industrial Sandy Hook village (1940 pop. 1,127). Settled c.1708, inc. 1711. **2** Town (pop. 287), Fountain co., W Ind., 18 mi. NW of Crawfordsville, in agr. and bituminous-coal area. **3** Town (pop. 231), Sullivan co., N Mo., 16 mi. NW of Milan. **4** Borough (pop. 2,095), Bucks co., SE Pa., 21 mi. NE of Philadelphia; lumber; textiles, metal products; agr. Settled 1684, laid out 1733, inc. 1838.

Newtown, Welsh *Trenewydd* (trĭnĕ'wĭdh), town (pop. 2,905) in Newtown and Llanllwchaiarn (lăn-thlōō-khī'ŭrn) urban district (1931 pop. 5,154; 1951 census 5,427), S Montgomery, Wales, on Severn R. and 8 mi. SW of Montgomery; woolen (flannel) milling, leather tanning, mfg. of electrical appliances and tools. Has 17th-cent. half-timbered inn and remains of anc. parish church. Robert Owen b. here. Just N is town of Llanllwchaiarn (pop. 2,249).

Newtown and Llanllwchaiarn, Wales: see NEWTOWN.

Newtownards (nū"tŭnärdz'), municipal borough (1937 pop. 10,546; 1951 census 12,237), NE Co. Down, Northern Ireland, near head of Strangford Lough, 10 mi. E of Belfast; linen and woolen milling, mfg. of lace curtains, hosiery. In 1244 Walter de Burgh founded a Dominican priory here; there are some remains. Just NE of town is village of Movilla, with remains of abbey church founded in 6th cent. by St. Finian.

Newtownbarry (nū"tŭnbă'rē), Gaelic *Bun Clóidighe,* town (pop. 699), NW Co. Wexford, Ireland, on Slaney R. and 11 mi. NNW of Enniscorthy, at foot of Mt. Leinster; agr. market (dairying; wheat, barley, potatoes, beets).

Newtown Battlefield Reservation, N.Y.: see ELMIRA.

Newtown Creek, SE N.Y., a tidal arm (c.4 mi. long) of East R., within New York city; partly separates Brooklyn and Queens boroughs. Carries much shipping for industrial NW Queens.

Newtowncunningham (nū"tŭnkŭ'nĭng-ŭm), Gaelic *Baile Nua an Mhaoil,* town (pop. 189), E Co. Donegal, Ireland, 8 mi. W of Londonderry; agr. market (flax, oats, potatoes; cattle, sheep).

Newtownhamilton (nū"tŭnhă'mĭltŭn), town (pop. 896), W Co. Armagh, Northern Ireland, 12 mi. SSE of Armagh; agr. market (flax, potatoes, oats; cattle).

Newtownstewart or **Newtown Stewart** (nū"tŭnstū'-ŭrt), town (pop. 682), NW Co. Tyrone, Northern Ireland, on Mourne R. and 9 mi. NNW of Omagh; agr. market (oats, flax, potatoes; cattle). Castle here was destroyed by James II on his retreat from Londonderry.

New Tredegar, England: see BEDWELLTY.

New Trier (trēr), village (pop. 73), Dakota co., SE Minn., near Mississippi R., 25 mi. SSE of St. Paul, in agr. area.

New Tupton, England: see TUPTON.

Newtyle (-tīl), agr. village and parish (pop. 831), SW Angus, Scotland, 10 mi. NW of Dundee.

New Ulm (ŭlm'), city (pop. 9,348), ⊙ Brown co., S Minn., on Minnesota R., near mouth of Cottonwood R., and 25 mi. WNW of Mankato; trade and mfg. center for diversified-farming area; dairy products, flour, beverages, bricks and tiles. Lutheran col. is here. Cottonwood State Park is near by. Founded 1854, inc. as village 1857, as city 1876. Harbored many refugees during Sioux uprising of 1862.

New Underwood, town (pop. 268), Pennington co., SW central S.Dak., 20 mi. E of Rapid City and on Boxelder Creek; trading point for farm region; grain, livestock, poultry.

New Vienna (vēē'nŭ). **1** Town (pop. 204), Dubuque co., E Iowa, 22 mi. WNW of Dubuque, in livestock area. **2** Village (pop. 807), Clinton co., SW Ohio, 14 mi. ESE of Wilmington and on East Fork of Little Miami R.

Newville. 1 Town (pop. 565), Henry co., SE Ala., 14 mi. NNE of Dothan. **2** Borough (pop. 1,788), Cumberland co., S Pa., 11 mi. WSW of Carlisle; clothing, beverages, flour. Laid out 1794, inc. 1817.

New Vineyard, town (pop. 447), Franklin co., W central Maine, 9 mi. NNE of Farmington; wood products; hunting, fishing.

New Virginia, town (pop. 342), Warren co., S central Iowa, 29 mi. S of Des Moines, in agr. area.

New Washington, town (1939 pop. 1,086; 1948 municipality pop. 13,370), Capiz prov., N Panay isl., Philippines, on Sibuyan Sea, 23 mi. WNW of Capiz; agr. center (tobacco, rice).

New Washington. 1 Village (pop. 910), Crawford co., N central Ohio, 21 mi. NW of Mansfield; aluminum utensils, food products. **2** Borough (pop. 65), Clearfield co., W central Pa., 11 mi. NNE of Barnesboro.

New Waterford, town (pop. 9,302), NE N.S., on NE coast of Cape Breton Isl., 10 mi. NNE of Sydney; coal-mining center; fishing port.

New Waterford, village (pop. 610), Columbiana co., E Ohio, 17 mi. S of Youngstown, in agr. and coal area; furniture, pottery.

New Waterway, Du. *Nieuwe Waterweg* (nē'vŭ wä'tŭrvākh), canal, South Holland prov., SW Netherlands; one of main Du. navigation routes; extends 5 mi. NW, from W end of the SCHEUR (4 mi. SE of Hook of Holland) to North Sea 1 mi. NW of Hook of Holland; average depth 35 ft. Forms part of Rotterdam–North Sea waterway. Entire length navigable by ocean-going ships. Built 1866–72. Sometimes the name New Waterway is applied to entire Rotterdam–North Sea route (16 mi. long).

New Waverly, village (1940 pop. 543), San Jacinto co., E Texas, 14 mi. S of Huntsville, in cotton-growing, lumbering area. Settled in 1830s as plantation center.

New Westminster, city (pop. 21,967), SW B.C., on N bank of the Fraser R. and 9 mi. ESE of Vancouver; 49°12'N 122°55'W; major port, open the year-round, shipping grain, lumber, metals, minerals, fruit, chemicals. Base of Fraser R. fishing fleet; has large grain elevator; oil refinery; salmon, fruit, and vegetable canneries; foundries; paper, lumber, and flour mills; meat-packing plants; distilleries; mfg. of machinery and leather and gypsum products. Site of Columbia and St. Louis colleges; has Anglican and R.C. cathedrals. Founded 1859 and originally named Queensborough, New Westminster was ⊙ B.C. until colonies of B.C. and Vancouver Isl. were united and ⊙ removed to Victoria. Parts of center of city were destroyed 1898 in large fire.

New Weston, village (pop. 136), Darke co., W Ohio, 16 mi. N of Greenville, in agr. area; ceramics.

New Willard, village (1940 pop. 929), Polk co., E Texas, c.40 mi. SSW of Lufkin; lumbering.

New Wilmington, borough (pop. 1,948), Lawrence co., W Pa., 8 mi. N of New Castle; tools; agr. Westminster Col. Inc. 1863.

New Windsor, England: see WINDSOR.

New Windsor (wĭn'zŭr). **1** Village, Ill.: see WINDSOR, village. **2** Town (pop. 707), Carroll co., N Md., 19 mi. ENE of Frederick, in agr. area (grain, apples). **3** Suburban village (pop. 2,754), Orange co., SE N.Y., on W bank of the Hudson, just S of Newburgh; mfg. (candles, handbags, heaters, paper products, felt, floating dry docks). Was home of George Clinton. De Witt Clinton was b. here.

New Witten, town (pop. 198), Tripp co., S S.Dak., 12 mi. NW of Winner and on Cottonwood Creek. Inc. 1938, absorbing most of Witten town (1940 pop. 9; 1930 pop. 307).

New Woodville, town (pop. 78), Marshall co., S Okla., near L. Texoma, 2 mi. N of Woodville.

New World Island (□ 62; pop. 1,979), in Notre Dame Bay, E N.F.; 20 mi. long, 8 mi. wide; 49°35'N 54°40'W. Fishing is chief occupation.

New Wortley, England: see ARMLEY AND NEW WORTLEY.

New Year's Islands, Sp. *Islas Año Nuevo* (ē'släs ä'nyō nwä'vō), small archipelago (□ 2.2) in the South Atlantic off the Argentine Tierra del Fuego, just N of Staten Isl.; 3 small isls., on largest of which (54°39'S 64°8'W) are lighthouse and observatory.

New Year's Point, Calif.: see AÑO NUEVO POINT.

New York, USSR: see NYU-YORK.

New York, state (land □ 47,929; with inland waters, but without □ 3,627 of Great Lakes, □ 49,576; 1950 pop. 14,830,192; 1940 pop. 13,479,142), NE U.S., in Middle Atlantic region; bordered E by Vt. (partly along L. Champlain), Mass., and Conn., SE by Long Isl. Sound, Atlantic Ocean, and N.J., S by Pa., W by L. Erie, Niagara R. (Ontario line), and L. Ontario, N by St. Lawrence R. (separating Ontario) and Quebec; 29th in area, 1st in pop.; one of original 13 states, the 11th to ratify (1788) the Constitution; ⊙ Albany. The "Empire State" extends c.300 mi. N-S, c.315 mi. E-W at its widest points; Long Isl. (SE) is 118 mi. long. The state includes parts of several physiographic provs. and has much varied scenery. Along the N border is the 10–20-mi.-wide St. Lawrence valley. S of this lowland rise the ADIRONDACK MOUNTAINS, a mass of Pre-Cambrian crystalline and metamorphic rocks, forming an extension of the Laurentian Plateau of Canada, to which they are joined by a narrow neck through the Thousand Isls. in the St. Lawrence R. The mts. have a subdued upland character in the W, becoming bolder in the E, where they are highest and include Whiteface Mtn. (4,872 ft.) and Mt. Marcy (5,344 ft.), highest point in N.Y. S of the Adirondacks is an E-W lowland trough drained by Mohawk R. An important transportation route, traversed by the old Erie Canal and its successor, the N.Y. State Barge Canal, it links the lake plains in the W with the HUDSON RIVER valley in the E. The latter, L. Champlain, and Wallkill valley form part of the Great Appalachian Valley, running N-S through E N.Y. E of the Hudson, along Mass. line, are the Taconic Mts. (c.2,000 ft.). The lake plains consist of a narrow strip along L. Erie and a 25–35-mi.-wide tract S of L. Ontario. Running W from near Rochester into Ont. is a limestone escarpment, over which the Niagara R. flows at Niagara Falls. S N.Y. lies on the ALLEGHENY PLATEAU, an extensive, well-dissected highland area of horizontal rock strata. Averaging 1,500–2,000 ft. in alt., it rises to 3,500–4,000 ft. in the CATSKILL MOUNTAINS in the E. Its N edge, the Helderberg Mts., overlooks the Mohawk valley. The region drains partly N (e.g., by Genesee R. and Schoharie Creek), but mostly S via the Allegheny, Susquehanna, and Delaware rivers. In SE N.Y. are Shawangunk Mtn.—a ridge of the Folded Appalachians—and, S of Newburgh, the Hudson Highlands. Jutting S bet. the Hudson and Long Isl. Sound is the so-called Manhattan prong, composed largely of hard crystalline rocks. LONG ISLAND and Staten Isl. are segments of the Atlantic coastal plain and consist of sand and gravel deposits, surfaced by morainic material and outwash plains. Almost all of the state was covered by continental glaciation, remains of which include the numerous Adirondack lakes (e.g., L. George, Saranac Lakes) and the picturesque Finger Lakes (W center). N.Y. has a humid continental climate, with annual rainfall exceeding 50 in. in the Adirondacks and Hudson highlands, c.30 in. in places in the W, but mostly over 35 in. throughout the state. New York city (SE) has mean temp. of 31°F. in Jan., 74°F. in July, and 42 in. of rainfall; Buffalo (W) has mean temp. of 24°F. in Jan., 70°F. in July, and 33 in. of rain. Growing season varies from 160–180 days in coastal and lakeside areas to less than 130 days in higher inland sections. Native vegetation consists mostly of maple, hemlock, birch, beech, with spruce, fir, white pine in the Adirondack area, oak chestnut, yellow poplar in the lake plains and SE and scrub oak and stunted pine on E Long Isl. commercial forest land amounts to some 11,000,000 acres. The state lies largely in the U.S. hay and dairying belt, with c.17,500,000 acres in farm and pasture land, of which c.6,500,000 acres are in crops. Dairying, concentrated in the lowlands and Allegheny Plateau country, is the most important agr. industry and milk (N.Y. ranks 2d in U.S.) and cheese production is considerable. Besides the large hay crop, oats, corn, wheat, barley, rye, and buckwheat are raised. N.Y. ranks 2d in apples and grapes; it also grows peaches, pears, cherries, plums and berries. Chief fruit-producing areas are the lake shores, Finger Lakes dist. (wine making), and Hudson valley. The state is 2d only to Vt. in maple sugar and syrup production. The demand of a large urban pop. make truck farming an important industry, especially in Long Isl., Orange co., and L. Ontario plain. Cabbages, onions, celery, cauliflower, snap beans, tomatoes, broccoli and other market crops are extensively cultivated Long Isl. is also noted for its potatoes and poultry (particularly ducks). Fish resources include oysters, clams, lobsters, cod, flounder, bluefish, and haddock from Long Isl. Sound and the Atlantic whitefish, shad, and herring from the Great Lakes N.Y. produces a wide variety of minerals, including petroleum (SW), rock salt (rich deposits S of L. Ontario to Pa. line), clay products (brick, porcelain), gypsum (W), zinc (St. Lawrence co.), natural gas, cement rock, sandstone, slate, granite, and pyrite. It ranks 1st in talc, abrasive garnets (in Adirondacks), emery, wollastonite, and ilmenite (from titaniferous deposits at Sanford L. in the Adirondacks). A small amount of iron ore (magnetite) is worked. The production of cement, coke pig iron, and ferro-alloys is large. Situated on both the Great Lakes and the Atlantic Ocean and favored by natural transportation routes, proximity to fuel and raw materials, and large urban market and labor supply (including numerous immigrants as well as by a long tradition of industry, N.Y. has been the leading mfg. state since 1840. It is primarily a processor of raw materials and producer of consumer goods. Clothing mfg. is easily the largest industry, followed by printing and publishing, food processing (meat packing, grain milling, fruit and vegetable canning, bakery and confectionery products), and the mfg. of machinery, fabricated metal products, rugs, carpets, and other textiles, transportation equipment, furniture, refined petroleum scientific instruments, electrical equipment, tobacco products, chemicals, paper, leather goods, and wide range of other items. Almost ⅔ of the mfg. output is concentrated in the New York city area centering in the great port of New York, which handles 25% of U.S. domestic wholesale trade and 50% of its foreign commerce. The nation's largest city and financial capital, it is noted for its garment industry and publishing firms. BUFFALO, on L. Erie, is the country's flour-milling center and has large meat-packing plants and iron- and steel-works. ROCHESTER produces photographic equipment, optical goods, and clothing; SYRACUSE type-writers, agr. machinery, and chinaware; YONKERS and UTICA textiles; SCHENECTADY electrical equipment and locomotives; NIAGARA FALLS has large hydroelectric plants, supplying W N.Y. industries. Other major cities are ALBANY, Binghamton, Troy, Mt. Vernon, New Rochelle, and Elmira. Important local industries are glass products (Corning), aluminum wire and cable (Massena), copper products (Rome), and gloves (Gloversville). The state has extensive rail and road networks and an important inland waterway in the NEW YORK STATE BARGE CANAL, which links the Hudson at Cohoes with the Niagara R. at Tonawanda; the Hudson is navigable for ocean-going ships to Albany. Although containing several large urban centers, up-state N.Y. has a predominantly rural character. The vast New York city metropolitan area (extending into Rockland, Westchester, Nassau, and Suffolk counties) accounts for the majority of the state's pop., which is 86% urban. N.Y.'s varied natural setting offers numerous recreational facilities. The Adirondacks (L. George, L. Placid, Saranac Lakes), the Catskills, Hudson highlands (Bear Mtn.), Thousand Isls., Finger Lakes, Long Isl., Niagara Falls, Saratoga Springs, and a fine system of state parks (e.g., Jones Beach, Palisades) are the principal resort areas. Leading educational institutions include Columbia Univ., N.Y. Univ., the City Col. of the City of New York, and numerous other institutions in N.Y. city (see the articles on the city and its boroughs); Cornell Univ. (at Ithaca); Syracuse Univ.; Univ. of Buffalo; Rensselaer Polytechnic Inst. (at Troy); U.S. Military Acad. (at West Point), U.S. Merchant Marine Acad. (at Kings Point), Vassar Col. (at Poughkeepsie), and Colgate Univ. (at Hamilton). In the 17th cent. the region was inhabited by the Five Iroquois Nations—the Mohawks, Oneidas, Onondagas, Cayugas, and Senecas—who had defeated the Algonquins and established a strong, well-organized confederacy. In 1609 Champlain explored L. Champlain and Henry Hudson sailed up the Hudson. The Dutch set up a fur-trading post near Albany in 1614 to which permanent settlers came in 1623. A fortified colony, called New Amsterdam, was made (1625) on Manhattan isl., purchased from the Indians by the Du. West India Co. Settlement of the Hudson valley was undertaken by means of patroonship grants, such as Rensselaerwyck. The English landed on Gardiners Isl. (off E Long Isl.) in 1639 and in 1664 forced the Dutch to surrender the New Netherland colony, which they renamed New York. From 1689 to 1763 N.Y. figured prominently in the Anglo-French wars, in which the Iroquois tribes played an important part as allies of the British. The influential merchant groups objected strongly to Br. trade restrictions and it was in New York city that the Stamp Act Congress met in 1765. However, during the Revolution, a large number of New Yorkers remained loyal to England. Major military actions of the war included Ethan Allen's capture of Ticonderoga, the battles of Long Isl., White Plains, and Harlem Heights, Burgoyne's surrender after Saratoga, Indian raids on the frontier, and the failure of Benedict Arnold's attempt to betray West Point. N.Y. was won over to the Federal Constitution largely through the efforts of Alexander Hamilton. The E boundary was defined with the admission of Vt. in 1791. In the War of 1812 there were several engagements along the Niagara and St. Lawrence rivers and the noted Amer. naval victory of Plattsburg took place on L. Champlain. The completion of the Erie Canal (1825) proved a major event in the opening of the West and in the development of N.Y. mfg. New York city grew rapidly as the nation's commercial and financial center. Large-scale immigration (at 1st from Ireland and Germany, later from S and E Europe) accompanied the industrial trend, which increased enormously after the Civil War. Fenian activities along the Canadian border (1866–70) seriously strained Anglo-Amer. relations. The state's large pop. early gave it an importance in national politics it has continued to maintain. See also articles on cities, towns, geographic features, and the 62 counties: ALBANY, ALLEGANY, BRONX, BROOME, CATTARAUGUS, CAYUGA, CHAUTAUQUA, CHEMUNG, CHENANGO, CLINTON, COLUMBIA, CORTLAND, DELAWARE, DUTCHESS, ERIE, ESSEX, FRANKLIN, FULTON, GENESEE, GREENE, HAMILTON, HERKIMER, JEFFERSON, KINGS, LEWIS, LIVINGSTON, MADISON, MONROE, MONTGOMERY, NASSAU, NEW YORK, NIAGARA, ONEIDA, ONONDAGA, ONTARIO, ORANGE, ORLEANS, OSWEGO, OTSEGO, PUTNAM, QUEENS, RENSSELAER, RICHMOND, ROCKLAND, SAINT LAWRENCE, SARATOGA, SCHENECTADY, SCHOHARIE, SCHUYLER, SENECA, STEUBEN, SUFFOLK, SULLIVAN, TIOGA, TOMPKINS, ULSTER, WARREN, WASHINGTON, WAYNE, WESTCHESTER, WYOMING, YATES.

New York, county (□ 22; pop. 1,960,101), SE N.Y., coextensive with MANHATTAN borough of New York city.

New York, city (□ 365.4, including water surface; □ 299, land only; 1950 pop. 7,891,957; 1940 pop. 7,454,995), SE N.Y., largest city and financial and commercial center of the U.S., on New York Bay at mouth of Hudson R.; alt. is from sea level to c.400 ft.; 40°42'N 74°W (City Hall). Composed of 5 boroughs, each coextensive with a county: Manhattan (New York co.), the heart of the city, on an isl.; the Bronx (Bronx co.), on the mainland NE of Manhattan and separated from it by Harlem R. and Spuyten Duyvil Creek; Queens (Queens co.), on W Long Isl., E of Manhattan and bordering East R.; Brooklyn (Kings co.), on SW Long Isl., on East R. adjoining Queens and on New York Bay; and Richmond (Richmond co.) on Staten Island SW of Manhattan and separated from it by Upper New York Bay. New York is focus of a vast metropolitan area (1950 census, preliminary total pop. 12,831,914) extending W into NE N.J., NW and N into Rockland and Westchester counties, and far E on Long Isl.; from this area, which is both residential and industrial, thousands of workers commute daily into city. With its cultural and educational resources—great museums, art galleries, musical organizations, universities and colleges—its great seaport, famous shops and restaurants, places of entertainment (including many of the nation's legitimate theaters), striking architecture, colorful nationality neighborhoods, parks and botanical gardens, and rich historic background, New York is almost unparalleled. For detailed descriptions of the boroughs, see the separate articles on The BRONX, BROOKLYN, MANHATTAN, QUEENS, STATEN ISLAND. Its location on a magnificent natural harbor (connected with the Great Lakes and the St. Lawrence by N.Y. State Barge Canal) has made it the nation's chief seaport, handling c.40% (by value) of U.S. foreign commerce over the docks of NEW YORK HARBOR (771 mi. of water front), which also embraces part of NE N.J. As the financial and commercial metropolis of U.S., it is a world center for banking and trade, and is in addition the focus of an industrial area producing c.10% (by value) of nation's industrial output, chiefly consumer goods. Chief industries are the mfg. of clothing (c.¼ of natl. output), largely concentrated in Manhattan, and the allied output of fur goods (c.90% of U.S. total), hats, leather goods and other accessories, and jewelry; printing and publishing (Manhattan has hq. of most of U.S. publishers), food processing (including meat packing, baking, brewing, sugar refining, preparation of coffee and spices), metalworking, mfg. of drugs and medicines, machinery, wood products, textiles, scientific instruments and equipment, automobile assembling, shipbuilding and repairing. Although Manhattan has mfg. industries, most of the industrial plants are in the other boroughs. Four of the 12 railroad systems serving New York enter the city's heart; other lines terminate at N.J. railheads. Served by La Guardia and New York International (Idlewild) airports (N.Y.) and Newark and Teterboro airports in N.J. (all administered by Port of N.Y.), truck freight lines, and many interstate and local bus lines. A system of express highways links New York with neighboring cities and the boroughs with each other. Internal transportation includes connected subway systems joining all the boroughs except Staten Isl., as well as bus lines, trolley lines (in outlying dists.), and nation's largest fleet of taxicabs. Among New York's bridges are George Washington, Henry Hudson, Brooklyn, Bronx-Whitestone, Triborough, Queensboro, Hell Gate, Williamsburg, Manhattan bridges; plans for a bridge bet. Brooklyn and Staten Isl. have long been under discussion. Lincoln and Holland tunnels and railroad tunnels pass under the North R. bet. N.J. and Manhattan; Queens-Midtown Tunnel, subway tubes, and Brooklyn-Battery Tunnel pass under East R. City's isls. include Welfare, Rikers, Randalls, Wards, Governors, Ellis, Bedloe's (with Statue of Liberty), and Hart isls. Many of the state's largest educational institutions are here; New York is also a medical treatment and research center, with more than 130 hosps. and several medical schools. The site of New York was possibly visited (1524) by Giovanni da Verrazano, and certainly by Henry Hudson in 1609. The history of the 5 boroughs began with a Dutch settlement at S tip of Manhattan; in 1624 Peter Minuit of the Dutch West India Co. purchased the isl. from the Indians according to legend, for trinkets worth $24. The settlement, known as New Amsterdam after 1625, grew as capital of the colony, schools were opened and the Dutch Reformed Church was established. The English, basing claims upon the 15th-cent. explorations of John Cabot, seized the colony (1664) during the Dutch Wars and renamed it for the Duke of York. The Dutch returned to power 1673–74, and the autocratic English rule, when re-established, was protested by a rebellion (1689–91) led by Jacob Leisler. The 1st permanent settlement on Staten Isl. was not made until 1661; Queens had been settled in 1635, Brooklyn in 1636, and the Bronx in 1641. New York's strategic site for commerce drew newcomers; by the end of the Revolution, its pop. was c.20,000, and increased rapidly thereafter. The 1st newspaper, the New York *Gazette*, appeared in 1725; in 1735 the trial of John Peter Zenger helped to establish the principle of a free press. After disturbances (1765) over the Stamp Act, the colony actively opposed British measures; in 1775, the N.Y. Sons of Liberty forced the Br. governors and soldiers from the city. Continental forces under Washington relinquished the city after the Americans' defeat in Aug., 1776, in battle of Long Isl.; the British remained until 1781. As the old provincial capital, New York remained ⊙ the new state until 1797, and was (1789–90) the 1st ⊙ the U.S. under the Constitution; President Washington was inaugurated at Federal Hall (built 1700 as 1st city hall), whose site in Manhattan is now a natl. monument. By 1790, N.Y. was largest city in the U.S., with over 33,000 inhabitants; its pop. had grown to more than 60,000 in 1800. The beginnings (1792) of the stock exchange, establishment (1784) of the Bank of N.Y. (under Alexander Hamilton), and of the N.Y. Chamber of Commerce (1768) foreshadowed the city's remarkable financial and commercial growth in the early 19th cent. Opening (1825) of the Erie Canal, which made New York the seaboard gateway for the Great Lakes region, together with coming of railroads (the N.Y. and Harlem RR was built in 1832) and the establishment of a favorable tariff policy, soon made New York the nation's leading port and commercial center. The great fire of 1835 destroyed much of the old Dutch town, but brought about new building laws and the construction (completed 1842) of the 1st Croton water-supply system. Even before the Civil War, floods of immigrants (at 1st chiefly from Ireland and Germany, later from S and E Europe) had created congestion which gave rise to notorious slums; after 1865, with increasing industrialization, more settlers came from abroad in a tide which reached its crest in the early 20th cent. Settling for the most part in distinct ethnic neighborhoods, the newcomers faced economic and political exploitation, particularly in the heyday of such plunderers as the early Tammany Hall and the notorious Tweed Ring. Until 1874, when portions of Westchester were annexed, city's boundaries were those of present-day Manhattan; with the adoption of a new charter in 1898, New York became Greater New York, a metropolis of 5 boroughs: New York city was split into present Manhattan and the Bronx boroughs, the independent city of Brooklyn was annexed, as were Queens co. and Staten Isl. Increased problems of transportation, urban planning, and water supply faced the enlarged city. The 1st subway was opened in 1904, supplementing the elevated railroads (1st one opened 1878) as the beginning of today's great (but still inadequate) system (mainly underground) of rapid transit. Scores of new bridges, tunnels, and highway connections have since been added to the interborough and interstate transportation systems. The Flatiron Bldg. (1902) foreshadowed Manhattan's skyscrapers, brought into being by the fabulous cost and scarcity of land. City's growing need for water has been met by enlargement (1890) of the Croton system, addition of a system of Catskill reservoirs, and the building (begun in 1940s) of an aqueduct tapping headstreams of Delaware R. The aspect of many parts of the 5 boroughs has been changed by the erection of publicly sponsored housing projects (since 1936) and large-scale privately financed ventures. New York World's Fair was held 1939–40 at Flushing Meadows on Long Isl. Manhattan was chosen (1946) as site for the UN's permanent hq., whose bldgs. were completed in 1951 on a site overlooking the East R. New York's climate, although temperate, is known for its generally high humidity; Jan. average temp. is 31°F., July average is 74°F.; average annual precipitation is 42 inches.

New York Bay, N.Y. and N.J., an arm of the Atlantic at junction of Hudson and East rivers, opening SE to the Atlantic bet. Sandy Hook and Rockaway Point; enclosed by the shores of N N.J., Staten Isl., Manhattan, and Brooklyn. Its Upper and Lower bays are connected by the Narrows (strait c.3 mi. long, 1 mi. wide), separating Staten Isl. from Brooklyn (W tip of Long Isl.). Upper Bay (c.6 mi. in diameter) is joined to Newark Bay (W) by Kill Van Kull and to Long Island Sound (NE) by East R.; the extensive port facilities of New York Harbor are on N.J., Manhattan, and Brooklyn shores. Its isls. include Ellis, Governors, and Bedloe's (site of Statue of Liberty Natl. Monument). The larger Lower Bay, including RARITAN BAY (W) and GRAVESEND BAY (NE), is joined to Newark Bay by Arthur Kill. Federally maintained Ambrose Channel crosses Sandy Hook bar at entrance to Lower Bay, and extends N into Upper Bay, where it is called Anchorage Channel; it connects with channels into East R., the Hudson, and Raritan and Newark bays. Buttermilk Channel leads into East R. bet. Governors Isl. and Brooklyn. U.S. forts Hamilton (in Brooklyn) and Wadsworth (on Staten Isl.) overlook the Narrows; Fort Jay is on Governors Isl.

New York Harbor, SE N.Y., great seaport (largest in U.S.) and port of entry of New York city and its metropolitan area, at mouth of Hudson R. on New

York Bay; connected with Great Lakes and the St. Lawrence by N.Y. State Barge Canal system, with Long Isl. Sound by East R. Port of N.Y. is legally-defined dist. (□ c.1,500) of N.Y. and N.J., administered by an interstate body (Port of N.Y. Authority) est. 1921, which also has jurisdiction over the New York municipal airports, Newark Airport and Teterboro Airport in N.J., George Washington Bridge, Holland and Lincoln tunnels, and the bridges bet. Staten Isl. and N.J. Port dist. embraces Upper and Lower New York bays, Raritan, Gravesend, Newark, Flushing, and Jamaica bays, waterfronts of the Hudson (North), East, Hackensack, Passaic, Raritan, and Harlem rivers, Newtown Creek, Arthur Kill, and Kill Van Kull. Has 771 mi. of dock frontage, of which more than 500 mi. are within New York city; its more than 2,000 piers, wharves, and quays include accommodations (chiefly along Manhattan shore of Hudson R. S of 59th St.) for largest passenger vessels afloat. Other principal port areas are those along N.J. shore of the Hudson (Jersey City, Hoboken, Weehawken, West New York, Edgewater); on Upper New York Bay (Staten Isl., Bayonne, N.J., and part of Brooklyn waterfront, including huge Bush and Atlantic terminals and Erie Basin); on Newark Bay (Port Newark, at Newark); on East R. waterfronts of Manhattan and Brooklyn (U.S. navy yard); and along Newtown Creek and Harlem R. The harbor, virtually landlocked and never severely affected by ice, is the leading U.S. passenger port, and handles c.40% (by value) of U.S. foreign trade as well as nation's greatest tonnages of intercoastal and East Coast shipments and heavy canal traffic. It is served by 12 railroad systems, most of which have their railheads on the N.J. shore, necessitating transshipment by lighterage and carfloats of much freight, and by hundreds of truck lines. Important exports are machinery and vehicles, grain, meat, and other foodstuffs, textiles, tobacco, clothing, metal products (iron, steel, and copper), chemicals, paper, and a wide variety of manufactured goods. Imports include petroleum and petroleum products, sugar, coffee, cocoa, spices, bananas and other fruits, copra, rubber, gypsum, copper, vegetable oils and oilseeds, woodpulp, vegetable fibers (hemp, sisal, jute), and luxury goods. From New York's earliest days, history of port and city have gone hand in hand. Its location directly on the Atlantic early gave city an advantage over Philadelphia and Baltimore, and opening (1825) of the Erie Canal made it the seaboard gateway for the vast Middle West. Fulton's *Clermont* made its 1st voyage (1807) on the Hudson, and in 1838 the 1st vessels to cross the Atlantic entirely under steam reached New York. In both World Wars the harbor was one of nation's most vital supply ports and ports of embarkation.

New York International Airport, SE N.Y., municipal airport (4,900 acres), part of Port of New York, at Idlewild on Jamaica Bay, in S Queens borough of New York city; seaplane, landplane facilities. Opened 1948. Sometimes called Idlewild Airport.

New York Mills. 1 Resort village (pop. 977), Otter Tail co., W Minn., 37 mi. NE of Fergus Falls, in grain, potato, and poultry area; dairy products, beverages, lumber. **2** Village (pop. 3,366), Oneida co., central N.Y., 3 mi. W of Utica; mfg. (wood products, textiles). Inc. 1922.

New York State Barge Canal or **Barge Canal,** N.Y., system (525 mi. long) of waterways connecting the Hudson with L. Erie, and with branches extending to L. Ontario, L. Champlain, and Cayuga and Seneca lakes. Main section (Erie Canal) extends from Troy (Hudson R.) to Tonawanda, whence Niagara R. connects with L. Erie; it follows canalized Mohawk R. W to Rome, beyond which it utilizes route of old Erie Canal. Champlain division of system joins Erie Canal at Waterford, follows canalized Hudson R. to Fort Edward, thence a land cut to L. Champlain, which is in turn connected with the St. Lawrence by Richelieu R. Oswego section (following canalized OSWEGO RIVER) extends to L. Ontario at Oswego; Cayuga and Seneca Canal (in SENECA RIVER) extends to Cayuga and Seneca lakes. A modification and improvement of the old ERIE CANAL, the toll-free Barge Canal was authorized (1903) by public vote, begun 1905, completed 1918. It has been improved to 12-ft. depth, minimum bottom width of 75 ft., minimum surface width of 123 ft. It has 310-ft. electrically operated locks and can accommodate 2,000-ton vessels.

New Zealand (zē'lund), British dominion (□ 103,416; pop. 1,702,298), 1,200 mi. SE of Australia, 34°15'–47°30'S 166°30'–178°45'E; comprises narrow 1,000-mi. isl. chain: NORTH ISLAND, SOUTH ISLAND, STEWART ISLAND, CHATHAM ISLANDS; ⊙ WELLINGTON. The 2 main isls. (North Isl. and South Isl.) are separated by narrow Cook Strait. Volcanoes on N.Isl., Ruapehu (alt. 9,175 ft.) being the highest; S.Alps on S.Isl. contain Mt. Cook (12,349 ft.), highest peak of New Zealand. Many glaciers, the longest being Tasman Glacier in S.Alps. Waikato R. (largest river) and Lake Taupo (largest lake) in N.Isl. are sources of hydroelectric power. SW coast of S.Isl. is indented by many sounds and fjords, surrounded by mts.; the best-known is Milford Sound. Large hot-springs dist. in N.Isl. is site of health resorts. Mean annual temp. 56°F. (N.Isl.), 51°F. (S.Isl.); rainfall, 35 in. Giant tree ferns, kauri pine, rata trees (*Metrosideros robusta*), edelweiss; virgin forest in S and N extremities of S.Isl. Native fauna include kiwi (*apteryx*), albatrosses, parrots, tuatara (survivor of prehistoric order of reptiles, *Rhynchocephalia*), poisonous spiders; no land snakes. Large oyster beds in Foveaux Strait bet. Stewart Isl. and S.Isl.; deep-sea fishing off NW peninsula of N.Isl. Several extensive natl. parks: Tongariro and Egmont parks on N.Isl., Arthur Pass, Tasman, Fiordland parks on S.Isl. Over 90% of Maori natives (pop. 95,000), Polynesian natives of New Zealand, are on N.Isl. Chief cities are Auckland and Wellington on N.Isl., Christchurch (agr. center of Canterbury plains) and Dunedin on S.Isl. The Univ. of New Zealand with hq. at Wellington comprises 4 univ. colleges at Wellington, Dunedin, Christchurch, and Auckland, and 2 agr. colleges at Lincoln and Palmerston North. Chief harbors of N.Isl. are Auckland and Wellington; on S.Isl., Lyttelton (port of Christchurch), Bluff (port of Invercargill), Port Chalmers (port of Dunedin). Chief products: sheep, cattle, wheat, fruits, kauri gum; some coal and gold. Small deposits of mercury, manganese, ore, tungsten, sulphur, asbestos, tin, platinum, phosphates. Chief exports: dairy products, frozen meat, wool, kauri gum. Dominion is divided into 9 provincial dists.: AUCKLAND, HAWKE'S BAY, TARANAKI, WELLINGTON, MARLBOROUGH, NELSON, WESTLAND, CANTERBURY, OTAGO. These dists., which represent the old provinces (abolished 1875), are used for census purposes. The 12 land dists. to which the provincial dists. roughly correspond are used for surveys and maps. Small outlying isls. belonging to New Zealand are AUCKLAND ISLANDS, CAMPBELL ISLAND, ANTIPODES ISLANDS, THREE KINGS ISLANDS, BOUNTY ISLANDS, SNARES ISLANDS, SOLANDER ISLAND. Dependencies are KERMADEC ISLANDS, COOK ISLANDS, TOKELAU, NIUE, ROSS DEPENDENCY. Western SAMOA is under N.Z. trusteeship; NAURU is under U.N. trusteeship held jointly by New Zealand, Great Britain, and Australia. Discovered 1642 by Tasman, visited 1769 by Cook; first missionary arrived 1814. Colony (established 1840) became dependency of New South Wales; became (1841) a separate Br. colony and in 1907 a dominion. The period 1854–64 was a bloody one, with a series of unsuccessful attempts to subdue the hostile Maori natives. By Treaty of Waitangi (1840) the Maoris were guaranteed full possession of their land in exchange for permission to admit Br. settlers. Social welfare laws have been notable. New Zealand was 1st to adopt (1898) noncontributary old-age pensions, to establish (1907) a national infant welfare system, and to set up (1941) a program for socialized medicine. In Second World War, New Zealand declared war on Germany in Sept., 1939, and on Japan in Dec., 1941. Joined the U.N. The administration is vested in a governor general (representing the Br. sovereign) and a Parliament, consisting of the House of Representatives and the Legislative Council.

Nexo, Denmark: see NEKSO.

Nexon (nĕksō'), village (pop. 1,160), Haute-Vienne dept., W central France, 11 mi. SSW of Limoges; brick- and tileworks; stud breeding.

Nextlalpan (nĕslăl'păn), officially Santa Ana Nextlalpan, town (pop. 1,556), Mexico state, central Mexico, 22 mi. N of Mexico city; cereals, livestock.

Ney (nā), village (pop. 301), Defiance co., NW Ohio, 10 mi. NW of Defiance; grain- and sawmills; sand, gravel.

Neya (nyä'ŭ), town (1948 pop. over 2,000), central Kostroma oblast, Russian SFSR, on Neya R. (right affluent of the Unzha), and 55 mi. E of Galich; sawmilling center.

Neyagawa (nāyä'gäwŭ) or **Neyakawa** (–käwŭ), town (pop. 28,033), Osaka prefecture, S Honshu, Japan, just NE of Osaka; commercial center for poultry and agr. area (rice, wheat).

Neybandan, Iran: see NAIBANDAN.

Neye, Germany: see WIPPERFÜRTH.

Neyland (nā'lŭnd), urban district (1931 pop. 2,157; 1951 census 2,204), S Pembroke, Wales, on Milford Haven, 3 mi. NW of Pembroke; bathing resort and small port. Formerly terminal of shipping services to Ireland.

Neyrac-les-Bains, France: see THUEYTS.

Neyriz, Iran: see NIRIZ.

Neyrolles, Les (lā nārôl'), village (pop. 353), Ain dept., E France, in the Jura, 2 mi. SE of Nantua; wood turning; plastics.

Neyshabur or **Neyshapur,** Iran: see NISHAPUR.

Neyva River, Russian SFSR: see NEIVA RIVER.

Neyvo-Rudyanka, Russian SFSR: see NEIVO-RUDYANKA.

Neyvo-Shaytanskiy, Russian SFSR: see NEIVO-SHAITANSKI.

Neyyattinkara (nāyä'tĭngkŭrŭ), city (pop. 13,830), S Travancore, India, 10 mi. SE of Trivandrum; mfg. of rope and mats of coconut and palmyra fiber, copra, jaggery; cassava and cashew-nut processing, hand-loom weaving.

Neyyur, India: see IRANIEL.

Nezametny, Russian SFSR: see ALDAN, city.

Nezeros, village, Greece: see KALLIPEUKE.

Nezeros, Lake, Greece: see XYNIAS, LAKE.

Nezhin (nyĕ'zhĭn), city (1926 pop. 37,990), S central Chernigov oblast, Ukrainian SSR, on Oster R. and 40 mi. SE of Chernigov; rail junction; agr. center in grain, potato, sugar-beet area. Has teachers col. with 100,000-volume library. Known since 11th cent.; passed 1667 to Russia; was important 18th-cent. trade and cultural center. In Second World War, held (1941–43) by Germans.

Nezib, Turkey: see NIZIP.

Nezinscot River (nĕzĭn'skŏt), W Maine, rises in 12-mi. E and W branches in Oxford co., joining at Buckfield; flows c.11 mi. E to the Androscoggin above Auburn.

Nez Perce (nĕz" pûrs'), county (□ 847; pop. 22,658), W Idaho; ⊙ Lewiston. Stock-raising and agr. area bounded W by Snake R. and Wash., drained by Clearwater R. Wheat, fruit, vegetables. Lumber milling at Lewiston. Mts. are in S, part of Nez Perce Indian Reservation in N. Formed 1861.

Nezperce, village (pop. 543), ⊙ Lewis co., W Idaho, 40 mi. ESE of Lewiston in wheat area; flour, lumber milling.

Nezpique, Bayou (bī'ō nĕzpēkā'), S La., rises in Evangeline parish, flows c.70 mi. S, joining Bayou Cannes near Mermentau village to form Mermentau R. Navigable for 23 mi. of lower course.

N'Fis, Oued (wĕd' nŭfēs'), stream of SW Fr. Morocco, a left tributary of the Tensift, rising at Tizi n'Test pass in the High Atlas; 70 mi. long. Dam (170 ft. high; 25 mi. SSW of Marrakesh), completed 1936, irrigates Haouz plain. Lalla Takerkoust hydroelectric plant built here 1938. Also Nfis.

N'Gabé (ŭng-gäbā'), village, SE Middle Congo territory, Fr. Equatorial Africa, on Congo R. and 100 mi. NNE of Brazzaville.

Ngahere (nähĕ'rē), township (pop. 254), W S.Isl., New Zealand, 13 mi. NE of Greymouth, on Grey R.; sawmills, coal mines.

Ngala (ŭng-gä'lä), town (pop. 1,523), N Br. Cameroons, administered as part of Bornu prov. of Nigeria, near L. Chad, 23 mi. NE of Dikwa, on road to Fort Lamy; peanuts, cotton, millet; cattle.

Ngambo, Zanzibar: see ZANZIBAR, town.

Ngami, Lake (ŭng-gä'mē), marsh region (40 mi. long, 4–8 mi. wide), NW Bechuanaland Protectorate, near South-West Africa border; 20°32'S 22°40'E; receives some of the waters of Okovangga R. (outflow obstructed). Formerly a lake covering □ 20,000; described (1849) by Livingstone as an inland sea. Batawana Reserve extends N.

Ngamiland, district (pop. 38,859), NW Bechuanaland Protectorate, bounded by South-West Africa (N and W); ⊙ Maun. Dist. includes Batawana native reserve, established 1899, and Chobe crown lands. Okovanggo Basin is in central part of dist.

Ngan-, for Chinese names beginning thus and not found here: see under AN-.

Ngandjoek, Indonesia: see NGANJUK.

Ngandong, Indonesia: see TRINIL.

Ngang Kong, Hong Kong: see SILVER MINE BAY.

Nganglaring Tso or **Nganglaring Tsho** (both: ŭng-găng'lärĭng tsō"), Chinese *Ang-la-ling Hu* (äng'lä'-lĭng' hōō'), lake in W central Tibet, 150 mi. E of Gartok, bet. Aling Kangri and Kailas ranges; 30 mi. long; 31°40'N 83°E.

Ngangtse Tso or **Ngangtse Tsho** (both: ŭng-găng'-tsĕ tsō), Chinese *I-ku-ch'i Hu* (yē'gōō'chē' hōō'), lake in central Tibet, 250 mi. WNW of Lhasa; 31°N 87°E.

Nganjuk or **Ngandjoek** (both: ŭng-änjōōk'), town (pop. 9,458), E central Java, Indonesia, 60 mi. WSW of Surabaya; trade center for agr. area (rice, cassava, corn, peanuts).

Nganson (ŭngän'shŭn'), village, Bachan prov., N Vietnam, at S end of Piaouac Range, 25 mi. SW of Caobang; mining of silver-lead-zinc ores.

Ngao-, for Chinese names beginning thus and not found here: see under AO-.

N'Gaoundéré or **N'Gaundere** (ŭng-goundĕ'rā), town, ⊙ Adamaoua region, N central Fr. Cameroons, 275 mi. NE of Yaoundé; alt. 3,670 ft.; 7°23'N 13°33'E. Large native market and agr. center; cattle, horses, sheep, goats, coffee plantations. Hosp., meteorological station, experimental farms, hydroelectric power plant.

Ngape (ŭngŭpĕ'), village, Minbu dist., Upper Burma, at foot of the Arakan Yoma, 27 mi. WSW of Minbu, on An Pass road.

Ngaputaw (ŭngŭpōōtô'), village, Bassein dist., SW Lower Burma, on Bassein R., 16 mi. S of Bassein.

Ngara (ŭng-gä'rä), village, Lake Prov., NW Tanganyika, near upper Kagera R. and Ruanda-Urundi border, 50 mi. WNW of Biharamulo; 2°30'S 30°39'E. Tobacco, coffee, corn; livestock. Tin deposits.

Ngare Nanyuki, Tanganyika: see ENGARE NANYUKI.

Ngari (ŭng-gä'rē), Chinese *A-li* (ä'lē'), westernmost historical province of Tibet; main town, Gartok.

Ngaruawahia (nä"rōōwä'hyŭ), borough (pop. 1,606), ⊙ Raglan co. (□ 936; pop. 10,617), N N.Isl., New Zealand, 60 mi. SSE of Auckland, at junction of Waipa R. with Waikato R.; agr. center. Coal mine at near-by Glen Massey.

Ngatea (nätē'ŭ), township (pop. 556), ⊙ Hauraki Plains co. (□ 233; pop. 4,795), N N.Isl., New Zealand, near Firth of Thames, 50 mi. SE of Auckland; dairy products.

Ngathainggyaung or **Ngathaingyaung** (ùng-ùthĭn'-joung), town (pop. 5,380), Bassein dist., Lower Burma, on Bassein R. (ferry) and 50 mi. NNE of Bassein.

Ngatik (ùng-ä'tĕk), atoll (pop. 383), Ponape dist., E Caroline Isls., W Pacific, 75 mi. SW of Ponape; 11 mi. long, 5 mi. wide; 8 low islets on triangular reef.

Ngau or **Gau** (both: ùng-ou'), volcanic island (□ 54; pop. 1,651), Fiji, SW Pacific, c.40 mi. E of Viti Levu; 13 mi. long; bananas, copra.

N'Gaundere, Fr. Cameroons: see N'GAOUNDÉRÉ.

Ngauruhoe (nourùhoi'), active volcanic peak (7,515 ft.) in Tongariro Natl. Park, central N.Isl., New Zealand. Erupted in 1948 for first time in 20 yrs.

Ngawi (ùng-ä'wē), town (pop. 10,193), E central Java, Indonesia, on Solo R. and 40 mi. ENE of Surakarta; trade center for agr. area (rice, corn, coffee, kapok, cassava).

Ngawun River, Burma: see BASSEIN RIVER.

Ngazun (ùngùzōōn'), village, Sagaing dist., Upper Burma, landing on left bank of Irrawaddy R. and 27 mi. WSW of Mandalay.

Ngchün (ùng'chün'), Mandarin *Wuchwan* or *Wu-ch'uan* (both: wōō'chwän'), town (pop. 3,810), ⊙ Ngchün co. (pop. 177,706), SW Kwangtung prov., China, at mouth of Foshan R., 17 mi. ENE of Chankiang; rice, wheat, pears.

Ngemda (ùng-gĕm'dä), Chinese *Enta* (ŭn'dä'), town, E Tibet, in Kham prov., 25 mi. WSW of Chamdo and on road to Lhasa. Silver mining near by.

Ngen-, for Chinese names beginning thus and not found here: see under EN-.

Ngerengere (ùng-gĕ"rĕng-gĕ'rā), town, Eastern Prov., Tanganyika, on railroad and 35 mi. E of Morogoro; sisal plantation; cotton gin.

Ngeu River, China: see WU RIVER.

Nggamea or **Quamia** (both: ùng-gämē'ä), volcanic island (□ 13; pop. 410), Fiji, SW Pacific, separated from Taveuni by Tasman Strait (1.5 mi. wide); 7 mi. long; copra.

Nghean, province, Vietnam: see VINH.

N'giri River, Belgian Congo: see GIRI RIVER.

Ngiva, Angola: see VILA PEREIRA DE EÇA.

Ngoenoet, Indonesia: see NGUNUT.

N'Goko River (ùng-gō'kō) or **Dja River** or **Ja River** (jä), in central and SE Fr. Cameroons and along Fr. Cameroons–Fr. Equatorial Africa border, rises SE of Abong-M'Bang, flows in a wide curve W, E, and SE past Moloundou to Sanga R. at Ouesso. Navigable year-round for small steamboats downstream (for c.80 mi.) from Moloundou.

Ngombezi (ùng-gōmbĕ'zē), village, Tanga prov., NE Tanganyika, on railroad and 3 mi. SW of Korogwe; sisal.

Ngomeni (ùng-gōmĕ'nē), village, Tanga prov., NE Tanganyika, on railroad and 15 mi. WSW of Tanga. Has sisal experimental station.

Ngong (ùng-gông'), town, Masai dist., S Kenya, on road and 13 mi. SW of Nairobi; stock raising; coffee, wheat, corn. Ngong Hills form E escarpment of Great Rift Valley.

Ngonshun Chau, Hong Kong: see STONECUTTERS ISLAND.

N'Gor (ùng-gôr'), fishing village and beach resort, W Senegal, Fr. West Africa, on NE Cape Verde peninsula, 6 mi. NW of Dakar.

Ngora (ùng-gō'rä), town, Eastern Prov., Uganda, 21 mi. SSE of Soroti; cotton, peanuts, sesame; livestock. Mission with hosp.

Ngornu (ùng-gôr'nōō), town (pop. 2,014), Bornu prov., Northern Provinces, NE Nigeria, 70 mi. NE of Maiduguri, 10 mi. from L. Chad; cassava, millet, gum arabic; salt; cattle, skins. An important center in Bornu kingdom until end of 19th cent. Sometimes written N'Gornu.

Ngorongoro Crater (ùng-gō"rông-gō'rō), in Great Rift Valley of N Tanganyika, 80 mi. W of Arusha; 3°15'S 35°30'E. Rim is 7,000 ft. high, crater's floor (□ 126; inhabited) is 2,000 ft. below rim. Has fantastic "crater-of-the-moon" appearance.

N'Gouça (nùgōōsä'), village and oasis, Saharan Oases territory, E central Algeria, 12 mi. N of Ouargla; date palms.

Ngouna, New Hebrides: see NGUNA.

N'Gounié, region, Fr. Equatorial Africa: see MOUILA.

N'Gounié River (ùng-gōōnyā'), central Gabon, Fr. Equatorial Africa, rises 25 mi. SE of M'Bigou, flows c.275 mi. SW and NW, past Mouila and Sindara, to Ogooué R. 12 mi. above Lambaréné. Navigable most of the year for 50 mi. below Sindara.

N'Gouri (ùng-gōōrē'), village, W Chad territory, Fr. Equatorial Africa, near E shore of L. Chad, 40 mi. S of Mao; military outpost with fort. Stud farm.

Ngozi (ùng-gō'zē), village, central Ruanda-Urundi, in Urundi, 36 mi. NNW of Kitega; market for food staples; cattle raising, mfg. of bricks, tiles.

Ngudu (ùng-gōō'dōō), village, Lake Prov., NW Tanganyika, 40 mi. SE of Mwanza; cotton, peanuts, corn.

N'Guigmi (ùng-gĕg'mē), town (pop. c.2,400), SE Niger territory, Fr. West Africa, on NW shore of L. Chad, on desert road, and 280 mi. W of Zinder; 14°14'N 13°8'E. Region produces millet, beans, peanuts, manioc, indigo, cotton, wheat, henna; livestock. Meteorological station; airfield.

Ngulu (ùngōōlōō'), atoll (pop. 45), Yap dist., W Caroline Isls., W Pacific, 59 mi. SSW of Yap; 19 mi. long, 12 mi. wide; coconut palms.

Nguna, Fr. *Ngouna* (both: ùng-ōō'nä), volcanic island (pop. 578), New Hebrides, SW Pacific, 4 mi. N of Efate; 5 mi. long, 2 mi. wide. Formerly Montague Isl.

Ngunut or **Ngoenoet** (both: ùng-ōōnōōt'), town (pop. 12,583), E Java, Indonesia, on Brantas R. and 10 mi. W of Blitar; trade center for agr. area (coffee, tobacco, rubber, corn, tea, cinchona bark).

Nguru (ùng'-gōō'rōō), town (pop. 3,003), Bornu prov., Northern Provinces, N Nigeria, 140 mi. ENE of Kano; rail terminus; cotton, peanuts, millet, durra; cattle raising; saltworks.

Nguyenbinh (ùngōōyĕn'bĭng), town, Caobang prov., N Vietnam, 20 mi. W of Caobang, at foot of Piaouac Range; tin, tungsten mining at Tinhtuc, 5 mi. W.

Ngwa (ùng'wä'), Mandarin *Wu-hua* (wōō'hwä'), town (pop. 10,129), ⊙ Ngwa co. (pop. 327,346), E Kwangtung prov., China, 50 mi. SW of Meihsien; textiles; cotton, rice; sericulture. Tin and tungsten mines near by. The name Ngwa was applied 1914–41 to Chonglok, Mandarin *Ch'ang-le,* 30 mi. N. Present Ngwa was called Onliu, Mandarin *Anliu,* until it became ⊙ in 1941.

Ngwaketse (ùng-gwäkĕ'tsā), district (pop. 38,790), SE Bechuanaland Protectorate; ⊙ Kanye; coextensive with Bangwaketse tribal reserve, established 1899. Near Kanye is irrigation dam.

Ngwato (ùng-gwä'tō), district (pop. 101,634), E Bechuanaland Protectorate, bounded E by Transvaal, U. of So. Afr.; ⊙ Serowe. Dist. includes Bamangwato native reserve, established 1899, and Tuli block of farms (E), granted to British South Africa Co.

Ngwerere (ùng-gwĕrĕ'rā), township (pop. 23), Central Prov., Northern Rhodesia, on railroad and 10 mi. N of Lusaka; agr., livestock.

Nhabe (nyä'bā'), town, Giadinh prov., S Vietnam, on Dongnai R. below confluence of Saigon R. and 8 mi. SSE of Saigon.

Nhamarrói, Mozambique: see NAMARRÓI.

Nhanam (nyä'näm'), town, Bacgiang prov., N Vietnam, 35 mi. NNE of Hanoi; road center.

Nhandeara (nyăndēä'rù), city (pop. 1,304), NW São Paulo, Brazil, 40 mi. W of São José do Rio Prêto; grain, cotton, coffee, fruit, cattle.

Nhatrang (nyä'träng'), town (1936 pop. 15,500), ⊙ Khanhhoa prov. (□ 2,100; 1943 pop. 146,600), S central Vietnam, in Annam, on South China Sea, on railroad (station 3 mi. W) and 200 mi. NE of Saigon, at mouth of the small Song Cai; trading center (rice, cotton, cattle, pigs); fisheries. Airport. Oceanographic institute, Pasteur institute; seaside resort. Brahmin shrines (7th cent.) of Ponagar are just N across Song Cai estuary. Nhatrang is served by 2 harbors (depending on the monsoon) of Chut (3 mi. NE) and Cauda (4 mi. S).

Nhill (nĭl), town (pop. 1,974), W Victoria, Australia, 210 mi. WNW of Melbourne, in agr. area (wheat, oats); flour mill.

Niafunké or **Niafounké** (both: nyäfōōng'kā), town (pop. c.4,100), S central Fr. Sudan, Fr. West Africa, in mid-Niger depression, 85 mi. SW of Timbuktu; market for livestock, wool, hides. Region also grows millet and rice.

Niagara, Ont.: see NIAGARA-ON-THE-LAKE.

Niagara (nīă'grù, –gùrù), county (□ 533; pop. 189,992), W N.Y.; ⊙ Lockport. Bounded W by Niagara R. and L. Erie, N by L. Ontario; crossed by the Barge Canal; drained by Tonawanda Creek. Includes Niagara Falls resort area. Agr. (fruit, truck, grain; dairy products) and industrial (extensive mfg.) area. Limestone quarries; oil refining. Contains Tuscarora and part of Tonawanda Indian reservations. Formed 1808.

Niagara. 1 Village (pop. 163), Grand Forks co., E N.Dak., 40 mi. WNW of Grand Forks and on Turtle R. **2** Village (pop. 2,022), Marinette co., NE Wis., at falls of Menominee R., 5 mi. SE of Iron Mountain (Mich.), in potato-growing area; paper milling. Inc. 1914.

Niagara, Fort, Niagara co., W N.Y., on E bank of Niagara R. at its mouth on L. Ontario, just N of Youngstown. Historic shrine and mus. of colonial frontier life. Restored French fort here was built c.1725 on site of earlier French fortifications, and enlarged 1756–57. Taken by British forces under Sir William Johnson in 1759; passed to U.S. in 1796; recaptured by the British in War of 1812, and restored to U.S. in 1815. On grounds of fort is Father Millet Cross Natl. Monument (established 1925), a memorial to 17th-cent. missionary who erected a cross here in 1688.

Niagara Falls, city (pop. 20,589), S Ont., on Niagara R. (railroad bridges), opposite Niagara Falls, N.Y., and 16 mi. NE of Buffalo, overlooking Niagara Falls; port of entry. Hydroelectric-power center; paper and pulp milling, food canning; mfg. of industrial machinery, railroad and electrical equipment, domestic appliances, leather, clothing, graphite, silverware, toilet articles, batteries, castings, cereal foods. Seat of Canadian branches of many U.S. firms. Queen Victoria Park extends 2½ mi. along gorge of Niagara R. Niagara Falls became important with building (1855) of 1st bridge, built by John Roebling.

Niagara Falls, industrial and resort city (pop. 90,872), Niagara co., W N.Y., on Niagara R. (here crossed by several bridges) at the falls, opposite Niagara Falls, Ont., and 15 mi. NNW of Buffalo; port of entry. Hydroelectric plants here supply power to much of state and to city's industries, which manufacture chemicals, paper, abrasives, flour and cereals, metal products, machinery, airplanes, graphite and grease, wood and steel products, corsets, electrical equipment. State Niagara Reservation (1885) near here includes Prospect Park and other areas along the river, and Luna, Goat, and other smaller isls. Niagara Falls Mus., moved here from the Canadian city across the river, is one of country's oldest. Niagara Univ. is in the suburb Niagara University. Tourist trade is one of city's earliest and most important industries.

Niagara Falls, cataract in W N.Y. and S Ont., one of the most famous spectacles in North America and an important source of hydroelectric power, in Niagara R. on international line bet. cities of Niagara Falls, N.Y., and Niagara Falls, Ont. Goat Isl. separates the American Falls (c.167 ft. high, c.1,000 ft. wide) from the Canadian or Horseshoe Falls (c.160 ft. high, c.2,500 ft. wide). Behind American Falls is Cave of the Winds, a natural chamber made by water action. Narrow gorge, with spectacular Whirlpool Rapids, has been formed below falls by gradual recession (now lessening) of crest; here is Rainbow Bridge (1941), bet. U.S. and Canada, replacing span destroyed by ice in 1938. The 2 govts. control appearance of surrounding area, much of which has been included in parks since 1885; colored lights illuminate falls at night. International agreements control diversion of water for power; weirs divert part of flow above Canadian Falls to supplement shallower American Falls. Cataract 1st described by Hennepin (1697) after he accompanied La Salle's expedition of 1678. Historical and natural-history material relating to falls region is in Niagara Falls Mus. in Niagara Falls city, N.Y.

Niagara-on-the-Lake or **Niagara,** town (pop. 1,541), S Ont., on L. Ontario, at mouth of Niagara R., 11 mi. NE of St. Catharines; fruit and vegetable canning, jam making, basket weaving; resort. Has historical mus. Settled by United Empire Loyalists, it was made ⊙ Upper Canada (1792) by Simcoe, and named Newark; ⊙ was moved (1796) to York (now Toronto). Town was subsequently named Niagara and, later, Niagara-on-the-Lake to distinguish it from Niagara Falls cities. Fort George, built in 1790s, was taken by the Americans in 1813, retaken by the British later in the same year. Opposite, in U.S., is Fort Niagara.

Niagara River, in W N.Y. and S Ont., issues from L. Erie bet. Buffalo (N.Y.) and Fort Erie (Ont.), flows c.34 mi. N, forming international line, around GRAND ISL. (American) and over NIAGARA FALLS, to L. Ontario. Navigable for c.20 mi. above falls; again navigable in lower 7 mi. from Lewiston, N.Y., to L. Ontario. N.Y. State Barge Canal enters river at Tonawanda, N.Y.; in Ont., Welland Ship Canal is lake-freighter route around falls. Many bridges cross Niagara R., notably Peace Bridge (1927) at Buffalo, bridges linking Grand Isl. with both shores (1935), and Rainbow Bridge (1941) below Niagara Falls.

Niagara University, N.Y.: see NIAGARA FALLS, city.

Niakornârssuk or **Niaqornârssuk** (both: nyäkôrnär'-shōōk), fishing settlement (pop. 135), Egedesminde dist., W Greenland, on Arfersiorfik fjord, near its mouth on Davis Strait, 30 mi. S of Egedesminde; 68°10'N 52°50'W.

Niakornat or **Niaqornat** (both: nyäkôr'nät), fishing and hunting settlement (pop. 95), Umanak dist., W Greenland, on N shore of Nugssuak peninsula, on Umanak Fjord, 35 mi WNW of Umanak; 70°47'N 53°39'W.

Niamati, India: see NYAMATI.

Niamey (nyämā'), city (pop. c.8,800, of which c.325 are Europeans), ⊙ Niger territory, Fr. West Africa, inland port on left bank of the Niger, and c.675 mi. E of Bamako (Fr. Sudan), c.500 mi. NNW of Lagos (Nigeria); 13°30'N 2°8'E. Linked by rail with Tillabery, 70 mi. NW. Airport, administrative and trading center. Exports onions, hides, skins, livestock (cattle, sheep, goats), mats. The region grows millet, corn, manioc, potatoes, rice, vegetables, melons. Limekiln, tannery; mfg. of pottery, plaited goods, charcoal. City has meteorological station, serological laboratory, R.C. and Protestant missions.

Niangara (nyäng-gä'rä), town (1946 pop. c.3,500), Eastern Prov., NE Belgian Congo, on Uele R., on Congo-Nile highway, and 220 mi. ENE of Buta; cotton ginning; cotton, coffee, sesame growing. Seat of vicar apostolic. Has R.C. and Protestant missions and schools, R.C. seminary for native priests, hosp. for Europeans.

Niangua (nīăng'gwù), city (pop. 344), Webster co., S central Mo., in the Ozarks, near Niangua R., 29 mi. ENE of Springfield.

Niangua River, central Mo., rises in the Ozarks near Marshfield, flows c.90 mi. N to an arm of L. of the Ozarks in Camden co.

Nia Nia (nyä' nyä'), village, Eastern Prov., NE Belgian Congo, near Ituri R., 125 mi. W of Irumu; communications point with airfield at junction of roads to Anglo-Egyptian Sudan and Uganda; repairing of motor vehicles.

Niantic (nīăn'tĭk). **1** Village, Conn.: see EAST LYME. **2** Village (pop. 625), Macon co., central Ill., 10 mi. W of Decatur; grain, livestock, dairy products.

Niaouli (nyou'lē), village, S Dahomey, Fr. West Africa, 35 mi. NW of Cotonou; experiment station for coffee cultivation.

Niaousta or **Niausta,** Greece: see NAOUSA.

Niapu (nyä'pōō), village, Eastern Prov., N Belgian Congo, near source of Rubi R., 110 mi. ESE of Buta; trading post in cotton area.

Niaqornârssuk, Greenland: see NIAKORNÂRSSUK.

Niaqornat, Greenland: see NIAKORNAT.

Niari, region, Fr. Equatorial Africa: see DOLISIE.

Niari River, Fr. Equatorial Africa: see KOUILOU RIVER.

Nias (nēäs'), volcanic island (□ 1,569; pop. 187,199), Indonesia, off W coast of Sumatra, 80 mi. SW of Sibolga; 1°5'N 97°35'E; 75 mi. long, 30 mi. wide. Hilly, rising to 2,907 ft. Isl. is subject to severe earthquakes. Agr. (coconuts, nutmeg, sago, rice), fishing, handicraft. Chief town and port is Gunungsitoli on E coast. The Dutch began trading here 1669.

Niassa (nīă'sŭ, nēă'sŭ), province (□ 107,328; 1950 pop. 2,073,213), N Mozambique; ⊙ Nampula. Bounded N by Tanganyika (along Ruvuma R.), W by Nyasaland (lakes Nyasa, Chiuta, and Chilwa form part of border), E by Mozambique Channel (Indian Ocean). Coast is marked by mangrove swamps and numerous coral isls. (site of 1st settlements) just offshore. The lowland (up to 80 mi. wide) rises in W to savanna hill country dotted with isolated higher peaks (especially in S and NW). Principal streams are the Lugenda and the Lúrio. Commercial agr. is concentrated in Nampula area. Chief crops are cotton, sisal, corn, beans, oilseeds, tobacco. There are mica and kaolin deposits near Ribáuè. Principal ports are Mozambique and Ibo (both on offshore isls.), Pôrto Amélia, and António Edes. Nampula and Entre Rios are on railroad leading from Lumbo (opposite Mozambique city) inland and projected to reach Vila Cabral near L. Nyasa. Territory N of Lúrio R. was administered by Nyassa Company 1893–1929. Prov. ⊙ was at Mozambique until 1930s. In 1946 prov. was divided into 3 dists. (Nampula, Cabo Delgado, Lago). Formerly spelled Nyassa.

Niassa, Lake, E Africa: see NYASA, LAKE.

Niau (nēä'ōō), atoll (pop. 204), N Tuamotu Isls., Fr. Oceania, S Pacific; 16°10'S 146°21'W; circular, 4 mi. in diameter. Formerly Greig Isl.

Nibbiano (nēb-byä'nô), village (pop. 492), Piacenza prov., Emilia-Romagna, N central Italy, on Tidone R. and 12 mi. SSW of Castel San Giovanni.

Nibe (nē'bü), city (pop. 2,149), Aalborg amt, N Jutland, Denmark, on Lim Fjord and 11 mi. WSW of Aalborg; glue mfg.; fisheries.

Nibionno (nēbyôn'nô), village (pop. 722), Como prov., Lombardy, S Italy, 9 mi. SW of Lecco; cotton-milling center.

Nibley, town (pop. 304), Cache co., N Utah, 4 mi. S of Logan.

Nibong Tebal (nēbông' tĕbäl'), town (pop. 4,118), Prov. Wellesley, Penang, NW Malaya, on KrianR. and 20 mi. SE of George Town; rubber plantations.

Nicaea, France: see NICE.

Nicaea, Turkey: see IZNIK.

Nicapa (nēkä'pä), town (pop. 444), Chiapas, S Mexico, in Gulf lowland, 45 mi. N of Tuxtla; fruit.

Nicaragua (nĭkürä'gwŭ) [Sp.,=water of Nicarao], republic (□ 57,145; 1940 pop. 983,160; 1950 pop. 1,053,189), Central America; ⊙ MANAGUA. On the E is a c.350-mi.-long swampy coast (MOSQUITO COAST) along the Caribbean, and on SW is c.200 mi. of shore line on the Pacific. Bounded N by Honduras, with which it disputes the N section of the Mosquito Coast, bet. Patuca and Coco rivers (the de facto boundary follows COLÓN MOUNTAINS to TEOTECANITE peak). Costa Rica borders S, partly along SAN JUAN RIVER. Numerous keys fringe the Caribbean coast, among them the CORN ISLANDS (Sp. *Islas del Maíz*), leased to U.S. Nicaragua shares with Salvador (NW) and Honduras frontage on Gulf of FONSECA. The country is situated roughly bet. 11°-15°10'N and 83°10'-87°40'W. Largely mountainous, it is traversed diagonally NW-SE by the main cordillera of Central America, rising to c.7,000 ft. There are several horizontal E-W spurs, such as Cordillera ISABELA, Cordillera DARIENSE, and HUAPI MOUNTAINS, sloping gradually to the wide Atlantic lowland, which is drained by several large rivers—the Coco (or Segovia), Río GRANDE, ESCONDIDO RIVER, and San Juan R. The last forms the Atlantic outlet for the great lacustrine depression, lying W of the principal mtn. divide, that consists of L. NICARAGUA (c.100 by 45 mi.), linked by TIPITAPA RIVER with L. MANAGUA (c.30 by 15 mi.). This navigable waterway has often been proposed for a trans-Nicaraguan canal from the Caribbean to the Pacific landing of BRITO near RIVAS. N of L. Managua and E upon the narrow isthmus (c.12 mi. wide) separating the 2 lakes from the Pacific extends a chain of volcanoes, some of them intermittently active; among them are COSIGÜINA (2,776 ft.), Monotombo (4,128 ft.), Las Pilas (3,514 ft.), and the cones of ZAPATERA (2,428 ft.) and OMETEPEC isls. (Concepción, 5,066 ft.; Madera, 4,350 ft.) in L. Nicaragua. Earthquakes occur frequently in this region, occasionally devastating the principal cities which are located at a low elevation near the W coast. The higher wooded *tierra templada* of the interior is—in contrast to other Latin American countries—little colonized; neither is the humid Caribbean lowland. While this tropical E section has about 200 inches of rainfall distributed almost equally over the whole year, the drier and more healthful W beyond the watershed has 2 seasons with c.60 inches rainfall during May-Dec. Nicaragua is rich in minerals, especially gold—from placers both in the Pacific (BONANZA and LA LUZ mines in Zelaya dept.) and Caribbean area—which in some years make up the leading export item. The same mines also produce a large volume of silver. There are also deposits of copper, limestone, and precious stones. Rich forest resources (mahogany, cedar, pine, guayacan, ñambar, crude rubber) are little exploited. Apart from its gold production, the country's economy is based on agriculture. The large foreign-owned banana plantations (worked by Jamaican Negroes) of the E plains, along Río Grande, Escondido, and Wawa rivers, have decreased because of plant disease, but cacao is increasingly taking its place. Products of the Mosquito Coast are shipped through PUERTO CABEZAS, BLUEFIELDS, and SAN JUAN DEL NORTE (Greytown). Bluefields is now linked by highway (*Carretera Roosevelt*), past inland port of RAMA on Escondido R., with W coast, where more than 90% of the people (almost entirely mestizo) live. Here coffee is by far the leading commercial crop, a mild variety chiefly grown on volcanic slopes N of L. Managua and centered on MATAGALPA. Also raised for export are sugar cane (near CHINANDEGA, a sugar-refining center), cotton, sesame (vegetable oil), cacao. For home consumption: corn, rice, wheat (Jinotega dept.), beans, tobacco (Masaya dept.), plantains, oranges, pineapples, yucca. There is much cattle raising in lake dist. (Chontales dept.). The trade balance is favorable, with the U.S. taking most of the exports (over ¾ in recent years) and supplying bulk of imports (textiles, iron and steel products, machinery, chemicals, pharmaceuticals). Nicaragua's foreign commerce is in value, however, one of the smallest in Latin America, particularly because of geographical drawbacks, but primarily because of the country's turbulent history. Industries, apart from processing, are negligible. Chief port for foreign trade is CORINTO, Pacific RR terminal. Lesser Pacific landings are PUERTO SOMOZA and SAN JUAN DEL SUR. PONELOYA is a favorite beach resort. Managua, the capital, is largest city and commercial hub, with consumer industries. It was chosen as capital in 1865 to terminate the rivalry bet. LEÓN and GRANADA, 2d and 3d cities of the country. The latter is the flourishing old conservative bastion of a rich agr. region, while the former is renowned for its liberal politics and intellectual life (seat of a univ.). About ⅓ of the Nicaraguan people are urban, concentrated in the W cities. The hinterland is underdeveloped, and communication remains poor. The government-owned Pacific RR (Granada-Corinto) is only 236 mi. long. Through Managua passes the Inter-American Highway, and it is served by natl. and international airlines. The nation has been torn by civil strife and has been subject to foreign intervention. Nicaragua probably takes its name from Nicarao, an Indian Cacique defeated in 1522 by Gil González de Ávila. León and Granada were founded in 1524 by Francisco Fernández de Córdoba. Region became part of captaincy general of Guatemala. After gaining independence from Spain (1821), Nicaragua was briefly part of Iturbide's Mexican empire and then (1823–38) a member of the Central American Federation. Br. influence on the E coast since 17th cent. led to Br. seizure (1848) of San Juan del Norte (Greytown). Gold rush in California heightened the U.S. interest in a transcontinental canal. Some of the issues were settled (1850) by the Clayton-Bulwer Treaty. Internal warfare reached a peak with activities of the filibuster William Walker (shot 1860 in Honduras). In 1912 U.S. marines were landed, staying on—apart from short interruption 1925–26—until 1933. The Bryan-Chamorro Treaty, giving the U.S. an option on a route for the Nicaragua Canal, was ratified in 1916. For further information see separate articles on towns, cities, and the following 16 depts.: BOACO, CARAZO, CHINANDEGA, CHONTALES, ESTELÍ, GRANADA, JINOTEGA, LEÓN, MADRÍZ, MANAGUA, MASAYA, MATAGALPA, NUEVA SEGOVIA, RÍO SAN JUAN, RIVAS, and ZELAYA (including territory of CABO GRACIAS A DIOS).

Nicaragua, Lake, largest lake (□ 3,100) of Nicaragua and Central America; over 100 mi. long, up to 45 mi. wide, 230 ft. deep, alt. 105 ft. Separated from Pacific Ocean by 12-mi.-wide isthmus; receives Tipitapa R. (outlet of L. Managua; NW); empties through San Juan R. into the Atlantic. Contains Zapatera and Ometepe isls. and Solentiname Isls. Fish and alligators abound. Principal ports: Granada (NW), San Jorge (linked by isthmian railroad with Pacific port of San Juan del Sur), San Carlos (at San Juan R. outlet), San Miguelito, Morrito, San Ubaldo, Puerto Díaz. Its Indian name is Cocibolca. Lake forms part of a long-proposed canal route across Nicaragua.

Nicaria, Greece: see ICARIA.

Nicaro (nēkä'rō) or **Lengua de Pájaro** (lĕng'gwä dā pä'härō), town (pop. 2,832), Oriente prov., E Cuba, on Levisa Bay (Atlantic), at base of small Lengua de Pájaro peninsula, 6 mi. E of Mayarí. Refining of nickel oxide, which is mined near by (S) at foot of Sierra del Cristal. Refining operations were started in 1943.

Nicastro (nēkäs'trô), town (pop. 16,273), Catanzaro prov., Calabria, S Italy, 16 mi. WNW of Catanzaro. Commercial center (wine, olive oil, wheat, fruit); alcohol distillery, bell foundry, soap factory. Bishopric. Has ruins of anc. castle. Frequently damaged by earthquakes.

Nicatous Lake (nĭ'kŭtŭs), Hancock co., E central Maine, 36 mi. NE of Bangor, in hunting, fishing area; 8.5 mi. long.

Nice (nēs), Ital. *Nizza* (nē'tsä), anc. *Nicaea,* city (pop. 181,984), ⊙ Alpes-Maritimes dept., SE France, port on the Baie des Anges of the Mediterranean at mouth of Paillon R., 420 mi. SE of Paris, near Ital. border; 43°42'N 7°17'E. Leading resort of Fr. Riviera, beautifully situated in small coastal plain sheltered (N) by a fan-like hill range dotted with villas and gardens, and dominated by Maritime Alps. Famed for its mild winter climate, Nice depends chiefly on tourist trade. Produces perfumes, olive oil, soap, furniture, automatic pianos, silk and cotton goods, brandy, electrical and viticultural equipment, straw hats, and tobacco. Principal exports: southern fruits, olives and flowers locally grown. Numerous festivals are held here, and the Mardi Gras of Nice marks the height of Riviera carnival season. Foremost in attractively laid out modern city is the Promenade des Anglais (built by English colony early in 19th cent.). Place Masséna is city's focal point. Nice is junction for lines to Marseilles, Genoa, and Turin (via Tenda Pass). Former episcopal town of Cimiez (1 mi. N of city center) has ruined Roman arena (A.D. 4th cent.), a fine church, luxurious hotels and gardens. Probably a Gr. colony established in 5th cent. B.C. on hill just W of present port, Nice became episcopal see in 3d cent. A.D. Passed under counts of Savoy in 14th cent. Ceded to France by Sardinia in 1796, restored to Sardinia in 1814, again ceded to France after a plebiscite in 1860. In Second World War, Italians occupied it in 1940. Garibaldi and Masséna b. here.

Nice, Turkey: see IZNIK.

Nicephorium, Syria: see RAQQA.

Niceville, town (pop. 2,497), Okaloosa co., NW Fla., c.45 mi. ENE of Pensacola, on Choctawhatchee Bay.

Nichelino (nēkēlē'nô), village (pop. 2,282), Torino prov., Piedmont, NW Italy, 6 mi. S of Turin.

Nichicun Lake or **Nichikun Lake** (both: nĭ'chĭkŭn) (□ 150), central Que., on St. Lawrence-Hudson Bay watershed, at foot of the Otish Mts.; 53°5'N 71°W; alt. 1,737 ft.; 20 mi. long, 12 mi. wide. Drained N by Fort George R. Just SE is Naokokan L. (18 mi. long, 12 mi. wide).

Nicholas. 1 County (□ 204; pop. 7,532), N Ky.; ⊙ Carlisle. Bounded NE by Licking R. Gently rolling upland agr. area (burley tobacco, grain), in Bluegrass region. Includes Blue Licks Battlefield State Park. Formed 1799. **2** County (□ 649; pop. 27,696), central W.Va.; ⊙ Summersville. On Allegheny Plateau; bounded SW by Gauley and Meadow rivers; drained by short Cherry R. Includes Carnifex Ferry Battlefield State Park and part of Monongahela Natl. Forest. Agr. (livestock, fruit, tobacco); bituminous-coal mining; limestone quarrying, lumbering. Formed 1818.

Nicholas Channel, strait off NW coast of Cuba, 90 mi. E of Havana and 80 mi. SE of Key West; extends c.100 mi. E, bounded N by Cay Sal Bank (20 mi. off Cuba). Continued E by Old Bahama Channel. Sometimes spelled Nicolas.

Nicholas II Land, Russian SFSR: see SEVERNAYA ZEMLYA.

Nicholasville, city (pop. 3,406), ⊙ Jessamine co., central Ky., 13 mi. SSW of Lexington, in Bluegrass agr. area (dairy products, livestock, poultry, burley tobacco, corn, wheat, truck); makes shoes. Early gristmill (1782) near by. Settled 1798.

Nicholls (nĭ'kŭlz), city (pop. 806), Coffee co., S central Ga., 13 mi. E of Douglas, in agr. area.

Nicholls' Town, town (pop. 441), W Bahama Isls., on NE shore of Andros Isl., 40 mi. W of Nassau; 25°8'N 77°59'W. Fishing. Submarine caverns near by.

Nichols. 1 Village, Conn.: see TRUMBULL. **2** Town (pop. 348), Muscatine co., SE Iowa, 13 mi. WNW of Muscatine, in agr. area. **3** Village (pop. 578), Tioga co., S N.Y., near the Susquehanna, 25 mi. WSW of Binghamton; wood products. **4** Town (pop. 380), Marion co., E S.C., 35 mi. E of Florence and on Lumber R., at its mouth on Little Pee Dee R.; tobacco.

Nichols Field, Philippines: see PARAÑAQUE.
Nichols Hills or **Nichols Hill,** residential town (pop. 2,606), Oklahoma co., central Okla., just N of Oklahoma City. Inc. 1929.
Nicholson (nĭ'kŭlsŭn). **1** Town (pop. 252), Jackson co., NE central Ga., 10 mi. N of Athens. **2** Borough (pop. 979), Wyoming co., NE Pa., 16 mi. NNW of Scranton; dairying; flagstone quarrying; wood products. Inc. 1875.
Nicholson River, N Australia, rises in Barkly Tableland in Northern Territory, flows 130 mi. generally E to Gulf of Carpentaria on NW coast of Queensland, near mouth of Albert R.; in generally arid area. Gregory R., main tributary.
Nickelsdorf (nĭk'ŭlsdôrf), village (pop. 2,324), Burgenland, E Austria, near Leitha R. and Hung. border, 14 mi. S of Bratislava, Czechoslovakia; vineyards.
Nickelsville, town (pop. 268), Scott co., SW Va., 25 mi. W of Abingdon.
Nickerie, district, Du. Guiana: see NIEUW NICKERIE.
Nickerie Point (nēkä'rēŭ), on Atlantic coast of NW Du. Guiana, at mouth of Nickerie R., 3 mi. NW of Nieuw Nickerie; 5°58'N 57°3'W.
Nickerie River, W Du. Guiana, rises in outliers of the Guiana Highlands at 4°13'N 56°54'W, flows c.200 mi. N and WNW to the Atlantic just below Nieuw Nickerie, at mouth of Courantyne R. Tropical forests rich in hardwood and gums along upper course; fertile alluvial land (rice grown on large scale) along lower course. Navigable for c.60 mi. upstream. Linked by natural waterway with Coppename R.
Nickerson. 1 City (pop. 1,013), Reno co., S central Kansas, on Arkansas R. and 10 mi. NW of Hutchinson, in grain and livestock area. Oil wells near by. Inc. 1879. **2** Village (pop. 140), Dodge co., E Nebr., 8 mi. N of Fremont and on Elkhorn R.
Nicobar Islands (nĭkōbär', nĭ'kōbär), group of islands (□ 635; pop. 12,452) in Indian Ocean, forming S part of Indian state of ANDAMAN AND NICOBAR ISLANDS; ⊙ Port Blair, in the Andamans. Consist of 19 isls., extending c.185 mi. NNW-SSE and divided roughly into 3 sections: in N is Car Nicobar Isl., lying 90 mi. S of Little Andaman Isl.; in center are Katchall, Comorta, Nancowry, and Chowra isls.; in S, across Sombrero Channel, are Great Nicobar (33 mi. long N-S; 16 mi. wide) and Little Nicobar isls., largest in the group. Highest point, a 2,105-ft. peak, is on Great Nicobar Isl. The Nicobars have heavy monsoon rainfall (90–130 in. annually); coconut palms are numerous and betel nut is cultivated in places. Chief occupations are woodworking, canoe building, fishing, palm-mat and basket weaving, pottery making (on Chowra); interisland trade centers at Nancowry Harbour and Chowra Isl. The Nicobarese tribes, who comprise bulk of pop., are of Mongoloid stock, wear very little clothing, and, despite persistent efforts of Christian missionaries, remain confirmed animists. In 18th and 19th cent., isls. were occupied for short periods by Danes, Austrians, British, and French, until 1869, when British took formal possession. In Second World War, held (1942–45) by Japanese.
Nicola River (nĭ'kōlŭ), S B.C., rises c.40 mi. SSE of Kamloops, flows generally W, through Nicola L. (14 mi. long), to Merritt, thence NW to Thompson R. just ENE of Spences Bridge; 100 mi. long.
Nicolás Bravo (nēkōläs' brä'vō), town (pop. 990), Puebla, central Mexico, 10 mi. N of Tehuacán; corn, sugar, fruit, stock.
Nicolas Channel, Atlantic Ocean: see NICHOLAS CHANNEL.
Nicolás Romero (nēkōläs' rōmä'rō), town (pop. 3,688), Mexico state, central Mexico, 18 mi. NW of Mexico city; rail terminus; agr. (grain, fruit, stock).
Nicolás Ruiz (rwēs'), town (pop. 725), Chiapas, S Mexico, at SW foot of Sierra de Hueytepec, 23 mi. SSE of San Cristóbal de las Casas; fruit, livestock.
Nicole (nēkôl'), village (pop. 312), Lot-et-Garonne dept., SW France, near influx of the Lot into Garonne R., 16 mi. NW of Agen; cementworks; apricot growing and shipping.
Nicolet (nēkōlā'), county (□ 626; pop. 30,085), S Que., on the St. Lawrence; ⊙ Bécancour.
Nicolet, town (pop. 3,751), S Que., on Nicolet R., near its mouth on the St. Lawrence, 9 mi. SSW of Trois Rivières; textile knitting, mfg. of optical equipment, hosiery, furniture; in dairying region. Seat of R.C. bishop; site of cathedral and seminary.
Nicolet, Lake (nĭ'kŭlĕt), E Upper Peninsula, Mich., an expansion of St. Marys R., 4 mi. SE of Sault Ste. Marie and W of Sugar Isl.; c.13 mi. long, 2 mi. wide. Formerly called Hay L.
Nicolet River, S Que., flows 100 mi. in a winding course generally NW, past Nicolet, to L. St. Peter.
Nicollet (nĭ'kŭlĕt), county (□ 459; pop. 20,929), S Minn.; ⊙ St. Peter. Agr. area bounded S and E by Minnesota R. Livestock, dairy products, corn, oats, barley, potatoes. Swan L., near center of co., once large body of water, now largely dry. Co. formed 1853.
Nicollet, village (pop. 493), Nicollet co., S Minn., near Minnesota R., 11 mi. NW of Mankato; dairy products.
Nicolosi (nēkôlô'zē), village (pop. 3,368), Catania prov., E Sicily, on S slope of Mt. Etna, 8 mi. NNW of Catania. Point of ascent for Mt. Etna.
Nicoma Park (nŭkō'mä), village (pop. c.1,200), Oklahoma co., central Okla., 10 mi. E of Oklahoma City, in oil-producing area; truck, berries.
Nicomedia, Turkey: see IZMIT.
Nico Pérez, Uruguay: see JOSÉ BATLLE Y ORDÓÑEZ.
Nicopolis, Bulgaria: see NIKOPOL.
Nicopolis (nĭkŏ'pŭlĭs, nī–), anc. city of S Epirus, Greece, 4 mi. N of modern Preveza, on peninsula bet. Ionian Sea and Gulf of Arta. Founded 31 B.C. by Octavian (Augustus) in memory of his victory at near-by ACTIUM, Nicopolis was the scene of the Actian Games. It was originally settled by the rounded-up pop. of near-by towns, including Ambracia (Arta), which it succeeded as regional center and as ⊙ Roman Epirus. St. Paul visited here (Titus 3.12). Destroyed A.D. 396 by the Goths, it was rebuilt by Justinian. In early Middle Ages it declined and was superseded by Preveza. A theater and amphitheater were excavated here.
Nicopolis, Palestine: see EMMAUS.
Nicopolis or **Nicopolis of Pontus** (pŏn'tŭs), anc. city in Pontus, Asia Minor, on Lycus (modern Kelkit) R. and 75 mi. NE of modern Sivas, Turkey. There Pompey defeated Mithridates, king of Pontus, in 66 B.C. Later it became Roman ⊙ Lesser Armenia.
Nicopolis ad Istrum, Bulgaria: see NIKYUP.
Nicopolis ad Nestos, Bulgaria: see NEVROKOP.
Nicoresti (nēkôrĕsht'), Rum. *Nicoreşti*, village (pop. 1,331), Putna prov., E Rumania, 5 mi. NW of Tecuci; winegrowing.
Nicosia (nĭkŭsē'ŭ), Gr. *Leukosia* or *Levkosia* (both: lĕfkôsē'ä), district (□ 1,053; pop. 145,965), central and NW Cyprus, on the Mediterranean; ⊙ NICOSIA. Mostly occupied by fertile MESSAORIA lowland, flanked N by the KYRENIA MOUNTAINS and S by the OLYMPUS MOUNTAINS. The latter and EVRYKHOU VALLEY (NW) have important mines, yielding pyrite, chromite, ocher, asbestos, gypsum. Economy is, however, predominantly agr.; wheat, barley, oats, almonds, wine, olive oil; sheep, hogs, goats, cattle. Processing industries centered at Nicosia, through which passes railroad from Famagusta. Among other towns are MORPHOU, LEFKA, KARAVOSTASI, and KYTHREA. There are several summer resorts in wooded Olympus Mts., such as KAKOPETRIA, PEDHOULAS, KALOPANOAYIOTIS. Anc. ruined city SOLI is NW on Morphou Bay.
Nicosia, Gr. *Leukosia* or *Levkosia*, Turk. *Lefkosha*, anc. *Ledrae*, city (pop. 34,485), ⊙ Cyprus and Nicosia dist., N central Cyprus, 150 mi. NW of Beirut (Lebanon) and 280 mi. NNE of Port Said. Linked by rail with its port Famagusta, 33 mi. E. Leading trade center in fertile MESSAORIA plain (wheat, wine, olive oil, almonds, citrus fruit; cattle, sheep, hogs). Mfg. of brandy, cigarettes, pottery, soap, leather, textiles, bricks, machine tools. Seat of Br. governor and patriarch of autonomous Church of Cyprus. Historic city with occidental and oriental features, it has circular walls, towered over by 11 bastions (built by Venetians). In center is the bazaar with covered arcades, where artisans have their workshops. Near by (E) is the former Church of St. Sophia (early 13th cent.), now a mosque, adjoined by ruins of Latin archbishop's palace. There are numerous other churches, mostly converted into mosques, a Venetian column, Paphos Portal, and the Cyprian Mus. with remarkable collection of antiquities. Nicosia was the residence of the Lusignan kings of Cyprus from 1192. Became a Venetian possession in 1489 and fell to the Turks in 1571 after short siege. Under Br. rule since 1878. Suffered several air raids during Second World War. A modern airfield is 5 mi. W. Sometimes spelled Nikosia.
Nicosia (nēkôzē'ä), town (pop. 15,382), Enna prov., N central Sicily, near Salso R., 14 mi. NNE of Enna, in livestock and cereal-growing region; alt. 2,340 ft. Rock salt and sulphur mines near by. Bishopric. Has 14th-cent. cathedral, ruins of Norman castle. Scene of heavy fighting (1943) in Second World War.
Nicotera (nēkô'tĕrä), town (pop. 4,003), Catanzaro prov., Calabria, S Italy, near Gulf of Gioia, 13 mi. SW of Vibo Valentia; wine, olive oil. Bishopric since 8th cent. Has baroque cathedral and 11th-cent. castle (rebuilt 18th cent.). Just S is bathing resort of **Nicotera Marina** (pop. 1,845).
Nicoya (nēkoi'ä), city (1950 pop. 1,625), Guanacaste prov., NW Costa Rica, 33 mi. S of Liberia. Agr. (coffee, plantains) and livestock center; lumbering. Connected by road with Puerto Jesús. Has 19th-cent. colonial-style church. One of oldest cities of Costa Rica.
Nicoya, Gulf of, inlet of the Pacific in W Costa Rica, bet. Nicoya Peninsula and the mainland; c.50 mi. long, c.10 mi. wide. Opening bet. Cabo Blanco and Cape Herradura, it penetrates inland in a right angle. Contains Chira and San Lucas isls. Chief port is Puntarenas, on E shore. Minor coastal trade ports are Puerto Jesús, Puerto Thiel, Jicaral, Manzanillo. Receives Tempisque, Abangares, and Tárcoles rivers.
Nicoya Peninsula, largest peninsula of Costa Rica, on the Pacific; 75 mi. long (NW-SE), 20–30 mi. wide. Separated from mainland by Gulf of Nicoya.
Nictheroy, Brazil: see NITERÓI.
Nida or **Nidah** (nē'dŭ), village (pop. 6,513), Girga prov., central Upper Egypt, on E bank of the Nile and 4 mi. NNW of Akhmim; cotton, cereals, dates, sugar cane.
Nida (nē'dä), Ger. *Nidden*, seaside resort (1941 pop. 847), W Lithuania, on Courland Spit, 28 mi. SSW of Memel. In Memel Territory, 1920–39.
Nidadavole (nĭdŭ'dŭvōl) or **Nidadavolu** (nĭdŭdŭvō'lōō), town (pop. 8,669), West Godavari dist., NE Madras, India, in Godavari R. delta, 9 mi. SW of Rajahmundry; rail junction; rice milling; oilseeds, tobacco, sugar cane. Sometimes spelled Nidadavol.
Nidamangalam, India: see MANNARGUDI, Tanjore.
Nida River (nē'dä). **1** In SE Poland, rises 6 mi. NE of Szczekociny, flows E and SSE, past Pinczow, to Vistula R. 13 mi. SSE of Busko Zdroj; c.90 mi. long. **2** In NE Poland: see WKRA RIVER.
Nidaros, Norway: see TRONDHEIM.
Nidau (nē'dou), town (pop. 2,454), Bern canton, W Switzerland, on Aar Canal, on NE shore of L. Biel, adjoining Biel; watches, metal products (pianos, bicycles). Has 14th-cent. church, old castle.
Nidda (nĭ'dä), town (pop. 4,055), central Hesse, W Germany, in former Upper Hesse prov., on the Nidda and 12 mi. ENE of Friedberg; lumber milling. Has 17th-cent. church and castle.
Nidda River, Hesse, W Germany, rises 3 mi. NNE of Schotten, flows 50 mi. generally SW to the Main, just W of Höchst.
Nidden, Lithuania: see NIDA.
Nidd River, central Yorkshire, England, rises on Great Whernside, flows 50 mi. SE, past Knaresborough, to Ouse R. 7 mi. NW of York. Valley of upper course is the Nidderdale.
Nideggen (nē'dĕ"gŭn), town (pop. 849), in former Prussian Rhine Prov., W Germany, after 1945 in North Rhine-Westphalia, near the Rur, 7 mi. S of Düren; summer resort. Has ruined 12th-cent. castle.
Nidelv, Norway: see NID RIVER.
Niderviller (nēdĕrvēlâr'), Ger. *Niederweiler* (nē'-dŭrvīlŭr), village (pop. 756), Moselle dept., NE France, on Marne-Rhine Canal, and 3 mi. SE of Sarrebourg; faïence and tileworks.
Nidhauli (nĭdou'lē), town (pop. 2,618), Etah dist., W Uttar Pradesh, India, on Upper Ganges Canal and 11 mi. W of Etah; wheat, pearl millet, barley, corn, oilseeds.
Nid River (nēd), Nor. *Nidelv*. **1** Largely in central Norway, rises (as the Nea, Swed. *Nean*) in Jamtland co., Sweden, 38 mi. NE of Roros, Norway; flows WNW through the Tydal to Selbu L., whence, as the Nid, it flows to Trondheim Fjord at Trondheim; 100 mi. long. Forms several falls, notably Hyttefoss and Leirfosse. **2** In S Norway, rises in Nisser L. in Telemark co., flows 60 mi. S into Aust-Agder co. to the Skagerrak at Arendal. Several falls furnish hydroelectric power. Railroad follows the river. Also called Nisser, Nea, and Arendal.
Nidubrolu, India: see PONNURU.
Nidwalden (nēd'väldŭn), Fr. *Nidwald* (nĕdväld'), half-canton (□ 106; 1950 pop. 19,459), Switzerland, part of UNTERWALDEN canton; ⊙ Stans. Pop. German speaking and Catholic. Meadowland, forests, and pastures, with Alpine mts. in S, orchards in N; resorts on S shore of L. of Lucerne. Woodworking; glass and cement works.
Nidze or **Nidzhe** (nē'jĕ), Serbo-Croatian *Nidže*, Gr. *Voras* (vô'rŭs), mountain massif on Yugoslav-Greek border. The name of its highest peak, the KAJMAKCALAN (8,280 ft.), 15 mi. NW of Edessa (Greece), is sometimes applied to the entire massif.
Nidzica (nējē'tsä), Ger. *Neidenburg* (nī'dŭnbŏŏrk), town (1939 pop. 9,201; 1946 pop. 2,852) in East Prussia, after 1945 in Olsztyn prov., NE Poland, on Wkra R. and 30 mi. S of Allenstein (Olsztyn); grain and cattle market; sawmilling. Teutonic Knights established castle, 1382. Historian Gregorovius b. here. In 1914, town heavily damaged in battle with Russians. In Second World War, c.90% destroyed.
Niebla (nyä'lvä), town (pop. 2,116), Huelva prov., SW Spain, on the Río Tinto, on railroad and 17 mi. ENE of Huelva; cereals, grapes, vegetables, olives, timber, goats, sheep. Known for its wines. Limestone quarries and limekilns. Has castle and medieval walls.
Niebüll (nē'bŭl"), village (pop. 5,738), in Schleswig-Holstein, NW Germany, 23 mi. W of Flensburg, in North Friesland; rail junction; market center for cattle region; spinning, weaving. Main village of Südtondern dist.
Nied, river, France: see NIED RIVER.
Niedenstein (nē'dŭn-shtīn), town (pop. 1,065), in former Prussian prov. of Hesse-Nassau, W Germany, after 1945 in Hesse, 9 mi. SW of Kassel; lumber.
Niederaltaich (nē'dŭräl'tīkh), village (pop. 1,372), Lower Bavaria, Germany, on the Danube and 6 mi. SSE of Deggendorf; gravel quarrying. Has Benedictine monastery founded c.731.
Niederbayern, Germany: see LOWER BAVARIA.
Niederbieber-Segendorf (–bē"bŭr-zä'gŭndôrf), village (pop. 4,215), in former Prussian Rhine Prov., W Germany, after 1945 in Rhineland-Palatinate, 2 mi. N of Neuwied.
Niederbipp (–bĭp"), residential town (pop. 2,690), Bern canton, NW Switzerland, 8 mi. NE of Solothurn. Oberbipp (pop. 917) is near by.

Niederbreisig (–brī'zĭkh), village (pop. 2,344), in former Prussian Rhine Prov., W Germany, after 1945 in Rhineland-Palatinate, on left bank of the Rhine (landing) and 7 mi. NW of Andernach; resort with thermal spring.

Niederbronn-les-Bains (nēdĕrbrôn'-lā-bē'), Ger. *Niederbronn* (nē'dûrbrôn), town (pop. 3,167), Bas-Rhin dept., E France, at E foot of the lower Vosges, 12 mi. NW of Haguenau; resort with mineral springs. Iron- and steelworks, sawmills.

Niedercorn, Ger. *Niederkorn* (both: nē'dûrkôrn'), town (pop. 3,457), SW Luxembourg, 5 mi. WNW of Esch-sur-Alzette; iron-mining center.

Niedere Tauern (nē'dûrŭ tou'ûrn), central Austria, range of Eastern Alps in SE Salzburg and SW Styria; extends 75 mi. ENE from headwaters of Enns and Mur rivers, bet. their valleys, rising to 9,393 ft. in the Hochgolling. Forested, with many small lakes and high peaks. Pastures on S slopes; chamois hunted on N slopes. Subranges are (W-E) the Radstadt Tauern, Schladming Tauern, Rottenmann Tauern.

Niederfeulen, Luxembourg: see FEULEN.

Niederfinow (nē"dûrfē'nō), village (pop. 1,517), Brandenburg, E Germany, on Hohenzollern Canal and 4 mi. NE of Eberswalde; ship elevator (118 ft. level difference), completed 1933, replaces earlier structure.

Niederfrohna (–frō'nä), village (pop. 3,973), Saxony, E central Germany, 3 mi. NNW of Oberfrohna; mfg. of textile machinery.

Niedergebra (–gā'brä), village (pop. 1,607), in former Prussian Saxony prov., central Germany, after 1945 in Thuringia, on the Wipper and 2 mi. SW of Bleicherode; potash mining.

Niedergösgen (–gûs"gûn), town (pop. 2,350), Solothurn canton, N Switzerland, on Aar R. and 5 mi. ENE of Olten; hydroelectric plant; shoes, rubber goods. R.C. church on site of former castle. With Obergösgen (W), it is known as Gösgen.

Niederhaslach (nēdĕr"äzläk', Ger. nē"dûrhäs'läkh), village (pop. 891), Bas-Rhin dept., E France, in the E Vosges, 7 mi. W of Molsheim; small woodworking center. Has restored 13th-cent. abbey church.

Niederhässlich, Germany: see FREITAL.

Nieder-Ingelheim, Germany: see INGELHEIM.

Nieder Jeutz, France: see BASSE-YUTZ.

Niederkassel, Germany: see DÜSSELDORF.

Niederkerschen, Luxembourg: see BASCHARAGE.

Niederkirchen (nē'dûrkĭr"khŭn), village (pop. 835), NE Saar, near Ger. border, 4 mi. E of St. Wendel; stock, grain. Formerly in Rhenish Palatinate, Germany; annexed to Saar in 1946.

Niederkorn, Luxembourg: see NIEDERCORN.

Niederlahnstein (–län'shtīn), town (pop. 5,256), in former Prussian prov. of Hesse-Nassau, W Germany, after 1945 in Rhineland-Palatinate, on Lahn R. at its confluence with the Rhine (landing), opposite Oberlahnstein; rail junction; machinery mfg. Cement works.

Niederlausitz, region, Germany and Poland: see LUSATIA.

Niederlehme (–lā"mû), village (pop. 2,567), Brandenburg, E Germany, on Dahme R. and 2 mi. NE of Königs Wusterhausen; basic-chemicals mfg.

Nieder Lindewiese, Czechoslovakia: see DOLNI LIPOVA.

Niederlössnitz, Germany: see RADEBEUL.

Niedermarsberg (–märs'bĕrk), town (pop. 8,033), in former Prussian prov. of Westphalia, W Germany, after 1945 in North Rhine-Westphalia, on the Diemel and 12 mi. W of Warburg; copper mining.

Niedermendig (–mĕn'dĭkh), village (pop. 3,699), in former Prussian Rhine Prov., W Germany, after 1945 in Rhineland-Palatinate, in the Eifel, 4 mi. NE of Mayen; noted for its large, subterranean basalt quarries (paving- and millstones), also used as beer cellars.

Niedermorschweiler, France: see MORSCHWILLER-LE-BAS.

Niedernhall (nē'dûrnhäl), town (pop. 1,498), N Württemberg, Germany, after 1945 in Württemberg-Baden, on the Kocher and 15 mi. SW of Mergentheim; wine.

Niederoderwitz (nē'dûrō'dûrvĭts), village (pop. 4,399), Saxony, E central Germany, near Czechoslovak border, in Upper Lusatia, 6 mi. NW of Zittau; linen and cotton milling. Just NW is Oberoderwitz.

Niederösterreich, Austria: see LOWER AUSTRIA.

Niederpfalz, Germany: see RHENISH PALATINATE.

Niederrad (nē'dûrät), SW district (pop. 13,774) of Frankfurt, W Germany, on left bank of the canalized Main; race track.

Nieder-Ramstadt (–räm'shtät), residential village (pop. 5,041), S Hesse, W Germany, in former Starkenburg prov., 4 mi. SSE of Darmstadt.

Niedersachsen, Germany: see LOWER SAXONY.

Niedersachswerfen (–zäks'vĕr"fûn), village (pop. 4,499), in former Prussian Saxony prov., central Germany, after 1945 in Thuringia, at S foot of the lower Harz, 4 mi. NNW of Nordhausen; gypsum quarrying; refrigerator mfg.

Niederschlema, Germany: see OBERSCHLEMA.

Niederschlesien, province, Germany: see SILESIA.

Niederschmalkalden (–shmäl'käl"dûn), village (pop. 955), in former Prussian Saxony prov. exclave, central Germany, after 1945 in Thuringia, at foot of Thuringian Forest, on small Schmalkalde R. and 4 mi. W of Schmalkalden; steelworks.

Niedersedlitz (–zād'lĭts), town (pop. 8,113), Saxony, E central Germany, near the Elbe, 6 mi. SE of Dresden; metalworking, paper milling; mfg. of electrical and optical equipment, chemicals, ceramics, furniture, machinery, chocolate, hats.

Niederselters (–zĕl"tûrs), village (pop. 2,089), in former Prussian prov. of Hesse-Nassau, W Germany, after 1945 in Hesse, 8 mi. SE of Limburg. Its mineral springs furnish well-known Seltzer water, which is bottled and exported.

Niedersprockhövel (–shprôk'hû"vûl), village (pop. 5,602), in former Prussian prov. of Westphalia, W Germany, after 1945 in North Rhine-Westphalia, in the Ruhr, 3 mi. SE of Hattingen.

Niederstetten (–shtĕ"tûn), town (pop. 1,670), N Württemberg, Germany, after 1945 in Württemberg-Baden, 9 mi. SE of Mergentheim; spelt, oats. Has 16th-cent. castle.

Niederstotzingen (–shtô'tsĭng-ûn), town (pop. 1,801), N Württemberg, Germany, after 1945 in Württemberg-Baden, 10 mi. SSE of Heidenheim; grain.

Niederurnen (–ŏŏr"nûn), town (pop. 2,572), Glarus canton, E central Switzerland, 6 mi. N of Glarus; cotton textiles, cement, asbestos products. With Oberurnen (pop. 1,107), just S, it is known as Urnen.

Niederwald (–vält), SW tip (1,080 ft.) of the Taunus, W Germany, on a bend of the Rhine, just W of Rüdesheim (rack-and-pinion railway). Vine-covered slopes. On summit, overlooking the Rhine, is the National Monument, with principal relief symbolizing the "Watch on the Rhine."

Niederwalluf (–vä'lŏŏf), village (pop. 2,288), in former Prussian prov. of Hesse-Nassau, W Germany, after 1945 in Hesse, in the Rheingau, on right bank of the Rhine and 4 mi. WSW of Wiesbaden; wine.

Niederwampach (–väm"päkh), village (pop. 146), NW Luxembourg, in the Ardennes 5 mi. NW of Wiltz, near Wiltz R.; lead mining.

Niederwartha (–vär'tä), village (pop. 749), Saxony, E central Germany, on the Elbe and 7 mi. NW of Dresden; hydroelectric power station.

Niederweiler, France: see NIDERVILLER.

Niederwiesa (–vē'zä), village (pop. 5,721), Saxony, E central Germany, 5 mi. ENE of Chemnitz; hosiery and glove knitting, woolen milling, woodworking; mfg. of musical instruments.

Niederwiltz, Luxembourg: see WILTZ.

Niederwürschnitz (–vür'shnĭts), village (pop. 5,634), Saxony, E central Germany, at N foot of the Erzgebirge, 2 mi. S of Lugau; coal mining; hosiery knitting, machinery mfg.

Nied River (nēd), Moselle dept., N France, and in the Saar, rises in several headstreams near Grostenquin, flows c.40 mi. generally N, past Faulquemont and Bouzonville, to Saar R. 5 mi. above Merzig.

Niefang or **Sevilla de Niefang** (sāvēl'yä dā nyä'fäng), town (pop. 490), continental Sp. Guinea, on Benito R. and 35 mi. E of Bata; 1°53'N 10°16'E. Coffee, cacao.

Niefern (nē'fûrn), village (pop. 4,377), N Baden, Germany, after 1945 in Württemberg-Baden, on N slope of Black Forest, on the Enz and 4 mi. NE of Pforzheim; metalworking, paper milling.

Niegocin, Lake (nyĕgô'tsēn), Ger. *Löwentin* (lû'vûntēn) (□ 10), in East Prussia, after 1945 in NE Poland, S of Gizycko; one of Masurian Lakes; 6 mi. long, 1–4 mi. wide; drains N into L. Mamry.

Nieheim (nē'hīm), town (pop. 2,713), in former Prussian prov. of Westphalia, NW Germany, after 1945 in North Rhine-Westphalia, 16 mi. ENE of Paderborn; grain.

Niehl (nēl), suburb of Cologne, W Germany, on left bank of the Rhine and 4 mi. N of city center; industrial harbor (lignite shipping). Race track just W.

Niel (nēl), town (pop. 10,820), Antwerp prov., N Belgium, near junction of Rupel R. and Scheldt R., 9 mi. SSW of Antwerp; mfg. (Portland cement, bricks, tiles).

Nielson Field, Philippines: see MAKATI.

Nielsville, village (pop. 189), Polk co., NW Minn., in Red R. valley, 19 mi. SW of Crookston; grain.

Niemba (nyĕm'bä), village, Katanga prov., E Belgian Congo, on railroad and 50 mi. W of Albertville; trading post; cotton.

Niemcza (nyĕm'chä), Ger. *Nimptsch* (nĭmpch), town (1939 pop. 3,523; 1946 pop. 3,075) in Lower Silesia, after 1945 in Wroclaw prov., SW Poland, 8 mi. E of Reichenbach (Dzierzoniow); metalworking, malt processing. First mentioned 11th cent.

Niemegk (nē'mĕk"), town (pop. 3,257), Brandenburg, E Germany, 25 mi. SSE of Brandenburg; linen milling; grain, potatoes, stock.

Niemen River, USSR: see NEMAN RIVER.

Niemes, Czechoslovakia: see MIMON.

Niemirow, Ukrainian SSR: see NEMIROV, Lvov oblast.

Niemodlin (nyĕmôd'lēn), Ger. *Falkenberg* (fäl'kûnbĕrk), town (1939 pop. 2,727; 1946 pop. 2,580) in Upper Silesia, after 1945 in Opole prov., SW Poland, 14 mi. W of Oppeln (Opole); agr. market (grain, sugar beets, potatoes, livestock). Has 16th-cent. palace.

Nienbergen (nēn'bĕr"gûn), village (pop. 269), in former Prussian prov. of Hanover, NW Germany, after 1945 in Lower Saxony, 8 mi. W of Salzwedel.

Nienburg (nēn'bŏŏrk). **1** or **Nienburg an der Saale** (än dĕr zä'lŭ), town (pop. 7,931), in former Anhalt state, central Germany, after 1945 in Saxony-Anhalt, on the Saxonian Saale, at mouth of the Bode, and 4 mi. NNE of Bernburg, in potash-mining region; mfg. (paper bags, cement). Has early-Gothic church; remains of former Benedictine monastery (founded 975; destroyed in Thirty Years War). **2** or **Nienburg an der Weser** (än dĕr vā'zûr), town (pop. 18,415), in former Prussian prov. of Hanover, W Germany, after 1945 in Lower Saxony, on right bank of the Weser and 28 mi. NW of Hanover; rail junction; mfg. of chemicals (dyes, phosphates, vulcanizing agents), furniture. Glassworks. Has Gothic church. Chartered 1025.

Nien-ch'ing T'ang-ku-la, Tibet: see NYENCHEN TANGLHA.

Nien-ch'u Ho, river, Tibet: see NYANG CHU.

Nienhagen (nēn'hä"gûn), village (pop. 1,692), in former Prussian prov. of Hanover, NW Germany, after 1945 in Lower Saxony, 5 mi. S of Celle; oil wells.

Niepolomice (nyĕpôwômē'tsĕ), Pol. *Niepołomice*, town (pop. 4,071), Krakow prov., S Poland, near the Vistula, 12 mi. E of Cracow; rail branch terminus; steam-power mill, tile kiln. Niepolomice Forest, Pol. *Niepołomska Puszcza* or *Niepołomicka Puszcza*, lies bet. Niepolomice and Raba R. (E).

Niepos (nyä'pōs), town (pop. 647), Cajamarca dept., NW Peru, on W slopes of Cordillera Occidental, 50 mi. ESE of Chiclayo; alt. 7,985 ft.; sugar cane, coffee, tobacco.

Nieppe (nyĕp), town (pop. 2,691), Nord dept., N France, near Belg. border, 2 mi. NW of Armentières; cotton and linen weaving and bleaching.

Nieppe Forest, France: see MERVILLE.

Nieriko, Fr. West Africa: see OUASSADOU.

Niers River (nērs), W Germany, rises 3 mi. S of Wickrath, flows c.80 mi. generally NNE, past Rheydt, crosses Dutch border 5 mi. NW of Goch, continuing to the Maas 1 mi. N of Gennep.

Nierstein (nēr'shtīn), village (pop. 5,044), Rhenish Hesse, W Germany, on left bank of the Rhine, 9 mi. SSE of Mainz; rail junction; noted for wine.

Niesen (nē'zûn), peak (7,762 ft.) in Bernese Alps, SW Switzerland, 10 mi. WSW of Interlaken.

Niesky (nē'skē), town (pop. 7,436), in former Prussian Lower Silesia prov., E central Germany, after 1945 in Saxony, in Upper Lusatia, 12 mi. NW of Görlitz; lignite and quartzite mining; mfg. (railroad cars, machinery, leather products). Founded 1742 by Moravian Brothers.

Niesky, U.S. Virgin Isls.: see NISKY.

Nieswiez, Belorussian SSR: see NESVIZH.

Nieszawa (nyĕ-shä'vä), Rus. *Neshava* (nyĭ-shä'vŭ), town (pop. 2,403), Bydgoszcz prov., central Poland, port on the Vistula, 14 mi. NNW of Wloclawek; flour milling, brewing. Monastery.

Niete Mountains (nīĕ'tä), SE Liberia, 85 mi. NNW of Harper; 5°35'N 8°10'W. Rise to 2,296 ft. Form divide bet. Cavalla R. (N) and coastal streams (Grand Cess, Nana Kru, and Sinoe rivers).

Nietleben (nēt'lā"bûn), village (pop. 5,208), in former Prussian Saxony prov., central Germany, after 1945 in Saxony-Anhalt, 3 mi. W of Halle, in lignite-mining dist.; mfg. (agr. machinery, cement).

Nieul (nyûl), village (pop. 380), Haute-Vienne dept., W central France, 8 mi. NNW of Limoges; wool spinning, cider making.

Nieuport (nyûpôr'), Flemish *Nieuwpoort* (nē'ŏŏpōrt"), town (pop. 5,062), West Flanders prov., W Belgium, on Yser R. and 10 mi. SW of Ostend; fishing port; oyster culture; mfg. (metallic pigments, bricks). An old town, besieged by French in 15th cent.; scene of Du. victory over Spanish in 1600. Has 15th-cent. cloth hall and 16th-cent. town hall, both considerably damaged in First World War; rebuilt since. Just NW, on North Sea, is seaside resort of Nieuport-Bains.

Nieuw Amsterdam (nēv' äm'stûrdäm), town (pop. 977), ⊙ Commewijne dist. (□ 2,014; pop. 22,740), N Du. Guiana, at confluence of Commewijne and Surinam rivers, near the Atlantic, 6 mi. NE of Paramaribo; 5°50'N 55°8'W. Fertile agr. region (sugar cane, coffee, rice). Formerly a Du. fort.

Nieuw-Amsterdam, village (pop. 3,017), Drenthe prov., NE Netherlands, on Overijssel Canal and 6 mi. NE of Coevorden; potato-flour milling. A fen colony founded in mid-19th cent. by citizens of Amsterdam.

Nieuw Beijerland or **Nieuw Beierland** (both: nē'ŏŏ bī'ûrlänt), village (pop. 1,149), South Holland prov., SW Netherlands, on NW Beijerland isl., on the Spui and 10 mi. SW of Rotterdam; large sugar refinery. Sometimes spelled Nieuw Beyerland.

Nieuwe Maas, Netherlands: see NEW MAAS RIVER.

Nieuwe Merwede, Netherlands: see NEW MERWEDE RIVER.

Nieuwenhoorn (nē'vûnhōrn), agr. village (pop. 541), South Holland prov., SW Netherlands, on Voorne isl. and 4 mi. S of Brielle.

Nieuwe Pekela (nē'vû pā'kûlä), town (pop. 4,439), Groningen prov., NE Netherlands, 5 mi. SW of Winschoten; cigar mfg., potato-flour milling, knitting mills; peat production.

Nieuwer-Amstel (nē'vůr-äm'stůl), residential town (pop. 17,511), North Holland prov., W Netherlands, 4 mi. S of Amsterdam.

Nieuwerkerk (nē'vůrkĕrk"). **1** or **Nieuwerkerk aan den Ijssel** (än důn ī'sůl), village (pop. 1,027), South Holland prov., W Netherlands, on Hollandsche Ijssel R. and 5 mi. WSW of Gouda; flower growing, meat packing, dairying. **2** Village (pop. 1,382), Zeeland prov., SW Netherlands, on Duiveland isl., 4 mi. E of Zierikzee; processes dairy products, chicory.

Nieuwerkerken (nē'vůrkĕrkůn), agr. village (pop. 4,498), East Flanders prov., N central Belgium, 2 mi. WSW of Alost.

Nieuwe Schans (nē'vů skhäns'), village (pop. 1,977), Groningen prov., NE Netherlands, 7 mi. ENE of Winschoten; frontier station on Ger. border; strawboard mfg.

Nieuwe Waterweg, Netherlands: see NEW WATERWAY.

Nieuwkerk, Netherlands: see NIJKERK.

Nieuwkoop (nē'ōōkōp), village (pop. 2,060), South Holland prov., W Netherlands, on small lake and 5 mi. NE of Alphen aan den Rijn; dairying, cattle raising, agr.

Nieuwkuyk or **Nieuwkuik** (both: nē'ōōkoik), village (pop. 1,738), North Brabant prov., S Netherlands, 5 mi. W of 's Hertogenbosch; mfg. (leather, baskets); cattle raising, agr.

Nieuw Nickerie (nē'ōō nĭkâ'rēů), town (pop. 3,100), ⊙ Nickerie dist. (□ 19,098; pop. 15,402), NW Du. Guiana, port on Nickerie R. 3 mi. from its mouth, and 40 mi. SE of New Amsterdam (Br. Guiana), 125 mi. W of Paramaribo; 5°56'N 57°2'W. Reached by medium-sized vessels; exports cacao, rice, lumber, balata. Rice-growing region.

Nieuwpoort, Belgium: see NIEUPORT.

Nieuwpoort (nē'ōōpōrt), town (pop. 845), South Holland prov., W central Netherlands, on Lek R. and 9 mi. NNW of Gorinchem; silverware mfg.; wood and stone processing.

Nieuwrhode, Belgium: see NIEUWRODE.

Nieuwrode (nē'ōōrōdů), village (pop. 1,939), Brabant prov., central Belgium, 7 mi. NE of Louvain; agr., lumbering. Formerly spelled Nieuwrhode.

Nieuwveld Range (nē'ōōfĕlt), S central Cape Prov., U. of So. Afr., at NW edge of the Great Karroo and on S side of the Northern Karroo, extends 120 mi. W from Beaufort West; rises to 6,422 ft. on Klaverfontein mtn., 20 mi. NW of Beaufort West. Continued W by Komsberg Escarpment.

Nieva (nyä'vä), town (pop. 681), Segovia prov., central Spain, 19 mi. WNW of Segovia; cereals, grapes. Lumbering; mfg. of boot polish.

Nieves (nyā'vĕs), town (pop. 3,081), Zacatecas, N central Mexico, on interior plateau, 14 mi. NE of Río Grande, 90 mi. NNW of Zacatecas; alt. 6,617 ft.; silver, gold, antimony mining.

Nieves, Puerto de las (pwĕr'tō dhä läs), small bay and landing, NW Grand Canary, Canary Isls., 17 mi. W of Las Palmas.

Nieves Negras Pass (nā'gräs) (12,500–13,000 ft.), in the Andes, on Argentina-Chile border, at S foot of San José Volcano, on road bet. San Carlos (Mendoza prov., Argentina) and El Volcán (Chile); 33°51'S 69°54'W.

Nièvre (nyĕ'vrů), department (□ 2,659; pop. 248,559), in old Nivernais prov., central France; ⊙ Nevers. Bounded by crest of the MORVAN (E), by Allier and Loire rivers (W); occupied by Nivernais Hills (center). Drained by the Loire and its tributaries (Allier, Aron, Nièvre), the Yonne, and the Cure. Crossed S–N by Nivernais Canal (from the Loire to the Yonne). Dept. is primarily agr., with important forest stands and extensive livestock industry. Chief crops are green vegetables and potatoes; good cereal yields. Noted vineyards on Loire R. slopes, especially at Pouilly. Iron and coal mines in Decize–La Machine area are of declining importance; kaolin quarries at Fleury-sur-Loire and Saint-Pierre-le-Moûtier. Metallurgy in Fourchambault-Nevers area, with steel mills at Imphy and forges at Guérigny. Ceramic (Nevers, Saint-Amand-en-Puisaye) and woodworking industries throughout dept. Chief towns are Nevers, Cosne, Clamecy, and Decize. Thermal springs at Pougues-les-Eaux and Saint-Honoré.

Nièvre River, Nièvre dept., central France, rises SW of Varzy, flows c.25 mi. S, past Guérigny, to the Loire at Nevers.

Nif, Turkey: see KEMALPASA.

Niffer, Iraq: see NIPPUR.

Nifisha or **Nifishah** (nĭfē'shů), village (1937 pop. 951; 1947 commune pop. 16,368), Sharqiya prov., Lower Egypt, on Ismailiya Canal, on Cairo-Ismailiya RR, and 2 mi. SW of Ismailiya. Here the Ismailiya Canal branches off (S) as the Suez Fresh Water Canal, and the Cairo-Ismailiya RR has a branch to Suez.

Nigata, Japan: see KURE, Hiroshima prefecture.

Nigde (nēdĕ'), Turk. *Niğde*, prov. (□ 5,891; 1950 pop. 331,061), S central Turkey; ⊙ Nigde. Drained by the Kizil Irmak. Lignite in N at Aksaray and Arapsun, lead in S at Ulukisla. Mohair goats; rye, legumes, potatoes, onions, walnuts, raisins.

Nigde, Turkish *Niğde*, town (1950 pop. 12,423), ⊙ Nigde prov., S central Turkey, on railroad 75 mi. NNW of Adana; tile making; rye, wheat, barley, legumes. Some of its bldgs. date from Middle Ages. Was important city of the Seljuk Turks; fell to Ottoman Turks in 15th cent.

Nigel (nī'jůl), town (pop. 30,731), S Transvaal, U. of So. Afr., 30 mi. WSW of Johannesburg; alt. 5,150 ft.; gold-mining center. Increased gold mining in region has resulted in recent growth of town.

Niger, river, W Africa: see NIGER RIVER.

Niger (nī'jůr), French overseas territory (□ 449,400; pop. c.1,873,000), NE Fr. West Africa, S of Tropic of Cancer; ⊙ NIAMEY. Borders N on Libya and Algeria, W on Fr. Sudan, SW on Upper Volta and Dahomey, S on Nigeria, E on Chad (with L. Chad). Its vast N section, covered by sand dunes, is part of the Sahara, though there are a few oases (e.g., Agadez) in the Aïr mtn. region (rises to 5,900 ft.). The Niger R. (obstructed by rapids) traverses the SW section, which is wooded and is the more heavily populated area. The climate is excessively hot. Practically all resources come from the narrow, fertile strips (c.100 mi. wide) along the Nigeria border and the Niger. Principal crops: millet, corn, manioc, rice, wheat, peanuts, dates, sugar cane, beans, tobacco, cotton, melons. Most important, however, is stock raising (goats, cattle, sheep, horses, donkeys). Meat, stock, hides, and millet are exported, chiefly to Nigeria. Some salt and sodium-phosphate deposits are worked. Chief trading towns are Zinder, Niamey, Maradi, and Birni-N'Konni. Racially the majority are of Negroid Hausa stock, though a Tuareg kingdom formerly occupied most of the N. French penetration began in the 1890s. The region was established (1900) by the French as a military territory, and became an autonomous territory in 1922.

Niger, province (□ 25,178; pop. 461,208), Northern Provinces, W central Nigeria; ⊙ Minna. Bounded W and S by Niger R.; savanna with well-wooded parklands along streams; drained by Kaduna R. Gold mining (Kuta, Minna, Kontagora), tin (Abuja). Agr. (shea nuts, cotton, peanuts, cassava); rope- and sackmaking. Chief centers: Minna, Bida, Abuja, Kontagora, Zungeru. Pop. largely Nupe (S).

Niger Coast, protectorate: see NIGERIA.

Nigeria (nījē'rēů), British colony and protectorate (including Br. Cameroons: □ 372,674; 1931 pop. 19,928,171 [believed underestimated by c.2,000,000]; 1949 pop. estimate 24,000,000), W Africa, along lower course of Niger R. and on Gulf of Guinea; ⊙ LAGOS. The colony (□ 1,381; 1931 pop. 325,020) consists of Lagos municipality and surrounding territory; the protectorate has 3 major administrative divisions, NORTHERN PROVINCES, EASTERN PROVINCES, and WESTERN PROVINCES. The part of CAMEROONS under Br. trusteeship (□ 34,081; 1931 pop. 778,352; 1948 pop. estimate 1,027,500) is (since 1923) administratively included in Nigeria. Lying bet. 4°N and 14°N and bet. 3°E and 14°E, Nigeria is the largest and most populous Br. possession in W Africa; it is bounded by Fr. territories of Dahomey (W) and Niger (N), and by Fr. Cameroons (E); in extreme NE it touches on L. Chad. The 4 distinct and roughly parallel physiographic and vegetational zones are, from S to N: (1) a belt of swamp and mangrove forests (10–60 mi. wide) along the coastline; it includes the huge delta (□ c.14,000) of the Niger and the braided course of minor coastal streams (Benin, Calabar, Cross, Imo, Kwa Ibo); (2) a belt of dense tropical forest with thick undergrowth (50–100 mi. wide) and few clearings; rolling topography; here grow the oil palm and the cacao tree; (3) a zone of hilly country with deciduous forests gradually merging with park and high-grass savanna; (4) a vast tableland (average alt. 2,000 ft.), which occupies N half of Nigeria N of Niger and Benue rivers; the region's highest section (to 6,000 ft.) around Bauchi and Jos is the tin-rich Bauchi Plateau. Along Nigeria's N border is a sandy strip of thorn and scrub vegetation marking the approaches of the Sahara. In E Nigeria, along Cameroons border, the belted pattern is altered by irregular mtn. ranges (Bamenda, Shebshi, Alantika; up to 7,000 ft. high) extending inland from coastal Mt. Cameroon. The Niger and its only important tributary, the Benue, drain most of Nigeria; NE, intermittent streams flow to the Chad depression. Nigeria's climate is influenced by the torrid harmattan (blowing S from the Sahara) during the dry season (Nov.–April), and by monsoon-type SW winds from the Gulf of Guinea during rainy season (May–Oct.). Mean temp. 82°F. Rainfall, decreasing from S to N, is 140 in. along SE coast, 50 in. in center, and 25 in. in N; Lagos, on SW coast, receives c.70 in. of rain per year. Nigeria's chief export crops are palm kernels, palm oil, cacao (Western Provs.), and peanuts (Northern Provs.); benni seed, shea nuts, raw cotton, bananas, and rubber are shipped in smaller quantities. Principal local food crops are yams, cassava, corn, millet, rice, beans, peanuts, and plantains. Animal husbandry is limited to N savanna where the tsetse fly has been partially controlled; hides and skins (especially goatskins) are a major export product (chiefly to U.S.). Timber shipments from hardwood forests are of increasing importance. The noted tin deposits of the Bauchi Plateau (mined at Jos, Bukuru, Naraguta, Bauchi, Pankshin) are nearing exhaustion and only lower-grade ores are being worked; some columbite has been recovered since Second World War. Although Nigeria has W Africa's only significant coal deposits, these are of low, non-coking quality; mines are at Enugu and Udi; widespread lignite deposits have been located. Some gold is dredged, and small quantities of silver, lead, and zinc are mined at Abakaliki. Industries consist predominantly of oil milling, cacao processing, and sawmilling; cotton weaving and dyeing, metal casting, wood carving, and mat making are leading native handicrafts. A cigarette factory at Ibadan, a brewery at Lagos, a peanut-expressing plant and a tannery at Kano, and a large plywood factory at Sapele are among the few modern mfg. plants. Nigeria's rail net (1,900 mi.) links Lagos and PORT HARCOURT with the interior; the W line (from Lagos) passes by the large Yoruba cities of Abeokuta, IBADAN, and Oshogbo, crosses the Niger at Jebba, meets the E rail branch at Kaduna, and continues NE to KANO and Nguru; Kaura Namoda is the NW terminus. The railroad from Port Harcourt leads to Enugu (coal) and Jos (tin). There are c.7,500 mi. of trunk roads. The Niger, navigable seasonally below Jebba, is an important waterway, especially for delta navigation. Over 30 all-season airports are served by internal and international airlines. The pop. of Nigeria falls into 2 major ethnological groups: the N group, predominantly Moslem, has a highly developed tribal organization; the S group, less highly organized, is partly pagan, partly Christianized, and partly Moslem (Yorubas). Most numerous are, in N, the Hausa (18% of total pop.), the Fulah or Fulani (10%), the Kanuri (5%), and in S, the Yoruba (16%) and the Ibo (16%). The annexation in 1861 of Lagos, a notorious slave depot, as a crown colony, marked the beginning of Br. administration in Nigeria. In 1885, Br. interests in the Niger delta were recognized at Berlin conference by creation of the Oil Rivers protectorate (renamed Niger Coast protectorate in 1893). Meanwhile, the Royal Niger Co., which had extended its activities northward in the Niger valley, was granted a charter in 1886; this charter was revoked by the crown in 1900, and the company's territories were divided into a protectorate of Northern Nigeria (roughly N of 9°N) and a protectorate of Southern Nigeria to which was joined the Niger Coast protectorate. Bet. 1898 and 1906, Br. expeditions under Lugard succeeded in subjugating the powerful Fulani empire (which had controlled the Hausa states). In 1906, Lagos colony was amalgamated with the protectorate of Southern Nigeria, the new designation being colony and protectorate of Southern Nigeria. In 1914, Northern and Southern Nigeria were in turn amalgamated into the colony and protectorate of Nigeria. Nigeria is ruled by an appointed governor with the aid of an executive and a legislative council. The colony is administered by a commissioner residing at Lagos. The 3 major administrative divisions of the protectorate, headed by chief commissioners residing at Kaduna (Northern Provs.), Enugu (Eastern Provs.), and Ibadan (Western Provs.), are in turn subdivided into the following provs.: ADAMAWA, BAUCHI, BENUE, BORNU, ILORIN, KABBA, KANO, KATSINA, NIGER, PLATEAU PROVINCE, SOKOTO, and ZARIA (all in Northern Provs.); CALABAR, Cameroons (in Br. Cameroons), OGOJA, ONITSHA, OWERRI (all in Eastern Provs.); ABEOKUTA, BENIN, IJEBU, OYO, ONDO, WARRI (all in Western Provs.).

Niger River (nī'jůr), W Africa, 3d longest (c.2,600 mi.) stream (after the Nile and the Congo) of the continent, rises in outliers of the Fouta Djallon near Sierra Leone–Fr. Guinea border at c.9°N 10°45'W, only 175 mi. from the Atlantic coast, and forms a great W–E arc, flowing NE through Fr. Sudan toward the Sahara, SE across Fr. Niger territory and into Nigeria, and S to the Gulf of Guinea. In its upper course it flows past Kouroussa, Siguiri, Bamako, Koulikoro, Ségou, and Sansanding. At Sansanding is an irrigation dam (completed 1946) just above a great lacustrine depression (c.300 mi. long) called the Macina; here the river splits into several braided arms enclosing isls. and marshes, and forming lakes (e.g., L. Debo); the famous old town of Djenné is in this area; at Mopti the Bani R. is received. Below the Macina the Niger passes Timbuktu (with its port, Kabara), and soon reaches its most northerly point (c.16°50'N), before turning SE at Bourem (where the trans-Saharan auto track reaches the valley). It then continues SE, past Gao, Ansongo, and Niamey, and, in Nigeria, past Gomba (mouth of Kebbi R.), Yelwa, Jebba, Mureji (mouth of Kaduna R.), Baro, Lokoja (where it receives its only large tributary, the Benue, from left), Idah, and Onitsha, to Abo (c.80 mi. from coast), where begins its large, marshy delta (c.200 mi. wide along coast; □ c.14,000) marked by extensive mangrove forests. Of the numerous arms and channels the Forcados, Nun, Brass, New Calabar, Sombrero, and Bonny rivers are navigable for shallow-draft vessels able to negotiate the sandbar near entrance. Since First World War, the Bonny channel has been dredged to provide access to Port Harcourt (30 mi. upstream), a rail terminus and major coal-shipping port. Minor ports in delta, chiefly engaged in palm oil and kernel trade, are Forcados, Akassa, Degema, Burutu, and Warri. The river is called Upper Niger (also Djoliba or Joliba) from source to northernmost part of the bend; Middle Niger to Bussa rapids or to Jebba in W Nigeria; and Lower Niger (also Kovarra, Kowarra, or Kwara) to the delta, whose channels are sometimes referred to as Oil Rivers. Though the Niger is, because of its great irrigation potentialities (drainage basin □ c.600,000), sometimes referred to as the "Nile of West Africa," it is as yet of little economic value. As an artery for shipping it is unsatisfactory, since only sections are seasonally navigable, such as the stretches bet. Kouroussa and Bamako (July–Dec.), Koulikoro and Mopti (Aug.–Nov.), Mopti and Timbuktu (Aug.–Dec.), Timbuktu and Ansongo (Oct.–March); interrupted by rapids bet. Ansongo and Say, navigation is again possible for 300 mi. bet. Say and Bussa (Nigeria), and, below Bussa rapids, from Jebba to the sea (July–Oct.). Since the Niger's waters traverse its great length at a leisurely pace, flooding large areas in mid-course, the high and low stages, which vary greatly, occur simultaneously in different sections of the river. A railroad from Dakar via Kayes to Bamako and Koulikoro links the Senegal and Niger basins. The course of the Niger long mystified geographers, and at one time it was even thought to be an arm of the Nile. It was 1st explored by Mungo Park in 1795–96 and 1805–6; other explorers included Clapperton (1827) and Lander (1827–34).

Nigg, village, Berbice co., NE Br. Guiana, in Atlantic coastland, 10 mi. E of New Amsterdam; rice, sugar cane.

Nigg. **1** Agr. parish in NE Kincardine, Scotland, on Nigg Bay of North Sea, 2 mi. SE of Aberdeen. On coast is experiment station of the Scottish Fishery Board. **2** Agr. village and parish (pop. 726), E Ross and Cromarty, Scotland, on Cromarty Firth, 3 mi. NNE of Cromarty.

Nighasan (nĭgä'sŭn), village, Kheri dist., N Uttar Pradesh, India, 20 mi. NNE of Lakhimpur; rice, wheat, gram, sugar cane.

Nighrita, Greece: see NIGRITA.

Nightcaps, town (pop. 602), S S.Isl., New Zealand, 25 mi. N of Invercargill; coal-mining center at rail terminus.

Nighthawk, village, Okanogan co., N Wash., port of entry at B.C. line, on Okanogan R. and c.40 mi. N of Okanogan.

Night Hawk Lake (13 mi. long, 6 mi. wide), E Ont., 15 mi. E of Timmins; drains N into Abitibi R.

Nightingale Islands, group of 3 uninhabited islets (largest 1 mi. long, ¾ mi. wide) in S Atlantic, 13 mi. SSW of Tristan da Cunha, with which it is (since 1938) a dependency of St. Helena; 37°25'S 12°30'W. It was named 1760 by a Br. naval officer. Tiny Stolten hoff and Middle isls. are just NNW of Nightingale Isl.

Nigliva, Nepal: see PADERIA.

Nigrita (nĭgrē'tŭ), town (pop. 8,921), Serrai nome, Macedonia, Greece, on road and 13 mi. S of Serrai; trading center for grain, cotton, sesame, tobacco, corn, barley. Noted sulphur springs near by. Also spelled Nighrita.

Nigtmute or **Nigtmuit** (both: nĭkt'myōōt), village (pop. 27), SW Alaska, on Nelson Isl., W of Bethel.

Nigüelas (nēgwā'läs), village (pop. 1,521), Granada prov., S Spain, 14 mi. SSE of Granada; olive-oil processing; wine, cereals, potatoes.

Nihavand, Iran: see NEHAVEND.

Nihing River, W Pakistan: see DASHT RIVER.

Nihoa (nēhō'ŭ), island (155 acres), T.H., 120 mi. NW of Niihau; uninhabited. Formerly Bird Isl.

Nihommatsu (nēhōm'mätsōō), town (pop. 11,819), Fukushima prefecture, central Honshu, Japan, on Abukuma R. and 12 mi. SSW of Fukushima, in horse-breeding and agr. area; mfg. (yarn, textiles, pottery). Hot springs near by. Sometimes spelled Nihonmatu.

Nihtaur (nē'tour), town (pop. 12,549), Bijnor dist., N Uttar Pradesh, India, 16 mi. ESE of Bijnor; road junction; sugar refining; rice, wheat, gram, sugar cane.

Nihuil (nēwēl'), village (pop. estimate 300), central Mendoza prov., Argentina, on Atuel R. and 40 mi. SW of San Rafael; irrigation dam begun here1942.

Niigata (nē'gätä), prefecture [Jap. *ken*] (□ 4,856; 1940 pop. 2,064,402; 1947 pop. 2,418,271), central and N Honshu, Japan; ⊙ Niigata, its port. Bounded W by Sea of Japan; includes Sado Isl. Partly mountainous terrain; Shinano R. drains large fertile plain producing rice and tea. Oil field in W coast area. Fishing, gold and silver mining (on Sado Isl.), raw-silk culture, mfg. of textiles and lacquer ware. Principal centers: Niigata, KASHIWAZAKI (oil refining), NAGAOKA (heavy industry), TAKADA, SANJO.

Niigata, city (1940 pop. 150,903; 1947 pop. 204,477), ⊙ Niigata prefecture, N Honshu, Japan, on Sea of Japan, 160 mi. NNW of Tokyo, at mouth of Shinano R.; 37°55'N 139°3'E. Principal port of W coast; industrial center (refined oil, machinery, textiles, metalwork, chemicals). Because it is poorly sheltered by low sand hills, the city's winter port is RYOTSU on Sado Isl. Principal exports: oil, machinery, textiles. Named in U.S.-Japanese treaty of 1858 as one of 3 ports to be opened to foreign trade; its opening delayed until 1868.

Niihama (nē'hämä), city (1940 pop. 42,392; 1947 pop. 51,930), Ehime prefecture, N Shikoku, Japan, port on Hiuchi Sea (central section of Inland Sea), 30 mi. ENE of Matsuyama. Industrial center for Besshi copper field, with copper refineries. Exports copper, fertilizer.

Niihau (nē'hou), island (□ 72; 1940 pop. 182), T.H., SW of Kauai, across Kaulakahi Channel; 18 mi. long, 6 mi. wide; privately owned. Mostly arid lowland, except on rocky E side. Cattle grazing; Niihau mats, made from rushes, are best in the Territory.

Nii-jima (nē'jĭmä), volcanic island (□ 11; pop. 5,012, including near-by isls.) of isl. group Izu-shichito, Greater Tokyo, Japan, in Philippine Sea, 19 mi. SSW of O-shima; 7 mi. long, 2 mi. wide. Hilly; rises to 1,404 ft. Produces camellia oil, charcoal, grain; stock raising, dairying. Honmura, on W coast, is chief settlement. Near-by Shikine-jima (2 mi. long, 1 mi. wide) has hot springs.

Niikura, Japan: see YAMATO, Saitama prefecture.

Niimi (nē'mē), town (pop. 7,374), Okayama prefecture, SW Honshu, Japan, 35 mi. NW of Okayama; rail junction in agr. area (rice, wheat, persimmons); sake, charcoal, *konnyaku* (paste made from devil's tongue).

Niirala (nē'rälä), village in Värtsilä commune (pop. 1,634), Kuopio co., SE Finland, 40 mi. SE of Joensuu; frontier station on USSR border, opposite Vyartsilya.

Niitaka-yama, Formosa: see MORRISON, MOUNT.

Niitoi, Russian SFSR: see NOVOYE.

Niitsu (nē'tsōō), town (pop. 36,053), Niigata prefecture, central Honshu, Japan, 9 mi. SSE of Niigata; distribution center for agr. area; textiles, sake. Oil field near by.

Níjar (nē'här), town (pop. 1,925), Almería prov., S Spain, 17 mi. NE of Almería; mfg. of porcelain, knitwear; olive-oil processing, flour milling. Esparto, cereals, almonds, lumber. Silver-bearing lead, gold, garnet mines, and clay quarries in vicinity.

Nijkerk (nī'kĕrk), town (pop. 6,652), Gelderland prov., central Netherlands, 6 mi. NE of Amersfoort, near the Ijsselmeer; mfg. (baskets, furniture, boxes, brooms); egg, poultry, dairy, and cattle market. Connected by canal with harbor on the Ijsselmeer. Town since 1413. Sometimes spelled Nykerk or Nieuwkerk.

Nijlen (nī'lŭn), town (pop. 7,121), Antwerp prov., N Belgium, 13 mi. ESE of Antwerp; agr. market (vegetables, potatoes).

Nijmegen (nī'măgŭn, Du. -khŭn), Ger. *Nimwegen* (nĭm'vāgŭn), anc. *Noviomagus*, city (pop. 106,523), Gelderland prov., E Netherlands, on Waal R. (bridge) and 10 mi. SSW of Arnhem, near Maas-Waal Canal; rail junction, frontier station on Ger. border; inland shipping center. Mfg. of ceramics, shoes, plastics, artificial silk, electrical and photographic equipment, clothing, agr. machinery, food products. Has 13th-cent. Groote Kerk, 16th-cent. town hall, the Kerkboog (vaulted passage), 16th-cent. Latin school, 17th-cent. weighhouse, remains of palace Valkhof (built 777 by Charlemagne, rebuilt 1165 by Frederick Barbarossa). Town chartered in 1184; became free imperial city (Reichsstadt); later joined Hanseatic League; subscribed (1579) to Union of Utrecht. The Treaty of Nijmegen, ending Third Dutch War, was negotiated here (1678–79) bet. the Netherlands, France, Spain, and the Holy Roman Empire. In Second World War, scene (1944) of U.S. airborne landing. Sometimes spelled Nijmwegen; formerly spelled Nimeguen, Nymegen, and Nymwegen.

Nijvel, Belgium: see NIVELLES.

Nijverdal (nī'vŭrdäl), town (pop. 9,614), Overijssel prov., E Netherlands, 19 mi. SE of Zwolle; cotton weaving and bleaching. Sometimes spelled Nyverdal, Nijverdaal, or Nyverdaal.

Nikaia, Greece: see NEA KOKKINIA.

Nikaria, Greece: see ICARIA.

Nikel or **Nikel'** (nyē'kĭl). **1** Rail station, Chkalov oblast, Russian SFSR: see ORSK. **2** Town (1946 pop. over 500), NW Murmansk oblast, Russian SFSR, 5 mi. SE of Salmiyarvi, in Pechenga dist.; nickel-mining center; developed after 1935. Called Kolosjoki until ceded (1944) by Finland to USSR.

Nikel-Tau or **Nikel'-Tau** (-tou'), village (1945 pop. over 500), N Aktyubinsk oblast, Kazakh SSR, on railroad and 45 mi. ENE of Aktyubinsk, in nickel-mining area. Junction of rail spur to Donskoye chromium mine.

Nikesiane or **Nikisiani** (both: nĭkē'sēänē), town (pop. 3,257), Kavalla nome, Macedonia, Greece, at E foot of Mt. Pangaion, 14 mi. W of Kavalla; tobacco, corn.

Niketsu, Formosa: see ERHKIEH.

Nikhab, Egypt: see KAB, EL.

Nikheila, El Nikheila, En Nikheila, or **Al-Nikhaylah** (all: ĕn-nĭkhā'lū), village (pop. 17,736), Asyut prov., central Upper Egypt, on W bank of the Nile, on railroad, and 2 mi. S of Abu Tig; pottery making, wood and ivory carving; cereals, dates, sugar cane. Also spelled Nekhela.

Nikiforovka (nyĭkē'fŭrŭfkŭ), village (1939 pop. over 500), W Tambov oblast, Russian SFSR, 10 mi. E of Michurinsk; cardboard mill.

Nikisiani, Greece: see NIKESIANE.

Nikitinka (nyĭkē'tyĭnkŭ), village (1939 pop. over 500), W East Kazakhstan oblast, Kazakh SSR, in Kalba Range, 35 mi. S of Ust-Kamenogorsk; gold mining.

Nikitovka (nyĭkē'tŭfkŭ). **1** Village (1939 pop. 283), W Kaliningrad oblast, Russian SFSR, 15 mi. NW of Kaliningrad; narrow-gauge rail junction. Until 1945, in East Prussia and called Marienhof (märē'-ŭnhōf). **2** Village (1926 pop. 6,111), SW Voronezh oblast, Russian SFSR, 17 mi. NE of Valuiki; wheat. **3** City (1939 pop. over 10,000), central Stalino oblast, Ukrainian SSR, in the Donbas, 3 mi. NNW (under jurisdiction) of Gorlovka; rail center; limestone (dolomite) quarries, chemical works; mercury refinery (mines 3 mi. W).

Nikitsch (nĭ'kĭch), village (pop. 1,922), Burgenland, E Austria, 11 mi. SSE of Sopron, Hungary; sugar beets.

Nikki (nĭ'kē), town (pop. c.3,000), E central Dahomey, Fr. West Africa, on motor road and 55 mi. NE of Parakou; ginning of kapok and cotton.

Nikko (nēk'kō), town (pop. 27,931), Tochigi prefecture, central Honshu, Japan, 20 mi. NW of Utsunomiya, in Nikko Natl. Park; tourist resort; religious center. Tosho-gu (17th-cent. shrine known for its architectural splendor) houses tomb of Ieyasu. His grandson Iemitsu is also buried here. Shrines on summits of near-by mts.

Nikko National Park (□ 220), central Honshu, Japan, in Tochigi and Gumma prefectures, in mtn. area with cryptomeria forests, scenic waterfalls, hot springs. L. Chuzenji is notable.

Nikla el 'Inab or **Nikla al-'Inab** (both: nĭklăl' ĭnăb'), village (pop. 7,885), Beheira prov., Lower Egypt, on Rosetta branch of the Nile and 6 mi. ENE of Teh el Barud; cotton, rice, cereals.

Niklasdorf (nĭ'kläsdôrf), town (pop. 3,141), Styria, SE central Austria, on Mur R. and 3 mi. E of Leoben; lumber and paper mills; cellulcse, paper products.

Nikolaev-, in Rus. names: see NIKOLAYEV-.

Nikolai (nĭ'kŭlī), village (pop. 64), S central Alaska, in upper reaches of Kuskokwim R., 45 mi. E of McGrath.

Nikolai, Poland: see MIKOLOW.

Nikolaiken, Poland: see MIKOLAJKI.

Nikolainkaupunki, Finland: see VAASA.

Nikolaistad, Finland: see VAASA.

Nikolaital (nē'kōlĭtäl"), valley in Pennine Alps, S Switzerland, extending along Mattervisp R. (a headstream of the Visp) from N of Zermatt to S of Visp.

Nikolayev (nyĭkŭlī'ŭf), oblast (□ 7,500; 1946 pop. estimate 800,000), S Ukrainian SSR; ⊙ Nikolayev. In Black Sea Lowland; bounded S by Black Sea; drained by lower Southern Bug and Ingul rivers; steppe region. Cotton and wheat are chief crops; castor beans and sunflowers (N); truck produce near Nikolayev; dairy farming. Nikolayev is major port and industrial center. Flour milling, dairying, sugar refining in rural areas. Formed 1937.

Nikolayev **1** Pol. *Mikolajów* (mēkôwĭ'ōōf), city (1931 pop. 3,630), NE Drogobych oblast, Ukrainian SSR, 24 mi. NE of Drogobych; ceramics (pottery, tiles, bricks). Has old town hall and churches. Founded in 1552; passed from Poland to Austria (1772); reverted to Poland (1919); ceded to USSR in 1945. **2** Village (1926 pop. 2,994), central Kamenets-Podolski oblast, Ukrainian SSR, 13 mi. NW of Proskurov; sugar beets, wheat. **3** City (1939 pop. 167,108), ⊙ Nikolayev oblast, Ukrainian SSR, port on lower Southern Bug R., at mouth of Ingul R., and 65 mi. NE of Odessa, 250 mi. SSE of Kiev; 46°58'N 32°E. Major Black Sea port; shipbuilding center; next to Leningrad, site of most extensive shipyards in USSR; flour mills; mfg. of road-building machines. Naval construction school, teachers col. Exports grain, sugar, iron ore, manganese ore. Founded 1784 by Russians on site of anc. Gr. colony of Olbia; rapidly grew into one of chief Rus. Black Sea naval bases. Opened to commercial trade in 1862, when it became a major grain port. Sometimes (in early 1930s) called Vernoleninsk. In Second World War, held (1941–43) by Germans.

Nikolayevka (nyĭkŭlī'ŭfkŭ). **1** Town (1948 pop. over 2,000), NE Jewish Autonomous Oblast, Russian SFSR, on Trans-Siberian RR and 13 mi. W of Khabarovsk; sawmilling. **2** Village (1939 pop. over 2,000), SW Ulyanovsk oblast, Russian SFSR, 25 mi. E of Kuznetsk; grain, legumes. Limestone and chalk quarries near by (S). **3** Town (1926 pop. 2,248), central Dnepropetrovsk oblast, Ukrainian SSR, on left bank of Dnieper R. and 10 mi. W of Dnepropetrovsk. **4** Town (1926 pop. 2,054), W Voroshilovgrad oblast, Ukrainian SSR, in the Donbas, 11 mi. SSW of Lisichansk; coal mines.

Nikolayevka Vtoraya (ftŭrī'ŭ) [Rus.,=Nikolayevka No. 2], village (1926 pop. 2,281), E central Odessa oblast, Ukrainian SSR, 22 mi. NNW of Berezovka; wheat.

Nikolayevsk (nyĭkŭlī'ŭfsk). **1** or **Nikolayevsk-on-Amur** (–ämōōr'), Rus. *Nikolayevsk-na-Amur*, city (1948 pop. over 50,000), ⊙ Lower Amur oblast, Khabarovsk Territory, Russian SFSR, port on Amur R. and 25 mi. above its mouth, 400 mi. NNE of Khabarovsk; 53°10'N 140°45'E. Center of fishing, gold-mining, and fur-collecting area; oil refining, shipbuilding, fish canning. An air-transport center and important port of Soviet Far East, although frozen 6½ months annually. Iron deposits near by. Founded 1850; leading Rus. city in Far East until rise of Khabarovsk after 1880; nearly destroyed (1920) during civil war. Naval base was transferred in 1920s to Sovetskaya Gavan. **2** City, Saratov oblast, Russian SFSR: see PUGACHEV. **3** Town, Stalingrad oblast, Russian SFSR: see NIKOLAYEVSKI.

Nikolayevskaya (–skīŭ). **1** Village (1939 pop. over 2,000), central Rostov oblast, Russian SFSR, on right bank of Don R. and 60 mi. E of Shakhty; metalworks; wheat, orchards, vineyards. **2** Town, Stalingrad oblast, Russian SFSR: see NIKOLAYEVSKI.

Nikolayevski or **Nikolayevskiy** (–skē), town (1926 pop. 19,225), NE Stalingrad oblast, Russian SFSR, on left bank of Volga R., opposite Kamyshin; dairying, sunflower-oil extraction. Until 1936, called Nikolayevsk, and, 1936–c.1940, Nikolayevskaya.

Nikolayevskoye (–skŭyŭ), village (1929 pop. over 500), N Adyge Autonomous Oblast, Krasnodar Territory, Russian SFSR, 7 mi. SW of Ust-Labinskaya; sunflower oil, tobacco.

Nikolo-Berezovka (nyĭkô'lŭ-bĕrĭzôf'kŭ), village (1948 pop. over 2,000), NW Bashkir Autonomous SSR, Russian SFSR, on left bank of Kama R. (landing) and 70 mi. NW of Birsk; flour milling, sawmilling. Formerly Nikolo-Berezovskoye.

Nikologory (nyĕkŭlŭgô'rē), town (1926 pop. 1,552), E Vladimir oblast, Russian SFSR, 10 mi. SW of Vyazniki; linen milling.

Nikolo-Pavdinski Zavod, Russian SFSR: see PAVDA.

Nikolopavlovskoye (nyĭkô'lŭpäv'lŭfskŭyŭ), village (1926 pop. 4,638), W central Sverdlovsk oblast, Russian SFSR, on Tagil R. and 10 mi. S of Nizhni Tagil, on railroad; truck, stock. Site until c.1928 of ironworks called Nikolaye-Pavlovski Zavod.

Nikolo-Svekhsvyatskoye, Russian SFSR: see NIKOLSKI.

Nikolsburg, Czechoslovakia: see MIKULOV.

Nikolsk or **Nikol'sk** (nyĭkôlsk'), city (1926 pop. 3,100), SE Vologda oblast, Russian SFSR, on Yug R. (head of navigation), on Sharya-Kotlas road and 90 mi. SSW of Veliki Ustyug, in flax area; dairying, metalworking. Chartered 1780.

Nikolskaya Pestravka or **Nikol'skaya Pestravka** (–kôl'skīŭ pyĭsträf'kŭ), town (1944 pop. over 10,000), NE Penza oblast, Russian SFSR, 55 mi. NE of Penza, in forested grain and hemp area; glassworking center; sawmilling.

Nikolski (nĭkŏl'skē), village (pop. 64), SW Umnak Isl., Aleutian Isls., SW Alaska, 80 mi. SW of Kashega; 52°55'N 168°47'W. Has church and school. Supply center for ships in the N Pacific and Bering Sea, and sheep ranchers and fox farmers on isl.; base for sealing operations in Pribilof Isls.

Nikolski or **Nikol'skiy** (nyĭkôl'skē), town (pop. over 500), central Moscow oblast, Russian SFSR, adjoining (NW of) Moscow, on SE bank of its N port. Until 1938, Nikolo-Svekhsvyatskoye.

Nikolski Khutor or **Nikol'skiy Khutor** (khōō'tŭr), town (1932 pop. estimated 5,200), E central Penza oblast, Russian SFSR, on Sura R. and 30 mi. ESE of Penza; woolen milling.

Nikolskoye or **Nikol'skoye** (nyĭkôl'skŭyŭ). **1** Village (1926 pop. 6,418), N Astrakhan oblast, Russian SFSR, on right bank of Volga R. (landing) and 120 mi. NNW of Astrakhan; fruit, cotton, wheat; cattle, sheep. **2** Village (1939 pop. over 500), N central Chkalov oblast, Russian SFSR, on Sakmara R. and 30 mi. NE of Chkalov; metalworking; wheat, livestock. **3** Chief village (1948 pop. over 500) of Komandorski Isls., Kamchatka oblast, Khabarovsk Territory, Russian SFSR, on NW Bering Isl. **4** Village (1939 pop. over 2,000), S Orel oblast, Russian SFSR, 8 mi. SSE of Livny; potatoes. **5** or **Nikolskoye na Cheremshane** or **Nikol'skoye na Cheremshane** (nŭ chĕrĭmshä'nyĭ), village (1926 pop. 2,535), NE Ulyanovsk oblast, Russian SFSR, on Greater Cheremshan R. and 38 mi. SE of Ulyanovsk; flour milling, distilling; wheat, orchards. **6** Village (1926 pop. 304), W central Vologda oblast, Russian SFSR, on railroad, on Sheksna R. and 22 mi. ENE of Cherepovets; flax retting, dairying.

Nikolsk-Ussuriski, Russian SFSR: see VOROSHILOV.

Nikopol (nĭkô'pŏl), anc. *Nicopolis*, city (pop. 5,409), Pleven dist., N Bulgaria, port on right bank of the Danube (Rum. border) opposite Turnu-Magurele, near mouth of Osam R., and 23 mi. NE of Pleven, in agr. area (grain, livestock). Has 13th-cent. church, ruins of fortifications. Founded A.D. 629 by Byzantine Emperor Heraclius. Sigismund, King of Hungary, defeated here (1396) by Turkish sultan Bajazet I. Became important cultural center during 2d Bulg. Kingdom. A city with c.10,000 pop., it was fortified under Turkish rule (15th–19th cent.); subjected to several 19th-cent. Rus. invasions. Declined following rise of Somovit. Sometimes identified with Nicopolis ad Istrum, which was located at present site of NIKYUP. Formerly spelled Nikopoli.

Nikopol or **Nikopol'** (nyĭkô'pŭl), city (1926 pop. 14,214; 1939 pop. 57,841) S Dnepropetrovsk oblast, Ukrainian SSR, on right bank of Dnieper R. and 65 mi. SSW of Dnepropetrovsk; center of major manganese-mining dist.; large pipe-rolling mills, machinery works (grain-elevator, transportation equipment), ship repair yards, iron foundry, flour mills. Teachers col. Manganese mines extend NW of Nikopol to ORDZHONIKIDZE and also center around MARGANETS (NE).

Nikosia, Cyprus: see NICOSIA.

Niksar (nĭksär'), anc. *Neocaesarea*, town (pop. 6,942), Tokat prov., N central Turkey, on Kelkit R. and 28 mi. NE of Tokat; grain. Anc. Neocaesarea was important town of Pontus. There are Roman and Byzantine remains.

Nikshahr (nēkshä'hŭr), village (1945 pop. 1,900), Eighth Prov., in Makran, SE Iran, 65 mi. N of Chahbahar; dates, rice, grain; camel grazing. Formerly known as Qasrqand.

Niksic or **Nikshich** (both: nēk'shĭch), Serbo-Croatian *Nikšić*, town (pop. 6,686), W Montenegro, Yugoslavia, near Zeta R., on narrow-gauge railroad and 28 mi. NNW of Titograd; local trade and cultural center. Has Roman bridge and a church built by Russian Emperor Nicholas II. Town probably dates from 6th cent. Once called Ogonoste; under Turkish rule (until 1878), in Herzegovina.

Nikumaroro, Phoenix Isls.: see GARDNER ISLAND.

Nikunau (nēkōōnou'), atoll (□ 7; pop. 1,592), N Gilbert Isls., W central Pacific; 1°23'S 176°26'E; discovered 1765 by Byron. Also called Nukunau; formerly Byron Isl.

Nikyup (nĭkyōōp'), village (pop. 1,824), Gorna Oryakhovitsa dist., N Bulgaria, 9 mi. NNW of Gorna Oryakhovitsa; flour milling; livestock raising. Site of ruins of anc. Roman town Nicopolis ad Istrum, which existed up to A.D. 600 and is sometimes identified with NIKOPOL.

Nilai (nēlī'), village (pop. 581), W Negri Sembilan, Malaya, on railroad and 11 mi. NW of Seremban, near Selangor line; rubber, rice.

Nilakkottai (nĭlŭk'kōt-tī), village, Madura dist., S Madras, India, 25 mi. NW of Madura; grain, sesame.

Nilambur, India: see SHORANUR.

Niland (nī'lŭnd), village (1940 pop. 627), Imperial co., S Calif., 18 mi. N of Brawley, at N end of IMPERIAL VALLEY; citrus fruit, truck.

Nilandu Atoll (nīlŭn'dōō), central group (pop. 3,670) of Maldive Isls., in Indian Ocean, bet. 2°40'N and 3°21'N; coconuts.

Nilanga (nĭlŭng'gŭ), town (pop. 5,234), Bidar dist., W central Hyderabad state, India, 50 mi. WNW of Bidar; millet, cotton, rice, sugar cane.

Nilaveli (nĭlŭvä'lē), village (pop. 1,555), Eastern Prov., Ceylon, on NE coast, 8 mi. N of Trincomalee; coconut-palm plantations, vegetable gardens. Has major saltern of NE coast.

Nil Desperandum (nĕl' dĕspŭrăn'dŭm), township (pop. 259), Gwelo prov., S central Southern Rhodesia, in Matabeleland, 2 mi. ESE of Shabani; asbestos mining.

Nile River (nīl), Arabic *Bahr en Nil*, *Bahr el Nil*, or *Bahr al-Nil* (all: bä'hŭr ĕn-nēl'), colloquially in Egypt *El Bahr*, Lat. *Nilus*, Gr. *Neilos*, longest river of Africa and, measured from its remotest headstream (Luvironza R.), the longest river in the world (over 4,150 mi.); from L. Victoria (often considered its source) its length is 3,485 mi. The Nile system drains a basin of over 1,100,000 sq. mi. bet. 4°S and 31°N in E central and NE Africa, the White Nile collecting the run-off of the well-watered lake region of Uganda, Ruanda-Urundi, and Tanganyika, and the Blue Nile draining the Ethiopian highlands. It flows N across the desert belt of N Anglo-Egyptian Sudan and Egypt to the E Mediterranean, where it forms a delta (100 mi. N–S, 150 mi. E–W) bounded by Cairo (S), Port Said (E), and Alexandria (W). The White Nile and the Blue Nile unite at Khartoum (1,875 mi. upstream) to form the main Nile, whose lower course and delta irrigate some 13,000 sq. mi., representing almost all of Egypt which is not desert. The White Nile is known by several names in its upper course. Above L. Victoria is the Kagera, which receives the Ruvuvu, in turn receiving the Luvironza; the Luvironza rises in Ruanda-Urundi just E of the Great Rift Valley (here containing L. Tanganyika) at 3°48'S 29°42'E. Issuing from L. Victoria (alt. 3,720 ft.; Africa's largest natural reservoir) at Jinja, the stream, now called the Victoria Nile, at once descends over RIPON FALLS and (1.5 mi. downstream) over OWEN FALLS; continuing generally NW, it traverses marshy L. Kyoga and, dropping over MURCHISON FALLS, reaches L. Albert (alt. 2,030 ft.) in W Great Rift Valley. It leaves N tip of L. Albert as the Albert Nile just W of influx of Victoria Nile and flows N (henceforth the Nile's dominant direction), crossing Uganda–Anglo-Egyptian Sudan border at Nimule, where it becomes the Bahr el Jebel. Beyond Juba, the river spreads out in the SUDD marshes, losing half of its waters through evaporation and dispersal. At L. No (9°30'N) it is joined by the Bahr el Ghazal, and is henceforth called only the White Nile; above Malakal it receives the Sobat (which drains E Ethiopian highlands) and continues N, past Kodok (formerly Fashoda), Kosti (railroad bridge), and the GEZIRA irrigation scheme to Khartoum. Here it meets the Blue Nile, which, over 900 mi. NNE of the White Nile's source, issues from SE end of L. Tana (alt. c.6,000 ft. in Ethiopian highlands) and, after an initial SE bend, flows 1,000 mi. NW, past SENNAR (dam, railroad bridge), Wad Medani, and the E edge of the Gezira, to Khartoum. The combined Nile then enters the arid portion of its course, flanked by the Nubian (E) and Libyan (W) deserts in Anglo-Egyptian Sudan, and by the Arabian (E) and Western deserts in Egypt. In this stretch, marked by a narrow entrenched valley as far as Aswan, the main Nile receives its only tributary, the Atbara (from N Ethiopian highlands), while still 1,675 mi. from the sea. Thence, in a great S-shaped bend it reaches Egyptian border below Wadi Halfa and continues 950 mi. N, past Aswan, the ruins of Luxor and Karnak (site of anc. Thebes), and, in a widening valley never exceeding 12 mi. in width, past Asyut, Minya, Beni Suef, Memphis, and Giza, to Cairo, at the head of the delta. The delta, which in anc. times had 7 major mouths, now consists of 2 main channels, the Rosetta (W) and Damietta (E), each c.150 mi. long. In its narrow valley bet. Khartoum (alt. 1,217 ft.) and Aswan (alt. 282 ft.) the Nile drops 935 ft. in a series of 6 rapids (called cataracts), numbered consecutively N–S: 1st at ASWAN (site of dam, locks), 2d above Wadi Halfa, 3d below Kerma (20°N), 4th above Kareima (18°N), 5th below Berber, and 6th (or Sabaluka Cataract) above Wad Hamid, 50 mi. N of Khartoum. Accordingly, bet. Wadi Halfa and Khartoum the river is not navigable (except for section bet. 3d and 4th cataracts). Elsewhere, however, the Nile is navigable at almost all seasons, direct steamship service existing bet. Alexandria (linked to Rosetta mouth by Mahmudiya Canal) and Wadi Halfa, and again bet. Khartoum and Juba on the White Nile. Bet. Juba and Nimule a road by-passes the rapids of the Bahr el Jebel, and above Nimule the Albert Nile is navigable to L. Albert. On the Victoria Nile navigation is limited to the L. Kyoga section. The Blue Nile can be ascended 400 mi. from Khartoum to Roseires (near Ethiopian border). The Nile is paralleled by a railroad bet. Cairo and Shallal (just above Aswan), and again bet. Wadi Halfa and Khartoum (cataract section), where the railroad cuts off the river's great bend across Nubian Desert. Down to 15th cent. the Nile's source, believed to be in the "Mountains of the Moon" (RUWENZORI), was a mystery, and no explanation existed for the river's periodic floods, when the flow in the main Nile at flood's peak (late Aug. and early Sept.) is 16 times that of its lowest stage, in April. Over ½ of yearly volume passes bet. mid-July and Sept. Bet. Jan. and July, when flow is ⅕ of yearly volume, no water passes the bars at delta's mouths. The flood stage is due to the abundant waters of the Blue Nile, which reflect the heavy precipitation of the monsoon season in Ethiopia. The White Nile's flow, regulated by the great lakes and the diversion in the Sudd, is even the year round. As a result, contributions of the branches to the main Nile volume vary as follows: at flood time, the Blue Nile contributes 68%, the White Nile and Sobat R. 10%, the Atbara 22%; at low water, 17% comes from the Blue Nile and 83% from the White Nile. Most of the fertile soil which for ages has been carried down the Nile and deposited in the valley during flood time originates, therefore, in the Ethiopian highlands. Attempts to harness the floodwaters date back to 4000 B.C. when the system of basin irrigation, still in use today, was 1st initiated. Storage of Nile waters for perennial irrigation is now effected in Aswan, Sennar, and Jebel Aulia reservoirs (combined capacity over 220,000,000,000 cu. yds.). A series of barrages (diversion dams) in Egypt (at Isna, Nag Hammadi, Asyut, Zifta, and at head of delta below Cairo) lead Nile waters into an extensive net of irrigation canals along the river's floodplain and into the Faiyum basin. These works are insufficient, however, to eliminate yearly fluctuations and to increase irrigable areas for the rapidly-increasing Egyptian pop. A project to create long-range storage reservoirs by damming outlets of great lakes in watershed area (lakes Victoria, Kyoga, Albert, Tana) was initiated in 1949 by the start of construction of a dam and hydroelectric plant at Owen Falls on the Victoria Nile. This project further envisages a drainage and diversion canal by-passing the Sudd bet. Jonglei and Malakal, and the construction of large dams along the entrenched course of the main Nile in N Anglo-Egyptian Sudan. The Nile's upper reaches were 1st explored by Portuguese travelers in 15th–17th cent. The source (L. Tana) of the Blue Nile was discovered c.1770 by James Bruce, that of the White Nile (L. Victoria) by John Speke in 1858. Sir Samuel Baker discovered L. Albert and Murchison Falls in 1864. The battle of the Nile was fought in ABUKIR BAY.

For further details of the Nile system see WHITE NILE, BLUE NILE, BAHR EL JEBEL, BAHR EL GHAZAL, BAHR EL ZERAF, ALBERT NILE, VICTORIA NILE, and articles on tributaries and lakes.

Niles (nīlz). **1** Village (pop. 1,519), Alameda co., W Calif., 23 mi. SE of Oakland, in dairying and fruit-growing area; tile and pottery works, cannery; large nursery. Niles Canyon (E) is recreational area. **2** Village (pop. 3,587), Cook co., NE Ill., NW suburb of Chicago, 7 mi. WSW of Evanston. Inc. 1899. **3** City (pop. 13,145), Berrien co., extreme SW Mich., 11 mi. N of South Bend (Ind.) and on St. Joseph R., in fruit- and grain-growing, and dairying area. Mfg. (refrigeration equipment, metal plating, furniture, wire, cable, leather and paper products, foodstuffs). Mushroom growing. Niles has existed under the flags of France, Britain, Spain, and U.S. A Jesuit mission was established here in 1690 and a Fr. fort in 1697; before its final abandonment, fort fell to British in 1761, to Indians (Pontiac's Rebellion) in 1763, and to Spanish and Indians in 1780–81. Settled permanently in 1827; inc. as village 1838, as city 1859. **4** Industrial city (pop. 16,773), Trumbull co., NE Ohio, on Mahoning R. at mouth of Mosquito Creek, and 8 mi. NW of Youngstown; iron and steel mills; also mfg. of electric-light bulbs, metal products, chemicals, railroad equipment. Has memorial to William McKinley, b. here in 1843. Settled 1806.

Niles Center, Ill.: see SKOKIE.

Nileshwar, India: see KASARAGOD.

Nilgiri (nēl′gĭrē), former princely state (□ 263; pop. 73,109) in Orissa States, India; ⊙ was Raj Nilgiri. Inc. 1949 into Balasore dist.

Nilgiri or **Nilgiris** (–rēs), Tamil *Nilagiri* [=blue hills], district (□ 989; pop. 209,709), SW Madras, India; ⊙ Ootacamund. Consists mainly of NILGIRI HILLS (E), with SE portion of the WYNAAD in NW. Numerous mtn. streams (trout, mahseer, carp) drain into Moyar (N) and Bhavani (on SE border) rivers. Temperate-zone flower and vegetable gardens and experimental farms; millet, wheat, barley, Pyrethrum. Important cinchona plantations (main quinine factory at Naduvattam); numerous eucalyptus, tea, and coffee estates. Headworks of hydroelectric system at Pykara. Main towns: Ootacamund, Coonoor, Kotagiri. Pop. 30% hill tribe (including Kotas and Todas). Formerly spelled Neilgherry.

Nilgiri Hills or **The Nilgiris,** steep plateau adjoining S Deccan Plateau at convergence of Eastern and Western Ghats, in SW Madras, India; form main (E) part of Nilgiri dist.; average height, 6,500 ft. Include several peaks over 8,000 ft.; rise to 8,640 ft. in Dodabetta mtn. Moyar R. rises on Mukurti peak. Extensive cinchona, eucalyptus, tea, and coffee plantations; teak, blackwood, bamboo; building-stone quarries, lignite deposits. Gold placers in mtn. streams. Game includes panther, Nilgiri ibex, antelope, and bear. Separated from Anaimalai Hills (S) by Palghat Gap. Formerly spelled Neilgherry.

Nilikluguk (nĭlĭ′klōō′gŏŏk), village (pop. 40), SW Alaska, near Bethel.

Nilkantha, Nepal: see KATMANDU.

Nilópolis (nēlô′pŏŏlēs), suburb (1950 pop. 31,192) of Rio de Janeiro, Brazil, Rio de Janeiro state, 15 mi. from city center, on Federal Dist. border. Metallurgical plants. Orange groves.

Nilphamari (nĭlpä′märē), town (pop. 8,201), Rangpur dist., N East Bengal, E Pakistan, 29 mi. WNW of Rangpur; trades in rice, jute, tobacco, oilseeds; hosiery mfg.

Nilufer River (nĭlüfĕr′), Turkish *Nilüfer*, NW Turkey, rises on Ulu Dag 11 mi. SE of Bursa, flows 60 mi. N and W, past Bursa, to Simav R. 7 mi. NE of Karacabey.

Nilus, Africa: see NILE RIVER.

Nilvange (nĕlväzh′), town (pop. 7,257), Moselle dept., NE France, 5 mi. WSW of Thionville; blast furnaces, forges.

Nilwood, town (pop. 321), Macoupin co., SW central Ill., 28 mi. SSW of Springfield, in agr. and bituminous-coal area.

Nima (nē′mä), town (pop. 3,375), Shimane prefecture, SW Honshu, Japan, on Sea of Japan, 26 mi. WSW of Matsue; silk textiles, rice, raw silk.

Nimach or **Neemuch** (nē′mŭch), town (pop., including cantonment area, 17,074), NW Madhya Bharat, India, 30 mi. NNW of Mandasor; trades in wheat, cotton, opium, building stone; hand-loom weaving; airport. In 1857, Sepoys stationed here rebelled. Formerly in Gwalior state.

Nimaj (nē′mäj), town (pop. 5,728), central Rajasthan, India, 60 mi. ESE of Jodhpur; millet, wheat, gram, oilseeds.

Nimar (nĭmär′). **1** District, SW Madhya Bharat, India; ⊙ Khargon. **2** District (□ 4,228; pop. 513,276), W Madhya Pradesh, India, on Deccan Plateau; ⊙ Khandwa. In broad valleys of Narbada R. (N) and Tapti R. (S); bordered N and W by Madhya Bharat. Cotton, millet, wheat, oilseeds in alluvial river valleys; mahua, date palms, mangoes. Teak, salai, and a hardwood tree (pulp used in newsprint plant at Chandni) in dense forests, largely on Satpura Range (S, SW); lac cultivation. Cotton ginning, sawmilling, oilseed milling; cattle raising; sandstone quarrying. Burhanpur (Deccan hq. of Mogul empire in early-17th cent.) is cotton-textile and -trade center. Industrial school and experimental farm (silk growing) at Khandwa, also a cotton-trade center. Noted temples at Godarpura. Enclave of dist. lies in Madhya Bharat. Pop. 64% Hindu, 22% tribal (Bhils, Gonds), 12% Moslem.

Nimbahera (nēm′bŭhä′rŭ), town (pop. 6,898), S Rajasthan, India, 65 mi. E of Udaipur; agr. market (millet, corn, wheat, oilseeds); cotton ginning; handicraft metal utensils. Sandstone quarries SW.

Nimba Mountains, in W African bulge along Liberia–Ivory Coast–Fr. Guinea border; highest alt., 6,000 ft.

Nimbi, Nigeria: see NEMBE.

Nimbschen, Germany: see GRIMMA.

Nimbus, Mount, Colo.: see NEVER SUMMER MOUNTAINS.

Nimeguen, Netherlands: see NIJMEGEN.

Nîmes (nēmz, Fr. nēm), anc. *Nemausus*, city (pop. 75,398), ⊙ Gard dept., S France, 60 mi. NW of Marseilles; commercial and industrial center well-known for its numerous Roman relics. Produces shoes, hosiery (cotton and silk), clothing, rugs, and upholstery. There are foundries, metalworks (agr. equipment, automobile chassis), tanneries, distilleries, and oil-processing plants. Active trade bet. CÉVENNES (metallurgy, textiles) and lower Rhone valley (fruit- and winegrowing) converges at Nîmes. Leading points of interest: the perfectly preserved Roman arena (1st cent. A.D.) still in use, and the Maison Carrée [square house], a remarkable Corinthian temple (1st or 2d cent. A.D.), which now houses a mus. of antiquities. The Tour Magne, a watchtower built c.50 B.C., overlooks the city from atop a hill. At its foot is an 18th-cent. park (Jardin de la Fontaine) which contains a temple of Diana (2d cent. A.D.) and the spring (dedicated to Nemausus by the Romans) to which the city owes its name. The famous PONT DU GARD is 12 mi. NE. Founded by Augustus, Nîmes became one of the finest cities of the Roman Empire. The medieval viscounty of Nîmes was incorporated into the royal domain in 1271. The city became a stronghold of Protestantism and suffered economically from the revocation of the Edict of Nantes. It was only slightly damaged during Second World War. Alphonse Daudet b. here. Old spelling, Nismes.

Nimfaion, Cape, Greece: see NYMPHAION, CAPE.

Nimis (nē′mēs), village (pop. 2,449), Udine prov., Friuli-Venezia Giulia, N Italy, 10 mi. N of Udine; alcohol distillery.

Nim-ka-Thana (nēm′-kä-tä′nŭ), town (pop. 6,967), E Rajasthan, India, 55 mi. N of Jaipur; millet, barley.

Nimkhar (nēm′kär) or **Nimsar** (nēm′sär), since 1948 officially **Naimisharanya** (nīmēshä′rŭnyŭ), town (pop. 1,736), Sitapur dist., central Uttar Pradesh, India, on the Gumti and 19 mi. SW of Sitapur; wheat, rice, gram, barley. Pilgrimage site.

Nimla (nĭm′lŭ), village, Eastern Prov., E Afghanistan, 26 mi. WSW of Jalalabad and on highway to Kabul; royal cypress garden.

Nimmons (nĭ′mŭnz). **1** Town (pop. 199), Clay co., extreme NE Ark., 28 mi. NE of Paragould. **2** Summer resort, Pickens co., NW S.C., in the Blue Ridge, 28 mi. WNW of Greenville.

Nimpkish River (nĭmp′kĭsh), SW B.C., on Vancouver Isl., rises near Victoria Peak, flows 80 mi. NW, through Nimpkish L. (□ 12), to Johnstone Strait opposite Alert Bay.

Nimptsch, Poland: see NIEMCZA.

Nimrod, village (pop. 112), Wadena co., central Minn., on Crow Wing R. and 19 mi. NE of Wadena; dairying.

Nimrod Bay, China: see SIANGSHAN BAY.

Nimrod Dam, Ark.: see FOURCHE LA FAVE RIVER.

Nimrud, Iraq: see CALAH.

Nimsar, India: see NIMKHAR.

Nimtita, India: see DHULIAN.

Nimule (nē′mōōlā), town, Equatoria prov., southernmost Anglo-Egyptian Sudan, on Uganda border, on right bank of the Bahr el Jebel (here also called Albert Nile), the upper course of the White Nile, and 95 mi. SSE of Juba (linked by road). N end of navigation on Albert Nile (from L. Albert); steamer-road transfer point for by-pass to Juba. Customs station. A dam here is planned for long-range storage of L. Albert waters.

Nimwegen, Netherlands: see NIJMEGEN.

Nimy (nēmē′), town (pop. 3,799), Hainaut prov., SW Belgium, 2 mi. N of Mons, near Canal du Centre; mfg. (steel tubing, cement, ceramics); glass-blowing industry.

Nin (nēn), Ital. *Nona* (nô′nä), anc. *Aenona*, village, W Croatia, Yugoslavia, on Adriatic Sea, 9 mi. N of Zadar, in Dalmatia. Ruins of Roman town and 8th–9th-cent. Croat churches. Medieval bishopric.

Ninacaca (nēnäkä′kä), town (pop. 526), Pasco dept., central Peru, in Cordillera Central of the Andes, on railroad and 15 mi. SE of Cerro de Pasco; alt. 13,930 ft.; grain, potatoes.

Nindirí (nēndērē′), town (1950 pop. 1,530), Masaya dept., SW Nicaragua, on railroad and 3 mi. NW of Masaya; agr. (tobacco, coffee, rice, sugar cane). Has archaeological mus. An important Indian center in pre-colonial times.

Nine (nē′nĭ), village (pop. 59), Braga dist., N Portugal, 8 mi. SW of Braga; rail junction; creosote mfg.

Nine Cantons, name of original component units of the Western Aden Protectorate; treaty relations with Britain were concluded bet. 1839 and 1904, when the Anglo-Turkish boundary was delimited bet. Yemen and the Nine Cantons. Include tribal dists. of Abdali, Amiri, Haushabi, Fadhli, Yafa, Subeihi, Aqrabi, Aulaqi, and Alawi.

Nine Degree Channel, channel of the Laccadives, India, in Arabian Sea, at 9°N, bet. Minicoy Isl. (S) and the Laccadives proper (N).

Ninette (nīnĕt′), village (pop. estimate 150), SW Man., 15 mi. N of Killarney, at NW end of Pelican L.; grain, stock.

Ninety Six, town (pop. 1,556), Greenwood co., W S.C., 7 mi. E of Greenwood; mfg. (brickworks, lumber, textile, and cottonseed-oil mills). Saluda R. (E) is dammed into L. Greenwood (hydroelectric power); state park here. Town settled around near-by trading post built c.1730; moved to present site with railroad's arrival 1855.

Nineveh (nĭ′nůvů), Gr. *Ninos*, Lat. *Ninus*, ancient city, ⊙ Assyrian Empire, on the Tigris opposite modern Mosul, N Iraq. The old capital Ashur or Assur was replaced by Calah, which seems to have been replaced by Nineveh. Nineveh was thereafter generally the capital, though Sargon built Dur Sharrukin as his capital. Nineveh reached its full glory under Sennacherib and Assur-bani-pal. It continued to be the leader of the anc. world until it fell in 612 B.C. to the attack of Cyaxares and Nabopolassar, and the Assyrian Empire came to an end. Excavations, begun in middle of 19th cent., have revealed a city more than 3 mi. long, the principal ruins being found at the mound named Kuyunjik. Buildings and inscriptions give much material on the history of Assyria. The library of Assur-bani-pal was at Nineveh. The city is mentioned often in the Bible. The book of Nahum tells of its fall.

Nineveh, village (pop. c.400), Broome co., S N.Y., 16 mi. NE of Binghamton; dairy products, poultry, livestock.

Ninga (nĭng′gů), village (pop. estimate 300), SW Man., 11 mi. WNW of Killarney; grain, stock.

Ningan (nĭng′än′), town (pop. 40,000), ⊙ Ningan co. (pop. 298,364), S Sungkiang prov., Manchuria, on left bank of Mutan R. and 17 mi. S of Mutankiang, and on railroad; wheat-growing center; flour and soybean milling, distilling; lumbering. One of the oldest cities of Manchuria, it was ⊙ Pohai kingdom (7th–10th cent.) and one of chief centers of Manchu settlement. It was not colonized by Chinese until 19th cent. Declined when by-passed by railroad. Formerly called Ninguta.

Ningcheng or **Ning-ch'eng** (nĭng′chŭng′), town, ⊙ Ningcheng co., central Jehol prov., Manchuria, 36 mi. S of Chihfeng. Until 1947 called Siaochengtze.

Ning-chiang, China: see NINGKIANG.

Ning-chin, China: see NINGTSIN.

Ning-ching, China: see NINGTSING.

Ning-chin T'ang-la, Tibet: see NYENCHEN TANGLHA.

Ningchow. **1** Town, Kansu prov., China: see NINGHSIEN. **2** Town, Yunnan prov., China: see HWANING.

Ningerh (nĭn′gŭr′), town, ⊙ Ningerh co. (pop. 45,574), S Yunnan prov., China, 170 mi. SW of Kunming and on road to Burma; alt. 4,495 ft.; major tea- and salt-producing center; rice, millet, beans. Until 1914 called Puerh.

Ninghai (nĭng′hī′). **1** Town (pop. 13,085), ⊙ Ninghai co. (pop. 228,828), E Chekiang prov., China, 40 mi. S of Ningpo, near Sanmen Bay of E.China Sea; fish- and salt-trading center; rice, wheat, peanuts, tea. **2** Town, Shantung prov., China: see MOWPING.

Ningho (nĭng′hŭ′), town, ⊙ Ningho co. (pop. 250,443), NE Hopeh prov., China, 40 mi. NE of Tientsin; salt-extracting center; wheat, kaoliang, millet.

Ning-hsia, China: see NINGSIA.

Ning-hsiang, China: see NINGSIANG.

Ninghsien (nĭng′shyĕn′). **1** City, Chekiang prov., China: see NINGPO. **2** or **Linghsien** (lĭng), town, ⊙ Ninghsien co. (pop. 86,951), SE Hunan prov., China, near Kiangsi line, 75 mi. ESE of Hengyang; tea, fruit. Tungsten mining (S). **3** Town, ⊙ Ninghsien co. (pop. 155,088), SE Kansu prov., China, on Wan R. and 34 mi. NE of Kingchwan; grain. Until 1913, Ningchow.

Ninghwa or **Ning-hua** (both: nĭng′hwä′), town (pop. 20,996), ⊙ Ninghwa co. (pop. 122,269), W Fukien prov., China, on Chekiang line, 35 mi. NNE of Changting, near source of Sha or Ninghwa R. (SW tributary of Min R.); rice, sweet potatoes, peanuts.

Ningkang (nĭng′gäng′), town (pop. 4,139), ⊙ Ningkang co. (pop. 29,017), W Kiangsi prov., China, 65 mi. WSW of Kian, near Hunan line; rice, wheat. The name Ningkang was applied during 1914–34 to a town 15 mi. E, which was called Yungning until 1914 and is now known as old Ningkang. Present Ningkang was called Lungshih until it became co. ⊙ in 1934.

Ningkiang. **1** or **Ning-ch'iang** (nĭng′chyäng′), town, ⊙ Ningkiang co. (pop. 113,636), SW Shensi prov., China, near Szechwan line, 45 mi. WSW of Nancheng; commercial center; tanning, paper mfg. Exports tung oil, medicinal herbs, potatoes, rice, wheat, kaoliang. **2** or **Ning-chiang** (nĭng'jyäng'), village, ⊙ Ningkiang dist. (pop. 7,255), S Yunnan prov., China, 60 mi. SSW of Ningerh and on right bank of Mekong R.; rice, millet, sweet potatoes, cotton, tea. Until 1935 called Mengwang.

Ningkwo or **Ning-kuo** (both: nĭng'gwô'), town, ⊙ Ningkwo co. (pop. 161,163), SW Anhwei prov., China, near Chekiang line, 65 mi. SE of Wuhu, and on railroad; rice, wheat. Until 1912, the name Ningkwo was applied to SÜANCHENG, 35 mi. SE of Wuhu.

Ninglang (nĭng'läng'), village, ⊙ Ninglang dist. (pop. 11,637), N Yunnan prov., China, 40 mi. NE of Likiang, near Sikang line; timber, rice, millet; kaolin quarrying. Until 1936 called Langchu.

Ningling (nĭng'lĭng'), town, ⊙ Ningling co. (pop. 161,172), NE Honan prov., China, 65 mi. WSW of Kaifeng; cotton weaving; wheat, kaoliang, beans, indigo.

Ningming (nĭng'mĭng'), town, ⊙ Ningming co. (pop. 27,955), SW Kwangsi prov., China, on railroad (junction for Lungtsin) and 75 mi. SW of Nanning; rice, wheat, peanuts, vegetable oil.

Ningnan (nĭng'nän'), town, ⊙ Ningnan co. (pop. 18,970), SE Sikang prov., China, 55 mi. SSE of Sichang; wax, honey, timber, wheat, rice. Until 1930 called Pisha. Before 1938 in Szechwan.

Ningpo (nĭng'pō', Chinese nĭng'bŭ'). **1** City (1942 pop. 249,633; 1948 pop. 210,377), NE Chekiang prov., China, on Yung (or Ningpo) R. and 90 mi. ESE of Hangchow (linked by railroad), 15 mi. from Hangchow Bay of E.China Sea; 29°54'N 121°32'E. Commercial and fishing center; fish processing; mfg. of straw mats and hats, furniture, lace. Ships tea, cotton, lumber, fish products. Through its outer port, CHINHAI, it trades largely with Shanghai. Dating from 8th cent., it was known as Chingyüan during the Ming dynasty. The Portuguese, who had a trading settlement here (1533–45), called city Liampo. Ningpo became (1842) one of the original treaty ports. During Sino-Japanese War, it was held (1941–45) by the Japanese. City passed in 1949 to Communist control. Called Ninghsien (1911–49) as ⊙ Ninghsien [Mandarin *Yinhsien*] co. (1948 pop. 617,657). It was created an independent municipality in 1949, and regained its old name of Ningpo. **2** Town, Tsinghai prov., China: see LOTU.

Ningpo River, China: see YUNG RIVER, Chekiang prov.

Ningshen or **Ningshan** (both: nĭng'shän'), town, ⊙Ningshen co. (pop. 35,275), S Shensi prov., China, 70 mi. SSW of Sian, in mtn. region; wheat, beans, millet, kaoliang.

Ningshuo, China: see NINGSO.

Ningsi, China: see KODJIGER.

Ningsia or **Ning-hsia** (both: nĭng'shyä'), province (□ 100,000; pop. 750,000) of NW China, largely in Inner Mongolia; ⊙ Yinchwan. Bounded N by Mongolian People's Republic, S by Kansu, SE by Shensi, and E by Suiyuan, Ningsia lies entirely on the Mongolian plateau, crossed in the extreme SE by the Yellow R. and in the NW by the Etsin Gol. The prov. divides into 2 natural regions, separated by the Alashan Mts.: the agr. Yellow R. valley (SE) and the Alashan Desert (NW). Settled by Chinese (speaking N Mandarin) since 13th cent. and protected by the Great Wall, the Yellow R. dist. is irrigated and produces wheat, kaoliang, beans, fruit, and vegetables in the shelter of the Alashan Mts. The Alashan Desert, inhabited by the 2 W.Mongol banners of the Alashan Eleut (Ölöt) and the Etsin Torgot (W of the Etsin Gol), has some grassland for nomadic grazing and salt extraction in Kilantai L. Wool weaving (noted rugs), camel's-hair felting, and fur processing are local industries. Ningsia is nearly coextensive with the Tangut kingdom (c.1000–1227), conquered by Jenghiz Khan. The "pacification" of this kingdom (known in Chinese as Sia or Hsia) is the origin of the name Ningsia [peaceful Sia]. The area remained tributary to China and became part of Kansu after 1914. In 1928 the new prov. of Ningsia was created.

Ningsia, city, China: see YINCHWAN.

Ningsiang or **Ning-hsiang** (both: nĭng'shyäng'). **1** Town, ⊙ Ningsiang co. (pop. 656,830), NE Hunan prov., China, 28 mi. WNW of Changsha; rice, tea. Coal mining (W). **2** Town, Shansi prov., China: see CHUNGYANG.

Ningso or **Ningshuo** (both: nĭng'shwô'), town, ⊙ Ningso co. (pop. 56,915), SE Ningsia prov., China, 40 mi. SSW of Yinchwan, and on Yellow R., opposite Kinki; furs, wool, wheat. Until 1942, Siaopapao.

Ningteh or **Ning-te** (both: nĭng'dŭ'), town (pop. 30,079), ⊙ Ningteh co. (pop. 170,256), NE Fukien prov., China, 40 mi. NNE of Foochow, on Samsa Bay of E.China Sea; rice, sweet potatoes, sugar cane. Kaolin quarrying in vicinity. Silver-lead, molybdenum, graphite mines near by.

Ningting (nĭng'dĭng'), town, ⊙ Ningting co. (pop. 90,455), SE Kansu prov., China, 40 mi. SSW of Lanchow; cotton weaving, tobacco processing; corn. Until 1919 called Taitzesze.

Ningtsin or **Ning-chin** (both: nĭng'jĭn'), town, ⊙ Ningtsin co. (pop. 321,901), SW Hopeh prov., China, 35 mi. SE of Shihkiachwang; cotton, wheat, kaoliang, beans. Old Ningtsin is 8 mi. SE.

Ningtsing or **Ning-ching** (both: nĭng'jĭng'). **1** Town, Shantung prov., China: see CHENHWA. **2** Town, Tibet: see MARKHAM.

Ningtu (nĭng'dōō'), town (pop. 32,493), ⊙ Ningtu co. (pop. 165,855), S Kiangsi prov., China, 65 mi. NE of Kanchow; iron mining.

Ningtung (nĭng'dŏŏng'), village, ⊙ Ningtung dist. (pop. 30,272), SE Sikang prov., China, 30 mi. NNE of Sichang; rice, wheat, kaoliang. Until 1938, called Mishih, and in Szechwan.

Ninguta, Manchuria: see NINGAN.

Ningwu (nĭng'wōō'), town, ⊙ Ningwu co. (pop. 70,130), N Shansi prov., China, near S section of Great Wall (Chahar line), 80 mi. N of Taiyüan, and on railroad; felt-producing center; wheat, millet, kaoliang, timber. Coal mines near by.

Ningyang (nĭng'yäng'). **1** Town, Fukien prov., China: see LENGYONG. **2** Town, ⊙ Ningyang co. (pop. 322,485), W Shantung prov., China, 15 mi. N of Tzeyang; cotton weaving; wheat, beans, ginger, persimmons.

Ningyüan (nĭng'yüän'). **1** Town, ⊙ Ningyüan co. (pop. 355,462), S Hunan prov., China, 50 mi. SSE of Lingling; rice, wheat, corn. Tin mining (E). **2** Town, Kansu prov., China: see WUSHAN. **3** Town, Liaosi prov., Manchuria, China: see HINGCHENG. **4** Town, Sikang prov., China: see SICHANG. **5** Town, Sinkiang prov., China: see KULDJA.

Ninhbinh (nĭng'bĭng'), town, ⊙ Ninhbinh prov. (□ 600; 1943 pop. 406,200), N Vietnam, in Tonkin, on the Song Dai, on railroad and 60 mi. S of Hanoi, in cotton- and coffee-growing region; cattle-trading center; sericulture.

Ninhchu (nĭng'chōō), village, Ninhthuan prov., S central Vietnam, minor South China Sea port, 3 mi. NE of Phanrang, which it serves as harbor; salines.

Ninhgiang (nĭng'zhäng'), town, Haiduong prov., N Vietnam, on the Song Cau, 45 mi. ESE of Hanoi; rice-trading center.

Ninhhoa (nĭng'hwä'), village, Khanhhoa prov., S central Vietnam, on railroad and 18 mi. N of Nhatrang; trading center and outlet for Banmethuot (linked by highway); served by Honecohe port on Bengoi Bay, 8 mi. NE.

Ninhthuan, province, Vietnam: see PHANRANG.

Ninhue (nēn'wā), village (1930 pop. 433), Ñuble prov., S central Chile, 22 mi. NW of Chillán, in agr. area (wine, grain, vegetables, potatoes, fruit, livestock); lumbering.

Ninigo Islands (nē'nēgō), coral group (pop. c.270), Manus dist., Bismarck Archipelago, Territory of New Guinea, SW Pacific, 150 mi. W of Admiralty Isls.; 1°16'S 144°19'E; comprise c.10 islets and atolls. Copra, trepang, tortoise shell.

Ninigret Pond, R.I.: see CHARLESTOWN.

Ninilchik (nĭnĭl'chĭk), village (pop. 67) on W coast of Kenai Peninsula, S Alaska, on Cook Inlet 75 mi. W of Seward; fur farming, fishing, fish processing. Founded c.1830 by employees of Russian America Co.

Ninnescah River (nĭ'nŭskä"), S Kansas, formed by confluence of its North Fork (87 mi. long) and South Fork (92 mi. long) in Sedgwick co. 6 mi. SE of Cheney, flows 49 mi. SE to Arkansas R. 19 mi. NNW of Arkansas City.

Ninnis Glacier Tongue (nĭ'nĭs) (75 naut. mi. long, 20 naut. mi. wide), Antarctica, off George V Coast; 67°40'S 148°E. Discovered 1913 by Sir Douglas Mawson.

Ninomiya (nēnō'mēyä). **1** (Town pop. 12,284), Chiba prefecture, central Honshu, Japan, just E of Funabashi, in agr. area (rice, wheat); poultry. **2** Town (pop. 12,302), Kanagawa prefecture, central Honshu, Japan, on N shore of Sagami Bay, 5 mi. W of Hiratsuka; seaside resort; fishing. Until 1935, called Azuma.

Niño Perdido (nē'nyō pĕr-dhē'dhō), suburb (pop. 2,506) of Villarreal, Castellón de la Plana prov., E Spain, 7 mi. SW of Castellón de la Plana, in orange-growing dist.; ships fruit, vegetables.

Ninove (nēnōv'), town (pop. 11,177), East Flanders prov., W central Belgium, on Dender R. and 15 mi. W of Brussels; textile center (cotton, artificial silk).

Nio (nē'ō), town (pop. 10,510), Kagawa prefecture, N Shikoku, Japan, on Hiuchi Sea, 11 mi. SW of Marugame; saltmaking center; mfg. (imitation pearls, tobacco).

Nioaque (nyōōä'kĭ), city (pop. 962), S Mato Grosso, Brazil, on upper Miranda R. and 90 mi. SW of Campo Grande; cattle shipping. In Ponta Porã territory, 1943–46. Formerly spelled Nioac.

Niobrara (nīūbrâ'rŭ), county (□ 2,613; pop. 4,701), E Wyo.; ⊙ Lusk. Grain, livestock region, bordering on S.Dak. and Nebr.; watered by branches of Cheyenne R. Petroleum, natural gas. Formed 1911.

Niobrara, village (pop. 577), Knox co., NE Nebr., on Missouri R. at mouth of Niobrara R., at S.Dak. line, and 60 mi. NNW of Norfolk; resort; dairying; poultry, livestock, grain. Santee and Ponca Indian reservations here.

Niobrara River, Wyo. and Nebr., rises in E Wyo., flows 431 mi. E, past Valentine, N Nebr., through dry-farming and cattle-raising area of N Nebr., to Missouri R. at Niobrara; drains □ 13,000. Used for hydroelectric power. Box Butte Dam (87 ft. high, 5,508 ft. long; built 1946 as unit in Mirage Flats irrigation project) is on stream near Marsland, NW Nebr. Much of its course is characterized by scenic beauty. Longest tributary is Keya Paha R.

Nioka (nyō'kä), village, Eastern Prov., NE Belgian Congo, 75 mi. NE of Irumu; alt. 5,904 ft.; center of agr. research, with model stock-breeding farm, plantations of coffee, tea, pyrethrum, cinchona, tobacco, aleurites, essential-oil plants, African staples; palm-oil milling. Kwandruma (kwändrōō'-mä), 7 mi. E, also known as Rheti or Rethy (rātē'), has Protestant mission, schools for European children. Nioka vicinity is noted as an area of European agr. settlement, supplying Stanleyville with vegetables.

Nioki (nyō'kē), village, Leopoldville prov., SW Belgian Congo, on right bank of Fimi R. and 70 mi. SW of Inongo; lumbering center; sawmilling, woodworking, rubber plantations.

Niono (nyō'nō), village (pop. c.800), S Fr. Sudan, Fr. West Africa, in mid-Niger depression (irrigation), 90 mi. NE of Ségou; cotton growing. Mfg. of vegetable oil, soap. Cotton experiment station.

Nioro (nyō'rō), town (pop. c.5,450), W Fr. Sudan, Fr. West Africa, 130 mi. NE of Kayes; gum, peanuts, kapok; also millet, corn, manioc, sweet potatoes, melons. Animal husbandry.

Nioro-du-Rip (nyō'rō-dü-rēp') or **Nioro-Rip**, town (pop. c.1,900), W Senegal, Fr. West Africa, near Br. Gambia border, 34 mi. SE of Kaolack. Experiment station for peanut growing.

Niort (nyôr), town (pop. 29,068), ⊙ Deux-Sèvres dept., W France, on Sèvre Niortaise R. and 34 mi. ENE of La Rochelle; commercial and transportation center producing leather goods (especially gloves); light metalworking, distilling, flour milling. Other mfg.: bicycles, pharmaceuticals, mustard. Niort preserves 2 towers of 12th–13th-cent. fortress and several Renaissance bldgs. A Huguenot stronghold in 16th–17th cent. Mme de Maintenon b. in jail here.

Nios, Greece: see IOS.

Niota (nīō'tŭ), town (pop. 956), McMinn co., SE Tenn., 45 mi. SW of Knoxville; makes hosiery.

Niotaze (nī'ūtāz, nē'–), city (pop. 162), Chautauqua co., SE Kansas, 22 mi. W of Coffeyville, near Okla. line, in livestock and grain area. Oil fields near by.

Nipani (nĭpä'nē), town (pop., including suburban area, 18,982), Belgaum dist., S Bombay, India, 37 mi. NNW of Belgaum; tobacco market; trades in chili, jaggery, corn; biri mfg.

Nipawin (nĭ'pŭwĭn"), town (pop. 2,211), E central Sask., on Saskatchewan R. and 75 mi. E of Prince Albert; flour milling, dairying.

Nipe, Sierra de (syĕ'rä dā nē'pā), range, Oriente prov., E Cuba, extends c.25 mi. S from Nipe Bay towards Santiago de Cuba, forming divide bet. Nipe (W) and Mayarí (E) rivers. Rises to c.3,200 ft. Iron mined in N (refined at Felton). Also called Los Pinales.

Nipe Bay (nē'pā), sheltered Atlantic inlet (14 mi. long, 8 mi. wide), Oriente prov., NE Cuba, 50 mi. N of Santiago de Cuba, and linked with sea by narrows. Receives Mayarí R. and small Nipe R. Preston is on E, Antilla on N shore.

Niphad (nĭ'päd"), village (pop. 5,106), Nasik dist., central Bombay, India, 22 mi. ENE of Nasik; market center for millet, wheat, gur, grapes; oilseed (peanuts) pressing.

Nipigon (nĭ'pĭgŏn), village (pop. estimate 750), W central Ont., on Nipigon Bay of L. Superior, at mouth of Nipigon R., 60 mi. NE of Port Arthur; lumbering.

Nipigon, Lake (□ 1,870), W central Ont., 80 mi. NE of Port Arthur; 66 mi. long, 46 mi. wide; alt. 852 ft. Contains many isls.; largest are Kelvin, Shakespeare, Geikie, Murchison isls. Drained S into L. Superior by Nipigon R. (40 mi. long). Gold mined in region.

Nipisiguit River (nĭpĭ'zĭgwĭt), N N.B., rises at foot of Mt. Carleton, flows E, turning NNE to Nipisiguit Bay, inlet of Chaleur Bay, at Bathurst; c.100 mi. long. Grand Falls, 20 mi. SSW of Bathurst, are 4 falls with total height of 140 ft.

Nipissing (nĭ'pĭsĭng"), district (□ 7,560; pop. 43,315), SE central Ont., on L. Nipissing; ⊙ North Bay.

Nipissing, Lake (□ 330), SE central Ont., midway between L. Huron and Ottawa R., extends W from North Bay; contains many islets. Drained SW into Georgian Bay of L. Huron by French R.

Nippersink Lake, Ill.: see CHAIN-O'-LAKES.

Nipple Top, peak (4,620 ft.) of the Adirondacks, in Essex co., NE N.Y., c.6 mi. ESE of Mt. Marcy and 16 mi. SE of Lake Placid village.

Nippur (nĭpŏŏr'), anc. city of Babylonia, a N Sumerian settlement on the Euphrates (now 25 mi. away), whose site (modern Niffer), 90 mi. SE of Babylon, is in SE central Iraq, in Diwaniya prov., 20 mi. ENE of Diwaniya. Was seat of cult of the god En-lil, flourishing above all others in Sumerian times. Excavations have yielded a large library and other valuable finds.

Niquelândia (nēkŭlän'dyŭ), city (pop. 533), central Goiás, central Brazil, 125 mi. N of Anápolis; nickel mining; electric smelter under construction. Extensive nickel, cobalt, and copper deposits in region. Until 1944, called São José do Tocantins.

Niquero (nēkä'rō), town (pop. 5,437), Oriente prov., E Cuba, port on SE Guacanayabo Bay, 35 mi. SW of Manzanillo, in fertile region (sugar cane, fruit, livestock, timber). Airfield.

Niquinohomo (nēkēnō-ō'mō) or **La Victoria** (lä vēktōr'yä), town (1950 pop. 1,670), Masaya dept., SW Nicaragua, on railroad and 5 mi. S of Masaya; health resort; coffee, rice, corn. Scene of govt. victory (1860) over rebel forces.

Niquitao (nēkētou'), town (pop. 999), Trujillo state, W Venezuela, at E foot of Teta de Niquitao (13,143 ft.), 19 mi. S of Trujillo; alt. 6,355 ft.; wheat, corn, potatoes.

Nir Am or **Nir 'Am** (both: nēr' äm'), settlement (pop. 200), SW Israel, in Judaean Plain, at NW edge of the Negev, on border of Egyptian-held Palestine, 6 mi. E of Gaza; dairying; vegetables, fruit. A center for the Negev (terminal pumping station of water pipe line; large hosp.). Founded 1943. Also spelled Nir'am. Formerly Shedmot.

Nira River (nē'rŭ), central Bombay, India, rises in Western Ghats S of Poona, flows 115 mi. ESE to Bhima R. 12 mi. SE of Indapur. Lloyd Dam (1½ mi. N of Bhor) supplies canal irrigation system, with headworks 16 mi. E. Right (S) canal extends 106 mi. ESE, past Phaltan, to point 5 mi. SE of Pandharpur; left (N) canal extends 100 mi. E, past Baramati, to point 4 mi. W of Indapur. System irrigates large sugar-cane area.

Nirasaki (nērä'-sä'kē), town (pop. 9,885), Yamanashi prefecture, central Honshu, Japan, 8 mi. WNW of Kofu; raw silk, rice.

Niravi (nē'rŭvē), Fr. *Néravy* (nārävē'), town (commune pop. 8,126), Karikal settlement, Fr. India, 2 mi. SW of Karikal.

Nir David (nēr' dävēd'), settlement (pop. 350), NE Israel, in SE part of Plain of Jezreel, at NE foot of Mt. Gilboa, 3 mi. W of Beisan; mixed farming, banana growing; fowl raising, fish breeding. Founded 1936.

Ñirehuau or **Ñirihuau** (nyērīwou'), village (1930 pop. 251), Aysén prov., S Chile, in the Andes, 40 mi. NE of Puerto Aysén; sheep-raising center. Also Nirehuao or Nirihuao.

Nirgajni, India: see MUZAFFARNAGAR, town.

Nirgua (nēr'gwä), town (pop. 4,284), Yaracuy state, N Venezuela, in coastal range, 39 mi. W of Valencia; agr. center (coffee, tobacco, cacao, sugar cane, cotton, cattle); liquor distilling, sugar milling. Copper, iron, salt, coal, and sulphur deposits near by.

Ñirihuau, Chile: see ÑIREHUAU.

Nirim (nērēm'), agr. settlement (pop. 100), SW Israel, in the Negev, near border of Egyptian-held Palestine, 12 mi. S of Gaza. Founded 1946; withstood heavy Egyptian attacks, 1948.

Nirin, Formosa: see ERHLIN.

Nirivilo (nērēvē'lō), village (1930 pop. 219), Maule prov., S central Chile, 32 mi. NE of Cauquenes; grain, potatoes, lentils, sheep; lumbering.

Niriz (nērēz'), **Neiriz,** or **Neyriz** (all: närēz'), town (1940 pop. 19,439), Seventh Prov., in Fars, S Iran, 110 mi. ESE of Shiraz and on road to Kerman; trade center; fruit, nuts, gums. Lead and iron deposits. Seat of Babist religious sect.

Niriz Lake (nērēz', närēz'), **Bakhtigan Lake,** or **Bakhtegan Lake** (both: bäkhtēgän'), salt marsh of S central Iran, in the Zagros ranges, 60 mi. E of Shiraz; c.60 mi. long, up to 10 mi. wide. Receives Kur R. (W).

Nirmal (nĭr'mŭl), town (pop. 14,499), Adilabad dist., NE Hyderabad state, India, 40 mi. SSW of Adilabad; road center in agr. area; cotton ginning, rice milling; noted toy handicrafts.

Niroemoar, Netherlands New Guinea: see KUMAMBA ISLANDS.

Nirsa (nĭr'sŭ), village, Manbhum dist., SE Bihar, India, in W Raniganj coal field, 39 mi. NE of Purulia; coal mining.

Nirumoar, Netherlands New Guinea: see KUMAMBA ISLANDS.

Nis or **Nish** (nēsh), Serbo-Croatian *Niš*, anc. *Naissus*, city (pop. 50,692), ⊙ Nis oblast (formed 1949), SE central Serbia, Yugoslavia, on Nisava R. and 125 mi. SSE of Belgrade. Important rail center (repair shops), with lines to Belgrade, Salonika, Sofia, and Negotin; also new line (begun 1947) to Caribrod, on Bulg. border. Mfg. of cut tobacco, cigarettes, textiles, leather, flour. Truck gardening, winegrowing in vicinity. Niska Banja, health resort, is ESE. Castle is near by, on the Southern Morava; just ESE is the "Tower of Skulls" (Serbo-Croatian *Cele Kula*), built to commemorate the Serbs massacred by the Turks in the uprising of 1809. Was site of a victory (A.D. 269) of Claudius II over the Ostrogoths and was birthplace of Constantine the Great. In Middle Ages, city passed back and forth bet. the Bulgarian and Serbian empires. The Turks, who captured it c.1386, were defeated here 1443 by John Hunyadi, but soon obtained a permanent hold over all Serbia. Nis was several times held, for brief periods, by Christian forces, but it permanently passed to Serbia only in 1878. Was a ⊙ Serbia until 1901. Damaged by air raids in Second World War. Formerly also called Nissa.

Nisa, town, Poland: see NEISSE.

Nisa (nē'zŭ), town (pop. 5,085), Portalegre dist., central Portugal, 19 mi. NW of Portalegre; agr. trade center; mfg. (cheese, hats, lace). Noted for its pottery industry. Ships lumber, cork, olives, livestock. Also spelled Niza.

Nisab (nĭsäb'), town (pop. 4,000), ⊙ Upper Aulaqi sultanate, Western Aden Protectorate, 70 mi. NNW of Ahwar; center of cotton-growing area; cotton weaving (shawls, turbans). Airfield.

Nisa River, Czechoslovakia: see NEISSE RIVER.

Nisava River or **Nishava River** (both: nē'shävä), Serbo-Croatian *Nišava*, NW Bulgaria and SE Yugoslavia, rises in Berkovitsa Mts. at S foot of Kom peak, flows c.100 mi. WNW, into Yugoslavia, past Dimitrovgrad, Pirot, Bela Palanka, Niska Banja, and Nis, to Southern Morava R. 7 mi. WNW of Nis. Sofia-Nis RR follows its course.

Niscemi (nēshā'mē), town (pop. 19,711), Caltanissetta prov., S Sicily, 9 mi. NE of Gela, in cork-growing region; wine.

Nish, Yugoslavia: see NIS.

Nishapur (nēshäpōōr') or **Neyshapur** (nā–), town (1941 pop. 24,270), Ninth Prov., in Khurasan, NE Iran, on road and railroad, and 45 mi. W of Meshed; alt. 4,008 ft. Center of irrigated agr. area; opium, cotton, wheat, rhubarb, gums; cotton ginning, soap mfg., cottonseed-oil processing; hides, rugs. Celebrated for fine turquoise mined at Madan (32 mi. NW). In suburb is tomb of Omar Khayyam. Built by Shapur I and expanded by Shapur II of Sassanian dynasty (3d and 4th cent. A.D.), it was one of the great cities of early Khurasan until it was destroyed by earthquakes and the Mongol invasion (13th cent. A.D.). Also spelled Nishabur and Neyshabur.

Nishava River, Bulgaria and Yugoslavia: see NISAVA RIVER.

Nishi-achi (nē'shē-ä'chē), town (pop. 5,070), Okayama prefecture, SW Honshu, Japan, just W of Kurashiki; rice, wheat, grapes, raw silk, rushes.

Nishi-aki (nē'shē-ä'kē), town (pop. 4,782), Oita prefecture, NE Kyushu, Japan, 15 mi. N of Oita; rice, poultry; lumbering.

Nishi-arie (nē'shē-ärē'ā), town (pop. 14,271), Nagasaki prefecture, W Kyushu, Japan, on SE Shimabara Peninsula, 24 mi. ESE of Nagasaki, near Arie; rice, wheat.

Nishi-biwajima (nē'shē-bēwä'jĭmä), town (pop. 10,829), Aichi prefecture, central Honshu, Japan, adjacent to Nagoya (E); agr. (rice, wheat, herbs, radishes).

Nishiichi (nēshē'chē), town (pop. 5,247), Yamaguchi prefecture, SW Honshu, Japan, 16 mi. NNE of Shimonoseki; rice, raw silk, poultry.

Nishi-ichiki, Japan: see ICHIKI.

Nishiki (nē'shĭkē). **1** Town (pop. 8,839), Fukushima prefecture, central Honshu, Japan, 12 mi. SW of Taira; coal-mining; fishing, agr. **2** Town (pop. 3,815), Mie prefecture, S Honshu, Japan, on Kumano Sea, 25 mi. SW of Uji-yamada; fishing; charcoal, lumber, raw silk.

Nishi-kuwana, Japan: see KUWANA.

Nishi-mizuhashi, Japan: see MIZUHASHI.

Nishimonai (nē'shĭmōnī"), town (pop. 6,857), Akita prefecture, N Honshu, Japan, 5 mi. ENE of Yuzawa; mining (gold, silver, copper, lead, zinc).

Nishimukai (nē'shĭmōōkī"), town (pop. 4,473), Wakayama prefecture, S Honshu, Japan, on Kumano Sea, on SE Kii Peninsula, 18 mi. SW of Shingu; fishing, agr. (rice, citrus fruit); raw silk.

Nishi-naibuchi, Russian SFSR: see ZAGORSKI.

Nishinasuno (nē'shĭnä'sōōnō), town (pop. 9,609), Tochigi prefecture, central Honshu, Japan, 3 mi. NW of Otawara; rice, wheat, barley.

Nishi-nomi-shima, Japan: see NOMI-SHIMA.

Nishinomiya (nē'shĭnō'mē-ŭ), city (1940 pop. 103,774; 1947 pop. 108,893), Hyogo prefecture, S Honshu, Japan, on Osaka Bay, bet. Kobe (W) and Amagasaki (E); sake-producing center; beer, vegetable oil. Kobe Women's Col. here. Sometimes spelled Nisinomiya.

Nishinoomote (nēshē'nō-ō'mōtā), chief town and port (pop. 23,281) on Tanega-shima, Kagoshima prefecture, Japan, on W coast of isl., on Osumi Strait; fishing and agr. center; rice, bran. Exports charcoal, livestock, lumber, sugar.

Nishi-no-shima (nēshē'-nō'shĭmä), largest island (□ 33; pop. 7,109, including offshore islets) of Dozen group of the Oki-gunto, Shimane prefecture, Japan, 8 mi. SW of Dogo; 12 mi. long, c.¼–4 mi. wide. Mountainous, forested; lumber, charcoal, rice. Sometimes called Nishi Shima.

Nishino Shima, Pacific Ocean: see ROSARIO ISLAND.

Nishi-notoro-saki, Russian SFSR: see CRILLON, CAPE.

Nishinoura, Cape, Japan: see NISHIURA, CAPE.

Nishio (nēshē'ō), town (pop. 24,295), Aichi prefecture, central Honshu, Japan, 22 mi. SSE of Nagoya; raw silk, textiles, sake; poultry.

Nishi-shakutan, Sakhalin: see BOSHNYAKOVO.

Nishi Shima, Japan: see NISHI-NO-SHIMA.

Nishiura (nēshē'ōōrä), town (pop. 6,922), Aichi prefecture, central Honshu, Japan, on W Chita Peninsula, on Ise Bay and 5 mi. WSW of Handa, in agr. area (rice, wheat, poultry); raw silk, pottery. Fishing; sandstone quarrying.

Nishi-ura, Japan: see KASUMI-GA-URA.

Nishiura, Cape, Jap. *Nishiura-misaki*, N Kyushu, Japan, forms W side of entrance to Hakata Bay (inlet of Genkai Sea); 33°40'N 130°13'E. Sometimes called Cape Nishinoura.

Nishiwaki (nēshē'-wäkē), town (pop. 12,624), Hyogo prefecture, S Honshu, Japan, 24 mi. NW of Kobe; agr. center (rice, wheat, tobacco, fruit, flowers, poultry). Home industries (woodworking, cutlery, leather goods, floor mats); tea processing.

Nishi-yamashiro, Japan: see YAMASHIRO, Saga prefecture.

Nishka Banya, Yugoslavia: see NISKA BANJA.

Nishnabotna River (nĭsh"nŭbōt'nŭ), in SW Iowa and NW Mo., formed by East and West Nishnabotna rivers rising in Carroll co., Iowa, both flowing c.100 mi. S and W, then joining near Hamburg to form Nishnabotna R., which flows c.12 mi. S to Missouri R. 2 mi. W of Watson in extreme NW Mo. Used for hydroelectric power. Tributaries and main stream are canalized for flood control.

Nisi, Greece: see MESSENE.

Nísia Floresta (nē'zyŭ flōōrĕ'stŭ), city (pop. 870), E Rio Grande do Norte, NE Brazil, near the Atlantic, 19 mi. S of Natal; sugar, cattle. Until 1948, called Papari.

Nisib, Turkey: see NIZIP.

Nisibin or **Nisibis,** Turkey: see NUSAYBIN.

Nisida (nē'zēdä), anc. *Nesis*, rocky islet (pop. 312), S Italy, in Bay of Naples, 3 mi. SE of Pozzuoli. Site of penal institution. Brutus had a villa here.

Nisinomiya, Japan: see NISHINOMIYA.

Nisiro, Nisiros, Greece: see NISYROS.

Niska Banja or **Nishka Banya** (both: nē'shkä bä'-nyä), Serbo-Croatian *Niška Banja*, village, E Serbia, Yugoslavia, on railroad and 6 mi. ESE of Nis, near Nisava R.; health resort.

Niskakoski, Russian SFSR: see PATS RIVER.

Niskayuna (nĭskĭyōō'nŭ), village, Schenectady co., E N.Y., on Mohawk R. and 5 mi. E of Schenectady. Site of 2 atomic research laboratories operated by General Electric Company.

Nisko (nē'skō), town (pop. 6,590), Rzeszow prov., SE Poland, on San R., on railroad and 33 mi. N of Rzeszow; brewing, lumber milling; brickworks.

Nisky (nĭ'skē), village, S St. Thomas Isl., U.S. Virgin Isls., 1½ mi. W of Charlotte Amalie. Site of a Moravian mission (founded 1755), in picturesque setting. Sometimes spelled Niesky.

Nisland (nĭs'lŭnd), town (pop. 216), Butte co., W S.Dak., 15 mi. E of Belle Fourche and on Belle Fourche R.; cucumbers. Butte co. fair takes place here.

Nismes (nĕm), village (pop. 1,650), Namur prov., S Belgium, 9 mi. S of Philippeville; lumber center.

Nismes, France: see NÎMES.

Níspero, El, Honduras: see EL NÍSPERO.

Nisporeny (nyēspŭrye'nē), Rum. *Nisporeni* (nĕspôrĕn'), village (1941 pop. 5,068), W Moldavian SSR, 30 mi. WNW of Kishinev; corn, wheat, fruit, wine.

Nisqually Glacier, Wash.: see MOUNT RAINIER NATIONAL PARK.

Nisqually River (nĭskwô'lē), W central Wash., fed by Nisqually Glacier on S slopes of Mt. Rainier, flows 81 mi. W and NW to Puget Sound 10 mi. ENE of Olympia. Alder Dam (completed 1944; 330 ft. high, 1,600 ft. long) and La Grande Dam (completed 1945; 215 ft. high, 710 ft. long) furnish power.

Nissa, Yugoslavia: see NIS.

Nissan (nēsā'), town (pop. 2,243), Hérault dept., S France, near the Canal du Midi, 6 mi. SW of Béziers; winegrowing.

Nissan (nĭsän'), atoll (pop. c.1,500), northernmost of Solomon Isls., SW Pacific, 100 mi. E of New Ireland; 4°31'S 154°11'E. Comprises 4 isls. (Nissan, Barahun, Sirot, Han) on reef 10 mi. long, 5 mi. wide; coconuts. In Second World War, Allied capture (1944) of isl. completed Solomons campaign. Sometimes called Green Isl.

Nissa River, Swedish *Nissan* (nĭ'sän"), SW Sweden, rises SW of Jonkoping, flows 100 mi. SW, past Gislaved and Oskarstrom, to the Kattegat at Halmstad.

Nissedal (nĭs'sŭdäl), village and canton (pop. 1,756), Telemark co., S Norway, on Nisser L., 40 mi. W of Skien; lumbering, fishing. From near Treungen, 11 mi. S of the village, is a rail line to Grimstad and Arendal.

Nissequogue (nĭ'sĭkwäg"), residential village (pop. 219), Suffolk co., SE N.Y., on N shore of Long Isl., near mouth of Nissequogue R., 12 mi. E of Huntington, in summer-resort area.

Nissequogue River, SE N.Y., rises in small lake just S of Smithtown Branch on Long Isl., flows c.8 mi. SW and NE, past Smithtown, to Smithtown Bay 4 mi. W of Stony Brook.

Nisser Lake (nĭs'sŭr), Telemark co., S Norway, 49 mi. W of Skien; 22 mi. long, 2 mi. wide; alt. 794 ft. Outlet: Nid R.

Nisser River, Norway: see NID RIVER.

Nissum Fjord (nĭ'sōōm), inlet (c.10 mi. long) of North Sea, W Jutland, Denmark, S of Lim Fjord. Stor R. flows into it.

Nisswa (nĭ'swä), village (pop. 578), Crow Wing co., central Minn., 13 mi. NNW of Brainerd, near Gull L. Fishing and boating resorts.

Nistelrode (nĭs'tŭlrōdŭ), agr. village (pop. 1,742), North Brabant prov., E central Netherlands, 11 mi. E of 's Hertogenbosch.

Nistru River, USSR: see DNIESTER RIVER.

Nisui, Formosa: see ERHSHUI.

Nisutlin River, S Yukon, headstream of Yukon R., rises in SE part of Pelly Mts., flows 150 mi. in wide arc W and S to Teslin L.

Nisyros or **Nisiros** (both: nē'sĭrôs), Ital. *Nisiro,* Aegean volcanic island (□ 16; pop. 2,605), in the Dodecanese, Greece, off Turkish Resadiye Peninsula and S of Kos; 36°35'N 27°10'E; 4 mi. long, 4 mi. wide, rises to 2,270 ft. Has dormant volcano (sulphur deposits; hot springs). Produces barley, olive oil, figs, almonds, wheat. Main town, Mandraki (pop. 1,352), is on NW shore.

Niterói (nētĭroi'), city (1950 pop. 174,535), ⊙ Rio de Janeiro state, SE Brazil, at mouth to Guanabara Bay, opposite Rio (2 mi. W; ferry), of which it is a residential suburb. Because of its proximity to the federal capital, city has not acquired great commercial and cultural importance. Its industries, however, are well-developed along water front (and on offshore isls.) and in N suburbs. These include shipbuilding and -repairing, metalworking (chiefly at Neves), textile milling, food processing. Other mfg.: flat glass, matches, tobacco products, furniture, chemicals (including explosives) and pharmaceuticals. Large cement mill near by. Railroad terminus. Harbor dist. of São Lourenço enlarged since 1920. City's fine residential dists. (Icaraí, Saco de São Francisco) are noted for their beaches. Institutions of higher learning include schools of pharmacy, dentistry, veterinary medicine, commerce. Known since end of 16th cent. as an Indian settlement. Planned by a Fr. architect, it became a town (1819) under the name of Villa Real da Praia Grande; has been ⊙ Rio de Janeiro state since 1835 (except for period 1894–1903, when ⊙ was at Petrópolis) under present name. Old spelling, Nictheroy.

Nith River, SW Ont., rises SE of Listowel, flows c.70 mi. SE, past New Hamburg, to Thames R. 9 mi. SW of Galt. Receives Millbank R.

Nith River (nĭth), Ayrshire and Dumfries, Scotland, rises 2 mi. NE of Dalmellington, flows NE to New Cumnock, E to Sanquhar, and SE past Thornhill and Dumfries to Solway Firth 11 mi. S of Dumfries; 80 mi. long. Below Dumfries it forms Dumfries-Kirkcudbright boundary. Its valley is called Nithsdale. Receives Afton R. at New Cumnock.

Nitinat Lake (□ 10), SW B.C., on SW Vancouver Isl., 70 mi. WNW of Victoria, in lumbering area; 13 mi. long, 1 mi. wide.

Niti Pass (nĭtē') (alt. 16,627 ft.), in SE Zaskar Range of Kumaun Himalayas, SW Tibet, near India (border undefined), 60 mi. SSW of Gartok, at 30°57'N 79°53'E. Also called Kiunglang.

Nitra (nyĭ'trä), Ger. *Neutra* (noi'trä), Hung. *Nyitra* (nyĭ'trŏ), town (pop. 19,712), ⊙ Nitra prov. (□ 3,076; pop. 689,853), SW Slovakia, Czechoslovakia, on Nitra R., on railroad and 45 mi. ENE of Bratislava, in fertile agr. region (wheat, barley, sugar beets); 48°19'N 18°5'E. Known for its agr. industries (flour milling, distilling, starch mfg.). Noted religious center; seat of R.C. bishopric since 9th cent. Has fine cathedral, old castle. Ruins of 11th-cent. monastery near by (N). First Christian church in Czechoslovak territory established here in 830.

Nitra River, Ger. *Neutra,* Hung. *Nyitra,* SW Slovakia, Czechoslovakia, rises on SE slope of the Lesser Fatra, 13 mi. N of Prievidza; flows c.150 mi. generally S, past Nitra and Nove Zamky, to Vah R. just N of Komarno.

Nitro (nī'trō), town (pop. 3,314), Putnam and Kanawha counties, W W.Va., on Kanawha R. and 11 mi. WNW of Charleston, in agr. and coal-producing area; mfg. of chemicals, rayon, pencils. A boom town in First World War; govt. explosives plant here was later abandoned. Inc. 1932.

Nitsanim or **Nitzanim** (both: nētsänēm'), settlement (pop. 175), W Israel, in Judaean Plain, near Mediterranean, 16 mi. SW of Rehovot; mixed farming. Founded 1943; captured (1948) by Egyptians, shortly afterwards retaken by Israeli forces.

Nitsa River (nē'tsŭ), Sverdlovsk oblast, Russian SFSR, formed 20 mi. ENE of Alapayevsk by confluence of Neiva and Rezh rivers; flows 100 mi. generally ESE, past Irbit and Yelan, to Tura R. 10 mi. SSE of Turinskaya Sloboda. Navigable below Irbit; lumber floating. Receives Irbit R.

Nittenau (nĭ'tŭnou), village (pop. 3,853), Upper Palatinate, E Bavaria, Germany, in Bohemian Forest, on the Regen and 15 mi. NE of Regensburg; brickworks; brewing.

Nitzanim, Israel: see NITSANIM.

Niuafoo (nēōō'äfô'ō), northernmost island of Tonga, S Pacific; 15°45'S 175°45'W; 3.5 mi. long, 3 mi. wide. Volcanic; large crater lake, hot springs. Isl. was evacuated 1946 because of volcanic eruptions. Popularly called Tin Can Isl.; formerly Proby Isl.

Niuatobutabu (nyōō'ätô'bōōtä'bōō), volcanic island, N Tonga, S Pacific; 16°S 173°48'W; c.3 mi. long, 1 mi. wide; rises to 350 ft. Formerly Keppel Isl.

Niuchwang, Manchuria: see NEWCHWANG.

Niue (nēōō'ā), coral island (□ c.100; pop. 4,253), S Pacific, belonging to New Zealand; 19°2'S 169°52'W. Rises to c.200 ft.; fertile soil on central plateau; poor harbors. Alofi is chief town. Exports copra, bananas. Also known as Savage Isl.

Niu-hsin-t'ai, Manchuria: see NIUSINTAI.

Niulakita (nyōōläkē'tä), atoll (104 acres; pop. 4,487), S Ellice Isls., SW Pacific; 10°45'S 179°30'E; 1 mi. long, ½ mi. wide. Also called Nurakita; formerly Sophia Isl.

Niusintai or **Niu-hsin-t'ai** (both: nyō'shĭn'tī'), town, W central Liaotung prov., Manchuria, on rail spur and 8 mi. E of Penki; coal- and alunite-mining center.

Niutao (nē'ōōtä'ō), atoll (625 acres; pop. 644), N Ellice Isls., SW Pacific; 6°6'S 177°16'E; copra. Formerly Speiden Isl.

Nivala (nĭ'välä), village (commune pop. 12,682), Oulu co., W Finland, near Kala R., 55 mi. E of Kokkola; nickel mining.

Niva River (nyē'vŭ), on SW Kola Peninsula, Russian SFSR, leaves L. Imandra (alt. 420 ft.) at Zasheyek, flows 22 mi. S, past Nivski (site of Niva hydroelectric plant), to Kandalaksha Bay at Kandalaksha. Its strong current keeps it from freezing during the winter.

Nivelle, Mount (nĭ'vŭl) (10,620 ft.), SE B.C., near Alta. border, in Rocky Mts., 50 mi. SSE of Banff; 50°31'N 115°11'W.

Nivelles (nēvĕl'), Flemish *Nijvel* (nī'vŭl), town (pop. 11,980), Brabant prov., S central Belgium, 17 mi. S of Brussels; steel center (blast furnaces, rolling mills); mfg. of railroad rolling-stock; paper and cotton industry. Has 11th-cent. church of St. Gertrude, rebuilt in 18th cent. Town originated in convent founded 645.

Nivenskoye (nyē'vyĭnskŭyŭ), village (1939 pop. 897), W Kaliningrad oblast, Russian SFSR, on railroad and 9 mi. SSE of Kaliningrad; junction of rail spur to Slavskoye. Until 1945, in East Prussia and called Wittenberg (vĭ'tŭnbĕrk).

Nive River (nēv), Basses-Pyrénées dept., SW France, formed by confluence of several branches near Saint-Jean-Pied-de-Port, flows 45 mi. NNW, past Cambo-les-Bains and Ustaritz (head of navigation), to the Adour at Bayonne. Its narrow valley is followed by a railroad.

Nivernais (nēvŭrnā'), region and former province of central France, coinciding roughly with present NIÈVRE dept.; ⊙ Nevers. A county after 10th cent., it passed (1384) to Philip the Bold of Burgundy, was raised to a duchy in 1539, and passed (1601) to house of Gonzaga. In 1659 Cardinal Mazarin bought the title, which remained with his family after duchy was inc. (1669) into royal domain.

Nivernais Canal, Yonne and Nièvre depts., central France, connects Decize (on the Loire) with Auxerre (on the Yonne), paralleling the Aron to its source, crossing W slopes of the Morvan near Châtillon-en-Bazois, and entering Yonne R. valley S of Corbigny. Runs alongside Yonne R. past Clamecy, merging with it above Auxerre. Total length, 108 mi. Lumber shipping.

Nivernais Hills, Nièvre dept., central France, bet. the Morvan (E) and the Loire (W) N of Nevers. Average alt. 1,000 ft. Cattle raising, lumbering.

Nivillers (nēvēlâr'), village (pop. 161), Oise dept., N France, 4 mi. NE of Beauvais.

Nivski or **Nivskiy** (nyēf'skē), town (1939 pop. over 2,000), SW Murmansk oblast, Russian SFSR, on Niva R., on Murmansk RR and 10 mi. N of Kandalaksha; hydroelectric station; metalworks.

Niwai, India: see NAWAI.

Niwas (nĭvŭs'), village, Mandla dist., NE Madhya Pradesh, India, 31 mi. N of Mandla; rice, wheat, oilseeds. Lac cultivation in near-by dense sal forests.

Niwase, Japan: see KIBI.

Nixa, town (pop. 509), Christian co., SW Mo., in the Ozarks, near James R., 12 mi. S of Springfield.

Nixon, city (pop. 1,875), Gonzales co., S central Texas, c.45 mi. ESE of San Antonio; poultry packing and shipping center; peanut-grading plant, hatcheries.

Niya or **Niya Bazar** (nēyä' bäzär'), Chinese *Ming-feng* (mĭng'fŭng'), town and oasis (pop. 9,791), S Sinkiang prov., China, 160 mi. E of Khotan, and on highway skirting S edge of Taklamakan Desert; 37°4'N 82°46'E. Sericulture; carpets, cotton textiles. Gold mines near by.

Niyodo River (nēyō'dō), Jap. *Niyodo-gawa,* W Shikoku, Japan, rises in mts. near Kuma, flows 82 mi. generally SE, through forested area, past Ochi, Ino, and Takaoka, to Tosa Bay 7 mi. SW of Kochi.

Niza, Portugal: see NISA.

Nizamabad (nĭzä'mäbäd), district (□ 2,992; pop. 647,043), N central Hyderabad state, India, on Deccan Plateau; ⊙ Nizamabad. Bordered N by Godavari R., W by Manjra R.; Nizam Sagar (reservoir) forms SW corner of dist. Mainly lowland (largely sandy red soil), drained by tributaries of the Godavari; rice, millet, oilseeds (chiefly peanuts, sesame), cotton, tobacco; sugar-cane grown along Nizam Sagar Canal. Rice and oilseed milling, cotton ginning, biri mfg., silk weaving. Main towns: Nizamabad (trade center), Bodhan (sugar factory). Part of Hyderabad since beginning (early 18th cent.) of state's formation. Pop. 75% Hindu, 10% Moslem, 2% Christian.

Nizamabad. 1 Town (pop. 32,741), ⊙ Nizamabad dist., N central Hyderabad state, India, 90 mi. NNW of Hyderabad; road and agr. trade center in sugar-cane area; rice milling, cotton ginning. Industrial school. **2** Town (pop. 3,878), Azamgarh dist., E Uttar Pradesh, India, on Tons R. and 8 mi. W of Azamgarh; pottery mfg.; rice, barley, wheat, sugar cane.

Nizamabad, village, Gujranwala dist., E Punjab, W Pakistan, 1 mi. S of Wazirabad; mfg. of cutlery, swords, walking sticks.

Nizampatam (nĭzäm'pŭtŭm), village, Guntur dist., NE Madras, India, 35 mi. SW of Masulipatam. Was English trading station, founded 1611 and called Pedapalle; soon outgrown by Masulipatam.

Nizam Sagar (nĭzŭm sä'gŭr), reservoir (15 mi. long, 10 mi. wide), in Medak dist., central Hyderabad state, India, NW of Hyderabad; impounded by 115-ft.-high dam across Manjra R., 32 mi. S of Bodhan; constructed in 1930s. Feeds **Nizam Sagar Canal,** which extends 70 mi. N and NE, past Rudrur (sugar-cane experimental farm) and Nizamabad, to just S of Armur, irrigating c.135,000 acres.

Nizam's Dominions, India: see HYDERABAD, state.

Nizankowice, Ukrainian SSR: see NIZHANKOVICHI.

Nizao (nēsou'), town (1950 pop. 2,039), Trujillo Valdez prov., S Dominican Republic, on the coast, 26 mi. SW of Ciudad Trujillo; coffee, rice, bananas.

Nizhankovichi (nyēzhŭnkô'vēchē), Pol. *Niżankowice,* town (1931 pop. 2,014), NW Drogobych oblast, Ukrainian SSR, on Pol. border, 7 mi. N of Dobromil; cement; sawmilling, grain processing.

Nizhegorod, Russian SFSR: see GORKI, oblast.

Nizhne-[Rus. combining form,=LOWER], in Rus. names: see also NIZHNEYE, NIZHNI, NIZHNIYE, NIZHNYAYA.

Nizhne-Amur, oblast, Russian SFSR: see LOWER AMUR.

Nizhne-Angarsk (nyēzh"nyĭ-ŭn-gärsk'), town (1948 pop. over 2,000), NW Buryat-Mongol Autonomous SSR, Russian SFSR, on L. Baikal, at mouth of Upper Angara R., 285 mi. NNE of Ulan-Ude; fish canneries. Until 1938, also called Kozlovo.

Nizhne-Chirskaya (–chēr'skīŭ), village (1926 pop. 7,320), SW Stalingrad oblast, Russian SFSR, on right bank of Don R., just below mouth of the Chir, and 65 mi. WSW of Stalingrad; flour milling, metalworks; wheat, cotton. Pop. largely Cossack.

Nizhnedevitsk (–dyĭvētsk'), village (1926 pop. 2,272), W Voronezh oblast, Russian SFSR, 35 mi. WSW of Voronezh; wheat.

Nizhne-Gnilovskoi or **Nizhne-Gnilovskoy** (–gnyēlŭfskoi'), town (1939 pop. over 2,000), SW Rostov oblast, Russian SFSR, on Don R. and 3 mi. SW of Rostov; shipbuilding.

Nizhne-Gniloye (–gnĭloi'ŭ), village (1939 pop. over 2,000), E Kursk oblast, Russian SFSR, 17 mi. NE of Stary Oskol; wheat, sugar beets.

Nizhnegorski or **Nizhnegorskiy** (–gôr'skē), town (1948 pop. over 2,000), NE Crimea, Russian SFSR, on railroad, on Salgir R. and 23 mi. SE of Dzhankoi; flour mill; wheat, cotton, orchards. Until 1944, Seitler.

Nizhne-Ilimsk (–ēlyēmsk'), village (1939 pop. over 500), W central Irkutsk oblast, Russian SFSR, on Ilim R. and 210 mi. NNE of Tulun. Iron-ore deposits near by.

Nizhne-Isetski, Russian SFSR: see SVERDLOVSK, city, Sverdlovsk oblast.

Nizhne-Kamchatsk (–kŭmchätsk'), village (1939 pop. under 500), Kamchatka oblast, Khabarovsk Territory, Russian SFSR, on E Kamchatka Peninsula, 255 mi. N of Petropavlovsk and on Kamchatka R. Founded 1700.

Nizhne-Kolosovskoye, Russian SFSR: see KOLOSOVKA, Omsk oblast.

Nizhne-Kolymsk (nyēzh"nyĭ-kŭlĭmsk'), village (1948 pop. over 500), NE Yakut Autonomous SSR, Russian SFSR, on Kolyma R., at mouth of Anyui R., and 200 mi. NE of Sredne-Kolymsk; river port; reindeer raising. Founded 1644; early center of Siberian exploration.

Nizhne-Saraninski, Russian SFSR: see SARANA.

Nizhne-Stalinsk (–stä'lyĭnsk), town (1948 pop. over 500), SE Yakut Autonomous SSR, Russian SFSR, on Yakutsk-Never highway and 5 mi. SSE of Aldan; gold mining.

Nizhne-Troitski or **Nizhne-Troitskiy** (–trô'yĭtskē), town (1926 pop. 2,348), W Bashkir Autonomous SSR, Russian SFSR, 95 mi. WSW of Ufa; woolen-milling center. Until 1928, Nizhnetroitski Zavod.

Nizhneudinsk (–ōōdyēnsk', –ōō'dyĭnsk), city (1926 pop. 10,342), SW Irkutsk oblast, Russian SFSR, on Trans-Siberian RR, on Uda R. and 285 mi. NW of Irkutsk; metalworking, lumbering, distilling, tanning sheepskin. Founded 1648, chartered 1764.

Nizhne-Uvelskoye, Russian SFSR: see UVELSKI.

Nizhnev (nyēzh'nyĭf), Pol. *Niżniów* (nyēzh'nyōōf), town (1931 pop. 4,720), E Stanislav oblast, Ukrainian SSR, on the Dniester and 17 mi. E of Stanislav; lime processing, basketmaking, flour milling, distilling.

Nizhneye (nyēzh'nyăŭ), town (1926 pop. 5,113), W Voroshilovgrad oblast, Ukrainian SSR, in the Donbas, on the Northern Donets and 15 mi. NE of Popasnaya; coal mines.

Nizhni or **Nizhniy** [Rus.,=LOWER], in Rus. names: see also NIZHNE- [Rus. combining form], NIZHNIYE, NIZHNYAYA.

Nizhni Baskunchak or **Nizhniy Baskunchak** (nyēzh"nyē bŭskōōnchäk'), town (1926 pop. 3,234), NE

Astrakhan oblast, Russian SFSR, on L. BASKUNCHAK, 140 mi. NNW of Astrakhan, on rail spur; major salt-extracting center; gypsum works.

Nizhni Ingash or **Nizhniy Ingash** (ēn-gäsh'), village (1948 pop. over 2,000), SE Krasnoyarsk Territory, Russian SFSR, 40 mi. E of Kansk and on Trans-Siberian RR (Ingashskaya station); lumber milling.

Nizhni Karanlug, Armenian SSR: see MARTUNI.

Nizhni Lomov or **Nizhniy Lomov** (lô'mŭf), city (1939 pop. over 10,000), N Penza oblast, Russian SFSR, 60 mi. WNW of Penza; rail spur terminus; road hub; match-mfg. center; distilling. Became city in 17th cent. Village of Verkhni Lomov is 6 mi. SW; match mfg.

Nizhni Nagolchik or **Nizhniy Nagol'chik** (nŭgôl'-chĭk), town (1939 pop. over 2,000), S Voroshilovgrad oblast, Ukrainian SSR, in the Donbas, 6 mi. S of Bokovo-Antratsit; silver-lead and coal mines.

Nizhni Naur, Russian SFSR: see NADTERECHNAYA.

Nizhni Novgorod, Russian SFSR: see GORKI, city.

Nizhni Pyandzh or **Nizhniy Pyandzh** (pyänj') [Rus.,=lower Panj], town (1939 pop. over 500), S Stalinabad oblast, Tadzhik SSR, on Panj R. (Afghanistan border) and 45 mi. S of Kurgan-Tyube (connected by narrow-gauge railroad); sheep, goats. Head of navigation on the Amu Darya system.

Nizhni Tagil or **Nizhniy Tagil** (tŭgēl'), city (1926 pop. 38,849; 1939 pop. 159,864; 1946 pop. estimate 250,000), W Sverdlovsk oblast, Russian SFSR, in the central Urals, on Tagil R. and 75 mi. NNE of Sverdlovsk. Rail junction (San-Donato station, 4 mi. N). Leading metallurgical center, based on magnetite and iron deposits of VYSOKAYA and LEBYAZHYE mts.; mfg. (railroad cars, aircraft, coke, machine tools, agr. machinery, building materials, chemicals, textiles, ceramics), woodworking, food processing. Has teachers col., mus. Within city limits are Vysokaya works (8 mi. WNW of city, on rail spur), noted railroad-car mfg. plant (established 1939) at Vagonozavod station (6 mi. NE of city), and Gorbunovo chemical and peat works (5 mi. S of city, on rail spur). Manganese, copper, gold, and building-stone deposits near by. Founded 1725, following development of Vysokaya works. Noted steel and sheet-metal mfg. center prior to First World War. Became city in 1917; expanded in 1930s and during Second World War.

Nizhni Tsasuchei or **Nizhniy Tsasuchey** (tsŭsōōchā'), village (1948 pop. over 500), S Chita oblast, Russian SFSR, on Onon R. and 125 mi. SE of Chita, near Mongolian border, in agr. area (wheat, livestock).

Nizhni Ufalei or **Nizhniy Ufaley** (ōōfŭlyā'), town (1926 pop. 4,864), NW Chelyabinsk oblast, Russian SFSR, in the central Urals, near upper Ufa R., 12 mi. SW (under jurisdiction) of Verkhni Ufalei; metalworking center. Iron-ore, refractory-clay deposits. Until 1928, Nizhne-Ufaleiski Zavod.

Nizhniye [Rus.,=LOWER], in Rus. names: see also NIZHNE- [Rus. combining form], NIZHNEYE, NIZHNI, NIZHNYAYA.

Nizhniye Kresty (nēzh"nyĕù kryĕstē'), village (1948 pop. over 500), NE Yakut Autonomous SSR, Russian SFSR, on Kolyma R. and 215 mi. NE of Sredne-Kolymsk; river port.

Nizhniye Sergi (syĕr'gē), city (1935 pop. estimate 12,000), SW Sverdlovsk oblast, Russian SFSR, in the central Urals, on small lake, on railroad and 55 mi. WSW of Sverdlovsk; metallurgical center (steel, pig iron). Developed prior to First World War; became city in 1943. Until c.1928, Nizhneserginski Zavod.

Nizhniye Serogozy (syĕrŭgô'zē), village (1926 pop. 8,209), E Kherson oblast, Ukrainian SSR, 45 mi. W of Melitopol; metalworks, flour mill.

Nizhniye Ustriki, Poland: see USTRZYKI DOLNE.

Nizhnyaya [Rus.,=LOWER], in Rus. names: see also NIZHNE- [Rus. combining form], NIZHNEYE, NIZHNI, NIZHNIYE.

Nizhnyaya Akhta (nyēzh"nyĭù äkh'tŭ), village (1932 pop. estimate 4,070), central Armenian SSR, near NW shore of L. Sevan, 25 mi. NNE of Erivan; rail terminus of branch from Erivan; wheat; metalworks. Sometimes called Akhta.

Nizhnyaya Akhtala, Armenian SSR: see AKHTALA.

Nizhnyaya Berezovka (bĭryô'zŭfkŭ), W suburb (1926 pop. 4,784) of Ulan-Ude, Buryat-Mongol Autonomous SSR, Russian SFSR.

Nizhnyaya Dobrinka, Russian SFSR: see DOBRINKA, NE Stalingrad oblast.

Nizhnyaya Duvanka (dōōvän'kŭ), village (1926 pop. 5,305), NW Voroshilovgrad oblast, Ukrainian SSR, 40 mi. NW of Starobelsk; wheat.

Nizhnyaya Krynka (krĭn'kŭ), town (1939 pop. over 2,000), E Stalino oblast, Ukrainian SSR, in the Donbas, 6 mi. N of Khartsyzsk; coal mines.

Nizhnyaya Omka (ôm'kŭ), village (1948 pop. over 500), E Omsk oblast, Russian SFSR, 30 mi. NE of Kalachinsk, in agr. area.

Nizhnyaya Pesha (pyĕ'shŭ), agr. village (1939 pop. under 500), W Nenets Natl. Okrug, Archangel oblast, Russian SFSR, on small Pesha R., near Chesha Bay of Barents Sea, and 115 mi. NE of Mezen; trading post.

Nizhnyaya Salda (sŭldä'), city (1926 pop. 15,166), W central Sverdlovsk oblast, Russian SFSR, in E foothills of the central Urals, on Salda R. (right tributary of Tagil R.), on railroad and 30 mi. ENE of Nizhni Tagil; metallurgical center (steel, pig iron); sawmilling; asbestos and talc quarrying. Regional mus. Founded 1760; developed prior to First World War; became city in 1938. Formerly called Nizhne-Saldinski Zavod.

Nizhnyaya Sarana, Russian SFSR: see SARANA.

Nizhnyaya Shakhtama (shŭkhtŭmä'), town (1939 pop. over 500), SE Chita oblast, Russian SFSR, 60 mi. S of Sretensk; gold mines; graphite deposits.

Nizhnyaya Suyetka (sōō'yĭtkŭ), village (1939 pop. over 500), NW Altai Territory, Russian SFSR, on Kulunda Steppe, 50 mi. ENE of Slavgorod; dairy farming.

Nizhnyaya Tavda (tŭvdä'), village (1948 pop. over 2,000), SW Tyumen oblast, Russian SFSR, on Tavda R. and 40 mi. NE of Tyumen, in agr. area (grain, livestock).

Nizhnyaya Tunguska River, SFSR: see LOWER TUNGUSKA RIVER.

Nizhnyaya Tura (tōōrä'), town (1926 pop. 5,428), W Sverdlovsk oblast, Russian SFSR, in the central Urals, on small lake formed by Tura R., 11 mi. SSW of Is, on rail spur; metallurgical center (steel, pig iron). Until 1929, Nizhne-Turinski Zavod.

Nizhnyaya Veduga (vyĭdōō'gŭ), village (1939 pop. over 2,000), W Voronezh oblast, Russian SFSR, 23 mi. WNW of Voronezh; wheat.

Nizi (nē'zē), village (1948 pop. 6,898), Eastern Prov., NE Belgian Congo, 4 mi. SE of Kilo-Mines; gold-mining and trading center; gold processing. Machine shops.

Nizip (nĭzĭp'), town (pop. 10,017), Gaziantep prov., S Turkey, 23 mi. E of Gaziantep; olives, pistachios, wheat. Here in 1839 Turks were defeated by Egyptians. Formerly sometimes spelled Nezib, Nisib.

Nizke Tatry, mountains, Czechoslovakia: see Low TATRA.

Nizna Slana, Czechoslovakia: see ROZNAVA.

Nizne Ruzbachy, Czechoslovakia: see VYSNE RUZBACHY.

Nizniow, Ukrainian SSR: see NIZHNEV.

Nizny Medzev (nyĭzh'nē mĕd'zĕf), Slovak *Nižný Medzev*, Hung. *Alsómecenzéf* (ŏl'shōmĕ"tsĕnzāf), village (pop. 2,076), S Slovakia, Czechoslovakia, on Bodva R. and 16 mi. W of Kosice; rail terminus. Iron mines of Vysny Medzev, Slovak *Vyšný Medzev*, are just NE.

Nizny Svidnik, Czechoslovakia: see SVIDNIK.

Nizovye or **Nizov'ye** (nyĕ'zŭvyĭ), village (1939 pop. 789), W Kaliningrad oblast, Russian SFSR, near Pregel R., 9 mi. E of Kaliningrad. Until 1945, in East Prussia and called Waldau (väl'dou).

Nizwa or **Nazwa** (both: nĭzwă'), town (pop. 6,000), Oman Proper, 20 mi. W of Izki, at S foot of the Jabal Akhdar; strategic and commercial center; fortress. Copper and brass working; leather, pottery, and weaving handicrafts. Noted *halwa* production. Was long ⊙ Oman.

Nizza, France: see NICE.

Nizza di Sicilia (nē'tsä dē sēchē'lyä), village (pop. 2,857), Messina prov., NE Sicily, port on Tyrrhenian Sea, 15 mi. SSW of Messina. Sometimes Nizza Sicilia.

Nizza Monferrato (mônfĕr-rä'tô), town (pop. 5,656), Asti prov., Piedmont, NW Italy, on Belbo R. and 12 mi. SE of Asti, in grape- and vegetable-growing region; rail junction; sulphur refining; artisan industries (wine making, wood- and metalworking).

Njakwa (ŭnjä'kwä), village, Northern Prov., Nyasaland, S of Nyika Plateau, 35 mi. SSW of Livingstonia; road junction; cassava, corn.

Njala (ŭnjä'lä), village (pop. 590), South-Western Prov., S central Sierra Leone, on Jong R. and 4 mi. N of Mano; palm oil and kernels, piassava, rice. Has agr. and teachers col., experimental farm; hq. govt. Dept. of Agr.

Njarasa, Lake, Tanganyika: see EYASI, LAKE.

Njegos or **Nyegosh** (both: nyĕ'gôsh), Serbo-Croatian *Njegoš*, mountain of Dinaric Alps, W Montenegro, Yugoslavia; highest point (5,658 ft.) is 14 mi. NW of Niksic.

Njegusi or **Nyegushi** (both: nyĕ'gōōshē), Serbo-Croatian *Njeguši*, village, S Montenegro, Yugoslavia, at NE foot of the Lovcen, 5 mi. NW of Cetinje; road junction.

N'Jolé, Fr. Equatorial Africa: see N'DJOLÉ.

Njombe (ŭnjōm'bā), town, Southern Highlands prov., S Tanganyika, 95 mi. ESE of Mbeya, in Livingstone Mts.; wheat, tea, coffee; livestock.

Njoro (ŭnjō'rō), village, Rift Valley prov., W Kenya, on railroad and 10 mi. WSW of Nakuru; alt. 7,113 ft. Corn, wheat, flax; dairy farming. Agr. school.

Njurunda (nyü'rŭn"dä), village (pop. 879), Västernorrland co., NE Sweden, on Ljunga R. and 8 mi. SSE of Sundsvall; lumber and pulp mills, sulphite works. Has old church.

Nkalago (ŭn-kä'lägō'), town, Ogoja prov., Eastern Provinces, SE Nigeria, 20 mi. E of Enugu; silver and lead-zinc mining. Limestone, salt deposits.

Nkana or **Nkana Mine** (ŭngkä'nä), mining township (pop. 13,851), Western Prov., N Northern Rhodesia, just W of Kitwe and 33 mi. WNW of Ndola; copper-mining center; smelter, electrolytic refinery. Also produces cobalt and gold, with silver and selenium as by-products.

Nkata Bay (ŭngkä'tä), town, Northern Prov., Nyasaland, port on W shore of L. Nyasa, 22 mi. NNE of Chinteche; fishing; cassava, corn. Tourist resort. Rubber plantation (S).

Nkawkaw (ŭngkô'kô), town, Eastern Prov., N Gold Coast colony, on railroad and 45 mi. NW of Koforidua; gold mining; cacao market. Mpraeso bauxite mine just NE.

N'Komi, Fr. Equatorial Africa: see FERNAN-VAZ.

N'Kongsamba (ŭng-kôngsäm'bä), town, ⊙ Mungo region, W Fr. Cameroons, 140 mi. NW of Yaoundé; commercial and tourist center, terminus of railroad from Douala; sawmilling, palm-oil plantations, repair shops. Has meteorological station, R.C. and Protestant missions, jr. col. Airfield. Seat of vicar apostolic. Djoungo (jōōng'gō), 8 mi. NNE, on railroad, has large banana plantations.

Nmai River (nmī'), native *Nmai Kka* (mā'kä), Chinese *En-mei-k'ai* (ŭn'mā'kī'), left (main) headstream of Irrawaddy R. in N Upper Burma, rises in high mts. on China's Sikang line, N of Putao, flows 300 mi. S, joining the Mali R. 25 mi. N of Myitkyina to form Irrawaddy R.

Nnewi (ŭn-nōō'wē), town, Onitsha prov., Eastern Provinces, Nigeria, 12 mi. SSE of Onitsha; palm oil and kernels, kola nuts. Sometimes Newi.

No, Lake (nō), in swampy SUDD region of the Nile system, S central Anglo-Egyptian Sudan, 80 mi. W of Malakal; of variable size (maximum □ 40), depending on season. Formed by flood waters of the BAHR EL GHAZAL and the BAHR EL JEBEL, on the White Nile. Navigable year-round.

Noailles (nôī'), village (pop. 1,147), Oise dept., N France, 9 mi. SE of Beauvais; mfg. of brushes, wood products.

Noakhali (nōäkä'lē), district (□ 1,658; 1951 pop. 2,294,000), East Bengal, E Pakistan; ⊙ Noakhali Bounded NE by Tripura state, W by Meghna R.; Ganges Delta in S part of dist.; includes Sandwip (SE) and Hatia (SW) isls., separating Meghna R. mouths from Bay of Bengal. Mainly alluvial soil; rice, jute, pulse, chili, oilseeds, sugar cane, extensive coconut and betel palm groves; hill tract NE (sal trees). Major cotton-weaving center at Chaumuhani; brassware mfg. at Noakhali, perfume mfg. at Fenny; coconut-oil milling. Dist. subject to severe cyclones (over half of Hatia Isl. pop. destroyed in 1876). Became part of Bengal under Afghan governors in 1353; figured in 17th-cent. struggle bet. Moguls and Portuguese; passed 1765 to English. Sandwip Isl. was 17th-cent. Port. and Arakanese pirate stronghold. Present dist. formed 1822. Part of former Br. Bengal prov., India, until inc. 1947 into new Pakistan prov. of East Bengal, following creation of Pakistan. Formerly called Bhulua.

Noakhali, town (pop. 18,575), ⊙ Noakhali dist., SE East Bengal, E Pakistan, on Meghna R. and 75 mi. SE of Dacca; trades in rice, jute, oilseeds; brassware mfg. Formerly called Sudharam.

Noale (nôä'lĕ), town (pop. 1,263), Venezia prov., Veneto, N Italy, 15 mi. NW of Venice; mfg. (agr. machinery, stoves, beads).

Noalejo (nōälā'hō), town (pop. 3,129), Jaén prov., S Spain, 18 mi. SSE of Jaén; flour milling; olive oil, cereals, vegetables, livestock.

Noamundi (nō'ŭmōōndē), town (pop. 6,389), Singhbhum dist., S Bihar, India, on railroad and 65 mi. SW of Jamshedpur; major hematite-mining center for Jamshedpur iron- and steelworks. Hematite mining near Gua (10 mi. WNW) and Bada Barabil (9 mi. WSW), both rail spur termini.

Noank, Conn.: see GROTON.

Noarlunga, village (pop. 188), SE South Australia, 19 mi. SSW of Adelaide; fruitgrowing and dairying center. Port Noarlunga (pop. 690) is near by on Gulf St. Vincent.

Noatak (nō'ŭtăk), Eskimo village (pop. 320), NW Alaska, on Noatak R. and 50 mi. NNW of Kotzebue; supply center for trappers and hunters.

Noatak River, NW Alaska, rises in Brooks Range, near 67°28'N 154°50'W, flows c.400 mi. W to Kotzebue Sound opposite Kotzebue.

Nobber, Gaelic *An Obair*, town (pop. 103), N Co. Meath, Ireland, on Dee R. and 13 mi. NNW of An Uaimh; agr. market (cattle, horses; potatoes). Turlough O'Carolan b. here.

Nobeoka (nōbā'ōkä), city (1940 pop. 79,426; 1947 pop. 73,742), Miyazaki prefecture, E Kyushu, Japan, on Hyuga Sea, at mouth of Gokase R., 47 mi. NNE of Miyazaki; industrial center (chemicals, rayon clothing). Important munitions center in Second World War. Bombed 1945.

Noble, Dominican Republic: see VICENTE NOBLE.

Noble. 1 County (□ 410; pop. 25,075), NE Ind.; ⊙ Albion. Agr. area (livestock, poultry, fruit, grain, soybeans, truck). Mfg., including dairy- and farm-products processing, at Kendallville, Albion, Ligonier. Gravel pits. Has many small lakes. Drained by Elkhart R. Formed 1835. **2** County (□ 404; pop. 11,750), E Ohio; ⊙ Caldwell. Drained by Wills Creek and small Duck and Seneca creeks. Includes Senecaville Reservoir. Agr. (livestock, grain, tobacco, poultry; dairy products); coal mines, oil wells, clay pits, limestone quarries. Formed 1851. **3** County (□ 744; pop. 12,156), N Okla.; ⊙ Perry. Bounded NE by Arkansas R.; drained by small Black Bear Creek. Agr. area (wheat, oats, livestock, cotton); dairying. Mfg. at Billings and Perry. Oil and natural-gas wells; gasoline plant. Includes Tonkawa and Ponca Otoe Indian reservations. Formed 1893.

Noble. 1 Village (pop. 776), Richland co., SE Ill., 7 mi. WSW of Olney, in agr. area (corn, wheat, livestock, apples). 2 Village (pop. 238), Sabine parish, W La., 57 mi. S of Shreveport; agr. Oil wells near by. 3 Town (pop. 724), Cleveland co., central Okla., 6 mi. SSE of Norman, and on Canadian R., in agr. area. 4 Village, Pa.: see ABINGTON.

Nobleboro or **Nobleborough,** town (pop. 654), Lincoln co., S Maine, on Damariscotta L. and 11 mi. NE of Wiscasset.

Nobleford, village (pop. 126), S Alta., 17 mi. NW of Lethbridge; wheat, dairying.

Noblejas (nōvlä'häs), town (pop. 3,100), Toledo prov., central Spain, on railroad and 33 mi. SSE of Madrid, in agr. region (cereals, olives, grapes, esparto). Olive-oil pressing, alcohol distilling, plaster mfg. Mineral springs.

Nobles, county (□ 712; pop. 22,435), SW Minn.; ⊙ Worthington. Agr. area bordering Iowa and watered by headwaters of Little Rock R. Corn, oats, barley, potatoes, livestock. Includes part of Coteau des Prairies. Co. formed 1857. Ocheda L. is in SE.

Noblestown, village (pop. 1,375, with adjacent Sturgeon), Allegheny co., W Pa., 11 mi. WSW of downtown Pittsburgh.

Noblesville, city (pop. 6,567), ⊙ Hamilton co., central Ind., on West Fork of White R. and 20 mi. NNE of Indianapolis, in livestock and grain area; mfg. (furniture, canned goods, jars, rubber goods, paper, flour); breeds draft horses. Settled 1823; inc. as town in 1851, as city in 1887.

Noboribetsu, Japan: see HOROBETSU.

Noboritate (nōbōrō'tätä), largest town (pop. 8,473) of Oyano-shima, Amakusa Isls., Japan, in Kumamoto prefecture, near E coast of isl.; rice, wheat; fishing. Coal.

Nobressart (nōbrĕsär'), Ger. *Elcherot* (ĕl'khürōt), agr. village (pop. 866), Luxembourg prov., SE Belgium, in the Ardennes, 6 mi. NW of Arlon. Pop. mainly German-speaking.

Nobska Point (nŏb'skŭ), SW Cape Cod, Mass., low promontory just SE of Woods Hole; extends into Vineyard Sound; lighthouse (41°31'N 70°39'W).

Nocatee (nŏ'kūtē"), village (1940 pop. 595), De Soto co., S central Fla., near Peace R., 4 mi. S of Arcadia; large crate factory.

Noccalula Falls (nŏkŭlōō'lŭ), in small Black Creek (c.15 mi. long), just NW of Gadsden, Ala.; drop of c.100 ft. over limestone ridge of Lookout Mtn.

Nocé (nôsā'), village (pop. 295), Orne dept., NW France, in the Perche hills, 8 mi. NW of Nogent-le-Rotrou; sawmilling, horse raising.

Nocera Inferiore (nôchā'rä ĕnfĕrēō'rĕ), anc. *Nuceria Alfaterna,* town (pop. 23,289), Salerno prov., Campania, S Italy, 8 mi. NW of Salerno; rail junction; tomato canneries, cotton and lumber mills; tinworking, candy mfg. Bishopric. Has ruins of Angevin castle. Destroyed by Hannibal (216 B.C.); rebuilt by Augustus.

Nocera Tirinese (tērēnā'zĕ), town (pop. 2,718), Catanzaro prov., Calabria, S Italy, near Savuto R., 10 mi. WNW of Nicastro, in agr. region (cereals, olives, fruit).

Nocera Umbra (ōōm'brä), village (pop. 1,152), Perugia prov., Umbria, central Italy, 9 mi. ENE of Assisi. Bishopric. Mineral baths near by.

Noce River (nô'chĕ), Trentino–Alto Adige, N Italy, rises in glaciers on Cima dei Tre Signori in Ortles group, flows ENE, through Val di Sole, and S to Adige R. 6 mi. N of Trent; 50 mi. long. Used for hydroelectric power (Mezzocorona).

Noceto (nôchā'tô), town (pop. 1,759), Parma prov., Emilia-Romagna, N central Italy, 7 mi. W of Parma; sausage.

Nochistlán (nōchēstlän'). 1 Town, Oaxaca, Mexico: see NOCHIXTLÁN. 2 City (pop. 4,151), Zacatecas, N central Mexico, on interior plateau, 50 mi. SW of Aguascalientes; alt. 6,232 ft.; agr. center (grain, sugar cane, beans, fruit, livestock).

Nochixtlán or **Nochistlán** (both: nōchēslän'), officially Asunción Nochixtlán, town (pop. 2,562), Oaxaca, S Mexico, in Sierra Madre del Sur, on Inter-American Highway and 45 mi. NW of Oaxaca; alt. 6,423 ft. Agr. center (cereals, coffee, sugar cane, beans, fruit; goats).

Nochrich (nō'krēk), Ger. *Leschkirch* (lĕsh'kĭrkh), Hung. *Ujegyház* (ōō'yĕdyŭhäs), village (pop. 1,393), Sibiu prov., central Rumania, on railroad and 15 mi. NE of Sibiu; agr. center.

Noci (nô'chē), town (pop. 10,595), Bari prov., Apulia, S Italy, 14 mi. SSW of Monopoli; olive oil, macaroni.

Nocona (nŭkō'nŭ), city (pop. 3,022), Montague co., N Texas, c.45 mi. E of Wichita Falls, in agr., ranching, oil-producing area; a leather-goods mfg. center (boots, saddles, sports equipment).

Nocupétaro (nōkōōpā'tärō), town (pop. 707), Michoacán, central Mexico, 28 mi. SE of Tacámbaro; rice, sugar cane, fruit.

Noda (nō'dä), town (pop. 24,028), Chiba prefecture, central Honshu, Japan, 20 mi. NNE of Tokyo; soy-sauce mfg.; raw silk, poultry, rice.

Noda, Russian SFSR: see CHEKHOV, city.

Nodaway (nŏ'dŭwā), county (□ 877; pop. 24,033), NW Mo.; ⊙ Maryville. Drained by Nodaway R., Little Platte R., and One Hundred and Two R. Agr. region (corn, wheat); stock raising (especially hogs). Formed 1845.

Nodaway, town (pop. 233), Adams co., SW Iowa, on East Nodaway R. and 9 mi. WSW of Corning.

Nodaway River, in SW Iowa and NW Mo., formed near Villisca in Montgomery co. (Iowa) by junction of Middle and West Nodaway rivers, flows to Missouri R. above St. Joseph. Total length, including Middle Nodaway R., is 188 mi. Receives East Nodaway R. (c.60 mi. long) near Shambaugh.

Nodoa (nō'dō'ä'), Mandarin *Nata* (nä'dä'), town (pop. 2,000), NW Hainan, Kwangtung prov., China, 20 mi. SE of Tanhsien; commercial center; exports rubber, coffee, sugar, ginger, peas, melon seeds, livestock.

Nodushan, Iran: see NUDUSHAN.

Noehoe, in Indonesian names: see NUHU.

Noel (nō'ŭl), town (pop. 685), McDonald co., extreme SW Mo., in the Ozarks, on Elk R. and 24 mi. SSW of Neosho; resort, fishing; strawberries, dairying.

Noemfoor, Netherlands New Guinea: see NUMFOR.

Noépé (nōĕ'pā), village, S Fr. Togoland, on railroad and 15 mi. NW of Lomé; palm oil and kernels, copra. R.C. and Protestant missions. Custom house.

Noesa, in Indonesian names: see NUSA.

Noetinger (nwĕtĭng-gâr'), town (pop. 2,482), E Córdoba prov., Argentina, 55 mi. E of Villa María; wheat, flax, corn, alfalfa, livestock.

Noeux-les-Mines (nû-lā-mēn'), town (pop. 12,643), Pas-de-Calais dept., N France, 4 mi. SSE of Béthune; coal-mining center. Sugar-beet distilling. In Br. front lines during First World War.

Noez (nōĕth'), town (pop. 1,041), Toledo prov., central Spain, 12 mi. SW of Toledo; wheat, barley, carobs, chick-peas, olives, grapes, livestock.

Nogaisk or **Nogaysk** (nŭgīsk'), town (1926 pop. 4,523), S Zaporozhe oblast, Ukrainian SSR, on Sea of Azov, 21 mi. W of Osipenko; fish canneries; metalworks. A center of Nogai Tatars in early-19th cent.

Nogales (nōgä'lĕs), town (pop. 2,245), Valparaiso prov., central Chile, on railroad and 33 mi. NE of Valparaiso; agr. center (grain, wine, fruit, hemp, stock). Lime and copper deposits near by.

Nogales (nōgä'lĭs, Sp. nōgä'lĕs). 1 City (pop. 13,866), Sonora, NW Mexico, on U.S. border adjoining Nogales (Ariz.), 160 mi. N of Hermosillo. Rail junction at terminus of Mexico's west coast railroad; international trading point in cattle-raising and mining area (graphite, manganese, silver, gold, lead, antimony). Exports winter vegetables of S Sonora and Sinaloa. 2 Town (pop. 8,479), Veracruz, E Mexico, in valley of Sierra Madre Oriental, at S foot of Pico de Orizaba, on railroad and 4 mi. WSW of Orizaba; textile-milling and agr. center (coffee, tobacco, sugar cane, fruit).

Nogales (nōgä'lĕs), town (pop. 2,079), Badajoz prov., W Spain, 23 mi. SE of Badajoz; cereals, vegetables, olives, livestock.

Nogales (nōgä'lĭs), city (pop. 6,153), ⊙ Santa Cruz co., S Ariz., c.60 mi. S of Tucson; contiguous with Nogales, Mexico; port of entry in mining (gold, silver, lead, copper, molybdenum), livestock area. Near by are ruined Guevavi mission (1692), Tumacacori (tōōmŭkä'kŭrē) mission (1696; now a natl. monument), and ruins of Tubac (1752; 1st white settlement in Ariz.). Founded 1880 as Isaactown, renamed 1882 with railroad's arrival, inc. 1893. Has rail connection with Guadalajara, 880 mi. SSE, in Mexico.

Nogal Peak, N.Mex.: see SIERRA BLANCA, range.

Nogal Valley (nōgäl'), in N Ital. Somaliland, extends 150 mi. ESE from Br. Somaliland border to Negro Bay of Indian Ocean; intermittent stream in lower section below Callis.

Nogami (nōgä'mē), town (pop. 9,470), Saitama prefecture, central Honshu, Japan, 16 mi. W of Kumagaya; raw silk, textiles.

Nogamut (nŏ'gŭmŭt), Indian village (1939 pop. 23), W Alaska, on Holitna R. and 75 mi. SE of Aniak; trapping, prospecting. Sometimes spelled Nugammute and Nogamiut.

Nogara (nôgä'rä), village (pop. 1,330), Verona prov.; Veneto, N Italy, 19 mi. S of Verona; rail junction, hemp mill.

Nogaro (nôgärō'), village (pop. 1,202), Gers dept., SW France, 25 mi. SW of Condom; winegrowing and Armagnac brandy distilling. Has 11th-cent. church.

Nogata (nōgä'tä), city (1940 pop. 47,026; 1947 pop. 47,521), Fukuoka prefecture, N Kyushu, Japan, 22 mi. NE of Fukuoka; rail junction; commercial center for agr. area (rice, wheat, sweet potatoes); steel mills, dairies; woodworking, sake brewing.

Nogatino (nŭgä'tyĭnŭ), town (1939 pop. over 500), central Moscow oblast, Russian SFSR, on S bank of S port of Moscow (SE); metalworking.

Nogat River (nō'gät), in East Prussia, after 1945 in N Poland, E arm of Vistula R. delta estuary, leaves the Vistula 11 mi. SW of Marienburg (Malbork), flows 35 mi. NE, past Marienburg, to Vistula Lagoon 9 mi. NW of Elbing. From 1919 to 1939, formed border bet. territory of Free City of Danzig and East Prussia.

Nogaysk, Ukrainian SSR: see NOGAISK.

Nogent-en-Bassigny (nôzhã'-ã-bäsēnyē'), town (pop. 3,161), Haute-Marne dept., NE France, 11 mi. SE of Chaumont; noted cutlery-mfg. center.

Nogent-l'Abbesse (–läbĕs'), village (pop. 314), Marne dept., N France, 6 mi. E of Rheims; winegrowing (champagne). Its fort and Fort de la Pompelle (3 mi. SSW) were key German-held strongholds in First World War.

Nogent-l'Artaud (–lärtō'), village (pop. 933), Aisne dept., N France, on the Marne and 7 mi. SSW of Château-Thierry; optical instruments. Silicate quarries near by.

Nogent-le-Roi (–lù-rwä), village (pop. 1,379), Eure-et-Loir dept., NW central France, on the Eure and 10 mi. SE of Dreux; optical factory; flour milling.

Nogent-le-Rotrou (–lù-rôtrōō'), town (pop. 6,439), Eure-et-Loir dept., NW central France, on the Huisne and 32 mi. WSW of Chartres; horse-breeding center and agr. market; mfg. of felt hats, tanning. Has ruins of 11th–16th-cent. castle and tomb of Sully. Old ⊙ Perche region.

Nogent-sur-Marne (–sür-märn'), town (pop. 20,969), Seine dept., N central France, E residential suburb of Paris, 6 mi. from Notre Dame Cathedral, on hill above right bank of the Marne, at E edge of Bois de Vincennes; mfg. (flour products, chemicals, padlocks, thermometers, brooms). Has 13th-cent. church and a curving railroad viaduct, 2,500 ft. long. Site of institute of colonial agronomy.

Nogent-sur-Oise (–sür-wäz'), town (pop. 6,353), Oise dept., N France, near Oise R., 7 mi. NW of Senlis; aluminum works, copper and bronze smelters, metalworks.

Nogent-sur-Seine (–sür-sĕn'), town (pop. 3,511), Aube dept., NE central France, on left bank of Seine R., and 11 mi. ESE of Provins; road center; mfg. (building material, hosiery); dairying. On farm (4 mi. ESE) once stood abbey of the Paraclete (Fr. *Le Paraclet*), founded 1123 by Abélard for Héloïse, its 1st abbess.

Nogent-sur-Vernisson (–sür-vĕrnēsõ'), village (pop. 1,111), Loiret dept., N central France, 11 mi. S of Montargis; enameled household articles. School of forestry.

Noginsk (nŭgēnsk'). 1 Village, W Evenki Natl. Okrug, Krasnoyarsk Territory, Russian SFSR, on lower Tunguska R. and 260 mi. W of Tura. Graphite mines near by. 2 City (1926 pop. 38,494; 1939 pop. 81,024), E Moscow oblast, Russian SFSR, on Klyazma R. and 32 mi. E of Moscow; major textile-milling center (cotton, silk, wool); metalworking, sawmilling. Glukhovo cotton mill is 2 mi. NE. Chartered 1791; until c.1930, called Bogorodsk.

Nogliki (nô'glyĭkē), village (1948 pop. over 2,000), N Sakhalin, Russian SFSR, on Sea of Okhotsk, at mouth of Tym R., on road and 75 mi. NE of Aleksandrovsk; fish cannery.

Nogoa River (nŭgō'ŭ), E central Queensland, Australia, rises in Great Dividing Range SW of Springsure, flows 180 mi. NE, joining Comet R. near Comet to form Mackenzie R.

Nogoyá (nōgoi-ä'), town (1947 pop. 11,914), ⊙Nogoyá dept. (□ 1,670; 1947 pop. 45,859), S central Entre Ríos prov., Argentina, near Nogoyá R., 60 mi. SE of Paraná; rail junction in agr. area (flax, wheat, corn, grapes, livestock); flour milling. Airport. Has col., agr. school.

Nograd (nō'gräd), Hung. *Nógrád,* town (pop. 1,811), Nograd-Hont co., N Hungary, 25 mi. N of Budapest. Fortress here, now in ruins, dates back to Arpad rulers.

Nograd-Hont (no'gräd-hônt'), Hung. *Nógrád-Hont,* county (□ 1,090; pop. 226,272), N Hungary; ⊙ Balassagyarmat. Heavily forested Börzsöny Mts. in W, Cserhat Mts. in S; drained by Zagyva R.; bounded W and N by the Ipoly. Grain, potatoes, hogs, sheep; coal and lignite mines near Salgotarjan, industrial center. Numerous distilleries and brickworks.

Nogradveröce (nō'grädvĕ"rû-tsĕ), Hung. *Nógrádverőce,* town (pop. 2,253), Nograd-Hont co., N Hungary, on the Danube and 5 mi. NW of Vac; summer resort; brickworks.

Nogueira, Serra de (sĕ'rŭ dĭ nōōgā'rŭ), range in Bragança dist., N Portugal, SW of Bragança; rises to 4,324 ft.

Noguera Pallaresa River (nōgā'rä pälyärä'sä), Lérida prov., NE Spain, rises N of Sort near Fr. border in the central Pyrenees, flows c.100 mi. S to the Segre above Camarasa. Forms the Tremp reservoir (with 300-ft. dam), feeding 2 hydroelectric plants. The Flamisell joins it at Pobla de Segur.

Noguera Ribagorzana River (rēvägōr-thä'nä), NE Spain, rises in the mts. of Valle de Arán in the central Pyrenees, flows 80 mi. S, forming Catalonia-Aragon border as far as Alfarrás, to the Segre 6 mi. above Lérida.

Nohant-Vic (nôä-vēk'), village (pop. 155), Indre dept., central France, near Indre R., 3 mi. NW of La Châtre; near-by home of George Sand is now a mus. Sometimes spelled Nohant-Vicq.

Nohar (nō'hŭr), town (pop. 9,607), N Rajasthan, India, 120 mi. NE of Bikaner; millet, gram; handloom weaving, cattle raising.

Nohara (nōhä'rä), town (pop. 4,976), Nara prefecture, S Honshu, Japan, just SE of Gojo; rice, wheat, raw silk. Bamboo groves.

Noheji (nōhä'jē), town (pop. 15,243), Aomori prefecture, N Honshu, Japan, on S Mutsu Bay, 20 mi. E of Aomori; rice growing, fishing, horse breeding.

Noho (nô'hŭ'), town, ⊙ Noho co. (pop. 275,534), NW Heilungkiang prov., Manchuria, on railroad and 85 mi. NNE of Tsitsihar; kaoliang, rye, millet, corn, hemp, tobacco, skins and hides.

Noicattaro (noikät'tärô), town (pop. 9,862), Bari prov., Apulia, S Italy, 9 mi. SE of Bari; hosiery.

Noichi (nōē'chē), town (pop. 5,154), Kochi prefecture, S Shikoku, Japan, 9 mi. E of Kochi; rice, raw silk, wheat.

Noir, Lac, Haut-Rhin dept., France: see ORBEY.

Noire, Montagne, France: see MONTAGNE NOIRE.

Noire, Rivière, Vietnam: see BLACK RIVER.

Noires, Montagnes, France: see MONTAGNES NOIRES.

Noirétable (nwärātä'blů), village (pop. 848), Loire dept., SE central France, in Monts du Forez, 11 mi. ESE of Thiers; cutlery mfg., woodworking.

Noir Island (nwär), in SW Tierra del Fuego, Chile, 30 mi. S of Santa Inés Isl.; 7 mi. long; rises to 600 ft. Terminates SW in rocky Cape Noir, 54°30'S 73°6'W.

Noirmont (nwärmō'), mountain (5,150 ft.) in the Jura, SW Switzerland, 9 mi. NW of Nyon.

Noirmoutier (nwärmōōtyä'), town (pop. 2,016), on NE shore of Île de Noirmoutier, Vendée dept., W France, 19 mi. S of Saint-Nazaire; bathing resort and fishing port; saltworks. Church of abbey (founded c.680) contains empty crypt of Saint-Philibert. Here, in 1794, the leader of the Vendée rebellion was captured and shot.

Noirmoutier, Île de (ēl dů), island (□ 22; pop. 7,432), in Bay of Biscay, off Vendée dept., W France, c.18 mi. S of Saint-Nazaire; 12 mi. long, 1–4 mi. wide, sheltering Bay of Bourgneuf (NE) and separated from mainland by Goulet de Fromentine. Consists of low, barren tracts, sand dunes, and salt marshes; produces fertilizer, salt, fruits, potatoes; fisheries. Port of Noirmoutier and bathing resort of Bois de la Chaize on NE shore.

Noisiel (nwäzyĕl'), village (pop. 1,000), Seine-et-Marne dept., N central France, on left bank of the Marne and 13 mi. E of Paris; chocolate factory.

Noisy-le-Grand (nwäzē'-lů-grā'), town (pop. 6,586), Seine-et-Oise dept., N central France, an outer E suburb of Paris, 9 mi. from Notre Dame Cathedral, on left bank of the Marne, opposite Neuilly-sur-Marne; mfg. (rubber, paints, surgical instruments).

Noisy-les-Bains (–lā-bē'), village (pop. 1,248), Oran dept., NW Algeria, 10 mi. SSW of Mostaganem; winegrowing; oil pressing, brick mfg. Mineral springs.

Noisy-le-Sec (–lů-sĕk'), town (pop. 16,103), Seine dept., N central France, a NE suburb of Paris, 6 mi. from Notre Dame Cathedral, on Ourcq Canal; rail center; plaster- and metalworks.

Nojima, Cape (nōjē'mä), Jap. *Nojima-saki*, Chiba prefecture, central Honshu, Japan, on S Chiba Peninsula, in the Pacific, near entrance to Tokyo Bay; 34°54'N 139°53'E; lighthouse.

Nokhar, W Pakistan: see CHUHARKANA.

Nokia (nō'kēä), town (pop. 14,922), Häme co., SW Finland, on L. Pyhä, at outflow of Kokemäki R. (52-ft.-high Emä Rapids, Finnish *Emäkoski*), 7 mi. W of Tampere; pulp, cellulose, paper, and knitting mills, rubber works. Hydroelectric station. Until 1938 called Pohjois-Pirkkala.

Nokilalaki, Mount (nōkēlälä'kē) (10,863 ft.), central Celebes, Indonesia, 45 mi. NNW of Poso.

Nokkeushi, Japan: see KITAMI.

Nok Kundi (nōk' kōōn'dē), village, Chagai dist., NW Baluchistan, W Pakistan, on railroad and 205 mi. WSW of Nushki. Sulphur-ore, gypsum, limestone deposits near by. Also called Kundi, Nokkundi, Kondi, Nok Kondi.

Nokomis (nōkō'mĭs), town (pop. 442), S central Sask., 22 mi. SE of Watrous; railroad junction; grain elevators, lumbering.

Nokomis, city (pop. 2,544), Montgomery co., S central Ill., 21 mi. ENE of Litchfield, in agr. and bituminous-coal area; dairy products, concrete blocks. Inc. 1867.

Nokoué, Lake (nō'kwā), coastal lagoon (12 mi. long, 5 mi. wide), S Dahomey, Fr. West Africa, just N of Cotonou; linked to adjoining (E) Porto-Novo lagoon. Fishing, duck shooting. Into it empties main arm of Ouémé R.

Nokrek Peak (nŏk'răk), highest point (c.4,630 ft.) in Garo Hills, W Assam, India, 7 mi. SE of Tura.

Nol (nōōl), village (pop. 863), Alvsborg co., SW Sweden, on Gota R. and 6 mi. NE of Kungalv; paper milling; mfg. of electrical equipment.

Nola (nōlä'), village, SW Ubangi-Shari, Fr. Equatorial Africa, at confluence of headstreams of Sanga R., 55 mi. SSE of Berbérati; coffee plantations, diamond mining.

Nola (nô'lä), town (pop. 10,733), Napoli prov., Campania, S Italy, 15 mi. ENE of Naples; agr. center; glass and macaroni factories. Bishopric. Seminary and 15th-cent. Franciscan convent near by. Has monument to Giordano Bruno, who was b. here. Of anc. origin, it became a flourishing Roman colony; Augustus died here in A.D. 14. Excavations have yielded fine Hellenistic vases and numerous coins.

Nolan, county (□ 921; pop. 19,808), W Texas; ⊙ SWEETWATER. Drained by Colorado R. and tributaries of the Colorado and the Brazos; alt. 2,100–2,700 ft. Ranching, agr., dairying area; cattle, sheep, goats, horses, hogs, poultry, cotton, corn, grain sorghums, oats, wheat, hay; some fruit, vegetables; some oil production; gypsum quarries. Recreation areas at Sweetwater and Trammel lakes. Formed 1876.

Nolay (nôlā'), village (pop. 1,355), Côte-d'Or dept., E central France, on S slope of the Côte d'Or, 11 mi. SW of Beaune; Burgundy wines. Meat preserving. Lazare Carnot b. here.

Nolby (nōōl'bü"), village (pop. 1,986), Vasternorrland co., NE Sweden, on Ljunga R., near its mouth on Gulf of Bothnia, 7 mi. SSE of Sundsvall; timber yards. Includes Kvissle (kvĭs'lů) village.

Nole (nô'lē), village (pop. 2,353), Torino prov., Piedmont, NW Italy, 13 mi. N of Turin; textile industry.

Noli (nô'lē), village (pop. 1,645), Savona prov., Liguria, NW Italy, port on Gulf of Genoa and 8 mi. SSW of Savona; fishing center; canneries. Bishopric. Has 12th-cent. church. Just SE is Cape Noli (44°12'N 8°26'E); quartz mines.

Noli, Tanganyika: see NACHINGWA.

Nolichucky River (nŏ"lĭchŭ'kē, nō'lĭchŭ"kē), N.C. and E Tenn., rises in the Blue Ridge in W N.C., flows NW into Tenn., past Erwin and Embreeville, and generally W to French Broad R. (Douglas Reservoir) 11 mi. N of Newport. Power dam 7 mi. SSW of Greeneville, Tenn., impounds narrow Davy Crockett L. (c.5 mi. long).

Nolin River (nō'lĭn), 105 mi. long, central Ky., rises in E Larue co., flows W past Hodgenville, and SSW through W part of Mammoth Cave Natl. Park, to Green R. 3 mi. NE of Brownsville; partly navigable.

Nolinsk, Russian SFSR: see MOLOTOVSK, Kirov oblast.

Nollendorf, Czechoslovakia: see NAKLEROV.

Nolso (nôl'sû), Dan. *Nolsø*, Faeroese *Nólsoy*, island (□ 4; pop. 316) of the E Faeroe Isls., separated from Stromo by Nolso Fjord. N part is flat; highest point 1,217 ft. Fishing; sheep; copper ores.

Noma (nō'mä), town (pop. 7,039), Aichi prefecture, central Honshu, Japan, on SW Chita Peninsula, on Ise Bay and 10 mi. SSW of Handa; rice, wheat, raw silk; fishing.

Noma, town (1940 pop. 344), Holmes co., NW Fla., near Ala. line, 14 mi. NNE of Bonifay, in agr. area.

Noma, Cape, Jap. *Noma-misaki*, SW Kyushu, Japan, on SW Satsuma Peninsula, Kagoshima prefecture, on E.China Sea; 31°25'N 130°7'E.

Nomachi (nō'mächē), town (pop. 4,830), Niigata prefecture, central Honshu, Japan, on Toyama Bay, 14 mi. W of Takada; fishing.

Nomad, Mich.: see BEAVER ISLAND.

No Mans Land, SE Mass., isl. in the Atlantic, 6 mi. S of Gay Head; c.2 mi. long, ½–1 mi. wide.

Nombela (nōmbā'lä), town (pop. 1,972), Toledo prov., central Spain, 21 mi. NE of Talavera de la Reina; grapes, cereals, livestock. Lumbering; flour milling. Mineral springs.

Nombre de Dios (nōm'brā dā dyōs'). **1** Town (pop. 966), Chihuahua, Mexico, in E outliers of Sierra Madre Occidental, on railroad and 3 mi. N of Chihuahua; alt. 4,662 ft. Corn, cotton, beans, fruit, cattle. Silver, lead, gold mines near by. **2** City (pop. 1,875), Durango, N Mexico, on interior plateau, 30 mi. ESE of Durango; alt. 5,689 ft.; grain, cotton, vegetables, livestock. Silver mines near by. First Sp. settlement in Durango.

Nombre de Dios, village (pop. 759), Colón prov., central Panama, railhead and port on Caribbean Sea, and 20 mi. NE of Colón, in banana area; also abacá, cacao, coconuts, livestock. Manganese deposits. Important port in 16th cent. for shipment of Sp. colonial riches.

Nombre de Dios, Sierra de (syĕ'rä dā), mountain range of N Honduras, on Atlántida-Yoro dept. border, S of Tela; rises to over 7,000 ft.

Nome (nōm), city (pop. 1,852), W Alaska, on S Seward Peninsula, on N shore of Norton Sound; 64°30'N 165°24'W; commercial and supply center for NW Alaska, serving important placer gold-mining region. Has Federal Bldg. (1938), several schools, and hosp. Frequented by tourists, it is center of Eskimo handicraft industry (ivory carving, needlework). Seaport (open May–Nov.), with steamer connection to Seattle; air base and commercial airport at Mark Field, just WNW. Fishing industry is being developed. Mean temp. range from 3.7°F. (Jan.) to 49.9°F. (July); average annual rainfall 17.26 inches. Established (1899) when gold was found on beach at locality known as Anvil City, Nome became center of gold rush in summer 1900, when pop. reached c.30,000, but many prospectors died or left because of the hardships of arctic conditions. Dredge mining was introduced later; fur farming and trapping became important recently. Amundsen arrived here (1906) after completing Northwest Passage.

Nome, village (pop. 217), Barnes co., SE N.Dak., 20 mi. SE of Valley City.

Nome, Cape, W Alaska, S Seward Peninsula, on N shore of Norton Sound, 12 mi. ESE of Nome; 64°27'N 165°W.

Nomeland (nō'mŭlän), village in Hylestad canton (pop. 693), Aust-Agder co., S Norway, on Otra R. and 70 mi. NNW of Kristiansand.

Nomelandsfoss (nō'mŭlänsfôs"), waterfall (66 ft.) on Otra R., Vest-Agder co., S Norway, 15 mi. N of Kristiansand; hydroelectric plant.

Nomeny (nômnē'), agr. village (pop. 639), Meurthe-et-Moselle dept., NE France, on Seille R. and 14 mi. N of Nancy; curtain mfg. Burned by Germans in Aug., 1914. Also spelled Noméný.

Nomexy (nômsē'), town (pop. 2,604), Vosges dept., E France, port on Moselle R. and Canal de l'Est, 10 mi. NNW of Épinal; cotton spinning.

Nominingue (nômēnĕg'), village (pop. 533), SW Que., on L. Nominingue (6 mi. long, 3 mi. wide), in the Laurentians, 45 mi. NW of Ste. Agathe des Monts; dairying.

Nomi-shima (nōmē'-shĭmä), island (□ 39; pop. 63,460), Hiroshima prefecture, Japan, in Hiroshima Bay, just S of Hiroshima and W of Kure; 10 mi. long, 3 mi. wide; has peninsula 8 mi. long, ½–4 mi. wide. S part is called Higashi-nomi-shima, NW part, Nishi-nomi-shima, and NE part, Etajima. Mountainous; fertile. Rice, tea, citrus fruit; livestock. Fishing.

Nomme or **Nymme,** Est. *Nõmme* (all: nŭ'mā), S residential suburb (pop. 15,105) of Tallinn, Estonia, within city limits.

Nomo, Cape (nō'mō), Jap. *Nomo-saki*, S extremity of Nomo Peninsula, NW Kyushu, Japan; forms NW side of entrance to Amakusa Sea; 32°34'N 129°44'E. Kaba-shima, islet, is near by.

Nomoi Islands (nō'moi) or **Mortlock Islands** (môrt'-lŏk), E Caroline Isls., W Pacific, 150 mi. SE of Truk; include ETAL, LUKUNOR, and SATAWAN atolls.

Nomonhan (nōmōnhän'), locality on NW Manchuria-Mongolia border, 120 mi. SSW of Hailar, at Khalka R. Scene (1939) of border incident.

Nomo Peninsula, NW Kyushu, Japan, S projection of Hizen Peninsula, bet. E.China Sea (W) and Amakusa Sea (E); 17 mi. long, 5 mi. wide; terminates (S) at Cape Nomo. Nagasaki is at NW corner of base, where peninsula joins Sonogi Peninsula.

Nomo-saki, Japan: see NOMO, CAPE.

Nomura (nōmōō'rä), town (pop. 7,842), Ehime prefecture, W Shikoku, Japan, 11 mi. NNE of Uwajima; paper, lime, raw silk. Gold, silver, copper mines near by.

Nomwin (nōm'wĭn), atoll (pop. 134), Hall Isls., Truk dist., E Caroline Isls., W Pacific, 45 mi. N of Truk; 15 mi. long, 9 mi. wide; 9 wooded islets.

Nona, Yugoslavia: see NIN.

Nonacho Lake (□ 305), SE Mackenzie Dist., Northwest Territories, E of Great Slave L.; 61°42'N 109°40'W; 30 mi. long, 1–20 mi. wide. Drained W into Great Slave L. by Taltson R.

Nonai (nōnī'), village (pop. 8,849), Aomori prefecture, N Honshu, Japan, on SE Aomori Bay, 8 mi. NE of Aomori; hot-springs resort. Aquarium of Tohoku Imperial Univ. here. Sometimes called Asamushi.

Nonamesset Island, Mass.: see ELIZABETH ISLANDS.

Nonancourt (nônäkōōr'), village (pop. 1,295), Eure dept., NW France, on the Avre and 8 mi. WNW of Dreux; sawmilling, rubber mfg.

Nonant-le-Pin (nônā'-lů-pē'), village (pop. 516), Orne dept., NW France, 11 mi. ESE of Argentan; horse breeding.

Nonantola (nônän'tôlä), town (pop. 2,096), Modena prov., Emilia-Romagna, N central Italy, near Panaro R., 6 mi. ENE of Modena. Has Romanesque abbey of San Silvestro (founded c.753).

Nonantum, Mass.: see NEWTON.

Nonceveux (nōsvû'), village, Liége prov., E central Belgium, on Amblève R. and 14 mi. SE of Liége; hydroelectric power station, with power plant at REMOUCHAMPS, 1.5 mi. NW.

Nondaburi, Thailand: see NONTHABURI.

Nondalton (nŏndôl'tŭn), village (pop. 99), S Alaska, at SW end of L. Clark, 190 mi. WSW of Anchorage; fishing resort.

None (nô'nĕ), village (pop. 1,917), Torino prov., Piedmont, NW Italy, 12 mi. SSW of Turin.

None (nō'nā), town (pop. 4,464), Kochi prefecture, SE Shikoku, Japan, on Philippine Sea, 42 mi. E of Kochi; rice, wheat, raw silk.

Nonesuch River, SW Maine, tidal stream; follows 12-mi. semi-circular course, NE above Saco, then SE and S to the Atlantic at Scarboro.

Nonget (nông'-ĕt'), village, Xiengkhouang prov., N Laos, 115 mi. ESE of Luang Prabang, on highway to Vinh.

Nongkhai (nông'kī'), town (1947 pop. 11,757), ⊙ Nongkhai prov. (□ 2,907; 1947 pop. 144,201), NE Thailand, on right bank of Mekong R. (Laos line), near Vientiane, 30 mi. N of Udon (linked by road and projected railroad); rice, beans, tobacco. Sometimes spelled Nongkay or Nongkhay.

Nongkhlaw (nông'klou), village, Khasi and Jaintia Hills dist., W Assam, India, on Shillong Plateau, 17 mi. WNW of Shillong; rice, sesame, cotton.

Nongson (nông'shŭn), village, Quangnam prov., central Vietnam, 20 mi. S of Faifo; anthracite mining.

Nongstoin (nông'stoin), village, Khasi and Jaintia Hills dist., W Assam, India, on Shillong Plateau, 39 mi. W of Shillong; rice, sesame, cotton.

Nonington, town and parish (pop. 4,326), E Kent, England, 8 mi. NNW of Dover; coal mining. Has 13th-cent. church.

Nonnenweier (nô'nŭnvī"ŭr), village (pop. 1,462), S Baden, Germany, on the Rhine and 5 mi. W of Lahr; tobacco.

Nonni River (nŏn-nē'), Chinese *Nen Kiang (Chiang)* (nŭn'jyäng') or *Nun Kiang (Chiang)* (nōōn'), chief tributary of Sungari R., in NW central Manchuria; rises in Ilkuri Mts., flows 740 mi. S, along E foot of the Great Khingan Mts., past Nunkiang (Mergen) and Tsitsihar, to Sungari R. 100 mi. WSW of Harbin. Frozen Nov.-April, it is navigable for shallow-draught vessels below Nunkiang and for regular shipping below Tsitsihar. Receives Tao R. (right). The Nonni R. Mongols (organized in the BUTEHA league), on the river's right bank, were joined in 1949 with Barga league to form Huna league within Inner Mongolian Autonomous Region.

Nonnweiler (nôn'vī"lŭr), village (pop. 518), NE Saar, on Prims R. and 19 mi. SE of Trier, opposite Hermeskeil, W Germany; rail junction; cattle, poultry, grain. Formerly part of Prussian Rhine Prov.; annexed to Saar in 1947.

Nono (nō'nō), village (pop. estimate 500), W Córdoba prov., Argentina, at foot of Sierra Grande, 55 mi. SW of Córdoba; resort in livestock and fruit area.

Nono, oil wells in Pichincha prov., N central Ecuador, in the Andes, N of Quito.

Nonoava (nōnōä'vä), town (pop. 617), Chihuahua, N Mexico, on affluent of Conchos R. and 90 mi. SW of Chihuahua; corn, cotton, beans, livestock; lumbering.

Nonoc Island (nōnŏk') (□ 19; 1939 pop. 902), Surigao prov., Philippines, just off NE tip of Mindanao, at S end of Dinagat Isl.; coconuts.

Nonogasta (nōnōgä'stä), town (pop. estimate 1,000), central La Rioja prov., Argentina, in Famatina Valley, on railroad and 40 mi. W of La Rioja; fruit- and winegrowing center; barium sulphate deposits.

Nonoichi (nōnō'ĕchē), town (pop. 2,873), Ishikawa prefecture, central Honshu, Japan, 3 mi. SW of Kanazawa; rice growing.

Nonouti (nōnō-ōō'tē), atoll (□ 9.8; pop. 2,004), Kingsmill group, S Gilbert Isls., W central Pacific; 0°41'S 174°23'E; reef is 24 mi. long. Produces copra. Formerly Sydenham Isl.

Nonquitt, Mass.: see DARTMOUTH.

Nonsan (nôn'sän'), Jap. *Ronzan,* town (1949 pop. 20,308), S.Chungchong prov., S Korea, 21 mi. SW of Taejon; rice-growing center. Has 11th-cent. Buddhist temple with 86-ft. granite Buddha.

Nonsuch Island (nŭn'–), small island (1,500 ft. long, 600 ft. wide) of E Bermuda, at SE entrance of Castle Harbour.

Nonthaburi or **Nontburi** (nôntä'bōōrē'), town (1947 pop. 8,897), ⊙ Nonthaburi prov. (□ 250; 1947 pop. 135,537), S Thailand, on Chao Phraya R. and 15 mi. N of Bangkok, in rice and fruitgrowing area. Sometimes spelled Nondaburi.

Nontron (nōtrō'), town (pop. 2,181), Dordogne dept., SW France, on Bandiat R. and 24 mi. N of Périgueux; mfg. (cutlery, clothing, footwear, biscuits); food processing (*pâté de foie gras* and truffles); lumber trade.

Nooitgedacht (nōō'ĭt-khŭdäkht"), locality, SW Transvaal, U. of So. Afr., at foot of Magaliesberg mts., 20 mi. NW of Krugersdorp. In South African War scene (1900) of battle in which Boers under Delarey defeated British force.

Nooksack, town (pop. 323), Whatcom co., NW Wash., 15 mi. NE of Bellingham and on Nooksack R., in agr. area.

Nooksack River, NW Wash., rises NE of Mt. Baker, flows c.75 mi. W and SW to Bellingham Bay at Lummi Indian Reservation; receives South Fork (c.40 mi. long) and Middle Fork (c.20 mi. long). Has power plant at falls near source.

Noonan, city (pop. 551), Divide co., NW N.Dak., port of entry 13 mi. E of Crosby; lignite mining; dairy products, poultry, wheat, corn, flax.

Noonmark, peak (3,552 ft.) of the Adirondacks, in Essex co., NE N.Y., c.8 mi. E of Mt. Marcy and 16 mi. SE of Lake Placid village.

Noord Beveland, Netherlands: see NORTH BEVELAND.

Noordbrabant, Netherlands: see NORTH BRABANT.

Noordervaart, Netherlands: see WESSEM-NEDERWEERT CANAL.

Noordholland, Netherlands: see NORTH HOLLAND.

Noord-Oost-Polder, Netherlands: see NORTH EAST POLDER.

Noord River (nōrt), SW Netherlands, formed by forking of LOWER MERWEDE RIVER into Noord R. and Old Maas River 1 mi. N of Dordrecht; flows 6 mi. NW, past Alblasserdam and Kinderdijk, joining Lek R. ½ mi. W of Krimpen aan den Lek to form NEW MAAS RIVER. Entire length navigable.

Noordwijk aan Zee (nōrt'vĭk än zā'), town (pop. 6,037), South Holland prov., W Netherlands, on North Sea and 7 mi. NNW of Leiden; seaside resort; flowers, medicinal herbs. Lighthouse. Village of Noordwijk-Binnen is 1 mi. E. Sometimes spelled Noordwyk.

Noordwijk-Binnen, Netherlands: see NOORDWIJK AAN ZEE.

Noordwijkerhout (–ŭrhout), town (pop. 5,770), South Holland prov., W Netherlands, 8 mi. N of Leiden; mfg. (chemicals, incubators); short-wave radio transmitter.

Noordwolde (nōrt-vŏl'dŭ), village (pop. 987), Friesland prov., N Netherlands, 10 mi. ESE of Heerenveen; chair- and basket-weaving; reed growing.

Noordwyk aan Zee, Netherlands: see NOORDWIJK AAN ZEE.

Noordzee Kanaal, Netherlands: see NORTH SEA CANAL.

Noormarkku (nōr'märk"kōō), Swedish *Noormark* (nôr'märk"), village (commune pop. 4,613), Turku-Pori co., SW Finland, 8 mi. NNE of Pori; a commercial seat of lumbering industry; machine shops.

Noorvik (nōr'vĭk), village (pop. 250), NW Alaska, on Kobuk R. and 45 mi. E of Kotzebue; supply point for prospectors and trappers in Kobuk R. region. Has govt. hospital for natives; airfield.

Nooseneck, R.I.: see WEST GREENWICH.

Nootka Island (nōōt'kŭ, nōōt'–) (□ 206), SW B.C., in the Pacific, off W central coast of Vancouver Isl., 45 mi. NW of Tofino; center near 49°45'N 126°45'W; 21 mi. long, 16 mi. wide. Fishing, lumbering. Nootka village on SE coast. **Nootka Sound,** washing isl.'s S and E coasts, stretches several long, narrow arms inland: Muchalat Inlet (E), Tahsis Inlet (N). Mouth of sound was 1st visited (1774) by Sp. explorer Juan Perez, explored and named (1778) by Capt. James Cook. John Meares built fort here (1788); it was seized by Spaniards in 1789. Ensuing controversy bet. Great Britain and Spain was settled by the Nootka Convention (1790), which opened way to British settlement along N Pacific coast of America. Spanish colony at Nootka Sound was abandoned in 1795.

Nopala (nōpä'lä), town (pop. 839), Hidalgo, central Mexico, on railroad and 25 mi. SE of San Juan del Río; alt. 7,693 ft.; corn, beans, maguey, stock.

Nopala, Cerro (sĕ'rō), peak (10,170 ft.), Hidalgo, central Mexico, 6 mi. SSE of Huichapan.

Nopaltepec (nōpältāpĕk'), officially Santa María Nopaltepec, town (pop. 918), Mexico state, central Mexico, on railroad and 35 mi. NE of Mexico city; cereals, maguey.

Nopalucan (nōpälōō'kän), officially Nopalucan de la Granja, town (pop. 2,187), Puebla, central Mexico, 28 mi. NE of Puebla; cereals, beans, maguey.

Nóqui (nō'kē), town (pop. 416), Congo prov., NW Angola, river port on the Congo (Belgian Congo border), 4 mi. S of Matadi; sesame.

Nor, river, Sweden; see NOR RIVER.

Nora (nōō'rä), city (pop. 3,168), Orebro co., S central Sweden, on Nora L., Swedish *Norasjön* (3 mi. long), 18 mi. NNW of Orebro; metalworking, brick mfg., sawmilling. Chartered 1643; until 18th cent. a trade center for Bergslagen mining region (N). In iron-mining region.

Nora (nô'rŭ). **1** Village (pop. 208), Jo Daviess co., NW Ill., 20 mi. NW of Freeport, in agr. area. Apple River Canyon State Park is near by. **2** Village (pop. 88), Nuckolls co., S Nebr., 10 mi. NNE of Superior. **3** Coal-mining village (1940 pop. 763), Dickenson co., SW Va., in the Cumberlands, 18 mi. SE of Jenkins, Ky.

Norak, Tadzhik SSR: see NUREK.

Noranda (nôrăn'dŭ), town (pop. 4,576), W Que., on Osisko L., just N of Rouyn and 140 mi. NNE of North Bay; gold, copper, and zinc mining center, with large smelting plant; lumbering, dairying. Airfield.

Norangdal (nō'rängdäl), valley in More og Romsdal co., W Norway; extends from Oye on Hjorund Fjord, SE of Alesund, c.10 mi. SE to Hellesylt; popular scenic region. A landslide in 1908 dammed the valley, forming a lake which submerged the surrounding farms.

Norashen (nŭrŭshĕn'), town (1926 pop. 508), NW Nakhichevan Autonomous SSR, Azerbaijan SSR, on the Eastern Arpa-Chai near its confluence with Aras R., and 30 mi. NW of Nakhichevan, on railroad; cotton ginning.

Nora Springs, town (pop. 1,257), Floyd co., N Iowa, on Shell Rock R. and 10 mi. E of Mason City; dairy products, concrete blocks. Limestone quarry, sand and gravel pits near by. Inc. 1875.

Norba Caesarea, Spain: see ALCÁNTARA.

Nor-Bayazet (nôr"-bĭŭzyĕt'), city (1926 pop. 8,447), central Armenian SSR, near W shore of L. Sevan, 35 mi. ENE of Erivan; wheat, potatoes; rug weaving. Formerly Novo-Bayazet.

Norberg (nōōr'bĕr"yŭ), village (pop. 1,285), Vastmanland co., central Sweden, in Bergslag region, 6 mi. NE of Fagersta; one of Sweden's oldest iron- and lead-mining centers; machinery works. Has 13th-cent. church, mining mus.

Norberto de la Riestra (nōrbĕr'tō dā lä rēĕs'trä), town (pop. 4,159), N central Buenos Aires prov., Argentina, 25 mi. ENE of Veinticinco de Mayo; cattle- and hog-raising center; seed cultivating; tanning.

Norbertville, village (pop. 236), S Que., 25 mi. W of Thetford Mines; dairying; cattle, wheat, potatoes.

Norbestos (nôrbĕ'stŭs), asbestos-mining village, S Que., 5 mi. NE of Asbestos.

Norborne (nôr'bŭrn), city (pop. 1,114), Carroll co., NW central Mo., near Missouri R., 10 mi. WSW of Carrollton; ships grain, livestock; coal. Laid out 1868.

Norbury, England: see CROYDON.

Norcatur (nôrkā'tŭr), city (pop. 368), Decatur co., NW Kansas, 15 mi. W of Norton; grain, cattle.

Nor Chichas, Bolivia: see COTAGAITA.

Norcia (nôr'chä), anc. *Nursia,* town (pop. 2,631), Perugia prov., Umbria, central Italy, near Monti Sibillini, 19 mi. ENE of Spoleto; rail terminus; mfg. (woolen textiles, metal furniture). Bishopric. Has 14th-cent. walls and a castle (1554–63). St. Benedict b. here.

Nor Cinti, Bolivia: see CAMARGO.

Norco. 1 Village (pop. 1,584), Riverside co., S Calif., on Santa Ana R. and 11 mi. WSW of Riverside; farming, poultry raising. **2** Village (pop. 3,366, with adjacent Goodhope), St. Charles parish, SE La., near E bank (levee) of the Mississippi, c.20 mi. W of New Orleans; oil refining.

Norcott Mills, textile-mill village (pop. 4,802, with adjacent Brown), Cabarrus co., S central N.C., just W of Concord.

Norcross. 1 City (pop. 1,340), Gwinnett co., N central Ga., 15 mi. NE of Atlanta; tanning. **2** Village (pop. 179), Grant co., W Minn., on Mustinka R. and 14 mi. SW of Elbow Lake village; dairy products.

Nord (nôr), department (□ 2,229; pop. 1,917,452), in French Flanders and Hainaut, N France; ⊙ LILLE. Northernmost Fr. dept., bounded by Belgium (N and E), with narrow frontage on North Sea, and abutting on Ardennes foothills (SE). Generally level (low and swampy near coast); drained by Sambre, Escaut, Scarpe, Lys, Deûle, and Yser rivers, interconnected by dense network of canals (collectively known as Flanders canals). A leading agr. dept., with fertile soils skillfully irrigated and cultivated. Chief crops: wheat, oats, sugar beets, flax, hops, chicory, tobacco, potatoes, vegetables. Cattle pastures. S central part of dept. crossed by important Franco-Belgian coal basin, with mining centers at Anzin, Aniche, Douchy, Denain. One of France's chief industrial depts., with numerous textile and metallurgical plants powered by locally mined coal. Leading textile towns are Lille (lisle thread and fabrics), ROUBAIX, Tourcoing, and Fourmies (all wool-mfg. centers), Armentières (linen weaving), Cambrai (cambric and miscellaneous fine textiles). Metalworks heavily concentrated in Lille conurbation (locomotive works at Fives-Lille), Denain (steel milling), and Douai. Other manufactures: glass and paper milling, chemical mfg., food processing (sugar, chicory, flour products, chocolates). Principal port: Dunkirk (heavily damaged in Second World War). Second in population only to Seine dept., Nord has attracted many foreigners (Poles, Belgians), especially to coal mines. Long a European battleground, Nord was ravaged in First World War. In 1940, over 300,000 Allied troops, cut off by Ger. drive to the Channel, were evacuated to England from Dunkirk.

Nord, Massif du (mäsēf' dü nôr'), range in N Haiti, bet. the Plaine du Nord (N) and Central Plain (S), continuing the Cordillera Central of the Dominican Republic; extends c.80 mi. SE from Port-de-Paix; rises to 2,525 ft. The Plaine du Nord continues the Cibao region of the Dominican Republic; grows sugar cane, coffee, cacao, tobacco, bananas, pineapples, sisal, fine wood.

Nord-Audnedal, Norway: see VIGMOSTAD.

Nord-Aurdal, Norway: see FAGERNES.

Nordaustlandet, Spitsbergen: see NORTHEAST LAND.

Nordborg (nôr'bôr), town (pop. 1,110), Aabenraa-Sonderborg amt, Denmark, on N Als isl. 10 mi. N of Sonderborg. Founded around 12th-cent. castle.

Nord-Cameroun (nôr-kämrōōn'), administrative region (□ 11,350; 1950 pop. 750,550), N Fr. Cameroons; ⊙ Maroua. Bordered W by Br. Cameroons, N by L. Chad, E by Fr. Equatorial Africa (along Shari and Logone rivers). Mostly savanna plain; Mandara Mts. in W. Marked dry and wet seasons. Stock raising (cattle, horses, sheep, goats), peanuts, cotton, millet. Moslem pop. of Fulahs and Hausas practices leather handicrafts.

Norddal, canton, Norway: see SYLTE.

Norddal Fjord, Norway: see STOR FJORD.

Norddeich (nôrt'dīkh"), seaside resort (commune pop. 1,338), in former Prussian prov. of Hanover, NW Germany, after 1945 in Lower Saxony, in East Friesland, on North Sea, 3 mi. NW of Norden; rail terminus; steamer connection to isls. of Baltrum, Juist, and Norderney. Commune is called Lintelermarsch (lĭn'tŭlŭrmärsh').

Nörde (nûr'dŭ), village (pop. 820), in former Prussian prov. of Westphalia, NW Germany, after 1945 in North Rhine-Westphalia, 4 mi. NW of Warburg; rail junction.

Nordegg (nûr'dĕg) or **Brazeau** (brā'zō), town (pop. estimate 1,000), SW Alta., in Rocky Mts., near North Saskatchewan R., 130 mi. SW of Edmonton; alt. 4,471 ft.; coal mining.

Norden, former urban district (1931 pop. 4,348), SE Lancashire, England, 2 mi. WNW of Rochdale; cotton weaving.

Norden (nôr'dŭn), town (pop. 16,854), in former Prussian prov. of Hanover, NW Germany, after 1945 in Lower Saxony, in East Friesland, near

North Sea, 15 mi. N of Emden; linked by canal with Ems R. estuary; rail junction; metalworking, distilling (brandy). Has 15th-cent. church, 16th-cent. town hall. Oldest town of East Friesland (1st mentioned 1124).

Norden, winter resort, Nevada co., E Calif., in the Sierra Nevada, 35 mi. SW of Reno (Nev.), on L. Van Norden; alt. 6,880 ft. Just E is Norden Tunnel (c.10,000 ft. long), carrying a railroad under the sierra summit at Donner Pass.

Nordenham (nôr′dùnhäm), town (pop. 25,669), in Oldenburg, NW Germany, after 1945 in Lower Saxony, port on left bank of the Weser (just above its estuary) and 30 mi. below Bremen, nearly opposite Bremerhaven; shipbuilding; lead and zinc refining; mfg. of transoceanic cables, phosphates, textiles. Dispatches deep-sea fishing fleet. Chartered 1908.

Nordenskjöld Archipelago or **Nordenskiöld Archipelago** (no͝or′dùn-shûl), Rus. *Arkhipelag Nordenshelda,* in Kara Sea of Arctic Ocean, 10–15 mi. off N Taimyr Peninsula, in Krasnoyarsk Territory, Russian SFSR; includes Vilkitski, Tsivolka, Pakhtusov, and Litke isl. groups. Northernmost isl., Russki or Russkiy, has govt. observation post. Named for 19th-cent. Swedish explorer.

Nordenskjöld Bay or **Nordenskiöld Bay,** on SW coast of Alexandra Land, Franz Josef Land, Russian SFSR, in Arctic Ocean.

Nordenskjöld Coast, Antarctica, E coast of Palmer Peninsula bet. Sjögren Fiord (64°10′S) and Drygalski Bay (64°40′S); c.70 naut. mi. long.

Nordenskjöld Glacier, Greenland: see ARFERSIORFIK.

Nordenskjöld Sea or **Nordenskiöld Sea,** Russian SFSR: see LAPTEV SEA.

Norden Tunnel, Calif.: see NORDEN.

Norderelbe, Germany: see ELBE RIVER.

Norderney (nôrdùrnī′), North Sea island (□ 9; pop. 6,452) of East Frisian group, Germany, 5 mi. N of Norddeich (steamer connection); 8 mi. long (E-W), c.1 mi. wide (N-S). Nordseebad Norderney (S tip) is Germany's most popular North Sea resort.

Nordeste (nôrdĕsh′tĭ), town (pop. 1,296), Ponta Delgada dist., E Azores, on NE shore of São Miguel Isl., 29 mi. ENE of Ponta Delgada; 37°50′N 25°9′W. Tea growing, beekeeping; woodworking.

Nord Fjord (nôrd′fyôrd″, Nor. nōr′fyōr″), inlet (70 mi. long) of North Sea, Sogn og Fjordane co., W Norway, 50 mi. SW of Alesund; 1–3 mi. wide, 1,850 ft. deep. Receives glacier streams of the Jostedalsbre at its head. Vagsoy and several other isls. protect mouth. Extends several small arms, noted for scenic beauty.

Nordfjordeid (nōr′fyōr-ād″), village (pop. 588) in Eid canton (pop. 3,409), Sogn og Fjordane co., W Norway, at head of a N branch of Nord Fjord, 38 mi. NE of Floro; fishing, lumbering, cattle raising. Frequently called Eid.

Nordfolda, Norway: see FOLDA.

Nordfriesland, Germany: see NORTH FRIESLAND.

Nord-Fron, Norway: see VINSTRA.

Nordhalben (nôrt′häl″bùn), village (pop. 2,600), Upper Franconia, N Bavaria, Germany, on the Rodach and 12 mi. NE of Kronach; rail terminus; mfg. of tobacco and chemicals, lumber milling.

Nordhausen (nôrt′hou″zùn), city (pop. 32,848), in former Prussian Saxony prov., central Germany, after 1945 in Thuringia, in the Goldene Aue, at S foot of the lower Harz, 40 mi. NNW of Erfurt, in potash-mining region; rail junction; cotton and linen milling, oil refining, distilling, printing, woodworking. Mfg. of machinery, glass, chewing tobacco. City was heavily damaged in Second World War (about 30% destroyed). Founded 927; chartered in 12th cent. Was free imperial city, 1253–1803; passed to Prussia, 1813.

Nordheim (nôrd′hīm). **1** City (pop. 477), De Witt co., S Texas, 38 mi. WNW of Victoria; rail point in cotton, corn, cattle area; cotton ginning. **2** Village (pop. 1,318), Winnebago co., E central Wis., near Oshkosh.

Nord-Helgeland, Norway: see HELGELAND.

Nordhordland, Norway: see HORDALAND.

Nordhorn (nôrt′hôrn), town (pop. 28,399), in former Prussian prov. of Hanover, NW Germany, after 1945 in Lower Saxony, on the Vechte (head of navigation), at junction of Almelo-Nordhorn, Ems-Vechte, and Süd-Nord canals, and 42 mi. WNW of Osnabrück, near Dutch border; textile center (cotton spinning and weaving, mfg. of artificial fiber, bleaching, dyeing). Has 15th-cent. church. First mentioned in 11th cent. Chartered 1379.

Nordhur-Mula, Iceland: see NORDUR-MULA.

Nord Islands (nōr), Nor. *Nordøyane* (nōr′ûüànü) [=north islands], island group in North Sea, More og Romsdal co., W Norway, paralleling the coast, and extending from mouth of Molde Fjord 30 mi. SW to Alesund; include isls. HAROY, HARAMSOY.

Nordkapp, Norway: see NORTH CAPE.

Nordkette (nôrd′kĕtù), range of Bavarian Alps in Tyrol, W Austria, forming N wall (c.20 mi. long) of Inn R. valley at Innsbruck. Highest peak, Hafelekar (7,657 ft.).

Nordkyn (nōr′chün), or **Kinnarodden** (chĭn′närôd″dùn), rocky cape (768 ft. high) on Barents Sea of Arctic Ocean, Finnmark co., N Norway, 95 mi. ENE of Hammerfest, 90 mi. NW of Vadso; 71°8′1″N 27°40′9″E. Northernmost point of European mainland. Sometimes spelled Nordkinn.

Nordland (nōr′län), county [Nor. *fylke*] (□ 14,797; pop. 215,972), N central and N Norway; ⊙ Bodo. On Arctic Circle, it comprises narrow mainland section bet. Swedish border and North Sea, and offshore isls., including the Lofoten and S part of Vesteralen groups. Coast line is deeply indented by numerous fjords; surface, generally mountainous, rises to 6,279 ft. in the Sulitjelma. There are rich forests and extensive marshes; little arable land. Chief regions are HELGELAND, SALTEN, and Ofoten. Largest city and port is NARVIK. Metals are mined in Sulitjelma village, Narvik, and Mo regions; steel plant at Mo. In Lofoten and Vesteralen groups are important fisheries (cod, herring, haddock, halibut, eel), centered at Svolvaer. Marble, slate, steatite are quarried. Stock raising (cattle, sheep, hogs, reindeer), oat and barley growing. In Second World War, Narvik and Bodo and surrounding waters were scene of heavy fighting; towns suffered considerable destruction.

Nördlingen (nûrt′lĭng-ùn), town (1950 pop. 13,268), Swabia, W Bavaria, Germany, 31 mi. SSW of Ansbach; rail junction; mfg. of textiles, precision instruments, paper, shoes; woodworking, printing, brewing. Wall (14th-15th cent.) surrounds Old City, which has 14th-cent. city hall and late-Gothic church (1427–1505). Founded in 9th cent., Nördlingen became free imperial city in 1217. Scene of several battles in Thirty Years War and in French Revolutionary Wars.

Nordmaling (no͝ord′mä″lĭng), village (pop. 656), Vasterbotten co., N Sweden, on small inlet of Gulf of Bothnia, 30 mi. SW of Umea; lumbering, dairying. Has medieval church.

Nordmark-Finnmossen (no͝ord′märk″-fĭn′mô″sùn), village (pop. 508), Varmland co., W Sweden, in Bergslag region, 8 mi. N of Filipstad; iron mining.

Nordmarsch-Langeness (nôrt′märsh″-läng′ùnĕs″) or **Langeness,** North Sea island (□ 5; pop. 397) of North Frisian group, NW Germany, in Hallig Isls., 6 mi. off Schleswig-Holstein coast (connected by dike); 5.5 mi. long (E-W), 1 mi. wide (N-S). Grazing.

Nordmor, Norway: see MORE.

Nordostlandet, Spitsbergen: see NORTHEAST LAND.

Nordost Rundingen, Greenland: see NORTHEAST FORELAND.

Nord-Ostsee-Kanal, Germany: see KIEL CANAL.

Nordoyane, Norway: see NORD ISLANDS.

Nord-Rana, Norway: see BASMOEN.

Nordre Bergenhus or **Nordre Bergenhuus,** county, Norway: see SOGN OG FJORDANE.

Nordre Isortoq (nôr′drù ĭsôkh′tôk), fjord (85 mi. long, 1–3 mi. wide) of Davis Strait, SW Greenland, 17 mi. N of Holsteinsborg; 67°15′N 52°30′W. Receives several glacier streams from inland icecap.

Nordre River, Sweden: see GOTA RIVER.

Nordre Strom Fjord (strûm′fyōr′), Dan. *Nordre Strømfjord,* inlet (110 mi. long, 1–16 mi. wide) of Davis Strait, W Greenland, 60 mi. S of Egedesminde; 67°40′N 52°W; extends inland to edge of icecap.

Nordre Trondhjem, Norway: see NORD-TRONDELAG.

Nordrhein-Westfalen, Germany: see NORTH RHINE-WESTPHALIA.

Nordseebad Sankt Peter, Germany: see SANKT PETER.

Nordslesvig, Denmark: see SCHLESWIG.

Nordstemmen (nôrt′shtĕ″mùn), village (pop. 3,089), in former Prussian prov. of Hanover, NW Germany, after 1945 in Lower Saxony, 7 mi. W of Hildesheim; rail junction; metal- and woodworking, sugar refining.

Nordstrand (nôrt′shtränt), North Sea island (□ 18; 1939 pop. 2,729; 1946 pop. 4,576) of North Frisian group, NW Germany, in Hallig Isls., 2 mi. off Schleswig-Holstein coast (connected by dike); 6 mi. wide (E-W), 4 mi. long (N-S). Grazing. Main village: Odenbüll. It is remainder of larger isl., which was partly flooded in 1634.

Nordstrand (nōr′strän), residential suburb (pop. 7,569) of Oslo, SE Norway, on Bonne Fjord (arm of Oslo Fjord), 4 mi. SSE of city center. Has sanitarium. Until 1948, in Akershus co.

Nord-Trondelag (nōr′trûn′nùläg), Nor. *Nord-Trøndelag,* county [Nor. *fylke*] (□ 8,657; pop. 105,679), central Norway; ⊙ Steinkjer. Bet. North Sea and Swedish border, around the inner Trondheim Fjord and the Namdal; coast indented by Nams Fjord, Folda, and many lesser fjords. Rises to the Borgefjell in NE. Chief occupations: agr. (hay, rye, potatoes), dairying, animal husbandry (horses, cattle, sheep, goats, hogs, fowl), lumbering, fishing (cod, herring, salmon). Pyrites mined around Grong and Meraker. Industries at Namsos, Grong, Levanger, Steinkjer. Railroad to Nordland passes through co., with spur to Namsos and branch line to Ostersund (Sweden). Before 1918, co. (then called *amt*) was named Nordre Trondhjem.

Nordur-Mula or **Nordhur-Mula** (nôr′dhür-mo͞o″lä), Icelandic *Norður-Múla,* county [Icelandic *sýsla*] (pop. 2,412), NE Iceland; ⊙ Seydisfjordur, a city in but independent of the co. Extends along NE coast of Iceland bet. Langanes peninsula (N) and Seydisfjordur (S). Drained by Jokuls a Bru and Lagarfljot rivers. Fishing.

Norduz River, Turkey: see BUHTAN RIVER.

Nord-Varanger, Norway: see VESTRE JAKOBSELV.

Nordvik (nôrd′vĕk), town (1947 pop. over 2,000), E Taimyr Natl. Okrug, Krasnoyarsk Territory, Russian SFSR, N of Arctic Circle, on Khatanga Gulf of Laptev Sea, 235 mi. NE of Khatanga; salt and petroleum extraction. Until 1943, the name Nordvik was applied to near-by village of KOZHEVNIKOVO.

Nordwalde (nôrt′väl″dù), village (pop. 6,010), in former Prussian prov. of Westphalia, NW Germany, after 1945 in North Rhine-Westphalia, 7 mi. SE of Burgsteinfurt; dairying.

Nore, canton, Norway: see RODBERG.

Nore, The, sandbank in the Thames estuary, SE England, bet. Shoeburyness and Sheerness. At E end, 4 mi. SE of Shoeburyness, is Nore Lightship (51°29′N 0°51′E). The name is also applied to part of the Thames estuary, a famous anchorage.

Norefjord, Norway: see LAGEN RIVER.

Noreña (nōrā′nyä), town (pop. 2,156), Oviedo prov., NW Spain, 7 mi. ENE of Oviedo; meat-processing center; apples, corn, cattle, hogs.

Nörenberg, Poland: see INSKO.

Nore River, Ireland, rises 6 mi. SW of Roscrea, N Co. Tipperary, flows a short distance NE into Co. Laoighis, then SSE through Co. Kilkenny to Barrow R. 2 mi. N of New Ross; 70 mi. long. Valley is noted for scenic beauty.

Noresund (nō′rùso͞on), village in Krodsherad (Nor. *Krødsherad*) canton (pop. 2,232), Buskerud co., SE Norway, on the lake Kroderen, 20 mi. W of Honefoss; tourist center noted for its scenery. Agr., lumbering. Nore Mts., Nor. *Norefjell,* rise to 4,810 ft. 10 mi. NW.

Norfolk (nôr′fùk), county (□ 634; pop. 35,611), S Ont., on L. Erie; ⊙ Simcoe.

Norfolk (nôr′fùk), county (□ 2,053.5; 1931 pop. 504,940; 1951 census 546,550), SE England; ⊙ Norwich. Bounded by The Wash, Lincolnshire and Cambridge (W), Suffolk (S), and the North Sea (E and N). Drained by Yare, Bure, Waveney and Ouse rivers. Mostly flat, with low coast lined by sand dunes; in NE of co. are The Broads, an extensive lake and marsh area (yachting resort). Soil is fertile, and area is known for its turkeys and horses. North Sea fishing, based on Yarmouth and other smaller ports, is the chief maritime industry. Besides Norwich, other important towns are Yarmouth, King's Lynn, Thetford, Cromer Fakenham, Diss, East Dereham, Wymondham. Co. has numerous literary and historical associations. In Second World War many bomber stations were located here.

Norfolk. 1 (nôr′fùk, nôr′fôk″) County (□ 398; pop. 392,308), E Mass.; ⊙ Dedham. S of Boston, with Quincy and Hingham bays on Boston Bay; bounded SW by R.I.; drained by Charles and Neponset rivers. NE area is thickly populated, with residential suburbs of Boston (e.g., Brookline, Milton). Mfg. (shoes, textiles, metal and wood products, building materials, machinery, paper products), printing and publishing, granite quarrying in its industrial towns, notably Quincy. Agr. in SW. Formed 1793. **2** (nôr′fùk) County (□ 364; pop. 99,937), SE Va.; co. courthouse is at PORTSMOUTH, which is, like NORFOLK, in but independent of co. Bounded N by Chesapeake Bay and great harbor of HAMPTON ROADS; indented by tidal inlets, including Elizabeth and Lafayette rivers. Much of DISMAL SWAMP (crossed by Dismal Swamp Canal) is in W and S. Sandy coastal plains support farming, dairying, poultry raising, growing of nursery plants and fruit. Commercial fisheries (especially oysters). Shore resorts. Sport fishing, waterfowl and game (deer, bear) hunting. Formed 1691.

Norfolk. 1 (nôr′fôk″, nôr′fùk) Resort town (pop. 1,572), Litchfield co., NW Conn., in Litchfield Hills, on Mass. line, 8 mi. NW of Winsted; agr., recreational area, with state parks; electrical products. Annual Litchfield co. choral concerts began here, 1899. William Henry Welch b. here. Settled 1755, inc. 1758. **2** (nôr′fùk, nôr′fôk″) Agr. town (pop. 2,704), Norfolk co., E Mass., 22 mi. SW of Boston. Norfolk Prison Colony here. Settled 1795, inc. 1870. **3** (nôr′fùk, nôr′fôk″) City (pop. 11,335), Madison co., NE Nebr., 90 mi. NW of Omaha and on Elkhorn R.; trade center, railroad division point in rich grain, livestock region; serums, beverages, flour, cereals; dairy and poultry produce. Jr. col. here. State hosp. for insane near by. Settled 1866, inc. 1881. **4** (nôr′fùk) Village (pop. 1,252), St. Lawrence co., N N.Y., on Raquette R. and 10 mi. SSW of Massena; paper. **5** (nôr′fùk) City (1940 pop. 144,332; 1950 pop. 213,513), in but independent of Norfolk co., SE Va., great port on Elizabeth R. and HAMPTON ROADS, opposite Portsmouth (W) and Newport News (NW), and 75 mi. SE of Richmond; 2d-largest (after Richmond) city of Va.; one of nation's leading seaports and a port of entry; shares with Portsmouth (site of Norfolk Navy Yard) major East Coast naval installations. Has Atlantic Fleet hq. (naval operating base), supply center, and naval air station

Harbor, served by belt-line railroad connecting 8 trunk lines, is N terminus of 2 sections (Dismal Swamp Canal, Albemarle and Chesapeake Canal) of Intracoastal Waterway, leading S to Albemarle Sound. Ships coal, farm products (tobacco, cotton, grain, meat, fruit, vegetables), seafood, lumber, textiles, chemicals, metals, minerals; receives oil, minerals, woodpulp, chemicals, hides, coffee, sugar, tapioca, timber. Large shipyards, railroad yards, foundries, smelter, automobile assembly plant; also mfg. of fertilizers, textiles, clothing, bags, wood products, farm equipment, drugs, cement, food products. Supply, shipping center for truck farms of coastal plain. Shore resorts of Ocean View (within city limits) and near-by Cape Henry and Virginia Beach. Has marine hosp., jr. col. Points of interest include St. Paul's Church (1739), Fort Norfolk (1794), Mus. of Arts and Sciences, Myers House (1791). City founded 1682; inc. as borough 1736, as city 1845. Burned (1776) by British in Revolution.

Norfolk Bay, Tasmania: see FREDERICK HENRY BAY.

Norfolk Broads, England: see BROADS, THE.

Norfolk Dam, Ark.: see NORTH FORK, Mo. and Ark.

Norfolk Island, volcanic island (□ 13; pop. 1,231), S Pacific, belonging to Commonwealth of Australia, 930 mi. NE of Sydney; 29°2'S 167°57'E; c.5 mi. long, 3 mi. wide. Fertile, hilly; rugged coast. Luxuriant vegetation; Norfolk Isl. pine trees (*Araucaria excelsa*). Large tourist trade. Exports citrus and passion fruit. Principal village, Kingston. Discovered 1774 by Capt. Cook; used as Br. penal colony (1788–1813; 1826–1855); annexed 1844 by Tasmania. Surplus pop. (descendants of *Bounty* mutineers) of Pitcairn Isl. was moved here in 1856, and settlement was placed 1896 under New South Wales (then a Br. colony); transferred 1913 to Commonwealth of Australia.

Norfork (nôr'fôrk), town (pop. 431), Baxter co., N Ark., c.45 mi. E of Harrison, at junction of White R. and the North Fork. Norfork Dam is near by, on NORTH FORK.

Norg (nôrkh), town (pop. 1,138), Drenthe prov., N Netherlands, 7 mi. NW of Assen; cattle market; dairying.

Norge: see NORWAY.

Norheimsund (nōr'hāmsōōn"), village (pop. 724) in Kvam canton, Hordaland co., SW Norway, on Hardanger Fjord, 10 mi. WSW of Alvik; tourism.

Noria (nōr'yä), town (pop. 1,337), Sinaloa, NW Mexico, in coastal lowland, 22 mi. NW of Mazatlán; agr. center (sugar cane, tobacco, cotton, corn, fruit, vegetables); lumbering.

Noria, La, Chile: see LA NORIA.

Noria de Ángeles (dā än'hĕlĕs) or **Alvaro Obregón** (älvä'rō ōbrēgōn'), town (pop. 1,088), Zacatecas, N central Mexico, 50 mi. SE of Zacatecas; alt. 7,523 ft. Maguey, fruit, livestock; silver and copper deposits. Exports bananas.

Noria de San Pantaleón (dā sän' päntälāōn'), mining settlement (pop. 3,461), Zacatecas, N central Mexico, 10 mi. ENE of Sombrerete; silver, gold, lead, copper deposits.

Noric Alps (nō'rĭk), Ger. *Norische Alpen*, division of Eastern Alps in S Austria, mainly along Styria-Carinthia line; extend E from Hohe Tauern at Katschberg Pass to the Mur valley near Graz; bounded N by upper Mur R., S by Drau R. valley. Consist of several ranges, of which the Gurktal Alps (W) are highest, rising to 8,008 ft. in the Eisenhut. Sometimes Styrian-Carinthian Alps.

Noricum (nŏ'rĭkům), province of the Roman Empire. It corresponded roughly to modern Austria S of the Danube and W of Vienna and included all or most of the later Upper Austria, Lower Austria, Styria, Carinthia, Salzburg, and the Tyrol. It was bordered W by Rhaetia, E by Pannonia. Noricum was conquered in the Roman thrust into Germany which began in 16 B.C. Thoroughly established by the death of Augustus (A.D. 14), it prospered as a frontier colony for centuries, then declined and was abandoned to the Germans in late 6th cent.

Norikura, Mount (nōrē'kōōrä), Jap. *Norikura-dake*, peak (9,925 ft.), central Honshu, Japan, on Gifu-Nagano prefecture border, in Chubu-sangaku Natl. Park, 17 mi. E of Takayama.

Norilsk or **Noril'sk** (nŭrēlsk'), town (1948 pop. over 2,000), W Taimyr Natl. Okrug, Krasnoyarsk Territory, Russian SFSR, N of Arctic Circle, 50 mi. E of Dudinka (port on the Yenisei; linked by railroad). Important nickel mines; also coal, gold, platinum, cobalt, copper; nonferrous smelter.

Norische Alpen, Austria: see NORIC ALPS.

Nor Lake (nōr), Nor. *Norsjå* (nōr'shô), formerly *Norsjø*, Telemark co., S Norway, just W and NW of Skien; □ 23; 18 mi. long, 1–3 mi. wide, 577 ft. deep; alt. 49 ft. Boats from Skien (via Skien R.) traverse the lake to Ulefoss, the E terminus of the BANDAK-NORSJA CANAL.

Norlina (nôrlī'nů), town (pop. 874), Warren co., N N.C., 14 mi. NE of Henderson; sawmilling.

Nor Lípez, Bolivia: see COLCHA "K."

Norma (nôr'mä), village (pop. 3,440), Latina prov., Latium, S central Italy, 8 mi. NW of Sezze, on hill near Pontine Marshes; livestock raising. In the plain below are ruins of Ninfa, a medieval town abandoned in 17th cent. because of malaria.

Normal. 1 Town (pop. c.100), Madison co., N Ala., 3 mi. N of Huntsville. Seat of Ala. Agr. and Mechanical Col. **2** Town (pop. 9,772), McLean co., central Ill., adjoining Bloomington (S); seat of Ill. State Normal Univ. and a home for children of soldiers and sailors; has canneries. Inc. 1865. Formerly North Bloomington.

Norman, county (□ 885; pop. 12,909), NW Minn.; ⊙ Ada. Agr. area bounded W by Red River of the North and N.Dak. and drained by Wild Rice R. Wheat, small grains, livestock, potatoes, dairy products, poultry. Formed 1881.

Norman. 1 Town (pop. 401), Montgomery co., W Ark., 35 mi. W of Hot Springs, in Ouachita Natl. Forest; lumbering. **2** Village (pop. 68), Kearney co., S Nebr., 7 mi. E of Minden. **3** Town (pop. 300), Richmond co., S N.C., 16 mi. NNE of Rockingham; lumber milling. **4** City (pop. 27,006), ⊙ Cleveland co., central Okla., 17 mi. S of Oklahoma City, near Canadian R. Seat of Univ. of Okla., and a distribution center for agr. area. Cotton ginning, cottonseed-oil milling, dairying. A state mental hosp. is here. Settled 1889, inc. 1902.

Norman, Cape, promontory at N extremity of N.F., on Strait of Belle Isle; 51°38'N 55°54'W; lighthouse.

Normanby. 1 Agr. village and parish (pop. 150), North Riding, E Yorkshire, England, 4 mi. WSW of Pickering. **2** Steel-milling town in ESTON urban dist., North Riding, NE Yorkshire, England.

Normanby Island, volcanic island (□ c.400), D'Entrecasteaux Isls., Territory of Papua, SW Pacific, 10 mi. SE of New Guinea, across Goschen Strait; 45 mi. long, 15 mi. wide; gold.

Normandie, France: see NORMANDY.

Normandin (nôrmãdē'), village (pop. 1,029), S central Que., 26 mi. NW of Roberval; lumbering; cheese, butter making.

Normandy, England: see ASH AND NORMANDY.

Normandy (nôr'můndē), Fr. *Normandie* (nôrmãdē'), region and former province of NW France; ⊙ Rouen. Forming NW part of Paris Basin, it borders on English Channel and extends from Brittany (SW) to Picardy (NE). Includes depts. of Manche, Orne, Calvados, Eure, and Seine-Inférieure. Regionally, it is broken up into Upper Normandy (area on both sides of lower Seine R. and its estuary), and Lower Normandy, which includes hedgerow country of Calvados and Cotentin Peninsula, and hilly area bet. Alençon (E) and Avranches (W). A rich agr. region, chiefly known for its dairy industry (Isigny butter, Camembert cheese), cider and apple brandy (Calvados). Horse breeding is principal activity in Perche hills around Mortagne. Coastal and Newfoundland fishing from numerous Channel ports. Widely scattered low-grade iron mines in Normandy Hills. Granite quarries. Textile milling is chief industry (centers at Rouen, Elbeuf, Lillebonne, Louviers). Lower Seine R. is a major commercial artery with important ports and industrial districts at LE HAVRE and ROUEN. Other seaports are CHERBOURG, CAEN (on Orne R.; ship canal), Dieppe, and Fécamp. Chief interior towns are Évreux, Alençon, and Lisieux. Numerous bathing resorts on Channel coast: Deauville, Trouville, Étretat, Cabourg, Houlgate. MONT-SAINT-MICHEL, Bayeux, and Second World War landing beaches (Omaha Beach, Utah Beach, etc.) provide chief tourist attraction. Conquered by Caesar, region became part of Lugdunensis prov., was Christianized in 3d cent., and conquered by Franks in 5th cent. Repeatedly devastated by heathen Norsemen (or Normans) after whom duchy (911) was named. In 1066, Duke William II invaded England. Normandy, contested by William's sons, passed to England in 1106. In 1144, Geoffrey of Anjou conquered it, his son, Henry Plantagenet (later Henry II of England) becoming duke in 1151. Seized (1204) by Philip II of France, Normandy was again devastated in Hundred Years War. Confirmed in Fr. possession by Treaty of Brétigny (1360); retaken by Henry V of England; and restored (1450) to France with exception of larger Channel Isls. Provincial *parlement* established at Rouen in 1499. The States-General was suppressed (1654) by Louis XIV. In 1790, prov. was broken up into present depts. On June 6, 1944, Allied troops landed along its N coast bet. Saint-Marcouf (Manche dept.) and Ouistreham (Calvados dept.) in Second World War. Ensuing Normandy campaign (June–Aug., 1944) was climaxed by American break-through at Saint-Lô and subsequently led to liberation of all of France from Ger. occupation. Most Norman towns were heavily damaged.

Normandy. 1 Town (pop. 2,306), St. Louis co., E Mo., just W of St. Louis. Inc. since 1940. **2** Town (pop. 159), Bedford co., central Tenn., on Duck R. and 13 mi. SE of Shelbyville.

Normandy Hills, Normandy, NW France, extend E–W in several irregular chains from Argentan-Falaise area to vicinity of Coutances. Average alt. 600 ft. Paralleled S by outlying hill-range extending from Alençon area to the Channel near Avranches. Covered by wooded tracts and hedgerows. Scattered low-grade iron mining. Scene of fighting during Normandy campaign of Second World War.

Normangee (nôr'můnjē), town (pop. 657), Leon and Madison counties, E central Texas, 29 mi. NE of Bryan; trade point in farm area (cotton, truck). State park near by.

Norman Island, islet, Br. Virgin Isls., 3 mi. E of St. John. Has old pirates' caves.

Norman Isles: see CHANNEL ISLANDS.

Norman Park, town (pop. 832), Colquitt co., S Ga., 9 mi. NE of Moultrie. Norman Col. here.

Norman River, N Queensland, Australia, rises in SE Gregory Range, flows WNW and NNW, past Normanton, to Gulf of Carpentaria; 260 mi. long. Navigable 30 mi. below Normanton by small craft. Yappar and Clara rivers, main tributaries.

Normans, Md.: see KENT ISLAND.

Norman's Woe, NE Mass., rocky headland on W side of entrance to Gloucester Harbor. Just offshore, to NE, is **Norman's Woe Rock,** islet with surrounding reefs, which figures in Longfellow's poem "The Wreck of the Hesperus."

Normanton, village and river port (pop. 234), N Queensland, Australia, on Norman R., 30 mi. from its mouth on Gulf of Carpentaria, and 390 mi. NNW of Townsville; terminus of railroad from Croydon; exports cattle.

Normanton (nôr'můntůn). **1** Town, Derby, England: see DERBY, city. **2** Urban district (1931 pop. 15,684; 1951 census 19,087), West Riding, S Yorkshire, England, 4 mi. ENE of Wakefield; railroad junction; coal-mining center.

Normantown, town (pop. 78), Toombs co., E central Ga., 7 mi. N of Vidalia.

Norman Wells, village (pop. estimate 600), W Mackenzie Dist., Northwest Territories, on Mackenzie R. (here 4 mi. wide), at foot of Franklin Mts., 45 mi. NW of Fort Norman; 65°18'N 126°51'W; oil-production center, site of oil refinery, storage tanks, machine shops. Trading post; airfield and govt. radio and meteorological station, hosp., Royal Canadian Mounted Police post. Oil is supplied to Mackenzie Dist. mining camps. Oil wells were discovered 1920, refinery built 1939. During Second World War Norman Wells was N terminus of the *Canol* pipeline system to Whitehorse and the Alaska Highway; closed down 1945.

Normetal, village (pop. estimate 500), W Que., 55 mi. NNW of Rouyn, near Ont. border; gold, copper, zinc mining.

Noroton, Conn.: see DARIEN.

Noroy-le-Bourg (nôrwä'-lů-bōōr'), village (pop. 486), Haute-Saône dept., E France, 7 mi. E of Vesoul; cheese mfg.

Norphlet (nôr'flĕt), town (pop. 653), Union co., S Ark., 7 mi. N of El Dorado; oil refinery.

Norquay (nôr'kwā), village (pop. 340), E Sask., near Man. border, 23 mi. NNW of Kamsack; mixed farming.

Ñorquin, Argentina: see EL HUECÚ.

Ñorquincó (nyôrkĕngkō'), village (pop. estimate 500), ⊙ Ñorquincó dept., SW Río Negro natl. territory, Argentina, on railroad and 55 mi. SSE of San Carlos de Bariloche; stock raising (sheep, cattle, goats). Coal deposits near by.

Norrahammar (nô'rähä"mär), town (pop. 4,169), Jonkoping co., S Sweden, 5 mi. S of Jonkoping; iron- and steelworks, sawmills; mfg. of household utensils.

Norrbotten (nôr'bô"tůn), northernmost and largest county [Swedish *län*] (□ 40,750; 1950 pop. 241,602) of Sweden; ⊙ Lulea. In LAPLAND, it is bounded by Norway (W and NW), Finland (NE and E), and Gulf of Bothnia (SE); comprises Norrbotten province [Swedish *landskap*] (□ 10,703; pop. 163,684) and N part of Lappland prov. More than half of co. is N of Arctic Circle, and pop. includes c.4,400 Lapps and c.40,000 Finns. E part of co. is fertile lowland, rising toward W, becoming mountainous on Norwegian border. Near border is Kebnekaise (6,965 ft.), Sweden's highest peak. Drained by large Pite, Lule, Torne, and Kalix rivers; contains several large lakes, including Torne, Stora Lule, Hornavan, and Uddjaur lakes. Lumbering and sawmilling are chief occupation; vast iron deposits are worked at Kiruna, Gallivare, and Malmberget, and the ore is shipped from Lulea and from Norwegian port of Narvik. Hydroelectric power from large stations at Porjus and Harspranget. Sheep and cattle are raised. Cities are Lulea, Boden, Kiruna, Haparanda, and Pitea.

Norrbyn (nôr'bün"), village (pop. 407), Vasterbotten co., N Sweden, on Gulf of Bothnia, 20 mi. SW of Umea; sawmilling, brick mfg.

Norre Aaby (nû'rů ô'bü), Dan. *Nørre Aaby*, town (pop. 1,120), Odense amt, Denmark, on NW Fyn isl. and 21 mi. WNW of Odense; mfg. (margarine, bicycles).

Norre Alslev (äl'slĕv), Dan. *Nørre Alslev*, town (pop. 1,325), Maribo amt, Denmark, on N Falster isl. and 17 mi. NE of Maribo; slaughterhouse; orchards.

Norrent-Fontes (nôrã'-fōt'), village (pop. 380), Pas-de-Calais dept., N France, 11 mi. WNW of Béthune; coal mining.

Norre Sundby (nû'rů sōōn'bü), Dan. *Nørre Sundby*, city (pop. 8,251) and port, Aalborg amt, N Jutland, Denmark, on Lim Fjord (here bridged) opposite Aalborg, 27 mi. S of Hjorring. Mfg. (cement, chemicals, textiles), machine shops, tanneries.

Formerly center of communication and commerce bet. Aalborg and Vendsyssel region.

Norrhult (nôr'hŭlt"), village (pop. 791), Kronoberg co., S Sweden, 20 mi. NE of Vaxjo; glass and mechanical works, foundry.

Norridge, village (pop. 3,428), Cook co., NE Ill., just W of Chicago. Inc. since 1940.

Norridgewock (nŏ'rĭjwŏk), town (pop. 1,784), Somerset co., W central Maine, on the Kennebec and 5 mi. above Skowhegan. Mfg. (shoes, boats, canoes), farm produce canned. In 17th cent. Norridgewock Indians here were visited by Jesuit missionaries; monument commemorates chapel of Sébastien Rasles who, with the Indians, was killed by English in 1724. Inc. 1788.

Norris. 1 Village (pop. 319), Fulton co., W central Ill., 5 mi. N of Canton, in agr. and bituminous-coal area. **2** Village (pop. c.100), Madison co., SW Mont., on branch of Madison R. and 50 mi. SE of Butte; corundum of gem quality mined here. **3** Town (pop. 325), Pickens co., NW S.C., 21 mi. WSW of Greenville. **4** City (pop. 1,134), Anderson co., E Tenn., on Clinch R. and 16 mi. NW of Knoxville. Built originally as residential community for construction workers on near-by Norris Dam; hq. of forestry div. of TVA and regional hq. of U.S. Bureau of Mines. Near by is Norris Park (resort) on Norris Reservoir. Inc. 1949.

Norris City, village (pop. 1,370), White co., SE Ill., 20 mi. NE of Harrisburg; trade center in agr. and bituminous-coal area; wheat, corn, oats, livestock. Inc. 1901.

Norris Dam, E Tenn., in Clinch R., near mouth of Powell R., 20 mi. NW of Knoxville. First major TVA dam (265 ft. high, 1,860 ft. long), it was completed 1936 for flood control and power. Forms irregularly-shaped Norris Reservoir (□ 53; capacity 2,567,000 acre-ft.; sometimes known as Norris L.) extending upstream 72 mi. along Clinch R., 56 mi. along Powell R.; drains parts of Anderson, Campbell, Union, and Claiborne counties. Norris Park (with TVA fish hatchery and facilities for picnicking, camping, and boating) is here. Norris city is just SE.

Norristown, borough (pop. 38,126), ⊙ Montgomery co., SE Pa., 15 mi. NW of Philadelphia and on Schuylkill R., near E end of Pennsylvania Turnpike; agr. shipping center; machinery, metal products, asbestos, furniture, hardware, textiles, plastics, clothing, drugs, food and dairy products, bricks, paper products. State hosp. for the insane here. Mineral deposits accounted for early growth. Laid out 1784, inc. 1812.

Nor River, Swedish *Norsälven* (nōōrs'ĕl"vŭn), W Sweden, rises in E Norway NE of Kongsvinger near Swedish border, flows 90 mi. generally S, through L. Fryk, past Sunne and Edsvalla (head of navigation), to L. Vaner 2 mi. E of Grums. Logging route.

Norrkoping (nôr'chû"pĭng), Swed. *Norrköping,* city (1950 pop. 84,939), Ostergotland co., SE Sweden, on Motala R., near its mouth on Bra Bay, Swedish *Bråviken,* 30-mi.-long inlet of Baltic, 80 mi. SW of Stockholm; 58°35'N 16°6'E. Seaport; chief textile-milling center of Sweden, with paper and lumber mills, shipyards; mfg. of rayon, rubber products, margarine, furniture. Has 16th-cent. castle and several other old bldgs. Known since 14th cent., industrial center since 17th cent., city was burned (1719) by Russians in Northern War.

Norrland, Sweden: see SWEDEN.

Norrland (nôr'länd), village (pop. 1,266), Vasternorrland co., NE Sweden, on Angerman R. estuary, 20 mi. N of Harnosand; sawmills. Includes villages of Lugnvik (lŭng"ŭnvēk'), Maland (mä'länd), Swedish *Måland,* and Hallsta (häl'stä").

Norrmark, Finland: see NOORMARKKU.

Norrsundet (nôr'sŭn"dût), village (pop. 1,331), Gavleborg co., E Sweden, on Gulf of Bothnia, 18 mi. N of Gavle; sawmills, sulphite works.

Norrtalje (nôrtĕl'yü), Swedish *Norrtälje,* city (pop. 5,806), Stockholm co., E Sweden, at head of Norrtalje Bay, Swedish *Norrtäljeviken,* 12-mi.-long inlet of the Baltic, 40 mi. NE of Stockholm; aircraft works; wood industry. Health resort, with mud baths. Trade center in Middle Ages; chartered 1622. Burned (1719) by Russians. Modern city dates from late-19th cent.

Norsalven, Sweden: see NOR RIVER.

Norseman, town (pop. 2,480), S central Western Australia, 100 mi. S of Kalgoorlie and on Kalgoorlie-Esperance RR; gold-mining center; also tin, silver, lead, pyrite.

Norsja, Norway: see NOR LAKE.

Norsjo (nôr'shû"), Swedish *Norsjö,* village (pop. 919), Vasterbotten co., N Sweden, on small Nor L., Swedish *Norsjö,* 40 mi. WNW of Skelleftea: stock; dairying.

Norsk (nôrsk), village, E Amur oblast, Russian SFSR, on Selemdzha R. and 175 mi. N of Blagoveshchensk; trading post. Gold mining near by.

Norskehavet: see NORWEGIAN SEA.

Norte, Cabo do (kä'bōō dōō nôr'tĭ), headland of Amapá territory, N Brazil, on the Atlantic, formed by NE tip of Maracá isl. just off mainland; 2°20'N 50°15'W. Lighthouse.

Norte, El, Honduras: see EL NORTE.

Norte, Sierra del (syĕ'rä dĕl nôr'tā), pampean mountain range of Sierra de Córdoba system, NW Córdoba prov., Argentina, extends c.35 mi. N from Deán Funes; rises to c.3,000 ft.

Norte de Santander (nôr'tā dā säntändär'), department (□ 8,297; 1938 pop. 346,181; 1950 estimate 433,390), N Colombia; ⊙ Cúcuta. Bounded E by Venezuela (Táchira R.), it is located in deeply dissected Cordillera Oriental and includes a narrow strip of Maracaibo lowlands. Watered by Zulia R., affluent of the Catatumbo. Tropical to temperate climate, depending on alt. Mineral resources include coal, kaolin, sulphur, gypsum, iron, talc, copper, tin, lead; rich Petrólea oil fields of the Barco concession are linked by pipe line with Coveñas (Bolívar dept.) on Caribbean coast. Forests yield fine lumber, balsam, resins, tagua nuts. Around Cúcuta is a rich coffeegrowing region; other products are cacao, sugar cane, tobacco, cotton, corn, wheat, fique fibers, livestock. Cúcuta, Pamplona, and Ocaña are its trading and processing centers. Sometimes called Santander Norte.

Nörten-Hardenberg (nûr'tùn-här'dùnbĕrk), village (pop. 3,866), in former Prussian prov. of Hanover, W Germany, after 1945 in Lower Saxony, on the Leine and 7 mi. N of Göttingen; sugar refining, distilling, woodworking. Large ruins of Hardenberg castle tower above village.

North, for names beginning thus and not found here: see under NORTHERN.

North, Northern, in Rus. names: see also SEVERNAYA, SEVERNIYE, SEVERNOYE, SEVERNY, SEVERO-.

North, town (pop. 954), Orangeburg co., W central S.C., 16 mi. NW of Orangeburg; lumber.

North, Cape, NE extremity of Cape Breton Isl., NE N.S. on Cabot Strait, 60 mi. NNW of Sydney; 47°2'N 60°25'W.

North Abington, Mass.: see ABINGTON.

North Adams. 1 City (pop. 21,567), Berkshire co., NW Mass., in the Berkshires, on Hoosic R. and 19 mi. NNE of Pittsfield, near W terminus of Hoosac Tunnel and Mohawk Trail; woolens, cottons, machinery, electrical goods, shoes, paper; printing. Has state teachers col. Includes state park and forest, and village of Blackinton. Mt. Greylock is SW. Settled c.1737, set off from Adams 1878, inc. as city 1895. **2** Village (pop. 499), Hillsdale co., S Mich., 6 mi. NE of Hillsdale, in agr. area; mfg. of chemicals.

North Albanian Alps, Albanian *Bjeshkë te Shqipnis së Veriut,* Serbo-Croatian *Prokletije* or *Prokletiye* [=the accursed (alps); Albanian *Bjeshkë te nemuna*], mountain group at S end of Dinaric Alps, on Albanian-Yugoslav border, extend c.60 mi. in an alpine arc bet. L. Scutari and White Drin R.; rises to 8,714 ft. in the Djaravica. A wild, precipitous highland region, more easily accessible from N (Yugoslav) slopes.

Northallerton (nôr-thă'lùrtùn), urban district (1931 pop. 4,786; 1951 census 6,087), ⊙ North Riding, N Yorkshire, England, 15 mi. N of Ripon, in valley of the Wiske; trade center, with dairying (milk canning, cheese making) and leather-tanning industries. Has 12th–13th-cent. church, remains of Roman station and of 12th-cent. palace. Standard Hill, 2 mi. N, was site of defeat (1138) of Scots by English in "battle of the Standard."

Northam (nôr'thùm), municipality (pop. 4,652), SW Western Australia, 50 mi. ENE of Perth and on Avon R.; rail junction; wheat center; flour mill. Agr. col. near by.

Northam (nôr'dhùm), urban district (1931 pop. 5,563; 1951 census 6,470), N Devon, England, on Torridge R., near its mouth on Barnstaple Bay of the Channel, and 2 mi. N of Bideford; agr. market. Scene of 9th-cent. battle bet. Saxons and Danes. Has 14th-cent. church. Urban dist. includes APPLEDORE and WESTWARD HO.

North America, continent (including Central America: □ c.8,443,600; pop. c.200,000,000; including Greenland and the West Indies: □ c.9,390,000; pop. c.215,000,000), northern of the 2 continents of the Western Hemisphere, connected with South America by the Isthmus of Panama (7°–9°N), and extending to 71°59'N at tip of Boothia Peninsula, northernmost mainland point, and to 83°7'N at N coast of Ellesmere Isl. Westernmost mainland point, Cape Prince of Wales, Alaska (168°4'W), is 55 mi. across Bering Strait from Cape Dezhnev (USSR); easternmost mainland point (Labrador coast) is c.55°W. Greatest length of mainland is c.4,500 mi., with Arctic Archipelago c.5,300 mi.; greatest width is c.4,000 mi. Continent is washed on W by the North Pacific and Bering Sea, N by the Arctic Ocean, E by the North Atlantic, Gulf of Mexico (SE), and the Caribbean Sea (bordering Central America, which is here considered part of North America). Greenland, across Baffin Bay E of the Arctic Archipelago, is northernmost region of Western Hemisphere. Off NW coast of the continent are many small isls. in the Bering Sea and the long chain of ALEUTIAN ISLANDS, stretching to USSR boundary near 172°E. In the Pacific are the Alexander Archipelago, Queen Charlotte Isls., and Vancouver Isl.; bet. the Caribbean and the Atlantic E of Central America are the WEST INDIES. Off the Atlantic coast are Newfoundland, Nova Scotia, Cape Breton and Prince Edward isls. (Canada), and Long Isl. (N.Y.). Continent's enormous coast line is indented in N by huge Hudson Bay; in E by Gulf of St. Lawrence, Bay of Fundy, Delaware and Chesapeake bays, and Gulf of Mexico; in W by Gulf of Calif., San Francisco Bay, Puget Sound, Gulf of Alaska and its inlets. Politically, North America is divided into CANADA, the largest nation in area, member of British Commonwealth of Nations; the UNITED STATES, greatest in pop. and in economic development; the U.S. territory of ALASKA; the republic of MEXICO; the 6 republics of CENTRAL AMERICA—GUATEMALA, HONDURAS, SALVADOR, NICARAGUA, COSTA RICA, and PANAMA (crossed by U.S.-administered PANAMA CANAL ZONE), and the colony BRITISH HONDURAS. Continent's highest point is Mt. McKinley (Alaska), 20,270 ft.; its lowest, 280 ft. below sea level, is in Death Valley, Calif. Topographically, North America is dominated by the ROCKY MOUNTAINS (8–14,000 ft.), globe's 2d-longest mtn. chain, extending from the Arctic Ocean to N.Mex., whence they are believed to be linked by connecting ranges with the SIERRA MADRE (Mexico) and thence by the Central American highlands (5–10,000 ft.) with the Andes of South America. The Rockies are the continental divide and the E belt of the North American cordillera, whose W members, in places rising abruptly from the sea, include (N–S) the lofty ALASKA RANGE (Mt. McKinley), the Coast Mts. of B.C., the COAST RANGES, CASCADE RANGE, and the SIERRA NEVADA (Mt. Whitney, 14,495 ft., highest peak in U.S.). Bet. the Rockies and these W ranges lie the Yukon plateau and interior plateau of the far NW (2–5,000 ft.), the Columbia and Colorado plateaus and the GREAT BASIN of the U.S.; in Mexico is the high (4–8,000 ft.) central plateau embraced by the main members of the Sierra Madre. The GREAT PLAINS (2–5,000 ft.) border the Rockies on the E for most of their length. To E of Great Plains in N Canada are the BARREN GROUNDS and W part of the LAURENTIAN PLATEAU, which swings in a wide arc from the Arctic Ocean to the Atlantic. From central Sask. S to the Gulf of Mexico coastal plain are the central (or interior) plains (500–1,000 ft.), a vast fertile lowland drained to Hudson Bay by SASKATCHEWAN RIVER, NELSON RIVER, and RED RIVER of the North; to the Gulf of Mexico by the vast MISSOURI RIVER-MISSISSIPPI RIVER system; and to the Atlantic by way of the Great Lakes and the SAINT LAWRENCE. In S central part of the plains rise the Ozark and Ouachita mts., the only uplands in the region. Highlands of E North America consist mainly of the APPALACHIAN MOUNTAINS (to c.6,700 ft.), flanked by lower plateaus to W and by the PIEDMONT to E, and extending from the St. Lawrence to Ala.; other E mts. are the LAURENTIAN MOUNTAINS (Canada), Adirondack Mts. (U.S.). Along E coast is a sandy plain, narrow in NE by widening S of New England, whence it is also fringed by sandy barrier isls. for much of its length; the Gulf of Mexico coastal plain (Fla., Ala., Miss., La., Texas) is continued in Mexico and Central America by the jungle-covered lowlands along the Gulf and the Caribbean. The W coast, except in scattered localities, lacks a coastal plain. The GREAT LAKES (□ 94,710; on U.S.-Can. line) contain L. Superior, largest body of fresh water in world; other large lakes of North America are Great Bear, Great Slave, Athabaska, Manitoba, and Winnipeg (Canada), Great Salt L. (U.S.), L. Nicaragua (Nicaragua). Besides those draining the central plains, continent's principal rivers include the Mackenzie (to Arctic Sea), the Yukon (to Bering Sea), the Columbia and the Colorado (to the Pacific), the Rio Grande (to Gulf of Mexico). Navigation far into the heart of the continent (chiefly to the Great Lakes) is carried by the Mississippi and Ohio systems and the St. Lawrence. Extending from far N of the Arctic Circle (which crosses Canada and Alaska) to far S of the Tropic of Cancer (across Mexico), North America has a wide range of climatic and vegetation zones, which are affected by local elevation and exposure to prevailing winds, and by ocean currents (especially the Labrador Current and the Gulf Stream on E, Japan Current on W) as well as by latitude. A polar-climate belt along Bering Strait and the Arctic Sea in N is characterized by tundra vegetation and, in parts, by scanty rainfall (under 10 inches); in this zone the normal Jan. temp. is from −20° F. to −40°F., July from c.30°F. to 50°F. Below this is the subarctic belt, extending from Alaska across central Canada, and, at higher alts., alpine vegetation; annual rainfall is 10–20 inches, Jan. normal temp. from −4°F. to −22°F., July normal temp. c.50°F. to 60°F. Along the W coast (including coastal Alaska) as far S as N Calif. is a marine-climate belt, mild (Jan., 50°–68°F. in S, 14°–32°F. in N; July temp. is fairly uniform N and S, 50°–c.70°F.), and moist, with 40 to 100 inches of rainfall; here are valuable coniferous forests containing a large share of continent's accessible saw timber. In SW Calif. is a mediterranean-climate belt (warm and dry, with c.10–20 inches rainfall), succeeded to the S and SW by the deserts (under 10 inches rain) of SW U.S. and W

Mexico; vegetation ranges from desert plants through scrub woodland to coniferous forests (at higher alts.). In the great W mtn. belt, with its enclosed arid basins and plateaus, precipitation varies from under 10 inches (as in the Great Basin) to the heavy snowfalls of the mtn. crests, temp. ranges vary similarly, and vegetation ranges from xerophytic plants in the arid tracts to the coniferous forests of the mtn. slopes and valleys; timber line in the Rockies is at 12,000 ft. in S, at level of the adjacent plains in extreme N. The Great Plains to E of the Rockies receive only 10–20 inches of rain and naturally support only short grass; generally cold winters (in Jan., from –4°F. to 14°F. in N, to c.30°F. in S) and hot summers are the rule here. The central plains (except subtropical Gulf coast and the lower Mississippi valley), the Great Lakes region, and SE Canada receive sufficient rainfall (20–40 inches) for agr., and before clearing supported good forests, mainly deciduous in S part, coniferous in Great Lakes region and Canada. The subtropical Gulf coast, the SE U.S., and much of the E coast of U.S. and E Canada receive 40–80 inches of rainfall; Jan. normal temperatures are from 50°–70°F. along the Gulf, to 14°–30°F. in the N; July temperatures (except for cooler coastal strips) are bet. c.68°F. and c.85°F. for most of region. An important pine belt, yielding naval stores, pulpwood, and saw timber, is along the Gulf coast and in S and SE U.S.; the Appalachians, Adirondacks, and the Laurentians contain large forest tracts (chiefly coniferous in N, hardwoods in S). Tropical S Mexico and Central America experience temp. and rainfall ranges governed largely by alt.; on central Mex. plateau rainfall is bet. 10 and 20 inches, and the mean annual temp. (at Mexico city) is 63°F. Up to 120 inches of rainfall supports the jungle vegetation of the lowlands along the Gulf and Caribbean; tropical forests here yield choice hardwoods, rubber, chicle, and naval stores, while the uplands have savannah and scrub vegetation. Highest recorded temp. on continent, 134°F., in Death Valley; lowest, –79°F., in Northwest Territories, Canada. Native fauna of North America, while clearly related to that of the other continents, includes such distinctive creatures as the Rocky Mtn. sheep and goats, the bison (now nearly extinct), mtn. lions (puma), the grizzly bear, certain antelopes, muskrats, raccoons, opossums, porcupines, and many rodents. Typical of the far N are the arctic birds in great variety, polar bears, and seals (Pribilof Isls. have great fur-seal herds); tundra creatures include the caribou and musk ox, while the great forests and lakes of the N wilderness harbor moose, deer, bears, wolves, and many fur-bearers, including the beaver, once enormously plentiful over most of the continent. Deer are widely distributed, as are squirrels, foxes, and many reptiles, including several poisonous varieties. The semi-tropical S U.S. has alligators, while in Mexico and Central America are animals (including monkeys, armadillos, peccaries, jaguars) and many colorful birds closely akin to those native to South America. Agr. regions of North America include 2 of world's great wheat regions—the spring-wheat belt in the prairie provs. of Canada (nation's principal agr. area, although there is diversified farming in S Que. and SE Ont., fruit-growing in B.C. and Ont.) and in the Plains States of the U.S., supplemented by smaller wheat areas in B.C. and E Wash. and E Ore.; and the winter-wheat belt farther S, extending from the E edge of the Great Plains into the central U.S. to meet the CORN BELT. The Corn Belt lies across the central states S of the hay-and-dairying region which borders the Great Lakes on the W, S, and SE. In S central and S U.S. is the COTTON BELT; along the Gulf coast and SE Atlantic coast are humid areas producing subtropical crops (including citrus), and along the Atlantic coast from S.C. northwards is the productive coastal-plains truck-, fruit-, and poultry-producing area. The Great Plains region, which includes the spring wheat belt in N, is the great dry-farming (grain) and stock-grazing (cattle, sheep, goats) region, with some irrigated agr. in many localities, chiefly in U.S. Mexico produces coffee, cacao, sugar cane, cotton, coconuts, fruit, corn, rice, henequen (c.50% of world's supply), maguey, istle fiber, tobacco, and cereals. Central America grows an important part of world's banana crop, as well as abaca, coffee, cacao, sugar cane, corn, beans, rice, cotton, coconuts, tobacco, vanilla, and some wheat; bananas, coffee, cacao, rubber, cotton, and some sugar are chief export crops. Alaskan agr. is of negligible, although increasing, importance; potatoes, truck, berries, and dairy products are produced for domestic consumption. In terms of acreage, most important North American crops are corn (more than ½ of world supply), hay, wheat, oats, cotton (c.½ of world supply), barley, soybeans (c.⅓ of world total), rye, flaxseed, potatoes, tobacco, rice, sweet potatoes. The U.S. and Canada together produce a large share of the world's meat. Vast irrigation projects in the U.S., chiefly in the W, have brought more than 20,000,000 arid acres under production. North American fisheries are a valuable resource; principal areas of production are Alaska, B.C., and Puget Sound ports (salmon and halibut); Calif. (sardines and tuna); Gulf of Calif. ports, Gulf of Mexico coast and Fla. ports (shrimp, sponges, shellfish, a wide variety of finfish); Chesapeake Bay area (shellfish, finfish); and the enormously valuable offshore fisheries of New England and the Maritime Provs. of Canada, yielding cod, sardines, herring, halibut, and lobsters. North America has enormous reserves and production of both metallic and non-metallic minerals. About ⅔ of world's crude petroleum is produced, mainly in U.S. and Canada, although there is considerable production in Mexico. Continent has more than ½ of world's coal reserves as well as high proportions of world supplies of iron ore, natural gas, copper, lead, zinc, and silver. Principal coal regions are in U.S. and Canada; in the U.S., bituminous coal is mined in the Appalachians (which also produce most of world's anthracite), Ill., Ind., Mich., Iowa, Mo., Ark., Okla., Kansas, Nebr., N.Mex., Ariz., Colo., Utah, Wyo., Mont., the Dakotas, and scattered areas in Pacific NW; the lower Mississippi valley and upper Gulf coastal plain produce lignite. Bituminous coal comes from Alta. and Sask. in Canada, and also from Coahuila, Mexico. Canadian petroleum comes from Alta., B.C., Northwest Territories, and other scattered localities; in U.S., chief oil and natural-gas fields are in the NE central, central (Okla.-Kansas), Gulf Coast (La.-Texas), and Rocky Mtn. regions, and along the W coast, particularly Calif.; Mex. oil fields center on Tampico, Tuxpan, and Coatzacoalcos. Iron dists. of Canada are led in importance by Ungava region, in U.S. by the great iron ranges of the L. Superior country (Minn., Mich.); there are also deposits in the Appalachian region (Pa. and Ala.); Mex. deposits are led in importance by Cerro de Mercado peak near Durango. Copper mines are operating in the Laurentian Plateau (Canada), Great Lakes region (Mich.), Mont. (Butte region), Utah, Ariz., N. Mex., Colorado, Nev., Calif., Wash., and Oregon; Mexico also produces some copper. Lead comes from Canada, Alaska, Mexico, and U.S. (SE Mo., Coeur d'Alene dist. of Idaho, Bingham dist. of Utah, Tri-State region of Kansas, SW Mo., and Okla., and other dists.); zinc from Mexico and from U.S. (Tri-State and Coeur d'Alene dists., E Tenn., and other areas). Mexico produces c.40% of world silver supply; other North American centers of production are in Canada and in W U.S. (Mont., Idaho, Utah, Nev., Ariz.), while some silver comes from Honduras, Salvador, Nicaragua, and Panama. Chief gold fields of the continent are in Alaska (Fairbanks, Juneau, Nome), Canada (Great Slave L. and Rouyn-Noranda fields), Mexico, Honduras, Salvador, Nicaragua, Costa Rica, Panama, and U.S. (Calif., Utah, Idaho, Nev., Ariz., Mont., Colo., S.Dak., Wash., Ore., N.Mex.). Other valuable mineral production includes nickel (Canada, U.S.), pitchblende (source of uranium) at Great Bear L. (Canada), asbestos (Que.), bauxite (U.S., Canada), mercury (U.S.), platinum (Canada, Alaska, U.S.), antimony, molybdenum, manganese, phosphate rock, cement rock, building stones, limestone, salt, sulphur (chiefly along Gulf coast of U.S.), borates, potassium salts, gypsum, clay, fluorspar, graphite. The rich agr., mineral, timber, and water-power resources of North America have given rise on the continent to the growth of some of the world's ranking industrial cities and centers, led by New York. The E seaboard of the U.S. has the continent's greatest pop. density; most of Canada's chief cities (except Winnipeg) and industries are in the St. Lawrence valley and Great Lakes regions, while the greatest concentration of pop. and industry of Mexico are in the Mexico city region. Location of industrial raw materials and ease of transportation has tended to concentrate heavy industries in such regions as that of the Great Lakes, the Mississippi and St. Lawrence valleys, and in the great seaports of the sea and Gulf coasts. First sure knowledge of North America came with Columbus' 1st landfall (1492) in the Bahamas and his later expeditions to the West Indies and Central America, although Leif Ericsson had visited (early 11th cent.) a region he called Vinland, now thought to be somewhere in New England. Cabot visited the Can. coast in 1497, and in 1604 the 1st settlement there (Port Royal, now Annapolis, N.S.) was made by the sieur de Monts and Champlain. Meantime, the 1st permanent settlement in the present U.S. had been made (1565) at St. Augustine, Fla., by Pedro Menéndez de Ávila, for the Spanish. The W coast of present Mexico was first visited (1517) by Francisco Fernández de Córdoba; shortly after, Cortés undertook the conquest of the Aztecs and established Sp. rule. Alaska was first visited by Vitus Bering and Alexsandr Chirikov in 1741, and the 1st permanent settlement was made 1784 on Kodiak Isl. by Grigori Shelekhov, for the Russians.

North Amherst, Mass.: see AMHERST.

Northampton (nôr″thămp′tŭn), town (pop. 626), W Western Australia, 30 mi. N of Geraldton; lead-mining center of state.

Northampton or **Northamptonshire** (nôr″thămp′tŭn, -shĭr), county (less Soke of Peterborough: □ 914.3; 1931 pop. 309,474; 1951 census 359,550; including Soke of Peterborough; □ 994.7; 1931 pop. 361,313; 1951 census 423,334), central England; ⊙ Northampton. Bounded by Warwick (W), Leicester, Rutland, and Lincolnshire (NW and N), Cambridge (NE), Huntingdon, Bedford, and Buckingham (E and SE), and Oxford (S). Drained by Nene, Welland, and Ise rivers. Hilly country, without major elevations; NE is reclaimed fenland, belonging to Bedford Level. NE part of the co. is administrative county of Soke of PETERBOROUGH. Chief industries are ironstone mining and quarrying, and leather, shoe, and allied industries (Northampton, Kettering, Wellingborough, Higham Ferrers, Raunds). There are remains of Roman settlements; co. was crossed by Watling Street and Ermine Street. Important Civil War battles were fought at Northampton and Naseby. Shortened form is Northants.

Northampton, county borough (1931 pop. 92,341; 1951 census pop. 104,429), ⊙ Northamptonshire, England, in center of co., on Nene R. and 60 mi. NW of London; 52°14′N 0°54′W. Important center of the leather industry, with tanneries, shoe factories, and other leather-goods works. Other industries include mfg. of machinery for leather industry, woolen milling, metalworking, mfg. of paint, plastics, soap, pharmaceuticals. St. Peter's Church has Norman interior, Perpendicular church of St. Giles has Norman door, and All Saints church has 14th-cent. tower. There is a Renaissance town hall (1682), St. John's Hosp. (founded 1138), and R.C. cathedral. St. Sepulchre's is one of 4 round churches in England. Just S, at Hardingstone, is an Eleanor Cross. Norman castle, erected when the town was an important settlement of the Angles and the Danes, was scene of the trial of Thomas à Becket (1164) and of 12th–14th-cent. parliaments; it is the locale of part of Shakespeare's *King John.* Henry VI was defeated here (1460). Town sided with Parliamentarians in the Civil War, and Charles II ordered castle and walls razed on his accession. Much of town destroyed by fire in 1675. In county borough (N) is shoe-mfg. town of Kingsthorpe (pop. 9,379).

Northampton (nôrth″hămp′tŭn, nôr″thămp′tŭn). **1** County (□ 540; pop. 28,432), NE N.C.; ⊙ Jackson. Bounded N by Va., SW by Roanoke R.; drained by Meherrin R. Piedmont agr. (peanuts, cotton, corn) and timber area. Formed 1741. **2** County (□ 374; pop. 185,243), E Pa.; ⊙ Easton. Industrial region; bounded E by Delaware R., NW by Lehigh R.; Blue Mtn. along N border. Settled first by English and Scotch-Irish, then by Germans. Mfg. (steel, cement, metal products, textiles, clothing); slate, limestone quarrying. Formed 1752. **3** County (□ 226; pop. 17,300), E Va.; ⊙ Eastville. At S end of Eastern Shore peninsula; Cape CHARLES is at S tip, at N side of entrance from the Atlantic to Chesapeake Bay. Many barrier and bay isls. lie off Atlantic coast. Fertile coastal plain truck-farming area, known for white and sweet potatoes; also tomatoes, cabbage, beans, other vegetables, strawberries, poultry, and dairy products. Pine timber. Ocean fisheries. Cape Charles, resort town, is a port, rail and ferry terminus. Several canneries process seafood, farm produce. Formed 1663.

Northampton. 1 City (pop. 29,063), ⊙ Hampshire co., W central Mass., on Connecticut R. and 15 mi. N of Springfield; hosiery, cutlery, brushes; tobacco, onions, potatoes. Best known as seat of Smith Col. Also has Clarke School for Deaf, state hosp. for insane. Inc. as town 1656, as city 1883. Includes villages of Leeds and FLORENCE. **2** Borough (pop. 9,332), Northampton co., E Pa., 5 mi. N of Allentown and on Lehigh R.; cement, textiles, beer; slate quarrying, agr. Settled c.1763, inc. 1901.

Northamptonshire, England: see NORTHAMPTON, county.

North Andaman Island: see ANDAMAN ISLANDS.

North Andover (ăn′dōvŭr), residential town (pop. 8,485), Essex co., NE Mass., on Merrimack R. just E of Lawrence; mfg. (woolens, textile machinery, chemicals). Settled c.1644, inc. 1855.

North Anna River, central Va., rises in the piedmont in Orange co., flows c.70 mi. SE, joining South Anna R. c.20 mi. N of Richmond to form Pamunkey River.

Northants, England: see NORTHAMPTON, county.

North Apollo, borough (pop. 1,502), Armstrong co., W central Pa., on Kiskiminetas R. opposite Vandergrift. Inc. 1930.

North Arcot (är′kŏt), Tamil *Vada Arkadu* (vŭdŭ ŭr′kŭdōō), district (□ 4,671; pop. 2,577,540), E central Madras, India; ⊙ Vellore. Bordered NW by S Eastern Ghats. Mainly lowland, except for Javadi Hills (W; sandalwood, hemp narcotics) and numerous isolated granite outcrops (quarries); drained by Palar R. and its tributary, the Cheyyar. Largely red ferruginous soil; alluvial soil along rivers. Mainly agr.: rice, peanuts (intensive cultivation), sesame, sugar cane, cotton, tobacco; mango and orange groves. Rice and sugar milling, peanut- and sesame-oil extraction. Gudiyattam is cotton-milling center. Tanneries at Ambur and Vaniyambadi; rail workshops at Akronam. Medical and psychiatric research center at Vellore. Under Chola kingdom and successive Indian powers, until it became main arena of 18th-cent. struggle bet. French, English, Mysore sultans, and nawabs of Arcot in French-English contest for supremacy in India (decisive English victory, 1760, at Wandiwash). Ceded to English 1801 by nawab of Arcot. Pop. 93% Hindu, 6% Moslem, 1% Christian.

North Arlington, borough (pop. 15,970), Bergen co., NE N.J., on Passaic R. and 4 mi. S of Passaic; mfg. (metal products, cement blocks; celluloid, bakelite, and rubber products; paint, toys, food products); nurseries. Inc. 1896.

North Atlanta, town (pop. 5,930), De Kalb co., N central Ga., suburb of Atlanta.

North Atlantic Current or **North Atlantic Drift,** terminal section of GULF STREAM system, in North Atlantic Ocean, formed by union of Labrador Current and the Gulf Stream proper in area of Grand Banks, SE of Newfoundland. It no longer has the characteristics of a well-defined warm current and has a surface temp. of 60°F. N of the Azores. It is often masked by shallow wind-drift surface movements caused by the prevailing westerlies. Its terminal branches are the IRMINGER CURRENT, the CANARIES CURRENT, and the NORWEGIAN CURRENT, which has considerable influence on the climate of NW Europe.

North Attleboro or **North Attleborough** (both: ă'tŭlbûrŭ), town (pop. 12,146), Bristol co., SE Mass., at R.I. line, 13 mi. NNE of Providence; jewelry (since late 18th cent.), silverware, jewelers' supplies, foundry products, electrical products. Settled 1669, set off from Attleboro 1887. Includes Attleboro Falls (1940 pop. 1,073).

North Auckland, New Zealand: see AUCKLAND, provincial dist.

North Augusta, village (pop. estimate 500), SE Ont., 12 mi. W of Brockville; dairying, mixed farming.

North Augusta, town (pop. 3,659), Aiken co., W S.C., on Savannah R. (bridged) opposite Augusta, Ga.; bricks, flower pots, veneer. Inc. 1906.

North Aurora (ûrô'rŭ), village (pop. 921), Kane co., NE Ill., on Fox R. (bridged here), just N of Aurora.

North Australia: see NORTHERN TERRITORY.

North Baldy. 1 Peak in Calif.: see SAN GABRIEL MOUNTAINS. **2** Peak in N.Mex.: see MAGDALENA MOUNTAINS.

North Baltimore (bôl'tĭmôr), village (pop. 2,771), Wood co., NW Ohio, 13 mi. S of Bowling Green, in diversified-farming area (corn, wheat, sugar beets); leather goods, machine-shop products, tools. Stone quarries, oil wells near by. Settled 1834.

North Bass Island, Ohio: see BASS ISLANDS.

North Battleford, city (pop. 5,717), W Sask., on North Saskatchewan R. at mouth of Battle R., and 80 mi. NW of Saskatoon, opposite BATTLEFORD; distributing center for W Sask.; grain elevators, cold-storage plants, tanneries. Resort.

North Bay, city (pop. 15,599), ⊙ Nipissing dist., SE central Ont., on L. Nipissing, 180 mi. N of Toronto; railroad center, with repair shops; lumbering, dairying, mining-machinery mfg.; distributing center for N Ont. mining and lumbering region.

North Bay, town (pop. 198), Dade co., S Fla., near Miami. Sometimes North Bay Village.

North Beach, summer-resort town (pop. 314), Calvert co., S Md., on Chesapeake Bay, 19 mi. S of Annapolis.

North Bellevernon (bĕlvûr'nŭn), borough (pop. 3,147), Westmoreland co., SW Pa., 22 mi. S of Pittsburgh and on Monongahela R. Inc. 1876.

North Bellmore, village (1940 pop. 3,519), Nassau co., SE N.Y., on W Long Isl., just N of Bellmore; mfg. of clothing.

North Bellport, village (pop. 1,605, with adjacent Hagerman), Suffolk co., SE N.Y., just E of Patchogue.

North Belmont or **Belmont Junction,** village (pop. 3,948), Gaston co., S N.C., 2 mi. N of Belmont.

North Bend. 1 City (pop. 906), Dodge co., E Nebr., 15 mi. W of Fremont and on Platte R.; livestock, poultry, grain. **2** Village (pop. 711), Hamilton co., extreme SW Ohio, on the Ohio and 11 mi. W of Cincinnati. Benjamin Harrison was b. here. William Henry Harrison Memorial State Park is near by. Village founded 1789. **3** City (pop. 6,099), Coos co., SW Oregon, on Coos Bay (of Pacific Ocean), c.70 mi. SW of Eugene; lumber milling, oyster packing and canning; fisheries. Has boat connections. Ships lumber, fish, fertilizer. Settled 1853, inc. 1903. City of Coos Bay just S. **4** Village (pop. c.800), Clinton co., N central Pa., on West Branch of Susquehanna R. and 20 mi. NW of Lock Haven; tannery. **5** Town (pop. 787), King co., W central Wash., 25 mi. ESE of Seattle and on South Fork Snoqualmie R.; lumber, farm and dairy products.

North Bennington, village (pop. 1,327) of BENNINGTON town, Bennington co., SW Vt., 4 mi. N of Bennington; wood products, paper, chemicals. Seat of Bennington Col. for women.

North Bergen (bûr'gŭn), residential suburban township (pop. 41,560), Hudson co., NE N.J., just NE of Jersey City; mfg. (ink, electrical equipment, radio parts, clothing, machinery, metal goods, batteries, buttons, pens and pencils, jewelry, paper boxes, knit goods). Annual German folk festival held here. Inc. 1861.

North Berwick (bĕ'rĭk), burgh (1931 pop. 3,473; 1951 census 4,001), N East Lothian, Scotland, on Firth of Forth, 20 mi. ENE of Edinburgh; seaside resort and fishing port, with noted golf course. Has remains of 12th-cent. Cistercian nunnery. Near by are ruins of Tantallon Castle. Offshore, in Firth of Forth, is BASS ROCK.

North Berwick (bûr'wĭk), town (pop. 1,655), including North Berwick village (pop. 1,019), York co., SW Maine, on Great Works R. and 10 mi. NE of Dover, N.H. Mfg. (wood and metal products, textiles), winter sports. Settled c.1630, set off from Berwick 1831.

North Bessemer (bĕ'sŭmûr), village (1940 pop. 2,410), Allegheny co., W Pa., 11 mi. NE of Pittsburgh.

North Beveland, Du. *Noord Beveland* (nōrt bā'vŭlänt), island (□35), Zeeland prov., SW Netherlands, WNW of Bergen op Zoom; bounded by the Zandkreek (S), the Veersche Gat (W), North Sea (N), the Eastern Scheldt (E); 10 mi. long, 3.5 mi. wide. Grows sugar beets, potatoes, winter wheat, peas, flax, grass. Many medieval castles. Chief villages: Kortgene, Colijnsplaat (or Kolijnsplaat).

North Billerica, Mass.: see BILLERICA.

North Bimini, Bahama Isls.: see BIMINI ISLANDS.

North Bonneville (bŏ'nŭvĭl), town (pop. 564), Skamania co., SW Wash., 30 mi. E of Vancouver and on Columbia R., at Wash. end of Bonneville Dam.

North Borden Island, Northwest Territories: see BORDEN ISLANDS.

North Borneo (bôr'nēō) or **British North Borneo,** British crown colony (□ 29,387; 1951 census pop. 331,236) comprising N part of Borneo and offshore isls. (the most important being LABUAN and the largest BANGGI), 600 mi. SSW of Manila; 7°20'–3°45'N 115°9'–119°16'E; ⊙ JESSELTON, chief port. Bounded W by S.China Sea, N by Sulu Sea, E by Celebes Sea, SW by Sarawak, S by Indonesian Borneo; roughly triangular in shape, 220 mi. wide at the base. Extensive coastline (c.800 mi.) is heavily indented. Largely mountainous terrain rises to 13,455 ft. at Mt. Kinabalu, highest peak of isl. Coastal areas are low and partly swampy. Largest rivers (Kinabatangan and Segama) are on E coast; rivers on W coast are short, but important for irrigation of major agr. area. Tropical climate, with annual temp. ranging from 66° to 88°F. Rainfall (60–180 in.) is heaviest Oct.-Feb. during NE monsoon period. Chief products: rubber, timber, copra, manila hemp, rice, sago, tobacco. Fishing industry is important; stock raising is on small scale. The most important of the Malay-speaking native groups are the Dusun (a Dyak tribe), who are largely pagan. Roughly 20% of pop. is Chinese. Chief centers: Jesselton, SANDAKAN (former ⊙ colony), KUDAT, BEAUFORT. Colony is divided into 3 residencies; WEST COAST, EAST COAST, and INTERIOR AND LABUAN. The area was ruled (16th to late 19th cent.) by sultan of Brunei. A large portion of N Borneo was ceded 1872 to group of Amer. and Br. traders; Br. North Borneo Co. took over (1881) the area and held it until Second World War, during which it was occupied (Jan., 1942–Sept., 1945) by the Japanese. In 1946 North Borneo became a crown colony, including Labuan isl.

Northboro. 1 Town (pop. 167), Page co., SW Iowa, near Mo. line, 12 mi. SSE of Shenandoah, in agr. region. **2** or **Northborough,** agr. town (pop. 3,122), including Northboro village (pop. 1,442), Worcester co., E central Mass., 10 mi. ENE of Worcester. Settled c.1672, inc. 1766.

North Bosque River, Texas: see BOSQUE RIVER.

Northbourne, town and parish (pop. 1,323), E Kent, England, 3 mi. W of Deal; coal mining. Has 12th-cent. church with tomb of Sir Edwin Sandys, whose home was 14th-cent. Northbourne Court.

North Brabant (brŭbănt', brä'bŭnt), Du. *Noord-brabant* (nōrt'bräbänt'), province (□ 1,893.6; pop. 1,180,133), S Netherlands; ⊙ 's Hertogenbosch. Bounded by Maas R. (N), Limburg prov. (E), Belgium (S), and Zeeland prov. (W). Low-lying, fertile land near Maas R.; mostly sandy heathland in all other areas; drained by Mark R., Dommel R., the Zuid-Willemsvaart, and Wilhelmina Canal. Some agr. and dairying. Chief industries: wool, cotton, and linen textiles (Tilburg, Helmond, Boxtel); electrical industry (Eindhoven); leather tanning and shoe mfg. (Waalwijk, Oisterwijk); pharmaceuticals (Oss); jute spinning (Goirke). Most of these industries benefit from an ample supply of pure water. Originally prov. formed, with Belg. prov. of Antwerp, duchy of Brabant. Although town of Breda played a part in uprising against Spain (1571), prov. was not one of original Seven United Provinces; it was ceded by Spain (1637) and directly administered by States-General. Joined United Provinces in 1648.

North Braddock, industrial borough (pop. 14,724), Allegheny co., SW Pa., ESE suburb of Pittsburgh, on Monongahela R.; steel. Inc. 1897.

North Branch. 1 Village (pop. 832), Lapeer co., E Mich., 14 mi. NNE of Lapeer, in area producing livestock, grain, dairy products; flour and feed milling. **2** Village (pop. 769), Chisago co., E Minn., near St. Croix R., 39 mi. N of St. Paul, in grain, livestock, and poultry area; dairy products, flour.

North Branford, town (pop. 2,017), New Haven co., S Conn., 9 mi. E of New Haven; agr., rock quarrying. Includes Northford village. Settled c.1680, inc. 1831.

North Brentwood, town (pop. 833), Prince Georges co., central Md., just NE of Washington.

Northbridge, town (pop. 10,476), Worcester co., S Mass., on Blackstone R. and 11 mi. SE of Worcester; cotton and rayon goods, coated paper. Settled 1704, inc. 1772. Includes villages of Linwood (pop. 854) and Whitinsville (pop. 5,662) (textiles).

North Bridgton, Maine: see BRIDGTON.

North Brisbane, suburb (pop. 27,983) of Brisbane, SE Queensland, Australia.

North Bromsgrove, England: see BROMSGROVE.

Northbrook, village (pop. 3,348), Cook co., NE Ill., NW suburb of Chicago, 8 mi. WNW of Evanston; makes oil burners, truck bodies; nurseries; truck and dairy farms. Inc. 1923.

North Brookfield, town (pop. 3,444), including North Brookfield village (pop. 2,599), Worcester co., central Mass., 14 mi. W of Worcester; rubber and asbestos goods, beverages, poultry feed; dairying, poultry, fruit. Settled 1664, inc. 1812.

Northbrook Island, in SW Franz Josef Land, Russian SFSR, in Arctic Ocean; 20 mi. long, 12 mi. wide; 80°N 51°E. Terminates W in Cape Flora. Discovered 1880 by Br. explorer Leigh Smith.

North Brother Island (13 acres), SE N.Y., in East R., off S shore of Bronx borough of New York city.

North Brother Mountain (4,143 ft.), Piscataquis co., N central Maine, 25 mi. NW of Millinocket, in Katahdin State Game Preserve.

North Broughton Island, B.C.: see BROUGHTON ISLAND.

North Bruny, Tasmania: see BRUNY.

North Buena Vista (bū'nŭ vĭ'stŭ), town (pop. 148), Clayton co., NE Iowa, on the Mississippi and 19 mi. NW of Dubuque, in agr., dairying region.

North Cachar Hills (kă'chär), autonomous district (□ 1,888; pop. 37,361), S central Assam, India; ⊙ Haflong. Largely coextensive with Barail Range; bordered E by Naga Hills and Manipur, W by Khasi and Jaintia Hills, S by Cachar dist., from which it was separated in 1950. Pop. 85% tribal (Kucharis, Kukis).

North Caicos (kī'kōs, kī'kŭs), island (□ 54.1; c.12 mi. long; pop. 1,703), Turks and Caicos Isls., dependency of Jamaica, NW of Middle Caicos isl.; 21°50'N 72°W. Most populous of the group, with Kew and Bottle Creek villages. Some agr. and fishing.

North Caldwell (kôld'wŭl), borough (pop. 1,781), Essex co., NE N.J., 6 mi. SW of Paterson. Inc. 1898.

North Canaan (kā'nŭn), resort town (pop. 2,647), Litchfield co., NW Conn., in Taconic Mts., on Mass. line and 17 mi. NW of Torrington; magnesium mining and reduction; agr.; limestone quarrying. Includes villages of CANAAN and East Canaan. Canaan town is S.

North Canadian River, S U.S., rises in high plateau area of NE N.Mex., flows E through NE N.Mex. and panhandle regions of Texas and Okla., thence SE through central Okla., past Oklahoma City, to Canadian R. just E of Eufaula; total length 843 mi.; used for irrigation. CANTON RESERVOIR is in Okla. Tributaries: Wolf Creek (Texas, Okla.), Deep Fork (Okla.). Sometimes known as Beaver R. in Okla., above mouth of Wolf Creek.

North Canara, India: see KANARA.

North Canton. 1 Village (pop. 1,913), Cherokee co., NW Ga., near Canton and Allatoona Reservoir. **2** Village (pop. 4,032), Stark co., E central Ohio, 5 mi. NNW of Canton; makes vacuum cleaners.

North Cape, N N.Isl., northernmost point of New Zealand proper; 34°25'S 173°5'E.

North Cape, Nor. *Nordkapp* (nŏr'käp), on Barents Sea of the Arctic Ocean, on isl. of Mageroy, Finnmark co., N Norway, 60 mi. NE of Hammerfest; 71°10'20"N 25°47'40"E; rises 1,007 ft. sheer from the sea. Popularly considered northernmost point of Europe, though Knivskjellodden, 4 mi. WNW, is actually farther N. NORDKYN is northernmost point on European mainland.

North Cape, Russian SFSR: see SHMIDT, CAPE.

North Caribou Lake (22 mi. long, 14 mi. wide), NW Ont., in NW Patricia dist., 52°49'N 90°46'W; alt. 1,060 ft. Drains N into Severn R.

North Carolina, state (land only □ 49,142; with inland waters □ 52,712; 1950 pop. 4,061,929; 1940 pop. 3,571,623), SE U.S., on the Atlantic, bordered by Va. (N), S.C. (S), Ga. (SW), and Tenn. (W); 27th in area, 10th in pop., one of the original 13 states; ⊙ Raleigh. The "Tarheel State" or "Old North State" extends 503 mi. E-W, 188 mi. N-S. Rises gradually from the coast to the Appalachians in broad steps: the low coastal plain (c.40% of state), the hilly piedmont (c.45% of state; alt. 500–1,500 ft.), and the rugged Appalachian region (2,000–5,000 ft.). The Catawba, Yadkin, Tar, Roanoke, Neuse, and Cape Fear rivers rise in the mts. and piedmont and flow SE to the Atlantic; the Hiwassee, Little Tennessee,

French Broad, Nolichucky, and Watauga flow from the mts. W into the Gulf of Mexico via the Mississippi R. system. N.C. has a humid subtropical climate of hot summers and mild winters. Snow is common only in the Appalachian highlands (average fall of 10–30 inches). The annual rainfall of 50 inches is fairly evenly distributed, with a summer maximum and fall minimum. Forests, both coniferous and hardwood, occupy ⅔ of N.C. Clay and sandy loams cover the crystalline rocks of the highlands and piedmont, while the sedimentary rocks of the coastal plain are surfaced by sandy soils. Erosion (especially in the uplands) and soil depletion are major problems. N.C. has c.10% of its area severely eroded and uses more fertilizer than any other state. Farming and mfg. are aided by abundant hydroelectric power. The growing season ranges from 200 days in the mts. to 240 days along the coast. Corn, a major food staple, occupies the largest acreage, but tobacco, cotton, and peanuts are the chief cash crops. The most industrialized state in the South, N.C. leads the U.S. in tobacco production and cigarette mfg. and marketing (Durham, Winston-Salem, Reidsville, Goldsboro, Greenville) and ranks high in pipe tobacco mfg. It is 1st in cotton milling (especially yarn, thread, fabrics, household goods) and wooden furniture mfg.; among its plants are the largest underwear, towel, denim, and hosiery mills in the country (Charlotte, Greensboro, Gastonia, Kannapolis, Burlington, Concord). Also important are the rayon, lumber, paper and pulp, fertilizer, brick and tile, fishing (menhaden, oysters, shrimp), and mining industries. Furniture mfg. at High Point, Hickory, Mt. Airy, Thomasville. N.C. is the chief U.S. producer of granite (Mt. Airy, Salisbury), feldspar, and mica, and also mines kaolin and clay. The piedmont and W part of the coastal plain contain c.50% of the state's pop. and its largest cities—Charlotte, Winston-Salem, Durham, Greensboro—and Raleigh, the capital. In its swift rivers are many dams which form lakes and supply power to the piedmont mfg. area. Badin has a large aluminum reduction plant. Corn is grown throughout the piedmont, tobacco is predominant in the N and cotton in the S; the central piedmont, where wheat, cotton, and tobacco are major crops, is the state's chief dairying and haying region. Along the E edge of the piedmont from Sanford SW into S.C. is the narrow sand-hills belt, a cotton- and peach-growing area with noted winter resorts (Southern Pines, Pinehurst). Bet. the piedmont and the coastal plain is the fall line, traversing the state from Northampton co. (NE) to Anson co. (SW). The coastal plain sustains lumbering industries (pine, cypress, tupelo, sweet gum). In the swampy tidewater area in the E are lakes Mattamuskeet, Waccamaw, and Phelps, and part of DISMAL SWAMP (N). The shore line (c.300 mi. long) is bordered by a chain of sandy barrier isls., from which capes Hatteras, Lookout, and Fear project into the Atlantic. Behind the isls. are sounds, notably Albemarle and Pamlico, traversed by the INTRACOASTAL WATERWAY. The coastal plain, with the exception of marshy coastal strip, is the chief agr. area of the state. Cotton, tobacco, peanuts, and corn are major crops throughout; truck crops, soybeans, and hogs, chiefly produced in E, are of lesser importance. In W part of the coastal plain are the tobacco and cotton markets and also textile and wood-processing centers (Fayetteville, Roanoke Rapids). The chief centers of the sparsely-settled tidewater area are at heads of estuaries; WILMINGTON and MOREHEAD CITY are ocean ports; Elizabeth City, New Bern, Washington, Beaufort and Edenton are fishing ports; boat building, fertilizer mixing, and sea-food canning are other industries. The coast and adjacent isls. are a recreation area. The state's mtn. region is part of the E Appalachian chain. Geologically, the N.C. mts. are included in the BLUE RIDGE province, but the name is applied within N.C. only to the SE escarpment. The Black Mts. culminate in Mt. Mitchell, the highest point (6,684 ft.) E of the Mississippi. The W part includes the GREAT SMOKY MOUNTAINS (site of a natl. park), UNAKA MOUNTAINS, and the Iron, Stone, Bald, and Unicoi ranges. The rivers rising in the SW highlands, the highest rainfall area (up to c.80 in. annually in Macon co.) in the state, are important sources of hydroelectric power. On them are the Hiwassee, Fontana, and Apalachia dams built by TVA, and the Cheoah, Santeetlah, Glenville, and Nantahala privately-built dams, each forming lakes also useful for flood control and recreation. The highlands are c.70% forest covered (oak, poplar, hickory, spruce, fir, pine). Much of the region is included in Nantahala, Pisgah, and Yadkin natl. forests. In the sparsely-settled Appalachian region highlands, the people have preserved old crafts, customs, songs and speech. General farming, stock raising, lumbering, and handicraft industries (wood carving, pottery making, weaving) are the traditional activities. The Asheville area supplies c.75% of all drug plants gathered in the U.S. Mfg. (textiles, furniture, paper, leather), mining (feldspar, kaolin, mica) and tourism have become increasingly important in recent years. The chief towns include ASHEVILLE (the principal center), Canton, Waynesville, Hendersonville, Brevard, Boone, Bryson City, and Murphy. Pisgah Forest is the chief manufacturer of cigarette paper in the U.S. Probably the 1st exploration of North Carolina's coast was that of Verrazano in 1524. Colonists sent by Sir Walter Raleigh landed on ROANOKE ISLAND in 1585, but the 1st lasting settlements were made in the 1650s around Albemarle Sound by colonials from Virginia. In the tidewater area are the oldest towns of the state—BATH (inc. 1705), Edenton, and New Bern. The Indians were gradually pushed to the Appalachians and beyond with the arrival of new settlers—German and Scotch-Irish from Pennsylvania, Highland Scots, and some Swiss, French, and Welsh. There has been little foreign immigration since colonial days. Negroes, imported to work the large plantations of the coastal plain and later for piedmont plantations, formed c.⅓ of the pop. by 1790; in 1940 they constituted c.28%. N.C. was made a royal colony in 1729, after the earlier govt. under proprietors had proved unsatisfactory. Conflicts bet. the colonists and the government were frequent, and in 1771 the Regulators, a group of backcountry farmers, fought a battle with the government militia. During the Revolutionary War, the territory was invaded by British troops in 1780–81. The tidewater planter aristocracy dominated the government until the 1830s when the small farmers of the uplands and W coastal plain became the more powerful group. Although considerable antislavery sentiment existed, the widespread adoption of the cotton gin created a greatly increased demand for cotton and, therefore, for slaves. In the Civil War, Wilmington was an important port for blockade runners. After the war, the piedmont began to experience a great rise in industry, but agr. was slower to recover. The state's widespread system of farm tenancy dates from this period. The turn of the century brought a new interest in developing the state's resources. Piedmont waterpower attracted numerous textile mills, and in the 1920s N.C. surpassed the New England states in cotton milling. The ante-bellum demand for tobacco, which created such "tobacco barons" as James B. Duke and R. J. Reynolds, was greatly increased during this period and new factories sprang up. With these industrial booms came an agr. revival. The state's abundant forests formed the basis of a large furniture and lumber industry, which received additional impetus from the earlier depletion of the Great Lakes forests. The historic rivalry bet. the E and W parts of the state now became one bet. the factory workers of the W and farmers of the E. The three major state educational institutions were merged into a greater Univ. of North Carolina (main campus at Chapel Hill) which became notable influence in the state's economic and social programs. Other leading educational institutions include Duke Univ. (at Durham), Davidson Col. (at Davidson), and Wake Forest Col. (at Wake Forest). In the Second World War many large military installations, most notably Fort Bragg (near Fayetteville), were active training centers. See also articles on cities, towns, geographic features, and the 100 counties: ALAMANCE, ALEXANDER, ALLEGHANY, ANSON, ASHE, AVERY, BEAUFORT, BERTIE, BLADEN, BRUNSWICK, BUNCOMBE, BURKE, CABARRUS, CALDWELL, CAMDEN, CARTERET, CASWELL, CATAWBA, CHATHAM, CHEROKEE, CHOWAN, CLAY, CLEVELAND, COLUMBUS, CRAVEN, CUMBERLAND, CURRITUCK, DARE, DAVIDSON, DAVIE, DUPLIN, DURHAM, EDGECOMBE, FORSYTH, FRANKLIN, GASTON, GATES, GRAHAM, GRANVILLE, GREENE, GUILFORD, HALIFAX, HARNETT, HAYWOOD, HENDERSON, HERTFORD, HOKE, HYDE, IREDELL, JACKSON, JOHNSTON, JONES, LEE, LENOIR, LINCOLN, MCDOWELL, MACON, MADISON, MARTIN, MECKLENBURG, MITCHELL, MONTGOMERY, MOORE, NASH, NEW HANOVER, NORTHAMPTON, ONSLOW, ORANGE, PAMLICO, PASQUOTANK, PENDER, PERQUIMANS, PERSON, PITT, POLK, RANDOLPH, RICHMOND, ROBESON, ROCKINGHAM, ROWAN, RUTHERFORD, SAMPSON, SCOTLAND, STANLY, STOKES, SURRY, SWAIN, TRANSYLVANIA, TYRRELL, UNION, VANCE, WAKE, WARREN, WASHINGTON, WATAUGA, WAYNE, WILKES, WILSON, YADKIN, YANCEY.

Northcarrollton or **North Carrollton,** town (pop. 506), Carroll co., central Miss., 15 mi. E of Greenwood and just N of Carrollton.

North Carver, Mass.: see CARVER.

North Catasauqua (kătüsô'kwü), borough (pop. 2,629), Northampton co., E Pa., 4 mi. N of Allentown. Inc. 1908.

North Caucasus, territory, Russian SFSR: see CAUCASUS.

North Central Province, administrative division (□ 4,009; pop., including estate pop., 139,565), N Ceylon; ⊙ Anuradhapura. Undulating, jungle-covered plain, with a few isolated peaks and short hill ranges extending NE-SW. Served by extensive irrigation tanks near Polonnaruwa, MINNERIYA, KALAWEWA, and Anuradhapura; agr. (rice, vegetables). Archaeological landmarks at ANURADHAPURA, POLONNARUWA, MIHINTALE. Created 1886.

North Channel, central Ont., N arm (120 mi. long, 1-20 mi. wide) of L. Huron, bet. N shore of lake and Manitoulin Isls.; connects St. Marys R. (W) and Georgian Bay (E). Crossed by road and rail bridge to Manitoulin Isl. at Little Current.

North Channel, strait bet. Scotland and NE Ireland, c.13 mi. wide at narrowest point (bet. the Mull of Kintyre, Argyll, Scotland, and Torr Head, Co. Antrim, Northern Ireland), connecting the Irish Sea with the Atlantic.

North Charleroi (shärlůroi', shär'lůroi), borough (pop. 2,554), Washington co., SW Pa., just below Charleroi on Monongahela R. Inc. 1894.

North Chatham, Mass.: see CHATHAM.

North Cheek, England: see ROBIN HOOD'S BAY.

North Chelmsford, Mass.: see CHELMSFORD.

North Chicago, industrial city (pop. 8,628), Lake co., extreme NE Ill., N of Chicago, on L. Michigan, adjacent to Waukegan; machinery, electrical equipment, auto parts, hardware, metal products, candy. Strike at a steel plant here in 1937 brought U.S. Supreme Court ruling in 1939 that sit-down strikes were illegal. Near by are Great Lakes Naval Training Station (S) and a veterans' hosp. Inc. 1909.

North Chili (chī'lī"), village, Monroe co., W N.Y., 10 mi. WSW of Rochester. Seat of Roberts Wesleyan Col.

North Chillicothe (chĭlĭkŏ'thē), village (pop. 1,741), Peoria co., central Ill., near Illinois R., 16 mi. NNE of Peoria, in agr. and bituminous-coal area. Inc. 1890.

North Cholla (chŭl'lä'), Korean *Cholla-pukdo*, Jap. *Zenra-hokudo*, province [Jap. and Korean *do*] (□ 3,302; 1949 pop. 2,050,485), S Korea, bounded W by Yellow Sea; ⊙ CHONJU. Chief port is KUNSAN. Partly mountainous, with fertile valleys drained by Kum R. and several small rivers. Primarily agr., the prov. produces rice, soy beans, cotton, ramie, tobacco, ginseng, and persimmons. Silk-cocoon production and lumbering are widespread. There are gold, silver, molybdenum, and iron mines. Handicraft is important.

North Chungchong (chōōng'chŭng'), Korean *Chung-chong-pukdo*, Jap. *Chusei-hokudo*, inland province [Jap. and Korean *do*] (□ 2,864; 1949 pop. 1,146,-509), S Korea; ⊙ CHONGJU. Largely mountainous terrain, drained by Kum and Han rivers. Agr. products include rice, barley, hemp, tobacco; gold, tungsten, and graphite are mined. Other products: silk cocoons, honey, textiles. The prov. has no heavy industry.

North City, village (pop. 513), Franklin co., S Ill., 13 mi. N of Herrin, in bituminous-coal and agr. area.

North Cohasset, Mass.: see COHASSET.

North College Hill, city (pop. 7,921), Hamilton co., extreme SW Ohio, a N suburb of Cincinnati. Clovernook Home for the Blind is here. Inc. 1916.

North Collins, village (pop. 1,325), Erie co., W N.Y., 22 mi. S of Buffalo, in fruitgrowing region; mfg. (chemicals, cheese, brick, canned foods); natural-gas wells. Settled c.1810, inc. 1911.

North Conway, village in Conway town, Carroll co., E N.H., on Saco R.; winter and summer resort at approach to White Mts.; grain, hay.

North Corbin, village (pop. 1,077), Laurel co., SE Ky., in Cumberland foothills near Laurel R., just N of Corbin.

Northcote, municipality (pop. 44,947), S Victoria, Australia, 4 mi. NNE of Melbourne, in metropolitan area; commercial center for agr., sheep region.

Northcote (nôrth'kōt), borough (pop. 2,651), N N.Isl., New Zealand, on N shore of Waitemata Harbour; residential suburb of Auckland.

North Cousin Island, one of the Seychelles, in Indian Ocean, off SW coast of Praslin Isl., 4°20'S 55°43'E; ⅓ mi. long, ⅛ mi. wide; granite formation. Copra; fisheries.

North Creake, England: see SOUTH CREAKE.

North Creek, resort village (1940 pop. 703), Warren co., E N.Y., in the Adirondacks, on the Hudson and 32 mi. NNW of Glens Falls; wood products; garnet mining. Just SW is Gore Mtn. (3,595 ft.), skiing center.

North Crimean Canal, canal project in the Crimea, Russian SFSR; S continuation of the SOUTH UKRAINIAN CANAL, extending from Sivash lagoon past Dzhankoi and through Crimean steppe to Kerch. Begun 1951.

North Crows Nest, town (pop. 46), Marion co., central Ind.

North Curry, agr. village and parish (pop. 1,246), central Somerset, England, 6 mi. E of Taunton. Has 13th–15th-cent. church.

North Dakota (dŭkō'tŭ), state (land □ 70,054; with inland waters □ 70,665; 1950 pop. 619,636; 1940 pop. 641,935), N U.S., bounded N by Canada (Man. and Sask.), S by S.Dak., W by Mont., and E by Minn. along Red River of the North; 16th in area, 41st in pop.; admitted 1889 as 39th state; ⊙ Bismarck. N.Dak. (the "Flickertail State"), rectangular in shape, extends c.200 mi. N–S, c.350 mi. E–W. The surface is generally flat, underlain by layers of sandstone and shale containing extensive veins of lignite and beds of bentonite. Rises in 3 broad steps from E to W and includes parts of central lowlands in E and Great Plains in W; lowest at Pembina (750 ft.) in NE, highest at

Area in square miles is indicated by the symbol □, capital city or county seat by the symbol ⊙.

Black Butte (3,468 ft.) in Slope co. (SW). In E is valley of Red R. of the North (alt. 800–1,000 ft.; valley is 40 mi. wide at international line, 10 mi. wide in S), once the floor of glacial L. Agassiz. Drift Prairie (alt. 1,300–1,600 ft.) is expanse of glacial drift extending S from Man. through central N.Dak. Missouri Plateau is in W, extending from Missouri escarpment (rising 400 ft. above Drift Prairie) to Rocky Mts. and including scenic Badlands area (now part of Theodore Roosevelt Natl. Memorial Park) along Little Missouri R. W and SW are drained by Missouri R. and tributaries (Little Missouri, Knife, Heart, Cannonball rivers), NE and SE by tributaries of the Red R., and N by large loop of Souris R.; James R., rising in central N.Dak., flows through SE. Devils L. (□ 30) is largest in state. In the geographical center of North America, N.Dak. is subject to the extremes of a dry continental climate; winters are generally severe (sometimes −45°F.), summers short and hot (sometimes 114°F.); average temp. for Jan. is 8.3°F., for July 70.5°F. Rainfall in SE is 22 in.; average for state is 16 in.; W is semiarid and subject to protracted droughts. Black-earth belt extends throughout E, where soil is derived from rich glacial materials. State is primarily agr., ranking 2d to Kansas in total wheat production and 1st in spring and durum wheat and flax. The Red River Valley, whose plains were transformed in 1870s and '80s into bonanza wheat farms that ranged in size from 3,000 to 65,000 acres, now holds farms of several hundred acres and produces wheat, flax, corn, barley, rye, alfalfa, sugar beets, and seed potatoes. Field crops are raised in fertile Drift Prairie, and corn (used for cattle feed) is grown in SE. W is grazing-forage region, scanty rainfall making extensive cultivation impossible except in irrigated areas and river valleys. Other sources of farm income are dairying and poultry raising. Most of state is in farms, 47% in harvested cropland, 29% in pasture. Principal industry is processing of farm products (flour and other mill products, butter and eggs, meat, poultry and bakery products, beet sugar). Manufactures are farm machinery, electrical equipment, brick and tile. Lignite is abundant in W, much of it so close to surface that strip mining is possible, and in SW are large deposits of clay suitable for pottery mfg. The SW yields bentonite, and sodium sulphate is produced from dry lake beds of NW. FARGO, the largest city, is food-processing center and distribution point for agr. products, farm machinery, and automobiles. Other cities include Grand Forks, Minot, Bismarck, Jamestown, Mandan, Devils Lake, Valley City, Dickinson, Williston. Disastrous droughts during 1930s demonstrated inadequacy of artesian water supply and gave rise to Federal and state program of dam construction, irrigation, soil conservation, and reforestation. Institutions of education are Univ. of N.Dak. and Wesley Col. at Grand Forks; N.Dak. Agr. Col. at Fargo; Jamestown Col. at Jamestown; N.Dak. State School of Science at Wahpeton; State Normal and Industrial Col. at Ellendale. There are 4 state teachers colleges (Dickinson, Mayville, Minot, Valley City), 2 jr. colleges (Bismarck, Devils Lake), and 1 school of forestry (Bottineau). Fort Berthold Indian Reservation is in W, near Sanish; Turtle Mtn. Indian Reservation is in N, near Turtle Mts.; Devils Lake Indian Reservation is in NE central N.Dak., at Devils L.; part of Standing Rock Indian Reservation is in S, on S.Dak. line. Souris Natl. Forest is in N, W of Rugby; Sheyenne Natl. Forest is in SE, W of Abercrombie. Region was 1st explored (c.1738) by Pierre de la Vérendrye (now honored by Verendrye Natl. Monument) and was much frequented by fur traders late in 18th cent. Lewis and Clark, in traveling to and from Pacific Northwest, twice (1804 and 1806) passed through area now included in N.Dak. and S.Dak. U.S. acquired parts of region from France in 1803 (Louisiana Purchase) and from Great Britain in 1818. Territory was organized in 1861 (⊙ Yankton 1861–83; ⊙ Bismarck 1883); states of N.Dak. and S.Dak. were formed from it 1889. Economy was dominated by fur-trading companies throughout 1st half of 19th cent. Early attempts at colonization were temporary settlements (1812, 1815, 1818) at Pembina; 1st permanent settlement, also at Pembina, was made in 1851. Further settlement was temporarily prevented by Civil War and by wars with Sioux Indians (1863–66). In 1880s, with construction of Northern Pacific RR, pop. was increased by influx of Scandinavians, Germans, and Russians, who worked on railroad or on bonanza wheat farms of valley of the Red River of the North and later established cooperatives which influenced development of state's economy. Last decade of 19th cent. was dominated by struggle in which railroads and big-business interests, represented by Alexander McKenzie, were opposed by the Farmers' Alliance; farmers objected to monopoly of grain-marketing facilities and pressed for publicly owned grain elevators. Intermittent efforts at reform (1892–1915) culminated in formation (1915) of Nonpartisan League and establishment (1919) of an industrial commission for the management of state-owned enterprises. The drought and depression of 1930s hurt the state severely, but by the late 1940s the recovery was widespread. Additional measures for flood control, irrigation, and power are included in proposed plan for development of basin of MISSOURI RIVER. See also articles on cities, towns, geographic features and the 53 counties: ADAMS, BARNES, BENSON, BILLINGS, BOTTINEAU, BOWMAN, BURKE, BURLEIGH, CASS, CAVALIER, DICKEY, DIVIDE, DUNN, EDDY, EMMONS, FOSTER, GOLDEN VALLEY, GRAND FORKS, GRANT, GRIGGS, HETTINGER, KIDDER, LA MOURE, LOGAN, MCHENRY, MCINTOSH, MCKENZIE, MCLEAN, MERCER, MORTON, MOUNTRAIL, NELSON, OLIVER, PEMBINA, PIERCE, RAMSEY, RANSOM, RENVILLE, RICHLAND, ROLETTE, SARGENT, SHERIDAN, SIOUX, SLOPE, STARK, STEELE, STUTSMAN, TOWNER, TRAILL, WALSH, WARD, WELLS, WILLIAMS.

North Darley, England: see DARLEY.

North Dartmouth, Mass.: see DARTMOUTH.

North Devon Island, Northwest Territories: see DEVON ISLAND.

North Dighton, Mass.: see DIGHTON.

North Dome. 1 Peak in Calif.: see YOSEMITE NATIONAL PARK. **2** Peak (3,593 ft.) in Greene co., SE N.Y., in the Catskills, 20 mi. WNW of Saugerties.

North Downs, England: see DOWNS.

Northeast or **North East,** town (pop. 1,517), Cecil co., NE Md., at head of navigation on Northeast R. (6 mi. long) and 24 mi. WSW of Wilmington, Del.; trade center for hay and grain area; sand, gravel pits; makes fireworks, firebrick. Yachting. Sandy Cove (summer resort), Elk Neck (site of state forest, state park) are near.

North East, borough (pop. 4,247), Erie co., NW Pa., 13 mi. NE of Erie, near L. Erie; center of Pa. grape industry; mfg. (metal and electrical products, grape juice, flour, canned goods), agr. (cherries, tomatoes). Settled c.1800, inc. 1834.

Northeast Billings, suburb (pop. 2,128) of Billings, Yellowstone co., S Mont.

Northeast Cape, Russian SFSR: see CHELYUSKIN, CAPE.

Northeast Cape Fear River, SE N.C., rises in N Duplin co., flows 130 mi. S to Cape Fear R. at Wilmington; lower c.50 mi. tidal.

North East Carry, village (pop. 7), Piscataquis co., W central Maine, on Moosehead L. and 28 mi. N of Greenville; hunting, fishing.

Northeast Foreland, Dan. *Nordost Rundingen* (nôr′-ōst′ ro͝o′nĭngŭn), cape, NE extremity of Greenland, on Greenland Sea, at E tip of Crown Prince Christian Land peninsula; 81°21′N 11°40′W.

North East Frontier Agency, India: see ASSAM.

North Eastham, Mass.: see EASTHAM.

Northeast Harbor, Maine: see MOUNT DESERT.

Northeast Land, Nor. *Nordaustlandet* (nôr″oust′-län′nů), formerly *Nordostlandet,* island (□ 5,710) of Spitsbergen group, in Barents Sea of Arctic Ocean, NE of West Spitsbergen, from which it is separated by Hinlopen Strait; 79°10′–80°31′N 17°35′–27°10′E. Isl. is 110 mi. long (E–W), 40–90 mi. wide. Almost wholly glaciated, its inland ice rises to over 2,000 ft. Coast line is irregular and deeply indented, especially on N and W coasts. Discovered in early 17th cent.; 1st charted (1707) by Van Keulen. Isl. explored (1873) by Nordenskjold; completely charted (1935–36) by British expedition. Off N coast are the Sjuoyane (sho͞o′-ůüänů), Nor. *Sjuøyane,* a group of 5 small mountainous isls.

North Easton, Mass.: see EASTON.

Northeast Passage. In the era of discovery that began in 15th cent. efforts were made to find some new passage to Cathay and India. Of these attempts most were devoted to seeking a NORTHWEST PASSAGE. Less important was the attempt to go through the cold seas N of Europe and Asia from the North Atlantic to the Pacific: this was the Northeast Passage. English, Russian, and Dutch navigators sought to sail along the N coast of Russia and far into arctic seas. William Barentz made notable attempts to locate the passage in 16th cent., as did Henry Hudson in 17th cent. In early 18th cent. Vitus Bering, in the service of Russia, sailed through Bering Strait and later made his way to Alaska. The Northeast Passage was not, however, traversed until N. A. E. Nordenskjold of Sweden did it in 1878–79. He rounded Cape Chelyuskin, the northernmost point of the Asian mainland, in 1878 and passed through Bering Strait in 1879. Several other explorers have repeated this exploit, among them Roald Amundsen in 1918–20. In recent years the passage has become a regular shipping route for Siberian ports. A fleet of Soviet icebreakers, aided by airplane reconnaissance and by radio weather stations, keeps the route navigable June–Sept.

North East Point, cape at NE extremity of Jamaica, on Jamaica Channel, 33 mi. ENE of Kingston; 18°9′N 76°20′W.

North East Polder, Du. *Noord-Oost-Polder* (nōrt′-ōst-pōl′důr), reclaimed area of the Ijsselmeer (□ 185) off W coast of Overijssel prov., N central Netherlands; 17 mi. long, 16 mi. wide. Includes isls. of Urk and Schokland.

Northeast Providence Channel, Atlantic strait, Bahama Isls., NE of the Great Bahama Bank, bounded by New Providence Isl. and Eleuthera Isl. (S) and Great Abaco Isl. (N); c.110 mi. long SW-NE. Leads through Northwest Providence Channel to Straits of Florida.

Northeast Vineland, village (pop. 5,646), Cumberland co., S N.J., near Vineland.

North Egremont, Mass.: see EGREMONT.

Northeim (nôrt′hīm), town (pop. 16,941), in former Prussian prov. of Hanover, W Germany, after 1945 in Lower Saxony, on the Leine and 12 mi. N of Göttingen; rail junction; food processing (flour products, canned goods, beer, spirits); mfg. of tobacco, feed, leather and wood products. Has late-Gothic church; remains of old fortifications. Was member of Hanseatic League.

North Elba, village, Essex co., NE N.Y., in the Adirondacks, just SE of Lake Placid village. Here are the farm, home (now a mus.), and grave of John Brown.

North Elmham, town and parish (pop. 889), central Norfolk, England, 5 mi. N of East Dereham; leather tanning. Site of naval training school. Has church dating from 13th–15th cent. It was seat of a Saxon bishopric and traces of its defenses remain. Also called Elmham.

North Elmsall, town and parish (pop. 2,368), West Riding, S Yorkshire, England, 6 mi. SSE of Pontefract; coal mining.

North Emporia, Va.: see EMPORIA.

Northenden, residential town and parish (pop. 3,236), NE Cheshire, England, on Mersey R. and 5 mi. S of Manchester; mfg.: chemicals, pharmaceuticals.

North English, town (pop. 853), Iowa co., E central Iowa, 39 mi. SSW of Cedar Rapids; creamery.

North Enid (ē′nĭd), town (pop. 219), Garfield co., N Okla., just N of Enid.

Northern, for names beginning thus and not found here: see under NORTH.

Northern, in Rus. names: see also SEVERNAYA, SEVERNIYE, SEVERNOYE, SEVERNY, SEVERO.

Northern Anyui Range, Russian SFSR: see ANYUI.

Northern Caucasus, territory, Russian SFSR: see CAUCASUS.

Northern Circars, India: see CIRCARS, NORTHERN.

Northern District (□ 2,548; pop. 12,293), Br. Honduras; ⊙ Corozal. Mostly level country, drained by New R. Agr. (sugar cane, corn, coconuts), stock raising (cattle, hogs); fisheries; lumbering. Sugar milling at Corozal. Main centers are Corozal and Orange Walk. Formed in early 1940s by union of Corozal and Orange Walk dists.

Northern Donets River, USSR: see DONETS RIVER.

Northern Dvina (dvē′nů), former government of N European Russian SFSR; ⊙ was Veliki Ustyug. Formed 1918 out of Vologda govt.; inc. 1929 into Northern Territory.

Northern Dvina Canal (dvēnä′), Rus. *Severo-Dvinskiy Kanal,* system of lakes, canals, and canalized rivers in W central Vologda oblast, Russian SFSR; 35 mi. long. Links Sheksna R. (W) with Kubeno L. (E); E section formed by canalized Porozovitsa R. Joins Mariinsk canal system with basin of Northern Dvina R. via Sukhona R. Formerly called Württemberg Canal.

Northern Dvina River, Russian SFSR: see DVINA RIVER.

Northern Frontier Province or **Northern Province** (□ 120,300; pop. c.194,000), N Kenya; ⊙ Isiolo. Includes (since 1946) Turkana dist. Bordered by Ethiopia (N), Uganda (W), and Ital. Somaliland (E), it comprises 3/5 of Kenya. Comparatively waterless, it consists of a vast undulating plain sloping upwards from the Indian Ocean; in NW is section of Great Rift Valley (here occupied by L. Rudolf) flanked by escarpments. Has mainly scrub grasslands. A nomadic stock-raising region (cattle, sheep and goats); some agr. (peanuts, sesame, corn, wild coffee). Main centers are Isiolo, Wajir, Moyale.

Northern Ireland, political division (□ 5,238; 1937 pop. 1,279,753; 1951 census pop. 1,370,709) of the UNITED KINGDOM OF GREAT BRITAIN AND NORTHERN IRELAND; ⊙ BELFAST. It occupies NE part of IRELAND and comprises the 6 counties of ANTRIM, ARMAGH, DOWN, FERMANAGH, LONDONDERRY, and TYRONE. It is frequently called ULSTER, name of northernmost of the anc. Irish provinces, of which it occupies greater part. Northern Ireland is bounded by republic of Ireland (S and W), the Atlantic (N), North Channel (NE and E), and the Irish Sea (SE). Coast line, rocky and rugged in N, is deeply indented by Lough Foyle (N), Belfast Lough (E), and Strangford Lough and Carlingford Lough (SE). Surface, in general, consists of plateau, volcanic in origin, c.500 ft. high, with higher hills at its edges; in SE part of region, near Irish border, Mourne Mts. rise to 2,796 ft. on Slieve Donard. In central part of Northern Ireland surface slopes down to Lough Neagh, largest lake in British Isles. On SW slope of plateau are upper and lower parts of Lough Erne. Region is drained by Lagan, Bann, Blackwater, Mourne, Foyle, and Main rivers. Among the few natural resources of Northern Ireland is bauxite, mined in Co. Antrim and refined at Larne. Linen milling is principal industry and is concentrated in region around Belfast and Lisburne. Belfast, one of largest British ports, is one of the principal shipbuilding centers of the British Isles. In Second World War an important aircraft industry was developed in Northern Ireland. Chief cities are Belfast, Londonderry, Bangor, Lurgan, Lisburn, Ballymena, Newry, Portadown, Larne, Newtonards, Coleraine, and Armagh. Agr. is principal occupation of Northern Ireland; potatoes and flax are grown; sheep, cattle, and poultry raising are important, and large quantities of dairy products and eggs are shipped to Great Britain. Chief mail-steamer routes to Great Britain are from Larne to Stranraer, and from Belfast to Heysham and Liverpool. Established (1920) by Government of Ireland Act, Northern Ireland is represented in the British Parliament; it has, at the same time, its own govt., responsible to Northern Irish Senate and House of Commons. The republic of Ireland does not recognize division of the country and the status of Northern Ireland. Relatively distinctive history of Northern Ireland dates from early 17th cent., when Scottish and English settlers were introduced into the region after rebellion (1607) and subsequent flight of the Irish earls. Later the growth of Protestantism and industrial development further separated character of the region from that of the rest of Ireland. Deeper split was induced by the various Home Rule bills, 1st of which was laid (1886) before Parliament by Gladstone; Northern Ireland feared that they would result in domination by Catholic majority of S Ireland and in set-backs to region's industries and close ties with British economy. Latent tension in Northern Ireland is created by steady growth of the Catholic minority, which threatens Protestant hegemony.

Northern Karroo (kŭrōō′) or **High Veld** (fĕlt′), N Cape Prov., Transvaal, and Orange Free State, U. of So. Afr., innermost and highest of Union's plateau regions, extends N from Great Karroo, bounded by Namaqualand (W), Komsberg and Roggeveld escarpments (SW), and Drakensberg and Stormberg ranges (E). Up to 4,000 ft. high in Cape Prov., it rises to c.6,000 ft. in Transvaal High Veld and to c.10,000 ft. in Basutoland. Forms main watershed of U. of So. Afr.

Northern Kearsarge Mountain, N.H.: see PEQUAWKET, MOUNT.

Northern Land, Russian SFSR: see SEVERNAYA ZEMLYA.

Northern Nafud, Arabia: see NAFUD.

Northern Neck, E Va., tidewater peninsula bet. the Potomac (N) and the Rappahannock, extending c.85 mi. SE from vicinity of Fredericksburg to Chesapeake Bay. Embraces 5 counties: King George, Westmoreland, Richmond, Northumberland, Lancaster.

Northern Oblast, Russian SFSR: see NORTHERN TERRITORY.

Northern Panhandle, NW W.Va., narrow arm (□ 584) of state, jutting N bet. Pa. (E) and Ohio R. (Ohio line) on N and W; includes Marshall, Ohio, Brooke, and Hancock counties. Largely industrial, due to proximity to Pittsburgh steel dist. (to E) and to region's abundant natural resources (especially coal, clay, natural gas, glass sand, salt). WEIRTON (steel) and WHEELING (diversified industries) are principal mfg. centers.

Northern Penner River, India: see PENNER RIVER.

Northern Province, administrative division (□ 236,200; 1948 pop. estimate 664,403), N Anglo-Egyptian Sudan; ⊙ Ed Damer. Bordered by Egypt (N), Libya (NW), and Fr. Equatorial Africa (W), it lies in S part of Libyan and Nubian deserts which are separated by the Nile. A strip ½–3 mi. wide on either side of river is cultivable. Agr.: cotton, wheat, barley, corn, fruits. Nomadic grazing (camels, goats, sheep). The Libyan Desert (W of the Nile) is uninhabited and waterless with the exception of a few oases. The Nubian Desert is crossed here by railroad from Abu Hamed to Wadi Halfa, cutting off great bend of the Nile. There are numerous anc. ruins (Meroë, Napata). Chief towns are Atbara, Berber, Shendi, Wadi Halfa, and Ed Damer. Prov. was formed in 1930s by amalgamation of Halfa, Dongola, Berber provs.

Northern Province, administrative division (□ 3,429; pop., including estate pop., 479,381) of N Ceylon; ⊙ Jaffna. Comprises 2 natural divisions, JAFFNA PENINSULA (N), with group of isls. lying off W coast, and mainland (dense jungle area in interior known as the Wanni); lagoons along E coast. Agr. (rice, tobacco, chili, yams, pan, millet); extensive coconut- and palmyra-palm plantations. Fishing (Jaffna Lagoon, Mannar Isl.); pearl banks in Gulf of Mannar. Main towns: Jaffna, Chavakachcheri, Mannar, Mullaitivu, Vavuniya. Large salterns at Jaffna and Elephant Pass; irrigation project at Kilinochchi. Created 1833.

Northern Provinces, major administrative division (□ 281,778; 1931 pop. 11,303,476) of Nigeria; ⊙ Kaduna. Prov. includes part (□ 17,350; 1931 pop. 395,851; 1948 pop. estimate 540,100) of Br. Cameroons. Bounded W and N by Dahomey and Niger territories of Fr. West Africa, E by Fr. Cameroons. Includes provs. of ADAMAWA, BAUCHI, BENUE, BORNU, ILORIN, KABBA, KANO, KATSINA, NIGER, PLATEAU, SOKOTO, and ZARIA. Situated largely in savanna zone; some deciduous forest along lower Niger R. (S), dry thorn and scrub vegetation (N). Bauchi Plateau (center) forms watershed bet. Niger R. and its left affluents (Kebbi, Kaduna, and Benue rivers; W and S) and the Komadugu Yobe flowing into L. Chad (NE). Produces shea nuts (S), cotton, rice, peanuts, ginger, and sesame for export. Main food crops are millet, cassava, durra, and in S, yams and corn. Livestock (cattle, sheep, goats) are bred largely by Fulah tribe. Area contains all tin mines of Nigeria, concentrated in Bauchi Plateau, with centers at Jos, Bukuru, Naraguta, and Bauchi; mining of gold and diamonds (W); limestone and salt workings. Main centers: Kano (chief trading and mfg. town), Kaduna and Zaria (rail junctions), Jos and Bauchi (in tin-mining zone), Sokoto, Maiduguri, and Ilorin. Pop. is largely Hausa and Fulah (N), Kanuri, Fulah, and Shuwa Arab (NE), Nupe and Yoruba (SW), and Tiv (S, along lower Benue). Railroads from Lagos and Port Harcourt meet at Kaduna; serve Jos tin region and Kano-Zaria agr. area. Territories now included in Northern Provinces came (c.1885) under Br. protection and were 1st administered by Royal Niger Company. Passed to the crown (1900); known as protectorate of Northern Nigeria until amalgamated (1914) with colony and protectorate of Southern Nigeria.

Northern Rhodesia (rōdē′zhŭ), Br. protectorate (□ 292,323; 1946 estimated pop. 1,565,547), SE central Africa; ⊙ Lusaka (since 1935). Bounded N by Tanganyika, E by Nyasaland, SE by Mozambique, S by Southern Rhodesia (along Zambezi R.) and by South-West Africa's Caprivi Strip, W by Angola, and NW by Belgian Congo. Although it is entirely within the tropics (bet. 8°S and 18°S), its elevation (3–5,000 ft.; over 5,000 ft. in NE and in Muchinga Mts.) gives it a climate almost subtropical and, on the whole, healthful, with moderate winters (May–Aug.). Mean temperatures vary from 55°F to 75°F. The river valleys have extremely hot summers. Average annual rainfall ranges from 50 in. (N) to 25–30 in. (S); Nov.–April is rainy season. Drained by the middle Zambezi (which traverses Barotseland N–S, then forms S boundary) and by its principal left affluents, Kafue and Luangwa. Luapula R., which rises in L. Bangweulu and receives the Chambezi, drains N areas. L. Mweru and S tip of L. Tanganyika are on N frontier. Waterfalls (especially VICTORIA FALLS in S and KALAMBO FALLS in N) are noted tourist attractions. The rolling upland is park-savanna; the extensive lowlands (Barotse plain, Kafue R. flats, L. Bangweulu marshes) are covered with tall grasses and are poorly drained. Tropical hardwoods are exploited in Barotseland. Principal crops are corn (on ⅔ of cultivated land), wheat (near Lusaka), tobacco and coffee (near Fort Jameson and Abercorn). Cattle raising is limited to uplands not infested by tse-tse fly. Mineral resources are chief source of export revenue. Rich copper deposits in belt adjoining Belgian Congo's Katanga prov. are mined at Roan Antelope, Nkana (electrolytic refinery), Mufulira, and Nchanga mines near NDOLA. BROKEN HILL mine yields lead, zinc, and vanadium. Chief towns and European settlements are found along the railroad which crosses the protectorate N–S from Belgian Congo border at Ndola to Southern Rhodesia line at Victoria Falls just S of LIVINGSTONE (former ⊙). Lusaka, near country's geographical center, is a hub of communications, with roads leading SE to Salisbury (Southern Rhodesia), ENE to Fort Jameson and Nyasaland (Great East Road), NNE to Kasama, Abercorn, and Tanganyika (Great North Road, a section of Cape-to-Cairo link). A secondary road leads W from Lusaka to Mongu in Barotseland (a native reserve). Main towns are served by airfields. Copper smelters use coal from Wankie basin in Southern Rhodesia. Hydroelectric potential has been harnessed to a limited extent at Victoria Falls and Mulungushi Dam (near Broken Hill). At Livingstone and Ndola are sawmilling, tobacco processing, leatherworking. Territory N of the Zambezi was 1st explored by Portuguese near end of 18th cent. David Livingstone, on his missionary journeys, 1st came in 1851. He traveled through Barotseland and in 1855 discovered Victoria Falls; he died in 1873 near Chitambo. Throughout 19th cent., the region (especially in N) was harassed by Arab slave traders who were finally driven out (1891–94) by Br. troops under Sir Harry Johnston. In 1889, it came under Br. South Africa Company, which administered it as 2 territories (Barotseland–North-Western Rhodesia and North-Eastern Rhodesia) until combined (1911) under the name of Northern Rhodesia. Company's control (with certain checks by Br. govt.) continued until 1924, when Br. rule was established with an appointed governor aided by an executive and a legislative council. The latter includes, since 1948, 2 African members. Local administration is vested in native authorities and subject to veto by prov. commissioners residing at Livingstone (⊙ Southern Prov.), Broken Hill (⊙ Central Prov.), Fort Jameson (⊙ Eastern Prov.), Kasama (⊙ Northern Prov.), Ndola (⊙ Western Prov.), and Mongu (⊙ Barotse Prov.). Pop. (1946) consisted of 21,919 Europeans, 1,119 Coloured (Mixed), 789 Asiatics, and an estimated 1,541,720 natives.

Northern Shan State, Burma: see SHAN STATE.

Northern Sosva River, Russian SFSR: see SOSVA RIVER, Tyumen oblast.

Northern Sporades, Greece: see SPORADES.

Northern Territories, British protectorate (□ 30,600; pop. 870,778), N Gold Coast, bet. 8°N and 11°N; ⊙ Tamale. Bounded W by Ivory Coast, N by Upper Volta, E by Togoland. Drained by Black Volta (W and S borders) and White Volta rivers which join to form Volta R. Hills (N and W) slope gently toward Volta basin. Savanna vegetation. Main products: shea nuts, cotton (near Tamale), hides and skins (N); extensive livestock raising (Pong Tamale experimental station). Food crops: millet, durra, yams. Iron deposits near Pudo. Roads radiate from Tamale. Divided into dists. (Dagomba, Gonja, Mamprusi, Krachi, Wa) named for principal tribes. N section (pop. 206,360) of Br. Togoland is administered as part of Northern Territories. Region came under Br. influence in 1897; made a protectorate in 1901.

Northern Territory (□ 523,620; pop. 10,868), territory of Commonwealth of Australia, N of parallel 26°S, bet. meridians 138° and 129°E, bounded by Timor and Arafura seas (N), South Australia (S), Gulf of Carpentaria (NE), Queensland (E), Western Australia (W); ⊙ DARWIN. Flat coastline indented by many bays. Grassy land on Barkly Tableland and W central plains. Simpson Desert in SE. Arnhem Land (N) is largest of 15 aboriginal reservations (total □ 67,244). Lakes usually dry. Victoria R. is largest stream; Mt. Zeil, in Macdonnell Ranges, highest peak. Gold, tungsten, mica. Mean annual temp. of N area, 84°F.; rainfall 59 in.; S area 70°F., 11 in. Wet season, Nov.–April; monsoons Dec.–Jan. Mangroves, eucalyptus, tropical vegetation. Marsupials, alligators, snakes, buffaloes, tropical birds. Produces livestock, gold, peanuts, pearl shell. N coast discovered 1623 by Dutch; 1st Br. settlement 1824. Northern Territory placed 1825 under New South Wales, 1863 under South Australia. Transferred 1911 to Commonwealth; subdivided 1926 into North Australia and Central Australia; recombined 1931 as Northern Territory.

Northern Territory, Rus. *Severny Krai* or *Severnyy Kray* (sĕ′vyĭrnē krī′), former administrative division of N European Russian SFSR; ⊙ was Archangel. Formed 1929 out of former govts. of Archangel, Vologda, Northern Dvina, and Komi Autonomous Oblast. It was converted (1936) into Northern Oblast [Rus. *Severnaya Oblast′*] following separation of Komi Autonomous SSR and entirely dissolved (1937) into oblasts of Archangel and Vologda.

Northern Uvals (ōōvälz′), Rus. *Severnyye Uvaly*, one of the moraine uplands [Rus. *uvaly*] in N European Russian SFSR; form watershed bet. Northern Dvina and Volga-Kama river basins; extend from area of Soligalich c.450 mi. E to upper Vychegda R.; rise to 695 ft.

North Esk River. 1 In Angus, Scotland, rises in the Grampians, flows 30 mi. SE, past Edzell, to North Sea 3 mi. N of Montrose. At its mouth are fisheries. **2** In Midlothian, Scotland: see ESK RIVER.

North Esk River, NE Tasmania, rises in mts. 15 mi. S of Scottsdale, flows 45 mi. S, W, and NW to Launceston, here joining South Esk R. to form Tamar R.

North Fabius River, Mo. and Iowa: see FABIUS RIVER.

North Fairfield, village (pop. 468), Huron co., N Ohio, 10 mi. S of Norwalk and on East Branch of Huron R.

North Falmouth, Mass.: see FALMOUTH.

North Ferriby, town and parish (pop. 1,489), East Riding, SE Yorkshire, England, on Humber R. and 7 mi. WSW of Hull; agr. market; cementworks.

Northfield. 1 Village (pop. 1,426), Cook co., NE Ill., N suburb of Chicago, just W of Winnetka. **2** Town (pop. 75), Washington co., E Maine, 9 mi. NW of Machias. **3** Town (pop. 2,246), Franklin co., N Mass., on Connecticut R. and 10 mi. NE of Greenfield, near N.H. line; a beautiful New England town. Dwight L. Moody, b. here, founded Northfield Seminary (now Northfield School) for girls and Mount Hermon School for boys. Hq. American Youth Hostels; 1st hostel opened here 1934. Town 1st settled 1672, permanently settled 1714, inc. 1723. Includes villages of East Northfield, South Vernon, and Mount Hermon. **4** City (pop. 7,487), Rice co., SE Minn., on Cannon R. and 35 mi. S of St. Paul; trade and mfg. center for grain, livestock, and poultry area; dairy products, breakfast foods, agr. equipment. St. Olaf Col. and Carleton Col. are here. City founded 1850. On Sept. 7, 1876, Jesse and Frank James attempted a bank robbery here which was frustrated and led to the breakup of the gang after several members were captured. **5** Town (pop. 1,561), including Northfield village (pop. 1,065), Merrimack co., central N.H., 15 mi. N of Concord and on Winnipesaukee R. opposite TILTON; wood products. **6** City (pop. 3,498), Atlantic co., SE N.J., 6 mi. W of Atlantic City; glass products. Inc. 1905. **7** Village (pop. 780), Summit co., NE Ohio, 15 mi. SSE of downtown Cleveland, near Cuyahoga R.; machine shops, foundries. Furnace Run Reservation (recreation) is near by. **8** Town (pop. 4,314), including Northfield village (pop. 2,262), Washington co., central Vt., 10 mi. SW of Montpelier. Textiles, hosiery; lumber, maple sugar; granite, slate. Winter sports. Seat of Norwich Univ. Chartered 1781, settled 1785, organized 1794.

Northfleet, urban district (1931 pop. 16,428; 1951 census 18,803), NW Kent, England, port on the Thames just W of Gravesend; shipbuilding; mfg. of brick, cement, foundry products, paper, paint. Has 14th-cent. church.

North Fond du Lac (fŏn' dū lăk", jōō lăk"), village (pop. 2,291), Fond du Lac co., E Wis., on L. Winnebago, just NNW of Fond du Lac, in farm area; railroad shops. Inc. 1903.

Northford, Conn.: see NORTH BRANFORD.

North Foreland, promontory at NE tip of Kent, England, on Isle of Thanet, on S shore of Thames estuary, just N of Broadstairs at N end of The Downs roadstead. Site of lighthouse, 51°22′N 1°27′E.

Northfork, town (pop. 994), McDowell co., S W.Va., on Tug Fork and 8 mi. E of Welch; trade center for semibituminous-coal-mining region.

North Fork. 1 River in Mo. and Ark., rises SE of Mountain Grove in Mo., flows c.100 mi. S, into Baxter co. in Ark., to White R. at Norfork. Impounded near Norfork by Norfork Dam (244 ft. high, 2,624 ft. long), built for flood control and power production, and completed in 1944; sometimes spelled Norfolk Dam. **2** River in Oregon, rises in SE corner of Grant co., E Oregon, flows 45 mi. S to Malheur R. at Juntura. Agency Valley Dam (110 ft. high, 1,850 ft. long; completed 1935), 12 mi. NNW of Juntura, forms Beulah Reservoir (2.5 mi. long, 1.5 mi. wide; capacity 59,900 acre-ft.). Unit in Vale irrigation project.

North Fork of Red River, N Texas and SW Okla., rises in the Llano Estacado near Lefors, Texas, flows generally E to Sayre, Okla., then SSE and S to Red R. 12 mi. N of Vernon, Texas; c.195 mi. long. On it is ALTUS DAM. Elm Fork (c.90 mi. long) enters from W, c.10 mi. E of Mangum, Okla.

North Fork of Wichita River, Texas: see WICHITA RIVER.

North Fork, Republican River, in Colo. and Nebr., formed by confluence of 2 forks in Yuma co., NE Colo., flows c.30 mi. E, past Wray, Colo., into Dundy co., SW Nebr., joining Arikaree R. at Haigler to form Republican R.

North Fork Virgin River, SW Utah, flows through Zion Canyon, in Zion National Park, joining East Fork Virgin R. to form Virgin R.; 40 mi. long.

North Fox Island, Mich.: see FOX ISLANDS.

North Freedom, village (pop. 611), Sauk co., S central Wis., on Baraboo R. and 6 mi. W of Baraboo, in dairy and livestock area; cannery.

North Friesland (frēz'lŭnd), Ger. *Nordfriesland* (nôrt'frēs'länt), region (□ 658; 1939 pop. 73,560; 1946 pop. 165,465) in Schleswig-Holstein, NW Germany, on North Sea, bet. Danish border and Eiderstedt peninsula; includes most of North Frisian isls. Low, level region, with reclaimed land along shore; noted cattle raising. Main town: Husum. Region came (1435) to duchy of Schleswig.

North Frisian Islands, Denmark and Germany: see FRISIAN ISLANDS.

North Gamboa, Panama Canal Zone: see GAMBOA.

Northgate, village, SE Sask., frontier station on N.Dak. border, 35 mi. ESE of Estevan.

Northgate, village, Burke co., NW N.Dak., port of entry at Can. line, 14 mi. N of Bowbells.

North Girard (jĭrärd'), borough (pop. 1,369), Erie co., NW Pa., 16 mi. SW of Erie, near L. Erie; agr. tools. Inc. 1926.

North Glenside, Pa.: see ABINGTON.

North Gower (gôr), village (pop. estimate 450), SE Ont., 18 mi. S of Ottawa; dairying, mixed farming.

North Grafton, Mass.: see GRAFTON.

North Grosvenor Dale, Conn.: see THOMPSON.

North Grove, town (pop. 126), Miami co., N central Ind., 12 mi. SSE of Peru, in agr. area.

North Guilford, Conn.: see GUILFORD.

North Haledon (hāl'dŭn), borough (pop. 3,550), Passaic co., NE N.J., 3 mi. N of Paterson; dairy products. Inc. 1901.

North Hamgyong (häm'gyông'), Jap. *Kankyo-hokudo*, Korean *Hamgyong-pukdo*, northernmost province [Jap. and Korean *do*] (□ 7,838; 1944 pop. 1,124,153) of Korea; ⊙ NANAM. Chief port is CHONGJIN. Bounded E by Sea of Japan, W by Tumen R. (on Manchurian and Rus. borders). Extremely mountainous interior rises to 8,337 ft. in Mt. Kwanmo. There are several hot-springs resorts, the best known being CHUURONJANG. Rivers (other than the Tumen) are small; they drain extensive lumbering and coal-mining area. Iron, graphite, and gold are mined in scattered areas. Fishing is an important industry. There is some stock raising; agr. is generally limited to the cultivation of soy beans, millet, and potatoes. Industrial centers are Chongjin and SONGJIN; NAJIN is a naval base.

North Hampton (nôrth' hămp'tŭn, nôr"thămp'tŭn). **1** Agr., resort town (pop. 1,104), Rockingham co., SE N.H., on the coast and 8 mi. SW of Portsmouth. Set off from Hampton 1742. **2** Village (pop. 424), Clark co., W central Ohio, 8 mi. NW of Springfield. **3** Suburb (pop. 5,924, with near-by South Hampton) of Hampton, Elizabeth City co., SE Va.

North Hangay, Mongolia: see NORTH KHANGAI.

North Hartsville, village (pop. 1,743), Darlington co., NE S.C., near Hartsville.

North Harwich, Mass.: see HARWICH.

North Hatley, village (pop. 472), S Que., on L. Massawippi, 9 mi. SSW of Sherbrooke; dairying.

North Haven. 1 Town (pop. 9,444), New Haven co., S Conn., on Quinnipiac R., just N of New Haven; truck farming, mfg. (bricks, hardware). Includes Montowese (mŏntŭwēs', mŏn'tŭwēz") village (1940 pop. 897). Settled c.1650, set off from New Haven 1786. **2** Resort town (pop. 410), Knox co., S Maine, on **North Haven Island** (8 mi. long, ½ to 2 mi. wide), in Penobscot Bay, and 12 mi. ENE of Rockland. Includes Pulpit Harbor village. **3** Resort village (pop. 153), Suffolk co., SE N.Y., on E Long Isl., just N of Sag Harbor, on peninsula just E of Noyack Bay.

North Haverhill, N.H.: see HAVERHILL.

North Helgeland, Norway: see HELGELAND.

North Henderson, village (pop. 1,873), Vance co., N N.C., a suburb of Henderson.

North Hero, island and town (pop. 407), ⊙ Grand Isle co., NW Vt., in L. Champlain, 10 mi. W of St. Albans. Isl. (c.12 mi. long) is bridged to Grand Isle (S) and Alburg (N).

North High Shoals, town (pop. 124), Oconee co., N central Ga.

North Hills, residential village (pop. 330), Nassau co., SE N.Y., on W Long Isl., c.2 mi. N of Mineola.

North Holland, Du. *Noordholland* (nōrt'hô'länt), province (□ 1,016.4; pop. 1,774,273), NW Netherlands; ⊙ HAARLEM. Includes West Frisian Isl. of TEXEL. Mainland peninsula bounded by North Sea (W), the Waddenzee (N), the Ijsselmeer (E), South Holland and Utrecht provs. (S). Mainly low fenland with sea and river clay or sand. Drained by Zaan, Amstel, and Vecht rivers and North Sea, North Holland, Ringvaart, and Merwede canals. Agr. (bread grains, sugar beets, cabbage, cauliflower, potatoes, strawberries); produces flower bulbs, flowers, seeds for truck gardening. Cattle raising in reclaimed areas of the Ijsselmeer; Edam and Alkmaar are celebrated cheese markets. Fishing on North Sea coast; Ijsselmeer fisheries declined after building of Ijsselmeer Dam. Industries centered at Amsterdam and ZAANSTREEK industrial area: steel (Velsen), machinery, shipbuilding, railroad equipment, building materials, paper, wood products, oil and feed cakes; sugar refining, food processing. Foreign trade centered at AMSTERDAM, chief commercial center. Other important towns: Haarlem, Ijmuiden, Zaandam, Alkmaar, Helder, Hilversum. Formed 1840 by division of Holland into North Holland and South Holland.

North Holland Canal, Du. *Noordhollandsch Kanaal*, North Holland prov., NW Netherlands, extends 50 mi. N–S, bet. Helder and the Ij at Amsterdam; c.30 ft. deep. Navigable along entire length by ships up to 800 tons capacity; crossed by 3 railroad swingbridges. Locks at Purmerend. Built (1819–24) to give Amsterdam direct access to sea; soon proved inadequate and was superseded by NORTH SEA CANAL.

North Hollywood, suburban community, now part of LOS ANGELES city, Los Angeles co., S Calif., in San Fernando Valley, 10 mi. NW of downtown Los Angeles; gravel pits; fruit farms. Formerly Lankershim.

North Hornell (hôrnĕl'), village (pop. 605), Steuben co., S N.Y., on Canisteo R., opposite Hornell.

North Horr (hôr), village, Northern Frontier Prov., N Kenya, on road and 210 mi. NNW of Isiolo, E of L. Rudolf; 3°21′N 36°58′E; stock raising; peanuts, sesame, corn. Airfield.

North Hsenwi (shĕnwē'), NE state (sawbwaship) (□ 6,422; pop. 243,499), Northern Shan State, Upper Burma; ⊙ Hsenwi. Bounded E and N by Chinese Yunnan prov. and NW by Shweli R., it is astride Salween R. Rice in valleys, cotton, sesame, corn, opium in hills. Served by Mandalay-Lashio RR and Burma Road. Pop.: Kachins and Chinese (N), Shans and Palaungs (S).

North Hsingan (shĭng'än'), former province (□ 60,320; 1940 pop. 132,426) of NW Manchukuo, in Inner Mongolia; ⊙ was Hailar. See HSINGAN prov. The region of North Hsingan was coextensive with Mongolian BARGA league.

North Hudson, village (pop. 787), St. Croix co., W Wis., on St. Croix R., just N of Hudson; dairying.

North Hyde Park, Vt.: see HYDE PARK.

Northill, agr. village and parish (pop. 1,228), E central Bedford, England, 3 mi. WNW of Biggleswade. Has 14th-cent. church.

North Irwin, borough (pop. 1,076), Westmoreland co., SW Pa., 16 mi. SE of Pittsburgh. Inc. 1894.

North Island (□ 44,281; pop. 1,146,292), NEW ZEALAND, the smaller but more populous of its 2 main isls.; separated from S.Isl. by Cook Strait. It is 510 mi. from N.Cape to Cape Palliser (S), 200 mi. wide at widest point. Seat of Wellington, ⊙ dominion. Irregularly shaped, with long peninsula projecting NW. Ruahine Range is largest of several mtn. chains. Volcanic mts.; Ruapehu (9,175 ft.) and Mt. Egmont (8,260 ft.) highest. Hot springs in N central area, site of health resorts. Fertile plains in coastal areas. Largest river and lake of New Zealand are Waikato R. and L. Taupo. Site of Tongariro and Egmont natl. parks. Chief centers: Auckland (seat of Auckland Univ. Col.), Wellington (seat of Victoria Univ. Col.); Massey Agr. Col. is near Palmerston North. Produces dairy foods, kauri gum, timber, coal, gold. Isl. is divided into provincial dists. of AUCKLAND, HAWKE'S BAY, TARANAKI, WELLINGTON.

North Island (525 acres; pop. 57), one of the Seychelles, in Indian Ocean, 20 mi. NNW of Victoria; 4°23′S 55°15′E; granite formation; copra.

North Island, S.C.: see WINYAH BAY.

North Island Naval Air Station, Calif.: see SAN DIEGO, city.

North Jay, Maine: see JAY.

North Johns or **Johns,** town (pop. 454), Jefferson co., N central Ala., 20 mi. SW of Birmingham.

North Judson, town (pop. 1,705), Starke co., NW Ind., c.40 mi. SW of South Bend; agr. (onions, grain, livestock).

North Kanara, India: see KANARA.

North Kansas City, town (pop. 3,886), Clay co., W Mo., on left bank of Missouri R., opposite Kansas City. Mfg. (flour, paint, metal products, bags, boxes); dairy, truck farms. Founded 1912.

North Kazakhstan (kä"zäkstän', Rus. kŭzŭkhstän'), Rus. *Severo-Kazakhstan*, oblast (□ 17,600; 1947 pop. estimate 400,000), N Kazakh SSR; ⊙ Petropavlovsk. On W.Siberian Plain; drained by Ishim R. Entirely agr. (wheat, millet, oats); cattle and sheep raising. Trans-Siberian RR crosses E–W, Trans-Kazakhstan RR N–S. Industry centered at Petropavlovsk. Pop.: Russians, Ukrainians, Kazakhs. Formed 1936.

North Kemmerer, Wyo.: see FRONTIER.

North Kennebunkport (kĕn"ŭbŭngkpôrt'), resort town (pop. 939), York co., SW Maine, 20 mi. SW of Portland. Formerly part of Kennebunkport; inc. 1915.

North Khangai or **North Hangay** (both: khäng'gī), Mongolian *Ara Khangai* or *Ara Hangay* (ä'rä), aimak (□ 18,500; pop. 80,000), central Mongolian People's Republic; ⊙ Tsetserlik. Situated on NE slopes of the Khangai Mts., the aimak lies in wooded steppe watered by right tributaries of Selenga R. Agr. and pastoral economy (high livestock density).

North Kingstown (kĭng'stŭn, kĭngz'toun"), town (pop. 14,810), Washington co., S central R.I., on Narragansett Bay, on Hunt and Potowomut rivers, and 18 mi. S of Providence; mfg. (woolens, webbing, elastic braid), agr., fisheries, resorts. Includes villages of Saunderstown, ALLENTON, Davisville (site of naval construction training center in Second World War), Hamilton, LAFAYETTE, Slocum, WICKFORD, and QUONSET POINT. Settled 1641, inc. 1674 as Kingstown, divided (1723) into North Kingstown and South Kingstown. Gilbert Stuart b. here.

North Kingsville, village (pop. 1,271), Ashtabula co., extreme NE Ohio, on L. Erie, 6 mi. ENE of Ashtabula; wood products.

North Koel River (kō'ăl), W Bihar, India, rises on Chota Nagpur Plateau c.25 mi. NE of Jashpurnagar, flows 140 mi. NNW past Daltonganj to Son R. 32 mi. SSW of Sasaram.

North Kyongsang (kyŭng'säng'), Korean *Kyongsang-pukdo*, Jap. *Keisho-hokudo*, province [Jap. and Korean *do*] (□ 6,930; 1949 pop. 3,206,201), S Korea, bounded E by Sea of Japan; ⊙ TAEGU. Partly mountainous and forested, with fertile lowlands drained by Naktong R. The prov. is a major producer of raw silk. Also important are stock raising and agr. (barley, cotton, hemp, ramie, fruit). There are many fishing ports and scattered salt fields. Gold, silver, coal, graphite, molybdenum, and tungsten are mined. The only important center is Taegu.

North La Junta (lŭ hōōn'tŭ, hŭn'tŭ), village (pop. 1,502), Otero co., SE Colo., just N of La Junta.

North Lake. 1 Village (pop. 4,361), Cook co., NE Ill., just W of Chicago. Inc. since 1940. **2** Village (1940 pop. 653), Marquette co., NW Upper Peninsula, Mich., 2 mi. NW of Ishpeming. **3** Village (pop. c.250), Waukesha co., SE Wis., on small North L., 24 mi. WNW of Milwaukee, in farm and lake-resort region.

North Lake, Greene co., SE N.Y., in the Catskills, 2 mi. E of Haines Falls; c.½ mi. long. State camp site.

North Lakhimpur (lŭkĭm'pōōr), town (pop. 2,790), Lakhimpur dist., E central Assam, India, in Brahmaputra valley, 50 mi. WSW of Dibrugarh; road center; tea, rice, jute, sugar cane, rape and mustard; tea processing. Extensive tea gardens near by.

North Lancing, England: see SOUTH LANCING.

North Land, Russian SFSR: see SEVERNAYA ZEMLYA.

North Laramie River (lă'rŭmē), SE Wyo., rises in Laramie Mts., flows 69 mi. S and E to Laramie R. 5 mi. N of Wheatland.

North Las Vegas (läs vā'gůs), residential town (pop. 3,875), Clark co., SE Nev., just N of Las Vegas.

Northleach, agr. village and parish (pop. 596), E Gloucester, England, 11 mi. ESE of Cheltenham. Has 15th-cent. church.

North Leigh (lē), agr. village and parish (pop. 682), W Oxfordshire, England, 3 mi. NE of Witney; limestone quarrying. Church has a Saxon tower.

North Lewisburg, village (pop. 854), Champaign co., W central Ohio, 13 mi. NE of Urbana, near Darby Creek, in agr. area.

North Liberty. 1 Town (pop. 1,165), St. Joseph co., N Ind., 13 mi. SW of South Bend; dairy products, grain. **2** Town (pop. 309), Johnson co., E Iowa, 7 mi. NNW of Iowa City. State park near by.

North Little Rock, city (pop. 44,097), Pulaski co., central Ark., on Arkansas R. (bridged) opposite LITTLE ROCK. Large railroad shops, timber-creosoting and cottonseed-oil processing plants, stockyards. Seat of Shorter Col. (jr.), Central Col. Near by are a veterans' hosp. and U.S. Camp Joseph T. Robinson. Settled c.1856, inc. 1903. Annexed Levy town in 1946.

North Logan, town (pop. 535), Cache co., N Utah, just N of Logan.

North Long Branch, N.J.: see LONG BRANCH.

North Loup (lōōp), village (pop. 526), Valley co., central Nebr., 10 mi. SE of Ord and on N.Loup R.; dairying, grain.

North Loup River, Nebr.: see LOUP RIVER.

North Lumberton, town (pop. 423), Robeson co., S N.C., just N of Lumberton.

North Madison, town (pop. 715), Jefferson co., SE Ind., just NW of Madison, in agr. area. State hosp. for insane here.

North Manchester, town (pop. 3,977), Wabash co., NE central Ind., on Eel R. and 34 mi. W of Fort Wayne, in agr. area (livestock, grain); makes furniture, electrical appliances, iron castings, water heaters, milk coolers, automobile parts. Seat of Manchester Col.

North Manistique Lake, Mich.: see MANISTIQUE LAKE.

North Manitou Island, Mich.: see MANITOU ISLANDS.

North Mankato (măn-kā'tō), city (pop. 4,788), Nicollet co., S Minn., on W bank of Minnesota R. opposite Mankato, in grain, livestock, and poultry area. Inc. 1922.

North Maroon Peak (14,000 ft.), W central Colo., in Elk Mts., Pitkin co.

North Meols (mēlz), agr. parish (pop. 2,197), W Lancashire, England, just ENE of Southport.

North Merrick, residential village (1940 pop. 2,072), Nassau co., SE N.Y., on W Long Isl., just N of Merrick.

North Miami (mīă'mē, -mů). **1** Town (pop. 10,734), Dade co., S Fla., a N suburb of Miami. Inc. 1926 as Miami Shores; renamed 1931. The present MIAMI SHORES village was separated from Miami in 1932. **2** Town (pop. 486), Ottawa co., extreme NE Okla., 3 mi. N of MIAMI.

North Miami Beach, resort city (pop. 2,129), Dade co., S Fla., 20 mi. N of Miami, on Atlantic coast. Formerly called Fulford.

North Middletown, town (pop. 319), Bourbon co., N central Ky., 9 mi. ESE of Paris, in Bluegrass horse-breeding region.

North Minch, Scotland: see MINCH, THE.

North Modesto (mōdě'stō), village (pop. 5,046, with near-by College Gardens), Stanislaus co., central Calif., near Modesto.

North Mountain, in Va. and W.Va., a ridge of the Alleghenies, extends c.50 mi. SW-NE, partly along border bet. Hardy co., W.Va., and Shenandoah co., Va.; c.2,000-3,300 ft. high.

North Mullins, town (pop. 297), Marion co., E S.C., 28 mi. E of Florence.

North Muskegon (můskē'gůn), city (pop. 2,424), Muskegon co., SW Mich., on Muskegon L., opposite Muskegon; truck farming. Inc. as village 1881, as city 1891.

North Natuna Islands (nůtōō'nů), small group of Natuna Isls., Indonesia, in S.China Sea, 40 mi. NW of Great Natuna; 4°42'N 108°E; comprises isl. of North Natuna surrounded by many islets. North Natuna (7 mi. long, 3 mi. wide) is also called Laut or Laoet. Coconuts are chief product of group.

North Negril Point (nĭgrĭl', nē-), cape at W end of Jamaica, 29 mi. WSW of Montego Bay; 18°21'N 78°22'W. South Negril Point, westernmost cape of the isl., is 6 mi. S.

North Newton, city (pop. 566), Harvey co., S central Kansas, just N of Newton. Seat of Bethel Col.

North Ogden (ŏg'důn), town (pop. 1,105), Weber co., N Utah; agr. suburb 3 mi. N of Ogden; alt. 4,275 ft. Inc. 1934.

North Olmsted (ŏm'stĕd), city (pop. 6,604), Cuyahoga co., N Ohio, 13 mi. WSW of downtown Cleveland; makes machine tools.

Northolt, residential town (pop. 3,047) in Ealing municipal borough, Middlesex, England, 11 mi. WNW of London. Site of major international airport; Royal Air Force station during Second World War. Has 14th-15th-cent. church. There is a race course.

Northome (nôr'thōm), village (pop. 349), Koochiching co., N Minn., c.40 mi. NE of Bemidji, in grain and livestock area; dairy products, lumber. State forests near by.

Northop (nôr'thůp), town and parish (pop. 2,812), Flint, Wales, 3 mi. S of Flint; agr. market. Has 15th-cent. church.

North Ossetian Autonomous Soviet Socialist Republic (ŏsē'shůn), Rus. *Severo-Osetinskaya Avtonomnaya SSR* (□ 3,550; 1946 pop. estimate 450,000), in S European Russian SFSR, on N slopes of the central Greater Caucasus; ⊙ Dzaudzhikau. Bordered (S) by South Ossetian Autonomous Oblast of Georgian SSR; extends N beyond Terek R. at Mozdok; drained by the Terek and its affluents, Gizeldon and Ardon rivers. Agr. concentrated in Terek lowland (orchards, corn, wheat, Indian hemp, soybeans); wine making, cotton growing near Mozdok. Livestock raising, lumbering, and hardy grain in mts. Agr. industry (corn processing at Beslan, canning). Lead, zinc, and silver mined at Sadon pass through Mizur concentrating mill to nonferrous metallurgical plants at Dzaudzhikau. Since 1944, republic contains important Malgobek oil fields. Served by branch of Rostov-Baku RR with spurs to Alagir and Dzaudzhikau, N termini of Ossetian and Georgian military roads. Originally part of Mountain Autonomous SSR, North Ossetia was constituted 1924 as autonomous oblast, 1936 as autonomous SSR. During Second World War, partly occupied (1942-43) by Germans.

Northowram, England: see HALIFAX.

North Oxford, Mass.: see OXFORD.

North Pacific Current or **North Pacific Drift,** warm ocean current in North Pacific Ocean, formed at c.38°N by convergence of Japan and Okhotsk currents, and flowing E to c.150°W before turning around toward S in the general clockwise circulation of the North Pacific.

North Pagi, Indonesia: see PAGI ISLANDS.

North Palisade, Calif.: see KINGS CANYON NATIONAL PARK.

North Park, village (pop. 1,239), Taylor co., W central Texas.

North Peak, Nev.: see BATTLE MOUNTAIN.

North Pease River, Texas: see PEASE RIVER.

North Pekin, village (pop. 1,758), Tazewell co., central Ill., suburb of Pekin. Inc. 1947.

North Pelham (pĕ'lům), residential village (pop. 5,046), Westchester co., SE N.Y., just N of Pelham and E of Mount Vernon, in New York city metropolitan area; mfg. (dishes, furniture). Settled 1851, inc. 1896.

North Perry, village (pop. 470), Lake co., NE Ohio, on L. Erie, 8 mi. NE of Painesville.

North Petherton, town and parish (pop. 3,011), central Somerset, England, 3 mi. SSW of Bridgwater; agr. market in dairying region. Has 14th-15th-cent. church. Site of radio-telegraph station.

North Phoebus (fē'bůs), village (pop. 3,437, with near-by East Hampton), Elizabeth City co., SE Va., near Hampton.

North Plainfield, residential borough (pop. 12,766), Somerset co., NE N.J., just NW of Plainfield; mfg. (metal products, electric motors, office equipment). Settled 1736, inc. 1885.

North Platte (plăt), city (pop. 15,433), ⊙ Lincoln co., central Nebr., 125 mi. W of Grand Island, at confluence of N.Platte and S.Platte rivers. A Great Plains shipping point on transcontinental railroad and air lines, in irrigated agr. and livestock region; railroad repair shops; flour, insulation material; dairy products, grain. Near by are state agr. experiment station, Scout's Rest Ranch (once home of Buffalo Bill), and Fort McPherson Natl. Cemetery. Laid out 1866 with the coming of the railroad; inc. 1871.

North Platte River, 680 mi. long, in N Colo., SE Wyo., and W Nebr., rises in several branches in Park Range, N Colo.; flows generally N, past Casper, Wyo., thence E and SE, past Douglas and Torrington, Wyo., and Scottsbluff, Nebr., to North Platte city, Nebr., here joining S.Platte R. to form Platte R. Principal tributaries: Sweetwater, Medicine Bow, and Laramie rivers in Wyo. Irrigation, power, and flood-control projects are part of comprehensive control plan for Missouri R. basin. KINGSLEY DAM, in main stream c.50 mi. W of North Platte, is used for power and irrigation. North Platte project, in SE Wyo. and W Nebr., irrigates 237,000 acres, supplements 175,000 privately developed acres. Principal activities in project area are agr. (sugar beets, alfalfa, barley) and livestock raising. Scottsbluff and Gering, W Nebr., and Lingle and Torrington, SE Wyo., are chief communities. Important units are PATHFINDER DAM, GUERNSEY DAM, and a diversion dam 6 mi. ESE of Guernsey that conducts water into irrigation canals; other features are 3 small reservoirs near Scottsbluff and 2 power plants at Lingle and Guernsey, Wyo. Kendrick project, on N.Platte R. in Wyo., supplies 66,000 acres near Casper; includes ALCOVA DAM, Casper Canal, and SEMINOE DAM. KORTES DAM, in S central Wyo. bet. Seminoe and Pathfinder dams, is power unit.

North Pleasanton, city (pop. 832), Atascosa co., SW Texas, on the Atascosa and 30 mi. S of San Antonio, in peanut, cotton, truck area.

North Pleasureville, town (pop. 198), Henry co., N Ky., 18 mi. NW of Frankfort, in Bluegrass agr. region.

North Plymouth, Mass.: see PLYMOUTH.

North Point, NW extremity of P.E.I., on the Gulf of St. Lawrence, 7 mi. NNE of Tignish; 47°4'N 63°59'W; lighthouse.

North Point, suburban village, Baltimore co., central Md., on North Point, extending into Chesapeake Bay at N side of Patapsco R. mouth (lighthouse), 12 mi. SE of downtown Baltimore; truck farms; steel plant. Fort Howard veterans' hosp. is here. British landing party was repulsed here (Sept. 12, 1814) in War of 1812.

North Polar Sea: see ARCTIC OCEAN.

North Pole, N end of earth's axis, at lat. 90°N long. 0°, in the ARCTIC REGIONS. The N magnetic pole is located on PRINCE OF WALES ISLAND at 73°N 100°W; it has earlier been located on BOOTHIA PENINSULA. The North Pole was 1st reached (1909) by R. E. Peary.

Northport. 1 City (pop. 3,885), Tuscaloosa co., W central Ala., on Black Warrior R. opposite Tuscaloosa; lumber. **2** Resort town (pop. 574), Waldo co., S Maine, on Penobscot Bay and just S of Belfast. **3** Village (pop. 582), Leelanau co., NW Mich., 25 mi. N of Traverse City, on W shore of Grand Traverse Bay, in cherry- and potato-producing area; fisheries, cherry canneries. Lighthouse and state park near by. **4** Resort and residential village (pop. 3,859), Suffolk co., SE N.Y., on N shore of W Long Isl., on Northport Bay, 5 mi. ENE of Huntington; oysters, clams; sand, gravel pits. Settled c.1683, inc. 1894. **5** City (pop. 487), Stevens co., NE Wash., port of entry 25 mi. NNE of Colville and on Columbia R., near B.C. line; lumber.

North Portal, village (pop. 146), SE Sask., frontier station on N.Dak. border, 23 mi. ESE of Estevan; mixed farming.

Northport Bay, SE N.Y., an arm of Long Island Sound indenting N shore of W Long Isl.; opens on E side of Huntington Bay, 2 mi. NE of Huntington; 3 mi. long N-S, 2½ mi. wide. Northport is on its E shore.

North Powder, town (pop. 403), Union co., NE Oregon, 22 mi. SSE of La Grande, near Powder R.; alt. 3,256 ft.

North Prairie, village (pop. 424), Waukesha co., SE Wis., 26 mi. WSW of Milwaukee, in dairying region; dairy products.

North Princeton, village (pop. 1,721), Mercer co., W N.J., near Princeton.

North Providence, town (pop. 13,927), Providence co., NE R.I., on Woonasquatucket R. and just NW of Providence; residential; mfg. (woolens, worsteds, yarns, machinery), food processing. Centerdale village is administrative center. Set off from Providence and inc. 1765.

North Pulaski (půlă'skē, pyů-), village (pop. 1,557), Pulaski co., SW Va., near Pulaski. Sometimes called Needmore.

North Pyongan (pyông'än'), Korean *Pyongan-pukdo*, Jap. *Heian-hokudo*, second largest province [Jap. and Korean *do*] (□ 10,982; 1944 pop. 1,881,352) of Korea; ⊙ Sinuiju. Includes SINMI ISLAND and several islets. Bounded N by Yalu R. (forming Manchurian border), S by Chongchon R., W by Korea Bay (arm of Yellow Sea). Largely mountainous, the prov. is sparsely settled except for NW corner. Extensive lumbering in the interior; gold and some coal are mined in W area. Agr. is limited to growing of potatoes, soy beans, and millet. Only important center is Sinuiju.

North Queensferry, Scotland: see INVERKEITHING.

North Quincy (kwĭn'sē), village (pop. 2,985), Adams co., W Ill., just N of Quincy.

North Randall, village (pop. 178), Cuyahoga co., N Ohio, a SE suburb of Cleveland.

North Reading (rě'dĭng), agr. town (pop. 4,402), Middlesex co., NE Mass., on Ipswich R. and 15 mi. N of Boston; makes slippers. Settled 1651, inc. 1853. Includes Martins Pond village (pop. 1,109).

North Red Deer, village (pop. 698), S central Alta., N suburb of Red Deer.

North Reddish, England: see REDDISH.

North Redwood, village (pop. 215), Redwood co., SW Minn., on Redwood R. at its mouth on Minnesota R. and just NE of Redwood Falls; corn, oats, barley.

North Regina (rŭjī'nů), village (pop. 682), S Sask., N suburb of Regina.

North Rhine-Westphalia (-wĕstfā'lyů), Ger. *Nordrhein-Westfalen* (nôrt'rīn-vĕstfä'lůn), state (□ 13,157; 1946 pop. 11,735,421, including displaced persons 11,797,092; 1950 pop. 13,147,066), W Germany; ⊙ Düsseldorf. Formed after 1945 through union of former Prussian prov. of WESTPHALIA, the state of LIPPE, and N portion (□ 4,880) of former Prussian RHINE PROVINCE, including Aachen, Cologne, and Düsseldorf. Bounded by Belgium (SW), the Netherlands (W,NW), Lower Saxony (N,E), Hesse (SE), and Rhineland-Palatinate (S). Situated in lower Rhine plain (W) and adjacent lowlands; hilly in SE (Rhenish Slate Mts.); includes the Rothaargebirge (SE) and Teutoburg Forest (E). Drained by Rhine, Ruhr, Wupper (all W), Lippe (E), and Ems (N) rivers. Highly industrialized region with large coal (Ruhr,

Aachen area) and lignite (Brühl, Frechen, Hürth) deposits; iron-ore mining around Siegen, and at Dortmund, Hattingen, Laasphe, and Warstein; lead and zinc mining in SW (Bensberg, Engelskirchen, Gressenich, Marienheide, Mechernich). Heavy industry (steel, chemicals) predominates in the Ruhr (Bochum, Castrop-Rauxel, Duisburg, Dortmund, Düsseldorf, Essen, Hagen, Herne, Lünen, Rheinhausen, Wanne-Eickel, Wattenscheid, Witten). Textile mfg. is concentrated at Krefeld, München Gladbach, Rheydt, Viersen, and Wuppertal; noted Westphalian linen mfg. in N and E (Bielefeld, Bocholt, Emsdetten, Gronau, Rheine). Other important industrial centers are Cologne, Detmold (furniture), Gelsenkirchen (glass, garments), Leverkusen (chemicals), Lüdenscheid (small metal goods), Neuss (food processing), Remscheid (tools), and Stolberg (a center of Ger. brass industry). Canals (Lippe-Lateral, Rhine-Herne, Dortmund-Ems, and Ems-Weser) of the great Mittelland Canal system provide cheap shipping facilities to and from North Sea and Baltic ports; Duisburg, Hagen, and Hamm are important transshipment points. Noted Westphalian ham and pumpernickel processed around Münster and Gütersloh; dairying and truck farming in N and E lowlands. Aachen is world-renowned spa, the Siebengebirge a frequented tourist center. Universities at Bonn, Cologne, and Münster. After capture (1944–45) by British, Canadian, and U.S. troops, the region (it has no historic unity) was constituted into new state of North Rhine-Westphalia in Br. occupation zone. Joined (1949) the German Federal Republic (West German state).

North Richland, village (pop. 3,067), Benton co., S Wash., near Richland.

Northridge or **North Ridge**, suburban section of Los ANGELES city, Los Angeles co., S Calif., in San Fernando Valley, 7 mi. SW of San Fernando.

North Ridgeville, village (1940 pop. 1,138), Lorain co., N Ohio, 18 mi. WSW of downtown Cleveland, in agr. area.

North Riding, administrative division of Yorkshire, England, covering N part of county. See YORK, county.

North River, SW Que., flows 75 mi. S and SW, past Ste. Agathe des Monts, St. Jérôme, and Lachute, to W end of L. of the Two Mountains.

North River, Chinese *Pei Kiang*, *Peh Kiang*, *Pe Kiang*, or *Pei Chiang* (all: bä'jyäng'), Kwangtung prov., China, formed at Kükong by union of Cheng (left) and Wu (right) rivers, flows 200 mi. S, past Yingtak, Tsingyün, and Samshui, to CANTON RIVER DELTA. At Samshui it joins a short arm of the West R. and gives rise to waterways flowing E to form CANTON RIVER. Navigable in entire course. Receives Linchow R. and an arm of Sui R. (right). Formerly, North R. was an important water route bet. S and N China. The name North R. is sometimes also applied to its 2 headstreams.

North River. **1** In W Ala., formed by confluence of 2 headstreams E of Fayette, flows c.70 mi. S to Black Warrior R. NE of Tuscaloosa. **2** In S central Iowa, rises near Menlo in Guthrie co., flows c.70 mi. E, to Des Moines R. 10 mi. SE of Des Moines. **3** In E Mass., rises in N Plymouth co., flows c.25 mi. NE, past Hanover, to Massachusetts Bay c.2 mi. S of Scituate. **4** In NE Mo., rises in Knox co., flows c.70 mi. SE and E to the Mississippi below Quincy, Ill. **5** In N.Y.: see HUDSON RIVER. **6** In Rockbridge co., W Va., formed SE of Goshen by junction of Calfpasture and Maury rivers; flows c.60 mi. generally S through Rockbridge co., past Lexington, to James R. at Glasgow. **7** In NW Va., rises in the Blue Ridge in Rockingham co., flows c.25 mi. generally SE, joining South R. near Port Republic to form South Fork of the Shenandoah. Receives Middle R.

North Riverside, residential village (pop. 3,230), Cook co., NE Ill., W suburb of Chicago. Inc. 1923.

North Robinson, village (pop. 252), Crawford co., N central Ohio, 6 mi. E of Bucyrus; machinery, lumber.

North Ronaldsay, island (pop. 298) of the Orkneys, Scotland, at NE extremity of the group, 3 mi. N of Sanday; 3 mi. long, 2 mi. wide. Sandy, fertile soil. On N tip is lighthouse (59°24'N 2°23'W).

Northrop, village (pop. 157), Martin co., S Minn., near Middle Chain of Lakes, 6 mi. N of Fairmont; dairy products.

North Roswell (rŏz'wŭl), suburb (pop. 1,239) of Roswell, Chaves co., SE N.Mex.

North Royalton, residential village (pop. 3,939), Cuyahoga co., N Ohio, 13 mi. SSW of downtown Cleveland. Inc. 1927.

North Sacramento (săkrŭmĕn'tō), city (pop. 6,029), Sacramento co., central Calif., suburb of Sacramento, across American R. Grant Technical Col. is here. Packed meat, brick, machinery. Inc. 1924.

North Saint Paul, village (pop. 4,248) and NE suburb of St. Paul, Ramsey co., E Minn., in dairying, truck-farming, and poultry area; resort; ice cream, furniture, hardware products. White Bear L. is 3 mi. N.

North Salem (sā'lŭm), town (pop. 544), Hendricks co., central Ind., on a fork of Eel R. and 26 mi. WNW of Indianapolis, in agr. area.

North Salt Lake, village (pop. 255), Davis co., N central Utah, just N of Salt Lake City, near Jordan R. and Great Salt L.; meat packing.

North Santee River, S.C.: see SANTEE RIVER.

North Saskatchewan River, Canada: see SASKATCHEWAN RIVER.

North Schleswig, Denmark: see SCHLESWIG.

North Scituate, Mass.: see SCITUATE.

Norths Coast, part of Wilkes Land, Antarctica, on Indian Ocean; c.127°45'E. Discovered 1840 by Charles Wilkes, U.S. explorer.

North Sea, arm (□ 222,000) of Atlantic Ocean, bet. Great Britain and the European continent, opening N on the Atlantic bet. the Orkney and Shetland isls. and on the Norwegian Sea bet. the Shetlands and Norway, and connected SW by Strait of Dover with English Channel; 600 mi. long (N–S), 400 mi. wide; average depth, 180 ft.; greatest depth, 2,165 ft. off Norway (N). It communicates with the Baltic Sea (E) via the Skagerrak, the Kattegat, and the Danish sounds, as well as by the Kiel Canal. Its N shores are deeply indented (fjords, firths) in Norway and Scotland; its S shores are low and smooth in Denmark, Germany, Netherlands, and Belgium. The sea's submarine topography is characterized by a series of banks rising to within 56 ft. of the surface in the Dogger Bank (S central part). These banks are known for their cod and herring fisheries. Tides enter through the N channel, reach a max. of 13–20 ft. off the English coast, and subside to 6–12 ft. in the German embayment. Its salinity is generally 34–35 per mill, and little ice forms during the winter, except for 15–30-day period in the coastal reaches. The principal North Sea ports—London, Antwerp, Rotterdam, Bremen, Hamburg — are among the greatest in the world. The North Sea was formerly also known as the German Ocean.

North Sea-Baltic Canal, Germany: see KIEL CANAL.

North Sea Canal, Du. *Noordzee Kanaal*, North Holland prov., W Netherlands, extends 18 mi. E–W, bet. the Ij at Amsterdam and North Sea at Ijmuiden; 400–425 ft. wide, 40 ft. deep. Entire length navigable by sea-going ships. Joined by Zaan R. and numerous side canals. Built 1865–76, it made Amsterdam a major seaport. Large sea locks at Ijmuiden destroyed during Second World War; later rebuilt.

North Sewickley (sŭwĭ'klē), village (pop. 1,501, with adjacent Frisco), Beaver co., W Pa., just SE of Ellwood City.

North Sheen, England: see RICHMOND.

North Shields, England: see TYNEMOUTH.

North Skunk River, Iowa: see SKUNK RIVER.

North Smithfield, industrial town (pop. 5,726), Providence co., N R.I., on Mass. line, on Branch R., and 13 mi. NW of Providence; wool and thread processing, textile weaving and finishing. Has several old inns. Includes villages of Forestdale and Slatersville (pop. 1,780; administrative center). Inc. 1871.

North Stack, Wales: see HOLYHEAD.

North Star, village (pop. 166), Darke co., W Ohio, 22 mi. NW of Piqua.

North Star Lake or **Potato Lake**, Itasca co., N central Minn., in state forest, 22 mi. N of Grand Rapids; 3 mi. long, 1 mi. wide. Fishing, boating, bathing resorts.

North Stonington (stō'nĭngtŭn), farming town (pop. 1,367), New London co., SE Conn., on R.I. line, 12 mi. SE of Norwich. State forest here. Settled before 1700, inc. 1807.

North Stradbroke Island (□ 123), in Pacific Ocean, just off SE coast of Queensland, Australia, S of Moreton Isl.; forms E shore of Moreton Bay; 24.5 mi. long, 7 mi. wide; rises to 700 ft. Sandy; hardwood timber. Sometimes called Stradbroke Isl.

North Stratford, N.H.: see STRATFORD.

North Sulphur Island, Volcano Isls.: see KITA-IWO-JIMA.

North Swansea, Mass.: see SWANSEA.

North Sydney, municipality (pop. 60,379), E New South Wales, Australia, ½ mi. N of Sydney, on N shore of Port Jackson, across Sydney Harbour Bridge; mfg. center (clothing factories, knitting mills); shipyards.

North Sydney, town (pop. 6,836), E N.S., on E Cape Breton Isl., on W side of Sydney Harbour, 6 mi. NW of Sydney; coal-shipping port for near-by Sydney Mines. Terminal of mail ships to Port aux Basques, Newfoundland. Winter base of Cape Breton fisheries; site of cable station.

North Syracuse (sĭ'rŭkūs, sĕ'–), village (pop. 3,356), Onondaga co., central N.Y., 6 mi. N of Syracuse, in agr. area; plating works; nurseries. Inc. 1925.

North Taranaki Bight (tă"rŭnă'kē), Tasman Sea, W N.Isl., New Zealand, separated from S.Taranaki Bight by Cape Egmont. Receives Mokau R. Near S extremity is New Plymouth.

North Tarryall Peak, Colo.: see TARRYALL MOUNTAINS.

North Tarrytown (tă'rētoun), residential village (pop. 8,740), Westchester co., SE N.Y., on E bank of the Hudson, just N of Tarrytown; mfg. (electrical products, automobiles). Castle Philipse (c.1683) of PHILIPSE MANOR has collections relating to Washington Irving and John D. Rockefeller, Sr. Here at Sleepy Hollow is old Dutch Reformed Church (c.1697) and cemetery. Capture here of the British spy John André revealed Benedict Arnold's treachery. Inc. 1875.

North Tawton, town and parish (pop. 1,280), central Devon, England, on Taw R. and 7 mi. NE of Okehampton; agr. market town; scene of annual horse and cattle fair. Has 13th-cent. church and many old houses.

North Tazewell (tăz'wŭl), town (pop. 816), Tazewell co., SW Va., in the Alleghenies, just N of Tazewell, 19 mi. WSW of Bluefield, in coal-mining and agr. area; lumber.

North Texarkana (tĕk"särkă'nŭ), city (pop. 1,328), Bowie co., NE Texas, suburb of Texarkana. Inc. after 1940.

North Thompson River, B.C.: see THOMPSON RIVER.

North Tidworth, town and parish (pop. 2,771), E Wiltshire, England, 13 mi. NNE of Salisbury; agr. market; important military center (usually called Tidworth). Has 15th-cent. church.

North Tisbury, Mass.: see WEST TISBURY.

North Tiverton, R.I.: see TIVERTON.

North Tonawanda (tŏnŭwŏn'dŭ), industrial city and lumber port (pop. 24,731), Niagara co., W N.Y., on Niagara R. at mouth of Tonawanda Creek, and 10 mi. N of Buffalo; W terminus of the Barge Canal. Mfg. of iron and steel products, boats, paper, musical instruments, radios, toys; stone, metal, and wood products; chemicals, airplanes, spark plugs; oil refining. Settled 1808; inc. as village in 1865, as city in 1897.

North Toronto (tŭrŏn'tō), N suburb of Toronto, S Ont.; merged with Toronto 1912.

North Troy, Vt.: see TROY.

North Truchas Peak, N.Mex.: see **TRUCHAS, peak.**

North Truro, Mass.: see TRURO.

North Turlock (tûr'lŏk), village (pop. 1,586), Stanislaus co., central Calif., near Turlock.

North Turtle Lake, Otter Tail co., W Minn., 10 mi. E of Fergus Falls; 6 mi. long, 1 mi. wide. Village of Underwood is at W end of lake.

North Twin Lake (□ 15.5), central N.F., 25 mi. WNW of Botwood; 8 mi. long, 4 mi. wide. Drains into Exploits R.

North Twin Lake, Vilas co., N Wis., 7 mi. NE of Eagle River city; c.5 mi. long, 1½ mi. wide. Phelps is on NE shore.

North Twin Mountain, N.H.: see FRANCONIA MOUNTAINS.

North Tyne River, England: see TYNE RIVER.

North Tyrol Alps, Austria: see BAVARIAN ALPS.

North Ubian Island (ōōbyän') (□ 6.5; 1939 pop. 844), Sulu prov., Philippines, in Pangutaran Group of Sulu Archipelago, 30 mi. WNW of Jolo Isl.

North Uist (yōō'ĭst, ōō'ĭst), island (pop. 2,349) and parish (□ 118; pop. 2,827, including surrounding small isls.), Outer Hebrides, Inverness, Scotland, bet. Benbecula (S) and Harris (N), separated from NW Skye by the Little Minch (15 mi. wide here). Isl. is 17 mi. long, 13 mi. wide; rises to 1,138 ft. in Mt. Eaval (SE). E part is hilly and boggy; there is fertile land in W, where crofting, chief occupation, is carried on. Fishing is also important. Coastline is indented, especially on E coast, where are inlets of Loch Maddy and Loch Eport. Lochmaddy, the chief town, is fishing port at head of Loch Maddy (5 mi. long), on NE coast of isl. At entrance to Loch Maddy is promontory of Weaver's Point, site of lighthouse (57°34'N 6°58'W). The term The Uists is sometimes used to include North and SOUTH UIST and BENBECULA.

Northumberland (nôr-thŭm'bŭrlŭnd). **1** County (□ 4,671; pop. 38,485), N central N.B., on the Gulf of St. Lawrence; ⊙ Newcastle. **2** County (□ 734; pop. 30,786), S Ont., on L. Ontario and on Rice L.; ⊙ Cobourg.

Northumberland, county (□ 2,018.7; 1931 pop. 756,782; 1951 census 798,175), most northerly co. of England, on Scottish border; ⊙ Newcastle-upon-Tyne. Bounded N by Scottish cos. of Roxburgh and Berwick, across Cheviot Hills and the Tweed; W by Cumberland, S by Durham, E by the North Sea. Drained by Tyne, Blyth, Aln, Coquet, and Till rivers. There are extensive coal deposits; lead and zinc are also mined. Heavy industry (including shipbuilding) is concentrated in the Tyneside area (SE) and metal-mfg. towns and ports of Newcastle, Wallsend, and Tynemouth. Other important towns are Berwick-on-Tweed, Blyth, Whitley and Monkseaton, Morpeth, Prudhoe, and Hexham. Co. includes Farne Isls. and Holy Isl. Northumberland formed part of the kingdom of Bernicia in Saxon times; later was included in the kingdom of Northumbria, from which its name derives. Its location on Scottish border made it scene of many border wars and disputes.

Northumberland. **1** County (□ 454; pop. 117,115), E central Pa.; ⊙ Sunbury. Anthracite-mining region; drained by Susquehanna R. and its West Branch, joining at Northumberland; mountainous in S. Anthracite; textiles, metal products, food products, beverages, crushed stone; agr. (truck, grain, poultry, livestock, dairy products). Formed 1772. **2** County (□ 200; pop. 10,012), E Va.; ⊙ Heathsville. On NE shore (Potomac R.) of Northern Neck peninsula; bounded by Chesapeake Bay (E); coast has many bays and inlets. Reedville (fish-processing center) is a port. Mainly agr. (grain, potatoes, truck, especially tomatoes; tobacco); livestock, poultry. Shore resorts (fishing, bathing). Oystering. Formed 1648.

Northumberland. **1** Town (pop. 2,779), Coos co., NW N.H., on the Connecticut just above Lancaster, at mouth of Upper Ammonoosuc R.; paper milling in its villages of Northumberland and Groveton (pop. 1,918). Settled 1767, inc. 1779. **2** Borough (pop. 4,207), Northumberland co., E central Pa., on Susquehanna R. just above Sunbury, at mouth of its West Branch. Mfg. (metal products, textiles), canning; coal dredging; railroad shops. Dr. Joseph Priestley lived here 1794–1804. Laid out c.1775, inc. 1828.

Northumberland, Cape, SE Alaska, S extremity of Duke Isl., 35 mi. SSE of Ketchikan; 54°52′N 131°21′W.

Northumberland, Cape, extreme SE South Australia, in Indian Ocean; forms W end of Discovery Bay (site of Port MacDonnell); 38°4′S 140°40′E.

Northumberland Islands, coral group in Coral Sea, bet. Great Barrier Reef and Shoalwater Bay, off E coast of Queensland, Australia. Comprise 80-mi. chain of 40 rocky isls. and scattered islets; largest, Prudhoe Isl. (2.3 mi. long, 1 mi. wide; rising to 1,074 ft.); generally wooded. Tourist resorts.

Northumberland Strait, channel of the Gulf of St. Lawrence, separating P.E.I. from N.B. and N.S.; 200 mi. long, 9–30 mi. wide.

Northumbria (nôrthŭm′brēŭ), kingdom of the Anglo-Saxon Heptarchy, formed by union of 2 kingdoms: Bernicia (including E Scotland, E Northumberland, and Durham co.) and Deira (including N and E Ridings of Yorkshire), both settled (c.500) by invading Angles. Æthelfrith of Bernicia (593–617) united both kingdoms; he was displaced by Edwin of Deira (617–33), who accepted (627) Roman Christianity and established Northumbrian supremacy in England. Christianity was introduced in late 7th cent., and in 8th and 9th cent. arts, learning, and literature flourished, but political discord was rife. Culture was wrecked by invading Danes after their victory (867) at York. They occupied S part of kingdom; English only kept region from the Tees N to the Firth of Forth and acknowledged (920) Edward the Elder of Wessex as overking.

North Utica (ū′tĭkŭ), village (pop. 985), La Salle co., N Ill., on Illinois R. and 8 mi. W of Ottawa, in agr. and bituminous-coal area. Inc. 1869. Also called Utica.

Northvale, borough (pop. 1,455), Bergen co., extreme NE N.J., 13 mi. NE of Paterson, at N.Y. line; makes artificial flowers, dresses. Inc. 1916.

North Valley Stream, residential village (1940 pop. 1,090), Nassau co., SE N.Y., on W Long Isl., just N of Valley Stream.

North Vancouver (vănkōō′vûr), city (pop. 8,914), SW B.C., on N side of Burrard Inlet of Strait of Georgia, opposite Vancouver (bridge, ferry); 49° 19′N 123°3′W; fishing base and seaport, with large drydock; shipbuilding, lumbering, woodworking; mfg. of electrical equipment, soap, umbrellas. Center of quarrying (granite, gravel, sand) region.

North Vandergrift, village (pop. 1,878), Armstrong co., W Pa., on Kiskiminetas R. opposite Vandergrift.

North Vernon (vûr′nŭn), city (pop. 3,488), Jennings co., SE Ind., on small Vernon Creek and 24 mi. NW of Madison; railroad and farm-trading center; furniture, lumber, household appliances, auto parts. Timber; limestone quarries. Platted 1854. Muscatatuck State Park is near by.

Northville. **1** Village (pop. 3,240), Wayne and Oakland counties, SE Mich., 23 mi. NW of Detroit, in diversified farm area; mfg. (auto parts, furnaces, furniture). Two tuberculosis sanatoriums and a U.S. fish hatchery are near by. Inc. 1867. **2** Resort village (pop. 1,114), Fulton co., E central N.Y., on NW arm of Sacandaga Reservoir, 15 mi. NE of Gloversville; leather gloves, lumber, wood products. Inc. 1873. **3** Village (pop. c.600), Suffolk co., SE N.Y., on NE Long Isl., 4 mi. NE of Riverhead, in summer-resort area; mfg. of machinery. **4** City (pop. 220), Spink co., NE central S.Dak., 20 mi. N of Redfield and on Snake Creek; trading point for agr. area.

North Vineland, village (pop. 1,013), Cumberland co., S N.J., 3 mi. N of Vineland.

North Virginia Beach, village (pop. 1,593), Princess Anne co., SE Va., near Virginia Beach.

North Vizagapatam, India: see VIZAGAPATAM, dist.

North Wales, borough (pop. 2,998), Montgomery co., SE Pa., 19 mi. NNW of Philadelphia; textiles, pottery, metal and paper products, asbestos; agr. Settled 1850, laid out 1867, inc. 1869.

North Walpole, N.H.: see WALPOLE.

North Walsham (wôl′shŭm), urban district (1931 pop. 4,137; 1951 census 4,733), NE Norfolk, England, 14 mi. NNE of Norwich; agr. market, with agr.-machinery works. Has 14th-cent. church, remains of a Saxon church tower, and 16th-cent. grammar school, attended by Lord Nelson. Wool-weaving industry was important in Middle Ages.

North Warren, residential village (1940 pop. 887), Warren co., NW Pa., on Conewango Creek, just N of Warren.

North Washington, town (pop. 159), Chickasaw co., NE Iowa, 14 mi. ENE of Charles City.

Northway, village (pop. 112), E Alaska, near Yukon border, on Nabesna R. and 110 mi. SW of Dawson; 62°57′N 141°57′W; air base; radio station.

North Waziristan, W Pakistan: see WAZIRISTAN.

North Weald Bassett (wēld), residential town and parish (pop. 1,642), W Essex, England, 3 mi. N of Epping.

North Webster, town (pop. 487), Kosciusko co., N Ind., c.40 mi. SE of South Bend, in agr. area.

Northwest Angle, Minn.: see LAKE OF THE WOODS.

Northwest Cape, NW Western Australia, in Indian Ocean, on peninsula forming W shore of Exmouth Gulf; 21°47′S 114°10′E.

North Westchester, Conn.: see COLCHESTER.

North West District (□ 8,507; pop. 6,358), NW Br. Guiana, on the Atlantic, bordering W on Venezuela; ⊙ Mabaruma. The NW section of Essequibo co., it is watered by gold-bearing Barima and Barama rivers and includes the inland landing of Morawhanna.

North Western Canal, irrigation canal of SUKKUR BARRAGE system, N Sind, W Pakistan; from right bank of Indus R. at Sukkur runs c.120 mi. W., through Sukkur and SW Sibi (Baluchistan) dists. Distributaries take off S. Waters crops of wheat, millet, gram.

North Western Province, administrative division (□ 3,016; pop., including estate pop., 668,000), W Ceylon; ⊙ Kurunegala. Bounded W by Indian Ocean and Gulf of Mannar; mainly lowland, with W foothills of Ceylon Hill Country in SE; drained by the Deduru Oya. Largely agr. (coconut palms, rice, vegetables, cacao, rubber, fruit, tobacco). Important govt. salterns (Puttalam, Palavi); graphite mines (Dodangaslanda, Ragedara). Land-reclamation project at Tobbowa. Main towns: Kurunegala, Puttalam, Chilaw. Archaeological remains at Yapahuwa and Dambadeniya; Ceylonese Christian pilgrimage center at St. Anna's Church. Created 1844.

North-Western Provinces, name given to former British presidency of Agra, now part of Uttar Pradesh, India. Created 1833 partly out of Mogul empire's AGRA PROVINCE; named North-Western Provinces in 1835.

Northwest Fork of Nanticoke River, Del. and Md.: see MARSHYHOPE CREEK.

North-West Frontier Province, province (□ 13,815; 1951 pop. 3,239,000; with tribal areas and princely states: □ 41,057; 1951 pop. 5,699,000) of W Pakistan; ⊙ Peshawar. On N and W is Afghanistan, on S Baluchistan, on E Punjab, on NE Kashmir; Indus R. forms part of E boundary. Crossed N by E Hindu Kush, NE by W Punjab Himalayas, W by N Sulaiman Range and Safed Koh Range. Aside from Derejat plain (SE) and Kabul and Kurram river basins (E), area is mostly mountainous, with several notable peaks, including Tirich Mir (N; 25,263 ft.), Sikaram (W; 15,620 ft.), and Takht-i-Sulaiman (S; 11,290 ft.). On W borders are noted Khyber and Gumal passes. Annual rainfall, 10–30 in. Agr. (wheat, corn, barley, millet, sugar cane) and livestock raising (sheep, goats, mules) are principal occupations; also some fruitgrowing (apricots, peaches, apples, pomegranates). Little mfg.; mainly handicraft cloth weaving, mat and basket making, leather- and metalworking; large sugar factory at Mardan. Exports grain, wool, ghee, hides, timber (deodar from N forests), and fruit; important caravan trade via KHYBER PASS. Mineral resources include rock salt from Kohat hills (center), gypsum, marble, limestone, antimony (Chitral), and lead. Hydroelectric works at Dargai and Warsak; Swat R. tapped for irrigation. Main centers: PESHAWAR, Nowshera, Dera Ismail Khan, Kohat, Bannu, Mardan, Abbottabad. Pakistan Military Acad. at Kakul. Early history of region was dominated by Iranians; anc. prov. of Gandhara (around present Peshawar) was inc. c.500 B.C. into Persian empire. Alexander the Great invaded NW India in 327 B.C., but by next century whole area was under Asokan empire (rock edicts near Mansahra and Mardan) and Buddhism became dominant religion. After short rule by Bactrian Greeks, Peshawar was center of strong Kushan kingdom (1st cent. B.C.–2d cent. A.D.). Mahmud of Ghazni raided India several times bet. 1001 and 1025 via the NW frontier; subsequent Moslem invaders were Muhammad of Ghor (1179), Genghiz Khan (early-13th cent.), Tamerlane (1398), and Baber (1505). In 16th and 17th cent., local Afghan tribes became powerful and engaged Mogul rulers of India in bitter conflict. Nadir Shah crossed frontier in 1738, followed by Ahmad Shah Durrani, who defeated Mahrattas at Panipat in 1761. Sikhs held control from 1818 to 1849, when British annexed area as part of the Punjab. Repeated disturbances among Pathan tribes led to Br. retaliatory measures and several shifts in administrative policy. Durand Line, which demarcates boundary with Afghanistan bet. Mt. Sikaram and Gumal Pass, was drawn in 1894. Area separated 1901 from Punjab and created a chief commissioner's prov.; made governor's prov. in 1932; part of Pakistan since 1947. Comprises 6 dists.: Bannu, Dera Ismail Khan, Hazara, Kohat, Mardan, Peshawar. Tribal agencies of Malakand (includes Dir, Swat, and Chitral states), Khyber, Kurram, North Waziristan, and South Waziristan lie within borders but are administered separately by Pakistan govt. Pop., which is 95% Moslem, 4% Hindu, and 1% Sikh, speaks mainly Pushtu. Chief tribes: Afridi, Mohmand, Waziri, Orakzai, Utman Khel. Commonly called the Frontier Prov.

Northwest Gander River, central N.F., headstream of GANDER RIVER.

North Westminster, Vt.: see WESTMINSTER.

Northwest Passage, the sea passage through the Arctic Archipelago of Canada, bet. the Atlantic and the Pacific. Southernmost route runs from the Atlantic via Davis Strait, Hudson Strait, Foxe Channel, Foxe Basin, Fury and Hecla Strait, the Gulf of Boothia, Prince Regent Inlet, Bellot Strait, Franklin Strait, Victoria Strait, Queen Maud Gulf, Dease Strait, Coronation Gulf, Dolphin and Union Strait, and Amundsen Gulf, to Beaufort Sea of the Arctic Ocean, thence to the Pacific. N of this is a passage via Baffin Bay, Lancaster Sound, Barrow Strait, Viscount Melville Sound, and McClure Strait. Northernmost route extends from N Baffin Bay, through Jones Sound, Norwegian Bay, and Belcher Channel, thence either through Maclean Strait and Prince Gustav Adolph Sea, or through Hazen Strait and Ballantyne Strait. These routes are interconnected by numerous N–S passages, providing for alternative routing. Through navigation is extremely difficult and only possible under very favorable circumstances; the various straits are rarely ice-free. E approaches to Northwest Passage were 1st explored by Frobisher, who reached S Baffin Isl., 1576, and again 1577 and 1578. Davis also reached Baffin Isl., 1585–87. Henry Hudson discovered Hudson Bay (1610) while searching for the passage. William Baffin discovered Baffin Bay (1616) aboard the *Discovery*, but decided that no E–W passage existed. Luke Foxe and Thomas James further explored Hudson Bay (1631–32). Samuel Hearne reached Coppermine R. overland, 1772, and an expedition under C. J. Phipps attempted the passage in 1773. Many noted 19th-cent. explorers charted the region or tried to complete a crossing; Sir John Ross rediscovered Baffin Bay, 1818. Sir William Parry reached Melville Isl. (1819–20) and Fury and Hecla Strait (1821–23), and visited Prince Regent Inlet, 1824–25. Sir John Franklin's expedition aboard the *Erebus* and *Terror* (1847–48) was lost on King William Isl. Robert J. Le M. McClure penetrated the passage from W aboard the *Investigator* and reached Viscount Melville Sound by land expedition; this, together with Parry's earlier approach from the E, proved the existence of a through passage. Other explorers who added to knowledge of various waterways of the passage were David Buchan, Joseph Bellet, F. W. Beechey, Sir George Back (who reached Great Fish R., now Back R.), and Sir Thomas Simpson. 1st successful voyage through Northwest Passage was made (1903–06) by Roald Amundsen aboard the *Gjoa*, through Lancaster Sound, along Boothia Peninsula, and thence along the S route.

North West Point, cape in Hanover parish, NW Jamaica, 19 mi. W of Montego Bay; 18°28′N 78°14′W.

North Westport, Mass.: see WESTPORT.

Northwest Providence Channel, Bahama Isls., just E of West Palm Beach, Fla., bet. Little Bahama Bank (N) and Great Bahama Bank (S); c.130 mi. long WNW–ESE, linking Straits of Florida (W) with Northeast Providence Channel (E).

North West River, village (pop. 341), SE Labrador, at W end of L. Melville, at mouth of Naskaupi R., 10 mi. NE of Goose Bay; lumbering.

Northwest Territories, region and administrative unit (land area □ 1,253,438, total □ 1,304,903; 1941 pop. 12,028; 1948 estimate 16,000) of N Canada, extending N from 60°N to the Arctic Ocean, bounded by Davis Strait and Baffin Bay (E and NE), Hudson Strait and Hudson Bay (SE), Man., Sask., Alta., and B.C. (S), and the Yukon (W). It also includes all isls. in Hudson, James, and Ungava bays and in Hudson Strait, and isls. bet. Canadian mainland and the North Pole. Administrative divisions are the provisional districts of MACKENZIE (SW), KEEWATIN (SE), and FRANKLIN (N). In W part of mainland section are the Mackenzie Mts., N range of the Rocky Mts., rising to 9,049 ft. on Mt. Sir James McBrien. Mackenzie R. valley and plain bet. Great Bear and Great Slave lakes lie E of mts., continued E by 350-mi.-wide plateau. Toward E coast of Hudson Bay terrain is low and level, dotted with numerous lakes; bet. Chesterfield Inlet and Boothia and Melville peninsulas lies another extensive plateau. S part of the Northwest Territories is covered by the BARREN GROUNDS, extensive arctic prairie region. Mainland section is drained by Mackenzie, Arctic Red, Great Bear, Liard, Hay, Slave, Coppermine, Anderson, Thelon, Kazan, and Dubawnt rivers; largest of the numerous lakes are Great Bear, Great Slave, Dubawnt, Garry, Baker, Yathkyed, Maguse, Aberdeen, and Nueltin lakes. Consisting mainly of wasteland, the region until recently yielded only large quantities of furs. Mineral development began in 1934, when gold deposits were discovered in Yellowknife region. Oil was struck at Norman Wells and a refinery erected here. Copper deposits near Coppermine are not worked because of transportation difficulties. Pitchblende deposits were discovered on E shore of Great Bear L., and Port Radium settlement was established here. Subsequently this region became important uranium supply source. The Arctic Archipelago extends to within 500 mi. of the North Pole; largest isls. are Baffin, Victoria, Ellesmere, Devon, Melville, Prince of Wales (location of magnetic north pole, 1948; 73°N 100°W), Axel Heiberg, and Somerset isls. Hunting of fur-bearing animals is chief occupation of native Eskimos in the isls. Numerous U.S.-Canadian meteorological stations have been established here, as well as air bases at Frobisher Bay, on Padloping Isl., and on Southampton Isl. Yellowknife is largest town of Northwest Territories; principal mainland trading posts are Fort Smith, Hay River, Fort Resolution, Reliance, Fort Providence, Fort Simpson, Wrigley, Fort Norman, Norman Wells, Fort Franklin, Fort Good Hope, Arctic Red River, Aklavik, Port Brabant, Chesterfield Inlet, Eskimo Point, and Baker Lake. Main trading posts in the Arctic Archipelago are Cambridge Bay on Victoria Isl.; Peterson Bay on King William Isl.; Fort Ross on Somerset Isl.; Lake Harbour, Frobisher Bay, Pangnirtung, River Clyde, Pond Inlet, and Arctic Bay on Baffin Isl.; Dundas Harbour on Devon Isl.; and Craig Harbour on Ellesmere Isl. There are extensive game reserves on mainland; the Arctic Archipelago constitutes a game reserve in its entirety. In SW part of Territories is N part of Wood Buffalo Natl. Park. Mainland climate is humid and continental, with very cold winters and comparatively warm summers; isls. have Arctic climate. Representative temp. ranges (Jan. and July) are; Fort Smith, −16°F., 60°F.; Fort Good Hope, −24°F., 46°F.; Craig Harbour, −22°F., 40°F.; and Fort Conger, −40°F., 37°F. Precipitation in Mackenzie R. valley is 10–13 inches annually, with 40–50 inches of snow; in the Arctic Isls. it averages 6–9 inches, mostly falling as snow. Trading posts on the isls. are visited annually by Hudson's Bay Co. supply steamer. Air transportation is used extensively. Territorial govt. consists of Commissioner of the Northwest Territories, a deputy commissioner, and 5 councillors, sitting at Ottawa; administrative hq. are at Fort Smith. Law enforcement is in hands of Royal Canadian Mounted Police. Designation of Northwest Territories was given to Hudson's Bay Co. territory (Rupert's Land and North West Territory) when it was acquired by Canada, 1870; area then included Man. (became prov. in same year), Sask. and Alta. (became provs. 1905), and parts of B.C. and Que.; Territory was organized under Northwest Territories Act, 1875; many border changes were made subsequently. Present form of administration was adopted 1905, and S border of 60°N was established 1912, when Ungava Peninsula was annexed to Que. Oil pipeline (closed 1945), from Norman Wells to Whitehorse, Yukon, was part of Canol project.

Northwest Territory, region awarded to the U.S. by the Treaty of Paris (1783), extending S from the Great Lakes to Ohio R. and W from Pa. line to the Mississippi. The 1st natl. territory of the U.S., established by Congress in Ordinance of 1787, it encompassed present states of OHIO, INDIANA, ILLINOIS, MICHIGAN, WISCONSIN, and part of MINNESOTA. Parts were claimed by Mass., Conn., N.Y., and Va., but these states had ceded their preserves to Federal govt. by 1786, except for the Conn. WESTERN RESERVE and Va. Military Dist. First settlement in the organized territory was MARIETTA, Ohio (1788). In 1800 W portion split off as Indiana Territory. By 1803 most of E portion was sufficiently populous to be admitted as a state (Ohio). Region was area of international dispute from early 17th cent. French claims were surrendered to the British at close of the French and Indian War (1763). Even after the Revolution unrest among the Indians and dissatisfaction of British fur traders persisted, and contributed to outbreak of War of 1812. Only with Treaty of Ghent (1814) was problem closed. Region, plus a little territory further W, has been generally known since 1803 as the Old Northwest to distinguish it from NW part of present U.S.

Northwest Vineland, village (pop. 3,827), Cumberland co., S N.J., near Vineland.

North Weymouth, Mass.: see WEYMOUTH.

Northwich (-wĭch), urban district (1931 pop. 18,732; 1951 census 17,480), N central Cheshire, England, on Weaver R. at mouth of Dane R., and 16 mi. ENE of Chester; long the center of England's salt industry; chemical engineering. Has salt mus. and library. Because of brine pumping, the town's soil is constantly subsiding. Northwich was site of a Roman station.

North Wilbraham, Mass.: see WILBRAHAM.

North Wildwood, resort city (pop. 3,158), Cape May co., S N.J., on barrier isl. (bridged to mainland) off Cape May Peninsula and 32 mi. SW of Atlantic City; ships seafood. Inc. 1917.

North Wilkesboro (wĭlks'bŭrō), town (pop. 4,379), Wilkes co., NW N.C., 50 mi. W of Winston-Salem and on Yadkin R.; poultry market; mfg. center (furniture, caskets, mirrors, hosiery, yarn, foundry products, leather goods); sawmilling. Founded 1890; inc. 1891.

North Windham, Conn.: see WINDHAM, town.

North Wingfield, town and parish (pop. 6,086), NE Derby, England, 4 mi. SE of Chesterfield; coal-mining center. Has 14th–15th-cent. church.

Northwood. 1 Agr. village and parish (pop. 1,517), on Isle of Wight, Hampshire, England, 2 mi. S of Cowes. Church dates from 13th cent. **2** Suburb, Middlesex, England: see RUISLIP NORTHWOOD.

Northwood. 1 Town (pop. 1,767), ⊙ Worth co., N Iowa, near Minn. line, on Shell Rock R. and 20 mi. N of Mason City; dairy products, insecticides. Settled 1853, inc. 1875. **2** Town (pop. 966), Rockingham co., SE N.H., 15 mi. W of Dover. Formerly a shoe-mfg. center. **3** City (pop. 1,182), Grand Forks co., E N.Dak., 28 mi. SW of Grand Forks; dairy products, wheat, flax, potatoes. Inc. 1892.

Northwoods, town (pop. 1,602), St. Louis co., E Mo., W of St. Louis. Inc. 1939.

North Woodstock, N.H.: see WOODSTOCK.

Northwye (nôrth'wī"), town (pop. 99), Phelps co., central Mo., in the Ozarks, just N of Rolla.

North Yarmouth (yär'mŭth), town (pop. 942), Cumberland co., SW Maine, on Royal R. and 15 mi. NNE of Portland; wood products. Inc. 1680, Yarmouth set off 1849.

North York, borough (pop. 2,445), York co., S Pa., just N of York.

North Zanesville, village (pop. 1,544), Muskingum co., SE central Ohio.

North Zulch, village (pop. c.400), Madison co., E central Texas, 22 mi. NE of Bryan, near Navasota R.; rail point in agr. area.

Norton, village, Central Prov., Ceylon, on Hatton Plateau, on right headstream of the Kelani Ganga and 5 mi. WNW of Hatton. Dam site for hydroelectric project.

Norton. 1 Residential town and parish (pop. 2,308), N Derby, England, 3 mi. S of Sheffield. **2** Suburb, Durham, England: see STOCKTON-ON-TEES. **3** Urban district (1931 pop. 3,935; 1951 census 4,814), East Riding, E Yorkshire, England, on Derwent R. just SE of Malton; steel milling. Race-horse training center.

Norton, township (pop. 1,164), Salisbury prov., central Southern Rhodesia, in Mashonaland, on railroad and 40 mi. NE of Hartley; alt. 4,499 ft. Tobacco, cotton, peanuts, citrus fruit, dairy.

Norton, county (□ 880; pop. 8,808), NW Kansas; ⊙ Norton. Rolling plain region, bordering N on Nebr.; watered by Prairie Dog Creek and North Fork Solomon R. Grain, livestock. Formed 1872.

Norton. 1 City (pop. 3,060), ⊙ Norton co., NW Kansas, on Prairie Dog Creek and c.70 mi. NNW of Hays; processing center for agr. region; flour milling, dairying, poultry and egg packing. Silica mines in vicinity. State tuberculosis sanitarium near by. Inc. 1885. **2** Town (pop. 4,401), Bristol co., SE Mass., 11 mi. SW of Brockton; dyeing, bleaching, wool finishing; wooden and paper boxes, jewelry, atomizers; turkeys. Wheaton Col., House in the Pines School here. Settled 1669, set off from Taunton 1711. **3** Town (pop. 279), Essex co., NE Vt., on Que. line, 21 mi. ENE of Newport; port of entry. Norton L. (c.3 mi. long; fishing) is S. **4** Town (pop. 4,315), Wise co., SW Va., in the Cumberlands, 9 mi. NE of Big Stone Gap. Trade, processing and shipping center in bituminous-coal and agr. area; coke works; lumber. Settled 1787; inc. 1894.

Norton Air Force Base, Calif.: see SAN BERNARDINO, city.

Norton Bay, W Alaska, NE arm (30 mi. long, 20 mi. wide) of Norton Sound, on S side of base of Seward Peninsula; 64°40'N 161°27'W; receives Koyuk R.

Norton Radstock, urban district (1931 pop. 11,112; 1951 census 11,934), NE Somerset, England. Includes coal-mining town of Radstock (pop. 3,622), 8 mi. SW of Bath, center of Somerset mining area and also agr. market; and (W) coal-mining town of Midsomer Norton (pop. 7,490), with paper and shoe industries.

Norton Sound, W Alaska, arm (130 mi. long, 90 mi. wide at mouth) of Bering Sea, on S shore of Seward Peninsula; 63°16'–64°55'N 160°45'–165°W. Norton Bay is NE arm. Nome city on N side of entrance of sound. Open to navigation May–Oct.

Nortonville. 1 City (pop. 568), Jefferson co., NE Kansas, 15 mi. SW of Atchison; shipping point in grain, dairy, and poultry area. **2** Town (pop. 909), Hopkins co., W Ky., 10 mi. SSE of Madisonville; coal mining, lumber milling.

Nortorf (nôr'tôrf), town (pop. 6,047), in Schleswig-Holstein, NW Germany, 14 mi. SW of Kiel; mfg. (shoes, leather goods, dried vegetables).

Nort-sur-Erdre (nôr-sür-âr'drū), town (pop. 2,066), Loire-Inférieure dept., W France, on Erdre R. and 16 mi. N of Nantes; tanning, shoe mfg., flour milling. Slate quarries (E).

Norusovo, Russian SFSR: see KALININO, Chuvash Autonomous SSR.

Norvell (nôr'vŭl), town (pop. 372), Crittenden co., E Ark., 3 mi. NW of Earle, near small Tyronza R.

Norvelt, village (pop. 2,155, with adjacent Calumet), Westmoreland co., SW Pa., 7 mi. SSE of Greensburg.

Norwalk (nôr'wôk"). **1** Unincorporated town (1940 pop. 3,749), Los Angeles co., S Calif., 14 mi. SE of Los Angeles; oil refining. State psychopathic hosp. here. **2** City (pop. 49,460), coextensive with Norwalk town, Fairfield co., SW Conn., on Long Isl. Sound, at mouth of Norwalk R., and 13 mi. SW of Bridgeport. Mfg. (hats, hardware, machinery, textiles, rubber, plastic, paper, and glass products, chemicals, clothing, food products); seafood; shore resorts. Seat of St. Mary's Seminary. Includes South Norwalk (railroad junction and mfg. center), villages of Winnipauk, Rowayton, and Silvermine (an artists' colony), several offshore isls. Settled 1649, town inc. 1651, city inc. 1893, South Norwalk and other communities annexed 1913. Burned by British in Revolution; industrial since late 18th cent. **3** Town (pop. 435), Warren co., S central Iowa, near North R., 9 mi. S of Des Moines, in agr. and bituminous-coal area; corn chips. **4** City (pop. 9,775), ⊙ Huron co., N Ohio, 15 mi. SSE of Sandusky, in agr. area (fruit, truck); wood products, rubber goods, canned foods. Founded 1816. **5** Village (pop. 519), Monroe co., W central Wis., on a branch of Kickapoo R. and 30 mi. E of La Crosse, in farm and dairy area.

Norwalk River (nôr'wôk"), SW Conn., rises just E of Ridgefield, flows N, then S, past Georgetown and Wilton, to Long Isl. Sound at Norwalk; c.30 mi. long.

Norway, Nor. *Norge* (nôr'gù), kingdom (□ 119,240; with water area □ 125,182; pop. 3,156,950), N Europe; ⊙ OSLO. Occupies narrow mountainous strip in W part of Scandinavian peninsula; bounded by the Skagerrak (S), the North Sea and the Norwegian Sea of the Atlantic (W), Barents Sea of the Arctic Ocean (N), USSR and Finland (NE), and Sweden (E), with which it has 1,030-mi.-long land frontier. Its greatest length, bet. Lindesnes (S) and North Cape (N) is c.1,100 mi. Coast line (c.2,100 mi. long) is deeply indented by numerous fjords; largest and best-known are Sogne, Hardanger, Oslo, Nord, Trondheim, Ofot, Lyng, Porsanger, and Varanger fjords. Coast is protected by many isls.; largest and economically most important are LOFOTEN ISLANDS and VESTERALEN group (fishing centers). From the coast, surface rises, generally precipitously, to high plateaus (DOVREFJELL, HARDANGERFJELL, and HARDANGERVIDDA) and mtn. ranges. In Jotunheim Mts. are Norway's highest peaks, Galdhoppigen (8,097 ft.) and Glittertind (8,048 ft.); W of this range is JOSTEDALSBRE, largest ice field in Europe. Mts. on Swedish border rise to 6,279 ft. in Sulitjelma range (copper-pyrite mines at foot). Ranges and plateaus are cut by fertile valleys, notably the GUDBRANDSDAL, HALLINGDAL, OSTERDAL, ROMSDAL, and NUMEDAL; these are inland pop. centers and form main routes of overland transportation. Numerous rapid rivers provide abundant hydroelectric power and are used for logging. The Glomma (S) is Norway's longest and most important river. Mjosa and Femund are largest lakes. While most of the land is unproductive and under 4% is under cultivation, extensive mtn. pastures are used for cattle and sheep raising; dairying is important. Norwegian counties of Nordland, Troms, and Finnmark, within the Arctic Circle, form W part of LAPLAND; among Finnish and partly-nomad Lapp pop. here, fishing and reindeer raising are main occupations. Large tracts of S and central Norway are forested, supporting extensive lumbering and woodworking industry, and numerous pulp and paper mills. Fishing is Norway's chief industry and fish and fish products are largest export item. Cod, herring, haddock, halibut, mackerel, and sardines form bulk of the catch and are exported fresh, salted, dried, or canned. Norway's whaling fleet is largest operating in antarctic waters. Norwegian merchant fleet ranks 3d after those of the United States and Great Britain and plays major part in world trade; large percentage consists of modern motor vessels and tankers. Mineral resources include pyrites, iron, copper, zinc, niobium, and lead; electrometallurgical (especially aluminum and magnesium) and electrochemical industries are important and are being expanded rapidly. Leading cities, almost all seaports, are Oslo, Bergen, Trondheim, Stavanger, Drammen, Kristiansand, Sarpsborg, Tonsberg, Arendal, Tromso, Horten, Narvik (port serving N Swedish iron mines), Hamar, and Hammerfest (world's northernmost city). There are universities at Oslo and Bergen. Magnificent scenery, especially in fjord regions, and midnight sun in N Norway, attract numerous tourists. Due to North Atlantic Drift, Norway has mild and humid climate. A constitutional monarchy, with legislative power vested in parliament (*Storting*), Norway is administratively divided into 20 counties [Nor. *fylker*]. State church is Lutheran. Norwegian language is developed from the Danish and is divided into 2 official and very similar idioms: *Rigsmaal*, the literary language, and *Landsmaal*, a more popular variant. Frequent spelling reforms account for variation in place-name spelling. Norwegian overseas possessions are SPITSBERGEN and Jan Mayen in the arctic, and Bouvet and Peter I isls. in the subantarctic, as well as claims in ANTARCTICA. First attempt to create a united Norway was made by Harold I, who, having defeated (872) the petty kings of the *fylker* at battle of Hafrsfjord, conquered the Shetland and Orkney isls. and raided Normandy, where Norse duchy was subsequently established. Many nobles displaced by Harold's unification of the country settled in Iceland. After Harold's death the country was again divided, except for brief interludes. Olaf II, who made Christianity Norway's official religion, was killed, and his forces defeated (1030) by King Canute of England and Denmark at Stiklestad, but his son, Magnus I, was restored (1035) to Norwegian throne and firmly established country's unity. In 12th cent. church influence increased and Nicholas Breakspear (later Pope Adrian IV) organized Norwegian hierarchy. Clerical power was finally broken by Haakon IV (1217–63); his reign, followed by that of Magnus VI (1263–80), was period of peaceful prosperity and cultural rise; Iceland and Greenland came under Norwegian control. Brief union with Sweden under Magnus VII lasted from 1319 to 1343. Margaret of Denmark became (1387) regent of Norway and Denmark, and later also of Sweden; in 1397 she initiated the Kalmar Union and had Eric of Pomerania proclaimed king of the 3 countries. Though union was a personal one, Norway was virtually reduced to status of Danish vassal. Its trade had previously been captured by Hanseatic League, which established (1445) its northern hq. at Bergen. Under Treaty of Kiel (1814), Denmark ceded Norway to Sweden; in the same year Norway adopted a constitution at Eidsvold, and made an abortive attempt to establish independent kingdom, but was forced to accept a Swedish king. In 1815 Norway was recognized as an independent kingdom, in personal union with Sweden. Growing national sentiment finally led to dissolution (1905) of the union by Norwegian *Storting*, and Prince Charles of Denmark was elected King Haakon VII of Norway. In late 19th and early 20th cent. there was large-scale emigration to the United States, rapid industrialization, and intensive arctic and antarctic exploration, led by Nansen, Amundsen, and Sverdrup. Cultural renaissance was symbolized by works of Ibsen, Grieg, Bjornson, Hamsun, Bull, Edvard Munch, Undset, and Vigeland. In First World War Norway remained neutral. Industrial development led to rise of Labor party, which formed its 1st govt. in 1928 and has since predominated in Norwegian politics. On April 8–9, 1940, German troops invaded Norway and occupied Oslo and other strategic points. Despite all Norwegian efforts, aided by small Anglo-French expeditionary force and strong British naval support, resistance collapsed in most of Norway by mid-April. Narvik, recaptured by Allies (May, 1940), had to be abandoned in June; at the same time King Haakon and his cabinet left Tromso, last seat of govt., and established a govt. in exile in London. Norwegian merchant fleet played major part throughout Allied war effort; Norwegian resistance at home defied terroristic measures by the Germans and their tool, the traitor Quisling. Sabotage efforts by Norwegian parachute troops paralyzed, among others, the German heavy-water plant at Rjukan. In Oct., 1944, Russian troops entered N Norway and captured Kirkenes; retreating Germans then devastated most of Norwegian Lapland, but remained in the rest of Norway until May, 1945. Post-war reconstruction was rapid, especially in replacement of the numerous vessels sunk during the war. Important social legislation, including family allowances, was introduced by post-war Labor govt. Norway was an original member of the U.N. and later joined the European Recovery Program and the North Atlantic Treaty. For further information, see separate articles on the physical features, cities, towns, and the following 20 counties: AKERSHUS, AUST-AGDER, BERGEN, BUSKERUD, FINNMARK, HEDMARK, HORDALAND, MORE OG ROMSDAL, NORDLAND, NORD-TRONDELAG, OPLAND, OSLO, OSTFOLD, ROGALAND, SOGN OG FJORDANE, SOR-TRONDELAG, TELEMARK, TROMS, VEST-AGDER, VESTFOLD.

Norway. 1 Town (pop. 441), Benton co., E central Iowa, 14 mi. WSW of Cedar Rapids, in agr. area. **2** Town (pop. 3,811), including Norway village (pop. 2,687), Oxford co., W Maine, 17 mi. NW of Auburn and on L. Pennesseewassee. Mfg. (shoes, moccasins, winter sports equipment, wooden articles), resort area. Settled 1786, inc. 1797. **3** City (pop. 3,258), Dickinson co., SW Upper Peninsula, Mich., 8 mi. ESE of Iron Mountain city, in iron-mining, lumbering, and farming region (fruit, truck, potatoes, poultry; dairy products). Trout hatchery near by. Settled c.1879, inc. 1891. **4** Town (pop. 476), Orangeburg co., W central S.C., 15 mi. WSW of Orangeburg; lumber.

Norway Islands, group of islets in Gulf of Tonkin, N Vietnam, 10 mi. SE of Catba Isl.; 20°37′N 107°9′E.

Norwegian Bay, N Franklin Dist., Northwest Territories, arm (c.100 mi. long, 90 mi. wide) of the Arctic Ocean, off SW Ellesmere Isl.; 77°N 90°W.

Norwegian Current, terminal branch of North Atlantic Current, in Norwegian Sea, flowing N along coast of Norway before branching into Barents Sea and past Spitsbergen. Has great moderating effect on climate of N Europe.

Norwegian Sea, Nor. *Norskehavet*, part of Atlantic Ocean, off coast of Norway, opening N on Greenland Sea, NE on Barents Sea, S on North Sea, and SW on the open Atlantic; 12,031 ft. deep (at 68°21′N 2°5′E). The Norwegian Sea is separated from the open Atlantic by a submarine ridge linking Greenland, Iceland, the Faeroes, and N Scotland, and is thus often associated with the Arctic Ocean. However, unlike the Arctic Ocean, it has generally ice-free conditions produced by the warm Norwegian Current.

Norwell (nôr′wŭl), town (pop. 2,515), Plymouth co., E Mass., on North R., near Coast, and 20 mi. SE of Boston; truck, poultry. Settled 1634, set off from Scituate 1888.

Norwich (nôr′wĭch, nŏ′rĭch), village (pop. 1,268), S Ont., 12 mi. SE of Woodstock; lumbering, milk canning, cider and vinegar making, broom mfg.

Norwich (nŏ′rĭj, –rĭch), county borough (1931 pop. 126,236; 1951 census 121,226) and city, ⊙ Norfolk, England, in E central part of co., on Wensum R. just above its mouth on the Yare, and 100 mi. NE of London; 52°38′N 1°17′E; has important leather and shoe industry, silk mills, and mfg. of chocolate, pharmaceuticals, electrical equipment, agr. machinery, asbestos; agr. market, notably for grain. Has great cathedral, founded 1096 by Bishop Losinga, with tomb of Edith Cavell; remains of anc. walls; gatehouses and tower (1294–1342); the keep of a Norman castle (now a mus.); and 36 old churches. Among old bldgs. destroyed by air raids in Second World War are the 15th-cent. Dolphin House, the Boar's Head Inn, and the 17th-cent. church of St. Mary's Baptist. There is 13th-cent. St. Giles's Hosp., 15th-cent. Strangers Hall (now a mus.), and 14th-cent. guildhall. In 1004 town was destroyed by Danes, but by end of 11th cent. it had become an important commercial and ecclesiastical center. A 14th-cent. immigration of Flemish weavers made it a center of the worsted industry. In 1348 and in 17th cent. the town was hit by the Black Death. It was site of Litester's (1381) and Kett's (1549) rebellions. In 18th and 19th cent. it was seat of the Norwich Society of Artists (including John Crome and John Sell Cotman) and has been the scene of a triennial music festival since 1824. In Second World War a large number of U.S. bomber stations were located in the vicinity. Among its suburbs are Mousehold (NE; pop. 12,421), Thorpe-next-Norwich (E; pop. 8,875), Catton (N; pop. 18,595), and Lakenham (S; pop. 7,711). Village of Caister St. Edmund, or Caistor, 3 mi. S, has remains of a large Roman encampment (*Venta Icenorum*).

Norwich (nôr′wĭch). **1** (also nŏ′rĭch) City (pop. 23,429), in Norwich town (pop. 37,633), a ⊙ New London co., SE Conn., at junction of Yantic and Shetucket (which form the Thames) rivers, 12 mi. N of New London. Mfg. center (thermos bottles, textiles, airplane parts, silverware, paper products, leather goods and shoes, chemicals, clothing, metal products, bedding, paint); truck farming. Norwich town includes villages of Norwichtown (pop. 2,916), industrial Taftville (pop. 3,598), and part of YANTIC. Thomas Danforth began making pewter here, 1730. Slater Memorial, art gall., school here; state tuberculosis sanatorium near by. Benedict Arnold b. here. Settled 1659–60, inc. 1784. **2** City (pop. 378), Kingman co., S Kansas, 33 mi. SW of Wichita; wheat-shipping point. **3** City (pop. 8,816), ⊙ Chenango co., central N.Y., on Chenango R. and 35 mi. NE of Binghamton, in dairying and farming area; mfg. (pharmaceuticals, dairy products, machinery, wood and metal products, knit goods). Gail Borden b. here. Settled 1788, inc. 1915. **4** Village (pop. 197), Muskingum co., central Ohio, 12 mi. ENE of Zanesville, in agr. area. **5** Town (pop. 1,532), Windsor co., E Vt., on the Connecticut, opposite Hanover, N.H., and 35 mi. ENE of Rutland, in agr. area; lumber. Includes Pompanoosuc village. Settled before 1775.

Norwood, Australia: see KENSINGTON AND NORWOOD.

Norwood, village (pop. 762), S Ont., on Ouse R. and 22 mi. E of Peterborough; dairying, feed milling, woodworking.

Norwood, England: see SOUTHALL.

Norwood, NE suburb of Johannesburg, S Transvaal, U. of So. Afr.

Norwood. 1 Town (pop. 294), San Miguel co., SW Colo., near San Miguel R., 30 mi. NW of Telluride, in diversified-farming area; alt. 7,017 ft.; grain. San Miguel Mts. just S. **2** Town (pop. 268), Warren co., E Ga., 12 mi. W of Thomson. **3** Village (pop. 414), East Feliciana parish, SE central La., near Miss. line, 35 mi. N of Baton Rouge. **4** Residential town (pop. 16,636), Norfolk co., E Mass., near Neponset R., 14 mi. SW of Boston; printing and publishing, tanning, knitting, foundries; roofing, ink. Norfolk Agr. School. Settled 1678, inc. 1872. **5** Village (pop. 749), Carver co., S Minn., 35 mi. WSW of Minneapolis, in agr. area; ice cream, flour. **6** Town (pop. 345), Wright co., S central Mo., in the Ozarks, 50 mi. E of Springfield; dairy, poultry farms. **7** Borough (pop. 1,792), Bergen co., extreme NE N.J., 12 mi. NE of Paterson, near N.Y. line. Inc. 1905. **8** Village (pop. 1,995), St. Lawrence co., N N.Y., on Raquette R. and 13 mi. SSW of Massena; paper products, crushed stone, lime. Inc. 1871. **9** Town (pop. 1,735), Stanly co., S central N.C., 10 mi. SSE of Albemarle, near L. Tillery; mfg. of yarn, furniture, store fixtures. Settled c.1800; inc. 1882. **10** City (pop. 35,001), Hamilton co., extreme SW Ohio, within but administratively independent of Cincinnati; makes motor vehicles, electrical apparatus, machinery, aircraft parts, metal products, tools, lithographs, paperboard products, office fixtures, footwear, railroad equipment, soap products. Settled as Sharpsburg; renamed Norwood and inc. as a village in 1888; inc. as a city in 1903. **11** Borough (pop. 5,246), Delaware co., SE Pa., SW suburb of Philadelphia. Inc. 1893. **12** Village, Kent co., R.I.: see WARWICK.

Norwood Court, town (pop. 72), St. Louis co., E Mo.

Norwoodville, village (1940 pop. 689), Polk co., central Iowa, just N of Des Moines, in bituminous-coal-mining and agr. area.

Norwottock, Mount, Mass.: see HOLYOKE RANGE.

Nor Yungas, Bolivia: see COROICO.

Norzagaray (nôrsägärī′), town (1939 pop. 3,839; 1948 municipality pop. 13,394), Bulacan prov., S central Luzon, Philippines, 21 mi. NNE of Manila; trade center for rice-growing and gold-mining area.

Nos (nōs), village (1930 pop. 509), Santiago prov., central Chile, on railroad and 13 mi. S of Santiago; black-powder plant (just W; in 1930 settlement pop. was 88).

Nosappu, Cape, Japan: see NOSHAPPU, CAPE.

Noshappu, Cape (nō′shäp′pōō), Jap. *Noshappu-saki*, 2 capes of Hokkaido, Japan. Sometimes called Nosappu and Nosshafu. **1** Easternmost point of isl., on narrow Nemuro peninsula, in Goyomai Strait; 43°23′N 145°49′E; lighthouse. **2** Cape just W of Cape Soya (northernmost point of isl.), in La Pérouse Strait; 45°27′N 141°39′E; lighthouse.

Noshiro (nōshē′rō), city (1940 pop. 37,054; 1947 pop. 46,416) Akita prefecture, N Honshu, Japan, port on Sea of Japan, 35 mi. N of Akita; collection center for lumber and fruit; exports lumber. Includes (since late 1930s) former town of Noshiro-minato. Sometimes spelled Nosiro.

Nosob River (nō′sŏb), intermittent stream, S Africa, rises in central South-West Africa NNE of Windhoek, flows SW, forms border bet. Bechuanaland Protectorate and Cape Prov. (U. of So. Afr.), through Kalahari Desert, to Molopo R. at 26°55′S 20°41′E; c.500 mi. long.

Nosovka (nŭsôf′kŭ), town (1926 pop. 12,955), SW Chernigov oblast, Ukrainian SSR, 15 mi. SW of Nezhin; sugar refining.

Noss, island (pop. 4) of the Shetlands, Scotland, just E of Bressay isl., 4 mi. E of Lerwick; 2 mi. long, 1 mi. wide; rises to 592 ft. Ponies are bred here and isl. is home of vast numbers of sea birds during breeding season.

Nossa Senhora da Glória (nô′sŭ sĭnyô′rŭ dä glô′ryŭ), city (pop. 1,335), W Sergipe, NE Brazil, 60 mi. NW of Aracaju; livestock, cotton.

Nossa Senhora das Dores (däs dô′rĭs), city (pop. 3,407), central Sergipe, NE Brazil, 32 mi. NNW of Aracaju; agr. trade center (cotton, corn, fruit, cattle).

Nossa Senhora do Livramento (dōō lēvrŭmĕn′tōō), city (pop. 1,063), central Mato Grosso, Brazil, 23 mi. SW of Cuiabá; sugar, medicinal plants, livestock. Until 1943, called Livramento; and, 1944–48, São José dos Cocais.

Nossebro (nô′sŭbrōō″), village (pop. 1,042), Skaraborg co., SW Sweden, 17 mi. ESE of Trollhattan; rail junction; foundry, mechanical workshop.

Nossen (nô′sŭn), town (pop. 8,505), Saxony, E central Germany, on the Freiberger Mulde and 11 mi. SW of Meissen; metalworking, paper and textile milling; mfg. of machinery, leather products, toys. Towered over by large castle. Near by are remains of 12th-cent. Cistercian monastery of Altzella.

Nosshafu, Cape, Japan: see NOSHAPPU, CAPE.

Nossi-Bé or **Nosy-Bé** (nōō′sē-bā′, nō′–), island (□ 115; 1948 pop. 16,900), in Mozambique Channel just off NW coast of Madagascar; part of Majunga prov.; 18 mi. long, 10 mi. wide; 13°20′S 48°15′E. Of volcanic origin. Sugar, rum, quality cacao, vanilla, black pepper, bitter oranges, and especially essential oils (ilang-ilang, lemon grass, palma rosa) are its chief products. Large sugar-cane fields. Has old Arab ruins (9th–14th cent.). Hellville, the ⊙, is on S shore. Isl. was ceded to France, 1840; attached to Madagascar, 1896.

Nosy-Bé, Madagascar: see NOSSI-BÉ.

Nosy-Boraha, island, Madagascar: see SAINTE-MARIE ISLAND.

Nosy-Varika (nōō′sē-värē′kŭ), town, Fianarantsoa prov., E Madagascar, on Indian Ocean coast and Canal des Pangalanes, 115 mi. NE of Fianarantsoa; coffee center. Meteorological station.

Notaresco (nōtärē′skō), village (pop. 1,040), Teramo prov., Abruzzi e Molise, S central Italy, 10 mi. E of Teramo; wrought-iron products. Has late-13th-cent. church.

Notasulga (nōtŭsŭl′gŭ), town (pop. 816), Lee and Macon counties, E Ala., 10 mi. N of Tuskegee; lumber.

Notec River (nô'tĕch), Pol. *Noteć*, Ger. *Netze* (nĕ'tsŭ), W central Poland, rises 11 mi. NNE of Kolo, flows W, NNW through Goplo and Pakosc lakes, past Naklo, and generally WSW past Czarnkow and Wielen to Warta R. 8 mi. E of Landsberg (Gorkow Wielkopolski); 273 mi. long. Navigable below L. Goplo; mostly canalized. Linked with Brda R. (E) via Bydgoszcz Canal. Extensive swamps on lower course have been drained.

Notero, Norway: see NOTTEROY.

Notium (nō'shēŭm), anc. town on Aegean coast of Asia Minor, just S of Colophon, for which it was the port, NE of Samos isl. Here in the Peloponnesian War the Athenian fleet suffered a disastrous defeat (407 or 406 B.C.) by the Spartan Lysander.

Notium Promontorium, Ireland: see MIZEN HEAD.

Noto (nô'tô), town (pop. 18,923), Siracusa prov., SE Sicily, 17 mi. SW of Syracuse; wine, olive oil, hemp; cement, soap, metal furniture. Limestone and lignite mined near by. Bishopric. Has churches, palaces, mus. Founded 1703, replacing anc. Netum or Neetum (5 mi. NW), largely destroyed by earthquake of 1693.

Notobe (nōtō'bā), town (pop. 4,678), Ishikawa prefecture, central Honshu, Japan, 10 mi. SW of Nanao; rice growing; textiles.

Notodden (nŏt'ŏd"dŭn), city (pop. 6,062), Telemark co., S Norway, at mouth of Tinne R. on Heddal L., 28 mi. NNW of Skien; industrial center. Hydroelectric plant, paper mills, sawmills, smelting works, chemical works (cellulose products, fertilizer, rayon), textile mills. Tourist center. Has teachers col. Inc. 1913.

Notogawa (nōtō'gäwŭ), town (pop. 16,340), Shiga prefecture, S Honshu, Japan, on E inlet of L. Biwa, 25 mi. NE of Kyoto, in agr. area (rice, wheat, tea); mfg. (rayon textiles, vegetable oil).

Noto Peninsula (nō'tō), Jap. *Noto-hanto*, Ishikawa prefecture, central Honshu, Japan, bet. Sea of Japan (W) and Toyama Bay (E); terminates at Nagate Point; 45 mi. long, 6–17 mi. wide; deeply indented E coast. Rugged terrain, with scattered rice fields. Lumbering and fishing are important. Nanao, principal center.

Noto-shima (nōtō'-shĭmä), island (□ 19; pop. 6,388), Ishikawa prefecture, central Honshu, Japan, in W inlet of Toyama Bay, N of Nanao; 7 mi. long, ½–3 mi. wide; flat, fertile. Rice growing, fishing.

Notre-Dame (nō'trŭ dăm', Fr. nô'trŭ däm'), village (pop. estimate c.350), E N.B., on Cocagne R. and 16 mi. N of Moncton; mixed farming.

Notre Dame, Ind.: see SOUTH BEND.

Notre Dame Bay, inlet (50 mi. long, 55 mi. wide at entrance) of the Atlantic, E N.F., extending S from Cape St. John; 49°5'–50°N 54°30'–56°10'W. W shore of bay, deeply indented by numerous small inlets, receives Exploits R. On shore are numerous fishing settlements, with lobster- and salmon-canning plants. Bay contains many isls.; largest are New World and Twillingate isls. Near entrance of bay is Fogo Isl. Chief town of district is Botwood, at head of Bay of Exploits.

Notre-Dame-de-Bondeville (nô'trŭ-däm-dŭ-bōdvēl'), town (pop. 3,509), Seine-Inférieure dept., N France, 4 mi. NW of Rouen; calico mfg.; textile dyeing and bleaching.

Notre-Dame-de-Briançon (–dŭ-brēäsō'), village (pop. 560), Savoie dept., SE France, in Alpine Tarentaise valley, on the Isère and 5 mi. NW of Moutiers; produces nitric acid, cyanamide, calcium carbide, and electrodes for steel mills of Maurienne valley. Spa of La Léchère-les-Bains (mineral springs) is 1 mi. SSE.

Notre-Dame-de-la-Salette, France: see CORPS.

Notre-Dame-de-Lorette (–dŭ-lôrĕt'), hill (541 ft.), Pas-de-Calais dept., N France, 8 mi. NNW of Arras, just NW of Vimy Ridge. Captured at great cost by French in May, 1915. Site of large Fr. military cemetery of First World War dead.

Notre-Dame-de-Monts (–dŭ-mō'), village (pop. 307), Vendée dept., W France, near Bay of Biscay, 29 mi. NNW of Les Sables-d'Olonne. Has bathing beach and pine forests.

Notre Dame de Portneuf, Que.: see PORTNEUF, village.

Notre Dame du Lac (nō'trŭ dăm' dū lăk', Fr. nô'trŭ däm dü läk'), village (pop. estimate 1,500), ⊙ Temiscouata co., SE Que., on L. Temiscouata, 40 mi. ESE of Rivière du Loup; dairying, lumbering.

Notre-Dame-du-Laus, France: see GAP.

Notre Dame Mountains, range (c.3,500 ft.) in E Que., continuation of the Green Mts. of Vt., extending NE to the St. Lawrence opposite Quebec, thence E into Gaspé Peninsula, where they are continued by the SHICKSHOCK MOUNTAINS.

Nottawa (nŏ'tŭwŭ), village (pop. estimate 200), S Ont., 3 mi. S of Collingwood; woolen milling, dairying, mixed farming.

Nottawasaga River (nŏ"tŭwŭsô'gŭ), S Ont., rises NNE of Toronto, flows 60 mi. N to Nottawasaga Bay, S arm of Georgian Bay, 11 mi. ENE of Collingwood.

Nottaway River (nŏ'tŭwā), W Que., issues from Mattagami L., flows 205 mi. NW to James Bay of the Hudson Bay, 10 mi. WNW of Rupert House. There are several rapids. Sturgeon fisheries. Waswanipi R., chief headstream, rises S of L. Mistassini, flows 195 mi. S and WNW to Mattagami L.

Nottely River (nŏt'lē), in N Ga. and W N.C., rises in Blue Ridge Mts. 17 mi. NE of Dahlonega, flows NW into Cherokee co., N.C., then NE to Hiwassee Reservoir (in Hiwassee R.) near Murphy; c.40 mi. long. Nottely Dam, in Ga., 9 mi. NW of Blairsville, is major TVA dam (184 ft. high, 2,300 ft. long) completed 1942; used for flood control. Forms Nottely Reservoir (□ 6.7; 20 mi. long, 1–3 mi. wide; capacity 184,400 acre-ft.) in Union co., Ga.

Notteroy (nût'tůr-ûü), Nor. *Nøtterøy*, island (□ 17), SE Norway, in Oslo Fjord just S of Tonsberg (bridge); 7 mi. long, 4 mi. wide. Shipyards; truck gardening, fishing, seafaring. Small section at N tip is part of Tonsberg city. Notteroy canton (pop. 11,082) includes some smaller isls. Formerly spelled Nottero (Nor. *Nøtterø*), sometimes Notero.

Nottingham or **Nottinghamshire** (nŏ'tĭng-ŭm, –shĭr), county (□ 843.8; 1931 pop. 712,731; 1951 census 841,083), central England; ⊙ Nottingham. Bounded by Derby (W), Yorkshire (NW), Lincolnshire (NE and E), and Leicester (S). Largely in the broad valley of the Trent, and drained also by Idle and Maun rivers, it is slightly hilly in W and NW (Sherwood Forest), lowland in E, and moorland (the Wolds) in S. Chief industries are coal mining (W); mfg. of textiles, lace, hosiery, pharmaceuticals (Nottingham); leather and shoe mfg. (Mansfield); metalworking and various light industries. Other important towns are Worksop, Newark, East Retford, and Southwell. The area of the Dukeries contains several large country estates. In Saxon times co. was part of kingdom of Mercia and later was an important Danish borough. Shortened form is Notts.

Nottingham, county borough (1931 pop. 268,801; 1951 census 306,008), ⊙ Nottinghamshire, England, in S part of co., on the Trent and 110 mi. NNW of London; 52°51'N 1°8'W; important modern industrial center with varied light industries. It dates from 9th cent., when it was an important Danish borough. Bet. 1330 and 1337 three parliaments were held here; in 1642 it was scene of raising of standard of Charles I, marking beginning of Civil War. The castle, built by William Peverel in Norman times on rock above the Trent, was prison of David II of Scotland, and hq. of Richard III before battle of Bosworth Field. It was dismantled by Cromwell, rebuilt in 1674, and burned in Reform Bill riots (1831). In 1878 it was restored by the city and now has art mus. The city has modern Council House; R.C. cathedral, built by Pugin; University Col.; art school; a grammar school founded in 1513; large public park; and arboretum. Nottingham is a textile-milling and tobacco-processing center, with mfg. also of lace, leather, shoes, hosiery, pharmaceuticals, motorcycles, bicycles, railroad rolling stock, and electrical equipment. Its lace-making industry was formerly of great importance. According to legend Robin Hood was b. here. Among industrial suburbs are Basford, Bulwell, Daybrook, Mapperley, and Radford.

Nottingham (nŏ'tĭng-hăm"), town (pop. 566), Rockingham co., SE N.H., 18 mi. WNW of Portsmouth. Includes Pawtuckaway State Forest on Pawtuckaway Pond (3 mi. long).

Nottingham Island (□ 441), SE Franklin Dist., Northwest Territories, in Hudson Strait, bet. Ungava Peninsula (S) and Southampton Isl. (WNW); 63°20'N 78°W; 38 mi. long, 11–22 mi. wide. At SW extremity is govt. radio direction-finding and meteorological station.

Nottinghamshire, England: see NOTTINGHAM, county.

Nottoway (nŏ'tŭwā), county (□ 308; pop. 15,479), central Va.; ⊙ Nottoway. Bounded S by Nottoway R. Agr. (mainly tobacco; also fruit, hay, grains), dairying, livestock, poultry; lumbering. Blackstone is commercial, processing center. Formed 1788.

Nottoway, village (pop. c.200), ⊙ Nottoway co., central Va., 37 mi. W of Petersburg.

Nottoway River, S Va., rises in N Lunenburg co., flows c.170 mi. generally SE past Courtland, joining Blackwater R. at N.C. line to form Chowan R.

Notts, England: see NOTTINGHAM, county.

Nottuln (nô'tōōln), village (pop. 6,710), in former Prussian prov. of Westphalia, NW Germany, after 1945 in North Rhine-Westphalia, 12 mi. W of Münster; dairying, hog raising (ham). Has late-Gothic church.

Notus, village (pop. 313), Canyon co., SW Idaho, 8 mi. NW of Caldwell and on Boise R., in dairying and agr. area served by Boise irrigation project.

Nouakchott (nwäkshôt'), village, W Mauritania, Fr. West Africa, near Atlantic coast, on desert trail and 150 mi. NNE of Saint-Louis; gum, millet, livestock.

Nouaseur (nwäsûr'), village, Fr. Morocco, 15 mi. S of Casablanca, U.S. air base.

Noua Sulita, Ukrainian SSR: see NOVOSELITSA.

Nouméa (nōōmā'ŭ, Fr. nōōmāä'), port town (1936 pop. 11,108), ⊙ Fr. colony of New Caledonia, SW Pacific, on SW coast of isl. Excellent landlocked harbor; steamship service to Sydney; air base on Calif.–New Zealand route. Exports nickel, chrome, copra. Site of isls.'s chief nickel-smelting plant, and Collège La Pérouse. In Second World War, site of U.S. air base. Formerly site of Fr. penal colony. Also spelled Numea; formerly Port de France.

Noun, Oued, Morocco: see ASACA RIVER.

Nouna (nōō'nä), village, NW Upper Volta, Fr. West Africa, 60 mi. WSW of Tougan; peanuts, cotton, sesame; cattle. Cheese making.

Nouveau Québec, Que.: see UNGAVA.

Nouveau Salaberry (nōōvō' să'lŭbĕ"rē), village (pop. 1,043), S Que., suburb of Valleyfield.

Nouvelle, La (lä nōōvĕl'), village (pop. 1,689), Aude dept., S France, port on Gulf of Lion, 11 mi. S of Narbonne (connected by canal); sulphur refining, fertilizer mfg. Saltworks.

Nouvelle-Amsterdam, island, Indian Ocean: see AMSTERDAM ISLAND.

Nouvelle-Anvers (nōōvĕl'-ävârs'), village, Equator Prov., W Belgian Congo, on right bank of Congo R. and 165 mi. WSW of Lisala; steamboat landing and trading center, with R.C. missions and schools. Formerly called Bangala. Founded 1884.

Nouvelle Calédonie: see NEW CALEDONIA.

Nouvelles Hébrides: see NEW HEBRIDES.

Nouvion or **Nouvion-en-Ponthieu** (nōōvyō'-ä-pōtyû'), village (pop. 719), Somme dept., N France, 8 mi. NNW of Abbeville; poultry raising.

Nouvion, Le, or **Le Nouvion-en-Thiérache** (lŭ nōōvyō'-ä-tyärăsh'), village (pop. 1,755), Aisne dept., N France, on the Sambre and 10 mi. SW of Avesnes; glassworks; cheese mfg. Lavisse b. here.

Nouvion-en-Ponthieu, Somme dept., France: see NOUVION.

Nouvion-en-Thiérache, Le, Aisne dept., France: see NOUVION, LE.

Nouvion-sur-Meuse (–sür-mûz'), town (pop. 2,411), Ardennes dept., N France, on right bank of the Meuse (canalized) and 5 mi. SE of Mézières; foundries.

Nouzonville (nōōzōvēl'), town (pop. 4,648), Ardennes dept., N France, in entrenched Meuse R. valley, 4 mi. NNE of Mézières; metallurgical center (iron and steel foundries, stamping and sheet-metal works).

Nouzov, Czechoslovakia: see UNHOST.

Nova Aliança (nô'vŭ älyā'sŭ), city (pop. 1,123), NW São Paulo, Brazil, 17 mi. SSW of São José do Rio Prêto; coffee, rice, beans, cattle.

Nova Almeida (nô'vŭ älmā'dŭ), town (pop. 593), central Espírito Santo, Brazil, on the Atlantic, 22 mi. NNE of Vitória. Founded by Jesuits in 16th cent.

Novabad (nŭvŭbät'). **1** City (1950 pop. over 2,000), ⊙ Garm oblast, Tadzhik SSR, 10 mi. WNW of Garm. Called Shulmak until 1950, when it replaced Garm as oblast capital. **2** Town (1945 pop. over 500), N Stalinabad oblast, Tadzhik SSR, near Stalinabad, in cotton and orchard area.

Nova Bana (nô'vä bä'nyä), Slovak *Nová Baňa*, Hung. *Ujbánya* (ōō'ēbä"nyŏ), town (pop. 5,083), S Slovakia, Czechoslovakia, on Hron R., on railroad and 32 mi. SW of Banska Bystrica; lumbering.

Nova Bystrice (nô'vä bĭs'tûrzhĭtsĕ), Czech *Nová Bystřice*, Ger. *Neubistritz* (noibĭ'strĭts), town (pop. 2,366), S Bohemia, Czechoslovakia, near Austrian border, 10 mi. SSE of Jindrichuv Hradec; rail terminus; bathing resort; mfg. cotton goods, hair nets. Fish ponds in vicinity.

Nova Chaves (nô'vŭ shä'vĭsh), town (pop. 293), Malange prov., NE Angola, on Luembe R. and 90 mi. SE of Vila Henrique de Carvalho; rubber manioc.

Novachene (nôvä'chĕnĕ), village (pop. 4,191), Pleven dist., N Bulgaria, on Osam R. and 9 mi. S of Nikopol; grain, livestock, truck.

Novaci (nôväch'), village (pop. 2,009), Gorj prov. SW Rumania, 20 mi. NE of Targu-Jiu; summer resort (alt. 2,231 ft.) in S foothills of the Transylvanian Alps. Asbestos production, cheese making. Includes *Novacii-Români* (rō'mûn) and Novacii-*Străini* (strû'ēn). Polovragi summer resort (alt. 2,161 ft.), with 17th-cent. monastery, is 5 mi. E.

Nova Cruz (nô'vŭ krōōs'), city (pop. 3,084), E Rio Grande do Norte, NE Brazil, on Paraíba border on Natal–João Pessoa RR and 50 mi. SSW of Natal; cotton, corn, hides.

Nova Dantzig, Brazil: see CAMBÉ.

Nova Era (nô'vŭ ā'rŭ), city (pop. 3,482), E central Minas Gerais, Brazil, on Piracicaba R. and 60 mi. ENE of Belo Horizonte; here rail spur from Itabira iron mine (15 mi. NW) joins main Belo Horizonte-Vitória line. Until 1930s, called São José da Lagoa and, until 1944, Presidente Vargas. Monlevade steel mill is 9 mi. SW.

Nova Friburgo (nô'vŭ frēbōōr'gō), locally called **Friburgo,** city (1950 pop. 29,258), Rio de Janeiro state, Brazil, in the Serra do Mar, on railroad and 60 mi. NE of Rio; alt. 2,779 ft. Popular mtn. resort built in Alpine style by Swiss who 1st settled here in 1818. Textile milling, stone cutting, soap mfg. In fertile agr. dist. growing potatoes, wine fruit, and flowers.

Nova Gaia (nô'vŭ gä'yŭ), town (pop. 1,427), Malange prov., N central Angola, on road and 90 mi. ESE of Malange; coffee, rubber; goat raising.

Novaglia, Yugoslavia: see PAG ISLAND.

Nova Goa, Portuguese India: see PANGIM.

Nova Gorica (nô'vä gō'rĭtsä), town, ⊙ Gorica oblast (formed 1949), W Slovenia, Yugoslavia, adjoining (E of) Gorizia, Italy; public buildings; furniture mfg. Developed after Italo-Yugoslav border settlement in 1947.

Nova Gradiska (nô′vä grä′dĭshkä), Serbo-Croatian *Nova Gradiška*, Hung. *Ujgradiska* (ōō′ĕgrŏdĭskŏ), village (pop. 5,852), N Croatia, Yugoslavia, on railroad and 32 mi. W of Slavonski Brod, at S foot of the Psunj, in Slavonia. Trade center for plum-growing region; brewing, furniture mfg. Petroleum and lignite deposits in vicinity.

Nova Granada (nô′vů grůnä′dů), city (pop. 3,770), NW São Paulo, Brazil, 20 mi. N of São José do Rio Prêto; rail terminus in pioneer settlement zone; pottery mfg., cotton ginning, coffee and rice processing.

Nova Iguaçu (nô′vů ēgwůsōō′), industrial suburb (1950 pop. 58,683) of Rio de Janeiro, Brazil, in Rio de Janeiro state, near Federal Dist. line, 18 mi. NW of city center. Fruit-preserving (marmalades) and vegetable-canning center. Has metalworks, paper mills, rubber factory. Also mfg. of chemicals, pharmaceuticals, soft drinks; coffee drying, cutting of semiprecious stones.

Nova Iorque (nô′vů yôr′kĭ), city (pop. 1,103), E Maranhão, Brazil, on left bank of Parnaíba R. (Piauí border) and 140 mi. SW of Teresina; ships cacao, medicinal plants, babassu nuts, lumber. Airfield. Formerly spelled Nova York.

Nova Kanjiza, Yugoslavia: see NOVI KNEZEVAC.

Nova Lamego (nô′vů lůmā′gōō), village, NE Port. Guinea, on road and 85 mi. ENE of Bissau; almonds, corn, coconuts; cattle raising. Until 1948, called Gabú or Gabú Sara.

Novalesa (nôvälā′zä), village (pop. 494), Torino prov., Piedmont, NW Italy, near Fr. border, 4 mi. N of Susa. Just SW is Benedictine abbey (founded 726; frequently rebuilt) which served as Charlemagne's hq. against Lombards in 774.

Nova Lima (nô′vů lē′mů), city (pop. 16,321), S central Minas Gerais, Brazil, near the Rio das Velhas, on SE slope of the Serra do Curral, 7 mi. SE of Belo Horizonte; alt. 2,760 ft. Brazil's leading gold-mining center (producing 90% of total output), with one of world's deepest mines (8,000 ft.), worked since 1834 and called Morro Velho [Port.,= old mountain]. Arsenic and silver are by-products. Bauxite exploited at Motuca mine near by. City has tile-roofed colonial houses and is surrounded by eucalyptus groves. Blast furnaces and iron-works at Rio Acima, 9 mi. SSE.

Nova Lisboa (nô′vů lēzhbō′ů), city (pop. 16,288), ⊙ Huambo dist. (□ 11,715; pop. 553,669), Benguela prov., W central Angola, on Bié Plateau, 150 mi. E of Lobito and 300 mi. SE of Luanda; 12°44′S 15°47′E; alt. 5,560 ft. Has chief railroad repair shops of Benguela RR. Agr. trade and processing center amidst European settlements. Ships corn, wheat, rice, fruits, hides and skins. Has moderately healthful climate (annual mean 66°F.; yearly rainfall c.50 in.). Hydroelectric plant 10 mi. SE. City, founded 1912, was to become ⊙ Angola in 1927 but has not yet supplanted Luanda. Has fine public bldgs., churches, radio transmitter, airport. Until 1928, called Huambo.

Novalja, Yugoslavia: see PAG ISLAND.

Novallas (nōvä′lyäs), village (pop. 1,535), Saragossa prov., NE Spain, 4 mi. NNE of Tarazona; olive-oil processing; wine, sugar beets, cherries, apricots.

Nova Lusitânia (nô′vů lōōzētä′nyů), village, Manica and Sofala prov., central Mozambique, on lower Buzi R. and 16 mi. W of Beira, amidst sugar plantations; pottery mfg.

Nova Paka (nô′vä pä′kä), Czech *Nová Paka*, Ger. *Neupaka* (noi′päkä), town (pop. 6,065), NE Bohemia, Czechoslovakia, on railroad and 23 mi. NNW of Hradec Kralove; textile mfg. Village of Stara Paka (rail junction) is 2 mi. NNW; 13th-cent. castle of Pecka is 4 mi. SE.

Nova Prata (nô′vů prä′tů), city (pop. 1,284), NE Rio Grande do Sul, Brazil, in the Serra Geral, 38 mi. NW of Caxias do Sul; winegrowing; wheat, corn. Until 1944, Prata.

Novar (nō′vär), village (pop. estimate 250), S Ont., 40 mi. E of Parry Sound; diatomite mining.

Novara (nôvä′rä), province (□ 1,393; pop. 395,730), Piedmont, N Italy; ⊙ Novara. Bordered N by Switzerland; drained by Toce, Agogna, and Anza rivers. Contains L. of Orta and part of Lago Maggiore. Mtn. terrain in N, including Lepontine Alps, which rise to over 9,500 ft. Highly irrigated plains in S, crossed by CAVOUR CANAL. A major rice region of Piedmont, producing also fodder crops and grapes; cattle raising. Quarries (granite, marble, limestone); several gold mines in Monte Rosa region (Pestarena). Industry at Novara, Domodossola, Intra, Pallanza, and Omegna. Important rice market at Novara. Area reduced in 1927 to form Vercelli prov.

Novara, anc. *Novaria*, city (pop. 52,269), ⊙ Novara prov., Piedmont, N Italy, bet. Agogna and Terdoppio rivers, 28 mi. W of Milan, in irrigated region (rice); 45°27′N 8°37′E. Important road and rail junction; a major rice market of Piedmont; producer of 80% of Italy's Gorgonzola cheese. Rice, flour, cotton, and silk mills; mfg. of cheese, biscuits, confectionery, bricks, shoes, hose; chemical plants (ammonia, nitrogen and sulphuric acids, superphosphates), iron works; printing; cartographical inst.; petroleum refinery; power station. Bishopric. Has cathedral (rebuilt 1863–69), baptistery of 9th–10th cent., church of San Gaudenzio (1577–1659), mus., picture gall., school of obstetrics. Here, in 1849, Austrians under Radetzky defeated Piedmontese forces led by Charles Albert, king of Sardinia.

Novara di Sicilia (nôvä′rä dē sēchē′lyä), village (pop. 3,473), Messina prov., NE Sicily, in Peloritani Mts., 16 mi. SSW of Milazzo. Sometimes Novara Sicilia.

Nova Russas (nô′vů rōō′sůs), city (pop. 2,306), W Ceará, Brazil, on Camocim-Crateús RR and 32 mi. N of Crateús, near Piauí border; stock raising. Graphite deposits.

Nova Scotia (nō′vů skō′shů), province (land area □ 20,743, total □ 21,068; 1941 pop. 577,962; 1948 estimate 635,000), E Canada, one of the Maritime Provinces; ⊙ HALIFAX. Comprises a peninsula (over 375 mi. long, 50–100 mi. wide) connected with mainland by isthmus of Chignecto; bounded by the Atlantic (E, S, W), Bay of Fundy (NW), New Brunswick and Northumberland Strait (N), and the Gulf of St. Lawrence (NE). Prov. includes CAPE BRETON ISLAND (NE), separated from mainland by 2-mi.-wide Strait of Canso. Coastline is deeply indented by numerous bays and inlets; largest are Chignecto Bay and Cumberland Basin, Minas Channel, Minas Basin, Cobequid Bay, Annapolis Basin, St. Mary Bay, Mahone Bay, Halifax Harbour, Chedabucto Bay, and George Bay. Low hill ranges extend bet. W extremity of prov. and the Minas Basin, and along N coast along Northumberland Strait. Climate is maritime, with annual rainfall of c.45 inches. Of the numerous lakes, lakes Rossignol, Ponhook, Malaga, Sherbrooke, and Shubenacadie are the largest on mainland; on Cape Breton Isl. is extensive Bras d'Or Lake. Prov. is drained by many small rivers. Forests cover over half of mainland area; lumbering and woodworking are major industry. Fishing and fish canning and curing are carried on on all coasts. Hay, oats, wheat, potatoes, turnips, and fruit (apples, berries) are grown; Annapolis and Cornwallis valleys have noted apple crops. Dairying is important. Coal is mined extensively in N part of prov. (Springhill and New Glasgow regions), and in NE part of Cape Breton Isl. (Sydney–Glace Bay area). Other minerals worked include gold, silica, fluorspar, gypsum, granite, sandstone, quartzite, salt. Steel making, shipbuilding, mfg. of railroad cars, steel parts, marine engines, furniture, and chemicals, and food processing and packing are main industries. Imperoyal, near Halifax, is site of major oil refinery. Important towns include Sydney, Glace Bay, Dartmouth, Truro, New Waterford, New Glasgow, Amherst, Sydney Mines, Yarmouth, Springhill, North Sydney, Stellarton, Westville, and Kentville. Halifax is chief Canadian Atlantic winter port. Grand Pré village is center of district celebrated in Longfellow's *Evangeline*. Early settled by the French and called ACADIA (Port Royal was established 1605), mainland of prov. was assigned to England by Treaty of Utrecht (1713), while Cape Breton Isl. remained French. British dominance in the area was established by foundation of Halifax (1749) and capture (1758) of French stronghold of Louisburg. Treaty of Paris (1763) handed Cape Breton Isl. to England, and, while it was separate prov. from 1784, isl. was reincorporated in Nova Scotia in 1820. Nova Scotia joined Canadian Confederation in 1867.

Nova Sintra (nô′vů sēn′trů), town (pop. 5,660), Cape Verde Isls., on Brava isl., 80 mi. W of Praia; 14°52′N 24°42′W. Straw-hat weaving. Furna (2 mi. NE) is its port.

Nova Sofala (nô′vů sōōfä′lů), village, Manica and Sofala prov., central Mozambique, on Mozambique Channel, 22 mi. S of Beira; ships sugar, copra. Formerly called Sofala, it was ⊙ Arab state prior to capture (1505) by Portuguese. Its small harbor is silting up and its trade declined after founding (1891) of Beira.

Novate Milanese (nôvä′tĕ mēlänā′zĕ), town (pop. 5,145), Milano prov., Lombardy, N Italy, 5 mi. NNW of Milan, in truck-gardening region.

Nova Timboteua (nô′vů tēmbōōtĕ′wů), city (pop. 1,139), E Pará, Brazil, near Belém-Bragança RR, 80 mi. ENE of Belém; rubber, cereals.

Novato (nōvä′tō), residential village (pop. 3,496), Marin co., W Calif., 10 mi. N of San Rafael, in dairying, and truck- and fruit-farming area. Hamilton Air Force Base is near by.

Nova Trento (nô′vů trĕn′tōō), city (pop. 1,649), E Santa Catarina, Brazil, 30 mi. NW of Florianópolis; textile mill; dairying, winegrowing. Settled after 1876 by Italians.

Nova Varos or **Nova Varosh** (nô′vä vä′rôsh), Serbo-Croatian *Nova Varoš*, village (pop. 2,073), W Serbia, Yugoslavia, 26 mi. S of Titovo Uzice, in the Sanjak.

Nova Venécia (nô′vů vĭnĕ′syů), town (pop. 521), N Espírito Santo, Brazil, 35 mi. W of São Mateus (linked by rail); coffee, oranges, bananas.

Nova Vicenza, Brazil: see FARROUPILHA.

Novaya [Rus.,=new], in Rus. names: see also Novo=[Rus. combining form], NOVOYE, NOVY, NOVYE.

Novaya Aleksandriya, Poland: see PULAWY.

Novaya Astrakhan or **Novaya Astrakhan'** (nô′vīŭ ä′strŭkhŭnyů), village (1926 pop. 5,797), central Voroshilovgrad oblast, Ukrainian SSR, 16 mi. SW of Starobelsk; wheat.

Novaya Basan or **Novaya Basan'** (bŭsän′yů), village (1926 pop. 8,715), SW Chernigov oblast, Ukrainian SSR, 37 mi. SSW of Nezhin; sugar beets.

Novaya Chigla (chēg′lŭ), village (1939 pop. over 2,000), central Voronezh oblast, Russian SFSR, 21 mi. ENE of Bobrov; wheat.

Novaya Eushta, Russian SFSR: see TIMIRYAZEVSKI.

Novaya Ivanovka (ēvä′nůfků), Rum. *Ivaneştii-Noui* (ēvänĕsh′tē-nô′ōōē), village (1941 pop. 3,202), central Izmail oblast, Ukrainian SSR, 40 mi. NNE of Izmail; agr. center.

Novaya Kalitva (kŭlyēt′vŭ), village (1926 pop. 2,859), S Voronezh oblast, Russian SFSR, on Don R. and 22 mi. ESE of Rossosh; metalworks.

Novaya Kazanka (kŭzän′kŭ), village (1939 pop. over 500), W West Kazakhstan oblast, Kazakh SSR, in Caspian Lowland, 170 mi. SW of Uralsk; millet, wheat; camel and cattle breeding. Natural-gas wells near by. Greater and Lesser Uzun rivers disappear into salt lakes (E).

Novaya Ladoga (lä′důgŭ), city (1926 pop. 3,931), N Leningrad oblast, Russian SFSR, port on S shore of L. Ladoga, at mouth of Volkhov R., 70 mi. ENE of Leningrad; fish canning, distilling. Has Suvorov mus. Chartered 1704.

Novaya Lyalya (lyä′lyŭ), city (1935 pop. estimate 15,000), W central Sverdlovsk oblast, Russian SFSR, on Lyalya R. and 80 mi. NNE of Nizhni Tagil, on railroad; major wood-pulp-processing center (paper, cellulose); sawmilling, wood cracking, fibrolite-plate mfg. Developed prior to First World War. Until c.1928, Novo-Lyalinski Zavod.

Novaya Mayachka (mīăch′kŭ), village (1926 pop. 12,641), SW central Kherson oblast, Ukrainian SSR, 28 mi. E of Kherson; metalworks, flour mill.

Novaya Mysh or **Novaya Mysh'** (mĭsh′), Pol. *Nowa Mysz*, village (1931 pop. 1,820), S central Baranovichi oblast, Belorussian SSR, 5 mi. W of Baranovichi; flour milling, pitch processing; bricks.

Novaya Odessa (ůdyĕ′sŭ), village (1926 pop. 6,355), central Nikolayev oblast, Ukrainian SSR, on the Southern Bug and 25 mi. NNW of Nikolayev, on railroad; metalworks; food processing.

Novaya Pismyanka or **Novaya Pis'myanka** (pĭsmyän′kŭ), village (1939 pop. over 500), SE Tatar Autonomous SSR, Russian SFSR, 13 mi. WNW of Bugulma, in petroleum area; wheat, livestock.

Novaya Praga (prä′gŭ), village (1926 pop. 13,096), E Kirovograd oblast, Ukrainian SSR, on road and 29 mi. E of Kirovograd; flour milling.

Novaya Shulba or **Novaya Shul'ba** (shōōlbä′), village (1939 pop. over 2,000), NE Semipalatinsk oblast, Kazakh SSR, 45 mi. E of Semipalatinsk; agr., cattle breeding.

Novaya Sibir Island or **Novaya Sibir' Island** (sēbēr′) [Rus.,=new Siberia], easternmost of Anjou group of NEW SIBERIAN ISLANDS, off Yakut Autonomous SSR, Russian SFSR; 75 mi. long, 35 mi. wide; rises to 330 ft. Discovered 1806.

Novaya Slobodka (slŭbôt′kŭ), town (1926 pop. 1,754), NE Ivanovo oblast, Russian SFSR, on Volga R., at mouth of Unzha R., opposite Yuryevets; sawmilling center for timber floated down Unzha R.

Novaya Ushitsa (ōōshē′tsŭ), town (1926 pop. 6,490), SE Kamenets-Podolski oblast, Ukrainian SSR, 33 mi. ENE of Kamenets-Podolski; fruit canning; tobacco, flour.

Novaya Usman or **Novaya Usman'** (ōō′smŭnyů), village (1939 pop. over 2,000), W central Voronezh oblast, Russian SFSR, 8 mi. ESE of Voronezh; metalworks.

Novaya Vodolaga (vŭdŭlä′gŭ), town (1926 pop. 11,509), W Kharkov oblast, Ukrainian SSR, 23 mi. SW of Kharkov; metalworking, flour milling.

Novaya Zemlya (zĭmlyä′) [Rus.,=new land], archipelago (□ 35,000; 1939 pop. c.400), in the Arctic Ocean, bet. Barents (W) and Kara (E) seas; part of Archangel oblast, Russian SFSR; hq. is Belushya Guba. Extends from the cape Kusov Nos (70°32′ N) 600 mi. N to Cape Zhelaniye (76°59′N), and is 35–90 mi. wide. Consists of a N isl. (□ 20,000) and a S isl. (□ 15,000), separated by the narrow strait Matochkin Shar, with many small offshore isls. Separated from Vaigach Isl. (S) by the strait Karskiye Vorota. Glaciated in N; mts. (continuation of the Urals) rise to 3,500 ft. (center); tundra lowland (S). Deeply indented W coast is site of most permanent settlements (Nentsy pop.) and govt. observation stations. Foggy, windy Arctic climate restricts economic activities to fishing, sealing, hunting of birds (for eggs and down) and fur-bearing animals. Deposits of copper, lead-zinc ores, pyrite, and asphaltite. Known since 16th cent.; explored by Russians (early 19th cent.) and W European expeditions (late 19th cent.). The name Novaya Zemlya, of which Nova Zembla is a corrupt form, is usually applied to the 2 main isls.

Nova York, Brazil: see NOVA IORQUE.

Nova Zagora (nô′vä zägō′rä), city (pop. 11,031), Stara Zagora dist., E central Bulgaria, near branch of Sazlika R., 19 mi. ENE of Stara Zagora; rail junction; agr. center (grain, cotton), livestock; produces textiles, tobacco. Health resort Banya (pop. 859) is 9 mi. N, near Tundzha R.

Nova Zembla, Russian SFSR: see NOVAYA ZEMLYA.

Novbaran, Iran: see NUBARAN.

Nove (nō'vĕ), village (pop. 1,375), Vicenza prov., Veneto, N Italy, near Brenta R., 14 mi. NE of Vicenza; hydroelectric station. Noted for its ceramic industry.

Nove Benatky, Czechoslovakia: see BENATKY NAD JIZEROU.

Novegradi, Yugoslavia: see NOVIGRAD.

Nove Hrady (nô'vā hrä'dĭ), Czech *Nové Hrady*, Ger. *Gratzen* (grä'tsŭn), town (pop. 775), S Bohemia, Czechoslovakia, on railroad and 21 mi. E of Cesky Krumlov, near Austrian border; glassmaking. Peat extraction from near-by marshes.

Novelda (nōvĕl'dä), city (pop. 9,798), Alicante prov., E Spain, in Valencia, 16 mi. WNW of Alicante; mfg. of essential oils, dyes, perfumes, textiles (vegetable fibers), footwear, tiles, cement; marble working, flour- and sawmilling, brandy and liqueur distilling, vegetable canning. Ships saffron, almonds, fruit, wine, olive oil. Marble and stone quarries.

Novellara (nôvĕl-lä'rä), town (pop. 2,842), Reggio nell'Emilia prov., Emilia-Romagna, N central Italy, 11 mi. NNE of Reggio nell'Emilia; motors, generators. Has a Gonzaga castle.

Novelty, town (pop. 188), Knox co., NE Mo., on North R. and 11 mi. S of Edina.

Nove Mesto nad Metuji (nô'vā myĕ'stô näd' mĕ"tŏŏyē), Czech *Nové Město nad Metují*, Ger. *Neustadt an der Mettau* (noi'shtät än dĕr mĕ'tou), town (pop. 3,839), NE Bohemia, Czechoslovakia, in foothills of the Adlergebirge, on railroad and 17 mi. NE of Hradec Kralove; summer resort; textile mfg., jute processing. Has picturesque castle, 16th-cent. church.

Nove Mesto nad Vahom (näd' vähôm), Slovak *Nové Mesto nad Váhom*, Hung. *Vágújhely* (vä'gōōhā), town (pop. 7,743), W Slovakia, Czechoslovakia, on Vah R. and 43 mi. NE of Bratislava; rail junction; grain-trading center; specializes in meat production, furniture mfg., fruit export. Has 15th-cent. Gothic church.

Nove Mesto na Morave (nä' mô"rävĕ), Czech *Nové Město na Moravě*, Ger. *Neustadl* (noi'städŭl), town (pop. 3,301), W Moravia, Czechoslovakia, in Bohemian-Moravian Heights, on railroad and 24 mi. NE of Jihlava; excursion center; shoemaking industry.

Nove Mesto pod Smrkem (pôd' smŭrkĕm), Czech *Nové Město pod Smrkem*, Ger. *Neustadt an der Tafelfichte* (noi'shtät än dĕr tä'fŭlfĭkh"tŭ), village (pop. 2,446), N Bohemia, Czechoslovakia, at NW foot of Smrk peak, on railroad and 13 mi. NNE of Liberec; oats, potatoes; textile mfg.

Nove Myasto, Poland: see NOWE MIASTO, Lodz prov.

Noventa di Piave (nôvĕn'tä dē pyä'vĕ), village (pop. 1,219), Venezia prov., Veneto, N Italy, on Piave R. and 18 mi. NE of Venice.

Noventa Padovana (pädōvä'nä), village (pop. 1,544), Padova prov., Veneto, N Italy, 3 mi. E of Padua; shoe factory, tannery.

Noventa Vicentina (vēchĕntē'nä), village (pop. 1,753), Vicenza prov., Veneto, N Italy, 18 mi. S of Vicenza, in cereal-growing region; liquor, agr. machinery.

Noves (nôv), village (pop. 1,691), Bouches-du-Rhône dept., SE France, on left bank of the Durance, and 7 mi. SE of Avignon; olive- and wine-growing, soap mfg. Petrarch's Laura b. here.

Novés (nōvās'), village (pop. 2,060), Toledo prov., central Spain, 19 mi. NW of Toledo; cereals, potatoes, sheep, hogs; sawmilling.

Nove Straseci (nô'vā strä'shĕtsĕ), Czech *Nové Strašecí*, Ger. *Neustraschnitz* (noi'sträshnĭts), town (pop. 2,764), W central Bohemia, Czechoslovakia, on railroad and 23 mi. WNW of Prague, in wheat and sugar-beet dist. Coal mining near by.

Nove Zamky (nô'vā zäm'kĭ), Slovak *Nové Zamky*, Hung. *Érsekújvár* (ār'shĕkōōēvōr), Ger. *Neuhäusel* (noi'hoizŭl), town (pop. 19,121), S Slovakia, Czechoslovakia, on Nitra R. and 15 mi. N of Komarno; rail junction; tanning center; mfg. of brushes and brooms, sugar refining. Intensive tobacco growing in vicinity. Former Hung. fortress, founded in 1561; played important part in Turkish wars. Held by Hungary, 1938–45.

Novgorod (nŏv'gŭrŏd, Rus. nôv'gŭrŭt), oblast (□ 20,750; 1946 pop. estimate 1,050,000) in NW European Russian SFSR; ⊙ Novgorod. Includes N Valdai Hills (E) and L. Ilmen depression (W); drained by Msta, Lovat, and Volkhov rivers; extensive forests (½ of total area) and marshes, clayey and sandy soils. Mineral resources around Borovichi (lignite at Komarovo and Zarubino, refractory clays, limestone). Chief crop is flax; wheat and potatoes in same areas. Dairy cattle raised extensively. Lumber industry is important: sawmilling, paper milling (Velgiya, Parakhino-Poddubye), match mfg. (Chudovo, Gruzino), veneering (Staraya Russa, Parfino). Glassworking (Malaya Vishera, Bolshaya Vishera, Imeni Kominterna, Proletari) and porcelain mfg. (Krasnofarforny). Main industrial centers: Borovichi, Novgorod, Chudovo, Staraya Russa. Formed 1944 out of Leningrad oblast.

Novgorod, city (1926 pop. 32,764), ⊙ Novgorod oblast, Russian SFSR, on Volkhov R., near its issuance from L. Ilmen, and 100 mi. SSE of Leningrad; 58°31'N 31°16'E. Road and rail center; agr. industries (distilling, meat packing, flour milling), clothing and shoe factories, lumber mills, metalworks. One of oldest cities (founded 862) of USSR, it has been dubbed the "museum city" because of its many architectural relics. The 12th-cent. kremlin on left bank contains Cathedral of St. Sophia (founded 1045), monument (erected 1862) commemorating 1000th anniversary of founding of Russia, historical mus., and seat of the oblast administration. On right bank (former commercial center) are numerous churches and cathedrals (12th–18th cent.), mus. of revolution and of old Rus. art. City governed by Kiev until 12th cent., when it became center of vast territory and acquired name of Novgorod Veliki [Rus.,=Novgorod the great]. An important economic and political center (pop. up to 400,000), it flourished in 13th and 14th cent. as a rival of Moscow and member of Hanseatic League. Escaped Tatar invasion and repulsed German and Scandinavian attacks, but fell to Moscow in 1478. Destruction by Ivan the Terrible (1570) and by Swedes (1616) completed its downfall. Was ⊙ Novgorod govt. until 1927. During Second World War, held (1941–44) by Germans; its architectural relics severely damaged.

Novgorodka (nôv'gŭrŭtkŭ), village (1926 pop. 9,648), central Kirovograd oblast, Ukrainian SSR, 20 mi. SE of Kirovograd; flour mill. Formerly also Novgorodkovka.

Novgorod-Severski or **Novgorod-Severskiy** (nôv'-gŭrŭt-sĕ'vyĭrskē), city (1932 pop. estimate 10,075), NE Chernigov oblast, Ukrainian SSR, on Desna R. (landing) and 90 mi. ENE of Chernigov; rail terminus; food processing, hemp milling; chalk quarries. Was ⊙ independent principality in 11th–13th cent.; passed (14th cent.) to Lithuania and (1503) to Muscovy. In Second World War, held (1941–43) by Germans.

Novgorodsk, Russian SFSR: see POSYET, town.

Novgradets (nôv'grädĕts), village (pop. 3,859), Stalin dist., E Bulgaria, in S part of Deliorman upland, 18 mi. WNW of Stalin; sheep raising, lumbering. Formerly Kozludzha; name changed from Novgradets to Suvorovo in 1950.

Novi (nôvē'), village (pop. 1,146), Alger dept., N central Algeria, on the Mediterranean, 4 mi. WSW of Cherchel; vineyards, olive groves.

Novi (nô'vē). **1** or **Bosanski Novi** (bô'sänskē), town (pop. 4,003), NW Bosnia, Yugoslavia, on Una R., at mouth of the Sana (Croatia border), and 45 mi. NW of Banja Luka; rail junction; local trade center. Gypsum deposits. Blast furnace at Beslinac, 6 mi. SW. **2** Village, NW Croatia, Yugoslavia, small port on Adriatic Sea, 23 mi. SE of Rijeka, opposite Krk Isl.; bathing resort; trade center for fruitgrowing region. Founded in 1288.

Novibazar, Yugoslavia: see NOVI PAZAR.

Novi Becej, Yugoslavia: see VOLOSINOVO.

Novice (nō'vĭs), town (pop. 252), Coleman co., central Texas, 15 mi. NW of Coleman.

Novichikha (nŭvĕchē'khŭ), village (1939 pop. over 2,000), SW Altai Territory, Russian SFSR, 50 mi. N of Rubtsovsk, in agr. area.

Novi di Modena (nô'vē dē mô'dĕnä), village (pop. 1,272), Modena prov., Emilia-Romagna, N central Italy, 8 mi. W of Mirandola; wine making.

Noviembre, 27 de (väntēsyä'tā dā nōvyĕm'brā), or **Gabino Mendoza** (gäbē'nō mĕndō'sä), military post (Fortín 27 de Noviembre or Fortín Gabino Mendoza), Santa Cruz dept., SE Bolivia, in the Chaco, 90 mi. ESE of Charagua, on Paraguay border. Boundary marker established (1938) in Chaco Peace Conference.

Novigrad, Trieste: see CITTANOVA.

Novigrad or **Novigrad Dalmatinski** (nô'vēgrät" dälmä'tĭnskē), Ital. *Novegradi* (nôvĕgrä'dē), village, W Croatia, Yugoslavia, on Novigrad Sea (inlet of Adriatic Sea), 15 mi. ENE of Zadar, in Dalmatia. Bauxite deposits. Also Novi Grad.

Novi Knezevac or **Novi Knezhevats** (nô'vē knĕ'zhĕ-väts), Serbo-Croatian *Novi Kneževac*, Hung. *Törökkanizsa* (tû'rûk-kŏ"nĭzhŏ), village (pop. 7,495), Vojvodina, N Serbia, Yugoslavia, on Tisa R., on railroad and 22 mi. E of Subotica, in the Banat; raw silk mfg. Formerly called Nova Kanjiza.

Novi Ligure (nô'vē lē'gōōrĕ), town (pop. 17,251), Alessandria prov., Piedmont, N Italy, 14 mi. SE of Alessandria; rail junction; industrial center; ironworks, textile mills (silk, cotton). Austro-Russian army under Suvarov defeated French here, 1799.

Noville-les-Bois (nōvē'-lā-bwä'), village (pop. 1,030), Namur prov., S central Belgium, 8 mi. NNE of Namur; agr., lumbering.

Novi Marof (nô'vē mä'rôf), village, N Croatia, Yugoslavia, 10 mi. S of Varazdin, in lignite area; local trade center; lumbering. Castle, castle ruins.

Novinger (nŏ'vĭnjŭr), city (pop. 734), Adair co., N Mo., on Chariton R. and 6 mi. W of Kirksville.

Noviodunum, France: see NEVERS; SOISSONS.

Noviomagus, France: see LISIEUX.

Noviomagus, Germany: see SPEYER.

Noviomagus, Netherlands: see NIJMEGEN.

Novion-Porcien (nōvyō-pôrsyē'), agr. village (pop. 579), Ardennes dept., N France, 7 mi. NNE of Rethel. Stone quarries.

Novi Pazar (nô'vē päzär') [=new market], city (pop. 5,461), Kolarovgrad dist., E Bulgaria, on headstream of Provadiya R. and 15 mi. ENE of Kolarovgrad; agr. center; porcelain mfg. Kaolin quarried near by. Called Yeni Pazar under Turkish rule.

Novi Pazar (nô'vē pä'zär), town (pop. 12,196), W Serbia, Yugoslavia, on Raska R. and 115 mi. S of Belgrade; carpet-weaving school. Oriental architecture. Ruins of medieval Serbian castle and cathedral. In Middle Ages, known as Raska or Rashka, anc. *Rascia*, original home of the Serbs; captured (15th cent.) by Turks; developed (17th cent.) as important trade center on Dubrovnik-Nis route; was seat of a Turkish sanjak. The name Sanjak is still applied to the adjoining Serbia-Montenegro frontier region (NW), occupied in part (1878–1908) by Austro-Hungarian troops. Under Turkish rule (until 1913), called Yeni-Pazar; formerly also Novibazar or Novipazar.

Novi Sad (sät'), Hung. *Újvidék* (ōō'ēvĭdāk), Ger. *Neusatz* (noi'zäts), city (pop. 77,127), ⊙ Vojvodina, N Serbia, Yugoslavia, port on left bank of the Danube, opposite Petrovaradin, on Belgrade-Budapest RR, on internatl. highway, and 45 mi. NW of Belgrade, in the Backa. Terminus of canal to Mali Stapar; airport; industrial center; mfg. of agr. machinery, electrochemical equipment, industrial porcelain, chocolate, and candy; flour milling, canning; grain trade. Vegetable and hemp growing, silkworm raising, natural-gas extracting in vicinity. Coal mining in FRUSKA GORA. Founded after 1690 as settlement for PETROVARADIN fortress, it rapidly developed as an economic center of the Backa. Became Orthodox Eastern bishopric in early-18th cent.; made a royal free city and named Novi Sad in 1748. Became seat of 1st Serbian theological seminar (1765) and 1st Serbian high school (1810); developed as Serbian literary center. Has commercial acad., women teachers col., state theater.

Novi Sad-Mali Stapar Canal (–mä'lē stä'pär), in the Backa, Vojvodina, N Serbia, Yugoslavia; runs bet. the Danube at Novi Sad and Danube-Tisa Canal at Mali Stapar; 43 mi. long. Until 1945, called Franz Joseph Canal in Hungary, King Alexander Canal in Yugoslavia.

Novi Seher or **Novi Shekher** (shĕ'hĕr, –khĕr), Serbo-Croatian *Novi Šeher*, village (pop. 5,729), N central Bosnia, Yugoslavia, 4 mi. SW of Maglaj.

Nóvita (nō'vētä), village (pop. 418), Chocó dept., W Colombia, landing on affluent of San Juan R. and 50 mi. S of Quibdó; gold- and platinum-placer mines.

Novka (nôf'kŭ), town (1926 pop. 919), N central Vitebsk oblast, Belorussian SSR, 20 mi. NNE of Vitebsk; glassworks.

Novo- [Rus. combining form,=new], in Rus. names: see also NOVAYA, NOVOYE, NOVY, NOVYE.

Novo-Aidar or **Novo-Aydar** (nô"vŭ-īdär'), village (1926 pop. 5,225), central Voroshilovgrad oblast, Ukrainian SSR, on Aidar R. and 22 mi. S of Starobelsk; wheat.

Novo-Aleksandrovka (–ŭlyĭksän'drŭfkŭ), town (1939 pop. over 500), SE Voroshilovgrad oblast, Ukrainian SSR, in the Donbas, 2 mi. W of Krasnodon; coal mines.

Novoaleksandrovsk, Lithuania: see ZARASAI.

Novo-Aleksandrovsk (–drŭfsk), village (1947 pop. over 500), S Sakhalin, Russian SFSR, on E coast railroad and 7 mi. N of Yuzhno-Sakhalinsk, in agr. area; rail junction (branch to Sinegorsk coal mines). Under Jap. rule (1905–45), called Konuma.

Novo-Aleksandrovskaya (–drŭfskīŭ), village (1926 pop. 10,747), NW Stavropol Territory, Russian SFSR, on railroad and 45 mi. NW of Stavropol; agr. center in wheat and livestock area; meat packing, flour milling; metalworking.

Novo-Alekseyevka (–ŭlyĭksyā'ŭfkŭ). **1** Village (1948 pop. over 2,000), NW Aktyubinsk oblast, Kazakh SSR, 70 mi. W of Aktyubinsk; millet, wheat. **2** Town (1939 pop. over 500), SE Kherson oblast, Ukrainian SSR, 55 mi. SW of Melitopol; rail junction (spur to Genichesk).

Novo-Annenski or **Novo-Annenskiy** (–ä'nyĭnskē), town (1944 pop. over 10,000), NW Stalingrad oblast, Russian SFSR, on railroad (Filonovo station), on Buzuluk R. and 150 mi. NW of Stalingrad; major flour-milling center; metalworks. Until c.1939, Novo-Annenskaya.

Novo-Arkhangelsk, Alaska: see SITKA.

Novo-Arkhangelsk or **Novo-Arkhangel'sk** (–ŭr-khän'gĭlsk), village (1926 pop. 7,120), W Kirovograd oblast, Ukrainian SSR, on road and 33 mi. E of Uman; metalworks.

Novoasbest (nŭ"vŭŭzbyĕst'), town (1939 pop. over 2,000), W central Sverdlovsk oblast, Russian SFSR, 18 mi. SE of Nizhni Tagil; asbestos-mining center. Developed in 1930s. Called Krasnouralski Rudnik until 1933.

Novo-Aydar, Ukrainian SSR: see NOVO-AIDAR.

Novo-Bayazet, Armenian SSR: see NOR-BAYAZET.

Novo-Belitsa, Belorussian SSR: see GOMEL, city.

Novo-Belokatai or **Novo-Belokatay** (nô"vŭ-byĕlŭ-kŭtī'), village (1948 pop. over 2,000), NE Bashkir Autonomous SSR, Russian SFSR, 45 mi. NNW of Zlatoust; grain, livestock; lumbering.

Novobogatinskoye (nŭ"vŭbŭgä'tyĭnskŭyŭ), village (1939 pop. over 500), N Guryev oblast, Kazakh SSR, on arm of Ural R. delta mouth and 35 mi. NW of Guryev, in petroleum area.

Novobratsevski or **Novobratsevskiy** (nŭ"vŭbrä'-tsyĭfskē), town (1939 pop. over 500), central Moscow oblast, Russian SFSR, 2 mi. NW of Tushino; textile milling.

Novo Brdo (nô'vô bûr'dô), mine, S Serbia, Yugoslavia, 14 mi. ESE of Pristina, in the Kosovo. Produces lead and zinc ores with some silver and gold. Flotation mill. A noted silver-mining center in 14th–15th cent.

Novocherkassk (nŭ"vŭchĭrkäsk'), city (1939 pop. 81,286), SW Rostov oblast, Russian SFSR, on hill on right bank of the Aksai (right affluent of the Don) and 20 mi. NE of Rostov; industrial center; mfg. (machines, explosives), lumber milling, agr. processing (wines, alcohol, meat); mfg. of locomotives (at Lokomotivstroi station, 6 mi. NW). A historic cultural center of the Don Cossacks, with former ataman's palace. Has polytechnic col., veterinary, swamp drainage, and teachers institutes. At Persianovka station (7 mi. N) is Azov-Black Sea agr. col. Founded 1805 as administrative hq. of Don Cossacks; acquired (1905–17) its higher schools and became a leading Rus. educational center. Held during civil war (1917–20) by Ger. and counter-revolutionary troops, during Second World War, by Germans (1942–43).

Novo-Chernorechenski or **Novo-Chernorechenskiy** (nô"vŭ-chĕrnŭrĭ'chĕn'skē), town (1949 pop. over 500), S Krasnoyarsk territory, Russian SFSR, near Kozulka, W of Krasnoyarsk.

Novo-Daryevka or **Novo-Dar'yevka** (nô"vŭ-där'-yĭfkŭ), town (1939 pop. over 500), S Voroshilovgrad oblast, Ukrainian SSR, in the Donbas, 8 mi. S of Rovenki; coal mines.

Novodevichye or **Novodevich'ye** (nŭ"vŭdyĭvē'chĭ), village (1926 pop. 3,616), W Kuibyshev oblast, Russian SFSR, grain port on right bank of the Volga and 35 mi. NNE of Syzran; grain, sunflowers. Chalk and cement-rock quarrying near by.

Novo-Druzheskoye (nô"vŭ-drōō'zhĭskŭyŭ), town (1939 pop. over 500), W Voroshilovgrad oblast, Ukrainian SSR, in the Donbas, N of Lisichansk; coal mines.

Novo-Dugino (–dōō'gēnŭ), village (1939 pop. over 500), NE Smolensk oblast, Russian SFSR, 13 mi. S of Sychevka; dairying.

Novo-Ekonomicheskoye (–ĕ"kŭnŭmē'chĭskŭyŭ), city (1939 pop. over 10,000), W Stalino oblast, Ukrainian SSR, in the Donbas, 4 mi. NE of Krasnoarmeiskoye; coal mines. Formerly called Novo-Ekonomicheski Rudnik.

Novogeorgievsk, Poland: see MODLIN.

Novo-Georgiyevsk (–gäōr'gēŭfsk), city (1926 pop. 5,085), N Kirovograd oblast, Ukrainian SSR, port on Tyasmin R., near its mouth on Dnieper R., and 15 mi. W of Kremenchug; furniture mfg.; dairying, distilling; shipbuilding.

Novo-Glukhov, Ukrainian SSR: see KREMENNAYA.

Novograd-Volynski or **Novograd-Volynskiy** (nŭvŭ-grät'-vŭlĭn'skē), city (1926 pop. over 14,897), W Zhitomir oblast, Ukrainian SSR, on Sluch R. and 50 mi. WNW of Zhitomir; rail junction; machine shops; distilling, furniture mfg. Lignite deposits. Passed (1793) from Poland to Russia; called Novograd-Volynsk until c.1928. Pop. 40% Jewish until Second World War, when city was held (1941–43) by Germans.

Novogrod, Poland: see NOWOGROD.

Novogroznenski or **Novogroznenskiy** (nŭvŭgrôz'-nyĭnskē), town (1946 pop. over 500), SE Grozny oblast, Russian SFSR, 9 mi. ESE of Gudermes; petroleum wells. Developed during Second World War. Until 1944, Oisungur.

Novogrudok (nŭvŭgrōō'dŭk), Pol. *Nowogródek* (nô-vôgrōō'dĕk), city (1948 pop. over 10,000), N central Baranovichi oblast, Belorussian SSR, 34 mi. NNW of Baranovichi, on rail spur, in woodland; agr. processing (powdered milk, grain, hides), mfg. (cement, concrete blocks, pottery, knitwear). Has ruins of 13th-cent. castle, several old churches, and house mus. of Pol. poet Adam Mickiewicz (b. here 1798). Founded by Kievan Russians prior to 12th cent.; was ⊙ independent Lith. duchy in 13th cent.; chartered 1444. Passed (1795) from Poland to Russia; reverted (1921) to Poland, where it was ⊙ Nowogrodek prov. (1921–39); ceded to USSR in 1945.

Novo Hamburgo (nō'vōō ămbōōr'gōō), city (pop. 12,954), E Rio Grande do Sul, Brazil, on railroad and 25 mi. N of Pôrto Alegre; livestock slaughtering, tanning, mfg. of musical instruments. Agr. trade. Settled by Germans in 19th cent.

Novo Horizonte (nō'vôrēzōn'tĭ), city (pop. 5,433), N central São Paulo, Brazil, near Tietê R., 37 mi. ENE of Lins; rail-spur terminus; coffee, rice, and cotton processing; pottery mfg.; cattle raising.

Novo-Ilinski or **Novo-Il'inskiy** (nô"vŭ-ēlyēn'skē), town (1942 pop. over 500), S central Molotov oblast, Russian SFSR, on right bank of Kama R. and 5 mi. SE of Nytva; petroleum deposits.

Novo-Izborsk (–ēzbôrsk'), Estonian *Irboska*, city (pop. 906), W Pskov oblast, Russian SFSR, on road and 20 mi. WSW of Pskov; gypsum-quarrying center. Castle ruins. Rail station (pop. 360) with gypsum works is 6 mi. NE of city. In Rus. Pskov govt. until 1920; in Estonia until 1945.

Novo-Kazalinsk (–kŭzŭlyēnsk'), town (1939 pop. over 10,000), NW Kzyl-Orda oblast, Kazakh SSR, on Trans-Caspian RR (Kazalinsk station) and 70 mi. SSE of Aralsk, in rice area. Developed after construction (1905) of railroad; superseded Kazalinsk as local trade center.

Novokhopersk (nŭ"vŭkhŭpyôrsk'), city (1926 pop. 7,437), E Voronezh oblast, Russian SFSR, on Khoper R. and 25 mi. SW of Borisoglebsk; distilling, sunflower-oil extraction. Beaver reserve near by. Novokhopersk station, with adjoining Novokhoperski town, lies 3 mi. SW. City dates from 1716; chartered 1762; site of shipyards under Catherine the Great.

Novo-Kiyevka (nô"vŭ-kē'ŭfkŭ), village (1939 pop. over 500), SE Amur oblast, Russian SFSR, near confluence of Zeya and Selemdzha rivers, 35 mi. NE of Svobodny, in agr. area (wheat, livestock).

Novokiyevskoye, Russian SFSR: see KRASKINO, Maritime Territory.

Novo-Kubanskaya (–kōōbän'skīŭ), village (1926 pop. 12,303), E Krasnodar Territory, Russian SFSR, near Kuban R., 7 mi. NW of Armavir; flour mill; wheat, sunflowers, castor beans.

Novo-Kurovka (–kōō'rŭfkŭ), village (1948 pop. over 500), S Khabarovsk Territory, Russian SFSR, on Kur R. and 40 mi. NW of Khabarovsk, in lumbering area.

Novo-Kuznetsk, Russian SFSR: see STALINSK, Kemerovo oblast.

Novo-Lakskoye (–läk'skŭyŭ), village (1939 pop. over 500), N Dagestan Autonomous SSR, Russian SFSR, 8 mi. SW of Khasavyurt; cotton, wheat, orchards. Until 1944 (in Chechen-Ingush Autonomous SSR), called Yaryksu-Aukh.

Novo-Leushkovskaya (–lyăōōsh'kŭfskīŭ), village (1926 pop. 9,626), N Krasnodar Territory, Russian SFSR, 12 mi. NW of Tikhoretsk; dairying, flour milling; wheat, sunflowers.

Novoli (nô'vôlē), town (pop. 7,721), Lecce prov., Apulia, S Italy, 7 mi. WNW of Lecce; wine-making center.

Novo-Lyubino, Russian SFSR: see LYUBINSKI.

Novo-Malorossiskaya, **Novo-Malorossiiskaya**, or **Novo-Malorossiyskaya** (nô"vŭ-mä"lŭrŭsē'skīŭ), village (1926 pop. 10,101), N central Krasnodar Territory, Russian SFSR, on Beisug R. and 18 mi. SW of Tikhoretsk; flour mill, metalworks. In late 1930s, also called Grazhdanskaya.

Novo-Malykla (–mŭlĭk'lŭ), village (1939 pop. over 2,000), NE Ulyanovsk oblast, Russian SFSR, 12 mi. E of Melekess; wheat, sunflowers. Sometimes called Novaya Malykla.

Novo-Mariinsk, Russian SFSR: see ANADYR, town.

Novo-Mariinsk Canal, Russian SFSR: see MARIINSK CANAL.

Novo-Melovatka (–myĕlŭvät'kŭ), village (1926 pop. 6,587), E Voronezh oblast, Russian SFSR, 11 mi. WNW of Kalach; wheat, sunflowers.

Novo Mesto (nô'vô mĕ'stô), Ger. *Rudolfswerth* (rōō'dôlfs-vĕrt"), formerly Ger. *Neustädtl* (noi'-shtĕt"ŭl), village (pop. 6,017), S Slovenia, Yugoslavia, on Krka R., on railroad and 36 mi. SE of Ljubljana. Trade center; terminus of rail spur to TOPLICE; hydroelectric plant. Founded 1365 by Duke Rudolf of Austria. Until 1918, in Carniola.

Novo Minsk, Poland: see MINSK MAZOWIECKI.

Novo-Minskaya (nô"vŭ-mĕn'skīŭ), village (1926 pop. 15,925), NW Krasnodar Territory, Russian SFSR, on railroad and 40 mi. SE of Yeisk; metalworks, flour mill; wheat, sunflowers, cotton.

Novo-Mirgorod (–mĕr'gŭrŭt), town (1926 pop. 8,734), NW Kirovograd oblast, Ukrainian SSR, 34 mi. NW of Kirovograd; metalworks.

Novo-Moskovsk (–mŭskôfsk'), city (1926 pop. 15,-167), N central Dnepropetrovsk oblast, Ukrainian SSR, on Samara R. and 15 mi. NNE of Dnepropetrovsk; rail junction; tin-plate milling; flour.

Novo-Nazyvayevka (–nŭzĭvī'ŭfkŭ), town (1948 pop. over 10,000), W Omsk oblast, Russian SFSR, on Trans-Siberian RR and 90 mi. NW of Omsk; peat extraction, dairy farming. Until c.1935 called Sibirski.

Novo-Nikolayevka (–nyĭkŭlī'ŭfkŭ). **1** Village, Dnepropetrovsk oblast, Russian SFSR: see CHKALOVO. **2** Town, Stalino oblast, Ukrainian SSR: see BUDENNOVKA. **3** Village (1926 pop. 3,547), N Zaporozhe oblast, Ukrainian SSR, 35 mi. ENE of Zaporozhe; flour.

Novonikolayevsk, Russian SFSR: see NOVOSIBIRSK, city.

Novo-Nikolayevskaya (–skīŭ), village (1926 pop. 2,461), NW Stalingrad oblast, Russian SFSR, 30 mi. SSE of Borisoglebsk; rail junction (Aleksikovo station; branch SW to Uryupinsk); flour milling, metalworking.

Novo-Omsk, Russian SFSR: see OMSK, city.

Novo-Orsk (nô"vŭ-ôrsk'), village (1926 pop. 3,935), E central Chkalov oblast, Russian SFSR, on Kumak R. (left tributary of Ural R.), on railroad and 20 mi. NE of Orsk; wheat, livestock. Limonite deposits near by. Until c.1935, Novo-Orskaya; sometimes written Novoorsk.

Novo-Pavlovka (–päv'lŭfkŭ). **1** Town (1948 pop. over 2,000), SW Chita oblast, Russian SFSR, on Trans-Siberian RR (near Tolbaga station) 20 mi. E of Petrovsk; lignite mining. **2** Town (1926 pop. 6,117), S Voroshilovgrad oblast, Ukrainian SSR, on Mius R., 5 mi. S of Krasny Luch; coal mines.

Novo-Pavlovskaya (–skīŭ), village (1926 pop. 5,143), S Stavropol Territory, Russian SFSR, on railroad (Apollonskaya station) and 15 mi. SE of Georgiyevsk, in wheat and sunflower area; metalworks.

Novo-Petrovskoye (–pĕtrôf'skŭyŭ), village (1939 pop. over 500), central Moscow oblast, Russian SFSR, on railroad (Ustinovka station) and 15 mi. WNW of Istra; dairying.

Novo-Pistsovo (–pĕstsô'vŭ), town (1939 pop. over 500), NE Ivanovo oblast, Russian SFSR, 9 mi. NNW of Vichuga; flour milling.

Novo-Pokrovka (–pŭkrôf'kŭ). **1** Village (1939 pop. over 500), N Semipalatinsk oblast, Kazakh SSR, on Turksib RR and 15 mi. NE of Semipalatinsk; livestock breeding. **2** Village (1926 pop. 2,490), E central Chkalov oblast, Russian SFSR, 37 mi. NW of Orsk, in Orsk-Khalilovo industrial dist.; flour milling, metalworking. Phosphorite deposits (S). Formerly Novo-Pokrovskoye. **3** Village (1939 pop. over 500), W Maritime Territory, Russian SFSR, 36 mi. E of Iman, in agr. area (grain, soybeans, perilla). **4** Town, Voronezh oblast, Russian SFSR: see LISKI. **5** Village (1939 pop. under 500), central Dnepropetrovsk oblast, Ukrainian SSR, 33 mi. SSW of Dnepropetrovsk; truck produce. **6** Town (1926 pop. 2,910), N central Kharkov oblast, Ukrainian SSR, 6 mi. W of Chuguyev, in Kharkov metropolitan area; flour milling.

Novo-Pokrovskaya (–skīŭ), village (1926 pop. 17,-235), E Krasnodar Territory, Russian SFSR, on Yeya R. and 27 mi. ENE of Tikhoretsk; flour milling, dairying; metalworks; wheat, sunflowers.

Novo-Pokrovskoye (–skŭyŭ), village (1926 pop. 3,158), SW Saratov oblast, Russian SFSR, 20 mi. ENE of Balashov; flour mill, metalworks; wheat, sunflowers.

Novo-Pskov (–pskôf'), town (1926 pop. 4,593), N Voroshilovgrad oblast, Ukrainian SSR, on Aidar R. and 10 mi. NNE of Starobelsk; metalworks.

Novoradomsk, Poland: see RADOMSKO.

Novo Redondo (nō'vōō rĭdōn'dōō), town (pop. 1,016), ⊙ Cuanza-Sul dist. (□ 24,250; pop. 288,914), Benguela prov., W Angola, on the Atlantic, 170 mi. SSE of Luanda; 11°11'S 13°52'E. Open roadstead. Ships sugar, coffee, palm oil. Airfield. R.C. mission.

Novo-Repnoye (nô"vŭ-ryĕp'nŭyŭ), village (1939 pop. over 2,000), E Saratov oblast, Russian SFSR, 20 mi. SSE of Yershov; flour mill; wheat, cattle.

Novorossisk, **Novorossiisk**, or **Novorossiysk** (nŭvŭ-rŭsēsk'), city (1939 pop. 95,280), W Krasnodar Territory, Russian SFSR, port on small Tsemes Bay of Black Sea, 60 mi. WSW of Krasnodar. Rail terminus; major grain port and cement-making center; cement plants here and at Gaiduk and Verkhne-Bakanski (NW); petroleum refining, rail and ship repair yards, slate works; mfg. (mechanical tools, agr. machinery, bicycles, clothing, furniture), food processing. Wine-making center of Abrau-Dyurso is 8 mi. WSW. Grain, petroleum, cement, lumber, and machinery exports. A center for surrounding resort area, including Anapa and Gelendzhik; industrial and port section is on E side of bay, residential part on W shore. A Genoese port in 13th–14th cent.; later a Turkish fortress, captured 1808 by Russians. Present city (founded 1838) developed rapidly as ⊙ Black Sea govt. after construction (1888) of railroad from Rostov. In Second World War, held (1942–43) by Germans.

Novorossiski, **Novorossiiski**, or **Novorossiyskiy** (–rŭsē'skē), village (1948 pop. over 2,000), N Aktyubinsk oblast, Kazakh SSR, 35 mi. E of Aktyubinsk; millet, wheat.

Novo-Ryazhsk (nô"vŭ-ryäshsk'), town (1926 pop. 1,932), S central Ryazan oblast, Russian SFSR, NE suburb of Ryazhsk; rail junction.

Novorzhev (nŭvŭrzhĕf'), city (1926 pop. 3,051), S Pskov oblast, Russian SFSR, 45 mi. SE of Ostrov, at N foot of Bezhanitsy Upland; flax retting. Dolomite quarries near by. Chartered 1777.

Novo-Selenginsk (nô"vŭ-sĕlyĭn-gēnsk'), village (1948 pop. over 2,000), SE Buryat-Mongol Autonomous SSR, Russian SFSR, on Selenga R. (landing), just N of Chikoi R. mouth, and 65 mi. SW of Ulan-Ude; highway center. Old Rus. colonization center of Selenginsk founded near by in 1666.

Novoselitsa (nŭvŭsyĕ'lyĭtsŭ), Rum. *Nouă Sulița* or *Sulița* (nô'ōōŭ sōō'lētsä), town (1930 pop. 12,143; 1941 pop. 7,937), S central Chernovtsy oblast, Ukrainian SSR, in Bessarabia, on Prut R., on railroad, and 15 mi. ESE of Chernovtsy; flour and oilseed milling, tanning. Passed (1812) to Russia; Russo-Austrian frontier station until 1918.

Novoselitskoye (nŭvŭsyĕ'lyĭtskŭyŭ), village (1926 pop. 8,452), central Stavropol Territory, Russian SFSR, 25 mi. S of Blagodarnoye; flour mill; wheat, sunflowers, castor beans.

Novo-selo (nô'vô-sĕ'lô), village (pop. 4,307), Vidin dist., NW Bulgaria, on the Danube and 11 mi. NNW of Vidin; grain, livestock, truck, vineyards; fisheries.

Novo Selo or **Banatsko Novo Selo** (bä'nätskô nô'vô sĕ'lô), Hung. *Révaújfalu* (rā'vŏ-ōō"ĕfôlōō), village (pop. 5,736), Vojvodina, NE Serbia, Yugoslavia, 10 mi. NE of Pancevo, in the Banat.

Novoselovka (nŭvŭsyô'lŭfkŭ), town (1926 pop. 3,292), N Stalino oblast, Ukrainian SSR, 8 mi. NW of Krasny Liman.

Novoselovo (–lŭvŭ), village (1948 pop. over 2,000), SW Krasnoyarsk Territory, Russian SFSR, 90 mi. SW of Krasnoyarsk and on Yenisei R.; dairy farming.

Novoselovskoye (–lŭfskŭyŭ), village (1939 pop. under 500), W central Crimea, Russian SFSR, 19 mi. NE of Yevpatoriya; metalworks; wheat, cotton. A Jewish settlement from c.1925 to Second World War. Until 1944, called Fraidorf.

Novoselskoye or **Novosel'skoye** (nŭvŭsĕl'skŭyŭ), village (1926 pop. 5,097), S Grozny oblast, Russian SFSR, on right branch of Sunzha R. and 22 mi. WSW of Grozny; corn, wheat. Lumbering (S). Until 1944, Achkhoi-Martan.

Novoseltsi (nôvôsĕl'tsē), village (pop. 3,586), Sofia dist., W Bulgaria, on right tributary of Iskar R. and 15 mi. E of Sofia; mfg. of porcelain and ceramics. Ironworks near by (N) in Yana (pop. 816).

Novoselye or **Novosel'ye** (–sĕ'lyĭ), village (1948 pop. over 500), central Pskov oblast, Russian SFSR, 28 mi. NE of Pskov; flax processing.

Novo-Sergiyevka (nô"vŭ-sĕr'gēŭfkŭ), village (1926 pop. 3,192), W central Chkalov oblast, Russian SFSR, on Samara R. and 30 mi. SE of Sorochinsk; wheat, livestock. Kumiss resort near by. Novo-Sergiyevskaya, town (1948 pop. over 2,000), is just S, on railroad; metalworks.

Novoshakhtinsk (nŭvŭshäkh'tyĭnsk), city (1926 pop. 6,709; 1939 pop. c.50,000), SW Rostov oblast, Russian SFSR, 35 mi. NNE of Rostov, 13 mi. W of Shakhty (linked by rail spur); major anthracite-mining center in E Donets Basin. Called Imeni III Internatsionala in 1920s and later (1929–39), Komintern.

Novo-Shepelichi (nô"vŭ-shĕpĭlyē'chē), village (1939 pop. over 500), N Kiev oblast, Ukrainian SSR, on Pripet R. and 70 mi. NNW of Kiev.

Novo-Sheshminsk (–shĭshmēnsk'), village (1926 pop. 5,317), central Tatar Autonomous SSR, Russian SFSR, on Sheshma R. and 32 mi. SE of Chistopol; wheat, livestock.

Novosibirsk (nŭvŭsēbērsk'), oblast (□ 69,000; pop. c.2,100,000) in S Siberian Russian SFSR; ⊙ Novosibirsk. Drained by middle Ob (E), Om and Tara rivers. L. Chany is in W. Includes low, marshy BARABA STEPPE (W) and hilly forest steppe (E of Ob R.), with continental climate. Except for highly industrialized NOVOSIBIRSK and its suburbs, economy of oblast is chiefly agr., with emphasis on dairy products, wheat, and livestock breeding. Trans-Siberian RR, site of largest towns (Novosibirsk, BARABINSK, TATARSK), traverses oblast E to W. Pop. chiefly Russians, with some Ukrainians and Tatars in Baraba Steppe. Created 1937 out of W.Siberian Territory; until 1943–44 it included areas now in oblasts of TOMSK and KEMEROVO.

Novosibirsk, city (1926 pop. 120,128; 1939 pop. 405,589; 1946 pop. estimate 750,000), ⊙ Novosibirsk oblast, Russian SFSR, on Trans-Siberian RR, on Ob R. and 1,750 mi. E of Moscow; 55°N 83°50'E. Industrial and river-rail transportation center of W Siberia; terminus of Turksib RR and of direct railroad to Kuznetsk Basin. One of largest USSR machine-mfg. centers (Diesel trucks, agr. and mining machinery, hydraulic presses, heavy machine tools), based on Kuzbas iron and steel production; produces cold-rolled steel for auto and tractor industries; cotton milling (raw cotton from Central Asia), shipbuilding, sawmilling; mfg. of bicycles, plastics, instruments, tools, abrasives, radios; food processing. Site of opera house, several higher technical institutes (rail transportation, construction, military engineering, geodetic survey), agr., medical, and teachers colleges, W.Siberian branch of Acad. of Sciences, regional mus. Situated largely on right bank of the Ob bet. 2 small tributaries, the Inya (S) and the Yeltsovka (N), with large park area (NW); extends to its left-bank suburb of Krivoshchekovo. SE of the city, across the Inya, is the rail junction of Inskaya, with extensive switchyards. City developed after 1893, during construction of Trans-Siberian RR; originally called Novonikolayevsk until 1925. Owing to its centralized location and its proximity to Kuznetsk Basin, it developed with exceptional rapidity (city has been called the "Chicago of Siberia") and supplanted (c.1930) Omsk as the leading city of Siberia. Became ⊙ Novonikolayevsk govt. (1920), ⊙ Siberian Territory (1925), ⊙ W.Siberian Territory (1930), and ⊙ Novosibirsk oblast (1937).

Novo-Sibirskiye Ostrova, Russian SFSR: see NEW SIBERIAN ISLANDS.

Novosil or **Novosil'** (nŭvŭsēl'), city (1926 pop. 2,733), N central Orel oblast, Russian SFSR, 37 mi. E of Orel; fruit and vegetable canning, hemp milling. Chartered 1155.

Novosokolniki (nŭ"vŭsŭkôl'nyĭkē), city (1926 pop. 4,676), S central Velikiye Luki oblast, Russian SFSR, 12 mi. W of Velikiye Luki; rail junction; metalworks.

Novo-Spasskoye (nô"vŭ-spä'skŭyŭ), village (1926 pop. 2,547), S Ulyanovsk oblast, Russian SFSR, on Syzran R. and 28 mi. W of Syzran; flour milling; wheat, potatoes.

Novostroyevo (nŭvŭstroi'ŭvŭ), village (1939 pop. 872), S Kaliningrad oblast, Russian SFSR, 7 mi. WNW of Ozersk. Until 1945, in East Prussia and called Trempen (trĕm'pŭn).

Novo-Subkhangulovo (nô"vŭ-sōōpkhän'gōōlŭvŭ), village (1926 pop. 260), S central Bashkir Autonomous SSR, Russian SFSR, in the S Urals, on Belaya R. and 70 mi. SE of Sterlitamak; lumbering; livestock.

Novo-Sukhotino (–sōōkhô'tyĭnŭ), village (1948 pop. over 2,000), N Kokchetav oblast, Kazakh SSR, near railroad, (Taincha station), 45 mi. NNE of Kokchetav; center of sunflower-growing area; metalworks.

Novo-Sventsyany, Lithuania: see SVENCIONELIAI.

Novo-Svetlovka (–svyĕt'lŭfkŭ), village (1939 pop. over 2,000), SE Voroshilovgrad oblast, Ukrainian SSR, in the Donbas, 10 mi. SE of Voroshilovgrad; truck produce.

Novo-Titarovskaya (–tyĕtŭrôf'skŭ), village (1926 pop. 15,756), central Krasnodar Territory, Russian SFSR, 15 mi. N of Krasnodar; flour mill, metalworks; dairying; wheat, sunflowers.

Novo-Troitsk (–trô'yĭtsk), city (1946 pop. estimate 20,000), SE Chkalov oblast, Russian SFSR, in S foothills of the S Urals, on right bank of Ural R., on rail spur and 10 mi. W of Orsk city center, in Orsk-Khalilovo industrial dist. Metallurgical center (high-quality steels); alloys (nickel, cobalt, chromium) mined here. Limonite shipped from Khalilovo (15 mi. NW), limestone from Izvestnyaki (just WSW; on rail spur). Construction of metallurgical plant began in 1942. Absorbed Akkermanovka (nickel mine, jasper quarries) and became city in 1945.

Novo-Troitskoye (–skŭyŭ). **1** Village (1948 pop. over 2,000), E Dzhambul oblast, Kazakh SSR, near Turksib RR, 130 mi. ENE of Dzhambul; cotton. **2** Village, Frunze oblast, Kirghiz SSR: see KAGANOVICH. **3** City, Chita oblast, Russian SFSR: see BALEI. **4** Village (1939 pop. over 500), W Kirov oblast, Russian SFSR, 45 mi. WNW of Kotelnich; flax processing. **5** Village (1926 pop. 4,621), SE Kherson oblast, Ukrainian SSR, 25 mi. NW of Genichesk; dairy farming. **6** Village (1926 pop. 7,403), W Stavropol Territory, Russian SFSR, on Yegorlyk R. (dam) and 33 mi. NW of Stavropol, in grain area; flour mill. Dam (3/4 mi. long) backs up main reservoir (□ 12) of Kuban-Yegorlyk irrigation system; feeds right and left Yegorlyk lateral canals. **7** Town (1926 pop. 5,100), central Stalino oblast, Ukrainian SSR, in the Donbas, 21 mi. SW of Stalino; kaolin and dolomite quarries.

Novo-Tulski or **Novo-Tul'skiy** (–tōōl'skē), town (1939 pop. over 10,000), central Tula oblast, Russian SFSR, on Upa R. and 3 mi. SE of Tula; metallurgical center; iron- and steelworks.

Novoturukhansk, Russian SFSR: see TURUKHANSK.

Novougolny or **Novougol'nyy** (nŭ"vŭōō'gŭlnē), town (1939 pop. over 500), S Moscow oblast, Russian SFSR, near Donskoi; lignite mining.

Novo-Ukrainka (nô"vŭ-ōōkrēn'kŭ), city (1926 pop. 16,431), SW Kirovograd oblast, Ukrainian SSR, 36 mi. WSW of Kirovograd; flour-milling center; dairying, distilling.

Novo-Urgench, Uzbek SSR: see URGENCH.

Novoutkinsk (nŭvŭōōt'kĭnsk), town (1935 pop. estimate 6,700), SW Sverdlovsk oblast, Russian SFSR, in the central Urals, near Chusovaya R., on railroad and 9 mi. WNW of Bilimbai; metalworking (electrical welding), sawmilling, mfg. of silicates.

Novouzensk (–ōō'zyĭnsk), city (1926 pop. 13,943), SE Saratov oblast, Russian SFSR, on Greater Uzen R. and 115 mi. SE of Saratov; agr. center; cattle market; metalworking, flour milling. Kumiss resort. Chartered 1835.

Novo-Varshavka (nô"vŭ-vŭrshäf'kŭ), village (1939 pop. over 500), SE Omsk oblast, Russian SFSR, 5 mi. W of Cherlak, across Irtysh R.; wheat, dairy.

Novo-Vasilyevka or **Novo-Vasil'yevka** (–vŭsē'lyĭfkŭ), village (1939 pop. over 2,000), S Zaporozhe oblast, Ukrainian SSR, 19 mi. E of Melitopol; cotton, wheat.

Novo-Vilnya, Lithuania: see NAUJA VILNIA.

Novo-Voikovo or **Novo-Voykovo** (–voi'kŭvŭ), town (1939 pop. over 10,000), central Stalino oblast, Ukrainian SSR, in the Donbas, 3 mi. SE of Makeyevka; coal mines. Formerly Kholodnaya Balka.

Novo-Vorontsovka (–vŭrŭntsôf'kŭ), village (1926 pop. 4,741), N Kherson oblast, Ukrainian SSR, 20 mi. WSW of Nikopol, on Dnieper R. arm; flour.

Novo-Voznesenovka (–vŭznyĭsyĕ'nŭfkŭ), village (1948 pop. over 500), NE Issyk-Kul oblast, Kirghiz SSR, 20 mi. ENE of Przhevalsk; wheat.

Novo-Vyazniki (–vyŭznyĭkē'), town (1939 pop. over 2,000), NE Vladimir oblast, Russian SFSR, 4 mi. SSE of Vyazniki; linen milling.

Novoye [Rus.,=new], in Rus. names: see also NOVAYA, Novo- [Rus. combining form], NOVY, NOVYE.

Novoye (nô'vŭyŭ), village (1947 pop. over 500), S Sakhalin, Russian SFSR, on E coast railroad and 23 mi. SSW of Poronaisk. Coal mining near by. Under Jap. rule (1905–45), called Niitoi.

Novoye Churilino (chōōrĭlyē'nŭ), town (1926 pop. 912), NW Tatar Autonomous SSR, Russian SFSR, on railroad and 15 mi. ENE of Arsk; summer resort; grain, legumes.

Novo-Yegoryevskoye or **Novo-Yegor'yevskoye** (nô"vŭ-yĭgô'ryĭfskŭyŭ), village (1926 pop. 6,535), SW Altai Territory, Russian SFSR, on small L. Peresheyechnoye and 20 mi. NW of Rubtsovsk; metalworks.

Novoye Leushino (nô"vŭyŭ lyāōō'shĭnŭ), town (1939 pop. over 500), central Ivanovo oblast, Russian SFSR, near railroad (Sakhtysh station), 4 mi. S of Teikovo; peat works.

Novoyelnya or **Novoyel'nya** (nŭvŭyĕl'nyŭ), Pol. *Nowojelnia*, town (1931 pop. 1,060), W Baranovichi oblast, Belorussian SSR, 15 mi. SW of Novogrudok; rail junction; flour milling.

Novo-Yerudinski or **Novo-Yerudinskiy** (nô"vŭ-yĕrōōdyēn'skē), town (1948 pop. over 2,000), central Krasnoyarsk Territory, Russian SFSR, on Yenisei Ridge, 80 mi. NE of Yeniseisk; gold mines.

Novoye Selo (nô"vŭyŭ syĭlô'), Pol. *Nowe Siolo*, village (1939 pop. over 500), E Ternopol oblast, Ukrainian SSR, 13 mi. E of Zbarazh; wheat, barley; beekeeping.

Novo-Zaimka (nô"vŭ-zīēm'kŭ), village (1926 pop. 2,385), SW Tyumen oblast, Russian SFSR, on Trans-Siberian RR and 25 mi. SE of Yalutorovsk; flour milling, dairying.

Novo-Zavidovski or **Novo-Zavidovskiy** (–zŭvē'dŭfskē), town (1948 pop. over 2,000), S Kalinin oblast, Russian SFSR, on Volga Reservoir, 27 mi. SE of Kalinin; cotton-milling center.

Novozybkov (nŭvŭzĭp'kŭf), city (1926 pop. 21,505), SW Bryansk oblast, Russian SFSR, 110 mi. SW of Bryansk; match-producing center; mfg. of match-making machinery, shoes; hemp milling, oil extraction. Agr. experimental station, teachers col. Peat works near by. Chartered 1809. During Second World War, held (1941–43) by Germans.

Novska (nôf'skä), village (pop. 4,130), N Croatia, Yugoslavia, 20 mi. SSW of Daruvar, in Slavonia, in lignite area; rail junction; local trade center.

Novy or **Novyy** [Rus.,=new], in Rus. names: see also NOVAYA, Novo- [Rus. combining form], NOVOYE, NOVYE.

Novy or **Novyy** (nô'vē), town (1948 pop. over 2,000), N Kemerovo oblast, Russian SFSR, 15 mi. ESE of Barzas; gold placers.

Novy Afon, Georgian SSR: see AKHALI-AFONI.

Novy Bohumin (nô'vē bô'hōōmēn), Czech *Nový Bohumín*, Ger. *Neuoderberg* (noi'ōdŭrbĕrk), town (pop. 8,439), NE Silesia, Czechoslovakia, on Oder R. and 6 mi. NNE of Ostrava, on Pol. border; noted for iron and chemical works producing steel, pig-iron, pipes, wire, cables, soap, candles, pharmaceuticals, and chemical reagents. Has major oil refinery and largest freight station in Czechoslovakia. Twin-town of Bohumin, Ger. *Oderberg*, is just SW. Both are part of TESCHEN territory.

Novy Bor (bôr"), Czech *Nový Bor*, Ger. *Haida* (hī'dä) town (pop. 3,480), N Bohemia, Czechoslovakia, on railroad and 24 mi. ENE of Usti nad Labem; noted glass industry (mainly artistic glassware). Now also includes commune of Arnultovice (är'nōōltôvĭtsĕ), Ger. *Arnsdorf*. Until 1946, called Bor u Ceske Lipy.

Novy Bug or **Novyy Bug** (bōōk"), village (1926 pop. 14,188), N Nikolayev oblast, Ukrainian SSR, 38 mi. WSW of Krivoi Rog; dairying, metalworking.

Novy Buyan or **Novyy Buyan** (bōōyän'), village (1926 pop. 2,614), W Kuibyshev oblast, Russian SFSR, 35 mi. N of Kuibyshev; wheat, potatoes.

Novy Bydzov (bĭ'jôf), Czech *Nový Bydžov*, Ger. *Neubidschow*, town (pop. 6,120), NE Bohemia, Czechoslovakia, on railroad and 15 mi. W of Hradec Kralove; tanning; oats, potatoes.

Novy Chardzhui, Turkmen SSR: see CHARDZHOU, city.

Novy Donbass or **Novyy Donbass** (dŭnbäs'), city (1940 pop. over 2,000), E Stalino oblast, Ukrainian SSR, in the Donbas, 4 mi. N of Snezhnoye; coal-mining center. Formerly called Shakhta No. 18.

Novy Dvor, Poland: see NOWY DWOR.

Novye or **Novyye** [Rus.,=new], in Rus. names: see also NOVAYA, Novo- [Rus. combining form], NOVOYE, NOVY.

Novye Aldy, Russian SFSR: see CHERNORECHYE.

Novye Burasy or **Novyye Burasy** (nô"vēŭ bōōrä'sē), village (1926 pop. 6,580), N Saratov oblast, Russian SFSR, 40 mi. N of Saratov; metalworks; wheat, sunflowers.

Novye Petushki or **Novyye Petushki** (pyĕtōōshkē'), town (1926 pop. 1,154), W Vladimir oblast, Russian SFSR, on Klyazma R. and 20 mi. ENE of Orekhovo-Zuyevo; woodworking center; peat works, cotton mill. Older village of Petushki (1939 pop. over 500) is just NE.

Novye Senzhary or **Novyye Senzhary** (syĭnzhä'rē), town (1926 pop. 4,195), SE Poltava oblast, Ukrainian SSR, on Vorskla R. and 20 mi. SSW of Poltava; clothing mfg., woodworking. Also called Novo-Senzhary.

Novye Strelishche or **Novyye Strelishche** (stryĕlyē'shchĭ), Pol. *Strzeliska Nowe*, agr. town (1939 pop. over 500), NE Drogobych oblast, Ukrainian SSR, 9 mi. NNE of Khodorov.

Novy Gorod, Russian SFSR: see ORSK.

Novy Hrozenkov (nô'vē hrô'zĕnkôf), Czech *Nový Hrozenkov*, Ger. *Neuhrosenkau* (noihrō'zŭnkou), village (pop. 4,792), E Moravia, Czechoslovakia, on the Horni Becva (headstream of Becva R.), on railroad and 25 mi. ENE of Gottwaldov, in the

Beskids; summer and winter resort, noted for skiing facilities, picturesque wooden cottages, and regional costumes.

Novy Jicin (yĭ'chēn), Czech *Nový Jičín*, Ger. *Neutitschein* (noi'tĭchīn), town (pop. 11,408), S central Silesia, Czechoslovakia, on railroad and 21 mi. SW of Ostrava; known for mfg. of men's hats; machinery, woolen textiles; tobacco processing. Hodslavice (hôt'slävĭtsĕ), birthplace of F. Palacky, is 4 mi. S.

Novy Kiner or **Novyy Kiner** (kēnyĕr'), village (1939 pop. over 500), NW Tatar Autonomous SSR, Russian SFSR, 22 mi. NNW of Arsk; grain, livestock.

Novy Margelan, Uzbek SSR: see FERGANA, city.

Novy Milyatin or **Novyy Milyatin** (mĕlyä'tyĭn), Pol. *Milatyn Nowy*, village (1939 pop. over 500), central Lvov oblast, Ukrainian SSR, 6 mi. W of Busk; grain, potatoes, flax.

Novy Oskol or **Novyy Oskol** (nô"vē ŭskôl'), city (1939 pop. over 10,000), SE Kursk oblast, Russian SFSR, on Oskol R. and 95 mi. SE of Voronezh; agr. center; sunflower-oil extraction, flour milling. Chartered 1655; scene of peasant revolt (1905). During Second World War, held (1942–43) by Germans.

Novy Pochayev, Ukrainian SSR: see POCHAYEV.

Novy Port or **Novyy Port** (pôrt"), settlement, N Yamal-Nenets Natl. Okrug, Tyumen oblast, Russian SFSR, port on Ob Bay, 190 mi. ENE of Salekhard; fish cannery; airport; supply port on Arctic sea route.

Novy Smokovec (smô'kôvĕts), Slovak *Nový Smokovec*, Ger. *Neuschmecks* (noi'shmĕks), Hung. *Ujtátrafüred* (ōō'ētätrŏfü"rĕd), village, N Slovakia, Czechoslovakia, on SE slope of the High Tatra, on rack-and-pinion railroad and 7 mi. NNW of Poprad; health resort (alt. 3,312 ft.) with leading sanatorium for tubercular patients. Part of commune of Vysoke Tatry.

Novy Svet; Novy Svet Pass, Czechoslovakia: see HARRACHOV.

Novy Toryal or **Novyy Tor'yal** (tŭryäl'), village (1948 pop. over 500), NE Mari Autonomous SSR, Russian SFSR, 40 mi. NE of Ioshkar-Ola; flax processing.

Novy Vasyugan, Russian SFSR: see VASYUGAN.

Novy Yarychev or **Novyy Yarychev** (yä'rĭchĭf), town (1931 pop. 2,555), central Lvov Oblast, W Ukrainian SSR, 13 mi. ENE of Lvov; lumbering; grain. Until 1940, called Yarychev Novy, Pol. *Jaryczów Nowy* (yärĭ'chōōf nô'vĭ).

Nowa Huta (nô'vä hōō'tä), city (pop. c.100,000), Krakow prov., S Poland, port on left bank of the Vistula and 5 mi. E of Cracow. Rail spur terminus; metallurgical center (construction begun 1949); blast furnaces, steel-rolling mills, coke ovens. Developed on site of villages of Mogila, Pol. *Mogiła* (môgē'wä), with 13th-cent. Cistercian monastery, and Pleszow, Pol. *Pleszów* (plĕ'shōōf). City inc. 1951 in Cracow.

Nowa Mysz, Belorussian SSR: see NOVAYA MYSH.

Nowa Ruda (rōō'dä), Ger. *Neurode* (noirō'dŏŏ), town (1939 pop. 10,059; 1946 pop. 11,342) in Lower Silesia, after 1945 in Wroclaw prov., SW Poland, near Czechoslovak border, at S foot of the Eulengebirge, 13 mi. NNW of Glatz (Klodzko); coal and clay mining, cotton milling, slate quarrying.

Nowa Sol (sōōl), Pol. *Nowa Sól*, Ger. *Neusalz* (noizälts'), town (1939 pop. 17,326; 1946 pop. 5,993) in Lower Silesia, after 1945 in Zielona Gora prov., W Poland, port on the Oder and 13 mi. SE of Grünberg (Zielona Gora); textile mills, foundries; oil refining, mfg. of chemicals, glue, paper-milling machinery.

Nowata (nōwä'tŭ), county (□ 577; pop. 12,734), NE Okla.; ⊙ Nowata. Bounded N by Kansas line; drained by Verdigris R. Stock raising, agr. (cotton, corn, wheat, oats). Oil and natural-gas fields; refineries. Some mfg. at Nowata. Timber. Formed 1907.

Nowata, city (pop. 3,965), ⊙ Nowata co., NE Okla., 20 mi. E of Bartlesville, in agr. and oil-producing area; mfg. (oil-field supplies and equipment, tin products, mattresses, dairy products, chemicals); timber. Settled 1888, inc. 1895.

Nowawes, Germany: see BABELSBERG.

Nowa Wilejka, Lithuania: see NAUJA VILNIA.

Nowe (nô'vĕ), Ger. *Neuenburg* (noi'ŭnbŏŏrk), town (pop. 4,137), Bydgoszcz prov., N Poland, port on the Vistula and 11 mi. N of Grudziadz; rail terminus; mfg. of agr. machinery, cement; sawmilling, distilling, flour milling.

Nowe Miasteczko (nô'vĕ myästĕch'kô), Ger. *Neustädtel* (noi'stĕ"tŭl), town (1939 pop. 1,708; 1946 pop. 604) in Lower Silesia, after 1945 in Zielona Gora prov., W Poland, 8 mi. S of Nowa Sol; agr. market (vegetables, grain, potatoes, livestock).

Nowe Miasto (myä'stô) [Pol.,=new town]. **1** or **Nowe Miasto nad Pilica** (näd pēlē'tsä), Rus. *Nove Myasto* (nô'vyĭ myä'stŭ), town (pop. 2,947), Lodz prov., central Poland, on Pilica R., opposite Drzewiczka R. mouth, and 25 mi. E of Tomaszow Mazowiecki; rail spur terminus; summer resort. **2** or **Nowe Miasto Lubawskie** (lōōbäf'skyĕ), Ger. *Neumark* (noi'märk), town (pop. 4,719), Olsztyn prov., N Poland, on Drweca R. and 12 mi. S of Ilawa; rail junction; mfg. of bricks, furniture; flour milling, sawmilling.

Nowe nad Drawa, Poland: see DRAWNO.

Nowe Siolo, Ukrainian SSR: see NOVOYE SELO.

Nowe Warpno (nô'vĕ värp'nô), Ger. *Neuwarp* (noi'värp), town (1939 pop. 2,056; 1946 pop. 2,154) in Pomerania, after 1945 in Szczecin prov., NW Poland, on small inlet of S Stettin Lagoon, 25 mi. NW of Stettin, on German border; fishing port; fish smoking.

Nowgong (nou'gông), district, central Assam, India; ⊙ Nowgong. Mainly in left-bank Brahmaputra valley; alluvial soil; agr. (rice, jute, rape and mustard, tea, sugar cane); silk and lac growing in dispersed forest areas; tea processing. Original dist. (□ 3,896; 1941 pop. 710,800; 40% Hindu, 35% Moslem, 23% tribal) reduced in 1950, when E area with tribal Mikir majority was separated to form Mikir Hills dist.

Nowgong. 1 Town (pop. 12,972), ⊙ Nowgong dist., central Assam, India, in Brahmaputra valley, on Kalang R. and 60 mi. ENE of Gauhati; trades in rice, jute, rape and mustard, tea, lac; tea processing. Rail junction 3 mi. SW, at Senchoa, with spur to Mairabari, 17 mi. WNW. Also spelled Naogaon. **2** Town (pop. 5,999), N Vindhya Pradesh, India, 14 mi. NW of Chhatarpur, in Bundelkhand; market center for grain, cloth fabrics, sugar, oilseeds; chemical and pharmaceutical works, distillery. Formerly a large Br. cantonment; Sepoys rebelled in 1857. Was hq. of former Bundelkhand Agency.

Nowimburk, Poland: see NOWOGRODZIEC.

Nowitna River (nôwĭt'nŭ), SW Alaska, rises N of upper Kuskokwim R., near 63°26'N 155°2'W, flows 250 mi. in a winding course generally N to Yukon R. at 64°56'N 154°20'W.

Nowogard (nôvô'gärt), Ger. *Naugard* (nou'gärt), town (1939 pop. 8,148; 1946 pop. 2,446) in Pomerania, after 1945 in Szczecin prov., NW Poland, 30 mi. NE of Stettin; flour milling, distilling, starch mfg. In Second World War, c.50% destroyed.

Nowogrod (nôvô'grōōt), Pol. *Nowógród*, Rus. *Novogrod* (nŭvŭgrôt'), town (pop. 1,125), Bialystok prov., NE Poland, on the Narew and 9 mi. WNW of Lomza.

Nowogrodek (nôvôgrōō'dĕk), Pol. *Nowogródek*, former province (□ 8,945; 1931 pop. 1,054,846) of E Poland; ⊙ NOVOGRUDOK [Pol. *Nowogródek*]. Formed 1921 out of Rus. govts.; occupied 1939 by USSR and became part of BARANOVICHI and Vileika (after 1944, MOLODECHNO) oblasts of Belorussian SSR.

Nowogrodek, city Belorussian SSR: see NOVOGRUDOK.

Nowogrodziec (nôvôgrô'jĕts), Ger. *Naumburg am Queis* (noum'bŏŏrk äm kvīs'), town (1939 pop. 2,240; 1946 pop. 872) in Lower Silesia, after 1945 in Wroclaw prov., SW Poland, on Kwisa (Queis) R. and 18 mi. E of Görlitz; ceramic mfg. Chartered 1233. Heavily damaged in Second World War. After 1945, briefly called Nowimburk.

Nowojelnia, Belorussian SSR: see NOVOYELNYA.

Noworadomsk, Poland: see RADOMSKO.

Nowo-Swieciany, Lithuania: see SVENCIONELIAI.

Nowra (nou'rŭ), municipality (pop. 3,551), E New South Wales, Australia, on Shoalhaven R. and 75 mi. SSW of Sydney; rail terminus; tourist center; dairy products, hogs.

Nowrangapur (nourŭng'gŭpŏŏr), village, Koraput dist., SW Orissa, India, 25 mi. N of Jeypore, near Indravati R.; rice milling. Sal forests near by.

Nowshahr, Iran: see NAUSHAHR.

Nowshera, Kashmir: see NAOSHERA.

Nowshera or **Naushahra** (both: nou'shŭrŭ), town (pop. 17,491; including cantonment area, 44,022), Peshawar dist., central North-West Frontier Prov., W Pakistan, on Kabul R. and 23 mi. E of Peshawar; rail junction; military station; agr. market (wheat, corn, barley); handicrafts (felt mats, saddlecloths, leather belts, copper products); tannery, ice factory, meat-dehydrating plant. Has Pakistan Artillery School. Slate quarried near by (SE).

Nowy Bytom (nô'vĭ bĭ'tôm), Ger. *Morgenroth* (môr'gŭnrōt), town (pop. 14,120), Katowice prov., S Poland, 4 mi. E of Hindenburg (Zabrze); rail junction; coal mines, zinc and chemical works.

Nowy Dwor (dvŏŏr'), Pol. *Nowy Dwór*. **1** or **Nowy Dwor Gdanski** (gŭdä'nyŭskē), Pol. *Nowy Dwór Gdański*, Ger. *Tiegenhof* (tē'gŭnhōf"), town (1946 pop. 1,247), Gdansk prov., N Poland, in Vistula R. delta, 22 mi. ESE of Danzig; rail junction. **2** or **Nowy Dwor Mazowiecki** (mäzôvyĕts'kē), Rus. *Novy Dvor* or *Novyy Dvor* (both: nô'vyĭ dvôr'), town (pop. 5,046), Warszawa prov., E central Poland, port on Vistula R., at Narew R. mouth, on railroad and 18 mi. NW of Warsaw. Naval base; brewing, sawmilling, flour milling, mfg. of earthenware, soap, sirup. Before Second World War, pop. 60% Jewish.

Nowy Port (pôrt'), Ger. *Neufahrwasser* (noi"fär'vä"sŭr), outer port of Danzig, Gdansk prov., N Poland, on Gulf of Danzig of Baltic Sea, at mouth of NW arm of the Vistula estuary, 3 mi. N of city center. Ocean-going vessels here tranship cargos to Vistula steamers. Port constructed in 1694. Just NW is former Westerplatte fortress.

Nowy Sacz (sŏch'), Pol. *Nowy Sącz*, Ger. *Neu Sandec* or *Neu-Sandec* (noi"-zän'dĕts), city (pop. 23,049), Krakow prov., S Poland, in the Carpathians, on Dunajec R. and 45 mi. SE of Cracow. Rail junction (repair shops); mfg. of agr. tools, chemicals, cement products, bricks; food processing, tanning, flour milling, lumbering; salmon hatchery. Brown-coal deposits near by. Has castle ruins. Founded 1294. In Austrian Poland, 1772–1919. During Second World War, under Ger. rule, called Neu Sandez.

Nowy Staw (stäf'), Ger. *Neuteich* (noi'tīkh), town (1946 pop. 1,560), Gdansk prov., N Poland, in Vistula R. delta, 21 mi. SE of Danzig; rail junction. After 1945, briefly called Nytych.

Nowy Targ (tärk'), town (pop. 8,144), Krakow prov., S Poland, on Dunajec R. and 40 mi. S of Cracow, in the Podhale. Rail junction; airport; lumbering, tanning, flour milling; stone quarries; salmon hatchery. Hydroelectric plant. Founded 13th cent. In Austrian Poland (until First World War), called Neumarkt.

Nowy Tomysl (tô'mĭ-shŭl), Pol. *Nowy Tomyśl*, Ger. *Neutomischel* (noi'tō'mĭ"shŭl), town (1946 pop. 2,700), Poznan prov., W Poland, 34 mi. WSW of Poznan; rail junction; brewing, flour milling, sawmilling, mfg. of lamps, baskets; trades in hops.

Noxapater (nŏk'sŭpā"tŭr), town (pop. 615), Winston co., E central Miss., 9 mi. S of Louisville; lumber milling.

Noxen, village (1940 pop. 795), Wyoming co., NE Pa., 21 mi. W of Scranton; tannery.

Noxon, village (pop. c.150), Sanders co., NW Mont., 35 mi. NW of Thompson Falls and on the Clark Fork, near Idaho line, in farming and trapping region; berries.

Noxubee (nŏksōō'bē, nŏk'shŭbē), county (□ 695; pop. 20,022), E Miss., bordering E on Ala.; ⊙ Macon. Drained by Noxubee R. Agr. (cotton, corn), dairying; lumbering. Formed 1833.

Noxubee River, in E Miss. and W Ala., formed by confluence of several forks in Noxubee co., flows c.140 mi. SE, past Macon, into Sumter co., Ala., entering Tombigbee R. near Gainesville.

Noya (noi'ä), town (pop. 3,149), La Coruña prov., NW Spain, in Galicia, fishing port on Noya Bay (inlet of the Atlantic), 18 mi. WSW of Santiago; shellfish and sardine fishing; boatbuilding, lace mfg., tanning, flour- and sawmilling. Has Gothic church. Tin and wolfram deposits near by.

Noyack Bay, SE N.Y., inlet indenting N shore of S peninsula of Long Isl., c.1 mi. W of Sag Harbor; c.2 mi. in diameter. In summer-resort area; yachting; fishing.

Noyan (nō'yän) or **Noyon** (nō'yōn), village, South Gobi aimak, S Mongolian People's Republic, at foot of Noyan Bogdo (7,884 ft.), 125 mi. WSW of Dalan Dzadagad.

Noyant (nwäyä'), village (pop. 845), Maine-et-Loire dept., W France, 20 mi. NNE of Saumur; olive-oil pressing. Sometimes called Noyant-sous-le-Lude.

Noyant-d'Allier (nwäyä'-dälyā'), village (pop. 1,428), Allier dept., central France, 11 mi. SW of Moulins; coal mining.

Noyelles-Godault (nwäyĕl'-gôdō'), town (pop. 4,164), Pas-de-Calais dept., N France, 5 mi. NW of Douai; coal mines. Zinc and lead smelters.

Noyelles-sous-Lens (–sōō-läs'), E suburb (pop. 7,765) of Lens, Pas-de-Calais dept., N France, in coal-mining dist.

Noyemberyan (nŭyĕmbĭryän'), village (1939 pop. over 2,000), NE Armenian SSR, 19 mi. ENE of Alaverdi, near Azerbaijan border; wheat. Also called Noyember.

Noyen (nwäyä'), village (pop. 1,160), Sarthe dept., W France, on the Sarthe and 12 mi. N of La Flèche; flour milling. Also called Noyen-sur-Sarthe.

Noyers (nwäyä'), agr. village (pop. 687), Yonne dept., N central France, on Serein R. and 11 mi. S of Tonnerre; woodworking.

Noyers-sur-Jabron (–sür-zhäbrō'), village (pop. 100), Basses-Alpes dept., SE France, on N slope of Montagne de Lure, 6 mi. WSW of Sisteron; orchards.

Noyes, village, Kittson co., extreme NW Minn., port of entry near Man. line, on 2 railroads and 20 mi. NW of Hallock.

Noyil River (noi'ŭl), SW Madras, India, rises on S spur of Nilgiri Hills, W of Coimbatore, flows 100 mi. E, past Coimbatore, Singanallur, and Tiruppur, to Cauvery R. 24 mi. SSE of Erode; supplies many irrigation channels in the W part of Coimbatore dist.

Noyo (noi'ō), fishing port (pop. c.75), Mendocino co., NW Calif., at mouth of Noyo R. on the Pacific, just S of Fort Bragg; fish canning.

Noyon (nwäyō'), anc. *Noviodunum Veromanduorum* or *Noviomagus*, town (pop. 5,900), Oise dept., N France, near Oise R. and its lateral canal, 14 mi. NE of Compiègne; agr. trade center (cereals, cherries, black currants, artichokes, sugar beets); mfg. (plumbing fixtures, cattle feed), woodworking. Tree nurseries. Here Charlemagne was crowned King of the Franks in 768, and Hugh Capet chosen king in 987. Treaty bet. France and Spain signed here in 1516. Occupied by Germans 1914–17, and devastated in both world wars. The 12th–13th-cent. cathedral was damaged but survived. The 15th-cent. town hall and birthplace of Calvin (now housing mus.) had to be completely restored after First World War.

Noyon, Mongolia: see NOYAN.

Noyo River (noi'ō), NW Calif., rises in central Mendocino co., flows c.30 mi. W to the Pacific at Noyo.

Nozawa (nōzä'wä). **1** Town (pop. 5,446), Fukushima prefecture, N central Honshu, Japan, 17 mi. WNW of Wakamatsu; mining (gold, silver, copper). **2** Town (pop. 8,613), Nagano prefecture, central Honshu, Japan, 17 mi. SE of Ueda; spinning, paper milling.

Nozay (nôzā'), village (pop. 1,613), Loire-Inférieure dept., W France, 14 mi. SW of Châteaubriant; cider making. Iron mined near by.

Nozeroy (nôzůrwä'), village (pop. 437), Jura dept., E France, 17 mi. SW of Pontarlier; diamond cutting, cheese mfg.

Nozhai-Yurt, Russian SFSR: see ANDALALY.

Nsanakang (ůnsänä'kän), town (pop. 156), S Br. Cameroons, administered as part of Eastern Provinces of Nigeria, on Cross R. and 25 mi. WNW of Mamfe; cacao, bananas, palm oil and kernels; hardwood, rubber. Salt deposits.

Nsawam (ůnsäwäm'), town, Eastern Prov., S Gold Coast colony, on railroad and 20 mi. NNW of Accra; road junction; major cacao center.

Nsok (nůsōk'), town (pop. 199), continental Sp. Guinea, near Gabon border, 120 mi. SE of Bata; 1°8'N 11°17'E. Coffee, cacao, hardwoods. Also spelled Nsork.

Nsukka (ůn-sōō'kä), town, Onitsha prov., Eastern Provinces, S Nigeria, 30 mi. N of Enugu; agr. trade center; palm oil and kernels, yams, cassava, corn. Coal deposits at Obolo (E).

Nsuta (ůnsōō'tä), town, Western Prov., SW Gold Coast colony, on railroad and 4 mi. S of Tarkwa. One of the world's leading manganese-mining centers; ore is exported via Takoradi (130 mi. SSE). Sometimes spelled Insuta.

Ntakataka (ůntäkätä'kä), village, Central Prov., Nyasaland, on railroad and 23 mi. NE of Dedza; tobacco, corn.

N'Tem (ůntĕm'), administrative region (□ 13,585; 1950 pop. 147,300), S Fr. Cameroons; ⊙ Ebolowa. Borders S on Sp. Guinea and Fr. Equatorial Africa (partly along N'Tem and Ivindo rivers). Lies in tropical rain-forest zone. Cacao production. Also coffee, palm oil and kernels, rubber.

N'Tem River, Fr. Equatorial Africa: see CAMPO RIVER.

Nu, China: see SALWEEN RIVER.

Nuages, Col des, Vietnam: see CLOUDS, PASS OF THE.

Nuanetsi (nōō"änĕt'sē), village, Victoria prov., SE Southern Rhodesia, in Mashonaland, on Nuanetsi R. (left tributary of Limpopo R.) and 90 mi. S of Fort Victoria; cattle, sheep, goats; corn. Hq. of native commissioner for Nuanetsi dist. Police post.

Nuanetsi River, S Southern Rhodesia, rises in high veld 20 mi. NE of Filabusi, flows c.250 mi. SE, past Nuanetsi, to the Limpopo in Mozambique.

Nuangola (nōō"ăng-gō'lů), borough (pop. 295), Luzerne co., NE central Pa., 8 mi. SW of Wilkes-Barre.

Nuatja (nwä'chä), village, S Fr. Togoland, on railroad and 55 mi. N of Lomé; cacao, palm oil and kernels; cotton gin. R.C. mission. Also Nouatja.

Nuba Mountains (nōō'bä), group of isolated hills in central Anglo-Egyptian Sudan, S of El Obeid; rise to 3,000–4,000 ft. Main centers are Dilling, Rashad, Talodi, Kadugli.

Nubaran or **Novbaran** (both: nōvbärän'), village, First Prov., in Saveh, W central Iran, 35 mi. WNW of Saveh and on the Qara Chai; cotton, wheat, fruit.

Nubia (nū'bēů), region and ancient country, NE Africa, now included in S Egypt and N Anglo-Egyptian Sudan. At its height it extended from 1st cataract of the Nile at Aswan to Khartoum. Its useful area is limited to the narrow irrigable strip along the Nile; there are no well-defined borders, for region includes sections of Libyan and Nubian deserts. Region came early under influence of the Pharaohs. Egypt was ruled briefly by conquering Nubian kings who established XXV dynasty. Expulsed from Egypt, Nubians established capital at NAPATA (c.750 B.C.), later moved it to MEROË. Under the Romans Nubia was settled by a Negro tribe who mixed with the indigenous Hamites and formed a powerful kingdom, with capital at DONGOLA. Converted to Christianity in A.D. 6th cent., the kingdom joined with Christian kingdom of Ethiopia and resisted Moslem encroachment until 14th cent., when Nubia broke up into many petty states. Conquered 1820–22 by Mohammed Ali. Held by Mahdists 1885–98.

Nubian Desert (nū'bēůn), in NE Anglo-Egyptian Sudan bet. Nile valley and Red Sea; largely a sandstone plateau trenched by many wadis flowing toward the Nile (but seldom reaching it) from the backslope of the coastal Etbai range. The Nile traverses several gorges and is cut by 5 cataracts bet. Khartoum and Wadi Halfa, at desert's W edge. The river here forms its great S-curve, which has been by-passed by a rail line (Abu Hamed–Wadi Halfa) across the desert.

Ñuble (nū'blā), province (□ 5,487; 1940 pop. 243, 185; 1949 estimate 221,341), S central Chile, bet. the Andes and the Pacific; ⊙ CHILLÁN. Watered by Itata and Ñuble rivers, it occupies part of the fertile central valley, has temperate climate. Mainly agr.: fruit, wine, wheat, sheep; also corn, rye, oats, flax, potatoes, lentils, beans, cattle. Lumbering, flour milling, dairying, wine making. Resorts: Termas de Chillán and Cobquecura. L. Laja borders prov. in SE. Area has suffered frequently from earthquakes, notably in 1939. Prov. was set up 1848.

Ñuble River, Ñuble prov., S central Chile, rises at foot of Nevados de Chillán at Argentina border, flows c.100 mi. W, through irrigated valley, to Itata R. 20 mi. W of Chillán.

Nubra River, Kashmir: see SIACHEN GLACIER.

Nuchek (nōō'chĕk), Indian fishing village, S Alaska, on W coast of Hinchinbrook Isl., 35 mi. WSW of Cordova.

Nu Chiang, China: see SALWEEN RIVER.

Nucía, La (länōō-thē'ä), town (pop. 1,609), Alicante prov., E Spain, 25 mi. ESE of Alcoy; olive pressing; wine, almonds, citrus and other fruit.

Nucice (nōō'chĭtsĕ), Czech *Nučice*, Ger. *Nutschitz* (nōōt'shĭts), village (pop. 1,108), central Bohemia, Czechoslovakia, 10 mi. SW of Prague; rail junction; iron and coal mining.

Nuckolls (nŭ'kůlz), county (□ 579; pop. 9,609), S Nebr.; ⊙ Nelson. Agr. region bounded S by Kansas; drained by Republican and Little Blue rivers. Livestock, grain. Formed 1871.

Nucla (nōō'klů), town (pop. 457), Montrose co., SW Colo., near San Miguel R., 39 mi. WSW of Montrose, in irrigated livestock, fruit, and vegetable area; alt. 5,916 ft. Near-by deposits of carnotite yield vanadium and uranium.

Nudushan or **Nodushan** (both: nōdōōshän'), village (1930 pop. estimate 2,500), Tenth Prov., in Yezd, central Iran, 50 mi. WNW of Yezd, in sheep-grazing area; grain, dairy products (especially cheese).

Nueces (nōōā'sĭs, nū–), county (□ 838; pop. 165,-471), S Texas; ⊙ CORPUS CHRISTI, deepwater port, industrial, commercial center. On Gulf plains; bounded N by Nueces R. and Nueces Bay, NE and E by Corpus Christi Bay and Laguna Madre, sheltered from Gulf of Mexico by Mustang and Padre Isls. A leading Texas oil and natural-gas producing co.; diversified agr. (cotton, grain sorghums, truck, some citrus), livestock, poultry, dairying. Resort beaches; fishing. Oil refining, diversified mfg. (especially chemicals), processing of farm products, seafood. Clay, sand mining; lime mfg. (from shells). Formed 1846.

Nueces Bay, Texas: see CORPUS CHRISTI BAY.

Nueces River, Texas, rises on Edwards Plateau in Edwards co., flows generally SE past Cotulla, NE to Three Rivers, thence again SE to Nueces Bay, a NW arm of Corpus Christi Bay; 315 mi. long. Receives combined Frio and Atascosa rivers at Three Rivers. Dam 32 mi. WNW of Corpus Christi impounds L. Corpus Christi (capacity 64,000 acre-ft.; for water supply; fishing).

Nueltin Lake (nūĕl'tĭn) (□ 336), S Keewatin Dist., Northwest Territories, and NW Manitoba, W of Hudson Bay; 60°N 100°W; 85 mi. long, 3–19 mi. wide. Drained NE by Thlewiaza R. into Hudson Bay.

Nuestra Senora de la Soledad, Mission, Calif.: see SOLEDAD.

Nueva Arica (nwā'vä ärē'kä), village (pop. 1,492), Lambayeque dept., NW Peru, in W foothills of Cordillera Occidental, on Saña R. and 3 mi. SW of Oyotún; rice, corn, alfalfa.

Nueva Armenia (ärmā'nyä), town (pop. 614), Francisco Morazán dept., S Honduras, 9 mi. SE of Sabanagrande; grain, livestock.

Nueva Australia, Paraguay: see COLONIA NUEVA AUSTRALIA.

Nueva Caceres, Philippines: see NAGA, Camarines Sur prov.

Nueva Carteya (kärtā'ä), town (pop. 5,878), Córdoba prov., S Spain, 8 mi. W of Baena; agr. trade center (wheat, grapes, vegetables); olive-oil processing, soap mfg.

Nueva Casas Grandes (kä'säs grän'dĕs), town (pop. 3,182), Chihuahua, N Mexico, on arid plateau, on Casas Grandes R. (irrigation) and 130 mi. SW of Ciudad Juárez; alt. 4,832 ft. Rail junction; agr. center (cotton, corn, beans, tobacco, cattle); tanning, flour milling, lumbering.

Nueva Chicago (chēkä'gō), W industrial section of Buenos Aires, Argentina.

Nueva Colombia (kōlōm'byä), town (dist. pop. 3,998), La Cordillera dept., S central Paraguay, 20 mi. NE of Asunción, in agr. area (fruit, tobacco, stock). Sometimes Colonia Nueva Colombia.

Nueva Concepción (kōnsĕpsyōn'), city (pop. 1,298), Chalatenango dept., W central Salvador, 18 mi. E of Santa Ana; agr., livestock raising.

Nueva Ecija (ā'sĕhä), province (□ 2,120; 1948 pop. 467,769), central Luzon, Philippines, drained by Pampanga R.; ⊙ CABANATUAN. Mountainous, with fertile valleys. Principal crop is rice; corn, tobacco, abacá, and sugar cane are also grown. After Second World War, the prov. was chief center of disturbances by rebellious Hukbalahaps.

Nueva España (ĕspä'nyä), town (pop. estimate 500), S central Tucumán prov., Argentina, 32 mi. S of Tucumán; agr. center (cotton, peanuts, sugar cane, livestock).

Nueva Esparta (ĕspär'tä), state (□ 444; 1941 pop. 69,195; 1950 census 76,035), Venezuela: see MARGARITA ISLAND.

Nueva Esperanza (ĕspärän'sä), village (pop. estimate 500), ⊙ Pellegrini dept. (□ 2,500; 1947 pop. 16,841), NW Santiago del Estero prov., Argentina, 75 mi. NE of Tucumán; agr. center (corn, alfalfa, livestock); lumbering.

Nueva Galicia (gälē'syä), Spanish colonial administrative region, W Mexico, comprising roughly the present states of Jalisco and Nayarit, with S Sinaloa. Conquered (1529–31) by Nuño de Guzmán, it was scene of the Mixtón War in 1541. In 1548 it was given an audiencia at Guadalajara, and, though nominally subject to viceroy of New Spain, was essentially a separate administration controlled from Spain. In 1563 it was given a presidential office of its own, but its independent character declined as colonial authority became centralized in Mexico city.

Nueva Germania (hĕrmä'nyä), town (dist. pop. 4,294), San Pedro dept., central Paraguay, 32 mi. NE of San Pedro; maté-growing center.

Nueva Gerona (hārō'nä), principal town (pop. 2,935) of Isle of Pines, SW Cuba, on small Las Casas R. and 90 mi. SSW of Havana; 21°53'N 82°48'W. Resort, trading and agr. center (citrus fruit, tobacco, potatoes, winter vegetables). Served by airline and linked through near-by landing (N) with Surgidero de Batabanó on main isl. A clean town of modern character, it has customhouse, industrial art center. Fine beaches (fishing, bathing) and caves are in picturesque surrounding region. Presidio Modelo penitentiary is 2 mi. E. Marble, copper, iron, and gold deposits in vicinity.

Nueva Helvecia (ĕlvā'syä), town, Colonia dept., SW Uruguay, on railroad and 37 mi. ENE of Colonia, in agr. region (grain, fruit, livestock). Serves as urban nucleus of Colonia Suiza agr. settlement.

Nueva Imperial (ēmpāryäl'), town (pop. 6,643), ⊙ Imperial dept. (□ 1,112; pop. 82,584), Cautín prov., S central Chile, on Imperial R., on railroad and 20 mi. W of Temuco; 38°45'S 72°57'W. Inland river port, trading and agr. center (cereals, livestock); flour milling, tanning, lumbering.

Nueva Island (□ 45.8), in Tierra del Fuego, at mouth of Beagle Channel on the Atlantic, 8 mi. S of main isl. of the archipelago; 55°15'S 66°35'W; 9 mi. long. Disputed by Chile and Argentina.

Nueva Italia (ētä'lyä), town (pop. 3,746), Michoacán, W Mexico, 35 mi. SSW of Uruapan; cereals, rice, sugar, fruit.

Nueva Lubecka (lōōbā'kä), village (pop. estimate 700), W Chubut natl. territory, Argentina, 100 mi. NW of Sarmiento; alfalfa, sheep, horses, goats.

Nueva Numancia, Spain: see PUENTE DE VALLECAS.

Nueva Ocotepeque (ōkōtāpā'kā) [Sp.,=new Ocotepeque], city (pop. 2,622), ⊙ Ocotepeque dept., W Honduras, on Lempa R. and 33 mi. SW of Santa Rosa de Copán, near Salvador border; 14°26'N 89°12'W; alt. 2,641 ft. Commercial center in agr. area; coffee, sugar cane, wheat, tobacco; livestock. Linked by road with San Salvador. Founded just NE of site of Ocotepeque, destroyed 1935 by flood of Marchala R. (small left affluent of the Lempa).

Nueva Palmira (pälmē'rä), town (pop. 8,000), Colonia dept., SW Uruguay, port on Uruguay R. (Argentina border) above its mouth on the Río de la Plata, 50 mi. NW of Colonia and 50 mi. N of Buenos Aires, in rich agr. region. Ships grain, livestock; flour milling.

Nueva Paz (päs'), town (pop. 3,202), Havana prov., W Cuba, 45 mi. SE of Havana; rice, sugar cane, vegetables, cattle. Rice mills. Sugar central near by.

Nueva Pompeya (pōmpĕ'yä), village (pop. estimate 300), N Chaco natl. territory, Argentina, on old bed of Bermejo R. and 24 mi. SW of El Pintado; desert outpost with Franciscan mission.

Nueva Rocafuerte (rōkäfwĕr'tä), village, Napo-Pastaza prov., E Ecuador, landing on Napo R. at mouth of the Yasuní, on Peru line, and 20 mi. W of Pantoja (Peru), 230 mi. ESE of Quito; 0°56'S 75°23'W. Cattle raising; collecting of rubber, balata, chicle, furs. Has a govt. sawmill. Founded after 1942 boundary settlement, replacing ROCAFUERTE. Near by on Napo R. are Puerto Miranda (military base; 10 mi. NW) and Tiputini airfield (at mouth of Tiputini R.; 20 mi. NW).

Nueva Rosita (rōsē'tä), mining city (pop. 25,551), Coahuila, N Mexico, in semiarid country, in Sabinas coal district, 170 mi. NW of Monterrey. Connected by rail with Saltillo, Monterrey, Piedras Negras. Developed as prominent industrial city of N Mexico in 1930s. Zinc smelter; mfg. (zinc sulphate and sulphuric acid). Sometimes called simply Rosita.

Nueva San Salvador (sän' sälvädōr') or **Santa Tecla** (sän'tä tā'klä), city (1950 pop. 19,601), ⊙ La Libertad dept., W Salvador, in coastal range, at S foot of volcano San Salvador, on Inter-American Highway and 7 mi. W of San Salvador; alt. 3,025 ft.; 13°41'N 89°18'W. Commercial and residential center noted for fine private homes and estates, in coffee and livestock area; mfg. (candles, soap, matches), tanning. Founded 1854 following destruction by earthquake of San Salvador; ⊙ Salvador 1855–59; named Nueva Ciudad de San Salvador. Became ⊙ La Libertad dept. in 1865.

Nueva Santa Rosa (sän'tä rō'sä), town (1950 pop. 1,468), Santa Rosa dept., S Guatemala, in Pacific piedmont, 1 mi. ESE of Santa Rosa, 8 mi. N of Cuilapa; coffee, corn, beans.

Nueva Segovia (sägō'vyä), department (□ 1,595; 1950 pop. 26,975), NW Nicaragua, on Honduras border; ⊙ Ocotal. Separated from Honduras by sierras de Dipilto and Jalapa; bounded SE by Coco R. Gold and silver mining at El Jícaro. Tobacco, sugar cane, coffee, livestock (N), cacao, corn, vegetables (S). Main centers: Ocotal, El Jícaro.

Nuevas Grandes (nwā'väs grän'dĕs), narrow inlet (8 mi. long) on N coast of Cuba, at Camagüey-Oriente prov. border, 20 mi. ESE of Nuevitas; receives small Cabreras R.

Nueva Vizcaya (vēskä'yä), province (□ 2,627; 1948 pop. 82,718), central Luzon, Philippines; ⊙ BAYOMBONG. Drained by the Cagayan and its tributary Magat R. Mountainous, with fertile valleys. Agr. (rice, corn, tobacco), stock raising.

Nueve de Julio. **1** Department, Río Negro natl. territory, Argentina: see SIERRA COLORADA. **2** Department, Santa Fe prov., Argentina: see TOSTADO.

Nueve de Julio or **9 de Julio** (nwā'vā dā hōō'lyō). **1** City (pop. 13,409), ⊙ Nueve de Julio dist. (□ 1,650; pop. 43,171), N central Buenos Aires prov., Argentina, 60 mi. SW of Chivilcoy; commercial center in stock-raising area; meat packing, dairying. **2** Town (pop. estimate 1,000), ⊙ Nueve de Julio dept. (□ c.50; 1947 pop. 2,497), S San Juan prov., Argentina, in San Juan R. valley (irrigation area), 12 mi. SSE of San Juan, in wine- and fruitgrowing area.

Nuevitas (nwävē'täs), town (pop. 11,303), Camagüey prov., E Cuba, N shore port on sheltered Nuevitas Bay (c.8 mi. long, 6 mi. wide), 45 mi. ENE of Camagüey. Rail terminus, trading and processing center for fertile agr. region (sugar cane, molasses, cacao, coffee, sisal, fruit). Agr. products shipped through the subsidiary ports Puerto Tarafa (N) and Pastelillo (E). Also a fishing and lumbering hq. Industries include sawmilling, sisal processing, coffee roasting, textile milling, sponge treating; mfg. of soap and furniture. Sugar mills are in vicinity. The site of Nuevitas was discovered by Columbus, who landed here on his 1st voyage (1492). During colonial era it was frequently raided, notably by Sir Henry Morgan in 1668. Chromium mined near by.

Nuevo, Golfo (gōl'fō nwā'vō), inlet of S Atlantic Ocean in E Chubut natl. territory, Argentina, S of Valdés Peninsula; 40 mi. W–E, 30 mi. N–S. Port of Puerto Madryn on W shore, Puerto Pirámides (on Valdés Peninsula) on NE.

Nuevo, Río (rē'ō), or **Gonzâlez River** (gōnsä'lĕs), in Tabasco, SE Mexico, arm of lower Grijalva R., formed 7 mi. ENE of Cárdenas; flows E, N, and NW, to Gulf of Campeche 6 mi. ENE of Paraíso; c.75 mi. long.

Nuevo Berlín (bĕrlēn'), town (pop. 2,500), Río Negro dept., W Uruguay, 18 mi. NE of Fray Bentos; commercial and shipping center; wheat, grapes, cattle, sheep.

Nuevo Chagres (chä'grĕs), village (pop. 156), Colón prov., central Panama, minor port on Caribbean Sea, and 14 mi. SW of Colón; corn, beans, rice, coconuts; stock raising. At mouth of Chagres R. 8 mi. NE, in Canal Zone, are remains of old town of Chagres, which flourished until rise of Colón.

Nuevo Laredo (lärā'dō), city (pop. 28,872), Tamaulipas, N Mexico, on Rio Grande (rail and highway bridges), opposite Laredo (Texas), and 140 mi. NE of Monterrey. Rail junction; N terminus of Inter-American Highway and point of entry for Amer. tourist traffic. Major custom station; trading and agr. center (cotton, sugar cane, cereals, cattle); cotton ginning, flour and textile milling, vegetable-oil pressing, fruit canning, coffee processing, lumbering, printing. Airport. Founded 1755; was part of Laredo until Texas was ceded (1848) to U.S. after Mexican War.

Nuevo Leôn (lāōn'), state (□ 25,136; 1940 pop. 541,147; 1950 pop. 743,297), N Mexico; ⊙ MONTERREY. Separated, except for small strip of land to the W, from the Rio Grande (N) by the panhandle of Tamaulipas, which also adjoins it E; San Luis Potosí is SW. The S and W are traversed (NW–SE) by the Sierra Madre Oriental. Watered by several tributaries of the Rio Grande: Río Salado, and Pesquería, Salinas, and San Juan rivers. Climate is hot and arid in N and NE, more temperate and humid toward mountainous S and SW. Mineral resources include silver, gold, lead, copper, and zinc, mined at Santa Catarina, Zaragoza, Villa García, Sabinas Hidalgo, and the Monterrey dist.; iron at Lampazos; extensive marble deposits in the mts. Predominantly agr.; produces cotton, wheat, corn, barley, tobacco; sugar cane grown on large scale in irrigated N cactus country. Linares and Montemorelos (S) are important orange and grain producers. The cacti of the arid plains yield istle fibers and mescal liquor. Livestock (cattle, sheep) in entire state. Nuevo León is one of the most industrialized states of Mexico, with Monterrey, a great metalworking center, 2d only to Mexico city in industrial importance. There are several thermal springs, best known being Topo Chico, near Monterrey. The old Sp. colonial province of Nuevo León, established 1579, included much of what is now E Coahuila; was scene of serious Indian uprisings. After Mex. independence, Nuevo León, much reduced in size, became (1824) a state. It was occupied by U.S. forces under Zachary Taylor during Mexican War.

Nuevo Morelos (mōrā'lōs), town (pop. 290), Tamaulipas, NE Mexico, in E foothills of Sierra Madre Oriental, 90 mi. WNW of Tampico; henequen, fruit, stock.

Nuevo Necaxa (nākä'hä), town (pop. 3,938), Puebla, central Mexico, in Sierra Madre Oriental, on Necaxa R. and 4 mi. NE of Huauchinango; sugar cane, coffee, fruit. Hydroelectric plant, on Necaxa Falls (c.540 ft. high) near by, supplies Mexico city. Sometimes called Necaxa.

Nuevo Progreso (prōgrā'sō), town (1950 pop. 621), San Marcos dept., SW Guatemala, in Pacific piedmont, 5 mi. NNW of Coatepeque; coffee, sugar cane, grain.

Nuevo Saltillo, Mexico: see GUADALUPE VICTORIA.

Nuevo San Carlos (sän kär'lōs), town (1950 pop. 398), Retalhuleu dept., SW Guatemala, in Pacific piedmont, on branch of Tilapa R. and 4 mi. N of Retalhuleu; sugar cane, corn, rice.

Nuevo Urecho (ōōrā'chō), town (pop. 805), Michoacán, central Mexico, 22 mi. SSE of Uruapan; alt. 5,754 ft.; fruit, cereals.

Ñuflo de Châvez, Bolivia: see CONCEPCIÓN, Santa Cruz dept.

Nufud, Arabia: see NAFUD.

Nugammute, Alaska: see NOGAMUT.

Nûgâtsiak or **Nûgâtsiaq** (both: nōōgät'syäk), fishing and hunting settlement (pop. 131), Umanak dist., W Greenland, on S Qeqertarssuaq Isl. (16 mi. long, 3–10 mi. wide), on Karrats Fjord, 65 mi. NNW of Umanak; 71°33'N 53°12'W. Radio station.

Nugegoda (nōōgăgō'dŭ), SE suburb (pop. 4,395) of Colombo, Western Prov., Ceylon, 5 mi. SE of Colombo city center; handicrafts (lace, pottery); trades in vegetables, rice, coconuts, cinnamon, rubber. Part of Kotte urban council.

Nugent (nū'jùnt), village (pop. 135), SE Tasmania, 25 mi. NE of Hobart; sawmills.

Nûgssuak or **Nûgssuaq** (both: nōōkh'shwäk). **1** Peninsula (110 mi. long, 18–30 mi. wide), W Greenland, extends from inland icecap NW into Davis Strait, bet. Umanak Fjord (N) and the Vaigat and head of Disko Bay (S); 70°20'N 52°30'W. Mountainous and partly glaciated, it rises to 7,340 ft. 12 mi. SW of Umanak. In center, bet. high mts., is Taserssuaq L. (26 mi. long, 1–2 mi. wide; alt. c.2,000 ft.). Peninsula has lignite deposits and petrified flora. Sometimes spelled Nugsuak. **2** Peninsula (30 mi. long, 1–4 mi. wide), NW Greenland, on Baffin Bay; 74°12'N 56°35'W. At base is Peary Lodge (74°19'N 56°13'W), N base of Univ. of Michigan expedition, 1932–33. Kraulshavn (krouls'houn"), fishing outpost, on S coast.

Nuguria Islands (nōōgōōrē'ä), coral group (□ c.2; pop. c.70), New Ireland dist., Bismarck Archipelago, Territory of New Guinea, SW Pacific, c.135 mi. E of New Ireland; 2 atolls of c.50 islets. Privately owned; coconut plantations.

Nuh (nōō), village, Gurgaon dist., SE Punjab, India, 24 mi. S of Gurgaon; millet, gram, wheat; handicraft cloth weaving. Stone (used for road metal) quarried in hills (SW).

Nuhu Chut, Nuhu Tjut, or **Noehoe Tjoet** (all: nōō'-hōōchōōt') or **Great Kai** (kī), largest island (□ 241; pop. 25,246) of KAI ISLANDS, S Moluccas, Indonesia, in Banda Sea, 180 mi. SE of Ceram; 5°37'S 133°2'E; 65 mi. long, 8 mi. wide. Wooded, mountainous, rising to 2,500 ft. Fishing; copra.

Nuhu Rowa or **Noehoe Rowa** (both: nōō'hōō rō'wù) or **Little Kai** (kī), island (30 mi. long, 10 mi. wide; pop. 13,285), KAI ISLANDS, S Moluccas, Indonesia, in Banda Sea, just W of Nuhu Chut, 175 mi. SE of Ceram; 5°37'S 132°44'E. Produces coconuts, trepang.

Nuhu Tjut, Indonesia: see NUHU CHUT.

Nui (nōō'ē), atoll (500 acres; pop. 490), N Ellice Isls., SW Pacific; 7°16'S 177°10'E; copra. Formerly Netherland Isl.

Nuia, Nuiya, or **Nuyya** (nōō'īyä), town (pop. 772, including adjoining Karksi), S Estonia, 18 mi. S of Viljandi; road junction; flax, livestock. Karksi is just E.

Nuits-Saint-Georges (nüē'-sē-zhôrzh'), town (pop. 2,987), Côte-d'Or dept., E central France, on E slope of the Côte d'Or, 13 mi. SSW of Dijon; renowned Burgundy winegrowing center. Liqueurs, fruit juices. The celebrated abbey of Cîteaux (founded 1098), mother house of the Cistercian monastic order, is 7 mi. E.

Nuits-sous-Ravières, France: see RAVIÈRES.

Nuiya, Estonia: see NUIA.

Nuka Bay (nōō'kù) (20 mi. long, 1–7 mi. wide), S Alaska, on SE coast of Kenai Peninsula, opens into Gulf of Alaska at 59°23'N 150°31'W.

Nukahiva, Marquesas Isls.: see NUKU HIVA.

Nuka Island (8 mi. long, 3 mi. wide; 1939 pop. 40), S Alaska, in Gulf of Alaska, off SE Kenai Peninsula, 65 mi. SW of Seward; 59°22'N 150°41'W. Entire isl. used as fox farm.

Nukatl Range or **Nukatl' Range** (nōōkä'tùl), N spur of the E Greater Caucasus, in S central Dagestan Autonomous SSR, Russian SFSR; extends in arc 30 mi. N, forming right watershed of the Avar Koisu; rises to 12,860 ft.

Nukerke (nü'kĕrkù), agr. village (pop. 1,836), East Flanders prov., W central Belgium, 3 mi. S of Oudenaarde.

Nukey Bluff, Australia: see GAWLER RANGES.

Nukha (nōōkhä'), city (1932 pop. estimate 37,000), N Azerbaijan SSR, on S slope of the Greater Caucasus, 150 mi. WNW of Baku, in rice and fruit dist.; major silk center; spinning and weaving, cocoon processing. Teachers col. Former ⊙ Nukha khanate conquered 1806 by Russians.

Nukualofa (nōō'kōōälō'fä), port town (pop. 7,000), N Tongatabu, S Tonga, S Pacific, ⊙ Tongatabu group and of Tongan kingdom; port of entry. Site of royal palace. Exports copra, bananas.

Nukufetau (nōō'kōōfĕtä'ōō), atoll (□ 1; pop. 524), central Ellice Isls., SW Pacific; 8°S 178°28'E; many islets on reef (circumference 24 mi.); airfield. Formerly Depeyster Isl.

Nuku Hiva (nōō'kōō hē'vä), volcanic island (□ 46; pop. 737), largest of MARQUESAS ISLANDS, Fr. Oceania, S Pacific, 70 mi. N of Hiva Oa; 8°52'S 140°8'W; circumference c.70 mi. Fertile valleys, wooded hills (highest peak c.4,000 ft.). Of its 8 harbors, best is Taiohae Bay on S coast. Exports copra, fruits. TAIOHAE was former ⊙ Marquesas Isls. Sometimes spelled Nukuhiva and Nukahiva.

Nukulaelae (nōō'kōōlī'lī), atoll (449 acres; pop. 282), S Ellice Isls., SW Pacific; 9°23'S 179°51'E; copra. Formerly Mitchell Isl.

Nukumanu (nōō'kōōmä'nōō), atoll (pop. c.100), Solomon Isls., SW Pacific, c.250 mi. ENE of Bougainville; 4°32'S 159°26'E; c.40 small isls. on reef 11 mi. long, 7 mi. wide. Largest isl. is Nukumanu (□ 1). Governed as part of Australian Territory of New Guinea under U.N. trusteeship. Sometimes called Tasman Isl.

Nukunau, Gilbert Isls.: see NIKUNAU.

Nukunono (nōōkōōnō'nō), central atoll (1,370 acres; pop. 367), TOKELAU, S Pacific, 35 mi. WNW of Fakaofo; 24 islets, village on SW isl.; produces copra. Formerly Duke of Clarence Isl.

Nukuoro (nōōkwō'rō), atoll (pop. 210), Ponape dist., E Caroline Isls., W Pacific, 115 mi. SE of Satawan; 3°51'N 154°58'E; c.4 mi. in diameter; rises to 12 ft.; comprises 48 low islets. Polynesian natives. Formerly Nuguor.

Nukus (nōōkōōs'), city (1935 pop. estimate 5,000), ⊙ Kara-Kalpak Autonomous SSR, Uzbek SSR, at head of the Amu Darya delta, 500 mi. WNW of Tashkent; 42°25'N 59°40'E. In irrigated cotton area; cotton spinning and weaving, tanning, brewing, motor repairing. A new city, developed in 1930s. Succeeded Turtkul as capital in 1939.

Nukuty (nōōkōō'tē), village (1948 pop. over 500), NW Ust-Orda Buryat-Mongol Natl. Okrug, Irkutsk oblast, Russian SFSR, 40 mi. NNW of Cheremkhovo, in agr. area.

Nulato (nōōlä'tō), Indian village (pop. 173), on W bank of Yukon R., W Alaska, 200 mi. E of Nome; 64°43'N 158°7'W; gold mining, fur breeding and trapping. Has R.C. mission. On Yukon R. boat line; airfield. Russian blockhouse built here 1838; garrison massacred by Indians 1851.

Nules (nōō'lĕs), town (pop. 5,925), Castellón de la Plana prov., E Spain, on irrigated plain near the Mediterranean, 12 mi. SW of Castellón de la Plana; agr. trade center (olive oil, almonds, rice, oranges, wine); sawmills. Hot mineral springs near by. Severely damaged during Sp. civil war (1936–39); now mostly rebuilt.

Nulhegan River (nŭl"hē'gùn), NE Vt., rises near Brighton, flows c.15 mi. E to the Connecticut at Bloomfield.

Nullagine, village, N Western Australia, 140 mi. SE of Port Hedland; gold mining.

Nullarbor Plain (nŭ'lùrbōr'), vast plateau of S Australia, extending c.300 mi. W from Ooldea, South Australia, into Western Australia, bet. Victoria Desert and Great Australian Bight; rises to 1,000 ft.; traversed by Trans-Australian RR. Sand dunes; sparse vegetation; few sheep.

Nulvand or **Nul'vand** (nōōlvänt'), village, SW Garm oblast, Tadzhik SSR, on Panj R. (Afghanistan border) and 55 mi. S of Garm; gold placers; goats.

Nulvi (nōōlvē), village (pop. 3,694), Sassari prov., NW Sardinia, 10 mi. ENE of Sassari.

Numa, town (pop. 248), Appanoose co., S Iowa, 6 mi. WSW of Centerville, in coal-mining area.

Numadate (nōōmä'dätā), town (pop. 6,379), Akita prefecture, N Honshu, Japan, 7 mi. W of Yokote; rice, silk cocoons.

Numakunai (nōōmä'kōōnī), town (pop. 4,794), Iwate prefecture, N Honshu, Japan, 19 mi. NNE of Morioka; horse trading.

Numan (nōōmä'), town (pop. 1,209), Adamawa prov., Northern Provinces, E Nigeria, on Benue R., at mouth of the Gongola, and 40 mi. NW of Yola; agr. trade center; peanuts, millet, durra, cassava, yams; cattle raising; saltworks.

Numana (nōōmä'nä), town (pop. 1,060), Ancona prov., The Marches, central Italy, port on the Adriatic, 9 mi. SE of Ancona; mfg. (religious articles, harmoniums, harmonicas). Bishopric.

Numantia (nōōmăn'shù, nūmăn'shēù), Sp. *Numancia* (nōōmän'thyä), ruined city and national monument, Soria prov., N central Spain, in Old Castile, on Garray hill near the Duero (Douro), 3 mi. N of Soria. Historic center of the Celtiberian Arevaci, who rose against the Romans and, after a long siege by Scipio Africanus Minor, set fire (133 B.C.) to their city rather than surrender. Excavations, begun in 1905, revealed, besides entrenchments of Scipio's troops, ornaments of great artistic merit, now treasured in the archaeological mus. of Soria. An obelisk commemorates the heroic defense, which has also been depicted in a tragedy by Cervantes.

Numarán (nōōmärän'), town (pop. 2,149), Michoacán, central Mexico, on Lerma R. and 7 mi. SW of La Piedad; cereals, fruit, livestock.

Numas, An Numas, or **Al Numas** (both: ăn nōōmăs'), village, S Hejaz, Saudi Arabia, in highlands, 80 mi. E of Qunfidha; grain (sorghum), vegetables, fruit. Formerly in Asir.

Numata (nōōmä'tä). **1** Town (pop. 19,977), Gumma prefecture, central Honshu, Japan, 18 mi. N of Maebashi, in agr. area (rice, wheat); spinning. **2** Town (pop. 16,707), W Hokkaido, Japan, 22 mi. WNW of Asahigawa; coal mining.

Numazu (nōōmä'zōō), city (1940 pop. 53,165; 1947 pop. 92,838), Shizuoka prefecture, central Honshu, Japan, port on NE shore of Suruga Bay, 28 mi. ENE of Shizuoka; commercial center for agr. and sericulture area; textile mills. Exports rice, sake, sugar, textiles, machinery.

Nümbrecht (nüm'brĕkht), village (pop. 5,235), in former Prussian Rhine Prov., W Germany, after 1945 in North Rhine-Westphalia, 9 mi. S of Gummersbach; forestry.

Numea, New Caledonia: see NOUMÉA.

Numedal (nōō'mūdäl), valley of Lagen R., SE Norway, extends from E slope of the Hardangervidda c.60 mi. SSE to Kongsberg. Agr., lumbering, fishing; silver mining near Kongsberg. Folk customs and dialect resemble those of the Hallingdal.

Numfor or **Noemfoor** (both: nōōmfôr'), island (pop. 4,729), Schouten Isls., Netherlands New Guinea, off NW coast of isl. at entrance to Geelvink Bay, 50 mi. E of Manokwari; 14 mi. long, 12 mi. wide; fishing. In Second World War isl. was taken July, 1944, by U.S. forces.

Ñumí (nyōōmē'), town (dist. pop. 4,487), Guairá dept., S Paraguay, 16 mi. SE of Villarrica; sugar cane, fruit, livestock.

Numidia (nūmĭ'dēŭ), anc. country of N Africa, roughly coextensive with E part of modern Algeria; its chief centers were Cirta (Constantine) and Hippo Regius (Bône). Part of Carthaginian empire, until Masinissa, ruler of E Numidia, took sides with Rome (206 B.C.) in Second Punic War. Country flourished after war's end (201 B.C.) and under Micipsa (148–118 B.C.); but Jugurtha brought about a civil war (111–106 B.C.). Region became a Roman prov. in 46 B.C.; it throve under Romans until Vandal invasion in 5th cent. A.D.

Nu Mountains, Chinese *Nu Shan* (nōō' shän'), outlier of Tibetan highlands, NW Yunnan prov., China, extends c.250 mi. N–S bet. Mekong (E) and Salween (W) rivers; mts. rise to 15,800 ft.

Numurkah (nŭmûr'kŭ), town (pop. 1,519), N Victoria, Australia, 120 mi. N of Melbourne; rail junction in agr. area (tobacco, wheat, oats).

Nun, Manchuria: see NONNI RIVER.

Nun, Cape (nōōn), Fr. *Noun*, headland on Atlantic, Ifni territory, NW Africa, 10 mi. SW of Sidi Ifni; 29°15'N 10°18'W. Formerly confused with Cape Dra, 60 mi. SW, in Fr. Morocco.

Nun, Uad, Morocco: see ASACA RIVER.

Nunachuak (nōō'nŭchŭk"), village (pop. 44), SW Alaska, on Nushagak R. and 60 mi. NE of Dillingham; supply base for trappers and sportsmen.

Nunapitchuk (nōō"näpē'chōōk), village (pop. 125), SW Alaska, 30 mi. SW of Bethel, near Kuskokwim R.; 60°30'N 162°25'W.

Nunarssuit (nōōnäkh'shwĭt), island (20 mi. long, 3–9 mi. wide), just off SW Greenland, near S side of mouth of Kobbermine Bay, 55 mi. W of Julianehaab; 60°47'N 48°W. Rises to 2,400 ft. On W coast is Cape Desolation (60°44'N 48°11'W), landmark for early explorers. Formerly called Desolation Isl.

Nuncheng, Manchuria: see NUNKIANG, town.

Nunda. 1 (nŭn'dŭ, –dä") Village (pop. 1,224), Livingston co., W central N.Y., 23 mi. NW of Hornell; mfg. (caskets, cutlery, canned foods, dairy and milk products, machinery); agr. (poultry, grain). Letchworth State Park along Genesee R. is NW. Inc. 1839. **2** (nŭn'dŭ) Town (pop. 102), Lake co., E S.Dak., 12 mi. NNE of Madison.

Nundle (nŭn'dŭl), village (pop. 388), E New South Wales, Australia, 110 mi. NNW of Newcastle; gold-mining center.

Nuneaton (nŭnē'tŭn), municipal borough (1931 pop. 46,291; 1951 census 54,408), NE Warwick, England, on Anker R. and 8 mi. NNE of Coventry; coal mining; woolen, cotton, silk, rayon milling; also produces leather, iron products, hats, clothing, concrete, brick and tile. Near by are granite quarries. Has remains of 12th-cent. convent, and church dating from 15th cent. In municipal borough are coal-mining town of Stockingford (W) and granite-quarrying town of Chilvers Coton (SW), birthplace of George Eliot.

Nuñez (nōō'nyĕs), NE residential section of Buenos Aires, Argentina, bordering on the Río de la Plata.

Nunez (nū'nĕz), town (pop. 82), Emanuel co., E central Ga., 7 mi. S of Swainsboro.

Nunez, Rio, Fr. West Africa: see RIO NUNEZ.

Nungan (nŏŏng'än'), town, ⊙ Nungan co. (pop. 341,400), NW Kirin prov., Manchuria, 38 mi. N of Changchun and on railroad; livestock, soybeans, grain; flour and oil processing; lumbering. Formerly called Lungwan.

Nungwa or **Nungua** (nŏŏng'gwä), town, Eastern Prov., SE Gold Coast colony, on Gulf of Guinea, 11 mi. ENE of Accra; fishing; coconuts, cassava, corn. Dairy farm.

Nunivak Island (nōō'nĭvăk) (56 mi. long, 40 mi. wide; 1939 pop. 225), W Alaska, in Bering Sea, NW of Kuskokwim Bay, separated from mainland and Nelson Isl. by Etolin Strait; 60°6'N 166°24'W; rises to 830 ft. (NW). Treeless; covered with lichens, sedge, and shrubs; fogbound most of the year. Primitive native culture; pottery and ivory carvings are made. Reindeer and musk oxen have been introduced. Discovered 1821 by Russians.

Nunkiang (nŏŏn'jyäng'), **Nünkiang** (nün'–), **Nenkiang,** or **Nen-chiang** (nŭn'–), former province (□ 25,885; pop. 3,308,906) of W central Manchuria, on lower Nonni R.; ⊙ was Tsitsihar. Formed 1946 by Nationalists after Second World War, it was largely inc. 1949 into new Heilungkiang prov.

Nunkiang, Nünkiang, Nenkiang, or **Nen-chiang,** town, ⊙ Nunkiang co. (pop. 80,540), NW Heilungkiang prov., Manchuria, on Nonni (Nun) R., on railroad, and 140 mi. NNE of Tsitsihar; agr. center (kaoliang, millet, corn, soybeans). Coal and gold mining near by. Originally called Mergen or Merghen (Chinese *Meierhken*), it is one of the oldest (early-17th cent.) Chinese posts in N Manchuria. It was also called Nuncheng in late 1940s.

Nunkiní (nōōngkēnē'), town (pop. 1,813), Campeche, SE Mexico, on NW Yucatan Peninsula, 50 mi. SW of Mérida; sugar cane, henequen, fruit, livestock. Anc. ruins near by.

Nunkun (nŏŏng'kōōn), peak (23,410 ft.) in central Punjab Himalayas, S central Kashmir, 40 mi. E of Pahlgam, at 34°N 76°E. Also written Nun Kun.

Nunn, town (pop. 182), Weld co., N Colo., 20 mi. N of Greeley; alt. 5,186 ft. Farm center in cattle-grazing area.

Nuñoa (nōōnyō'ä), town (pop. 1,627), Puno dept., SE Peru, on the Altiplano, 28 mi. N of Ayaviri; alt. 13,222 ft.; barley, quinoa, livestock.

Nun River (nōōn), a main outlet of Niger R., S Nigeria, in middle section of delta; enters Gulf of Guinea at Akassa.

Nun's Island (2 mi. long, 1 mi. wide), S Que., in the St. Lawrence, opposite Montreal, near the Lachine Rapids.

Nunspeet (nŭn'spăt), village (pop. 4,308), Gelderland prov., N central Netherlands, 13 mi. NW of Apeldoorn, near the Ijsselmeer; tourist resort; egg market; paint mfg.

Nuoro (nwô'rô), province (□ 2,808; pop. 224,643), central Sardinia; ⊙ Nuoro. Least populous, most mountainous region of Sardinia, with Monti del Gennargentu and Catena del Marghine; drained by Tirso and Flumendosa rivers. Deposits of chalcopyrite, anthracite, talc and steatite, granite, barite, lignite. Fisheries. Forestry (cork plantations in Tirso valley, wood carving in Gennargentu villages). Livestock raising in E and NW. Corn, barley, potatoes, vineyards in E and NW; olives and fruit in NW; industry at Macomer and Bosa. Served by main N–S railroad, forking at Macomer to Bosa and Nuoro. Nuraghi in NW. Formed 1927 from Sassari and Cagliari provs.

Nuoro, town (pop. 10,820), ⊙ Nuoro prov., E central Sardinia, 50 mi. SE of Sassari; 40°19'N 9°20'E. Rail terminus; bishopric. Prehistoric rock tombs (E).

Nupe, former native kingdom, W Africa: see BIDA.

Nuporanga (nōōpōōräng'gŭ), city (pop. 1,091), NE São Paulo, Brazil, 30 mi. N of Ribeirão Prêto; coffee, rice, cotton, grain.

Nuqub (nŏŏkōōb'), town, ⊙ Beihan tribal area, Western Aden Protectorate, on Yemen hinterland border, 18 mi. N of Beihan al Qasab; airfield.

Nuquí (nōōkē'), village (pop. 437), Chocó dept., W Colombia, minor port on the Pacific, 40 mi. W of Quibdó; rice, corn, coconuts, oranges; fishing.

Nurakita, Ellice Isls.: see NIULAKITA.

Nuraminis (nōōrä'mēnēs), village (pop. 2,290), Cagliari prov., S Sardinia, 16 mi. N of Cagliari.

Nura River (nōōrä'), in N Karaganda and S Akmolinsk oblasts, Kazakh SSR, rises in Kazakh Hills SE of Karaganda, flows 445 mi. generally NW, past Temir-Tau (site of reservoir and power plant) and Kurgaldzhino, through L. Kurgaldzhin, to the Tengiz (lake); intermittent connection with Ishim R. SW of Akmolinsk.

Nurata (nōōrŭtä'), village (1926 pop. 8,185), NW Samarkand oblast, Uzbek SSR, in W foothills of the Ak-Tau, 55 mi. NNW of Katta-Kurgan; wheat, sheep.

Nura-Tau (nōōrŭ-tou'), range in N Samarkand oblast, Uzbek SSR; extends 100 mi. E–W; rises to 6,300 ft.

Nürburg (nür'bōōrk), village (pop. 173), in former Prussian Rhine Prov., W Germany, after 1945 in Rhineland-Palatinate, in the Eifel, 12 mi. W of Mayen; scene of auto races (track opened 1927).

Nurek (nōōryĕk'), village, NE Stalinabad oblast, Tadzhik SSR, on Vakhsh R. and 32 mi. ESE of Stalinabad; wheat; salt deposits, gold placers. Until 1937, Norak.

Nuremberg (nyŏŏ'rŭmbûrg), Ger. *Nürnberg* (nürn'bĕrk), city (1939 pop. 423,383; 1946 pop. 312,338; 1950 pop. 360,017), Middle Franconia, N central Bavaria, Germany, on Pegnitz R. and Ludwig Canal, and 92 mi. NNW of Munich; 49°27'N 11°05'E. Communications, industrial, and cultural center, long known for its toys and gingerbread. Has metal industry (cranes, motors, steam engines, transformers, turbines, vehicles, machine tools, armatures). Mfg. of precision instruments (drawing, measuring, and optical goods; radio parts, photoelectric cells), office equipment (typewriters, calculating machines, pencils, fountain pens); chemicals, paint brushes, leather articles, textiles. Breweries and distilleries. Hops trade. Seat of state col. for economics and sociology, acad. of fine arts, Ohm polytechnic institute. The producer, before 1945, of about 50% of Germany's airplane engines and Diesel engines for submarines and tanks, Nuremberg suffered severe destruction (about 75%) in Second World War. Its historic old town, which had completely preserved its medieval appearance, is now in ruins; and the 14th–15th-cent. wall surrounding it was heavily damaged. Completely destroyed were the 13th-cent. St. Catherine church, 14th-cent. Holy Ghost church, Peller House, Topler House, and the Bratwurstglöcklein, an anc. restaurant and a landmark of Nuremberg. Badly damaged were the 13th–14th-cent. St. Sebaldus church, 13th–15th-cent. St. Lorenz church, 14th-cent. St. Jacob church, the anc. Hohenzollern fortress, 14th-cent. city hall, and Albrecht Dürer House. Germanic Mus. (founded 1852) was damaged, but the valuable collections are preserved. Noteworthy 20th-cent. structures are (SE outskirts) the Party Rally Grounds with huge Luitpold Arena, and the Stadium. Nuremberg is 1st mentioned in 1050; created free imperial city in 1219. Rose to importance as trade center on route from Italy to N Germany. In 15th and 16th cent. Nuremberg was a center of Ger. culture. Dürer, Krafft, Vischer, and Stoss adorned city with their works. Hans Sachs and other meistersingers lived here. Peter Hele here made the 1st pocket watches, long called "Nuremberg eggs"; Regiomontanus built a noted observatory; Koberger here established his 1st printery (1470). Nuremberg early adopted the Reformation, and still retains its Protestant character. Declined after Thirty Years War. First Ger. railroad opened (1835) bet. here and neighboring Fürth. City again rose as an industrial center in 1870s. The National Socialists made it a natl. shrine and held annual party congresses here; at 1935 congress the violently anti-Semitic Nuremberg Laws were promulgated. Became seat of international tribunal on war crimes in 1945, after capture by U.S. troops in Second World War.

Nure River (nōō'rĕ), N central Italy, rises in Ligurian Apennines on Monte Maggiorasca, flows 40 mi. NNE, past Ferriere, Bettola, and Ponte dell'Olio, to Po R. 5 mi. E of Piacenza.

Nuri (nōō'rē), village, Northern Prov., Anglo-Egyptian Sudan, on the Nile, just above Kareima, near anc. Napata. Site of pyramid field with tombs of Ethiopian kings (after 7th cent. B.C.).

Nuriootpa (nūrēōōt'pŭ), town (pop. 1,257), SE South Australia, 40 mi. NNE of Adelaide; wheat, fruit, livestock; mfg. (cream of tartar).

Nuristan (nōō'rĭstän"), formerly called **Kafiristan** (kä'fĭ–), wooded, mountainous district (□ 5,000; pop. 100,000) of Eastern Prov., Afghanistan, on S slopes of the Hindu Kush, bounded E by Pakistan. A remote, undeveloped region, it consists of a series of deep, narrow valleys separated by rugged outliers of the Hindu Kush and drained by left tributaries of Kabul R. It furnishes 80% of Afghanistan's timber production (ASMAR FOREST). Some agr. (wheat, barley, millet, fruit) and stock raising in valleys. Pop., of uncertain origin, is thought to be remnant of an early Iranian people. Long referred to as Kafirs [=infidels], they came under Afghan control in 1890s. Following their conversion to Islam, Kafiristan [=land of the infidels] was renamed Nuristan [=land of the enlightened].

Nurlat (nōōrlät'), town (1948 pop. over 2,000), S Tatar Autonomous SSR, Russian SFSR, on railroad and 65 mi. S of Chistopol; metalworking, food processing; wheat.

Nurlaty (–lä'tē), village (1932 pop. estimate 2,320), W Tatar Autonomous SSR, Russian SFSR, near Sviyaga R., 33 mi. WSW of Kazan; grain, livestock.

Nurmahal (nōōr'mŭhŭl), town (pop. 8,324), Jullundur dist., central Punjab, India, 16 mi. S of Jullundur; wheat, cotton, gram; handicrafts (cotton cloth, shell buttons).

Nurmes (nōōr'mĕs), town (pop. 1,515), Kuopio co., E Finland, at NW end of L. Pielinen, 60 mi. NE of Kuopio; lumber milling, woodworking.

Nur Mountains, Turkey: see AMANOS MOUNTAINS.

Nürnberg, Germany: see NUREMBERG.

Nurpur (nōōr'pōōr), village, Kangra dist., N Punjab, India, 26 mi. WNW of Dharmsala; market for grain, fiber; handwoven woolen shawls.

Nurpur (no͞or'po͝or). **1** Village, Jhelum dist., N Punjab, W Pakistan, in Salt Range, 65 mi. WSW of Jhelum. Several rock-salt mines are just S. **2** Town (pop. 5,013), Shahpur dist., W central Punjab, W Pakistan, in Thal region, 50 mi. WSW of Sargodha; market center for grain, cattle, wool.

Nurri (no͞or'rē), village (pop. 3,223), Nuoro prov., S central Sardinia, 34 mi. NNE of Cagliari. Nuraghi, extinct volcano near by.

Nürschan, Czechoslovakia: see NYRANY.

Nursingpur, India: see NARSINGHPUR, Madhya Pradesh.

Nürtingen (nür'tĭng-ŭn), town (pop. 16,142), N Württemberg, Germany, after 1945 in Württemberg-Baden, on the Neckar and 8 mi. S of Esslingen; mfg. (machinery, machine tools, textiles, furniture). Has late-Gothic church. Chartered in 13th cent.

Nuruhak Dag (no͞orōōhäk' dä), Turkish *Nuruhak Dağ*, peak (9,850 ft.), S central Turkey, in Malatya Mts., 50 mi. WSW of Malatya.

Nurzec River (no͞o'zhĕts), Rus. *Nurzhets* (no͞or'-zhĭts), Bialystok prov., E Poland, rises SW of Kleszczele, near USSR border, flows WNW past Bransk, and SSW past Ciechanowiec to Bug R. 7 mi. SSW of Ciechanowiec; 64 mi. long.

Nurzhets River, Poland: see NURZEC RIVER.

Nus (no͞os), village (pop. 385), Val d'Aosta region, NW Italy, on Dora Baltea R. and 7 mi. E of Aosta. Near by is restored chateau of Fénis, built 1330.

Nus, Ras (räs' no͞os'), cape on SE Oman coast, at SW side of Kuria Muria Bay of Arabian Sea; 17°15'N 55°18'E. Marks E limit of Dhofar dist. of Oman.

Nusa Barung or **Noesa Baroeng** (both: no͞o'so͝o bärōōng'), uninhabited island (10 mi. long, 4 mi. wide) of Indonesia, in the Indian Ocean, off SE coast of Java, 55 mi. ESE of Malang; 8°28'S 113°21'E. Rocky, hilly, with steep coastal cliffs. Edible birds' nests are collected here. Pop. was removed 1776 to Java.

Nusa Besi, Portuguese Timor: see JACO.

Nusa Kambangan or **Noesa Kambangan** (both: no͞o'so͝o kämbäng'ŭn), island (□ c.45; 20 mi. long, 3 mi. wide) in Indian Ocean, just off S coast of Java, Indonesia, sheltering Chilachap harbor; 7°45'S 108°59'E. Rubber trees.

Nusa Laut or **Noesa Laoet** (both: no͞o'so͝o läōōt'), island (□ 24; pop. 4,593), Uliaser Isls., Indonesia, in Banda Sea, just SE of Saparua, near SW coast of Ceram; 3°40'S 128°47'E. Roughly circular, c.5 mi. in diameter. Coconuts, cloves, sago.

Nusantara: see INDONESIA.

Nusaybin or **Nisibin** (no͞osibĭn', nĭsĭ-), anc. *Nisibis*, village (pop. 2,311), Mardin prov., SE Turkey, rail terminus at Syrian border, 32 mi. ESE of Mardin; barley, wheat. In anc. times the residence of kings of Armenia.

Nusco (no͞o'skô), village (pop. 2,148), Avellino prov., Campania, S Italy, 16 mi. E of Avellino; lime and cementworks.

Nusfjord, Norway: see FLAKSTAD.

Nushagak (no͞o'shōōgăk), village (1939 pop. 41), SW Alaska, on Nushagak Bay, inlet of Bristol Bay, 8 mi. S of Dillingham; fishing; cannery.

Nushagak Bay (50 mi. long, 4–20 mi. wide), SW Alaska, on N shore of Bristol Bay; 58°37'N 158°31'W. Receives Nushagak R. Fishing and canning region. Dillingham village, N.

Nushagak River, SW Alaska, rises in Alaska Range near 60°50'N 154°W, flows 280 mi. SW, past Nunachuak and Ekwok, to Nushagak Bay, inlet of Bristol Bay, just E of Dillingham. Salmon stream. Upper course called Mulchatna R.

Nu Shan, China: see NU MOUNTAINS.

Nushki (no͞osh'kē), village, ⊙ Chagai dist., N Baluchistan, W Pakistan, 75 mi. SW of Quetta; road center; trades in carpets, salt, camels. Near-by rock quarries produce road metal and ballast.

Nusle (no͞o'slĕ), SSE suburb of Prague, Czechoslovakia; workers' homes.

Nussdorf (no͞os'dôrf), village (pop. 1,590), Rhenish Palatinate, W Germany, 2 mi. N of Landau; wine.

Nussdorf am Attersee (äm ä'tŭrzā), village (pop. 1,140), S Upper Austria, on W shore of the Attersee and 12 mi. W of Gmunden; summer resort (alt. 1,630 ft.); brewery.

Nussfjord, Norway: see FLAKSTAD.

Nussloch (no͞os'lôkh), village (pop. 4,993), N Baden, Germany, after 1945 in Württemberg-Baden, 2 mi. N of Wiesloch; mfg. of cigars and cigarettes. Limestone quarrying.

Nutarawit Lake (no͞otŭrô'wĭt) (□ 350), S central Keewatin Dist., Northwest Territories, just NW of Yathkyed L.; 62°55'N 98°50'W. Drains SE into Kazan R. through Yathkyed L.

Nutfield, residential town and parish (pop. 2,129), E central Surrey, England, 3 mi. E of Reigate; quarries fuller's earth. Has 15th-cent. church.

Nutley, residential town (pop. 26,992), Essex co., NE N.J., 5 mi. N of Newark; mfg. (chemicals, metal products, drugs, paper, beverages, textiles, insulating materials); poultry, truck, dairy products. Has early 18th cent. buildings. Inc. as township 1874, as town 1902.

Nutrias or **Ciudad de Nutrias** (syōōdädh'dä no͞o'-trēäs), town (pop. 318), Barinas state, W Venezuela, just N of Puerto de Nutrias on Apure R., 70 mi. ESE of Barinas, in cattle-raising region.

Nutschitz, Czechoslovakia: see NUCICE.

Nuttall Lane, England: see RAMSBOTTOM.

Nutter Fort, town (pop. 2,285), Harrison co., N W.Va., 3 mi. SE of Clarksburg; mfg. of pottery, glassware, stone products. Settled 1770; inc. 1924.

Nutzotin Mountains (nŭtsō'tĭn), E Alaska and SW Yukon, NW extension of St. Elias Mts., bet. Wrangell Mts. (SW) and upper Tanana R. (NE); extend 75 mi. bet. upper Nabesna R. (NW) and upper White R., Yukon (SE); rise to 9,489 ft. (62°15'N 142°8'W). Continued NW by Mentasta Mts.

Nuuanu Pali (no͞o-ä'no͞o pä'lē), cliff and mountain pass, Koolau Range, SE Oahu, T.H., 7 mi. N of Honolulu; alt. c.1,200 ft. **Nuuanu Valley,** just N of Honolulu, terminates in Nuuanu Pali; it is fertile and beautiful; site of the royal mausoleum.

Nuutajärvi (no͞o'täyăr"vē), village in Urjala commune (pop. 9,835), Häme co., SW Finland, in lake region, 30 mi. SSW of Tampere; glassworks.

Nuwakot (no͞ov' äkōt), town, central Nepal, 9 mi. SW of Pokhara; rice, corn, wheat, millet, vegetables, fruit. Nepalese military post.

Nuwara Eliya (no͞o'vŭrŭ ā'lĭyŭ, no͞orä'lēŭ), town (pop. 9,840), ⊙ Nuwara Eliya dist. (□ 462; pop., including estate pop., 268,397), Central Prov., Ceylon, in Ceylon Hill Country, 25 mi. SSE of Kandy; road and trade (tea, rubber, vegetables, rice) center; pisciculture. Meteorological observatory. Hill resort (alt. 6,199 ft.; average temp. 57° F.); sanatorium. Site 1st discovered 1827 by English.

Nuwuk, Alaska: see POINT BARROW.

Nuyts Archipelago (nūts), in Great Australian Bight, 5 mi. off S coast of South Australia; shelters Denial and Smoky bays. It is a 40-mi. chain comprising SAINT PETER ISLAND (largest), Franklin Isls. (easternmost), Isles of St. Francis, Lacy Isles, Purdie Isls. (westernmost), and scattered islets. Sandy, hilly; petrels, geese.

Nuyya, Estonia: see NUIA.

Nuzi (no͞o'zē), site 5 mi. SW of Kirkuk, N Iraq. Hundreds of clay tablets unearthed here bear inscriptions said to have been made by the Horims (or Horites) of the Bible. One of them has map dating from c.2500 B.C.

Nuzvid (no͞oz'vēd), town (pop. 14,184), Kistna dist., NE Madras, India, 24 mi. NE of Bezwada; rice milling; hand-loom woolen blankets; coconut and mango groves. Nuzvid rail station 12 mi. SE.

Nyabarongo River, Ruanda-Urundi: see NYAWARONGO RIVER.

Nyabira (nyäbē'rä), village, Salisbury prov., NE central Southern Rhodesia, in Mashonaland, on railroad and 20 mi. NW of Salisbury; tobacco, wheat, corn, citrus fruit, dairy products. Gold deposits.

Nyac (nī'ăk), village (pop. 64), W Alaska, 70 mi. ENE of Bethel; placer gold mining. Airfield.

Nyack (nī'ăk"), residential village (pop. 5,889), Rockland co., SE N.Y., on W bank of Tappan Zee (widening of the Hudson; ferry), opposite Tarrytown; mfg. of clothing, leather goods, organs, sewing machines, air-conditioning equipment; boatbuilding. Seat of Missionary Training Inst. Hook Mountain Park (c.650 acres; a section of Palisades Interstate Park) is just N. Settled 1684, inc. 1833.

Nyah, village (pop. 460), N Victoria, Australia, on Murray R. and 200 mi. NNW of Melbourne, on New South Wales border; agr. (citrus fruit, grapes); dried fruit.

Nyakrom (nyäkrōm'), town, Western Prov., S Gold Coast colony, 20 mi. NNW of Winneba; cacao, palm oil and kernels, cassava. Sometimes spelled Nyakrum.

Nyaksimvol or **Nyaksimvol'** (nyŭksēmvôl'), village, W Khanty-Mansi Natl. Okrug, Tyumen oblast, Russian SFSR, on (Northern) Sosva R. (head of navigation) and 280 mi. NW of Khanty-Mansisk.

Nyak Tso, Kashmir and Tibet: see PANGONG TSO.

Nyala (nyä'lä), town, Darfur prov., W Anglo-Egyptian Sudan, 115 mi. SSW of El Fasher; road and trade center (gum arabic).

Nyalam (nyä'läm'), town [Tibetan *dzong*], S Tibet, in N Nepal Himalayas, on Katmandu-Lhasa trade route and 50 mi. SW of Tingri.

Ny-Alesund (nü"-ô'lŭsōōn) or **New Alesund,** Nor. *Ny-Ålesund*, coal-mining settlement (pop. 174) and port, NW West Spitsbergen, Spitsbergen group, on S shore of Kings Bay, 70 mi. NW of Longyear City; 78°55'N 12°E. Starting point of Amundsen's polar flight in airship *Norge* near by.

Nyamandhlovu (nyämändlō'vo͞o), township (pop. 181), Bulawayo prov., SW Southern Rhodesia, in Matabeleland, on railroad and 30 mi. NW of Bulawayo; alt. 3,942 ft. Tobacco, peanuts, corn; cattle, sheep, goats.

Nyamati (nyä'mŭtē), town (pop. 4,455), Shimoga dist., NW Mysore, India, 15 mi. N of Shimoga; local trade in grain, betel nuts, jaggery. Also spelled Nyamti; formerly Niamati.

Nyamina (nyämē'nä), village, S Fr. Sudan, Fr. West Africa, on the Niger and 80 mi. NE of Bamako; peanuts, shea nuts, livestock. Market.

Nyamjang Chu, river, Tibet and Bhutan: see MANAS RIVER.

Nyamlagira (nyämläḡē'rä) or **Nyamuragira** (nyämo͞oräḡē'rä), active volcano (c.10,000 ft.) of the Virunga range, E Belgian Congo, N of L. Kivu and 15 mi. NE of Sake, in S part of Albert Natl. Park. Before 1938, main point of volcanic activity was the central crater, a large lake of incandescent lava. In 1938, further eruption opened new outlet on SW slopes, bringing previous center to a stop. Streams of lava reached L. Kivu and closed Sake bay to NW of the lake.

Nyando, N.Y.: see ROOSEVELTTOWN.

Nyandoma (nyŭndô'mŭ), city (1939 pop. over 10,000), SW Archangel oblast, Russian SFSR, on railroad and 200 mi. S of Archangel; sawmilling center; metalworking, dairying. City since 1939.

Nyanga, region, Fr. Equatorial Africa: see TCHIBANGA.

Nyanga River (nyäng-gä'), SW Gabon, Fr. Equatorial Africa, rises 50 mi. E of M'Bigou, flows 240 mi. SW, NW, and WSW, past Tchibanga, to the Atlantic 40 mi. NW of Mayumba. Many rapids.

Nyang Chu or **Nyang Chhu** (nyäng' cho͞o'), Chinese *Nien-ch'u Ho* (nyĕn'cho͞o' hŭ'), river, SE Tibet, right tributary of upper Brahmaputra R., rises in small lake (alt. c.14,800 ft.) in NW Assam Himalayas, 21 mi. S of Kangmar; flows c.110 mi. N and NW, along main India-Tibet trade route, past Gyangtse, Penam, and Shigatse, to the Brahmaputra 2 mi. NE of Shigatse. In upper course, called Tumbayung (or Trumbayung) Chu.

Nyangwe (nyäng'gwā), village, Kivu prov., E Belgian Congo, on right bank of the Lualaba and 30 mi. NW of Kasongo; center of native trade, in cotton-growing area. Former center of Arab slave-traders in central Africa, established 1863. It was reached by David Livingstone and V. L. Cameron in 1870. Stanley began the 1st upstream voyage on Congo R. here in 1874. Nyangwe fell to the Belgians in 1893.

Nyanza (nīăn'zŭ, nē–, nyän'zä) [Bantu,=lake]. Generic name sometimes applied to lakes VICTORIA, ALBERT, and EDWARD, in E central Africa.

Nyanza, province (□ 11,240, including 1,457 sq. mi. of lake area; pop. 1,865,677), W Kenya; ⊙ Kisumu. Bordered W by L. Victoria, N by Mt. Elgon and Uganda, S by Tanganyika. Consists of savanna plateau sloping toward the lake. Agr. (cotton, peanuts, sesame, sugar cane, corn), stock raising. Sorghum and millet are chief food crops. Dairy and poultry farming; lake fisheries. Gold mining in Kakamega area. Main centers are Kisumu, Londiani, Kisii.

Nyanza (nyän'zä), village, central Ruanda-Urundi, in Ruanda, 35 mi. SW of Kigali; center of native trade and residence of *mwami* (sultan) of Ruanda; cinchona plantations, dairying. R.C. mission.

Nyanza Migera (mēḡĕ'rä), village, S Ruanda Urundi, in Urundi, on NE shore of L. Tanganyika, near Tanganyika territory border, 65 mi. SSW of Kitega; small port exporting palm kernels and native food staples. Sometimes called Nyanza-Lac.

Nyaradszereda, Rumania: see MERCUREA-NIRAJ.

Nyasa, Lake (nīă'sŭ, nē–), Port. *Niassa*, formerly *Nyassa*, 3d-largest (□ c.11,000) and southernmost of E Africa's great lakes, on border bet. Nyasaland (W and S), Mozambique (E), and Tanganyika (NE); 360 mi. long, 15–50 mi. wide, 2,316 ft. deep (near N end); alt. c.1,550 ft. Occupies deep trough (S part of Great Rift Valley); has steep, mountainous shores, especially in N. Receives short streams from W (Songwe, Dwangwa, Bua), and the Ruhuhu (NE). Its only outlet (at S tip) is SHIRE RIVER, a tributary of the Zambezi. Lake is everywhere navigable, with chief landing places at Fort Johnston (on Shire R. just below efflux from lake), Chipoka (rail-steamer transfer point), Kota Kota, Chinteche, Karonga (all in Nyasaland); Mwaya, Manda, and Mbamba Bay in Tanganyika; and Mtangula in Mozambique. Chisamula and Likoma isls. near E shore belong to Nyasaland. Highlands near W shore and at N tip are densely populated. Lake was explored by Portuguese early in 17th cent. Rediscovered (1859) by David Livingstone. Lake level undergoes seasonal (up to 6 ft.) and periodic variations in 11-yr. cycles, which affect volume of Shire R.

Nyasaland, Br. protectorate (land area □ 36,829 or 37,374; including water □ 47,949; 1949 pop. 2,314,000), SE Africa; ⊙ Zomba. Territory (c.520 mi. long; 50–130 mi. wide) includes all of L. Nyasa, a narrow strip of land W of lake, and a wedge (S of lake) which penetrates Mozambique to within 130 mi. of Mozambique Channel of Indian Ocean. Bounded W by Northern Rhodesia, N and NE by Tanganyika. Lies in the Great Rift Valley, flanked by high savanna-covered plateaus; in N the Nyika Plateau rises sharply from lake shore to 8,000 ft.; in S, the Shire Highlands (alt. c.3,500 ft.; area of European settlement) and Mlanje Mts. (alt. 9,843 ft.) rise high on E edge of SHIRE RIVER valley. In the low, marshy SE frontier area are lakes Chilwa and Chiuta. Nyasaland lies entirely within the tropics (bet. 9°S and 17°S) but has 2 distinct climatic zones. In the hot, unhealthful Rift Valley temperatures reach 120°F. before Nov. rains. Highlands have a considerable seasonal temp. range (40°F.–95°F.) and receive well over 40 in. of rainfall. Almost entire economy is based on agr. Chief cash crops are tobacco (represents ⅓ of total export volume), tea (especially from Mlanje Mts. and Cholo dist.), tung, cotton (cultivated in Shire valley), sisal (Cholo dist.), peanuts. Minor export products are soybeans, rubber (from Chinteche dist.), chili, cottonseed, potatoes. Corn, cassava, rice, wheat, coffee, and pulses are grown for local consumption. Livestock industry has been enhanced by tsetse control work since 1946. Lake fishing, lumbering (tropical hardwoods, cedar). Coal, gold, bauxite, and corundum deposits are unexploited. Local industries (mfg. of tobacco products, soap, sisal rope) grew up during Second World War. Nyasaland is served by railroad from Beira (Mozambique) to Shire Highlands (Blantyre, Limbe) and S shore of L. Nyasa (present terminus at Salima, in resort area). From Blantyre (chief commercial center) roads lead to Salisbury (Southern Rhodesia), Fort Jameson (Northern Rhodesia), Quelimane (Mozambique). Two main airports are at Chileka (serving Blantyre and Limbe) and Lilongwe. Steamer navigation on L. Nyasa (Chipoka, near S end, is rail-ship transfer point). The African pop. is of Bantu stock (chief tribes: Nyanja, Chewa, Yao, Ngoni). Some 140,000 natives are usually employed outside of Nyasaland. Estimated European pop. (1948), 3,000; Asiatics, 4,000. Nyasaland was visited by Portuguese explorers in 17th–18th cent. It was rediscovered 1859 by David Livingstone. Other Scottish missionaries founded a mission (1874) in his honor at Blantyre. European settlement in Blantyre-Limbe area began in 1880s. British troops subdued (1888–96) Arab slavers in area and defeated (1889) a Port. attempt to annex S uplands to Mozambique. Territory became (1891) a Br. protectorate named British Central Africa; renamed Nyasaland in 1907. In 1914, N Nyasaland was briefly threatened by German invasion from Tanganyika (then German East Africa). Nyasaland is ruled by an appointed governor aided by an executive and a legislative council (which includes 2 African members). Native local govt. dates from 1933. Country is administratively divided into 3 provinces: Southern (⊙ Blantyre), Central (⊙Lilongwe), Northern (⊙ Mzimba).

Nyasoso (nyä'sōsō), village (pop. 578), S Br. Cameroons, administered as part of Eastern Provinces of Nigeria, near Fr. Cameroons border, 23 mi. NE of Kumba; cacao, bananas, palm oil and kernels.

Nyassa, Lake, E Africa: see NYASA, LAKE.

Nyaunglebin (nyoung"lă'bĭn), town (pop. 7,790), Pegu dist., Lower Burma, on Rangoon-Mandalay RR, near Sittang R. and 90 mi. NNE of Rangoon, in rice-growing area.

Nyaungu or **Nyaung-u** (nyoung'ōō'), town (pop. 8,118), Myingyan dist., Upper Burma, on left bank of Irrawaddy R. and 15 mi. SW of Pakokku; lacquer works.

Nyawarongo River (nyäwärông'gō), Ruanda-Urundi, rises E of L. Kivu, flows c.250 mi. generally E, joining the Ruvuvu at Tanganyika border to form KAGERA RIVER. Formerly considered the remotest headstream of the Nile, this distinction is now given to the Luvironza, the longest branch of the Ruvuvu. Also spelled Nyavarongo, Nyabarongo, Nyawarungu.

Nyazepetrovsk (nyŭzyĭpĕtrôfsk'), city (1938 pop. estimate 11,500), NW Chelyabinsk oblast, Russian SFSR, in the central Urals, on upper Ufa R. and 65 mi. SW of Sverdlovsk, near railroad (repair shops); metalworking and metallurgical center; mfg. (construction and crushing machinery, steel, bricks); sawmilling. Iron deposits. Became city in 1944. Formerly called Nyazepetrovski Zavod.

Nyborg (nü'bôr), city (1950 pop. 10,775) and port, Svendborg amt, E Fyn isl., Denmark, on the Great Belt and 18 mi. ESE of Odense, on Nyborg Fjord (c.4 mi. long). Shipbuilding; textiles, hardware, leather tanning. Ferry to Korsor (Zealand). Was important medieval trade center and fort.

Nybro (nü'brōō"), city (pop. 6,043), Kalmar co., SE Sweden, 19 mi. WNW of Kalmar; rail junction; glass and crystal mfg., paper milling, woodworking; health resort with chalybeate springs.

Nyby bruk (nü"bü" brük'), village (pop. 496), Sodermanland co., E Sweden, 4 mi. NNW of Eskilstuna; iron- and steelworks.

Nyda (nĭdä'), village, central Yamal-Nenets Natl. Okrug, Tyumen oblast, Russian SFSR, just N of Arctic Circle, on Ob Bay, at mouth of short Nyda R., 170 mi. E of Salekhard; fish cannery; reindeer raising.

Nydalen (nü'dälŭn), suburb (pop. 873) of Oslo, SE Norway, 4 mi. ENE of city center; steel milling, metalworking. Until 1948, in Akershus co.

Nye, county (□ 18,064; pop. 3,101), S and central Nev.; ⊙ Tonopah. Mtn. region bordering on Calif. Sections of Toiyabe Natl. Forest are in N, in Monitor, Toiyabe, and Toquema ranges; Pahute Mesa, Amargosa Desert, and part of Death Valley Natl. Monument are in S. Mining (silver, copper, gold), ranching. Formed 1863.

Nyegosh, mountain, Yugoslavia: see NJEGOS.

Nyegushi, Yugoslavia: see NJEGUSI.

Nyenchen Tanglha or **Nyenchhen Thanglha** (nyĕn'-chĕn täng'glä), Chinese *Ning-chin T'ang-la* or *Nien-ch'ing T'ang-ku-la* (nyĕn'chĭng' täng'gōō'-lä'), mountain range of the SE Trans-Himalayas, in SE Tibet, N of the Brahmaputra; extends c.550 mi. E–W. Highest point, Nyenchen Tanglha peak (23,255 ft.), is 60 mi. NW of Lhasa. S central area drained by the Kyi Chu.

Nyer (nyâr), village (pop. 160), Pyrénées-Orientales dept., S France, in CONFLENT valley, 10 mi. SW of Prades; iron and manganese mining.

Nyergesujfalu (nyĕr'gĕ-shōōĭfôlōō), Hung. *Nyergesújfalu,* town (pop. 2,719), Komarom-Esztergom co., N Hungary, on the Danube and 9 mi. W of Esztergom; silk mfg., cement and brickworks.

Nyeri (nyĕ'rē), town (pop. c.2,500), S central Kenya, bet. Aberdare Range and Mt. Kenya, on road and 60 mi. N of Nairobi; alt. 5,900 ft.; 0°25'S 36°57'E. Hunting resort and agr. trade center; coffee, sisal, wheat, corn; dairying. Airfield. R.C. mission. Nyeri rail station is 5 mi. ENE.

Nygard (nü'gär), village in Vardal canton (pop. 7,867), Opland co., SE Norway, 3 mi. SW of Gjovik; paper and cellulose milling; mfg. of chemicals, tanning extract.

Nyhammar (nü'hä"mär), village (pop. 675), Kopparberg co., central Sweden, in Bergslag region, 11 mi. NW of Ludvika; ironworks, sawmills.

Nyhamn, Sweden: see ESSVIK.

Nyika (nyē'kä), arid steppe in E Kenya, bet. tropical coastal lowland and central highlands; alt. 500–3,000 ft. Watered by Tana R.

Nyika Plateau, grassy highland in N Nyasaland, W of Livingstonia; rises to 7–8,000 ft. Wild game.

Nyimba (nyēm'bä), village (village area pop. 917), Eastern Prov., E Northern Rhodesia, on Great East Road and 180 mi. ENE of Lusaka; tobacco, corn, wheat.

Nyirabrany (nyē'räbränyŭ), Hung. *Nyírábrány,* town (pop. 6,246), Hajdu co., E Hungary, 18 mi. E of Debrecen, near Rumanian line; distilleries; excellent wine raised near by.

Nyiracsad (nyē'rō-chäd), Hung. *Nyíracsád,* town (pop. 4,369), Szabolcs co., E Hungary, 16 mi. ENE of Debrecen; distilleries; grain, sugar beets, cattle, horses.

Nyirad (nyĭ'räd), Hung. *Nyirád,* town (pop. 1,786), Zala co., W Hungary, 22 mi. SSW of Veszprem; wine, cattle, sheep. Bauxite mined near by.

Nyiradony (nyē'rōdônyŭ), Hung. *Nyíradony,* town (pop. 5,890), Szabolcs co., E Hungary, 17 mi. NE of Debrecen; potatoes, tobacco, cattle.

Nyiragongo (nyērägông'gō) or **Tshaninagongo** (chänēnägông'gō), active volcano (c.11,400 ft.) of the Virunga range in E Belgian Congo, near Ruanda-Urundi border, NE of L. Kivu and 12 mi. N of Goma, in S part of Albert Natl. Park. Central crater is c.1.3 mi. in diameter, 800 ft. deep. There are several old craters, easily accessible and noted for their picturesque scenery and flora. In 1948, some cones opened at WSW base and lava flows issued, one reaching L. Kivu and obstructing Sake-Goma road. Native legends associate the volcano with the place of expiation of guilty souls.

Nyirbator (nyēr'bätôr), Hung. *Nyírbátor,* town (pop. 11,808), Szabolcs co., NE Hungary, 21 mi. ESE of Nyiregyhaza; rail junction; mfg. (vegetable oil, soap); tobacco warehouses, brickworks, distilleries, flour mills. Agr., dairy farming in vicinity.

Nyirbeltek (nyēr'bāltĕk), Hung. *Nyírbéltek,* town (pop. 3,126), Szabolcs co., NE Hungary, 25 mi. ENE of Debrecen; rye, wheat, cattle.

Nyirbogat (nyēr'bôgät), Hung. *Nyírbogát,* town (pop. 3,599), Szabolcs co., NE Hungary, 19 mi. SE of Nyiregyhaza; petroleum refinery, distillery; corn, potatoes, hogs, cattle.

Nyirbogdany (nyēr'bôgdänyŭ), Hung. *Nyírbogdány,* town (pop. 2,519), Szabolcs co., NE Hungary, 10 mi. NE of Nyiregyhaza; oil refinery.

Nyiregyhaza (nyē'rĕdyŭhä"zŏ), Hung. *Nyíregyháza,* city (pop. 59,156), ⊙ Szabolcs co., NE Hungary, 29 mi. N of Debrecen; rail, mfg., market center. Produces furniture, vegetable oil, cement, soap, candles, tile, bricks, flour; tobacco warehouses. Mus. with gold relics of Avar times. Two teachers cols. Small salt lake near by, with baths. Farms, vineyards, stock raising in vicinity.

Nyirlugos (nyēr'lōōgōsh), Hung. *Nyírlugos,* town (pop, 3,569), Szabolcs co., NE Hungary, 23 mi. SE of Nyiregyhaza; beans, rye, corn, hogs.

Nyirmada (nyēr'mŏdŏ), Hung. *Nyírmada,* town (pop. 4,331), Szabolcs co., NE Hungary, 23 mi. ENE of Nyiregyhaza; flour; wheat, beans, rye, hogs.

Nyirpazony (nyēr'pŏzônyŭ), Hung. *Nyírpazony,* town (pop. 3,027), Szabolcs co., NE Hungary, 4 mi. NE of Nyiregyhaza; potatoes, tobacco, peaches.

Nyirseg (nyēr'shāg), Hung. *Nyírség,* section of the Alföld, NE Hungary; main town is Nyiregyhaza. A section of sandy soils, largely anchored by vegetation; barley, rye cultivation.

Nyitra, Czechoslovakia: see NITRA.

Nykarleby (nü'kärl'übü"), Finnish *Uusikaarlepyy* (ōō'sĭkär"lĕpü), city (pop. 1,066), Vaasa co., W Finland, on 100-mi.-long Lapua R. (lä'pōōä), Finnish *Lapuan joki,* Swedish *Nykarleby älv,* near its mouth on Gulf of Bothnia, 40 mi. NE of Vaasa; trade center in lumbering, woodworking region. Pop. is largely Swedish-speaking. Site of Swedish teachers seminary. Has church (1708). Poet Topelius b. here.

Nykerk, Netherlands: see NIJKERK.

Nykirke, Norway: see BORRE.

Nykobing (nü'kûbĭng), Dan. *Nykøbing,* formerly *Nykjøbing.* **1** City (1950 pop. 4,453) and port, Holbaek amt, N Zealand, Denmark, on Nykobing Bay of Ise Fjord and 38 mi. NW of Copenhagen; 55°55'N 11°41'E. Meat cannery, egg-packing plant, brewery. **2** City (1950 pop. 17,192), Maribo amt, Denmark, port on Falster isl., on Guldborg Sound (here bridged to Lolland isl.) and 65 mi. SSW of Copenhagen; rail junction; commercial, industrial center. Sugar refining, mfg. (machinery, tobacco), meat canning; shipbuilding, fishing. Founded around 12th-cent. castle (ruins still extant). Seat of bishop; has Gothic church, used as Franciscan monastery until 1532. **3** City (1950 pop. 9,187), Thisted amt, N Jutland, Denmark, on E Mors isl., in Lim Fjord, and 43 mi. WSW of Aalborg; iron foundry, mfg. (textiles, tobacco); oyster fisheries.

Nykobing Bay, Denmark: see ISE FJORD.

Nykoping (nü'chû"pĭng), Swedish *Nyköping,* city (1950 pop. 20,477), ⊙ Sodermanland co., E Sweden, on small Baltic bay at mouth of short Nykoping R., 50 mi. SW of Stockholm; 58°45'N 17°1'E. Seaport, shipping iron ore; rail junction; automobile and furniture works, textile and lumber mills. Has 12th-cent. church, 17th-cent. town hall, mus., and remains of 12th-cent. castle. Major port and trade center in Middle Ages; burned 1665, and again, 1719, by Russians.

Nykroppa (nü"krô'pä), village (pop. 2,028), Varmland co., W Sweden, in Bergslag region, on Oster L., Swedish *Östersjön* (ûs'tûr-shûn") (5 mi. long), 7 mi. SE of Filipstad; rail junction; ironworks.

Nykvarn (nü'kvärn"), village (pop. 960), Stockholm co., E Sweden, 6 mi. W of Sodertalje; paper mills.

Nyland, county, Finland: see UUSIMAA.

Nyland (nü'länd), village (pop. 560), Vasternorrland co., NE Sweden, on Angerman R. estuary, 25 mi. N of Harnosand; metal- and woodworking, shoe and glove mfg.

Nylga (nĭlgä'), village (1926 pop. 544), S central Udmurt Autonomous SSR, Russian SFSR, 30 mi. W of Izhevsk; wheat, rye, oats, livestock. Formerly Nylga-Zhikya.

Nylstroom (näl'strōōm), village (pop. 3,707), central Transvaal, U. of So. Afr., on upper Magalakwin R. and 75 mi. N of Pretoria; rail junction; agr. center (wheat, tobacco, peanuts).

Nymagee, village (pop. 197), central New South Wales, Australia, 285 mi. E of Broken Hill; copper-mining center.

Nymburk (nĭm'bŏŏrk), Ger. *Neuenberg an der Elbe* (noi'ûnbĕrk än dĕr ĕl'bĕ), town (pop. 11,442), central Bohemia, Czechoslovakia, on Elbe R. and 19 mi. NNW of Kutna Hora; rail junction (large railroad workshops); hydroelectric power station. Noted for production of liqueurs. Has 13th-cent. church, remains of fortifications. Founded in Middle Ages; laid waste during Hussite wars.

Nymegen, Netherlands: see NIJMEGEN.

Nymme, Estonia: see NOMME.

Nymphaion, Cape, or **Cape Nimfaion** (both: nĭmfā'ôn), Lat. *Nymphaeum* (nĭmfē'ŭm), a SE extremity of Akte (Athos) prong of Chalcidice peninsula, on Aegean Sea, at S foot of Mt. Athos; 40°7'N 24°23'E. Darius' fleet was wrecked off this cape, 492 B.C. Formerly called St. George [Gr. *Hagios Georgios* or *Ayios Yeoryios*].

Nymphenburg (nüm'fûnbŏŏrk), W suburb of Munich, Upper Bavaria, Germany; has noted porcelain factory founded 1761. Contains castle, begun 1664, situated in splendid park.

Nymphio, Turkey: see KEMALPASA.

Nymwegen, Netherlands: see NIJMEGEN.

Nynashamn (nü"nĕs"hä'mŭn), Swedish *Nynäshamn,* city (pop. 6,883), Stockholm co., E Sweden, on the Baltic, 25 mi. S of Stockholm; seaport, terminus of steamers to Visby; shipbuilding, oil refining, metalworking, electrical-equipment mfg. Developed rapidly after construction (1901) of railroad; inc. as town 1911; as city 1946. Near by is 15th-cent. manor house.

Nyngan (nĭng'gŭn), municipality (pop. 1,802), central New South Wales, Australia, on Bogan R. and 290 mi. NW of Sydney; rail junction; mining center (copper, gold).

Nyon (nēō'), anc. *Noviodunum* or *Civitas Julia Equestris,* town (pop. 5,326), Vaud canton, SW Switzerland, on L. Geneva and 13 mi. NNE of Geneva; chemicals, leather products, pastry; metalworking. Has 16th-cent. castle with mus.

Nyondo, Ruanda-Urundi: see KISENYI.

Nyong et Sanaga (nyông' ā sänägä'), administrative region (□ 10,930; 1950 pop. 410,750), central Fr. Cameroons; ⊙ Yaoundé. Drained by Nyong and Sanaga rivers. Lies in tropical rain-forest zone and produces palm oil and kernels, coffee (along Nyong R.), cacao, rice. Hardwood lumbering is also important. Some titanium deposits. Secondary industries at Yaoundé.

Nyong River, tributary of Gulf of Guinea in central and W Fr. Cameroons, rises c.25 mi. E of Abong-M'Bang, flows c.400 mi. generally W, past Abong-M'Bang, Ayos, Akonolenga, M'Balmayo, and Eséka, to the Atlantic 40 mi. SSW of Edéa. Its middle course (Abong-M'Bang to M'Balmayo) is navigable for small steamboats April–Nov.

Nyons (nyõ'), town (pop. 2,545), Drôme dept., SE France, on the Aygues and 33 mi. NNE of Avignon; agr. trade center (truffles, lavender essence, black olives, wines, almonds, honey); fruit processing and shipping, olive-oil pressing, silk milling. Has 14th-cent. bridge and picturesque old quarter.
Nyord (nü'ôr), island (□ 2; pop. 207), Denmark, bet. Moen and Zealand isls., bet. Stege Bay (SE) and Fakse Bay (NW).
Nyrany (nĕr'zhänĭ), Czech *Nýřany*, Ger. *Nürschan* (nür'shän), village (pop. 4,073), W Bohemia, Czechoslovakia, 8 mi. WSW of Pilsen; rail junction; coal mining, clay quarrying; optical-glass mfg.
Nyrob (nĭrôp'), village (1948 pop. over 2,000), N Molotov oblast, Russian SFSR, near Kolva R., 25 mi. NNE of Cherdyn; wheat, rye, livestock.
Nyrsko (nĕr'skô), Czech. *Nýrsko*, Ger. *Neuern* (noi'ûrn), town (pop. 2,559), SW Bohemia, Czechoslovakia, in foothills of Bohemian Forest, on railroad, on Uhlava R. and 10 mi. SW of Klatovy, near Ger. border; iron mining, lumbering.
Nysa, town, Poland: see NEISSE.
Nysa Klodzka River, Poland: see NEISSE RIVER.
Nysa Luzycka River, Poland: see NEISSE RIVER.
Nysa River, Poland: see NEISSE RIVER.
Nyslott, Finland: see SAVONLINNA.
Nyson (nĭ'sŭn), rural township (pop. 65) of Umvuma, Gwelo prov., central Southern Rhodesia.
Nyssa (nĭ'sŭ), name of several anc. cities devoted to worship of Dionysus. Best known is town of Cappadocia, Asia Minor, near the Halys (modern Kizil Irmak), residence of Gregory of Nyssa.
Nyssa (nĭ'sŭ), town (pop. 2,525), Malheur co., E Oregon, on Snake R., near mouth of Owyhee R., and c.45 mi. NW of Boise, Idaho; alt. 2,178 ft.; beet-sugar refining, flour milling, fruit and vegetable packing. Town is market for irrigation projects on Owyhee and Boise rivers and for Vale project. Owyhee Dam is 20 mi. SW. Inc. 1903.
Nystad, Finland: see UUSIKAUPUNKI.
Nysted (nü'stĕdh), city (pop. 1,637) and port, Maribo amt, Denmark, on Lolland isl., and 12 mi. SE of Maribo, on Baltic Sea; brewing, shipbuilding.
Nytva (nĭt'vŭ), city (1926 pop. 5,199), W central Molotov oblast, Russian SFSR, near Kama R., 45 mi. WSW of Molotov and on rail spur; metallurgical center, producing quality steels. Became city in 1942. Called Nytvinski prior to First World War. Landing at Ust-Nytva, 5 mi. S, on left bank.
Nytych, Poland: see NOWY STAW.
Nyudo, Cape (nū'dō), Jap. *Nyudo-saki*, Akita prefecture, N Honshu, Japan, at NW tip of Oga Peninsula, in Sea of Japan; 40°N 139°42'E.
Nyugawa (nū'gäwä), town (pop. 10,241), Ehime prefecture, N Shikoku, Japan, on Hiuchi Sea, 19 mi. ENE of Matsuyama; rice, raw silk, shellfish, edible seaweed. Artisan umbrella industry.
Nyuksenitsa (nyŏŏksĭnyē'tsŭ), village (1939 pop. over 500), NE Vologda oblast, Russian SFSR, on Sukhona R. and 75 mi. WSW of Veliki Ustyug; flax processing.
Nyul (nyōōl), Hung. *Nyúl*, town (pop. 3,487), Györ-Moson co., NW Hungary, 6 mi. S of Györ; grain, peaches, horses.
Nyundo, Ruanda-Urundi: see KISENYI.
Nyurba (nyōōrbä'), village (1948 pop. over 500), SW Yakut Autonomous SSR, Russian SFSR, on Vilyui R., 100 mi. WSW of Vilyuisk, in agr. area.
Nyustya, Czechoslovakia: see HNUSTA.
Nyuvchim (nyōōfchēm'), town (1926 pop. 715), SW Komi Autonomous SSR, Russian SFSR, on Sysola R. and 20 mi. S of Syktyvkar; iron mines; foundry (dating from 1756).
Nyu-York, N'yu-York, or **New York**, town (1939 pop. over 500), central Stalino oblast, Ukrainian SSR, in the Donbas, 5 mi. S of Dzerzhinsk; agr.-machinery works.
Nyuzen (nū'zän), town (pop. 7,278), Toyama prefecture, central Honshu, Japan, on Sea of Japan, 11 mi. NE of Uozu, in agr. area (rice, pears); mfg. (straw goods, sake).
Nyverdaal, Netherlands: see NIJVERDAL.
Nzega (ŭnzĕ'gä), town, Western Prov., W central Tanganyika, on road and 60 mi. NNE of Tabora; agr. trade center; cotton, peanuts, corn; cattle, sheep, goats.
N'zérékoré (ŭnzĕrĕkō'rā), town (pop. c.5,700), SE Fr. Guinea, Fr. West Africa, near Liberia border, 165 mi. NE of Monrovia (road); agr. center (rice, palm kernels, coffee, tobacco, pepper, kola nuts, pimento; sheep, goats). Mfg. of cigars. Missions. Gold and iron deposits in vicinity.
Nzi River (ŭnzē'), Ivory Coast, Fr. West Africa, rises SE of Ferkéssédougou, flows c.280 mi. in meandering course generally S to Bandama R. near Tiassalé.
Nzoia River (ŭnzō'yä), SW Kenya, rises in Cherangani Hills, flows c.150 mi. SW, past Mumias, to L. Victoria just S of Port Victoria. Its right affluents (from Mt. Elgon) drain the Trans-Nzoia region (chief town, Kitale).
N'zoro, Belgian Congo: see WATSA.

O

O, Japan: see O-o.
Oacalco (wäkäl'kō), town (pop. 1,146), Morelos, central Mexico, 13 mi. E of Cuernavaca; sugar, rice, fruit, stock.
Oacoma (ōŭkō'mŭ), town (pop. 231), Lyman co., S central S.Dak., 4 mi. W of Chamberlain, across Missouri R.; manganese deposits near by.
Oadby, urban district (1931 pop. 4,724; 1951 census 6,206), central Leicester, England, 3 mi. SE of Leicester; hosiery, shoes. Has church dating from 13th cent.
Oadweina, Br. Somaliland: see ODWEINA.
Oahe Dam (ōwä'hē), S.Dak., a major flood-control unit of MISSOURI RIVER Basin project, in the Missouri 6 mi. above Pierre; 230 ft. high, 9,300 ft. long.
Oahu (ōä'hōō), island (□ 589; pop. 347,529), T.H., 3d largest of HAWAIIAN ISLANDS, commercially most important; separated from Molokai by Kaiwi Channel, from Kauai by Kauai Channel; 21°27'N 158°W; seat of HONOLULU, Territorial capital. Isl. is 40 mi. long, 26 mi. wide. Has 2 mtn. ranges, WAIANAE RANGE and KOOLAU RANGE, and several fertile valleys, notably Manoa and NUUANU VALLEY. Has no active volcanoes, but many extinct craters, among which Diamond Head, Koko Head, and Punchbowl are most important. Site of Univ. of Hawaii, Punahou Acad., Mid-Pacific Inst. It is vital defense area, with PEARL HARBOR naval base, SCHOFIELD BARRACKS, and HICKAM FIELD. Pineapple and sugar plantations, coral gardens, and fine bathing beaches, of which WAIKIKI is most famous. Chief exports, sugar and pineapples.
Oak, village (pop. 131), Nuckolls co., S Nebr., 17 mi. NNE of Superior and on Little Blue R.
Oakbank, village in Kirknewton parish, NW Midlothian, Scotland, just S of Mid Calder; shale-oil mining.
Oak Bay, SE suburb of Victoria, SW B.C., at SE extremity of Vancouver Isl., on Juan de Fuca Strait.
Oak Bluffs, town (pop. 1,521), Dukes co., SE Mass., on NE Martha's Vineyard, 23 mi. SE of New Bedford; summer resort. Steamer connections with Woods Hole. Settled 1642, set off from Edgartown as Cottage City in 1880, renamed 1907.
Oakboro, town (pop. 631), Stanly co., S central N.C., 11 mi. SW of Albemarle; cotton and lumber mills.
Oak City. 1 Town (pop. 518), Martin co., E N.C., 28 mi. E of Rocky Mount. **2** Town (pop. 334), Millard co., W central Utah, 12 mi. E of Delta; alt. 4,700 ft.
Oak Creek, town (pop. 1,488), Routt co., NW Colo., on branch of Yampa R., in SW foothills of Park Range, and 110 mi. WNW of Denver; alt. 7,401 ft.; dairy products. Coal mines in vicinity. Part of Routt Natl. Forest near by. Inc. 1907.
Oakdale. 1 City (pop. 4,064), Stanislaus co., central Calif., in San Joaquin Valley, 25 mi. ESE of Stockton, and on Stanislaus R.; dairying, irrigated farming (fruit, almonds), horticulture. Inc. 1906. **2** Village, New London co., Conn.: see MONTVILLE. **3** City (pop. 5,598), Allen parish, SW central La., 52 mi. NE of Lake Charles city, in lumber and agr. (truck, strawberries, citrus fruit, livestock) region; sawmills; naval stores; cotton gin. Laid out 1886. **4** Village, Worcester co., Mass.: see WEST BOYLSTON. **5** Village (pop. 502), Antelope co., NE central Nebr., 5 mi. SE of Neligh and on Elkhorn R.; livestock, dairy and poultry produce, grain. **6** Resort village, Suffolk co., SE N.Y., on S shore of Long Isl., 2 mi. NW of Sayville. Heckscher State Park is near by. **7** Borough (pop. 1,572), Allegheny co., SW Pa., 11 mi. WSW of Pittsburgh; oil. Inc. 1872. **8** Town (pop. 718), Morgan co., NE central Tenn., 35 mi. W of Knoxville, in the Cumberlands.
Oakengates, urban district (1931 pop. 11,190; 1951 census 11,659), E Shropshire, England, 4 mi. E of Wellington; coal mining, steel milling.
Oakenholt, Wales: see FLINT.
Oakes (ōks), city (pop. 1,774), Dickey co., SE N. Dak., 27 mi. SW of Lisbon, near James R.; railroad junction, agr. shipping center; dairy products, grain. Platted 1886, inc. 1888.
Oakesdale, town (pop. 576), Whitman co., SE Wash., 18 mi. NNE of Colfax; wheat, oats, peas.
Oakes Field, airport just E of Nassau, New Providence Isl., N central Bahama Isls.
Oakey, town (pop. 1,432), SE Queensland, Australia, 80 mi. W of Brisbane; agr. center (wheat, corn).
Oakfield. 1 Town (pop. 108), Worth co., S central Ga., 20 mi. NE of Albany, near Flint R. **2** Agr. town (pop. 1,009), Aroostook co., E Maine, 15 mi. W of Houlton. Inc. 1897. **3** Village (pop. 1,781), Genesee co., W N.Y., 7 mi. NW of Batavia, in wheat and truck area; gypsum quarrying and processing, food canning. Summer resort. Settled 1850, inc. 1858. **4** Village (pop. 697), Fond du Lac co., E central Wis., 8 mi. SSW of Fond du Lac, in dairy and farm region; mfg. of bricks, electrical apparatus; vegetable cannery.
Oakford, village (pop. 281), Menard co., central Ill., near Sangamon R., 26 mi. NW of Springfield, in agr. and bituminous-coal area.
Oak Forest, village (pop. 1,856), Cook co., NE Ill., suburb S of Chicago. Inc. 1947.
Oak Grove. 1 Town (pop. 1,796), ⊙ West Carroll parish, NE La., near Ark. line, 50 mi. NE of Monroe, in agr. area (cotton, corn, livestock, seed oats); cotton gins; concrete products; lumber. Inc. as village in 1908, as town in 1928. **2** City (pop. 761), Jackson co., W Mo., 25 mi. SE of Kansas City; corn, wheat, oats.
Oakham (ō'kŭm), urban district (1931 pop. 3,191; 1951 census 3,537), ⊙ Rutland, England, 17 mi. E of Leicester; mfg. of hosiery, shoes. Has public school founded 1584, 12th-cent. castle, and 14th-cent. church.
Oakham, town (pop. 455), Worcester co., central Mass., 13 mi. WNW of Worcester; dairying.
Oakharbor or **Oak Harbor**, village (pop. 2,370), Ottawa co., N Ohio, 23 mi. ESE of Toledo and on Portage R.; baskets, food products, cement blocks, barrels; ships fruit.
Oak Harbor, town (pop. 1,193), Island co., NW Wash., on Whidbey Isl. and 30 mi. NW of Everett; dairy products, wheat, poultry, truck. Site of naval air station.
Oakhaven, town (pop. 81), Hempstead co., SW Ark., 4 mi. N of Hope.
Oak Hill. 1 Town (pop. 683), Volusia co., NE Fla., 27 mi. SSE of Daytona Beach, near the Atlantic; citrus-fruit packing; beekeeping. **2** or **Oakhill**, city (pop. 92), Clay co., N central Kansas, 14 mi. SW of Clay Center, in grain and livestock area. **3** Village, Middlesex co., Mass.: see NEWTON. **4** Resort village, Greene co., SE N.Y., in Catskill Mts., on Catskill Creek and 20 mi. NW of Catskill. **5** Village (pop. 1,615), Jackson co., S Ohio, 28 mi. ENE of Portsmouth; firebrick, sponge rubber, foundry products, food products; coal mines, gas wells. **6** City (pop. 4,518), Fayette co., S central W.Va., 14 mi. N of Beckley; bituminous-coal mines; timber; stock raising. Settled 1820.
Oakhill, town (pop. 123), Wilcox co., SW central Ala., 35 mi. S of Selma.
Oakhurst. 1 Village (pop. 2,388), Monmouth co., E N.J., near the coast, 3 mi. N of Asbury Park; makes tools; truck farming. **2** Village (1940 pop. 679), San Jacinto co., E Texas, 14 mi. E of Huntsville, in Sam Houston Natl. Forest; trade point in timber, agr. area.
Oak Island, islet in Mahone Bay, S N.S., 4 mi. SW of Chester; 44°31'N 64°18'W. The treasure of Captain Kidd is reputedly hidden here; many unsuccessful attempts have been made to recover it.
Oak Island, village, Minn.: see LAKE OF THE WOODS, lake.
Oak Island, St. Lawrence co., N N.Y., one of the Thousand Isls., in the St. Lawrence, near Ont. line, just SW of Chippewa Bay; c.2 mi. long; max. width c.½ mi.
Oak Knoll, town (pop. 3,930), Tarrant co., N Texas. Inc. since 1940.
Oak Lake, town (pop. 479), SW Man., near Assiniboine R., 30 mi. W of Brandon; mixed farming, stock; muskrat farms.
Oakland, county (□ 877; pop. 396,001), SE Mich.; ⊙ Pontiac. Drained by Shiawassee, Huron, and Clinton rivers, and by the River Rouge. Fruit growing (apples, peaches, cherries), agr. (truck, grain, beans, corn, alfalfa, livestock, poultry; dairy products; nurseries, poultry hatcheries. Mfg. at Pontiac, Ferndale, and Royal Oak. Many small lakes (resorts). Organized 1820.
Oakland. 1 City (pop. 384,575), ⊙ Alameda co., W Calif., 3d-largest city in state, port and industrial center on E shore of San Francisco Bay (spanned by SAN FRANCISCO-OAKLAND BAY BRIDGE), opposite San Francisco and the Golden Gate; Oakland harbor is estuary bet. Alameda (on an isl.; bridge and tube connections with Oakland) and E bay shore. From its harbor, industrial, and downtown dists., city rises inland to Berkeley Hills (here up to 1,550 ft.). Extensive residential sections include PIEDMONT. Adjoining towns on N are Emeryville (industrial) and Berkeley; San Leandro is S. L. Merritt, landscaped salt-water lagoon (with a waterfowl refuge), is in city's heart. Oakland airport is in SW. Has naval air station. Served by 4 rail lines, for 2 of which it is W transcontinental terminus, has port facilities (Oakland Army Base) of San Francisco Port of Embarkation. Industries include large canneries, automobile assembly and truck plants, lumber mills, oil refineries, shipyards, drydocks; and plants producing glass, cereals and feeds, beer, wine, chemicals, building materials, food products. Served (with

other cities of E bay region) by 150-mi. aqueduct from Mokelumne R. Seat of Mills Col., Col. of the Holy Names, Calif. Col. of Arts and Crafts, Chabot Observatory; has fine parks, museums, an art gall. St. Mary's Col. is 10 mi. E (near Moraga). Founded 1850; inc. as town in 1852, as city in 1854. Trans-bay ferry service (1850) and railroad's arrival (1863) stimulated growth. San Francisco earthquake (1906) brought heavy influx of residents. Posey Tube to Alameda was completed in 1928, the bridge to San Francisco in 1936; Broadway Tunnel, a link with cities across hills to E, was completed in 1937. **2** Town (pop. 548), Orange co., central Fla., 15 mi. W of Orlando, near L. Apopka; ships truck produce and citrus fruit. **3** City (pop. 980), Coles co., E Ill., near Embarrass R., 22 mi. ENE of Mattoon, in rich agr. area (corn, wheat, oats, broomcorn, livestock, poultry). Inc. 1855. **4** Town (pop. 1,296), Pottawattamie co., SW Iowa, on West Nishnabotna R. and 25 mi. E of Council Bluffs, in livestock, grain, poultry area; rendering works. Inc. 1882. **5** Town (pop. 195), Warren co., S Ky., 12 mi. ENE of Bowling Green, in agr. area. **6** Town (pop. 2,679), including Oakland village (pop. 1,605), Kennebec co., S Maine, just W of Waterville and on Messalonskee L.; tools, hardware, machinery, wood products, paper, textiles. Set off from Waterville 1873. **7** Town (pop. 1,640), ⊙ Garrett co., extreme W Md., in the Alleghenies near W.Va. line, c.40 mi. WSW of Cumberland; trade center in resort and agr. area (dairy products, truck, grain); wood products, maple sugar. Swallow Falls State Forest is just NW. Area settled 1790; town laid out 1849, inc. 1861. **8** Town (pop. 551), Yalobusha co., N central Miss., 20 mi. NNW of Grenada. **9** Town (pop. 1,041), St. Louis co., E Mo., W of St. Louis. **10** City (pop. 1,456), Burt co., E Nebr., 45 mi. NNW of Omaha and on Logan Creek, near Missouri R.; trade, shipping point for rich agr. area; livestock, dairy and poultry produce, grain, corn. Settled 1863, inc. 1881. **11** Residential borough (pop. 1,817), Bergen co., NE N.J., near Ramapo R., 8 mi. NW of Paterson; makes silk labels. **12** Town (pop. 293), Marshall co., S Okla., 20 mi. ESE of Ardmore, in farm area. **13** City (pop. 829), Douglas co., SW Oregon, 15 mi. N of Roseburg and on a tributary of Umpqua R.; livestock, lumber. **14** Village (pop. 1,909), Lawrence co., W Pa., just SW of New Castle. **15** Borough (pop. 871), Susquehanna co., NE Pa., on Susquehanna R. opposite Susquehanna Depot. **16** Village, Providence co., R.I.: see BURRILLVILLE. **17** Town (pop. 236), Fayette co., SW Tenn., 29 mi. ENE of Memphis. **18** Village (pop. 1,241, with adjacent Brownwood), Orange co., SE Texas.

Oakland Beach. **1** Section of New York city, N.Y.: see SOUTH BEACH. **2** Village, Kent co., R.I.: see WARWICK.

Oakland City, residential town (pop. 3,539), Gibson co., SW Ind., 28 mi. NNE of Evansville; bituminous-coal mines; grain farms. Seat of Oakland City Col.

Oakland Park, city (pop. 1,295), Broward co., S Fla., on Atlantic coast, just N of Fort Lauderdale; vegetable packing.

Oaklawn. or **Oak Lawn,** residential village (pop. 8,751), Cook co., NE Ill., suburb just SW of Chicago; nurseries; truck farms. Inc. 1909. **2** Village (pop. 1,567, with adjacent Beechwood), Ottawa co., W Mich.

Oakleigh (ōk'lē), municipality (pop. 15,979), S Victoria, Australia, 9 mi. SE of Melbourne, in metropolitan area; commercial center for agr. region.

Oakley, village in Carnock parish, SW Fifeshire, Scotland, 4 mi. W of Dunfermline; coal mining.

Oakley. **1** Village (pop. c.2,000), Contra Costa co., W Calif., near San Joaquin R., 6 mi. E of Antioch; fruit, vegetable packing. **2** Village (pop. 684), Cassia co., S Idaho, on small affluent of Goose Creek and 20 mi. SSW of Burley, in agr. area (potatoes, sugar beets, wheat); alt. 4,191 ft.; flour milling. Oakley Dam (145 ft. high, 1,025 ft. long) is on Goose Creek 4 mi. SSW; forms Goose Creek Reservoir (6 mi. long, .5 mi. wide), used for irrigation. **3** City (pop. 1,915), Logan co., NW Kansas, 21 mi. SSE of Colby; rail junction, trading point in grain, livestock region; dairying. Inc. 1887. **4** Village (pop. 333), Saginaw co., E central Mich., 22 mi. SW of Saginaw, near Shiawassee R. **5** Town (pop. 58), Pitt co., E N.C., 11 mi. NNE of Greenville. **6** Town (pop. 264), Summit co., N Utah, 15 mi. SSE of Coalville and on Weber R.; alt. 6,517 ft.; flour mills, sawmills, creamery.

Oaklyn, residential borough (pop. 4,889), Camden co., SW N.J., 4 mi. SE of Camden. Settled 1682 by Friends, laid out c.1890, inc. 1905.

Oakman. **1** Town (pop. 1,022), Walker co., NW central Ala., 10 mi. SW of Jasper. **2** Town (pop. 127), Gordon co., NW Ga., 15 mi. ENE of Calhoun.

Oakmont. **1** Residential borough (pop. 7,264), Allegheny co., SW Pa., NE suburb of Pittsburgh, on Allegheny R.; metal products, paper, boilers, paints, railroad supplies; agr. National tournaments have been held at golf links here. Inc. 1889. **2** Village, Montgomery co., Pa.: see HAVERFORD.

Oakmulgee Creek (ōkmŭl'gē), central Ala., rises in SE Bibb co., flows c.40 mi. S to Cahaba R. 9 mi. NW of Selma.

Oak Orchard Creek, W N.Y., rises in N central Genesee co., flows c.60 mi. N, W, again N, and NE, crossing the Barge Canal at Medina, to L. Ontario 9 mi. N of Albion.

Oak Park. **1** Town (pop. 308), Emanuel co., E central Ga., 16 mi. S of Swainsboro. **2** Residential village (pop. 63,529), Cook co., NE Ill., W suburb of Chicago; one of largest U.S. communities with village form of govt. Mfg.: candy and food products, tools and dies, transformers, veneer-making machinery. Has a number of churches and denominational schools and fine bldgs., many of them designed by Frank Lloyd Wright, who lived here. Ernest Hemingway b. here. Settled 1833, inc. 1901. **3** Village (pop. 1,364, with adjacent Level Park), Calhoun co., S Mich., 7 mi. NW of Battlecreek. **4** City (pop. 5,267), Oakland co., SE Mich., residential suburb just N of Detroit. Inc. as village 1927, as city 1945.

Oak Point, village (pop. estimate 150), S Man., on L. Manitoba, 55 mi. NW of Winnipeg; fishing.

Oak Point, resort village, St. Lawrence co., N N.Y., on the St. Lawrence and 18 mi. SW of Ogdensburg.

Oak Ridge, village (pop. 396), on S coast of Roatán Isl., Bay Islands dept., N Honduras, 16 mi. ENE of Roatán; shipbuilding; exports coconuts.

Oak Ridge. **1** Town (pop. 474), St. Clair co., central Ala., near Pell City. **2** Village (pop. 287), Morehouse parish, NE La., 14 mi. SSE of Bastrop; agr.; cotton gins. **3** Town (pop. 202), Cape Girardeau co., SE Mo., bet. Mississippi and Whitewater rivers, 9 mi. NNW of Jackson. **4** Area (59,000 acres; pop. 30,299), on Anderson-Roane co. line, E Tenn., on Clinch R. and 17 mi. WNW of Knoxville, on an E ridge of the Cumberlands. Here are a nuclear research center (Oak Ridge Natl. Laboratory; until 1948 called Clinton Natl. Laboratory) and plants, controlled by Atomic Energy Commission, which produce radioactive isotopes (for medical and industrial uses) and U-235, which may be used in atomic bombs. In 1942, this site was chosen for work of "Manhattan District," which developed materials of the atomic bomb; existence and purpose of community (then called Clinton Engineer Works) were kept secret until July, 1945. Control of project passed (Dec., 1946) from U.S. Corps of Engineers to Atomic Energy Commission. In 1948, Oak Ridge Inst. of Nuclear Studies was organized by 14 member universities.

Oakridge, town (pop. 1,562), Lane co., W Oregon, 38 mi. SE of Eugene and on Middle Fork of Willamette R. Inc. 1934.

Oak River, village (pop. estimate 200), SW Man., on Oak R. and 30 mi. NW of Brandon; grain, stock.

Oaktown, town (pop. 763), Knox co., SW Ind., 14 mi. NNE of Vincennes; shipping center for rich fruit and general farming area; oil and natural-gas wells; fruit-packing plant.

Oak Vale or **Oakvale,** village (pop. 136), on Jefferson Davis-Lawrence co. line, S central Miss., 15 mi. NNW of Columbia.

Oakvale, town (pop. 239), Mercer co., S W.Va., 8 mi. ESE of Princeton, in coal-mining area.

Oak View or **Oakview,** village (pop. 1,648), Ventura co., S Calif., 20 mi. E of Santa Barbara.

Oakville. **1** Village (pop. estimate 200), S Man., 14 mi. ESE of Portage la Prairie; grain, stock; dairying. **2** Town (pop. 4,115), S Ont., on L. Ontario, 20 mi. SW of Toronto; port; boat bldg., woodworking, mfg. of automobiles, aluminum products, paint.

Oakville. **1** Village (pop. c.225), Napa co., W Calif., wine-making center in Napa R. valley, 6 mi. SE of St. Helena. U.S. Dept. of Agr. experimental vineyard here. **2** Village, Litchfield co., Conn.: see WATERTOWN. **3** Town (pop. 360), Louisa co., SE Iowa, on Iowa R. and 22 mi. S of Muscatine. **4** Town (pop. 372), Grays Harbor co., W Wash., 20 mi. SW of Olympia and on Chehalis R.; fruit, dairy products, lumber, poultry.

Oakwood. **1** Village, Madison co., Ala.: see HUNTSVILLE. **2** Town (pop. 225), Hall co., NE Ga., 5 mi. SW of Gainesville. **3** Village (pop. 641), Vermilion co., E Ill., 7 mi. W of Danville, in agr. and bituminous-coal area. Kickapoo State Park is near by. **4** City (pop. 9,691), Montgomery co., W Ohio, just S of Dayton. Inc. as village in 1907; became city after 1930. **5** Village (pop. 542), Paulding co., NW Ohio, on Auglaize R. and 13 mi. S of Defiance, in agr. area. **6** Town (pop. 161), Dewey co., W Okla., 17 mi. WNW of Watonga, in agr. area (cotton, grain, livestock). **7** Village (pop. 2,267), Lawrence co., W Pa. **8** Town (pop. 759), Leon co., E central Texas, 17 mi. SW of Palestine, near Trinity R.; lumbering center.

Oakworth, former urban district (1931 pop. 3,983), West Riding, W Yorkshire, England, 9 mi. NNW of Halifax; woolen milling. Inc. 1938 in Keighley.

Oamaru (ŏmŭrōō'), borough (pop. 7,481), ⊙ Waitaki co. (□ 2,392; pop. 9,047), E S.Isl., New Zealand, 60 mi. NNE of Dunedin; grain, wool, sheep, Oamaru stone (limestone). Small harbor (formed by concrete breakwater) is used to ship limestone. Oamaru is in, but independent of, Waitaki co.

Oami (ōä'mē), town (pop. 4,414), Chiba prefecture, central Honshu, Japan, on N central Chiba Peninsula, 3 mi. SW of Togane; rice, poultry, raw silk. Agr. school.

Oas (ōäs'), town (1939 pop. 5,294; 1948 municipality pop. 27,824), Albany prov., SE Luzon, Philippines, on railroad and 8 mi. WNW of Legaspi; abacá-growing center.

Oasa (ōä'sä), town (pop. 4,588), Hiroshima prefecture, SW Honshu, Japan, 26 mi. N of Hiroshima; raw silk, lumber, livestock.

Oasis Sahariennes, Algeria: see SAHARAN OASES.

Oates Coast, part of Antarctica, W of Victoria Land, bet. 157° and 164°E. Discovered 1912 by R. F. Scott, Br. explorer.

Oathlaw, agr. village and parish (pop. 362), central Angus, Scotland, on South Esk R. and 4 mi. N of Forfar.

Oatlands, England: see WALTON AND WEYBRIDGE.

Oatlands, town (pop. 679), E central Tasmania, 40 mi. N of Hobart; coal-mining center; also has flax mill.

Oatman, village (1940 pop. 737), Mohave co., W Ariz., 20 mi. SW of Kingman; gold-mining town in foothills of Black Mts.

Oaxaca or **Oaxaca de Juárez** (wŭhä'kŭ, Sp. wähä'kä dä hwä'rĕs), state (□ 36,375; 1940 pop. 1,196,381; 1950 pop. 1,444,929), S Mexico; ⊙ Oaxaca. On the Pacific coast and its inlet the Gulf of Tehuantepec, bounded by Guerrero (W), Puebla (NW), Veracruz (N), Chiapas (E). Traversed by Inter-American Highway. Apart from the narrow coastal strip along the Pacific, the S part of the Isthmus of Tehuantepec, and the lowlands near Veracruz border, it is an extremely mountainous region of the Sierra Madre del Sur, with high ridges (Sierra de las Mixtecas, Cerro Zempoaltépetl), plateaus (Mixtecapán), and deep, fertile valleys. The rugged, long coast line has many lagoons, including Laguna Inferior, Laguna Superior, and Mar Muerto at head of Gulf of Tehuantepec. Oaxaca is drained by Atoyac, Tehuantepec, and Tuxtepec rivers. Climate varies: cool in high sierras, subtropical-humid in upland valleys, tropical along coast and on Isthmus of Tehuantepec. Its abundant mineral resources, not extensively exploited, include silver, gold, copper, and lead, mined at Ixtlán, Ocotlán, Progreso, Tlacolula, Teojomulco; antimony at San Juan Mixtepec, deposits of coal near Tlaxiaco and Huajuápan, petroleum near Pochutla, marble near TEHUANTEPEC, onyx near Etla. The state is particularly rich in medicinal plants, rubber, resins, fine cabinet- and dyewoods. It is, however, predominantly agr.; produces corn, wheat, rice, alfalfa, coffee, indigo, tobacco, cotton, vanilla, cacao, sugar cane, fruit. Valle Nacional is famed for its coffee and tobacco; pineapples at Loma Bonita. Considerable stock raising (cattle, hogs). Rural industries: mining, lumbering, flour milling, mescal distilling, cochineal extracting, native handicrafts (pottery, serapes), textile processing, and silverware mfg. concentrated at Oaxaca, Tehuantepec, Juchitán, Tlaxiaco, and Huajuápan. Salina Cruz on Gulf of Tehuantepec is its main port. The most thoroughly Indian of the Mex. states, with a pop. predominantly Mixtec and Zapotec, Oaxaca has famous archaeological ruins at MITLA and MONTE ALBÁN. Conquered 1522 by the Spanish. It became a state of the Mexican Federation in 1824, and its constitution was promulgated in 1851. Benito Juárez was b. in a village near Oaxaca city.

Oaxaca or **Oaxaca de Juárez,** city (pop. 29,306), ⊙ Oaxaca, S Mexico, in Atoyac R. valley, surrounded by the Sierra Madre del Sur, 230 mi. SE of Mexico city (linked by rail and by Inter-American Highway); alt. 5,034 ft.; 17°3'N 96°43'W. The chief city of S Mexico, it is a trade, stock-raising, mfg., coffee-growing, and mining center; lumbering, flour milling, vegetable-oil extracting, tanning, cotton ginning, silversmithing; ceramics, pottery, porcelain, footwear, textile goods (famed for serapes), chocolate, gold and silver filigree. Airfield. It is a charming old city with fine colonial architecture. Has convents and churches of Santo Domingo and Soleda; civic bldgs. ornamented with carved stonework and lofty balconies; univ.; mus. Alleged to have been founded 1486 by Aztecs as the military outpost Huasyacac. Upon Sp. conquest renamed Antequera (1524), but Indian name was later restored. The city was severely damaged (1727 and 1787) by earthquakes; and was repeatedly captured in Mexico's many wars and revolutions. It is the birthplace of the dictator Porfirio Díaz. Benito Juárez b. in village near by. Monte Albán, site of fine Zapotec ruins, is 3 mi. SW.

Ob or **Ob'** (ōb, Rus. ôp), town (1948 pop. over 2,000), E Novosibirsk oblast, Russian SFSR, on Trans-Siberian RR and 5 mi. W of Novosibirsk.

Ob or **Ob',** river, Russian SFSR: see OB RIVER.

Oba (ō'bŭ), village (pop. estimate 100), central Ont., on Oba L. (12 mi. long, 2 mi. wide), 100 mi. SW of Kapuskasing; gold mining.

Obabika Lake (ōbŭbē'kŭ) (15 mi. long, 2 mi. wide), SE central Ont., 50 mi. NE of Sudbury, in gold-mining region. Drains E into L. Timagami.

Obah, Afghanistan: see OBEH.

Obal, Yemen: see UBAL.

Obalski Lake (ōbäl'skē) (7 mi. long, 2 mi. wide), W Que., on Harricanaw R., 11 mi. NE of Amos. On shore are gold and copper deposits; airfield.

Obama (ōbä'mä). **1** Town (pop. 16,446), Fukui prefecture, central Honshu, Japan, port on Wakasa Bay, 35 mi. N of Kyoto; mfg. center (lacquer ware, silk textiles, noodles); fishing. Exports straw products. **2** Town (pop. 7,587), Fukushima prefecture, N central Honshu, Japan, 14 mi. S of Fukushima; raw silk. **3** Town (pop. 14,104), Nagasaki prefecture, W Kyushu, Japan, on W coast of Shimabara Peninsula, 19 mi. E of Nagasaki, across Tachibana Bay; health resort (hot springs) in agr. area.

Oban (ō'băn), township (pop. 228) and port, NE STEWART ISLAND, New Zealand, 22 mi. SSW of Bluff, S.Isl., across Foveaux Strait, and on N shore of Paterson Inlet (8 mi. E–W, 5 mi. N–S); ⊙ Stewart Isl. co. Fisheries. Until early 1940s, called Half-moon Bay.

Oban (ô'bän), town, Calabar prov., Eastern Provinces, SE Nigeria, 30 mi. NE of Calabar; agr. trade center; hardwood, rubber, palm oil and kernels, cacao, kola nuts. Oban Hills are N.

Oban (ō'bŭn), burgh (1931 pop. 5,759; 1951 census 6,227), W Argyll, Scotland, on the Firth of Lorne, in Lorne dist., 60 mi. NW of Glasgow; 56°22'N 5°22'W; tourist resort and port for Mull and other isls. of the Hebrides. Scene of annual (Sept.) Argyllshire Highland Gathering. Port entrance is sheltered by Kerrera isl. Oban has R.C. and Protestant cathedrals, and ruins of 12th- or 13th-cent. Dunolly Castle, former stronghold of lords of Lorne. In castle ground is rock called Dog Stone; according to legend Fingal here fastened his dog Bran. Town became important with rise of tourist trade in 19th cent. There are whisky distilleries. Oban figures in Scott's *Lord of the Isles*.

Obanazawa (ōbänä'zäwù), town (pop. 8,983), Yamagata prefecture, N Honshu, Japan, 13 mi. SSE of Shinjo; horse trading.

Obando (ōbän'dō), town (1939 pop. 1,041; 1948 municipality pop. 11,957), Bulacan prov., S central Luzon, Philippines, 7 mi. NNW of Manila, near Manila Bay; rice growing.

Oban Hills (ô'bän), in SE Nigeria, N of Oban; 30 mi. long (N–S); rise to c.3,500 ft. Calabar R. rises on W slopes.

Obara (ōbä'rä), town (pop. 682), Kanagawa prefecture, central Honshu, Japan, 8 mi. WSW of Hachioji; mineral springs.

Obata (ōbä'tä). **1** Town (pop. 6,211), Gumma prefecture, central Honshu, Japan, just SE of Tomioka; rice, wheat, raw silk. **2** or **Kobata** (kōbä'tä), town (pop. 8,841), Mie prefecture, S Honshu, Japan, just NW of Uji-yamada; agr. (rice, wheat, bamboo shoots), livestock; fishing; mfg. of cotton textiles. Sericulture school.

Ob Bay or **Ob Gulf** (ōb) Rus. *Obskaya Guba*, shallow estuary of Ob River, NW Siberian Russian SFSR; forms inlet of Kara Sea, bet. Yamal and Gyda peninsulas; 500 mi. long, 35–50 mi. wide; fresh water, low shores. W bend called Nadym Bay. Receives Ob, Nadym, and Nyda rivers (S). Has E arm called TAZ BAY. Abounds in fish. Chief port, Novy Port.

Obbe, Scotland: see HARRIS.

Obbia (ŏb'byä), town (pop. 3,000), in the Mudugh, central Ital. Somaliland, port on Indian Ocean, 360 mi. NE of Mogadishu; 5°21'N 48°32'E; road junction; fishing, weaving (mats, baskets). Has old native fort.

Obbola (ôbōō'lä), village (pop. 1,290), Vasterbotten co., N Sweden, on Obbola isl. (□ 8.5) in Gulf of Bothnia, at mouth of Ume R., 9 mi. SSE of Umea; pulp and cellulose mills.

Obbrovazzo, Yugoslavia: see OBROVAC.

Obdorsk, Russian SFSR: see SALEKHARD.

Obecse, Yugoslavia: see BECEJ.

Obedovo, Russian SFSR: see OKTYABRSKI, Ivanovo oblast.

Obeh or **Obah** (ō'bù), town (pop. over 500), Herat prov., NW Afghanistan, 55 mi. E of Herat, and on the Hari Rud at E end of its irrigated valley; stock-raising center; felt and coarse woolen goods. Old walled town.

Obeid, El (ĕl ōbād'), city (pop. 70,100), ⊙ Kordofan prov., central Anglo-Egyptian Sudan, 230 mi. SW of Khartoum; 13°10'N 30°14'E. Communications and commercial center; rail terminus tapping oilseed and gum-arabic region of W Sudan; airport. Junction of roads and caravan routes. Hq. of Sudan camel corps. Here, in 1883, the Mahdi defeated Hicks Pasha's Egyptian forces. Railroad from Khartoum completed 1912.

Obeid, Tell el, excavation site near the lower Euphrates, in Muntafiq prov., SE Iraq, c.15 mi. WSW of Nasiriya, c.4 mi. WNW of site of anc. Ur. Finds of Sumerian kings have been made.

Obejo (ōvā'hō), town (pop. 1,324), Córdoba prov., S Spain, 17 mi. N of Córdoba; olive-oil processing; cereals, peas, livestock.

Obelya (ôbĕ'lyä), village (pop. 5,470), Sofia dist., W Bulgaria, just N of Sofia; poultry raising, dairying, truck.

Oberá (ōvärä'), town (1947 census pop. 4,686), S Misiones natl. territory, Argentina, 50 mi. E of Posadas; lumbering and farming center (maté, tobacco, hardwood); corn and rice milling, maté processing; sawmills. Formerly Yerbal Viejo.

Oberaar Glacier, Switzerland: see AAR RIVER.

Oberaarhorn (ō"bùrär'hôrn), peak (11,949 ft.) in Bernese Alps, S central Switzerland, 13 mi. S of Meiringen.

Oberachern (–ä'khùrn), village (pop. 2,474), S Baden, Germany, at W foot of Black Forest, 5.5 mi. SSW of Bühl; mfg. of chemicals, textiles, paper; lumber milling, woodworking.

Oberägeri (–ā'gùrē), town (pop. 2,255), Zug canton, N central Switzerland, on the Aegerisee, 5 mi. SE of Zug.

Oberalp Pass (ō'bùrälp") (6,716 ft.), in the Alps, S central Switzerland, on border of Grisons and Uri cantons; forms divide bet. headwaters of Vorderrhein and Reuss rivers; crossed by road and railway which join Disentis and Andermatt.

Oberalpstock (–shtôk), mountain (10,925 ft.) in Glarus Alps, S central Switzerland, 5 mi. NW of Disentis.

Oberammergau (ō"bùrä'mùrgou"), village (pop. 5,101), Upper Bavaria, Germany, in Bavarian Alps, on the Ammer and 7.5 mi. NNW of Garmisch-Partenkirchen; rail terminus; lumber milling, wood carving. Summer resort and winter-sports center (alt. 2,739 ft.). Has rococo church. Noted for Passion play performed here by peasants every decade in fulfillment of vow made during plague of 1633; it attracts many foreign tourists.

Oberaudorf (–ou'dôrf), village (pop. 2,565), Upper Bavaria, Germany, on E slope of the Bavarian Alps, near the Inn, 4 mi. N of Kufstein, near Austrian border; textiles; summer and winter resort (alt. 1,585 ft.).

Oberbayern, Germany: see UPPER BAVARIA.

Oberbipp, Switzerland: see NIEDERBIPP.

Oberbruch (ō'bùrbrōōkh"), village (pop. 3,748), in former Prussian Rhine Prov., W Germany, after 1945 in North Rhine-Westphalia, on the Rur and 7 mi. W of Erkelenz; mfg. of synthetic fiber.

Oberburg (–bōōrk"), town (pop. 2,923), Bern canton, NW central Switzerland, 1 mi. S of Burgdorf; linen textiles, tiles; metal- and woodworking.

Oberburg, Yugoslavia: see GORNJI GRAD.

Obercorn, Ger. *Oberkorn* (both: ō'bùrkôrn'), town (pop. 3,485), SW Luxembourg, 4 mi. W of Esch-sur-Alzette; iron-mining center.

Oberdan (ôbĕrdän'), village (pop. 1,600), W Cyrenaica, Libya, 17 mi. NE of Barce, on a plateau; agr. settlement (cereals, olives, grapes) founded 1938–39 by the Italians.

Oberdollendorf (ō'bùrdô'lùndôrf), village (pop. 3,202), in former Prussian Rhine Prov., W Germany, after 1945 in North Rhine-Westphalia, near right bank of the Rhine, 5 mi. SE of Bonn; wine.

Oberdorf, Russian SFSR: see REMENNIKOVO.

Oberdorla (ō"bùrdôr'lä), town (pop. 3,348), in former Prussian Saxony prov., central Germany, after 1945 in Thuringia, 4 mi. SSW of Mühlhausen; woolen and cotton milling.

Oberegg (ō'bùrĕk"), town (pop. 2,233), Appenzell Inner Rhoden half-canton, NE Switzerland, 8 mi. E of St. Gall; embroideries, silk textiles.

Oberehnheim, France: see OBERNAI.

Obereisenheim (ō"bùrī'zùnhīm), village (pop. 581), Lower Franconia, NW Bavaria, Germany, on the Main (canalized) and 13 mi. NE of Würzburg; rye, barley, hogs.

Oberentfelden (–ĕnt'fĕldùn), town (pop. 2,381), Aargau canton, N Switzerland, on Suhr R. and 3 mi. S of Aarau; shoes, rubber products; woodworking. With Unterentfelden (N), it is known as Entfelden.

Oberfeulen, Luxembourg: see FEULEN.

Oberfranken, Germany: see UPPER FRANCONIA.

Oberfrohna (–frō'nä), town (pop. 11,101), Saxony, E central Germany, 8 mi. W of Chemnitz; hosiery knitting, chemical mfg.

Oberg (ō'bĕrk), village (pop. 2,744), in former Prussian prov. of Hanover, NW Germany, after 1945 in Lower Saxony, 4 mi. SSE of Peine; oil wells.

Obergabelhorn (ō'bùrgä'bùlhôrn), peak (13,340 ft.) in Pennine Alps, S Switzerland, 4 mi. WNW of Zermatt, NW of the Matterhorn. The Untergabelhorn (11,138 ft.) is SE.

Oberglogau, Poland: see GLOGOWEK.

Obergrafendorf (–grä'fùndôrf), town (pop. 3,574), central Lower Austria, 5 mi. SW of Sankt Pölten; rail junction.

Obergrombach (–grôm'bäkh), town (pop. 1,593), N Baden, Germany, after 1945 in Württemberg-Baden, 3.5 mi. SSW of Bruchsal; fruit, hops.

Obergünzburg (–günts'bōōrk), village (pop. 2,884), Swabia, SW Bavaria, Germany, 10 mi. NE of Kempten; textile mfg., dairying. Summer resort (alt. 2,417 ft.). Chartered 1407.

Obergurgl (ō'bùrgōōrgùl), village, Tyrol, W Austria, in Ötztal Alps, on the Ötztaler Ache and 31 mi. SW of Innsbruck; highest village (6,320 ft.) in Austria; winter-sports center.

Oberhaag (ō'bùrhäg), village (pop. 2,825), Styria, SE Austria, 17 mi. WNW of Maribor, Yugoslavia; rye, potatoes, poultry; vineyards.

Oberhalbstein (–hälp'shtīn), Romansh *Sursès* (sōōrsās'), valley and circle (pop. 2,412), Grisons canton, E Switzerland, S of Tiefencastel. Road leads to Julier Pass.

Oberharmersbach (–här'mùrsbäkh"), village (pop. 2,003), S Baden, Germany, in Black Forest, 10 mi. SE of Offenburg; rail terminus; lumber milling. Summer resort.

Oberhasle (–häs"lē), district (pop. 7,466), Bern canton, S central Switzerland, comprising upper Aar R. valley and surrounded by peaks of Bernese Alps. Largest town, Meiringen. In the valley Hasletal, here, is **Oberhasli** hydroelectric works, supplied by water from near-by Grimsel L. and small Gelmersee; power stations at Handegg and Innertkirchen.

Oberhauenstein, peak, Switzerland: see HAUENSTEIN.

Oberhausen (–hou"zùn). **1** Village (1946 pop. 4,804), N Baden, Germany, after 1945 in Württemberg-Baden, on an arm of the Rhine and 4.5 mi. SE of Speyer; potteries. Asparagus, strawberries, tobacco. **2** City (□ 30; 1939 pop. 191,842; 1946 pop. 174,117; 1950 pop. 202,343), in former Prussian Rhine Prov., W Germany, after 1945 in North Rhine-Westphalia, in the Ruhr, port on Rhine-Herne Canal, adjoining Duisburg (SW), Mülheim (S), and Essen (E); 51°28'N 6°50'E. Rail hub; coal-mining and industrial center; foundries, zinc refineries; mfg. of steam boilers, cables, chemicals (fertilizer, detergents, varnish), furniture, glass, cigars. Cement works, breweries. Founded 1862; chartered 1874. In 1929 it inc. neighboring (N) towns of OSTERFELD and STERKRADE.

Oberhessen, Germany: see UPPER HESSE.

Oberhof (ō"bùrhōf'), village (pop. 1,263), Thuringia, central Germany, in Thuringian Forest, 17 mi. S of Gotha; popular health, winter-sports resort.

Oberhofen am Thunersee (ō'bùrhōfùn äm tōō'nùrzā"), village (pop. 1,300), Bern canton, central Switzerland, on L. of Thun and 2 mi. SSE of Thun; resort. Old castle.

Oberhomburg, France: see HOMBOURG-HAUT.

Ober-Ingelheim, Germany: see INGELHEIM.

Oberkassel (–kä'sùl). **1** Village (pop. 4,617), in former Prussian Rhine Prov., W Germany, after 1945 in North Rhine-Westphalia, on right bank of the Rhine and 3 mi. SE of Bonn; cement works. Has 12th–13th-cent. church, 18th-cent. château. Poet Kinkel b. here. **2** Suburb, Rhine Prov., Germany: see DÜSSELDORF.

Oberkaufungen (–kou'fōōng-ùn), village (pop. 4,509), in former Prussian prov. of Hesse-Nassau, W Germany, after 1945 in Hesse, 6 mi. ESE of Kassel; lumber.

Oberkirch (–kĭrkh"), town (pop. 5,690), S Baden, Germany, at W foot of Black Forest, 7 mi. NE of Offenburg; noted for its wine. Mfg. of water turbines, sawing machines, costume jewelry, cigarettes; woodworking, paper milling, printing. Summer resort.

Oberkorn, Luxembourg: see OBERCORN.

Oberkotzau (–kō'tsou), village (pop. 4,898), Upper Franconia, NE Bavaria, Germany, on the Saxonian Saale, at mouth of small Schwesnitz R., and 4 mi. S of Hof; rail junction; textile mfg., glass- and metal-working, brewing.

Oberkreuzberg (–kroits'bĕrk), village (commune pop. 1,928), Lower Bavaria, Germany, in Bohemian Forest, 10 mi. SE of Zwiesel; cellulose mfg. at Louisenfels (pop. 61), 1.5 mi. NNE.

Oberlaa (–lä"), town (pop. 3,299), after 1938 in Schwechat dist. of Vienna, Austria, 5 mi. S of city center.

Oberlahn, Germany: see WEILBURG.

Oberlahnstein (ō'bùrlän'shtīn), town (pop. 8,992), in former Prussian prov. of Hesse-Nassau, W Germany, after 1945 in Rhineland-Palatinate, port on right bank of the Rhine (landing), at mouth of Lahn R., and 4 mi. S of Coblenz; machinery mfg., paper milling. Has 14th-cent. castle, a former residence of electors of Mainz.

Oberlaibach, Yugoslavia: see VRHNIKA.

Oberland, Bernese, Switzerland: see BERNESE ALPS.

Oberlandischer Kanal, Poland: see WARMIA CANAL.

Oberlausitz, region, Germany: see LUSATIA.

Oberleutensdorf, Czechoslovakia: see LITVINOV.

Oberlin (ō'bùrlĭn). **1** City (pop. 2,019), ⊙ Decatur co., NW Kansas, on Sappa Creek and 32 mi. W of Norton; trading point in grain, poultry, and livestock area; dairying. State park near by. Laid out 1878, inc. 1885. **2** Village (pop. 1,544), ⊙ Allen parish, SW central La., 38 mi. NE of Lake Charles city; agr. (rice, cotton, corn, citrus fruit); timber; cotton gin, sawmill. **3** Village (pop. 7,062), Lorain co., N Ohio, 7 mi. SW of Elyria, in truck, dairy, and poultry area. Seat of Oberlin Col.

Oberlind (ō'bùrlĭnt"), town (pop. 4,529), Thuringia, central Germany, in Thuringian Forest, 2 mi. S of Sonneberg; toy and china mfg., wood carving.

Oberlössnitz, Germany: see RADEBEUL.

Oberlungwitz (–lōōng'vĭts), town (pop. 10,335), Saxony, E central Germany, 9 mi. WSW of Chemnitz; coal mining; textile milling, hosiery knitting, machinery mfg.

Obermarsberg (–märs'bĕrk), town (pop. 1,710), in former Prussian prov. of Westphalia, W Germany, after 1945 in North Rhine-Westphalia, just S of Niedermarsberg. Has 13th-cent. church.

Obermatt, Switzerland: see ENGELBERG.

Obermoschel (–mô'shùl), town (pop. 1,406), Rhenish Palatinate, W Germany, 9 mi. SW of Bad Kreuznach; mercury mining. Vineyards; fruit, cattle. Ruined castle. Limestone quarries in area.

Obernai (ōbĕrnĕ'), Ger. *Oberehnheim* (ō"bùrān'hīm), town (pop. 3,924), Bas-Rhin dept., E France, at E foot of the Vosges, 15 mi. SW of Strasbourg; winegrowing and distilling; cotton spinning, sauerkraut mfg. Has picturesque market square with 16th-cent. town hall, historical mus., and many old houses. St. Odile b. here in 7th cent. Seat of early dukes of Alsace.

Obernau (ō'bůrnou), village (pop. 2,332), Lower Franconia, NW Bavaria, Germany, on the Main (canalized) and 4 mi. S of Aschaffenburg; hydroelectric station; textiles, precision instruments.

Obernbreit (ō'bůrnbrīt), village (pop. 1,495), Lower Franconia, W Bavaria, Germany, 6 mi. S of Kitzingen; brewing, lumber and flour milling. Has 16th-cent. town hall.

Obernburg (–bŏŏrk), town (pop. 3,317), Lower Franconia, NW Bavaria, Germany, on the Main (canalized) and 9 mi. S of Aschaffenburg; mfg. of synthetic fiber, cider, sparkling wine, fruit preserves; printing. Built on site of Roman camp; chartered 1317. Has Romanesque church; portions of medieval wall still surround town.

Oberndorf (–dôrf), town (pop. 3,015), Salzburg, W Austria, 11 mi. NNW of Salzburg; processes magnesite.

Oberndorf or **Oberndorf am Neckar** (äm nĕ'kär), town (pop. 7,845), S Württemberg, Germany, after 1945 in Württemberg-Hohenzollern, at W foot of Black Forest, on the Neckar and 9 mi. NNW of Rottweil; mfg. (office equipment, machinery). Site (until 1945) of well-known arms factory. Damaged in Second World War.

Oberneukirchen (ō"bůrnoi'kĭrkhůn), town (pop. 2,726), N Upper Austria, 11 mi. NNW of Linz, N of the Danube; rye, potatoes.

Obernick, Poland: see OBORNIKI.

Obernigk, Poland: see OBORNIKI SLASKIE.

Obernkirchen (ō'bůrnkĭr"khůn), town (pop. 6,419), in former Prussian prov. of Hanover, W Germany, after 1945 in Lower Saxony, 9 mi. E of Minden; coal mining. Has 14th-cent. church. Belonged to former Prussian prov. of Hesse-Nassau until 1932.

Obernzell (ō'bůrntsĕl"), village (pop. 2,392), Lower Bavaria, Germany, on the Danube and 8 mi. E of Passau; mfg. of melting pots, tanning, woodworking. Graphite mining in area. Chartered c.1300. Has been metalworking center since 16th cent. Formerly called Hafnerzell (häf'nůrtsĕl").

Obernzenn (–tsĕn"), village (pop. 1,134), Middle Franconia, W Bavaria, Germany, on small Zenn R. and 5 mi. SE of Windsheim; oats, wheat, hops.

Oberoderwitz (ō'bůrō'důrvĭts), village (pop. 4,290) Saxony, E central Germany, in Upper Lusatia, 7 mi. NW of Zittau, near Czechoslovak border; linen and cotton milling. Just SE is Niederoderwitz.

Oberon, village (pop. 834), E central New South Wales, Australia, 80 mi. WNW of Sydney; rail terminus; gold mines, granite quarries. Jenolan (jŭnō'lŭn) limestone caves 12 mi. SE in Blue Mts.

Oberon (ō'bůrŏn", ō'brŭn), city (pop. 238), Benson co., N central N.Dak., 20 mi. SW of Devils Lake.

Oberösterreich: see UPPER AUSTRIA.

Oberpahlen, Estonia: see POLTSAMAA.

Oberpfalz, Germany: see UPPER PALATINATE.

Oberpfälzer Wald, Germany: see BOHEMIAN FOREST.

Oberplan, Czechoslovakia: see HORNI PLANA.

Oberpleis (ō'bůrplīs"), village (pop. 5,813), in former Prussian Rhine Prov., W Germany, after 1945 in North Rhine-Westphalia, 8 mi. ESE of Bonn; orchards.

Oberpullendorf (ō"bůrpŏŏ'lŭndôrf), village (pop. 1,286), Burgenland, E Austria, 14 mi. SSW of Sopron, Hungary; sugar beets. Large Hung. pop. in vicinity.

Oberradkersburg, Yugoslavia: GORNJA RADGONA.

Ober-Ramstadt (–räm'shtät), village (pop. 7,267), Hesse, W Germany, in former Starkenburg prov., 5 mi. SE of Darmstadt; leather- and woodworking.

Oberriet (ō'bůrēt), town (pop. 5,220), St. Gall canton, NE Switzerland, 7 mi. E of Appenzell, near the Rhine and the Austrian border; embroideries, metalworking.

Oberriexingen (–rēks'ĭng-ůn), town (pop. 1,244), N Württemberg, Germany, after 1945 in Württemberg-Baden, on the Enz and 5 mi. WSW of Bietigheim; grain, cattle.

Oberröblingen or **Oberröblingen am See** (–rû'blĭng-ůn äm zā'), village (pop. 3,706), in former Prussian Saxony prov., central Germany, after 1945 in Saxony-Anhalt, 8 mi. SE of Eisleben; lignite mining. Small near-by lake was drained in 1890s.

Ober-Roden (–rō'důn), village (pop. 4,154), S Hesse, W Germany, in former Starkenburg prov., 10 mi. NE of Darmstadt; grain.

Oberscheld (–shĕlt), village (pop. 2,168), in former Prussian prov. of Hesse-Nassau, W Germany, after 1945 in Hesse, in the Westerwald, 3 mi. E of Dillenburg; blast furnace.

Oberschlema or **Radiumbad Oberschlema** (rä'dyŏŏmbät" ō'bůr-shlā'mä), village (pop. 2,606), Saxony, E central Germany, in the Erzgebirge, 2.5 mi. NW of Aue, in uranium- and cobalt-mining region; resort with radioactive mineral springs. Paper milling, knitting, pigment mfg. Mining industry dates from 16th cent. Just NE is Niederschlema village (pop. 2,630).

Oberschlesien, province, Germany: see SILESIA.

Obersee, Austria, Germany, Switzerland: see CONSTANCE, LAKE OF.

Obersee, Switzerland: see ZURICH, LAKE OF.

Obershagen (ō'bůrs-hä"gůn), village (pop. 928), in former Prussian prov. of Hanover, NW Germany, after 1945 in Lower Saxony, 8 mi. S of Celle; oil wells.

Obersiggenthal (ō"bůrzĭ'gůntäl), town (pop. 2,340), Aargau canton, N Switzerland, near Limmat R., 2 mi. NW of Baden; resort; metal products. With Untersiggenthal (NW), it is known as Siggenthal.

Oberstdorf (ō'bůrstdôrf), village (pop. 8,197), Swabia, SW Bavaria, Germany, in Allgäu Alps, 7 mi. S of Sonthofen; rail terminus; dairying, spinning, weaving. Well-known climatic health resort (alt. 2,640 ft.). Chartered 1495.

Oberstein, Germany: see IDAR-OBERSTEIN.

Obersuhl (ō"bůrzōōl'), village (pop. 3,424), in former Prussian prov. of Hesse-Nassau, W Germany, after 1945 in Hesse, 11 mi. E of Bebra, opposite Gerstungen and 9 mi. SW of Wartha, Thuringia.

Obert (ō'bůrt), village (pop. 91), Cedar co., NE Nebr., 12 mi. ENE of Hartington, near Missouri R.

Obertaunus, Germany: see BAD HOMBURG.

Oberthulba (ō"bůrt-hŏŏl'bä), village (pop. 1,042), Lower Franconia, NW Bavaria, Germany, on small Thulba R. and 4 mi. W of Bad Kissingen; rye, peas, lentils; winegrowing; sheep.

Obertin (ŭbyĕr'tyĭn), Pol. *Obertyn* (ôbĕr'tĭn), town (1931 pop. 4,670), E Stanislav oblast, Ukrainian SSR, on left tributary of Prut R. and 13 mi. NNE of Kolomyya; flour milling, tile mfg. Scene of defeat (1531) of Walachians by Pol. hetman Jan Tarnowski.

Obertraun (ō'bůrtroun), village (pop. 763), S Upper Austria, in the Salzkammergut, near E shore of L. of Hallstatt, 11 mi. SSE of Bad Ischl; tourist center (alt. 1,640 ft.).

Obertyn, Ukrainian SSR: see OBERTIN.

Oberurbach (ō'bůrŏŏr'bäkh), village (pop. 3,030), N Württemberg, Germany, after 1945 in Württemberg-Baden, 2 mi. ENE of Schorndorf; wine.

Oberursel (–zůl), town (pop. 15,021), in former Prussian prov. of Hesse-Nassau, W Germany, after 1945 in Hesse, on S slope of the Taunus, 7 mi. NNW of Frankfurt (tramway connection); mfg. of machinery. Has Gothic church. Already mentioned at time of Carolingians. Belonged to electors of Mainz (1581–1803).

Oberuzwil (–ōōts'vēl), town (pop. 3,666), St. Gall canton, NE Switzerland, 12 mi. W of St. Gall; cotton textiles, leather, shoes. Uzwil, NE of town, has aluminum and woodworking industries. Niederuzwil is NE of Uzwil.

Obervellach (–fĕ'läkh), village (pop. 2,463), Carinthia, S Austria, on Möll R. and 21 mi. NE of Lienz; hydroelectric station; tannery; summer resort (alt. 2,250 ft.).

Oberviechtach (–fēkh'täkh), village (pop. 2,607), Upper Palatinate, E Bavaria, Germany, in Bohemian Forest, 17 mi. NE of Schwandorf; grain, cattle. Has rococo church. Chartered 1337.

Oberwampach (–väm"päkh), village (pop. 227), NW Luxembourg, in the Ardennes, 5 mi. NW of Wiltz; lead mining.

Oberwart (ō'bůrvärt), town (pop. 4,284), Burgenland, E Austria, 20 mi. WNW of Szombathely, Hungary; rail junction. Hung. pop. in vicinity engaged in agr., horse breeding.

Oberweissbach (ō'bůrvīs'bäkh), town (pop. 2,598), Thuringia, central Germany, in Thuringian Forest, 11 mi. WSW of Saalfeld; mfg. of glass, china, light bulbs; woodworking, medicinal-herb processing. Fröbel b. here.

Oberwesel (–vā'zůl), town (pop. 3,668), in former Prussian Rhine Prov., W Germany, after 1945 in Rhineland-Palatinate, on left bank of the Rhine (landing) and 10 mi. SE of Boppard; wine. Has 14th-cent. walls and towers, several Gothic churches. Modern castle Schönberg and ruins of 12th-cent. castle Schönburg tower above town.

Oberwesterwald, Germany: see WESTERBURG.

Oberwiesenthal or **Kurort Oberwiesenthal** (kŏŏr'ôrt" ō'bůrvē'zůntäl"), town (pop. 2,946), Saxony, E central Germany, in the Erzgebirge, 11 mi. S of Annaberg; frontier point on Czechoslovak border, 5 mi. NE of Jachymov, in uranium-mining region. Lace, ribbon, and glove mfg.; wood carving. Winter-sports center at foot of the Fichtelberg (funicular railway). Inc. (in 1927) Unterwiesenthal.

Oberwil (ō'bůrvēl), town (pop. 2,128), Basel-Land half-canton, N Switzerland, on Birsig R. and 4 mi. SSW of Basel; tiles, woodworking.

Oberwinter (ō'bůrvĭn'tůr), village (pop. 2,136), in former Prussian Rhine Prov., W Germany, after 1945 in Rhineland-Palatinate, on left bank of the Rhine (winter harbor) and 9 mi. SSE of Bonn. Remains of anc. castle Rolandseck are 1 mi. N.

Obetz (ō'bĕts), village (pop. 1,049), Franklin co., central Ohio, 5 mi. SSE of Columbus.

Obey River (ō'bē), N Tenn., rises in E Putnam co., flows 58 mi. NW and W to Cumberland R. at Celina; DALE HOLLOW DAM, 7 mi. above mouth, impounds 51-mi.-long Dale Hollow Reservoir.

Obi (ō'bē), town (pop. 11,558), Miyazaki prefecture, SE Kyushu, Japan, 20 mi. SSW of Miyazaki; agr. center (rice, wheat); lumber; livestock.

Óbidos (ô'bĕdŏŏsh), city (pop. 2,726), W Pará, Brazil, on height above left bank of the lower Amazon (which here narrows down to 1¼ mi.), and 65 mi. NW of Santarém; port of call of river steamer and hydroplanes; ships tobacco, cacao, coffee, sugar, lumber, oil seeds, and cattle. Chocolate mfg., fruit preserving, jute processing. Founded 1697, and fortified in colonial period, Óbidos occupies a strategic site on the Amazon just below influx of Trombetas R. Formerly also spelled Obydos.

Óbidos, town (pop. 705), Leiria dist., W central Portugal, on railroad and 3 mi. SSW of Caldas da Rainha; mfg. (chemical fertilizer, wax candles), resin processing, clay quarries. Surrounded by walls of well-preserved 14th-cent. castle. Recaptured from Moors 1148.

Obi-Dzhuk, Tadzhik SSR: see VARZOB.

Obi-Garm (ô'bē-gärm"), village (1939 pop. over 500), W Garm oblast, Tadzhik SSR, on Vakhsh R. and 40 mi. SW of Garm; wheat, cattle.

Obihiro (ōbē'hĭrō), city (1940 pop. 36,555; 1947 pop. 46,774), S central Hokkaido, Japan, on Tokachi R. and 95 mi. E of Sapporo; rail junction; commercial center for agr., horse-breeding area; beet-sugar refining, butter making.

Obi Islands or **Ombi Islands** (ō'bē, ōm'–), group (pop. 3,391), N Moluccas, Indonesia, in Ceram Sea, bet. Halmahera (N) and Ceram (S); 1°20'S 127°38'E. Comprise Obir or Obira (pop. 3,476; 52 mi. long, 28 mi. wide) and several small offshore isls. Obir is largely mountainous, rising to 4,321 ft., with narrow coastal plain. Chief village is Laiwui (līwōō'ē), on N coast. Other isls. of group are Bisa (N; 15 mi. long), Obi Latu (W; 8 mi. long), Tobalai (E; 7 mi. long). Principal products of group: resin, sago. Obi Isls. became Du. possession in 1682.

Obi-Khingou River (ô"bē-khēn-gŭōō'), central Tadzhik SSR, rises in several branches in Darvaza Range, flows c.120 mi. W, past Sangvor and Tavil-Dara, joining Surkhab R. near Komsomolabad to form VAKHSH RIVER.

Obilic or **Obilich** (both: ô'bĭlĭch), Serbo-Croatian *Obilić*, village (pop. 5,192), SW Serbia, Yugoslavia, on railroad and 5 mi. WNW of Pristina, in the Kosovo; mfg. of explosives.

Obion (ōbī'ůn), county (□ 550; pop. 29,056), NW Tenn.; ⊙ Union City. Bounded N by Ky., NW by Reelfoot L.; drained by Obion R. and its tributaries. Fertile farm region, producing chiefly cotton, livestock; some mfg. at Union City. Formed 1823.

Obion, town (pop. 1,212), Obion co., NW Tenn., on Obion R. and 14 mi. SSW of Union City; shipping point for fertile farm area (cotton, livestock); makes work shirts.

Obion Creek, SW Ky., rises in central Graves co., flows c.50 mi. NW and SW to Mississippi R. 3 mi. NE of Hickman.

Obion River, W Tenn., formed in Obion co. by confluence of canalized North Fork (c.45 mi. long), South Fork (c.55 mi. long), and Rutherford Fork (c.50 mi. long); flows c.50 mi. SW past Obion, to Mississippi R. 13 mi. NW of Ripley. Receives Forked Deer R.

Obiou, France: see DÉVOLUY.

Obir, Austria: see HOCHOBIR.

Obir, Indonesia: see OBI ISLANDS.

Obiralovka, Russian SFSR: see ZHELEZNODOROZHNY, Moscow oblast.

Obi River, Russian SFSR: see OB RIVER.

Öbisfelde, Germany: see OEBISFELDE.

Obispos (ōbē'spōs), town (pop. 318), Barinas state, W Venezuela, in llanos, 7 mi. E of Barinas; cattle.

Obispo Santiesteban, Bolivia: see MONTERO.

Obispo Trejo (ōbēs'pō trā'hō), town (pop. estimate 1,000), N Córdoba prov., Argentina, 65 mi. NE of Córdoba; flax, alfalfa, cotton, livestock; lumber.

Obitoke (ōbē'tōkā), town (pop. 3,180), Nara prefecture, S Honshu, Japan, just S of Nara; rice, wheat, raw silk.

Objat (ôb-zhä'), village (pop. 1,307), Corrèze dept., S central France, 9 mi. NW of Brive-la-Gaillarde; agr. trade (fruit, vegetable, truffles, chestnuts, hogs). Mfg. (rattan furniture, bicycles).

Oblatos, Barranca de, Mexico: see BARRANCA DE OBLATOS.

Oblivskaya (ŭblyēf'skŭĭ), village (1926 pop. 2,506) E Rostov oblast, Russian SFSR, on Chir R., on railroad and 35 mi. ENE of Morozovsk; flour mill, metalworks; wheat, sunflowers, livestock.

Oblong (ŏ'blông), village (pop. 1,639), Crawford co., SE Ill., 21 mi. NNE of Olney; mfg. (stationery, flour, feed); oil, natural-gas wells; timber. Agr. (livestock, poultry, corn, wheat, oats). Inc. 1883.

Obluchye or **Obluch'ye** (ŭblōō'chyĭ), city (1939 pop. over 10,000), NW Jewish Autonomous Oblast, Khabarovsk Territory, Russian SFSR, on Trans-Siberian RR and 85 mi. W of Birobidzhan; metalworks; food industry.

Obnova (ôbnô'vä), village (pop. 4,890), Pleven dist., N Bulgaria, 9 mi. ENE of Levski; flour milling; livestock, poultry, truck.

Obo (ōbō'), village, SE Ubangi-Shari, Fr. Equatorial Africa, near Anglo-Egyptian Sudan and Belgian Congo borders, 260 mi. ENE of Bangassou; trade center. Protestant mission.

Obock or **Obok** (ōbŏk'), town (pop. 250), Fr. Somaliland, port on N shore of Gulf of Tadjoura, 26 mi. NNE of Djibouti; fisheries. Hot springs.

Ceded 1862 to France; was ⊙ Fr. Somaliland 1884–92, until transfer to Djibouti.

Obodovka (ŭbúdôf'kŭ), village (1926 pop. 8,603), SE Vinnitsa oblast, Ukrainian SSR, 25 mi. SE of Tulchin; sugar mill. Lignite deposits.

Obok, Fr. Somaliland: see OBOCK.

Obokum (ōbō'ko͝om), town, Ogoja prov., Eastern Provinces, SE Nigeria, on Cross R. (Br. Cameroons border) and 12 mi. ESE of Ikom; hardwood, rubber; palm oil and kernels, cacao.

Obolo, Nigeria: see NSUKKA.

Obolon or **Obolon'** (ô'bŭlŭnyŭ), town (1926 pop. 3,993), central Poltava oblast, Ukrainian SSR, 28 mi. S of Lubny; wheat, flax, mint.

Obón (ōvōn'), town (pop. 1,054), Teruel prov., E Spain, 32 mi. WSW of Alcañiz; cereals, olive oil, saffron, sheep.

Obonai (ōbō'nī), village (pop. 6,051), Akita prefecture, N Honshu, Japan, near L. Tazawa, 32 mi. E of Akita; rail terminus; rice growing, horse breeding; copper mining. Hot springs.

Öbör Hangay, aimak, Mongolia: see SOUTH KHANGAI.

Öbör Hangayin, town, Mongolia: see ARBAI KHERE.

Oborniki (ôbôrnē'kē), Ger. *Obornik* (ōbŭrnĕk'), town (1946 pop. 5,266), Poznan prov., W Poland, on Warta R., at Welna R. mouth, and 17 mi. N of Poznan; rail junction; mfg. of wooden shoes; flour milling, sawmilling; cementworks. Tuberculosis sanatorium. During Second World War, called Obernick.

Oborniki Slaskie (shlō'skyĕ), Pol. *Oborniki Śląskie,* Ger. *Obernigk* (ōbŭrnĕk'), town (1939 pop. 4,383; 1946 pop. 1,463) in Lower Silesia, after 1945 in Wroclaw prov., SW Poland, 14 mi. NNW of Breslau (Wroclaw); agr. market (grain, sugar beets, potatoes, livestock). Heavily damaged in Second World War.

Oborona, Russian SFSR: see MORDOVO.

Obourg (ōbo͞or'), town (pop. 2,631), Hainaut prov., SW Belgium, on Canal du Centre and 3 mi. ENE of Mons; mfg. (artificial silk, Portland cement).

Oboyan or **Oboyan'** (ŭbŭyän'yŭ), city (1926 pop. 12,200), central Kursk oblast, Russian SFSR, on Psel R. and 35 mi. S of Kursk; rail terminus; road center; meat packing, flour milling, fruit and vegetable canning. Chartered 1672.

Obozerskaya (ŭbŭzyôr'skīŭ), village (1926 pop. 516) W Archangel oblast, Russian SFSR, on railroad and 75 mi. S of Archangel; junction of line to Onega and Belomorsk.

Obrajes (ōbrä'hĕs), SE suburb of La Paz, La Paz dept., W Bolivia, on La Paz R.; alt. 11,007 ft. Residential and climatic resort of La Paz.

Obra River (ôb'rä), W Poland, rises 3 mi. N of Kozmin, flows generally WNW past Koscian, W and N past Zbaszyn and Miedzyrzecz to Warta R. at Skierzyna; c.150 mi. long. Just below Koscian, its W course divides into 3 parallel canals; the longest (N) canal (Obra Canal, Pol. *Kanał Obry*), extends E to Warta R. near Mosina; canals drain Obra Marshes, Pol. *Łegi Oberskie.*

Obraztsovo-Travino (ŭbrŭstsô"vŭ-trŭvē'nŭ), village (1926 pop. 2,077), E Astrakhan oblast, Russian SFSR, in Volga R. delta area, 25 mi. S of Astrakhan; fisheries; fruit, cotton. Formerly called Obraztsovoye or Obraztsovo.

Obree, Mount, New Guinea: see OWEN STANLEY RANGE.

Obregón, Ciudad, Mexico: see CIUDAD OBREGÓN.

Obregón, Villa, Mexico: see VILLA OBREGÓN.

Obrenovac or **Obrenovats** (both: ôbrĕ'nôväts), village (pop. 5,805), N central Serbia, Yugoslavia, on Kolubara R. and 17 mi. SW of Belgrade, near the Sava; rail junction.

O'Brien, Argentina: see GENERAL O'BRIEN.

O'Brien, county (□ 575; pop. 18,970), NW Iowa; ⊙ Primghar. Prairie agr. area (hogs, cattle, poultry, corn, oats, barley) drained by Little Sioux and Floyd rivers. Has state park. Formed 1851.

O'Brien, village (1940 pop. 544), Suwannee co., N Fla., 18 mi. S of Live Oak, in agr. area.

O'Brien Island, Tierra del Fuego, Chile, bet. the main isl. and Londonderry Isl.; 54°50'S 70°40'W.

O'Brien's Bridge or **O'Briensbridge,** Gaelic *Droichead Uí Bhriain,* town (pop. 129), SE Co. Clare, Ireland, on the Shannon (bridged) and 8 mi. NE of Limerick; agr. market (potatoes, grain; dairying).

Obrighoven-Lackhausen (ō'brĭkh-hō"vŭn-läk'hou"-zŭn), commune (pop. 5,671), in former Prussian Rhine Prov., W Germany, after 1945 in North Rhine-Westphalia, in the Ruhr; includes Obrighoven (3 mi. E of Wesel) and Lackhausen (1.5 mi. N of Wesel). Tobacco.

Ob River or **Ob' River** (ōb, Rus. ôp), one of largest rivers of Asiatic Russian SFSR, in W Siberia; 2,113 mi. long (with the Katun, 2,494 mi.). Formed by union of BIYA RIVER and KATUN RIVER SW of Bisk, Altai Territory; flows generally NW, past Barnaul, Kamen, and Novosibirsk (in rich agr. area), through swampy forests (Tomsk oblast), past Kolpashevo and Narym, then E, past Surgut, to mouth of Irtysh R. near Khanty-Mansisk. Here the Ob turns N, dividing into many arms and flowing past Kondinskoye, Kushevat, Salekhard, and Aksarka, to OB BAY, an inlet of the Kara Sea, 75 mi. ENE of Salekhard. Basin lies entirely in W.Siberian Plain. Chief tributaries: Tom, Chulym, Ket, Vakh, and Kazym (right) and Vasyugan, Irtysh (its main affluent), Konda, and Northern Sosva (left) rivers. Its width varies from ½ mi. at Barnaul to 12 mi. in lower course. Navigation begins at Bisk (on the Biya). River has low gradient, is subject to spring floods, and freezes for 6 months. In winter its water assumes characteristic iron-red coloring (due to plant decay), mainly in its swampy middle course. Important trade route. Sometimes called Obi. The length of the Ob-Irtysh waterway, 3,230 mi., is second only to that of the Yangtze R. in Asia.

Obrovac or **Obrovac Dalmatinski** (ô'brôväts dälmä'-tĭnskē), Ital. *Obbrovazzo* (ôb-brôvät'tsô), village, W Croatia, Yugoslavia, on Zrmanja R. and 22 mi. ENE of Zadar, in Dalmatia. Center of bauxite-mining area which extends along Adriatic Sea.

Obruchevo (ŭbro͞o'chĭvŭ), town (1939 pop. over 500), NE Samarkand oblast, Uzbek SSR, on Trans-Caspian RR and 35 mi. E of Dzhizak; fiber plants, sheep.

Obry, Kanal, Poland: see OBRA RIVER.

Observatory Inlet, W B.C., long narrow arm (45 mi. long, 1–4 mi. wide) of Portland Inlet (arm of Dixon Entrance), extending inland near and parallel to the S tip of the Alaska panhandle. Alice Arm extends E to Alice Arm village. On W side of Observatory Inlet is copper-mining center of Anyox.

Obshchi Syrt or **Obshchiy Syrt** (ôp'shchē sērt'), SW foothills of the S Urals, in SE European Russian SFSR, N of Ural R., rise to c.1,400 ft.

Obstruction Mountain (10,394 ft.), SW Alta., in Rocky Mts., near SE edge of Jasper Natl. Park, 60 mi. SE of Jasper; 52°23'N 116°53'W.

Obu (ō'bo͞o), town (pop. 19,234), Aichi prefecture, central Honshu, Japan, 10 mi. SSE of Nagoya; commercial center for cattle and agr. area; cotton textiles.

Obuasi (ōbwä'sē), town (pop. 15,833), Ashanti, S central Gold Coast, on railroad and 33 mi. S of Kumasi; major gold-mining center.

Obubra (ôbo͞obrä'), town (pop. 811), Ogoja prov., Eastern Provinces, SE Nigeria, port on Cross R. and 25 mi. SE of Abakaliki; palm oil and kernels, cacao, kola nuts.

Obuda, Hungary: see BUDAPEST.

Obudu (ôbo͞odo͞o'), town (pop. 706), Ogoja prov., Eastern Provinces, SE Nigeria, 29 mi. E of Ogoja; shea nuts, sesame.

Obukhov (ŭbo͞o'khŭf), agr. town (1926 pop. 9,773), central Kiev oblast, Ukrainian SSR, 23 mi. S of Kiev; truck produce.

Obukhovka, Ukrainian SSR: see KIROVSKI, Dnepropetrovsk oblast.

Obukhovo (–khŭvŭ), town (1926 pop. 3,905), E central Moscow oblast, Russian SFSR, on Klyazma R. and 7 mi. WSW of Noginsk; cotton-milling center.

Obwalden (ôp'väldŭn), Fr. *Obwald* (ôbväld'), half-canton (□ 190; 1950 pop. 22,075), Switzerland; ⊙ Sarnen. Commune of Engelberg is separated from it by Nidwalden half-canton which forms, together with Obwalden half-canton, UNTERWALDEN canton. Dairying region, with meadows, forests, and pastures; the Alps rise in S. Several resorts (e.g., ENGELBERG) and hydroelectric plants (e.g., at L. of LUNGERN). Woodworking industry. Pop. German speaking and Catholic.

Obyachevo or **Ob"yachevo** (ŭbyä'chĭvŭ), village (1926 pop. 275), SW Komi Autonomous SSR, Russian SFSR, on navigable Luza R. and 120 mi. N of Kirov; flax, potatoes.

Obydos, Brazil: see ÓBIDOS.

Ob-Yenisei Canal System (ôp"-yĕnyĭsyā'), in Tomsk oblast and Krasnoyarsk Territory, Russian SFSR, 70-mi. waterway joining Ob and Yenisei rivers. Kas R. (tributary of the Yenisei) and Ket R. (tributary of the Ob) are joined by means of their dredged branches (with locks) and a 5-mi. canal across the watershed. Built 1882–91 for small craft; fell into disuse.

Obzor, Bulgaria: see BYALA, Stalin dist.

Oca, Montes de (mōn'tĕs dhā ō'kä), Andean range on Colombia-Venezuela border, an offshoot of Cordillera Oriental, extending c.30 mi. NE from Serranía de Valledupar; rises to c.3,500 ft.

Oca, Montes de, low range, Burgos prov., N Spain, 10 mi. E of Burgos; extends c.30 mi. NW–SE; rises to c.3,250 ft.

Ocala (ōkă'lŭ), city (pop. 11,741), ⊙ Marion co., N central Fla., 33 mi. SSE of Gainesville; trade and shipping center; citrus-fruit packing and canning; limestone, phosphate, and wood processing; mfg. of fertilizer, concrete products, lumber, crates, millwork, shirts, soap, sausage, marmalade. City grew around Fort King, army post in Seminole War, near site of an Indian village visited by De Soto in 1539. Silver Springs near by.

Ocallí (ōkäyē'), town (pop. 666), Amazonas dept., N Peru, on E Andean slopes, 32 mi. W of Chachapoyas; cacao, coca, coffee.

Ocampo, Argentina: see VILLA OCAMPO.

Ocampo (ōkäm'pō). **1** Town (pop. 947), Chihuahua, N Mexico, in Sierra Madre Occidental, 145 mi. WSW of Chihuahua; alt. 5,682 ft.; silver, gold, lead, copper mining. Airfield. **2** Town (pop. 1,217), Coahuila, N Mexico, on plateau E of Sierra Madre Oriental, 145 mi. NNE of Torreón; alt. 3,497 ft.; gold, silver, lead, zinc mining. **3** Town (pop. 2,145), Guanajuato, central Mexico, in Sierra Madre Occidental, 21 mi. NW of Doctor Hernández Alvarez; alt. 7,342 ft.; beans, wheat, corn, mescal, livestock. **4** Town, Mexico state, Mexico: see MELCHOR OCAMPO. **5** Town (pop. 875), Michoacán, central Mexico, on railroad and 16 mi. SE of Hidalgo; corn, livestock. **6** City (pop. 2,006), Tamaulipas, NE Mexico, in E foothills of Sierra Madre Oriental, 60 mi. SSW of Ciudad Victoria; cereals, henequen, livestock.

Ocampo, Villa, Mexico: see VILLA OCAMPO.

Ocaña (ōkä'nyä), town (pop. 9,937), Norte de Santander dept., N Colombia, in W valley of Cordillera Oriental, 65 mi. WNW of Cúcuta, on cableway to Gamarra (Magdalena R.); alt. 3,940 ft. Trading and agr. center (coffee, cacao, tobacco, sugar cane, corn, wheat, tagua nuts, indigo, vanilla, livestock); coffee and hides shipped to Magdalena R. and Barranquilla. Mfg. of cigars. Airfield. Old colonial town, formerly a cinchona-growing center. A triumphal arch commemorates an independence convention held here 1828.

Ocaña, town (pop. 9,806), Toledo prov., central Spain, in New Castile, on railroad and 8 mi. SE of Aranjuez. Communications, processing, and agr. center (olives, grapes, cereals, livestock). Olive-oil pressing, alcohol and liquor distilling, flour milling, meat packing, cheese processing, tanning, printing; mfg. of sandals, ceramics, plaster, pottery, soap. Site of Fr. victory (Nov., 1809) in Peninsular War.

Occhieppo Inferiore (ôk-kyĕp'pô ēnfĕrēô'rĕ), village (pop. 2,917), Vercelli prov., Piedmont, N Italy, 2 mi. W of Biella. **Occhieppo Superiore** (pop. 989) is 1 mi. NW. Both have woolen mills.

Occhiobello (ôk"kyôbĕl'lô), village (pop. 900), Rovigo prov., Veneto, N Italy, on Po R. and 6 mi. N of Ferrara, in hemp-growing region.

Occidental, Cordillera (kôrdĭyā'rä ôksēdĕntäl') [Sp.,=western cordillera], name applied to several mtn. ranges in Spanish-speaking countries, notably in the Andes. In Bolivia, term refers to main range of the Andes, bounding the Altiplano on W. In Peru, it is the westernmost (main) range bet. Nudo de VILCANOTA and Nudo de PASCO, and beyond; its highest section here is known as Cordillera Blanca. In Ecuador, it forms the western of 2 ranges enclosing the central tableland. In Colombia, it is again the westernmost of the 3 main cordilleras which fan out from near Ecuador border N to the Caribbean.

Occimiano (ôt-chēmyä'nô), village (pop. 1,389), Alessandria prov., Piedmont, N Italy, 12 mi. NNW of Alessandria.

Occoquan (ŏ'kŭkwän), town (pop. 317), Prince William co., N Va., on Occoquan Creek near the Potomac and 20 mi. SW of Washington, D.C.

Occoquan Creek, N Va., formed SE of Manassas by junction of 2 headstreams, Bull Run and Cedar Run; flows c.20 mi. SE past Occoquan, to Occoquan Bay (an inlet of Potomac R. estuary), 15 mi. SE of Manassas; partly navigable. Dammed to form L. JACKSON.

Occumster (ŏkŭm'stŭr), fishing village, S Caithness, Scotland, on Moray Firth, just E of Lybster.

Ocean, county (□ 639; pop. 56,622), E N.J.; ⊙ Toms River. Bounded E by Barnegat Bay; Long Beach isl. and Island Beach peninsula, bet. bay and the Atlantic, have many popular summer resorts, fisheries. Inland agr. area produces truck, poultry, dairy products, fruit. Part of co. is in pine barrens region (timber, cranberries, huckleberries), here including Lebanon State Forest. Drained by Toms and Metedeconk rivers and Cedar Creek. Formed 1850.

Oceana (ō"shēă'nŭ), county (□ 536; pop. 16,105), W Mich.; ⊙ Hart. Bounded W by L. Michigan; drained by White R. and short Pentwater R. Fruitgrowing (apples, peaches), stock and poultry raising, dairying, agr. (truck, potatoes, beans). Some mfg. at Hart, Shelby, and Pentwater. Fisheries. Resort. Includes part of Manistee Natl. Forest, and 2 state parks. Organized 1855.

Oceana, town (pop. 1,373), Wyoming co., S W.Va., on Clear Fork and 9 mi. NW of Pineville.

Ocean Beach. 1 Section of SAN DIEGO city, Calif. **2** Village, Suffolk co., N.Y.: see FIRE ISLAND.

Ocean Bluff, Mass.: see MARSHFIELD.

Ocean Cape, SE Alaska, on Gulf of Alaska, on E shore of entrance to Yakutat Bay; 59°32'N 139°52'W. Near by are a native fishing and an air strip built in Second World War.

Ocean City. 1 Resort town (pop. 1,234), Worcester co., SE Md., on barrier beach off the Atlantic shore, 28 mi. E of Salisbury. Only ocean shore resort (summer pop. up to 30,000) and oceanside port in Md.; important shipping point for seafood. Noted for sport fishing (surf and deep-sea), yachting; has boating and bathing facilities; boardwalk, amusement dist. Ocean City Inlet (just S) connects Assawoman and Sinepuxent bays with the ocean. Laid out 1872; 1st hotel was built 1875. **2** Resort city (pop. 6,040), Cape May co., SE N.J., on Peck Beach bet. Great Egg Harbor Bay and the Atlantic, and 10 mi. SW of Atlantic City; boatbuilding; truck. Noted fishing and summer resort since late 19th cent. Laid out 1879, inc. 1897.

Ocean Drive Beach, resort town (pop. 255), Horry co., E S.C., on the coast 20 mi. E of Conway.

Ocean Falls, town (pop. estimate 1,500), W B.C., on inlet of the Pacific, 300 mi. NW of Vancouver; 52°22′N 127°41′W; paper milling and shipping center; hydroelectric power.

Ocean Gate, borough (pop. 452), Ocean co., E N.J., on Toms R. and 4 mi. SE of Toms River village, in fishing and resort area.

Ocean Grove. 1 Village, Bristol co., Mass.: see SWANSEA. **2** Resort village (pop. 3,806), Monmouth co., E N.J., on the coast just S of Asbury Park; owned and controlled by Methodist camp meeting assn. Agr. (dairy products, poultry, fruit, truck). Tent city for summer camp meetings and auditorium seating 9,000 here. Founded 1869.

Oceania (ōshēă′nēū, –ā′nēū, –nyū), collective name of islands and island groups in Pacific Ocean. Includes MICRONESIA (U.S. Trust Territory of the PACIFIC ISLANDS, GUAM, NAURU, GILBERT ISLANDS), POLYNESIA (French Oceania; the NIUE, COOK, and TOKELAU isls. of New Zealand; ELLICE ISLAND, TONGA, SAMOA, HAWAII), and MELANESIA (NEW CALEDONIA, SOLOMON ISLANDS and, FIJI ISLANDS, NEW HEBRIDES) with NEW GUINEA and the BISMARCK ARCHIPELAGO. Australia and New Zealand are sometimes included in Oceania.

Ocean Island, phosphate island (□ 2.2; pop. 2,060), W central Pacific, c.250 mi. SW of Tarawa, Gilbert Isls.; 0°52′S 169°35′E; former ⊙ Br. colony of GILBERT AND ELLICE ISLANDS. Central phosphate mass rises to c.265 ft. Discovered 1804 by British; annexed 1915. In Second World War it was occupied (1942–45) by Japanese. Formerly Banaba.

Ocean Island, T.H.: see KURE ISLAND.

Oceanlake, town (pop. 700), Lincoln co., W Oregon, on Pacific Ocean and 25 mi. N of Toledo; logging, woodworking.

Oceano (ōshēă′nō), village (pop. 1,446), San Luis Obispo co., SW Calif., on coast 12 mi. S of San Luis Obispo; ships flower, vegetable seed; resort.

Ocean Park, Calif.: see SANTA MONICA.

Ocean Pond, lake (4 mi. long, 2 mi. wide), E N.F., 30 mi. SW of Bonavista; 48°19′N 53°39′W. Drains into Trinity Bay.

Oceanport, borough (pop. 7,588), Monmouth co., E N.J., on Shrewsbury R. estuary (head of navigation) and 3 mi. NW of Long Branch. U.S. Fort Monmouth near by. Inc. 1920.

Ocean Ridge, town (pop. 67), Palm Beach co., SE Fla., 13 mi. S of West Palm Beach. Set off (1931) as Boynton Beach from Boynton town (now called Boynton Beach); renamed Ocean Ridge 1937.

Oceanside. 1 City (pop. 12,881), San Diego co., S Calif., beach resort 35 mi. N of San Diego, at mouth of San Luis Rey R.; trade center for agr. region (lima beans, citrus fruit, avocados, truck). Seat of Oceanside-Carlsbad Col. Old mission at near-by SAN LUIS REY. U.S. Camp Pendleton (Marine base) in vicinity. Inc. 1888. **2** Resort village (1940 pop. 9,744), Nassau co., SE N.Y., on S shore of W Long Isl., near Rockville Centre, 9 mi. ESE of Jamaica; mfg. (awnings, machinery, greeting cards).

Ocean Springs, resort town (pop. 3,058), Jackson co., extreme SE Miss., 3 mi. E of BILOXI across Biloxi Bay (bridged); canned sea food, lumber, pottery. Seat of marine research laboratory (1948). Town established on site of Old Biloxi, founded in 1699 by Iberville as 1st white settlement in lower Mississippi valley.

Ocean View. 1 Town (pop. 450), Sussex co., SE Del., near Indian River Bay, 16 mi. SSE of Lewes, in poultry-raising region. **2** Resort, Va.: see NORFOLK, city.

Ochagavía (ōchägävē′ä), town (pop. 1,056), Navarre prov., N Spain, 30 mi. ENE of Pamplona; sawmilling; wheat, potatoes, cattle, sheep.

Ochakov (ŭchä′kŭf), city (1939 pop. over 10,000), SW Nikolayev oblast, Ukrainian SSR, port on Black Sea, at mouth of Dnieper Liman, and 30 mi. SW of Nikolayev; flour milling, fish canning. Former Turkish naval fortress, it fell (1788) to Russia in the Russo-Turkish War of 1787–92.

Ochandiano (ōchändyä′nō), village (pop. 792), Vizcaya prov., N Spain, 20 mi. SE of Bilbao. Destroyed (April, 1937) in fighting in Sp. civil war.

Oche or **Okhi** (both: ô′khē), Lat. *Ocha*, mountain in SE Euboea, Greece, extends c.10 mi. from Karystos NE to Cape Kaphereus, rises to 4,585 ft. at the Hagios Elias [=St. Elias], 4 mi. NNE of Karystos.

Oche, Dent d', France: see DENT D'OCHE.

Ocheda Lake (ō-chē′dū), Nobles co., SW Minn., 3 mi. S of Worthington; 7 mi. long, 5 mi. wide. Drains into Ocheyedan R.

Ochelata (ō″chūlā′tū), town (pop. 357), Washington co., NE Okla., 30 mi. N of Tulsa, in farm and ranch area.

Ochemchiri (ŭchĭmchē′rē), city (1939 pop. over 10,000), S Abkhaz Autonomous SSR, Georgian SSR, port on Black Sea, 30 mi. SE of Sukhumi; tobacco and tea center; woodworking, mfg. (tanning materials, rubber goods). Port for Tkvarcheli coal fields (linked by rail spur). Formerly spelled Ochemchiry.

Ocheng or **O-ch'eng** (ŭ′chŭng′), town (pop. 11,324), ⊙ Ocheng co. (pop. 330,715), E Hupeh prov., China, on Yangtze R., opposite Hwangkang, and 38 mi. ESE of Hankow; cotton weaving; wine-growing. Until 1914 called Showchang.

Ocher (ô′chĭr), town (1926 pop. 4,839), W Molotov oblast, Russian SFSR, on Ocher R. (short right tributary of Kama R.) and 60 mi. WSW of Molotov; agr.-machine mfg. center (threshers, scutchers). Teachers col. Until 1929, Ocherski Zavod.

Ocheyedan (ō-chē′dŭn), town (pop. 700), Osceola co., NW Iowa, near Ocheyedan R., 11 mi. E of Sibley; makes popcorn. Near by is Ocheyedan Mound, highest point (1,675 ft.) in Iowa.

Ocheyedan River, rises in Nobles co., SW Minn., flows SE into NW Iowa to Little Sioux R. at Spencer; 58 mi. long. Receives S outlet of L. Ocheda.

Ochi (ō′chē), sometimes spelled Oti. **1** Town (pop. 6,755), Ishikawa prefecture, central Honshu, Japan, 13 mi. SW of Nanao; raw silk, rice. **2** Town (pop. 7,260), Kochi prefecture, S Shikoku, Japan, on Niyodo R. and 17 mi. W of Kochi; commercial center in agr. area (rice, wheat); lumber, raw silk. **3** Town (pop. 12,377), Saga prefecture, NW Kyushu, Japan, on N Hizen Peninsula, 21 mi. NE of Sasebo; rail junction; rice, wheat, raw silk.

Ochiai (ōchēī′), town (pop. 6,552), Okayama prefecture, SW Honshu, Japan, 14 mi. WSW of Tsuyama, in agr. area (rice, wheat, persimmons); raw silk, charcoal, yarn, sake. Sometimes spelled Otiai.

Ochiai, Russian SFSR: see DOLINSK.

Ochil Hills (ōkh′ĭl), mountain range of volcanic origin in Perthshire, Clackmannan, Kinross, and Fifeshire, Scotland, extends 25 mi. ENE–WSW bet. Stirling and the Firth of Tay. There are mineral deposits, and silver was formerly mined here. Highest points are Ben Cleuch (bĕn klōōkh′) (2,363 ft.), 3 mi. N of Tillicoultry, and King's Seat (2,111 ft.), 2 mi. NNE of Tillicoultry. Devon R. rises in Ochil Hills.

Ochiltree (ōkh′ĭltrē). **1** Agr. village and parish (pop. 2,023), central Ayrshire, Scotland, on Lugar Water and 4 mi. W of Cumnock. George Douglas (George Douglas Brown) b. here. DRONGAN is in parish. **2** Village in Linlithgow parish, NW West Lothian, Scotland, 3 mi. SE of Linlithgow; shale-oil mining.

Ochiltree (ŏk′ŭltrē), county (□ 905; pop. 6,024), extreme N Texas; ⊙ Perryton. On high plains of the Panhandle, and bounded N by Okla. line; alt. c.2,600-3,100 ft. Drained by tributaries of Canadian and North Canadian rivers. A leading wheat-producing co. of U.S.; also cattle ranching, some dairying, sheep, hogs, horses. Includes a state park. Formed 1876.

Ochlockonee (ōklŏk′nē), town (pop. 503), Thomas co., S Ga., 10 mi. NNW of Thomasville. Also spelled Ochlochnee.

Ochlockonee River, in Ga. and Fla., rises SW of Sylvester in SW Ga., flows generally S, across NW Fla., into W end of Apalachee Bay of the Gulf of Mexico, 14 mi. SSW of Crawfordville; c.150 mi. long. W of Tallahassee, a dam forms L. Talquin (tăl′kwĭn), c.14 mi. long, 1–4 mi. wide.

Ochoco Creek (ō′chūkō), central Oregon, rises in mtn. region of Crook co., flows c.40 mi. W to Crooked R. near Prineville. Ochoco Reservoir (4 mi. long) is formed by small dam in upper course. Used for irrigation.

Ochomogo Pass (ōchōmō′gō) (alt. 5,138 ft.), on continental divide, in central Costa Rica, connecting San José and Cartago (Guarco Valley) sections of central plateau. Used by railroad bet. San José and Limón and by Inter-American Highway.

Ocho Rios (ō″chō rē′ōs, ō″chū rē′ŭs), town (pop. 2,660), St. Ann parish, N Jamaica, 6 mi. E of St. Ann's Bay; resort with well-protected harbor, in agr. region (citrus fruit, corn, pimento, cattle). In its vicinity (W), along small Dunn's and Roaring rivers, are noted waterfalls. In early 1950s became bauxite-shipping port for new mines opened 6–8 mi. inland (tramway link).

Ochre River, village (pop. estimate 300), W Man., on Ochre R., near Dauphin L., 14 mi. ESE of Dauphin; grain; mixed farming.

Ochrida or **Okhrida** (both: ō′krĭdū), Serbo-Croatian *Ohrid* (ô′khrĭd), Turkish *Okhri*, anc. *Lychnidus*, town (pop. 11,419), Macedonia, S Yugoslavia, on L. Ochrida, 70 mi. SSW of Skoplje. Terminus of narrow-gauge railroad to Skoplje; trade and tourist center; fishing. Cherries and chestnuts grown in vicinity. Notable churches include partly ruined Sveta Sofia (9th cent.; originally a cathedral), Sveti Kliment (cathedral; 1295), 14th-cent. Sveti Nikola Bolnicki and Sveti Jovan. Walls and towers of former Turkish castle remain. On site of Greek colony which fell (A.D. 168) to Romans; was important traffic center and bishopric. Became Slav settlement in 9th cent.; developed into a center of Christianity and Slav culture. Long contested bet. Serbia, Bulgaria, and Byzantine Empire; finally passed to Serbia in 1334. Sometimes spelled Ochrid or Okhrid.

Ochrida, Lake, or **Lake Okhrida,** Serbo-Croatian *Ohridsko Jezero* (ô′khrĭdshô yĕ′zĕrô), Albanian *Liqen i Ohrit* (lē′kyĕn ē ô′hrēt), deepest lake (□ 134; alt. 2,280, depth 938 ft.) in the Balkans, on Yugoslav-Albanian border, W of the Galicica. Connected with L. Prespa by underground channels. Water, received from coastal and bottom springs, is unusually transparent (sometimes down to 72 ft.). Fishing (carp, eel, trout) is important source of local livelihood; fish hatchery. Noted for its beauty, the lake is surrounded by beaches and historic buildings (e.g., monastery at SVETI NAUM). Coastal towns (STRUGA, OCHRIDA, POGRADEC) are connected by boat lines. Outlet: the Black Drin. Sometimes spelled Ochrid or Okhrid.

Ochsen (ôk′sŭn), peak (7,192 ft.) in Bernese Alps, W central Switzerland, 11 mi. SW of Thun; resort of Schwefelbergbad at N foot.

Ochsenfurt (–fōōrt), town (pop. 6,213), Lower Franconia, W Bavaria, Germany, on the Main (canalized) and 10 mi. SE of Würzburg; rail junction; mfg. of textiles, and of wood, food, and metal products; printing, brewing. Partly surrounded by 14th-cent. walls. Has church from 2d half of 14th cent.; late-Gothic chapel; town hall (1497–1513).

Ochsenkopf (–kôpf), peak (3,356 ft.) of the Fichtelgebirge, Bavaria, Germany, 8 mi. W of Wunsiedel. Separated from neighboring (NE) Schneeberg by a wide moor.

Ochtrup (ôkh′trōōp), village (pop. 11,609), in former Prussian prov. of Westphalia, NW Germany, after 1945 in North Rhine-Westphalia, 7 mi. E of Gronau; cattle.

Ocilla (ōsĭ′lū), city (pop. 2,697), ⊙ Irwin co., S central Ga., 8 mi. S of Fitzgerald; agr. trade center; mfg. (turpentine, lumber, cottonseed products). Inc. 1897.

Ockbrook, agr. village and parish (pop. 2,971), SE Derby, England, 4 mi. E of Derby; site of 18th-cent. Moravian settlement and school. Has church with 12th-cent. tower.

Ockelbo (ô′kŭlbōō″), village (pop. 1,275), Gavleborg co., E Sweden, 20 mi. NW of Gavle; rail junction; lumber and flour mills; metal- and woodworking.

Ockero (ŭ′kûrû″), Swedish *Öckerö*, fishing village (pop. 1,422), Goteborg och Bohus co., SW Sweden, on islet of same name in the Skagerrak, 12 mi. W of Goteborg. Has 18th-cent church.

Ocker River, Germany: see OKER RIVER.

Ocland (ôk′lănd), Hung. *Okländ* (ôk′länt), village (pop. 1,069), Stalin prov., central Rumania, 11 mi. SE of Odorhei; mfg. of bricks and tiles. In Hungary, 1940–45.

Ocmulgee National Monument (ōkmŭl′gē) (683.48 acres; established 1936), central Ga., on Ocmulgee R. just E of Macon. Mounds, pyramids, artifacts, and village remains of early Indian civilization.

Ocmulgee River, central Ga., c.255 mi. long, formed c.40 mi. SE of Atlanta by confluence of South, Yellow, and Alcovy rivers in LLOYD SHOALS RESERVOIR, flows SSE, past Macon, Hawkinsville, and Abbeville, thence E to junction with Oconee R. 7 mi. NNE of Hazelhurst, forming the Altamaha.

Ocna, Ukrainian SSR: see OKNA.

Ocna-Dejului, Rumania: see DEJ.

Ocna-Muresului (ôk′nä-mōōrĕ′shōōlwē), Rum. *Ocna-Mureşului*, Hung. *Marosújvár* (mŏ′rôshōō″-ĕvär), village (pop. 5,004), Cluj prov., central Rumania, in Transylvania, on Mures R. and 24 mi. NNE of Alba-Iulia; salt-production center and health resort with saline springs and baths; extensive vineyards in vicinity.

Ocna-Sibiu (ôk′nä-sēbē′ōō), Ger. *Salzburg* (zälts′-bōōrk), Hung. *Vizakna* (vē′zŏknŏ), village (pop. 3,752), Sibiu prov., central Rumania, on railroad and 7 mi. NW of Sibiu; health resort with saline lakes; saltworking, mfg. of cutlery and steel products. Has two old churches. Known as spa in Roman times. Also spelled Ocna-Sibiului.

Ocna-Sugatag (ôk′nä-shōōgä), Rum. *Ocna-Şugatag* Hung. *Aknasugatag* (ŏk′nŏshōō″gŏtŏk), village (pop. 1,583), Baia-Mare prov., NW Rumania, on W slopes of the Carpathians, 10 mi. S of Sighet; rail terminus and salt-mining center; also a summer resort (alt. 1,608 ft.) with alkaline springs. In Hungary, 1940–45.

Ocnele-Mari (ôk′nĕlĕ-mä′rē), town (1948 pop. 6,159), Valcea prov., S central Rumania, in Walachia, on railroad and 3 mi. SW of Ramnicu-Valcea; major salt-production center and health resort on salt lake. Has 16th-cent. church. Ocnita (Rum. *Ocniţa*) or Ocnitsa bathing resort is just W.

Ocnita, Moldavian SSR: see OKNITSA.

Ocoa Bay (ōkō′ä), inlet of the Caribbean, S Dominican Republic, 45 mi. W of Ciudad Trujillo.

Ocobamba (ōkōbäm′bä), agr. town (pop. 280), Cuzco dept., S central Peru, on affluent of Urubamba R. and 35 mi. NNW of Urubamba.

Ococingo, Mexico: see OCOSINGO.

Ocoee (ōkō′ē), city (pop. 1,370), Orange co., central Fla., 10 mi. W of Orlando, near L. Apopka; ships citrus fruit and truck produce.

Ocoee River, in N Ga. and SE Tenn., formed in Blue Ridge Mts. 9 mi. SE of Blue Ridge city, Ga., by confluence of 2 headstreams; flows NW through Fannin co. (here called Toccoa R.), into Tenn., past Copper Hill, through Polk co., and N to Hiwassee R. 2 mi. N of Benton; 90 mi. long. Drains forest area in both states. Dammed in upper course by BLUE RIDGE DAM, forming L. Toccoa. Three other dams are in Tenn. Ocoee No. 1 (135 ft. high, 840 ft. long; completed 1912) is in lower course, 6 mi. S of Benton; forms L. Ocoee (7 mi. long, .5 mi. wide; also known as Parksville Reservoir). Ocoee No. 2 (30 ft. high, 450 ft. long; completed 1913) is further upstream, 6 mi. NW of Copperhill. Ocoee No. 3 (110 ft. high, 612 ft. long; completed 1943) is at Copperhill, just N of Ga. line. All 3 owned by TVA and used for power development; Nos. 1 and 2 were privately constructed, No. 3 built by TVA.

Ocoña (ōkō'nyä), town (pop. 932), Arequipa dept., S Peru, minor Pacific port, at mouth of Ocoña R., on Pan American Highway and 100 mi. W of Arequipa; cotton, sugar cane, olives, grapes, grain; wine and liquor distilling.

Ocoña River, Arequipa dept., S Peru, rises as Cotahuasi R. at S foot of Cordillera de Huanzo on Apurímac dept. border, flows c.110 mi. S to the Pacific at Ocoña. Used for irrigation.

Oconee (ōkō'nē). **1** County (□ 186; pop. 7,009), NE central Ga.; ⊙ Watkinsville. Piedmont area drained by Apalachee and Oconee rivers. Agr. (cotton, corn, grain, sorghum, fruit). Formed 1875. **2** County (□ 670; pop. 39,050), extreme NW S.C.; ⊙ Walhalla. Bounded NW by Chattooga R., SW by Tugaloo R., E by Keowee and Seneca rivers. Includes much of S.C. part of the Blue Ridge; summer-resort area, with part of Sumter Natl. Forest. Produces timber, cotton, corn, wheat; cotton mills. Formed 1868.

Oconee (ō"kŭnē'), village (pop. 256), Shelby co., central Ill., 22 mi. N of Vandalia, in agr. and bituminous-coal area.

Oconee River (ōkō'nē), Ga., rises near Lula, NE Ga., flows 282 mi. SSE, past Athens, Milledgeville (head of navigation), and Dublin, to confluence with Ocmulgee R., forming the Altamaha 7 mi. NNE of Hazelhurst.

Oconee State Park, S.C.: see WALHALLA.

Ocongate (ōkōng-gä'tā), town (pop. 513), Cuzco dept., S central Peru, in Cordillera de Vilcanota, 40 mi. E of Cuzco, in agr. region (potatoes, wheat, alfalfa); gold washing; silver, coal deposits.

O'Connor, Bolivia: see ENTRE RÍOS.

Oconomowoc (ōkŏ'nŭmúwôk", ŭkŏ'nŭmúwŏk), city (pop. 5,345), Waukesha co., SE Wis., on Oconomowoc R. (tributary of Rock R.), bet. small Fowler and La Belle lakes, and 28 mi. W of Milwaukee; resort with mineral springs. Dairy-products processing; mfg. of boats, machine tools, chemicals, canned vegetables, beer. Seat of Immaculate Conception Seminary. Has annual winter-sports carnival. Rogers Memorial Sanitarium is near by. Inc. 1875.

Oconto (ōkŏn'tō), county (□ 1,106; pop. 26,238), NE Wis.; ⊙ Oconto. Bounded E by Green Bay; drained by Oconto R. Primarily a dairying and lumbering area. Contains part of Menominee Indian Reservation. Formed 1851.

Oconto. 1 Village (pop. 258), Custer co., central Nebr., 20 mi. SSW of Broken Bow and on Wood R. **2** City (pop. 5,055), ⊙ Oconto co., NE Wis., at mouth of Oconto R., on W shore of Green Bay, 28 mi. NNE of Green Bay city; commercial center for lumbering and dairying area; mfg. (wood products, knit goods, beer). Has fisheries. Father Allouez founded a mission here in 1669; the 1st Christian Science church was built here in 1886. Was important lumbering center. Inc. 1869.

Oconto Falls, city (pop. 2,050), Oconto co., NE Wis., on Oconto R. and 26 mi. NNW of Green Bay city; paper milling, vegetable canning, butter and cheese making. Inc. 1919.

Oconto River, NE Wis., rises in several small lakes in Forest co., flows 87 mi. S and E, past Oconto Falls, to Green Bay at Oconto city.

Ocós (ōkōs'), town (1950 pop. 340), San Marcos dept., SW Guatemala, port on Pacific coast, 25 mi. SW of Coatepeque, at mouth of Naranjo R.; 14°30'N 92°11' W. Rail terminus; exports coffee, sugar, lumber. Saltworks near by. Flourished (19th cent.) in indigo and cochineal trade; declined after rise of Puerto Barrios.

Ocosingo (ōkōsēng'gō), town (pop. 980), Chiapas, S Mexico, on N plateau of Sierra Madre, 36 mi. NE of San Cristóbal de las Casas; corn, rice, mangoes, oranges. Anc. Maya ruins of great interest and artistic merit near by. Sometimes Ococingo.

Ocosito River, Guatemala: see TILAPA RIVER.

Ocotal or **El Ocotal** (ĕl ōkōtäl'), village (pop. 262), Chiapas, S Mexico, on Inter-American Highway and 40 mi. SSE of Comitán, on Guatemala border.

Ocotal, city (1950 pop. 2,807), ⊙ Nueva Segovia dept., NW Nicaragua, on branch of Inter-American Highway and 105 mi. NNW of Managua, near Coco R.; commercial center; mfg. (shoes, furniture, beverages), agr. processing (coffee, sugar cane, tobacco).

Ocotepec (ōkōtāpĕk'). **1** Town (pop. 1,433), Chiapas, S Mexico, in N spur of Sierra Madre, 30 mi. N of Tuxtla; cereals, sugar cane, fruit. **2** Town (pop. 661), Puebla, central Mexico, 33 mi. SE of Zacatlán; corn, maguey.

Ocotepeque (ōkōtāpā'kā), department (□ 859; 1950 pop. 50,240), W Honduras, on Salvador and Guatemala borders; ⊙ Nueva Ocotepeque. Largely mountainous (sierras de Metapán and del Merendón); drained by Lempa R. (W) and upper Jicatuyo R. (E). Agr. (wheat, corn, coffee, tobacco, rice, fruit); cattle, hogs. Local industries: flour milling, mat weaving, cigar mfg. Main centers: Nueva Ocotepeque, San Marcos. Active international trade. Formed 1906 from Copán dept.

Ocotepeque, city, Honduras: see NUEVA OCOTEPEQUE.

Ocotlán (ōkōtlän'). **1** Town (pop. 14,289), Jalisco, central Mexico, on NE shore of L. Chapala, at outlet of Santiago (Lerma) R., and 45 mi. SE of Guadalajara; rail junction; processing and agr. center (grain, vegetables, fruit, livestock); milk canneries, rayon-yarn plants. Point of departure for L. Chapala resort dist. Airfield. **2** Officially Ocotlán de Morelos, city (pop. 4,270), Oaxaca, S Mexico, in Sierra Madre del Sur, on railroad and 19 mi. S of Oaxaca; agr. center (cereals, sugar cane, coffee, fruit, livestock, timber); silver and gold deposits. **3** Town (pop. 1,759), Puebla, central Mexico, 8 mi. NW of Puebla; cereals, maguey, livestock. **4** Officially Ocotlán de Betancourt, town (pop. 2,421), Puebla, central Mexico, 11 mi. W of Teziutlán; sugar cane, coffee, vegetables, fruit.

Ocoyoacac (ōkoiwäkäk'), town (pop. 3,133), Mexico state, central Mexico, 12 mi. E of Toluca; rail junction; agr. center (cereals, livestock); dairying.

Ocoyucan (ōkoiōō'kän), officially Santa Clara Ocoyucan, town (pop. 926), Puebla, central Mexico, 8 mi. SW of Puebla; cereals, fruit, livestock.

Ocozocoautla (ōkōsōkwout'lä), officially Ocozocoautla de Espinosa, city (pop. 4,496), Chiapas, S Mexico, in Sierra Madre, 18 mi. W of Tuxtla; agr. center (corn, beans, sugar cane, coffee, tobacco, fruit).

Ocracoke (ō'krúkōk"), fishing and resort village, Hyde co., E N.C., 27 mi. WSW of Cape Hatteras, on SW shore of Ocracoke Isl., a barrier beach (c.12 mi. long) bet. the Atlantic and Pamlico Sound. An important port before Civil War.

Ocracoke Inlet, E N.C., passage connecting Pamlico Sound with the Atlantic, at SW end of Ocracoke Isl.

Ocros (ō'krōs), town (pop. 1,321), Ancash dept., W central Peru, in Cordillera Occidental, 60 mi. S of Huarás; cereals, livestock.

Ocsa (ō'chŏ), Hung. *Ócsa*, town (pop. 6,153), Pest-Pilis-Solt-Kiskun co., N central Hungary, 15 mi. SSE of Budapest. Has Romanesque church.

Öcseny (û'chānyû), Hung. *Öcsény*, town (pop. 3,927), Tolna co., S Hungary, 4 mi. SE of Szekszard; wheat, corn.

Öcsöd (û'chûd), town (pop. 8,189), Bekes co., SE Hungary, 17 mi. NNE of Szentes; flour mills; grain, cattle. Town dates back to medieval times.

Octa (ŏk'tú), village (pop. 87), Fayette co., S central Ohio, 10 mi. WNW of Washington Court House.

Octavia, village (pop. 103), Butler co., E Nebr., 15 mi. ESE of Columbus, near Platte R.

Octay, Chile: see PUERTO OCTAY.

Octeville (ôktvēl'), SW suburb (pop. 3,619) of Cherbourg, Manche dept., NW France; horse breeding.

October 11, Russian SFSR: see OKTYABRYA, IMENI 11.

October Revolution Island, Russian SFSR: see OKTYABRSKAYA REVOLYUTSIYA ISLAND.

Octoraro Creek (ŏktúrô'rú), in SE Pa. and NE Md., rises near Parkesburg, Pa., flows c.40 mi. SSW to the Susquehanna below Conowingo Dam in Md.

Octubre, 10 de (dyās' dā ōktōō'brā), military post, Tarija dept., SE Bolivia, in the Chaco, on Paraguay border, 80 mi. ENE of Villa Montes.

Ocú (ōkōō'), village (pop. 807), Herrera prov., S central Panama, 18 mi. WSW of Chitré; corn, rice, beans, livestock.

Ocucaje (ōkōōkä'hā), village (pop. 2,238), Ica dept., SW Peru, on Ica R. and 20 mi. S of Ica; cotton center; vineyards.

Ocuilan (ōkwē'län), officially Ocuilan de Arteaga, town (pop. 2,926), Mexico state, central Mexico, 27 mi. SW of Mexico city; cereals, sugar cane, vegetables, stock.

Ocuitico (ōkwētē'kō), town (pop. 1,769), Morelos, central Mexico, 12 mi. NE of Cuautla; grain, sugar, fruit, stock.

Ocumare (ōkōōmä'rā). **1** or **Ocumare de la Costa** (dā lä kō'stä), town (pop. 931), Aragua state, N Venezuela, at N foot of coastal range, in narrow lowland, on small river and 16 mi. E of Puerto Cabello; cacao, fruit. Its port is 3 mi. N on the Caribbean. **2** or **Ocumare del Tuy** (dĕl twē'), town (pop. 2,409), Miranda state, N Venezuela, in valley of coastal range, on Tuy R., and 28 mi. SSE of Caracas, (linked by railroad); agr. center (coffee, cacao, sugar cane, cereals).

Ocuri (ōkōō'rē), town (pop. c.4,200), Potosí dept., W central Bolivia, on road and 16 mi. SE of Colquechaca; corn, alpaca, sheep.

Ocussi, Timor: see OE-CUSSE.

Oda (ō'dä), town (pop. 8,341), Eastern Prov., central Gold Coast colony, on railroad and 45 mi. NNW of Winneba; diamond-mining center.

Oda (ō'dä) or **Ota** (ō'tä), town (pop. 7,651), Shimane prefecture, SW Honshu, Japan, 28 mi. WSW of Matsue, at foot of extinct volcanic peak. Agr. center; summer resort; rice, sake, soy sauce, raw silk; livestock; sawmilling.

Oda, Jebel (jĕ'bĕl ō'dú), peak (7,412 ft.) in the Etbai range bordering Red Sea, NE Anglo-Egyptian Sudan, 70 mi. NNW of Port Sudan.

Odadahraun, Iceland: see ASKJA.

Odaejin (ŭ'dă'jĕn'), Jap. *Gyotaishin*, town (1944 pop. 9,083), N.Hamgyong prov., N Korea, on Sea of Japan, 23 mi. S of Chongjin; fishing.

Odaid, Khor al, Qatar: see ODEID, KHOR EL.

Odaka. 1 (ō'däkä) Town, Aichi prefecture, Japan: see OTAKA. **2** (ōdä'kä) or **Otaka** (ōtä'kä), town (pop. 9,205), Fukushima prefecture, N central Honshu, Japan, on the Pacific, 6 mi. SSE of Haranomachi; raw silk.

Odakra (û'dōkrä"), Swedish *Ödåkra*, village (pop. 725), Malmohus co., SW Sweden, 5 mi. NE of Halsingborg; distilling; grain, potatoes, cattle.

Odanah (ōdä'nú), Indian village (1940 pop. 920), Ashland co., extreme N Wis., 9 mi. E of Ashland, in Bad River Reservation (for Chippewa Indians), in barren, marshy area; wild rice.

Odate ō'dātā), town, (pop. 22,036), Akita prefecture, N Honshu, Japan, 29 mi. E of Noshiro; rail junction; lumbering center; aluminum and zinc products.

Odawara (ōdä'wärú), city (1940 pop. 27,860; 1947 pop. 68,911), Kanagawa prefecture, central Honshu, Japan, on NW shore of Sagami Bay, 30 mi. WSW of Yokohama, in agr. area (oranges, potatoes, wheat); tourist resort (hot springs). Produces raw silk, celluloid goods. Has large Zen-Buddhist temple founded in 15th cent. Site of 16th-cent. castle of Hojo clan. Includes (since early 1940s) former village of Ashigara (1940 pop. 16,807) and 3 smaller villages.

Odawara Bay, Japan: see SAGAMI SEA.

Odayd, Khawr al-, Qatar: see ODEID, KHOR EL.

Odda (ôd'dä), village (pop. 4,800; canton pop. 8,267), Hordaland co., SW Norway, at head of Sor Fjord (an arm of Hardanger Fjord), at foot of Folgefonn glacier, 50 mi. SE of Bergen; zinc-mining and -smelting center; also produces cadmium and carbide; superphosphate plant. Tourist center. EITRHEIM is in canton. Formerly spelled Odde.

Odden, Denmark: see FANO.

Odder (ô'dhûr), town (pop. 4,961), Aarhus amt, E Jutland, Denmark, 8 mi. S of Aarhus; meat, fruit packing; machinery mfg.

Oddernes, Norway: see MOSBY.

Odderoy (ôd'dûr-ûü), Nor. *Odderøy*, island (□ c.1; pop. 52) in an inlet of the Skagerrak, Vest-Agder co., S Norway, 1 mi. SE of Kristiansand; lumber mills, veneer works. Has fortifications for Kristiansand. Formerly spelled Odderö.

Oddur, Ital. Somaliland: see HODUR.

Ode or **Ode Remo** (ōdā' rāmō'), town, Ijebu prov., Western Provinces, SW Nigeria, 20 mi. WNW of Ijebu-Ode; road center; cacao industry; cotton weaving, indigo dyeing; palm oil and kernels, rice.

Odebolt (ō'dúbōlt"), town (pop. 1,279), Sac co., W Iowa, c.60 mi. ESE of Sioux City; popcorn. Inc. 1877.

Odegardens Verk (û'dúgôrdûns vărk"), Nor. *Ødegårdens Verk*, village (pop. 226) in Bamble canton (pop. 4,712), Telemark co., S Norway, near the coast, 16 mi. S of Skien; apatite mining. Near by are zinc, lead, and nickel mines. Lumbering region, with many sawmills and a cellulose plant.

Odeid, Khor el, Khor al Odaid, or **Khawr al-Odayd** (all: khōr' ĕl ōdīd'), inlet of Persian Gulf, at base of Qatar peninsula, marking S limit of Qatar sheikdom; 24°35'N 51°25'E.

Odell, village and parish (pop. 226), NW Bedford, England, on Ouse R. and 7 mi. NW of Bedford; leatherworks. Has 15th-cent. church.

Odell (ōdĕl'). **1** Village (pop. 908), Livingston co., NE central Ill., 10 mi. NNE of Pontiac, in agr. and bituminous-coal area; mfg. of clothing. **2** Village (pop. 420), Gage co., SE Nebr., 15 mi. S of Beatrice and on branch of Big Blue R., near Kansas line; grain, livestock, dairy and poultry produce. **3** Town (pop. 238), Wilbarger co., N Texas, 15 mi. NNW of Vernon, near Red R. (Okla. line), in agr. area.

Odem (ō'dŭm), city (pop. 1,680), San Patricio co., S Texas, 15 mi. NW of Corpus Christi, near Nueces R.; trade, shipping point in farm area. Inc. as city 1929.

Odemira (ōōdĭmē'rú), town (pop. 2,231), Beja dist., S Portugal, river port on the Mira, 12 mi. from its mouth, on railroad and 52 mi. SW of Beja; cork-producing center; grain milling.

Odemis (ûdĕmĭsh'), Turkish *Ödemiş*, town (1950 pop. 22,662), Smyrna prov., W Turkey, rail terminus 45 mi. ESE of Smyrna; emery, mercury, antimony, arsenic, iron; olives, figs, valonia, tobacco, barley, potatoes.

Oden (ō'dún). **1** Town (pop. 133), Montgomery co., W Ark., c.40 mi. WNW of Hot Springs. **2** Resort village, Emmet co., NW Mich., on Crooked L. and 6 mi. NE of Petoskey; has large state fish hatchery.

Odenbüll, Germany: see NORDSTRAND.

Ödenburg, Hungary: see SOPRON, city.

Odendaalsrust (ō"dündälsrûst'), town (pop. 1,097), W Orange Free State, U. of So. Afr., 35 mi. WSW of Kroonstad, 90 mi. NNE of Bloemfontein; alt. 4,420 ft.; center of gold field discovered 1946. Airfield.

Odenheim (ō'dúnhīm), village (pop. 3,048), N Baden, Germany, after 1945 in Württemberg-Baden, 8 mi. NE of Bruchsal; mfg. of cigars and cigarettes.

Odenkirchen (ō'dŭnkĭr"khŭn), S suburb of Rheydt, W Germany, on the Niers. Inc. 1929 with München Gladbach and Rheydt to form Gladbach-Rheydt. Since 1933, part of RHEYDT.

Odenpäh, Estonia: see OTEPAA.

Odense (ō'dŭnsĕ), amt (□ 699; 1950 pop. 245,864), Denmark, largely on N Fyn isl.; includes BAAGO, FAENO isls. in the Little Belt, several smaller isls.; ⊙ Odense. Divided into Odense (E) and Assens (W) dists. Other cities: Middelfart, Assens. Grain, dairy, sugar-beet farming. Drained by Odense R.

Odense, city (1950 pop. 100,940), 3d largest city of Denmark, ⊙ Odense amt, port on N Fyn isl. and Odense R. and 85 mi. WSW of Copenhagen; 55°23'N 10°24'E. Important commercial and industrial center; mfg. (machinery, rubber, tobacco, textiles, sugar, glass); iron foundries; shipyard; meat and fish canning. Has 14th-cent. cathedral, 12th-cent. church. Birthplace of Hans Christian Andersen. City dates from 10th cent.

Odense Fjord (c.10 mi. long), inlet of the Kattegat, N Fyn isl., Denmark; connects with Odense through Odense R. and Odense Canal.

Odense River, largest on Fyn isl., Denmark; rises in Arreskov L.; flows c.40 mi. N, past Odense, to Odense Fjord.

Odenthal (ō'dŭntäl), village (pop. 6,148), in former Prussian Rhine Prov., W Germany, after 1945 in North Rhine-Westphalia, 3.5 mi. S of Burscheid.

Odenton (ō'dŭntŭn), village (pop. 1,059), Anne Arundel co., central Md., 14 mi. WNW of Annapolis, in truck-farm area; plastics plant. Fort George G. Meade is just NW.

Odenville, town (pop. 302), St. Clair co., NE central Ala., 30 mi. NE of Birmingham.

Odenwald (ō'dŭnvält), hills in W Germany, bet. the Neckar (S), the Tauber (E), the Main (N), and the Rhine plain (W); rise to 2,054 ft. in the Katzenbuckel. Fruit and wine grown on the Bergstrasse (W slope). Chief town: Michelstadt. Red porphyry quarried at Dossenheim (W foot).

Oder, river, Germany and Poland: see ODER RIVER.

Öderan, Germany: see OEDERAN.

Oderberg, Czechoslovakia: see NOVY BOHUMIN.

Oderberg or **Oderberg in der Mark** (ō'dŭrbĕrk ĭn dĕr märk'), town (pop. 3,768), Brandenburg, E Germany, on Hohenzollern Canal, at NE edge of Oder Marshes, 10 mi. E of Eberswalde; lumbering; sugar-beet market; tile mfg. Has remains of 12th-cent. castle. Was a center of lumber trade with Russia and Poland.

Oderbruch, East Germany: see ODER MARSHES.

Oder-Danube Canal, Poland and Czechoslovakia: see DANUBE-ODER CANAL.

Ode Remo, Nigeria: see ODE.

Oderfurt, Czechoslovakia: see OSTRAVA.

Odergebirge, Czechoslovakia: see ODER MOUNTAINS.

Oderin Island (ōdĕr'ĭn,-dĕ'rĭn) (pop. 221; 2 mi. long), SE N.F., in Placentia Bay, 40 mi. W of Argentia; 47°18'N 54°49'W. Fishing.

Oder Marshes (ō'dŭr), Ger. *Oderbruch* (ō'dŭrbrŏŏkh), Pol. *Bagna Odry* (bäg'nä ō'drĭ), in E Germany, extend c.30 mi. N–S along W bank of the lower Oder, bet. Küstrin (Kostrzyn) and Oderberg. The old Oder, Ger. *Alte Oder* (äl'tŭ ō'dŭr), Pol. *Odrzyca* (ôjĭ'tsä) arm of the river runs along W edge to Hohenzollern Canal. The marshes were drained by Frederick the Great.

Oder Mountains, Czech *Oderské Vrchy* (ô'dĕrskā vŭr'khĭ), Ger. *Odergebirge* (ō'dŭrgŭbĭr"gĕ), easternmost range of the Sudetes, N central Moravia, Czechoslovakia; extend c.30 mi. W–E, bet. Olomouc and Odry. Highest point (2,234 ft. is 10 mi. E of Olomouc. Oder R. rises in S.

Oder River (ō'dŭr), Czech and Pol. *Odra* (ô'drä), one of the chief rivers (563 mi. long) of central Europe and 2d-longest river of Poland, rises in Czechoslovakia in Oder Mts., 10 mi. ENE of Olomouc; flows generally NE, through Moravian Gate, along W outskirts of Ostrawa past Novy Bohumin into Poland, thence generally NW past Ratibor (Raciborz), KOZLE (head of navigation), Oppeln (Opole), Brieg (Brzeg), Breslau (Wroclaw), Scinawa, Glogav (Glogow), and Nowa Sol, W past Krosno Odrzanskie, and N past Frankfurt and Küstrin (Kostrzyn), here entering Oder Marshes and paralleled (W) by the Old Oder arm. At N end of marshes river enters estuarial section, splitting into 2 arms, the East Oder or Reglitz and the West Oder (Berlin-Stettin Canal); both arms flow N, past Gartz and Gryfino, to Stettin, here entering Damm L. and rejoining just SE of Police; the canalized Oder drains into Stettin Lagoon 15 mi. N of Stettin; lagoon empties into the Baltic via Peene, Swine, and Dievenow rivers. River is navigable for ocean-going vessels below Stettin, especially via the Swine. Above Stettin (navigable for ships up to 700 tons), it is connected with the Havel by Berlin-Stettin Canal, with the Spree by Oder-Spree Canal, and with the Vistula via Warta (Warthe) and Notec rivers, Bydgoszcz Canal, and Brda R. From Warta R. mouth at Küstrin (Kostrzyn) to Breslau (Wroclaw) canalization has been done since Second World War. Bet. Breslau and Kozle, river is canalized by locks; water level is maintained by reservoirs on its tributaries (as on the Glatzer Neisse at Otmuchow). At Kozle, where construction of N end of DANUBE-ODER CANAL was begun c.1950, the Oder is also linked via Gleiwitz (Gliwice) Canal with Upper Silesian industrial region around Katowice. Barges carry chiefly iron upstream, coal and coke downstream. River shipyards at Stettin, Breslau, Oppeln, and Kozle. Main tributaries are (right) Olza, Klodnica (Klodnitz), Baryz (Bartsch), Warta (Warthe), and Ihna (Ina) rivers and (left) Glatzer Neisse (Nysa Klodzka), Olawa (Ohle), Katzbach, Bobrawa (Bober), and Lusatian Neisse (Nysa Luzycka) rivers. Bet. mouth of the Lusatian Neisse and Gryfino the Oder forms N part of the Oder-Neisse Line, provisional border bet. Poland and E. Germany as determined in 1945 by the Potsdam Conference. Bet. First and Second World Wars, part of the Oder was internationalized under Treaty of Versailles.

Oderske Vrchy, Czechoslovakia: see ODER MOUNTAINS.

Oder-Spree Canal (ō'dŭr-shprā'), E Germany, extends 57 mi. E–W bet. the Oder at Fürstenberg and Seddin L., whence it is connected via Dahme R. with the Spree at Köpenick; 7 locks; navigable for ships up to 600 tons. Utilizes 13-mi.-long section of Spree R. near Fürstenwalde. Opened 1892, it inc. greater part of the Friedrich-Wilhelm Canal (built 1662–68 by Elector Frederick William), which leaves the Oder 5 mi. S of Frankfurt. Sometimes called Spree-Oder Canal.

Oderzo (ôdĕr'tsô), anc. *Opitergium,* town (pop. 3,995), Treviso prov., Veneto, N Italy, 15 mi. ENE of Treviso, bet. Piave and Livenza rivers, in silk- and tobacco-growing region; alcohol distillery, bicycle factory, lime- and cementworks. Has church dating partly from 10th cent.

Odeshog (û'dŭs-hûg"), Swedish *Ödeshög,* village (pop. 1,566), Ostergotland co., S Sweden, near W shore of L. Vatter, 18 mi. WSW of Mjolby; foundry; woodworking.

Odessa (ōdĕ'sŭ). **1** Village (pop. estimate 600), SE Ont., 12 mi. WNW of Kingston; woolen milling, cheese making. **2** Village (pop. 209), S Sask., 40 mi. ESE of Regina; wheat, dairying.

Odessa (ōdĕ'sŭ, Rus. ŭdyĕ'sŭ), oblast (□ 10,800; 1946 pop. estimate 1,800,000), S Ukrainian SSR; ⊙ Odessa. In Black Sea Lowland, rising (N) to Volyn-Podolian Upland; bounded S by Black Sea, W by Moldavian SSR; drained by the Southern Bug (N) and numerous intermittent streams. Agr. steppe region with sugar beets (extreme N), wheat and sunflowers (center), cotton (S), truck produce (near Odessa); lesser crops include corn and fruit (W), castor beans. Chief industrial center and port is Odessa; mfg. also at Pervomaisk, Balta, Kotovsk, Ananyev. Sugar refining, flour milling, dairying, wine making. Formed 1932.

Odessa, city (1939 pop. 604,223), ⊙ Odessa oblast, Ukrainian SSR, port on Odessa Gulf of Black Sea, 275 mi. S of Kiev; 46°29'N 30°45'E. One of chief ports of USSR; industrial and cultural center; sea and rail transfer point bet. mouths of Dnieper and Dniester rivers. Machine mfg. (agr. implements, lathes, cranes, transportation, printing, food-processing, and grain-elevator equipment); automobile assembly; petroleum refining (Caucasus oil), agr. processing (flour, sugar, fruit, hides, sacks and ropes); also produces superphosphate, iodine, linoleum, steel cables, shoes, garments. A major educational center, with state univ., polytechnical, agr., medical, and teachers colleges, maritime acad., conservatory, and numerous trade schools (marine engineering, communications, meteorology, food canning, flour milling, building trades). Has museums devoted to 1941 defense of city and to revolutionary movement, art, industry, and archaeology. In picturesque location on slope of hill, descending in terraces (including notable stairway) to the sea, city is laid out on rectangular, tree-lined pattern. Industrial suburbs include Peresyp (N), Krasnaya Slobodka (formerly Slobodka-Romanovka; NW), and Bugayevka (W). Port (including several harbors, extensive docks, and warehouses) exports grain, lumber, sugar; imports petroleum, coal, iron, cotton. Along the sea (N and S of city) are famous health resorts with mineral and mud baths (Luzanovka, Khadzhibei Liman, Kugalnik Liman, Arkadiya, Fontan). Site of city was 1st occupied by Gr. colony (Odessos or Ordyssos); later replaced by Turkish village Khadzhi-Bei, which belonged successively to Lithuanians (15th cent.), Tatars, and Turks (16th cent.). After Russian annexation (Treaty of Jassy, 1792), port and naval base were built and city named Odessa (1795). Became free port (1822–59); grew rapidly as chief Russian grain-exporting center. Revolt of 1905 and mutiny on battleship *Potemkin* led to severe pogroms and heavy emigration (pop. was 35% Jewish). During civil war, repeatedly occupied (1918–20) by foreign troops. In Second World War, Odessa fell (Oct., 1941) to German and Rumanian troops following 2-month siege; many bldgs. were damaged or destroyed, and 280,000 civilians, mostly Jews, are said to have been massacred or deported during Axis occupation. Placed under Rumanian administration and ⊙ Transnistria until taken (1943) by Russians.

Odessa. 1 Town (pop. 467), New Castle co., N central Del., 20 mi. S of Wilmington, in agr. region. Has 18th-cent. homes; Friends meetinghouse dates from 1783. **2** Village (pop. 283), Big Stone co., SW Minn., on Minnesota R., near S.Dak. line, and 7 mi. ESE of Ortonville, in grain area. **3** City (pop. 1,969), Lafayette co., W central Mo., near Missouri R., 33 mi. E of Kansas City; processes and ships farm products. Platted 1878. **4.** Resort village (pop. 526), Schuyler co., W central N.Y., in Finger Lakes region, 15 mi. WSW of Ithaca. **5** City (pop. 29,495), ⊙ Ector co., W Texas, 115 mi. WNW of San Angelo. An important oil center, with great oil fields (S), a huge carbon-black plant, refineries, and plants producing oil-field equipment, chemicals, foundry products. Ships livestock. Seat of a jr. col. Airport (NE) handles transcontinental traffic. Huge meteor crater is c.8 mi. S. Founded 1881, inc. 1927. **6** Town (pop. 1,127), Lincoln co., E Wash., 32 mi. SW of Davenport, in Columbia basin agr. region; ships wheat, cattle.

Odessadale, town (pop. 55), Meriwether co., W Ga., 12 mi. ESE of La Grange.

Odesskoye (ŭdyĕ'skŭyŭ), village (1926 pop. 1,327), S Omsk oblast, Russian SFSR, near Kazakh SSR border, 55 mi. S of Omsk, in agr. area.

Odet River (ôdā'), Finistère dept., W France, rises in Montagnes Noires 5 mi. SE of Châteauneuf-du-Faou, flows 35 mi. SW and S, past Quimper (head of navigation), through a drowned valley to the Atlantic 5 mi. E of Pont l'Abbé.

Odeypore, India: see UDAIPUR, former princely state, city, Rajasthan.

Odia Island, Marshall Isls.: see AILINGLAPALAP.

Odiel River (ō-dhyĕl'), Huelva prov., SW Spain, rises in the Sierra Morena 4 mi. ESE of Aracena, flows c.90 mi. SW and S in wide estuary to the Atlantic. Joined by the Río Tinto 3 mi. S of Huelva. Only the estuary is navigable.

Odienné (ōdyĕ'nā), town, (pop. c.6,500), NW Ivory Coast, Fr. West Africa, road junction and market 130 mi. ESE of Kankan, communicating with Fr. Guinea and Fr. Sudan. Climatological and medical station.

Odiham (ō'dēŭm), town and parish (pop. 2,647), NE Hampshire, England, 7 mi. E of Basingstoke; agr. market. Has 13th-cent. church. Near by is Odiham Castle, with 12th-cent. keep. David II of Scotland was imprisoned here after battle of Neville's Cross (1346).

Odilienberg, France: see SAINTE-ODILE, MONT.

Odin (ō'dĭn). **1** Village (pop. 1,341), Marion co., S central Ill., 7 mi. NNE of Centralia, in agr., bituminous-coal, and oil-producing area. Inc. 1865. **2** Village (pop. 208), Watonwan co., S Minn., on fork of Watonwan R. and 10 mi. SW of St. James; dairy products.

Odin, Mount (9,751 ft.), SE B.C., in Monashee Mts., 30 mi. S of Revelstoke; 50°33'N 118°8'W.

Odinkovka (ŭdyĭnkôf'kŭ), E suburb (1939 pop. over 2,000) of Dnepropetrovsk, Dnepropetrovsk oblast, Ukrainian SSR, near Samara R., 7 mi. ENE of city center and on left bank of the Dnieper.

Odintsovo (ŭdyĭntsô'vŭ), town (1939 pop. over 10,000), central Moscow oblast, Russian SFSR, 14 mi. WSW of Moscow; brickworks.

Odioñgan (ōdyō'nyŭgän), town (1939 pop. 1,631; 1948 municipality pop. 18,401), Romblon prov., Philippines, on W Tablas Isl., on Tablas Strait; agr. center (rice, coconuts).

Odiorne's Point (ō'dēôrnz), SE N.H., small peninsula near mouth of the Piscataqua, bet. Portsmouth and Rye; site of state's 1st settlement (1623).

Odoben (ōdōbĕn'), town, Western Prov., S Gold Coast colony; 5 mi. W of Nyakrom; cacao, palm oil and kernels, cassava.

Odobesti (ôdôbĕsht'), Rum. *Odobeşti,* town (1948 pop. 4,482), Putna prov., E Rumania, on railroad and 7 mi. NW of Focsani; wine center, with school of viticulture. Has 18th-cent. church.

Odolanow (ôdôlä'nŏŏf), Pol. *Odolanów,* Ger. *Adelnau* (ä'dŭlnou), town (1946 pop. 2,339), Poznan prov., W Poland, on Barycz R. and 22 mi. SW of Kalisz; flour milling, sawmilling.

Odomez (ōdŭmĕz'), village (pop. 637), Nord dept., N France, on Escaut R., 7 mi. N of Valenciennes; rayon mfg.

Odon (ō'dŭn), town (pop. 1,177), Daviess co., SW Ind., 31 mi. ENE of Vincennes, in agr. area; mfg. of dairy products, monuments, brick, tile; lumber and flour milling.

O'Donnell, city (pop. 1,473), Lynn and Dawson counties, NW Texas, on the Llano Estacado 45 mi. S of Lubbock; shipping point for agr. area (grain, cotton, livestock); chemical plant processes local sodium sulphate, magnesium sulphate. Settled 1916, inc. 1923.

Odon River (ōdō'), Calvados dept., NW France, rises in Normandy Hills above Aunay-sur-Odon, flows 25 mi. NE to the Orne at Caen. Heavy fighting along its banks, 1944, in Second World War (Normandy campaign).

Odorhei (ôdôrhā'), Hung. *Székelyudvarhely* (sā'kĕ-ŏŏdvōr"hŏ), town (1948 pop. 10,366), Stalin prov., central Rumania, in Transylvania, on railroad and

100 mi. NNW of Bucharest; distilling, brewing, tanning, mfg. of bricks and tiles; trade in lumber and livestock. Has ruins of Roman and medieval citadels, 17th-cent. Franciscan monastery and R.C. church. Mineral springs near by (SW). Over 90% pop. are Magyars. In Hungary, 1940–45.

Odoyevo (ŭdoi'ŭvŭ), village (1926 pop. 3,583), W Tula oblast, Russian SFSR, on Upa R. and 40 mi. SW of Tula; flour milling, fruit canning.

Odrabash (ŭdrŭbäsh'), village (1945 pop. over 500), SW Kemerovo oblast, Russian SFSR, near Mundybash; iron mining.

Odra Port (ô'drä pôrt') or **Odra-Warszow** (–vär'shōōf), Pol. *Odra-Warszów*, Ger. *Ostswine* (ôst'svē'nŭ), village in Pomerania, after 1945 in Szczecin prov., NW Poland, at W end of Wolin isl., on Swine mouth of the Oder, opposite Swinemünde, and 35 mi. NNW of Stettin; fishing port. Terminus since 1948 of train ferry across Baltic Sea to Trelleborg, Sweden.

Odra River, central Europe: see ODER RIVER.

Odra River, N Croatia, Yugoslavia, formed by several headstreams joining 13 mi. SE of Zagreb; flows c.25 mi. SE to Kupa R. just NW of Sisak.

Odrau, Czechoslovakia: see ODRY.

Odra-Warszow, Poland: see ODRA PORT.

Odra Zachodnia River, Poland: see WEST ODER RIVER.

Odrin, Turkey: see ADRIANOPLE, city.

Odry (ô'drĭ), Ger. *Odrau* (ôd'rou), town (pop. 3,183), S central Silesia, Czechoslovakia, on railroad, on Oder R. and 26 mi. ENE of Olomouc, in oat-growing area.

Odrzyca River, Poland: see ODER MARSHES.

Ödt, Germany: see OEDT.

Odum (ō'dŭm), town (pop. 389), Wayne co., SE Ga., 10 mi. NW of Jesup, in agr. area.

Odweina (ŏdwā'nä), village, central Br. Somaliland, in Ogo highland, on road and 35 mi. WSW of Burao; camels, sheep, goats. Formerly spelled Oadweina.

Odzaci or **Odzhatsi** (both: ô'jätsĭ), Serbo-Croatian *Odžaci*, Hung. *Hódság* (hōd'shäg), village (pop. 6,477), Vojvodina, NW Serbia, Yugoslavia, 31 mi. NW of Novi Sad, in the Backa; rail-junction; hemp processing.

Odzak or **Odzhak** (both: ô'jäk), Serbo-Croatian *Odžak*, village (pop. 3,792), N Bosnia, Yugoslavia, on Bosna R. and 8 mi. WSW of Samac.

Odzhak; Odzhatsi, Yugoslavia: see ODZAK; ODZACI.

Odzi (ŏd'zē), village (pop. 145), Umtali prov., E Southern Rhodesia, in Mashonaland, on Odzi R. (left affluent of Sabi R.), on railroad and 20 mi. W of Umtali. Gold, copper, lead, tin, and tungsten mining.

Oea, Tripolitania: see TRIPOLI, city.

Oebisfelde (û'bĭsfĕl"dŭ), town (pop. 6,968), in former Prussian Saxony prov., central Germany, after 1945 in Saxony-Anhalt, on the Aller and 20 mi. NW of Haldensleben, 6 mi. E of Vorsfelde; agr. market (grain, sugar beets, vegetables, livestock); food canning. Until 1938 called Oebisfelde-Kaltendorf. Sometimes spelled Öbisfelde.

Oebroeg, Indonesia: see UBRUG.

Oe-Cusse (ōkōō'sē) or **Ambeno** (ämbĕ'nō), Portuguese enclave (□ 310; pop. 16,281) in Indonesian section of TIMOR, on N coast of isl., on Savu Sea; 9°17'S 124°19'E; 31 mi. E-W, 19 mi. N-S. Has sandalwood forests and coconut groves. Rice growing. Its port and chief center is PANTE MACASSAR. Sometimes spelled Ocussi and Okusi.

Oedanes, river, S Asia: see BRAHMAPUTRA RIVER.

Oedelem (û'dŭlŭm), agr. village (pop. 4,986), West Flanders prov., NW Belgium, 6 mi. ESE of Bruges; brick mfg.

Oederan (û'dŭrän), town (pop. 7,774), Saxony, E central Germany, in the Erzgebirge, 11 mi. E of Chemnitz; produces textiles (hosiery, cotton, wool, carpets), machinery, precision instruments, electrical equipment. Sometimes spelled Öderan.

Oedjoeng, Indonesia: see SURABAYA.

Oedjoengbatoe, Indonesia: see BANYAK ISLANDS.

Oedt (ût), village (pop. 5,358), in former Prussian Rhine Prov., W Germany, after 1945 in North Rhine-Westphalia, on the Niers and 3 mi. SW of Kempen; cattle. Sometimes spelled Ödt.

Oehringen, Germany: see ÖHRINGEN.

Oeiras (wā'rŭsh). **1** City, Pará, Brazil: see ARATICU. **2** City (pop. 3,038), central Piauí, Brazil, near Canindé R., 140 mi. SSE of Teresina; road junction and cattle-raising center; ships carnauba wax, cotton. Airfield. Was ⊙ Piauí prov. until 1852.

Oeiras, town (pop. 4,011), Lisboa dist., W central Portugal, on N shore of Tagus estuary at its influx into the Atlantic, 9 mi. W of Lisbon; fishing port and bathing resort; mfg. (paper, biscuits). Has dismantled fort.

Oel (ō'äl), town (pop. 4,644), Kheri dist., N Uttar Pradesh, India, 8 mi. SSW of Lakhimpur; sugar milling; rice, wheat, gram, corn, oilseeds.

Oelde (ûl'dŭ), town (pop. 10,269), in former Prussian prov. of Westphalia, NW Germany, after 1945 in North Rhine-Westphalia, 11 mi. ENE of Ahlen; dairying, hog raising; pumpernickel.

Oeleëlheuë, Indonesia: see ULE-LUE.

Oeliaser Islands, Indonesia: see ULIASER ISLANDS.

Oella (ōĕ'lŭ), suburban village (pop. c.750), Baltimore co., central Md., on Patapsco R. and 10 mi. W of downtown Baltimore; large woolen mill, established c.1845. Patapsco State Park is near.

Oelrichs (ōl'rĭks), town (pop. 168), Fall River co., SW S.Dak., 20 mi. SE of Hot Springs and on Horsehead Creek.

Oels, Poland: see OLESNICA.

Oelsburg (ûls'bōōrk), village (pop. 1,884), in former Prussian prov. of Hanover, NW Germany, after 1945 in Lower Saxony, 3.5 mi. S of Peine; oil wells. In Brunswick exclave until 1941.

Oël Sina Point, Timor: see OISINA POINT.

Oelsnitz or **Ölsnitz** (ûl'snĭts). **1** Town (pop. 20,034), Saxony, E central Germany, at N foot of the Erzgebirge, 9 mi. E of Zwickau; coal-mining center. Power station. **2** Town (pop. 16,024), Saxony, E central Germany, at N foot of the Erzgebirge, on the White Elster and 6 mi. SSE of Plauen, in the Vogtland; textile milling (cotton, wool, lace, furnishing fabrics, carpets, clothing); mfg. of machinery, leather. River-pearl fisheries. Has 13th-cent. church. Town largely destroyed by fire in 1859.

Oelwein (ōl'wīn), city (pop. 7,858), Fayette co., NE Iowa, 25 mi. ENE of Waterloo; rail center, with repair shops; poultry-packing plant; feed, wood products, beverages. Inc. 1888.

Oembilin, Indonesia: see OMBILIN.

Oenaoena, Indonesia: see TOGIAN ISLANDS.

Oene (ōō'nŭ), village (pop. 291), Gelderland prov., E central Netherlands, 10 mi. NNE of Apeldoorn; wooden-shoe mfg.

Oengar, Indonesia: see KARIMUN ISLANDS.

Oengaran, Indonesia: see UNGARAN.

Oeno Island: see PITCAIRN ISLAND.

Oensingen (ûn'zĭng-ŭn), town (pop. 2,176), Solothurn canton, N Switzerland, 10 mi. ENE of Solothurn.

Oenussae Islands, Greece: see OINOUSAI ISLANDS.

Oer-Erkenschwick (ûr'-ĕr'kŭn-shvĭk), village (pop. 16,931), in former Prussian prov. of Westphalia, W Germany, after 1945 in North Rhine-Westphalia, in the Ruhr, 3 mi. NE of Recklinghausen; truck produce.

Oerle, Belgium: see OREYE.

Oerlikon (ûr'lĭkôn), suburb of Zurich, N Switzerland; noted for its production of firearms. Absorbed by Zurich 1934.

Oerlinghausen (ûr"lĭng-hou'zŭn), town (pop. 4,515), in former Lippe, NW Germany, after 1945 in North Rhine-Westphalia, in Teutoburg Forest, 9 mi. WNW of Detmold; woodworking. Sometimes spelled Örlinghausen.

Oescus River, Bulgaria: see ISKAR RIVER.

Oesede or **Ösede** (both: û'zŭdŭ), village (pop. 6,153), in former Prussian prov. of Hanover, NW Germany, after 1945 in Lower Saxony, on N slope of Teutoburg Forest, 6 mi. SSE of Osnabrück; forestry.

Oestringen, Germany: see HEIDMÜHLE.

Oeta (ē'tŭ), Gr. *Oite* or *Oiti* (both: ē'tē), mountain massif in E central Greece, on Phthiotis-Phocis border, rises to 7,063 ft. 12 mi. SW of Lamia. Bauxite deposits. In legend, Hercules died here on a pyre after being poisoned by Nessus' robe.

Oetling (wĕt'lĭng), town (pop. estimate 500), S Chaco natl. territory, Argentina, 50 mi. SSE of Presidencia Roque Sáenz Peña; rail terminus; agr. center (corn, cotton, livestock).

Oetrange (ûtrãzh'), village (pop. 281), SE Luxembourg, on Syre R. and 6 mi. E of Luxembourg city; plums, cherries.

Oettingen, Germany: see ÖTTINGEN.

Oetz, Austria: see ÖTZ.

Oever, Den, Netherlands: see DEN OEVER.

Oeynhausen, Bad, Germany: see BAD OEYNHAUSEN.

Of (ôf), village (pop. 1,227), Trebizond prov., NE Turkey, on Black Sea 28 mi. E of Trebizond; corn, beans, vetch.

O'Fallon. 1 City (pop. 3,022), St. Clair co., SW Ill., 12 mi. E of East St. Louis, in bituminous-coal and agr. area (corn, wheat, livestock); flour mill, stove factory. Inc. 1865. Scott Air Force Base is near by. **2** City (pop. 789), St. Charles co., E Mo., 25 mi. WNW of St. Louis; R.C. convent.

O'Fallon Creek, SE Mont., rises in NW Carter co., flows c.90 mi. N, past Ismay, to Yellowstone R. near Terry.

Ofanto River (ôfän'tô), anc. *Aufidus*, S Italy, rises in the Apennines near Torella de' Lombardi, flows E, N, and NE to Adriatic Sea 4 mi. NW of Barletta; 83 mi. long. Southernmost river on E coast; below it are only a few small streams. Forms boundary bet. Campania, Basilicata, and Apulia regions in upper course, bet. Bari and Foggia provs. in lower course.

Ofen, Hungary: see BUDAPEST.

Ofena (ôfā'nä), village (pop. 2,025), Aquila prov., Abruzzi e Molise, S central Italy, near Gran Sasso d'Italia, 19 mi. E of Aquila; ironworking.

Ofen Pass (ō'fŭn) (7,070 ft.), in the Rhaetian Alps, E Switzerland, 11 mi. S of Schuls; Ofen Pass Road leads from Lower Engadine through Swiss Natl. Park and the Münstertal into Italy.

Offa (ôfä'), town (pop. 13,649), Ilorin prov., Northern Provinces, SW Nigeria, on railroad and 25 mi. SSE of Ilorin; agr. trade center; shea-nut processing, cotton weaving; cassava, yams, corn; cattle.

Offa, Wales: see WREXHAM.

Offaly (ŏ'fŭlē), Gaelic *Ua bhFailghe*, formerly Co. King's, county (□ 771.2; pop. 53,686), Leinster, central Ireland; ⊙ Tullamore. Bounded by cos. Laoighis (S), Tipperary (SW and W), Galway and Roscommon (NW), Westmeath (N), Meath (NE), and Kildare (E). Drained by Shannon, Barrow, Nore, and Brosna rivers. Co. is served by Grand Canal. Surface is generally level, partly boggy (Bog of Allen covers NE part of co.), and rises to Slieve Bloom mts. in SW. Peat is produced extensively. Cattle raising and growing of hops, barley, and potatoes chief occupations. Industries include malting, woolen and jute milling, alcohol distilling, mfg. of shoes, rope, fish nets. Besides Tullamore, other towns are Birr (formerly Parsonstown), Portarlington, Daingean (formerly Philipstown), Banagher, Clara, and Edenderry. There are several Danish raths; Clonmacnoise is important religious center, site of the Seven Churches; and Durrow has anc. abbey.

Offanengo (ôf-fänĕng'gô), village (pop. 2,836), Cremona prov., Lombardy, N Italy, near Serio R., 3 mi. NE of Crema.

Offa's Dyke (ŏ'fŭ), ancient intrenchment bet. England and Wales, extending from mouth of Dee R. S to Severn R. just SE of Chepstow. Built in 8th cent. by Offa, king of Mercia; parts are well preserved. Paralleled, 2 mi. away, by Watt's Dyke.

Offenbach or **Offenbach am Main** (ô'fŭnbäkh äm mīn'), city (1946 pop. 60,528, including suburbs 75,479; 1950 pop. 88,528), S Hesse, W Germany, on left bank of the canalized Main, just E of Frankfurt; 50°6'N 8°45'E. Mfg. center with noted leather industry (luggage, handbags, shoes; tanning); other products: machinery, chemicals. Metalworking, printing. Renaissance castle was damaged in Second World War. An anc. settlement, Offenbach was residence of Isenburg family from mid-16th cent. until annexed to Hesse in 1816. Grew rapidly in late-19th and early-20th cent.; proximity of metropolitan Frankfurt arrested further development after First World War.

Offenburg (ô'fŭnbōōrk), town (pop. 19,574), S Baden, Germany, at W foot of Black Forest, on the Kinzig and 32 mi. N of Freiburg; rail junction; mfg. of machinery, textiles, rubber, tobacco; metal-, leather-, and woodworking; paper milling. Glassworks. Market center for truck-farming (fruit, vegetables) and winegrowing region. Has remnants of old fortifications; 18th-cent. town hall. Created free imperial city in 1289. Destroyed by French in 1689.

Offerle (ô'fŭrlē), city (pop. 269), Edwards co., S central Kansas, 27 mi. ENE of Dodge City, in wheat region.

Officer River, N South Australia, rises in SE Musgrave Ranges, flows 100 mi. S and SE, disappearing in arid central area; usually dry.

Offida (ôf-fē'dä), town (pop. 2,592), Ascoli Piceno prov., The Marches, central Italy, 8 mi. NE of Ascoli Piceno; woolen mill. Has 14th-cent. church.

Offleben (ôf'lā"bŭn), village (pop. 2,594), in Brunswick, NW Germany, after 1945 in Lower Saxony, 6 mi. SSE of Helmstedt, opposite Völpke, in lignite region; sugar refining.

Offranville (ôfrãvēl'), village (pop. 1,429), Seine-Inférieure dept., N France, 4 mi. SSW of Dieppe; metalware, flour.

Offutt Air Force Base, Nebr.: see OMAHA.

Oficina, oil field, Venezuela: see EL TIGRE.

Ofidousa, Ofidusa, Greece: see OPHIDOUSA.

Ofin River (ōfēn'), S Gold Coast, rises in Ashanti 20 mi. NW of Mampong, flows 150 mi. SW, S, and E, past Dunkwa, to Pra R. 20 mi. ESE of Dunkwa. Logging in wet season to Dunkwa lumber mill.

Ofot Fjord (ō'fôt), inlet (45 mi. long, 3–6 mi. wide) of Vest Fjord, Nordland co., N Norway, opposite Lofoten and Vesteralen isls. Narvik is near its head. In Second World War, the fjord and its E arm, Rombakken Fjord, were scene (April-June, 1940) of repeated naval action for control of Narvik. Surrounding region called Ofoten.

Oftersheim (ôf'tŭrs-hīm), village (pop. 5,010), N Baden, Germany, after 1945 in Württemberg-Baden, 1.5 mi. SSE of Schwetzingen; asparagus, hops, tobacco.

Oftringen (ôf'trĭng'ŭn), town (pop. 4,837), Aargau canton, N Switzerland, 2 mi. SSE of Olten; paper, watches.

Ofu (ō'fōō), island and county (pop. 575), MANUA dist., American Samoa, S Pacific, c.60 mi. from Tutuila; rises to c.1,585 ft.; thick vegetation.

Ofuna (ō'fōōnä), town (pop. 20,989), Kanagawa prefecture, central Honshu, Japan, just SW of Yokohama, in agr. area (rice, wheat); meat processing.

Ofunato (ō'fōōnätō), town (pop. 7,237), Iwate prefecture, N Honshu, Japan, on the Pacific, 17 mi. SW of Kamaishi; fishing, agr.; cement making.

Ogaden (ōgä'dĕn), region in Harar prov., SE Ethiopia, bounded by Br. Somaliland (E), Ital. Somaliland (S), and the Webi Shebeli (SW and W). An arid plateau (1,500–3,000 ft. high), intermittently watered by Fafan and Jerer rivers. Inhabited by the Somali, a Moslem people engaged in nomadic grazing (camels, sheep, goats). Chief villages: Gabredarre, Daghabur, Sassabaneh, Wardere, and Wal Wal (where an incident in 1934 precipitated

Italo-Ethiopian War). Acquired by Ethiopia 1891. Incorporated 1936–48 into Ital. Somaliland; under Br. military administration 1941–48.

Ogago (ōgä′gō′), village (pop. 3,756) on Hachijo-jima, of isl. group Izu-shichito, Greater Tokyo, Japan, on W coast of isl.; sake brewing, condensed-milk canning.

Ogaki (ō′gäkē). **1** City (1940 pop. 56,117; 1947 pop. 63,830), Gifu prefecture, central Honshu, Japan, on Ibi R. and 22 mi. NW of Nagoya; mfg. (textiles, chemicals, metal products, fish nets). Has feudal castle. Bombed 1945 in Second World War. **2** Town (pop. 13,885) on Nomi-shima, Hiroshima prefecture, Japan, on S coast of isl.; fishing and agr. center; citrus fruit, livestock.

Ogallala (ō″gŭlä′lŭ), city (pop. 3,456), ⊙ Keith co., SW central Nebr., 50 mi. W of North Platte city and on S.Platte R.; electrical equipment; livestock, dairy and poultry produce, grain. Near by, on N.Platte R., are Kingsley Dam and L. McConaughy (Kingsley Reservoir). City laid out 1875, inc. 1930.

Ogano (ōgä′nō), town (pop. 6,094), Saitama prefecture, central Honshu, Japan, 6 mi. WNW of Chichibu; spinning; rice, wheat.

Oga Peninsula (ō′gä), Jap. *Oga-hanto*, Akita prefecture, N Honshu, Japan, in Sea of Japan; 13 mi. long, 8 mi. wide; mountainous, with rocky shores. At its base is lagoon Hachiro-gata; Funakawaminato is on S shore.

Ogarevka (ô′gŭryĭfkŭ), town (1939 pop. over 2,000), central Tula oblast, Russian SFSR, on rail spur and 21 mi. S of Tula; iron and lignite mining.

Ogasawara (ōgä″sä′wärŭ), town (pop. 8,129), Yamanashi prefecture, central Honshu, Japan, 7 mi. WSW of Kofu; rice, raw silk; woodworking, soy-sauce making.

Ogasawara-gunto: see BONIN ISLANDS.

Ogata (ō′gätä), town (pop. 11,786), Kochi prefecture, SW Shikoku, Japan, 26 mi. ESE of Uwajima; commercial center for agr. area (rice, melons, raw silk). Formed 1943 by combining former villages of Nanasato, Irino, and Tanokuchi.

Ogawa (ōgä′wä). **1** Town (pop. 6,835), Ibaraki prefecture, central Honshu, Japan, 5 mi. ESE of Ishioka; rice, soybeans, tobacco; silk cocoons, agr. implements. **2** Town (pop. 5,399), Kumamoto prefecture, W Kyushu, Japan, 15 mi. S of Kumamoto; produces tea; paper mill. **3** Town (pop. 10,664), Saitama prefecture, central Honshu, Japan, 9 mi. SW of Kumagaya; paper milling; rice, wheat, raw silk. **4** Town (pop. 8,538), Tochigi prefecture, central Honshu, Japan, 20 mi. NE of Utsunomiya; rice, tobacco.

Ogawara, Japan: see OKAWARA.

Ogawara-numa (ōgä′wärä-nōōmä), lagoon (□ 25), Aomori prefecture, N Honshu, Japan, 16 mi. NNW of Hachinohe, near E coast; 9 mi. long, 3 mi. wide; stream connects with the Pacific.

Ogbomosho (ōb-bō′mōshō), town (pop. 86,744), Oyo prov., Western Provinces, SW Nigeria, on road and 55 mi. NNE of Ibadan; cotton-weaving center; shea-nut processing; agr. (cotton, yams, cassava, corn, plantains). Has teachers col., American Baptist mission.

Ogburntown, village (pop. 3,653), Forsyth co., N central N.C., 3 mi. N of Winston-Salem.

Ogdem, Turkey: see YUSUFELI.

Ogden (ŏg′dŭn). **1** Town (pop. 296), Little River co., extreme SW Ark., 11 mi. N of Texarkana and on Red R. **2** Village (pop. 436), Champaign co., E Ill., 15 mi. E of Champaign, in agr. area; feed mill, poultry hatchery. **3** Town (pop. 1,486), Boone co., central Iowa, 7 mi. W of Boone, in bituminous-coal-mining and agr. area. Inc. 1878. **4** City (pop. 845), Riley co., NE central Kansas, on Kansas R. and 9 mi. SW of Manhattan; grazing, agr. **5** City (pop. 57,112), ⊙ Weber co., N Utah, on Weber R. at mouth of Ogden R. and 32 mi. N of Salt Lake City, just W of Wasatch Range, near Great Salt L.; 41°13′N 111°58′W; alt. 4,300 ft. Second largest city in state; intermountain railroad junction (chief station bet. Rockies and Pacific coast) and industrial and distribution center for irrigated agr. area. Ships livestock and has meat-packing plants, canneries, and creameries. Produces beet sugar, flour, candy; manufactures clothing, iron castings. Seat of Weber jr. col., state industrial school, state school for deaf and blind, and Mormon tabernacle; dist. hq. of U.S. Forest Service. Has livestock coliseum and city stadium. Near by are U.S. ordnance depot, Transportation Corps railroad shops, and Hill Air Force Base. Just E, in Wasatch Range, are Ogden Canyon (formed by Ogden R.; used as recreational area) and municipally developed ski center (Snow Basin), on E ridge of Ogden Peak (9,592 ft.). City first settled c.1845, colonized by Mormons after 1847, renamed from Brownsville 1850, inc. 1851. Growth stimulated by completion (1869) of transcontinental rail line through city.

Ogden, Mount (7,441 ft.), on Alaska-B.C. border, in Coast Range, 40 mi. ENE of Juneau; 58°26′N 133°23′W.

Ogden Dunes, town (pop. 429), Porter co., NW Ind., on L. Michigan, just E of Gary; residential suburb.

Ogden Island, St. Lawrence co., N N.Y., in the St. Lawrence (rapids here), at Ont. line, just N of Waddington, N.Y.; c.2¾ mi. long, ½–1½ mi. wide; connected to N.Y. shore by bridge.

Ogden Peak, Utah: see OGDEN.

Ogden River, formed by confluence of 2 forks in Wasatch Range, N Utah, flows c.35 mi. W to Weber R. at Ogden. Pine View Dam (103 ft. high, 480 ft. long; completed 1937), in Ogden Canyon, 7 mi. E of Ogden, is used for irrigation and power.

Ogdensburg. 1 Borough (pop. 1,169), Sussex co., NW N.J., on Wallkill R. and 3 mi. S of Franklin; cellulose products. Inc. 1914. **2** City (pop. 16,166), St. Lawrence co., N N.Y., port on the St. Lawrence, opposite Prescott, Ont. (ferry), at mouth of Oswegatchie R., 34 mi. SW of Massena; port of entry; trade center for agr. and timber area. Mfg.: paper, wood, and metal products; paint, mattresses, clothing, flour. Summer resort. Remington Art Memorial, with works of Frederic Remington and a collection of Indian relics, is here. Near by are St. Lawrence State Hosp. and a state fish hatchery. Settled 1749; inc. as village in 1817, as city in 1868. **3** Village (pop. 221), Waupaca co., central Wis., 7 mi. N of Waupaca, in farm area.

Ogeechee River (ōgē′chē), E Ga., rises E of Greensboro, flows c.250 mi. SE, past Louisville and Millen, to the Atlantic Ocean through Ossabaw Sound, (15 mi. S of Savannah.

Ogema (ō′gŭmä), village (pop. 249), Becker co., W Minn., in White Earth Indian Reservation, 20 mi. N of Detroit Lakes; dairy products.

Ogemaw (ō′gŭmô), county (□ 574; pop. 9,345), NE central Mich.; ⊙ West Branch. Drained by Au Gres and Rifle rivers. Agr. (livestock, poultry, potatoes, grain, fruit; dairy products); oil wells. Part of Huron Natl. Forest, and a state forest, game refuge, and many small lakes (fishing, hunting; resorts) are in co. Organized 1875.

Oger, Latvia: see OGRE.

Ogerlistye, Rumania: see RUDARIA.

Oge-shima (ōgā′shĭmä), island (□ 4; pop. c.7,000), Tokushima prefecture, Japan, just off NE coast of Shikoku, in Naruto Strait opposite SW coast of Awaji-shima; 3.5 mi. long, 2.5 mi. wide, with deeply indented W coast. Hilly, fertile. Produces salt, rice. Fishing.

Ogge Lake (ŏg′gŭ), Nor. *Oggevatn*, formerly *Augevand*, Aust-Agder co., S Norway, 18 mi. N of Kristiansand; □ 4. Skirted by railroad.

Oggersheim (ô′gŭrs-hīm), W district (since 1938) of Ludwigshafen, Rhenish Palatinate, W Germany; iron foundries. Mfg. of machinery, cotton, cigars; malting, brewing, distilling, flour milling. Has 18th-cent. church.

Oggiono (ôd-jô′nô), village (pop. 3,036), Como prov., Lombardy, N Italy, 13 mi. E of Como, on small lake; mfg. (silk textiles, bedspreads, machinery). Octagonal baptistery (11th–12th cent.).

Ogi (ō′gē). **1** Town (pop. 5,423), Ishikawa prefecture, central Honshu, Japan, on NE Noto Peninsula, on Sea of Japan, 20 mi. NE of Nanao; rice, wheat. **2** Town (pop. 6,615) on S Sado Isl., Niigata prefecture, Japan, 30 mi. W of Niigata; fishing port; agr., lumbering. **3** Town (pop. 17,672, Saga prefecture, NW Kyushu, Japan, 7 mi. NW of Saga; agr. center (rice, wheat); raw silk.

Ogida (ō′gēdä) or **Ogita** (ō′gētä), town (pop. 6,115), Akita prefecture, N Honshu, Japan, 4 mi. ESE of Noshiro; rice, silk cocoons.

Ogidi (ôgēdē′), town, Onitsha prov., Eastern Provinces, S Nigeria, 5 mi. E of Onitsha; road junction; palm oil and kernels, kola nuts.

Ogíjares (ōhē′härĕs), S suburb (pop. 1,519) of Granada, Granada prov., S Spain; olive oil, wine, truck produce, hemp, tobacco.

Ogilvie (ō′gŭlvē), village (pop. 362), Kanabec co., E Minn., 7 mi. WSW of Mora, in grain, livestock, poultry area; dairy products.

Ogilvie Range, E Yukon, range at NW end of MACKENZIE MOUNTAINS, extends c.150 WNW from Yukon–Northwest Territories border.

Oginski Canal or **Oginskiy Canal** (ŭgēn′skē), Pol. *Kanał Ogińskiego*, SW Belorussian SSR, in Pripet Marshes, bet. Yaselda R. (S) and Vygonovo L. (N); 34 mi. long; built 1777. Telekhany on W shore. Part of Dnieper-Neman waterway.

Ogita, Japan: see OGIDA.

Oglangli or **Oglangly** (ŭglän′glyē, –glē), oil town (1941 pop. over 500), W Ashkhabad oblast, Turkmen SSR, 25 mi. N of Nebit-Dag, at N foot of Greater Balkhan Range; bentonite deposits.

Ogle (ō′gŭl), county (□ 757; pop. 33,429), N Ill.; ⊙ Oregon. Agr. (livestock, poultry; dairy products; corn, oats, barley, hay, truck). Food-processing plants; also other mfg. at Oregon and Rochelle. Drained by Rock, Leaf, and Kyte rivers, and by small Pine Creek. Includes a state park. Formed 1836.

Oglesby (ō′gŭlzbē). **1** City (pop. 3,922), La Salle co., N Ill., on Illinois R. at mouth of Vermilion R., just SE of La Salle; bituminous coal, limestone, slate; makes cement; river shipping. Inc. 1902. **2** Village (pop. c.500), Coryell co., central Texas, near Leon R., 23 mi. WSW of Waco; rail point in cattle, farm area.

Oglethorpe (ō′gŭlthôrp), county (□ 432; pop. 9,958), NE Ga.; ⊙ Lexington. Piedmont agr. (cotton, corn, grain, fruit) and timber area. Formed 1793.

Oglethorpe, city (pop. 1,204), ⊙ Macon co., W central Ga., c.45 mi. SW of Macon and on Flint R. opposite Montezuma, in farm area. Inc. 1849.

Oglethorpe, Mount (alt. 3,290), Pickens co., N Ga., 6 mi. NE of Jasper, at S end of the Blue Ridge; at SW terminus of Appalachian Trail. A white marble shaft has been erected at its summit as a memorial to Gen. James E. Oglethorpe, founder of Ga. Called Grassy Mountain until 1929.

Oglinzi (ôglēnz′), village (pop. 1,953), Bacau prov., NE Rumania, 4 mi. NW of Targu-Neamt; health resort (alt. 1,608 ft.) with alkaline springs.

Oglio River (ô′lyô), anc. *Ollius*, Lombardy, N Italy, formed at Ponte di Legno by union of several glacial streams rising in S Ortles mtn. group; flows SSW, past Edolo, through Val Camonica and Lago d'Iseo, S, past Palazzolo sull'Oglio, and SE, across Lombard plain, to Po R. 10 mi. SW of Mantua; 175 mi. long. Receives Mella and Chiese rivers (left) and waters from Adamello mtn. glaciers. Navigable for 20 mi. in lower course; forms boundary bet. Brescia and Cremona provs. Extensively used for hydroelectric power in Val CAMONICA and for irrigation in Lombard plain.

Ogmore and Garw (ŏg′môr, gă′rōō), urban district (1931 pop. 26,981; 1951 census 22,638), central Glamorgan, Wales, bet. Ogwr R. and Garw R., 7 mi. N of Bridgend. Includes coal-mining towns of PONTYCYMMER, BETTWS AND PONTYRHYL, BLAENGARW, NANTYMOEL.

Ogmore River, Wales: see OGWR RIVER.

Ogmore Vale, Wales: see NANTYMOEL.

Ognon River (ônyō′), E France, rises in the S Vosges near Le Thillot, flows 115 mi. SW, past Villersexel, Montbozon, Marnay, and Pesmes, to the Saône above Pontailler-sur-Saône. Through most of its course it forms border bet. Haute-Saône and Doubs depts.

Ogo (ō′gō), highland of Br. Somaliland, rising steeply from Gulf of Aden and merging in S with the Haud plateau. Rises to 7,900 ft.

Ogo (ō′gō), town (pop. 9,912), Gumma prefecture, central Honshu, Japan, 5 mi. ENE of Maebashi; raw-silk center; radishes.

Ogoe (ōgō′ä), town (pop. 5,713), Fukushima prefecture, central Honshu, Japan, 14 mi. E of Koriyama; rice.

Ogoja (ôgô′jä), province (□ 7,529; pop. 726,233), Eastern Provinces, SE Nigeria, in forest belt; ⊙ Ogoja. Bounded E by Br. Cameroons; deciduous forest (S), savanna (N); drained by Cross R. Silver and lead-zinc mining near Abakaliki; salt and limestone deposits (NW). Main forest products: hardwood, rubber, palm oil and kernels, cacao, kola nuts. Yams, cassava, corn, and plantains are chief food crops. Main centers: Ogoja, Abakaliki, Afikpo. Pop. largely Ibo (in W).

Ogoja, town (pop. 1,314), ⊙ Ogoja prov., Eastern Provinces, SE Nigeria, 85 mi. ENE of Enugu; 6°39′N 8°43′E. Trade center; shea nuts, palm oil and kernels, sesame, yams, cassava, corn.

Ogoki River (ōgō′kē), NW Ont., rises in lake region NW of L. Nipigon, flows 300 mi. NE to Albany R. at 51°38′N 85°57′W. At Waboose Rapids (50°46′N 87°59′W) is a dam (50 ft. high, 1,700 ft. long at crest) which forms a 30-mi.-long reservoir, draining via L. Nipigon into L. Superior; construction begun in 1940.

Ogoño, Cape (ōgō′nyō), on Bay of Biscay, in Vizcaya prov., N Spain, 19 mi. NE of Bilbao; 43°26′N 2°38′W.

Ogontz, Pa.: see ELKINS PARK.

Ogooué-Ivindo, Fr. Equatorial Africa: see BOOUÉ.

Ogooué-Maritime, Fr. Equatorial Africa: see PORT-GENTIL.

Ogooué River or **Ogowe River** (ōgōwā′), Gabon, Fr. Equatorial Africa, rises c.5 mi. S of Zanaga, flows NW past Franceville and Lastoursville, thence W and SW past Booué, N'Djolé, and Lambaréné, draining a region of lakes and splitting into several arms E and SE of Port-Gentil to form a delta on the Gulf of Guinea; total length, 560 mi. Navigable most of the year for c.375 mi. below N'Djolé and year-around below Lambaréné. Receives Ivindo R. (right), N'Gounié R. (left).

Ogose (ōgō′sā), town (pop. 6,600), Saitama prefecture, central Honshu, Japan, 11 mi. WNW of Kawagoe; silk textiles; rice.

Ogosta River (ôgô′stä), NW Bulgaria, rises W of Berkovitsa in Chiporov mts., flows 91 mi. generally NE, past Mikhailovgrad, to the Danube 5 mi. W of Oryakhovo. Receives Botunya R. (right).

Ogowe River, Fr. Equatorial Africa: see OGOOUÉ RIVER.

Ogradena (ôgrädänä′), village (pop. 1,167), Severin prov., SW Rumania, on the Danube and 5 mi. SW of Orsova; chromium and nickel mining. Includes *Ogradena-Nouă* (nō′ŭ) (Hung. *Ujasszonyrét*) and *Ogradena-Veche* (vä′kĕ) (Hung. *Óasszonyrét*).

Ogradiska, Yugoslavia: see STARA GRADISKA.

Ograzden or **Ograzhden** (ô′grăzhdĕn), Serbo-Croatian *Ogražden*, mountain on Yugoslav-Bulgarian border, bet. Struma (E) and Strumica (S, W) rivers; heavily forested. Highest peak (5,717 ft.) is 14 mi. NE of Strumica.

Ogre (ō′grā), Ger. *Oger*, city (pop. 1,727), central Latvia, in Vidzeme, on right bank of the Western Dvina, at mouth of the Ogre and 20 mi. ESE of

Riga; health and summer resort; sawmilling. Kegums hydroelectric plant is 6 mi. SE.

Ogreyak, peak, Bulgaria and Yugoslavia: see KADIJICA.

Ogualik Island, Labrador: see COD ISLAND.

Ogulin (ô'gōōlĭn), village (pop. 7,624), NW Croatia, Yugoslavia, on Dobra R. (which here disappears underground) and 20 mi. SW of Karlovac; rail junction; local trade center. Castle.

Ogumali, Nigeria: see IGUMALE.

Oguni (ōgōōnē). **1** Town (pop. 14,634), Kumamoto prefecture, N central Kyushu, Japan, 30 mi. WSW of Oita, near Aso Natl. Park; sawmills. **2** Town (pop. 10,061), Yamagata prefecture, N Honshu, Japan, 35 mi. WSW of Yamagata; rice, silk cocoons, charcoal. Until late 1930s, called Oguni-moto.

Oguni-moto, Japan: see OGUNI, Yamagata prefecture.

Ogunquit (ōgŭn'kwĭt), village (1940 pop. 615) in Wells town, York co., SW Maine, on the coast, 35 mi. SSW of Portland; summer resort frequented especially by artists; summer playhouse.

Ogun River (ōgōōn'), SW Nigeria, rises in Oyo prov. NE of Shaki, flows c.200 mi. S, past Olokemeji and Abeokuta, to Lagos Lagoon N of Lagos. Drains rich cacao-growing region.

Ogusu, Japan: see YOKOSUKA, Kanagawa prefecture.

Oguta (ôgōōtä'), town, Owerri prov., Eastern Provinces, S Nigeria, on arm of Niger R., near head of delta, and 25 mi. NW of Owerri; palm oil and kernels, kola nuts. Lignite deposits.

Ogwashi Uku or **Ugwashi Uku** (ōgwä'shē ōō'kōō, ōōg–), town (pop. 6,638), Benin prov., Western Provinces, S Nigeria, 60 mi. E of Benin City; palm oil and kernels, hardwood, rubber, kola nuts, yams, cassava, corn, plantains. Lignite deposits.

Ogwen, Wales: see BETHESDA.

Ogwr River (ô'gōōr) or **Ogmore River,** Glamorgan, Wales, rises just N of Nantymoel, flows 16 mi. S and SW, past Bridgend and Newcastle, to Bristol Channel 3 mi. ESE of Porthcawl. Receives Garw R. 3 mi. N of Bridgend.

Ogyalla, Czechoslovakia: see HURBANOVO.

Ohain (ōhē'), village (pop. 2,200), Brabant prov., central Belgium, 11 mi. SSE of Brussels; agr., lumbering.

Ohakune (ō'äkōōnē), borough (pop. 1,411), W central N Isl., New Zealand, 75 mi. ESE of New Plymouth; rail junction; dairy plants, sawmills.

Ohama (ō'hämä). **1** Town (pop. 12,117), Aichi prefecture, central Honshu, Japan, 3 mi. SE of Handa; cotton-textile mills; rice, wheat, raw silk, poultry. **2** Town (pop. 3,728), Kumamoto prefecture, W Kyushu, Japan, on Shimabara Bay, 11 mi. NW of Kumamoto; rice, wheat, edible seaweed.

Ohama, town (1950 pop. 8,039), on S Ishigaki-shima, in the Ryukyus, 5 mi. SE of Ishigaki; fishing port.

Ohanes (ōä'nĕs), town (pop. 1,785), Almería prov., S Spain, 20 mi. NW of Almería; flour mills; cherries, grapes, wine.

Ohara (ō'härä). **1** Town (pop. 11,866), Chiba prefecture, central Honshu, Japan, on E coast of Chiba Peninsula, 36 mi. NE of Tateyama; rail junction; agr. center (rice, wheat, corn); raw-silk production; fishing. **2** Town (pop. 7,350), Iwate prefecture, N Honshu, Japan, 15 mi. ENE of Ichinoseki; rice, wheat, charcoal. **3** Town (pop. 3,088), Okayama prefecture, SW Honshu, Japan, 19 mi. ENE of Tsuyama, in agr. area (rice, wheat); charcoal, persimmons, sake.

Ohasama (ō'häsämä), town (pop. 3,438), Iwate prefecture, N Honshu, Japan, 18 mi. SSE of Morioka; rice, tobacco, raw silk.

Ohata (ō'hätä), town (pop. 11,139), Aomori prefecture, N Honshu, Japan, on Tsugaru Strait, 8 mi. NNW of Tanabu; northernmost rail terminus; fishing center. Hot springs near by.

Ohaton (ōhä'tŭn), village, central Alta., 9 mi. ESE of Camrose; coal mining.

Ohau, Lake (ō'ou) (□ 23), central S.Isl., New Zealand, 65 mi. W of Timaru; 10 mi. long, 3 mi. wide. Outlet: Ohau R., which flows E to Tekapo R.

O'Higgins, inland province (□ 2,746; 1940 pop. 200,297; 1949 estimate 209,866), central Chile; ⊙ RANCAGUA. The Andes (E) give way to the fertile central valley (W), watered by Cachapoal R.; on SW is Rapel R. Has mild climate. Predominantly agr.: wheat, corn, beans, potatoes, fruit, wine, livestock (mainly milch cows; also sheep). Flour milling, wine making, dairying, lumbering. At El Teniente are some of largest copper mines in Chile. Cauquenes is a spa resort. Prov. was set up 1883.

O'Higgins Land, Antarctica: see PALMER PENINSULA.

Ohinemuri, New Zealand: see PAEROA.

Ohio (ōhī'ō), state (land □ 41,122; with inland waters, but without □ 3,457 of L. Erie, □ 41,222; 1950 pop. 7,946,627; 1940 pop. 6,907,612), NE central U.S., bordered N by Mich. and L. Erie, NE by Pa., SE by W.Va., SW by Ky., W by Ind.; 34th in area, 5th in pop.; admitted 1803 as 17th state; ⊙ Columbus. The "Buckeye State" extends 215 mi. N–S, 225 mi. E–W. The Ohio R. flows 435 mi. along its SE and S boundaries, separating it from W.Va. and Ky. The whole E part of Ohio, E of Columbus, is a section of the ALLEGHENY PLATEAU, hilly country (alt. c.900–1,400 ft.) of generally moderate relief, consisting of horizontal carboniferous strata (shales, sandstones). W Ohio is part of the interior lowlands, where the gently rolling topography is characterized by till plains and ground moraine (continental glaciation covered all of Ohio except the central and S Appalachian Plateau areas). Campbell Hill (1,550 ft.), near Bellefontaine, is highest point in state. Bordering L. Erie, in the N, is a narrow strip of former lake plain which widens in the W to include most of the NW counties. Ohio drains largely S to the Ohio R. via the Muskingum, Scioto, and Great Miami rivers, while L. Erie receives the Maumel and the Sandusky. The state has a continental climate with 33–40 in. of annual rainfall (slight spring-summer max.). Cleveland (NE) has mean temp. of 25°F. in Jan., 72°F. in July, and 33 in. of annual rainfall; Cincinnati (SW) has mean temp. of 33°F. in Jan., 77°F. in July, and 37 in. of rain. The growing season varies from 140 to 180 days (NE–SW). Present commercial forest area totals 4,779,000 acres, chief species being oak, ash, maple, walnut, basswood, hickory, and beech; natl. forest reserves comprise 1,466,000 acres. Ohio has a diversified agr. production. Corn, hay, winter wheat, oats, and soybeans are the major field crops, mostly fed to livestock, while potatoes, tobacco, sugar beets, and grapes are grown on a more localized and commercial scale. Farm and range land comprise 22,000,000 acres, of which over 11,000,000 acres are in crops. Corn occupies the largest acreage, the W half of the state forming the E end of the Midwest corn belt; hog raising is extensive here. Wheat is grown chiefly in the W and N central parts, oats in NW and N, soybeans in NW and W center, tobacco in SW, and potatoes in NE. The lake counties, with less frost hazard than elsewhere, are noted for grapes (used largely in winemaking) and other fruit (apples, peaches) and truck crops. The production of sugar beets (NW), maple syrup (Geauga co.), and honey is important. Livestock includes (1950) milch cows (1,060,000), hogs (3,176,000), sheep (1,195,000), beef cattle, and horses. Dairying is important, especially in W and N, and there is a large annual wool clip. Much of the hilly, woodland area (S and SE) is in pasture. Bituminous coal is Ohio's principal mineral resource, mined from easily accessible seams in the E and SE sectors, which are part of the rich Appalachian coal field; Belmont, Harrison, Jefferson, Perry, Tuscarawas, Athens, and Muskingum counties are large producers. The state ranks 1st in clay products (pottery, fire bricks, tile) and lime, and produces large amounts of sandstone, limestone, sand and gravel, and silica (quartz). Rock salt is worked in the NE section. Petroleum fields occur in the NW (around Lima) and SE; refineries at Toledo. Valuable natural gas deposits are located in many areas, particularly E center, SE, and NW. Ohio's position as a leading industrial state is based largely on its coal, gas, oil, and other natural resources, as well as on its good transportation facilities and proximity to Midwestern and Middle Atlantic markets. Iron ore from L. Superior mines is received via Great Lakes at CLEVELAND, TOLEDO, and the smaller ports of Lorain, Ashtabula, and Conneaut. Iron- and steelworks—the state's leading industry—are centered in Cleveland (largest city in state), CANTON, and, predominantly, in the Mahoning valley near Pa. line at Youngstown, Warren, and Niles. Ohio ranks high in the production of coke, pig iron, and steel products. Other important industries produce machinery (including electrical apparatus and appliances), rubber products (notably at Akron), motor vehicles and parts, other metal goods, paper, printed matter, processed and packed meat and other foods, clothing, chemicals, cement, transportation equipment, glass, and boats; noted products include cash registers and refrigerators (from Dayton), soap and playing cards (from Cincinnati), stoves, matches, and tableware. Other cities with diversified mfg. are Columbus, Springfield, Lakewood, Hamilton, Lima, Mansfield, Portsmouth, Steubenville, Zanesville, Norwood, Sandusky, Massillon, and East Liverpool. Navigable waterways are the Ohio R., Muskingum R. (for c.100 mi.), and L. Erie (230-mi. shore line). Flood dams have been built on several rivers, especially in the E; Mosquito Creek, Berlin, Tappan, and Senecaville are among the largest reservoirs. Other lakes (e.g., Grand, Portage, Buckeye, Indian), as well as the L. Erie shore, have resort facilities. Leading educational institutions: Ohio State Univ. (at Columbus), Western Reserve Univ. (at Cleveland), Univ. of Cincinnati, Kent State Univ. (at Kent), Miami Univ. (at Oxford), and Ohio Univ. (at Athens). Ohio contains many earthenwork remains of the prehistoric Mound Builders' culture, notably Serpent Mound and those remnants preserved at MOUND CITY GROUP NATIONAL MONUMENT, Fort Ancient State Memorial Park, Miamisburg, and Newark. One of the earliest Indian tribes in the region was the Erie, later succeeded by the Miami, Shawnee, Delaware, and certain Iroquois tribes. Although the French laid claim to the Ohio valley after 1670, the British were active in making Indian alliances, and the region—valuable for its fur trade—was the scene of continuous Anglo-French conflict until 1763, when the British were ceded all Fr. territory E of the Mississippi. By the Quebec Act of 1774 England sought to annex the region to Canada and continue the fur trade at the expense of colonial settlement. The Ohio country was ceded to the U.S. after the Revolution, and when the states had relinquished most of their claims to the area it was inc. (1787) into the NORTHWEST TERRITORY by the Federal govt. The 1st permanent settlement was made at Marietta in 1788; Cincinnati was founded 1789. At battle of Fallen Timbers in 1794 the Indians were defeated by Gen. Anthony Wayne, who negotiated with them the Treaty of Greenville (1795). Ohio became a territory (1800) which included the former Conn. WESTERN RESERVE. The 1st settlers, including the celebrated Johnny Appleseed, arrived mainly via the Ohio R. on flatboats and, later, steamboats. Although the War of 1812 generally went badly for the West, Perry's victory at PUT-IN-BAY on L. Erie was a decisive American triumph. Ohio's development was furthered by the building of the Erie Canal (1825) and several state canals. Cincinnati early became the commercial center of the Ohio valley. In the 1840s and 1850s the railroads opened up the N plains to agr. Antislavery sentiment was strong, and the state figured prominently in the "Underground Railroad" activities. During the Civil War Gen. John Morgan's Confederate raiders ravaged S Ohio, but were finally captured near Salineville (E). The development of iron- and steelworks and oil refining shifted industrial activity from the Ohio valley to the N part of the state and attracted many European immigrants. In the late 19th cent. big business became dominant, and boss govt., particularly under Mark Hanna and George Cox, gave rise to political corruption—later exposed by the muckrakers Lincoln Steffens and Ida Tarbell. However, the growth of the labor movement and the efficient administrations of municipal leaders, such as Samuel ("Golden Rule") Jones and Tom Johnson, began a trend toward reform. The state has experienced some disastrous floods. The expansion and diversification of industry was especially marked during the First and Second World Wars. Ohio's native sons include William Dean Howells, Sherwood Anderson, Thomas Edison, Orville Wright, and Presidents Grant, Hayes, Garfield, Benjamin Harrison, McKinley, Taft, and Harding. See also articles on the cities, towns, geographic features, and the 88 counties: ADAMS, ALLEN, ASHLAND, ASHTABULA, ATHENS, AUGLAIZE, BELMONT, BROWN, BUTLER, CARROLL, CHAMPAIGN, CLARK, CLERMONT, CLINTON, COLUMBIANA, COSHOCTON, CRAWFORD, CUYAHOGA, DARKE, DEFIANCE, DELAWARE, ERIE, FAIRFIELD, FAYETTE, FRANKLIN, FULTON, GALLIA, GEAUGA, GREENE, GUERNSEY, HAMILTON, HANCOCK, HARDIN, HARRISON, HENRY, HIGHLAND, HOCKING, HOLMES, HURON, JACKSON, JEFFERSON, KNOX, LAKE, LAWRENCE, LICKING, LOGAN, LORAIN, LUCAS, MADISON, MAHONING, MARION, MEDINA, MEIGS, MERCER, MIAMI, MONROE, MONTGOMERY, MORGAN, MORROW, MUSKINGUM, NOBLE, OTTAWA, PAULDING, PERRY, PICKAWAY, PIKE, PORTAGE, PREBLE, PUTNAM, RICHLAND, ROSS, SANDUSKY, SCIOTO, SENECA, SHELBY, STARK, SUMMIT, TRUMBULL, TUSCARAWAS, UNION, VAN WERT, VINTON, WARREN, WASHINGTON, WAYNE, WILLIAMS, WOOD, WYANDOT.

Ohio. 1 County (□ 87; pop. 4,223), SE Ind.; ⊙ Rising Sun. Bounded E by Ky., line, here formed by Ohio R.; drained by small Laughery Creek. Agr. area (livestock, truck, tobacco); mfg. (flour, dairy and food products, furniture, construction machinery and materials). Formed 1844. **2** County (□ 596; pop. 20,840), W Ky.; ⊙ Hartford. Bounded W and S by Green R.; crossed by Rough R. and South Fork of Panther Creek. Rolling agr. area (livestock, grain, burley tobacco, hay, strawberries); bituminous coal mines, oil wells, limestone quarries; timber. Formed 1798. **3** County (□ 107; pop. 71,672), W.Va., in Northern Panhandle; ⊙ WHEELING, industrial and commercial center of the Panhandle. Bounded W by Ohio R. (Ohio line), E by Pa.; drained by Wheeling Creek and other short streams. Coal mines, natural-gas wells. Iron, steel, and metal-working industries and other mfg. at Wheeling. Agr. (livestock, dairy products, tobacco, truck); nurseries. Formed 1776.

Ohio. 1 Town (pop. 40), Gunnison co., W central Colo., just W of Sawatch Mts., 17 mi. E of Gunnison; alt. 8,556 ft. **2** Village (pop. 561), Bureau co., N Ill., 19 mi. S of Dixon, in agr. and bituminous-coal area; dairy products.

Ohio Caverns, Ohio: see WEST LIBERTY.

Ohio City, village (pop. 861), Van Wert co., W Ohio, 7 mi. SSW of Van Wert; dairy products, canned foods, grain products. An Ohio City in Cuyahoga co. was annexed (1854) by Cleveland.

Ohiopyle (ōhī'ūpīl"), borough (pop. 345), Fayette co., SW Pa., 12 mi. E of Uniontown and on the Youghiogheny.

Ohio River (ōhī'ō), 981 mi. long, E central U.S., formed by confluence of Allegheny and Monongahela rivers at Pittsburgh, Pa.; chief E tributary of the Mississippi; to the farthest headstream of the Allegheny, it is 1,306 mi. long. Flowing NW out of Pa., the Ohio then flows generally SW, forming several state boundaries: Ohio-W.Va., Ohio-Ky., Ind.-Ky., and Ill.-Ky. to the Mississippi at Cairo, Ill. Chief tributaries: Beaver, Muskingum, Hocking, Scioto, Miami, Wabash from the right; Kanawha, Guyandot, Big Sandy, Licking, Kentucky, Salt, Green, Cumberland, and the Tennessee from the left. The drainage area (□ 203,900) includes a region of concentrated population and great industrial establishments. Cities on the Ohio include, besides Pittsburgh and Cairo: Steubenville, Marietta, Gallipolis, Ironton, Portsmouth, and Cincinnati, Ohio; Madison, Jeffersonville, New Albany, Evansville, and Mt. Vernon, Ind.; Wheeling, Parkersburg, and Huntington, W.Va.; and Ashland, Maysville, Covington, Louisville, Owensboro, and Paducah, Ky. Spring floods have long caused great havoc, those of 1913, 1936, and 1937 being particularly destructive, and Federal action has been taken to construct dams, levees, wells, and reservoirs to control the river. Navigation has been improved to allow a slackwater navigable depth of 9 ft. A hydroelectric plant is at the Falls of the Ohio (rapids at Louisville), where occurs the only obstacle to navigation. A dam and canal (opened 1830) with locks circumvent the rapids. A dam at Montgomery Isl., 31 mi. below Pittsburgh, aids navigation. The Ohio carries much coal, coke, sand, gravel, cement, iron, steel, oil, lumber. La Salle is said to have found the Ohio in 1669, and the fork at Pittsburgh attracted the attention of both French and British. Fort Duquesne, built here, was a prize of the French and Indian War. Settlers, especially in early 19th cent., poured down the Ohio to the Middle West lands. Commerce expanded, and the set-back caused in the late 1820s by the opening of the Erie Canal was later compensated for by improvement of navigability in 1827. The construction of the railroads cut its trade sharply, but it still carries much freight.

Ohiowa (ōhī'ùwù), village (pop. 253), Fillmore co., SE Nebr., 10 mi. SE of Geneva.

Ohito (ō'hētō), town (pop. 10,016), Shizuoka prefecture, central Honshu, Japan, on N central Izu Peninsula, 8 mi. SE of Numazu; mining center (gold, silver).

Ohiya (ō'hīyŭ), town (pop. 284), Uva Prov., S central Ceylon, in Ceylon Hill Country, near Horton Plains, 34 mi. SSE of Kandy.

Ohlau, Poland: see OLAWA.

Ohle River, Poland: see OLAWA RIVER.

Ohligs (ō'lĭkhs), outer suburb (1925 pop. 29,768) of Solingen, W Germany, 3.5 mi. W of city center. Inc. 1929 into Solingen.

Ohlsdorf (ōls'dôrf), town (pop. 2,594), S central Upper Austria, 3 mi. N of Gmunden; wheat, cattle.

Ohlsdorf, outer district of Hamburg, NW Germany, on left bank of the Alster, 5 mi. NNE of city center; site of Hamburg's main cemetery (founded 1877).

Ohm River (ōm), Hesse, W Germany, rises 6 mi. NE of Schotten, flows 35 mi. generally NW to the Lahn, 2 mi. N of Marburg.

Ohogamiut (ōhō'gùmūt), village (pop. 27), W Alaska, on lower Yukon R. and 55 mi. N of Bethel; 61°35'N 161°56'W; supply point for gold prospectors. Sometimes spelled Ohogamut. Also called Iguak.

Ohoka (ōhō'kù), township (pop. 246), ⊙ Eyre co. (□ 175; pop. 1,691), E S.Isl., New Zealand, 13 mi. NNW of Christchurch, in agr. area.

Ohoopee (ōhōō'pē), village (pop. 53), Toombs co., E central Ga., 10 mi. E of Vidalia.

Ohoopee River, E central Ga., rises S of Sandersville, flows c.100 mi. SE to Altamaha R. 13 mi. S of Reidsville. Receives Little Ohoopee River (c.45 mi. long).

Ohori, Japan: see AOHORI.

Ohrdruf (ōr'drōōf), town (pop. 7,474), Thuringia, central Germany, at N foot of Thuringian Forest, 9 mi. S of Gotha; mfg. of machinery, toys, china, leather, cardboard; metal- and woodworking. Has 18th-cent. church on site of 1st Christian chapel in Thuringia (built 724 by St. Boniface); 16th-cent. Ehrenstein castle, on site of early monastery. J. S. Bach attended school here. During Second World War, town was site of notorious concentration camp and of extensive subterranean Ger. army hq.

Ohre River, Czechoslovakia: see EGER RIVER.

Ohre River (ō'rù), central Germany, rises 6 mi. NW of Gardelegen, flows 65 mi. generally SE, past Calvörde, Haldensleben, and Wolmirstedt, to the Elbe 5 mi. NW of Burg.

Ohrid; Ohridsko Jezero, Yugoslavia: see OCHRIDA, town; OCHRIDA, LAKE.

Ohrigstad (ō'rĭkhstät"), town (pop. 1,159), E Transvaal, U. of So. Afr., on Ohrigstad R. and 25 mi. NNE of Lydenburg; cotton, wheat, tobacco, sheep. Founded 1845 by Boer trekkers, who established *Volksraad* (people's council) here; abandoned 1850 because of fever outbreak, later resettled.

Öhringen (û'rĭng-ùn), town (pop. 6,976), N Württemberg, Germany, after 1945 in Württemberg-Baden, 13 mi. ENE of Heilbronn; mfg. of agr. machinery, tinware, furniture, shoes, stockings and knitwear; leather- and woodworking. Has late-Gothic church, Renaissance castle. Was Roman settlement. Chartered c.1240. Sometimes spelled Oehringen.

Ohura (ōhōō'rù), town (pop. 474), ⊙ Ohura co. (□ 416; pop. 1,691), W N.Isl., New Zealand, 50 mi. ENE of New Plymouth; sawmills.

Oi (ō'ē), town (pop. 8,100), Gifu prefecture, central Honshu, Japan, 18 mi. NE of Tajimi; commercial center for agr. area (rice, wheat, herbs); bamboo ware. Has radioactive mineral springs.

Oiapoque (oi-ùpô'kĭ), city, northernmost Amapá territory, N Brazil, on right bank of Oiapoque R. (Fr. Guiana border) and 85 mi. SSE of Cayenne. Gold found in area.

Oiapoque River, Brazil–Fr. Guiana: see OYAPOCK RIVER.

Oich, Loch (lŏkh oikh'), lake in central Inverness, Scotland, extending 4 mi. NE-SW along the Great Glen of Scotland bet. Loch Ness and Loch Lochy, forming highest section of the Caledonian Canal. Drained by Oich R., which flows 7 mi. NE to Loch Ness at Fort Augustus.

Oie, Norway: see OYE.

Oies, Île aux (ēlōzwä'), or **Goose Island** (6 mi. long, 1 mi. wide), in the St. Lawrence, S Que., 40 mi. ENE of Quebec. Just SW is Île aux Grues.

Oignies (wänyē'), village (pop. 850), Namur prov., S Belgium, 13 mi. SSE of Philippeville; agr., lumbering.

Oignies, town (pop. 7,317), Pas-de-Calais dept., N France, 8 mi. NW of Douai; coal-mining center.

Oihama (ōē'hämù), town (pop. 5,631), Chiba prefecture, central Honshu, Japan, on NW Chiba Peninsula, on Tokyo Bay, just S of Chiba; rice growing, poultry raising; beach resort.

Oil City, village (pop. estimate 200), S Ont., 5 mi. SSE of Petrolia; oil production.

Oil City. 1 Village (pop. 422), Caddo parish, extreme NW La., 20 mi. NW of Shreveport, on Caddo L.; center of oil field discovered in 1906. **2** City (pop. 19,581), Venango co., NW central Pa., 50 mi. SSE of Erie and on Allegheny R., at mouth of Oil Creek; oil refining and distribution center since 1860. Oil-well supplies and machinery, bituminous coal; metal products, paint, glass; natural gas, timber; railroad shops. Grew after discovery of oil at near-by TITUSVILLE. Laid out c.1860, inc. as borough 1862, as city 1871, reinc. 1881.

Oil Creek. 1 In central Colo., rises in several branches W of Pikes Peak, flows 46 mi. S to Arkansas R. just E of Canon City. Drains oil-producing region. **2** In NW Pa., rises in headstreams in N Crawford co., flows SE, past Titusville, and S, through oil-producing region to Allegheny R. at Oil City; c.45 mi. long. On its banks near Titusville first successful oil well in U.S. was drilled in 1859.

Oildale, village (pop. 16,615), Kern co., S central Calif., oil-field center just N of Bakersfield, across Kern R.

Oil Hill, village (1940 pop. 501), Butler co., SE Kansas, near Arkansas R., 23 mi. ENE of Wichita; NW suburb of El Dorado.

Oil Rivers, protectorate: see NIGERIA.

Oil Springs, village (pop. 458), S Ont., 7 mi. SSE of Petrolia; oil production.

Oilton, city (pop. 1,109), Creek co., central Okla., 34 mi. W of Tulsa, and on Cimarron R., in petroleum and agr. area (grain, cotton, corn); oil and natural-gas wells; cotton ginning. Founded c.1915.

Oil Trough, village (pop. c.600), Independence co., NE central Ark., 14 mi. SE of Batesville and on White R., in agr. area.

Oimyakon or **Oymyakon** (oimyŭkôn'), village (1948 pop. over 500), E Yakut Autonomous SSR, Russian SFSR, on Indigirka R. and 430 mi. ENE of Yakutsk; one of world's coldest spots. Formerly Oimekon.

Oimyakon Plateau or **Oymyakon Plateau**, NE Yakut Autonomous SSR, Russian SFSR, at junction of Verkhoyansk, Kolyma, and Dzhugdzhur ranges; alt. 3–4,000 ft.; gives rise to Kolyma and Indigirka rivers. Formerly Oimekon plateau.

Oinousa (ēnōō'sù), Greek Aegean island (□ 6; pop. 2,321), largest of the Oinousai group, in Chios nome, bet. NE Chios isl. and Turkish Karaburun Peninsula; 38°32'N 26°15'E; 5 mi. long, 1.5 mi. wide; livestock, fisheries. Also called Agnousa and Ignusi.

Oinousai Islands (–sā), Lat. *Oenussae*, archipelago in Ionian Sea, off Cape Akritas, SW Peloponnesus, Greece; part of Messenia nome. Constitute shipping hazard. Include isls. of SCHIZA and SAPIENTZA.

Oirat or **Oirot**, in Rus. names: see GORNO-ALTAI.

Oirschot or **Oorschot** (both: ōr'skhōt), town (pop. 2,717), North Brabant prov., S Netherlands, on Wilhelmina Canal and 11 mi. ESE of Tilburg; mfg. (chairs, wooden shoes).

Oisans (wäzä'), valley of Romanche R., Hautes-Alpes and Isère depts., SE France, in the Dauphiné Alps, extending from Col du Lautaret (E) to Séchilienne (W). Chief pop. center: Le Bourg-d'Oisans. Numerous dams (including huge Chambon Dam) and hydroelectric plants power its electrochemical and electrometallurgical industries. Alpinism (ascent of Massif du Pelvoux peaks).

Oise (wäz), department (□ 2,273; pop. 396,724), N France, occupying parts of Île-de-France and of Picardy; ⊙ Beauvais. Generally level, with large wooded tracts (Forests of Compiègne, Chantilly) in S. Drained NE–SW by the Oise, which receives the Aisne, its principal tributary, near Compiègne. A leading agr. dist. (wheat, sugar beets, oats, feed crops, apples, cherries, black currants, vegetables) with important cattle-raising and dairying industry. Numerous clay and sandstone quarries. Principal industries: metallurgy (in Creil area), woolen milling (noted tapestry manufactures formerly at Beauvais), woodworking (in Compiègne and Senlis area), and food processing (sugar refining, cider distilling, fruit and vegetable preserving for Paris market). Méru is center of mother-of-pearl and bone industry. Chief towns: Beauvais (large cathedral), Compiègne, Creil, Senlis, and Chantilly (horse racing).

Oise-Aisne Canal (–ān'), Aisne dept., N France, connects Oise R. (below Chauny) with Aisne R. (above Vailly); c.40 mi. long. Follows course of Ailette R., pierces Chemin des Dames ridge in tunnel.

Oisemont (wäzmō'), village (pop. 930), Somme dept., N France, 11 mi. SSW of Abbeville; beet-sugar refining.

Oise River, N France, rises in the Ardennes of S Belgium S of Chimay, enters France N of Hirson, flows 186 mi. generally SW, past La Fère, Compiègne, Creil, and Pontoise, to the Seine above Andrésy. Navigable upstream to Compiègne, thence paralleled by lateral canal. Connected with Somme and Escaut rivers by SAINT-QUENTIN CANAL, and with the Sambre by OISE-SAMBRE CANAL, both originating above Chauny. Chief tributary: AISNE RIVER. Oise R. banks were scene of several battles (1918) in First World War.

Oise-Sambre Canal (wäz-sä'brù), Aisne and Nord depts., N France, begins at Chauny, follows the Oise upstream, past Fargniers (where it is joined by SAINT-QUENTIN CANAL), La Fère, and Ribemont, crosses watershed W of Wassigny and follows upper Sambre R. to Landrecies; 50 mi. long. In battle line during First World War.

Oishida (ō'ē'shĭdä), town (pop. 4,569), Yamagata prefecture, N Honshu, Japan, on Mogami R. and 13 mi. SSE of Shinjo; rice, silk cocoons.

Oisina Point (oisē'nù), westernmost point of Timor, in Roti Strait, opposite SE end of Semau isl.; 10°21'S 123°28'E. Sometimes spelled Oël Sina.

Oiso (ō'ēsō), town (pop. 15,189), Kanagawa prefecture, central Honshu, Japan, on N shore of Sagami Bay, just W of Hiratsuka; seaside resort. Sandstone quarrying.

Ois River, Austria: see YBBS RIVER.

Oissel (wäsĕl'), town (pop. 6,861), Seine-Inférieure dept., N France, port on left bank of the Seine and 7 mi. S of Rouen; cotton-spinning center; metal- and woodworking (railroad equipment), mfg. of textile dyes, mattresses, and cushions. Damaged in Second World War.

Oisterwijk or **Oosterwijk** (both: ōst'ùrvīk), town (pop. 7,043), North Brabant prov., S Netherlands, 6 mi. ENE of Tilburg; leather tanneries. Sometimes spelled Oisterwyk or Oosterwyk.

Oistins or **Oistins Town** (oi'stĭnz), village, S Barbados, B.W.I., 5 mi. ESE of Bridgetown; fisheries, fish market. Sometimes Oistin's or Oistin's Town.

Oisungur, Russian SFSR: see NOVOGROZNENSKI.

Oita (ō'ētä), prefecture [Jap. *ken*] (□ 2,447; 1940 pop. 972,975; 1947 pop. 1,233,651), NE Kyushu, Japan; chief port and ⊙ Oita. Bounded N by Suo Sea (W section of Inland Sea), NE by Iyo Sea (SW section of Inland Sea), SE by Hoyo Strait. Mountainous terrain; rises to 5,850 ft. in Mt. Kuju, highest peak of Kyushu. Kunisaki Peninsula is NE projection. Drained by Chikugo R. (largest river of isl.). Numerous hot springs at BEPPU and vicinity. Volcanic area around Mt. Kuju is part of Aso Natl. Park. Densely forested (cedar, pine, bamboo). Gold, silver, tin mined in S, with refineries at SAGANOSEKI. Rice, wheat, soybeans grown in coastal region and in valleys of interior. Widespread production of raw silk, charcoal, lumber. Thriving fishing industry. Produces silk textiles, paper, sake. Mfg. centers: Oita (E), NAKATSU (N).

Oita, city and port (1940 pop. 76,985; 1947 pop. 86,570), ⊙ Oita prefecture, NE Kyushu, Japan, 65 mi. SE of Yawata, on S shore of Beppu Bay; 33°14' N 131°37'E. Rail junction; mfg. center; paper mills, cotton-thread factory; straw mats, raw silk, livestock. Exports paper, raw silk, rice. Airfield. Bombed (1945) in Second World War.

Oital or **Oytal** (oitäl'), town (1948 pop. over 2,000), SW Dzhambul oblast, Kazakh SSR, on branch of Turksib RR (Merke station) and 90 mi. E of Dzhambul; beet-sugar refinery.

Oite or **Oiti**, Greece: see OETA.

Oiticica (wētēsē'kù), village, N central Piauí, Brazil, near Ceará border, 33 mi. W of Crateús. Present terminus of railroad from Camocim and Crateús.

Oituz Pass (oitōōz') (alt. 2,837 ft.), in the Moldavian Carpathians, E central Rumania, 15 mi. NE of Targu-Sacuesc; highway corridor bet. Moldavia and Transylvania.

Oizu (ō'ēzōō) or **Oyodo** (ō'yōdō), town (pop. 3,657), Mie prefecture, S Honshu, Japan, on SW shore of Izu Bay, 5 mi. NW of Uji-yamada; agr. (rice, wheat); fishing; raw silk.

Oizumi, Japan: see INABE.

Oizumihara, Japan: see INABE.

Ojai ō'hī), city (pop. 2,519), Ventura co., S Calif., 12 mi. N of Ventura, in fertile Ojai Valley in Coast Ranges; seat of several private schools. Year-round resort. Inc. 1921.

Oje, Norway: see OYE.

Ojén (ōhĕn'), town (pop. 1,456), Málaga prov., S Spain, in coastal spur of the Cordillera Penibética, 27 mi. WSW of Málaga, in picturesque setting known for its Ojén liqueur, containing anise. Also has iron mines and a nickel foundry. Among agr. produce of the region are oranges, carob beans, olives, corn; also livestock.

Ojestad, Norway: see RYKENE.

Oji (ō'jē), town (pop. 8,252), Nara prefecture, S Honshu, Japan, on NW Kii Peninsula, 12 mi. E of Osaka; commercial center for rice-growing area.

Ojibwa (ōjĭb'wā), village, Sawyer co., N Wis., on Chippewa R. and 24 mi. SE of Hayward; lumbering, dairying. Relics of early logging days are exhibited here. Near by is Ojibwa State Roadside Park.

Ojika Peninsula (ōjē'kä), Jap. *Ojika-hanto,* Miyagi prefecture, N Honshu, Japan, bet. Ishinomaki Bay (W) and the Pacific (E); 12 mi. long, 1–6 mi. wide; mountainous. Chief town, Onagawa. Just off SE tip of peninsula is sacred Kinkazan Isl., a small wooded islet with popular shrine and lighthouse.

Ojika-shima (ō"jĭkä'shĭmä), island (□ 10; pop. 10,753, including offshore islets) of isl. group Goto-retto, Nagasaki prefecture, Japan, in E.China Sea, 26 mi. W of Kyushu; 3.5 mi. long, 2.5 mi. wide; hilly. Fishing. Sometimes spelled Ozika-shima.

Ojima (ōjē'mä), town (pop. 12,531), Gumma prefecture, central Honshu, Japan, 8 mi. ESE of Isezaki; mulberry and rice fields.

Ojinaga (ōhēnä'gä), town (pop. 2,227), Chihuahua, N Mexico, on the Rio Grande, opposite Presidio (Texas), at mouth of Conchos R., 120 mi. NE of Chihuahua; border trade; cotton and cattle center. Airport.

Ojitlán (ōhētlän'), town (pop. 1,643), Oaxaca, S Mexico, near Tuxtepec R., 19 mi. E of Tuxtepec; cereals, sugar cane, coffee, tobacco, tropical fruit, livestock.

Ojiya (ōjē'yä), town (pop. 21,987), Niigata prefecture, central Honshu, Japan, on Shinano R. and 10 mi. SSW of Nagaoka; textile center (hemp).

Ojo Caliente, Chihuahua, Mexico: see CAMARGO.

Ojocaliente (ō'hō kälyĕn'tā), city (pop. 4,566), Zacatecas, N central Mexico, on central plateau, 23 mi. SE of Zacatecas; alt. 6,896 ft.; rail terminus; mining center (gold, silver, lead).

Ojo Caliente (ō'hō kälyĕn'tā), village (pop. c.700), Rio Arriba and Taos counties, N N.Mex., on branch of Rio Chama and 28 mi. WSW of Taos, in corn and bean area; alt. 6,290 ft. Health resort with hot mineral springs. Magnesite, meerschaum, mica mined in vicinity. Pueblo ruins and part of Carson Natl. Forest near by, Sangre de Cristo Mts. E.

Ojo de Agua or **Villa Ojo de Agua** (vē'yä ō'hō dhä ä'gwä), town (pop. estimate 1,500), ⊙ Ojo de Agua dept. (□ 2,485; 1947 pop. 14,798), S Santiago del Estero prov., Argentina, at NE slopes of Sierra de Córdoba, 120 mi. SSE of Santiago del Estero; agr. center (corn, alfalfa, grapes, livestock). Manganese mines near by.

Ojo de Agua, Costa Rica: see SAN RAFAEL, Alajuela prov.

Ojo del Toro (dhĕl tō'rō), peak (1,749 ft.), Oriente prov., E Cuba, near W end of the Sierra Maestra, 22 mi. E of the Cape Cruz.

Ojojona (ōhōhō'nä), town (pop. 489), Francisco Morazán dept., S central Honduras, in Sierra de Lepaterique, on road and 13 mi. SSW of Tegucigalpa; alt. 4,383 ft. Summer resort; pottery and ropemaking; grain, coffee, livestock. A gold- and silver-mining center in colonial times.

Ojos del Guadiana (ō'hōs dhĕl gwädh-yä'nä), marshes and ponds, Ciudad Real prov., S central Spain, 20 mi. NE of Ciudad Real, in low basin into which flow the Gigüela, Záncara, and Azuer, and from which emerges the Guadiana.

Ojos del Salado, Cerro (sĕ'rō, sälä'dō), Andean peak (c.22,550 ft.) on Argentina-Chile border, 15 mi. WSW of Cerro Incahuasi; 27°7'S; 2d highest peak (the Aconcagua is higher) in the Western Hemisphere.

Ojos Negros (nā'grōs), village (pop. 1,415), Teruel prov., E Spain, 35 mi. NW of Teruel; center of rich iron-mining region of Sierra Menera; connected by mining railroad with Mediterranean port of Sagunto.

Ojstro, Yugoslavia: see HRASTNIK.

Ojuelos de Jalisco (ōwhā'lōs dā hälē'skō), town (pop. 2,543), Jalisco, central Mexico, in Sierra Madre Occidental, near Zacatecas border, 45 mi. SW of San Luis Potosí; alt. 7,395 ft.; corn, beans, chili, livestock.

Ojus, village (1940 pop. 1,176), Dade co., S Fla., 12 mi. NNE of Miami; dairy products; limestone quarries.

Ok (ôk), glacier, W Iceland, 45 mi. NE of Reykjavik; rises to 3,743 ft. at 64°36'N 20°53'W.

Oka (ō'kû), village (pop. estimate 1,000), S Que., on L. of the Two Mountains of Ottawa R., 25 mi. WSW of Montreal; dairying. Near by is Trappist monastery, famed for cheese made here. Agr. institute here is affiliated with Univ. of Montreal.

Oka, Formosa: see YINGKO.

Oka (ō'kä). **1** Town (pop. 4,283), E Mie prefecture, S Honshu, Japan, 5 mi. S of Matsuzaka; rice, raw silk. **2** Town, S Mie prefecture, Japan: see AIGA.

Oka (ôkä'), town, Ondo prov., Western Provinces, S Nigeria, 25 mi. NE of Owo; cacao, palm oil and kernels, kola nuts.

Oka, river, Russian SFSR: see OKA RIVER.

Okabe (ōkä'bā), town (pop. 6,463), Shizuoka prefecture, central Honshu, Japan, 7 mi. ESE of Shizuoka; rice, tea.

Okabena (ōkûbē'nû), village (pop. 236), Jackson co., SW Minn., near Heron L., 19 mi. WNW of Jackson; dairy products.

Okabena Lake, Nobles co., SW Minn., at Worthington; 2 mi. long, 1 mi. wide. Drains into Ocheda L., 3 mi. S.

Okachi (ōkä'chē) or **Okatsu** (ōkä'tsōō), town (pop. 10,270), Miyagi prefecture, N Honshu, Japan, on the Pacific, 11 mi. NE of Ishinomaki; fishing; slate quarrying. Until late 1930s, called Jugohama.

Okada (ōkä'dä), town (pop. 4,891), Aichi prefecture, central Honshu, Japan, on W Chita Peninsula, on Ise Bay and 6 mi. NW of Handa; rice.

Okahandja (ō"kûhän'jû), town (pop. 1,739), N central South-West Africa, 40 mi. NNW of Windhoek; alt. 4,398 ft.; stock-raising center; site of govt. training school.

Okahukura (ō"kähōōkōōr'û), village (pop. 186), W N.Isl., New Zealand, 65 mi. ENE of New Plymouth; rail junction.

Okaihau (ōkī'ou), township (pop. 494), N N.Isl., New Zealand, 120 mi. NNW of Auckland; northernmost rail terminus; sawmills, limonite quarries, coal.

Okak Islands (ō'kăk), group of 2 adjoining islands, NE Labrador, at entrance of Okak Bay on the Atlantic; 57°21'–57°33'N 61°36'–62°1'W. Each isl. is 10 mi. long, 10 mi. wide. On NW isl. is fishing settlement of Nutak (pop. 66). Adjacent are several islets. Formerly sometimes spelled Okkak.

Okaloosa (ōkûlōō'sû), county (□ 938; pop. 27,533), NW Fla., bounded by Ala. line (N) and Gulf of Mexico (S); ⊙ Crestview. Rolling agr. area (corn, peanuts, cotton, hogs, cattle, poultry) drained by Blackwater, Yellow, and Shoal rivers. Also forestry (lumber, naval stores) and some fishing. Includes part of Choctawhatchee Natl. Forest and Choctawhatchee Bay. Formed 1915.

Okanagan Lake (ō"kûnŏ'gûn) (□ 127), S B.C., extends 69 mi. N from Penticton, 2–4 mi. wide. Drained S by Okanagan R. On E shore is Kelowna.

Okanagan Landing, village (pop. estimate 200), S B.C., on Okanagan L., 5 mi. SW of Vernon; fruit, vegetables.

Okanagan River, U.S. and Canada: see OKANOGAN RIVER.

Okanogan (ō"kûnŏ'gûn), county (□ 5,295; pop. 29,131), N Wash., on British Columbia line; ⊙ Okanogan. Bounded S by Columbia R.; drained by Okanogan and Methow rivers. Cascade Mts. in W. Includes parts of Chelan and Colville natl. forests and Colville Indian Reservation. Apples, timber, wheat; gold, silver, copper. Formed 1888.

Okanogan, town (pop. 2,013), ⊙ Okanogan co., N Wash., 38 mi. NW of Grand Coulee Dam and on Okanogan R.; center of Okanogan irrigation project. Settled 1886, c.20 mi. from Fort Okanogan, which was 1st American settlement in Wash.; inc. 1907. Silver, copper; timber, apples (in irrigated Okanogan R. valley), wheat. Gateway to Chelan Natl. Forest (NW).

Okanogan River (ō"kûnŏ'gûn) (in Canada, **Okanagan**), N Wash. and S B.C., issues from S end of Okanagan L. at Penticton (Canada), flows S, through Skaha L., past Oliver, through Osoyoos L., in which it crosses B.C.-Wash. border, past Omak and Okanogan, to Columbia R. 2 mi. E of Brewster; 115 mi. long. Receives Similkameen R.

Okany (ô'kányû), Hung. *Okány,* town (pop. 5,129), Bihar co., E Hungary, 10 mi. N of Sarkad; corn, tobacco, cattle, poultry.

Okara (ōkä'rû), town (pop. 19,315), Montgomery dist., SE Punjab, W Pakistan, 23 mi. NE of Montgomery; cotton ginning and milling center; trades in grain, cloth fabrics, ghee, saltpeter; flour milling, metal-box mfg. Technical school. Dairy farm 5 mi. W.

Okarche (ōkär'chē), town (pop. 532), on Kingfisher-Canadian co. line, central Okla., 30 mi. WNW of Oklahoma City, in grain, cotton, and livestock area; cotton ginning.

Oka River (ŭkä'). **1** In central European Russian SFSR, principal right affluent of Volga R., rises in Central Russian Upland W of Maloarkhangelsk, flows N past Orel, Belev, Chekalin (head of shallow-draught navigation), and Kaluga, generally E past Serpukhov, Kolomna, and Ryazan, and NE past Kasimov and Murom, to Volga R. at Gorki; 918 mi. long. Floods in spring; shallow in summer; frozen 225–240 days a year. Navigable for large vessels (grain, lumber) below Kolomna, 550 mi. above mouth; flows through densely populated area. Receives Zhizdra, Ugra, Moskva, and Klyazma (left) and Upa, Pronya, and Moksha (right) rivers. **2** In SW Buryat-Mongol Autonomous SSR and S Irkutsk oblast, Russian SFSR, rises in Eastern Sayan Mts., flows 500 mi. N, past Zima, to Angara R. at Bratsk.

Okatsu, Japan: see OKACHI.

Okauchee (ōkô'chē), resort village (pop. 1,673), Waukesha co., SE Wis., on Okauchee L. (c.3 mi. long), 26 mi. W. of Milwaukee.

Okavango River, Africa: see OKOVANGGO RIVER.

Okawa (ō'käwä), town (pop. 17,665), Fukuoka prefecture, NW Kyushu, Japan, on Chikugo R. and 11 mi. WSW of Kurume; timber, grain, raw silk.

Okawara (ō'käwärä) or **Ogawara** (ō'gä–), town (pop. 11,304), Miyagi prefecture, N Honshu, Japan, 17 mi. SW of Sendai; agr., poultry raising.

Okawville (ō'kôvĭl), village (pop. 855), Washington co., SW Ill., 25 mi. WSW of Centralia; health resort, with mineral springs.

Okay, town (pop. 427), Wagoner co., E Okla., 7 mi. NNE of Muskogee, in agr. area.

Okaya (ōkä'yä), city (1940 pop. 40,033; 1947 pop. 36,491), Nagano prefecture, central Honshu, Japan, on W shore of L. Suwa, 13 mi. SSE of Matsumoto, near efflux of Tenryu R.; raw-silk center. Sericulture school.

Okayama, Formosa: see KANGSHAN.

Okayama (ōkä'yämû), prefecture [Jap. *ken*] (□2,721; 1940 pop. 1,329,358; 1947 pop. 1,619,622), SW Honshu, Japan; ⊙ Okayama. Bounded S by Hiuchi and Harima seas (central and E sections of Inland Sea). Includes many offshore isls.; largest, KONO-SHIMA and KITAGI-SHIMA. Mountainous terrain, drained by many small streams. Chief products: rice, wheat, peppermint, fruit (persimmons, pears, watermelons). Prefecture is major production area for floor mats made from rushes. Widespread stock raising; saltmaking on shores of Inland Sea. Mfg. (textiles, pottery). Chief centers: Okayama, KURASHIKI, TSUYAMA, TAMANO.

Okayama, city (1940 pop. 163,552; 1947 pop. 140,-631). ⊙ Okayama prefecture, SW Honshu, Japan, at mouth of small Asahi R., on Kojima Bay (inlet of Inland Sea), 70 mi. W of Osaka; 34°39'N 133°56' E. Rail junction; mfg. (porcelain ware, cotton textiles, flour, fancy matting). Has medical univ., ruins of feudal castle. Known for Koraku-en, a 22-acre park laid out in 18th cent. Bombed (1945) in Second World War.

Okazaki (ōkä'zä'kē), city (1940 pop. 84,073; 1947 pop. 85,361), Aichi prefecture, central Honshu, Japan, 20 mi. SE of Nagoya; cotton-textile center. Has feudal castle. Ieyasu (founder of Tokugawa shogunate) b. here.

O'Kean (ōkēn'), town (pop. 165), Randolph co., NE Ark., 20 mi. WNW of Paragould.

Okecie (ôkĕ'tsyĕ), Pol. *Okęcie,* residential suburb of Warsaw, Warszawa prov., E central Poland, 4 mi. SW of city center; principal Warsaw airport.

Okeechobee (ō"kēchō'bē), county (□ 780; pop. 3,454), central Fla., bounded W by Kissimmee R. and S by L. Okeechobee; ⊙ Okeechobee. Cattle-raising area of grassy plains with many small lakes and some swamps; also poultry and truck farming. Formed 1917.

Okeechobee, city (pop. 1,849), ⊙ Okeechobee co., central Fla., 35 mi. WSW of Fort Pierce, near N end of L. Okeechobee; shipping center for vegetables, poultry, fish, frogs legs, and palm fronds.

Okeechobee, Lake, S central Fla., at N edge of the EVERGLADES, c.37 mi. WNW of West Palm Beach; the 2d largest fresh-water lake (□ c.730) wholly within U.S., it is c.35 mi. long, 30 mi. wide, and 15 ft. deep; contains some small isls. Receives Kissimmee R. (N). Reclamation of the Everglades and adjacent lands led to diking of S shore to prevent periodic overflows, such as destructive flood accompanying 1926 hurricane, and to the building of drainage canals (also used for light navigation) from the lake to the Atlantic; larger boats use OKEECHOBEE WATERWAY. Drained, fertile muck lands along S shore support a major truck-produce and sugar-cane region; cattle raising is important on grasslands W and N of the lake; and the lake itself is a favorite fishing resort area with some commercial fisheries. Lake Okeechobee probably originated during late Pleistocene era as a slight depression in the sea bottom.

Okeechobee Waterway, S Fla., system of linked canals, rivers, and lakes extending for 155 mi. across the Fla. peninsula; from E terminus (near Stuart) at St. Lucie Inlet of the Atlantic, it passes through St. Lucie R. estuary, St. Lucie Canal, across L. Okeechobee into Caloosahatchee Canal, thence across L. Hicpochee and into Caloosahatchee R., which it follows to the Gulf of Mexico (W terminus) c.15 mi. SW of Fort Myers. Minimum Channel depth is 6 ft.; has 4 locks. Used as flood-time outlet for L. Okeechobee, and as commercial and pleasure-boat waterway. Sometimes called Cross-Florida waterway or Lake Okeechobee–Cross Florida waterway.

Okeene (ōkēn'), town (pop. 1,170), Blaine co., W central Okla., 31 mi. SW of Enid, near Cimarron

R.; wheat, cotton, corn, poultry, livestock; flour milling.

Okefenokee Swamp (ō″kŭfŭnōk′, –nō′kē) (□ c.700), mostly in SE Ga. (Charlton, Ware, Clinch, Brantley counties) and partly in NE Fla. (Baker, Columbia counties). One of the most famous and primitive swamps in the U.S., it is a saucer-shaped depression (c. 45 mi. long, 30 mi. wide) broken by low ridges and covered by brush, vines, cypress forests, wet savannas, and stretches of water. Contains many small isls. (hammocks) surrounded by marshes, and is habitat of deer, bear, raccoons, alligators, and a great variety of birds, including ibises. The part in SE Ga. is largely included in Okefenokee Natl. Wildlife Refuge (established 1937), with hq. at Waycross.

Okegawa (ōkā′gäwŭ), town (pop. 9,822), Saitama prefecture, central Honshu, Japan, 7 mi. NW of Omiya; cotton textiles; wheat, sweet potatoes.

Okehampton (ōk′hăm′tŭn), municipal borough (1931 pop. 3,352; 1951 census 3,897), W central Devon, England, on Okement R., at N edge of Dartmoor, and 15 mi. NNE of Tavistock; agr. market; mfg. (shoes, agr. machinery, fertilizer); limestone and slate quarries. Has remains of Norman castle.

Okemah (ōkē′mŭ), city (pop. 3,454), ⊙ Okfuskee co., central Okla., 22 mi. SW of Okmulgee, in agr. area (grain, pecans, cotton, sweet potatoes, corn); oil fields. Mfg. of petroleum products, mattresses, feed, tile; cotton ginning. A state training school for boys is here. Settled 1902.

Okement River, Devon, England, rises in 2 headstreams near center of Dartmoor, 5 mi. S of Okehampton; flows 13 mi. N to Torridge R. 2 mi. NE of Hatherleigh.

Okene (ōkĕ′nē), town (pop. 27,592), Kabba prov., Northern Provinces, S central Nigeria, 40 mi. WSW of Lokoja; agr. trade center; shea-nut processing, cotton weaving, sackmaking; palm oil and kernels, durra, corn, plantains.

Oker (ō′kŭr), village (pop. 7,220), in Brunswick, NW Germany, after 1945 in Lower Saxony, in the upper Harz, at NE foot of the Rammelsberg, on Oker R. and 3 mi. E of Goslar; rail junction; smelting of nonferrous metals; paint mfg.

Oker, Yugoslavia: see ZMAJEVO.

Oker River, NW Germany, rises in the upper Harz S of Goslar, flows c.70 mi. N, past Brunswick, to the Aller 8 mi. WNW of Gifhorn. Formerly also spelled Ocker.

Oketo (ōkē′tō), city (pop. 169), Marshall co., NE Kansas, on Big Blue R. and 9 mi. NNE of Marysville, near Nebr. line; grain.

Okfuskee (ōfŭ′skē, ōkfŭ′skē), county (□ 638; pop. 16,948), central Okla.; ⊙ Okemah. Intersected by North Canadian R. Agr. (watermelons, peaches, apples, cotton, grain, pecans, peanuts), stock raising, dairying. Oil and natural-gas fields; gasoline mfg. Formed 1907.

Okha or **Port Okha** (ō′kŭ), town (pop. 4,664), Amreli dist., NW Bombay, India, on W end of Kathiawar peninsula, at mouth of Gulf of Cutch, 17 mi. NNE of Dwarka; rail terminus; trade center; fishing, salt mfg.; automobile assembly plant. Lighthouse (NE). Large chemical works (mfg. of soda ash, bleaching powder) 5 mi. SW, at Mithapur.

Okha (ŭkhä′), city (1948 pop., including suburbs, over 50,000), N Sakhalin, Russian SFSR, on Sea of Okhotsk, 185 mi. NNE of Aleksandrovsk. Major petroleum-producing center, linked by rail and pipe line to MOSKALVO on W coast; sawmilling; asphalt deposits. Became city in 1938.

Okhaldhunga (ō′kŭldŏŏng″gŭ), town, E central Nepal, 80 mi. ESE of Katmandu; Nepalese military station. Formerly called Wakhaldunga. Copper mines 6 mi. N, at Jantra Khani village.

Okhansk (ŭkhänsk′), city (1935 pop. estimate 4,100), W central Molotov oblast, Russian SFSR, port on right bank of Kama R. and 40 mi. SW of Molotov; trade center in grain, livestock, lumber area. Founded 1781 as Rus. colonization outpost.

Okhi, Greece: see OCHE.

Okhota River (ŭkhô′tŭ), Khabarovsk Territory, Russian SFSR, rises in highland S of Oimyakon Plateau, flows 220 mi. S to Sea of Okhotsk near Okhotsk.

Okhotsk (ōkŏtsk′, Rus. ŭkhôtsk′), town (1948 pop. over 10,000), NE Lower Amur oblast, Khabarovsk Territory, Russian SFSR, on Sea of Okhotsk, near mouth of Okhota R., 440 mi. N of Nikolayevsk. Fishing port; gold mines. Highway leads to Yakutsk. Founded 1649. Formerly an administrative and trading center of Okhotsk Sea coast.

Okhotsk, Sea of, Rus. *Okhotskoye More,* NW arm of Pacific Ocean W of Kamchatka Peninsula and Kurile Isls.; connected with Sea of Japan (SW) by Tatar and La Pérouse straits, with Pacific Ocean (SE) through passages bet. Kurile Isls. Includes Shantar Isls. and Shelekhov Gulf (noted for high tides). Area is □ 590,000, has mean depth of 2,750 ft., deepest point is 11,060 ft. (near the Kuriles). Main ports: Nagayevo (harbor of Magadan), Okhotsk, Ayan, Gizhiga, Abashiri. Icebound (N) Nov.-June, with floating ice fields in extreme S. Heavy fogs are common. Fishing and crabbing off W coast of Kamchatka Peninsula.

Okhotsk Current (ōkŏtsk′), Jap. *Oyashio* [=parent stream], cold ocean current flowing S from Bering Sea along E Kurile Isls., Hokkaido, and N Honshu; meets Japan Current in the Pacific at about 38°N. A branch of Okhotsk Current enters Sea of Japan through Sea of Okhotsk and Tatar Strait and flows S along E shores of Korea, meeting Tsushima Current (branch of Japan Current) at about 40°N. Okhotsk Current chills shores of N Japan.

Okhri, Yugoslavia: see OCHRIDA, town.

Okhrid; Okhrida, Yugoslavia: see OCHRIDA.

Okhta (ôkh′tŭ), E suburb of Leningrad, Russian SFSR, on right bank of Neva R.; includes Bolshaya Okhta (N) and Malaya Okhta (S); mfg. of chemicals, sawmilling.

Okierabu-shima, Ryukyu Isls.: see OKINOERABU-SHIMA.

Oki-gunto (ō′kē-gōōn′tō), island group (□ 145; pop. 42,400), Shimane prefecture, Japan, in Sea of Japan, 35 mi. N of Matsue, off SW Honshu; includes DOGO (largest isl.) and DOZEN (group of 3 isls.). Generally mountainous and forested. Cattle raising, lumbering, fishing. Produces rice, raw silk. Emperor Gotoba exiled here in 1239. Saigo (on Dogo), chief town and port. Anglicized as Oki Isls.; sometimes called Oki-no-shima.

Okigwi (ôkē′gwē), town (pop. 2,290), Owerri prov., Eastern Provinces, S Nigeria, 35 mi. NE of Owerri; trade center; palm-oil milling; kola nuts. Has hosp.

Oki Islands, Japan: see OKI-GUNTO.

Okikeska Lake (ōkĭkĕ′skŭ) (7 mi. long, 3 mi. wide), W Que., on Harricanaw R., 22 mi. NW of Val d'Or, in gold-mining region.

Okinawa (ō″kĭnä′wä, Jap. ōkē′näwä), largest island (□ 467; 1950 pop. 517,634, including offshore islets) of Okinawa Islands, in Ryukyu Islands, bet. E.China Sea (W) and Philippine Sea (E), 330 mi. S of Kyushu; 26°30′N 127°55′E; 60 mi. long, 9 mi. wide. Volcanic; mountainous; rises to 1,600 ft., with dense vegetation over wide areas. Buckner Bay (SE) is largest harbor. Malarial region. Produces sugar cane, sweet potatoes, lumber, charcoal. Kadena and Yontan airfields are on W coast. NAHA (SW) is chief town and port; other centers are SHURI and ITOMAN. Scene of last great U.S. amphibious campaign (April–June, 1945) of Second World War. It was, until 1945, seat of governor of Okinawa prefecture (included isl. groups Okinawa and Sakishima isls.), Japan. These isls. were placed (Aug., 1945) under U.S. military governor. Formerly called Great Nansei.

Okinawa Islands, Jap. *Okinawa-gunto,* central group (□ 579; 1950 pop. 579,791) of RYUKYU ISLANDS, bet. East China Sea (W) and Philippine Sea (E), 325 mi. S of Kyushu; 26°4′–27°3′N 127°40′–127°59′E. Its 70-mi. chain comprises volcanic isls. of OKINAWA (largest), KERAMA-RETTO, IE-JIMA, KUME-SHIMA, DAITO-SHIMA, IHEYA-SHOTO, and scattered coral islets. Generally mountainous and fertile; in typhoon zone. Pine and oak forests. Agr. (sweet potatoes, sugar cane, bananas, pineapples); livestock-breeding. Produces textiles, lacquer ware, pottery. Naha on Okinawa is chief center.

Okino-daito-shima, Ryukyu Isls.: see DAITO-SHIMA.

Okinoerabu-shima (ōkĭnō′wäräbōō″shĭmä) or **Okierabu-shima** (ōkē′äräbōō″shĭmä), island (□ 37; 1950 pop. 28,309) of isl. group Amami-gunto, in Ryukyu Islands, bet. East China Sea (W) and Philippine Sea (E), 35 mi. N of Okinawa; 12 mi. long, 6 mi. wide. Hilly; fertile (sugar cane, sweet potatoes). Also called Erabu-shima. Chief town, Wadomari.

Okino-oagari-shima, Ryukyu Isls.: see DAITO-SHIMA.

Oki-no-shima, island group, Shimane prefecture, Japan: see OKI-GUNTO.

Okino-shima (ōkē′nō-shĭmä), island (□ 5; pop. 2,669, including offshore islets), Kochi prefecture, Japan, in Hoyo Strait just off SW coast of Shikoku; 3 mi. long, 2 mi. wide; hilly, fertile. Agr. (barley, sweet potatoes); raw silk, ornamental coral. Fishing.

Oki Shima, Japan: see DOGO.

Okitipupa (ōkēchēpōō′pä), town, Ondo prov., Western Provinces, S Nigeria, 40 mi. S of Ondo; agr. trade, center; cacao, palm oil and kernels, rubber, timber.

Okitsu (ōkē′tsōō). **1** Town (pop. 8,170), Chiba prefecture, central Honshu, Japan, on E Chiba Peninsula, 4 mi. W of Katsuura; beach resort; fishing. **2** Town (pop. 14,228), Shizuoka prefecture, central Honshu, Japan, on NW shore of Suruga Bay, 4 mi. NE of Shimizu; spinning, paper milling, tea processing. Has horticultural experiment station. Near by is temple founded in 7th cent. Sometimes spelled Okitu.

Okitu, Japan: see OKITSU, Shizuoka prefecture.

Okkak Islands, Labrador: see OKAK ISLANDS.

Oklahoma (ōklŭhō′mŭ), state (land □ 69,283; with inland waters □ 69,919; 1950 pop. 2,233,351; 1940 pop. 2,336,434), S central U.S., bordered S by Texas, E by Ark. and Mo., N by Kansas and Colo., W by N.Mex. and Texas; 17th in area, 25th in pop.; admitted 1907 as 46th state; ⊙ Oklahoma City. The "Sooner State" has a NW panhandle (165 mi. long E–W, 34 mi. wide N–S); the main body of state averages 205 mi. N–S, 305 mi. E–W. RED RIVER forms its entire S boundary. The whole region is essentially plains country, sloping SE, and interrupted in places by low, hilly tracts. The Arkansas R. receives Cimarron, North Canadian, and Canadian rivers; the Red R. receives the Washita R. Average elevation is c.1,300 ft., ranging from 4,978 ft. (Black Mesa) in extreme NW to c.320 ft. in extreme SE. The W counties, including those in the Panhandle, lie in the Great Plains, level and mostly treeless, descending, in the E, over a broken escarpment to a dissected plains region, marked by gypsum ledges and saline flats. This in turn gives way to an extensive prairie land of underlying shale formations, broken by low sandstone and limestone hills. In the E, extending into the state from Ark., are the Boston Mts.—the S part of the Ozarks—and, S of Arkansas R., the Ouachita Mts., the former a rugged plateau area, the latter a series of E–W folded ridges. Rising above the plain in the S are the Arbuckle Mts. and Wichita Mts. (2,464 ft.). In the extreme SE is a small strip (sand and clay soils) of the Gulf coastal plain. Okla. lies astride the vague climatic boundary bet. the humid subtropical SE U.S. and the dry continental W, the division being determined by the 20-in. rainfall line which passes through the W part of the state. W of this line the sparsely populated plains, covered with short buffalo grass, with sagebrush and yuccas in places, are subject to droughts, such as those of the 1930s in the Dust Bowl region. Most of Okla., however, has an adequate rainfall (25–50 in., W–E). The center of the state is prairie grassland (tall bluestem grass), while in the E oak-hickory and, in the Ouachitas, oak-pine woodlands predominate. Oklahoma City (center) has mean temp. of 37°F. in Jan., 81°F. in July, and annual rainfall of 32 in. The growing season varies from 180 days in the Panhandle to 230 days in the Red R. valley. Much of the land suffers from severe soil erosion. Farm acreage totals 36,000,000, with over 14,000,000 acres under crops; large-scale commercial farming is becoming dominant, especially in W. Chief crops are wheat (mainly hard winter wheat grown in N center and Panhandle), corn (throughout state, but especially E), grain sorghums (W and NW), hay, cotton (SW), oats (center, E), peanuts (S center), broomcorn (mostly NW; usually ranks 1st in U.S. output), truck crops, fruit (peaches, apples), and pecans (E center). There are nearly 2,500,000 head of cattle in the state; dairy and poultry farming are concentrated around the larger cities. Commercial forests comprise c.4,000,000 acres; natl. forest land (in Ouachita Mts.) is less than 350,000 acres. Okla. has considerable mineral wealth, especially in petroleum, ranking 4th in crude oil production in U.S. Main oil fields, many with natural gas, are located in N–S zone running through center of state, with large refineries at TULSA ("oil capital of the world"), Ponca City, Duncan, Cushing, and Enid. Bituminous coal is mined in the E, and the Tri-State Region (Okla.–Kansas–Mo.) in NE corner is a major zinc-lead producing area. Other deposits include natural gasoline, asphalt, gypsum, selenite, granite (Wichita and Arbuckle mts.), limestone, glass sand, and gravel. Next to refined petroleum and petroleum by-products, the chief manufactures are flour, grain and oilseed products, cotton goods, packed meat, oil-field equipment, cement, glass, bricks and tiles, and dairy and lumber products. Oklahoma City and Tulsa are the principal industrial centers, while other mfg. and trading cities include Muskogee, Enid, Shawnee, Lawton, Ardmore, Ada, Bartlesville, Okmulgee, Chickasha, Guthrie, and McAlester. Educational institutions include Univ. of Okla. (at Norman and Oklahoma City), Okla. Agr. and Mechanical Col. (at Stillwater), Univ. of Tulsa, and Langston Univ. (for Negroes). The Indian pop. (in 1940, 63,125; 19% of all U.S. Indians) is the largest of any state, comprising members of some 30 tribes. Osage co. (N) is coextensive with the Osage Indian Reservation. Indian dances and festivals, including an annual exhibition at Anadarko, are picturesque events in Oklahoman life. Principal recreation areas are the hilly Ozark, Ouachita, Arbuckle, and Wichita sections, PLATT NATIONAL PARK (near Sulphur), L. of the Cherokees, and L. Texoma, impounded by DENISON DAM on Red R. Excavations in the Panhandle and Ozarks have uncovered remains of several pre-Columbian Indian cultures. The Spaniards, including Coronado (1541) and de Oñate (1601), in search for gold, were perhaps the 1st explorers of the region, but in the 1680s the whole area was claimed by France. Spain regained possession in 1762, France in 1800, and, in 1803, it was sold to the U.S. as part of the Louisiana Purchase. The 1st white settlement was made at Salina in the early 19th cent., and in 1824 FORT GIBSON and Fort Towson were established. About this time the Five Civilized Tribes—Cherokee, Choctaw, Chickasaw, Creek, Seminole—were forced by the govt. to leave their lands in the SE states and settle in the country now comprising the state of Okla. This area, except for the Panhandle, became known as Indian Territory and was administered by the 5 Indian "nations" in treaty relations with the U.S. As punishment for joining the Confederacy during the Civil War the Tribes lost the W part of their territory, in which the Federal govt. erected forts and assigned lands to several plains Indians (Osage, Comanche, Cheyenne) and other tribes (Delaware, Shawnee) who were forced to emigrate from the NE states. Agitation for opening the unused Indian lands to white settlement—intensified by cattlemen seeking grazing land along the Texas-Kansas cattle trails and by the advent of the railroads in the '70s and '80s—led Congress to open a tract of "unassigned land" near the center of the Indian territory in the famous "run" of April 22, 1889. Thousands waited at the border for the signal to rush in and stake their claims, but a few illegally crossed over ahead of time and became known as the "Sooners." This area was organized in 1890 as Okla. Territory (⊙ Guthrie) and to it was added the Territory of CIMARRON, a public-land strip, now the state's Panhandle. Other Indian lands were soon made available to white men by runs or lotteries, including the large CHEROKEE STRIP in 1893. Although Indian Territory and Okla. Territory sought admission to the Union as separate states, the 2 were united as one state in 1907; since 1910, ⊙ Oklahoma City. Originally dependent on stock raising and agr., Okla.'s economy changed radically at the turn of the century with the discovery of extensive oil deposits. In the '30s NW Okla., along with other areas in the Dust Bowl, suffered from serious drought, and many tenant farmers were forced to go west as migrant laborers. However, irrigation and modern farming methods, as well as the food demands of the Second World War, brought back a degree of prosperity to agr. See also articles on the cities, towns, geographic features, and the 77 counties: ADAIR, ALFALFA, ATOKA, BEAVER, BECKHAM, BLAINE, BRYAN, CADDO, CANADIAN, CARTER, CHEROKEE, CHOCTAW, CIMARRON, CLEVELAND, COAL, COMANCHE, COTTON, CRAIG, CREEK, CUSTER, DELAWARE, DEWEY, ELLIS, GARFIELD, GARVIN, GRADY, GRANT, GREER, HARMON, HARPER, HASKELL, HUGHES, JACKSON, JEFFERSON, JOHNSTON, KAY, KINGFISHER, KIOWA, LATIMER, LE FLORE, LINCOLN, LOGAN, LOVE, MCCLAIN, MCCURTAIN, MCINTOSH, MAJOR, MARSHALL, MAYES, MURRAY, MUSKOGEE, NOBLE, NOWATA, OKFUSKEE, OKLAHOMA, OKMULGEE, OSAGE, OTTAWA, PAWNEE, PAYNE, PITTSBURG, PONTOTOC, POTTAWATOMIE, PUSHMATAHA, ROGER MILLS, ROGERS, SEMINOLE, SEQUOYAH, STEPHENS, TEXAS, TILLMAN, TULSA, WAGONER, WASHINGTON, WASHITA, WOODS, WOODWARD.

Oklahoma, county (□ 709; pop. 325,352), central Okla.; ⊙ OKLAHOMA CITY, capital of state. Intersected by North Canadian R. and the Deep Fork. Dairying, stock raising, agr. (wheat, poultry, oats). Mfg. at Oklahoma City. Oil fields; refineries, gasoline plants. Formed 1890.

Oklahoma, borough (pop. 930), Westmoreland co., W central Pa., on Kiskiminetas R. just above Vandergrift.

Oklahoma City, city (pop. 243,504), ⊙ Okla. and Oklahoma co., central Okla., on North Canadian R. and c.300 mi. SW of Kansas City, Mo.; largest city of state, at its geographical center in plains region; 35°28'N 97°31'W; alt. 1,195 ft. Important industrial, commercial, and distribution center for rich oil-producing and agr. area, with oil fields lying within city limits. Petroleum refining, mfg. of oil-field equipment, printing and publishing, flour milling, meat packing; also mfg. of steel and iron products, wood products, building materials, industrial gases, sporting goods, furniture, clothing, electrical equipment, pottery, bedding, paint. Seat of Oklahoma City Univ., the medical school of the Univ. of Okla., and Okla. City Col. of Law. Points of interest: Civic Group (1937), the capitol, the state historical society bldg., and several parks. A "pioneer city," settled in one day when area was opened to homesteaders in 1889; inc. 1890; made ⊙ Okla. in 1910. Development of city's oil pool began in 1928. Became important air base in Second World War. Tinker Air Force Base is near.

Okland, Rumania: see OCLAND.

Oklaunion (ō'klŭ-ū'nyŭn), town (pop. 129), Wilbarger co., N Texas, near Okla. line c.40 mi. WNW of Wichita Falls, in agr. area.

Oklawaha River (ŏklŭwô'hô), central and N Fla., rises in extensive central Fla. lake system (with L. Apopka at its upper end), flows N, receiving outlets of Silver Springs and Orange L., then turns E, converging with St. Johns R. near Welaka; total length c.140 mi. The upper course, extremely tortuous, is dredged to Leesburg (head of steamboat navigation) and has a dam and lock (completed 1925) 19 mi. N of Leesburg.

Oklee (ō'klē), village (pop. 494), Red Lake co., NW Minn., on Lost R. and 19 mi. E of Red Lake Falls; dairy products.

Okmulgee (ōkmŭl'gē), county (□ 700; pop. 44,561), E central Okla.; ⊙ Okmulgee. Intersected by the Deep Fork; includes Okmulgee and Henryetta lakes (recreation). Agr. (grain, cotton, livestock, pecans, peanuts, corn; dairy products). Mfg. at Okmulgee and Henryetta. Oil and natural-gas fields; oil refining, gasoline mfg. Coal mining. Formed 1907.

Okmulgee, city (pop. 18,317), ⊙ Okmulgee co., E central Okla., near the Deep Fork, 37 mi. S of Tulsa; trade and industrial center for oil-producing and agr. area (grain, livestock, cotton, corn; dairy products). Oil refining, glass-making, cotton ginning, meat packing; mfg. of oil-field equipment, furniture, mattresses, leather goods, canvas products; peanut and pecan processing. Coal mines. Near by is L. Okmulgee. An old Creek council house, and laboratories for study of hog cholera are in vicinity. Settled c.1889 on the site of ⊙ Creek Nation (1868–1907); inc. 1908. Boomed after discovery of oil (1907).

Okmulgee, Lake, Okmulgee co., E central Okla., 6 mi. WSW of Okmulgee, to which it supplies water; c.5 mi. long. Recreation area.

Okna (ôk'nŭ), Rum. *Ocna* (ôk'nä), village (1941 pop. 1,650), N Chernovtsy oblast, Ukrainian SSR, in N Bukovina, on Dniester R. and 20 mi. N of Chernovtsy; rail terminus; quartz-sand quarry.

Oknitsa (ŭknyē'tsŭ), Rum. *Ocnița* (ôknē'tsä), town (1941 pop. 2,698), N Moldavian SSR, 16 mi. WSW of Mogilev-Podolski, near Ukrainian border; flour and oilseed milling. Phosphorite deposits near by. Oknitsa rail junction (1941 pop. 1,531) is 2 mi. NE.

Okny, Ukrainian SSR: see KRASNYE OKNY.

Oko, Russian SFSR: see YASNOMORSKI.

Okoboji (ō"kōbō'jē), town (pop. 336), Dickinson co., NW Iowa, 17 mi. N of Spencer, bet. lakes East Okoboji (c.5 mi. long) and West Okoboji (c.6 mi. long); makes rowboats. Situated in popular resort area containing several state parks on West Okoboji L. and one, with a fish hatchery, on East Okoboji L.

Okodongwe (ōkōdông'gwā), village, Eastern Prov., NE Belgian Congo, 230 mi. ENE of Buta; cotton ginning.

Okolona (ōkŭlō'nŭ). **1** Town (pop. 458), Clark co., S central Ark., 18 mi. WSW of Arkadelphia, in agr. area. **2** Village (pop. 1,047), Jefferson co., N Ky., 10 mi. SE of Louisville. **3** City (pop. 2,167), a ⊙ Chickasaw co., NE central Miss., 18 mi. S of Tupelo, in agr., dairying, livestock, and timber area; bricks, tiles, lumber, clothing, cheese. Seat of Okolona Col. Founded 1848; burned in Civil War. Has a Confederate cemetery. Near by is a U.S. game preserve.

Okonek (ôkô'nĕk), Ger. *Ratzebuhr* (rä'tsŭbōōr), town (1939 pop. 2,940; 1946 pop. 1,799) in Pomerania, after 1945 in Koszalin prov., NW Poland, 14 mi. SSE of Szczecinek; woolen milling, dairying. Until 1938, in former Prussian prov. of Grenzmark Posen-Westpreussen. After 1945, briefly called Raciborz.

Okoneshnikovo (ŭkô'nyĭshnyĕkŭvŭ), village (1939 pop. over 2,000), SE Omsk oblast, Russian SFSR, 23 mi. SE of Kalachinsk; flour milling, metalworks.

Ökörmezö, Ukrainian SSR: see VOLOVO, Transcarpathian Oblast.

Okoshi (ōkō'shē), town (pop. 21,410), Aichi prefecture, central Honshu, Japan, on Kiso R. and 3 mi. W of Ichinomiya; silk textiles.

Oko-shima, Japan: see O-SHIMA, Nagasaki prefecture.

Okotoks (ō'kŭtŏks), town (pop. 694), SW Alta., at foot of Rocky Mts., 23 mi. S of Calgary; alt. 3,448 ft.; oil-shipping center for Turner Valley field; natural-gas and oil production, oil refining, pharmaceuticals mfg.

Okoudja (ōkōōjä'), village, E Gabon, Fr. Equatorial Africa, 75 mi. NNE of Franceville. Until 1946, in Middle Congo colony.

Okovanggo River or **Okovango River** (ōkōväng'gō), Port. *Cubango* (kōōbäng'gō), SW Africa, rises in central Angola on Bié Plateau E of Nova Lisboa, flows SE to South-West Africa border, then turns E and SE, crossing Caprivi Zipfel, into Bechuanaland Protectorate, where it loses itself in the Okovanggo Basin (or Okovanggo Marshes) NW of Maun; c.1,000 mi. long. One of its terminal arms reaches L. Ngami. Also spelled Okavango.

Okpara River (ōkpä'rä), E Dahomey, Fr. West Africa, rises N of Parakou, flows c.160 mi. S, mostly along Nigeria border, to Ouémé R. 25 mi. NNE of Zagnando.

Okrilla, Germany: see OTTENDORF-OKRILLA.

Oksarka, Russian SFSR: see AKSARKA.

Oksendal (ŭk'sŭndäl), Nor. *Øksendal*, village and canton (pop. 537), More og Romsdal co., W Norway, 5 mi. from head of Sunndals Fjord, 40 mi. E of Molde. Cattle raising in mts. near by. Formerly spelled Oxendal, Nor. *Øxendal*.

Oksfjordhamn (ŏks'fyŏrhäm"ŭn), fishing village in Skiervoy canton, Troms co., N Norway, on Nordreisa (small fjord of Norwegian Sea), 60 mi. ENE of Tromso.

Oksino (ôk'sēnŭ), village, central Nenets Natl. Okrug, Archangel oblast, Russian SFSR, on W arm of Pechora R. delta mouth and 22 mi. WSW of Naryan-Mar; trading post; fisheries; reindeer raising.

Oksoy (ôks'ūū), Nor. *Oksøy*, small island at the Skagerrak approach to Kristiansand, Vest-Agder co., S Norway; beacon light. Sometimes Oxö.

Oktaha (ŏk'tŭhä), town (pop. 207), Muskogee co., E Okla., 13 mi. SSW of Muskogee; cotton ginning.

Oktemberyan (ŭktyĕmbĭryän'), city (1947 pop. over 2,000), W Armenian SSR, in irrigated Aras R. valley, on railroad and 27 mi. W of Erivan; cotton ginning, fruit canning, metalworking, tanning; geranium-oil press. Orchards, vineyards, cotton, sugar beets, tobacco. Site of children's colony. Until c.1935, Sardarabad; sometimes called Oktember. Developed in 1930s, in irrigated desert zone.

Oktibbeha (ŏktĭ'bēhô), county (□ 454; pop. 24,569), E Miss.; ⊙ Starkville. Drained by Noxubee R. and small Oktibbeha R. Farming (cotton, corn, hay), dairying, stock raising; lumbering. Formed 1833.

Oktwin (ouk"twĭn'), village, Toungoo dist., Lower Burma, on railroad and 8 mi. S of Toungoo.

Oktyabr or **Oktyabr'** (ŭktyä'bŭr), town (1947 pop. over 500), NE Kashka-Darya oblast, Uzbek SSR, near Shakhrizyabz, in cotton area.

Oktyabrsk or **Oktyabr'sk** (–bŭrsk), village, S Stalinabad oblast, Tadzhik SSR, in Vakhsh valley, 5 mi. SSE of Kurgan-Tyube; long-staple cotton. Formerly Chichka.

Oktyabrskaya Revolyutsiya Island or **Oktyabr'skaya Revolyutsiya Island** (–bŭrskŭŭ rĕvŭlyōō'tsēŭ) [Rus., =October revolution], central island (□ 5,400) of Severnaya Zemlya archipelago, in Arctic Ocean, in Krasnoyarsk Territory, Russian SFSR; 45% covered by glaciers.

Oktyabrski or **Oktyabr'skiy** (–bŭrskē). **1** Suburb (1948 pop. over 500) of Tokmak, Frunze oblast, Kirghiz SSR; beet-sugar refining. **2** Town (1939 pop. over 500), NW Amur oblast, Russian SFSR, 110 mi. N of Zeya; gold mining. **3** City (1946 pop. over 2,000), W Bashkir Autonomous SSR, Russian SFSR, on Ik R. and 100 mi. WSW of Ufa, on rail spur from Urussu; major petroleum center in Tuimazy oil field (pipe lines to Chernikovsk and Urussu). Developed in 1940s through urbanization of Naryshevo and near-by villages; became city in 1946. **4** Town (1942 pop. over 500), W Chelyabinsk oblast, Russian SFSR, near (under jurisdiction of) Miass, in gold-mining region. **5** Town, NW Ivanovo oblast, Russian SFSR, 24 mi. WNW of Ivanovo; peat works. Until 1941, Obedovo. **6** Town (1940 pop. over 500), NW Kirov oblast, Russian SFSR, on railroad and 4 mi. NNW of Murashi; lumber milling. **7** Town (1946 pop. over 500), NE Komi Autonomous SSR, Russian SFSR, outer NE suburb of Vorkuta; coal mines. **8** Town (1939 pop. over 500), central Kostroma oblast, Russian SFSR, on railroad and 70 mi. E of Galich; sawmilling. Until 1939, Brantovka. **9** Town (1926 pop. 3,319), central Moscow oblast, Russian SFSR, on rail spur and 6 mi. SE of Lyubertsy; limestone quarries. **10** E suburb (1939 pop. over 500) of Shakhty, SW Rostov oblast, Russian SFSR, 10 mi. E of city center; anthracite mining. **11** Town (1939 pop. over 2,000), W central Ryazan oblast, Russian SFSR, 4 mi. SW of Skopin, in Moscow Basin; lignite mining. **12** Town (1926 pop. 972), W Ryazan oblast, Russian SFSR, 5 mi. W of Mikhailov; cement-making center; limestone works. Until 1927, Sapronovo. **13** Town (1948 pop. over 10,000), N Sakhalin, Russian SFSR, on Tatar Strait, 13 mi. S of Aleksandrovsk; coal mines. **14** Town (1943 pop. over 500), S Sverdlovsk oblast, Russian SFSR, 15 mi. NNE (under jurisdiction) of Berezovski; lumbering, peat digging. **15** Town (1941 pop. over 500), NW Stalinabad oblast, Tadzhik SSR, on railroad (Cheptura station) and 23 mi. W of Stalinabad; cotton.

Oktyabrskoi Revolyutsii, Imeni, or **Imeni Oktyabr'skoy Revolyutsii** (ē'mĭnyē ŭktyä'bŭrskoi rĕvŭlyōō'tsēē), N iron-mining suburb (1939 pop. over 10,000) of Krivoi Rog, Dnepropetrovsk oblast, Ukrainian SSR, 7 mi. NNE of city center and on right bank of Saksagan R. Until c.1926, called Rostkovski Rudnik.

Oktyabrskoye or **Oktyabr'skoye** (–skŭyŭ). **1** Village (1939 pop. over 2,000), SW Dzhalal-Abad oblast, Kirghiz SSR, near railroad (Bagysh station), 11 mi. NE of Dzhalal-Abad; walnut processing. **2** Village (1939 pop. over 500), E Chelyabinsk oblast, Russian SFSR, 50 mi. NE of Troitsk; wheat, livestock. **3** Village (1926 pop. 5,887), N Chkalov oblast, Russian SFSR, 45 mi. SSW of Meleuz; metalworking; wheat, livestock. Originally called Isayevo-Dedovo, and from 1923 until 1937 Kashirinskoye. **4** Village (1939 pop. under 500), NE Chuvash Autonomous SSR, Russian SFSR, 15 mi. SSE of Mariinski Posad; wheat, rye, oats. Until 1939, Ismeli. **5** Village (1948 pop. over 2,000), central Crimea, Russian SFSR, on railroad and 22 mi. N of Simferopol; flour mill, metalworks; wheat, barley, cotton. Pop. largely Tatar prior to Second World War. Until 1944, called Biyuk-Onlar. **6** Town (1926 pop. 7,178), S Nikolayev oblast, Ukrainian SSR, at mouth of the Southern Bug, 4 mi. S of Nikolayev (linked by railroad); metalworks; limestone quarries. Until 1938, Bogoyavlensk. **7** Village, Odessa oblast, Ukrainian SSR: see ZHOVTEN, village.

Oktyabrya, Imeni 11 (ē'mĭnyē ŭdyē'nŭtsŭ"tŭvŭ ŭktyŭbryä') [Rus., =in the name of 11th of October], village, N Chita oblast, Russian SFSR, 215 mi. NW of Skovorodino; former gold-mining town (1930–42).

Oku (ō'kōō), town (pop. 8,212), Aichi prefecture, central Honshu, Japan, on Kiso R. and 3 mi. NW of Ichinomiya; cotton textiles.

Okubo (ō'kōōbō). **1** Town, Akita prefecture, Japan: see SHOWA. **2** Town (1940 pop. 10,070; 1947 pop.

23,567), Hyogo prefecture, S Honshu, Japan, on Harima Sea, just W of Akashi, 10 mi. W of Kobe; sake-producing center. Hot springs. 3 Town (pop. 3,823), Toyamo prefecture, central Honshu, Japan, 5 mi. S of Toyama; rice growing; medicine, raw silk. Mineral springs.

Okucani (ô'kōōchänē), Serbo-Croatian *Okučani*, village, N Croatia, Yugoslavia, on railroad and 20 mi. S of Daruvar, at SW foot of the Psunj, in Slavonia, in lignite area.

Okuchi (o'kōōchē), town (pop. 17,952), Kagoshima prefecture, W central Kyushu, Japan, 33 mi. N of Kagoshima; rail junction; agr. center (rice, wheat); raw silk. Agr. and forestry schools. Site of feudal castle.

Okujiri-jima, Japan: see OKUSHIRI-SHIMA.

Okulovka (ŭkōō'lŭfkŭ), town (1926 pop. 2,923), E central Novgorod oblast, Russian SFSR, 22 mi. W of Borovichi; rail junction. Paper mill at Parakhino-Poddubye, just N.

Okulovski, Russian SFSR: see KAMENKA, Archangel oblast.

Okuma (ō'kōōmä), town (pop. 9,741), Fukuoka prefecture, N Kyushu, Japan, 19 mi. E of Fukuoka; coal-mining center.

Okushiri-shima (ōkōō'shĭrē-shĭmä) or **Okujiri-jima** (ōkōō'jĭrē-jĭmä), island (□ 56; pop. 7,618), Japan, in Sea of Japan, just W of SW peninsula of Hokkaido, in Hokkaido administrative unit; 42°9'N 139°28'E; 15 mi. long, 5 mi. wide. Mountainous, with fertile coastal area; hot springs. Rice growing, lumbering, fishing. Sometimes spelled Okushirisima.

Okusi, Timor: see OE-CUSSE.

Okuta (ôkōō'tä), town (pop. 1,122), Ilorin prov., Northern Provinces, W Nigeria, 65 mi. SW of Kaiama; road center; customs depot on Dahomey border; shea-nut processing, cotton weaving; cassava, yams, corn.

Okuura, Japan: see TOMOOKU.

Olá (ōlä'), village (pop. 170), Coclé prov., central Panama, 15 mi. WSW of Penonomé; corn, rice, beans, sugar cane, livestock.

Ola (ŭlä'), village (1926 pop. 271), N Khabarovsk Territory, Russian SFSR, on Sea of Okhotsk, 17 mi. E of Magadan; fisheries.

Ola (ō'lů), town (pop. 880), Yell co., W central Ark., 18 mi. SSW of Russellville; sawmilling.

Olaa (ō'lä'), also called **Keaau** (kā'ů-ou'), town (pop. 1,620), E Hawaii, T.H., 7 mi. SSE of Hilo. Large sugar plantation here employs workers in near-by villages of Kurtistown, Mountain View, and Nine Miles.

Olafsfjordur or **Olafsfjordhur** (ō'läfsfyûr"dhür), Icelandic *Ólafsfjörður*, city (pop. 941), in but independent of Eyjafjardar co., N Iceland, on SW arm of Eyja Fjord, 160 mi. NE of Reykjavik; 66°4'N 18°39'W; fishing port.

Olafsvik (ō'läfsvēk"), Icelandic *Ólafsvík*, village (pop. 458), Snaefellsnes co., W Iceland, NW Snaefellsnes peninsula, on Breidi Fjord; 64°53'N 23°43'W; cod fisheries.

Olamon, Maine: see GREENBUSH.

Olan, Pic d' (pēk dôlā'), peak (11,739 ft.) of the Massif du Pelvoux, Dauphiné Alps, SE France, on Isère–Hautes-Alpes dept. border, 10 mi. NE of Saint-Firmin, overlooking Valgodemar valley (S). Glacier. Difficult ascent.

Olanchab or **Ulanchap** (both: ōlänchäp'), Chinese *Wu-lan-ch'a-pu* (wōō'län'chä'bōō'), Mongolian league in Suiyuan section of Inner Mongolia, China; bounded E by Kalgan–Ulan Bator highway, S by Yin Mts., N by Mongolian People's Republic; main town is Polingmiao. Largely desert, the area has some grasslands used for sheep and cattle grazing.

Olancha Peak (ōlän'chů) (12,135 ft.), E Calif., in the Sierra Nevada, on Inyo-Tulare co. line, 24 mi. S of Lone Pine.

Olanchito (ōlänchē'tō), city (pop. 2,785), Yoro dept., N Honduras, in Olanchito valley, near Aguán R., 27 mi. SE of La Ceiba; commercial center in banana area; linked by rail with ports of La Ceiba, Trujillo, and Puerto Castilla; dairy farming. Airfield. Founded in early 17th cent.

Olancho (ōlän'chō), department (□ 12,986; 1950 pop. 105,450), E central Honduras; ⊙ Juticalpa. Bounded SE by Oro R. and Nicaragua; largely mountainous (sierras de Esperanza and de Agalta, Colón mts.); drained by Patuca R. and its 2 headstreams (Guayapa and Guayambre rivers) and by Sico R. Livestock raising and dairying, mainly in Olancho Valley; agr. (coffee, tobacco, sugar cane, rice). Gold placers in principal rivers. Pop. is concentrated in W half of dept. E half is covered by largely unexplored tropical forest; hardwood lumbering only activity. Tanning, sugar milling, cigar mfg. are lesser industries. Liquidambar oil is produced. Main centers (linked by road with Tegucigalpa): Juticalpa, Catacamas. Formed 1825.

Olancho Valley, in Olancho dept., central Honduras, extends c.50 mi. along middle course of Guayape R.; over 10 mi. wide; major livestock and dairying area. Main centers: Juticalpa, Catacamas.

Oland (û'länd), Swedish *Öland*, island (□ 519; pop. 26,230), Kalmar co., SE Sweden, in the Baltic; 56°12'–57°22'N 16°23'–17°9'E. Separated from mainland by Kalmar Sound (4–14 mi. wide). Together with surrounding islets forms Oland province [Swedish *landskap*] (□ 520); ⊙ Borgholm. Isl. is 85 mi. long, 2–9 mi. wide. Surface is generally level and fertile; sugar beets, rye, potatoes are grown, cattle raised. Chief industries are limestone and alum quarrying, sugar refining, cement mfg. Borgholm, Morbylanga, Degerhamn, and Haga are centers of pop. Isl. is popular summer resort. Islanders are called *Öningar*. Inhabited since Stone Age, isl. was historic Scandinavian battleground; there are remains of Viking fortifications.

Olanesti (ôlŭnĕsht'), Rum. *Olăneşti*, village (pop. 1,448), Valcea prov., S central Rumania, 8 mi. NW of Ramnicu-Valcea; health and summer resort (alt. 1,312 ft.) in S foothills of the Transylvanian Alps, noted for its iodine and sulphurous springs.

Olanesti, Moldavian SSR: see OLONESHTY.

Olanga (ô'lŭn-gŭ), Finnish *Oulanka* (ō'längkä), village, NW Karelo-Finnish SSR, on NW lake Pyaozero, 65 mi. W of Loukhi; iron deposits.

Olanpi, Cape, Formosa: see OLWANPI, CAPE.

Olanta (ōlăn'tů), town (pop. 586), Florence co., E central S.C., 22 mi. SSW of Florence; tobacco.

Olar (ō'lůr), town (pop. 414), Bamberg co., W central S.C., 29 mi. SW of Orangeburg; wood products.

Olargues (ôlärg'), village (pop. 606), Hérault dept., S France, at foot of the Monts de l'Espinouse, 21 mi. NW of Béziers; lumber. Has 15th-cent. bridge.

Olary, village, E South Australia, 140 mi. ENE of Port Pirie, on Port Pirie–Broken Hill RR; sheep. Uranium at near-by Radium Hill.

Olascoaga (ōläskwä'gä), town (pop. 2,027), central Buenos Aires prov., Argentina, 10 mi. SW of Bragado; rail junction and agr. center (corn, wheat, hogs, cattle).

Olaszfalu (ô'lŏsfŏlŏŏ), town (pop. 1,659), Veszprem co., NW central Hungary, in Bakony Mts., 10 mi. N of Veszprem; manganese and bauxite mined at near-by Epleny (ĕp'lānyů), Hung. *Eplény*.

Olathe (ōlā'thē). 1 Town (pop. 810), Montrose co., W Colo., on Uncompahgre R. and 45 mi. SE of Grand Junction; alt. 5,346 ft. Shipping point in livestock region; potatoes, onions. 2 City (pop. 5,593), ⊙ Johnson co., E Kansas, 19 mi. SW of Kansas City, Kansas; trade center for agr. and oil-producing area; mfg. (flour, boots, shoes). Has a naval air station and state school for deaf. Founded 1857 on Santa Fe Trail; inc. 1858.

Olavakkot, India: see PALGHAT, city.

Olavarría (ōläväré'ä), city (pop. 24,326), ⊙ Olavarría dist. (□ 2,959; pop. 52,739), S central Buenos Aires prov., Argentina, on the Arroyo Tapalqué and 175 mi. SW of Buenos Aires. Rail junction and agr. center; sheep and cattle raising; flour milling, dairying, meat packing; mfg. of chocolate, shoes, soap. Limestone and stone quarries (SE) feed cement mills at Sierras Bayas and Loma Negra.

Olawa (ôwä'vä), Pol. *Oława*, Ger. *Ohlau* (ō'lou), town (1939 pop. 13,136; 1946 pop. 6,410) in Lower Silesia, after 1945 in Wroclaw prov., SW Poland, port bet. Oder and Olawa rivers (here linked by canal), 17 mi. SE of Breslau (Wroclaw); chemical mfg., metalworking, zinc and lead refining, sawmilling. Gothic church, 16th-cent. castle (former seat of Pol. Piast princes). Town suffered heavily in Thirty Years War.

Olawa River (ôlä'vä), Ger. *Ohle* (ō'lů), in Lower Silesia, after 1945 in SW Poland, rises E of Zabkowice, flows N past Ziebice and Strzelin, NNE past Wiazow and Olawa (here linked by canal to the Oder), and NW to the Oder at Breslau (Wroclaw); 62 mi. long.

Olazagutía (ōläth-ägōōtē'ä), village (pop. 1,559), Navarre prov., N Spain, 28 mi. W of Pamplona; cement mfg., sawmilling; stock raising.

Ölberg, Grosser, Germany: see SIEBENGEBIRGE.

Olbernhau (ôl'bůrnhou), town (pop. 11,133), Saxony, E central Germany, in the Erzgebirge, 23 mi. SE of Chemnitz, near Czechoslovak border; toy-mfg. center; tin-plate and paper milling, woodworking, hosiery knitting; also mfg. of electrical equipment, radios, furniture.

Olbersdorf, Czechoslovakia: see ALBRECHTICE.

Olbersdorf (ôl'bůrsdôrf), town (pop. 6,674), Saxony, E central Germany, in Upper Lusatia, at foot of Lusatian Mts., 2 mi. SW of Zittau, near Czechoslovak border; lignite mining; mfg. of steel products, porcelain, linen; paper milling. Power station.

Olbia (ôlbē'ä), town (pop. 7,799), Sassari prov., NE Sardinia, port on Gulf of Terranova and 50 mi. NE of Sassari. Sardine fishing, corkworking. Passenger port (main service to mainland at Civitavecchia). Has Pisan church of San Simplicio. Originally Greek colony of Olbia. Called Terranova Pausania until early 1940s.

Olbia, Ukrainian SSR: see NIKOLAYEV, city, Nikolayev oblast.

Olca, Cerro (sĕ'rō ōl'kä), Andean peak (17,420 ft.) on Chile-Bolivia border; 20°54'S.

Olching (ôl'khĭng), village (pop. 7,249), Upper Bavaria, Germany, on the Amper and 12 mi. WNW of Munich; mfg. (precision instruments, textiles, paper).

Olcott, resort village (1940 pop. 772), Niagara co., W N.Y., on L. Ontario, 30 mi. NNE of Buffalo; makes cider, vinegar.

Old Aberdeen, Scotland: see ABERDEEN.

Old Albuquerque, N.Mex.: see ALBUQUERQUE.

Old Alresford, England: see NEW ALRESFORD.

Old Andreafsky, village (1939 pop. 11), W Alaska, on Yukon R. and 100 mi. NW of Bethel; formerly important trading center (salmon fishing and packing) and port with dock installations now destroyed. Has Russian Orthodox church. Fortified post established by Russians, c.1853.

Old Bahama Channel (bůhä'mů, bůhä'mů), strait (c.100 mi. long, 15 mi. wide) off N coast of Cuba, S of Great Bahama Bank.

Old Baldy. 1 Peak in Ariz.: see WRIGHTSON, MOUNT. 2 Peak in Calif.: see SAN ANTONIO PEAK. 3 Peak (14,125 ft.) in S Colo., in Sierra Blanca of Sangre de Cristo Mts., just NE of Blanca Peak. 4 Peak in Mont.: see GRAVELLY RANGE. 5 Peak in Texas: see LIVERMORE, MOUNT.

Old Bennington, Vt.: see BENNINGTON, town.

Old Bight, town (pop. 574), central Bahama Isls., on SW Cat Isl., 140 mi. SE of Nassau; 24°22'N 75°22'W. Sisal, fruit.

Oldbridge, agr. village in NE Co. Meath, Ireland, on the Boyne and 3 mi. W of Drogheda; scene (1690) of the battle of the Boyne, in which William of Orange and Schomberg defeated army of James II. Schomberg was killed here; James was forced to flee to France.

Old Bridge, village (1940 pop. 1,302), Middlesex co., E N.J., on South R. and 7 mi. SE of New Brunswick; bricks, concrete and cinder blocks.

Old Bridgeport, coal-mining village, NE N.S., on NE coast of Cape Breton Isl., 9 mi. NE of Sydney.

Old Brookville, village (pop. 644), Nassau co., SE N.Y., on W Long Isl., 4 mi. SE of Glen Cove.

Oldbury. 1 Village, Shropshire, England: see BRIDGNORTH. 2 Municipal borough (1931 pop. 35,926; 1951 census 53,895), N Worcester, England, 5 mi. WNW of Birmingham; glass-mfg. center (specializing in lighthouse lenses); steel and aluminum milling; mfg. of machinery, machine tools, plastics, chemicals, railroad cars. Near by are coal and iron mines and limestone quarries.

Old Cairo, Egypt: see FUSTAT, EL.

Old Calabar, Nigeria: see CALABAR, town.

Old Castile, Spain: see CASTILE.

Oldcastle, Gaelic *Sean-Chaisleán an Fhásaigh*, town (pop. 637), NW Co. Meath, Ireland, 21 mi. WNW of An Uaimh; agr. market (cattle, horses; potatoes). Many anc. cairns excavated near by.

Old Chitambo, Northern Rhodesia: see CHITAMBO.

Old Cleeve, agr. village and parish (pop. 1,435), W Somerset, England, 2 mi. WSW of Watchet. Has 15th-cent. church.

Old Cold Harbor, Va.: see COLD HARBOR.

Old Corinth, Greece: see CORINTH.

Old Cristobal, Panama Canal Zone: see CRISTOBAL.

Old Crow, village, N Yukon, on Porcupine R., at mouth of Old Crow R. and 250 mi. N of Dawson; 67°35'N 139°50'W; trading post, Royal Canadian Mounted Police station.

Old Cumnock (kŭm'nůk), parish (pop. 5,637), E central Ayrshire, Scotland. Parish includes burgh of CUMNOCK AND HOLMHEAD.

Old Dailly, Scotland: see DAILLY.

Old Deer or **Deer,** agr. village and parish (pop. 3,380), NE Aberdeen, Scotland, 10 mi. W of Peterhead. Of monastery founded here by St. Columba in 6th cent., the "Book of Deer," now in Cambridge Univ. Library, is sole relic. There are ruins of 13th-cent. Cistercian abbey. Village of New Deer is 6 mi. W.

Old Delhi, India: see DELHI, city; MAHRAULI.

Old Dongola, Anglo-Egyptian Sudan: see DONGOLA.

Oldeani (ōldĕä'nē), village, Northern Prov., Tanganyika, 35 mi. N of Mbulu; coffee, mixed farming.

Oldebroek (ôl'dübrōōk), village (pop. 842), Gelderland prov., central Netherlands, 3 mi. E of Elburg; graphite smelting; dairying.

Oldehove (ôl'dühōvů), agr. village (pop. 646), Groningen prov., N Netherlands, 9 mi. NW of Groningen. Also spelled Oldenhove.

Olde Lake (ôl'dů), Nor. *Oldevatn*, lake (□ 3) in a fissure of the glacier Jostedalsbre, Sogn og Fjordane co., W Norway; extends 8 mi. S from Olden village in Innvik canton (pop. 3,159), 60 mi. ENE of Floro. Tourist center.

Oldenburg (ôl'důnbûrg, Ger. ôl'dŭnbŏŏrk), former state (□ 2,084; 1939 pop. 577,648), NW Germany, after 1945 included as an administrative division [Ger. *Verwaltungsbezirk*] (□ 2,085; 1946 pop. 745,182) in Lower Saxony; ⊙ was Oldenburg. Until 1937 state was composed of 3 separate portions: Oldenburg proper, situated in N German lowlands on North Sea, forming an enclave in former Prussian prov. of Hanover; BIRKENFELD, forming an enclave in former Prussian Rhine Prov., after 1945 in Rhineland-Palatinate; and dist. of Lübeck (excluding Lübeck city), now in Schleswig-Holstein. Originally part of Saxony, Oldenburg became a county in 11th cent. Count Christian became (1448) king of Denmark; his brother Gerard and his successors continued to rule the county. Upon extinction (1667) of Ger. line, Oldenburg passed to Denmark. In 1773 it was exchanged for ducal Holstein, belonging to Grand Duke (later Emperor)

Peter I of Russia. Peter gave Oldenburg to his great-uncle, the bishop of Lübeck, who assumed (1777) ducal title. After Napoleonic Wars, Oldenburg, in 1815, acquired Birkenfeld and became a grand duchy. Joined (1871) German Empire. Last grand duke abdicated in 1918; Oldenburg joined Weimar Republic. Birkenfeld and Lübeck dist. were annexed by Prussia in 1937.

Oldenburg. 1 or **Oldenburg in Oldenburg,** city (1950 pop. 121,643), ⊙ Oldenburg, NW Germany, after 1945 in Lower Saxony, on the Hunte, at its junction with Ems-Hunte Canal, and 25 mi. WNW of Bremen; rail and water transshipment point; foundries. Mfg. of agr. machinery, dyes, varnish, soap, stearine, wax, cosmetics, ceramics; pipe and chewing tobacco, snuff; textile milling (cotton, wool), food processing (meat products, fruit and vegetable preserves, beer). Glassworks. Trades in lumber, grain, cattle, horses. Has Gothic church; former grand-ducal residence (17th cent.) now houses mus. Seat of Lutheran bishop. First mentioned in 12th cent. Chartered 1345. Seat of counts of Oldenburg until 1667, when it passed (with county) to Denmark (until 1773). Residence (1777–1918) of dukes, later grand dukes (since 1815), of Oldenburg. Captured by Canadian troops in May, 1945. 2 or **Oldenburg in Holstein** (ĭn hôl'-shtīn), town (1946 pop. 9,493), in Schleswig-Holstein, NW Germany, 15 mi. NE of Eutin; mfg. of machinery, pharmaceuticals, toys, mirrors, pressed peat; flour milling. Has 13th-cent. church. Was seat (948–1163) of bishop. Chartered 1235.

Oldenburg, town (pop. 591), Franklin co., SE Ind., 33 mi. ESE of Shelbyville, in agr. area. Seat of Acad. of the Immaculate Conception, a nunnery, and a Franciscan monastery.

Oldendorf, Germany: see MARKOLDENDORF.

Oldendorf, Hessisch, Germany: see HESSISCH OLDENDORF.

Oldendorf, Preussisch, Germany: see PREUSSISCH OLDENDORF.

Old England, town (pop. 1,110), Manchester parish, S Jamaica, 4 mi. SSE of Mandeville, in agr. region (tropical spices and fruit, livestock).

Oldenhorn (ōl'dŭnhôrn"), or **Becca d'Audon** (bĕkä' dōdō'), peak (10,256 ft.) in the Diablerets of the Bernese Alps, SW Switzerland, 9 mi. NW of Sion.

Oldenhove, Netherlands: see OLDEHOVE.

Oldenswort (ôl'dŭnsvôrt), village (pop. 2,068), in Schleswig-Holstein, NW Germany, on Eiderstedt peninsula, 8 mi. SW of Husum; cattle, horses. Has large church.

Oldenzaal (ōl'dŭnzäl), town (pop. 12,173), Overijssel prov., E Netherlands, on branch of Twente Canal and 7 mi. ENE of Hengelo; frontier station near Ger. border; textile center (cotton and linen spinning and weaving, dyeing, clothing mfg.); rope, furniture; building stone; dairy products. Has 10th–11th-cent. church (*Plechelmuskerk*).

Oldernes, Norway: see LAKSEVAG.

Oldesloe, Bad, Germany: see BAD OLDESLOE.

Old Factory River, village, NW Que., on Old Factory Bay, on E side of James Bay; 52°36'N 78°43'W. Hudson's Bay Co. trading post.

Old Faithful, Wyo.: see YELLOWSTONE NATIONAL PARK.

Old Field, village (pop. 238), Suffolk co., SE N.Y., on N shore of Long Isl., overlooking Smithtown Bay and 5 mi. NW of Port Jefferson, in resort, truck, and poultry area.

Old Field Point, SE N.Y., promontory with lighthouse (40°59'N 73°7'W), on N shore of W Long Isl., at W side of entrance to Port Jefferson Harbor.

Old Fletton. 1 Urban district (1931 pop. 7,481; 1951 census 8,955), N Huntingdon, England, just S of Peterborough; brickmaking center. Includes towns of Fletton (pop. 2,935), with Saxon and Norman church, New Fletton, Woodston (pop. 2,421), and Stanground (pop. 2,125). 2 Town, Northampton, England: see PETERBOROUGH.

Old Forge. 1 Resort village (1940 pop. 780), Herkimer co., N central N.Y., in the Adirondacks, on a lake of Fulton Chain of Lakes, c.45 mi. NNE of Utica, in winter-sports (skiing) and summer-resort area; logging; hunting, fishing. 2 Borough (pop. 9,749), Lackawanna co., NE Pa., 5 mi. SW of Scranton and on Lackawanna R.; anthracite; textiles. Settled 1798, inc. 1895.

Old Fort, town (pop. 771), McDowell co., W central N.C., on Catawba R. and 21 mi. E of Asheville.

Old Glory, village (pop. c.250), Stonewall co., NW central Texas, c.50 mi. NNW of Abilene, in cotton and grain area.

Old Goa, Portuguese India: see GOA, town.

Old Grand Port or **Vieux Grand Port** (vyû' grã' pôr'), village (pop. 1,024), SE Mauritius, on the Grand Port (inlet of Indian Ocean), on road and 3 mi. NNE of Mahébourg; sugar cane; limekiln.

Old Greenwich, Conn.: see GREENWICH.

Oldham (ōl'dŭm), county borough (1931 pop. 140,314; 1951 census 121,212), SE Lancashire, England, 7 mi. NE of Manchester; 53°33'N 2°7'W; major cotton-milling center; also leather tanning, engineering, mfg. of light metals and plastics. Has art gall. with large collection of 19th- and 20th-cent. English paintings. Site of "Oldham Wakes," an annual folk holiday. Linen weaving, originally introduced in 1630, gave way to milling of cotton (joined, later, by silk and wool) with the mechanization of spinning and weaving processes. Oldham is favored by its nearness to coal fields, its moist climate, and an adequate water supply.

Oldham. 1 County (□ 184; pop. 11,018), N Ky.; ⊙ La Grange. Bounded W by Ohio R. (Ind. line); drained by Floyds Fork. Rolling upland agr. area (burley tobacco, dairy products, oats, corn), in outer Bluegrass region. Formed 1823. 2 County (□ 1,466; pop. 1,672), extreme N Texas; ⊙ Vega. In high plains of Panhandle; alt. 3,200–4,100 ft. Wheat and cattle ranching; some fruit, truck; hogs, sheep, poultry, dairy products. Drained by Canadian R. and tributaries. Formed 1876.

Oldham, city (pop. 349), Kingsbury co., E S.Dak., 16 mi. SE of De Smet; dairy products, livestock, grain.

Old Hamilton, Alaska: see HAMILTON.

Oldhamstocks (ōld-hăm'stŏks), agr. village and parish (pop. 405), E East Lothian, Scotland, 7 mi. SE of Dunbar.

Old Harbor, village (pop. 122), Alaska, on SE Kodiak Isl., 60 mi. SW of Kodiak; fishing, fish processing. Site of THREE SAINTS BAY, Russian settlement in Alaska, established 1784.

Old Harbour, town (pop. 1,930), St. Catherine parish, S Jamaica, in coastal lowland, on railroad and 20 mi. W of Kingston; sugar cane, tropical fruit, coffee. The minor port Old Harbour Bay (2 mi. S), on bay of the same name, was once noted for shipbuilding. U.S. naval base (leased in 1940) near by.

Old Harbour Bay, Caribbean inlet of S Jamaica, bounded by Clarendon and St. Catherine parishes, c.20 mi. SW of Kingston; at its SW gate is Portland Ridge peninsula. The bay is dotted with many islets, such as Great Goat Isl. and Pigeon Isl., which, together with sections of the shore line, were leased to the U.S. for naval bases in 1940. The minor port of Old Harbour Bay is at its head. Sometimes called Portland Bight.

Old Head, cape (348 ft. high) on S shore of Clew Bay, SW Co. Mayo, Ireland, 2 mi. NE of Louisburgh; 53°47'N 9°48'W.

Old Head of Kinsale (kĭnsāl'), Atlantic cape, S Co. Cork, Ireland, 7 mi. S of Kinsale; lighthouse (51°36'N 8°31'W).

Old Hickory, industrial village (1940 pop. 5,993), Davidson co., N central Tenn., on Cumberland R. and 10 mi. NNE of Nashville. Owned by E. I. du Pont de Nemours and Co.; produces rayon, cellophane, chemicals. Until 1923, called Jacksonville.

Old Hill, town (pop. 12,079) in Rowley Regis municipal borough, S Stafford, England; mfg. of machinery, wire, aluminum products, shoes.

Oldhorn Mountain (10,125 ft.), W Alta., near B.C. border, in Rocky Mts., in Jasper Natl. Park, 11 mi. SW of Jasper; 52°46'N 118°13'W.

Old Ijssel River or **Old Yssel River,** Du. *Oude IJssel* or *Oude IJsel* (both: ou'dŭ ī'sŭl), Ger. *Issel* (ĭ'sŭl), in NW Germany and E Netherlands, rises 3 mi. SW of Borken, flows 45 mi. SW and NE, past Anholt, forms border bet. Germany and Netherlands (for 2 mi.), enters the Netherlands just SSE of Ulft (head of navigation), continuing, past Terborg, Doetinchem, and Doesburg, to Ijssel R. just SSW of Doesburg.

Old Iliamna, Alaska: see ILIAMNA.

Oldisleben (ôl'dĭslā"bŭn), village (pop. 3,262), Thuringia, central Germany, on the Unstrut and 14 mi. ESE of Sondershausen; wheat, rye, sugar beets, livestock. Has remains of 12th-cent. Sachsenburg castle.

Old Kasaan National Monument (kŭsăn') (38 acres), SE Alaska, on E Prince of Wales Isl., 30 mi. WNW of Ketchikan; includes historic ruins of abandoned Haida Indian village, with grave houses and totem poles. Established 1916.

Old Kilpatrick or **West Kilpatrick,** town and parish (pop. 55,641, including Clydebank burgh), SE Dumbarton, Scotland, on the Clyde and 5 mi. ESE of Dumbarton; shipbuilding, ironworking. Roman Wall of Antoninus passes town. Old Kilpatrick is one of places claiming to be birthplace of St. Patrick.

Oldland, town and parish (pop. 2,125), SW Gloucester, England, 5 mi. E of Bristol; shoe industry.

Old Leighlin (lē'lĭn), Gaelic *Sean-Leithghlin,* agr. village (district pop. 415), W Co. Carlow, Ireland, 8 mi. SSW of Carlow; wheat, potatoes, beets; sheep. Monastery was founded here in 7th cent. by St. Laserian; site of Protestant cathedral, founded c.1185, rebuilt 1529–49, seat of bishop of Ossory, Ferns, and Leighlin. Town is also seat of R.C. bishop of Kildare and Leighlin. Sometimes called Leighlin.

Old Lighthouse Island or **Lighthouse Island,** islet in the Irish Sea at SE entrance to Belfast Lough, Co. Down, Northern Ireland, 4 mi. N of Donaghadee.

Old Luce, parish (pop. 2,052), S central Wigtown, Scotland. Includes GLENLUCE.

Old Lyme (līm), residential town (pop. 2,141), New London co., SE Conn., at mouth of the Connecticut, 11 mi. WSW of New London; furniture mfg. Formerly part of Lyme town (N); includes village of Lyme, near the Connecticut. Has art gall., fine old buildings, restored Congregational church (1817). Settled c.1665, inc. 1855.

Old Maas River, Du. *Oude Maas* (ou'dŭ mäs'), SW Netherlands, formed by forking of LOWER MERWEDE RIVER into Noord R. and Old Maas R. 1 mi. N of Dordrecht; flows 19 mi. WNW, joining New Maas R. 7 mi. WSW of Rotterdam to form the SCHEUR and BRIELSCHE MAAS RIVER. Dortsche Kil R. branches from it 1 mi. SW of Dordrecht; Spui R. branches from it 6 mi. SSW of Rotterdam. Forms N boundary of Beijerland and Putten isls. Entire length navigable.

Old Malda or **Malda** (mäl'dŭ), town (pop. 3,845), Malda dist., N West Bengal, India, on the Mahananda and 2 mi. N of English Bazar; rice, wheat, oilseeds, jute. Has 16th-cent. mosque. Site of former Dutch and French factories.

Old Malton, England: see MALTON.

Old Man of Coniston, England: see CONISTON.

Old Man of Hoy, Scotland: see HOY.

Old Man of the Mountain, N.H.: see PROFILE MOUNTAIN.

Oldman River, Alta., headstream of South Saskatchewan R., rises in several headstreams in Rocky Mts. near Coleman, flows in a winding course E, past Macleod and Lethbridge, to confluence with Bow R. 45 mi. W of Medicine Hat, here forming South Saskatchewan R.; 250 mi. long from source of Crowsnest R., its principal headstream. Receives Belly, St. Mary, and several minor rivers.

Oldmans Creek, SW N.J., rises SW of Glassboro, flows c.25 mi. generally NW, forming Gloucester-Salem co. line, to Delaware R. above Penns Grove. Navigable for c.11 mi. above mouth. Chief freight, farm produce.

Old Man's Pond, lake (8 mi. long, 1 mi. wide), W N.F., 10 mi. NNE of Corner Brook.

Old Marissa (mŭrĭ'sŭ), village (pop. 200), St. Clair co., SW Ill., 32 mi. SE of East St. Louis, just N of Marissa, in bituminous-coal and agr. area.

Old Meldrum, burgh (1931 pop. 980; 1951 census 1,104), E central Aberdeen, Scotland, 15 mi. NNW of Aberdeen; cotton milling. Has 17th-cent. church. Just S is Barra Hill (634 ft.), with prehistoric fort.

Old Mission Peninsula, Mich.: see GRAND TRAVERSE BAY.

Old Mobeetie, Texas: see MOBEETIE.

Old Monkland, town and parish (pop. 62,843, including Coatbridge burgh), N Lanark, Scotland, just S of Coatbridge; coal mining.

Old Monroe, town (pop. 268), Lincoln co., E Mo., on Cuivre R., near the Missouri, and 13 mi. ESE of Troy.

Old Mulkey Meeting House State Park, Ky.: see TOMPKINSVILLE.

Old Mystic, Conn.: see GROTON.

Old Northwest, U.S.: see NORTHWEST TERRITORY.

Old Orchard Beach, town (pop. 4,707), York co., SW Maine, on the coast 10 mi. SSW of Portland; resort with 4-mi.-long beach, amusement equipment. Resort development began in early 19th cent. Trading post here before 1630, inc. 1883.

Old Oswestry, England: see OSWESTRY.

Old Oyo (ôyô'), town, Oyo prov., Western Provinces, SW Nigeria, 38 mi. WSW of Jebba; cotton weaving, shea-nut processing; cattle raising. Sometimes called Katunga. Was ⊙ of Yoruba tribe in 17th–18th cents.

Old Paphos, Cyprus: see KOUKLIA.

Old Perlican (pûr'lĭkŭn), village (pop. 694), SE N.F., on E side of Trinity Bay, 25 mi. NNE of Carbonear; fishing. Just offshore is Perlican Isl.

Old Point Comfort, shore resort, Elizabeth City co., SE Va., on small peninsula (Old Point Comfort) at N side of entrance to Hampton Roads, SE of Phoebus and Hampton and opposite Norfolk; postoffice name is Fort Monroe. Ferries to Norfolk, Cape Charles city. Bathing, fishing resort since 1830s. Here is U.S. Fort Monroe (long known as Fortress Monroe), built 1819–34 on site of 17th-cent. fortifications. Held by Union throughout Civil War; Jefferson Davis imprisoned here, 1865–67. Long a coast artillery post, it became (1946) hq. of U.S. army field forces.

Old Providence Island, Sp. *Providencia* or *Vieja Providencia* (vyä'hä prōvēdĕn'syä), island (pop. 2,267) in Caribbean Sea, 145 mi. off Mosquito Coast of Nicaragua, belonging to Colombia, part of SAN ANDRÉS Y PROVIDENCIA intendancy, c.50 mi. NNE of St. Andrews Isl.; 13°19'N 81°23'W. Of volcanic origin, it is 4½ mi. long and rises to 1,190 ft. The village (pop. 184) of Providencia or Isabel, on its NW coast, has chief anchorage. Main products: coconuts, oranges; also corn, sugar cane, bananas, cotton, livestock. Populated by Protestant English-speaking Negroes.

Old Radnor, Wales: see NEW RADNOR.

Old Rampart, Indian village (1939 pop. 6), NE Alaska, near Yukon border, on Porcupine R. and 110 mi. ENE of Fort Yukon; 67°10'N 141°40'W; trapping. Established 1869 as trading post of Hudson's Bay Co.

Old Rayne, agr. village in Rayne parish (pop. 921), central Aberdeen, Scotland, on Urie R. and 8 mi. NW of Inverurie.

Old Rhine River, Du. *Oude Rijn* (ou'dŭ rīn'), arm of the Rhine in central and W Netherlands, a continuation of CROOKED RHINE RIVER at Utrecht; flows 42 mi. W past Woerden, Bodegraven, Alphen aan den Rijn, and Leiden, to North Sea at Katwijk aan Zee. Crossed by Merwede Canal 1 mi. WSW of Utrecht. Navigable bet. Utrecht and Woerden by ships to 50 tons, to Bodegraven by ships to 200 tons, to Leiden by ships to 700 tons, below Leiden by ships to 300 tons.

Old Rhodes Key (c.2½ mi. long), one of the Florida Keys, S Fla., in the Atlantic (E), 28 mi. S of Miami, partly sheltering Biscayne Bay (W).

Old Ripley, village (pop. 135), Bond co., SW central Ill., 26 mi. W of Vandalia, in agr. area (corn, wheat; dairy products; poultry, livestock).

Old River, Br. Honduras: see BELIZE RIVER.

Old River, La.: see RED RIVER.

Old Road, village, W St. Kitts, B.W.I., 5 mi. WNW of Basseterre; sugar cane, sea-island cotton. Here landed (1623) Sir Thomas Warner with Br. settlers.

Olds, town (pop. 1,521), S central Alta., 50 mi. N of Calgary; grain elevators, dairying, stock. Site of prov. school of agr.

Olds, town (pop. 187), Henry co., SE Iowa, 12 mi. N of Mount Pleasant, in livestock area.

Old Sarum (sâ'rŭm), anc. *Sorbiodunum*, ancient city, SE Wiltshire, England, 2 mi. N of Salisbury. Hilltop was fortified by anc. Britons, Romans, and Saxons in turn. Normans built cathedral, city, and castle here. Seat of bishopric was moved here (1075) from Sherborne. Declined in early 13th cent., after seat of bishopric was moved (1220) to New Sarum (Salisbury). Many relics and foundations have been excavated.

Old Saybrook, resort town (pop. 2,499), Middlesex co., S Conn., on Long Isl. Sound, at mouth of the Connecticut (here bridged), and 28 mi. E of New Haven; agr., fishing, mfg. (hardware, boats, food products). Includes Fenwick (resort borough; pop. 16), Old Saybrook village (1940 pop. 801; formerly Saybrook), and Saybrook Point (summer colony). Collegiate School of America here (early 18th cent.) was nucleus of Yale Univ. Settled 1635 as Saybrook colony, inc. 1854 as Old Saybrook. A town formerly named Saybrook (now DEEP RIVER) is N.

Old Scone, Scotland: see SCONE.

Old Sennar, Anglo-Egyptian Sudan: see SENNAR.

Oldsmar, city (pop. 345), Pinellas co., W Fla., 10 mi. ENE of Clearwater, near Old Tampa Bay.

Old Sodbury, agr. village and parish (pop. 837), SW Gloucester, England, 12 mi. ENE of Bristol, in the Cotswold Hills. Has church dating from 12th cent. Site of anc. Br. camp, later one of largest Roman camps in Britain. Just N is agr. village and parish of Little Sodbury (pop. 129), with manor house in which William Tyndale was tutor (1521) to family of Sir John Walsh and where he translated Erasmus' *Enchiridion* and began translation of New Testament.

Old Spec Mountain (4,180 ft.), Oxford co., W Maine, near N.H. line, 20 mi. W of Rumford; has state's highest lookout station.

Old Tampa Bay, Fla.: see TAMPA BAY.

Old Tappan (tăpăn'), borough (pop. 828), Bergen co., extreme NE N.J., 12 mi. NE of Paterson, near Hackensack R. and N.Y. line.

Old Town. 1 Town (pop. 40), Dickinson co., NW Iowa. **2** City (pop. 8,261), Penobscot co., S central Maine, on the Penobscot and 13 mi. above Bangor. Mfg. (canoes, shoes, pulp, paper; other lumber-product mills; woolen mills). On small isl. N of Old Town village is a reservation for Penobscot Indians. Maine's 1st railroad (1836) connected Old Town with Bangor. Includes villages of Stillwater and Great Works. Settled 1774, inc. 1840, city chartered 1891.

Oldtown. 1 Village (pop. 358), Bonner co., N Idaho, at state line adjacent to Newport, Wash. **2** Village (pop. c.200), Allegany co., W Md., on North Branch of the Potomac (bridged) and 11 mi. SE of Cumberland. Near by is Green Ridge State Forest. Settled 1741 by Thomas Cresap, on old Indian trail.

Old Trafford, S suburb (pop. 8,766) of Manchester, SE Lancashire, England, in Stretford urban dist.; mfg. of machine tools, electrical equipment, pharmaceuticals, oleomargarine.

Old Tupton, England: see TUPTON.

Old Uppsala, Sweden: see GAMLA UPPSALA.

Old Washington, Ohio: see WASHINGTON.

Old Westbury, residential village (pop. 1,160), Nassau co., SE N.Y., on W Long Isl., 3 mi. NE of Mineola. Inc. 1924.

Old Windsor (wĭn'zŭr), residential town and parish (pop. 2,347), E Berkshire, England, on the Thames just SE of Windsor. Church dates from 13th cent. Edward the Confessor had castle here.

Old Yssel River, Netherlands and Germany: see OLD IJSSEL RIVER.

Olean. 1 (ō'lēăn") Town (pop. 165), Miller co., central Mo., 5 mi. N of Eldon. **2** (ō'lēăn", ōlēăn') Industrial city (pop. 22,884), Cattaraugus co., W N.Y., on Allegheny R. at mouth of Olean Creek, near Pa. line, and 60 mi. SSE of Buffalo; oil-storage center; mfg. of carbon black, clothing, chemicals, machinery, metal and wood products, dairy products, feed, tile, glass, cutlery; printing. Sand and gravel pits. Oil fields near by. Settled 1804, inc. 1893.

Olean Creek, N.Y.: see ISCHUA CREEK.

Olecko (ôlĕts'kô), Ger. *Treuburg* (troi'bŏŏrk), town (1939 pop. 7,114; 1946 pop. 1,413) in East Prussia, after 1945 in Bialystok prov., NE Poland, in Masurian Lakes region, on small lake, 18 mi. W of Suwalki; rail junction; grain and cattle market. Founded 1560. In First World War, important flank position of Russian lines in 1st stage (Sept., 1914) of battle of Masurian Lakes. In Second World War, c.90% destroyed. Until 1928, called Marggrabowa.

Oledo (ŏŏlā'dŏŏ), village (pop. 1,509), Castelo Branco dist., central Portugal, 15 mi. NE of Castelo Branco; grain, corn, horse beans. Oak woods.

Oleggio (ôlĕd'jô), village (pop. 3,068), Novara prov., Piedmont, N Italy, 11 mi. N of Novara; rail junction; cotton and hosiery mills. Has Romanesque church with 10th-cent. frescoes.

Oleh (ō'lĕ), tribal confederation of Western Aden Protectorate, astride the Kaur al Audhilla. Although centered on Mudia plain of DATHINA dist., it also includes tribes on N slopes of the Kaur range in Upper Aulaqi country.

Olehleh, Indonesia: see ULE-LUE.

Oleiros (ŏŏlā'rŏŏsh), town (pop. 601), Castelo Branco dist., central Portugal, 23 mi. WNW of Castelo Branco; lumbering, resin and pitch extracting. Has 16th-17th-cent churches.

Olekma River (ŭlyĕk'mŭ), in N Chita oblast and S Yakut Autonomous SSR, Russian SFSR, rises in Yablonovy Range, flows 794 mi. N, through gold-mining area, to Lena R. below Olekminsk. Receives Nyukzha and Tungir (right), Chara (left) rivers.

Olekminsk (–mĭnsk), city (1926 pop. 2,285), S Yakut Autonomous SSR, Russian SFSR, on Lena R., near mouth of Olekma R., and 325 mi. SW of Yakutsk, in agr., cattle-raising area; flour mill.

Olen (ō'lŭn), town (pop. 5,663), Antwerp prov., N Belgium, 3 mi. SSE of Herentals; copper, cobalt, and pitchblende refining; radium production. Formerly spelled Oolen.

Olen (û'lŭn), Nor. *Ølen*, village and canton (pop. 2,048), Hordaland co., SW Norway, on a S inlet of Hardanger Fjord, 24 mi. ENE of Haugesund; canneries.

Olenek (ŭlyĭnyôk'), village (1948 pop. over 500), NW Yakut Autonomous SSR, Russian SFSR, on Olenek R. and 350 mi. S of Nordvik; trading post. Formerly Olenekskaya Kultbaza.

Olenek River, NW Yakut Autonomous SSR, Russian SFSR, rises on central Siberian plateau, flows 1,500 mi. E and N in zig-zag course, past Olenek, to Laptev Sea of Arctic Ocean at Ust-Olenek. Navigable for c.500 mi. Abounds in fish.

Olenino (ŭlyĕ'nyĭnŭ), town (1948 pop. over 2,000), SW Kalinin oblast, Russian SFSR, 30 mi. W of Rzhev; flax processing.

Olentangy River (ō"lŭntăn'jē), central Ohio, rises near Galion in Crawford co., flows NW, then S, past Delaware and Worthington, to Scioto R. at Columbus; c.75 mi. long.

Óleo (ô'lēŏŏ), city (pop. 608), W central São Paulo, Brazil, 35 mi. E of Ourinhos; coffee and cotton processing, sawmilling, pottery mfg.

Oléron, Île d' (ēl dôlārō'), largest island (□ 68; pop. 12,820) in Bay of Biscay, part of Charente-Maritime dept., W France; extends NW-SE opposite mouth of Charente R.; separated from mainland by the Pertuis de Maumusson (1 mi. wide) and from Île de Ré by the Pertuis d' Antioche; 18 mi. long, 6 mi. wide; generally level and sandy with pine-covered dunes in S. Produces early vegetables, forage crops, wines (for distilling); oyster beds. Tourist trade. Principal localities are Le Château-d'Oléron, Saint-Pierre, Saint-Trojan-les-Bains.

Olesa de Montserrat (ōlā'sä dhä mōnsĕrät'), town (pop. 5,651), Barcelona prov., NE Spain, in Catalonia, on the Llobregat and 17 mi. NW of Barcelona; mfg. of cotton and wool textiles, felt, cement, dyes; olive-oil processing; lumbering. Livestock, wine, cereals, fruit in area. Warm sulphur springs near by.

Olesko (ŭlyĕs'kŭ), town (1931 pop. 3,824), E Lvov oblast, Ukrainian SSR, 14 mi. SW of Brody; cement mfg. Has ruins of 16th-cent. castle.

Olesnica (ôlĕshnē'tsä), Pol. *Oleśnica*, Ger. *Oels* or *Öls* (ûls), town (1939 pop. 18,183; 1946 pop. 4,246) in Lower Silesia, after 1945 in Wroclaw prov., SW Poland, 17 mi. ENE of Breslau (Wroclaw); linen and paper milling, mfg. of shoes, chemicals, furniture, food products; brewing, distilling, flour milling, sawmilling. Mentioned 1214 as trade center; chartered 1255. Was (1312–1492) ⊙ duchy under branch of Piast dynasty. Passed 1884 to Prussia. Considerably damaged in Second World War; 13th-cent. tower, medieval gate, and remains of old town walls survived.

Olesno (ôlĕs'nô), Ger. *Rosenberg* (rō'zŭnbĕrk), town (1939 pop. 7,263; 1946 pop. 6,058) in Upper Silesia, after 1945 in Opole prov., S Poland, 25 mi. NE of Oppeln (Opole); linen milling; agr. market (grain, potatoes, livestock). Old church is object of pilgrimage.

Oletta (ôlĕtä', It. ôlĕt'tä), village (pop. 1,008), N Corsica, 7 mi. SW of Bastia; olives, sericulture.

Oletta (ōlĕ'tä) or **Holetta** (hō–), village (pop. 1,500), Shoa prov., central Ethiopia, 17 mi. W of Addis Ababa. Agr. settlement (cereals, fruit, vegetables) founded here (1937) by Italians; mills (flour, lumber).

Olette (ôlĕt'), village (pop. 599), Pyrénées-Orientales dept., S France, in CONFLENT valley, on Têt R. and 9 mi. WSW of Prades; hot sulphur springs. Iron mines near by.

Oleum (ō'lēŭm), oil-refining and -shipping point, Contra Costa co., W Calif., on San Pablo Bay, 9 mi. NE of Richmond; tanker docks.

Olevano Romano (ôlā'vänô rômä'nô), town (pop. 6,615), Roma prov., Latium, central Italy, 6 mi. SW of Subiaco. Has remains of anc. walls and old castle.

Olevsk (ŭlyĕfsk'), town (1926 pop. 5,060), NW Zhitomir oblast, Ukrainian SSR, on Ubort R. (right tributary of the Pripet) and 45 mi. WNW of Korosten; ceramics; lumbering. USSR-Poland frontier station (1921–39).

Oley, village (1940 pop. 605), Berks co., SE central Pa., 7 mi. ENE of Reading; hosiery mfg.

Olfen (ôl'fŭn), town (pop. 3,603), in former Prussian prov. of Westphalia, NW Germany, after 1945 in North Rhine-Westphalia, on Dortmund-Ems Canal and 5 mi. SW of Lüdinghausen; grain, cattle, hogs.

Olfusa (ûl'vüsou"), Icelandic *Ölfusá*, wide river, SW Iceland, formed 10 mi. NE of Eyrarbakki by confluence of Hvita and Sog rivers, flows 18 mi. SW to Atlantic 2 mi. WNW of Eyrarbakki. Noted for its salmon.

Olga or **Ol'ga** (ŏlgä'), town (1947 pop. over 2,000), SE Maritime Territory, Russian SFSR, port on small Olga Gulf of Sea of Japan, 175 mi. ENE of Vladivostok; fishing flotilla base; fish canneries. Important iron mines near by.

Olga (ŏl'gŭ), village, Plaquemines parish, extreme SE La., on E bank (levee) of the Mississippi and c.55 mi. SE of New Orleans, in the delta; ships oysters.

Olgiate Comasco (ôljä'tĕ kômä'skô), village (pop. 3,698), Como prov., Lombardy, N Italy, 6 mi. WSW of Como; silk mills.

Olgiate Olona (ôlô'nä), village (pop. 2,996), Varese prov., Lombardy, N Italy, on Olona R. and 2 mi. NE of Busto Arsizio; mfg. (textile machinery, alcohol, candy).

Olginate (ôljēnä'tĕ), village (pop. 2,059), Como prov., Lombardy, N Italy, near Adda R., 16 mi. E of Como.

Olginka or **Ol'ginka** (ôl'gĭn-kŭ), agr. town (1926 pop. 3,783), central Stalino oblast, Ukrainian SSR, in the Donbas, 25 mi. SW of Stalino.

Olgino or **Ol'gino** (–gĭnŭ), village (1939 pop. over 2,000), SW Omsk oblast, Russian SFSR, on Trans-Siberian RR (Moskalenki station) and 55 mi. W of Omsk; metalworks.

Olgod (ûl'gōdh), Dan. *Ølgod*, town (pop. 1,862), Ribe amt, SW Jutland, Denmark, 24 mi. N of Esbjerg; bricks, margarine.

Olgopol or **Ol'gopol'** (ŭlgô'pŭl), town (1926 pop. 5,707), SE Vinnitsa oblast, Ukrainian SSR, 17 mi. NNW of Balta; metalworks.

Olhão (ŏŏlyã'ō), town (pop. 13,627), Faro dist., S Portugal, port on the Atlantic (S coast), on railroad and 5 mi. E of Faro; major fishing and fish-canning center (sardines and tuna); saltworks; mfg. of fertilizer and pottery.

Ölheim, Germany: see EDEMISSEN.

Ôlho Marinho (ō'lyŏŏ mŭrē'nyŏŏ), village (pop. 1,142), Leiria dist., W central Portugal, 8 mi. SW of Caldas da Rainha; wine, beans.

Oliana (ōlyä'nä), town (pop. 866), Lérida prov., NE Spain, on Segre R. (dam) and 20 mi. SSW of Seo de Urgel; livestock, agr. products.

Oliarus, Greece: see ANTIPAROS.

Olías (ōlē'äs), town (pop. 603), Málaga prov., S Spain, 6 mi. ENE of Málaga; wine, olive oil, almonds. Inc. into Málaga city after 1940.

Olías del Rey (dhĕl rā'), town (pop. 1,181), Toledo prov., central Spain, 6 mi. NNE of Toledo; cereals, grapes, olives, olive oil, cherries.

Olib Island (ô'lĭp), Ital. *Ulbo* (ŏŏl'bô), Dalmatian island in Adriatic Sea, W Croatia, Yugoslavia, 29 mi. NNW of Zadar; c.5 mi. long, c.2 mi. wide. Chief village, Olib.

Olicana, England: see ILKLEY.

Oliena (ôlyā'nä), town (pop. 5,316), Nuoro prov., E central Sardinia, 5 mi. SE of Nuoro; wine; nuraghe.

Oliete (ōlyā'tā), town (pop. 1,850), Teruel prov., E Spain, 28 mi. W of Alcañiz; olive-oil processing, flour milling; saffron, beans, potatoes. Irrigation reservoir near by.

Olifants River (ŏ'lĭfŭnts). **1** Port. *Rio dos Elefantes* (rē'ŏŏ dŏŏs ĕlĕfăn'tĕsh), U. of So. Afr. and Mozambique, rises in S Transvaal W of Witbank, flows in a wide arc NE and E, crossing into Mozambique at 23°39'S 31°57'E, to Limpopo R. 130 mi. N of Lourenço Marques; 350 mi. long. **2** In S Cape Prov., U. of So. Afr., rises in Outeniqua Mts. E of Uniondale, flows 130 mi. W, along N slope of Outeniqua Mts., past Uniondale and Oudtshoorn, to confluence with Gamka R. 10 mi. S of Calitzdorp, forming Gouritz R. **3** In SW Cape Prov., U. of So. Afr., rises NNW of Worcester, flows 170 mi. NNW, past Clanwilliam, to the Atlantic 30 mi. NNW of Lamberts Bay. On lower course are extensive irrigation works.

Olimar, Uruguay: see Santa Clara.

Olimarao (ō'lĕmärou'), uninhabited atoll, Yap dist., W Caroline Isls., W Pacific, 21 mi. WNW of Elato; 7°41'N 145°52'E; 2.3 mi. long, 1.5 mi. wide; 2 wooded islets.

Olimar River (ōlēmär'), Treinta y Tres dept., E central Uruguay, rises in the Cuchilla Grande Principal SW of Santa Clara, flows c.100 mi. E, past Treinta y Tres, to the Cebollatí, 6 mi. SW of General Enrique Martínez.

Olimbos, Greece: see Olympus.

Olímpia (ŏŏlēm'pyŭ), city (pop. 8,694), N São Paulo, Brazil, on railroad and 30 mi. ENE of São José do Rio Prêto; livestock market; butter, beverages, macaroni products, coffee. Formerly Olympia.

Olimpo (ŏŏlēm'pŏŏ), town (pop. 2,511), SE Rio Grande do Sul, Brazil, on railroad and 30 mi. W of Pelotas; cattle and sheep raising.

Olimpo (ōlēm'pō), department (□ 7,882; pop. 3,678), N Paraguay, in the Chaco; ⊙ Fuerte Olimpo. Bounded E by Brazil (Paraguay R.), NE and N by Bolivia. Covered by jungle, scrub forests, and low grasslands. Largely inhabited by primitive Indian tribes. Some quebracho lumbering and cattle raising along Paraguay R. centered at Fuerte Olimpo. Dept. was set up 1944 out of Paraguayan Chaco.

Olimpo, town, Paraguay: see Fuerte Olimpo.

Olimtepeque, Guatemala: see Olintepeque.

Olin, town (pop. 626), Jones co., E Iowa, 27 mi. E of Cedar Rapids; dairy products.

Olinalá (ōlēnälä'), town (pop. 2,339), Guerrero, SW Mexico, in Sierra Madre del Sur, 30 mi. ENE of Chilapa; alt. 4,642 ft.; cereals, sugar cane, coffee, fruit, forest products (resin, vanilla).

Olinda (ŏŏlēn'dŭ), city (1950 pop. 38,981), Pernambuco, NE Brazil, on hill overlooking the Atlantic, just N of Recife (linked by streetcar); sugar milling, cigar mfg. Founded in 1530s, it was ⊙ Pernambuco captaincy until superseded by Recife (its one-time port) in mid-17th cent. Of old Dutch character, it has fine bldgs., notably the monastery of São Francisco, the prefecture (seat of colonial captains general), and several churches. It is a favorite suburban bathing resort of Recife.

Olinda (ōlĭn'dŭ), village (pop. c.500), Orange co., S Calif., 12 mi. N of Santa Ana; oil field here (since 1890s).

Olintepeque (ōlēntāpā'kā), town (1950 pop. 1,538), Quezaltenango dept., SW Guatemala, on headstream of Samalá R. and 3 mi. N of Quezaltenango; alt. 8,051 ft. Cotton weaving; corn, wheat, fodder grasses, livestock. Sometimes spelled Olimtepeque.

Olintla (ōlēn'tlä), town (pop. 2,220), Puebla, central Mexico, 23 mi. ESE of Huauchinango; sugar, coffee, fruit.

Olishevka (ŭlyĭshĕf'kŭ), town (1926 pop. 4,952), W central Chernigov oblast, Ukrainian SSR, 18 mi. S of Chernigov; flax, potatoes; brickworks.

Olisipo, Portugal: see Lisbon.

Olita, Lithuania: see Alytus.

Olite (ōlē'tā), city (pop. 2,818), Navarre prov., N Spain, 23 mi. S of Pamplona, in winegrowing area; brandy and chocolate mfg. Has 15th-cent. castle (temporary residence of kings of Navarre) and 2 Gothic churches (12th and 13th cent.).

Olitsikas, Greece: see Tomaros.

Oliva (ōlē'vä), town (pop. 4,871), ⊙ General Belgrano (former Tercero Arriba) dept. (□ 1,800; pop. 60,716), central Córdoba prov., Argentina, 90 mi. SE of Córdoba; dairy products (casein, cheese), furniture; trading in grain. Corn, wheat, flax, peanuts, livestock. Nutria are bred.

Oliva or **Villa Oliva** (vē'yä), town (dist. pop. 4,129), Ñeembucú dept., S Paraguay, on Paraguay R. (Argentina border) and 50 mi. SSW of Asunción; lumbering, cattle raising.

Oliva (ōlē'vŭ, –vä), Pol. *Oliwa* (ôlē'vä), residential village, Gdansk prov., N Poland, near Gulf of Danzig of Baltic Sea, 5 mi. NW of Danzig city center. Has former abbatial church (begun c.1175; completed 1836); now serves as cathedral of R.C. bishop of Danzig. At Peace of Oliva (1660), John II of Poland renounced claim of his line to Swedish throne and confirmed Swedish possession of N Livonia. Frederick William, elector of Brandenburg, was recognized in full sovereignty over East Prussia and in turn confirmed Pol. possession of West Prussia.

Oliva (ōlē'vä), city (pop. 17,557), Valencia prov., E Spain, near the Mediterranean, SE of Gandía and 42 mi. SSE of Valencia; agr. trade center in rich truck-farming area; mfg. of colored tiles, soap; sawmilling, olive-oil processing; hog raising. Mineral springs.

Oliva, La (lä), village (pop. 383), Fuerteventura, Canary Isls., 9 mi. NNW of Puerto de Cabras; barley, cochineal, chick-peas, cereals; sheep, goats, camels. Jasper quarrying; limekilns. Embroidery.

Oliva de la Frontera (ōlē'vä dhä lä frōntä'rä) or **Oliva de Jerez** (hĕrĕth'), town (pop. 10,766), Badajoz prov., W Spain, in Estremadura, in mtn. country near Port. border, 8 mi. WSW of Jerez de los Caballeros. Stock-raising and agr. center (cereals, acorns, olives, cork). Flour milling, olive-oil distilling. Galena deposits near by.

Oliva de Mérida (mä'rē-dhä), town (pop. 2,641), Badajoz prov., W Spain, 15 mi. SE of Mérida; olives, livestock; mfg. of tiles, pottery.

Olivar (ōlēvär'), village (1930 pop. 721), O'Higgins prov., central Chile, on Cachapoal R. and 5 mi. SW of Rancagua, in agr. area (alfalfa, wheat, beans, potatoes, wine, cattle). Formerly also Olivar Alto. Near by is Olivar Bajo (1930 pop. 796).

Olivares (ōlēvä'rĕs), town (pop. 4,460), Seville prov., SW Spain, on Seville-Huelva RR and 9 mi. W of Seville; agr. center (olives, grain, grapes, fruit, livestock). Its church is noted for paintings by Roelas, who died here (1625). Has palace of counts of Olivares.

Olivares, Cerro de (sĕ'rō dhā), Andean peak (20,512 ft.) on Argentina-Chile border, 40 mi. WSW of Rodeo, Argentina; 30°17'S.

Olivares de Júcar (hōō'kär), town (pop. 1,679), Cuenca prov., E central Spain, 25 mi. SSW of Cuenca; olives, saffron, grapes, cereals, potatoes, truck produce, sheep; apiculture; lumbering.

Olive Branch, village (pop. 534), De Soto co., extreme NW Miss., near Tenn. line, 15 mi. SE of Memphis (Tenn.), in agr. area.

Olivebridge, resort village, Ulster co., SE N.Y., in the Catskills, near Ashokan Reservoir, 11 mi. W of Kingston.

Olive Bridge Dam, N.Y.: see Ashokan Reservoir.

Olive Cove, fishing village (1939 pop. 11), SE Alaska, on N shore of Etolin Isl., 20 mi. S of Wrangell; 56°11'N 132°19'W.

Olive Hill, town (pop. 1,351), Carter co., NE Ky., on Tygarts Creek and 32 mi. WSW of Ashland, in agr., clay, glass-sand, and gravel, and coal-mining area; mfg. of firebrick, crushed limestone, cement, lumber, clothing. Near by are limestone Carter Caves (in a state park) and Cascade Caves, and several natural bridges.

Olivehurst, village (pop. 3,588), Yuba co., N central Calif., just SSE of Marysville.

Oliveira (ŏŏlēvā'rŭ), old city (pop. 6,630), S central Minas Gerais, Brazil, on railroad and 45 mi. NW of São João del Rei, and on Belo Horizonte–São Paulo highway (under construction); alt. 3,150 ft. Produces textiles, dried meat, lard; coffee and rice processing, dairying.

Oliveira de Azeméis (dĭ äzĭmĕ'ĕsh), town (pop. 1,709), Aveiro dist., N central Portugal, 16 mi. NNE of Aveiro; mfg. (glass, paper, shoes, pottery); dairying.

Oliveira de Frades (frä'dĭsh), town (pop. 975), Viseu dist., N central Portugal, on Vouga R. and 14 mi. WNW of Viseu; resin extracting.

Oliveira do Bairro (dōō bī'rōō), town (pop. 708), Aveiro dist., N central Portugal, on railroad and 12 mi. SE of Aveiro; winegrowing; textile milling, brick mfg.

Oliveira do Conde (kōn'dĭ), agr. village (pop. 788), Viseu dist., N central Portugal, on railroad and 16 mi. S of Viseu; sawmilling.

Oliveira do Douro (dō'rōō), town (pop. 3,284), Pôrto dist., N Portugal, SE suburb of Oporto, on left bank of Douro R.; footwear, hosiery, paper.

Oliveira do Hospital (ôshpĕtäl'), town (pop. 857), Coimbra dist., N central Portugal, on N slope of Serra da Estrêla, 31 mi. ENE of Coimbra; cheese mfg. Has 13th-14th-cent. chapel.

Oliveira Fortes (fôr'tĭs), town (pop. 772), S Minas Gerais, Brazil, on rail spur, and 20 mi. SE of Barbacena; rutile and nickel deposits. Until 1944, called Livramento.

Olivenza (ōlēvĕn'thä), city (pop. 8,367), Badajoz prov., W Spain, in Estremadura, near Port. border, 15 mi. SW of Badajoz; processing and agr. center on fertile plain (olives, grapes, cereals, acorns, livestock). Mfg. of olive oil, flour, liquor, soft drinks, meat products, tiles, soap. Has notable church. Formerly fortified, it belonged until 1801 to Portugal.

Oliver, village (pop. estimate 1,000), S B.C., near Wash. border, on Okanagan R. and 22 mi. S of Penticton, in irrigated farming region; fruit and vegetable packing, canning. Gold, silica mining.

Oliver, county (□ 720; pop. 3,091), central N.Dak.; ⊙ Center. Agr. area watered by Square Butte Creek; bounded E by Missouri R. Coal mines; farming; livestock, poultry, grain, potatoes. Formed 1885.

Oliver. **1** Town (pop. 223), Screven co., E Ga., 15 mi. SSE of Sylvania; sawmilling. **2** Village (pop. 2,180), Fayette co., SW Pa., just NE of Uniontown. **3** Village (pop. 210), Douglas co., extreme NW Wis., 4 mi. SW of Superior; grain growing.

Oliverea (ŏ''lĭvûrē'ŭ), resort village, Ulster co., SE N.Y., in the Catskills, 26 mi. WNW of Kingston.

Oliveros (ōlēvā'rōs), town (pop. estimate 1,000), SE Santa Fe prov., Argentina, 30 mi. NNW of Rosario, in agr. area (corn, wheat, flax, livestock).

Oliver Springs, town (pop. 1,089), Roane and Anderson counties, E Tenn., 23 mi. WNW of Knoxville, in coal-mining area.

Olives, Mount of, or **Olivet** (ŏ'lĭvĕt), hill (2,680 ft.), central Palestine, just E of Old City of Jerusalem. Closely associated with story of the New Testament, and, in Old Testament, with David's flight, it is site (W) of garden of Gethsemane. Near E foot are biblical localities of Bethany, Bethpage.

Olivet (ôlēvā'), S residential suburb (pop. 1,779) of Orléans, Loiret dept., N central France, on left bank of Loiret R. (which rises 2 mi. SE); cheese and wax mfg. Tree nurseries.

Olivet. **1** (ŏ'lĭvĕt) City (pop. 127), Osage co., E central Kansas, near Marais des Cygnes R., 24 mi. ENE of Emporia, in livestock and grain area. **2** (ŏ'lĭvĕt) Village (pop. 887), Eaton co., S central Mich., 16 mi. NE of Battle Creek, in farm area. Seat of Olivet Col. **3** (ŏ'–) Town (pop. 202), ⊙ Hutchinson co., SE S.Dak., 35 mi. SSE of Mitchell.

Oliveti (ōlēvā'tē), village (pop. 700), W Tripolitania, Libya, on Mediterranean coast, 23 mi. WSW of Tripoli; agr. settlement (grain, lucerne, olives, almonds) founded 1938–39 by Italians.

Oliveto Citra (ōlēvā'tô chē'trä), village (pop. 1,427), Salerno prov., Campania, S Italy, near Sale R., 25 mi. E of Salerno. Hot mineral springs near by.

Olivette (ŏ'lĭvĕt), town (pop. 1,761), St. Louis co., E Mo., W of St. Louis. Inc. 1930.

Olive View, outlying section of Los Angeles city, Los Angeles co., S Calif., in San Fernando Valley, just N of San Fernando. Co. tuberculosis sanatorium here.

Olivia (ōlĭ'vēŭ), village (pop. 2,012), ⊙ Renville co., SW Minn., 28 mi. E of Granite Falls, in grain, livestock, poultry area; dairy products, beverages, canned corn. Platted 1878, inc. 1881.

Olivos (ōlē'vōs), city (pop. 24,675) in Greater Buenos Aires, Argentina, on the Río de la Plata and 10 mi. NW of Buenos Aires; residential suburb, popular beach resort, and mfg. center. Industries: frozen meat, liqueur, food preserves, medical instruments, cement articles, combs, perfumes. Fishing and yachting ground, with small port facilities. Theater. Country residence of Argentine president.

Oliwa, Poland: see Oliva.

Ol Joro Orok (ōl' jō'rō ō'rōk), village, Rift Valley prov., W central Kenya, on rail spur and 25 mi. NNE of Nakuru; coffee, wheat, corn.

Ol Kalou (ōl' kälō'), village, Rift Valley prov., W central Kenya, on rail spur and 20 mi. E of Nakuru; coffee, wheat, corn.

Olkhon Island or **Ol'khon Island** (ŭlkhôn'), largest island in L. Baikal, in E Irkutsk oblast, Russian SFSR; 46 mi. long, 7 mi. wide. Highest point, Izhimei (4,254 ft.). Manganese deposits.

Olkhovatka or **Ol'khovatka** (ŭlkhô'vŭtkŭ). **1** Village (1926 pop. 3,959), S Voronezh oblast, Russian SFSR, 12 mi. WNW of Rossosh; sugar refinery, flour mill. **2** Village (1926 pop. 4,231), NE Kharkov oblast, Ukrainian SSR, 33 mi. N of Kupyansk; metalworks. **3** Town (1926 pop. 2,238), E Stalino oblast, Ukrainian SSR, in the Donbas, 9 mi. E of Yenakiyevo.

Olkhovchik or **Ol'khovchik** (ŭlkhôf'chĭk), town (1926 pop. 2,838), E Stalino oblast, Ukrainian SSR, in the Donbas, 6 mi. WNW of Chistyakovo; coal mines.

Olkhovka or **Ol'khovka** (–kŭ). **1** Village (1926 pop. 1,421), NW Kurgan oblast, Russian SFSR, 20 mi. N of Shadrinsk; flour mill, dairy plant. **2** Village (1926 pop. 4,295), N central Stalingrad oblast, Russian SFSR, on Ilovlya R. and 40 mi. SW of Kamyshin; metalworks; wheat. **3** Town (1926 pop. 3,216), S Voroshilovgrad oblast, Ukrainian SSR, in the Donbas, 13 mi. SW of Voroshilovgrad; chemical works. Until c.1940, Olkhovski Zavod.

Olkhovski, Russian SFSR: see Artemovsk, Krasnoyarsk Territory.

Olkusz (ōl'kōōsh), Rus. *Olkush* (ôl'kōōsh), town (pop. 7,921), Krakow prov., S Poland, on railroad and 22 mi. NW of Cracow, at W foot of Cracow Jura; iron-ore mining; sawmilling, mfg. of enameled products. Center of one of oldest Pol. mining dists.; mining of lead ore (containing some silver) flourished in 14th cent.; site of silver mint in 17th cent. Mining declined in 18th cent.; redeveloped in 19th cent. following building of local railroad; included zinc mines. At present, lead and zinc mining concentrated near Boleslaw, Pol. *Bolesław*, 4 mi. W of town. Dolomite and lime deposits (used as flux and for cement mfg.) in vicinity. Castle ruins just NE. In Second World War, under Ger. rule, called Ilkenau.

Olla (ŏ'lŭ), village (pop. 1,115), La Salle parish, central La., c.45 mi. NNE of Alexandria; cotton ginning, lumber milling.

Ollachea (ōyächā'ä), town (pop. 806), Puno dept., SE Peru, on N slopes of Cordillera Oriental, 17 mi. NNW of Macusani; alt. 8,596 ft. Gold and silver mining; potatoes, corn, coca, livestock.

Ollagüe (ōyä'gwā), village (1930 pop. 441), Antofagasta prov., N Chile, at NW foot of Ollagüe Volcano, in the Andes, last Chilean stop on railroad to Bolivia, and 95 mi. NE of Calama; alt. 12,125 ft. Sulphur mining and refining.

Ollagüe, Cerro (sĕ'rō), Andean peak (19,260 ft.) on Chile-Bolivia border; 21°18'S.

Ollantaytambo or **Ollantaitambo** (both: ōyäntītäm'bō), town (pop. 939), Cuzco dept., S central Peru, in a canyon on Urubamba R., on railroad and 32 mi. NW of Cuzco, in agr. region (cereals, potatoes); silver, gold, copper deposits. Has remains of anc. pre-Columbian fortress, famed for its massive structure.

Ollería (ōlyärē'ä), town (pop. 3,715), Valencia prov., E Spain, 6 mi. SSW of Játiva; mfg. of glass and crystal, baskets; meat processing; olive oil, wine, cereals, vegetables.

Ollerton, town and parish (pop. 3,912), central Nottingham, England, on Maun R. and 8 mi. NE of Mansfield; coal mines, hosiery mills.

Ollie, town (pop. 298), Keokuk co., SE Iowa, 15 mi. NNW of Fairfield. Limestone quarries near by.

Olliergues (ôlyârg'), village (pop. 639), Puy-de-Dôme dept., central France, on Dore R. and 10 mi. NNW of Ambert; makes rosaries, cutlery, insecticides. Near-by Giroux has paper mill.

Ollioules (ôlyōōl'), town (pop. 3,280), Var dept., SE France, 5 mi. WNW of Toulon, in flower-growing area; mfg. (flour products, olive oil). Gorge (used by Marseilles-Toulon road) just N.

Ollomont (ôlômō'), village (pop. 71), Val d'Aosta region, NW Italy, S of the Grand Combin, 8 mi. N of Aosta; copper mines.

Ollon (ôlō'), town (pop. 3,708), Vaud canton, SW Switzerland, 23 mi. SE of Lausanne; vineyards and orchards.

Ollur (ō'lōōr), town (pop. 4,975), central Cochin, India, suburb (3 mi. SW) of Trichur; timber-trade center; sawmilling, rice and oilseed milling, tile mfg.

Olmeda del Rey (ōlmā'dhä dhĕl rā'), town (pop. 915), Cuenca prov., E central Spain, 18 mi. S of Cuenca; cereals, saffron, chick-peas, grapes, sheep, goats. Flour milling; lumbering (pine).

Olmedo (ōlmā'dhō), town (pop. 3,234), Valladolid prov., N central Spain, 25 mi. S of Valladolid; mfg. of resins, sandals, awnings; flour- and sawmilling. Wine, cereals, fruit in area. Has anc. walls and towers and several churches and former convents. In Middle Ages played notable role in history of Castile and was seat of powerful noble families.

Olmen (ŏl'mŭn), agr. village (pop. 2,275), Antwerp prov., N Belgium, near Grande Nèthe R., 3 mi. SSE of Mol.

Olmeto (ôlmā'tō), village (pop. 1,044), SW Corsica, 8 mi. NNW of Sartène; olive-oil mfg.

Olmito (ōlmē'tŭ, -tō), village, Cameron co., extreme S Texas, 8 mi. N of Brownsville; rail point in irrigated agr. area of lower Rio Grande valley. State fish hatchery.

Olmitz, city (pop. 125), Barton co., central Kansas, 14 mi. NW of Great Bend, in wheat region. Gas and oil fields near by.

Olmos (ōl'mōs), town (pop. 2,163), Lambayeque dept., NW Peru, in W foothills of Cordillera Occidental, at E edge of Olmos desert, on Pan American Highway and 50 mi. NNE of Lambayeque, corn, cotton, sugar cane; cattle raising in algarroba area.

Olmos, Lake, salt lake (□ 31), SE Córdoba prov., Argentina, formed by the Río Cuarto, 10 mi. E of La Carlota; c.25 mi. long.

Olmos Dam, Texas: see OLMOS PARK.

Olmos Desert, Lambayeque dept., NW Peru, in W foothills of Cordillera Occidental, N of Leche R. and just E of Olmos; 25 mi. wide, 35 mi. long. It is continued by SECHURA DESERT (NW) and MÓRROPE DESERT (SW). Some agr. (corn, cotton) and cattle raising in irrigated areas.

Olmos Park (ŏl'mŭs), city (pop. 2,841), Bexar co., S central Texas, N suburb of San Antonio. Olmos Dam (flood control) built here across small Olmos Creek (a tributary of San Antonio R.) after 1921 flood. Inc. 1939.

Olmsted (ŏm'stĕd), county (□ 655; pop. 48,228), SE Minn.; ⊙ Rochester. Agr. area drained by Root R. and branches of Zumbro R. Livestock, dairy products, corn, oats, barley, potatoes. Mayo Clinic at Rochester. Co. formed 1855.

Olmsted, village (pop. 525), Pulaski co., extreme S Ill., 13 mi. NNE of Cairo, in agr. area.

Olmsted Air Force Base, Pa.: see MIDDLETOWN.

Olmsted Falls, village (pop. 1,137), Cuyahoga co., N Ohio, 14 mi. SW of downtown Cleveland and on Rocky R.; makes machine tools.

Olmstedville, resort village, Essex co., NE N.Y., in the Adirondacks, 35 mi. NNW of Glens Falls.

Olmué (ōlmwā'), town (pop. 1,088), Valparaiso prov., central Chile, 25 mi. ENE of Valparaiso; resort in fruitgrowing area.

Olmütz, Czechoslovakia: see OLOMOUC.

Olna Firth, Scotland: see SWARBACKS MINN.

Olne (ōln), village (pop. 2,332), Liége prov., E Belgium, 9 mi. ESE of Liége; textile industry; agr.

Olney (ō'nē, ŏl'nē, ŏl'–), town and parish (pop. 2,438), N Buckingham, England, on Ouse R. and 17 mi. N of Leighton Buzzard; leather tanning, shoe mfg., flour milling. Near by are limestone quarries. Olney was home of William Cowper, whose house is now mus. Has 14th-cent. church.

Olney. 1 (ŏl'nē) City (pop. 8,612), ⊙ Richland co., SE Ill., 30 mi. W of Vincennes, Ind.; trade and shipping center in agr. (corn, wheat, livestock, poultry, apples) and timber area; mfg. (shoes, flour, butter, handles, vinegar). Univ. of Chicago bird sanctuary here. Inc. 1841. **2** (ŏl'nē) Residential village, Montgomery co., central Md., 17 mi. N of Washington, D.C.; seat of co. hosp. **3** (ŏl'nē) N residential section of Philadelphia, Pa. **4** (ŏl'nē) City (pop. 3,765), Young co., N Texas, 40 mi. S of Wichita Falls; commercial center for oil, livestock, agr. area (wheat, cotton, poultry, dairy products), oil refining. Settled 1891, inc. 1909.

Olney Springs (ŏl'nē), town (pop. 279), Crowley co., SE central Colo., near Arkansas R., 10 mi. WSW of Ordway, in irrigated sugar-beet region; alt. 4,400 ft.

Olocuilta (ōlōkwēl'tä), city (pop. 3,285), La Paz dept., S Salvador, on road and 11 mi. SE of San Salvador, on Pacific slope of coastal range; market center; mfg. (hats, baskets); grain. Has colonial Sp. church.

Olofstrom (ōō'lôfstrûm"), Swedish *Olofström*, town (pop. 3,266), Blekinge co., S Sweden, 20 mi. NE of Kristianstad; steel and paper milling; mfg. of automobile bodies, hardware. Power station.

Ölögey, Mongolia: see ULEGEI.

Olokemeji (ôlō'kämĕjē), town, Abeokuta prov., Western Provinces, SW Nigeria, on railroad, on Ogun R., and 20 mi. NNE of Abeokuta; cotton weaving, indigo dyeing; cacao, palm oil and kernels, cotton. Has agr. experiment station.

Olombrada (ōlōmbrä'dhä), town (pop. 1,426), Segovia prov., central Spain, 33 mi. N of Segovia; cereals, grapes, chick-peas, vetch.

Olomega, Lake (ōlōmā'gä), or **Lake Camalotal** (kämälōtäl') (□ c.15), in San Miguel dept., SE Salvador, 12 mi. SSE of San Miguel; 5 mi. long, 2 mi. wide. Abounds in fish.

Olomouc (ô'lômōts), Ger. *Olmütz* (ôl'müts), city (pop. 20,817; metropolitan area pop. 58,617), ⊙ Olomouc prov. (□ 2,399; pop. 584,973), N central Moravia, Czechoslovakia, on Morava R. and 40 mi. NE of Brno; 49°36'N 17°15'E. Trade, industrial, and railroad center of HANA region; airport. Specializes in food industries (confectionery, chocolate, smoked meats); exports fine-quality malt (Hana malt); iron- and steelworks produce mainly agr. machinery; saltworks, distilleries, cementworks. An archiepiscopal see; noted for old Cyril-Methodius theological faculty and newly reopened Palacky Univ. Rich in historic landmarks: 12th-cent. St. Wenceslaus cathedral with 3 towers (restored in 19th cent.); 13th–15th-cent. St. Maurice church; 13th-cent. town hall with famous astronomical clock; a Renaissance loggia; and an old chapel (now a mus.); 17th-cent. baroque convent of Hradisko (now military hosp.); archbishop's palace. Founded in 1050; R.C. bishopric since 1062; until 1640, alternated with Brno as ⊙ Moravia. Here Wenceslaus II of Bohemia defeated Mongols in 1242 and Wenceslaus III, last of Premyslides, was murdered in 1306. Devastated by Swedes in 1642; rebuilt in 18th cent. as Austrian fortress against Prussia; Lafayette was imprisoned in fortress, 1794–97. Scene of treaty of 1478, which ceded Czech lands to king of Hungary, and of convention of 1850 which restored Ger. confederation. Much-frequented pilgrimage center of Svaty Kopecek (svä'tē kô'pĕchĕk), Czech *Svatý Kopeček*, with 17th–18th-cent. baroque church, is 5 mi. NE.

Olona River (ôlō'nä), Lombardy, N Italy, rises 4 mi. N of Varese, flows c.65 mi. SSE, past Legnano and Milan, to Lambro R. at Sant'Angelo Lodigiano. At Milan part of its waters are canalized and flow S to Pavia, with a branch past Cortedona, continuing to the Po 4 mi. NE of Stradella.

Oloneshty (ŭlŭnyĕsh'tē), Rum. *Olăneşti* (ôlŭnĕsht'), village (1941 pop. 3,374), SE Moldavian SSR, on Dniester R. and 31 mi. SE of Bendery; red-wine-making center.

Olonets (ŭlŭnyĕts', ŭlō'nyĭts), Finnish *Aunus* (ou'nōōs), city (1926 pop. 1,766), S Karelo-Finnish SSR, near L. Ladoga, on rail branch and 90 mi. SE of Sortavala, on Olonets Isthmus; grain; light mfg. Sawmilling at Ilinski, Finnish *Alavoinen*, 5 mi. W. Former Olonets govt. (abolished 1922; ⊙ Petrozavodsk) extended E beyond Onega R., N nearly to White Sea.

Olonets Isthmus, in NW European USSR, bet. lakes Ladoga (W) and Onega (E); 100 mi. long, 80–100 mi. wide; bounded S by Svir R. Crossed by Russian SFSR–Karelo-Finnish SSR line. Olonets city in SW portion.

Olongapo (ōlông"gäpō'), village (1939 pop. 8,644) in Subic municipality, Zambales prov., central Luzon, Philippines, on E shore of Subic Bay, at base of Bataan Peninsula, 50 mi. WNW of Manila; U.S. naval station.

Olonki (ŭlŭnkē'), village (1939 pop. over 500), SE Irkutsk oblast, Russian SFSR, on Angara R. and 32 mi. SE of Cheremkhovo.

Olonne-sur-Mer (ôlôn'-sür-mâr'), village (pop. 742), Vendée dept., W France, near Bay of Biscay, 3 mi. N of Les Sables-d'Olonne; saltworks, limekilns. Has 11th–12th-cent. church.

Olonos, Greece: see ERYMANTHOS.

Olonzac (ôlōzäk'), village (pop. 1,905), Hérault dept., S France, near the Canal du Midi, 15 mi. WNW of Narbonne; winegrowing, coal mining.

Oloron, Gave d' (gäv dôlôrō'), river in Basses-Pyrénées dept., SW France, formed by confluence of the Gave d'ASPE and Gave d'OSSAU at Oloron-Sainte-Marie, flows 75 mi. NW, past Navarrenx and Sauveterre, to the Gave de Pau above Peyrehorade. Receives Saison R. (left).

Oloron-Sainte-Marie (ôlôrō'-sĕt-märē'), anc. *Iluro*, town (pop. 8,601), Basses-Pyrénées dept., SW France, at junction of Gave d'Ossau and Gave d'Aspe rivers, 14 mi. SW of Pau; road center and N terminus of trans-Pyrenean highway to Spain via Somport pass. Has important livestock and wool trade, and textile industries (berets, blankets, slippers). Tanning, cheese and chocolate mfg. Has former 11th–14th-cent. cathedral (fine Romanesque portal). Seat of a bishop, 4th–18th cent. Was ⊙ Basses-Pyrénées dept., 1795–96.

Olosega (ōlōsĕng'ä), island and county (pop. 544), MANUA dist., American Samoa, S Pacific, c.60 mi. from Tutuila; rises to 2,095 ft.; mountainous, fertile. Sometimes written Olosenga.

Olot (ôlôt'), city (pop. 13,029), Gerona prov., NE Spain, in Catalonia, 22 mi. NW of Gerona; road center; wool and cotton spinning, tanning, paper- and sawmilling, meat processing, hat mfg. Trades in livestock, cereals, potatoes. In region of dormant volcanoes. Completely destroyed (1427) by earthquake. A prosperous textile center until 18th cent. Has art school and mus. Carlist hq. in last Carlist War (19th cent.).

Olovyannaya (ŭlŭvyä'nĭŭ), town (1948 pop. over 10,000), SE Chita oblast, Russian SFSR, on Onon R., on branch of Trans-Siberian RR and 120 mi. SE of Chita; tin-mining center; metalworks.

Olpad (ōl'päd), village, Surat dist., N Bombay, India, 11 mi. NNW of Surat; rice; fishing (pomfrets), cotton ginning. Sometimes spelled Olphad.

Olpe (ôl'pŭ), town (pop. 9,316), in former Prussian prov. of Westphalia, W Germany, after 1945 in North Rhine-Westphalia, 15 mi. SE of Lüdenscheid; ironworks; copper refining. Lister dam and reservoir 3 mi. NNW.

Olpe (ŏl'pē), city (pop. 293), Lyon co., E central Kansas, 10 mi. S of Emporia; cattle, grain.

Olperer (ôl'pŭrŭr), highest peak (11,414 ft.) of Tuxer Alps, in Tyrol, W Austria, 8 mi. ENE of Brenner Pass.

Öls, Poland: see OLESNICA.

Olsburg, city (pop. 140), Pottawatomie co., NE Kansas, 15 mi. N of Manhattan.

Olse River, Czechoslovakia and Poland: see OLZA RIVER.

Olshana or **Ol'shana** (ŭlshä'nŭ), village (1926 pop. 6,738), SE Kiev oblast, Ukrainian SSR, 40 mi. WSW of Cherkassy; sugar refining.

Olshanka or **Ol'shanka** (ŭlshän'kŭ), village (1926 pop. 5,740), NE Odessa oblast, Ukrainian SSR, 13 mi. N of Pervomaisk; metalworks.

Olshany or **Ol'shany** (ŭlshä'nē), city (1926 pop. 12,896), NW Kharkov oblast, Ukrainian SSR, 12 mi. WNW of Kharkov; furniture mfg., tanning, food processing.

Ölsnitz, Germany: see OELSNITZ.

Olst (ôlst), town (pop. 2,083), Overijssel prov., E Netherlands, on Ijssel R. and 6 mi. N of Deventer; mfg. (asphalt, roofing paper, plastics, machinery); meat canning.

Olsztyn (ôl'shtĭn), province [Pol. *województwo*] (□ 8,106; pop. 441,651), NE Poland; ⊙ Allenstein (Olsztyn). Borders N on USSR, NW on the Baltic. Agr. region of low rolling hills, partly forested, and dotted with numerous small lakes. In E part is extensive MASURIAN LAKES region. Drained by Pasleka (Passarge), Lyna (Alle), and Angerapp rivers. Principal crops are rye, potatoes, oats, barley; livestock. Sawmilling and woodworking are chief industries; fishing. Principal cities: Allenstein, Ketrzyn (Rastenburg), Dzialdowo. Until 1945, in East Prussia, Germany; subsequently briefly called Mazury. In 1950 prov. was enlarged by small sections of Bydgoszcz and Warszawa provs. Ger. pop. expelled after 1945 and replaced by Poles.

Olsztyn, city, Poland, see ALLENSTEIN.

Olsztynek (ôlsh-tĭ'nĕk), Ger. *Hohenstein* (hō'ŭnshtīn), town (1939 pop. 4,245; 1946 pop. 1,438) in East Prussia, after 1945 in Olsztyn prov., NE Poland, in Masurian Lakes region, 16 mi. SSW of Allenstein (Olsztyn); grain and cattle market. In 14th cent., Teutonic Knights built castle. In First World War, heavily damaged during battle of Tannenberg.

Olta (ōl'tä), village (pop. estimate 500), ⊙ General Belgrano dept. (□ 888; 1947 pop. 5,750), SE La Rioja prov., Argentina, at E foot of Sierra de los Llanos, 55 mi. W of Serrezuela (Córdoba prov.); agr. center (grain, fruit, wine, livestock).

Olte, Sierra de (syĕ'rä dā ōl'tā), subandean range in W central Chubut natl. territory, Argentina, 30 mi. WNW of Paso de los Indios; c.35 mi. N–S; rises to c.3,500 ft.

Oltedal, Norway: see ALGARD.

Olten (ōl'tŭn), town (1950 pop. 16,492), Solothurn, N Switzerland, on Aar R. and 20 mi. SSE of Basel; railway junction with railroad shops. Metal products (notably aluminumware), shoes, soap, chocolate, leather; printing.

Oltenia (ôltā'nyŭ) or **Lesser Walachia** (wŭlā'kēŭ, wŭ–), the W part (□ 9,305; 1948 pop. 1,717,882) of WALACHIA, Rumania.

Oltenita or **Oltenitsa** (ôltānē'tsä), Rum. *Olteniţa*, town (pop. 10,284), Bucharest prov., S Rumania, on Danube R. (Bulg. border) opposite Tutrakan, at mouth of Arges R., and 35 mi. SE of Bucharest; rail terminus and inland port, trading in fish, fowl, eggs, cheese, and wool; woodworking, flour milling, tanning, brickmaking.

Oltis, France: see LOT RIVER.

Olton (ŏl'tŭn), city (pop. 1,201), Lamb co., NW Texas, on the Llano Estacado, 25 mi. W of Plainview; makes tile, brick. ⊙ Lamb co. until 1946.

Oltovsk (ŭltôfsk′), city (1945 pop. 55,000), S Krasnoyarsk Territory, Russian SFSR, on right bank of Yenisei R. and 55 mi. N of Krasnoyarsk, on spur of Trans-Siberian RR; industrial center supplying near-by Yenisei gold fields with machinery and industrial equipment. Ships refined gold and silver. Mining col. Founded 1929 on site of 16th-cent. Rus. fur-trading post destroyed by the Tatars, Oltovsk boomed in 1930s and became a leading economic center of S Siberia. Originally called Slovetsky, 1929–30; known as Kyz-Kurt, 1931–39.

Oltre Giuba, Ital. Somaliland: see JUBALAND.

Olt River (ôlt) or **Oltul** (ôl′tōōl), Ger. *Aluta* (älōō′-tä), central and S Rumania, in Transylvania and Walachia, rises on W slopes of the Moldavian Carpathians, 7 mi. E of Gheorgheni, flows S past Mercurea-Ciuc and Sfantu-Gheorghe, thence wends its way W past Fagaras and cuts S across the Transylvanian Alps through Turnu-Rosu Pass, passing Ramnicu-Valcea and joining the Danube just S of Turnu-Magurele, opposite Nikopol, Bulgaria. Total length, 348 mi. Used for logging in upper and middle courses; navigable for small craft in lower course, below Slatina. Forms boundary bet. Oltenia and Muntenia.

Oltu (ôltōō′), village (pop. 3,241), Erzurum prov., NE Turkey, on Oltu R. and 60 mi. NE of Erzurum; coal, grain.

Oltu River, NE Turkey, rises in Coruh Mts. 8 mi. SE of Tortum, flows 80 mi. NE and WNW, past Oltu, to Coruh R. 12 mi. NE of Yusufeli.

Oluanpi, Cape, Formosa: see OLWANPI, CAPE.

Olublo, Czechoslovakia: see STARA LUBOVNA.

Olula del Río (ōlōō′lä dhĕl rē′ō), town (pop. 1,492), Almería prov., S Spain, on Almanzora R. and 18 mi. WSW of Huércal-Overa; marble cutting and shipping. Olive oil, cereals, esparto.

Olustee (ōlŭ′stē). **1** Village (pop. c.400), Baker co., N Fla., 13 mi. E of Lake City; ships naval stores obtained from near-by Osceola Natl. Forest, and is site of U.S. naval stores experiment station. Scene of chief Civil War battle (1864) fought in Fla., a Confederate victory. **2** Town (pop. 455), Jackson co., SW Okla., 8 mi. SW of Altus, near Salt Fork of Red R., in cotton and grain area.

Oluta (ōlōō′tä), town (pop. 2,197), Veracruz, SE Mexico, on Isthmus of Tehuantepec, 2 mi. SE of Acayucan; rice, coffee, fruit, livestock.

Olutanga Island (ōlōōtäng′gä) (□ 78; 1939 pop. 1,749), Zamboanga prov., Philippines, just off W coast of Mindanao, across Sibuguey Bay from Zamboanga Peninsula.

Olvega (ōl′vāgä), town (pop. 1,598), Soria prov., N central Spain, 25 mi. E of Soria; stock raising; meat packing.

Olvenstedt (ôl′vŭn-shtĕt), residential village (pop. 6,322), in former Prussian Saxony prov., central Germany, after 1945 in Saxony-Anhalt, 4 mi. WNW of Magdeburg.

Olvera (ōlvā′rä), city (pop. 8,478), Cádiz prov., SW Spain, in spur of the Cordillera Penibética, 15 mi. NNW of Ronda; processing, lumbering, and agr. center (cereals, vegetables, olives, acorns, livestock). Olive-oil pressing, flour milling, sawmilling, alcohol distilling. Sulphur springs. An old city, taken (1327) by Alfonso XI.

Olveston (ôl′vĕstŭn, ōlvz′–), town and parish (pop. 1,369), SW Gloucester, England, 9 mi. N of Bristol; agr. market. Church dates from 12th cent.

Olviopol, Ukrainian SSR: see PERVOMAISK, Odessa oblast.

Olwanpi, Cape, or **Cape Oluanpi** (both: ŭ′lwän′bē′), Chinese also *Nan Chia* (nän′ jyä′) [=south cape], Jap. *Garanbi* (gäräm′bē), southernmost point of Formosa; 21°54′N 120°51′E. Lighthouse (built 1882), radio station, seaplane anchorage. Sometimes spelled Olanpi.

Olyka (ŭlĭ′kŭ), Pol. *Ołyka* (ôwĭ′kä), town (1931 pop. 5,785), E Volyn oblast, Ukrainian SSR, 22 mi. E of Lutsk; lumber- and grain-trading center; agr. processing (cereals, vegetable oils, hops), sawmilling, brick mfg. Has ruins of town hall, 16th-cent. castle. An old Ruthenian settlement; became (16th cent.) residence of Pol. gentry; sacked (1648) by Cossacks. Passed to Russia in 1795; reverted to Poland in 1921; ceded to USSR in 1945.

Olymbos, Greece: see OLYMPUS.

Olympia, Brazil: see OLÍMPIA.

Olympia (ōlĭm′pēŭ), anc. city of Elis in W Peloponnesus, Greece, in plain of Olympia, on Alpheus R. at mouth of the Cladeus, 10 mi. E of Pyrgos. Site of ruins of temple of Zeus with the Olympian Zeus (by Phidias), one of the Seven Wonders of the World; ruins of Stadium, Gymnasium, Treasuries, and other temples within Altis enclosure. Founded c.1000 B.C., Olympia became a political and religious center of Greece, the place of worship of Zeus, and scene of the Olympic Games. Controlled mainly by Pisa until 572 B.C., it was then under the rule of Elis until suppression of Olympic Games (A.D. 394). Near site across the Cladeus, on rail spur, is modern village of Olympia or Olimbia (pop. 644), with mus. housing excavated bronze and marble sculptures, including the Hermes of Praxiteles and the Victory of Paeonius.

Olympia, city (pop. 15,819), ⊙ Wash. and Thurston co., 25 mi. SW of Tacoma, at S end of Puget Sound, at mouth of Deschutes R.; 47°3′N 122°54′W; alt. c.25 ft. Seaport and port of entry; ships and processes lumber, fish, oysters, and agr. products; mfg. of metal products, farm machinery, cannery equipment. Noteworthy are old capitol (1893) and new capitol group (1911–35). Seat of St. Martin's Col. Olympia was founded 1850 at end of Oregon Trail after homesteads were staked out in 1848; became ⊙ Wash. Territory in 1853.

Olympia Fields, village (pop. 160), Cook co., NE Ill., S suburb of Chicago, just W of Chicago Heights.

Olympic Hot Springs, NW Wash., health resort (alt. c.2,000 ft.), in Olympic Mts., N of Mt. Olympus and 15 mi. SW of Port Angeles.

Olympic Mountains (3–8,000 ft.), NW Wash., part of Coast Ranges, on Olympic Peninsula S of Juan de Fuca Strait and W of Puget Sound. Mt. Olympus (7,954 ft.), highest peak, is in OLYMPIC NATIONAL PARK.

Olympic National Park (□ 1,313.8; established 1938), NW Wash., c.50 mi. W of Seattle, on Olympic Peninsula. Mt. Olympus (7,954 ft.; highest peak of Olympic Mts.), with 7 large glaciers, is the center of this wild, rainy mountainous area, which abounds in wild life (especially Roosevelt Elk) and magnificent virgin forests of Sitka spruce, Douglas fir, western red cedar, and hemlock. Rainfall (c.140 in. annually) in rain forest of W slope of park is heaviest in continental U.S. Lake and stream fishing, hiking and bridle paths, campgrounds, winter sports facilities. Mt. Olympus was 1st set aside (1909) in Mt. Olympus Natl. Monument, extended in 1938 and reestablished as Olympic National Park.

Olympic Peninsula, NW Wash., peninsula bounded E by Puget Sound and Hood Canal, W by Pacific Ocean, N by Juan de Fuca Strait; includes Olympic Mts. and Olympic Natl. Park.

Olympus (ōlĭm′pŭs), Gr. *Olymbos* or *Olimbos* (both: ô′lĭmbôs), highest mountain of Greece, on Macedonia-Thessaly line, at Aegean coast; rises to 9,570 ft. in the Mytikas (Mitikas) or Scholeion (Skholion), 16 mi. SW of Katerine. Its summit, snow-covered and hidden in the clouds, was in Gr. religion the home of the Olympian gods. Barring the access from Macedonia to Thessaly, Olympus has always been of strategic importance and can be bypassed only by the Petra Pass (at NW foot) and the Vale of Tempe. It is sometimes known as the higher (upper) Olympus [Gr. *Ano Olymbos*] as opposed to the lower Olympus [Gr. *Kato Olymbos*], an adjacent range (S), rising to 5,141 ft. in the Metamorphosis (Metamorfosis), 22 mi. S of Katerine, and separated from Ossa by the Vale of Tempe (Peneus R.)

Olympus, Mount (10,132 ft.), SW Alta., near B.C. border, in Rocky Mts., in Jasper Natl. Park, 50 mi. SE of Jasper: 52°28′N 117°2′W.

Olympus, Mount, Tasmania: see SAINT CLAIR, LAKE.

Olympus, Mount, Turkey: see ULU DAG.

Olympus, Mount, Wash.: see OLYMPIC NATIONAL PARK.

Olympus Mountains, range of S Cyprus, extending c.70 mi. from Cape Arnauti (W) to environs of Larnaca (E); forms S flank of Messaoria basin. Rises in Mt. TROODOS or Olympus to isl.'s highest elevation (6,406 ft.). Largely forested and of a healthful summer climate, it is a popular vacation area with several resorts (Troodos, PANO PLATRES, PRODHROMOS, KAKOPETRIA, KALOPANAYIOTIS); skiing in winter. The range is rich in minerals, particularly pyrites, asbestos (Amiandos), chromite, ocher, gold, silver, gypsum, and terra umbra. For the mts. and its highest peak, the names Olympus and Troodos are often used interchangeably.

Olynthus (ōlĭn′thŭs), one of leading anc. Gr. cities on Chalcidice peninsula, in Macedonia, 7 mi. SW of modern Polygyros. Became head (late 5th cent. B.C.) of Chalcidian League, briefly dissolved by Sparta (370s B.C.). Siding first with Philip II of Macedon and then with Athens, was besieged (occasion of Demosthenes' Olynthiac orations) and destroyed 348 B.C. by Philip. Near site is modern Gr. village of Olynthos or Olinthos (pop. 827), formerly called Mariana.

Olyphant (ŏ′lĭfŭnt, ō′–), borough (pop. 7,047), Lackawanna co., NE Pa., 5 mi. NE of Scranton and on Lackawanna R.; anthracite mining; silk mill, iron foundries. Settled 1858, inc. 1877.

Olytsikas, Greece: see TOMAROS.

Olyutorskoye (ŭlyōō′tŭrskŭyŭ), village, NE Koryak Natl. Okrug, Kamchatka oblast, Khabarovsk Territory, Russian SFSR, fishing port on Olyutorski Gulf of Bering Sea, at mouth of Apuka R., 350 mi. NE of Palana; fisheries; canning plant. Across Apuka R. is village of Apuka or Ust-Apuka.

Olza River (ôl′zä), Czech *Olše* (ôl′shĕ), S Poland and Silesia, Czechoslovakia, rises in Poland in the W Beskids, 8 mi. E of Jablunkov (Czechoslovakia); flows E and NNW, partly along Czechoslovak-Pol. border, past Cieszyn, Cesky Tesin, and Frystat, to Oder R. just NW of Novy Bohumin; c.40 mi. long. Supplies most of water power for metallurgical industry of Ostrava area.

Oma (ō′mä), town (pop. 6,274), Aomori prefecture, at northernmost tip of Honshu, Japan, 20 mi. NW of Tanabu; fishing port on E Tsugaru Strait. Until early 1940s, called Ooku.

Oma, Cape, Jap. *Oma-zaki,* northernmost point of Honshu, Japan, in Tsugaru Strait, opposite Hakodate peninsula of Hokkaido; 41°32′N 140°55′E.

O-machi (ō′mächē), town (pop. 16,256), Nagano prefecture, central Honshu, Japan, 20 mi. NNW of Matsumoto, rice growing.

Omachi (ō′mächē), town (pop. 22,594), Saga prefecture, NW Kyushu, Japan, on E Hizen Peninsula, 10 mi. WSW of Saga; agr. center (rice, wheat); raw silk.

Omagari (ō′mägärē), town (pop. 14,630), Akita prefecture, N Honshu, Japan, 26 mi. SE of Akita; rice-collection center; woodworking, textile mfg. Agr. school.

Om Ager, Eritrea: see UMM HAJAR.

Omagh (ō′mä), urban district (1937 pop. 5,741; 1951 census pop. 6,620), ⊙ Co. Tyrone, Northern Ireland, in W central part of co., on Strube R. and 55 mi. W of Belfast; agr. market (cattle, potatoes, flax, oats); dairy-products processing. Has ruins of castle besieged 1509 and again 1641, when it was destroyed. In 8th cent., site of an abbey.

Omaha (ō′mŭhä, –hô). **1** Town (pop. 91), Boone co., N Ark., 15 mi. NNW of Harrison, near Mo. line. **2** Town (pop. 217), Stewart co., SW Ga., 14 mi. WNW of Lumpkin, near Chattahoochee R. **3** Village (pop. 394), Gallatin co., SE Ill., 17 mi. NE of Harrisburg, in agr. area. **4** City (pop. 251,117), ⊙ Douglas co., E Nebr., 425 mi. W of Chicago and on W bank of Missouri R., opposite Council Bluffs, Iowa; 41°15′N 95°56′W; alt. 1,041 ft. Largest city of state, in heart of a rich agr. region, it is an important transportation, shipping, and industrial center, served by several railroads, transcontinental air lines, and bus lines, and on the Lincoln Highway. Port of entry. Industries include oil refining, lead smelting, and meat packing; mfg. includes farm implements, paint, mechanical appliances, boxes, beverages, flour, cereals, and dairy products. There are large stockyards and grain elevators. The city has a municipal airport, Offutt Air Force Base, and numerous parks and churches, and is connected with Council Bluffs by 3 highway and 2 railroad bridges across the Missouri. Points of interest are BOYS TOWN (just SW), Fort Omaha and Fort Crook (near-by military stations), Union Passenger Terminal, courthouse, St. Cecilia's Cathedral (R.C.), Levi Carter Park, smelting plant, and Joslyn Memorial, which contains a concert hall and art collections. Also: Creighton Univ., Univ. of Nebr. Col. of Medicine and School of Nursing, Municipal Univ. of Omaha, Duchesne Col., Col. of St. Mary, Grace Bible Inst., state school for the deaf, and various preparatory and denominational schools. Founded 1854 on site visited by Lewis and Clark and inc. 1857, the city grew as a river port and supply station for pioneers and served (1855–67) as territorial capital. Greatest factor in city's growth was transportation. Following extension of the Union Pacific RR (1865) to Omaha, mfg. increased, and the meat-packing and grain-refining industries of the city developed rapidly. **5** Town (pop. 735), Morris co., NE Texas, c.45 mi. WSW of Texarkana; trade, shipping point in cotton, truck, fruit area.

Omaha Beach, name given to section of Normandy coast, Calvados dept., NW France, bet. Grandcamp-les-Bains (W) and Port-en-Bessin (E), NW of Bayeux, where units of American First Army landed on June 6, 1944, in invasion of France during Second World War. Heavy fighting especially at Colleville-sur-Mer and Saint-Laurent-sur Mer.

Omai, gold mine in Essequibo co., central Br. Guiana, on left bank of Essequibo R. and 70 mi. S of Rockstone. Also tungsten deposits.

Omak (ō′măk), town (pop. 3,791), Okanogan co., N Wash., on Okanogan R. and 4 mi. above Okanogan; lumber, wood products, apples, grain, tomatoes. Settled 1907, inc. 1911.

Omalur (ō′mŭlōōr), town (pop. 4,525), Salem dist., S central Madras, India, 10 mi. NW of Salem, on rail branch to Mettur Dam; cotton weaving; steatite culinary vessels. Magnesite and chromite mines in Chalk Hills (SE); magnetite, magnesite, and chromite mines in Kanjamalai hill (S).

Omama (ō′mämä), town (pop. 11,736), Gumma prefecture, central Honshu, Japan, 4 mi. WNW of Kiryu; agr. center (rice, wheat); silk textiles.

Oman, 'Oman (ōmän′, ō′măn), or **'Uman** (ōōmăn′), name applied in its broadest sense to the coastal region of the eastward projecting butt of the Arabian Peninsula, bounded N by Persian Gulf, NE by Gulf of Oman, SE by Arabian Sea, and inland by the great Arabian desert Rub' al Khali. It thus includes the TRUCIAL OMAN, a group of sheikdoms, on Trucial Coast of Persian Gulf, bound by truces with Great Britain; the so-called "Independent Oman," not subject to any recognized ruler and consisting of the oases of Jau (⊙ BARAIMI) and MAHADHA; and the independent sultanate of Oman, an absolute monarchy bound to Britain by treaty last reaffirmed in 1939. The sultanate of **Oman** or **Muscat and Oman** (mŭs′kăt) (□ 82,000; 1949 pop. estimate 550,000; ⊙ Muscat) fronts on the Gulf of Oman bet. the Oman Promontory (Masandam Peninsula) and the cape Ras al Hadd (with the exception of the coastal section bet. Dibba and Khor Kalba belonging to the Trucial sheikdoms of KALBA and FUJAIRA) and on the Arabian Sea bet. the capes Ras al Hadd and Ras Dharbat 'Ali, which marks the E limit of Aden Protectorate. Physiographically, the sultanate is dominated by the HAJAR hill country, which extends along the entire coast of the Gulf of Oman and rises to 9,900 ft. in the Jabal AKHDAR. It is divided into the Western Hajar and Eastern Hajar by the Wadi Sama'il, the largest of a series of steep-walled wadies cutting SW–NE across the Hajar range. At the N tip of the Oman Promontory is the detached dist. of RUUS AL JIBAL, separated by the Kalba and Fujaira sheikdoms from the rest of the sultanate. Bet. the Western Hajar and the Gulf of Oman lies the fertile, populous BATINA date-growing plain; while the Eastern Hajar hills approach closer to the coast SE of Muscat. On the landward side of the Hajar hill country lies a sandy tableland (alt. 4,000 ft.) extending to the margins of the desert Rub' al Khali and including the dists. of DHAHIRA, OMAN PROPER, SHARQIYA, and JA'LAN. Off the desolate Arabian Sea coast are Masira isl. (belonging to Oman) and the Kuria Muria Isls. (forming part of Aden Colony). In the extreme S, the DHOFAR dist. of Oman adjoins Aden Protectorate. The climate of the coastal belt is relatively pleasant during Nov.–March, when temperature falls to 60°–70°F., but high humidity is coupled with high temperatures (to 110°F.) during the rest of the year. A fresher temperate climate is found in the Hajar hill country. Rainfall averages 5 inches annually, and agr. depends on irrigation, largely derived from wells (as in the Batina date belt) or from streams in the hilly tracts. Dates are the leading agr. product grown for export; other fruit trees are the plantain, mango, pomegranate, lime, olive, and almond. Walnuts, figs, wine, and the mulberry flourish in the cooler Hajar hills, and the coconut palm grows in Dhofar. Common subsistence crops are grain (wheat, barley, millet), melons, and sugar cane; while alfalfa is sown for cattle feed. Fishing and pearling are important along the coast. In addition to dates, the major export item, Oman ships pearls, dried limes, fresh fruit, and salted fish. Because of its desert-backed location, Oman has few contacts with the interior and has primarily maritime interests, trading chiefly with India and Iraq. Her ship-borne trade passes through Muscat, its commercial suburb Matrah, and to a lesser extent through Sohar, Sur, and Khabura. With the exception of the Dhofar dist. on the Arabian Sea, most of the pop. is concentrated in the coastal belt of the Gulf of Oman and adjoining interior dists. Arabs compose the bulk of the pop., the rest consisting of Persians, Baluchi, Indians, and Negroes (in part still slaves). The Arab pop. is split into 2 major groups: the predominant earlier settlers (Yemeni), mainly in SE, who belong to the so-called Hinawi political faction and are of the Abadite (Ibadite) sect of Islam; and the later immigrants (Nizari), mainly in NW, who belong to the ruling Ghafiri faction and are orthodox Sunnis, though a few are Wahabites. Converted to Islam under Mohammed and inc. (7th–10th cent.) into the caliphate, Oman was occupied by the Portuguese from 1508 until they were expelled by the Persians in mid-17th cent. The present dynasty seized power in 1741, when, with the aid of inland tribesmen from Oman Proper, Ahmed ibn Said, the dynasty's founder, expelled his predecessor with his Persian allies from Muscat. British treaty relations with Oman began in 1798; and in 1st half of 19th cent., Oman became the most powerful state of the Arabian Peninsula. At its peak, under the great ruler Said ibn Sultan (1804–56), the dominions of Oman encompassed Zanzibar on E African coast, the Persian littoral of the Persian Gulf, and ports on the coast of Baluchistan, of which GWADAR has remained a dependency of Oman. Following the death of Said, the realm was divided bet. his 2 sons, the Persian possessions were lost in 1875, and Oman declined. Since 1891, the sultan has been under a binding agreement with the Indian (after 1947, directly with the British) govt. In return for the exclusive rights granted to Britain, the sultan receives an annual subsidy and a guarantee of protection. British interests are represented by a consul residing in Muscat.

Oman, Gulf of, NW arm of Arabian Sea, bet. Oman section of Arabian Peninsula and Makran coast of Iran; 350 mi. long, 200 mi. wide bet. Ras al Hadd and Gwatar Bay. Ports of Muscat and Matrah are on S coast, Jask and Chahbahar on N coast. Connects NW with Persian Gulf via Strait of Hormuz.

Oman Promontory or **Masandam Peninsula** (mŭsăn'dăm), northward projection of Oman region of Arabian Peninsula, bet. Persian Gulf and Gulf of Oman, terminating in rocky Cape Masandam on Strait of Hormuz. Except for Ruus al Jibal, detached dist. of Oman sultanate at N point, Oman Promontory belongs to the sheikdoms of Trucial Oman. The towns of Sharja and Dibai are on W coast.

Oman Proper, interior district of Oman, on landward side of the Jabal Akhdar; main towns: Nizwa, Bahla, and Izki. Until transfer of sultan's residence to Muscat and coastal belt in 1741, Oman Proper was principal seat of political power and most prosperous dist. in Oman.

Omar, mining village (pop. 3,073, with adjoining Barnabus), Logan co., SW W.Va., 7 mi. S of Logan, in coal region.

Omaruru (ō"mŭrōō'rōō), town (pop. 1,947), NW South-West Africa, on Omaruru R. and 110 mi. NW of Windhoek, in tin-, gold-mining region. During Herero campaign German force was besieged here (1904). Reserve of Bergdamara tribe is 40 mi. W.

Omasuyos, Bolivia: see ACHACACHI.

Omata (ōmä'tä), town (pop. 6,646), Tochigi prefecture, central Honshu, Japan, 3 mi. SE of Kiryu; rice, silk cocoons; rayon textiles.

Omate (ōmä'tā), town (pop. 620), ⊙ General Sánchez Cerro prov. (□ 1,545; pop. 17,916), Moquegua dept., S Peru, at S foot of the Huaina Putina or Omate volcano, on affluent of Tambo R. and 30 mi. NNE of Moquegua; alt. 7,086 ft. Grain, fruit, stock. Thermal springs.

Omate, volcano, Peru: see HUAINA PUTINA.

Ombai, Indonesia: see ALOR.

Ombai Strait (ōmbī'), channel connecting Banda Sea (NE) and Savu Sea (SE), bet. Timor (S) and Alor Isls. (N); 20–50 mi. wide. Pante Macassar is on S shore. Also called Matua Strait.

Ombella-M'Poko, Fr. Equatorial Africa: see BANGUI.

Ombella River (ōmbĕlä'), S Ubangi-Shari, Fr. Equatorial Africa, rises 40 mi. WSW of Fort-Sibut, flows c.100 mi. generally SE to Ubangi R. 20 mi. WSW of Fort-de-Possel. Also called Yambéré.

Ombi Islands, Indonesia: see OBI ISLANDS.

Ombilin (ōmbĭlĭn'), **Umbilin,** or **Oembilin** (both: ōōmbĭlĭn'), region in Padang Highlands, central Barisan Mts., W Sumatra, Indonesia. Major coal fields; mining center at Sawahlunto.

Ombo (ôm'bô), island (□ 22; pop. 628) in Bokn Fjord, Rogaland co., SW Norway, at mouth of Josen Fjord, 25 mi. ESE of Haugesund; 6 mi. long (WSW–ESE), 4 mi. wide; fishing, lumbering.

Ombret-Rawsa (ōbrā'-rävzä'), village (pop. 926), Liége prov., E central Belgium, on Meuse R. and 5 mi. ENE of Huy; mfg. of mining explosives. Formerly spelled Ombret-Rausa.

Ombrone River (ômbrô'nĕ), Tuscany, central Italy, rises in S Monti Chianti 10 mi. ENE of Siena, flows 100 mi. generally SW, past Buonconvento, to Tyrrhenian Sea 10 mi. SW of Grosseto. Chief tributaries: Orcia R. (left), Arbia R. (right).

Ombúes de Lavalle (ōmbōō'ĕs dā lävä'yä), town, Colonia dept., SW Uruguay, 38 mi. N of Colonia; agr. center (livestock, wheat, corn, tobacco, fruit). Founded 1890.

Omdurman (ŏmdûrmăn', Arabic ōmdōōrmăn'), city (□ 15; pop. 125,300), Khartoum prov., central Anglo-Egyptian Sudan, on left bank of the Nile where it is formed by confluence of White Nile and Blue Nile, 5 mi. NW of Khartoum (linked by tramway); largest city of the Sudan. Native commercial and agr. center; cotton, grain, fruit, livestock. Radio station. Extending 5 mi. along the Nile, it includes town proper (S), Christian quarter with R.C. and Coptic churches (N), and Abu Ruf residential quarter (NE). Omdurman proper contains Mosque Square with ruins of the Mahdi's tomb (destroyed 1898 by British), the Khalifa house (now a mus.), and large native market. Has Maahad el Ilmi (Islamic school), technical school (building trades), women's teachers col. An insignificant village until 1884, when the Mahdi made it his military hq., Omdurman developed rapidly in 1880s and 1890s as residence of the Mahdi and his successor, the Khalifa. It was captured (1898) by Kitchener following final defeat of Khalifa's troops at Kerreri, 6 mi. N.

Ome (ō'mā), town (pop. 15,187), Greater Tokyo, central Honshu, Japan, 10 mi. NW of Tachikawa, in agr. area; mfg. (textiles, umbrellas).

Omealca (ōmääl'kä), town (pop. 1,350), Veracruz, E Mexico, in Sierra Madre Oriental foothills, 14 mi. SE of Córdoba; coffee, sugar cane, fruit.

Omega (ōmē'gŭ), town (pop. 966), Tift co., S central Ga., 9 mi. SW of Tifton, in farm area.

Omegna (ōmā'nyä), town (pop. 6,650), Novara prov., Piedmont, N Italy, port at N end of L. of Orta, 17 mi. SSE of Domodossola; iron- and steelworks, aluminum factory, tanneries, cotton and paper mills. Marble quarries near by.

Omei (ō'mā', ŭ'mā'), town (pop. 14,409), ⊙ Omei co. (pop. 169,622), SW Szechwan prov., China, 15 mi. W of Loshan; paper milling, Chinese-wax processing; rice, millet, wheat, beans, rapeseed. Rock-crystal quarrying, coal and copper deposits near by. It lies at NE foot of the **Omei Shan** (shän') (9,957 ft.), a sacred mtn., and center of a noted Buddhist summer resort area; there are numerous pagodas and monasteries on its slopes.

Omemee (ōmē'mē), village (pop. 620), S Ont., near S end of Pigeon L., 12 mi. W of Peterborough; dairying, mixed farming.

Omemee, village (pop. 60), Bottineau co., N N.Dak., 9 mi. SSE of Bottineau.

Omena (ōmē'nŭ), resort village, Leelanau co., NW Mich., 19 mi. N of Traverse City, on W shore of Grand Traverse Bay. Has Indian cemetery.

Omeo, village (pop. 461), E central Victoria, Australia, 150 mi. ENE of Melbourne; tin mines; sheep, cattle.

Omer, city (pop. 321), Arenac co., E Mich., 30 mi. N of Bay City and on Rifle R. near its mouth on Saginaw Bay, in farm area; fishing. Settled 1873, inc. as city 1903.

Ometepec (ōmātāpĕk'), city (pop. 4,643), Guerrero, SW Mexico, in Pacific lowlands, 100 mi. E of Acapulco; agr. center (cereals, sugar cane, tobacco, cotton, fruit, livestock). Airfield.

Ometepec Bay, small inlet of Gulf of California, on NE coast of Lower California, NW Mexico, near mouth of Colorado R., 85 mi. SE of Mexicali. Large deposits of pure salt.

Ometepe Island (ōmātā'pā), SW Nicaragua, in L. Nicaragua, 5 mi. offshore, 8 mi. ENE of Rivas. Consists of 2 isls. connected by 2-mi. isthmus. Larger (N) is 12 mi. long, 10 mi. wide; smaller (S) is circular (7 mi. across). Rises to 5,066 ft. in volcano Concepción (N), to 4,350 ft. in volcano Madera (S). Coffee, tobacco. Main centers: Alta Gracia, Moyogalpa.

Omi (ō'mē), former province in S Honshu, Japan; now Shiga prefecture.

Omi, town, Japan: see AOMI.

Omigawa (ōmē'gäwŭ) or **Omikawa** (–käwŭ), town (pop. 9,130), Chiba prefecture, central Honshu, Japan, on Tone R. and 7 mi. ESE of Sawara; agr., fishing, raw-silk production.

Omileiho, China: see DURBULDJIN.

Omin, China: see DURBULDJIN.

Ominato (ō'mēnätō), town (pop. 14,252), Aomori prefecture, N Honshu, Japan, on N Mutsu Bay, 3 mi. WSW of Tanabu; rail terminus; fishing, agr., lumbering.

Omine (ō'mēnā), town (pop. 13,778), Yamaguchi prefecture, SW Honshu, Japan, 17 mi. W of Yamaguchi; mining center (anthracite coal).

Omis (ô'mĭsh), Serbo-Croatian *Omiš*, Ital. *Almissa* (älmēs'sä), village, S Croatia, Yugoslavia, port on Adriatic Sea, at Cetina R. mouth, 14 mi. ESE of Split, in Dalmatia. Seaside resort; electrochemical industries; mfg. (phosphates, artificial fertilizers, flour products); wine trade. Sometimes spelled Omish. Dugirat, village, is 2 mi. W; mfg. (calcium carbide, cyanamid).

Omisalj (ô'mĭshäl), Serbo-Croatian *Omišalj*, Ital. *Castelmuschio* (kästĕlmōō'skyō), village, NW Croatia, Yugoslavia, on Krk Isl., on Adriatic Sea, 1[illegible] mi. N of Krk; seaside resort. Has old church, castle ruins.

Omish, Yugoslavia: see OMIS.

Omi-shima (ō'mē-shĭmä). **1** Island (□ 26; pop. 23,338, including offshore islets), Ehime prefecture, Japan, in W Hiuchi Sea off N coast of Shikoku, N of Cape Osumi, 10 mi. N of Imabari; 6 mi. long, 3.5 mi. wide; broad peninsula in SW. Mountainous; rises to 1,430 ft. Fishing. Site of anc. Shinto shrine. **2** or **Aomi-shima** (ä'ōmē shĭmä), island (□ c.7; pop. 13,021, including offshore islets), Yamaguchi prefecture, Japan, in Sea of Japan, just off SW Honshu, N of Senzaki; 5 mi. long, 2 mi. wide; long, narrow E peninsula. Mountainous; scenic. Produces citrus fruit; fishing. Know for anc. temple.

Omitlán (ōmētlän'), officially Omitlán de Juárez, town (pop. 1,229), Hidalgo, central Mexico, 6 mi. NE of Pachuca; corn, maguey, beans, livestock.

Omiya (ō'mēä). **1** Town (pop. 5,909), Ibaraki prefecture, central Honshu, Japan, 13 mi. NNW of Mito; mining (gold, silver, copper). **2** City (194[illegible] pop. 39,291; 1947 pop. 91,378), Saitama prefecture, central Honshu, Japan, adjacent to Urawa (S), 17 mi. NNW of Tokyo; rail junction; commercial center for agr. area (rice, wheat, raw silk). Known for anc. Shinto shrine dedicated to Susa-no-wo, brother of the sun goddess. **3** Town, Shizuoka prefecture, Japan: see FUJIMIYA.

Omizo, Japan: see TAKASHIMA.

Omlouj, Saudi Arabia: see UMM LAJJ.

Ommaney, Cape (ō'mŭnē), SE Alaska, S tip of Baranof Isl., on W shore of S entrance to Christian Sound, 7 mi. S of Port Alexander; 56°10'N 134°40'W.

Ommen (ô'mŭn), town (pop. 2,287), Overijssel prov., E Netherlands, on Vecht R. and 14 mi. E of Zwolle; market center; powder milk and other dairy products; cattle market.

Ommersheim (ô'mŭrs-hīm), village (pop. 1,339), SE Saar, 5 mi. SSW of St. Ingbert; stock, grain.

Omo (ō'mû), Dan. *Omø*, island (□ 1.7; pop. 283), Denmark, in Smaalandsfarvand strait, just SW of Zealand isl.

Omo (ō'mō), village, Kaffa prov., SW Ethiopia, near Omo R., on Mt. Mai Gudo, 40 mi. ESE of Jimma; iron mining.

Omoa (ōmō'ä), town (pop. 507), Cortés dept., NW Honduras, minor port on Omoa Bay of Gulf of Honduras, 8 mi. WSW of Puerto Cortés; 15°45'N 88°3'W. Coastal trade; coconuts, rice, fruit, livestock. Pop. largely Negro. Site of San Fernando fort (completed 1795; now a state prison). Founded 1752; flourished until rise of Puerto Cortés (after 1870).

Omoa, Scotland: see CLELAND.

Omoa, Sierra de (syĕ'rä dā), N section of Sierra de Merendón system, NW Honduras; extends c.3[illegible] mi. from Santa Barbara dept. border NE to Gulf of Honduras near Puerto Cortés; forms left watershed of Chamelicon R.; rises to 7,310 ft. at peak San Ildefonso.

Omoa Bay, NW Honduras, S inlet of Gulf of Honduras, SW of Puerto Cortés; 12 mi. wide bet. Motagua R. mouth (W) and port of Omoa (E), 6 mi. long.

Omodeo, Lake, Sardinia: see TIRSO, LAKE.

Omoldova, Rumania: see MOLDOVA-VECHE.

Omolon River (ŭmŭlôn'), NW Khabarovsk Territory and NE Yakut Autonomous SSR, Russian SFSR, rises in Kolyma Range, flows 715 mi. N to Kolyma R. 60 mi. SW of Nizhne-Kolymsk.

Omon (ō'mŏn'), town, Cantho prov., S Vietnam, near Bassac R., in Mekong delta, 12 mi. NW of Cantho; rice center.

Ömönö Gobi, Mongolia: see SOUTH GOBI.

Omont (ômô'), village (pop. 96), Ardennes dept., N France, 11 mi. S of Mézières; barrelmaking.

Omori (ō'mōrē). **1** Town (pop. 3,330), Akita prefecture, N Honshu, Japan, 8 mi. WNW of Yokote; rice, peaches; lumber, charcoal. **2** Town (pop. 5,407), Chiba prefecture, central Honshu, Japan, 9 mi. NW of Sakura; rice, poultry, raw silk. **3** Town (pop. 1,816), Shimane prefecture, SW Honshu, Japan, 25 mi. SW of Izumo; rice, sake, raw silk. Silver mine near by.

Omo River (ō'mō), Ital. *Omo Bottego,* central and S Ethiopia, rises in highlands S of Mt. Goroken 40 mi. ENE of Nakamti, flows c.500 mi. generally S to L. Rudolf. Receives Gojab and Gibbe rivers.

Omorphita, Cyprus: see KAIMAKLI KUTCHUK.

Omortag (ômôrtäk'), city (pop. 4,215), Kolarovgrad dist., E central Bulgaria, on N slope of Lisa Mts., 28 mi. WSW of Kolarovgrad; market center; sawmilling, parquet mfg. Until 1934, Osman Pazar.

Ompompanoosuc River (ŏm"pŏmpŭnōō'sŭk), E Vt., rises in E Orange co., flows c.25 mi. S to the Connecticut near Norwich.

Om River or **Om' River** (ôm), in N Novosibirsk and SE Omsk oblasts, Russian SFSR, rises in Vasyuganye marshes, flows 475 mi. W, past Kuibyshev, Ust-Tarka, and Kalachinsk, to Irtysh R. at Omsk. Navigable 200 mi. above mouth.

Omro (ŏm'rō), city (pop. 1,470), Winnebago co., E central Wis., on Fox R. and 10 mi. W of Oshkosh; butter, cheese, flour, feed. Settled 1845; inc. as village in 1857, as city in 1944.

Omsk (ŏmsk, Rus. ômsk), oblast (□ 53,800; 1946 pop. estimate c.1,500,000) in SW Siberian Russian SFSR; ⊙ Omsk. Drained by middle Irtysh R. Economy is wholly agr., with wheat on S steppe, dairy farming on central wooded steppe; flax grown around Tara. Lumbering in N forests. Industry concentrated at Omsk. Trans-Siberian RR crosses oblast, with 2 W branches joining at Omsk. Other urban centers: Isil-Kul, Tara, Tyukalinsk. Formed 1934 out of W.Siberian territory. Major portion of original area organized into TYUMEN oblast (1944).

Omsk, city (1939 pop. 280,716; 1946 pop. estimate 450,000), ⊙ Omsk oblast, Russian SFSR, on Irtysh R., at mouth of Om R., on Trans-Siberian RR and 380 mi. W of Novosibirsk, 1,400 mi. E of Moscow; 55°N 73°20'E. Major transportation and industrial center in W Siberia; mfg. (agr. machinery, locomotives, rolling stock, tires, auto cord), auto assembling, agr. processing (meat, flour, dairy products, leather, animal feed), lumber milling. Important rail-river transfer point for Irtysh R. goods (lumber from N; melons, livestock products from S). Has medical, agr., and teachers colleges and technical schools (machine, road construction, river navigation). Located on treeless, level terrain, Omsk developed around old fortress (founded 1716) on right bank of Om R. It expanded along right bank of Irtysh R. from rail depot (S) to agr. research institute (N; founded 1827). Following construction of Trans-Siberian RR, its left-bank suburb of Kulomzino or Novo-Omsk developed and is now the junction of railroads from Tyumen and Chelyabinsk. Omsk was chartered in 1804; in 1824 succeeded Tobolsk as administrative center of W Siberia. Noted agr.-processing center (butter, livestock, agr. implements) in early 20th cent.; seat of counter-revolutionary Kolchak govt. (1918–19). Industrialization under Soviet regime was greatly intensified during Second World War. After c.1900, it was largest Siberian city until rise of Novosibirsk.

Omsnijding Canal, Netherlands: see VAN STARKENBORGH CANAL.

Omuda, Japan: see OMUTA.

Omulew River (ômōō'lĕf), Rus. *Omulev* (ŭmōō'lyĭf), NE Poland, rises in L. Omulew 11 mi. NNE of Nidzica, flows 65 mi. SE to Narew R. opposite Ostroleka.

Omu Peak or **Omul Peak** (ō'mōō,–l), highest mtn. (8,236 ft.) of the Bucegi group, S central Rumania, 6 mi. NW of Sinaia.

Omura (ō'mōōrä), city (1940 pop. 33,390; 1947 pop. 56,851), Nagasaki prefecture, W Kyushu, Japan, port on Omura Bay, 13 mi. NNE of Nagasaki, in agr. area; fishery; sake breweries. Principal exports: sake, fish. Had aircraft plant during Second World War; bombed 1944.

Omura Bay, landlocked gulf of E.China Sea, W Hizen Peninsula, W Kyushu, Japan; sheltered W by Sonogi Peninsula; 20 mi. long, 8 mi. wide. Connected N to Sasebo harbor by 2 narrow channels.

Omuta (ō'mōōtä) or **Omuda** (ō'mōōdä), city (1940 pop. 124,266; 1947 pop. 166,438), Fukuoka prefecture, W Kyushu, Japan, port on the Ariakenoumi, 19 mi. S of Kurume. Industrial center; zinc refinery, chemical plants, coke ovens; mfg. (dyes, nitrate fertilizer, cotton thread). Includes (since early 1940s) former adjacent towns of Miike (1940 pop. 6,905) and Hayame (1940 pop. 21,870). Large coal mines in vicinity. Chief export, coal. Heavily bombed (1945) in Second World War.

Omutinskoye (ô'mōōtyĭnskŭyŭ), village (1939 pop. over 2,000), S Tyumen oblast, Russian SFSR, on Trans-Siberian RR and 50 mi. ESE of Yalutorovsk; metalworks; grain, livestock.

Omutninsk (ô'mōōtnyĭnsk), city (1939 pop. over 10,000), E Kirov oblast, Russian SFSR, on railroad and 90 mi. E of Kirov; metallurgical center, producing high-grade steels from local ores. Teachers col. Satellite plants at KIRS, PESKOVKA, CHERNAYA KHOLUNITSA.

On, Egypt: see HELIOPOLIS.

Oña (ō'nyä), village, Azuay prov., S Ecuador, in the Andes, on Pan American Highway and 10 mi. NNE of Saraguro; alt. 9,580 ft.; cereals, potatoes, livestock.

Oña (ō'nyä), town (pop. 1,430), Burgos prov., N Spain, in the Ebro valley, 31 mi. NNE of Burgos; fruit, truck produce, stock. Flour- and sawmilling; mfg. of charcoal, resins, turpentine. Known for Jesuit San Salvador col., founded as a monastery in 10th cent. by Benedictines and in Middle Ages one of the most famed in Spain.

Ona, city (pop. 89), Hardee co., central Fla., 8 mi. WSW of Wauchula; has cattle experiment station.

Onada, Japan: see TAKAYAMA.

Onaga (ōnä'gŭ), city (pop. 882), Pottawatomie co., NE Kansas, 40 mi. NW of Topeka; trade and shipping point in livestock and grain region.

Onagawa (ōnä'gäwŭ) or **Onakawa** (–käwŭ), town (pop. 16,398), Miyagi prefecture, N Honshu, Japan, at base of Ojika Peninsula, on the Pacific, 7 mi. E of Ishinomaki; rail terminus; fishing center; rice, raw silk.

Onaght, townland (pop. 201), SW Co. Galway, Ireland, on NW shore of Inishmore, Aran Isls., 5 mi. WNW of Kilronan; fishing port. Site of prehistoric circular fort and of St. Brecan's grave. Near by are remains of 7 anc. churches, chief of which (St. Brecan's) has been restored.

Onahama (ōnä'hämŭ), town (pop. 24,310), Fukushima prefecture, central Honshu, Japan, on the Pacific, 7 mi. S of Taira; chief fishing center of prefecture; canneries.

Onaka (ōnä'kŭ), town (pop. 158), Faulk co., N central S.Dak., 20 mi. NW of Faulkton.

Onakawa, Japan: see ONAGAWA.

Onakawana (ŏnäkŭwä'nŭ), village, NE Ont., on Abitibi R. and 110 mi. NNW of Cochrane; lignite deposits.

Onalaska (ŏnŭlă'skŭ), city (pop. 2,561), La Crosse co., W Wis., on Black R., just N of La Crosse, in farm and dairy area; dairy products, canned vegetables, pickles; limestone quarries; summer resort. Hamlin Garland b. near by. Settled 1854, inc. 1887.

Onamia (ōnă'mēŭ), resort village (pop. 704), Mille Lacs co., E central Minn., on Rum R., just S of Mille Lacs L., and 35 mi. N of Princeton, in grain, livestock, and poultry area; dairy products. Mille Lac Indian Reservation here.

Onancock (ōnăn'kŏk), town (pop. 1,353), Accomack co., E Va., on tidewater inlet (Onancock R.) and 26 mi. SSW of Pocomoke City, Md.; oyster dredging and canning; trade center for truck-farming and lumbering (pine) region. Rail station at Tasley, just E. Founded 1680.

Onaping Lake (ō'nŭpĭng) (35 mi. long, 3 mi. wide), SE central Ont., 40 mi. NW of Sudbury; drains S into Wanapitei L.

Onaqui (ōnă'kwē), town (pop. 333), Tooele co., N central Utah, 20 mi. NW of Eureka.

Onaqui Mountains, range (6–9,000 ft.) in Tooele co., W Utah; forms S extension of Stansbury Mts.

Onarga (ōnär'gŭ), village (pop. 1,455), Iroquois co., E Ill., 30 mi. SSW of Kankakee, in rich agr. area (corn, oats, wheat, soybeans, livestock, poultry; dairy products); canned foods. A military school is here. Inc. 1867.

Ona River, Russian SFSR: see BIRYUSA RIVER.

Oñate (ōnyä'tā), town (pop. 2,895), Guipúzcoa prov., N Spain, 18 mi. SW of Tolosa; metalworking (wire, electrical equipment); other mfg. (dyes, furniture). Formerly seat of univ. Was hq. of Don Carlos in Carlist Wars (19th cent.). Aranzanzu monastery is 4 mi. S.

Onavas (ōnä'väs), town (pop. 321), Sonora, NW Mexico, on Yaqui R. and 100 mi. SE of Hermosillo; cereals, fruit, livestock.

Onawa (ŏ'nŭwŭ). **1** City (pop. 3,498), ⊙ Monona co., W Iowa, near the Mississippi, c.40 mi. SSE of Sioux City; trade center for grain, livestock area; dairying, mfg. of farm equipment, leather goods. State park near by. Platted 1857, inc. 1858. **2** Village, Piscataquis co., Maine: see ELLIOTTSVILLE.

Onaway (ŏ'nŭwā). **1** Village, Latah co., Idaho: see POTLATCH. **2** Resort city (pop. 1,421), Presque Isle co., NE Mich., 20 mi. WSW of Rogers City, in lake-resort and farm area (livestock, potatoes; dairy products); mfg. (clothing, lumber). Fishing on near-by Black L. State forest and state park near by. Settled c.1880; inc. as village 1899, as city 1903.

Oncativo (ōngkätē'vō), town (pop. 4,509), central Córdoba prov., Argentina, 50 mi. SE of Córdoba; flour milling, linseed-oil pressing; grain, flax, peanuts, potatoes, livestock.

Onchan (ŏng'kŭn), village district (1939 pop. 2,675), on E coast of Isle of Man, England, 2 mi. NE of Douglas; seaside resort. Has governor's official residence.

Onda (ōn'dä), town (pop. 6,483), Castellón de la Plana prov., E Spain, near Mijares R., 13 mi. WSW of Castellón de la Plana (linked by branch railroad). Important ceramics center (colored tiles); alcohol distilling, varnish mfg. Rice, oranges, wine, olive oil in area. Mineral springs. Clay quarries and bituminous schists near by. Irrigation reservoir on Mijares R.

Ondaine River (ōdĕn'), Loire dept., SE central France, rises N of Saint-Genest-Malifaux, flows 10 mi. W, through W part of Saint-Étienne coal-mining and industrial dist., past Le Chambon-Feugerolles and Firminy, to the Loire near Unieux.

Ondal, India: see ANDAL.

Ondangua (ōndäng'gwŭ), village, ⊙ Ovamboland, N South-West Africa, near Angola border; 17°58'S 16°1'E; center of cattle-raising, grain-growing region. Airfield.

Ondara (ōndä'rä), town (pop. 2,317), Alicante prov., E Spain, 15 mi. SE of Gandía; artificial flowers; olive-oil processing; raisins, oranges, cereals.

Ondárroa (ōndä'rōä), town (pop. 5,329), Vizcaya prov., N Spain, fishing port on Bay of Biscay, 26 mi. ENE of Bilbao; fish processing (anchovies), mfg. of fishing supplies, boatbuilding, cider distilling. Bathing resort.

Ondava River (ôn'dävä), E Slovakia, Czechoslovakia, rises on S slope of the Beskids, 6 mi. NE of Bardejov; flows 85 mi. S, joining Latoritsa R. in Tisa lowlands, 11 mi. SSE of Trebisov, to form Bodrog R. Receives Topla R.

Onderneeming (ŏn"dŭrnā'mĭng), village (pop. 512), Essequibo co., N Br. Guiana, on coast at mouth of Essequibo R., 30 mi. NW of Georgetown; site of govt. farm and agr. experiment station.

Onderstepoort (ŏn'dŭrstŭpōōrt"), N suburb of Pretoria, S central Transvaal, U. of So. Afr.; site of Veterinary Research Foundation.

Ondo (ōn'dō), town (pop. 22,030) on Kurahashijima, Hiroshima prefecture, Japan, opposite Kure; agr. center (rice, wheat); raw silk, heavy rope.

Ondo (ŏn'dō), province (□ 8,211; pop. 462,560), Western Provinces, S Nigeria, in equatorial forest belt; ⊙ Akure. On Gulf of Guinea; extends from coastal swamp forest, through rain forest (major vegetation type), to deciduous woods (N). Chief products: hardwood, rubber, cacao, palm oil and kernels, cotton, kola nuts. Food crops: yams, corn, cassava, plantains. Pop. is largely Yoruba.

Ondo, town (pop. 20,859), Ondo prov., Western Provinces, S Nigeria, 28 mi. WSW of Akure; agr. trade center; cacao industry; palm oil and kernels, timber, rubber, cotton.

Ondores (ōndō'rĕs), town (pop. 299), Junín dept., central Peru, in Cordillera Central of the Andes, on L. Junín and 12 mi. WNW of Junín; barley, potatoes, livestock. Salt mining near by.

Öndör Haan, Mongolia: see UNDUR KHAN.

Ondozero (ô'ndōzyĭrŭ), Finnish *Ontajärvi,* lake (□ 65) in central Karelo-Finnish SSR, 60 mi. SW of Belomorsk; 15 mi. long, 5 mi. wide. Frozen Nov.–Apr. Outlet: Onda R. (E), an affluent of Vyg R.

One and a Half Degree Channel, seaway of Indian Ocean, roughly along 1°30'N, bet. Haddummati Atoll (N) and Suvadiva Atoll (S) of Maldive Isls.; c.55 mi. wide.

Oneco, Conn.: see STERLING.

Onega (ōnē'gŭ, ōnä'gŭ, Rus. ŭnyä'gŭ), city (1939 pop. over 10,000), NW Archangel oblast, Russian SFSR, lumber port on White Sea, at mouth of Onega R., on rail spur and 80 mi. WSW of Archangel; sawmilling center; plywood mfg., fish canning. Chartered 1780.

Onega, Lake, Rus. *Onezhskoye Ozero* (ŭnyĕsh'skŭyŭ ô'zyĭrŭ), Finnish *Ääninen* (ă'nĭnĕn), second largest lake (□ c.3,800) in Europe, in NW European USSR, bet. L. Ladoga (SW) and White Sea (NE); 140 mi. long, 50 mi. wide, max. depth 400 ft.; alt. 108 ft. Low, sandy shores (S); deeply indented rocky coast (N), with narrow bays extending up to 70 mi. inland (Povenets Gulf). Lesser inlets (NW) include Petrozavodsk, Kondopoga, Lizhma, and Unitsa. Receives Vytegra (S), Shuya and Suna (W), and Vodla (E) rivers; drains via Svir R. (SW) into L. Ladoga. Onega Canal (45 mi. long), along its S coast, joins Vytegra and Svir rivers as part of Mariinsk canal system. Main ports: Petrozavodsk, Voznesenye (at Svir R. outlet), Velikaya Guba, and Povenets (at S end of White Sea–Baltic Canal). Frozen Nov.–May.

Onega Bay, S inlet of White Sea, W of Onega Peninsula, in NW European USSR; 30–50 mi. wide, 100 mi. long; receives Kem, Vyg, and Onega rivers.

Main ports: Kem, Belomorsk (N end of White Sea–Baltic Canal), Onega. Solovetskiye Isls. are at its entrance.

Onega Peninsula, N Archangel oblast, Russian SFSR, on White Sea, bet. Onega and Dvina bays; 15–60 mi. wide, 80 mi. long; marshy lowland. Fisheries along coast.

Onega River, Archangel oblast, Russian SFSR, rises in L. Lacha, flows 252 mi. N, past Kragopol, to Onega Bay at Onega. Navigable (May–Nov.) in upper course and for 100 mi. above mouth; rapids in middle course.

Oneglia, Italy: see IMPERIA, town.

One Hundred and Two River, in SW Iowa and NW Mo., rises in S Iowa, flows c.90 mi. S to Little Platte R. 6 mi. E of St. Joseph.

Onehunga (ōnĕhŭng'gŭ), borough (pop. 13,872), and port N N.Isl., New Zealand, 5 mi. SSE of Auckland, on NE shore of Manukau Harbour; woolen mills, tanneries, sawmills.

Oneida (ōnī'dŭ). **1** County (□ 1,191; pop. 4,387), SE Idaho; ⊙ Malad City. Mtn. region bordering on Utah and crossed in SE by Malad R. and tributaries. Stock raising, agr. (wheat, alfalfa, sugar beets). Part of Caribou Natl. Forest in SE. Co. formed 1864. **2** County (□ 1,227; pop. 222,855), central N.Y.; ⊙ ROME and UTICA. Partly bounded W by Oneida L.; rises to the Adirondacks in E and NE; drained by Mohawk and Black rivers, and by Oneida, Oriskany, and West Canada creeks. Traversed by the Barge Canal. Dairying, stock raising, farming; extensive mfg. (especially textiles, brass- and copperware) at Rome, Utica. Limestone quarries. Resorts on lakes and in Adirondacks. Formed 1798. **3** County (□ 1,114; pop. 20,648), N Wis.; ⊙ Rhinelander. Drained by Wisconsin R. Largely a resort area with numerous lakes; contains American Legion State Forest and a section of Nicolet Natl. Forest. Lumbering; dairying and farming (mostly potatoes) on cutover forest land. Formed 1885.

Oneida. 1 (ōnē'dŭ, ōnī'dŭ) City (pop. 554), Knox co., NW central Ill., 10 mi. NE of Galesburg, in agr. and bituminous-coal area. **2** (ōnī'dŭ) Town (pop. 75), Delaware co., E Iowa, 6 mi. NE of Manchester. **3** (ōnī'dŭ) City (pop. 138), Nemaha co., NE Kansas, 7 mi E of Seneca; livestock, grain. **4** (ōnī'dŭ) City (pop. 11,325), Madison co., central N.Y., SE of Oneida L., on Oneida Creek and 26 mi. E of Syracuse, in dairying area; mfg. (silverware, fertilizers, electrical supplies, caskets, plaster and paper products). Silverware industry and some others are outgrowth of activities of Oneida Community, a religious communistic society established here in 1848 by J. H. Noyes and reorganized in 1881 as a stock company. Community bldgs. survive in suburban Kenwood. Inc. as city in 1901. **5** (ōnī'dŭ) Village (pop. 2,248), Butler co., SW Ohio. **6** (ōnī'dŭ, ōnē'dŭ) City (pop. 1,304), Scott co., N Tenn., 50 mi. NW of Knoxville, in the Cumberlands; ships timber, coal, farm produce, livestock; mfg. of wood products, hosiery. Settled 1868; inc. 1914.

Oneida Castle (ōnī'dŭ), village (pop. 596), Oneida co., central N.Y., on Oneida Creek and just SE of Oneida, on site of chief settlement of Oneida Indians.

Oneida Creek, central N.Y., rises c.20 mi. E of Syracuse, flows c.35 mi. E, N, and NW, forming boundary of Oneida and Madison counties, to SE end of **Oneida Lake** (□ c.80; 20 mi. long, 1–5 mi. wide), 12 mi. NE of Syracuse; resorts. The Barge Canal enters E end of lake, linking it with Mohawk R. (E), and follows part of course of **Oneida River,** which drains Oneida L. from W end and flows c.20 mi. generally W, joining Seneca R. to form Oswego R. near Phoenix.

O'Neill, city (pop. 3,027), ⊙ Holt co., N Nebr., 70 mi. NW of Norfolk and on Elkhorn R.; shipping point for grain and livestock region; dairy products. Important hay-baling center. Founded 1874.

Onejime, Japan: see ONESHIME.

Onekama (ōnĕ'kŭmŭ), village (pop. 435), Manistee co., NW Mich., 9 mi. NNE of Manistee, on Portage L. and near L. Michigan, in cucumber-growing area; mfg. (paper, food products); resort.

Onekotan Island or **Onnekotan Island** (ŭnyĕkŭtän') (□ 121), one of N main Kurile Isls. group, Russian SFSR; separated from Paramushir Isl. (N) by Fourth Kurile Strait, from Kharimkotan Isl. (S) by Sixth Kurile Strait; 49°25'N 154°45'E; 27 mi. long, 7 mi. wide. Krenitsyn Peak [Jap. *Kuroishi-yama*], secondary volcanic cone in S part of isl., rises to 4,350 ft. in circular crater lake. Small fishing pop.

Onemen Gulf, Russian SFSR: see ANADYR BAY.

Onemen River, Russian SFSR: see BOLSHAYA RIVER, Chukchi Natl. Okrug.

Oneonta. 1 (ŏnēŏn'tŭ, ō–) Town (pop. 2,802), ⊙ Blount co., N central Ala., 35 mi. NE of Birmingham, in cotton and truck area; children's wear and work clothes, lumber, cotton, canned goods. **2** (ōnēŏn'tŭ) City (pop. 13,564), Otsego co., central N.Y., in foothills of the Catskills, on Susquehanna R. and 50 mi. ENE of Binghamton; railroad shops, flour mills; mfg. of clothing, gloves, machinery, wood products, trailers. Seat of a state teachers col., Hartwick Col. (coeducational), and a state tuberculosis hosp. Gilbert Lake State Park is NW; Goodyear L. is 5 mi. NE. Settled c.1780; inc. as village in 1848, as city in 1909.

Oneshime (ō'nāshĭmā) or **Onejime** (–jĭmā), town (pop. 14,064), Kagoshima prefecture, S Kyushu, Japan, on W Osumi Peninsula, port on E shore of Kagoshima Bay, 27 mi. SE of Kagoshima; agr. center (rice, wheat), livestock; raw silk, lumber. Exports wood products, livestock.

One Tree Hill, borough (pop. 11,648), N N.Isl., New Zealand; residential suburb of Auckland. Site of Hahunga Cave (burial place of anc. Maoris).

Onewhero (ōnēfĕ'rō), village (pop. 484), N N.Isl., New Zealand, 32 mi. S of Auckland; dairying; phosphate.

Ong, village (pop. 173), Clay co., S Nebr., 30 mi. SE of Hastings.

Onga (ông'gŏ), town (pop. 2,157), Abauj co., NE Hungary, 5 mi. E of Miskolc; grain, potatoes, cattle, sheep.

Ongar or **Chipping Ongar** (ŏng'gŭr), residential town and parish (pop. 1,062), W Essex, England, on Roding R. and 9 mi. NNE of Romford. Has 12th-cent. church and remains of anc. castle. Just NE is residential town and parish (pop. 1,419) of High Ongar, with partly Norman church.

Ongin Gol or **Ongiin Gol** (ông'gēn gōl'), river in central Mongolian People's Republic, rises on SE slopes of the Khangai Mts., flows 270 mi. SE, past Arbai Khere, to lake Ulan Nor in Gobi desert. Intermittent in lower course.

Ongjin (ông'jĕn'), Jap. *Oshin*, town (1949 pop. 32,965), Hwanghae prov., central Korea, S of 38°N, on small peninsula in Yellow Sea, 90 mi. WNW of Seoul; gold-mining center.

Ongole (ŏngōl'), city (pop. 21,184), Guntur dist., NE Madras, India, 60 mi. SSW of Guntur; road junction; tobacco-curing center; rice and oilseed milling, ghee processing; leather goods. Salt refining at Kanuparti, 12 mi. NE.

Ongudai or **Onguday** (ŭn-gōōdī'), village (1948 pop. over 2,000), central Gorno-Altai Autonomous Oblast, Altai Territory, Russian SFSR, 85 mi. S of Gorno-Altaisk and on Chuya highway.

Onguren (ŭn-gōōryĕn'), village, SE Irkutsk oblast, Russian SFSR, on L. Baikal, 70 mi. ESE of Kachuga; fisheries.

Oni (ô'nyē), city (1926 pop. 2,932), N Georgian SSR, on Rion R., on Ossetian Military Road and 40 mi. NE of Kutaisi; trading center in agr. area (vineyards, orchards, sericulture, corn); woolen handicrafts. Has medieval Imeretian castle.

Onida (ōnī'dŭ), city (pop. 822), ⊙ Sully co., central S.Dak., 27 mi. NNE of Pierre; dairy produce, livestock, poultry, grain.

Oniishi, Japan: see ONISHI.

Onikshty, Lithuania: see ANYKSCIAI.

Onil (ōnēl'), town (pop. 2,460), Alicante prov., E Spain, 12 mi. WSW of Alcoy; toy and footwear mfg., olive-oil processing; cereals, wine, almonds. Has palace of dukes of Dos Aguas.

Onilahy River (ōōnēlä'hē), Tuléar prov., SW Madagascar, rises c.20 mi. S of Betroka, flows c.250 mi. generally W to St. Augustin Bay on Mozambique Channel, just N of Soalara. Navigable year-round for shallow-draught boats in its lower course. Used for irrigation.

Onishi (ōnē'shē), town (pop. 7,032), Gumma prefecture, central Honshu, Japan, 12 mi. SSE of Takahashi; hot-springs resort; raw silk, charcoal. Sometimes called Oniishi.

Onitsha (ônēchä'), province (□ 4,937; pop. 1,096,323), Eastern Provinces, S Nigeria, in forest belt; ⊙ Onitsha. Bounded W by Niger R., deciduous forest (S), savanna (N). Mineral resources include extensive coal field (mines at Enugu and Udi), lignite, limestone, and salt deposits. Produces palm oil and kernels, kola nuts. Chief centers: Enugu (on railroad) and Onitsha. Pop. largely Ibo.

Onitsha, town (pop. 18,084), ⊙ Onitsha prov., Eastern Provinces, S Nigeria, on left bank of Niger R., opposite Asaba (ferry), and 50 mi. WSW of Enugu; 6°9'N 6°47'E. Trade center; palm oil and kernels, kola nuts, corn, cassava, yams. Has leper settlement and leprosy control station, R.C. mission, women's teachers col. A Br. commercial post in 19th cent.

Onival, France: see AULT.

Onjo, Korea: see ONSONG.

Onjuku (ōn'jōōkōō), town (pop. 6,592), Chiba prefecture, central Honshu, Japan, on E Chiba Peninsula, 4 mi. SSW of Ohara; fishing, rice growing, poultry raising.

Onk, Djebel (jĕ'bĕl ŏk'), mountain (4,390 ft.), Constantine dept., NE Algeria, near Tunisia border, 50 mi. SSW of Tebessa; its large phosphate deposits (not yet commercially exploited) are continuation of Tunisia's deposits in Gafsa area.

Onkhor, Br. Somaliland: see ANKHOR.

Onley (ŏn'lē), village (1940 pop. 884), Accomack co., E Va., 3 mi. SW of Accomac; cooperative produce-marketing center.

Onliu, China: see NGWA.

Onnaing (ônē'), town (pop. 5,809), Nord dept., N France, 4 mi. NE of Valenciennes, near Belg. border; engineering works (factory and mining equipment, washing machines), breweries; tile mfg.

Onnekotan Island, USSR: see ONEKOTAN ISLAND.

Onnekotan-kaikyo, USSR: see KURILE STRAIT.

Onnestad (ŭ'nŭstäd"), Swedish *Önnestad*, village (pop. 490), Kristianstad co., S Sweden, 5 mi. WNW of Kristianstad; grain, potatoes, livestock.

Ono (ō'nō), volcanic island (□ 12; pop. 499), Fiji, SW Pacific, c.4 mi. NE of Kandavu; 4.5 mi. long, 3.5 mi. wide; rises to 1,160 ft.; copra.

Ono (ō'nō). **1** Town (pop. 4,285), Aichi prefecture, central Honshu, Japan, on W Chita Peninsula, on Ise Bay, 7 mi. WNW of Handa; textiles. Hot springs. **2** Town (pop. 2,058), Aichi prefecture, central Honshu, Japan, 18 mi. NE of Toyohashi; lumber, raw silk, rice. **3** Town (pop. 17,558), Fukui prefecture, central Honshu, Japan, 16 mi. ESE of Fukui; silk-textile center. **4** Town (pop. 4,774), Gifu prefecture, central Honshu, Japan, 7 mi. W of Gifu; agr. (rice, persimmons). **5** Town (pop. 10,008), Hyogo prefecture, S Honshu, Japan, 14 mi. E of Himeji; commercial center for agr. area (rice, wheat, tobacco, fruit, market produce); woodworking; soy sauce, paper. **6** Town, Ishikawa prefecture, Japan: see KANAZAWA. **7** Village, Kanagawa prefecture, Japan: see SAGAMIHARA. **8** Town (pop. 12,793), Oita prefecture, E Kyushu, Japan, 50 mi. NNE of Nobeoka; agr. center; raw silk; spinning mill.

Onod (ō'nôd), Hung. *Ónod*, town (pop. 2,369), Borsod-Gömör co., NE Hungary, on Sajo R. and 9 mi. SE of Miskolc; flour mills; vineyards, grain, tobacco, cattle.

Onoda (ōnō'dä). **1** Town (1947 pop. 12,008), Miyagi prefecture, N Honshu, Japan, 22 mi. NNW of Sendai; rice, raw silk. **2** City (1940 pop. 46,484; 1947 pop. 48,957), Yamaguchi prefecture, SW Honshu, Japan, port on Suo Sea, 12 mi. E of Shimonoseki. Rail terminus; mfg. center (cement, pottery, patent medicine) in coal-mining area. Exports cement, fertilizer. Includes (since early 1940s) former village of Takachiho (1940 pop. 15,101).

Onoe (ōnō'ā), town (pop. 8,713), Aomori prefecture, N Honshu, Japan, 6 mi. E of Hirosaki; rice, poultry, sake.

Onomichi (ōnō'mēchē), city (1940 pop. 48,726; 1947 pop. 59,891), Hiroshima prefecture, SW Honshu, Japan, on Hiuchi Sea, 43 mi. E of Hiroshima, just E of Mihara; sheltered by Mukai-shima. Transportation center; mfg. (sailcloth, floor mats). Site of Senko-ji, anc. Buddhist temple. Since 1937, includes former town of Kurihara.

Onon, river, Mongolia and USSR: see ONON RIVER.

Onondaga (ŏnŭndô'gŭ), village (pop. estimate 200), SE Ont., 8 mi. E of Brantford; oil production.

Onondaga (ŏnŭndä'gŭ, –dô'gŭ), county (□ 792; pop. 341,719), central N.Y.; ⊙ SYRACUSE. Situated in Finger Lakes region; drained by Seneca and Oswego rivers and by Onondaga and small Chittenango creeks; crossed by the Barge Canal. Includes Onondaga Indian Reservation. Resorts on Oneida and Skaneateles lakes. Dairying and farming area (poultry, corn, truck, potatoes, hay), with extensive mfg.; saltworks. Formed 1794.

Onondaga Creek, N.Y.: see ONONDAGA LAKE.

Onondaga Lake, Onondaga co., central N.Y., salt lake just W of Syracuse; 5 mi. long, 1 mi. wide. Drains N through short outlet to Seneca R. Receives short Onondaga Creek from S. Purchased by state in 1795 from Onondaga Indians; site of early salt industry, relics of which are in Salt Mus. near Liverpool. Reconstruction of French fort (1656) is in park on shore near Syracuse.

Ononiimachi (ōnōnē'māchē), town (pop. 7,822), Fukushima prefecture, central Honshu, Japan, 15 mi. SE of Koriyama; agr. (rice, soybeans, tobacco), horse breeding.

Onon River (ō'nŏn), westernmost headstream of Amur R., in NE Mongolian People's Republic and USSR; rises in the Kentei Mts., flows 592 mi. E and NE, past Aksha and Olovyannaya (in Chita oblast), joining the Ingoda 15 mi. SW of Shilka to form navigable Shilka R. Used for logging. Lower course forms S and E border of Aga Buryat-Mongol Natl. Okrug. Receives Borzya and Aga rivers.

Ono San Pietro (ô'nô sän pyā'trô), village (pop. 546), Brescia prov., Lombardy, N Italy, near Oglio R., 11 mi. S of Edolo; iron mining.

Onota, Lake (ŭnŏ'tŭ), W Mass., in the Berkshires, just NW of Pittsfield; c.1.5 mi. long.

Onoto (ōnō'tō), town (pop. 825), Anzoátegui state, NE Venezuela, landing on Unare R. (navigable in rainy season) and 50 mi. SW of Barcelona; cotton, sugar cane, fruit, cattle; collects hides, timber.

Onotoa (ōnōtō'ä), atoll (□ 5.2; pop. 1,491), Kingsmill Group, S Gilbert Isls., W central Pacific; 1°50'S 175°33'E; copra. Formerly Clerk Isl.

Onoway (ŏ'nōwā), agr. village (pop. 175), central Alta., 30 mi. WNW of Edmonton.

Onsen (ōn'sän), town (pop. 5,606), Hyogo prefecture, S Honshu, Japan, 15 mi. ENE of Tottori; hot-springs resort; skiing. Rice, raw silk; sawmilling. Sometimes called Yumura.

Onset, Mass.: see WAREHAM.

Onslow (ŏnz'lō), port (pop. 180), NW Western Australia, 490 mi. N of Geraldton, at mouth of Ashburton R., near NE entrance to Exmouth Gulf; airport; exports gold, livestock.

Onslow, county (□ 756; pop. 42,047), E N.C., on the Atlantic; ⊙ Jacksonville. Bounded S by Onslow Bay; drained by New R. Heavily forested and partly swampy tidewater area; farming (tobacco, corn), sawmilling, fishing. U.S. Camp Lejeune (Marine base) in E. Formed 1734.

Onslow, town (pop. 244), Jones co., E Iowa, 14 mi. E of Anamosa, in livestock and grain area.

Onslow Bay, SE N.C., bight of the Atlantic bet. Cape Lookout (NE) and Cape Fear (SW); c.100 mi. long, 25 mi. wide.

Onsong (ôn'sông'), Jap. *Onjo*, township (1944 pop. 10,116), N.Hamgyong prov., N Korea, near Manchurian border, 45 mi. NNW of Unggi, in coal-mining and stock-raising area.

Onsoy (ôns'ûü), Nor. *Onsøy*, village and canton (pop. 8,532), Ostfold co., SE Norway, 5 mi. NW of Fredrikstad; center of stone-quarrying region (granite, paving stone); construction industry.

Onsted, village (pop. 486), Lenawee co., SE Mich., 12 mi. NW of Adrian, in farm area.

Onstmettingen (ônst"mĕ'tĭng-ùn), village (pop. 3,364), S Württemberg, Germany, after 1945 in Württemberg-Hohenzollern, in Swabian Jura, 5 mi. N of Ebingen; rail terminus; mfg. (knitwear, precision instruments).

Onstwedde (ōnst'vĕdù), town (pop. 16,892), Groningen prov., NE Netherlands, 5 mi. ENE of Stadskanaal; biscuits, synthetic fertilizer, potato flour; sheep raising.

On-take (ōn'täkā), peak (10,108 ft.), central Honshu, Japan, on Gifu-Nagano prefecture border, 36 mi. SW of Matsumoto. On its summit are a 14th-cent. Shinto shrine and several small lakes.

Ontario (ŏntâ'rēō), province (land area □ 363,282, total □ 412,582; 1941 pop. 3,787,655; 1948 estimate 4,297,000), SE Canada; ⊙ Toronto. Bounded by Que. (E), N.Y., L. Ontario, and L. Erie (SE), Mich., L. Huron, L. Superior, and Minn. (S), Man. (W)., and Hudson and James bays (N). Drained by the Severn, Winisk, Attawapiskat, Albany, Moose, and Abitibi rivers, flowing into Hudson and James bays; Ottawa R., flowing into the St. Lawrence; and the Rainy, Nipigon, Kaministikwia, Agwa, Montreal, Thames, Trent, Grand, Saugeen, Niagara, and St. Clair rivers, flowing into the Great Lakes. Of the numerous lakes, other than the Great Lakes, the largest are L. of the Woods and lakes Nipigon, Seul, des Mille Lacs, St. Joseph, Nipissing, Abitibi (partly in Que.), Simcoe, and Muskoka. N part of prov. is sparsely populated, densely wooded, and studded with lakes; part of the Laurentian Plateau extends here. Central Ont. is one of world's richest mining regions (gold, silver, nickel, copper, cobalt, arsenic, bismuth, pitchblende); timber stands supply pulp and paper mills. There is ample hydroelectric power. Chief towns in this region are Timmins, Sudbury, Sault Ste. Marie, Kirkland Lake, Cobalt, Cochrane, Kapuskasing, Haileybury, Blind River. Area near Man. border is rich in timber and minerals; here are important grain and iron ports of Fort William and Port Arthur. Center of pop. of prov. is its S part, on lakes Huron, Erie, and Superior. Agr. (stock raising, dairying, grains, fruit, vegetables, tobacco) is intensive; industries, supplied with abundant hydroelectric power, include metalworking, mfg. of machinery, railroad equipment, automobiles, trucks, textiles, leather, and wide range of consumer goods. Many U.S. firms have branch works here. Chief towns, besides Toronto, are Ottawa (⊙ Canada), London, Windsor, Kitchener, Guelph, Kingston, Chatham, Hamilton, Peterborough, St. Catharines, St. Thomas, Niagara Falls, and Owen Sound. Champlain 1st penetrated into interior of Ont. in 1615; area was subsequently visited by Frontenac and other French explorers, followed by missionaries and fur traders; but settlement took place only in S part. French cession (1763) of Canada to Great Britain was followed, after American Revolution, by influx of United Empire Loyalists. Constitution of 1791 divided Canada into Upper Canada (Ont.) and Lower Canada (Que.). Upper Canada was invaded by American forces in War of 1812 and was scene of several battles. Separatist rebellion took place 1837–38; subsequent Union Act of 1840 joined Upper and Lower Canada. Prov. of Ontario came into being upon establishment of the confederation in 1867. Part of Keewatin Dist. of the Northwest Territories was added to Ont., 1912.

Ontario, county (□ 853; pop. 65,718), S Ont., on L. Ontario and L. Simcoe; ⊙ Whitby.

Ontario, county (□ 649; pop. 60,172), W central N.Y.; ⊙ Canandaigua. Situated in Finger Lakes region, and partly bounded E by Seneca L.; includes Canandaigua, Honeoye, and Canadice lakes. Drained by small Honeoye, Mud, and Flint creeks and Canandaigua Outlet. Fruit- and truck-growing area; diversified mfg., especially at Geneva, Canandaigua, Naples; nurseries. Agr. (grain, hay, potatoes; dairy products; poultry). Formed 1789.

Ontario. 1 City (pop. 22,872), San Bernardino co., S Calif., 35 mi. E of Los Angeles, in the foothill citrus-fruit belt; processes citrus fruit, olives, wine. Mfg. of electrical equipment, furniture, aircraft parts; aircraft testing. Chaffey Jr. Col. here. Founded 1882, inc. 1891. **2** Village (1940 pop. 654), Wayne co., W N.Y., 16 mi. ENE of Rochester, in agr. area; canned foods, condiments. **3** City (pop. 4,465), Malheur co., E Oregon, on Snake R., at mouth of Malheur R., and c.45 mi. NW of Boise, Idaho; alt. 2,154 ft.; rail, trade, and highway center for large irrigated area (apples, sugar beets, potatoes, livestock, grain) in Owyhee R. project; lumber milling, dairying; concrete products. City is gateway to Oregon cattle country. Inc. 1914. **4** Village (pop. 527), Vernon co., SW Wis., on Kickapoo R. and 32 mi. ESE of La Crosse, in farm and dairy area.

Ontario, Fort, N.Y.: see OSWEGO, city.

Ontario, Lake, in U.S. and Canada, smallest and most easterly of the GREAT LAKES; 193 mi. long, 53 mi. wide, 778 ft. deep, it lies c.246 ft. above sea level and covers □ 7,540, of which □ c.3,725 are in Canada. It is bordered N, W, and partly S by Ont., S and E by N.Y. It receives the drainage of entire Great Lakes system through Niagara R. (SW), its connection with L. Erie, and discharges (NE) through the St. Lawrence. Receives Black, Oswego, Genesee rivers (N.Y.), Trent R. (Ont.). Welland Canal (Ont.) carries shipping around the barrier of Niagara Falls; lake is connected with the Hudson by a branch (terminating at Oswego) of N.Y. State Barge Canal system and with Georgian Bay of L. Huron by Trent Canal; Rideau Canal connects port of Kingston (Ont.) and Ottawa. Other Canadian ports are Hamilton, Toronto, and Cobourg; in N.Y. are Rochester and Oswego. Navigation is never seriously impeded by ice. Along its shores is a productive agr. belt whose climate is modified by lake; the N.Y. shore is particularly known for its fruit and truck farms. The lake was 1st seen (1615) by Étienne Brulé, and was visited later the same year by Champlain.

Onteniente (ōntĕnyĕn'tā), city (pop. 11,712), Valencia prov., E Spain, 14 mi. SSW of Játiva; textile center; also mfg. of cigarette paper, knit-goods, bleaching powder, footwear, hats, furniture, wax, brandy, candy; olive-oil processing. Wine and cereals in area.

Ontiñena (ōntēnyā'nä), village (pop. 1,281), Huesca prov., NE Spain, 17 mi. NW of Fraga; wine, olive oil, figs, livestock.

Ontonagon (ŏntùnô' gùn, –nä'gùn),county(□ 1,321; pop. 10,282), NW Upper Peninsula, Mich.; ⊙ Ontonagon. Bounded N by L. Superior; drained by Ontonagon R. and by small Iron and Firesteel rivers. Porcupine Mts. (copper mining) are in NW. Includes part of Ottawa Natl. Forest and part of Gogebic L. (S). Has Indian reservation. Lumber and agr. area (livestock, potatoes, hay, grain, dairy products); commercial fishing; resorts. Organized 1848.

Ontonagon, village (pop. 2,307), ⊙ Ontonagon co., NW Upper Peninsula, Mich., 40 mi. SW of Houghton, on L. Superior at mouth of Ontonagon R. Mfg. (lumber, paper products); shipping center; commercial fishing. Resort. The Ontonagon boulder, a huge copper mass, was found near the river, and was moved to the Smithsonian Institution. Established on site of Indian village; inc. 1885.

Ontonagon River, W Upper Peninsula, Mich., formed by several branches uniting in Ontonagon co., c.6 mi. SW of Mass, flows c.22 mi. NNW to L. Superior at Ontonagon. East Branch rises in NW Iron co., flows c.35 mi. NNW. Middle Branch rises near Wis. line, flows generally c.55 mi. N past Watersmeet. South Branch rises at Wis. line, flows c.55 mi. NNE, past Ewen. Victoria Dam (power) is on the South Branch just below the influx of West Branch (c.20 mi. long), which flows from N end of Gogebic L.

Ontong Java (ôn'tông jä'vä) or **Lord Howe Island,** atoll (pop. c.750), Solomon Isls., SW Pacific, c.160 mi. N of Santa Isabel; 5°25'S 159°30'E; 4 isls. on reef 30 mi. long, 20 mi. wide; coconuts. Polynesian natives.

Ontur (ōntōōr'), town (pop. 3,224), Albacete prov., SE central Spain, 14 mi. NE of Hellín; olive-oil processing, flour milling; cereals, wine, saffron, fruit.

Onufriyevka (ŭnōō'frēŭfkŭ), village (1926 pop. 3,430), E Kirovograd oblast, Ukrainian SSR, 12 mi. S of Kremenchug; flour mill.

Onuki (ō'nōōkē). **1** Town (pop. 9,926), Chiba prefecture, central Honshu, Japan, on W Chiba Peninsula, on Uraga Strait, 8 mi. SW of Kisarazu; rice growing, fishing. **2** Town (pop. 5,182), Ibaraki prefecture, central Honshu, Japan, just SW of Isohama; rice growing.

Onverdacht (ônfŭrdäkht'), village (pop. 151), Surinam dist., N Du. Guiana, on Surinam R. just N of Paranam, and 15 mi. SSE of Paramaribo. Commonly called Billiton, for the new (1942) bauxite plant.

Onverwacht (–väkht'), village (pop. 350), Surinam dist., N Du. Guiana, on Paramaribo-Dam RR and 17 mi. S of Paramaribo; coffee, rice, fruit.

Onward, town (pop. 140), Cass co., N central Ind., 10 mi. ESE of Logansport, in agr. area.

Onzaga (ōnsä'gä), town (pop. 758), Santander dept., N central Colombia, in Cordillera Oriental, 25 mi. SSW of Málaga; alt. 6,673 ft.

Onzain (ōzē'), village (pop. 1,017), Loir-et-Cher dept., N central France, on Cisse R. and 10 mi. SW of Blois; dairying; winegrowing.

Onze Lieve Vrouw-Waver (ō'zù lē'vù vrou-vä'vùr), Fr. *Wavre-Notre Dame* (vä'vrù-nôt'rù däm'), town (pop. 4,510), Antwerp prov., N Belgium, 5 mi. ENE of Mechlin; agr. market (vegetables, potatoes).

Oô (ō), village (pop. 143), Haute-Garonne dept., S France, in central Pyrenees, 5 mi. W of Luchon, near Sp. border. Near-by Lake of Oô (alt. 4,912 ft.), fed by waterfall (850 ft. high), has hydroelectric station.

O-o (ō) or **Aioi** (ī-oi'), city (1940 pop. 24,110; 1947 pop. 26,191), Hyogo prefecture, S Honshu, Japan, port on Harima Sea (E section of Inland Sea), 13 mi. W of Himeji; shipbuilding; exports coal, metalwork, lumber. Includes (since early 1940s) former town of Naba. Sometimes spelled O; sometimes called Sosei.

Oodeypore, India: see UDAIPUR, former princely state, city, Rajasthan.

Oodla Wirra (ōōd'lù wēr'ù), village, S South Australia, 65 mi. ENE of Port Pirie, on Port Pirie–Broken Hill RR; wool, some wheat. Sometimes spelled Oodlawirra.

Oodnadatta (ōōd"nùdă'tù), village (pop. 130), N central South Australia, 405 mi. NNW of Port Pirie and on Neales R., on Port Pirie–Alice Springs RR; cattle.

Ookala (ōkä'lä), coast village (pop. 663), E Hawaii, T.H., 23 mi. NW of Hilo; sugar plantation.

O'Okiep (ōkēp'), town (pop. 1,017), Little Namaqualand, NW Cape Prov., U. of So. Afr., 300 mi. N of Cape Town, 5 mi. N of Springbok; 29°36'S 17°53'E; copper-mining center. Ore shipped via Port Nolloth.

Ooku, Japan: see OMA.

Oola (ōō'lù), Gaelic *Ubhla*, town (pop. 346), E Co. Limerick, Ireland, 6 mi. NW of Tipperary; agr. market (dairying, cattle raising; grain, potatoes).

Oolagah, Okla.: see OOLOGAH.

Ooldea (ōōldē'ù), settlement, S South Australia, at E edge of Nullarbor Plain, 410 mi. NW of Port Pirie, on Trans-Australian RR; railway station.

Oolen, Belgium: see OLEN.

Oolitic (ōōlĭ'tĭk, ō–), town (pop. 1,125), Lawrence co., S Ind., on Salt Creek and 4 mi. NNW of Bedford; limestone quarrying.

Oologah or **Oolagah** (both: ōō'lùgä"), town (pop. 242), Rogers co., NE Okla., 25 mi. NE of Tulsa, in stockraising and agr. area. Will Rogers' birthplace is bet. here and Claremore. Near by on Verdigris R. is site of Oologah Reservoir, for flood control, hydroelectric power.

Ooltgensplaat (ōlt'khĕnsplät), agr. village (pop. 2,135), South Holland prov., SW Netherlands, on Overflakkee isl., 9 mi. SE of Middelharnis.

Oorgaum, India: see KOLAR GOLD FIELDS.

Oorschot, Netherlands: see OIRSCHOT.

Ooru, India: see KHARAGHODA.

Oos (ōs), NW suburb of Baden-Baden, S Germany, on the Oos; airport.

Oos-Londen, U. of So. Afr.: see EAST LONDON.

Oos River (ōs), S Baden, Germany, rises on W slope of the Black Forest, flows 15 mi. WNW and N, past Baden-Baden, to the Murg at Rastatt.

Oostakker (ōs'täkùr), agr. village (pop. 7,523), East Flanders prov., NW Belgium, 3 mi. NNE of Ghent, near Ghent-Terneuzen Canal. Formerly spelled Oostacker.

Oostanaula River (ōō"stùnô'lù), NW Ga., formed by confluence of Conasauga and Coosawattee rivers 3 mi. NE of Calhoun, flows c.45 mi. SSW to Rome where it unites with Etowah R. to form the Coosa.

Oostburg (ōst'bûrkh), town (pop. 2,313), Zeeland prov., SW Netherlands, on Flanders mainland and 6 mi. SSW of Breskens; trade center, with small industries. Town chartered in 13th cent.; reached its zenith as trading center in Middle Ages.

Oostburg (ōōst'bûrg), village (pop. 895), Sheboygan co., E Wis., 10 mi. SSW of Sheboygan, in dairy and farm area; mfg. (dairy products, canned vegetables, raincoats); fishing. Terry Andrae State Park (on L. Michigan) near by.

Oostcamp, Belgium: see OOSTKAMP.

Oostduinkerke (ōstdoin'kĕrkù), town (pop. 3,934), West Flanders prov., W Belgium, near North Sea, 3 mi. W of Nieuport. Just NNW, on North Sea, is seaside resort of Oostduinkerke-Bains.

Oosteeklo (ō'stäklō"), agr. village (pop. 2,331), East Flanders prov., NW Belgium, 6 mi. E of Eekloo. Formerly spelled Oost-Eecloo or Oost-Eekloo.

Oostende, Belgium: see OSTEND.

Oosterbeek (ōst'ùrbāk), residential village (pop. 9,819), Gelderland prov., central Netherlands, on Lower Rhine R. and 3 mi. W of Arnhem; furniture mfg. Allied airborne landing here (1944), and subsequent battle.

Oosterhout (–hout), town (pop. 13,618), North Brabant prov., SW Netherlands, 12 mi. WNW of Tilburg, at junction of Wilhelmina and Mark canals; straw and hay trade, mfg. (leather, shoes, cigars, tobacco, cement, biscuits, wood products, strawboard), iron foundry.

Oosterland (–länt), agr. village (pop. 1,121), Zeeland prov., SW Netherlands, on Duiveland isl., 5 mi. E of Zierikzee.

Ooster Schelde, Netherlands: see EASTERN SCHELDT.

Oosterwijk, Netherlands: see OISTERWIJK.

Oosterzele (–zā″lů), agr. village (pop. 3,122), East Flanders prov., NW Belgium, 8 mi. SSE of Ghent. Formerly spelled Oosterzeele.

Oosthaven, Indonesia: see PANJANG.

Oostkamp (ōst′kämp), village (pop. 7,791), West Flanders prov., NW Belgium, 4 mi. S of Bruges; agr., lumbering. Formerly spelled Oostcamp.

Oostmahorn (ōstmä′hôrn), village (pop. 130), Friesland prov., N Netherlands, on Lauwers Zee and 8 mi. ENE of Dokkum; port; fishing. Ferry to Schiermonnikoog isl.

Oostmalle (ōst′mälů), village (pop. 2,735), Antwerp prov., N Belgium, 9 mi. W of Turnhout; agr., lumbering.

Oostnieuwkerke (ōstnē′ŏŏkĕrků), village (pop. 3,089), West Flanders prov., W Belgium, 3 mi. W of Roulers; flax and tobacco growing.

Oostrozebeke (ōstrō′zůbāků), town (pop. 5,541), West Flanders prov., W Belgium, 7 mi. NNE of Courtrai; textile industry; agr. market. Formerly spelled Oostroosebeke or Oostroozebeke.

Oost-Vlaanderen, Belgium: see EAST FLANDERS.

Oostvleteren (ōst-vlā′tůrůn), agr. village (pop. 1,491), West Flanders prov., W Belgium, 8 mi. NW of Ypres.

Oost-Vlieland, Netherlands: see VLIELAND.

Oostvoorne (ōst′fōrnů), village (pop. 2,421), South Holland prov., SW Netherlands, on North Sea coast of Voorne isl., 7 mi. NNW of Hellevoetsluis; crate mfg.; truck gardening, dairy industry.

Ootacamund (ōō′tůkůmŭnd), city (pop. 29,850), ⊙ Nilgiri dist., SW Madras, India, in Nilgiri Hills, 60 mi. S of Mysore. Terminus of rail spur from Coimbatore; well-known hill resort on scenic plateau (alt. over 7,000 ft.; annual mean temp., 57°); summer hq. of Madras govt. Noted botanical gardens; fine motor roads. Big-game hunting in surrounding hills. Near-by lake (constructed 1825) has fisheries (trout research). Extensive cinchona plantations in hills just E (rise to 8,640 ft. in Dodabetta peak) supply quinine factory at Naduvattam. Eucalyptus estates produce fuel and distilled oil. Often popularly called Ooty.

Ootegem (ō′tů-khům), agr. village (pop. 1,765), West Flanders prov., W Belgium, 7 mi. E of Courtrai. Formerly spelled Ooteghem.

Ootmarsum (ōtmär′sŭm), town (pop. 1,886), Overijssel prov., E Netherlands, 11 mi. ENE of Almelo, near Ger. border; mfg. (cotton and linen textiles, bricks); summer resort.

Ootsa Lake (ōōt′sů) (□ 50), W central B.C., on N boundary of Tweedsmuir Park, 120 mi. WSW of Prince George. Drains ESE into Nechako R. by short Ootsa R.

Ooty, India: see OOTACAMUND.

Opaka (ô′päkä), village (pop. 4,927), Kolarovgrad dist., NE Bulgaria, on Cherni Lom R. and 7 mi. NNW of Popovo; grain, poultry, oil-bearing plants.

Opal (ō′pŭl), town (pop. 67), Lincoln co., SW Wyo., on Hams Fork and 11 mi. E of Kemmerer; alt. c.6,660 ft. Shipping point for sheep and wool.

Opala (ōpä′lä), village, Eastern Prov., central Belgian Congo, on left bank of Lomami R. and 110 mi. SW of Stanleyville; steamboat landing in rice- and fiber-growing area. R.C. mission.

Opalaca, Sierra de (syĕ′rä dā ōpälä′kä), section of main Andean divide, in Intibuca dept., W Honduras; extends c.20 mi. NW–SE of La Esperanza; rises to over 5,000 ft. Forms divide bet. upper Ulúa R. (N) and Guarajambala R. (S).

Opalenica (ôpälĕnē′tsä), Ger. *Opalenitza* (ōpälůnĭ′-tsä), town (1946 pop. 4,366), Poznan prov., W Poland, 23 mi. WSW of Poznan; rail junction; beet-sugar and flour milling, tanning.

Opalescent River (ōpůlĕ′sůnt), NE N.Y., name given to main headstream of HUDSON RIVER.

Opa-Locka (ō″pů-lŏ′ků), city (pop. 5,271), Dade co., S Fla., just N of Miami.

Opanake (ō′pŭnůkä), village (pop., including near-by villages, 1,299), Sabaragamuwa Prov., S central Ceylon, 16 mi. ESE of Ratnapura; rail terminus; rubber, tea, vegetables, rice.

Opari (ōpä′rē), town, Equatoria prov., S Anglo-Egyptian Sudan, near Uganda border, on road and 70 mi. SSE of Juba; cotton, corn, durra; livestock. Leper settlement.

Oparino (ŭpä′rēnů), town (1948 pop. over 2,000), NW Kirov oblast, Russian SFSR, on railroad and 100 mi. NNW of Kirov; dairying, lumbering.

Oparo, Fr. Oceania: see RAPA.

Opatija (ô′pätēä), Ital. *Abbazia* (äb-brä′tsēä), town (pop. 11,737), NW Croatia, Yugoslavia, on Kvarner gulf of Adriatic Sea, on railroad and 7 mi. W of Rijeka, in NE Istria, at NE foot of the Ucka. Noted summer and winter resort; sea bathing. Includes suburbs of Lovran, Ital. *Laurana* (S), and Volosko, Ital. *Volosca* (N).

Opatoro (ōpätō′rō), town (pop. 150), La Paz dept., SW Honduras, in Sierra de Guajiquiro, 13 mi. SE of Marcala; coffee, wheat; mfg. (palm hats, rope, pottery).

Opatoro, Sierra de, Honduras: see GUAJIQUIRO, SIERRA DE.

Opatow (ôpä′tōōf), Pol. *Opatów*, Rus. *Opatov* (ŭpä′-tŭf), town (pop. 5,459), Kielce prov., E Poland, 35 mi. ESE of Kielce; mfg. (chemicals, cement products, brushes). Known from 1040; flourished at end of 14th cent., trading with Greece, Persia, Armenia, Nuremberg, and Holland. Has old church and town gate.

Opava (ô′pävä), Ger. *Troppau* (trô′pou), city (pop. 20,441; metropolitan area pop. 30,191), N Silesia, Czechoslovakia, on Opava R. and 16 mi. WNW of Ostrava; rail junction; industrial center in fertile agr. dist. (sugar beets, barley, oats); mfg. of knit goods and textiles (notably woolens), food and jute processing, tanning. Has 15th-cent. church, medieval remains. Main part of city is on right bank; KATERINKY suburb is on left bank. Tourist center of Hradec or Hradec u Opavy is on Moravice R., 4 mi. S; has paper mills of Zimrovice (zhĭm′-rôvĭtsĕ), Czech *Žimrovice*. Opava was former ⊙ Austrian Silesia. Major European powers conferred here, in 1820 (Troppau protocol).

Opava River (ô′pävä), Ger. *Oppa* (ô′pä), Pol. *Opawa* (ôpä′vä), central Silesia, Czechoslovakia, formed by 3 headstreams joining at Vrbno; flows SE, then NE past Krnov and SE along Czechoslovak-Pol. border for c.12 mi., past Opava, to Oder R. at W outskirts of Ostrava; 70 mi. long. Receives Moravice R. (right).

Opazova, Yugoslavia: see STARA PAZOVA.

Opbrakel (ô′bräkůl), agr. village (pop. 1,738), East Flanders prov., W central Belgium, 7 mi. ESE of Oudenaarde.

Opcine, Free Territory of Trieste: see OPICINA.

Opdal (ôp′däl). **1** Village and canton, Buskerud co., Norway: see UVDAL. **2** Village, More og Romsdal co., Norway: see OPDOL. **3** Village and canton (pop. 5,181), Sor-Trondelag co., central Norway, on Driva R., on railroad and 40 mi. NNE of Dombas; slate quarry; skiing center in the Dovrefjell. Also spelled Oppdal. At village of Engan (ĕng′än), 8 mi. S, is mfg. of paving materials.

Opdol (ôp′dûl), Nor. *Opdøl*, village in Alvundeid (Nor. *Ålvundeid*) canton (pop. 448), More og Romsdal co., W Norway, on Sunndals Fjord, 45 mi. E of Molde; tourist center, starting point for trips to Trollheimen mts. Formerly spelled Opdal.

Opechenski Posad or **Opechenskiy Posad** (ŭpyĕ′-chĭnskē pŭsät′), village (1926 pop. 666), E Novgorod oblast, Russian SFSR, on Msta R. and 10 mi. SE of Borovichi; flax.

Opecska, Rumania: see PECICA.

Opelika (ōpůlī′ků), city (pop. 12,295), ⊙ Lee co., E Ala., 60 mi. ENE of Montgomery, N of Chattahoochee R.; trade center for cotton and corn area; mfg. (cotton fabrics and clothing, cottonseed oil, fertilizer, wood products), dairying, meat processing. Settled 1836, inc. 1854 as town, 1899 as city.

Opelousas (ŏpůlōō′sůs), city (pop. 11,659), ⊙ St. Landry parish, S central La., c.55 mi. W of Baton Rouge; commercial, processing and shipping center for agr. and stock-raising area; rice, cotton, sugar cane, corn, sweet potatoes, pecans. Cottonseed-oil mills, cotton gins; rice, lumber, and sugar mills; canneries, creameries; mfg. of drugs, machine-shop products, mattresses. One of oldest towns in state. Founded 1765, inc. 1821; made ⊙ La. for a short time during Civil War.

Open Door, town (pop. 5,293), NE Buenos Aires prov., Argentina, 5 mi. NNE of Luján; agr. center (alfalfa, grain, flax). Site of insane asylum using "open door" cure method.

Open Lake, Tenn.: see RIPLEY.

Openshaw (ō′pŭn-shô), E suburb (pop. 23,240) of Manchester, SE Lancashire, England; steel milling, electrical engineering, textile printing; mfg. of chemicals (for textile industry), abrasives, industrial belting.

Opeongo Lake (ōpēŏng′gō) (20 mi. long, 5 mi. wide), S Ont., in Algonquin Provincial Park, 60 mi. W of Pembroke; alt. 1,323 ft.; drained by Madawaska R.

Opheim (ŏp′hīm), town (pop. 383), Valley co., NE Mont., near Sask. line, 48 mi. N of Glasgow; port of entry and marketing point in fertile wheat area.

Ophel, Palestine: see JERUSALEM.

Opheusden (ôp-hûz′důn), village (pop. 1,992), Gelderland prov., central Netherlands, near Lower Rhine R., 9 mi. ENE of Tiel; tree nurseries.

Ophidousa or **Ofidousa** (both: ôfēdhōō′sů), Ital. *Ofidusa* (ôfēdōō′zä), westernmost island of the Dodecanese, Greece; 36°33′N 26°10′E.

Ophir (ō′fůr), village (pop. 43), SW central Alaska, 30 mi. WNW of McGrath; trapping; placer gold mining. Air strip.

Ophir. 1 Town (pop. 2), San Miguel co., SW Colo., in San Juan Mts., 5 mi. S of Telluride, in gold-mining region; alt. 9,800 ft. **2** Town (pop. 199), Tooele co., N central Utah, 12 mi. S of Tooele, in Oquirrh Mts.; alt. 6,498 ft.; silver, gold, lead deposits.

Ophir, Mount (ō′fůr), peak (9,554 ft.), W central Sumatra, Indonesia, in Padang Highlands of Barisan Mts., 75 mi. NNW of Padang.

Ophir, Mount, Malay *Gunong Ledang* (gōōnōōng′ lůdäng′), highest peak (4,187 ft.) in Johore, S Malaya, 100 mi. NW of Johore Bharu, near Malacca line; 2°21′N 102°39′E.

Ophirton (ō′vůrtůn), S suburb of Johannesburg, S Transvaal, U. of So. Afr.; gold mining.

Ophoven (ôp′hōvůn), agr. village (pop. 1,881), Limburg prov., NE Belgium, on Meuse R., near Netherlands border, and 2 mi. N of Maaseik.

Opichén (ōpēchĕn′), town (pop. 1,222), Yucatan, SE Mexico, 33 mi. SSW of Mérida; henequen, sugar cane, fruit.

Opicina (ōpēchē′nä), Slovenian *Opčine* (ôp′chēnā), N suburb (pop. 2,458) of Trieste, Free Territory of Trieste, on the Karst above the city, near Yugoslav border; rail junction (Poggioreale Campagna) and frontier station; fine views.

Opico or **San Juan Opico** (sän whän′ ōpē′kō), city (pop. 2,721), La Libertad dept., W central Salvador, 14 mi. NNW of Nueva San Salvador; sugar cane, grain, coffee.

Opien (ŭ′byĕn′), town (pop. 3,628), ⊙ Opien co. (pop. 47,522), SW Szechwan prov., China, near Sikang line, 50 mi. SW of Loshan, in mtn. region; rice, millet, wheat.

Opienge (ōpyĕng′gä), village, Eastern Prov., E Belgian Congo, 125 mi. ESE of Stanleyville; trading post with Protestant mission; rice processing.

Opiskoteo Lake (ō″pĭskō′tēō) (22 mi. long, 15 mi. wide), E central Que., near Labrador border; 53°10′N 68°10′W; alt. 2,025 ft.

Opladen (ôp′lä″důn), town (pop. 22,645), in former Prussian Rhine Prov., W Germany, after 1945 in North Rhine-Westphalia, on the Wupper and 3 mi. N of Leverkusen; rail junction; railroad repair shops; mfg. of bicycles and dyes.

Opland (ôp′län), county [Nor. *fylke*] (□ 9,775; pop. 154,734), S central Norway; ⊙ Lillehammer. Central and N parts of co. are alpine in character and include major portions of the Jotunheim, Dovrefjell, and Rondane mts.; the Galdhopiggen (8,097 ft.) is highest peak in Scandinavia. Co. is transected (N-S) by the GUDBRANDSDAL, its economic, ethnological, and cultural center. Slate, steatite, and talc are quarried. Grain growing, stock raising, dairying are chief occupations. Mfg. industries at Lillehammer and Gjovik. On one of Norway's most important inland trade routes since earliest times, co. is setting of numerous sagas and folk legends, including that of Peer Gynt. It is noted for its scenery and healthful climate and is a tourist center. Until 1918, co. (then called *amt*) was named Kristians. In Second World War, it was scene (April, 1940) of heavy fighting.

Oploca (ōplō′kä), village (pop. c.1,000), Potosí dept., SW Bolivia, on Tupiza R. and 10 mi. NNW of Tupiza, on Villazón-Uyuni RR, in agr. area; corn, orchards; flour mill. Oploca tin mines lie 45 mi. NW, near Chocaya, on W slopes of Cordillera de Chichas.

Opobo (ōpō′bō), town (pop. 1,609), Calabar prov., Eastern Provinces, SE Nigeria, port on Gulf of Guinea, on mouth of Imo R. (here called Opobo R.), at E end of coastal lagoon waterway of Niger delta and 40 mi. ESE of Port Harcourt; fisheries; palm oil and kernels, rubber, kola nuts, hardwood. Sometimes called by its native name Egwanga. Opobo Town, a 19th-cent. Br. commercial station, is 4 mi. SSW, across Opobo R.

Opochka (ŭpôch′kŭ), city (1948 pop. over 10,000), NW Velikiye Luki oblast, Russian SFSR, on Velikaya R. and 65 mi. NW of Nevel; road center; woodworking, flax and food processing.

Opochno, Poland: see OPOCZNO.

Opocno (ô′pôchnô), Czech *Opočno*, town (pop. 2,415), E Bohemia, Czechoslovakia, 13 mi. ENE of Hradec Kralove; rail junction; textile industry.

Opoczno (ôpôch′nô), Rus. *Opochno* (ŭpôch′nů), town (pop. 7,433), Kielce prov., central Poland, on Drzewiczka R., on railroad and 45 mi. SE of Lodz; clay pit, limekiln; ironworks; glass, porcelain; flour milling, brewing. Small electric plant.

Opodepe (ōpōdā′pā), town (pop. 654), Sonora, NW Mexico, on San Miguel R. and 60 mi. NNE of Hermosillo; corn, beans, cattle.

Opogodó (ōpōgōdō′), village, Chocó dept., W Colombia, 50 mi. S of Quibdó; gold- and platinum-placer mines.

Opol (ōpōl′), town (1939 pop. 4,429) in Cagayan municipality, Misamis Oriental prov., N Mindanao, Philippines, near Macajalar Bay, 6 mi. NW of Cagayan; agr. center (corn, coconuts). Chromite deposits.

Opole (ôpô′lĕ), province [Pol. *województwo*] (□ 3,633; pop. 792,234), S Poland; ⊙ Oppeln (Opole). Borders S on Czechoslovakia. Surface rises from fertile Oder valley SW to the Sudetes range, which slopes down (SE) toward Moravian Gap. Drained by Oder and Glatzer Neisse (Nysa Klodzka) rivers. Principal industries: leather-goods mfg., tanning, textile milling, sugar refining. Heavy industry (mfg. of machinery, electrical equipment) concentrated at Ratibor (Raciborz). Iron, galena, tetrahedryte are worked. Chief crops: rye, potatoes, oats, wheat, sugar beets, flax. Principal cities: Oppeln, Ratibor, Neisse (Nysa), Brieg (Brzeg), and Kozle (Cosel). Until 1945, in Ger. Upper SILESIA prov. Prov. created 1950 when Slask, Pol. *Śląsk*, prov., established 1945 and briefly called Slask Dabrowski, Pol. *Śląsk Dąbrowski*, was divided bet. Opole prov. (W) and Katowice prov. (E); it also received small part (W) of Wroclaw prov. Ger. pop. expelled after 1945 and replaced by Poles.

Opole, town, Poland: see OPPELN.

Opolye, Russian SFSR: see VLADIMIR, oblast.

Opon (ō′pōn, ōpōn′), chief town (1939 pop. 2,173; 1948 municipality pop. 37,280) of Mactan Isl., Cebu prov., Philippines, on W coast of isl., 3 mi. E of Cebu city across narrow channel; coconut-growing and fishing center. Near by is a monument dedicated to Magellan, killed here in 1521.

Oporto (ŭpôr′tō, ō–), Port. *Pôrto* (pōr′to͝o), anc. *Portus Cale*, city (1950 pop. 279,738), ⊙ Pôrto dist. and Douro Litoral prov., N Portugal, on bank of Douro R. 3 mi. above its mouth on the Atlantic, and 175 mi. NNE of Lisbon; 41°8′N 8°35′W; Portugal's second city, world-famous for its port wine. City is built in terraces on steep slopes above deep, rock-bound Douro gorge; it is linked to its S suburb, Vila Nova de Gaia (noted for its wine storehouses), by two-storied Dom Luís I bridge. Since a sand bar prevents entrance of vessels above 2,000 tons, an artificial harbor (LEIXÕES) was built (1890) on the Atlantic, 5 mi. NW. In addition to port wine, Oporto ships fruits, olive oil, salt, building materials. Diversified industry is represented by textile mills (cotton, wool, linen, silk, and lace), foundries, sugar refineries, glass and pottery works. Other mfg.: preserves, paper, soap, tobacco products, oilcloth, perfumes, jewelry, leather goods. The Torre dos Clérigos (an 18th-cent. tower 245 ft. high) is city's most conspicuous landmark. Also noteworthy are the Gothic cathedral (called Sé), the episcopal palace, and several churches. Univ. was established 1911. The port wine trade, begun in late 17th cent. by Br. merchants, was considerably advanced by Methuen Treaty (1703) which give Port. wines preferential treatment over French. City was held by French 1805–09. It has been repeatedly hit by flash winter floods. Prince Henry the Navigator b. here.

Oposhnya (ŭpôsh′nyŭ), town (1926 pop. 8,608), NE Poltava oblast, Ukrainian SSR, on Vorskla R. and 25 mi. N of Poltava; ceramic industry.

Opotiki (ōpŭtē′kē), borough (pop. 1,571), ⊙ (Opotiki co. (□ 1,537; pop. 4,672), N N.Isl., New Zealand, at mouth of short Waioeka R., on Bay of Plenty and 60 mi. NW of Gisborne; center of corn-raising area; dairy products, sheep.

Opp, city (pop. 5,240), Covington co., S Ala., 15 mi. E of Andalusia; cotton fabrics, peanut butter, lumber. Inc. 1902.

Oppach (ô′päkh), village (pop. 3,987), Saxony, E central Germany, in Upper Lusatia, at N foot of Lusatian Mts., near the Spree, 9 mi. SSE of Bautzen, near Czechoslovak border; textile milling (cotton, linen, jute), distilling.

Oppa River, Czechoslovakia and Poland: see OPAVA RIVER.

Oppau (ô′pou), N district (since 1938) of Ludwigshafen; mfg. of chemicals (nitrogen compounds, dyestuffs, synthetic fiber).

Oppdal, Norway: see OPDAL, Sor-Trondelag co.

Oppegard (ôp′pŭgôr), Nor. *Oppegård*, residential village (pop. 1,505); canton pop. 5,217), Akershus co., SE Norway, on E shore of Bunde Fjord (SE arm of Oslo Fjord), 9 mi. S of Oslo. Sometimes spelled Oppegaard.

Oppeln (ô′pŭln) or **Opole** (ôpô′lĕ), town (1939 pop. 52,977; 1946 pop. 27,666) in Upper Silesia, after 1945 ⊙ Opole prov., S Poland, port on the Oder and 50 mi. SE of Breslau (Wroclaw), in porphyry- and quartzite-quarrying region. Rail junction; trade center; mfg. of cement, lime, agr. machinery, textiles; flour milling, woodworking; grain market. Seat of R.C. bishopric. Was (1163–1532) ⊙ duchy under branch of Pol. Piast dynasty; passed (1532) to Hapsburgs and (1742) to Prussia. Was (1919–45) ⊙ former Prussian Upper Silesia prov. Heavily damaged in Second World War.

Oppenau (ô′pŭnou), town (pop. 2,222), S Baden, Germany, in Black Forest, 10 mi. E of Offenburg; chemical mfg. (carbon black, lacquer, varnish), lumber milling, woodworking. Climatic health resort (alt. 879 ft.) and tourist center.

Oppenheim (ô′pŭnhīm), town (pop. 4,674), Rhenish Hesse, W Germany, on left bank of the Rhine and 11 mi. SE of Mainz; noted for its wine. Brickworks. Ruins of former imperial fortress Landskron (destroyed 1689 by French) tower above town. On site of Roman settlement; was free imperial city.

Oppido Lucano (ôp′pēdô lo͞okä′nô), village (pop. 3,834), Potenza prov., Basilicata, S Italy, 13 mi. NE of Potenza; wine, olive oil, cheese. Formerly Palmira.

Oppido Mamertina (mämĕrtē′nä), town (pop. 4,981), Reggio di Calabria prov., Calabria, S Italy, on N slope of the Aspromonte, 9 mi. ESE of Palmi, in lumbering and stock-raising region. Bishopric. Rebuilt after earthquakes of 1783 and 1908.

Oppidum Batavorum, Netherlands: see BATENBURG.

Opponitz (ôp′pōnĭts), village (pop. 983), SW Lower Austria, on Ybbs R. and 6 mi. SSE of Waidhofen; hydroelectric plant; mfg. of scythes.

Optima (ŏp′tĭmŭ), town (pop. 97), Texas co., extreme NW Okla., 10 mi. NE of Guymon, in wheat-growing area; carbon-black mfg. Near by is site of Optima Reservoir, for flood control, irrigation in North Canadian R. valley.

Opua (ōpo͞o′ŭ), township (pop. 190), N N.Isl., New Zealand, 110 mi. NNW of Auckland and on S shore of Bay of Islands; rail terminus; in agr. area. Deep-sea fishing.

Opunake (ōpo͞onä′kē), borough (pop. 935), W N.Isl., New Zealand, on small bay of S.Taranaki Bight and 30 mi. SSW of New Plymouth; dairying center.

Opuntian Locris, Greece: see LOCRIS.

Oputo (ōpo͞o′tō), town (pop. 1,505), Sonora, NW Mexico, on W slopes of Sierra Madre Occidental, on Bavispe R. and 125 mi. NE of Hermosillo; cattle; wheat, corn.

Opuzen (ô′po͞ozĕn), village, S Croatia, Yugoslavia, on Neretva R., near its mouth, on railroad and 4 mi. SW of Metkovic, in Dalmatia. Former Austrian strongpoint called Fort Opus.

Opwijk (ōp′vīk), town (pop. 8,305), Brabant prov., central Belgium, 11 mi. NW of Brussels; textile industry; agr. market. Formerly spelled Opwyck.

Opzullik, Belgium: see SILLY.

Oqair or **Al 'Uqayr** (ăl ōkīr′), town (pop. 5,000) in Hasa, Saudi Arabia, port on Gulf of Bahrein, on road and 45 mi. ENE of Hofuf; fishing, pearling; grain, vegetables, fruit. An important port until development of oil industry and rise of Dammam. Kuwait–Saudi Arabia frontier was agreed to here, in 1922. Identified with *Gerrha*, anc. Chaldean colony.

Oquaga Lake (ōkwä′gŭ), resort village, Broome co., S N.Y., near Pa. line, 25 mi. ESE of Binghamton, on small Oquaga L.

Oquawka (ōkwô′kŭ), village (pop. 929), ⊙ Henderson co., W Ill., on the Mississippi and 11 mi. NNE of Burlington, Iowa; summer resort; agr. (truck, livestock, poultry; dairy products); hardwood timber; limestone quarries, button mfg.

Oquirrh Mountains (ō′kwŭr), NW Utah, extend c.30 mi. S from Great Salt L.; rise to c.11,000 ft. Copper, lead, zinc, gold, and silver mined near Bingham Canyon.

Oquitoa (ōkētō′ä), town (pop. 406), Sonora, NW Mexico, on affluent of Magdalena R. and 60 mi. SW of Nogales; wheat, corn, cotton, beans, cattle.

Oquossoc, village, Maine: see RANGELEY.

Oquossoc Lake, Maine: see RANGELEY LAKES.

Or, Mont d' (mō dôr′), summit (4,800 ft.) of the E Jura, on Franco-Swiss border, 11 mi. S of Pontarlier (France), overlooking Vallorbe (Switzerland). Pierced by international railroad tunnel (4 mi. long).

Or, Mont d', peak (7,145 ft.) in Bernese Alps, SW Switzerland, 7 mi. NE of Aigle.

Ora (ô′rä), Ger. *Auer*, town (pop. 1,919), Bolzano prov., Trentino–Alto Adige, N Italy, near Adige R., 11 mi. SSW of Bolzano; rail junction; canned foods, marmalade.

Oracabessa (ō″rŭkŭbbĕ′sŭ), town (pop. 2,360), St. Mary parish, N Jamaica, banana port on fine Caribbean bay, 4 mi. WNW of Port Maria.

Oradea or **Oradea-Mare** (ôrä′dyä-mä′rĕ), Hung. *Nagyvárad* (nŏ′dyŭvärŏt), Ger. *Grosswardein* (grōs-vär′dīn), city (1948 pop. 82,282), ⊙ Bihor prov., W Rumania, in Crisana, on Rapid Körös R., near Hung. border and 275 mi. NW of Bucharest, 135 mi. ESE of Budapest; 47°3′N 21°56′E. Commercial and industrial center in winegrowing region; rail hub with locomotive repair shops. Airport. Mfg. of machinery (notably agr. equipment), clay products, glass, textiles, clothing, shoes, toilet articles, liquor, beer, confectionery, candles, flour, wooden products, malt, yeast. Brisk trade in livestock, grain, wool, wine, and fruit. Educational establishments include law school, 2 theological seminaries, several teachers' colleges, business academy. R.C. and Greek Uniate bishoprics. Most of city's architecture is baroque and dates from Maria Theresa. Worthy of note are 12th-cent. St. Ladislas church which contains his remains, 18th-cent. Orthodox cathedral with frescoes and astronomical clock, 18th-cent. R.C. cathedral and rococo episcopal residence, former fortress (now barracks), archaeological and historical mus. Presumably built on site of a Roman settlement, Oradea was made R.C. bishopric by St. Ladislas in 1083. Destroyed (1241) by the Tatars, it was rebuilt in 14th cent. and prospered under Mathias Corvinus. Held by Turks (1660–92). Ceded to Rumania 1919. Hungary held it, 1940–45. More than half of its pop. are Magyars. Noted health resorts of Baile Episcopiei (bŭ′ēlĕ yĕpēskôpyā′), Rum. *Băile Episcopiei*, and Baile Felix (fā′lĕks), Rum. *Băile Felix*, both with sulphurous thermal springs, lie c.5 mi. SE.

Oradell (ô′rŭdĕl), residential borough (pop. 3,665), Bergen co., NE N.J., on Hackensack R., at SW end of Oradell Reservoir, and 5 mi. N of Hackensack; makes gummed-tape dispensers. Settled by Dutch before the Revolution, inc. 1894.

Oradell Reservoir, N.J.: see HACKENSACK RIVER.

Oradna, Rumania: see RODNA.

Oradour-sur-Glane (ôrädo͞or′-sür-glän′), village (1936 pop. 1,574; 1946 pop. 15), Haute-Vienne dept., W central France, 12 mi. NW of Limoges. Burnt down and population massacred by the Germans June 10, 1944.

Oradour-sur-Vayres (–sür-vâr′), agr. village (pop. 408), Haute-Vienne dept., W central France, near Tardoire R., 6 mi. SSE of Rochechouart.

Oraefajokull, Iceland: see HVANNADALSHNJUKUR.

Orahovac or **Orakhovats** (both: ôrä′hôväts,–khô–), village (pop. 5,480), SW Serbia, Yugoslavia, 14 mi. N of Prizren, in the Metohija.

Orahovica or **Slavonska Orahovica** (slävôn′skä ôrä′hôvĭtsä), village (pop. 3,259), N Croatia, Yugoslavia, 31 mi. SE of Virovitica, at E foot of the Papuk, in Slavonia; rail terminus; local trade center. There are castle ruins. First mentioned in 1228.

Orai (ō′rī), town (pop. 17,242), ⊙ Jalaun dist., S Uttar Pradesh, India, 65 mi. SW of Cawnpore; road center; trades in gram, wheat, oilseeds, jowar.

Oraibi (ōrī′bē), Indian pueblo, Hopi Indian Reservation, NE Ariz., on high mesa and c.60 mi. N of Winslow; alt. 6,497 ft. Built c.1150, discovered 1540 by Coronado expedition; site of mission of San Francisco (established 1629, destroyed in Pueblo revolt of 1680). Sometimes considered oldest continually inhabited town in U.S., it was long the most important pueblo of the Hopis, but has been gradually abandoned because of economic disturbances and internal dissensions. At foot of mesa is Lower Oraibi village.

Oraison (ôrāzō′), village (pop. 1,527), Basses-Alpes dept., SE France, near left bank of Durance R., 20 mi. SW of Digne, in Provence Alps; market; flour milling, canning, toy mfg.

Orakhovats, Yugoslavia: see ORAHOVAC.

Oran (ōrăn′, Fr. ôrä′), northwesternmost department (□ 25,970; 1948 pop. 1,990,729) of Algeria, on the Mediterranean, bordering W on Fr. Morocco; ⊙ Oran. Traversed SW-NE by parallel ranges of the Tell Atlas (Tlemcen, Tessala, Saïda mts., Ouarsenis Massif), and further inland by the semi-arid High Plateaus. The main range (Djebel Amour) of the Saharan Atlas crosses the southernmost extension of dept. In the TELL (N), climate is typically Mediterranean; semi-arid to arid subtropical in High Plateaus. Short streams (Tafna, Mékerra, Hammam, Mina), draining northward from the Tell Atlas, are dammed in upper course to irrigate sub-coastal lowlands (Sig, Habra, Marnia). The lower Chéliff valley (E of Mostaganem) is also irrigated. Principal crops are hard and soft wheat (grown throughout the Tell), oats, and barley; wine along the coast, in interior basins (Tlemcen, Sidi-bel-Abbès, Mascara), and on N mtn. slopes; citrus fruit, cotton, and truck produce in irrigated valleys; olive groves, especially on N slope of Tlemcen Mts. In the High Plateaus sheep and goats are raised and esparto grass grown. The Atlas ranges S of the coastal area are densely forested (oak, Aleppo pine). Only important mineral deposit is iron, mined near Béni-Saf. From the E-W trunk railroad linking Fr. Morocco with Tunisia, spurs extend S from Nemours (across E Fr. Morocco) and from Perrégaux, meeting at Colomb-Béchar (Aïn-Sefra Territory). The Tell has a dense net of good roads. Agr. processing is carried on in chief seaports (Oran, Mostaganem) and in towns of the interior (Sidi-bel-Abbès, Mascara, Relizane). Tlemcen is a picturesque center of native handicraft industries. Dept. has 40% of Algeria's non-Moslem pop. Dept. was created 1848, when Fr. occupation of Algeria was completed.

Oran, city (pop. 244,594), ⊙ Oran dept., NW Algeria, on Oran Bay (semicircular inlet of the Mediterranean) and 220 mi. WSW of Algiers; 35°42′N 0°39′W. Second largest city and seaport of Algeria and, with adjacent MERS-EL-KEBIR, Algeria's chief naval station. Principal commercial center of the W TELL, linked by rail with Algiers (ENE), Fr. Morocco (SW), the immediate hinterland (Sidi-bel-Abbès, Mascara, Aïn-Témouchent), and the High Plateaus of the interior (Colomb-Béchar). Airport at La Sénia, just S. Leading exports are wine, alcohol, wheat, and early vegetables (all grown in the Tell); sheep, wool, and esparto grass from the semi-arid and arid High Plateaus. Industries, of secondary importance, include foundries and metalworks (based on scrap and imported pig iron and steel), glass mill, cigarette factory, chemical works (fertilizer), and processing plants (flour milling, fruit preserving, fish salting and canning, distilling, olive-oil pressing). Footwear, woolens, wine barrels, brooms, and brushes are also made. The harbor (protected by breakwater 1½ mi. long) extends E along entire waterfront from foot of hill (topped by Santa Cruz fort, Oran's landmark). The old town, bet. hill and the Château-Neuf (former residence of Spanish governors and of beys of Oran), centers on Kléber Square. Here is the 18th-cent. chief mosque and the casbah (rebuilt by Spaniards in 16th–17th cent.) Elsewhere, the sprawling city is reminiscent of French towns in layout and appearance, and reflects the numerical predominance of the European (Franco-Spanish) element. Suburbs (Eckmühl, Saint-Eugène, Gambetta, Montplaisant) have grown S and E along trunk railroads. Oran was founded in 10th cent. by Andalusian sailors. It was held by Spaniards (1509–1708), by Turks (1708–32), and again by Spaniards until after the disastrous earthquake of 1791. Occupied by French in 1831. City's rapid growth, coinciding with port development, dates from last decades of 19th cent. During naval engagement of Oran Bay (July 3, 1940), which actually took place at Mers-el-Kebir, most of Fr. fleet anchored there was destroyed by Br. warships. In Nov., 1942, Oran was one of the main landing areas of the Allied invasion forces.

Orán (ōrän′), town (1947 pop. 6,834), ⊙ Orán dept. (□ 10,660; 1947 pop. 60,715), N Salta prov., Argentina, 95 mi. NE of Jujuy; railhead; farming, lumbering, and mining center. Oil wells, sawmills, woodworking plants, grain mills. Citrus fruit, watermelons, papayas. Gold, silver, copper, bismuth, kaolin, and nickel deposits.

Oran (ōrăn′), city (pop. 1,156), Scott co., SE Mo., in Mississippi flood plain, 16 mi. SW of Cape Girardeau. Platted 1869.

Orange, municipality (pop. 13,780), E central New South Wales, Australia, 130 mi. WNW of Sydney; rail junction; gold-mining center; woolen and knitting mills; marble quarries.

Orange (ôräzh′), anc. *Arausio*, town (pop. 8,145), Vaucluse dept., SE France, near the Aygues and the Rhone, 13 mi. N of Avignon; agr. processing center with flour and sugar mills, alcohol distilleries, broom factories, fruit canneries. Other mfg.: woolens, jewelry, footwear, honey. Important trade in wines, early fruits, broomcorn, truffles. Rich in Roman remains, it has a triumphal arch (1st cent. A.D.), theater (A.D. c.120), and gymnasium. Atop isolated hill of Saint-Eutrope, just S of amphitheater, was castle (demolished 17th cent.) of princes of Orange. In 11th cent. town became ⊙ of county, later principality of Orange, which passed (1544) to William the Silent of the house of Nassau, among whose descendants is the ruling family of the Netherlands. Orange was conquered (1672) by Louis XIV. Confirmed in Fr. possession by treaties of Ryswick (1697) and Utrecht (1713), though title remained with Dutch princes of Orange.

Orange (ŏ′rĭnj). **1** County (□ 782; pop. 216,224), S Calif.; ⊙ Santa Ana. Coastal plain and foothill region, drained by Santa Ana R.; rises to Santa Ana Mts. (over 5,000 ft.) along E border. Includes part of Cleveland Natl. Forest. A leading Calif. citrus-fruit co.; also avocados, truck, lima beans, alfalfa, sugar beets, dairy products, poultry. Extensive petroleum and natural-gas fields in N and offshore. Coast has resorts (Newport Beach, Balboa, Laguna Beach), state parks, lagoons and marshes (waterfowl hunting). Large packing, canning, and processing industries; oil refining. Clay, sand quarrying. Formed 1889. **2** County (□ 916; pop. 114,950), central Fla., bounded E by St. Johns R.; ⊙ Orlando. Hilly lake region in W includes part of L. Apopka; lowland in E. A major citrus-fruitgrowing area; also truck farming, dairying, poultry raising. Mfg. of food products, naval stores; lumber milling. Peat beds and sand pits. Formed 1824. **3** County (□ 405; pop. 16,879), S Ind.; ⊙ Paoli. Drained by Lick, Lost, and Patoka rivers. Mainly agr. (grain, fruit, livestock, poultry; dairy products); stone quarrying, bituminous-coal mining. Mineral springs (notably FRENCH LICK) are resorts. Mfg. at Paoli. Formed 1815. **4** County (□ 829; pop. 152,255), SE N.Y.; ⊙ Goshen. Bounded E by the Hudson, SW by N.J. and Pa. lines and Delaware R.; includes parts of the Hudson highlands, the Ramapos, and the Shawangunk range. Drained by small Wallkill and Ramapo rivers and by Shawangunk Kill. An important dairying region; farming (truck, fruit, hay, poultry). Many mtn. and lake resorts. Includes West Point military reservation and part of Palisades Interstate Park. Mfg. at Newburgh, Middletown. Formed 1683. **5** County (□ 398; pop. 34,435), N central N.C.; ⊙ Hillsboro. Piedmont area; agr. (tobacco, corn, dairy products, poultry), timber (pine, oak); mfg. of textiles, furniture; sawmilling. Formed 1753. **6** County (□ 356; pop. 40,567), SE Texas; ⊙ Orange, deepwater port, industrial center. Bounded E by Sabine R. (here the La. line), W and SW by Neches R., S by Sabine L. Gulf coastal plains in S; wooded (chiefly pine; lumbering) in N. Agr. (rice, wheat, potatoes, fruit, truck, pecans); livestock (cattle, poultry, hogs); dairying. Hunting, fishing, fur trapping. Oil, natural-gas wells. Formed 1852. **7** County (□ 690; pop. 17,027), central and E Vt., bounded E by the Connecticut; ⊙ Chelsea. Dairying, lumbering; mfg. (machinery, wood products, paper, printing); maple sugar. Drained by White, Waits, and Ompompanoosuc rivers. Organized 1781. **8** County (□ 354; pop. 12,755), N central Va.; ⊙ Orange. In the piedmont; bounded N by Rapidan R., S by North Anna R. Agr. (grain, fruit, legumes, sweet potatoes, tobacco, truck), livestock, dairying, poultry; oak timber. Has many fine estates, including "Montpelier," near Orange. Formed 1734.

Orange. 1 City (pop. 10,027), Orange co., S Calif., just N of Santa Ana, in orange-growing area; citrus-fruit packing and processing plants; mfg. of wire, rope, concrete products. Founded 1868, inc. 1888. **2** Town (pop. 3,032), New Haven co., SW Conn., on the Housatonic and 5 mi. W of New Haven; printing, mfg. (burial vaults, tools, machinery); farming, dairy products. Set off from Milford 1822. **3** Town (pop. 5,894), including Orange village (pop. 4,048), Franklin co., N Mass., on Millers R. and 15 mi. E of Greenfield; precision tools, shoes, clothing, castings; truck. Settled c.1746, inc. 1810. **4** Town (pop. 82), Grafton co., W central N.H., 15 mi. SW of Plymouth; chalk, ochre deposits. Includes solitary Mt. Cardigan (3,121 ft.) in Cardigan State Forest; skiing. **5** Industrial city (pop. 38,037), Essex co., NE N.J., 4 mi. NW of Newark; mfg. (clothing, chemicals, metal products, machinery, auto accessories, brushes, textiles, cement and concrete products, malted beverages). Orange and surrounding municipalities of East Orange, West Orange, South Orange, and Maplewood are known as a suburban community called "The Oranges." Settled c.1675, set off from Newark 1806, city inc. 1872. **6** Village (pop. 897), Cuyahoga co., N Ohio, a SE suburb of Cleveland. **7** City (pop. 21,174), ⊙ Orange co., SE Texas, 22 mi. E of Beaumont, at head of deep-water Sabine R. channel (an arm of Sabine-Neches Waterway) to Gulf of Mexico; ships oil, lumber, paper, cotton, rice, fruit; port of entry. Shipyards (boomed pop. to c.17,000 in Second World War); railroad shops; paper, lumber, rice mills; oil refining, mfg. (nylon, salt and other chemicals, steel products, wood and creosoted wood products, food products, beverages). Founded 1836, inc. 1858. **8** Town (pop. 410), Orange co., E central Vt., 5 mi. SE of Barre, in agr. region. **9** Town (pop. 2,571), ⊙ Orange co., N central Va., 25 mi. NE of Charlottesville; rail junction; trade center for agr. area; textile and lumber milling, mfg. of metal cabinets, clothing, wood products. "Montpelier," the home (built c.1760) of James Madison, is 4 mi. W; Madison and his wife are buried near by. Settled c.1810; inc. 1856.

Orange, Cape, northernmost point of Amapá territory, N Brazil, on the Atlantic at mouth of Oiapoque R. (Fr. Guiana border); 4°20′N 51°30′W. Lighthouse.

Orange, Cape, headland at N tip of main isl. of Tierra del Fuego, Chile, on Strait of Magellan 3 mi. SE of Point Anegada; 52°28′S 69°23′W.

Orange Bay, small inlet of Nassau Gulf, in SE coast of Hardy Peninsula (Hoste Isl.), Tierra del Fuego, Chile, 45 mi. NW of Cape Horn; 55°30′S 68°2′W; excellent harbor.

Orangeburg, county (□ 1,120; pop. 68,726), S central S.C.; ⊙ Orangeburg. Bounded SW by South Fork of Edisto R., E by Marion; drained by North Fork of the Edisto. One of leading agr. counties in the South (cotton, corn, sweet potatoes, truck), hogs, cattle. Mfg. at Orangeburg. Formed 1785.

Orangeburg. 1 Village (1940 pop. 582), Rockland co., SE N.Y., 3 mi. SSW of Nyack; mfg. (pharmaceuticals, metal and paper products, fiber conduits). U.S. Camp Shanks here was converted after Second World War into Shanks Village for temporary veterans' housing. **2** City (pop. 15,322), ⊙ Orangeburg co., central S.C., on North Fork of Edisto R. and 37 mi. SSE of Columbia, in cotton area; lumber, cotton milling, printing, grain processing, meat packing, canning; foundry and machine-shop products, chemicals. Seat of Claflin Col. (Negro) and S.C. State Agr. and Mechanical Col. (Negro). Settled c.1735, inc. as city 1884. Edisto Gardens and U.S. fish hatchery near by.

Orange City. 1 Town (pop. 797), Volusia co., NE Fla., 24 mi. SW of Daytona Beach; known for its pure water, bottled here and shipped all over Fla. Near by are hot springs. **2** Town (pop. 2,166), ⊙ Sioux co., NW Iowa, 37 mi. NNE of Sioux City; mfg. (oil furnaces, heaters). Sand and gravel pits near by. Northwestern Jr. Col. is here. Holds annual Tulip Day. Founded 1869 by Dutch settlers; inc. 1884.

Orange Cove, city (pop. 2,395), Fresno co., central Calif., 27 mi. ESE of Fresno, in sheltered valley of Sierra Nevada foothills; citrus fruit, avocados, olives, grapes. Inc. 1948.

Orange Free State, Afrikaans *Oranje Vrystaat* (ôrä′-nyŭ frä′stät), province (□ 49,647; pop. 879,071), E central U of So. Afr., bounded by Cape Prov. (SW and W), Vaal R. and Transvaal (N), Natal (E), and Basutoland (SE); Orange R. forms S border; ⊙ Bloemfontein. Surface consists of high plateau (c.4–5,000 ft.) and is drained by tributaries of Orange and Vaal rivers, including Modder, Riet, Wilge, and Caledon rivers. Corn and wheat are major crops; cattle, sheep (wool), horse raising; fruit, vegetable, tobacco growing; dairying, malting. Diamond mining (W); some coal is mined near Vaal R. Major gold field in Odendaalsrust region came into operation 1946. There are some small mfg. industries. Main towns are Kroonstad, Bethlehem, Harrismith, Ficksburg, Heilbron, Ladybrand, Parys, Senekal, and Vrede. Settlement by Europeans, mainly Boers from Cape Prov., began c.1824; more settlers arrived during Great Trek period (1836–38) and drove out the Matabele. Though part of territory was claimed by British, 1842, its status remained undetermined. Following hostilities (1845) bet. Boers and Griquas a British resident was appointed 1846. Orange River Sovereignty under British rule was proclaimed 1848 by Sir Harry Smith, governor of Cape Colony; this was opposed by Andries Pretorius, who was defeated (Aug. 29, 1848) by Smith at Boomplaats and subsequently led Boer exodus across Vaal R. Orange Free State Republic established 1854. Subsequent to treaty of alliance (1897) with Transvaal, Orange Free State entered South African War (1899–1902) on Boer side. Britain annexed the territory, which became Orange River Colony; it acquired self-govt. in 1907 and became a prov. of U. of So. Afr. 1910, resuming name of Orange Free State.

Orange Grove, city (pop. 935), Jim Wells co., S Texas, 35 mi. WNW of Corpus Christi, near Nueces R.; trade, shipping point in area producing oil, natural gas, dairy products, truck, cotton.

Orange Lake (c.16 mi. long), Alachua co., N Florida, 10 mi. SE of Gainesville; drains into Oklawaha R. (E) via Orange Creek (c.6 mi. long).

Orange Mountains, N.J.: see WATCHUNG MOUNTAINS.

Orange Park, town (pop. 1,502), Clay co., NE Fla., on St. Johns R. and 12 mi. SSW of Jacksonville.

Orange Range, Du. *Oranje*, central New Guinea, forms E section of Snow Mts., extends c.200 mi. E from Nassau Range to border of Australian territories. Rises to c.15,585 ft. in Mt. Wilhelmina.

Orange River, Afrikaans *Oranjerivier* (ôrä″nyŭrĭ-fēr′), Basutoland, U. of So. Afr., and South-West Africa, rises in Drakensberg Range on Mont-aux-Sources in NE Basutoland, flows SW across Basutoland, thence W and NW, forming border bet. Orange Free State and Cape Prov., to mouth of Vaal R., then SW to Prieska, where it turns NW, flows to Upington, and finally, in winding course generally W, forms border bet. South-West Africa and Cape Prov. and reaches the Atlantic at Alexander Bay at 28°38′S 16°29′E; 1,300 mi. long. Near mouth are extensive diamond deposits; here river navigation is blocked by sand bar and many shoals. On lower course are several high falls, notably AUGHRABIES FALLS. Receives Caledon, Vaal, Molopo, and many smaller streams.

Orange River Colony, U. of So. Afr.: see ORANGE FREE STATE.

Orange Town, Du. West Indies: see ORANJESTAD.

Orangeville, town (pop. 2,718), ⊙ Dufferin co., S Ont., on Credit R. and 40 mi. WNW of Toronto; knitting mills; flour milling, dairying.

Orangeville. 1 Village (pop. 460), Stephenson co., N Ill., near Wis. line, 11 mi. N of Freeport, in agr. area. **2** Village (pop. 367), Trumbull co., NE Ohio, 17 mi. NNE of Youngstown, and on Pymatuning Creek, at Pa. line. **3** Borough (pop. 424), Columbia co., E central Pa., 6 mi. NNE of Bloomsburg. **4** City (pop. 589), Emery co., central Utah, 2 mi. NW of Castle Dale; alt. 5,772 ft.; agr.

Orange Walk, district, Br. Honduras: see NORTHERN DISTRICT.

Orange Walk, town (pop. 1,395), Northern Dist., Br. Honduras, on New R. and 50 mi. NNW of Belize. Lumbering (mahogany); rubber (sapodilla gum); sugar and rum mfg. Raided (1872) by Indians. Declined with fall in demand for mahogany.

Orango, Port. Guinea: see BIJAGÓS ISLANDS.

Orani (ōrä′nē), town (1939 pop. 7,628; 1948 municipality pop. 12,718), Bataan prov., S Luzon, Philippines, on Manila Bay, at base of Bataan Peninsula, 33 mi. WNW of Manila, sheltered by small Tubutubu Isl.

Orani (ôrä′nē), village (pop. 3,083), Nuoro prov., central Sardinia, 9 mi. SW of Nuoro; sulphur springs. Talc and steatite mines near by.

Oranienbaum (ōrä′nyŭnboum), town (pop. 5,484), in former Anhalt state, central Germany, after 1945 in Saxony-Anhalt, 9 mi. ESE of Dessau; tobacco processing, distilling, glass and brush mfg. Has 17th-cent. palace.

Oranienbaum, Russian SFSR: see LOMONOSOV.

Oranienburg (–bŏŏrk), town (1939 pop. 29,232; 1946 pop. 18,633), Brandenburg, E Germany, on Havel R., at junction of Hohenzollern Canal, and 18 mi. NNW of Berlin, in fruitgrowing region; mfg. of chemicals, pharmaceuticals, gas mantles, food products; metal- and woodworking. Airfield (SW). Has 17th-cent. palace. Founded c.1200 by Ascanians. Site (1933–45) of notorious concentration camp. Bombed in Second World War (c.30% destroyed).

Oranje Mountains (ôrän′yŭ), S Du. Guiana, NE spur of the Guiana Highlands; extend c.60 mi. NW from Tumuc-Humac Mts. (Brazil line); rise to 2,430 ft.

Oranje Range, New Guinea: see ORANGE RANGE.

Oranjerivier, U. of So. Afr.: see ORANGE RIVER.

Oranjestad (ôrä′nyŭstät″). **1** Town, chief town of ARUBA, Du. West Indies, port on isl.'s W coast, 80 mi. WNW of Willemstad, Curaçao; 12°32′N 70°3′W. Only 20 mi. N of Venezuela coast, it is an important petroleum-transshipping and -refining point, at which most of the isl.'s pop. is concentrated. The oil refineries are in NW outskirts. **2** or **Orange Town**, principal settlement of SAINT EUSTATIUS, Du. West Indies, in the Leewards, 8 mi. NW of St. Kitts, c.530 mi. NE of Willemstad, Curaçao; 17°29′N 62°58′W. Yams, cotton, corn, livestock raised in vicinity. Has 2 old forts.

Oranje Vrystaat, U. of So. Afr.: see ORANGE FREE STATE.

Oranmore (ôrŭnmôr′), Gaelic *Uarán Mór*, town (pop. 140), S central Co. Galway, Ireland, at head of Galway Bay, 6 mi. E of Galway; fishing port.

Oran Sebkha (ōrän′ sĕbkä′), salt flat in Oran dept., NW Algeria, just S of Oran city; 25 mi. long, 5 mi. wide. Filled with shallow lake after rainfall.

Orany, Lithuania: see VARENA.
Oranzherei (ŭrănzhĭryä'), town (1939 pop. over 500), E Astrakhan oblast, Russian SFSR, in Volga R. delta area, 40 mi. SSW of Astrakhan; fish-processing center; metalworking.
Oras (ōräs'), town (1939 pop. 5,557; 1948 municipality pop. 19,300), E Samar isl., Philippines, on small inlet of Philippine Sea, 45 mi. NE of Catbalogan; agr. center (rice, corn, coconuts).
Orasac or **Orashats** (both: ôrä'shäts), Serbo-Croatian *Orašac*, hamlet, central Serbia, Yugoslavia, 33 mi. S of Belgrade, in the Sumadija; brown-coal mine.
Orasheny (ŭrŭshĕ'nē), Rum. *Oraşeni* (ôräshĕn'), village (1941 pop. 2,614), W Chernovtsy oblast, Ukrainian SSR, in N Bukovina, on Prut R. and 15 mi. WNW of Chernovtsy; rail junction; sawmilling. Pol.–Rum. frontier station (1921–39).
Orasje or **Orashye** (both: ôräsh'yĕ), Serbo-Croatian *Orašje*, village, NW Macedonia, Yugoslavia, in outlier of Sar Mts., on left bank of Vardar R. and 13 mi. WNW of Skoplje; rail terminus for Radusa chromium mine, 2 mi. SE (across the Vardar).
Orastie (ôrŭshtē'ĕ), Rum. *Orăştie*, Ger. *Broos* (brōs), Hung. *Szászváros* (säs'värōsh), town (1948 pop. 8,817), Hunedoara prov., W central Rumania, in Transylvania, near Mures R., on railroad and 13 mi. E of Deva; mfg. of soap, candles, footwear for alpinists, alcohol, tiles, bricks, printed matter; flour milling, woodworking, fur and medicinal herb processing. Trade in livestock, grain, charcoal, fruit, wine. Has large cemetery of First World War. Founded by Ger. colonists (13th cent.). Early printing works established here (1582) published first church books in Rumanian.
Orasul Stalin, Rumania: see STALIN.
Oratorio or **El Oratorio** (ĕl ōrätōr'yō), town (1950 pop. 1,175), Santa Rosa dept., S Guatemala, in Pacific piedmont, near Inter-American Highway, 8 mi. ESE of Cuilapa; coffee, sugar cane, livestock.
Oratov (ŭrä'tŭp), town (1926 pop. 2,764), E Vinnitsa oblast, Ukrainian SSR, 45 mi. E of Vinnitsa; metalworks.
Orava, castle, Czechoslovakia: see ORAVSKY PODZAMOK.
Oravais (ô'rävīs), Finnish *Oravainen* (ō'rävī"nĕn), village (commune pop. 3,762), Vaasa co., W Finland, on inlet of Gulf of Bothnia, 30 mi. NE of Vaasa; woolen mills.
Orava River (ô'rävä), Hung. *Árva* (är'vŏ), Pol. *Orawa* (ôrä'vä), N Slovakia, Czechoslovakia, formed by junction of its headstreams (Biela Orava and Cierna Orava rivers) on S slope of the Beskids, 2 mi. NW of Trstena; flows c.70 mi. SW, past Oravsky Podzamok, to Vah R. at Kralovany. Major reservoir at conflux of its 2 headstreams. Part of territory N and NE of Trstena was appropriated by Poland (1938) after Munich Pact and returned by Germany to Slovakia after partition (1939) of Pol. state.
Oravita (ô'rävētsä), Rum. *Oraviţa*, Hung. *Oravicabánya* (ŏ'rŏvētsŏbä"nyŏ), Ger. *Orawitza* (ô'rävētsä), town (1948 pop. 6,974), Severin prov., SW Rumania, in Banat, 215 mi. WNW of Bucharest, 60 mi. ENE of Belgrade; rail junction; iron mining, iron working, flour milling, mfg. of gloves. Formerly had a large Ger. pop. Known as mining center since Roman times (notably for gold, silver, and iron). Sometimes spelled Oravitsa.
Oravsky Podzamok (ô'räfskē pôd'zämôk), Slovak *Oravský Podzámok*, Hung. *Árvaváralja* (är'vŏvä"rŏlyŏ), village (pop. 433), N Slovakia, Czechoslovakia, on right bank of Orava R., on railroad, and 28 mi. ENE of Zilina; tourist center at foot of Orava castle. The castle, built on 360-ft. high cliff in 13th cent. and enlarged in 15th and 16th cent., dominates the river; has extensive natural-science collections, Gothic chapel.
Orawa River, Czechoslovakia: see ORAVA RIVER.
Orawia (ōrä'wēŭ), village (pop. 218), S S.Isl., New Zealand, 35 mi. NW of Invercargill; agr. rail terminus.
Orawitza, Rumania: see ORAVITA.
Orb, river, France: see ORB RIVER.
Orb, Bad, Germany: see BAD ORB.
Orbassano (ôrbäs-sä'nô), village (pop. 2,774), Torino prov., Piedmont, NW Italy, 8 mi. SW of Turin; textiles.
Orbe (ôrb), town (pop. 3,558), Vaud canton, W Switzerland, on Orbe R. and 15 mi. NNW of Lausanne; flour, beer, chocolate. Known in Roman times (*Urba*), some anc. architecture still stands 1 mi. N.
Orbec (ôrbĕk'), town (pop. 2,328), Calvados dept., NW France, 12 mi. SE of Lisieux; cider distilling, metalworking, dairying, ribbon mfg. Has 15th- and 16th-cent. houses.
Orbe River (ôrb), W Switzerland, rises in small lake in the Jura, just inside Fr. line; flows NE into Vaud canton, entering Lac de Joux (S) and leaving Lac Brenet (N), thence to L. of Neuchâtel at Yverdon (here called Thièle R.). La Dernier hydroelectric plant, N of Lac Brenet, is on it. Length, 35 mi.
Orbetello (ôrbĕt-tĕl'lô), town (pop. 5,528), Grosseto prov., Tuscany, central Italy, on spit in lagoon of Orbetello (□ 10; 5 mi. long, 3 mi. wide) formed by 2 tombolos connecting Monte ARGENTARIO with mainland. Bathing resort; fishing center; canned foods, macaroni, explosives, agr. machinery. Has school of aerial navigation. From its seaplane base Italo Balbo led mass transatlantic flights to Rio de Janeiro (1931) and Chicago (1933). Badly damaged by air bombing (1944) in Second World War.
Orbey (ôrbā'), Ger. *Urbeis* (ōōrbīs'), town (pop. 1,846), Haut-Rhin dept., E France, resort in the Vosges, 10 mi. WNW of Colmar; alt. 1,620 ft. Cotton milling, dairying. Damaged in First World War. Scenic lakes Blanc (□ ¾; alt. 3,458 ft.) and Noir (□ ½; alt. 3,117 ft.; hydroelectric station) are 3 mi. W, near crest of the Vosges.
Órbigo River (ôr'vēgō), Leon and Zamora provs., NW Spain, rises on S slopes of the Cantabrian Mts. 8 mi. SE of Villablino, flows 67 mi. SSE, past La Bañeza, to the Esla near Benavente.
Orbisonia, borough (pop. 648), Huntingdon co., S central Pa., 10 mi. S of Mount Union; railroad shops; bituminous coal.
Orbliston, agr. village, NE Moray, Scotland, 6 mi. ESE of Elgin.
Orbó (ôrvō'), mining village (pop. 939), Palencia prov., N central Spain, on S slopes of the Cantabrian Mts., 44 mi. SW of Santander. Anthracite and bituminous-coal mines.
Orbost (ôr'bŏst), town (pop. 1,726), Victoria, Australia, 190 mi. E of Melbourne, near SE coast; rail terminus in agr. region (corn, potatoes).
Orb River (ôrb), Hérault dept., S France, rises in the Cévennes near Le Caylar, flows 71 mi. S, past Bédarieux, to the Gulf of Lion 9 mi. below Béziers.
Orbyhus (ûr"bühüs'), Swedish *Örbyhus*, village (pop. 1,141), Uppsala co., E Sweden, on Fyris R. and 25 mi. N of Uppsala; rail junction; wood- and metalworking, ski mfg. Has medieval castle, rebuilt in 17th cent.
Orcadas del Sur, Islas, Antarctic region: see SOUTH ORKNEY ISLANDS.
Orcades, Scotland: see ORKNEY.
Orcas Island, Wash.: see SAN JUAN ISLANDS.
Orce (ôr'thā), town (pop. 2,535), Granada prov., S Spain, 23 mi. NE of Baza; ships hemp, esparto. Stock raising, lumbering; wine, cereals, sugar beets.
Orcera (ôr-thā'rä), town (pop. 3,144), Jaén prov., S Spain, in mountainous region, near Guadalimar R., 27 mi. NE of Villacarrillo; olive-oil processing, flour- and sawmilling, soap mfg. Truck produce; lumber. Gypsum quarries.
Orchanie, Bulgaria: see BOTEVGRAD.
Orchard. 1 Town (pop. 114), Mitchell co., N Iowa, near Cedar R., 4 mi. SSE of Osage. Limestone quarries, sand and gravel pits in vicinity. **2** Village (pop. 458), Antelope co., NE Nebr., 17 mi. NW of Neligh; dairy center; grain, livestock.
Orchard Beach, village (pop. 1,203), Anne Arundel co., central Md., 10 mi. SE of downtown Baltimore, near Chesapeake Bay.
Orchard Beach, N.Y.: see PELHAM BAY PARK.
Orchard City, town (pop. 956), Delta co., W Colo., on branch of Gunnison R. and 9 mi. NE of Delta; alt. 5,300 ft. Postoffice name is Eckert.
Orchard Hill, town (pop. 82), Spalding co., W central Ga., 6 mi. SE of Griffin.
Orchard Lake, village (pop. 696), Oakland co., SE Mich., 4 mi. SW of Pontiac, in lake-resort and farm area. Seat of St. Mary's Col.
Orchard Park, residential village (pop. 2,054), Erie co., W N.Y., 10 mi. SE of Buffalo; summer and winter resort; mfg. (caskets; wood, metal, and clay products; cutlery, machinery); agr. (vegetables, wheat). Inc. 1921. Until 1934, called East Hamburg.
Orchards, Idaho: see LEWISTON ORCHARDS.
Orchha (ōr'chŭ), former princely state (□ 1,999; pop. 363,405) of Central India agency; ⊙ was Tikamgarh. A Rajput state, founded c.1500. Since 1948, merged with Vindhya Pradesh.
Orchha, village, W Vindhya Pradesh, India, on Betwa R. and 7 mi. SE of Jhansi; has large fortress and fine 17th-cent. palace. Until 1783, was ⊙ former princely state of Orchha.
Orchies (ôrshē'), town (pop. 4,294), Nord dept., N France, 10 mi. NE of Douai; rail junction; seed-growing and shipping center (especially sugar beets and potatoes). Mfg. (faïence tiles, chicory, cotton fabrics).
Orchila Island (ôrchē'lä), in the Caribbean, belonging to Venezuela, 105 mi. NE of Caracas; 7 mi. long, 4 mi. wide. Some goat grazing. Guano deposits. Sometimes Orchilla (ôrchē'yä).
Orchilla, Cape (ôrchē'lyä), westernmost point of HIERRO isl. and of Canary Isls., 16 mi. WSW of Valverde; 27°42'N 18°10'W. Through it was once drawn the prime meridian.
Orchomenus (ôrkŏ'mĭnŭs), anc. city of Boeotia, central Greece, 7 mi. NE of Levadia, on Cephisus R., at edge of drained L. Copais. Associated in Gr. tradition with the mythical Minyans, a prehistoric tribe, Orchomenus was an early leader in the Boeotian League, later supplanted by Thebes, which destroyed it several times in 4th cent. B.C. Here the Roman general Sulla defeated (85 B.C.) an army of Mithridates VI of Pontus. On site is modern town of Orchomenus or Orkhomenos (1951 pop. 5,442), formerly called Skripou. Mycenaean remains have been excavated here by Schliemann.
Orchy River (ôr'kē), N Argyll, Scotland, issues from Loch Tulla (2½ mi. long, 1 mi. wide), flows 16 mi. SW, past Dalmally, to head of Loch Awe.
Orciano di Pesaro (ôrchä'nô dē pä'zärô), village (pop. 1,053), Pesaro e Urbino prov., The Marches, central Italy, 8 mi. ESE of Fossombrone; agr. tools.
Orcières (ôrsyâr'), village (pop. 99), Hautes-Alpes dept., SE France, on the Drac and 15 mi. NE of Gap, in the Champsaur.
Orcival (ôrsēväl'), village (pop. 144), Puy-de-Dôme dept., central France, in Auvergne Mts., 13 mi. WSW of Clermont-Ferrand; makes religious articles. Has 12th-cent. Romanesque pilgrimage church.
Orco River (ôr'kô), in Piedmont, NW Italy, rises in glaciers of Gran Paradiso region, 7 mi. NW of Ceresole Reale; flows 50 mi. SE, past Cuorgnè, to Po R. 1 mi. W of Chivasso. Used for hydroelectric power and irrigation.
Orcotuna (ôrkōtōō'nä), town (pop. 3,400), Junín dept., central Peru, in Mantaro R. valley, on road, and 16 mi. SE of Jauja; weaving of native textiles; agr. products (wheat, grain); livestock.
Orcutt, village (pop. 1,001), Santa Barbara co., SW Calif., 6 mi. S of Santa Maria, in oil field.
Ord, village, on SW coast of Isle of Skye, Inverness, Scotland; fishing port.
Ord, city (pop. 2,239), ⊙ Valley co., central Nebr., 55 mi. NW of Grand Island and on N.Loup R.; flour; livestock, dairy and poultry produce, grain. Surveyed 1874.
Ord, Fort, Calif.: see MONTEREY, city.
Ord, Mount (7,155 ft.), central Ariz., in Mazatzal Mts., c.50 mi. NE of Phoenix.
Orda (ŭrdä'), village (1926 pop. 755), SE Molotov oblast, Russian SFSR, 16 mi. S of Kungur; wheat, flax, clover, livestock.
Ordelos, Greece-Bulgaria: see ALIBOTUSH MOUNTAINS.
Órdenes (ôr'dhĕnĕs), town (pop. 1,129), La Coruña prov., NW Spain, 20 mi. SSW of La Coruña; tanning; lumbering, stock raising; cereals, potatoes.
Orderville, town (pop. 371), Kane co., SW Utah, 18 mi. NNW of Kanab and on Virgin R.; alt. 5,250 ft.; agr. Settled 1864 as Mormon economic experiment.
Ordhilos, Greece-Bulgaria: see ALIBOTUSH MOUNTAINS.
Ording, Germany: see SANKT PETER.
Ordino (ôrdē'nō), village (pop. c.500), Andorra, on headstream of Valira R. and 3 mi. N of Andorra la Vella; forges. Grazing. Moorish ruins.
Ord of Caithness (kăthnĕs', kāth'nĕs), headland, 652 ft. high, on Moray Firth, on borders of Caithness and Sutherland, Scotland, 3 mi. NE of Helmsdale; 58°9'N 3°37'W.
Ordos Desert (ôr'dŏs), Chinese *O-erh-to-ssu* (ŭr'dŭ'sŭ), sandy plateau in Yellow R. bend, Suiyuan prov., China, bounded S by the Great Wall; slopes from 5,000 ft. (S) to 3,000 ft. near Yellow R. (N). A desolate region, it has some grasslands (E) and is coextensive with the Yeghe Jo (Ikh Chao; Chinese *I-k'o-chao*) or Ordos league of the Mongols. The salt lake YENHAI TZE yields natron.
Ord River, NE Western Australia, rises SE of Hall's Creek, flows 300 mi. N, through mountainous area, to Cambridge Gulf near Wyndham.
Ordsall, SE suburb (pop. 16,305) of Salford, SE Lancashire, England; cotton milling.
Ordu (ôrdōō'), prov. (□ 2,076; 1950 pop. 372,492), N Turkey, on Black Sea; ⊙ Ordu. Bordered S by Canik Mts.; drained by Melet R. Zinc, copper, iron deposits near coast. Filberts, hazelnuts, hemp. Well forested.
Ordu. 1 Village, Hatay. Turkey: see YAYLADAGI. **2** anc. *Cotyora*, town (1950 pop. 11,913), ⊙ Ordu prov., N Turkey, port on Black Sea near mouth of Melet R., 100 mi. W of Trebizond, 95 mi. NNE of Sivas; market for local crop of hazelnuts, corn. Founded by Greek colonists from Sinope.
Ordubad (ŭrdōōbät'), city (1926 pop. 3,739), SE Nakhichevan Autonomous SSR, Azerbaijan SSR, near Aras R., 38 mi. SE of Nakhichevan; fruit canning, silk milling. Silk-cocoon collecting station. Until c.1940, spelled Ordubat.
Orduña (ôr-dhōō'nyä), city (pop. 4,594), Vizcaya prov., N Spain, on Nervión R. and 19 mi. SSW of Bilbao, in an enclave bet. Álava and Burgos provs.; cement mfg., tanning. Cereals, beans, potatoes in area. Mineral springs near by.
Ordway. 1 Town (pop. 1,290), ⊙ Crowley co., SE central Colo., near Arkansas R., 45 mi. E of Pueblo; alt. 4,300 ft. Melon-shipping point in agr. region; alfalfa meal, dairy products, sugar beets, turkeys. Small lake near by. Inc. 1900. **2** Village and township (pop. 229), Brown co., N S.Dak., 10 mi. NNE of Aberdeen.
Ordynskoye (ŭrdĭn'skŭyŭ), village (1926 pop. 3,333), SE Novosibirsk oblast, Russian SFSR, on Ob R. and 55 mi. SW of Novosibirsk; metalworks.
Ordzhonikidze, territory, Russian SFSR: see STAVROPOL, territory.
Ordzhonikidze (ŭrjŭnyĭkē'dzĭ), district of Greater Baku, Azerbaijan SSR, on central Apsheron Peninsula, ENE of Baku; oil fields. Main centers: Surakhany, Amiradzhany, Byul-Byuly.
Ordzhonikidze. 1 Town (1939 pop. over 500), S Azerbaijan SSR, on railroad (Dashburun station)

Area in square miles is indicated by the symbol □, capital city or county seat by the symbol ⊙.

and 50 mi. SW of Sabirabad; cotton-ginning center; shipping point for Zhdanovsk cotton dist. **2** Agr. town (1939 pop. over 500), N Azerbaijan SSR, 22 mi. NE of Yevlakh; livestock grazing. **3** Town (1932 pop. estimate 590), W central Georgian SSR, on railroad and 30 mi. SE of Kutaisi; distilling; corn, vineyards. Marble deposits near by. Until 1949, Kharagouli. **4** Town (1939 pop. over 500), SW Crimea, Russian SFSR, on Black Sea coast, 8 mi. SW of Feodosiya; produces trass (hydraulic cement rock) for Novorossisk mills. **5** City, North Ossetian Autonomous SSR, Russian SFSR: see DZAUDZHIKAU. **6** Town (1939 pop. over 500), S Dnepropetrovsk oblast, Ukrainian SSR, on road and 17 mi. WNW of Nikopol; manganese. Until 1939, called Aleksandrovka. **7** Town, Stalino oblast, Ukrainian SSR: see YENAKIYEVO. **8** Town (1926 pop. 2,505), N Tashkent oblast, Uzbek SSR, just NE of Tashkent, in orchard area; metalworks. Until c.1935, Lunacharskoye.

Ordzhonikidzeabad (–kē"dzĭŭbät'), town (1948 pop. over 2,000), N Stalinabad oblast, Tadzhik SSR, on Kafirnigan R. and 12 mi. E of Stalinabad (linked by railroad) cotton, sericulture; flour milling, metalworking. Until 1937, Yangi-Bazar.

Ordzhonikidzegrad, Russian SFSR: see BEZHITSA.

Ordzhonikidzevskaya (–kē'dzyĭfskŭ), village (1926 pop. 7,598), SW Grozny oblast, Russian SFSR, on railroad, on left bank of Sunzha R. and 32 mi. W of Grozny; junction of lumber railroad to Pervomaiskoye (S); wheat, corn, fruit, vegetables. Until 1939, Sleptsovskaya.

Ordzhonikidzevski or **Ordzhonikidzevskiy** (–skē). **1** Town (1948 pop. over 2,000), NW Khakass Autonomous oblast, Krasnoyarsk Territory, Russian SFSR, 110 mi. NW of Abakan; gold mines. **2** Town (1939 pop. over 500), SW Stavropol Territory, Russian SFSR, in the W Greater Caucasus, on Kuban R. and 33 mi. SSW of Cherkessk. Coal mining here and at Khumarinski (just N).

Orea (ōrā'ä), town (pop. 801), Guadalajara prov., central Spain, near Teruel prov. border, 21 mi. SE of Molina; wheat, potatoes, livestock; flour milling. Copper mining.

Orealla, village, Berbice co., E Br. Guiana, on Courantyne R. (Du. Guiana border) and 65 mi. SSE of New Amsterdam, at head of navigation for large vessels. Bauxite and kaolin deposits.

Oreamuno, San Rafael de, Costa Rica: see SAN RAFAEL, Cartago prov.

Orebic (ô'rĕbĭch), Serbo-Croatian *Orebić*, Ital. *Sabbioncello* (säb-byônchĕl'lô), village, S Croatia, Yugoslavia, on Adriatic Sea, on S coast of Peljesac peninsula, 3 mi. NE of Korcula, in Dalmatia. Seaside resort; center of olive- and winegrowing region. Sometimes spelled Orebich.

Orebro (û"rübrōō'), Swedish *Örebro*, county [Swedish *län*] (□ 3,559; 1950 pop. 247,990), S central Sweden; ⊙ Orebro. Includes Narke, SE Varmland, and E Vastmanland provs. Low and level with fertile soil (S), becomes undulating highland in N. Drained by Arboga, Let, Svart, and Hork rivers, region is dotted with numerous small lakes. There are important iron, zinc, and copper mines, and timber stands. Leading industries are steel, paper, pulp, and lumber milling, metal smelting, shoe mfg. Cities are Orebro, Karlskoga, Kumla, Lindesberg, and Nora.

Orebro, Swedish *Örebro*, city (1950 pop. 66,548), ⊙ Orebro co., S central Sweden, at W end of L. Hjalmar, at mouth of Svart R., 100 mi. W of Stockholm; 59°17'N 15°13'E. Rail junction; Sweden's chief shoe-mfg. center, with paper mills, soap-mfg. and woodworking plants. Has 14th-cent. castle (now mus.), on isl. in river; 13th-cent. church; and several other old bldgs. Known since 11th cent., it is one of Sweden's oldest cities, and scene of several parliaments; in 1810 Bernadotte was here elected king of Sweden.

Ore City, village (pop. c.500), Upshur co., NE Texas, 27 mi. NW of Marshall; farm market.

Oredezh (ŭrўĭdyĕsh'), village (1948 pop. over 2,000), S Leningrad oblast, Russian SFSR, 19 mi. ENE of Luga and on Oredezh R. (left tributary of Luga R.; 100 mi. long).

Oregon (ŏ'rĭgŭn, –gŏn, ŏ'rĭ–), state (land □ 96,350; with inland waters □ 96,981; 1950 pop. 1,521,341; 1940 pop. 1,089,684), NW U.S., in the Pacific Northwest; bordered by Pacific Ocean (W), Wash. (N), Idaho (E), and Nev. and Calif. (S); 9th in area, 32d in pop.; admitted 1859 as 33d state; ⊙ Salem. Oregon averages 300 mi. E–W, 260 mi. N–S. The COLUMBIA RIVER forms most of the N boundary, while the SNAKE RIVER, flowing through a deep gorge, forms N half of E boundary. The state varies from the moist coast-mtn.-valley region in the W to the dry upland plateau in the E. Along the Pacific is a long, narrow coastal strip with a temperate marine climate, modified by warm ocean currents, and an annual rainfall of c.75 in. The only important town here is ASTORIA, at the mouth of the Columbia. Running parallel to the coast bet. the Columbia R. and Calif. line are low (2,000–3,000 ft.) rolling hills of the COAST RANGES. About 100 mi. inland is the great CASCADE RANGE, which divides the state into contrasting E and W sections. Running N–S, with an average elevation of 5,000–7,000 ft., its most prominent peaks are Mt. Hood (11,245 ft.; highest point in Oregon), Mt. Jefferson (10,495 ft.), and the Three Sisters (c.10,000 ft.). The Cascades region is one of rugged grandeur with glaciers and picturesque mtn. lakes, notably the remarkable CRATER LAKE. Bet. the Coast and Cascade ranges is the fertile trough of the WILLAMETTE RIVER valley, extending c.170 mi. S from the Columbia R. with an average width of 60 mi. Favored with a mild climate (yearly rainfall 40–50 in.), it is the leading agr., commercial, and industrial area of Oregon and is its most populous section; PORTLAND (N) is the largest city in the state. S of the Willamette valley the Coast and Cascade ranges merge in the KLAMATH MOUNTAINS, a dissected plateau, drained in Oregon by the Rogue and Umpqua rivers; on the Calif. line are the Siskiyou Mts. The major portion of E Oregon lies in the Columbia Plateau, a broad expanse underlain by horizontal lava beds and having a dry continental climate with an annual rainfall of 10–20 in. In the Columbia basin (N) are the rolling plains of the INLAND EMPIRE, drained by the Deschutes, John Day, and Umatilla rivers. The Blue Mts. and Wallowa Mts. in the NE rise to elevations of 6,000–10,000 ft. S of these mts. settlement is sparse as the land merges gradually with the almost desert-like Great Basin; low, block ridges, buttes, and playa lakes are the dominant features. Public lands comprise 53% of state's area. Agr. is the main occupation and the state has c.20,000,000 acres of farm land, ranging in size from the small truck farms W of the Cascades to the large wheat and cattle ranches in the E parts. Oregon is a major producer of prunes, pears, apples, strawberries, filberts, walnuts, wheat, hay, hops, potatoes, and barley; other crops include oats, rye, corn, flax, cherries, and cranberries. The Willamette valley, where there is a growing season of 160–200 days, is a region of intensive fruit and vegetable cultivation; there are also large orchards in the Rogue (pears), Hood (apples), Umpqua (prunes), and Tualatin (nuts) river valleys. Wheat is the great field crop of E Oregon, especially in the Columbia-Deschutes basin, where dry farming is practiced and the growing season averages 200 days. Over 1,000,000 acres of dry land have been reclaimed by irrigation, the chief projects being along the Deschutes, John Day, and Umatilla rivers, the OWYHEE RIVER, MALHEUR RIVER, and KLAMATH RIVER. Other E areas, too dry for cultivation, have been given over to cattle and sheep raising. Peas are grown and canned in the Blue Mts. dist. The moist climate on the Pacific coast is especially suitable for dairying; poultry farming is common in the Willamette valley. Oregon is the leading lumber-producing state, with c.29,755,000 acres of total forest land, including 11,000,000 acres of natl. forests. The chief species of timber (predominantly softwoods) are Douglas fir (Cascade, Klamath, and Coast ranges), spruce and hemlock (coast), ponderosa pine (E slopes of Cascades, and in Blue and Wallowa Mts.), and lesser stands of lodgepole pine, larch, alder, ash, juniper, maple, and oak. Processing of its agr. and forest resources is Oregon's principal industry, with the Willamette valley the center of industrial activity. Here—in Portland, Salem, Eugene, Oregon City, Corvallis, and other towns—are fruit and vegetable canneries, sawmills, pulp and paper mills, meat-packing plants, and furniture factories. Other mfg. towns in the state include Medford (fruit, lumber), Pendleton (food, woolen products), Klamath Falls (lumber), Nyssa (food, beet-sugar refining), and The Dalles (flour, lumber). Mfg. of lumbering equipment, agr. machinery, tin cans, and chemicals, and publishing are subsidiary industries. The fishing industry (salmon, halibut, pilchards, oysters, tuna) is centered in Astoria; there are also fisheries at The Dalles on the Columbia and at Coos Bay and other towns on the Pacific coast. Gold, copper, and silver are mined in Baker co. (NE), some manganese ore is worked in the Klamath Mts., and bauxite deposits are NW of Portland, but the state's total mineral output is relatively small. Deposits of quicksilver ore, diatomite, chromite, and limonite are known to exist. Increased hydroelectric power, mainly from BONNEVILLE DAM on the Columbia, and the needs of natl. defense led to the development of such industries as shipbuilding, electrochemical and metallurgical works, and aluminum plants during the Second World War. Among the many recreational sites in Oregon are CRATER LAKE NATIONAL PARK, OREGON CAVES NATIONAL MONUMENT, the snow-capped peaks and mtn. lakes in the Cascades, and the fine bathing beaches along the Pacific coast. Educational institutions include Oregon State Col. (at Corvallis), Univ. of Oregon (at Eugene and Portland), Univ. of Portland, and Willamette Univ. (at Salem). The coast of the Pacific Northwest was 1st visited by Sp. explorers in the 16th and 18th cent. In 1792 the American Robert Gray discovered and named the Columbia R., but for many years afterwards it was known as the Oregon R. and the surrounding region as the Oregon country. Amer. claims to the area were strengthened by the Lewis and Clark expedition (1804–6), which explored the lower reaches of the Snake and Columbia rivers, and by the establishment (1811) of a fur-trading post by John Jacob Astor on the site of present Astoria. The Oregon country was jointly occupied by the U.S. and Great Britain from 1818 to 1846, when the 49th parallel became (by treaty) the international boundary; Oregon was made a territory in 1848; the N part was organized as Wash. Territory in 1853. Oregon obtained statehood and present boundaries in 1859. As a result of the great influx of white settlers via the Oregon Trail after 1842, there were periodic clashes with the resentful Indians bet. the 1840s and '70s. With the completion of the transcontinental railroads in the late 19th cent. lumbering and agr. prospered and the state's pop. grew rapidly. See also articles on the cities, towns, geographic features, and the 36 counties: BAKER, BENTON, CLACKAMAS, CLATSOP, COLUMBIA, COOS, CROOK, CURRY, DESCHUTES, DOUGLAS, GILLIAM, GRANT, HARNEY, HOOD RIVER, JACKSON, JEFFERSON, JOSEPHINE, KLAMATH, LAKE, LANE, LINCOLN, LINN, MALHEUR, MARION, MORROW, MULTNOMAH, POLK, SHERMAN, TILLAMOOK, UMATILLA, UNION, WALLOWA, WASCO, WASHINGTON, WHEELER, YAMHILL.

Oregon, county (□ 784; pop. 11,978), S Mo.; ⊙ Alton. In the Ozarks; drained by Eleven Point R. and Spring R. Agr., notably livestock, dairying; oak, hickory, walnut timber. Part of Clark Natl. Forest is here. Formed 1845.

Oregon. 1 City (pop. 3,205), ⊙ Ogle co., N Ill., on Rock R. (bridged) and 21 mi. SW of Rockford; trade and industrial center in rich agr. area; mfg. (pianos and piano parts, coal stokers, sprinklers, tanks, silica products). Near by is Eagle's Nest Art Colony, founded 1898 by Lorado Taft and others; Taft's soldiers' monument is in the city, and his great *Black Hawk* statue is on bluff overlooking Rock R. The public library has art gall. A state park is near by. Inc. 1843. **2** City (pop. 870) ⊙ Holt co., NW Mo., near Missouri R., 22 mi. NW of St. Joseph; agr. (corn, apples, wheat), livestock. Big Lake state park near by. **3** Village (pop. 1,341), Dane co., S Wis., 10 mi. S of Madison, in dairying and farming area (poultry, hogs, tobacco); creamery. Settled 1842, inc. 1883.

Oregon Caves National Monument (480 acres; established 1909), SW Oregon, in Siskiyou Mts. near Calif. line, c.30 mi. SW of Medford. Labyrinth (on 4 levels) of subterranean chambers and corridors formed by dissolution of limestone by ground water; contain varied and beautiful stalactite and stalagmite formations. Discovered 1874.

Oregon City, city (pop. 7,682), ⊙ Clackamas co., NW Oregon, at falls (c.40 ft. high); by-passed by locks) of Willamette R., 11 mi. S of Portland. Processing center (pulp, paper, and woolen mills) in dairying and fruit area. Laid out 1842, inc. 1849. Territorial ⊙ until late in 1851. Had 1st newspaper (*Oregon Spectator*; 1846) W of the Missouri. Edwin Markham b. here (1852). McLoughlin House Natl. Historic Site (established 1941) preserves home (1846–57) of Dr. John McLoughlin, who had city platted and who, as chief factor of Hudson's Bay Company, was influential figure in early development of Pacific Northwest.

Oregon Inlet, E N.C., channel (c.1 mi. wide) through the Outer Banks, c.40 mi. N of Cape Hatteras and at N end of Pea Isl.; connects Pamlico Sound with the Atlantic.

Oregon River, NW U.S.–SW Canada: see COLUMBIA RIVER.

Oregon Trail, in W U.S., overland emigrant trail from the Missouri R. to the Columbia R. country, traveled by thousands of pioneers after the 1840s. From vicinity of Independence, Mo., it generally followed valleys of the Platte, North Platte (past Fort Laramie), and Sweetwater rivers to the Rockies, where it crossed the Continental Divide at South Pass; from Fort Bridger (Wyo.), near here, the Mormon Trail branched off to Salt Lake City and the Oregon Trail swung NW; at Soda Springs (Idaho), the California Trail parted to the SW, while main trail followed the Snake R. valley (from Fort Hall to Fort Boise, Idaho), whence it struck out over the Blue Mts. to Fort Walla Walla on the Columbia. Many of the travelers transferred here to boats going downstream. The Astoria expedition of 1811–12 followed W part of the route, but not until 1832 did "mountain men" get wagons across South Pass. The 1st emigrant wagon train reached Oregon in 1842.

Oregrund (û"rügrŭnd'), Swedish *Öregrund*, city (pop. 1,275), Stockholm co., E Sweden, on Oregrund Strait, Swedish *Öregrundsgrepen*, 20-mi.-long strait of Gulf of Bothnia, opposite Graso isl., 45 mi. NE of Uppsala; port, with shipyards; seaside resort. Chartered 1491; for some time shipping center for Uppland prov. iron mines.

Ore Hill, Conn.: see SALISBURY.

Orei, Greece: see OREOI.

Orekhi-Vydritsa, Belorussian SSR: see OREKHOVSK.

Orekhov (ŭryĕ'khŭf), city (1939 pop. over 10,000), N Zaporozh oblast, Ukrainian SSR, on Konka R. and 30 mi. SE of Zaporozh; food processing (flour, dairy products), metalworks.

Orekhovo, Bulgaria: see ORYAKHOVO.

Orekhovo (-khŭvŭ), village, W Kostroma oblast, Russian SFSR, near railroad, 17 mi. E of Bui; flax.

Orekhovo-Zuyevo (-zōō'yĭvŭ), city (1939 pop. 99,329), E Moscow oblast, Russian SFSR, on Klyazma R. and 50 mi. E of Moscow. Rail junction; major cotton-milling center; weaving and dyeing plants; plastics mfg., flour milling, sawmilling, metalworking. Has peat-fed power station. Teachers col. Formed 1917 out of neighboring towns of Orekhovo and Zuyevo.

Orekhovsk (ŭryĕ'khŭfsk), town (1946 pop. over 500), SE Vitebsk oblast, Belorussian SSR, 14 mi. NNE of Orsha; sawmilling. Large peat-fed power plant (*Belgres*) here. Until 1946, Orekhi-Vydritsa.

Orekhovski or **Orekhovskiy** (-skē), town (1939 pop. over 500), E Stalino oblast, Ukrainian SSR, in the Donbas, 4 mi. W of Snezhnoye; coal mines. Formerly called Shakhta No. 8.

Orel (ōrĕl', Rus. ŭryôl'), oblast (□ 12,200; 1946 pop. estimate 1,500,000) in SW central European Russian SFSR; ⊙ Orel. In Central Russian Upland; drained by Sosna and upper Oka rivers; black-earth, wooded steppe. Basic crops: hemp (W), potatoes (E); also wheat, coarse grain, rubber-bearing plants, sugar beets; orchard products, truck gardens important. Hogs extensively raised. Rural industries: hemp processing and milling, distilling, starch making. Metalworking, food processing (Orel, Yelets, Livny). Formed 1937 out of Kursk and Western oblasts.

Orel. 1 Town (1939 pop. over 500), N central Molotov oblast, Russian SFSR, port on left bank of Kama R., opposite Yaiva R. mouth, and 8 mi. SW of Berezniki; lumbering. Mineral springs. Founded 1564 as Rus. stronghold of Kergedan. **2** City (1939 pop. 110,567), ⊙ Orel oblast, Russian SFSR, on Oka R. and 200 mi. SSW of Moscow; 52°58'N 36°4'E. Rail, road, and industrial center; iron foundry; mfg. (tractor parts, textile machinery), flour milling, meat packing, distilling, brewing; knitting and hemp mills, shoe factory. Has triumphal arch (1786), Turgenev mus., mus. of revolution and of natural history. Teachers col. Founded 1564 as S outpost of Moscow domain. Place of exile (1860s) for Polish revolutionaries. Northernmost point reached (1919) by Denikin. Was ⊙ Orel govt. until 1928. During Second World War, held (1941–43) by Germans, and the center of heavy fighting.

Orellana (ōrĕyä'nä). **1** Village, Amazonas dept., N Peru, landing on upper Marañón R. and 90 mi. NE of Jaén (Cajamarca dept.); 4°39'S 78°4'W. **2** or **Francisco de Orellana** (fränsē'skō dā), town (pop. 853), Loreto dept., E central Peru, landing on Ucayali R. and 29 mi. NNW of Contamana; sugar cane, fruit.

Orellana la Sierra (ōrĕlyä'nä lä syĕ'rä) or **Orellanita** (ōrĕlyänē'tä), town (pop. 1,294), Badajoz prov., W Spain, 16 mi. E of Villanueva de la Sierra; cereals, olives, oranges, grapes.

Orellana la Vieja (vyā'hä), town (pop. 4,833), Badajoz prov., W Spain, 14 mi. E of Villanueva de la Serena; cereals, grapes, livestock; olive-oil pressing, flour milling; mfg. of tiles and textile goods.

Orellanita, Spain: see ORELLANA LA SIERRA.

Orelle (ôrĕl'), village (pop. 185), Savoie dept., SE France, in Alpine Maurienne valley, on the Arc and 11 mi. ESE of Saint-Jean-de-Maurienne; aluminum and explosives made at near-by Prémont.

Orel River or **Orel' River** (ŭryĕl'), E Ukrainian SSR, rises S of Kharkov in outlier of Central Russian Upland, flows 110 mi. W in S-shaped course, past Nekhvoroshcha, to Dnieper R. N of Verkhne-Dneprovsk.

Orem (ô'rŭm), town (pop. 8,351), Utah co., N central Utah, near Utah L., just N of Provo; alt. 4,760 ft.; vegetable-canning center in truck-gardening area served by irrigation works on Provo R. Inc. 1925. Large Geneva plant of U.S. Steel Corporation is 3 mi. W on Utah L.; Wasatch Range E.

Ore Mountains, Czechoslovakia and Germany: see ERZGEBIRGE.

Orenburg, Russian SFSR: see CHKALOV, city.

Orense (ōrĕn'sā), town (pop. 2,071), SE Buenos Aires prov., Argentina, 36 mi. SE of Tres Arroyos; wheat, oats, sheep, cattle; dairying. Beach resort on Atlantic coast 9 mi. S.

Orense, province (□ 2,691; pop. 458,272), NW Spain, in Galicia; ⊙ Orense. Bounded S by Portugal; crossed by Galician Mts., here reaching highest point (Cabeza de Manzaneda, 5,833 ft.). Drained by the Miño and its tributaries (e.g., the Sil), and by Limia and Támega rivers, flowing into Portugal. Tin and tungsten mines (richest in Spain), noted since anc. times, are now little exploited. Numerous mineral springs. Principally agr., with extensive forests (lumbering) and pastures (cattle and hog raising); fertile valleys, favored by sufficient rainfall, have vineyards, orchards, vegetable gardens; also cereals, potatoes, flax, honey. Industries limited to domestic type. Trade hampered by poor communications. Pop. widely scattered, with few towns: Orense, Celanova, Ribadavia.

Orense, anc. *Aureum*, city (pop. 17,866), ⊙ Orense prov., NW Spain, in Galicia, road center on Miño R., and 80 mi. SSE of La Coruña, at foot of hill, circled by vineyards, orchards, and vegetable gardens; 42°20'N 7°53'W. Brandy distilling, sawmilling, furniture mfg. Agr. trade. Episcopal see. Has 12th-cent. bridge (restored) across Miño; Gothic cathedral (13th cent.; restored in 16th–17th); and provincial mus. with prehistoric and Roman antiquities. Was occupied by Romans; ⊙ of Suevi tribes (5th–6th cent.); destroyed by Moors (8th cent.), rebuilt by Alfonso III of Asturias (9th cent.). In center of city are warm sulphur springs (*Las Burgas*), noted since Roman times.

Oreoi (ôrāē'), village (pop. 1,266), NW Euboea, Greece, port on Oreos Channel, 45 mi. NW of Chalcis; wheat, wine; fisheries. Also spelled Oreï.

Oreos Channel (ôrāôs'), arm of Aegean Sea, Greece, bet. Euboea (SE) and mainland of central Greece (NW) joins Trikeri Channel (NE) and Malian Gulf (SW); 20 mi. long, 2–4 mi. wide. Village of Oreoi on S shore.

Orepuki (ōrĕpōō'kē), township (pop. 347), S S.Isl., New Zealand, 30 mi. W of Invercargill; agr. center; oil shale, gold.

Ore River, Suffolk, England: see ALDE RIVER.

Oresh (ô'rĕsh), village (pop. 3,404), Pleven dist., N Bulgaria, on Svishtov L. and 5 mi. WSW of Svishtov; rail junction; grain, hemp, livestock.

Orestes (ôrĕ'stŭs), town (pop. 482), Madison co., E central Ind., 7 mi. E of Elwood, in agr. area.

Orestia, Turkey: see ADRIANOPLE, city.

Orestias (ôrĕstēäs'), town (pop. 12,047), Hevros nome, W Thrace, Greece, on railroad and 12 mi. S of Adrianople (Edirne), near Maritsa R. (Turkish line); trade center for fertile agr. lowland; silk, wheat, cotton, rice, sesame; dairy products. Named for Byzantine name of Adrianople; sometimes called Nea Orestias.

Orestias, Lake, Greece: see KASTORIA, LAKE.

Oresund or **The Sound**, Swedish *Öresund* (û'rŭsŭnd'), Dan. *Øresund* (ûr'ŭsōōn) or *Sundet*, strait (87 mi. long), bet. Zealand (Denmark) and Sweden, connecting the Kattegat with Baltic Sea, to which it is the deepest channel (minimum depth, 23 ft.). Average width (Copenhagen to Malmo), 17 mi.; narrowest bet. Helsingor and Halsingborg, 2½ mi. Hven, Amager, and Saltholm isls. are in it; Saltholm splits The Sound into Drogden (W) and Flinterenden (E) straits. Until 1857, ship tolls were collected at Helsingor.

Oret (ôrā'), village (pop. 578), Namur prov., S Belgium, 11 mi. SE of Charleroi; kaolin-earth quarrying.

Oretana, Cordillera, Spain: see TOLEDO, MONTES DE.

Oreti River, New Zealand: see NEW RIVER.

Oreye (ôrā'), Flemish *Oerle* (ōōr'lŭ), village (pop. 932), Liége prov., E Belgium, 12 mi. NW of Liége; beet-sugar refining.

Orezza, Corsica: see PIEDICROCE.

Orfa, Turkey: see URFA.

Orfani, Gulf of, Greece: see STRYMONIC GULF.

Orford. 1 Town, Lancashire, England: see POULTON WITH FEARNHEAD. **2** Oyster-fishing village and parish (pop. 706), E Suffolk, England, on Alde R. (which here becomes Ore R.), and 17 mi. ENE of Ipswich, separated from North Sea by narrow spit of land (Orford Beach). Has remains of Norman castle. Church dates from 14th cent. On North Sea, 2 mi. E, is promontory of Orford Ness.

Orford (ôr'fŭrd), town (pop. 726), Grafton co., W N.H., on the Connecticut (here bridged) opposite Fairlee, Vt. and 25 mi. NW of Plymouth; site of fine early houses. Mt. Cube is ESE.

Orfordville, village (pop. 543), Rock co., S Wis., 12 mi. WSW of Janesville, in tobacco, dairying, and grain area; condensed milk, butter, feed.

Organ Cave, W.Va.: see RONCEVERTE.

Organ Mountains, Brazil: see ORGÃOS, SERRA DOS.

Organ Mountains, S N.Mex., in Dona Ana co., just E of Rio Grande and Las Cruces. Prominent points: Organ Peak (8,870 ft.), Organ Needle (9,012 ft.). Just N is San Augustin Pass, separating range from San Augustin Mts.

Órganos, Sierra de los (syĕ'rä dā lōs ôr'gänōs), mountain range, Pinar del Río prov., W Cuba, extending c.60 mi. NE from Mantua to the Sierra del Rosario; rises to c.1,350 ft. Rich in copper and lumber. Sometimes considered to include the Sierra del Rosario.

Organ Pipe Cactus National Monument (□ 512.7; established 1937), SW Ariz., at Mex. line and 100 mi. SSW of Phoenix. Mtn. and desert region, with fine tracts of Organ Pipe Cactus, Sinita Cactus, and many other desert plants. Papago Indian Reservation adjoins on E.

Orgãos, Serra dos (sĕ'rŭ dōōs ôrgã'ōs) [Port.,= Organ Mountains], range in central Rio de Janeiro state, Brazil, forming part of the great coastal escarpment (Serra do Mar) overlooking Guanabara Bay, and extending E from Petrópolis to beyond Teresópolis. Highest peaks are Pedra do Sino (7,365 ft.) and Pedra Açu (7,323 ft.). One of its many serrate heights, the sheer Dedo de Deus [Port.,=finger of God] (5,561 ft.) is a landmark seen from Rio (30 mi. SSW). A leading tourist area, part of which was set aside (1939) as a natl. park (□ 9).

Orgaz or **Orgaz con Arísgotas** (ôrgäth' kōn ärēz'gōtäs), town (pop. 3,252), Toledo prov., central Spain, in New Castile, 16 mi. SSE of Toledo; agr. center in picturesque mtn. terrain; olives, grapes, cereals, goats, sheep. Wool and tanning industry; also olive-oil extracting, sawmilling; limekilns. Unexploited copper mine. Agr. station. Has noteworthy Santo Tomás church and ruins of castle.

Orgelet (ôrzhlā'), village (pop. 1,091), Jura dept., E France, in the Revermont, 11 mi. SSE of Lons-le-Saunier; wood turning, tanning, plastics mfg. Near-by Mont Orgier (2,100 ft.) is topped by giant statue of the Virgin.

Orgéo (ôrgāō'), village (pop. 1,371), Luxembourg prov., SE Belgium, in the Ardennes, 6 mi. W of Neufchâteau; potato-seed nurseries; agr. experiment station.

Orgères-en-Beauce (ôr-zhâr'-ã-bōs'), agr. village (pop. 574), Eure-et-Loir dept., N central France, in the Beauce, 19 mi. NNW of Orléans.

Orgeyev (ŭrgyā'ŭf), Rum. *Orhei* (ôrhā'), city (1930 pop. 18,034; 1941 pop. 10,504), central Moldavian SSR, on Reut R. and 25 mi. N of Kishinev, in rich agr. dist. (orchards, vineyards, tobacco plantations); home industry (sewing, shoemaking); flour milling, fruit and tobacco processing, brewing, mfg. of felt hats. Has 17th-cent. church. An anc. settlement, it flourished under Moldavian and Turkish rule (15th–18th cent.), trading with N Moldavia and Tatar lands across the Dniester. While in Rumania (1918–40; 1941–44), it was ⊙ Orhei dept. (□ 1,639; 1941 pop. 276,944).

Orgiano (ôrjä'nô), village (pop. 381), Vicenza prov., Veneto, N Italy, in Monti Berici, 14 mi. SSW of Vicenza; basalt quarries.

Órgiva, Spain: see ÓRJIVA.

Orgon (ôrgõ'), village (pop. 934), Bouches-du-Rhône dept., SE France, on left bank of the Durance and 16 mi. SE of Avignon; limekilns; carton and olive-oil mfg.

Orgosolo (ôrgô'zôlô), village (pop. 3,563), Nuoro prov., E central Sardinia, 8 mi. S of Nuoro. Nuraghe near by.

Orgtrud (ŭrgtrōōt'), town (1926 pop. 2,482), N central Vladimir oblast, Russian SFSR, on Klyazma R., at mouth of the Nerl, and 8 mi. NE of Vladimir; cotton-milling center. Called Lemeshenski (1927–c.1940).

Orgun, Afghanistan: see URGUN.

Orhaneli (ôrhän'ĕlē), village (pop. 1,439), Bursa prov., NW Turkey, 20 mi. SSW of Bursa; cereals; rich chromium deposits. Formerly Atranos.

Orhangazi (ôrhän'gäzē), village (pop. 3,214), Bursa prov., NW Turkey, near W end of L. Iznik, 25 mi. NE of Bursa; olives, potatoes, vetch, cereals. Formerly Pazarkoy.

Orhei, Moldavian SSR: see ORGEYEV.

Orhon River, Mongolia: see ORKHON RIVER.

Oria (ô'rēä), anc. *Uria*, town (pop. 10,610), Brindisi prov., Apulia, S Italy, 19 mi. SW of Brindisi; agr. center (olives, grapes, figs, vegetables). Bishopric. Has cathedral, castle (1227–33; restored), several palaces.

Oria (ō'ryä), town (pop. 1,187), Almería prov., S Spain, 18 mi. SW of Vélez Rubio; lumbering, stock raising; olive oil, cereals, esparto, fruit.

Orica (ōrē'kä), town (pop. 634), Francisco Morazán dept., central Honduras, 15 mi. NE of Cedros and on headstream of Sulaco R.; corn, wheat, coffee.

Orichi (ŭrē'chē), village, central Kirov oblast, Russian SFSR, 25 mi. WSW of Kirov; grain; dairying (butter).

Orient. 1 City (pop. 801), Franklin co., S Ill., 8 mi. NNE of Herrin, in bituminous-coal-mining and agr. area. **2** Town (pop. 427), Adair co., SW Iowa, 11 mi. N of Creston, in agr. region. **3** Agr. town (pop. 176), Aroostook co., E Maine, on Grand L. and 22 mi. S of Houlton, in recreational area. **4** Resort village (1940 pop. 572), Suffolk co., SE N.Y., NE Long Isl., overlooking Orient Harbor (inlet of Gardiners Bay), 24 mi. NE of Riverhead. To E are: Orient Point resort village, with ferry connections with New London, Conn.; Orient Point promontory at tip of N peninsula of Long Isl.; and Orient Beach State Park (342 acres). **5** Town (pop. 206), Faulk co., N central S.Dak., 10 mi. S of Faulkton. **6** Village (pop. 1,788), Wichita co., N Texas, near Iowa Park.

Orient, L', France: see LORIENT.

Oriental (ōryĕntäl'), town (pop. 2,883), Puebla, central Mexico, on central plateau, 45 mi. NE of Puebla; alt. 7,693 ft.; corn, maguey.

Oriental, fishing town (pop. 590), Pamlico co., E N.C., on Neuse R. and 20 mi. SE of New Bern.

Oriental, Cordillera (kôrdĭyā'rä ōryĕntäl') [Sp.,= eastern cordillera], name applied to several mtn. ranges in Spanish-speaking countries, notably in the Andes. In Bolivia, term refers to a branch range of the Andes, bounding the Altiplano on E; its highest section is known as Cordillera Real or Cordillera de la Paz. In Peru, it is the easternmost range bet. Nudo de VILCANOTA and Nudo de PASCO and beyond. In Ecuador, it forms the eastern of 2 ranges enclosing the central tableland. In Colombia, it is again the easternmost of the 3 main cordilleras which fan out from near Ecuador border N to the Caribbean.

Orient Beach State Park, N.Y.: see ORIENT.

Oriente (ōryĕn'tā), town (pop. 2,191), S Buenos Aires prov., Argentina, on Quequén Salado R. (hydroelectric station) and 37 mi. E of Coronel Dorrego, in wheat-growing dist.

Oriente (ōŏryĕn'tĭ), city (pop. 1,812), W central São Paulo, Brazil, on railroad and 10 mi. WNW of Marília, in pioneer agr. zone (cotton, sugar cane, fruit, coffee); sugar milling.

Oriente (ōryĕn'tā), province (□ 14,132; pop. 1,356,489), E Cuba; ⊙ SANTIAGO DE CUBA. The largest and most populous prov. of the isl., occupying its easternmost section. Coast line has many sheltered inlets in N and S, but rises abruptly SW in the Sierra Maestra, which includes Cuba's highest elevation, the Pico Turquino (6,560 ft.). The W shore line along Gulf of Guacanayabo is marshy, drained by Cauto R., longest of the isl. Prov. has agr. and mineral riches. It mines iron (Sierra Maestra, Sierra de Nipe, Caney), copper (Cobre), chromium and iron near Mayarí (refined at Felton); nickel refined at Nicaro. Also contains large manganese deposits and mercury, asphalt, and marble. Sugar cane is leading crop, milled at numerous centrals; cattle raising and tobacco growing rank next. Other agr. products are coffee, cacao, coconuts, bananas, citrus fruit, rice, corn, beeswax, honey. The forested ranges yield fine timber (mahogany, cedar, ebony, etc.). Apart from sugar milling, chief industries are mining, lumbering, rum distilling, brewing, tobacco processing, dairying, coconut-oil extracting, tanning, mfg. of cigars; foundries. These are concentrated in trading centers such as Holguín, Banes, Guantánamo, Palma Soriano, Bayamo, and the major ports Santiago de Cuba, Baracoa, Manzanillo, Gibara, and Puerto Padre. The prov. is rich in historical associations. On its N shore, near Gibara, Columbus made his 1st landing (1492) in Cuba. Baracoa was the 1st white settlement on the isl. (1511–12). In Oriente were fought the major battles of Cuban struggle for independence. San Juan Hill, famed for Theodore Roosevelt's exploits, is just E of Santiago de Cuba. A U.S. naval base is maintained (since 1903) at Guantánamo Bay. Prov. was formerly named (until 1905) Santiago de Cuba.

Oriente, former province of Ecuador comprising all its territory E of the Andes, in Amazon basin; divided 1925 into NAPO-PASTAZA and SANTIAGO-ZAMORA provs., separated by Pastaza R. The region's boundaries, long disputed by Peru and Ecuador, were settled 1942 at Rio de Janeiro.

Orient Point, N.Y.: see ORIENT.

Orignac (ōrēnyäk'), village (pop. 290), Hautes-Pyrénées dept., SW France, 4 mi. N of Bagnères-de-Bigorre; lignite mining.

Origny or **Origny-en-Thiérache** (ōrēnyē'-ā-tyārăsh'), village (pop. 1,091), Aisne dept., N France, 7 mi. NE of Vervins; basket making.

Origny-Sainte-Benoîte (-sĕt-bünwät'), village (pop. 1,735), Aisne dept., N France, on the Oise and Oise-Sambre Canal, and 9 mi. E of Saint-Quentin; Portland cement mfg., cotton weaving.

Orihuela (ōrēwä'lä), city (pop. 11,983; commune pop. 43,619), Alicante prov., E Spain, in Valencia, on Segura R. and 32 mi. SW of Alicante; hemp-production and -processing center. Other mfg.: shoes, toys, tiles, furniture, insecticides, candy; flour- and sawmilling, vegetable-fiber processing. Irrigation of surrounding garden region (oranges and other fruit, olive oil, cereals, vegetables, pepper) dates from Moorish times; sericulture. Marble quarries. Mineral springs. Bishopric; and formerly seat (1568–1835) of univ. On side of hill above city is large seminary. Has cathedral (14th–15th cent.; restored), several old mansions, and 16th-cent. churches of Santiago and Santo Domingo (with adjoining 17th-cent. former univ. bldg.). Was held by Romans, Visigoths, and Moors; liberated (1264) by Christians. Partly destroyed (1829) by earthquake.

Orijärvi (ô'rĭyăr"vē), village in Kisko commune (pop. 4,082), Turku-Pori co., SW Finland, in lake region, 45 mi. ESE of Turku, 17 mi. NNE of Ekenas; copper, zinc, lead, and silver mines.

Orillia (ôrĭl'yů), town (pop. 9,798), S Ont., on Couchiching L. at N end of L. Simcoe, 70 mi. N of Toronto; boat building, woodworking, flour milling; mfg. of mining, lumbering machinery, agr. implements; in fruitgrowing region. Resort. Site of Ont. Hosp. for the Feebleminded. Has memorial (1925) to Champlain, commemorating 300th anniversary of explorer's visit here.

Orimattila (ō'rĭmät"tĭlä), village (commune pop. 14,462), Uusimaa co., S Finland, 13 mi. SSE of Lahti; woolen mills.

Orinda (ōrĭn'dů), residential village (1940 pop. 782), Contra Costa co., W Calif., just E of Berkeley, across Berkeley Hills.

Orinin (ŭrē'nyĭn), town (1932 pop. estimate 1,820), SW Kamenets-Podolski oblast, Ukrainian SSR, 9 mi. NW of Kamenets-Podolski; clothing and metal industries.

Orinoco River (ôrĭnō'kō, Sp. ōrēnō'kō), Venezuela, one of the great streams of South America; rises in Parima mts. (part of Guiana Highlands) on Brazil border at 2°18'N 63°15'W, winds in large semicircle, flowing NW to Colombia and N along Colombia border, then through center of Venezuela, running NNE to mouth of Apure R., and finally E to the Atlantic in a wide delta S of Trinidad. A vast stream, with a great flow of water varying considerably in volume and length with the seasons, it has been estimated to be 1,200 to 1,700 mi. long. It flows through tropical rain forests and vast savannas, called llanos, in a sparsely populated region. Navigable for c.1,000 mi., the Orinoco is separated into an upper and lower course by Atures and Maipures rapids (circumvented by highway) along Colombia border S of Puerto Ayacucho. The CASIQUIARE, a 140-mi.-long natural waterway of good navigability, links the upper Orinoco with the Amazon via the Río NEGRO. Among its main, mostly navigable, affluents are, left: Guaviare, Vichada (Colombia), Meta (Colombia and Colombia-Venezuela border), Capanaparo, Arauca (Colombia and Venezuela), Apure; right: Ventuari, Caura, Caroní, Paragua. The huge delta (□ 7,745) begins 100 mi. from the sea, near Barrancas; its many arms include the Mánamo, Macareo, Araguao, and the wide Río Grande which forms Boca Grande (or Boca de Navíos) estuary. Along the middle course extends good grazing land; however, the vast lowland expanses, especially near the delta, are, during the rainy season (beginning in April and continuing into Oct.) reduced to swamps. Communication and commercial center for the entire basin is the port Ciudad Bolívar (262 mi. upstream); the tide reaches to this point in the low-water season), port of call for ocean-going vessels. Other important landings are: San Fernando de Atabapo at mouth of Guaviare and Atabapo rivers; Puerto Ayacucho N of Atures Rapids and terminus for lower Orinoco shipping; Puerto Carreño at Meta confluence in Colombia; Caicara; Soledad opposite Ciudad Bolívar; San Félix, with iron deposits near by; Barrancas at head of delta; and Tucupita on Mánamo delta arm. The Orinoco was 1st sighted (1498) by Columbus on his 3d voyage. The 1st European to navigate it was Diego de Ordaz, who ascended the stream to its confluence with the Meta in 1530–31. The Orinoco was probably 1st traveled for most of its length by Lope de Aguirre in 1560. Alexander von Humboldt explored upper reaches, establishing the linkage of the Orinoco and Amazon systems. Not until recent years, however, as a result of expeditions in 1931, 1943, and 1951, has the location of the source of the Orinoco been established.

Orio (ō'ryō), town (pop. 1,650), Guipúzcoa prov., N Spain, 8 mi. WSW of San Sebastián; mfg. (ceramics, dyes, burlap) corn, apples, cattle.

Oriolo (ōrēô'lô), town (pop. 4,475), Cosenza prov., Calabria, S Italy, 21 mi. NNE of Castrovillari; wine, olive oil.

Oriolo Romano (rômä'nô), village (pop. 1,635), Viterbo prov., Latium, central Italy, near L. Bracciano, 30 mi. NNW of Rome; resort (alt. 1,411 ft.); foundry.

Orion (ōrēōn'), town (1939 pop. 6,753; 1948 municipality pop. 8,721), Bataan prov., S Luzon, Philippines, on E Bataan Peninsula, on Manila Bay, 28 mi. W of Manila; agr. center (sugar cane, rice).

Orion (ōrī'ŭn). **1** Village (pop. 829), Henry co., NW Ill., 12 mi. SE of Moline, in agr. and bituminous-coal-mining area. **2** Village, Oakland co., Mich.: see LAKE ORION.

Oriska, village (pop. 135), Barnes co., E N.Dak., 10 mi. E of Valley City.

Oriskany (ûrĭ'skůnē), village (pop. 1,346), Oneida co., central N.Y., near mouth of Oriskany Creek on Mohawk R., 7 mi. NW of Utica; mfg. (felt, dies). Obelisk at Oriskany Battlefield (NW) marks site of an engagement (Aug. 6, 1777) of the Saratoga campaign. Inc. 1914.

Oriskany Creek, central N.Y., rises in Madison co. S of Oneida, flows c.30 mi. S and NNE to Mohawk R. 6 mi. NW of Utica.

Oriskany Falls, village (pop. 893), Oneida co., central N.Y., on Oriskany Creek and 16 mi. SW of Utica; mfg. of clothing; crushed stone.

Orissa (ůrĭ'sů, ō–), constituent state (□ 59,869; 1951 census pop. 14,644,293), E India; ⊙ Bhubaneswar (⊙ was Cuttack). Bounded E by Bay of Bengal, S by Madras, W by Madhya Pradesh, N by Bihar, NE by West Bengal. Mostly a hilly region (c.1,500–3,000 ft. high; several peaks over 4,000 ft.), with N end of Eastern Ghats in S half and outliers of Chota Nagpur Plateau in N. Fertile coastal strip is well watered by several mtn. streams and by large deltas of Mahanadi, Brahmani, and Baitarani rivers, whose flood waters are utilized for canal irrigation. Annual rainfall, 40–60 in. Rice is extensively cultivated; also oilseeds, sugar cane, millet, jute, turmeric. Dense tropical forests produce timber (sal), bamboo, lac, and honey; sericulture. Elephants, tigers, and leopards are common. Major iron-ore (hematite) deposits worked in Mayurbhanj and Keonjhar dists. (N); also manganese, coal, and limestone. Although predominantly agr., state has important factories at Rayagada and Aska (sugar), Barang (glassworks), Brajrajnagar (paper), and Titlagarh (graphite products). Rice milling, biri mfg., handicraft cloth weaving and metalworking, and basket making are widespread local industries; along coast are salt panning and fishing (pomfrets, mackerel, hilsa, mullet). Hydroelectric projects under construction on Mahanadi and Machkund rivers. Principal towns: CUTTACK, Berhampur, Puri, Balasore, Sambalpur, Parlakimedi; lack of good ports due to offshore silting and inland rail traffic. From anc. Ayran times to early Middle Ages, area was center of strong Kalinga kingdom, although conquered c.250 B.C. by Asoka (rock edicts at Dhauli and Jaugada) and held for almost a century by Mauryas. Upon gradual decline of Kalingas, several Hindu dynasties arose and built famous temples at BHUBANESWAR, PURI, and Konarak. About this time many petty states were established in hills by Rajput chieftains and aboriginal tribes; their semi-independence tolerated by subsequent invaders of Orissa. After long resistance to Moslems, country was finally overcome by Afghans (1568); later annexed to Mogul empire; in 1751 ceded to Mahrattas; conquered 1803 by British. Was subdivision of Bengal until 1912, when prov. of Bihar and Orissa was created; princely states in meantime had entered into treaty engagements with British and were grouped into a political agency (Orissa Tributary States). Desire on part of Oriya-speaking peoples for unification led to creation of Orissa as separate autonomous prov. in 1936, comprising original dists. of Balasore, Cuttack, Puri, Sambalpur, and Ganjam and Koraput (the latter 2 dists. having been formerly in Madras prov.). In 1948–49, the original prov. (□ 32,198; 1941 census pop. 8,728,544) was enlarged by the merger of most of the ORISSA STATES (of Eastern States Agency), Kalahandi and Patna (of Chhattisgarh States), and Mayurbhanj (of Bengal States), which were inc. into existing or newly-created dists. Became constituent state of Indian republic in 1950. Now comprises 13 dists.: Balasore, Baudh, Bolangir, Cuttack, Dhenkanal, Ganjam, Kalahandi, Keonjhar, Koraput, Mayurbhanj, Puri, Sambalpur, Sundargarh. Pop. 74% Hindu, 24% tribal (chiefly Khonds, Santals, Saoras, Gonds), 1% Moslem.

Orissa States, subordinate agency (□ 18,151; pop. 3,023,731) of former Eastern States agency, India; hq. were at Sambalpur. Comprised princely states of Athgarh, Athmallik, Bamra, Baramba, Baudh, Bonai, Daspalla, Dhenkanal, Gangpur, Hindol, Keonjhar, Khandpara, Kharsawan, Narsinghpur, Nayagarh, Nilgiri, Pal Lahara, Rirakhol, Ranpur, Saraikela, Sonepur, Talcher, and Tigiria. In 1948 Kharsawan and Saraikela were inc. into Bihar, while rest of states merged with Orissa.

Oristano (ōrēstä'nô), town (pop. 9,454), Cagliari prov., W Sardinia, near mouth of Tirso R., 55 mi. NNW of Cagliari, in the Campidano; potteries, canneries (fish, fruit), olive-oil and macaroni factories, flour mills; domestic embroidery, netting. Archbishopric. Has 18th-cent. cathedral (replacing one built in 13th cent.; 2 of its towers remain), medieval fortifications. Pisan church of Santa Giusta (12th cent.) is 1 mi. S.

Oristano, Gulf of, W Sardinia, inlet of Mediterranean Sea, bet. Cape San Marco (N) and Cape Frasca (S); 13 mi. long, 6 mi. wide. Fisheries (tunny, lobster). Receives Tirso R.

Orituco River (ōrētōō'kō), Guárico state, central Venezuela, rises on S slopes of coastal range near Miranda state border, flows c.150 mi. SSW and SW, past Altagracia de Orituco, to Guárico R. 13 mi. S of Calabozo.

Orivesi (ō'rĭvĕ"sē), village (commune pop. 8,481), Häme co., SW Finland, on small L. Ori, Finnish *Orivesi*, 25 mi. ENE of Tampere; rail junction; grain, potatoes, livestock.

Oriximiná (ōōrĕshēmēnä'), city (pop. 1,847), W Pará, Brazil, on Trombetas R. and 25 mi. NW of Óbidos, in marshy flood area; rubber, Brazil nuts, medicinal plants.

Orizaba (ōrēsä'bä), city (pop. 47,910), Veracruz, E Mexico, in Maltrata valley of Sierra Madre Oriental, at SE foot of Pico de Orizaba, on railroad and 65 mi. SW of Veracruz; alt. c.4,000 ft. Resort and cotton-milling center. Mild climate, abundant rainfall, and water power. Mexico's leading textile factories; and railroad shops, breweries, paper mill, cement plant, jute factory, other processing plants. Situated in fertile agr. area (coffee, cotton, sugar cane, tobacco, fruit). Has many churches, city hall, federal school, beautiful parks. Rincón Grande Cascade and hydroelectric plant near by. First Sp. flour mill dates from 1553; an Indian village, allegedly conquered (1457) by Aztecs, existed long before. Benito Juárez called conference here (1862) in unsuccessful attempt to ward off foreign invasion; French made Orizaba their headquarters shortly afterward. Suburb Jalapilla became favorite residence of Emperor Maximilian.

Orizaba, Pico de (pē'kō dā), or **Citlaltépetl** (sētlältā'pĕtůl), peak (18,700 ft.), E Mexico, on Veracruz-Puebla border, 60 mi. E of Puebla; 19°2'N 97°16'W. Highest in Mexico and 2d only to Mt. McKinley and Mt. Logan in North America; has well-shaped, snow-covered cone, with several smaller craters. Inactive since 1687. First ascended 1848.

Orizatlán (ōrēsätlän'), officially San Felipe Orizatlán, town (pop. 1,653), Hidalgo, central Mexico, in foothills of Sierra Madre Oriental, 13 mi. WNW of Huejutla; corn, rice, tobacco, coffee, fruit; cigars.

Orizona (ōōrēzō'nů), city (pop. 1,002), S Goiás, central Brazil, 60 mi. SE of Anápolis; lard, cereals. Rutile deposits. Until 1944, Campo Formoso.

Orjen or **Oryen** (both: ôr'yĕn), mountain in Dinaric Alps, on Montenegro–Herzegovina border, Yugoslavia; highest point (6,216 ft.) is 10 mi. N of Herceg Novi.

Órjiva or **Órgiva** (both: ôr'hēvä), city (pop. 3,852), Granada prov., S Spain, chief center of Alpujarras dist., 22 mi. SSE of Granada; olive-oil and cheese processing, brandy distilling. Oranges, cereals, livestock. Silver-bearing lead mines near by. Starting point for the ascent of the MULHACÉN.

Orkanger (ôrk'äng-ûr), village and canton (pop. 2,634), Sor-Trondelag co., central Norway, at head of Orkdal Fjord (inlet of Trondheim Fjord), at mouth of Orkla R., on railroad and 20 mi. SW of Trondheim; industrial center. Lumber floated down the Orkla is processed here; wood pulp, lumber, wood products are exported. Herring-oil, canning, cement factories. THAMSHAMN is in canton.

Orkdal, Norway: see FANNREM.

Orkedalen, Norway: see FANNREM.

Orkelljunga (ûr"kùlyŭng'ä), Swedish *Örkelljunga* village (pop. 2,401), Kristianstad co., SW Sweden, 16 mi. E of Angelholm; grain, potatoes, livestock.

Örkeny (ûr'kānyù), Hung. *Örkény*, town (pop. 7,396), Pest-Pilis-Solt-Kiskun co., central Hungary, 29 mi. NNW of Kecskemet; distilleries; grain, horses, cattle.

Orkhaniye, Bulgaria: see BOTEVGRAD.

Orkhomenos, Greece: see ORCHOMENUS.

Orkhon River or **Orhon River** (both ôr'kŏn), main right tributary of Selenga R., in N central Mongolian People's Republic; rises in the E Khangai Mts., flows 700 mi. E and N, past site of anc. Karakorum, and NE to Selenga R. at Sukhe Bator city. Navigable at high water (July-Aug.) for shallow-draught vessels for 190 mi. (below mouth of Tola R.). Also receives Khara and Iro rivers. The Orkhon inscriptions, discovered 1889 by Russian explorer N. M. Yadrintsev on site of KARAKORUM, are old Turkic and Chinese writings dating from 8th cent. They were further examined (1891) by the Russian Turkologist V. V. Radlov and deciphered (1896) by Vilhelm Thomsen.

Orkland, Norway: see SVORKMO.

Orkla River (ôr'klä), central Norway, rises in the NE Dovrefjell of Sor-Trondelag co. 40 mi. NE of Dombas, flows E to Kvikne in Hedmark co., then NW to Sor-Trondelag co., past Rennebu, Meldal, Orkland, and Orkdal, to an inlet of Trondheim Fjord at Orkanger; 100 mi. long.

Orkney, insular county (□ 376.4; 1931 pop. 22,077; 1951 census 21,258) of Scotland, consisting of the **Orkney Islands,** anc. *Orcades*, an archipelago 50 mi. long and 35 mi. wide, separated from Caithness mainland by the Pentland Firth; 59°N 3°W. Of the 90 isls. and islets 29 are inhabited. Larger isls. are POMONA (or Mainland), South Ronaldsay, Westray, Sanday, Stronsay, and Hoy. Kirkwall, the ⊙, is on Pomona isl.; the only other burgh is Stromness. With the exception of Hoy the surface of the isls. is level; soil is shallow and barren, with many lakes. Climate is mild. Fishing (herring, cod, ling) and fish curing are main occupations; sheep and cattle raising, farming, egg production, and woolen weaving are other industries. There are numerous vestiges of anc. habitation; the most famous are monuments of Maeshowe and Stenness, on Pomona isl. In 875 Harold Fairhair (Harold I), 1st king of Norway, annexed the Orkneys and Shetlands to his Scandinavian possessions; they were ruled by Norse jarls in behalf of Norwegian crown. In 1468 Christian I of Norway and Denmark pledged isls. to James III of Scotland as security for dowry of Margaret, James's queen. As pledge was not redeemed, the Orkneys and Shetlands were annexed to Scotland in 1472. Most place names are of Scandinavian origin; inhabitants are of Scandinavian and Scottish stock. In the S Orkneys is naval base of Scapa Flow.

Orkney, formerly Eastleigh, town (pop. 7,119), SW Transvaal, U. of So. Afr., on Schoon Spruit R. near its mouth on Vaal R., 6 mi. S of Klerksdorp; alt. 4,275 ft.; rail junction; gold mining.

Orkney Springs, health resort, Shenandoah co., NW Va., near W.Va. line, 23 mi. N of Harrisonburg, in foothills of the Alleghenies; mineral springs.

Orlamünde (ôr"lämün'dù), town (pop. 2,411), Thuringia, central Germany, on the Thuringian Saale, at mouth of Orla R., and 11 mi. SSW of Jena; toy mfg., woodworking. Remains of medieval castle.

Orland, canton, Norway: see AUSTRATT.

Orland. 1 Town (pop. 2,067), Glenn co., N central Calif., in Sacramento Valley, c.90 mi. NNW of Sacramento; shipping, processing center. Hq. of U.S. Bureau of Reclamation irrigation project begun in 1910; water from reservoirs impounded in Stony Creek. Founded 1881, inc. 1909. **2** Town (pop. 386), Steuben co., NE Ind., near Mich. line, 55 mi. E of South Bend. **3** Town (pop. 1,155), Hancock co., S Maine, near Bucksport, 16 mi. S of Bangor. Settled 1764.

Orlândia (ôrlăn'dyù), city (pop. 3,460), NE São Paulo, Brazil, on railroad and 31 mi. N of Ribeirão Prêto; corn meal, beverages, macaroni products, butter.

Orlando, residential town (pop. 57,660), S Transvaal, U. of So. Afr., on Witwatersrand, 8 mi. WSW of Johannesburg. A separate municipality, but under jurisdiction of Johannesburg city; almost entire pop. consists of native mine workers.

Orlando (ôrlăn'dō). **1** City (pop. 52,367), ⊙ Orange co., central Fla., c.75 mi. ENE of Tampa; citrus-fruit shipping center; packing houses, canneries, nurseries; railroad shops; mfg. of machinery, sheet-metal and concrete products, fertilizer, mirrors, boxes. A noted resort, it has many small lakes within city limits. Air Force base here. Founded near Fort Gatlin (1837–48). Inc. 1875. Recent rapid growth has made it state's largest inland city. **2** Town (pop. 262), Logan co., central Okla., 19 mi. N of Guthrie; trade center for farming area.

Orlandovtsi (ôrlän'dôftsē), village (pop. 6,299), Sofia dist., W Bulgaria, just N of Sofia; livestock, fruit, truck.

Orland Park, village (pop. 788), Cook co., NE Ill., SW suburb of Chicago, 12 mi. NE of Joliet; dairy farms.

Orla River (ôr'lä), central Germany, rises ESE of Triptis, flows 20 mi. W, past Triptis and Neustadt, to the Thuringian Saale at Orlamünde.

Orle (ôr'lĕ), mountain, Macedonia, Yugoslavia, along left bank of the lower Crna Reka; highest peak (4,966 ft.) is 17 mi. E of Prilep.

Orleães (ôrlĭā'ĭs), city (pop. 1,817), SE Santa Catarina, Brazil, on railroad and 35 mi. WNW of Laguna, in coal-mining area; livestock. Formerly spelled Orleans.

Orléanais (ôrlāänā'), region and former province of N central France, on both sides of the middle Loire; ⊙ was ORLÉANS. It now forms Loiret and Loir-et-Cher depts., and parts of Eure-et-Loir and Yonne depts. Primarily agr., it includes the rich BEAUCE (N), the Gâtinais (E), the poorly drained SOLOGNE (S), and the extensive Forest of Orléans (center). Along the huge bend of the Loire are vineyards, orchards, and truck farms. Chief towns are Orléans, Chartres, Blois, and Montargis. Nucleus of Orléanais was part of royal domain since 1st kings of France; its history is that of Orléans.

Orleans, Brazil: see ORLEÃES.

Orléans (ôr'lēunz, ôrlēnz', Fr. ôrlāā'), anc. *Cenabum* or *Genabum*, later *Aurelianum*, city (pop. 64,755), ⊙ Loiret dept., N central France, on right bank of Loire R. and 70 mi. SSW of Paris; 47°54'N 1°55'E. Important commercial and transportation center, with food-processing and textile industries. Chief products are blankets and ready-to-wear clothing, agr. and electrical equipment, vinegar, mustard, candies, chocolate, biscuits, liqueurs, and pharmaceuticals. There are tanneries, distilleries, breweries, and flour mills. Important trade in sparkling wines and cereals. Railroad station of Les Aubrais (1½ mi. N of city center) is junction of 5 major lines. The old city, hugging right bank of the Loire, is surrounded by extensive modern suburbs. During Ger. advance across France in 1940, entire sections of Orléans were ravaged by fire. Some additional damage was inflicted in 1944. The cathedral of Sainte-Croix, rebuilt (17th–19th cent.) after its destruction by Huguenots in 1568, was heavily damaged; the Place du Martroi (center of Orléans), with statue of Joan of Arc, and the Joan of Arc mus. were virtually leveled. However, numerous Renaissance bldgs. remain intact, including the mus. of painting and sculpture and the town hall, where Francis II died in 1560. The feast of Joan of Arc is celebrated here each May with great ceremony. The town, the Gallic *Cenabum*, was burned by Julius Caesar and rebuilt by Aurelian, after whom it was later named. Taken by Clovis I (5th cent.) it became ⊙ of Frankish kingdom of Orléans. In 7th cent. it became, next to Paris, the chief residence of French kings. Together with surrounding ORLÉANAIS, Orléans formed nucleus of royal domain. By lifting the English siege of Orléans (1428–29), Joan of Arc was instrumental in turning tide of Hundred Years War. As the Huguenot hq. during Wars of Religion, city was besieged (1563) by Catholics under François de Guise, who was assassinated under its walls. In 1652, Orléans was seized for the Fronde by Mlle de Montpensier. It was occupied by Prussians in 1815 after battle of Waterloo, and again during Franco-Prussian War (1870–71).

Orleans. 1 (ôr'lēùnz) Parish (□ 199; pop. 570,445), SE La., coextensive with NEW ORLEANS. **2** (ôr'-lēnz") County (□ 396; pop. 29,832), W N.Y.; ⊙ Albion. Bounded N by L. Ontario; crossed by the Barge Canal; drained by Oak Orchard Creek. Fruitgrowing area; also truck, dairy products. Diversified mfg. at Albion, Medina, Lyndonville. Formed 1824. **3** (ôrlēnz') County (□ 715; pop. 21,190), N Vt., on Que. line; ⊙ Newport. Dairying, lumbering; wood products; granite, asbestos; maple sugar. Resorts on L. Memphremagog, L. Willoughby, and smaller lakes; winter sports. Drained by Barton, Missisquoi, Black, and Clyde rivers. Organized 1792.

Orleans (ôrlēnz'). **1** Town (pop. 1,531), Orange co., S Ind., near Lost R., 14 mi. S of Bedford, in dairy, fruit, and grain area; butter, feed, lumber. Settled 1815. **2** Resort town (pop. 317), Dickinson co., NW Iowa, on Spirit L., 22 mi. N of Spencer. **3** (also ôr'lēnz) Town (pop. 1,759), Barnstable co., SE Mass., near elbow of Cape Cod, 17 mi. ENE of Barnstable; summer resort; agr. Transatlantic cable to Brest, France. Includes villages of East Orleans, Rock Harbor, South Orleans. Settled 1693, set off from Eastham 1797. **4** City (pop. 956), Harlan co., S Nebr., 6 mi. WNW of Alma and on Republican R., near Kansas line; dairy products, grain. **5** Village (pop. 1,261) in BARTON town, Orleans co., N Vt., 9 mi. S of Newport and on Barton R.; wood products, chemicals. Settled c.1821.

Orléans, Forest of, one of largest (□ c.150) in France, extends 40 mi. E and ESE of Orléans, Loiret dept., N of the Loire. Consists of oak, birch, and hornbeam stands.

Orleans, Isle of, or **Île d'Orléans** (ēl), island (□ 72; pop. 4,293), S Que., in the St. Lawrence, 5 mi. NE of Quebec; 20 mi. long, 5 mi. wide, rises to 293 ft. Agr. (dairying; vegetables, fruit, poultry). Main settlements are Ste. Famille and St. Jean d'Orléans. Essentially French in character, isl. was 1st settled 1651. During attack (1759) on Quebec Wolfe established part of his camp here. Highway bridge to mainland (1935).

Orléans Canal, Loiret dept., N central France, one of waterways connecting Loire and Seine rivers; begins just above Orléans, traverses Forest of Orléans, and joins BRIARE CANAL below Montargis, whence both are continued by LOING CANAL to the Seine. Total length, 45 mi.

Orléansville (ôrlāävēl'), town (pop. 12,455), Alger dept., N central Algeria, in irrigated Chéliff valley, on trunk railroad and 105 mi. WSW of Algiers; agr. trade center (cereals, wine, citrus fruit, cotton); leather-working, printing. Linked by rail spur with Ténès, its port on the Mediterranean (24 mi. N). Zinc and lead mine at Bou-Caïd and Molière (c.25 mi. SE, in Ouarsenis Massif). Founded 1843 by French, on site of anc. *Castellum Tingitanum*. An early Christian basilica (paved in mosaic) has been excavated.

Orlice River (ôr'lĭtsĕ), Ger. *Adler* (äd'lùr), E Bohemia, Czechoslovakia, formed by junction of 2 headstreams, DIVOCHA ORLICE (right) and TICHA ORLICE (left), 1 mi. above Tyniste nad Orlici; flows c.20 mi. NW to Elbe R. at Hradec Kralove.

Orlicke, Hory, and **Gory Orlickie,** Czechoslovakia and Poland: see ADLERGEBIRGE.

Orlik, Czechoslovakia: see PISEK.

Örlik (ôr'lyĭk), village, SW Buryat-Mongol Autonomous SSR, Russian SFSR, on Oka R. and 130 mi. S of Tulun, in Eastern Sayan Mts.; alt. 5,250 ft.; gold mining.

Orlinghausen, Germany: see OERLINGHAUSEN.

Orljava River (ôr'lyävä), N Croatia, Yugoslavia, in Slavonia; rises on NE slope of the Psunj, flows SE past Pozega and Pleternica, and SSW to Sava R. 15 mi. WSW of Slavonski Brod; c.50 mi. long. Receives Londza R.

Orlod, Yugoslavia: see ORLOVAT.

Orlov, Russian SFSR: see KHALTURIN.

Orlova (ôr'lôvä), Czech *Orlová*, town (pop. 8,572; urban commune pop. 20,201), NE Silesia, Czechoslovakia, 6 mi. E of Ostrava; rail junction; major coal-mining center of Ostrava-Karvina coal basin; iron mining, metallurgical industries.

Orlovat (ôr'lôvät), Hung. *Orlód* (ôr'lōd), village, Vojvodina, N Serbia, Yugoslavia, on Tamis R. and 13 mi. SSE of Zrenjanin, in the Banat; rail junction.

Orlovo (ŭrlô'vù), village (1940 pop. 3,926), Sakhalin, Russian SFSR, on Tatar Strait, 17 mi. SSW of Uglegorsk; fishing. Under Jap. rule (1905–45), called Ushiro (ōō"shē'rō).

Orlovskaya (ŭrlôf'skīù), village (1926 pop. 4,402), S Rostov oblast, Russian SFSR, on railroad (Dvoinaya station) and 38 mi. NE of Salsk; flour mill, metalworks; wheat, cotton, livestock.

Orlu or **Awlu** (ô'lōō), town, Owerri prov., Eastern Provinces, S Nigeria, 20 mi. N of Owerri; palm oil and kernels, kola nuts.

Orly (ôrlē'), town (pop. 6,006), Seine dept., N central France, outer SSE suburb of Paris, 8 mi. from Notre Dame Cathedral. Villeneuve-Orly airport is 1 mi. SSW.

Ormara (ōrmä'rù), village, Las Bela state, S Baluchistan, W Pakistan, on promontory in Arabian Sea, 150 mi. WNW of Karachi; fishing; some coastal trade.

Orme (ôrm), town (pop. 230), Marion co., S Tenn., near Ala. line, 29 mi. W of Chattanooga.

Ormea (ôrmā'ä), village (pop. 1,576), Cuneo prov., Piedmont, NW Italy, on Tanaro R. and 18 mi. S of Mondovì; rail terminus; paper mfg.; resort.

Ormenion (ôrmĕn'ēôn), village (pop. 1,978), Hevros nome, W Thrace, Greece, on railroad and 18 mi. WNW of Adrianople (Edirne), on Maritsa R. (Bulg. line); border post opposite Svilengrad.

Ormesby (ôrmz'bē), residential village and parish (pop. 789), North Riding, NE Yorkshire, England, 3 mi. SE of Middlesbrough.

Ormesson-sur-Marne (ôrmĕsō'-sür-märn'), town (pop. 3,307), Seine-et-Oise dept., N central France, on left bank of the Marne and 10 mi. SE of Paris; metalworking, mfg. of pharmaceuticals. Has fine 17th–18th-cent. château with garden laid out by Le Nôtre.

Ormiston (ôr'mĭstùn), village, S Sask., near small Shoe L., 45 mi. S of Moose Jaw; sodium-sulphate production.

Ormiston, town and parish (pop. 2,032), W East Lothian, Scotland, on Tyne R. and 2 mi. S of Tranent; coal mining. Just E is coal-mining village of Elphinstone (ĕl′fĭnstŭn), with remains of Elphinstone Tower, 14th-cent. border fortress.

Ormoc, city, Philippines: see MACARTHUR.

Ormoc Bay (ôrmŏk′), inlet of Camotes Sea, W Leyte, Philippines; 13 mi. E-W, 16 mi. N-S. MacArthur (formerly Ormoc) is at head of bay.

Ormond, resort city (pop. 3,418), Volusia co., NE Fla., on Halifax R. lagoon and 5 mi. N of Daytona Beach. Founded c.1875, inc. 1929. Across lagoon (bridged here) is Ormond Beach, with part of the famous Daytona Beach speedway. "The Casements," former winter home of John D. Rockefeller, is here.

Ormont-Dessous (ôrmō′-dŭsōō′) and **Ormont-Dessus** (–dŭsü′), Alpine communes (total pop. 2,445), Vaud canton, SW Switzerland, 6–10 mi. E of E shore of L. of Geneva.

Ormoz (ôr′môsh), Slovenian *Ormož*, Ger. *Friedau* (frē′dou), village, NE Slovenia, Yugoslavia, on Drava R. and 23 mi. SE of Maribor, on Croatia frontier, in brown-coal mining and winegrowing region. Rail junction; tuberculosis sanatorium. In Styria until 1918.

Ormsby, county (□ 141; pop. 4,172), W Nev.; ⊙ Carson City, the state capital. Irrigated area bordering on Calif., drained by Carson R. Dairy products, livestock, grain. Part of L. Tahoe in W. Formed 1854.

Ormsby, village (pop. 190), Martin and Watonwan counties, S Minn., 18 mi. NW of Fairmont; grain, livestock, poultry.

Ormskirk, urban district (1931 pop. 17,118; 1951 census 20,554), SW Lancashire, England, 12 mi. NNE of Liverpool; cotton and silk milling, flour milling; mfg. of synthetic fertilizer, metal products. The church, with 15th-cent. tower, contains a vault of the earls of Derby. Near by is 15th-cent. mansion of Rufford Old Hall. Urban dist. includes town of Burscough (bûr′skō), 2 mi. NE of Ormskirk, with metalworking, biscuit baking. Has ruins of Norman priory.

Ormstown, village (pop. 887), S Que., on Châteauguay R. and 12 mi. SE of Valleyfield; dairying.

Ormuz, Iran: see HORMUZ.

Ornain River (ôrnĕ′), in Meuse and Marne depts., NE France, rises above Gondrecourt, flows 75 mi. NW, past Ligny-en-Barrois, Bar-le-Duc, and Revigny, to the Saulx at Pargny-sur-Saulx. Paralleled in most of its course by Marne-Rhine Canal.

Ornans (ôrnā′), town (pop. 2,741), Doubs dept., E France, on the Loue and 11 mi. SE of Besançon, in the Jura; metallurgy (mfg. of electrical equipment, nails); hosiery knitting, distilling. Gustave Courbet b. here.

Ornavasso (ôrnäväs′sô), village (pop. 1,732), Novara prov., Piedmont, N Italy, near Toce R., 12 mi. SSE of Domodossola; foundry, cotton mill.

Ornbau (ôrn′bou), town (pop. 1,047), Middle Franconia, W Bavaria, Germany, on the Altmühl and 10 mi. SSE of Ansbach; tanning, brewing, flour milling. Has well-preserved medieval fortifications.

Orne (ôrn), department (□ 2,372; pop. 273,181), in Normandy, NW France; ⊙ Alençon. Rolling area traversed by Perche hills (E), with wooded heights (Forest of Écouves) and Alençon plain (center), and hedgerow country (W). Watershed bet. Loire R. tributaries flowing S (Mayenne, Sarthe, Huisne), and streams (Orne, Dives, Vie, Touques, Risle) draining into English Channel. Chief crops: cereals, potatoes, colza, hemp, apples, pears. Camembert cheese mfg. (especially in Vimoutiers area). Percheron horses reared chiefly in Perche dist.; cattle fattened for Paris market. Poultry shipping. Iron mines at Saint-Clair-de-Halouze, Le Châtellier, and La Ferrière-aux-Étangs (all in Domfront area). Metal industry at Laigle (pins and needles), Tinchebray (hardware), and Alençon. Textile milling at Flers, La Ferté-Macé, Alençon (lace). Bagnoles-de-l'Orne and Tessé-la-Madeleine are thermal stations. Heavy fighting occurred here during battle of Argentan-Falaise pocket (Aug., 1944) in Second World War.

Orne River. 1 In Meuse, Meurthe-et-Moselle, and Moselle depts., NE France, rises in Côtes de Meuse, flows c.45 mi. E. past Étain, Conflans, and through Briey iron basin, to the Moselle 5 mi. S of Thionville. Also called Orne de Woëvre. **2** In Orne and Calvados depts., NW France, rises just E of Sées, flows 95 mi. NW and N in an arc, past Argentan, Thury-Harcourt, and Caen, to the Channel at Ouistreham. Crosses Normandy Hills in gorge-like valley. Receives the Odon (left). Below Caen paralleled by ship-canal to its mouth. Along its banks heavy fighting took place in Normandy campaign (June–July, 1944) of Second World War.

Ornes or **Ornes i Sogn** (ôr′năs ē sông′ŭn), village in Hafslo canton, Sogn og Fjordane co., W Norway, on E shore of Luster Fjord (an arm of Sogne Fjord), 9 mi. NE of Sogndal. Norway's oldest stave church, built c.1090, is well preserved. Formerly spelled Urnaes or Urnes.

Orneta (ôrnĕ′tä), Ger. *Wormditt* (vôrm′dĭt), town (1939 pop. 7,817; 1946 pop. 2,109) in East Prussia, after 1945 in Olsztyn prov., NE Poland, near Pasleka R., 30 mi. E of Elbing; grain and cattle market. Founded by Silesian colonists; chartered 1312.

Ornsay, Isle of (pop. 2), Inner Hebrides, Inverness, Scotland, just off SE coast of Skye, opposite Loch Hourn; ½ mi. long, ½ mi. wide. At S extremity is lighthouse (57°10′N 5°44′W).

Ornskoldsvik (ûrn″shŭltsvēk′), Swedish *Örnsköldsvik*, city (pop. 6,731), Vasternorrland co., NE Sweden, on Gulf of Bothnia, at mouth of Angerman R., 75 mi. NE of Sundsvall; seaport (ice-bound in winter), shipping timber and wood products; shipbuilding, woodworking; mfg. of aircraft, wallboard, shoes. Has mus. Inc. 1894.

Orny, Pointe d' (pwĕt dôrnē′), peak (10,751 ft.) in Pennine Alps, SW Switzerland, 7 mi. S of Martigny-Ville.

Oro, Denmark: see ISE FJORD.

Oro, Conca d', Sicily: see PALERMO, prov.

Oro, El, Ecuador: see EL ORO.

Oro, El, Mexico: see EL ORO.

Oro, Río de, Sp. West Africa: see RÍO DE ORO.

Oro, Río del (rē′ō dĕl ō′rō), or **Sestín River** (sĕstēn′), Durango, N Mexico, rises in Sierra Madre Occidental 25 mi. W of Villa Ocampo, flows c.100 mi. SE, joining Ramos R. to form Nazas R. near El Palmito (irrigation dam).

Oro Bay (ō′rō), inlet, NE Papua, New Guinea, c.20 mi. S of Buna; Allied base in 1943.

Orobayaya (ōrōbīä′yä), village (pop. c.450), Beni dept., NE Bolivia, on Río Blanco and 27 mi. NE of Magdalena; cotton, rice, rubber.

Orochen (ŭrŭchĕn′), town (1939 pop. over 2,000), SE Yakut Autonomous SSR, Russian SFSR, on Yakutsk-Never highway and 10 mi. S of Aldan; gold mines.

Orocovis (ōrōkō′vēs), town (pop. 2,674), central Puerto Rico, in Cordillera Central, 23 mi. SW of San Juan; alt. 1,430 ft.; summer resort; tobacco.

Orocué (ōrōkwā′), village (pop. 598), Casanare intendancy, E Colombia, landing on navigable Meta R. and 150 mi. ESE of Tunja; stock raising. Airfield.

Orocuina (ōrōkwē′nä), town (pop. 952), Choluteca dept., S Honduras, near Choluteca R., 12 mi. NE of Choluteca; corn, beans, livestock.

Orofino (ôrōfē′nō), city (pop. 1,656), ⊙ Clearwater co., N Idaho, on Clearwater R. and 40 mi. E of Lewiston; lumber-milling point and gateway to one of country's largest stands of white pine; also dairy products, cement. Limestone quarries near by. Founded 1898 (c.25 mi. from original site, established in gold rush of 1860), inc. 1906.

Orog Nuur, Mongolia: see OROK NOR.

Oro Grande (ō″rō grăn′dē), village (pop. c.475), San Bernardino co., S Calif., 35 mi. N of San Bernardino, in Mojave Desert; cement.

Orohena, Mount (ōrōhā′nä), peak (7,618 ft.), W Tahiti, Society Isls., S Pacific; highest mtn. of isl. group.

Orok Nor, Orok Nur, or **Orog Nuur** (all: ō′rōkh nōr, nōōr), lake (□ 50) in SW central Mongolian People's Republic, in Gobi desert, 170 mi. SSW of Tsetserlik, at foot of the Ikhe Bogdo; 17 mi. long, 5 mi. wide; alt. 3,930 ft. Receives the Tuin Gol.

Orolaunum, Belgium: see ARLON.

Oroluk (ō′rōlōōk′), atoll, Ponape dist., E Caroline Isls., W Pacific, 165 mi. WNW of Ponape; 7°38′N 155°10′E; 18 mi. in diameter. Jap. air base in Second World War.

Oromocto (ōrōmŏk′tō), village (pop. estimate c.375), S central N.B., on St. John R. at mouth of Oromocto R. and 11 mi. ESE of Fredericton, in fruit-growing and lumbering region.

Oromocto Lake (□ 15.6; 8 mi. long, 4 mi. wide), SW N.B., 16 mi. WSW of Fredericton.

Oromocto River, SW N.B., rises in 2 branches, one issuing from Oromocto L., the other from South Oromocto L., joining 21 mi. S of Fredericton; flows thence 20 mi. N to St. John R. at Oromocto.

Oron or **Idua Oron** (ēd′wä ō′rôn), town, Calabar prov., Eastern Provinces, Nigeria, port at mouth of Cross R., 12 mi. SSW of Calabar (ferry service); palm oil and kernels, hardwood, rubber. Fisheries.

Orona, Phoenix Isls.: see HULL ISLAND.

Orong (ōrông′), town (1939 pop. 5,118) in Kabankalan municipality, Negros Occidental prov., W central Negros isl., Philippines, 18 mi. S of Binalbagan; agr. center (rice, hemp).

Orono (ŏ′rōnō), village (pop. estimate 800), S Ont., 15 mi. ENE of Oshawa; apple canning, dairying, flour milling.

Orono (ô′rŭnō), town (pop. 7,504), including Orono village (pop. 3,634), Penobscot co., S Maine, on the Penobscot and 8 mi. above Bangor. Seat of Univ. of Maine. Mfg. (textiles, wood products, paper). Settled c.1775, called Stillwater until inc. 1806, included Old Town until 1840.

Oronoco (ōrŭnō′kō), village (pop. c.200), Olmsted co., SE Minn., 10 mi. NNW of Rochester, in livestock area; dairy products.

Oronogo (ō′rŭnō″gō), city (pop. 519), Jasper co., SW Mo., near Spring R., 8 mi. N of Joplin; lead, zinc mines.

Oronsay (ŏ′rŭnsā, ŏ′rŭnzā). **1** Island (pop. 6) of the Inner Hebrides, Argyll, Scotland, just S of COLONSAY; 3 mi. long, 2 mi. wide; rises to 304 ft. There are ruins of 14th-cent. priory founded by the Lord of the Isles, and sculptured cross. **2** Island (2 mi. long, 1 mi. wide) at mouth of Loch Sunart, Argyll, Scotland, 25 mi. NW of Oban. **3** Island, Outer Hebrides, Inverness, Scotland, just E of N peninsula of Barra; ½ mi. long.

Orontes, Iran: see ALWAND.

Orontes River (ōrŏn′tēs), Arabic *'Asi*, Turkish *Asi* (both: ä′sē), SW Asia, rises in Lebanon in the Bekaa valley near Baalbek, flows N bet. the Lebanon and Anti-Lebanon mts., swings into W Syria, passing Homs and Hama, forms parts of Lebanon-Syria and Syria-Turkey borders, and curves abruptly W into Turkey, where it turns SW, past Antioch, to the Mediterranean at Suveydiye, 13 mi. SW of Antioch; c.240 mi. long. Unnavigable. Used for irrigation, particularly in Syria, where L. Homs is formed by damming the Orontes, and where it waters the fertile valley El Ghab.

Oropa, Santuario di, Italy: see BIELLA.

Oropesa (ōrōpā′sä), town (pop. 1,553), Cuzco dept., S central Peru, on railroad and 16 mi. ESE of Cuzco; grain, vegetables, alfalfa. Archaeological remains near by.

Oropesa River, Peru: see VILCABAMBA RIVER.

Oropesa y Corchuela (ē kôr-chwä′lä), town (pop. 3,316), Toledo prov., central Spain, on railroad and highway to Cáceres, and 18 mi. W of Talavera de la Reina; cereals, acorns, olives, grapes, sheep, hogs. Olive-oil extracting, sawmilling, charcoal burning, tile mfg.; limekilns. Town of medieval character, actually consisting of Oropesa and small Corchuela section. Known for its traditional Toledan customs.

Oropeza, Bolivia: see YOTALA.

Oropus (ōrō′pŭs), anc. town of Attica, Greece, on Asopus R. and 24 mi. E of Thebes, near S arm of Gulf of Euboea. Frequently mentioned in frontier wars bet. Athenians and Boeotians. Near by was oracle of Amphiaraüs. On site is modern village of Oropos (pop. 436), and, just NE, on the gulf, is its harbor, Skala Oropou (pop. 756); lignite mining.

Oroquieta (ōrōkyā′tä), town (1939 pop. 5,771; 1948 municipality pop. 22,837), ⊙ MISAMIS OCCIDENTAL prov., W Mindanao, Philippines, port on Iligan Bay, 50 mi. NE of Pagadian; agr. center (corn, coconuts); ships copra.

Orós (ōōrôs′), town (pop. 1,122), SW Ceará, Brazil, 28 mi. ENE of Iguatu; terminus of rail spur from Alencar. Magnesite deposits. Site of dam impounding waters of Jaguaribe R. for irrigation and flood control.

Oros (ô′rôsh), town (pop. 6,979), Szabolcs co., NE Hungary, 4 mi. E of Nyiregyhaza; corn, wheat, tobacco, hogs.

Orosei (ōrôzā′), village (pop. 2,633), Nuoro prov., E Sardinia, near Gulf of Orosei, 20 mi. ENE of Nuoro. Has medieval castle. Port (Marina di Orosei) is 2 mi. E.

Orosei, Gulf of, inlet of Tyrrhenian Sea, E Sardinia, bet. Cape Comino and Cape Monte Santo; 31 mi. wide, 8 mi. deep; fisheries. Chief port, Orosei.

Orosh (ô′rôsh) or **Oroshi** (ô′rôshē), village (1930 pop. 1,059), N Albania, 32 mi. ESE of Scutari, in the Mirditë tribal region.

Oroshaza (ô′rôsh-häzŏ), Hung. *Orosháza*, city (pop. 27,062), Bekes co., SE Hungary, 22 mi. WSW of Bekescsaba; rail, agr. center; pottery, shoe mills, flour mills, wineries, brickworks; ships poultry. Grain, tobacco, vineyards, cattle raising in area. Resort of Gyoparosfürdö is near by.

Oroshi (ōrō′shē), town (pop. 6,189), Gifu prefecture, central Honshu, Japan, 4 mi. E of Tajimi; ceramic products.

Orosi (ōrō′sē), town (pop. 3,747), Cartago prov., central Costa Rica, on Reventazón R. and 3 mi. SSE of Paraíso; coffee, sugar cane, livestock. Has 18th-cent. colonial church. Founded by Franciscans; an old mission town.

Orosi, extinct volcano (5,056 ft.) in NW Costa Rica, at NW end of the Cordillera de Guanacaste, 12 mi. SE of La Cruz; slopes are covered with dense rain forest.

Orosi (ōrō′sū), village (pop. c.1,200), Tulare co., S central Calif., in San Joaquin Valley, 15 mi. N of Visalia; ships fruit.

Oroszvar, Czechoslovakia: see RUSOVCE.

Orotava, La (lä ōrōtä′vä), town (pop. 5,635), Tenerife, Canary Isls., 18 mi. WSW of Santa Cruz de Tenerife, in Orotava Valley (world's most beautiful, according to Humboldt), famed for its luxuriant vegetation. Served by its port Puerto de la Cruz, 2 mi. NW. A noted health resort and among archipelago's most prosperous town. Region produces chiefly bananas; also tomatoes, cereals, grapes, tobacco, cochineal. Flour milling.

Orotelli (ôrōtĕl′lē), village (pop. 2,787), Nuoro prov., central Sardinia, 12 mi. W of Nuoro.

Orotina (ōrōtē′nä), city (pop. 1,286), Alajuela prov., W central Costa Rica, in Tárcoles valley, on railroad and 22 mi. ESE of Alajuela; grading center; grain, fruit; lumbering. Developed in 20th cent. with construction of railroad.

Orotukan (ŭrŭtōōkän′), village (1948 pop. over 2,000), N Khabarovsk Territory, Russian SFSR, on short Orotukan R. (right branch of Kolyma R.) and 190 mi. N of Magadan (linked by road); gold mines. Formerly Urutukan.

Oroua, New Zealand: see FEILDING.

Oroville (ô′rōvĭl). **1** City (pop. 5,387); ⊙ Butte co., N central Calif., on Feather R., in Sacramento Valley, at base of the Sierra Nevada, 65 mi. N of Sacramento; canning, processing, and shipping center for citrus fruit, olives, vegetables. W gateway to Feather R. recreational and placer-mining region; Feather River Canyon and Feather Falls are near by. Settled 1849 as gold camp (Ophir City); inc. 1857. **2** Town (pop. 1,500), Okanogan co., N Wash., port of entry near British Columbia line, 40 mi. N of Okanogan and on Okanogan R.; gold, silver, clay; timber, apples, grain; fruit canning. Inc. 1908.

Oroya, La, Peru: see La Oroya.

Orphane, Gulf of, Greece: see Strymonic Gulf.

Orphir (ôr'fûr), village on S coast of Pomona, Orkneys, Scotland.

Orpierre (ôrpyâr'), village (pop. 219), Hautes-Alpes dept., SE France, in S Dauphiné Alps, 15 mi. NW of Sisteron; beekeeping, winegrowing.

Orpington, urban district (1951 census pop. 63,344), NW Kent, England, on Cray R. and 4 mi. ESE of Bromley. Has church with Roman and Saxon foundations. The town gives its name to Orpington chickens. In parish, 5 mi. SW, is Biggin Hill, major Royal Air Force fighter station in Second World War.

Orp-le-Grand (ôrp-lü-grã'), town (pop. 1,941), Brabant prov., central Belgium, 8 mi. SSE of Tirlemont; cement. Just SSW is village of Orp-le-Petit.

Orr. 1 Village (pop. 309), St. Louis co., NE Minn., on Pelican L., in state forest area, 40 mi. NNW of Virginia; trading point for resorts; grain, potatoes. **2** Textile-mill village (pop. 2,625), Anderson co., NW S.C., just S of Anderson.

Orrefors (ŏ"rŭfôrs', -fôsh'), village (pop. 641), Kronoberg co., S Sweden, 9 mi. NW of Nybro; site of one of best-known Swedish crystal and glass works, founded 1726.

Orrell (ŏ'rŭl), urban district (1931 pop. 6,949; 1951 census 9,317), SW Lancashire, England, 3 mi. WSW of Wigan; cotton milling. Includes (N) coal-mining village of Kit Green.

Orrery and Kilmore (ŏ'rŭrē, ô'rē, kĭlmôr'), anc. barony covering part of N Co. Cork, Ireland; formerly held by the Boyles.

Orrick (ôr'ĭk), city (pop. 675), Ray co., NW Mo., near Missouri R., 9 mi. SW of Richmond; agr. (corn, wheat, potatoes); coal mines.

Orrington (ŏ'rĭngtŭn), town (pop. 1,895), Penobscot co., S Maine, on the Penobscot and 8 mi. below Bangor in orchard area. Settled 1770, inc. 1788.

Orrin River, Ross and Cromarty, Scotland, rises 18 mi. E of Lochcarron, flows 26 mi. NE, through Glen Orrin valley, past Urray, to Conon R. just NE of Urray.

Or River or **Or' River** (ôr), in NW Kazakh SSR and SE Chkalov oblast, Russian SFSR, rises in central Mugodzhar Hills, flows 206 mi. generally N and W to Ural R. at Orsk; nonnavigable.

Orroli (ôr-rô'lē), village (pop. 2,620), Nuoro prov., SE central Sardinia, 33 mi. NNE of Cagliari.

Orroroo, village (pop. 638), S South Australia, 45 mi. NE of Port Pirie; wheat, wool; dairying; wine.

Orrs Island, Maine: see Harpswell.

Orrstown, borough (pop. 295), Franklin co., S Pa. on Conodoguinet Creek and 9 mi. NNE of Chambersburg.

Orrum (ŏ'rŭm), town (pop. 162), Robeson co., S N.C., 10 mi. S of Lumberton.

Orrville. 1 Town (pop. 416), Dallas co., S central Ala., 15 mi. SW of Selma. **2** City (pop. 5,153), Wayne co., N central Ohio, 20 mi. W of Canton, in agr. area; food and dairy products, machinery, chemicals, motor vehicles, wood products, leather goods, mattresses. Settled c.1850, inc. 1864.

Orsa (ōōr'sä"), village (pop. 1,135), Kopparberg co., central Sweden, on N shore of L. Orsa, Swedish *Orsasjön* (7 mi. long, 2–4 mi. wide), 50 mi. NW of Falun; rail junction; lumber, woolen, and flour mills; mfg. of saw blades, crisp bread. Has 14th-cent. church.

Orsa, Lake, Sweden: see Silja, Lake.

Orsago (ôrsä'gô), village (pop. 1,460), Treviso prov., Veneto, N Italy, 7 mi. SE of Vittorio Veneto, in cereal- and grape-growing region; mfg. (silk textiles, agr. tools).

Orsara di Puglia (ôrsä'rä dē pōō'lyä), town (pop. 6,665), Foggia prov., Apulia, S Italy, 5 mi. WNW of Bovino, in stock-raising region.

Orsaro, Monte (môn'tě ôrsä'rô), peak (6,004 ft.) in Etruscan Apennines, N central Italy, on Parma–Massa e Carrara prov. border, 6 mi. ENE of Pontremoli.

Orsay (ôrsā'), town (pop. 4,989), Seine-et-Oise dept., N central France, on small Yvette R. and 13 mi. SSW of Paris; pharmaceuticals.

Orsay, Scotland: see Oversay.

Orsett (ôr'–), town and parish (pop. 1,771), S Essex, England, 4 mi. N of Tilbury. Has church of Norman origin.

Orsha (ôr'shŭ), city (1926 pop. 22,011), S Vitebsk oblast, Belorussian SSR, on Dnieper R. and 50 mi. S of Vitebsk; major rail junction; metal- and woodworking, mfg. (linen textiles, clothing, machine tools); meat packing, flour milling. Teachers col., agr. mus. Has 11th-cent. castle. Sewing-machine mfg. at near-by Baran. Belgres power plant at Orekhovsk, 14 mi. NNE. During Second World War, held (1941–44) by Germans.

Orshanka (ŭrshän'kŭ), village (1932 pop. estimate 800), N Mari Autonomous SSR, Russian SFSR, 18 mi. N of Ioshkar-Ola; flax processing.

Orshütz River, Poland: see Orzyc River.

Orsières (ôrsyâr'), town (pop. 2,231), Valais canton, SW Switzerland, on Drance R. and 17 mi. SW of Sion, N of Great St. Bernard Pass; rail terminus; hydroelectric plant.

Orsino, Fla.: see Merritt Island.

Orsk (ôrsk), city (1926 pop. 13,581; 1939 pop. 65,799; 1946 pop. estimate 100,000), S Chkalov oblast, Russian SFSR, on Ural R., at mouth of Or R., on railroad and 150 mi. ESE of Chkalov. Major center of Orsk-Khalilovo industrial dist. (other centers: Novo-Troitsk, Mednogorsk, Khalilovo); machine mfg. (locomotives, agr. implements), nickel refining, nonferrous (aluminum) metalworking, oil cracking (550-mi.-long pipe line from Emba oil field); meat packing, flour milling, distilling, canning (fruit, tomatoes). Old city is on left bank of the Ural; new industrial city, on right bank, includes rail junction at Nikel (3 mi. W of old city; nickel works) and Novy Gorod [Rus.,= new city]. Just NE of old city is Gudron station; refractory-clay quarry. Orenburg (now Chkalov), originally founded here in 1735, moved to its present location in 1743, but the Russians here maintained a frontier stronghold called Orsk, which was chartered in 1866. Industrialization and development of new city began prior to Second World War.

Orskog, Norway: see Sjoholt.

Orsogna (ôrsô'nyä), town (pop. 4,689), Chieti prov., Abruzzi e Molise, S central Italy, 6 mi. W of Lanciano; furniture mfg. In Second World War almost completely destroyed (1943) by heavy fighting and air bombing.

Orsova (ôr'shôvä), Rum. *Orşova*, town (1948 pop. 5,107), Severin prov., SW Rumania, in Banat, on Danube R. near the Iron Gates and opposite Tekija (Yugoslavia), on railroad and 70 mi. SSE of Lugoj; transshipment point; petroleum refining; mfg. of woolen textiles, cloth, underwear, furniture. Built on the ruins of a Roman citadel, it played a prominent part in the Turco-Austrian wars (17th–18th cent.).

Orsoy (ôr'zoi), town (pop. 2,481), in former Prussian Rhine Prov., W Germany, after 1945 in North Rhine-Westphalia, in the Ruhr, port on left bank of the Rhine and 7 mi. NNW of Duisburg.

Orstavik (ûr'stävĭk), Nor. *Ørstavik*, village (pop. 1,887) in Orsta (Nor. *Ørsta*) canton (pop. 4,556), More og Romsdal co., W Norway, at head of Orsta Fjord (6-mi. inlet of North Sea), 18 mi. S of Alesund; mfg. (furniture, hosiery); mountaineering center. Formerly Orstenvik, Nor. *Ørstenvik*.

Örszallas, Yugoslavia: see Stanisic.

Orta, Lake of (ôr'tä), Novara prov., Piedmont, N Italy, 24 mi. NNW of Novara; □ 7; 8 mi. long, 1.5 mi. wide, alt. 951 ft., max. depth 469 ft. Discharges into Lago Maggiore, 7 mi. E, through outlet (N) to Toce River. Furnishes water to industries of Omegna, on N shore. Contains islet of San Giulio. Sometimes called L. Cusio.

Ortaklar (ôrtäklär'), village (pop. 2,819), Aydin prov., SW Turkey, 11 mi. NNE of Soke; rail junction.

Orta-koi, Bulgaria: see Ivailovgrad.

Orta Nova (ôr'tä nô'vä), town (pop. 9,997), Foggia prov., Apulia, S Italy, 13 mi. SE of Foggia; paper.

Orta Novarese (nôvärä'zě), village (pop. 508), Novara prov., Piedmont, N Italy, port on E shore of L. of Orta, opposite isl. of San Giulio, 23 mi. SSE of Domodossola; resort; glove mfg. Has palace (1582). On near-by hill is sanctuary (started 1590) comprising 20 chapels with frescoes and terra cottas of 16th–17th cent.

Orta San Giulio (sän jū'lyô), commune (pop. 1,068), Novara prov., Piedmont, N Italy, on L. of Orta. Comprises Orta Novarese and San Giulio. Formed in early 1930s.

Orte (ôr'tě), town (pop. 3,087), Viterbo prov., Latium, central Italy, on the Tiber and 15 mi. E of Viterbo, in cereal- and grape-growing region. Travertine quarries near by.

Ortega (ôrtā'gä), town (pop. 2,243), Tolima dept., W central Colombia, in E foothills of Cordillera Central, 36 mi. S of Ibagué; agr. center (coffee, corn, rice, tobacco, cattle). Founded 1572.

Ortegal, Cape (ôrtāgäl'), on Atlantic coast of Galicia, La Coruña prov., NW Spain, 38 mi. NE of La Coruña; generally considered southwesternmost limit of Bay of Biscay; 43°45'N 7°54'W.

Orteguaza River (ôrtāgwä'sä), Caquetá commissary, S Colombia, rises in Cordillera Oriental, flows c.100 mi. SSE, past Florencia, to Caquetá R. at Tres Esquinas.

Ortelsburg, Poland: see Szczytno.

Ortenberg (ôr'tŭnbĕrk), village (pop. 1,761), S Baden, Germany, at W foot of Black Forest, on the Kinzig and 1.5 mi. SW of Offenburg; noted for its wine. Castle, destroyed by French in 1668, was rebuilt 1834–40.

Ortenburg (-bŏŏrk), village (pop. 1,857), Lower Bavaria, Germany, 10 mi. WSW of Passau; brewing. Wheat, cattle, horses. Has Gothic church, and 16th–17th-cent. castle.

Orthez (ôrtěz'), town (pop. 4,609), Basses-Pyrénées dept., SW France, on the Gave de Pau and 24 mi. NW of Pau; market (important trade in hams) and mfg. center; electrometallurgy; produces furniture, copperware, linen goods, slaked lime; flour milling, meat preserving and salting, casein mfg. Has 13th–14th-cent. bridge, the tower of a medieval castle, and picturesque old houses. Was ⊙ Béarn until 1460. Here Wellington defeated the French in 1814.

Orthon River, Bolivia: see Orton River.

Ortiga, Cordillera de la (kôrdĭyä'rä dhä lä ôrtē'gä), Andean range in NW San Juan prov., Argentina, near Chile border; extends c.30 mi. N–S; rises to c.18,860 ft. at 29°13'S.

Ortigueira or **Santa Marta de Ortigueira** (sän'tä mär'tä dhā ôrtēgā'rä), town (pop. 1,479), La Coruña prov., NW Spain, fishing port on inlet of Bay of Biscay, SE of Cape Ortegal, and 24 mi. NE of El Ferrol; fish processing (sardines), boatbuilding; lumbering, stock raising.

Orting, town (pop. 1,299), Pierce co., W central Wash., 17 mi. SE of Tacoma and on Puyallup R.; bulbs, timber, fruit, dairy products. A state soldiers' home and a fish hatchery are here. Inc. 1889.

Ortisei (ôrtēsā'), Ger. *Sankt Ulrich*, town (pop. 1,687), Bolzano prov., Trentino–Alto Adige, N Italy, in Val Gardena, 16 mi. NE of Bolzano. Resort (alt. 4,050 ft.); wood-carving center (toys, religious articles). Has wood-carving school.

Ortiz (ôr'tĭz), village (1940 pop. 558), Conejos co., S Colo., on branch of Conejos R., in SE foothills of San Juan Mts., at N.Mex. line, and 6 mi. SSW of Conejos; alt. c.8,000 ft.

Ortiz (ôrtēs'), town (pop. 423), Guárico state, N central Venezuela, 22 mi. SSE of San Juan de los Morros; cattle raising; coffee, tobacco, hides, cheese.

Ortiz Mountains (ôr'tĭs, -tĭz), N central N.Mex., in Santa Fe co., E of Rio Grande, 25 mi. SSW of Santa Fe. Highest point, Placer Peak (8,928 ft.). Coal is mined.

Ortles (ôrtlěs'), Ger. *Ortler* (ôr'tlûr), mountain group of S zone of Ötztal Alps, in N Italy, near Swiss border, N of Adamello group, E of upper Valtellina. Highest peaks are Ortles, Ger. *Ortlerspitze* (12,792 ft.), 9 mi. ENE of Bormio, Gran Zebrù (12,661 ft.), and Monte Cevedale (12,350 ft.); Corno dei Tre Signori (11,020 ft.) is in S. Contains c.60 glaciers, largest (□ 7), 5 mi. long. Waters carried to Po R. by Adda and Oglio rivers. Sometimes considered E outliers of Rhaetian Alps.

Ortley, town (pop. 144), Roberts co., NE S.Dak., 24 mi. SSW of Sisseton.

Ortoire River (ôr'twär), SE Trinidad, B.W.I., flows 31 mi. E to the Atlantic; not navigable. Formerly called Guataro R.

Ortona (ôrtô'nä), town (pop. 9,215), Chieti prov., Abruzzi e Molise, S central Italy, port on the Adriatic, 12 mi. SE of Pescara. Fishing center; mfg. (soap, hats, macaroni, olive oil, bricks). Exports asphalt, bricks, fruit, cereals. Bishopric. Has 12th-cent. cathedral (rebuilt 18th cent.; war damage restored) and castle (1452; severely damaged). A major port from 11th to mid-15th cent., when its flotilla and arsenal were destroyed (1447) by Venetians. Severely damaged by heavy fighting (1943) in Second World War. Near by is a Br. military cemetery with c.1,600 dead. From c.1938–47 called Ortona a Mare.

Orton River (ôr'tōn), Pando dept., N Bolivia, formed by confluence of Tahuamanu River and Manuripi River at Puerto Rico; flows 120 mi. E, through tropical forest (rubber), past Ingavi and Humaitá, to Beni R. 10 mi. N of Riberalta. Navigable for entire course. Also spelled Orthon.

Ortonville. 1 Village (pop. 702), Oakland co., SE Mich., 17 mi. NNW of Pontiac, in farm area. **2** City (pop. 2,577), ⊙ Big Stone co., W Minn., on S.Dak. line, at S end of Big Stone L. (at outlet of Minnesota R.), and c.70 mi. WNW of Willmar. Resort; food-processing point (dairy products, canned corn, beverages); monuments. Granite quarries near by. Settled 1872, laid out 1873.

Orto-Tokoi or **Orto-Tokoy** (ŭrtô"-tŭkoi'). **1** Reservoir (□ 15) on Chu R., in SE Frunze oblast, Kirghiz SSR, in Boom Gorge, bet. Kirghiz Range and Kungei Ala-Tau, 15 mi. W of Rybachye; 7 mi. long. Constructed in late 1940s. **2** Reservoir, Uzbek SSR: see Kassansai.

Ortrand (ôr'tränt), town (pop. 2,518), in former Prussian Saxony prov., central Germany, after 1945 in Saxony-Anhalt, 12 mi. NE of Grossenhain; grain, potatoes, livestock.

Ortuella (ôrtwě'lyä), village (pop. 2,834), Vizcaya prov., N Spain, 8 mi. NW of Bilbao, in iron-mining region.

Ortulu (ûrtülü'), Turkish *Örtülü*, village (pop. 1,440), Erzurum prov., NE Turkey, 75 mi. NE of Erzurum; grain.

Ortygia, Sicily: see Syracuse.

Oru (ōrōō'), town, Ijebu prov., Western Provinces, SW Nigeria, 10 mi. N of Ijebu-Ode; road center; cacao and hardwood industry; rubber, palm oil and kernels, rice.

Orune (ôrōō'ně), village (pop. 4,491), Nuoro prov., E central Sardinia, 6 mi. NNE of Nuoro.

Oruro (ōrōō'rō), department (□ 20,386; 1949 pop. estimate 215,000), W Bolivia; ⊙ Oruro. Includes L. Poopó (E) and Salar de Coipasa (SW). Western Cordillera of the Andes (W) separates dept. from Chile, Cordillera de Azanaques (part of the Eastern Cordillera; E) from Potosí dept. The Altiplano (alt. over 12,000 ft.), bet. ranges, is drained by Desaguadero and Lauca rivers. Severe climate and arid soil conditions permit raising only of potatoes, *oca*, and quinoa; alpaca, sheep, and llama breeding. One of richest mineral dists. of Bolivia lies in E mtn. ranges, with main tin mines at Huanuni, Morococala, Avicaya, and Antequera. Salt, saltpeter, and sulphur deposits near Salinas de Garci Mendoza. Mfg. centered at Oruro. E part of dept. served (N–S) by Oruro-Uyuni RR.

Oruro, city (1949 pop. estimate 52,600), ⊙ Oruro dept. and Cercado prov., W Bolivia, in the Altiplano, 120 mi. SE of La Paz; 17°58′S 67°7′W; alt. 12,159 ft. Third largest city and rail hub of Bolivia, at junction of lines from La Paz, Cochabamba, and Uyuni. Ore-trading and commercial center in tin-mining region; flour milling, brewing, distilling, clothing and shoe mfg.; tin-smelting plant, railroad shops; airport. Site of govt. house, palace of justice, and other public buildings, univ. with school of mines, and mineralogical mus. Fortress (center) built 1820 by Spaniards. First settled 1595; city originally known as Real Villa de San Felipe de Austria; renamed Oruro in 1826. In colonial times, a flourishing silver-mining center (pop. c.75,000) rivaling Potosí. After a decline, Oruro again assumed importance with building of railroads and start of tin-mining industry. Tin is mined at San José (just W) and at Morococala (ESE).

Orusco (ōrōō′skō), town (pop. 1,087), Madrid prov., central Spain, on Tajuña R., on railroad and 27 mi. ESE of Madrid; olives, grain, grapes, truck produce. Mfg. of woolen goods.

Orust (ōō′rŭst″), island (□ 133; pop. 13,910), SW Sweden, in the Skagerrak, 25 mi. N of Goteborg; separated from mainland by a channel 1–3 mi. wide. Isl. is 18 mi. long, 7–9 mi. wide. Hallevikstrand (W) is chief fishing village; also several fishing ports and seaside resorts. Fish canning.

Orval (ôrväl′), village, Luxembourg prov., SE Belgium, on S slopes of the Ardennes, 10 mi. WNW of Virton; cheese-mfg. center. Remains of abbey destroyed by French in 1794. Just SSW, near Fr. frontier, is commune center of Villers-devant-Orval (vēlĕrs″-dŭvä–) (pop. 745).

Orval. 1 Town, Cher dept., France: see SAINT-AMAND-MONTROND. **2** Village (pop. 116), Manche dept., NW France, 3 mi. SSW of Coutances; paper milling, alcohol distilling.

Orvieto (ôrvyā′tō), anc. *Urbs Vetus*, town (pop. 8,883), Terni prov., Umbria, central Italy, NE of L. Bolsena, on an isolated rock (alt. 1,033 ft.) near Paglia R., opposite mouth of the Chiana, 21 mi. N of Viterbo. Agr. center; noted for its white wine; mfg. (agr. machinery, metal furniture, pottery, soap, macaroni, alcohol, chemicals). Bishopric. Has notable Romanesque, Gothic, and Renaissance bldgs. Its beautiful cathedral (begun 1290) has black and white marble façade and a chapel (Cappella Nuova) frescoed by Fra Angelico and Luca Signorelli. In Palazzo dei Papi (1297–1304; restored) is mus. with Etruscan antiquities. Probably occupies site of Etruscan town of Volsinii. Extensive remains of Etruscan necropolis near by.

Orviken (ûr′vē″kŭn), Swedish *Örviken*, village (pop. 587), Vasterbotten co., N Sweden, on islet in Gulf of Bothnia, at mouth of Skellefte R., 8 mi. SE of Skelleftea; sulphite works.

Orvinio (ôrvē′nyō), village (pop. 1,405), Rieti prov., Latium, central Italy, 17 mi. NNE of Tivoli.

Orwell, parish (pop. 1,997), Kinross, Scotland. Includes MILNATHORT.

Orwell. 1 Village (pop. c.500), Oswego co., N central N.Y., 27 mi. NE of Oswego; furniture mfg. **2** Village (pop. 759), Ashtabula co., extreme NE Ohio, c.40 mi. E of Cleveland, in fruit, dairy, grain, and poultry area. **3** Town (pop. 902), Addison co., W Vt., on L. Champlain and 21 mi. NW of Rutland; wood and dairy products; poultry, fruit, truck.

Orwell Bay, inlet (10 mi. long, mouth 4 mi. wide, S P.E.I., opening SE from Hillsborough Bay.

Orwell River, Suffolk, England, rises as Gipping R. in several headstreams near Stowmarket, flows 21 mi. SE, past Stowmarket, Needham Market, and Ipswich (where it becomes Orwell R.), to Stour R. estuary opposite Harwich.

Orwigsburg (ôr′wĭgzbûrg), borough (pop. 2,309), Schuylkill co., E central Pa., 5 mi. ESE of Pottsville; shoes, textiles. Settled 1747, laid out 1796, inc. 1813.

Oryakhovitsa (ôryä′khôvētsä), village (pop. 4,554), Pleven dist., N Bulgaria, on Iskar R. and 17 mi. NW of Pleven; wheat, corn, livestock.

Oryakhovo (ôryä′khôvô), city (pop. 6,972), Vratsa dist., N Bulgaria, port on right bank of the Danube (Rum. border), opposite mouth of Jiu R., and 40 mi. NNE of Vratsa; rail terminus; agr. center (grain and fruit exports). Has ruins of Roman castles. Scene of defeat of Turks by Stephen the Great (1475). Formerly Rakhovo (later spelled Rahova), and Orekhovo or Oryekhovo until 1945.

Oryen, mountain, Yugoslavia: see ORJEN.

Oryokko, Korea and Manchuria: see YALU RIVER.

Orzhitsa (ŭrzhē′tsŭ), village (1926 pop. 3,654), W central Poltava oblast, Ukrainian SSR, 20 mi. SW of Lubny; wheat. Peat bogs.

Orzhits River, Poland: see ORZYC RIVER.

Orzinuovi (ôrtsēnwô′vē), town (pop. 4,340), Brescia prov., Lombardy, N Italy, near Oglio R., 17 mi. SW of Brescia; foundries. Built 1193 by Brescia as fortress against Cremona.

Orzyc River (ô′zhĭts), Ger. *Orschütz* (ôr′shüts), Rus. *Orzhits* (ôr′zhĭts), N Poland, rises 4 mi. ENE of Mlawa, flows NNE and SSE, past Chorzele and Makow Mazowiecki, to Narew R. 7 mi. NE of Pultusk; 84 mi. long.

Orzysz (ô′zhĭsh), Ger. *Arys* (ä′rĭs), town (1939 pop. 3,553; 1946 pop. 795) in East Prussia, after 1945 in Olsztyn prov., NE Poland, in Masurian Lakes region, 17 mi. W of Elk; grain, cattle; sawmilling. Chartered 1726.

Os, Netherlands: see OSS.

Os (ōs), village (pop. 717; canton pop. 4,993), Hordaland co., SW Norway, port on Bjorna Fjord, 15 mi. SSE of Bergen; terminus of narrow-gauge railroad to Nesttun. Mfg. of furniture.

Osa, canton, Costa Rica: see PUERTO CORTÉS.

Osa, Norway: see BYGLAND.

Osa (ŭsä′). **1** Village (1948 pop. over 500), central Ust-Orda Buryat-Mongol Natl. Okrug, Irkutsk oblast, Russian SFSR, 35 mi. NE of Cheremkhovo; dairy farming. **2** City (1926 pop. 5,876), SW Molotov oblast, Russian SFSR, port on left bank of Kama R. and 60 mi. SW of Molotov; metal- and woodworking, sawmilling, shoe mfg. Teachers col. An old Khanty (Ostyak) village; became Rus. town of Nikolskaya Sloboda in 1557; fortified and renamed Osa in 1737; captured (1744) by peasant rebels under Yemelyan Pugachev.

Osa de la Vega (ō′sä dhā lä vā′gä), town (pop. 1,380), Cuenca prov., E central Spain, in La Mancha, 45 mi. SW of Cuenca; cereals, grapes, olives, saffron, sheep, goats.

Osage (ōsāj′, ō′sāj). **1** County (□ 721; pop. 12,811), E Kansas; ⊙ Lyndon. Gently rolling plains area, drained by Marais des Cygnes R. (mûrā″ dŭ sēn′, mĕ″rŭ). Livestock, grain. Bituminous-coal mining. Formed 1859. **2** County (□ 601; pop. 11,301), central Mo.; ⊙ Linn. In Ozark region, on Missouri (N) and Osage (W) rivers; drained by Gasconade R. Agr. (corn, wheat, hay, potatoes), livestock; fire-clay, lead mines. Formed 1841. **3** County (□ 2,293; pop. 33,071), coextensive with Osage Indian Reservation, N Okla.; ⊙ Pawhuska, Osage agency hq. Largest co. in Okla.; bounded N by Kansas line, SW by Arkansas R.; drained by Caney R. and Bird Creek; hilly in W. Cattle-ranching and petroleum-producing area, with some agr. (wheat, cotton; dairy products); oil refineries, gasoline plants; some farm-products processing, mfg. Includes Osage Hills State Park. Formed 1907.

Osage. 1 City (pop. 3,436), ⊙ Mitchell co., N Iowa, near Cedar R. and 22 mi. ENE of Mason City; dried eggs, dressed poultry, feed, woolen mittens, lime, wood products. Limestone quarries, sand and gravel pits near by. Settled 1853, inc. 1871. **2 or Osage City**, town (pop. 425), Osage co., N Okla., 25 mi. WNW of Tulsa, and on Arkansas R., in agr. area. **3** Village, Weston co., NE Wyo., 14 mi. NW of Newcastle; alt. c.4,300 ft.; oil refining.

Osage City, city (pop. 1,919), Osage co., E Kansas, 30 mi. SSW of Topeka; trade center for livestock, grain, and coal-mining area. Settled 1865 near Santa Fe Trail; inc. 1872.

Osage River, Mo., formed SE of Rich Hill, W Mo., by junction of Marais des Cygnes R. and Little Osage R., flows SE and E, past Osceola, then NE, widening into LAKE OF THE OZARKS (c.130 mi. long) impounded by BAGNELL DAM (head of navigation), thence NE to Missouri R. E of Jefferson City; c.360 mi. long (including lake); c.500 mi. long, including the Marais des Cygnes. Power plants at Bagnell, Osceola.

Osa Gulf, Costa Rica: see DULCE, GOLFO.

Osaka (ō′säkä), prefecture [Jap. *fu*] (□ 700; 1940 pop. 4,792,966; 1947 pop. 3,334,659), S Honshu, Japan; ⊙ Osaka, its principal port. Bounded W by Osaka Bay (E arm of Inland Sea). Interior has rugged terrain; coastal area is generally flat and fertile, with most of urban centers on wide Osaka plain. Engineering works, chemical plants, textile mills, celluloid and rubber-goods factories. Important home industries are weaving, woodworking. Extensive production of rice, wheat, fruit (peaches, citrus fruit, pears); poultry raising, flour milling, lumbering, raw-silk production. Chief centers: Osaka, SAKAI, FUSE, KISHIWADA, SUITA, TOYONAKA, KAIZUKA, IKEDA, TAKATSUKI.

Osaka. 1 (ō′säkä) Town (pop. 6,376), Gifu prefecture, central Honshu, Japan, 13 mi. S of Takayama; rice, raw silk, charcoal, lumber. Hot springs. **2** (ōsä′kŭ, ō′säkä) Second largest city (□ 71; 1940 pop. 3,252,340; 1947 pop. 1,559,310) of Japan, ⊙ Osaka prefecture, S Honshu, port on Osaka Bay, at mouth of Yodo R., 250 mi. WSW of Tokyo; 34°40′N 135°31′E. Principal industrial and commercial center of Japan. Focal point of a continuous industrial belt on N and NE shores of Osaka Bay comprising Kobe, Nishinomiya, Amagasaki (adjacent to Osaka), and several smaller cities. Has shipyards, textile mills, blast furnaces, steel mills, metallurgical and chemical plants. Exports cotton textiles, machinery, woolen yarn, metal (copper, gold, silver, aluminum) products. Situated on a wide, fertile plain, intersected by many canals. A major transportation center; terminus of important railroads connecting it with all other major centers and of electric railways from surrounding towns. Air transport service bet. Tokyo and Osaka. Seat of Osaka Imperial Univ., Kansai Univ., and Osaka Univ. of Commerce. City is a theatrical center, known particularly for puppet shows at the Bunrakuza. Has 6th-cent. Buddhist temple and ruins of Hideyoshi's castle (16th cent.). Tennoji Park (57 acres) contains botanical gardens, art and science mus. Known as Naniwa, Osaka was ⊙ Japan in 4th cent. Its importance as a commercial center dates from 16th cent., when Hideyoshi made it his hq. Port was open (1868) to foreign trade. City heavily bombed (1945) in Second World War.

Osaka (ōsä′kŭ, ōsä′kŭ), village (pop. 1,822, with near-by Roda), Wise co., SW Va., 5 mi. N of Big Stone Gap in coal-mining region of the Cumberlands.

Osaka Bay (ōsä′kŭ, ō′säkä) E arm of Inland Sea, Japan, bet. Awaji-shima (W) and S coast of Honshu; merges with Harima Sea (W); connected with Philippine Sea (S) by Kii Channel; 35 mi. long, 20 mi. wide. Osaka is on NE shore. Part of Kii Peninsula forms E shore.

Osakabe (ōsä′kä′bā), town (pop. 3,407), Okayama prefecture, SW Honshu, Japan, 25 mi. W of Tsuyama, in agr. area (rice, wheat); raw silk, persimmons, sake, *konnyaku* (paste made from devil's tongue).

Osakarovka (ŭsŭkä′rŭfkŭ), village, NE Karaganda oblast, Kazakh SSR, on railroad and 50 mi. NNW of Karaganda, in cattle area.

Osaki (ō′säkē), town (pop. 17,973), Kagoshima prefecture, S Kyushu, Japan, on E Osumi Peninsula 29 mi. ESE of Kagoshima; agr. center (rice, sweet potatoes). Town of BANSEI, SW of Kagoshima, is sometimes called Osaki.

Osaki-kami-shima (ō′säkē-kä′mē-shĭmä), island (□ 16; pop. 24,277 including offshore islets), Hiroshima prefecture, Japan, in Hiuchi Sea, 3 mi. S of Takehara on SW Honshu, just W of Omi-shima; 5 mi. long, 4 mi. wide. Mountainous, fertile (fruitgrowing). Kinoe (E) is chief town.

Osakis (ōsā′kĭs), resort village (pop. 1,488), Douglas and Todd counties, W Minn., at S end of L. Osakis, 11 mi. E of Alexandria, in grain, poultry area; dairy products.

Osakis, Lake (□ 10), in Todd and Douglas counties, W Minn., 10 mi. E of Alexandria; 8 mi. long, 2 mi. wide. Drains into small affluent of Long Prairie R. Fishing, boating, bathing.

Osaki-shimo-shima (ō′säkē-shĭmō″-shĭmä), island (□ 6; pop. c.11,500, including offshore islets), Hiroshima prefecture, Japan, in Hiuchi Sea, just SW of Osaki-kami-shima, 10 mi. SE of Kure; 4 mi. long, 2 mi. wide. Hilly, fertile (fruitgrowing). Fishing.

Osam River (ô′säm), N Bulgaria, formed N of Troyan by confluence of Beli Osam and Cherni Osam rivers, which rise in Troyan Mts.; flows N, past Lovech, NE, and NW, past Levski, to the Danube 3 mi. W of Nikopol; 207 mi. long. Sometimes called Osma R.

Osa Peninsula (ō′sä), on the Pacific in S Costa Rica; 35 mi. long, 10–15 mi. wide. Separated from the mainland by the Golfo Dulce (E).

Osarizawa (ōsärē′zäwŭ), town (pop. 9,234), Akita prefecture, N Honshu, Japan, just W of Hanawa; mining center (gold, copper).

Osasco (ōōsä′skōō), W suburb of São Paulo city, SE São Paulo, Brazil, on Tietê R., and on railroad to Sorocaba; meat packing, mfg. of rolling stock.

Osawa (ō′säwä), town (pop. 5,258), Saitama prefecture, central Honshu, Japan, 8 mi. E of Urawa; rice, wheat.

Osawano (ō′säwänō), town (pop. 8,973), Toyama prefecture, central Honshu, Japan, 8 mi. S of Toyama, in agr. area (rice, wheat); patent medicine.

Osawatomie (ō″sŭwŏ′tŭmē, ō″sŭ–), city (pop. 4,347), Miami co., E Kansas, on Marais des Cygnes R., at mouth of Pottawatomie Creek, and c.45 mi. SSW of Kansas City; trade center, with railroad repair shops, in diversified agr. and fruitgrowing region. Oil and gas wells near by. Has state hosp. for insane. Founded 1855, inc. 1883. Was once a station on Underground Railroad. Memorial park includes statue of John Brown and cabin occupied by him (1856). A marble shaft honors 5 of Brown's men who were killed in battle with proslavery men.

Osborn (ŏz′bûrn). **1** Town (pop. 237), De Kalb and Clinton counties, NW Mo., 26 mi. E of St. Joseph; ships cattle, grain. **2** Former village, Ohio: see FAIRBORN.

Osborne (ŏz′bûrn), district of Cowes, on Isle of Wight, Hampshire, England, just E of the town; site of Osborne House (1846), summer residence and place of death of Queen Victoria. Presented to nation by Edward VII, it is now convalescent home.

Osborne, county (□ 898; pop. 8,558), N central Kansas; ⊙ Osborne. Rolling plain, drained by South Fork Solomon R. Livestock, grain. Formed 1871.

Osborne. 1 City (pop. 2,068), ⊙ Osborne co., N Kansas, on South Fork of Solomon R. and 70 mi. NW of Salina; shipping center for livestock and grain area; monument works. Founded 1871, inc. 1879. **2** Borough (pop. 496), Allegheny co., SW Pa., opposite Coraopolis on Ohio R., NW of Pittsburgh.

Osborne Park, town (pop. 4,546), SW Western Australia, N suburb of Perth; dairying center.

Osbornsville, village (pop. 1,619, with near-by Breton Woods), Ocean co., E N.J., 7 mi. NNE of Toms River. Sometimes Osbornville.

Osby (ōōs′bü″), town (pop. 2,755), Kristianstad co., S Sweden, on N side of Osby L. (3 mi. long), 18 mi. NNE of Hassleholm; paper- and sawmilling, furniture mfg.; tourist resort. Agr. col. Has Danish fortifications, built 1611.

Osca, Spain: see HUESCA, city.

Oscarsborg (ôs′kärsbôr″), fortress on islet at N end of Oslo Fjord narrows, Akershus co., SE Norway, 18 mi. S of Oslo. During German invasion (April, 1940), its guns sank cruiser *Blücher*. Sometimes spelled Oskarsborg.

Oscarville, village (pop. 27), SW Alaska, near Bethel.

Oscawana (ŏskuwä′nu), summer-resort village, Putnam co., SE N.Y., on Oscawana L. (2 mi. long, c.½ mi. wide), 8 mi. NNE of Peekskill, in dairying and farming area.

Oscela, Italy: see DOMODOSSOLA.

Osceola. 1 (ŏsēō′lu) County (□ 1,325; pop. 11,406), central Fla.; ⊙ Kissimmee. Lowland area with many lakes (notably Kissimmee, Tohopekaliga, and East Tohopekaliga), and streams of Kissimmee R. system. Citrus fruit, truck, cattle, lumber. Formed 1887. **2** (ōsēō′lu, ōsē–) County (□ 398; pop. 10,181), NW Iowa, on Minn. line; ⊙ Sibley. Prairie agr. area (hogs, cattle, poultry, corn oats, wheat), rising to highest alt. (1,675 ft.) in Iowa near OCHEYEDAN; drained by Ocheyedan R. Formed 1851. **3** (ōsēō′lu) County (□ 581; pop. 13,797), central Mich.; ⊙ Reed City. Intersected by Muskegon R. and drained by small South Branch of Manistee R. Agr. (livestock, grain, potatoes, corn, hay; dairy products). Some mfg. at Reed City. Resorts; hunting, fishing. Part of Manistee Natl. Forest is in W. Organized 1869.

Osceola. 1 (ōsēō′lu) City (pop. 5,006), a ⊙ Mississippi co., NE Ark., 15 mi. S of Blytheville and on Mississippi R., in rich cotton area; mfg. of cottonseed-oil pressing, cotton ginning, sawmilling. Inc. 1838. **2** (ōsēō′lu) Town (pop. 1,091), St. Joseph co., N Ind., 10 mi. E of South Bend and on St. Joseph R. **3** (ōsēō′lu, ōsē–) City (pop. 3,422), ⊙Clarke co., S Iowa, near Whitebreast Creek, c.40 mi. SSW of Des Moines; mfg. (lingerie, dairy products). Settled 1850, inc. 1859. **4** (ōsēō′lu, ō′sēōlu) City (pop. 1,082), ⊙ St. Clair co., W Mo., on Osage R. (hydroelectric plant) and 85 mi. SSE of Kansas City; resort; agr.; coal mines. **5** (ōsēō′lu) City (pop. 1,098), ⊙ Polk co., E central Nebr., 50 mi. NW of Lincoln and on branch of Big Blue R.; brooms; livestock, dairy and poultry produce, grain. Founded c.1872. **6** or **Osceola Mills** (ōsēō′lu), borough (pop. 1,992), Clearfield co., central Pa., 25 mi. NNE of Altoona; bituminous coal; clay, lumber, and metal products; field crops. Laid out c.1857, inc. 1864. There is a village, Osceola, in Tioga co. **7** (ōsēō′lu) Resort village (pop. 700), Polk co., W Wis., on St. Croix R. and 19 mi. NNE of Stillwater (Minn.), in dairying and stock-raising area; cheese, wooden boxes, linseed oil.

Osceola, Mount (ŏsēō′lu), peak (4,326 ft.) of White Mts., Grafton co., central N.H., near Waterville Valley.

Osceola Park (ōsēō′lu), village (pop. 1,392, with adjacent Pine Tree Park), Broward co., S Fla.

Oschatz (ô′shäts, ō′–), town (pop. 15,331), Saxony, E central Germany, 30 mi. E of Leipzig; woolen and felt milling, sugar refining; mfg. of shoes, furniture, electrical equipment, chemicals, glass, paper products, scales. Has 15th-cent. church, 16th-cent. town hall.

Oschersleben (ô′shursla″bun), town (pop. 21,011), in former Prussian Saxony prov., central Germany, after 1945 in Saxony-Anhalt, on the Bode and 19 mi. WSW of Magdeburg, 14 mi. ESE of Jerxheim; sugar refining, malting; mfg. of light metals, agr. machinery, chemicals, cigars, food products.

Oschiri (ô′skērē), village (pop. 3,098), Sassari prov., N Sardinia, 28 mi. E of Sassari, near mouth of Mannu d'Oschiri R.

Oscoda (ŏskō′du), county (□ 565; pop. 3,134), NE central Mich.; ⊙ Mio. Intersected by Au Sable R., and drained by Upper South Branch of Thunder Bay R. Stock raising and agr. (potatoes, grain); dairy products; hardwood timber. Recreational area (hunting, fishing). Includes part of Huron Natl. Forest and several small lakes. Organized 1881.

Oscoda, village (pop. c.600), Iosco co., NE Mich., c.45 mi. SE of Alpena, on L. Huron at mouth of Au Sable R. Trade center for resort and farm area (poultry, truck, potatoes; dairy products); fisheries. U.S. Air Force base near by.

Oscura Peak (ŏskōō′ru) (8,732 ft.), highest point in SIERRA OSCURA, S central N.Mex., 29 mi. W of Carrizozo. First atomic bomb was exploded (July 16, 1945) near by.

Oscuro, Cerro (sĕ′rō ōskōō′rō), peak (over 7,000 ft.) in main Andean divide, on Guatemala-Honduras border, 10 mi. E of Esquipulas, Guatemala.

Ose, Norway: see BYGLAND.

Oseberg (ō′sùbûrg″, –băr″), village in Sem canton, Vestfold co., SE Norway, 3 mi. NE of Tonsberg; scene (1903) of excavation of well-preserved, 9th-cent. viking ship, now in Oslo mus.

Ösede, Germany: see OESEDE.

Osek (ô′sĕk), Ger. *Osseg* (ô′sùk), town (pop. 5,852), NW Bohemia, Czechoslovakia, in NE foothills of the Erzgebirge, on railroad and 6 mi. WSW of Teplice; deep-shaft coal mining. Has famous Cistercian abbey founded in 12th cent.

Osek, Germany: see HOHER BOGEN.

Osel, Estonia: see SAARE.

Osen (ō′sun), canton (pop. 1,684), Sor-Trondelag co., central Norway, on North Sea, 60 mi. N of Trondheim; fishing center; beacon light.

Oseras, Altos de las (äl′tōs dā läs ōsä′räs), Andean massif (12,565 ft.), W central Colombia, in Cordillera Oriental, 60 mi. SSW of Bogotá; S point of Páramo de Sumapaz.

Osetia: see NORTH OSSETIAN AUTONOMOUS SOVIET SOCIALIST REPUBLIC, Russian SFSR; SOUTH OSSETIAN AUTONOMOUS OBLAST, Georgian SSR.

Osetrovo (ŭsyĭtrô′vù), town (1939 pop. over 500), N Irkutsk oblast, Russian SFSR, on Lena R. just NE of Ust-Kut; shipbuilding.

Osgood (ŏz′gŏŏd). **1** Town (pop. 1,228), Ripley co., SE Ind., 18 mi. SE of Greensburg; farm trading center, with some mfg. (wood and cement products, polo balls, condensed milk); timber; limestone quarries. **2** Town (pop. 173), Sullivan co., N Mo., 12 mi. W of Milan. **3** Village (pop. 194), Darke co., W Ohio, 18 mi. NNE of Greenville, in agr. area.

Osgoode Station, village (pop. estimate 400), SE Ont., near Rideau R. and Rideau Canal, 20 mi. S of Ottawa; dairying, mixed farming.

Osgood Mountains, N Nev., in E Humboldt co.; Adam Peak (8,651 ft.), 25 mi. NE of Winnemucca, is highest point. Gold mining, tungsten deposits.

Osh (ôsh), oblast (□ 17,000; 1946 pop. estimate 400,000), SW Kirghiz SSR; ⊙ Osh. On N slopes of Alai and Turkestan ranges, except for Alai Valley, which is on S slope of Alai Range; includes S fringe of Fergana Valley (N; site of cotton area). Wheat and livestock in mtn. valleys. Extensive coal mining (Sulyukta, Kizyl-Kiya, Uzgen), antimony and mercury (Frunze, Khaidarkan, Chauvai); sericulture near Osh. Pop.: Kirghiz, Uzbeks. Formed 1939.

Osh, city (1939 pop. 33,315), ⊙ Osh oblast, Kirghiz SSR, 30 mi. SE of Andizhan, 185 mi. SW of Frunze (linked by road), on Uzbek border; 40°32′N 72°48′E. Largest city in Kirghiz section of Fergana Valley; rail terminus; end of Pamir mtn. highway to Khorog; freight transfer point. Major silk-milling center; spinning, mfg. of silk goods, cocoon production, food processing (meat, flour, canned goods), tobacco products; lime and brickworks. Teachers col. Sanatorium near by (climatic cures). Consists of lower old Oriental city and higher new Rus. section, 2 mi. apart. Contains odd-shaped rock, Tash-Suleiman [Solomon's throne], once visited by pilgrims. One of oldest towns of Central Asia, Osh became a leading silk center after 8th cent.

Oshamambe (ōshä′-mäm′bā), town (pop. 13,055), SW Hokkaido, Japan, on NW shore of Uchiura Bay, 34 mi. WNW of Muroran; gold and silver mining, agr. (wheat, potatoes, soybeans).

Oshan (ŭ′shän′), town (pop. 5,209), ⊙ Oshan co. (pop. 40,718), S central Yunnan prov., China, 60 mi. SSW of Kunming and on road to Burma; alt. 5,387 ft.; iron smelting; rice, wheat, millet, beans. Until 1929 called Siwo.

Osha River (ô′shù), central Omsk oblast, Russian SFSR, rises in small L. Saltaim, 25 mi. NW of Tyukalinsk, flows c.150 mi. ENE, past Staro-Soldatskoye and Kolosovka, and N to Irtysh R. below Znamenskoye.

O'Shaughnessy Dam, Calif.: see HETCH HETCHY VALLEY.

Oshawa (ŏ′shuwu), city (pop. 26,813), S Ont., on L. Ontario, 30 mi. ENE of Toronto; automobile works, woolen mills, foundries; mfg. of steel products, glass, pottery, radios, leather.

Oshchepkovo, Russian SFSR: see PYSHMA, town.

Oshi (ō′shē), town (pop. 31,075), Saitama prefecture, central Honshu, Japan, 4 mi. E of Kumagaya; produces *tabi* (a kind of sock); rice, wheat, raw silk.

Oshima (ō′shĭmä), fishing town (pop. 4,859), Kumamoto prefecture, W Kyushu, Japan, 4 mi. W of Kumamoto, on Shimabara Bay.

O-shima (ō′shĭmä). **1** Island (□ 17; pop. 20,045), Ehime prefecture, Japan, in Hiuchi Sea, just off N coast of Shikoku, NE of Imabari; 6 mi. long, 3 mi. wide; hilly, fertile (rice, wheat, fruit). Sake brewery, fishery. **2** Largest and northernmost island (□ 35; pop. 11,627) of isl. group Izu-shichito, Greater Tokyo, Japan, at entrance to Sagami Bay of central Honshu, 50 mi. SSW of Tokyo; 34°44′N 139°24′E; 9 mi. long, 5 mi. wide. Mountainous; rises to 2,477 ft. at Mt. MIHARA. Dense vegetation. Oshima Park, on N end of isl., is maintained by city of Tokyo. Dairying, fishing, agr. Produces camellia oil, charcoal, raw silk. Isl. used as penal colony until c.1870. MOTOMURA is principal town. Formerly sometimes called Vries Isl., for 17th-cent. Du. navigator Maarten Gerritz Vries. **3** Island (□ 6; pop. 5,323, including offshore islets), Nagasaki prefecture, Japan, in E. China Sea, 22 mi. NNW of Sasebo, Kyushu, N of Hirado-shima; 33°28′N 129°33′E; 5 mi. long, 3 mi. wide. Fishing. Sometimes called Oko-shima. **4** Island (□ 5; pop. 11,164, including offshore islets), Nagasaki prefecture, Japan, in E.China Sea just off NNW coast of Sonogi Peninsula, Kyushu, 9 mi. SW of Sasebo; 33°3′N 129°37′E; 3.5 mi. long, 1.5 mi. wide; fishing. **5** Island, Ryukyu Isls.: see AMAMI-O-SHIMA. **6** Island (□ 1.5; pop. 3,271), Wakayama prefecture, Japan, in Kumano Sea, just E of Shio Point on S Kii Peninsula in S Honshu; shelters Kushimoto harbor; 3 mi. long, 1 mi. wide; tourist resort. **7** Island (□ 54; pop. 64,928, including offshore islets), Yamaguchi prefecture, Japan, in Iyo Sea, just SE of Yanai on SW Honshu; 8 mi. long (with narrow E peninsula 11 mi. long), 6 mi. wide. Mountainous; rises to 2,280 ft. Fertile soil; agr. (rice, wheat, oranges). Fishing. Agenosho, on S coast, is chief town.

Oshin, Korea: see ONGJIN.

Oshio (ō′shēō), town (pop. 6,591), Hyogo prefecture, S Honshu, Japan, on Harima Sea, 5 mi. SE of Himeji; rice, wheat; saltmaking.

Oshkosh (ŏsh′kŏsh″). **1** Village (pop. 1,124), ⊙ Garden co., W Nebr., 75 mi. ESE of Scottsbluff and on N.Platte R., in irrigated sugar-beet region; livestock, grain. **2** City (pop. 41,084), ⊙ Winnebago co., E central Wis., on W shore of L. Winnebago, at mouth of Upper Fox R. and 75 mi. NNW of Milwaukee, in resort area; industrial center (woodwork, machinery, automobile parts, clothing, leather goods). A state teachers col. is here. Has a mus. Father Allouez visited the site in 1670; a French fur-trading post was set up here in early-19th cent. Settled 1836; inc. as village in 1846, as city in 1853.

Oshkurya or **Oshkur'ya** (ŭshkōōr′yŭ), town (1946 pop. over 500), N Komi Autonomous SSR, Russian SFSR, on Pechora R. (landing) and 8 mi. NW of (opposite) Ust-Usa.

Oshmyany (ŭshmyä′nē), Pol. *Oszmiana* (ŏshmyä′-nä), city (1931 pop. 7,334), W Molodechno oblast, Belorussian SSR, 28 mi. ESE of Vilna; agr.-processing center (hides, grain, potatoes, hops); sawmilling, brick mfg. Has ruins of 17th-cent. churches. Old Rus. settlement; successively captured by Lithuanians, Teutonic Knights (1384), and Poles. Passed (1795) from Poland to Russia; reverted (1921) to Poland; ceded to USSR in 1945.

Oshnuiyeh, Iran: see USHNUIYEH.

Oshogbo (ōshōb′bō), town (pop. 49,599), Oyo prov., Western Provinces, SW Nigeria, on railroad and 50 mi. NE of Ibadan; major cacao-industry center; cotton weaving; tobacco products, palm oil and kernels; agr. (cotton, yams, cassava, corn, plantains). Has hosp.

Oshta (ôsh′tŭ), village (1939 pop. over 500), NW Vologda oblast, Russian SFSR, near L. Onega, 32 mi. WSW of Vytegra; coarse grain.

Oshwe (ōsh′wā), village, Leopoldville prov., W Belgian Congo, on left bank of Lukenie R. and 130 mi. SE of Inongo; steamboat landing and trading center; fibers, copal.

Osicala (ōsēkä′lä), city (pop. 910), Morazán dept., E Salvador, 9 mi. NNW of San Francisco; henequen, sugar cane, coffee, livestock raising. Dept. ⊙, 1875–87.

Osieczna (ô-shĕch′nä), Ger. *Storchnest* (shtôrkh′-nĕst), town (1946 pop. 1,323), Poznan prov., W Poland, 6 mi. NE of Leszno; cement mfg., flour milling; trades in horses, pigs.

Osierfield, town (pop. 147), Irwin co., S central Ga., 8 mi. ESE of Fitzgerald.

Osijek (ô′sĭyĕk), Hung. *Eszék* (ĕs′āk), Ger. *Esseg* (ĕs′ĕk), anc. *Mursa Major*, city (pop. 50,398), ⊙ Osijek oblast (formed 1949), NE Croatia, Yugoslavia, port on Drava R. (head of passenger navigation) and 130 mi. E of Zagreb, across river from the Baranja. Chief city of Slavonia and of the Podravina; trade and transportation center, a hub of several rail lines; industrial center; petroleum refinery (gasoline, kerosene, lubricants), electrical plant; woodworking (lumber, furniture, matches), sugar milling (sugar, molasses, dried beet pulp), flour milling, machine mfg., chemicals. Anc. Roman colony; became bishopric in 4th cent.; 1st mentioned as Osijek in 12th cent.

Osilo (ô′zēlô), village (pop. 4,903), Sassari prov., NW Sardinia, 6 mi. E of Sassari; home weaving.

Osimo (ô′zēmô), anc. *Auximum*, town (pop. 6,817), Ancona prov., The Marches, central Italy, 9 mi. S of Ancona; mfg. (harmoniums, harmonicas, silk textiles, metal products, plastics, soap, macaroni). Bishopric. Has cathedral and remains of Roman walls.

Osinniki (ŭsē′nyĭkē), city (1939 pop. over 10,000), SW Kemerovo oblast, Russian SFSR, on branch of Trans-Siberian RR (Kandalep station) and 14 mi. SE of Stalinsk; coal-mining center in Kuznetsk Basin. Developed in 1930s. Large coal-fed power plant (Rus. abbr. *Yuzhkuzbassgres*), serving S Kuznetsk Basin and the Gornaya Shoriya, is on Kondoma R. near Shushtalep coal field, 5 mi. SW of Osinniki.

Osintorf (ŭsēntôrf′), town (1939 pop. over 2,000), SE Vitebsk oblast, Belorussian SSR, 13 mi. NE of Orsha; peat works supply Belgres power plant at Orekhovsk (W).

Osio Sotto (ô'zyô sôt'tô), village (pop. 2,850), Bergamo prov., Lombardy, N Italy, 7 mi. SSW of Bergamo.

Osipee or **Ossipee** (ŏ'sĭpē), village (1940 pop. 693), Alamance co., N central N.C., on Haw R. and 7 mi. NNW of Burlington; rayon mfg.

Osipenko (Rus. ŭsē'pyĭnkŭ, Ukr. ŭsĭpyĕn'kô), city (1939 pop. 51,664), SE Zaporozhe oblast, Ukrainian SSR, port on Sea of Azov, 100 mi. SE of Zaporozhe; rail terminus; mfg. (agr. machinery, road-building equipment), vegetable canning, tanning, flour milling. Teachers col. Exports grain, imports petroleum. Developed in 19th cent.; until 1939, called Berdyansk. Health and beach resort (mud baths) is on sandspit S of city.

Osipovichi (ô'sĭpŭvēchē), city (1948 pop. over 10,000), N Bobruisk oblast, Belorussian SSR, near Svisloch R., 60 mi. SE of Minsk; rail junction (repair shops); lumber center; wood distilling, food and light industries.

Osisko Lake (ōsĭ'skō) (2 mi. long, 2 mi. wide), W Que. On W shore are mining centers of Rouyn and Noranda.

Osjecenica or **Osyechenitsa** (both: ô'syĕchĕ"nētsä), Serbo-Croatian *Osječenica*, mountain in Dinaric Alps, W Bosnia, Yugoslavia, along lower right bank of Unac R.; highest point (5,888 ft.) is 7 mi. WSW of Bosanski Petrovac.

Oskaloosa (ŏskùlōō'sù). **1** City (pop. 11,124), ⊙ Mahaska co., S central Iowa, 23 mi. NNW of Ottumwa, bet. Des Moines and Skunk rivers; trade and processing center for farm and livestock area. Mfg. of overalls, tile, brick, valves, feeds, metal and wood products; food packing (soups, poultry, dairy products); music publishing. Many musicians and composers, including Thurlow Lieurance, b. here. Scene of annual Quakers' meeting and regional fair. City contains William Penn Col. (1873) and statue (by Sherry Fry) of Indian chief Mahaska. Kletzing Col. is at adjacent University Park. Settled by Quakers 1843; inc. 1853. **2** City (pop. 721), ⊙ Jefferson co., NE Kansas, 23 mi. NE of Topeka; trading point in grain, livestock, and dairy region.

Oskarsborg, Norway: see OSCARSBORG.

Oskarshamn (ôs"kärs-hä'mŭn), city (1950 pop. 10,707), Kalmar co., SE Sweden, on Kalmar Sound (Baltic), 40 mi. N of Kalmar; 57°16'N 16°28'E. Seaport, with shipyards, copper smelters, paper mills, stone quarries; mfg. of machinery, storage batteries. Inc. 1856.

Oskarstrom (ôs'kärstrûm"), Swedish *Oskarström*, village (pop. 2,653), Halland co., SW Sweden, on Nissa R. and 10 mi. NNE of Halmstad; linen, jute, and paper mills.

Oskol River (ŭskôl'), in W central European USSR, rises ESE of Kursk in Central Russian Upland, flows 285 mi. S, past Stary Oskol, Novy Oskol, Valuiki, and Kupyansk, to Northern Donets R. E of Izyum. High right bank; timber floating in spring.

Osku, Iran: see USKU.

Öslau (ûs'lou), village (pop. 2,219), Upper Franconia, N Bavaria, Germany, on Itz R. and 4 mi. ENE of Coburg; mfg. (precision instruments, pottery). Clay pits near by.

Oslavany (ô'slävänĭ), Ger. *Oslawan*, village (pop. 3,802), S Moravia, Czechoslovakia, 13 mi. WSW of Brno; rail terminus; coal-mining center; large power plant. Graphite and asbestos deposits in vicinity.

Osler (ōs'lùr, ŏz'–), village (pop. estimate 200), central Sask., 18 mi. NNE of Saskatoon; mixed farming, dairying.

Oslo (ŏs'lō, ŏz'lō, Nor. ôs'lô, ŏŏs'lōō), city (□ 175; pop. 417,238) and a county in itself, ⊙ Norway, in SE part of country, on hill slope at head of Oslo Fjord, an inlet of the Skagerrak; 59°55'N 10°45'E. Largest city in Norway, and the chief industrial, commercial, and cultural center; seaport, ice-free the year round; rail and airline hub (airports at GARDERMOEN and FORNEBU). Seat of univ. (founded 1811), Lutheran bishopric, and the Nobel Institute. Oslo is modern in design and character, and its planned residential sections make it a slumless city. Karl Johans Gate, its main thoroughfare, leads from main railroad station (E), past the Storting (parliament) bldg., the univ., and the natl. theater, to the royal palace (built 1848). City hall, inaugurated 1950 during city's 900th anniversary celebrations, and Akershus fortress (c.1300; royal residence, 1319–80) overlook harbor. Of Oslo's many museums, the best-known are City Mus. in 18th-cent. manor house of FROGNERSETEREN, with adjacent Ski Mus. and surrounded by Frogner Park; Vigeland Mus. and Vigeland Park, where works of the sculptor Vigeland, who was sponsored by Oslo municipality, are shown; and several permanent exhibits at BYGDOY, showing viking ships excavated at Oseberg and Gokstad, and Nansen's ship *Fram*. Here also are Norwegian Folk Mus., with reconstructions of old timber houses, and Nautical Mus. Other museums specialize in art, the theater, history, geology, engineering, and natural history. There are numerous statues throughout the city; univ. auditorium has noted murals by Munch. Oslo's social institutions are municipally operated; they include numerous modern hospitals, homes for infants and the aged, bathing beaches, public baths, libraries, children's summer camps, and all Oslo moving-picture theaters. Chief industries are metalworking; mfg. of electrical equipment, machinery, chemicals, clothing, paper and food products; brewing, distilling; handicrafts. Port ships lumber, wood products, paper, stone, fish; imports metals, coal, textiles, fats. Oslo's pop. was 286,222 until 1948, when it absorbed Aker canton (formerly in Akershus co.), an area embracing numerous industrial localities lining head of Oslo Fjord. Among chief suburbs are Holmenkollen (NW), popular ski resort; Ulleval (N), Nordstrand and Bekkelaget (SE), Bestun and Smestad (W), and the islet Hovedoy (S). City was founded c.1050 by Harold III (Harold Fairhair); his son established bishopric and built a cathedral. Haakon V made Oslo the royal residence (c.1300) and built Akershus fortress. Under dominance of Hanseatic League in 14th cent., city flourished as port; but after union (1397) bet. Denmark and Norway, its importance dwindled. After destructive fire (1624), it was rebuilt by Christian IV of Denmark and Norway and renamed Christiania or Kristiania. Occupied (1716) by Charles XII of Sweden. Economic and cultural renascence took place in 19th cent.; in literary field it was led by Ibsen and Bjornson (Nor. *Bjørnson*), both buried here. In 1905 city again became ⊙ independent Norway; reassumed name of Oslo in 1925. In Second World War, Oslo fell easily to the Germans, on April 9, 1940, and was occupied throughout the war; though the city suffered no war damage, the occupation brought great hardship.

Oslo (ŏz'lō), village (pop. 440), Marshall co., NW Minn., on Red R. and 20 mi. N of Grand Forks, N.Dak.; grain.

Oslob (ōslōb'), town (1939 pop. 1,659; 1948 municipality pop. 13,614), S Cebu isl., Philippines, on Bohol Strait, 19 mi. E of Tanjay; agr. center (corn, coconuts).

Osma (ō'zmä), city (pop. 824), Soria prov., N central Spain, in Old Castile, near the Duero (Douro), 35 mi. WSW of Soria, 1 mi. W of the cathedral town El Burgo de Osma, in agr. region; sugar refining, flour milling. Was anc. Celtiberian settlement *Uxama*. Heavily disputed during Moorish wars. Adjoined by ruins and Mudejar watchtower.

Osma Kalugerovo (ô'smä kälōō'gĕrôvô), village (pop. 3,147), Pleven dist., N Bulgaria, on Osam R. and 4 mi. SSW of Levski; flour milling; livestock, poultry.

Osmanabad (ōs"mänäbäd'), district (□ 3,526; pop. 748,691), W Hyderabad state, India, on Deccan Plateau; ⊙ Osmanabad. Enclave of Bombay (in W portion of dist.) includes cotton-milling center of Barsi. Bordered N by Manjra R.; highland (NE); lowland (SW). In black-soil area; millet, wheat, cotton, oilseeds (chiefly peanuts). Cotton ginning, flour and oilseed milling, road-metal quarrying. Main trade centers: Latur (rail terminus), Osmanabad. Became part of Hyderabad during state's formation in 18th cent. Pop. 85% Hindu, 13% Moslem. Called Naldrug for its former ⊙ until c.1900. Sometimes spelled Usmanabad.

Osmanabad, town (pop. 14,414), ⊙ Osmanabad dist., W Hyderabad state, India, 35 mi. N of Sholapur; trade center for grain (chiefly millet, wheat, rice), cotton, oilseeds (chiefly peanuts). Anc. Jain and Vishnuite caves near by. Sometimes spelled Usmanabad; formerly called Dharaseo.

Osmancik (ôsmän"jĭk"), Turkish *Osmancık*, village (pop. 4,295), Corum prov., N central Turkey, on the Kizil Irmak and 30 mi. N of Corum; grain, cotton, mohair goats. Sometimes spelled Osmanjik.

Osmaneli (ôsmän'ĕlē), village (pop. 2,436), Bilecik prov., NW Turkey, on Sakarya R., on railroad, and 15 mi. N of Bilecik; cereals.

Osmaniye (ôsmän'ĭyĕ), town (1950 pop. 13,076), Seyhan prov., S Turkey, near Ceyhan R., on railroad, 50 mi. E of Adana; wheat, cotton. Formerly Cebelibereket (Jebel-Bereket).

Osmannagar, India: see SULTANABAD.

Osman Pazar, Bulgaria: see OMORTAG.

Osma River, Bulgaria: see OSAM RIVER.

Osmino or **Os'mino** (ôs'mēnŭ), village (1948 pop. over 500), SW Leningrad oblast, Russian SFSR, 32 mi. NW of Luga; dairying.

Osmond, village (pop. 732), Pierce co., NE Nebr., 10 mi. N of Pierce and on branch of Elkhorn R., in grain and livestock area; dairy and poultry produce.

Osnabrock (ŏz'nùbrŏk), village (pop. 284), Cavalier co., NE N.Dak., 12 mi. ESE of Langdon.

Osnabrück (ŏz'nùbrŏŏk, Ger. ôs"näbrük), city (1939 pop. 107,081; 1946 pop. 88,663; 1950 pop. 108,900), in former Prussian prov. of Hanover, NW Germany, after 1945 in Lower Saxony, bet. Teutoburg Forest (S) and Wiehen Mts. (N), on the Haase and 58 mi. NE of Dortmund; port linked by 9-mi.-long canal with Ems-Weser Canal (NW); 52°17'N 8°8'E. Rail and industrial center; steel milling (pig iron, rolled products, cables, wire, nails); mfg. of machinery, lifting appliances, turbines, boilers, railroad equipment, auto bodies, hardware, textiles (Osnaburg fabrics, artificial fiber, garments), paper and paper products, celluloid. Food processing, woodworking. Cathedral (consecrated c.785; burned 1254) was rebuilt in late-Romanesque style; has Gothic additions. Second World War destruction (about 65%) included heavily damaged Gothic church of St. Mary; and Gothic old town hall, where Treaty of Westphalia was signed in 1648. Was anc. Saxon settlement. Created bishopric by Charlemagne after 783. Was member of Hanseatic League. Accepted Reformation in 1543, but cathedral remained Catholic. Under provisions of Treaty of Westphalia, see was ruled (from 1650 until secularized and given to Hanover in 1803) alternately by Protestant and R.C. bishops. R.C. diocese was reconstituted in 1858. Formerly sometimes called Osnaburg by English writers.

Osnaburg, Germany: see OSNABRÜCK.

Osnaburgh, Scotland: see DAIRSIE.

Osnaburgh House (ŏz'nùbûrg), village, NW Ont., in Patricia dist., on L. St. Joseph, 23 mi. SSW of Pickle Lake and 100 mi. NE of Sioux Lookout; gold mining. Near by is hydroelectric station.

Osne-le-Val (ōn-lù-väl'), village (pop. 368), Haute-Marne dept., NE France, 15 mi. SE of Saint-Dizier. Blast furnace and foundries at near-by Val-d'Osne.

Osno (ôsh'nô), Pol. *Ośno*, Ger. *Drossen* (drô'sùn), town (1939 pop. 5,664; 1946 pop. 1,194) in Brandenburg, after 1945 in Zielona Gora prov., W Poland, 16 mi. ENE of Frankfurt, in lignite-mining region; vegetable and flower market. Has 13th- and 15th-cent. churches, remains of 15th-cent. town walls. Founded c.1150 by bishops of Lebus.

Oso, Mount, peak (13,706 ft.), in Rocky Mts., La Plata co., SW Colo.

Osoblaha (ô'sôblähä), Ger. *Hotzenplotz* (hô'tsùnplôts), village (pop. 421), N Silesia, Czechoslovakia, 13 mi. N of Krnov, near Pol. border; rail terminus; produces smoked meats, liqueurs.

Osogov Mountains (ô'sôgôf) or **Osogovo Mountains** (–vô), Bulg. and Serbo-Croatian *Osogovska Planina*, on Yugoslav-Bulgarian border; form divide bet. Vardar (W) and Struma (E) rivers and bet. the Kriva Reka (N) and Bregalnica R. (S). Rise to c.7,390 ft. at Rujen peak. Crossed by Velbazh Pass at Gyuyeshevo (Bulgaria). Scattered copper, lead, zinc, silver, gold, and iron deposits (mined at KRATOVO and ZLETOVO). Heavily forested.

Osoppo (ôzôp'pô), town (pop. 1,987), Udine prov., Friuli–Venezia Giulia, NE Italy, on Tagliamento R. and 15 mi. NNW of Udine; mfg. (automobile chassis, soap). Has fort (damaged in Second World War) in which Friulians resisted Austrians for 6 months in 1848.

Osor, Yugoslavia: see CRES ISLAND.

Osório (ŏŏzô'ryŏŏ), city (pop. 2,337), E Rio Grande do Sul, Brazil, near the Atlantic, amidst coastal lagoons, 60 mi. ENE of Pôrto Alegre; linked by rail with Emílio Meyer (30 mi. SSW on the Lagoa dos Patos), and by road with Araranguá (Santa Catarina); brandy distilling, fish drying, livestock slaughtering, wool processing. Airfield. Formerly called Conceição do Arroio.

Osorno (ōsôr'nō), province (□ 3,507; 1940 pop. 107,341, 1949 estimate 109,013), S central Chile; ⊙ Osorno. Situated bet. the Andes and the Pacific, it includes part of the Chilean lake dist., notably lakes Rupanco and Puyehue and N tip of L. Llanquihue. The volcanoes Osorno and Puntiagudo are in SE. Has a temperate, wet climate. Contains an agr. valley (of which Osorno city is the center), engaging in wheat growing and cattle and sheep raising. Also rich in timber. Fresh-water fishing in Andean lakes. Major resorts: Termas de Puyehue, Puerto Octay.

Osorno, city (1940 pop. 25,075, 1949 estimate 22,772), ⊙ Osorno prov. and Osorno dept. (□ 2,728; 1940 pop. 79,618), S central Chile, in heart of the Chilean lake dist., on railroad and 55 mi. SSE of Valdivia, 500 mi. SSW of Santiago; 40°35'S 73°8'W. Situated in an agr. valley, it is distributing and processing center. Wheat, livestock, timber; dairies, flour mills, meat canneries, brewery; wood products, agr. implements. Founded 1558, it was subsequently destroyed by the Araucanian Indians and was refounded 1776 by order of Ambrosio O'Higgins. There was a large influx of Ger. immigrants in latter half of 19th cent.

Osorno, town (pop. 1,805), Palencia prov., N central Spain, 30 mi. NNE of Palencia; cereals, wine, vegetables.

Osorno Volcano, Andean peak (8,725 ft.) on Osorno-Llanquihue prov. border, S central Chile, bet. L. Llanquihue (W) and L. Todos los Santos (E), in Chilean lake dist.; 41°7'S 72°30'W. Winter sports. Known for its symmetrical cone.

Osoyoos (ōsōō'yùs), village (pop. estimate 1,000), S B.C., near Wash. border, on Osoyoos L. (12 mi. long), 30 mi. S of Penticton, in irrigated-farming region (fruit, vegetables).

Ospedaletti (ôspĕdälĕt'tē), village (pop. 1,568), Imperia prov., Liguria, NW Italy, port on Gulf of Genoa and 3 mi. WSW of San Remo, in flower-growing region; winter resort, flower market; fisheries.

Ospino (ôspē'nō), town (pop. 507), Portuguesa state, W Venezuela, in llanos, 27 mi. NE of Guanare; cotton, cattle.

Ospitaletto (ôspētälĕt'tô), town (pop. 3,554), Brescia prov., Lombardy, N Italy, 7 mi. WNW of Brescia; hosiery mfg.

Osroene or **Osrhoene** (ŏsrōē'nē, ŏz–), anc. principality of NW Mesopotamia, E of the Euphrates, in present SE Turkey and NE Syria; ⊙ was Edessa (modern Urfa). One of the semi-Hellenistic states that replaced the Seleucid empire (2d cent. B.C.), it came under Roman rule late in 2d cent. A.D.

Oss (ôs), town (pop. 17,070), North Brabant prov., E central Netherlands, 11 mi. ENE of 's Hertogenbosch; mfg. of pharmaceuticals, tannin, oleomargarine, meat products, electrical products, cotton, wool, kapok products, boxes, metalware. Chartered as town 1399. Also spelled Os.

Ossa (ŏ'sŭ, Gr. ô'sŭ), mountain massif in E Thessaly, Greece, on Gulf of Salonika (Aegean Sea), separated by Vale of Tempe from the Olympus; rises to 6,490 ft. in the Prophet Elias [Gr. *Prophetes Elias* or *Profitis Ilias*] 18 mi. NE of Larissa. Formerly called Kissavos. The Aloadae were the giants who tried to pile Pelion on Ossa.

Ossa, Serra de (sĕ'rŭ dĭ ô'sŭ), hills in S central Portugal, bet. Évora and Elvas. Rise to 2,150 ft. Iron deposits on N slopes.

Ossabaw Island (ŏ'sŭbô"), one of the Sea Isls., just off SE Ga. coast, in Chatham co., 15 mi. S of Savannah; c.9 mi. long, 7 mi. wide; marshy. Ossabaw Sound (c.5 mi. long and wide), at N end of isl., receives Ogeechee R.

Ossa de Montiel (ō'sä dhä mōntyĕl'), town (pop. 2,606), Albacete prov., SE central Spain, 22 mi. SSW of Villarrobledo; plaster mfg., flour milling. Cereals, wine, honey. Gypsum quarries. From chain of lagoons SW of here originates one of the Guadiana's headstreams.

Ossau, Gave d' (gäv dôsō'), river in Basses-Pyrénées dept., SW France, rises in central Pyrenees near Pourtalet pass (Sp. border), flows 40 mi. NW, through picturesque Ossau valley (winter-sports area), past Gabas, Les Eaux-Chaudes, Laruns, and Arudy, joining the Gave d'Aspe at Oloron-Sainte-Marie to form the Gave d'Oloron. Used for hydroelectric power.

Ossau, Pic du Midi d', France: see PIC DU MIDI D'OSSAU.

Osseg, Czechoslovakia: see OSEK.

Osséja (ōsāzhä'), village (pop. 807), Pyrénées-Orientales dept., S France, in CERDAGNE, near Sp. border, 3 mi. ESE of Puigcerdá (Spain); alt. 4,114 ft.; resort. Sanatoriums.

Osseo (ŏ'sēō). **1** Village (pop. 1,167), Hennepin co., E Minn., near Mississippi R., 12 mi. NNW of Minneapolis; poultry- and potato-shipping point; ice cream, cattle feed. **2** City (pop. 1,126), Trempealeau co., W Wis., on Buffalo R. and 21 mi. SE of Eau Claire, in dairy, livestock, and poultry area; cheese, pickles, condensed milk, canned vegetables. Settled 1851; inc. as village in 1893, as city in 1941.

Ossero, Yugoslavia: see CRES ISLAND.

Ossetia: see NORTH OSSETIAN AUTONOMOUS SOVIET SOCIALIST REPUBLIC, Russian SFSR; SOUTH OSSETIAN AUTONOMOUS OBLAST, Georgian SSR.

Ossetian Military Road (ŏsē'shŭn), road (c.120 mi. long) across the Greater Caucasus, linking Kutaisi (Georgian SSR) and Alagir (Russian SFSR). Uses Ardon and Rion river valleys, crossing Caucasian crest via Mamison Pass (alt. 9,550 ft.) as a trail.

Ossett (ŏ'sĭt), municipal borough (1931 pop. 14,838; 1951 census 14,576), West Riding, S Yorkshire, England, 8 mi. S of Leeds; woolen milling; mfg. of leather and leather products, textile machinery, paint, pharmaceuticals.

Ossi (ôs'sē), village (pop. 4,072), Sassari prov., NW Sardinia, 4 mi. SSE of Sassari.

Ossiachersee (ô'sēäkhŭrzā"), lake (□ 4) in Carinthia, S Austria, 3 mi. NE of Villach; 7 mi. long, 1 mi. wide, average depth 59 ft. Abounds in fish. Site of tourist resorts (Ossiach, Steindorf).

Ossian. **1** (ŏ'sēŭn) Town (pop. 761), Wells co., E Ind., on small Longlois Creek and 14 mi. S of Fort Wayne. **2** (ŏ'shŭn) Town (pop. 804), Winneshiek co., NE Iowa, 11 mi. S of Decorah, in grain and dairy area. Limestone quarries near by.

Ossineke (ŏsĭnēk'), fishing village (pop. c.100), Alpena co., NE Mich., on Thunder Bay of L. Huron, 10 mi. S of Alpena; Indian basketmakers live here.

Ossining (ŏ'sŭnĭng), residential and industrial village (pop. 16,098), Westchester co., SE N.Y., on E bank of the Hudson and 5 mi. N of Tarrytown; mfg. (plumbing and electrical equipment, machinery, wire, surgical and scientific instruments, chemicals, maps and timetables, lime, wallpaper, clothing, plaster). Has St. Johns School for boys. Seat of Sing Sing state prison. Settled c.1750; inc. as Sing Sing 1813; renamed 1901.

Ossipee (ŏ'sĭpē). **1** Resort town (pop. 1,412), ⊙ Carroll co., E N.H., 28 mi. N of Rochester and on Ossipee L.; lumber, furniture. Inc. 1785. Includes villages of Ossipee, West Ossipee (where Whittier spent many summers), and Center Ossipee, latter on **Ossipee Lake,** resort lake 3.5 mi. long, drained by short Ossipee R. (dam at Kezar Falls, Maine), which flows E to Saco R. **Ossipee Mountains,** to SW, rise to 2,975 ft. in Mt. Shaw. **2** Village, N.C.: see OSIPEE.

Ossipee Mountain (1,054 ft.), SW Maine, in Waterboro resort area; camp site, ski trail.

Ossmannstedt (ôs'män-shtĕt), village (pop. 1,462), Thuringia, central Germany, on Ilm R. and 5 mi. NE of Weimar. Has former estate of Wieland, who is buried here with his wife and his friend Sophie Brentano.

Ossora (ŭsô'rŭ), town (1949 pop. over 500), S Koryak Natl. Okrug, Kamchatka oblast, Khabarovsk Territory, Russian SFSR, on neck of Kamchatka Peninsula, 110 mi. ENE of Palana; fish canning.

Ossu (ô'sōō), town, Portuguese Timor, in E Timor, 55 mi. ESE of Dili; palm oil, copra.

Ossun (ôsŭ'), village (pop. 1,598), Hautes-Pyrénées dept., SW France, 6 mi. SW of Tarbes; horse raising, sawmilling.

Ostafyevo, Russian SFSR: see SHCHERBINKA.

Ostana (ŭs'tänō"), Swedish *Östanå*, village (pop. 946), Uppsala co., E Sweden, on Dal R., near its mouth on Gulf of Bothnia, 13 mi. SE of Gavle; grain, potatoes, livestock.

Ostanbo (–bōō"), Swedish *Östanbo*, village (pop. 1,428), Gavleborg co., E Sweden, on Gulf of Bothnia, 4 mi. SE of Soderhamn; sawmills.

Ostansjo (–shû"), Swedish *Östansjö*, village (pop. 647), Orebro co., S central Sweden, 17 mi. SSW of Orebro; shoe mfg., sawmilling.

Ostashevo (ŭstä'shĭvŭ), village, W Moscow oblast, Russian SFSR, on Ruza R. (left tributary of Moskva R.) and 12 mi. S of Volokolamsk; hog farming.

Ostashkov (ŭstäsh'kŭf), city (1926 pop. 12,900), W Kalinin oblast, Russian SFSR, in Valdai Hills, on L. Seliger (fisheries), 105 mi. WNW of Kalinin; tanning center; boatbuilding; sawmills, brickworks; net making. Tourist resort. Chartered 1770. During Second World War, held (1941–42) by Germans.

Ostellato (ôstĕl-lä'tô), village (pop. 984), Ferrara prov., Emilia-Romagna, N central Italy, on NW shore of Valli di Comacchio, 17 mi. ENE of Ferrara; rail junction.

Ostenburg, Poland: see PULTUSK.

Ostend (ŏ'stĕnd), Fr. *Ostende* (ôstād'), Flemish *Oostende* (ōstĕn'dŭ), town (pop. 50,255), West Flanders prov., NW Belgium, on North Sea, at W end of Ostend-Bruges Canal, and 14 mi. W of Bruges; 51°14'N 2°56'E. Second largest Belg. port; exports cement, bricks, tiles, chemicals, coke, fish; imports coal, timber, pit props, wool, nitrate, barrels. Terminus of cross-channel boats from Dover (England); bunker station; fishing port; fish curing, oyster culture. Popular seaside resort. Central point of a dike and roadway along Belgium's North Sea coast. Fishing village since 9th cent.; fortified (1583) by Prince William of Orange. Became last Du. stronghold in Belgium; captured by Spaniards (1604) after 3-year siege. In 1854 Ostend Manifesto was drawn up here. In First World War, captured by Germans in 1914; became a major submarine base until it was sealed (1918) by sinking of a Br. blockship at its entrance.

Ostend-Bruges Canal, NW Belgium, runs 16 mi. E-W, bet. Bruges and North Sea at Ostend.

Ostende, Belgium: see OSTEND.

Ostenfeld (ô'stŭnfĕlt"), village (pop. 1,829), in Schleswig-Holstein, NW Germany, 7 mi. ESE of Husum; grain, cattle. Has 18th-cent. church.

Oster (ŏstyôr'), town (1926 pop. 6,837), SW Chernigov oblast, Ukrainian SSR, on Desna R., at mouth of Oster R., and 40 mi. SSW of Chernigov; lumber center; wood distilling, hemp milling, food processing.

Oster, river, Ukrainian SSR: see OSTER RIVER.

Osteras (ŭs'tŭrōs"), Swedish *Österås*, residential village (pop. 846), Vasternorrland co., NE Sweden, on Angerman R., at mouth of Fax R., Swedish *Faxälven* (fäks'ĕl"vŭn), 4 mi. NW of Solleftea; site of sanitarium.

Osterburg (ô'stŭrbŏŏrk), town (pop. 6,893), in former Prussian Saxony prov., central Germany, after 1945 in Saxony-Anhalt, 13 mi. NNW of Stendal; mfg. of lenses, eyeglass frames, bricks. Has church rebuilt in 15th cent.

Osterburken (ô"stŭrbŏŏr'kŭn), town (pop. 2,302), N Baden, Germany, after 1945 in Württemberg-Baden, 16 mi. WSW of Mergentheim; rail junction; fruit, wheat. Was Roman castrum.

Osterby (ŭs'tŭrbü") or **Osterbybruk** (ŭs"tŭrbü"-brük'), Swedish *Osterby* or *Osterbybruk*, village (pop. 1,504), Uppsala co., E Sweden, 20 mi. NNE of Uppsala; iron- and steelworks. Founded in 17th cent. by Dutch industrialists, the works mainly employ descendants of workers originally brought here from Low Countries.

Osterbygd, anc. Norse settlement, Greenland: see GREENLAND.

Osterdal (ŭs'tŭrdäl), Nor. *Østerdal*, valley (100 mi. long) of Glomma R., Hedmark co., E Norway, extends from E slope of the Dovrefjell SSE to Rena. Pyrites mined in the Folldal, a tributary valley (NW). Lumbering, agr., stock raising are carried on. Valley is traversed by secondary railroad linking Oslo and Trondheim. Noted for its low precipitation.

Osterdalalven, Sweden: see DAL RIVER.

Osterdock (ŏ'stŭrdŏk), town (pop. 51), Clayton co., NE Iowa, on Turkey R. and 4 mi. SW of Guttenberg, in dairying area.

Osterfeld (ō'stŭrfĕlt"). **1** Industrial suburb (1925 pop. 32,592) of OBERHAUSEN, in former Prussian Rhine Prov., W Germany, after 1945 in North Rhine-Westphalia, N of Rhine-Herne Canal, 2 mi. N of city center. Until inc. (1929) into Oberhausen, it was in former Prussian prov. of Westphalia. **2** Town (pop. 2,851), in former Prussian Saxony prov., central Germany, after 1945 in Saxony-Anhalt, 7 mi. SE of Naumburg; sugar beets, grain; brick mfg.

Oster Fjord (ôs'tŭr), inlet of the North Sea in Hordaland co., SW Norway; c.20 mi. long, 1 mi. wide; extends NE from coast, separating the isl. Osteroy from mainland; joins with Sor Fjord at head, 25 mi. NNE of Bergen.

Ostergotland (ûs'tŭryût"länd), Swed. *Östergötland*, county [Swed. *län*] (□ 4,266; 1950 pop. 347,996), SE Sweden; ⊙ Linkoping. Comprises Ostergotland province [Swedish *landskap*] (□ 4,239; pop. 332,228) and small section of Sodermanland prov., bet. the Baltic and L. Vatter. Fertile plain is dotted with lakes (Rox, Gla, Somme); drained by Motala, Svart, and Stang rivers. Partly wooded. Agr. (rye, wheat, oats, sugar beets), stock raising, dairying. There are deposits of iron, zinc, lead, and copper; stone quarries. Cities are Norrkoping, Linkoping, Motala (industrial centers), Mjolby (railroad center), Vadstena, Soderkoping, and Skanninge.

Osterhofen (ô"stŭrhō'fŭn), town (pop. 2,761), Lower Bavaria, Germany, near the Danube, 9 mi. SE of Plattling; textile mfg., brewing, tanning.

Osterholz-Scharmbeck (ō'stŭrhôlts-shärm'bĕk), town (pop. 12,059), in former Prussian prov. of Hanover, NW Germany, after 1945 in Lower Saxony, 9 mi. N of Bremen; foundry; mfg. of tobacco products, furniture, shoes, apparel, soap, paint; woodworking, food processing.

Oste River (ō'stŭ), NW Germany, formed 7 mi. SW of Zeven, flows c.80 mi. N, past Bremervörde, to Elbe R. estuary 3 mi. N of Neuhaus. Navigable in lower course.

Osterley, England: see HESTON AND ISLEWORTH.

Ostermycklang, Sweden: see ALVDALEN.

Ostermyra, Finland: see SEINÄJOKI.

Osternienburg (ôstĕr'nyünbŏŏrk), village (pop. 3,078), in former Anhalt state, central Germany, after 1945 in Saxony-Anhalt, 4 mi. NE of Köthen; lignite mining; chemical mfg.

Ostero (ôs'dŭrû), Dan. *Østerø*, Faeroese *Eysturoy*, second largest island (□ 111; pop. 6,811) of the Faeroe Isls., separated from Stromo by c.600-ft.-wide Sundene strait (W), from Kalso by Djupene strait, and from Bordo by Kalso Fjord. E coast has many inlets, including Funding Fjord (6 mi. long); from S, Skaale Fjord (10 mi. long; Faeroese *Skála*) comes to within 4 mi. of head of Funding Fjord. Terrain is mountainous; in N is Slaettaratinde (Faeroese *Slaettaratindur*), highest point in the Faeroes (2,894 ft.). Less than 4% of area is cultivated; fishing, sheep raising.

Osterode or **Osterode am Harz** (ô"stŭrō'dŭ äm härts'), town (pop. 13,407), in former Prussian prov. of Hanover, W Germany, after 1945 in Lower Saxony, at W foot of the upper Harz, 19 mi. NE of Göttingen; mfg. of chemicals (especially white lead), textiles, machinery, furniture; copperworking, food processing. Has 16th-cent. church and town hall. Sculptor Riemenschneider b. here. Gypsum quarries near by.

Osterode, Poland: see OSTRODA.

Osteroy (ôs'tŭr-ûü), Nor. *Osterøy*, island (□ 127; pop. 6,271), Hordaland co., SW Norway, NE of Bergen, separated from mainland by very narrow Sor Fjord on SW, S, and E, and by Oster Fjord on NW; 19 mi. long (N-S), 12 mi. wide. Fishing, agr., lumbering industries at Bruvik, Lonevag, Hosanger, Haus, Skafta.

Österreich: see AUSTRIA.

Osterrisor, Norway: see RISOR.

Oster River (ŏstyôr'), in Chernigov oblast, Ukrainian SSR, rises SSW of Bakhmach, flows 100 mi. generally WSW, past Nezhin and Kozelets, to Desna R. at Oster.

Ostersund (ûs'tŭrsŭnd'), Swedish *Östersund*, city (1950 pop. 21,378), ⊙ Jamtland co., N central Sweden, on E Stor L., 100 mi. NW of Sundsvall; 63°11'N 14°40'E. Rail junction; tourist center. Mfg. of machinery, chemicals, furniture, leather goods; handicrafts. Has co. mus. Founded 1786.

Osterville, Mass.: see BARNSTABLE, town.

Osterwieck (ō"stŭrvēk'), town (pop. 6,283), in former Prussian Saxony prov., central Germany, after 1945 in Saxony-Anhalt, at N foot of the upper Harz, 10 mi. NNW of Wernigerode; mfg. (leather goods, paint, gloves). Has 16th-cent. church and town hall; many half-timbered houses.

Ostfold (ûst'fôl), Nor. *Østfold*, county [Nor. *fylke*] (□ 1,614; pop. 178,449), SE Norway, bet. Swedish border (E and S) and Oslo Fjord (W); ⊙ Moss. Generally level, surface rises toward E; drained by Glomma R. Besides Moss, cities are Fredrikstad, Sarpsborg, and Halden. Lumbering and paper milling are chief industries; there are textile mills, shipyards, fish canneries, chemical plants. Granite quarrying and agr. are extensively carried on. Abundant hydroelectric power. Until 1918, co. (then called *amt*) was named Smaalenene.

Ostfriesland, Germany: see EAST FRIESLAND.

Ostgeim, Ukrainian SSR: see TELMANOVO.

Osthammar (ûst'hä"mär), Swedish *Osthammar*, city (pop. 1,283), Stockholm co., E Sweden, on Gran

Fjord, Swedish *Granfjärden*, 12-mi.-long inlet of Gulf of Bothnia, 35 mi. NE of Uppsala; port and seaside resort. Has 18th-cent. town hall, mus. Chartered in 14th cent.; destroyed 1719 by Russians.

Ostheim or **Ostheim vor der Rhön** (ôst'hīm fôr dĕr rûn'), town (pop. 2,992), Lower Franconia, N Bavaria, Germany, 11 mi. SW of Meiningen; mfg. of textiles and precision instruments; woodworking, tanning. Was in Thuringian exclave until 1945.

Ostheim, Ukrainian SSR: see TELMANOVO.

Osthofen (ôst-hō'fŭn), village (pop. 4,893), Rhenish Hesse, W Germany, 5 mi. NNW of Worms; mfg. of machinery, furniture, bottle tops, paper; brickworks. Vineyards; sugar beets.

Ostia (ŏ'stēŭ), anc. city of Latium and once port of Rome, central Italy, at S mouth of the Tiber. A new harbor was built by Claudius and enlarged by Trajan; the town, which had important saltworks, declined from 3d cent.; revived in Middle Ages. Its ruins have been excavated systematically since 1854. Present village (pop. 1,160), founded 830 by Gregory IV, is adjacent to the ruins, which now lie 4 mi. above the mouth of the Tiber; produces agr. machinery. Has Renaissance castle (1483–86).

Ostiano (ôstyä'nô), town (pop. 3,206), Cremona prov., Lombardy, N Italy, on Oglio R. and 13 mi. NE of Cremona.

Ostiglia (ôstē'lyä), anc. *Hostilia*, town (pop. 5,276), Mantova prov., Lombardy, N Italy, on Po R. and 18 mi. ESE of Mantua; rail junction; agr. center; beet-sugar and hemp mills; foundries; cheese, macaroni, soap.

Ostional (ōstyōnäl'), village, Rivas dept., SW Nicaragua, 22 mi. S of Rivas, on the Pacific; livestock; coffee.

Ostotitlán (ōstōtētlän'), town (pop. 2,017), Guerrero, SW Mexico, 32 mi. SW of Iguala; cereals, sugar cane, coffee, fruit.

Ostpreussen, Germany: see EAST PRUSSIA.

Ostra (ô'strä), town (pop. 1,975), Ancona prov., The Marches, central Italy, 18 mi. W of Ancona; macaroni mfg.

Ostra Aros, Sweden: see UPPSALA.

Ostraat, Norway: see AUSTRATT.

Ostrander (ō'străn"dŭr). **1** Village (pop. 191), Fillmore co., SE Minn., near Iowa line, 28 mi. S of Rochester, in grain area. **2** Village (pop. 408), Delaware co., central Ohio, 7 mi. WSW of Delaware; leather products.

Ostrava or **Moravska Ostrava** (mô'räfskä ô'strävä), Czech *Moravská Ostrava*, Ger. *Mährish Ostrau* (mâ"rĭsh ô'strou), city (pop. 116,225), ⊙ Ostrava prov. (□ 1,747; pop. 790,285), NE Moravia, Czechoslovakia, bet. Oder and Ostravice rivers, just above their junction, 170 mi. E of Prague; 49°51'N 18°18'E. Rail junction; leading metallurgical center of most industrialized region of Czechoslovakia. Its noted heavy industry, geared for world-wide export, smelts Moravian, Slovak, and Swedish ores. Ostrava-Karvina coalfield (SE part of Upper Silesian basin, of which it forms c.1/10 of total area) produces anthracite and bituminous coal. Moravska Ostrava includes Vitkovice, Privoz, and Marianske Hory, while Greater Ostrava (pop. c.180,000) extends across Oder and Ostravice rivers into E Silesia to include SLEZSKA OSTRAVA, HRUSOV, MICHALKOVICE, and PETRKOVICE. Vitkovice (vĕt'kôvĭtsĕ), Czech *Vítkovice*, Ger. *Witkowitz*, iron- and steelworks produce not only iron and steel, but also finished and semi-finished products (ship parts, bridge parts, railroad rolling stock, cranes, boilers, etc.); also large tar works and power plants. Privoz (pŭrzhē'vôs), Czech *Přívoz*, Ger. *Oderfurt*, rolling mills and workshops specialize in tin plate, dies, lithographic plates, dry-cell containers, light aluminum alloys. Marianske Hory (mä'rēänskä hô'rĭ), Czech *Mariánské Hory*, Ger. *Marienberg*, has synthetic nitrogen installations. Ostrava area is also known for its chemical by-products industry (notably metallurgical coke) and for mfg. of house-building materials, foodstuffs, wearing apparel, furniture, and petroleum products. First foundry was built 1829 in Vitkovice, but large-scale expansion occurred only in 20th cent. Some industrial plants were badly damaged in Second World War, and post-war expulsion of Ger. inhabitants caused temporary shortage in specialists. Has mining acad. transferred (1945) from Pribram.

Ostra Vansbro, Sweden: see VANSBRO.

Ostra Vetere (ô'strä vä'tĕrĕ), village (pop. 1,069), Ancona prov., The Marches, central Italy, 11 mi. SW of Senigallia; agr. tools.

Ostravice River (ô'strävĭtsĕ), E Silesia, Czechoslovakia, formed in the Beskids, by 2 headstreams joining 22 mi. E of Valasske Mezirici; flows NNW, past Frydlant nad Ostravici, forming part of Moravia-Silesia border, past Frydek-Mistek and Ostrava, to Oder R. at Hrusov; c.40 mi. long.

Ostredok (ô'strĕdôk), highest mountain (5,218 ft.) of the Greater Fatra, W central Slovakia, Czechoslovakia, 16 mi. SW of Ruzomberok.

Ostrica (ŏ'strĭkŭ), village, Plaquemines parish, extreme SE La., on E bank (levee) of the Mississippi and c.50 mi. SE of New Orleans, in the delta; oyster culture; hunting, fishing. Ostrica Canal, with lock through levee here, connects the Mississippi with Breton Sound (E).

Östrich (ûs'trĭkh). **1** Village (pop. 3,864), in former Prussian prov. of Hesse-Nassau, W Germany, after 1945 in Hesse, in the Rheingau, on right bank of the Rhine and 11 mi. WSW of Wiesbaden; mfg. of chemicals. **2** Village (pop. 8,428), in former Prussian prov. of Westphalia, W Germany, after 1945 in North Rhine-Westphalia, 2 mi. W of Iserlohn; forestry.

Ostricourt (ôstrēkōōr'), commune (pop. 6,578), Nord dept., N France, 6 mi. NNW of Douai; coal mines. Cité du Bois-Dion (pop. 1,195) and Cité Saint-Éloi (pop. 1,181) are miners' communities with large Polish pop.

Östringen (ûs'trĭng-ŭn), village (pop. 4,592), N Baden, Germany, after 1945 in Württemberg-Baden, 9 mi. NE of Bruchsal; mfg. of cigars and cigarettes.

Ostritz (ô'strĭts), town (pop. 4,945), Saxony, E Germany, in Upper Lusatia, on the Lusatian Neisse and 10 mi. S of Görlitz; linen and cotton milling, leather mfg., stone quarrying.

Ostroda (ôstrōō'dä), Pol. *Ostróda*, Ger. *Osterode* (ôstŭrō'dŭ), town (1939 pop. 19,519; 1946 pop. 6,769) in East Prussia, after 1945 in Olsztyn prov., NE Poland, in Masurian Lakes region, on Drweca R. and 20 mi. WSW of Allenstein (Olsztyn); rail junction; trade center; grain and cattle market; sawmilling. In First World War, Ger. army hq. here during battle of Tannenberg. In Second World War, c.50% destroyed.

Ostrog (ŭstrôk'), Pol. *Ostróg* (ô'strōōk), city (1931 pop. 12,955), SE Rovno oblast, Ukrainian SSR, on Goryn R. and 22 mi. SSE of Rovno; agr. and mfg. center; food processing (cereals, meat, fruit, vegetables), textile and leather industries, sawmilling. Lignite deposits near by. Has ruins of old castle. Founded in 9th cent.; was ⊙ independent principality until 17th cent. Passed (1793) from Poland to Russia; reverted (1921) to Poland; ceded to USSR in 1945.

Ostrogozhsk (ŭstrŭgôshsk'), city (1926 pop. 22,990), W Voronezh oblast, Russian SFSR, on Tikhaya Sosna R. and 55 mi. S of Voronezh; fruit canning, flour milling, tanning, metalworking (motor-repair shops). Teachers and veterinary institutes. Regional mus. with picture gall. Founded 1652 as fortress. During Second World War, held (1942–43) by Germans.

Ostroleka (ôstrôwē'kä), Pol. *Ostrołęka*, Rus. *Ostrolenka* (ŭstrŭlyĕn'kŭ), town (pop. 9,279), Warszawa prov., NE central Poland, on Narew R., opposite Omulew R. mouth, and 65 mi. NNE of Warsaw. Rail junction; flour and groat milling, brewing, tanning; pulp, paper. Scene of Rus. victory (1831) over Pol. insurgents. During Second World War, under administration of East Prussia, called Scharfenwiese.

Ostropol or **Ostropol'** (ŭstrô'pŭl), town (1926 pop. 3,746), E Kamenets-Podolski oblast, Ukrainian SSR, on Sluch R. and 15 mi. ENE of Staro-Konstantinov; flour mill.

Ostrorog (ôstrô'rōōk), Pol. *Ostroróg*, Ger. *Scharfenort* (shär'fŭnôrt), town (1946 pop. 1,170), Poznan prov., W Poland, on railroad and 25 mi. NW of Poznan; flour milling; cattle trade.

Ostrov (ôstrôf'), village (pop. 4,573), Vratsa dist., N Bulgaria, near the Danube, 12 mi. ESE of Oryakhovo; vineyards, livestock; fisheries.

Ostrov (ô'strôf). **1** Ger. *Schlakenwerth* (shlä'kŭnvĕrt), village (pop. 1,893), W Bohemia, Czechoslovakia, 6 mi. NNE of Carlsbad; rail junction; health resort. **2** Village, W central Moravia, Czechoslovakia: see MORAVIAN KARST.

Ostrov, island, Slovakia, Czechoslovakia: see SCHÜTT.

Ostrov, Poland: see OSTROW, Lublin prov.

Ostrov (ô'strôv), town (1948 pop. 4,015), Constanta prov., SE Rumania, in Dobruja, on Danube R. and 60 mi. WSW of Constanta; trade in grain, livestock, animal products, fish, grapes, wine.

Ostrov (ô'strŭf), city (1939 pop. over 10,000), SW Pskov oblast, Russian SFSR, on Velikaya R. and 32 mi. S of Pskov; road center in flax region; flax processing, dairying; metalworking. Peat works near by. Founded 1342 as outpost of Pskov; later border fortress of Moscow domain. Border station on Latvian frontier (1920–40). During Second World War, held (1941–44) by Germans.

Ostrovets (ŭstrŭvyĕts'), Pol. *Ostrowiec*, village (1939 pop. over 500), W Molodechno oblast, Belorussian SSR, 13 mi. N of Oshmyany; flour milling; bricks.

Ostrovnoye (ô'strŭvnŭyŭ), village (1948 pop. over 500), NW Chukchi Natl. Okrug, Kamchatka oblast, Khabarovsk Territory, Russian SFSR, on Lesser Anyui R. and 425 mi. NW of Anadyr; reindeer farms; trading post, airfield.

Ostrovo (ô'strôvô), village (pop. 3,663), Ruse dist., NE Bulgaria, 12 mi. NNE of Razgrad; wheat, rye, sunflowers. Formerly Golyama-ada.

Ostrovon, village, Greece: see ARNISSA.

Ostrovon, Lake, Greece: see VEGORITIS, LAKE.

Ostrow (ô'strōōf), Pol. *Ostrów*. **1** or **Ostrow Lubelski** (lōōbĕl'skē), Pol. *Ostrów Lubelski*, Rus. *Ostrov* (ô'strŭf), town (pop. 2,604), Lublin prov., E Poland, on Tysmienica R. and 21 mi. NNE of Lublin; tanning, flour and groat milling; brickworks. Sometimes called Ostrow Siedlecki. **2** or **Ostrow Wielkopolski** (vyĕlkôpôl'skē), Pol. *Ostrów Wielkopolski*, Ger. *Ostrowo* (ôstrō'vō), city (1946 pop. 30,808), Poznan prov., W central Poland, 65 mi. SSE of Poznan. Rail junction; trade center; mfg. of railroad cars, agr. machinery, chemicals, furniture, bricks; brewing, flour milling, sawmilling. Passed (1793, 1815) to Prussia; returned to Poland in 1919. **3** or **Ostrow Mazowiecka** (mäzôvyĕts'kä), Pol. *Ostrów Mazowiecka*, town (pop. 12,304), Warszawa prov., E central Poland, on railroad and 55 mi. NE of Warsaw; mfg. of bricks, cement, knit goods, hosiery; brewing, flour milling. Before Second World War, pop. 50% Jewish.

Ostrowiec or **Ostrowiec Swietokrzyski** (ôstrô'vyĕts shvyĕtôk-zhĭ'skē), Pol. *Ostrowiec Świętokrzyski*, Rus. *Ostrovets* (ŭstrô'vyĭts), town (pop. 19,211), Kielce prov., E Poland, on Kamienna R., on railroad and 33 mi. ENE of Kielce, in brown-coal and iron-ore mining region; linked by pipe line with Jaslo-Krosno natural-gas field. Ironworks; mfg. of munitions, firebricks, cement products; food processing, sawmilling, tanning, brewing. Development in 1920s (1931 pop. 25,983) because of existence of local iron ore. Before Second World War, pop. was ⅔ Jewish.

Ostrowiec, Belorussian SSR: see OSTROVETS.

Ostrozhets (ŭstrô'zhĭts), Pol. *Ostrożec* (ôstrô'zhĕts), village (1939 pop. over 2,000), W Rovno oblast, Ukrainian SSR, 11 mi. SE of Lutsk; rye, wheat.

Ostryna (ô'strĭnŭ), town (1931 pop. 1,570), N Grodno oblast, Belorussian SSR, 29 mi. E of Grodno; tanning, flour milling, brick mfg.

Ostrzeszow (ôs-chĕ'shōōf), Pol. *Ostrzeszów*, Ger. *Schildberg* (shĭlt'bĕrk), town (1946 pop. 5,403), Poznan prov., SW central Poland, on railroad and 25 mi. SSW of Kalisz; mfg. (bricks, machinery, chemicals, cement, flour).

Ostsee: see BALTIC SEA.

Ostseebad Wustrow, Germany: see WUSTROW, Mecklenburg.

Ostswine, Poland: see ODRA PORT.

Osttirol, Austria: see TYROL.

Ostuacán (ōstwäkän'), town (pop. 164), Chiapas, S Mexico, 45 mi. NW of Tuxtla; cacao, rice.

Ostuncalco or **San Juan Ostuncalco** (sän hwän' ōstōōngkäl'kō), town (1950 pop. 3,060), Quezaltenango dept., SW Guatemala, on Inter-American Highway and 6 mi. WNW of Quezaltenango, in agr. region; alt. 8,185 ft. Market center; coffee, sugar cane, grain, livestock.

Ostuni (ôstōō'nē), town (pop. 21,826), Brindisi prov., Apulia, S Italy, 20 mi. WNW of Brindisi; agr. center (wine, olive oil, fruit, vegetables). Bishopric. Has cathedral.

Ostvaagoy, Norway: see AUSTVAGOY.

Ostwald (ōstväld', Ger. ōst'vält), outer SSW suburb (pop. 3,134) of Strasbourg, Bas-Rhin dept., E France, on the Ill.

Ostyako-Vogulsk, Russian SFSR: see KHANTY-MANSISK.

Ostyak-Vogul National Okrug, Russian SFSR: see KHANTY-MANSI NATIONAL OKRUG.

Osumacinta (ōsōōmäsēn'tä), town (pop. 323), Chiapas, S Mexico, 10 mi. NNE of Tuxtla; corn, fruit, livestock.

Osumi (ō'sōōmē), former province in S Kyushu, Japan; now part of Kagoshima prefecture.

Osumi, Cape, Jap *Osumi-bana*, N Shikoku, Japan, in Hiuchi Sea (central section of Inland Sea), W of O-shima; 34°8'N 132°57'E; lighthouse.

Osumi Peninsula, Jap. *Osumi-hanto*, S Kyushu, Japan, in Kagoshima prefecture, bet. Kagoshima Bay (W) and Ariake Bay (E); 45 mi. long (terminating S at Cape Sata), 20 mi. wide. SAKURA-JIMA (formerly an isl.) is NW projection.

Osumi Strait, Jap. *Osumi-kaikyo*, channel connecting E.China Sea (W) with Philippine Sea (E), bet. S coast of Kyushu and Tanega-shima; 35 mi. long, 20 mi. wide. Cape Sata of Osumi Peninsula forms NW side. Formerly sometimes called Van Diemen Strait.

Osum River (ô'sōōm) or **Osumi River** (ô'sōōmē), S central Albania, rises in the Grammos (Gr. border) near Ersekë, flows c.70 mi. W and NW, past Berat, joining Devoll R. 8 mi. NW of Berat to form Seman R.

Osuna (ōsōō'nä), town (pop. 19,552), Seville prov., SW Spain, on fertile Andalusian plain, on railroad and 50 mi. E of Seville; trading and processing center for agr. region (olives, cereals, vegetables, grapes, truck produce, fruit, livestock). Sawmilling, vegetable-oil processing, dairying, flour milling; lime, stone, and gypsum quarrying; apiculture. Also mfg. of soap, esparto goods, baskets. An anc. town with many historic relics. Above it is a noted 16th-cent. collegiate church containing a *Crucifixion* by Ribera. A restored crypt contains graves of the dukes of Osuna. The univ., founded in 1549 and dissolved in early 19th cent., was a noted cultural center. Osuna was an important Roman colony, alternatively called *Urso*, *Gemina Urbanorum*, or *Orsona*. Taken in 711 by the Moors (who spelled it Oxuna), it was recaptured in 1239.

Osvaldo Cruz (ōōzväl'dōō krōōs'), city, W São Paulo, Brazil, 60 mi. WNW of Marília, in region of pioneer agr. settlements; cotton, coffee.

Osveya (ŭsvā'ŭ), town (1926 pop. 1,771), N Polotsk oblast, Belorussian SSR, on Osveya L., 45 mi. NW of Polotsk; flax.

Oswaldtwistle (ŏz'wŭltwĭsŭl, -wŭld-), urban district (1931 pop. 14,218; 1951 census 12,133), central Lancashire, England, 3 mi. E of Blackburn; cotton milling, coal mining, mfg. of pottery.

Oswayo (ŏswā'ō), borough (pop. 167), Potter co., N Pa., 10 mi. N of Coudersport.

Oswegatchie River (ŏswĭgŏ'chē, -gă'chē), N N.Y., rises in small lakes of the W Adirondacks, flows N, entering and issuing from Cranberry L., thence generally NW, past Gouverneur, beyond which it turns sharply SW and again NE in a bend, then continues NE and N to the St. Lawrence at Ogdensburg; c.150 mi. long. West Branch (c.45 mi. long) enters from S 7 mi. SE of Gouverneur.

Oswego (ŏswē'gō), county (□ 968; pop. 77,181), N central N.Y.; ⊙ Oswego and Pulaski. Bounded NW by L. Ontario, S by Oneida L. and Oneida R.; crossed by the Barge Canal; drained by Oswego and Salmon rivers. Dairying area, with diversified mfg. especially at Oswego; gas wells. Farming (strawberries and other truck), poultry and stock raising. Lake and canal shipping. Resorts on lakes. Formed 1816.

Oswego. 1 (ŏswā'gō, ŏswē'gō) Village (pop. 1,220), Kendall co., NE Ill., on Fox R. (bridged here) and 4 mi. SSW of Aurora, in agr. area. **2** (ŏswē'gō) City (pop. 1,997), ⊙ Labette co., extreme SE Kansas, on Neosho R. and 14 mi. SSE of Parsons; trading point in livestock, grain, and poultry area; cheese, feed. Founded 1865, inc. 1870. **3** (ŏswē'gō) City (pop. 22,647), a ⊙ Oswego co., N central N.Y., on harbor on L. Ontario, at mouth of Oswego R., 34 mi. NW of Syracuse; N terminus of Oswego R. section of the Barge Canal, a port of entry, and important lake port, handling oil, coal, lumber, grain, cement, pulpwood. Mfg.: machinery, textiles, matches, clothing, metal and paper products, oil-well supplies, tools, confectionery, plasterboard, chemicals, feed, cement. Seat of a state teachers col. Founded by English in 1722; inc. as village in 1828, as city in 1848. As an early trading post and fort, it was held alternately by French and English in the colonial wars. Fort Ontario (1755), now in U.S. military reservation, is still garrisoned. **4** (ŏswē'gō) City (pop. 3,316), Clackamas co., NW Oregon, on the Willamette, bet. Portland and Oregon City; cement, neckwear. Seat of Marylhurst Col. and girls' orphan home. Founded c.1850, inc. 1909.

Oswego River (ŏswē'gō), N central N.Y., formed by confluence of Oneida and Seneca rivers just S of Phoenix, flows c.23 mi. NW, past Fulton, to L. Ontario at Oswego (water power). Part of N.Y. State Barge Canal system; has locks at Oswego.

Oswestry (ŏz'wŭstrē), municipal borough (1931 pop. 9,654; 1951 census 10,713), NW Shropshire, England, 17 mi. NW of Shrewsbury; mfg. of machinery, leather, light metal products; agr. market. Town named after St. Oswald, Christian king of Northumbria, killed here (642) in a battle with Penda, king of Mercia. In 12th cent. town was fortified by Normans and played a part in wars with Wales. Fragments of the walls remain. Church dates from 13th cent., and there is a 15th-cent. grammar school. Just N is Old Oswestry, site of an anc. British fort.

Oswiecim (ôshvyĕ'chĕm), Pol. *Oświęcim*, Ger. *Auschwitz* (oush'vĭts), town (pop. 6,708), Katowice prov., S Poland, on Sola R. near its mouth, and 32 mi. W of Cracow. Rail junction; trade center; mfg. of chemicals, metalware, cardboard; distilling, canning. Major power station. Coal deposits and fish hatcheries (dating from 13th cent.) in vicinity. During Second World War, the Germans here organized one of their most infamous concentration-camp systems; it included the base camp (*Auschwitz I*) at near-by Owsianka, an extermination camp (*Auschwitz II*) at near-by Brzezinka, Ger. *Birkenau*, and c.40 supplementary camps scattered throughout a wide area. At the huge Brzezinka extermination camp were gas chambers where victims were killed and crematoria where corpses were burned. About 4,000,000 inmates, mostly Jews, were annihilated, mainly by gassing, but also by phenol injections, shooting, hanging, malnutrition, and disease. Poland led the list of 27 nations represented among the prisoners. Until 1951 in Krakow prov.

Osyechenitsa, mountain, Yugoslavia: see OSJECENICA.

Osyka (ōsī'kŭ), town (pop. 724), Pike co., SW Miss., on Tangipahoa R. and 16 mi. S of McComb, at La. line.

Oszmiana, Belorussian SSR: see OSHMYANY.

Ota (ō'tä). **1** Town (pop. 6,450), Gifu prefecture, central Honshu, Japan, on Kiso R. and 10 mi. NW of Tajimi; rice, wheat, raw silk. **2** Town (pop. 49,943), Gumma prefecture, central Honshu, Japan, 8 mi. S of Kiryu; agr. center (rice, wheat); aircraft plant. **3** Town (pop. 11,256), Ibaraki prefecture, central Honshu, Japan, 9 mi. SW of Hitachi; agr. center (tobacco, rice, wheat); sawmilling, spinning. **4** Town, Shimane prefecture, Japan: see ODA. **5** Town (pop. 4,068), Yamaguchi prefecture, SW Honshu, Japan, 9 mi. NW of Yamaguchi; agr. center (rice, wheat). Copper, cobalt mined near by.

Otaci, Moldavian SSR: see ATAKI.

Otáez or **Santa María de Otáez** (sän'tä märē'ä dā ōtīs'), town (pop. 329), Durango, N Mexico, in W foothills of Sierra Madre Occidental, 45 mi. SW of Santiago Papasquiaro; corn, cotton, chick-peas.

Otago, Japan: see YATSUSHIRO.

Otago (ōtä'gō), provincial district (□ 25,220; pop. 214,213), S S.Isl., New Zealand. Chief cities are Dunedin (seat of Univ. of Otago) and Invercargill. Fertile coastal plain in SE; Otago Peninsula on E coast. Fiordland Natl. Park in SW contains many lakes and sounds surrounded by mts. Produces wool, fruits, Oamaru limestone, some quartz and gold. Chief ports: Bluff, Port Chalmers. Area roughly divided into 2 land dists., Otago and Southland.

Otago Harbour, inlet of S Pacific, SE S.Isl., New Zealand; 13 mi. long, 1 mi. wide at mouth; Port Chalmers on W shore. Flanked by **Otago Peninsula** (E), 14 mi. long, 5 mi. wide; Dunedin is at its base.

Otahara, Japan: see OTAWARA.

Otahuhu (ō"tŭhōō'), borough (pop. 7,161), NW N.Isl., New Zealand, SE suburb of Auckland, on Tamaki R., chemical plants, soap and candle factories, abattoirs.

Otaka. 1 (ō'täkä) or **Odaka** (ō'däkä), town (pop. 9,278), Aichi prefecture, central Honshu, Japan, just S of Nagoya; rice, wheat, raw silk. **2** (ōtä'kä) Town, Fukushima prefecture, Japan: see ODAKA.

Otake (ō'täkä), town (pop. 14,047), Hiroshima prefecture, SW Honshu, Japan, on Hiroshima Bay, 18 mi. SW of Hiroshima; commercial center for agr. area (rice, wheat); paper milling.

Otaki (ō'täkē), town (pop. 5,970), Chiba prefecture, central Honshu, Japan, on central Chiba Peninsula, 8 mi. WNW of Ohara; rice, wheat, raw silk, poultry.

Otaki (ōtä'kē), borough (pop. 2,042), S N.Isl., New Zealand, 40 mi. NNE of Wellington; dairying center. Maori col.

Otamatea, New Zealand: see PAPAROA.

Otani, Russian SFSR: see SOKOL, Sakhalin oblast.

Otar (ŭtär'), town (1948 pop. over 2,000), E Dzhambul oblast, Kazakh SSR, on Turksib RR and 90 mi. W of Alma-Ata.

Ota River, Japan: see HIROSHIMA.

Otaru (ōtä'rōō), city (1940 pop. 164,282; 1947 pop. 164,934), W Hokkaido, Japan, on Ishikari Bay, 20 mi. WNW of Sapporo. Principal coal-loading port of isl.; fishing center; herring processing; paper milling, rubber-goods mfg., sake brewing.

Otaru Bay, Japan: see ISHIKARI BAY.

Otatitlán (ōtätētlän'), town (pop. 2,595), Veracruz, SE Mexico, on Papaloápam R. and 28 mi. SE of Tierra Blanca; sugar cane, coffee, fruit.

Otautau (ōtou'tou), town (pop. 227), ⊙ Wallace co. (□ 3,727; pop. 8,625), S S.Isl., New Zealand, 27 mi. NW of Invercargill; sawmill, dairy plant.

Otava (ō'tävä), village in Mikkeli rural commune (pop. 13,383), Mikkeli co., SE Finland, in Saimaa lake region, 7 mi. WSW of Mikkeli; sawmills. Site of agr. school.

Otavalo (ōtävä'lō), town (1950 pop. 8,379), Imbabura prov., N Ecuador, on Pan American Highway, on railroad, 35 mi. NNE of Quito, in magnificent setting, surrounded by Andean peaks; alt. 8,441 ft. Health resort (thermal springs), textile and agr. center (coffee, cotton, sugar cane, tobacco, cereals, potatoes, fruit, livestock). Mfg. of woolen goods (ponchos, carpets), cotton textiles, leather goods, soap, native jewelry; flour milling. Its weekly Indian fair is one of the most colorful in South America, and Indians predominate in the whole region. The town was largely destroyed by the 1868 earthquake. Iron deposits near by.

Otava River (ô'tävä), S Bohemia, Czechoslovakia, formed 4 mi. SW of Kasperske Hory by junction of 2 headstreams rising in foothills of Bohemian Forest; flows NNE, past Susice, E, past Strakonice, and N, past Pisek, to Vltava R. at historic ruins of Zvikov; c.55 mi. long.

Otavi (ōtä'vē), village, N South-West Africa, 50 mi. WSW of Grootfontein; alt. 4,658 ft.; rail junction in cattle-raising, copper-, lead-mining region.

Otawara (ō'täwärŭ) or **Otahara** (-härŭ), town (pop. 16,132), Tochigi prefecture, central Honshu, Japan, 23 mi. NNE of Utsunomiya; commercial center for agr. area (rice, wheat); silk cocoons.

Otay (ō'tī), village (pop. 1,774), San Diego co., S Calif., near Chula Vista.

Otay River (ō'tī), S Calif., rises in SW San Diego co., flows c.25 mi. generally W to S end of San Diego Bay. Savage Dam (172 ft. high, 750 ft. long; completed 1919) impounds a water-supply reservoir for San Diego city.

Otdykh, Russian SFSR: see ZHUKOVSKI.

Oteapan (ōtäă'pän), town (pop. 2,358), Veracruz, SE Mexico, on Isthmus of Tehuantepec, 8 mi. WNW of Minatitlán; fruit, livestock.

Otego (ōtē'gō), village (pop. 699), Otsego co., central N.Y., on the Susquehanna and 7 mi. SW of Oneonta, in dairying and grain-growing area; summer resort.

Oteiza (ōtā'thä), town (pop. 1,301), Navarre prov., N Spain, 5 mi. SE of Estella; grain, wine.

Otélé (ōtĕ'lā), village, Nyong et Sanaga region, SW central Fr. Cameroons, 30 mi. SW of Yaoundé; rail junction and native market; cacao and coffee plantations in vicinity.

Otepaa or **Otepya**, Est. *Otepää* (all: ō'tăpă), Ger. *Odenpäh*, city (pop. 2,015), SE Estonia, 24 mi. SSW of Tartu, in Otepaa hills (rising to 804 ft.); agr. market; oats, dairy farming. Dates from 13th cent.

Otero (ōtâ'rō). **1** County (□ 1,267; pop. 25,275), SE Colo.; ⊙ La Junta. Irrigated agr. area, drained by Purgatoire, Apishapa, and Arkansas rivers. Livestock, sugar beets, feed. Formed 1889. **2** County (□ 6,638; pop. 14,909), S N.Mex.; ⊙ Alamogordo. Livestock-grazing area bordering on Texas; lumber. Mescalero Indian Reservation in N; ranges of Sacramento Mts. in N and SE, in parts of Lincoln Natl. Forest. Part of White Sands Natl. Monument in W. Formed 1899.

Otero de Herreros (ōtā'rō dhā ĕrā'rōs), town (pop. 791), Segovia prov., central Spain, 9 mi. SW of Segovia; wheat, rye, barley, oats, livestock. Nickel and copper mining.

Otford, town and parish (pop. 1,314), W Kent, England, on Darent R. and 3 mi. N of Sevenoaks; agr. market. Has 14th-cent. church and remains of palace of archbishops of Canterbury, built 1070, rebuilt 1501.

Othello, town (pop. 526), Adams co., SE Wash., 65 mi. ENE of Yakima, in Columbia basin agr. region.

Othfresen (ôt'frā"zŭn), village (pop. 3,415), in Brunswick, NW Germany, after 1945 in Lower Saxony, 7 mi. N of Goslar; sugar refining; feed. Until 1941 in former Prussian prov. of Hanover.

Otho (ō'thō), village, Webster co., central Iowa, near Des Moines R., 5 mi. S of Fort Dodge; brick and tile plant.

Othonoi (ô-thônoi'), island (□ 3.4; pop. 747) in Ionian Sea, Greece, in Corfu nome, 13 mi. off NW Corfu; 39°50'N 19°26'E; 3.5 mi. long, 1.5 mi. wide; largely mountainous. Fisheries. Also called Phanos or Fanos.

Othrys or **Othris** (both: ô'thrĭs), mountain massif in E central Greece, on Thessaly-Phthiotis line, bet. Malian Gulf (S) and Gulf of Volos (NE); rises to 5,773 ft. in the Gerakovouni (Yerakovouni), 17 mi. ENE of Lamia. Copper deposits. Also called Orthrys or Orthris.

Oti, Japan: see OCHI.

Otiai, Japan: see OCHIAI.

Ötigheim (ŭ'tĭkh-hīm), village (pop. 2,661), S Baden, Germany, 3 mi. N of Rastatt; corn, horse-radish.

Otira (ōtĭ'rŭ), township (pop. 237), W central S.Isl., New Zealand, 70 mi. NW of Christchurch, at W end of Otira tunnel (5.25 mi. long), near Arthur's Pass. Tunnel through Southern Alps is only rail route bet. E and W coasts. Winter sports.

Oti River (ō'tē), chiefly in Togoland, rises in S Upper Volta near Fr. Togoland border, flows 320 mi. S in meandering course, past Sansanné-Mango to Volta R. 12 mi. SSE of Kete-Krachi. Forms part (c.60 mi.) of border bet. Br. and Fr. Togoland.

Otis (ō'tĭs). **1** Town (pop. 532), Washington co., NE Colo., 13 mi. E of Akron; grain, livestock, dairy and poultry products. **2** City (pop. 410), Rush co., central Kansas, 18 mi. NW of Great Bend, in wheat area. Gas and oil fields near by. **3** Town (pop. 109), Hancock co., S Maine, 16 mi. SE of Bangor, in recreational area; paper mill. **4** Agr. town (pop. 359), Berkshire co., SW Mass., 19 mi. SSE of Pittsfield.

Otis Air Force Base, Mass.: see FALMOUTH.

Otisco Lake (ōtĭ'skō), Onondaga co., central N.Y., one of the Finger Lakes, 14 mi. SW of Syracuse; 6 mi. long, ½–1 mi. wide. Drains NE to Onondaga L. via small Otisco Outlet.

Otisfield, resort town (pop. 599), Cumberland co., SW Maine, bet. Crooked R. and Thompson L. 16 mi. W of Auburn.

Otish Mountains, range in central Que., c.50 mi. long, on N side of the Laurentian Plateau; rises to 3,700 ft.; 52°20'N 70°40'W. Eastmain, Peribonca, and Outardes rivers rise here. Range is part of the St. Lawrence–Hudson Bay watershed.

Otisville. 1 Village (pop. 592), Genesee co., SE central Mich., 14 mi. NE of Flint, in farm area. **2** Resort village (pop. 911), Orange co., SE N.Y., 7 mi. WNW of Middletown, in the Shawangunk range; stone quarries.

Otivar (ōtēvär'), village (pop. 1,812), Granada prov., S Spain, 10 mi. WNW of Motril; sugar milling, brandy distilling, olive-oil processing. Sugar cane, esparto, honey, figs.

Otjiwarongo (ōchēwärông'gō), town (pop. 2,488), N South-West Africa, 150 mi. NNW of Windhoek, alt. 4,774 ft.; rail junction; distributing center for N part of country, in cattle-raising region. Fluorspar deposits. Reserve (□ c.1,300) of Herero and Damara tribes is 30 mi. E.

Otley, urban district (1931 pop. 11,034; 1951 census 11,568), West Riding, central Yorkshire, England, on Wharfe R. and 8 mi. NNE of Bradford; woolen and paper milling; also mfg. of leather, biscuits, printing machinery. Has church of 15th-cent. origin.

Otley (ŏt'lē), village (pop. c.200), Marion co., S central Iowa, 31 mi. ESE of Des Moines, in bituminous-coal-mining area.

Otmuchow (ôtmōō'khōōf), Pol. *Otmuchów*, Ger. *Ottmachau* (ôtmä'khou), town (1939 pop. 4,964; 1946 pop. 3,075) in Upper Silesia, after 1945 in Opole prov., S Poland, near Czechoslovak border, at N foot of Reichenstein Mts., on the Glatzer Neisse and 8 mi. W of Neisse (Nysa); textile and paper milling, mfg. of glass, furniture. Just W, on the Glatzer Neisse, is dam and irrigation reservoir (□ 8; 5 mi. long, 3 mi. wide), completed 1933. Hydroelectric station. Town was residence of prince-bishops of Breslau. Has 17th-cent. church, remains of 15th-cent. castle.

Oto (ō'tō), town (pop. 302), Woodbury co., W Iowa, on Little Sioux R. and 31 mi. ESE of Sioux City, in livestock and grain area.

Otocac (ôtô'chäts), Serbo-Croatian *Otočac*, village (pop. 3,503), W Croatia, Yugoslavia, on Gacka R. and 19 mi. ESE of Senj; local trade center. First mentioned in 12th cent.

Otoe (ō'tō), county (□ 613; pop. 17,056), SE Nebr.; ⊙ Nebraska City. Agr. and commercial region bounded E by Missouri R. at Iowa-Mo. line; drained by Little Nemaha R. and its branches. Mfg. at Nebraska City. Livestock, feed, grain, fruit, dairy and poultry produce. Formed 1855; lost territory (1943) to Fremont co., Iowa.

Otoe, village (pop. 230), Otoe co., SE Nebr., 13 mi. W of Nebraska City and on branch of Little Nemaha R.

Otomari, Russian SFSR: see KORSAKOV.

Oton (ōtōn'), town (1939 pop. 4,467; 1948 municipality pop. 21,306), Iloilo prov., SE Panay isl., Philippines, near Panay Gulf, 6 mi. W of Iloilo; rice-growing center.

Otopeni (ôtôpān'), village (pop. 3,136), Bucharest prov., S Rumania, 7 mi. N of Bucharest; corn, wheat. Includes Otopeni-de-Sus and Otopeni-de-Jos. Also spelled Otopenii.

Otoque Island (ōtō'kā) (pop. 954), in Bay of Panama of the Pacific, Panama prov., E Panama, 24 mi. SSW of Panama city; 2 mi. long, 1 mi. wide.

Otori, Japan: see SAKAI, Osaka prefecture.

Otorohanga (ō"tûrōhäng'û), town (pop. 934), ⊙ Otorohanga co. (□ 600; pop. 5,880), W central N.Isl., New Zealand, 95 mi. SSE of Auckland; dairy plants.

Otradnaya (ŭträd'nĭŭ), village (1926 pop. 12,553), SE Krasnodar Territory, Russian SFSR, on Urup R., in N foothills of the Greater Caucasus, and 45 mi. SSE of Armavir; flour mill, metalworks; bast-fiber processing (sunn hemp).

Otradnoye (-nŭyŭ). **1** Town (1940 pop. over 500), central Leningrad oblast, Russian SFSR, on Neva R. and 21 mi. SE of Leningrad; brickworks. **2** Town (1939 pop. 791), W Kaliningrad oblast, Russian SFSR, just W of SVETLOGORSK; Baltic seaside resort. Until 1945, in East Prussia and called Georgenswalde (gäôr'gûnsväldû).

Otranto (ōtrăn'tō, It. ô'träntô), anc. *Hydruntum*, town (pop. 2,507), Lecce prov., Apulia, S Italy, fishing port on Strait of Otranto, 22 mi. SE of Lecce. Rail terminus; agr. center (olives, grapes, figs, vegetables). Archbishopric. Has cathedral (begun 1080; fine mosaic floor) and ruins of an imposing castle, the setting of Horace Walpole's novel, *The Castle of Otranto*. An important seaport until devastated by Turks in 1480.

Otranto, Cape, easternmost point of Italy, in Apulia, on "heel" of Ital. peninsula, at W end of Strait of Otranto, 3 mi. SSE of Otranto; 40°7'N 18°31'E.

Otranto, Strait of, connects Adriatic Sea (N) with Ionian Sea (S); extends c.43 mi. bet. Cape Otranto (S Italy) and Cape Linguetta (Albania).

Otrar, Kazakh SSR: see SHAULDER.

Otra River (ôt'rä), Nor. *Otra*, *Otterå*, or *Ottra*, Aust-Agder co., S Norway, rises in lakes in the Bykle Mts., flows S through the Setesdal and the Byglandsfjord to the Skagerrak at Kristiansand. Length, 150 mi. Below the Byglandsfjord it is sometimes called the Torridal.

Otricoli (ôtrē'kôlē), village (pop. 818), Terni prov., Umbria, central Italy, near the Tiber, 13 mi. SW of Terni. Near by are remains of anc. Ocriculum.

Otrokovice (ô'trôkôvĭtsĕ), town (pop. 7,830), E Moravia, Czechoslovakia, 6 mi. E of Gottwaldov; rail junction; tanning center producing mainly semi-finished goods for Gottwaldov workshops; mfg. of textiles, paper, chemicals, woodworking. Municipal airport of Gottwaldov area here.

Otrozhka (ŭtrôsh'kŭ), N suburb of Voronezh, Voronezh oblast, Russian SFSR, on left bank of Voronezh R., near railroad (Otrozhka junction); mfg. (locomotives, railroad cars). Inc. c.1940 into Voronezh. Sometimes called Otrozhenski.

Otsego (ŏtsē'gō). **1** County (□ 530; pop. 6,435), N Mich.; ⊙ Gaylord. Drained by Sturgeon and Black rivers, and by North Branch of Au Sable R. Agr. (livestock, potatoes, fruit; dairy products); hardwood timber; sawmilling. Year-round resort area (hunting, fishing, boating). Includes many small lakes, a state park, and state forest. Organized 1875. **2** County (□ 1,013; pop. 50,763), central N.Y.; ⊙ Cooperstown. Bounded W by Unadilla R.; drained by the Susquehanna, issuing here from Otsego L. Dairying area; also poultry, livestock, grain, hay. Mfg. at Oneonta, Unadilla, Worcester. Resorts on Canadarago L. and several small lakes. Mineral springs at Richfield Springs. Formed 1791.

Otsego, city (pop. 3,990), Allegan co., SW Mich., 13 mi. NW of Kalamazoo and on Kalamazoo R. (water power), in agr. area; paper milling, mfg. of shoes. Settled 1832; inc. as village 1865, as city 1918.

Otsego Lake. **1** Lake (4 mi. long), Otsego co., N Mich.; at Send, 7 mi. S of Gaylord, is Otsego Lake village (pop. c.50); resort with fine beaches. A state park is here. **2** Lake (8 mi. long, c.1 mi. wide), E central N.Y., 28 mi. SE of Utica, in a resort area. The Susquehanna issues from its S end at Cooperstown. It is the Glimmerglass of James Fenimore Cooper's tales.

Otselic River (ŏtsē'lĭk), central N.Y., rises in S Madison co., flows c.45 mi. SW, past Cincinnatus, to Tioughnioga R. at Whitney Point.

Otsu (ō'tsōō). **1** Village (pop. 5,184), S Hokkaido, Japan, on the Pacific, at mouth of Tokachi R., 28 mi. SE of Obihiro; fishing. **2** Town (pop. 7,392), Ibaraki prefecture, central Honshu, Japan, on the Pacific, 18 mi. NNE of Hitachi; fishing port. **3** Town (pop. 9,078), Kumamoto prefecture, W central Kyushu, Japan, 11 mi. NE of Kumamoto; agr. center (rice, wheat). Sometimes spelled Otu. **4** City, Osaka prefecture, Japan: see IZUMI-OTSU. **5** City (1940 pop. 67,532; 1947 pop. 81,426), ⊙ Shiga prefecture, S Honshu, Japan, on S shore of L. Biwa, 5 mi. E of Kyoto; tourist center; mfg. (textiles, staple fibers, hemp cloth). Port for excursion steamers. Imperial seat in 2d and 7th cent. Site of Mii-dera (7th-cent. Buddhist temple). Bombed (1945) in Second World War. Sometimes Otu.

Otsuki (ō'tsōōkē). **1** Town (pop. 6,003), Fukushima prefecture, central Honshu, Japan, 3 mi. W of Koriyama; rice growing. Copper formerly mined here. **2** Town (pop. 10,510), Yamanashi prefecture, central Honshu, Japan, near Fujiyama, 22 mi. E of Kofu; mfg. of silk textiles; agr. (rice, wheat).

Otta (ô'tä), town, Abeokuta prov., Western Provinces, SW Nigeria, 20 mi. SE of Ilaro; road junction; cotton weaving, indigo dyeing; cacao, palm oil and kernels. Phosphate deposits.

Otta (ôt'tä), village (pop. 903) in Sel canton (pop. 3,036), Opland co., S central Norway, in the Gudbrandsdal, on Lagen R. at mouth of Otta R., on railroad and 60 mi. NW of Lillehammer; slate and steatite quarries; stock raising. Tourist resort. Near-by monument celebrates defeat (1612) of Scottish mercenaries in Swedish service by Otta peasants. In Second World War, scene (April, 1940) of engagement bet. Anglo-Norwegian and German forces. Sel village, 2 mi. N, has talc quarries.

Ottaiano, Italy: see OTTAVIANO.

Ottakring (ô'tŭkrĭng), outer W district (□ 3; pop. 117,361) of Vienna, Austria.

Ottappalam (ŏtŭpä'lŭm), town (pop. 8,281), Malabar dist., SW Madras, India, on Ponnani R. and 50 mi. SE of Calicut; rice, cassava, pepper, ginger. Sometimes spelled Ottapalam.

Otta River (ôt'tä), Opland co., S central Norway, rises on NW slope of Jotunheim Mts. near head of Geiranger Fjord, flows 70 mi. generally ESE, past Skjak, through expansion (25 mi. long) of Vagavatn, Nor. *Vågåvatn*, past Vagamo, to Lagen R. at Otta.

Ottauquechee River (ŏ"tûkwē'chē), E Vt., rises in Green Mts. NE of Rutland, flows c.40 mi. generally E, past Woodstock (dam here), to the Connecticut S of White River Junction. Formerly Quechee R.

Ottaviano (ôt"tävyä'nô), town (pop. 6,088), Napoli prov., Campania, S Italy, at NE foot of Vesuvius, 11 mi. E of Naples; textile mfg. (cotton, linen). Formerly Ottaiano.

Ottawa (ŏ'tûwû), city (pop. 154,951), ⊙ Canada and Carleton co., SE Ont., on Ottawa R. (bridge), opposite Hull (Que.), and 100 mi. WSW of Montreal; 45°24'N 75°42'W. Founded 1826 by Colonel By and named Bytown, its named was changed (1854) to Ottawa. It was chosen as ⊙ Canada by Queen Victoria in 1858, and became ⊙ of new dominion of Canada in 1867. Features include Parliament bldgs., built 1859–65, burned 1916 and later rebuilt; Victoria Memorial Mus.; Royal Mint; Dominion Observatory; Natl. Art Gall.; Public Archives; Anglican and R.C. cathedrals; and Rideau Hall, official residence of governor general of Canada. City is site of Ottawa Univ., founded 1848, several other educational institutions, and Central Canadian Experimental Farm. Chaudière Falls of Ottawa R., within city limits, supply hydroelectric power. Near by is N end of Rideau Canal. City's industries include paper milling, woodworking, watchmaking.

Ottawa. **1** County (□ 723; pop. 7,265), N central Kansas; ⊙ Minneapolis. Rolling prairie region, intersected by Solomon R. and drained in SW by Saline R. Grain, livestock. Formed 1866. **2** County (□ 564; pop. 73,751), SW Mich.; ⊙ Grand Haven. Bounded W by L. Michigan; drained by Grand and Black rivers. Livestock, poultry, fruit, truck, grain, celery, potatoes, sugar beets; dairy products; tulip growing. Mfg. at Grand Haven and Zeeland. Oil refineries, commercial fisheries. Has resorts, two state parks. Organized 1837. **3** County (□ 263; pop. 29,469), N Ohio; ⊙ Port Clinton. Bounded NE by L. Erie; drained by Portage R. and small Toussaint and Packer creeks. Includes Perry's Victory and International Peace Memorial Natl. Monument. Agr. area (grain, fruit, sugar beets, truck, dairy products); mfg. at Genoa, Oakharbor, Port Clinton. Limestone quarries; fisheries. Bass Isls. are resorts. Formed 1840. **4** County (□ 483; pop. 32,218), extreme NE Okla.; ⊙ Miami. Bounded N by Kansas line, E by Mo. line; part of the Ozarks are in E. Drained by Neosho and Spring rivers; includes section of L. of the Cherokees (recreation). Contains part of rich lead and zinc-mining region (centering on Picher) extending into Kansas and Mo. Also stock raising, dairying, agr. (corn, grain, poultry), some mfg. (mining equipment, food products). Formed 1907.

Ottawa. **1** City (pop. 16,957), ⊙ La Salle co., N Ill., at confluence of Illinois and Fox rivers (both bridged here), c.40 mi. SW of Aurora; mfg. (glass, tile, clay products, farm machinery, asphalt, radium dials, zinc, cement). Bituminous-coal mines; clay, silica-sand pits. Agr. (corn, wheat, oats, soybeans, livestock, poultry; dairy products) in region. Near by are Starved Rock State Park and Buffalo Rock State Park. Laid out 1830, but settled 1832 after Black Hawk War; inc. as village in 1837, as city in 1853. First Lincoln-Douglas debate held here in 1858. **2** City (pop. 10,081), ⊙ Franklin co., E Kansas, on Marais des Cygnes R. and 50 mi. SW of Kansas City; trade, shipping center for grain and poultry area. Flour milling, dairying; mfg. of brooms, gas engines; railroad shops; rock quarries. Seat of Ottawa Univ. Site was settled in 1832 by Ottawa Indians. Baptist mission was established here in 1837 by Jotham Meeker. City founded 1864, inc. 1866. Extensively damaged by great flood of July, 1951. **3** Village (pop. 2,962), ⊙ Putnam co., NW Ohio, 18 mi. N of Lima and on Blanchard R.; beet-sugar refining; mfg. of television tubes, food and dairy products, clay and wood products. Oil wells, stone quarries. Founded 1833.

Ottawa Hills, residential village (pop. 2,333), Lucas co., NW Ohio, just W of Toledo. Settled 1916, inc. 1924.

Ottawa Islands, SE Keewatin Dist., Northwest Territories, group of 24 small isls. and islets in Hudson Bay, off NW Ungava Peninsula; 60°N 80°W. Group covers area c.70 mi. long, 50 mi. wide. Main isls. are Booth, Bronson, Gilmour (rises to over 1,800 ft.), Perley, J. Gordon, Paltee, and Eddy.

Ottawa River, in Ont. and Que., largest tributary of the St. Lawrence, rises in the Laurentian Plateau, issuing from Grand Lake Victoria 120 mi. NE of North Bay; flows W through Lac Simard and Lac des Quinze to L. Timiskaming, thence S and SE, over the Long Sault Rapids, to Mattawa, and then generally ESE, past Chalk River, Petawawa, Pembroke, Ottawa, and Cornwall, to the St. Lawrence W of Montreal; 696 mi. long. Forms border bet. Ont. and Que. over most of its course. Lower course consists largely of a series of expansions, including Allumette, Chats, Deschênes lakes, and Lac des Deux Montagnes. There are numerous rapids, among them Des Joachims, Chats, and Chaudière falls, supplying hydroelectric power. Chief tributaries are Rouge, North Nation, Lièvre, Gatineau, Coulonge (N), Mattawa, South Nation, Mississippi, Madawaska, Petawawa, and Rideau rivers (S). Rideau Canal connects the Ottawa with L. Ontario. Navigable to Ottawa for vessels with 9-ft. draught. Valley was 1st visited by Étienne Brûlé (1610); explored (1613–15) by Champlain to the Mattawa R. Later became important highway for explorers, fur traders, and missionaries. Settlement of valley began in 19th cent.; subsequently lumbering industry along the Ottawa became important.

Ottawa River, W Ohio, rises in Hardin co., flows NW and W, past Lima, then N, past Elida, to Auglaize R. in Putnam co.; c.50 mi. long.

Ottbergen (ôt'bĕr"gûn), village (pop. 1,881), in former Prussian prov. of Westphalia, NW Germany, after 1945 in North Rhine-Westphalia, 5 mi. SW of Höxter; rail junction.

Ottendorf-Okrilla (ô'tûndôrf-ôkrĭ'lä), town (pop. 5,735), Saxony, E central Germany, 12 mi. NNE of Dresden; mfg. (glass, brake linings).

Ottenheim (-hīm), village (pop. 1,621), S Baden, Germany, near the Rhine (Fr. border; road bridge) and 6 mi. NW of Lahr; customs station; woodworking. Tobacco.

Ottenhöfen or **Ottenhöfen im Schwarzwald** (ô"tûnhû'fûn ĭm shvärts'vält), village (pop. 2,272), S Baden, Germany, in Black Forest, 11 mi. NE of Offenburg; rail terminus; woodworking, lumber milling. Fruitgrowing. Climatic health resort (alt. 1,020 ft.) and tourist center.

Ottensen, Germany: see ALTONA.

Otter, Peaks of, Va., 2 summits in the Blue Ridge, on Bedford-Botetourt co. line, c.25 mi. W of Lynchburg. Flat Top (N) is 4,001 ft., Sharp Top (S) 3,875 ft. high.

Ottera, Norway: see OTRA RIVER.

Otterbach (ô'tûrbäkh), village (pop. 2,592), Rhenish Palatinate, W Germany, on the Lauter and 3 mi. N of Kaiserslautern; grain, potatoes.

Otterbein (ŏ'tûrbīn), town (pop. 641), Benton co., W Ind., 13 mi. WNW of Lafayette.

Otterberg (-bĕrk), town (pop. 3,261), Rhenish Palatinate, W Germany, 4 mi. N of Kaiserslautern; rye, oats, potatoes. Has 13th-cent. church.

Otterbourne (ŏ'tûrbûrn), agr. village and parish (pop. 1,147), central Hampshire, England, near Itchen R., 5 mi. SSW of Winchester.

Otterburn, village and parish (pop. 361), central Northumberland, England, on Rede R. and 18 mi. N of Hexham; woolen milling. Scene of battle (1388) in which Scots defeated the English; sometimes called the battle of Chevy Chase, after the ballad.

Otterburne, village (pop. estimate 350), SE Man., on Rat R. and 27 mi. S of Winnipeg; grain; dairying.

Otter Creek, village (1940 pop. 632), Levy co., N Fla., 34 mi. SW of Gainesville.

Otter Creek. 1 In S central Utah, rises in Fish Lake Plateau, flows 30 mi. SSW, past Sevier Plateau, to Otter Creek Reservoir (5.5 mi. long), formed by dam on East Fork Sevier R. Creek is dammed near source. **2** In W Vt., rises in Green Mts. near Dorset, flows c.100 mi. generally NW, past Rutland, Proctor, Middlebury, and Vergennes, to L. Champlain near Ferrisburg. In upper course, flows bet. the Taconics (W) and Green Mts.

Otter Creek Recreational area, Ky.: see MEADE, co.

Otter Lake. 1 Village (pop. 523), on Lapeer-Genesee co. line, E Mich., 18 mi. NE of Flint, in farm and lake region. **2** Resort village, Oneida co., central N.Y., in the W Adirondacks, on small Otter L., 35 mi. N of Utica.

Otterndorf (ô′tûrndôrf), town (pop. 6,909), in former Prussian prov. of Hanover, NW Germany, after 1945 in Lower Saxony, near Elbe estuary, 9 mi. SE of Cuxhaven; agr. market center; food processing (flour and dairy products, canned goods, spirits); feed.

Otteroy (ôt′tûr-ûü), Nor. *Otterøy*, island (□ 29; pop. 1,540) at mouth of Molde Fjord, More og Romsdal co., W Norway, 7 mi. W of Molde; 10 mi. long, 4 mi. wide; fisheries.

Otter River, Devon, England, rises near Somerset border at Otterford, flows 24 mi. SW, past Honiton, to the Channel at Budleigh Salterton.

Otter River, Mass.: see GARDNER.

Ottersberg (ô′tûrsbĕrk), village (pop. 3,074), in former Prussian prov. of Hanover, NW Germany, after 1945 in Lower Saxony, 14 mi. E of Bremen; sawmilling.

Otterstadt (ô′tûr-shtät), village (pop. 1,814), Rhenish Palatinate, W Germany, on an oxbow lake of the Rhine and 4 mi. N of Speyer; corn, tobacco.

Otter Tail, county (□ 2,000; pop. 51,320), W Minn.; ⊙ Fergus Falls. Extensively watered agr. area drained by Pelican, Pomme de Terre, and Otter Tail rivers, and numerous lakes. Dairy products, livestock, poultry, grain, potatoes; deposits of marl and peat. Chief lakes are L. Lida in NW, and Dead L. and Otter Tail L., NE of Fergus Falls. Co. formed 1858.

Ottertail or **Otter Tail,** resort village (pop. 237), Otter Tail co., W Minn., just E of Otter Tail L., 27 mi. NE of Fergus Falls; dairy products.

Otter Tail Lake (□ 23), Otter Tail co., W Minn., 17 mi. ENE of Fergus Falls; 9 mi. long, 3 mi. wide. Fishing resorts. Lake is fed and drained by Otter Tail R.

Otter Tail River, rises in S part of Clearwater co., W Minn., flows 150 mi. S, through Pine, Rush, and Otter Tail lakes, then W, past Fergus Falls, to Breckenridge (opposite Wahpeton, N.Dak.), where it joins Bois de Sioux R. to form Red River of the North.

Otterup (ô′tûro͝op), town (pop. 1,246), Odense amt, Denmark, on N Fyn isl. and 8 mi. N of Odense; machinery, explosives, furniture.

Otterville, village (pop. estimate 500), S Ont., on Otter Creek and 16 mi. SE of Woodstock; lumbering, dairying, tobacco growing.

Otterville. 1 Town (pop. 118), Jersey co., W Ill., 15 mi. NW of Alton, in applegrowing area. **2** Town (pop. 414), Cooper co., central Mo., near Lamine R., 12 mi. E of Sedalia.

Ottery Saint Mary (ŏ′tûrē), urban district (1931 pop. 3,713; 1951 census 4,015), E Devon, England, on Otter R. and 11 mi. E of Exeter; agr. market. Has 13th-cent. church and Tudor mansion. Coleridge b. here.

Ottignies (ōtēnyē′), town (pop. 3,893), Brabant prov., central Belgium, on Dyle R. and 15 mi. SE of Brussels; agr. market.

Ottine (ŏ′tēn″), village (pop. c.200), Gonzales co., S central Texas, on San Marcos R. and 10 mi. NW of Gonzales; health resort, with mineral springs and hospitals for crippled children. Palmetto State Park, known for tropical plants, is here.

Öttingen or **Öttingen in Bayern** (û′tĭng-ŭn ĭn bī′ûrn), town (pop. 3,634), Swabia, W Bavaria, Germany, on the Wörnitz and 9 mi. NE of Nördlingen; organ mfg., woodworking. Potatoes, cabbage, ducks, hogs. Has 16th–18th-cent. castle. Chartered 12th cent. Sometimes spelled Oettingen.

Ottmachau, Poland: see OTMUCHOW.

Ottnang (ôt′näng), town (pop. 4,346), central Upper Austria, 6 mi. N of Vöcklabruck; rye, potatoes.

Otto, Cerro (sĕ′rō ŏ′tō), Andean peak (4,600 ft.) SW Río Negro natl. territory, Argentina, in Nahuel Huapí natl. park, 5 mi. WSW of San Carlos de Bariloche; popular skiing ground.

Otto Beit Bridge: see CHIRUNDU, Southern Rhodesia.

Ottobeuren (ô″tōboi′rŭn), village (pop. 4,748), Swabia, SW Bavaria, Germany, 6 mi. SE of Memmingen; metal- and woodworking, brewing, meat preserving, tanning. Church of former Benedictine abbey (764–1803) is one of outstanding baroque bldgs. of Germany. Kneipp b. here.

Ottobiano (ôt-tôbyä′nô), village (pop. 1,802), Pavia prov., Lombardy, N Italy, 8 mi. SSE of Mortara.

Ottoman Empire (ŏ′tŭmŭn), a vast state preceding the present-day republic of TURKEY (the term Turkey and Ottoman Empire are, however, often used interchangeably in a historical sense). Founded by the Ottoman or Osmali Turks, last of the Turkish people to invade the Middle East from Central Asia, it rose in 14th cent. when Osman (1288–1326), who had been given a fief by the Seljuk Turks, made himself an independent ruler upon dissolution of the Seljuk empire. His younger son Orkhan captured most of Anatolia and gained a foothold in Europe, thus engulfing the dwindling Byzantine Empire, whose fate was sealed a century later by the fall of Constantinople (1453). The great Turkish victories of Kossovo (1389) and Nikopol (1397) placed large parts of the Balkan Peninsula under Turkish rule. In 15th cent. the Ottoman Empire included practically the whole Balkan Peninsula with Rumelia, Bulgaria, Macedonia, Thessaly, Serbia, Herzegovina, and Albania, and the despotats of Athens, Mistra, and Patras, as well as some of the Venetian and Genoese possessions in the Aegean and E Mediterranean. Within a century the Ottomans had changed from a nomadic horde to a great imperial nation. The Empire reached its peak in the 16th cent. under Sultan Suleiman I, called Suleiman the Magnificent (1494–1566). He conquered Belgrade (1521), expelled (1522) the Knights Hospitalers from Rhodes, and defeated (1526) the Hungarians at Mohacs, thus paving way for the absorption of the major part of Hungary. Transylvania became a tributary principality, as did Walachia and Moldavia. Other dependencies included Bessarabia and the Khanate of the Crimea (made a vassal in 1478). Vienna was repeatedly threatened. The Asiatic borders of the empire were pushed deep into Persia and Arabia. Cairo and Algiers fell in 1517 and 1518 respectively, while all of Tripoli, Egypt, Syria, Mesopotamia, Kurdistan, Armenia, Georgia, and Azerbaijan were inc. by the 17th cent. Cyprus was conquered from Venice in 1571 and Crete in 1699. After the capture of Egypt, the Ottomans assumed the title of caliph, which they retained until 1924. The Ottoman state was founded on 2 basic institutions—the army and religion. The clergy or *ulemas* exercised the functions of judges and teachers. Another typical institution were the *Janizaries*, originally recruited from Christian youth, who became an élite corps of the army. However, the military and civil virtues of the ruling class were soon to disappear in the progressive decay that followed Suleiman's death. Economically, socially, and militarily Turkey remained a medieval state, little affected by the advancement of the rest of Europe. Court and administration became prey to vice and corruption. First serious blow was the naval defeat of Lepanto (1571). The expansion of Russia became increasingly a serious challenge. During 19th cent. disintegration of the Empire was in full swing. The Treaties of Kuchuk-Kainarji (1784), Jassy (1792), and Bucharest (1812) cost Turkey the N and NE coast of the Black Sea. In the wake of Greek War of Independence and its sequel, the Russo-Turkish War (1828–29), Greece became independent. Mohammed Ali of Egypt threatened Turkey itself. The rebellion (1875) of Bosnia and Herzegovina precipitated the Russo-Turkish War of 1877–78, in which Turkey was defeated. Only foreign intervention mitigated the peace terms. Nevertheless, Rumania (i.e., Walachia and Moldavia), Serbia, and Montenegro were declared fully independent and Bosnia and Herzegovina passed under Austrian administration. Bulgaria, made a virtually independent principality, annexed (1885) Eastern Rumelia. Reforms of the political system came too late. The 1st Turkish parliament, opened in 1877, was soon again dismissed by the sultan. Massacres inflicted on the large Armenian minority in the late 19th cent. alienated world opinion. In the meantime, the Young Turk nationalistic movement gained strength, forcing (1908) return of constitutional order. Interior disputes offered Bulgaria a chance to proclaim its independence. At the same time (1908) Austria-Hungary annexed Bosnia and Herzegovina, while disorders broke out in Albania and Arabia. A war with Italy (1911–12) resulted in the loss of Libya, and in the 2 successive Balkan Wars (1912–13) Turkey lost nearly its entire territory in Europe to Bulgaria, Serbia, Greece, and newly reconstituted Albania. This "Sick Man of Europe" was in fact dying. In 1913, Enver Pasha, leader of the Young Turks, gained virtual control by a coup d'état. The outbreak (1914) of the First World War found Turkey on the side of the Central Powers, since German interests (which had been developing the BAGHDAD RAILWAY) were strongly entrenched. Ottoman troops were successful against the Allies in the Gallipoli Campaign (1915). In 1917, however, the British occupied Baghdad and Jerusalem. Arabia rose against Turkish rule, and in 1918 resistance collapsed in Europe and Asia. With the armistice (Oct., 1918) the Ottoman Empire came to an end. Anatolia itself was salvaged by Turkish nationalists under leadership of Kemal Pasha, who ousted (1922) the sultan and became the father of modern TURKEY.

Ottone (ôt-tô′nĕ), village (pop. 371), Piacenza prov., Emilia-Romagna, N central Italy, on Trebbia R. and 11 mi. S of Bobbio.

Ottosen (ŏ′tŭsŭn), town (pop. 127), Humboldt co., N central Iowa, 30 mi. NNW of Fort Dodge; dairy products.

Ottoville, village (pop. 543), Putnam co., NW Ohio, 18 mi. NW of Lima, and on Auglaize R.

Ottra, Norway: see OTRA RIVER.

Ottumwa (ōtŭm′wŭ, ō–), city (pop. 33,631), ⊙ Wapello co., SE Iowa, on both banks of Des Moines R. (hydroelectric plant) and c.75 mi. ESE of Des Moines; industrial, commercial, and rail center in farm and coal-mining area. Meat- and poultry-packing plants, foundries, ironworks; farm and mining machinery, tools, millwork, dairy products, confectionery. Has monument to Indian chief Wapello, whose grave is near by. Ottumwa Heights jr. col. for women is here. Settled 1843, inc. 1851.

Ottweiler (ôt′vī″lŭr), city (pop. 8,016), E Saar, on Blies R. and 15 mi. NE of Saarbrücken; coal mining; iron and steel industry; mfg. of chemicals, tobacco products, ceramics; brewing.

Ottynia, Ukrainian SSR: see OTYNYA.

Otu, Japan: see OTSU, Kumamoto and Shiga prefectures.

Otumba (ōto͞om′bä), officially Otumba de Gómez Farías, city (pop. 1,560), Mexico state, central Mexico, 30 mi. NE of Mexico city; maguey, corn, stock. Cortés fought on plains near by a fierce battle (1520) in which 20,000 Indians are said to have been slain.

Otuquis, Bañados del (bänyä′dōs dĕl ōto͞o′kēs), marshy area in Santa Cruz dept., E Bolivia, in the Chaco, c.35 mi. WSW of Puerto Suárez; c.45 mi. long, 20 mi. wide. Formed by Otuquis R.

Otuquis River, Santa Cruz dept., E Bolivia, formed by confluence of TUCAVACA RIVER and SAN RAFAEL RIVER c.3 mi. S of Tucavaca; flows c.100 mi. SSE, across the NE Chaco, through the Bañados del Otuquis to the Paraguay near Bahía Negra (Paraguay).

Otura (ōto͞o′rä), town (pop. 2,072), Granada prov., S Spain, 6 mi. S of Granada; cereals, olive oil, wine.

Oturkpo (ōto͞ork′pō), town (pop. 1,367), Benue prov., Northern Provinces, S central Nigeria, on railroad and 45 mi. SW of Makurdi; agr. trade center; shea-nut processing; sesame, cassava, durra.

Otusco or **Otuzco** (both: ōto͞o′skō), city (pop. 3,726), ⊙ Otusco prov. (□ 1,343; pop. 82,938), Libertad dept., NW Peru, in Cordillera Occidental of the Andes, 34 mi. ENE of Trujillo; alt. 8,645 ft. Agr. products (wheat, coca); cattle raising.

Otvazhny, Russian SFSR: see ZHIGULEVSK.

Otvotsk, Poland: see OTWOCK.

Otway, village (pop. 229), Scioto co., S Ohio, 13 mi. WNW of Portsmouth; sawmills.

Otway, Cape, S Victoria, Australia, on N side of W approach to Bass Strait; 38°51′S 143°31′E; lighthouse.

Otway Bay, inlet of the Pacific in Tierra del Fuego, Chile, bet. Santa Inés Isl. and Desolation Isl.

Otway Sound, large inlet of Strait of Magellan, in S Magallanes prov., Chile, bet. Brunswick Peninsula and Riesco Isl.; 50 mi. long, 12–20 mi. wide.

Otwock (ôt′vôtsk), Rus. *Otvotsk* (ôt′vŭtsk), town (pop. 12,592), Warszawa prov., E central Poland, near the Vistula, on railroad and 14 mi. SE of Warsaw; cement mfg., flour milling; health resort (notably for tubercular). Meteorological station.

Otynya (ŭtĭn′yŭ), Pol. *Ottynia* (ôtĭn′yä), town (1931 pop. 4,777), central Stanislav oblast, W Ukrainian SSR, on right tributary of the Bystritsa and 15 mi. SSE of Stanislav; pottery, bricks; vegetable-oil extracting.

Ötz or **Oetz** (both: ûts), village (pop. 1,547), Tyrol, W Austria, on Ötztaler Ache R. and 23 mi. W of Innsbruck; summer resort. Chestnut trees, vineyards in vicinity.

Otze (ô′tsŭ), village (pop. 1,757), in former Prussian prov. of Hanover, NW Germany, after 1945 in Lower Saxony, 9 mi. SSW of Celle, in oil dist.

Otzolotepec, Mexico: see VILLA CUAUHTÉMOC, Mexico state.

Ötztal (ûts′täl), valley of Tyrol, W Austria, extending 30 mi. S from Inn R. along the Ötztaler Ache, which rises in the Ötztal Alps. Flanked by peaks and glaciers of the Ötztal Alps (SW) and Stubai Alps (NE), the valley is known for its scenic beauty. Flax and corn grown in fertile lower valley. Also spelled Ötzthal.

Ötztal Alps, Ger. *Ötztaler Alpen*, Ital. *Alpi Venoste*, E division of Central Alps along Austro-Ital. border, but principally in S Tyrol (Austria); extend E from Rhaetian Alps at Passo di Resia to Zillertal Alps at Brenner Pass. Bounded by Inn R. valley (N) and by upper Adige R. valley (S). Highest peak, Wildspitze (12,379 ft.). Divided by Ötztal (valley of Ötztaler Ache R.) into Ötztal Alps proper (SW) and STUBAI ALPS (NE). The Ortles group (in Italy, S of Val Venosta) is sometimes considered S outlier of Ötztal Alps. Also spelled Ötzthal.

Ou-, for Chinese names beginning thus and not found here: see under Ow-.

Ou, river, China: see WU RIVER.

Ouachita (wŏ'shĭtô", wô'-). **1** County (□ 738; pop. 33,051), S Ark.; ⊙ Camden. Drained by Ouachita and Little Missouri rivers. Agr.: cotton, corn, poultry. Mfg. at Camden. Oil wells; timber; gravel, asphalt. Lumbering. Formed 1844. **2** Parish (□ 642; pop. 74,713), NE central La.; ⊙ Monroe. Bounded E by Bayou Lafourche; intersected by Ouachita R. and Bayou D'Arbonne. Stock raising, fruitgrowing, lumbering in W; cotton and corn growing, dairying in E. Large natural-gas fields, gas pipelines. Some mfg., including processing of farm products. Formed 1805.

Ouachita Mountains, in E Okla. and W Ark., a series of E-W ridges (c.220 mi. long, 60 mi. wide) extending W from Little Rock (Ark.) to Atoka (Okla.), and lying bet. the Red and Arkansas rivers. Elevations range from bet. 500 to 700 ft. near Little Rock to c.2,900 ft. in Le Flore co. (Okla.). Part of Ouachita Natl. Forest is here.

Ouachita River. 1 In Ark. and La., rises in the Ouachita Mts. in W Ark., flows c.605 mi. SE and S, past Hot Springs, Arkadelphia (head of navigation), and Camden (Ark.), into La., past Monroe, to Red R. c.35 mi. above its mouth. Formerly called Washita R. In La., the section (57 mi. long) from its mouth on Red R. to influx of the Tensas at Jonesville is called Black R. Near Hot Springs, Carpenter Dam (1931) impounds L. HAMILTON, Remmel Dam (1924) impounds L. CATHERINE; these, with proposed Blakely Dam above L. Hamilton, are units of Federal flood-control project. **2** In Texas and Okla.: see WASHITA RIVER.

Ouadaï, state, Fr. Equatorial Africa: see WADAI.

Ouadda (wäd-dä'), village, E Ubangi-Shari, Fr. Equatorial Africa, 260 mi. N of Bangassou; trading post.

Ouaddaï, state, Fr. Equatorial Africa: see WADAI.

Ouadi-Rimé (wä'dē-rēmā'), village, central Chad territory, Fr. Equatorial Africa, 55 mi. N of Ati; oasis on caravan road.

Ouagadougou or **Wagadugu** (wägädōō'gōō), city (pop. c.20,700), ⊙ Upper Volta, Fr. West Africa, road junction in central Upper Volta, on road from Bamako (420 mi. W), Fr. Sudan, to Niamey (250 mi. ENE), Niger territory; 12°22'N 1°31'W. Projected terminus of railroad from Abidjan (c.500 mi. SSW), Fr. Ivory Coast. Administrative and commercial center in agr. region (shea nuts, peanuts, millet, sesame, beans; livestock). Shea-nut butter processing, vegetable-oil extracting, cotton ginning; mfg. of soap, soda water, rugs, textiles. Has airfield; garrison; hospitals; orphanage; R.C. and Protestant missions; administrative offices.

Ouagbo (wäg'bō), village, S Dahomey, Fr. West Africa, on railroad and 37 mi. NW of Porto-Novo; palm kernels, palm oil.

Ouahigouya (wähēgōō'yä), town (pop. c.7,300), N Upper Volta, Fr. West Africa, near Fr. Sudan border, 100 mi. NW of Ouagadougou. Stock-raising center. Grows chiefly shea nuts and cotton for export; also millet, corn, beans, manioc, potatoes, sesame. Has daily market; climatological station; landing field; R.C. and Protestant missions.

Ouaka-Kotto, Fr. Equatorial Africa: see BAMBARI.

Ouakam (wäkäm'), military and air base in W Senegal, Fr. West Africa, on Cape Verde peninsula, 5½ mi. NW of Dakar. Its civil air functions have been moved to Yoff. Adjoined W by Mamelles lighthouse.

Ouaka River (wäkä'), central and S Ubangi-Shari, Fr. Equatorial Africa, rises 30 mi. W of Bria, flows 225 mi. SW and S, past Bambari, to Ubangi R. at Kouango. Also known as Kouango (kwäng-gō') in its middle and lower courses.

Oualata (wälä'tä), village, SE Mauritania, Fr. West Africa, in Oualata range of the Sahara, 320 mi. N of Bamako, Fr. Sudan, linked by rail. Prehistoric remains near by.

Ouallam (wäläm'), village (pop. c.1,800), SW Niger territory, Fr. West Africa, 70 mi. NNW of Niamey; stock raising.

Ouanaminthe (wänämĕt'), town (1950 census pop. 2,378), Nord dept., NE Haiti, on Massacre R. (Dominican Republic border), opposite Dajabón, 34 mi. ESE of Cap-Haïtien; coffee.

Ouanary (wänärē'), town (commune pop. 258), NE Fr. Guiana, near mouth of small Ouanary R., 70 mi. SE of Cayenne.

Ouango (wäng-gō'), village, E Ubangi-Shari, Fr. Equatorial Africa, on Bomu R. (Belgian Congo border) and 30 mi. SSE of Bangassou; customs station, trading center; coffee plantations.

Ouanne River (wän'), Yonne and Loiret depts., N central France, rises 8 mi. above Toucy, flows c.45 mi. NW, past Charny and Châteaurenard, to the Loing above Montargis.

Ouaouizarhte (wäwēzärt'), village, Marrakesh region, central Fr. Morocco, at SW extremity of the Middle Atlas, 30 mi. S of Kasba Tadla; oak forests. Also spelled Ouaouizert.

Ouara or **Wara** (wärä'), village, E Chad territory, Fr. Equatorial Africa, 25 mi. N of Abéché; burial site of sultans of Wadai.

Ouargla (wärglä'), town (pop. 5,461), ⊙ Saharan Oases territory, E central Algeria, 90 mi. SSW of Touggourt, 31°58'N 5°20'E. Caravan center at junction of desert tracks from Touggourt, Ghardaïa (WNW), El-Goléa (SW), and Fort Lallemand (SE). Principal product: high-quality dates. Oasis watered by artesian wells from underground Oued Mya. Fr. military post. Airfield. Pop. is of mixed Berber and Negro origin. Formerly also spelled Wargla.

Ouarsenis Massif (wärsnēs' mäsēf'), section of the Tell Atlas, in N central Algeria; extends c.120 mi. E-W bet. Boghari and Relizane. Bounded by the Chéliff valley (N and E), by the Oued Mina (W) and by the High Plateaus (S). Rises to 6,512 ft. in the Kef-Sidi-Amar (also called Djebel Ouarsenis). Well-watered N slopes are covered with oak and pine trees. Around Téniet-el-Haâd is a well-known cedar forest. Here, at its main pass, the massif is crossed by Affreville-Tiaret road.

Ouarzazate (wärzäzät'), town (pop. 3,468), Marrakesh region, SW Fr. Morocco, oasis on S slope of the High Atlas, 80 mi. SE of Marrakesh (linked by road via Tizi n'Tichka pass); 30°56'N 6°55'W. Military center of region not pacified by French until 1930. Date palms. Noted *casbah.* Tourist hotel. High-grade manganese deposits along Imini (c.30 mi. NW) and Iriri or Irhir (20 mi. W) stream beds. Important Bou Azzer cobalt mine 27 mi. S.

Ouassadou (wäsä'dōō) or **Nieriko** (nyĕrĕ'kō), village, S Senegal, Fr. West Africa, on Gambia R. and 35 mi. SE of Tambacounda; sisal growing. Sometimes Ouassadou-Nieriko.

Ouassou (wä'sōō), village, W Fr. Guinea, Fr. West Africa, on Konkouré R. and 36 mi. N of Conakry; bananas, palm kernels.

Oubangui-Chari, Fr. Equatorial Africa: see UBANGI-SHARI.

Oubari, Fezzan: see UBARI.

Oubatche (ōōbäch'), village (dist. pop. 1,254), New Caledonia, on NE coast, 185 mi. NW of Nouméa; agr. products.

Ouche (ōōsh), old district of NW France, now included in NE Orne and SW Eure depts. Cattle.

Ouche River, Côte-d'Or dept., E central France, rises just above Bligny-sur-Ouche in the Côte d'Or, flows c.60 mi. E in a great arc, past Dijon, to the Saône above Saint-Jean-de-Losne. Above Dijon it is accompanied by a section of Burgundy Canal.

Ou Chiang, Chekiang prov., China: see WU RIVER.

Ouchtata (ōōshtätä'), village, Béja dist., N Tunisia, on Mateur-Tabarka RR and 14 mi. E of Tabarka; cork oaks. Iron mines near by.

Ouchy (ōō-shē'), village, Vaud canton, W Switzerland, on L. Geneva; port for Lausanne, connected by cable railway; resort. Once residence of Byron and Shelley.

Oucques (ōōk), village (pop. 1,147), Loir-et-Cher dept., N central France, 11 mi. E of Vendôme; mfg. (hosiery, agr. machinery).

Ouda (ō'dä), town (pop. 12,837), Nara prefecture, S Honshu, Japan, 15 mi. SSE of Nara; commercial center in rice-growing area. Formed in early 1940s by combining former town of Matsuyama (1940 pop. 1,951) and 3 former villages, largest being Kambe (1940 pop. 5,215).

Oud Beijerland or **Oud Beierland** (both: oud bī'ürlänt), town (pop. 6,259), South Holland prov., SW Netherlands, on N Beijerland isl., near Old Maas R., and 8 mi. SSW of Rotterdam; woodworking, mfg. of cement, synthetic fertilizer, paint. Sometimes spelled Oud Beyerland.

Oude Ijssel, Netherlands: see OLD IJSSEL RIVER.

Oude Maas, Netherlands: see OLD MAAS RIVER.

Oudenaarde (ou"dünär'dü), Fr. *Audenarde* (ōdnärd'), town (pop. 6,567), East Flanders prov., W central Belgium, on Scheldt R. and 15 mi. SSW of Ghent; brewing, textiles (wool). Here English under Marlborough and Austrians under Prince Eugene defeated (1708) French under Vendôme. American memorial commemorates First World War battle.

Oudenbosch (ou'dünbôs), town (pop. 5,782), North Brabant prov., SW Netherlands, 5 mi. NE of Roosendaal; strawboard mfg.; tree nurseries.

Oudenburg (-bûrkh), town (pop. 3,459), West Flanders prov., NW Belgium, 5 mi. SE of Ostend; fruit, vegetable, and flower market for Ostend. Textile center in Middle Ages.

Oude Pekela (ou'dü pā'külä), town (pop. 5,702), Groningen prov., NE Netherlands, 3 mi. SSW of Winschoten; mfg. of bricks, strawboard, rope; peat production.

Oudergem, Belgium: see AUDERGHEM.

Oude Rijn, Netherlands: see OLD RHINE RIVER.

Ouderkerk or **Ouderkerk aan den Ijssel** (ou'dürkĕrk än dün ī'sül), village (pop. 3,484), South Holland prov., W Netherlands, on Hollandsche Ijssel R. and 7 mi. E of Rotterdam; explosives plant.

Oudeschild, Netherlands: see TEXEL.

Oudewater (ou'düvätür), town (pop. 3,517), South Netherlands prov., W Netherlands, on Hollandsche Ijssel R. and 6 mi. E of Gouda; mfg. (rope, machinery, vegetable oil), dairy products. Many 16th- and 17th-cent. houses. Site (1575) of massacre by Spaniards.

Oud-Gastel (oud-khäs'tĕl), village (pop. 3,749), North Brabant prov., SW Netherlands, 4 mi. N of Roosendaal; chemicals (nicotine).

Oudh (oud), historic region in E central Uttar Pradesh, N India. Early history centers around anc. Kosala kingdom, with ⊙ at AJODHYA (Awadh), from which prov. receives its name. After Ramayana times, Buddhist kingdom of *Sravasti* dominated Oudh N of the Gogra. It was under Gupta empire in 4th cent. A.D. Rajput clans arose to form KANAUJ kingdom (1019–1194); defeat by Afghans marked fall of last great Hindu kingdom in Oudh. Became a prov. (16th cent.) of Mogul empire, governed by Nawabs of Oudh, with capitals at Fyzabad (1724–75) and (after Nawabs declared their independence from empire) at Lucknow (1775–1856). The annexation of Oudh (1856) as a Br. prov. (⊙ LUCKNOW) was a major cause of the Sepoy Rebellion (1857–58). Joined (1877) with presidency of Agra, and the union was named United Provs. of Agra and Oudh in 1902. Name Oudh now designates central portion (□ 24,071; pop. 14,114,470) of Uttar Pradesh, nearly coextensive with area of anc. Kosala kingdom.

Oudiane, El- (ĕl-ōōdyän'), oasis in Tozeur dist., SW Tunisia, in the Bled-el-Djerid, at NW edge of the Chott Djerid, on railroad and 7 mi. NE of Tozeur; olives, dates, and citrus fruit. Contains villages of Degache and Kriz.

Oudjda, Fr. Morocco: see OUJDA.

Oudna (ōōdnä'), agr. village, Tunis dist., N Tunisia, on railroad and 12 mi. S of Tunis; winegrowing. Near by are ruins of *Uthina,* once a prosperous Roman settlement.

Oudong (ōōdông'), town, Kompong Speu prov., central Cambodia, near Tonle Sap R., 20 mi. NNW of Pnompenh; was anc. ⊙ Cambodia (1618–1866), site of monasteries, pagodas, and 16th-cent. ruins. Formerly spelled Udong.

Oudon River (ōōdō'), in Mayenne and Maine-et-Loire depts., W France, rises 3 mi. W of Loiron, flows 40 mi. SE, past Craon and Segré, to the Mayenne 1 mi. SE of Le Lion-d'Angers.

Oudref (ōōdrĕf'), village, Gabès dist., E Tunisia, 10 mi. NW of Gabès; date palms; nomadic sheep grazing.

Oud Schoonebeek (out" skhō'nübāk), village (pop. 744), Drenthe prov., NE Netherlands, 6 mi. E of Coevorden; oil wells; drilling installations.

Oudtshoorn (outs'hōōrn), town (pop. 16,103), S Cape Prov., U. of So. Afr., near Olifants R., 200 mi. W of Port Elizabeth, 40 mi. N of Mossel Bay, at foot of Great Swartberg range; agr. center (tobacco, grain, fruit, vegetables; dairying, wine and brandy making, fruit drying, ostrich farming). Has teachers col. Airfield. The CANGO CAVES are 15 mi. N.

Oued [Fr. transliteration of Arabic for wadi], for names in Fr. North Africa beginning thus and not found here, see under following part of the name.

Oued, El- (ĕl-wĕd'), town (pop. 13,489) and Saharan oasis, Touggourt territory, E Algeria, amidst high sand dunes, 50 mi. NE of Touggourt; 33°22'N 6°52'E. Largest of the Souf oases, noted for its fine Deglet Nur dates. Also grows tobacco. Handicraft industries (silk and woolen cloth; carpets). Called the town of cupolas because of its rounded, windowless houses.

Oued-Amizour (wĕd'-ämēzōōr'), village (pop. 1,991), Constantine dept., NE Algeria, in Oued Soummam valley, 13 mi. SW of Bougie; olives, wine, citrus fruit.

Oued-Athménia (-ätmänyä'), village (pop. 1,364), Constantine dept., NE Algeria, on railroad and 20 mi. SW of Constantine, in cereal-growing region.

Oued-el-Alleug, (-ĕl-älûg'), village (pop. 763), Alger dept., N central Algeria, in the Mitidja plain, 6 mi. NNW of Blida; winegrowing; processing of essential oils. Citrus tree nursery.

Oued-Fodda (-fôd-dä'), village (pop. 2,663), Alger dept., N central Algeria, on railroad and 11 mi. E of Orléansville, in cotton-growing section of the Chéliff valley. Oued-Fodda Dam (292 ft. high) on small left tributary of the Chéliff 5 mi. S, used for hydroelectric power (since 1941) and irrigation.

Oued-Imbert (-ēbâr'), village (pop. 1,601), Oran dept., NW Algeria, on NE slope of Tessala Mts., on railroad and 14 mi. NNE of Sidi-bel-Abbès; wheat, wine.

Oued Ksob Dam, Algeria: see M'SILA.

Oued-Méliz (-mälēz'), village, Souk-el-Arba dist., NW Tunisia, on the Medjerda, on railroad and 21 mi. NNW of Le Kef; cereal and livestock market; iron mines. Near-by Chemtou marble quarries, worked since pre-Roman times, are now abandoned. Roman ruins.

Oued-Taria (-täryä'), village (pop. 1,827), Oran dept., NW Algeria, on railroad and 20 mi. S of Mascara; cereals, wine.

Oued Yquem (ēkĕm'), locality, Rabat region, NW Fr. Morocco, on Casablanca-Rabat road, 15 mi. SW of Rabat; marble quarries.

Oued-Zarga (-zärgä'), village, Tunis dist., N Tunisia, on the Medjerda, 13 mi. ESE of Béja; cereals, wine, cattle.

Oued Zem (zĕm'), town (pop. 12,223), Casablanca region, W central Fr. Morocco, 80 mi. SE of Casablanca; rail terminus; agr. trade center (grain, livestock); flour milling. Iron mined at Aït Amar (15 mi. NNW) and phosphates in Khouribga-André Delpit area (W).

Oued-Zenati (-zĕnätē'), town (pop. 4,507), Constantine dept., NE Algeria, on the High Plateaus, on railroad and 31 mi. E of Constantine; agr. market in cereal-growing region; mfg. of flour products.

Ouégoa (wāgōä'), village (dist. pop. 1,133), NE New Caledonia, 185 mi. NW of Nouméa; agr. products, livestock.

Ouémé (wĕ'mā), village, S central Dahomey, Fr. West Africa, on Ouémé R. (crossed here by railroad to Parakou), 100 mi. N of Port-Novo; cotton.

Ouémé River, Dahomey, Fr. West Africa, rises in Atakora Mts. at about 10°N, flows c.300 mi. S, past Carnotville and Ouémé, to the Gulf of Guinea in delta near Cotonou, emptying largely into L. Nokoué. Impeded by rapids, though partly navigable during rainy season. Sometimes spelled Weme. Main affluent is the Okpara.

Ouenza, Djebel (jĕ'bĕl wĕnzä'), mountain (4,226 ft.) in Constantine dept., NE Algeria, near Tunisia border, 37 mi. N of Tebessa. Has Algeria's leading iron mine, linked by railroad with Bône (shipping port) via Souk-Ahras. Djebel bou Kadra mine is 13 mi. S.

Ouenzerig, Fezzan: see UENZERICH.

Ouergha, Oued (wĕd' wĕrgä'), stream of N Fr. Morocco, rises in Rif Mts. near Sp. Morocco border, flows c.120 mi. WSW to the Sebou in the Rharb lowland 15 mi. N of Petitjean. Navigable in lower course. Also spelled Ouerrha.

Ouessant, France: see USHANT.

Ouesso (wĕsō'), town, ⊙ Sangha region (formed 1949; pop. 28,000), NW Middle Congo territory, Fr. Equatorial Africa, on Sanga R. at mouth of N'Goko R., on Fr. Cameroons border, and 400 mi. NNE of Brazzaville; trading center, terminus of year-round steam navigation on the Sanga; palm products, hides, copal, rubber, African mahogany. Customs, meteorological stations. Founded 1891.

Ouezzane (wĕzän'), Arabic *Wazzan* or *Wezzan*, city (pop. 23,509), Rabat region, N Fr. Morocco, on SW slope of the Rif, near Sp. Morocco border, 60 mi. NNW of Fez. A sacred pilgrimage place, seat of an important Moslem brotherhood.

Ouffet (ōōfā'), village (pop. 1,549), Liége prov., E central Belgium, 11 mi. ESE of Huy; granite quarrying.

Oughter, Lough (lŏkh ou'tûr), shallow lake (7 mi. long, 4 mi. wide), W Co. Cavan, Ireland, on Erne R., W and NW of Cavan. On one of the many isls. is 11th-cent. round tower of Cloughoughter Castle of the O'Reillys. Lake receives Annalee R. at N end; on W shore is town of Killeshandra.

Oughterard (ōōtûrärd'), Gaelic *Uachtarárd*. **1** Town (pop. 498), W Co. Galway, Ireland, on W shore of Lough Corrib, 16 mi. NW of Galway; agr. market (sheep; beets, potatoes); angling resort. Near by, in Lough Corrib, is Inchagoill isl. **2** Agr. village (district pop. 357), NE Co. Kildare, Ireland, 6 mi. NE of Naas; cattle, horses; potatoes. Has remains of anc. round tower.

Oughterside and Allerby (ou'tûrsīd, ă'lûrbē), parish (pop. 586), W Cumberland, England. Includes coal-mining village of Oughterside, on Ellen R. and 6 mi. NE of Maryport, and dairying village of Allerby, 4 mi. NE of Maryport.

Oughtibridge (ōō'tĭbrĭj, ou'–, ō'–), town in Sheffield county borough, West Riding, S Yorkshire, England, on Don R. and 5 mi. NW of Sheffield; steel and paper milling.

Ougrée (ōōgrā'), town (pop. 20,130), Liége prov., E Belgium, on Meuse R. and 3 mi. SW of Liége; coal mines; blast furnaces; mfg. (cables, chemicals, cement, textiles).

Ouham, region, Fr. Equatorial Africa: see BOSSANGOA.

Ouham-Pendé, Fr. Equatorial Africa: see BOZOUM.

Ouham River, Fr. Equatorial Africa: see BAHR SARA.

Ouiatchouanish River (wē"ûchwä'nĭsh), S central Que., outlet of Commissioners L., flows N past Lac Bouchette to L. St. John at Val Jalbert. Just above its mouth are 236-ft. falls.

Ouidah (wē'dä), town (pop. c.14,600), S Dahomey, Fr. West Africa, minor port on Gulf of Guinea, on railroad and 37 mi. W of Porto-Novo. Commercial and agr. center (palm kernels, palm oil, kopra, coffee, corn, manioc, beans, tomatoes, onions). Trades in cured and dried fish. Mfg. of vegetable oil. Has cathedral, Saint Gallus seminary, Protestant church, mosque; garrison. In a tiny Portuguese enclave here is the Port. fort of São João Baptista de Ajudá, founded 1788. Ouidah beach is 2 mi. S. Sometimes spelled Whydah or Wida.

Ouistreham (wēstrā'), town (pop. 3,504), Calvados dept., NW France, on English Channel, at mouth of Orne R. and Caen maritime canal, and 8 mi. NE of Caen; small seaport and resort; boatbuilding. Near-by Riva-Bella has fine beach.

Oujda or **Oudjda** (ōōjdä'), city (pop. 88,658), ⊙ Oujda region (□ 19,782; pop. 396,131), NE Fr. Morocco, near Algerian border, 180 mi. ENE of Fez; 34°41'N 1°54'W. Major agr. trade center and important rail junction, where Morocco-Tunisia trunk line meets trans-Saharan RR completed to Colomb-Béchar (Algeria) across Morocco territory. Trade in wines, citrus fruit, early vegetables, wheat and barley (all grown in area); sheep, wool, and esparto from the arid interior. City is also supply depot for E Morocco's mining areas: Bou Beker (just S; lead), Djérada (coal), Bou Arfa (manganese). Old native town (*Medina*) is surrounded by bastioned walls, has a *casbah* and numerous mosques. Modern European city has grown up in W and N. Military camp and airport are S. Founded end of 10th cent., city was ruled by successive Berber and Arab dynasties. Taken temporarily by French in 1844 (after battle of the Isly, fought just W of city) and in 1859, it was permanently occupied in 1907; it is one of Morocco's fastest growing cities (1936 pop. 34,523).

Oukaïmeden, Fr. Morocco: see ASNI.

Oulad-Naïl Mountains, Algeria: see OULED-NAÏL MOUNTAINS.

Oulad Saïd (ōōläd' säēd'), village, Casablanca region, W Fr. Morocco, 12 mi. WSW of Settat; wheat, barley.

Oulainen (ō'lĭ'nûn), Swedish *Oulais* (ō'lĭs), village (commune pop. 8,448), Oulu co., W Finland, on Pyhä R. and 30 mi. SSE of Raahe; light industries.

Oulanka, Karelo-Finnish SSR: see OLANGA.

Oulchy-le-Château (ōō-shē'-lû-shätō'), agr. village (pop. 506), Aisne dept., N France, 13 mi. S of Soissons. Partly destroyed in Franco-American advance of July, 1918. On near-by Chalmont hill is monument to 2d victory of the Marne (1918).

Ouled-Djellal (ōōlĕd'-jĕläl'), town (pop. 9,363) and Saharan oasis, Touggourt territory, N central Algeria, on the Oued Djedi and 50 mi. SW of Biskra; dates, wool. Handicraft blankets.

Ouled-Fayet (–fäyĕt'), village (pop. 647), Alger dept., N central Algeria, 7 mi. SW of Algiers; winegrowing.

Ouled-Naïl Mountains or **Oulad-Naïl Mountains** (–näēl'), range of the Saharan Atlas in N central Algeria, extending c.100 mi. across N Ghardaïa territory and southernmost Alger dept. from the Djebel Amour (SW) to the Hodna depression (NE). Rises to c.5,000 ft. Traversed by N–S road from Djelfa to Laghouat.

Ouled-Rahmoun (–rämōōn'), village (pop. 799), Constantine dept., NE Algeria, 14 mi. SSE of Constantine; rail junction. Cereals.

Oulgaret (ōōlgärĕt'), town (commune pop. 35,311), Pondicherry settlement, Fr. India; suburb of Pondicherry, 3 mi. W of city center; hand-loom cotton weaving; pottery.

Oulili, Fr. Morocco: see VOLUBILIS.

Oullins (ōōlē'), outer SSW suburb (pop. 17,728) of Lyons, Rhône dept., E central France, near right bank of the Rhone; metalworks (agr. machinery, aircraft parts), tanneries, textile mills; candy, perfume, and carton mfg. Railroad yards.

Oulmès (ōōlmĕs'), village, Rabat region, W central Fr. Morocco, on a high tableland (alt. 4,100 ft.), 40 mi. SW of Meknès; tin and antimony mining. The mineral waters of near-by Oulmès-les-Thermes are bottled.

Oulton Broad, England: see LOWESTOFT.

Oulu (ō'lōō), Swedish *Uleåborg* (ü'lăōbôr"yů), county [Finnish *lääni*] (□ 21,886; including water area □ 23,626; pop. 352,158), N central Finland, bet. Gulf of Bothnia (W) and USSR border (E); ⊙ Oulu. Low and level in coastal region, becomes hilly in E part of co.; drained by Ii, Oulu, Kala, Pyhä, and several smaller rivers. Of the many lakes in SE part of co., L. Oulu is largest. Lumbering and woodworking (plywood, wallboard, bobbin, and spindle milling) are chief industries. Grain growing, cattle raising. Minerals worked include iron, nickel (Nivala), granite, kaolin, feldspar, and fossil meal. Cities are Oulu, Raahe, and Kajaani. Co. formerly included all of Finnish Lapland, created a separate co. 1938.

Oulu, Swedish *Uleåborg*, city (pop. 36,073), ⊙ Oulu co., W Finland, on Gulf of Bothnia, at mouth of Oulu R., 280 mi. N of Helsinki; 65°1'N 25°29'E. Rail junction and seaport, shipping lumber, cellulose, tar, and fish. Lumber and cellulose-milling center, with shipyards, flour mills, tanneries, soap works, machine shops; fisheries, dairying. Radio and power station; dist. hospital. Seat of Lutheran bishop (since 1900). Has cathedral (1830–32) and mus. of history and ethnography. Rapids at mouth of Oulu R. are tourist attraction. City grew around castle built (1375) by Swedes as outpost against Russia. Inc. 1610. Destroyed (1822) by fire; harbor installations shelled by British during Crimean War.

Oulu, Lake, Finnish *Oulujärvi* (ō'lōōyăr"vē), Swedish *Ule träsk* (ü'lů trĕsk") (□ 387), N central Finland, 50 mi. SE of Oulu; 40 mi. long (SE–NW), 2–18 mi. wide. Contains several isls. (total □ 44). Drained (NW) by Oulu R. On SE arm of lake is Kajaani city. A chain of small lakes, connected with L. Oulu, extends E to USSR border.

Oulu River, Finnish *Oulujoki* (ō'lōōyō"kē), Swedish *Ule älv* (ü'lů ĕlv"), N central Finland, issues from NW end of L. Oulu, flows 60 mi. NW, over Pyhä Falls, Finnish *Pyhäkoski* (pü'hăkōs"kē) (105 ft. high; hydroelectric plant), 20 mi. SE of Oulu, to Gulf of Bothnia at Oulu. Important logging route.

Oulx, Italy: see ULZIO.

Oum-Douil (ōōm'-dwēl'), village, Grombalia dist., NE Tunisia, in Cape Bon Peninsula, 36 mi. E of Tunis; lignite mining.

Oumé (ōō'mā), village (pop. c.1,000), S central Ivory Coast, Fr. West Africa, 120 mi. NW of Abidjan; coffee, cacao, palm kernels.

Oum er Rbia (ōōm'ĕr rûbyä'), chief river of W Fr. Morocco, rises in the Middle Atlas 20 mi. NE of Khénifra, flows SW, past Kasba Tadla and Dar Ould Zidouh, then NW in entrenched meanders to the Atlantic just below Azemmour; 345 mi. long. Harnessed for hydroelectric power and irrigation at Kasba Zidania Dam (11 mi. SW of Kasba Tadla; completed 1936); Im Fout Dam (360 ft. high; 12 mi. NW of Mechra Benabbou; built 1939–44, improved after Second World War); Daourat Dam (30 mi. below Im Fout Dam; built 1945–49); and Sidi Saïd Machou Dam (20 mi. above river mouth; completed 1929). On the Oued el Abid (left tributary), Bin el Ouidane Dam (largest in Morocco) was begun 1948. Sometimes spelled Oum er Rebia.

Oum-Hadjer (ōōm-häjĕr'), village, central Chad territory, Fr. Equatorial Africa, on Batha R. and 90 mi. E of Ati; trading post on caravan road to Darfur; vegetable raising.

Oum-Theboul, Algeria: see CALLE, LA.

Ounas River, Finnish *Ounasjoki* (ō'näsyō"kē), Lapland, N Finland, rises on Norwegian border W of L. Inari, near 68°40'N 24°E, flows 210 mi. in winding course generally S to Kemi R. at Rovaniemi. Logging route.

Oundle (oun'dûl), urban district (1931 pop. 2,001; 1951 census 2,224), NE Northampton, England, on Nene R. and 12 mi. SW of Peterborough; agr. market. Has public school founded 1554, 14th-cent. church, several old inns, and 16th-cent. bridge over the river.

Our, river: see OUR RIVER.

Ouray (ōōrā', yōōrā'), county (□ 540; 2,103), SW central Colo.; ⊙ Ouray. Livestock-grazing and mining region, drained by Uncompahgre R. Gold, silver, lead, copper. Includes part of Uncompahgre Natl. Forest and ranges of Rocky Mts. Formed 1883.

Ouray, city (pop. 1,089), ⊙ Ouray co., SW central Colo., on Uncompahgre R., in San Juan Mts., and 85 mi. SE of Grand Junction; alt. 7,800 ft. Health resort with mineral hot springs, in grain, livestock, potato region. Gold, silver, lead, copper mines in vicinity. State game refuge and Wetterhorn Peak near by. Settled 1875, inc. 1884.

Ouray Peak (13,955 ft.), central Colo., in S tip of Sawatch Mts., 18 mi. SW of Salida.

Ource River (ōōrs), Côte-d'Or and Aube depts., N Central France, rises in the Plateau of Langres 3 mi. NW of Grancey-le-Château, flows 55 mi. NW, past Recey-sur-Ource and Essoyes, to the Seine above Bar-sur-Seine.

Ourcq River (ōōrk), Aisne and Seine-et-Marne depts., N central France, rises NNW of Dormans, flows 50 mi. SW in an arc across First World War Château-Thierry battlefield, past Fère-en-Tardenois and La Ferté-Milon, to the Marne just below Lizy-sur-Ourcq. Paralleled in lower course by Ourcq Canal.

Ourém (ōrān'), city (pop. 383), easternmost Pará, Brazil, head of navigation on Guamá R. and 105 mi. ESE of Belém; tobacco, manioc, cotton, hides.

Ouricia, El- (ĕl-ōōrēsyä'), village (pop. 879), Constantine dept., NE Algeria, 7 mi. N of Sétif; wheat.

Ouricuri (ōrēkōōrē'), city (pop. 942), W Pernambuco, NE Brazil, 110 mi. NNE of Juàzeiro (Bahia); cotton, corn, livestock. Formerly spelled Ouricury.

Ourinhos (ōrē'nyōōs), city (pop. 6,666), W central São Paulo, Brazil, near Paranapanema R. (Paraná border), 200 mi. WNW of São Paulo; important rail junction with spur to recently settled agr. dist. of N Paraná. Food-processing center (macaroni, lard, candy), with trade in coffee, cotton, alfalfa, fruit, livestock, and timber.

Ourique (ōrē'kĭ), town (pop. 1,378), Beja dist., S Portugal, 32 mi. SW of Beja; cheese mfg. The battle of Ourique (1139), in which the Moors were decisively beaten by Alfonso I, actually took place at an as yet undetermined near-by location.

Ou River, China: see WU RIVER.

Ourlal (ōōrläl'), village (pop. 3,224), Touggourt territory, NE Algeria, oasis in the Ziban region of the N Sahara, on rail spur and 18 mi. SW of Biskra; date palms.

Ouro Fino (ō'rōō fē'nōō), city (pop. 7,149), SW Minas Gerais, Brazil, near São Paulo border, on railroad and 35 mi. SSE of Poços de Caldas; agr. trade center; coffee- and tea growing.

Ouro Prêto (prā'tōō) [Port.,=black gold], city (pop. 8,819), SE central Minas Gerais, Brazil, in offshoot of the Serra do Espinhaço, on branch railroad and 45 mi. SE of Belo Horizonte; alt. 3,515 ft. Founded c.1700 as Villa Rica, a short-lived gold-rush town, it has since been preserved as a living mus. of 18th-cent. Brazilian baroque architecture. Site was decreed a natl. monument in 1933. Here the famous sculptor Aleijadinho decorated many of city's 15 churches. Also noteworthy are the old govt. palace (now housing school of mines), mus. of Inconfidência (in former penitentiary), Brazil's oldest theater (restored 1861), the colonial Casa dos Contos (old mint; now post office), statue of the patriot Tiradentes, several monumental fountains, and the picturesque cobblestone streets winding up the hills. Gold is still mined on a small scale E of city, but chief economic activity today is mining of iron pyrites which supply sulphur for Piquete (São Paulo) munitions plant. Manganese, bauxite, ocher, and marble also found in area. Industries include electrometallurgy, textile milling, shoe mfg. Has school of pharmacy, founded 1839. Ouro Prêto was ⊙ Minas Gerais until 1897, when, because of its relative inaccessibility to modern transport and limited opportunity for expansion, seat of govt. was transferred to newly laid out Belo Horizonte.

Ouro Verde, Brazil: see CANOINHAS.

Our River (o͞or), E Belgium and E Luxembourg, rises 10 mi. NE of St-Vith (Belgium), flows 50 mi. S, forming Luxembourg-German border for greater part of its course, past Vianden, to Sûre R. 6 mi. E of Diekirch.

Ourthe River (o͞ort), E Belgium, rises in 2 branches joining 5 mi. W of Houffalize, flows 100 mi. NW and N, past Esneux, Tilff, and Angleur, to Meuse R. at Liége. Receives Amblève R. just N of Comblain-au-Pont, Vesdre R. at Angleur.

Ourville-en-Caux (o͞orvēl-ā-kō'), agr. village (pop. 341), Seine-Inférieure dept., N France, 25 mi. SW of Dieppe.

Ousa, India: see AUSA.

Ouse (o͞oz), town (pop. 178), central Tasmania, 40 mi. NW of Hobart and on Ouse R.; zinc-lead mines; cattle.

Ouse River (o͞oz). **1** or **Great Ouse River,** flowing through Northampton, Buckingham, Bedford, Huntingdon, Cambridge, and Norfolk, England. Rises 3 mi. NW of Brackley, Northampton, flows 156 mi. E, NE, and finally N, past Buckingham, Olney, Bedford, St. Neots, Huntingdon, Ely, Downham Market, and King's Lynn, to the Wash 3 mi. NNW of King's Lynn. Navigable for two-thirds of its course. **2** In Sussex, England, rises 6 mi. ESE of Horsham, flows 30 mi. E and S, past Lewes, to the Channel at Newhaven. Navigable in its lower course. **3** In Yorkshire, England, formed by confluence of Ure and Swale rivers 13 mi. NW of York, flows 45 mi. SE, past York, Tadcaster, Selby, and Goole, to confluence with Trent R. 7 mi. E of Goole, forming the Humber. It is navigable below York; receives Wharfe, Nidd, Derwent, Aire, and Don rivers.

Ouse River, central Tasmania, rises in small lakes WNW of Great L., flows 62 mi. SE, past Waddamana (hydroelectric plant) and Ouse, to Derwent R. just S of Ouse.

Ousseltia (o͞osĕltyä'), village, Kairouan dist., central Tunisia, 30 mi. WNW of Kairouan; silos; lumbering and cork gathering. Zinc mine near by.

Oussouye (o͞oso͞o'yä), town (pop. c.600), SW Senegal, Fr. West Africa, in Casamance R. delta and 20 mi. W of Ziguinchor; peanuts, hardwoods. R.C. mission.

Oust (o͞ost), village (pop. 293), Ariège dept., S France, in central Pyrenees, on the Salat and 8 mi. SSE of Saint-Girons; whetstone mfg., cheese making.

Oust River, Brittany, W France, rises in Armorican Massif 4 mi. NE of Corlay (Côtes-du-Nord dept.), flows 80 mi. SE into Morbihan dept., past Rohan, Josselin, and Malestroit, to Vilaine R. 1 mi. SW of Redon. Its course through Morbihan dept. forms part of Brest-Nantes Canal.

Outagamie (outúgă'mē), county (□ 634; pop. 81,722), E Wis.; ⊙ Appleton. Drained by Wolf, Fox, and Embarrass rivers. Dairying and paper milling are principal industries. Some stock raising and farming (oats, corn). Formed 1851.

Outardes, Rivière aux (rēvyâr' ōzo͞otärd'), central Que., rises in Otish Mts., flows 300 mi. S, through Pletipi L., to the St. Lawrence 18 mi. SW of Baie Comeau. Several waterfalls.

Outarville (o͞otärvēl'), agr. village (pop. 361), Loiret dept., N central France, in the Beauce, 11 mi. WNW of Pithiviers.

Outeïba, Syria: see 'ATEIBE, EL.

Outeniqua Mountains (outúnē'kwú), S Cape Prov., U. of So. Afr., extend 170 mi. E from Gouritz R. valley and E end of Langeberg range S of Calitzdorp to W side of St. Francis Bay. Range parallels Indian Ocean coast; rises to 5,503 ft. on Formosa Peak, 35 mi. ESE of Uniondale. W part of range crossed by railroad and road on Montagu Pass (2,348 ft.), 5 mi. N of George.

Outer Banks or **The Banks,** E N.C., chain of sandy barrier isls. stretching length of N.C. coast and separating the sounds from the Atlantic; marked by dangerous capes (Hatteras, Lookout, Fear) and shoals to seaward, the banks are inhabited by hardy fishermen and farmers ("bankers"), among whom some remote ways of life have persisted despite contact with sport fishermen, hunters, and vacationers attracted by the beaches and abundant wildlife.

Outer Brewster Island, Mass.: see BREWSTER ISLANDS.

Outerbridge Crossing, N.Y. and N.J., highway bridge across Arthur Kill, bet. Tottenville, Staten Isl., and Perth Amboy, N.J. Completed 1928 by Port of N.Y. Authority, it is a cantilever structure; total length of truss spans is 2,100 ft., and main span is 750 ft. long and 142 ft. above water.

Outer Hebrides, Scotland: see HEBRIDES.

Outer Mongolia: see MONGOLIA.

Outjo (out'yō), town (pop. 1,412), NW South-West Africa, 180 mi. NNW of Windhoek, 40 mi. NW of Otjiwarongo; alt. 4,139 ft.; rail terminus in cattle-raising region. Airfield. Fransfontein reserve of Swartbooi Hottentots is 75 mi. W.

Outlook, town (pop. 614), S central Sask., on South Saskatchewan R. and 50 mi. SSW of Saskatoon; wheat. Site of Outlook Col. (Norwegian Lutheran Church of Canada).

Outlook, town (pop. 235), Sheridan co., NE Mont., near Sask. line, 13 mi. NW of Plentywood.

Outokumpu (ō'tōko͝om"po͞o), village in Kuusjärvi commune (pop. 11,804), Kuopio co., SE Finland, in Saimaa lake region, 25 mi. WNW of Joensuu; rail terminus; copper-mining and smelting center. Sulphur, zinc, and iron are important by-products. Refineries at Harjavalta and Pori.

Outreau (o͞otrō'), S industrial suburb (pop. 6,620) of Boulogne, Pas-de-Calais dept., N France; blast furnaces, steel mills, tar- and Portland cement works. Mfg. of ceramic products. Damaged in Second World War.

Outremont (o͞o'trúmŏnt, o͞otrúmō'), city (pop. 30,751), S Que., on Montreal Isl., NW residential suburb of Montreal. Inc. 1895; became city 1915.

Out Skerries, group of small islands, easternmost of the Shetlands, Scotland. Largest isl., Housay (hou'sā) (pop. 68), 22 mi. NE of Lerwick, is 2 mi. long, 1 mi. wide. Just E of Housay are islets of Bruray (bro͞o'rā) (pop. 34) and Grunay or Gruna (grŭ'nú) (pop. 6). Just E of Grunay is Bound islet (pop. 2), site of the Out Skerries light (60°25' N 0°43'W). Fishing is chief occupation.

Outwood, coal-mining parish (pop. 2,195), SE Lancashire, England. Includes coal-mining village of Ringley Road, 4 mi ESE of Bolton.

Ouvéa, Loyalty Isls.: see UVEA.

Ouvéze River (o͞ovĕz'), Drôme and Vaucluse depts., SE France, rises near Le Buis-les-Baronnies, flows c.40 mi. generally SW, past Vaison-la-Romaine and Bédarrides, to the Rhone 5 mi. above Avignon. Receives the Sorgue (left).

Ouyen (o͞o'yún), town (pop. 1,141), NW Victoria, Australia, 240 mi. NW of Melbourne; rail junction; agr. center (wheat, oats).

Ouzinkie or **Uzinki** (ūzĭng'kē), village (pop. 178), S Alaska, on Spruce Isl., in Gulf of Alaska, 9 mi. NNW of Kodiak; salmon fishing and canning, fur farming. Has a Greek Orthodox church, Baptist mission, territorial school. Shipyard established here by Russians c.1800.

Ouzouer-le-Marché (o͞ozwā'-lú-mär-shā'), village (pop. 684), Loir-et-Cher dept., N central France, 17 mi. W of Orléans; beet-sugar and flour milling.

Ouzouer-sur-Loire (–sür-lwär'), village (pop. 408), Loiret dept., N central France, near right bank of Loire R., 9 mi. NW of Gien; sawmilling.

Ovacik (ôväjŭk'), Turkish *Ovacık,* village (pop. 749), Tunceli prov., E central Turkey, on Monzur R. and 29 mi. SW of Erzincan; grain. Formerly Zerenik and Marasalcakmak.

Ovada (ôvä'dä), town (pop. 5,294), Alessandria prov., Piedmont, N Italy, 19 mi. S of Alessandria; rail junction; wine market; textiles.

Ovadno (ŭvăd'nú), Pol. *Owadno,* village (1939 pop. over 500), W Volyn oblast, Ukrainian SSR, 5 mi. NNE of Vladimir-Volynski; wheat, barley, livestock.

Ovalau (ō'välou'), volcanic island (□ 39; pop. 4,280), Fiji, SW Pacific, 10 mi. E of Viti Levu; 8 mi. long, 5 mi. wide; rises to 3,000 ft.; bananas, pineapples. Site of Levuka, former ⊙ colony.

Ovalle (ōvä'yä), town (pop. 14,807), ⊙ Ovalle dept. (□ 4,678; pop. 77,772), Coquimbo prov., N central Chile, on Limarí R. (irrigation) and 50 mi. S of La Serena; rail junction; fruitgrowing and sheep-raising center. Copper mill, tannery, shoe factory. Hydroelectric plant; airport. Founded 1831 by President Ovalle.

Ovamboland (ōvăm'bōlănd), district (□ c.16,220; total pop. 156,588; native pop. 156,496), N South-West Africa, extends W from Okovanggo R., along Angola border; native reserve, inhabited by Ovambos and several other tribes; ⊙ Ondangua. Cattle raising, grain growing are chief occupations. In S part of dist. is Etosha Pan, salt-water filled depression.

Ovando, village (pop. c.100), Powell co., W Mont., near Blackfoot R., 60 mi. NW of Helena; supply point for hay and sheep region; timber. Fish hatchery.

Ovar (o͞ovär'), fishing town (pop. 6,844), Aveiro dist., N central Portugal, on railroad and 15 mi. N of Aveiro, at N end of Aveiro lagoon; mfg. (hardware, paper, felt, pottery); sardine processing.

Ovaro (ôvä'rô), village (pop. 470), Udine prov., Friuli–Venezia Giulia, NE Italy, 9 mi. NW of Tolmezzo; paper mill.

Ovcar or **Ovchar** (both: ôf'chär), Serbo-Croatian *Ovčar,* mountain (3,231 ft.) in Dinaric Alps, W Serbia, Yugoslavia, 7 mi. W of Cacak. Ovcar Banja or Ovcarska Banja, health resort, is at W foot, on railroad.

Ovce Polje or **Ovche Polye** (both: ôf'chĕ pôl'yĕ), Serbo-Croatian *Ovče Polje,* wide valley in N Macedonia, Yugoslavia; extends c.15 mi. NW from lower Bregalnica R.; sheep raising. Chief village, SVETI NIKOLA.

Ovcha-mogila (ôf'chä-môgē'lä), village (pop. 3,714), Pleven dist., N Bulgaria, 12 mi. SSW of Svishtov; grain, livestock.

Ovchar, mountain, Yugoslavia: see OVCAR.

Ovcharets (ôfchä'rĕts), peak (9,085 ft.) in E Rila Mts., W Bulgaria, 11 mi. S of Samokov. Formerly called Yurushki-chal.

Ovche Polye, valley, Yugoslavia: see OVCE POLJE.

Oveja, Cerro (sĕ'rō ōvä'hä), peak (7,237 ft.) in W Córdoba prov., Argentina, 50 mi. WSW of Río Tercero, in N Sierra de Comechingones, a range of the Sierra de Córdoba.

Ovejas (ōvä'häs), town (pop. 3,371), Bolívar dept., N Columbia, 15 mi. SSW of Carmen; tobacco-growing center.

Ovejería (ōvāhārē'ä), town (pop. 1,817), Osorno prov., S central Chile, 7 mi. SE of Osorno; wheat and livestock center; dairying, flour milling, lumbering.

Ovelgönne (ō'fúlgû"nú), village (commune pop. 6,123), in Oldenburg, NW Germany, after 1945 in Lower Saxony, 3 mi. WNW of Brake; wool mfg.

Ovenden, England: see HALIFAX.

Ovens Peninsula (3 mi. long, 1 mi. wide), SW N.S., 4 mi. SSE of Lunenburg. Former gold-mining area.

Ovens River, NE Victoria, Australia, rises in Australian Alps near Mt. Hotham, flows 110 mi. generally NW, past Bright, Myrtleford, and Wangaratta (hydroelectric plant), to Murray R. 14 mi. E of Yarrawonga. King R., main tributary.

Over, England: see WINSFORD.

Overath (ō'vúrät), village (pop. 10,553), in former Prussian Rhine Prov., W Germany, after 1945 in North Rhine-Westphalia, 14 mi. E of Cologne; rail junction.

Overbrook, city (pop. 387), Osage co., E Kansas, 20 mi. SSE of Topeka; livestock, grain.

Overflakkee (ō'vúrflăkā), island, South Holland prov., SW Netherlands; bounded by Goeree isl. (NW), with which it forms isl. of Goeree-Overflakkee, by the Grevelingen (W), the Krammer (S), the Volkerak (SE), the Haringvliet (NE). Chief village: Middelharnis. Isl. flooded in Second World War.

Overhalla, Norway: see OYSVOLL.

Overijse (ō'vúrī"sú), town (pop. 9,810), Brabant prov., central Belgium, 9 mi. SE of Brussels; market center for grape-growing area. Formerly spelled Overyssche, Overijssche, or Overijsche.

Overijssel or **Overyssel** (–súl), province (□ 1,254.6; pop. 638,797), NE Netherlands, bet. the Ijsselmeer and Ijssel R. on W and Germany on E; ⊙ Zwolle. Sandy soil and hilly heathland; some fenland near the Ijsselmeer coast and Drenthe prov. border (N). Besides the Ijssel, it is drained by Vecht and Zwatewater rivers and Twente and Overijssel canals. Dairy cattle; fruit, vegetables, some flax. Important center of Netherlands textile industry (in Twente area, SE); machine building (Deventer, Hengelo, Enschede). Chief towns: Zwolle, Hengelo, Deventer, Enschede, Oldenzaal, Almelo. In Middle Ages the lordship of Overijssel belonged to the bishops of Utrecht but was sold (1527) to Emperor Charles V. It joined (1579) the Union of Utrecht and became one of the 7 United Provinces of the Netherlands.

Overijssel Canal, network of canals, mainly in Overijssel prov., NE Netherlands, joining towns of Zwolle, Deventer, Raalte, Almelo, Vriezenveen, Coevorden, and Nieuw Amsterdam; connected with Ijssel R., the Zwartewater, and ALMELO-NORDHOORN CANAL. Total length, 73 mi.

Overkalix (û'vúrkä"lĭks), Swedish *Överkalix,* village (pop. 827), Norrbotten co., N Sweden, on Kalix R. and 50 mi. NW of Haparanda; market center in lumbering, stock-raising region.

Overland, residential city (pop. 11,566), St. Louis co., E Mo., W of St. Louis. City inc. 1939.

Overland Park, village (1940 pop. 2,563), Johnson co., E Kansas, 10 mi. S of Kansas City (Kansas), near Mo. line, in dairying region.

Overlea (ō'vúrlē), village (pop. c.6,000), Baltimore co., central Md., 6 mi. NE of downtown Baltimore.

Overly, village (pop. 90), Bottineau co., N N.Dak., 17 mi. SE of Bottineau.

Overmere (ō'vúrmĕrú), agr. village (pop. 3,423), East Flanders prov., NW Belgium, 9 mi. E of Ghent. Formerly spelled Overmeire.

Overo, Cerro (sĕ'rō ōvā'rō), Andean volcano (15,630 ft.) Mendoza prov., Argentina, near Chile border, 45 mi. SE of Rancagua (Chile); 34°35'S. Sulphur deposits.

Overod, Denmark: see HOLTE.

Overpelt (ō'vúrpĕlt), town (pop. 7,133), Limburg prov., NE Belgium, 20 mi. N of Hasselt; zinc and lead processing. Town of Neerpelt (pop. 6,157) is just N, on Scheldt–Meuse Junction Canal.

Oversay or **Orsay** (both: ôr'sā), island (pop. 14) of the Inner Hebrides, Argyll, Scotland, off SW end of Islay, just SW of Portnahaven; 1 mi long; lighthouse (55°40'N 6°29'W).

Overschie (ō"vúrskhē'), South Holland prov., W Netherlands, NW suburb of Rotterdam.

Overseal, town and parish (pop. 2,112), S Derby, England, 6 mi. SE of Burton-upon-Trent; coal mining.

Overstrand, village and parish (pop. 473), N Norfolk, England, on North Sea, 2 mi. ESE of Cromer; seaside resort.

Overton, town and parish (pop. 1,885), N Hampshire, England, on Test R. and 8 mi. W of Basingstoke; paper milling. A sheep and lamb fair is held here. At village of Steventon, 2 mi. ESE, Jane Austen was born.

Overton, county (□ 442; pop. 17,566), N Tenn.; ⊙ Livingston. In the Cumberlands; drained by affluents of Obey and Cumberland rivers. Includes part of Dale Hollow Reservoir. Bituminous-coal mining, pine and hardwood lumbering, agr. (corn, hay, tobacco, livestock, poultry, dairy products). Formed 1806.

Overton. 1 Village (pop. 497), Dawson co., S central Nebr., 15 mi. ESE of Lexington, near Platte R.; grain, livestock, dairy and poultry produce, sugar beets. **2** Village (1940 pop. 529), Clark co., SE Nev., on Muddy R., near its mouth in N arm of L. Mead, and c.45 mi. NE of Las Vegas. Mus. here has Pueblo Indian relics. **3** Town (pop. 2,001), Rusk co., E Texas, 19 mi. ESE of Tyler; an oil center in East Texas field; oil refineries, lumber milling. Boomed after oil discovery (1930).

Overton, town and parish (pop. 1,099), in detached section of Flint, Wales, near the Dee, 6 mi. SW of Wrexham; agr. market. Has 15th-cent. church.

Overtornea, Finland: see YLITORNIO.

Overtornea (û'vûrtōr"nāō), Swedish *Övertorneå*, or **Matarengi** (mä"tärĕng'ē), village (pop. 929), Norrbotten co., N Sweden, on Torne R. (Finnish border) and 40 mi. NNW of Haparanda; lumbering; stock raising. Has high school and sanitarium, serving Torne R. valley.

Overtown, village in Cambusnethan parish, N Lanark, Scotland, 2 mi. S of Wishaw; coal mining.

Overum (û'vûrŭm"), Swedish *Överum*, village (pop. 1,376), Kalmar co., SE Sweden, 20 mi. NW of Vastervik; mfg. of agr. machinery; woodworking.

Overveen (ō'vûrvān), residential town (pop. 4,751), North Holland prov., W Netherlands, just W of Haarlem.

Overyssche, Belgium: see OVERIJSE.

Overyssel, Netherlands: see OVERIJSSEL.

Ovett (ŏvĕt'), town (pop. 357), Jones co., SE Miss., 18 mi. SSE of Laurel.

Ovetum, Spain: see OVIEDO, city.

Ovid (ō'vĭd). **1** (also ŏ'vĭd) Town (pop. 664), Sedgwick co., NE Colo., on S.Platte R., near Nebr. line, 6 mi. WSW of Julesburg; trade point in grain, livestock region; beet sugar, dairy and poultry products. **2** Village (pop. 1,410), Clinton co., S central Mich., 21 mi. NNE of Lansing and on Maple R., in agr. area. Platted 1857, inc. 1869. **3** Village (pop. 646), a ⊙ Seneca co., W central N.Y., 23 mi. NW of Ithaca, bet. Seneca and Cayuga lakes, in agr. area (dairy products, poultry, fruit, grain). Willard State Hosp. is at Willard (W).

Ovidiopol or **Ovidiopol'** (ŭvĕdyēō'pŭl), village (1926 pop. 4,774), S Odessa oblast, Ukrainian SSR, on the Dniester Liman, 18 mi. SW of Odessa (linked by railroad); flour mill, metalworks. Once identified with site of anc. Tomis, where Ovid was exiled.

Oviedo (ōvyā'dhō), province (□ 4,207; pop. 836,642), NW Spain, on Bay of Biscay; ⊙ Oviedo. Coextensive with the historic region ASTURIAS, which see.

Oviedo, anc. *Ovetum*, city (pop. 51,410), ⊙ Oviedo prov. and Asturias, NW Spain, 230 mi. NW of Madrid, 55 mi. NNW of Leon, and 15 mi. SW of port of Gijón; 43°22'N 5°51'W. Industrial and communications center in fertile agr. area circled by mts. Its important metallurgical industries are based on near-by Asturian iron-mining basin. Has govt. armaments plant in old Benedictine convent; chemical works (explosives, fertilizers), brewery, match factory, distilleries (brandy, liqueurs, cider); also produces coal briquettes, cement, ceramics, and dairy products. Bishopric; and seat of univ. (founded 1604). Has 14th-cent. Gothic cathedral (damaged in 1937) with tombs of early Asturian kings. Near-by *Cámara Santa* (1st built 9th–11th cent. as chapel) contains precious treasures and relics. Also notable are univ. palace (16th cent.) with art collection, town hall (17th cent.), and some anc. churches and palaces. Founded in 8th cent., Oviedo flourished as ⊙ Asturian kingdom (9th–10th cent.), but declined after its transfer to Leon. Was plundered (1809) by French. Suffered in Sp. civil war of 1936–39. On Naranço hills near by are two 9th-cent. churches. Mineral springs.

Oviedo (ōvē'dō), town (pop. 1,601), Seminole co., E central Fla., 14 mi. NE of Orlando, near L. Jessup; ships truck, citrus fruit; makes fertilizer. Inc. 1925.

Ovindoli (ôvēn'dôlē), village (pop. 1,508), Aquila prov., Abruzzi e Molise, S central Italy, in the Apennines, 8 mi. NE of Avezzano; resort (alt. 4,511 ft.). Bauxite mines.

Ovoca, Ireland: see AVOCA.

Ovrebo (ûv'rúbû), Nor. *Øvrebø*, village and canton (pop. 1,004), Vest-Agder co., S Norway, 12 mi. NW of Kristiansand. At Mushom, near by, the oldest ski in Scandinavia was found, said to date from 2000 B.C.

Ovre Eiker, Norway: see VESTFOSSEN.

Ovre Fryken, Sweden: see FRYK, LAKE.

Ovre Sandsvaer, Norway: see HEDENSTAD.

Ovre Sirdal (ûv'rú sĭr'däl), Nor. *Øvre Sirdal*, village and canton (pop. 630), Vest-Agder co., S Norway, on the Sira and 37 mi. N of Flekkefjord; fishing, deer and grouse hunting; tourist center.

Ovruch (ô'vrōōch), city (1948 pop. over 10,000), N Zhitomir oblast, Ukrainian SSR, on S edge of Pripet Marshes, 25 mi. NNE of Korosten; rail junction; lumber center; furniture mfg., food processing. Dates from 9th cent.; originally called Vruchi.

Owada (ō'wädä). **1** Town (pop. 6,116), Chiba prefecture, central Honshu, Japan, 8 mi. N of Chiba; rice, wheat, poultry, raw silk. **2** Town (pop. 6,700), Saitama prefecture, central Honshu, Japan, 9 mi. W of Kawaguchi; rice, wheat, sweet potatoes, raw silk.

Owadno, Ukrainian SSR: see OVADNO.

Owaneco (ōwŏ'nŭkō), village (pop. 343), Christian co., central Ill., 27 mi. SSW of Decatur, in agr. and bituminous-coal-mining area.

Owani (ō'wänē), town (pop. 10,805), Aomori prefecture, N Honshu, Japan, 8 mi. SE of Hirosaki, in apple-growing area; hot-springs resort. Near by is Mt. Ajara (3,200 ft.); ski meet held annually.

Owari Bay, Japan: see ISE BAY.

Owasa (ōwä'sŭ), town (pop. 100), Hardin co., central Iowa, 7 mi. NW of Eldora, in agr. area.

Owasco (ōwä'skō), resort village (pop. c.300), Cayuga co., W central N.Y., in Finger Lakes region, between Owasco and Skaneateles lakes, 8 mi. SE of Auburn.

Owasco Lake, Cayuga co., W central N.Y., one of the Finger Lakes, bet. Cayuga L. (W) and Skaneateles L. (E); extends c.11 mi. SSE from Auburn, at its outlet. Fillmore Glen State Park is near S end.

Owashi (ōwä'shē), or **Owase** (ōwä'sä), town (pop. 18,214), Mie prefecture, S Honshu, Japan, port on Kumano Sea, on E Kii Peninsula, 42 mi. SW of Ujiyamada; fishing center (dried bonito, fish canning); woodworking. Exports fish, lumber, charcoal.

Owasso (ōwä'sō), town (pop. 431), Tulsa co., NE Okla., 11 mi. NE of Tulsa.

Owatonna (ōwŭtŏ'nŭ), city (pop. 10,191), ⊙ Steele co., SE Minn., on Straight R. and c.60 mi. S of St. Paul; trade and industrial center for poultry, livestock, and truck-farming area; resort with mineral spring; dairy products, canned vegetables, beverages; mfg. (farm equipment, tools, leather goods, cement, tile). Natl. Farmers Bank Bldg. (1908) was designed by Louis Sullivan. State park just S. Settled in early 1850s.

Owchihkow or **Ou-ch'ih-k'ou** (both: ō'chû'kō'), town, S Hupeh prov., China, near Hunan line, port on canal linking Yangtze R. (near by) with Tungting L., and 130 mi. SW of Hankow.

Owego (ōwē'gō), village (pop. 5,350), ⊙ Tioga co., S N.Y., on the Susquehanna at mouth of Owego Creek, and 18 mi. W of Binghamton; railroad junction; mfg. (feed, shoes, furniture, polishes and waxes); agr. (dairy products; poultry). Settled 1787 and inc. 1827 on site of Indian village destroyed (1779) in Sullivan campaign. Thomas C. Platt b. here.

Owego Creek, S N.Y., rises in S Cortland co., flows c.35 mi. generally SSW to the Susquehanna at Owego.

Owel, Lough (lŏkh), lake (4 mi. long, 2 mi. wide), central Co. Westmeath, Ireland, 2 mi. NNW of Mullingar. Reservoir for Royal Canal.

Owen, village (pop. 199), SE South Australia, 45 mi. N of Adelaide; agr. center.

Owen (ō'vŭn), town (pop. 1,945), N Württemberg, Germany, after 1945 in Württemberg-Baden, at W foot of the Teck, 4 mi. S of Kirchheim; grain. Has Gothic church with tombs of dukes of Teck.

Owen (ō'ĭn). **1** County (□ 391; pop. 11,763), SW central Ind.; ⊙ Spencer. Agr. (grain, fruit, livestock). Mfg. of cement products, dairy and other food products, drugs, typewriter ribbons; lumber milling. Limestone quarrying; timber. Drained by West Fork of White R. and Mill Creek. Formed 1818. **2** County (□ 351; pop. 9,755), N Ky.; ⊙ Owenton. Bounded W by Kentucky R.; drained by Eagle Creek. Rolling upland agr. area (burley tobacco, corn, wheat), in Bluegrass region. Lead and zinc mines, limestone quarries. Formed 1819.

Owen, city (pop. 1,034), Clark co., central Wis., on small Poplar R. and 45 mi. W of Wausau, in dairying, stock-raising, and lumbering area; cheese, evaporated milk, wooden boxes, canned peas. Settled c.1890; inc. as village 1904, as city 1925.

Owen, Mount, Wyo.: see GRAND TETON NATIONAL PARK.

Owendale, village (pop. 307), Huron co., E Mich., 32 mi. ENE of Bay City, near Saginaw Bay.

Owendo (ōwĕndō'), village, NW Gabon, Fr. Equatorial Africa, on N shore of Gabon River, part of and 5 mi. SSE of Libreville; ships hardwoods (notably *okume* wood). Seaplane base. Experimental stock-raising station.

Owenea River, W Co. Donegal, Ireland, rises in Croaghgorm mts., flows 14 mi. W, past Glenties, to the Atlantic 5 mi. W of Ardara.

Owen Falls, SE Uganda, on the Victoria Nile just NW of Jinja, below its outlet from L. Victoria. Here in 1949 was begun construction of a dam (2,725 ft. long, 85 ft. high) to raise level of L. Victoria and provide long-range storage for Nile waters; a major hydroelectric installation is part of the project. The development, financed jointly by Egypt and Uganda, was scheduled for completion in 1952.

Owensboro (ō'ĭnz-), city (pop. 33,651), ⊙ Daviess co., NW Ky., on left bank (levee) of the Ohio (toll bridge) and 29 mi. ESE of Evansville, Ind., in area of agr., oil and gas wells, coal mines, clay, sand, and gravel pits, and timber. Important oil center, tobacco market, and shipping point, with boat connections; mfg. of radio tubes, electric-light bulbs, furniture, cellulose, wood products, building materials, machinery, foodstuffs, tobacco products, clay and metal products; distilleries. Airport. Scene of several Civil War skirmishes. Near by are small lake (fishing) and Mt. St. Joseph convent (Ursuline; established 1874), with acad. and jr. col. Settled c.1800 as Yellow Banks; renamed Rossborough in 1815; inc. 1866 as Owensboro.

Owens Lake, Calif.: see OWENS RIVER.

Owen Sound, city (pop. 14,002), ⊙ Grey co., S Ont., on Owen Sound (15-mi.-long inlet of Georgian Bay of L. Huron), 100 mi. NW of Toronto at base of Saugeen Peninsula; lake port, with large grain elevators; mfg. of agr. implements, furniture; center of dairying, mixed-farming region. Near by is hydroelectric power station.

Owens River (ō'ĭnz), E Calif., rises in the Sierra Nevada in SW Mono co., flows c.120 mi. SE and S, through trough-like Owens Valley bet. the Sierra Nevada (W) and White and Inyo mts. (E), to Owens L. (now nearly dry; borax deposits) just S of Lone Pine. At a point c.43 mi. above lake, river is tapped by Los Angeles Aqueduct (completed 1913), which leads 233 mi. S and SW, flowing entirely by gravity, along E base of the Sierra Nevada and through Mojave Desert, to San Fernando Reservoir N of Los Angeles. Other reservoirs in course of river are L. Crowley (or Long Valley Reservoir), 8 mi. long, near source of Owens R.; Tinemaha Reservoir (tĭnēmä'hä), c.4 mi. long, at aqueduct intake; Haiwee Reservoirs (hā'wā) (Upper Haiwee, Lower Haiwee), each c.3 mi. long, just below Owens L. Much of Owens Valley, formerly a productive irrigated region, has been taken out of cultivation since acquisition of water rights by Los Angeles.

Owen Stanley Range, SE New Guinea, contains Mt. Victoria (13,240 ft., highest peak of Territory of Papua), Mt. Albert Edward (c.13,000 ft.), Mt. Scratchley (12,860 ft.), Mt. Obree (10,200 ft.); largely jungle. Several small rivers rise in the range and empty into Coral Sea. In Second World War, Jap. drive (1942) on Port Moresby through mtn. pass at Kokoda was checked by Allied forces.

Owens Valley, Calif.: see OWENS RIVER.

Owensville (ō'ĭnzvĭl). **1** Town (pop. 1,110), Gibson co., SW Ind., 22 mi. NNW of Evansville; agr.; gas and oil wells, bituminous-coal mines; timber; feed and lumber mills. Settled 1817, inc. 1881. **2** City (pop. 1,946), Gasconade co., E central Mo., 40 mi. SE of Jefferson City; agr.; mfg. (shoes, corncob pipes, flour); clay, flint, diaspore mining. Inc. 1900. **3** Village (pop. 419), Clermont co., SW Ohio, 20 mi. E of Cincinnati; limestone quarry.

Owenton, town (pop. 1,249), ⊙ Owen co., N Ky., 24 mi. N of Frankfort, in Bluegrass agr. area (burley tobacco, corn, wheat); makes cheese. Fishing near by.

Owerri (ôwä'rē), province (□10,374; pop. 1,616,072), Eastern Provinces, S Nigeria, in equatorial forest belt; ⊙ Port Harcourt. Includes E part of Niger R. delta; mangrove forest (S), rain forest (N); drained by arms (Nun, Brass, Sombrero, and Bonny rivers) of Niger R. delta and by Imo R. Main forest products: palm oil and kernels, hardwood, rubber, kola nuts. Food crops are yams, corn, cassava. Lignite deposits (N) bet. Oguta and Bende. Chief centers: Port Harcourt (major port and railhead), Owerri, Aba, Bende, Okigwi. Pop. largely Ijo in Niger R. delta, Ibo in N.

Owerri, town (pop. 2,069), Owerri prov., Eastern Provinces, S Nigeria, 35 mi. NW of Aba; trade center; palm oil and kernels; kola nuts. Has hosp.

Owey, island (306 acres; 1 mi. long) off NW Co. Donegal, Ireland, 4 mi. NE of Aran Isl.

Owings (ō'ĭngz), village, Laurens co., NW S.C., 22 mi. SE of Greenville, near Gray Court.

Owings Mills, village, Baltimore co., N Md., 12 mi. NW of downtown Baltimore; seat of Rosewood State Training School for the insane.

Owingsville, city (pop. 929), ⊙ Bath co., NE Ky., 28 mi. ESE of Paris, in outer Bluegrass agr. region; wood products, flour, feed. Near by are ruins of Slate Creek iron furnace (built 1790) and Olympian Springs (used since 1791) most important of once-famous mineral springs and baths for which co. is named.

Owl Creek Mountains, central Wyo., a range of the Rockies, bet. Bridger Mts. (E), Absaroka Range (NW); partly encloses Bighorn Basin (N). Highest point, 9,665 ft.

Owl Head Mountain (3,425 ft.), S Que., on W side of L. Memphremagog, near Vt. border, 30 mi. SE of Granby.

Owls Head, resort and fishing town (pop. 784), Knox co., S Maine, just S of Rockland on Owls Head peninsula; includes Ash Point village. Lighthouse (1826) near by.

Owo (ō'wō), town, Ondo prov., Western Provinces, S Nigeria, 25 mi. ESE of Akure; agr. trade center; cacao, palm oil and kernels, kola nuts, rubber, timber.

Owode (ôwō'dā), town, Abeokuta prov., Western Provinces, SW Nigeria, 18 mi. SSE of Abeokuta; cotton weaving, indigo dyeing; cacao, palm oil and kernels.

Owosso (ōwŏ'sō), city (pop. 15,948), Shiawassee co., S central Mich., 26 mi. NE of Lansing and on Shiawassee R., in farm area (livestock, grain, truck). Mfg. (machinery, stoves, boilers, auto parts, metal and wood products, plumbing supplies); railroad shops. Coal mines. A log cabin built 1836 is now a historical mus. Settled c.1835, inc. 1859.

Owpu or **Ou-p'u** (both: ō'pōō'), town, ⊙ Owpu co. (pop. 4,202), N Heilungkiang prov., Manchuria, 140 mi. NNW of Aigun and on Amur R. (USSR line); gold-mining center.

Owsa, India: see AUSA.

Owschlag (ō'shläk), village (pop. 2,615), in Schleswig-Holstein, NW Germany, 6 mi. NNW of Rendsburg; mfg. of concrete ware.

Owsianka, Poland: see OSWIECIM.

Owsley (ouz'lē), county (□ 197; pop. 7,324), E central Ky.; ⊙ Booneville. In the Cumberlands; drained by South Fork of Kentucky R. and several creeks. Includes part of Cumberland Natl. Forest. Mtn. agr. region (livestock, fruit, tobacco); bituminous-coal mines, timber. Formed 1843.

Owyhee, T.H.: see HAWAII.

Owyhee (ōwī'ē, ōwī'hē), county (□ 7,648; pop. 6,307), SW Idaho; ⊙ Murphy. Hilly region bordering on Oregon and Nev. and bounded N by Snake R. Irrigated areas are in E along Bruneau R., and in SW along forks of Owyhee R. Stock raising, dairying, agr. (hay, sugar beets, fruit, truck), mining (lignite, quartz). Part of Duck Valley Indian Reservation is in S on Nev. line. Co. formed 1863.

Owyhee, village (pop. c.200), Elko co., N Nev., on East Fork Owyhee R., near Idaho line, and c.80 mi. NNW of Elko; alt. 5,400 ft. Here is Western Shoshone Agency, hq. for South Fork Indian Reservation in Nev., Duck Valley Indian Reservation in Nev. and Idaho, Goshute Indian Reservation in Nev. and Utah, and Skull Valley Indian Reservation in Utah.

Owyhee Dam, SE Oregon, in canyon of Owyhee R., c.50 mi. W of Boise, Idaho. Dam (417 ft. high, 833 ft. long; constructed 1928–32), main unit in Owyhee power and irrigation project (established 1928), forms Owyhee Reservoir (48 mi. long, average width 1 mi.). Project area is W of Snake R. (including 82,000 acres in Oregon and 30,500 acres in Idaho) and is contiguous with Boise project in Idaho and with Vale project, in Oregon. Chief communities in Oregon are Ontario and Nyssa; in Idaho, Homedale and Marsing. Beet-sugar refining, dairying, and stock raising are important activities. **Owyhee River,** rising in several branches in SW Idaho, N Nevada, and SE Oregon, is formed in Malheur co., SE Oregon, by confluence of several headstreams and flows 170 mi. NW, N, and NNE, through Owyhee Reservoir, to Snake R. S of Nyssa. Total length, including South Fork, is c.300 mi.

Oxapampa (ōksäpäm'pä), town (pop. 796), ⊙ Oxapampa prov., Pasco dept., central Peru, in Cordillera Oriental, 60 mi. NNE of Tarma; coffee, cacao, fruit; tea cultivation.

Oxbow, town (pop. 576), SE Sask., on Souris R. and 40 mi. ENE of Estevan; grain elevators; stock raising, dairying.

Oxbow. 1 Plantation (pop. 189), Aroostook co., NE Maine, on the Aroostook and 30 mi. SW of Presque Isle; hunting, fishing. **2** Village (pop. 1,722), Oakland co., SE Mich.

Oxbow Lake, S Hamilton co., E central N.Y., in the Adirondacks, 3 mi. SW of Lake Pleasant village; c.2 mi. long. Resort.

Oxchuc (ōschōōk'), town (pop. 404), Chiapas, S Mexico, 18 mi. ENE of San Cristóbal de las Casas; wheat, fruit.

Oxeia, Greece: see OXYA.

Oxelosund (ōōk"sŭlŭsŭnd'), Swedish *Oxelösund*, village (pop. 3,057), Sodermanland co., E Sweden, on the Baltic, 6 mi. SE of Nykoping; 58°40'N 17°6'E; major seaport, ice-free the year round, ships iron ore from central Sweden. Important iron- and glassworks, coke ovens.

Oxendal, Norway: see OKSENDAL.

Oxenhope, former urban district (1931 pop. 2,277), West Riding, W Yorkshire, England, 7 mi. NNW of Halifax; woolen milling; textile-machinery works. Stone quarries near by. Inc. 1938 in Keighley.

Oxford, county (□ 765; pop. 50,974), S Ont., on Thames R.; ⊙ Woodstock.

Oxford, town (pop. 1,297), N N.S., on Philip R. and 20 mi. ESE of Amherst; woolen-milling center; also furniture and machinery mfg.

Oxford or **Oxfordshire** (-shĭr), county (□ 748.8; 1931 pop. 209,621; 1951 census 275,765), S central England; ⊙ Oxford. Bounded by Gloucester (W), Warwick (NW), Northampton (NE), Buckingham (E), Berkshire (S). Drained by Thames (or Isis), Cherwell, Evenlode, and Thame rivers. The co. is level and undulating, rising in SE (Chilterns), and has fertile soil. Chief industries are automobile mfg. (Oxford), light metals (Banbury), woolen milling, leather and paper mfg. Oxford is seat of Oxford Univ. Other important towns are Banbury, Henley-on-Thames, Chipping Norton, and Woodstock (Blenheim Park). The co. was important in Roman times; it was crossed by Akeman Street and Icknield Street; there are Roman ruins at Dorchester and Alchester.

Oxford, county borough (1931 pop. 80,539; 1951 census 98,675), ⊙ Oxfordshire, England, in S center of co., on the Thames (or Isis) R. at mouth of the Cherwell, and 50 mi. WNW of London; 51°45'N 1°15'W. Famous as seat of Oxford Univ. In 8th cent. the town was site of a shrine of St. Frideswide; in 10th cent. it became a frontier fort and later suffered Danish raids. In 12th cent. a castle, royal palace, and abbey were built here, and Oxford Univ. established. Town grew as a trading, educational, and religious center. In Civil War it was Royalist capital and was besieged by Parliamentarians. Among best-known colleges are Baliol, New, Magdalen, Merton, Oriel, and Corpus Christi. Famous bldgs. include Radcliffe Camera (1737), Radcliffe Observatory (1772), Sheldonian Theatre (1668; designed by Wren), Christ Church Chapel (12th cent.), St. Mary the Virgin Church (13th cent.), St. Michael's Church (11th cent.), and Bodleian Library (1602). In recent years the city has undergone considerable industrial development: the SE suburb of Cowley and Iffley (pop. 12,174) has large factories producing automobiles and pressed-steel products, and there are also paper mills and works mfg. electrical and heating equipment. Other important suburbs are Headington (E) and Summertown and Wolvercote (N). Oxford's Latin name is *Oxonia.*

Oxford, township (pop. 756), ⊙ Oxford co. (□ 318; pop. 1,494), E S.Isl., New Zealand, 30 mi. NW of Christchurch; head of rail spur; dairy products, sheep.

Oxford, county (□ 2,085; pop. 44,221), W Maine, bordering on N.H. and Que.; ⊙ Paris. Mfg. at RUMFORD on the Androscoggin, Paris on the Little Androscoggin, and Norway. Shoes, paper, winter sports equipment, wood products; lumber and textile mills, canneries, feldspar mines, agr., dairying. Winter sports at Rumford and Fryeburg; summer resorts in Rangeley Lakes region. Part of White Mtn. Natl. Forest at N.H. line. Formed 1805.

Oxford. 1 Town (pop. 1,697), Calhoun co., E Ala., just S of Anniston, in farm area; cotton products. Settled 1855. **2** Town (pop. 79), Izard co., N Ark., 22 mi. N of Melbourne. **3** Town (pop. 2,037), New Haven co., SW Conn., on the Housatonic and 13 mi. NW of New Haven, in agr. region. Part of state forest here. Settled c.1680, inc. 1798. **4** Town (pop. 304), Sumter co., central Fla., 19 mi. SSE of Ocala. **5** Town (pop. 817), Newton co., N central Ga., 2 mi. NNW of Covington. Seat of Emory Jr. Col. **6** Town (pop. 110), Franklin co., SE Idaho, 17 mi. NNW of Preston. **7** Town (pop. 888), Benton co., W Ind., 21 mi. WNW of Lafayette, in agr. area (grain, soybeans, livestock). **8** Town (pop. 543), Johnson co., E Iowa, 14 mi. WNW of Iowa City, in livestock and grain area. **9** City (pop. 798), Sumner co., S Kansas, on Arkansas R. and 30 mi. SSE of Wichita, in wheat area; grain milling. Oil wells near by. **10** Town (pop. 1,569), Oxford co., SW Maine, on Thompson L. and 15 mi. W of Auburn; resorts; wood products, textiles. Settled 1794, set off from Hebron and inc. 1829. **11** Fishing town (pop. 757), Talbot co., E Md., on the Eastern Shore 9 mi. NNW of Cambridge, and on Tred Avon R.; boatyards (c.250 years old). Popular sport-fishing and yachting resort; annual (Aug.) regatta. **12** Town (pop. 5,851), including Oxford village (pop. 3,238), Worcester co., S Mass., 11 mi. SSW of Worcester; woolens, wooden boxes, monuments. Settled 1687, inc. 1693. Includes village of North Oxford. **13** Village (pop. 2,305), Oakland co., SE Mich., 14 mi. N of Pontiac, in lake and farm area (potatoes, fruit, poultry); mfg. (tools, flour); gravel pits; resort. Settled 1836, inc. 1876. **14** City (pop. 3,956), ⊙ Lafayette co., N Miss., c.60 mi. SSE of Memphis, Tenn.; seat of Univ. of Mississippi (at adjacent University); trade center for agr. area (cotton, corn, truck, poultry); lumber, dairy-products processing. Sardis Reservoir is NW. Home of William Faulkner is here. Settled 1835, inc. 1837. **15** Village (pop. 1,270), Furnas and Harlan counties, S Nebr., 50 mi. E of McCook and on Republican R.; grain. Fall festival takes place here. Inc. 1879. **16** Village (pop. 1,041), Warren co., NW N.J., on N slope of Scotts Mtn. and 26 mi. W of Morristown, in iron-mining region; cement rock deposits; makes screw drivers. **17** Village (pop. 1,811), Chenango co., central N.Y., on Chenango R. and 28 mi. NE of Binghamton, in agr. area (dairy products, poultry); summer resort. Site of N.Y. State Woman's Relief Corps Home. Settled 1788, inc. 1808. **18** Town (pop. 6,685), ⊙ Granville co., N N.C., 28 mi. NE of Durham; tobacco market and processing (stemming, redrying) center; mfg. of yarn, furniture, boxes, lumber, sawmilling. Has Negro and white orphanages. Settled 1760; laid out 1811; inc. 1816. **19** City (pop. 6,944), Butler co., extreme SW Ohio, 12 mi. NW of Hamilton. Seat of Miami Univ. and of Western Col. Laid out 1810, inc. 1830. **20** Borough (pop. 3,091), Chester co., SE Pa., 23 mi. W of Wilmington, Del.; dairying; mushrooms; tourist center; furniture mfg. Inc. 1833. **21** Village (pop. 509), Marquette co., central Wis., on small Neenah Creek and 17 mi. NNW of Portage, in livestock and dairy area.

Oxford, Mount, peak (14,000 ft.) in Rocky Mts., Chaffee co., central Colo.

Oxford Junction, town (pop. 663), Jones co., E Iowa, near Wapsipinicon R., 37 mi. E of Cedar Rapids, in livestock and grain area.

Oxford Lake (□ 155), NE central Man., on Hayes R.; 38 mi. long, 9 mi. wide; 54°52'N 95°35'W.

Oxford Lake, N.C.: see CATAWBA RIVER.

Oxfordshire, England: see OXFORD, county.

Oxhey, England: see WATFORD.

Oxia, Greece: see OXYA.

Oxilithos, Greece: see OXYLITHOS.

Oxkutzcab (ōskōōts'käb), town (pop. 5,030), Yucatan, SE Mexico, on railroad and 10 mi. SE of Ticul; agr. center (henequen, sugar cane, tobacco, corn, tropical fruit, timber). Remarkable Maya ruins are at Labná, 7 mi. SW, and interesting grottoes are near by.

Ox Mountains, Ireland: see SLIEVE GAMPH.

Oxna (ŏks'nŭ), island (1 mi. long) of the Shetlands, Scotland, off SW coast of Mainland isl., at S end of the Deeps, 4 mi. WSW of Scalloway; rises to 115 ft.

Oxnam (ŏks'nŭm), agr. village and parish (pop. 522), E Roxburgh, Scotland, 3 mi. SE of Jedburgh, at foot of Cheviot Hills.

Oxnard (ŏks'närd), city (pop. 21,567), Ventura co., S Calif., near the coast, c.55 mi. WNW of Los Angeles and near Ventura; farming (notably sugar beets); ships citrus fruit, walnuts, seed, truck. Beet-sugar refining, mfg. of farm equipment, oil refining. Founded 1898, inc. 1903.

Oxö, Norway: see OKSOY.

Oxon Hill, village (pop. c.200), Prince Georges co., central Md., S suburb of Washington. Oxon Hill Manor has notable gardens.

Oxonia, England: see OXFORD.

Oxted, residential town and parish (pop. 3,799), E Surrey, England, 9 mi. E of Reigate; agr. market. Has 13th-15th-cent. church, 15th-cent. inn, and other old bldgs.

Oxton, agr. village in Channelkirk parish, W Berwick, Scotland, in Lauderdale at foot of Lammermuir Hills, on Leader Water and 4 mi. NNW of Lauder; angling resort.

Oxus River, Central Asia: see AMU DARYA.

Oxya or **Oxia** (both: ôkseä'), uninhabited island (□ 1.9) in Ionian Sea, Greece, in Acarnania nome, at mouth of Achelous R.; 38°18'N 21°6'E; 3 mi. long, 5 mi. wide. Naval battle of Lepanto (1571) took place at mouth of Gulf of Patras (S). Sometimes spelled Oxeia.

Oxylithos or **Oxilithos** (both: ôksĭ'lĭthôs), town (pop. 2,107), E central Euboea, Greece, port on Aegean Sea, S of Kyme and 30 mi. ENE of Chalcis; fisheries.

Oxyrhyncus or **Oxyrhynchus** (ŏk"sĭrĭng'kŭs), excavation site, Minya prov., Upper Egypt, at village (pop. 4,606) of El Bahnasa or Al-Bahnasa (both: ĕl bä'năsä) (also spelled Behnesa), on the Bahr Yusuf near the Nile, 9 mi. WNW of Beni Mazar. Here in 1896–97 and 1906–07 were made some of the largest finds of papyri, partly Ptolemaic in date, but mostly Roman and Byzantine. They tell of a Greek colony 1st and a large Christian monastic center later.

Oyabu (ō'yäbōō), town (pop. 2,747), Gifu prefecture, central Honshu, Japan, 5 mi. SSE of Ogaki; rice.

Oyama. 1 (ōyä'mä) Town (pop. 16,658), Shizuoka prefecture, central Honshu, Japan, 20 mi. NNE of Numazu, in rice-growing area; textiles, dyes. Sometimes called Koyama. **2** (ōyä'mä) Town (pop. 20,785), Tochigi prefecture, central Honshu, Japan, 6 mi. SE of Tochigi; spinning and flour mills. **3** (ōyä'mä) Town (pop. 12,707), Toyama prefecture, central Honshu, Japan, just E of Toyama, in rice-growing area; paper milling, sake brewing. Includes (since early 1940s) former town of Gohyakkoku (1940 pop. 3,921). **4** (ō'yämä) Town (pop. 8,179), Yamagata prefecture, N Honshu, Japan, 4 mi. WNW of Tsuruoka, in rice-growing area; textiles, soy sauce.

Oyano-shima (ō'yänō-shĭmä), island (□ 12; pop. 21,979, including offshore islets) of Amakusa Isls., in E.China Sea, Japan, in Kumamoto prefecture, off W coast of Kyushu just N of Kami-shima; 5.5 mi. N-S, 3.5 mi. E-W; mountainous, fertile. Coal mining, fishing; rice, wheat. Chief town, Noboritate (E).

Oyapock, district of Inini territory, and commune, Fr. Guiana: for the commune see SAINT-GEORGES; for the dist., MARIPA.

Oyapock River (ôyäpôk'), in Brazil **Oiapoque** (ôyŏopô'kĭ), river, NE South America, forms Brazil–Fr. Guiana boundary throughout its northeasterly course of c.260 mi. and empties into the Atlantic at Cape Orange. Towns on Brazilian bank: Oiapoque, Ponta dos Índios; on Fr. Guiana bank: Saint-Georges.

Oyash (ŭyăsh'), village (1939 pop. over 2,000), E Novosibirsk oblast, Russian SFSR, on Trans-Siberian RR and 45 mi. NE of Novosibirsk; metalworks.

Oyashio: see OKHOTSK CURRENT.

Oyat River or **Oyat' River** (ô'yŭtyŏŏ), NW European Russian SFSR, rises in lake region S of L. Onega, flows 150 mi. generally W, past Andronovskoye and Alekhovshchina (Leningrad oblast), to Svir R. 5 mi. E of Sviritsa; lumber floating.

Oye (ŏŏ'üŭ), Nor. *Øye*, village in Hjorundfjord (Nor. *Hjørundfjord*) canton (pop. 1,914), More og Romsdal co., W Norway, on Hjorund Fjord, at foot of the Norangdal, 25 mi. SE of Alesund; tourist and mountaineering center. Formerly spelled Oie or Oje (Nor. *Øie* or *Øje*).

Oyem (ōyĕm'), town, ⊙ Woleu-N'Tem region (□ 14,700; pop. 71,500), N Gabon, Fr. Equatorial Africa, near Sp. Guinea border, 170 mi. NE of Libreville; cacao, coffee, and experimental rubber plantations; potato growing. Customs station. Has R.C. mission and agr. school.

Oyen (oi'ŭn), village (pop. 339), SE Alta., near Sask. border, 60 mi. W of Kindersley; grain elevators.

Oyens (oi'ŭnz), town (pop. 95), Plymouth co., NW Iowa, 6 mi. ENE of Le Mars, in livestock area.

Oyer, canton, Norway: see TRETTEN.

Oyeren Lake (ŏŏ'ürŭn), Nor. *Øyeren*, expansion (□ 34) of Glomma R., Akershus co., SE Norway, 12 mi. E of Oslo; 21 mi. long, 1–4 mi. wide.

Oyestad, Norway: see RYKENE.

Oyesvold, Norway: see OYSVOLL.

Oykell Bridge or **Oykel** (oi'kĕl), agr. village, N Ross and Cromarty, Scotland, on Sutherland border, on Oykell R. and 13 mi. WSW of Lairg.

Oykell River, Sutherland co. and Ross and Cromarty co., Scotland, rises on Ben More Assynt, flows 25 mi. SE, through Loch Ailsh (1 mi. long, 1 mi. wide), along border bet. Sutherland and Ross and Cromarty, to Dornoch Firth at Bonar Bridge. Just above its mouth it widens into Kyle of Sutherland, a lake 2 mi. long, ½ mi. wide. Receives Shin and Carron rivers.

Oymyakon, Russian SFSR: see OIMYAKON.

Oyne, agr. village and parish (pop. 630), central Aberdeen, Scotland, 7 mi. WNW of Inverurie. Near by are ruins of Harthill Castle, built 1600, burned after Covenanters' uprising.

Oyo (ôyô'), province (□ 14,216; pop. 1,339,609), Western Provinces, SW Nigeria, on Dahomey border; ⊙ Oyo. Mainly in savanna, with some deciduous forest (W and SE); drained by Ogun R. Gold mining (Ife, Ilesha). Native textile industry (cotton weaving, indigo dyeing), metalworking. Agr.: cacao (S), shea nuts, cotton, yams, corn, cassava, plantains. Main centers: Ibadan, Iwo, Ede, and Oshogbo (along railroad); Oyo, Ogbomosho, Ife. Pop. (largely Yoruba) is concentrated in large towns.

Oyo, town (pop. 48,733), ⊙ Oyo prov., Western Provinces, SW Nigeria, 35 mi. N of Ibadan; 7°52'N 3°56'E. Agr. trade and textile center; cotton weaving; cacao, palm oil and kernels; agr. (cotton, yams, corn, cassava, plantains); poultry development center. Seat of the Alafin, political ruler of Yoruba tribe. Church of England mission.

Oyodo (ō'yōdō). **1** Town, Mie prefecture, Japan: see OIZU. **2** Town (pop. 13,660), Nara prefecture, S Honshu, Japan, on N central Kii Peninsula, 24 mi. SE of Osaka, in agr. area (rice, wheat); drugs, raw silk.

Oyolo (oiō'lō), town (pop. 1,316), Ayacucho dept., S Peru, in Cordillera Occidental, 34 mi. E of Coracora; grain, alfalfa.

Oyón (oiōn'), town (pop. 1,202), Lima dept., W central Peru, in Cordillera Occidental, 21 mi. ESE of Cajatambo, on highway from Huacho; coal fields.

Oyón, town (pop. 1,163), Ávila prov., N Spain, 4 mi. N of Logroño; olive-oil processing; wine, cereals, lumber, sheep.

Oyonnax (ôyônäks'), town (pop. 9,694), Ain dept., E France, in the Jura, 21 mi. ENE of Bourg; France's leading plastics mfg. center, producing great variety of celluloid and bakelite objects in hundreds of workshops. Traditionally known for its comb industry.

Oyotún (oiōtōōn'), town (pop. 2,245), Lambayeque dept., NW Peru, on W slopes of Cordillera Occidental, 38 mi. E of Chiclayo; agr. products (rice, corn, tobacco).

Oyrat or **Oyrot,** in Rus. names: see GORNO-ALTAI.

Oyster Bay, inlet of Tasman Sea formed by E coast of Tasmania (W) and Freycinet Peninsula and Schouten Isl. (E); 17 mi. long, 14 mi. wide; opens N into lagoons. Swansea on NW shore.

Oyster Bay, village (pop. 5,215), Nassau co., SE N.Y., on N shore of W Long Isl., on Oyster Bay Harbor, 5 mi. E of Glen Cove; part of Oyster Bay town (pop. 42,594). Residential; summer resort. A terminus of Long Isl. R.R. Has historic bldgs. Near by are grave of Theodore Roosevelt, a bird sanctuary and a park commemorating him, and "Sagamore Hill," his home at Cove Neck. Region settled 1653.

Oyster Bay, SE N.Y., irregular inlet of Long Island Sound indenting N shore of W Long Isl., with entrance (c.2 mi. wide) bet. Rocky Point (W) and Lloyd Point (E). Cold Spring Harbor (c.3 mi. long) is SE arm. Oyster Bay Harbor, with irregular branches, is W arm; Oyster Bay village is on its S shore.

Oyster Bay Cove, residential village (pop. 561), Nassau co., SE N.Y., on NW Long Isl., just ESE of Oyster Bay village, in shore-resort area. Inc. 1931.

Oyster Island (32 acres; 1 mi. long) in Sligo Bay, N Co. Sligo, Ireland, 4 mi. NW of Sligo; lighthouse.

Oystermouth, Wales: see SWANSEA.

Oyster River, Strafford co., SE N.H., rises W of Dover, flows c.12 mi. SE, past Durham, to Great Bay.

Oystese (ŏŏ'üstā"sŭ), Nor. *Øystese*, village (pop. 271) in Kvam canton, Hordaland co., SW Norway, on N shore of Hardanger Fjord, 8 mi. WSW of Alvik; Norway's largest suspension bridge (1,131 ft. long) spans an inlet of the fjord (W).

Oystre-Slidre, Norway: see BYGDIN.

Oysvoll (ŏŏ'üsvôl), Nor. *Øysvoll*, village in Overhalla canton (pop. 3,326), Nord-Trondelag co., central Norway, on Nams R., on railroad and 11 mi. E of Namsos; makes agr. machinery. Formerly spelled Oyesvold, Nor. *Øyesvold*.

Oytal, Kazakh SSR: see OITAL.

Oyu (ō'yōō), town (pop. 7,529), Akita prefecture, N Honshu, Japan, 14 mi. E of Odate; agr., lumbering, stock raising. Copper mine near by.

Ozaki (ōzä'kē), town (pop. 4,799), Osaka prefecture, S Honshu, Japan, 10 mi. NNE of Wakayama, in agr. area (rice, wheat); domestic weaving.

Ozalj, Yugoslavia: see KUPA RIVER.

Ozalp (ŭzälp'), Turkish *Özalp*, village (pop. 1,903), Van prov., SE Turkey, 45 mi. ENE of Van, 6 mi. W of Iran frontier; grain. Also called Karakalli; formerly Kazim Pasa and Saray.

Ozama River (ōsä'mä), S central and S Dominican Republic, rises in the Cordillera Central SE of Monseñor Nouel, flows c.65 mi. E and S to the Caribbean at Ciudad Trujillo; navigable for c.15 mi. upstream. Sometimes Ozuma R.

Ozamiz (ōsä'mēs), city (1939 pop. 7,856; 1948 metropolitan area pop. 35,262) in but independent of Misamis Occidental prov., N Mindanao, Philippines, port on Panguil Bay, 35 mi. NE of Pagadian; trade center for agr. area (corn, coconuts); ships copra. Until 1940s, called Misamis (mēsä'mēs).

Ozan (ō'zăn"), town (pop. 124), Hempstead co., SW Ark., 14 mi. NNW of Hope.

Ozarichi (ŭzä'rēchē), village (1926 pop. 1,669), N Polesye oblast, Belorussian SSR, 28 mi. N of Mozyr; furniture mfg. Formerly also spelled Azarichi.

Ozark (ō'zärk"), county (□ 756; pop. 8,856), S Mo.; ⊙ Gainesville. In the Ozarks; drained by North Fork of White R. Agr. (corn, wheat, oats, cotton), especially livestock. Parts of Mark Twain Natl. Forest here. Formed 1841.

Ozark. **1** City (pop. 5,238), ⊙ Dale co., SE Ala., 22 mi. NW of Dothan, near Choctawhatchee R., in diversified farming area; cotton products, peanuts, lumber. U.S. Camp Rucker is near. **2** City (pop. 1,757), a ⊙ Franklin co., NW Ark., 33 mi. ENE of Fort Smith and on Arkansas R. (here bridged); agr. (corn, cotton, peanuts, dairy products); coal mining. Ozark Natl. Forest and a game refuge are near by. Settled 1836, inc. as city 1938. **3** City (pop. 1,087), ⊙ Christian co., SW Mo., in the Ozarks, near James R., 14 mi. S of Springfield; resort; cheese, flour.

Ozark Mountains, S central U.S., highlands lying S of the Missouri in Mo. (covering c.⅓ of state) and extending SW into N Ark. (N of Arkansas R. and W of Black R.) and into NE Okla.; an outlier (Illinois Ozarks) extends into S Ill. Representing a dissected plateau (□ c.50,000; alt. generally 1–1,200 ft.) of horizontal limestone and dolomite strata overlying Pre-Cambrian igneous rocks, the Ozarks are highest in Arkansas (BOSTON MOUNTAINS), where there are several summits over 2,000 ft. In SE Mo. are the mineral-rich SAINT FRANCOIS MOUNTAINS, an outcrop of the underlying igneous rocks, in which is Taum Sauk Mtn. (1,772 ft.), highest point in Mo. Osage, Gasconade, White, and Black rivers drain the Ozarks. Poor soil (except in a few stream valleys and several fruit-growing areas) and poor communications have hampered the Ozarks; region is known for its ruggedness, isolation, timber (mainly hardwoods), underground streams, and springs, and has fishing and vacation resorts. Bagnell Dam (Mo.), impounding Lake of the Ozarks, produces hydroelectric power.

Ozarks, Lake of the, Mo.: see LAKE OF THE OZARKS.

Ozaukee (ōzô'kē), county (□ 235; pop. 23,361), E Wis.; ⊙ Port Washington. Bounded E by L. Michigan; drained by Milwaukee R. Dairying, stock-raising, and truck-farming area, with dairy-products processing, vegetable canning, other mfg. at Cedarburg and Port Washington. Fisheries. Formed 1853.

Ozd (ōzd), Hung. *Ózd*, city (pop. 21,277), Borsod-Gömör co., NE Hungary, 23 mi. WNW of Miskolc; steel and pig-iron mills, fireproof bricks. Lignite mines near by.

Ozdziutycze, Ukrainian SSR: see OZYUTICHI.

Ozea, Greece: see PARNES.

Ozernaya, Armenian SSR: see SEVAN, town.

Ozernovski or **Ozernovskiy** (ŭzyôr'nŭfskē), town (1948 pop. over 500), Kamchatka oblast, Khabarovsk Territory, Russian SFSR on S Kamchatka Peninsula, on Sea of Okhotsk, just S of Ozernoye; fish cannery.

Ozernoye (ŭzyôr'nŭyŭ), village (1947 pop. over 500), Kamchatka oblast, Khabarovsk Territory, Russian SFSR, on S Kamchatka Peninsula, on Sea of Okhotsk, 135 mi. SW of Petropavlovsk; fisheries. Fish canning at near-by Ozernovski.

Ozeros, Lake (ôzĕrôs') (□ 3.8), in Acarnania nome, W central Greece, off Achelous R., 11 mi. NW of Missolonghi; 3 mi. long, 1.5 mi. wide.

Ozersk (ŭzyôrsk'), city (1939 pop. 4,336), S Kaliningrad oblast, Russian SFSR, on the Angerapp (left headstream of Pregel R.) and 18 mi. SE of Chernyakhovsk; iron foundry, metalworking. Until 1945, in East Prussia where it was called Darkehmen (där'kāmŭn) and, later (1938–45), Angerapp (äng'gĭräp).

Ozerski or **Ozerskiy** (–skē), town (1940 pop. 3,380), S Sakhalin, Russian SFSR, on Aniva Gulf, 17 mi. E of Korsakov; fisheries. Under Jap. rule (1905–45), called Nagahama (nägä'hämŭ).

Ozery (ŭzyô'rē). **1** Pol. *Jeziory* (yĕzyô'rĭ), town (1937 pop. 2,700), NW Grodno oblast, Belorussian SSR, on small lake, 13 mi. E of Grodno; rail spur terminus; sawmilling center. **2** City (1926 pop. 14,131), SE Moscow oblast, Russian SFSR, port on Oka R. and 19 mi. SSW of Kolomna; rail spur terminus; cotton-milling center, machine mfg. Became city in 1925.

Ozherelye or **Ozherel'ye** (ŭzhĭrĕ'lyĭ), town (1939 pop. over 500), SE Moscow oblast, Russian SFSR, 5 mi. SE of Kashira; rail junction; lumber mills, brickworks.

Ozieri (ôtsyā'rē), town (pop. 9,091), Sassari prov., N central Sardinia, 25 mi. SE of Sassari, near Mannu d'Ozieri R.; a major livestock center of Sardinia; bishopric.

Ozika-sima, Japan: see OJIKA-SHIMA.

Ozinki (ŭzēn'kē), town (1948 pop. over 2,000), E Saratov oblast, Russian SFSR, on railroad and 65 mi. E of Yershov, in the Obshchi Syrt; oil-shale mining; metalworks.

Ozolaean Locris, Greece: see LOCRIS.

Ozona (ōzō'nŭ), village (pop. 2,885), ⊙ Crockett co., W Texas, c.70 mi. SW of San Angelo; trading center for oil and livestock region (sheep, goats, cattle).

Ozone Park (ō'zōn), SE N.Y., a residential section of SW Queens borough of New York city; some mfg. (clothing, chemicals, stone products, furniture, leather goods, machinery).

Ozora (ô'zôrŏ), town (pop. 4,311), Tolna co., W central Hungary, on Sio R. and 30 mi. S of Szekesfehervar; grain, wine, cattle.

Ozorkow (ôzôr'kōōf), Pol. *Ozorków*, Rus. *Ozyurkov* (ŭzyōōr'kŭf), town (pop. 11,296), Lodz prov., central Poland, on Bzura R. and 15 mi. NNW of Lodz; mfg. (textiles, agr. tools, flour). Before Second World War, pop. was 50% Jewish.

Ozren Mountains (ô'zrĕn). **1** In Dinaric Alps, SE Bosnia, Yugoslavia, in Sarajevo coal area; c.10 mi. long; highest peak (5,025 ft.) is 5 mi. N of Sarajevo. **2** In Dinaric Alps, NE Bosnia, Yugoslavia, bet. Bosna and lower Spreca rivers; highest point (3,008 ft.) is 10 mi. SE of Doboj.

Ozu (ō'zōō), town (pop. 18,319), Ehime prefecture, W Shikoku, Japan, 27 mi. WSW of Matsuyama; mfg. center (paper, silk textiles). Sometimes called Iyo-ozu.

Ozuakoli, Nigeria: see UZUAKOLI.

Ozuchi (ō'zōōchē), town (pop. 15,195), Iwate prefecture, N Honshu, Japan, on the Pacific, 5 mi. N of Kamaishi; fishing center; fish hatcheries.

Ozuka, Japan: see URAYASU.

Ozuki, Japan: see SHIMONOSEKI.

Ozuluama (ōsōōlwä'mä), city (pop. 1,916), Veracruz, E Mexico, in Gulf lowland, 38 mi. S of Tampico; cereals, coffee, sugar cane, fruit, livestock.

Ozuma River, Dominican Republic: see OZAMA RIVER.

Ozumba (ōsōōm'bä), officially Ozumba de Alzate, town (pop. 3,403), Mexico state, central Mexico, at W foot of Popocatepetl, 35 mi. SE of Mexico city; rail junction; agr. center (cereals, fruit, stock). Has old Franciscan church with 17th-cent. historical painting. Chimal Falls near by.

Ozun (ô'zōōn), Hung. *Uzon* (ōō'zôn), village (pop. 2,201), Stalin prov., central Rumania, 5 mi. SE of Sfantu-Gheorghe; mfg. of alcohol; lumbering. In Hungary, 1940–45.

Ozurgeti or **Ozurgety,** Georgian SSR: see MAKHARADZE.

Ozyutichi (ŭzyōō'tyĭchē), Pol. *Oździutycze*, town (1939 pop. over 500), S central Volyn oblast, Ukrainian SSR, 26 mi. WNW of Vladimir-Volynski; flour milling, brick mfg.; cattle trade.

P

Paal (päl), agr. village (pop. 4,828), Limburg prov., NE Belgium, 11 mi. NW of Hasselt. Formerly spelled Pael.

Paama (pä"ä'mä), Fr. *Paou Ouma* (pä͞o͞o'o͞omä'), volcanic island (pop. c.2,500), New Hebrides, SW Pacific, 5 mi. S of Ambrym; 6 mi. long, 2 mi. wide; rises to 1,490 ft.; copra. Also called Pauuma.

Pa-an (pŭ-än'), village, Thaton dist., Lower Burma, in Tenasserim, on left bank of Salween R. and 27 mi. N of Moulmein.

Paan (bä'än'), Tibetan *Batang* (bä'täng'), town, ⊙ Paan co. (pop. 10,565), in W Sikang prov., China, on left bank of Yangtze R. and 190 mi. W of Kangting; alt. 9,000 ft.; trade center on Tibetan border, in agr. area (wheat, barley). Silver found near by. Until 1913, officially called Batang; sometimes spelled Baan. Placed 1950 in Tibetan Autonomous Dist.

Paardeberg (pär'dŭbûrg, –bĕrkh), agr. village, W Orange Free State, U. of So. Afr., on Modder R. and 25 mi. SE of Kimberley; scene (Feb., 1900) in South African War of surrender of Gen. Cronje to Gen. French.

Paardekraal (–kräl"), locality, S Transvaal, U. of So. Afr., on Witwatersrand, just E of Krugersdorp; scene (1880) of meeting of burghers at which re-establishment of South African Republic was decided; prelude to Transvaal revolt (1880–81).

Paarl (pärl), town (pop. 27,286), SW Cape Prov., U. of So. Afr., on Great Berg R. and 35 mi. ENE of Cape Town; wine-making center; fruit, tobacco, olive growing, jam making, fruit canning, textile milling, granite quarrying. Founded 1690 by Huguenot settlers; original rectory now Huguenot Mus. Site of Athlone Training School.

Paar River (pär), Bavaria, Germany, rises in marshy region c.3 mi. NW of the Ammersee, flows 73 mi. N and NE to the Danube, 5 mi. E of Ingolstadt.

Pabay or **Paby** (both: pă'bē), island (pop. 3), Inner Hebrides, Inverness, Scotland, in Broadford Bay, just off E coast of Skye, at S end of the Inner Sound; 1 mi. long, 1 mi. wide.

Pabbay (pă'bā). **1** Island (pop. 3), Outer Hebrides, Inverness, Scotland, in the Sound of Harris, 5 mi. SW of Harris; 2½ mi. long, 2 mi. wide; rises to 844 ft. **2** Island, Outer Hebrides, Inverness, Scotland, bet. isls. of Sandray (N) and Mingulay (S); 1½ mi. long, 1 mi. wide; rises to 560 ft.

Pabellón (päbĕyōn'), village (1930 pop. 94), Atacama prov., N central Chile, on railroad, on Copiapó R. (irrigation) and 22 mi. SSE of Copiapó; alfalfa, clover, corn, goats.

Pabellón de Pica (dā pē'kä), abandoned village, Tarapacá prov., N Chile, on the coast, former minor Pacific port, 50 mi. S of Iquique; exported guano (deposits near by).

Pabhosa, India: see KOSAM.

Pabianice (päbyänē'tsĕ), Rus. *Pabyanitse* or *Pab'yanitse* (both: pŭbyŭnē'tsĕ), city (pop. 37,140), Lodz prov., central Poland, on railroad and 8 mi. SW of Lodz; mfg. of textiles, dyes, furniture, machinery, electric bulbs, bricks, paper. Formerly spelled Pabjanice. During Second World War, under Ger. rule, called Pabianitz.

Pabillonis (päbēl-lô'nēs), village (pop. 1,983), Cagliari prov., S Sardinia, 20 mi. SSE of Oristano.

Pabjanice, Poland: see PABIANICE.

Pablo (pă'blō), village (pop. c.150), Lake co., NW Mont., near Flathead L., 50 mi. N of Missoula; trading point in ranching region. Migratory waterfowl refuge at near-by Pablo Reservoir.

Pabna (päb'nŭ), district (□ 1,836; 1951 pop. 1,588,000), East Bengal, E Pakistan; ⊙ Pabna. Bounded E by the Jamuna (main course of the Brahmaputra), S by the Padma (Ganges); drained by Atrai and tributaries of Padma rivers. Alluvial soil; rice, jute, rape and mustard, wheat, sugar cane, tobacco; swamps in SW area. Jute pressing, rice, flour, and cotton milling; cotton-cloth dyeing; soap and brick mfg. at Sirajganj; a major hosiery-mfg. center at Pabna; rail workshops at Ishurdi (tobacco processing). Col. at Pabna. Part of former Br. Bengal prov., India, until inc. 1947 into new Pakistan prov. of East Bengal, following creation of Pakistan. Pop. 77% Moslem, 22% Hindu.

Pabna, town (1941 pop. 32,299), ⊙ Pabna dist., East Bengal, E Pakistan, on distributary of the Padma and 75 mi. WNW of Dacca; a major hosiery-mfg. center; trades in rice, jute, rape and mustard, wheat; soap mfg., rice milling; general engineering factory. Has col.

Pabrade (päbrädä'), Lith. *Pabradė*, Pol. *Podbrodzie*, Rus. *Podberezye*, city (1931 pop. 2,588), E Lithuania, 28 mi. NE of Vilna; rail junction; tanning, sawmilling. In Rus. Vilna govt. until it passed to Poland in 1921; to Lithuania in 1939.

Pab Range (pŭb), mountain system in SE Baluchistan, W Pakistan; from peak (c.7,730 ft. high) in central Kalat state it extends fanwise, in 4 main ridges, c.190 mi. S to Arabian Sea; 20–70 mi. wide. Watered by Hab R. (E), Porali R. (center), and left tributaries of Hingol R. (W). Encloses central lowland of Las Bela. Partly inhabited by pastoral tribes.

Paby, Scotland: see PABAY.

Pabyanitse, Poland: see PABIANICE.

Pacaca, Costa Rica: see VILLA COLÓN.

Pacaipampa (päkīpäm'pä), town (pop. 1,050), Piura dept., NW Peru, on W slopes of Cordillera Occidental, 24 mi. S of Ayabaca; wheat, corn, potatoes.

Pacajá River (pŏŏkŭzhä'), E Pará, Brazil, enters Pará R. (S branch of Amazon delta) near 2°S 51°W after a N course of c.150 mi. Numerous rapids.

Pacajes, Bolivia: see COROCORO.

Pacajes y Carangas, Cordillera de (kôrdĭyā'rä dā päkä'hĕs ē käräng'gäs), section of Western Cordillera of the Andes, on Chile-Bolivia border; extends c.140 mi. S from Peru frontier to Isluga Volcano; rises to 21,390 ft. in the Sajama.

Pacajús (pŏŏkŏŏzho͞os'), city (pop. 1,194), N Ceará, Brazil, 30 mi. S of Fortaleza; manioc, sugar, cotton, coffee. Until 1944, called Guarani or Guarany.

Pacanga (päkäng'gä), village (pop. 1,281), Libertad dept., NW Peru, on coastal plain, 5 mi. N of Guadalupe, in irrigated rice and sugar-cane area.

Pacaraima, Sierra (syĕ'rä päkärī'mä), in Brazil **Serra Pacaraima** (sĕ'rŭ päkärī'mŭ), in Br. Guiana **Pakaraima Mountains**, range of the Guiana Highlands, extending W-E along approximate latitude 4°N, forming Venezuela-Brazil and Br. Guiana–Brazil border; c.500 mi. long. Culminates in Mt. Roraima (9,219 ft.). Forms drainage divide bet. Orinoco and Amazon basins.

Pacaraos (päkärous'), town (pop. 821), Lima dept., W central Peru, in Cordillera Occidental, 15 mi. N of Canta, in agr. region (potatoes, grain, stock). Thermal springs.

Pacasmayo, province, Peru: see SAN PEDRO, Libertad dept.

Pacasmayo (päkäzmī'ō), town (pop. 6,615), Libertad dept., NW Peru, Pacific port on Pacasmayo Bay, NE of Pacasmayo Point (7°26'S 79°37'W), 4 mi. WNW of San Pedro. Connected by railroad with Guadalupe and Chilete; airport. Shipping center for rice, sugar cane, cotton, hides, cattle. Rice mills, railroad shops; fisheries.

Pacatuba (pŏŏkŏŏtō͞o'bŭ), city (pop. 1,723), N Ceará, Brazil, on Fortaleza-Crato RR and 20 mi. S of Fortaleza; coffee, sugar, fruit. Manganese deposits.

Pacaudière, La (lä päkōdyâr'), village (pop. 607), Loire dept., E central France, on E slope of Montagnes de la Madeleine, 13 mi. NW of Roanne; agr. market (cattle, horses, poultry); cotton weaving.

Pacaya (päkī'ä), extinct volcano (8,346 ft.), S central Guatemala, on Escuintla-Guatemala dept. border, 6 mi. SSE of Amatitlán. Last erupted 1775.

Pacayas (päkī'äs), town (pop. 209), ⊙ Alvarado canton, Cartago prov., central Costa Rica, at SE foot of Irazú volcano, 8 mi. NE of Cartago; trading center; potatoes, corn, grain; stock raising, lumbering.

Paccha (päk'chä), village (pop. 1,204), Piura dept., NW Peru, in irrigated Piura R. valley, 7 mi. NW of Chulucanas; rice; cattle raising.

Pace, town (pop. 422), Bolivar co., NW Miss., 29 mi. NNE of Greenville, in cotton-growing area.

Paceco (pächä'kô), town (pop. 6,759), Trapani prov., W Sicily, 3 mi. SE of Trapani, in fruit- and vegetable-growing region.

Pace del Mela (pä'chĕ dĕl mä'lä), village (pop. 2,688), Messina prov., NE Sicily, 5 mi. SE of Milazzo. Glycerin factory in commune.

Pacentro (pächĕn'trô), village (pop. 3,993), Aquila prov., Abruzzi e Molise, S central Italy, 4 mi. E of Sulmona.

Pachacamac (pächäkämäk'), town (pop. 1,114), Lima dept., W central Peru, on coastal plain, on Lima–Lurín RR and 15 mi. NW of Lima. Site of ruins of pre-Incan temple. Is believed to have been religious center of great pre-Incan civilization. Marble quarries near by. Pachacamac Isls., in Pacific Ocean, are 2 small isls. 5 mi. SW of Pachacamac, 2 mi. offshore; 12°17'S 76°55'W.

Pachachaca (pächächä'kä), village (pop. 53), Junín dept., central Peru, in Cordillera Occidental, on railroad and 10 mi. SW of La Oroya. Hydroelectric plant (fed by Pomacocha reservoir and connected with LA OROYA).

Pachachaca River, Apurímac dept., S central Peru, rises in Cordillera de Huanzo near Ayacucho dept. border, flows c.110 mi. N to Apurímac R. NW of Abancay.

Pachaconas (pächäkō'näs), town (pop. 781), Apurímac dept., S central Peru, in high Andean valley, 40 mi. SSW of Abancay; gold washing; grain, livestock.

Pachai, China: see TANCHAI.

Pachaimalai Hills (pŭchī'mŭlī"), outlier of S Eastern Ghats, S central Madras, India, SE of Salem, separated from Kollaimalai Hills (W) by river valley; c.20 mi. long, up to c.20 mi. wide; rise to over 3,500 ft.; sandalwood, teak, bamboo; magnetite mines. Also spelled Pachchaimalai.

Pachangará (pächäng-gärä'), town (pop. 602), Lima dept., W central Peru, in Cordillera Occidental, 36 mi. N of Sayán; thermal springs.

Pachao Island (bä'jou'), Chinese *Pachao Hsü* (shü), Jap. *Hatto-to* (hät'tō-tō'), one of the Pescadores, 12 mi. S of Makung; 2.5 mi. long, 1 mi. wide.

Pachas (pä'chäs), town (pop. 1,214), Huánuco dept., central Peru, on E slopes of Cordillera Blanca, 20 mi. NNE of Huallanca; corn, potatoes; sheep raising.

Pachaug, Conn.: see GRISWOLD.

Pachbhadra (pŭch'bŭdrŭ), town (pop. 2,178), W central Rajasthan, India, 55 mi. SW of Jodhpur. Rail spur terminus, brine springs, and salt evaporation pans are just W; salt largely exported by rail. Summer heat is intense. Sometimes spelled Pachpadra or Pachbadra.

Pachchaimalai Hills, India: see PACHAIMALAI HILLS.

Pachelma (pŭchĭlmä'), town (1926 pop. 2,145), W Penza oblast, Russian SFSR, on railroad and 65 mi. W of Penza, in grain area.

Pachhar (pŭchär'), town (pop. 7,571), central Madhya Bharat, India, 26 mi. ESE of Guna; local trade in millet, oilseeds, wheat, gram; cotton gins.

Pachía (pächē'ä), town (pop. 344), Tacna dept., S Peru, in Andean foothills, 10 mi. NE of Tacna; sugar cane, wine, fruit, sheep. Thermal springs.

Pachikhani, India: see RHENOK.

Pachin, Thailand: see PRACHINBURI.

Pachino (päkē'nô), town (pop. 18,324), Siracusa prov., SE Sicily, NW of Cape Passero, 14 mi. S of Avola; rail terminus; tunny canneries; wine, olive oil. Saltworks (SE).

Pachitea, province, Peru: see PANAO.

Pachitea River (pächētä'ä), in Pasco, Huánuco, and Loreto depts., E central Peru, rises E of Cerro de Pasco, flows c.220 mi. N, past Puerto Victoria, to join the Ucayali 23 mi. S of Pucallpa. Its main headstream is the navigable Pichis R. (pē'chēs), on which lies Puerto Bermúdez.

Pachiza (pächē'sä), town (pop. 825), San Martín dept., N central Peru, on affluent of Huallaga R. and 27 mi. S of Saposoa; coca, tobacco, yucca.

Pachmarhi (pŭch'mŭrhē), town (pop. 6,696), Hoshangabad dist., NW Madhya Pradesh, India, 50 mi. ESE of Hoshangabad. Climatic health resort (alt. c.3,500 ft.) with military sanatorium, in scenic location on wooded plateau (sal, teak) in central Satpura Range; summer hq. of Madhya Pradesh govt. Plateau has sandstone quarries on slopes and is fringed by peaks; Dhupgarh (4,429 ft.) is highest. Big-game hunting.

Pacho (pä'chō), town (pop. 3,155), Cundinamarca dept., central Colombia, in Cordillera Oriental, 38 mi. N of Bogotá; alt. 6,100 ft. Trading and tourist center in picturesque setting of rocks and lakes; agr. products are coffee, sugar cane, tobacco, fruit. Iron deposits near by.

Pachor (pŭchōr'), village, central Madhya Bharat, India, 22 mi. W of Narsinghgarh; agr. market (cotton, wheat, millet); cotton ginning.

Pachora (pä'chōrŭ), town (pop. 10,474), East Khandesh dist., E Bombay, India, 27 mi. SW of Jalgaon; trade center for cotton, millet, peanuts; cotton ginning, oilseed milling, chemical mfg.; ironworks.

Pachow. 1 Town, Hopeh prov., China: see PAHSIEN. **2** Town, Szechwan prov., China: see PACHUNG.

Pachpadra, India: see PACHBHADRA.

Pachrukhi (pŭ'chro͝okē), village, Saran dist., NW Bihar, India, 5 mi. SE of Siwan; sugar milling.

Pachu, China: see MARALBASHI.

Pachuca (pächo͞o'kä), officially Pachuca de Soto, city (pop. 53,354), ⊙ Hidalgo, central Mexico, on central plateau, in foothills of Sierra Madre Oriental, 55 mi. NE of Mexico city; 20°7'N 98°44'W; alt. 7,956 ft. Railhead. Major silver-mining center, with one of largest production outputs in world; one of oldest mining towns in Mexico. Silver and gold refining; also tanneries, woolen mills, pulque distilleries, soapworks, soft-drink factories, iron foundries. Airport. Inter-American Highway passes 5 mi. W of city. Mountain scenery. Has fine colonial bldgs., including La Caja, built 1670 as storehouse for royal tribute; Casas Coloradas (1785), now court of justice; and Franciscan convent (built 1576–1732). Has theater and scientific-literary institute. Silver mines date from pre-Spanish Aztec period. Founded 1534 on anc. Toltec site. Severely damaged by inundation 1949.

Pachung (bä'jo͝ong'), town (pop. 15,992), ⊙ Pachung co. (pop. 510,483), N Szechwan prov., China, 60 mi. NNW of Tahsien, and on the Nan Kiang (headstream of Chü R.), in mtn. region; cotton textiles; rice, sweet potatoes, wheat, beans, indigo. Until 1913 called Pachow.

Pachungsan, Ryukyu Isls.: see ISHIGAKI-SHIMA.

Pachuta (pŭ-cho͞o'tŭ), town (pop. 273), Clarke co., E Miss., 25 mi. SSW of Meridian; lumbering (pulpwood).

Pacific, county (□ 925; pop. 16,558), SW Wash.; ⊙ South Bend. Bounded W by Pacific Ocean and Willapa Bay; includes Shoalwater Indian Reservation. Timber, fruit, fish, shellfish, dairy products. Formed 1851.

Pacific. 1 City (pop. 1,985), Franklin and St. Louis counties, E Mo., on Meramec R., near Missouri R., and 25 mi. W of St. Louis; ships sand, gravel, silica products. State arboretum near by. Laid out 1852. **2** Town (pop. 755), King co., W central Wash., 10 mi. E of Tacoma, in agr. region.

Pacific Beach, Calif.: see SAN DIEGO, city.

Pacific Grove, residential and resort city (pop. 9,623), Monterey co., W Calif., on Monterey Bay, adjacent to Monterey. Seat of Hopkins Marine Laboratory of Stanford Univ. Founded 1874 by Methodists; inc. 1889.

Pacific Highway, scenic inland route on W coast of North America. Road (U.S. and Canadian highway No. 99) extends c.1,675 mi. N-S from Vancouver (B.C.) to Calexico (Calif.) at Mex. border.

Pacific Islands, Trust Territory of the (□ 685; 1948 pop. 53,900), consists of CAROLINE ISLANDS, MARSHALL ISLANDS, and MARIANAS ISLANDS, held by U.S. under U.N. trusteeship. Before First World War, they belonged to Germany. Occupied 1914 by the Japanese; mandated 1922 to Japan. In Second World War, occupied 1944 by U.S. forces and governed by naval govt. in Guam. In 1947, U.N. approved U.S. trusteeship of isls., and in July, 1951, they passed from military (Navy) control to civilian (Dept. of the Interior) administration.

Pacific Junction, town (pop. 550), Mills co., SW Iowa, 17 mi. S of Council Bluffs; feed milling.

Pacific Ocean, largest (□ 64,000,000; with adjoining seas, □70,000,000) of the oceans of the world, bet. the Americas (E) and Asia and Australia (W); known as South Sea or South Seas in its southern part. It extends from the Arctic to the Antarctic regions, merging with the Atlantic S of Cape Horn via Drake Passage, and with Indian Ocean N and S of Tasmania via Bass Strait and across 147°E. Its greatest width is 11,000 mi. along the equator, which divides it into the North Pacific Ocean (□ 28,000,000) and the South Pacific Ocean (□ 36,000,000). The Pacific is connected with the Arctic Ocean by Bering Strait, with the Atlantic by the Panama Canal, and with the Indian Ocean by passages in the Malay Archipelago. Its principal subsidiary seas are along its W margins; they are, from N to S: Bering Sea, Sea of Japan; Yellow, East China, and South China seas; the seas (Java, Flores, Celebes, Molucca, Ceram, Banda, Timor, Arafura) of Indonesia; the seas (Sulu, Mindanao, Visayan, Sibuyan) of the Philippines; and the Philippine, Coral, and Tasman seas. One of the most distinguishing features of the Pacific is the great number of isls., of volcanic and coral origin, concentrated in S and W—they are primarily the isls. comprising OCEANIA. Along the N and W continental margins are the Aleutian, Pribilof, and Komandorski isls.; and the Kuriles, Sakhalin, Japan, the Ryukyus, Formosa, Hainan, and the Malay Archipelago. The world's deepest ocean, the Pacific has an average depth of 14,000 ft. Its greatest known depth (34,440 ft.) occurs in the MINDANAO TRENCH off NE Mindanao in the Philippines. The Pacific is skirted by a series of deep trenches along the South American continental margins and along the convex side of its W isl. arcs. Of unknown origin, these depressions give rise to many of the world's earthquakes and tidal waves. Typical of Pacific submarine topography are isolated, flat-topped, conical seamounts (guyots) rising from the ocean floor bet. Hawaii and the Marianas. The Pacific current circulation is counterclockwise S of the equator, and consists of the Peru (Humboldt), South Equatorial, and East Australian currents. It is clockwise N of the equator, where it consists of the California, North Equatorial, and Japan currents. The meeting of the Japan and Okhotsk currents at 38°N off Japan to form the North Pacific Current is analogous to the merger of the Gulf Stream and the Labrador Current in the North Atlantic. Prevailing winds of the central Pacific are the trade winds (from NE in N hemisphere and SE in S hemisphere). In the monsoon regime off the Asiatic littoral, the summer monsoon brings warm, moist marine air from the Pacific to the continent. Here also is one of the world's tropical cyclone (typhoon) regions. The Pacific isls. of the S and W were populated by migrants who crossed long distances of open sea in primitive boats. European travelers, including Marco Polo, had reported an ocean off Asia, and by late-15th cent. trading ships had sailed around Africa to the W rim of the Pacific. However, definite recognition of the Pacific as distinct from the Atlantic dates from Balboa's discovery (1513) of the ocean's E shore in the Isthmus of Panama. Balboa 1st named the ocean South Sea (Sp. *Mar del Sur*). It received its present name from Magellan because of its calmness during his voyage (1520–21) to the Philippines. His crossing initiated a series of explorations, including those of Drake, Tasman, Dampier, Cook, Bering, and Vancouver, which, by end of 18th cent., had disclosed the coast line and the major isls. In 16th cent., supremacy in the Pacific area was shared by Spain and Portugal. The English and Dutch established a foothold in 17th cent., France and Russia in 18th, and Germany, Japan, and the U.S. in 19th. Sealers and whalers sailed the Pacific from late-18th cent., and Yankee clippers entered Pacific trade in early-19th cent. The desire to exploit Pacific commerce was a factor in the westward expansion of the U.S., which, by 20th cent., had extended its interest through the purchase of Alaska, trade agreements with Japan, and acquisition of the Hawaiian Isls., the Philippines, and Guam. Japan's growing hegemony in the Pacific area before and during Second World War was ended with its defeat in 1945, and leadership passed to the U.S. in the postwar period. The strategic importance of the area has become paramount since development of the airplane. Scheduled crossings by air date from 1935.

Pacific Palisades, W residential section of Los ANGELES city, Los Angeles co., S Calif., on hills above the Pacific, just NW of Santa Monica; a chautauqua center.

Pacijan Island (päsē'hän) (□ 34; 1948 pop. 19,286), in Camotes Isls., Cebu prov., Visayan Isls., Philippines, in Camotes Sea, just W of Poro Isl., 17 mi. E of Cebu isl.; 9 mi. long, 6 mi. wide. Generally low; rises to 811 ft. In N area is brackish L. Lanao, 3 mi. long, 2 mi. wide. Coconut growing, fishing. The isl. is coextensive with San Francisco municipality.

Packalpe (päk'älpů), range of the Noric Alps in S Austria, extending c.15 mi. along Styria-Carinthia line, S of Knittelfeld. Highest point, Amering Kogel (7,165 ft.). Crossed by Graz-Klagenfurt road.

Packard Homesite, village (pop. 1,096), Washtenaw co., SE Mich.

Packwood, town (pop. 211), Jefferson co., SE Iowa, 11 mi. NW of Fairfield; livestock, grain.

Paclín, Argentina: see LA MERCED, Catamarca prov.

Pacocha, Peru: see ILO.

Paço de Arcos (pä'sōō dĭ är'kōōsh), town (pop. 3,502), Lisboa dist., central Portugal, on N shore of Tagus estuary near its influx into the Atlantic; popular bathing resort; fisheries.

Pacoima (pŭkoi'mŭ), outlying section of Los ANGELES city, Los Angeles co., S Calif., in San Fernando Valley, just SE of San Fernando. Near by on Pacoima R. (an intermittent tributary of Los Angeles R.) is Pacoima or Reagan Dam (372 ft. high, 640 ft. long; completed 1928; for flood control).

Pacolet (pă'kŭlĭt), town (pop. 455), Spartanburg co., NW S.C., 10 mi. ESE of Spartanburg; granite quarry. Just NE is Pacolet Mills village (pop. 2,170), with textile mills.

Pacolet River, NW S.C., formed 10 mi. NNE of Spartanburg by short North and South Pacolet rivers; flows 50 mi. SE to Broad R. 4 mi. N of Lockhart.

Pácora (pä'kōrä), town (pop. 3,223), Caldas dept., W central Colombia, in Cordillera Central, 31 mi. N of Manizales; alt. 6,037 ft.; coffeegrowing center.

Pacora (päkō'rä), village (pop. 604), Panama prov., central Panama, in Pacific lowland, on Inter-American Highway, on Pacora R. (15-mi.-long coastal stream) and 18 mi. ENE of Panama city; coconuts; stock raising, lumbering.

Pacora, town (pop. 1,469), Lambayeque dept., NW Peru, on coastal plain, on Pan-American Highway and 20 mi. NNE of Lambayeque, in irrigated Leche R. valley; rice, corn, alfalfa; cattle raising, apiculture.

Paços de Ferreira (pä'sōōsh dĭ fĕrā'rŭ), town (pop. 253), Pôrto dist., N Portugal, 15 mi. NE of Oporto; agr. trade.

Pacoti (pŭkōōtē'), city (pop. 1,093), N Ceará, Brazil, in hills 10 mi. NNW of Baturité; coffee, fruit. Formerly spelled Pacoty.

Pacov (pä'tsôf), Ger. *Patzau* (pä'tsou), town (pop. 2,816), E Bohemia, Czechoslovakia, on railroad and 22 mi. N of Jindrichuv Hradec; barley, oats, potatoes; furniture mfg.

Pacsa (pŏ'chŏ), town (pop. 2,406), Zala co., W Hungary, 11 mi. SSE of Zalaegerszeg; wine; wheat, rye, cattle.

Pactolus (păktō'lŭs), small river of anc. Lydia, W central Asia Minor (now Turkey), joining the Hermus (modern Gediz) after passing Sardis. Was famous for the gold washed from its sands, a source of wealth to the kings of Lydia.

Pactolus, town (pop. 265), Pitt co., E N.C., 9 mi. E of Greenville.

Pacuarito (päkwärē'tō), village dist. (pop. 2,440), Limón prov., E Costa Rica, 3 mi. E of Siquirres, on railroad; abacá, cacao, rubber, bananas.

Pacú-cuá, Paraguay: see ENCARNACIÓN.

Pacula (päkōō'lä), town (pop. 511), Hidalgo, central Mexico, 8 mi. NW of Jacala; cereals, beans, sugar, stock.

Pacy-sur-Eure (päsē-sür-ûr'), village (pop. 1,900), Eure dept., NW France, on the Eure and 11 mi. E of Évreux; chocolate and confection mfg. Has 12th–16th-cent. church.

Paczkow (päch'kōōf), Pol. *Paczków*, Ger. *Patschkau* (päch'kou), town (1939 pop. 7,522; 1946 pop. 6,955) in Upper Silesia, after 1945 in Opole prov., SW Poland, near Czechoslovak border, on the Glatzer Neisse and 15 mi. E of Glatz (Klodzko); woodworking, soap mfg. Has medieval town walls, 14th-cent. church.

Padada (pädhä'dhä), town (1939 pop. 7,587), Davao prov., S Mindanao, Philippines, 30 mi. SSW of Davao, on Davao Gulf; abacá, coconuts.

Padanaram, Mass.: see DARTMOUTH.

Padang (pŭdăng', pädäng'), town (pop. 52,054), W Sumatra, Indonesia, port on Indian Ocean, at mouth of small Padang R., 350 mi. SSE of Medan, at foot of Padang Highlands of central Barisan Mts.; 0°58'S 100°21'E. Trade center for coal-mining and agr. area (coffee, copra). Railroad connects Padang with centers in Padang Highlands. Port of Padang is outlet for important Ombilin coal field; it includes small Padang harbor (sheltered by islet of Pisang), and the more important harbor of Telukbayur or Telukbajur (tĕlōōk' bäyōōr), formerly Emmhaven (ĕ"mŭhä'vŭn), 4 mi. S of town proper. Exports (besides coal) are coffee, copra, rubber, tea, spices, cinchona bark, resin, tobacco, rattan. Airport. In 1663 Du. East India Co. gained trading monopoly in region and established (1680) trading post here. Town came under Br. control 1781–84. Held briefly by the French in 1793, it was recaptured by the British in 1795 and returned to the Dutch in 1819. Padang area was included in original Republic of Indonesia when it was set up in 1945. Seat of Panchasila Univ. (1951).

Padang. 1 Island off Borneo, Indonesia: see KARIMATA ISLANDS. **2** Island (35 mi. long, 18 mi. wide), Indonesia, in Strait of Malacca, just off E coast of Sumatra, c.80 mi. W of Singapore, adjacent to Bengkalis isl. (N) and Tebingtinggi isl. (SE); 1°10'N 102°20'E. Low, swampy.

Padang Besar (Malay bĕsär'), Thai *Padang Besa*, railroad station, Perlis, NW Malaya, on Thailand border, 38 mi. N of Alor Star, on W coast railroad; Malay and Thai customs stations.

Padang Highlands, mountainous region in W central Sumatra, Indonesia, forming part of Barisan Mts., near Padang; contains many peaks, highest being Mt. Marapi (9,485 ft.). Healthful climate with heavy rainfall. Here are the important OMBILIN coal fields. The region also has fertile areas producing rice, coconuts, tobacco, and coffee, shipped by rail to Padang. Chief centers: Bukittinggi and Sawahlunto.

Padangpanjang or **Padangpandjang** (both: pädäng'-pänjäng'), town (pop. 9,609), W Sumatra, Indonesia, near L. Singkarak, in Padang Highlands, 33 mi. N of Padang, on railroad; alt. 2,536 ft.; rice and rubber-growing center. Has heavy rainfall.

Padang Serai (sŭrī'), village (pop. 1,464), S Kedah, Malaya, 16 mi. ENE of George Town, near Penang line; rubber plantations.

Padangsidempuan or **Padangsidempoean** (both: pädäng"sĭdĕmpwän'), town (pop. 5,709), W central Sumatra, Indonesia, 40 mi. SE of Sibolga; trade center for rubber-growing region. Virtually destroyed (1885) by fire; subsequently rebuilt.

Padany (pä'dŭnē), Finnish *Paatene*, village (1926 pop. 363), S central Karelo-Finnish SSR, on lake Segozero, 40 mi. NW of Medvezhyegorsk; dairying.

Padas River (pädäs'), NW Borneo, rises in mts. in central part of isl., flows 150 mi. N, past Beaufort, turning W to Brunei Bay 15 mi. W of Beaufort; navigable 20 mi. by small craft; scenic gorge.

Padaung (pŭdoung'), village, Prome dist., Lower Burma, on Irrawaddy R. and 12 mi. SSW of Prome.

Padborg, Denmark: see FROSLEV.

Padcaya (pädh-kī'ä), town (pop. c.1,600), ⊙ Arce prov., Tarija dept., S Bolivia, 32 mi. S of Tarija, on road; corn, sheep.

Paddington, municipality (pop. 24,681), E New South Wales, Australia, on S shore of Port Jackson, 2 mi. SE of Sydney, in metropolitan area; mfg. center (cigarettes, rubber goods, chemicals).

Paddington. 1 Town, Lancashire, England: see WARRINGTON. **2** Residential metropolitan borough (1931 pop. 144,923; 1951 census 125,281) of London, England, N of the Thames, 2.5 mi. WNW of Charing Cross. Here is Paddington Station, principal railroad terminus for W England. Near the Marble Arch was site of Tyburn, scene of London executions until 1783. Robert Browning lived in Paddington; Mrs. Siddons is buried here.

Paddock, England: see HUDDERSFIELD.

Paddock Wood, town in parish of Brenchley (pop. 4,076), SW Kent, England, 6 mi. NE of Tunbridge Wells; agr. market in hop-growing region; fruit canning; mfg. of agr. machinery, leather. Market town of Brenchley, 2 mi. S, has 14th-cent. church.

Paden (pā'dŭn). **1** Village (pop. 158), Tishomingo co., extreme NE Miss., 11 mi. SSW of Iuka, in timber and agr. area. **2** Town (pop. 426), Okfuskee co., central Okla., 20 mi. NNE of Seminole, in agr. area; cotton ginning.

Paden City, town (pop. 2,588), Tyler and Wetzel counties, NW W.Va., on the Ohio and 35 mi. SSW of Wheeling, in livestock, tobacco, truck area; makes bottles. Settled 1790.

Paderborn (pädŭrbôrn'), town (1939 pop. 42,490; 1946 pop. 29,033), in former Prussian prov. of Westphalia, NW Germany, after 1945 in North Rhine-Westphalia, 23 mi. SSE of Bielefeld; rail junction; cultural center. Some mfg.: agr. machinery, precision instruments, textiles, organs; also leather- and woodworking. Cement and lime works. Market and export center for agr. region (noted Paderborn bread, cattle, beer). Second

World War destruction (75–90%) included Romanesque-Gothic cathedral, noted baroque former Jesuit church, and late-Renaissance town hall (gutted). Has theological acad. and seminary (was univ. 1614–1819). Created bishopric by Charlemagne c.800. Town developed rapidly in 11th cent.; joined Hanseatic League in 13th cent. Was residence of powerful prince-bishops of the Holy Roman Empire until 1803. Raised to archbishopric 1930. Captured by Allied forces in April, 1945.

Paderia (pŭdär'yŭ), village, S Nepal, in the Terai, 10 mi. WNW of Nautanwa (India). In anc. Lumbini (or Rummindei) Garden, here, a 3d-cent. B.C. Asokan pillar was discovered (1895), erected on site of birthplace (c.563 B.C.) of Gautama Siddhartha of the Sakya clan, who later became the Buddha; one of 8 great anc. Buddhist pilgrimage centers. Near by (W) was Kapilavastu, ⊙ Sakya kingdom. Near Nigliva village, 15 mi. WNW, is Asokan pillar erected c.250 B.C.

Paderno (pädĕr'nô), village (pop. 1,577), Cremona prov., Lombardy, N Italy, 8 mi. NNW of Cremona; hemp and woolen mills. Also called Paderno Ponchielli; until 1950, Paderno Ossolaro.

Paderno Dugnano (dōōnyä'nô), town (pop. 5,169), Milano prov., Lombardy, N Italy, 7 mi. N of Milan; furniture-mfg. center; aluminum, glass.

Padgate, England: see Poulton with Fearnhead.

Padiham (pă'dēŭm), urban district (1931 pop. 11,633; 1951 census 10,031), E Lancashire, England, on Calder R. and 3 mi. WNW of Burnley; cotton and rayon milling, metalworking, mfg. of chemicals, coal mining.

Padilla (pädē'yä), town (pop. c.10,800), ⊙ Tomina prov., Chuquisaca dept., S central Bolivia, c.65 mi. ESE of Sucre; *ají* production center, straw hat mfg. Until 1900s, Laguna.

Padilla, town (pop. 1,115), Tamaulipas, NE Mexico, 32 mi. NE of Ciudad Victoria; cereals, sugar cane, fruit, livestock.

Padina (pä'dĭnä), Hung. *Nagylajosfalva* (nŏ'dyŭlŏ"yŏshfŏlvŏ), village (pop. 5,074), Vojvodina, NE Serbia, Yugoslavia, 17 mi. NNE of Pancevo, in the Banat.

Padlei, trading post, S Keewatin Dist., Northwest Territories, W of Maguse L.; 61°57'N 96°40'W; radio station.

Padloping Island (4 mi. long, 1 mi. wide), SE Franklin Dist., Northwest Territories, in Merchants Bay of Davis Strait, off Cumberland Peninsula, SE Baffin Isl.; 67°3'N 62°45'W. Site of Crystal III air base.

Padmanabhapuram (pŭdmŭnä'bŭpōōrŭm), city (pop. 11,936), S Travancore, India, 30 mi. SE of Trivandrum; mfg. of coir rope and mats, copra, palmyra jaggery. Monazite and ilmenite workings near by.

Padma River (pŭd'mŭ), in West Bengal (India) and East Bengal (E Pakistan), main channel of the Ganges below its bifurcation into Bhagirathi (leaves the Ganges 5 mi. NE of Jangipur; until c.16th cent., main course of the Ganges) and Padma rivers. Flows c.190 mi. SE, past Rajshahi and mouth of Jamuna R. (main channel of lower Brahmaputra R.), joining Meghna River NE of Chandpur; combined streams continue S as the Meghna. Main tributary, Mahananda R.; principal distributary, Madhumati R. Navigable for entire course by river steamer.

Padova (pä'dôvä), province (□ 827; pop. 668,025), Veneto, N Italy; ⊙ Padua. Consists largely of Po plain, with Euganean Hills (c.12% of area) in W. Watered by Adige, Brenta, and Bacchiglione rivers. Agr. (wheat, corn, sugar beets, tobacco); stock raising (cattle, horses, swine). Trachyte quarries in Euganean Hills. Mfg. at Padua, Este, Monselice, and Montagnana.

Padova, city, Italy: see Padua.

Padra (pä'drŭ), town (pop. 12,858), Baroda dist., N Bombay, India, 8 mi. SW of Baroda; trades in cotton, tobacco, millet, pulse; handicraft cloth weaving, calico printing, dyeing.

Padrauna (pŭdroun'ŭ), town (pop. 9,399), Gorakhpur dist., E Uttar Pradesh, India, 40 mi. ENE of Gorakhpur; trades in rice, wheat, barley, oilseeds, sugar cane. Sugar processing 9 mi. W, at Ramkola.

Padre Burgos (pä'dhrä bōōr'gōs), town (1939 pop. 874; 1948 municipality pop. 10,029), Quezon prov., S Luzon, Philippines, on railroad and 14 mi. E of Lucena, on Tayabas Bay opposite small Pagbilao Grande Isl.

Padre Island (pä'drē), S Texas, narrow barrier isl. bet. Laguna Madre and Gulf of Mexico, extends c.115 mi. along coast from Brazos Santiago Pass (S) to channel separating it from Mustang Isl. (N), SE of Corpus Christi; generally less than 2 mi. wide.

Padrela, Serra (sĕ'rŭ pŭdrä'lŭ), range in Vila Real dist., N Portugal, S of Chaves; rises to 3,760 ft.

Padre Las Casas (pä'dhrä läs kä'säs), town (pop. 2,631), Cautín prov., S central Chile, on Cautín R., just SW of Temuco; agr. center (cereals, potatoes, fruit, livestock); lumbering, flour milling.

Padre Las Casas, town (1950 pop. 1,053), Azua prov., SW Dominican Republic, 20 mi. NW of Azua; tobacco- and coffeegrowing, lumbering. Until 1928, Túbano.

Padre Miguelinho, Brazil: see Santo Antônio, Rio Grande do Norte.

Padrón (pä-dhrōn'), town (pop. 1,372), La Coruña prov., NW Spain, port on Ulla R. estuary and 12 mi. SW of Santiago; fishing and boatbuilding; mfg. of lamps, linen and cotton cloth. Has collegiate church founded in 11th cent.

Padstow (păd'stō), urban district (1931 pop. 1,919; 1951 census 2,852), N central Cornwall, England, at mouth of Camel R., on Padstow Bay (1 mi. wide) of the Atlantic, and 11 mi. NW of Bodmin; fishing port and tourist resort. Has 15th-cent. church and Elizabethan manor.

Padua (pă'dūŭ), Ital. *Padova* (pä'dôvä), anc. *Patavium*, city (pop. 90,325), ⊙ Padova prov., Veneto, N Italy, on Bacchiglione R. and 22 mi. W of Venice; joined by canals with Brenta, Adige, and Po rivers; 45°24'N 11°53'E. Commercial, industrial, and transportation center; mfg. (machinery, automobile chassis, motorcycles, refrigerators, aluminum products, furniture, plastics, macaroni, canned tomatoes, liquor). Bishopric. Its 13th-cent. churches include the basilica of St. Anthony, with tomb of St. Anthony of Padua and equestrian statue and bronze reliefs by Donatello, and the Eremitani church (largely destroyed in 1944; being restored) with frescoes by Mantegna. In Scuola del Santo are frescoes by Titian; Cappella degli Scrovegni has frescoes by Giotto. Other interesting bldgs. are the 12th-cent. Palazzo della Ragione, Renaissance Loggia del Consiglio, and Palazzo del Capitano. The palace called Il Bo houses the university of Padua, founded 1222 by teachers and students from Bologna; here Galileo taught, 1592–1610. The city has an acad. of science, letters, and arts (1599), astronomical observatory (1761), sericulture institute, and the oldest (1545) botanical gardens in Europe. In Roman times one of the richest cities of N Italy. Flourished as an independent commune of great importance from 12th to 14th cent. and later (1318–1405) under the Carrara family. Passed (1405) to Venice, which held it until 1797. Birthplace of Livy and Mantegna, and a residence of Dante. Heavily bombed (1943–45) in Second World War.

Padua Bank, India: see Bassas de Pedro.

Paducah. **1** (pŭdū'kŭ, pŭdōō'kŭ) City (pop. 32,828), ⊙ McCracken co., SW Ky., port on left bank (levee) of the Ohio (bridged here to Brookport, Ill.), at Tennessee R. mouth, and 85 mi. SW of Evansville, Ind. A principal dark-tobacco market of U.S.; rail, river, and air transportation focus and trade, industrial, and distributing center of W Ky.; shipyards, drydocks, railroad shops; mfg. of clothing, textile machinery, shoes, cooperage, concrete products, radios, chemicals, batteries, machine-shop products; packed meat, dairy products, beverages; flour and lumber mills. West Ky. Vocational Training School for Negroes, jr. col. here. Former Kentucky Ordnance Works (W) chosen 1950 by Atomic Energy Commission as site of atomic plant. Region produces dark tobacco, strawberries, apples, peaches, corn, livestock, dairy products, clay, fluorspar, coal, timber. Kentucky Dam and Kentucky Reservoir are SE. Settled 1821 as Pekin, on site visited 1778 by George Rogers Clark; laid out and renamed 1827; inc. as town 1831, as city 1856. Taken by Grant (1861) in Civil War and held throughout war as Union supply depot; in 1864, objective of raid by Forrest. **2** (pŭdōō'kŭ) Town (pop. 2,952), ⊙ Cottle co., NW Texas, in rolling plains 30 mi. S of Childress; trade and shipping center for cotton, livestock region; cotton gins and compress, mfg. of mattresses, agr. implements. Settled 1885, inc. 1910.

Padul (pä-dhōōl'), town (pop. 5,640), Granada prov., S Spain, 10 mi. S of Granada; produces aromatic plants and extracts. Olive-oil and cheese processing. Cereals, esparto, sugar beets.

Padula (pädōō'lä), town (pop. 4,462), Salerno prov., Campania, S Italy, 5 mi. SSE of Sala Consilina. Large Carthusian convent (14th–18th cent.) near.

Paduli (–lē), village (pop. 2,123), Benevento prov., Campania, S Italy, 6 mi. ENE of Benevento.

Padus, Italy: see Po River.

Paektu-san, Korea and Manchuria: see Changpai Mountains.

Pael, Belgium: see Paal.

Paengnyong Island (pyăng'yông'), Korean *Paengnyong-do*, Jap. *Hakurei-to*, island (□ 18), Hwanghae prov., Korea, in Yellow Sea, just W of Ongjin peninsula; 37°57'N 124°40'E; 7 mi. long, 5 mi. wide, with deeply indented E coast. Generally low and fertile; produces rice, wheat, millet, tobacco. Fishing, whaling.

Pa-erh-k'o, Tibet: see Barkha.

Paeroa (pī'rōŭ), borough (pop. 2,253), ⊙ Ohinemuri co. (□ 237; pop. 3,056), N N.Isl., New Zealand, 65 mi. SE of Auckland and on Thames R.; agr. center.

Paesana (päĕzä'nä), village (pop. 1,221), Cuneo prov., Piedmont, NW Italy, on Po R. and 11 mi. WNW of Saluzzo. Graphite mines, gneiss quarries near by.

Paese (päā'zĕ), village (pop. 1,108), Treviso prov., Veneto, N Italy, 4 mi. W of Treviso; mfg. (macaroni, scales).

Paestum (pĕ'stŭm), anc. city of Campania, S Italy, 22 mi. SSE of Salerno. Founded c.600 B.C. by Sybarites and called Posidonia. Taken by Lucanians c.400 B.C.; passed to Rome in 273 B.C. and renamed Paestum. Remarkable ruins near modern village of Paestum (pop. 325), formerly Pesto, include 3 well-preserved Doric temples and remains of Roman amphitheater.

Paete (päā'tā, pī'tā), town (1939 pop. 4,212; 1948 municipality pop. 5,546), Laguna prov., S Luzon, Philippines, on Laguna de Bay, 23 mi. NNE of San Pablo; agr. center (rice, coconuts, sugar cane).

Paet Riu, Thailand: see Chachoengsao.

Páez, Colombia: see Belalcázar, Cauca dept.

Paffenthal, Luxembourg: see Luxembourg, city.

Pafuri (päfōō'rē), village, Sul do Save prov., SW Mozambique, on Limpopo R. where it enters colony, on Transvaal and Southern Rhodesia border, and 260 mi. NNW of Lourenço Marques.

Pag (päk), Ital. *Pago* (pä'gô), Dalmatian island (□ 114) in Adriatic Sea, W Croatia, Yugoslavia; 35 mi. long NW–SE; separated from mainland (E) by narrow Velebit Channel. Bauxite deposits; fishing; winegrowing, saltmaking. Produces dried meat, cheese, fine embroideries and lace; noted for beautiful costumes. Chief village, Pag, is 17 mi. WSW of Gospic; trade center. Village of Novalja, Ital. *Novaglia*, is 18 mi. W of Gospic. Both are seaside resorts.

Pagadian (pägädē'än), town (1939 pop. 11,917; 1948 municipality pop. 57,913), Zamboanga prov., W Mindanao, Philippines, port on Illana Bay, 115 mi. ENE of Zamboanga; 7°49'N 123°26'E. Coconuts, corn, rice. Fishing, lumbering.

Pagai Islands, Indonesia: see Pagi Islands.

Pagala (pägä'lä), village, S central Fr. Togoland, near railroad and 45 mi. NNW of Atakpamé; cacao, palm oil and kernels, cotton; Pagala railroad station is c.6 mi. ESE.

Pagan (pŭgän'), village, Myingyan dist., Upper Burma, on left bank of Irrawaddy R. and 20 mi. SW of Pakokku; pilgrimage center; lacquer school. Founded 847, rose under Burmese king Anawratha and flourished as ⊙ early Burmese dynasty (11th–13th cent.); fell to Kublai Khan 1287. Ruins of imposing brick shrines and pagodas cover wide area.

Pagan (pägän'), volcanic island (□ 19), Saipan dist., N Marianas Isls., W Pacific, 27 mi. N of Alamagan; 18°8'N 145°47'E; 8.5 mi. long, 3.5 mi. wide; 3 volcanoes; hot springs. Mt. Pagan (1,870 ft.) in NW; Apaan Bay on W coast. U.S. airfield. Formerly Paygan.

Pagani (pägä'nē), town (pop. 16,448), Salerno prov., Campania, S Italy, 1 mi. W of Nocera Inferiore; canned tomatoes, macaroni, cotton textiles, pharmaceuticals.

Paganica (pägä'nēkä), town (pop. 3,387), Aquila prov., Abruzzi e Molise, S central Italy, 4 mi. E of Aquila.

Paganini (pägänē'nē), town (pop. estimate 500), SE Santa Fe prov., Argentina, on Paraná R. and 7 mi. NNW of Rosario; agr. center (corn, wheat, flax, grapes, horses, cattle).

Pagan River (pā'gŭn), SE Va., tidal stream flowing c.10 mi. NE through Isle of Wight co., past Smithfield (head of navigation), to James R.

Pagasae, Greece: see Volos.

Pagasaean Gulf or **Sinus Pagasaeus,** Greece: see Volos, Gulf of.

Pagasai, Greece: see Volos.

Pagasai, Gulf of, Greece: see Volos, Gulf of.

Pagasetikos Kolpos or **Pagasitikos Kolpos,** Greece, see Volos, Gulf of.

Pagbilao (pägbēlou'), town (1939 pop. 4,733; 1948 municipality pop. 12,978), Quezon prov., S Luzon, Philippines, on railroad and 5 mi. NE of Lucena; agr. center (coconuts, rice).

Pagbilao Grande Island (grän'dā), small island (□ 8; 1939 pop. 1,367), Quezon prov., Philippines, in Tayabas Bay, off Luzon, 8 mi. E of Lucena, opposite town of Padre Burgos; 4 mi. long, 3 mi. wide, with E peninsula 2 mi. long; fishing, coconut growing.

Page. **1** County (□ 535; pop. 23,921), SW Iowa, on Mo. line; ⊙ Clarinda. Prairie agr. area (corn, hogs, cattle, poultry) drained by Nodaway, East Nodaway, Tarkio, and East Nishnabotna rivers. Bituminous-coal deposits mined in E. Formed 1847. **2** County (□ 316; pop. 15,152), N Va.; ⊙ Luray. In Shenandoah Valley; Massanutten Mtn. in W, Blue Ridge in E; drained by South Fork of Shenandoah R. Includes part of Shenandoah Natl. Park and Luray Caverns. Mtn. resorts. Fertile valley agr. area (grain, hay, fruit, poultry, livestock, dairy products); some timber. Some mfg. at Luray. Formed 1831.

Page. **1** Village (pop. 275), Holt co., N Nebr., 12 mi. ESE of O'Neill. **2** Village (pop. 482), Cass co., E N.Dak., 25 mi. NW of Casselton. **3** Village (pop. 1,360, with adjacent Kincaid), Fayette co., S central W.Va., 30 mi. SE of Charleston.

Pagedale, town (pop. 3,866), St. Louis co., E Mo., just W of St. Louis. Inc. since 1940.

Pagegiai, Pagegyai, or **Pagegyay** (pägā'gyī), Lith. *Pagėgiai*, Ger. *Pogegen* (pōgā'gŭn), city (1941 pop. 2,761), SW Lithuania, 4 mi. N of Sovetsk; rail junction. In Memel Territory, 1920–39.

Pageland, town (pop. 1,925), Chesterfield co., N S.C., 22 mi. ENE of Lancaster, in the piedmont; cotton, lumber; granite.

Pagenema, Caroline Isls.: see PAKIN.
Pages Mill, S.C.: see LAKEVIEW.
Paget (pă'jĭt), parish (1939 pop. 2,590), central Bermuda, S of Hamilton.
Paget Island (2/5 mi. long, 1/5 mi. wide), E Bermuda, at E entrance to St. George's Harbour.
Pageton, village (pop. 1,116), McDowell co., S W.Va., 9 mi. SE of Welch, in bituminous-coal area.
Pagham (pă'gům), town and parish (pop. 2,038), SW Sussex, England, on a small inlet of the Channel, 3 mi. WSW of Bognor Regis; seaside resort. Has 12th-cent. church and fragments of archbishops' palace.
Paghman (pŭgmän'), town (pop. 15,000), Kabul prov., E Afghanistan, at foot of Paghman Mts., 15 mi. WNW of Kabul; alt. 7,300 ft.; one of country's leading summer resorts; royal summer residence. Hydroelectric station.
Paghman Mountains, S outlier of the Hindu Kush, in E Afghanistan; rises to 15,417 ft. 22 mi. NW of Kabul. Forms watershed bet. Helmand and Kabul river basins; Paghman summer resort at E foot.
Pagi Islands (pä'gē), small group belonging to Mentawai Isls., Indonesia, off W coast of Sumatra, just SE of Sipora; 3°S 100°20'E; comprises 2 hilly isls. (North Pagi and South Pagi) surrounded by many islets. North Pagi (pop. 2,872) is 25 mi. long, 17 mi. wide; South Pagi (pop. 2,071) is 42 mi. long, 12 mi. wide. Agr. (sago, sugar, tobacco, coconuts), fishing. Sometimes spelled Pagai.
Paglia River (pä'lyä), central Italy, rises on E slope of Monte Amiata, 6 mi. W of Radicofani, flows 35 mi. SE to Tiber R. 4 mi. SE of Orvieto. Receives the Chiana (here called Chiani) opposite Orvieto.
Paglieta (pälyā'tä), village (pop. 1,895), Chieti prov., Abruzzi e Molise, S central Italy, 7 mi. SE of Lanciano.
Pagny-sur-Meuse (pänyē-sür-mûz'), village (pop. 668), Meuse dept., NE France, on Meuse R. at junction of Marne-Rhine Canal, 8 mi. W of Toul; Portland cement mfg.
Pagny-sur-Moselle (–sür-môzĕl'), town (pop. 2,693) Meurthe-et-Moselle dept., NE France, on left bank of Moselle R. and 12 mi. SW of Metz; rail junction; mfg. (electrical equipment, cartons). Vineyards.
Pago, Yugoslavia: see PAG ISLAND.
Pagoda, Chinese *Losingtah* or *Lo-hsing-t'a* (both: lŭ'shĭng'tä'), town, E Fukien prov., China, port on isl. in Min R. near its mouth, 12 mi. SE of Foochow; deepwater anchorage of Foochow, and transshipment point.
Pagoda (pŭgō'dŭ), peak (13,491 ft.) in Front Range, N Colo.; rises on SW slope of Longs Peak, 25 mi. NW of Boulder.
Pagoda Point, SW headland of Burma, on Andaman Sea, at S end of Arakan Yoma; 15°12'N 97°46'E.
Pagopago (păng'gō-păng'gō, päng'ō-päng'ō), coast village (pop. 1,610), SE Tutuila, American SAMOA; landlocked harbor, only port of call in American Samoa; powerful wireless station, naval hospital. Ceded 1872 to U.S. as naval and coaling station. Sometimes written Pango Pango.
Pagosa Peak (pŭgō'sŭ) (12,674 ft.), SW Colo., in San Juan Mts., Mineral co., 12 mi. NNW of Pagosa Springs.
Pagosa Springs, town (pop. 1,379), ⊙ Archuleta co., SW Colo., on San Juan R., in SW foothills of San Juan Mts., and 50 mi. E of Durango; alt. 7,077 ft. Resort with mineral hot springs; livestock, grain, dairy and poultry products. Pagosa Peak is 12 mi. NNW. Chimney Rock, with ruins of anc. cliff dwellings, is 4 mi. W. Platted 1880, inc. 1891.
Pagsanjan (pägsänhän'), town (1939 pop. 3,566; 1948 municipality pop. 9,282), Laguna prov., S Luzon, Philippines, 16 mi. NNE of San Pablo, near Laguna de Bay, on small Pagsanjan R.; rail terminus; tourist center. Near by are scenic rapids, waterfall (c.200 ft. high), and Caliraya Reservoir (4 mi. long, 1 mi. wide).
Paguate (pŭwä'tē), village (1940 pop. 520), Valencia co., W central N.Mex., 40 mi. W of Albuquerque; sheep raising.
Pahala (pŭhä'lŭ), village (pop. 1,607), S Hawaii, T.H.; sisal cultivation.
Pahang (pŭhăng', pähäng'), largest state (□ 13,873; pop. 250,178; including transients 250,240) of Malaya, on South China Sea; ⊙ Kuala Lipis. Bounded N by Trengganu and Kelantan, W by Perak and Selangor, S by Negri Sembilan and Johore, it consists essentially of the vast Pahang R. basin enclosed W by central Malayan range and N by mts. rising to 7,186 in the Gunong Tahan on Kelantan line. Coast (130 mi. long) is flat and sandy. Forest produce (rattan, gutta percha), rubber, rice, coconuts; tin mining at Sungei Lembing, gold at Raub. Served by E coast railroad, few highways, and port of Kuantan. Hill stations at Fraser's Hill and Cameron Highlands. Pop.: 50% Malay, 40% Chinese, aboriginal Sakais. Ruled until 16th cent. by the various powers that in turn dominated Malay Peninsula, Pahang formed part of kingdom of Johore after fall of Malacca (1511). The agents of Johore (and later, Riouw) gradually established themselves as independent rulers. Pahang accepted Br. protection in 1888. Ruled by a sultan (residence at Pekan), it became (1895) one of the Federated Malay States and joined the Federation of Malaya after Second World War.
Pahang River, main river (200 mi. long) of Malaya, in Pahang, rises in 2 headstreams (Jelai and Tembeling rivers) uniting 10 mi. N of Jerantut, flows S, past Temerloh, and E to South China Sea below Pekan. Navigable for shallow-draught boats.
Paharpur (pŭhär'pŏor), anc. *Somapura* (sō'mŭpŏorŭ), village, Rajshahi dist., W East Bengal, E Pakistan, 40 mi. N of Nator; site of remains of one of largest Buddhist monuments in Indian subcontinent. Temple (built late-8th cent. A.D.; antiquities include a copper plate dated A.D. 479) is decorated with thousands of terra-cotta and stone plaques representing Buddhist and Brahmanic figures; surrounded by extensive monastic complex (822 ft. long on sides). Earliest known center of Krishna worship in E India. First excavations 1923.
Pahartali (pŭhär'tŭlē), village, Chittagong dist., SE East Bengal, E Pakistan, 5 mi. NW of Chittagong; railway workshops.
Pahasu (pŭhä'sōō), town (pop. 5,609), Bulandshahr dist., W Uttar Pradesh, India, on tributary of the Ganges and 19 mi. SE of Bulandshahr; wheat, barley, oilseeds, cotton, corn, jowar, sugar cane.
Pahiatua (pä"yŭtōō'ŭ), borough (pop. 1,749), ⊙ Pahiatua co. (□ 285; pop. 3,596), S N.Isl., New Zealand, 80 mi. NE of Wellington; dairy center.
Pahlevi, Pahlavi, or **Bandar Pahlavi** (bändär' pälŭvē'), town (1940 pop. 37,511), First Prov., in Gilan, N Iran, Caspian port 15 mi. NW of Resht, on spit of Murdab Lagoon; leading Iranian port on Caspian Sea; naval base; fishing, rice milling, silkworm-cocoon breeding. Has royal palace. Airfield. Built in 19th cent.; modernized c.1910. Used by Soviet troops during Second World War. Formerly called Enzeli.
Pahlevi Dezh (dĕzh), town, Second Prov., in Gurgan, NE Iran, on Gurgan R. and 13 mi. N of Gurgan; cotton, wheat, rice; rugmaking. Formerly known as Ak Kaleh or Aq Qaleh.
Pahlgam (päl'gäm), village, Anantnag dist., W central Kashmir, 30 mi. E of Srinagar; popular hill resort. Sometimes spelled Pailgam. Amarnath Cave (alt. c.12,730 ft.), a noted Hindu pilgrimage center in Pir Panjal Range, is 16 mi. NNE; its frozen spring is central object of worship.
Pahoa (pähō'ŭ), coast village (pop. 988), N Maui, T.H.; sugar mill.
Pahokee (pŭhō'kē), town (pop. 4,472), Palm Beach co., SE Fla., c.40 mi. WNW of West Palm Beach, on SE shore of L. Okeechobee; shipping center for large truck-farming area. Inc. 1922.
Pahou (pä'hōō), village, S Dahomey, Fr. West Africa, rail junction 28 mi. W of Porto-Novo; palm kernels, palm oil, copra, coffee. R.C. mission.
Pahra (pä'rŭ), former petty state (□ 27; pop. 4,062) of Central India agency, W of Karwi; one of the CHAUBE JAGIRS. In 1948, merged with Vindhya Pradesh.
Pah-rum Peak, Nev.: see LAKE RANGE.
Pahsien (bä'shyĕn'). **1** Town, ⊙ Pahsien co. (pop. 148,975), N central Hopeh prov., China, 45 mi. W of Tientsin; wheat, kaoliang, corn. Until 1913 called Pachow. **2** Town (pop. 20,842), ⊙ Pahsien co. (pop. 828,352), S central Szechwan prov., China, 6 mi. SSW of Chungking city (a former seat of the co.); rice, wheat, millet, beans, rapeseed. Iron mining, oil deposits and large coal deposits near by. The name Pahsien was applied to CHUNGKING until 1936, when the co. seat was moved to present location, previously known as Likiato.
Pahtavaara, Finland: see KITTILÄ.
Pahuatlán (päwätlän'), officially Pahuatlán de Valle, town (pop. 2,262), Puebla, central Mexico, 8 mi. NW of Huauchinango; corn, coffee, sugar cane, fruit.
Pahute Mesa (pī'yōōt), S Nev., tableland (6–7,000 ft. high) in S Nye co.; Amargosa R. rises here.
Pai, China: see PAI RIVER.
Paia (pä-ē'ŭ), town (pop. 3,195), E Maui, T.H., 8 mi. ENE of Wailuku; starting point for ascent of Haleakala; sugar.
Paiania (päyŭnē'ŭ), town (pop. 4,590), Attica nome, E central Greece, on railroad and 7 mi. E of Athens; wine center; wheat, olive oil; stock raising (sheep, goats). Formerly called Liopesi.
Pai-Aryk or **Pay-Aryk** (pī'-ŭrĭk"), village (pop. over 500), S Samarkand oblast, Uzbek SSR, near the Ak Darya (S arm of Zeravshan R.), 19 mi. NNW of Samarkand; cotton; metalworks.
Paicheng. 1 or **Paichengtze,** town, Heilungkiang prov., Manchuria: see TAOAN. **2** Town and oasis, Sinkiang prov., China: see BAI.
Paichüan or **Pai-ch'üan** (bī'chüän'), town, ⊙ Paichüan co. (pop. 349,050), central Heilungkiang prov., Manchuria, 130 mi. NNW of Harbin; road junction; corn, millet, hemp; cattle raising. Formerly called Tapaotze.
Paide or **Payde** (pī'dā), Ger. *Weissenstein* (vī'sŭnshtīn), city (pop. 3,285), central Estonia, on Parnu R. and 45 mi. SE of Tallinn; mfg. (matches, cigarettes, tiles); machine shops. Castle hill. Founded (13th cent.) by Danes; passed in 1346 to Livonian Knights, in 1561 to Sweden; occupied (1710) by Russia.
Paige, village (pop. c.500), Bastrop co., S central Texas, 37 mi. E of Austin, in cattle-ranching, agr. area.
Paignton (pān'tŭn), urban district (1931 pop. 18,414; 1951 census 25,369), S Devon, England, on Tor Bay of the Channel and 3 mi. SW of Torquay; seaside resort and fishing port. Has 15th-cent. church and zoological gardens. The 14th-cent. Bible Tower is relic of anc. bishops' palace; residence of Miles Coverdale.
Paiguano, Chile: see PAIHUANO.
Paiho (bī'hŭ'), town, ⊙ Paiho co. (pop. 64,923), SE Shensi prov., China, 55 mi. ENE of Ankang and on Han R. (Hupeh line).
Pai Ho, China: see PAI RIVER.
Pai-hsiang, China: see PAISIANG.
Paihuano or **Paiguano** (both: pīwä'nō), village (1930 pop. 630), Coquimbo prov., N central Chile, in Andean foothills, on the Río Claro (an affluent of Elqui R.) and 45 mi. ESE of La Serena; fruitgrowing and mule-raising center.
Paiján (pīhän'), city (pop. 2,977), Libertad dept., NW Peru, on coastal plain, on Pan American Highway and 33 mi. NW of Trujillo, in irrigated sugarcane and rice area; rice milling.
Päijänne, Lake (pī'yăn"nä) (□ 557), S central Finland, extends 85 mi. bet. Lahti (S) and Jyväskylä (N); 2–20 mi. wide; maximum depth 305 ft. Largest single lake of Finland, it consists of series of rocky basins, with numerous isls. (total □ 128). Drained S into Gulf of Finland by Kymi R. In lumbering region, it is important timber-transportation route. Steamers ply lake. Fisheries. Many country houses line low S shore; hilly N shore sparsely populated. Päijänne lake system comprises numerous adjacent small lakes.
Paikara, India: see PYKARA.
Pai-Khoi or **Pay-Khoy** (pī'-khoi), mountain range in N European Russian SFSR, on Yugor Peninsula, bet. Kara and Barents seas; forms N extension of the N Urals (separated by 25-mi.-wide tundra belt); 100 mi. long; rises to 1,560 ft. at peak Mor-Pai. Consists mainly of eroded pre-Cambrian schists.
Paikon (pä'ēkôn), mountain massif in Greek Macedonia, N of Giannitsa lowland, near Yugoslav border; rises to 5,413 ft. 13 mi. NNW of Giannitsa. Sometimes called Poglet.
Paikwan, Chekiang prov., China: see POKWAN.
Pail (pīl), town (pop. 4,708), N central Patiala and East Punjab States Union, India, 34 mi. NNW of Patiala; millet, sugar cane, wheat; woodworking. Sometimes spelled Payal.
Pailahueque (pīläwā'kā), village (1930 pop. 669), Malleco prov., S central Chile, on railroad and 30 mi. SE of Angol, in agr. area (wheat, oats, fruit, wine, livestock); lumbering.
Pailgam, Kashmir: see PAHLGAM.
Pailin (pīlĭn'), town (1941 pop. 2,281), Battambang prov., W Cambodia, at foot of Cardamom Mts., on Thailand frontier, 40 mi. SW of Battambang; sapphire and topaz deposits; Brahman sanctuary. In Thailand, 1941–46.
Pailingmiao, China: see POLINGMIAO.
Paillaco (pīyä'kō), town (pop. 2,980), Valdivia prov., S central Chile, 27 mi. SE of Valdivia; agr. center (cereals, livestock); flour milling, dairying, lumbering.
Paillon River (pīō'), Alpes-Maritimes dept., SE France, rises in 2 branches in Maritime Alps, flows c.15 mi. to the Mediterranean at Nice.
Pailolo Channel (pī'lō'lō), bet. Maui and Molokai isls., T.H., 8 naut. mi. wide.
Paimawan, China: see KANGHSIEN.
Paimboeuf (pēbûf'), town (pop. 2,567), Loire-Inférieure dept., W France, on Loire R. estuary 8 mi. E of Saint-Nazaire; chemical fertilizer mfg., iron founding, rope making. Its harbor is silted up.
Paimio (pī'mēō), Swedish *Pemar* (pā'mär), village (commune pop. 6,904), Turku-Pori co., SW Finland, 14 mi. E of Turku; site of tuberculosis sanitarium. Has 17th-cent. church.
Paimiut (pī'mūt), Eskimo village (1939 pop. 8), W Alaska, on lower Yukon R. and 20 mi. SW of Holy Cross; trading point for trappers and fishermen.
Paimpol (pĕpôl'), town (pop. 2,577), Côtes-du-Nord dept., W France, port on English Channel, 22 mi. NW of Saint-Brieuc; engages in cod fishing off Iceland and Newfoundland. Attracts artists and tourists en route to Bréhat isl. (offshore).
Paimpont, Forest of (pĕpõ') (□ 23), in Ille-et-Vilaine dept., W France, c.25 mi. SW of Rennes; last relic of the primeval forest of Armorica, containing 14 lakes and ponds. Cited in Arthurian legend under the name of Brocéliande.
Paine, town (pop. 1,461), Santiago prov., central Chile, 25 mi. S of Santiago; rail junction and agr. center (wheat, alfalfa, fruit, wine, livestock).
Paine Range, Patagonian mountains in Magallanes prov., S Chile, 55 mi. NW of Puerto Natales, near Argentina border; rises to 8,800 ft. Sometimes spelled Payne.
Painesdale (pānz'dāl), village (pop. 1,360, with adjacent Trimountain), Houghton co., NW Upper Peninsula, Mich., 7 mi. SW of Houghton, in copper-mining area of Keweenaw Peninsula.
Painesville (pānz'vĭl), city (pop. 14,432), ⊙ Lake co., NE Ohio, 25 mi. NE of Cleveland, and on Grand R. near its mouth on L. Erie; trade and distribution point for fruit, truck, and dairying area; chemicals (chlorine, caustic soda), rayon,

machinery, magnesium. Nursery center. Seat of Lake Erie Col. for women. Laid out c.1805; inc. as village in 1832, as city in 1902.

Paingakmiut (pān-gäk'myōōt), village (pop. 44), SW Alaska, near Bethel.

Painswick (pānz'wĭk), town and parish (pop. 2,542), central Gloucester, England, 5 mi. SE of Gloucester; agr. market. Has 15th-cent. church.

Paint, borough (pop. 1,547), Somerset co., SW central Pa., just W of Windber.

Paint Creek, S central Ohio, rises in Madison co., flows c.106 mi. S, past Washington Court House and Greenfield, to Bainbridge, then E to Scioto R. just below Chillicothe. Near its mouth, it receives North Fork (c.47 mi. long). Rattlesnake Creek (c.43 mi. long) enters 5 mi. S of Greenfield.

Painted Canyon, Calif.: see MECCA.

Painted Desert, large arid area extending generally SE from mouth of Little Colorado R. in Grand Canyon, N Ariz., along right bank of river into Apache co., E Ariz. Predominance of lemonite, hematite, gypsum, and fossil material in soil, lack of water, and extreme heat combine to create great variety of color effects. Desert dust makes the air glow with a pink mist or purple haze. Petrified Forest National Monument is in SE.

Painted Post, village (pop. 2,405), Steuben co., S N.Y., at junction of Tioga and Cohocton rivers here forming Chemung R., 15 mi. WNW of Elmira; mfg. (wood and metal products, machinery). Settled before 1790, inc. 1893.

Painten (pīn'tŭn), village (pop. 1,641), Upper Palatinate, central Bavaria, Germany, 13 mi. W of Regensburg; brewing. Chartered 1576. Limestone quarried in area.

Painter, Mount, Australia: see FLINDERS RANGES.

Paint River, SW Upper Peninsula, Mich., formed by two branches in Iron co., flows c.45 mi. SE, past Crystal Falls, to Brule R. 12 mi. NW of Iron Mountain.

Paint Rock. 1 Town (pop. 276), Jackson co., NE Ala., on Paint Rock R. and 15 mi. ESE of Huntsville; woodworking. **2** Village (pop. c.800), ⊙ Concho co., W central Texas, on Concho R. and 30 mi. E of San Angelo; wool, mohair market, in sheep, goat, cattle ranching area. Prehistoric rock paintings, hunting, fishing near by.

Paint Rock River, in S Tenn. and NE Ala., rises in Franklin co., Tenn., flows 65 mi. S into Jackson co., Ala., entering Wheeler Reservoir, in Tennessee R., 13 mi. NW of Guntersville.

Paintsville, city (pop. 4,309), ⊙ Johnson co., E Ky., near Levisa Fork, 45 mi. SSW of Huntington, W.Va., in mtn. agr. area (livestock, poultry, truck, grain, fruit); bituminous-coal mines, oil wells; oil refining, mfg. of soft drinks, staves. Has Mayo State Vocational School. Old trading post called Paint Lick Station was here.

Paipa (pī'pä), town (pop. 1,006), Boyacá dept., central Colombia, in Cordillera Oriental, on railroad, on Pan-American Highway and 23 mi. NE of Tunja; alt. 8,455 ft.; thermal springs. Site of battle in War of Independence.

Paiporta (pīpôr'tä), SW suburb (pop. 3,111) of Valencia, Valencia prov., E Spain, in rich truck-farming area; furniture and silk-textile mfg.

Paipote (pīpō'tā), SE suburb of Copiapó, Atacama prov., N Chile, on left bank of Copiapó R.; copper smelter.

Pai River, Chinese *Pai Ho* (bī' hŭ'). **1** In Hopeh prov., China, rises at Great Wall SE of Kuyüan in Chahar prov., flows 300 mi. SE, past Miyün and Tunghsien (E of Peking), joins Yungting R., Huto R., and Grand Canal in area of Tientsin, then flows to Gulf of Chihli bet. Taku and Tangku. Called Hai R. (Chinese *Hai Ho*) below Tientsin. Also spelled Pei and Peh (Chinese *Pei Ho* and *Peh Ho*). **2** In W central China, rises in Funiu Mts. of W Honan prov., flows over 150 mi. generally S, past Nanyang (head of navigation), and into NW Hupeh prov., where it joins Tang R. before entering Han R. near Fancheng.

Pairumani, Bolivia: see VINTO.

Paise, China: see POSEH.

Paisha (bī'shä'). **1** Town, Kwangtung prov., China: see PAKSHA. **2** Town, S Szechwan prov., China, 40 mi. SW of Chungking city and on right bank of Yangtze R.; winegrowing center.

Paisha Island (bī'shä'), Chinese *Pai-sha Tao* (dou'), Jap. *Hakusa-to* (hä'kōōsä-tō'), one of the Pescadores, N of Penghu Isl. (linked by causeway); 4 mi. long, 1 mi. wide.

Paishambe, Uzbek SSR: see KARA-DARYA, village.

Pai-shou, China: see POSHOW.

Paishui (bī'shwā'), town, ⊙ Paishui co. (pop. 62,296), central Shensi prov., China, 70 mi. NE of Sian; wheat, kaoliang, beans.

Paisiang or **Pai-hsiang** (both: bī'shyäng'), town, ⊙ Paisiang co. (pop. 60,995), SW Hopeh prov., China, 40 mi. SSE of Shihkiachwang, near Peking-Hankow RR; cotton, wheat, millet, kaoliang.

Paisley (pāz'lē), village (pop. 709), S Ont., on Saugeen R., at confluence of North and South Saugeen rivers, 25 mi. SW of Owen Sound; dairying, flour and alfalfa milling, woodworking.

Paisley, burgh (1931 pop. 86,445; 1951 census 93,704), NE Renfrew, Scotland, on White Cart Water near its mouth on the Clyde, and 7 mi. W of Glasgow; 55°51'N 4°25'W; thread-mfg. center; also woolen and silk milling, bleaching, and printing; tanning; mfg. of chemicals, soap, boilers. It was formerly famous for silk gauze and Paisley shawls (no longer produced). A Cluniac priory was founded here c.1163 and became abbey in 1219; in 1307 it was destroyed by the English. Present abbey dates from 15th cent. and contains tomb of Marjory, daughter of Robert the Bruce. Paisley is site of an observatory. Alexander Wilson and John Wilson ("Christopher North" of *Blackwood's Magazine*) b. here.

Paisley, town (pop. 214), Lake co., S Oregon, 35 mi. NNW of Lakeview; alt. 4,369 ft.; ranching.

Païta (päētä'), village (dist. pop. 1,317), SW New Caledonia, 10 mi. NW of Nouméa; livestock, agr. products.

Paita (pī'tä), city (pop. 7,177), ⊙ Paita prov. (□ 2,211; pop. 72,582), Piura dept., NW Peru, Pacific port on Paita Bay, and 34 mi. W of Piura (connected by railroad); 5°5'S 81°7'W. Shipping center for cotton; storage of cotton products and petroleum; cottonseed-oil mills, cotton gins; mfg. (soap, candles); railroad shops. Airfield. The area was formerly a yellow-fever zone.

Paita Bay, inlet of the Pacific in Piura dept., NW Peru; 5 mi. long, 30 mi. wide. City of Paita is on SE coast.

Paithan (pī'tŭn), town (pop. 7,167), Aurangabad dist., NW Hyderabad state, India, on Godavari R. and 29 mi. S of Aurangabad; millet, wheat, oilseeds; cotton ginning. Weaving school. Was a major inland center of trade with Alexandria in 3d cent. B.C. Paleolithic artifacts discovered near by. Sometimes spelled Pattan or Patan.

Pai-ti, Tibet: see PEDE.

Paitok or **Paytok** (pītôk'), village (1926 pop. 4,993), N Andizhan oblast, Uzbek SSR, on railroad and 7 mi. NW of Andizhan; cotton ginning.

Pai-t'ou Shan, Korea and Manchuria: see CHANGPAI MOUNTAINS.

Paituk, Tadzhik SSR: see KOLKHOZABAD.

Paitzepa, China: see FAIZABAD.

Paiwar Pass or **Peiwar Pass** (pī'wŭr) (alt. 8,531 ft.), on Afghanistan-Pakistan line, 55 mi. SE of Kabul, at W end of the Safed Koh; crossed by road bet. Gardez and Parachinar.

Paiyentsing, China: see YENFENG.

Pai-Yer or **Pay-Yer** (pī'yâr'), peak (5,900 ft.) in N Urals, Russian SFSR; 65°40'N.

Paiyü (bī'yü'), town, ⊙ Paiyü co. (pop. 12,452), W Sikang prov., China, 70 mi. WSW of Kantse and on Yangtze R. (Tibet border); cattle raising; timber. Copper found near by. Also spelled Beyü. Placed 1950 in Tibetan Autonomous Dist.

Paja (pä'hä), village (pop. 570), Panama prov., central Panama, 13 mi. NW of Panama city, on Canal Zone border; bananas, oranges, livestock.

Pajacuarán (pähäkwärän'), town (pop. 3,805), Michoacán, central Mexico, 20 mi. SE of Ocotlán; agr. center (cereals, fruit, vegetables, livestock).

Pajakoemboeh, Indonesia: see PAYAKUMBUH.

Pajakombo, Indonesia: see PAYAKUMBUH.

Pajakumbuh, Indonesia: see PAYAKUMBUH.

Pajala (pä'yälä), village (pop. 1,270), Norrbotten co., N Sweden, on Torne R. and 70 mi. E of Gallivare, near Finnish border; market center (leather, reindeer hides, timber, salmon).

Pajapan (pähä'pän), town (pop. 2,299), Veracruz, SE Mexico, in Gulf lowland, on Isthmus of Tehuantepec, 19 mi. NW of Coatzacoalcos; fruit, livestock.

Pajapita (pähäpē'tä), town (1950 pop. 1,047), San Marcos dept., SW Guatemala, in Pacific coastal plain, on Naranjo R. and 12 mi. WNW of Coatepeque, on railroad; livestock, grain, sugar cane.

Pájara (pä'härä), village (pop. 328), Fuerteventura, Canary Isls., 18 mi. SW of Puerto de Cabras; cochineal, chick-peas, alfalfa, corn, wheat, tomatoes, barley, almonds. Tanning, cheese processing, lime and plaster mfg.

Pajaral, Ciénaga (syā'nägä pähäräl'), lagoon in Magdalena dept., N Colombia, near Caribbean Sea, in alluvial lowlands of lower Magdalena R., linked through narrow channel with Ciénaga Grande de Santa Marta (E), 12 mi. SE of Barranquilla; c.6 mi. in diameter.

Pajares (pähä'rēs), town (pop. 284), Oviedo prov.; NW Spain, 23 mi. S of Oviedo; anthracite mines.

Pajares de la Lampreana (dhä lä lämprä'nä), town (pop. 1,308), Zamora prov., NW Spain, 14 mi. NNE of Zamora; cereals, wine, livestock.

Pajares Pass (4,475 ft.), in the Cantabrian Mts., N Spain, on Leon-Oviedo prov. border, 27 mi. NNE of Leon city. Crossed by highway and railroad.

Pajarito Peak, N.Mex.: see NACIMIENTO MOUNTAINS.

Pajarito Plateau (pä"hārē'tō), high tableland (6–8,000 ft.) in N central N.Mex., W of Santa Fe; extends 50 mi. S from Rio Chama along Rio Grande (E) and forms E extremity of Valle Grande Mts. Cut by numerous small canyons once occupied by Pueblo Indians. Parts of area included in BANDELIER NATIONAL MONUMENT.

Pajaro (pä'hŭrō), village (pop. 1,487), Monterey co., W Calif., just S of Watsonville.

Pajaro River, W Calif., formed near Gilroy in Santa Clara co., flows c.30 mi. generally W to Pacific near Watsonville; applegrowing in valley. A tributary, San Benito R., drains S part of Santa Clara Valley.

Pajaros (pä'hārōs), **Farallon de Pajaros** (färäyōn' dā), or **Uracas** (ōōrä'käs), northernmost of Marianas Isls., Saipan dist., W Pacific, 20°32'N 144°54' E; 1 mi. in diameter; active volcano (1,047 ft.).

Pájaros Islands (pä'härōs), archipelago of small islets off coast of Coquimbo prov., N central Chile, 30 mi. NW of La Serena; guano deposits.

Pak, China: see HUNGSHUI RIVER.

Paka, Malaya: see KUALA PAKA.

Pakala, India: see CHITTOOR, city.

Pakaraima Mountains, Br. Guiana–Brazil–Venezuela: see PACARAIMA, SIERRA.

Pakbanang, Thailand: see PAK PHANANG.

Pakchan River (päk'chän'), on Thailand-Burma border, at W side of Isthmus of Kra, rises in S Tenasserim Range, flows 40 mi. S, past Pakchan, forming a 40-mi.-long estuary below Kraburi which opens on Andaman Sea at Victoria Point. Also called Kra R. in upper course.

Pakchon (päk'chŭn'), Jap. *Hakusen*, town (1944 pop. 17,184), N.Pyongan prov., N Korea, 50 mi. NNW of Pyongyang; commercial center in agr. area (soybeans, potatoes); textiles.

Pakefield, town and parish (pop. 1,774), NE Suffolk, England, near North Sea, 2 mi. SSW of Lowestoft; agr. market and fruit-packing center. Church bombed in Second World War.

Pakenham (pă'kŭnŭm), village (pop. estimate 500), SE Ont., on Mississippi R. and 28 mi. W of Ottawa; dairying, lumbering, mixed farming.

Pakha (päk'khä'), town, Laokay prov., N Vietnam, 23 mi. E of Laokay, near China border.

Pakhal Lake (pă'käl), reservoir (□ 13) in Warangal dist., E Hyderabad state, India, ESE of Warangal; feeds numerous irrigation canals; built 12th cent.

Pak Hin Boun (päk' hĭn' bōōn'), village, Khammouene prov., central Laos, 18 mi. NW of Thakhek, on left bank of Mekong R. (Thailand line) at mouth of the Nam Hin Boun; tin-shipping center for Nam Patene tin-mining dist. (mines at BONENG and PHONTIOU). Founded 1895.

Pakhna (päkh'nä), village (pop. 1,500), Limassol dist., SW Cyprus, 15 mi. WNW of Limassol; grapes, wheat, carobs; sheep, goats.

Pak Ho, China: see HUNGSHUI RIVER.

Pakhoi (bäk'hoi'), Mandarin *Peihai* (bā'hī'), town (pop. c.36,000), SW Kwangtung prov., China, port on Gulf of Tonkin S of Lim R. delta, 20 mi. SSW of Hoppo; exports aniseed, hides, indigo, tin, hog bristles. Supplanted Hoppo as deep-water port; flourished c.1890 as port for W Kwangtung, Kwangsi, and Yunnan, but declined following rise of Chankiang, Wuchow, and Mengtsz.

Pakhotny or **Pakhotnyy** (pä'khŭtnē), town (1945 pop. over 500), NE East Kazakhstan oblast, Kazakh SSR, in Altai Mts., 30 mi. N of Leninogorsk.

Pakhra River (päkh'rŭ), Moscow oblast, Russian SFSR, rises NNE of Naro-Fominsk, flows 60 mi. E, past Krasnaya Pakhra and Podolsk, to Moskva R. 10 mi. W of Ramenskoye.

Pakhtaabad (pŭkhtŭbät'), village (1939 pop. over 500), NW Stalinabad oblast, Tadzhik SSR, near Uzbek SSR border, on railroad and 35 mi. W of Stalinabad; cotton.

Pakhta-Aral, Kazakh SSR: see ILICH.

Pakhta-Gisar (pŭkhtä"-gēsär'), town (1939 pop. over 500), S Surkhan-Darya oblast, Uzbek SSR, on the Amu Darya just SE of Termez; river port. Until 1937, Patta-Gisar.

Pakhtakor (pŭkhtŭkôr'), village, SW Samarkand oblast, Uzbek SSR, on Trans-Caspian RR and 34 mi. WNW of Samarkand; cotton; metalworks. Until 1937, Ziyautdin.

Pakhtusov Islands (pŭkhtōō'sŭf), island group off E coast of N isl. of Novaya Zemlya, Russian SFSR; 74°20'N 59°E. Settlement of Pakhtusovo (trading post) is on main isl. of group.

Paki, Nigeria: see FAIKI.

Pakiachen. 1 Town, Kirin prov., Manchuria: see HWAITE. **2** Town, Liaotung prov., Manchuria: see TSINGYÜAN.

Pakin (pä'kēn), small atoll, Senyavin Isls., Ponape dist., E Caroline Isls., W Pacific, 18 mi. WNW of Ponape; 4 mi. long; 9 low islets. Formerly Pagenema.

Pakiotai, Manchuria: see TAIAN, Liaosi prov.

Pakistan (pă'kĭstăn", päkĭstän'), dominion (□ 365,907; pop., based on 1941 census, c.70,200,000; 1951 census pop. 75,687,000; all figures without Kashmir) of Br. Commonwealth of Nations, S Asia; ⊙ KARACHI. Consists of 2 parts, separated by c.900 mi. of Indian territory. West Pakistan (□ 311,406; 1951 pop. 33,568,000) comprises BALUCHISTAN, NORTH-WEST FRONTIER PROVINCE (along with adjacent princely states), PUNJAB, SIND, BAHAWALPUR, KHAIRPUR, and the Karachi administrative area; bordered S by Arabian Sea, W by Iran, NW and N by Afghanistan, NE by Kashmir, and E by India. East Pakistan (□ 54,501; 1951 pop. 42,119,000) is coextensive with East BENGAL; bordered S by Bay of Bengal, W, N, and E by India, and SE by Burma. The 2 sections differ considerably in their natural setting, the one a region of snow-capped mts., arid deserts, and broad alluvial plains, the other a humid, low-lying deltaic tract. The dominant feature of W Pakistan is the Indus River, which flows over 1,000 mi. through the country from Kashmir to the Arabian Sea SE of Karachi. To E is Thar Desert and, farther N, the Punjab plains, drained by Jhelum, Chenab, Ravi, and Sutlej rivers. To W lies a series of rugged mtn. ranges, including (N–S) the E Hindu Kush (culminating in Tirich Mir, 25,263 ft.), Safed Koh range (rising to 15,620 ft. in Mt. Sikaram), Sulaiman Range (rising to 11,290 ft. in Takht-i-Sulaiman), and Kirthar Range (4–6,000 ft.). Behind the Sulaiman and Kirthar ranges in Baluchistan are the Toba-Kakar, Central Brahui, Pab, and Makran ranges, with intervening stony valleys and sandy wastes. W Pakistan has a dry climate with extremes of temp. ranging from below 40°F. in winter to 90°–120°F. in summer; Jacobabad, in Sind, is one of the hottest places in Asia. Annual rainfall varies from less than 5 in. in SW to c.25 in. in NE. The Indus and its Punjab and North-West Frontier Prov. affluents are perennial streams, but the rivers of the S and SW are mostly seasonal; W Baluchistan is an inland-drainage basin. E Pakistan lies largely in the fertile Ganges-Brahmaputra delta, a vast alluvial tract intersected by numerous streams and tidal creeks, all throwing off distributaries and merging with one another in a confused network of waterways. Most of the land is not more than 300 ft. above sea level, but in the SE the Chittagong Hills rise to 600–2,000 ft. The climate is monsoon tropical, with a mean temp. of 67°F. in Jan. and 83°F. in May; annual rainfall averages 80 in., with 100 in. in the Sundarbans and 140 in. in Sylhet dist. All of Pakistan is predominantly agr. (c.85% of pop.) and has some 45,000,000 acres under cultivation. Irrigation is vital in the dry W Pakistan, where extensive canal systems, such as the Chenab and Jhelum river canals in Punjab and the Sukkur Barrage in Sind, have been built; altogether almost 20,000,000 acres are artificially watered. Wheat is the most important crop in the W, followed by cotton (long-staple variety), rice, gram, millet, corn, barley, sugar cane, and oilseeds. Citrus fruits are grown in Punjab, melons, dates, apricots, and apples in Baluchistan, and grapes, plums, quinces, peaches, and pomegranates in North-West Frontier Prov. Cattle (best breed in Sind), sheep, goats, horses, mules, and camels are raised in large numbers. In E Pakistan, where floods have caused severe damage to crops and property, too much water is the problem rather than too little. Rice is the great food staple here, comprising 88% of Pakistan's output; jute (75–80% of world's production) is the important cash crop; sugar cane, tobacco, tea (mostly in Sylhet dist.), oilseeds, and chilies are also grown. Fruits include mangoes, pineapples, bananas, and oranges; coconut and areca palms are common. Cattle and goats are raised, and in the Sundarbans much wild life (tigers, wild hogs, snakes) is found. The chief products from Pakistan's small forest area (□ c.11,000) are deodar and pine (in the NW) and bamboos, sal, resin, and silkworms (in the E). Fish resources—marine, estuarine, and inland fresh water—are abundant; principal species are prawn, hilsa, shrimp, mullet, pomfret, Indian salmon, shark, shad, mahseer, and oysters. Virtually all of the mineral wealth is concentrated in W Pakistan, where rock salt (Salt Range, Kohat hills), gypsum (Salt Range), natural salt (S Sind), coal (Salt Range, NE Baluchistan), chromite (NE Baluchistan), limestone, and sulphur are worked; there are also petroleum fields in NW Punjab (refinery at Rawalpindi), granite and marble quarries, and deposits of fuller's earth, alluvial gold, copper, antimony, alkalis, and steatite; in E Pakistan salt is obtained from sea water. Several hydroelectric projects were begun after 1947 in Punjab and East Bengal to supplement the total power capacity generated by plants in North-West Frontier Prov., but these and the small output of coal and oil are insufficient resources for large-scale industrial expansion. The main industries (mostly in W Pakistan) are agr. processing (cotton, rice, flour, oilseeds, sugar, tea, jute), railway workshops, general engineering, cement mfg., ordnance works, sawmills, and fruit canneries; also glassworks, a soda-ash plant, and the noted sports goods and surgical instruments made at Sialkot. Among the many fine handicraft products are the muslins and silver filigree work of Dacca; Baluchistan embroidery; Frontier turbans, shoes, knives, and rifles; wax cloth and copperware of Peshawar; and pottery, leather goods, carved ivory, and metalware. Pakistan's principal cities are Lahore, Karachi, Peshawar, Rawalpindi, Multan, Hyderabad, Sialkot, Quetta, and Sukkur in the W and Dacca, Chittagong, Mymensingh, and Narayanganj in the E. Railways are fairly well developed in the plains of W Pakistan and in East Bengal, and most of the major cities are linked by air; in East Bengal there is considerable river traffic. Karachi, an important international air center, is also the only port for W Pakistan's foreign trade, exporting cotton, wheat, wool, hides and skins, bone fertilizer, and oilseeds, and importing textiles, machinery, iron and steel, coal, and liquid fuel. Chittagong handles the bulk of E Pakistan's exports (jute, tea, tobacco) and imports (metals, machinery, coal, sugar, textiles); Port Jinnah or Chalna Anchorage is an important jute port. Commerce with Afghanistan is via the frontier railheads of Landi Khana in Khyber Pass and Chaman in Baluchistan. The leading schools are Punjab Univ. (at Lahore), Sind Univ. (at Karachi), and Dacca Univ. Although E Pakistan is less than ⅙ the size of W Pakistan, it has over 55% of the total pop., with a density of 773 as compared with only 108 in the W. The majority (c.85%) of Pakistanis are Moslems, but the country is not racially or linguistically homogeneous. The main racial types are Bengalis (mixed Aryans, Mongolians, and Dravidians), Punjabis (Indo-Aryans), Sindhis (Scytho-Dravidians), Pathans or Afghans (Indo-Iranians), and Baluchis (Turko-Iranians). Though Urdu is the national language, Bengali, Punjabi, Lahnda, Pushtu, Sindhi, Baluchi, and Brahui are the provincial vernaculars, and English is still in official usage. The NW of the Indian subcontinent, which now comprises W Pakistan, lies athwart the historic invasion routes through Khyber, Gumal, and Bolan passes from central Asia to Hindustan. The Arabs, who conquered Sind in A.D. 712, were the 1st Moslems to establish themselves in India, and by the 10th cent. Islam had spread to central Asia and Afghanistan. There followed a long succession of incursions into India by zealous Turk and Afghan adventurers, Mongols, and Moguls, who, from the 14th to early-18th cent., brought most of the country under their control. In mid-18th cent. the British East India Co. annexed Moslem-ruled Bengal, but not until a century later did Br. influence extend to the NW regions. Unlike previous settlers in India, the Moslem immigrants, with their well-defined, monotheistic religion, were not absorbed into the Hindu society; but the 2 cultures, existing side by side, were strongly influenced by each other and several attempts (unsuccessful) at a synthesis were made. Although there were instances of religious friction, it was largely economic and social factors that stimulated the demand for a separate Moslem state. Under the British, especially after the Sepoy Rebellion of 1857, the status of Moslems declined, while those Hindus (and other non-Moslems) who took to Western ways gradually assumed dominant positions in industry, the professions, education, and administration. Another grievance was the fact that in many Moslem rural areas the powerful and hated money-lender (*banya*) was very often a Hindu. The idea of a Moslem homeland in India was introduced in 1930 by the poet Sir Mohammed Iqbal, and was ardently supported by a group of Moslem students in England, who 1st used the name Pakistan, which is composed of the initial letters of Punjab, Afghania (North-West Frontier Prov.), Kashmir, and Sind, plus the ending *stan* (=land); since *pak* is the Urdu word for spiritually pure or clean, Pakistan also means "land of the pure." Later Bengal and Assam (or "Bangistan") were included in the separatist claims. Many Moslems regarded the Indian Natl. Congress as a communal party and were concerned lest the rights of the Moslem community (24% of total pop.) be ignored by the Hindu majority (66%) in an independent India. Accordingly, in 1940 the Moslem League, headed by Mohammed Ali Jinnah, officially demanded the establishment of Pakistan in the NW and E areas of India where Moslems were in a numerical majority. Congress reluctantly accepted the partition plan, and, on Aug. 15, 1947, the Br. govt. formally handed over authority to the 2 independent dominions of India and Pakistan, after having set up a commission to divide Punjab and Bengal into contiguous Moslem and non-Moslem areas. Pakistan's territory included the provs. of Baluchistan, North-West Frontier Prov., Sind, and parts of Punjab and Bengal (plus most of Sylhet dist. of Assam), and the acceding princely states of Bahawalpur, Khairpur, Kalat, Kharan, Las Bela, Makran, Dir, Swat, and Chitral. The immediate problems facing the new state were the suppression of rioting in Punjab, the rehabilitation of millions of Moslem refugees from India, and the replacement of the non-Moslem, experienced administrative personnel who had departed for India upon partition. Foreign affairs were dominated by the Kashmir dispute with India and by trouble with recalcitrant Pathan tribes along the Afghan border. Pakistan is a member of the U.N.

Pakkai (bäk'gī'), Mandarin *Pei-chieh* (bā'jyĕ'), town, S Kwangtung prov., China, port on West R. branch of Canton R. delta, just NE of Sunwui; railroad terminus; commercial center.

Paklay, Laos: see Sayaboury.

Pakli (bŭk'lī'), Mandarin *Peili* (bā'lē'), town, W Hainan, Kwangtung prov., China, 13 mi. NE of Kumyan and on coastal railway. Sometimes spelled Bakli. Paso, 4 mi. SW, is port for Shekluk (Shihlu) iron mines.

Paklow (bŭk'lou'), Mandarin *Peiliu* (bā'lyō'), town, ⊙ Paklow co. (pop. 368,911), SE Kwangsi prov., China, on Jung R. (head of navigation) and 15 mi. NE of Watlam; tobacco processing; rice, wheat, peanuts, melons, fruit.

Paknam, Thailand: see Samutprakan.

Paknampho or **Paknampo**, Thailand: see Nakhon Sawan.

Pakokku (pŭkō'kōō), N district (□ 5,350; 1941 pop. 559,671) of Magwe div., Upper Burma; ⊙ Pakokku. Bet. Chin Hills and Irrawaddy R.; in dry zone (annual rainfall 26 in.). Agr. (rice, millet, corn, tobacco, catechu, toddy plant, beans, cotton, peanuts; extensive teak forests. Oil at Yenangyat and Lanywa. Coal deposits and salt extraction along Yaw R. Served by Irrawaddy and Chindwin steamers. Pop. 95% Burmese, 5% Chin.

Pakokku, town (pop. 23,115), ⊙ Pakokku dist., Upper Burma, port on right bank of Irrawaddy R., SW of Chindwin R. mouth and 75 mi. SW of Mandalay. Downstream head of Chindwin R. service; linked by road with Chindwin R., Myittha and Kabaw valleys; trades in palm sugar, hides, beans, cotton. Timber-shipping point; boat landing; silk weaving, palm-sugar mfg.

Pakosc (pä'kôshch), Pol. *Pakość*, Ger. *Pakosch* (pä'kôsh), town (pop. 3,351), Bydgoszcz prov., central Poland, on Notec R. and 7 mi. W of Inowroclaw; rail junction; sawmilling, flour and sugar milling, tanning, machine mfg. **Pakosc Lake**, just S, is 12 mi. long, 1 mi. wide.

Pakpattan (päk'pŭt-tŭn), town (pop. 17,852), Montgomery dist., SE Punjab, W Pakistan, near Pakpattan Canal, on railroad (workshop) and 26 mi. SE of Montgomery; trade center for wheat, cotton, millet, rice, cloth fabrics; cotton ginning, handloom weaving; lacquered woodwork. Visited by Timur in 1398. Moslem pilgrimage center.

Pakpattan Canal, irrigation channel (opened 1926) in SE Punjab, W Pakistan; from right bank of Sutlej R. at Sulaimanke runs c.165 mi. WSW; irrigates parts of Montgomery and Multan dists. in Bari Doab.

Pak Phanang (päk' pŭnäng'), village (1937 pop. 6,391), Nakhon Sithammarat prov., S Thailand, on E coast of Malay Peninsula, Gulf of Siam port for Nakhon Sithammarat; ships coconuts, rubber. Also spelled Pakbanang and Pakpenang.

Pak Phrieo, Thailand: see Saraburi.

Pak Preo or **Pakpriew**, Thailand: see Saraburi.

Pakrac (pä'kräts), village (pop. 4,828), N Croatia, Yugoslavia, on Pakra R., on railroad and 9 mi. S of Daruvar, at W foot of the Psunj, in Slavonia; local trade center. Petroleum and lignite deposits in vicinity. First mentioned in 13th cent.; Orthodox Eastern bishopric since 1708.

Pakra River (pä'krä), N Croatia, Yugoslavia, in Slavonia; rises 10 mi. ENE of Pakrac, flows c.40 mi. WSW, past Pakrac and Lipik, to Lonja R. 6 mi. S of Kutina.

Paks (pŏksh), market town (pop. 11,776), Tolna co., W central Hungary, on the Danube and 20 mi. NNE of Szekszard; rail terminal; woolen mills, distilleries, brickworks, fisheries. Large Ger. pop. near by raises wheat, cattle.

Paksane (päksän'), village, Vientiane prov., N Laos, on left bank of Mekong R. (Thailand line) and 70 mi. NE of Vientiane; R.C. mission.

Pakse (päk'sä'), town (1936 pop. c.5,000), ⊙ Champassak (Bassac) prov. (□ 10,200; 1947 pop. 170,000), S Laos, port on left bank of Mekong R. at mouth of the Se Done, and 115 mi. SE of Savannakhet. Communication and trading center for Boloven Plateau, on road from Ubon (Thailand); cardamoms, cotton, hemp, tobacco, cattle. Airport.

Paksey, E Pakistan: see Sara.

Paksha (Cantonese bäk'sä'), Mandarin *Paisha* (bī'-shä'). **1** Town, ⊙ Paksha co. (pop. 153,479), central Hainan, Kwangtung prov., China, 80 mi. SW of Kiungshan; grain. Gold mining near by. **2** Town, S Kwangtung prov., China, near Tam R., 12 mi. W of Toishan; rail terminus; commercial center.

Pakshitirtham, India: see Tirukkalikkunram.

Paksong (päk'sông'), village (1936 pop. c.250), Champassak prov., S Laos, 25 mi. NE of Pakse, in Boloven Plateau; hill resort and coffeegrowing center.

Pak Thong Chai (päk' tông' chī'), village (1937 pop. 5,511), Nakhon Ratchasima prov., E Thailand, in Dong Phaya Yen Range, on road and 18 mi. S of Nakhon Ratchasima. Pop. is largely Mon.

Pakwach (pä'kwäch), town, Northern Prov., NW Uganda, landing on the Albert Nile and 50 mi. SE of Arua; cotton, coffee, tobacco; livestock; fishing.

Pala, Belgian Congo: see M'Pala.

Pala (pälä'), village, SW Chad territory, Fr. Equatorial Africa, 70 mi. SSW of Bongor; cotton ginning.

Pala (pä'lū), village (pop. c.250), San Diego co., S Calif., in Pala Indian Reservation, 21 mi. NE of Oceanside. Here are restored bldgs. of San Antonio de Pala, founded 1816 as an *asistencia* of Mission San Luis Rey.

Palacagüina (päläkägwē'nä), town (1950 pop. 311), Madriz dept., NW Nicaragua, 15 mi. SE of Somoto; agr. center (tobacco, sugar cane, rice). Gold and nitrate deposits.

Palacios (pŭlă'shŭs), town (pop. 2,799), Matagorda co., S Texas, on Matagorda Bay and 25 mi. SW of Bay City; fishing port and resort, in area producing rice, cotton, flax, cattle; seafood canning, packing. Military camp here was active in Second World War. Settled 1903, inc. 1909.

Palacios, Lake (pälä'syōs), Patagonian lake (□ 27) in N Comodoro Rivadavia military zone, Argentina, 30 mi. N of L. Musters; 8½ mi. long, 3 mi. wide.

Palacios, Los, Cuba: see Los Palacios.

Palacios, Los, or **Los Palacios y Villafranca** (lōs pälä'thyōs ē vēlyäfräng'kä), town (pop. 9,465), Seville prov., SW Spain, 17 mi. S of Seville; agr. center (olives, grapes, cereals, cattle). Sawmilling, olive-oil pressing. Bull and horse raising. Sometimes Villafranca y Los Palacios.

Palacios de Goda (dhä gō'dhä), town (pop. 880), Ávila prov., central Spain, 33 mi. N of Ávila; winegrowing; stock raising (sheep, goats).

Palacios de la Sierra (lä syĕ'rä), town (pop. 1,230), Burgos prov., N Spain, 38 mi. WNW of Soria; cereals, potatoes, livestock; timber, naval stores. Flour- and sawmills.

Palacole, India: see Palakollu.

Paladru (pälädrü'), village (pop. 169), Isère dept., SE France, in the Pre-Alps, 8 mi. SE of La Tour-du-Pin, on N shore of Paladru L. (4 mi. long, 1 mi. wide); makes flashlight batteries.

Palaeopolis, Greece: see Elis, city.

Palafrugell (päläfrōōgĕl'), town (pop. 6,502), Gerona prov., NE Spain, 17 mi. E of Gerona, near the Mediterranean; a center of cork industry. Cereals, olive oil, wine.

Palagiano (pälăjä'nô), town (pop. 4,972), Ionio prov., Apulia, S Italy, 13 mi. WNW of Taranto.

Palagonia (pälägônē'ä), town (pop. 9,495), Catania prov., E Sicily, 14 mi. NE of Caltagirone, in citrus-fruit and cereal region; linen. Believed to be anc. Palica, founded 453 B.C.; 3 mi. W is L. Naftia or Palici, anc. *Lacus Palicorum,* c.500 ft. in circumference. Emits carbonic-acid gas from 2 apertures. Siculians erected temple here to twin gods, Dii Palici; no traces remain.

Palai, Monte, Sardinia: see Marghine, Catena del.

Palaia (pälä'yä), village (pop. 875), Pisa prov., Tuscany, central Italy, 8 mi. SE of Pontedera.

Palaia Epidauros, Greece: see Epidaurus.

Palaiochora or **Palaiokhora** (both: pälăôkhô'rŭ), town (pop. 2,310), Canea nome, W Crete, port on S coast 30 mi. SSW of Canea; wheat, carobs, olive oil. Formerly called Selino.

Palaiokhorion (pälăôkhô'rēôn), town (pop. 2,634), Kavalla nome, Macedonia, Greece, 13 mi. W of Kavalla, at E foot of Mt. Pangaion; tobacco, corn. Also spelled Palaiochorion. Formerly called Antiphilippoi (Andifilippoi), a name now applied to a village (pop. 832), 2 mi. E, previously known as Dranitsi (Dhranitsi).

Palaion Phaleron or **Palaion Faliron** (both: pälăôn' fä'lērôn) [=old Phaleron], S suburb (pop. 9,087) of Athens, Greece, on E shore of Phaleron Bay opposite Neon Phaleron; seaside resort.

Palaiopanagia, Greece: see Ascra.

Palaiopolis, Greece: see Elis, city.

Palaiovouna, Greece: see Helicon.

Palairos (pä'lĕrôs), village (pop. 2,126), Aetolia and Acarnania nome, W central Greece, small port on Bay of Palairos of Ionian Sea, 9 mi. S of Vonitsa; livestock raising; fisheries. Formerly called Zaverda or Zaverdha.

Palais, Le (lü pälĕ'), village (pop. 1,254), Morbihan dept., W France, port on N shore of Belle-Île, 28 mi. SW of Vannes; sardine and tunny fishing; canning, vegetable preserving. Has 16th-cent. citadel (now penal institution) and town walls.

Palaiseau (pälăzō'), town (pop. 5,147), Seine-et-Oise dept., N central France, outer SSW suburb of Paris, 11 mi. from Notre Dame Cathedral; chocolate factory.

Palais-sur-Vienne, Le (lü pälĕ'-sür-vyĕn'), ENE suburb (pop. 402) of Limoges, Haute-Vienne dept., W central France, on Vienne R.; electrolytic copper refining, porcelain mfg.

Palaiyampatti, India: see Palayampatti.

Palakollu (pä'lŭkōlōō), city (pop. 19,869), West Godavari dist., NE Madras, India, in Godavari R. delta, on rail spur and 45 mi. ESE of Ellore; road and agr. trade center; rice and oilseed milling; tobacco, sugar cane, coconuts; orange orchards. Dutch trading station established in 1652; finally ceded 1825 to English. Also spelled Palakol or Palacole.

Palam, airport, Delhi, India: see Delhi, city.

Palam (pä'lŭm), village (pop. 3,935), Parbhani dist., NW Hyderabad state, India, 14 mi. ENE of Gangakher; cotton, millet, oilseeds.

Palamartsa (pälămär'kä), village (pop. 3,162), Kolarovgrad dist., NE Bulgaria, 4 mi. NW of Popovo; poultry, grain, oil-bearing plants, truck.

Palamas (pälämäs'), town (pop. 4,776), Karditsa nome, central Thessaly, Greece, in Trikkala lowland, 10 mi. NE of Karditsa; vegetables, corn, livestock.

Palamau (pŭlä'mou), district (□ 4,901; pop. 912,-734), W Bihar, India, in Chota Nagpur div.; ⊙ Daltonganj. Mainly in foothills of Chota Nagpur Plateau (S, W); bounded N by Son R.; drained by its tributaries. Agr. (rice, corn, gram, oilseeds, barley, wheat); bamboo, mahua, teak in dispersed forest areas. Lac and silk growing; shellac and Portland-cement mfg. Coal mining in central section. Main towns: Daltonganj, Garwa.

Palamcottah (pä"lŭmkōt'tŭ), city (pop. 30,967), ⊙ Tinnevelly dist., S Madras, India, on Tambraparni R. opposite Tinnevelly (bridge) and 85 mi. SSW of Madura, in cotton- and palmyra-growing area; mfg. of palmyra products. Has cols. affiliated with Madras Univ. A chief center of Christian missions in S India.

Palamós (pälämōs'), town (pop. 4,966), Gerona prov., NE Spain, 18 mi. ESE of Gerona; port and bathing resort on the Mediterranean. Cork processing and exporting; fishing. Has 14th-cent. parochial church. Was important fortified port from late Middle Ages. Sacked and burned (1543) by Turks, bombed (1742) by British; twice captured and lost by French in Peninsular War. Seriously damaged in Sp. civil war (1936–39).

Palampet, India: see Mulug.

Palampur (pä'lŭmpŏŏr), village, Kangra dist., N Punjab, India, 15 mi. SE of Dharmsala; tea, wheat, corn, pears, apples; tea processing. Annual Hindu festival fair.

Palana (pŭlä'nŭ), village, N central Rajasthan, India, 11 mi. SSW of Bikaner; coal mining; fuller's earth deposits worked.

Palana (pŭlŭnä'), village (1948 pop. over 500), ⊙ Koryak Natl. Okrug, Kamchatka oblast, Khabarovsk Territory, Russian SFSR, on NW Kamchatka Peninsula, 425 mi. NNW of Petropavlovsk; 59°8'N 160°2'E. In reindeer-raising area; fisheries.

Palanan Point (pälä'nän), Isabela prov., N Luzon, Philippines, on small peninsula in Philippine Sea; 17°10'N 122°30'E.

Palancia River (pälän'thyä), Castellón de la Plana and Valencia provs., E Spain, rises 8 mi. WNW of Viver, flows 37 mi. generally SE to the Mediterranean near Sagunto. Used for irrigation.

Palandoken Dag (pälän"dükĕn'dä), Turkish *Palandöken Dağ,* peak (10,249 ft.), E central Turkey, 10 mi. SSW of Erzurum.

Palandri (pŭlŭn'drē), village, Punch jagir, W Kashmir, in S Punjab Himalaya foothills, 24 mi. WSW of Punch; corn, wheat, rice, pulse.

Pa-lang, Tibet: see Penam.

Palanga (päläng'gä), Ger. *Polangen,* city (pop. 2,513), W Lithuania, on Baltic Sea (landing), 14 mi. NNW of Memel; noted bathing resort and amber-processing center; concrete ware, flour milling. Airport. Has castle ruins. Dates from 13th cent.; in Courland until 1920.

Palanka (pä'län-kä). **1** or **Palanka Smederevska** or **Smederevska Palanka** (smĕ'dĕrĕfskä), village (pop. 8,662), central Serbia, Yugoslavia, on railroad and 38 mi. SSE of Belgrade; mfg. of rolling stock. **2** or **Backa Palanka** or **Bachka Palanka** (both: bäch'kä), Serbo-Croatian *Bačka Palanka,* Hung. *Palánka* (pŏ'länkŏ), village (pop. 12,522), Vojvodina, NW Serbia, Yugoslavia, on the Danube and 21 mi. W of Novi Sad, in the Backa; rail terminus.

Palanpur (pä'lŭnpŏŏr), city (pop. 21,643), ⊙ newly-created Banas Kantha dist., N Bombay, India, 80 mi. N of Ahmadabad; rail junction; trade center (grain, cloth fabrics, ghee, oilseeds, sugar cane); hand-loom weaving, oilseed milling, embroidering; metal goods. Was ⊙ former princely state of Palanpur (□ 1,794; pop. 315,855) in Rajputana States; state inc. 1949 into Banas Kantha dist.

Palapag (pälä'päg), town (1939 pop. 3,986; 1948 municipality pop. 17,021), NE Samar isl., Philippines, 55 mi. NNE of Catbalogan; agr. center (corn, rice).

Palá Palá (pälä' pälä'), town (pop. estimate 500), central Tucumán prov., Argentina, on railroad and 16 mi. S of Tucumán; sugar refinery, mfg. of soft drinks.

Palapatti, India: see Pallapatti.

Palapye or **Palapye Road** (pälä'pyā), agr. village (pop. 1,042), Ngwato dist., E Bechuanaland Protectorate, 30 mi. WSW of Serowe, on railroad, in Bamangwato Reserve. Airfield. Old Palapye, 10 mi. E, is former hq. of paramount chief of Bamangwato tribe, now moved to Serowe.

Palar River (pä'lär, pälär'), mainly in SE Madras, India, rises on Deccan Plateau E of Kolar (Mysore), flows SSE, NE past Vaniyambadi and Ambur, and generally ESE past Vellore, Arcot, Conjeeveram, and Chingleput, to Coromandel Coast of Bay of Bengal 11 mi. SSW of Mahabalipuram; 230 mi. long. Receives Cheyyar R.

Palasa, India: see Kasibuggapalasa.

Palasan Island (pälä'sän) (□ 6), one of the Polillo Isls., Quezon prov., Philippines, in Philippine Sea, bet. Polillo Isl. (W) and Patnanongan Isl. (E); 14°51'N 122°2'E; 5 mi. long, 2 mi. wide; rises to 222 ft. Fishing.

Palasbari (pŭläs'bärē), town (pop. 3,692), Kamrup dist., W Assam, India, on Brahmaputra R. and 13 mi. WSW of Gauhati; rice, mustard, jute. Lac growing near by. Also spelled Palashbari.

Palat (pälät'), village (pop. 879), Oran dept., N Algeria, on S slope of the Tell Atlas, 10 mi. SSW of Tiaret; winegrowing.

Palatinate (pŭlă'tĭnĭt), Ger. *Pfalz* (pfälts), name given to domain of counts, later electors palatine, high officials of Holy Roman Empire. Consisted of 2 geographically separate territories: major portion (called Rhenish Palatinate, Lower Palatinate, or simply Palatinate) was situated along the Rhine, reaching S beyond Heidelberg (old ⊙) and Mannheim; E portion, the Upper Palatinate (⊙ Amberg), was constituted 1329 under senior Wittelsbach line of Bavaria, to which Rhenish Palatinate had passed in 1214. In 1356, electoral dignity, which had alternated bet. Palatinate and Bavarian Wittelsbachs, was settled upon counts palatine. Elector Rupert became (1400) Holy Roman Emperor; after his death, Palatine line divided into several collateral branches which, after extinction (1559) of direct line, succeeded in turn to electoral dignity. Electors palatine accepted Reformation; election (1619) of Elector Frederick V (Frederick the Winter King) to Bohemian throne precipitated Thirty Years War, and resulted in loss of Upper Palatinate and electoral vote to Bavaria. At Peace of Westphalia (1648), new electoral vote was created for Palatine line, which succeeded, at extinction (1777) of Bavarian line, to Bavaria. Elector Maximilian of Pfalz-Zweibrücken united (1799) all Wittelsbach lands; became (1806) king of Bavaria. Rhenish Palatinate was lost (1803) to Baden, Hesse, and Nassau; some territory W of the Rhine was recovered at Congress of Vienna. In 1837, Rhenish Palatinate (⊙ Speyer) and Upper Palatinate (⊙ Regensburg) were constituted as administrative divisions [Ger. *Regierungsbezirk*] of Bavaria. After Second World War, Rhenish Palatinate was inc. into newly formed state of Rhineland-Palatinate in Fr. occupation zone.

Palatinate, Upper, Germany: see Upper Palatinate.

Palatine (pă'lŭtĭn), village (pop. 4,079), Cook co., NE Ill., NW suburb of Chicago, 12 mi. ENE of Elgin; makes fuses; grain, dairy, poultry, truck farms. Inc. 1869.

Palatine Bridge, village (pop. 592), Montgomery co., E central N.Y., on Mohawk R. (bridged), opposite Canajoharie, and 20 mi. W of Amsterdam; cider, vinegar, feed.

Palatine Hill (pă'lŭtĭn), one of the 7 hills of Rome.

Palatka (pŭlăt'kŭ), city (pop. 9,176), ⊙ Putnam co., N Fla., port on St. Johns R. (bridged here) and 26 mi. SW of St. Augustine; shipping and wood-processing center; lumber milling; mfg. of barrels, boxes, furniture, prefabricated bldgs., metal products; sea-food canning, citrus-fruit packing. Noted for its azalea gardens. Founded as a trading post in 1821, it was a military post in the Seminole War, and developed as an important river port and resort in 2d half of 19th cent.

Palattsy (pŭlä'tsē), town (1947 pop. over 500), central East Kazakhstan oblast, Kazakh SSR, c.25 mi. NE of Samarskoye; gold-mining center.

Palau (pälou'), island group (□ 188; pop. 5,900), W Caroline Islands, W Pacific, c.550 mi. E of Philippines; 7°30'N 134°30'E. Includes 4 volcanic isls. (Babelthuap, largest isl., Arakabesan, Koror, Malakal), 4 coral isls. (Angaur, Aurapushekaru, Peleliu, Urukthapel), and Kayangel atoll. Produces tapioca, copra, dried bonito, bauxite. In Second World War, Palau was major Jap. naval base in W Carolines, and only important stronghold in group to be taken (1944) by U.S. Palau dist. (□ 190; pop. 6,207), ⊙ Koror, includes Merir, Pulo Anna, Sonsorol, Tobi. Sometimes spelled Pelew.

Palau (pälou'), mining settlement (pop. 5,116), Coahuila, N Mexico, in Sabinas coal dist., E of Múzquiz; coal mines; coke oven; coal-tar products.

Palau (pä'lou), village (pop. 906), Sassari prov., NE Sardinia, 50 mi. NE of Sassari, on coast; port and rail terminus; granite quarries.

Palâu de Anglesola (pälou' dhā äng-glāsō'lä), village (pop. 1,379), Lérida prov., NE Spain, 13 mi. ENE of Lérida, on irrigated Urgel plain; olive-oil and wine processing; livestock (cattle, donkeys, goats), cereals.

Palaui Island (pälou'ē), islet just off Escarpada Point peninsula, Cagayan prov., NE Luzon, Philippines, in SE side of entrance to Babuyan Channel; 4 mi. long, 3 mi. wide. Northernmost point of isl. is Cape Engaño, 18°35'N 122°8'E.

Palavas-les-Flots (pälävä'-lā-flō), village (pop. 1,260), Hérault dept., S France, on tongue of land bet. lagoon and Gulf of Lion, 6 mi. SSE of Montpellier; fishing port and bathing resort. Damaged in Second World War.

Palavi (pŭl'ŭvē), village, North Western Prov., Ceylon, on Puttalam Lagoon, 4 mi. S of Puttalam; govt. salterns along lagoon; coconut plantations.

Palaw (pŭlô'), village, Mergui dist., Lower Burma, in Tenasserim, on Andaman Sea, on road and 35 mi. N of Mergui; tin, tungsten mines, and rubber plantations near by.

Palawai, Mount (pä'lŭwī'), peak (3,370 ft.), SE Lanai, T.H.; highest on isl.

Palawan (pälä'wän), province (□ 5,693; 1948 pop. 106,269), Philippines; ⊙ Puerto Princesa. Includes Palawan isl., Cuyo Islands, Calamian Islands, Cagayan Islands, Dumaran Island, Balabac Island, and numerous islets off Palawan.

Palawan, island (□ 4,550; 1939 pop. 43,813), Palawan prov., the most westerly of the large isls. of the Philippines, c.125 mi. SW of Mindoro, extends SW bet. Sulu Sea (E) and S.China Sea (W) to within 100 mi. of Borneo; c.275 mi. long, max. width c.25 mi. A rugged mtn. chain traverses its length, rising to 6,839 ft. in Mt. Mantalingajan (S). Offshore are numerous isls. and rocks, and the coast is indented by many bays, especially in N. At St. Paul Bay, on W central coast, is the outlet of a remarkable underground river which has been ascended in small boats for several miles; the river tunnel is 80 ft. wide, 30 ft. high. On Palawan are great stands of timber, and the soil is fertile. Coconuts, rice, rubber, sugar, lumber, livestock are produced. Manganese mines (N). Visayans inhabit the N, Moros the S. Of the towns (all small), Puerto Princesa, the largest, on E central coast, is chief trading and shipping center. A former name of Palawan was Paragua (pärä'gwä).

Palayampatti or **Palaiyampatti** (pŭlŭyŭm'pŭt-tē), town (pop. 5,400), Ramnad dist., S Madras, India, 2 mi. N of Aruppukkottai, in cotton area; hand-woven cotton fabrics.

Palazuelo de Vedija (pälä-thwā'lō dhā vā-dhē'hä), town (pop. 1,010), Valladolid prov., N central Spain, 7 mi. NW of Medina de Ríoseco; hog and sheep raising; cereals, vegetables.

Palazzo Adriano (pälä'tsô ädrēä'nô), village (pop. 4,162), Palermo prov., SW central Sicily, 10 mi. SSE of Corleone, in stock-raising, cereal-growing region. Mostly built by Albanian colonists in 1482.

Palazzolo Acreide (pälätsô'lô äkrā'dĕ), town (pop. 11,387), Siracusa prov., SE Sicily, on Anapo R. and 21 mi. W of Syracuse; hydroelectric plant. Largely destroyed by earthquake of 1693. SW are ruins of anc. Acrae (founded 664 B.C. by Syracusans), including small Greek theater, baths, tombs (Greek and early Christian).

Palazzolo sull'Oglio (sōōlô'lyô), town (pop. 6,600), Brescia prov., Lombardy, N Italy, on Oglio R. and 17 mi. WNW of Brescia. Rail junction; mfg. center (button factories, foundries, silk and cotton mills, textile and printing machinery, chemicals, rope, macaroni).

Palazzolo Vercellese (vĕrchĕl-lā'zĕ), village (pop. 1,973), Vercelli prov., Piedmont, N Italy, near Po R., 13 mi. SW of Vercelli.

Palazzo San Gervasio (pälä'tsô sän jĕrvä'zyô), town (pop. 7,743), Potenza prov., Basilicata, S Italy, 18 mi. ESE of Melfi, in agr. region (cereals, grapes, olives).

Palca (päl'kä), town (pop. c.3,900), ⊙ Murillo prov., La Paz dept., W Bolivia, on Palca R. (branch of La Paz R.) and 13 mi. ESE of La Paz, on SW slopes of Cordillera de La Paz; alt. 14,216 ft.; fodder crops.

Palca, town (pop. 946), Junín dept., central Peru, on E slopes of Cordillera Central, 11 mi. ENE of Tarma; corn, potatoes, wheat.

Palca Grande (grän'dā), village (pop. c.1,160), Chuquisaca dept., S Bolivia, at confluence of Cinti and Cotagaita rivers, 8 mi. S of Camargo; corn, wheat.

Palcamayo (pälkämī'ō), town (pop. 1,891), Junín dept., central Peru, in Cordillera Central of the Andes, 8 mi. NNW of Tarma; grain, fruit, vegetables.

Palco, city (pop. 405), Rooks co., NW central Kansas, 14 mi. W of Plainville, in wheat and livestock area.

Paldeo (päldā'ō), former petty state (□ 52; pop. 9,820) of Central India agency, W of Karwi; one of the CHAUBE JAGIRS. In 1948, merged with Vindhya Pradesh.

Paldiski (päl'dĕskē) or **Baltic Port,** Ger. *Baltischport* (bäl'tĭshpôrt), Rus. (until 1917) *Baltiski* (*Baltiiski, Baltiyskiy*) or *Baltiski Port,* city (pop. 851), NW Estonia, ice-free port on Baltic Sea, near entrance to Gulf of Finland, 25 mi. WSW of Tallinn (connected by rail); major Soviet naval base; serves as winter port for Tallinn. Was free port (1920–39).

Pale (pŭlā'), village, Lower Chindwin dist., Upper Burma, 20 mi. SW of Monywa.

Pale, Greece: see LEXOURION.

Pale (pä'lĕ), village (pop. 5,543), SE Bosnia, Yugoslavia, on railroad and 8 mi. ESE of Sarajevo; mtn. resort bet. Romanija and Jahorina mts.

Palej (pä'lāj), village, Broach dist., N Bombay, India, 17 mi. NNE of Broach; trades in cotton, millet, wheat; cotton ginning.

Palekh (pä'lyĭkh), town (1948 pop. over 2,000), S central Ivanovo oblast, Russian SFSR, 18 mi. E of Shuya; noted wood-carving center; caskets, snuff-boxes, book illustrations, decorated porcelain. Has art mus.

Palel (pŭlāl'), village, Manipur, NE India, on Manipur R. and 25 mi. SSE of Imphal; rice, mustard, sugar cane. Figured in Jap. invasion of India in 1944.

Palembang (pälĕm"bäng'), largest city (pop. 108,145) of Sumatra, Indonesia, in SE Sumatra, port on Musi R., 55 mi. S of its mouth on Bangka Strait, 260 mi. NW of Jakarta; 3°S 104°44'E. Terminus of railroad to port of Telukbetung, major commercial center for S Sumatra, trade center for area producing rubber and oil. Has large refineries in E suburbs of PLAJU and SUNGAIGERONG. Port ships petroleum products, rubber, timber, coffee, tea, resin, spices, cinchona bark, rattan, pepper. Has machine shops, shipyards, iron foundries. There is an airport. Has large stone mosque (1740) with minaret (1753). Palembang was ⊙ Hindu-Sumatran kingdom of Sri Vijaya which flourished in 8th cent. The Du. East India Co. began trading here in 1617 and built (1659) a fort. Intermittently (1812–14; 1818–21) town was under Br. rule. Sultanate of Palembang was abolished 1825 by the Dutch. In Aug., 1948, Palembang became ⊙ of temporary autonomous state of South Sumatra which was included (1950) in Indonesia.

Palena (pälā'nä), town (pop. 3,251), Chieti prov., Abruzzi e Molise, S central Italy, on S slope of Maiella mts., 22 mi. SSW of Lanciano, in stock-raising region; hardware mfg. Severely damaged in Second World War.

Palena River (pälā'nä), rises in Argentina as the Carrenleufú from E end of L. General Paz, flows in a wide curve N and W into Chile, as the Palena, to Gulf of Corcovado; 180 mi. long. Navigable 25 mi. upstream.

Palencia (pälĕn'syä), town (1950 pop. 2,627), Guatemala dept., S central Guatemala, 10 mi. E of Guatemala; alt. 4,690 ft.; coffee, sugar cane; cattle.

Palencia (pälĕn'thyä), province (□ 3,096; pop. 217,108), N central Spain, in Leon; ⊙ Palencia. Bounded N by crest of the Cantabrian Mts. sloping S to high plain of Tierra de Campos; drained by Pisuerga and Carrión rivers and their affluents; irrigated by Canal of Castile. Abundant rainfall in N (forests and pastures); fertile valleys alternating with barren areas in S. Essentially agr.: cereals, wine, vegetables, fruit, some flax and sugar beets; stock raising (cattle and sheep). Ships cereals and flour. Important anthracite and bituminous-coal mines in Cantabrian Mts. (Barruelo de Santullán, Guardo, Orbó); also some copper and iron. Anc. flourishing wool industry only survives (blankets, textiles) in Palencia, Astudillo, and a few other towns. Other industries all derived from agr. (flour- and sawmilling, tanning, dairy-products processing), except for some metalworking and chemical mfg. in Palencia, only important city of prov. Other centers are Venta de Baños, Barruelo de Santullán, Paredes de Nava, and Dueñas. Though long connected with Castile, and often considered part of Old Castile, Palencia is now usually placed in the region of Leon.

Palencia, anc. *Pallantia,* city (pop. 30,127), ⊙ Palencia prov., N central Spain, on Carrión R., on fertile plain, and 120 mi. NNW of Madrid, 27 mi. NNE of Valladolid; 42°N 4°32'W. Agr. trade center (cereals, livestock, wine, sugar beets, fruit) Its anc. woolen industry has declined, but new activities have recently developed. Metal foundries, railroad repair shops, chemical works (turpentine oil, resins, pharmaceuticals), tanneries, flour- and sawmills; mfg. of woolen blankets and textiles, leather goods, ceramics, tiles. Episcopal see. Has Gothic cathedral (14th–16th cent.) rich in works of art, 13th-cent. parochial church, and 15th-cent. Dominican church. Was occupied by Romans; devastated by Visigoths (6th cent.) and Moors (8th cent.); liberated (10th cent.) by Christians, prospered as favorite residence of kings of Leon (12th–13th cent.). First Sp. univ. is said to have been founded here (c.1212), removed to Salamanca (1238). City declined after 16th cent.

Palenciana (pälĕn-thyä'nä), town (pop. 2,892), Córdoba prov., S Spain, near the Genil, 13 mi. SW of Lucena; olive-oil processing. Cereals, vegetables, wine. Sandstone, grinding stone, gypsum quarries.

Palenque (pälĕng'kā), village, Los Ríos prov., W central Ecuador, landing on Vinces R. (Guayas system), in tropical lowlands, and 10 mi. N of Vinces, in fertile agr. region (cacao, sugar cane, rice, tropical fruit); rice milling.

Palenque, town (pop. 560), Chiapas, S Mexico, in jungle lowland, 21 mi. SW of Emiliano Zapata; in lumbering area. Famous Palenque ruins, remains of a Mayan city extending some 20 mi. are near by (4 mi. SW). Mayan city reached peak in its development in 692 and is believed to have been abandoned in 12th cent.; noted for sculptures and palatial secular bldgs. decorated with delicate stucco and carved stonework; ruins discovered 1750.

Palenque, village (pop. 285), Colón prov., central Panama, on Caribbean Sea, 37 mi. ENE of Colón; cacao, abacá, coconuts, livestock.

Palenville (pā'lŭnvĭl), resort village, Greene co., SE N.Y., at E base of the Catskills, at entrance to Kaaterskill Clove, 8 mi. WSW of Catskill. Legendary home of Rip Van Winkle; Sleepy Hollow, where he reputedly slept for 20 years, is near by.

Palenzuela (pälĕn-thwā'lä), town (pop. 1,041), Palencia prov., N central Spain, 22 mi. ENE of Palencia; cheese processing; livestock, cereals, wine, honey.

Paleomylos or **Paliomilos** (both: pälēô'mĭlôs), village (1928 pop. 186), Larissa nome, SE Thessaly, Greece, 11 mi. E of Pharsala; chromite mining. Formerly called Ineli.

Palered, Indonesia: see PLERED.

Palermo (pälĕr'mō), NW residential section of Buenos Aires, Argentina; has zoological garden, parks, racecourse.

Palermo, town (pop. 1,983), Huila dept., S central Colombia, on affluent of Magdalena R. and 10 mi. WSW of Neiva; rice, cacao, coffee, stock.

Palermo (pŭlûr'mō, pälĕr'mô), province (□ 1,922; pop. 890,752), N and NW Sicily; ⊙ Palermo. Mtn. terrain, including Madonie Mts. (rising to 6,480 ft.) in E; drained by Belice, Torto, and Grande rivers. Chief lowland is fertile Conca d'Oro (□ 40) around Palermo (NW). Agr. (citrus fruit, grapes, olives in Conca d'Oro; wheat in interior); livestock (cattle about Palermo; sheep and goats elsewhere); mining (sulphur, rock salt, marble). Tunny fisheries. A major hydroelectric station at L. Piana dei Greci. Industry at Palermo.

Palermo, anc. *Panormus* and *Panhormus,* largest city (pop. 339,497; metropolitan area pop. 411,879) and port of Sicily; ⊙ Sicily and Palermo prov., on Gulf of Palermo, at edge of fertile plain, the Conca d'Oro, and 200 mi. SSW of Naples; 38°7'N 13°22'E. Transportation and industrial center; produces steel, furniture, glass, cement, chemicals, textiles, paper, soap, cork, perfume, macaroni, canned goods (fruit juices, tomatoes, fish), wine, leather, antimony, tobacco products; publishing industry. Has large shipyards, quarantine station. Archbishopric. Buildings representing Saracen-Byzantine, Norman, Renaissance, and Spanish baroque styles of architecture include 12th-cent. cathedral with tombs of Norman kings, palace chapel (Cappella Palatina) built 1132–40 by Roger II, several palaces, particularly 14th-cent. Palazzo Chiaramonte. Has acad. of medical science (1621) and acad. of science, letters, and arts (founded 1568; reestablished 1621), univ., observatory, natl. library (bldg. destroyed in Second World War), natl. mus. (badly damaged in Second World War), gall. of modern art, famous botanical garden. Founded by Phoenicians, city became a military base under Carthaginians, who lost it to Romans in 254–53 B.C. Ruled by Byzantines from 535 to 831. Its prosperity began under Saracens (831); continued under Normans (1072), who made it capital of the kingdom of Sicily. Achieved greatest splendor under Roger II and later under Emperor Frederick II. In 1282 was scene of the Sicilian Vespers, a massacre of French in retaliation for cruelties of Charles of Anjou. Thereafter it was under Aragon, Savoy, and, finally, the Bourbon house of Naples, until freed by Garibaldi in 1860. Heavily bombed (1943) in Second World War.

Palermo. 1 Town (pop. 511), Waldo co., S Maine, 20 mi W of Belfast; agr , lumber mills. **2** Village (pop. 150), Mountrail co., NW central N.Dak., 45 mi. W of Minot Near-by lakes contain large amounts of sodium sulphate.

Palermo, Gulf of, inlet of Tyrrhenian Sea, NW Sicily, bet. Cape Gallo (NW) and Cape Zaffarano (SE); 10 mi. long, 4 mi. wide. Chief port, Palermo.

Palermo, Port, Albanian *Portë e Palermos,* Ital. *Porto Palermo,* inlet of Strait of Otranto, in S Albania, 4 mi. SSE of Himarë; natural harbor serving Himarë and Gusmar. Was naval base under Venetian and Turkish rule.

Palestina (pŭlĭstē'nŭ). **1** City, Minas Gerais, Brazil: see JORDÂNIA. **2** City (pop. 1,917), NW São Paulo, Brazil, 30 mi. N of São José do Rio Prêto; rice, manioc, coffee; pottery mfg.

Palestina (pälĕstē'nä), town (pop. 1,509), Caldas dept., W central Colombia, in Cauca valley, 8 mi. SW of Manizales; coffeegrowing; sericulture.

Palestina, town (1950 pop. 1,076), Quezaltenango dept., SW Guatemala, on Inter-American Highway and 13 mi. WNW of Quezaltenango; alt. 8,500 ft.; corn, wheat, fodder grasses, livestock.

Palestine (pă'lŭstīn) [ultimately from Philistine], country on E shore of the Mediterranean. In the Bible it is called Canaan (kā'nŭn) before the invasion of Joshua; the usual Hebrew name is Eretz Israel [land of Israel]. Palestine is the Holy Land, of the Jews as having been promised them by God, of Christians because it was the home of Christ, and of Moslems as heirs of Jews and Christians. While its geographical boundaries have varied through history, it has always included the region (c.140 mi. long, c.30–c.70 mi. wide) bet. the Mediterranean and Jordan R., bordering SW on Egypt. Outside of these bounds are such biblical lands as EDOM, GILEAD, MOAB, and HAURAN. The area of Palestine (□ 10,434; 1946 pop. 1,845,559) in the British mandate (established 1920) included the Negev, a 100-mi.-long desert area reaching to the Gulf of Aqaba. This article covers the history of the region up through the formation of the state of ISRAEL in 1948. For the economy, for more geographical details, and for the further history of the region see that article and the article on the kingdom of JORDAN. Palestine under the British mandate was bounded by Sinai Peninsula of Egypt (SW), Saudi Arabia (S and E), Iraq (NE), and Syria and Lebanon (N). In 1923 the semi-independent emirate of Trans-Jordan (later renamed Jordan) was formed from the region E of the Jordan R. Palestine on the whole has a dry, hot climate. From E to W the country comprises 3 zones: the depression—the northernmost extension of the GREAT RIFT VALLEY—in which lie the Jordan and the DEAD SEA; a ridge rising steeply from this cleft; and a coastal plain a dozen miles wide. In N Palestine the ridge is interrupted by the Plain of Jezreel (Esdraelon) and the connecting valley of Beisan. The highland area to N is called GALILEE; its chief centers are SAFAD and NAZARETH, near which rises Mt. TABOR. To the S the broad ridge stretches to the Negev. First there are the hills of SAMARIA, with northward prongs (Gilboa, Mt. CARMEL), fronting on Haifa Bay. The center of Samaria is NABLUS, which lies between Mt. EBAL and Mt. GERIZIM. The mts. of JUDAEA are W of the mouth of the JORDAN. Here are JERUSALEM, BETHLEHEM, and HEBRON. In the Negev lies BEERSHEBA. The coastal plain of Palestine has water, but since great sand dunes block drainage, this was formerly a zone of swamps, desolate and unused; the land, now reclaimed, is fertile and productive. Towns of the littoral are ACRE, HAIFA, TEL AVIV, PETAH TIQVAH, LYDDA, and REHOVOT. To the S is old GAZA. The plain is diversely named; it is the Valley of Zevulun (Zebulun) S of Acre, Sharon S of Mt. Carmel, and the Shephelah in extreme S. Agr. in the Jordan valley centers around the lakes, including L. Hula and the Sea of GALILEE, and in the Beisan area. The chief town is TIBERIAS, and there is an important hydroelectric plant just S of the Sea of Galilee. The surface of the Dead Sea, into which the Jordan empties, is 1,292 ft. below sea level. Before the Jewish colonization of Palestine in the 20th cent. the rural people were Arab peasants (fellahin). In cities there were important groups of Christians (at Nazareth, Bethlehem, and Jerusalem) and of Jews (at Safad, Tiberias, Jerusalem, Jericho, and Hebron). Otherwise the population was Moslem Arab. The Holy Land has a special character as a place of pilgrimage. Shrines cluster most numerously about Jerusalem, Bethlehem, Nazareth, and Hebron; they are commonly shared by several religions. The earliest-known inhabitants of Palestine were Neanderthallike and used Mousterian tools. By 4th millennium B.C. a civilization of troglodytic herders and farmers had arisen. Due to its strategic location on coastal route bet. Egypt, Mesopotamia, and Persia, Palestine was the sought-after prize of whichever empire was ascendant in E Mediterranean; the Plain of Jezreel, near MEGIDDO, is noted as one of world's great battlegrounds since earliest times. After 1000 B.C. the Hebrew kingdom was well established; profiting from decline of the New Empire in Egypt, Hebrews set up their own state, which was consolidated under kings Saul and David, who defeated the Philistines, seafaring people who had colonized S part of Palestine's Mediterranean coast. After expansive reign of Solomon, whose dominion extended to Gulf of Aqaba, the kingdom fell into 2 states: Israel (⊙ Samaria) and Judah (⊙ Jerusalem) under house of David. Both came under pressure of empires expanding from Mesopotamia; Israel was destroyed (c.722 B.C.) by Assyria and Judah (586 B.C.) by Babylonia. Under Persian aegis, a new Jewish community was soon reestablished in Jerusalem by Zerubbabel, Ezra, and Nehemiah. In 4th cent. B.C. Alexander the Great conquered Palestine; subsequent effort to impose Hellenism led to Jewish revolt under the Maccabees, who established (141 B.C.) new Jewish state which ruled Palestine for 70 years but finally yielded to Rome. At time of Christ Palestine was under the Herods, Roman puppet kings. After Jewish revolt (A.D. 66) Romans destroyed (A.D. 70) the Temple and expelled Jews from Judaea; another revolt (A.D. 132) was brutally suppressed. Tiberias and Caesarea (Caesarea Palaestinae) became Jewish centers, while Jaffa and Nablus were Roman strongholds. With Constantine I Palestine became a center of Christian pilgrimage; under Justinian, the country flourished and agr. was encouraged, even in the Negev. Palestine soon came under the ascendant Moslems and, by 640, was under control of the caliph Omar. Centuries of Moslem domination led to drastic decline; cultivated valleys and hill slopes became swamps and grazing land, highlands were deforested. In 9th cent. Palestine passed to Fatimite rulers of Egypt, who destroyed Church of the Holy Sepulcher and molested pilgrims, thus provoking the Crusades. Latin Kingdom of Jerusalem, established 1099, lasted less than 100 years and Palestine came under the Mamelukes. Numerous Norman fortresses and Moslem monuments are relics of these eras. In 1516 Mamelukes were defeated by Ottoman Turks, under whose rule the country fell into further decay. Jewish colonization from Europe began (1870) with establishment of agr. school; 1st Jewish settlement, Petah Tiqva, was founded 1878. Bet. 1882 and 1914 immigrants, sponsored by private organizations, arrived from Russia; the Zionist movement, founded 1897 as political body, entered colonizing field in 1906. At this stage Palestine was comprised within the sanjaks of Acre and Nablus, both part of the vilayet of Beirut, and the independent sanjak of Jerusalem. The Balfour Declaration (Feb., 1917) marked Palestine for establishment of a Jewish national home. Bet. Oct., 1917, and Sept., 1918, country was conquered from the Turks by British under Allenby; in 1920 British civil administration was established (⊙ Jerusalem) under League of Nations mandate; it functioned through a high commissioner and an executive council. Jewish pop. was officially represented by the Jewish Agency; Moslem religious affairs were regulated by a supreme council. Jewish land purchases, economic development, and social services progressed, sponsored by various Jewish organizations abroad. Strife bet. Jews and Arabs soon developed; there were clashes (1928) over the Wailing Wall and (1929) at Safad, Hebron, and elsewhere. In 1930s, when advent of Hitler led to increased Jewish immigration from Germany and other central European countries, Arab attacks on Jewish settlements were stepped up. A British Royal Commission (1936–37) proposed partition of Palestine into Jewish and Arab territories. In 1939 the British issued a White Paper, announcing their intention to create a predominantly Arab independent Palestine and limiting Jewish immigration to 1,500 persons per month, cutting it off entirely in 1944. Outbreak of Second World War led to lessening of political tension; Palestine became important supply base for the Middle East, her industries supplied Allied armies, and a Jewish brigade fought with British in N Africa and Italy. With the end of the war, Jewish demands for greater immigration were refused by the British. This led to a vast stream of illegal immigrants, who entered country under protection of the Haganah (Jewish defense army, created by British during 1930s, later outlawed); at the same time Jewish extremists attacked British troops and installations. British counter measures were severe; whole settlements were punished for possession of arms, wholesale internment took place, illegal immigrants, when intercepted, were sent to detention camps on Cyprus or, in the case of the ship *Exodus 1947*, returned to Germany. In 1946–47 the Palestine problem was subject of Anglo-American Commission of Inquiry, and on Nov. 29, 1947, the United Nations General Assembly recommended establishment of independent Jewish and Arab states in Palestine. British authorities withdrew (May 14, 1948) after a further period of violence, and on same date state of ISRAEL was proclaimed. Area allocated to proposed Arab state subsequently passed under control of Jordan, except for the GAZA strip, which came under control of Egypt.

Palestine. **1** (pă'lŭstĭn, –stēn) Town (pop. 420), St. Francis co., E Ark., 7 mi. WSW of Forrest City. **2** (pă'lŭstĭn) Village (pop. 1,589), Crawford co., SE Ill., near the Wabash, 22 mi. NNW of Vincennes (Ind.), in agr. area (livestock, wheat, corn); flour mill, railroad shops. Settled 1811, laid out 1816, inc. 1855. **3** (pă'lŭstĭn) Village (pop. 207), Darke co., W Ohio, 7 mi. WSW of Greenville, near Ind. line. **4** (pă'lŭstēn) City (pop. 12,503), ⊙ Anderson co., E Texas, c.45 mi. SSW of Tyler; rail, highway junction (with railroad shops), and industrial center of rich petroleum, agr. (cotton, truck), poultry area; ships produce; cottonseed-oil milling, woodworking; recycling plant; mfg. of glass products, mattresses, clothing. Large salt dome here; lignite, coal, clay deposits in area. Settled 1846, inc. 1871.

Palestrina (pälĕstrē'nä), town (pop. 6,517), Roma prov., Latium, central Italy, 22 mi. ESE of Rome; macaroni mfg.; limestone quarrying. Occupies site of anc. *Praeneste*; has Roman remains, including a temple of Fortune, and 17th-cent. Barberini palace. Severely damaged (1943–44) in Second World War.

Palestro (pälĕstrō'), village (pop. 2,285), Alger dept., N central Algeria, on the Oued Isser, on railroad and 33 mi. SE of Algiers; vineyards, olive groves; oil pressing, soap mfg. Iron and zinc deposits near by. Founded 1851; sacked during Kabylian revolt (1871).

Palestro (pälĕs'trô), village (pop. 2,485), Pavia prov., Lombardy, N Italy, near Sesia R., 11 mi. NW of Mortara; agr. center (rice, dairy products, silkworm cocoons); mfg. (rayon, cellophane).

Paletwa (pŭlĕt'wä''), village, S.Chin Hills dist., Upper Burma, on Kaladan R. and 80 mi. NNW of Akyab; hosp. and post office. Former ⊙ Arakan Hill Tracts.

Palfrey Lake, Maine and N.B.: see CHIPUTNETICOOK LAKES.

Palghar (päl'gŭr), town (pop. 4,101), Thana dist., W Bombay, India, near Arabian Sea, 45 mi. N of Bombay; market center for rice, fish, sugar cane.

Palghat (päl'gät), city (pop. 55,160), Malabar dist., SW Madras, India, on Ponnani R., in Palghat Gap, and 70 mi. SE of Calicut; trade center (agr. products, timber); tobacco processing, rice milling, coir-yarn weaving, mfg. of biri, railway sleepers. Tileworks here and just N, across river, at rail junction of Olavakkot. Seat of Victoria Col. (affiliated with Madras Univ.). Fort (built 1766 by Hyder Ali) finally captured from Mysore sultans in 1790 and used as base of operations against Tippoo Sahib. Products of foothills of Western Ghats (N, S) include cassava, coffee, rubber, and pepper.

Palghat Gap, major opening (c.20 mi. wide) in Western Ghats, SW India, bet. Nilgiri Hills (N) and Anaimalai Hills (S); main trade route (highways, railroad) bet. Malabar Coast and E side of peninsular India; affords entry for climatic advantages of SW monsoon and outlet for storms of Bay of Bengal.

Palguín (pälgēn') village (1930 pop. 65), Cautín prov., S central Chile, in Chilean lake dist., at N foot of Villarrica Volcano, 55 mi. SE of Temuco; alt. 1,475 ft.; health resort; thermal springs.

Palhoça (pŭlyô'sŭ), city (pop. 1,690), E Santa Catarina, Brazil, on the Atlantic, opposite Santa Catarina Isl., and 8 mi. SW of Florianópolis; hog raising, meat processing, mfg. of flour products. Founded in 18th cent. by Portuguese.

Pali (pä'lē). **1** Town (pop. 12,356), ⊙ Pali dist., central Rajasthan, India, 39 mi. SSE of Jodhpur; trades in grain, cotton, oilseeds, cloth fabrics, wool; cotton milling, oilseed pressing, handicraft cloth weaving, dyeing, and printing; ivory products, metalwork. Marwar, rail junction, is 18 mi. ESE. **2** Town (pop. 5,511), Hardoi dist., central Uttar Pradesh, India, on tributary of the Ramganga and 10 mi. SSW of Shahabad; wheat, gram, barley, oilseeds, sugar cane. Founded 12th cent. Sometimes called Pali Khas.

Pali, Cape (pä'lē), Albanian *Kep i Palit*, in W Albania, on the Adriatic, 7 mi. NNW of Durazzo; 41°25'N 19°24'E. Forms northernmost outlier of Mt. Durazzo.

Palia (pŭl'yŭ), town (pop. 5,551), Kheri dist., N Uttar Pradesh, India, 35 mi. NNW of Lakhimpur; rice, wheat, gram, corn, oilseeds, turmeric. Sometimes called Palia Kalan.

Paliano (pälyä'nô), town (pop. 4,092), Frosinone prov., Latium, S central Italy, 9 mi. S of Subiaco; fireworks mfg.

Paliat, Indonesia: see KANGEAN ISLANDS.

Palibothra, India: see PATNA, city.

Palic or **Palich** (both: pä'lĭch), Serbo-Croatian *Palić*, Hung. *Palics* (pŏ'lĭch), village, Vojvodina, N Serbia, Yugoslavia, on railroad and 5 mi. E of Subotica, on Palic L. (c.4 mi. long); health resort with mineral waters.

Pa-li-chiao, China: see PALIKAO.

Palici, Sicily: see PALAGONIA.

Palics, Yugoslavia: see PALIC.

Palikao (pälēkou'), town (pop. 5,772), Oran dept., NW Algeria, in the Tell, 11 mi. E of Mascara; agr. trade center (cereals, wine, livestock).

Palikao, Palikiao, or **Pa-li-chiao** (all: bä'lē'jyou'), locality, N Hopeh prov., China, 2 mi. W of Tunghsien. Here a combined British and French force defeated (1860) the Chinese and invested Peking. The victorious commander, Cousin-Montauban, subsequently adopted the title of count of Palikao.

Palikea (pä'lĕkä'ū), peak (3,111 ft.), W Oahu, T.H., in Waianae Range.

Pali Khas, India: see PALI, Uttar Pradesh.

Palimé (pälē'mā), town, S Fr. Togoland, rail terminus 3 mi. SE of Klouto and 65 mi. NW of Lomé; agr. center (cacao, palm oil and kernels, cotton); cotton ginning. Has agr. station, customhouse, hosp., R.C. and Protestant missions. Pop. 2,714.

Palín (pälēn'), town (1950 pop. 3,586), Escuintla dept., S Guatemala, in Pacific piedmont, on Michatoya R. and 9 mi. NE of Escuintla, on railroad; alt. 3,724 ft. Market center; kapok, coffee, sugar, pineapples. Just S are falls (200 ft. high) and hydroelectric station of San Pedro Mártir.

Palinges (pälēzh'), village (pop. 698), Saône-et-Loire dept., E central France, on Bourbince R. and Canal du Centre, 9 mi. NNW of Charolles; pottery and fertilizer mfg.

Palinuro, Cape, (pälēnōō'rô), promontory, Campania, S Italy, on Tyrrhenian Sea, 8 mi. WNW of Punta degli Infreschi; 40°2'N 15°16'E.

Paliomilos, Greece: see PALEOMYLOS.

Paliouri, Cape, Greece: see KANASTRION, CAPE.

Palisade. **1** Town (pop. 861), Mesa co., W Colo., on Colorado R. and 11 mi. ENE of Grand Junction; alt. 4,740 ft. Fruit-shipping point in Grand Valley. Coal mines in vicinity. **2** Village (pop. 212), Aitkin co., central Minn., on Mississippi R. and 16 mi. NE of Aitkin; dairy products. **3** Village (pop. 694), Hitchcock and Hayes counties, S Nebr., 27 mi. WNW of McCook and on Frenchman Creek; livestock, grain. **4** Village (pop. c.200), Eureka co., N central Nev., on Humboldt R. and 27 mi. SW of Elko; alt. 4,821 ft.; ships livestock. Emigrant Pass (6,121 ft.) is near.

Palisades, The (pălĭsādz'), in NE N.J. and SE N.Y., bluffs along W bank of the Hudson, extending from region N of Jersey City, N.J., N to vicinity of Piermont, N.Y.; general alt. 350–550 ft. Much of the most scenic section, N of Fort Lee (N.J.), is included in Palisades Interstate Park (more than 47,070 acres), a chain of wooded, hilly, recreational areas on or near W bank of the Hudson bet. Fort Lee, N.J. (S), and Newburgh, N.Y. (N). Park's sections (S to N) are: Palisades section (mostly in N.J.), with 12-mi. frontage on the Hudson; Tallman Mtn. section, SE of Piermont, N.Y.; Blauvelt section, SW of Nyack, N.Y.; Hook Mtn. section, N of Nyack; BEAR MOUNTAIN–Harriman section (c.41,000 acres), opposite Peekskill; Stony Point Battlefield Reservation near STONY POINT; and STORM KING section N of West Point.

Palisades Park, residential borough (pop. 9,635), Bergen co., NE N.J., 3 mi. SE of Hackensack; amusement park; mfg. of soap, screens, clothing. Inc. 1899.

Palisades Interstate Park, N.Y. and N.J.: see PALISADES, THE.

Palisades Peaks, Calif.: see KINGS CANYON NATIONAL PARK.

Palisadoes, The (pălĭsā'dōz), peninsula, Port Royal parish, SE Jamaica, a narrow spit (c.7½ mi. long) bounding Kingston Harbour. On its W tip is the once prosperous town of Port Royal. In center, opposite Kingston, is the Palisadoes airport. The peninsula is coextensive with Port Royal parish, usually included in Kingston.

Paliseul (pälēzûl'), town (pop. 1,405), Luxembourg prov., SE Belgium, in the Ardennes, 14 mi. WNW of Neufchâteau; market center for lumber area.

Palisse, La, France: see LAPALISSE.

Palissy (pälēsē'), village (pop. 1,303), Oran dept., NW Algeria, on the Mékerra, on railroad and 7 mi. SSW of Sidi-bel-Abbès; winegrowing, cattle raising.

Palitana (pälĭtä'nŭ), town (pop. 18,134), SE Saurashtra, India, on Kathiawar peninsula, 27 mi. SW of Bhaunagar; market center for millet, cotton, wheat, sugar cane; cotton ginning, hand-loom weaving; horse breeding. Just SW is noted hill of Satrunjaya (or Shetrunja), whose summit (c.1,900 ft.) is covered with numerous Jain temples, most of which are modern, although some date from 11th cent.; a very sacred place of Jain pilgrimage. Town was ⊙ former princely state of Palitana (□ 300; pop. 76,432) of Western India States agency; state merged 1948 with Saurashtra.

P'a-li-tsung, Tibet: see PHARI.

Paliuri, Cape, Greece: see KANASTRION, CAPE.

Palizada (pälēsä'dä), town (pop. 1,348), Campeche, SE Mexico, on SW Yucatan Peninsula, 32 mi. SSW of Carmen; corn, sugar cane, tobacco, henequen, fruit, livestock; dairying, furniture making.

Palizada River, Mexico: see USUMACINTA RIVER.

Palkino (päl'kēnŭ). **1** Village (1926 pop. 404), W central Kostroma oblast, Russian SFSR, 23 mi. ESE of Galich; flax. **2** Village (1939 pop. over 500), W Pskov oblast, Russian SFSR, 20 mi. SW of Pskov; flax, dairying.

Palkonda (pälkōn'dŭ), town (pop. 12,414), Vizagapatam dist., NE Madras, India, on Nagavali R. and 40 mi. NE of Vizianagaram; rice and oilseed milling; sugar cane, millet.

Palk Strait (pôk, pôlk), inlet of Bay of Bengal bet. S Madras, India, and N coast of Ceylon; bounded S by Rameswaram Isl., Adam's Bridge, and Mannar Isl.; 40–85 mi. wide, 85 mi. long. Receives Vaigai R. Includes numerous Ceylonese isls. S part of strait is sometimes called Palk Bay.

Palla Bianca, peak on Austro-Ital. border: see WEISSKUGEL.

Palladam (pŭ'lŭdŭm), town (pop. 7,654), Coimbatore dist., SW Madras, India, 9 mi. SSW of Tiruppur; road center in tobacco area; cotton pressing.

Pal Lahara (päl' lŭ'hŭrŭ), village, Dhenkanal dist., N Orissa, India, 60 mi. NNW of Dhenkanal. Was ⊙ former princely state of Pal Lahara (□ 450; pop. 34,130) in Orissa States; state inc. 1949 into newly-created Dhenkanal dist.

Pallantia, Spain: see PALENCIA, city.

Pallanza (päl-län'tsä), town (pop. 4,515), Novara prov., Piedmont, N Italy, port on W shore of Lago Maggiore, opposite Borromean Isls., 1 mi. SW of Intra; resort. Mfg. (rayon, cotton, and jute textiles, paper, beer, chemicals, flour, leather goods). Has Romanesque church of San Remigio (11th cent.), 17th-cent. palace, and mus.

Pallapatti or **Pallappatti** (pŭl'lŭpŭt-tē), town (pop. 11,263; 90% Moslem), Trichinopoly dist., S Madras, India, 55 mi. WSW of Trichinopoly; tanning, sesame-oil extraction; hides, leather goods, millet, tobacco. Also spelled Palapatti.

Pallas (pă'lŭs), hamlet, S Co. Longford, Ireland, 3 mi. ENE of Ballymahon; childhood home and probably the birthplace of Oliver Goldsmith.

Pallasca, province, Peru: see CABANA, Ancash dept.

Pallasca (päyä'skä), city (pop. 1,949), Ancash dept., W central Peru, in Cordillera Occidental, 10 mi. N of Cabana; grain, alfalfa. Lead, silver, copper mining near by.

Pallaskenry (pă"lŭskĕn'rē), Gaelic *Pailis Caonraighe*, town (pop. 348), N Co. Limerick, Ireland, 10 mi. W of Limerick; agr. market (grain, potatoes; dairying).

Pallas Mountains, Finnish *Pallastunturi* (päl'lästo͞on"to͞orē), small range in Lapland, N Finland, overlooking upper Ounas R. Rises to 2,693 ft. on Taivaskero (tī'väskĕ"rō) or Himmelriiki (hĭm'mĕlrē"kē), 25 mi. SE of Enontekiö. Winter-sports center. Region forms a natl. park.

Pallasovka (pŭlä'sŭfkŭ), town (1926 pop. 3,764), NE Stalingrad oblast, Russian SFSR, on railroad and 60 mi. S of Krasny Kut, near Kazakh SSR border; metalworks, flour mill.

Pallattur or **Pallatur** (pŭl-lŭto͞or'), town (pop. 6,315), Ramnad dist., S Madras, India, 6 mi. NNE of Karaikudi; residence of Chetty merchant community.

Pallavaram (pŭlä'vŭrŭm), town (pop. 9,879), Chingleput dist., E Madras, India, outer suburb of Madras, 10 mi. SW of city center; has dispersed residential areas. Large tanning and leather-goods industry near by was greatly increased (1920s) by introduction of chrome tanning; tanning settlement was named Chromepet. Pallavaram cantonment area is administered as part of St. Thomas Mount. Extensive road-metal and building-stone quarrying in near-by hill. Minambakkam, airport for Madras city, is just NE. Large annual Moslem festival in vicinity.

Pallene, peninsula, Greece: see KASSANDRA.

Pallewella or **Pallewela** (pŭl"ĕvĕl'ŭ), village, Western Prov., Ceylon, 24 mi. NNE of Colombo; garnet mining; coconut palms, rice. Graphite mines (E).

Pallice, La, France: see ROCHELLE, LA.

Pallikonda (pŭl"lĭkōn'dŭ) or **Pallikondai** (-dī), town (pop. 9,454), North Arcot dist., central Madras, India, on Palar R. and 5 mi. ESE of Gudiyattam; trades in agr. products (rice, sugar, peanuts) of Palar R. valley.

Pallion, England: see SUNDERLAND.

Palliser Bay (pă'lĭsŭr), inlet of Cook Strait, S N.Isl., New Zealand, near Wellington harbor; 20 mi. long, 10 mi. wide; summer resort. Cape Palliser is at SE end.

Palliser Islands, Tuamotu Isls.: see APATAKI.

Pallivasal, India: see MUNNAR.

Pall Mall (pĕl' mĕl', păl' măl'), street in City of Westminster, W London, England, running along N side of St. James's Park, from St. James's Palace to the Haymarket, near W end of Trafalgar Square. Laid out by Charles II for purpose of playing the game pall-mall, it is famous as a street of clubs.

Palluau (pälwō'), village (pop. 410), Vendée dept., W France, 13 mi. NW of La Roche-sur-Yon; truck farming.

Palma or **Palma de Mallorca** (päl'mä dhä mälyôr'kä), city (pop. 97,009, with suburbs 114,405), ⊙ Majorca isl. and Baleares prov., and chief city of Balearic Isls., Spain, major seaport for the archipelago, at head of Bay of Palma, in the W Mediterranean, 125 mi. SSE of Barcelona and 160 mi. E of Valencia; 39°34'N 2°38'E. Picturesquely situated along bay, with its outskirts nestling among surrounding hills, and favored by a year-round mild climate, it has become one of Europe's most renowned resorts. Also an important industrial and commercial center, shipping almonds, apricots, figs, olive oil, wine, apricot purée. Among its industrial plants are cement and paper mills, iron foundries, brewery; also mfg. of shoes, woolen goods, pottery, crystal and glass, chemicals, pharmaceuticals, matches, hardware, ship engines. Has shipyards; airport Son San Juan (E). From it radiate railroads and highways. Handsome, historic city enhanced by notable bldgs., such as Gothic cathedral (begun 1229), Almudaina castle (once a Moorish palace), and fortress-like 15th-cent. Lonja (exchange). There are several churches, notably San Francisco (13th cent.) with fine cloister and tomb of Raymond Lull. Bellver Castle built (in 14th cent.) c.400 ft. above the bay (W), a former royal residence, now serves as jail. Imposing gates remain of the old town walls. City was founded 276 B.C. as Roman colony by the consul Metellus. Known as Mallorca during Moslem rule, it was conquered in 1229 by James I of Aragon. During the Sp. civil war (1936–39), Palma was an important naval and air base of the Nationalists.

Palma. 1 City, Ceará, Brazil: see COREAÚ. **2** City, Goiás, Brazil: see PARANÃ.

Palma or **La Palma** (lä päl'mä), island (□ 281; pop. 60,533) of the NW Canary Isls., in Santa Cruz de Tenerife prov., Spain; chief town and port, SANTA CRUZ DE LA PALMA. Situated NW of Gomera and 55 mi. W of Tenerife; extends 26 mi. N-S bet. 28°28'N 17°49'W and 28°50'N 17°46'W; up to 15 mi. wide. Has a year-round mild, semitropical climate, but suffers from droughts. The rugged, volcanic isl. rises to greatest elevations (7,730 ft.) of the archipelago, after Tenerife; 2 roughly parallel ranges traverse the isl., enclosing a vast old crater, called La Caldera. Most of the settlements are in the fertile coastal regions. Produce include bananas, tobacco, sugar cane, tomatoes, potatoes, almonds, cereals, grapes, cochineal. Wine, sugar, and flour are produced. Lumbering, fishing, and embroidery mfg. are also important. Leading towns, apart from Santa Cruz de la Palma, are Los Llanos, El Paso, and Los Sauces. Known since anc. times, isl. was unsuccessfully coveted by Mauretanians, Carthaginians, Romans, and Moors. Conquered in 1492 for Spain. Isl. is sometimes called San Miguel de la Palma.

Palma (päl'mŭ), village, Niassa prov., northernmost Mozambique, on Mozambique Channel, near Tanganyika border, just SW of Cape Delgado, 150 mi. N of Pôrto Amélia; coconuts.

Palma, La, in Latin America: see LA PALMA.

Palma, La, or **La Palma del Condado** (lä päl'mä dhĕl kōndä'dhō), city (pop. 7,905), Huelva prov., SW Spain, in Andalusia, on railroad and 24 mi. ENE of Huelva; viticultural center (alcohol, vinegar, wine, vermouth, *mistela*, brandy). Mfg. of barrels; olive oil.

Palma, Rió de la (rē'ō dhä), river, Matanzas prov., W Cuba, rises S of Los Arabos, flows c.60 mi. N to Santa Clara Bay. Poor navigability.

Palma Campania (päl'mä kämpä'nyä), town (pop. 6,544), Napoli prov., Campania, S Italy, 4 mi. SSE of Nola; wine making.

Palma de Gandía (päl'mä dhä gändē'ä), village (pop. 1,450), Valencia prov., E Spain, 3 mi. SW of Gandía, in truck-farming area; olive oil.

Palma del Condado, La, Spain: see PALMA, LA., Huelva prov.

Palma del Río (dhĕl rē'ō), city (pop. 11,973), Córdoba prov., S Spain, in Andalusia, near confluence of Guadalquivir and Genil rivers, 14 mi. NW of Écija; fruit-shipping center (oranges, cherries, apples). Processes vegetable fibers; soap mfg., flour- and sawmilling. Livestock, cereals, sugar beets.

Palma di Montechiaro (päl'mä dē môntĕkyä'rô), town (pop. 15,456), Agrigento prov., S Sicily, near coast, 13 mi. SE of Agrigento, in almond-growing region; agr. center; sulphur mines. Ruins of castle near by.

Palmaner (pŭl'mŭnār), town (pop. 5,298), Chittoor dist., W Madras, India, 24 mi. W of Chittoor; road center; peanut milling, silk growing. Sandalwood, dyewood (red sanders) in near-by forests (cattle grazing).

Palmanova (pälmänō'vä), town (pop. 3,237), Udine prov., Friuli–Venezia Giulia, NE Italy, 12 mi. SSE of Udine; rail junction. Formerly a Venetian fortress (begun 1593) against Turks and Austrians. Has cathedral.

Palmar or **Palmar de Bravo** (pälmär' dā brä'vō), town (pop. 1,630), Puebla, central Mexico, 13 mi. SW of Serdán; cereals, maguey, livestock.

Palmar, El, in Latin America: see EL PALMAR.

Palmar, El (ĕl), SW suburb (pop. 3,016) of Murcia, Murcia prov., SE Spain; meat and fruit canning, liqueur distilling, mfg. of cement pipes.

Palmar de Bravo, Mexico: see PALMAR.

Palmar de las Islas (dā läs ē'släs), ravine in Santa Cruz dept., SE Bolivia, in the Chaco, 10 mi. S of Ravelo, on Paraguay border; intersection of Ravelo-Ingavi (Paraguay) road. Boundary marker established (1938) in Chaco Peace Conference.

Palmar de Varela (värā'lä), town (pop. 3,403), Atlántico dept., N Colombia, on Magdalena R., in Caribbean lowlands, and 20 mi. S of Barranquilla; cotton-growing center.

Palmares (pŭlmä'rĭs). **1** City (pop. 7,223), E Pernambuco, NE Brazil, on railroad and 60 mi. SW of Recife, in sugar-growing area; sugar refining, alcohol distilling. **2** Town, Rio Grande do Sul, Brazil: see EMÍLIO MEYER.

Palmares (pälmä'rēs), city (pop. 671), Alajuela prov., W central Costa Rica, on central plateau, on Inter-American Highway and 15 mi. WNW of Alajuela; tobacco and coffee center.

Palmaria (pälmärē'ä), triangular islet (1 mi. long) in Ligurian Sea, N Italy, at SW end of Gulf of Spezia; separated from promontory of Portovenere by channel (125 yd. wide); rises to 650 ft. Notable for its black marble. Agr. (grapes, olives); tunny fishing. Formerly fortified. Just S are smaller islets of Tino (marble; lighthouse) and Tinetto. Total area of 3 islets, □ .6.

Palmarito (pälmärē'tō), town (pop. 1,223), Oriente prov., E Cuba, on Cauto R., on railroad and 23 mi. NNW of Santiago de Cuba; manganese mining. Sometimes Palmarito de Cauto.

Palmarito. 1 Town (pop. 630), Apure state, W central Venezuela, landing on Apure R. and 45 mi. NE of Guadualito, in cattle-raising region. **2** Town (pop. 579), Mérida state, W Venezuela, on SE shore of L. Maracaibo, 5 mi. SW of Bobures (Zulia state); sugar growing; mica mining. Petroleum deposits near by.

Palmar Point (pälmär'), on Atlantic coast of Rocha dept., SE Uruguay, 23 mi. SSW of Chuy; 34°5'S 53°22'W.

Palmas (päl'mŭs), city (pop. 2,151), S Paraná, Brazil, 60 mi. WSW of União da Vitória; cattle-raising center; sawmills, tanneries; sugar, grapes.

Palmas, island, Indonesia: see MIANGAS.

Palmas, Cape (päl'mŭs), headland of SE Liberia, on Atlantic Ocean; 4°22'N 7°43'W. Site of Harper. Marks W limit of Gulf of Guinea.

Palmas, Gulf of (päl'mäs), inlet of Mediterranean Sea, bet. SW Sardinia and Sant'Antioco Isl.; 9 mi. wide. Nearly closed off (N) by isl. chain crossed by road and rail causeway. Fisheries (coral, mussels, oysters).

Palmas, Isla de las (ē'slä dä läs päl'mäs), small island off Pacific coast of W Colombia, in Chocó Bay, 20 mi. W of Buenaventura.

Palmas, Las, Argentina: see LAS PALMAS.

Palmas, Las, province (pop. 320,524), CANARY ISLANDS, Spain, in the Atlantic; ⊙ Las Palmas. Includes the 3 major eastern isls. of the archipelago, GRAND CANARY, FUERTEVENTURA, and LANZAROTE, as well as several adjacent islets, among them Lobos, Graciosa, Alegranza. Prov. was set up in 1927. Two variant official figures for its area are □ 1,569.5 and □ 1,583.

Palmas, Las, officially **Las Palmas de Gran Canaria** (dhä grän' känä'ryä), city (pop. 97,856, with suburbs 119,595), ⊙ Las Palmas prov., Spain, principal town and port of Canary Isls., on Grand Canary, 155 mi. W of Cape Juby (NW Africa) and 830 mi. SW of Cádiz; 28°6'N 15°24'W. On transatlantic crossroads of 3 continents, its adjoining (N) port, Puerto de la Luz, is a fuel and supply base for ocean vessels. Also exports great amount of products from the fertile isl.: tomatoes, bananas, tobacco, cochineal, salted and dried fish, canned food. Fishing and fish processing are the principal industries; there are also breweries, wineries, shipyards; mfg. of fertilizer, matches, sweets, ceramics, cement articles, textile goods. Las Palmas possesses a mild, semitropical climate with little seasonal change, the temp. ranging from summer mean of 82°F. to mean of 57°F. in winter. The gay, cosmopolitan city has become a famed tourist resort, particularly in winter. Has fine, palm-lined beaches and luxuriant parks. Outstanding bldgs. include the cathedral (begun 1497), bishop's palace, Our Lady of Carmen church, art mus., Canary mus., theater, institutions of higher learning, and several other interesting churches, hermitages, and convents. House where Columbus stopped on his 1st voyage is still preserved. Las Palmas was founded in 1478.

Palmas, Las, Panama: see LAS PALMAS.

Palmas, Las, Venezuela: see EL MENE.

Palmas de Gran Canaria, Las, Canary Isls.: see PALMAS, LAS, city.

Palma Sola (päl'mä sō'lä), rail junction in Yaracuy state, N Venezuela, on Aroa R. and 22 mi. NE of San Felipe, 39 mi. WNW of Puerto Cabello.

Palma Soriano (sōryä'nō), town (pop. 15,743), Oriente prov., E. Cuba, on Cauto R., on Central Highway and on railroad, and 18 mi. NW of Santiago de Cuba. Processing and trading center for agr. region (sugar cane, cacao, coffee, corn, fruit, beeswax and honey, cattle); coffee roasting, mfg. of furniture and soft drinks. Has airfield. Manganese deposits near by.

Palmas Suergiu (päl'mäs swĕr'jū), village (pop. 2,652), Cagliari prov., SW Sardinia, 14 mi. S of Iglesias, adjacent to San Giovanni Suergiu; rail junction.

Palm Beach, town (pop. 612), E New South Wales, Australia, on S inlet of Broken Bay and 21 mi. NNE of Sydney; summer resort.

Palm Beach, county (□ 1,978; pop. 114,688), SE Fla., on the Atlantic; ⊙ West Palm Beach. Everglades truck, dairy, and poultry area, with noted resort section (West Palm Beach, Palm Beach, Delray Beach), and citrus groves along coast. Mfg. of food and wood products. Fishing. Includes L. Okeechobee (NW) and is crossed by several drainage canals from lake to the Atlantic. Formed 1909.

Palm Beach, town (pop. 3,886), Palm Beach co., SE Fla., on a long, narrow barrier beach bet. the Atlantic (E) and L. Worth (W), a lagoon spanned here by bridges to West Palm Beach. The area, settled mainly after 1871, was named Palm Beach in 1887. With the arrival of Henry M. Flagler in 1893, it developed rapidly into a wealthy and exclusive winter resort with many beautiful estates.

Palm Beach Harbor, town (1940 pop. 27), Palm Beach co., SE Fla., across Lake Worth Inlet from Palm Beach.

Palm Canyon, Calif.: see PALM SPRINGS.

Palmdale, village (1940 pop. 913), Los Angeles co., S Calif., in irrigated Antelope Valley (W Mojave Desert), 35 mi. N of Los Angeles. Has airfield for jet-aircraft testing; chosen 1951 as site of aircraft assembly plant.

Palmeira (pŭlmā'rŭ). **1** City (pop. 2,041), S Paraná, Brazil, on railroad and 45 mi. W of Curitiba; sawmilling, furniture mfg., maté processing; rye, oats. **2** City, Rio Grande do Sul, Brazil: see PALMEIRA DAS MISSÕES.

Palmeira das Missões (däs mēsō'ĭs), city (pop. 2,342), N Rio Grande do Sul, Brazil, in the Serra Geral, 50 mi. NNE of Cruz Alta; maté, tobacco, lard. Agates and amethysts exploited here. Airfield. In area settled by Jesuit missionaries. Until 1944, called Palmeira.

Palmeira dos Índios (dŏŏs ēn'dyŏŏs), city (pop. 5,433), central Alagoas, NE Brazil, W terminus (1949) of railroad from Maceió (60 mi. ESE) projected to reach Pôrto Real do Colégio on São Francisco R. (Sergipe border). Ships cotton, corn, castor beans.

Palmeirais (pŭlmărä'ĭs), city (pop. 378), central Piauí, Brazil, on right bank of Parnaíba R. (Maranhão border) and 60 mi. S of Teresina; babassu nuts, hides, cotton. Until 1944, Belém.

Palmeiras (pŭlmā'rŭs). **1** City (pop. 3,114), central Bahia, Brazil, on the Chapada Diamantina, 25 mi. NW of Andaraí; state's leading diamond-mining center. Formerly called Villa Bella das Palmeiras. **2** City, São Paulo, Brazil: see SANTA CRUZ DAS PALMEIRAS.

Palmeiras de Goiás (dĭ goi-äs'), city (pop. 1,227), S Goiás, central Brazil, 40 mi. WSW of Goiânia; tobacco, cattle. Diamond washing in area. Until 1944, called Palmeiras; and, 1944–48, Mataúna.

Palmeirinhas Point (pŭlmărē'nyŭsh), low headland of NW Angola, 12 mi. SW of Luanda; 9°5'S 12°59'E.

Palmela (pŭlmā'lŭ), town (pop. 3,189), Setúbal dist., S central Portugal, on railroad and 3 mi. N of Setúbal; mfg. (pottery, textiles, cheese). Preserves medieval walls and a castle (alt. 780 ft.; magnificent view of Lisbon Bay area) recaptured from the Moors (1147) by Alfonso I.

Palmer (pä'mŭr), village (pop. 879), S Alaska, on Matanuska R. and 40 mi. NE of Anchorage, on Alaska RR spur, on Glenn Highway; market for MATANUSKA VALLEY agr. development. Cold-storage facilities (cooperative); airport. Hq. of Matanuska Valley Farmers' Cooperating Association. Site of agr. experiment station of Univ. of Alaska.

Palmer. **1** (pŏl'mŭr) Village (pop. 335), Christian co., central Ill., 25 mi. SSE of Springfield, in agr. and bituminous-coal-mining area. **2** (pä'mŭr) Town (pop. 296), Pocahontas co., N central Iowa, 23 mi. WNW of Fort Dodge; livestock, grain. **3** (pä'mŭr) City (pop. 150), Washington co., N Kansas, 13 mi. SSW of Washington; grain, livestock. **4** (pä'mŭr) Town (pop. 9,533), including Palmer village (pop. 3,440), Hampden co., S Mass., 14 mi. ENE of Springfield; wire cloth and rope, brushes, metal culverts; dairying, poultry, apples. Has state fish hatchery. Settled 1716, inc. 1775. Includes villages of Bondsville (1940 pop. 1,080), Thorndike (1940 pop. 1,167), and Three Rivers (pop. 2,359), at junction of Ware and Quaboag rivers to form Chicopee R. **5** (pä'mŭr) Village (1940 pop. 853), Marquette co., NW Upper Peninsula, Mich., 4 mi. S of Negaunee, in iron-mining region. **6** (pä'mŭr) Village (pop. 434), Merrick co., E central Nebr., 14 mi. NW of Central City, near Loup R.; dairying; grain, stock. **7** (pä'mŭr) Town (pop. 871), Grundy co., SE central Tenn., in the Cumberlands, 27 mi. NW of Chattanooga, in coal-mining region. **8** (pä'mŭr) Town (pop. 647), Ellis co., N Texas, 25 mi. SSE of Dallas; shipping point in cotton, truck area; brick making.

Palmer Archipelago, group of isls. (including Liége, Brabant, Anvers, and Wiencke isls.), Antarctica, SW of the South Shetlands, off NW coast of Palmer Peninsula, from which they are separated by De Gerlache and Bismarck straits; 64°S 62°W. Discovered 1898 by Adrien de Gerlache, Belgian explorer. Sometimes called Antarctic Archipelago.

Palmerganj, India: see AURANGABAD.

Palmer Goldfield, Australia: see PALMERVILLE.

Palmer Lake (pä'mŭr), town (pop. 263), El Paso co., central Colo., on Monument Creek, in SE foothills of Front Range, and 40 mi. S of Denver; alt. 7,237 ft.; resort. Small lake near by.

Palmer Peninsula, Antarctica, extends c.800 mi. from its base (c. 73°S) toward South America bet. 59° and 67°W; its tip (c.63°S 56°40'W), 650 mi. from Cape Horn, is farthest point of the Antarctic continent from the South Pole. Forms W shore of Weddell Sea. Mostly mountainous, rising to 13,750 ft. in Mt. Andrew Jackson, in S. Numerous isls. are off its coast, e.g.: Palmer Archipelago (NW), Biscoe Isls. and Adelaide Isl. (W), Alexander I Isl. and Charcot Isl. (SW), Ross Isl. (NE), Robinson, Hearst, and Dolleman isls. (E). Marguerite Bay indents W coast. First considered as part of Antarctic continent, it was later thought to be a group of isls.; subsequent exploration proved it to be indeed a peninsula of Antarctica, surrounded by numerous isls. Just off its N tip are the South Shetlands, across Bransfield Strait. The whole peninsula is covered with shelf ice. Named for Capt. N. B. Palmer, an American who explored part of its W coast in 1820. Also called Graham Land (especially by the British, who claim it as part of Falkland Isls. Dependencies) and Trinity Peninsula. Argentina and Chile (which calls it O'Higgins Land) also claim it.

Palmerston, Australia: see DARWIN.

Palmerston, town (pop. 1,418), S Ont., 32 mi. NW of Kitchener; railroad shops; dairying; gristmills.

Palmerston or **Palmerstown** (pä'mŭrstŭn), Gaelic *Baile Pámar*, town (pop. 214), Co. Dublin, Ireland, on the Liffey 4 mi. W of Dublin.

Palmerston, atoll (□ c.1; pop. 65), Manihiki group, S Pacific, 270 mi. NW of Rarotonga; 18°4'S 163°10' W. Under N.Z. COOK ISLANDS administration since 1901; natives part Polynesian, part English. Missionary school. Coconut and pandanus groves; copra. Also known as Avarau (ävärou').

Palmerston, borough (pop. 735), ⊙ Waihemo co. (□ 338; pop. 1,030), SE S.Isl., New Zealand, 22 mi. NNE of Dunedin; agr. center. Tuberculosis sanatorium near by.

Palmerston North, city (pop. 25,277; metropolitan Palmerston North 27,294), ⊙ Kairanga co. (□ 187; pop. 5,669), S N.Isl., New Zealand, 80 mi. NNE of Wellington and on Manawatu R.; agr. center; mfg. (clothing, furniture). Seat of Massey Agr. Col. Rail junction; airport near by. Settled 1871 by Scandinavians. Palmerston North is in, but independent of, Kairanga co.

Palmerstown, Ireland: see PALMERSTON.

Palmerstown House (pä'mŭrstŭn), agr. village, NE Co. Kildare, Ireland, 4 mi. NE of Naas; cattle, horses; potatoes. Mansion is natl. memorial to 6th earl of Mayo.

Palmerton (pä'mŭrtŭn), borough (pop. 6,646), Carbon co., E Pa., 15 mi. NNW of Allentown and on Lehigh R.; zinc refining, chemicals, paint; sand quarries; agr. Settled 1737, laid out 1898, inc. 1912.

Palmerville, village, N Queensland, Australia, 125 mi. NW of Cairns; cattle; limited gold mining. Formerly important center of Palmer Goldfield.

Palmetto (pălmĕ'tō). **1** City (pop. 4,103), Manatee co., SW Fla., on Manatee R. near its mouth on Tampa Bay, and connected by bridge with Bradenton; boating and fishing resort; packing and shipping of vegetables and citrus fruit; mfg. of furniture, concrete products. **2** Town (pop. 1,257), Fulton and Coweta counties, NW central Ga., 22 mi. SW of Atlanta; textile mfg. Inc. 1854. **3** Village (pop. 457), St. Landry parish, S central La., 16 mi. NE of Opelousas; cotton and moss gins, sawmills.

Palmetto Point (pälmĕ'tō, păl–), town (pop. 454), central Bahama Isls., on E central shore of Eleuthera Isl., opposite Governor's Harbour, 75 mi. E of Nassau; 25°10'N 76°9'E. Tomato growing.

Palmi (päl'mē), town (pop. 13,590), Reggio di Calabria prov., Calabria, S Italy, at N foot of the Aspromonte, 20 mi. NNE of Reggio di Calabria, in orange and olive groves. Just below, on Gulf of Gioia, is its port, Marina di Palmi; olive-oil refining, wine making, furniture mfg.; fishing. Severely damaged by earthquakes of 1783 and 1908.

Palmietfontein (päl'mĭtfôntān"), international airport for Witwatersrand, S Transvaal, U. of So. Afr., 13 mi. SE of Johannesburg; 29°19'S 28°9'E; alt. 5,080 ft.

Palmilla (pälmē'yä), village (1930 pop. 467), Colchagua prov., central Chile, on railroad, on Tinguiririca R. and 21 mi. W of San Fernando, in agr. area (grain, potatoes, peas, fruit, livestock).

Palmilla, village (pop. 185), Matanzas prov., W Cuba, 10 mi. ESE of Colón; fruit, honey, cattle. Sometimes Palmillas.

Palmillas (pälmē'yäs), town (pop. 1,107), Tamaulipas, NE,Mexico, in Sierra Madre Oriental, 40 mi. SW of Ciudad Victoria; alt. 4,242 ft.; cereals, livestock.

Palmira (pälmē'rä), town (pop. estimate 1,500), N Mendoza prov., Argentina, on Mendoza R. (irrigation area) and 20 mi. SE of Mendoza; rail junction and agr. center (wine, alfalfa, livestock); wine making.

Palmira, city (pop. 21,235), Valle del Cauca dept., W Colombia, in Cauca valley, on Cali-Manizales RR, on highway, and 15 mi. ENE of Cali; alt. 3,497 ft. Resort; communication, trading, and agr. center (tobacco, coffee, sugar cane, corn, rice, vegetables, cattle). Has natl. research station and experimental farm. Town founded c.1794. La Manuelita, 3 mi. NNE, is site of large sugar plantation and refinery.

Palmira, village (dist. pop. 841), Guanacaste prov., NW Costa Rica, on Tempisque R. and 5 mi. NNW of Filadelfia; lumbering, stock raising.

Palmira, town (pop. 5,865), Las Villas prov., central Cuba, on railroad and 7 mi. NNE of Cienfuegos; sugar-growing center; several adjoining centrals.

Palmira, village, Chimborazo prov., S central Ecuador, on Quito-Guayaquil RR, on Pan American Highway at one of its high Andean crests (10,617 ft.), and 28 mi. SSW of Riobamba; stock grazing. Sometimes Palmyra.

Palmira, Italy: see OPPIDO LUCANO.

Palmira (pälmē'rä), town (pop. 901), Táchira state, W Venezuela, in Andean spur, 5 mi. N of San Cristóbal; coffeegrowing.

Palm Islands, coral group in Coral Sea, 7 mi. off E coast of Queensland, Australia, within Great Barrier Reef, at entrance to Halifax Bay. Consists of 20 isls. and rocks; largest, GREAT PALM ISLAND; wooded, fertile. Sheep, agr. products (peanuts, pineapples, sugar cane).

Palmital (pŭlmētäl'), city (pop. 3,182), W São Paulo, Brazil, on railroad and 25 mi. WNW of Ourinhos, in coffee zone; lead smelting, tile mfg., manioc milling, sawmilling.

Palmitas (pälmē'täs), village (pop. 150), Soriano dept., SW Uruguay, on railroad and highway, and 20 mi. SE of Mercedes; wheat, oats, corn, sheep, cattle.

Palmito (pälmē'tō), town (pop. 2,082), Bolívar dept., N Colombia, in Caribbean lowlands, 20 mi. ENE of Lorica; corn, fruit, livestock.

Palmito, El, Mexico: see EL PALMITO.

Palmnicken, Russian SFSR: see YANTARNY.

Palmoli (päl'mōlē), village (pop. 2,251), Chieti prov., Abruzzi e Molise, S central Italy, 14 mi. SSW of Vasto.

Palms, SW residential section of LOS ANGELES city, Los Angeles co., S Calif., adjoining Culver City (SE).

Palms, Isle of, S.C.: see ISLE OF PALMS.

Palm Springs, winter-resort city (pop. 7,660), Riverside co., S Calif., in N Coachella Valley, at E base of Mt. San Jacinto, 40 mi. ESE of Redlands; surrounded by Agua Caliente Indian Reservation, which has sulphur springs. Near by are Palm Canyon, with ancient grove of native palms, and Tahquitz Bowl, a natural amphitheater. Founded 1876, inc. 1938; developed as luxurious desert resort in early 1930s.

Palmyra, Brazil: see SANTOS DUMONT.

Palmyra, Ecuador: see PALMIRA.

Palmyra (pălmī'rŭ), atoll (pop. 32), comprising 55 islets; in Line Isls., central Pacific, 1,100 mi. SSW of Honolulu, T.H.; 5°52'N 162°6'W; under jurisdiction of City and County of Honolulu. An American discovery (1802); annexed by U.S. (1912); U.S. naval air base authorized (1939). In 1947 Supreme Court ruled against govt.'s claim on isl., which is owned by private citizens.

Palmyra, anc. city of central Syria, an oasis at N edge of the Syrian Desert, 130 mi. NE of Damascus, 90 mi. E of Homs. Was important in Syrian-Babylonian trade by 1st cent. B.C. Tradition says it was founded by Solomon, and it appears in the Bible as Tadmor [city of palms]. Became of true importance only after Roman control was established, probably in the reign of Tiberius. Local tribes vied for control, which fell to the Septimii by

3d cent. A.D. The greatest of them, Septimius Odenathus, built Palmyra into a strong autonomous state that practically embraced the Eastern Empire, with Syria, NW Mesopotamia, and W Armenia. After his death his widow, Zenobia, briefly increased the territory by conquering Egypt and most of Asia Minor, making Palmyra one of the great cities of the empire. But her ambition brought on (A.D. 272) attack by Aurelian, who was victorious (at Homs) and partly destroyed the city. Palmyra, in decline, was taken by the Arabs and sacked by Tamerlane and fell into ruin. Even the ruins were forgotten until 17th cent. The great temple dedicated to Baal and other remains show the oriental splendor of Palmyra at its prime. A small village (pop. c.2,000), called Tadmor or Tadmur in Arabic, is on the site, with orchards, palm trees, olives, dates. The Kirkuk-Tripoli oil pipe line passes through Palmyra.

Palmyra. 1 Village (pop. 746), Macoupin co., SW central Ill., 30 mi. SW of Springfield, in agr., coal, and timber area. **2** Town (pop. 327), Harrison co., S Ind., 18 mi. WNW of New Albany; stone quarries; timber. **3** Agr. town (pop. 965), Somerset co., central Maine, on the Sebasticook and 18 mi. ENE of Skowhegan. **4** City (pop. 2,295), ⊙ Marion co., NE Mo., on North R., near Mississippi R. and 10 mi. NW of Hannibal; agr.; lumber products. Settled c.1819. **5** Village (pop. 372), Otoe co., SE Nebr., 17 mi. ESE of Lincoln and on branch of Little Nemaha R. **6** Borough (pop. 5,802), Burlington co., SW N.J., on Delaware R. (bridged here) opposite Philadelphia and 5 mi. NE of Camden; mfg. (machinery, metal products, clothing); canning. Inc. 1923. **7** Village (pop. 3,034), Wayne co., W N.Y., on the Barge Canal and 20 mi. ESE of Rochester, in fruit- and truck-growing area; mfg. (packings, machine parts, canned foods, paper boxes). Agr. (dairy products; potatoes, fruit, truck). Joseph Smith lived and published The Book of Mormon here. **8** Town (pop. 67), Halifax co., NE N.C., 15 mi. NE of Tarboro, near Roanoke R. **9** Borough (pop. 5,910), Lebanon co., SE central Pa., 14 mi. ENE of Harrisburg; limestone; mfg. (textiles, leather goods, paper boxes). Settled 1749, inc. 1913. **10** Village, ⊙ Fluvanna co., central Va., on Rivanna R. and 16 mi. SE of Charlottesville. **11** Village (pop. 862), Jefferson co., SE Wis., 26 mi. NE of Janesville, in agr. and resort region; flour milling.

Palmyras Point (pălmī'rŭz), headland on Bay of Bengal, Cuttack dist., E Orissa, India, 75 mi. ENE of Cuttack, at mouth of combined outlet of Baitarani and Brahmani rivers; 20°45'N 87°E.

Palni (pŭl'nē), city (pop. 24,706), Madura dist., S Madras, India, 55 mi. NW of Madura, in tobacco and grain area; trade center for products (coffee, cardamom, turmeric, fruit) of Palni Hills (S) and Sirumalai Hills (SW); silk weaving; cattle market. Anc. Sivaite temple.

Palni Hills, E spur of S Western Ghats, SW Madras, India; extend c.50 mi. NE to area of Dindigul; up to 25 mi. wide; rise to 8,263 ft. in Ibex peak, to 8,221 ft. in Vembadi Shola peak. Mainly forested; produce subtropical agr. products (coffee, cardamom, rubber); eucalyptus, bamboo, fruit trees; rice on terraced slopes, irrigated by mtn. streams; cattle grazing. Kodaikanal lies on central plateau. S slopes sometimes called Kodaikanal Hills.

Palo (pă'lō), village, W Sask., near Whiteshore L. (11 mi. long), 40 mi. S of North Battleford; sodium-sulphate production.

Palo (pä'lō), town (1939 pop. 5,555; 1948 municipality pop. 27,253), E Leyte, Philippines, 6 mi. SSW of Tacloban; agr. center (rice, hemp).

Palo (pă'lō), town (pop. 285), Linn co., E Iowa, on Cedar R. and 9 mi. NW of Cedar Rapids, in agr. area.

Palo, El (ĕl pä'lō), E residential section of Málaga, Málaga prov., S Spain. Has Jesuit col.

Palo Alto (pă"lō ăl'tō, pă"lō), county (□ 561; pop. 15,891), NW Iowa; ⊙ Emmetsburg. Prairie agr. area (cattle, hogs, poultry, corn, oats, soybeans) drained by West Des Moines R. Has lake region with state parks. Sand and gravel pits. Formed 1851.

Palo Alto (pă"lō ăl'tō). **1** Residential city (pop. 25,475), Santa Clara co., W Calif., 30 mi. SSE of San Francisco, near S end of San Francisco Bay, which is crossed near here by Dumbarton Bridge (c.1½ mi. long over water) to Alameda co. (E). Seat of Stanford Univ. Founded 1891; inc. as town 1894, as city 1909. **2** Borough (pop. 1,767), Schuylkill co., E central Pa., on Schuylkill R. opposite Pottsville. Laid out c.1844, inc. 1854. **3** Town, Texas: see BROWNSVILLE.

Palo Blanco (pä'lō blăng'kō), village (pop. 1,444), Piura dept., NW Peru, on W slopes of Cordillera Occidental, 30 mi. SSE of Ayabaca; wheat, corn.

Palo del Colle (pä'lô dĕl kôl'lĕ), town (pop. 11,897), Bari prov., Apulia, S Italy, 10 mi. SW of Bari; wine, olive oil.

Palo Duro Canyon (pă'lů dû'rō, dū'rů), extreme N Texas, in the Panhandle, c.15 mi. SE of Amarillo. A colorful gorge gashed in Cap Rock escarpment by Prairie Dog Town Fork of Red R., it reveals 4 geologic ages. Here is a state park (c.15,000 acres), with camping and other recreational facilities. Explored by Coronado's expedition, 1541; in 19th cent., Col. Charles Goodnight drove a herd through canyon to establish 1st Panhandle ranch.

Palo Duro Creek or **Paloduro Creek,** extreme N Texas, in the Panhandle, rises in Deaf Smith co., flows c.60 mi. generally E to join Tierra Blanca Creek near Canyon to form Prairie Dog Town Fork of Red R., whose scenic gorge, beginning just E of Canyon, is called PALO DURO CANYON.

Palo Gordo (pä'lō gôr'dō), village (pop. 120), Suchitepéquez dept., SW Guatemala, in Pacific piedmont, 6 mi. ESE of Mazatenango, on railroad; sugar milling. Rail junction of branch to San Antonio (N).

Palo Grande (pä'lō grän'dā), village, Chinandega dept., W Nicaragua, on Río Negro (Honduras border) and 8 mi. WSW of Somotillo; sugar cane, rice, corn, beans.

Paloh (pälō'), town (pop. 1,571), central Johore, Malaya, on railroad and 65 mi. NW of Johore Bharu, rubber plantations.

Paloma, La, Uruguay: see LA PALOMA.

Paloma, La, Venezuela: see LA PALOMA.

Palomaní (pälōmänē'), Andean peak (18,924 ft.) in the Nudo de Apolobamba, on Peru-Bolivia border, 45 mi. SW of Huancané; 14°43'S 69°15'W.

Palomar, El, Argentina: see EL PALOMAR.

Palomar, Mount (pă'lōmär) (6,126 ft.), S Calif., 45 mi. NNE of San Diego. Site of Mt. Palomar Observatory, operated jointly by Calif. Inst. of Technology and the Carnegie Institution; the 200-inch disk of its reflecting telescope, largest in world, was installed in 1947–48. Palomar Mountain State Park (c.1,700 acres; recreational facilities) is on mtn. slope.

Palomares del Campo (pälōmä'rĕs dhĕl käm'pō), town (pop. 1,933), Cuenca prov., E central Spain, 26 mi. WSW of Cuenca; wheat, grapes, olives, livestock; flour milling, olive-oil pressing.

Palomares del Río (rē'ō), town (pop. 679), Seville prov., SW Spain, 6 mi. SW of Seville; olives, cereals.

Palomas (pälō'mäs), town (pop. 949), Badajoz prov., W Spain, 15 mi. E of Almendralejo; olive growing.

Palomas, village, Salto dept., NW Uruguay, on railroad and 29 mi. NE of Salto, in agr. region (cereals, cattle, sheep, horses).

Palombara Sabina (pälômbä'rä säbē'nä), town (pop. 4,771), Roma prov., Latium, central Italy, 7 mi. N of Tivoli.

Palombe (pälōm'bā), road center, Southern Prov., SE Nyasaland, in Fort Lister Gap, N of Mlanje Mts., 45 mi. E of Blantyre, in agr. area; cotton, tea, coffee, tobacco. Just E is Fort Lister, a former Br. military post (founded 1893), used in slave-trade suppression.

Palomo, Cerro del (sĕ'rō dĕl pälō' mō), Andean peak (15,930 ft.), O'Higgins prov., central Chile, 40 mi. SE of Rancagua.

Palompon (pälōmpōn'), town (1939 pop. 4,290; 1948 municipality pop. 30,858), W Leyte, Philippines, port on Camotes Sea, 45 mi. WSW of Tacloban; agr. center (rice, sugar cane).

Paloncha (pä'lōnchŭ), town (pop. 5,593), Warangal dist., SE Hyderabad state, India, 4 mi. NE of coal-mining center of Kottagudem; rice, oilseeds.

Palo Negro (pä'lō nä'grō), town (pop. 3,147), Aragua state, N Venezuela, on small Aragua R., near E shore of L. Valencia, and 6 mi. SSE of Maracay; agr. center (coffee, cacao, sugar cane, corn, fruit, cattle).

Palo Pinto (pă'lů pĭn'tů), county (□ 982; pop. 17,154), N central Texas; ⊙ Palo Pinto. Crossed NW–SE by Brazos R.; part of Possum Kingdom L. is in NW. Palo Pinto Mts. (c.1,450 ft.) in W. Agr., ranching, resort region (includes MINERAL WELLS); peanuts, corn, grain sorghums, wheat, fruit, truck, pecans; cattle, horses, hogs, sheep, goats (wool, mohair marketed), poultry; dairying. Oil, natural gas, coal, clay. Ships mineral salts. Hunting, fishing. Timber (mainly cedar). Formed 1856.

Palo Pinto, village (pop. c.500), ⊙ Palo Pinto co., N central Texas, 55 mi. W of Fort Worth, near the Brazos, in farm, ranch area.

Palopo (pŭlō'pō), town (pop. 4,208), central Celebes, Indonesia, port on Gulf of Boni, at base of SW peninsula, 160 mi. NNE of Macassar; 2°59'S 120°12'E. Trade center for rice-growing region; exports copra, rattan.

Palos (pä'lōs), town (pop. 3,665), Havana prov., W Cuba, on railroad and 45 mi. SE of Havana, in sugar-growing region.

Palos or **Palos de la Frontera** (pä'lōs dhā lä frōntā'-rä), city (pop. 1,856), Huelva prov., SW Spain, in Andalusia, on estuary of the Río Tinto and 3½ mi. SE of Huelva, in winegrowing region. From its port (now silted up) Columbus sailed on his 1st voyage (Aug. 3, 1492), and returned here in March, 1493. Cortés landed here (1528) after his conquest of Mexico. Near La Rábida monastery (2 mi. SW), where Columbus laid out his plans, is a monument to him. Palos is sometimes also called Palos de Moguer.

Palos, Cape (pä'lōs), on the Mediterranean, in Murcia prov., SE Spain, 16 mi. ENE of Cartagena; 37°38'N 0°40'W. Lighthouse.

Palosco (pälō'skô), village (pop. 2,017), Bergamo prov., Lombardy, N Italy, near Oglio R., 11 mi. SE of Bergamo; mfg. (compasses, agr. tools).

Palos de la Frontera, Spain: see PALOS.

Palo Seco (pä'lō sĕ'kō), leper colony, Balboa dist., S Panama Canal Zone, on Panama Bay, near Pacific entrance of the Canal, 3½ mi. SW of Panama city.

Palo Seco (pä'lō sĕ'kō), village (pop. 1,063), SW Trinidad, B.W.I., 15 mi. SW of San Fernando; petroleum wells.

Palos Park (pā'lŭs, pä'lōs), village (pop. 854), Cook co., NE Ill., SW suburb of Chicago, 15 mi. NE of Joliet. Argonne Natl. Laboratory for atomic research is here.

Palos Verdes Estates (pă"lŭs vûr'dĭs), suburban residential city (pop. 1,963), Los Angeles co., S Calif., in Palos Verdes Hills near the Pacific, 16 mi. SSE of Santa Monica. Palos Verdes Col. is at near-by Rolling Hills. Inc. 1939.

Palos Verdes Hills, S Calif., low rolling range (up to 1,300 ft.) occupying peninsula bet. Santa Monica Bay (NW) and San Pedro Bay (SE); San Pedro city at SE base. Sometimes called San Pedro Hills.

Palourde, Lake (pŭlōōrd'), SE La., just NE of Morgan City; c.6 mi. long, 3 mi. wide. Entered from N by Grand R., and crossed by channel of Plaquemine–Morgan City Waterway; joined by waterways to Grand L. (W) and L. Verret (N).

Palouriotissa (pälōōryô'tēsä), E suburb (pop. 2,369) of Nicosia, N central Cyprus; vegetables; sheep, cattle.

Palouse (pŭlōōs', pă–), city (pop. 1,036), Whitman co., SE Wash., 12 mi. E of Colfax and on Palouse R., near Idaho line; wheat, peas, oats, lumber; canneries. Settled 1876, inc. 1889.

Palouse Falls, Wash.: see PALOUSE RIVER.

Palouse River, in N Idaho and SE Wash., rises in Latah co., Idaho, flows c.140 mi. generally W, past Palouse and Colfax, Wash., to Snake R. 22 mi. NW of Dayton. Drops over Palouse Falls (198 ft. high) a few miles above mouth. Lumbering and agr. (wheat, livestock) in river basin.

Palo Verde. 1 Village, Imperial co., Calif.: see PALO VERDE VALLEY. **2** Town, Lincoln co., N.Mex.: see GREEN TREE.

Palo Verde Valley (pă"lō vûr'dē), SE Calif., irrigated desert basin in Imperial and Riverside counties, extending c.40 mi. bet. Colorado R. (E) and low desert ranges (W). Blythe is chief town; in valley also are Midland (gypsum mining), Ripley (pop. c.125; in Riverside co.), Palo Verde (pop. c.100; in Imperial co.). Alfalfa, grain, cotton, fruit, truck, dairy products.

Palpa (päl'pŭ) or **Tansing** (tän'sĭng), town, S Nepal, in Mahabarat Lekh range, 12 mi. NNE of Butwal; trades in corn, wheat, millet, buckwheat, barley, rice, fruit, vegetables. Nepalese military post.

Palpa (päl'pä). **1** City (pop. 2,171), Ica dept., SW Peru, on Palpa R. (affluent of the Río Grande), on highway, and 60 mi. SE of Ica; cotton, grain, livestock. **2** Village (pop. 1,466), Lima dept., W central Peru, 5 mi. ENE of Huaral; rail terminus; cotton-growing center.

Palpalá (pälpälä'), village (pop. estimate 500), SE Jujuy prov., Argentina, on railroad and 7 mi. SE of Jujuy, in agr. area. Has blast furnace, brick-works; iron deposits near by.

Palpana, Cerro (sĕ'rō pälpä'nä), Andean peak (19,815 ft.), N Chile, near Bolivia border; 21°32'S.

Palsana (pŭlsä'nŭ), town (pop. 3,192), Surat dist., N Bombay, India, 11 mi. SE of Surat; cotton, millet grown.

Palsboda (pōls'bōō"dä), Swedish *Pålsboda*, village (pop. 942), Orebro co., S central Sweden, 15 mi. SSE of Orebro; rail junction; metalworking.

Paltamo (päl'tämō), village (commune pop. 8,201), Oulu co., central Finland, on L. Oulu, 5 mi. NW of Kajaani, in lumbering region. Site of agr. and domestic-science school. Has church (1726).

Paltinis, Rumania: see RASINARI.

Palti Tso, Tibet: see YAMDROK TSO.

Palu (pälōō'), village (pop. 7,487), Elazig prov., E central Turkey, on railroad, on Murat R., and 40 mi. E of Elazig; grain, lentils, fruit.

Palua (päl'wä), river port, Bolívar state, SE Venezuela, on Orinoco R. near San Félix; ore transshipment point for El Pao mines (S), connected by rail line; developed in 1940s.

Palud, La (lä pälüd'), village (pop. 107), Basses-Alpes dept., SE France, 10 mi. SW of Castellane, in Provence Alps. Starting point for excursion through Verdon R. canyon.

Paluoja or **Paluoya,** Estonia: see ABJA-PALUOJA.

Palur, India: see PANRUTI.

Palus Maeotis: see AZOV, SEA OF.

Paluxy Creek (pŭlŭk'sē), N central Texas, rises in several streams NE of Stephenville, flows 25 mi. generally ESE, past Glen Rose, to the Brazos.

Palvantash (pŭlvŭntäsh'), town (1947 pop. over 500), S Andizhan oblast, Uzbek SSR, c.10 mi. SE of Leninsk, near Markhamat; oil wells developed in mid 1940s.

Palwal (pŭl'vŭl), town (pop. 13,606), Gurgaon dist., SE Punjab, India, 28 mi. SE of Gurgaon; trade center for cotton, grain, sugar, oilseeds; cotton ginning, hand-loom weaving.

Pamalang, Indonesia: see PEMALANG.

Pamalombe, Lake, Nyasaland: see MALOMBE, LAKE.
Pamangkat (pùmäng-kät'), town (pop. 4,292), W Borneo, Indonesia, port at mouth of small Sambas R., on S.China Sea, 18 mi. N of Singkawang; 1°11'N 108°59'E. Trade center, shipping copra, rubber, pepper. Also spelled Pemangkat.
Pamarru (pä'mŭrōō), town (pop. 7,696), Kistna dist., NE Madras, India, in Kistna R. delta, 17 mi. NW of Masulipatam; rice, tobacco, coconuts. Sometimes spelled Pamaru.
Pambak (pŭmbäk'), NE suburb (1939 pop. over 2,000) of Kirovakan, Armenian SSR; granite quarries. Formerly spelled Bambak. Inc. c.1940 into Kirovakan.
Pamban (päm'bŭn), village (pop. 2,569), Ramnad dist., S Madras, India, on Pamban Channel, 85 mi. SE of Madura, on W shore of Rameswaram Isl.; exports coral.
Pamban Channel, in Indian Ocean bet. peninsular India and Rameswaram Isl.; joins Palk Strait (N) and Gulf of Mannar (S); 1⅓ mi. wide; crossed by rail causeway (drawbridge just W of Pamban). Admits shallow-draught vessels.
Pamban Island, India: see RAMESWARAM ISLAND.
Pambotis, Lake, Greece: see IOANNINA, LAKE.
Pambrun, Mount (10,400 ft.), SE B.C., in Selkirk Mts., 50 mi. NE of Nelson; 50°6'N 116°35'W.
Pamekasan (pämĕkùsän'), chief town (pop. 13,403) of Madura, Indonesia, near S coast of isl., 50 mi. E of Surabaya; 7°10'S 113°28'E; trade center for agr. area (tobacco, rice, corn, peanuts); textile mills.
Pamel (pä'mùl), village (pop. 4,907), Brabant prov., central Belgium, on Dender R. and 12 mi. W of Brussels; strawberries.
Pamhagen (päm'hägùn), village (pop. 2,125), Burgenland, E Austria, 15 mi. E of Sopron, Hungary, across Neusiedler L.; sugar beets.
Pamidi (pä'mĭdē), town (pop. 5,807), Anantapur dist., NW Madras, India, on Penner R. and 18 mi. N of Anantapur; hand-printed chintz; rice, cotton, oilseeds.
Pamiers (pämyā'), town (pop. 9,641), Ariège dept., S France, on Ariège R. and 34 mi. SSE of Toulouse; commercial and road center; electrometallurgical plants, hosiery and carton factories. Hydroelectric plant inaugurated 1950. Cathedral has fine 14th-cent. octagonal tower.
Pamiongchi, India: see NAMCHI.
Pamir or the **Pamirs** (pämērz'), elevated region of Central Asia, forming part of PAMIR-ALAI mtn. system; bordered N by Trans-Alai Range, W by Panj R., S by the Hindu Kush, E by Sarikol Range. Major part of territory is in USSR, E and S edges in China and Afghanistan. High plains (alt. 11–13,000 ft.) in E, deeply dissected mtn. country in W; drained by affluents of Panj R. and by inland basins (Kara-Kul, Rang-Kul). Highest peaks (over 20,000 ft.) are in AKADEMIYA NAUK RANGE (USSR). Stalin Peak (24,590 ft.) is highest in USSR. Dry, continental climate; quartz and gold deposits. USSR section is contained in Gorno-Badakhshan Autonomous Oblast, Tadzhik SSR. Called by natives Bam-i-Dunya [roof of the world].
Pamir-Alai or **Pamir-Alay** (pŭmēr"-ŭlī'), one of main mountain systems of Central Asia, in USSR (major portion), China, and Afghanistan; extends from the Tien Shan (N) to the Hindu Kush and Kunlun mts. (S). Includes the PAMIR, TRANS-ALAI RANGE, PETER THE FIRST RANGE, and AKADEMIYA NAUK RANGE. The southwesternmost outlier of the Tien Shan, the parallel Turkestan, Zeravshan, and Gissar ranges, are sometimes considered part of the Pamir-Alai system.
Pamir River, right headstream of Panj R., on USSR-Afghanistan border; rises in Zor-Kul (lake); flows c.65 mi. WSW, joining Wakhan R. near Qala Panja to form PANJ RIVER.
Pamirski Post, Tadzhik SSR: see MURGAB.
Pamisos River (pä'mĭsôs), Lat. *Pamisus,* in SW Peloponnesus, Greece, rises in Minthis mts., flows 27 mi. SSE, past Messene, to Gulf of Messenia, 5 mi. W of Kalamata; nonnavigable. Formerly Pirnatsa R.
Pamlico (păm'lĕkō, -lĭkō), county (□ 341; pop. 9,993), E N.C., on the Atlantic; ⊙ Bayboro. Forested and swampy tidewater area; bounded by Pamlico Sound (E), Neuse R. (S). Farming (potatoes, corn, tobacco), fishing, lumbering. Formed 1872.
Pamlico River, N.C.: see TAR RIVER.
Pamlico Sound, E N.C., separated from the Atlantic by narrow barrier beaches, the easternmost of which terminates in Cape Hatteras; c.80 mi. long N–S, 25 mi. wide; joins Albemarle Sound (N). Receives Pamlico (Tar) and Neuse rivers.
Pa-mo Hu, Tibet: see BAM TSO.
Pampa or **Pampas** (păm'pù, -pùz, Sp. päm'pä, -päs), vast, treeless, fertile plain of S South America, particularly in central E Argentina. Bounded W by the Andean piedmont, N by the Chaco, E by the Atlantic, and S (along the Río Colorado) by Patagonia. Gradually rising from E to W, the region includes the humid Pampa, the economic heart (cattle, flax, grain) of Argentina, which extends W to c.64°W (20-inch isohyet). Its rich agr. products are shipped through Buenos Aires and Bahía Blanca. Bet. the humid Pampa and the Andean piedmont lies the dry Pampa, a more arid section with low, scrubby trees and grass (*monte*) vegetation. The humid Pampa, once covered by tall prairie grass but now largely under cultivation, includes Buenos Aires, Santa Fe, and Córdoba provs., and sections of San Luis and Santiago del Estero provs. The natl. territory of LA PAMPA is largely in the dry Pampa.
Pampa (păm'pù), city (pop. 16,583), ⊙ Gray co., extreme N Texas, in rich Panhandle oil, natural-gas field, c.55 mi. NE of Amarillo; railroad junction, shipping and distributing center for wheat and livestock region, with oil and gas wells and refineries, carbon-black plants; mfg. of oil-well equipment and supplies, chemicals; cotton gins, grain elevators.
Pampa Aullagas (päm'pä ouyä'gäs), town (pop. c.1,400), Oruro dept., W Bolivia, in the Altiplano near SW shore of L. Poopó, 55 mi. SW of Poopó; alt. 12,155 ft. Name sometimes applied to L. POOPÓ.
Pampa Baja (päm'pä bä'hä), town (pop.1,377), Coquimbo prov., N central Chile, near the Pacific, on railroad and 2 mi. SW of La Serena; agr. center (grain, vegetables, fruit, wine, livestock).
Pampa Blanca (päm'pä bläng'kä), town (pop. estimate 500), SE Jujuy prov., Argentina, on railroad and 28 mi. SE of Jujuy; lumbering and agr. center (sugar cane, cotton, rice, alfalfa, wine, tobacco, vegetables, livestock); cotton ginning.
Pampachiri (pämpächē'rē), town (pop. 712), Apurímac dept., S central Peru, in Andean spur, on affluent of Pampas R. and 35 mi. SSW of Andahuaylas; grain, livestock. Coal deposits.
Pampacolca (pämpäkōl'kä), town (pop. 1,969), Arequipa dept., S Peru, at S foot of the Nudo Coropuna, 95 mi. NW of Arequipa; fruit, grapes, grain, livestock.
Pampa de las Salinas (päm'pä dā läs sälē'näs), salt desert (□ 1,050) in La Rioja and San Luis provs., Argentina, NW of the Sierra de San Luis, extends c.60 mi. N–S (c.18 mi. wide); contains sodium and potassium salts.
Pampa del Castillo (dĕl kästē'yō), village (pop. estimate 500), E Comodoro Rivadavia military zone, Argentina, on railroad and 29 mi. W of Comodoro Rivadavia; sheep-raising and oil-producing center.
Pampa del Chañar (chänyär') town (pop. estimate 1,000), N central San Juan prov., Argentina, 13 mi. N of Jachal; wheat, corn, alfalfa, wine, fruit, onions, livestock; apiculture. Lime deposits, limekilns. Sometimes called Chañar.
Pampa del Infierno (ĭnfyĕr'nō), town (pop. estimate 500), W Chaco natl. territory, Argentina, on railroad and 50 mi. NW of Presidencia Roque Sáenz Peña; lumbering, stock raising, cotton growing.
Pampa de los Silva (dā lōs sĕl'vä), town (pop. 1,121), Piura dept., NW Peru, in lower Piura valley, 12 mi. SSW of Piura, in irrigated cotton area.
Pampa del Sacramento (dĕl säkrämĕn'tō), highlands in San Martín and Loreto depts., E Peru, E Andean outliers W of upper Ucayali R. and running parallel to Cordillera Azul; c.60 mi. NW–SE.
Pampa Grande (päm'pä grän'dā), town (pop. c.1,900), Santa Cruz dept., central Bolivia, in E foothills of Cordillera de Cochabamba, 20 mi. WNW of Samaipata, on Cochabamba–Santa Cruz road; corn.
Pampa Grande, village (pop. 1,687), Lambayeque dept., NW Peru, in W foothills of Cordillera Occidental, on Chancay R. and 25 mi. E of Chiclayo; rice, corn.
Pampán (pämpän'), town (pop. 1,969), Trujillo state, W Venezuela, 5 mi. NNW of Trujillo; coffee, sugar cane, corn.
Pampana River (pämpä'nä), headstream of Jong R., central Sierra Leone. Gold dredgings in Tonkolili dist.
Pampanga (pämpäng'gä), province (□ 827; 1948 pop. 416,583), central Luzon, Philippines, bounded S by Manila Bay; ⊙ SAN FERNANDO. Largely a plain, drained by Pampanga R. Rising in central part of prov. is Mt. Arayat (3,378 ft.). Agr. (rice, sugar cane), fishing. The prov. is known for handmade buri-palm hats.
Pampanga River or **Rio Grande de la Pampanga** (rē'ō grän'dā dā lä), second largest river of Luzon, Philippines, in central area, rises in several branches in mts. in Nueva Ecija prov. near Carranglan, flows 120 mi. generally SW, past Cabanatuan, Arayat, and Candaba, thence through marshy area to Manila Bay 25 mi. NW of Manila; has wide delta. Navigable c.45 mi. by small craft, but no longer important as transportation route.
Pampanito (pämpänē'tō), town (pop. 2,158), Trujillo state, W Venezuela, on transandine highway and 5 mi. NW of Trujillo, in agr. region (coffee, corn, sugar cane, cacao, tobacco).
Pampas, plain, South America: see PAMPA.
Pampas (päm'päs). **1** Town (pop. 1,826), Ancash dept., W central Peru, in Cordillera Occidental, 15 mi. NNE of Cabana; mining center (copper, lead, silver, tungsten). **2** City (pop. 1,761), ⊙ Tayacaja prov. (□ 1,654; pop. 91,263), Huancavelica dept., S central Peru, in Cordillera Central, on highway, and 30 mi. NNE of Huancavelica; alt. 10,725 ft. Distilling, mfg. of native leather goods; sugar cane, grain, cattle, sheep.
Pampas River, S central Peru, rises in Andean lakes in Cordillera Occidental 10 mi. ENE of Castrovirreyna, flows 200 mi. generally E, past Cangallo, to the Apurímac 26 mi. WNW of Abancay. Receives the San Miguel (left). Forms Ayacucho–Apurímac dept. border in lower course.
Pampatar (pämpätär'), town (pop. 2,177), port on Margarita Isl. (SE), Nueva Esparta state, NE Venezuela, on the Caribbean, 6 mi. SE of La Asunción; main export and import center of isl.; exports pearls; fishing.
Pampa Vieja (päm'pä vyā'hä), town (pop. estimate 500), N central San Juan prov., Argentina, 6 mi. N of Jachal; wine making, lime processing, flour milling.
Pampelonne (päpùlôn'), village (pop. 412), Tarn dept., S France, near the Viaur, 15 mi. NNE of Albi; dairying. Hydroelectric plant at Tanus (3 mi. E).
Pampeluna, Spain: see PAMPLONA.
Pamphylia (pămfĭ'lēù), anc. region of S Asia Minor, occupying W part of S Anatolian coast, in present Turkey; its cities included Perga and Aspendus. Lycia was on SW, Pisidia on N, and Cilicia on SE. It was not a political entity except in the provincial administration of Rome.
Pampichuela (pämpēchwā'lä), village (pop. estimate 500), ⊙ Valle Grande dept. (□ 390; 1947 census 2,128), E central Jujuy prov., Argentina, 50 mi. NE of Jujuy, in corn and livestock area.
Pampilhosa or **Pampilhosa do Botão** (pämpēlyô'zù dōō bōōtā'ō), village (pop. 1,015), Aveiro dist., N central Portugal, 9 mi. N of Coimbra; rail junction; pottery mfg. Has restored Gothic church.
Pampilhosa da Serra (dù sĕ'rù), town (pop. 676), Coimbra dist., N central Portugal, 27 mi. ESE of Coimbra; lumbering, resin extracting.
Pamplemousses (päplùmōōs'), town (pop. 947), N Mauritius, on railroad and 6 mi. NE of Port Louis; sugar milling. Site of botanical gardens and Royal Alfred Observatory.
Pamplico (păm'plĭkō), town (pop. 728), Florence co., E central S.C., 17 mi. SE of Florence; tobacco, lumber, veneer.
Pampliega (pämplyā'gä), town (pop. 1,047), Burgos prov., N Spain, on Arlanzón R. and 17 mi. SW of Burgos; wheat, grapes, vegetables, potatoes, sheep. In vicinity was old monastery of San Vicente, where Visigothic king Wamba retired.
Pamplin or **Pamplin City** (păm'plĭn), town (pop. 370), Appomattox and Prince Edward counties, S central Va., 27 mi. ESE of Lynchburg; rail junction.
Pamplona (pämplō'nä), town (pop. 13,126), Norte de Santander dept., N Colombia, in Cordillera Oriental, on W bank of Pamplonita R., on Bogotá-Caracas highway and 36 mi. S of Cúcuta; alt. 7,677 ft. Lumbering, textile-milling, processing, and agr. center (coffee, cacao, wheat, corn, tobacco, livestock); distilling, flour milling; brewery. Gold, copper, tin, and coal deposits near by. Old colonial town, founded 1548. Bishopric. Has cathedral, archives, mus., ruins of monasteries. Severely damaged by 1644 and 1875 earthquakes.
Pamplona, town (1939 pop. 6,468) in Tanjay municipality, Negros Oriental prov., SE Negros isl., Philippines, near Tañon Strait, 2 mi. SW of Tanjay; trade center for agr. area (corn, coconuts, sugar cane).
Pamplona (pămplō'nù, Sp. pämplō'nä), sometimes **Pampeluna** (pămpùlōō'nù, Sp. pämpälōō'nä), anc. *Pompaelo,* city (pop. 45,885), ⊙ Navarre prov., N Spain, in strategic position at exit of Pyrenean valleys, on Arga R. and 90 mi. WNW of Saragossa, and only 20 mi. from France; 42°49'N 1°39'W. A historic, fortified Basque town, now an industrial, commercial, and communications center. Industries, largely developed in 20th cent., include sugar milling, wine making, brewing, tanning, canning, meat packing, textile (cotton, hemp) milling; mfg. of firearms, viticultural machinery, furniture, shoes, fertilizers, flour products, chocolate, candies. Episcopal see. Notable are: Gothic cathedral (chiefly 14th–15th cent.), also noted for its modern (1780) façade and for its magnificent cloisters, where the Cortes of Navarre assembled; Gothic church of San Saturnino; 17th-cent. town hall with Sasarate mus.; and a 15th-cent. citadel. There are some remains of the recently demolished massive walls. The *Pompaelo* of the Romans, named for its probable founder Pompey, the city was repeatedly occupied (1st in 476) by the Visigoths, and sacked (778) by Charlemagne. It fell for a short time during 8th cent. to the Moors. Upon its reconquest it served as ⊙ kingdom of Navarre until taken (1512) by Ferdinand the Catholic, who united Navarre with Castile and Aragon, and installed a viceroy. Fortifications, built 1571 by Philip II, made it strongest fortress in Spain. During Peninsular War it was in possession of the French until taken (1813) by the duke of Wellington.
Pamplonita River (pämplōnē'tä), Norte de Santander dept., N Colombia, near Venezuela border, rises in Cordillera Oriental S of Pamplona, flows c.100 mi. N, past Pamplona and Cúcuta, to Zulia R. at Puerto Villamizar, 5 mi. from Venezuela line. Receives Táchira R.

Pampur (pămʹpŏŏr), anc. *Padmapura*, town (pop. 4,446), Anantnag dist., W central Kashmir, in Vale of Kashmir, on Jhelum R. and 8 mi. SE of Srinagar city center; hand-loom woolen weaving; rice, corn, oilseeds, saffron, wheat. Founded early-9th cent. A.D.; has 9th cent. Vishnuite temple ruins, anc. mosque. Extensive saffron growing near by.

Pamunkey River (pŭmŭngʹkē), E Va., formed c.20 mi. N of Richmond by junction of North Anna and South Anna rivers; flows c.90 mi. SE, joining Mattaponi R. at West Point to form York R. Navigable for 50 mi. above mouth; chief cargoes are grain, lumber.

Pamyati 13 Bortsov (pămʹyŭtyē trēnăʹtsŭtyē bŭrtsôfʹ) [Rus.,=in memory of 13 fighters], town (1926 pop. 3,121), SW Krasnoyarsk Territory, Russian SFSR, 25 mi. WNW of Krasnoyarsk; glass industry. Formerly Znamenski.

Pamyat Parizhskoi Kommuny or **Pamyat' Parizhskoy Kommuny** (–yŭtyŭ pŭrēshʹskoi kŭmōōʹnē), town (1939 pop. over 2,000), central Gorki oblast, Russian SFSR, on Volga R. and 25 mi. SE of Gorki; metalworks.

Pan, India: see PEN.

Pana (pāʹnŭ), city (pop. 6,178), Christian co., central Ill., 32 mi. SSW of Decatur; shipping center for bituminous-coal and agr. area (dairy products; poultry, grain); oil refinery; commercial rose growing. Inc. 1857.

Panabá (pänäbäʹ), town (pop. 1,191), Yucatan, SE Mexico, 12 mi. NW of Tizimín; henequen, chicle.

Panacachi (pänäkäʹchē), town (pop. c.4,200), Potosí dept., W central Bolivia, on E slopes of Eastern Cordillera of the Andes, 9 mi. ENE of Chayanta; truck produce, grain.

Panachaikon or **Panakhaikon** (both: pänäkhīkônʹ), Lat. *Panachaicus*, mountains in NW Peloponnesus, Greece, extend 15 mi. from Selinous R. NW to Cape Drepanon; rise to 6,317 ft. Formerly called Voidhias or Voidia.

Panache, Lake (pănăshʹ) (20 mi. long, 5 mi. wide), SE central Ont., 20 mi. SW of Sudbury.

Panadure (pŭnʹŭdōōrŭ), town (pop. 16,562), Western Prov., Ceylon, on SW coast, 15 mi. S of Colombo; trade (coconuts, cinnamon, tea, rubber, areca nuts, rice, arrack, pan) center; mfg. of coir rope, mats, brassware, silverware, agr. implements. Tamil invaders defeated here (12th cent. A.D.) by Singhalese and Portuguese and (17th cent.) by Dutch.

Panaetolius, Greece: see PANAITALIKON.

Panagyurishte (pänägyōōʹrĭshtĕ), city (pop. 12,015), Plovdiv dist., W central Bulgaria, in central Sredna Gora, on Luda Yana R. and 37 mi. NW of Plovdiv; rail spur terminus; agr. center; exports mutton and cheese; carpet mfg., woodworking, dairying. Copper mining near by (E). Developed as cloth-weaving center under Turkish rule; site of Bulg. uprising in 1876. Sometimes spelled Panagiurishte. Health resort Banya (pop. 1,715), 4 mi. SW, has thermal springs.

Panaitan, Indonesia: see PRINSEN.

Panaitolikon (pänĕtôlĭkônʹ), anc. *Panaetolius* (pănētōʹlyŭs), mountain range in W central Greece, on Acarnania-Eurytania line; 30 mi. long; rises to 6,313 ft. 10 mi. NE of Agrinion.

Panaitolion (pänĕtōʹlēōn), village (pop. 2,876), Acarnania nome, W central Greece, 3 mi. SE of Agrinion, near L. Trichonis; wheat, oats, tobacco; wine; livestock. Formerly called Moustafouli.

Panajachel (pänähächĕlʹ), market town (1950 pop. 1,901), Sololá dept., SW central Guatemala, on Inter-American Highway and 3 mi. SE of Sololá, near N shore of L. Atitlán, alt. 5,184 ft. Coffee, vegetables, sugar cane, corn, wheat. Just SW are lake ports and summer resorts of Tzunjuyú and Monterrey.

Panakhaikon, Greece: see PANACHAIKON.

Panaloya (pänäloiʹä), village, Granada dept., SW Nicaragua, on L. Nicaragua, at mouth of Tipitapa R., 13 mi. NNE of Granada; lumber; livestock.

Panama (păʹnŭmä″), Sp. *Panamá* (pänämäʹ), republic (□ 28,575, excluding Panama Canal Zone; 1940 pop. 622,576, including 55,987 tribal Indians; 1950 pop. 801,290), Central America; ⊙ PANAMA. Occupies the Isthmus of Panama, the narrowest section of the Americas bet. the Atlantic (Caribbean) and the Pacific oceans, and links Central America with South America. Bounded W by Costa Rica, E by Colombia, of which it was a dept. until 1903. Roughly bet. 7°15′–9°10′N and 77°15′–82°55′W, it forms a curved ribbon of land c.450 mi. in length E–W, varying from 32 to 113 mi. in width. AZUERO PENINSULA juts c.75 mi. S into the Pacific. Heavily indented coasts are fringed by numerous keys and isls., among them, in the Pacific, SAN MIGUEL ISLAND and PEARL ISLAND in the shallow Gulf of Panama, and COIBA ISLAND, a penal colony, in Gulf of Chiriquí. On the Caribbean side, in NW, is the MOSQUITO GULF. Tides are weak (c.2 ft.) on the Atlantic side but rise as much as 20 ft. on the Pacific. Narrow lowlands adjoin both shores. Largely mountainous and overlaid by fertile volcanic soil, the isthmus is traversed E–W by several ranges (Serranía de TABASARÁ, Cordillera de SAN BLAS, Serranía del Darién), rising in the inactive volcano CHIRIQUÍ to 11,410 ft. near the Costa Rican border. The center of the country is lower, with hills 200–1,500 ft., but rises again towards Colombian border. The PANAMA CANAL and transisthmian railroad use a low depression in the Latin American cordillera system. The climate is, apart from a few lofty upland areas, tropical throughout, with a mean annual temp. of 80°F. Seasonal (mid-May to mid-Dec.) rainfall is much heavier on the Caribbean side (c.150 inches) than on the Pacific (70 inches). All kinds of minerals (aluminum, iron, mercury, lead, nickel, cobalt, uranium, coal, limestone, silica, sulphur, asbestos) have been reported, but only gold (near SANTIAGO), silver, and manganese (near MANDINGA and NOMBRE DE DIOS) are mined. Salt is evaporated from the sea at AGUADULCE. Fishing (tuna, mackerel, snappers, corvina, sponges, pearls, tortoise shells, etc.) is excellent. The country is covered by vast, luxuriant forests (almost untapped) which yield fine hardwoods, cabinet woods, sasarparilla, ipecacuahu, vanilla. Although Panama depends to a large degree on the income from Panama Canal traffic, and despite its highly urbanized population—¼ live in Panama city and COLÓN alone—its economy is basically agricultural. Bananas (about 85% of all exports, but declining because of plant disease), coconuts, rubber, abacá (Bocas del Toro prov.), and cacao are grown for foreign trade. For home consumption and personnel of the Canal Zone: rice (the largest crop), coffee (chiefly from slopes of productive Chiriquí prov.), corn, sugar cane, beans, fresh vegetables, citrus, peanuts, yucca. Cattle are grazed exclusively in upland savannas. Small-scale industries include food processing, alcohol and whisky distilling, brewing; mfg. of cement, nails, plywood, furniture, ceramics, soap, shoes, perfumes. Unfavorable trade balance is somewhat compensated for by tourism, commerce resulting from canal traffic, and employment in the U.S. zone. Bulk of trade (overwhelmingly with the U.S.) passes through Panama city (also seat of 2 universities) and Colón, both enclaves at S and N gates of the 10-mi.-wide Panama Canal Zone. Minor ports are: on the Pacific—Aguadulce, PEDREGAL (the port of the W agr. center DAVID), PUERTO ARMUELLES, PUERTO MUTIS (serving Santiago), LA PALMA in Darién prov.; on the Atlantic—offshore isl. BOCAS DEL TORO. Apart from transisthmian railroad and highway, and the partly completed Inter-American Highway, communication in the underdeveloped hinterland is poor. There are a few local railroads in plantation areas of the W. Tocumen is airport near Panama city. The people are racially heterogeneous. Birth increase is relatively low, largely due to unhealthful conditions and economic hazards. About ⅔ are mestizo, 15% are Negro (principally from Jamaica), 10% are Indian. The people are overwhelmingly R.C. First European to disembark (1501) on the coast was Rodrigo de Bastidas, followed by Columbus who dropped anchor (1502) off the site of future PORTOBELO. In 1513 Vasco Núñez de Balboa made his momentous trip across the isthmus to the Pacific. Since then the region has played a major part as roadway. Panama became the route by which the treasure of the Inca empire went to Spain. In 1740 authority was transferred from viceroyalty of Peru to New Granada. A Scottish colonization plan (the Darien Scheme) in late 18th cent. failed. The immense wealth carried through its harbors attracted raids of Br. buccaneers, among them Sir Francis Drake and Sir Henry Morgan. With fall of Sp. empire, Panama became part of the federation of Greater Colombia and after the latter's dissolution (1830) of Colombia (originally called republic of New Granada). The settlement of the U.S. Northwest and the gold rush in California made the short route from Atlantic to Pacific of new importance. A railroad was built across 1848–55, and the question of a canal became paramount. A treaty with Colombia had already granted (1846) the U.S. transit rights. But the project ultimately led to a revolution which established a separate republic (Nov., 1903) with U.S. support. In 1914 Colombia recognized its independence. The American-controlled canal became the determinant of Panama history. Internal politics remained turbulent. Panama is a member of the United Nations. For further information see separate articles on PANAMA CANAL, towns, cities, physical features, and the following 9 provinces: BOCAS DEL TORO, COCLÉ, COLÓN, CHIRIQUÍ, DARIÉN, HERRERA, LOS SANTOS, Panama, VERAGUAS.

Panama, province (□ 4,452; 1950 pop. 247,027) of central Panama, on Pacific coast; ⊙ Panama. Divided into W and E sections by Panama Canal Zone; drained by Chepo and upper Chagres rivers. Includes Pearl Isls. (pearl fisheries) in Gulf of Panama of the Pacific (S). Agr.: plantains, coffee, citrus fruit, coconuts. Stock raising, lumbering. Gold mining (La Campana); manganese, iron, agate, chrome, limestone deposits. Fishing in Gulf of Panama. Prov. is served by Inter-American Highway and Panama RR. Main centers are Panama, La Chorrera, Chepo, Río Abajo, and San Francisco Formed originally in 1719, when it covered entire E section of Panama.

Panama, city (1950 pop. 122,693), ⊙ Panama and Panama prov., on Bay of Panama, near Pacific end of Panama Canal, 38 mi. SE of Colón; 8°57′N 79°32′W. Industrial and transportation center of Panama, on Inter-American Highway; linked with Colón by Panama RR and Trans-Isthmian Highway. Its port is Balboa, in the Canal Zone. Mfg. of beer, furniture, shoes, clothing, bakery products, beverages. Located on slopes of Ancon Hill, the city is geographically within Panama Canal Zone, but separated administratively from adjoining (W) Ancon. Panama city consists of old San Felipe section on rocky, rectangular peninsula (site of cathedral, San José church with golden altar, and other churches) of Santa Ana (developed in 18th cent.), and of the 20th-cent. residential sections of Chorrillo (S), Calidonia (N; developed by West Indian pop. employed in Panama Canal construction), and Bella Vista. Seat of Natl. Univ. and Inter-American Univ. Panama city was originally founded 5 mi. NE of present site, in 1519. It was a Sp. exploration base and transshipment point for Sp. colonial riches across the isthmus. Destroyed 1671 by Br. pirate Morgan, it was rebuilt 1673 on present site. City declined when gold shipments ceased (1746), but revived after 1848, during California gold rush and building (1848–55) of Panama RR. Became ⊙ Panama in 1903, and developed rapidly with construction of Panama Canal.

Panama. 1 Village (pop. 520), on Bond-Montgomery co. line, SW central Ill., 36 mi. ENE of Alton, in agr. area (corn, wheat, poultry; dairy products). **2** Town (pop. 230), Shelby co., W Iowa, on Mosquito Creek and 9 mi. WNW of Harlan. **3** Village (pop. 168), Lancaster co., SE Nebr., 16 mi. SSE of Lincoln. **4** Village (pop. 456), Chautauqua co., extreme W N.Y., 13 mi. W of Jamestown; lumber. **5** Town (pop. 1,027), Le Flore co., SE Okla., 20 mi. SW of Fort Smith (Ark.), and on Poteau R., in coal-mining, stock-raising, and farming area; makes hardware.

Panama, Bay of, N section of Gulf of Panama of the Pacific, E Panama, at S side of Isthmus of Panama; 75 mi. wide, 30 mi. long.

Panama, Gulf of, inlet of the Pacific in E Panama, at S side of Isthmus of Panama and E of Azuero Peninsula; 115 mi. wide, c.100 mi. long. It forms Parita Gulf (W), Bay of Panama (N), and San Miguel Gulf (E), and includes Pearl Isls. Fisheries.

Panama, Isthmus of, central Panama, bet. the Caribbean and Gulf of Panama of the Pacific, and bet. 79° and 80° W; crossed by Panama Canal. In a wider sense, the name is applied to the entire link bet. North America and South America, corresponding to the republic of Panama and including the isthmuses of Chiriquí (W) and Darien (E).

Panama Canal, waterway across the Isthmus of Panama in Central America, connecting the Atlantic (the Caribbean part) and the Pacific oceans, built by the U.S. on territory (Panama Canal Zone) leased in perpetuity from the republic of Panama. A lock-and-lake type of canal, it was built (1904–14) across the narrowest section of the Americas, where the great continental divide reaches one of its lowest points (c.275 ft.). It uses the valleys of CHAGRES RIVER and the Rio Grande, which lead to the Caribbean and Pacific respectively. The canal runs generally SE from its Atlantic ports, COLÓN (Panama) and CRISTOBAL on Limón Bay, to BALBOA (a suburb of Panama city), the Pacific terminus on Panama Bay. It is 40.27 mi. long from shore to shore and 50.72 mi. long bet. the 2 channel entrances. The Pacific entrance is therefore, paradoxically, 27.02 mi. E of the Atlantic entrance. The minimum depth is 41 ft., the bottom of the waterway at least 300 ft. wide. Transit averages 7–8 hrs. Traffic moves in both directions, since all locks are double; the locks are each 1,000 ft. long, 110 ft. wide, 70 ft. deep. From Limón Bay a ship is raised by the 3 sets of the Gatun Locks near GATUN to 85 ft. above sea level, traverses artificial L. GATUN (formed by impounding of Chagres R. by Gatun Dam) for c.24 mi., passing bet. JUAN GALLEGOS ISLAND (N) and BARRO COLORADO ISLAND (S), crosses the continental divide through the 8-mi.-long GAILLARD CUT (300 ft. wide; 45 ft. deep; formerly called Culebra Cut), is lowered 31 ft. by the single set of PEDRO MIGUEL Locks and finally by the 2 sets of the Miraflores Locks to the short sea-level canal which leads to the Pacific. The approaches to both ends of the canal are protected by breakwaters. Tidal range on the Pacific side averages 12.6 ft. and occasionally exceeds 20 ft., while the average is less than 1 ft. on the Atlantic. Since the canal's inauguration, a few additional features have been installed, foremost the construction of Madden Dam (completed 1935), which impounds L. MADDEN on upper Chagres R.; this helps to maintain level of L. Gatun in dry season. During the fiscal year 1949-50 the canal was used by 5,448 vessels with a cargo of 28,013,236 long tons. Plans for an interoceanic canal go back to early Sp. colonial era. The U.S., interested since late 18th cent. in trading voyages to the Pacific Northwest, became more concerned after settlers poured into Oregon, and the California gold rush attracted numerous migrants. A treaty with Colombia (then New Granada) granted (1846) the U.S. transit rights, and a railroad was built (1848-55) across the isthmus. At the same time another waterway, the Nicaragua Canal, was seriously considered both by Great Britain and the U.S., who came to an agreement by signing (1850) the Clayton-Bulwer Treaty, which guaranteed neutrality of any canal here; this was superseded 1901 by Hay-Pauncefote Treaty. Meanwhile a Fr. company, encouraged by completion of the Suez Canal, bought (1878) rights from Colombia and began construction under Ferdinand de Lesseps. But disease and mismanagement led (1889) to bankruptcy. A new company was formed (1894), later selling its rights to the U.S. The Hay-Herrán Treaty (signed Jan., 1903) with Colombia, which would have given the U.S. an isthmus strip, was not ratified by the Colombian senate. An insurrection (Nov. 3, 1903) set up a separate republic of Panama with U.S. support. The U.S. was granted (Hay-Bunau-Varilla Treaty) exclusive control of a canal zone in perpetuity, besides other sites necessary for defense, and sanitary supervision over Panama city and Colón. Panama received initial cash payment of $10,000,000 and an annuity of $250,000 (increased in 1939 to $430,000). Work was begun in 1904, when stamping out of yellow fever became the 1st great task, ably carried out by W. C. Gorgas. Actual construction, directed by Col. G. W. Goethals, took 7 years. Total cost amounted to $336,650,000 and about 240,000,000 cubic yards of earth were excavated. First ship passed the canal in Aug., 1914. Landslides have several times blocked (1915 and 1916) passage of Gaillard Cut. The limited capacity of the canal has long worried the U.S., and in Aug., 1939, Congress approved the building of a 3d set of locks. This plan was shelved with the outbreak of the Second World War, and post-war controversy centered on a sea-level route.

Panama Canal Zone or **Canal Zone,** administrative area (land area only, □ 372.49; with inland water surface, □ 558.56; including tidewater, □ 648; 1940 pop. 28,189; 1950 pop. 52,822) of the U.S., consists of a 10-mi.-wide strip astride the PANAMA CANAL, bounded by the Caribbean (NW) and the Pacific (SE), and forming a c.40-mi.-long NW-SE corridor in the republic of Panama. It is situated approximately bet. 8°50′–9°25′N and 79°30′–80°W. The zone is administered by a governor appointed by the president of the U.S., but in war time the governor is subordinate to the military commander. Seat of the civil administration is at BALBOA HEIGHTS. The zone is administratively divided into Cristobal and Balboa dists. Although all the area is government owned, sites may be leased to companies or individuals. Climate is tropical, with high rainfall on Atlantic side. Limited agr. activities include stock raising, growing of tropical fruit and sugar cane. Military and naval reservations guard the canal, at whose heads are the ports of CRISTOBAL on the Atlantic and BALBOA on the Pacific—virtually suburbs of Colón and Panama city respectively, in Panama. Region is crossed by the trans-isthmian Panama Railroad. Control over the Trans-Isthmian Highway—largely outside the zone—was transferred (1950) to Panama. History of the Panama Canal Zone is that of the canal.

Panama City, city (pop. 25,814), ⊙ Bay co., NW Fla., c.95 mi. ESE of Pensacola; port of entry on St. Andrew Bay; lumber- and paper-milling, fishing, and resort center. Peat mines, Tyndall Air Force Base near by. Inc. as city in 1909 after merger with adjacent Millville and St. Andrew.

Panama City Beach, resort village (pop. c.500), Bay co., NW Fla., on St. Andrew Bay, just W of Panama City.

Pan American Highway, projected system of roads, 15,714 mi. long, to link the nations of the Western Hemisphere. Suggested at the Fifth International Conference of American States (1923), the system was in 1950 more than 80% complete. A few gaps remained in the section, called the INTER-AMERICAN HIGHWAY, bet. the U.S. and the Panama Canal; the route from the Panama Canal through South America is complete except for an unsurveyed stretch in S Ecuador. Climatic zones along the highway vary from lush jungle to cold mtn. passes nearly 15,000 ft. high. Under consideration is a ferry service from Key West to Cuba and the West Indies and from Cuba to Yucatan peninsula.

Panamint Range (pă′nŭmĭnt) (c.6–11,000 ft.), desert range mainly in Inyo co., E Calif., near Nev. line, along W side of Death Valley; rises to 11,045 ft. at TELESCOPE PEAK. Ghost mining towns (Panamint, Skidoo). Barren Panamint Valley is at W base.

Panan or **P'an-an** (pän′än′), town (pop. 1,332), ⊙ Panan co. (pop. 82,090), SE central Chekiang prov., China, 45 mi. E of Kinhwa; corn, beans, tea, medicinal herbs, tung oil.

Panao (pänä′ō), city (pop. 1,027), ⊙ Pachitea prov. (□ 5,151; enumerated pop. 22,849, plus estimated 15,000 Indians), Huánuco dept., central Peru, in Cordillera Oriental, near Huallaga R., 17 mi. ENE of Huánuco; alt. 6,037 ft. Coca, cotton, coffee, grain, cattle.

Panaon Island (pänäōn′) (□ 78; 1939 pop. 24,769), Leyte prov., Philippines, bet. Surigao Strait and Canigao Channel, just off S coast of Leyte isl., forms SE shore of Sogod Bay; 21 mi. long, 7 mi. wide. Mountainous, rising to 2,814 ft. Coconut growing, fishing.

Panapakkam)pŭnŭpäk′kŭm), town (pop. 6,245), North Arcot dist., E central Madras, 29 mi. E of Vellore, in irrigated agr. area; cotton, rice, peanuts.

Panaquire (pänäkē′rā), town (pop. 810), Miranda state, N Venezuela, on Tuy R. and 50 mi. ESE of Caracas; cacao growing.

Panarago, Indonesia: see PONOROGO.

Panarea, Sicily: see PANARIA.

Panaria (pänärē′ä) or **Panarea** (pänärā′ä), anc. *Hicesia* or *Euonymus,* smallest island (□ 1.3; pop. 579) of Lipari Isls., in Tyrrhenian Sea off NE Sicily, NE of Lipari, 30 mi. NNW of Milazzo; 2 mi. long; rises to 1,378 ft. in W. Has fumaroles, hot springs. Agr. (corn, vegetables, olives). Exports fish.

Panaro River (pänä′rô), N central Italy, rises in 2 headstreams on Monte Cimone in Etruscan Apennines, flows 103 mi. N, past Vignola, Finale nell'Emilia, and Bondeno, to Po R. 12 mi. WNW of Ferrara.

Panasoffkee, Lake (pănŭsŏf′kē), Sumter co., central Fla., 13 mi. W of Leesburg; c.7 mi. long, 1 mi. wide, and shallow; has short outlet in W to Withlacoochee R.

Panasqueira (pŭnŭshkā′rŭ), village, Santarém dist., central Portugal, near Rio Maior; wolfram deposits.

Panay (pänī′). **1** Island (□ 4,446; 1939 pop. 1,291,548) of Visayan Isls., Philippines, bounded by Sibuyan Sea (N), Sulu Sea (S), Visayan Sea (E), Cuyo East Pass (W), and situated c.10 mi. NW of Negros isl. across Guimaras Strait, c.40 mi. SE of Mindoro isl. across Tablas Strait; 10°26′–11°56′N 121°50′–123°9′E. Just off SE coast is Guimaras Isl. Panay is c.95 mi. long, c.75 mi. wide. Largely mountainous, with broad fertile valleys. Produces rice, sugar cane, coconuts, citrus fruit, tobacco. Horses are bred in the mountainous interior. Copper mining. Panay is densely populated, particularly in coastal areas. With adjacent isls., the isl. comprises 3 provs.: ILOILO, CAPIZ, and ANTIQUE. **2** Small island (□ 4; 1939 pop. 449) of Catanduanes prov., Philippines, in Philippine Sea, just off E coast of Catanduanes isl., 5 mi. NE of Viga; 3.5 mi. long, 2 mi. wide; coconuts.

Panay, town (1939 pop. 1,384; 1948 municipality pop. 16,648), Capiz prov., N Panay isl., Philippines, 3 mi. SE of Capiz; rice-growing center.

Panay Gulf, wide arm of Sulu Sea, bet. Panay and Negros isls., Philippines, and leading NE into Guimaras Strait; c.50 mi. N-S, c.55 mi. E-W. On E shore is Binalbagan.

Panbride, fishing village, S Angus, Scotland, on North Sea, just N of Carnoustie. Near-by Panmure Castle is on site of 12th-cent. fort destroyed 1651 by General Monk.

Pancajché (pängkakh-chā′), village, Alta Verapaz dept., central Guatemala, on Polochic R. and 5 mi. E of Tucurú. W terminus of Verapaz RR, connecting at PANZÓS with L. Izabal water route.

Pancalieri (päng-kälyā′rē), village (pop. 2,017), Torino prov., Piedmont, NW Italy, near Po R., 17 mi. SSW of Turin; alcohol distilleries.

Pancasán (pängkäsän′), peak (4,920 ft.) in Cordillera Dariense, central Nicaragua, 5 mi. NW of Matiguás.

Pancevo or **Panchevo** (both: pän′chĕvô), Serbo-Croatian *Pančevo,* Hung. *Pancsova* (pŏn′chôvŏ), city (pop. 30,816), Vojvodina, N Serbia, Yugoslavia, port on the Danube, at Tamis R. mouth, and 10 mi. ENE of Belgrade, in the Banat. Rail junction; construction industry, glassworks; raw-silk mfg., flour milling, fishing. Sericulture in vicinity. Has old church with fine iconostasis. Linked with Belgrade by a bridge (nearly 1 mi. long) over the Danube.

Pancharevo (pŭnchä′rĕvô), village (pop. 1,026), Sofia dist., W Bulgaria, on Iskar R. and 8 mi. SSE of Sofia; health resort with thermal springs; grain, livestock, truck.

Panchevo, Yugoslavia: see PANCEVO.

Panchgani (pänch′gŭnē), town (pop. 3,691), Satara North dist., W central Bombay, India, in Western Ghats, 10 mi. E of Mahabaleshwar; climatic health resort; strawberry, coffee, and vegetable gardening. Several boarding schools.

Pan-ch'iao, Formosa: see PANKIAO.

Panchimalco (pänchēmäl′kō), town (pop. 3,343), San Salvador dept., S Salvador, in coastal range, 8 mi. S of San Salvador; grain, coffee, sugar cane; poultry farming; hand-woven textiles. Pop. is largely Indian. Has old colonial church noted for its wood carving.

Panch Mahals (pänch′ mŭhäls′), district, N Bombay, India; ⊙ Godhra. Bordered (S, SW) by Baroda dist.; drained NW by Mahi R. Agr. (maize, rice, gram, peanuts, cotton); exports grain, timber (teak). Manganese and bauxite mining (SW). Main towns: Godhra, Dohad. Raided 1535 by Humayun; in 18th cent., under Mahrattas. In 1930s, temporarily merged with Broach dist. Original Panch Mahals dist. (□ 1,608; 1941 pop. 527,326) was enlarged 1949 by inc. of former Gujarat states of Sunth, Lunavada, Bariya, Sanjeli, and Jambughoda.

Panchor (pŭn-chōr′), village (pop. 594), NW Johore, Malaya, on Muar R., and 13 mi. NE of Bandar Maharani; rubber plantations.

Panchow, China: see PANHSIEN.

Panchupur (pŭn′chŏŏpŏŏr), village, Rajshahi dist., W East Bengal, E Pakistan, on Atrai R. and 30 mi. NE of Rajshahi; ganja-growing center; rice, jute, oilseeds, wheat.

Panciu (pän′chōō), town (1948 pop. 4,523), Putna prov., E Rumania, 16 mi. NW of Focsani; wine center; distilling. Vizantea health resort (alt. 1,312 ft.), with mineral springs and 16th-cent. monastery, is 15 mi. NW.

Pancorvo or **Pancorbo** (both: päng-kôr′vō), town (pop. 1,108), Burgos prov., N Spain, on affluent of the Ebro, on Burgos-Irún RR and highway (cut through near-by gorge), and 9 mi. ENE of Miranda de Ebro; cereals, fruit, livestock; timber. Ceramics, plaster mfg; cheese processing.

Pancota (pŭng′kôtä), Rum. *Pâncota,* Hung. *Pankota* (pŏng′kôtŏ), village (pop. 5,224), Arad prov., W Rumania, on railroad and 22 mi. NE of Arad; grain and wine market; mfg. of vinegar, furniture, leather goods.

Pancsova, Yugoslavia: see PANCEVO.

Panda, Belgian Congo: see JADOTVILLE.

Panda (pän′dä), village, Sul do Save prov., SE Mozambique, on road and 50 mi. SW of Inhambane; pottery mfg.

Pandai, Indonesia: see PANTAR.

Pandaklii, Bulgaria: see TERVEL.

Pandalkudi (pŭn′dŭlkŏŏdē), town (pop. 7,185), Ramnad dist., S Madras, India, 8 mi. S of Aruppukkottai, in cotton area; hand-woven cotton fabrics. Also spelled Pandalugudi.

Pandan (pändän′). **1** Town (1939 pop. 2,657; 1948 municipality pop. 21,532), Antique prov., NW Panay isl., Philippines, 45 mi. WNW of Capiz; agr. center (rice, tobacco). **2** Town (1939 pop. 3,631; 1948 municipality pop. 10,253), N Catanduanes isl., Philippines, 32 mi. NNW of Virac; fishing and agr. center (coconuts, hemp). Also called Caramoran.

Pandan, village (pop. 1,346), W central Singapore isl., 2 mi. W of Bukit Timah; rubber, pineapples. Pop. is Chinese.

Pan de Azúcar (pän′ dā äsōō′kär), Andean peak (15,320 ft.), SW Colombia, in Cordillera Central adjoining Los Coconucos massif, 25 mi. SE of Popayán.

Pan de Azúcar, town (pop. 2,900), Maldonado dept., S Uruguay, at N foot of the low Cerro Pan de Azúcar, 17 mi. WNW of Maldonado; rail junction in winegrowing dist.

Pan de Azúcar Island, small islet on Pacific coast of Atacama prov., N Chile; 26°10′S 70°43′W; 2 mi. long.

Pan de Guajaibón (gwähībōn′), highest peak (2,533 ft.) in the Sierra del Rosario, W Cuba, 35 mi. NE of Pinar del Río.

Pan de Matanzas (mätän′säs), peak (1,149 ft.), Matanzas prov., W Cuba, in hilly range, 6 mi. W of Matanzas.

Panderma, Turkey: see BANDIRMA.

Pandharkawada (pŭndŭr′kŭvŭdŭ), town (pop. 8,386), Yeotmal dist., SW Madhya Pradesh, India, 37 mi. SE of Yeotmal; cotton ginning, oilseed milling.

Pandharpur (pŭn′dŭrpŏŏr), town (pop. 33,329), Sholapur dist., E central Bombay, India, on Bhima R. and 39 mi. W of Sholapur; road junction; markets rice, millet, wheat; cotton ginning, chemical mfg. Hindu pilgrimage center (3 annual fairs); has noted Vishnuite temple. Sometimes spelled Pondharpur.

Pandhurna (pän′dŏŏrnŭ), town (pop. 13,078), Chhindwara dist., central Madhya Pradesh, India, 40 mi. SW of Chhindwara; cotton ginning, oilseed milling; sunn-hemp products (mats, cordage).

Pan di Zucchero, peak on Austro-Ital. border: see ZUCKERHÜTL.

Pandjang, Indonesia: see PANJANG.

Pando (pän′dō), department (□ 23,876; 1949 pop. estimate 19,500), NW Bolivia; ⊙ Cobija. Bounded by Acre and Abuná rivers (N) and Madeira R. (E) along Brazil border, by Peru (W), by Madre de Dios R. (SW), and Beni R. (E). Drained by Tahuamanu, Manuripi, Orton, and Madre de Dios rivers. Bolivia's main rubber-producing region, covered with tropical forests along rivers; also produces rice, bananas, timber, furs. Served by river traffic on its main streams and by highway bet. Cobija and Puerto Rico, its 2 main centers. Dept. created 1938 from Colonias natl. territory.

Pando, city (pop. 9,600), Canelones dept., S Uruguay, on small Pando R., on railroad and 20 mi. NE of Montevideo; trades in agr. produce (grain, wine, stock).

Pando, Cerro (sĕ′rō), peak (10,375 ft.) in continental divide, on Panama–Costa Rica border.

Pandora (păndō′rŭ), village (pop. 717), Putnam co., NW Ohio, 16 mi. NNE of Lima, in diversified-farming area; stone quarries.

Pandrethan (pŭndrā′tän), Sanskrit *Puranadhishtana* [=old capital], former village, Anantnag dist.,

W central Kashmir, in Vale of Kashmir, on Jhelum R. and 5 mi. SE of Srinagar city center. Has ruins of Sivaite temple (built A.D. c.900 or c.1135), noted for stone-carved ceiling. Buddhist remains include stupa and monastery ruins, c.7th-cent. A.D. Gupta-style sculptures (now in Srinagar Mus.). Reputedly built (3d cent. B.C.) by Asoka as a ⊙ Kashmir, before foundation (6th cent. A.D.) of Srinagar.

Pandu (pän'dōō), village, Equator prov., NW Belgian Congo, on Ubangi R. (Fr. Equatorial Africa border) opposite Fort de Possel, and c.240 mi. NW of Lisala; cotton ginning.

Pandu (pŭn'dōō), village, Kamrup dist., W Assam, India, on Brahmaputra R. and 4 mi. W of Gauhati, opposite Amingaon (rail ferry).

Pandua (pŭnd'wŭ), ruined city, Malda dist., N West Bengal, India, 9 mi. N of English Bazar. Site of 14th-cent. Adina Masjid, largest mosque in Bengal, built by Sikander Shah. Was ⊙ Bengal (14th cent.) under Afghans and independent Moslem rulers.

Panducan Island (pändōō'kän) (□ 7.5; 1939 pop. 664), Sulu prov., Philippines, in Pangutaran Group of Sulu Archipelago, 25 mi. NW of Jolo Isl.

Pandu Mewas, India: see GUJARAT STATES.

Paneas, Palestine: see BANIYAS, Syria.

Panega River (pänĕ'gä), N Bulgaria, rises in central Balkan Mts. c.15 mi. SW of Lukovit, flows E and N, past Lukovit (hydroelectric station), and WNW, past Cherveni Bryag, to Iskar R. just W of Cherveni Bryag; 30 mi. long.

Panelas (pŏnā'lŭs), city (pop. 1,237), E Pernambuco, NE Brazil, 29 mi. W of Palmares; coffee, cotton, corn. Formerly spelled Panellas.

Panevezys or **Panevezhis** (pänyĕvĕzhēs'), Lith. *Panevėžys*, Rus. *Ponevezh*, city (pop. 26,653), N central Lithuania, on Nevezys R. and 60 mi. NNE of Kaunas; rail junction (repair shops); industrial center; machine shops, foundries; mfg. of paints, turpentine, linen, woolen, and cotton textiles, shoes, cement, soap; large flour-milling industry; sugar refining, meat packing, tobacco processing; beer, alcohol, yeast, honey. Dates from 16th cent.; in Rus. Kovno govt. until 1920.

Panfilov (pŭnfē'lŭf), city (1926 pop. 11,148), SE Taldy-Kurgan oblast, Kazakh SSR, near China frontier, on highway from Sary-Uzek and 100 mi. SE of Taldy-Kurgan, in irrigated agr. (cotton, rice, opium) and livestock-breeding area; cotton ginning; metalworks. Until 1942, called Dzharkent or Jarkent.

Panfilovo (-lŭvŭ). **1** Town (1944 pop. over 500), S Ivanovo oblast, Russian SFSR, 13 mi. SSW of Shuya; peat works. **2** Village (1939 pop. over 2,000), NW Stalingrad oblast, Russian SFSR, on railroad and 12 mi. SE of Novo-Annenski; wheat, sunflowers.

Panfilovskaya (-skĭŭ), village (1939 pop. over 500), W Frunze oblast, Kirghiz SSR, in Chu valley, near railroad (Kainda station), 45 mi. W of Frunze; sugar beets (refinery at Molotovsk, just N). Until 1942, Staro-Nikolayevka.

Panfilovski or **Panfilovskiy** (-skē), town (1948 pop. over 2,000), S Alma-Ata oblast, Kazakh SSR, 30 mi. W of Alma-Ata; tobacco factory. Also called Imeni Panfilova.

Pang, Nam (näm päng'), river in Shan State, Upper Burma; rises on Shan Plateau near Mong Yai, flows 200 mi. S to Salween R. 20 mi. SW of Takaw.

Panga (päng'gä), village, Eastern Prov., NE Belgian Congo, on Aruwimi R. just below rapids and 115 mi. NE of Stanleyville, in palm and cotton area; cotton ginning. Has R.C. mission. Gold is mined in vicinity (E).

Pangaion (päng-gä'ôn), Lat. *Pangaeus*, mtn. range in Macedonia, Greece, W of Kavalla, 20 mi. long bet. Struma R. (W) and Philippi marshes (E); rises to 6,418 ft. 16 mi. W of Kavalla. Gold was mined in anc. times here by Athens. Called Pilav Dagh under Turkish rule and Kushnitsa by Slavs.

Pangala (päng-gälä'), village, SE Middle Congo territory, Fr. Equatorial Africa, 80 mi. NW of Brazzaville; native trade center.

Pangalanes, Canal des (känäl' dā pägälän'), waterway in E Madagascar, along Indian Ocean Coast, extends 460 mi. from Farafangana (S) to Foulpointe (N). Collects produce of E Madagascar destined for Tamatave seaport. Now navigable mainly for shallow-draught craft, it is being deepened. Main towns on canal are Tamatave, Fénérive, Brickaville, Vatomandry, Nosy-Varika, Mananjary, Manakara. Laid out (1896–1901) by Galliéni.

Pangani (päng-gä'nē), town (pop. c.2,500), NE Tanganyika, small port on Pemba Channel of Indian Ocean, at mouth of Pangani R., 25 mi. SSW of Tanga. Commercial center; exports sisal, copra, cotton, sugar. Once a major slave-trading station at terminus of caravan routes from the interior.

Pañganiban (pä"nyōōgänē'bän), town (1939 pop. 3,303; 1948 municipality pop. 12,385), E Catanduanes isl., Philippines, 25 mi. ENE of Virac; fishing and agr. center (coconuts, hemp).

Pangani River, NE Tanganyika, rises on S slope of the Kilimanjaro, flows 250 mi. SE, past Korogwe, to Pemba Channel of Indian Ocean at Pangani. Pangani Falls (25 mi. W of Pangani) are source of hydroelectric power for Tanga area. Also known as Ruvu R.

Pangaon (pän'goun), town (pop. 5,574), Bir dist., NW Hyderabad state, India, 16 mi. SSE of Parli; millet, cotton, oilseeds.

Pangasinan (päng"gäsēnän'), province (□ 2,021; 1948 pop. 920,491), central Luzon, Philippines; ⊙ LINGAYEN. Bounded N by Lingayen Gulf, W by South China Sea and Dasol Bay; includes CABARRUYAN ISLAND and SANTIAGO ISLAND. Watered by the Agno, the prov. is one of richest agr. areas in the Philippines. Chief products: rice, copra, corn. Prov. is known for buri-palm hats. There are chromite deposits. Chief towns: Lingayen, DAGUPAN, SAN CARLOS.

Pangasun, Mount, Philippines: see BABUYAN ISLAND.

Pangbourne (-bôrn), town and parish (pop. 1,920), E Berkshire, England, on the Thames and 5 mi. WNW of Reading; agr. market, with flour mills. Site of a nautical col.

Pangburn, town (pop. 669), White co., central Ark., 12 mi. NNW of Searcy and on Little Red R.

Pange (päzh), village (pop. 190), Moselle dept., NE France, 8 mi. ESE of Metz.

Pangerango, Mount, Indonesia: see GEDEH, MOUNT.

Pang-fou or **Pangfow,** China: see PENGPU.

Panggong Tso, Kashmir and Tibet: see PANGONG TSO.

Pangi (päng'gē), village, Kivu prov., E Belgian Congo, near Elila R., 80 mi. NNE of Kasongo; trading center.

Pangim (pän-zhēm', pän'zhĭm) or **New Goa,** Port. *Nova Goa* (nô'vŭ gō'ŭ), city (pop. 14,213), ⊙ PORTUGUESE INDIA and GOA dist., port on small inlet of Arabian Sea at NW end of Tissuari Isl., 255 mi. SSE of Bombay, India; road center; trades in rice, copra, fish, salt, cashew nuts, coconuts; wood carving, soap mfg. Saltworks near by. Commercial and medical schools, agr. research station. Upon decline of Goa (Old Goa), became (c.1760) seat of govt. and (c.1843) ⊙ Port. India. Also spelled Panjim.

Pangkalanbrandan (pŏongkŏolän'brän'dŏon), town (dist. pop. 22,050), NE Sumatra, Indonesia, near Aru Bay of Strait of Malacca, 40 mi. NW of Medan; 4°2'N 98°17'E; trade center for area producing rubber and palm oil. Has important oil refinery, linked by pipe line with oil fields at Perlak and in Aru Bay region. Its port is PANGKALANSUSU, 8 mi. NW.

Pangkalansusu or **Pangkalansoesoe** (both: pŏongkŏolän'sōō'sōō), town, N Sumatra, Indonesia, on Aru Bay of Strait of Malacca, 45 mi. NW of Medan; port for Pangkalanbrandan (8 mi. SE). Exports oil, rubber, palm oil. Mfg. of oil drums.

Pangkalpinang (pŏongkŏolpē"näng'), chief town (pop. 11,970) of Bangka, Indonesia, on E coast of isl., on Java Sea; tin-shipping port. Has airport.

Pangkong Tsho, Tibet and Kashmir: see PANGONG TSO.

Pangkor (päng"kôr'), village (pop. 2,079) on E coast of Pangkor Isl., W Perak, Malaya, in the Dindings; fisheries.

Pangkor Island, in Strait of Malacca, W Perak, Malaya, in the Dindings, 1 mi. off Dindings R. mouth (separated by Dindings Channel); 6 mi. long, 2 mi. wide. Main fishing villages are Pangkor and Sungei Pinang Kechil. Originally part of Perak; ceded 1826 (confirmed 1874) to Great Britain; was part of Penang settlement until retroceded 1935 to Perak as part of the Dindings.

Panglao Island (päng-glä'ō, -glou') (□ 35; 1948 pop. 23,577), Bohol prov., Philippines, at E side of entrance to Bohol Strait, just off SW coast of Bohol isl., opposite Tagbilaran; 9 mi. long, 4.5 mi. wide. Generally flat, rising to 646 ft. Rice and coconut growing. Centers are Dauis (dä'wēs) (1939 pop. 1,876; 1948 municipality pop. 12,303) on E coast, and Panglao (1939 pop. 1,948; 1948 municipality pop. 11,274) on W coast.

Pangmi (päng'mē), W state (ngegunhmu) (□ 30; pop. 2,789), Southern Shan States, S Upper Burma; ⊙ Pinhmi, village 25 mi. SW of Taunggyi.

Pangnga, Thailand: see PHANGNGA.

Pangnirtung (păng'nûrtŭng, păng"nûrtŭng'), trading post (1941 pop. c.65), E Baffin Isl., SE Franklin Dist., Northwest Territories, on N side of Cumberland Sound; 66°9'N 65°44'W. Radio and meteorological station; Royal Canadian Mounted Police post. Site of Anglican mission. Medical center for Baffin Isl., with hosp. Has whale-blubber rendering plant; on opposite side of Pangnirtung Fjord is Hudson's Bay Co. fox farm. Post was established 1921.

Pangojin (päng'ŭ'jĭn'), Jap. *Hogyoshin*, town (1949 pop. 16,897), S.Kyongsang prov., S Korea, on Sea on Japan, 32 mi. NE of Pusan; fishing and whaling port.

Pangong Range (pän'gông) or **Pankong Range** (-kông), SE extension of Kailas-Karakoram Range, E Kashmir and W Tibet; extends c.170 mi. WNW-ESE, bet. Pangong Tso (lake; N) and Ladakh Range (S); rises to 22,060 ft. in W. Main town is Rudok (Tibet).

Pangong Tso (pän'gông tsō') or **Pangkong Tsho** (pän'kông tsō'), Chinese *Pan-kung Hu* (bän'gōōng' hōō'), lake (□ 230) in SE Kashmir and W Tibet, bet. Chang Chenmo Range (N) and Pangong Range (S); c.130 mi. long E–W; alt. 13,930 ft. Contains brackish water, except for fresh water in extreme E end (called Nyak Tso) in Tibet. Sometimes Panggong Tso.

Pango Pango, American Samoa: see PAGOPAGO.

Pangrango, Mount, Indonesia: see GEDEH, MOUNT.

Pangsau Pass (päng'-sô) major crossing (4,000 ft.) on India-Burma border, in Patkai Range, 35 mi. E of Ledo (Assam); 27°15'N 96°10'E. Used by Ledo (Stilwell) Road (built in Second World War).

Pangtara (päng'tŭrä), W state (ngegunhmu) (□ 86; pop. 13,139), Southern Shan State, Upper Burma; ⊙ Pangtara, village 25 mi. NW of Taunggyi.

Panguil Bay (päng-gēl'), SW arm (25 mi. long, 2–6 mi. wide) of Iligan Bay, N Mindanao, Philippines. Near its entrance is port of Ozamiz.

Panguipulli (päng-gēpōō'yē), village (1930 pop. 163), Valdivia prov., S central Chile, on NW shore of L. Panguipulli, in Chilean lake dist., 55 mi. ENE of Valdivia; resort in picturesque landscape towered over by several volcanoes. Fishing, lumbering. Copper deposits near by.

Panguipulli, Lake (□ 55), Valdivia prov., S central Chile, in Chilean lake dist., bet. L. Calafquén and L. Riñihue; c.15 mi. long, c.3 mi. wide. Fishing, lumbering.

Panguitch (păn'gwĭch), city (pop. 1,501), ⊙ Garfield co., SW Utah, on Panguitch Creek and 32 mi. SSE of Beaver; alt. 6,624 ft.; trading point for livestock and grain area; dairy products. State fish hatchery near by. Part of Dixie Natl. Forest is just W, in Markagunt Plateau. Settled c.1865 by Mormons, abandoned 1867, resettled 1871.

Panguitch Creek, rises in Markagunt Plateau, SW Utah, flows c.30 mi. generally NE, through Panguitch L. (1.5 mi. long), and joins Assay Creek just N of Panguitch to form Sevier R.

Pangutaran Group (päng"ōōtä'rän), coral island group (1948 pop. 8,536), Sulu prov., Philippines, in Sulu Archipelago, 25 mi. NW of Jolo Isl.; 6°20'N 120°30'E. Largest is Pangutaran Isl. (□ 36.7), 11 mi. long. Other isls. include Panducan, North Ubian, and Usada.

Panhai, India: see MAU, Banda district.

Panhala (pŭnhä'lŭ), village, Kolhapur dist., S Bombay, India, in Western Ghats, 11 mi. NW of Kolhapur; noted hill fortress, captured 1659 by Sivaji. Just E is Jotiba's Hill, with several temples; iron-ore and bauxite deposits.

Panhandle, in U.S., name of narrow territorial extensions, such as those in IDAHO, OKLAHOMA, TEXAS, WEST VIRGINIA, and ALASKA.

Panhandle, town (pop. 1,406), ⊙ Carson co., extreme N Texas, 27 mi. ENE of Amarillo, in the Panhandle natural-gas and oil field; pipelines, oil wells; ships wheat, cattle. Settled 1896, inc. 1909.

Panhormus, Sicily: see PALERMO, city.

Panhsien or **P'an-hsien** (both: pän'shyĕn'), town (pop. 16,922), ⊙ Panhsien co. (pop. 202,858), SW Kweichow prov., China, near Yunnan line, 135 mi. SW of Kweiyang and on main road to Yunnan; alt. 5,312 ft.; cotton- and wool-textile, paper mfg.; rice, wheat, beans. Coal deposits near by. Until 1913 called Panchow.

Pania Mutombo (pän'yä mōōtōm'bō), village, Kasai prov., central Belgian Congo, on right bank of Sankuru R. and 80 mi. NNW of Kabinda; terminus of steamboat navigation and trading center; rice fields, coffee plantations in vicinity.

Panié, Mount (pänēā'), highest mountain (5,412 ft.) of New Caledonia, SW Pacific; in NE.

Panihati (pänēhä'tē), town (pop. 27,410), 24-Parganas dist., SE West Bengal, India, on Hooghly R. and 8.5 mi. N of Calcutta city center; cotton milling, mfg. of chemicals, pottery, cement, glass, paint, rubber goods; tanneries. Includes S suburb of Agarpara.

Pani Kota, Portuguese India: see SIMBOR.

Panimávida or **Baños de Panimávida** (bä'nyōs dā pänēmä'vēdä), village (1930 pop. 459), Linares prov., S central Chile, on railroad and 13 mi. NE of Linares; health resort; thermal springs.

Pani Mines (pä'nē), village, Baroda dist., N Bombay, India, 38 mi. ENE of Baroda; rail terminus; manganese mining; small deposits of lead and copper.

Panindícuaro (pänēndē'kwärō), officially Panindícuaro de la Reforma, town (pop. 3,681), Michoacán, central Mexico, on central plateau, on railroad and 33 mi. E of Zamora; alt. 6,135 ft. Agr. center (grain, sugar cane, fruit, stock).

Paninka, Ukrainian SSR: see PONINKA.

Panino (pä'nyĭnŭ), village (1926 pop. 2,938), central Voronezh oblast, Russian SFSR, on railroad (Tulinovo station) and 40 mi. E of Voronezh; metalworks. Insect pest-control station.

Panipat (pä'nēpŭt), town (pop. 37,837), Karnal dist., E Punjab, India, 20 mi. S of Karnal, 55 mi. NNW of Delhi; rail junction; trade center (grain, wool, cotton, salt); woolen milling, cotton ginning, saltpeter refining, mfg. of glass, electric appliances, bricks; handicrafts (copper and brass utensils, cloth fabrics, pottery, baskets). Famous site of 3 decisive battles in N India: in 1526, Baber defeated Ibrahim Lodi, king of Delhi; in 1556, Akbar overcame Afghans under Hindu general of Muhammad

Adil Shah; in 1761, Mahratta confederacy crushed by Ahmad Shah Durani.

Paniqui (pänē'kē, pänēkē'), town (1939 pop. 5,225; 1948 municipality pop. 27,554), Tarlac prov., central Luzon, Philippines, 12 mi. N of Tarlac; rail junction; trade center for agr. area (coconuts, rice, sugar cane). Sugar mill, distillery.

Panissières (pänēsyâr'), village (pop. 1,794), Loire dept., SE central France, in Monts du Beaujolais, 18 mi. NE of Montbrison; textile milling (linen, silk), cabinetmaking.

Panitan (pänē'tän, pänētän'), town (1939 pop. 1,568; 1948 municipality pop. 15,179), Capiz prov., N Panay isl., Philippines, on small Panay R. and 3 mi. SE of Capiz; rice-growing center.

Panitao (pänētou'), village (1930 pop. 501), Llanquihue prov., S central Chile, on NW shore of Reloncaví Sound, 9 mi. SW of Puerto Montt; wheat, potatoes, apples, livestock; dairying, lumbering. Sometimes Punitao.

Paniza (pänē'thä), town (pop. 1,249), Saragossa prov., NE Spain, 13 mi. NE of Daroca, in wine-growing area; cereals, sheep.

Panj, Afghanistan and USSR: see PANJ RIVER.

Panjab, Afghanistan: see PANJAO.

Panjab, India and Pakistan: see PUNJAB.

Panjang or **Pandjang** (both: pänjäng'), formerly **Oosthaven** (ōst'hä"vün), port, extreme S Sumatra, Indonesia, on Lampung Bay, 5 mi. SE of Telukbetung; terminus of railroad from Palembang. Ferry service to Merak, Java. Also called East Harbor.

Panjang, island, Indonesia: see GORAM ISLANDS.

Panjang, Pulau, Thailand: see YAO YAI, KO.

Panjao (pŭnjou') or **Panjab** (–jäb'), town, Kabul prov., central Afghanistan, 125 mi. W of Kabul and on central highway to Herat; administrative hq. of Dehzangi (Dayzangi) dist. and main town of the Hazarajat. Has fortress; radio station.

Panjdeh (pänjdĕ'), former district in Turkmenia, USSR, at confluence of Murgab and Kushka rivers. Scene of Russo-Afghan incident (1885) that resulted in settlement of the frontier boundary.

Panjgur (pŭnj'gōōr), town (pop. 473), Makran state, W Baluchistan, W Pakistan, on Rakhshan R. and 230 mi. NW of Karachi; famous for its dates; markets wheat, barley; palm-mat weaving.

Panjhra River (pänj'rŭ), in West Khandesh dist., N Bombay, India, rises in N Western Ghats near Sakri, flows E, past Dhulia, and N to Tapti R. 4 mi. NNE of Betawad; c.100 mi. long.

Panjim, Portuguese India: see PANGIM.

Panjkora River (pŭnjkō'rŭ), N central North-West Frontier Prov., W Pakistan, rises on SE spur of the Hindu Kush, flows c. 90 mi. generally SSW through Dir state, to Swat R. 12 mi. WNW of Malakand.

Panjnad Canal (pŭnj'nŭd), irrigation channel in Bahawalpur state, W Pakistan; from headworks on Panjnad R., just below confluence of Sutlej and Chenab rivers, runs c.110 mi. SW, along left bank of the Indus, to c.12 mi. NW of Ahmadpur Lamma; has several S branches. Irrigates wheat, cotton, rice, and millet fields.

Panjnad River, combined waters of 5 rivers of the Punjab, in W Pakistan, on Bahawalpur state–Muzaffargarh dist. border; formed by confluence of Sutlej and Chenab rivers just E of Alipur; flows c.50 mi. SW to the Indus 15 mi. ESE of Rajanpur.

Panj River (pänj), Pashto *Ab-i-Panj* (ä'bēpänj'), Rus. *Pyandzh* (pyänj), a headstream of the Amu Darya, on USSR-Afghanistan frontier, formed by junction of Pamir and Wakhan rivers in Wakhan panhandle of Afghanistan near Qala Panja; flows W and N along W edge of the Pamir, past Khorog, and through Darvaza Gorge, then WSW, past Parkhar and Nizhni Pyandzh, joining Vakhsh R. to form the Amu Darya; c.400 mi. long. Navigable below Nizhni Pyandzh, rail terminus and head of navigation of Amu Darya system. Receives Gunt, Bartang, Vanch, and Kyzyl-Su rivers (right) and Kokcha R. (left). Established 1873 as international frontier, separating Afghan and Russian Badakhshan in upper course; finally delimited in mid-1890s.

Panjshir River (pŭnj-shēr'), E Afghanistan, rises in the Hindu Kush at foot of Khawak Pass, flows over 100 mi. SW, past Gulbahar, and SE, to Kabul R. 30 mi. E of Kabul. Receives Ghorband R. (right).

Pankakoski (päng'käkōs"kē), village in Pielisjärvi commune (pop. 21,968), Kuopio co., E Finland, near USSR border, near E shore of L. Pieli, 50 mi. NNE of Joensuu; pulp and board mills. Founded and chartered (1653) as Brahea, Swedish *Braheå*, it was sacked (1656) by Russians and lost its charter, 1681.

Pankiao or **Pan-ch'iao** (both: bän'chyou'), Jap. *Itabashi* (ētä'bäshē) or *Bankyo* (bäng'kyō), officially *Taipei* (dī'bā'), town (1935 pop. 5,100), N Formosa, on railroad and 4 mi. SW of Taipei, on Tanshui R.; coal mining, distilling. The oriental garden of the Linpenyüan mansion here is visited by tourists.

Pankota, Rumania: see PANCOTA.

Pankow (päng'kō), workers' residential district (1939 pop. 154,725; 1946 pop. 143,962), N Berlin, Germany, 5 mi. NNE of city center. Mfg. (food products, electrical equipment). After 1945 in Soviet sector.

Pankrushikha (pŭnkrōōshē'khŭ), village (1926 pop. 3,302), NW Altai Territory, Russian SFSR, on Burla R. and 38 mi. W of Kamen; flour milling, dairy farming.

Pankshin (pŭng'-chĕng), town (pop. 5,654), Plateau Prov., Northern Provinces, central Nigeria, 55 mi. SE of Jos; tin mining; cassava, millet, durra. Sometimes spelled Pankishin.

Pan-kung Hu, Tibet and Kashmir: see PANGONG TSO.

Panmunjom (păn"mōōnjŏm', pän'mōōn'jŭm'), village, central Korea, 6 mi. SE of Kaesong; in the Korean War, scene of 2d series of truce negotiations, beginning Oct., 1951.

Panna (pŭn'nŭ), town (pop. 13,375), ⊙ Panna dist., central Vindhya Pradesh, India, 70 mi. WNW of Rewa; trade center for millet, wheat, gram, timber, cloth fabrics; hand-loom weaving. Diamonds mined in near-by hill range. Was ⊙ former princely state of Panna (□ 2,580; pop. 231,170) of Central India agency; state (founded mid-17th cent.) merged since 1948 with Vindhya Pradesh.

Panna Maria (pă'nŭ mŭrē'ŭ), village (pop. c.100), Karnes co., S Texas, c.45 mi. SE of San Antonio; an old Polish settlement.

Pannanich or **Pannanich Wells** (pă'nŭnĭkh), village, SW Aberdeen, Scotland, near the Dee 2 mi. ENE of Ballater; resort with chalybeate springs.

Panne, De (dŭ pä'nŭ), Fr. *La Panne* (lä pän'), town (pop. 5,550), West Flanders prov., W Belgium, on North Sea, 7 mi. WSW of Nieuport, near Fr. border; seaside resort.

Pannerden Canal, Netherlands: see LOWER RHINE RIVER.

Panni (pän'nē), village (pop. 4,347), Foggia prov., Apulia, S Italy, 4 mi. SW of Bovino, in stock-raising region.

Pannonhalma, Hungary: see GYÖRSZENTMARTON.

Pannonia (pănō'nēŭ), anc. Roman province, central Europe, S and W of the Danube, including parts of modern Austria, Hungary, and Yugoslavia. Its natives were identified by the Romans with Illyrians. Their final subjugation took place in A.D. 10. Later there were provs. of Upper Pannonia and Lower Pannonia. Important centers were Carnuntum, Vindobona (Vienna), Aquincum (Budapest), and Sirmium. Pannonia was abandoned by the Romans after 395.

Pano Akil (pŭnō' ä'kĭl), village, Sukkur dist., NE Sind, W Pakistan, 19 mi. NE of Sukkur; local agr. market (wheat, millet); tanning.

Pano Amiandos, Cyprus: see AMIANDOS.

Panola (pŭnō'lŭ). **1** County (□ 704; pop. 31,271), NW Miss.; ⊙ Batesville and Sardis. Drained by Tallahatchie and Yocona rivers. Agr. (cotton, corn, hay, livestock, poultry; dairy products). Timber; clay and gravel deposits. Formed 1836. **2** County (□ 880; pop. 19,250), E Texas; ⊙ Carthage. Bounded E by La. line; drained by Sabine R. Rolling wooded region (pine, gum, cypress; extensive lumbering). Huge natural-gas field is tapped by interstate pipelines; some oil wells. Agr. (cotton, truck, corn, peanuts, pecans, forage crops, fruit), livestock (cattle, hogs, sheep, horses, poultry). Clay, iron, lignite deposits. Formed 1846.

Panola, village (pop. 52), Woodford co., central Ill., 20 mi. N of Bloomington, in agr. and coal area.

Pano Lefkara, Cyprus: see LEFKARA.

Pano Platres, Cyprus: see PLATRES, PANO.

Panopolis, Egypt: see AKHMIM.

Panora (pănô'rŭ), town (pop. 1,062), Guthrie co., W central Iowa, near Middle Raccoon R., c.40 mi. WNW of Des Moines; livestock, grain. Inc. 1872.

Panormus, Sicily: see PALERMO, city.

Panormus, Turkey: see BANDIRMA.

Panotla or **San Nicolás Panotla** (sän nēkōläs' pänōt'lä), town (pop. 1,485), Tlaxcala, central Mexico, 2½ mi. W of Tlaxcala; grain, maguey, beans, livestock.

Panpu, China: see KWANYÜN.

Panquehue (pängkā'wā), village (1930 pop. 64), Aconcagua prov., central Chile, on railroad and 6 mi. SW of San Felipe; fruit, hemp, livestock. Largest vineyards in Chile.

Panqueua (pängkā'wä), town (pop. estimate 500), N Mendoza prov., Argentina, 5 mi. N of Mendoza; rail junction; cement mfg., wine- and fruitgrowing. Limestone deposits.

Panruti (pŭn'rōōtē), town (pop. 16,429), South Arcot dist., SE Madras, India, on Gadilam R. and 15 mi. W of Cuddalore; trade center for cashew nuts, peanuts, grain; peanut-oil and cassava-starch extraction; ceramics. Industrial school. Experimental farm 5 mi. E, at Palur.

Panshan or **P'an-shan** (pän'shän'), town, ⊙ Panshan co. (pop. 285,207), S Liaosi prov., Manchuria, on Liao plain, 50 mi. E of Chinchow, and on railroad; saltworks; kaoliang, wheat, millet, cotton. Formerly called Shwangtaitze.

Panshih or **P'an-shih** (pän'shŭ'), town, ⊙ Panshih co. (pop. 249,308), S Kirin prov., Manchuria, on railroad and 65 mi. SSW of Kirin, on Liaotung line; limestone quarrying, copper mining (smelter).

Pantabangan (päntäbä'nyŭgän), town (1939 pop. 1,799; 1948 municipality pop. 5,132), Nueva Ecija prov., central Luzon, Philippines, 27 mi. NNE of Cabanatuan; rice, corn; mineral pigments.

Pantai Remis (päntī' rĕmĭs'), village (pop. 1,469), W Perak, Malaya, in the Dindings, 15 mi. N of Lumut; coconuts.

Pantaleón (päntälāōn'), village (pop. 1,480), Escuintla dept., S Guatemala, on railroad and 2 mi. ESE of Santa Lucía; sugar-milling center.

Pantaleón Dalence, Bolivia: see HUANUNI.

Pantalica, Sicily: see SORTINO.

Pantanaw (păn'tŭnô"), village, Maubin dist., Lower Burma, on Pantanaw R. (arm of Irrawaddy delta) and 50 mi. ENE of Bassein.

Pantar (päntär') or **Pandai** (pändī'), island (□ 281; pop. 18,141), Alor Isls., Lesser Sundas, Indonesia, 45 mi. N of Timor across Ombai Strait; 30 mi. long, 7–18 mi. wide. Generally level except for hilly NE area rising to c.3,300 ft. Fishing, agr. (corn, cotton, rice, coconuts).

Panteg (păntāg'), former urban district (1931 pop. 11,499), central Monmouth, England, just SE of Pontypool. Steel-milling towns of Griffithstown and Llanfihangel Pontymoel (lănvē-hăng'ĕl pŏntŭmoil') here. Panteg inc. (1935) in Pontypool.

Pantego (păn'tĭgō, păntē'gō). **1** Town (pop. 275), Beaufort co., E N.C., 22 mi. E of Washington. **2** Town (pop. 646), Tarrant co., N Texas.

Panteleimonovka or **Panteleymonovka** (pŭntyĭlyā'-mŭnŭfkŭ), town (1939 pop. over 2,000), central Stalino oblast, Ukrainian SSR, in the Donbas, 12 mi. N of Makeyevka; ceramics mfg. (Dinas bricks).

Pantelho (päntĕlō'), town (pop. 877), Chiapas, S Mexico, 40 mi. ENE of Tuxtla; cereals, fruit.

Pantelimon (päntĕlē'mōn), outer E rural suburb (1948 pop. 4,975) of Bucharest, S Rumania, on left bank of Colentina R.; dairying center. Has 18th-cent. church with historic tombstones. Near by is Cernica monastery with seminary and printing works.

Pantelleria (päntĕl-lĕrē'ä), anc. *Cossyra,* island (□ 32; pop. 9,306) in Mediterranean Sea 65 mi. SW of Cape Granitola, Sicily, in Trapani prov.; 9 mi. long, 5 mi. wide. Volcanic, with numerous fumaroles, hot mineral springs, and extinct crater of Magna Grande (last eruption 1891), rising to 2,743 ft. Fertile, though fresh water is scarce. Agr. (grapes, barley, oats, cotton); livestock (sheep, asses); fisheries. Chief port, Pantelleria (pop. 3,804), on NW coast; site of penal colony. Neolithic sepulchers in NW. Settled by Phoenicians 7th cent. B.C.; followed by Romans 217 B.C. In Second World War, destroyed by aerial bombardment (1943). Sometimes spelled Pantellaria.

Pante Macassar (păn'tĕ mäkä'sär), port in Portuguese enclave of Oe-Cusse in Indonesian Timor, on Ombai Strait, 95 mi. WSW of Dili; 9°12'S 124°22'E; ships copra, sandalwood. Has airport.

Panten (pän'tŭn) or **Patnow Legnicki** (pŏt'nōōf lĕgnēts'kē), Pol. *Pątnów Legnicki,* village in Lower Silesia, after 1945 in Wroclaw prov., SW Poland, near the Katzbach, 4 mi. NE of Liegnitz (Legnica). Here Prussians under Frederick the Great defeated (1760) Austrians under Loudon.

Pantepec (päntāpĕk'). **1** Town (pop. 568), Chiapas, S Mexico, in N spur of Sierra Madre, 29 mi. N of Tuxtla; alt. 4,855 ft.; cereals, fruit. **2** Town (pop. 1,811), Puebla, central Mexico, 25 mi. NNE of Huauchinango; coffee, sugar cane, tobacco, fruit.

Pantepec River, Mexico: see TUXPAN RIVER.

Panther Creek, NW Ky., formed SSE of Owensboro by junction of North and South forks; flows c.35 mi. generally W to Green R. 12 mi. WSW of Owensboro. North Fork rises in Hancock co., flows c.22 mi. generally W; South Fork rises in Breckinridge co., flows c.40 mi. SW and W.

Panther Mountain. 1 Peak (3,865 ft.) in Hamilton co., NE central N.Y., in the Adirondacks, 35 mi. SW of Mt. Marcy and 7 mi. WSW of Indian Lake village. **2** Peak (3,760 ft.) in Ulster co., SE N.Y., in the Catskills, 22 mi. WNW of Kingston.

Panther Peak (4,448 ft.), Essex co., NE N.Y., in the Adirondacks, 10 mi. W of Mt. Marcy and 14 mi. SSW of Lake Placid village.

Panth Piploda (pŭnt' pĭplō'dŭ), former chief commissioner's prov. (□ 25; pop. 5,267), India; comprised 5 small detached areas within Central India agency, E of Jaora; in 1950, inc. into Madhya Bharat.

Panticapaeum, Russian SFSR: see KERCH, city.

Panticosa (päntēkō'sä), village (pop. 583), Huesca prov., NE Spain, in the central Pyrenees, 20 mi. NE of Jaca; alt. c.5,500 ft.; health resort noted for its sulphur baths.

Pantin (pãtē'), industrial town (pop. 35,969), Seine dept., N central France, just NE of Paris, 4 mi. from Notre Dame Cathedral, on Ourcq Canal; rail freight yards and workshops, natl. tobacco factory; other mfg. (electrical equipment, machine tools, rubber, chemicals, sewing thread, margarine, chocolate, sauerkraut, jam); flour milling, petroleum refining, distilling. Pantin cemetery just N.

Pantoja (päntō'hä), military post (pop. 192), Loreto dept., N Peru, landing on Napo R. at mouth of Aguarico R. (Ecuador line); 0°58'S 75°10'W. Airfield. Following 1942 border settlement, the near-by Ecuadorian post of Rocafuerte was replaced by NUEVA ROCAFUERTE.

Pantoja, town (pop. 751), Toledo prov., central Spain, 26 mi. SSW of Madrid; cereals, olives, grapes, hogs.

Panton, town (pop. 332), Addison co., W Vt., on L. Champlain and 12 mi. NW of Middlebury. Burned by British in Revolution; site of grounding of Arnold's fleet (1776).

Pant River, England: see BLACKWATER RIVER.

Pantukan, Philippines: see KINGKING.

Pánuco (pä'nōōkō). **1** Officially Panuco de Coronado, town (pop. 1,301), Durango, N Mexico, 40 mi. NE of Durango; silver, gold, lead, copper deposits. **2** Town (pop. 1,328), Sinaloa, W Mexico, in W outliers of Sierra Madre Occidental, 38 mi. NE of Mazatlán; silver, gold, copper mining. **3** City (pop. 5,942), Veracruz, E Mexico, in Gulf lowland, on Pánuco R. and 23 mi. SW of Tampico; rail terminus; agr. center (corn, wheat, fruit, cattle). Petroleum wells near by. **4** Town (pop. 526), Zacatecas, N central Mexico, on interior plateau, 9 mi. NNE of Zacatecas; alt. 7,277 ft.; silver mining; agr. (maguey, corn, livestock).

Pánuco River, NE central Mexico, formed in N Veracruz by headstreams rising in San Luis Potosí, meanders c.100 mi. ENE, past Pánuco (Veracruz) and Tampico (7 mi. upstream, in Tamaulipas), to Gulf of Mexico, near which it joins Tamesí R. by means of coastal lagoons. Main headstreams are MOCTEZUMA RIVER and Tamuin R. (lower course of SANTA MARÍA RIVER). Santa María–Pánuco R. is 316 mi. long, navigable over 200 mi. Irrigates fertile La Huasteca lowlands and drains, by artificial means, central plateau and interior valleys. Tampico can accommodate ocean vessels; the river here is c.1,200 ft. wide, 300 ft. deep.

Panu Khani (pä'nōō kä'nē), village, N central Nepal, on right tributary of the Trisuli and 27 mi. ENE of Pokhara; salt extraction from brine springs.

Panulcillo (pänōōlsē'yō), village (1930 pop. 152), Coquimbo prov., N central Chile, 16 mi. NNW of Ovalle; rail terminus; copper mining and smelting.

Panvel (pŭn'vāl), town (pop., including suburban area, 11,984), Kolaba dist., W Bombay, India, 17 mi. E of Bombay; port on small river; agr. market (rice, millet, ghee, oilseeds); mfg. of cart wheels, salt, drugs and chemicals. Transmission station for power lines from Khopoli and Bhira hydroelectric plants.

Panyam (pänyäm'), town, Plateau Prov., Northern Provinces, central Nigeria, 40 mi. SSE of Jos; tin mining.

P'an-yü, China: see PUNYÜ.

Panyutino (pŭnyōō'tyĭnŭ), town (1926 pop. 4,563), S Kharkov oblast, Ukrainian SSR, 3 mi. NW of Lozovaya; metalworks.

Panza Island (pän'sä), in center of L. Poopó, Oruro dept., W Bolivia, 30 mi. SW of Poopó; 5 mi. long, 1–2 mi. wide. Home of remaining families of the Urus, an old Indian group.

Panzós (pänsōs'), town (1950 pop. 573), Alta Verapaz dept., central Guatemala, port on Polochic R. and 37 mi. E of Cobán. E terminus of Verapaz RR; transfer point for Polochic R.–L. Izabal water route; coffee, grain.

Pao, El, Venezuela: see EL PAO.

Paoan. 1 Town, Chahar prov., China: see CHOLU. **2** Town, Kwangtung prov., China: see POON. **3** Town, Shensi prov., China: see CHIHTAN.

Paocheng or **Pao-ch'eng** (bou'chŭng'), town (pop. 5,696), ⊙ Paocheng co. (pop. 147,355), SW Shensi prov., China, 10 mi. NW of Nancheng; grain.

Pao-chi, China: see PAOKI.

Pao-ching or **Pao-ch'ing,** China: see PAOTSING.

Pão de Açúcar (pã'ō dĭ äsōō'kŭr), city (pop. 2,909), W Alagoas, NE Brazil, on left bank of navigable São Francisco R. (Sergipe border) and 70 mi. NW of Penedo; ships rice, cotton, sugar. Has new hosp.

Pão de Açúcar, peak, Brazil: see SUGAR LOAF MOUNTAIN.

Paofeng (bou'fŭng'), town, ⊙ Paofeng co. (pop. 191,963), NW central Honan prov., China, on road and 65 mi. SSE of Loyang; wheat, millet, beans.

Paohing or **Pao-hsing** (bou'shĭng'), town, ⊙ Paohing co. (pop. 19,033), E Sikang prov., China, near Szechwan line, 50 mi. ENE of Kangting; rice, wheat, corn. Called Muping until 1929. Until 1938 in Szechwan.

Paokang or **Pao-k'ang** (bou'käng'), town (pop. 9,514), ⊙ Paokang co. (pop. 113,679), NW Hupeh prov., China, 45 mi. W of Siangyang; timber, millet, wheat.

Paoki or **Pao-chi** (both: bou'jē'), town (pop. 56,289), ⊙ Paoki co. (pop. 270,454), SW Shensi prov., China, on Wei R. and 100 mi. W of Sian, and on Lunghai RR; commercial center; cotton weaving; wheat, beans, millet.

Paoking, China: see SHAOYANG.

Paola (pä'ôlä), town (pop. 7,021), Cosenza prov., Calabria, S Italy, near Tyrrhenian Sea, 13 mi. WNW of Cosenza. Agr. trade center (olive oil, wine, fruit, livestock). St. Francis of Paula (Paola) b. here.

Paola or **Pawla** (both: pou'lä), town (pop. 14,793), SE Malta, residential suburb 2 mi. S of Valletta. Suffered severely during Second World War, but most monuments survived, among them troglodyte temple, unfinished old parish church (1626), 18th-cent. palaces. Founded 1626 by grand master De Paula. Sometimes spelled Paula.

Paola (pāō'lŭ), city (pop. 3,972), ⊙ Miami co., E Kansas, 36 mi. SSW of Kansas City, Kansas; trade and rail center for grain, poultry, and livestock region. Oil wells near by. Seat of Ursuline Col. of Paola. Laid out 1855, inc. as city 1860.

Paoli (pāō'lē). **1** Town (pop. 91), Phillips co., NE Colo., on Frenchman Creek, near Nebr. line, and 8 mi. W of Holyoke; trade and supply point in grain region. Inc. 1930. **2** Town (pop. 2,575), ⊙ Orange co., S Ind., on Lick R. and 22 mi. S of Bedford; trade center for agr. area; mfg. (furniture, wood products, canned foods, dairy products); timber; mineral springs. Settled 1807, inc. 1869. **3** Town (pop. 353), Garvin co., S central Okla., 6 mi. NNW of Pauls Valley, in agr. area; cotton ginning. **4** Residential village (pop. 3,029), Chester co., SE Pa., 18 mi. WNW of Philadelphia; railroad shops. Near here is birthplace of Gen. Wayne and scene of his defeat by British, 1777.

Paonia (pāō'nēŭ), town (pop. 1,257), Delta co., W Colo., on branch of Gunnison R., just W of West Elk Mts., and 27 mi. ENE of Delta; alt. 5,696 ft. Fruit-shipping point; dairy and poultry products. Coal mines near by. Inc. 1902.

Paoning, China: see LANGCHUNG.

Paonta (poun'tŭ), village, S Himachal Pradesh, India, on Jumna R. and 22 mi. ESE of Nahan; agr. market (wheat, corn, rice).

Pao River (pä'ō), N Venezuela, rises in coastal range NW of Valencia, flows c.150 mi. S, through llanos, to Portuguesa R. 28 mi. NW of La Unión. Navigable for small craft.

Paoshan (bou'shän'). **1** Town (pop. 7,233), ⊙ Paoshan co. (pop. 122,640), S Kiangsu prov., China, 14 mi. N of Shanghai, on estuary of Yangtze R.; cotton spinning; rice, wheat, beans, rapeseed. Shanghai's outer port of Woosung is just S. **2** Town (pop. 11,847), ⊙ Paoshan co. (pop. 283,309), W Yunnan prov., China, on Burma Road and 220 mi. W of Kunming; alt. 5,463 ft.; cotton textiles; rice, wheat, beans, millet, figs. Copper, iron, and sulphur mines near by. Until 1914, Yungchang.

Paosintsi, China: see SIHSIEN, Honan prov.

Paoteh or **Pao-te** (bou'dŭ'), town, ⊙ Paoteh co. (pop. 53,304), NW Shansi prov., China, 60 mi. W of Ningwu, and on Yellow R. (Shensi border), opposite Fuku; corn, wheat, kaoliang.

Paoti (bou'dē), town, ⊙ Paoti co. (pop. 328,250), NE Hopeh prov., China, 45 mi. ESE of Peking; cotton, wheat, millet, kaoliang.

Paoting. 1 (bou'dĭng') City (1947 pop. estimate 130,000), ⊙ Hopeh prov., China, 90 mi. SW of Peking and on railroad to Hankow; administrative and cultural center; cotton-weaving industry. Has univ. (1901); military acad. An old city, dating from Sung dynasty (13th cent.), it became ⊙ Hopeh after Chinese revolution (1911). Paoting was known as Tsingyüan (jing'yüän') from 1913, when it became ⊙ Tsingyüan co. (1935 pop. 409,745), until 1949, when it became an independent municipality. **2** or **Pao-t'ing** (bou'tĭng', Cantonese bō'–), town, ⊙ Paoting co. (pop. 71,840), S Hainan, Kwangtung prov., China, 25 mi. WNW of Lingshui; wheat, rice, sweet potatoes.

Paotow or **Pao-t'ou** (bou'tō'), city (1948 pop. 81,613), central Suiyuan prov., China, port on Yellow R. and 85 mi. W of Kweisui, and on railroad from Peking; major trading center and entrepôt for Mongolian products; flour milling, soap mfg., rug weaving, oilseed pressing, brewing. Trades in wool, hides, grain (wheat, millet), licorice. Its Yellow R. landing is Nanhaitze (just SE). An important hub of Mongolian caravan routes, Paotow developed greatly after 1923, when it was reached by railroad from Peking. During Sino-Japanese War, it was held (1937–45) by the Japanese. Became an independent municipality in 1933.

Paotsing. 1 or **Pao-ching** (bou'jĭng'), town, ⊙ Paotsing co. (pop. 133,867), NW Hunan prov., China, near Szechwan line, on branch of Yüan R. and 33 mi. NW of Yüanling; tung oil, rice, wheat. Coal mining (W). **2** or **Pao-ch'ing** (bou'chĭng'), town, ⊙ Paotsing co. (pop. 75,000), NE Sungkiang prov., Manchuria, China, 90 mi. E of Kiamusze; grain, timber.

Paoua (päwä'), village, NW Ubangi-Shari, Fr. Equatorial Africa, 110 mi. N of Bozoum, in cotton-growing region.

Paou Ouma, New Hebrides: see PAAMA.

Paoying (bou'yĭng'), town (1935 pop. 59,102), ⊙ Paoying co. (1946 pop. 494,174), N Kiangsu prov., China, 55 mi. N of Yangchow, and on Grand Canal, near N end of Kaoyu L.; rice center; wheat, beans.

Paoyüan (bou'yüän'), town, ⊙ Paoyüan co. (pop. 22,974), NE Chahar prov., China, on upper Lwan R. and 65 mi. NE of Kalgan, and on road to Tolun; cattle raising; agr. products. Until 1950, Kuyüan.

Pap (päp), village (1926 pop. 3,049), SW Namangan oblast, Uzbek SSR, on the Syr Darya, on railroad, and 30 mi. WSW of Namangan; metalworks. Mining at near-by Uigursai.

Papa (pä'pŏ), Hung. *Pápa,* city (pop. 23,735), Veszprem co., NW Hungary, 25 mi. SSW of Györ; rail, market center; mfg. (shoes, cigars, textiles); distilleries. Truck farming, extensive flax growing in area. Has late-18th-cent. castle built by Count Maurice Eszterhazy.

Papaaloa (pä'päūlō'ŭ), coast village (pop. 597), E Hawaii, T.H., 19 mi. NNW of Hilo; sugar plantation and mill.

Papagaios Islands (pŭpŭgī'ōōs), a group of islets off the SE coast of Rio de Janeiro, Brazil, just E of Cabo Frio.

Papagayo Gulf (päpägī'ō), inlet of Pacific Ocean on Costa Rica–Nicaragua border, N of Santa Elena Peninsula; 25 mi. wide, 15 mi. long. It forms Salinas and Santa Elena bays (E). Noted for strong winds, called *Papagayo.* The name Papagayo is also applied to the CULEBRA GULF, S of Santa Elena Peninsula.

Papagayo Point, southernmost cape of Lanzarote, Canary Isls., 16 mi. SW, of Arrecife; 28°50'N 13°46'W.

Papaikou (pä'pīkō'), coast village (pop. 1,430), E Hawaii, T.H., 3 mi. N of Hilo; sugar plantation.

Papakura (păpŭkōōr'ŭ), borough (pop. 2,239), N N.Isl., New Zealand, on SE shore of Manukau Harbour and 18 mi. SSE of Auckland; agr. center; dairy plant.

Papallacta (päpäyäk'tä), village, Napo-Pastaza prov., N central Ecuador, at N foot of Antisana volcano, 38 mi. ESE of Quito; corn, fruit, stock.

Papaloápam River (päpälwä'päm), Veracruz, SE Mexico, one of Mexico's most important rivers, formed by Tuxtepec R. and other headstreams on Oaxaca-Veracruz border, 4 mi. N of Tuxtepec; flows c.75 mi. NE in meandering course, past Tlacojalpan, Tuxtilla, Cosamaloapan, and Tlacotalpan, to Alvarado Lagoon 10 mi. ESE of Alvarado; c.200 mi. long, with the Tuxtepec; navigable for 150 mi. upstream. Receives San Juan R. Fertile tropical vegetation of Sotavento lowlands along course. Irrigation project. Site of Maya ruins.

Papalotla (päpälōt'lä). **1** Town (pop. 815), Mexico state, central Mexico, 20 mi. NE of Mexico city; maguey. **2** Officially San Francisco Papalotla, town (pop. 2,478), Tlaxcala, central Mexico, 8 mi. N of Puebla; cereals, alfalfa, beans, livestock.

Papal States or **States of the Church,** former independent territory under the temporal rule of the popes, with ROME as its center. Of varying size, it extended before its absorption (2d half of 19th cent.) by the Kingdom of Italy across the Italian peninsula from the lower Po southward bet. the Adriatic and Tyrrhenian seas, thus roughly including the present regions of LATIUM, UMBRIA, the MARCHES, and E EMILIA-ROMAGNA. There were also some minor enclaves, such as the Comtat VENAISSIN (1274–1791) around Avignon in S France, and Pontecorvo and Benevento in S Italy. The nucleus of the states consisted of endowments given to the popes from the 4th cent. in and around Rome, the Italian mainland, Sicily, Sardinia, and other lands. These came to be called the *Patrimony of St. Peter.* While authority over more distant possessions was gradually lost, papal power increased in the duchy of Rome. In 754 Pepin the Short gave Pope Stephen II the Exarchate of Ravenna and Pentapolis. Charlemagne continued (774) his father's grants. Papal claims to Naples, Sicily, and Sardinia were based on the forged *Donation of Constantine.* In 1115 Countess Matilda of Tuscany left her territories to the Church. In Rome itself the pope's temporal sway, almost nonexistent in 10th cent., remained until 14th cent., greatly limited—in spite of the vigorous regime of Innocent III—by interference of the emperors, by the power of the nobles, and by the ambitions of the commune of Rome. In 14th cent. the emperors, however, renounced their claims to duchy of Spoleto, the Romagna, and the March of Ancona. During "Babylonian Captivity" at Avignon and the Great Schism (14th–15th cent.) the Papal States were in a chaotic state, temporarily relieved by efforts of Cardinal Albornoz. Cesare Borgia, son of Pope Alexander VI, conquered in 16th cent. the petty states of the Romagna and the Marches; after his fall (1503), most of them passed directly under papal rule, consolidated and expanded by Julius II to its pre-1860 limits. The Papal States were invaded (1796) by the French under Napoleon Bonaparte and consecutively abolished. Fully restored (1815) by Congress of Vienna, they were placed under Austrian protection. During the *Risorgimento* (struggle for Italy's unification) only Fr. intervention temporarily prevented total annexation. Ancona and Romagna both joined (1860) Kingdom of Sardinia, as did the Marches and Umbria. Because of intervention of Napoleon III, the greatly reduced papal domain maintained its independence despite Garibaldi's incursions, until the fall (1870) of Napoleon made it safe for Victor Emmanuel II of Italy to seize Rome. Pope Pius IX and his successors chose nominal "imprisonment" in the Vatican, refusing to recognize their loss of secular power. Impasse bet. Italy and the Church was resolved (1929) by the Lateran Treaty, granting the papacy political control of VATICAN CITY.

Papan (päpän'), town (pop. 763), central Perak, Malaya, 7 mi. SW of Ipoh, at foot of Kledang Range; tin mining.

Papanasam (päpŭnä'sŭm). **1** Town (pop. 7,635), Tanjore dist., SE Madras, India, on arm of Cauvery R. delta and 13 mi. NE of Tanjore; betel-trade center; rice milling. **2** Village (pop., including surrounding work settlements, 5,303), Tinnevelly dist., S Madras, India, at foot of Western Ghats, on Tambrapani R. and 22 mi. W of Tinnevelly. Site of major hydroelectric works and irrigation dams, built (1940–44) to develop varied industries (paper, textile, and rice milling, electroplating, sugar refining). Project has furthered industrial development in AMBASAMUDRAM and VIKRAMSINGAPURAM; linked at Madura with Pykara system and at Shencottah with Pallivasal (MUNNAR) system of Travancore-Cochin. Falls and Agastya temple are noted Hindu places of pilgrimage. Sometimes spelled Papanasham.

Papanoa Point (päpänō'ä), headland on Pacific coast of Guerrero, SW Mexico, 27 mi. W of Tecpan; 17°16'N 101°5'W.

Papantla (päpän'tlä), officially Papantla de Olarte, city (pop. 6,644), Veracruz, E Mexico, in Sierra Madre Oriental foothills, 37 mi. S of Tuxpan; agr. center (coffee, tobacco, fruit, vanilla, livestock); coffee and vanilla processing. Famed for yearly fiesta with picturesque dances. Archaeological remains near by include anc. pyramid described by Humboldt.

Papanui (păpŭnōō'ē), NW residential suburb (pop. 1,695) of Christchurch, E S.Isl., New Zealand; ⊙ Waimairi co. (□ 48; pop. 17,928).

Papao, China: see KILIEN.

Papar (päpär'), town (pop. 1,000, including environs), West Coast residency, Br. North Borneo, near W coast, 20 mi. SSW of Jesselton; on railroad; agr. center (fruit, rice, sago); rice mills.

Papari, Brazil: see NÍSIA FLORESTA.

Paparoa (păpŭrō'ŭ), township (pop. 260), ⊙ Otamatea co. (□ 421; pop. 5,313), N N.Isl., New Zealand, near Kaipara Harbour, 60 mi. NW of Auckland; agr. center.

Paparoa Range, W S.Isl., New Zealand, parallel with W coast; extends from Westport 25 mi. S to lower course of Grey R.; coal, gold.

Paparua, New Zealand: see SOCKBURN.

Papas, Cape, or **Cape Pappas** (both: pä'pŭs), anc. *Araxus* (ărăk'sŭs), NW point of Peloponnesus, Greece, on Ionian Sea bet. Gulf of Patras (E) and Ionian Sea (W); 38°13'N 21°20'E. Also called Cape Araxos; formerly Cape Kalogria.

Papa Stour (pä'pŭ stoor'), island (pop. 100) of the Shetlands, Scotland, just off W extremity of Mainland isl., in St. Magnus Bay, 23 mi. NW of Lerwick; 3 mi. long, 2 mi. wide; rises to 288 ft. Coastline, much indented, is precipitous and has many beautiful caves. Isl. is one of the most fertile of the Shetlands and is important fishing station.

Papa Stronsay (pä'pŭ strŏn'zā), island (pop. 18) of the Orkneys, Scotland, just off NE coast of Stronsay isl.; 1 mi. long, 1 mi. wide. At N end is lighthouse (59°10'N 2°36'W).

Papatlatla (päpätlät'lä), town (pop. 1,289), Hidalgo, central Mexico, 17 mi. SSW of Huejutla; corn, rice, tobacco, sugar cane, livestock.

Papatoetoe (pä"pŭtoitoi'), town (pop. 3,683), N N.Isl., New Zealand, 11 mi. SSE of Auckland; agr., dairying.

Papa Westray (pä'pŭ wĕ'strā), island (2,039 acres; pop. 237), most northerly of the Orkneys, Scotland, just NE of Westray isl.; 5 mi. long, 1 mi. wide; rises to 157 ft. Has fertile soil. Isl. was once site of many hermits' cells and has remains of anc. chapel of St. Tredwall. Just off E coast is islet of Holm of Papa, last Br. abode of the great auk.

Papaya (päpä'yä), town (1939 pop. 4,506; 1948 municipality pop. 8,645), Nueva Ecija prov., central Luzon, Philippines, 14 mi. SW of Cabanatuan; agr. center (rice, corn); marble quarrying.

Papcastle, village and parish (pop. 549), W Cumberland, England, on Derwent R. just W of Cockermouth; dairy farming.

Papeete (pŭpē'tē, päpēä'tē), town (pop. 12,428) and port, ⊙ Tahiti and French Establishments in Oceania, Society Isls., S Pacific, on NW coast of Tahiti. Exports copra, vanilla, phosphates, mother-of-pearl; sugar refinery, soap factory. Residence of governor.

Papelpampa (päpĕlpäm'pä), town (pop. c.3,400), La Paz dept., W Bolivia, in the Altiplano, on road and 50 mi. WNW of Oruro; barley, sheep.

Papenburg (pä'pŭnbŏŏrk), town (pop. 13,986), in former Prussian prov. of Hanover, NW Germany, after 1945 in Lower Saxony, port near the Ems (linked by canal), 10 mi. S of Leer, in drained fenland region (former peat bogs) now used for agr.; metalworking. Founded 1630 (Germany's oldest fen colony). Chartered 1861.

Papendrecht (pä'pŭndrĕkht), town (pop. 3,227), South Holland prov., SW Netherlands, on Lower Merwede R. and 1 mi. NE of Dordrecht; mfg. (aircraft, machinery); shipbuilding.

Paperville, Pa.: see MODENA.

Paphlagonia (pă"flŭgō'nēŭ), anc. region of N Asia Minor, on Black Sea bet. Bithynia (W) and Pontus (E); Galatia was to S. Chief city was Sinope. Its chief river was the Halys (modern Kizil Irmak). It was not a political unit; the kings of Pontus annexed it and finally lost it to the Romans, 63 B.C.

Paphos (pā'fŏs), district (□ 539; pop. 53,891), W Cyprus, on the Mediterranean; ⊙ PAPHOS or New Paphos, which now includes Ktima as N suburb. Mostly mountainous, crossed by outliers of the Olympus Mts. Principal occupations are agr. (flax, almonds, carobs, wine, olive oil, grain), stock raising (sheep, goats, donkeys), and fishing. Center of Cyprian sericulture. Flax-fiber mfg. at YEROSKIPOU. KOUKLIA or Old Paphos contains ruins of famous Aphrodite temple. Sometimes called Baffo.

Paphos or **New Paphos**, city (pop., including Ktima, 5,803), ⊙ Paphos dist., SW Cyprus, minor Mediterranean port, 60 mi. WSW of Nicosia. Trades in almonds, carobs, wine, olives. Sericulture, stock-raising (hogs, donkeys, mules). Most activities carried on in adjoining N suburb of Ktima. Founded near an older city (Old Paphos or KOUKLIA is 10 mi. ESE), Paphos flourished under Roman administration, when it was ⊙ Cyprus. Here St. Paul converted the Roman governor Sergius Paulus to Christianity. Paphos was destroyed 960 by Saracen invaders. Rich in Roman and Byzantine ruins. Paphos is sometimes called Baffo.

Papigno (päpē'nyō), village (pop. 1,528), Terni prov., Umbria, central Italy, on Nera R. and 3 mi. E of Terni; carbide and cyanamide factory.

Papillion (pŭpĭl'yŭn), village (pop. 1,034), ⊙ Sarpy co., E Nebr., 10 mi. SW of Omaha; grain.

Papineau (pă'pĭnō, Fr. päpēnō'), county (□ 1,581; pop. 27,551), SW Que., on Ont. border and on Ottawa R.; ⊙ Papineauville.

Papineau, village (pop. 157), Iroquois co., E Ill., 14 mi. SSE of Kankakee, in agr. area.

Papineau, Lake (8 mi. long, 3 mi. wide), S Que., 25 mi. NW of Lachute; drains S into Ottawa R.

Papineauville (pă'pĭnōvĭl"), village (pop. 1,023), ⊙ Papineau co., SW Que., on Ottawa R. and 35 mi. ENE of Ottawa; dairying, lumbering.

Papinsville (pă'pĭnzvĭl), town (pop. 55), Bates co., W Mo., on Marais des Cygnes R. and 8 mi. E of Rich Hill.

Paplaya, Honduras: see PLAPLAYA.

Paposo (päpō'sō), village (1930 pop. 56), Antofagasta prov., N Chile, minor port on the Pacific, 28 mi. N of Taltal; 25°2'S; ships nitrates. Copper deposits.

Papozze (päpô'tsĕ), village (pop. 1,441), Rovigo prov., Veneto, N Italy, on Po R. and 5 mi. S of Adria.

Pappas, Emmanouil Pappas, or **Emmanuil Pappas** (ĕmänōōēl' pŭpäs'), town (pop. 2,620), Serrai nome, Macedonia, Greece, 8 mi. E of Serrai, at foot of the Menoikion. Formerly Dovista or Dhovista.

Pappas, Cape, Greece: see PAPAS, CAPE.

Pappenheim (pä'pŭnhīm), town (pop. 2,367), Middle Franconia, W central Bavaria, Germany, on the Altmühl and 7 mi. S of Weissenburg; mfg. of precision instruments and glass, woodworking; summer resort. Has late-16th-cent. castle. Chartered 1288. Limestone quarries in area.

Paps of Jura (jŏŏr'ŭ), 3 peaks on Jura isl., Inner Hebrides, Argyll, Scotland, in S part of isl. Beinn-an-Oir (bĕn"-ŭn-oir') [mount of gold], 8 mi. SW of Tarbert, is the highest (2,571 ft.).

Papua, island: see NEW GUINEA.

Papua, Gulf of (pă'pū-ŭ, pä'pōōä), indentation of SE New Guinea, on Coral Sea; 225 mi. E-W, 95 mi. N-S; receives Fly and Purari rivers.

Papua, Territory of, Australian territory (□ 90,540; pop. 373,000), SW Pacific, includes SE New Guinea, TROBRIAND ISLANDS, WOODLARK ISLAND, D'ENTRECASTEAUX ISLANDS, LOUISIADE ARCHIPELAGO; ⊙ PORT MORESBY, which is also the new ⊙ Territory of New Guinea. It was annexed 1883 by Queensland; became 1884 Br. protectorate, annexed 1888 to Great Britain as colony of British New Guinea; became 1906 territory of Commonwealth of Australia, divided (since 1950) into Central Highlands, Western, Delta, Gulf, Central, Milne Bay, and Northern divs. See NEW GUINEA.

Papudo (päpōō'dō), village (1930 pop. 644), Aconcagua prov., central Chile, minor port on the Pacific (Papudo Bay) S of mouth of Ligua R., 40 mi. NNE of Valparaiso; rail terminus and beach resort. Salt deposits.

Papuk (pä'pŏŏk), mountain (3,126 ft.), N Croatia, Yugoslavia, 20 mi. E of Daruvar, in Slavonia.

Papun (pä'pōōn), village, ⊙ Salween dist., Lower Burma, on Yunzalin R. and 110 mi. N of Moulmein, near Thailand line. Pop. are Karens.

Papury River (päpōōrē') or **Capury River** (kä–), Port. *Papuri*, in Colombia and Brazil, rises in SE Vaupés commissary (Colombia), flows E almost its entire length (c.100 mi.) along Brazil-Colombia line to Vaupés (or Uaupés) R. at Iauaretê (Brazil).

Papworth Everard (ĕ'vŭrärd), village and parish (pop. 842), central Cambridge, England, 6 mi. SSW of St. Ives; site of colony of tubercular patients, with small handicraft industries.

Paquera (päkā'rä), village (dist. pop. 2,517), Puntarenas prov., W Costa Rica, small Pacific port on Gulf of Nicoya, on Nicoya Peninsula, and 12 mi. SW of Puntarenas; lumbering, stock raising.

Paquetá Island (pŭkĭtä'), in Guanabara Bay, SE Brazil, 10 mi. NNE of downtown Rio de Janeiro (ferry service), and in Federal Dist. Area, 270 acres. Shrimp fishing. Has numerous residences along fine beaches and in hilly terrain covered with abundant vegetation. Here are a sanitarium and a seamen's institute. Isl.'s beauty has been celebrated by Braz. poets.

Paquette (păkĕt'), village (pop. estimate 150), S Que., on N.H. border, 30 mi. SE of Sherbrooke; dairying, lumbering, stock raising.

Par, town, E Cornwall, England, on St. Austell Bay of the Channel and 4 mi. E of St. Austell; fishing port, resort; China-clay mines, granite quarries.

Pará (pŭrä'), state (□ 469,778; 1940 pop. 944,644; 1950 census 1,142,846), N Brazil; ⊙ Belém. Bounded by Br. Guiana and Du. Guiana (N); and by Amapá territory and the Atlantic (NE), states of Maranhão and Goiás (E and SE), Mato Grosso (S), Amazonas (W), and Rio Branco territory (NW). Third largest state of Brazil. Lies entirely within Amazon basin, which is covered by tropical rain forest. Crossed E-W by the equator and by lower Amazon R., which forms an enormous delta composed of 2 main distributaries—Amazon proper and Pará R.—separated by large Marajó isl. Chief Amazon tributaries in this state are the Tapajós, Xingu, and Tocantins (right), and the Trombetas and Jari (left). Warm and humid climate, with small diurnal temperature range and heavy, almost daily, precipitation. Agr. only in clearings along streams and in pioneer areas bet. Belém and Bragança; includes cotton, cacao, manioc, sugar, rice, corn, and tobacco growing. Brazil nuts, oil-bearing seeds, fibers, medicinal plants and rubber are gathered in their wild state. Experimental rubber plantations were established in 1927 along Tapajós R. at Fordlândia and later at Belterra. Cattle and horse raising on grasslands of E Marajó isl. Diamonds found in Tocantins R. and gold in Gurupi R. along Maranhão border. Pará state's products (primarily rubber, Brazil nuts, medicinal plants, tropical hardwood, jute) are exported via Belém, chief commercial and communications center of the Amazon area. Other important cities are Santarém and Óbidos on the lower Amazon. Pará has less than 300 mi. of railroads: one linking Belém and Bragança (with several spurs), and one under construction around the rapids of Tocantins R. above Tucuruí. Chief means of transport are hydroplanes and river steamers. There are few hard-surfaced roads. Pará was made a prov. after creation of Brazilian Empire (early 19th cent.), and a state when Brazil became a federal republic in 1889. Early 20th-cent. rubber boom in state was followed by economic decline; renewed efforts at growing rubber on plantations have not yet brought large-scale results. Amapá territory was carved out of Pará in 1943. An area (□ 1,232) along W border of state is disputed (1949) by Pará and Amazonas.

Pará, city, Pará state, Brazil: see BELÉM.

Para, La, Argentina: see LA PARA.

Parabel or **Parabel'** (pŭrŭbyĕl'), village (1948 pop. over 500), central Tomsk oblast, Russian SFSR, on Ob R., at mouth of Parabel R., and 15 mi. S of Narym, in agr. area; river port.

Parabel River or **Parabel' River**, central Tomsk oblast, Russian SFSR, formed by junction of Kenga and Chuzik rivers; flows c.80 mi. N and ENE to Ob R. at Parabel.

Parabiago (päräbyä'gô), town (pop. 8,453), Milano prov., Lombardy, N Italy, near Olona R., 13 mi. NW of Milan; industrial center; shoe factories, foundries, cotton mills.

Parabita (pärä'bētä), town (pop. 7,091), Lecce prov., Apulia, S Italy, 8 mi. E of Gallipoli; wine, olive oil.

Paracale (päräkä'lā), town (1939 pop. 5,776; 1948 municipality pop. 11,801), Camarines Norte prov., SE Luzon, Philippines, on small inlet of Philippine Sea, just E of Jose Pañganiban, 100 mi. NW of Legaspi; mining center (iron, topaz, amethyst).

Paracambi (pŭrŭkăm'bē), town (pop. 3,278), W Rio de Janeiro state, Brazil, in the Serra do Mar, 10 mi. SSE of Barra do Piraí; rail terminus; corn, rice, coffee.

Paracas Peninsula (pärä'käs), on the Pacific, in Ica dept., SW Peru, 10 mi. SW of Pisco; 7 mi. wide, 9 mi. long. Has pre-Columbian ruins. Paracas Bay (a S inlet of Pisco Bay) is N.

Paracatu (pŭrŭkŭtōō'), city (pop. 4,287), NW Minas Gerais, Brazil, near Goiás border, 120 mi. W of Pirapora; cattle-raising center; coffee- and sugar-growing. Abandoned gold and diamond mines. Road to Pôrto do Buriti, head of navigation on Paracatu R.

Paracatu River, W Minas Gerais, Brazil, rises in 2 headstreams on Goiás border, flows over 200 mi. generally E to the São Francisco (left bank) above São Romão. Navigable from Pôrto do Buriti (25 mi. E of Paracatu city).

Paracel Islands (pärăsĕl'), Chinese *Sisha* or *Hsi-sha* (both: shē'shä') [western reefs], extensive group of low coral islands and reefs, in S.China Sea, part of Kwangtung prov., China, 150 mi. SE of Hainan, bet. 15°46'–17°8'N and 111°11'–112°54'E. Includes Amphitrite Group (NE) with Woody Isl. (radio station), Crescent Group (W), Lincoln Isl. (E), Triton Isl. (SW). Edible birds' nests, also turtles, guano deposits. Prior to Second World War, under vague control of Fr. Indochina. Occupied 1939–45 by Japan. Passed to Chinese after Second World War.

Parachilna (părŭchĭl′nŭ), settlement, E central South Australia, 130 mi. NNE of Port Pirie, on Port Pirie–Alice Springs RR; sheep center.

Parachinar (pä″rŭchĭnär′), village, hq. of Kurran agency, W North-West Frontier Prov., W Pakistan, 80 mi. W of Peshawar, at foot of Safed Koh Range; rice, wheat, corn; handicraft cloth weaving. Apples and pears grown near by. Linked via Paiwar Pass with Gardez, Afghanistan.

Paracho (pärä′chō), officially Paracho de Verduzco, town (pop. 3,304), Michoacán, central Mexico, on central plateau, 18 mi. N of Uruapan; corn, sugar cane, fruit, tobacco, livestock; mfg. of stringed instruments.

Paracin or **Parachin** (both: pä′rächĭn), Serbo-Croatian *Paraćin*, town (pop. 10,120), central Serbia, Yugoslavia, 80 mi. SSE of Belgrade, near the Morava. Rail junction; center of woolen textile industry dating from 1921; glassworks, construction industry.

Paraclete, France: see NOGENT-SUR-SEINE.

Paracotos (päräkō′tōs), town (pop. 659), Miranda state, N Venezuela, in coastal range, 8 mi. SE of Los Teques; coffee, sugar cane, cacao, corn.

Parácuaro (pärä′kwärō). **1** Town (pop. 3,134), Guanajuato, central Mexico, on railroad and 6 mi. NNE of Acámbaro; grain, alfalfa, sugar cane, vegetables, livestock. **2** Officially Parácuaro de Morelos, town (pop. 1,500), Michoacán, W Mexico, 10 mi. NE of Apatzingán; sugar cane, rice, fruit.

Paracuellos de Jarama (päräkwĕ′lyōs dhä härä′mä), town (pop. 649), Madrid prov., central Spain, on Jarama R. and 10 mi. NE of Madrid; cereals, olives, chick-peas, sheep; lumbering. Has palace of dukes of Medinaceli.

Parad (pŏ′räd), Hung. *Parád*, resort town (pop. 2,715), Heves co., N Hungary, on N slope of Matra Mts. and 16 mi. W of Eger; hot springs in vicinity.

Parada Arapey, Uruguay: see ARAPEY.

Parada Esperanza, Uruguay: see ESPERANZA.

Paradas (pärä′dhäs), town (pop. 8,204), Seville prov., SW Spain, 22 mi. E of Seville; processing and agr. center (olives, cereals, grapes, livestock). Liquor distilling, olive-oil pressing, flour milling, mfg. of soap.

Pará de Minas (pŭrä′ dĭ mē′nŭs), city (pop. 6,710), S central Minas Gerais, Brazil, on railroad and 45 mi. W of Belo Horizonte; textiles, coffee, tobacco, brandy, dairy products. Talc and soapstone quarries. Has model state farm.

Paradís, Dominican Republic: see PARAÍSO.

Paradise, village (pop. 726), Berbice co., E Br. Guiana, head of navigation on lower Berbice R. (100 mi. upstream), just S of Takama, 55 mi. SSW of New Amsterdam.

Paradise (pärädē′zŭ), village (pop. 1,367), Nickerie dist., NW Du. Guiana, on Nickerie R. and 5 mi. SE of Nieuw Nickerie; rice-growing center.

Paradise (pă′rŭdīs). **1** Village (1940 pop. 2,859), Butte co., N central Calif., in Sierra Nevada foothills, 12 mi. E of Chico; citrus fruit, grape juice. **2** Village (pop. 4,426), Stanislaus co., central Calif. **3** City (pop. 145), Russell co., N central Kansas, on small affluent of Saline R. and 16 mi. NNW of Russell; livestock, wheat. **4** Village (pop. c.250), Sanders co., W Mont., near confluence of Flathead R. and the Clark Fork, 50 mi. NW of Missoula; railroad div. point. **5** Town (pop. 401), Cache co., N Utah, 10 mi. NE of Brigham City; alt. 4,860 ft.; agr.

Paradise Harbor, wide embayment in Danco Coast, Palmer Peninsula, Antarctica. Site of Chilean air base (Presidente González Videla Base) established (1951) at 64°49′S 62°52′W. Also called Paradise (Sp. *Paraíso*) Bay.

Paradise Lake, Ill.: see LITTLE WABASH RIVER.

Paradise Valley, village (pop. estimate 200), E Alta., near Sask. border, 30 mi. SW of Vermilion; mixed farming, grain, stock.

Paradox Lake, Essex co., NE N.Y., in the Adirondacks, just NE of Schroon L. and 14 mi. W of Ticonderoga; c.4 mi. long, ¼–½ mi. wide. State camp site.

Paragon, town (pop. 463), Morgan co., central Ind., near West Fork of White R., 16 mi. N of Bloomington, in agr. area.

Paragonah (pârŭgō′nŭ), town (pop. 404), Iron co., SW Utah, 4 mi. NE of Parowan; alt. 5,897 ft.; alfalfa, grain.

Paragould (pă′rŭgōōld), city (pop. 9,668), ⊙ Greene co., NE Ark., 34 mi. WNW of Blytheville, in agr. area; mfg. of wood products, feed, flour, clothing; cotton ginning; cold storage plants, canneries, bottling works, railroad shops. Crowley's Ridge State Park (swimming, boating, camping) near by. Inc. 1882.

Paragua, a former name of PALAWAN isl., Philippines.

Paragua, La, Venezuela: see LA PARAGUA.

Paraguaçu or **Paraguassú** (both: pŭrŭgwŭsōō′). **1** City (pop. 2,334), SW Minas Gerais, Brazil, 20 mi. W of Varginha, in coffeegrowing dist. **2** City, São Paulo, Brazil: see PARAGUAÇU PAULISTA.

Paraguaçu Paulista (poulē′stŭ), city (pop. 4,440), W São Paulo, Brazil, on railroad and 55 mi. ESE of Presidente Prudente; processes cotton, coffee, corn, lumber. Until 1944, called Paraguaçu (old spelling, Paraguassú); and, 1944–48, Araguaçu.

Paraguaçu River, central and E Bahia, Brazil, rises on N slope of the Serra do Sincorá, flows c.300 mi. E, past Andaraí, Itaetê, and Cachoeira (head of navigation), to Todos os Santos Bay of the Atlantic below Maragogipe. Crossed by railroad bridge bet. Cachoeira and São Félix. Region along its upper course is a leading source of black industrial diamonds. Formerly spelled Paraguassú R.

Paraguaipoa (pärägwīpō′ä), town (pop. 604), Zulia state, NW Venezuela, landing on W shore of Gulf of Venezuela, 55 mi. NNW of Maracaibo; fishing.

Paraguai River, Brazil: see PARAGUAY RIVER.

Paraguaná Peninsula (pärägwänä′), Falcón state, NW Venezuela, bet. the Caribbean and Gulf of Venezuela; linked S with mainland by narrow Isthmus of Médanos, at the base of which lies Coro; c.40 mi. long (N-S), 33 mi. wide. Gulf of Coro is S. Consists of arid plains with lagoons along coast. Main activities are goat grazing and fishing (pearls, mackerel, tuna, mullet, shrimp, sharks). Cariubana on SW coast has oil wells, and Las Piedras serves as port for transshipment of oil. Pueblo Nuevo is main settlement.

Paraguarí (pärägwärē′), department (□ 3,187; pop. 152,250), S Paraguay; ⊙ Paraguarí. Bordered S by Tebicuary R. Fertile forested lowlands, with hills in NE; subtropical climate. Predominantly a lumbering and agr. area (oranges, cotton, sugar cane, peanuts, corn, rice, tobacco, cattle). Processing at its centers: Paraguarí, Carapeguá, Quiindy, Acahay, Ybycuí. Its iron deposits are largely unexploited.

Paraguarí, city (dist. pop. 12,691), ⊙ Paraguarí dept., S Paraguay, on railroad and 40 mi. SE of Asunción; 25°37′S 57°8′W. Commercial, industrial, and agr. center (cotton, tobacco, oranges, corn, rice, cattle); potteries, distilleries, tanneries, rice and flour mills; oil of petitgrain extracting. Once a Jesuit mission (founded 1775), it has also an old Franciscan church. The Santo Tomás grottoes, with renowned hieroglyphs, are near by.

Paraguá River (pärägwä′), Santa Cruz and Beni depts., NE Bolivia, rises near San Ignacio, flows 260 mi. N to the Guaporé at Brazil border. Receives the Tarvo (right). Navigable for c.110 mi., below mouth of Tarvo R., to Puerto Frey.

Paragua River (pärä′gwä), Bolívar state, SE Venezuela, rises in Pacaraima mts. near Brazil border, flows 300 mi. N and NNE, through tropical forests, to Caroní R., 100 mi. SSE of Ciudad Bolívar, at 6°55′N 62°55′W. Not navigable.

Paraguassú, city, Brazil: see PARAGUAÇU, Minas Gerais.

Paraguassú River, Brazil: see PARAGUAÇU RIVER.

Paraguay (pă′rŭgwā, –gwī, Sp. pärägwī′), republic (□ 157,047; 1947 pop. estimate 1,259,826), S central South America; ⊙ ASUNCIÓN. One of the continent's 2 inland republics, it is largely surrounded by rivers of the Río de la Plata system, giving it access to the sea. Its entire S section is embedded in N Argentina, from which it is separated by the Paraná R. (S and SE), Paraguay R. (joining the Paraná at S boundary), and Pilcomayo R. (W). It borders Brazil on E (Paraná R., Cordillera de Amambay) and NE (Apa R., Paraguay R.). Bolivia, the other inland republic, with whom it shares part of the once vehemently disputed CHACO, is on N and NW. The country is divided into 2 well-defined halves by the Paraguay R., which crosses it N-S and is navigable by 12-ft.-draft ships from the Atlantic to Asunción (625 mi. N of Buenos Aires) and by 7-ft.-draft vessels further upstream to Corumbá in Brazil. The Paraná can be navigated to the GUAÍRA FALLS on Brazil line. All the eastern land in the fork of the Paraguay and Paraná rivers is Paraguay proper, sometimes referred to as *Paraguay Oriental*. The vast, backward W part consists of torrid grasslands and hardwood forests, drained by several affluents of the Paraguay. Here quebracho (for tannin) and petroleum are its chief resources; the region is well adapted to cattle raising, and some crops (cotton, corn, manioc, peanuts, tobacco) are grown on a limited scale by immigrants, chiefly Mennonites. There are a few scattered military outposts. Practically all the country's pop., however, lives E of the Paraguay. This is a fertile lowland, composed of *tierra colorada* and watered by numerous streams bordered by swamplands. Densely forested ridges, partly cleared, are in the N. The principal crop is cotton, the leading export, followed by tobacco and oranges; also sugar cane, tangerines, grapefruit, corn, rice, wheat, barley, beans, coffee, mandioca, indigo, grapes, bananas, pineapples, olives. Paraguay furnishes c.¾ of the world's supply of oil of petitgrain (bitter oranges), used in perfumes and flavorings. Forest products, making up about ⅓ of all exports (another ⅓ comes from agr., and roughly ⅓ is animal products), include quebracho extract, maté, timber, vanilla, cinnamon, dye, fiber-producing and medicinal plants. The extensive cattle industry yields meat (frozen, jerked, canned), beef extract, hides, fats, tallow. Meat-packing plants, stationed in the major cities, play an important part in the economy. Industries are chiefly devoted to the processing of grazing and agr. produce (cotton ginning, maté milling, sugar refining, mfg. of alcohol, rum, molasses, cigars). Paraguay's lace is highly esteemed. Protective duties, yielding about ½ of the country's revenues, are levied on consumer goods and other imports, such as textiles, clothing, vehicles, foodstuffs, wines, chemicals and pharmaceuticals, machinery. Paraguay is rich in mineral deposits, which have so far been little exploited; foremost are iron and manganese, and there are copper, mercury, limestone, kaolin, gold, and zinc deposits. All important cities are in the E. The capital, Asunción, dominates the nation's entire social and economic life. Here live 10% of all the inhabitants, and the bulk of foreign trade passes through its port. A railroad now links the city with Buenos Aires across the Paraná (by ferry) via ENCARNACIÓN. Aviation solves some of the country's transportation difficulties. The 2d city, also on railroad to Buenos Aires, and a trading and processing center, is VILLARRICA. The pop. of Paraguay is predominantly mestizo, with some Spanish, Italian, German, Russian, Anglo-Saxon, and French elements due to more recent immigration. There are hardly any Negroes. The language of the native Guaranís is still widely used, even in literature, though Spanish is the official language. The Guaranís had achieved a high material civilization in pre-Columbian times, and the Jesuit reductions (*reducciones*), operating from late-16th to 18th cent., helped to blend them with Sp. culture. Paraguay's "discovery" is closely linked with that of the Río de la Plata, though the 1st European to visit (about 1524) the region is believed to have been the Portuguese Alejo García, who set out from the Brazilian coast. The Paraguay R., promising access to Peru, was explored (1527) by Sebastian Cabot. Asunción was founded in 1536 or 1537, and soon emerged, notably under Irala, as the center of the La Plata region, from which the new Buenos Aires and other Argentine cities (e.g., Santa Fe and Corrientes) were founded. In 1617 Paraguay became a colony separate from Argentina and was placed immediately under viceroyalty of Peru until the viceroyalty of La Plata was set up in 1776 with Buenos Aires as capital. The flourishing colonization (leaving many remarkable monuments) under Jesuit guidance came to an abrupt end (1767) when the fathers were recalled. Though early revolts against Sp. rule took place, Paraguay stood aside when the struggle for independence broke out in Buenos Aires, and the expedition sent out (1810) by the Argentine patriots under Manuel Belgrano remained unsuccessful. Paraguay quietly ousted the Sp. officials next year, but soon embarked on a disastrous political course. Three dictators shaped her destiny successively: José Gaspar Rodríguez Francia (1814–40), known as El Supremo, Carlos Antonio López (1844–62), and the latter's son Solano López, who by his megalomaniac designs drove Paraguay into the War of the Triple Alliance (1865–70) against the combined forces of Brazil, Argentina, and Uruguay. The little country fought stubbornly until more than ½ of its pop. (and virtually all healthy males) were killed. Short-lived dictatorships followed. A promising recovery was disrupted by the outbreak of the Chaco War (1932–35) with Bolivia, which left victorious Paraguay exhausted. Apart from the Higinio Morínigo dictatorship (1940–48), which itself had to face civil warfare, the country went through a rapid succession of governments and coups d'état. Paraguay sided (1945) during Second World War with the Allies, and soon after signed the U.N. charter. For further information see separate articles on cities, towns, physical features, and the following 16 departments: ALTO PARANÁ, AMAMBAY, BOQUERÓN, CAAGUAZÚ, CAAZAPÁ, CENTRAL, CONCEPCIÓN, GUAIRÁ, ITAPÚA, LAS CORDILLERAS, MISIONES, ÑEEMBUCÚ, OLIMPO, PARAGUARÍ, PRESIDENTE HAYES, SAN PEDRO.

Paraguay Grande (pärägwī′ grän′dā), village (1930 pop. 502), Llanquihue prov., S central Chile, 19 mi. NW of Puerto Montt, in agr. area (cereals, potatoes, livestock); dairying, lumbering. Paraguay Chico (1930 pop. 565) is 5 mi. S.

Paraguay River (pă′rŭgwā, –gwī, Sp. pärägwī′), Port. *Paraguai* (pŭrŭgwī′), central South America, chief tributary of the Paraná; rises in Brazil in central Mato Grosso on SE slopes of the Serra dos Parecis near Diamantino, flows S, past Cáceres, Corumbá, and Coimbra (old fort), beyond which it forms Brazil-Bolivia line (for 25 mi.), then Brazil-Paraguay line, passing Puerto Guaraní and Pôrto Murtinho. It enters Paraguay at influx of Apa R., divides that country into the Chaco (W Paraguay) and more densely populated E Paraguay, flows past Concepción and Asunción, then forms Paraguay-Argentina border until its influx into the Paraná just above Corrientes (Argentina). Length, c.1,300 mi. In its Braz. course (bet. Cáceres and Paraguay border) it traverses a marshy flood plain (locally called *Pantanal*) inundated Nov.–April. Chief tributaries are Pilcomayo and Bermejo rivers (right), and São Lourenço (which receives Cuiabá R.), Taquari, Miranda, Jejuí-guazú, and Tebicuary rivers (left). The Paraguay is an important shipping lane serving the interior of S. America. It is regularly ascended by steamers from Buenos Aires to Asunción and Corumbá, and thence to the influx of São Lourenço R. (which is ascended to Cuiabá, head of navigation on Cuiabá R.). The Paraguay proper is navigable for smaller vessels to Cáceres. First ascended by Sebastian Cabot in 1526. In 1536–37, Asunción (1st permanent settlement on the Paraná-Paraguay) was founded by members of Pedro de Mendoza's party.

Parahiba, state, Brazil: see PARAÍBA.

Parahiba do Sul, city, Brazil: see PARAÍBA DO SUL.

Parahiba River, Brazil: see PARAÍBA RIVER.

Parahoué (pärä'hwā), village (pop. c.500), S Dahomey, Fr. West Africa, near Fr. Togoland border, 70 mi. WNW of Porto-Novo; palm kernels, palm oil, cotton. Cotton gin. R.C. mission.

Parahyba, state, Brazil: see PARAÍBA.

Parahyba, city, Brazil: see JOÃO PESSOA, Paraíba.

Parahyba do Sul, city, Brazil: see PARAÍBA DO SUL.

Parahyba River, Brazil: see PARAÍBA RIVER.

Parahybuna. 1 City, Minas Gerais, Brazil: see JUIZ DE FORA. **2** City, São Paulo, Brazil: see PARAIBUNA.

Parahybuna River, Brazil: see PARAIBUNA RIVER.

Paraíba (pŭräē'bŭ), state (□ 21,730; 1940 pop. 1,422,282; 1950 census 1,730,784), NE Brazil; ⊙ João Pessoa. Bounded N by Rio Grande do Norte, W by Ceará, S by Pernambuco, and E by the Atlantic. Consists of narrow coastal plain drained by intermittent-flowing streams (chiefly the Paraíba), of the Borborema Plateau (center), and of a semiarid interior (*sertão*) drained northward by upper Piranhas R. Dams and storage reservoirs permit irrigation agr. in the interior. It is a leading cotton-growing state, supplying textile mills in Recife. Other crops are sugar cane, tobacco, corn, and pineapples. State also ships agave fibers, cottonseed and oiticica oil, hides and skins. Highly mineralized Borborema Plateau yields copper, tin ore, columbite, tantalite, and beryls. Growing industries include textile milling (especially at Rio Tinto), sugar refining; and mfg. of Portland cement, footwear, and tobacco products. Chief cities are João Pessoa and its seaport of Cabedelo, Campina Grande, Cajàzeiras, and Patos. E part of state is linked by rail with Natal (N) and Recife (S). W part has rail line extending into Ceará and is therefore commercially tributary to Fortaleza. Economy suffers from periodic droughts. Several federal water-storage and irrigation projects under construction. Settled 1584, territory was originally part of Itamaracá captaincy, then was briefly (end of 18th cent.) a dependency of Pernambuco, and afterward became a prov. (1820s) of the Brazilian empire, and a state of the federal republic (1889). Formerly spelled Parahyba or Parahiba and sometimes called Parahyba do Norte.

Paraíba do Norte River, Brazil: see PARAÍBA RIVER, Paraíba.

Paraíba do Sul (do͞o so͞ol'), city (pop. 3,516), N central Rio de Janeiro state, Brazil, on Paraíba R. and 5 mi. WSW of Três Rios; rail junction; has large textile mill; ships dairy produce, lard, coffee, brandy. Nickel deposits. Formerly spelled Parahyba (or Parahiba) do Sul.

Paraíba do Sul River, Brazil: see PARAÍBA RIVER, São Paulo and Rio de Janeiro.

Paraíba River. 1 or **Paraíba do Norte River** (do͞o nôr'tĭ), Paraíba state, NE Brazil, rises in the Serra dos Cariris Velhos on Pernambuco border, flows c.180 mi. generally ENE, past João Pessoa (head of navigation), to the Atlantic at Cabedelo. Intermittent-flowing stream. Formerly spelled Parahyba or Parahiba. **2** or **Paraíba do Sul River** (do͞o so͞ol'), SE Brazil, chief stream of Rio de Janeiro state (which it traverses in length) entering the Atlantic below Campos. Length, over 600 mi. Rises as the Paraitinga in the Serra da Bocâina (São Paulo) 30 mi. NW of Angra dos Reis (Rio de Janeiro), flows SW to Guararema (where it is but 40 mi. from São Paulo city), then turns sharply NE, forming an ever-widening valley bet. the Serra da Mantiqueira (N) and Serra do Mar (S), and passing São José dos Campos, Taubaté, Cruzeiro (São Paulo), and Barra Mansa, Volta Redonda, Barra do Piraí (Rio de Janeiro); below Três Rios the river enters narrow rocky gorge, and forms Rio de Janeiro–Minas Gerais border as far as its lower valley, which begins above influx of Pomba R. The poorly drained delta, beginning at Campos and protruding into the Atlantic at São Tomé Cape, is filled with lagoons and crisscrossed by canals. The river proper enters the sea at São João da Barra. The Paraíba valley figures prominently in the economic development of SE Brazil. The coffee cycle, which began here early in 19th cent., has spread to central and W São Paulo. More recently, the land has been reclaimed for stock raising and for localized commercial cultivation of rice and citrus fruit. The valley forms the chief traffic artery bet. Rio de Janeiro and São Paulo, and as such has been the scene of recent industrialization (steel mill at Volta Redonda). Sugar is extensively grown in lower valley and delta. River's left tributaries (especially the Paraibuna) provide access to the central plateau of Minas Gerais. The SANTA CECÍLIA reservoir above Barra do Piraí forms part of the Paraíba-Piraí diversion project, designed to bring water from the Paraíba R. via the Piraí R. (SANTANA reservoir) to the Forçacava power plants. Formerly spelled Parahyba or Parahiba.

Paraibuna (pŭräēbo͞o'nŭ), city (pop. 1,793), E São Paulo, Brazil, on Paraibuna R. and 60 mi. ENE of São Paulo; dairying, distilling; mica, kaolin, graphite deposits. Formerly Parahybuna.

Paraibuna River, S Minas Gerais, Brazil, rises in the Serra da Mantiqueira S of Santos Dumont, flows c.75 mi. SSE, past Juiz de Fora, into Rio de Janeiro state, entering the Paraíba below Três Rios. Paralleled by Belo Horizonte–Rio de Janeiro road and railroad. Formerly spelled Parahybuna.

Paraim River, Brazil: see GURGUEIA RIVER.

Parainen, Finland: see PARGAS.

Paraíso (pärä'ē'sō), town (pop. 1,759), Cartago prov., central Costa Rica, on branch of Inter-American Highway, on railroad and 4 mi. SE of Cartago. Corn, manioc, beans, livestock. Radio station. Founded 1823 by pop. of colonial center of Ujarrás or Ujarraz (ruins 3 mi. SE in Reventazón R. valley), which was abandoned because of malarial and flood conditions.

Paraíso, town (1950 pop. 1,230), Barahona prov., SW Dominican Republic, on the coast, 17 mi. SSW of Barahona; coffee, sugar cane, timber. Formerly Paradís.

Paraíso, city (pop. 1,753), Tabasco, SE Mexico, on inlet of Gulf of Campeche, 32 mi. NNW of Villahermosa; cacao-growing center.

Paraíso, village (pop. 306), Los Santos prov., S central Panama, in Pacific lowland, 2 mi. W of Pocrí; sugar cane, coffee, yucca, livestock.

Paraiso, Sp. *Paraíso,* military reservation (pop. 1,503), Balboa dist., S Panama Canal Zone, on Gaillard Cut, near Pedro Miguel Locks, 8 mi. NW of Panama city. Airfield.

Paraíso, El, Honduras: see EL PARAÍSO.

Paraíso Bay, Antarctica: see PARADISE HARBOR.

Paraíso de Chavasquén (dā chäväskĕn'), town (pop. 679), Portuguesa state, W Venezuela, in Andean spur, 30 mi. NNW of Guanare; alt. 6,476 ft.; coffeegrowing.

Paraisópolis (pŭrīzô'po͝olēs), city (pop. 4,542), SW Minas Gerais, Brazil, on N slope of the Serra da Mantiqueira, near São Paulo border, 22 mi. SW of Itajubá; alt. 2,840 ft. Rail-spur terminus; agr. trade center (livestock, sugar cane, coffee, tobacco); sugar milling, dairying. Formerly spelled Paraizopolis.

Paraíso River, Bolivia: see SAN MARTÍN RIVER.

Paraitinga River, headstream of PARAÍBA RIVER in SE São Paulo, Brazil.

Parajd, Rumania: see PRAID.

Parakhino-Poddubye or **Parakhino-Poddub'ye** (pŭrä'khēnŭ-pŭdo͞o'byĭ), town (1939 pop. over 10,000), E central Novgorod oblast, Russian SFSR, 22 mi. W of Borovichi; paper-milling center.

Parakou (pärä'ko͞o), town (pop. c.5,000), central Dahomey, Fr. West Africa, rail terminus 190 mi. N of Porto-Novo; agr. center (cotton, peanuts, castor beans, shea nuts, shea-nut butter, kapok, rice, soya; goats, sheep, cattle); cotton and kapok ginning. Animal husbandry.

Parakrama Samudra, Ceylon: see POLONNARUWA.

Paralimne, Lake, or **Lake Paralimni** (both: pärŭlĭm'nē) (□ 5.8), in Boeotia nome, E central Greece, 7 mi. NE of Thebes, on Cephisus R.; 6 mi. long.

Paralimni (pärälēm'nē), village (pop. 2,720), Famagusta dist., SE Cyprus, 6 mi. SSE of Famagusta; wheat, potatoes, vetches, olives; sheep, cattle, hogs. Frequently visited by earthquakes. Near by was L. Paralimni, formerly isl.'s largest lake, now drained for irrigation.

Paraloma (pă'rŭlō'mŭ), town (pop. 186), Sevier co., SW Ark., 11 mi. NNE of Ashdown.

Paramagudi (pŭr"ŭmŭgo͝od'ē) or **Paramakudi** (–ko͝od'ē), town (pop. 17,758), Ramnad dist., S Madras, India, on Vaigai R. and 40 mi. SE of Madura; silk weaving.

Paramaribo (pă"rŭmă'rĭbō, Du. pärämä'rēbō), city (□ 5.5; pop. 76,466), ⊙ Du. Guiana and ⊙ (but independent of) Surinam dist. (□ 8,036; pop. 62,741), on left bank of Surinam R. 15 mi. upstream from its mouth on the Atlantic, and c.200 mi. ESE of Georgetown; 5°50'N 55°13'W. Largest town and chief port of the colony, connected by sea and air with U.S., Brazil, and the Netherlands. Terminus of railroad inland to Dam (80 mi S). As trade center and principal outlet for the interior, it exports sugar cane, rice, coffee, cacao, rum, balata, tropical timber, bauxite, and gold. Mfg. of matches and soft drinks; sawmills. A clean city of Du. character, intersected by canals, it has wharves, warehouses, customhouse, botanical gardens, agr. research station, and the old Fort Zeelandia. An anc. Indian village, selected by the French for early settlement in 1540, it was made capital of the English Surinam colony by Lord Willoughby in 1650, a status which it retained when finally placed (1816) under Du. rule.

Paramé (pärämā'), town (pop. 6,357), Ille-et-Vilaine dept., W France, on English Channel and 2 mi. ENE of Saint-Malo; well-known bathing resort with 2-mi.-long beach and boardwalk; truck gardens, fishing.

Paramillo (pärämē'yō), Andean massif (12,992 ft.) in Antioquia dept., NW central Colombia, 60 mi. NW of Medellín, in Cordillera Occidental; from it branch off northward the Serranía de Ayapel, Serranía de San Jerónimo, and Serranía de Abibe.

Paramillos, Sierra de los (syĕ'rä dā lōs pärämē'yōs), or **Sierra de Uspallata** (o͞ospäyä'tä), subandean range in Mendoza prov., Argentina, W and NW of Mendoza; extends c.70 mi. S from San Juan prov. border; rises to over 11,000 ft. Rich in coal (Salagasta), limestone (Capdevila, Panqueua), serpentine, lead, zinc (Uspallata), sulphur springs (Villavicencio, Cacheuta), and other minerals.

Paramirim (pŭrŭmērēn'), city (pop. 1,055), central Bahia, Brazil, 75 mi. SW of Andaraí, and on Paramirim R. (right tributary of São Francisco R.); gold mining.

Paramithia, Greece: see PARAMYTHIA.

Páramo Cendé (pä'rämō sĕndā'), peak (11,653 ft.) on Trujillo-Lara border, NW Venezuela, in N Andean spur, 11 mi. SW of Humocaro Alto.

Páramo Frontino, Colombia: see FRONTINO, PÁRAMO.

Paramonga (pärämōng'gä), village (pop. 4,985), Lima dept., W central Peru, on the Pacific, on Pan-American Highway and 6 mi. NW of Barranca. Major sugar-cane plantation; sugar and paper milling; mfg. of furniture. Airfield. Ruins of the anc. Paramonga fortress of pre-Incan (Mochica or Chimu) and Incan civilizations are near by.

Paramus (pŭră'mŭs), residential borough (pop. 6,268), Bergen co., NE N.J., 6 mi. NE of Paterson; cement and cinder blocks; truck farming. Early Dutch buildings. Settled 1666, inc. 1922.

Paramushir Island (pŭrŭmo͞oshēr'), Jap. *Paramushiru-to* (pärä'mo͞oshē'rōōtō'), third largest (□ 954) of main Kurile Isls. group, Russian SFSR; separated from Shumshu Isl. (N) by Second Kurile Strait, from Onekotan Isl. (S) by Fourth Kurile Strait; 50°20'N 155°45'E; 60 mi. long (NE-SW), 12 mi. wide. Very mountainous, with several volcanic ranges rising to 5,898 ft. in Mt. Fuss [Jap. *Shiriyajiri*]. Sulphur deposits; fish canning, iodine processing. Main centers: Severo-Kurilsk (N), Shelekhovo (W).

Paramushiru-kaikyo, Russian SFSR: see KURILE STRAIT.

Paramushiru-to, Russian SFSR: see PARAMUSHIR ISLAND.

Paramythia or **Paramithia** (both: pärŭmĭthēä'), town (pop. 2,642), Thesprotia nome, S Epirus, Greece, 13 mi. ESE of Egoumenitsa; barley, olive oil, corn, rice, timber, livestock. Also called Aidonat or Aidunat under Turkish rule.

Paraná (pärä̈nä'), city (pop. 83,824), ⊙ Entre Ríos prov. and Paraná dept. (□ 1,840; 1947 pop. 146,754), E Argentina, on left bank of Paraná R., opposite Santa Fe, on railroad and 235 mi. NW of Buenos Aires; 31°44'S 60°32'W. River port (BAJADA GRANDE); commercial, educational, industrial, and agr. center. Mfg. of cement, lime, ceramics, soap, matches, furniture, shoes; frozen meat, lard, dairy products; railroad workshops. Trading in beef and grain. Agr. products: cereals, potatoes, tomatoes, fruit, livestock, poultry. Fishing and lumbering. Lime and gypsum deposits near by. Airport. Has administrative bldgs., governor's palace, cathedral, mus. of fine arts, observatory, agr. school, Litoral Univ. (faculty of science and education). Founded 1730, it was ⊙ Argentine confederation, 1853–62. Formerly called Bajada de Santa Fe.

Paraná (pŭrŭnä'), state (□ 77,717; 1940 pop. 1,236,276; 1950 census 2,149,509), S Brazil; ⊙ Curitiba. Bounded by São Paulo (N) and Mato Grosso (NW) states, by Paraguay (W) and Argentina (SW), and by Santa Catarina state (S), and the Atlantic (E). Its narrow coastal lowland, with short but indented shore line (Paranaguá Bay), is separated from interior upland by the great coastal escarpment, Serra do Mar, rising to 3,000 ft. The plateau, sloping westward, is dissected by numerous tributaries and subtributaries of the Paraná (Paranapanema, Ivaí, Piquiri, Iguassú). The Paraná proper forms state's W boundary. The mild, subtropical climate, tempered by alt., is considered the finest in Brazil, and has attracted numerous immigrants. Only coastal zone is warmer and humid. Fertile soil and extensive timber stands (Paraná pine) constitute Paraná's great natural wealth. Hog raising and lumbering are chief occupations in Ponta Grossa–Curitiba area. N Paraná, recently penetrated by a railroad from São Paulo, is Brazil's latest region of pioneer settlement. Here immigrants and native Brazilians from N drought areas are growing coffee on S extension of São Paulo's famed *terra roxa* [Port.,= purple soil]. Their other crops include cotton, citrus, bananas, grain, and potatoes. Londrina, regional commercial center, trades primarily with São Paulo. Central and W Paraná produces maté and livestock. Chief industries are woodworking, paper milling (large newsprint plant at Monte Alegre), meat packing (especially at Jaguariaíva and Ponta Grossa), and maté processing (Curitiba). State's products are exported via Paranaguá. the port of Curitiba. Paraná is connected by rail and road with São Paulo and Santa Catarina. W part, however, is difficult of access, except by air; here, only rail line links Pôrto Guaíra with Pôrto Mendes, circumventing the GUAÍRA FALLS on the Paraná. Near SW corner, along Argentine border, are the famed IGUASSÚ FALLS, a tourist attraction. Long a part of São Paulo, Paraná became a separate prov. in 1853, and a state of federal republic in 1889. Large-scale immigration of Italians, Germans, and Slavs has boosted Paraná's pop. and prosperity in last 50 years. Extensive W areas still await settlement. The westernmost portion of state was detached in 1943 to form part of Iguaçu federal territory, but was restored to Paraná in 1946.

Paranã (pŭrŭnä'), city (pop. 440), central Goiás, central Brazil, on Paranã R. and 130 mi. SSE of Pôrto Nacional; manioc meal, rice. Airfield. Until 1944, called Palma.

Paraná, river, Brazil-Paraguay-Argentina: see PARANÁ RIVER.

Paraná Bravo River, Argentina and Uruguay: see PARANÁ RIVER.

Paraná de las Palmas River (pärä'nä' dā läs päl'-mäs), navigable S distributary of Paraná R. delta, N Buenos Aires prov., Argentina; formed ESE of Baradero, flows c.60 mi. SE, past Zárate and Campana, to the Río de la Plata 20 mi. NNW of Buenos Aires.

Paranaguá (pŭrŭnŭgwä'), city (pop. 12,930), SE Paraná, Brazil, port on Paranaguá Bay of the Atlantic, at foot of Serra do Mar, and 50 mi. E of Curitiba. Rail terminus and chief export center of Paraná; ships maté, lumber (pine), coffee, bananas, sugar. Sawmilling, woodworking, coffee roasting and grinding, maté processing; mfg. of matches, pencils, soap, and waxes. Kaolin and manganese deposits near by. Founded c.1600 by Portuguese.

Paranaguá Bay, deep inlet of the Atlantic in Paraná, SE Brazil; 30 mi. long, 15 mi. wide. Paranaguá, the port for Curitiba, is on S shore; Antonina is at head of bay. Entrance, marked by lighthouses, is by means of a channel bet. 2 sheltering isles.

Paraná Guazú River (pärä'nä' gwäsōō'), navigable N distributary of Paraná R. delta, on Buenos Aires–Entre Ríos prov. border, Argentina; formed 14 mi. NE of Zárate, flows c.25 mi. ESE to the Río de la Plata opposite Carmelo (Uruguay).

Paranaíba (pŭrŭnäē'bŭ), city (pop. 861), SE Mato Grosso, Brazil, near Paranaíba R. (Minas Gerais border), 80 mi. NNE of Três Lagoas; cattle; lead deposits. Until 1939, called Santana do Paranaíba (old spelling, Sant' Anna do Paranahyba).

Paranaíba River, one of the headstreams of the Paraná, in E central Brazil, rises in W Minas Gerais near São Gotardo, flows c.500 mi. W and SW, forming part of Goiás–Minas Gerais and Mato Grosso–Minas Gerais border, to its confluence with the Rio Grande near 17°S 51°W where the Paraná is formed. Interrupted by falls. Important diamond washings along its course and along those of its left tributaries in the Triângulo Mineiro. Formerly Paranahyba or Paranahiba.

Paraná Ibicuy River (pärä'nä' ēbēkwē'), N arm of Paraná R. delta, Argentina, bet. Lechiguanas Isls. (S) and Entre Ríos prov. (N); formed 25 mi. SW of Gualeguay by confluence of Gualeguay and Paraná Pavón rivers, flows c.50 mi. SE, past Ibicuy, joining an arm of main Paraná stream to form the Paraná Guazú.

Paranam (pärä'näm'), village (pop. 659), Surinam dist., N Du. Guiana, landing on left bank of Surinam R. and 16 mi. SSE of Paramaribo; bauxite-mining center, with a new plant begun 1941. The mineral is loaded here on ocean-going vessels for export, mainly to U.S. The Billiton bauxite mine and plant is just N, at Onverdacht.

Paranamí, Laguna, Paraguay: see YPOÁ, LAKE.

Paranapanema River (pŭrŭnä''pŭnä'mŭ), SE Brazil, rises in the Serra Paranapiacaba 50 mi. S of Itapetininga (São Paulo), flows c.500 mi. WNW, past Piraju, and, after receiving the Itararé (left), it forms São Paulo–Paraná line to its mouth on the Paraná at 22°37'S 53°7'W. Numerous rapids. Navigable only in lower 50 mi. Chief tributaries: Rio das Cinzas, Tibagi R. (left). Paralleled by railroad bet. Salto Grande and Ourinhos (São Paulo), where it is crossed by line leading to S Brazil and to agr. colonies of N Paraná. Coffee grown on fertile plateau just S of river.

Paraná Pavón River (pärä'nä' pävōn'), N arm of Paraná R. delta, Argentina, bet. Lechiguanas Isls. (S) and Entre Ríos prov. (N), branches off main stream at Villa Constitución, flows c.60 mi. E, joining Gualeguay R. to form PARANÁ IBICUY RIVER.

Paranapiacaba (pŭrŭnä''pyŭkä'bŭ), town (pop. 2,279), SE São Paulo, Brazil, on crest of Serra do Mar, on São Paulo–Santos RR; alt. 4,510 ft.

Paranapiacaba, Serra (sĕ'rŭ), mountain range (average alt. 3,200 ft.) in E Paraná and S São Paulo, Brazil, extends c.200 mi. NE from Ponta Grossa (Paraná) to a point c.50 mi. SW of São Paulo city. Constitutes a section of the great coastal escarpment Serra do Mar. Forms divide bet. coastal Ribeira R. and tributaries of the Paraná (Paranapanema) draining W. Highly mineralized (lead, copper, gold).

Parañaque (pärän'yä'kä), town (1939 pop. 21,125; 1948 pop. 28,884), Rizal prov., S Luzon, Philippines, on Manila Bay, 7 mi. S of Manila; trade center for agr. area (rice, sugar cane, fruit); embroidery. Near-by Nichols Field (important airport serving Manila) was formerly U.S. base. The Philippines acquired it by pact (1947) with U.S.

Paraná River (Sp. pärä'nä', Port. pŭrŭnä'), a major river of South America forming, with its tributaries—notably the PARAGUAY—and with the URUGUAY, that continent's 2d largest drainage system and economically most important artery of inland communications. Rising on the plateau of SE central Brazil, it flows generally S, along Paraguay's E and S border, into Argentina where, after a course of c.2,050 mi., it joins the Uruguay to form the huge Río de la PLATA estuary on the Atlantic. Assuming the name Alto (upper) Paraná at junction (20°S 51°W) of its 2 headstreams (PARANAÍBA and Rio GRANDE), it flows SSW along Mato Grosso–São Paulo and Mato Grosso–Paraná line, cutting a deep channel into the diabase Paraná tableland. Below the URUBUPUNGÁ FALLS, it is crossed by São Paulo–Corumbá RR bridge, and becomes navigable for small barges to the GUAÍRA FALLS, which are circumvented by Pôrto Guaíra–Pôrto Mendes RR. Bet. the falls and influx of Iguassú R., it forms Brazil-Paraguay border, then turns SW and W, separating Argentina (Misiones natl. territory, Corrientes prov.) from Paraguay. Below Posadas (Argentina) and Encarnación (Paraguay), it is divided into several branches by large riverine isls., and traverses c.50 mi. of rapids (named Apipé rapids). Joined by the Paraguay above Corrientes, the Paraná (now in its middle course) assumes the former's direction of flow (N-S) and enters Argentina's N lowlands. Overflowing its low W banks at flood stage, and paralleled by numerous arms, it separates the Chaco region (W) from Mesopotamia (E). The intricate delta, which forms N limit of the Argentine Pampa, begins below Paraná (city) and Santa Fe. The Paraná Pavón, a N distributary, branches off at Villa Constitución and receives the Gualeguay to form the Paraná Ibicuy, while the main stream breaks up below San Pedro into the Paraná de las Palmas and into an arm which rejoins the Paraná Ibicuy to form the Paraná Guazú. The Paraná Bravo, branching off (N) from the Paraná Guazú, enters the Uruguay (flowing N-S) opposite Nueva Palmira (Uruguay) and at a point marking the head of the Río de la Plata. Most of the other distributaries flow directly into the Río de la Plata bet. this point and Buenos Aires, depositing large amounts of silt at their mouths. The Paraná's chief tributaries, in addition to the mighty Paraguay, are the Tietê, Paranapanema, Ivaí, Iguassú all (left) and the Rio Verde, Rio Pardo, Ivinhema, Amambaí all (right), in Brazil; the Salado and Carcarañá (right), in Argentina. Since the Paraná and Paraguay rise in tropical and subtropical areas of max. summer rainfall, the volume of the combined streams is subject to seasonal fluctuations, causing variations of level up to 15 ft. in lower course. Navigation at low stage (Sept.-Oct.) depends on regular dredging of main channel. The Paraná delta (especially the Paraná Bravo branch) is ascended by ocean-going vessels (20-ft. draught) to Rosario, Paraná, and Santa Fe, the channel being marked by lighted buoys for night travel. Smaller boats (up to 17 ft. draught) maintain year-round navigation to Corrientes, and up the Paraguay to Asunción. Shipping on the Alto Paraná (above Corrientes) is seasonal and difficult. Sebastian Cabot 1st ascended the Paraná and Paraguay in 1526. He was shortly followed by Diego García. In 1536, Pedro de Mendoza, after founding Buenos Aires, ascended the river, but did not establish a permanent settlement on the Paraná. By 1543, the middle Paraná had been reached overland from Peru, and later from Chile. Juan de Garay, during his down-river expeditions from Asunción in 1570s and '80s, founded several of today's important cities on the Paraná. In 17th and early 18th cent., Jesuit missions flourished along the Paraná as far N as Brazil. Today the river transports maté from Brazil and Paraguay, quebracho from the Chaco, corn from Rosario, and livestock, wheat, alfalfa, and flax from the N Pampa and S Mesopotamia to the Río de la Plata and overseas.

Paranã River (pŭrŭnä'), central Goiás, central Brazil, rises near Formosa, flows 250 mi. NNW to the Tocantins below Paranã city. Sometimes considered one of the headstreams of the Tocantins.

Paranestion (pärŭnĕ'stēōn), town (pop. 3,488), Drama nome, Macedonia, Greece, on railroad and 20 mi. ENE of Drama; tobacco, potatoes; wine. Formerly Boukia.

Parang, W Pakistan: see PRANG.

Parang (pä'räng), town (1939 pop. 1,393; 1948 municipality pop. 13,413), Cotabato prov., central Mindanao, Philippines, on Polloc Harbor of Illana Bay, 10 mi. N of Cotabato, for which it is a port; copra, rice, corn.

Paranga or **Paran'ga** (pŭrŭnyŭgä'), village (1932 pop. estimate 3,900; largely Tatars), E Mari Autonomous SSR, Russian SFSR, 55 mi. E of Ioshkar-Ola; wheat, rye, oats.

Parangaba (pŭrăng-gä'bŭ), residential town (1940 pop. 1,910; 1950 pop. 25,239), N Ceará, Brazil, SW suburb of Fortaleza; cotton. Airfield. Old Indian village. Formerly spelled Porangaba.

Parangaricutiro (päräng-gärēkōōtē'rō), town (1940 pop. 1,895), Michoacán, central Mexico, in Sierra de los Terascos, 20 mi. WNW of Uruapan, in agr. area. After eruption (1943) of PARICUTÍN volcano, 5 mi. SSW, town was largely engulfed by lava flow. Sometimes San Juan Parangaricutiro.

Parang Pass (päräng') (alt. 18,300 ft.), in SE Punjab Himalayas, Kangra dist., NE Punjab, India, 105 mi. ENE of Dharmsala, on mule path leading NE to W Tibet.

Parantij (pŭrän'tēj), town (pop. 8,035), Sabar Kantha dist., N Bombay, India, 12 mi. SSW of Himatnagar; trades in millet, ghee, wheat, rice, leather goods; soap mfg., tanning. Also spelled Prantij.

Paraopeba (pŭroupĕ'bŭ), city (pop. 2,907), central Minas Gerais, Brazil, near railroad, 50 mi. NW of Belo Horizonte; cotton milling.

Paraopeba River, central Minas Gerais, Brazil, rises on W slope of the Serra do Espinhaço near Conselheiro Lafaiete, flows 160 mi. NNW to the São Francisco. Not navigable. Iron deposits are along the valley.

Paraparaumu (pä''rŭpŭrŭm'), township (pop. 486), S N.Isl., New Zealand, 30 mi. NNE of Wellington; dairying center; manganese.

Parapetí, Bañados del, Bolivia: see IZOZOG, BAÑADOS DE.

Parapetí River (päräpätē'), Chuquisaca and Santa Cruz depts., SE central Bolivia, rises E of Azurduy, flows 220 mi. E, past Camiri (petroleum region), San Francisco del Parapetí, and San Antonio del Parapetí, and NE to Bañados de Izozog 70 mi. E of Cabezas.

Parapitinga (pŭrŭpētĕng'gŭ), city (pop. 1,199), NE Sergipe, NE Brazil, on right bank of São Francisco R. just above its mouth on the Atlantic, and 13 mi. SE of Penedo (Alagoas); rice. Until 1944, called São Francisco.

Parapoungia, Greece: see LEUKTRA.

Parapuã (pŭrŭpwä'), city, W São Paulo, Brazil, 60 mi. WNW of Marília, in recently settled cotton-growing region.

Pará River (pŭrä'), E Pará, Brazil, navigable SE arm of the Amazon delta, S of Marajó isl., extending from a point (1°50'S 50°40'W) where it receives the waters of the Amazon via a network of narrow, irregular channels, to the Atlantic off Cape Maguari. Length, c.200 mi.; width, 5–40 mi. Receives (right) the Tocantins (8 mi. wide at its mouth), of which it is sometimes considered the estuary. On its right bank, at influx of Guamá and Guajará rivers, is city of Belém. The famous Amazon delta tidal bore is strong here.

Parás (pärás'), town (pop. 1,123), Nuevo León, N Mexico, in alluvial plains of Rio Grande, 75 mi. NE of Monterrey; cotton, corn, sugar cane, cactus fibers.

Parasan Island (päräsän', pärä'sän) (□ 3.4; 1939 pop. 1,471), Samar prov., Philippines, in Samar Sea, near W coast of Samar isl., just NE of Daram Isl.; 11°43'N 124°45'E; 3 mi. long, 1.5 mi. wide. Coconut growing.

Parasnath Hill (pŭrŭsnät'), E outlier (4,480 ft.) of Chota Nagpur Plateau, E central Bihar, India, 50 mi. E of Hazaribagh; sacred Jain pilgrimage center, with several fine temples.

Parati (pŭrŭtē'). **1** City (pop. 1,554), southwesternmost Rio de Janeiro state, Brazil, on Ilha Grande Bay of the Atlantic, 28 mi. SW of Angra dos Reis; fish processing, sugar and manioc-flour milling. Formerly spelled Paraty. **2** City, Santa Catarina, Brazil: see ARAQUARI.

Paratinga (pŭrŭtĕng'gŭ), city (pop. 2,055), W Bahia, Brazil, on right bank of São Francisco R. (navigable) and 110 mi. S of Barra; irrigation agr. Sulphur springs near by. Airfield. Until 1944, called Rio Branco.

Paratwada (pŭrŭtvä'dŭ), town (pop. 11,156), Amraoti dist., W Madhya Pradesh, India; suburb (3 mi. N) of cotton-trade center of Ellichpur. Site of former cantonment. Sometimes called Ellichpur Camp.

Paraty, Brazil: see PARATI, Rio de Janeiro.

Paraúna (pŭräōō'nŭ), city (pop. 629), SW Goiás, central Brazil, 60 mi. W of Goiânia; livestock.

Parauta (pärou'tä), town (pop. 849), Málaga prov., S Spain, 6 mi. SSE of Ronda; chestnuts, esparto, olives, cereals, sheep, goats.

Paray-le-Monial (pärā'-lŭ-mônyäl'), town (pop. 6,240), Saône-et-Loire dept., E central France, on Bourbince R. and Canal du Centre, 28 mi. N of Roanne; mfg. of pottery and refractories. Next to Lourdes most frequented pilgrimage center in France; acquired special fame in reign of Louis XIV from visions of a nun, Marguerite Marie Alacoque (canonized 1920), out of which grew cult of Sacred Heart of Jesus. Site of 12th-cent. Romanesque church of Notre Dame and of eucharistic mus.

Paray-Vieille-Poste (–vyā-pōst'), town (pop. 4,166), Seine-et-Oise dept., N central France, 10 mi. S of Paris; mfg. (fire extinguishers, rubber soles). Orly airport just E.

Parbatipur, E Pakistan: see PARVATIPUR.

Parbati River (pär'bŭtē), W central India, rises in Vindhya Range c.19 mi. SSW of Ashta (W Bhopal), flows c.275 mi. N, through central Madhya Bharat and SE Rajasthan, to Chambal R. 15 mi. NW of Sheopur. Headworks of small irrigation canal near Atru.

Parbhani (pŭr'bŭnē), district (□ 5,125; pop. 911,886), NW Hyderabad state, India, on Deccan Plateau; ⊙ Parbhani. Bordered NE by Penganga R., SW by Godavari R., which crosses S portion. Highland (N) and lowland (S), drained by Purna R. (tributary of Godavari R.). In black-soil area; cotton, wheat, millet, oilseeds (chiefly peanuts, flax). Cotton ginning, flour and oilseed milling; cattle raising. Main trade centers: Parbhani (rail junction; experimental farm), Basmat. Became part of Hyderabad during state's formation in 18th cent. Pop. 83% Hindu, 13% Moslem.

Parbhani, town (pop. 21,683), ⊙ Parbhani dist., NW Hyderabad state, India, 170 mi. NW of Hyderabad; rail junction; trade center for cotton, millet, wheat, oilseeds (chiefly peanuts); cotton ginning. Experimental farm. Industrial school.

Parbig (pŭrbĕk'), village (1948 pop. over 500), S Tomsk oblast, Russian SFSR, on Parbig R. (headstream of Chaya R.) and 95 mi. SSW of Kolpashevo; lumbering.

Parbig River, Russian SFSR: see CHAYA RIVER.

Parbold, agr. village and parish (pop. 688), SW Lancashire, England, 7 mi. NW of Wigan. Includes village of Appley Bridge, 5 mi. NW of Wigan; mfg. of chemicals, concrete.

Parchev, Poland: see PARCZEW.

Parchim (pär'khĭm), town (pop. 19,948), Mecklenburg, N Germany, on the regulated Elde and 22 mi. SE of Schwerin; rail junction; paper milling, distilling, woodworking, food canning; asparagus market. Has 13th-cent. churches and many half-timbered houses. Founded 1218. Field Marshal von Moltke b. here.

Parchment, city (pop. 1,179), Kalamazoo co., SW Mich., 3 mi. NNE of Kalamazoo; parchment-paper factories. Founded 1909, inc. as city 1939.

Parchonice, Poland: see PROCHOWICE.

Parchwitz, Poland: see PROCHOWICE.

Parco, Sicily: see ALTOFONTE.

Parco, Wyo.: see SINCLAIR.

Parcoy (pärkoi'), town (pop. 428), Libertad dept., N central Peru, in Cordillera Central, 15 mi. NW of Tayabamba; alt. 10,535 ft.; barley, corn. Gold mining near by.

Parcq, Le (lù pärk'), agr. village (pop. 613), Pas-de-Calais dept., N France, 11 mi. W of Saint-Pol.

Parczew (pär'chĕf), Rus. *Parchev* (pär'chĭf), town (pop. 6,173), Lublin prov., E Poland, 32 mi. NNE of Lublin; mfg. of glass, bricks, tiles, cement, soap, hats; flour and groat milling; swine trade. Before Second World War, pop. 50% Jewish.

Pardee Dam; Pardee Reservoir, Calif.: see MOKELUMNE RIVER.

Pardeeville (pär'dēvĭl"), village (pop. 1,112), Columbia co., S central Wis., on Fox R. and 32 mi. N of Madison, in farm area (livestock, poultry, melons); cheese and other dairy products, canned foods; nursery stock. Inc. 1894.

Pardelhas (pŭrdā'lyŭsh), fishing village (pop. 1,963), Aveiro dist., N central Portugal, on Aveiro lagoon, 7 mi. N of Aveiro; trade in sardines and fertilizer.

Pardes Hanna or **Pardess Hanna** (both: pärdĕs' hänä'), settlement (pop. 3,500), W Israel, in Plain of Sharon, 25 mi. S of Haifa; mfg. of plastics, cosmetics, cheese; mineral-water bottling; mixed farming, citriculture. Health resort. Has agr. school; site of large immigrants' reception camp. Founded 1929.

Pardi (pär'dē), town (pop. 6,565), Surat dist., central Bombay, India, 50 mi. S of Surat; market center for rice, fish, millet; metalworks.

Pardo, El (ĕl pär'dhō), town (pop. 2,997), Madrid prov., central Spain, on the Manzanares and 9 mi. NW of Madrid. Important for its palace (built 1543 by Charles V, rebuilt by Philip IV), where the royal family frequently lived in winter; residence of Franco. Several Sp. treaties were signed here. The town is surrounded by forests of the Monte del Pardo.

Pardo, Rio (rē'ŏŏ pär'dŏŏ). **1** River in SE Mato Grosso, Brazil, rises N of Campo Grande, flows 220 mi. SE, past Ribas do Rio Pardo, to the Paraná (right bank) opposite Presidente Epitácio (São Paulo). Navigable in lower course. **2** River in NE Minas Gerais and SE Bahia, rises in the Serra do Espinhaço near 15°S 42°30'W, flows c.400 mi. E, past Rio Pardo de Minas and Itambé, to a joint delta on the Atlantic with Jequitinhonha R. just S of Canavieiras. Cacao grown in lower valley. **3** River in E São Paulo, Brazil, rises in Minas Gerais NW of Pouso Alegre, flows c.300 mi. NW, past São José do Rio Pardo, to the Rio Grande 27 mi. N of Barretos. Not navigable. Receives the Mogi-Guaçu (left).

Pardubice (pär'dŏŏbĭtsĕ), Ger. *Pardubitz* (pär'dŏŏbĭts), city (pop. 31,420), ⊙ Pardubice prov. (□ 1,634; pop. 422,950), NE Bohemia, Czechoslovakia, on Elbe R., at mouth of Chrudimka R., and 60 mi. E of Prague; 50°3'N 15°45'E. Rail junction; industrial center; produces beer, liquor, refined sugar, gingerbread, coffee substitutes; mfg. of radio and telegraph equipment, milling machinery, footwear; large oil refinery. Well-known as horse-breeding center and for its horse races and motorcycle competitions. In its layout the only purely Renaissance town in Bohemia, with 14th-cent. Annunciation church, 13th-cent. cathedral (rebuilt in 15th cent.), 16th-cent. gates, and castle (now used as mus.). Remains of 15th-cent. castle of Kunetice (kŏŏ'nĕtyĭtsĕ) 3 mi. NE.

Pare or **Paree** (both: pŭrē', -ā'), town (pop. 22,388), E central Java, Indonesia, 50 mi. SW of Surabaya, at foot of Mt. Arjuno; trade center for agr. area (rice, corn, cassava, peanuts); railroad workshops.

Parece Vela (pŭrē'sē vē'lŭ), reef in W Pacific Ocean, W of the Marianas; 20°20'N 136°E. Formerly a Jap. possession, it passed to U.S. administration after Second World War. Sometimes called Douglas Reef.

Parecis, Serra dos (sĕ'rŭ dŏŏs pŭrā'sĭs), range in Guaporé territory and central Mato Grosso, Brazil, forming W section of the Amazon-Paraguay drainage divide; extends 500 mi. NW–SE from 10°30'S, near Bolivia border, to vicinity of Diamantino near headwaters of the Paraguay. A rolling plateau in NW, it rises above 2,300 ft. in SE. On its N and W slopes rise Juruena and Guaporé rivers flowing into Amazon basin; on S slope rise the Paraguay and its tributaries.

Parede (pŭrā'dĭ), town (pop. 4,603), Lisboa dist., on the Atlantic, 12 mi. W of Lisbon; bathing and health resort; fisheries.

Paredes, Bolivia: see MAX PAREDES.

Paredes (pŭrā'dĭsh). **1** Town (pop. 1,105), Pôrto dist., N Portugal, on railroad and 14 mi. ENE of Oporto; winegrowing; olives, figs, almonds. **2** Village (pop. 1,650), Viseu dist., N central Portugal, 20 mi. SW of Viseu; sheep and goat raising.

Paredes, Las, Argentina: see LAS PAREDES.

Paredes de Coura (pŭrā'dĭsh dĭ kō'rŭ), town (pop. 373), Viana do Castelo dist., N Portugal, 20 mi. NE of Viana do Castelo; winegrowing; cattle.

Paredes de Nava (pärā'dhĕs dhä nä'vä), town (pop. 4,581), Palencia prov., N central Spain, on Canal of Castile and 13 mi. NW of Palencia; tanning, flour milling; agr. trade (cereals, wine, sheep).

Paredón, Bolivia: see ANZALDO.

Paredones (pärädhō'nĕs), village (1930 pop. 617), Colchagua prov., central Chile, 16 mi. SW of San Fernando, in agr. area (grain, fruit, wine, livestock); dairying.

Paree, Indonesia: see PARE.

Pareja (pärä'hä), town (pop. 748), Guadalajara prov., central Spain, on affluent of the Tagus and 28 mi. E of Guadalajara; olives, grapes, cereals, fruit, honey, livestock. Lumbering; olive-oil pressing; lime quarrying. Mineral springs.

Parejas, Las, Argentina: see LAS PAREJAS.

Parel, India: see BOMBAY, city.

Parelhas (pŭrā'lyŭs), city (pop. 1,657), S Rio Grande do Norte, NE Brazil, on Borborema Plateau, 120 mi. SW of Natal; mining center for columbite, tantalite, and tin. Beryl deposits.

Pare Mountains (pä'rā), volcanic range in NE Tanganyika, bet. Kilimanjaro and Usambara Mts. Rise to 6,000 ft. Sisal and coffee plantations. Tanga RR runs along W base.

Parenda (pŭrān'dŭ), village (pop. 4,802), Osmanabad dist., W Hyderabad state, India, 16 mi. W of Barsi; millet, oilseeds, wheat. Has 15th-cent. fort. Sometimes spelled Paronda.

Parent, Lac (läk pärä'), lake (32 mi. long, 4 mi. wide), W Que., extends NE from Senneterre; alt. 990 ft. Drains N into Nottaway R.

Parentis-en-Born (pärätē'-ā-bôrn'), village (pop. 998), Landes dept., SW France, 40 mi. SSW of Bordeaux; lumbering, extracting of resinous products. Lignite mined near by.

Parenzo, Yugoslavia: see POREC, village.

Parepare (pŭrā-pŭrā'), town (pop. 6,273), SW Celebes, Indonesia, on Macassar Strait, 80 mi. N of Macassar; 4°1'S 119°37'E. Trade center and port, shipping copra. Brought under Du. control in 1824.

Parera (pärä'rä), town (pop. estimate 1,000), ⊙ Rancul dept., NE La Pampa natl. territory, Argentina, 60 mi. NW of General Pico; wheat, flax, alfalfa, livestock; dairying.

Paréts (pärĕts'), village (pop. 1,521), Barcelona prov., NE Spain, 13 mi. NNE of Barcelona; livestock, wine, hemp, vegetables.

Parfenovo (pŭrfyĕ'nŭvŭ), village (1926 pop. 5,144), central Altai Territory, Russian SFSR, 20 mi. N of Aleisk, in agr. area. Formerly called Mokhovoye.

Parfenyevo or **Parfen'yevo** (pŭrfyĕ'nyĭvŭ), village (1926 pop. 1,302), central Kostroma oblast, Russian SFSR, on Neya R. (right affluent of Unzha R.) and 22 mi. WNW of Neya; flax processing.

Parfino (pär'fēnŭ), town (1926 pop. 1,186), S Novgorod oblast, Russian SFSR, 10 mi. E of Staraya Russa; veneering center; mfg. of prefabricated houses.

Parga (pär'gŭ), village (pop. 1,722), Thesprotia nome, S Epirus, Greece, port on Ionian Sea opposite Paxos isl., and 16 mi. S of Egoumenitsa, near S entrance to Strait of Corfu; olives, olive oil; goat raising, fisheries. A flourishing town in Middle Ages, Parga sought (1401) Venetian protection against the Turks, and kept it until fall of Venice (1797). Under French rule until 1814, it then passed to the British and was ceded (1819) to the Turks against wish of local pop., which abandoned the town for British-protected Ionian Isls.

Parganas, 24-, India: see TWENTY-FOUR PARGANAS.

Pargas (pär'gäs), Finnish *Parainen* (pä'rĭnĕn), town (pop. 5,835), Turku-Pori co., SW Finland, on inlet of Gulf of Bothnia, 10 mi. S of Turku; cement and lime mfg. center; limestone quarries.

Parghelia (pärgä'lyä), village (pop. 1,448), Catanzaro prov., Calabria, S Italy, near Tyrrhenian Sea, 1 mi. ENE of Tropea; kaolin quarrying.

Pargi or **Purgi** (both: pŭr'gē), village (pop. 3,430), Mahbubnagar dist., S central Hyderabad state, India, 31 mi. NNW of Mahbubnagar; millet; cattle raising, woolen weaving.

Pargny-sur-Saulx (pärnyē'-sür-sō'), village (pop. 812), Marne dept., N France, at confluence of the Saulx and the Ornain, 12 mi. ENE of Vitry-le-François, on Marne-Rhine Canal; brickworks.

Pargolovo (pär'gŭlŭvŭ), town (1926 pop. 4,187), W Leningrad oblast, Russian SFSR, 10 mi. N of Leningrad; metalworks; peat digging.

Parham (pă'rŭm), village, NE Antigua, B.W.I., 5 mi. E of St. John's. Sites near by were leased (1941) to U.S. for military and naval base.

Parham (pă'rŭm), agr. village and parish (pop. 310), E Suffolk, England, 2 mi. SE of Framlingham. Has old moated mansion and 14th-15th-cent. church with medieval stocks.

Paria (pär'yä), town (pop. c.3,600), Oruro dept., W Bolivia, in the Altiplano, on railroad and 10 mi. NE of Oruro; potatoes, sheep.

Paria, Gulf of (pär'yä), inlet (c.100 mi. long, c.40 mi. wide) of the Caribbean, bet. Trinidad (E) and coast of Venezuela, separated from the Caribbean by Paria Peninsula. Linked with the Caribbean by Dragon's Mouths (N), and with the Atlantic by Serpent's Mouth (S). Receives San Juan R. and several arms of Orinoco R. delta, including Caño Mánamo. Main ports on its coast are Port of Spain (Trinidad), and Güiria, Irapa, and Pedernales (Venezuela).

Pariaguán (päryägwän'), town (pop. 3,747), Anzoátegui state, NE Venezuela, 32 mi. W of El Tigre; agr. center (cotton, cacao, sugar cane, coffee, corn, cattle). Airfield.

Paria Peninsula (pär'yä), Sucre state, NE Venezuela, on the Caribbean, N of Gulf of Paria, separated (E) by Dragon's Mouths from Trinidad; 75 mi. long, 3–14 mi. wide. Traversed by spur of coastal range. On S coast are ports of Güiria, Irapa, and Macuro (or Cristóbal Colón).

Paria River (pŭrē'ŭ), in S Utah and N Ariz., rises in Paunsaugunt Plateau near Tropic, Utah, flows c.75 mi. SE to Colorado R. at N end of Marble Gorge, Ariz.

Parichhatgarh (pŭrē'chŭtgŭr), town (pop. 6,586), Meerut dist., NW Uttar Pradesh, India, on distributary of Upper Ganges Canal and 13 mi. E of Meerut; wheat, gram, jowar, sugar cane, oilseeds. Founding attributed to Arjuna's grandson.

Parichi (pä'rēchē), town (1926 pop. 3,549), SE Bobruisk oblast, Belorussian SSR, on Berezina R. (landing) 25 mi. SSE of Bobruisk; food products.

Paricutín (pärēkŏŏtēn') [from Tarascan *Parícuti*], active volcano (c.8,200 ft.), Michoacán, W central Mexico, just N of Tancítaro volcano, 20 mi. WNW of Uruapan. The earth's youngest mtn. and a remarkable example of a growing volcano, it erupted Feb. 20, 1943, from a cultivated field, its lava burying the little village of Paricutín and threatening Parangaricutiro, 5 mi. NNE. From its base (c.7,380 ft. above sea level) it had risen c.820 ft. (mostly in its 1st year) by 1950, when its activity had declined considerably. Its name is sometimes given as Parícutin (pärē'kŏŏtĕn), taking the accent from the Tarascan.

Parida, La, Venezuela: see BOLÍVAR, CERRO.

Parihasapura, Kashmir: see SRINAGAR.

Parika (pärē'kŭ), village (pop. 577), Demerara co., N Br. Guiana, landing on right bank of Essequibo R. estuary, terminus of railroad from Vreed-en-Hoop, and 18 mi. W of Georgetown, in rice-growing region; ships timber.

Parikkala (pä'rĭk-kä"lä), village (commune pop. 8,702), Kymi co., SE Finland, near USSR border, in lake region, 30 mi. SE of Savonlinna; lumbering.

Parima, Sierra (syĕ'rä pärē'mä), Port. *Serra Parima* (sĕ'rŭ pŭrēmä'), outlying range of the Guiana Highlands, N South America, extending c.200 mi. NNW-SSE along Brazil-Venezuela border; rises to c.5,000 ft.; largely unexplored. Here rise the Orinoco and headstreams of the Rio Branco. Range is connected with Sierra Pacaraima (NE).

Parinacochas, province, Peru: see CORACORA.

Parinacochas, Lake (pärēnäkō'chäs), Ayacucho dept., S Peru, in Cordillera Occidental of the Andes, 15 mi. SSE of Coracora; 9 mi. long, 3 mi. wide; alt. c.9,800 ft.

Parinacota, Cerro de, Chile-Bolivia: see PAYACHATA, NEVADOS DE.

Pariñas Point (pärē'nyäs), westernmost point of South America, on the Pacific, in Piura dept., NW Peru, 7 mi. SSW of Talara, at S end of Negritos oil fields; 4°40'S 81°20'W.

Parincea (pŭrēn'chä), Rum. *Pǎrincea*, village (pop. 794), Bacau prov., E Rumania, 11 mi. SE of Bacau.

Parintins (pŭrēntēns'), city (pop. 3,219), E Amazonas, Brazil, steamer and hydroplane landing on right bank of the Amazon, near Pará border, and 220 mi. E of Manaus; boatbuilding; ships guarana, rubber, Brazil nuts, jute, copaiba oil, cacao, and hides. Old names: Villa Nova da Rainha, later Villa Bella da Imperatriz.

Paripiranga (pŏorēpĕrāng'gŏo), city (pop. 3,540), NE Bahia, Brazil, on Sergipe border, 55 mi. WNW of Aracaju; coffee, tobacco, cotton; leatherworking. Formerly called Patrocínio do Coité or Coité.

Paris (pă'rĭs), town (pop. 4,637), S Ont., on Grand R., at mouth of Nith R., and 7 mi. NW of Brantford in dairying, gypsum-quarrying region; woolen-milling center; mfg. of alabastine products, refrigerators, hardware.

Paris (pă'rĭs, Fr. pärē'), largest city (□ 41; pop. 2,691,473) and ⊙ France, on both banks of Seine R. just below influx of the Marne, in the heart of the Paris Basin; 48°50'N 2°20'E. Cultural, administrative, commercial, industrial, and communications center of France. The term Greater Paris is commonly applied to the wholly urbanized area of SEINE dept. (□ 185; pop. 4,775,711)—of which Paris is ⊙—and more recently has come to include the rapidly growing outer suburbs in Seine-et-Oise dept. City is administered by 2 govt.-appointed prefects, the prefect of Seine dept. and the prefect of police, and by an elected municipal council. Paris is divided into 20 *arrondissements* (each headed by a state-appointed mayor), each further subdivided into 4 *quartiers* of approximately equal size. Located at junction of the natural routes from Spain and Aquitaine to N central Europe, and from the Mediterranean to England, Paris is at the hub of a net of communications. Within city limits are 7 leading rail termini (gares de l'Est, du Nord, de Lyon, d'Austerlitz, de Montparnasse, d'Orsay, de Saint-Lazare) interconnected by 2 rail circuits (*ceintures*) surrounding city. Principal highways leave Paris at the former city gates. Chief metropolitan airports are at LE BOURGET and ORLY. Along the Seine, which traverses Paris in a great arc for nearly 8 mi., are the tree-lined *quais*, at the foot of which are landings for small passenger boats. The river port of Paris handles largest volume of all Fr. ports. The Seine is navigable for ships up to 800 tons below Paris. The Scheldt, Meuse, Rhine, Rhone, and Loire can be reached by barges via connecting canals. Within city limits the Seine is spanned by 33 bridges of which the Pont-Neuf (at W end of Île de la Cité) is oldest (built 1578) and carries heaviest traffic. Other bridges include Pont Alexandre III (built 1900), Pont de la Concorde (1787–91), Pont Royal with 5 stone arches (1685–89), Pont du Carroussel (1831–34), and Pont d'Austerlitz (1804–06). Besides busses and trolleys, there is a network of subways (*métropolitain* or *métro*), 1st opened 1900. Paris sewers (*égouts*), 1st built under Louis XIII, discharge into the Gennevilliers peninsula, fertilizing the soil there. Boat-trips through the sewers are a leading tourist attraction. Though specializing in luxury products or *articles de Paris* (fashions, perfumes, cosmetics, jewelry, leather goods), Paris has almost every kind of Fr. industry. The dressmakers, perfumers, and luxury stores are on the Rue de la Paix, Place Vendôme, Rue Royale, Rue de Rivoli, Avenue and Place de l'Opéra; Faubourg Saint-Antoine is furniture quarter; tanners and leather dealers are concentrated on left bank along course of the Bièvre (which now flows mostly underground); chief publishing houses are in Boulevard Saint-Germain district; financial houses, large business houses, and newspapers are grouped around the Bourse; and the Rue du Sentier, in same quarter, is center of textile trade. Mfg. of automobiles and other heavy industry is in outlying Grenelle, Boulogne-Billancourt, Issy-les-Moulineaux, Levallois-Perret, Puteaux, and Suresnes. Known as the "city of light" (*Ville Lumière*) both because of the lavish illumination of its wide arteries and numerous monuments and because of its intellectual leadership, Paris was planned on an unequaled grand scale. While picturesque and fashionable districts alternate with drab and squalid ones, the city nevertheless has an undefinable unity of appearance and atmosphere that has impressed writers, painters, and visitors for centuries. The Île de la CITÉ (Notre Dame Cathedral, Palais de Justice) and its immediate environs remain the city's judicial and administrative center. It is linked by bridge with the Île Saint-Louis (just SE) occupied by elegant 17th–18th-cent. houses. The N, or right bank, part of Paris is the larger one and the center of business activity and amusements. Here is the Louvre with its famous art galleries, the Place du Carroussel (with an arch of triumph, 48 ft. high, erected 1804–06 in memory of Napoleon's victories), Tuileries garden, Place de la Concorde (city's finest square, with Obelisk of Luxor, 75 ft. high, presented 1831 to Louis Philippe by Mohamed Ali), Avenue des CHAMPS-ELYSÉES, and the Place de l'Étoile (where 12 avenues converge) with the Arc de Triomphe. The Arc de Triomphe (161 ft. high, 148 ft. wide), the largest of its kind, is richly adorned with sculptures (notably "The Marseillaise"). Begun by Napoleon I, it was completed 1836 by Louis Philippe. Under the arch is the tomb of the Unknown Soldier. Also on right bank are the Place de la Bastille (site of Bastille fortress destroyed at beginning of Fr. Revolution) with July Column (154 ft. high) erected 1831–40 in honor of Revolution of 1830; the Place Vendôme (planned by Mansart and once adorned with equestrian statue of Louis XIV) with a column (143 ft. high) topped by a statue of Napoleon I. The classical Place des Vosges with equestrian statue of Louis XIII is situated in the old Marais dist., a piece of 17th-cent. Paris. The Théatre-Français (or Comédie-Française) occupies a wing of the Palais-Royal, which encloses an arcade-lined garden. From it to the impressive Opéra (covering nearly 3 acres; built 1862–74) leads the broad Avenue de l'Opéra. On the N, MONTMARTRE, highest point of Paris, topped by church of Sacré-Coeur, dominates the city. To the E and N of it are crowded workers' residential districts. The W and NW sections of Auteuil and Passy are the city's most fashionable residential quarters. At the E and W city limits are the BOIS DE VINCENNES and BOIS DE BOULOGNE respectively, each over 2,000 acres. The left bank, lined by the famous open-air book stalls, is the intellectual, governmental, and military section. Here are the Sorbonne (Univ. of Paris); Collège de France; Institut de France (embracing the French Acad.); the Panthéon (a secularized church of grandiose design noted for its lofty dome); the 17th-cent. Luxembourg Palace and gardens (seat of upper legislative chamber); the Paris Observatory; the Chamber of Deputies (also known as Palais Bourbon); the Hôtel des Invalides (containing a military mus. and Napoleon's Tomb); and the Quai d'Orsay (with govt. agencies, notably the ministry of foreign affairs). Montparnasse quarter, S of the Luxembourg, has replaced Montmartre as the center of Parisian artistic life. The Latin Quarter (oldest in Paris next to Île de la Cité), the haunt of univ. students and teachers, is also on the left bank. Adjoining it W is the Faubourg Saint-Germain, until recently Paris' most aristocratic quarter, in which the church of Saint-Germain-des-Prés is most noteworthy. The Eiffel Tower (984 ft. high; built 1887–89), chief landmark of Paris, stands on left bank of the Seine in the CHAMP DE MARS. SE of the tower is the École Militaire, and NW, on right bank, is the Palais de Chaillot, a modern structure which has replaced the unsightly Palais du Trocadéro. Other parks are the Jardin des Plantes (botanical garden, with natural history mus.), and parks of Montsouris, Monceau, and Buttes-Chaumont. Paris is an old city, whose development can be traced outward, in approximately concentric rings, from the Gallo-Roman nucleus on the Île de la Cité. The Grands Boulevards have replaced in great part the 14th–17th-cent. ramparts and enclose most of old Paris. The *faubourgs*, outside the Grands Boulevards, are the old suburbs around which another ring of boulevards (*boulevards extérieurs*) represents the 18th-cent. ramparts. Beyond these lie the more modern suburbs incorporated into the city in 1860 as *arrondissements* 12–20. In 1919, the outermost fortifications were abolished and replaced by modern housing developments, parks, and, in S, by the *Cité Universitaire*. After Caesar's conquest, the Gallic fishing village on Île de la Cité became a town (*Lutetia Parisiorum*), which spread to left bank and grew under the later emperors. St. Denis, semi-legendary 1st bishop of Paris, was martyred on Montmartre. In late 5th cent. St. Genevieve, patron of Paris, by her prayers preserved city from destruction by the Huns. Clovis I and other Merovingians had their capital in Paris, which became a center of learning under Charlemagne. Devastated by Norsemen's raids (845–61), city was refortified and successfully defended (885–87) by Eudes and Gozlin. City's growth resumed when Hugh Capet, count of Paris, became (987) King of France, firmly establishing Paris as Fr. capital. Bet. 12th and 14th cent. churches of Saint-Germain-des-Prés, Notre Dame, and Sainte-Chapelle, as well as the 1st Louvre were built; streets were paved, walls enlarged, and the *Parlement* of Paris and *States-General* established. Left-bank schools, merged in the Sorbonne, became center of theological learning. Greatest prosperity was reached in early 14th cent. when merchants and guilds obtained their own municipal government. In 1358, under leadership of Étienne Marcel, Paris became independent commune and rebelled against the Dauphin (later Charles V). The Hundred Years War brought civil strife, English occupation, and the Black Death. Reconquered 1436 from English. During the Renaissance, the Louvre was rebuilt and the Tuileries, Luxembourg, and Hôtel de Ville added to the city. In Wars of Religion, Parisians, siding with Catholics, perpetrated Massacre of St. Bartholomew's Day (1572), forced Henry III to leave city, and allowed Henry IV to enter only after his conversion to Catholicism. Under Louis XIII, Richelieu made Paris the intellectual and political center of Europe. Archiepiscopal see established 1622. As a result of the Fronde, in which Paris defied royal authority, Louis XIV transferred his court to Versailles in 1682. In 17th–18th cent., Mansart, Soufflot, and Gabriel planned some of the city's most majestic prospects, while its cultural life flourished (Molière, Racine, Diderot, d'Alembert, Lavoisier, Buffon). While the lavishness of the court increased under Louis XV, growing popular unrest among an ever-growing proletariat crowded into the *faubourgs* pointed toward an upheaval. In 1789, the royal family was brought to Paris by mobs which stormed the Bastille and formed the revolutionary commune. Later, Napoleon I replanned the city and enriched its museums with captured art treasures. Twice occupied (1814, 1815) by Allies, Paris again expanded after the Restoration. Its pop. grew from 714,000 in 1817 to 1,696,000 in 1861. Both the July (1830) and February (1848) revolutions took place here. In letters, music, and painting Paris also led; Balzac, Hugo, Chopin, Liszt, Berlioz, Wagner, Ingres, Delacroix, Daumier are but random names out of the Paris of the romantic era. Most of modern Paris dates from Napoleon III. The great avenues, boulevards, and parks are the work of Haussmann. Captured by Prussians after a siege (1870–71), Paris lived through the Commune of 1871 and its reprisal. Recovery and modernization proceeded rapidly under Third Republic. Though shelled by long-range guns, Paris was never reached by Germans in First World War. Occupied by Germans on June 14, 1940, Paris was liberated by its own resistance forces aided by American and Fr. troops. Its Ger. garrison surrendered Aug. 25, 1944. Only outlying districts suffered damage in Second World War. Important treaties concluded here were in 1763 (Seven Years War), 1783 (American Revolutionary War), 1814 and 1815 (Napoleonic Wars), 1856 (Crimean War), 1898 (Spanish-American War), 1919–20 (First World War peace conference; treaty signed at Versailles and Saint-Germain), and 1947 (Second World War treaties with Italy and Axis satellites). Mean annual temp. 50.5°F.; mean for January 36.5°F., for July 65.5°F. Average yearly rainfall is 21 inches.

Paris. 1 City (pop. 3,731), a ⊙ Logan co., W Ark., 38 mi. E of Fort Smith, in Ouachita foothills; coal mining, lumbering, farming. Subiaco Col. and Abbey (Benedictine) are near by. Laid out 1874. **2** City (pop. 774), ⊙ Bear Lake co., SE Idaho, 27 mi. ENE of Preston; alt. 5,967 ft. Sugar beets, grain, livestock, dairy products. **3** City (pop. 9,460), ⊙ Edgar co., E Ill., 17 mi. NW of Terre Haute, Ind.; trade, rail, and industrial center in agr. and bituminous-coal-mining area; mfg. of shoes, brooms, farm machinery, metal products, streetcars, buses; meat packing. Inc. 1853. Lincoln practiced law here. **4** City (pop. 6,912), ⊙ Bourbon co., N central Ky., on South Fork of Licking R. and 18 mi. NE of Lexington, in Bluegrass region. Largest U.S. bluegrass-seed market; burley-tobacco and livestock shipping point; airport; mfg. of men's shorts, radiators, canned goods, soft drinks, concrete products; lumber and feed mills; limestone quarries. Early distillery here (1790) was one of 1st in Ky.; its whisky was called bourbon, after the co. Among fine old bldgs. in vicinity is "Mt. Lebanon" (1786). Near-by Cane Ridge Meeting House was scene of founding of Christian denomination of Disciples of Christ in 1804. City founded as Hopewell 1789; inc. 1893. **5** Town (pop. 4,358), ⊙ Oxford co., W Maine, on the Little Androscoggin and 17 mi. NW of Auburn. Settled 1779, inc. 1793. Includes villages of South Paris (pop. 2,067) (mfg., wood and leather products, sports equipment), West Paris (wood products; ships feldspar), and Paris Hill (residential; Hannibal Hamlin b. here). **6** City (pop. 1,407), ⊙ Monroe co., NE central Mo., on Middle Fork of Salt R. and 38 mi. WSW of Hannibal; agr. center. Laid out 1831. **7** City (pop. 8,826), ⊙ Henry co., NW Tenn., 40 mi. ESE of Union City; trade center for agr., clay, and timber-producing area; mfg. of cosmetics, work shirts, pottery; railroad shops, cotton gins. Kentucky Reservoir is E. Laid out and inc. 1823. **8** City (pop. 21,643), ⊙ Lamar co., NE Texas, c.95 mi. NE of Dallas; trade, shipping, industrial center of rich blackland agr. area (cotton, truck, dairy products, poultry); woodworking, flour and cottonseed-oil milling, meat packing, mfg. of vinegar and other food products, furniture, leather goods; hatcheries. Seat of a jr. col. U.S. Camp Maxey (N) was active in Second World War. Paris and Crook lakes (recreation) are near. Settled as Pinhook; renamed 1844; planned rebuilding followed fire, 1916.

Paris, Lake, Texas: see PINE CREEK.

Paris Basin, chief depression of N and N central France, bounded by English Channel (NW), Armorican Massif (W), Massif Central (S), plateaus of Langres and of Lorraine (E). Formed by Jurassic sediments which cover a granitic substratum, it is roughly circular and shaped like a huge amphitheater with concentric escarpments (most distinguishable in E) surrounding its lowest middle portion, at the center of which is Paris. Drained SE-NW by the Seine and its tributaries. Fertility, low in outlying Champagne, increases toward center where Beauce and Brie districts are breadbaskets of France. Freestone, limestone, and gypsum, laid bare in places by erosion, provide building materials.

Parish, village (pop. 574), Oswego co., N central N.Y., 19 mi. ESE of Oswego; mfg. (brooms, brushes, canned foods); agr. (dairy products; poultry, vegetables).

Parish (pärēsh'), village, Durazno dept., central Uruguay, in the Cuchilla Grande del Durazno, on railroad and 10 mi. S of Paso de los Toros; grain, sheep.

Paris Hill, Maine: see PARIS.

Parismina River, Costa Rica: see REVENTAZÓN RIVER.

Paris Mountain (2,054 ft.), NW S.C., c.4 mi. N of Greenville, in state park (1,275 acres); forested recreational area (lakes, trails, camp and picnic grounds).

Parit (pŭrĭt'), village (pop. 1,662), central Perak, Malaya, on Perak R. and 14 mi. SW of Ipoh; rice, rubber.

Parita (pärē'tä), village (pop. 982), Herrera prov., S central Panama, in Pacific lowland, on branch of Inter-American Highway, on small Parita R. and 6 mi. NW of Chitré. Corn, rice, beans, livestock. Founded 1556.

Parita Gulf, W section of Gulf of Panama of the Pacific, in central Panama, E of Azuero Peninsula; 20 mi. wide, 10 mi. long. Receives Parita R., which flows 25 mi. NE, past Pesé and Parita.

Parit Buntar (pŭrĭt' bŏŏn'tär), town (pop. 3,475), NW Perak, Malaya, on railroad and 25 mi. NW of Taiping, on Krian R. (Kedah line) opposite Bandar Bharu, at Penang border; a center of Krian rice dist.

Paritilla (pärētē'yä), village (pop. 968), Los Santos prov., S central Panama, in Pacific lowland, 2 mi. SW of Pocrí; sugar cane, coffee, yucca, livestock.

Parit Jawa (pŭrĭt' jä'wä), town (pop. 1,967), NW Johore, Malaya, on Strait of Malacca, 8 mi. SE of Bandar Maharani; rubber, coconuts.

Parit Raja (rä'jä), village (pop. 1,179), Johore, SW Malaya, 18 mi. ESE of Bandar Penggaram; rubber, coconuts.

Parit Sulong (sōō"lŏŏng'), village (pop. 401), NW Johore, Malaya, 9 mi. NW of Bandar Penggaram; rubber.

Parizhskaya Kommuna (pŭrēsh'skīŭ kŭmōō'nŭ), city (1926 pop. 3,393), SW Voroshilovgrad oblast, Ukrainian SSR, in the Donbas, 3 mi. SSE of Voroshilovsk; coal mines. Until c.1926, called Seleznevski Rudnik.

Park. 1 County (□ 2,166; pop. 1,870), central Colo.; ⊙ Fairplay. Mining and livestock-grazing region, drained by headwaters of South Platte R. Gold, silver, lead. Includes part of Park Range and of Arapaho, Cochetopa, and Pike natl. forests. Antero and Eleven Mile reservoirs in S are units in Denver water-supply system. Formed 1861. **2** County (□ 2,627; pop. 11,999), S Mont.; ⊙ Livingston. Agr. region drained by Yellowstone R.; borders on Wyo. and Yellowstone Natl. Park. Livestock. Absaroka Natl. Forest and Absaroka Range in S. Formed 1887. **3** County (□ 5,217; pop. 15,182), NW Wyo.; ⊙ Cody. Irrigated agr. area, bordering on Mont. and Yellowstone Natl. Park; watered by Shoshone and Greybull rivers and Shoshone Reservoir. Sugar beets, grain, beans, livestock; oil, coal. Shoshone Natl. Forest and part of Absaroka Range in W; Shoshone Cavern Natl. Monument near Cody. Formed 1909.

Park, city (pop. 223), Gove co., W central Kansas, 12 mi. NNE of Gove.

Parkal (pŭrkäl'), village (pop. 4,519), Karimnagar dist., E Hyderabad state, India, 40 mi. ESE of Karimnagar; rice, oilseeds.

Parkan, Czechoslovakia: see STUROVO.

Park City. 1 Town (pop. 448), Barren co., S Ky., 10 mi. NW of Glasgow; a tourist center for Ky. limestone-cave region and SE gateway to MAMMOTH CAVE NATIONAL PARK. Diamond Caverns, beautiful small caves, are near by. Until 1938, called Glasgow Junction. **2** Village (pop. 300), Stillwater co., S Mont., on Yellowstone R. and 23 mi. SW of Billings; fruits and vegetables marketed during summer. Tourist camp here. **3** City (pop. 2,254), Summit co., N central Utah, 20 mi. ESE of Salt Lake City, in Wasatch Range; alt. 7,000 ft.; mining center (silver, gold, copper, lead, zinc) and resort with skiing facilities. Growth followed discovery of ore (1869).

Park Cone, peak (12,102 ft.) in Rocky Mts., Gunnison co., W central Colo.

Parkdale, town (pop. 385), Ashley co., SE Ark., 23 mi. E of Crossett.

Parke, county (□ 451; pop. 15,674), W Ind.; ⊙ Rockville. Bounded W by Wabash R.; drained by Sugar and Raccoon creeks. Agr. and bituminous-coal mining area, with some mfg. at Montezuma and Rockville. Timber, clay and gravel pits, mineral springs, fisheries. Formed 1821.

Parkent (pŭrkyĕnt'), village (1926 pop. 7,722), N Tashkent oblast, Uzbek SSR, 20 mi. E of Tashkent; wheat.

Parker, county (□ 904; pop. 21,528), N Texas; ⊙ Weatherford. Partly hilly; drained by Brazos R. and Clear Fork of Trinity R. Rich, diversified agr., ranching, dairying area; melons, peaches, other fruits, truck, peanuts, corn, grains, pecans; beef cattle, poultry, horses. L. Mineral Wells (recreation) is in W. Processing, mfg. at Weatherford. Formed 1855.

Parker. 1 Town (pop. 1,201), Yuma co., W Ariz., on Colorado R. (Calif. line) and 100 mi. NNE of Yuma; trade center for mining and grazing area and hq. of several Indian reservations (Fort Yuma and Chemehuevi in Calif., Fort Mohave and Colorado River in Calif. and Ariz., and Cocopah in Ariz.). Inc. since 1940. **2** Village (pop. 306), Fremont co., E Idaho, 3 mi. W of St. Anthony and on Henrys Fork river; alt. 4,991 ft. Shipping point in agr., dairy area. **3** or **Parker City,** town (pop. 915), Randolph co., E Ind., 9 mi. E of Muncie, in agr. area. **4** City (pop. 251), Linn co., E Kansas, 11 mi. S of Osawatomie, in general-farming area. **5** or **Parker City,** city (pop. 979), Armstrong co., W Pa., 20 mi. NE of Butler and on Allegheny R.; glass products; bituminous coal, oil; timber. Inc. as city 1873. Also called Parkers Landing. **6** City (pop. 1,148), ⊙ Turner co., SE S.Dak., 23 mi. SW of Sioux Falls; trade center for farm area; livestock, dairy produce, grain, poultry. Founded 1879.

Parker, Cape, E extremity of Devon Isl., E Franklin Dist., Northwest Territories, on Baffin Bay; 75°20'N 79°41'W.

Parker City. 1 Town, Ind.: see PARKER. **2** City, Pa.: see PARKER.

Parker Dam, in Colorado R. (Calif.-Ariz. line), c.50 mi. SSE of Needles, Calif., just below mouth of Bill Williams R.; concrete arch dam (320 ft. high, 856 ft. long; completed 1938). Used for power, water supply, and some irrigation. Forms HAVASU LAKE and diverts water through COLORADO RIVER AQUEDUCT to Los Angeles metropolitan dist.

Parker Head, Maine: see PHIPPSBURG.

Parker Islands, N group of Chusan Archipelago, in E.China Sea, Kiangsu prov., China. The largest is Raffles Isl., 6 mi. long, 3 mi. wide; 30°45'N 122°25'E.

Parker Pond, S Maine, northernmost lake of 12-mi. chain extending N from Androscoggin L. in W Kennebec co.; 4 mi. long.

Parkersburg. 1 Village (pop. 288), Richland co., SE Ill., 10 mi. S of Olney, in agr. area (corn, wheat, livestock, apples). **2** Town (pop. 1,300), Butler co., N central Iowa, 24 mi. WNW of Waterloo; shipping center (livestock, grain); creamery. Beaver Meadow State Park near by. Inc. 1874. **3** Town (pop. 114), Sampson co., S central N.C., 13 mi. SW of Clinton. **4** City (pop. 29,684), ⊙ Wood co., W W.Va., port on the Ohio (bridged), at Little Kanawha R. mouth, 60 mi. W of Clarksburg. Shipping, distribution, mfg., and rail center (repair shops), in region producing oil, natural gas, bituminous coal, clay, livestock, tobacco, truck, and timber. Large plants produce rayon, shovels and other implements; mfg. of oil-field equipment, steel, glassware, porcelain, tiles, shoes, paper. Near by, in the Ohio, is Blennerhassett Isl. City settled 1785; chartered 1820.

Parkers Landing, Pa.: see PARKER.

Parkers Prairie, village (pop. 900), Otter Tail co., W Minn., 37 mi. ESE of Fergus Falls, in grain, livestock, poultry area; dairy products. Small lakes near by.

Parkerton, village, Converse co., E central Wyo., on N.Platte R. and 18 mi. E of Casper; alt. 5,123 ft. Big Muddy oil field near by.

Parkerville, city (pop. 78), Morris co., E central Kansas, on headstream of Neosho R. and 21 mi. SSE of Junction City; grazing, agr.

Parkes, municipality (pop. 6,897), E central New South Wales, Australia, 185 mi. WNW of Sydney; rail junction; gold-mining center; wheat, wool.

Parkesburg, agr. borough (pop. 2,611), Chester co., SE Pa., 5 mi. WSW of Coatesville; clothing, metal products; stone quarries. Inc. 1872.

Parkeston Quay, England: see HARWICH.

Park Falls, city (pop. 2,924), Price co., N Wis., on Flambeau R. and 50 mi. SSE of Ashland, in wooded area; paper milling, woodworking. Near by are resort lakes. Inc. 1912.

Park Forest, village (pop. 8,138), Cook co., NE Ill., just S of Chicago. Inc. since 1940.

Parkgate, England: see NESTON.

Parkha, Tibet: see BARKHA.

Parkhar (pŭrkhär'), village (1939 pop. over 500), SW Kulyab oblast, Tadzhik SSR, on Panj R. (Afghanistan border) and 35 mi. SW of Kulyab; cotton ginning.

Parkhill, town (pop. 947), S Ont., on Parkhill R. and 26 mi. WNW of London; woodworking, lumbering; mfg. of bricks, tiles.

Park Hills, residential town (pop. 2,577), Kenton co., N Ky., just W of Covington, within Cincinnati metropolitan dist. Inc. 1927.

Parkhurst, England: see NEWPORT, Hampshire.

Parkin, city (pop. 1,414), Cross co., E Ark., 32 mi. WNW of Memphis (Tenn.) and on St. Francis R., in farm area (cotton, corn, hay); hardwood timber; mfg. of buttons, building machinery, concrete products.

Parkland, village (pop. 1,292), Bucks co., SE Pa., 6 mi. NW of Bristol.

Parkman. 1 Town (pop. 590), Piscataquis co., central Maine, 10 mi. WSW of Dover-Foxcroft, in farming, lumbering area. **2** Village, Sheridan co., N Wyo., near Mont. line and Bighorn Mts., 20 mi. NW of Sheridan; alt. c.4,300 ft. Supply point in ranching region.

Parkmore (pärkmôr'), village, NE Co. Antrim, Northern Ireland, 16 mi. NW of Larne; iron mining.

Parknasilla (pärk"nŭsĭ'lŭ), seaside resort, SW Co. Kerry, Ireland, on Kenmare R. and 2 mi. SE of Sneem.

Park Place, residential suburb (pop. 3,723, with adjacent Poe), Greenville co., NW S.C., just N of Greenville.

Park Range, Colo. and Wyo., in Rocky Mts.; extends c.200 mi. NNW from NW Park co., central Colo., into Carbon co., S Wyo. Watered in Colo. by headstreams of Colorado and South Platte rivers; lies largely within natl.-forest area. Includes GORE RANGE in N central Colo., SIERRA MADRE in S Wyo., and parts of Continental Divide in both states. Highest peaks rise in S tip (sometimes known as Mosquito Range), near Leadville, central Colo. They are Ptarmigan Peak (13,736 ft.), Mosquito Peak (13,784 ft.), Mt. Buckskin (13,800 ft.), Mt. SHERMAN (14,037 ft.), Mt. DEMOCRAT (14,142 ft.), Mt. BROSS (14,169 ft.), Mt. CAMERON (14,233 ft.), QUANDARY PEAK (14,256 ft.), and Mt. LINCOLN (14,284 ft.; highest point in range). Coal is mined near Oak Creek and Steamboat Springs, NW Colo.; gold, silver near Leadville; molybdenum at Climax.

Park Rapids, resort village (pop. 3,027), ⊙ Hubbard co., central Minn., on Fish Hook R., near Fish Hook L., and c.55 mi. NW of Brainerd; dairy products, beverages. Founded 1880.

Park Ridge. 1 Residential city (pop. 16,602), Cook co., NE Ill., NW suburb of Chicago, 8 mi. WSW of Evanston; truck farms. O'Hare Field–Chicago International Airport, which is also a U.S. military airfield, is near by. Inc. 1910. **2** Borough (pop. 3,189), Bergen co., NE N.J., near small Woodcliff L., 9 mi. N of Hackensack; mfg. (office supplies, clothing, silk labels); fruit farming. Settled c.1770, inc. 1894. **3** Town (pop. 314), Portage co., central Wis., just SE of Stevens Point.

Park River, city (pop. 1,692), Walsh co., NE N.Dak., 15 mi. W of Grafton and on Park R. Trading center; dairy products, potatoes, grain. Seat of co. agr. school and center of soil conservation project. Inc. 1896.

Park River, NE N.Dak., formed by confluence of 3 branches in Walsh co., flows 35 mi. E, past Grafton, to Red River of the North S of Drayton; 80 mi. long, including S branch.

Parks, village (1939 pop. 11), SW Alaska, on Kuskokwim R. and 50 mi. SE of Flat; fur trapping, prospecting.

Parks, village (pop. 460), St. Martin parish, S central La., 10 mi. E of Lafayette, near Bayou Teche.

Parkside, borough (pop. 1,637), Delaware co., SE Pa., just NW of Chester.

Parksley, town (pop. 883), Accomack co., E Va., 20 mi. S of Pocomoke City, Md., in truck-farming region; shirt mfg.

Park Slope, SE N.Y., a residential section of Brooklyn borough of New York city, lying immediately W of Prospect Park.

Parkstein (pärk'shtīn), village (pop. 1,515), Upper Palatinate, NE Bavaria, Germany, 6 mi. NW of Weiden; cranberries, rye, cattle. Chartered 1435.

Parkston, city (pop. 1,354), Hutchinson co., SE S.Dak., 22 mi. S of Mitchell; farm trading point; cattle feed, grain, livestock, dairy products, poultry. Founded 1886.

Parkstone, England: see POOLE.

Parksville, village (pop. estimate 450), SW B.C., on E Vancouver Isl., 20 mi. NW of Nanaimo; farming, lumbering.

Parksville. 1 Village (1940 pop. 512), Boyle co., central Ky., 7 mi. WSW of Danville, in berry-growing region. **2** Resort village, Sullivan co., SE N.Y., in the Catskills, 4 mi. N of Liberty. **3** Town (pop. 198), McCormick co., W S.C., 28 mi. S of Greenwood; lumber.

Parksville Reservoir, Tenn.: see OCOEE RIVER.

Parkton, town (pop. 527), Robeson co., S N.C., 13 mi. SSW of Fayetteville; lumber milling.

Parkview, village (pop. 661), Cuyahoga co., N Ohio, a SW suburb of Cleveland.

Park View Peak (12,433 ft.), in Front Range, bet. Grand and Jackson counties, N Colo.

Parkville. 1 Suburban village, Baltimore co., central Md., 6 mi. NNE of downtown Baltimore. **2** City (pop. 1,186), Platte co., W Mo., on Missouri R. and 10 mi. NW of Kansas City; agr., tobacco. Park Col. here. **3** Village (pop. 3,299), York co., S Pa., just W of Hanover.

Parkway Village or **Parkway,** town (pop. 1,036), Jefferson co., N Ky., a suburb of Louisville.

Parla (pär'lä), town (pop. 1,013), Madrid prov., central Spain, on railroad and 12 mi. S of Madrid; cereals, olives, grapes, livestock.

Parlakimedi (pŭrlä"kĭmā'dē), town (pop. 21,042), Ganjam dist., S Orissa, India, 55 mi. SW of Berhampur; trades in rice, sal timber; rice milling, handicrafts (palm mats, baskets). Col. Sometimes spelled Parlakimidi.

Parli or **Purli** (both: pŭr'lē), town (pop. 9,528), Bir dist., NW Hyderabad state, India, 34 mi. SSW of Parbhani; agr. trade center (chiefly cotton, millet, peanuts, wheat); cotton ginning. Hindu place of pilgrimage. Rail station called Purli-Vaijnath.

Parlier (pär'lēr), city (pop. 1,419), Fresno co., central Calif., in San Joaquin Valley, near Kings R., 17 mi. SE of Fresno; agr. trade center.

Parlin, N.J.: see SAYREVILLE.

Parlita (pûr'lĕtsä), Rum. *Pârliţa*, village (pop. 677), Ilfov dept., S Rumania, 25 mi. E of Bucharest.

Parma (pär'mŭ, It. pär'mä), province (□ 1,333; pop. 381,771), Emilia-Romagna, N central Italy; ⊙ Parma. Extends from Apennines N to Po R.; bounded E by Enza R. Largely mountainous, with Po plain in N. Drained by Taro, Ceno, and Parma rivers. Agr. (cereals, grapes, fodder, tomatoes), livestock raising. With adjacent Piacenza prov. (W), produces most of Italy's petroleum (wells at Salsomaggiore, Fontevivo, Fornovo di Taro). Talc mining at Borgo Val di Taro. Has extensive food industry (Parmesan cheese, sausage, canned tomatoes).

Parma, city (pop. 65,126), ⊙ Parma prov., Emilia-Romagna, N central Italy, near the Apennines, on Parma R. and 55 mi. WNW of Bologna; on the Aemilian Way; 44°48'N 10°19'E. Rail junction; chief center of Emilia-Romagna after Bologna. Produces machinery (agr., cannery), food products (canned tomatoes, macaroni), glass, shoes, furniture, pharmaceuticals, alcohol, paper, fertilizer, clocks, cork products. Noted for Parmesan cheese. Bishopric. Rich in works of Correggio, who painted frescoes for Romanesque cathedral (12th cent.) and convent of St. Paul. Octagonal baptistery (1196–1260) ranks among finest in Italy; also has churches of San Giovanni Evangelista (1510) and Madonna della Steccata (1521–39; bomb damage repaired), wooden Farnese theater (begun 1618; severe bomb damage being repaired), and unfinished Palazzo della Pilotta (started 1583; severe bomb damage being repaired), housing mus., picture gall., and Palatina library. A center of learning in the Middle Ages; university dates officially from 1502. Roman colony after 183 B.C. From 1545 to 1860, when it passed to Italy, it was chief city of duchy of Parma and Piacenza. Severely bombed (1944).

Parma. **1** Village (pop. 1,369), Canyon co., SW Idaho, near Oregon line, on Boise R. and 15 mi. NW of Caldwell in truck-farming area served by Boise irrigation project. Ships fruit and agr. produce. Inc. 1904. **2** Village (pop. 680), Jackson co., S Mich., 10 mi. W of Jackson, in farm area (fruit, poultry; dairy products). **3** City (pop. 1,163), New Madrid co., extreme SE Mo., in Mississippi flood plain, 22 mi. SW of Sikeston; cotton gins. Inc. 1906. **4** City (pop. 28,897), Cuyahoga co., N Ohio, a S suburb of Cleveland. Inc. as village in 1925, as city in 1931.

Parmachenee Lake (pär"mŭchē'nē), N Oxford co., W Maine; c.3 mi. long. Receives N and discharges S Magalloway R.

Parma Heights, village (pop. 3,901), Cuyahoga co., N Ohio, a S suburb of Cleveland, just W of Parma. Settled 1818, inc. 1912.

Parma River (pär'mä), N central Italy, rises in Etruscan Apennines 8 mi. E of Pontremoli, flows N, past Parma, and E, past Colorno, to Po R. 4 mi. SSE of Casalmaggiore; 50 mi. long.

Parmele (pär'mūlē), town (pop. 406), Martin co., E N.C., 14 mi. SE of Tarboro.

Parmentier (pärmätyā'), village (pop. 2,295), Oran dept., NW Algeria, 12 mi. SW of Sidi-bel-Abbès; cereal and winegrowing.

Parmer, county (□ 859; pop. 5,787), W Texas; ⊙ Farwell. On N.Mex. line (W), and on Llano Estacado; alt. 3,800–4,100 ft. Agr., especially wheat; also grain sorghums, hay, barley, peanuts, cotton, cattle, hogs, sheep; some dairying, poultry raising. Formed 1876.

Parnaguá (pŭrnŭgwä'), city (pop. 315), southernmost Piauí, Brazil, on marshy L. Parnaguá and 250 mi. SSW of Floriano, at N foot of Serra da Gurgueia; mineral springs.

Parnaíba (pŭrnäē'bŭ). **1** City (1950 pop. 30,900), N Piauí, Brazil, near Parnaíba R. mouth on the Atlantic, 170 mi. ESE of São Luís (Maranhão); 2°54'S 41°45'W. Its seaport is LUÍS CORREIA (9 mi. ENE; connected by railroad). Commercial center of Parnaíba valley, shipping carnauba wax, cotton, babassu oil, sugar, cattle and hides. Soap and oil factories. Projected railroad to Teresina (170 mi. SSW) now reaches Piripiri (90 mi. S). Airport. Founded 1761. Formerly spelled Parnahyba. **2** City, São Paulo, Brazil: see SANTANA DE PARNAÍBA.

Parnaíba River, NE Brazil, rises in the Serra da Tabatinga near 10°15'S 45°57'W, flows NNE to the Atlantic, forming Maranhão-Piauí border throughout its course. Length, c.750 mi. On it are Alto Parnaíba, Santa Filomena, Uruçuí, Nova Iorque, Floriano (head of regular navigation), Amarante, and Teresina. It enters the Atlantic in several branches. In delta are ports of Tutóia and Luís Correia, and city of Parnaíba. Chief tributaries are Balsas R. (left), and Gurgueia, Canindé, Poti, and Longá rivers (right). The Parnaíba drainage basin, the largest bet. Amazon (NW) and São Francisco (SE) rivers, covers all of Piauí and Maranhão states. Products of Parnaíba valley are tobacco, rice, cotton, and carnauba. River is crossed by railroad bridge connecting Timon and Teresina. Formerly spelled Parnahyba.

Parnamirim (pŭrnŭmērēn'), city (pop. 673), W Pernambuco, NE Brazil, 110 mi. NE of Juàzeiro (Bahia); cotton, corn. Until 1944, Leopoldina.

Parnamirim, airport, Rio Grande do Norte, Brazil: see NATAL.

Parnarama (pŭrnŭrä'mŭ), city (pop. 1,507), E Maranhão, Brazil, near left bank of Parnaíba R. (Piauí border), 40 mi. SW of Teresina; cattle, babassu nuts. Until 1944, called São José dos Matões; and, 1944–48, Matões.

Parnassus (pärnă'sŭs), Gr. *Parnassos* (pärnŭsôs'), one of highest massifs in central Greece, N of Gulf of Corinth, on borders of Phocis, Phthiotis, and Boeotia nomes; rises to 8,062 ft. 16 mi. NW of Livadia. A barren, limestone mass, it is commonly ascended from Delphi or Arachova (at S foot) for a magnificent view that commands all central Greece, the Gulf of Corinth, and the N Peloponnesus. Bauxite deposits. It was sacred to Apollo, Dionysus, and the Muses and an inspiring source of letters and art. The Corycian stalactite grotto, associated with Bacchic festivals, and the sacred Castalian spring of Delphi are on its slopes. Formerly called Liakura (Liakoura) or Likeri.

Parnassus, Pa.: see NEW KENSINGTON.

Parndorf (pärn'dôrf), town (pop. 2,569), Burgenland, E Austria, 15 mi. SW of Bratislava, Czechoslovakia; cattle.

Parnell (pärnĕl'). **1** Town (pop. 206), Iowa co., E central Iowa, 33 mi. SSW of Cedar Rapids, in agr. area. **2** City (pop. 362), Nodaway co., NW Mo., on Little Platte R. and 14 mi. NE of Maryville.

Parner (pär'nār), village (pop. 6,087), Ahmadnagar dist., E Bombay, India, 20 mi. WSW of Ahmadnagar; local trade center for millet, cotton, wheat.

Parnes or **Parnis** (both: pär'nēs), mountain massif in Attica-Boeotia border, E central Greece, rises to 4,635 ft. 13 mi. N of Athens. Sanitarium on S slope. Formerly called Ozea.

Parnon (pär'nôn), mountain range in SE Peloponnesus, Greece, extends 30 mi. along Laconia-Arcadia border, parallel to coast of Gulf of Argolis; rises to 6,346 ft. 17 mi. NE of Sparta. Formerly called Malevon, for Mt. Malevon (5,914 ft.), 15 mi. NE of Sparta.

Parnu or **Pyarnu**, Est. *Pärnu* (all: păr'nōō), Ger. *Pernau* (pĕr'nou), Rus. (until 1917) *Pernov* (pĕr'nôf), city (pop. 20,334), SW Estonia, port on Parnu Bay (inlet of Gulf of Riga), 75 mi. S of Tallinn, at mouth of Parnu R.; 58°23'N 24°30'E. Second seaport of Estonia; exports timber, flax, potatoes; sawmilling center; mfg. of linen goods, shoes, leather products, matches, furniture, chocolate; shipbuilding, machine repairing, brewing. Peat deposits worked near by. Summer resort (mud baths). Founded c.1250 by Livonian Knights on right side of Parnu R.; became a Hanseatic city; passed in 1561 to Poland, in 1629 to Sweden; occupied 1710 by Russia and inc. into govt. of Livonia until 1920.

Parnu-Jagupi or **Pyarnu-Yagupi**, Est. *Pärnu-Jaagupi* (all: păr'nōō-yä'gōō pē), town (pop. 276), W Estonia, 15 mi. N of Parnu; fodder crops, flax, livestock. Formerly spelled Parnu-Jakobi.

Parnu River or **Pyarnu River**, Est. *Pärnu* (all: păr'nōō), Ger. *Pernau* (pĕr'nou), SW Estonia, rises in several marshy branches near Paide, flows 90 mi. SW, past Turi and Sindi (head of navigation), to Parnu Bay at Parnu.

Paro (pä'rô), fortified town [Bhutanese *dzong*], W Bhutan, on right tributary of the Raidak and 30 mi. WSW of Punakha; lamasery (annual festival). After Punakha, chief town of W Bhutan.

Paroikia, Greece: see PAROS.

Parol (pŭrōl'), town (pop. 2,966), Kathua dist., SW Kashmir, 6 mi. WSW of Kathua; wheat, rice, corn, bajra.

Parola (pä'rōlŭ), town (pop. 15,247), East Khandesh dist., NE Bombay, India, 31 mi. WSW of Jalgaon; road center; trades in cloth fabrics, millet, wheat, cattle; cotton ginning.

Parole, village (pop. 1,032), Anne Arundel co., central Md., 2 mi. W of Annapolis. Sometimes called Camp Parole.

Paronda, India: see PARENDA.

Paropamisus Mountains (pă"rŭpŭmī'sŭs), W outlier of the Hindu Kush, in NW Afghanistan, extending c.300 mi. along right (N) watershed of the Hari Rud bet. Iran line (61°E) and the Koh-i-Baba (67°E); rises to more than 11,000 ft. 50 mi. ENE of Herat. Crossed by Ardewan and Zarmast passes. The name SAFID KOH is sometimes applied to the E section of the range. Silver-lead and crystal deposits.

Paros (pā'rŏs), Aegean island (□ 77; pop. 8,993) of the Cyclades, Greece, W of Naxos; 37°5'N 25°10'E; 12 mi. long, 10 mi. wide; rises to 2,530 ft. in the Prophet Elias (anc. *Marpessa*). On N slope of mtn. are the quarries of the beautiful white Parian marble, used by sculptors since 6th cent. B.C. Isl. produces wine, olive oil, cotton, figs, tobacco; granite is also quarried. Main town is Paros (pop. 3,264), the former Paroikia or Parikia, on NW shore. Settled by Ionians, Paros became a maritime power and a center of Aegean trade, and colonized Thassos. Became tributary to Athens in 5th cent. B.C. In Middle Ages it belonged until 15th cent. to Naxos and after 1537 to the Turks.

Parow (părou'), residential town (pop. 18,096), SW Cape Prov., U. of So. Afr., 7 mi. E of Cape Town. Site of St. Augustine's Training Col. Just N is Wingfield Airport.

Parowan (pă'rŭwăn", pä'-), city (pop. 1,455), ⊙ Iron co., SW Utah, 17 mi. NE of Cedar City; alt. 5,990 ft.; flour and lumber milling; cheese. Settled 1851 by Mormons, nominal capital of Utah Territory 1858–59. Part of Dixie Natl. Forest is near by. Little Salt L. (dry) is N.

Parpaillon, Chaîne du (shĕn dü pärpäyõ'), offshoot range of Cottian Alps, in SE France, along Basses-Alpes–Hautes-Alpes dept. border bet. Durance (N) and Ubaye (S) valleys, extending c.30 mi. from Savines (W) to Ital. border SW of Monte Viso. Rises to 11,057 ft. at the Pointe de la Font-Sancte. Crossed by Col de Vars.

Parra, La (lä pä'rä), town (pop. 1,918), Badajoz prov., W Spain, 31 mi. SE of Badajoz; olives, cereals, acorns, livestock.

Parral (päräl'), town (pop. 10,225), ⊙ Parral dept. (□ 928; pop. 36,756), Linares prov., S central Chile, in the central valley, 25 mi. SSW of Linares; rail junction; commercial and agr. center (wheat, vegetables, chick-peas, wine, livestock); flour mills, wineries, tanneries.

Parral, Mexico: see HIDALGO DEL PARRAL.

Parral (pă'rŭl), village (pop. 199), Tuscarawas co., E Ohio, 5 mi. NNW of New Philadelphia; clay products.

Parramatta (pă"rŭmă'tŭ), municipality and port (pop. 20,816), E New South Wales, Australia, near head of Parramatta R. and 13 mi. WNW of Sydney, in metropolitan area; mfg. center (woolen and leather goods, bicycles).

Parramatta River, W arm of Port Jackson, E New South Wales, Australia; 15 mi. long. Suburbs of Sydney on shores: Balmain, Drummoyne, and Concord on S shore; Parramatta, Ermington and Rydalmere, Ryde, and Hunter's Hill on N shore.

Parramore Island (pă'rŭmôr), E Va., barrier island (c.8 mi. long) off Atlantic shore of Accomack co., 10 mi. SSE of Accomac. Wachapreague Inlet is at N, Little Machipongo Inlet at S end.

Parramos (pärä'mōs), town (1950 pop. 1,658), Chimaltenango dept., S central Guatemala, on Guacalate R. and 3 mi. SSW of Chimaltenango; alt. 5,610 ft.; corn, wheat, beans.

Parras or **Parras de la Fuente** (pä'räs dā lä fwĕn'tā), city (pop. 15,555), Coahuila, N Mexico, in semiarid irrigated Laguna Dist., on railroad and 115 mi. WSW of Monterrey; alt. 5,548 ft. Processing and agr. center (wine, cotton, cereals, fruit); known for wines and brandies; cotton gins, flour mills, guayule plants. Occupied (1846) by U.S. troops during Mexican War. Site of Fr. defeat 1866. Francisco I. Madero lived here.

Parreiras, Brazil: see CALDAS.

Parrett River or **Parret River**, Dorset and Somerset, England, rises just N of Beaminster (Dorset), flows 35 mi. N and NW, past Langport and Bridgwater, to Bridgwater Bay at Burnham-on-Sea. Receives Yeo R. at Langport, Tone R. at Isle of Athelney.

Parrillas (pärē'lyäs), town (pop. 1,489,) Toledo prov., central Spain, 13 mi. WNW of Talavera de la Reina; olives, grapes, cereals; timber.

Parrish, town (pop. 757), Walker co., NW central Ala., 7 mi. S of Jasper.

Parrish Court, Va.: see IDLEWILDE.

Parris Island (pă'rĭs), Beaufort co., S S.C., one of Sea Isls., in Port Royal Sound just S of Port Royal Isl., c.30 mi. NE of Savannah, Ga.; 5.5 mi. long. Occupied by U.S. Marine Corps training camp. Scene of attempted settlement by Fr. Huguenots under Jean Ribaut in 1562.

Parrita (pärē'tä), town (dist. pop. 808), Puntarenas prov., W Costa Rica, shallow Pacific port 50 mi. SE of Puntarenas at mouth of Parrita R. (50 mi. long). Center of banana region (developed in 1930s), connected by rail with deep-water port of Quepos; cacao, livestock.

Parrott, town (pop. 291), Terrell co., SW Ga., 8 mi. NW of Dawson.

Parrottsville, town (pop. 115), Cocke co., E Tenn., 7 mi. NE of Newport.

Parrsboro (pärz'bŭrŭ), town (pop. 1,971), N N.S., on N shore of Minas Basin, 30 mi. SSW of Amherst; port, shipping coal, lumber; shipbuilding, furniture mfg.

Parr Shoals Dam, S.C.: see BROAD RIVER.

Parry, Cape, NW Mackenzie Dist., Northwest Territories, N extremity of Parry Peninsula (50 mi. long, 4–30 mi. wide), on Amundsen Gulf, bet. Franklin Bay (W) and Darnley Bay (E); 70°8'N 124°35'W.

Parry Cape. **1** NW Greenland, on N Baffin Bay, 50 mi. NW of Thule; 77°1'N 71°10'W; rises steeply to 1,200 ft. **2** E extremity of Traill Isl., NE Greenland, on Greenland Sea; 72°18'N 21°55'W.

Parry Island, Cook Isls.: see MAUKE.

Parry Islands, Jap. *Muko-jima-retto*, northernmost group of Bonin Isls., W Pacific, c.20 mi. NE of Chichi-jima; 27°40'N 142°10'E; 21-mi. chain of small volcanic isls.; the largest isl. is Muko-jima (□ 1.3).

Parry Islands, archipelago, W central Franklin Dist., Northwest Territories, in the Arctic Ocean; includes MELVILLE ISLAND, BATHURST ISLAND, DEVON ISLAND, PRINCE PATRICK ISLAND, CORNWALLIS ISLAND, and numerous smaller isls.

Parry Sound, district (□ 4,336; pop. 30,083), SE central Ont., on Georgian Bay; ⊙ Parry Sound.

Parry Sound, town (pop. 5,765), ⊙ Parry Sound dist., SE central Ont., on Parry Sound, inlet of Georgian Bay, 120 mi. NNW of Toronto; railroad shops; lumbering, woodworking; resort. In copper and feldspar mining region.

Parryville, borough (pop. 598), Carbon co., E Pa., 3 mi. NW of Palmerton and on Lehigh R.

Parsberg (pärs'bĕrk), village (pop. 3,424), Upper Palatinate, central Bavaria, Germany, 20 mi. NW of Regensburg; paper milling, tanning. Has 16th-cent. castle.

Parscov (pûr'skôv), Rum. *Pârscov*, village (pop. 2,191), Buzau prov., SE central Rumania, on Buzau R. and 17 mi. NW of Buzau.

Parseierspitze (pärsī'ürshpĭtsü), highest peak (9,965 ft.) of Lechtal Alps, in Tyrol, W Austria, 5 mi. WNW of Landeck.

Parshall, city (pop. 935), Mountrail co., NW central N.Dak., 45 mi. SW of Minot; coal mines; dairy produce, poultry, grain, vegetables.

Parsippany (pärsĭ'pünē), village, Morris co., N N.J., 6 mi. NNE of Morristown, at S end of **Parsippany Reservoir** (c.2 mi. long; formed by Boonton Dam in Rockaway R.), supplying water to Jersey City.

Parsnip River, NE B.C., rises in Rocky Mts. near 54°20'N 121°20'W, flows 160 mi. NW to confluence with Finlay R. at Finlay Forks, forming Peace R. Discovered 1793 by Sir Alexander Mackenzie.

Parsons. 1 City (pop. 14,750), Labette co., SE Kansas, on small affluent of Neosho R. and 31 mi. WSW of Pittsburg; shipping center, with railroad repair shops, for grain-growing and dairying region; grain milling; foundry work; rock crushing, shirt mfg. Has jr. col., Army ordnance plant, and state hosp. for epileptics. Laid out 1870, inc. 1871. **2** Town (pop. 1,640), Decatur co., W Tenn., 40 mi. E of Jackson, near Kentucky Reservoir (Tennessee R.), in timber, cotton, corn, livestock area; work clothes, lumber. **3** City (pop. 2,009), ⊙ Tucker co., NE W.Va., at junction of Black and Shavers forks to form Cheat R., 25 mi. SE of Grafton, in coal, timber, and farm area. Mfg. of textiles, wood products; lumber mill, tannery. U.S. tree nursery. Battle of Corrick's (or Carrick's) Ford, a Union victory, was fought here in 1861. Inc. 1893.

Parsonsfield, town (pop. 958), York co., SW Maine, on the Ossipee and 32 mi. WNW of Portland. Includes villages of Kezar Falls (kē'zür) (bobbins, textiles), partly in Oxford co., and East Parsonfield. Inc. 1785.

Parsonstown, Ireland: see BIRR.

Partabgarh (pŭrtäb'gŭr), former princely state (□ 873; pop. 91,967) in Rajputana States, India; ⊙ was Partabgarh. Founded 15th cent.; in 1948, merged with union of Rajasthan. Sometimes called Pratapgarh or Kanthal.

Partabgarh, since 1948 officially **Pratabgarh** (prŭ–), district (□ 1,457; pop. 1,041,024), SE Uttar Pradesh (Oudh), India; ⊙ Bela. On Ganges Plain; bounded S by the Ganges; drained by Sai R. Agr. (rice, barley, wheat, gram, rape and mustard, millets, sugar cane); extensive mango and mahua groves. Main towns: Bela, Manikpur, Partabgarh.

Partabgarh. 1 Town (pop. 13,505), S Rajasthan, India, 75 mi. SE of Udaipur; market center (maize, millet, cotton, wheat); cotton ginning, hand-loom weaving. Was ⊙ former Rajputana state of Partabgarh, whose early ⊙ was at Deolia, 8 mi. W. **2** Since 1948 officially **Pratabgarh,** town (pop. 4,197), Partabgarh dist., SE Uttar Pradesh, India, 4 mi. WSW of Bela; trades in grains, oilseeds. Founded c.1617.

Partanna (pärtän'nä), town (pop. 12,459), Trapani prov., W Sicily, 6 mi. NE of Castelvetrano, in cereal-growing region; olive oil, wine, soap. Gypsum deposits near by.

Partenkirchen, Germany: see GARMISCH-PARTENKIRCHEN.

Partenstein (pär'tünshtīn), village, N Upper Austria, on Grosse Mühl R., near its mouth on the Danube, and 16 mi. NW of Linz; hydroelectric plant.

Parthenay (pärtnā'), town (pop. 6,860), Deux-Sèvres dept., W France, on Thouet R. and 25 mi. NNE of Niort; commercial center and livestock market of Gâtine dist.; woodworking, meat preserving, mfg. (hosiery, porcelain, flour products). A picturesque medieval stronghold with ramparts and 15th-cent. houses. Given to Dunois in 1458, it remained in his family until 1641.

Parthenen (pärtā'nün), village, Vorarlberg, W Austria, on Ill R. and 28 mi. SE of Feldkirch; hydroelectric works.

Parthenope, Italy: see NAPLES.

Parthe River (pär'tü), E central Germany, rises 3 mi. E of Bad Lausick, flows 30 mi. generally NW, past Naunhof and Taucha, to the White Elster at Leipzig.

Parthia (pär'thēü), province of anc. Persian Empire, corresponding roughly to modern Khurasan. Under the Diadochi, Parthia broke away in c.250 B.C. from the Seleucid kingdom and extended its rule over all Persia westward to the Euphrates. Led by the Arsacid dynasty, Parthia challenged Roman expansion (1st cent. B.C.). Parthian capitals were Hecatompylus, Ctesiphon, and Seleucia. The Parthian kingdom was overthrown in A.D. 226 by the Sassanids, a native Persian dynasty.

Partick, W suburb (pop. 52,271) of Glasgow, Lanark, Scotland, on N bank of the Clyde and on Kelvin R.; shipyards, textile and flour mills.

Partido (pärtē'dō), tobacco- and coffeegrowing region, W Cuba, in hills of central Havana prov.

Partille (pärtĭ'lü), village (pop. 2,641), Goteborg och Bohus co., SW Sweden, on Save R. and 5 mi. ENE of Goteborg; electrical and mechanical works.

Partington, town and parish (pop. 816), N Cheshire, England, on Manchester Ship Canal and 4 mi. NW of Altrincham; mfg. of paper, paint.

Partinico (pärtēnē'kô), town (pop. 22,282), Palermo prov., NW Sicily, 14 mi. WSW of Palermo; wine, olive oil, macaroni.

Partizanske (pär'tyĭzänskĕ, Slovak *Partizánske*, town (pop. 3,171), W Slovakia, Czechoslovakia, on Nitra R., on railroad and 26 mi. NE of Nitra; footwear mfg. Until 1947, known as Simonovany (shĭ'mônôvänĭ), Slovak *Šimonovany*, Hung. *Simony*, and, 1947–49 as Batovany (bä'tyôvänĭ), Slovak *Bat'ovany*.

Partizanskoye (pŭrtyēzän'skŭyŭ), village (1948 pop. over 2,000), SE Krasnoyarsk Territory, Russian SFSR, 65 mi. ESE of Krasnoyarsk, in agr. area. Until 1930s, called Perovo.

Parton, town and parish (pop. 1,470), W Cumberland, England, just N of Whitehaven; coal mining.

Partridge, city (pop. 221), Reno co., S central Kansas, 11 mi. SW of Hutchinson, in wheat region.

Partur (pŭrtōōr'), town (pop. 7,216), Parbhani dist., NW Hyderabad state, India, 45 mi. NW of Parbhani; agr. market (chiefly cotton, millet, wheat, peanuts); cotton ginning.

Paruna (pürōō'nü), village, SE South Australia, 120 mi. ENE of Adelaide; wheat, wool.

Parur (pŭrōōr'), city (pop. 16,179), NW Travancore, India, near Periyar R. mouth, 45 mi. NNW of Kottayam; coir mats and rope, copra; cashew-nut processing; rice, sugar cane.

Paru River (pōōrōō'), N central Pará, Brazil, rises on S slope of the Serra de Tumucumaque, flows c.370 mi. SSE to the lower Amazon (left bank) above Almeirim. Navigable in lower 50 mi.

Paruro (pärōō'rō), town (pop. 2,316), ⊙ Paruro prov. (□ 767; pop. 32,358), Cuzco dept., S central Peru, in the Andes, 18 mi. SSE of Cuzco; alt. 10,100 ft.; wheat-growing and flour-milling center.

Parvatipur (pär'vŭtēpōōr"), town (pop. 6,521), Dinajpur dist., NW East Bengal, E Pakistan, 17 mi. E of Dinajpur; rail junction (workshops); trades in rice, jute, rape and mustard, sugar cane; rice and oilseed milling. Also spelled Parbatipur.

Parvatipuram (pär'vŭtēpōōrŭm), town (pop. 19,456); Vizagapatam dist., NE Madras, India, 45 mi. N of Vizianagaram; agr. trade center (rice, oilseeds, sugar cane, jute) at junction of roads serving forested hills (N; sal, teak, bamboo, tanning bark, lac). Also called Parvatipur.

Parvin Lake, Salem co., SW N.J., small artificial lake in state park, 7 mi. NNE of Bridgeton; recreational center.

Parvomai or **Parvomay** (pŭr"vômī'), city (pop. 5,027), Plovdiv dist., S central Bulgaria, on Maritsa R. and 25 mi. E of Plovdiv; agr. center in Plovdiv Basin; exports grain and tobacco; winegrowing, truck gardening. Originally Khadzhi Eles; known as Borisovgrad, 1891–1944. Also spelled Pervomai or Pervomay.

Paryd (pō'rüd"), Swedish *Påryd*, village (pop. 695), Kalmar co., SE Sweden, 20 mi. WSW of Kalmar; furniture mfg., woodworking.

Parys (pärās'), town (pop. 6,467), N Orange Free State, U. of So. Afr., on Transvaal border, on Vaal R. (bridge) and 35 mi. SE of Vereeniging; alt. 4,647 ft.; agr. center (fruit, tobacco, stock); fruit preserving, jam making, basket weaving. Resort. Site of textile school.

Parys Mountain (pä'rĭs), hill (c.500 ft.), NE Anglesey, Wales, 2 mi. S of Amlwch; former copper-mining center.

Pas (pä) or **Pas-en-Artois** (päzänärtwä'), village (pop. 854), Pas-de-Calais dept., N France, 16 mi. SW of Arras; dairying.

Pas, The, Manitoba: see THE PAS.

Pasadena (păsüdē'nü). **1** Residential city (pop. 104,577) and resort, Los Angeles co., S Calif., NE suburb of Los Angeles, in foothills of San Gabriel Mts. Seat of Calif. Inst. of Technology, Pasadena Col., Pasadena City Col., John Muir Col., Fuller Theological Seminary, Southern Calif. Bible Col., a fine community playhouse, an art gall., and Busch Gardens (noted for rare plants). Mt. Wilson and Mt. Lowe observatories are near by, as is Henry E. Huntington Library and Art Gall. (at San Marino). Arroyo Seco (üroi'ō sĕ'kō), intermittent water-course entering Los Angeles R., has several parks. City's annual Tournament of Roses (1st held in 1890) developed from a small village fiesta. The East-West football game, started in 1902, was discontinued until 1916; since then it has been held annually (Jan. 1), from 1923 on in famous Rose Bowl, seating over 85,000 spectators. City has light industries (notably mfg. of precision instruments). Founded 1874, inc. 1886, chartered 1901. **2** Industrial town (pop. 22,483), Harris co., S Texas, just E of Houston, on Houston Ship Channel; oil refining, paper milling. Inc. 1928.

Pasadena Hills, town (pop. 1,102), St. Louis co., E Mo., W of St. Louis. Inc. 1937.

Pasadena Park, town (pop. 682), St. Louis co., E Mo., W of St. Louis.

Pasado, Cape (päsä'dō), on Pacific coast of Manabí prov., W Ecuador, 17 mi. NNW of Bahía de Caráquez; 0°21'S 80°30'W.

Pasaje (päsä'hā), town (1950 pop. 4,864), El Oro prov., S Ecuador, in lowlands, on Jubones R. 12 mi. ESE of Machala (connected by rail spur); agr. center (cacao, coffee, corn, tagua nuts, fruit, cattle).

Pasaje, village (pop. 1,706), Pontevedra prov., NW Spain, on Miño R. estuary (Port. border); fishing; sawmilling. Wine, lumber in area.

Pasaje River, N Argentina: see SALADO, Río.

Pasajes (päsä'hĕs), chief port and industrial area of Guipúzcoa prov., N Spain, in the Basque Provs., on Bay of Biscay, 3 mi. E of San Sebastián; includes dists. of Pasajes Ancho (pop. 3,243), Pasajes San Juan (E; pop. 1,575) and Pasajes San Pedro (W; pop. 4,838). Fine natural harbor with dry docks, in protected bay dominated by Mt. Ulía; exports minerals, wine, fish, cement. Fishing and fish processing; metalworking (marine motors, hardware). Oil refinery. Other mfg.: brandy and liqueurs, flour products, paper articles.

Pa Sak River (pä'säk'), central Thailand, rises in N Phetchabun Range at 17°10'N 101°20'E, flows 250 mi. S, parallel to Dong Phaya Yen Range, past Lomsak, Phetchabun, and Saraburi, to Lopburi R. (arm of the Chao Phraya) at Ayutthaya. Barrage near Tha Rua feeds extensive irrigation canal network.

Pasalimanli (pä-shä'lĭmän"lü), Turkish *Paşalimanlı*, island (pop. 208), NW Turkey, in Sea of Marmara S of Marmara Isl.

Pasanauri (pŭsŭnŭōō'rē), village, N central Georgian SSR, on slope of central Greater Caucasus, on Georgian Military Road, in Aragva R. valley, and 45 mi. N of Tiflis; auto service station.

Pasaquina (päsäkē'nä), city (pop. 1,669), La Unión dept., E Salvador, near Inter-American Highway and Honduras border, 16 mi. N of La Unión; livestock; salt extraction.

Pasarel Dam, Bulgaria: see STALIN DAM.

Pasargadae (püsär'güdē), anc. city of S Persia, 60 mi. NE of modern Shiraz, along road to Isfahan, and on Pulvar R. Built by Cyrus the Great as residence of Persian Empire, it was later supplanted by Persepolis. Among the ruins, the tomb of Cyrus is best preserved.

Pasarón (päsärōn'), town (pop. 1,925), Cáceres prov., W Spain, 14 mi. E of Plasencia; olive oil, cereals, pepper, wine; stock raising.

Pasay, Philippines: see RIZAL, city.

Pasbrug (päs'brükh), agr. village, Antwerp prov., N central Belgium, just E of Mechlin.

Pascagoula (păskügōō'lü), city (pop. 10,805), ⊙ Jackson co., extreme SE Miss., on Pascagoula Bay of Mississippi Sound, at mouth of Pascagoula R., 20 mi. E of Biloxi; seaport, port of entry, resort; fishing and boatbuilding center. Has U.S. dry docks and a coast guard base. Mfg. of kraft paper, fish oil and meal, clothing. Grew around "Old Spanish Fort" (extant), built in 1718. Peak of its lumber-shipping industry was in late-19th cent.

Pascagoula River, SE Miss., formed in N George co. by confluence of Leaf and Chickasawhay rivers, flows c.90 mi. S to Mississippi Sound at Pascagoula, where its mouth is a seaport; partly navigable.

Pascalis (päskälē'), village (pop. 823), W Que., 14 mi. ENE of Val d'Or; gold mining.

Pascani (päsh-kän'), Rum. *Paşcani*, town, (1948 pop. 10,857), Jassy prov., NE Rumania, in Moldavia, 25 mi. SE of Falticeni; rail junction and commercial center with trade in grain, livestock, lumber; flour milling, tanning. Has 17th-cent. church.

Paschoal, Monte, Brazil: see PASCOAL, MONTE.

Pasco (pä'skō), department (□ 11,654; enumerated pop. 96,949, plus estimated 20,000 Indians), central Peru, in the Andes; ⊙ Cerro de Pasco. Bounded W by Cordillera Occidental, S by Cordillera Oriental, E by N outlier of the Gran Pajonal; includes Nudo de Pasco (W). Drained by the upper Huallaga and the headstreams of the Pachitea. Peru's chief mining dist., with mining centers of Cerro de Pasco and Huarón (copper, silver, gold, lead, and zinc), Goyllarisquizga and Quishuarcancha (coal), and Mina Ragra (vanadium). Grain, potatoes, livestock in mts.; cacao, coffee, tropical fruit in valleys on E slopes of the Andes. Main centers: Cerro de Pasco, Chacayán, Huachón, Oxapampa. Served by railroad and highway from Lima. Formed 1944 out of part of Junín dept.

Pasco (pă'skō), county (□ 751; pop. 20,529), W central Fla., on Gulf of Mexico (W); ⊙ Dade City. Citrus-fruit, poultry, and cattle area, with sawmilling industry. Has many small lakes. Formed 1887.

Pasco, city (1940 pop. 3,913; 1950 pop. 10,228), ⊙ Franklin co., S Wash., 35 mi. WNW of Walla Walla, near junction of Snake and Columbia rivers; rail center and river port (barges) in wheat, livestock, truck region. Settled c.1880, inc. 1891; pop. boomed during Second World War with influx of residents employed at atomic-energy works near Richland (NW).

Pasco, Nudo de (nōō'dō dā pä'skō), high mountain knot of the Andes in Pasco dept., central Peru, considered to be junction of the cordilleras Occidental, Central, and Oriental converging from N and S; the massif, consisting of several peaks, rises to 15,118 ft. In its vicinity are the sources of Marañón and Huallaga rivers (N), Pachitea and Perené rivers (E), and Mantaro R. (S). City of Cerro de Pasco is here.
Pascoag, village, R.I.: see BURRILLVILLE.
Pascoag River (pă'skōg), NW R.I., rises in W Glocester town, flows c.6 mi. generally NE, through Burrillville town, joining Chepachet R. near Oakland to form Branch R. Dammed S of Pascoag village to form Pascoag Reservoir (c.2 mi. long).
Pascoal, Monte (mŏn'tĭ pŭskōäl') [Port.,=Easter Mountain], isolated hill (alt. 1,716 ft.) in coastal lowland of SE Bahia, Brazil, 40 mi. SSW of Pôrto Seguro. First land sighted by Cabral in 1500. Formerly spelled Monte Paschoal.
Pascola (păskō'lŭ), town (pop. 242), Pemiscot co., extreme SE Mo., near Mississippi R., 11 mi. NW of Caruthersville.
Pascua, Isla de, Chile: see EASTER ISLAND.
Pascuales (päskwä'lĕs), village, Guayas prov., W Ecuador, on navigable Daule R. and 9 mi. NNW of Guayaquil, in agr. region (cacao, rice, fruit); iron deposits.
Pascua Village, Ariz.: see PASQUA VILLAGE.
Pas-de-Calais (pä-dŭ-kälā', pätkälā'), department (□ 2,607; pop. 1,168,545), in Artois and part of Picardy, N France; ⊙ Arras. Extends inland from Strait of Dover (Fr. *Pas de Calais*) and English Channel. Drained by short coastal streams (Aa, Canche, Authie). Traversed WNW-ESE by low chain of hills (Artois hills). High agr. yields (wheat, oats, sugar beets, flax, tobacco, colza, potatoes, chicory) due to modern cultivation methods. Cattle, horse, and hog-raising area. Important fisheries based on Boulogne. Crossed by westernmost part of Franco-Belgian coal basin, Pas-de-Calais is France's leading coal-mining dept., with centers at Lens, Liévin, Hénin-Liétard, Noeux-les-Mines, and in Béthune area. Metallurgy (steel milling, lead and zinc smelting, machinery and auto chassis mfg.) and textile milling (cotton and linen cloth, famous Calais lace) are chief industries. Other mfg.: food processing (sugar, biscuits, dairy produce) and canning, paper milling (in Aa R. valley). Chief towns: Calais and Boulogne (seaports), Arras, Béthune, Saint-Omer, and Lens, all heavily damaged in Second World War. Bathing resorts: Le Touquet-Paris-Plage, Berck. Large foreign pop. (mostly Polish) engaged in coal mining. Ravaged during First World War (especially in Lens-Arras-Bapaume area).
Pas de Calais, France and England: see DOVER, STRAIT OF.
Pas de Morgins, France: see CHÂTEL.
Pas-des-Lanciers, France: see SAINT-VICTORET.
Pas-en-Artois, Pas-de-Calais dept., France: see PAS.
Pasewalk (pä'zŭvälk), town (pop. 10,977), in former Prussian Pomerania prov., N Germany, after 1945 in Mecklenburg, on Uecker R. and 25 mi. W of Stettin; rail junction; mfg. of machinery, electrical equipment, food products; metalworking, lumbering, potato-flour milling. Has 13th–15th-cent. church; remains of old town walls and gates. Passed to Sweden in 1648, to Prussia in 1720.
Pashichevo, Yugoslavia: see ZMAJEVO.
Pashiya (pä'shēŭ), town (1926 pop. 3,506), E Molotov oblast, Russian SFSR, 18 mi. NE (under jurisdiction) of Chusovoi, on rail spur; metallurgical center (pig iron). Bauxite deposits near by. Until 1929, Arkhangelo-Pashiski Zavod.
Pashkovo, Russian SFSR: see SALTYKOVO.
Pashkovskaya (päsh'kŭfskīŭ), village (1926 pop. 17,996), central Krasnodar Territory, Russian SFSR, 3 mi. E of Krasnodar (linked by tramway); flour milling, woodworking; truck produce.
Pashmakli, Bulgaria: see SMOLYAN.
Pashman, Yugoslavia: see PASMAN ISLAND.
Pashski Perevoz or **Pashskiy Perevoz** (päsh"skē-pĕrĭvôs'), village (1939 pop. over 500), NE Leningrad oblast, Russian SFSR, on Pasha R. (right affluent of Svir R.) and 30 mi. SW of Lodeinoye Pole; sawmilling.
Pashtrik, peak, Yugoslavia: see PASTRIK.
Pashupati (pŭsh'ōōpŭtē), town, central Nepal, in Nepal Valley, on the Baghmati, just E of Katmandu. Regarded as the Benares of Nepal by Nepalese; has anc. wooden Sivaite temple of Pashupatinath, the most important Hindu shrine of Nepal, and burning and bathing ghats. Hindu pilgrimage center. Also spelled Pashpati and Pasupati.
Pasian di Prato (päsyän' dē prä'tô), village (pop. 1,906), Udine prov., Friuli-Venezia Giulia, NE Italy, 2 mi. WSW of Udine; alcohol distillery.
Pasian Schiavonesco, Italy: see BASILIANO.
Pasicevo, Yugoslavia: see ZMAJEVO.
Pasig (pä'sēg), town (1939 pop. 1,121; 1948 municipality pop. 35,407), ⊙ RIZAL prov., S Luzon, Philippines, on Pasig R., on railroad and 7 mi. SE of Manila, in agr. area (rice, fruit).
Pasighat (pŭs'ĭgät), village, NE frontier tract of Assam, India, on Dihang section of the Brahmaputra, in foothills of Abor Hills, and 25 mi. NW of Sadiya; rice, tea, rape and mustard, sugar cane. It is ⊙ Abor Hills tribal dist.
Pasig River (pä'sēg), small but commercially important river in S Luzon, Philippines, rises in Laguna de Bay, flows 14 mi. generally NW, past Pasig and through Manila (dividing city into 2 sections), to Manila Bay. Navigable 1 mi. by steamer.
Pasinler (päsĭnlĕr'), town (pop. 5,759), Erzurum prov., NE Turkey, near source of Aras R., on railroad and 22 mi. E of Erzurum; wheat, barley. Formerly Hasankale.
Pasión River (päsyōn'), Petén dept., N Guatemala, rises as Santa Isabel R. near San Luis, flows c.220 mi. W, N, and W in winding course, past Sayaxché, joining Chixoy R. at Mex. border to form USUMACINTA RIVER. Navigable for c.150 mi. Called Cancuén R. in middle course.
Pasir Mas (pŭsēr' mäs'), town (pop. 3,051), N Kelantan, Malaya, on Kelantan R. and 9 mi. SW of Kota Bharu; rail junction on E coast line (spur to Tumpat port); rice. Agr. station.
Pasir Panjang (pänjäng'), village (pop. 603), SW Negri Sembilan, Malaya, on Strait of Malacca, 20 mi. S of Seremban; coconuts, rubber; fisheries.
Pasir Panjang, fishing village (pop. 1,114), Singapore isl., on SW coast, 6 mi. W of Singapore; coconuts.
Pasir Penambang (pŭnäm"bäng'), village (pop. 764), W Selangor, Malaya, on Selangor R., just E of Kuala Selangor; coconuts, rubber.
Pasir Puteh (pōōtē'), town (pop. 1,688), NE Kelantan, Malaya, 23 mi. SSE of Kota Bharu; road junction near Trengganu line; rice.
Paskal (päskäl'), peak (6,665 ft.) in Teteven Mts., N central Bulgaria, 9 mi. S of Teteven.
Paskallavik (pōskä"lävēk'), Swedish *Påskallavik*, town (pop. 233), Kalmar co., SW Sweden, on Kalmar Sound of the Baltic, near mouth of Em R., 6 mi. S of Oskarshamn; stone quarrying.
Paslek (päs'wĕk), Pol. *Pasłęk*, Ger. *Preussisch Holland* (proi'sĭsh hŏ'länt), town (1939 pop. 6,345; 1946 pop. 3,278) in East Prussia, after 1945 in Olsztyn prov., NE Poland, 12 mi. SE of Elbing; sawmilling; grain and cattle market. Founded 13th cent. by Dutch colonists sponsored by Teutonic Knights; chartered 1297. Fortified in Middle Ages. In Second World War, c.50% destroyed.
Pasleka River (päswĕ'kä), Pol. *Pasłęka*, Ger. *Passarge* (päsär'gŭ), in East Prussia, after 1945 in NE Poland, rises NE of Olsztynek, flows 75 mi. generally NNW, through several small lakes, past Braniewo, to Vistula Lagoon 5 mi. NW of Braniewo (head of navigation).
Pasley, Cape (păz'lē), S Western Australia, in Indian Ocean, at W end of Great Australian Bight; 33°56'S 123°32'E.
Pasley Bay, inlet (c.10 mi. long), W Boothia Peninsula, S Franklin Dist., Northwest Territories, on Franklin Strait; 70°35'N 96°32'W.
Pasman Island (päsh'män), Serbo-Croatian *Pašman*, Ital. *Pasmano* (päzmä'nô), Dalmatian island (□ 21) in Adriatic Sea, W Croatia, Yugoslavia, WNW of Biograd; 13 mi. long; rises to 900 ft. Sometimes spelled Pashman.
Pasni (pŭs'nē), town (pop. 3,616), Makran state, SW Baluchistan, W Pakistan, on Arabian Sea, 220 mi. WNW of Karachi; small port (open roadstead); some trade in dates, salt, wheat, leather goods; fishing. Sometimes called Pasni Fort.
Paso, China: see PAKLI.
Paso, El, Bolivia: see EL PASO.
Paso, El (ĕl pä'sō), city (pop. 3,671), Palma, Canary Isls., 8 mi. W of Santa Cruz de la Palma; agr. center (almonds, tobacco, fruit, grapes, cochineal). Ships also hides, silk, cheese, wine. Taburiente crater near by.
Paso Ataques (pä'sō ätä'kĕs), village, Rivera dept., NE Uruguay, on railroad and 14 mi. SSW of Rivera; grain, vegetables, livestock; viticulture.
Paso Caballos (pä'sō käbä'yōs), village (pop. 85), Petén dept., N Guatemala, 35 mi. NW of Flores, near San Pedro R.; airfield; chicle-shipping center.
Paso Caballos, Nicaragua: see CORINTO.
Pasochoa, Cerro (sĕ'rō päsōchō'ä), or **Cerro Pasuchoa** (–sōō–), extinct Andean volcano (13,776 ft.), Pichincha prov., N central Ecuador, 18 mi. S of Quito.
Paso de Indios, Argentina: see PASO DE LOS INDIOS.
Paso de la Cruz (pä'sō dā lä krōōs'), village (pop. 1,000), Río Negro dept., W Uruguay, on the Arroyo Don Esteban and 11 mi. S of Algorta, 65 mi. NE of Fray Bentos; grain, corn, cattle, sheep.
Paso de la Patria (pä'trēä), village (pop. estimate 500), NW Corrientes prov., Argentina, on Paraná R., opposite Paraguayan town of Paso de Patria, and 17 mi. NE of Corrientes; agr. (cotton, corn, livestock).
Paso del Borracho, Uruguay: see EL BORRACHO.
Paso del Cerro (dĕl sĕ'rō), village, Tacuarembó dept., NE Uruguay, near Tacuarembó R., on railroad and 18 mi. NE of Tacuarembó; ships cattle.
Paso del Macho, Mexico: see VILLA JARA.
Paso del Norte, Mexico: see CIUDAD JUÁREZ.
Paso de los Andes, Argentina: see CHACRAS DE CORIA.
Paso de los Indios (dā lōs ēn'dyōs), town (pop. estimate 500), ⊙ Paso de los Indios dept., central Chubut natl. territory, Argentina, on Chubut R. and 200 mi. WSW of Rawson; stock-raising center (sheep, cattle). Sometimes called Paso de Indios.
Paso de los Libres (lē'brĕs), town (pop. 12,507), ⊙ Paso de los Libres dept. (□ c.1,700; pop. 30,251), SE Corrientes prov., Argentina, port on Uruguay R. (Brazil border), opposite Uruguaiana, on railroad and 80 mi. SSE of Mercedes. Commercial and agr. center, trading with Uruguay and Brazil. Sawmills, rice and maté mills; grows rice and corn; stock raising. Bridge across Uruguay R. Seat of Jesuit mission in 18th cent.; refounded 1843 by Argentine Gen. Madariaga during war against Brazil. Sometimes called Libres.
Paso de los Toros (tō'rōs), city (pop. 9,000), Tacuarembó dept., central Uruguay, on the Río Negro, on railroad (railroad bridge) and 80 mi. SSW of Tacuarembó; river port, rail junction, trade center for grain, vegetables, cattle, sheep. Airport. Called Santa Isabel until early 1930s. Hydroelectric dam at RINCÓN DEL BONETE (E).
Paso de Ovejas (ōvā'häs), town (pop. 1,523), Veracruz, E Mexico, in Gulf lowland, 20 mi. WNW of Veracruz; fruit, livestock.
Paso de Patria (pä'trēä), town (dist. pop. 2,718), Ñeembucú dept., S Paraguay, on Paraná R. near confluence with Paraguay R., opposite Paso de la Patria (Argentina), and 32 mi. SW of Pilar; fruit, corn, cattle.
Paso de Sotos, Mexico: see VILLA HIDALGO, Jalisco.
Paso de Tempisque (tĕmpē'skā), village, Guanacaste prov., NW Costa Rica, on Tempisque R. and 4 mi. NNW of Filadelfia; sugar mill.
Pasoeroean, Indonesia: see PASURUAN.
Paso Flores (pä'sō flō'rĕs), village (pop. estimate 500), SW Río Negro natl. territory, Argentina, on Limay R. and 50 mi. NE of San Carlos de Bariloche, in sheep-raising area.
Paso Grande (pä'sō grän'dā), village (pop. estimate 500), NE San Luis prov., Argentina, 50 mi. NE of San Luis; mining (beryllium), agr. (corn, alfalfa, wheat, livestock).
Pasorapa (päsōrä'pä), town (pop. c.4,800), Cochabamba dept., central Bolivia, near Mizque R., on S outliers of Cordillera de Cochabamba, 36 mi. ESE of Aiguile; alt. 7,743 ft.; wheat growing, sheep raising.
Paso Real or **Paso Real de San Diego** (pä'sō rääl' dā sän' dyā'gō), town (pop. 1,434), Pinar del Río prov., W Cuba, on railroad and 26 mi. ENE of Pinar del Río; tobacco, fruit, livestock. Station for San Diego de los Baños spa, 8 mi. NNE.
Paso Río Mayo (pä'sō rē'ō mī'ō), village (pop. estimate 500), ⊙ Paso Río Mayo dept. (1947 census pop. 2,427), central Comodoro Rivadavia military zone, Argentina, 60 mi. W of Sarmiento; customhouse, radio station, airport.
Paso Robles (pă'sō rō'bŭlz, pä'sō rō'blĕs), city (pop. 4,835), San Luis Obispo co., SW Calif., on Salinas R. and 25 mi. N of San Luis Obispo; resort noted for its hot sulphur springs. U.S. Camp Roberts near by was active in Second World War. Ships almonds; produces dried fruit, grain, dairy foods, cattle. Old mission near by, at SAN MIGUEL. Inc. 1889.
Paspébiac (päspābyäk'), village (pop. estimate 750), E Que., on S Gaspé Peninsula, on Chaleur Bay, 50 mi. E of Dalhousie; fishing port, resort; lumbering.
Pasqua Village or **Pascua Village** (both: pă'skwä), suburb (pop. 5,466, with near-by El Rio) of Tucson, Pima co., SE Ariz.; a Yaqui Indian community.
Pasque Island, Mass.: see ELIZABETH ISLANDS.
Pasquotank (pă'skwŭtăngk"), county (□ 229; pop. 24,347), NE N.C.; ⊙ Elizabeth City. Bounded S by Albemarle Sound, E by Pasquotank R. Forested tidewater area, partly in Dismal Swamp (N); farming (truck, soybeans, corn), livestock raising (cattle, hogs), sawmilling, fishing; mfg. at Elizabeth City. Formed 1672.
Pasquotank River, NE N.C., rises in Dismal Swamp, flows c.50 mi. SE past Elizabeth City, to Albemarle Sound, forming estuary mouth (3–5 mi. wide) below Elizabeth City. In middle course, forms part of DISMAL SWAMP CANAL.
Pasrur (pŭsrōōr'), town (pop. 10,523), Sialkot dist., E Punjab, W Pakistan, 17 mi. SSE of Sialkot; market center (wheat, rice); mfg. of chemicals, brushes, cutlery, pencils; handicraft cloth weaving and printing, glazed pottery.
Passaconaway, Mount, N.H.: see SANDWICH RANGE.
Passadumkeag (păsŭdŭm'kēg), town (pop. 331), Penobscot co., central Maine, on the Penobscot, at mouth of small Passadumkeag R., and c.28 mi. above Bangor; hunting, fishing area.
Passagassawakeag River (pă"sŭgă'sŭwŭkēg), Waldo co., S Maine, tidal stream c.11 mi. long; flows SW to Belfast Bay to form part of harbor.
Passage, Le, or **Le Passage-d'Agen** (lŭ päsäzh'-däzhä'), W suburb (pop. 1,945) of Agen, Lot-et-Garonne dept., SW France, bet. Garonne R. and Garonne Lateral Canal; fertilizer mfg.
Passage-d'Agen, Le, France: see PASSAGE, LE.
Passage East or **Passage**, Gaelic *Pasáiste*, town (pop. 365), E Co. Waterford, Ireland, near Suir R. estuary, 5 mi. ESE of Waterford; agr. market (dairying, cattle raising; potatoes). Just S was site of New Geneva, Genevese settlement established 1785, dissolved 1798.

Passagem Franca (pŏŏsä'zhăn frăng'kŏŏ), city (pop. 719), E central Maranhão, Brazil, road junction 100 mi. SW of Teresina; ships cotton, alcohol, hides.

Passage West, Gaelic *Pasáiste*, urban district (pop. 2,442), SE Co. Cork, Ireland, 6 mi. ESE of Cork, at NW end of Cork Harbour, on Lee estuary opposite Great Isl.; seaport for Cork, with dock facilities. Iron foundries. Just S is small port of Monkstown, with fortified mansion (1636).

Pass-a-Grille Beach, resort town (pop. 1,000), Pinellas co., W Fla., 8 mi. SW of St. Petersburg, on Long Key.

Passaic (pŏŏsā'ĭk, pŏŏsāk'), county (□ 194; pop. 333,093), N N.J., on N.Y. line; ⊙ Paterson. Highly industrialized in SE (steel, rugs, woolens, clothing, textiles, rubber goods, textile machinery, baked goods, aircraft motors and parts, explosives, chemicals); agr. (dairy products, poultry, truck, fruit). Includes part of Ramapo Mts. Many lakes (including Greenwood L., with state park) have resorts. Drained by Passaic, Ramapo, and Pequannock rivers; Wanaque Reservoir is here. Co. formed 1837.

Passaic, city (pop. 57,702), Passaic co., NE N.J., on Passaic R. and 8 mi. N of Newark; textile, metal-products center; also mfg. of woolens, clothing, radio and telegraph equipment, rubber goods, railroad cars, brakes, leather products, chemicals, paper products, biscuits. Settled 1678 by Dutch traders as Acquackanonk, named Passaic 1854, inc. 1873, adopted commission govt. 1911. Occupied by Americans and British in Revolution. Developed industrially in late 19th cent. Famous strike here (1926), against a wage cut, involved right of free assembly. Park, here, has old burial vault built as morgue c.1690.

Passaic River, NE N.J., rises SW of Morristown; flows S, past Millington, thence N and NE to Paterson (here c.70-ft. falls furnish power), thence S and E, past Passaic and Newark, to head of Newark Bay; c.80 mi. long. Navigable below rapids above Passaic. River's power aided early growth of industry in NE N.J., especially in Paterson area.

Passais or **Passais-la-Conception** (päsā'-lä-kōsĕp-syō'), village (pop. 515), Orne dept., NW France, 7 mi. SW of Domfront; horse raising.

Passamaquoddy Bay (păsŏŏmŏŏkwŏ'dē), inlet (30 mi. long, 20 mi. wide at entrance) of Bay of Fundy, bet. NE Maine and SW N.B., at mouth of St. Croix R.; mostly in Canada, it contains N.B. isls. of Campobello and Deer; near entrance is Grand Manan Isl. Chief Maine towns on bay are Eastport and Lubec (at entrance); N.B. towns are St. Andrews and St. George. Herring, quahaug, pollock, sardine, and lobster fisheries. Passamaquoddy (or Quoddy) power project, begun 1935 in U.S. part of bay to convert heavy tides (18 ft. average range) into hydroelectric power, was suspended after Congress refused funds in 1936, and govt.-built workers' village was sold in 1949. Proposals have been made to revive project under U.S.-Canadian sponsorship.

Passa Quatro (pä'sŏŏ kwä'trŏŏ), city (pop. 3,957), southernmost Minas Gerais, Brazil, on railroad pass across the Serra da Mantiqueira, and 12 mi. N of Cruzeiro (São Paulo); alt. 3,000 ft. Wine- and tobacco-growing. Resort.

Passara (pŭs'sŭrŭ), town (pop. 765), Uva Prov., SE central Ceylon, in Uva Basin, 8 mi. SE of Badulla; extensive tea gardens; rice. Rubber plantations, limestone deposits near by.

Passarge River, Poland: see PASLEKA RIVER.

Passaro, Cape, Sicily: see PASSERO, CAPE.

Passarowitz, Yugoslavia: see POZAREVAC.

Passa Tempo (pä'sŏŏ tĕm'pŏŏ), city (pop. 1,923), S central Minas Gerais, Brazil, 22 mi. E of Oliveira; dairying center.

Passau (pä'sou), anc. *Castra Batava*, city (1950 pop. 34,338), Lower Bavaria, Germany, on Austrian border, port on the Danube (head of passenger navigation), at mouth of the Inn (right) and the Ilz (left), and 68 mi. SE of Regensburg; 48°34'N 13°28'E. Communications and tourist center; metal industry (agr. machinery, cogwheels); textiles, tobacco; lumber and paper milling, woodworking, brewing. Trades in coal, grain, and wood. Cathedral, in late-Gothic and baroque style, has one of world's largest organs. Anc. former Benedictine nunnery contains tomb of Hungary's 1st queen (died 1060). Fortress Oberhaus was started in 1219, completed in 15th and 16th cent. City also contains late-Gothic town hall with tower rebuilt in late 19th cent., and baroque episcopal residence. Site of theological acad. An anc. Celtic settlement, Passau is associated with the Nibelungen legend and is frequently called the "Nibelungen Town." Colonized by the Romans; was capital of powerful episcopal see (founded by St. Boniface) from 8th cent. until secularized in 1803. Treaty of Passau (1552) bet. Emperor Charles V and Maurice of Saxony secured liberation of captive Protestant princes and led to Peace of Augsburg. Bishopric reestablished 1817.

Passavant-la-Rochère (päsävä'-lä-rōshâr'), village (pop. 836), Haute-Saône dept., E France, near the Canal de l'Est, 25 mi. NNW of Vesoul; tileworks, brewery.

Pass Cavallo, Texas: see MATAGORDA BAY.

Pass Christian (păs" krĭs"chēăn'), city (pop. 3,383), Harrison co., SE Miss., 10 mi. WSW of Gulfport, on Mississippi Sound; summer and winter resort; packs and ships seafood; lumber milling. Settled in 18th cent.

Passendale (pä'sŭndälŭ), village (pop. 3,260), West Flanders prov., W Belgium, 7 mi. ENE of Ypres. Site of battle (1917) in First World War. Formerly spelled Passchendaele or Passchendale.

Passenheim, Poland: see PASYM.

Passero, Cape (päs'sĕrō), anc. *Pachynum Promontorium*, NE tip of islet in Ionian Sea, just off SE Sicily, 4 mi. SE of Pachino; 36°41'N 15°7'E; large lighthouse. Sometimes spelled Passaro.

Passi (pä'sē), town (1939 pop. 2,294; 1948 municipality pop. 30,918), Iloilo prov., E central Panay isl., Philippines, 29 mi. NNE of Iloilo; agr. center (rice, tobacco, sugar cane).

Passignano sul Trasimeno (päs-sēnyä'nō sŏŏl träzēmā'nō), village (pop. 1,266), Perugia prov., Umbria, central Italy, port on N shore of lake Trasimeno, 14 mi. WNW of Perugia; bathing resort. Formerly Passignano.

Pass Island (pop. 213; 1 mi. long), S N.F., at entrance of Hermitage Bay, 70 mi. E of Burgeo; 47°30'N 56°13'W.

Pass Mountain, peak (11,400 ft.) in Rocky Mts., Park co., central Colo.

Passo Bormann, Brazil: see CHAPECÓ.

Passo de Camaragibe (pä'sŏŏ dĭ kŭmŭrŭzhē'bĭ), city (pop. 1,810), E Alagoas, NE Brazil, near the Atlantic, 30 mi. NE of Maceió, in sugar-growing dist.; sugar mills. Has early-18th-cent. church.

Passo Fundo (pä'sŏŏ fōōn'dŏŏ), city (1950 pop. 25,232), Rio Grande do Sul, Brazil, in Serra Geral, on railroad and 140 mi. NW of Pôrto Alegre; agr. trade center; livestock slaughtering, meat and maté processing, lumbering and sawmilling. Manganese deposits near by. Has wheat experiment station; airfield. Settled in 1830s.

Passos (pä'sŏŏs), city (pop. 11,336), SW Minas Gerais, Brazil, near left bank of the Rio Grande, on railroad and 80 mi. NE of Ribeirão Prêto (São Paulo); cattle and sugar-shipping center. Cement plant at Itaú de Minas just W.

Passumpsic, village of BARNET town, Caledonia co., NE Vt., is on **Passumpsic River,** which rises in N Caledonia co. and flows c.40 mi. S, past St. Johnsbury, to the Connecticut at Barnet.

Passy (päsē'). **1** W residential district of Paris, France, on right bank of the Seine, forming 16th *arrondissement*. It includes the Bois de Boulogne. **2** Alpine village (pop. 84), Haute-Savoie dept., SE France, in Faucigny valley, 9 mi. W of Chamonix. At Plateau d'Assy (alt. 3,450 ft.) are numerous sanatoriums and a modern church (consecrated 1950).

Pastaza River (pästä'sä), in Ecuador and Peru, affluent of the Marañón, formed in the Ecuadorian Andes by Patate and Chambo rivers 4 mi. W of Baños, flows c.400 mi. SE and S, through tropical forest lowland, to the Marañón in Peru at 4°52'S 76°20'W; good navigability. Main affluent, Bobonaza R. It forms border bet. Napo-Pastaza and Santiago-Zamora provs. of the Ecuadorian Oriente.

Pastelillo (pästĕlē'yō), E port of NUEVITAS, Camagüey prov., E Cuba.

Pastena (pä'stĕnä), village (pop. 2,143), Salerno prov., Campania, S Italy, on Gulf of Salerno, 2 mi. ESE of Salerno; tannery.

Pasterze (päs'tĕr'tsŭ), large glacier (□ 12.16; over 5 mi. long, almost 3 mi. wide) in the Hohe Tauern of the Eastern Alps, on borders of Salzburg, Carinthia, and Tyrol, S Austria; fed by snows of the GROSSGLOCKNER. Drained by Möll R. Its base is reached by a spur of the Grossglocknerstrasse, a highway connecting Heiligenblut and Bruck.

Pasto (pä'stō), city (pop. 27,564), ⊙ Nariño dept., SW Colombia, on high Andean plateau, at E foot of Galeras Volcano, on Pan American Highway and 140 mi. NE of Quito (Ecuador), 330 mi. SW of Bogotá; alt. 8,510 ft.; 1°13'N 77°16'W. Commercial, communication, and processing center in agr. area (coffee, wheat, corn, cacao, sugar cane, tobacco, fruit, potatoes, vanilla, livestock); dairying, brewing, flour milling, tanning, sugar refining, liquor distilling, textile milling; mfg. of chocolate, honey, cheese, tobacco products, soap, bricks, furniture, straw hats. Active trade with Quito, Ecuador. Known for its polychrome wooden bowls finished with local gums (Pasto varnish). An old colonial city, founded 1539, it has a cathedral and small univ., and was one of the last strongholds of Sp. royalists in the War of Independence. Occupied for a short period in 1831 by Ecuadorian forces, Pasto was the scene of a treaty (1832) by which Colombia (then called New Granada) and Ecuador became separate states, and Pasto with its adjacent territory was confirmed as Colombian.

Pastol Bay (pă'stŭl) (50 mi. wide), W Alaska, on S Norton Sound, W Alaska, E of Yukon R. delta; 63°10'N 163°14'W. Pastolik village on S shore.

Pastolik (păstō'lĭk), Eskimo village, W Alaska, on Pastol Bay of Norton Sound, 50 mi. SW of St. Michael. Important under Russians in 19th cent., now almost deserted.

Pastora Peak (păstô'rŭ) (9,420 ft.), NE corner of Ariz., c.55 mi. W of Farmington, N.Mex.; highest point in Carrizo Mts.

Pastores (pästō'rĕs), town (1950 pop. 1,284), Sacatepéquez dept., S central Guatemala, on Guacalate R. and 3 mi. NW of Antigua; alt. 5,118 ft.; coffee, grain.

Pastor Ortiz (pästōr' ōrtēs'), town (pop. 1,656), Michoacán, central Mexico, on Lerma R. (Guanajuato border) and 17 mi. NNW of Puruándiro; cereals, stock. Formerly Zurumuato.

Pastos Bons (päs'tŏŏs bōs'), city (pop. 1,700), E Maranhão, Brazil, 140 mi. SW of Teresina, in cattle-raising area; babassu nuts, sugar, coffee, cotton.

Pastos Grandes, department, Argentina: see SANTA ROSA DE PASTOS GRANDES.

Pastos Grandes, Sierra de (syĕ'rä dā päs'tōs grän'dĕs), subandean mountain range in W Salta prov., Argentina, W of Poma; extends c.35 mi. N–S. The peak Nevado Pastos Grandes, 28 mi. WSW of San Antonio de los Cobres, rises to 20,175 ft. Along SE foot of the range extends the Salar Pastos Grandes, a salt desert (□ 24).

Pasto Volcano, Colombia: see GALERAS VOLCANO.

Pastra, Greece: see PATERA.

Pastrana (pästrä'nä), town (pop. 2,971), Guadalajara prov., central Spain, on fertile Alcarria plain, 40 mi. E of Madrid; agr. center (olives, truck produce, livestock); apiculture. Olive-oil pressing, flour milling, dairying, tile mfg. Has 16th-cent. palace of princes of Éboli; and convent founded by St. Theresa.

Pastrik or **Pashtrik** (both: päsh'trĭk), Serbo-Croatian *Paštrik*, Albanian *Mal i Pushtrikut*, peak (6,506 ft.) on Yugoslav-Albanian frontier, 11 mi. W of Prizren, Yugoslavia.

Pasubio, Monte (mōn'tĕ päsŏŏ'byō), peak (7,335 ft.), N Italy, N of Monti Lessini, 9 mi. SE of Rovereto. Scene of heavy fighting (1915–18) in First World War.

Pasuchoa, Cerro, Ecuador: see PASOCHOA, CERRO.

Pasupati, Nepal: see PASHUPATI.

Pasuquin (päsŏŏkēn'), town (1939 pop. 4,129; 1948 municipality pop. 12,407), Ilocos Norte prov., NW Luzon, Philippines, 9 mi. N of Laoag; rice-growing center.

Pasur, Turkey: see KULP.

Pasuruan or **Pasoeroean** (both: päsōōrōōän'), town (pop. 36,973), E Java, Indonesia, port on Madura Strait, 30 mi. SSE of Surabaya; 7°38'S 112°54'E; exports sugar, rubber, coffee, fish; tanneries, machine shops, railroad shops. Sugar-research station.

Pasvalys or **Pasvalis** (päsvälēs'), Rus. *Posvol*, city (pop. 2,793), N Lithuania, 16 mi. SW of Birzai; flour milling. In Rus. Kovno govt. until 1920.

Pasvik River, Norway and USSR: see PATS RIVER.

Pasym (pä'sĭm), Ger. *Passenheim* (pä'sŭnhīm), town (1939 pop. 2,431; 1946 pop. 619) in East Prussia, after 1945 in Olsztyn prov., NE Poland, in Masurian Lakes region, 16 mi. SE of Allenstein; grain and cattle market; limestone quarries. Church, founded 1391 by Teutonic Knights.

Paszto (päs'tō), Hung. *Pásztó*, town (pop. 6,574), Heves co., N Hungary, on Zagyva R. and 17 mi. N of Hatvan; agr., vineyards.

Pata (pä'tŭ), village, SE South Australia, 110 mi. ENE of Adelaide; wheat, wool.

Pata (pä'tä), village, La Paz dept., NW Bolivia, near Tuichi R., 19 mi. NNW of Apolo; oil deposits.

Pata, town, Philippines: see CLAVERIA.

Patacamaya (pätäkämī'ä), village (pop. c.6,850), La Paz dept., W Bolivia, in the Altiplano, 50 mi. S of La Paz, on La Paz–Oruro RR; alt. 12,500 ft.; barley, sheep.

Patagones, Argentina: see CARMEN DE PATAGONES.

Patagonia (pătŭgō'nēŭ, –nyŭ, Sp. pätägō'nyä), originally the southernmost region of South America, comprising the S part of both Argentina and Chile; the name is, however, usually applied only to the Argentine portion. Argentine Patagonia (□ 300,000), lying E of the Andes and extending c.1,000 mi. S from the Río Colorado (38°–39°S) to Cape Horn, includes the natl. territories of RÍO NEGRO, NEUQUÉN, CHUBUT, COMODORO RIVADAVIA, SANTA CRUZ, and TIERRA DEL FUEGO (sometimes considered a separate region). Patagonia is essentially a semiarid grass and scrub plateau, with a dry, windy, marine climate, where sheep raising is the dominant occupation of the scant pop. (many Anglo-Saxon elements). Petroleum is produced near Comodoro Rivadavia. First visited 1520 by Magellan, the region was not colonized until after c.1880, following the wars against the local Tehuelche Indians. Disputed by Chile and Argentina, Patagonia was divided by treaty (1881; final settlement, 1902).

Patagonia, town (pop. 700), Santa Cruz co., S Ariz., 18 mi. NE of Nogales; alt. 4,050 ft.; center of mining (silver, lead, copper, zinc) and cattle area. Santa Rita Mts. are N, Patagonia Mts. S.

Patagonia Mountains, W spur of Huachuca Mts., in section of Coronado Natl. Forest, Santa Cruz co., SE Ariz.; extends S into Sonora, Mexico, and rises to 7,300 ft. in Ariz., near international line. There are deposits of lead, silver, zinc, and copper.

Pataholm (pä"tähōlm'), town (pop. 62), Kalmar co., SE Sweden, on Kalmar Sound of the Baltic, at mouth of Alster R., 17 mi. N of Kalmar; fishing port. Founded in 17th cent.

Pataias (pŭtä'yūsh), village (pop. 1,556), Leiria dist., W central Portugal, on railroad and 11 mi. SW of Leiria; mfg. of glass bottles, ceramics; resin processing, sawmilling. Pine forests (N).

Pata Island (pä'tä) (□ 18; 1948 pop., including offshore islets, 6,795), Sulu prov., Philippines, in Sulu Archipelago, just off S coast of Jolo Isl.

Pata Kesar (pŭ'tŭ kä'sŭr), village, Mazar-i-Sharif prov., N Afghanistan, 34 mi. N of Mazar-i-Sharif and on the Amu Darya (USSR line); frontier post opposite Pakhta-Gissar (port for Termez); ferry connection. Sometimes spelled Patta-Gisar.

Pataliputra, India: see PATNA, city.

Patalung, Thailand: see PHATTHALUNG.

Patamari (pŭtä'märē), village, Goalpara dist., W Assam, India, on the Brahmaputra and 8 mi. WSW of Dhubri; jute-trade center; rice, mustard.

Patamban (pätäm'bän), town (pop. 2,333), Michoacán, W central Mexico, at NE foot of Cerro Patamban, 16 mi. S of Zamora; cereals, sugar cane, fruit, stock.

Patamban, Cerro, peak (12,303 ft.), Michoacán, N central Mexico, 18 mi. SSW of Zamora.

Patan (pä'tŭn). **1** Town (pop. 39,549), Mehsana dist., N Bombay, India, on Saraswati R., and 24 mi. NW of Mehsana; trade center (millet, cotton, oilseeds); cotton milling, handicrafts (cloth weaving, embroidering, wood and ivory carving), mfg. of pottery, swords. Site of anc. Anhilvada, sacked 1024 by Mahmud of Ghazni. **2** Village, Satara North dist., W central Bombay, India, 22 mi. SSW of Satara; local market for millet, peanuts, rice. **3** Town, Hyderabad state, India: see PAITHAN. **4** Village, Jubbulpore dist., N Madhya Pradesh, India, 20 mi. NW of Jubbulpore; wheat, gram, rice, oilseeds. **5** Town, SE Rajasthan, India: see JHALRAPATAN. **6** Town, SE central Rajasthan, India: see KESHORAI PATAN. **7** Town, S Saurashtra, India: see SOMNATH.

Patan or **Pattan** (both: pŭtŭn'), anc. *Sankarapura-pattana*, town (pop. 3,032), Baramula dist., W central Kashmir, in Vale of Kashmir, 15 mi. WNW of Srinagar; rice, corn, wheat, oilseeds. Founded mid-9th cent. A.D. Ruined 9th-cent. Sivaite temples near by.

Patan (pä'tŭn), city (1920 pop., including environs, 104,928), central Nepal, in NEPAL VALLEY, near the Baghmati, 2 mi. S of Katmandu city center; barley, rice, wheat, millet, vegetables, fruit. Numerous temples, including Buddhist temple of Machendranath (built 1408; annual festival) and 16th-cent. Mahabuddha temple, built in imitation of famous temple at Buddh Gaya. Has 4 Asokan cardinal-point stupas around city and 1 in center, built 3d cent. B.C. Founded A.D. c.650. Was ⊙ Dharmakar, traditional 1st king of Nepal. Former petty kingdom, long ruled by Newars of Malla dynasty under suzerainty of Bhadgaon; in 1480, after division of valley, became a principality; soon inc. into Katmandu; again became independent (1639) under Patan dynasty. Conquered 1768 by Gurkhas under Prithwi Narayan, who partially sacked and ruined city. Damaged by earthquake of 1934. Pop. mainly Newar. Sacred springs 7 mi. SE, at Godavari village, with Hindu shrines (pilgrimage site) near by.

Patangata, New Zealand: see WAIPUKURAU.

Patani (pätä'nē), town, Warri prov., Western Provinces, S Nigeria, in Niger R. delta, 37 mi. ESE of Warri; trade center; palm oil and kernels, hardwood, rubber.

Patani, Thailand: see PATTANI.

Patan Somnath, India: see SOMNATH.

Pâtapo (pä'täpō), village (pop. 2,714), Lambayeque dept., NW Peru, on coastal plain, on Taimi Canal (irrigation) and 13 mi. ENE of Chiclayo; rail terminus; sugar milling, distilling.

Patapsco River (pŭtăp'skō), Md., formed c.20 mi. W of Baltimore by junction of N and S branches; flows c.65 mi. generally SE to Chesapeake Bay bet. Bodkin Point (S) and North Point. Baltimore is at head of its estuary (river's lower 14 mi.; up to 3 mi. wide; dredged deep-water channel); city's harbor installations and industrial suburbs (notably Sparrows Point) are on its shores and on inlets (Northwest Branch, Middle Branch, Curtis Bay). On man-made isl. W of Sparrows Point is Fort Carroll (never finished) and a lighthouse. Along river W of Baltimore is Patapsco State Park, recreational area. North Branch (c.45 mi. long) rises in NE Carroll co., flows generally S. South Branch (c.30 mi. long) rises in S Carroll co., flows generally E.

Patara (pă'tŭrŭ), anc. seaport city of Lycia, SW Asia Minor (now Turkey), on Mediterranean Sea 4 mi. E of mouth of Koca R.; colonized by Dorians, dedicated to Apollo, visited by Paul. Ruins.

Patarlagele (pŭtŭrläge̱'lä), Rum. *Pătârlagele*, village (pop. 850), Buzau prov., SE central Rumania, on Buzau R., on railroad and 27 mi. WNW of Buzau.

Patarrá (pätärä'), village (dist. pop. 975), San José prov., central Costa Rica, on central plateau, 2 mi. SE of Desamparados; limestone quarries, limekilns.

Patás, province, Peru: see TAYABAMBA.

Patás or **Pataz** (both: pätäs'), town (pop. 214), Libertad dept., N central Peru, on W slopes of Cordillera Central, 50 mi. NW of Tayabamba; alt. 8,130 ft. Wheat, corn, coca, cattle, sheep. Gold mining near by.

Patascoy de Santa Lucía, Cerro (sĕ'rō pätäskoi' dā sän'tä lōōsē'ä), Andean peak (c.13,000 ft.) in Putumayo commissary, SW Colombia, 25 mi. SE of Pasto.

Pataskala (pŭtă'skŭlŭ), village (pop. 928), Licking co., central Ohio, 15 mi. WSW of Newark, and on South Fork of Licking R., in fruit and dairy area.

Patate River (pätä'tā), central Ecuador, Andean stream joining Chambo R. 4 mi. W of Baños to form the Pastaza.

Pataudi (pŭtou'dē), town (pop. 4,105), Gurgaon dist., SE Punjab, India, 17 mi. SW of Gurgaon; market center for grain, oilseeds, cotton. Was ⊙ former princely state of Pataudi (□ 53; pop. 21,520) of Punjab States, India; since 1948, state inc. into Gurgaon dist.

Patavium, Italy: see PADUA.

Patay (pätā'), agr. village (pop. 1,313), Loiret dept., N central France, in the Beauce, 14 mi. NW of Orléans. Here Joan of Arc defeated the English in 1429.

Pataz, province, Peru: see TAYABAMBA.

Pataz, town, Peru: see PATÁS.

Patcham, England: see BRIGHTON.

Patch Grove, village (pop. 203), Grant co., extreme SW Wis., 11 mi. SE of Prairie du Chien.

Patchogue (pă'chăg", –chôg"), resort and fishing village (pop. 7,361), Suffolk co., SE N.Y., on S Long Isl., on Great South Bay, 30 mi. E of Freeport; mfg. of clothing, lace, hair preparations; wood, leather, and metal products; concrete blocks, lamp shades, floor coverings; boatbuilding. Nurseries. Inc. 1893.

Patchogue Highlands, village (pop. 1,159), Suffolk co., SE N.Y.

Patdi (pät'dē), former Eastern Kathiawar state (□ 39; pop. 3,147) of Western India States agency, near SE edge of Little Rann of Cutch. Since 1948, merged with Saurashtra. Sometimes spelled Patri.

Patea (pătē'ŭ), borough (pop. 1,486), ⊙ Patea co. (□ 591; pop. 3,490), on W coast of N.Isl., New Zealand, at mouth of Patea R., 55 mi. SSE of New Plymouth; small artificial harbor exporting dairy products. Iron ore.

Pategi (pächä'jē), town (pop. 4,350), Ilorin prov., Northern Provinces, W central Nigeria, on Niger R. opposite Mureji, at mouth of the Kaduna, and 85 mi. ENE of Ilorin; shea-nut processing; cotton weaving, raffia matting; cassava, yams, corn.

Pateley Bridge, town in parish of High and Low Bishopside (pop. 1,846), West Riding, W central Yorkshire, England, on Nidd R. and 10 mi. WSW of Ripon; agr. market.

Patene, Nam, Laos: see PAK HIN BOUN.

Pater, Wales: see PEMBROKE, municipal borough.

Patera (pŭtĕ'rŭ) or **Pateras** (pŭtĕ'rŭs), mountain in Attica nome, E central Greece, rises to 3,714 ft. 6 mi. N of Megara. An alternate name, Pastra, is properly applied to a mtn. 14 mi. N of Megara.

Paterna (pätĕr'nä). **1** or **Paterna del Río** (dhĕl rē'ō), town (pop. 1,348), Almería prov., S Spain, on S slopes of the Sierra Nevada, 12 mi. N of Berja; olive-oil processing; lumbering. Cereals, sugar beets, nuts, grapes. **2** Outer W suburb (pop. 9,394) of Valencia, Valencia prov., E Spain, in truck-farming area; flour milling, tanning, silk spinning, mfg. of furniture and blankets. On site of Roman military camp. Was famous in 14th-15th cent. for its pottery. Wireless station.

Paterna del Campo (dhĕl käm'pō), town (pop. 3,650), Huelva prov., SW Spain, 32 mi. ENE of Huelva; olives, cereals, chick-peas, grapes, livestock; olive-oil extracting, flour milling.

Paterna de Rivera (dhā rēvä'rä), town (pop. 2,888), Cádiz prov., SW Spain, 25 mi. E of Cádiz; spa in grain-growing region; apiculture; sawmilling. Sometimes Paterna de la Rivera.

Paternion (pätĕr'nēōn), town (pop. 9,111), Carinthia, S Austria, on the Drau and 12 mi. NW of Villach; resort (alt. 1,722 ft.).

Paternò (pätĕrnô'), town (pop. 28,533), Catania prov., E Sicily, at S foot of Mt. Etna, 11 mi. NW of Catania, in grape and citrus-fruit region; wine, fireworks. Hot chalybeate springs. Has cathedral, medieval castle. Believed to be near or on site of Siculian town of Hybla or Hybla Major. Heavily bombed (1943) in Second World War.

Paternosters, Channel Isls.: see PIERRES DES LECQ.

Pateros (pŭtă'rŭs), town (pop. 866), Okanogan co., N central Wash., 25 mi. SSW of Okanogan, near junction of Methow and Columbia rivers, in mining, agr. region; asbestos.

Paterson (pă'tŭrsŭn), city (pop. 139,336), ⊙ Passaic co., NE N.J., at falls of Passaic R., 12 mi. N of Newark; 3d largest N.J. city, and a leading U.S. silk-weaving and dyeing center, mfg. also textile machinery, metal and rubber goods, furniture, plastics, clothing, chemicals, mirrors. State teachers col., vocational schools. Founded 1791 as industrial community by Alexander Hamilton, inc. 1851. Water power used for cotton spinning after 1794; industry giving Paterson the name "The Silk City" began 1839; 1st loom for silk fabric built here 1842. Early cotton industry had one of 1st factory strikes in U.S. (1828); silk industry, with many small "family" shops, has had many strikes, notably in 1912–13, 1933, and 1936. Fire, flood, and a tornado devastated city in 1902. In Second World War, nylon, rubber, aircraft, and metal industries employed many former silk workers. Points of interest: mus., with natural-history and Indian collections and submarine built 1878 by John P. Holland; library and art gall. designed by Henry Bacon; Garret Mtn. park, with co. historical society mus.

Paterson Inlet, New Zealand: see OBAN.

Patgram (păt'gräm), village, Dinajpur dist., N East Bengal, E Pakistan, on tributary of the Jaldhaka and 43 mi. NNW of Rangpur; rice, tobacco, mustard, jute. Until 1947, in Jalpaiguri dist. of Br. Bengal prov.

Pathalkati, India: see GAYA, city.

Pathankot (pŭtän'kōt), town (pop. 12,354), Gurdaspur dist., NW Punjab, India, 21 mi. NE of Gurdaspur; trade center for wheat, corn, sugar cane, gram, wool, timber, hides; hand-loom weaving; fruit-preserving factory.

Pathardi (pä'tŭrdē), town (pop. 7,336), Ahmadnagar dist., E Bombay, India, 28 mi. ENE of Ahmadnagar; local trade in cotton, millet; handicraft cloth weaving.

Pathari (pŭtä'rē), village, E Madhya Bharat, India, 38 mi. NE of Bhilsa; wheat, millet. Just E is sandstone pillar with medieval inscription. Was ⊙ former princely state of Pathari (□ 30; pop. 4,171) of Central India agency; since 1948, state merged with Madhya Bharat.

Patharkandi (pä'tŭrkändē), village, Cachar dist., S Assam prov., India, on tributary of the Kusiyara and 34 mi. WSW of Silchar; rice, tea, mustard. Until 1947, in Sylhet dist. Rail spur terminus 1 mi. S, at Kalkali Ghat.

Pathead, Scotland: see KIRKCALDY.

Pathfinder Dam, S central Wyo., in deep canyon of N.Platte R., 40 mi. SW of Casper; masonry dam 214 ft. high, 1,070 ft. long; completed 1913. Used for irrigation. Pathfinder Reservoir (□ 35; 23 mi. long, 1 mi. wide; capacity 1,070,000 acre-ft.) is main reservoir of North Platte project; furnishes supplemental water to Seminoe and Alcova dams in Kendrick project.

Pathfork, mining village (1940 pop. 711), Harlan co., SE Ky., in the Cumberlands, 17 mi. NE of Middlesboro; bituminous coal.

Pathri (pä'trē), **1** Town (pop. 5,728), Parbhani dist., NW Hyderabad state, India, 22 mi. W of Parbhani; cotton, millet, oilseeds. **2** Village, Uttar Pradesh, India: see HARDWAR.

Pathrot (păt'rōt), town (pop. 5,370), Amraoti dist., W Madhya Pradesh, India, 5 mi. NE of Anjangaon; cotton, millet, wheat.

Pathumthani (pätōōm'tä'nē'), town (1947 pop. 2,353), Pathumthani prov. (□ 592; 1947 pop. 139,339), S Thailand, on right bank of Chao Phraya R. and 20 mi. N of Bangkok, in rice-growing area; rice milling; fisheries. Sometimes spelled Pradum or Pradumdhani; also Prathum Thani.

Pati (pätē'), town (pop. 22,444), NW Java, Indonesia, 20 mi. W of Rembang; trade center for agr. area (sugar, rice, peanuts, cassava).

Patía (pätē'ä), town (pop. 1,224), Cauca dept., SW Colombia, on Patía R., on Pasto Popayán highway and 40 mi. SW of Popayán, in agr. region (cacao, sugar cane, tobacco, coffee, corn, fique, cattle, horses).

Patiala (pŭtyä'lŭ), former princely state (□ 5,942; pop. 1,936,259) of Punjab States, India; ⊙ was Patiala. Comprised large main body, with detached areas E (in Kumaun Himalaya foothills) and S, and several scattered enclaves in surrounding princely states and Punjab dists. Formed 1763 by Sikh confederacy on breakup of Mogul empire. Since 1948, merged with Patiala and East Punjab States Union. Sometimes spelled Puttiala.

Patiala, city (pop. 69,850), ⊙ Patiala and East Punjab States Union and Patiala dist., India, on E branch of Sirhind Canal and 125 mi. NNW of New Delhi, 22 mi. WSW of Ambala. Trade center for cotton, grain, cloth fabrics, hardware; mfg. of electrical appliances, shoes, flour, ice; hand-loom cotton and silk weaving; metalworks. Cols., clinical research laboratory. Was ⊙ former Punjab state of Patiala. Sometimes spelled Puttiala.

Patiala and East Punjab States Union, abbr. **PEPSU** or **Pepsu**, constituent state (□ 10,099; 1951 census pop. 3,468,631), NW India; ⊙ Patiala. Consists of several detached areas surrounded by or bordering on Punjab state (India); large central body lies in plain bet. Sutlej R. (N, W) and Jumna R. (E); N sections are within Bist Jullundur Doab, bet. Beas and Sutlej rivers; E sections lie in outer Kumaun Himalayas and are bordered E by Himachal Pradesh; S sections, on NE edge of Thar Desert, are bordered S by Rajasthan. With average rainfall less than 25 in., agr. (gram, wheat, millet, corn, cotton) depends heavily on irrigation, particularly by branches of Sirhind and Western Jumna canal systems, which extend throughout central portion of state. Sugar mill at Hamira, cementworks at Surajpur, biscuit factory at Rajpura; also cotton ginning, handicraft cloth and metalware mfg. Patiala, Phagwara, Kot Kapura, Kapurthala, and Bhatinda are trade centers. State formed 1948 by merger of former princely states of PUNJAB STATES of Patiala, Jind,

Nabha, Kapurthala, Faridkot, and Maler Kotla, and former Punjab Hill states of Kalsia and Nalagarh. Comprises 8 dists.: Barnala, Bhatinda, Fatehgarh Sahib, Kapurthala, Kohistan, Narnaul, Patiala, and Sangrur. Has large Sikh community (c.40% of pop.).

Patiali (pŭt'yŏŏlē), town (pop. 4,088), Etah dist., W Uttar Pradesh, India, on tributary of the Ganges and 23 mi. ENE of Etah; wheat, pearl millet, barley, corn, oilseeds. Important in 13th cent. under Afghans.

Patía River (pätē'ä), in Cauca and Nariño depts., SW Colombia, continues southward the Andean valley of Cauca R. bet. Cordillera Occidental and Cordillera Central; rises SW of Popayán (Cauca), flows SSW into Nariño, and cuts W through the mts. to the Pacific by several mouths N of Tumaco; c.200 mi. long. Navigable up to Barbacoas, on a left affluent.

Pati dos Alferes (pŏŏtē' dŏŏs älfĕ'rĭs), town (pop. 1,393), W central Rio de Janeiro, Brazil, in the Serra do Mar, on railroad and 25 mi. E of Barra do Piraí; resort. Marble deposits. Formerly spelled Paty dos Alferes.

Patillas (pätē'yäs), town (pop. 2,241), SE Puerto Rico, 6 mi. E of Guayama (linked by rail), in irrigated area (large sugar plantations).

Patillos (pätē'yōs), abandoned village, Tarapacá prov., N Chile, former minor Pacific port, 40 mi. S of Iquique; shipped nitrates.

Patiño, department, Argentina: see KILÓMETRO 642.

Patiño, Estero (ĕstä'rō pätē'nyō), swamp area in the Chaco region, on Argentina-Paraguay border, extends c.70 mi. (c.30 mi. wide) along Pilcomayo R., which here splits into 2 arms, the Brazo Norte and Brazo Sud. The Río Confuso, in Paraguay, rises here. It is a wild jungle area. Border, disputed bet. Paraguay and Argentina, was finally delimited 1945.

Pativilca (pätēvēl'kä), town (pop. 1,142), Lima dept., W central Peru, on coastal plain, on Pativilca R. (irrigation) and 4 mi. NNW of Barranca. Sugarcane plantations near by.

Patkai Range (pät'kī), culminating section of Naga Hills, on Burma-India border, extends SW-NE bet. 25°30'N and 27°30'N; rises to 12,553 in the Saramati. Crossed in Pangsau Pass by Ledo (Stilwell) Road.

Patmos (păt'mŏs), Ital. *Patmo* (pät'mō), Aegean island (□ 13; pop. 2,428) in the N Dodecanese, Greece, SSW of Samos; 37°20'N 26°34'E; 8 mi. long, 1–4 mi. wide; rises to 748 ft. Produces wheat, tomatoes, wine, olive oil. Main town, Patmos (pop. 952), is on SE shore. Here, according to Rev. 1.9., the exiled John the Divine wrote the Revelation.

Patna (pŭt'nŭ, păt'nŭ), former princely state (□ 2,530; pop. 632,220) in Chhattisgarh States, India; ⊙ was Bolangir. Ruling chiefs were Rajputs. Inc. 1949 into newly-created dist. of Bolangir, Orissa.

Patna, district (□ 2,164; pop. 2,162,008), N central Bihar, India; ⊙ Bankipore (within area of PATNA city). Mainly on Ganges Plain (isolated hills in S); bounded N by Ganges, W by Son rivers; drained by tributaries of the Ganges; served by Patna Canal (W). Mainly alluvial soil; rice, gram, barley, wheat, oilseeds, corn, sugar cane, millet. Silk weaving, jasmine-oil extracting, rice, oilseed, and sugar milling. Chief industrial center is Patna; other centers, Barh, Dinapore, Khagaul, Fatwa. Univ. and major radium research institute at Patna. Silica mining near Bihar. Ruins of Buddhist Nalanda Univ. at Baragaon; cave sculpture, Buddhist ruins in hills near Rajgir.

Patna, city (including areas of Bankipore, New Patna, and Patna City, □ 30; pop. 196,415), Patna dist., ⊙ Bihar, India, on Ganges Plain, extending 9 mi. along right (S) bank of the Ganges, and 290 mi. NW of Calcutta; 25°35'N 85°10'E. Bankipore (central section of Patna) is ⊙ Patna dist.; New Patna (SW; adjoining Bankipore) is administrative ⊙ Bihar. Patna City, major mfg. area, is E, adjoining Bankipore. Rail and road junction; airport; trade (rice, gram, wheat, oilseeds, barley, corn, sugar cane, millet) and industrial center; noted for handicrafts; glassware, brass utensils, furniture, carpets, brocades, toys, fireworks, gold and silver wire and leaf, boots and shoes, ice, aerated water, pottery; hemp-narcotics; pisciculture. Patna Univ., Bihar Col. of Engineering, medical col., radium research institute, Pasteur Inst., and Hindi Inst. are here. Has Sikh temple, mosque of Sher Shah. As *Pataliputra* (*Palibothra*) or *Kusumapura*, an anc. city now buried beneath Patna city and Bankipore, it was ⊙ Magadha kingdom in 6th cent. B.C., was important under Mauryas, Chandragupta and Asoka, and was ⊙ Gupta empire until it fell in 5th cent. A.D. Fr. trading post established here 1732; rights renounced in 1947. Buddhist ruins near by. Also called Azimabad.

Patna (păt'nŭ), village, S central Ayrshire, Scotland, on Doon R. and 9 mi. SE of Ayr; coal mining.

Patna Canal, India: see SON CANALS.

Patna City, India: see PATNA, city.

Patnagarh (pŭt'nŭgŭr), village, Bolangir dist., W Orissa, India, 23 mi. W of Bolangir.

Patnanongan Island (pätnänông'gän) (□ 34), one of the Polillo Isls., Quezon prov., Philippines, in Philippine Sea, bet. Palasan Isl. (NW) and Jomalig Isl. (SE); 14°47'N 122°11'E; 14 mi. long, 1–4 mi. wide; rises to 279 ft. Fishing.

Patnoñgon (pätnōnyŭgōn'), town (1939 pop. 2,582; 1948 municipality pop. 23,145), Antique prov., W Panay isl., Philippines, 40 mi. WNW of Iloilo; rice-growing center.

Patnos (pätnôs'), village (pop. 1,266), Agri prov., E Turkey, 36 mi. SSW of Karakose.

Patnow Legnicki, Poland: see PANTEN.

Patnus, India: see BHIRA.

Pato Branco (pä'tŏŏ brāng'kŏŏ), town (pop. c.1,000), SW Paraná, Brazil, on road, and 23 mi. NW of Clevelândia; rum distilling, grain milling, wine making, lard processing.

Patoda (pä'tōdŭ), village (pop. 4,189), Bir dist., NW Hyderabad state, India, 23 mi. SW of Bir; millet, wheat, cotton.

Patoka (pŭtō'kŭ). **1** Village (pop. 602), Marion co., S central Ill., 16 mi. N of Centralia, in oil-producing and agr. area. **2** Town (pop. 626), Gibson co., SW Ind., on Patoka R. and 19 mi. S of Vincennes; shipping center for fruit, grain, and vegetables.

Patoka River, S Ind., rises in SE Orange co., flows 138 mi. generally W, past Jasper, Winslow, and Patoka, to the Wabash opposite Mount Carmel, Ill.

Patom Plateau (pŭtôm'), NE Irkutsk oblast, Russian SFSR, bet. Vitim and Lena rivers; rises to over 5,000 ft. Gold-mining region centered on Bodaibo.

Paton (pā'tŭn), town (pop. 404), Greene co., central Iowa, 24 mi. S of Fort Dodge, in agr. area.

Patones (pätō'nĕs), village (pop. 335), Madrid prov., central Spain, on Isabel II or Lozoya Canal (which here forms several reservoirs), and 3 mi. NE of Torrelaguna; cereals, grapes, livestock. Limestone quarrying.

Patos (pä'tôs) or **Patosi** (pä'tôsē), village (1930 pop. 341), S central Albania, in Mallakastër range, 8 mi. SE of Fier; petroleum and asphalt deposits.

Patos (pä'tŏŏs), city (pop. 7,760), W central Paraíba, NE Brazil, 170 mi. W of João Pessoa; E terminus (1949) of railroad from Cedro and Fortaleza (Ceará); agr. trade center shipping cotton, sugar, corn, beans, and livestock.

Patos, Cerro (sĕ'rō pä'tōs), Andean volcano (18,900 ft.) in N Catamarca prov., Argentina, 15 mi. NW of Antofalla volcano.

Patos, Cerro de los (dā lōs), Andean peak (15,960 ft.) on Argentina-Chile border; 30°43'S.

Patos, Lagoa dos (lŭgō'ŭ dŏŏs pä'tŏŏs) [Port.,= lake of the ducks], tidal lagoon (□ 3,917) in SE Rio Grande do Sul, Brazil; c.150 mi. long, up to 30 mi. wide. Separated from the Atlantic by a low sand bar (20 mi. wide in N, narrowing southward), it communicates with the open sea by a channel (1 mi. wide) at its S end, near port of Rio Grande. At Pelotas it receives the overflow of MIRIM LAKE via São Gonçalo Canal. The Guaíba estuary (on which Pôrto Alegre is located) forms lagoon's northernmost inlet. Generally shallow, but a dredged channel permits vessels drawing 15 ft. to ply bet. Rio Grande and Pôrto Alegre. Extensive fishing. Rice cultivation on low W shore.

Patos, Río de los (rē'ō dā lōs pä'tōs), river in SW San Juan prov., Argentina, rises in the Andes near Chile border, curves SE, then flows NNE, past Tamberías and Calingasta, joining Castaño R. 6 mi. N of Calingasta to form San Juan R.; 125 mi. long.

Patos de Minas (pä'tŏŏs dĭ mē'nŭs), city (pop. 6,943), W Minas Gerais, Brazil, in the Triângulo Mineiro, 120 mi. NE of Uberaba; agr. trade center; has experimental wheat-growing station. Airfield. Diamond washings in area. Until 1944, called Patos.

Patos Island (pä'tōs), islet off Venezuela in the Gulf of Paria, in the Dragon's Mouth, bet. Paria Peninsula (W) and Trinidad, B.W.I. (E), 23 mi. W of Port of Spain. Long disputed, it became part of Venezuela by Anglo-Venezuelan Treaty (1942). Sometimes called Goose Isl.

Patquia (pät'kyä), village (pop. estimate 500), ⊙ Independencia dept. (□ 3,140; 1947 census pop. 1,628), S central La Rioja prov., Argentina, at SE end of Famatina Valley, 40 mi. S of La Rioja; rail junction, farming and lumbering center; corn, alfalfa, wine, livestock (goats, cattle, sheep).

Patras (pă'trăs'), Gr. *Patrai* (pä'trĕ), Lat. *Patrae* (pă'trē), city (1951 pop. 88,414), ⊙ Achaea nome, N Peloponnesus, Greece, port on Gulf of Patras, on railroad, and 110 mi. W of Athens; 38°15'N 21°44'E. Third largest city of Greece; commercial and industrial center; has cotton, flour, and paper mills and distilleries powered by hydroelectric works along rivers (E). Exports large quantities of Zante currants and, in addition, olive oil, wine, citrus fruit, skins. Airport. Has church of St. Andrew (patron-saint), Venetian-Turkish castle, remains of Roman aqueduct. Founded by Achaeans on site of anc. Aroe, anc. Patrae was member of Achaean League and became Roman commercial center under Augustus. One of earliest centers of Christianity. From here, the French began (1205) their conquest of Peloponnesus. For a short time in 15th cent. it was under Venetian rule and later passed to the Turks. After its destruction (1821) during Gr. war of independence, it was rebuilt in rectangular plan.

Patras, Gulf of, inlet of Ionian Sea, Greece, bet. Peloponnesus (S) and central Greece (N), and bet. capes Rion (E) and Papas (W); 25 mi. wide, 10 mi. long. Connects E with Gulf of Corinth through Rion Strait. Patras is on SE shore.

Patrasaer (pä'trŭsīr), town (pop. 5,731), Bankura dist., W central West Bengal, India, 30 mi. E of Bankura; cotton weaving, metalware mfg.; rice, wheat, pulse, mustard, potatoes. Also spelled Patrasayar or Patrasair.

Patreksfjordur or **Patreksfjordhur** (pä'trĕkhsfyûr"-dhür), Icelandic *Patreksfjörður*, town (pop. 901), ⊙ Bardastrandar co., NW Iceland, on Vestfjarda Peninsula, 40 mi. SW of Isafjordur, on Patrek Fjord, 20-mi. inlet of Denmark Strait; fishing port.

Patri, former state, India: see PATDI.

Patri (pä'trē), town (pop. 7,082), Ahmadabad dist., N Bombay, India, 50 mi. WNW of Ahmadabad; market center for cotton, millet, molasses, salt; cotton ginning.

Patriarsheye, Russian SFSR: see VODOPYANOVO.

Patricia, district (pop. 9,613), NW Ont., N portion of Kenora co., bounded by Manitoba (W) and Hudson Bay (N); drained by Severn, Winisk, and Attawapiskat rivers. There is abundant water power. Contains numerous lakes, including Big Trout, St. Joseph, and North Caribou lakes. Gold is mined in Pickle Crow and Central Patricia region. Formerly part of Northwest Territories, dist. was disputed bet. Man. and Ont. It was added to Ont. by The Ontario Boundaries Extension Act of 1912; named after Princess Patricia, daughter of the duke of Connaught, governor general at the time. Annexed 1927 for judicial purposes to Kenora co.

Patricio Lynch Island (pätrē'syō lēnch'), off coast of Aysén prov., S Chile, just NW of Wellington Isl., N of 48°50'S; 27 mi. long, 3–10 mi. wide.

Patrick, county (□ 469; pop. 15,642), S Va.; ⊙ Stuart. Partly in the piedmont; rises to Blue Ridge in W and NW; includes Fairy Stone Mtn. (in Fairy Stone State Park) and Pinnacles of Dan. Blue Ridge Parkway, Appalachian Trail traverse co. Drained by Mayo, Smith, and Dan rivers. Agr. (corn, wheat, tobacco, fruit), livestock raising, lumbering; mfg. (especially furniture and wood products). Formed 1790.

Patrick, town (pop. 310), Chesterfield co., N S.C., 35 mi. NW of Florence; naval stores, lumber.

Patricroft, town in Eccles borough, SE Lancashire, England, 5 mi. W of Manchester, cotton and silk milling, locomotive building; mfg. of textile machinery, textile soap, plastics.

Patrie, La (lä pătrē'), village (pop. 343), S Que., on Salmon R., a tributary of St. Francis R. and 30 mi. E of Sherbrooke, at foot of Megantic Mtn.; dairying, stock raising.

Patrimônio União, Brazil: see AMAMBAÍ.

Patrington, town and parish (pop. 1,121), East Riding, SE Yorkshire, England, 14 mi. ESE of Hull; agr. market. Has large cruciform 14th-cent. church.

Patriot, town (pop. 315), Switzerland co., SE Ind., on Ohio R. and 25 mi. SW of Cincinnati (Ohio), in agr. area. Suffered during flood of 1937.

Patrocínio (pŏŏtrŏŏsē'nyŏŏ). **1** City (pop. 6,078), W Minas Gerais, Brazil, on railroad and 85 mi. NE of Uberaba; alt. 3,120 ft. Livestock-shipping center; dairying. Has healthful climate and mineral springs. **2** City, Piauí, Brazil: see PIO NÔNO. **3** Town, Rio Grande do Sul, Brazil: see ABOLIÇÃO.

Patrocínio do Coité, Brazil: see PARIPIRANGA.

Patrocínio do Muriaé (dŏŏ mŏŏryä-ĕ'), town (pop. 2,162), SE Minas Gerais, Brazil, 10 mi. E of Muriaé; rail junction.

Patrocínio Paulista (poulē'stŭ), city (pop. 1,447), NE São Paulo, Brazil, 10 mi. SE of Franca; distilling, dairy-products processing; tobacco, sugar cane, coffee. Until 1948, called Patrocínio do Sapucaí.

Patroclus, Greece: see PATROKLOU.

Patroha (pät'rôhŏ), Hung. *Pátroha*, town (pop. 3,180), Szabolcs co., NE Hungary, 20 mi. NE of Nyiregyhaza; rye, beans, potatoes, cattle.

Patroklou (pätrô'klŏŏ), Lat. *Patroclus* (pŭtrō'klŭs), uninhabited island (□ 1.23) in Aegean Sea at mouth of Saronic Gulf, Attica nome, E central Greece, 1 mi. off S tip of Attica Peninsula; 1½ mi. long, ¾ mi. wide. Also called Gaidaros or Gaidharos, and Gaidouronesi or Gaidhouronisi.

Patsaliga Creek (pătsă'lĭgŭ), S Ala., rises in S Montgomery co., flows c.60 mi. S and SW to Conecuh R. 4 mi. NW of Andalusia.

Patscherkofel (pä'chŭrkōfŭl), peak (7,373 ft.) of Tuxer Alps, in Tyrol, W Austria, 5 mi. SSE of Innsbruck. Reached by cable car from Igls (at NW foot). Fine view of Inn R. valley (N) and Wipptal (W).

Patschkau, Poland: see PACZKOW.

Pats River, Finnish *Patsjoki* (päts'yō"kē), Russian *Paz* (päz), Nor. *Pasvik* (päs'vēk) or *Pasvikelv* (–ĕlv"), outlet of L. Inari, on USSR-Norwegian border, emerges 25 mi. NE of Ivalo, flows 88 mi. NE, past Salmiyarvi, to Bok Fjord, arm of Varanger Fjord, at Kirkenes. Upper course, bet. L. Inari and Norwegian border, including areas of

Jäniskoski (Yaniskoski) and Niskakoski (hydroelectric stations supplying Nikel mines), was ceded (1947) by Finland to USSR.

Patta (pŭt'tŭ), village, W Himachal Pradesh, India, 19 mi. SW of Simla; corn, rice, wheat. Was ⊙ former Punjab Hill state of Mailog.

Pattada (pät-tä'dä), village (pop. 4,846), Sassari prov., N central Sardinia, 31 mi. SE of Sassari, near Mannu d'Oschiri R.

Patta-Gisar, Afghanistan: see PATA KESAR.

Patta-Gisar, Uzbek SSR: see PAKHTA-GISAR.

Patta Island (pä'tä), in Indian Ocean, just off Kenya coast, 10 mi. NNE of Lamu Isl.; 15 mi. long; 6 mi. wide. Copra, fisheries.

Pattamadai (pŭt-tä'mŭdī), town (pop. 8,205), Tinnevelly dist., S Madras, India, 8 mi. WSW of Tinnevelly; grass-mat weaving.

Pattambi, India: see SHORANUR.

Pattan, India: see PAITHAN.

Pattan, Kashmir: see PATAN.

Pattani or **Patani** (both: pät'tänē'), town (1947 pop. 8,969), ⊙ Pattani prov. (□ 753; 1947 pop. 199,253), S Thailand, on E coast of Malay Peninsula, at mouth of small Pattani R., port (sheltered by Cape Pattani) on Gulf of Siam, 150 mi. ESE of Songkhla; large coconut, tobacco, and rubber plantations; fisheries. The region has tin deposits and grows spices. Pop. mostly Malay. Was 1st Thai port opened (16th cent.) to foreign trade; had Portuguese, British, and Dutch factories.

Pattani, Cape, S Thailand, on E coast of Malay Peninsula, at entrance of Gulf of Siam, off Pattani town; 70°N 101°20'E.

Patten, town (pop. 1,536), including Patten village (pop. 1,032), E central Maine, 30 mi. WSW of Houlton; lumbering, hunting, fishing area. Settled 1828, inc. 1841.

Pattensen (pä'tŭnzŭn), town (pop. 3,541), in former Prussian prov. of Hanover, W Germany, after 1945 in Lower Saxony, 8 mi. S of Hanover; cattle.

Patterdale, village and parish (pop. 817), NW Westmorland, England, at S end of Ullswater, 7 mi. N of Ambleside; sheep.

Patterson. 1 Town (pop. 357), Woodruff co., E central Ark., 7 mi. E of Augusta. Also called Jelks. **2** City (pop. 1,343), Stanislaus co., central Calif., on San Joaquin R. and 35 mi. S of Stockton, in irrigated fruitgrowing, farming, and dairying area. Inc. 1919. **3** Town (pop. 656), Pierce co., SE Ga., 18 mi. NE of Waycross. **4** Town (pop. 112), Lemhi co., E Idaho, c.45 mi. SSE of Salmon. **5** Village, Greene co., Ill.: see WILMINGTON. **6** Town (pop. 133), Madison co., S central Iowa, 22 mi. SW of Des Moines, in agr. area. **7** Town (pop. 1,938), St. Mary parish, S La., 7 mi. W of Morgan City, in sugar-cane-growing area; sugar and lumber milling; sea food; water-tank mfg. Settled in late-18th cent.; inc. 1907. **8** Village (1940 pop. 538), Putnam co., SE N.Y., 11 mi. NW of Danbury (Conn.), in dairying and farming area. **9** Town (pop. 195), Caldwell co., W central N.C., 5 mi. N of Lenoir; cotton milling. **10** Village (pop. 189), Hardin co., W central Ohio, 10 mi. NNE of Kenton.

Patterson, Mount (10,490 ft.), SW Alta., near B.C. border, in Rocky Mts., in Banff Natl. Park, 60 mi. NW of Banff; 51°45'N 116°35'W.

Patterson Creek Mountain, NE W.Va., a ridge of the Appalachians, in Eastern Panhandle; from South Branch of the Potomac near Petersburg extends 31 mi. NNE; highest point (2,774 ft.) is 8 mi. NNE of Petersburg. Patterson Creek (49 mi. long) rises in N Grant co., flows E and NNE along W base to North Branch of the Potomac.

Patterson Gardens, village (pop. 1,548), Monroe co., SE Mich.

Patterson Heights, borough (pop. 678), Beaver co., W Pa., on Beaver R. just below Beaver Falls.

Patti (pŭt'tē). **1** Town (pop. 17,595), Amritsar dist., W Punjab, India, 23 mi. S of Amritsar; trades in grain, cotton, oilseeds, rice, cloth fabrics; handloom weaving, cotton ginning. **2** Village, Partabgarh dist., E Uttar Pradesh, India, 12 mi. E of Bela; rice, barley, wheat, gram, mustard.

Patti (pät'tē), town (pop. 5,490), Messina prov., NE Sicily, SE of Cape Calava, 16 mi. SW of Milazzo; pottery, wine, olive oil. Bishopric. Has 14th-cent. cathedral (damaged in Second World War) and monasteries. Antimony mines near by. Its port, Marina di Patti, is 1 mi. N on Gulf of Patti; tunny fishing, mfg. (machinery, clocks, ladders).

Patti, Gulf of, inlet of Tyrrhenian Sea in NE Sicily, bet. Cape Milazzo (E) and Cape Calava (W); 18 mi. long, 8 mi. wide; tunny fisheries. Chief port, Marina di Patti.

Pattikonda (pŭtĭkŏn'dŭ), town (pop. 6,195), Kurnool dist., N Madras, India, 46 mi. SW of Kurnool; cotton ginning, oilseed (peanut) milling. Bamboo, dyewood in near-by forests.

Pattison State Park (1,140 acres), Douglas co., extreme NW Wis., near Superior. Principal feature is Big Manitou Falls or Manitou Falls (165 ft. high), highest in Wis., in Black R. Established 1920.

Pattoki (pŭt-tō'kē), town (pop. 11,114), Lahore dist., E Punjab, W Pakistan, 45 mi. SW of Lahore; market center for cotton, wheat, oilseeds, gram; cotton ginning, sugar milling, hand-loom weaving. Sometimes called Mandi Pattoki.

Patton, parish (pop. 67), S Westmorland, England. Includes wool-weaving village of Mealbank, 3 mi. NE of Kendal.

Patton. 1 Village (pop. c.1,000), San Bernardino co., S Calif., 4 mi. NE of San Bernardino; citrus fruit. **2** Borough (pop. 3,148), Cambria co., SW central Pa., 25 mi. NE of Johnstown; bituminous coal; clay products, lumber, ribbons; agr.

Pattonsburg, city (pop. 883), Daviess co., NW Mo., on Grand R. and 42 mi. NE of St. Joseph; dairy products; ships grain, cattle, lumber; limestone quarries.

Pattukkottai (pŭt"to͝ok-kōt'tī), town (pop. 12,709), Tanjore dist., SE Madras, India, on branch of Grand Anicut Canal, 27 mi. SSE of Tanjore, in agr. area; rail junction; sugar cane, peanuts, soybeans, and cotton at experimental farm.

Patu (po͞otoo'), city (pop. 945), SW Rio Grande do Norte, NE Brazil, on railroad and 65 mi. SSW of Mossoró; livestock, cotton, sugar.

Patuakhali (pŭtwä'kälē), town (pop. 10,847), Bakarganj dist., S East Bengal, E Pakistan, in the Sundarbans, on Patuakhali R. (distributary of Arial Khan R.) and 34 mi. S of Barisal; trades in rice, jute, oilseeds, sugar cane, betel nuts; match mfg., rice milling.

Patuakhali River, E Pakistan: see ARIAL KHAN RIVER.

Patuca Point (päto͞o'kä), on Mosquito Coast of NE Honduras, on Caribbean Sea, just W of Patuca R. mouth; 15°51'N 84°18'W.

Patuca River, in Mosquito region of E Honduras, formed 23 mi. SE of Juticalpa by union of Guayape (left) and Guayambre (right) rivers; flows c.200 mi. NE, past Portal del Infierno (rapids), Gualpatanta, and Cropunta, to Caribbean Sea at Patuca Point 60 mi. ESE of Iriona, sending a left arm (Tom-Tom Creek or Toom-Toom Creek) to Brus Lagoon. Navigable below Portal del Infierno; used for timber floating.

Patulul (päto͞olo͞ol'), town (1950 pop. 2,466), Suchitepéquez dept., SW Guatemala, in Pacific piedmont, 24 mi. ESE of Mazatenango; coffee, sugar cane, grain, fodder grasses; livestock.

Patung (bä'do͝ong'), town (pop. 16,493), ⊙ Patung co. (pop. 214,960), W Hupeh prov., China, on right bank of Yangtze R. (gorges) and 15 mi. W of Tzekwei, in rice-growing area. Coal deposits near.

Patur (pä'to͞or), town (pop. 7,307), Akola dist., W Madhya Pradesh, India, 18 mi. SSW of Akola; millet, cotton, oilseeds.

Pâturages (pätürăzh'), town (pop. 10,559), Hainaut prov., SW Belgium, 5 mi. SW of Mons; coal.

Patusha Mountains, Bulgaria and Yugoslavia: see VLAKHINA MOUNTAINS.

Patuxent River (pŭtŭk'sŭnt), Md., rises in NW Howard co., flows c.100 mi. generally SE and S, past Laurel and Solomons, to Chesapeake Bay bet. Cove (N) and Cedar points. Estuary (c.5 mi. wide at mouth) is deep-water anchorage. Navigable for c.45 mi., tidal for 56 mi. Small reservoir is impounded in upper course on Howard-Montgomery co. line. Patuxent Naval Air Test Center is along right bank at mouth.

Paty dos Alferes, Brazil: see PATI DOS ALFERES.

Patzau, Czechoslovakia: see PACOV.

Pátzcuaro (päts'kwärō), city (pop. 9,557), Michoacán, central Mexico, on central plateau, on S shore of L. Pátzcuaro, 30 mi. SW of Morelia; alt. 6,995 ft. Resort; fishing, processing, and agr. center (cereals, sugar cane, fruit, livestock); canning, tanning, flour- and sawmilling, liquor distilling; processing of forest products (resins). Known for native lacquer ware. Old Tarascan town, with 16th-cent. colonial character.

Pátzcuaro, Lake (□ 100), Michoacán, central Mexico, 25 mi. SW of Morelia; 14 mi. long, 4–12 mi. wide. Situated in beautiful mtn. setting (alt. 6,706 ft.); abounds in fish. Popular resort. Native Indian villages upon its indented shores and green isls. (Janitzio, Jarácuaro).

Patzicía (pätsēsē'ä), town (1950 pop. 5,015), Chimaltenango dept., S central Guatemala, on Inter-American Highway and 7 mi. W of Chimaltenango; alt. 6,998 ft.; market center (corn, wheat). Flour milling at La Sierra, 3 mi. WNW.

Patzún (pätso͞on'), town (1950 pop. 5,135), Chimaltenango dept., S central Guatemala, on Inter-American Highway and 12 mi. W of Chimaltenango; alt. 7,300 ft. Market center; grain, coffee. Has 16th-cent. church. Sawmilling near by. Formerly spelled Patzum.

Pau (pō), city (pop. 40,604), ⊙ Basses-Pyrénées dept., SW France, on right bank of the Gave de Pau and 95 mi. WSW of Toulouse, beautifully situated at foot of the Pyrenees; important tourist center, known for its mild winters; produces hosiery, table linen, handkerchiefs; ships hams, *pâté de foie gras,* and wines. Tanning, flour milling, meat preserving, brewing. Has recently restored castle (birthplace of Henry IV) and fine public bldgs. Old capital of BÉARN and residence of French kings of Navarre. Charles XIV of Sweden b. here.

Pau, Gave de (gäv dü pō'), river in Hautes-Pyrénées and Basses-Pyrénées depts., SW France, rises in the Cirque de GAVARNIE of central Pyrenees, flows N and NW, past Luz, Lourdes, Pau, and Orthez, to the Adour below Peyrehorade; 110 mi. long. Receives the Gave d'Oloron (left). Used for hydroelectric power.

Pauca (pou'kä), village (pop. 2,058), Cajamarca dept., NW Peru, in Cordillera Occidental, 35 mi. ENE of Cajamarca; barley, potatoes; sheep and cattle raising.

Paucarbamba (poukärbäm'bä), town (pop. 1,173), Huancavelica dept., S central Peru, in Cordillera Central, 24 mi. ESE of Pampas; distilling; sugar cane, grain, cattle, sheep.

Paucartambo (poukärtäm'bō). **1** Town (pop. 1,930), ⊙ Paucartambo prov. (□ 927; enumerated pop. 23,298, plus estimated 7,000 Indians), Cuzco dept., S Peru, at NW foot of Cordillera de Carabaya, on Paucartambo R. and 27 mi. NE of Cuzco, in agr. region (cotton, sugar cane); liquor distilling; alt. 9,980 ft. Kaolin deposits. Has archaeological remains. **2** Town (pop. 1,382), Pasco dept., central Peru, in Cordillera Central of the Andes, at source of Paucartambo R. (a left headstream of the Perené), 25 mi. ESE of Cerro de Pasco; grain, potatoes, livestock.

Paucartambo River. 1 In Cuzco dept., S central Peru, rises at W foot of the peak Asungate, flows c.200 mi. NW and W, past Paucartambo, to Urubamba R. at 12°6'S 72°57'W. Its lower course is also called the Yavero. **2** In central Peru, rises in Cordillera Central of the Andes at Paucartambo (Pasco dept.), flows 60 mi. E and S, past San Luis de Shuaro, joining the Chanchamayo at Puerto Wertheman to form PERENÉ RIVER.

Paudalho (poudä'lyo͞o), city (pop. 4,248), E Pernambuco, NE Brazil, on railroad and 25 mi. NW of Recife, in sugar-growing region. Formerly spelled Pau d'Alho.

Pau d'Alho, São Paulo, Brazil: see IBIRAREMA.

Pau dos Ferros (pou'do͞os fĕ'ro͞os), city (pop. 1,789), SW Rio Grande do Norte, NE Brazil, near Ceará border, 85 mi. SW of Mossoró; cattle raising; cotton, hides. Aquamarines found in area.

Pau Gigante, Brazil: see IBIRAÇU.

Paugus, Lake (pô'gŭs), Belknap co., central N.H., just N of Laconia; joined by Winnipesaukee R. to L. Winnipesaukee (N) and Winnisquam L. (SW); 3.5 mi. long.

Pauhunri, peak, India and Tibet: see DONGKYA RANGE.

Pauillac (pōyäk'), town (pop. 2,320), Gironde dept., SW France, port on W shore of the Gironde and 26 mi. NNW of Bordeaux; petroleum refineries. Its vineyards, including Château-Lafite and Château-Latour, produce the finest Médoc red wines.

Pauk (pouk), village, Pakokku dist., Upper Burma, near Yaw R., 40 mi. W of Pakokku, on road to Gangaw and Myittha R. valley.

Paukkaung (pouk"koun'), village, Prome dist., Lower Burma, 21 mi. ENE of Prome.

Pauktaw (pouktô'), village, Akyab dist., Lower Burma, in the Arakan, on tidal creek, 11 mi. ENE of Akyab.

Paul, former urban district (1931 pop. 5,814), SW Cornwall, England, near Mounts Bay of the Channel, 2 mi. SSW of Penzance; agr. market. Church, said to date from 10th cent., rebuilt after burning (1595) by Spaniards. Inc. 1934 in Penzance.

Paúl (päo͞ol'), village (pop. 1,720), Castelo Branco dist., central Portugal, on SE slope of Serra da Estrêla, 9 mi. SW of Covilhã; olives, livestock.

Paul (pôl), village (pop. 560), Minidoka co., S Idaho, 5 mi. W of Rupert; alt. 4,200 ft.; beet sugar, cheese.

Paula, Malta: see PAOLA.

Paular Pass (poulär') (alt. 6,004 ft.), in Castile, central Spain, across Sierra de Guadarrama bet. Segovia and Madrid provs., 30 mi. NNW of Madrid. Near by is the monastery Santa María del Paular, founded 1390.

Paulatuk, trading post, N Mackenzie Dist., Northwest Territories, at head of Darnley Bay (50 mi. long, 23–40 mi. wide) of Amundsen Gulf; 69°23'N 123°59'W; site of R.C. mission.

Paulaya River (poulī'ä), in Mosquito region of E Honduras, rises in NE outliers of Sierra de Agalta, flows c.50 mi. NE to Sico R. 9 mi. SE of Iriona. Lower valley is used by banana railroad.

Paúl da Serra (päo͞ol' dä sĕ'rŭ), basalt tableland (alt. c.5,000 ft.) on W part of Madeira, forming part of isl.'s central range. Waterfalls at plateau's edges.

Paulding (pôl'dĭng). **1** County (□ 318; pop. 11,752), NW Ga.; ⊙ Dallas. Piedmont agr. (cotton, corn, grain, fruit) and timber area; mfg. at Dallas. Formed 1832. **2** County (□ 416; pop. 15,047), NW Ohio; ⊙ Paulding. Bounded W by Ind. line; drained by Auglaize and Maumee rivers. Agr. area (wheat, sugar beets, corn, oats, livestock); clay pits, limestone quarries. Formed 1839.

Paulding. 1 Village (pop. c.150), a ⊙ Jasper co., E central Miss., 30 mi. SW of Meridian. **2** Village (pop. 2,352), ⊙ Paulding co., NW Ohio, 14 mi. SW of Defiance; corn, wheat, sugar beets, oats; sugar refining, alfalfa milling, mfg. of abrasive and asbestos products.

Paulenfoss, Norway: see KRINGSJA.

Paulesti (poulĕsht'), Rum. *Paulesti*, NW suburb of Ploesti, S central Rumania, in oil region.

Paulhaguet (pōlyägĕ'), village (pop. 1,116), Haute-Loire dept., S central France, in Monts du Velay, 9 mi. SE of Brioude; tile factory; barite quarries. Near-by castle of Chavaniac is birthplace of Lafayette.

Paulhan (pōlyā'), town (pop. 2,161), Hérault dept., S France, near Hérault R., 15 mi. SSE of Lodève; fruit and vegetable preserving and shipping, wine-growing.

Paulilatino (poulēlä'tēnô), village (pop. 3,183), Cagliari prov., central Sardinia, 15 mi. NNE of Oristano. Nuraghi near by.

Pauline, Lake, Hardeman co., N Texas, reservoir (capacity c.7,000 acre-ft.) impounded by power dam in a small S tributary of Prairie Dog Town Fork of Red R., c.5 mi. SE of Quanah. Fishing; hunting near by.

Paulins Kill (pô'lĭnz), NW N.J., stream rising in Kittatinny Mtn. ridge in NW Sussex co.; flows c.35 mi. SW, past Blairstown, to the Delaware at Columbia (hydroelectric dam here). Dammed W of Newton to form Paulins Kill L. (c.3 mi. long; boating, summer homes).

Paulinzella (pou"lĭntsĕ'lä), village (pop. 203), Thuringia, central Germany, 11 mi. W of Rudolstadt; climatic health resort. Has remains of noted Benedictine abbey, founded c.1100; plundered 1525 in Peasants' War; dissolved 1534 after Reformation. Its church (1112–32) was restored in late-19th cent. Near-by 17th-cent. hunting lodge is associated with Goethe.

Paulis (pōlēs'), town (1948 pop. 5,114), Eastern Prov., NE Belgian Congo, on railroad and 185 mi. E of Buta; commercial center in cotton-producing area. Cotton ginning; palm products; repair shops for automobiles. Also native center of Mangbettu tribe. Has Dominican mission, hosp. for Europeans. Formerly called Isiro. Gossamu-lez-Paulis (gôsämōō'-lā-pōlēs') cotton center is 2 mi. E. Nala (nä'lä) coffee plantations and Protestant mission are 6 mi. N.

Paul Isnard, Fr. Guiana: see P.I.

Paulista (poulē'stŏŏ), city (1951 pop. 21,944), E Pernambuco, NE Brazil, N suburb of Olinda, 8 mi. N of Recife; sugar milling; coconuts, tobacco.

Paulistana (poulēstä'nŏŏ), city (pop. 735), SE Piauí, Brazil, 100 mi. SE of Oeiras; N terminus of railroad from Petrolina (Pernambuco). Until 1944, called Paulista.

Paullina (pôlē'nŭ), town (pop. 1,289), O'Brien co., NW Iowa, 17 mi. NNW of Cherokee; concrete products, farm equipment. Sand and gravel pits near by. State park just E. Inc. 1883.

Paulo Affonso, city, Brazil: see MATA GRANDE.

Paulo Afonso Falls (pou'lŏŏ äfō'sŏŏ), on lower São Francisco R., NE Brazil, along Bahia-Alagoas border, c.190 mi. above river's mouth and 240 mi. SW of Recife (Pernambuco); 9°25'S 38°12'W. Consist of a series of impressive rapids, and of 3 cataracts totaling 275 ft. in height. Width of river at head of main falls is less than 60 ft. New hydroelectric installations, begun in late 1940s as part of a TVA-like project for the São Francisco valley, will supply power to much of NE Brazil. River is navigable above and below falls. A railroad circumvents falls bet. Petrolândia (Pernambuco) and Piranhas (Alagoas). Falls best reached by rail and car from Recife. Formerly spelled Paulo Affonso.

Paulo de Faria (dĭ fŏŏrē'ŭ), city (pop. 1,319), N São Paulo, Brazil, near the Rio Grande (Minas Gerais border), 55 mi. N of São José do Rio Prêto; butter processing; coffee, cotton, grain, cattle.

Paulpietersburg (poul"pē'tŭrsbûrkh"), town (pop. 2,006), N Natal, U. of So. Afr., near Transvaal border, near Pongola R., 25 mi. N of Vryheid; coal.

Paul Roux (rōō'), town (pop. 1,142), SE Orange Free State, U. of So. Afr., 20 mi. W of Bethlehem; grain, stock, dairying.

Paulsboro, borough (pop. 7,842), Gloucester co., SW N.J., on Mantua Creek and 10 mi. SW of Camden, near the Delaware; oil refineries; mfg. (fertilizer, chemicals, cigars), oil refining; agr. (truck, fruit, poultry). Steel plant at Thorofare (E) begun 1951. Settled 1681, inc. 1904. Fortified in the Revolution.

Paul Smiths, resort village, Franklin co., NE N.Y., on Lower St. Regis L., in the Adirondacks, 10 mi. NNW of Saranac Lake village. Site of Paul Smith's Col. of Arts and Sciences. Founded 1859 as one of 1st wilderness resorts in region.

Pauls Valley, city (pop. 6,896), ⊙ Garvin co., S central Okla., 31 mi. SW of Ada, and on Washita R., in rich farm, orchard, and dairy area. Oil refining, cotton ginning; mfg. of oilfield equipment, feed, food products, furniture. A state hosp. for epileptics is near by. Settled c.1887, inc. 1899.

Paulton, town and parish (pop. 2,498), NE Somerset, England, 3 mi. WNW of Radstock; coal mining, shoe mfg.

Paulus Hook, N.J.: see JERSEY CITY.

Paumotu: see TUAMOTU ISLANDS.

Paung (poung, Burmese pŏŏng'), village, Thaton dist., Lower Burma, in Tenasserim, on Pegu-Martaban RR and 15 mi. NW of Moulmein.

Paungbyin (poun"-byĭn'), village, Upper Chindwin dist., Upper Burma, on left bank of Chindwin R. and 80 mi. NNE of Kalewa; 24°16'N 94°49'E; trading center. In Second World War, recaptured (Nov., 1944) from Japanese by Br. forces.

Paungde (poung'dĕ), town (pop. 13,479), Prome dist., Lower Burma, on Rangoon-Prome RR and 30 mi. SE of Prome; center of rice dist.

Pauni (pou'nē), town (pop. 13,691), Bhandara dist., central Madhya Pradesh, India, on Wainganga R. and 26 mi. S of Bhandara; rice milling, handicraft cotton and silk weaving; wheat, oilseeds, mangoes. Sal and bamboo in near-by forests. Pauni Road (rail station) is 6 mi. SW.

Paunsaugunt Plateau (pôn'sŭgŭnt"), SW Utah, high tableland (7,000–9,300 ft.) in Garfield and Kane counties; extends S from Sevier Plateau along East Fork Sevier R., terminating in Pink Cliffs on S and E. Unusually dissected part of plateau and cliffs now included in BRYCE CANYON NATIONAL PARK (E).

Pauri (pou'rē), town (pop. 2,813), ⊙ Garhwal dist., N Uttar Pradesh, India, in central Kumaun Himalayas, 23 mi. NNE of Lansdowne, on N slope of hill; wheat, barley, rice, buckwheat.

Paurito (pourē'tō), town (pop. c.1,200), Santa Cruz dept., central Bolivia, c.17 mi. SE of Santa Cruz; road junction.

Pausa (pou'zä), town (pop. 4,503), Saxony, E central Germany, 9 mi. NW of Plauen; textile milling (cotton, muslin, curtains, lace); mfg. of china, rubber products.

Pausa (pou'sä), town (pop. 1,480), Ayacucho dept., S Peru, in Cordillera Occidental, 29 mi. ESE of Coracora; alfalfa, barley, livestock.

Pausula, Italy: see CORRIDONIA.

Pautalia, Bulgaria: see KYUSTENDIL.

Paute (pou'tā), town (1950 pop. 1,342), Azuay, S central Ecuador, in high Andean valley of Paute R., 18 mi. ENE of Cuenca, on road to trans-Andean Amazon basin; fruitgrowing center; sugar cane, cereals.

Paute River, SE central Ecuador, rises in the Andes S of Cuenca, flows NE, past Paute, then SE to join the Zamora, forming the Santiago at 3°S; c.125 mi. long. Its lower course is called Namangoza (nämäng-gō'sä).

Pauuma, New Hebrides: see PAAMA.

Pavagada (pä'vŭgŭdŭ), town (pop. 3,534), Tumkur dist., NE Mysore, India, 55 mi. NNE of Tumkur, in area detached from rest of dist. and almost surrounded by Madras state; goat raising, tanning. Formerly also spelled Pavugada.

Pavant Mountains (pă'vănt'), in Fishlake Natl. Forest, Millard and Sevier counties, SW central Utah; extend c.45 mi. N from Tushar Mts. along W bank of Sevier R. Rise to 10,082 ft. in Mt. CATHERINE.

Pavda (pŭvdä'), town (1926 pop. 1,695), W Sverdlovsk oblast, Russian SFSR, in the central Urals, on Lyalya R. and 33 mi. NNE of Is; lumbering. Gold placers near by. Former site of ironworks called Nikolo-Pavdinski Zavod.

Paveh (pävĕ'), town, Fifth Prov., in Kermanshah, W Iran, 60 mi. NW of Kermanshah, near Iraq border; orchards (pomegranates, figs, walnuts, berries).

Pavelets (pä'vĭlyĭts), town (1926 pop. 831), W Ryazan oblast, Russian SFSR, 12 mi. W of Skopin; rail junction; lignite mines.

Pavelsko (pä'vĕlskô), village (pop. 2,339), Plovdiv dist., S Bulgaria, in central Rhodope Mts., on Asenovitsa R. and 19 mi. N of Smolyan; mining center (copper, silver, tin, and lead deposits).

Pavia (pŭvē'ŭ, It. pävē'ä), province (□ 1,145; pop. 492,303), Lombardy, N Italy; ⊙ Pavia. Drained by Po and Ticino rivers; fertile, irrigated Po plain comprises over 75% of area; N spur of Ligurian Apennines in S, rising to 4,889 ft. Produces 25% of Italy's rice. A chief rice-growing region is the LOMELLINA. Other crops: cereals, fodder, grapes. Livestock raising (cattle, swine, horses) widespread. Mfg. at Pavia, Vigevano, Voghera.

Pavia, anc. *Ticinum*, city (pop. 40,208), ⊙ Pavia prov., Lombardy, N Italy, on Ticino R., near its confluence with the Po, and 20 mi. S of Milan; 45°11'N 9°9'E. Rail junction; linked by large canal with Milan. A major agr. market (cereals, rice, wine, livestock) of Po valley; mfg. center (textiles, sewing machines, agr. machinery, scales, furniture, glass, hosiery, macaroni, cheese). Bishopric. Has Lombard-Romanesque church of San Michele (rebuilt 12th cent.) where early kings of Italy were crowned, castle (1360–65), medieval covered bridge (severely damaged in 1944), cathedral (begun 1488), mus., and one of best universities in Italy. An anc. city; capital of Lombards and Carolingians. In Middle Ages seat of famous law school (c.825) which became the university in 1361. Near here in 1525 Emperor Charles V defeated and captured Francis I of France. Successively under Spanish, French, and Austrian domination; liberated in 1859. In Second World War suffered air bombing (especially 1944). Near by is celebrated Carthusian monastery, Certosa di Pavia.

Pavia d'Udine (pävē'ä dōō'dēnĕ), village (pop. 1,055), Udine prov., Friuli–Venezia Giulia, NE Italy, 6 mi. SSE of Udine; mfg. (alcohol, agr. tools)

Pavillier (pävēlyā), village, Kairouan dist., central Tunisia, on railroad, 21 mi. SW of Kairouan; agr. settlement with olive groves. Lead and zinc mine near by.

Pavillion, town (pop. 241), Fremont co., W central Wyo., on branch of Bighorn R. and 28 mi. N of Lander.

Pavillons-sous-Bois, Les (lā pävēyō'-sōō-bwä'), town (pop. 15,093), Seine dept., N central France, a residential outer NE suburb of Paris, 8 mi. from Notre Dame Cathedral, just N of Le Raincy; mfg. (toys, paper bags, soap).

Pavilly (pävēyē'), town (pop. 2,474), Seine-Inférieure dept., N France, 11 mi. NW of Rouen; cotton spinning.

Pavino (pä'vēnŭ), village, NE Kostroma oblast, Russian SFSR, 25 mi. WNW of Vokhma; flax processing.

Pavione, Monte (môn'tĕ pävyô'nĕ), peak (7,657 ft.) in the Dolomites, N Italy, 7 mi. NW of Feltre.

Pavlikeni (pä'vlĭkĕnē), city (pop. 6,610), Gorna Oryakhovitsa dist., N Bulgaria, 17 mi. NE of Sevliyevo; market center; flour milling, wine making; poultry, truck.

Pavlitsa, Greece: see PHIGALIA.

Pavlodar (pŭvlŭdär'), oblast (□ 53,600; 1946 pop. estimate 300,000), NE Kazakh SSR; ⊙ Pavlodar. Chiefly dry steppe with wooded black-earth area (N) and Kazakh Hills (SW). Drained by Irtysh R. Agr. (wheat, millet), dairying in Kulunda Steppe (E of Irtysh R.); many salt lakes (salt extraction); sheep breeding. Coal (at Ekibastuz), gold and copper (at Maikain) in Kazakh Hills. Chemical industry, food processing at Pavlodar. Pop.: Kazakhs, Ukrainians, Russians. Crossed by S.Siberian RR (E–W). Formed 1938.

Pavlodar, city (1933 pop. estimate 28,800), ⊙ Pavlodar oblast, Kazakh SSR, on Irtysh R. on S.Siberian RR and 250 mi. ENE of Akmolinsk, 670 mi. N of Alma-Ata; 52°18'N 77°E. Rail-river transfer point; chemical works (based on local salt extraction); meat and dairy plants, flour mills, grain elevator, metalworks. Founded 1720 as Rus. frontier post.

Pavlof or **Pavlof Harbor** (păv'lŏf), village (pop. 39), SW Alaska, on E shore of Pavlof Bay, on SW Alaska Peninsula; 55°29'N 161°29'W; fishing. Near by is Pavlof Volcano.

Pavlof Bay, inlet (21 mi. long, 10 mi. wide at mouth) of N Pacific, SW Alaska, on SW Alaska Peninsula; 55°24'N 161°36'W. On E shore is Pavlof village; Pavlof Volcano on W shore.

Pavlof Islands, group of 7 small islands, SW Alaska, off SW Alaska Peninsula, at entrance of Pavlof Bay; 55°6'N 161°38'W. Largest is Dolgoi Isl. (10 mi. long, 7 mi. wide).

Pavlof Volcano (8,900 ft.), SW Alaska, at W end of Alaska Peninsula, on W shore of Pavlof Bay; 55°25'N 161°54'W. Active volcano; frequent eruptions in recent years.

Pavlograd (pŭvlŭgrät'), city (1926 pop. 18,766), E Dnepropetrovsk oblast, Ukrainian SSR, near confluence of Volchya and Samara rivers, 35 mi. ENE of Dnepropetrovsk; rail junction; flour-milling center; distilling, fruit canning, dairying, furniture making.

Pavlogradka (–kŭ), village (1939 pop. over 2,000), S Omsk oblast, Russian SFSR, near Kazakh SSR border, 55 mi. S of Omsk; flour milling; also has metalworks.

Pavlogradskiye Khutora, Pervyye (pyĕr'vēŭ pŭvlŭgräd'skēŭ khōōtŭrä'), SE suburb (1926 pop. 8,371) of Pavlograd, E Dnepropetrovsk oblast, Ukrainian SSR.

Pavlovac or **Pavlovats** (both: päv'lôväts), village (pop. 5,478), NW Bosnia, Yugoslavia, 2 mi. NW of Banja Luka.

Pavlovka (päv'lŭfkŭ). **1** Village (1926 pop. 2,123), central Chkalov oblast, Russian SFSR, 15 mi. WNW of Chkalov, near railroad; wheat, truck, livestock. **2** Village (1932 pop. estimate 5,900), E Kuibyshev oblast, Russian SFSR, on Samara R., on railroad (Bogatoye station) and 50 mi. ESE of Kuibyshev; sunflower-oil extracting. Flour milling at Marychevka, 6 mi. E. **3** Village (1939 pop. over 2,000), SW Ulyanovsk oblast, Russian SFSR, 37 mi. SE of Kuznetsk; flour milling; wheat, sunflowers. **4** Town (1939 pop. over 500), SE Voroshilovgrad oblast, Ukrainian SSR, in the Donbas, 7 mi. NW of Sverdlovsk; coal.

Pavlovo (–lŭvŭ), city (1926 pop. 16,289), W Gorki oblast, Russian SFSR, on Oka R. and 45 mi. SW of Gorki; center of extensive industrial and handicraft metalworking area; tractor and automobile parts, scissors, locks, surgical instruments; flour milling.

Pavlovsk (päv'lŭfsk). **1** Town (1939 pop. over 10,000), N Altay Territory, Russian SFSR; on S.Siberian RR and 32 mi. W of Barnaul, in agr. area. **2** City (1939 pop. over 10,000), central Leningrad oblast, Russian SFSR, just SE of Pushkin; shoe mfg. Popular summer resort. Site of palace (built 1782) with art gall. and library, surrounded by English gardens, statues, and pavilions. Chartered 1796 as Pavlovsk; called Slutsk after revolution, until 1944. During Second World War, held (1941–44) by Germans in siege of Leningrad. **3** City (1948 pop. over 10,000), S central Voronezh oblast, Russian SFSR, on Don R. and 90 mi. SSE of Voronezh; shipyards, flour mills; woodworking, chemical plants. Kaolin quarried near by. Shipbuilding site under Peter the Great and Catherine the Great. Became city in 1931.

Pavlovskaya (–skīŭ), village (1926 pop. 12,125), N Krasnodar Territory, Russian SFSR, 25 mi. NW of Tikhoretsk; rail junction; flour milling, dairying; wheat, sunflowers, essential oils.

Pavlovskaya Sloboda (slŭbŭdä′), village (1926 pop. 2,399), central Moscow oblast, Russian SFSR, on Istra R. and 20 mi. WNW of Moscow; metalworks, clothing mills.

Pavlovski or **Pavlovskiy** (päv′lŭfskē), town (1926 pop. 2,646), W Molotov oblast, Russian SFSR, on Ocher R. (short right tributary of Kama R.) and 3 mi. SE of Ocher; metalworking.

Pavlovski Posad or **Pavlovskiy Posad** (pŭsät′), city (1926 pop. 20,844), E Moscow oblast, Russian SFSR, on Klyazma R. and 40 mi. E of Moscow; textile-milling center (mainly cotton goods); silk and linen milling; peat works. Chartered 1844.

Pavlucebel, Turkey: see SUTCULER.

Pavlysh (pä′vlĭsh), town (1926 pop. 4,330), E Kirovograd oblast, Ukrainian SSR, 11 mi. SSW of Kremenchug; metalworks.

Pavo (pā′vō), town (pop. 806), Thomas and Brooks counties, S Ga., 17 mi. ENE of Thomasville.

Pavón Arriba (pävōn′ärē′bä), town (pop. estimate 1,000), SE Santa Fe prov., Argentina, 27 mi. SSW of Rosario; agr. center (corn, wheat, flax, peas, potatoes, fruit); grain elevator.

Pavugada, India: see PAVAGADA.

Pavullo nel Frignano (pävōōl′lô nĕl frēnyä′nô), town (pop. 2,066), Modena prov., Emilia-Romagna, N central Italy, 22 mi. SSW of Modena; resort (alt. 2,238 ft.); woolen mill, sausage factory.

Pavy (pä′vē), village (1939 pop. over 500), E Pskov oblast, Russian SFSR, 20 mi. N of Porkhov; flax.

Pawa (pä′wä), village, Eastern Prov., NE Belgian Congo, 210 mi. ESE of Buta; center of leprosy research, with large leprosarium for natives.

Pawayan (pŭvä′yän), town (pop. 6,072), Shahjahanpur dist., central Uttar Pradesh, India, 17 mi. NNE of Shahjahanpur; road junction; wheat, rice, gram, sugar cane. Founded 18th cent.

Pawcatuck, village, Conn.: see STONINGTON.

Pawcatuck River (pô′kŭtŭk″, –tŭk), in R.I. and Conn., rises in Worden Pond, S R.I.; flows W and SW, past Shannock, Carolina, and Bradford, then NW, W, and S, past Potter Hill and Westerly, forming part of state line, to Little Narragansett Bay 13 mi. E of New London; c.30 mi. long. Furnishes water power to several mfg. villages. Formerly called Charles R. bet. source and mouth of Wood R. NNE of Bradford.

Pawhuska (pôhŭ′skŭ), city (pop. 5,331), ⊙ Osage co., N Okla., 39 mi. NNW of Tulsa, in oil-producing, agr., cattle-ranching region. The Osage Indian capital, city is agency hq. for the Osage Reservation, which is coextensive with co. Oil and natural-gas wells. Mfg. of oil-field equipment, dairy products, beverages, mattresses, clothing, sheet-metal and canvas products; cotton ginning. Has an Osage tribal mus. Settled 1872, inc. 1906.

Pawik, Alaska: see NAKNEK.

Pawla, Malta: see PAOLA.

Pawlet (pô′lĭt), town (pop. 1,156), Rutland co., SW Vt., on Mettawee R. and 20 mi. SW of Rutland; slate, lumber. Settled in 1760s.

Pawleys Island, summer resort, Georgetown co., E S.C., on Atlantic coast and 10 mi. ENE of Georgetown. Small Pawleys Isl. is just offshore.

Pawling, village (pop. 1,430), Dutchess co., SE N.Y., 20 mi. SE of Poughkeepsie, in resort and diversified-farming area; leather goods, lumber. Seat of Trinity-Pawling School for boys. Settled by Quakers c.1740; inc. 1893.

Pawn, Nam (näm pôn), river in Southern Shan State, Upper Burma, rises in hills near Loilem, flows c.300 mi. S through flat country, past Mongpawn, thence in deep valley through Karenni State to Salween R. E of Mawchi.

Pawnee (pô″nē′). **1** County (□ 749; pop. 11,041), SW central Kansas; ⊙ Larned. Rolling plain area, drained by Arkansas and Pawnee rivers. Wheat, livestock. Formed 1872. **2** County (□ 433; pop. 6,744), SE Nebr.; ⊙ Pawnee city. Farm area bounded S by Kansas; drained by branches of Nemaha R. Livestock, grain, dairy and poultry produce. Formed 1857. **3** County (□ 591; pop. 13,616), N Okla.; ⊙ Pawnee. Bounded NE by Arkansas R.; drained by Cimarron R. and small Black Bear Creek. Agr. area (cotton, barley, broomcorn, corn, fruit); stock raising, dairying; some mfg. Oil and natural-gas wells; oil refining, gasoline mfg. Formed 1893.

Pawnee. 1 Village (pop. 974), Sangamon co., central Ill., 13 mi. SSE of Springfield, in agr. and bituminous-coal area; grain, livestock, dairy products. Inc. 1891. **2** City (pop. 2,861), ⊙ Pawnee co., N Okla., c.45 mi. WNW of Tulsa, in cotton, grain, and dairying area; cotton ginning, grain milling; mfg. of food products, machine-shop products; Indian curios. Has a U.S. school for Indians and an Indian hosp. The home and mus. of Pawnee Bill (Gordon W. Lillie), one of the Wild West heroes, is here. Founded c.1893 on site of trading post and Indian agency.

Pawnee City, city (pop. 1,606), ⊙ Pawnee co., SE Nebr., 55 mi. SSE of Lincoln and on branch of Nemaha R., near Kansas line; building materials; livestock, grain. Inc. 1858.

Pawnee Creek, NE Colo., rises in N Weld co., flows 57 mi. SE to South Platte R. 6 mi. S of Sterling.

Pawnee River, SW central Kansas, formed by confluence of several headstreams in Finney co. WNW of Jetmore, flows 118 mi. E, past Rozel, to Arkansas R. at Larned.

Pawnee Rock, city (pop. 359), Barton co., central Kansas, 13 mi. SW of Great Bend, near Arkansas R., in grain area. State park near by.

Pawohumri, peak, India and Tibet: see DONGKYA RANGE.

Paw Paw. 1 or **Pawpaw,** village (pop. 594), Lee co., N Ill., 20 mi. SW of De Kalb, in rich agr. area; brick and tile mfg. **2** Village (pop. 2,382), ⊙ Van Buren co., SW Mich., 16 mi. SW of Kalamazoo and on a branch of Paw Paw R., in fruitgrowing area (grapes, apples); mfg. (packed and canned foods, wine, fish lures, baskets, trailers); resort. Indian earthworks near by. Settled 1832, inc. 1859. **3** Town (pop. 820), Morgan co., NE W.Va., in Eastern Panhandle, on the Potomac and 27 mi. WNW of Martinsburg; ships fruit.

Paw Paw Lake, village (pop. 1,625), Berrien co., extreme SW Mich., just NE of Coloma, on Paw Paw L. (3 mi. long); resort.

Paw Paw River, SW Mich., formed by branches W of Kalamazoo, flows W and SW, past Lawrence, Hartford, Watervliet, and Coloma, to St. Joseph R. just above its mouth on L. Michigan at Benton Harbor; c.55 mi. long.

Pawtuckaway Pond, N.H.: see NOTTINGHAM.

Pawtucket (pŭtŭ′kĭt), industrial city (pop. 81,436), Providence co., NE R.I., on Mass. line, on Blackstone R. at Pawtucket Falls, and 6 mi. NE of Providence; 2d largest city in state. Mfg. (textiles, thread, yarns, tape, webbing, electrical equipment, machinery, metal products, paper and wood products, sports equipment, glass, laundry and cleaning equipment, food products); textile bleaching, dying, and finishing. Area deeded to Roger Williams in 1638; in Mass. until 1862, when Pawtucket inc. as town; chartered as city 1885. Samuel Slater built here (1790) the 1st successful water-power cotton mill in U.S.; the 1793 Slater mill is now a mus. Narragansett race track is in Pawtucket and East Providence.

Pawtucket River, R.I.: see BLACKSTONE RIVER, Mass. and R.I.

Pawtuxet, village, R.I.: see CRANSTON.

Pawtuxet River (pŭtŭk′sĭt), central R.I., formed in West Warwick town by junction of Southwest Branch (8 mi. long; drains Flat R. Reservoir) and North Branch (7 mi. long; dammed to form SCITUATE RESERVOIR) at River Point; flows c.11 mi. generally NE, bet. Cranston and Warwick, furnishing water power for mfg. area, to Narragansett Bay at Pawtuxet village.

Pax, town (pop. 561), Fayette co., S central W.Va., 14 mi. SW of Fayetteville, in coal-mining and agr. region.

Pax, Cerro (sĕ′rō päks′), Andean peak (10,990 ft.) on Ecuador-Colombia border, in the Andes, 33 mi. SSE of Ipiales.

Pax Augusta, Spain: see BADAJOZ, city.

Paxico, city (pop. 196), Wabaunsee co., NE central Kansas, 26 mi. W of Topeka, in cattle, poultry, and grain region.

Paximadi, Cape, or **Cape Paximadhi** (both: päksēmä′dhē), SE Euboea, Greece, on Aegean Sea, bet. Bay of Karystos (E) and Gulf of Petalion (W); 37°57′N 24°24′E.

Pax Julia, Portugal: see BEJA, city.

Paxos (păk′sŏs) or **Paxoi** (päksē′), smallest (□ 7; 1940 pop. 3,050) of main Ionian Isls., Greece, in Corfu nome, 7.5 mi. SE of Corfu isl.; 39°12′N 20°12′E; 5.5 mi. long, 2 mi. wide, rises to 809 ft. Largely flatland covered with olive plantations; fisheries along shore; sulphur springs; oil-shale deposits. Main town is Gaios (1928 pop. 530), on E coast. Formerly also called Paxo.

Paxtang (păk′stăng″), borough (pop. 1,857), Dauphin co., S central Pa., just E of Harrisburg; limestone. Here occurred (1763) uprising of Paxtang (Paxton) Boys against Indians.

Paxton. 1 City (pop. 3,795), ⊙ Ford co., E Ill., 24 mi. NNE of Champaign, in rich agr. area (corn, oats, wheat, soybeans, livestock); mfg. (canned foods, clothing). Settled by Swedes in 1850s; inc. 1865. **2** Town (pop. 1,066), Worcester co., central Mass., 7 mi. WNW of Worcester. Settled c.1749, inc. 1765. **3** Village (pop. 606), Keith co., SW central Nebr., 30 mi. W of North Platte city and on S.Platte R.; grain, livestock, poultry produce, sugar beets.

Paxville, town (pop. 208), Clarendon co., central S.C., 12 mi. S of Sumter.

Payachata, Nevados de (nävä′dōs dā pīächä′tä), Andean massif on Chile-Bolivia border, 80 mi. WNW of Arica; 18°10′S 69°10′W. Includes 2 snow-capped peaks: Cerro de Pomarepe (sĕ′rō dā pōmärā′pā) (20,472 ft.) and Cerro de Parinacota (pärēnäkō′tä) (20,767 ft.).

Payakumbuh, Pajakumbuh, or **Pajakoemboeh** (all: päyäkōōm″bōō′), town (pop. 5,914), W Sumatra, Indonesia, in Padang Highlands, 50 mi. NNE of Padang; alt. c.1,650 ft.; terminus of railroad from Padang; agr. center (coffee, tea, tobacco, rubber). Airfield. Also spelled Pajakombo.

Payal, India: see PAIL.

Paya Lebar (pä′yä lā′bär), NE suburb (pop. 10,415) of Singapore, Singapore isl., on city line, 4 mi. NNE of city center. Pop. is Chinese.

Payar, Kashmir: see AWANTIPUR.

Pay-Aryk, Uzbek SSR: see PAI-ARYK.

Payde, Estonia: see PAIDE.

Payen (bä′yĕn′). **1** Town, ⊙ Payen co. (pop. 340,217), W Sungkiang prov., Manchuria, China, 45 mi. NE of Harbin, near left bank of Sungari R. Until rise of Harbin (after 1900), it was a leading center of the middle Sungari valley. **2** Town, Tsinghai prov., China: see HWALUNG.

Payenyungko, China: see HWALUNG.

Payerbach (pī′ŭrbäkh), town (pop. 3,175), SE Lower Austria, on Schwarza R. and 10 mi. WSW of Neunkirchen; rail junction; summer resort (alt. 1,575 ft.).

Payerne (päärn′), Ger. *Peterlingen* (pā′tŭrlĭng″ŭn), town (pop. 5,178), Vaud canton, W Switzerland, on Broye R. and 9 mi. W of Fribourg; flour, tobacco, tiles, clothes; metalworking. Has 11th-cent. church formerly belonging to a Benedictine abbey, a 16th-cent. church with tombs of Burgundian kings.

Payette (päĕt′), county (□ 403; pop. 11,921), W Idaho; ⊙ Payette. Farming region bounded W by Snake R. and Oregon, irrigated in valley of Payette R. Dairying, agr. (hay, sugar beets, fruit, truck). Formed 1917.

Payette, city (pop. 4,032), ⊙ Payette co., W Idaho, on Payette R. at its mouth in Snake R. (here forming Oregon line) and 50 mi. NW of Boise; trade and shipping center for fruit, dairy, and poultry area in Boise irrigation project (Idaho) and in Vale project (Oregon). Food processing (dairy products, canned fruits and vegetables, vinegar, cider), mfg. of wood products, bricks. Settled 1883, inc. 1901.

Payette River, W Idaho, formed by confluence of North Fork and South Fork in NW corner of Boise co., flows S, then W, past Emmett, to Snake R. near Payette at Oregon line; c.70 mi. long. North Fork rises above Payette L. (6 mi. long, 1 mi. wide; just N of McCall), flows c.110 mi. S, through lake and past Cascade, to junction with South Fork, which rises in Camas co. and flows 70 mi. W. BLACK CANYON DAM, on main stream, and CASCADE DAM, on North Fork, are units in Payette div. of Boise irrigation project.

Pay-Khoy, Russian SFSR: see PAI-KHOI.

Paymogo (pīmō′gō), town (pop. 2,865), Huelva prov., SW Spain, in W foothills of the Sierra Morena, near Port. border, 40 mi. NW of Huelva; wheat, olives, acorns, honey, timber, charcoal, livestock; flour milling.

Payne, county (□ 697; pop. 46,430), N central Okla.; ⊙ Stillwater. Intersected by Cimarron R.; includes L. Carl Blackwell. Stock raising, dairying, diversified agr. (grain, corn, cotton), poultry raising. Mfg., farm-products processing at Stillwater and Cushing. Oil and gas fields; oil refineries, gasoline plants. Formed 1890.

Payne. 1 or **Paynes,** city (pop. 520), Bibb co., central Ga., just NW of Macon. **2** Village (pop. 1,062), Paulding co. NW Ohio, on small Flatrock Creek, near Ind. line, and 24 mi. SW of Defiance; grain, livestock, sugar beets.

Payneham (pā′nŭm), town (pop. 9,636), SE South Australia, 3 mi. NE of Adelaide, in metropolitan area; agr. center.

Payne Lake (□ 300), NW Que., on Ungava Peninsula; 59°25′N 74°W; 55 mi. long, 10 mi. wide. Drained by Payne R. into Ungava Bay.

Payne Range, Chile: see PAINE RANGE.

Payne River, NW Que., issues from Payne L., flows 200 mi. NNE and E to W side of Ungava Bay. Near its mouth is Payne Bay (60°2′N 70°2′W), Hudson's Bay Co. trading post.

Paynes, Ga.: see PAYNE.

Paynesville (pānz′vĭl), town, Montserrado co., W Liberia, 9 mi. ESE of Monrovia; palm oil and kernels, cassava, rice.

Paynesville, resort village (pop. 1,503), Stearns co., S central Minn., on North Fork Crow R., near L. Koronis, and 30 mi. SW of St. Cloud, in agr. area (grain, livestock, poultry, fruit); dairy products. Inc. 1887.

Payo, El (ĕl pī′ō), town (pop. 1,551), Salamanca prov., W Spain, 24 mi. SW of Ciudad Rodrigo; livestock, lumber, potatoes, rye. Tungsten mining near by.

Payo Obispo, Mexico: see CHETUMAL.

Payrac (pārăk′), village (pop. 331), Lot dept., SW France, 6 mi. NE of Gourdon; sheep, truffles.

Paysandú (pīsändōō′), department (□ 5,117; pop. 84,265), NW Uruguay; ⊙ Paysandú. Bordered by Argentina (W, across Uruguay R.), Daymán R. (N), the Cuchilla de Haedo (E and S), and the Río Negro (S). Drained by Queguay R. Produces wheat, vegetables, fruit; vineyards; cattle and sheep raising. Centers are Paysandú, Guichón, Merinos, Porvenir. Steamer traffic on the Uruguay. Dept. was formed 1837, containing former territories of Salto and Tacuarembó.

Paysandú, city (pop. 46,000), ⊙ Paysandú dept., W Uruguay, on Uruguay R. and 55 mi. NNE of Fray Bentos, 200 mi. NNW of Montevideo, 15 mi. above Concepción del Uruguay (Argentina); 32°18′S

58°7′W. Second largest city of Uruguay, important port (reached by ocean-going ships), with rail, road, and air connections, it is an industrial and commercial center, known for its meat-packing (much of its produce is exported). Also flour milling, mfg. of noodles, bakery products, soap, candles, wooden and steel furniture, shoes, leather; shipyards, machine shops, tileworks, sawmills. Agr. products: fruit, vegetables; viticulture. Fisheries. Customhouse. Has library, theater. Founded 1772.

Payson. 1 Village (pop. c.300), Gila co., E central Ariz., 70 mi. NE of Phoenix, in stock-raising area. Holds annual rodeo. **2** Village (pop. 490), Adams co., W Ill., 12 mi. SE of Quincy, in agr. area; limestone quarries. **3** City (pop. 3,998), Utah co., central Utah, near Utah L., 13 mi. S of Provo; alt. c.4,600 ft.; trade center and egg-shipping point in agr. area (sugar beets, onions, alfalfa, fruit); beet sugar, flour. Settled 1850 by Mormons, inc. 1865. Surrounding region served by irrigation works on Strawberry R.

Paytok, Uzbek SSR: see PAITOK.

Payung, China: see HWALUNG.

Payún Plateau (pä-yōōn′), subandean highland in S Mendoza prov., Argentina, E of the Río Grande; generally over 5,000 ft., rising to 12,075 ft.

Pay-Yer, Russian SFSR: see PAI-YER.

Paz (päs), town (pop. estimate 1,000), S Santa Fe prov., Argentina, 40 mi. SSW of Rosario, in agr. area (wheat, flax, corn, potatoes, peas, livestock, poultry).

Paz, La, in Latin America: see LA PAZ.

Paz, Río de la (rē′ō dā lä päs′), on Guatemala-Salvador border, rises on slopes of volcano Chingo, flows c.60 mi. SW along border to the Pacific 24 mi. NW of Acajutla. Navigable for 14 mi. above mouth.

Pazanun (päzänōōn′), town, Sixth Prov., in Khuzistan, SW Iran, 18 mi. W of Behbehan and 100 mi. E of Abadan; center of natural-gas field.

Pazar (päzär′), village (pop. 1,823), Rize prov., NE Turkey, on Black Sea 24 mi. NE of Rize; maize. Formerly Atina.

Pazarcik (päzärjĭk′), Turkish *Pazarcık*, village (pop. 1,806), Maras prov., S central Turkey, on railroad and 23 mi. E of Maras; wheat, rice, chick-peas, pistachios.

Pazardzhik (pä″zärjĕk′), city (pop. 30,430), Plovdiv dist., W central Bulgaria, on Maritsa R. and 20 mi. W of Plovdiv; rail junction; agr.-processing center in rice, hemp, winegrowing Plovdiv Basin; textiles, rubber and leather goods. Agr. col. Has old church with collection of icons. Under Turkish rule (15th–19th cent.) called Tatar-Pazari; later Tatar Bazarjik or Tatar Pazarjik. Sometimes spelled Pazarjik.

Pazarkoy, Turkey: see ORHANGAZI.

Paz del Río (päs′ dĕl rē′ō), village (pop. 194), Boyacá dept., central Colombia, in Cordillera Oriental, 24 mi. NNE of Sogamoso; large iron deposits. Hydroelectric plant and steel-mill project.

Pazin (pä′zĭn), Ital. *Pisino* (pēzē′nô), Ger. *Mitterburg* (mĭt′ûrbōōrk), village (pop. 5,224), NW Croatia, Yugoslavia, on railroad and 27 mi. W of Rijeka (Fiume), in Istria; cultural center of Istrian Croats. Has cathedral (1266) and castle (1539).

Pazña (päs′nyä), village (pop. c.1,900), Oruro dept., W Bolivia, in the Altiplano, 45 mi. SSE of Oruro, on Oruro-Uyuni RR; alt. 12,149 ft. Shipping point for tin mines of Antequera, Totoral, Avicaya (E).

Paznauntal (pätsnoun′täl), valley in Rhaetian Alps of Tyrol, W Austria, extending c.20 mi. SW from the Inn at Landeck along Trisanna R.; cattle. Main town, Kappl.

Paz River, Russian SFSR: see PATS RIVER.

Pcinja River or **Pchinya River** (both: pchē′nyä), Serbo-Croatian *Pčinja*, SE Yugoslavia, rises c.20 mi. ESE of Vranje, flows c.80 mi. SW to Vardar R. 10 mi. NNW of Titov Veles. Receives the Kriva Reka (left).

Pe, China: see NORTH RIVER.

Peabody (pē′bŏdē, –bŭdē). **1** City (pop. 1,194), Marion co., SE central Kansas, 32 mi. NNE of Wichita, in grain and livestock area; poultry and dairy products, flour. Platted 1871, inc. 1878. **2** City (pop. 22,645), Essex co., NE Mass., just N of Lynn. Its tanning industry dates from early 18th cent.

Peabody River, Coos co., N central N.H., rises just E of Mt. Washington, flows c.15 mi. E and NNE to the Androscoggin at Gorham.

Peace Dale, industrial village (pop., with adjacent Wakefield, 5,224), in South Kingstown town, Washington co., S R.I., just N of Wakefield; textiles, rubberized fabrics.

Peacehaven, residential town and parish (pop. 2,007), S Sussex, England, on the Channel, 4 mi. E of Brighton.

Peace River, town (pop. 997), W Alta., on Peace R., just below mouth of Smoky R., 250 mi. NW of Edmonton; 56°14′N 117°17′W; fur-trading center, distributing point for Great Bear L. mineral regions, and transportation center for the Far North. Industries include woodworking, lumbering, meat packing, brick and lime mfg., dairying. Formerly site of Fort Fork, where Sir Alexander Mackenzie wintered, 1792–93.

Peace River, W Canada, rises as Finlay R. in N B.C., in Stikine Mts. at about 57°30′N 126°30′W, flows SE to Finlay Forks, where it is joined by Parsnip R. and becomes Peace R. proper; then flows E, crossing into Alta., to town of Peace River, whence it flows generally N to Fort Vermilion (rapids), and finally ENE to Slave R. near its outflow from L. Athabaska; 1,054 mi. long to head of Finlay R. Its valley is noted for its fertility; settlement here dates from early 20th cent. There are deposits of coal, gypsum, and salt. At Fort St. John (B.C.) a 2,275-ft. suspension bridge was built, 1943. Probably discovered (1779–81) by Peter Pond, river was explored by Sir Alexander Mackenzie, 1792–93; it later became important fur-trade artery.

Peace River, central and SW Fla., rises in L. Hancock, flows c.80 mi. S, past Bartow and Arcadia, into Charlotte Harbor near Punta Gorda; for its last 10 mi. it is an estuary.

Peach, county (□ 151; pop. 11,705), central Ga.; ⊙ Fort Valley. Bounded W by Flint R. Coastal plain peach-growing and timber area; also produces cotton, corn, truck, peanuts, and pecans. Mfg. at Fort Valley. Formed 1924.

Peacham, town (pop. 501), Caledonia co., NE Vt., 10 mi. SW of St. Johnsbury; summer resort; agr.

Peach Creek, village (1940 pop. 1,034), Logan co., SW W.Va., on Guyandot R. just N of Logan, in coal-mining region.

Peach Island, islet, S Ont., in SW part of L. St. Clair 4 mi. NE of Windsor.

Peach Lake, SE N.Y., resort lake (c.1¼ mi. long) near Conn. line, 3 mi. SE of Brewster.

Peachland, village (pop. estimate 500), S B.C., on W shore of Okanagan L., 20 mi. NNW of Penticton; peach growing and packing.

Peachland, town (pop. 485), Anson co., S N.C., 11 mi. W of Wadesboro; lumber milling.

Peach Orchard. 1 Town (pop. 327), Clay co., extreme NE Ark., 19 mi. NW of Paragould. **2** Town (pop. 59), Pemiscot co., E Mo., 11 mi. NNE of Independence.

Peacock. 1 Village (pop. 1,462, with near-by Medford), Burlington co., W central N.J., c.15 mi. E of Camden. **2** Town (pop. 165), Stonewall co., NW central Texas, 60 mi. NW of Abilene, near Salt Fork of Brazos R.; shipping point for cattle and agr. area. Inc. 1938.

Peacock Mountains: see HUALPAI MOUNTAINS.

Péage-de-Rousillon, Le (lù pääzh′-dù-rōōsēyō′), town (pop. 2,304), Isère dept., SE France, near left bank of the Rhone, 11 mi. SSW of Vienne; mfg. (silk goods, furniture, toys); fruit shipping. Chemical works at near-by Roussillon.

Pea Island, E N.C., section (c.8 mi. long) of the Outer Banks, bet. Pamlico Sound and the Atlantic; Oregon Inlet (crossed by ferry) is at N end, New Inlet (bridged to Hatteras Isl.) at S end. Natl. wildlife refuge; coast guard station.

Peak, town (pop. 134), Newberry co., NW central S.C., on Broad R. and 25 mi. NW of Columbia.

Peak, The, or **Peak District,** hilly section of the Pennine Chain, N Derby, England, rising to 2,088 ft. in the Kinder Scout or Kinderscout. The name is applied also to the surrounding region bounded roughly by Glossop (N), Ashbourne (S), Buxton (W) and Chesterfield (E). S of Kinder Scout is High Peak (c.1,980 ft.). In the area are limestone caves (notably at Castleton), fertile valleys, and craggy hills.

Peak Hill. 1 Municipality (pop. 1,144), E central New South Wales, Australia, on Bogan R. and 195 mi. WNW of Sydney; gold mines. **2** Village, W central Western Australia, 335 mi. NE of Geraldton, N of Robinson Ranges; gold mining.

Peak Island, SW Maine, residential isl. (717 acres) off Portland; pioneer summer resort of Casco Bay area; amusement center since 1890s.

Peaks of Otter, Va.: see OTTER, PEAKS OF.

Peal de Becerro (pääl′ dhā bā-thĕ′rō), town (pop. 5,791), Jaén prov., S Spain, 15 mi. SE of Úbeda; olive-oil processing, flour milling, plaster mfg. Agr. trade (cereals, wine). Saltworks.

Peale, Mount, highest peak (13,089 ft.) in La Sal Mts., E Utah, 20 mi. SE of Moab, near Colo. line.

Peapack-Gladstone (pē′păk–), residential borough (pop. 1,450), Somerset co., N central N.J., 11 mi. SW of Morristown; limestone quarries. Settled before 1776, inc. 1912.

Pea Patch Island, New Castle co., N Del., in Delaware R. just NE of Delaware City; c.1 mi. long. Site of U.S. Fort Delaware (1814), part of river and bay defenses.

Peard Bay (pērd), NW Alaska, inlet (18 mi. long, 8 mi. wide) of Chukchi Sea, 20 mi. NE of Wainwright; 70°48′N 158°30′W.

Pea Ridge, town (pop. 268), Benton co., extreme NW Ark., 8 mi. N of Rogers, near Mo. line, near Pea Ridge in the Ozarks. Battle of Pea Ridge (or battle of Elkhorn Tavern), principal Civil War engagement on Ark. soil, was fought here (March 7–8, 1862); victory of Union troops prevented Confederates from carrying war into Mo.

Pearisburg (pâ′rĭsbûrg), town (pop. 2,005), ⊙ Giles co., SW Va., in the Allegheniеs, on New R. and 45 mi. W of Roanoke; large rayon plant. Settled 1782; inc. 1914.

Pea River, SE Ala., rises in Bullock co., E of Union Springs, flows SW, past Elba, then S and E to Choctawhatchee R. below Geneva; c.140 mi. long.

Pearl. 1 Village (pop. 38), Gem co., SW Idaho, 8 mi. E of Emmett. **2** Village (pop. 472), Pike co., W Ill., on Illinois R. (ferry here) and 28 mi. SW of Jacksonville, in agr. area.

Pearl and Hermes Reef (hûr′mēz), atoll, N Pacific, 1,050 mi. NW of Honolulu, T.H.; 27°50′N 157°55′W; oblong with 7 sand islets; discovered 1822, annexed 1857 by Hawaiian kingdom; now belongs to U.S. Formerly worked for guano.

Pearl City, village (pop. 2,663), S Oahu, T.H., on Pearl R. and 9 mi. NW of Honolulu, near Pearl Harbor; sugar industry.

Pearl City, village (pop. 491), Stephenson co., N Ill., 10 mi. W of Freeport, in agr. area; dairy products.

Pearl Harbor, S Oahu, T.H., 7 mi. NW of Honolulu; large U.S. naval base. It has 3 lochs with 10 sq. mi. of navigable water and hundreds of anchorages; Fords Isl. is in harbor. U.S. was permitted (1887) to maintain coaling and repair station here, which became (1900) a naval station. Channel was improved after 1908, a drydock was formally opened in 1919, further improvements were made after 1940. The Japanese attack on Pearl Harbor (Dec. 7, 1941) touched off the Pacific phase of the Second World War. The U.S. fleet and the harbor (along with Hickam Field, Wheeler Field, Fords Isl., and naval air station at Kaneohe Bay) were badly damaged. Within a year most of the damage was repaired, and Pearl Harbor became major Pacific base for U.S. military operations.

Pearl Harbor, village (pop. 1,372), St. Clair co., SW Ill.

Pearl Island (3 mi. long, 2 mi. wide), W N.F., on N side of the Bay of Islands, 25 mi. NW of Corner Brook; 49°14′N 58°18′W.

Pearl Islands, Sp. *Archipiélago de las Perlas* (ärchēpyā′lägō dā läs pĕr′läs), group of islands in Gulf of Panama of the Pacific, c.40 mi. SE of Panama city, consisting of 183 (including 39 large) isls. Principal isls. are San Miguel, San José, Pedro González, Saboga. Pearl fisheries are important.

Pearl Lagoon, Sp. *Laguna de Perlas,* E Nicaragua, 20 mi. N of Bluefields; separated by swampy isthmus from Caribbean Sea; 30 mi. long, c.5 mi. wide. Receives Curinhuás R. (NW); connected by channel with sea (S); off entrance are Pearl Keys.

Pearl River, China: see CANTON RIVER.

Pearl River, county (□ 828; pop. 20,641), SE Miss.; ⊙ Poplarville. Bounded W by Pearl R., here the La. line; also drained by small Hobolochitto R. and by Wolf R. Agr. (cotton, corn; tung and pecan groves); lumbering. Formed 1890.

Pearl River. 1 Village (pop. 637), St. Tammany parish, SE La., 36 mi. NE of New Orleans and on West Pearl R.; lumber. **2** Village (1940 pop. 3,416), Rockland co., SE N.Y., at N.J. line, 8 mi. SE of Suffern, in fruit- and vegetable-growing area; mfg. (machinery, wood and metal products, pharmaceuticals, clothing, wine).

Pearl River, in Miss. and La., rises in E central Miss., flows SW to Jackson, thence generally S, past Columbia, into La., passing near Bogalusa (head of navigation near here), and dividing into 2 streams W of Picayune, Miss.: East Pearl R., the main channel, empties into L. Borgne; West Pearl R. enters the Rigolets 5 mi. W of mouth of East Pearl R. Total length, 485 mi.; forms Miss.-La. line for 116 mi. Bet. East and West Pearl rivers lies Honey Isl. Swamp (25 mi. long), a 19th-cent. outlaw refuge, and now a hunting and fishing area.

Pear Ridge, town (pop. 2,029), Jefferson co., SE Texas, N suburb of Port Arthur. Inc. 1935.

Pearsall (pēr′sôl), city (pop. 4,481), ⊙ Frio co., SW Texas, c.50 mi. SW of San Antonio, near Frio R.; a processing, trade center for irrigated Winter Garden area (peanuts, watermelons, corn, truck, dairy products); cattle ranches, oil fields near. Makes agr. equipment. Settled 1881, inc. 1909.

Pearse Canal (pērs), SE Alaska and NW B.C., natural waterway bet. mainland and Pearse Isl.; SW channel of Portland Canal; forms international boundary bet. Alaska and Canada. Extends 25 mi. NE from N end of Chatham Sound.

Pearse Island (□ 81; 20 mi. long, 6 mi. wide), W B.C., in Portland Inlet, 35 mi. N of Prince Rupert, separated from Alaska mainland by Pearse Canal (1 mi. wide).

Pearson, Mexico: see JUAN MATA ORTÍZ.

Pearson (pēr′sŭn), city (pop. 1,402), ⊙ Atkinson co., S Ga., 30 mi. W of Waycross; mfg. (naval stores, lumber).

Pearson Islands, Australia: see INVESTIGATOR ISLANDS.

Pearston (pēr′stŭn), town (pop. 2,081), SE Cape Prov., on Vogel R. and 40 mi. SE of Graaff Reinet; sheep, goats, dairying, citrus fruit; wool, mohair production.

Peary Channel (pē′rē), N Franklin Dist., Northwest Territories, arm (120 mi. long, 60 mi. wide) extending SE from the Arctic Ocean bet. Meighen Isl. (N) and Amund Ringnes and Ellef Ringnes isls. (S); 79°-80°N 96°-104°W.

Peary Channel, an arctic strait long thought to separate Peary Land from N Greenland in about 82°-83°N. Air photographs taken by Danish explorers in 1938 showed Peary Land to be connected with Greenland by an isthmus. The E entrance to

"Peary Channel" was renamed Frederick E. Hyde Fjord, the W entrance J. P. Koch Fjord.

Peary Land, region, N Greenland; extends c.200 mi. E-W along Arctic Ocean bet. Victoria Fjord and Greenland Sea; 81°30'-83°39'N 20°-47°20'W. It is c.150 mi. wide. Cape MORRIS JESUP is N extremity. Northernmost land region of the world, it is Greenland's largest ice-free part; surface is generally mountainous, rising to 6,398 ft. (E). Coast line is deeply indented by J. P. Koch Fjord and Frederick E. Hyde Fjords. Uninhabited; vegetation supports herds of musk oxen. Coast line charted by Peary, 1892.

Peary Lodge, Greenland: see NÛGSSUAK.

Pease, village (pop. 179), Mille Lacs co., E Minn., near Rum R., 10 mi. NNW of Princeton; dairy products.

Pease River, NW Texas, formed in NE Cottle co. by North Pease R. (c.80 mi. long) and Middle Pease R. (c.70 mi. long), both heading as intermittent streams draining E-facing Cap Rock escarpment; flows c.75 mi. generally E from their junction to Red R. 9 mi. E of Vernon. Middle Pease R. receives South Pease R. (c.60 mi. long) 17 mi. WSW of its junction with the North Pease.

Pebane (pĕbä'nä), village, Zambézia prov., central Mozambique, on Mozambique Channel, 95 mi. NE of Quelimane; copra, cashew nuts.

Pebas (pä'bäs), town (pop. 504), Loreto dept., NE Peru, landing on left bank of the upper Amazon and 115 mi. ENE of Iquitos; 3°17'S 71°49'W. Fueling station for river boats, in tropical forest region (rubber, vanilla, timber); banana growing.

Pebble Beach, resort village (pop. c.400), Monterey co., W Calif., on shore of Monterey Peninsula, 3 mi. SW of Monterey.

Pec, Czechoslovakia: see MARSOV.

Pec or **Pech** (both: pĕch), Serbo-Croatian *Peć*, anc. *Pescium*, town (pop. 17,175), SW Serbia, Yugoslavia, 45 mi. W of Pristina, in the Metohija. Rail terminus; handicraft (jewelry); fruit and vegetable processing. Seat (14th-18th cent.) of Serbian patriarchs. Noted for its 13th-cent. patriarchal church, mosques, and Turkish houses. Damaged in Second World War. Under Turkish rule (until 1913), called Ipek; formerly also Pecha. In Montenegro 1913-29; in Albania 1941-44.

Peca, peak, Austria and Yugoslavia: see PETZEN.

Pecalongan, Indonesia: see PEKALONGAN.

Pecan Bayou (pēkän' bī'ō), central Texas, rises in Callahan co., flows c.100 mi. generally SE, past Brownwood, to the Colorado 15 mi. N of San Saba. N of Brownwood, dam impounds L. Brownwood (141,800 acre-ft.); irrigation, recreation; state parks here.

Pecan Gap (pēkän'), city (pop. 319), Delta co., NE Texas, 22 mi. SW of Paris, near North Sulphur R., in agr. area.

Peçanha (pĭsä'nyŭ), city (pop. 2,378), E central Minas Gerais, Brazil, 65 mi. ESE of Diamantina; mica and semiprecious-stone deposits.

Pecan Island (pēkän'), Vermilion parish, S La., low ridge (c.18 mi. long) surrounded by sea marshes, c.45 mi. SW of New Iberia; pop. c.500. Short canal leads to White L. (N). Oil and natural-gas wells and pipeline; agr. (sugar cane, cotton, cattle); hunting, fishing, fur trapping. Indian mounds here have yielded many relics.

Pecatonica (pĕ'kŭtŏ'nĭkŭ), village (pop. 1,438), Winnebago co., N Ill., on Pecatonica R. (bridged here) and 13 mi. W of Rockford, in agr. area; condensed milk, canned foods. Inc. 1869.

Pecatonica River, in S Wis. and N Ill., rises near Cobb in Iowa co., Wis., flows generally SE, past Darlington, and into Ill. to Freeport, then ENE to Rock R. at Rockton; c.120 mi. long. Receives short East Branch just W of Browntown.

Pecaya (pākī'ä), town (pop. 722), Falcón state, NW Venezuela, 26 mi. SSW of Coro; coffee, cacao.

Peccioli (pĕt'chôlē), town (pop. 2,163), Pisa prov., Tuscany, central Italy, near Era R., 20 mi. SE of Pisa; furniture mfg.

Pecel (pä'tsĕl), Hung. *Pécel*, town (pop. 7,372), Pest-Pilis-Solt-Kiskun co., N central Hungary, on Rakos R. and 12 mi. E of Budapest; corn, potatoes, hogs, poultry.

Pech, Yugoslavia: see PEC.

Pechatkino, Russian SFSR: see SOKOL, Vologda oblast.

Pechea (pä'kyä), agr. village (pop. 5,825), Galati prov., E Rumania, 15 mi. NE of Galati.

Péchelbronn, France: see MERKWILLER-PÉCHELBRONN.

Pechenegi (pyĕchĭnyĕ'gē), village (1926 pop. 7,298), central Kharkov oblast, Ukrainian SSR, on the Northern Donets and 30 mi. ESE of Kharkov; metalworks.

Pechenezhin (pyĕchĭnyĕ'zhĭn), Pol. *Peczeniżyn* (pĕchĕnyĕ'zhĭn), town (1931 pop. 6,839), central Stanislav oblast, Ukrainian SSR, at N foot of East Beskids, 8 mi. WSW of Kolomyya; petroleum refining, lumbering; flour milling. Has old castle.

Pechenga (pyĕ'chĭn-gŭ), Finnish *Petsamo* (pĕt'sämô), town (1948 pop. over 2,000), NW Murmansk oblast, Russian SFSR, near Norwegian border, at head of Pechenga Fjord (narrow inlet of Barents Sea), 60 mi. NW of Murmansk, on Arctic highway from Rovaniemi; fisheries. Consists of several adjoining villages, including lower Luostari (S; govt. offices) and Parkkina (N; commercial section). In Second World War, supply base in unsuccessful Ger. Murmansk campaign; captured 1944 by Soviet troops. **Pechenga,** a dist. (□ 4,050; 1940 pop. c.5,000) of Finland, was ceded (1920) by Russia; reverted (1944) to USSR, confirmed (1947) by Finnish peace treaty: Includes NIKEL mines.

Pêcherie, La (lä pĕshrē'), SW suburb of Bizerte, Bizerte dist., N Tunisia, on N shore of L. of Bizerte; olive groves, truck-farms.

Pechiguera Point (pāchēgā'rä), SW cape of Lanzarote, Canary Isls., 21 mi. WSW of Arrecife; 28°52'N 13°51'W.

Pechili, China: see HOPEH.

Pechina (pāchē'nä), town (pop. 2,089), Almería prov., S Spain, 6 mi. N of Almería; flour milling, chocolate mfg.; ships grapes. Mining of silver-bearing lead.

Pech Morena, India: see MORENA.

Pechora (pyĭchô'rŭ), city (1949 pop. over 2,000), E central Komi Autonomous SSR, Russian SFSR, on left bank of Pechora R. and 20 mi. N of Kozhva, 160 mi. NE of Ukhta, in Pechora coal basin.

Pechora Bay, inlet of Barents Sea at mouth of Pechora R., in N European USSR; 40 mi. wide, 50 mi. long, up to 30 ft. deep; frozen Oct.-June.

Pechora River, N European Russian SFSR, rises in the N Urals at c.62°10'N, flows 1,110 mi. generally N, through forest and tundra regions, past Troitsko-Pechorsk, Kozhva, Ust-Usa, and Ust-Tsilma, to Pechora Bay of Barents Sea, forming delta mouth (50 mi. long, 20 mi. wide) at Naryan-Mar. Navigable for 470 mi. below Ust-Usa during summer, for 1,040 mi. in high-water seasons (spring, autumn). Receives Ilych, Shchugor, Usa rivers (right), Kozhva, Izhma, and Tsilma rivers (left). Fisheries, alluvial agr., and livestock raising along its course. Pechora coal basin, mainly in basin of Usa R., has mining centers at Vorkuta and Inta.

Pechora Sea, USSR: see BARENTS SEA.

Pechory (-rē), Estonian *Petseri* (pĕ'tsĕrē), Ger. *Petschur* (pĕ'chŏor), city (pop. 4,274), W Pskov oblast, Russian SFSR, 27 mi. W of Pskov, near Estonian border; flax-growing center; rail junction. Has large 13th-cent. cave monastery (fortified in 16th cent.). In Rus. Pskov govt. until 1920; in Estonia until 1945.

Pechos, Los (lōs pä'chōs), highest point (c.6,400 ft.) of volcanic massif in central Grand Canary, Canary Isls.

Pechtelsgrün (pĕkh'tŭlsgrün"), village (pop. 364), Saxony, E central Germany, in the Erzgebirge, 3 mi. NE of Lengenfeld; wolframite mining.

Pecica (pä'chēkä), Hung. *Ópécska* (ō'päch-kŏ), village (pop. 8,207), Arad prov., W Rumania, on railroad and 11 mi. W of Arad; poultry-breeding center; flour milling, sawmilling, mfg. of furniture. Noted for colorful local costumes.

Peck. 1 Village (pop. 170), Nez Perce co., NW Idaho, 8 mi. W of Orofino; agr. **2** Village (pop. 471), Sanilac co., E Mich., 27 mi. NW of Port Huron, in farm area; condensed-milk factory.

Pecka, Czechoslovakia: see NOVA PAKA.

Peck Beach, SE N.J., barrier beach along Atlantic bet. Great Egg Harbor Inlet (N) and Corsons Inlet (S); Ocean City at N tip. Separated from mainland by Great Egg Harbor Bay (bridged) and Intracoastal Waterway channel (bridged).

Peckelsheim (pĕ'kŭls-hīm), village (pop. 1,887), in former Prussian prov. of Westphalia, NW Germany, after 1945 in North Rhine-Westphalia, 7 mi. N of Warburg.

Peckham (pĕ'kŭm), residential district of Camberwell, London, England, S of the Thames, 4 mi. SE of Charing Cross.

Pecky (pĕch'kĭ), Czech *Pečky*, town (pop. 3,187), E central Bohemia, Czechoslovakia, on railroad and 14 mi. NW of Kutna Hora; glue mfg.

Peconic (pēkŏ'nĭk, pĭ-), village (1940 pop. 608), Suffolk co., SE N.Y., on N peninsula of E Long Isl., 12 mi. NE of Riverhead, in summer-resort area.

Peconic Bay, N.Y.: see GREAT PECONIC BAY.

Peconic River, SE N.Y., rises on E Long Isl. S of Wading R., flows c.15 mi. generally E, past Calverton and Riverhead, to Flanders Bay of Great Peconic Bay; navigable to Riverhead.

Pecora, Cape (pä'kôrä), point on SW coast of Sardinia; 39°27'N 8°23'E.

Pecos (pā'kŭs), county (□ 4,736; pop. 9,939), extreme W Texas; ⊙ Fort Stockton. Second-largest co. in state, extending from Glass Mts. (SW) to Pecos R. (NE boundary); alt. 2,200-5,200 ft. Large-scale ranching (cattle, sheep, goats). Some irrigated agr. (alfalfa seed, melons, truck) near Fort Stockton and in Pecos valley (water from Red Bluff L., c.85 mi. NW). Large oil production. Tourist trade. Formed 1871.

Pecos. 1 Village (pop. 1,241), San Miguel co., N central N.Mex., on Pecos R., in Sangre de Cristo Mts., and 16 mi. ESE of Santa Fe; alt. c.7,000 ft. Trading point in livestock, dude-ranch region. Fish hatchery and Sante Fe Natl. Forest near by. Pecos State Monument, 2 mi. S, consists of ruins of mission church and 2 communal dwellings that once contained 585 and 517 rooms each. Pueblo founded c.1348; abandoned 1838 because of epidemics. **2** City (pop. 8,054), ⊙ Reeves co., extreme W Texas, c.75 mi. WSW of Odessa and on Pecos R.; trade, shipping center (rail junction) in cattle-ranching and irrigated agr. region (water from Red Bluff L., c.40 mi. NW); cotton, alfalfa, melons. Oil wells, refinery; cotton ginning. Founded in 1880s as a cow town.

Pecos River, in N.Mex. and Texas, rises in Mora co., N N.Mex., near North Truchas Peak; flows SE past Santa Rosa, and S past Carlsbad, thence generally SE through Texas, past Pecos city, to the Rio Grande 35 mi. NW of Del Rio; length, 926 mi.; drains □ 38,300. Traverses extensive canyon in lower course in Texas; near N.Mex. line Red Bluff Dam creates RED BLUFF LAKE. Important dams on river in N.Mex. are Alamogordo, Avalon, and McMillan, units in Carlsbad project for land reclamation. Largest is Alamogordo Dam (finished 1937), 12 mi. NW of Fort Sumner; earthfill dam (148 ft. high, 3,084 ft. long); forms Alamogordo Reservoir (capacity 156,800 acre-ft.). Others, just above Carlsbad, form Avalon Reservoir (capacity 7,000 acre-ft.) and L. McMillan (capacity 38,700 acre-ft.). Long-standing disputes bet. N.Mex. and Texas over use of water for irrigation were settled 1949. In the heyday of ranching in W Texas, "west of the Pecos" was the term for the distinct wild and mountainous region of the W tip of the state.

Pecq, Le (lŭ pĕk'), town (pop. 5,038), Seine-et-Oise dept., N central France, port on the Seine (bridges) at foot of Saint-Germain-en-Laye escarpment, and 11 mi. WNW of Paris; mfg. (machine tools, perfumes, cement pipes).

Pecquencourt (pĕkākōōr'), residential town (pop. 3,311), Nord dept., N France, 6 mi. E of Douai, in coal-mining dist.

Pecs (pāch), Hung. *Pécs*, Ger. *Fünfkirchen*, city (pop. 73,000), ⊙ but independent of Baranya co., S Hungary, at S foot of MECSEK MOUNTAINS, in coal-mining area, 106 mi. SSW of Budapest; rail, industrial, wine center. Agr. chemical experiment station. Mfg. (vegetable oil, champagne, tobacco products, organs, leather goods, soap, candles); flour mills, brickworks, breweries, tanneries. Ceramics exported. Was Roman settlement, Sopinae. Seat of R.C. bishop; has 11th-cent. cathedral, rebuilt in late-19th cent. Under Turkish rule, 1543-1686; 2 of its 3 mosques were converted into churches. Univ., 1st in Hungary, founded 1367 by Louis the Great. Hungarian univ. of Pozsony transferred here in 1921.

Pecsvarad (pāch-värŏd), Hung. *Pécsvárad*, town (pop. 2,691), Baranya co., S Hungary, 10 mi. NE of Pecs; wine.

Peculiar, town (pop. 267). Cass co., W Mo., near South Grand R., 8 mi. NW of Harrisonville.

Peczenizyn, Ukrainian SSR: see PECHENEZHIN.

Pedalium, Cape, Cyprus: see GRECO, CAPE.

Pedana (pä'dŭnŭ), town (pop. 9,585), Kistna dist., NE Madras, India, in Kistna R. delta, on rail spur and 6 mi. N of Masulipatam; rice, coconuts. Sometimes spelled Pedannah.

Pedapalle, India: see NIZAMPATAM.

Pedapalli, India: see PEDDAPALLI.

Pedara (pĕdä'rä), village (pop. 3,577), Catania prov., E Sicily, on S slope of Mt. Etna, 6 mi. W of Acireale.

Pedasí (pādäsē'), village (pop. 676), Los Santos prov., S central Panama, in Pacific lowland, 18 mi. SE of Las Tablas; road terminus; sugar cane, coffee, livestock.

Pedaso (pĕdä'zô), village (pop. 923), Ascoli Piceno prov., The Marches, central Italy, port on the Adriatic, near mouth of Aso R., 8 mi. SE of Fermo; bathing resort; vegetable oils.

Pedda Ganjam (pĕ'dŭ gŭnjäm'), village, Guntur dist., NE Madras, India, 15 mi. NE of Ongole; here Buckingham Canal joins navigable irrigation-canal system of Kistna R. delta.

Peddapalli (pĕdŭpŭ'lē), town (pop. 10,731), Karimnagar dist., E Hyderabad state, India, 20 mi. NE of Karimnagar; cotton ginning, rice milling; agr. market. Also spelled Pedapalli.

Peddapuram (pĕ'dŭpōōrŭm), city (pop. 20,835), East Godavari dist., NE Madras, India, 11 mi. NNW of Cocanada; silk weaving, rice milling; sugar cane, oilseeds. Also called Peddapur.

Pedda Vegi, India: see ELLORE.

Peddocks Island, E Mass., in Boston Bay just off W tip (Windmill Point) of Nantasket Peninsula and E of Quincy; c.1½ mi. long.

Pede (pĕ'dĕ), Chinese *Pai-ti* (bī'dē'), town [Tibetan *dzong*], S Tibet, on lake Yamdrok Tso, on main India-Lhasa trade route and 55 mi. SW of Lhasa. Pede peak (17,699 ft.) is 2 mi. N.

Pedee River, N.C. and S.C.: see PEE DEE RIVER.

Pedegral or **El Pedegral** (ĕl pādägräl'), village (1930 pop. 300), Coquimbo prov., N central Chile, 35 mi. SE of Ovalle; fruitgrowing. Copper deposits near by.

Pedegral or **El Pedegral,** lava field (□ c.15) in Federal Dist., central Mexico, S of church of El Carmen in Villa Obregón; dates from eruption of Cerro Ajusco, c.5,000 B.C. Excavations have revealed archaeological remains believed to be contemporary with Cuicuilco pyramid (1½ mi. W of Tlalpan).

Pedegral River, Mexico: see TONALÁ RIVER.

Pedernales (pādĕrnä'lĕs), town (pop. 2,087), N central Buenos Aires prov., Argentina, 32 mi. ENE of Veinticinco de Mayo; cattle-raising and grain-growing center; cider mfg.

Pedernales, town (1950 pop. 947), Barahona prov., SW Dominican Republic, on the coast, on Haiti border opposite Anse-à-Pitre, 40 mi. WSW of Barahona, in irrigated region yielding coffee, sugar cane, corn, tubers. Has a fort. Founded 1915.

Pedernales, town (pop. 712), Delta Amacuro territory, NE Venezuela, landing on Gulf of Paria at mouth of Caño Pedernales (arm of Orinoco R. delta), 70 mi. SW of Port of Spain, Trinidad; petroleum and asphalt wells. Airfield.

Pedernales, Caño (kä'nyō), W arm of Orinoco R. delta, Delta Amacuro territory, NE Venezuela; branches off from the Caño Mánamo 5 mi. NW of Tucupita, flows c.75 mi. N to Gulf of Paria at Pedernales.

Pedernales, Salar de (sälär' dā), salt desert (alt. 11,500 ft.) in S Atacama Desert, Atacama prov., N Chile, extends c.20 mi. NNE-SSW (c.10 mi. wide) at N end of Cordillera Claudio Gay. Borax deposits.

Pedernales River (pûr"dŭnă'lĭs, pē"dûr–), S central Texas, rises in springs on Edwards Plateau in Gillespie co., flows c.105 mi. generally E to Marshall Ford L. in the Colorado WNW of Austin.

Pederneiras (pĭdĕrnā'rŏs), city (pop. 5,115), central São Paulo, Brazil, 20 mi. E of Bauru; rail junction; mfg. of soft drinks, pottery; coffee, cotton, and rice processing; tanning.

Pedernera, Argentina: see MERCEDES.

Pedernoso, El (ĕl pā-dhĕrnō'sō), town (pop. 1,835), Cuenca prov., E central Spain, 5 mi. S of Belmonte; cereals, einkorn, saffron, grapes, livestock. Lumbering; alcohol distilling, plaster mfg. Has mineral springs.

Pederobba (pĕdĕrôb'bä), village (pop. 1,926), Treviso prov., Veneto, N Italy, on Piave R. and 2 mi. SW of Valdobbiadene.

Pedhoulas (pĕdhōōläs'), summer resort (pop. 1,322), Nicosia dist., E central Cyprus, at NW foot of Mt. Olympus, 33 mi. WSW of Nicosia; alt. c.3,600 ft. Grows deciduous fruit (cherries, apricots, apples).

Pedias River (pēdhyäs'), largest river of Cyprus, rises in E section of Olympus Mts., flows NE and E, past Nicosia, draining into irrigation reservoirs of Akhyritou and Kouklia, c.5 mi. W of Famagusta. Formerly flowed to Famagusta Bay near anc. Salamis. Not navigable.

Pedley, village (pop. 2,226), Riverside co., S Calif., 13 mi. W of Riverside.

Pedra (pĕ'drŭ). **1** Town, Alagoas, Brazil: see DELMIRO. **2** City (pop. 1,197), central Pernambuco, NE Brazil, 40 mi. NW of Garanhuns; cotton, corn, tobacco, livestock.

Pedra Açu, peak, Brazil: see ORGÃOS, SERRA DOS.

Pedra Azul (pĕ'drŭ äzōōl'), city (pop. 3,927), NE Minas Gerais, Brazil, on Rio de Janeiro–Bahia highway and 110 mi. N of Teófilo Otoni; semi-precious stones found here. Until 1944, called Fortaleza.

Pedra Branca (brăng'kŭ), city (pop. 1,438), central Ceará, Brazil, in hills 25 mi. WNW of Senador Pompeu; livestock, cotton. Graphite deposits.

Pedra do Sino, peak, Brazil: see ORGÃOS, SERRA DOS.

Pedraja de Portillo (pā-dhrä'hä dhā pôrtē'lyō), town (pop. 1,005), Valladolid prov., N central Spain, 14 mi. SSE of Valladolid; sugar beets, cereals.

Pedrajas de San Estebán (–häs dhā sän' ĕstävän'), town (pop. 1,920), Valladolid prov., N central Spain, 23 mi. SSE of Valladolid; resin mfg., sawmilling; cereals, wine. Gypsum quarries.

Pedra Lavrada (pĕ'drŭ lŭvrä'dŭ), town (pop. 403), central Paraíba, NE Brazil, on Borborema Plateau, 18 mi. SSW of Picuí; copper mines. Tin ore and rose quartz deposits.

Pedralba (pā-dhräl'vä), city (pop. 2,542), Valencia prov., E Spain, on Turia R. and 6 mi. WSW of Liria; lumbering; agr. trade (olive oil, wine, cereals).

Pedra Lume (pĕ'drŭ lōō'mĭ), village, Cape Verde Isls., port on E coast of Sal isl., 11 mi. N of Santa Maria; 16°46'N 22°54'W. Saltworks 1 mi. NW.

Pedrão Point (pĭdrā'ō), headland of NW Angola, forming S limit of Congo R. estuary; 6°2'S 12°19'E. Just S is Santo António do Zaire.

Pedras Brancas, Brazil: see GUAÍBA.

Pedras de Fogo (pĕ'drŭs dĭ fô'gōō), town (pop. 1,775), E Paraíba, NE Brazil, on Pernambuco border, opposite També and 25 mi. SW of João Pessoa; sugar, cotton.

Pedras Negras (nā'grŭs), town, S Guaporé territory, W Brazil, on right bank of Guaporé R. (Bolivia border) and 290 mi. S of Pôrto Velho; 12°47'S 62°55'W.

Pedras Point (pĕ'drŭs), headland on Atlantic coast of Pernambuco, NE Brazil, 30 mi. N of Recife; 7°37'S 34°47'W. Lighthouse. Together with Cabo Branco (32 mi. N), it is considered easternmost point of South America.

Pedraza (pädrä'sä), town (pop. 1,939), Magdalena dept., N Colombia, on Magdalena R. and 5 mi. S of Calamar; corn.

Pedraza (pā-dhrä'thä), town (pop. 142), Segovia prov., central Spain, 21 mi. NE of Segovia; grain growing, stock raising, lumbering. Has imposing ruined castle where sons of Francisco I were held prisoner (1526–30) and modern Sp. painter Zuloaga had his studio for some time.

Pedraza, Venezuela: see CIUDAD BOLIVIA.

Pedregal (pā-dhrāgäl'), town (pop. estimate 500), N Mendoza prov., Argentina, in Mendoza R. valley (irrigation area), 10 mi. SE of Mendoza; rail junction, wine-making center.

Pedregal, village (pop. 309), Chiriquí prov., W Panama, on the Pacific, seaport of David (4 mi. N); road and rail terminus. Exports coffee, bananas, cacao. Flourished until construction of Inter-American Highway.

Pedregal, town (pop. 1,944), Falcón state, NW Venezuela, 40 mi. SW of Coro; coffee, cacao, sugar cane, stock.

Pedregal Grande (grän'dā), village (pop. 1,807), Piura dept., NW Peru, in lower Piura valley, 3 mi. SSW of Catacaos, in irrigated cotton area.

Pedreguer (pā-dhrāgĕr'), town (pop. 3,977), Alicante prov., E Spain, 16 mi. SE of Gandía; agr. trade center (almonds, raisins, oranges and other fruit); cotton and silk milling, vegetable-fiber processing (baskets and hats), olive pressing.

Pedregulho (pĭdrĭgōō'lyōō), city (pop. 2,462), NE São Paulo, Brazil, on railroad and 20 mi. N of Franca; processing of dairy products and tobacco, pottery mfg., distilling.

Pedreira (pĭdrā'rŭ), city (pop. 2,111), E central São Paulo, Brazil, on railroad and 15 mi. NE of Campinas; china mfg.; coffee, grain, fruit.

Pedreiras (pĭdrā'rŭs), city (pop. 4,760), central Maranhão, Brazil, head of navigation on Mearim R. and 140 mi. S of São Luís; agr. trade center in dist. growing cotton, sugar, and tobacco.

Pedrera (pā-dhrā'rä), town (pop. 3,335), Seville prov., SW Spain, in N Sierra de Yeguas, on railroad and 12 mi. E of Osuna; cereals, olives. Has sulphur springs.

Pedricktown, village, Salem co., SW N.J., near the Delaware 3 mi. NE of Penns Grove. Near by is U.S. ordnance depot.

Pedro II, Brazil: see PEDRO SEGUNDO.

Pedro II, Canal, Bolivia: see UBERABA, LAKE.

Pedro Abad (pā'dhrō ävädh'), town (pop. 3,306), Córdoba prov., S Spain, near the Guadalquivir, 20 mi. ENE of Córdoba; olive-oil processing, sawmilling.

Pedro Afonso (pĕ'drōō äfô'sōō), city (pop. 1,243), N Goiás, N central Brazil, on right bank of Tocantins R. at influx of Somno R., and 120 mi. SSW of Carolina (Maranhão); manioc meal, rice, corn, skins, feathers. Rock crystals found near by. Airfield. Formerly spelled Pedro Affonso.

Pedro Avelino (pĕ'drōō ävĭlē'nōō), city (pop. 693), central Rio Grande do Norte, NE Brazil, terminus (1949) of rail spur from Itaretama, projected to reach Macau (32 mi. NNW). Until 1948, called Epitácio Pessoa.

Pedro Bank (pē'drō), Caribbean shoal, 45 mi. S of Jamaica, B.W.I., extends c.110 mi. E-W, up to 65 mi. wide. Fringed by coral reefs, chiefly PEDRO CAYS (E).

Pedro Bay (pē'drō), village (pop. 44), SW Alaska, on NE shore of Iliamna L.; 59°46'N 154°9'W.

Pedro Bernardo (pā'dhrō bĕrnär'dō), town (pop. 3,196), Ávila prov., central Spain, in valley of Sierra de Gredos, 29 mi. SSW of Ávila; potatoes, grapes, olives, livestock. Flour mills, olive presses, woolen mills. Hydroelectric plant.

Pedro Betancourt (bātänkōrt'), town (pop. 6,030), Matanzas prov., W Cuba, on railroad and 28 mi. SE of Matanzas; agr. center (sugar cane, rice, cattle). Near by are the refineries and sugar centrals of Cuba (W) and Dolores (NW). Stone quarries in vicinity.

Pedro Cays (pē'drō kāz'), group of 4 Caribbean islets and a number of smaller reefs, dependency of Jamaica, B.W.I., 55 mi. off S coast of the main isl. On the SE fringes of Pedro Bank, they are situated bet. 16°58'–17°3'N and 77°45'–77°49'W. Include Northeast, Middle, Southwest, and South Cays. Yield some guano and coconuts. They were occupied by the British in 1863 and made a Jamaica dependency in 1882. Uninhabited. Sometimes called, together with Morant Cays (120 mi. ENE), Guano Isls.

Pedroche (pā-dhrō'chā), town (pop. 3,518), Córdoba prov., S Spain, 6 mi. NE of Pozoblanco; olive-oil processing, flour milling; hog raising. Cereals, wine. Stone quarries.

Pedro de Valdivia (pā'dhrō dhā väldē'ryä), mining settlement (1930 pop. 8,654), Antofagasta prov., N Chile, 85 mi. NNE of Antofagasta, on the edge of a desert; rail terminus; major nitrate- and iodine-producing center.

Pedrógão (pĭdrô'gā̃ō). **1** Village (pop. 1,692), Beja dist., S Portugal, 14 mi. NE of Beja; olives, oranges, wine. **2** Village (pop. 1,341), Castelo Branco dist., central Portugal, 22 mi. NE of Castelo Branco; wheat, corn, olives; oak woods.

Pedrogão Grande (grā̃n'dĭ), town (pop. 1,014), Leiria dist., central Portugal, on Zêzere R. and 25 mi. SE of Coimbra; resin processing; olives, potatoes. Has several medieval churches.

Pedro G. Méndez (pā'dhrō, mĕn'dēs), town (pop. estimate 500), central Tucumán prov., Argentina, 7 mi. ENE of Tucumán; agr. center (sugar cane, corn, alfalfa, livestock); sugar refining.

Pedro González (gōnsä'lĕs), town (dist. pop. 3,588), Ñeembucú dept., S Paraguay, near Paraná R., 25 mi. SE of Pilar; agr. center (tobacco, fruit, cattle).

Pedro González, town (pop. 1,189), on Margarita Isl. (NE), Nueva Esparta state, NE Venezuela, 5 mi. NW of La Asunción; sugar cane, corn, fruit.

Pedro Juan Caballero (hwän' kävävä'rō), town (dist. pop. 8,130), ⊙ Amambay dept., E Paraguay, in Sierra de Amambay, adjoining Ponta Porã (Brazil), 125 mi. NE of Concepción; 22°29'S 55°45'W; alt. 2,135 ft. Trade center in cattle area.

Pedrola (pā-dhrō'lä), town (pop. 1,787), Saragossa prov., NE Spain, on Imperial Canal and 20 mi. NW of Saragossa; olive-oil processing; sugar beets, cereals, wine, fruit, livestock.

Pedro Leopoldo (pĕ'drōō lēōōpōl'dōō), city (pop. 3,336), S central Minas Gerais, Brazil, on railroad and 22 mi. NNW of Belo Horizonte; cattle-raising center.

Pedro Martínez (pā'dhrō märtē'nĕth), town (pop. 3,296), Granada prov., S Spain, 15 mi. NNW of Guadix; lumbering, sheep raising; cereals, vegetables.

Pedro Miguel (mēgĕl'), town (pop. 812), Balboa dist., S Panama Canal Zone, on MIRAFLORES LAKE of the Canal, on transisthmian railroad, and 6 mi. NW of Panama city. Site of Pedro Miguel Locks, which consist of 1 set of locks at S end of Gaillard Cut, raising and lowering vessels 31 ft. Stock raising, dairying.

Pedro Montoya (mōntoi'ä), town (pop. 2,907), San Luis Potosí, N central Mexico, in outliers of Sierra Madre Oriental, near Guanajuato border, 23 mi. SE of Río Verde; alt. 2,897 ft. Agr. center (grain, beans, cotton, fruit, livestock). Formerly San Ciro.

Pedro Muñoz (mōōnyōth'), town (pop. 6,456), Ciudad Real prov., S central Spain, in New Castile, road junction 12 mi. E of Alcázar de San Juan. Agr. center on La Mancha plain (cereals, grapes, olives, sheep). Liquor distilling, sawmilling, flour milling, cheese processing; mfg. of plaster, sandals.

Pedroñeras, Las (läs pā-dhrōnyä'räs), town (pop. 4,619), Cuenca prov., E central Spain, in La Mancha region of New Castile, on Madrid-Alicante highway, and 50 mi. SW of Cuenca. Agr. center (grapes, saffron, garlic, licorice, fruit, livestock). Lumbering; flour milling.

Pedro Santana (pā'dhrō säntä'nä), village (1950 pop. 399), San Rafael prov., W Dominican Republic, on Haiti border, on Artibonito R., adjoining Bánica; rice, cotton, goats.

Pedro Segundo or **Pedro II** (pĕ'drōō sĭgōōn'dōō), city (pop. 2,036), N Piauí, Brazil, 27 mi. SE of Piripiri, in Serra Pedro Segundo (a dome rising to 2,330 ft.); sugar milling, distilling; ships carnauba wax, hides and skins. Formerly called Itamaraty.

Pedroso, El (ĕl pā-dhrō'sō), town (pop. 4,245), Seville prov., SW Spain, in the Sierra Morena, on railroad and 33 mi. NNE of Seville; iron-mining, lumbering, and agr. center (olives, cork, livestock). Granite quarries; limekilns.

Pedroso, Sierra del (syĕ'rä dhĕl), low W spur of the Sierra Morena, W Spain, extends c.25 mi. SW along Badajoz-Córdoba prov. border; rises to 2,782 ft.

Pedrosoengoe (pĕdrôsōōng'ōō), waterfalls, E Du. Guiana, on Marowijne or Maroni R. (Fr. Guiana border) and 33 mi. E of Dam.

Pedrotalagala, peak, Ceylon: see PIDURUTALAGALA.

Pedro Valley (pē'drō), village (pop. c.150), San Mateo co., W Calif., near the Pacific, c.12 mi. S of downtown San Francisco, in fertile San Pedro Valley (artichoke growing). Point San Pedro juts into the Pacific near by.

Pedro Vargas (pā'dhrō vär'gäs), town (pop. estimate 500), central Mendoza prov., Argentina, on Diamante R. (irrigation area), on railroad, and 7 mi. WSW of San Rafael. Wine, potatoes, fruit, livestock; dried-fruit processing, wine making, sawmilling.

Pedro Velho (pā'drōō vĕ'lyōō), city (pop. 1,965), E Rio Grande do Norte, NE Brazil, on railroad and 40 mi. S of Natal; cattle, sugar.

Peebinga (pē'bĭng-ŭ), village (pop. 67), SE South Australia, 130 mi. E of Adelaide, near Victoria border; rail terminus; wheat, wool.

Peebles or **Peeblesshire** (pē'bŭlz, pē'bŭlshĭr), sometimes called Tweeddale, county (□ 347.2; 1931 pop. 15,051; 1951 census 15,226), S Scotland; ⊙ Peebles. Bounded by Dumfries (S), Lanark (W), Midlothian (N and E), and Selkirk (E and SE). Drained by the Tweed and its tributaries. Surface is hilly, becoming mountainous in S, rising to 2,754 ft. in Broad Law. Sheep raising is main agr. occupation; slate and limestone are quarried. Chief industry is woolen milling (Peebles, Innerleithen, Walkerburn). Co. is scene of works of Allan Ramsay, James Hogg, Laidlaw, and Scott; home of the "Black Dwarfs" was near Peebles. There are numerous remains of anc. hilltop camps and forts.

Peebles, burgh (1931 pop. 5,853; 1951 census 6,013), ⊙ Peeblesshire, Scotland, in central part of co., on the Tweed (15th-cent. bridge) and 20 mi. S of Edinburgh; woolen milling, mfg. of leather-processing machinery; agr. market and resort. Chambers Institution (library and mus.) dates from 1644 and was home of Queensberry family. There are remains of 12th-cent. St. Andrews church and of 13th-cent. Cross Kirk; also fragment of anc. town walls. Just W are remains of anc. Neidpath Castle.

Peebles, village (pop. 1,498), Adams co., S Ohio, 26 mi. WNW of Portsmouth, in agr. area; sawmilling. Serpent Mound State Park is near by.

Peeblesshire, Scotland: see PEEBLES, county.

Pee Dee River (pē'dē), in N.C. and S.C., rises in the Blue Ridge in NW N.C., S of Boone, as Yadkin (yăd'kĭn) R.; flows NE past Wilkesboro, North Wilkesboro, and Elkin, and SSE, past Badin, becoming Pee Dee R. after a course of 204 mi. As the Pee Dee it continues for 231 mi. generally SSE, into S.C., to Winyah Bay just E of Georgetown; total length, 435 mi. In N.C., dammed to form High Rock and Badin lakes (as the Yadkin) and Tillery and Blewett Falls lakes (as the Pee Dee), with power plants. In lower course, navigable for 91 mi. Also called Great Pee Dee R. and Pedee R.

Peekamoose Mountain (3,863 ft.), Ulster co., SE N.Y., in the Catskills, 20 mi. W of Kingston.

Peekskill, city (pop. 17,731), Westchester co., SE N.Y., on E bank of the Hudson and 10 mi. N of Ossining, in truck-farm and resort area; mfg. (yeast, food products, alcohol, gin, jewelry, leather products, textiles, clothing, buttons, machinery); stone quarrying. Peekskill Military Acad. and St. Mary's School for girls are here. Camp Smith military reservation is just N. Bear Mountain Bridge crosses the Hudson 4 mi. NW. Inc. as village 1816, as city 1940.

Peekskill Lake, N.Y.: see LAKE PEEKSKILL.

Peel, county (□ 469; pop. 31,539), S Ont., on L. Ontario; ⊙ Brampton.

Peel, town district (1939 pop. 2,523), on W coast of Isle of Man, England, 10 mi. WNW of Douglas; fishing port and seaside resort, with brickworks. Has remains of 13th–14th-cent. cathedral and of 9th-cent. chapel. There are several other very old bldgs. Just W, in Irish Sea, is St. Patrick's Isle, with remains of anc. castle enclosed by 16th-cent. wall; site of lighthouse (54°13'N 4°44'W). Castle figures in Scott's *Peveril of the Peak.*

Peel, De, Netherlands: see DE PEEL.

Peelamedu (pē'lŭmĕdōō), town (pop. 8,297), Coimbatore dist., SW Madras, India, 3 mi. NE of Coimbatore; cotton-milling center. Industrial school (textiles). Formerly spelled Pilamedu.

Peel Island, Bonin Isls.: see CHICHI-JIMA.

Pe Ell, town (pop. 787), Lewis co., SW Wash., 18 mi. SW of Centralia; lumbering.

Peel Point, NW Victoria Isl., SW Franklin Dist., Northwest Territories, on Viscount Melville Sound, at N end of Prince of Wales Strait; 73°22'N 113°45'W.

Peel River, Australia: see NAMOI RIVER.

Peel River, Northwest Territories, rises in the Yukon near 65°30'N 140°W, flows E to 66°N 134°W, thence generally N, crossing into Mackenzie Dist., to Mackenzie R. 40 mi. SSE of Aklavik; 365 mi. long. Its lower course is W boundary of Peel River Preserve, game sanctuary (□ 3,300) set up 1923.

Peel Sound, S central Franklin Dist., Northwest Territories, arm (110 mi. long, 15–50 mi. wide) of the Arctic Ocean, bet. Barrow Strait (N) and Franklin Strait (S); 73°N 97°W. Separates Somerset Isl. (E) and Prince of Wales Isl. (W).

Peely, Pa.: see WARRIOR RUN.

Peenemünde (pā"nŭmün'dŭ), village (pop. 255), in former Prussian Pomerania prov., N Germany, after 1945 in Mecklenburg, on NW Usedom isl., at mouth of Peene R. estuary on the Baltic, 6 mi. N of Wolgast; guided-missile research and testing station established here during Second World War; power station. Gustavus Adolphus landed here in 1630.

Peene River (pā'nŭ), N Germany, formed by several headstreams in Malchin area of Mecklenburg; flows 97 mi. generally E, through Kummerow L., past Demmin (head of navigation) and Anklam; below Anklam, flowing in 25-mi.-long N–S estuary, it separates mainland and Usedom isl., emptying into the Baltic at Peenemünde. Receives the Tollense (right).

Peer (pār), village (pop. 4,204), Limburg prov., NE Belgium, 15 mi. W of Maaseik; agr., lumbering.

Peerless Park, town (pop. 119), St. Louis co., E Mo., on Meramec R., near the Mississippi, and SW of St. Louis.

Peetz, town (pop. 232), Logan co., NE Colo., 24 mi. NNE of Sterling, near Nebr. line; alt. 4,300 ft.; grain.

Peever, city (pop. 221), Roberts co., NE S.Dak., 10 mi. SSE of Sisseton; trading point for farming area.

Pegalajar (pāgälähär'), town (pop. 6,459), Jaén prov., S Spain, 8 mi. ESE of Jaén; olive-oil processing, flour milling, soap and plaster mfg. Corn and wine; sheep raising.

Pegasus Bay, inlet of S Pacific, E S.Isl., New Zealand, N of Banks Peninsula; 40 mi. N–S, 15 mi. E–W. Receives Waimakariri R. Lyttelton is on SW shore.

Pegau (pā'gou), town (pop. 6,754), Saxony, E central Germany, on the White Elster and 14 mi. SW of Leipzig; shoe and felt mfg., tanning. Has 12th-cent. church, 15th-cent. town hall. Developed around Benedictine abbey founded 1096.

Peggau (pĕ'gou), village (pop. 1,384), Styria, SE central Austria, on Mur R. and 10 mi. N of Graz; hydroelectric station; ironworks; summer resort.

Peggs, town (pop. 51), Cherokee co., E Okla., 14 mi. NNW of Tahlequah, in farm area.

Pegli (pä'lyē), town (pop. 16,294), Genova prov., Liguria, N Italy, port on Gulf of Genoa and 6 mi. W of Genoa, within Greater Genoa; iron industry (railroad bridges, storage tanks, electrical machinery), shipyards. Resort noted for villas and famous Pallavicini gardens (1837).

Pegnitz (päg'nĭts), town (pop. 6,378), Upper Franconia, N Bavaria, Germany, on the Pegnitz and 13 mi. SSW of Bayreuth; iron foundry; mfg. of heavy machinery, precision instruments, textiles, porcelain, paper; brewing. Iron ore and kaolin worked in area. Chartered 1574.

Pegnitz River, Bavaria, Germany, rises 6 mi. SSW of Bayreuth, flows S and then W, through Nuremberg, to Fürth, where it joins REDNITZ RIVER to form REGNITZ RIVER; 50 mi. long.

Pego (pā'gōō), town (pop. 2,674), Santarém dist., central Portugal, near left bank of the Tagus, 3 mi. E of Abrantes; wine, olives, cork.

Pego (pā'gō), town (pop. 8,547), Alicante prov., E Spain, 10 mi. SE of Gandía; agr. trade center (raisins, oranges, rice, beans, corn). Mfg. of essential oils, tiles; olive-oil processing, rice milling; sericulture. Gypsum quarries near by.

Pegswood, England: see MORPETH.

Pegu (pĕgōō', pŭgōō'), administrative division (□ 20,223; 1941 pop. 3,436,107) of Lower Burma, bet. Irrawaddy R. (W) and Sittang R. (E), on Gulf of Martaban; ⊙ Rangoon. An alluvial plain divided by S Pegu Yoma, drained by Myitmaka and Pegu rivers. Includes dists. of Hanthawaddy, Insein, Rangoon, Pegu, Tharrawaddy, Toungoo, Prome. Rice and sugar cane in plains, teak forests in mts. Served by Rangoon-Prome RR (paralleled by Rangoon-Chauk oil pipe line) and by Rangoon-Mandalay RR. Pop. is 70% Burmese, 15% Indian, 7% Karen. Settled 6th cent. by the Mons (or Talaings, as the Burmese call them), the area formed the nucleus of the Mon Pegu kingdom which flourished in 16th cent. and was finally crushed 1757 by the Burmese under Alaungpaya. Annexed 1852 by Britain in 2d Anglo-Burmese War; constituted 1862 as a div. of Lower Burma.

Pegu, district (□ 4,114; 1941 pop. 582,959), of Pegu div., Lower Burma, bet. Pegu Yoma (W) and Sittang R. (E); ⊙ Pegu. Drained by Pegu R. N part hilly and wooded; SE part in Sittang delta is constantly increasing because of sedimentation. Rice fields and fisheries. Served by Rangoon-Mandalay and Thongwa-Pegu-Martaban railroads, and by Pegu-Sittang canal. Pop. is 75% Burmese, 10% Indian, 8% Karen.

Pegu, town (pop. 21,712), ⊙ Pegu dist., Lower Burma, on Pegu R. and 45 mi. NNE of Rangoon, on Rangoon-Mandalay RR; head of railroads to Martaban and Thongwa. Produces pottery and bronze statuettes. Its large pagodas (some ruined, some restored) and a huge recumbent figure of Buddha are places of pilgrimage. Founded A.D. 573 by Mon emigrants from Thaton, it was a port until silting closed the river to seagoing vessels. From late 13th cent., it was center of one of the three chief states of Burma, and, in 16th cent., it succeeded Toungoo as ⊙ united Burmese kingdom until transfer (1635) of seat of govt. to Ava. Following a Mon rebellion against Burmese, Pegu was destroyed 1757 by Alaungpaya and later rebuilt as prov. capital. Passed under Br. rule in 1852. Damaged in 1931 earthquake.

Pegu River, Lower Burma, rises in the Pegu Yoma W of Pyu, flows 125 mi. SSE, past Pegu, and SSW to Rangoon where it joins the Myitmaka R. (here called Hlaing R.) to form Rangoon R. Navigable in lower course; linked to Sittang R. by 38-mi. navigable canal.

Pegu Yoma (yō'mä), mountain chain, S central Burma, bet. Irrawaddy R. and Sittang R. Forming a plateau (alt. c.500 ft.) S of Irrawaddy R. bend in Myingyan dist., the chain proper extends SSE from c.20°30'N to Insein and Pegu dists., ending in a ridge at Rangoon. Highest point is Mt. POPA (4,981 ft.); most peaks are below 2,000 ft. Teak forests, mostly govt. reserves.

Peh, China: see NORTH RIVER.

Pehan or **Peian** (both: bā'än'), town (pop. c.25,000), ⊙ Pehan co. (pop. 70,032), N central Heilungkiang prov., Manchuria, 175 mi. N of Harbin and on railroad to Aigun; rail junction for Tsitsihar; industrial center with railroad shops, power plant. Developed in early 1930s with railroad construction. Was (1937–43) ⊙ Pehan prov. (□ 29,415; 1940 pop. 2,318,957) in Manchukuo, and was briefly an independent municipality (1947–49) as ⊙ Heilungkiang prov. (1946–49).

Pehchen or **Peichen** (bā'jŭn'), town, ⊙ Pehchen co. (pop. 275,159), S central Liaosi prov., Manchuria, 50 mi. NE of Chinchow; soybeans, millet, corn, fruit. Until 1914 called Kwangning.

Pehchwan or **Pei-ch'uan** (both: bā-chwän'), town (pop. 6,061), ⊙ Pehchwan co. (pop. 38,508), NW Szechwan prov., China, 70 mi. NW of Santai; medicinal plants, tea, millet, beans. Until 1914 called Shihchwan.

Peh Ho, China: see PAI RIVER, Hopeh prov.

Peh Kiang, China: see NORTH RIVER.

Pehkiao, China: see SHANGHAI.

Pehpei or **Pei-p'ei** (both: bā'pā'), town (pop. 18,110), ⊙ Pehpei co. (pop. 92,885), S central Szechwan prov., China, 22 mi. NW of Chungking city and on right bank of Kialing R. Sometimes called Pehpeichang.

Pehpiao, Peipiao, or **Pei-p'iao** (all: bā'pyou'), town, ⊙ Pehpiao co., E Jehol prov., Manchuria, 50 mi. NNW of Chinchow and on rail spur; major coal-mining center. Was in Manchukuo's Chinchow prov. (1934–46).

Pehtaiho or **Peitaiho** (bā'dī'hŭ'), town, NE Hopeh prov., China, on railroad and 10 mi. SW of Chinwangtao; China's leading seaside resort.

Pehtang, Peitang, or **Pei-t'ang** (all: bā'täng'), village, N Hopeh prov., China, on Gulf of Chihli, 7 mi. N of Tangku. A combined British and French expeditionary force landed here in 1859 en route to Peking.

Pehtatung, China: see WEIYÜAN, Tsinghai prov.

Pehtwanlintze, Manchuria: see SUIHWA.

Pehuajó (pāwähō'), city (pop. 13,324), ⊙ Pehuajó dist. (□ 2,150; pop. 41,539), W central Buenos Aires prov., Argentina, 200 mi. WSW of Buenos Aires; agr. center (grain and livestock); dairying, flour milling. Founded 1883.

Pehuenches, Argentina: see BUTA RANQUIL.

Pei, China: see NORTH RIVER.

Peian, Manchuria: see PEHAN.

Peichen, Manchuria: see PEHCHEN.

Pei Chiang, China: see NORTH RIVER.

Pei-chiang, Formosa: see PEIKANG.

Pei-chieh, China: see PAKKAI.

Pei-ching, China: see PEKING.

Peichow, China: see PIHSIEN, Shantung prov.

Pei-ch'uan, China: see PEHCHWAN.

Peifeng, Manchuria: see SIAN.

Peigneur, Lake (pĕnyōōr', pĕnyōō'), S La., 9 mi. W of New Iberia; c.1½ mi. in diameter. Jefferson Isl. (salt dome) is on E shore; a dredged channel joins lake with Gulf Intracoastal Waterway to S.

Peihai, China: see PAKHOI.

Pei Ho, China: see PAI RIVER, Hopeh prov.

Peihsien or **P'ei-hsien** (both: pā'shyĕn'), town (pop. 68,889), ⊙ Peihsien co. (pop. 418,283), SW Shantung prov., China, 35 mi. NNW of Süchow, near Pingyuan line; kaoliang, beans, wheat, cotton. Until 1949 in Kiangsu.

P'ei-hsien, Shantung prov., China: see PIHSIEN.

Peikang (bā'gäng') or **Pei-chiang** (bā'jyäng'), Jap. *Hokko* (hōk'kō), town (1935 pop. 15,269), W central Formosa, 11 mi. NW of Kiayi; sugar-milling center. Its religious shrine attracts pilgrims.

Pei Kiang, China: see NORTH RIVER.

Peili, China: see PAKLI.

Peiling, Manchuria: see MUKDEN.

Peiliu, China: see PAKLOW.

Peilstein im Mühlviertel (pīl'shtīn ĭm mül'fĕrtŭl), village (pop. 1,766), N Upper Austria, near Kleine Mühl R., 28 mi. NW of Linz, near Czechoslovak line; linen mfg.

Peimen (bā'mŭn'), Jap. *Hokumon* (hō'kōōmōn), town (1935 pop. 5,552), W central Formosa, on W coast, 19 mi. NNW of Tainan; salt-producing center; hatmaking; fish hatchery.

Peinado, Cerro (sĕ'rō pānä'dō), Andean volcano (18,830 ft.) in W Catamarca prov., Argentina, 30 mi. NNE of Cerro Incahuasi, at SW tip of Sierra de Calalaste.

Peine (pī'nŭ), town (pop. 23,640), in former Prussian prov. of Hanover, NW Germany, after 1945 in Lower Saxony, on Weser-Elbe Canal and 20 mi. ESE of Hanover, in oil dist.; rolling mill, foundry; food processing (flour products, canned goods, sugar, malt, wine), silk spinning and weaving. Poet Bodenstedt b. here.

Pei-p'ei, China: see PEHPEI.

Peipiao, Manchuria: see PEHPIAO.

Peiping, China: see PEKING.

Peipu or **Pei-p'u** (bā'pōō), Jap. *Hoppo* (hŏp'pō), village (1935 pop. 3,027), NW Formosa, 9 mi. SE of Sinchu; natural-gas deposits.

Peipus, Lake (pī'pŭs, Ger. pī'pōōs), Est. *Peipsi Järv* (pā'psĭ yärv), Rus. *Chudskoye Ozero* (chōōt'skŭyŭ ô'zyĭrŭ), third largest lake (□ c.1,400, with L. PSKOV) of Europe, bet. Estonia and Russian SFSR; 48 mi. long, 20–30 mi. wide; 50 ft. deep; alt. c.100 ft. Shores are marshy meadows and sand dunes; weak northward current; frozen Dec.–March. Receives Ema R. (W); empties N through Narva R. into Gulf of Finland. Shore pop. largely Rus.; fishing. Main ports: Mustvee, Vasknarva, Gdov. Lake connected by 15-mi.-long strait with L. Pskov, to which the term Peipus is sometimes extended. On the frozen strait, the Livonian Knights were defeated (1242) by Alexander Nevski.

Peira-Cava, France: see LUCÉRAM.

Peiraieus, Greece: see PIRAEUS.

Peirce City or **Pierce City,** city (pop. 1,156), Lawrence co., SW Mo., in the Ozarks, 30 mi. ESE of Joplin; agr. center (grain growing, dairying); lime products. Founded c.1870.

Peishambe, Uzbek SSR: see KARA-DARYA, village.
Peiskretscham, Poland: see PYSKOWICE.
Peissenberg (pī'sŭnbĕrk), village (pop. 7,667), Upper Bavaria, Germany, at N foot of the Bavarian Alps, 4 mi. SW of Weilheim; lignite-mining center.
Peitaiho, China: see PEHTAIHO.
Peitang, China: see PEHTANG.
Peita River, Chinese *Pei-ta Ho* (bā'dä' hŭ'), NW Kansu prov., China, rises in the Nan Shan, flows over 200 mi. NW and NE, past Kiuchüan, joining Hei R. at Tingsin to form the Etsin Gol. Also called Lin Shui.
Peita Shan, China and Mongolia: see BAITAK BOGDO.
Peitaying, Manchuria: see MUKDEN.
Peiting (pī'tĭng), village (pop. 6,681), Upper Bavaria, Germany, 11 mi. WSW of Weilheim; lignite-mining center.
Peitow. 1 or **Pei-tou** (bā'dō), Jap. *Hokuto* (hō'kōō-tō), town (1935 pop. 14,300), W central Formosa, 20 mi. SSW of Taichung; rice, sugar cane, ramie, peanuts. **2** or **Pei-t'ou** (bā'tō'), Jap. *Hokuto*, town (1935 pop. 6,850), N Formosa, on railroad and 6 mi. N of Taipei, at foot of Tatun Shan; noted health resort (sulphur springs); sulphur mining and refining; mfg. (tile, pottery, rush mats).
Peitz (pīts), town (pop. 5,045), Brandenburg, E Germany, in Lower Lusatia, at SE edge of Spree Forest, on Malxe R. and 8 mi. NE of Cottbus; woolen milling, tanning, glass mfg. Has remains of 16th-cent. fortifications. Just S are large carp ponds.
Peiwar Pass, Afghanistan and Pakistan: see PAIWAR PASS.
Peixe (pā'shĭ), city (pop. 618), central Goiás, central Brazil, on left bank of Tocantins R. and 90 mi. S of Pôrto Nacional; mangabeira rubber, corn, manioc flour, tobacco. Rock crystals found in area. Airfield.
Peixe River. 1 In central Santa Catarina, Brazil, rises 20 mi. S of Pôrto União, flows c.140 mi. SW to the Uruguay (right bank) at Marcelino Ramos. Sometimes considered one of the headstreams of the Uruguay. Followed throughout course by São Paulo–Rio Grande do Sul RR. **2** In W São Paulo, Brazil, rises near Garça, flows 180 mi. WNW to Paraná R. NNW of Presidente Venceslau. Not navigable.
Pejepscot, Maine: see TOPSHAM.
Pekalongan (pŭkälông'än), town (pop. 65,982), central Java, Indonesia, on Java Sea, 210 mi. ESE of Batavia; 6°54'S 109°40'E; chief port for central Java, shipping sugar, rubber, tea. Tobacco processing, sugar milling, batik printing, textile milling. Has a fort built in 1753. Sometimes spelled Pecalongan.
Pekan (pŭkän'), town (pop. 1,695), E Pahang, Malaya, port at mouth of Pahang R., 5 mi. from South China Sea, and 23 mi. S of Kuantan; sultan's residence; domestic weaving of silk and cotton goods.
Pekela, Nieuwe, Netherlands: see NIEUWE PEKELA.
Pekela, Oude, Netherlands: see OUDE PEKELA.
Pe Kiang, China: see NORTH RIVER.
Pekiin, Israel: see PEQIIN.
Pekin, Albania: see PEQIN.
Pekin (pē'kĭn). **1** City (pop. 21,858), ⊙ Tazewell co., central Ill., on Illinois R. (bridged here) and 10 mi. S of Peoria; trade, shipping, and industrial center in agr. and bituminous-coal area; corn, oats, soybeans, wheat, livestock, poultry. Mfg.: dairy and food products, beverages, leather products, steel tanks, burial vaults, barrels, metal castings, organs, chip board, yeast, malt, alcohol. Settled 1829, inc. 1839. Lincoln practiced law here. Fishing, hunting near by along Mackinaw R. **2** Village (pop. 221), Nelson co., E central N.Dak., 18 mi. S of Lakota, near Sheyenne R.
Peking (pē'kĭng'), Chinese *Pei-ching* or *Peking* (both: bā'jĭng') [northern capital], formerly called (1928–49) **Peiping** or **Pei-p'ing** (pā'pĭng', bā'–) [northern peace], city (1946 pop. 1,672,438; 1947 pop. 1,603,324), ⊙ China, in N Hopeh prov., 70 mi. NW of Tientsin, its Yellow Sea port on Gulf of Chihli; 39°36'N 116°24'E. Peking is China's political, cultural, and intellectual center, situated at the junction of railroads to Hankow and Canton (SW), Suiyuan and Ningsia (NW), Jehol (NE), and Tientsin (SE), and within 40 mi. of the Great Wall. It is situated on the N China plain, bet. the Yungting and Pai rivers; on the latter is Tunghsien, an anc. river port of Peking. Among Peking's industrial plants are iron- and steelworks (at Shihkingshan) and a railroad rolling-stock mfg. plant; produces also woolens, leather, matches, glass, liquors, and processed foods. It is an important publishing center, and the seat of numerous higher educational institutions, including Peking, Tsinghwa, and Yenching universities; teachers and medical colleges, and natl. library. Peking proper (□ 25) is a square consisting of 2 contiguous walled cities: the Inner City or Tatar City (N) and the Outer City or Chinese City (S). The Inner City (walled in 15th cent.) includes the Forbidden City (former imperial palace), the Imperial City (which includes govt. offices), the legation quarter (SE), and numerous temples (of Confucius and of the Lamas) and parks. The Outer City is the commercial quarter and includes within its 16th-cent. walls the Temple of Heaven, set in a large park, and the Temple of Agriculture. In Peking's suburbs are the Manchu emperors' summer palace (7 mi. NW), and the civil airport, in the former imperial hunting grounds of Nanyüan (7 mi. S). Several bones of Peking Man (*Sinanthropus pekinensis*) were discovered at Chowkowtien, 30 mi. SW. The earliest record of a city on Peking's site is that of Chi, ⊙ Yen kingdom (222–110 B.C.) under the Chou dynasty. The city is again known as Chi under the Han dynasty (200 A.D.) and as Yuchow under the Tang dynasty (7th–10th cent.). It 1st became a great capital, named Yenking, in 920, following its capture by the Khitan Tatars (Liao dynasty). In 1122 it fell to the Golden Horde, and was greatly enlarged as the ⊙ Kin (Chin) dynasty, known as Chungtu. Its greatest period, however, was in the 13th cent., when Kublai Khan moved his capital here (1267) from Karakorum. During the reign of Kublai Khan, the city was called Cambaluc (rendered as Khanbalik by the Mongols) by Marco Polo, who visited here c.1275, and Tatu by the Chinese; it continued as ⊙ China under the Mongol Yüan dynasty until 1368. Under the early Mings, it was briefly replaced by Nanking, but was again chosen capital in 1421 and renamed Peking. It continued as China's capital through the Manchu dynasty (1644–1911) and under the new republic until the govt. was transferred (1928) by the Nationalists to Nanking. Then it was called Peiping, a name it had previously under the early Ming emperors. The Marco Polo Bridge incident at Wanping, 7 mi. SW of Peking, marked the beginning of the Sino-Japanese War (1937–45), during which Peking remained occupied by the Japanese. In 1949, the city fell to the Chinese Communists, who made it once more the ⊙ China under its historical name, formerly also spelled Pekin.
Pekini or **Pekinj,** Albania: see PEQIN.
Peklevskaya, Russian SFSR: see TROITSKI, Sverdlovsk oblast.
Peksha, Russian SFSR: see KOLCHUGINO, Vladimir oblast.
Pektubayevo (pyĕktōōbī'ŭvŭ), village (1939 pop. under 500), N Mari Autonomous SSR, Russian SFSR, on Lesser Kokshaga R. and 33 mi. NE of Ioshkar-Ola; flax.
Pelada, La, Argentina: see LA PELADA.
Pelagatos, Nevado (nävä'dō pälägä'tōs), peak (16,168 ft.) in Ancash dept., W central Peru, in Cordillera Occidental of the Andes, 30 mi. WSW of Buldibuyo (Libertad dept.). Tungsten deposits.
Pelageyevka (pyĕlŭgyä'ŭfkŭ), N suburb (1939 pop. over 2,000) of Chistyakovo, E Stalino oblast, Ukrainian SSR; coal mines.
Pelagie Islands (pĕlä'jē) (□ 10; pop. 3,482), in Mediterranean Sea, bet. Malta and Tunis, 105–135 mi. off SW Sicily, in Agrigento prov. Comprise LAMPEDUSA, LINOSA, and Lampione (uninhabited) isls.; fisheries (sponges, coral, sardines).
Pelagio B. Luna, Argentina: see SAN BLAS.
Pelago (pä'lägô), village (pop. 800), Firenze prov., Tuscany, central Italy, 12 mi. E of Florence; woolen mill.
Pelagonesi or **Pelagonisi** (both: pĕ"lŭgônē'sē), uninhabited Aegean island (□ 8.9), in the Northern Sporades, Magnesia nome, Greece, 40 mi. off Thessalian mainland, 39°20'N 24°4'E; 5 mi. long, 2.5 mi. wide; fisheries. Sometimes called Pelagos; also Kyra Panagia (Kira Panyia) for its N and S capes.
Pelagonija or **Pelagoniya** (both: pĕlägônē'ä), fertile valley in Macedonia, Yugoslavia; extends from Greek border c.25 mi. N, along the Crna Reka; includes Bitolj Plain. Chief town, BITOLJ (Monastir), which gave its name to Monastir Gap, a historic invasion route at S end of the valley.
Pelagos, island, Greece: see PELAGONESI.
Pelagosa, islands, Yugoslavia: see PELAGRUZ ISLANDS.
Pelagruz Islands (pĕ'lägrōōsh), Serbo-Croatian *Pelagruž*, Ital. *Pelagosa* (pĕlägô'zä), group of several small isls. in Adriatic Sea, S Croatia, Yugoslavia, c.90 mi. WSW of Dubrovnik. In Zara prov., Italy (1920–47). Sometimes spelled Pelagruzh.
Pelahatchie (pĕlŭhă'chē), town (pop. 867), Rankin co., central Miss., 23 mi. E of Jackson, in agr. and timber area. Sometimes Pelahatchee.
Pelahustán (päläōōstän'), town (pop. 1,238), Toledo prov., central Spain, 18 mi. NE of Talavera de la Reina; cereals, olives, grapes, livestock.
Pelam, Tibet: see PENAM.
Pelarco (pälär'kō), village (1930 pop. 311), Talca prov., central Chile, 13 mi. ENE of Talca; wheat, barley, wine, livestock.
Pelat, Mont (mō pülä'), highest peak (10,017 ft.) of Provence Alps, in Basses-Alpes dept., SE France, 4 mi. NE of Allos.
Pelaw, England: see FELLING.
Pelczyce (pĕōō-chĭ'tsĕ), Pol. *Pełczyce*, Ger. *Bernstein* (bĕrn'shtīn), town (1939 pop. 2,581; 1946 pop. 1,712) in Brandenburg, after 1945 in Szczecin prov., W Poland, 20 mi. N of Landsberg (Gorzow Wielkopolski); agr. market (grain, potatoes, livestock). After 1945, briefly called Bursztynowo.
Pelechuco (pälächōō'kō), town (pop. c.1,720), La Paz dept., W Bolivia, at N foot of Cololo peak, 50 mi. N of Puerto Acosta and on Pelechuco R. (headwater of Tuichi R.); alt. 11,890 ft.; agr. center for Pelechuco valley.
Peleco (pälā'kō), village (1930 pop. 128), Arauco prov., S central Chile, on L. Lanalhue, on railroad and 25 mi. SE of Lebu; tourist resort; lumbering. Sometimes Puerto Peleco.
Peledui or **Peleduy** (pyĕlyĭdōō'ē), town (1948 pop. over 2,000), SW Yakut Autonomous SSR, Russian SFSR, on Lena R. and 130 mi. NNW of Bodaibo; lumbering, shipbuilding.
Pelée, Île (ēl pülā'), rocky shoal in English Channel, just off Cherbourg, Manche dept., NW France. Fortified in 19th cent., it forms part of the *digue* (breakwater system) protecting the harbor.
Pelée, Mont (mō pülā') [Fr.,=bald mountain], volcano (4,429 ft.), N Martinique, 15 mi. NW of Fort-de-France; 14°48'N 61°10'W. Famed for its destructive eruption on May 8, 1902 (one day after the eruption of SOUFRIÈRE on St. Vincent isl.), when the town of Saint-Pierre at its W foot, then the principal commercial center of the isl., was completely destroyed, and an avalanche of flame and lava killed all but one of its c.28,000 inhabitants and several thousand more in neighboring towns. Minor eruptions occurred in 1792 and 1851. The volcano is sometimes called Mont Pelé or Montagne Pelée.
Pelee Island (pē'lē) (□ 18; pop. 644), S Ont., in L. Erie, 8 mi. SW of Pelee Point and 16 mi. S of Kingsville, near Ohio boundary; 9 mi. long, 4 mi. wide. Winegrowing. Southernmost point of Canada is tiny Middle Isl. (41°41'N), off S coast.
Pelee Point, cape, S Ont., on L. Erie, 12 mi. SSE of Leamington, at S extremity of 10-mi.-long peninsula. Here is Point Pelee Natl. Park. Offshore is Pelee Isl.
Pele La (pä'lä lä'), pass (alt. 11,055 ft.) in Black Mountain Range, central Bhutan, 19 mi. W of Tongsa.
Peleliu (pĕ'lĕlyōō, pĕ"lūlē'ōō), coral island, Palau group, W Caroline Isls., W Pacific, 6 mi. N of Angaur; 6 mi. long, 2 mi. wide. In Second World War, isl. (site of Jap. airfield) was taken (1944) by U.S. marines.
Pelendria (pĕlĕn'drēä), village (pop. 1,504), Limassol dist., central Cyprus, on S slopes of Olympus Mts., 30 mi. SW of Nicosia; wine, olives, almonds; sheep, goats. Sometimes Pelendri.
Peleng (pŭlĕng'), largest island (□ 929; pop. 37,862) of Banggai Archipelago, Indonesia, 12 mi. E of Celebes across Peleng Strait, at NE side of entrance to Gulf of Tolo; 1°25'S 123°10'E; 50 mi. long, 1–32 mi. wide. Deeply indented by 3 deep bays; mountainous, rising to 3,228 ft. Chief products: ebony, resin, rattan, tortoise shell.
Peleng Strait, Indonesia: see TOLO, GULF OF.
Pelequén (pälākĕn'), town (pop. 1,033), O'Higgins prov., central Chile, 22 mi. SSW of Rancagua; rail junction and agr. center (grain, beans, potatoes, wine, cattle); flour milling, dairying, lumbering.
Pèlerin, Mont (pälŭrē'), peak (3,556 ft.) in the Alps, W Switzerland, 2 mi. NNW of Vevey; winter sports.
Pelew, Caroline Isls.: see PALAU.
Pelgrimsrus, U. of So. Afr.: see PILGRIMS REST.
Pelham (pĕ'lŭm). **1** City (pop. 4,365), Mitchell co., SW Ga., 22 mi. NNW of Thomasville; processing and market center for agr. and timber area; mfg. (thread, cottonseed oil, fertilizer, wood products). Settled 1870, inc. 1881. **2** Town (pop. 579), Hampshire co., W central Mass., 12 mi. ENE of Northampton, near Quabbin Reservoir; lumber. **3** Town (pop. 1,317), Hillsboro co., S N.H., 7 mi. E of Nashua. **4** Residential village (pop. 1,843), Westchester co., SE N.Y., just E of Mount Vernon, in New York city metropolitan area. Settled in 17th cent.; inc. 1896.
Pelham Bay Park (c.2,000 acres), SE N.Y., in Bronx borough of New York city; park is in 2 divisions connected by causeway across Eastchester Bay. Includes Rodman's Neck peninsula, Orchard Beach (bathing), Hunter's Isl., and small Twin Isls. Golfing, picnicking; sports stadium.
Pelham Manor, residential village (pop. 5,306), Westchester co., SE N.Y., on N shore of Long Island Sound, just N of the Bronx, in New York city metropolitan area. Settled in mid-17th cent.; inc. 1891.
Pelhrimov (pĕl'hŭrzhĭmôf), Czech *Pelhřimov*, Ger. *Pilgram* (pĭl'gräm), town (pop. 6,191), SE Bohemia, Czechoslovakia, on railroad and 22 mi. NE of Jindrichuv Hradec, in barley- and oat-growing region; mfg. of brooms, brushes, paint brushes, knitwear; distilling.
Pelican City, village (pop. 177), SE Alaska, on W part of Chichagof Isl., on Lisianski Inlet, 38 mi. W of Hoonah; fishing center; sawmill, hydroelectric plant, cannery, cold-storage plant. Established 1939.
Pelican Lake, resort village (pop. c.200), Oneida co., N Wis., on small Pelican L., 15 mi. SE of Rhinelander, in cutover farm area.
Pelican Lake. 1 In Crow Wing co., central Minn., in state forest. 13 mi. N of Brainerd; □ 15; 5.5 mi. long, 4 mi. wide. Fishing resorts. **2** In Grant co.,

W Minn., just W of Christina L., 19 mi. SE of Fergus Falls; 3.5 mi. long, 2.5 mi. wide. **3** In Otter Tail co., W Minn., 9 mi. SSW of Detroit Lakes city; 5 mi. long, 2 mi. wide. Resorts. Drains into Pelican R. **4** In St. Louis co., NE Minn., in state forest c.40 mi. N of Hibbing; □ 19; 7 mi. long, max. width 5.5 mi. Includes small bay in SE and several small islands. Drains into affluent of Vermilion R. Orr village is on E shore. **5** In Codington co., E S.Dak., near Watertown; 5 mi. long, 1 mi. wide.

Pelican Lakes, village (pop. 154), Crow Wing co., central Minn., on Pelican L. and 17 mi. N of Brainerd; grain, potatoes.

Pelican Point, cape, Walvis Bay enclave, W South-West Africa, on the Atlantic, N extremity of promontory (6 mi. long) sheltering W side of Walvis Bay, 7 mi. NW of Walvis Bay town; 22°53'S 14°26'E; lighthouse.

Pelican Rapids, resort village (pop. 1,676), Otter Tail co., W Minn., on Pelican R. and 19 mi. N of Fergus Falls, in lake region; trade center and shipping point for grain and livestock; dairy products, poultry. Inc. 1882. "Minnesota man," human skeleton believed to be prehistoric, was found near by in 1932.

Pelican River, rises in lake region near Detroit Lakes city, W Minn., flows 60 mi. S, past Pelican Rapids, to Otter Tail R. just W of Fergus Falls. Drains Pelican L. and L. Lizzie.

Peligros (pālē'grōs), NW suburb (pop. 1,669) of Granada, Granada prov., S Spain; liqueur mfg.; olive oil, wine, sugar beets.

Pelileo (pālĕlā'ō), town (1950 pop. 2,299), Tungurahua prov., Ecuador, in the Andes, on railroad spur, and 10 mi. SSE of Ambato; agr. center (sugar cane, wheat, barley, corn, potatoes); *aguardiente* distilling. Leveled by 1949 earthquake, with heavy loss of life. Obsidian deposits near by.

Pelion or **Pilion** (pē'lēōn, Gr. pē'lēōn), range on Magnesia peninsula, SE Thessaly, Greece, bet. Aegean Sea and Gulf of Volos; rises to 5,252 ft. in the Pliassidi, 8 mi. NE of Volos. In Gr. legend, the home of Chiron, the centaur; the Aloadae were the giants that tried to pile Pelion on Ossa. Under Turkish rule, 24 villages on its slopes formed a semi-independent league.

Pelion (pē'lēŭn), town (pop. 196), Lexington co., central S.C., 20 mi. SSW of Columbia. Food products.

Pelister, peak, Yugoslavia: see PERISTER.

Peliyagoda (pălĭyŭgō'dŭ), town (pop. 3,711), Western Prov., Ceylon, on the Kelani Ganga and 3 mi. NE of Colombo city center; vegetables, rice. Administered by urban council (pop. 12,419) jointly with WATTALA (1.5 mi. N), Mabole (3 mi. N).

Peljesac (pĕ'lyĕshäts), Serbo-Croatian *Pelješac*, Ital. *Sabbioncello* (säb-bēōnchĕl'lō), peninsula, S Croatia, Yugoslavia, in Dalmatia; extends c.30 mi. W into Adriatic Sea, bet. Korcula and Hvar isls. Ston and Orebic are chief villages. Sometimes spelled Pelyeshats.

Pella (pĕ'lŭ), nome (□ 1,082; pop. 120,850), Macedonia, Greece; ⊙ Edessa. Bounded N by Yugoslavia along the Voras massif, it is largely mountainous and includes Ardea (N) and Giannitsa (SE) lowlands. Agr.: cotton, wheat, tobacco, silk, wine, fruit (cherries). Industry is centered on Edessa, served by Salonika-Phlorina RR. Named for anc. Macedonian ⊙ of Pella.

Pella, anc. city of Greek Macedonia, 6 mi. ESE of modern Giannitsa. Became ⊙ Macedonian empire under Philip II (359–336 B.C.) and declined after Roman conquest (168 B.C.). Alexander the Great b. here, 356 B.C. Near by is modern Gr. village of Pella (pop. 1,673).

Pella, anc. town of Gilead, Palestine, just E of the Jordan, 18 mi. S of Sea of Galilee. One of the Decapolis.

Pella, city (pop. 4,427), Marion co., S central Iowa, 38 mi. ESE of Des Moines; mfg. and trade center; tomato cannery, overall factory; Venetian blinds, screens, hybrid seed corn, foundry and wood products. Ships coal and livestock. Central Col. is here. Settled by Dutch in 1847; inc. 1855.

Pellaro, Cape (pĕl'lärō), on toe of Italy, at SW end of Strait of Messina, 6 mi. S of Reggio di Calabria; 38°1'N 15°39'E. Site of Pellaro (pop. 869).

Pell City, town (pop. 1,189), ⊙ St. Clair co., NE central Ala., 29 mi. ENE of Birmingham; textiles, lumber.

Pellecchia, Monte (môn'tĕ pĕl-lĕk'kyä), highest peak (4,488 ft.) in Sabine Mts., central Italy, 25 mi. NE of Rome.

Pellegrini, department, Argentina: see NUEVA ESPERANZA.

Pellegrini (pĕlāgrē'nē), town (pop. 2,247), ⊙ Pellegrini dist. (□ 1,491; pop. 18,919), W Buenos Aires prov., Argentina, near La Pampa natl. territory line, 80 mi. SW of Pehuajó, in agr. region (wheat, corn, cattle, hogs).

Pellegrini, Lake (□ 10), N Río Negro natl. territory, Argentina, N of Neuquén; c.6 mi. long, 3 mi. wide. Originally a depression, it has been made a lake through irrigation scheme in lower Neuquén R. valley.

Pellegrue (pĕlgrü'), village (pop. 334), Gironde dept., SW France, in Entre-deux-Mers, 17 mi. NNW of Marmande; wheat, wine.

Pellerin, Le (lŭ pĕlŭrĕ'), village (pop. 1,675), Loire-Inférieure dept., W France, on Loire R. and 9 mi. W of Nantes; truck, livestock.

Pellestrina (pĕl-lĕstrē'nä), town (pop. 3,676), Venezia prov., Veneto, N Italy, on isl. in isl. chain separating Lagoon of Venice from the Adriatic, 3 mi. N of Chioggia; sea bathing, fishing; lacemaking. Has mus. with collection of laces.

Pellezzano (pĕl-lĕtsä'nō), village (pop. 980), Salerno prov., Campania, S Italy, 3 mi. N of Salerno; cotton and woolen mills, tannery.

Pellston, village (pop. 442), Emmet co., NW Mich., on small Maple R. and 15 mi. NE of Petoskey; lumber mill.

Pelluhue (pĕyōō'wā), village (1930 pop. 127), Maule prov., S central Chile, on the Pacific coast, 21 mi. NW of Cauquenes; popular seaside resort.

Pellworm (pĕl'vôrm), North Sea island (□ 14; pop. 2,556) of North Frisian group, NW Germany, in Hallig Isls., 10 mi. off Schleswig-Holstein coast; 4 mi. wide (E-W), c.5 mi. long (N-S). Grazing. It is remainder of larger isl., which was partly flooded in 1634.

Pelly, village (pop. 358), E Sask., near Man. border, 20 mi. N of Kamsack; mixed farming.

Pelly, former city, Harris co., S Texas; now a part of BAYTOWN.

Pelly, Lake (□ 331), NW Keewatin Dist. and NE Mackenzie Dist., Northwest Territories, just W of L. Garry; 66°N 102°W; 60 mi. long, 2–23 mi. wide. Drained E by Back R.

Pelly Bay, R.C. mission station, N Keewatin Dist., Northwest Territories, at head of Pelly Bay, inlet (75 mi. long, 10–40 mi. wide) of the Gulf of Boothia; 68°24'N 89°12'W.

Pelly Mountains, S Yukon, N range of Rocky Mts., extends c.200 mi. NW-SE bet. upper course of Liard R., near B.C. border NW of Watson Lake, and Pelly R. valley. Rises to c.9,500 ft. (NW).

Pelly River, S central Yukon, rises in Mackenzie Mts. near 62°10'N 129°25'W, flows generally WNW, past Ross River, to confluence with Lewes R. (upper course of the Yukon) at Fort Selkirk, forming Yukon R. proper; 330 mi. long. Receives Ross and Macmillan rivers. Discovered 1840 by Robert Campbell.

Pelmadulla (pĕlmŭdōōl'lŭ), village, Sabaragamuwa Prov., S central Ceylon, 11 mi. ESE of Ratnapura; precious and semi-precious stone-mining center (including ruby, sapphire, aquamarine, topaz).

Pelmonostor, Yugoslavia: see BELI MANASTIR.

Peloche (pālō'chā), village (pop. 636), Badajoz prov., W Spain, 4 mi. NW of Herrera del Duque; cereals, cork, honey, livestock.

Peloncillo Mountains (pĕlŭnsĭ'lō), in Graham and Greenlee counties, SE Ariz., S of Clifton; rise to c.6,000 ft. in N.

Peloponnesus (pĕ"lŭpŭnē'sŭs), Gr. *Peloponnesos* or *Peloponnisos* (both: pĕlôpô'nĭsôs) S peninsula (□ 8,400; pop. 1,200,000) of Greece, bet. Ionian Sea (W) and Aegean Sea (E), separated from central Greece by gulfs of Patras and Corinth and the Saronic Gulf, and linked to it by Isthmus of Corinth; it is roughly 140 mi. N-S and E-W. Mainly mountainous, it includes Taygetus, Parnon, Kyllene, Aroania, and Erymanthos mts., and is drained by Eurotas and Alpheus rivers. Deeply indented S and E coasts terminate in capes Akritas, Matapan, Malea, and Skyllaion, separated by gulfs of Messenia, Laconia, and Argolis. Main offshore isls. are Hydra, Spetsai, Dokos, and Elaphonesos. Mediterranean climate with rainfall decreasing W to E. Politically, the Peloponnesus is divided into 6 nomes: ARGOLIS AND CORINTHIA, ARCADIA, ACHAEA, ELIS, LACONIA, MESSENIA. Agr. (NW, W, S) produces Zante currants, dried and citrus fruits, tobacco, olives, wine. Sericulture (SW). Livestock raising (sheep, goats) in center and E. Fisheries along coast. Deposits of pyrite, manganese, lignite. Industries at Patras and Kalamata (main ports), Tripolis, and Pyrgos. Other important centers are Sparta, Argos, Nauplia, and Corinth. Tourist trade. Original pop. of Leleges and Pelasgians (said to have been the builders of MYCENAE and TIRYNS), was displaced and absorbed by the Ionians and Achaeans (c.1300 B.C.) and by Dorians (c.1100 B.C.). City-states of Sparta, Argos, Elis flourished 8th–5th cent. B.C. With exception of Achaea and Argolis, the Peloponnesus participated in Persian Wars (500–449 B.C.). Sparta defeated Athens in Peloponnesian War (431–404 B.C.). Divided in Achaean and Aetolian leagues (3d cent. B.C.), the Peloponnesus later came largely under Macedonian rule. It was conquered (146 B.C.) by Romans and became part of Roman prov. of Achaea, later in Byzantine Empire. Following Slav inroads (6th–8th cent.), the peninsula (except Venetian-ruled Methone, Korone, and other ports) was occupied (13th cent.) by French Crusaders and divided into several feudal states. Annexed (1460) by Turkey, it remained under Turkish rule until Gr. war of independence (1821–28), except for brief Venetian occupation (1699–1718). Formerly known as Morea (mŭrē'ŭ); also Peloponnese.

Peloris, Sicily: see FARO, PUNTA DEL.

Peloritani Mountains (pĕlôrĕtä'nē), anc. *Pelorus* and *Neptunius*, NE Sicily, range extending 30 mi. NE from Nebrodi Mts. to Punta del Faro; rise to 4,219 ft. in Pizzo di Polo.

Peloro, Cape, Sicily: see FARO, PUNTA DEL.

Pelorum, Sicily: see FARO, PUNTA DEL.

Pelorus Sound (pŭlô'rŭs), inlet of Cook Strait, NE S.Isl., New Zealand; 20 mi. long; broken into many small bays.

Pelotas (pĭlō'tŭs), city (1950 pop. 79,649), SE Rio Grande do Sul, Brazil, seaport on São Gonçalo Canal near its entrance into the Lagoa dos PATOS, and 135 mi. SSW of Pôrto Alegre, of which it is an outport. Commercial center and Brazil's largest producer of jerked beef. Has large meat-packing and -canning plants, flour mills, tanneries, and animal by-product industries (lard, soap, candles); mfg. of footwear and furniture. Exports meat products, hides, wool, rice, dairy produce, and timber. Linked by rail with Rio Grande (20 mi. SSE), with cattle-raising interior, and with Uruguay (via Jaguarão). Transfer point for shipping on Lagoa dos Patos and Mirim L. Airfield. Has Jesuit col., veterinary and agr. schools.; also schools of law, pharmacy, dentistry, and commerce; and agr. experiment station. Founded 1789.

Pelotas River, chief headstream of Uruguay R. in S Brazil, rises onW slope of the Serra do Mar W of Urussanga (Santa Catarina), flows c.200 mi. NW, forming Santa Catarina–Rio Grande do Sul border; after receiving the Canoas and Peixe rivers, it becomes the Uruguay near Marcelino Ramos.

Pelplin (pĕl'plēn), town (1946 pop. 4,210), Gdansk prov., N Poland, on Wierzyca R., on railroad and 8 mi. ESE of Starogard; mfg. of furniture, mineral water; sugar, and flour milling. Seat of bishop of Chelmno; cathedral.

Pelsart Islands (pĕl'sŭrt), in Indian Ocean, one of coral groups of HOUTMAN ABROLHOS, 36 mi. off W coast of Western Australia. Consist of Pelsart Isl. (largest; 6 mi. long), Middle Isl., several smaller islets and reefs surrounding a lagoon; mangrove forests. Tourist resort.

Pelto, Lake, lagoon (c.12 mi. long E-W, 5 mi. wide) in Terrebonne parish, S La., lying bet. marshy coast and Isles Dernieres (S); underwater oil wells in E part. Connected by passages to Caillou Bay (W), Terrebonne Bay (E).

Peltosalmi (pĕl'tōsäl"mē), village in Iisalmi rural commune (pop. 13,922), Kuopio co., S central Finland, in lake region, 3 mi. SE of Iisalmi; site of agr. col.

Pelusium (pĭlōō'shēŭm), anc. city of Egypt, in NW Sinai, on easternmost branch of the Nile (long since silted up) and c.20 mi. SE of Port Said, 3 mi. from the coast. Here supposedly Sennacherib's Assyrians were struck by a pestilence, and Cambyses' Persians overthrew Psamtik II (525 B.C.). Ptolemy reputedly b. here. The present ruins date from Roman period. Mentioned in Bible as Sin. The Pelusiac branch of the Nile emptied into the Mediterranean at the bay, just N, called Bay of Pelusium or Tina Bay. Avaris, ⊙ Hyksos dynasty, is sometimes identified with Pelusium.

Pélussin (pālüsĕ'), village (pop. 1,544), Loire dept., SE central France, on NE slope of Mont Pilat, 14 mi. E of Saint-Étienne; silk milling, cabinetmaking.

Pelvoux, Massif du (mäsēf dü pĕlvōō'), largest mtn. group of Dauphiné Alps, in Isère and Hautes-Alpes depts., SE France, bounded by Oisans valley (N), the Guisane and upper Durance R. valley (E), the Champsaur (S and SW). Almost circular formation, with a diameter of 25 mi., culminating in glacier-covered crest. Highest peaks: Barre des Écrins (13,461 ft.), Meije (13,081 ft.), and Mont Pelvoux (12,920 ft.). Alpinism.

Pelvoux, Mont, peak (12,920 ft.) of the Massif du Pelvoux, Dauphiné Alps, SE France, in Hautes-Alpes dept., 12 mi. W of Briançon and 3 mi. ESE of the Barre des Écrins; glacier.

Pelyeshats, peninsula, Yugoslavia: see PELJESAC.

Pelzer, village (pop. 2,692), Anderson co., NW S.C., on Saluda R. and 15 mi. S of Greenville, in agr. area; contiguous with inc. town of West Pelzer (pop. 578). Textile mill.

Pemadumcook Lake (pĕ"mŭdŭm'kŏŏk), in Piscataquis and Penobscot counties, central Maine, 8 mi. WNW of Millinocket; c.13 mi. long. West Branch of Penobscot R. flows through.

Pemalang (pŭmŭläng'), town (pop. 29,249), central Java, Indonesia, near Java Sea, 60 mi. E of Cheribon; trade center for agr. area (sugar, rice, tobacco, peanuts). Also spelled Pamalang.

Pemangkat, Indonesia: see PAMANGKAT.

Pemaquid (pĕ'mŭkwĭd), peninsula, Lincoln co., S Maine, 16 mi. E of Bath; site of town of BRISTOL. Gives name to fishing and resort villages of **Pemaquid** and **Pemaquid Beach; Pemaquid Harbor, Pemaquid Neck, Pemaquid Point** (lighthouse here built 1827), and **Pemaquid Pond,** lake (5.5 mi. long) near Bremen.

Pemar, Finland: see PAIMIO.

Pematangsiantar (pŭmŭtäng"syäntär'), town (pop. 15,328), N Sumatra, Indonesia, 50 mi. SE of Medan, in Deli region; terminus of railroad from Medan; trade center for agr. area (rubber, tobacco, tea, fiber, palm oil, rice). Town's rapid development dates from 1900.

Pemayangtse, India: see NAMCHI.

Pemba (pĕm'bä), coral island (□ 380, including offshore islets; pop. 114,859), in Indian Ocean, off E coast of Africa, 30 mi. NNE of Zanzibar isl., facing Tanganyika across Pemba Channel (40 mi. wide); 5°S 39°45'E; 42 mi. long, 14 mi. wide. It is part of the Br. protectorate of Zanzibar. Has tropical monsoon climate; annual rainfall, 73 in.; mean high and low temperatures are 86.3°F. and 76.1°F. World's leading clove-growing area, outproducing near-by Zanzibar. Also produces copra; livestock raising. Chief towns are Wete, Chake Chake, Mkoani. Isl. has ruins of Persian origin (10th–16th cent.). Notorious slave-trading center until end of 19th cent. Noted for its bullfights.

Pemba, township (pop. 189), Southern Prov., Northern Rhodesia, on railroad and 55 mi. SW of Mazabuka; corn-growing center.

Pemba Bay, sheltered inlet of Mozambique Channel, on NE coast of Mozambique (13°S); Pôrto Amélia is on S shore.

Pemberton, town (pop. 1,042), SW Western Australia, 170 mi. S of Perth; sawmills; karri eucalyptus forests, tobacco.

Pemberton, England: see WIGAN.

Pemberton. 1 Village (pop. 152), Blue Earth co., S Minn., 15 mi. SE of Mankato, near Le Sueur R.; dairying. **2** Borough (pop. 1,194), Burlington co., central N.J., on Rancocas Creek and 6 mi. E of Mt. Holly; textiles; poultry, wheat, dairy products. Settled by Quakers before 1690.

Pemberville, village (pop. 1,099), Wood co., NW Ohio, 10 mi. ENE of Bowling Green and on Portage R.; grain, food products. Settled 1834, inc. 1876.

Pembina (pĕm'bĭnŭ), county (□ 1,124; pop. 13,990), extreme NE N.Dak.; ⊙ Cavalier. Agr. area drained by Tongue and Pembina rivers; bounded E by Red River of the North and N by Canada. Flour milling, farming; grain, livestock, dairy products, potatoes. Earliest settled co. of N.Dak. Formed 1867.

Pembina, city (pop. 640), Pembina co., extreme NE N.Dak., 22 mi. NE of Cavalier and on Red River of the North, at mouth of Pembina R. Dairy produce, livestock, grain, poultry. Port of entry. Oldest town in N.Dak.; lowest point (750 ft.) in state. Settled 1819, inc. 1885.

Pembina Mountains (pĕm'bĭnŭ), range, S Man., extends c.60 mi. NW-SE bet. Assiniboine R. and N.Dak. border; rises to c.2,000 ft.

Pembina River, Alta., rises in Rocky Mts. on E edge of Jasper Natl. Park, flows 350 mi. in a winding course generally NE to Athabaska R. 40 mi. W of Athabaska.

Pembina River, in N.Dak. and Canada, rises in Turtle Mts. of N N.Dak. and in Drift Prairie of S Manitoba; flows NE, then SE, into N.Dak., near Walhalla, then E to Pembina and Red River of the North; c.275 mi. long.

Pembrey (pĕmbrā'), town and parish (pop. 6,104), S Carmarthen, Wales, near Carmarthen Bay of Bristol Channel at mouth of Loughor R. estuary just W of Burry Port; copper smelting.

Pembridge, town and parish (pop. 954), NW Hereford, England, on Arrow R. and 14 mi. NNW of Hereford; agr. market known for its breed of Hereford cattle. Has 14th-cent. church.

Pembroke, parish (1939 pop. 11,851), central Bermuda. Hamilton is on S shore.

Pembroke (pĕm'brōk), town (pop. 11,159), ⊙ Renfrew co., SE Ont., on Ottawa R. (where it widens to form L. Allumette) and 75 mi. WNW of Ottawa; pulp, paper, wool, lumber, and flour milling, tanning, dairying; mfg. of shoes, gloves, tools. Gateway to Algonquin Provincial Park.

Pembroke (pĕm'brŏŏk), Gaelic *Cill Fionntan,* SE suburb (pop. c.35,000) of Dublin, Co. Dublin, Ireland. Includes DONNYBROOK.

Pembroke (pĕm'brōk). **1** City (pop. 1,171), ⊙ Bryan co., SE Ga., 31 mi. W of Savannah, near Canoochee R., in agr. and timber area; sawmilling. **2** Town (pop. 532), Christian co., SW Ky., 9 mi. SE of Hopkinsville. **3** Town (pop. 998), Washington co., E Maine, 16 mi. S of Calais, near Eastport, on an inlet of Cobscook Bay; packs sardines, blueberries. Settled 1770, inc. 1832. **4** Town (pop. 2,579), Plymouth co., E Mass., on North R. and 23 mi. SE of Boston; resort. Settled 1650, set off from Duxbury 1712. **5** Town (pop. 3,094), Merrimack co., S N.H., SE suburb of Concord; granted 1727 as Suncook, inc. 1759 as Pembroke. Includes Suncook village, mfg. center (textiles, wood products) on the Merrimack, at mouth of Suncook R. **6** Town (pop. 1,212), Robeson co., S N.C., 11 mi. WNW of Lumberton, in agr. area; sawmilling. Seat of Pembroke State Col. **7** Town (pop. 1,010), Giles co., SW Va., in the Alleghenies, on New R. and 40 mi. W of Roanoke, in agr., timber, resort area. Mountain Lake village is 6 mi. ENE.

Pembroke or **Pembrokeshire** (pĕm'brŏŏk, –shĭr), county (□ 614; 1931 pop. 87,206; 1951 census 90,896), SW Wales, on the Irish Sea and the Bristol Channel; ⊙ Pembroke. Bounded by Cardigan (NE) and Carmarthen (E). Has rugged coast line with several indentations (Milford Haven, St. Brides Bay, Fishguard Bay); hilly terrain with fertile valleys, rising in E to Mynydd Prescelly (1,760 ft.). Drained by Teifi R. and minor tributaries of Milford Haven. There is some coal mining, but main industries are agr., fishing, woolen milling. Besides Pembroke, main towns are Milford Haven, Fishguard (port), Tenby, Narberth, Haverfordwest, Neyland, Goodwick. St. David's has notable cathedral; there are many remains of anc. forts and megalithic monuments. Co. is much frequented by tourists. It was settled by Flemings in 12th cent., who introduced woolen industry.

Pembroke, Welsh *Penbroch* (pĕnbrōkh'), municipal borough (1931 pop. 12,009; 1951 census 12,296), ⊙ Pembrokeshire, Wales, in S part of co., on short Pembroke R. and 42 mi. W of Swansea; agr. market. Pembroke Castle (dating from 1090), on a ridge, has subterranean passage (the *Wogan*) to the harbor. In 1648 castle was taken by Cromwell. There are remains of Monkton Priory, founded 1098, and of 13th-cent. town walls; church was rebuilt in 14th cent. Henry VII b. here. On Milford Haven, 2 mi. NW, is port of Pembroke Dock (51°42'N 4°56'W), formerly called Pater; dockyard was established 1814, closed down in 1926, and turned over to Royal Air Force as coastal station in 1930.

Pembroke, Cape, NE extremity of Coats Isl., E Keewatin Dist., Northwest Territories, on Hudson Bay; 62°55'N 81°54'W.

Pembroke Dock, Wales: see PEMBROKE, municipal borough.

Pembroke Peak, New Zealand: see MILFORD SOUND.

Pembrokeshire, Wales: see PEMBROKE, county.

Pembury, town and parish (pop. 2,277), SW Kent, England, 3 mi. E of Tunbridge Wells; agr. market. Has church with Norman tower.

Pemigewasset River (pĕmĭjuwä'sĭt), central N.H., rises in Franconia Notch, flows c.70 mi. generally S to Franklin, here joining Winnipesaukee R. to form Merrimack R. Its East Branch (16 mi. long) joins the Pemigewasset near North Woodstock. On main stream N of Franklin is Franklin Falls Dam (136 ft. high, 1,740 ft. long; for flood control), completed 1943.

Pemiongchi, India: see NAMCHI.

Pemiscot (pĕ'mĭskŏt, –skō), county (□ 488; pop. 45,624), extreme SE Mo.; ⊙ Caruthersville. On Mississippi R. (levees); drainage canals. Agr. (corn, wheat, oats, hay), dairying; grows and processes cotton; gum, oak timber. Formed 1861.

Pemuco (pāmōō'kō), town (pop. 1,703), Ñuble prov., S central Chile, on railroad and 25 mi. S of Chillán; agr. center (wheat, corn, wine, potatoes, livestock); flour milling, dairying, lumbering.

Pen (pān), town (pop. 7,317), Kolaba dist., W Bombay, India, 22 mi. SE of Bombay, in the Konkan; agr. market center (chiefly rice); saltworks; cutlery mfg., rice milling. Also spelled Pan.

Peña (pā'nyä), town (1950 pop. 1,687), Santiago prov., N Dominican Republic, in fertile Cibao valley, on railroad and 5 mi. NE of Santiago; tobacco growing. Formerly Tamboril.

Peña, La, Panama: see LA PEÑA.

Peña, La (lä pā'nyä), village (pop. 1,255), Oviedo prov., NW Spain, 8 mi. SSE of Oviedo; coal and iron mines.

Peña Blanca (pā'nyä bläng'kä). **1** Village (1930 pop. 27), Atacama prov., N Chile, minor Pacific port, 20 mi. SW of Huasco; 28°44'S. **2** Town (pop. 2,480), Valparaiso prov., central Chile, on railroad and 15 mi. E of Valparaiso; agr. center (grain, fruit, vegetables, cattle); lumbering.

Peña Blanca, village, Rivas dept., SW Nicaragua, on Inter-American Highway, 23 mi. SE of Rivas; customs station on Costa Rica border.

Peña Blanca, peak (4,920 ft.) in Cordillera Isabelia, W central Nicaragua, 24 mi. ENE of Jinotega.

Peña Blanca, village (pop. 327), Los Santos prov., S central Panama, in Pacific lowland, 4 mi. SSW of Las Tablas; sugar cane, livestock.

Penablanca or **Pena Blanca** (pä"nyŭblŏng'kŭ), village (pop. c.500), Sandoval co., N central N.Mex., on Rio Grande, in Cochiti Pueblo land grant, and 24 mi. WSW of Santa Fe; alt. c.5,100 ft.; grain. Cochiti Pueblo Indian village 2 mi. N, part of Bandelier Natl. Monument 9 mi. N. Settled by Spaniards in early 17th cent.

Peña Blanca, Cerros (sĕ'rōs pā'nyä bläng'kä), Andean massif (19,750 ft.) in Atacama prov., N Chile, near Argentina border; 26°49'S.

Peña-Castillo (–kästē'lyō), suburb (pop. 7,230) of Santander, N Spain; liqueur and candy mfg.

Penacook (pĕ'nŭkŏŏk), village, Merrimack co., S central N.H., at junction of Contoocook and Merrimack rivers, partly in Concord and Boscawen. Produces electrical instruments, textiles, flour, mica and leather products, briar pipes. Monument on isl. in the Merrimack commemorates Hannah Dustin's escape from Indian captors, 1697.

Penacova (pĭnŭkô'vŭ), town (pop. 624), Coimbra dist., N central Portugal, on the Mondego and 9 mi. ENE of Coimbra; resort amidst steep forested hills; mfg. (toothpicks, matches).

Penafiel (pĭnŭfyĕl'), town (pop. 3,992), Pôrto dist., N Portugal, on railroad and 18 mi. E of Oporto; shoe mfg., textile dyeing, dairying, wine making.

Peñafiel (pānyäfyĕl'), town (pop. 4,216), Valladolid prov., N central Spain, on the Duero (Douro) and 32 mi. ESE of Valladolid; brandy distilling, woolen-cloth mfg., tanning, cheese processing, flour milling. Agr. trade (cereals, wine, fruit; lumber). Dominated by 15th-cent. fort on hill.

Peñaflor (pānyäflôr'), town (pop. 4,957), Santiago prov., central Chile, on railroad and 15 mi. SW of Santiago; resort in agr. area (alfalfa, grain, fruit, wine, livestock).

Peñaflor. 1 Village (pop. 1,274), Saragossa prov., NE Spain, near Gállego R., 8 mi. NNE of Saragossa; flour milling; cereals. **2** Town (pop. 3,373), Seville prov., SW Spain, on the Guadalquivir (rapids), on railroad and 40 mi. NE of Seville; cereals, peas, olives, livestock. Fishing; sawmilling, olive-oil pressing. Has fine church.

Penaga (pŭnä'gä), village, Prov. Wellesley, Penang, NW Malaya, on N Penang Channel, 8 mi. N of Butterworth; major radio transmitting station. Formerly spelled Penanga.

Penal (pä'näl, pä'nyäl), village (pop. 1,204), SW Trinidad, B.W.I., on railroad and 7 mi. S of San Fernando; petroleum wells. Sometimes spelled Peñal.

Peñalara (pānyälä'rä), highest peak (7,972 ft.) of the Sierra de Guadarrama, in Castile, central Spain, on Madrid-Segovia prov. border, 11 mi. ESE of Segovia. Near its top is a megalithic monument. The Navacerrada Pass, on old Madrid-Segovia road, is at its S foot.

Penalosa (pĕnŭlō'sŭ), city (pop. 71), Kingman co., S Kansas, 12 mi. WNW of Kingman; wheat.

Peñalsordo (pānyälsôr'dhō), town (pop. 4,449), Badajoz prov., W Spain, 38 mi. ESE of Villanueva de la Serena; olives, cereals, sheep; lumbering; flour milling.

Penalva (pĭnäl'vŭ), city (pop. 2,228), N central Maranhão, Brazil, 70 mi. SW of São Luís, in rice, cotton, and sugar dist.

Penalva do Castelo, Portugal: see CASTENDO.

Penam (pĕ'näm) or **Pelam** (pĕ'läm), Chinese *Pa-lang* (bä'läng), town [Tibetan *dzong*], S Tibet, on route to Gyangtse and 20 mi. SE of Shigatse, and on the Nyang Chu.

Penamacor (pĭnŭmŭkôr'), town (pop. 2,818), Castelo Branco dist., central Portugal, 29 mi. NE of Castelo Branco, near Sp. border; mfg. of textiles, soap, ceramics; woodworking. Has remains of 12th-cent. fortress.

Peñamiller (pānyämēyĕr'), town (pop. 120), Querétaro, central Mexico, 13 mi. NE of Tolimán; alt. 4,468 ft.; antimony mining; cereals, fruit.

Peña Negra Pass (pä'nyä nä'grä) (14,100 ft.), in the Andes, on Argentina-Chile border, on road bet. San Juan (Argentina) and Coquimbo (Chile); 28°12'S 69°28'W.

Peña Nevada (nävä'dä), peak (11,955 ft.) of Sierra Madre Oriental, N Mexico, on Nuevo León–Tamaulipas border, 45 mi. W of Ciudad Victoria.

Penang (pĕnăng'), settlement (pop. 292), N Viti Levu, Fiji, SW Pacific, 55 mi. NNW of Suva; sugar mill.

Penang (pŭnăng', pē–, pĕ'–, –näng) [Malay *Pinang,*=betel nut], island section (□ 110, including small adjacent isls.; pop. 262,705) of Penang settlement, NW Malaya, in Strait of Malacca off PROVINCE WELLESLEY (separated by Penang Channel); ⊙ George Town (Penang municipality) on NE coast. Largely covered with wooded hills rising to 2,722 ft. in Western Hill, it is 15 mi. long and 9 mi. wide; has extensive rice, rubber, coconut, and fruit plantations; fisheries at Tanjong Tokong and Telok Kumbar. Next to George Town, its largest center is Ayer Itam. Airport at Bayan Lepas. Pop. is 70% Chinese, 18% Malay, 12% Indian. Formerly called Prince of Wales Isl., it was ceded 1786 by Kedah and is oldest Br. settlement of Malay Peninsula. With the mainland strip known as Prov. Wellesley, it constitutes the **Settlement of Penang** (□400; pop. 446,321; including transients, 447,707; ⊙ George Town), originally (1806–26) a presidency of East India Company, later one of the Straits Settlements, and since 1946 a member of the Federation of Malaya. The DINDINGS (with Pangkor and Sembilan isls.) formed part of Penang settlement (1826, 1874–1935).

Penang, municipality, Malaya: see GEORGE TOWN.

Penanga, Malaya: see PENAGA.

Penang Channel, arm of Strait of Malacca, separating Penang isl. and Prov. Wellesley on Malay Peninsula; 2–10 mi. wide. Penang harbor, at channel's narrowest point bet. George Town and Butterworth-Prai (ferry services), is leading anchorage of Federation of Malaya.

Penang Hill, hilly residential section of Penang isl., NW Malaya, 4 mi. W of George Town, on NE slope of Government Hill (2,423 ft.); health resort; bungalows, hotel. Reached by 1-mi.-long cable railway.

Peñaparda (pānyäpär'dhä), town (pop. 1,815), Salamanca prov., W Spain, 20 mi. SSW of Ciudad Rodrigo; rye, potatoes, flax, lumber.

Peñaplata (pānyäplä'tä), chief town (1939 pop. 2,198) of Samal Isl., Davao prov., Philippines, just off Davao, Mindanao; abacá, coconuts.

Penápolis (pĭnä'pŏŏlēs), city (pop. 6,428), NW São Paulo, Brazil, on railroad and 27 mi. NW of Lins, in coffee zone; agr.-processing center (coffee, cotton, grain, fruit); dairying, manioc-flour milling, distilling, tanning. Airfield. Avanhandava hydroelectric plant 16 mi. NNE. Formerly Pennapolis.

Peñaranda (pānyärän'dä), town (1939 pop. 3,873; 1948 municipality pop. 9,623), Nueva Ecija prov., central Luzon, Philippines, 6 mi. SE of Cabanatuan; rice-growing center.

Peñaranda de Bracamonte (dhā bräkämōn'tä), city (pop. 4,652), Salamanca prov., W Spain, 25 mi. ESE of Salamanca; mfg. of cotton and woolen cloth, sandals, furniture, wax; tanning, meat processing. Cereals, vegetables in area.

Peñaranda de Duero (dhwā'rō), town (pop. 1,417), Burgos prov., N Spain, on affluent of the Douro (Duero) and 11 mi. E of Aranda de Duero; cereals, vegetables, grapes, sheep.

Pen Argyl (pĕn" är'jĭl), borough (pop. 3,878), Northampton co., E Pa., 12 mi. NNW of Easton; slate quarries; textiles. Founded 1868, inc. 1882.

Peñarroya-Pueblonuevo (pānyäroi'ä-pwĕ"blōnwā'vō), city (pop. 19,105), Córdoba prov., S Spain, in Andalusia, railroad junction in the Sierra Morena, near Guadiato R., 34 mi. NW of Córdoba; center of rich mining dist. (anthracite, bituminous coal, lignite, silver-bearing lead). Metal foundries (lead and silver, iron, zinc), chemical works (fertilizers, soap), paper mill. Burlap mfg., sawmilling, cheese processing. Near by is dist. of Peñarroya (pop. 7,330).

Peñarrubia (pānyäroo'vyä), town (pop. 1,502), Málaga prov., S Spain, on affluent of the Guadalhorce and 24 mi. NE of Ronda; cereals, olives.

Penarth (pĕnärth'), urban district (1931 pop. 17,719; 1951 census 18,528), SE Glamorgan, Wales, port on Bristol Channel at mouth of Taff R., 4 mi. SSW of Cardiff; 51°26'N 3°10'W; exports coal; imports pit props, wood pulp, iron ore. Also residential town and bathing resort.

Peñas (pā'nyäs), town (pop. c.5,300), La Paz dept., W Bolivia, in the Altiplano, 27 mi. NW of La Paz; potatoes, barley, sheep.

Peñas, Cape, on E coast of main isl. of Tierra del Fuego, Argentina, 9 mi. SE of Río Grande; 53°51'S 67°33'W.

Peñas, Cape, on Bay of Biscay, in Oviedo prov., NW Spain, 12 mi. NW of Gijón; 43°39'N 5°52'W.

Peñas, Gulf of, inlet on coast of Aysén prov., S Chile, bet. Taitao Peninsula (N) and Guayaneco Isls. (S), S of 47°S; 50 mi. long, c.40 mi. wide.

Peñas, Las, Argentina: see LAS PEÑAS.

Peñas, Las, Mexico: see PUERTO VALLARTA.

Penasco (pĭnă'skō), village (1940 pop. 627), Taos co., N N.Mex., in Picuris Pueblo land grant, in Sangre de Cristo Mts., near Rio Grande, 36 mi. NNE of Santa Fe; alt. c.7,500 ft.; agr., sheep raising, weaving. Part of Carson Natl. Forest near by.

Peñas de San Pedro (dhā sän' pā'dhrō), town (pop. 1,661), Albacete prov., SE central Spain, 19 mi. SSW of Albacete; alcohol distilling, mfg. of flour products; lumbering; wine, saffron, cereals.

Peñas Point, cape in Sucre state, NE Venezuela, at E tip of Paria Peninsula, on Dragon's Mouth channel of the Caribbean, opposite Trinidad, and 23 mi. WNW of Port of Spain; 10°44'N 61°51'W.

Penasse (pŭnăs'), northernmost village (pop. c.25) in continental U.S., in Lake of the Woods co., N Minn., in the Northwest Angle in LAKE OF THE WOODS.

Penboyr (pĕnboir'), agr. village and parish (pop. 1,127), NW Carmarthen, Wales, 4 mi. SE of Newcastle Emlyn.

Penbroch, Wales: see PEMBROKE.

Penbrook, borough (pop. 3,691), Dauphin co., S central Pa., just NE of Harrisburg.

Penbryn (pĕnbrĭn'), town and parish (pop. 1,053), SW Cardigan, Wales, on Cardigan Bay of Irish Sea, 8 mi. ENE of Cardigan; woolen milling; seaside resort.

Pencahue (pĕngkä'wā). **1** Town (pop. 1,390), O'Higgins prov., central Chile, on Cachapoal R. and 30 mi. SW of Rancagua; agr. center (alfalfa, wheat, potatoes, beans, fruit, wine, livestock); flour milling, dairying. **2** Village (1930 pop. 489), Talca prov., central Chile, 9 mi. WNW of Talca; agr. center (wheat, barley, wine, livestock).

Pencaitland (pĕnkāt'lŭnd), town and parish (pop. 1,398), W East Lothian, Scotland, on Tyne R. and 4 mi. SE of Tranent; agr. market. Has 13th-cent. church. Coal mines near by.

Pen-ch'i, Manchuria: see PENKI.

Penchot, France: see VIVIEZ.

Pench River, central Madhya Pradesh, India, rises in central Satpura Range, in 2 forks joining c.20 mi. NW of Chhindwara; flows E through coalfield area, and S to Kanhan R. 11 mi. NE of Nagpur; 140 mi. long.

Penclawdd (pĕn-kloudh'), town in Llanrhidian Higher (lănrĭ'dēŭn) parish (pop. 4,717), W Glamorgan, Wales, on Loughor R. estuary and 7 mi. W of Swansea; coal mining.

Penco (pĕng'kō), town (pop. 6,803), Concepción prov., S central Chile, on Concepción Bay, on railroad and 7 mi. NNE of Concepción; beach resort, minor port, and coal-mining center. Sugar refinery, ceramics works (pottery, tableware, sanitary fixtures). Damaged in 1939 earthquake. Penco was site of the city of Concepción before 1730 earthquake.

Pencoed (pĕn-koid'), town and parish (pop. 2,791), S central Glamorgan, Wales, 4 mi. ENE of Bridgend; mfg. of colliery equipment.

Pendapolis, Greece: see PENTAPOLIS.

Pend d'Oreille, Idaho: see PEND OREILLE.

Pendeen, England: see SAINT JUST.

Pendelikon, Greece: see PENTELIKON.

Pendembu (pĕndĕm'boo), town (pop. 2,203), South-Eastern Prov., E Sierra Leone, 175 mi. E of Freetown, near Liberian border; rail terminus; palm oil and kernels, cacao, coffee. Trade with Fr. Guinea (N).

Pendência (pĕndän'syŭ), town (pop. 1,771), N Rio Grande do Norte, NE Brazil, on Piranhas (or Açu) R. and 12 mi. S of Macau; saltworks. Until 1944, called Independência.

Pender (pĕn'dŭr), county (□ 857; pop. 18,423), SE N.C., on the Atlantic; ⊙ Burgaw. Bounded SE by Onslow Bay; drained by Northeast Cape Fear R. Forested tidewater area with Holly Shelter and Angola swamps in E. Farming (tobacco, corn, vegetables), sawmilling, fishing. Formed 1875.

Pender, village (pop. 1,167), ⊙ Thurston co., NE Nebr., 70 mi. NNW of Omaha and on Logan Creek; farm implements. Inc. 1886.

Pendergrass, town (pop. 189), Jackson co., NE central Ga., 12 mi. SE of Gainesville.

Pender Island, North (□ 10), Gulf Isls., SW B.C., in Strait of Georgia, bet. Saltspring Isl. (W) and Saturna Isl. (E), 25 mi. N of Victoria; 7 mi. long, 1–3 mi. wide; mixed farming. South Pender Isl. (4 mi. long) is just SE.

Pendé River (pĕndā'), E headstream of Logone R. in NW Ubangi-Shari and SW Chad territories, Fr. Equatorial Africa, rises 25 mi. SSW of Bocaranga, flows c.225 mi. N, past Doba, to join M'Béré R. (W branch of Logone) 28 mi. SSE of Laï. Also called Eastern Logone.

Penderyn (pĕndĕ'rĭn), agr. village and parish (pop. 1,858), S Brecknock, Wales, 5 mi. NW of Aberdare.

Pendhat (pän'dŭt), village, Mainpuri dist., W Uttar Pradesh, India, on Upper Ganges Canal and 27 mi. WNW of Mainpuri; pilgrimage center for shrine of a Bhungi deity.

Pendik (pĕndĭk'), village (pop. c.4,000), Istanbul prov., NW Turkey in Asia, on Gulf of Izmit, on railroad, and 3 mi. ESE of Kartal; cement, vaccines.

Pendlebury, England: see SWINTON AND PENDLEBURY.

Pendle Hill, England: see CLITHEROE.

Pendleton, N suburb of Salford, SE Lancashire, England; cotton milling, mfg. of machinery, asphalt, chemicals, soap, glass, wall paper, electrical equipment.

Pendleton. 1 County (□ 279; pop. 9,610), N Ky.; ⊙ Falmouth. NE corner bounded by Ohio R. (Ohio line); drained by Licking R. and its South Fork. Gently rolling upland agr. area (burley tobacco, dairy products, poultry, hay, corn, honey), mostly in outer Bluegrass region. Some mfg. at Falmouth. Formed 1798. **2** County (□ 695; pop. 9,313), E W.Va., in Eastern Panhandle; ⊙ Franklin. Bounded E, S, and SW by Va.; Allegheny Front traverses co. in W. Spruce Knob (4,860 ft.) in W is highest point of state. Shenandoah Mtn. is along Va. line on E. Drained by South Branch of the Potomac (here flowing through the SMOKE HOLE) and its tributaries. Includes Seneca Caverns, Smoke Hole Caverns, Seneca Rocks, and parts of George Washington and Monongahela natl. forests. Agr. (livestock, dairy products, fruit); timber. Summer resorts. Formed 1788.

Pendleton. 1 Town (pop. 2,082), Madison co., E central Ind., on small Fall Creek and 27 mi. NE of Indianapolis, in agr. area (stock, grain, dairy, and poultry farms); mfg. (clothing, canned foods, metal products). State reformatory. Settled 1826. **2** City (pop. 11,774), ⊙ Umatilla co., NE Oregon, on Umatilla R. and 35 mi. SW of Walla Walla, Wash. Trade and shipping center, with railroad repair shops, for wheat, sheep, and livestock area; hq. for near-by Umatilla Natl. Forest and Umatilla Indian Reservation; food processing (flour, dairy products, canned peas), woolen milling; mfg. of blankets, leather and wood products. Agr. experiment station of Oregon State Col. and Eastern Oregon State Hosp. for insane are here. Indians from reservation take part in annual Pendleton Roundup (Sept.). Founded 1869 on old Oregon Trail, laid out 1870, inc. 1880. **3** Town (pop. 1,432), Anderson co., NW S.C., 13 mi. NW of Anderson, in agr. area noted for its livestock; textile (rayon) and cottonseed-oil mills. Oldest settlement in S.C. piedmont; founded in late 18th cent.

Pendleton, Camp, Calif.: see OCEANSIDE.

Pend Oreille (pŏn"dŭrā'), county (□ 1,406; pop. 7,413), NE Wash., on Idaho line (E), British Columbia line (N); ⊙ Newport. Drained by Clark Fork R.; includes Kalispell Indian Reservation and part of Kaniksu Natl. Forest. Lumber; gold, silver, copper, lead; mfg. (cement, matches); agr. Formed 1911.

Pend Oreille Lake, in mtn. and natl.-forest area of Bonner co., N Idaho; largest lake (□ 125; c.40 mi. long, average width 4 mi.; c.2,500 ft. deep) in state. Receives Clark Fork (E), which, on leaving lake (NW), becomes Pend Oreille R. Lake is spanned by Sandpoint Bridge (c.2 mi. long) in NW corner. Sometimes spelled Pend d'Oreille. Farming, lumbering, and mining are chief activities in surrounding region.

Pend Oreille River, in Idaho and Wash., leaves NW corner of Pend Oreille L. at Sandpoint, N Idaho, flows W, past Newport, Wash., thence N, through Pend Oreille co., NE Wash., to Columbia R. at British Columbia line; 119 mi. long. Sometimes called part of CLARK FORK, which enters Pend Oreille L. on E from Mont. Sometimes spelled Pend d'Oreille.

Pendroy, village (pop. c.100), Teton co., N Mont., 20 mi. N of Choteau, in irrigated region; grain-shipping point.

Pendulum Island or **Little Pendulum Island** (8 mi. long, 3–5 mi. wide), in Greenland Sea, E Greenland; 74°40'N 18°30'W. Site (1823) of Sabine's observatory.

Pendzhikent (pyĕnjĭkyĕnt'), town (1926 pop. 3,847), SW Leninabad oblast, Tadzhik SSR, on Zeravshan R. and 35 mi. E of Samarkand; wheat, truck produce; wine making.

Penedo (pĭnā'doo), city (pop. 12,651), E Alagoas, NE Brazil, head of ocean navigation on left bank of lower São Francisco R. (Sergipe border) 25 mi. above its mouth on the Atlantic, and 70 mi. SW of Maceió. Important trade in hides, rice, and cotton. Mfg.: cotton spinning and weaving, vegetable-oil processing, rice husking. Has airport and recently improved harbor facilities.

Penedono (pĭnĭdō'noo), town (pop. 736), Viseu dist., N central Portugal, 36 mi. NE of Viseu; wine, figs, olives, almonds, oranges. Has medieval castle and noteworthy Romanesque church.

Peneios River, Greece: see PENEUS RIVER.

Penela (pĭnā'lŭ), town (pop. 578), Coimbra dist., N central Portugal, 12 mi. S of Coimbra; wood industry (resin, paper), oil-pressing.

Penelope (pĕ'nŭlōp, pŭnĕ'lŭpē), town (pop. 243), Hill co., central Texas, 25 mi. NNE of Waco, in cotton area.

Penetanguishene (pĕ"nŭtăng"gŭ-shēn',-gwŭ-shēn'), town (pop. 4,521), S Ont., on Georgian Bay of L. Huron, 80 mi. NNW of Toronto; port; tanning, lumbering; mfg. of leather goods, boxes, stoves, truck bodies. Resort. Naval base built here 1813. Prov. establishment for the criminal insane here.

Peneus River (pĭnē'ŭs), Gr. *Pineios* or *Pinios* (both: pēnēōs'). **1** In NW Peloponnesus, Greece, rises in Erymanthos mts., flows 48 mi. W, past ruins of Pylos and Elis, and past Gastoune, to Ionian Sea 14 mi. NW of Pyrgos. Non-navigable. Formerly called Gastoune, Gastouni, or Gastuni R. **2** Chief river of Thessaly, Greece, rises in Pindus Mts. just E of Metsovon, flows 135 mi. SE and E, past Kalambaka, Trikkala, and Larissa, and NE through Vale of Tempe (bet. Lower Olympus and Ossa mts.) to Gulf of Salonika of Aegean Sea. Formerly Salambria or Salamvria.

Penfield. 1 Town (pop. 74), Greene co., NE central Ga., 7 mi. N of Greensboro; sawmilling. **2** Village (pop. 1,013), Monroe co., W N.Y., on small Irondequoit Creek and 7 mi. ESE of Rochester. **3** Village (1940 pop. 673), Clearfield co., central Pa., 14 mi. NW of Clearfield, in bituminous-coal area. There is also a village, Penfield, in HAVERFORD township.

Penfield Junction, village (pop. 1,830), Lorain co., N Ohio, just S of Lorain.

Pengam, England: see BEDWELLTY.

Pengan or **P'eng-an** (pŭng'än'), town (pop. 13,265), ⊙ Pengan co. (pop. 370,192), N central Szechwan prov., China, 24 mi. NE of Nanchung and on right bank of Kialing R.; rice, sweet potatoes, sugar cane, kaoliang, tobacco, cotton. Until 1913 called Pengchow.

Penganga River (pĕng-gŭng'gŭ), largely on Hyderabad–Madhya Pradesh border, central India, rises in Ajanta Hills W of Buldana, Madhya Pradesh; flows ESE, past Mehkar, and generally E to Wardha R. 10 mi. SW of Chanda; c.340 mi. long.

P'eng-ch'i, China: see PENGKI.

Pengchow, China: see PENGAN.

Penge (pĕnj), residential urban district (1931 pop. 27,771; 1951 census 25,009), NW Kent, England, 3 mi. W of Bromley, suburb of London.

Pengerang (pŭng-ŭrăng'), village (pop. 793), S Johore, Malaya, 25 mi. ESE of Johore Bahru, on Singapore Strait; coconuts; fisheries.

Penghsien or **P'eng-hsien** (pŭng'shyĕn'), town (pop. 26,368), ⊙ Penghsien co. (pop. 365,162), W Szechwan prov., China, 23 mi. NNW of Chengtu, on Chengtu plain; rice, wheat, millet, rapeseed, beans. Copper mining (N).

Penghu, town, Pescadores: see MAKUNG.

P'eng-hu Ch'ün-tao, Formosa: see PESCADORES.

Penghu Island (pŭng'hoo'), Chinese *P'eng-hu Tao* (dou), Jap. *Boko-to* (bō'kō-tō') or *Hoko-to* (hō'–), largest island of the Pescadores, off W Formosa; 23°34'N 119°37'E. Much indented, it is 9 mi. long, 2–4 mi. wide. The naval base of Makung is on W shore. The isl. is linked by causeway with Paisha Isl. (N).

P'eng-hu Lieh-tao, Formosa: see PESCADORES.

P'eng-hu Tao, Formosa: see PENGHU ISLAND.

Pengilly, resort village (pop. c.350), Itasca co., NE central Minn., on Mesabi iron range, at N end of Swan L., and 17 mi. ENE of Grand Rapids. Iron mines near by.

Pengkalan Bharu or **Pengkalan Bahru** (pĕngkä'län' bä'rōō), village (pop. 246), W Perak, Malaya, in the Dindings, 16 mi. N of Lumut; coconuts.
Pengkalan Chepa, Malaya: see KOTA BHARU.
Pengkalan Kempas (kĕm"päs'), village (pop. 285), SW Negri Sembilan, Malaya, near Malacca line, minor port on Linggi R., and 19 mi. S of Seremban; rubber plantations.
Pengki or **P'eng-ch'i** (both: pŭng'chē'), town (pop. 9,265), ⊙ Pengki co. (pop. 624,625), central Szechwan prov., China, 22 mi. W of Nanchung; rice, sweet potatoes, wheat, millet, kaoliang. Oil deposits and saltworks near by.
Penglai or **P'eng-lai** (pŭng'lī'), town (1922 pop. estimate 60,000), ⊙ Penglai co. (1946 pop. 355,757), NE Shantung prov., China, on N coast of Shantung peninsula, 40 mi. NW of Chefoo, on strait linking Yellow Sea and Gulf of Chihli; winegrowing; noodle processing. Gypsum, talc deposits near by. Formerly one of Shantung's leading port cities, it silted up and declined, being superseded by Lungkow (W) and Chefoo (E). Called Tengchow until 1913.
Pen Gogarth, Wales: GREAT ORMES HEAD.
Pengpu (bŭng'bōō'), city (1934 pop. 105,237; 1947 pop. 200,743), N Anhwei prov., China, 110 mi. NW of Nanking; rail and industrial center of N Anhwei; tanning, food-processing, textile, and vegetable-oil industries. Coal mining at Hwaiyüan (W). Became independent municipality in 1947. Passed 1949 to Communist control. Sometimes written Pangfow (or Pang-fou).
Pengshan or **P'eng-shan** (pŭng'shän'), town (pop. 18,105), ⊙ Pengshan co. (pop. 147,971), W Szechwan prov., China, 35 mi. SSW of Chengtu and on Min R.; rice, tobacco, sugar cane, wheat. Thenardite deposits near by. Just N, the irrigation canals of the Chengtu plain unite again to form lower Min R.
Pengshui or **P'eng-shui** (pŭng'shwā'), town (pop. 10,654), ⊙ Pengshui co. (pop. 287,148), SE Szechwan prov., China, 50 mi. SE of Fowling and on Kien R.; rice-growing center; millet, wheat, sweet potatoes, beans. Iron deposits, saltworks near by.
Pengtseh or **P'eng-tse** (pŭng'dzŭ'), town (pop. 6,018), ⊙ Pengtseh co. (pop. 85,075), northernmost Kiangsi prov., China, 35 mi. NE of Kiukiang and on right bank of Yangtze R. (Anhwei line); cotton-growing center; tobacco, rice, hemp.
Penguin, town and port (pop. 938), N Tasmania, 60 mi. WNW of Launceston and on Bass Strait; dairying and agr. center.
Penguin Islands, group of 7 islets just off S N.F., 15 mi. SW of Cape La Hune. Largest is Harbour Isl., 47°23'N 56°59'W.
Penha, Serra da (sĕ'rŭ dä pā'nyŭ), range in E central Minas Gerais, Brazil, an outlier of the Serra do Espinhaço extending c.60 mi. NE of Diamantina; rises to 3,500 ft. Forms watershed bet. Araçuaí (N) and Suaçuí (S) rivers.
Penhalonga (pĕn'yŭlông-gŭ), village (pop. 3,189), Umtali prov., E Southern Rhodesia, in Mashonaland, near Mozambique border, 8 mi. N of Umtali; major gold-mining center. Near by is noted Rezende Mine.
Penhars (pĕnärs'), SW suburb (pop. 5,882) of Quimper, Finistère dept., W France; canning, household articles mfg.
Penhold (pĕn'hōld), village (pop. 134), S central Alta., near Red Deer R., 10 mi. SSW of Red Deer; mixed farming.
Penhsihu, Manchuria: see PENKI.
Penibética, Cordillera (kôr-dhĕlyā'rä pānēvā'tēkä), mountain system of Andalusia, in SE and S Spain, a wide arc (c.600 mi.) along the Mediterranean coast from Cape Nao (Alicante prov.) to Point Marroquí (Cádiz prov.), forming S divide of Guadalquivir valley, which separates it from the SIERRA MORENA. Consisting of many rugged subranges, its principal chain is the snow-capped SIERRA NEVADA, which rises in the Mulhacén to highest peak (11,411 ft.) of continental Spain. Other subranges are the Sierra de Ronda (W) and the Sierra de Yeguas (NW). Apart from a few interior valleys (*vegas*) and a narrow coastal strip, it is generally infertile, though rich in minerals, especially in Sierra de Ronda (iron, antimony, lead, copper, zinc, bismuth, gold, mercury). Also called Baetic Cordillera.
Peniche (pĭnĕ'shĭ), town (pop. 8,761), Leiria dist., W central Portugal, port on a peninsula jutting into the Atlantic, 45 mi. NNW of Lisbon; important sardine-fishing and canning center. Formerly of great strategic importance, it has 16th-cent. fortifications. Cape Carvoeiro (2 mi. W) is W tip of rugged peninsula. Offshore are Berlenga and Farilhões isls.
Penicuik (pĕn'ĭkwĭk), burgh (1931 pop. 2,750; 1951 census 4,255), central Midlothian, Scotland, on North Esk R. and 9 mi. S of Edinburgh; paper-milling center, with iron foundries.
Penida or **Penide** (both: pünē'dŭ), island (12 mi. long, 8 mi. wide; pop. 22,292), Indonesia, in Lombok Strait, bet. Bali (W) and Lombok (E); 8°44'S 115°32'E; corn, cattle raising. Also called Besar.
Penielheugh (pē'nŭlhē'ōōkh), hill (774 ft.), E Roxburgh, Scotland, 4 mi. N of Jedburgh; site of 150-ft.-high Waterloo Column (1815).
Penig (pā'nĭkh), town (pop. 9,480), Saxony, E central Germany, on the Zwickauer Mulde and 12 mi. NW of Chemnitz; woolen and paper milling, textile printing, hosiery knitting, metalworking; mfg. of machinery, enamelware, bricks. Has late-Gothic church.
Penikese Island, Mass.: see ELIZABETH ISLANDS.
Peninsula, Ont.: see MARATHON.
Peninsula, New Zealand: see PORTOBELLO.
Peninsula, village (pop. 636), Summit co., NE Ohio, 10 mi. N of Akron and on Cuyahoga R.
Peninsula Point, Mich.: see BIG BAY DE NOC.
Peninsular Ranges, Calif.: see COAST RANGES.
Peninsula State Park (3,388 acres), Door co., NE Wis., on Door Peninsula, near Ephraim, on Green Bay; wooded, with bathing beaches.
Peñíscola (pānyē'skōlä), city (pop. 2,833), Castellón de la Plana prov., E Spain, on the Mediterranean, 9 mi. SSW of Vinaroz, on rocky promontory connected with mainland by narrow, sandy isthmus; fishing and boatbuilding. Cereals, olive oil, wine in area. Dominated by remains of fortified castle where antipope Benedictus XIII (Pedro de Luna) took refuge after his deposition.
Penistone, urban district (1931 pop. 3,264; 1951 census 6,389), West Riding, S Yorkshire, England, on Don R. and 12 mi. NW of Sheffield; steel mills, foundries; cattle market.
Peñita Point, Colombia: see CRUCES POINT.
Penitentes, Cordón de los (kōrdōn' dā lōs pānētĕn'tĕs), Andean range in NW Mendoza and SW San Juan provs., Argentina, extends c.20 mi. N of Aconcagua massif; a number of peaks are over 18,000 ft.
Penjamillo (pĕnhämē'yō), officially Penjamillo de Degollado, town (pop. 2,779), Michoacán, central Mexico, on central plateau, 18 mi. SSE of La Piedad; alt. 8,550 ft.; cereals, stock.
Pénjamo (pĕn'hämō), city (pop. 8,795), Guanajuato, central Mexico, on central plateau, 30 mi. SW of Irapuato; alt. 5,817 ft. Agr. center (corn, wheat, alfalfa, beans, fruit, sugar cane, stock). Rail station 4 mi. SE. Founded 1542.
Penjwin (pĕnj'wĕn), village, Sulaimaniya prov., in Kurdistan, NE Iraq, 30 mi. E of Sulaimaniya, near Iran border; tobacco, fruit, livestock.
Penketh, residential village and parish (pop. 1,980), S Lancashire, England, 3 mi. W of Warrington; leather tanning; truck gardening.
Penki or **Pen-ch'i** (both: bŭn'chē'), city (1940 pop. 98,203), ⊙ but independent of Penki co. (1946 pop. 337,273), W central Liaotung prov., Manchuria, 35 mi. SE of Mukden; rail junction; leading metallurgical center (2d only to Anshan) of Manchuria and China; center of Penki coal field extending to Tienshihfu, 30 mi. E. Pig-iron and quality-steel production; coking, cement mfg.; power plant. Coal and iron have been worked here since 18th cent. A modern mill was 1st built in 1915, on the basis of local coal and iron-ore deposits of Miaoerhkow (15 mi. SE) and Waitowshan (15 mi. NW). In late 1930s, a new plant was built in Kungyüan, a S suburb. Penki became an independent municipality in 1949. Formerly called Penkihu, Penchihu, or Penhsihu.
Penkridge, town and parish (pop. 2,550), central Stafford, England, on short Penk R. (tributary of the Trent) and 5 mi. S of Stafford, on edge of Cannock Chase; agr. market. Has 13th–15th-cent. church.
Penkun (pĕng'kōōn), town (pop. 2,595), in former Prussian Pomerania prov., N Germany, after 1945 in Mecklenburg, 16 mi. SW of Stettin; grain, tobacco, sugar beets, stock.
Penland, village (pop. c.100), Mitchell co., W N.C., just NW of Spruce Pine; handicraft center (pottery making, weaving). Mining (quartz, feldspar, mica, clay) near by.
Penmachno (pĕnmäkh'nō), town and parish (pop. 1,253), SE Caernarvon, Wales, 4 mi. S of Bettws-y-Coed; woolen milling.
Penmaen Dewi, Wales: see SAINT DAVID'S HEAD.
Penmaenmawr (pĕnmĭnmour'), urban district (1931 pop. 4,021; 1951 census 4,218), N Caernarvon, Wales, on Conway Bay of Irish Sea, 4 mi. WSW of Conway, at foot of mountain of Penmaenmawr (1,550 ft.); seaside resort, with stone quarrying and concrete mfg. Includes districts of Capelulo (E; pop. 769) and Penmaenan (WSW; pop. 1,473). Near by is Druidical circle and anc. fortress of Dinas Penmaen.
Pen Mar, resort village, Franklin co., S Pa. and Washington co., W Md., in the Blue Ridge on state line and 4 mi. SE of Waynesboro, Pa.
Penmarch (pĕnmär'), Breton *Penmarc'h*, village (pop. 800), Finistère dept., W France, on Pointe de Penmarch, 16 mi. SW of Quimper; sardine fishing, iodine extracting. Flourished 14th–16th cent. until decline of cod-fishing industry.
Penmarch, Pointe de (pwĕt dŭ), rocky cape on Atlantic Ocean, in Finistère dept., W France, 16 mi. SW of Quimper; lighthouse; 47°48'N 4°23'W.
Penmark (pĕnmärk'), agr. village and parish (pop. 804), SE Glamorgan, Wales, 4 mi. W of Barry. Has ruins of 13th-cent. castle, destroyed by Owen Glendower. Near by are remains of Norman keep, with early-17th-cent. house added.
Penn, agr. village and parish (pop. 1,767), S Buckingham, England, 3 mi. E of High Wycombe. Has 14th-cent. church.
Penn, borough (pop. 987), Westmoreland co., SW Pa., just W of Jeannette. Laid out 1859, inc. 1865.
Pennabilli (pĕn"nābĕl'lē), town (pop. 750), Pesaro e Urbino prov., The Marches, central Italy, near Marecchia R., 20 mi. WNW of Urbino; woolen mill.
Pennadam (pĕn-nä'dŭm), town (pop. 5,961), South Arcot dist., SE Madras, India, on Vellar R. and 9 mi. SW of Vriddhachalam; rice, plantain, cassava.
Pennant, village (pop. 234), SW Sask., 26 mi. NW of Swift Current; wheat.
Pennant Hills, town (pop. 2,302), E New South Wales, Australia, 12 mi. NW of Sydney, near Hornsby; coal-mining center. Koala-bear park near by.
Pennapolis, Brazil: see PENÁPOLIS.
Pennar River, India: see PENNER RIVER; PONNAIYAR RIVER.
Penn Creek, central Pa., rises in E Centre co., flows c.75 mi. E and S to Susquehanna R. just S of Selinsgrove. Marker on its bank N of Selinsgrove commemorates massacre (1755) of settlers by Indians.
Penndel, borough (pop. 1,100), Bucks co., SE Pa., 19 mi. NE of Philadelphia. Formerly South Langhorne. Inc. 1889.
Penne (pĕn'nĕ), anc. *Pinna*, town (pop. 4,498), Pescara prov., Abruzzi e Molise, S central Italy, 15 mi. W of Pescara; rail terminus; mfg. (aqueduct sections, soap). Bishopric. Has 17th-cent. cathedral (badly damaged), medieval remains. Damaged by air bombing (1944) in Second World War.
Penne-d'Agenais (pĕn-däzhŭnā'), village (pop. 621), Lot-et-Garonne dept., SW France, on the Lot and 5 mi. E of Villeneuve-sur-Lot; fruit.
Pennell, Mount, Utah: see HENRY MOUNTAINS.
Penner River (pĕ'nŭr), in E Mysore and E central Madras, India, rises on Deccan Plateau 7 mi. WSW of Chik Ballapur, flows N past Goribidnur, E past Pamidi and Tadpatri, and generally ESE past Jammalamadugu and Nellore, to Coromandel Coast of Bay of Bengal 100 mi. N of Madras; c.350 mi. long. Also called Northern Penner; sometimes spelled Pennar. Southern Penner is name sometimes given to Ponnaiyar R.
Penneshaw, village (pop. 149), Kangaroo Isl., South Australia, on N shore of E peninsula, 17 mi. ESE of Kingscote; barley, sheep, wool; eucalyptus oil. Sometimes called Hog Bay.
Pennesseewassee, Lake (pĕ'nĭsēwä'sē), Oxford co., W Maine, in summer resort area; c.3 mi. long. Drains S, past Norway, to Little Androscoggin R.
Penney Farms, town (pop. 445), Clay co., NE Fla., 26 mi. SSW of Jacksonville. Founded 1927 by J. C. Penney as a home for retired religious leaders.
Pennfield, village (pop. estimate c.250), SW N.B., 18 mi. ENE of St. Andrews; granite quarrying. Site of airfield.
Pennine Alps (pĕ'nīn), Ital. *Alpi Pennine*, Fr. *Alpes Pennines*, SW division of Central Alps, along Italo-Swiss border; extend from Great St. Bernard Pass (SW) to Simplon Pass (NE). Bounded by Mont Blanc group along Fr.-Ital. border (W), by upper Rhone valley (N), by Lepontine Alps (ENE), by Dora Baltea valley (S). Culminate in Monte Rosa group, of which the Dufourspitze (15,203 ft.) is highest peak. Other peaks are the Mischabelhörner, the Matterhorn (14,701 ft.), and the Weisshorn (14,792 ft.). Of numerous glaciers, found chiefly on N (Swiss) slope, the Gorner (just above Zermatt) is best known. Called Valais Alps in Switzerland.
Pennine Chain or **Pennine Range,** long hill range, sometimes called "the backbone of England," extending from the Cheviot Hills (N) to S Midlands and appearing in counties of Cumberland, Northumberland, Lancashire, York, Cheshire, Derby, Stafford, and Nottingham. Range consists of a series of upland blocks, separated by transverse valleys. The North Pennines are bounded N by the Tyne valley, and are separated from the Central Pennines by the Tees valley. The Aire valley separates Central and South Pennines, which extend S to the Trent valley. Higher regions of the Pennines are mostly moorland or rough pasture; lower slopes have fertile arable land. There are few lakes, but several caves and deep chasms. Highest peak is CROSS FELL (2,930 ft.). Upper regions of the Central Pennines are site of large number of reservoirs, supplying industrial areas on E and W flanks.
Penninghame (pĕn'ĭng-hŭm), parish (pop. 2,924), E Wigtown, Scotland. Includes burgh of NEWTON STEWART.
Pennington, village and parish (pop. 1,436), N Lancashire, England, on Furness peninsula 2 mi. WSW of Ulverston; sheep raising, agr. Just SW is village of Lindal, site of abandoned iron mines.
Pennington. **1** County (□ 622; pop. 12,965), NW Minn.; ⊙ Thief River Falls. Agr. area drained by Red Lake and Thief rivers. Dairy products, grain, potatoes, livestock; peat. Formed 1910. **2** County (□ 2,776; pop. 34,053), SW S.Dak., on Wyo. line; ⊙ Rapid City. Farming and ranching region rich in minerals; crossed W by Black Hills; traversed E by Cheyenne R. Tourist trade; mfg. at Rapid City; gold, granite, timber, grain, livestock. Places

of interest: Harney Peak, Stratosphere Bowl (from which balloon ascents have been made), Mt. Rushmore Natl. Memorial, Custer State Park, Black Hills Natl. Forest, and Badlands Natl. Monument. Formed 1875.

Pennington, borough (pop. 1,682), Mercer co., W N.J., 7 mi. N of Trenton. Pennington School for boys (1838) here. Settled 1708, inc. 1890.

Pennington Gap, town (pop. 2,090), Lee co., extreme SW Va., in the Cumberlands near Ky. line, 15 mi. SW of Big Stone Gap; trade center for area producing bituminous coal, grain, tobacco, limestone, timber. Inc. 1891 or 1892.

Pennino, Monte (môn'tĕ pĕn-nē'nô), peak (5,151 ft.) in the Apennines, central Italy, 9 mi. WSW of Camerino. Source of Potenza R.

Pennock, village (pop. 238), Kandiyohi co., SW central Minn., 7 mi. W of Willmar; dairy products.

Pennock Island (3 mi. long; 1939 pop. 79), in Alexander Archipelago, SE Alaska, in Revillagigedo Channel bet. Annette Isl. (S) and Revillagigedo Isl. (N), just S of Ketchikan; fishing.

Pennsauken (pĕnsô'kĭn), township (pop. 22,767), Camden co., SW N.J., just NE of Camden; bricks, terra cotta, beer. Settled 1840, inc. 1892. Formerly sometimes spelled Pensauken.

Pennsboro, town (pop. 1,753), Ritchie co., NW W.Va., on North Fork of Hughes R. and 30 mi. E of Parkersburg. Market, shipping, and trade center for livestock, fruit, tobacco, natural-gas, and oil region; mfg. of clothing, glassware, marble products; lumber milling. Co. fairgrounds here. Settled in early 1800s.

Pennsburg, borough (pop. 1,625), Montgomery co., SE Pa., 15 mi. S of Allentown; clothing, textiles, furniture. Settled 1840, inc. 1887.

Penns Grove, residential borough (pop. 6,669), Salem co., SW N.J., on Delaware R. opposite Wilmington, Del. (ferry); mfg. (dyes, clothing, lumber products); dairy products, poultry, fruit, truck. U.S. army ordnance depot near by. Settled 1675, inc. 1894.

Pennsuco, town (pop. 133), Dade co., S Fla., 13 mi. NW of Miami.

Pennsville, residential village (1940 pop. 1,864), Salem co., SW N.J., on Delaware R., opposite New Castle, Del. (ferry), with bridge near by. Settled by Swedes after 1640.

Pennsylvania (pĕnsĭlvā'nyŭ), state (land □ 45,045; with inland waters, but without □ 735 of L. Erie, □ 45,333; 1950 pop. 10,498,012; 1940 pop. 9,900,180), NE U.S., in the Middle Atlantic region, bordered N by L. Erie and N.Y., E (along Delaware R.) by N.Y. and N.J., S by Del., Md., and W.Va., W by W.Va. and Ohio; 32d in area, 3d in pop.; one of original 13 states, the 2d to ratify (1787) the Constitution; ⊙ Harrisburg. From the N.Y. to Md. lines the state measures 158 mi.; greatest E–W distance, 312 mi. Pa. is almost wholly within the Appalachian mtn. system. The largest natural feature is the ALLEGHENY PLATEAU, which comprises all of the W and N parts, except for a narrow lake plain along L. Erie. Composed of horizontal carboniferous strata, the plateau region (generally 1,000–2,000 ft. high) has been considerably dissected by streams, producing such rounded heights as the Pocono Mts. (NE) and ALLEGHENY MOUNTAINS (SW). Mt. Davis (3,213 ft.), in the Allegheníes, is the highest point in the state. The E edge of the plateau, called the Allegheny Front, overlooks the ridge and valley terrain of the Folded Appalachians, a 40–60-mi.-wide belt in the center of the state curving roughly NE–SW bet. the Poconos and the Md. border. It consists of a series of parallel ridges (e.g., Blue, Tuscarora, Jacks, Bald Eagle mts.) of resistant rock (sandstone, conglomerate), with the intervening valleys developed on weaker limestone and shale. Flanking this section on the E is the Great Appalachian Valley, in Pa. represented by the Cumberland and Lebanon valleys (c.20 mi. wide). Extending N from Md. to a point S of Carlisle is South Mtn., northernmost part of the Blue Ridge, a complex of anc. crystalline rocks. An extension of the N.J. Highlands runs SW from Easton to Reading. SE Pa. is crossed (NE–SW) by the Piedmont region, consisting of the fertile Triassic Lowland (shales, sandstones) and a subdued upland belt. S of Trenton, along the Delaware, is a narrow strip of the Atlantic coastal plain. The state is drained by the Delaware, Lehigh, Schuylkill, Susquehanna, and Juniata rivers in the center and E, in the W by the Ohio R., formed at Pittsburgh by the junction of the Allegheny and Monongahela (with tributary Youghiogheny). The larger streams have cut deep, narrow valleys in the plateau area and flow transversely through the Folded Appalachians via scenic water gaps. Glaciers covered the NW and NE parts of the state. Pa. has a humid continental climate, marked by an annual rainfall of 35–50 in., well distributed throughout the year and slightly higher in the E and W than in the center. Philadelphia (SE) has mean temp. of 33°F. in Jan., 77°F. in July, and 42 in. of rain; Pittsburgh (W) has mean temp. of 29°F. in Jan., 74°F. in July, and 35 in. of rain. The growing season averages 150–180 days over most of the state, c.200 days in the extreme SE, and less than 130 days in the N. There are some 15,000,000 acres of forest land, in which hardwoods predominate, principally oak, chestnut, hemlock, maple, beech, birch, hickory, and poplar; natl. forest reserves comprise 747,000 acres. The best farming areas are in the Piedmont and in the valleys of the Folded Appalachians, where terrain, soil, and climate are conducive to specialized crop production. In all, c.15,000,000 acres are in farm and range land, of which 6,600,000 acres are in crops. Hay accounts for ⅓ of the harvested cropland and is widely grown throughout the state. In the Allegheny Plateau section there is extensive pasture; corn (for silage), winter wheat, oats, barley, buckwheat (ranks 1st in U.S. output), and rye are the chief crops. In the lower areas to the E and S of the plateau, grains (mainly wheat) are also grown, but market gardening and fruitgrowing are of most importance—potatoes, tomatoes, sweet corn, apples (especially Adams co.), and peaches. There is some soybean production. Lancaster co., one of the richest agr. areas in the U.S., is noted for its cigar leaf tobacco. Chester and Delaware counties grow most of the country's mushrooms. Grapes are important in the L. Erie sector. Dairying is the largest agr. industry, and milk production for urban markets is considerable. Much poultry is raised. The L. Erie fish catch includes lake herring (cisco), whitefish, pike, and perch. Pa. is 2d only to Texas in the total value of its mineral output, over 75% of which is from coal. In the W part of the state, on the Allegheny Plateau, are vast bituminous deposits, characterized by easily accessible, horizontal seams, worked extensively by machinery. Fayette, Washington, Allegheny, Cambria, Westmoreland, and Indiana counties, in the SW, are major producers. Almost all of the country's anthracite comes from the E part of the state, at the N end of the Folded Appalachians. Seams are difficult of access and the mines generally deep. Chief centers are Scranton, Wilkes-Barre, and Nanticoke in the Wyoming Valley, Hazleton, Shenandoah, and Pottsville. Most of the bituminous coal is consumed by railroads and industries in the Pittsburgh area, while anthracite is used largely for domestic heating in the cities of the East. Petroleum production is important, principally in the Bradford and Kane dists. and in Venango, Warren, Butler, and Washington counties; natural gas and gasoline are associated. Slate (from Lehigh and Northampton counties), sandstone, and traprock are quarried; limestone is widely used in cement mfg. (centered in Lehigh valley area) and for fluxing. Iron ore (magnetite) and cobalt are mined at Cornwall. Other workings include sand and gravel, clay, feldspar, and graphite, and there are extensive deposits of rock and brine salt in the W counties. Pa. usually ranks 2d to N.Y. in total value of manufactured goods. It is favored by abundant fuel resources, good transportation facilities (rail, river, canal), large labor supply, and near-by urban markets. Most important is the great iron and steel industry, producing c.30% of the nation's steel and large quantities of coke, pig iron, and ferro-alloys. PITTSBURGH, at confluence of Allegheny and Monongahela rivers, is the center of one of the world's largest steel-producing areas, which includes McKeesport, Munhall, Duquesne, Carnegie, Aliquippa, and Monessen. Sharon, near Youngstown in Ohio, and Johnstown, in the Alleghenies, are important centers, and, in E Pa., Bethlehem, Allentown, Reading, and Harrisburg are notable. Other leading products are textiles (apparel, hosiery, carpets, yarns, cloths; Philadelphia is chief center), petroleum products (large oil refineries at Marcus Hook and Philadelphia), food, machinery, fabricated metal products, chemicals, glass, transportation equipment, paper, tobacco products, packed meat, electrical apparatus, and household appliances. On the lower Delaware is PHILADELPHIA, 3d largest city and one of the largest ports in U.S. A major commercial center, it has miscellaneous industries, including printing and publishing and, along with Chester to the S, important shipbuilding facilities. In addition to the large steel centers, which produce a variety of other goods, mfg. takes place at Erie (state's only Great Lakes port), Scranton, Wilkes-Barre, Altoona (railroad shops), Lancaster, York, New Castle (aluminum products), Williamsport, Norristown, and Easton. Besides a good rail net, the state has a fine highway system, including the Philadelphia-Pittsburgh Pennsylvania Turnpike. There are a number of resort areas in the Poconos and other mts. and along L. Erie. Leading educational institutions are Univ. of Pa. and Temple Univ. (at Philadelphia), Univ. of Pittsburgh, Duquesne Univ. and Carnegie Inst. of Technology (at Pittsburgh), Pa. State Col. (at State College), Lehigh Univ. (at Bethlehem), Bucknell Univ. (at Lewisburg), Lafayette Col. (at Easton), Villanova Col. (at Villanova), Muhlenberg Col. (at Allentown), Franklin and Marshall Col. (at Lancaster), Swarthmore Col. (at Swarthmore), and Bryn Mawr Col. (at Bryn Mawr). Before the coming of the white man, the region was inhabited by Algonquian tribes—Delaware, Shawnee—who later came under Iroquoian influence. Étienne Brulé explored the Susquehanna R. in 1615. The 1st permanent settlement was made (1643) by Swedes at Tinicum Isl., one of their New Sweden colonies, later taken over (1655) by the Dutch. In 1681 William Penn received a grant of land, including most of present Pa., and in the next year acquired "the lower counties" (Delaware). Land was purchased from the Indians, Philadelphia was platted (1682), and a constitution guaranteeing religious freedom and universal suffrage was drawn up. The Del. counties formed their own govt. in 1703, though Pa.'s governor was retained. Religious freedom attracted thousands to the new colony, particularly Welsh Quakers, Germans (the so-called Pennsylvania Dutch), English, Scotch-Irish, and French Huguenots. Farming, iron mining, and lumbering developed early. Resentful of English encroachment on their lands, the Indians allied themselves with the French, who were building forts in W Pa. Skirmishes at the forks of the Ohio precipitated the French and Indian War (1754–63), during which Braddock's defeat (1755) was redeemed by the successful campaign of Gen. Forbes, who eliminated Fr. power from the upper Ohio region and laid the foundations of Fort Pitt on the site of former Fort Duquesne. The S boundary with Md. was determined 1763–67 by the Mason-Dixon line; its W extension in 1779 marked the boundary with Va. The "Keystone State" figured prominently during the Revolution. Philadelphia was the scene of the 1st and 2d Continental Congresses and the signing of the Declaration of Independence. Military actions included the Br. occupation of Philadelphia, battles of Brandywine and Germantown (1777), Washington's winter encampment at Valley Forge (1777–78), and the Wyoming Valley massacre. Pa.'s present boundaries were acquired in 1792. Rural hostility to certain Federal taxes was expressed in the Whisky and Fries rebellions (1794, 1798). In the War of 1812 Philadelphia felt the pinch of the Br. naval blockade. Road, canal, and rail construction speeded settlement and developed industry. The 1st successful oil well in the U.S. was sunk near Titusville in 1859. Pa.'s regiments played an active part in the Civil War, and the decisive battle of Gettysburg was fought (July, 1863) on the state's soil. In the postwar period steel and coal dominated the industrial scene— marred by occasional violent strikes and riots, such as the Homestead strike (1892). A major calamity was the Johnstown flood of 1889, which took over 2,000 lives; in 1936 extensive floods caused great damage in the W part of the state. See also articles on the cities, towns, geographic features, and the 67 counties: ADAMS, ALLEGHENY, ARMSTRONG, BEAVER, BEDFORD, BERKS, BLAIR, BRADFORD, BUCKS, BUTLER, CAMBRIA, CAMERON, CARBON, CENTRE, CHESTER, CLARION, CLEARFIELD, CLINTON, COLUMBIA, CRAWFORD, CUMBERLAND, DAUPHIN, DELAWARE, ELK, ERIE, FAYETTE, FOREST, FRANKLIN, FULTON, GREENE, HUNTINGDON, INDIANA, JEFFERSON, JUNIATA, LACKAWANNA, LANCASTER, LAWRENCE, LEBANON, LEHIGH, LUZERNE, LYCOMING, MCKEAN, MERCER, MIFFLIN, MONROE, MONTGOMERY, MONTOUR, NORTHAMPTON, NORTHUMBERLAND, PERRY, PHILADELPHIA, PIKE, POTTER, SCHUYLKILL, SNYDER, SOMERSET, SULLIVAN, SUSQUEHANNA, TIOGA, UNION, VENANGO, WARREN, WASHINGTON, WAYNE, WESTMORELAND, WYOMING, YORK.

Pennsylvania Turnpike, toll superhighway in Pa.; extends E–W across the state from just E of Norristown to Ohio line 13 mi. WNW of Ellwood City. First portion (with several long mtn. tunnels) bet. Carlisle (E) and Irwin was completed 1940. E extension opened late 1950, W extension about a year later.

Pennville, town (pop. 626), Jay co., E Ind., on Salamonie R. and 24 mi. NNE of Muncie, in agr. area.

Penn Wynne, Pa.: see LOWER MERION.

Penn Yan (pĕn"yăn'), resort village (pop. 5,481), ⊙ Yates co., W central N.Y., in Finger Lakes region, on E arm of Keuka L., 15 mi. SSW of Geneva; mfg. (flour, wine, fruit juices, machinery, auto bodies, baskets, wood and paper products, boats, clothing). Agr. (grain, grapes, potatoes). Keuka Col. is at near-by Keuka Park. Named for Pennsylvanians and New Englanders ("Yankees") who settled here; inc. 1833. Jemima Wilkinson established her short-lived "Jerusalem" near here in late-18th cent.

Peno (pyô'nŭ), town (1948 pop. over 2,000), NE Velikiye Luki oblast, Russian SFSR, on L. Peno (one of upper Volga R. lakes; 6 mi. long, 1 mi. wide), 90 mi. ENE of Velikiye Luki; sawmilling.

Penobscot (pŭnŏb'skŭt, –skŏt), county (□ 3,408; pop. 108,198), S and central Maine; ⊙ Bangor. Agr., mfg. (pulp, paper, wood products, textiles, canoes) in S, lumbering, hunting, fishing in N. Numerous lakes. Drained by Penobscot R. Formed 1816.

Penobscot, town (pop. 699), Hancock co., S Maine, on Penobscot Bay and 24 mi. SSE of Bangor, in resort area.

Penobscot Bay, S Maine, inlet of the Atlantic at mouth of the Penobscot, 70 mi. NE of Portland; 27 mi. wide, 35 mi. deep; with many isls., sheltered harbors, summer resorts.

Penobscot Lake, Somerset co., W Maine, 19 mi. NNE of Jackman, near Que. line; 3 mi. long.

Penobscot River, Maine, c.350 mi. long (from head of longest branch), formed by headstreams draining many lakes of central and W Maine; West Branch (c.110 mi. long) and shorter East Branch join at Medway to flow E, then generally S, past Lincoln, Howland, Old Town, and Bangor, to Penobscot Bay near Bucksport; water power. Navigable to Bangor; principal freight, lumber. Explored by English voyager 1603 and by Champlain 1604; CASTINE region at mouth colonized c.1626.

Penobsquis (pĕnŏb'skwĭs), village, SE N.B., on Kennebecasis R. and 8 mi. NW of Sussex; gypsum quarrying.

Penoeba, Indonesia: see LINGGA ARCHIPELAGO.

Penokee-Gogebic Range, Mich. and Wis.: see GOGEBIC RANGE.

Penokee Range, Wis.: see GOGEBIC RANGE.

Peñol (pānyōl'), town (pop. 1,456), Antioquia dept., NW central Colombia, in Cordillera Central, 24 mi. E of Medellín; alt. 6,194 ft.; corn, yucca, potatoes, coffee; lumbering.

Penola, village (pop. 864), SE South Australia, 210 mi. SSE of Adelaide, near Victoria border, and on Naracoorte–Mt. Gambier RR; dairy products, livestock.

Peñón Blanco (pānyōn' blăng'kō). **1** Town (pop. 2,649), Durango, N Mexico, 65 mi. NE of Durango; agr. center (corn, cotton, alfalfa, chick-peas). **2** City, San Luis Potosí, Mexico: see SALINAS.

Peñón del Rosario, Mexico: see ROSARIO, PEÑÓN DEL.

Peñón de Vélez de la Gomera (dā bā'lĕth dā lä gōmä'rä), rocky islet (pop. 51) in the W Mediterranean, just off Sp. Morocco, 22 mi. WSW of Villa Sanjurjo; 35°11'N 4°18'W; 1,100 ft. long, 200 ft. wide. A possession of Spain since 1508, it is under direct Sp. administration. It is of little strategic value today.

Penong (pē'nông'), village (pop. 118), S South Australia, 250 mi. NW of Port Lincoln; terminus of railroad from Port Lincoln; wheat, wool.

Penonomé (pānōnōmā'), town (1950 pop. 3,531), ⊙ Coclé prov., central Panama, in Pacific lowland, on Inter-American Highway and 60 mi. SW of Panama city. Commercial center; mfg. of soap, Panama hats. Exports rubber, coffee, cacao. Has normal school. Its port, Puerto Posada, 13 mi. SSW, on the Río Grande, was active until construction of Inter-American Highway.

Penrhiwceiber (pĕnrūkī'bûr), town (pop. 8,906) in Mountain Ash urban district, NE Glamorgan, Wales, on Taff R.; coal mining.

Penrhyn (pĕn'rĭn) or **Tongareva** (tŏng"ūrē'vū, tōng'ärävä), atoll (4,000 acres; pop. 654), Manihiki group, S Pacific, c.735 mi. NE of Rarotonga; 9°S 158°3'W; circumference c.40 mi.; pearls. Discovered 1788 by British, placed 1901 under N.Z. COOK ISLANDS administration. Exports copra, pearl and *pipi* shells, native handicraft.

Penrhyn, town and parish (pop. 1,471), N Caernarvon, Wales, resort on Colwyn Bay of Irish Sea, 3 mi. ESE of Llandudno.

Penrhyn, Port, Wales: see BANGOR.

Penrhyndeudraeth (pĕn'rĭn-dī'drīth), town and parish (pop. 2,022), NW Merioneth, Wales, 3 mi. E of Portmadoc; agr. market; stone quarries.

Penrith (pĕn'rĭth), municipality (pop. 4,961), E New South Wales, Australia, on Hawkesbury R. and 30 mi. W of Sydney; dairying, fruitgrowing.

Penrith, urban district (1931 pop. 9,066; 1951 census 10,490), E Cumberland, England, 17 mi. SSE of Carlisle, in the Lake District, for which it is a tourist center; agr. market; mfg. of agr. machinery and implements. Has grammar school founded in 14th cent. and refounded in Elizabeth's reign; ruins of 15th-cent. castle. The churchyard has 2 anc. monuments, "Giant's Grave" and "Giant's Thumb." The town was anc. capital of Cumbria. Just NE is mtn. of Penrith Beacon (937 ft.).

Penryn (pĕnrĭn'), municipal borough (1931 pop. 3,414; 1951 census 4,088), SW Cornwall, England, on inlet of Carrick Roads and 2 mi. NW of Falmouth; agr. market and port; center of Cornish granite industry. Church dates from 15th cent.

Pensacola (pĕnsūkō'lū). **1** City (pop. 43,479), ⊙ Escambia co., extreme NW Fla., on Pensacola Bay (bridged here), c.55 mi. ESE of Mobile, Fla.; port of entry with fine natural harbor sheltered by Santa Rosa Isl.; site of a major U.S. naval air station. Shipping, fishing, and wood-processing center; base for red-snapper fishing fleet operating mostly off Yucatan. Products include paper, wood products (lumber, furniture, creosoted wood), naval stores, ramie fiber, temperature instruments, beverages, concrete blocks, tile; has shipbuilding and seafood canning industries. Nylon plant near by (begun 1951). Exports wood and food products. Short-lived Spanish settlement was made here, 1559–61; it was recolonized by Spaniards in 1698, and a fort was erected on Santa Rosa Isl. After 1719, Spain and France alternated in its possession; town passed to the British in 1763, but was returned to Spain (1783) after capture by Bernardo de Gálves in 1781; was ⊙ West Florida until 1822. British troops were based here in War of 1812, though city was still Spanish. Andrew Jackson seized Pensacola in 1814 and again in 1818; U.S. took formal possession in 1821. Inc. as city, 1822. In Civil War, Confederate and Union forces held it at various times, but Fort Pickens on Santa Rosa Isl. remaining under Federal control throughout war. Harbor development in late-19th cent. and establishment of the large U.S. naval air station in 1914 greatly influenced city's economic life. Fort Barrancas, SE of city, is only garrisoned fort in area now; there are ruins of old forts Barrancas (built in 1780s), and Pickens and McRae (built in 1830s). Points of interest in city: Seville Square, the 18th-cent. Barclay House, and Walton House, now a mus. **2** Town (pop. 48), Mayes co., NE Okla., 13 mi. S of Vinita. Grand River Dam (sometimes called Pensacola Dam) is c.5 mi. E. Inc. 1938.

Pensacola Bay, NW Fla., irregular inlet of the Gulf of Mexico, with its entrance (c.1 mi. wide) bet. W end of Santa Rosa Isl. and the mainland; Pensacola (seaport) is on its shores. Bay proper (c.13 mi. long, 2½ mi. wide) is extended by several arms: to NW is Escambia Bay, receiving Escambia R.; to E is East Bay, in turn communicating with Blackwater Bay (NE arm), which receives Blackwater and Yellow rivers. Linked by Gulf Intracoastal Waterway to Choctawhatchee Bay (E), Perdido Bay (W).

Pensacola Dam, Okla.: see GRAND RIVER DAM.

Pensarn, Wales: see ABERGELE AND PENSARN.

Pensauken, township, N.J.: see PENNSAUKEN.

Pensauken Creek (pĕnsô'kĭn), SW N.J., rises E of Camden in North Branch (c.10 mi. long) and South Branch (c.15 mi. long), which join NW of Maple Shade and flow c.5 mi. NW to Delaware R. 5 mi. above Camden.

Pense (pĕns), village (pop. 275), S Sask., 16 mi. W of Regina; wheat.

Penshurst (pĕnz'hûrst), village (pop. 742), SW Victoria, Australia, 140 mi. W of Melbourne; flax, cattle; dairy plant.

Penshurst (pĕnz'hûrst), town and parish (pop. 1,673), SW Kent, England, on Medway R. and 4 mi. NW of Tunbridge Wells; agr. market, farm-implement works. Site of Penshurst Place, with mansion dating from 1340; Sir Philip Sidney b. here. Church dates from c.1200.

Pensilvania (pĕnsēlvä'nyä), town (pop. 2,936), Caldas dept., central Colombia, on E slopes of Cordillera Central, 45 mi. NE of Manizales; alt. 6,299 ft. Coffeegrowing and gold mining; limekiln.

Pentadaktylon, Greece: see TAYGETUS.

Pentagon Building: see ARLINGTON, Va.

Pentapadu Agraharam (pĕntŭpä'dōō ŭgrŭ'hŭrŭm), town (pop. 7,508), West Godavari dist., NE Madras, India, in Godavari R. delta, 27 mi. E of Ellore; rice milling; oilseeds, tobacco, sugar cane. Also called Pentapadu.

Pentapolis (pĕntă'pŭlĭs) [Gr.,=five cities], collective name anciently applied to several groups of 5 cities. The most important was that of the chief cities of Cyrenaica (Apollonia, Arsinoë, Berenice, Cyrene, and Ptolemaïs), which were called the Pentapolis from 4th cent. B.C. to 7th cent. A.D. In Italy the cities of Rimini, Ancona, Fano, Pesaro, and Senigallia on the Adriatic were called the Pentapolis from 5th cent. to 11th cent. A Pentapolis in Asia Minor was Cnidus, Cos, Lindus, Camirus, and Ialysus. There was also a Pentapolis in Palestine.

Pentapolis or **Pendapolis** (pĕntă'pŭlĭs, Gr. pĕndä'-pôlĭs), town (pop. 3,574), Serrai nome, Macedonia, Greece, 7 mi. ESE of Serrai; cotton, corn, beans, tobacco. Formerly Sarmousakli or Sarmusakli.

Pentecost (pĕn'tūkôst), Fr. *Pentecôte* (pătūkōt'), volcanic island (□ c.190; pop. c.4,400), New Hebrides, SW Pacific, c.60 mi. E of Espiritu Santo; 35 mi. long, 6 mi. wide; copra, coffee.

Pentecoste (pĕntĭkô'stĭ), city (pop. 470), N Ceará, Brazil, 55 mi. W of Fortaleza; mfg. of cheese; livestock, cotton.

Pentecôte, New Hebrides: see PENTECOST.

Pentelikon or **Pendelikon** (both: pĕndĕlĭkôn'), Lat. *Pentelicus* (pĕntĕ'lĭkŭs), mountain in Attica nome, E central Greece, rises to 3,637 ft. 11 mi. NE of Athens. Mining of white architectural marble; pine forests. Formerly called Penteli and Mendeli.

Penteuleu Peak (pĕntäōōlā'ōō), peak (5,822 ft.) in Buzau Mts., SE central Rumania, Muntenia, 35 mi. NW of Ramnicul-Sarat. Known for its pastures and the ewe-cheese made in the area.

Penthièvre (pătyĕv'rū), village (pop. 505), Constantine dept., NE Algeria, 20 mi. SW of Bône; tobacco, wine, cereals.

Penticton (pĕntĭk'tŭn), town (pop. estimate 9,000), S B.C., on Okanagan R., at S end of Okanagan L., and 180 mi. E of Vancouver; fruitgrowing center (apples, peaches, apricots), with canning and packing plants; lumbering, sheet-metal and chemicals mfg. Resort.

Pentima, Italy: see CORFINIO.

Pentir (pĕntēr'), agr. village and parish (pop. 1,925), N Caernarvon, Wales, 4 mi. S of Bangor.

Pentland Firth (pĕnt'lŭnd fûrth), navigation channel (14 mi. long, 6–8 mi. wide) bet. mainland of Scotland and the Orkneys, linking the North Sea and Atlantic. In the firth are isls. of Stroma, Swona, and the Pentland Skerries. Its tides and currents make navigation dangerous to small vessels.

Pentland Hills, uplands in SE Scotland, extending 16 mi. NE-SW bet. Carstairs, Lanark, and Edinburgh, Midlothian, forming E part of border bet. Peebles and Midlothian. Range is 4–6 mi. wide; highest peaks are Carnethy (1,890 ft.), 8 mi. S of Edinburgh, and Scald Law (1,898 ft.), 8 mi. SSW of Edinburgh. At foot of Carnethy is Rullion Green, scene of battle (1666) in which Covenanters were defeated by General Dalyell. In hills are several reservoirs of Edinburgh water-supply system.

Pentland Skerries (skĕ'rēz), group of islets (pop. 5), southernmost of the Orkneys, Scotland, at E entrance to Pentland Firth. Largest, 4½ mi. NE of Duncansbay Head, has lighthouse (58°41'N 2°54'W).

Pentre, Wales: see RHONDDA.

Pentrecwrt, Wales: see LLANGELER.

Pentrobin, Wales: see BUCKLEY.

Pentwater, village (pop. 1,097), Oceana co., W Mich., 12 mi. S of Ludington, and on L. Michigan at mouth of short Pentwater R., in resort and farm area; ships fruit; has fisheries. Sand dunes and state park near by. Inc. 1867.

Pentyrch (pĕntĭrkh'), town and parish (pop. 2,267), SE Glamorgan, Wales, 7 mi. NW of Cardiff; agr. market. Important in early days of iron industry.

Penuba, Indonesia: see LINGGA ARCHIPELAGO.

Peñuelas (pānyōōā'läs), village (1930 pop. 86), Coquimbo prov., N central Chile, seaside resort on the Pacific (Coquimbo Bay), on railroad and 4 mi. SW of La Serena. Fruitgrowing. Has casino, racecourse.

Peñuelas, town (pop. 2,330), S Puerto Rico, 7 mi. WNW of Ponce; rail terminus in sugar-growing region; mfg. of cigars. The Garzas falls and hydroelectric plant are 2½ mi. N.

Peñuelas, Lake (□ 7), Valparaiso prov., central Chile, 8 mi. SE of Valparaiso; c.7 mi. long.

Penugonda (pā'nōōgōndū), town (pop. 10,557), West Godavari dist., NE Madras, India, in Godavari R. delta, 15 mi. N of Narasapur; rice and oilseed milling, coir-rope mfg.; tobacco, sugar cane. Sometimes spelled Penukonda.

Penukonda (pĕnōōkōn'dū), town (pop. 5,906), Anantapur dist., W Madras, India, 40 mi. S of Anantapur; cotton, peanuts, castor beans. Sheep grazing in near-by forested hills (satinwood, tanbark). Picturesque hill fortress (alt. c.3,000 ft.) was refuge of Vijayanagar kings after their defeat (1565) at battle of Talikota.

Penwell, village (pop. c.900), Ector co., W Texas, 15 mi. SW of Odessa; an oilfield center; gasoline refining.

Penwortham, residential village and parish (pop. 5,586), W Lancashire, England, on Ribble R. and 2 mi. SW of Preston; truck gardening. Has ruins of Penwortham Priory.

Pen-y-Cae or **Penycae** (pĕnūkī'), town and parish (pop. 2,078), SE Denbigh, Wales, 5 mi. SW of Wrexham; coal mining, brick mfg.

Pen-y-Fan, Wales: see BRECON BEACONS.

Pen-y-Gader, Wales: see CADER IDRIS.

Pen-y-Gader Fawr, Wales: see BLACK MOUNTAINS.

Penygraig, Wales: see RHONDDA.

Penza (pyĕn'zŭ), oblast (□ 16,700; 1946 pop. estimate 1,500,000) in central European Russian SFSR; ⊙ Penza. Situated W of Volga Hills, in basin of Sura R.; hilly terrain, especially on sandy and wooded right bank of deep Sura R. valley. Left-bank section has treeless black soils. Pop. includes non-Russian elements (Tatars, Chuvash, Mordvinians). Mainly agr., with rye, oats, wheat, potatoes, hemp (N), sugar beets (NW; mill at Zemetchino), sunflowers; beef cattle, hogs. Industry largely on agr. basis (flour, starch, meat); coarse woolens milled E of Penza (Nikolski Khutor, Zolotarevka, Verkhozim, Sosnovoborsk). Match mfg. (Nizhni Lomov); glassworking (Nikolskaya Pestravka); sawmilling in wooded right-bank section. Main industrial centers: Penza (machine mfg.), Kuznetsk (tanning). Formed 1939 out of Tambov and Kuibyshev oblasts.

Penza, city (1939 pop. 157,145), ⊙ Penza oblast, Russian SFSR, on left bank of Sura R. and 350 mi. SE of Moscow; 53°10'N 45'E. Rail junction; airport; industrial center in grain-growing area; mfg. (machine tools, washing, calculating, and printing machines, agr. implements, watches, bicycles, medical instruments, aircraft parts, paper, matches, cement); agr. processing (meat, flour, alcohol, starch, biscuits, oilseeds). Has industrial and teachers colleges, agr. and regional mus. Rail yards and factories concentrated in N section. Founded 1663 as Moscow fortress on SE border; chartered 1682; developed as a commercial and political center in 18th cent. Was ⊙ Penza govt. until 1928.

Penzance (pĕnzăns'), municipal borough (1931 pop. 11,331; 1951 census 20,648), SW Cornwall, England, at head of Mounts Bay of the Channel, 9 mi. NE of Land's End; 50°7'N 5°32'W. Port, fishing center, and tourist resort; knitting mills. Exports tin, copper, kaolin, granite, vegetables. Port for Scilly Isls., whose flowers are transshipped here by rail to London. Has esplanade, 2 piers, mus., and libraries; known for its mild climate. Sacked by Spanish in 1595; subjected to pirate raids until 18th cent. Sir Humphrey Davy b. here.

Penzberg (pĕnts'bĕrk), town (pop. 8,702), Upper Bavaria, Germany, at N foot of the Bavarian Alps, on the Loisach and 28 mi. SSW of Munich; lignite-mining center.

Penzhina Bay (pyĭnzhē'nŭ), NE arm of Shelekhov Gulf of Sea of Okhotsk, NE Siberian Russian SFSR; separated from Gizhiga Bay by Taigonos Peninsula; extends 185 mi. deep into mainland; 60 mi. wide at mouth; high tides. Receives **Penzhina River,** which rises in Kolyma Range, flows 446 mi. ESE and SSW, through Koryak Natl. Okrug, past Penzhino and Kamenskoye.

Penzhino (–nŭ), village (1948 pop. over 500), N Koryak Natl. Okrug, Kamchatka oblast, Khabarovsk Territory, Russian SFSR, on Penzhina R. and 400 mi. N of Palana; reindeer farms.

Penzing (pĕnt'sĭng), outer W district (□ 25; pop. 95,871) of Vienna, Austria. Site of insane asylum. Its former area (□5; pop. 85,055) was enlarged (1938) by inc. of 2 towns, including Purkersdorf.

Penzlin (pĕntslēn'), town (pop. 3,811), Mecklenburg, N Germany, on small lake, 8 mi. WSW of Neubrandenburg; agr. market (grain, potatoes, stock). Has remains of medieval castle.

Peoria (pēō'rēŭ), county (□ 624; pop. 174,347), central Ill.; ⊙ Peoria. Bounded E and S by Illinois R. and L. Peoria; drained by Spoon R. and Kickapoo Creek. Agr. (corn, wheat, oats, soybeans, livestock, poultry, truck, fruit; dairy products). Bituminous-coal mines; sand, gravel deposits; timber; commercial fisheries. Diversified mfg., food processing and packing. Includes state parks. Formed 1825.

Peoria. 1 Village (1940 pop. 701), Maricopa co., central Ariz., 15 mi. NW of Phoenix; trading point for agr. area (truck, citrus, cotton). Settled 1897. **2** City (pop. 111,856), ⊙ Peoria co., central Ill., on Illinois R. at S end of its widening into L. Peoria, and 60 mi. N of Springfield; 40°42'N 89°35'W. Second-largest city (after Chicago) in Ill.; air, rail, highway, and river transportation center and port of entry, near large bituminous-coal field and in extensive agr. area; grain and livestock market, and a leading distilling center. Mfg. of farm and road machinery, food products, furnaces, washing machines, hardware and tools, sheet metal, wire, foundry products, caskets, cordage, brick, tile, pottery, cotton goods, strawboard, barrels, transparent wrappers, chemicals, corn products, feed; oil refineries. Bradley Univ. is here. Near by are Fort Creve Coeur State Park and Jubilee Col. State Park. La Salle established Fort Creve Coeur in this region in 1680; spot later became trading post (1691), was abandoned during American Revolution, became site of Fort Clark in 1813; American settlers came in 1818. Inc. as town in 1835, as city in 1845. Lincoln denounced slavery here in speech answering Douglas (1854). **3** Town (pop. 201), Ottawa co., extreme NE Okla., 12 mi. ENE of Miami, near Mo. line, in lead- and zinc-mining region.

Peoria, Lake, central Ill., widened section (c.20 mi. long) of Illinois R. immediately above Peoria.

Peoria Heights, village (pop. 5,425), Peoria co., central Ill., just N of Peoria. Inc. 1898.

Peosta (pēŏ'stŭ), town (pop. 60), Dubuque co., E Iowa, 9 mi. WSW of Dubuque.

Peotillos (pēōtē'yōs), village (pop. 1,520), San Luis Potosí, N central Mexico, on interior plateau, 34 mi. NE of San Luis Potosí; alt. 5,446 ft.; corn, wheat, beans, cotton. Cooperative settlement. Railroad station 3 mi. SE.

Peotone (pē'ūtōn), village (pop. 1,395), Will co., NE Ill., 19 mi. SE of Joliet, in agr. and bituminous-coal area; mfg. of steel products. Inc. 1869.

Pepacton Reservoir (pē'păk"tŭn), SE N.Y., artificial lake (18 mi. long), for water supply to New York city; impounded in East Branch of Delaware R. near Downsville by Downsville Dam (2,450 ft. long, 200 ft. high; begun 1947). A 25-mi. water tunnel leads to Rondout Reservoir, whence DELAWARE AQUEDUCT continues to New York.

Peparethus, island, Greece: see SKOPELOS.

Pepel (pĕpĕl'), town (pop. 1,309), Northern Prov., W Sierra Leone, at mouth of Sierra Leone R., 13 mi. ENE of Freetown, 22 mi. SW of Port Loko. Ships iron ore from Marampa mines (linked by rail); modern loading facilities for ocean-going vessels.

Peperpot (pā'pŭrpôt), coffee plantations, Surinam dist., N Du. Guiana, on Surinam R. and 3 mi. SE of Paramaribo.

Pepillo Salcedo (pāpē'yō sälsä'dhō), town (1950 pop. 2,927), Monte Cristi prov., NW Dominican Republic, port on Manzanillo Bay of the Atlantic, at mouth of Massacre (Dajabón) R. (Haiti border), 12 mi. SW of Monte Cristi; exports bananas. Renamed 1949 from Manzanillo. Includes Puerto Libertador or Libertador, a port developed 1945.

Pepin (pĕ'pĭn), county (□ 237; pop. 7,462), W Wis., bounded SW by L. Pepin; ⊙ Durand. Hilly region, drained by Chippewa R.; dairy and livestock area. Produces processed dairy products, canned vegetables; also agr. implements. Fishing and resorts on L. Pepin (a widening of the Mississippi). Formed 1858.

Pepin, village (pop. 840), Pepin co., W Wis., on L. Pepin, 31 mi. SSW of Menomonie, in dairy and farm area; mfg. of agr. implements, dairy-products processing; fishing and lake resort.

Pepin, Lake, natural widening of Mississippi R. bet. Minn. and Wis., SE of Minneapolis; 21 mi. long, 1–2.5 mi. wide. Formed by damming effect of silt deposited by Chippewa R., entering from Wis. Red Wing, Minn., is at NW end, Wabasha, Minn., at SE. There are fishing villages and resorts on its shores.

Pepinster (pŭpĕstâr'), town (pop. 3,023), Liége prov., E Belgium, on Vesdre R. and 3 mi. SW of Verviers; rail junction; wool spinning and weaving; machine-tool mfg.

Pepiri Guaçu River (pĭpĕrē' gwŭsōō'), Sp. *Pepirí Guazú,* right tributary of Uruguay R., forms Brazil-Argentina border throughout its length of 100 mi. Old Braz. spelling, Pepery Guassú.

Pepperell (pĕ'pŭrŭl). **1** Village (pop. 1,166), Lee co., E Ala., 3 mi. SW of Opelika; cotton milling. **2** Town (pop. 3,460), Middlesex co., N Mass., on Nashua R., near N.H. line, and 14 mi. W of Lowell; mfg. (paper, paper products, shoe laces, yarn); apples, peaches, poultry, dairying. Settled 1720, inc. 1753. Includes East Pepperell village (1940 pop. 1,694).

Pepper Pike, village (pop. 874), Cuyahoga co., N Ohio, an E suburb of Cleveland.

Pepperton, town (pop. 572), Butts co., central Ga., just SE of Jackson.

PEPSU, India, see PATIALA AND EAST PUNJAB STATES UNION.

Peqiin, Peqi'in, or **Pekiin** (all: pĕkē-ēn'), village, Upper Galilee, N Israel, at NW foot of Mt. Heidar, 10 mi. W of Safad. Noted for having had Jewish pop. continuously since destruction of Second Temple. Has old synagogue.

Peqin (pĕkyēn') or **Peqini** (pĕkyē'nē), town (1945 pop. 2,317), W central Albania, on Shkumbî R. and 20 mi. SSW of Tirana, on Durazzo-Elbasan RR, at SW foot of the Krrabë; agr. center (olives, rice); coal mining near by. Sometimes spelled Pekin, Pekini, or Pekinj.

Pequabuck, village, Conn.: see PLYMOUTH.

Pequabuck River (pĭkwô'bŭk, pē–), W central Conn., rises NW of Bristol, flows c.25 mi. S, E, and NE, past Bristol and Plainville, to Farmington R. near Farmington.

Pequannock River (pĭkŏ'nŭk, –kwŏ'nŭk, pē–), NE N.J., rises in E Sussex co., flows c.20 mi. generally ESE, forming part of Passaic-Morris co. line, joining Ramapo R. near Pompton Plains to form Pompton R. Near source, dams form Canistear and Oak Ridge reservoirs.

Pequawket, Mount (pĭkwô'kĭt, pē–), peak (3,260 ft.) of White Mts., N Carroll co., N.H., NE of Conway; formerly called Northern Kearsarge Mtn. (kēr'-särj").

Pequení River (pākānē'), tiny river in E central Panama, rises SE of Nombre de Dios in Cordillera de San Blas; formerly a right affluent of Chagres R., it flows to Madden L. of the Panama Canal system.

Pequest River (pē'kwĕst), NW N.J., rises SE of Newton, flows c.35 mi. SW and W, bet. ridges of the Appalachians, to Delaware R. at Belvidere.

Pequiri River (pĭkērē'), S central Mato Grosso, Brazil, rises near Goiás border, flows 200 mi. W to São Lourenço R., which it joins in Paraguay flood plain. Receives Itiquira R. Formerly spelled Pequiry.

Pequop Mountains (pē'kwŏp), NE Nev., in E Elko co., E of Ruby Mts. Spruce Mtn. (11,041 ft.) is in SW spur, c.50 mi. ESE of Elko.

Pequot Lakes (pē'kwŏt), resort village (pop. 552), Crow Wing co., central Minn., near Pelican L., in state forest, 18 mi. NNW of Brainerd; dairy products. Known as Pequot until 1939.

Pera (pĕ'rŭ), suburb of Constantinople, Turkey, on heights above the Golden Horn; under the sultans it was reserved for foreigners; now modern residential section of Istanbul.

Perachora, Greece: see LOUTRAKION.

Pérade, La, Que.: see SAINTE ANNE DE LA PÉRADE.

Peradeniya (pərŭdā'nĭyŭ), suburban section (pop. 2,755) of Kandy, Central Prov., Ceylon, on the Mahaweli Ganga and 3.5 mi. SW of Kandy; rail junction. Has noted botanical gardens with avenues of palms, spice gardens, fernery, orchid house, floricultural section, one of largest pineta in the tropics, and a mus. Central experiment station near by. Building of new university started in 1948.

Perak (pä'răk, Malay pĕräk'), most populous state (□ 7,890; pop. 953,938; including transients, 955,707) of Malaya, on Strait of Malacca; ⊙ Taiping. Bounded N by Thailand along Kalakhiri Range, NW by Kedah and Penang, E by Kelantan and Pahang along central Malayan range (7,160 ft. in the Gunong Korbu), and S by Selangor along Bernam R.; consists essentially of the large fertile Perak R. basin. Agr.: rice (chiefly in Krian dist.), rubber, and coconuts (on Strait near Bagan Datoh and Kuala Gula); fishing along mangrove coast. The leading tin-mining state of Malaya, Perak includes the Kinta Valley (major mines at Ipoh, Tanjong, Rambutan, Batu Gajah, and Kampar) and the Taiping tin dist. Served by W coast railroad with spurs to ports of Telok Anson and Port Weld. Pop.: 45% Chinese, 35% Malay, 15% Indian, and aboriginal Sakais. Ruled by a sultan (residence at Kuala Kangsar) whose dynasty claims descent from sultans of old Malacca, Perak had its first European contacts with Dutch after 1650. British influence began early in 19th cent. with trade treaty (1818). Following disorders among Chinese tin miners and acts of Malay piracy, a Br. protectorate was declared (1874). One of the former Federated Malay States, Perak joined the Federation of Malaya after the Second World War.

Perakhora, Greece: see LOUTRAKION.

Perak River, second longest river (170 mi. long) of Malaya, in Perak; rises on Thailand border in Kalakhiri Range, at Kelantan line, flows S past Kuala Kangsar, Parit, and Telok Anson (head of coastwise navigation) to Strait of Malacca at Bagan Datoh. Used for irrigation and hydroelectric power (CHENDEROH dam). Receives Kinta R. (right).

Peral (päräl') or **Los Molinos** (lōs mōlē'nōs), N suburb (pop. 4,938) of Cartagena, Murcia prov., SE Spain; boatbuilding.

Peral, El (ĕl päräl'), town (pop. 1,044), Cuenca prov., E central Spain, 36 mi. N of Albacete; cereals, grapes, saffron, livestock.

Perala, India: see CHIRALA.

Peralam (pä'rŭlŭm), village (pop. 2,605), Tanjore dist., SE Madras, India, in Cauvery R. delta, 18 mi. NW of Negapatam; rail junction for Fr. port of Karikal, 13 mi. ESE.

Peralba, Monte (môn'tĕ pĕräl'bä), peak (8,835 ft.) in Carnic Alps, N Italy, near Austrian border, 21 mi. NW of Tolmezzo. Source of Piave R.

Peraleda de la Mata (pārälā'dhä dhä lä mä'tä), town (pop. 2,956), Cáceres prov., W Spain, 36 mi. ESE of Plasencia; woolen-cloth mfg.; lumbering, stock raising; cereals, olive oil, wine, fruit.

Peraleda de San Román (sän' rōmän'), village (pop. 1,430), Cáceres prov., W Spain, 35 mi. NE of Trujillo; olive-oil processing; cereals.

Peraleda de Zaucejo (thou-thā'hō) or **Zaucejo,** town (pop. 1,434), Badajoz prov., W Spain, 16 mi. S of Castuera; cereals, olives, acorns, livestock.

Peraleja, La (lä pärälā'hä), town (pop. 1,078), Cuenca prov., E central Spain, 25 mi. WNW of Cuenca; wheat, barley, olives, grapes, anise, saffron, sheep. Lumbering; gypsum quarrying.

Perales del Puerto (pärä'lĕs dhĕl pwĕr'tō), village (pop. 1,674), Cáceres prov., W Spain, 34 mi. WNW of Plasencia; olive-oil processing, flour milling; cereals, figs.

Perales de Tajuña (tähōō'nyä), town (pop. 1,830), Madrid prov., central Spain, on Tajuña R., on railroad and 21 mi. SE of Madrid; cereals, vegetables, grapes, sugar beets, sheep, goats. Olive-oil extracting, soap mfg.

Peralillo (pärälē'yō), town (1930 pop. 721), Colchagua prov., central Chile, on railroad and 27 mi. WNW of San Fernando; fruit- and winegrowing center; livestock.

Peralta (päräl'tä), village (pop. 3,048), Cartago prov., central Costa Rica, on Reventazón R., on railroad and 6 mi. NE of Turrialba; trading center; grain, livestock.

Peralta, town (pop. 3,713), Navarre prov., N Spain, on Arga R. and 22 mi. NNW of Tudela; agr. center (wine, cereals, livestock); vegetable canning, mfg. of brandy and plaster.

Perambalur (pä"rŭmbŭlōōr'), town (pop. 6,998), Trichinopoly dist., S Madras, India, 30 mi. NNE of Trichinopoly; cotton weaving; sheep grazing. Gypsum, limestone, phosphate deposits near by.

Perambavoor, India: see PERUMPAVUR.

Perambur, India: see SEMBIYAM.

Peranai Dam, India: see PERIYAR LAKE; VAIGAI RIVER.

Peranambattu, India: see PERNAMBUT.

Perast (pĕ'räst), Ital. *Perasto* (pĕrä'stô), village, SW Montenegro, Yugoslavia, on E shore of Gulf of Kotor, bet. bays of Risan and Kotor, 6 mi. NW of Kotor. Old Venetian palaces, mostly in ruins. Until 1921, in Dalmatia.

Percé (pĕrsā'), village (pop. estimate 750), ⊙ Gaspé East co., E Que., E Gaspé Peninsula, on the Gulf of St. Lawrence, 25 mi. SSE of Gaspé, at foot of Percé Mtn. (1,230 ft.), opposite Bonaventure Isl.; fishing center. Just offshore is **Percé Rock,** 290 ft. high, sea-bird sanctuary and tourist attraction.

Perche (pârsh), region of NW France, mostly in W Maine and S Normandy, in E Orne, W Eure-et-Loir, and SW Eure depts.; traversed by arc-shaped hill range (average alt. 950 ft.) bet. Argentan (NW) and Nogent-le-Rotrou (SE). Important horse-breeding area which has given its name to the Percheron. Alençon and Mortagne are chief trade centers.

Perche, Col de la (kôl dŭ lä pârsh'), pass (alt. 5,135 ft.) in E Pyrenees, Pyrénées-Orientales dept., S France, on road bet. Mont-Louis and Puigcerdá (Spain).

Perches or **Les Perches** (lā pĕrsh'), town (1950 census pop. 935), Nord dept., NE Haiti, 25 mi. SE of Cap-Haïtien; coffeegrowing.

Perchtoldsdorf (pĕrkh'tōltsdôrf), town (pop. 10,668), after 1938 in Liesing dist. of Vienna, Austria, 7 mi. SW of city center; wine.

Percy (pĕrsē'), village (pop. 506), Manche dept., NW France, 14 mi. SSW of Saint-Lô; cider distilling, stock raising.

Percy (pûr'sē). **1** Village (pop. 933), Randolph co., SW Ill., c.50 mi. SSE of East St. Louis, in agr. and coal area. **2** Village, Coos co., N.H.: see STARK.

Percy Islands, coral group in Coral Sea, bet. Great Barrier Reef and Northumberland Isls., 50 mi. off E coast of Queensland, Australia. Consists of 12 isls. surrounded by reefs; largest, Pine Peak Isl. (5 mi. long, 2.5 mi. wide; rising to 224 ft.); wooded. Some sheep raising.

Perdasdefogu (pĕr"däsdĕfô'gōō), village (pop. 1,375), Nuoro prov., SE Sardinia, 37 mi. NNE of Cagliari; anthracite mines.

Perdices, Las, Argentina: see LAS PERDICES.

Perdido, Arroyo (äroi'ō pĕrdē'dō), Patagonian river in central Chubut natl. territory, Argentina, rises in salt desert 20 mi. SSE of Gastre, flows c.150 mi. SE and NE to lose itself in swamps 30 mi. SSW of Telsen.

Perdido, Monte (mōn'tā), Fr. *Mont Perdu* (mōpĕr-dü'), peak (10,997 ft.) in central Pyrenees, NE Spain (Huesca prov.), near Fr. border, 14 mi. SSE of Luz (France).

Perdido River (pûrdē'dō), in Ala. and Fla., rises 8 mi. NW of Atmore, S Ala., flows c.60 mi. S, forming SW Ala.–NW Fla. line, to Perdido Bay (15 mi. long, 1–5 mi. wide) of Gulf of Mexico, 11 mi. WNW of Pensacola, Fla.

Perdigão (pĕrdēgã'ō), town (pop. 641), S central Minas Gerais, Brazil, near railroad, 70 mi. W of Belo Horizonte. Newly discovered manganese deposits now mined. Until 1944, called Saúde.

Perdigón (pĕr-dhēgōn'), village (pop. 1,210), Zamora prov., NW Spain, 7 mi. S of Zamora; cereals, wine.

Perdizes, Brazil: see VIDEIRA.

Perdões (pĕrdō'ĭs), city (pop. 2,787), S Minas Gerais, Brazil, on railroad and 14 mi. SE of Campo Belo; coffee, tobacco.

Perdriel (pĕr-dhrē-ĕl'), town (pop. estimate 500), N Mendoza prov., Argentina, in Mendoza R. valley, on railroad, and 13 mi. SSW of Mendoza; winegrowing center; apiculture; petroleum refining.

Perdu, Mont, Spain: see PERDIDO, MONTE.

Perdue (pûr'dū), village (pop. 327), S central Sask., on small Van Scoy L., 40 mi. W of Saskatoon; grain elevators, dairying.

Perebory, Russian SFSR: see SHCHERBAKOV.

Perechin (pĕrĭchēn'), Czech. *Perečin* (pĕ'rĕchĭn), Hung. *Perecseny* (pĕ'rĕchĕnyŭ), town (1941 pop. 3,667), W Transcarpathian Oblast, Ukrainian SSR, on Uzh R., on railroad and 11 mi. NE of Uzhgorod; wood cracking.

Peredelkino (pĕrĭdyĕl'kēnŭ), town (1947 pop. over 500), central Moscow oblast, Russian SFSR, 6 mi. SW of Kuntsevo; summer resort.

Peredniye Traki, Russian SFSR: see KRASNOARMEISKOYE, Chuvash Autonomous SSR.

Pereginsko (–gēn'skŭ), Pol. *Perehińsko* (pĕrĕhē'-nyŭskô), town (1931 pop. 5,910), W central Stanislav oblast, Ukrainian SSR, on Lomnitsa R. and 25 mi. WSW of Stanislav, in petroleum dist.; flour and sawmilling.

Péreille (pārā'), village (pop. 42), Ariège dept., S France, 10 mi. ESE of Foix; bauxite and lignite mining.

Pereira (pĕrā'rä), city (pop. 30,762), Caldas dept., W central Colombia, on affluent of Cauca R., in W foothills of Cordillera Central, on railroad and highway, and 23 mi. SW of Manizales; alt. 4,840 ft. Communication, trading, and processing center for a rich coffee region, also trading in livestock; mfg. of chocolate, sweets, cigars. Other agr.: sugar, tobacco, fruit, yucca, cacao, corn, bamboo.

Pereira Barreto (pĭrā'rŭ bŭrā'tōō), city (pop. 1,258), NW São Paulo, Brazil, near right bank of Tietê R., 60 mi. WNW of Araçatuba; sericulture; coffee, rice, cotton. Settled by Japanese. Terminus of rail spur at Lussanvira (3 mi. S) across river.

Pereiras (–rŭs), city (pop. 1,124), S central São Paulo, Brazil, 40 mi. NW of Sorocaba; cotton, beans, corn, cattle.

Pereiro (–rōō), city (pop. 1,038), E Ceará, Brazil, near Rio Grande do Norte border, 65 mi. NE of Iguatu; hides, feathers, cotton.

Perejil (pārāhēl'), uninhabited islet in the Strait of Gibraltar, just off Sp. Morocco, 6 mi. WNW of Ceuta. Belongs to Spain.

Perekop (pĕrĭkôp'), crossroads village on Perekop Isthmus, N Crimea, Russian SFSR, on railroad and 45 mi. NW of Dzhankoi; grain, livestock. Has ruins of anc. Gr. and Tatar fortifications (ditches, ramparts). Located at strategic site on only overland route to Crimea; formerly a fortified trade center, but declined after 1900, following construction of Kharkov-Sevastopol rail route (E) across Sivash lagoon.

Perekop Gulf, inlet of Karkinit Gulf in NW Crimea, Russian SFSR, W of Perekop Isthmus; 10 mi. wide, 12 mi. long.

Perekop Isthmus, connects Crimea (Russian SFSR) with mainland of Ukrainian SSR; separates Perekop Gulf of Black Sea (W) from Sivash lagoon (E); 4–15 mi. wide, c.20 mi. long. Salt lakes (S). Site of small villages (former trade centers) of Perekop and Armyansk. Here Red Army inflicted final defeat (1920) on General Wrangel in Rus. civil war.

Père-Lachaise (pâr-läshĕz'), largest cemetery of Paris, France, located in city's 20th *arrondissement*. It is the resting place of many famous personages.

Perelada (pārālä'dhä), town (pop. 1,028), Gerona prov., NE Spain, 4 mi. NE of Figueras; livestock, olive oil, wine. Has fine 14th-cent. castle (restored 19th cent.), with glass collection.

Perelazovski or **Perelazovskiy** (pĕrĭlä'zŭfskē), village (1939 pop. over 500), W Stalingrad oblast, Russian SFSR, 25 mi. SW of Kletskaya; wheat, dairy farming.

Perelló (pārälyō'), village (pop. 2,275), Tarragona prov., NE Spain, near the Mediterranean, 10 mi. NE of Tortosa; processes and ships olive oil and honey. Wheat, almonds, wine in area.

Perelyub (pĕrĭlyōōp'), village (1926 pop. 2,840), E Saratov oblast, Russian SFSR, 65 mi. ESE of Pugachev, in the Obshchi Syrt; wheat, cattle. Oil-shale deposits near by.

Pere Marquette River (pēr" märkĕt'), W Mich., rises in N Newaygo co., flows generally NW c.50 mi., past Scottville, to L. Michigan at Ludington. Chief tributary: South Branch (c.35 mi. long).

Pere Marquette State Park, Ill.: see GRAFTON.

Peremetnoye (pĕrĭmyôt'nŭyŭ), village, N West Kazakhstan oblast, Kazakh SSR, on railroad and 20 mi. W of Uralsk, in wheat area; metalworks.

Peremyshl or **Peremyshl'** (–mĭ'shŭl), village (1948 pop. over 2,000), E Kaluga oblast, Russian SFSR, on the Oka, at Zhizdra R. mouth, and 18 mi. SSW of Kaluga; flour mill.

Peremyshlyany (pĕrĭmĭsh'lyŭnē), Pol. *Przemyślany* (pshĕmĭshlä'nē), city (1931 pop. 5,391), S Lvov oblast, Ukrainian SSR, on Gnilaya Lipa R. and 26 mi. SE of Lvov; flour and sawmilling, distilling.

Pereña (pārā'nyä), village (pop. 1,180), Salamanca prov., W Spain, near Duero (Douro) R., 50 mi. WNW of Salamanca; olive-oil processing; lumbering; livestock, wine, cereals.

Pérenchies (pārāshē'), residential town (pop. 4,359), Nord dept., N France, 5 mi. NW of Lille; textile weaving. Heavily damaged in First World War.

Perené River (pārānyā'), Junín dept., central Peru, formed by confluence of Chanchamayo R. and Paucartambo R. at Puerto Wertheman, flows 80 mi. ESE, joining Ene R. at Puerto Prado to form TAMBO RIVER. Coffee grown in valley.

Pereruela (pārārwā'lä), village (pop. 1,041), Zamora prov., NW Spain, 10 mi. SW of Zamora; ceramics mfg.; cereals, vegetables, livestock.

Pererva, Russian SFSR: see LYUBLINO.

Peresechnaya (pĕrĭsyĕch'nīŭ), town (1926 pop. 5,921), N central Kharkov oblast, Ukrainian SSR, on railroad and 11 mi. WNW of Kharkov city center.

Pereshchepino (–shchĕ'pēnŭ), village (1926 pop. 9,213), N Dnepropetrovsk oblast, Ukrainian SSR, 40 mi. NNE of Dnepropetrovsk; hemp, wheat.

Peresinthos, Greece: see DESPOTIKON.

Pereslavl-Zalesski or **Pereslavl'-Zalesskiy** (–slä'-vŭl-zŭlyĕs'kē), city (1936 pop. 16,900), S Yaroslavl oblast, Russian SFSR, on PLESHCHEYEVO LAKE, on road and 70 mi. SSW of Yaroslavl; cotton-milling center; chemicals, flour milling, clothing mfg. Has kremlin with oldest cathedral (1152) of NE Russia, Nikolski convent (1392), and mus. Several monasteries near by. Founded 1152; became ⊙ principality, passing 1302 to Moscow. Formerly called Pereyaslavl-Zalesski.

Perevoloki, Russian SFSR: see SAMARA BEND.

Perevolotskoye (pĕrĭvŭlôt'skŭyŭ), village (1948 pop. over 2,000), central Chkalov oblast, Russian SFSR, on Samara R., on railroad, and 35 mi. W of Chkalov; metalworking; wheat, livestock. Formerly called Perevolotsk.

Pereyaslavka (pĕrĭyŭslăf'kŭ), village (1948 pop. over 2,000), S Khabarovsk Territory, Russian SFSR, on Trans-Siberian RR (Verino station) and 35 mi. S of Khabarovsk; wheat, perilla; lumbering.

Pereyaslav-Khmelnitski or **Pereyaslav-Khmel'nitskiy** (pĕrĭyŭslăf'-khmĭlnyĕt'skē), city (1935 pop. 17,468), E Kiev oblast, Ukrainian SSR, on Trubezh R. (left affluent of the Dnieper) and 50 mi. SE of Kiev; clothing and leather industry; metalworking, flour milling. Known since 10th cent.; was ⊙ principality (11th–12th cent.). Formerly called Pereyaslavl and, c.1928–44, Pereyaslav; renamed for Bohdan Chmielnicki (Khmelnitski), who proclaimed here (1654) union of the Ukraine with Russia.

Pereyaslavl-Zalesski, Russian SFSR: see PERESLAVL-ZALESSKI.

Pérez (pā'rĕs), town (pop. estimate 2,000), SE Santa Fe prov., Argentina, 7 mi. WSW of Rosario; agr. and mfg. center, with railroad shops and glass factory; alfalfa, corn, flax, wheat, grapes, livestock (cattle, sheep).

Perez, town (1939 pop. 1,082; 1948 municipality pop. 3,507), Quezon prov., Philippines, on NW coast of Alabat Isl., off Luzon, 9 mi. NW of Alabat town; fishing.

Pérez Island, Mexico: see ALACRÁN ARRECIFE.

Pérez Rosales Pass (pā'rĕs rōsä'lĕs) (3,300 ft.), in the Andes, on Argentina-Chile border, at N foot of Monte Tronador, on road from San Carlos de Bariloche (Argentina) to Puerto Montt (Chile); 41°4'S 71°52'W.

Pérez Zeledón, canton, Costa Rica: see UREÑA.

Perg (pĕrk), town (pop. 3,837), NE Upper Austria, on short Naarn R. and 15 mi. E of Linz, N of the Danube; breweries.

Perga (pûr'gŭ), anc. town of Pamphylia, S Asia Minor, 10 mi. NE of Antalya (Adalia), Turkey. It was famous for its temple of Artemis, and there are extensive Roman ruins. Paul's first labors in Asia Minor here.

Pergamino (pĕrgämē'nō), city (pop. 30,904), ⊙ Pergamino dist. (□ 1,028; pop. 72,591), N Buenos Aires prov., Argentina, on branch of the Arrecifes and 65 mi. S of Rosario. Agr. and rail center (8 lines join here), with railroad shops; flour milling, dairying. Has art school, agr. research station, natl. col.

Pergamum or **Pergamon,** –**os,** –**us** (pûr'gŭmŭm, –mŏn, –mŏs, –mŭs), anc. Greek city of Asia Minor in the fertile Caicus (modern Bakir) valley at site of present-day BERGAMA, W Turkey, 50 mi. N of Smyrna. There are extensive ruins of the anc. city, which reached its greatest splendor in 3d cent. B.C. as ⊙ kingdom of Pergamum and as seat of great library which rivaled that of Alexandria. Passed to Romans c.130 B.C., became ⊙ Roman prov. of Asia; was early Christianized; one of the "seven churches of Asia." Parchment takes its name from Pergamum. Galen lived here.

Pergine Valsugana (pĕr'jēnĕ välsōōgä'nä), town (pop. 3,895), Trento prov., Trentino–Alto Adige, N Italy, 6 mi. E of Trent; lumber and silk mills, furniture and macaroni factories. Has castle (now a hotel).

Pergola (pĕr'gôlä), town (pop. 1,985), Pesaro e Urbino, The Marches, central Italy, 8 mi. S of Fossombrone; silk mill, tannery. Bishopric.

Pergusa, Lake, Sicily: see ENNA, city.

Perham (pŭ'rŭm). **1** Town (pop. 572), Aroostook co., NE Maine, 15 mi. NW of Presque Isle, in agr. region. **2** Resort village (pop. 1,926), Otter Tail co., W Minn., near Pine L., 32 mi. NE of Fergus Falls, in grain, livestock, poultry area; dairy products, flour.

Perhentian Islands, 2 islands (pop. 344) in South China Sea, N Trengganu, Malaya, 10 mi. off Kuala Besut; banana plantations.

Periam (pâ'ryäm), Hung. *Perjámos* (pĕr'yämôsh), village (pop. 5,050), Timisoara prov., W Rumania, 5 mi. NW of Timisoara; rail junction; mfg. of felt hats and knitwear; textile dyeing, flour milling, woodworking.

Periana (päryä'nä), town (pop. 2,724), Málaga prov., S Spain, 19 mi. NE of Málaga; olives, cereals, fruit; flour milling, liquor distilling. Has medicinal springs, with Baños de Vila 2 mi. N.

Periapatna, India: see PERIYAPATNA.

Peribán (pārēbän'), officially Peribán de Ramos, town (pop. 2,185), Michoacán, central Mexico, at W foot of Sierra de los Terascos, 33 mi. WNW of Uruapan; sugar cane, tobacco, coffee, fruit, stock.

Peribonca River (pĕ"rĭbŏng'kŭ), central Que., rises in the Otish Mts., flows 300 mi. S, through Peribonca L. (20 mi. long), to L. St. John. Near its mouth are 25-ft. falls.

Perico (pārē'kō), town (pop. estimate 1,500), SE Jujuy prov., Argentina, 17 mi. SE of Jujuy; rail junction and agr. center (corn, wine, alfalfa, citrus fruit, olives, livestock). Experimental farm, agr. school. Irrigation dam near by.

Perico, town (pop. 4,508), Matanzas prov., W Cuba, on Central Highway and 40 mi. ESE of Matanzas; rail junction and sugar-growing center. Near by are the sugar centrals of España (N), Tinguaro (E).

Perico del Carmen, Argentina: see EL CARMEN.

Perico Island, islet in Panama Bay of Panama Canal Zone guarding Pacific entrance of the Panama Canal, 3 mi. S of Panama city. Joined to Naos Isl. (W) and mainland by mole.

Pericos (pārē'kōs), town (pop. 1,269), Sinaloa, NW Mexico, in coastal lowland of Gulf of California, 23 mi. NW of Culiacán; chick-peas, corn, sugar cane, fruit, vegetables.

Périers (pārēā'), village (pop. 1,182), Manche dept., NW France, 15 mi. WNW of Saint-Lô; road junction. Dairying. Damaged during American Saint-Lô offensive (July, 1944) in Second World War.

Périgord (pārēgôr'), old division of Guienne, SW France, and former countship, now included in Dordogne and part of Lot-et-Garonne depts.; ⊙ Périgueux. Consists of arid limestone plateaus dissected by fertile valleys of Dordogne and Isle rivers. Region noted for its truffles and goose livers. Chief towns: Périgueux and Bergerac. Numerous cave dwellings and prehistoric remains have been found near Les Eyzies. Countship of Périgord (originated 9th cent.) was enfeoffed to dukes of Aquitaine. Wrested from the English in 14th cent. it passed to the house of Bourbon, and became part of royal domain when Henry of Navarre became (1589) King of France.

Périgotville (pārēgōvēl'), village (pop. 795), Constantine dept., NE Algeria, in Little Kabylia (Babor range), 13 mi. NNE of Sétif; cereals.

Périgueux (pārēgû'), anc. *Vesunna*, city (pop. 37,287), ⊙ Dordogne dept., SW France, on the Isle and 50 mi. SW of Limoges; known for its *pâté de foie gras* and truffles. Communications center and leading hog market; mfg. (hardware, cutlery, chemicals, textiles, leather goods); vegetable preserving, woodworking. Of considerable historical and architectural interest. Périgueux has 2 old districts: the old Roman city (W) and medieval Puy-Saint-Front section (E, overlooking river). Chief bldgs. are the restored 12th-cent. cathedral of Saint-Front; the cloister (only remnant of powerful medieval abbey); and 12th-cent. church of St. Étienne (former cathedral). Roman relics include tower of Vésone, amphitheater, and baths. Anc. stronghold of Gallic Petrucorii. Devastated by barbarians in 3d cent. Repulsed English repeatedly during Hundred Years War but ceded to them in 1360. Returned to France under Charles V. Protestant stronghold in 16th cent. Was old ⊙ Périgord.

Perijá, Venezuela: see MACHIQUES.

Perijá, Sierra de (syĕ'rä dā pārēhä'), Andean range on Colombia-Venezuela border, N spur of Cordillera Oriental; comprises Serranía de los Motilones, Serranía de Valledupar, and Montes de Oca; extends c.190 mi. NNE-SSW from 9° to 11°10'N; rises to 12,300 ft.

Peril Strait, SE Alaska, bet. Chichagof Isl. (N) and Baranof Isl. (S), extends c.50 mi. from Salisbury Sound to Chatham Strait on the Pacific.

Perim (pûrĭm'), Arabic *Barim*, island dependency (□ 5; 1946 pop. 360) of Aden Colony, in the strait Bab el Mandeb, 100 mi. W of Aden town; 12°39'N 43°25'E. Rocky, barren, and rising to 214 ft., it lies just off southwesternmost point of Arabian Peninsula, opposite Sheikh Said. On SW side is good small harbor, site of former coaling station (1883-1936), lighthouse, and telegraph station. Airfield (N); some fishing. Isl. was occupied in 1738 by the French; and held briefly (1799) by the British, who' reoccupied it in 1857 and placed it under the administration of Aden. Perim flourished (1921 pop. 2,075) while a coaling station, but declined after 1936 when coaling operations were transferred to Aden. The Aden commissioner of police is administrator of the isl.

Peri Mirim (pĭrē' mērēn'), city (pop. 1,590), N Maranhão, Brazil, near W shore of São Marcos Bay, 25 mi. WSW of São Luís; sugar, cotton, cereals, tobacco. Until 1944, called Macapá.

Perinaldo (pĕrēnäl'dô), village (pop. 1,242), Imperia prov., Liguria, NW Italy, 6 mi. N of Bordighera.

Perinet (pĕrēnā'), village, Tamatave prov., E central Madagascar, on railroad and 85 mi. SW of Tamatave; sawmilling, graphite mining.

Perintalmanna (pĕrĭn'tŭlmŭnŭ), village, Malabar dist., SW Madras, India, 14 mi. N of Shoranur; rice, cassava, pepper, ginger.

Perinthus, Turkey: see EREGLI.

Periperi, city, Brazil: see PIRIPIRI.

Periperi, Serra do (sĕ'rŭ dŏŏ pĭrēpĭrē'), range in S Bahia, Brazil, extends c.100 mi. ENE from Vitória da Conquista; rises to 3,300 ft. Forms watershed bet. the Rio de Contas (N) and Rio Pardo (S). Formerly spelled Serra do Peripery.

Peri River (pĕrē'), E central Turkey, rises on Saksak Dag 25 mi. S of Erzurum, flows 145 mi. W and SW, past Kigi, to Munzur R. 14 mi. E of Pertek. Sometimes spelled Piri.

Perister (pĕrĭstĕr'), highest peak (8,530 ft.) of Baba range in Pindus system, in Yugoslav Macedonia, 8 mi. WSW of Bitolj. Also called Pelister.

Peristera (pĕrĭstĕ'rä), uninhabited Aegean island (□ 5.3) in Northern Sporades, Magnesia nome, Greece, off E coast of Halonnesos isl.; 39°12'N 23°58'E; 5 mi. long, 1-2 mi. wide. Also called Evonymos (Evonimos) and Xeronesi (Xeronisi).

Peristeri (pĕrĭstĕ'rē), NW suburb (1951 pop. 35,656) of Athens, Greece, 3 mi. from city center.

Peristeri, peak, Greece: see LAKMOS.

Peristeri, island, Greece: see LIKOREMA.

Periyakulam (pä"rĭyŭkŏŏlŭm'), city (pop. 25,882), Madura dist., S Madras, India, 40 mi. WNW of Madura; trade center for products (timber, cardamom, tea, coffee, fruit) of Palni Hills (N), Cardamom Hills (W), and Kambam Valley (SW). Health resort of Kodaikanal is 9 mi. NNW.

Periyapatna (pĕ'rĭyäpŭtnŭ) or **Piriyapatna** (pĭ'-), town (pop. 3,957), Mysore dist., SW Mysore, India, 37 mi. W of Mysore; tobacco curing; grain and mango trade. Also spelled Periapatna; formerly also Periyapattana.

Periyar Lake (pārēyär'), reservoir (□ c.12) in Western Ghats, in E Travancore-Cochin, India, near Madras border; alt. c.2,800 ft.; surrounded by peaks rising to over 4,000 ft. Formed by dam (c.1,240 ft. long, 175 ft. high; completed 1895) across upper Periyar R. From N arm of lake a 5,700-ft. tunnel conducts water, via Suruli R. in Kambam Valley, Madras, to Vaigai R. mouth 8 mi. SSW of Periyakulam. From the Vaigai, irrigation canals (main channel, c.45 mi. long, begins at Peranai Dam, 8 mi. WNW of Solavandan) irrigate over 100,000 acres, formerly subject to famine, in Madura dist.

Periyar River, in Travancore-Cochin, India, rises in Western Ghats 60 mi. NNE of Trivandrum, flows N (here dammed to form Periyar L.), generally NNW, and W past Alwaye and Parur to Malabar Coast of Arabian Sea 15 mi. NNW of Cochin; length, 140 mi.

Perjamos, Rumania: see PERIAM.

Perkasie (pûr'kŭsē), borough (pop. 4,358), Bucks co., SE Pa., 28 mi. NNW of Philadelphia; textiles, metal products, cigars, bricks; sandstone, traprock quarrying; agr. Inc. 1876.

Perkata (pĕr'kätō), Hung. *Perkáta*, town (pop. 4,948), Fejer co., W central Hungary, 20 mi. SE of Szekesfehervar; hemp, potatoes, corn; cattle, horses.

Perkins. 1 County (□ 885; pop. 4,809), SW central Nebr.; ⊙ Grant. Agr. area bounded W by Colo. Wheat, small grains, livestock. Formed 1887. **2** County (□ 2,866; pop. 6,776), NW S.Dak., on N.Dak. line; ⊙ Bison. Farming and ranching region drained by North Fork Grand R., Moreau R., and several artificial lakes. Lignite deposits and mines; livestock, grain. Formed 1908.

Perkins. 1 Island township, Maine: see SWAN ISLAND. **2** Village (pop. c.500), Delta co., S Upper Peninsula, Mich., 9 mi. NNW of Gladstone, in farm and resort area. **3** Town (pop. 164), Scott co., SE Mo., in Mississippi flood plain, 7 mi. W of Oran. **4** Town (pop. 706), Payne co., N central Okla., 10 mi. S of Stillwater, and on Cimarron R.; wheat, cotton, corn, livestock.

Perkins Bay, inlet of Bass Strait, NW Tasmania; formed by Robbins Isl. (W), Circular Head peninsula (E), and Perkins Isl. (S); 10 mi. long, 8 mi. wide. Connects S with Duck Bay (6 mi. long, 2 mi. wide; site of Smithton).

Perkins Peak (9,880 ft.), SW B.C., in Coast Mts., 200 mi. NNW of Vancouver; 51°48'N 125°5'W.

Perkinston, village (pop. c.200), Stone co., SE Miss., 28 mi. N of Gulfport; lumber milling. Has dist. jr. col.

Perkinsville, Vt.: see WEATHERSFIELD.

Perkiomen Creek (pûrkēō'mŭn), SE Pa., rises in several branches in S Berks and Lehigh counties, flows c.35 mi. S to Schuylkill R. 6 mi. WNW of Norristown.

Perkovic (pĕr'kôvĭch), Serbo-Croatian *Perković*, Ital. *Percovio* (pĕrkô'vēô), village, S Croatia, Yugoslavia, 12 mi. ESE of Sibenik, in Dalmatia; rail junction. Sometimes spelled Perkovich.

Perl, Luxembourg: see PERLÉ.

Perl (pĕrl), village (pop. 964), NW Saar, near Moselle R., 16 mi. SE of Luxembourg city, 13 mi. NE of Thionville; frontier station on Luxembourg and Fr. borders, opposite Remerschen and Apach; viticulture. Formerly part of Prussian Rhine Prov.; annexed to Saar in 1946.

Perla, La, Mexico: see LA PERLA.

Perla, La, Peru: see BELLAVISTA, Callao constitutional prov.

Perlak (pûrläk'), **Peureulak,** or **Purulak** (both: pûrŭläk'), region of N Sumatra, Indonesia, on Strait of Malacca, c.30 mi. NNW of Langsa; site of important oil fields, connected by pipe line with Pangkalanbrandan. Also called Porola, Peureula.

Perlak, Yugoslavia: see PRELOG.

Perlas, Laguna de, Nicaragua: see PEARL LAGOON.

Perlé (pĕrlā'), Ger. *Perl* (pĕrl), village (pop. 603), W Luxembourg, in the Ardennes, 6 mi. WNW of Redange, near Belg. border; slate quarrying; rye, oats, pulse, potatoes.

Perleberg (pĕr'lûbĕrk), town (pop. 13,701), Brandenburg, E Germany, on Stepenitz R. and 7 mi. NE of Wittenberge; food canning, chemical mfg.; market center for asparagus- and fruitgrowing region. Has 14th-cent. church, 15th-cent. town hall.

Perlepe, Yugoslavia: see PRILEP.

Perles-et-Castelet (pârl-ā-kästŭlā'), village (pop. 91), Ariège dept., S France, in central Pyrenees, on the Ariège and 18 mi. SSE of Foix; calcium carbide and electrometallurgical plants. Pyrite mining near by.

Perlesreuth (pĕr'lŭsroit), village (pop. 2,725), Lower Bavaria, Germany, in Bohemian Forest, 14 mi. N of Passau; grain, tobacco, livestock.

Perley, village (pop. 204), Norman co., W Minn., on Red R. and 20 mi. N of Fargo, N.Dak.; dairy products.

Perlican Island (pûr'lĭkŭn), islet on E side of Trinity Bay, SE N.F., just NW of Old Perlican; 48°5'N 53°1'W; lighthouse.

Perlis (pĕrlĭs'), smallest and northwesternmost state (□ 310; pop. 70,490) of Malaya, on Strait of Malacca; ⊙ Kangar (raja's residence is at Arau). Enclosed NE and NW by Thailand along the Kalakhiri Range (rising to 2,370 ft. in the Gunong China) and bounded SE by Kedah; consists of alluvial plain (drained by Perlis R.), one of chief rice-growing areas of Malaya, and interior limestone hills (tin mining near Kaki Bukit). Rubber and coconuts are lesser crops. Fisheries along coast (minor ports at Kuala Perlis and Sanglang). State is traversed by W coast railroad crossing into Thailand at Padang Besar. Pop.: 80% Malay, 16% Chinese. Part of Kedah until 1821, it was set up (1841) as separate state under a raja. Thai suzerainty rights passed (1909) to Great Britain and Perlis became one of nonfederated Malay States. After Second World War, when it was temporarily annexed (1943-45) by Thailand, it joined Federation of Malaya.

Perlis River, chief river of Perlis, NW Malaya, formed by several branches at Kangar (head of navigation), flows 7 mi. SW to Strait of Malacca at Kuala Perlis.

Perm, Russian SFSR: see MOLOTOV, oblast, city.

Permanente, Calif.: see CUPERTINO.

Përmet (pûrmĕt') or **Përmeti** (pûrmĕ'tē), Tosk *Prëmet* or *Prëmeti*, town (1945 pop. 2,201), S Albania, on Vijosë R. and 40 mi. SE of Berat; commercial center. Pop. largely Orthodox.

Perna (pĕr'nō), Swedish *Pernå*, Finnish *Pernaja* (pĕr'näyä), residential village (commune pop. 8,286), Uusimaa co., S Finland, on bay of Gulf of Finland, 6 mi. W of Lovisa. Mikael Agricola b. here.

Pernambuco (pûrnŭmbōō'kō, Port. pĕrnãmbōō'kŏŏ), state (□ 37,458; 1940 pop. 2,688,240; 1950 census pop. 3,430,630), NE Brazil; ⊙ Recife. Largest of "finger states" on Brazilian bulge. Bounded N by Paraíba and Ceará, W by Piauí, S by Bahia and Alagoas, and E by the Atlantic. Has narrow coastal zone with damp tropical climate (somewhat relieved by SE trade winds), a drier intermediate zone giving access to Brazilian plateau, and the arid interior (*sertão*) which suffers from prolonged droughts. Average temp. 78°F. Only perennial stream is the São Francisco, which forms part of state's S border. Pernambuco is leading agr. and industrial state of the NE. Sugar cane is by far the leading crop in humid coastal strip (rainy season, March-June), which also grows tobacco, coffee, rice, castor beans, coconuts, and tropical fruit (pineapples, mangoes, cashews, avocados). Chief products of the interior are cotton, manioc, and vegetables (especially near Pesqueira). Here cattle, sheep, and horses are raised extensively. Main industries (primarily agr. processing) are sugar refining, alcohol distilling, cotton milling; mfg. of tobacco products, leather goods, pharmaceuticals, cement, furniture, paper; and processing of caroa fibers. Principal cities are Recife and its N suburb Olinda, Caruaru, Garanhuns, and Limoeiro, all in the densely populated E part of the state. Recife, hub of rail communications to the interior and to adjacent states, is state's only seaport. Through it are exported sugar, lumber, hides, fruit, and drugs. First permanent settlement (1530s) at Olinda, which became ⊙ Pernambuco captaincy. Occupied by Dutch (1630-54), it prospered under enlightened rule of Maurice of Nassau-Siegen. Originally embracing most of Brazil's NE bulge, Pernambuco lost (1799) territory of present states of Ceará, Rio Grande do Norte, Paraíba, and (1817) Alagoas. After creation of Brazilian Empire, Pernambuco prov. participated in several separatist revolts (1824, 1831, 1848). In 1889 it became a state of the federal republic. State's name sometimes given to its capital.

Pernambuco, city, Brazil: see RECIFE.

Pernambut (pĕrnäm'bŭt) or **Peranambattu** (pārŭnäm'bŭt-tōō), town (pop. 12,319), North Arcot dist., central Madras, India, 10 mi. W of Gudiyattam; hides and skins. Sometimes spelled Pernambathi.

Pernand-Vergelesses (pĕrnã'-vĕrzhŭlĕs'), commune (pop. 305), Côte-d'Or dept., E central France, on E slope of the Côte d'Or, 4 mi. N of Beaune; Burgundy wines.

Pernarec (pĕr'närĕts), Ger. *Pernharz* (pĕrn'härts), village (pop. 468), SW Bohemia, Czechoslovakia, 14 mi. NW of Pilsen; barite mining.

Pernau, Estonia: see PARNU.

Pernegg (pĕr'nĕk), village (pop. 3,003), Styria, SE central Austria, on Mur R. and 11 mi. E of Leoben; place of pilgrimage (church of Maria Pernegg); summer resort. Château (built 1582); ruins of Alt-Pernegg.

Perném (pĕrnĕm'), town, N Goa dist., Portuguese India, 15 mi. N of Pangim, on Goa-India border; local market for timber, fish, coconuts, rice; cattle raising.

Pernes or **Pernes-en-Artois** (pârn'-änärtwä'), village (pop. 1,472), Pas-de-Calais dept., N France, 10 mi. SW of Béthune; Portland cement mfg.

Pernes (pĕr'nĭsh), village (pop. 1,578), Santarém dist., central Portugal, 10 mi. N of Santarém; precision metalworking (blades).

Pernes-en-Artois, Pas-de-Calais dept., France: see PERNES.

Pernes-les-Fontaines (pârn-lā-fōtĕn'), town (pop. 2,019), Vaucluse dept., SE France, 13 mi. ENE of Avignon; agr. trade center; fruit and vegetable preserving, winegrowing.

Pernharz, Czechoslovakia: see PERNAREC.

Pernik, Bulgaria: see DIMITROVO.

Perniö (pĕr'nēŭ), Swedish *Bjärnå* (byĕr'nō), village (commune pop. 10,026), Turku-Pori co., SW Finland, 35 mi. ESE of Turku, in dairying and lumbering region. Has 15th-cent. church.

Pernis (pĕr'nĭs), town (pop. 848), South Holland prov., W Netherlands, on Ijsselmonde isl., on New Maas R., opposite Schiedam; 2 mi. W are large petroleum refineries, oil storage tanks, and docks. Mfg. (synthetic fertilizers, chemicals); oil bunkering station.

Pernitz (pĕr'nĭts), village (pop. 2,255), E Lower Austria, on Piesting R. and 8 mi. SW of Berndorf; poultry, vineyards.

Pernov, Estonia: see PARNU.

Pernstejn (pĕrn'shtān), Czech *Pernštejn*, village (pop. 152), W Moravia, Czechoslovakia, 5 mi. SSE of Bystrice nad Pernstejnem. Its famous 3-storied castle, partly cut in solid rock, founded in 13th cent., was completed in 17th cent., withstood

Swedish siege in 1645; has extensive fortifications, watchtowers, gates, and arms collections.

Perobolinggo, Indonesia: see PROBOLINGGO.

Peron, Cape (pĕ'rŭn), SW Western Australia, W end of headland forming S shore of Cockburn Sound; 32°16'S 115°42'E.

Péronne (pārôn'), town (pop. 3,669), Somme dept., N France, on Somme R. (canalized) and 17 mi. WNW of Saint-Quentin; agr. trade center with large flour mills. Truck farming and fishing in marshy valley. Formerly fortified. Here in 1468 took place the "interview" bet. Louis XI of France and Charles the Bold of Burgundy. Rebuilt after virtual destruction in First World War (changed hands 4 times), Péronne was again damaged 1939–45.

Péronnes (pārôn'), town (pop. 6,385), Hainaut prov., S Belgium, 9 mi. E of Mons; coal mining.

Peron Peninsula (pĕ'rŭn), W Western Australia, bet. Denham Sound (W) and Hopeless Reach (E) of Shark Bay; 50 mi. long, 19 mi. wide. Denham on W coast.

Perosa Argentina (pĕrō'zä ärjĕntē'nä), village (pop. 1,999), Torino prov., Piedmont, NW Italy, 8 mi. NW of Pinerolo; silk mill. Graphite and talc mines near by.

Peros Banhos (pā'rōōs bä'nyōōs), coral atoll (□ 4; pop. 332) in Chagos Archipelago of Indian Ocean, a dependency of Mauritius; 5°20'S 71°50'E. Encloses lagoon, 15 mi. long, 11 mi. wide. Copra.

Perote (pārō'tā), town (pop. 4,072), Veracruz, E Mexico, at NW foot of Cofre de Perote, in Sierra Madre Oriental, 22 mi. W of Jalapa; agr. center (corn, coffee, maguey); pulque distilling, sawmilling. Fortress of San Carlos de Perote (built 1770–77) near by was occupied 1847 by Amer. forces under Gen. Worth and heavily disputed during Fr. intervention; has been restored as military prison.

Perote, Canyón de, Peru: see SANTA RIVER.

Perote, Cofre de (kō'frā dā), peak (14,048 ft.) in Veracruz, E Mexico, 15 mi. W of Jalapa; extinct volcano. Called also Nauhcampatépetl or Naucampatépetl (noukämpätā'pĕtŭl).

Pêro Viseu (pā'rōō vēzē'ōō), village (pop. 1,450), Castelo Branco dist., central Portugal, 6 mi. SSE of Covilhã; lumbering, wool processing.

Perovo (pyĭrō'vŭ). **1** Village, Krasnoyarsk Territory, Russian SFSR: see PARTIZANSKOYE. **2** City (1926 pop. 23,711; 1939 pop. 77,727), central Moscow oblast, Russian SFSR, adjoining (E of) Moscow; important rail junction; locomotive repair shops; machine mfg. Includes Kuskovo (just E), with chemical plant (turpentine, rosin, formaldehyde), and former countryseat (now a mus.) of Count Sheremetyev.

Perovsk, Kazakh SSR: see KZYL-ORDA, city.

Perparim or **Perparimi**, Albania: see POGRADEC.

Perpendicular, Point, E New South Wales, Australia, forms NE end of entrance to Jervis Bay; 35°5'S 150°50'E. Rises sharply to c.265 ft.; lighthouse.

Perpetua, Cape, (pŭrpĕ'chōōŭ), W Oregon, coastal promontory 10 mi. S of Waldport; recreational area.

Perpignan (pĕrpēnyä'), city (pop. 64,358), ⊙ Pyrénées-Orientales dept., S France, near Gulf of Lion and Sp. border, on right bank of Têt R. and 95 mi. SE of Toulouse; 42°43'N 2°53'E. Regional commercial center with important trade in fruits (apricots, peaches, cherries), Roussillon wines, and olives. Has few industries (brickworks, carriage workshops). Architecture shows Sp. influence. Notable are: 14th-cent. *Loge*, which housed the merchants' exchange; 14th–16th-cent. Gothic cathedral of St. Jean; 14th-cent. Castillet (fortified gate); and castle of the kings of Mallorca which forms part of huge 16th–17th-cent. citadel. Founded in 11th or 12th cent., Perpignan was ⊙ of kingdom of Mallorca and, after 1642, of Roussillon prov. Became episcopal see in 1602. Pop. tripled since 1870, largely due to influx of Spaniards.

Perquenco (pârkĕng'kō), town (pop. 1,259), Cautín prov., S central Chile, on railroad and 27 mi. NNE of Temuco; agr. center (wheat, oats, potatoes, livestock); flour milling, lumbering.

Perquilauquén River (pĕrkēlouken'), S central Chile, rises in the Andes, flows c.80 mi. NW and N, along Linares-Ñuble and Linares-Maule prov. borders, to join Longaví R. 10 mi. WNW of Linares, forming Loncomilla R.

Perquimans (pŭrkwĭ'mŭnz), county (□ 261; pop. 9,602), NE N.C.; ⊙ Hertford. Bounded S by Albemarle Sound; drained by Perquimans R. Partly forested tidewater area, with Dismal Swamp in NE; farming (peanuts, cotton, corn), fishing, sawmilling. Formed 1672.

Perquimans River, NE N.C., rises in Dismal Swamp, flows c.30 mi. S and SE to Albemarle Sound 14 mi. SE of Hertford.

Perranzabuloe (pĕ"rŭnză'būlō), agr. village and parish (pop. 2,745), W Cornwall, England, 6 mi. NW of Truro. Oratory of St. Piran (6th cent.) discovered 2 mi. N in 1835 after being buried in sands 1,000 years, is considered one of oldest Christian churches in England. In parish, 2 mi. NW, on the Atlantic, is fishing village and seaside resort of Perranporth (pĕrŭnpôrth').

Perrégaux (pĕrāgō'), town (pop. 11,098), Oran dept., NW Algeria, in the Tell, 24 mi. S of Mostaganem; rail hub (junction of E-W line and of spur inland to Colomb-Béchar) with railroad workshops; center of irrigated Habra lowland (dams on Hammam and Fergoug rivers), growing citrus fruit, cotton, truck. Agr. experiment station near by.

Perreux (pĕrû'), village (pop. 352), Loire dept., SE central France, near Loire R., 2 mi. E of Roanne; tar processing, winegrowing.

Perreux-sur-Marne, Le (lŭ pĕrû'-sür-märn'), town (pop. 22,950), Seine dept., N central France, E suburb of Paris, 7 mi. from Notre Dame Cathedral, on right bank of Marne R.; road center; mfg. (furniture, clothing, toys, brushes); printing.

Perriers-sur-Andelle (pĕrēā'-sür-ädĕl'), village (pop. 1,034), Eure dept., NW France, on the Andelle and 13 mi. E of Rouen; cotton weaving.

Perrigny (pĕrēnyē'), village (pop. 937), Jura dept., E France, 2 mi. E of Lons-le-Saunier; clockmaking, gem cutting.

Perrigny-lès-Dijon (-lā-dēzhō'), outer S suburb (pop. 373) of Dijon, Côte-d'Or dept., E central France; important railroad yards.

Perrin Air Force Base, Texas: see SHERMAN, city.

Perrine, town (pop. 2,859), Dade co., S Fla., 13 mi. SW of Miami.

Perrinton, village (pop. 383), Gratiot co., central Mich., 8 mi. SSW of Ithaca, in agr. and dairying area.

Perris, city (pop. 1,807), Riverside co., S Calif., 16 mi. SSE of Riverside, bet. San Jacinto Mts. (E) and Santa Ana Mts. (W). Gold mining, fruit-growing, general farming (potatoes, truck) in area. Platted 1885, inc. 1911.

Perron (pĕrō'), village (pop. estimate 1,000), W Que., 11 mi. ENE of Val d'Or; gold mining.

Perros-Guirec (pĕrōs'-gērĕk'), town (pop. 3,867), Côtes-du-Nord dept., W France, small fishing port on English Channel, 6 mi. N of Lannion; summer resort. Granite quarries. Near-by Ploumanach noted for pink-granite formations.

Perrot Island or **Île Perrot** (ēl pĕrō') (7 mi. long, 3 mi. wide), S Que., at W end of L. St. Louis, 18 mi. SW of Montreal; dairying, potato growing. Bounded by channels of Ottawa R.; linked with Montreal Isl. and mainland by bridges.

Perrunal, El (ĕl pĕrōōnäl'), N suburb (pop. 1,288) of Calañas, Huelva prov., SW Spain; mines pyrite.

Perry. 1 County (□ 734; pop. 20,439), W central Ala.; ⊙ Marion. In the Black Belt; drained by Cahaba R. and Oakmulgee Creek. Cotton, livestock. Part of Talladega Natl. Forest in NE. Formed 1819. **2** County (□ 556; pop. 5,978), central Ark.; ⊙ Perryville. Bounded NE by Arkansas R. Nimrod Dam in Fourche La Fave R. is here. Agr. (cotton, corn, hay, truck, livestock); lumber milling. Formed 1840. **3** County (□ 443; pop. 21,684), SW Ill.; ⊙ Pinckneyville. Bounded partly E by Little Muddy R.; drained by small Beaucoup and Galum creeks. Agr. area (corn, wheat; dairy products; livestock, poultry), with bituminous-coal mining; oil wells. Mfg. (flour, explosives, cigars, machinery). Formed 1827. **4** County (□ 384; pop. 17,367), S Ind.; ⊙ Cannelton. Bounded S and partly E by Ohio R., here forming Ky. line; drained by small Anderson R., a tributary of the Ohio. Bituminous-coal mining and agr. area (dairy products; poultry, livestock), with mfg. at Cannelton and Tell City. Timber; sandstone quarries. Formed 1814. **5** County (□ 343; pop. 46,566), SE Ky.; ⊙ Hazard. In the Cumberlands; drained by North Fork of Kentucky R. and several creeks. Important bituminous-coal-mining area; oil and gas wells, timber; some agr. (dairy products, livestock, poultry, apples, corn, sweet and Irish potatoes, soybeans, tobacco). Some mfg. at Hazard. Formed 1820. **6** County (□ 653; pop. 9,108), SE Miss.; ⊙ New Augusta. Drained by Leaf R.; by Black, Thompsons, and Tallahala creeks; and by small Bogue Homo. Agr. (cotton, corn); lumbering. Includes part of De Soto Natl. Forest. Formed 1820. **7** County (□ 476; pop. 14,890), E Mo.; ⊙ Perryville. Bounded E by Mississippi R. Grain, livestock, lumber; iron deposits. Formed 1820. **8** County (□ 409; pop. 28,999), central Ohio; ⊙ New Lexington. Drained by small Rush, Sunday, Jonathan, and Moxahala creeks. Includes part of Buckeye L. (resort). Agr. (livestock, grain, fruit, truck); mfg. at New Lexington and Crooksville; coal mining, fire-clay quarrying. Formed 1817. **9** County (□ 550; pop. 24,782), S central Pa.; ⊙ Bloomfield. Mtn. area; bounded E by Susquehanna R.; drained by Juniata R. Tuscarora Mtn. along N, Blue Mtn. along S border. Grist-mill products, clothing, hardware, flour, milk products, textiles. Formed 1820. **10** County (□ 419; pop. 6,462), W central Tenn.; ⊙ Linden. Bounded W by Tennessee R.; drained by Buffalo R. Includes part of Kentucky Reservoir. Livestock raising, dairying, agr. (corn, hay, peanuts); timber. Formed 1821.

Perry. 1 Town (pop. 284), Perry co., central Ark., 35 mi. NW of Little Rock, near Arkansas R.; ships lumber. **2** Town (pop. 2,797), ⊙ Taylor co., N Fla., c.50 mi. ESE of Tallahassee; rail junction; sawmilling center (lumber; crates). **3** City (pop. 3,849), ⊙ Houston co., central Ga., 26 mi. S of Macon, in diversified agr. and quarrying area; mfg. (cement, lumber, baskets). Settled c.1820, inc. 1824. **4** Village (pop. 444), Pike co., W Ill., 28 mi. W of Jacksonville, in agr. area. **5** City (pop. 6,174), Dallas co., central Iowa, 30 mi. NW of Des Moines, bet. Raccoon R. and Beaver Creek; processing and trade center, with meat- and poultry-packing plants, fertilizer and shovel factories, foundry, railroad shops. Settled in 1860s. **6** City (pop. 399), Jefferson co., NE Kansas, on Delaware R. near its mouth on Kansas R., and 14 mi. E of Topeka; shipping point for grain, livestock, potatoes. **7** Town (pop. 613), Washington co., E Maine, on Passamaquoddy Bay and 5 mi. NW of Eastport. Passamaquoddy Indian Reservation near by. **8** Village (pop. 1,203), Shiawassee co., S central Mich., 18 mi. NE of Lansing, in farm area (livestock, poultry, truck, grain, beans; dairy products). **9** City (pop. 813), Ralls co., NE Mo., near Salt R., 25 mi. SW of Hannibal; grain, poultry; coal. **10** Village (pop. 4,533), Wyoming co., W N.Y., 27 mi. SSE of Batavia, near Silver L.; summer resort. Letchworth State Park is just SE. Mfg.: knit goods, metal products, food products. Settled 1815, inc. 1830. **11** Village (pop. 665), Lake co., NE Ohio, 6 mi. NE of Painesville, near L. Erie. **12** City (pop. 5,137), ⊙ Noble co., N Okla., 34 mi. ESE of Enid, in agr. area; flour milling, dairy-products processing; mfg. of concrete and sheet-metal products, leather, pottery. Oil wells. Founded 1893, inc. 1894. **13** Town (pop. 133), Aiken co., W central S.C., 28 mi. SSW of Columbia. **14** Town (pop. 449), Box Elder co., N Utah, just S of Brigham City.

Perry, Camp, Ohio: see PORT CLINTON.

Perry Hall, village (1940 pop. 897), Baltimore co., N Md., 11 mi. NE of downtown Baltimore.

Perryman, village (pop. c.300), Harford co., NE Md., 26 mi. ENE of Baltimore; cannery.

Perryopolis, village (pop. 1,125), Fayette co., SW Pa., 13 mi. N of Uniontown.

Perry Point, Md.: see PERRYVILLE.

Perry River, trading post, NW Keewatin Dist., Northwest Territories, on Queen Maud Gulf, at mouth of Perry R.; 67°48'N 101°40'W.

Perrysburg. 1 Village (pop. 361), Cattaraugus co., W N.Y., 18 mi. E of Dunkirk; mfg. (wooden containers, furniture). **2** Village (pop. 4,006), Wood co., NW Ohio, suburb of Toledo, across Maumee R. from SW outskirts of Toledo; metal stampings, furniture, playground equipment, tile, meat products. Laid out 1816.

Perrysville. 1 Town (pop. 462), Vermillion co., W Ind., on the Wabash and 40 mi. N of Terre Haute, in agr. and bituminous-coal area. **2** Village (pop. 674), Ashland co., N central Ohio, 13 mi. ESE of Mansfield and on Black Fork of Mohican R.; pottery. Pleasant Hill Reservoir (capacity 87,700 acre-ft.; for flood control), impounded in Clear Fork of Mohican R., is near by.

Perryton, city (pop. 4,417), ⊙ Ochiltree co., extreme N Texas, in high plains of the Panhandle, near Okla. line, 100 mi. NNE of Amarillo; market center for rich wheat-producing co.; ships cattle, feed; mfg. (dairy products, machinery and parts, canvas products, concrete blocks, truck and trailer bodies). Perryton State Park (recreation center) is near. Founded 1919, inc. 1920.

Perryville, village (1939 pop. 92), SW Alaska, on SE Alaska Peninsula, N of Kupreanof Point; 55°54'N 159°8'W; fishing, trapping. Established 1912 when natives from Katmai Volcano dist. were moved here.

Perryville. 1 Town (pop. 674), ⊙ Perry co., central Ark., 33 mi. WNW of Little Rock and on Fourche La Fave R., in stock-raising and agr. area; sawmilling. **2** Town (pop. 660), Boyle co., central Ky., 9 mi. W of Danville. Near by is Perryville Battlefield State Park, scene of Civil War battle (Oct. 8, 1862) bet. Confederates under Gen. Braxton Bragg and Union forces under Gen. D. C. Buell; battle, though indecisive, marked end of Bragg's invasion of Ky. Halfway Inn (built c.1792) and a natl. cemetery in vicinity. **3** Town (pop. 679), Cecil co., NE Md., at mouth of the Susquehanna (bridged 1940), opposite Havre de Grace; railroad shops. Seat of Perry Point hosp. (for veterans). **4** City (pop. 4,591), ⊙ Perry co., E Mo., near Mississippi R., 34 mi. NW of Cape Girardeau; shoes, cigars, grain, wood, dairy products. St. Mary's Seminary (Catholic) near by. Founded c.1821. **5** Village, R.I.: see SOUTH KINGSTOWN.

Persan (pĕrsä'), town (pop. 3,726), Seine-et-Oise dept., N central France, on right bank of Oise R., opposite Beaumont-sur-Oise, and 21 mi. N of Paris; metalworking center (forges, foundries); mfg. (rubber, absorbent cotton, chemicals). Damaged in Second World War.

Persante River, Poland: see PROSNICA RIVER.

Persberg (pĕrs'bĕr"yŭ, pĕsh'-), village (pop. 688), Varmland co., W Sweden, in Bergslag region, on Yng L., Swedish *Yngen* (6 mi. long, 4 mi. wide), 4 mi. ENE of Filipstad; largest iron mines of Varmland have been in operation here since 15th cent.

Perseigne, Forest of, France: see ALENÇON.

Persembe (pĕr-shĕmbĕ'), Turkish *Perşembe*, village (pop. 2,011), Ordu prov., N Turkey, on Black Sea, 8 mi. NW of Ordu; hazel-nuts, filberts. Formerly Vona and Babali.

Persenk, Bulgaria: see Chernatitsa Mountains.

Persepolis (pûrsĕ′pùlĭs), Persian *Takht-i-Jamshid* or *Takht-e-Jamshid* (both: täkht′ĕjămshēd′) [=throne of Jamshid], anc. city of Persia, 30 mi. NE of modern Shiraz, on Marvdasht plain, near confluence of Kur and Pulvar rivers. Founded by Darius, it was the ceremonial capital of the Persian Empire under the Achaemenids; the administrative capitals were Ecbatana (Hamadan) and Susa. Ruins stand on large platform at foot of mtn. façade (E) and are reached by great staircase (W). They include Hall of 100 Columns, and palaces of Darius, Xerxes, and later successors. In mtn. wall are 3 rock-hewn sepulchers of anc. Persian kings. Four more Achaemenian tombs, including that of Darius, and Sassanian bas-reliefs are on a mountainside, NNE across Pulvar R. Persepolis was ruined (330 B.C.) by Alexander the Great and declined through Seleucid and Parthian neglect. The Sassanids moved their official residence to near-by Istakhr (Estakhr, Stakhr), which flourished until arrival of Arabs in 7th cent. and its subsequent eclipse by Shiraz.

Pershing (pûr′shĭng), county (□ 5,993; pop. 3,103), NW central Nev.; ⊙ Lovelock. Mtn. region crossed (N-S) by Humboldt R. Chief ranges are Humboldt, Seven Troughs, and Trinity. Part of Black Rock Desert is in NW. Mining (quicksilver, tungsten, gold, copper). Agr. (alfalfa, barley, oats, sugar beets, wheat), livestock raising, and dairying in Humboldt irrigation project (N of Lovelock). Formed 1919.

Pershing. 1 (pûr′zhĭng, –shĭng) Village (1940 pop. 668), Marion co., S central Iowa, c.40 mi. ESE of Des Moines, in bituminous-coal-mining and agr. area. **2** (pûr′shĭng) Town (pop. 62), Osage co., N Okla., 6 mi. SSE of Pawhuska.

Pershore (pär′shùr), town in parishes of Pershore Holy Cross (pop. 2,394) and Pershore Saint Andrew (pop. 1,049), S Worcester, England, on Avon R. and 8 mi. SE of Worcester; agr. market; bacon and ham curing and packing. Has remains of abbey founded 689, a 15th-cent. church, and 14th-cent. bridge.

Pershotravensk (pyĕrshŭtră′vyĭnsk), town (1939 pop. over 500), W Zhitomir oblast, Ukrainian SSR, on Sluch R. and 3 mi. S of Baranovka; ceramics; kaolin.

Pershotravnevoye (–vnyĭvŭyù), village (1926 pop. 5,699), S Stalino oblast, Ukrainian SSR, 10 mi. WSW of Zhdanov; truck produce. Until 1946, Mangush.

Pershyttan (pĕrs″hü′tän, pĕsh″–), village (pop. 499), Orebro co., S central Sweden, 2 mi. SW of Nora; iron mining and smelting.

Persia: see Iran.

Persia, town (pop. 373), Harrison co., W Iowa, on Mosquito Creek and 27 mi. NNE of Council Bluffs.

Persian Gulf, anc. *Sinus Persicus*, Arabic *Khalij al 'Ajam*, Persian *Khalij-i-Fars*, shallow arm (□ 90,000) of Arabian Sea, bet. Iran and Arabia, extends c.600 mi. from the Shatt al Arab (mouth of the Tigris and Euphrates rivers) to the Strait of Hormuz, which links it with the Gulf of Oman; 600 mi. long, 230 mi. wide, up to 300 ft. deep. Chief ports are: Bandar Abbas, Bushire, Bandar Shahpur, Abadan, and Khurramshahr in Iran; Basra on the Shatt al Arab in Iraq; Kuwait; Ras Tanura and Dammam in Hasa (Saudi Arabia); Manama on main Bahrein isl.; Doha (Qatar); Sharja and Dibai (Trucial Oman). The Persian Gulf is a major oil-shipping lane (from Abadan and Ras Tanura) and was used as a route for lend-lease supplies going to USSR via Iran during Second World War. It is noted for an oppressively hot, humid summer climate. Its pearl fisheries are well known.

Persianovka, Russian SFSR: see Novocherkassk.

Persis, Iran: see Fars.

Person (pûr′sùn), county (□ 400; pop. 24,361), N N.C., on Va. line; ⊙ Roxboro. Piedmont tobacco and timber area; textile mfg. (Roxboro), sawmilling. Formed 1791.

Perstorp (pĕrs′tôrp″, pĕsh′–), village (pop. 2,223), Kristianstad co., S Sweden, 14 mi. W of Hassleholm; metalworking; mfg. of furniture, vinegar.

Pertang (pùrtäng′), village (pop. 611), N Negri Sembilan, Malaya, 25 mi. NE of Seremban; rubber.

Pertek (pĕrtĕk′), village (pop. 2,527), Tunceli prov., E central Turkey, near Murat R., 13 mi. NNE of Elazig; onions, tobacco.

Perth, municipality (pop. 98,924; metropolitan Perth 272,586), ⊙ Western Australia, on N bank of Perth Water and Swan Estuary, 12 mi. from its mouth; 31°57′S 115°52′E. Commercial and cultural center of state; its port, Fremantle, is 9 mi. SW. Mfg. of clothing, furniture, automobiles, fertilizer, Portland cement, sandalwood oil; govt. munitions plant, flour mills, confectionaries. St. George's Cathedral (Anglican), St. Mary's Cathedral (R.C.), mus., art gall. Seaside resorts in W suburbs. Univ. of Western Australia at near-by Crawley. City founded 1829.

Perth, county (□ 840; pop. 49,694), S Ont., on Thames R.; ⊙ Stratford.

Perth. 1 Village (pop. estimate c.700), NW N.B., on St. John R. and 22 mi. S of Grand Falls; lumbering, woodworking, canoe mfg. **2** Town (pop. 4,458), ⊙ Lanark co., SE Ont., on Tay R. and 45 mi. SW of Ottawa; woolen milling and knitting, woodworking; mfg. of shoes, felt, chemicals, soap, hardware.

Perth or **Perthshire** (–shĭr), county (□ 2,493.4; 1931 pop. 120,793; 1951 census 128,072), central Scotland; ⊙ Perth. Bounded by Kinross, Clackmannan, and Dumbarton (SW), Argyll (W), Inverness (N), Aberdeen (NE), Angus (E), and Fifeshire (SE). Drained by the Tay, Forth, Earn, Tummel, Garry, Isla, Lyon, and Teith rivers. Surface is mountainous, leveling toward SE, and includes Grampian Mts., Ochil Hills, and Sidlaw Hills; highest peaks are Ben Lawers, Ben More, Schiehallion, Ben Vorlich, Ben Ledi, and Ben Venue. Among the numerous lakes are lochs Earn, Ericht, Katrine, Tay, Rannoch, Achray, and Vennachar. Many glens are noted for their scenic beauty, and there are numerous tourist resorts, among them the famous Trossachs. The Tay fisheries are important; there are extensive deer forests. Agr. and sheep grazing are carried on; Strathearn and the Carse of Gowrie are especially fertile. Hydroelectric power is used; coal, copper, ironstone, and slate are worked; other industries are woolen, cotton, and linen milling. Besides Perth, other towns are Dunblane, Dunkeld, Blairgowrie, Crieff, Auchterarder, and Coupar-Angus. Cathedrals at Dunkeld and Dunblane; numerous anc. castles. Scone figures large in Scottish history. There are associations with Ossianic legend and with many of Scott's works. Co. was scene of battles of Dupplin Moor, Tibbermore or Tippermuir, Methven, Killiecrankie, and Sheriffmuir.

Perth, burgh (1931 pop. 34,807; 1951 census 40,466), ⊙ Perthshire, Scotland, in SE part of co., on right bank of the Tay (18th-cent. bridge) and 35 mi. NNW of Edinburgh; agr. market, with mfg. of textile machinery, agr. machinery, carpets. Beautifully situated at foot of Moncreiffe, Kinnoull, and other hills, with parks on banks of the Tay. Notable bldgs. include Hosp. of St. James (1569), now workers' tenement, on site of old Carthusian monastery (1429) in which James I was buried; 15th-cent. Church of St. John, in which John Knox delivered famous sermon against idolatry in 1559; Natural History Mus.; and General Prison for Scotland (1812). Perth or St. Johnstoun was site of 4 important monasteries and was ⊙ Scotland until murder here of James I in 1437, after which it was superseded by Edinburgh. Perth was involved in frequent conflicts, including battle (1396) bet. 2 clans on the North Inch (now a park) described in Scott's *Fair Maid of Perth*. In 1600 the Gowrie conspiracy took place here and in 1644 Tippermuir or Tibbermore, 4 mi. W of Perth, was scene of defeat of the Covenanters by Montrose. Just NNE, across the Tay, is suburb of Bridgend, where John Ruskin spent part of his childhood.

Perth, town (pop. 558), NE central Tasmania, 10 mi. S of Launceston and on S.Esk R.; agr. and dairying center.

Perth, village (pop. 124), Towner co., N N.Dak., 20 mi. NW of Cando.

Perth Amboy (ăm′boi), city (pop. 41,330), Middlesex co., NE N.J., 16 mi. S of Newark, with good harbor at mouth of Raritan R. (bridged) on Raritan Bay, at S end of Arthur Kill (here bridged, 1928, to Staten Isl.). Copper smelting, oil refining (also at Barber, just N), mfg. (metal products, clay and terra cotta products, plastics, asbestos, clothing, chemicals); shipyards, drydocks; clay deposits. Port of entry. Settled 1683, inc. 1718. Was ⊙ East Jersey (1686–1702); then alternate ⊙ N.J. for a time. Grew after coming of Lehigh Valley RR in 1876; became coal-shipping center. Points of interest: mansion of Gov. William Franklin, used as a British hq. in Revolution (now a hotel); Parker Castle (1723), St. Peter's Church (1722; Episcopal), and Lawrence Kearny's house (now occupied by local historical society). William Dunlap b. here.

Perthshire, Scotland: see Perth, county.

Perthus, Le (lù pĕrtüs′), village (pop. 569), Pyrénées-Orientales dept., S France, on Perthus pass (Sp. border), in the Monts Albères, 16 mi. S of Perpignan; alt. 915 ft. Custom station. Mispickel quarries near by. The pass (lowest in the Pyrenees), on Perpignan-Barcelona highway, is dominated by the fort of Bellegarde, rebuilt by Vauban in 1679.

Perth Water, Australia: see Swan River.

Perticara (pĕrtēkä′rä). **1** Village (pop. 1,916), Forlì prov., Emilia-Romagna, N central Italy, near Marecchia R., 16 mi. S of Cesena. Sulphur mines near by. **2** Village (pop. 1,916), Pesaro e Urbino prov., The Marches, central Italy, 20 mi. SW of Rimini; sulphur mining.

Pertominsk (pyĕrtŭmĕnsk′), village, NW Archangel oblast, Russian SFSR, on Dvina Bay, 60 mi. WNW of Archangel; sawmilling; fisheries.

Pertosa (pĕrtô′zä), village (pop. 771), Salerno prov., Campania, S Italy, on right bank of Tanagro R. and 22 mi. ESE of Eboli. The stalactite Grotta di Pertosa and a hydroelectric plant partly fed by stream issuing from the grotto lie across the river.

Pertuis (pĕrtwē′), town (pop. 4,498), Vaucluse dept., SE France, near the Durance, 12 mi. N of Aix-en-Provence; early fruit- and vegetable-shipping center; pyrotechnics. Has restored Gothic church and belfry.

Pertuis Breton, France: see Breton, Pertuis.

Pertuis d'Antioche, France: see Antioche, Pertuis d'.

Pertuis de Maumusson, France: see Maumusson, Pertuis de.

Pertunmaa (pĕr′tōōnmä″), village (commune pop. 4,595), Mikkeli co., S Finland, in lake region, 30 mi. WSW of Mikkeli; graphite mines.

Pertusato, Cape (pĕrtōōzä′tô), southernmost tip of Corsica, on Strait of Bonifacio, 2 mi. SE of Bonifacio; 41°21′N 9°11′E. Lighthouse.

Pertusola, Italy: see Muggiano.

Peru (pùrōō′), Sp. *Perú* (pārōō′), republic (in 1949: □ 514,059, pop. estimate 8,277,031; in 1940: □ 482,257, pop. 7,023,111, including c.3,000,000 Indians), W South America; ⊙ Lima. Third largest country of the continent and stretching S from the equator for 18° of latitude, it has a 1,400-mi. Pacific coastline from which it extends E in 3 parallel but utterly different regions—the arid coastal plain, the towering Andean cordilleras, and the E slope forested montaña descending to the jungle of the upper Amazon basin. It is bordered N by Ecuador, NE by Colombia along the Putumayo R. and E by Brazil, partly along Yavarí or Javari R.; in SE it shares the Altiplano and L. Titicaca with Bolivia. In the extreme S its coastal desert is continued by the Atacama Desert of Chile. Off the coast are a few isls., some of them, such as Chincha Islands and Lobos Islands, formerly important for their guano. Varying conditions of climate and topography have profoundly affected the economic, racial, and social pattern of Peru's people. Most distinctive physical feature is the Andean backbone of giant ranges, customarily divided into eastern, central, and western cordilleras, but really more a complex mass of disconnected ridges, separating the major rivers and converging upon so-called knots (Nudo de Pasco, Nudo de Vilcanota). Though the continental divide lies in the westernmost chain, where rises, only 85 mi. from the Pacific, the Marañón River, principal Amazon headstream, the E rim, on the edge of the montaña, represents the most formidable, deeply dissected barrier, drenched by heavy rainfall; here rises the other great headstream of the Amazon, the Ucayali River. Gorges such as Pongo de Manseriche obstruct access to the Amazon basin. The Andes rise to the Huascarán (22,205 ft.) in the snow-clad Cordillera Blanca. Volcanic peaks lie near Arequipa in SE (El Misti, Chachani, Pichu Pichu). More than 60% of the entire pop., mostly native Indians, still speaking *Quechua* and *Aymara*, live high in the Andes above 10,000 ft., able to engage in feats of physical labor impossible, in these heights, to others. Here, in the large upland basins, they raise corn and alfalfa, at higher altitudes potatoes, wheat, and barley; some sugar on lower slopes. Crops are cultivated on terraces. Coffee and cacao growing is pushed in Perené River valley. Stock raising, particularly in S, is devoted mostly to sheep; also cattle, goats, and—bred in the high, inhospitable *puna* or *páramos*—the characteristic Andean alpaca, vicuñas, guanacos, and llamas, which serve as beasts of burden and supply fine wool, collected at Arequipa and shipped through Mollendo and the new port of Matarani. Among the leading agr. centers are, N-S, Cajamarca, Huarás, Jauja, Huancayo, Ayachucho (site of ultimate Sp. defeat, 1824, in South America), Cuzco (the old Inca ⊙), and Sicuani. Puno, also a livestock and wool center, is the Peruvian port on the large L. Titicaca, considered the globe's highest navigable water body. However, the Andean region's chief economic importance lies in its vast mineral resources, for which Peru has been famed since Inca days. The country leads the world in production of bismuth and vanadium (from Minas Ragra), though far more copper (third in Latin America) is mined, centered at Cerro de Pasco, Morococha, and Casapalca, and smelted at La Oroya, which is supplied by coal from near-by Goyllarisquizga. Along with the copper, substantial amounts of silver and gold are mined. Peru also produces lead, zinc, tin, antimony (Puno dept.), mercury (Huancavelica), nickel, manganese, tungsten, molybdenum. Arsenic, cadmium, and indium are by-products of the copper-refining process. Iron mining is carried on at Marcona. The coal and iron deposits of the Santa River valley are being developed for a new steel industry based at the Pacific port of Chimbote. All these mineral products are, however, surpassed in quantity and value by petroleum, the leading export (mainly to Bolivia and Chile) after cotton and sugar cane. Oil wells are concentrated in N coastland of Tumbes and Piura provs. (Zorritos, Lobitos, Talara, Negritos). The same region of the Sechura desert yields salt. Petroleum is now also drilled in the montaña, principally in Ganso Azul field, and refined at Agua Caliente. This vast, partly unexplored section E of the Andes, covering more than 60% of Peru and extending far into the Amazon basin, is humid tropical lowland with a lush vegetation, where savannas and rain forests alternate. Only a small part of the Peruvian people live here, predominantly backward Indian tribes. The region is intersected by a vast net of streams, foremost the Ucayali and Marañón which form the Amazon S of IQUITOS. That city, c.2,300 mi. from the mouth of Amazon, and farthest inland port of major size in the world, can be reached by ocean-going vessels, and is thus, as is the entire area, oriented toward the Atlantic. A once-renowned rubber center (there was a boom here from the 1880s to 1912), it still trades in forest products (rubber, balata, gums, cinchona, coca, barbasco, medicinal plants, tagua nuts, timber); also some hides; cotton, rice, coffee grown in cleared ground. Flourishing agr. centers are farther W—the anc. town MOYOBAMBA and the river ports YURIMAGUAS on the Huallaga and PUCALLPA on the Ucayali, now linked by highway (completed 1943) with Lima via TINGO MARÍA and Cerro de Pasco. PUERTO MALDONADO on the MADRE DE DIOS (affluent of the BENI RIVER) has become a center for Japanese settlers. Entirely different conditions prevail in the Pacific lowland, a strip c.10–40 mi. wide wedged bet. the steep coastal escarpment and the western Andes. This desert belt has, in spite of an unfavorable climate, achieved pre-eminence in the nation's economy. Wholly within the Tropics, it nevertheless has none of the wetness usually associated with equatorial areas; because of the cold north-flowing Peru or Humboldt Current, rainfall is less than 2 inches annually. Lima has an average annual temp. of 66°F. Heavy fogs, called locally *garúa*, occur during winter (May-Nov.), but the southwesterly winds hardly ever drop rain. However, this regime is occasionally upset when once within 3 or 4 decades torrential rains cause untold havoc to the desert mode of life. Frequent earthquakes are another curse of this region as well as of the interior. The arid belt is crossed by numerous small rivers, of which only about 20 larger streams, plunging down from the Andes, have a permanent flow. As agr. is impossible here without irrigation, several isolated oases were developed (since pre-Colombian and probably pre-Incan times) along the alluvial fans. These highly productive oases, though covering approximately 1% of the country's surface, are responsible for the principal goods for foreign trade —cotton (a variety of long hard fibers) and sugar cane, making up about 50% of the export value. For home consumption are grown rice, alfalfa, corn, tobacco, beans, fruit, vegetables. Among the leading agr. districts are those of CHICLAYO in CHICAMA valley, shipping through PIMENTEL and PUERTO EDEN; the TRUJILLO dist., with its port SALAVERRY; HUACHO; HUARAL, with the port of CHANCAY. Around Lima and the great port of CALLAO truck gardening becomes prominent, while the region of ICA, PISCO, and MOQUEGUA are noted for their viticulture. Arequipa in the S lies within one of the largest oases. Most of the cultivated land consists of large estates owned by a politically prominent oligarchy, and generally worked by destitute Indian labor. Lima, a city of great colonial traditions and seat of San Marcos Univ. (founded 1551), is the commercial and social center for the nation, linked by several railroads and boulevards with Callao. In these 2 largest cities are some of the leading industries, mainly processing and textile milling. Through Callao passes the bulk of foreign imports, such as textile goods, electrical appliances, pharmaceuticals, metalware, paper, cardboard, dyes, machinery and vehicles, and foodstuffs. The Pan American Highway through Lima follows the coast. From Callao begins a railroad which is among the most remarkable engineering feats of its kind. The Central RR to La Oroya operates a branch to MOROCOCHA, where it reaches a height of 15,865 ft., said to be the highest of any standard-gauge railroad. From La Oroya a line leads to Cerro de Pasco (above 12,000 ft.), with several branches radiating to near-by mines. La Oroya is also linked with Jauja, Hunancayo, and Huancavelica. The port of Mollendo is the terminus of the Southern RR, which extends via Arequipa to Puno on L. Titicaca, where it connects by steamer with the Bolivian port Guaqui on the railroad to Buenos Aires. Another branch from JULIACA junction turns NW to Cuzco and the outstanding pre-Inca ruins of MACHUPICCHU. This anc. citadel city of pre-Inca origin is one of the many outstanding archaeological remains (Cuzco, Kencco, Chan Chan, Paramonga, etc.) of Peru which attract tourists and scientists from all over the world. During the period of the great Inca Empire (which covered almost half of South America) as well as in the colonial epoch, Peru was the leading cultural and political power of the continent. The Inca civilization came to an end when a small band of adventurers under Francisco Pizarro began (1532) the conquest of Peru, trapped the Inca monarch Atahualpa at Cajamarca, and executed him. The conquerors, spurred by greed for precious metals, instituted the notorious *economienda* and *repartimiento* system, forcing the Indians to work in mines. From Peru were sent expeditions to present-day Colombia, Ecuador, and Chile. The viceroyalty of Peru became, together with New Spain, the most valuable and influential Sp. possession, with all cultural and political activities of Sp. South America gravitating to fabulous Lima. The struggle for independence therefore found Sp. forces more securely intrenched here. Although the Argentine liberator San Martín entered Lima and proclaimed independence (1821), the power of the viceroy was not broken until 1824. San Martín withdrew in 1822 in favor of Bolívar and Sucre. A Peru-Bolivia confederation soon fell apart, and Peru embarked upon the characteristic course of Latin American politics—a vicious circle of civil strife, strong-man rule, military revolts—while the oligarchic pattern of Sp. colonial aristocracy was retained. A war with Spain (1864–71) in which Peru was assisted by Chile, Bolivia, and Ecuador did not go beyond minor naval engagements. Far more serious was the War of the Pacific with Chile (1879–84) over the Atacama Desert, in which Peru joined Bolivia. Lima was occupied during the hostilities, and the S coastal provs. of Tacna and Tarapacá, containing the cities of Tacna and Arica, were lost, though Tacna was at last returned in 1929. The League of Nations settled boundary disputes with Colombia over the *Leticia Trapezium* in 1934, and with Ecuador in 1942. Outstanding presidents of the early 20th cent. were Augusto Bernardino Leguía and Oscar Raimundo Benavides, who introduced social and economic measures. The famous Apra (Alíanza Popular Revolucionaria Americana), founded in 1924 by Raúl Haya de la Torre, evolved as an autochthonous Latin American political force of great significance, advocating agrarian reforms, particularly to the oppressed Indians, and ultimately aiming at a South American union. Peru declared war on the Axis powers in 1945. For further information, see separate articles on cities, regions, physical features, CALLAO constitutional prov. (with departmental status), and the following 23 depts.: AMAZONAS, ANCASH, APURÍMAC, AREQUIPA, AYACUCHO, CAJAMARCA, CUZCO or Cusco, HUANCAVELICA, HUÁNUCO, ICA, JUNÍN, LA LIBERTAD, LAMBAYEQUE, LIMA, LORETO, MADRE DE DIOS, MOQUEGUA, PASCO (set up 1944), PIURA, PUNO, SAN MARTÍN, TACNA, and TUMBES

Peru, Gilbert Isls.: see BERU.

Peru. 1 City (pop. 8,653), La Salle co., N Ill., on Illinois R. (bridged), adjoining La Salle; ships grain by barge. Zinc smelters, foundry; mfg. of clocks, glass, cement, farm vehicles, beverages, furniture, metal products). Seat of St. Bede Col. Bituminous-coal mines, agr., stock raising, dairying in region. Founded 1835, inc. 1845. **2** City (pop. 13,308), ⊙ Miami co., N central Ind., on the Wabash and 15 mi. E of Logansport; winter quarters for circuses here. Mfg. of electrical equipment, heaters, furniture, canned foods, baskets, clothing, fertilizer, paper products; railroad shops. Has historical mus. Naval air base. Laid out 1825. **3** City (pop. 368), Chautauqua co., SE Kansas, 26 mi. W of Coffeyville, in stock-, grain-, and oil-producing area. **4** Town (pop. 1,080), Oxford co., W Maine, on the Androscoggin and 10 mi. SE of Rumford, in farming, recreational area. Settled 1793, inc. 1821. **5** Rural town (pop. 143), Berkshire co., W Mass., 11 mi. E of Pittsfield. Highest town in state (alt. 2,295 ft.). **6** Village (pop. 1,265), Nemaha co., SE Nebr., 55 mi. SE of Lincoln and on Missouri R.; fruit-shipping point; timber, grain, livestock, dairy and poultry produce. State teachers col. here. Indian mounds near by. Inc. 1860. **7** Village (1940 pop. 737), Clinton co., extreme NE N.Y., 8 mi. SSW of Plattsburg; lumber, wood products. **8** Town (pop. 197), Bennington co., SW Vt., in Green Mtn. Natl. Forest, 10 mi. NE of Manchester.

Peru Current or **Humboldt Current** (hŭm'bōlt), a cold ocean current in South Pacific Ocean moving N along coast of N Chile and Peru to S Ecuador. It determines the dry climate W of the Andes, making the coastal belt one of the most arid regions in the world. The regime is, however, occasionally upset by oceanic irregularities. Sometimes also called Peruvian Current.

Perugia (pûrōō'jēŭ, It. pĕrōō'jä), province (□ 2,444; pop. 530,985), UMBRIA, central Italy; ⊙ Perugia. Comprises all but SW portion of Umbria. Mtn. and hill terrain, watered by Tiber and Nera rivers. Contains lake Trasimeno (W). Agr. (wheat, corn, olives, grapes); stock (sheep, cattle). Mining at Costacciaro (iron) and Branca (coal). Mfg. at Foligno, Perugia, Spoleto, Città di Castello. Area decreased to form provs. of Rieti (1923) and Terni (1927).

Perugia, anc. *Perusia*, city (pop. 31,839), ⊙ Umbria and Perugia prov., central Italy, 40 mi. SE of Arezzo, E of lake Trasimeno, on hill overlooking Tiber valley; 43°7'N 12°23'E. Agr. trade center noted for its chocolate; mfg. (macaroni, canned foods, furniture, glass, pottery, pharmaceuticals, metal goods). Archbishopric. Has Gothic cathedral (14th-15th cent.) with fine white and red marble façade, church of Sant'Angelo (5th or 6th cent.), Renaissance churches of San Bernardino and San Pietro. Its pinnacled town hall, which houses fine Umbrian art collection, and its university both date from 13th cent. Has well-preserved medieval quarters and city walls of Etruscan, Roman, and medieval origin. Near by, important Etruscan tombs have been found. An Umbrian and later (4th cent. B.C.) Etruscan center; fell to Romans in 3d cent. B.C. Became free commune (12th cent.) and soon gained hegemony over other Umbrian cities. Seat of Umbrian school of painting (13th-16th cent.), which reached its greatest splendor with Perugino and Pinturicchio.

Perugia, Lake of, Italy: see TRASIMENO, LAKE.

Perumpavur (pĕrōōmpä'vōōr), town (pop. 7,764), N Travancore, India, 35 mi. N of Kottayam; match mfg., rice milling, cashew-nut and cassava processing; coir rope and mats. Also spelled Perambavoor.

Perundurai, India: see ERODE.

Perur, India: see COIMBATORE, city.

Perus (pĭrōōs'), NNW suburb of São Paulo city, São Paulo, Brazil, 12 mi. from city center, and on railroad to Jundiaí; has large cement plant.

Perushitsa (pĕrōōshē'tsä), village (pop. 5,965), Plovdiv dist., S central Bulgaria, at N foot of W Rhodope Mts., 11 mi. SW of Plovdiv; agr. center; exports grapes; tobacco, sericulture; wine making.

Perusic (pĕ'rōōshĭch), Serbo-Croatian *Perušić*, village (pop. 2,683), W Croatia, Yugoslavia, on railroad and 7 mi. N of Gospic, in the Lika; local trade center.

Peruvian Current: see PERU CURRENT.

Péruwelz (pärüvä'), town (pop. 7,704), Hainaut prov., SW Belgium, near Fr. border, 11 mi. SE of Tournai; textile center.

Pervari (pĕrvärē'), village (pop. 1,236), Siirt prov., SE Turkey, on Buhtan R. and 34 mi. E of Siirt; grain. Sometimes spelled Perveri; formerly Hashir.

Pervenchères (pĕrvāshâr'), village (pop. 191), Orne dept., NW France, 8 mi. SW of Mortagne; horse breeding.

Pervoavgnstovski or **Pervoavgustovskiy** (pyĕr″-vŭäv'gōōstŭfskē), town (1926 pop. 1,323), NW Kursk oblast, Russian SFSR, 5 mi. N of Dmitriyev-Lgovski; paper mill, sugar refinery. Formerly Deryugino.

Pervomai or **Pervomay**, Bulgaria: see PARVOMAI.

Pervomaika or **Pervomayka** (pyĕrvŭmī'kŭ), town (1939 pop. over 500), SE Voroshilovgrad oblast, Ukrainian SSR, in the Donbas, near Krasnodon; coal mines.

Pervomaisk or **Pervomaysk** (pyĕrvŭmīsk'). **1** City (1926 pop. 31,683), NE Odessa oblast, Ukrainian SSR, on the Southern Bug and 105 mi. N of Odessa; agr.-machine mfg.; flour milling, distilling, meat packing, baking, sunflower-oil extraction. Regional mus. Until c.1920, called Olviopol. In Second World War, held (1941–43) by Germans. **2** City (1926 pop. 10,028), W Voroshilovgrad oblast, Ukrainian SSR, in the Donbas, 8 mi. E of Popasnaya; coal-mining center; machine works. Formerly Varvaropolye.

Pervomaiski or **Pervomayskiy** (–skē). **1** Suburb (1944 pop. over 500) of Ust-Kamenogorsk, East Kazakhstan oblast, Kazakh SSR. **2** Town (1941 pop. over 500), W Frunze oblast, Kirghiz SSR, in Chu valley on railroad (Belovodskaya station), adjacent to Stalinskoye; and 25 mi. W of Frunze; beet-sugar refinery. **3** Town (1939 pop. over 500), NE Bashkir Autonomous SSR, Russian SFSR, in the S Urals, 25 mi. ESE of Maloyaz; mining center, based on bauxite deposits. Until 1943, Kukshik. **4** Town (1940 pop. over 500), central Chkalov oblast, Russian SFSR, on Donguz R. (left tributary of Ural R.), on Trans-Caspian RR (Donguzskaya station) and 17 mi. S of Chkalov; truck; dairying. **5** Town (1948 pop. over 500), W Gorki oblast, Russian SFSR, near Balakhna; peat works. **6** Town (1939 pop. over 2,000), E Kemerovo oblast, Russian SFSR, 60 mi. SSW of Tyazhin, near Kiya R.; gold mines. **7** Suburb (1939 pop. over 500) of Slobodskoi, N central Kirov oblast, Russian SFSR; match mfg. Called Spas until 1938. **8** Town (1939 pop. over 500), E Stalino oblast, Ukrainian SSR, in the Donbas, 3 mi. SW of Snezhnoye; coal mines. Formerly called Shakhta No. 2.

Pervomaiskoye or **Pervomayskoye** (–skŭyŭ). **1** Village (1939 pop. over 500), SE Chuvash Autonomous SSR, Russian SFSR, on left tributary of Sviyaga R. and 30 mi. SSW of Kanash; flour milling. Until 1939, Bolshiye Arabuzy. **2** Village (1939 pop. under 500), N Crimea, Russian SFSR, 25 mi. W of Dzhankoi; wheat, barley, sheep. Dist. pop. largely Jewish prior to Second World War. Until 1944, Dzurchi. **3** Village (1926 pop. 2,018), SW Grozny oblast, Russian SFSR, on Assa R. and 15 mi. E of Dzaudzhikau; rail terminus in lumbering area; sawmill. Until 1944, Muzhichi. **4** Village (1939 pop. over 500), N central Rostov oblast, Russian SFSR, 40 mi. ESE of Millerovo; wheat, sunflowers, castor beans. Until 1940, Golodayevka. **5** Village (1939 pop. over 500), E central Saratov oblast, Russian SFSR, 28 mi. WNW of Yershov; wheat, cattle. Until 1941 (in German Volga Autonomous SSR), called Gnadenflyur or Gnadenflur.

Pervouralsk or **Pervoural'sk** (pyĕr″vŭōōrälsk'), city (1926 pop. 9,176; 1935 pop. estimate 49,000), S Sverdlovsk oblast, Russian SFSR, in the central Urals, on Chusovaya R. and 26 mi. WNW of Sverdlovsk; rail junction (Podvoloshnaya station); mfg. center (steel pipes, fireproof bricks); metalworking, sawmilling. Chromium salt mines and dichromate plant 4 mi. E, at Khrompik [Rus.,=dichromate] station. Developed as ironworks of Shaitanski Zavod prior to First World War. Called Pervouralski from 1928 until 1933, when it became city.

Pervoye Sadovoye, Russian SFSR: see Sadovoye, Pervoye.

Perwez (pĕrvā'), Flemish *Perwijs* (pĕr'vīs), town (pop. 2,598), Brabant prov., central Belgium, 11 mi. SE of Wavre; market center for horse-breeding region.

Perwez-lez-Andenne (–lā-ädĕn'), village (pop. 381), Namur prov., S central Belgium, 5 mi. SE of Andenne, in horse-breeding region.

Perwijs, Belgium: see Perwez.

Pesariis (pĕză'rēs), village (pop. 563), Udine prov., Friuli–Venezia Giulia, NE Italy, 8 mi. N of Ampezzo; electric clocks, watches.

Pesa River (pā'zä), Tuscany, central Italy, rises in Monti Chianti 7 mi. SW of Figline Valdarno, flows 30 mi. NW to Arno R. at Montelupo Fiorentino.

Pesaro (pā'zärô), anc. *Pisaurum*, town (pop. 24,163), ⊙ Pesaro e Urbino prov., The Marches, central Italy, port on the Adriatic, at mouth of Foglia R., 20 mi. SE of Rimini; 43°55'N 12°55'E. Bathing resort; mfg. (agr. machinery, hydraulic presses, tank cars, canned foods, soap, pharmaceuticals); sulphur refining. Noted for its majolica industry, dating from 15th cent.; mus. here contains richest collection in Italy. Bishopric. Has several churches and palaces, and a conservatory of music named after Rossini, who was b. here. Anciently a Roman colony. From 13th cent. until 1631, when it passed directly under the papacy, it was ruled by houses of Malatesta and Sforza, and dukes of Urbino. In Second World War badly damaged by fighting, air bombing, and a naval shelling (1944).

Pesaro e Urbino (ā o͞orbē'nô), province (□ 1,117; pop. 311,916), The Marches, central Italy, bordering on the Adriatic; ⊙ Pesaro. Crossed by the Apennines; watered by Metauro, Foglia, and Marecchia rivers. Agr. (cereals, raw silk, wine, olive oil, fruit, cheese), stock raising (cattle, sheep), and forestry. Sulphur mining at Perticara. Mfg. at Pesaro, Fano, Urbino, and Fossombrone.

Pesca (pĕ'skä), town (pop. 1,143), Boyacá dept., central Colombia, in Cordillera Oriental, 14 mi. SSW of Sogamoso; alt. 8,786 ft. Wheat, potatoes, corn, stock; flour milling, mfg. of woolen goods. Asphalt mines, petroleum deposits near by.

Pescadero (pĕskădâ'rō), village (pop. c.525), San Mateo co., W Calif., near the Pacific, in canyon of short Pescadero Creek, 35 mi. S of San Francisco; truck farming, dairying, stock raising. Butano Forest (redwoods) near by.

Pescado, Bolivia: see Villa Serrano.

Pescadores (pĕskŭdō'rŭz, –rĕs, –rēz), Chinese *P'eng-hu Ch'ün-tao* (pŭng'ho͞o' chün'dou') or *P'eng-hu Lieh-tao* (lyĕ'-dou), Jap. *Boko-retto* (bō'-kō-răt'tō) or *Hoko-retto* (hō'–), island group (□ 49; 1935 pop. 66,843) off W Formosa, in Formosa Strait, separated from Formosa by the 30-mi.-wide Pescadores Channel, and consisting of 64 isls., astride the Tropic of Cancer. The largest isls. are Penghu (site of Makung naval base) and Paisha (both linked by causeway), Yüweng, and Pachao. Isls. have phosphate deposits. Fishing and fish processing are the chief industries. Corn, fruit, peanuts, and sugar cane are grown. The group was named (16th cent.) Pescadores (=fishermen's isls.) by the Portuguese. Occupied 1622–24 by the Dutch, the isls. then reverted to China and became (late-17th cent.) a dependency of Formosa, whose subsequent history they have shared.

Pescadores Point (pĕskädōr'ĕs), Pacific cape, Arequipa dept., S Peru, 37 mi. WNW of Ocoña; 16°23'S 73°17'W.

Pescaglia (pĕskä'lyä), village (pop. 320), Lucca prov., Tuscany, central Italy, 10 mi. NNW of Lucca; paper mills.

Pescantina (pĕskäntē'nä), town (pop. 3,371), Verona prov., Veneto, N Italy, on Adige R. and 7 mi. WNW of Verona. Has fruit-packing plant, factories (chocolate, marmalade, sausage), tannery, cotton mill. Noted for its peaches.

Pescara (pĕskä'rä), province (□ 473; pop. 211,561), Abruzzi e Molise, S central Italy; ⊙ Pescara. Mtn. and hill terrain with Gran Sasso d'Italia in W; extends E to Adriatic Sea; watered by Pescara R. Agr. (wheat, potatoes, vegetables, olives, grapes); stock raising (sheep, cattle). Fishing. Has asphalt mines, oil wells (Tocco da Casauria). Hydroelectric plants (Piano d'Orta, Bussi sul Tirino). Mfg. at Pescara and Bussi sul Tirino. Formed 1927 from provs. of Aquila, Chieti, and Teramo.

Pescara, city (pop. 35,877), ⊙ Pescara prov., Abruzzi e Molise, S central Italy, port on the Adriatic, at mouth of Pescara R., 95 mi. ENE of Rome; 42°28'N 14°13'E. Fishing center; rail junction; mfg. (furniture, dyes, soap, glass, scales, majolica, woolen textiles, liquor, macaroni); sulphur refinery. Bathing beach. Includes, since 1927, Castellammare Adriatico, on left bank of river. G. D'Annunzio b. here. Badly damaged by air bombing (1943–44) in Second World War.

Pescara River, S central Italy, rises in the Apennines 4 mi. S of Amatrice; flows SW, past Aquila, and NE, past Popoli, to the Adriatic at Pescara; 90 mi. long. Receives Sagittario and Orte (right) and Tirino (left) rivers. Used for hydroelectric power. In upper course, above Popoli, called Aterno River.

Peschana (pyĭshchä'nŭ), village (1926 pop. 6,686), NW Odessa oblast, Ukrainian SSR, 13 mi. NNE of Balta; metalworks. In Moldavian Autonomous SSR (1924–40).

Peschanka (–shchän'kŭ), town (1926 pop. 3,112), S Vinnitsa oblast, Ukrainian SSR, 50 mi. ESE of Mogilev-Podolski; woodworking, food processing.

Peschanokopskoye (–shchä'nŭkôp'skŭyŭ), village (1926 pop. 12,091), S Rostov oblast, Russian SFSR, on railroad and 30 mi. SW of Salsk; flour mill, metalworks; wheat, cotton, livestock. Formerly also Peschanokopskaya.

Peschanoye (–nŭyŭ), village (1939 pop. over 500), W central Astrakhan oblast, Russian SFSR, 55 mi. E of Stepnoi; millet, mustard; sheep. Until 1944 (in Kalmyk Autonomous SSR), Yashkul.

Peschany Brod or **Peschanyy Brod** (pyĭshchä'nē brôt''), village (1926 pop. 6,794), SW Kirovograd oblast, Ukrainian SSR, on road and 25 mi. NE of Pervomaisk; wheat, sugar beets.

Peschany Island or **Peschanyy Island,** in Caspian Sea, off S shore of Apsheron Peninsula, Azerbaijan SSR, in Kaganovich dist. of Greater Baku, 9 mi. ESE of Baku; oil wells.

Peschici (pā'skēchē), town (pop. 3,559), Foggia prov., Apulia, S Italy, port on Adriatic Sea, on N shore of Gargano promontory, 10 mi. WNW of Vieste; bathing resort; fishing.

Peschiera del Garda (pĕskyā'rä dĕl gär'dä), village (pop. 1,056), Verona prov., Veneto, N Italy, port at SE end of Lago di Garda, at efflux of Mincio R., 14 mi. W of Verona; rail junction. Fish hatchery. Was NW fortress of the "Quadrilateral." Formerly Peschiera sul Garda.

Pescia (pā'shä), town (pop. 7,855), Pistoia prov., Tuscany, central Italy, at foot of Etruscan Apennines, 12 mi. W of Pistoia. Agr. and industrial center; large paper industry (dating from 15th cent.); tanneries, silk mills, paper- and oil-mill machine mfg.; food cannery, fertilizer factory. Market for flowers, asparagus, and olive plants from near-by nurseries. Bishopric. Has anc. cathedral (rebuilt 1693), 14th-cent. church, mus., agr. school.

Pescina (pĕshē'nä), town (pop. 4,853), Aquila prov., Abruzzi e Molise, S central Italy, near reclaimed Lago Fucino area, 12 mi. E of Avezzano, in cereal-growing, sheep-raising region. Cardinal J. Mazarin b. here.

Pescocostanzo (pĕs''kôkôstän'tsô), village (pop. 2,041), Aquila prov., Abruzzi e Molise, S central Italy, in the Apennines, 13 mi. SSE of Sulmona. Resort (alt. 4,577 ft.); lacemaking, goldworking, dairying. Damaged in Second World War.

Pescopagano (pĕ''skôpägä'nô), town (pop. 3,951), Potenza prov., Basilicata, 18 mi. SW of Melfi; cheese making.

Pesé (pāsā'), village (pop. 948), Herrera prov., S central Panama, in Pacific lowland, on Parita R. and 12 mi. WSW of Chitré; road center. Corn, rice, beans, livestock. Was ⊙ Herrera prov. (1855–64).

Peseux (pŭzû'), town (pop. 3,123), Neuchâtel canton, W Switzerland, near L. of Neuchâtel, adjacent to and W of Neuchâtel; watches, metalworking.

Peshawar (pŭshä'wŭr, pā'shävŭr), district (□ 1,547; 1951 pop. 901,000), North-West Frontier Prov., W Pakistan; ⊙ Peshawar. Bordered E by Indus R., W and S by E offshoots of Safed Koh Range; drained by Kabul and Swat rivers (canal-irrigation systems). Agr. (wheat, corn, barley, sugar cane, cotton, rice); handicrafts (cloth fabrics, felts, pottery, baskets, copper and leather goods); poultry farming, fruitgrowing (grapes, apricots, peaches, pomegranates, quinces). Slate and pottery-clay deposits worked. Chief towns: Peshawar, Nowshera, Charsadda. Part of anc. Gandhara kingdom; ruled by Kushans (1st–2d cent. A.D.); in 11th–12th cent., under Ghaznevids; occupied by Sikhs in early-19th cent. Dist. exercises political control over adjoining tribal area (pop. 139,000). Pop. 90% Moslem, 6% Hindu, 3% Sikh.

Peshawar, city (1951 pop. 114,000; 1941 pop. 130,967; including the cantonment area, pop. in 1941 was 173,420), ⊙ North-West Frontier Prov. and Peshawar dist., W Pakistan, 235 mi. NW of Lahore, 10 mi. E of Khyber Pass; 34°N 71°34'E. Major trade center of frontier region; military station; road junction (W terminus of Grand Trunk Road); airport. Goods (silk, gold thread, fruit, carpets, jewelry) brought through Khyber Pass from Afghanistan are mainly re-exported here to the Punjab and India, while reverse trade (piece goods, sugar, tea, salt) is re-exported W and N. Markets local agr. produce (wheat, corn, cotton, barley). Cotton ginning, rice and fodder milling, fruit processing, mfg. of ordnance, pharmaceuticals, ice; noted handicrafts (silk, cotton, and woolen fabrics; woodwork, knives, glazed earthenware, copper and leather goods). Fruitgrowing in suburbs; poultry farming. Islamia Col. (opened 1915; affiliated with Punjab Univ. in Lahore) is just W. City was ⊙ anc. Gandhara prov. and a Graeco-Buddhist cultural center; has ruins (E) of large stupa (2d cent. A.D.) which contained inscription of Kanishka (noted Kushan ruler) and relics of the Buddha (now in city's mus.). Allegedly given present name [Peshawar=frontier town] by Akbar; briefly under Sikhs in early-19th cent.; occupied 1849 by British. Long a center for caravans and merchants from Kabul, Bokhara, and Samarkand.

Peshkopi (pĕshkô'pē) or **Peshkopija** (pĕshkô'pēyä), town (1945 pop. 2,009), E central Albania, near Macedonian (Yugoslav) border, 40 mi. NE of Tirana, on W slopes of the Korab; road center, linked with Elbasan, Debar, and Kukës; tourist trade (thermal springs); airport.

Peshkovskoye (pyĭshkôf'skŭyŭ), village (1926 pop. 2,636), NW Kustanai oblast, Kazakh SSR, on railroad and 60 mi. NW of Kustanai; wheat, cattle.

Peshtera (pĕ'shtĕrä), city (pop. 8,946), Plovdiv dist., S central Bulgaria, at N foot of W Rhodope Mts., on Stara R. (right tributary of Maritsa R.) and 23 mi. WSW of Plovdiv; rail spur terminus; tobacco-processing, wine-making center; cotton milling, lumber exports. Has school for tobacco growers.

Peshtigo (pĕsh'tĭgō), city (pop. 2,279), Marinette co., NE Wis., on Peshtigo R. and 6 mi. SW of Marinette, in dairying and lumbering area; paper milling, boatbuilding. Near by is a memorial of the 1871 fire which ravaged NE Wis. Inc. 1903.

Peshtigo River, NE Wis., rises in Forest co., flows c.80 mi. through forested area, past Peshtigo, to Green Bay 8 mi. S of Marinette.

Peski (pyĭskē'). **1** Town (1939 pop. over 500), E central Moscow oblast, Russian SFSR, on Moskva R. and 7 mi. N of Kolomna; cement works. **2** Village (1926 pop. 13,889), E Voronezh oblast, Russian SFSR, on Khoper R. and 17 mi. ESE of Borisoglebsk; flour milling, metalworking.

Peskovka (pyĭskôf'kŭ). **1** Town (1926 pop. 3,406), NE Kirov oblast, Russian SFSR, on railroad, on Vyatka R. and 27 mi. N of Omutninsk; iron milling. **2** Town (1939 pop. over 500), W Kiev oblast, Ukrainian SSR, 40 mi. WNW of Kiev; ceramics.

Pesmes (pĕm), village (pop. 815), Haute-Saône dept., E France, on Ognon R. and 12 mi. S of Gray; forges.

Pesochenski or **Pesochenskiy** (pyĕsŭchĕn'skē), town (1926 pop. 1,223), W Tula oblast, Russian SFSR, 7 mi. NW of Chekalin; ironworks. Formerly Pesochenski Zavod.

Pesochin (pyĭsô'chĭn), town (1926 pop. 4,008), NW Kharkov oblast, Ukrainian SSR, on railroad and 7 mi. WSW of Kharkov city center.

Pesochnoye (–sôch'nŭyŭ), town (1926 pop. 2,245), central Yaroslavl oblast, Russian SFSR, on Volga R. and 12 mi. ESE of Shcherbakov; porcelain mfg.

Pesochny or **Pesochnyy** (–nē), town (1939 pop. over 2,000), N Leningrad oblast, Russian SFSR, 14 mi. NNW of Leningrad; brickworks.

Pesochnya, Russian SFSR: see Kirov, Kaluga oblast.

Pêso da Régua (pā'zo͞o dŭ rĕ'gwŭ), town (pop. 4,996), Vila Real dist., N Portugal, on right bank of Douro R. at influx of Corgo R. and 10 mi. SSW of Vila Real; center of region (*País do Vinho*) in which the famous port wine grape is grown. Ships wine to Oporto storage houses by rail and flat-bottomed barges on the Douro. Other products: olives, figs, almonds, oranges. Sometimes called Régoa.

Pesotum (pŭsō'tŭm), village (pop. 415), Champaign co., E Ill., 13 mi. S of Champaign, in agr. area; ships grain.

Pespire (pĕspē'rä), city (pop. 1,142), Choluteca dept., S Honduras, on Pespire R. (middle course of Nacaome R.), on Interoceanic Highway and 10 mi. NE of Nacaome; transit center for mule teams; light mfg. (pottery, beverages); grain, livestock.

Pesqueira (pĭskā'rŭ), city (pop. 8,472), central Pernambuco, NE Brazil, on railroad (Arcoverde spur) and 50 mi. W of Caruaru, in fertile agr. region; fruit and vegetable (especially tomato) canning and preserving; livestock, cotton, and coffee shipped to Recife. Soil conservation practiced here.

Pesqueira or **Villa Pesqueira** (vē'yä pĕskā'rä), town (pop. 703), Sonora, NW Mexico, on railroad and 23 mi. N of Hermosillo; sugar cane, corn, wheat, fruit.

Pesquera, La (lä), town (pop. 768), Cuenca prov., E central Spain, 45 mi. SE of Cuenca; saffron, grapes, olives, cereals, truck produce, fruit, sheep, goats. Lumbering; coal mining.

Pesquera de Duero (dhā dhwā'rō), town (pop. 1,296), Valladolid prov., N central Spain, on the Duero (Douro) and 29 mi. E of Valladolid; sheep raising; cereals, sugar beets, wine.

Pesquería Chica (pĕskärē'ä chē'kä), town (pop. 1,104), Nuevo León, N Mexico, on Pesquería R. and 18 mi. ENE of Monterrey; chick-peas, grain, cotton, stock.

Pesquería River, Nuevo León, N Mexico, rises in Sierra Madre Oriental W of Monterrey, flows 110 mi. E, past Apodaca, Pesquería Chica, and Los Herreras, to San Juan R. 1 mi. S of Doctor Coss. Receives Salinas R. Used for irrigation.

Pessac (pĕsäk'), W suburb (pop. 16,850) of Bordeaux, Gironde dept., SW France, on Bordeaux-Irún RR.; produces noted red wines at Château-Haut-Brion vineyards. Brick- and glassworks. Furniture, footwear, and biscuit mfg.

Pessinus (pĕ'sĭnŭs), anc. town of Galatia (now in central Turkey), 5 mi. S of Sivrihisar; was ⊙ of a Roman prov., with rich temple of Cybele.

Pest, Hungary: see BUDAPEST.

Pestarena (pĕstärā′nä), village (pop. 177), Novara prov., Piedmont, N Italy, near Monte Rosa, on Anza R. and 17 mi. SW of Domodossola. Chief Ital. gold-mining center.

Pesteana-Jiu (pĕshtyä′nä-zhōō′), Rum. *Peşteana-Jiu*, village (pop. 1,488), Gorj prov., SW Rumania, on Jiu R. and 12 mi. S of Targu-Jiu; agr. center.

Pestel (pĕstĕl′), town (1950 census pop. 717), Sud dept., SW Haiti, on N coast of Tiburon Peninsula, 23 mi. ESE of Jérémie; coffeegrowing.

Pesterzsebet, Hungary: see PESTSZENTERZSEBET.

Pesthidegkut (pĕsht′hĭdĕk-kōōt), Hung. *Pesthidegkút*, residential NW suburb (pop. 8,258) of Budapest, Pest-Pilis-Solt-Kiskun co., N central Hungary, in Buda Mts., 6 mi. NW of city center.

Pesto, Italy: see PAESTUM.

Pestovo (pyĕ′stŭvŭ), town (1935 pop. c.6,600), E Novgorod oblast, Russian SFSR, on Mologa R. (head of navigation) and 70 mi. E of Borovichi; sawmilling, mfg. of prefabricated houses.

Pest-Pilis-Solt-Kiskun (pĕsht′-pĭ′lĭsh-shôlt′-kĭsh′-kōōn), county (□ 4,487; pop. 1,537,884), central Hungary; ⊙ BUDAPEST. Level region except for Buda Mts. and Pilis Mts. in NW; includes part of the ALFÖLD, Danubian isls. of Szentendre and Csepel; bounded W by the Danube. Agr. (grain, potatoes), livestock (cattle, hogs, horses); intensive fruit (apricots, cherries, apples, mahalebs), vineyard cultivation around KECSKEMET and NAGYKÖRÖS. Large industries in Budapest and its suburbs; other industrial centers at Kecskemet, Szentendre, VAC. Some lignite mined in BUDA MOUNTAINS.

Pestravka (pyĭsträf′kŭ), village (1926 pop. 3,769), S Kuibyshev oblast, Russian SFSR, on Greater Irgiz R. and 40 mi. SSE of Chapayevsk; road center; wheat, sunflowers; cattle, sheep.

Pestretsy (pĭstryĕ′tsĕ), village (1926 pop. 2,416), W central Tatar Autonomous SSR, Russian SFSR, on right tributary of Kama R. and 20 mi. E of Kazan; woodworking; truck.

Pestszenterzsebet (pĕsht′sĕntĕr″zhäbĕt), Hung. *Pestszenterzsébet*, city (pop. 76,876), Pest-Pilis-Solt-Kiskun co., N central Hungary, 5 mi. SSE of Budapest city center; petroleum refineries, iron and steel plants; metal- and food-processing plants; textile mills (cotton, jute), flour mills, soap- and candleworks. Called Erzsebetfalva until 1924, then Pesterzsebet until 1932.

Pestszentimre (pĕsht′sĕntĭ″mrĕ), town (pop. 12,057), Pest-Pilis-Solt-Kiskun co., N central Hungary, 8 mi. SSE of Budapest; state housing projects for civil servants.

Pestszentlörinc (pĕsht′sĕntlûr″ĭnts), Hung. *Pestszentlőrinc*, city (pop. 42,075), Pest-Pilis-Solt-Kiskun co., N central Hungary, 7 mi. SE of Budapest city center; iron and steel plants; mfg. (machines, railroad cars, cotton, mineral oil); brickworks.

Pestujhely (pĕsh′tōōĭhĕĭ), Hung. *Pestújhely*, residential NE suburb (pop. 11,736) of Budapest, Pest-Pilis-Solt-Kiskun co., N central Hungary.

Pestyaki (pĭstyŭkē′), village (1926 pop. 1,149), SE Ivanovo oblast, Russian SFSR, 50 mi. ESE of Shuya; flax; linen goods.

Pet or **Petfürdö** (pāt′fürdû), Hung. *Pétfürdő*, town (pop. 462), Veszprem co., W central Hungary, 11 mi. NE of Veszprem; chemical industry (nitrogen basis).

Peta (pä′tŭ), town (pop. 2,519), Arta nome, Epirus, Greece, 2 mi. E of Arta; corn, barley, citrus fruits; olive oil.

Petah Tiqva or **Petah Tikva** (both: pĕ′tä tĭk′vä, pĕ′täkh), town (1950 pop. estimate 38,000), W Israel, in Plain of Sharon, near the Yarkon, on railroad and 7 mi. E of Tel Aviv; industrial center; textile mills; mfg. of chemicals, pharmaceuticals, pumps, asbestos cement, roofing felt, insulating materials, furniture, paper and rubber products; metalworking, food canning, distilling, canning; center of citricultural region; viticulture. Limestone quarrying. Has several large parks. First modern Jewish settlement in Palestine, founded 1878. Sometimes spelled Petach Tikva. Near by are ruins of anc. city of Antipatris.

Petal, village (pop. 2,148), Forrest co., SE Miss., just NE of Hattiesburg across Leaf R.

Petalcingo (pātälsĕng′gō), town (pop. 1,566), Chiapas, S Mexico, in N outliers of Sierra Madre, 45 mi. NNE of San Cristóbal de las Casas; cereals, sugar cane, fruit.

Petalia, Gulf of, Greece: see PETALION, GULF OF.

Petalia Islands (pĕtä′lēŭ), Gr. *Petalioi* (pĕtälyē′), Lat. *Petaliae*, group (□ 10; 1928 pop. 77) in Gulf of Petalion of Aegean Sea, Euboea nome, Greece, off SE Euboea. Includes MEGALO, XERO, and 4 smaller isls. Also called Petali Isls.

Petalidi, Greece: see KORONE.

Petaling (pŭtä′lĭng), village (pop. 725), N Negri Sembilan, Malaya, just NW of Kuala Klawang; rice, rubber.

Petalion, Gulf of (pĕtälyôn′), inlet of Aegean Sea, Greece, bet. SE Euboea (E) and Attica (W); 30 mi. wide, 30 mi. long; connects N with S arm of Gulf of Euboea. Contains Petalia Isls. and Styra isl. Laurion on SW shore. Also called Gulf of Petalia and Gulf of Petali.

Petaluma (pĕtŭlōō′mŭ), city (pop. 10,315), Sonoma co., W Calif., 35 mi. N of San Francisco, and on navigable Petaluma Creek (barges), c.15 mi. above an arm of San Francisco Bay; center of large poultry and egg industry; has chicken hatcheries; also plants producing poultry equipment and feed, dairy products, cord and twine, work clothing. Founded 1852; inc. as town in 1858, as city in 1884.

Pétange (pātäzh′), town (pop. 5,398), SW Luxembourg, on Chiers R. and 6 mi. NW of Esch-sur-Alzette; iron-mining center.

Petare (pätä′rā), town (pop. 4,045), Miranda state, N Venezuela, in coastal range, on railroad and highway, and 7 mi. ESE of Caracas; agr. center (coffee, sugar cane, cacao); mfg. of cardboard. Airfield.

Petarnitsa (pĕtŭrnē′tsä), village (pop. 3,325), Pleven dist., N Bulgaria, 10 mi. SW of Pleven; wheat, corn, legumes.

Petas, Las, Bolivia: see LAS PETAS.

Petatlán (pätätlän′), town (pop. 3,088), Guerrero, SW Mexico, in Pacific lowland, 100 mi. NW of Acapulco; rice, sugar cane, tobacco, fruit, forest products (rubber, vanilla, resin), livestock.

Petatlán River, Mexico: see SINALOA RIVER.

Petauke (pĕtou′kä), township (pop. 524), Eastern Prov., E Northern Rhodesia, 120 mi. WSW of Fort Jameson; tobacco, corn.

Petawawa (pĕtŭwä′wŭ), village (pop. estimate 300), SE Ont., on Ottawa R. and 10 mi. NW of Pembroke; paper, pulp milling. Site of military camp. A heavy-water pilot-plant established here, 1944.

Petchaburi, Thailand: see PHETBURI.

Petchaburn, Thailand: see PHETCHABUN.

Petegem (pā′tŭ-khŭm), town (pop. 5,174), East Flanders prov., W central Belgium, on Lys R. and 10 mi. SSW of Ghent; textiles, furniture, wood products.

Petén or **El Petén** (ĕl pātĕn′), department (□ 13,843; 1950 pop. 15,908), N Guatemala; ⊙ Flores. Forms a large panhandle; bordered N and W by Mexico, E by Br. Honduras. It is a low, vast, humid expanse of dense, tropical, hardwood forests interrupted by savannas and crisscrossed by ranges of hills not exceeding 1,000 ft. Drained by San Pedro and Pasión rivers and other affluents of Usumacinta R. (W border), and by Río Azul (NE). There are large lakes, notably L. Petén; heavy seasonal rains (annually, 70 in. in N, 150 in. in S) bring floods and temporary lakes. Inaccessibility has left the region economically undeveloped, but there are lumbering and chicle collecting, and, near L. Petén, some agr. (grain, sugar cane, rubber, cacao, fruit). Chicle is exported by air. Sparsely settled, with most of the Indians (unenumerated) deep in the forests, Petén was once center of the Maya Old Empire; there are rich archaeological ruins, notably TIKAL and UAXACTÚN. In 1697 the Itzá, last of the independent Mayas, were routed from their stronghold at L. Petén.

Petén, Lake, or **Lake Petén-Itzá** (-ētsä′), Petén dept., N Guatemala, 160 mi. NNE of Guatemala; 15 mi. long, 2 mi. wide, 165 ft. deep. FLORES is on one of its several small isls. San Benito is on S shore, San Andrés on W shore.

Peterboro or **Peterborough,** town (pop. 2,556; village pop. 1,506), Hillsboro co., S N.H., on the Contoocook, bet. Keene and Nashua. Resort, mfg. (textiles, baskets). Seat of MacDowell Colony for creative artists, developed (1907) by Marian Nevins MacDowell in memory of Edward MacDowell who lived here from 1896. Ski trails. First free tax-supported public library in U.S. founded here 1833. Granted 1738, settled 1749, inc. 1760.

Peterborough, town (pop. 2,890), S South Australia, 50 mi. ENE of Port Pirie; rail junction; wool, sheep, wheat; cyanide works. Formerly Petersburg.

Peterborough, county (□ 1,415; pop. 47,392), S Ont., on Buckhurst, Stony, and Rice lakes; ⊙ Peterborough.

Peterborough, city (pop. 25,350), ⊙ Peterborough co., S Ont., at falls on Otonabee R. (which connects, via Trent Canal, with L. Ontario and L. Huron) and 70 mi. NE of Toronto; rail and mfg. center; woolen and silk milling and knitting, meat packing; mfg. of electrical and dairy machinery, castings, hardware, motors, fire-fighting equipment, paper, shoes, carpets, food products, and Peterborough canoes. Has normal school and several institutes.

Peterborough, city and municipal borough (1931 pop. 43,551; 1951 census 53,412), NE Northampton, England, on Nene R. and 36 mi. NE of Northampton; ⊙ administrative co. of the Soke of Peterborough (53,464 acres; 1931 pop. 51,839; 1951 census 63,784), representing the former area of jurisdiction (soke) of the Benedictine abbey here founded 655 by Saxulf. The city, at edge of fen country on Huntingdon-Cambridge border, is a rail, industrial, and market center with railroad shops, leatherworks, foundries, machine shops, pharmaceutical works, beet-sugar refineries. In 1930s river was deepened, making city accessible to North Sea shipping. The abbey was destroyed by Danes (870), rebuilt in 10th cent., plundered in 11th cent., and burned in 1116. The cathedral, begun in 12th cent., was partly sacked by Cromwell's troops in 1643. Katherine of Aragon is buried here and the cathedral contained the original tomb of Mary Queen of Scots. Peterborough also has early-15th-cent. church of St. John the Baptist, a school founded 1541, bishop's palace, and remains of old abbey. The town's original name was Medeshamstede. In municipal borough (S) are brickmaking towns of New Fletton and Old Fletton.

Peterborough, N.H.: see PETERBORO.

Peterculter (pētŭrkōō′tŭr, pē′tŭrkōōtŭr), town and parish (pop. 6,309), SE Aberdeen, Scotland, on the Dee and 7 mi. SW of Aberdeen; paper milling. Just SW are remains of Roman camp.

Petergof, Russian SFSR: see PETRODVORETS.

Peterhead (pētŭrhĕd′), burgh (1931 pop. 12,545; 1951 census 12,765), NE Aberdeen, Scotland, on North Sea at mouth of Ugie R., 27 mi. NE of Aberdeen; 57°30′N 1°46′W; easternmost burgh of Scotland, on small peninsula. Herring-fishing port, with fish canneries, whisky distilleries, woolen mills, boilerworks. Burgh was founded 1593 by George Keith, 5th earl marischal of Scotland. There is a statue of James Keith, who, with his brother George Keith, 10th and last earl marischal, were exiled for permitting secret landing (1715) of the Old Pretender at Peterhead. Adjoining the burgh are fishing ports of Buchanhaven (N) and Burnhaven (S).

Peterhof, Russian SFSR: see PETRODVORETS.

Peterhofen, Czechoslovakia: see PETRKOVICE.

Peter I Island (□ c.100; 14 naut. mi. long, 5 naut. mi. wide), off Antarctica, in Bellingshausen Sea, NE of Thurston Peninsula; 68°50′S 90°35′W. Discovered 1821 Thaddeus von Bellingshausen, leader of Russian expedition. Claimed 1929 by Norway, placed 1931 under Nor. sovereignty, made dependency 1933.

Peter Island, islet, Br. Virgin Isls., 4 mi. S of Tortola isl.; 18°20′N 65°35′W.

Peterlee, town (1951 pop. 298), E Durham, England, near North Sea, 10 mi. ESE of Durham, in coal-mining area. Formed after Second World War as nucleus of projected model residential community.

Peterlingen, Switzerland: see PAYERNE.

Petermann Glacier (pā′tŭrmän), *Petermann Brae* or *Petermanns Gletscher*, NW Greenland, extends from inland icecap 60 mi. NW to Hall Basin near 81°7′N 62°W; 6–20 mi. wide.

Petermann Land, island in Arctic Ocean, reported (1874) by Austrian explorer Payer as being N of Franz Josef Land; proved to be nonexistent by Rus. Brusilov expedition (1912–13).

Petermann Peak, Dan. *Petermanns Bjaerg* or *Petermanns Fjaeld*, mountain (9,645 ft.), E Greenland, near head of Franz Josef Fjord; 73°4′N 28°40′W.

Peteroa Volcano (pātärō′ä), Andean peak (13,420 ft.) on Argentina-Chile border, 40 mi. ESE of Curicó; 35°16′S.

Peter Pond Lake (□ 302), NW Sask., 200 mi. N of North Battleford, on main headwater of Churchill R.; 40 mi. long, 14 mi. wide.

Peterreve, Yugoslavia: see PETROVO SELO.

Petersberg (pē′tŭrzbûrg, Ger. pā′tŭrsbĕrk), village, in former Prussian Rhine Prov., W Germany, after 1945 in North Rhine-Westphalia, on right bank of the Rhine, just N of Königswinter. After 1949, hq. of Allied High Commission for German Federal Republic.

Petersburg, town (pop. 1,605), SE Alaska, on N tip of Mitkof Isl., Alexander Archipelago, 120 mi. SSE of Juneau; trading, fishing, fur farming, lumbering; port of entry. Has cannery and Univ. of Alaska experimental fur-farm. Municipally-owned hydroelectric plant. Settled 1897 by Norwegian fishermen; inc. 1910.

Petersburg, Australia: see PETERBOROUGH.

Petersburg. **1** City (pop. 2,325), ⊙Menard co., central Ill., on Sangamon R. (bridged here) and 16 mi. NNW of Springfield, in agr. and bituminous-coal-mining area; corn, wheat, soybeans, livestock; mfg. (canned foods, beverages, brick, tile). Founded c.1836, inc. 1841. Ann Rutledge's grave is here. NEW SALEM (now a state park) is S. **2** City (pop. 3,035), ⊙ Pike co., SW Ind., near White R., 19 mi. SE of Vincennes; ships produce; bituminous-coal mines, oil wells; timber. Flour, lumber milling; mfg. of concrete blocks. Laid out 1817, inc. 1924. **3** Town (pop. 356), Boone co., N Ky., on the Ohio and 2 mi. SW of Lawrenceburg, Ind. **4** Village (pop. 1,001), Monroe co., extreme SE Mich., 17 mi. W of Monroe and on Raisin R., in grain-growing and dairying area; mfg. of auto parts. **5** Village (pop. 507), Boone co., E central Nebr., 12 mi. N of Albion; livestock, poultry produce, grain. **6** Village (pop. c.500), Rensselaer co., E N.Y., on Hoosic R. and 7 mi. WNW of Williamstown, Mass.; mfg. of clothing. **7** Village (pop. 318), Nelson co., E central N.Dak., 17 mi. E of Lakota. **8** Borough (pop. 621), Huntingdon co., central Pa., 6 mi. NNW of Huntingdon, near Juniata R. **9** Town (pop. 497), Lincoln and Marshall counties, S Tenn., 12 mi. NNW of Fayetteville, in timber and farm area. **10** Town (pop. 777), Hale co., NW Texas, on the Llano Estacado, 25 mi. NE of Lubbock, in agr. area. **11** City (pop. 35,054), in but independent of Dinwiddie co., SE Va., on Appomattox R. (head of navigation; bridged) and 22 mi. S of Richmond. Port of entry; rail-steamer transfer point; highway focus; shipping, processing, mfg. center in agr.

(peanuts, tobacco) area; water power supplied by river's falls here. Large tobacco- and peanut-processing industries; lumber milling, mfg. of luggage, clothing, textiles, optical goods, fountain pens. Seat of Virginia State Col. Points of interest: Blandford Church (1735); Golden Ball Tavern (c.1750); Center Hill Mansion (1825; now a U.S. mus.), "Battersea" (18th-cent. house); Wallace-Seward House, scene (1865) of conference bet. Grant and Lincoln; Blandford Cemetery, with graves of 30,000 Confederate dead. Poplar Grove Natl. Cemetery (8.7 acres; established 1866), 3 mi. S, contains c.6,000 Federal graves. U.S. Fort Lee (formerly Camp Lee) is just E. City founded 1646 as military post (Fort Henry) on site of Indian village; grew as trading point. Petersburg and Blandford villages were laid out in 1748, Pocahontas village in 1752; combined and inc. as Petersburg town 1784, as city 1850. In Revolution, taken (1781) by Br. troops under Benedict Arnold; starting point for Cornwallis' campaign which ended with his surrender at Yorktown. In Civil War, its position on S approach to Richmond made it a Federal objective. In June, 1864, after Wilderness campaign, Grant's assaults on city were repulsed by Beauregard, soon joined by Lee. Grant then established partial siege (which lasted until April, 1865), and began to push his left flank SW in order to cut off Lee's supplies. In Battle of the Crater (July 30, 1864), Federals exploded large mine under Confederate works, but were again driven off. After many hard-fought actions (including decisive Federal victory at Five Forks near Dinwiddie, April 1, 1865) and a general assault on the lines before the city, Petersburg fell (April 3, 1865); Richmond's fall the same day was followed by Lee's surrender (April 9) at Appomattox Court House. Petersburg Natl. Military Park (1,324.6 acres; established 1926) encloses much of battle area. **12** Town (pop. 1,898), ⊙ Grant co., NE W.Va., in Eastern Panhandle on South Branch of the Potomac and 32 mi. SSW of Keyser; trade center for livestock, fruit, tobacco, grain, and truck area; lumber, flour, and feed mills, tannery. State trout hatchery here. Holds annual co. rodeo. Settled c.1745.

Petersburg, Saint, Russia: see LENINGRAD, city.

Peters Dome, mountain (10,500 ft.), S central Alaska, in Alaska Range, in Mt. McKinley Natl. Park, 140 mi. NNW of Anchorage; 63°8'N 151°12'W.

Petersdorf or **Petersdorf auf Fehmarn** (pā'tūrsdôrf ouf fā'märn), village (pop. 3,527), in Schleswig-Holstein, NW Germany, on Fehmarn isl., 6 mi. NW of Burg; grain, potatoes, cabbage, beets.

Petersfield, village (pop. estimate 200), SE Man., near S end of L. Winnipeg, 30 mi. NNE of Winnipeg; grain; dairying.

Petersfield, urban district (1931 pop. 4,387; 1951 census 6,616), E Hampshire, England, 15 mi. NNE of Portsmouth; agr. market; mfg. of agr. machinery and rubber products. Town chartered in 12th cent. Once had important woolen mills.

Petersfield, town (pop. 2,370), Westmoreland parish, SW Jamaica, 5 mi. NE of Savanna-la-Mar; rice, sugar cane, breadfruit, livestock.

Petersgrat (pā'tūrs-grät"), ridge (10,532 ft.) in Bernese Alps, S central Switzerland, 8 mi. SW of Mürren.

Petershagen (pā"tūrs-hä'gūn). **1** Village (pop. 6,047), Brandenburg, E Germany, 15 mi. E of Berlin; market gardening; starch mfg. **2** Town (pop. 2,993), in former Prussian prov. of Westphalia, NW Germany, after 1945 in North Rhine-Westphalia, on left bank of the Weser and 7 mi. NNE of Minden; grain.

Petersham (pē'tūr-shŭm), municipality (pop. 29,451), E New South Wales, Australia, 4 mi. SW of Sydney, in metropolitan area; mfg. (pottery, furniture), brass foundries.

Petersham, England: see RICHMOND.

Petersham, town (pop. 814), Worcester co., N central Mass., 19 mi. NW of Worcester.

Petershausen (pā"tūrs-hou'zūn), N suburb of Constance, S Baden, Germany, on right bank of the Rhine; airport.

Peterskon, Greece: see PETRAIS.

Peter's Mine, gold-mining center, Essequibo co., N central Br. Guiana, on affluent of Mazaruni R., on road from Kartabo, and 50 mi. W of Bartica.

Peters Mountain, in SE W.Va. and SW Va., ridge of the Alleghenies; from gorge of New R. at Va.-W. Va. border extends 50 mi. NE, mostly along state line, to W Alleghany co., Va.; 3-4,000 ft. high. Its SW continuation is East River Mtn.

Peterson. 1 Town (pop. 589), Clay co., NW Iowa, on Little Sioux R. and 16 mi. NE of Cherokee, in livestock and grain area; sand and gravel pits. **2** Village (pop. 318), Fillmore co., SE Minn., on Root R. and 30 mi. W of La Crosse, Wis.; dairy products.

Peterson Bay or **Gjoa Haven,** trading post, SE King William Isl., S Franklin Dist., Northwest Territories, at junction of Simpson and Rae straits; 68°38'N 95°55'W; site of winter quarters of Roald Amundsen's Northwest Passage expedition, 1903-6.

Peterstal, Bad, Germany: see BAD PETERSTAL.

Peterston-super-Montem, town and parish (pop. 1,679), central Glamorgan, Wales, 4 mi. WNW of Llantrisant; coal mining.

Peterstown, town (pop. 571), Monroe co., SE W.Va., at Va. line, 17 mi. E of Princeton.

Peterswald, Czechoslovakia: see PETRVALD.

Peter the First Range, Rus. *Khrebet Petra Pervogo,* branch of Pamir-Alai mountain system, Tadzhik SSR; extends from Stalin Peak 90 mi. W, bet. Surkhab and Obi-Khingou rivers, to area of Garm; rises to 20,840 ft. at Kirov Peak and to 24,590 ft. at Stalin Peak (at junction with Akademiya Nauk Range). Many glaciers. Formerly also known as Peter the Great Mts.

Peter the Great Bay or **Peter the Great Gulf,** Rus. *Zaliv Petra Velikogo,* inlet of Sea of Japan, in SW Maritime Territory, Russian SFSR, bet. mouth of Tumen R. (SW) and Cape Povorotny (NE); 42°30'N 132°E; 115 mi. wide, 55 mi. long. Its main inlets are Amur and Ussuri bays (N; separated by Muravyev-Amurski Peninsula and Russian Isl.) and Posyet Bay (SW). Main ports: Vladivostok, Nakhodka, Posyet. Discovered 1852; named Victoria Bay (1855); changed in honor of Peter the Great (1859).

Peter the Great Mountains, Tadzhik SSR: see PETER THE FIRST RANGE.

Petervarad, Yugoslavia: see PETROVARADIN.

Peterwardein, Yugoslavia: see PETROVARADIN.

Petfürdö, Hungary: see PET.

Pethapur (pātä'pŏŏr), town (pop. 5,187), Mehsana dist., N Bombay, India, on Sabarmati R. and 29 mi. SSE of Mehsana; local market for millet, pulse, wheat; dye mfg.

Petilia Policastro (pētē'lyä pôlēkä'strô), town (pop. 6,847), Catanzaro prov., Calabria, S Italy, 18 mi. NE of Catanzaro; woolen mill; lumbering.

Pétionville or **Pétion-Ville** (pātyōvēl'), town (1950 pop. 9,570), Ouest dept., S Haiti, on N hills of the Massif de la Selle, 3½ mi. ESE of Port-au-Prince; residential suburb and resort.

Petit (pŭtē'), village (pop. 508), Constantine dept., NE Algeria, on railroad and 4 mi. E of Guelma; wine, truck, olives.

Petit-Bassam, Fr. West Africa: see PORT-BOUET.

Petit Bois Island (pě'tē bwä"), SE Miss., one of isl. chain in the Gulf of Mexico, partly sheltering Mississippi Sound (N), 13 mi. SE of Pascagoula; c.8 mi. long.

Petit-Bourg (pŭtē'-bŏŏr'), town (commune pop. 5,223), E Basse-Terre, Guadeloupe, 5 mi. SW of Pointe-à-Pitre (linked by rail), in agr. region (coffee, cacao); sugar milling, distilling.

Petit Buëch River, France: see BUËCH RIVER.

Petit Caillou, Bayou (bī'ō pě'tē käyōō', kälōō'), SE La., navigable waterway extending 35 mi. generally N-S, bet. Bayou Terrebonne c.3 mi. SE of Houma and a W arm of Terrebonne Bay; navigable; partly canalized as a branch of Gulf Intracoastal Waterway.

Petit-Canal (pŭtē'-känäl'), town (commune pop. 9,267), W Grande-Terre, Guadeloupe, 10 mi. NNE of Pointe-à-Pitre, in sugar-growing region.

Petitcodiac (pětēkō'dĭăk), village (pop. estimate c.1,000), SE N.B., on Petitcodiac R. and 22 mi. WSW of Moncton; lumbering, dairying, gypsum quarrying.

Petitcodiac River, SE N.B., rises NE of Sussex, flows ENE to Moncton, thence SSE, past Hillsborough, to Shepody Bay at Hopewell Cape; 80 mi. long. Navigable below Moncton, it carries the region's mineral resources. Bay of Fundy tidal bore ascends to Moncton.

Petit-Couronne, Le (lŭ pŭtē'-kōōrôn'), town (pop. 2,108), Seine Inférieure dept., N France, on left bank of Seine R. and 5 mi. SSW of Rouen; petroleum refinery.

Petit Cul de Sac (pŭtē' küdsäk'), bay in S Guadeloupe, Fr. West Indies, bet. Basse-Terre and Grande-Terre, and linked by 4-mi.-long Rivière Salée with Grand Cul de Sac. At its head (NE) is Pointe-à-Pitre.

Petit-de-Grat Island (pŭtē'-dŭ-grä') (3 mi. long, 2 mi. wide), E N.S., off S Cape Breton Isl., just E of Madame Isl.

Petite-Anse (pŭtēt-äs'), village (1950 pop. 706), Nord dept., N Haiti, 2 mi. SE of Cap-Haïtien. On near-by sandbank Columbus's flagship, the *Santa Maria,* was lost (Christmas Day, 1492). The navigator built here La Navidad Fort.

Petite Creuse River (pŭtēt' krûz'), Creuse dept., central France, rises 2 mi. SE of Lavaufranche, flows c.40 mi. W, past Boussac, to the Creuse 7 mi. SE of Éguzon.

Petite Flandre (flä'drŭ), marshy area (□ c.100) surrounding Rochefort, Charente-Maritime dept., W France, on both sides of lower Charente R. Reclaimed by medieval monks and (in 17th cent.) by Dutch engineers, it is now a fertile truck-gardening and cattle-raising dist.

Petite-Forêt (-fôrĕ'), W suburb (pop. 2,258) of Valenciennes, Nord dept., N France; ironworks.

Petite-Île, La (lä ēlptēt'), town (pop. 5,069; commune pop. 6,140), near S coast of Réunion isl., 6 mi. E of Saint-Pierre; sugar cane, vanilla.

Petite Martinique (pŭtēt' märtŭnēk', pě'tē), **Petit Martinique** (pě'tē, pŭtē'), or **Little Martinique,** islet (pop. 479, including near-by islet of Petite Dominique), S Grenadines, dependency of Grenada, B.W.I., 3 mi. E of Carriacou isl., 40 mi. NE of St. George's; 12°21'N 61°23'W.

Petite Nèthe River (pŭtēt' nĕt'), Flemish *Kleine Nete* (klī'nŭ nā'tŭ), N Belgium, rises 7 mi. N of Mol, flows 32 mi. W, joining Grande Nèthe R. at Lierre to form NÈTHE RIVER.

Petit-Enghien (-āgyē'), Flemish *Lettelingen* (lĕ'tŭlĭng"ŭn), town (pop. 2,759), Hainaut prov., SW central Belgium, 2 mi. E of Enghien; metal industry; sugar refining; agr. market.

Petite-Pierre, La (lä pŭtēt'-pyâr'), Ger. *Lützelstein* (lüt'sŭl-shtīn), village (pop. 630), Bas-Rhin dept., E France, in the N Vosges, 9 mi. NNW of Saverne; resort; pharmaceuticals.

Petite Rivière (rēvyâr'), village (pop. 1,715), W Mauritius, on railroad and 5 mi. SW of Port Louis; hemp milling.

Petite-Rivière-de-l'Artibonite (-dŭ-lärtēbônēt'), town (1950 census pop. 4,377), Artibonite dept., central Haiti, on Artibonite R. and 14 mi. E of Saint-Marc; agr. center (cotton, coffee, bananas). Has old palace and fort.

Petite-Rivière-de-Nippes (-nēp'), town (1950 census pop. 643), Sud dept., SW Haiti, on the N coast of Tiburon Peninsula, 40 mi. W of Léogane, in agr. region (cotton, rice, coffee).

Petite-Rosselle (-rôsĕl'), Ger. *Klein Rosseln* (klīn rô'sŭln), town (pop. 8,306), Moselle dept., NE France, on the Rosselle (Saar border), 2 mi. NW of Forbach; coal-mining center.

Petites-Dalles, Les, France: see SASSETOT-LE-MAUCONDUIT.

Petite-Synthe (-sēt'), outer WSW suburb (pop. 5,670) of Dunkirk, Nord dept., N France; railroad equipment and chicory mfg., jute spinning, sawmilling of imported lumber. Damaged in Second World War.

Petite Terre (târ'), group of 2 small islets (□ 1.2), Guadeloupe dept., Fr. West Indies, 27 mi. ESE of Pointe-à-Pitre, Guadeloupe; 16°10'N 61°6'W. Consists of Terre-de-Bas and Terre-de-Haut. Lighthouse.

Petit-Fort-Philippe, France: see GRAVELINES.

Petit-Goâve (pŭtē-gwäv'), town (1950 census pop. 5,536), Ouest dept., S Haiti, port on S arm of the Gulf of Gonaïves, at N base of Tiburon Peninsula, 36 mi. WSW of Port-au-Prince; coffee- and cacao-shipping center. Trades also in other agr. products (cotton, sweet potatoes, coconuts, oranges, bananas, mangoes). Has wharf and customhouse.

Petitjean (pŭtēzhä'), town (pop. 11,678), Rabat region, NW central Fr. Morocco, at S edge of Rharb lowland, 40 mi. WNW of Fez; important rail junction; agr. trade center (cereals, wool, livestock). Petroleum from near-by Bou Draa and Tselfat (10 mi. E) wells refined here (since 1939).

Petit Jean River (pě'tē jēn'), W and W central Ark., rises in Sebastian co., flows 113 mi. E, past Booneville and Danville, to Arkansas R. 10 mi. W of Morrilton. Impounded W of Danville by Blue Mountain Dam (1947), for flood control; the dam 115 ft. high, 2,800 ft. long) forms Blue Mountain L. (7½ mi. long, 1 mi. wide; flood-control storage, 233,000 acre-ft.), used for boating and fishing.

Petit Jean State Park, central Ark., recreational area on Petit Jean Mtn., c.10 mi. W of Morrilton; waterfalls, canyons, caves, lakes (bathing, boating, fishing), bridle and foot trails; cabins, lodge.

Petit Manan Island (pŭtēt' mŭnăn'), Washington co., E Maine, small lighthouse isl. 3 mi. SE of Petit Manan Point, W of entrance to Pleasant Bay.

Petit Manan Point, Washington co., E Maine, peninsula 28 mi. SE of Ellsworth and on E side of Dyer Bay.

Petit Martinique, Grenadines, B.W.I.: see PETITE MARTINIQUE.

Petit-Morin River (pŭtē'-môrē'), Marne and Seine-et-Marne depts., N central France, rises in Marshes of Saint-Gond, flows c.35 mi. W, past Montmirail, to the Marne at La Ferté-sous-Jouarre. Classical example of river capture.

Petit Nord Peninsula, N.F.: see GREAT NORTHERN PENINSULA.

Petit Piton, St. Lucia, B.W.I.: see PITONS, THE.

Petit-Popo, Fr. Togoland: see ANÉCHO.

Petit Pré (pŭtē' prā'), village, S Que., on the St. Lawrence and 12 mi. NE of Quebec; mica mining.

Petit-Quevilly, Le (lŭ pŭtē'-kŭvēyē'), WSW industrial suburb (pop. 19,857) of Rouen, Seine-Inférieure dept., N France, on left bank of the Seine; chemical plants, metalworks, cotton mills, rubber factory; canning, mfg. of explosives, flour products, and porcelain.

Petit-Rechain (pŭtē'-rŭshē'), town (pop. 2,346), Liége prov., E Belgium, 2 mi. NNW of Verviers; wool spinning and weaving. Village of Grand-Rechain (pop. 736) is 1.5 mi. WSW.

Petit Rhône, France: see RHONE RIVER.

Petit-Sable, Réunion: see SALAZIE.

Petit-Saint-Bernard, France: see LITTLE SAINT BERNARD PASS.

Petit Trianon, France: see TRIANON.

Petit-Trou-de-Nippes (pŭtē'-trōō-dŭ-nēp'), town (1950 census pop. 773), Sud dept., SW Haiti, on N coast of Tiburon Peninsula, 55 mi. W of Léogane; coffee, cotton.

Petlad (pāt'läd), town (pop. 23,928), Kaira dist., N Bombay, India, 20 mi. SSE of Kaira; rail junction; tobacco market; agr.-distributing center (millet, rice, pulse); cotton milling, hand-loom weaving, dyeing, mfg. of matches, bobbins, pencils, copper and brass utensils; chemical works. Col. Formerly in Baroda state.

Petlalcingo (pätlälsĕng'gō), town (pop. 2,348), Puebla, central Mexico, on Inter-American Highway and 13 mi. SE of Acatlán; sugar cane, fruit, corn, livestock.

Peto (pä'tō), town (pop. 5,104), Yucatan, SE Mexico, 70 mi. SE of Mérida; rail terminus; agr. center (henequen, sugar cane, corn, fruit, timber).

Petőhaza (pĕ'tûhăzō), Hung. *Petőháza*, town (pop. 871), Sopron co., W Hungary, on Ikva R. and 15 mi. ESE of Sopron; sugar refinery.

Petone (pŭtō'nē), borough (pop. 10,877), S N.Isl., New Zealand, on N shore of Wellington harbor; mfg. (woolen goods, soap, machinery).

Petorca, department, Chile: see La Ligua.

Petorca (pātôr'kä), town (pop. 1,098), Aconcagua prov., central Chile, on Petorca R. (a Pacific coastal stream) and 23 mi. NE of La Ligua; rail terminus in agr. area (fruit, tobacco, potatoes, livestock). Gold, gypsum deposits. Old colonial town.

Petoskey (pētŏ'skē), resort city (pop. 6,468), ⊙ Emmet co., NW Mich., on Little Traverse Bay of L. Michigan, and c.55 mi. NE of Traverse City, in lake and farm area (potatoes, apples). Limestone quarrying, mfg. of Portland cement; also mfg. of leather, lumber, wood products, paper pulp, flour, limestone quarries. Site of Magnus State Park. A winter carnival and summer Indian pageant are held here. Settled c.1860; inc. as village 1879, as city 1895.

Petra (pā'trä), town (pop. 2,832), Majorca, Balearic Isls., on railroad and 25 mi. E of Palma; stock raising, grain- and winegrowing; stone quarrying; cement mfg.

Petra (pē'trů, pĕ'–), anc. rock city of Jordan, just W of the village of Wadi Musa, 16 mi. NW of Ma'an, near foot of Jebel Harun (Mt. Hor). It was ⊙ of the Edomites and is sometimes identified with Sela of the Old Testament. Once a wealthy and celebrated city, with a great caravan trade, it declined with the rise of Palmyra, was subdued by the Nabataeans, and fell to the Romans, who included it in Arabia Petraea. An early seat of Christianity, it was conquered by the Moslems in 7th cent. and by the Crusaders in 12th cent. The ruins, discovered 1812 by John L. Burckhardt, and including a great theater, dwellings, temples, and altars, are carved (not built) from rock stratified in a soft profusion of colors, in which rose, crimson, purple, and saffron mingle with black and white.

Petrais (pĕ'trĕs), village (pop. 797), Phlorina nome, Macedonia, Greece, 3 mi. N of Amyntaion, on W shore of L. Petrais (□ 4.6). Formerly called Peterskon.

Petralia Sottana (pĕträlē'ä sôt-tä'nä), town (pop. 5,760), Palermo prov., N central Sicily, in Madonie Mts., near head of Salso R., 17 mi. S of Cefalù; wine, olive oil, macaroni. Mineral products include sulphur, iron pyrite, asphalt, petroleum. One mi. SE is **Petralia Soprana** (pop. 2,105); tourist resort; wine, cheese.

Petra Pass (pĕ'trů), 7-mi.-long defile on Thessaly-Macedonia line, N central Greece, bet. the Olympus (E) and the Pieria massif (W), on main Salonika-Larissa highway, 13 mi. SW of Katerine. Of strategic importance as by-pass of the Olympus.

Petra Pervogo, Khrebet, Tadzhik SSR: see Peter the First Range.

Petrel (pātrĕl'), town (pop. 4,467), Alicante prov., E Spain, 18 mi. NW of Alicante; mfg. (cement, pottery, shoes, furniture, knit goods). Olive oil, almonds, fruit, cereals. Gypsum, clay, and stone quarries. Has ruined Moorish castle.

Petrelë (pĕtrĕ'lů) or **Petrela** (pĕtrĕ'lä), village (1930 pop. 596), central Albania, 5 mi. SSE of Tirana, off road to Elbasan; has ruins of 15th-cent. castle.

Petreto-Bicchisano (pĕträtô-bēkēzänô), village (pop. 1,249), S central Corsica, 12 mi. N of Sartène; olives, fruits.

Petrey (pē'trē), town (pop. 171), Crenshaw co., S Ala., 14 mi. WNW of Troy.

Petrich (pĕ'trĕch), city (pop. 13,456), Gorna Dzhumaya dist., SW Bulgaria, in Macedonia, in Struma R. valley, 40 mi. S of Gorna Dzhumaya, on rail spur; market center; processes oil-bearing plants and tobacco. Once a Turkish commercial town; rebuilt in modern fashion after its destruction during First World War.

Petrified Forest National Monument (□ 133.2; established 1906), E Ariz., in Painted Desert, 18 mi. E of Holbrook. Area rich in colorful petrified flora, including huge agate logs and fossilized leaves and plants. Ancient ruins and petroglyphs remain from prehistoric Indian occupation. Museums, cabins.

Petrikau, Poland: see Piotrkow.

Petrikov (pyĕtrĭkôf'), city (1926 pop. 5,693), central Polesye oblast, Belorussian SSR, on Pripet R. and 33 mi. W of Mozyr; wood- and metalworking.

Petrikovka (–kŭ), village (1926 pop. 26,050), NW Dnepropetrovsk oblast, Ukrainian SSR, 25 mi. NW of Dnepropetrovsk; clothing industry.

Petrila (pĕtrē'lä), Hung. *Petrilla* (pĕ'trĕl-lŏ), village (pop. 10,555), Hunedoara prov., W central Rumania, in the Transylvanian Alps, 3 mi. NE of Petrosani; coal-mining center; woodworking, tar and pitch production.

Petrinja (pĕ'trĭnyä), village (pop. 5,261), N Croatia, Yugoslavia, on Kupa R., on railroad and 6 mi. SW of Sisak; trade center in plum-growing region; meat packing, woodworking, soap mfg. Chartered in 1242.

Petriu, Petriev, or **Petriew**, Thailand: see Chachoengsao.

Petrkovice (pĕ'tûrshkôvĭtsĕ), Czech *Petřkovice*, Ger. *Peterhofen* (pā'tûrhō″fŭn), village (pop. 3,482), E central Silesia, Czechoslovakia, on Oder R., just NNW of and across from Ostrava; rail terminus; coal-mining center, part of industrial complex of Greater Ostrava.

Petro-Aleksandrovsk, Uzbek SSR: see Turtkul.

Petroc, Yugoslavia: see Petrovac, Vojvodina, Serbia.

Petrodvorets (pyĕ″trůdvŭryĕts'), city (1935 pop. 28,000), W Leningrad oblast, Russian SFSR, on Gulf of Finland, 14 mi. WSW (under jurisdiction) of Leningrad; stone cutting. Site of Great Palace (built 1715; expanded 1750), Monplaisir castle (1st residence of Peter the Great), and several smaller palaces (such as Marly; built 1714) surrounded by extensive parks with fountains and cascades, including the Great Cascade. Founded by Peter the Great; city became one of most brilliant and extensive summer residences of Rus. tsars, reflecting architectural styles of 2 centuries. Called Petergof, Ger. *Peterhof*, until 1944, except for short period in 1930s, when it was named Leninsk. Petrodvorets was restored, following its destruction in Second World War, when city was held (1941–44) by Germans during siege of Leningrad.

Petro-Golinishchevo (–gŭlyĭnyē'shchĭvů), town (1939 pop. over 500), W Voroshilovgrad oblast, Ukrainian SSR, in the Donbas, 3 mi. from Irmino station; coal mines.

Petrograd, Russian SFSR: see Leningrad, city.

Petrograd, Yugoslavia: see Zrenjanin.

Petrogrado-Donetskoye (pyĕtrůgrä″dů-dŭnyĕts'-kŭyů), town (1939 pop. over 2,000), SW Voroshilovgrad oblast, Ukrainian SSR, in the Donbas, 10 mi. N of Kadiyevka; coal mines.

Petrohué (pātrōwā'), village (1930 pop. 124), Llanquihue prov., S central Chile, resort on W bank of L. Todos los Santos, at SE foot of Osorno Volcano, 35 mi. NE of Puerto Montt. Lumbering, fishing. The health resort Baños de Petrohué (1930 pop. 236) is 15 mi. SSE.

Petrokamenskoye (–kä'myĭnskŭyů), village (1926 pop. 2,491), S central Sverdlovsk oblast, Russian SFSR, on Neiva R. and 27 mi. SE of Nizhni Tagil; woodworking, lumbering. Gold placers near by.

Petrokhan Pass (pĕtrôkhän') (alt. 4,743 ft.), NW Bulgaria, in Berkovitsa Mts., 7 mi. S of Berkovitsa, on highway to Sofia.

Petrokov, Poland: see Piotrkow.

Petrokrepost or **Petrokrepost'** (–kryĕ'pûstyů), city (1926 pop. 6,412), N Leningrad oblast, Russian SFSR, port on L. Ladoga, at issuance of Neva R., 25 mi. E of Leningrad, on rail spur from Mga; cotton mill at Imeni Morozova (SW). On isl. opposite city is historic fortress, built 1323 by Novgorod and called Oreshek. Long a prize in Russo-Swedish wars, fortress was named (1661) Noteborg by Swedes and Shlisselburg, Ger. *Schlüsselburg*, after reconquest (1702) by Peter the Great. From 18th cent. until 1917, members of royal family (including wife and daughter of Peter the Great; Ivan IV), noblemen (including D. M. Golitsyn, E. J. Biron), and Rus. revolutionaries were imprisoned or executed here. Renamed Petrokrepost (1944) from Shlisselburg. During Second World War, taken (1941) by Germans. Its recapture (1943) by Russians opened land route to besieged Leningrad.

Pétrola (pā'trōlä), town (pop. 1,683), Albacete prov., SE central Spain, 21 mi. SE of Albacete; wine, saffron, cereals.

Petrolândia (pĭtrōolän'dyů), city (pop. 1,460), central Pernambuco, NE Brazil, on left bank of São Francisco R. (not navigable here; Bahia border) and 120 mi. WSW of Garanhuns; W terminus of railroad to Piranhas (Alagoas) around Paulo Afonso Falls; agr. settlement. Hydroelectric plant. Lignite deposits near by. Called Jatobá until 1939; and Itaparica, 1939–43.

Petrólea (pātrō'lēä), town, Norte de Santander dept., N Colombia, in lowlands near Venezuela border, 40 mi. N of Cúcuta; oil-drilling center in Barco petroleum concession; refinery. From here runs a 236-mi. pipe line to Coveñas on Caribbean coast of Bolívar dept.

Petroleum, county (□ 1,664; pop. 1,026), central Mont.; ⊙ Winnett. Agr. area drained by branches of Musselshell R.; bounded N by Missouri R., E by Musselshell R. Livestock, grain; petroleum, natural gas. Formed 1924.

Petrolia (pĕtrō'lēů), town (pop. 2,801), S Ont., on Bear Creek and 15 mi. ESE of Sarnia; oil-production center, with refineries, tank farms; also dairying, fruitgrowing region. Clay quarries near by.

Petrolia. 1 Borough (pop. 571), Butler co., W Pa., 15 mi. NE of Butler. **2** Town (pop. 606), Clay co., N Texas, near Red R., 18 mi. ENE of Wichita Falls; trade point in farm area.

Petrolina (pĭtrōolē'nů), city (pop. 4,568), W Pernambuco, NE Brazil, on left bank of São Francisco R., opposite Juàzeiro (Bahia; reached by ferry); S terminus of railroad to Paulistana (Piauí); ships cotton, tobacco, sugar. Airfield. Railroad bridge to Juàzeiro built 1951.

Petromagoula (pĕtrůmůgōo'lů), town (pop. 3,417), Boeotia nome, E central Greece, 7 mi. ENE of Levadia, on edge of drained L. Copais; wheat, tobacco; wine. Also spelled Petromaghoula.

Petronà (pĕtrônä'), village (pop. 2,665), Catanzaro prov., Calabria, S Italy, 13 mi. NE of Catanzaro.

Petropavlovka (pĕtrůpäv'lůfků). **1** Village (1939 pop. under 500), S Buryat-Mongol Autonomous SSR, Russian SFSR, 135 mi. SW of Ulan-Ude, near Dzhida R.; grain, livestock. **2** Village (1926 pop. 4,371), SE Voronezh oblast, Russian SFSR, 22 mi. SSW of Kalach; wheat. **3** Village (1926 pop. 9,926), E Dnepropetrovsk oblast, Ukrainian SSR, on Samara R. and 25 mi. ESE of Pavlograd; metalworks, flour mill.

Petropavlovsk (–lůfsk). **1** City (1939 pop. 91,678), ⊙ North Kazakhstan oblast, Kazakh SSR, on Ishim R., on Trans-Siberian RR and 875 mi. NNW of Alma-Ata. N terminus of Trans-Kazakhstan RR; center of agr. area (wheat); meat-packing plant, flour mills, tannery, agr.-machinery works. Teachers col. Pop. mainly Russians. Founded 1752 as Rus. fortress. Once a caravan trading center for silk, carpets, skins. Formerly also called Kyzyl-Dzhar. **2** or **Petropavlovsk-Kamchatski** (–kŭmchät'skē), city (1939 pop. over 20,000), ⊙ Kamchatka oblast, Khabarovsk Territory, Russian SFSR, on SE coast of Kamchatka Peninsula, on Avacha Bay, 1,700 mi. NE of Vladivostok; 53°N 158°45'E. Naval base and largest Soviet port in N.Pacific Ocean (ice-free for 9 months); shipyards (in suburb of Industrialny); fish canning, sawmilling, tin-can mfg., brickworking; cold-storage plants. Has monuments to La Pérouse and Bering; Bering founded it (1740) and named it for his ships, *St. Peter* and *St. Paul.* Attacked (1854) by Franco-British naval squadron during Crimean War.

Petropavlovski or **Petropavlovskiy** (–skē). **1** Suburb of Petropavlovsk, North Kazakhstan oblast, Kazakh SSR. **2** Town, Astrakhan oblast, Russian SFSR: see Vladimirovka, village. **3** Village, Chelyabinsk oblast, Russian SFSR: see Kusa. **4** Village, Sverdlovsk oblast, Russian SFSR: see Severouralsk.

Petropavlovskoye (–skŭyů). **1** Village (1926 pop. 6,076), central Altai Territory, Russian SFSR, 55 mi. WSW of Bisk, in agr. area. **2** Village, Chkalov oblast, Russian SFSR: see Sara.

Petrópolis (pĭtrô'pōolēs), city (1950 pop. 61,843), Rio de Janeiro state, Brazil, in valley on N slope of Serra da Estrêla, 26 mi. N of Rio; alt. 2,700 ft. Fashionable resort and unofficial summer capital of Brazil, noted for its healthful climate and mtn. scenery. Its industries include textile mills, chemical works, tobacco factories, breweries; diamond cutting, mfg. of ceramics. Dairying center. Ships flowers (carnations, orchids), fruit, vegetables, and poultry. First settled 1845 by Bavarian immigrants, it became the favorite summer residence of Dom Pedro II (after whom city is now named). Bet. 1894 and 1903, it was ⊙ Rio de Janeiro state. Notable bldgs. are the cathedral (in Fr. Gothic style) which contains the tomb of Dom Pedro II and his queen, Acad. of Letters, old imperial palace, Renaissance summer residence of Braz. presidents, and imperial mus. Petrópolis is linked to Rio by rail and modern highway. The luxurious new Quitandinha hotel (just SW, near crest of great escarpment) was scene of 1947 Inter-American Conference.

Petros (pē'trŏs), village (1940 pop. 1,109), Morgan co., NE central Tenn., 30 mi. WNW of Knoxville, in a valley of the Cumberlands.

Petrosani (pĕtrôshän'), Rum. *Petroşani*, Hung. *Petrozsény* (pĕ'trôzhānyů), town (1948 pop. 14,138), Hunedoara prov., W central Rumania, in the Transylvanian Alps, on headstream of Jiu R., on railroad and 40 mi. SE of Deva; leading coal-mining center of Rumania; also mfg. of coal by-products; cabinetmaking. Founded in 17th cent. Has large Hung. pop. Sometimes spelled Petroseni and Petroshan.

Petroskoi, Karelo-Finnish SSR: see Petrozavodsk.

Petrousa (pĕtrōo'sů), town (pop. 3,636), Drama nome, Macedonia, Greece, 8 mi. WNW of Drama; tobacco, barley; olive oil. Sometimes spelled Petroussa; formerly called Plevna.

Petrovac, Petrovats (both: pĕ'trôväts). **1** or **Bosanski Petrovac** or **Bosanski Petrovats** (bô'sänskē), town (pop. 3,515), W Bosnia, Yugoslavia, 45 mi. WSW of Banja Luka; local trade center. **2** or **Petrovac na Moru** or **Petrovats na Moru** (nä mô'rōo), village, S Montenegro, Yugoslavia, on the Adriatic, 23 mi. SW of Titograd, in fruitgrowing area. Summer resort. Until 1921, in Dalmatia. **3** or **Backi Petrovac**, or **Bachki Petrovats** (both: (băch'kē), Serbo-Croatian *Bački Petrovac*, Hung. *Petrőc* (pĕt'rûts), village (pop. 7,379), Vojvodina, NW Serbia, Yugoslavia, on Novi Sad–Mali Stapar Canal, on railroad and 14 mi. NW of Novi Sad, in the Backa. Hops grown in vicinity. Pop. largely Slovak. **4** or **Petrovac Pozarevacki** or **Petrovats Pozharevachki** (both: pô'zhärĕ″vächkē), Serbo-

Croatian *Petrovac Požarevački*, village (pop. 4,169), central Serbia, Yugoslavia, on Mlava R. and 21 mi. SSE of Pozarevac; rail terminus.

Petrova Gora (pĕ'trôvä gô'rä), mountain in Dinaric Alps, NW Croatia, Yugoslavia; highest point, the Petrovac (1,663 ft.) is 5 mi. E of Vojnic. Iron-ore deposits.

Petrovaradin (pĕ'trôvärä"dĭn), Hung. *Pétervárad* (pā'tĕrvä"rŏd), Ger. *Peterwardein* (pā'tŭrvärdīn"), S suburb of Novi Sad, Vojvodina, N Serbia, Yugoslavia, across the Danube, in the Srem; rail junction. Has old fortress. Allegedly named after Peter the Hermit, who assembled (1096) an army here for the First Crusade. Scene of victory (1716) of Prince Eugene of Savoy over Turks.

Petrovats, Yugoslavia: see PETROVAC.

Petroverovka, Ukrainian SSR: see ZHOVTEN, Odessa oblast.

Petrov Glacier (pĕ'trŏv, Rus. pētrôf'), on S slope of Terskei Ala-Tau, in Kirghiz SSR; 41°55'N 78°10'E. Site of meteorological observation post (alt. 12,045 ft.), 25 mi. S of Pokrovka. Source of the Yaak-Tash, a headstream of NARYN RIVER.

Petrovgrad, Yugoslavia: see ZRENJANIN.

Petrovka (pētrôf'kŭ). **1** Village (1939 pop. over 500), W Frunze oblast, Kirghiz SSR, in Chu valley, on railroad and 33 mi. W of Frunze; fiber-plant processing. **2** Village (1939 pop. over 500), E Kuibyshev oblast, Russian SFSR, on Lesser Kinel R. and 28 mi. ENE of Pavlovka; metalworking; wheat, sunflowers. **3** Village (1939 pop. over 500), W Tambov oblast, Russian SFSR, near railroad (Izberdei station), 20 mi. SSW of Michurinsk; grain, potatoes. Formerly called Petrovskoye.

Petrovka-Romenskaya (-rŭmyĕn'skŭ), village (1939 pop. over 500), N Poltava Oblast, Ukrainian SSR, on Khorol R. and 28 mi. SE of Romny; sugar beets.

Petrovo (pētrô'vŭ), village (1926 pop. 7,964), E Kirovograd oblast, Ukrainian SSR, on Ingulets R. and 45 mi. ESE of Kirovograd; wheat, sugar beets. Graphite deposits.

Petrovo-Krasnoselye or **Petrovo-Krasnosel'ye** (-krŭsnŭsĕ'lyĭ), town (1939 pop. over 2,000), SW Voroshilovgrad oblast, Ukrainian SSR, in the Donbas, 11 mi. NNW of Krasny Luch; coal mines.

Petrovo Selo, Backo Petrovo Selo, or **Bachko Petrovo Selo** (all: pĕ'trôvô sĕ'lô, bäch'kô), Serbo-Croatian *Bačko Petrovo Selo*, Hung. *Péterréve* (pā'tĕr-rāvĕ), village (pop. 9,792), Vojvodina, N Serbia, Yugoslavia, on the Tisa and 6 mi. NNE of Becej, in the Backa.

Petrovsk (pētrôfsk'). **1** or **Petrovsk-Zabaikalski** or **Petrovsk-Zabaykal'skiy** (-zŭbīkäl'skē), city (1933 pop. estimate 12,100), SW Chita oblast, Russian SFSR, on Trans-Siberian RR and 200 mi. WSW of Chita. Metallurgical center; produces pig iron, cast-iron products; sawmilling, glassworking. Iron ore is obtained from Balyaga mine (15 mi. NW). Original ironworks (established 1790; called Petrovski Zavod) were place of exile (1830s) of many Decembrists; modernized in 1930s. **2** City, Dagestan Autonomous SSR, Russian SFSR: see MAKHACHKALA. **3** City (1926 pop. 19,192), N Saratov oblast, Russian SFSR, on Medveditsa R. and 60 mi. NNW of Saratov; agr. center; mfg. (tractor parts, flour, starch); fruit, vegetable, and oilseed processing, poultry farming. Dates from c.1690.

Petrovskaya (pētrôf'skŭ), village (1926 pop. 10,886), W Krasnodar Territory, Russian SFSR, in Kuban R. delta mouth region, 55 mi. NW of Krasnodar; cotton, wheat, ambary hemp, rice; flour mill. Near-by village of Chernoyerkovskaya (1926 pop. 2,327) lies 8 mi. W, amid coastal lagoons of Sea of Azov.

Petrovskaya Sloboda, Russian SFSR: see LOSINO-PETROVSKI.

Petrovski or **Petrovskiy** (-skē). **1** Town (1939 pop. over 500), SW Ivanovo oblast, Russian SFSR, on Nerl R. and 10 mi. NE of Gavrilov-Posad; sawmilling, distilling. **2** Town (1937 pop. 2,900), NW Tula oblast, Russian SFSR, on Oka R. and 5 mi. SW of Aleksin; agr.-machine mfg., brick making.

Petrovski Zavod, Russian SFSR: see PETROVSK, Chita oblast.

Petrovskogo, Imeni G. I., Ukrainian SSR: see GORODISHCHE, Kiev oblast.

Petrovskoye (-skŭyŭ). **1** Village (1926 pop. 2,608), central Bashkir Autonomous SSR, Russian SFSR, 19 mi. E of Sterlitamak; grain, livestock. **2** Village (1926 pop. 14,732), central Stavropol Territory, Russian SFSR, 45 mi. ENE of Stavropol; rail junction; agr. center in wheat and cotton area; meat, flour, dairy goods; metalworks; quarry. **3** Town (1926 pop. 1,926), SE Yaroslavl oblast, Russian SFSR, 13 mi. SSW of Rostov. **4** Village (1926 pop. 6,389), SE Kharkov oblast, Ukrainian SSR, near the Northern Donets, 17 mi. W of Izyum; metalworks. Formerly called Petrovskaya.

Petrozavodsk (pyĕ"trŭzŭvôtsk'), Finnish *Petroskoi*, city (1926 pop. 27,105; 1939 pop. 69,728; 1941 pop. 80,000), ⊙ Karelo-Finnish SSR, port on L. Onega, on Murmansk RR (junction of branch to Suoyarvi) and 185 mi. NE of Leningrad, 61°47'N 34°23'E. Economic and cultural center; machine mfg. (lumber tractors, steam engines, lumbering tools); shipbuilding (fishing boats), mfg. of furniture, cement, bricks, alcohol. Sawmilling, mica processing; railroad shops. Ski factory at Lososinoye (SW). Site of Karelian regional mus., state univ. (1940), teachers col. Founded 1703 under Peter the Great as ironworking center; named Petrozavodsk in 1777. Became (1802) ⊙ Olonets govt. and (1920) ⊙ Karelian Workers' Commune (after 1923, Karelian Autonomous SSR). In 1930s also known as Kalininsk. In Second World War, held (1941–44) by Finns and Germans.

Petrusburg (pĕ'trŭsbûrkh), town (pop. 1,514), W Orange Free State, U. of So. Afr., 50 mi. W of Bloemfontein; alt. 4,161 ft.; stock, grain, feed crops. Rail station is called Petrus.

Petrus Steyn (pĕ'trŭs stān'), town (pop. 1,748), E Orange Free State, U. of So. Afr., 40 mi. NNW of Bethlehem; alt. 5,510 ft.; grain, stock.

Petrvald (pĕ'tŭrzhvält), Czech *Petřvald*, Ger. *Peterswald* (pā'tŭrsvält), town (pop. 9,461), NE Silesia, Czechoslovakia, on railroad and 5 mi. E of Ostrava; intensive coal and iron mining; ironworks.

Petryaksy (pētryäk'sē), village (1926 pop. 6,255), SE Gorki oblast, Russian SFSR, 23 mi. ESE of Sergach; wheat, hemp.

Petrzalka (pĕ'tŭrzhälkä), Slovak *Petržalka*, Hung. *Pozsonyligetfalu* (pô'zhônyŭlĭ"gĕtfŏlōō), Ger. *Engerau* (ĕng'ŭrou), town (pop. 11,618), SW Slovakia, Czechoslovakia, on railroad, on right bank of Danube R. opposite Bratislava, near Austrian border; mfg. of rubber goods; steelworks; extensive gardens and parks.

Petsamo, Russian SFSR: see PECHENGA.

Petschau, Czechoslovakia: see BECOV.

Petschur, Russian SFSR: see PECHORY.

Petseri, Russian SFSR: see PECHORY.

Pettau, Yugoslavia: see PTUJ.

Petten (pĕ'tŭn), village (pop. 130), North Holland prov., NW Netherlands, on North Sea, 10 mi. NNW of Alkmaar; fishing.

Pettenbach (pĕ'tŭnbäkh), town (pop. 4,347), S central Upper Austria, 10 mi. ENE of Gmunden; tanning.

Pettigo or **Pettigoe** (pĕ'tĭgō), Gaelic *Paite Gobha*, town (pop. 250), S Co. Donegal, Ireland, 14 mi. ESE of Donegal; frontier station on Northern Ireland border; agr. market (oats, potatoes; cattle, sheep). Near by is Lough Derg.

Pettis (pĕ'tĭs), county (□ 679; pop. 31,577), central Mo.; ⊙ Sedalia. Agr. (corn, wheat, oats, hay, potatoes), livestock; mfg. at Sedalia; barite, coal mines, limestone quarries. Formed 1833.

Pettorano sul Gizio (pĕt-tôrä'nô sōōl jē'tsyô), village (pop. 2,458), Aquila prov., Abruzzi e Molise, S central Italy, 5 mi. SSE of Sulmona.

Pettus, village (1940 pop. 643), Bee co., S Texas, 15 mi. N of Beeville; oil wells and refinery; mfg. of oil-well supplies.

Petty's Island (c.1 mi. long), Camden co., SW N.J., in Delaware R. just above Camden; oil refinery.

Petukhovo (pyĕtōōkhô'vŭ), city (1926 pop. 4,881), E Kurgan oblast, Russian SFSR, on Trans-Siberian RR and 50 mi. WNW of Petropavlovsk; agr. center; farm machinery, dairy products. Until 1944, Yudino.

Petuna, Manchuria: see FUYÜ, Kirin prov.

Petushki, Russian SFSR: see NOVYE PETUSHKI.

Petworth (pĕ'tŭrth), town and parish (pop. 2,362), W Sussex, England, 13 mi. NE of Chichester; agr. market. The 14th-cent. church contains monuments of Percy family; Petworth House (originally 12th cent.) has noted collection of paintings.

Petzen (pĕ'tsŭn), Slovenian *Peca* (pĕ'tsä), peak (8,162 ft.) in E Karawanken, on Austro-Yugoslav border, 6 mi. SW of Prevalje, Yugoslavia; lead, zinc, and brown-coal mines on slopes.

Peuerbach (poi'ŭrbäkh), town (pop. 2,323), central Upper Austria, 24 mi. W of Linz; market center for agr., livestock area.

Peulla (pĕōō'yä), village (1930 pop. 62), Llanquihue prov., S central Chile, resort on L. Todos los Santos, 50 mi. NE of Puerto Montt, on road to San Carlos de Bariloche, Argentina.

Peumo (pĕōō'mō), town (pop. 3,507), ⊙ Cachapoal dept. (□ 254; pop. 18,672), O'Higgins prov., central Chile, on Cachapoal R., in the central valley, on railroad and 30 mi. SW of Rancagua; agr. center (alfalfa, wheat, potatoes, beans, fruit, wine, livestock); dairying, flour milling, lumbering.

Peunasoe, Indonesia: see PUNASU.

Peureulak, Indonesia: see PERLAK.

Pevek (pĕvyĕk'), village (1948 pop. over 500), NW Chukchi Natl. Okrug, Kamchatka oblast, Khabarovsk Territory, Russian SFSR, on Chaun Bay of E.Siberian Sea, 400 mi. NW of Anadyr; reindeer farms; trading post, airfield.

Pevely (pĕ'vlē), town (pop. 416), Jefferson co., E Mo., on Mississippi R. and 25 mi. S of St. Louis.

Pevensey (pĕ'vŭnzē), agr. village and parish (pop. 793), SE Sussex, England, on the Channel, 4 mi. NE of Eastbourne. Site of Roman fort *Anderida* (there are remains of Roman walls), built toward end of 3d cent. as defense against the Saxons, who took it in 491. In 1066 William the Conqueror landed here; there are remains of a Norman castle. In Middle Ages town was a port and corporate member of the CINQUE PORTS, attached to Hastings; it declined when the sea receded. Has 13th-cent. church. Many Roman remains have been excavated here.

Peveragno (pĕvĕrä'nyô), village (pop. 1,807), Cuneo prov., Piedmont, NW Italy, 5 mi. SE of Cuneo; macaroni.

Pewamo (pēwä'mō), village (pop. 432), Ionia co., S central Mich., 11 mi. E of Ionia.

Pewaukee (pĭwô'kē), village (pop. 1,792), Waukesha co., SE Wis., at E end of Pewaukee L. (c.4½ mi. long), 17 mi. W of Milwaukee, in dairy- and poultry-farm area; farm trade center; resort (summer and winter lake sports). Inc. 1876.

Pewee Valley (pē'wē), town (pop. 687), Oldham co., N Ky., 18 mi. ENE of downtown Louisville, in outer Bluegrass region.

Pewsey (pū'zē), town and parish (pop. 1,574), E central Wiltshire, England, 6 mi. SSW of Marlborough; agr. market in dairying region. Has 13th-15th-cent. church. Pewsey Hill (705 ft.), with anc. earthworks, is 2 mi. SE.

Peyia (pā'yä), village (pop. 1,409), Paphos dist., W Cyprus, 8 mi. N of Paphos; wheat, barley, carobs, olive oil; sheep, goats.

Peyrano (pārä'nō), town (pop. estimate 1,500), S Santa Fe prov., Argentina, 40 mi. SSW of Rosario; rail junction and agr. center (wheat, corn, flax, potatoes, livestock).

Peyrat, Le (lŭ pārä'), village (pop. 261), Ariège dept., S France, on Hers R. and 16 mi. E of Foix; plastics (chiefly combs).

Peyrat-le-Château (pārä'-lŭ-shätō'), village (pop. 864), Haute-Vienne dept., W central France, in Monts du Limousin, 25 mi. E of Limoges; mfg. of varnishes.

Peyrehorade (pārôräd'), village (pop. 1,571), Landes dept., SW France, on Gave de Pau R. and 11 mi. S of Dax; shoe mfg.

Peyreleau (pārlō'), village (pop. 152), Aveyron dept., S France, at foot of the Causse Noir, on the Tarn (S end of Tarn gorge) at mouth of Jonte R., and 9 mi. NE of Millau; blue-cheese mfg.; ewe's milk is shipped to Roquefort.

Peyriac-Minervois (pārēäk'-mēnĕrvwä'), village (pop. 970), Aude dept., S France, 12 mi. ENE of Carcassonne; distilling, fruit- and winegrowing.

Peyrolles-en-Provence (pārôl'-ā-prôväs'), village (pop. 879), Bouches-du-Rhône dept., SE France, near the Durance, 11 mi. NE of Aix-en-Provence; rabbit breeding (for furs).

Peyruis (pārüē'), village (pop. 655), Basses-Alpes dept., SE France, near right bank of Durance R., 15 mi. WSW of Digne; olive-oil, lavender pressing.

Pezas (pyĭzäs'), town (1948 pop. over 2,000), E central Kemerovo oblast, Russian SFSR, in Kuznetsk Ala-Tau, 80 mi. SE of Kemerovo; gold mining.

Pézenas (pāzŭnä'), town (pop. 5,761), Hérault dept., S France, near Hérault R., 13 mi. NE of Béziers; commercial center (wines, alcohol, truck produce); iron foundry, shoe factory; distilling, fruit preserving.

Pezinok (pĕ'zĭnôk), Hung. *Bazin* (bŏ'zĭn), town (pop. 6,436), W Slovakia, Czechoslovakia, on railroad and 12 mi. NNE of Bratislava; wine making. Copper and antimony mines. Extensive vineyards in vicinity.

Pezuela de las Torres (pāth-wā'lä dhä läs tô'rĕs), town (pop. 921), Madrid prov., central Spain, 26 mi. E of Madrid, in grain-growing and stock-raising region. Limekilns.

Pezzana (pĕtsä'nä), village (pop. 2,247), Vercelli prov., Piedmont, N Italy, 5 mi. SSE of Vercelli.

Pfäfers (pfĕ'fŭrs), town (pop. 2,010), St. Gall canton, E Switzerland, near Tamina R., S of Bad Ragaz. Has Benedictine abbey (founded 8th cent.; 17th-cent. bldgs.). **Pfäfers Bad,** on the Tamina and S of town, is noted for its curative hot spring (discovered c.1038; 1st bathhouse erected c.1465).

Pfaffenberg (pfä'fŭnbĕrk), village (pop. 2,023), Lower Bavaria, Germany, on Kleine Laaber R. and 17 mi. SW of Straubing; brewing, tanning.

Pfaffenhausen (pfä"fŭnhou'zŭn), village (pop. 1,708), Swabia, SW Bavaria, Germany, on Mindel R. and 5 mi. NNW of Mindelheim; German wheat, oats, cattle, sheep.

Pfaffenhofen (fäfĕnôfĕn', Ger. pfä"fŭnhō'fŭn), village (pop. 1,455), Bas-Rhin dept., E France, on the Moder and 9 mi. WNW of Haguenau; brewing.

Pfaffenhofen (pfä"fŭnhō'fŭn). **1** or **Pfaffenhofen an der Roth** (än dĕr rōt'), village (pop. 922), Swabia, W Bavaria, Germany, on small Roth R. and 9 mi. ESE of Ulm; grain, cattle. Chartered 1479. **2** or **Pfaffenhofen an der Ilm** (än dĕr ĭlm'), town (pop. 6,844), Upper Bavaria, Germany, on Ilm R. and 17 mi. S of Ingolstadt; textile mfg., metal- and woodworking, printing, brewing. Has late-Gothic church. Chartered 1393.

Pfaffenreuth (pfä'fŭnroit), village (pop. 730), Upper Palatinate, NE Bavaria, Germany, in Bohemian Forest, 3 mi. SSE of Waldsassen; graphite and magnetic-pyrite mining.

Pfaffenthal, Luxembourg: see LUXEMBOURG, city.

Pfäffikersee (pfĕ'fĭkŭrzä'), lake (□ 1), Zurich canton, N Switzerland, E of Zurich. Pfäffikon is on lake (N).

Pfäffikon (pfĕ'fēkôn), town (pop. 4,058), Zurich canton, N Switzerland, on Pfäffikersee and 11 mi. E of Zurich; cables, tires, woolen textiles; printing.

Pfaffnau (pfäf'nou), town (pop. 2,407), Lucerne canton, N Switzerland, 9 mi. S of Olten.

Pfaffstätten (pfäf'shtĕtŭn), village (pop. 2,173), E Lower Austria, just ENE of Baden; excellent wine.

Pfalz, Germany: see PALATINATE; RHENISH PALATINATE.

Pfalzburg, France: see PHALSBOURG.

Pfalzel (pfäl'tsŭl), village (pop. 3,382), in former Prussian Rhine Prov., W Germany, after 1945 in Rhineland-Palatinate, on the Mosel and 3 mi. NE of Trier; wine. Has Romanesque church.

Pfannspitze, peak on Austro-Ital. border: see VANSCURO, CIMA.

Pfarrkirchen (pfär'kĭr"khŭn), town (pop. 5,788), Lower Bavaria, Germany, on Rott R. and 25 mi. SW of Passau; brewing, tanning, metal- and woodworking. Has late-Gothic church, and pilgrimage church. Chartered 1317.

Pfastatt (făstăt', Ger. pfä'shtät), NW suburb (pop. 3,448), of Mulhouse, Haut-Rhin dept., E France; textile dyeing; tanning.

Pfeddersheim (pfĕ'dŭrs-hīm), village (pop. 3,676), Rhenish Hesse, W Germany, 4 mi. W of Worms; machinery; fruit preserves. Sugar beets.

Pfeffenhausen (pfĕ'fŭnhou'zŭn), village (pop. 2,406), Lower Bavaria, Germany, on Great Laaber R. and 12 mi. NW of Landshut; brewing, tanning. Chartered 1402.

Pfeiffer State Redwood Park, Calif.: see BIG SUR.

Pfetterhouse (fĕtĕrōōz'), Ger. *Pfetterhausen* (pfĕ'tŭrhouzŭn), village (pop. 860), Haut-Rhin dept., E France, in the N Jura, 9 mi. SSW of Altkirch; custom station on Swiss border; mfg. of watch cases and leggings.

Pfinz River (pfĭnts), N Baden, Germany, rises on N slope of Black Forest 2 mi. W of Neuenbürg, flows 40 mi. generally NW, past Durlach, to the Rhine opposite Germersheim.

Pfirt, France: see FERRETTE.

Pflugerville (flōō'gŭrvĭl), village (pop. c.500), Travis co., S central Texas, 14 mi. NE of Austin; rail point in cotton, grain, truck area.

Pförring (pfû'rĭng), village (pop. 1,648), Upper Bavaria, Germany, near the Danube, 12 mi. E of Ingolstadt; grain, livestock. Chartered 1318. Roman coins found in area.

Pforta, Germany: see SCHULPFORTE.

Pforzheim (pfôrts'hīm), city (1939 pop. 79,011; 1946 pop. 46,752; 1950 pop. 53,942), N Baden, Germany, after 1945 in Württemberg-Baden, at N foot of Black Forest, on the Enz at mouth of Nagold R., and 16 mi. SE of Karlsruhe; 48°54'N 8°42'E. Rail junction; a center of Ger. jewelry industry (gold, silver, and costume jewelry; watches, precious stones). Mfg. of machinery, tools, precision instruments, radios, chemicals; paper milling. Jewelry trade and export. Second World War destruction (about 80%) caused damage to all noteworthy bldgs., including two 13th-cent. churches. Has school for precious metalworking. Of anc. origin, Pforzheim repeatedly changed hands until it came to margraves of Baden in 13th cent. Important wood-trading center in Middle Ages; seat of noted humanist school. Suffered severely in Thirty Years War; burned by French in 1689. Humanist Reuchlin b. here.

Pfraumberg, Czechoslovakia: see PRIMDA.

Pfreimd (pfrīmt), town (pop. 2,826), Upper Palatinate, E Bavaria, Germany, in Bohemian Forest, on the Nab and 13 mi. S of Weiden; brewing. Has 17th-cent. baroque church. Chartered 1497.

Pfronten (pfrôn'tŭn), commune (pop. 6,476), Swabia, SW Bavaria, Germany, at E foot of Allgäu Alps, 6 mi. WNW of Füssen; includes villages of Pfronten-Ried, Pfronten-Steinach, and Pfronten-Weissbach. Mfg. of electrical machinery and equipment, drawing instruments; woodworking. Summer and winter resort (alt. 2,885 ft.).

Pfullendorf (pfŏŏ'lŭndôrf), town (pop. 2,972), S Baden, Germany, 11 mi. NNE of Überlingen; woodworking, lumber milling.

Pfullingen (pfŏŏ'lĭng-ŭn), S suburb (pop. 9,453) of REUTLINGEN, S Württemberg, Germany, at N foot of Swabian Jura. Mfg. of textiles (cotton, thread; spinning), machines, shoes; leatherworking, tanning, brewing. Has late-Gothic church. Inc. into Reutlingen in 1945.

Pfunds (pfŏŏnts), village (pop. 1,632), Tyrol, W Austria, on the Inn and 12 mi. S of Landeck, bet. Ötztal Alps and Silvretta Group; sheep.

Pfungstadt (pfŏŏng'shtät), town (pop. 9,606), S Hesse, W Germany, in former Starkenburg prov., 5 mi. SSW of Darmstadt; mfg. of cigars and matches; brewing, brickmaking.

Phachi, Ban, Thailand: see BAN PHACHI.

Phadisana, Turkey: see FATSA.

Phaéton (fäātō'), village (1950 pop. 2,584), Nord dept., NE Haiti, on inlet of the Atlantic, 4 mi. W of Fort Liberté; mfg. of sisal fibers. Airfield.

Phagwara (pŭgvä'rŭ), town (pop. 16,194), N Patiala and East Punjab States Union, India, 25 mi. ESE of Kapurthala; rail junction; trade center (grain, sugar, salt); markets wheat, gram, millet, maize; sugar mill, chemical and metalworks. Has col. Formerly in princely state of Kapurthala.

Phalakron or **Falakron** (both: fälŭkrôn'), mountain massif in Macedonia, Greece, W of Mesta R.; rises to 7,198 ft. 9 mi. N of Drama. Crossed by Angites R. in underground channel. Also called Boz Dag or Boz Dagh and Vardena.

Phalane (pä'län'), town, Sawannakhet prov., central Laos, 50 mi. E of Savannakhet, on highway to Dongha (central Vietnam).

Phalanx, N.J.: see RED BANK.

Phalauda (pŭlou'dŭ), town (pop. 5,558), Meerut dist., NW Uttar Pradesh, India, 15 mi. NNE of Meerut; wheat, gram, jowar, sugar cane, oilseeds. Annual religious fair, connected with tomb of Moslem saint.

Phalempin (fälāpē'), town (pop. 2,449), Nord dept., N France, 8 mi. SSW of Lille; metalworks.

Phalera or **Phulera** (pŏŏlā'rŭ), village, E central Rajasthan, India, 4 mi. SE of Sambhar; rail junction (workshops).

Phaleron, Bay of, or **Bay of Faliron** (both: fä'lĭrôn), Lat. *Phalerum* (fŭlēr'ŭm), inlet of Saronic Gulf of Aegean Sea, in Attica nome, E central Greece, E of Piraeus; 1.5 mi. wide, 1 mi. long. Receives Athenian Cephisus R. Was port of Greece until early 5th cent. B.C.

Phalodi (pŭlō'dē), town (pop. 17,689), W central Rajasthan, India, 70 mi. NW of Jodhpur, on Thar Desert; trades in camels, hides, salt, sheep; handicrafts (metal utensils, camel's-hair mats, pottery). Camel breeding near by. Saline depression lies 10 mi. N.

Phalsbourg (fälzbōōr'), Ger. *Pfalzburg* (pfälts'bŏŏrk), village (pop. 1,481), Moselle dept., NE France, in the N Vosges just N of Saverne Gap, 5 mi. WNW of Saverne; brewing, hosiery mfg. Fortified by Vauban, it held out against Germans for 4 months in 1870. Erckmann b. here.

Phaltan (pŭl'tŭn), town (pop., including suburban area, 13,523), Satara North dist., central Bombay, India, on S canal of Nira R. irrigation system and 36 mi. NE of Satara; trade center for millet, sugar cane, wheat, cotton, timber; cotton milling, handicraft cloth weaving. Was ⊙ former princely state of Phaltan (□ 391; pop. 71,473) in Deccan States, Bombay; state inc. 1949 into Satara North dist.

Phan (pän'), village (1937 pop. 18,361), Chiangrai prov., N Thailand, 30 mi. S of Chiangrai; trading and teak-production center; petroleum deposits.

Phanagoria, Russian SFSR: see TAMAN, village.

Phanar or **Fanar** (both: fänär'), Turkish *Fener*, quarter (pop. 48,491) of Istanbul (Constantinople), Turkey, which under the Ottoman Empire was residence of privileged Greek families called Phanariots. These came into prominence in late 17th cent. and held some of the most influential positions until 1821, after which they played an important part in Greek fight for independence.

Phanarion or **Fanarion** (both: fŭnä'rēōn), town (pop. 2,293), Karditsa nome, SW Thessaly, Greece, on narrow-gauge railroad and 7 mi. NW of Karditsa; vegetables, corn; livestock.

Phanariotikos River, Greece: see ACHERON RIVER.

Phangan, Ko (kô' päng-än'), island (□ 65) in Gulf of Siam, Suratthani prov., S Thailand, 55 mi. NE of Suratthani; 9°45'N 100°E; rises to 2,057 ft.; lead deposits. Phangan Passage (10 mi. wide), separates isl. from Ko Samui (S).

Phangnga (phäng'ngä'), town (1947 pop. 3,496), ⊙ Phangnga prov. (□ 1,530; 1947 pop. 61,014), S Thailand, in Malay Peninsula, near W coast, 45 mi. NNE of Phuket; leading tin-mining center; coal and lead mining near by. Also spelled Banga, Bangnga, Bhangnga, or Pangnga.

Phanme (fän'mā'), village, Thainguyen prov., N Vietnam, 10 mi. NW of Thainguyen; coal mines; coking plant. Linked by railroad with river loading port of Minhli.

Phanos, Greece: see OTHONOI.

Phanrang (fän'räng'), town, ⊙ Ninhthuan prov. (□ 1,300; 1943 pop. 81,200), S central Vietnam, in Annam, on railroad (TOURCHAM station) and 170 mi. ENE of Saigon; rice, tobacco, castor beans; salt extraction. Its port is Ninhchu.

Phanri (fän'rē'), town, Binhthuan prov., S central Vietnam, on South China Sea, 35 mi. NE of Phanthiet. Fishing port, salt extraction, fish curing; lime factory. Anc. ⊙ of 9th-cent. kingdom. Formerly called Binhthuan.

Phanthiet (fän'tyĕt'), town, ⊙ Binhthuan prov. (□ 2,500; 1943 pop. 145,900), S central Vietnam, South China Sea port on Phanthiet Bay, on spur of Saigon-Hanoi RR and 100 mi. E of Saigon; airport. Seaside resort and fish-processing center; salt extraction and fisheries (fish curing).

Phao River (pou'), E Thailand, in Korat Plateau, SE of Udon, flows 85 mi. SE past Kalasin, through agr. area (rice, cotton, tobacco, cattle), to Chi R., E of Mahasarakham.

Phaoson, Vietnam: see SEPT PAGODES.

Phaphund (pŭpōōnd'), town (pop. 5,864), Etawah dist., W Uttar Pradesh, India, 30 mi. ESE of Etawah; pearl millet, wheat, barley, corn, oilseeds. Pilgrimage site, connected with tomb and mosque of Moslem saint.

Pharah, India: see PHARHA.

Pharay, Orkneys, Scotland: see FARA.

Pharendra (pŭrān'drŭ), village, Gorakhpur dist., E Uttar Pradesh, India, 24 mi. NNW of Gorakhpur; sugar processing; rice, wheat, barley. Terminus of rail spur to Nautanwa on Nepal border. Sugar processing 5 mi. S, at village of Campierganj.

Pharha (pŭr'hŭ), town (pop. 1,655), Mainpuri dist., W Uttar Pradesh, India, 34 mi. WNW of Mainpuri; wheat, gram, pearl millet, barley. Also spelled Phariha and Pharah.

Phari (pä'rē), Chinese *P'a-li-tsung* (pä'lē'dzōōng'), town [Tibetan *dzong*], S Tibet, in Chumbi Valley, near undefined Bhutan border, 60 mi. NE of Kalimpong, India; alt. 14,300 ft. Important junction of trade routes from India (via Natu La and Jelep La passes) and from Bhutan (via Paro); trade center (wool, barley, salt, borax, wheat, vegetables, cotton goods).

Pharos (fâ'rŏs, fā–), peninsula at Alexandria, Egypt. Originally an isl. just offshore, it was united to mainland by a mole built by order of Alexander the Great. On it stood the celebrated lighthouse completed (c.280 B.C.) by Ptolemy II which was in anc. times usually included among the Seven Wonders of the World. It was 100 ft. square and perhaps twice as high. Demolished by earthquake in 14th cent.

Pharpar (fär'pŭr), river of Damascus, mentioned in the Bible. It may be the A'WAJ, a stream c.10 mi. S of Damascus, Syria; or it may be a branch of the Barada.

Pharr (fär), city (pop. 8,690), Hidalgo co., extreme S Texas, in lower Rio Grande valley, 3 mi. E of McAllen; a shipping, processing point in irrigated cotton, fruit, truck area; canneries, packing plants. Founded c.1909.

Pharsala or **Farsala** (both: fär'sŭlŭ), anc. *Pharsalus* (färsā'lŭs), town (pop. 4,811), Larissa nome, S Thessaly, Greece, on narrow-gauge railroad and 24 mi. S of Larissa; road center; corn, wheat, barley, legumes; livestock. Chromite mining 12 mi. E. The home of Achilles. Caesar's decisive victory (48 B.C.) over Pompey on the Pharsalian plain is the subject of Lucan's epic *Pharsalia.* Known as Chatalja under Turkish rule (until 1881).

Phaselis (fŭsē'lĭs), anc. town of Lycia (now S Turkey), port on Gulf of Antalya (Adalia), 20 mi. SSW of Antalya; founded by Dorian colonists, later the base of pirates and therefore destroyed.

Phasis: see RION RIVER, Georgian SSR.

Phatnitic, branch of the Nile: see DAMIETTA.

Phatthalung (pät'tŭlōōng'), town (1947 pop. 5,180), ⊙ Phatthalung prov. (□ 1,462; 1947 pop. 149,469), S Thailand, in Malay Peninsula, on railroad and 45 mi. NE of Songkhla, in large, fertile plain: rice, coconuts, betel nuts; fisheries in Thale Sap (E). Also spelled Badalung and Patalung.

Phayao (päyou'), village (1937 pop. 8,253), Chiangrai prov., N Thailand, on Lampang-Kengtung (Burma) road and 50 mi. S of Chiangrai; rice, coffee, gold mining near by.

Phazania, N Africa: see FEZZAN.

Pheasant Island, France and Spain: see BIDASSOA RIVER.

Pheba (fē'bŭ, fē'bē), town (1940 pop. 351), Clay co., E Miss., 17 mi. W of West Point.

Phelps. 1 County (□ 677; pop. 21,504), central Mo.; ⊙ Rolla. In the Ozarks; drained by Meramec and Gasconade rivers. Agr. (grapes, apples, melons, berries), livestock; oak, hickory, cottonwood, elm timber; pyrite, fire-clay mining. Part of Mark Twain Natl. Forest is here. Formed 1857. **2** County (□ 545; pop. 9,048), S Nebr.; ⊙ Holdrege. Farm area bounded N by Platte R. Flour; livestock, grain, dairy produce. Formed 1873.

Phelps. 1 Town (pop. 926), Pike co., E Ky., in the Cumberlands, 13 mi. SSE of Williamson, W.Va., in bituminous-coal-mining area. **2** Village (pop. 1,650), Ontario co., W central N.Y., in Finger Lakes region, on Canandaigua Outlet and 7 mi. NW of Geneva; mfg. (sauerkraut, trucks, lumber, farm machinery, tinware, chemicals, paint, flour); sand and gravel pits, stone quarries. Agr. (cabbage, wheat, potatoes). Inc. 1855. **3** Village (pop. c.500), Vilas co., N Wis., on North Twin L., 33 mi. NNE of Rhinelander, in wooded lake region; sawmilling, mfg. of chemicals.

Phelps City, town (pop. 139), Atchison co., NW Mo., bet. Missouri and Nishnabotna rivers, 11 mi. WSW of Tarkio.

Phelps Lake, Washington co., E N.C., 17 mi. NE of Belhaven; c.7 mi. long, 5 mi. wide. Included in Pettigrew State Park.

Phenice, anc. country: see PHOENICIA.

Phenice, anc. town, Crete: see PHOENIX.

Phenicia: see PHOENICIA.

Phenix (fē'nĭks). **1** Village (pop. c.2,500) in West Warwick town, Kent co., central R.I., on North Branch of Pawtuxet R. and 10 mi. SW of Providence; lace goods, textile dyeing and finishing. **2** Town (pop. 290), Charlotte co., S Va., 31 mi. SE of Lynchburg. Also spelled Phoenix. Inc. 1930.

Phenix City, city (pop. 23,305), a ⊙ Russell co., E Ala., on Chattahoochee R. opposite Columbus, Ga.; trade and mfg. center; cotton ginning, dairying; mfg. of bricks and tiles, lumber, candy. Grew next to Girard (co. seat 1832–39). Named Phenix City 1890, annexed Girard 1923. Site of Fort Mitchell (1811–37) near by.

Pherae, Greece: see VELESTINO.

Pherrai or **Ferrai** (both: fĕ'rā), town (pop. 3,708), Hevros nome, W Thrace, Greece, on railroad and 15 mi. ENE of Alexandroupolis, on Maritsa R. (Turkish line); cotton, wheat, barley, silk, tobacco, cattle, sheep. Sulphur springs near by. Known as Feredjik or Ferejik under Turkish rule.

Phetburi or **Phetchburi** (both: pĕt'bōōrē'), town (1947 pop. 16,279), ⊙ Phetburi prov. (□ 2,436; 1947 pop. 180,509), S Thailand, on Phetburi R., on railroad, and 60 mi. SW of Bangkok; rice, coconuts, palm sugar. An anc. town, it possesses old Brahmin and Buddhist temples and palaces. Sometimes spelled Bejaburi, Bejrburi, and Petchaburi.

Phetburi River, S Thailand, rises in Tenasserim Range on Burma frontier at 13°10'N, flows 100 mi. E and NNE, past Phetburi, to Gulf of Siam. Navigable by small craft.

Phetchabun or **Phetchbun** (pĕt'chăbōōn'), town (1947 pop. 2,984), ⊙ Phetchabun prov. (□ 4,908; 1947 pop. 162,730), central Thailand, on Pa Sak R. and 190 mi. NNE of Bangkok, W of Phetchabun Range; rice, tobacco, teak. Sometimes spelled Bejaburn, Bejrburn, and Petchaburn.

Phetchabun Range, N central Thailand, S extension of Luang Prabang Range, on W edge of Korat Plateau; densely wooded; rises to 5,840 ft.

Phetchburi, Thailand: see PHETBURI.

Phichit (pē'chĭt), town (1947 pop. 4,791), ⊙ Phichit prov. (□ 1,727; 1947 pop. 237,241), N Thailand, on Nan R., on Bangkok-Chiangmai RR, and 190 mi. N of Bangkok, in rice-growing region; spices, tobacco, corn. Also spelled Bichitr and Pichitr.

Phidaris River, Greece: see EVENOS RIVER.

Phigalia (fĭgā'lyŭ), anc. city of Elis nome, W Peloponnesus, Greece, on S slope of Minthes Mts., 30 mi. SE of Pyrgos. There are ruins of city walls and temples. On site is modern village of Figalia or Phygalia (pop. 378), formerly called Pavlitsa; it has vineyards.

Philadelphia, England: see HOUGHTON-LE-SPRING.

Philadelphia, Jordan: see AMMAN, city.

Philadelphia, anc. city of Lydia, W Asia Minor, at foot of Mt. Tmolus, on site of present-day ALASEHIR, Turkey. Founded by Attalus II Philadelphus of Pergamum. Here was one of the "Seven Churches in Asia."

Philadelphia. 1 City (pop. 4,472), ⊙ Neshoba co., E central Miss., 36 mi. NW of Meridian, in agr. and timber area; lumber milling, glove mfg., cotton ginning. Seat of Choctaw Indian Agency; Choctaw reservation is NW. **2** Village (pop. 870), Jefferson co., N N.Y., on Indian R. and 16 mi. NE of Watertown. **3** City coextensive with Philadelphia co. (□ 127, land only; 1950 pop. 2,071,605; 1940 pop. 1,931,334), SE Pa., c.80 mi. SW of New York city and on Delaware R. at mouth of Schuylkill R., c.100 mi. above the Atlantic; 40°N 75°9'W; alt. is from sea level to 440 ft. Largest city in Pa. and 3d largest in U.S., and one of chief ports (generally ranking 2d only to New York) of U.S.; a natl. commercial, industrial, cultural, and educational center and focus of a metropolitan area (1950 census, preliminary total pop. 3,660,676) extending into Bucks, Chester, Delaware, and Montgomery counties (Pa.) and Burlington, Camden, and Gloucester counties (N.J.). Served by 4 railroad systems, several airlines, and a highway network. Important industries of Philadelphia and environs are oil refining and manufacture of petroleum-derived chemicals, metalworking, printing and publishing, shipbuilding, and mfg. of railroad cars, busses, textiles, clothing and hats, alcohol, leather products, paper, tobacco products, electrical supplies tools, machinery, rugs, glass, medicines, and processing of foodstuffs, including sugar and meat. Chief industrial areas are in S, W, and NE. City's fine deep-water harbor (connected with ocean by 40-ft. channel) ships oil and petroleum products, coal, grain, flour, textiles, railroad equipment, lumber and other building materials, and manufactured goods; port receipts include petroleum, iron and manganese ore, sugar, sulphur, nitrates, and general merchandise. There is a large navy yard (at League Isl.), a U.S. mint, and U.S. arsenals. Delaware R. Bridge (one of world's largest suspension bridges; opened 1926) crosses river to Camden, N.J.; at Tacony (in NE Philadelphia) is Tacony-Palmyra Bridge to N.J. Lying on both sides of the Schuylkill, Philadelphia has expanded from original area of settlement near the Delaware to include formerly independent communities, some of which retain their own shopping and business dists., and others whose names only remain. Among fine residential dists. are GERMANTOWN and CHESTNUT HILL; the NE industrial dist. centers on Frankford and Kensington; other sections include Nicetown, Oak Lane, Rosehill, Roxborough, Manayunk, Tacony, Olney, West Philadelphia, Mount Airy. The "Main Line" is a wealthy outlying dist., so called for its location along the Pennsylvania RR. At city's heart is City Hall, topped by statue of William Penn and standing at intersection of Broad (N-S) and Market Streets, the best-known thoroughfares. From City Hall, Benjamin Franklin Parkway extends NW to the Art Mus., beyond which is Fairmount Park (3,845 acres along the Schuylkill R. and Wissahickon Creek), one of largest municipal parks in U.S., containing Robin Hood Dell, setting for outdoor concerts; numerous historic monuments and shrines; the central branch of the public library; the Rodin Mus.; the aquarium; the zoological and botanical gardens; and the bldgs. of the 1876 Centennial Exposition. Around Broad and Market is the downtown dist. of department stores and shops, banks and office bldgs., and 3 railroad terminals; to E is the historic heart of old Philadelphia, containing such shrines as Independence Hall, where the Declaration was signed (1776) and where the Liberty Bell is kept; Congress Hall; the old City Hall (1791); Carpenters' Hall, where the 1st Continental Congress met; Betsy Ross House, where, according to one story, the 1st American flag was made; Christ Church (completed 1754); the old Custom House; the Edgar Allen Poe House, containing a Poe mus. Other points of interest in Philadelphia are Gloria Dei (Old Swedes') Church (1700; now a natl. historic site); the Acad. of Music, home of the famous Philadelphia Orchestra; St. Peter's Church (1758–61); St. Paul's Church (1761); Pennsylvania Hosp., founded 1751 as 1st hosp. in country; Historical Society of Pa.; Arch St. Friends' Meetinghouse (1804); Pennsylvania Acad. of the Fine Arts (1805); Cathedral of SS. Peter and Paul (R.C.); Acad. of Natural Sciences (established 1812); Bartram's Gardens, noted botanical gardens, established c.1731; Morris Arboretum (in Germantown). Philadelphia is the seat of the Univ. of Pennsylvania, Franklin Inst. (1824; with Fels Planetarium, 1933), Temple Univ., Drexel Inst. of Technology, Dropsie Col. for Hebrew and Cognate Learning, La Salle Col., Chestnut Hill Col., St. Joseph's Col., Girard Col., Curtis Inst. of Music, Hahnemann Medical Col., Jefferson Medical Col., Philadelphia Mus. School of Art, and colleges of optometry, osteopathy, pharmacy, and occupational therapy. The city's site was 1st occupied by Lenni-Lenape Indians, and in the 17th cent. there was a Swedish settlement. In 1682 Philadelphia, the "City of Brotherly Love," was founded as a Quaker colony by William Penn—hence the nickname Quaker City. Its commercial, industrial, and cultural growth was rapid. Except for the British occupation (Oct., 1777–June, 1778) after the battle of Brandywine, it was the American capital during the Revolution. It was ⊙ of the new republic, 1790–1800, as well as ⊙ Pa. (to 1799). It was an important trading and mfg. center before the Revolution and became a shipbuilding center in early 19th cent. It was a nucleus of American culture in colonial times, when among its prominent citizens was the scientist and statesman Benjamin Franklin; it early became the seat of philosophical, artistic, dramatic, musical, and scientific societies, many of which still exist. First magazine in America was published here 1741, 1st daily newspaper 1784. In 1948, a project for Independence Natl. Historical Park (20 acres) was authorized to include Independence Hall, the Custom House (now both natl. historic sites), Christ Church, and other historic sites and buildings. Philadelphia's distinctive atmosphere is compounded of elements of Quaker influence, of general conservatism (expressed in its comparative lack of places of public entertainment, and by the survival on its books of "blue laws"), of domesticity (its nickname "the city of homes" grew from the preponderance of single-family dwellings, a large proportion of them owned by their occupants), and the continuing interest in the arts, philosophy, and the sciences which was manifested so early in city's history.

Philae (fī'lē), island of the Nile, S Egypt, above ASWAN DAM; 1,200 ft. long, 500 ft. wide. Site of the temples of Isis and Hathor. Isl. and its temples are submerged, Nov.–June, when the sluices of the dam are closed.

Phil Campbell (kă'mŭl), farming town (pop. 469), Franklin co., NW Ala., 28 mi. S of Tuscumbia; lumber.

Philiates or **Filiates** (both: fēlēä'tĭs), town (pop. 2,082), Thesprotia nome, S Epirus, Greece, near Albanian line, 8 mi. NNE of Egoumenitsa; grain, timber; olive oil. Its port is Sagiada.

Philiatra or **Filiatra** (both: fēlēäträ'), city (pop. 10,658), Messenia nome, SW Peloponnesus, Greece, 25 mi. WNW of Kalamata; wheat, Zante currants, olives, olive oil, livestock.

Philip, city (pop. 810), ⊙ Haakon co., central S.Dak., 70 mi. WSW of Pierre and on Bad R.; trading center for farming and ranching area; dairy products, livestock, grain.

Philiphaugh (fĭ'lĭp-hôkh), mansion and estate in Selkirk parish, E Selkirk, Scotland, on Yarrow Water and 2 mi. W of Selkirk. Near by David Leslie and the Covenanters defeated Montrose in 1645. Battle is commemorated by monument.

Philippe-Thomas, Tunisia: see METLAOUI.

Philippeville (fĭ'lĭpvĭl, Fr. fēlēpvēl'), city (pop. 40,647), Constantine dept., NE Algeria, on the Gulf of Stora (Mediterranean Sea), 40 mi. NNE of Constantine, for which it is the seaport; 36°53'N 6°55'E. Rail terminus. A leading export center of Algeria's agr. products, it ships wine, citrus fruit, peaches, apricots, and early vegetables from Oued Saf-Saf valley (extending c.20 mi. S from here; irrigated by Zardézas Dam), sheep, and wheat. Also exports dates from the Saharan oases. Mineral shipments include iron and marble (quarried at Djebel Filfila, 10 mi. E). Industries: fish preserving (sardines, tuna), flour and olive-oil milling, mfg. of aluminum articles, burlap bags and cordage, chocolate, fruit preserves and juices. Built on site of anc. *Rusicade*, modern Philippeville, laid out by French after 1838 along a rectilinear pattern, owes present importance to its artificially sheltered harbor. Stora (3 mi. NW) is city's outport. Pop., c.50% Moslem, has large French, and smaller Italian and Maltese, colonies.

Philippeville, town (pop. 1,348), Namur prov., S Belgium, 17 mi. WSW of Dinant; market and highway center; marble quarrying. Established in 1555 by a Spanish governor; ceded to France in 1659; returned to United Netherlands by Treaty of Paris (1815).

Philippeville, Gulf of, inlet of the W Mediterranean, NE Algeria, bet. Cape Bougaroun (W) and Cap de Fer (E); 40 mi. wide, 15 mi. deep. Southernmost indentation (on which Philippeville is located) is called Gulf of Stora.

Philippi (fĭlĭ'pī), anc. city of Macedonia, Greece, 10 mi. NW of its Aegean port Neapolis (modern Kavalla), in marshy plain E of the Pangaion massif. Founded 358 B.C. by Philip II of Macedon, it developed as the center for the Pangaion gold and silver mines. It was scene of defeat (42 B.C.) of Brutus and Cassius by Octavian and Antony. Here St. Paul first preached in Europe, addressing one of his Epistles to his converts. The modern Gr. village of Philippoi or Filippoi (pop. 1,445), just E, was formerly known as Mesorrema and Seliane (Seliani).

Philippi (fĭ'lĭpē, fĭlĭ'pē), city (pop. 2,531), ⊙ Barbour co., E W.Va., on Tygart R. and 13 mi. S of Grafton; coal mines, gas and oil wells, timber; mfg. of drugs, beverages. Alderson-Broaddus Col. here. Civil War battle (a Union victory) was fought here, June 3, 1861. Settled c.1780.

Philippi, Lake, salt lake (□ 126), SW Queensland, Australia, 260 mi. SSW of Cloncurry; 14 mi. long, 14 mi. wide; usually dry.

Philippias, Greece: see NEA PHILIPPIAS.

Philippine or **Filippine** (fĭlĭpē'nŭ), village (pop. 1,068), Zeeland prov., SW Netherlands, on Flanders mainland, 5 mi. SSW of Terneuzen, on inlet of the Western Scheldt; mussel fishing; agr.

Philippine Deep: see MINDANAO TRENCH.

Philippine Islands (fĭ'lŭpēn), group of some 7,000 islands and rocks in the SW Pacific off SE Asia, in the Malay Archipelago, constituting the Republic of the Philippines (□ 114,830 land; □ 115,600 total; 1948 pop. 19,234,182), proclaimed July 4, 1946; ⊙ QUEZON CITY, an E suburb of MANILA, which it replaced officially in 1948 as ⊙. Over 4,000 of the isls. are unnamed, only 463 have over □ 1, and only some 400 are permanently inhabited. The largest, in decreasing order, are: LUZON (□ 40,420), MINDANAO, SAMAR, NEGROS, PALAWAN, PANAY, MINDORO, LEYTE, CEBU, BOHOL, MASBATE, CATANDUANES, BASILAN, MARINDUQUE, JOLO, BUSUANGA, and DINAGAT (□ 309). The isls. extend 1,152 mi. N-S bet. Formosa and Borneo, and 688 mi. E-W, and are bounded by Philippine Sea (E), Celebes Sea (S), S.China Sea (W), and Bashi Channel (N); 4°27'–21°7'N 116°56'–126°36' E. The isls. are in 3 natural divisions: the northern, which includes Luzon and Mindoro; the central, occupied by VISAYAN ISLANDS; and the southern, containing Mindanao and the SULU ARCHIPELAGO. Administratively, the republic is divided into 51 provs. (including the administratively separate city of Manila). Isls. are mostly of volcanic origin, being the higher portions of a partly submerged mtn. (the MINDANAO TRENCH, off E coast, is deepest-known ocean trough in the world), but some isls. are overlaid with coral. The larger isls. have great mtn. ranges, some of them with active volcanoes, such as Mt. Apo (9,690 ft., highest in Philippines) on Mindanao, and Mt. Mayon (7,926 ft.) in SE Luzon. There are numerous lakes, the largest being Laguna de Bay and L. Taal on Luzon, and lakes Lanao and Mainit on Mindanao. Cagayan R. (c.220 mi. long) on Luzon is largest river; other rivers of importance are Pampanga and Agno on Luzon, and Agusan and Pulangi (or Rio Grande de Mindanao) on Mindanao. The Philippines are entirely within the tropical zone. Manila's climate, with a mean daily temp. of 79.5°F., is typical of that of the lowland areas throughout the group—warm, humid, and enervating. The highlands, however, have a bracing climate; e.g., BAGUIO, the summer capital, on Luzon, has a mean annual temp. of 64°F. The seasons generally fall into 2 periods, that of the NE monsoon, bringing rain to the E coasts of the isls., and that of the SW monsoon, which marks the rain season on the W coasts; some areas have as much as 250 inches of rainfall annually. Rainfall in the S isls., however, is evenly distributed over the year, and this region is not in the typhoon belt which embraces the rest of the isls. With their tropical climate and naturally fertile soil, much of which is still uncultivated, the Philippines are predominantly agr. Principal food crops are rice and corn; the great central valley of Luzon grows much of the rice. Important are sugar cane, abacá (Manila hemp), coconuts (from which come coconut oil and copra, leading exports), and tobacco. Other exports include embroideries and canned pineapples (grown and canned largely in N Mindanao). There are great stands of virgin timber, which, besides fine cabinet and construction wood (mahogany, ebony, cedar, banyan, pine, palm, etc.), yield rubber, quinine, kapok, lumbang nuts (for tung oil). Cotton, and citrus and other fruit are also grown, but as yet have no significant markets. Fishing is widespread, and the Sulu Archipelago is known for its pearls and mother-of-pearl. The raising of carabao, cattle, pigs, goats, and ponies is important to the economy. The isls. abound in mineral resources, much of which are unexploited. Gold has been mined for centuries, and there are exports of chromite, manganese, iron, copper; also some coal deposits and silver, lead, sulphur, molybdenum, zinc, and asbestos. There are no large industrial establishments in the Philippines, industry being limited mainly to processing plants (except for a few producers of domestic needs, such as the cement plant at Naga on Cebu): sawmills, coconut-processing plants, sugar mills, hemp-treating plants, rope factories etc. Besides Manila, other important cities include TACLOBAN on Leyte, DAVAO and ZAMBOANGA on Mindanao, and ILOILO on Panay. Most of the people belong to the Malay racial group and are known as Filipinos; they constitute the only Christian nation in this part of the world. Roman Catholicism, a heritage from their Spanish conquerors, is professed by more than ⅔ of the people; and there are an estimated 1,000,000 Aglipayans, members of the Philippine Independent Church. Mohammedans (the Moros) are concentrated on Mindanao and the Sulu Archipelago. Next come the pagan peoples and the Protestants. The Christian Filipinos of all sects are divided into 8 ethnographic groups, differing from each other in habitat, speech, and other cultural elements. Largest of these groups are the Visayan, in the Visayan Isls., the Tagalog, native to the 8 provs. adjacent to Manila, and the Ilokano, of NW Luzon. Indonesian and Mongoloid elements have been blended with the dominant Malay strain in almost every one of the 8 groups, and the presence of Chinese and Spanish blood in the leading people of every Christian area is obvious. There are some 85 different dialects, most of them belonging to the Malayo-Polynesian linguistic group; Tagalog has been made (1946) the base for a natl. language. English is spoken by many Filipinos and Spanish by a much smaller number. The 1st Malayans (who are thought to have originated in SE Asia) to reach the Philippines represented an early and crude epoch of Malayan culture, which has apparently survived to this day among certain groups, such as the Igorot. Later came the invasions of Malayan tribes which possessed more highly developed cultures. The 1st Europeans to visit (1521) the Philippines were those in the world-circling Spanish expedition led by the Portuguese Magellan, who was killed here. Other Sp. expeditions followed, including one from New Spain (Mexico) under López de Villalobos, who, in 1542, named the isls. Las Felipinas for the child who was later to become Philip II. However, Sp. conquest of the Filipinos did not really begin until 1564, when another expedition from New Spain, commanded by Miguel López de Legaspi, arrived. Legaspi founded Manila in 1571, and by the end of 16th cent. it was the foremost commercial center of the Far East. There followed conflict with English freebooters, with the Dutch (1600–63), and with the Moro pirates; and the Spanish slew thousands of the Chinese, who had long traded here and were well established. With Spain's decline, the Philippines sank into obscurity. The British held them briefly, 1762–64. The Moros were not subdued by the Spaniards until the late 19th cent. The independence movement began before the U.S. acquired the isls. (1898) in the Spanish-American War, during which Dewey defeated the Sp. fleet in Manila Bay. José Rizal, the great early leader, was succeeded by Aguinaldo, and agitation for independence never ceased. In 1935, the Commonwealth of the Philippines was established, with Manuel Quezon as 1st president. The isls. began a 10-year transition period of controlled autonomy, and on July 4, 1946, the Republic of the Philippines came into being. In Second World War, the isls. fell swiftly to the Japanese after their surprise attack in Dec., 1941, and were recaptured 1944–45. See also the articles on the separate provs., which, besides those which have the same names as some of the isls. mentioned above, are: ABRA, AGUSAN, ALBAY, ANTIQUE, BATAAN, BATANES, BATANGAS, BUKIDNON, BULACAN, CAGAYAN, CAMARINES NORTE, CAMARINES SUR, CAPIZ, CAVITE, COTABATO, DAVAO, ILOCOS NORTE, ILOCOS SUR, ILOILO, ISABELA, LAGUNA, LANAO, LA UNION, MISAMIS OCCIDENTAL, MISAMIS ORIENTAL, MOUNTAIN PROVINCE, NEGROS OCCIDENTAL, NEGROS ORIENTAL, NUEVA ECIJA, NUEVA VIZCAYA, PAMPANGA, QUEZON, RIZAL, ROMBLON, SORSOGON, SURIGAO, TARLAC, ZAMBALES, ZAMBOANGA.

Philippine Sea, part of W Pacific bordering E coast of Philippine Isls. and extending N towards coast of Japan. In it is the MINDANAO TRENCH or Philippine Trench, deepest (34,440 ft.) trough of any sea. In Second World War, 2 great battles were fought here. The 1st battle of Philippine Sea was carried on by carrier planes, June 19–20, 1944; the 2d battle of Philippine Sea, bet. the bulk of both Jap. and U.S. fleets (Oct. 23–26, 1944), is also called battle of LEYTE GULF. Both were great U.S. victories.

Philippine Trench, Pacific Ocean: see MINDANAO TRENCH.

Philippolis, town (pop. 1,755), SW Orange Free State, U. of So. Afr., near Cape Prov. border, 100 mi. SW of Bloemfontein; sheep-raising center.

Philippopolis, Bulgaria: see PLOVDIV, city.

Philippopolis, Syria: see SHAHBA.

Philippsburg (fē'lĭpsbŏork), town (pop. 3,567), N Baden, Germany, after 1945 in Württemberg-Baden, on an arm of the Rhine at mouth of the Saalbach, and 4 mi. ENE of Germersheim, in tobacco area; mfg. of cigars and cigarettes. Formerly a fortress, it was repeatedly captured in wars of 17th and 18th cent.

Philippsthal or **Philippsthal an der Werra** (fē'lĭpstäl än dĕr vĕ'rä), village (pop. 2,401), in former Prussian prov. of Hesse-Nassau, W Germany, after 1945 in Hesse, on the Werra and 13 mi. E of Hersfeld, opposite Vacha in potash-mining region; building materials.

Philipsburg, Que.: see PHILLIPSBURG.

Philipsburg, principal settlement of Du. section of SAINT MARTIN, in the Leewards, West Indies, 3 mi. SE of Marigot; 18°2'N 63°3'W. Principal products: salt, cotton, livestock. Has good harbor.

Philipsburg. 1 City (pop. 1,048), ⊙ Granite co., W Mont., 45 mi. NW of Butte and on Flint Creek, just W of Flint Creek Range; manganese, silver, coal mines; timber; livestock, dairy products, grain, potatoes. Inc. 1890. **2** Borough (pop. 3,988), Centre co., central Pa., 14 mi. SE of Clearfield; metal products, bricks, clothing, confectionery; bituminous coal, clay; agr. Laid out 1797, inc. 1864.

Philipsburg Manor, N.Y.: see PHILIPSE MANOR.

Philipse Manor (fĭ'lĭps) or **Philipsburg Manor,** SE N.Y., former colonial estate (chartered 1693), once the property of Frederick Philipse and extending bet. Hudson and Bronx rivers from the present North Tarrytown (N) to the present Yonkers (S). At Yonkers is the southern manor hall (c.1682), now state-owned, with historical collections; at North Tarrytown is Castle Philipse (c.1683; restored; now a mus.), the northern manor seat.

Philipsland, Sint, Netherlands: see SINT PHILIPSLAND.

Philipstown, Ireland: see DAINGEAN.

Philistia (fĭlĭs'tyŭ), anc. region of SW Palestine, comprising a fertile plain along the Mediterranean and including a part of S Canaan. The 5 chief cities, Gaza, Ashkelon, and Ashdod (on the coast), and Ekron and Gath (inland), strategically located on the great commercial route from Egypt to Syria, formed a confederacy.

Phillack (fĭ'lŭk), former urban district (1931 pop. 3,233), W Cornwall, England, on St. Ives Bay of the Atlantic and 3 mi. ESE of St. Ives; agr. market (vegetables). Has 15th-cent. church.

Phillaur (pĭl'lour), town (pop. 9,011), Jullundur dist., central Punjab, India, near Sutlej R., 24 mi. SE of Jullundur; rail junction; trades in timber, grain, cotton; mfg. of pencils, crockery, crucibles, metal goods; handicraft cloth. Police training col.

Phillip, Port, Australia: see PORT PHILLIP BAY.

Phillip Island (□ 36; pop. 1,108), S Victoria, Australia, in Western Port of Bass Strait, S of French Isl., at mouth of inlet; separates W.Passage from E.Passage; 12 mi. long E-W, 5.5 mi. wide N-S; tourist resort. Koala bears, penguins, seals. Cowes, main village.

Phillippy (fĭl'ĭpē), resort village, Lake co., extreme NW Tenn., on Reelfoot L., 15 mi. W of Union City.

Phillips. 1 County (□ 704; pop. 46,254), E Ark.; ⊙ Helena. Bounded E by Mississippi R.; drained by White and St. Francis rivers and by small Lick Creek. Includes part of Crowley's Ridge. Agr. (fruit, cotton, feed crops, truck, soybeans, livestock; dairy products. Mfg. at Helena and West Helena. Timber; gravel. Formed 1820. **2** County (□ 680; pop. 4,924), NE Colo.; ⊙ Holyoke. Agr. area, bordering on Nebr.; drained by Frenchman Creek. Wheat, small grains. Formed 1889. **3** County (□ 906; pop. 9,273), N Kansas; ⊙ Phillipsburg. Rolling prairie region, bordering N on Nebr.; drained by North Fork Solomon R. Corn, livestock. Formed 1872. **4** County (□ 5,264; pop. 6,334), N Mont.; ⊙ Malta. Agr. area bordering on Sask.; bounded S by Missouri R.; drained by Milk R. Grain, dairy products, livestock; natural gas. Small part of Lewis and Clark Natl. Forest in SW. Formed 1915.

Phillips. 1 Town (pop. 1,088), Franklin co., W central Maine, on Sandy R. and 15 mi. NW of Farmington, in recreational area; farming, mfg. (wood products, textiles). Diatomaceous earth found here. Settled 1791, inc. 1812. **2** Village (pop. 190), Hamilton co., SE central Nebr., 7 mi. E of Grand Island and on Platte R. **3** Town (pop. 181), Coal co., S central Okla., 2 mi. S of Coalgate, in agr. and coal-mining area. **4** Village (pop. 4,105), Hutchinson co., extreme N Texas, 25 mi. NW of Pampa; an oil-refining center in great Panhandle oil and natural-gas region. **5** City (pop. 1,775), ⊙ Price co., N Wis., 48 mi. W of Rhinelander, in wooded lake region; sawmilling, woodworking; dairying; mfg. of electrical apparatus. Settled 1874, inc. 1891.

Phillipsburg or **Philipsburg,** village (pop. 457), S Que., on Missisquoi Bay of L. Champlain, 20 mi. SE of St. Jean, near Vt. border; marble quarrying, dairying.

Phillipsburg. 1 Village (pop. 2,770, with adjoining Unionville), Tift co., S Ga., near Tifton. **2** City (pop. 2,589), ⊙ Phillips co., N Kansas, 60 mi. N of Hays; shipping and trade center for corn and livestock area; oil refinery. Rodeo takes place here yearly in Aug. Platted 1872, inc. 1880. **3** Town (pop. 170), Laclede co., S central Mo., in the Ozarks, 11 mi. SW of Lebanon. **4** Industrial city (pop. 18,919), Warren co., NW N.J., on Delaware R. (bridged here) opposite Easton, Pa.; mfg. (metal products, chemicals, cement, clothing, beverages, textiles, bobbins); grain, dairy products. Settled 1739, inc. 1868. Peter Cooper introduced Bessemer steel process here, 1856; town grew with iron and steel industry. **5** Village (pop. 609), Montgomery co., W Ohio, 15 mi. NW of Dayton, in agr. area.

Phillipsdale, R.I.: see EAST PROVIDENCE.

Phillips Island, Tuamotu Isls.: see MAKEMO.

Phillips Pass, Wyo.: see TETON RANGE.

Phillipsport, resort village, Sullivan co., SE N.Y., just W of the Shawangunk range, 12 mi. E of Monticello.

Phillipston, agr. town (pop. 638), Worcester co., N Mass., 17 mi. WSW of Fitchburg.

Phillipstown, village (pop. 102), White co., SE Ill., 23 mi. SW of Mount Carmel, in agr. area.

Phillipsville, village (pop. 1,271), Haywood co., W N.C., residential suburb of Canton.

Philmont (fĭl'mŏnt), village (pop. 1,792), Columbia co., SE N.Y., 8 mi. E of Hudson; mfg. (clothing, textiles). A tuberculosis hosp. is near by. Village inc. 1892.

Philo (fī'lō). **1** Village (pop. 525), Champaign co., E Ill., 8 mi. SSE of Champaign, in agr. area. **2** Village (pop. 881), Muskingum co., central Ohio, 7 mi. SE of Zanesville, and on Muskingum R., in agr. area; coal mining. Also called Taylorsville.

Philomath (fĭ'lŭmăth), city (pop. 1,289), Benton co., W Oregon, 5 mi. SW of Corvallis in valley of Willamette R.; lumber milling.

Philomelion, Turkey: see AKSEHIR.

Philoteria, Palestine: see DEGANIYA.

Philpots Island (18 mi. long, 14 mi. wide), E Franklin Dist., Northwest Territories, in Baffin Bay, just off E Devon Isl.; 75°N 80°W.

Philpott Dam, Va.: see SMITH RIVER.

Philpstoun (fĭlp'stŭn, fŭlp'–), village in Abercorn parish, N West Lothian, Scotland, 4 mi. E of Linlithgow; shale-oil mining.

Phimai (pē'mī'), village (1937 pop. 2,569), Nakhon Ratchasima prov., E Thailand, in Korat Plateau, on Mun R. and 30 mi. ENE of Nakhon Ratchasima; ruins of Khmer temple dating from 11th-12th cent.

Phi Pan Nam Mountains (pē' pän' näm'), mtn. system of N Thailand, bet. Khun Tan Range (W) and Luang Prabang Range (E); its jungle-covered ranges (average alt. 2,000 ft.) enclose valleys of Wang, Nam, and Yom rivers (headstreams of the Chao Phraya).

Phippsburg, town (pop. 1,134), Sagadahoc co., SW Maine, just S of Bath, at mouth of the Kennebec. Includes resort villages of Parker Head and Sebasco and Popham Beach, resort at end of peninsula. Fort Popham, begun 1861, was never finished. Town was site (1607) of Fort St. George, a Plymouth Company colony (led by George Popham) destroyed by Indians and resettled c.1737. Inc. 1814.

Phirangipuram (pĭrŭng'gĭpŏorŭm), town (pop. 6,633), Guntur dist., NE Madras, India, 12 mi. W of Guntur; rice milling, cotton ginning. Steatite mines near by.

Phitsanulok or **Phitsnulok** (both: pēt'sänōō'lōk'), town (1947 pop. 14,494), ⊙ Phitsanulok prov. (□ 3,691; 1947 pop. 202,249), N Thailand, on Nam R. and Bangkok–Chiangmai RR, 215 mi. N of Bangkok; airport. Center of intensive rice-growing region; cotton, tobacco, sesame. Noted for temple and 15th-cent. statue of Buddha. Dates from 13th cent. Sometimes spelled Bisnulok, Bhitsanulok, and Pitsanulok.

Phlambouron, Greece: see PIERIA.

Phlegraean Fields (flĕgrē'ŭn), Ital. *Campi Flegrei,* volcanic region of S Italy, W of Naples. Contains lakes Agnano (drained), Averno, and Fusaro and many craters, including Solfatara and Monte Nuovo (formed 1538). Legendary scene of battle bet. giants and gods. In Roman times the cities of Cumae, Baiae, and Puteoli were fashionable watering places.

Phlorina or **Florina** (both: flô'rĭnŭ), nome (□ 733; pop. 92,233), Macedonia, Greece; ⊙ Phlorina. Bordered N by Yugoslavia, W by Albania, and S by the Vernon, it includes Gr. portion of the Prespa lakes. Agr. (grain, apples), lumbering, charcoal burning, stock raising. Lignite mining (Veve, Amyntaion).

Phlorina or **Florina,** city (pop. 12,562), ⊙ Phlorina nome, Macedonia, Greece, on railroad and 80 mi. WNW of Salonika, 18 mi. S of Bitolj, Yugoslavia; trading center for cereals, apples; wine, timber, livestock; bishopric. Has agr. school.

Phnom Dek, Cambodia: see PNOM DEK.

Phnompenh, Cambodia: see PNOMPENH.

Phobinhgia (fō'bĭng'zhä'), town, Langson prov., N Vietnam, 25 mi. WNW of Langson.

Phocaea (fōsē'ů, fō'sēů), anc. town, northernmost of the Ionian cities on W coast of Asia Minor, near site of modern FOCA, W Turkey, on Gulf of Candarli. Founded by Phocian colonists, it became a great maritime state, establishing Massillia (Marseilles) in Gaul. Abandoned 540 B.C. under Persian siege.

Phocatba, Vietnam: see CATBA ISLAND.

Phocis (fō'sĭs) Gr. *Phokis* or *Fokis* (both: fôkēs'), nome (□ 870; pop. 65,552), W central Greece, on N shore of Gulf of Corinth; ⊙ Amphissa. Bounded W by Aetolia, N by Phthiotis, and E by Boeotia, it is very mountainous (Parnassus, Giona, Vardousia, Oeta) and contains the small plain of Crisa. Livestock raising is chief occupation; wheat, olive oil, and wine are produced. Bauxite deposits on S slopes of Parnassus. The chief towns are Amphissa and Lidorikion, connected by roads with Gulf of Corinth ports of Itea and Galaxeidion. The modern nome includes anc. DORIS and W (Ozolean) LOCRIS. Anc. Phocis included the centers of Delphi, Elatea, and Daulis, and contained the entire Parnassus massif. Its chief river was the Cephissus. Deprived of Delphi in first Sacred War (c.590 B.C.), it briefly regained control (c.448 B.C.) in the second. Phocis achieved its greatest power (350 B.C.) in 3d Sacred War under Philomelus and Onomarchus, when it revolted against the Theban hegemony, but finally succumbed to Philip II of Macedon. After 1204 the area was part of the Duchy of Athens, fell 1458 to the Turks, and became part of independent Greece in 1832.

Phoebus (fē'bůs), town (pop. 3,694), Elizabeth City co., SE Va., on Hampton Roads opposite Norfolk, adjacent to Hampton (NW) and Old Point Comfort (S); residential; fishing. Just NE is Buckroe Beach (pop. 1,977), a shore resort. Near by is Kecoughtan (kē'kůtăn", kěkůtăn') site of U.S. veterans' home. Settled c.1840; inc. 1900.

Phoenice (fēnī'sē), anc. city of N Epirus, in modern Albania, 3 mi. SW of Delvinë. Probably founded by Corcyra (Corfu), it flourished 4th-3d cents. B.C. After 230 B.C. it became ⊙ Epirote League. It was a large, populous city under Byzantine rule but was destroyed in the Turkish conquest (early 15th cent.). Remains of acropolis were excavated (1926–27) by Italians. The Albanian village of Finiq or Finiqi (1930 pop. 379) is near by.

Phoenicia (fĭnē'shů, fĭnĭ'shů), territory occupied by the peoples of Phoenician civilization. Because the city-states of the Phoenicians were not continuous, the name is a vague one geographically and may be used to mean all those spots on shores of the E Mediterranean where the Phoenicians established colonies. More often it is used for the heart of the territory where the great Phoenician cities, notably TYRE and Sidon (modern SAIDA) stood. The core of this region roughly was coast of present-day Lebanon. The region was included in the general heading of Syria in anc. times. Phoenicia also appears as Phenice and Phenicia. Some time at the dawn of history in the Middle East, a people speaking a Semitic language moved westward and occupied the coast of E Mediterranean. This may have been as early as 2000 B.C. Certainly by 1250 B.C. the people who have come to be known as Phoenicians were well established as the navigators and traders of the Mediterranean world. Besides Tyre and Sidon, other city states were TRIPOLI, ARADUS, and BYBLOS. These were the home cities, but where the Phoenicians ranged across the Mediterranean they founded posts and colonies, which later became independent states. Of these the most important were CARTHAGE and UTICA; Carthage seems to have paid a form of rent to the Phoenicians as late as the 6th cent. B.C. The Phoenicians had a language and culture like those of other Semitic peoples in the general area and may be said to have been identical with the Canaanites of N Palestine except for the development of their seagoing culture. They worshiped fertility gods and goddesses generally denominated by the terms Baal and Baalat. The Phoenicians were more or less under the intermittent influence and control of the Egyptians, but with the weakening of Egyptian power in the 12th cent., Phoenician seamen came to dominate the Mediterranean. They went out to the edges of the known world, trading briskly from the Iberian Peninsula to the Dardanelles. They may have sailed as far as the British Isles and have obtained tin there. There is evidence that in Egyptian service they may have sailed down the coast of Africa, and possibly their little ships even rounded Africa and reached the East Indies. Their carrying trade was enormous, and their wares were varied. They had a monopoly on the great cedars of Lebanon from their homeland, they manufactured glassware and metal articles, and they colored cloth the famous Tyrian purple with dye obtained from shellfish. They were skilled architects and artisans. The greatest contribution of the Phoenicians to Western civilization was, however, the invention of an alphabet, an idea taken over by the Greeks. The Phoenicians were able to withstand most of the attacks of the Assyrian kings. To the tolerant empire of the Persians, however, they submitted in the 6th cent. B.C. The individuality of the Phoenician cities dwindled, and with the rise of Greek naval and maritime power the importance of the Phoenicians disappeared. They were, however, able in 4th cent. to offer serious resistance to Alexander the Great, who was able to take Tyre only after a long and hard siege (333–332 B.C.). After that time and into Roman days the cities remained important and had some autonomy, but Hellenistic culture had eliminated the last traces of Phoenician civilization.

Phoenicia (fĭnĭ'shů), summer-resort village (pop. c.400), Ulster co., SE N.Y., in the Catskills, on Esopus Creek and 19 mi. NW of Kingston; mfg. of kitchen utensils, lumber milling.

Phoenix (fē'nĭks) or **Phenice** (fē'nĭs), anc. harbor town, a port on SW coast of Crete, W of Sphakia, probably the modern Lutro or Loutro; mentioned in the Bible (Acts 27.12).

Phoenix, residential town (pop. 1,491), W central Mauritius, in central plateau, on railroad and 3 mi. NNW of Curepipe; soft-drink mfg. Founded after 1835 by freed slaves. Sugar mill at Highlands (on rail spur; E).

Phoenix. 1 City (pop. 106,818), ⊙ Ariz. and Maricopa co., S central Ariz., on Salt R., near its junction with Gila R., and c.360 mi. E of Los Angeles; 33°27'N 112°4'W; alt. 1,090 ft. Second-largest city in state, transportation and commercial center for rich irrigated region (Salt River valley) producing citrus fruits, long-staple cotton, dates, alfalfa, and green vegetables. There are creameries, food-packing plants (meat, vegetables), fruit canneries, brewery, and flour mill. Manufactures include wood, steel, and aluminum products, rock wool, aircraft equipment, air-conditioning apparatus, leather goods, and Indian novelties. City is health and tourist resort with warm, dry climate (annual rainfall, 7.8 in.; Jan. temp. 52°F, July 90°F; low wind velocity). Has airport, U.S. Indian school, Episcopalian cathedral, Phoenix Col., The Amer. Inst. for Foreign Trade. Points of interest are state capitol (completed 1900), Ariz. Mus. (state antiquities), Heard Mus. (prehistoric relics), and La Ciudad (ruins of anc. Indian dwelling). There are several Indian reservations in vicinity. Phoenix South Mountain Park (with small gold mine) is scenic area in Salt River Mts., c.10 mi. S. City was settled c.1867, inc. 1881. Succeeded Prescott as territorial capital (1889) and became state capital 1912. Growth stimulated by irrigation of Salt R. valley. Annual events are rodeo (Feb.) and Festival of the Sun (March). **2** Residential village (pop. 3,606), Cook co., NE Ill., S suburb of Chicago, just S of Harvey. Inc. 1900. **3** Village (pop. 1,917), Oswego co., central N.Y., on Oswego R. and the Barge Canal, and 15 mi. NNW of Syracuse; mfg. (paper, furniture, metal products). Agr. (dairy products; poultry, fruit). Inc. 1849. **4** Town (pop. 746), Jackson co., SW Oregon, 5 mi. SE of Medford. **5** Town, Charlotte co., Va.: see PHENIX.

Phoenix Islands, group of 8 coral islands (□ 11; pop. 984), S Pacific; 3°35'S 171°31'W. Include CANTON ISLAND, ENDERBURY ISLAND, MCKEAN ISLAND, BIRNIE ISLAND, Phoenix Isl., GARDNER ISLAND, HULL ISLAND, SYDNEY ISLAND; 2 most important, Canton and Enderbury isls., were placed 1939 under Anglo-American control. The other isls. were annexed 1937 to Br. colony of GILBERT AND ELLICE ISLANDS. Canton Isl., the largest atoll, is transpacific air-line base. Isls. formerly worked for guano; now produce copra. Uninhabited Phoenix Isl. (121 acres), 80 mi. SE of Canton Isl., is most fertile of group; discovered 1859 by Americans.

Phoenix Mountains, central Ariz., NE of Phoenix; rise to 2,700 ft. in CAMELBACK MOUNTAIN.

Phoenix Prince Mine, Southern Rhodesia: see BINDURA.

Phoenixville (fē'nĭksvĭl), borough (pop. 12,932), Chester co., SE Pa., 21 mi. NW of Philadelphia and on Schuylkill R.; ironworks; meat packing, mfg. (textiles, paper boxes, paint, abrasives). Large steam power plant. Valley Forge military and veterans' hosp. built 1942. Most western point in Pa. reached 1777 by British in Revolution. Settled 1720, inc. 1849.

Phokis, Greece: see PHOCIS.

Pholegandros or **Folegandros** (both: fôlě'gändrôs), Lat. *Pholegandrus* (fōlēgăn'drůs), Aegean island (□ 13; pop. 1,095) in the Cyclades, Greece, E of Melos isl.; 36°36'N 24°56'E; 8 mi. long, 2.5 mi. wide; barley, cotton, wine. Main town, Pholegandros (pop. 618), is on SE shore. Also called Polykandros or Polikandros.

Phon (pôn), village (1937 pop. 22,730), Khonkaen prov., E Thailand, in Korat Plateau, on railroad and 50 mi. SSW of Khonkaen.

Phongsaly (pông'sälē'), town, ⊙ Phongsaly prov., (□ 6,100; 1947 pop. 30,000), N Laos, 120 mi. N of Luang Prabang. Market center, served by river port of Hatsa on the Nam Hou. Formerly called Muong Hou. The prov. was constituted until 1947 as a military dist.

Phongtho (fông'tô'), town, Laokay prov., N Vietnam, near China border, 40 mi. W of Laokay.

Phontiou (pông'tyōō'), village, Khammouane prov., central Laos, on the small Nam Patene and 20 mi. N of Pak Hin Boun; tin-mining center (founded 1923).

Phournoi or **Fournoi** (both: fōōr'nē), Greek Aegean island (□ 18.5; pop. 1,093), SW of Samos, in Samos nome, forming with Phymaina and lesser isls. the Phournoi group (□ c.30; pop. 1,240); 37°34'N 26°30'E; 9 mi. long, 2 mi. wide. Sometimes spelled Furni.

Phrae (pră), town (1947 pop. 11,900), ⊙ Phrae prov. (□ 2,301; 1947 pop. 213,351), N Thailand, on Yom R., 10 mi. from railroad (Den Chai station) and 90 mi. SE of Chiangmai, in valley S of Phi Pan Nam Mts.; produces rice, cotton (weaving), and teak. Also spelled Prae.

Phra Nakhon, Thailand: see BANGKOK.

Phra Nakhon Si Ayutthaya, Thailand: see AYUTTHAYA.

Phra Pathom, Thailand: see NAKHON PATHOM.

Phra Phuttabat (prä' pōōt'tůbät'), village (1937 pop. 3,378), Saraburi prov., S Thailand, on rail spur from Tha Rua and 70 mi. NNE of Bangkok; noted pilgrimage center; has natural rock depression (discovered 17th cent.) venerated by Buddhists as imprint of foot of Buddha.

Phrygia (frĭ'jēů), anc. region, W central Asia Minor (now central Turkey). The Phrygians, who settled here c.1200 B.C., came from Europe and apparently spoke an Indo-European language. Nothing is known of their history; from c.700 B.C., Lydia dominated the area. The Greeks told of Phrygian kings named Gordius and Midas; they knew Phrygia best as a source of slaves and as a center of the cult of Cybele. N Phrygia became Galatia with the invasion of the Gauls (3d cent. B.C.). Much of it was ruled by kings of Pergamum, and when it passed to the Romans most of it was assigned to prov. of Asia. Cities included Laodicea, Apamea, and Celaenae.

Phthiotis or **Fthiotis** (thīō'tĭs, Gr. fthēō'tēs), nome (□ 1,597; pop. 143,528), E central Greece, ⊙ Lamia. Bordered N by Thessaly, E by the Malian Gulf and Gulf of Euboea, S by Boeotia and Phocis, and W. by Eurytania. It is largely mountainous (Oeta, Kallidromon), except for the Spercheios R. valley (center), where agr. (wheat, tobacco, cotton, almonds) is carried on. Bauxite is mined on Oeta massif, nickel and limonite at Larymna. Traversed by Athens-Salonika RR; chief town and road center is Lamia, with its port, Stylis. In anc. times the area corresponded to MALIS and Eastern LOCRIS, while the name Phthiotis (or Achaia Phthiotis) was applied to SE district of Thessaly on N slopes of the Othrys massif.

Phucyen (fōōk'yěn'), town, ⊙ Phucyen prov. (□ 300; 1943 pop. 202,100), N Vietnam, in Tonkin, on railroad and 15 mi. NW of Hanoi; rice, corn, castor beans, manioc, tea.

Phuket (pōō'kĕt'), island and prov. (□ 206; 1947 pop. 49,324), on S Thailand, off W coast of Malay Peninsula, in Andaman Sea; 8°N 98°20'E; 25 mi. long, 10 mi. wide; ⊙ Phuket. Flat with isolated hills (highest point, 1,700 ft.), it has large tin deposits and is one of leading tin-mining regions of Thailand. Rubber, coconut, and pepper plantations. Pop. Chinese and Thai. Known to Malays as Ujong [cape] Salang, corrupted by Thai to Thalang, by Europeans to Junkceylon. Long disputed bet. Thailand and Burma, isl. was inc. with Thailand only in 19th cent.

Phuket, town (1947 pop. 18,759), ⊙ Phuket prov., on SE coast of Phuket isl., S Thailand, off Malay Peninsula and 430 mi. SSW of Bangkok; 7°55'N 98°25'E. Port and largest tin-mining center of Thailand; ore is shipped to Penang and Singapore. Founded 1st cent. B.C. by colonists from India, received (15th cent.) large Chinese influx, destroyed (19th cent.) by Burmese. Developed as tin center in late 19th cent. Sometimes spelled Puket and Bhuket; also known as Tongka or Tongkah.

Phuket Range, S Thailand, S continuation of Tenasserim Range, in Malay Peninsula, extends 150 mi. from Isthmus of Kra to Phuket isl.; jungle-covered hills rising up to 4,658 ft.; tin mining.

Phul (pōōl), town (pop. 9,515), central Patiala and East Punjab States Union, India, 70 mi. W of Patiala; local market center for millet, gram, cotton; hand-loom weaving; food processing.

Phulangthuong (fōō'läng'twŭng), town, ⊙ Bacgiang prov. (□ 2,000; 1943 pop. 311,800), N Vietnam, in Tonkin, on Hanoi-Nacham RR and 30 mi. NE of Hanoi, on the Song Thuong (tributary of the Song Cau); silk center; sericulture, silk weaving; castor-bean plantations. Following Fr. conquest (1884), it was transportation center on route to Langson.

Phularwan (pōōlůrvän'), town (pop. 5,030), Shahpur dist., central Punjab, W Pakistan, 37 mi. NE of Sargodha; market center for wheat, oilseeds, cotton, wool, ghee; cotton ginning, oilseed and sugar milling, salt mfg., rice husking, hand-loom weaving. Sometimes called Phularwan Mandi.

Phulbani (po͝olbä′nē), village, Baudh dist., central Orissa, India, 25 mi. SSW of Baudh Raj.

Phulbari (–rē), village, Garo Hills dist., W Assam, India, on tributary of the Brahmaputra and 28 mi. NNW of Tura; rice, cotton, mustard. Coal deposits near by.

Phulbari, village, Dinajpur dist., NW East Bengal, E Pakistan, on Jamuna R. (tributary of the Atrai) and 22 mi. ESE of Dinajpur; rice milling; rice, jute, sugar cane.

Phulera, India: see PHALERA.

Phulien, Vietnam: see KIENAN.

Phulji (po͞ol′jē), village, Dadu dist., W Sind, W Pakistan, 11 mi. NNW of Dadu; rice, millet; handicraft carpet weaving.

Phulkian States (po͞ol′kyän), former Punjab states of PATIALA, JIND, and NABHA, whose ruling chiefs had common ancestor, Phul (d. 1652).

Phuloc (fo͞o′lŏk′), town, Soctrang prov., S Vietnam, 10 mi. N of Baclieu; rice.

Phulpur (po͞ol′po͝or). **1** Town (pop. 5,677), Allahabad dist., SE Uttar Pradesh, India, 16 mi. ENE of Allahabad; trades in gram, rice, barley, wheat, oilseeds, sugar cane, cotton. **2** Town (pop. 2,509), Azamgarh dist., E Uttar Pradesh, India, 20 mi. W of Azamgarh; rice, barley, wheat, sugar.

Phulra (po͞ol′rŭ), petty state (□ 36; pop. 8,739), NE North-West Frontier Prov., W Pakistan, in Malakand agency, NW of Abbottabad.

Phultala (po͞ol′tŭlŭ), village, Khulna dist., SW East Bengal, E Pakistan, on river arm of Ganges Delta and 13 mi. NNW of Khulna; trades in rice, jute, oilseeds, betel leaf.

Phulwaria, India: see BARAUNI.

Phuly (fo͞o′lē′), town (1936 pop. 5,000), ⊙ Hanam prov. (□ 500; 1943 pop. 596,200), N Vietnam in Tonkin, on the Song Dai (arm of Red R. delta), on railroad and 35 mi. S of Hanoi; coffee plantations, silk spinning.

Phunghiep (fo͞ong′hyĕp′), town, Cantho prov., S Vietnam, in Mekong delta, 17 mi. NW of Soctrang; rice center.

Phunhoquan (fo͞o′nyô′kwän), town, Ninhbinh prov., N Vietnam, 50 mi. S of Hanoi; coal mining, timber trading.

Phüntshog Ling, Tibet: see PINDZOLING.

Phuphong (fo͞o′fông′), village, Binhdinh prov., S central Vietnam, 22 mi. WNW of Quinhon, on road to Kontum; silk-milling center.

Phuqui (fo͞o′kwē′), town, Nghean prov., N central Vietnam, 45 mi. NNW of Vinh; coffee and tea plantations; forestry.

Phuquoc (fo͞o′kwôk′), island (□ 230; pop. c.7,000), in Gulf of Siam, S Vietnam, 25 mi. W of Hatien; 10°15′N 104′E; 30 mi. long, 2–17 mi. wide. Chief town, Duongdong, on W coast of isl. Very fertile and partly forested, it is flat save for low range of hills along E coast. Agr.: coconuts, pepper, cocoa, coffee, betel nuts. Rubber. Hardwood lumbering. Jet and anthracite mines. Fisheries, fish curing. Pop.: Thais and Annamese.

Phutho (fo͞o′tô′), town, ⊙ Phutho prov. (□ 1,400; 1943 pop. 351,700), N Vietnam, in Tonkin, on Red R. and Hanoi-Kunming RR, 45 mi. NW of Hanoi; agr. center; coffee, tea; lac, sericulture; forestry experimental station.

Phuyen, province, Vietnam: see SONGCAU.

Phygalia, Greece: see PHIGALIA.

Phyllis or **Filis** (both: filēs′), region of Greek Macedonia, in Serrai nome, E of lower Struma R.; main town, Nea Zichna.

Phymaina or **Fimaina** (both: fē′mänŭ), Greek Aegean island (□ 6.4; pop. 146), Samos nome, SW of Samos isl.; 37°35′E 26°26′E; 3 mi. long, 2 mi. wide; fisheries. Sometimes called Themina.

Phyong-yang, Korea: see PYONGYANG.

Pi, China: see PI RIVER.

P.I. or **Paul Isnard** (pôl ēznär′), town, ⊙ Moyenne-Mana dist. (pop. 481), Inini territory, W central Fr. Guiana, on affluent of Mana R. and 115 mi. W of Cayenne; 4°47′N 54°W. Gold placer mines in vicinity.

Piacenza (pēächĕn′tsä), province (□ 998; pop. 294,648), Emilia-Romagna, N central Italy; ⊙ Piacenza. Extends from Ligurian Apennines N to the Po. Largely mountainous, with Po plain occupying less than 1/3 of area. Drained by Trebbia, Nure, Arda, Tidone, and Chiavenna rivers. Agr. (cereals, grapes, sugar beets, tomatoes, tobacco); livestock raising. With adjacent Parma prov. (E), produces most of Italy's petroleum. Petroleum region extends bet. Podenzano and Bettola; wells at Cortemaggiore, Velleia, and Montechino. Iron and copper mining at Ferriere. Mfg. at Piacenza and Fiorenzuola d'Arda. Extensive tomato canning and sausage making.

Piacenza, anc. *Placentia*, city (pop. 49,527), ⊙ Piacenza prov., Emilia-Romagna, N central Italy, on Po R., near mouth of Trebbia R., and 40 mi. SE of Milan; 45°3′N 9°42′E. Transportation and agr. center; canned tomatoes, macaroni; mfg. (agr. machinery, leather goods, paper, cellophane, glass, chemicals, wax, buttons, metal products). Bishopric. Its notable churches include Lombard-Romanesque cathedral (1122–1233; restored 1898–1901), Sant'Antonino (11th cent.; former cathedral), San Savino (consecrated 1107), San Sisto (1499–1511; original home of the Sistine Madonna), and Madonna di Campagna (1522–28; frescoes by Pordenone and B. Gatti). Has Palazzo Municipale (begun 1281), Palazzo dei Tribunali (1484), and unfinished Palazzo Farnese (1588). In its main square are bronze equestrian statues (1620–25) of dukes Alessandro and Ranuccio Farnese. Founded by Romans, 218 B.C. Joined Lombard League in 12th cent. In 1545 passed to Parma, with which it formed duchy of Parma and Piacenza. In Second World War suffered many air raids (1944–45).

Piadena (pyä′dĕnä), village (pop. 2,027), Cremona prov., Lombardy, N Italy, near Oglio R., 17 mi. E of Cremona; rail junction; flour and silk mills, mfg. (irrigation pumps, hardware, soap).

Piaggine (pyäd-jē′nĕ), village (pop. 2,941), Salerno prov., Campania, S Italy, 10 mi. NNE of Vallo di Lucania.

Piai, Tanjong (tänjo͝ong′ pēī′), cape, Johore, S Malaya, southernmost point of continent of Asia, W of Singapore; 1°16′N 103°31′E. Sometimes called Tanjong Bulus.

Piako, New Zealand: see TE AROHA.

Piali, Greece: see TEGEA.

Piamonte (pyämōn′tā), town (pop. estimate 1,500), W Santa Fe prov., Argentina, 80 mi. WSW of Santa Fe; corn, wheat, flax.

Piana or **Piana-Mwanga** (pyä′nä-mwäng′gä), village, Katanga prov., SE Belgian Congo, on Luvua R. and 50 mi. SE of Manono; large hydroelectric plant supplies MANONO area; also tin mining.

Piana, village (pop. 729), W Corsica, near Gulf of Porto, 23 mi. NNW of Ajaccio; orchards. Near by, sheer red granite cliffs known as Calanche di Piana rise 1,300 ft. above the sea.

Piana dei Greci (dā grā′chē), town (pop. 7,153), Palermo prov., NW Sicily, 9 mi. S of Palermo, in cereal- and grape-growing region; olive oil. Founded 1488 by Albanians; it is their largest colony in Sicily and a diocese of Greek Orthodox church. L. Piana dei Greci (2 mi. long, 1 mi. wide) is 1 mi. SE; formed by dam (886 ft. long, 124 ft. high) on upper right branch of Belice R. Furnishes hydroelectric power to Palermo and irrigation for its fertile plain, the Conca d'Oro.

Piana Island, in Mediterranean Sea, bet. San Pietro Isl. and SW Sardinia; major tunny fisheries.

Piancastagnaio or **Pian Castagnaio** (pyän″kästänyä′yô), town (pop. 2,983), Siena prov., Tuscany, central Italy, on E slope of Monte Amiata, 2 mi. S of Abbadia San Salvatore. Resort (alt. 2,533 ft.); ore-processing center for near-by mercury mines.

Piancó (pyängkô′), city (pop. 1,462), W Paraíba, NE Brazil, 45 mi. SE of Cajàzeiras; cotton, rice, livestock. Gold field. Irrigation dams and reservoirs recently built in municipality.

Pian di Scò (pyän′ dē skô′), village (pop. 804), Arezzo prov., Tuscany, central Italy, on W slope of Pratomagno, 17 mi. SE of Florence; silk mill.

Pianella (pyänĕl′lä), town (pop. 2,167), Pescara prov., Abruzzi e Molise, S central Italy, 7 mi. NW of Chieti.

Pianello Val Tidone (–lô väl tēdō′nĕ), village (pop. 1,524), Piacenza prov., Emilia-Romagna, N central Italy, 8 mi. S of Castel San Giovanni.

Pianezza (pyänĕ′tsä), village (pop. 2,287), Torino prov., Piedmont, NW Italy, on Dora Riparia R. and 7 mi. WNW of Turin; metalware.

Piankatank River (pēăng′kĭtăngk), SE Va., irregular inlet (c.7 mi. long) of Chesapeake Bay, bordering Middlesex (N) and Mathews (S) counties; receives short stream (Dragon Run) from W.

Piano di Sorrento (pyä′nô dē sôr-rĕn′tô), commune (pop. 6,911), Napoli prov., Campania, S Italy, on Bay of Naples, just E of Sorrento. Consists of a small, beautiful plain, noted for its fine climate and luxuriant vegetation.

Piano d'Orta (dôr′tä), village (pop. 588), Pescara prov., Abruzzi e Molise, S central Italy, on Orte R. (branch of Pescara R.) and 14 mi. SW of Chieti. Hydroelectric plant furnishes power for its chemical industry (calcium carbide, chlorine, soda).

Pianoro (pyänô′rô), village (pop. 1,115), Bologna prov., Emilia-Romagna, N central Italy, 8 mi. S of Bologna and on Savena R. (branch of Idice R.). Badly damaged in Second World War.

Pianosa (pyänô′zä). **1** Anc. *Planasia*, island (□ 4; pop. 912) in Tuscan Archipelago, in Tyrrhenian Sea, Italy, in Livorno prov., 8 mi. S of W extremity of Elba; 3.5 mi. long, 3 mi. wide. Flat terrain, rising to c.90 ft. Has agr. penal colony. **2** Small island, Italy, in the Adriatic 14 mi. NE of Tremiti Isls.

Pianura (pyäno͞o′rä), village (pop. 5,625), Napoli prov., Campania, S Italy, 5 mi. W of Naples.

Piaouac Range or **Piaoac Range** (both: pyä′wäk′), in N Vietnam, in Tonkin, 25 mi. W of Caobang; extends c.40 mi. N–S, rising to 6,335 ft. Has Vietnam's chief source of tin and tungsten; principal mines at Tinhtuc. Lead, zinc, and silver mined at Nganson.

Piapot (pī′ŭpŏt), village (pop. 259), SW Sask., in the Cypress Hills, on Piapot Creek and 17 mi. ENE of Maple Creek; ranching, wheat growing.

Piarco (pēär′kō), village (pop. 615), N central Trinidad, B.W.I., 12 mi. ESE of Port of Spain; international airport.

Pias (pē′ŭsh), town (pop. 4,941), Beja dist., S Portugal, on railroad and 22 mi. E of Beja; trades in grain, olives, oranges, sheep.

Piaseczno (pyäsĕch′nô), Rus. *Pyasechno* (pyŭsĕch′nŭ), town (pop. 6,579), Warszawa prov., E central Poland, 12 mi. S of Warsaw; rail junction; mfg. of silk textiles, tanning, flour milling. Before Second World War, pop. 50% Jewish.

Piassabussu (pyŭsŭbo͞oso͞o′), city (pop. 3,180), E Alagoas, NE Brazil, on left bank of lower São Francisco R. 6 mi. above its mouth on the Atlantic, and 15 mi. SE of Penedo; ships rice, coconuts, castor beans, watermelons.

Piatã (pyŭtã′), city (pop. 581), central Bahia, Brazil, 40 mi. SW of Andaraí; diamond and gold mining. Until 1944, called Anchieta.

Piatra (pyä′trä), village (pop. 2,363), Arges prov., S Rumania, near Olt R., 18 mi. N of Caracal; rail junction and agr. center. Sometimes called Piatra-Olt.

Piatra-Craiului (–krä′yo͞olo͞oē), mountain group of the Transylvanian Alps, in SE central Rumania, partly in Transylvania, partly in Walachia, bet. the Bucegi and Fagaras mts.; rises to 7,360 ft.

Piatra-Neamt or **Piatra** (–nyämts′), Rum. *Piatra-Neamț*, town (1948 pop. 26,303), Bacau prov., NE Rumania, in Moldavia, on Bistrita R. and 175 mi. N of Bucharest; rail terminus and industrial center. Woodworking (construction materials, furniture, paper, cellulose); food processing, mfg. of textiles, brushes, pharmaceuticals, cosmetics, liquor, soap; brewing, tanning, metalworking. Also a noted resort and point of departure for excursions to numerous historic monasteries along Bistrita R. valley. Has 15th-cent. church repeatedly restored, regional mus. Bistrita monastery (2 mi. to W), 1st founded in 1402, destroyed by an earthquake, and again rebuilt in 1554, was formerly one of the cultural centers of Moldavia.

Piatt (pī′ŭt), county (□ 437; pop. 13,970), central Ill.; ⊙ Monticello. Agr. (corn, oats, soybeans, wheat, livestock, poultry; dairy products. Some mfg. (fiber tile, patent medicines, health foods). Drained by Sangamon R. Formed 1841.

Piauí (pyou-ē′), state (□ 96,261; 1940 pop. 817,601; 1950 census 1,064,438), NE Brazil; ⊙ Teresina. Separated from Ceará and Pernambuco (E) by the Serra Grande and Serra dos Dois Irmãos; from Bahia (S) by Tabatinga, Gurgueia, and Piauí ranges; and from Maranhão (W) by Parnaíba R., which forms border along its entire course. Piauí has shortest coast line (c.50 mi.) of all maritime Braz. states. It is drained by right tributaries of Parnaíba R. Land rises from narrow coastal plain (N) and Parnaíba valley (W) to E and S frontier ranges. Situated in transitional climate zone bet. tropical rain-forest and monsoon regions (NW) and semiarid uplands (SE); precipitation decreases from N to S (the latter is in a drought area). Piauí has extensive livestock pastures on short-grass uplands. Agr. in river valleys includes cotton, tobacco, rice, sugar, beans, and manioc. State ships large quantities of babassu nuts; also carnauba wax, oiticica oil, castor beans, maniçoba rubber, hides and skins. Chief cities are: Teresina (S terminus of railroad to São Luís); Parnaíba, with its seaport of Luís Correia; Floriano (head of regular navigation on the Parnaíba); and Oeiras (old ⊙). Piauí is served by 4 unconnected railroad systems, chief of which penetrates inland to Piripiri from Luís Correia on the coast. Piauí became a subordinate captaincy under Maranhão in 1718. Assuming independence in 1811, it became a prov. of the Brazilian empire after 1822, and a state of the federal republic in 1889. Its ⊙ was transferred from Oeiras to Teresina in 1852. Formerly spelled Piauhy.

Piauí, Serra do (sĕ′rŭ do͞o), range of NE Brazil, extending c.150 mi. along Piauí-Bahia border NE of the Serra da Gurgueia; rises to 2,000 ft. Forms watershed bet. Piauí R. (N) and São Francisco R. (SE). Formerly spelled Serra do Piauhy.

Piauí River, Piauí, NE Brazil, rises in the Serra do Piauí (Piauí-Bahia border), flows 250 mi. generally N, past São João do Piauí, to the Canindé above the latter's influx into the Parnaíba. Not navigable. Carnauba palms in valley. Formerly spelled Piauhy.

Piave River (pyä′vĕ), N Italy, rises in Carnic Alps on Monte Peralba, flows S and SSW, past Belluno, and SE, past San Donà di Piave, to the Adriatic 20 mi. NE of Venice; 137 mi. long. Navigable for 20 mi. Receives Boite and Cordevole rivers (right). Used for hydroelectric power (Lago di SANTA CROCE) and irrigation. In First World War, following defeat at Caporetto (1917), Italians withdrew to the Piave; despite fierce onslaughts by Austrians, the line was held until, in Oct., 1918, Austrians were routed by a combined Allied attack.

Piaxtla (pyä′slä), town (pop. 1,347), Puebla, central Mexico, 30 mi. SE of Matamoros; corn, sugar cane, fruit, stock.

Piaxtla River, W Mexico, rises on W slopes of Sierra Madre Occidental in Durango near Sinaloa border, flows c.150 mi. SW through fertile coastal lowlands of Sinaloa, past San Ignacio, to the Pacific 45 mi. NW of Mazatlán.

Piazza Armerina (pyä′tsä ärmĕrē′nä), town (pop. 22,815), Enna prov., SE central Sicily, 18 mi. SE of Caltanissetta. Bishopric, with 17th-cent. cathedral. Norman church of 1096 just N. Rich sulphur mines near by.

Piazzi Island (pyä'sē), off coast of S Chile, 60 mi. W of Puerto Natales, separated from Rennell Isls. by Smyth Channel; 25 mi. long, 3–12 mi. wide; uninhabited.

Piazzola sul Brenta (pyätsô'lä sōōl brĕn'tä), town (pop. 2,723), Padova prov., Veneto, N Italy, near Brenta R., 10 mi. NNW of Padua; silk, jute, and rice mills, fertilizer factory.

Pibanshur or **Piban'shur** (pēbŭnyŭshōōr'), rail junction, N Udmurt Autonomous SSR, Russian SFSR, 5 mi. SE of Balezino; line running S to Izhevsk was built during Second World War.

Piber (pē'bŭr), village (pop. 779), Styria, S Austria, 15 mi. W of Graz; stud farm. Lignite mines in vicinity.

Pibor (pē'bôr), village, Upper Nile prov., S Anglo-Egyptian Sudan, on Pibor R. and 215 mi. SE of Malakal; head of small-craft navigation. Also called Pibor Post.

Pibor River, Upper Nile prov., E Anglo-Egyptian Sudan, formed at Pibor by several branches which rise in E Sudd region, flows 172 mi. N, past Akobo, joining the Baro on Ethiopian border to form Sobat River. Navigable below Pibor for small craft. Floods after mid-June.

Pibrans, Czechoslovakia: see Pribram.

Pica (pē'kä), village (pop. 946), Tarapacá prov., N Chile, 55 mi. SE of Iquique; an oasis in subandean desert, its subterranean wells supply Iquique and near-by nitrate refineries. Wine- and fruitgrowing. Village was settled by Sp. soldiers in 16th cent.

Picacho (pēkä'chō), village (pop. c.200), Lincoln co., S central N.Mex., on Rio Hondo, E of Sacramento Mts., and 36 mi. W of Roswell; alt. c.5,000 ft. Trading point in livestock, fruit, truck region. Mescalero Indian Reservation, part of Lincoln Natl. Forest near by.

Picacho Butte (7,250 ft.), NW central Ariz., 10 mi. SE of Seligman.

Picacho del Carmen, Cerro (sĕ'rō pēkä'chō dĕl kär'mĕn), peak (10,925 ft.) in Guanajuato, central Mexico, in Sierra Madre, 14 mi. ENE of Alvaro Obregón; highest mtn. in Guanajuato.

Picadome (pĭ'kŭdōm), suburb (pop. 7,352) of Lexington, Fayette co., central Ky.

Picaña (pēkä'nyä), SW outer suburb (pop 2,280) of Valencia, Valencia prov., E Spain.

Picardie, France: see Picardy.

Picardy (pĭ'kŭrdē), Fr. *Picardie* (pēkärdē'), region and former province, N France, now in Somme dept. and parts of Pas-de-Calais, Oise, and Aisne depts.; historical ⊙ was Amiens. Abutting on English Channel bet. Calais (N) and Tréport (S), it extends eastward along Somme R. valley and upper Oise R. valley to Belg. border S of the Sambre, thus separating Artois and Flanders plain (N) from Île-de-France (S). Rich and diversified agr. region (grain, sugar beets, potatoes, flax, truck produce). Long known for textile industry centered at Amiens. Other towns: Saint-Quentin, Abbeville, and Channel ports of Calais and Boulogne. The name Picardy, unknown until 13th cent., came to designate numerous small feudal holdings (Vermandois, Ponthieu, Calaisis, etc.) added to crown by Philip II. Ceded to Burgundy in Treaty of Arras (1435); reverted to France (1477) and became prov. under jurisdiction of Paris parlement. In a more general regional sense, Picardy is said to embrace NE part of Île-de-France and Artois as well. Scene of 3 major battles (1914 and 1918) during First World War, especially along Somme and Ancre rivers, and of brief French stand during "battle of France" (1940) in Second World War.

Picasent (pēkäsĕnt'), town (pop. 5,483), Valencia prov., E Spain, 10 mi. SSW of Valencia, in rich truck-farming area; olive-oil processing; plaster.

Picatinny Arsenal, N.J.: see Dover.

Picayune (pĭkŭyōōn'), city (pop. 6,707), Pearl River co., SE Miss., 36 mi. WNW of Gulfport, in agr. and timber area; trade and shipping center; naval stores, lumber and wood products, creosoted lumber, tung oil; mfg. of clothing. Settled 1885, inc. 1906.

Picazo, El (ĕl pēkä'thō), town (pop. 1,669), Cuenca prov., E central Spain, on Júcar R. and 35 mi. NNW of Albacete; grapes, olives, truck, cereals, saffron, stock. Alcohol distilling; lumbering.

Piccadilly (pĭ'kŭdĭlē), famous street in W London, England, running W from Piccadilly Circus (traffic, theater, and amusement center) along Green Park (extension of St. James's Park), to Hyde Park Corner (W), forming boundary of Mayfair. There are numerous hotels, shops, clubs. Noted bldgs. include Burlington House; Royal Academy of Arts; and the Albany. Several bldgs., including Burlington House, suffered air-raid damage in 1940–41; St. James's Church (1684) by Wren was almost wholly destroyed.

Piccolo San Bernardo, France: see Little Saint Bernard Pass.

Pic d'Anie, France: see Anie, Pic d'.

Pic de Ger, France: see Ger, Pic de.

Pic de Montcalm, France: see Montcalm, Pic de.

Pic du Midi de Bigorre (pēk dü mēdē' dŭ bēgôr'), peak (9,439 ft.) in the central Pyrenees, Hautes-Pyrénées dept., SW France, 9 mi. S of Bagnères-de-Bigorre. Meteorological observatory at summit. Tourmalet pass is S.

Pic du Midi d'Ossau (dôsō'), 2-pronged summit (9,465 ft.) in the central Pyrenees, Basses-Pyrénées dept., SW France, near Sp. border, 25 mi. SSE of Oloron-Sainte-Marie. Winter sports area. At its foot lies Gabas.

Picerno (pēchĕr'nô), town (pop. 3,956), Potenza prov., Basilicata, S Italy, 9 mi. W of Potenza, in agr. region (cereals, grapes, olives).

Pichachén Pass (pēchächĕn') (6,950 ft.), in the Andes, on Argentina-Chile border, near SE bank of L. Laja, 65 mi. E of Los Angeles, Chile; 37°27'S 71°8'W.

Pichan, China: see Shanshan.

Picháturo (pēchä'tārō), town (pop. 1,877), Michoacán, central Mexico, 13 mi. NE of Uruapan; cereals, sugar cane, coffee, fruit.

Pichayevo (pēchī'ŭvŭ), village (1926 pop. 9,649), NE Tambov oblast, Russian SFSR, 20 mi. SE of Morshansk; grain.

Picher (pĭ'chŭr), city (pop. 3,951), Ottawa co., extreme NE Okla., 20 mi. WSW of Joplin (Mo.), near Kansas and Mo. lines; a center of lead- and zinc-mining region extending into the 3 states; has hq. for mining companies, smelters and refineries, and plants producing mining machinery and equipment.

Pichhor (pĭchōr'), town (pop. 3,747), NE Madhya Bharat, India, 21 mi. SE of Lashkar; agr. (millet, gram, wheat, rice). Also spelled Pichhore. Sugar milling 6 mi. SW, at Dabra.

Pi-chiang, China: see Pikiang.

Pichidegua (pēchēdā'gwä), village (1930 pop. 656), O'Higgins prov., central Chile, on Cachapoal R. and 35 mi. SW of Rancagua; agr. center (wheat, alfalfa, beans, wine, cattle); dairying.

Pichieh (bē'jyĕ'), town (pop. 36,440), ⊙ Pichieh co. (pop. 298,924), NW Kweichow prov., China, 100 mi. NW of Kweiyang, near Yunnan-Szechwan line; cotton weaving, papermaking, lacquer and tobacco processing; hides, hog bristles, timber, medicinal herbs, grain. Coal deposits, saltworks near by.

Pichigua (pēchē'gwä), town (pop. 598), Cuzco dept., S Peru, in Cordillera Occidental, 32 mi. SSW of Sicuani, in agr. region (potatoes, grain, stock); dairying and mining (gold, cinnabar); petroleum deposits. Sometimes Pichihua.

Pichilemu (pēchēlā'mōō), village (1930 pop. 774), Colchagua prov., central Chile, on the coast, 55 mi. WNW of San Fernando; rail terminus, minor port and resort.

Pichilinque Bay (pēchēlēng'kā), small inlet of La Paz Bay, SE Lower California, NW Mexico, 8 mi. N of La Paz; good deep-sea harbor.

Pichi Mahuida, Argentina: see Río Colorado, Río Negro natl. territory.

Pichincha (pēchēn'chä), province (□ 6,347; 1950 pop. 394,240), N central Ecuador, in the Andes, crossed by the equator; ⊙ Quito. Mountainous region including many high volcanic peaks, among them Pichincha, Cotopaxi, Antisana, Corazón, Rumiñahui, Cayambe. It slopes W to the lowlands. Frequently subjected to earthquakes and eruptions. Watered by Guaillabamba R. Climate is generally cool and temperate, with a mean temp. of c.55°F. Main rains: Oct.–May. Among its mineral resources are oil (Nono), alabaster (near Quito), manganese (San Antonio), and sulphur deposits. Predominantly agr., its fertile valleys produce wheat, corn, barley, potatoes, fruit, vegetables, sugar cane, and cattle. Dairying and flour milling are main rural industries. Quito, the cultural and political center of Ecuador, has textile mills and processing plants. Resorts and spas: Tingo, Thesalia, Cunuc-Yacu, Guápulo.

Pichincha, Cerro (sĕ'rō), Andean volcano (15,423 ft.) in Pichincha prov., N central Ecuador, 6 mi. NW of Quito, c.11 mi. S of the equator. Of little activity, though emitting gases. Last erupted 1881. Easily climbed from Quito and Lloa. On its lower slopes was fought the decisive battle of Pichincha (May 24, 1822), when patriot forces under Sucre, with aid of troops sent by San Martín, routed the Sp. royalists and, entering Quito following day, freed the territory that was to become Ecuador.

Pichi-Pellahuén (pēchē-pĕyäwĕn'), village (1930 pop. 235), Malleco prov., S central Chile, 40 mi. SSW of Angol, in agr. area (wheat, oats, potatoes, fruit, livestock); lumbering.

Pichis River, Peru: see Pachitea River.

Pichitr, Thailand: see Phichit.

Pichl (pē'khŭl), village (pop. 1,930), SE Upper Austria, 22 mi. SSW of Steyr, in the Sengsengebirge; summer resort (alt. 1,900 ft.).

Pichola Lake, India: see Udaipur, city.

Pichon (pēshō'), village, Kairouan dist., central Tunisia, 24 mi. W of Kairouan; Fr. agr. colony. Olive-oil pressing. Scene of fighting (April, 1943) in Tunisian campaign.

Pichucalco (pēchōōkäl'kō), city (pop. 2,016), Chiapas, S Mexico, in Gulf lowland, near Tabasco border, 35 mi. SSW of Villahermosa; rubber- and cocoa-growing center. Petroleum deposits near.

Pichu Pichu, Nevado de (nävä'dō dā pē'chōō pē'chōō), volcanic massif, Arequipa dept., S Peru, just SE of El Misti, E of Arequipa; comprises several peaks, rising to c.18,400 ft. At its N foot are the borax deposits of Laguna de Salinas.

Pickaway (pĭ'kŭwā), county (□ 507; pop. 29,352), S central Ohio; ⊙ Circleville. Intersected by Scioto R. and by Darby, Paint, and small Salt and Little Walnut creeks. Agr. (livestock, grain, poultry, soybeans); mfg. at Circleville; sand and gravel pits. Formed 1810.

Pick City, village (pop. 294), Mercer co., central N.Dak., on Missouri R. and 10 mi. SW of Garrison.

Pickens. 1 County (□ 887; pop. 24,349), W Ala.; ⊙ Carrollton. In Black Belt, bordering on Miss.; drained by Tombigbee and Sipsey rivers. Cotton, poultry; lumber milling. Formed 1820. **2** County (□ 225; pop. 8,855), N Ga.; ⊙ Jasper. Blue Ridge farming (corn, cotton, hay, fruit, livestock), marble quarrying, sawmilling, and resort area. Mt. Oglethorpe (NE). Formed 1853. **3** County (□ 501; pop. 40,058), NW S.C.; ⊙ Pickens. Bounded E by Saluda R., W by Keowee and Seneca rivers; borders N on N.C. Part of the Blue Ridge is in N; also includes Table Rock State Park and part of Sumter Natl. Forest. Agr. (cotton, corn, poultry) and summer-resort area; timber; mfg. (especially textiles); limestone quarries. Formed 1826.

Pickens. 1 Town (pop. 638), Holmes co., central Miss., c.45 mi. NNE of Jackson and on Big Black R.; lumber milling. **2** Town (pop. 1,961), ⊙ Pickens co., NW S.C., 17 mi. W of Greenville; summer resort; sawing machines, lumber, corn meal; cotton, corn. Settled 1868, inc. 1908. Near by are sites of Old Pickens (1828–68) and Fort Prince George (1753), the latter a center of conflict in the Cherokee War, 1760–62.

Pickerel Lake (14 mi. long, 4 mi. wide), W Ont., 100 mi. W of Port Arthur; alt. 1,338 ft. Drains SW into Rainy L.

Pickerel Lake, Emmet co., NW Mich., 10 mi. ENE of Petoskey; c.2½ mi. long, 1 mi. wide; resorts; fishing. Joined to Crooked L. (NW) by short stream.

Pickering, village (pop. estimate 650), S Ont., near L. Ontario, 20 mi. NE of Toronto; dairying, woodworking, mixed farming.

Pickering, urban district (1931 pop. 3,668; 1951 census 4,332), North Riding, NE Yorkshire, England, 8 mi. N of Malton; stone quarrying. Has remains of castle dating from Norman times, where Richard II was imprisoned.

Pickering, town (pop. 213), Nodaway co., NW Mo., on One Hundred and Two R. and 7 mi. N of Maryville.

Pickerington, village (pop. 433), Fairfield co., central Ohio, 13 mi. ESE of Columbus; dairy products.

Pickersgill, village (pop. 334), Essequibo co., N Br. Guiana, on navigable Pomeroon R. and 17 mi. WNW of Queenstown.

Picket Hill, highest peak (2,912 ft.) of Sierra Leone Colony, on Sierra Leone Peninsula, 17 mi. SE of Freetown. Offers views of almost entire peninsula.

Pickett, county (□ 174; pop. 5,093), N Tenn.; ⊙ Byrdstown. On Cumberland Plateau; bounded N by Ky.; drained by Obey and short Wolf rivers. Includes part of Dale Hollow Reservoir. Lumbering (hardwood, pine), bituminous-coal mining, agr. (livestock, tobacco, corn). Formed 1879.

Pickett, Camp, Va.: see Blackstone.

Picket Wire River, Colorado: see Purgatoire River.

Pickford, village (pop. c.500), Chippewa co., E Upper Peninsula, Mich., 24 mi. S of Sault Ste. Marie and on Munuscong R.; market center for flax-growing region.

Pickle Crow, village (pop. estimate 350), NW Ont., in Patricia dist., 6 mi. ENE of Pickle Lake and 130 mi. NE of Sioux Lookout; gold mining.

Pickle Lake, village, NW Ont., in Patricia dist., on Pickle L. (5 mi. long), 120 mi. NE of Sioux Lookout; gold mining. Seaplane base, radio station.

Pickleville, town (pop. 96), Rich co., N Utah, near Idaho line, 2 mi. S of Garden City.

Pickrell (pĭ'krŭl), village (pop. 161), Gage co., SE Nebr., 7 mi. N of Beatrice and on branch of Big Blue R.

Pickstown, village (pop. 2,217), Charles Mix co., S S.Dak., 7 mi. S of Lake Andes, near site of Fort Randall Dam on Missouri R.

Pickwick Landing Dam or **Pickwick Dam,** SW Tenn., in Tennessee R., c.50 mi. SE of Jackson, Tenn., 53 mi. downstream from Wilson Dam. Major TVA dam (113 ft. high, 7,715 ft. long; completed 1938); concrete construction, earthfill wings. Used for flood control and power; has lock (600 ft. long, 110 ft. wide) providing max. lift of 63 ft. Forms Pickwick Landing Reservoir (□ 67; 53 mi. long, .5–2 mi. wide; capacity 1,091,400 acre-ft.; sometimes known as Pickwick L.) in Hardin co., Tenn., in Colbert and Lauderdale counties, Ala., and in Tishomingo co., Miss. Recreation facilities (boating, fishing, cabins).

Pico (pē'kōō), active volcano and highest peak (7,611 ft.) of the Azores, on Pico Isl., 13 mi. ESE of Horta (on Faial Isl.); 38°28'N 28°24'W. Of perfect cone shape (except for small crater on W slope), it is often shrouded in clouds and therefore a great flying hazard. Principal eruptions occurred in 1562 and 1718.

Pico (pē'kō), unincorporated town (1940 pop. 2,594), Los Angeles co., S Calif., suburb 10 mi. ESE of downtown Los Angeles; oil refining; citrus-fruit, avocado packing. Seat of Whittier School for boys.

Pico Blanco (pē'kō bläng'kō) peak (11,696 ft.) in the Cordillera de Talamanca, SE Costa Rica, 22 mi. E of Buenos Aires.

Pico Island (pē'kō͞o), southern island (□ 167; 1950 pop. 22,344) of the central Azores, in the Atlantic, separated from Faial Isl. (4 mi. W) by Faial Channel. Madalena (38°32'N 28°32'W), its largest town, is on W shore. Isl. is 28 mi. long, up to 9 mi. wide. Pico (alt. 7,611 ft., highest in the Azores), an active cone-shaped volcano, occupies isl.'s W half. Lesser volcanoes dot narrower E part. Wine is grown on slopes of Pico volcano. Cattle raising, dairying. Whaling is carried on from Lajes do Pico (S shore) and São Roque do Pico (N shore). Administratively isl. is part of Horta dist.

Picón (pēkōn'), town (pop. 874), Ciudad Real prov., S central Spain, near the Guadiana, 8 mi. NW of Ciudad Real; grapes, cereals, olives, cattle, sheep.

Pico Peak (3,967 ft.), in Green Mts., W central Vt., 7 mi. NE of Rutland; ski lifts and trails.

Picos (pē'ko͞os). **1** City, Maranhão, Brazil: see COLINAS. **2** City (pop. 2,943), central Piauí, Brazil, 45 mi. E of Oeiras; cotton ginning; ships carnauba wax, cotton, hides and skins. Airfield.

Pico Salamanca (pē'kō sälämäng'kä), village (pop. estimate 500), E Comodoro Rivadavia military zone, Argentina, 32 mi. N of Comodoro Rivadavia; sheep-raising center.

Picota (pēkō'tä), town (pop. 847), San Martín dept., N central Peru, on Huallaga R. and 25 mi. S of Tarapoto; sugar cane, rice.

Pico Truncado (pē'kō tro͞ongkä'dō), village (pop. estimate 500), SE Comodoro Rivadavia military zone, Argentina, on railroad and 70 mi. SSW of Comodoro Rivadavia; sheep-raising center; also horses, hogs, goats. Airport.

Picquigny (pēkēnyē'), village (pop. 1,033), Somme dept., N France, on the Somme and 8 mi. WNW of Amiens; truck farming, linen bag mfg. Has ruins of medieval castle. Here, in 1475, a peace was signed by Edward IV and Louis XI.

Picton, town (pop. 1,091), E New South Wales, Australia, 40 mi. SW of Sydney; dairying. Silver-lead mines near by.

Picton, town (pop. 3,901), ⊙ Prince Edward co., SE Ont., on Adolphus Reach (an arm of L. Ontario leading to Bay of Quinte), 16 mi. SE of Belleville; fruit and vegetable canning center; textile and lumber milling, dairying.

Picton, borough (pop. 1,577) and port, NE S.Isl., New Zealand, 40 mi. W of Wellington across Cook Strait, on Queen Charlotte Sound; port for Blenheim; northernmost rail terminus of S. Isl. Exports fruit, grain, wool.

Pictón Island (pēktōn') (□ 35.4), in Tierra del Fuego, at mouth of Beagle Channel on the Atlantic, near 55°S 67°W; 13 mi. long, 3–4 mi. wide. Disputed by Chile and Argentina.

Pictou (pĭk'tō, –to͞o, pĭkto͞o'), county (□ 1,124; pop. 40,789), N N.S., on Northumberland Strait; ⊙ Pictou. Has rich coal and iron deposits.

Pictou, town (pop. 3,069), ⊙ Pictou co., N N.S., on Pictou Harbour, inlet of Northumberland Strait, 80 mi. NE of Halifax; shipbuilding, mfg. of steel products, furniture; fishing port. Site of Pictou Academy (1818). Terminal of car ferry to Wood Isl., P.E.I. Land was granted here (1762) to a Philadelphian group, including Benjamin Franklin; settlement was begun 1763. Near by are important coal fields.

Pictou Island (5 mi. long, 2 mi. wide), in Northumberland Strait, bet. N N.S., and SE P.E.I., 10 mi. NE of Pictou.

Picture Butte, village (pop. 689), S Alta., 14 mi. N of Lethbridge; coal mining, beet-sugar refining.

Pictured Rocks, N Upper Peninsula, Mich., cliff (generally 50–80 ft. high) along S shore of L. Superior, in Alger co., extends E of Munising for c.20 mi.; varicolored sandstone is here carved by action of wind and water into caves, columns, and fantastic figures.

Picture Rocks, borough (pop. 569), Lycoming co., N central Pa., 17 mi. ENE of Williamsport; furniture.

Picuí (pēkwē'), city (pop. 1,450), central Paraíba, NE Brazil, on Borborema Plateau, near Rio Grande do Norte border, 110 mi. NW of João Pessoa; center of important mining area yielding copper, tin ore, and several rare minerals (beryl, tantalite, columbite, scheelite). Airfield. Formerly spelled Picuhy.

Picunches, Argentina: see LAS LAJAS.

Picún-Leufú (pēko͞on'-lĕo͞ofo͞o'), village (pop. c.300), ⊙ Picún-Leufú dept. (pop. 1,672), Neuquén natl. territory, Argentina, on Limay R. and 70 mi. SW of Neuquén, in agr. area (wheat, alfalfa, livestock).

Picún-Leufú, Arroyo (äroi'ō), river in Neuquén natl. territory, Argentina, rises in N outliers of Sierra de Catán-Lil 15 mi. ENE of Aluminé, flows c.100 mi. ESE to Limay R. at Picún-Leufú.

Picuris (pĭkūrēs'), pueblo (□ 23.4), Taos co., N N.Mex. Picuris village (1948 pop. 132) is in Sangre de Cristo Mts., near the Rio Grande, 38 mi. NNE of Santa Fe; alt. c.8,000 ft. Agr., livestock, pottery making, weaving. Important holiday is San Lorenzo's day (Aug. 10), accompanied by Mass in San Lorenzo de Picurís Church (c.1692), followed by traditional dances. Mission established 1598 by Juan de Oñate. Village participated in general Pueblo revolt of 1680.

Piddig (pĭdĭg', pēdēg'), town (1939 pop. 2,309; 1948 municipality pop. 10,496), Ilocos Norte prov., NW Luzon, Philippines, 9 mi. ESE of Laoag; rice-growing center.

Piduru Ridges (pĭd'o͝oro͞o), S central Ceylon, in central Ceylon Hill Country, around Nuwara Eliya; consist of various ridges alternating with deep valleys, one extending NW to Pussellwara. Rise to 8,291 ft. in the Pidurutalagala, highest peak in Ceylon. Average rainfall, 75–100 in.; extensive tea and rubber plantations.

Pidurutalagala (pĭdo͝oro͝otŭlŭg'ŭlŭ), highest peak (8,291 ft.) of Ceylon, in Piduru Ridges, 2 mi. N of Nuwara Eliya. Corrupted name, Pedrotalagala.

Piedad, La, Mexico: see LA PIEDAD.

Piedade (pyĭdä'dĭ), city (pop. 1,642), S São Paulo, Brazil, 16 mi. S of Sorocaba; cattle, cotton, beans; graphite deposits.

Piedecuesta (pyādākwā'stä), town (pop. 6,974), Santander dept., N central Colombia, on W slopes of Cordillera Oriental, 10 mi. SSE of Bucaramanga; alt. 3,222 ft. Agr. center (sugar cane, coffee, tobacco, vegetables, stock); mfg. of tobacco products, footwear, fique bags; tanneries. Sericultural school.

Pie de Palo (pyā'dā'pä'lō), town (pop. estimate 500), S San Juan prov., Argentina, in San Juan R. valley, at S foot of Sierra del Pie de Palo, on railroad and 19 mi. SE of San Juan; alfalfa, corn, wheat, wine, livestock; wine making.

Pie de Palo, Sierra del (syĕ'rä dĕl), pampean range in E San Juan prov., Argentina, E of San Juan; extends c.40 mi. N–S; rises to c.10,000 ft. Coal, graphite, asbestos deposits.

Piedicroce (pyĕdĕkrō'chĕ), village (pop. 251), E central Corsica, 12 mi. NE of Corte; asbestos mining. Spa of Orezza 1 mi. W.

Piediluco (pyĕdēlo͞o'kō), village (pop. 104), Terni prov., Umbria, central Italy, on small lake (2 mi. long), 6 mi. ESE of Terni; pottery making. Has late 13th-cent. church. On near-by hill is ruined 14th-cent. castle.

Piedimonte d'Alife (pyĕdĕmōn'tĕ dälē'fĕ), town (pop. 5,997), Caserta prov., Campania, S Italy, at foot of Apennines, S of Lago di MATESE, 20 mi. N of Caserta. Rail terminus; paper and cotton mills, macaroni factory. Hydroelectric plant.

Piedimonte Etneo (ĕtnā'ō), village (pop. 3,794), Catania prov., E Sicily, at NE foot of Mt. Etna, 13 mi. N of Acireale.

Piedimonte San Germano (sän jĕrmä'nō), village (pop. 1,186), Frosinone prov., Latium, S central Italy, 4 mi. W of Cassino. Destroyed during battle of Cassino (1943–44) in Second World War.

Piedimulera (pyĕ"dēmo͞olā'rä), village (pop. 793), Novara prov., Piedmont, N Italy, on Anza R. and 7 mi. SSW of Domodossola; aluminum factory.

Piedmont (pēd'mŏnt), village (pop. estimate 300), S Que., in the Laurentians, on North R. and 40 mi. NW of Montreal; dairying; ski resort.

Piedmont Ital. *Piemonte* (pyĕmōn'tĕ), region (□ 9,817; pop. 3,418,300), N and NW Italy; ⊙ Turin. Borders on Val d'Aosta (NW), Switzerland (NE), Lombardy (E), Liguria (S), and France (W). Comprises 6 provs.: ALESSANDRIA, ASTI, CUNEO, NOVARA, TORINO, VERCELLI. Consists of fertile Po plain encircled on 3 sides by the Alps and Apennines. Lago Maggiore forms NE border. Drained by the upper Po and its tributaries, chiefly Dora Riparia, Dora Baltea, Sesia, and Tanaro rivers. Climate a transition bet. Mediterranean and continental types, with hot summers and cold winters prevailing (average annual temp. 52°–55°F.). Rainfall (heaviest in spring and autumn) averages 28 in. yearly in plains, 39–47 in. in Alpine margins and Apennines, and 63 in. in the Alps. Area c.20% forested. Irrigation widespread, especially in Vercelli and Novara provs. Wheat, corn, forage, fruit, and vegetables are prevailing crops, with sericulture (Cuneo), rice (Vercelli, Novara), grapes (Asti), and hemp (Torino) important provincial specialties. Stock raising (cattle, hogs, in plains; sheep, goats in mts.). Mining (graphite, talc, gold, iron). Quarrying (gypsum, limestone). Leads Italy in hydroelectric power development with numerous plants, especially in Dora Riparia valley. Industry at Alessandria (hats), Asti (wine), Biella (woolen), Casale Monferrato (lime and cement), Cuneo (silk), Novara (rice), Pinerolo (railroad equipment), and Vercelli (rice), with chief center at Turin (automobiles). Its alpine valleys contain many tourist resorts. Has important communication routes with France (Mont Cenis, Montgenèvre, Maddalena, Tenda passes) and Switzerland (Simplon Pass). Region came to be known as Piedmont by 13th cent. Was a major battefield in the Italian wars (16th cent.), wars of Louis XIV, and French Revolutionary Wars. From 11th cent. on, its history was closely associated with the house of Savoy, whose dukes in 1720 became kings of Sardinia, and by 1798 had acquired all of present Piedmont. In 19th cent., after its annexation (1798–1814) to France, Piedmont was the nucleus of the Risorgimento, which established the kingdom of Italy in 1861. After Second World War, its area was reduced by detachment (1945) of Aosta prov., which became VAL D'AOSTA autonomous region, and by loss (1947 Treaty of Peace) of territory in Cuneo and Torino provs. to France.

Piedmont, E U.S., generally rolling upland region (□ c.80,000) bordering the Older APPALACHIAN MOUNTAINS (of which it is physiographically the non-mountainous part) on the E, from N.J. on the NE to central Ala. on the SW. Inner boundary is E base of the Blue Ridge, except in S Pa. and at SW end, where it directly adjoins the Great Appalachian Valley; alt. of inner edge is low in N (under 300 ft. in N.J.) and rises southward to c.1,800 ft. in Ga. Its E boundary is the transition zone (the FALL LINE) where it meets the coastal plain. Piedmont soils, generally clayey, are moderately fertile, but have suffered much from erosion and over-cropping, particularly in S Piedmont (from central N.C. across S.C. and Ga.), where cotton is the chief crop. From central N.C. to central Va. tobacco dominates; northward lies a belt producing fruit (especially apples), fine livestock (especially horses), and general farm crops; northernmost section (Md. and Pa.) has prosperous general farming and dairying.

Piedmont. 1 City (pop. 4,498), Calhoun co., NE Ala., 12 mi. ESE of Gadsden, in dairying, fruit, and grain area; cotton yarn and textiles, lumber. Iron mines near by. Part of Talladega Natl. Forest just S. **2** City (pop. 10,138), Alameda co., W Calif., residential community surrounded by Oakland. Inc. 1907. **3** Town (pop. 34), Lamar co., W central Ga., 6 mi. WSW of Barnesville. **4** City (pop. 1,548), Wayne co., SE Mo., near Black R., 32 mi. NW of Poplar Bluff; agr. center; lumber mills. Clearwater Dam is SW. **5** Town (pop. 120), Canadian co., central Okla., 17 mi. NW of Oklahoma City. **6** Textile-mill village (pop. 2,673), Anderson and Greenville counties, NW S.C., on Saluda R. and 10 mi. S of Greenville. **7** Village (pop. c.175), Meade co., W S.Dak., 15 mi. NW of Rapid City, in Black Hills; alt. 3,463 ft. Supply point for ranching region; tourist trade. Near by are a petrified forest and Crystal and Wonderland caves. **8** City (pop. 2,565), Mineral co., NE W.Va., in Eastern Panhandle, on North Branch of the Potomac (bridged) opposite Westernport (Md.); trade center for coal and agr. (livestock, dairy products, fruit) area; foundry products. Chartered 1856.

Piedmont Reservoir, Ohio: see STILLWATER CREEK.

Piedra Blanca (pyā'dhrä bläng'kä), village (pop. estimate 500), ⊙ Fray Mamerto Esquiú dept. (□ 100; pop. 4,367), SE Catamarca prov., Argentina, on the Río del Valle (irrigation) and 8 mi. NNE of Catamarca (connected by rail); agr. area (grain, alfalfa, wine, livestock).

Piedra Blanca, village (1935 pop. 853), La Vega prov., central Dominican Republic, in the Cordillera Central, 9 mi. SE of Monseñor Nouel, in agr. region (tobacco, cacao, cereals). Manganese deposit near by.

Piedrabuena (pyā"dhräbwā'nä), town (pop. 5,289), Ciudad Real prov., S central Spain, in New Castile, 14 mi. W of Ciudad Real; agr. center (cereals, chick-peas, olives, grapes, livestock); apiculture; lumbering. Olive-oil pressing, food canning, tanning, cheese processing. Mfg. of X-ray apparatus. Silver-bearing lead deposits near by.

Piedra del Aguila (dhĕl ä'gēlä), village (pop. c.200), ⊙ Collón Curá dept. (pop. 1,897), S Neuquén natl. territory, Argentina, on Limay R. and 80 mi. S of Zapala, in grain and livestock area.

Piedra Grande (grän'dā), town (pop. 531), Falcón state, NW Venezuela, 29 mi. W of Churuguara; coffee, cacao, corn.

Piedrahita (pyā"dhräē'tä), town (pop. 1,857), Ávila prov., central Spain, on N slopes of the Sierra de Gredos, on Ávila-Plasencia highway, and 36 mi. WSW of Ávila. Resort in picturesque alpine surroundings. Fertile region, producing cereals, vegetables, potatoes, fruit, livestock. Flour milling, dairying; mfg. of shoes, fabrics, and tiles. Hydroelectric plant. Has palace of dukes of Alba.

Piedralaves (–lä'vĕs), town (pop. 2,128), Ávila prov., central Spain, in Sierra de Gredos, in fertile Tiétar valley, 23 mi. S of Ávila; grapes, cork, chestnuts, livestock. Mfg. of bottle corks. Hydroelectric plant. Sometimes spelled Piedralabes.

Piedra Negra (nä'grä), cape in Oaxaca, S Mexico, 4 mi. W of Puerto Angel; 15°58'N 96°35'W.

Piedra Pomez, Campo de (käm'pō dā, pōmĕs'), subandean plateau (c.13,000 ft.) in Puna de Atacama, N Catamarca prov., Argentina, at SE foot of Sierra de Calalaste.

Piedras (pyā'dhräs), village, El Oro prov., S Ecuador, at foot of the Andes, 27 mi. S of Machala, at terminus of rail spur; cacao, coffee, fruit.

Piedras, Las, in Latin America: see LAS PIEDRAS.

Piedras, Punta (po͞on'tä), headland on the Río de la Plata, NE Buenos Aires prov., Argentina, forms N head of Samborombón Bay, 60 mi. SE of La Plata; 35°28'S 57°7'W.

Piedras, Río de las (rē'ō dā läs), or **Tacuatimanu River** (täkwätēmä'no͞o), SE Peru, rises at approximately 11°5'S 72°20'W, flows c.260 mi. SE to Madre de Dios R. 6 mi. NNW of Puerto Maldonado. Navigable for small craft in lower course; numerous cascades in upper course.

Piedras Albas (äl'väs), village (pop. 1,269), Cáceres prov., W Spain, 36 mi. NW of Cáceres; Sp. customs station near Port. border, opposite Segura; olive oil, livestock, lumber.

Piedras Blancas (blăng'käs), Andean massif (15,623 ft.) in Mérida state, W Venezuela, in Sierra Nevada de Mérida, 22 mi. NNE of Mérida.

Piedras Blancas, Point (pēā'drŭs blăng'kŭs), SW Calif., promontory on the Pacific, c.35 mi. W of Paso Robles; lighthouse.

Piedras Coloradas (pyā'dhräs kōlōrä'däs), town (pop. 200), Paysandú dept., NW Uruguay, on railroad, and 30 mi. E of Paysandú; grain, cattle, sheep.

Piedras Negras (nā'gräs), village, Petén dept., NW Guatemala, on Usumacinta R. and 90 mi. WNW of Flores. Here are ruins of Piedras Negras, a city of the Maya Old Empire noted for its fine stone carvings by aboriginals, reaching a peak of sculptural achievement bet. 731 and 795.

Piedras Negras, city (pop. 15,663), Coahuila, N Mexico, on Rio Grande opposite Eagle Pass (Texas) and 210 mi. N of Monterrey, on railroad. Hub for international rail and road traffic; custom station; agr., commercial, and industrial center. Has open-hearth furnace, zinc smelters, cement plant, flour and textile mills, lard factory, lumber works. Uses natural gas from Zapata co., Texas. Exports cattle, sheep, hides, wheat, bran, istle fibers, candelilla wax. Coal, silver, gold and zinc mines in vicinity. Founded 1849. Renamed (1888) Ciudad Porfirio Díaz, for the dictator; with his downfall former name was restored.

Piedra Sola (pyā'dhrä sō'lä), village, Tacuarembó dept., N central Uruguay, in the Cuchilla de Haedo, 31 mi. SW of Tacuarembó, rail junction of lines from Tres Árboles (SW) and Paso de los Toros (S).

Piedrecitas (pyādrāsē'täs), town (pop. 1,134), Camagüey prov., E Cuba, on railroad and 31 mi. NW of Camagüey; sugar cane, cattle.

Piedrecitas, Las, Nicaragua: see MANAGUA, city.

Piegaro (pyĕgä'rō), village (pop. 457), Perugia prov., Umbria, central Italy, 18 mi. SW of Perugia; glass factories.

Pieh-pang Ssu, Tibet: see DREPUNG.

Pie Island (8 mi. long, 4 mi. wide), W Ont., in L. Superior, at entrance of Thunder Bay, 10 mi. SE of Fort William.

Piekary or **Piekary Slaskie** (pyĕkä'rĭ shlō'skyĕ), Pol. *Piekary Śląskie,* Ger. *Piekar* or *Deutsch-Piekar* (doich' pē'kär), city (21,467), Katowice prov., S Poland, 3 mi. N of Beuthen (Bytom); coal-mining center.

Pieksämäki (pē'ĕksămă"kē), town (pop. 7,256), Mikkeli co., SE Finland, in Saimaa lake region, 45 mi. SSW of Kuopio; rail junction; trade center for lumbering region.

Pielinen (pē'ĕlĭ"nĕn) or **Pielisjärvi** (pē'ĕlĭsyăr"vē), lake (□ 364), E Finland, near USSR border, extends 62 mi. SSE from Nurmes; 1–18 mi. wide. Drained S into Saimaa lake system by 50-mi.-long Pielinen R., Finnish *Pielisjoki.*

Pielisjärvi (pē'ĕlĭsyăr"vē), village (commune pop. 21,968), Kuopio co., E Finland, near USSR border, near E shore of the lake Pielinen 50 mi. N of Joensuu; rail terminus; molybdenum mines.

Pieman River, W Tasmania; formed by junction of 2 headstreams 5 mi. NE of Rosebery; flows 40 mi. generally W to Indian Ocean 40 mi. N of Macquarie Harbour.

Piemonte, Italy: see PIEDMONT.

Pieniny (pyĕnē'nĭ), mountain range in the Beskids, Krakow prov., S Poland, along upper Dunajec R. and Czechoslovak border; highest point (3,222 ft.) is 15 mi. SW of Stary Sacz. Health resort of Kroscienko (krôshchĕn'kô), Pol. *Krościenko,* lies on SE slope.

Pienkwan or **P'ien-kuan** (both: pyĕn'gwän'), town, ⊙ Pienkwan co. (pop. 38,767), NW Shansi prov., China, 50 mi. NW of Ningwu, near Yellow R. (Shensi border); wheat, kaoliang. Coal mining near by.

Piennes (pyĕn), town (pop. 3,353), Meurthe-et-Moselle dept., NE France, 8 mi. NW of Briey; iron mining; furniture mfg.

Pienza (pyĕn'zä), town (pop. 1,191), Siena prov., Tuscany, central Italy, 5 mi. W of Montepulciano; agr. center (wine, olive oil, cereals). Lignite mines near by. Bishopric, with seminary. Pope Pius II, who was b. here, had cathedral and Piccolomini Palace, designed by B. Rossellino, built in mid-15th cent.

Piera (pyä'rä), town (pop. 1,818), Barcelona prov., NE Spain, 8 mi. SE of Igualada; cotton milling, knit-goods mfg.; lumbering; agr. trade (olive oil, wine, fruit).

Pierce. 1 County (□ 342; pop. 11,112), SE Ga.; ⊙ Blackshear. Bounded S by Satilla R., NE by Little Satilla R.; drained by small Alabaha R. Coastal plain farming (tobacco, cotton, corn, sweet potatoes), stock raising, and sawmilling area. Formed 1857. **2** County (□ 573; pop. 9,405), NE Nebr.; ⊙ Pierce. Agr. region drained by branches of Elkhorn R. Grain, livestock, dairy and poultry produce. Formed 1856. **3** County (□ 1,053; pop. 8,326), N central N.Dak.; ⊙ Rugby. Agr. area watered by numerous small lakes. Dairy products, poultry, grain, livestock. Formed 1887. **4** County (□ 1,680; pop. 275,876), W central Wash.; ⊙ Tacoma. Includes parts of Mt. Rainier Natl. Park and Columbia Natl. Forest; drained by White and Puyallup rivers. Rich agr. area (fruit, nuts, bulbs, truck); dairy products, timber, coal, livestock; food processing, copper and gold smelters. Formed 1852. **5** County (□ 591; pop. 21,448), W Wis.; ⊙ Ellsworth. Bounded W by St. Croix R., SW and S by the Mississippi and L. Pepin, all forming Minn. line. Generally rugged terrain, with dairying and stock raising as chief industries. Lumbering; poultry raising; some mfg. at River Falls. Formed 1853.

Pierce. 1 Town (pop. 372), Weld co., N Colo., 15 mi. N of Greeley, in irrigated sugar-beet area; alt. 5,041 ft. **2** Village (1940 pop. 1,006), Polk co., central Fla., 15 mi. S of Lakeland; phosphate mining. **3** Village (pop. 544), Clearwater co., N Idaho, 22 mi. E of Orofino; summer resort and outfitting point in elk-hunting region. **4** City (pop. 1,167), ⊙ Pierce co., NE Nebr., 13 mi. NNW of Norfolk and on branch of Elkhorn R.; grain, livestock, dairy and poultry produce, fruit. Settled 1870.

Pierce, Mount, N.H.: see PRESIDENTIAL RANGE.

Pierce Bridge, N.H.: see BETHLEHEM.

Pierce City, Mo.: see PEIRCE CITY.

Pierceton, town (pop. 973), Kosciusko co., N Ind., 30 mi. WNW of Fort Wayne, in agr. area; baby chicks; lumber. Resort lakes near by.

Pieria (pīē'rēŭ, Gr. pēē'rēŭ), anc. *Pierus* (pī'ŭrŭs), mountain in Greek Macedonia, bet. Aliakmon R. valley (W) and Katerine (Pieria) lowland, NW of Olympus; rises to 7,198 ft. 19 mi. WSW of Katerine. Sometimes called Phlambouron or Flambouron.

Piermont. 1 Town (pop. 511), Grafton co., W N.H., on the Connecticut and 26 mi. NW of Plymouth. L. Tarleton (resorts) is E. **2** Residential village (pop. 1,897), Rockland co., SE N.Y., on W bank of the Hudson and 3 mi. S of Nyack; mfg. (paperboard, silk ribbons). Pier (1 mi. long) from which village takes its name was used for debarkation of troops in Second World War. Tallman Mountain State Park is near by. Inc. 1847.

Pierpont, town (pop. 326), Day co., NE S.Dak., 18 mi. NW of Webster; livestock, dairy products, poultry, grain.

Pierre or **Pierre-de-Bresse** (pyâr-dŭ-brĕs'), village (pop. 1,269), Saône-et-Loire dept., E central France, 18 mi. SW of Dôle; poultry shipping.

Pierre (pēr), city (pop. 5,715), ⊙ S.Dak. and Hughes co., central S.Dak., 190 mi. WNW of Sioux Falls and on E bank of Missouri R., opposite Fort Pierre; 44°22'N 100°22'W; alt. 1,441 ft. Trade and distribution center for farming and ranching area; railroad shops, airport; beverages, dairy products; livestock, wheat, corn, barley. U.S. Indian school and hosp. are here. Points of interest: capitol, Memorial Hall, State Mus. Founded 1880, inc. 1883; capital since 1889.

Pierre, Bayou (bī'ō pēâr'). **1** In NW La., rises NW of Shreveport, flows c.85 mi. generally SE, through Shreveport, to Red R. c.5 mi. N of Natchitoches. NE of Mansfield, it widens into L. Cannisnia (7 mi. long) and Bayou Pierre L. (c.10 mi. long). Formerly an auxiliary channel of Red R. **2** In SW Miss., formed by forks joining in NW Copiah co., flows c.50 mi. WSW, past Port Gibson, to the Mississippi in SW Claiborne co.

Pierre-Bénite (pyâr-bānēt'), outer suburb (pop. 4,565) of Lyons, Rhône dept., E central France, near right bank of the Rhone, 4 mi. S of city center; electrochemical works.

Pierre-Buffière (–büfyâr'), village (pop. 869), Haute-Vienne dept., W central France, on Briance R. and 10 mi. SSE of Limoges; hog market; brewing. Has ruined feudal castle and a Romanesque chapel.

Pierre-de-Bresse, Saône-et-Loire dept., France: see PIERRE.

Pierrefitte-Nestalas (pyĕrfēt'-nĕstälä'), village (pop. 1,180), Hautes-Pyrénées dept., SW France, on Gave de Pau R. and 3 mi. SSE of Argelès-Gazost; has electrometallurgical (ferrosilicon) and electrochemical (fertilizer) plants. Iron mines near by.

Pierrefitte-sur-Aire (–sür-âr'), agr. village (pop. 317), Meuse dept., NE France, on the Aire and 12 mi. NE of Bar-le-Duc.

Pierrefitte-sur-Seine (–sĕn'), town (pop. 12,100), Seine dept., N central France, an outer N suburb of Paris, 8 mi. from Notre Dame Cathedral, just N of Saint-Denis; agr. machinery.

Pierrefonds (pyĕrfō'), village (pop. 1,171), Oise dept., N France, at E edge of Forest of Compiègne, 8 mi. SE of Compiègne; resort (mineral springs); pottery and sugar mfg., sawmilling, mushroom shipping. Site of monumental feudal castle, built c.1400 by Louis I of Orleans and magnificently restored by Viollet-le-Duc at expense of Napoleon III.

Pierrefontaine or **Pierrefontaine-les-Varans** (pyĕrfōtĕn'-la-värä'), village (pop. 846), Doubs dept., E France, in the central Jura; tile and cheese mfg.

Pierrefort (pyĕrfôr'), village (pop. 676), Cantal dept., S central France, on S slope of Massif du Cantal, 19 mi. E of Aurillac; cattle market; wool spinning.

Pierrelatte (pyĕrlät'), town (pop. 1,964), Drôme dept., SE France, near left bank of the Rhone, 14 mi. S of Montélimar; market; sericulture; fruit, vegetable shipping.

Pierrelaye (pyĕrlā'), town (pop. 2,647), Seine-et-Oise dept., N central France, 3 mi. SE of Pontoise; truck.

Pierrepont (pyĕrpō'), village (pop. 859), Meurthe-et-Moselle dept., NE France, 7 mi. SSW of Longwy; flour milling.

Pierrerue (pyĕrürü'), village (pop. 240), Hérault dept., S France, 13 mi. WNW of Béziers; bauxite mining.

Pierres-des-Lecq (pyâr-dā-lĕk') or **Paternosters,** group of dangerous rocks, 4 mi. NE of Grosnez Point, NW extremity of Jersey, Channel Isls.

Pierreville (pyâr'vĭl), village (pop. 1,302), S Que., on St. Francis R., near its mouth on the St. Lawrence, 15 mi. E of Sorel; lumbering, woodworking, metal stamping, pump mfg., dairying.

Pierron (pēâ'rŏn), village (pop. 371), on Bond-Madison co. line, SW central Ill., 32 mi. ENE of East St. Louis, in agr. area (corn, wheat; dairy products; poultry). Until 1939, called Millersburg.

Pierry (pyĕrē'), S suburb (pop. 1,090) of Épernay, Marne dept., N France; noted vineyards (champagne).

Pierson. 1 Town (pop. 657), Volusia co., NE Fla., near L. George, 27 mi. W of Daytona Beach. **2** Town (pop. 453), Woodbury co., W Iowa, 27 mi. E of Sioux City; livestock, grain. **3** Village (pop. 169), Montcalm co., central Mich., 26 mi. NNE of Grand Rapids, in lake and farm area.

Pierz (pērz), village (pop. 856), Morrison co., central Minn., 14 mi. E of Little Falls, in agr. area; dairy products.

Piestany (pyĕsh'tyänĭ), Slovak *Piešťany,* Hung. *Pöstyén* (pûsh'tyān), town (pop. 14,367), W Slovakia, Czechoslovakia, on isl. in Vah R., 44 mi. NE of Bratislava; local rail junction; popular health resort, with hot sulphur springs (152°F.) and sulphurous mud baths, treating mostly rheumatic diseases. Lace making, tanning. Has airport, mus., large children's sanatorium. Known as spa since 12th cent.; modern development dates from 1918.

Piesteritz (pē'stŭrĭts), town (pop. 9,419), in former Prussian Saxony prov., central Germany, after 1945 in Saxony-Anhalt, on the Elbe, just W of Wittenberg; chemical-mfg. center (nitrogen, nitrates, pharmaceuticals, plastics); mfg. of rubber products, pottery.

Piesting River (pēs'tĭng), E Lower Austria, rises on the Schneeberg, flows 38 mi. E and NE to Fischa R. SW of Ebergassing.

Pieta (pyĕtä'), Maltese *Pietà,* residential town (pop. 3,626), E Malta, on S shore of Msida Creek (inlet of Marsamuscetto Harbour), 1½ mi. W of city of Valletta.

Pietarsaari, Finland: see JAKOBSTAD.

Pieter Both, Mauritius: see MOKA RANGE.

Pietermaritzburg (pē"tŭrmä'rĭtsbûrkh), popularly called **Maritzburg,** city (pop. 60,609; including suburbs 63,333), ⊙ Natal prov., U. of So. Afr., in central part of prov., on Umsunduzi R. and 45 mi. WNW of Durban, surrounded by hills rising to c.3,000 ft. Rail center; mfg. of wattle extract, metal, rubber, and canvas products, bricks, tiles, furniture, blankets, shoes, leather. Iron mined near by. Site of Natal Univ. Col. (1909; affiliated with Univ. of South Africa), technical institute, and teachers col. Has Natal Mus. (1903), Voortrekker Mus. (1912), art gallery, Anglican and R.C. cathedrals, botanical gardens. Near by is Fort Napier, established 1843 by British garrison. City was founded 1838 by Boers from the Cape.

Pietersburg (pē'tŭrzbûrg, Afrikaans pē'tŭrsbûrkh"), town (pop. 15,620), N Transvaal, U. of So. Afr., at foot of Strydpoort Mts., near Sand R., 150 mi. NE of Pretoria; 23°54'S 29°28'E; alt. 4,269 ft.; mining center (gold, asbestos, cryolite, corundum), in rich agr. region (fruit, cattle); distributing center for N Transvaal. Seat of Native Local Council with jurisdiction of dist. (□ 5,796; total pop. 201,994; native pop. 189,229). Airport. Town named after General Piet Joubert.

Pietole (pyā'tôlē), anc. *Andes,* village (pop. 580) in Virgilio commune, Mantova prov., Lombardy, N Italy, near Mincio R., 3 mi. S of Mantua. Vergil b. here, 70 B.C.

Pietracatella (pyĕ"träkätĕl'lä), village (pop. 3,301), Campobasso prov., Abruzzi e Molise, S central Italy, 11 mi. ENE of Campobasso.

Pietragalla (pyĕträgäl'lä), village (pop. 4,906), Potenza prov., Basilicata, S Italy, 8 mi. NNE of Potenza; wine, olive oil.

Pietra Ligure (pyĕ'trä lē'gŏŏrĕ), town (pop. 2,881), Savona prov., Liguria, NW Italy, port on Gulf of Genoa and 8 mi. NNE of Albenga; shipbuilding; fishing. Marble quarries near by.

Pietramelara (pyĕträmĕlä'rä), town (pop. 2,877), Caserta prov., Campania, S Italy, 11 mi. N of Capua.

Pietra Montecorvino (pyĕ'trä môn"tĕkôrvē'nô), village (pop. 4,709), Foggia prov., Apulia, S Italy, 11 mi. WNW of Lucera; flour milling.

Pietraperzia (pyĕ"träpĕr'tsyä), town (pop. 11,886), Enna prov., S central Sicily, 6 mi. SE of Caltanissetta, in cereal- and almond-growing region. Gypsum mines near by.

Pietrasanta (pyĕ″träsän′tä), town (pop. 5,907), Lucca prov., Tuscany, central Italy, at SW foot of Apuane Alps, 10 mi. SE of Carrara; marble-quarrying and -processing center. Has cathedral (founded 1303) and ruined citadel (1324). Marina di Pietrasanta (pop. 1,796), on Ligurian Sea, 3 mi. WSW, is a bathing resort.

Pietravairano (pyĕträvīrä′nô), village (pop. 2,167), Caserta prov., Campania, S Italy, 16 mi. N of Capua; paper mill.

Pietrelcina (pyĕtrĕlchē′nä), village (pop. 2,233), Benevento prov., Campania, S Italy, 6 mi. NE of Benevento.

Piet Retief (pēt rŭtēf′), town (pop. 4,716), SE Transvaal, U. of So. Afr., near Natal and Swaziland borders, 60 mi. SE of Ermelo; alt. 4,171 ft.; agr. center (tobacco, fruit, mealies, wattles). Gold deposits in region.

Pietrosu or **Pietrosu-Rodnei** (pyātrôs′-rôdnā′), highest mountain (alt. 6,660 ft.) in the Rodna Mts., N Rumania, on Transylvania-Maramures border, 22 mi. NNE of Nasaud.

Pieux, Les (lā pyû′), village (pop. 558), Manche dept., NW France, near W coast of Cotentin Peninsula, 12 mi. SW of Cherbourg; pharmaceuticals.

Pieve a Nievole (pyā′vĕ ä nyā′vôlĕ), village (pop. 669), Pistoia prov., Tuscany, central Italy, 1 mi. E of Montecatini Terme; agr. machinery, brooms.

Pieve del Cairo (dĕl kī′rô), village (pop. 2,001), Pavia prov., Lombardy, N Italy, near Po R., 20 mi. WSW of Pavia; agr. center.

Pieve di Cadore (dē kädô′rĕ), village (pop. 789), Belluno prov., Veneto, N Italy, near Piave R., 22 mi. NNE of Belluno. Resort (alt. 2,880 ft.); mfg. (spectacles, celluloid, soap). Titian b. here.

Pieve di Cento (chĕn′tô), town (pop. 3,241), Bologna prov., Emilia-Romagna, N central Italy, on Reno R. opposite Cento; hemp mill.

Pieve di Soligo (sôlē′gô), village (pop. 2,371), Treviso prov., Veneto, N Italy, 17 mi. N of Treviso, in fruit-growing region; mfg. (wine, scales). Rebuilt after First World War.

Pieve di Teco (tā′kô), village (pop. 1,403), Imperia prov., Liguria, NW Italy, on Arroscia R. and 18 mi. NNW of Imperia, in leading cereal-growing region.

Pieve Fosciana (fôshä′nä), village (pop. 1,337), Lucca prov., Tuscany, central Italy, 2 mi. N of Castelnuovo di Garfagnana; paper mill.

Pievepelago (pyĕ″vĕpĕ′lägô), village (pop. 865), Modena prov., Emilia-Romagna, N central Italy, near Monte Cimone, 14 mi. SW of Pavullo nel Frignano; resort (alt. 2,562 ft.).

Pieve Porto Morone (pyā′vĕ pôr′tô môrô′nĕ), village (pop. 2,478), Pavia prov., Lombardy, N Italy, near Po R., 15 mi. ESE of Pavia.

Pieve Santo Stefano (sän′tô stā′fänô), town (pop. 1,354), Arezzo prov., Tuscany, central Italy, on the Tiber and 16 mi. NE of Arezzo; tannery.

Pigeon, village (pop. 1,015), Huron co., E Mich., 35 mi. NE of Bay City and on small Pigeon R.; grain, vegetables, sugar beets; dairy products.

Pigeon Cove, Mass.: see ROCKPORT.

Pigeon Creek. 1 In S Ala., formed by confluence of several headstreams E of Greenville, flows c.55 mi. SSW to Sepulga R. 13 mi. W of Andalusia. **2** In NE Ind. and S Mich., rises in extreme NE Steuben co. near Mich. line, flows SW, NW, and W, and widens into several small lakes, reaching reservoir in N Lagrange co. Issues from reservoir as Pigeon R., flows NW into Mich., thence SW into Ind., to St. Joseph R. just N of Bristol. Total length, c.65 mi.

Pigeon Island, tiny islet (c.50 acres) off S Jamaica, at entrance of Old Harbour Bay, 22 mi. SW of Kingston. Leased to U.S. in 1940.

Pigeon Island, islet (½ by ¾ mi.; alt. 334 ft.) off NW St. Lucia, B.W.I., 6 mi. NNE of Castries; 14°6′N 60°58′W. Uninhabited, but a popular picnic resort. Historic point, from whence Rodney watched movements of the Fr. fleet.

Pigeon Key, Fla.: see FLORIDA KEYS.

Pigeon Lake (18 mi. long, 1–5 mi. wide), Kawartha Lakes, S Ont., 10 mi. WNW of Peterborough; drained E by Trent Canal.

Pigeon Point, headland, SW Tobago, B.W.I., 12 mi. W of Scarborough; 11°10′N 60°50′W. Has isl.'s principal bathing beach.

Pigeon Point, coastal promontory, W Calif., 25 mi. NW of Santa Cruz; lighthouse.

Pigeon River. 1 In Ind.: see PIGEON CREEK. **2** In Minn. and Ont., rises in Mountain L., NE Minn. and W Ont., flows 49 mi. SE and E, along Can. line, to L. Superior near Grand Portage. Drains several small lakes in its course; used for logging. It was the terminus of the Grand Portage. **3** In N.C. and Tenn., rises in the Blue Ridge on Black Mtn., in Haywood co., W N.C.; flows c.100 mi. NNW, past Canton and Clyde, around E edge of Great Smoky Mts. Natl. Park, into Cocke co., E Tenn., past Newport, to French Broad R. near its mouth in Douglas Reservoir. WATERVILLE DAM is in N.C. section of river. Sometimes called Big Pigeon R.

Piggott (pĭ′gŭt), city (pop. 2,558), a ⊙ Clay co., extreme NE Ark., 28 mi. NE of Paragould, on E slope of Crowley's Ridge, in farm and orchard area. Mfg. of shoes, wood and clay products; cotton ginning; nursery.

Piggs Peak, village, N Swaziland, 25 mi. NNE of Mbabane; asbestos mine, gold.

Piglio (pē′lyô), village (pop. 3,234), Frosinone prov., Latium, S central Italy, 7 mi. SSE of Subiaco; hosiery mfg.

Pigna (pē′nyä), village (pop. 1,933), Imperia prov., Liguria, NW Italy, 11 mi. N of Bordighera, in cattle- and sheep-raising region.

Pignans (pēnyä′), village (pop. 1,373), Var dept., SE France, on NW slope of Monts des Maures, 19 mi. NE of Toulon; cork mfg., sawmilling.

Pignon (pēnyõ′), town (1950 census pop. 1,546), Nord dept., N central Haiti, in Massif du Nord, 31 mi. SSE of Cap-Haïtien; coffee, timber.

Pigüé (pēgwā′), town (pop. 5,975), ⊙ Saavedra dist. (□ 1,367; pop. 16,599), W Buenos Aires prov., Argentina, in Sierra de Puán, 75 mi. N of Bahía Blanca; grain, livestock; flour milling.

Pihani (pĭhä′nē), town (pop. 13,101), Hardoi dist., central Uttar Pradesh, India, 16 mi. NNE of Hardoi; wheat, gram, barley, pearl millet, sugar cane. Mosques and tomb of 16th-cent. Moslem leader. Formerly noted for mfg. of sword blades.

Pihij (pĭ′hĭj), town (pop. 5,028), Kaira dist., N Bombay, India, 10 mi. SE of Kaira; local market for tobacco, millet, pulse. Sometimes spelled Pij.

Pi Ho, China: see PI RIVER.

Pihsien. 1 or **P'ei-hsien** (pā′shyĕn′), town, ⊙ Pihsien co. (pop. 642,641), SW Shantung prov., China, near Kiangsu line, 45 mi. ENE of Süchow; wheat, kaoliang, hemp. Called Peichow until 1912. Until 1949 in Kiangsu prov. **2** or **P'i-hsien** (pē′shyĕn′), town (pop. 16,882), ⊙ Pihsien co. (pop. 178,366), W Szechwan prov., China, 10 mi. NW of Chengtu, on Chengtu plain; winegrowing; rice, wheat, rapeseed, sugar cane, sweet potatoes.

Pihuamo (pēwä′mō), town (pop. 2,107), Jalisco, W Mexico, 23 mi. E of Colima; corn, sugar cane, chick-peas, fruit.

Pijao (pēhou′), town (pop. 1,807), Caldas dept., W central Colombia, in Cordillera Central, 12 mi. S of Armenia; alt. 7,323 ft.; corn, rice, sugar cane, bananas.

Pijijiápam (pēhēhyä′päm), town (pop. 2,125), Chiapas, S Mexico, in Pacific lowland, on railroad and 45 mi. SE of Tonalá; cacao, sugar cane, tobacco, fruit, stock.

Pijnacker or **Pijnakker** (both: pī′näkûr), town (pop. 3,869), South Holland prov., W Netherlands, 4 mi. E of Delft; market center for vegetable-growing area; mfg. (welding and cutting apparatus). Sometimes spelled Pynacker or Pynakker.

Pikalevo (pē′kŭlyĭvŭ), town (1947 pop. over 500), SE Leningrad oblast, Russian SFSR, 19 mi. ESE of Tikhvin; cement mfg.

Pike. 1 County (□ 673; pop. 30,608), SE Ala.; ⊙ Troy. Coastal plain drained by Conecuh R., Pea R., and Patsaliga Creek. Cotton, peanuts, poultry. Formed 1821. **2** County (□ 615; pop. 10,032), SW Ark.; ⊙ Murfreesboro. Bounded S by Little Missouri R.; drained by Antoine Creek. Agr. (peaches, strawberries, cotton, truck, livestock). Manganese and quicksilver mines; diamond mines (now inactive); gypsum quarries; lumbering. Formed 1833. **3** County (□ 230; pop. 8,459), W central Ga.; ⊙ Zebulon. Bounded W by Flint R. Piedmont agr. (cotton, peaches, truck) and timber area; food canning, sawmilling. Formed 1822. **4** County (□ 829; pop. 22,155), W Ill.; ⊙ Pittsfield. Bounded W and SW by Mississippi R. and E by Illinois R.; drained by small Bay and McCraney creeks. Agr. (corn, wheat, hay, apples, livestock, poultry); timber. Some mfg. (flour, cheese and other dairy products, shoes, costume jewelry, marble and granite products). Formed 1821. **5** County (□ 335; pop. 14,995), SW Ind.; ⊙ Petersburg. Bounded N by White R. and its East Fork; drained by Patoka R. Bituminous-coal mines, oil wells, clay pits; timber; agr. (grain, tobacco); mfg. of concrete blocks and wood products, flour and lumber milling; nursery stock. Formed 1816. **6** County (□ 786; pop. 81,154), E Ky.; ⊙ Pikeville. In the Cumberlands; bounded NE by Tug Fork (W.Va. line), SE by Va. line; drained by Levisa and Russell forks. Mtn. coal-mining region; co. ranks 2d in Ky. in coal production. Agr. (dairy products, poultry, cattle, apples, Irish and sweet potatoes, soybeans for hay, corn, tobacco); some timber; some mfg. at Pikeville. Includes Breaks of Sandy and part of Pine Mtn. Formed 1821. **7** County (□ 410; pop. 35,137), SW Miss.; ⊙ Magnolia. Bordered S by La.; drained by the Bogue Chitto and Tangipahoa R. Agr. (cotton, corn, truck), dairying; lumbering. Formed 1815. **8** County (□ 681; pop. 16,844), E Mo.; ⊙ Bowling Green. Bounded E by Mississippi R.; crossed by Salt R. Agr. (wheat, corn, oats, soybeans, fruit, especially apples), livestock; limestone; mfg. at Bowling Green and Louisiana. Formed 1818. **9** County (□ 443; pop. 14,607), S Ohio; ⊙ Waverly. Intersected by Scioto R. and small Sunfish and Beaver creeks. Includes Lake White State Park (resort). Agr. area (livestock, grain, poultry); hardwood timber; sawmilling. Formed 1815. **10** County (□ 545; pop. 8,425), NE Pa.; ⊙ Milford. Forested lake region, bounded E by Delaware R. Textile mfg.; timber; recreational area. Formed 1814.

Pike. 1 or **Pike City**, town (pop. 123), Pike co., SW Ark., 30 mi. W of Arkadelphia. **2** Village, N.H.: see HAVERHILL. **3** Village (pop. 286), Wyoming co., W N.Y., 17 mi. S of Warsaw, and on small Wiscoy Creek, in agr. area; cheese, butter, canned foods; timber.

Pike, Fort, SE La., old U.S. fortification built in early-19th cent., on bank of Rigolets pass, 30 mi. ENE of New Orleans. Surrounded by state park; partly restored.

Pike City, Ark.: see PIKE.

Pikelot (pē′kĕlŏt), uninhabited coral island, Yap dist., W Caroline Isls., W Pacific, c.50 mi. E of W. Fayu; 2.5 mi. long, 1.75 mi. wide.

Pike o' Stickle, England: see LANGDALE PIKES.

Pikes Peak (14,110 ft.), central Colo., in S part of FRONT RANGE of Rocky Mts., 60 mi. S of Denver and 10 mi. W of Colorado Springs. Exceeded in alt. by many other peaks in Colo., but conspicuous because it is isolated from other peaks and located on edge of Great Plains. Cog railroad ascends mtn. from Manitou Springs; automobile race to summit takes place annually on Pikes Peak Highway. Summit House is observation point at top of mtn., a level, stony area often covered with snow. Named for Lt. Zebulon Pike, by whom it was discovered in 1806.

Pikesville, suburban village (pop. c.3,500), Baltimore co., central Md., 8 mi. NW of downtown Baltimore; woodworking. Mt. Wilson state tuberculosis sanatorium is near by.

Piketberg, U. of So. Afr.: see PIQUETBERG.

Piketon, village (pop. 768), Pike co., S Ohio, on Scioto R. and 18 mi. S of Chillicothe; grain products, lumber.

Pikeville. 1 Town (pop. 5,154), ⊙ Pike co., E Ky., in the Cumberlands, on Levisa Fork and 18 mi. SW of Williamson, W.Va.; trade and shipping center for bituminous-coal-mining and timber region; mfg. of cement blocks, beverages, packed meat, food products; lumber mills; airport. Jr. col. here. **2** Town (pop. 464), Wayne co., E central N.C., 7 mi. N of Goldsboro. **3** Town (pop. 882), ⊙ Bledsoe co., central Tenn., on Sequatchie R. and 40 mi. NNE of Chattanooga, in timber and farm region; hosiery, wood products, cheese, flour.

Pikhtovka (pēkh′tŭfkŭ), village (1926 pop. 600), NE Novosibirsk oblast, Russian SFSR, 65 mi. N of Novosibirsk.

Pikiang or **Pi-chiang** (both: bē′jyäng′), village (pop. 233), ⊙ Pikiang dist. (pop. 14,903), NW Yunnan prov., China, 85 mi. N of Paoshan, and on Mekong R., in mtn. region; timber, rice, millet. Until 1934 called Yingpankai.

Pikmiktalik (pĭkmĭtä′lĭk), Eskimo village (1939 pop. 14), W Alaska, near Pastol Bay, 22 mi. SW of St. Michael; fishing, trapping.

Pila (pē′lä), town (pop. estimate 1,000), ⊙ Pila dist. (□ 1,333; pop. 3,995), E Buenos Aires prov., Argentina, 34 mi. NW of Dolores, in agr. region (corn, flax, livestock); dairying.

Pila, town (1939 pop. 2,372; 1948 municipality pop. 13,606), Laguna prov., S Luzon, Philippines, near Laguna de Bay, 12 mi. NNE of San Pablo; agr. center (rice, coconuts, sugar cane).

Pila, Poland: see SCHNEIDEMÜHL.

Pilagá, Argentina: see LAGUNA BLANCA, Formosa natl. territory.

Pilaia, Greece: see PYLAIA.

Pilamedu, India: see PEELAMEDU.

Pilancones (pēlängkō′nĕs), village (pop. 200), Cajamarca dept., NW Peru, in Cordillera Occidental, 2 mi. NW of Hualgayoc; hydroelectric plant.

Pilani (pĭl′ŭnē), village, NE Rajasthan, India, 20 mi. NNE of Jhunjhunu. Engineering col.; Association Montessori Internationale (founded 1940).

Pilão Arcado (pēlã′ō ärkä′dō͝o), city (pop. 1,026), NW Bahia, Brazil, on left bank of São Francisco R. (navigable) and 80 mi. NE of Barra; saltworks; livestock, manioc.

Pilar (pēlär′). **1** Town (pop. 4,923), ⊙ Pilar dist. (□ 214; pop. 21,674), NE Buenos Aires prov., Argentina, 30 mi. WNW of Buenos Aires; rail junction; corn, flax, cattle. **2** Town (pop. 2,568), central Córdoba prov., Argentina, on the Río Segundo and 22 mi. SE of Córdoba; rail junction and agr. center (cereals, peanuts, pears, figs). Natl. magnetic observatory here. **3** Town (pop. estimate 1,500), central Santa Fe prov., Argentina, 35 mi. WNW of Santa Fe; rail junction; agr. (wheat, corn, flax, livestock) and processing center (flax-fiber factory, dairy industry).

Pilar. 1 City (pop. 5,734), E Alagoas, NE Brazil, at N end of Manguaba Lagoon, 12 mi. NE of Maceió, in sugar- and cotton-growing region; sugar refining, textile milling, cigar mfg. Called Manguaba, 1944–48. **2** Town, Goiás, Brazil: see ITACÉ. **3** City (pop. 1,418), E Paraíba, NE Brazil, on railroad and 28 mi. WSW of João Pessoa; cotton, sugar, fruit, agave fibers. Founded 1670 by Jesuits. **4** City, São Paulo, Brazil: see PILAR DO SUL.

Pilar or **Central Pilar** (sĕnträl′), sugar-mill village (pop. 1,204), Camagüey prov., E Cuba, 15 mi. ESE of Ciego de Ávila.

Pilar, city (dist. pop. 10,282), ⊙ Ñeembucú dept., S Paraguay, port on Paraguay R. (Argentina border) opposite Bermejo R. mouth, and 115 mi. SSW of Asunción; 26°50′S 58°22′W. Commercial, processing, and agr. center (cotton, sugar cane, corn, oranges, onions). Outlet for fertile S Paraguayan hinterland, trading also in hides and timber. Cotton gins, lumber mills, textile mills, distilleries. Docks. Founded 1778 as Ñeembucú.

Pilar. **1** Town (1939 pop. 3,721; 1948 municipality pop. 5,805), Bataan prov., S Luzon, Philippines, on E Bataan Peninsula, 29 mi. W of Manila; agr. center (sugar cane, rice). **2** Town (1939 pop. 1,404; 1948 municipality pop. 25,720), Capiz prov., NE Panay isl., Philippines, on small inlet of Jintotolo Channel, 18 mi. ESE of Capiz; sugar milling. Chrysocolla is mined. **3** Municipality, Cebu prov., Philippines: see PONSON ISLAND. **4** Town (1939 pop. 2,304; 1948 municipality pop. 25,600), Sorsogon prov., extreme SE Luzon, Philippines, on small inlet of Burias Pass, 15 mi. SSW of Legaspi; agr. center (abacá, coconuts, rice).

Pilar, Cape, Chile: see PILLAR, CAPE.

Pilar, El, Venezuela: see EL PILAR.

Pilar do Sul (pēlär' dŏŏ sōōl'), city (pop. 809), S São Paulo, Brazil, 25 mi. SW of Sorocaba; sawmilling; grain, cotton, cattle. Until 1944, Pilar.

Pilas (pē'läs), town (pop. 6,111), Seville prov., SW Spain, near Huelva prov. border, 18 mi. WSW of Seville; agr. center (olives, cereals, grapes processed here); mfg. of boilers, baskets, soap.

Pilas, Las, volcano, Nicaragua: see LAS PILAS.

Pilas Islands, small group (1939 pop. 1,016), Zamboanga prov., Philippines, off SW tip of Mindanao, just W of Basilan Isl.; Pilas Isl. (□ 9.6) is largest.

Pilat, Mont (mō pēlä'), mountain of Massif Central, SE central France, at N end of Monts du Vivarais in SE Loire dept. Rises to c.4,700 ft. Long the site of artisan silk weaving, it has now become a winter-sports resort (ski lifts).

Pilate (pēlät'), town (1950 census pop. 1,280), Nord dept., N Haiti, in the Massif du Nord, on Les Trois Rivières and 23 mi. WSW of Cap-Haïtien; coffee, tropical fruit.

Pilatus (pēlä'tōōs), mountain in the Alps of the Four Forest Cantons, central Switzerland, 5–7 mi. SSW of Lucerne; ascended by rack-and-pinion railway passing through several tunnels. Main peak, Esel (6,965 ft.); highest peak, Tomlishorn (6,994 ft.). Known until 15th cent. as the Frakmunt or Frackmünd. According to medieval legend, the corpse of Pontius Pilate was received by a small lake on the mtn., after the Tiber and the Rhone had rejected it.

Pilav Dagh, Greece: see PANGAION.

Pilaya River (pēlī'ä), S Bolivia; formed just below Villa Abecia by confluence of San Juan and Cotagaita rivers; flows 120 mi. E to Pilcomayo R. 12 mi. E of El Palmar. Forms Tarija-Chuquisaca border in lower course. Also called Camblaya R. in upper course.

Pilbara Goldfield (pĭlbä'rŭ) (□ 32,000), N Western Australia; mining center is Marble Bar. Gold discovered here 1888; area placed (1889) under govt. control and leased to mining interests.

Pilcaniyeu (pēlkänē-ĕ'ōō), village (pop. estimate 500), ⊙ Pilcaniyeu dept., SW Río Negro natl. territory, Argentina, on railroad and 35 mi. E of San Carlos de Bariloche; resort and stock-raising center (sheep, goats, cattle).

Pilcante (pēlkän'tē), village (pop. 603), Trento prov., Trentino–Alto Adige, N Italy, on Adige R. opposite Ala and 9 mi. SSW of Rovereto; alcohol distillery.

Pilcaya (pēlkī'ä), town (pop. 1,820), Guerrero, SW Mexico, on S slope of central plateau, on Mexico state border, 13 mi. NNW of Taxco; cereals, sugar cane, coffee, fruit.

Pilchowice (pēl-chôvē'tsĕ), Ger. *Mauer* (mou'ŭr), village in Lower Silesia, after 1945 in Wroclaw prov., SW Poland, 6 mi. NW of Hirschberg (Jelenia Gora) and on Bobrawa R. (reservoir).

Pilcomayo, department, Argentina: see CLORINDA.

Pilcomayo, village, Argentina: see PUERTO PILCOMAYO.

Pilcomayo River (pēlkōmī'ō), chief right affluent of Paraguay R., in S central South America; over 700 mi. long. Rises at c.13,000 ft. in the Cordillera de los Frailes (E Andes) of Bolivia NNE of Río Mulato, flows SE through the Chaco, past Yocalla and Villa Montes, to Paraguay R. at Puerto Pilcomayo, just S of Asunción. Receives Pilaya R. (right) in Bolivia. Its lower, braided, shifting course (410 mi.) forms Paraguay-Argentina border, which, though fixed 1876, was not delimited until 1945 in the swampy Estero PATIÑO area. Shallow-draught navigation in lower course.

Pile Bay, village (pop. 48), SW Alaska, on E shore of Iliamna L.; 59°43'N 154°4'W.

Pileh Savar, Iran: see BELYASUVAR.

Piles (pē'lĕs), village (pop. 1,709), Valencia prov., E Spain, near the Mediterranean, 2 mi. SE of Gandía; corn and truck produce; sheep and cattle raising; orange shipping. Bathing beaches.

Pilesavar, Iran: see BELYASUVAR.

Pilger (pĭl'gŭr), village (pop. 512), Stanton co., NE Nebr., 10 mi. ENE of Stanton and on Elkhorn R., in hog-raising area; dairy, poultry produce, grain.

Pilgram, Czechoslovakia: see PELHRIMOV.

Pilgrim Springs, village (1939 pop. 60), NW Alaska, on Seward Peninsula, 45 mi. NNE of Nome; supply point for placer gold-mining dist. Air strip.

Pilgrims Rest, Afrikaans *Pelgrimsrus* (pĕl"khrĭmsrŭs'), village (pop. 747), E Transvaal, U. of So. Afr., on Blyde R. and 25 mi. ENE of Lydenburg; gold-mining center in important field discovered 1869.

Pili, Greece: see PYLI.

Pili (pē'lē), town (1939 pop. 2,039; 1948 municipality pop. 25,300), Camarines Sur prov., SE Luzon, Philippines, on railroad and 8 mi. SE of Naga; agr. center (rice, abacá, corn).

Pilibhit (pē'lēbēt), district (□ 1,353; pop. 490,718), Rohilkhand div., N Uttar Pradesh, India; ⊙ Pilibhit. On W Ganges Plain; irrigated by branches of Sarda Canal. Agr. (rice, wheat, gram, sugar cane, oilseeds, pearl millet, barley, jowar); sal (N) and dhak (S) forests. A major Indian sugar-processing dist. Main towns: Pilibhit, Bisalpur, Neoria Husainpur.

Pilibhit, town (pop. 44,709), ⊙ Pilibhit dist., N Uttar Pradesh, India, on tributary of the Ramganga and 30 mi. NE of Bareilly; sugar processing; trade depot for Nepal goods; trades in rice, wheat, gram, sugar cane, oilseeds. Large 18th-cent. mosque. Residence of 18th-cent. Rohilla leader.

Pilica River (pēlē'tsä), Rus. *Pilitsa* (pyĭlē'tsŭ), E central Poland, rises 7 mi. NW of Wolbrom, flows N past Szczekociny, Przedborz, Sulejow, and Tomaszow Mazowiecki, and ENE past Nowe Miasto and Warka to Vistula R. 19 mi. S of Warsaw; 195 mi. long.

Pilion, Greece: see PELION.

Pilis (pĭ'lĭsh), town (pop. 7,384), Pest-Pilis-Solt-Kiskun co., N central Hungary, 14 mi. NW of Cegled; flour mills. Ger. pop. near by; grain, potatoes, dairy farming.

Pilis Mountains (pĭ'lĭsh), N central Hungary, extend 19 mi. bet. Szentendre and Esztergom along the Danube, rising to 2,483 ft. at Mt. Pilis. Forested slopes; limestone quarries.

Pilisvörösvar (pĭ'lĭsh-vûr"ûsh-vär), Hung. *Pilisvörösvár*, town (pop. 8,392), Pest-Pilis-Solt-Kiskun co., N central Hungary, in Buda Mts., 11 mi. NNW of Budapest; Slovak pop. Lignite mine near.

Pilitsa River, Poland: see PILICA RIVER.

Pilkhana (pĭl'kŭnŭ), town (pop. 4,041), Aligarh dist., W Uttar Pradesh, India, 12 mi. ESE of Aligarh; wheat, barley, pearl millet, gram, cotton.

Pilkhua (pĭlk'wŭ), town (pop. 8,520), Meerut dist., NW Uttar Pradesh, India, 19 mi. S of Meerut; cotton weaving; trades in wheat, millet, sugar cane, oilseeds, leather.

Pillager (pĭ'lŭjŭr), village (pop. 362), Cass co., central Minn., on Crow Wing R., in state forest, and 13 mi. W of Brainerd; dairy products, lumber. Gull L. near by.

Pillahuincó, Sierra (syĕ'rä pĭyäwēngkō'), hill range (c.2,500 ft.) in S Buenos Aires prov., Argentina, SW of Coronel Pringles; extends c.30 mi. on right bank of Sauce Grande R.

Pillanlelbún (pĭyänlĕlbōōn'), village (1930 pop. 995), Cautín prov., S central Chile, on railroad, on Cautín R. and 12 mi. NE of Temuco; agr. (wheat, oats, potatoes, livestock).

Pillao (pĭyou'), town (pop. 1,189), Pasco dept., central Peru, in Cordillera Central of the Andes, 26 mi. NW of Cerro de Pasco; grain, livestock.

Pillar, Cape, or **Cape Pilar** (pēlär'), on NW Desolation Isl., Tierra del Fuego, Chile, on the Pacific at W entrance to Strait of Magellan; 52°42'S 74°41'W.

Pillar, Cape, Tasmania: see TASMAN PENINSULA.

Pillar Mountain (2,927 ft.), in the Cumbrians, S Cumberland, England, 13 mi. ESE of Whitehaven.

Pillaro (pē'yärō), town (1950 pop. 2,814), Tungurahua prov., Ecuador, in the Andes, 8 mi. NE of Ambato; agr. center (cereals, potatoes, fruit). Heavily damaged by 1949 earthquake.

Pillar Point, Calif.: see HALF MOON BAY.

Pillars of Hercules, 2 headlands flanking E entrance of Strait of Gibraltar. They are usually identified with Gibraltar (anc. *Calpe*) in Europe and with Mt. Acho (anc. *Abyla*) on narrow peninsula E of Ceuta, near Point Almina. The Jebel Musa (just W of Ceuta) is also often considered as one of the pillars, marking the end of the known world.

Pillau, Russian SFSR: see BALTISK.

Pilley's Island (□ 17; pop. 469), E N.F., in Notre Dame Bay, 40 mi. W of Twillingate; 6 mi. long, 4 mi. wide; 49°32'N 55°43'W. Fishing.

Pilling, village and parish (pop. 1,444), W Lancashire, England, near Lancaster Bay 4 mi. E of Fleetwood; dairy farming, wheat, potato, and barley growing.

Pillkallen, Russian SFSR: see DOBROVOLSK.

Pillnitz (pĭl'nĭts), village (pop. 1,597), Saxony, E central Germany, on the Elbe and 7 mi. ESE of Dresden; mfg. (cameras, photographic equipment, mirrors). Summer palace (18th cent.) of former kings of Saxony was scene of treaty (1791) defining Prussian and Austrian attitude toward French Revolution.

Pillon, Col du (kôl dü pēyō'), pass (5,085 ft.) in the Bernese Alps, SW Switzerland, 2 mi. N of the Oldenhorn; leads from SW Bern canton to Vaud canton.

Pillow, Pa.: see UNIONTOWN, Dauphin co.

Pillsbury, village (pop. 119), Barnes co., E central N.Dak., 22 mi. NNE of Valley City.

Pillsbury, Lake, NW Calif., in a valley of the Coast Ranges, 25 mi. N of Lakeport; c.5 mi. long; fishing. Entered and drained by Eel R.

Pillsbury Sound, Caribbean channel (2½ mi. wide) bet. St. Thomas Isl. (W) and St. John Isl. (E), U.S. Virgin Isls. Good navigability; adjoined by fine harbors.

Pilltown or **Piltown,** Gaelic *Baile an Phuill*, town (pop. 234), S Co. Kilkenny, Ireland, 4 mi. E of Carrick-on-Suir; agr. market (cattle; barley, potatoes).

Pillupönen, Russian SFSR: see NEVSKOYE.

Pilmaiquén (pēlmīkĕn'), village (1930 pop. 21), Osorno prov., S central Chile, in Chilean lake dist., 30 mi. ESE of Osorno, near W bank of L. Puyehue. Site of waterfalls on Pilmaiquén R., several cascades 100 ft. high; noted tourist attraction. Hydroelectric plant.

Pilna or **Pil'na** (pēl'nŭ), village (1926 pop. 4,192), SE Gorki oblast, Russian SFSR, on Pyana R. and 17 mi. E of Sergach; wheat, hemp.

Pilões, Serra dos (sĕ'rŭ dŏŏs pēlō'ĭs), mountain range of central Brazil, extends c.70 mi. N–S along Goiás–Minas Gerais border bet. 17° and 18°S lat.; rises to c.3,300 ft. Rutile deposits.

Pilos, Greece: see PYLOS.

Pilot Grove, city (pop. 635), Cooper co., central Mo., near Missouri R., 12 mi. SW of Boonville; agr.

Pilot Knob, town (pop. 582), Iron co., SE central Mo., just NNW of Ironton. Civil War battle of Pilot Knob, fought Sept. 27, 1864, resulted in reverse for Confederates under Sterling Price.

Pilot Mound, village (pop. 479), S Man., in Pembina Mts., 60 mi. SW of Portage la Prairie; grain elevators.

Pilot Mound, town (pop. 246), Boone co., central Iowa, near Des Moines R., 10 mi. NW of Boone. State park near by.

Pilot Mountain, town (pop. 1,092), Surry co., NW N.C., 23 mi. NNW of Winston-Salem; hosiery mfg. Just S is Pilot Mtn. (2,415 ft.).

Pilot Point, village (pop. 70), SW Alaska, on Alaska Peninsula, on Ugashik Bay, E arm (10 mi. long) of Bristol Bay, 45 mi. S of Egegik; 57°34'N 157°35'W; supply point for trappers; fishing (cannery at Ugashik, 6 mi. E).

Pilot Point, town (pop. 1,176), Denton co., N Texas, c.45 mi. NNW of Dallas; trade, shipping point in agr. area (cotton, grain, peanuts); oil wells. Settled 1835, inc. 1906.

Pilot Rock, city (pop. 847), Umatilla co., NE Oregon, 13 mi. S of Pendleton; wheat.

Pilot Station, village (pop. 52), W Alaska, on lower Yukon R. and 90 mi. NW of Bethel; supply base for trappers and prospectors. School.

Pilottown, village, Plaquemines parish, extreme SE La., 6.75 mi. SE of New Orleans and on E bank of the Mississippi, in the delta just above Head of the Passes (head of river's distributaries); hq. for river and bar pilots. Hunting, fur trapping, fishing near by.

Pilot Village, village, W Alaska, on Yukon R. and 90 mi. NNW of Bethel; supply point.

Pilsen (pĭl'sŭn, –zŭn, Ger. pĭl'zŭn), Czech *Plzeň* (pŭl'zĕnyŭ), city (pop. 103,767), ⊙ Plzen prov. (□ 3,045; pop. 549,913), W Bohemia, Czechoslovakia, in a fertile valley, at meeting point of Mze, Radbuza, Uhlava, and Uslava rivers, 50 mi. WSW of Prague; 49°45'N 13°22'E. Rail junction; industrial center; noted for its beer, exported throughout the world, and for its huge Skoda metallurgical works (now nationalized), based on local hard-coal and iron deposits and producing armaments, aircraft, locomotives, automobiles, machinery; mfg. of clothing, ceramics, chemicals, hardware, paper. Has medical school, trade schools, radio station. Though largely a modern city, Pilsen has 15th-cent. Gothic church with spire, 3-storied Renaissance town hall, baroque St. Anne church, and 18th-cent. Franciscan convent. One of earliest printing presses, 1st in Bohemia, established here in 1476. Pilsen remained a center of Catholicism throughout Hussite wars, sustaining long sieges. Its modern development dates from early-20th cent. In Second World War, taken by U.S. troops in May, 1945.

Pilsen, Poland: see PILZNO.

Pilshum, Cerro (sĕ'rō pēlshōōm'), Andean mountain in Cañar prov., S central Ecuador, 11 mi. E of Tambo; 2°33'S 78°45'W; rich gold and silver deposits. Sometimes spelled Pillzhum.

Pilsley, town and parish (pop. 2,821), NE Derby, England, 6 mi. SSE of Chesterfield; coal mining.

Pilsting (pĭl'stĭng), village (pop. 1,604), Lower Bavaria, Germany, 13 mi. SSE of Straubing; grain, livestock.

Piltdown or **Pilt Down,** locality, Sussex, England, 2 mi. NW of Uckfield; parts of skull and jawbone of so-called Piltdown man (*Eoanthropus dawsoni*) found here 1911–12 by Dawson and Smith-Woodward.

Piltene (pēl'tĕnä), Ger. *Pilten* (pĭl'tŭn), city (pop. 737), NW Latvia, in Kurzeme, on Venta R. and 12 mi. SSE of Ventspils; flour mill. Has ruins of castle. Seat (1561–1795) of semi-independent Piltene state.

Pilteng, Lake, Manchuria: see KINGPO LAKE.

Piltown, Ireland: see PILLTOWN.

Pilu, Nam (năm pēlōō'), Burmese *Balu Chaung* (bŭlōō' choung), river in Southern Shan State, Upper Burma, rises in Inle L., flows c.85 mi. SE in deep valley to the Nam Pawn.

Pilzno (pĭlz'nô), town (pop. 2,920), Rzeszow prov., SE Poland, on Wisloka R. and 32 mi. W of Rzeszow; mfg. of cement ware, flour milling; brickworks. In Second World War, under Ger. rule, called Pilsen.

Pima (pē'mŭ), county (□ 9,241; pop. 141,216), S Ariz.; ⊙ Tucson. Mtn. area bordering on Mexico. Santa Catalina Mts. in NE, Growler Mts. in W, Baboquivari Mts. SW of Tucson. Saguaro Natl. Monument is E of Tucson; Organ Pipe Cactus Natl. Monument and Papago Indian Reservation are in W. Irrigated farming (cotton, alfalfa, citrus fruit, truck) along Santa Cruz R. (E); copper, gold, silver, lead mines near Ajo (NW); health resorts around Tucson. Formed 1864.

Pima, town (pop. 824), Graham co., SE Ariz., on Gila R. and 8 mi. NW of Safford; agr. trade center.

Pimba, settlement, central South Australia, 105 mi. NW of Port Augusta, on transcontinental railroad, in arid area.

Pimentel (pēmĕntĕl'), town (1950 pop. 3,313), Duarte prov., E central Dominican Republic, in fertile La Vega Real valley, on railroad and 13 mi. SE of San Francisco de Macorís; cacao growing.

Pimentel, town (pop. 4,125), Lambayeque dept., NW Peru, port on the Pacific, and 7 mi. WSW of Chiclayo. Railhead. Shipping point for sugar, rice, cotton, hides; weaving of native textiles; fisheries. Summer resort for Chiclayo.

Pimienta (pēmyĕn'tä), city (pop. 1,228), Cortés dept., NW Honduras, in Sula Valley, on Ulúa R. (head of shallow-draught navigation) and 16 mi. S of San Pedro Sula, on railroad (bridged). Commercial center in banana zone. Partly destroyed by flood (1935); rebuilt a short distance upstream.

Pim Island (8 mi. long, 4 mi. wide), NE Franklin Dist., Northwest Territories, in Smith Sound, off Cape Sabine, E Ellesmere Isl.; 78°44'N 74°40'W. Donald MacMillan here erected (1924) memorial tablet to members of Greely expedition who died at Cape Sabine, 1884.

Pimlico (pĭm'lĭkō), district of Westminster, London, England, on N bank of the Thames, 1.5 mi. SW of Charing Cross. Residential area, with commercial and industrial quarter along the river, it contains Buckingham Palace and Victoria Station, principal railroad terminal for S England and the Continent.

Pimlico Race Track, Md.: see BALTIMORE.

Pimville, residential town (pop. 16,623), S Transvaal, U. of So. Afr., on Witwatersrand; WSW suburb of Johannesburg. Entire pop. consists of native mineworkers.

Pina (pē'nä), town (pop. 1,919), Saragossa prov., NE Spain, on the Ebro and 22 mi. SE of Saragossa; sugar beets, cereals, licorice.

Pinahat (pĭnä'hŭt), town (pop. 4,441), Agra dist., W Uttar Pradesh, India, near Chambal R., 31 mi. SE of Agra; pearl millet, gram, wheat, barley, oilseeds. Also spelled Pinhat.

Pinal (pēnăl'), county (□ 5,378; pop. 43,191), S central Ariz.; ⊙ Florence. Plateau and mesa region. San Carlos Reservoir (in NE) holds water from Gila and San Carlos rivers for irrigation. Co. includes Maricopa Indian Reservation in W and parts of Papago and Gila River Indian reservations in the SW and W, respectively. Casa Grande Natl. Monument is near Florence. Copper mining and processing at Ray and Superior. Cotton, alfalfa, citrus fruits, truck products, figs; cotton ginning. Formed 1875.

Pinal de Amoles, Mexico: see AMOLES.

Pinaleno Mountains (pēnălăn'yō), SE Ariz., range (40 mi. long, 8 mi. wide) in Graham co., SW of Safford, in part of Crook Natl. Forest. Chief peaks: Merrill Peak (9,285 ft.), HAWK PEAK (10,600 ft.), and Mt. GRAHAM (10,713 ft.; highest).

Pinal Mountains (pēnăl'), in section of Crook Natl. Forest, SE central Ariz., bet. Gila and Salt rivers; rise to 7,850 ft. in Pinal Peak, 8 mi. S of Globe.

Pinamalayan (pēnämälä'yän), town (1939 pop. 2,103; 1948 municipality pop. 21,756), on E coast of Mindoro isl., Philippines, 33 mi. SE of Calapan; agr. center (rice, copra).

Pinamungajan (pēnämōōng-gä'hän), town (1939 pop. 2,373; 1948 municipality pop. 20,364), central Cebu isl., Philippines, on Tañon Strait, 21 mi. W of Cebu city; agr. center (corn, coconuts).

Pinan, Formosa: see TAITUNG.

Pinar (pēnär'), mountain (5,426 ft.), Cádiz prov., SW Spain, in NW spur of the Cordillera Penibética, 2 mi. W of Grazalema.

Pinarbasi (pŭnär'bä-shŭ), Turkish *Pınarbaşı*, village (pop. 2,942), Kayseri prov., central Turkey, on Yenice R. and 50 mi. E of Kayseri; wheat, barley. Formerly Aziziye.

Pinar del Río (pēnär' dĕl rē'ō), province (□ 5,212; pop. 398,794), W Cuba; ⊙ Pinar del Río. Occupying westernmost section of the isl., it borders E on Havana prov.; in W, Cape San Antonio (Guanahacabibes Peninsula) is on Yucatan Channel. N coast is fringed by numerous coral keys, the Los Colorados archipelago. Along S coast stretches marshland. Its rolling, calcareous plain is crossed SW–NE by low ranges (Sierra de los Órganos, Sierra del Rosario) rising in the Pan de Guajaibón to 2,533 ft. On the slopes—the noted Vuelta Abajo region—some of the world's best tobacco is grown; coffee in W hills; sugar cane, bananas, pineapples, and citrus fruit in lowland. The prov. is rich in timber and in mineral deposits such as iron, lead, manganese, coal, asphalt, and petroleum, but only copper (Matahambre) is of economic importance. Sulphurous springs at San Diego de los Baños and San Vicente. Main industries: tobacco processing (San Juan y Martínez, Pinar del Río), sugar milling, lumbering, stock raising, fishing (also sponge, lobsters), fish canning. Prov. is traversed by the Central Highway, terminating at Pinar del Río city, the chief trading center.

Pinar del Río, city (pop. 26,241), ⊙ Pinar del Río prov., W Cuba, on railroad and 100 mi. SW of Havana; 22°25'N 83°42'W. Terminus of Central Highway and center of rich Vuelta Abajo tobacco-growing region. Mfg. of cigars, cigarettes, furniture, pharmaceuticals.

Pinarejo (pēnärā'hō), town (pop. 1,230), Cuenca prov., E central Spain, 35 mi. SSW of Cuenca; cereals, grapes, olives, livestock.

Pina River (pē'nŭ), in Pripet Marshes, W Belorussian SSR, part of Dnieper-Bug waterway bet. Dnieper-Bug Canal (W) and the Pripet (here called Strumen; E); 54 mi. long. Lower course flows ENE, past Pinsk, beyond confluence with the Pripet to Yaselda R. at Gorodishche.

Piñas (pē'nyäs), town (1950 pop. 2,126), El Oro prov., S Ecuador, in Andean foothills, 37 mi. SE of Machala; agr. center (cacao, coffee, cereals, stock).

Pin-au-Haras, Le (lü pē-ō-ärä'), commune (pop. 540), Orne dept., NW France, 7 mi. E of Argentan; stud farm.

Pinawa (pĭnä'wŭ), village, SE Man., on Pinawa Channel, branch of Winnipeg R., bet. Natalie L. and Lac du Bonnet, 60 mi. ENE of Winnipeg; hydroelectric power.

Pinced, Yugoslavia: see PIVNICE.

Pincehely (pĭn'tsĕhĕĭ), town (pop. 3,958), Tolna co., W central Hungary, on Kapos Canal and 26 mi. NNW of Szekszard; wine.

Pincher Creek, town (pop. 1,148), SW Alta., on Pincher Creek and 50 mi. WSW of Lethbridge; coal mining, lumbering, cattle raising.

Pinchi Lake (pĭn'chē) (□ 17), central B.C., just NE of Stuart L., 40 mi. NNW of Vanderhoof; 14 mi. long, 2 mi. wide. Drains S into Stuart L. Mercury mining on NE shore.

Pinchov, Poland: see PINCZOW.

Pinchow. 1 Town, Kwangsi prov., China: see PINYANG. **2** Town, Shantung prov., China: see PINHSIEN. **3** Town, Shensi prov., China: see PINHSIEN.

Pinchwan or **Pin-ch'uan** (both: bĭn'chwän'), town, ⊙ Pinchwan co. (pop. 92,577), NW central Yunnan prov., China, 25 mi. E of Tali; alt. 4,906 ft.; salt-mining center; cotton-textile mfg., tung-oil processing. Rice, wheat, millet, beans, fruit.

Pinckard, town (pop. 515), Dale co., SE Ala., 10 mi. NW of Dothan.

Pinckney, village (pop. 695), Livingston co., SE Mich., 16 mi. NW of Ann Arbor, in lake-resort and farm area (hay, wheat, corn, livestock; dairy).

Pinckneyville, city (pop. 3,299) ⊙ Perry co., SW Ill., on Beaucoup Creek and 33 mi. SSW of Centralia, in bituminous-coal (large strip mine) and agr. area; food processing (flour, dairy products); wheat, corn, livestock, poultry. Inc. 1861.

Pinçon, Mont (mõ pĕsõ'), height (1,210 ft.) in Normandy Hills, Calvados dept., NW France, 19 mi. SW of Caen, S of Aunay-sur-Odon. Heavily contested in Normandy campaign (June–July, 1944) of Second World War.

Pinconning (pĭn-kŏ'nĭng), city (pop. 1,223), Bay co., E Mich., 18 mi. NNW of Bay City, near Saginaw Bay. Agr. trade center (sugar beets, chicory, beans, livestock); makes pickles, cheese, prepared chicory. Summer resort. Settled c.1866; inc. as village 1877, as city 1931.

Pinczow (pē'nyŭ-chōōf), Pol. *Pińczów*, Rus. *Pinchov* or *Pin'chov* (both: pē'nyŭ-chŭf), town (pop. 3,701), Kielce prov., SE Poland, on Nida R. and 25 mi. S of Kielce; food processing.

Pindamonhangaba (pĕndŭmōōnyăng-gä'bŭ), city (pop. 8,642), SE São Paulo, Brazil, on Paraíba R. and 85 mi. NE of São Paulo; rail junction on São Paulo–Rio de Janeiro RR (spur to Campos do Jordão). Mfg. of paper, cardboard, buttons, starch, artificial flowers, shoes; rice processing, dairying. Peat bogs and graphite deposits in area.

Pindaré Mirim (pĕndŭrĕ' mērēn'), city (pop. 1,125), N central Maranhão, Brazil, head of navigation on Pindaré R. and 100 mi. SW of São Luís, in sugar- and cotton-growing region. Formerly called São Pedro or Engenho Central.

Pindaré River, Maranhão, NE Brazil, rises near 4°50'S 46°30'W, flows NE, past Pindaré Mirim (head of navigation) and Monção, to the Mearim above Anajatuba. Length, c.250 mi.

Pindar River, India: see CHAMOLI.

Pind Dadan Khan (pĭnd' dä'dŭn khän'), town (pop. 11,445), Jhelum dist., N Punjab, W Pakistan, near Jhelum R., 45 mi. SW of Jhelum, trades in wheat, millet, oilseeds, cloth fabrics; handloom weaving, mfg. of pottery, soap; boat building; metalware, leather goods.

Pindhos, Greece: see PINDUS.

Pindi Bhattian (pĭn'dē bŭt'tyän), town (pop. 5,653), Gujranwala dist., E central Punjab, W Pakistan, 55 mi. WSW of Gujranwala; local trade in wheat, rice, gram, ghee; leather products. Also spelled Pindi Bhatian.

Pindigheb (pĭn'dĭgāb), town (pop. 12,641), Attock dist., NW Punjab, W Pakistan, 36 mi. SSW of Campbellpur; market center (wheat, millet, horses); wood products; hand-loom weaving. Also written Pindi Gheb.

Pindo, El (ĕl pēn'dō), village (pop. 1,127), La Coruña prov., NW Spain, fishing port on the Atlantic, 28 mi. W of Santiago; fish processing.

Pindorama (pēndōōrä mŭ), city (pop. 2,949), N central São Paulo, Brazil, on railroad and 5 mi. SE of Catanduva; mfg. of pottery, tile; macaroni, coffee, and rice processing. Airfield.

Pindus (pĭn'dŭs), Gr. *Pindos* or *Pindhos* (both: pĭn'dhôs), mountain-system in W central and NW Greece, on Epirus-Thessaly border, extending 100 mi. NNW from c.39°N, at the Tymphrestos massif of central Greece, to the Albanian border at c.41°N, where it joins the Sar Mts.; rises to 8,650 ft. in the Smolikas massif, in N section. Other massifs and sub-ranges are (from N to S) the Grammos, Tymphe, Lakmos, and Tzoumerka (Athamanika). A continuation of the Dinaric Alps, the Pindus has far less limestone and is made up largely of schists and eruptive rocks (serpentine). It forms a considerable barrier for the humid westerlies, placing the Thessalian plain in its rain shadow. The only important pass is the Metsovon gap (4,800 ft.) at 39°45'N. Heavily forested, mainly with oak and beech stands. In anc. times restricted to the range on the Epirus-Thessaly border, the name Pindus (in conjunction with the Sar Mts. in Yugoslavia) has been applied in modern times to the more extensive system bet. the Dinaric Alps and the mts. of central Greece.

Pindushi (pēn'dōōshē), village (1939 pop. over 500), S central Karelo-Finnish SSR, port at head of Povenets Gulf of L. Onega, on Murmansk RR and 5 mi. E of Medvezhyegorsk; shipbuilding center.

Pindzoling (pĭn'dzōlĭng) or **Phüntshog Ling** (pün'-tsōg lĭng'), Chinese *P'ing-chuang-ling* (pĭng'jwäng'-lĭng'), lamasery, SE Tibet, on the Brahmaputra, on main Leh-Lhasa trade route and 50 mi. W of Shigatse.

Pine, county (□ 1,412; pop. 18,223), E Minn.; ⊙ Pine City. Agr. area bounded E by St. Croix R. and Wis., drained by Kettle R. Dairy products, livestock, grain, potatoes; deposits of sandstone and peat. Co. formed 1856.

Pine Apple, town (pop. 445), Wilcox co., S Ala., c.40 mi. S of Selma; lumber.

Pine Barrens, region (□ c.3,000) of coastal plain of S and SE N.J., occupies parts of Atlantic, Cumberland, Ocean, and Burlington counties. Characterized by sandy soils, and with swamplands along its streams, it supports extensive pine stands and tracts of cranberries and blueberries (now cultivated, with other truck crops).

Pine Beach, borough (pop. 495), Ocean co., E N.J., on Toms R. and 2 mi. SE of Toms River village, in resort, fishing area.

Pine Bluff, city (pop. 37,162), ⊙ Jefferson co., central Ark., c.40 mi. SSE of Little Rock and on Arkansas R.; industrial, rail, and market center for cotton-growing region; cotton and lumber processing, chemical mfg. (caustic soda, chlorine); mfg. of steel, wood, and cottonseed products; railroad shops, stockyards. Seat of Ark. Agr., Mechanical, and Normal Col. for Negroes. U.S. Pine Bluff Arsenal and a chemical depot (at Arsenal), a state park for Negroes, and a state prison farm are near. Settled 1819; 1st called Mount Marie, renamed 1832; inc. as town 1846.

Pinebluff, town (pop. 575), Moore co., central N.C., 6 mi. SSW of Southern Pines; winter resort.

Pine Bluffs, town (pop. 846), Laramie co., SE Wyo., on Lodgepole Creek, at Nebr. line, and 40 mi. E of Cheyenne; alt. c.5,050 ft. Grain, seed potatoes, livestock, dairy products, sugar beets.

Pine Bush, resort village (1940 pop. 687), Orange co., SE N.Y., on Shawangunk Kill and 13 mi. NNE of Middletown; mfg. of rayon cloth.

Pine Camp, N.Y.: see GREAT BEND.

Pine City, village (pop. 1,937), ⊙ Pine co., E Minn., on Snake R., near Wis. line, and c.60 mi. N of St. Paul, in grain, potato, livestock area; dairy products, beverages. Platted 1869, inc. 1881.

Pinecliff Lake, N.J.: see WEST MILFORD.

Pine Creek, settlement (dist. pop. 201), NW central Northern Territory, Australia, 115 mi. SSE of Darwin, on Darwin–Birdum RR; gold mines.

Pinecreek or **Pine Creek,** village, Roseau co., NW Minn., port of entry near Man. line, 11 mi. NNW of Roseau.

Pine Creek. 1 In N Pa., rises in E Potter co., flows 75 mi. generally SSE, through gorge (c.1,000 ft. deep; called Grand Canyon of Pennsylvania), to West Branch of Susquehanna R. just S of Jersey Shore. Once important for lumber transport. **2** In Lamar co., NE Texas, rises W of Paris, flows c.30 mi. NE to Red R. Just NW of Paris, dams impound L. Paris (capacity c.11,000 acre-ft.) and L. Crook (capacity 3,600 acre-ft.).

Pinecrest, Calif.: see STRAWBERRY LAKE.

Pineda (pēnä'dhä), town (pop. 2,479), Barcelona prov., NE Spain, on the Mediterranean, and 8 mi. NE of Arenys de Mar; knit-goods mfg.; fishing; olive oil, wine, cereals, livestock.

Pinedale. 1 Village (pop. 2,220), Fresno co., central Calif., 7 mi. N of Fresno; large lumber mill. **2** Town (pop. 770), ⊙ Sublette co., W Wyo., on branch of Green R. and c.95 mi. NNW of Rock Springs; alt. 7,175 ft. Resort; livestock, dairy products, timber.

Pine Falls, village (pop. estimate 600), SE Man., on Winnipeg R. (waterfalls), near its mouth on L. Winnipeg, 60 mi. NE of Winnipeg; hydroelectric-power center; paper milling.

Pine Flat Dam, Calif.: see KINGS RIVER.

Pine Flat Mountain, N.Mex.: see MIMBRES MOUNTAINS.

Pine Forest Mountains (9,000 ft.), NW Nev., in NW Humboldt co., near Oregon line.

Pinega (pēnyĕ'gŭ), village (1926 pop. 1,376), central Archangel oblast, Russian SFSR, on Pinega R. and 80 mi. E of Archangel; sawmilling, shipbuilding, dairying.

Pinega River, Archangel oblast, Russian SFSR, rises 65 mi. N of Kotlas, flows NW, past Karpogory, turning SW at Pinega, to Northern Dvina R. near Kholmogory; length, 407 mi. Navigable for 235 mi.; logging.

Pine Grove. 1 Borough (pop. 2,237), Schuylkill co., E central Pa., 13 mi. SW of Pottsville; tanning; clothing. Settled 1771, laid out 1830, inc. 1832. **2** Town (pop. 877), Wetzel co., NW W.Va., 27 mi. WNW of Fairmont, in petroleum-producing and agr. region.

Pinegrove, village (pop. 1,078, with adjacent Project City), Shasta co., N Calif., near Shasta L., 8 mi. NE of Redding.

Pine Hall, village, Stokes co., N N.C., 18 mi. NNE of Winston-Salem and on Dan R.; mfg. of bricks and other clay products.

Pine Hill. 1 Town (pop. 408), Wilcox co., SW Ala., near Alabama R., 45 mi. SW of Selma; lumber. **2** Borough (pop. 2,546), Camden co., SW N.J., 14 mi. SE of Camden. Inc. 1929. **3** Resort village (pop. 233), Ulster co., SE N.Y., in the Catskills, 28 mi. NW of Kingston. Belle Ayr Mtn. (skiing) is near by.

Pinehurst. 1 Town (pop. 430), Dooly co., central Ga., 15 mi. N of Cordele. **2** Village, Mass.: see BILLERICA. **3** Winter resort (pop. 1,016), Moore co., central N.C., 5 mi. W of Southern Pines. Noted for its golf courses and as a training center for horses. Developed after 1895; chartered 1911. **4** Village (pop. 1,419, with adjacent Sheppard Park), Dorchester co., S.C. **5** Village, Snohomish co., NW Wash., 4 mi. S of Everett.

Pineios River, Greece: see PENEUS RIVER.

Pine Island, village (pop. 1,298), Goodhue co., SE Minn., on branch of Zumbro R. and 15 mi. NW of Rochester; cheese-shipping center; dairy products, poultry equipment, cement blocks. Settled 1854, inc. 1878.

Pine Island, off coast of SW Fla., c.15 mi. W of Fort Myers; c.15 mi. long, 1–3 mi. wide, it has causeway to mainland. Mostly pine-clad, with orange groves in W; site of small resort and fishing villages of Pineland and St. James City. Isl. is bordered W by Pine Island Sound (c.15 mi. long, 5 mi. wide), sheltered from the Gulf of Mexico by a chain of barrier isls.—Lacosta, Captiva, Sanibel—and opening into Charlotte Harbor (N) and San Carlos Bay (S).

Pine Lake, town (pop. 566), De Kalb co., NW central Ga., 10 mi. E of Atlanta.

Pine Lake. 1 Lake in Ind.: see LA PORTE, city. **2** Lake in Otter Tail co., W Minn., 35 mi. NE of Fergus Falls; 5 mi. long, 2 mi. wide. Sometimes known as Big Pine L. Has fishing, boating, and bathing resorts. Fed and drained by Otter Tail R.

Pineland. 1 Village, Fla.: see PINE ISLAND. **2** Town (pop. 1,454), Sabine co., E Texas, c.45 mi. ESE of Lufkin; large lumber mill. Inc. after 1940.

Pinelands Garden City, residential town (pop. 4,472), SW Cape Prov., U. of So. Afr., 5 mi. ESE of Cape Town.

Pine Lawn, town (pop. 6,425), St. Louis co., E Mo., just W of St. Louis. Inc. since 1940.

Pine Level, town (pop. 602), Johnston co., central N.C., 5 mi. E of Smithfield; cottonseed-oil and lumber milling.

Pinellas (pīnĕ'lŭs), county (□ 264; pop. 159,249), W Fla.; ⊙ Clearwater. Largely a peninsula (Pinellas peninsula), bet. Gulf of Mexico (W) and Tampa Bay (E); bordered W by chain of barrier isls., including Long Key; has L. Butler in N. Citrus-fruit growing, dairying, and tourist area, with canning, wood processing, and sponge-fishing industries. Formed 1911.

Pinellas Park, town (pop. 2,924), Pinellas co., W Fla., 7 mi. NW of St. Petersburg; poultry farms, nurseries. Inc. 1913.

Pinell de Bray (pēnăl' dhä brī'), town (pop. 1,418), Tarragona prov., NE Spain, 5 mi. SE of Gandesa. Pine woods; and livestock (sheep, goats), olive oil, wine, almonds in area.

Pine Meadow, Conn.: see NEW HARTFORD.

Pine Mountain, ridge of the Cumberlands, mostly in SE Ky., partly along Va. border; from Russell Fork SE of Praise, Ky., extends c.125 mi. SW into Campbell co., Tenn.; rises to 2,100–2,300 ft. in SW, to 2,600–2,800 ft. in NE half, with sections rising above 3,000 ft. Extensive timber tracts and coal deposits. Trail of the Lonesome Pine (scenic highway) passes over part of ridge. POUND GAP (highway pass) is in N section, near Jenkins, Ky. Pine Mtn. State Park (2,500 acres; recreational facilities) near Pineville, Ky., is scene of state's annual mountain laurel festival.

Pine Mountain State Park, Ga.: see WARM SPRINGS.

Pine Nut Mountains, W Nev., E of Carson City; extend c.35 mi. S from Carson R.; rise to 9,550 ft. in S.

Pine Orchard, Conn.: see BRANFORD.

Pine Park, town (pop. 126), Grady co., SW Ga., 7 mi. ESE of Cairo.

Pine Plains, village (1940 pop. 665), Dutchess co., SE N.Y., 25 mi. NE of Poughkeepsie, in diversified agr. area.

Piñera (pēnyä'rä), town (pop. 1,000), Paysandú dept., NW Uruguay, on N slopes of Cuchilla de Haedo, on railroad and 65 mi. E of Paysandú; road junction. Sometimes called Beisso.

Pine Ridge, village (1940 pop. 1,007), Shannon co., SW S.Dak., 80 mi. SSE of Rapid City, near Nebr. line, and on branch of White R.; hq. for Pine Ridge Indian Reservation.

Pine River, resort village (pop. 835), Cass co., central Minn., on fork of Pine R., near Whitefish L., 27 mi. NNW of Brainerd, in livestock, poultry area; dairy products, pickles.

Pine River. 1 In Colo. and N.Mex.: see LOS PINOS RIVER. **2** In central Mich., rises in SE Mecosta co., flows SE into Gratiot co., then NE, past Alma and St. Louis, to Chippewa R. just W of Midland; c.80 mi. long. **3** In NE Mich., rises in central Alcona co., flows c.25 mi. SE, through Huron Natl. Forest, widening into Van Ettan L. (c.4 mi. long) c.4 mi. above its confluence with Au Sable R., 2 mi. NW of Oscoda. **4** In central Minn., rises in lake region N of Pine River village, flows S, then E, through Whitefish L., and SE, through Cross L., to Mississippi R. near Crosby; c.50 mi. long. Stream is dammed at outlet of Cross L. **5** In SW Wis., formed by several streams rising N of Richland Center, flows c.30 mi. generally S, past Richland Center, to Wisconsin R. c.45 mi. ENE of Prairie du Chien.

Pinerolo (pēnĕrô'lô), town (pop. 15,363), Torino prov., Piedmont, NW Italy, at foot of Cottian Alps, 21 mi. SW of Turin, in sericulture region. Commercial center; mfg. (silk and cotton textiles, railroad equipment, scales, paper, leather goods, fertilizers). Graphite mines near by. Bishopric since 1159. Has cathedral (1044), palace (built 1318; later modernized), 15th-cent. houses. Formerly possessed strong citadel where the Man with the Iron Mask was imprisoned in 17th cent.

Pines, Isle of, Sp. *Isla de Pinos* (ē'slä dā pē'nōs), island (□ 1,182; pop. 9,812), off SW Cuba, to which it belongs, separated by c.30-mi.-wide Gulf of Batabanó; bet. 21°26'–21°57'N and 82°32'–83°11'W. Principal town, Nueva Gerona. It is 35 mi. N–S, up to 40 mi. E–W. Has equable, subtropical climate; mean annual temp. c.75°F.; rains, May–Oct. Generally a low plateau, with swamps and extensive forests in S, it has in its N, more fertile, section several hilly ranges, rising to 1,017 ft. Apart from natural resources (marble, construction wood, and sponge in coastal waters), it yields chiefly agr. products (citrus fruit, tobacco, pineapples, watermelons, potatoes, winter vegetables). Because of its mild climate it has also become a popular tourist resort. There are fine beaches and mineral springs. Discovered 1494 by Columbus, who called it Evangelista (Evangelist), it was in colonial times a refuge for pirates and buccaneers and served as a penal settlement. The isl. is largely settled by American residents, who claimed it for the U.S. since it was surrendered by Spain in 1899 and was omitted from the Platt Amendment, which defined Cuba's boundaries. The claim was rejected, however, by the U.S. Supreme Court (1907). A treaty confirmed (1925) the isl. as Cuban. It is administratively a municipality of Havana prov.

Pines, Isle of, or **Kunie** (kōōnē'ā), island (□ 58; pop. 600), SW Pacific, 30 mi. SE of New Caledonia, of which it is a dependency; forested, mountainous; tourist resort. Deer, wild goats, pigs. Produces shrimp, oysters. Formerly penal colony.

Pinetops, town (pop. 1,031), Edgecombe co., E central N.C., 13 mi. SE of Rocky Mount, in agr. area.

Pinetown, residential town (pop. 5,481), SE Natal, U. of So. Afr., 10 mi. W of Durban, in fruitgrowing region.

Pinetown, town (pop. 301), Beaufort co., E N.C., 12 mi. ENE of Washington; lumber milling.

Pine Tree Park, village (pop. 1,392, with adjacent Osceola Park), Broward co., S Fla.

Pine Valley. 1 Borough (pop. 39), Camden co., SW N.J., 13 mi. SE of Camden. **2** Village (1940 pop. 745), Le Flore co., SE Okla., 28 mi. SSW of Poteau, and on Kiamichi R., in the Ouachita Mts.; lumber milling.

Pine Valley Mountains, in Dixie Natl. Forest, Washington co., SW Utah, N of St. George; rise to 10,324 ft.

Pineview, town (pop. 310), Wilcox co., S central Ga., 19 mi. ENE of Cordele.

Pine View Dam, Utah: see OGDEN RIVER.

Pine Village, town (pop. 311), Warren co., W Ind., on small Big Pine Creek and 20 mi. W of Lafayette, in agr. area.

Pineville. 1 City (pop. 3,890), ⊙ Bell co., SE Ky., in the Cumberlands, on Cumberland R., and 11 mi. N of Middlesboro. Resort and tourist center (alt. c.1,000 ft.); shipping point for bituminous-coal-mining and hardwood-timber area; food products; lumbering. Holds annual (May) Cumberland valley music festival. Town settled on old Wilderness Road around tollgate (1797–1830) at gap (the Narrows) in Pine Mtn. Near by is Pine Mtn. State Park, where annual mtn. laurel festival is held. **2** Town (pop. 6,423), Rapides parish, central La., on Red R., opposite ALEXANDRIA, its sister city; marble and granite monuments, pulpwood, wood products; commercial fishing. Louisiana Col., a natl. cemetery, and a state hosp. are here. U.S. Camp Beauregard, a veterans hosp., a state colony for the feeble-minded, and an industrial school for girls are near by. Settled in early-18th cent.; inc. 1878. **3** Town (pop. 464), ⊙ McDonald co., extreme SW Mo., in the Ozarks, on Elk R. and 19 mi. S of Neosho; resort; dairy, grain products. **4** Town (pop. 1,373), Mecklenburg co., SW N.C., 10 mi. SSW of Charlotte, near S.C. line; cotton milling. James K. Polk b. near by. **5** Town (pop. 1,082), ⊙ Wyoming co., S W.Va., on Guyandot R. and 24 mi. SW of Beckley; trade center for coal-mining, lumbering, agr. (stock, fruit, tobacco) area.

Pinewood, town (pop. 578), Sumter co., central S.C., 13 mi. SSW of Sumter.

Piney (pēnā'), agr. village (pop. 829), Aube dept., NE central France, 12 mi. ENE of Troyes; toy mfg.

Piney Fork, village (1940 pop. 1,270), Jefferson co., E Ohio, 9 mi. E of Cadiz, in coal-mining area.

Piney Park, town (pop. 21), Franklin co., E central Mo.

Piney Point, resort, St. Marys co., S Md., on the Potomac and 12 mi. SE of Leonardtown; duck hunting, fishing. Lighthouse here.

Piney River, mining village, Nelson co., central Va., on small Piney R. and 22 mi. N of Lynchburg; mining of titanium ores, apatite; chemical plant.

Piñeyro (pēnyā'rō), residential town (pop. estimate 40,000) in SE Greater Buenos Aires, Argentina, adjoining Avellaneda.

Pingchang or **P'ing-ch'ang** (pĭng'chäng'), town (pop. 19,274), NE Szechwan prov., China, 25 mi. SE of Pachung and on Chü R.; cotton, rice, sweet potatoes, wheat, beans. Until 1944 called Kiangkow.

Ping Chau (pĭng' jou'), small island of the New Territories of Hong Kong colony, off E coast of Lan Tao isl., 8 mi. W of Victoria; 1 mi. long, ½ mi. wide. Match factory.

Pingchen or **P'ing-chen** (both: pĭng'jŭn'), Jap. *Heichin* (hā'jĭn'), village, N Formosa, on railroad and 10 mi. SW of Taoyüan; tea-processing center.

P'ing-ch'i, Formosa: see PINGKI.

P'ing-chiang, China: see PINGKIANG.

Pingchih or **P'ing-chih** (pĭng'jŭ'), town, ⊙ Pingchih co. (pop. 95,339), W Kwangsi prov., China, 60 mi. ESE of Poseh. Called Panghü or Pangsü until 1936.

Pingchüan or **P'ing-ch'üan** (pĭng'chüän'), town, ⊙ Pingchüan co. (pop. 374,043), S Jehol prov., Manchuria, 38 mi. E of Chengteh and on railroad; trade center; millet, kaoliang, livestock, furs, skins, and hides; mfg. (wool blankets and other woolen goods, liquor). Gold mining. Colonized by Chinese in early-18th cent., it was then called Pakow (1729–78).

P'ing-chuang-ling, Tibet: see PINDZOLING.

Pingelap (pĭng'ŭläp'), atoll (pop. 685), Ponape dist., E Caroline Isls., W Pacific, 144 mi. WNW of Mokil; 6°15'N 160°40'E; 2 mi. long, 1.5 mi. wide; 3 low isls.

Pingfan, China: see YUNGTENG.

Pinggau (pĭng'gou), village (pop. 2,729), Styria, E Austria, 19 mi. S of Neunkirchen; machine factory.

P'ing-ho, China: see PINGHWO.

P'ing-hsiang, China: see PINGSIANG.

Pinghu or **P'ing-hu** (pĭng'hōō'), town (pop. 20,576), ⊙ Pinghu co. (pop. 268,136), NE Chekiang prov., China, near Kiangsu line, 60 mi. NE of Hangchow; rice, wheat.

Pinghwo or **P'ing-ho** (both: pĭng'hŭ'), town (pop. 19,603), ⊙ Pinghwo co. (pop. 207,862), S Fukien prov., China, 70 mi. WSW of Amoy, on Kwangtung line; rice, sugar cane, wheat. Copper and iron mines near by.

Pingi or **P'ing-i** (both: pĭng'yē'), town, ⊙ Pingi co. (pop. 119,744), E Yunnan prov., China, 25 mi. ENE of Kütsing, near Kweichow line; alt. 6,168 ft.; iron smelting, chemical mfg., tung-oil processing; timber, rice, buckwheat, millet, beans. Coal and sulphur mines, gypsum quarrying near by.

Pingki or **P'ing-ch'i** (both: pĭng'chē'), Jap. *Heikei* (hā'kā), village, N Formosa, 7 mi. S of Keelung and on railroad; coal mining.

Pingkiang or **P'ing-chiang** (both: pĭng'jyäng'), town, ⊙ Pingkiang co. (pop. 357,525), NE Hunan prov., China, 50 mi. NE of Changsha; rice, wheat. Gold and copper mining near by.

Pingku or **P'ing-ku** (pĭng'gōō'), town, ⊙ Pingku co. (pop. 66,508), N Hopeh prov., China, 40 mi. NE of Peking, near Great Wall; kaoliang, millet.

Pingla (pĭng'glŭ), village, Midnapore dist., SW West Bengal, India, 20 mi. ESE of Midnapore; cotton weaving; rice, pulse, jute, sugar cane; silk growing. Regional cotton-cloth distributing center near by.

Pingli or **P'ing-li** (pĭng'lē'), town (pop. 2,391), ⊙ Pingli co. (pop. 108,097), S Shensi prov., China, near Hupeh line, 28 mi. SE of Ankang, in mtn. region; wheat, millet, beans. Gold washing, asbestos mining near by.

Pingliang or **P'ing-liang** (pĭng'lyäng'), town, ⊙ Pingliang co. (pop. 135,964), SE Kansu prov., China, on King R. and 80 mi. NE of Tienshui; wool weaving, tobacco processing, match mfg.; hides, grain.

Pinglin or **P'ing-lin** (pĭng'lĭn'), Jap. *Heirin* (hā'rēn), village (1935 pop. 956), N Formosa, 14 mi. SE of Taipei; mercury deposits; lumbering.

Pinglo or **P'ing-lo** (pĭng'lŭ'). **1** Town, ⊙ Pinglo co. (pop. 171,551), NE Kwangsi prov., China, 55 mi. SSE of Kweilin and on Kwei R.; tung-oil processing; rice, wheat, beans, fruit, melons. Mercury mines near by. **2** Town (pop. 4,814), ⊙ Pinglo co. (pop. 60,092), SE Ningsia prov., China, on railroad and 35 mi. NNE of Yinchwan, near Yellow R.; cattle raising; rice, wheat, kaoliang. Exports wool, hides, licorice.

Pinglu or **P'ing-lu** (pĭng'lōō'). **1** Town, ⊙ Pinglu co. (pop. 33,212), SW Chahar prov., China, 60 mi. WSW of Tatung, near Great Wall (Suiyuan border); millet, kaoliang. Until 1949 in N Shansi. **2** Town, ⊙ Pinglu co. (pop. 87,056), SW Shansi prov., China, 20 mi. S of Anyi, and on Yellow R. (Honan border), opposite Shanhsien; wheat, kaoliang, corn.

Pingmin or **P'ing-min** (pĭng'mĭn'), town, ⊙ Pingmin co. (pop. 22,905), E Shensi prov., China, on W bank of Yellow R. (Shansi line), opposite Yüngtsi, and 85 mi. ENE of Sian; rice, wheat, beans.

Pingnam (pĭng'näm'), Mandarin *P'ing-nan* (–nän'), town, ⊙ Pingnam co. (pop. 378,573), SE Kwangsi prov., China, 60 mi. W of Wuchow and on Sün R.; silk- and rice-growing center; millet, peanuts.

Pingnan or **P'ing-nan** (pĭng'nän'), town (pop. 3,014), ⊙ Pingnan co. (pop. 69,088), N Fukien prov., China, 50 mi. E of Kienow; rice, sweet potatoes, wheat. Lead mines near by.

P'ing-nan, Kwangsi prov., China: see PINGNAM.

Pingpa or **P'ing-pa** (both: pĭng'bä'), town (pop. 8,563), ⊙ Pingpa co. (pop. 96,619), SW central Kweichow prov., China, 30 mi. WSW of Kweiyang and on main road to Yunnan; alt. 4,122 ft.; cotton-textile mfg., tobacco processing, pottery making; embroideries; wheat, millet, beans.

Pingpien or **P'ing-pien** (both: pĭng'byĕn'), town, ⊙ Pingpien co. (pop. 46,070), SE Yunnan prov., China, 25 mi. SE of Mengtsz, near Vietnam line; rice, millet. Until 1933, Tsingpien.

Pingree, village (pop. 161), Stutsman co., central N.Dak., 20 mi. NNW of Jamestown.

Pingree Grove, village (pop. 162), Kane co., NE Ill., c.40 mi. WNW of Chicago, in agr. area (dairy products; livestock).

Ping River (pĭng), one of headstreams of Chao Phraya R. in N Thailand, rises in Daen Lao Range on Burma line at 19°50'N 98°5'E, flows 300 mi. S, past Chiangmai, Tak, and Kamphaengphet, joining the combined Nam and Yom rivers near Nakhon Sawan to form Chao Phraya R. Navigable in most of its course. Receives Wang R. (right).

Pingshan or **P'ing-shan** (pĭng'shän'). **1** Town, ⊙ Pingshan co. (pop. 232,638), SW Hopeh prov., China, 20 mi. NW of Shihkiachwang; cotton, ramie, peaches. **2** Town (pop. 16,024), ⊙ Pingshan co. (pop. 129,252), SW Szechwan prov., China, 28 mi. WSW of Ipin and on left bank of Yangtze R. (Yunnan border); paper milling; rice, wheat, millet, potatoes, rapeseed. Iron deposits near by.

Pingshek (pĭng'sĕk'), Mandarin *P'ing-shih* (pĭng'shû'), town, N Kwangtung prov., China, on Canton-Hankow RR, on Wu R. and 50 mi. NW of Kükong, near Hunan border; commercial center; exports vegetable oil and cotton cloth.

Pingshun or **P'ing-shun** (pĭng'shōōn'), town, ⊙ Pingshun co. (pop. 92,090), SE Shansi prov., China, 20 mi. E of Changchih, in Taihang Mts.; wheat, kaoliang, medicinal herbs.

Pingsiang or **P'ing-hsiang** (both: pĭng'shyäng'). **1** Town, ⊙Pingsiang co. (pop. 108,565), SW Hopeh prov., China, 22 mi. ESE of Singtai; wheat, kaoliang, millet, beans. **2** City (1948 pop. 22,040), ⊙, but independent of, Pingsiang co. (1948 pop. 408,580, W Kiangsi prov., China, near Hunan line, on Chekiang-Kiangsi RR and 65 mi. SE of Changsha; major coal-mining center, producing coking coal for Hanyang steel mill. Mines are here and at Anyüan (ESE). City became an independent municipality in 1949. **3** Town, ⊙ Pingsiang co. (pop. 22,058), SW Kwangsi prov., China, on railroad and 95 mi. SW of Nanning, near Vietnam line, just N of Chennankwan.

Pingtan, China: see HAITAN ISLAND.

Pingtang or **P'ing-t'ang** (pĭng'täng'), town (pop. 3,623), ⊙ Pingtang co. (pop. 92,555), S Kweichow prov., China, 70 mi. SSE of Kweiyang; pottery making; embroideries; wheat, millet. Until 1942 called Tungchow.

Pingting or **P'ing-ting** (pĭng'dĭng'), town, ⊙ Pingting co. (pop. 316,129), E Shansi prov., China, 55 mi. E of Taiyüan and on highway to Peking; one of the earliest ironworking centers of China, near coal and iron mines, it is also known for its pottery, and gold- and silverware. An anc. city, dating from 13th cent., it has been largely superseded by the modern rail town of Yangchüan, just NW.

Pingtu or **P'ing-tu** (pĭng'dōō'), town, ⊙ Pingtu co. (pop. 868,317), E Shantung prov., China, 45 mi. E of Weifang; gold-mining center; wheat, rice, beans, cotton.

Pingtung or **P'ing-tung** (pĭng'dōōng'), Jap. *Heito* (hā'tō), town (1940 pop. 54,756), S Formosa, on railroad and 14 mi. ENE of Kaohiung, near Lower Tanshui R. (5,000-ft. rail bridge); center of agr. dist. (sugar cane, rice, bananas, fruit); one of leading sugar-milling centers of Formosa. Military air base. Until 1920, called Akow (Jap. *Ako*).

Pinguente, Yugoslavia: see BUZET.

Pingüicas, Cerro (sĕ'rō pĭng-gwē'käs), peak (10,469 ft.) in Querétaro, central Mexico, 3 mi. WNW of Amoles.

Pingwu or **P'ing-wu** (pĭng'wōō'), town (pop. 2,637), ⊙ Pingwu co. (pop. 56,728), N Szechwan prov., China, on Fow R., and 125 mi. NNE of Chengtu, near Kansu border; medicinal plants, millet, rice, beans, wheat. Graphite quarrying, gold deposits near by. Until 1913 called Lungan.

Pingyang or **P'ing-yang** (pĭng'yäng'). **1** Town (pop. 13,585), ⊙ Pingyang co. (pop. 710,667), SE Chekiang prov., China, 24 mi. SSW of Wenchow, near E.China Sea; rice, wheat, tea, fruit. Alum mining. **2** Town, Shansi prov., China: see LINFEN.

Pingyang, Korea: see PYONGYANG.

Pingyao or **P'ing-yao** (pĭng'you'), town, ⊙ Pingyao co. (pop. 240,061), central Shansi prov., China, on railroad and 50 mi. SSW of Taiyüan; junction for Fenyang, 20 mi. E; trading center. Coal mines near by.

Pingyin or **P'ing-yin** (pĭng'yĭn'), town, ⊙ Pingyin co. (pop. 181,308), W Shantung prov., China, on Yellow R. and 40 mi. SW of Tsinan, near Pingyuan line; rice, wheat, millet, peanuts.

Pingyuan, Pingyüan, or **P'ing-yüan** (all: pĭng'yüän') [Chinese, =level plain], province (□ 18,000; pop. 13,000,000) of N central China, astride Yellow R.; ⊙ Sinsiang. Bounded N by Hopeh, NW by Shansi along Taihang Mts., S by Honan (in part along Yellow R.), and E by Shantung along Grand Canal, Pingyuan lies entirely on the level N China plain at SE foot of Shansi plateau. It is traversed by a section of Yellow R., by Tsin R. (W), and by Wei R. (center), in whose valley the pop. and the main industries are concentrated. These last-mentioned are coal mining (at Tsiaotso and Liuhokow), cotton milling, and the processing of food products (mainly wheat, millet, kaoliang) and medicinal herbs (*tihwang* at Tsinyang). Main urban centers are Sinsiang, Anyang (site of Bronze Age excavations), Liaocheng (on Grand Canal). Prov. is traversed by Peking-Hankow RR, with coal-mine spurs joining at Sinsiang and near Anyang. Pop. speaks N Mandarin dialect. Pingyuan was constituted in 1949 from sections of Honan, Hopeh, and Shantung provs.

Ping-yüan or **P'ing-yüan** (both: pĭng'yüän'). **1** Town, Kwangtung prov., China: see PINGYÜN. **2** Town, Kweichow prov., China: see CHIHKIN. **3** Town, ⊙ Pingyüan co. (pop. 210,276), NW Shantung prov., China, near Hopeh-Pingyuan line, 45 mi. NW of Tsinan, and on Tientsin-Pukow RR; beans, kaoliang, peanuts, fruit.

Pingyüeh or **P'ing-yüeh** (both: pĭng'yüĕ'), town (pop. 4,058), ⊙ Pingyüeh co. (pop. 71,461), central Kweichow prov., China, 45 mi. ENE of Kweiyang; lacquer-producing center; cotton weaving, papermaking, embroidering. Wine growing; tobacco, rice, wheat, millet, beans. Iron, bauxite, and coal found near by.

Pingyün (pĭng'yün'), Mandarin *P'ing-yüan* (pĭng'yüän'), town (pop. 2,675), ⊙ Pingyün co. (pop. 104,363), NE Kwangtung prov., China, 38 mi. NNW of Meihsien, near Kiangsi-Fukien border; grain.

Pinhal (pēnyäl'), city (pop. 9,320), E São Paulo, Brazil, near Minas Gerais border, 50 mi. NNE of Campinas; rail-spur terminus. Cotton ginning and milling; mfg. of agr. equipment, macaroni products; coffee, cotton, rice processing; sawmilling. Airfield. Formerly Espírito Santo do Pinhal.

Pinhal Novo (nō'vōō), village (pop. 873), Setúbal dist., S central Portugal, 13 mi. ESE of Lisbon; rail junction.

Pinhat, India: see PINAHAT.

Pinheiro (pēnyā'rōō). **1** City (pop. 3,756), N Maranhão, Brazil, 55 mi. W of São Luís; ships cotton, sugar, babassu nuts. Airfield. **2** Town, Pará, Brazil: see ICORACI.

Pinheiro Machado (mŭshä'dōō), city (pop. 1,995), S Rio Grande do Sul, Brazil, in the Serra dos Tapes, 60 mi. WNW of Pelotas; wool; wheat; limestone quarries. Formerly Cacimbinhas.

Pinhel (pēnyĕl'), city (pop. 1,899), Guarda dist., N central Portugal, 20 mi. NE of Guarda; agr. trade center (rye, potatoes, wheat, livestock); metalworking. Has several old churches. Important fortress in Middle Ages.

Pinhmi, Burma: see PANGMI.

Pinhoe (pĭn'hō), agr. village and parish (pop. 1,653), E central Devon, England, 3 mi. NE of Exeter. Scene of Danish victory (1001) over Saxons. Has 15th-cent. church.

Pinhsien (bĭn'shyĕn'). **1** Town, ⊙ Pinhsien co. (pop. 300,000), N Shantung prov., China, 27 mi. E of Hweimin, near Yellow R.; cotton center; wheat, peanuts; saltworks. Until 1913 called Pinchow. **2** Town (pop. 6,259), ⊙ Pinhsien co. (pop. 78,391), W Shensi prov., China, on King R., and 75 mi. NW of Sian, and on road to Lanchow; wool weaving; pears, dates, honey. Until 1913 called Pinchow, it was one of the oldest Chinese capitals (1796–1327 B.C.). **3** Town, ⊙ Pinhsien co. (pop. 301,575), W Sungkiang prov., Manchuria, China, 40 mi. E of Harbin; barley, rye, soybeans, kaoliang; soybean and flour milling. Town was formerly called Weitzekow.

Pini (pē'nē), island (23 mi. long, 7 mi. wide), Batu Isls., Indonesia, off W coast of Sumatra, 12 mi. ENE of Tanahmasa; low, forested. Copra, resin, fish.

Pinilla de Toro (pēnē'lyä dhā tō'rō), village (pop. 1,141), Zamora prov., NW Spain, 8 mi. N of Toro; cereals, sheep.

Pinios River, Greece: see PENEUS RIVER.

Pinjainen, Finland: see BILLNAS.

Pinjarra (pĭnjă'rŭ), town (pop. 644), SW Western Australia, 45 mi. S of Perth and on Murray R.; rail junction; orchards.

Pinjaur (pĭnjour'), village, E Patiala and East Punjab States Union, India, in Siwalik Range, 45 mi. NE of Patiala; wheat, corn. Sacred bathing tank. Cement works just SW, at Surajpur.

Pinkafeld (pĭng'kŭfĕlt), Hung. *Pinkafő* (pĭng'kŭfû"), town (pop. 3,492), Burgenland, E Austria, 37 mi. NE of Graz; blanket mfg.

Pink Cliffs, SW Utah, series of rugged precipices (800–2,000 ft. high) extending in great arc through parts of Garfield, Kane, and Iron counties; form escarpments of Paunsaugunt Plateau on E and S, of Markagunt Plateau on S. Unusually dissected areas in Garfield and Iron counties now included in BRYCE CANYON NATIONAL PARK and CEDAR BREAKS NATIONAL MONUMENT.

Pinkham Notch (pĭng'kŭm), N central N.H., scenic pass in White Mts. running N–S bet. Presidential Range (W) and Carter-Moriah Range (E); Peabody R. flows N, Ellis R. S, from Notch. Area bought (1911) by U.S. as part of White Mtn. Natl. Forest. Winter sports.

Pink Hill, town (pop. 386), Lenoir co., E central N.C., 17 mi. SSW of Kinston.

Pinkiang, Manchuria: see HARBIN.

Pinkie, locality in NE Midlothian, Scotland, near Edinburgh, just SE of Musselburgh; site of battle (1547) in which the English under the duke of Somerset defeated the Scots.

Pinkney, N.C.: see SOUTH GASTONIA.

Pinlaung, Burma: see LOILONG.

Pinlebu (pĭn"-lĕ-bōō'), village, Katha dist., Upper Burma, on Mu R. and 60 mi. WSW of Katha; coal mining.

Pinnacle Mountain. **1** Peak (c.2,860 ft.) in Bell co., SE Ky., one of most beautiful summits of the Cumberlands, near Va. line, just E of Middlesboro. Rises above N side of Cumberland Gap, whence Skyland Highway ascends mtn. Ruins of Fort Lyon, strategic Civil War point, are on mtn. **2** Peak in S.C.: see TABLE ROCK.

Pinnacles, village, San Benito co., W Calif., 25 mi. SSE of Hollister. Pinnacles Natl. Monument is just SW.

Pinnacles National Monument (□ 20; established 1908), W Calif., c.30 mi. SE of Salinas, in Coast Ranges. Region of colorful spires, crags, and narrow canyons formed in Tertiary period by violent volcanic action. Rises to 3,287 ft. in S. Includes numerous caves.

Pinnacles of Dan, Va.: see DAN RIVER.

Pinnaroo (pĭ'nŭrōō'), town (pop. 621), SE South Australia, 135 mi. ESE of Adelaide, near Victoria border; wheat.

Pinne, Poland: see PNIEWY.

Pinneberg (pĭ'nŭbĕrk), town (pop. 23,932), in Schleswig-Holstein, NW Germany, 11 mi. NW of Hamburg city center; mfg. of machinery, motors, chemicals, raincoats, precision and optical instruments, leather goods; metal stamping, flour milling, dairying; enameling works. Horticulture (roses). A Baltic univ. here, founded 1947. Chartered 1875.

Pinner, residential town and parish (pop. 23,082), Middlesex, England, 2 mi. W of Harrow-on-the-Hill; mfg. of electrical equipment; metal foundries. Has 13th-cent. church.

Pinogana (pēnōgä'nä), village (pop. 347), Darién prov., E Panama, on Tuira R. and 3.5 mi. ENE of El Real; gold placers; lumbering.

Pino Hachado Pass (pē'nō ächä'dō) or **Hachado Pass** (c.6,100 ft.), in the Andes, on Argentina-Chile border, at N foot of Cerro Chucán; 38°40'S 70°55'W. Projected route for new transandine railway.

Pinola, Mexico: see LAS ROSAS.

Pinola (pīnō'lŭ), village (pop. 143), Simpson co., S central Miss., 32 mi. SSE of Jackson, near Strong R.

Pinole (pēnōl'), residential town (pop. 1,147), Contra Costa co., W Calif., near San Pablo Bay, 6 mi. NE of Richmond. Explosives plant near by.

Pinols (pēnôl'). village (pop. 295), Haute-Loire dept., S central France, on E slope of Montagnes de la Margeride, 15 mi. E of Saint-Flour; livestock raising, cheese making.

Piñón (pēnyōn'), town (pop. 2,861), Magdalena dept., N Colombia, on Magdalena R. and 40 mi. S of Barranquilla; corn, rice, livestock.

Pinopolis (pīnŏ'pŭlĭs), village, Berkeley co., SE S.C., on L. Moultrie and 30 mi. N of Charleston. Near by are Pinopolis Dam and hydroelectric plant.

Pinopolis Dam, S.C.: see SANTEE RIVER.

Pinos (pē'nōs), city (pop. 4,670), Zacatecas, N central Mexico, on interior plateau, 40 mi. WNW of San Luis Potosí; alt. 8,330 ft.; silver- and gold-mining center.

Pinos, Isla de, Cuba: see PINES, ISLE OF.

Pinos, Los, Argentina: see LOS PINOS.

Pinos, Los, town, Cuba: see LOS PINOS.

Pinos, Mount (8,831 ft.), S Calif., a peak of the Coast Ranges, in S wall of San Joaquin Valley, 40 mi. S of Bakersfield.

Pinos, Point, Calif.: see MONTEREY PENINSULA.

Pinos Altos (äl'tōs), village (pop. c.150), Grant co., SW N.Mex., in Pinos Altos Mts., 7 mi. NNE of Silver City; alt. c.7,000 ft. Gold and silver mines.

Pinos Altos Mountains, in Grant co., SW N.Mex., near Gila R., NE of Silver City, largely within Gila Natl. Forest. Highest point, Black Peak (9,020 ft.). Silver and copper are mined.

Pinoso (pēnō'sō), town (pop. 3,256), Alicante prov., E Spain, 20 mi. NW of Elche; agr. trade center (wine, olive oil, almonds, esparto). Salt mines and gypsum quarries near by.

Pino Solo, Cerro (sĕ'rō pē'nō sō'lō), Andean peak (c.9,000 ft.) on Argentina-Chile border; 38°32'S.

Pinos Puente (pē'nōs pwĕn'tā), city (pop. 7,499), Granada prov., S Spain, 10 mi. NW of Granada; terminus of tramway from Granada. Sugar milling, brandy distilling, olive-oil processing, vegetable canning; linen-cloth mfg. Livestock, lumber, cereals, tobacco in area. Limestone quarry. Scene of defeat (1319) of Christians by Moors. Near here Columbus was overtaken (1492) by Queen Isabella's messenger, recalling him after failure of first negotiations.

Pinotepa Nacional (pēnōtā'pä näsyōnäl'), town (pop. 3,985), Oaxaca, S Mexico, in Pacific coast lowland, 16 mi. WNW of Jamiltepec; cereals, sugar cane, fruit, livestock.

Pinsdorf (pĭns'dôrf), village (pop. 2,094), S central Upper Austria, 2 mi. NW of Gmunden; truck farming.

Pinsk (pĭnsk, Rus. pēnsk), oblast (□ 6,300; 1946 pop. estimate 500,000), W Belorussian SSR; ⊙ Pinsk. In W part of Pripet Marshes; drained by upper Pripet R. and its tributaries. Humid continental climate (short summers). Scattered peat deposits. Heavily forested; agr. (flax, potatoes, rye, oats) in limited dry areas (N, W); fisheries. Industries based on timber (sawmilling, veneering) and agr. (flax processing, flour milling). Light mfg. and handicrafts in urban centers (Pinsk, David-Gorodok, Luninets, Stolin). Has dense network of navigable rivers and canals which form W part of Dnieper-Bug and Dnieper-Neman waterways (chiefly lumber shipments). Formed (1939) out of E part of Pol. Polesie prov., following Soviet occupation of E Poland. Held by Germany (1941–44); ceded to USSR in 1945.

Pinsk, Pol. *Pińsk* (pēnsk), city (1931 pop. 31,913), ⊙ Pinsk oblast, Belorussian SSR, in Pripet Marshes, port on left bank of Pina R., near the Pripet (here called Strumen), 140 mi. SSW of Minsk; 52°6'N 26°5'E. Fish and lumber-trading center; shipyards, ironworks; mfg. of paper, matches, plywood, soap, candles, glass; tanning, distilling, brewing, flour milling, sawmilling. Has teachers col., ruins of 17th-cent. temple. Base of Pripet R. naval flotilla. Founded (1097) by Kievan Russians; passed to Lithuania in 13th cent. Developed by Pol. queen Bona in 16th cent.; chartered 1581. Subjected to several Tatar and Cossack assaults; destroyed (1706) by Swedes. Passed (1793) from Poland to Russia; reverted (1921) to Poland; ceded to USSR in 1945. Larger part of pop. was Jewish until Second World War, when they were virtually exterminated during German occupation.

Pinsonfork or **Pinson,** village (pop. 1,114), Pike co., E Ky., 15 mi. ENE of Pikeville.

Pintada, La, Panama: see LA PINTADA.

Pintada Peak (pĭntä'dŭ) (13,176 ft.), in San Juan Mts., Rio Grande co., S Colo.

Pintado, El, Argentina: see EL PINTADO.

Pintados, Salar de (sälär' dā pēntä'dōs), salt desert (alt. c.3,000 ft.), Tarapacá prov., N Chile, on the Pampa del Tamarugal, 6 mi. SE of Pozo Almonte; c.30 mi. long, 13–15 mi. wide. Contains borax and other salts.

Pinta Island (pēn'tä) or **Abingdon Island** (□ 20), N Galápagos Isls., Ecuador, in the Pacific, 125 mi. NW of Puerto Baquerizo (San Cristóbal Isl.); 0°35'N 90°45'W.

Pinte, De (dŭ pĭn'tŭ), or **La Pinte** (lä pĕt'), village (pop. 2,357), East Flanders prov., NW Belgium, 6 mi. SW of Ghent; fruitgrowing.

Pinto or **General Pinto** (hānäräl' pēn'tō), town (pop. estimate 1,000), ⊙ Aguirre dept. (□ 1,605; 1947 census 10,805), SE Santiago del Estero prov., Argentina, on railroad and 135 mi. SE of Santiago del Estero; agr. center (corn, wheat, alfalfa, livestock). Sometimes called General Mitre.

Pinto (pĭn'tō), village, SE Sask., on Souris R. and 15 mi. ESE of Estevan, near N.Dak. border; coal.

Pinto (pēn'tō), village (1930 pop. 820), Ñuble prov., S central Chile, on railroad and 14 mi. SE of Chillán; agr. (wine, grain, potatoes, lentils, livestock); timber.

Pinto, town (pop. 3,258), Madrid prov., central Spain, 10 mi. S of Madrid; agr. center (cereals, vegetables, grapes, olives, sheep, goats). Olive pressing; mfg. of chocolate, ceramics, aeronautical equipment.

Pinto (pĭn'tō), village, Allegany co., W Md., on North Branch of the Potomac, c.12 mi. above Cumberland, in apple-growing area.

Pinto Butte, mountain (3,350 ft.), SW Sask., near Mont. border, 70 mi. SSE of Swift Current.

Pintolá (pēntōlä'), city (pop. c.70,000), Amazonas prov., NW Brazil, on the Amazon and 500 mi. W of Manaus, in a rich jungle-rubber region. One of earliest settlements (1803) on the upper Amazon. Grew as hardwood lumbering center until development (early 1940s) as rubber plantation center. Airport, R.C. mission. Formerly São Paolo.

Pintsch (pĭnch), village (pop. 111), N Luxembourg, 4 mi. ENE of Wiltz; mfg. of tanning fluid; potatoes, rye, pulse.

Pintuaria, Canary Isls.: see TENERIFE.

Pinxton, town and parish (pop. 5,285), E Derby, England, 3 mi. E of Alfreton; coal mining. Has 13th-15th-cent. church. Town was formerly famous for its china.

Pinyang (bĭn'yäng'), town, ⊙ Pinyang co. (pop. 299,809), S central Kwangsi prov., China, 45 mi. NE of Nanning, at road junction; porcelain center; mfg. of fans, mats, hats, bamboo articles, cotton textiles. Rice, peanuts, beans, sweet potatoes, timber. Tungsten, antimony, and bismuth deposits near by. Until 1912 called Pinchow.

Pinyug (pēnyōōk'), town (1946 pop. over 500), NW Kirov oblast, Russian SFSR, on railroad and 75 mi. SE of Kotlas.

Pinzano al Tagliamento (pēntsä'nō äl tälyämĕn'tō), village (pop. 830), Udine prov., Friuli-Venezia Giulia, NE Italy, on Tagliamento R. and 16 mi. NW of Udine; rail junction; shoe factory.

Pinzgau (pĭnts'gou), valley of the upper Salzach, Salzburg, W central Austria, at S foot of the Hohe Tauern, extending c.35 mi. W from Lend; noted for horse breeding.

Pio IX, Brazil: see PIO NÔNO.

Pioche (pēōch'), village (pop. 1,392), ⊙ Lincoln co., E Nev., c.130 mi. NNE of Las Vegas; alt. 6,100 ft.; zinc, lead, silver, gold; livestock, truck.

Piojó (pyōhō'), town (pop. 1,621), Atlántico dept., N Colombia, on low hill on Caribbean plains, 27 mi. SW of Barranquilla; cotton growing.

Piolenc (pyôlăk'), village (pop. 826), Vaucluse dept., SE France, near left bank of the Rhone, 4 mi. NW of Orange; winegrowing. Lignite mines and sand quarries near by.

Piombino (pyōmbē'nō), town (pop. 19,966), Livorno prov., Tuscany, central Italy, port on small promontory opposite Elba (SW), 32 mi. NW of Grosseto. Rail terminus; industrial center; iron- and steelworks (supplied by Elba ores), shipyards, stearin factory (candles); mfg. (soap, glass, boxes, brooms). Has 14th-cent. church (restored). Etruscan remains at near-by Populonia. Badly damaged by air bombing (1943–44) in Second World War.

Pioneer. 1 Town (pop. 83), Humboldt co., N central Iowa, 15 mi. NW of Fort Dodge; livestock, grain. **2** Village (pop. 696), Williams co., extreme NW Ohio, near St. Joseph R. and Mich. line, 15 mi. N of Bryan; toys, sporting goods, flour, wood novelties.

Pioneer Memorial State Park (28 acres; established 1934), in Harrodsburg, Mercer co., central Ky. Commemorates 1st permanent English settlement W of the Alleghenies, made here in 1774 by Capt. James Harrod. On site of old Fort Harrod, park includes reproduction of fort and pioneer cabins, George Rogers Clark memorial, cabin in which Nancy Hanks and Thomas Lincoln were married, pioneer cemetery, and a mus.

Pioneer Mine, village (pop. estimate 450), SW B.C., in Coast Mts., on Cadwallader Creek and 110 mi. N of Vancouver; gold mining.

Pioneer Mountains. 1 In Blaine and Custer counties, S central Idaho, bet. Big Wood R. and Big Lost R. Include parts of Challis and Sawtooth natl. forests. Sun Valley is on W slope. Chief peaks: Smiley Mtn. (11,505 ft.), Ryan Peak (11,900 ft.), and Mt. HYNDMAN (12,078 ft.), highest point in range. **2** In SW Mont., rise in NW part of Beaverhead co. as spur of Bitterroot Range of Rocky Mts.; extend N to Continental Divide. Drained by branches of Big Hole R., which surround range on 3 sides. Prominent peaks: Sheep Mtn. (9,590 ft.), Torrey Mtn. (11,170 ft.).

Pioner (pēŭnyĕr'), SW suburb of Kemerovo, Kemerovo oblast, Russian SFSR, in Kuznetsk Basin; coal mining. Until 1936, called Ishanovo.

Pioner Island, W island (□ 636) of Severnaya Zemlya, in Arctic Ocean, in Krasnoyarsk Territory, Russian SFSR.

Pionerski or **Pionerskiy** (pēŭnyĕr'skē), town (1939 pop. 4,779), W Kaliningrad oblast, Russian SFSR, on railroad and 20 mi. NW of Kaliningrad; Baltic seaside resort; fisheries. Until 1945, in East Prussia and called Neukuhren (noi'kōōrŭn).

Pio Nôno or **Pio IX** (pē'ōō nō'nōō), city (pop. 610), E Piauí, Brazil, near Ceará border, 100 mi. E of Oeiras; cattle, hides. Until 1944, called Patrocínio.

Pionsat (pyōsä'), village (pop. 716), Puy-de-Dôme dept., central France, in Combrailles, 17 mi. SSE of Montluçon; cattle raising, dairying.

Pioraco (pyōrä'kō), village (pop. 1,340), Macerata prov., The Marches, central Italy, on Potenza R. and 12 mi. SSE of Fabriano; paper milling.

Piornal (pyōrnäl'), village (pop. 1,873), Cáceres prov., W Spain, 14 mi. NE of Plasencia; wine, olive oil, potatoes; stock raising. Summer resort (alt. 5,000 ft.).

Piossasco (pyōs-säs'kō), village (pop. 1,871), Torino prov., Piedmont, NW Italy, 12 mi. SW of Turin.

Piotrkow or **Piotrkow Trybunalski** (pyō'trŭkōōf trĭbōōnäl'skē), Pol. *Piotrków Trybunalski*, Ger. *Petrikau* (pā'trēkou), Rus. *Petrokov* (pyĭtrŭkôf'), city (pop. 40,141), Lodz prov., central Poland, on railroad and 26 mi. SSE of Lodz. Textile-milling center; mfg. of agr. machinery, chemicals, glass, bricks; tanning, flour milling, sawmilling. Quartzite slates and glass-sand deposits near by. Older and poorer part of city lies in muddy lowland (E); new sections lie higher (S, W), along the railroad. Has ruins of medieval castle. Founded 12th cent.; seat of several diets (15th–16th cent.) and tribunals (16th–18th cent.). When in Rus. Poland, 1815–1919, it was ⊙ Petrokov govt. City's growth dates from end of 19th cent.; in 1827, pop. was 4,200; grew to 51,000 before Second World War.

Piottino (pēōt-tē'nō), ravine of Ticino R., Ticino canton, S Switzerland, 8 mi. ESE of Airolo; spiral railway tunnels, Piottino hydroelectric plant here.

Piove di Sacco (pyō'vĕ dē säk'kō), town (pop. 4,399), Padova prov., Veneto, N Italy, 11 mi. SE of Padua, in irrigated agr. region; cereals, raw silk, tobacco, sugar beets; macaroni and vinegar factories.

Piovene Rocchette (pyōvā'nĕ rōk-kĕt'tĕ), town (pop. 4,072), Vicenza prov., Veneto, N Italy, 5 mi. NE of Schio; breweries, foundry, woolen mills. Sandstone quarries near by. Formed in mid-1930s by combining adjacent towns of Piovene and Rocchette.

Pipanaco, Salar de (sälär' dā pēpänä'kō), salt lake (□ 180) in S Catamarca prov., Argentina, extends c.40 mi. NNE–SSW from a point 17 mi. S of Andalgalá along Sierra de Ambato. Main inlet: Andalgalá R. Contains sodium chloride, sodium sulphate, magnesium and potassium salts.

Pipar (pē'pär), town (pop. 8,917), central Rajasthan, India, 32 mi. E of Jodhpur; agr. market (millet, wheat, oilseeds, cotton); handicraft cloth weaving and dyeing. Pipar Road, rail junction for the town, is 7 mi. NW.

Piparia (pĭpŭr'yŭ), town (pop. 5,874), Hoshangabad dist., NW Madhya Pradesh, India, 40 mi. E of Hoshangabad; flour, oilseed, and dal milling; transfer point for health resort of Pachmarhi, 20 mi. S. Sometimes spelled Pipariya.

Piper City (pī'pŭr), village (pop. 735), Ford co., E Ill., 30 mi. SSW of Kankakee, in agr. area (grain, soybeans, livestock).

Piperi (pēpā'rē), uninhabited Aegean island (□ 2.2) in the Northern Sporades, Magnesia nome, Greece, 50 mi. off Thessalian mainland; 39°19'E; 24°21'E; 3 mi. long, 1 mi. wide.

Piperno, Italy: see PRIVERNO.

Piper Peak, Nev.: see SILVER PEAK MOUNTAINS.

Piper's Brook, village (pop. 132), N Tasmania, 24 mi. N of Launceston; sheep center.

Pipe Spring National Monument (40 acres; established 1923), NW Ariz., in Kaibab Indian Reservation, 18 mi. SW of Kanab, Utah. Early Mormon settlement consisting of stone fort (completed 1873) and auxiliary bldgs. is preserved to commemorate westward migration of pioneers.

Pipestone, village (pop. estimate 250), SW Man., 50 mi. WSW of Brandon; grain, stock.

Pipestone, county (□ 464; pop. 14,003), SW Minn.; ⊙ Pipestone. Agr. area bordering on S.Dak. and drained by headwaters of Rock R. Livestock, corn, oats, barley. Pipestone Natl. Monument is just N of Pipestone. Co. formed 1857. Includes part of Coteau des Prairies.

Pipestone, city (pop. 5,269), ⊙ Pipestone co., SW Minn., on Coteau des Prairies, 38 mi. NE of Sioux Falls, S.Dak.; trade center for grain, livestock, and poultry area; dairy products, beverages, poultry; granite, pipestone quarries. Pipestone Natl. Monument, Pipestone Indian Training School, and Pipestone Indian Reservation are just N.

Pipestone National Monument (115.6 acres; established 1937), Pipestone co., SW Minn., at city of Pipestone. Quarries of red stone here were used for centuries by Indians in making calumets; they were first described by George Catlin, in whose honor the stone is also known as catlinite.

Pipinas (pēpē'näs), village (pop. estimate 100), E Buenos Aires prov., Argentina, 33 mi. SSE of Magdalena; railhead; cement-milling center.

Piplia (pē'plēŭ), village, W Madhya Bharat, India, 10 mi. NNW of Mandasor; slate factory.

Piploda (pĭplō'dŭ), village, W Madhya Bharat, India, 12 mi. W of Jaora; gur and sugar milling, cotton ginning. Was ⊙ former princely state of Piploda (□ 66; pop. 11,578) of Central India agency; since 1948, state merged with Madhya Bharat.

Pippapass, Ky.: see HINDMAN.

Pipraich (pĭp'rīch), town (pop. 4,679), Gorakhpur dist., E Uttar Pradesh, India, 12 mi. NE of Gorakhpur; sugar milling; rice, wheat, barley, sugar cane.

Pipriac (pēprēäk'), village (pop. 662), Ille-et-Vilaine dept., W France, 12 mi. NNE of Redon; dairying.

Piqua (pĭ'kwā), city (pop. 17,447), Miami co., W Ohio, 27 mi. N of Dayton and on Great Miami R.; mfg. of fabrics, machinery, tools, motor vehicles, metal products, aircraft parts, food products, wood specialties; meat-packing plant; stone quarries. Settled 1797 as Washington; named Piqua 1816; inc. as town 1823, as city 1850.

Piquetberg or **Piketberg** (pĭkĕt'bûrg, –bĕrkh), town (pop. 2,400), SW Cape Prov., U. of So. Afr., 40 mi. N of Malmesbury; agr. center (wheat, fruit, tobacco); cement mfg.

Piquete (pēkā'tā). **1** or **Piquete de Anta** (dā än'tä), village (pop. estimate 500), ⊙ Anta dept. (□ 8,840; 1947 pop. 20,605), E central Salta prov., Argentina, on the Río del Valle and 60 mi. E of Salta, in lumbering, corn-growing, stock-raising area. **2** Town (pop. estimate 500), E central Santa Fe prov., Argentina, on railroad (Las Flores station) and 4 mi. NNW of Santa Fe, in grain area.

Piquete (pēkĕ'tĭ), city (pop. 5,001), SE São Paulo, Brazil, at foot of the Serra da Mantiqueira, 12 mi. N of Guaratinguetá; rail-spur terminus. Munition works here are supplied by iron pyrites from Ouro Prêto area (Minas Gerais). Cattle, coffee, fruit, timber.

Piquiri River (pēkērē'), central Paraná, Brazil, rises NW of Guarapuava, flows c.350 mi. W and NW to the Paraná above Pôrto Guaíra. Not navigable.

Piracaia (pērŭkī'ŭ), city (pop. 2,204), SE São Paulo, Brazil, at W foot of the Serra da Mantiqueira, 40 mi. NNE of São Paulo; rail terminus; processes dairy products, coffee, rice, corn; distilling. Black-granite deposits.

Piracanjuba (pērŭkäzhōō'bŭ), city (pop. 1,709), S Goiás, central Brazil, 45 mi. SE of Goiânia; chromite mines, rutile deposits. Ships tobacco, dairy products, cattle. Until 1944, called Pouso Alto.

Piracicaba (pērŭsĕkä'bŭ), city (1950 pop. 46,611), central São Paulo, Brazil, on Piracicaba R. and 85 mi. NW of São Paulo; rail junction. Sugar-milling and brandy-distilling center; cotton ginning, coffee and rice processing, tanning, paper and flour milling. Has noted agr. col.

Piracicaba River. **1** In E central Minas Gerais, Brazil, rises on E slope of the Serra do Espinhaço S of Rio Piracicaba city, flows 90 mi. NE, past Nova Era, to the Rio Doce at 19°29'S 42°27'W. Harnessed for hydroelectric power. Followed by Rio Doce RR. **2** In E São Paulo, Brazil, formed by junction near Americana of 2 headstreams, both rising in the Serra da Mantiqueira at Minas Gerais border; flows past Piracicaba to the Tietê 20 mi. NNE of Botucatu. Length (including the Jaguari), c.200 mi. Navigable in lower course.

Piracuruca (pērăkōōrōō'kŭ), city (pop. 2,476), N Piauí, Brazil, on Luís Correia–Piripiri RR and 70 mi. S of Parnaíba; cotton-growing and -processing center; carnauba wax, babassu nuts. Airfield. Has 18th-cent. church.

Piraeus (pīrē'ŭs), Gr. *Peiraieus* or *Piraievs* (both: pērăĕfs'), city (1940 pop. 205,404; 1951 census pop. 184,802), Attica nome, Greece, in Athens metropolitan area; port on Saronic Gulf, 5 mi. SW of Athens (linked by interurban railroad), with which it forms a continuous urbanized area; 37°57'N 23°38'E. Leading port of Greece and the country's foremost industrial center, Piraeus handles half of Greece's imports. Shipbuilding and repair yards, flour mills, machinery works (ploughs, pumps); mfg. of chemical fertilizer, cotton textiles, rugs, glass, tiles and bricks, pharmaceuticals, soap, paper, cigarettes. Railhead of main Gr. trunk line to Salonika. Has trade, naval training, and music schools. Industry is powered by coal-fed electric stations at near-by Hagios Georgios Keratsiniou and Neon Phaleron. Located on hilly Acte peninsula, Piraeus extends in rectangular layout across an isthmus to the mainland. W of the isthmus is the land-locked harbor (the anc. Kantharos) with quayside railroad stations. On E side are the small oval Zea and Munichia harbors, the anc. ports of Athens prior to the construction (493–492 B.C.) of anc. Piraeus under Themistocles. The port was developed first as a naval base during the Persian Wars, subsequently as a commercial port, and the city was laid out (c.450 B.C.) in rectangular plan. The parallel Long Walls, providing a sheltered link with Athens, were built 461–456 B.C., razed by Spartans in 404, rebuilt 393, and were finally destroyed with all Piraeus by Sulla in 86 B.C. In 1834, the fishing village of Monte Leone, on site of anc. Piraeus, was chosen as the port for the modern Athens, was renamed Piraeus, and shared the rapid 19th-cent. development of the Gr. capital. It was heavily damaged by bombing in Second World War, but was rebuilt after its liberation with U.S. aid. It is sometimes spelled Pireefs.

Pirahy, **1** City, Paraná, Brazil: see PIRAÍ DO SUL. **2** City, Rio de Janeiro, Brazil: see PIRAÍ.

Piraí (pērăē'). **1** City, Paraná, Brazil: see PIRAÍ DO SUL. **2** City (pop. 1,754), W Rio de Janeiro state, Brazil, in the Serra do Mar, 11 mi. SSW of Barra do Piraí; rice processing, paper milling, dairying. Ribeirão das Lajes hydroelectric plant supplying Rio is 8 mi. SE. Formerly spelled Pirahy.

Piraí do Sul (dōō sōōl'), city (pop. 2,108), E Paraná, Brazil, on railroad and 75 mi. NW of Curitiba; road junction and lumbering center in Paraná pine dist. Distilling, grain and rice milling. Iron deposits and mineral springs near by. Until 1944, called Piraí (old spelling, Pirahy); and, 1944–48, Piraí-Mirim.

Piraieus, Greece: see PIRAEUS.

Piraí River, SW Rio de Janeiro state, Brazil, rises in coastal range N of Angra dos Reis, flows c.50 mi. NE, past Piraí, to the Paraíba at Barra do Piraí. The Paraíba-Piraí diversion project includes Tocos dam in upper course and SANTANA dam in lower course.

Pirajaí, Brazil: see CABRÁLIA PAULISTA.

Piraju (pērŭzhōō'), city (pop. 4,593), SW São Paulo, Brazil, on Paranapanema R., on railroad and 33 mi. SE of Ourinhos; coffee, rice, cotton, and corn processing; tanning. Hydroelectric plant.

Pirajuí (pērŭzhwē'), city (pop. 5,150), W central São Paulo, Brazil, 33 mi. NW of Bauru; coffee-growing center, processing coffee and cotton.

Pirambóia (pērămbô'yŭ), town (pop. 702), S central São Paulo, Brazil, on railroad and 18 mi. E of Botucatu; cotton, grain, cattle. Asphalt extracted at Anhembi (10 mi. N; pop. 475).

Pirámides, Argentina: see PUERTO PIRÁMIDES.

Pirámides, Cordón de las (kōrdōn' dā läs pērä'mēdĕs), Andean range in W Chubut natl. territory, Argentina, S of L. Menéndez; extends c.15 mi. SE from Chile border; rises to c.8,000 ft.

Piram Island, India: see GOGHA.

Piran, Turkey: see EGIL.

Pirané (pērănā'), town (pop. estimate 1,500), ⊙ Pirané dept. (□ c.3,500; 1947 pop. 20,330), E Formosa natl. territory, Argentina, on railroad and 65 mi. NW of Formosa; agr. center (corn, cotton, sugar cane, livestock).

Piranga (pērăng'gŭ), city (pop. 1,696), S Minas Gerais, Brazil, in the Serra do Espinhaço, 25 mi. SE of Ouro Prêto; agr., and mica mining. Has early-18th-cent. cathedral and other old churches.

Pirangi (pērăzhē'), city (pop. 1,659), N São Paulo, Brazil, 20 mi. E of Catanduva; coffee, cotton, grain, rice, cattle.

Piranhas (pērä'nyŭs). **1** City (pop. 880), W Alagoas, NE Brazil, on left bank of São Francisco R. and 90 mi. NW of Penedo; SE terminus of railroad from Petrolândia (Pernambuco) around Paulo Afonso Falls, and head of navigation on lower São Francisco R. Called Marechal Floriano, 1939–48. **2** Town (pop. 780), central Bahia, Brazil, on Paraguaçu R. and 20 mi. E of Andaraí; black diamonds found here.

Piranhas River, in Paraíba and Rio Grande do Norte, NE Brazil, rises near 7°20'S 38°30'W, flows c.250 mi. NE, past Açu, to the Atlantic, which it enters by 4 distributaries just W of Macau. Intermittent in upper and middle course. Important salt deposits near mouth. Also called Açu R. in lower course.

Pirano (pērä'nō), Slovenian *Piran* (pē'rän), town (pop. 5,740), S Free Territory of Trieste, fishing port on promontory at N side of Pirano Bay (Adriatic inlet of the Gulf of Trieste), 13 mi. SW of Trieste; boat building, mfg. of soap and crystal soda. Resort and salines of Portorose 2 mi. SE. An old Venetian town, with remains of 15th-cent. fortress and several 16th–17th cent. churches. Placed 1947 under Yugoslav administration.

Pirapora (pērŭpô'rŭ). **1** City (pop. 7,365), N central Minas Gerais, Brazil, on right bank of upper São Francisco R. and 190 mi. NNW of Belo Horizonte; 17°22'S 44°58'W. Rail terminus; head of regular navigation to Juàzeiro (Bahia), 850 mi. downstream. Agr. trade center; cotton milling. Airfield. Suburb of Buritizeiro (pop. 1,067) is on opposite bank. **2** Town, São Paulo, Brazil: see PIRAPORA DO BOM JESUS.

Pirapora do Bom Jesus (dōō bō zhā'zōōs) town (pop. 1,241), SE São Paulo, Brazil, on Tietê R. and 25 mi. NW of São Paulo; cement mill. Until 1944, Pirapora.

Piraquara (pērŭkwä'rŭ), city (pop. 1,238), SE Paraná, Brazil, on railroad and 18 mi. E of Curitiba; sawmilling, pottery mfg., corn milling. Until c.1935, called Deodoro.

Pirarajá, Santa María, or **Santa María del Pirarajá** (sän'tä märē'ä dĕl pērärähä'), town (pop. 1,000), Lavalleja dept., SE Uruguay, on highway, and 55 mi. NNE of Minas; wheat, corn, oats, livestock.

Pirassununga (pērŭsōōnōōng'gŭ), city (pop. 10,050), E central São Paulo, Brazil, 65 mi. NNW of Campinas; rail junction; cotton textiles, tiles, bricks, rum. Agr. (coffee, sugar). Has 18th-cent. church.

Pirasthan, Kashmir: see URI.

Pirate Coast, Arabia: see TRUCIAL OMAN.

Pirates, Isles des (ēl' dā pērät'), small group of islets in Gulf of Siam, 10 mi. SW of Hatien, S Vietnam.

Pirates' Well, town (pop. 104), SE Bahama Isls., on NW Mayaguana Isl., 10 mi. NW of Abraham's Bay; 22°28'N 73°5'W. Salt panning. Sometimes Pirate Well.

Piratini (pērŭtēnē'), city (pop. 945), S Rio Grande do Sul, Brazil, in the Serra dos Tapes, 50 mi. WNW of Pelotas; cattle and sheep raising. Formerly spelled Piratiny.

Piratininga (pērŭtēnēng'gŭ). **1** City (pop. 2,553), W central São Paulo, Brazil, on railroad and 8 mi. SSW of Bauru; cotton processing, pottery mfg.; grain, cotton, coffee. **2** City, SE São Paulo, Brazil: see SÃO PAULO, city.

Piratini River (pērŭtēnē'). **1** In NW Rio Grande do Sul, S Brazil, rises in the Serra Geral, flows c.120 mi. NW to the Uruguay 50 mi. NE of São Borja. **2** In S Rio Grande do Sul, S Brazil, rises in the Serra dos Tapes near Pinheiro Machado, flows 75 mi. SE to São Gonçalo Canal 20 mi. SSW of Pelotas. Unnavigable. Old spelling, Piratiny R.

Piratú (pērŭtōō'), village, Rio Branco territory, northernmost Brazil, near Venezuela border, on Uraricoera R. and 140 mi. WNW of Boa Vista.

Pirawa (pĭrä'vŭ), town (pop. 5,041), SE Rajasthan, India, 70 mi. SSE of Kotah; millet, cotton, maize; cotton ginning.

Piray River (pērī'), Santa Cruz dept., central Bolivia, rises near Samaipata, flows 160 mi. N, past W outskirts of Santa Cruz city and Cuatro Ojos, to Río Grande c.20 mi. above its mouth. Navigable for 30 mi. in lower course, below Cuatro Ojos.

Pirayú (pērīōō'), town (dist. pop. 10,044), Paraguarí dept., S Paraguay, on railroad and 32 mi. ESE of Asunción; agr. center (cotton, peanuts, corn, cattle); flour, vegetable oils, starch.

Pirbright (pûr'–), residential town and parish (pop. 3,096), W Surrey, England, 5 mi. NW of Guildford. Near by are military camps. Just W is Pirbright Common, an extensive heath area.

Pircas Pass (pēr'käs) (16,000 ft.), in the Andes, on Argentina-Chile border, on road bet. Tupungato (Argentina) and El Volcán (Chile); 33°16'S 70°3'W.

Pirchevan (pērchĭvän'), village (1932 pop. estimate 580), S Azerbaijan SSR, on rail spur and 65 mi. SSW of Agdam, near Aras R. (Iran border); cotton, silk, grain, livestock. Until c.1940, Pirchevany SSW of Agdam, near Aras R. (Iran border); cotton, silk, grain, livestock. Until c.1940, Pirchevany.

Pirdop (pĕr'dôp), city (pop. 3,813), Sofia dist., W central Bulgaria, in Zlatitsa Basin, 45 mi. E of Sofia; market and dairying center; butter and cheese exports; carpet mfg. Has dairying school. Once a commercial Turkish town (cloth weaving, lacemaking); declined under Bulg. rule.

Pirdop Basin, Bulgaria: see ZLATITSA BASIN.

Piré or **Piré-Goureye** (pē'rā-gōōrĕ'yā), village, W Senegal, Fr. West Africa, on railroad and 50 mi. ENE of Dakar; peanut growing.

Pireefs, Greece: see PIRAEUS.

Piré-Goureye, Fr. West Africa: see PIRÉ.

Pirehueico, Lake (pērĕwä'kō), Valdivia prov., S central Chile, in Chilean lake dist., near Argentina border, SE of lakes of Panguipulli and Riñihue; c.15 mi. long, c.2 mi. wide. Surrounded by forests and volcanic Andean peaks. Resort.

Pireneus, Serra dos (sĕ'rŭ dōōs pērĭnĕ'ōōs), mountain range in E central Goiás, central Brazil, E of Pirenópolis; drainage divide bet. Tocantins R. (N) and Paranaíba R. (S). Rises to 4,500 ft. Occupies area set aside for future federal ⊙ Brazil. Formerly spelled Serra dos Pyreneos.

Pirenópolis (pērĭnô'pōōlĕs), city (pop. 1,848), S central Goiás, central Brazil, 32 mi. NNW of Anápolis; ships tobacco, cattle, mangabeira rubber. Rutile deposits, and gold washings in area. Has two 18th-cent. churches. Formerly spelled Pyrenópolis. Old name, Meiaponte.

Pires do Rio (pē'rĭs dōō rē'ōō), city (pop. 2,447), SE Goiás, central Brazil, on railroad and 80 mi. SE of Anápolis; livestock, lard, tobacco, manioc. Rutile deposits. Near by (W) is old gold-mining town of Corumbalina (until 1944, Santa Cruz).

Pirford (pûr'–), agr. village and parish (pop. 1,401), W central Surrey, England, on Wey R. and 3 mi. E of Woking.

Pirgos, Greece: see PYRGOS.

Pirgovo (pĕr'gôvô), village (pop. 3,632), Ruse dist., NE Bulgaria, on the Danube and 9 mi. SW of Ruse; sugar beets, sunflowers, vineyards. Formerly Pirgos.

Piriac-sur-Mer (pērēäk'-sür-mâr'), village (pop. 528), Loire-Inférieure dept., W France, fishing port on Bay of Biscay, 17 mi. NW of Saint-Nazaire.

Piriápolis (pēryä'pōlēs), town (pop. 8,600), Maldonado dept., S Uruguay, on the Atlantic at mouth of the Río de la Plata, 50 mi. E of Montevideo; served by railroad from Pán de Azúcar, 6 mi. NNE. One of the country's major beach resorts, in beautiful wooded setting with parks, boardwalk, casino, and large hotels. Also mineral springs. Vineyards;

porphyry and lime quarries in vicinity. Piriápolis was an important trading post in colonial era, when it was known as Puerto del Inglés.

Piribebuy (pērēbäbwē'), town (dist. pop. 15,844), La Cordillera dept., S central Paraguay, in Cordillera de los Altos, 40 mi. ESE of Asunción; agr. center (sugar cane, maté, fruit, livestock); liquor and alcohol distilling; apiculture. Founded 1640. Has anc. church. Site of decisive battle (Aug. 12, 1869) in War of the Triple Alliance.

Pirin (pē'rēn), village, Puno dept., SE Peru, on the Altiplano, near Puno; oil fields.

Pirineos, Spanish name of the PYRENEES.

Pirin Mountains (pērēn'), W section of Rhodope system, SW Bulgaria, S of Rila Mts., forming divide bet. Struma (W) and Mesta (E) rivers. Subdivided into 3 sections: N Pirin Mts. (highest; rise to 9,558 ft. at Vikhren peak), central Pirin Mts. (rise to 9,351 ft. at Polezhan peak), and S Pirin Mts., extending to Alibotush Mts. on Greek border. Lignite mines near Simitli and in Brezhani (NW). Copper, manganese, and iron deposits (once exploited) concentrated near Nevrokop (SE). Horticulture, truck, and legumes in valleys on E slopes. Lumbering, woodworking, stock raising in Bansko and Razlog areas (NE).

Piripiri or **Periperi** (pērēpērē'), city (pop. 4,520), N Piauí, Brazil, present S terminus of railroad from Luís Correia and Parnaíba, slated to reach Teresina (90 mi. SW); cattle-shipping center; carnauba wax, cotton. Airfield. Formerly spelled Peripery.

Piripirituba (pērēpē"rētōō'bū), town (pop. 2,422), E Paraíba, NE Brazil, on rail spur to Bananeiras, and 4 mi. N of Guarabira; cotton, rice, tobacco.

Piri River, Turkey: see PERI RIVER.

Píritu (pē'rētōō). **1** Town (pop. 1,026), Anzoátegui state, NE Venezuela, near Caribbean coast, just S of Puerto Píritu, 24 mi. WSW of Barcelona; coconuts, cotton, sugar cane, livestock. **2** Town (pop. 1,033), Falcón state, NW Venezuela, 37 mi. E of Coro; sugar cane, corn, fruit. **3** Town (pop. 1,191), Portuguesa state, W Venezuela, in llanos, 13 mi. S of Acarigua; cotton, cattle.

Píritu Islands, two islets in the Caribbean, off Anzoátegui NE Venezuela, 15 mi. W of Barcelona.

Pi River or **P'i River,** Chinese *Pi Ho* or *P'i Ho* (pē' hŭ'), Anhwei prov., China, rises in Tapieh Mts. N of Yosi, flows 140 mi. N, past Hwoshan and Liuan, to Hwai R. at Chengyangkwan.

Piriyapatna, India: see PERIYAPATNA.

Pirkkala (pĭrk'kälä), village (commune pop. 3,642), Häme co., SW Finland, on L. Pyhä, 7 mi. WSW of Tampere, in lumbering region. Of anc. origin, it had (12th–14th cent.) extensive fur trade, with interests reaching into Lapland, where Finnish traders were known as *pirkkalaiset,* Swedish *birkarlar.*

Pir Mangho (pēr' mŭng'gō), village, Karachi administration area, W Pakistan, in S offshoot of Kirthar Range, 9 mi. N of Karachi. Hot springs near by; leper asylum. Also called Magar Pir.

Pirmasens (pĭrmäzĕns'), city (1939 pop. 50,401; 1946 pop. 37,859; 1950 pop. 41,852), Rhenish Palatinate, W Germany, 18 mi. SW of Kaiserslautern; 49°12'N 7°37'E. Rail terminus; noted shoemaking and leather-goods-mfg. center. Founded in 8th cent. by St. Pirmin. Belonged to counts of Hanau-Lichtenberg until 1736, then to Hesse Darmstadt. Chartered 1763. Passed to Bavaria in 1816. Developed as center of Ger. shoe industry in 19th cent. Captured by U.S. troops in March, 1945. Second World War destruction c.65%.

Pirna (pĭr'nä), town (pop. 37,426), Saxony, E central Germany, in Saxonian Switzerland, on the Elbe and 11 mi. SE of Dresden; rayon and paper milling, metal- and woodworking; mfg. of electrical equipment, enamelware, ceramics, glass, musical instruments, soap. Health resort. Sandstone quarries and power station near by. Has 16th-cent. church and town hall. Towered over by old Sonnenstein castle, now insane asylum. First mentioned 1233; passed to Bohemia in 1298. Went to margraves of Meissen in 1405. Saxonians surrendered (1756) here to Prussia in Seven Years War.

Pirnatsa River, Greece: see PAMISOS RIVER.

Piro, Mount. 1 In central Korea: see DIAMOND MOUNTAINS. **2** In N Korea: see MYOHYANG, MOUNT.

Pirogovski or **Pirogovskiy** (pērŭgôf'skē), town (1938 pop. 4,200), central Moscow oblast, Russian SFSR, on Klyazma R., at E end of Klyazma Reservoir, and 5 mi. NNW of Mytishchi; hydroelectric plant. Until 1928, Proletarskaya Pobeda.

Pirojpur (pĭrōj'pōōr), town (pop. 13,771), Bakarganj dist., S East Bengal, E Pakistan, on lower Madhumati (Baleswar) R. and 27 mi. WSW of Barisal; rice, jute, oilseeds, sugar cane.

Pirot (pē'rôt), town (pop. 13,033), E Serbia, Yugoslavia, on Nisava R., on railroad and 37 mi. ESE of Nis, near Bulg. border; produces carpets, cheese, and dried meat. Under Turkish rule until 1878. Held by Bulgaria 1885–86; 1941–44.

Pirovano (pērōvä'nō), town (pop. estimate 2,000), W central Buenos Aires prov., Argentina, 32 mi. SW of Bolívar, in cattle-raising and dairying area; agr. research station.

Pirovskoye (pērôf'skŭyŭ), village (1926 pop. 1,443), SW Krasnoyarsk Territory, Russian SFSR, 110 mi. NNW of Krasnoyarsk.

Pir Panjal Range (pēr' pŭnjäl'), S lateral range of Punjab Himalayas, SW Kashmir and NW India; from Jhelum R. extends c.200 mi. SE to upper Beas R.; forms W border of Vale of Kashmir; rises to over 19,000 ft. in S. Traversed by Chenab R. Sometimes regarded as extending N, beyond Jhelum and Kishanganga rivers, to Kashmir-Pakistan border N of Muzaffarabad. Pir Panjal Pass (alt. 11,462 ft.) is 35 mi. SSW of Srinagar.

Pirque (pēr'kā), village (1930 pop. 697), Santiago prov., central Chile, 17 mi. SSE of Santiago, in agr. area (grain, fruit, wine, livestock).

Pirquitas, Argentina: see MINA PIRQUITAS.

Pirri (pēr'rē), town (pop. 7,386), Cagliari prov., S Sardinia, just NNE of Cagliari; distilling (beer, wine, denatured alcohol), lead mining.

Pirsagat (pērsŭgät'), town (1945 pop. over 500), E Azerbaijan SSR, on Caspian Sea, 40 mi. SW of Baku; oil wells (developed 1937).

Pirshagi (pērshä'gē), town (1939 pop. over 500) in Greater Baku, Azerbaijan SSR, on N shore of Apsheron Peninsula, 13 mi. NNE of Baku; seaside resort; vineyards, orchards.

Pirsopolis, Greece: see PROSOTSANE.

Pirtleville, old ranch and mining village (1940 pop. 898), Cochise co., SE Ariz., near Mex. line, 1 mi. NW of Douglas.

Pirton, Lake, Manchuria: see KINGPO LAKE.

Piru (pīrōō'), village (1940 pop. 733), Ventura co., S Calif., 7 mi. E of Fillmore. Oil fields, orange groves near by.

Piryatin (pēryä'tyĭn), city (1926 pop. 12,212), NW Poltava oblast, Ukrainian SSR, on Udai R. and 100 mi. WNW of Poltava; flour-milling center; machinery works, tobacco products. Peat bogs near.

Piryi, Greece: see PYRGI.

Pisa (pī'sŭ), anc. town of Peloponnesus, Greece, near Olympia. It controlled the Olympic games until 572 B.C. when, together with the surrounding region (*Pisatis*), it passed to Elis.

Pisa (pē'zŭ, Ital. pē'sä), province (□ 945; pop. 341,428), Tuscany, central Italy; ⊙ Pisa. On Ligurian Sea; mtn. and hill terrain occupies 75% of area, enclosing Era R. valley and plains of the lower Arno and Serchio. Agr. (grapes, olives, cereals, fruit, vegetables) and livestock raising (cattle, sheep) predominate. Mining at Volterra (alabaster, salt), San Dalmazio (copper), Canneto (lignite), and Lari (marble). In S, around Pomarance, are many *soffioni* (Larderello, Castelnuovo di Val di Cecina, Serrazzano), which yield boric acid and thermoelectric power. Mfg. at Pontedera, Pisa, San Miniato, and Cascina. Area reduced by transfer of territory to Livorno prov. in 1925.

Pisa, city (pop. 49,471), ⊙ Pisa prov., Tuscany, central Italy, on both banks of the Arno, 6 mi. from its mouth in Ligurian Sea, 12 mi. NNE of Leghorn. Mfg. (railroad equipment, motorcycles, bicycles, cotton textiles, glass, pottery, pharmaceuticals, macaroni, matches); marble statues. Archbishopric. Probably a Gr. colony; later an Etruscan town; grew under Roman rule. Developed into a powerful maritime republic by end of 11th cent., rivalling Genoa and Venice. Naval power crushed by Genoa at battle of Meloria (1284); in 1406 city fell to Florence. In 13th and 14th cent. had flourishing school of sculpture, founded by Nicola Pisano. Its 14th-cent. university had, as a student and later a teacher, Galileo, who was b. here. Before Second World War, in which it suffered from much air bombing (1943–44) and heavy fighting (1944), city was a marvel of Romanesque and Gothic architecture. Anc. houses lining the Arno were badly damaged, and all but one of its bridges blown up. In the *camposanto* (cemetery), fine 14th- and 15th-cent. tracery and frescoes by Gozzoli and others were virtually ruined. Celebrated square of Pisa also has anc. cathedral with fine marble façade and rich art works, baptistery, and the famous Leaning Tower (180 ft. high; 14 ft. out of perpendicular), which were only slightly damaged. Of its other anc. churches, only Santa Maria della Spina (14th cent.) escaped heavy damage.

Pisac (pēsäk'), town (pop. 1,105), Cuzco dept., S central Peru, in the Andes, on upper Urubamba R. and 11 mi. NE of Cuzco, in agr. region (grain, vegetables); alt. 9,775 ft. Market for Indian textile goods. Here are ruins of an Inca fortress, with remains of anc. solar observatory.

Pisaflores (pēsäflō'rēs), town (pop. 879), Hidalgo, central Mexico, 18 mi. NE of Jacala; corn, sugar, coffee, fruit.

Pisagua (pēsä'gwä), town (pop. 419), ⊙ Pisagua dept. (□ 4,085; pop. 4,957), Tarapacá prov., N Chile, rail terminus, and port on the Pacific, 45 mi. N of Iquique, 80 mi. S of Arica; 19°37'S 70°13'W. Former nitrate-shipping center at N edge of the great Chilean nitrate fields. Originally belonging to Peru, it was bombarded (1879) by the Chilean navy during the War of the Pacific and was annexed (1883) to Chile. Flourished c.1900.

Pisania, Gambia: see KARANTABA.

Pisanino, Monte (môn'tĕ pēzänē'nô), highest peak (6,384 ft.) in Apuane Alps, Tuscany, central Italy, 7 mi. NE of Carrara.

Pisano, Monte (môn'tĕ pēzä'nô), mountain group (□ 60), Tuscany, central Italy, S of Apuane Alps, bet. Serchio and Arno rivers, near Pisa; rises to 3,012 ft. in Monte Serra (S). Excellent olives and grapes grown on lower slopes.

Pisarevo (pēsärĕ'vô), village (pop. 3,232), Pleven dist., N Bulgaria, 18 mi. W of Pleven; grain, legumes, livestock.

Pisarovina (pēsä'rôvēnä), village, N Croatia, Yugoslavia, 17 mi. S of Zagreb, near Kupa R.; local trade center.

Pisaurum, Italy: see PESARO, town.

Piscadera Bay (pĭskädā'rä), inlet and beach resort, W Curaçao, Du. West Indies, 3 mi. WNW of Willemstad.

Piscataqua River (pĭskă'tŭkwŭ), Maine and N.H., formed by Salmon Falls and Cocheco rivers at Dover, N.H.; flows SSE, forming c.11 mi. of state line, past Kittery, Maine, and Portsmouth, N.H., to Portsmouth Harbor. First visited (1603) by English voyager; explored 1614 by Capt. John Smith.

Piscataquis (pĭskă'tŭkwĭs), county (□ 3,948; pop. 18,617), N central Maine; ⊙ Dover-Foxcroft. Agr., mfg. (wood products, textiles); potatoes shipped. Lumbering and wilderness recreational area of N has state's largest lake (Moosehead), highest mtn. (Katahdin) and 112,945-acre Baxter State Park; hundreds of lakes are resort and camp sites for hunting, fishing, canoeing. Drained by Piscataquis and Pleasant rivers and West Branch of the Penobscot. Formed 1838.

Piscataquis River, central Maine, rises in 2 branches just S of Moosehead L., flows c.78 mi. S and E, past Dover-Foxcroft (water power), to the Penobscot at Howland.

Piscataquog River (pĭskă'tŭkwäg), S N.H., rises in N Hillsboro co., flows c.30 mi. SE to the Merrimack just below Manchester; dam at Goffstown forms Glen L.; hydroelectric power. South Branch (18 mi. long) enters river just W of Goffstown.

Piscataway (pĭskă'tŭwā). **1** Village (pop. 77), Prince Georges co., S Md., 14 mi. SSE of Washington. Near by is site of Moyaone, Indian village visited by Capt. John Smith, where archaeological excavations have been made. **2** Village in Piscataway township (pop. 10,180), Middlesex co., NE N.J., on Raritan R. opposite New Brunswick; mfg. (chemicals, metal products, leather). St. James Episcopal Church (1837), here, is reproduction of earlier church destroyed by tornado in 1835. Township inc. 1693.

Pisciotta (pēshôt'tä), village (pop. 1,413), Salerno prov., Campania, S Italy, near Tyrrhenian Sea, 9 mi. SSW of Vallo di Lucania.

Pisco (pē'skō), city (pop. 14,609), ⊙ Pisco prov. (□ 2,413; pop. 25,944), Ica dept., SW Peru, Pacific port near mouth of Pisco R., 42 mi. NW of Ica (connected by highway and railroad); 13°44'S 76°13'W. Shipping center in irrigated cotton and wine region; cotton ginning, cottonseed-oil milling, mfg. of oil cake, soap; trade in fruit, wine. Noted particularly for its Pisco brandy, which it exports. Fishing. Airport. Pisco port (connected by rail) on Pisco Bay (12 mi. wide, 4 mi. long) is near by, 1 mi. NW.

Piscopi, Greece: see TELOS.

Pisco River, Ica dept., SW Peru, rises in Cordillera Occidental, flows 150 mi. SW and W, past Humay and Pisco, to the Pacific 2 mi. NNW of Pisco, watering cotton- and winegrowing region.

Piscoyacu (pēskoiä'kōō), town (pop. 672), San Martín dept., N central Peru, 2 mi. SSE of Saposoa; sugar cane, rice, cotton.

Pisechai, China: see PISHIHCHAI.

Piseco (pĭsē'kō), resort village, Hamilton co., E central N.Y., in the Adirondacks, on Piseco L., c.45 mi. NE of Utica. Has airport.

Piseco Lake, Hamilton co., E central N.Y., in the Adirondacks, 37 mi. NW of Amsterdam; c.5 mi. long, ½–1 mi. wide. State camp site here.

Pisek (pē'sĕk), Czech *Písek,* town (pop. 16,858), S Bohemia, Czechoslovakia, on Otava R. and 27 mi. NNW of Budweis; rail junction; processing of tobacco, raw furs and hides; mfg. of paper, cotton goods, musical instruments. Popular summer resort. Forestry school. Has 12th-cent. cathedral, 13th-cent. castle, 13th-cent. bridge, baroque city hall. Originally a gold-mining settlement. Historic ruins of 13th-cent. Zvikov castle (keep, arcaded court, murals) are 9 mi. NNE, on Vltava R. at mouth of Otava R. Remains of Orlik castle are 14 mi. N, also on the Vltava.

Pisek (pē'zŭk, pē'shŭk), village (pop. 215), Walsh co., NE N.Dak., 15 mi. SW of Grafton.

Pisgah, Jordan: see NEBA, JEBEL.

Pisgah (pĭz'gŭ). **1** Town (pop. 217), Jackson co., NW Ala., 11 mi. E of Scottsboro. **2** Town (pop. 327), Harrison co., W Iowa, on Soldier R. and 40 mi. N of Council Bluffs. **3** Village (1940 pop. 504), Charles co., S Md., 26 mi. SSW of Washington, in agr. area. Near by is Doncaster State Forest.

Pisgah, Mount. 1 Peak (10,085 ft.) in Front Range, bet. Clear Creek and Gilpin counties, central Colo. **2** Peak (3,365 ft.) of the Catskills, Delaware co., S N.Y., 14 mi. SW of Stamford. **3** Peak (2,885 ft.) of the Catskills, Greene co., SE N.Y., 18 mi. E of Stamford. **4** Peak (5,749) of the Blue Ridge, W N.C., 16 mi. SW of Asheville, in Pisgah Natl. Forest.

Pisgah Forest, village (1940 pop. 597), Transylvania co., W N.C., 25 mi. SSW of Asheville, near French Broad R. Paper mill here is chief U.S. producer of cigarette paper (from fibers of seed flax plant) and exports much of the world supply.

Pisha, China: see NINGNAN.

Pishan. 1 (bē'shän') Town (pop. 9,169), ⊙ Pishan co. (pop. 342,472), S central Szechwan prov., China, 22 mi. WNW of Chungking city; paper milling; rice, sweet potatoes, wheat, beans. Coal mines near by. **2** Town and oasis, Sinkiang prov., China: see GUMA.

Pishihchai or **Pisechai** (both: bē'shŭ'jī'), village, SE Yunnan prov., China, 120 mi. SSE of Kunming; junction of railroad to Hanoi, serving Mengtsz and Kokiu.

Pishin, district, Pakistan: see QUETTA-PISHIN.

Pishin (pĭshĭn'), town (pop. 1,890), Quetta-Pishin dist., NE Baluchistan, W Pakistan, 23 mi. N of Quetta; wheat; carpet weaving.

Pishin Lora (lō'rŭ), river, W Pakistan and S Afghanistan, rises in central Toba-Kakar Range, NE Baluchistan, NW of Hindubagh; flows c.250 mi. generally SW, through SW Afghanistan, to the Hamun-i-Lora in Chagai dist. (Baluchistan); seasonal.

Pishpek, Kirghiz SSR: see FRUNZE, city, Frunze oblast.

Pisida (pēzē'dä), frontier station, W Tripolitania, Libya, near Tunisian border, on highway and 25 mi. WNW of Zuara, on Mediterranean coast; sponge fishing. Has a Turkish fort. Near by are large salt deposits. Formerly Bu Chemmasc.

Pisidia (pĭsĭ'dēŭ, pī–), anc. country of S central Asia Minor (now Turkey), bounded NW by Phrygia, NE by Lycaonia, SE by Cilicia, S by Pamphylia, SW by Lycia. An independent country until it became a Roman prov.

Pisino, Yugoslavia: see PAZIN.

Piskavica or **Piskavitsa** (both: pē'skävētsä), village (pop. 5,503), NW Bosnia, Yugoslavia, 12 mi. NW of Banja Luka.

Pismo Beach (pĭz'mō), resort city (pop. 1,425), San Luis Obispo co., SW Calif., on the coast, 10 mi. S of San Luis Obispo; fine beach; clams, fish. Oil and natural-gas field near by. Inc. 1946.

Pisogne (pēzô'nyě), village (pop. 1,825), Brescia prov., Lombardy, N Italy, port on NE shore of Lago d'Iseo, near influx of Oglio R., 19 mi. NNW of Brescia. Fishing center; cutlery mfg. Iron mine near by.

Pis Pis Mountains, Nicaragua: see BONANZA.

Pis Pis River, Nicaragua: see HUASPUC RIVER.

Pissa River (pĭ'sŭ), formerly in East Prussia, in E Kaliningrad oblast, Russian SFSR, rises in L. Vistytis on Lith. border, flows N and W, past Gusev, to the Angerapp above Chernyakhovsk; c.50 mi. long.

Pissevache, Switzerland: see VERNAYAZ.

Pissis, Monte (mōn'tä pē'sēs), Andean peak (22,240 ft.) on Catamarca–La Rioja prov. border, Argentina, 73 mi. W of Fiambalá; 27°45'S 68°40'W.

Pissos (pēsō'), village (pop. 612), Landes dept., SW France, on the Leyre and 32 mi. NNW of Mont-de-Marsan; brick- and tileworks; mfg. of resinous products.

Pistakee Lake, Ill.: see CHAIN-O'-LAKES.

Pisticci (pēstēt'chē), town (pop. 11,145), Matera prov., Basilicata, S Italy, on hill bet. Basento and Cavone rivers, 19 mi. S of Matera; agr. center; wine, olive oil, cheese; cereals, fruit; brickworks. Has 16th-cent. church and ruined castle. Heavily damaged by landslide (*frana*) in 1688.

Pistoia (pēstô'yä), province (□ 372; pop. 211,150), Tuscany, central Italy; ⊙ Pistoia. Etruscan Apennines in N, valleys in S; watered by Lima and upper Reno rivers. Agr. (grapes, fruit, vegetables), livestock raising; forestry. Resorts at Montecatini Terme and Abetone. Industry at Pistoia (food processing, ironworking) and Pescia (paper mill). Formed 1927 from provs. of Firenze and Lucca.

Pistoia, city (pop. 29,532), ⊙ Pistoia prov., Tuscany, central Italy, at foot of Etruscan Apennines, 20 mi. NW of Florence; 43°56'N 10°56'E. Agr. and industrial center; mfg. (macaroni, canned foods, agr. and bakery machinery, textiles, hats, musical instruments); foundries, tanneries, alcohol distillery. Bishopric since 5th cent. Has fine marble cathedral (12th cent.), churches of Sant'Andrea (12th cent.) and San Paolo (completed 1302), octagonal baptistery (started 1337), 14th-cent. Palazzo Pretorio (enlarged 19th cent.), and Ospedale del Ceppo (founded 1277; has frieze by G. della Robbia). Catiline was killed in battle (62 B.C.) near here. Important in Middle Ages; fell under rule of Florence in 14th cent. Pistols, 1st manufactured here in 1515, were named after Pistoia. Became capital of prov. in 1927. Badly damaged (1943–44) by air and artillery bombing in Second World War.

Pistsovo (pēs-tsô'vŭ), town (1926 pop. 3,621), NW Ivanovo oblast, Russian SFSR, 20 mi. NW of Ivanovo; cotton and flour mills.

Pistyll Cain (pĭ'stĭl kīn), falls (150 ft.) of Prysor R., N Merioneth, Wales, 9 mi. S of Ffestiniog.

Pistyll Rhaiadr (rī'ūdŭr), falls (230 ft.) of Rhaiadr R., S Denbighshire, Wales.

Pisuerga River (pēswĕr'gä), in Palencia and Valladolid provs., N central Spain, rises in the Cantabrian Mts. near Peña Labra, flows 176 mi. S (forming in part border bet. Palencia and Burgos provs.) and SW, past Valladolid, to the Duero (Douro) 13 mi. below city. Receives the Carrión and feeds Canal of Castile.

Pisz (pēsh), Ger. *Johannisburg* (yōhä'nĭsbŏŏrk), town (1939 pop. 6,322; 1946 pop. 1,028) in East Prussia, after 1945 in Olsztyn prov., NE Poland, in Masurian Lakes region, 35 mi. NNW of Lomza, at SW end of L. Ros, on edge of extensive forest lands; cattle and grain market; sawmilling. In First World War, occupied (1914–15) by Russians; center of final Ger. counterattack (Feb., 1915) under Hindenburg during battle of Masurian Lakes. In Second World War, c.90% destroyed.

Pita (pē'tä), town (pop. c.1,250), W central Fr. Guinea, Fr. West Africa, resort in Fouta Djallon mts., 140 mi. NE of Conakry; alt. c.2,750 ft. Cattle raising. Piscicultural station. Landing field.

Pitahaya (pētäī'ä), village (dist. pop. 1,843), Puntarenas prov., W Costa Rica, 3 mi. N of Puntarenas; corn, grain, livestock.

Pitäjänmäki (pĭ'täyänmä"kē), Swedish *Sockenbacka* (sô'kŭnbä"kä), village in Helsinki rural commune (pop. 13,678), Uusimaa co., S Finland, 3 mi. NNW of Helsinki city center; electrical-equipment works.

Pitalito (pētälē'tō), town (pop. 3,135), Huila dept., S central Colombia, in upper Magdalena valley, on highway, and 90 mi. SW of Neiva; alt. 4,232 ft. Cotton, rice, cacao, coffee; horse and mule breeding. Airfield. The Guácharos Caves (gwä'chärōs), impressive natural caverns, are 12 mi. S.

Pitanga (pētăng'gŭ), city (pop. 874), central Paraná, Brazil, 50 mi. NNW of Guarapuava; meat packing, processing of coffee and brown sugar.

Pitangueiras (pētăng-gā'rŭs), city (pop. 2,521), N São Paulo, Brazil, near Mogi-Guaçu R., on railroad and 27 mi. WNW of Ribeirão Prêto; distilling, dairy and rice processing, tanning.

Pitangui (pētăng-gē'), city (pop. 4,484), central Minas Gerais, Brazil, 65 mi. WNW of Belo Horizonte; rail junction; cotton, lard, butter. Iron and manganese deposits. Picturesque colonial town. Formerly spelled Pitanguy.

Pitcairn (pĭt'kârn), industrial borough (pop. 5,857), Allegheny co., SW Pa., E suburb of Pittsburgh; railroad shops, brickworks; bituminous coal, natural gas, clay; agr. Laid out c.1890, inc. 1891.

Pitcairn Island, volcanic island (□ 2; pop. 126) and Br. colony, S Pacific; 25°S 130°5'W; 2 mi. long; rises to 1,000 ft. Breadfruit, coconut, pandanus, banana groves; goats. Adamstown, only village, is near Bounty Bay. Discovered 1767 by British; settled 1790 by *Bounty* mutineers with Polynesian natives from Tahiti. Colony discovered 1808 by Americans. Overpopulation caused removal (1856) of inhabitants to NORFOLK ISLAND, but many returned to Pitcairn. Isl. placed 1898 under Br. High Commission of W Pacific at Suva, Fiji. Included in Pitcairn Isl. Dist. are uninhabited near-by Henderson, Ducie, Oeno isls., annexed 1902.

Pitch Lake (114 acres), SW Trinidad, B.W.I., at N side of SW peninsula, near Gulf of Paria, 11 mi. WSW of San Fernando; a vast basin of pitch, c.½ mi. in diameter. Refined and crude asphalt is exported through adjoining La Brea and Brighton. The site is visited by tourists. It is surrounded by petroleum deposits and is said to owe its origin to oil seepages. The lake is up to 285 ft. deep. It contains fossils of prehistoric animals.

Pitea (pē'tŭō"), Swedish *Piteå*, city (pop. 4,895), Norrbotten co., N Sweden, on Pite R., near its mouth on Gulf of Bothnia, 25 mi. SW of Lulea; seaport, timber-shipping center; sawmilling, metalworking. Has 17th-cent. church. Chartered in 17th cent.; burned (1716 and 1721) by Russians.

Piteglio (pētā'lyô), village (pop. 367), Pistoia prov., Tuscany, central Italy, 10 mi. NW of Pistoia; paper mill.

Pitelino (pĕtyĕ'lyĭnŭ), village (1926 pop. 1,791), E Ryazan oblast, Russian SFSR, 16 mi. N of Sasovo; coarse grain, hemp. Also spelled Petelino.

Pite River, Swedish *Pite älv* (pē'tŭ ĕlv"), Lapland, N Sweden, rises near Norwegian border at foot of Mt. Sulitelma, flows 230 mi. SE, over several falls (power stations), past Alvsbyn and Pitea, to Gulf of Bothnia just below Pitea. Important logging route; salmon fishing.

Piterka (pē'tyĭrkŭ), village (1926 pop. 4,863), SE Saratov oblast, Russian SFSR, on Lesser Uzen R. and 27 mi. SE of Krasny Kut; metalworks; wheat, cattle, sheep.

Pitesti (pētēsht'), Rum. *Piteşti*, town (1948 pop. 29,007), ⊙ Arges prov., S central Rumania, in Walachia, on Arges R. and 65 mi. NW of Bucharest; rail junction and commercial center; mfg. of textiles, earthenware, lacquers, varnishes, barrels; flour milling, distilling. Extensive orchards (mainly cherries) and vineyards in vicinity. Has several 17th-cent. churches. Textile mills of Gavana (gŭ'vänä), Rum. *Găvana*, are 2 mi. NW.

Pit-Gorodok (pēt"-gŭrŭdôk'), town (1939 pop. over 500), central Krasnoyarsk Territory, Russian SFSR, on Yenisei Ridge, on Pit R. and 40 mi. NE of Yeniseisk; gold mines.

Pithapuram (pĭ'täpŏŏrŭm), town (pop. 18,174), East Godavari dist., NE Madras, India, 12 mi. N of Cocanada; road center; rice milling; copra, coir, metalware. Beekeeping in near-by fruit orchards.

Pithion, Greece: see PYTHION.

Pithiviers (pētēvyā'), town (pop. 6,416), Loiret dept., N central France, 25 mi. NE of Orléans; noted for its lark pies, gingerbread, and almond cakes. Trade center for saffron, honey, wool, potatoes, wheat, wine. Sugar refining, fertilizer mfg.

Pitholm, Sweden: see MUNKSUND.

Pithom, Egypt: see ABU SUWEIR.

Pithoragarh (pĭtō'rŭgŭr), town (pop. 1,519), Almora dist., N Uttar Pradesh, India, 33 mi. E of Almora, in E Kumaun Himalaya foothills; rice, wheat, barley. Fort ruins.

Pithoro (pĭtō'rō), village, Thar Parkar dist., E central Sind, W Pakistan, 25 mi. WNW of Umarkot; rail junction; cotton, rice; cotton ginning.

Piti (pē'tē), town (pop. 778), and municipality (pop. 1,892), SW Guam; port town; in rice-farming area.

Pitigliano (pētēlyä'nô), town (pop. 4,103), Grosseto prov., Tuscany, central Italy, 29 mi. ESE of Grosseto, in agr. region (cereals, grapes, olives); macaroni mfg. Bishopric. Has cathedral (restored 16th cent.) and 14th-cent. castle.

Pitillas (pētē'lyäs), town (pop. 1,096), Navarre prov., N Spain, 28 mi. S of Pamplona, in winegrowing area; brandy mfg.; wheat, livestock.

Pitiquito (pētēkē'tō), town (pop. 1,472), Sonora, NW Mexico, on lower Magdalena R. and 80 mi. SW of Nogales; agr. center (wheat, cotton, corn, fruit, cattle); copper and zinc mining.

Pitkälahti (pĭt'kälä'tē, –läkh'tē), village in Kuopio rural commune (pop. 9,261), Kuopio co., central Finland, near L. Kalla, 5 mi. SW of Kuopio; power station, serving Kuopio; sawmills.

Pitkas Point (pĭt'kŭz), Eskimo village (pop. 84), W Alaska, on Yukon R. and 100 mi. NW of Bethel.

Pitkin, county (□ 974; pop. 1,646), W central Colo.; ⊙ Aspen. Livestock-grazing and mining area, drained by branches of Colorado R. Silver, lead. Holy Cross Natl. Forest throughout. Part of Sawatch Mts. in E. Formed 1881.

Pitkin, town (pop. 152), Gunnison co., W central Colo., on branch of Gunnison R., in Sawatch Mts., and 23 mi. ENE of Gunnison; alt. 9,200 ft.

Pitkyaranta (pēt'kyŭrŭntŭ), Finnish *Pitkäranta* (pĭt'käräntä), city (1948 pop. over 2,000), SW Karelo-Finnish SSR, on L. Ladoga, on railroad and 28 mi. ESE of Sortavala; mining and sawmilling center; smelting of iron and nonferrous metals (tin, copper, zinc); cellulose mill. In Finland until 1940.

Pitlochry (pĭtlŏkh'rē), burgh (1951 census pop. 2,384), N Perthshire, Scotland, on Tummel R. and 25 mi. NNW of Perth; fashionable resort. Also has woolen mills and whisky distilleries. Near by is Pass of KILLIECRANKIE.

Pitman, borough (pop. 6,960), Gloucester co., SW N.J., 15 mi. S of Camden; summer resort; fruit, truck, dairy and nursery products. Settled 1871 as place for Methodist camp meetings, inc. 1905.

Pitminster, agr. village and parish (pop. 1,066), S Somerset, England, 4 mi. S of Taunton.

Pitoa (pētō'ä), village, Benoué region, N Fr. Cameroons, 8 mi. NE of Garoua; cotton ginning, mfg. of cottonseed and peanut oils.

Pitogo (pētō'gō), town (1939 pop. 2,340; 1948 municipality pop. 7,668), Quezon prov., S Luzon, Philippines, on Tayabas Bay, 34 mi. ESE of Lucena; fishing, agr. (coconuts, rice).

Piton des Neiges, Réunion: see NEIGES, PITON DES.

Pitones, Madeira: see Selvagens.

Pitons, The (pētōnz'), twin peaks, SW St. Lucia, B.W.I., on S Soufrière Bay, 13 mi. SSW of Castries. Petit Piton (pŭtē') (N) rises to 2,461 ft. and Gros Piton (grōs) to 2,619 ft. They form remarkable, pyramidical cones, detached from other mts.

Pito Solo (pē'tō sō'lō), village (pop. 52), Comayagua dept., W central Honduras, port on S shore of L. Yojoa, 65 mi. NW of Tegucigalpa (linked by road). Ferry service to El Jaral is link in Tegucigalpa-Caribbean coast route.

Pit River (pēt), central Krasnoyarsk Territory, Russian SFSR, rises on SW border of Evenki Natl. Okrug, flows 245 mi. generally SW, through Yenisei Ridge, to Yenisei R. below Yeniseisk.

Pit River, NE Calif., rises in GOOSE LAKE, flows c.200 mi. SW, past Alturas, to Shasta L., backed up by SHASTA DAM on the Sacramento, into which the Pit formerly emptied.

Pitrufquén (pētrŏŏfkĕn'), town (pop. 5,193), ⊙ Pitrufquén dept. (□ 812; pop. 43,610), Cautín prov., S central Chile, on Toltén R., on railroad, and 17 mi. S of Temuco; agr. center (wheat, barley, vegetables, potatoes, livestock); tanning, flour milling, dairying, lumbering.

Pitsani (pētsä'nē), locality, SE Bechuanaland Protectorate, near U. of So. Afr. border, 25 mi. N of Mafeking, on railroad; alt. 4,421 ft. Starting point (Dec. 30, 1895) of Jameson Raid.

Pitsanulok, Thailand: see PHITSANULOK.

Pitsburg, village (pop. 359), Darke co., W Ohio, 11 mi. SE of Greenville. Also spelled Pittsburg.

Pitschen, Poland: see BYCZYNA.

Pitsea, residential town and parish (pop. 3,414), S Essex, England, 10 mi. NE of Tilbury; mfg. of electrical equipment and textile-machinery parts.

Pitsligo (pĭtslĭ'gō), parish (pop. 2,987, including Rosehearty burgh), N Aberdeen, Scotland. Includes SANDHAVEN. Pitsligo parish church dates from 1633. New Pitsligo is S.

Pitsunda (pētsōōn'dŭ), village (1948 pop. over 500) and wooded cape in NW Abkhaz Autonomous SSR, Georgian SSR, port on Black Sea, 35 mi. WNW of Sukhumi; mfg. of essential oils. Has 10th-cent. church.

Pitt, county (□ 656; pop. 63,789), E central N.C.; ⊙ Greenville. Coastal plain, drained by Tar R. Largely agr. (especially tobacco) and timber (pine, gum) area; sawmilling. Formed 1760.

Pittem (pĭ'tŭm), agr. village (pop. 4,620), West Flanders prov., W Belgium, 2 mi. W of Tielt. Formerly spelled Pitthem.

Pitten River (pĭ'tŭn), SE Lower Austria, rises in the Wechsel group, flows 25 mi. N, joining Schwarza R. just NE of Erlach to form Leitha R.

Pittenweem (pĭtŭnwēm'), burgh (1931 pop. 1,619; 1951 census 1,642), E Fifeshire, Scotland, on the Firth of Forth, near its mouth on the North Sea, 11 mi. E of Leven; port and seaside resort. Has remains of 12th-cent. priory. Near by are remains of 16th-cent. Kellie Castle.

Pitthem, Belgium: see PITTEM.

Pitt Island (□ 528), W B.C., in Hecate Strait, separated from mainland by Grenville Channel and from Banks Isl. (W) by Principe Channel; 53°30'N 130°W. It is 56 mi. long, 5–14 mi. wide; rises to 3,155 ft. Chino Hat Indian village on W coast. Lumbering; magnesite and iron deposits.

Pitt Island, Gilbert Isls.: see MAKIN.

Pitt Island, New Zealand: see CHATHAM ISLANDS.

Pitt Lake (17 mi. long, 1–2 mi. wide), SW B.C., 20 mi. ENE of Vancouver, on Pitt R. (52 mi. long), which flows to the Fraser.

Pittock, Pa.: see STOWE, Allegheny co.

Pitt Passage, Indonesia: see CERAM SEA.

Pitts, town (pop. 397), Wilcox co., S central Ga., 13 mi. E of Cordele.

Pittsboro. **1** Town (pop. 599), Hendricks co., central Ind., 18 mi. NW of Indianapolis, in agr. area. **2** Village (pop. 246), ⊙ Calhoun co., N central Miss., 29 mi. ENE of Grenada, in agr. and timber area. **3** Town (pop. 1,094), ⊙ Chatham co., central N.C., 31 mi. WSW of Raleigh; cotton and lumber mills. Settled 1771.

Pittsburg (pĭts'bûrg), county (□ 1,359; pop. 41,031), SE Okla.; ⊙ McAlester. Bounded N by Canadian R.; drained by small Gaines Creek; Ouachita Mts. are in SE corner. Agr. (cotton, corn, vegetables, peanuts; dairy products; cattle, hogs). Mfg. at McAlester. Coal mining; natural-gas and oil wells; rock quarries; lumbering. Formed 1907.

Pittsburg. **1** Industrial city (pop. 12,763), Contra Costa co., W Calif., at junction of Sacramento R. and San Joaquin R., 25 mi. NE of Oakland; steelworks (open-hearth furnaces; foundries; sheet, plate, and wire mills), here, are among largest in West; planing mills, canneries (asparagus, fruit, fish). Mfg. also of chemicals, asbestos and rubber products, brick; boat yards. U.S. Camp Stoneman near by. Laid out 1849; inc. 1903 as Black Diamond (because of short-lived coal mines near by); renamed c.1910 with coming of steel industry. **2** Village (pop. 612), Williamson co., S Ill., 10 mi. ESE of Herrin, in bituminous-coal-mining and agr. area. **3** City (pop. 19,341), Crawford co., extreme SE Kansas, 25 mi. NNW of Joplin, Mo.; trade and coal-mining center, with railroad repair shops. Mfg. of coal by-products, fertilizer, mining equipment; foundry work; dairying, meat packing, flour milling. Coal, lead, and zinc mines in vicinity. Has state teachers col. Quail hatchery is near by. Founded 1872 as mining town; inc. 1880. **4** Town (pop. 697), Coos co., N N.H., on Que. line. Pittsburg village, on Connecticut R., is 9 mi. NE of Colebrook. Hunting, fishing; includes L. Francis and Connecticut Lakes. Independent "Republic of Indian Stream," formed here by settlers in 1832; functioned until occupation by N.H. militia in 1835; inc. with N.H. in 1840. **5** Village, Darke co., Ohio: see PITSBURG. **6** Town (pop. 278), Pittsburg co., SE Okla., 17 mi. SSW of McAlester, in agr. area. **7** City (pop. 3,142), ⊙ Camp co., NE Texas, 45 mi. NW of Marshall, in agr., lumbering area; processes sweet potatoes, black-eyed peas; also cottonseed oil, lumber, soap, canned foods. Settled 1854. Indian artifacts found near by.

Pittsburgh (pĭts'bûrg), city (pop. 676,806), ⊙ Allegheny co., SW Pa., c.250 mi. W of Philadelphia, at confluence of Allegheny and Monongahela rivers, meeting in city at tip of "Golden Triangle" and forming Ohio R.; 40°27'N 80°W. One of nation's most important industrial cities, and a center of rail and river transportation; on the Pa. Turnpike; port of entry; 2d largest city in Pa., 12th largest in U.S. Termed the "Steel City" or "Smoky City," it is center of rich bituminous-coal region producing also natural gas, oil, and limestone; a large part of U.S. steel and iron is produced here and in adjacent industrial communities (notably Munhall, Homestead, Duquesne, Braddock, Carnegie, McKeesport, McKees Rocks, Clairton, Rankin, Blawnox). Other mfg. includes coke, aluminum, petroleum products, tin plate, electrical equipment, industrial machinery, clay products, air brakes and other railroad equipment, plate glass, chemicals, hardware, leather, cork products, food products; printing; railroad shops, shipyards, industrial laboratories, atomic-energy research laboratory. Seat of Univ. of Pittsburgh, Carnegie Inst. of Technology, Duquesne Univ., Pennsylvania Col. for Women; seminaries include Pittsburgh-Xenia, Reformed Presbyterian, and Western Theological. Here are Carnegie Mus., Music Hall, Carnegie Library (with library school), other museums, art galleries, municipal parks (notably Schenley Park), Buhl Planetarium, conservatories; has noted symphony orchestra. Built on plateau dissected by 3 rivers, city's sections are joined by many bridges. Fort Duquesne built here in mid-18th cent. on site of Indian village and fur-trading post; later seized by British and renamed Fort Pitt. Its blockhouse (1764) is extant. Settlement grew up 1775 around fort, in present-day "Golden Triangle" business dist. River commerce and mfg. promoted early growth; railroad came 1834, mining of bituminous coal and iron mfg. began c.1840. City's position on E–W transportation arteries and availability of local raw materials and iron ore from Lake Superior region led to present-day industrial importance. Severe floods inundated city in 1936 and 1937. Inc. as borough 1794, as city 1816.

Pittsburg Landing, village, Hardin co., SW Tenn., on Tennessee R. and 45 mi. SE of Jackson, at entrance to SHILOH NATIONAL MILITARY PARK.

Pittsfield. **1** City (pop. 3,564), ⊙ Pike co., W Ill., 32 mi. WSW of Jacksonville, in agr. area (corn, wheat, livestock, poultry, apples, hay); mfg. (flour, cheese and other dairy products, shoes, costume jewelry). Laid out 1833, inc. 1869. **2** Town (pop. 3,909), including Pittsfield village (pop. 3,012), Somerset co., central Maine, on the Sebasticook and 16 mi. E of Skowhegan; agr. trade center; textiles, shoes. Maine Central Inst., preparatory school, here. Settled 1794, inc. 1819 as Warsaw, renamed 1824. **3** City (pop. 53,348), ⊙ Berkshire co., W Mass., in the Berkshires, on headstreams of the Housatonic (water power) and 45 mi. NW of Springfield. Main center of the Berkshires; produces electrical machinery, woolen goods, paper, foundry and machine-shop products, clothing, plastics; printing; tourist trade. Settled 1752, inc. as town 1761, as city 1889. Includes village of West Pittsfield. **4** Town (pop. 2,321), including Pittsfield village (pop. 1,342), Merrimack co., S central N.H., on the Suncook and 14 mi. NE of Concord; shoes, textiles, lumber; agr. (corn, potatoes, fruit). Settled 1768, inc. 1782. **5** Town (pop. 225), Rutland co., central Vt., 14 mi. NE of Rutland, partly in Green Mtn. Natl. Forest.

Pittsford. **1** Residential village (pop. 1,668), Monroe co., W N.Y., on the Barge Canal, just SE of Rochester; mfg. (pickles, condiments, machinery); truck farming. Fish hatchery here. Inc. 1827. **2** Town (pop. 2,076), including Pittsford village (pop. 622), Rutland co., W central Vt., on Otter Creek and 8 mi. N of Rutland; marble, dairy products, lumber. Settled 1769; 2 forts here during Revolution. Site of sanatorium, tuberculosis preventorium, U.S. trout hatchery.

Pittsound Island (5 mi. long, 1 mi. wide), E N.F., in Bonavista Bay; 48°52'N 53°45'W.

Pittston. **1** Agr. town (pop. 1,258), Kennebec co., S Maine, on the Kennebec, near Gardiner. Settled c.1759, inc. 1779. **2** City (pop. 15,012), Luzerne co., NE central Pa., 7 mi. NE of Wilkes-Barre and on Susquehanna R., near mouth of Lackawanna R.; mfg. (textiles, clothing, metal products, paper, cigars); anthracite; railroad shops. Settled 1770, laid out 1772, inc. as borough 1853.

Pittsville. **1** Town (pop. 497), Wicomico co., SE Md., 10 mi. E of Salisbury, in truck-farm area; ships Christmas evergreens; tomato-packing plant. **2** City (pop. 636), Wood co., central Wis., near Yellow R., 14 mi. W of Wisconsin Rapids, in dairy and farm area; canned foods, cheese, pottery.

Pittsworth, town (pop. 1,252), SE Queensland, Australia, 90 mi. W of Brisbane; wheat-raising center.

Pittsylvania (pĭtsĭlvā'nyū), county (□ 1,022; pop. 66,096), S Va.; ⊙ Chatham. In the piedmont; bounded S by N.C., N by Roanoke R.; drained by Dan and Banister rivers. DANVILLE is in but independent of co. Rich tobacco-growing area, producing also corn and timber. Formed 1767.

Pitt Water, Tasmania: see FREDERICK HENRY BAY.

Pitumarca (pētōōmär'kä), town (pop. 2,162), Cuzco dept., S Peru, in Vilcanota R. valley, 45 mi. SE of Cuzco, in agr. region (grain, potatoes).

Pitvaros (pĭt'vŏrōsh), town (pop. 2,843), Csanad co., SE Hungary, 14 mi. NE of Mako; wheat, hemp, hogs, horses.

Pityusae (pĭ"tēū'sē), Sp. *Las Pitiusas* (läs pētyōō'säs), anc. name for IVIZA and FORMENTERA, Balearic Isls., Spain, derived from Greek word for pine trees.

Pitzewo or **Pitzuwo**, Manchuria: see SINKIN.

Pitzthal, Austria: see SANKT LEONHARD.

Piu (pū), peak (5,900 ft.) in Cordillera Isabelia, N central Nicaragua, 50 mi. WSW of Bonanza.

Piũi (pyōōn-ē'), city (pop. 4,887), SW Minas Gerais, Brazil, near source of São Francisco R., 50 mi. NE of Passos; dairying. Chromite mines. Formerly spelled Piumhy.

Piuka (pēōō'kä) or **Bifuka** (bēfōō'kä), town (pop. 12,455), N Hokkaido, Japan, on Teshio R. and 11 mi. NNW of Nayoro; agr. center (grain, soybeans, sugar beets, hemp).

Piumhy, Brazil: see PIŨI.

Piuquenes Pass (pyōōkā'nĕs) (13,220 ft.), in the Andes, on Argentina-Chile border, 20 mi. SSW of Tupungato peak, on road bet. Tunuyán (Argentina) and El Volcán (Chile); 33°38'S 69°54'W. The mtn. Piuquenes (19,685 ft.) is 8 mi. N.

Piura (pū'rä), department (□ 15,239; pop. 431,487), NW Peru; ⊙ Piura. Bordered by Ecuador (NE) and the Pacific (W). Includes Sechura Desert. Cordillera Occidental crosses dept. N–S. The mountainous section (E) is drained by Huancabamba R., the coastal plain by Chira and Piura rivers. Dept. is Peru's main cotton and petroleum region. Irrigated cotton areas in lower Piura and Chira valleys. Also sugar cane, rice, grapes, wheat, corn. Cattle are raised in mtn. valleys. Petroleum fields are located on the Pacific, in area of Talara, Negritos, and Lobitos. Salt is mined at Sechura and Colán. Dept. is served by Pan American Highway; narrow-gauge railroads in oil fields.

Piura, city (pop. 20,093), ⊙ Piura dept. and Piura prov. (□ 4,632; pop. 113,547), NW Peru, on coastal plain, on Piura R., on Pan American Highway and 540 mi. NNW of Lima; 5°12'S 80°57'W. Terminus of railroad from Paita. Important cotton market and commercial center for agr. products (corn, rice, sugar cane), cattle, hides; cottonseed-oil mills, cotton gins; mfg. (soap, candles, tiles). Airport. Bishopric. Residence of planters of near-by cotton estates. Founded 1532 by Pizarro in area NW of present site and originally named San Miguel de Piura, it is the oldest Sp. settlement in Peru and was moved several times until it was established at its present site. In 1912 it was largely destroyed by earthquake.

Piura River, Piura dept., NW Peru, rises on W slopes of Cordillera Occidental near Huarmaca, flows 150 mi. NW and SW, through major cotton region, past Chulucanas, Tambo Grande, and Piura, to Sechura Bay of the Pacific 3 mi. NW of Sechura. In rainy season it feeds numerous irrigation channels along its lower course.

Piute (pīūt'), county (□ 753; pop. 1,911), SW central Utah; ⊙ Junction. Mtn. and plateau area crossed by Sevier R. Piute Reservoir, on Sevier R., is near Junction. Parts of Fishlake Natl. Forest in W and N. Livestock; gold, antimony. Formed 1865.

Piute Reservoir, Utah: see SEVIER RIVER.

Piuthan or **Pyuthan** (pyōōtän'), town, S Nepal, 150 mi. WNW of Katmandu; corn, wheat, millet, buckwheat, barley, vegetables, rice. Nepalese military post. Former mfg. center (muskets, gunpowder).

Pivan, Russian SFSR: see KOMSOMOLSK, Ivanovo.

Piva River (pē'vä), SW Yugoslavia, rises in several branches joining at SW foot of the Durmitor, at Savnik; flows 54 mi. past Goransko, joining Tara R. 10 mi. S of Foca to form Drina R. Navigable for 12 mi.

Pivijay (pēvēhī'), town (pop. 3,135), Magdalena dept., N Colombia, on arm of Magdalena R., in Caribbean lowlands, and 33 mi. SSE of Barranquilla; road center in agr. region (cotton, fruit, livestock).

Pivnice or **Pivnitse** (pēv'nĭtsĕ), Hung. *Pincéd* (pĭn'tsād), village (pop. 5,289), Vojvodina, N Serbia, Yugoslavia, 25 mi. NW of Novi Sad, in the Backa.

Piwniczna (pēvnēch'nä), town (pop. 4,046), Krakow prov., S Poland, in the Carpathians, on Poprad R. and 12 mi. S of Nowy Sacz, near Czechoslovak border; health resort; flour milling, tanning.

Pixaria, Greece: see PYXARIA.

Pixley, village (1940 pop. 1,625), Tulare co., S central Calif., 17 mi. S of Tulare; cotton, fruit, alfalfa.

Piyang, China: see MIYANG.

Pizarra (pē-thä'rä), town (pop. 2,290), Málaga prov., S Spain, on Guadalhorce R., on railroad and 15 mi. W of Málaga; oranges, lemons, olives, figs.

Pizarro (pēsä'rō), town, Chocó intendancy, W Colombia, at mouth of Baudó R. on Pacific coast, 60 mi. SW of Quibdó; lumber and other forest products (chicle, rubber, vegetable oils).

Piz Bargias, Switzerland: see RINGELSPITZ.

Piz Bernina, Switzerland: see BERNINA, PIZ.

Piz Buin (pēts bwē'), peak (10,880 ft.) in SILVRETTA GROUP of Rhaetian Alps, on Swiss-Austrian border, E of Klosters.

Piz Curvèr (pēts kōōrvĕr'), peak (9,764 ft.) in Rhaetian Alps, SE Switzerland, 10 mi. NE of Splügen Pass.

Piz d'Err (pēts dĕr'), peak (11,094 ft.) in Rhaetian Alps, SE Switzerland, 8 mi. WNW of St. Moritz.

Piz Duan (pēts dwän'), peak (10,279 ft.) in Rhaetian Alps, SE Switzerland, 9 mi. SW of Sils im Engadin.

Pizhanka (pēzhän'kŭ), village (1939 pop. over 500), S Kirov oblast, Russian SFSR, 27 mi. ENE of Yaransk; flax processing.

Pizhma (pēzh'mŭ), town (1947 pop. over 500), NE Gorki oblast, Russian SFSR, 20 mi. NE of Shakhunya; sawmilling center.

Piz Julier (pēts zhülyā'), peak (11,103 ft.) in Rhaetian Alps, SE Switzerland, 4 mi. W of St. Moritz.

Piz Kesch (pēts kĕsh'), highest peak (11,223 ft.) in Albula Alps (division of Rhaetian Alps), SE Switzerland, 9 mi. N of St. Moritz.

Piz Languard (pēts län'gvärt), peak (10,715 ft.) in Rhaetian Alps, SE Switzerland, 2 mi. E of Pontresina.

Piz Linard (pēts lēnär'), peak (11,200 ft.) in Rhaetian Alps, E Switzerland, 11 mi. E of Davos; highest in SILVRETTA GROUP.

Piz Lischanna (pēts lēshä'nä), peak (10,202 ft.) in the Rhaetian Alps, E Switzerland, 3 mi. SE of Schuls, in Lower Engadine.

Piz Medel (pēts mā'dŭl), peak (10,542 ft.) in Lepontine Alps, E central Switzerland, 6 mi. SSE of Disentis.

Piz Ot (pēts ōt'), peak (10,662 ft.) in Albula Alps (part of Rhaetian Alps), SE Switzerland, 3 mi. NNW of St. Moritz.

Piz Quatervals (pēts kvä'tŭrväls), peak (10,396 ft.) in Rhaetian Alps, E Switzerland, 9 mi. W of Ofen Pass.

Piz Rusein, Switzerland: see TÖDI.

Piz Sesvenna (sĕsvĕ'nä), peak (10,523 ft.) in Rhaetian Alps, E Switzerland, on Ital. border, 7 mi. NE of Ofen Pass.

Piz Sol (sôl), peak (9,342 ft.) in Grauehörner group of Glarus Alps, E Switzerland, 10 mi. NW of Chur.

Pizzighettone (pētsēgĕt-tō'nĕ), town (pop. 2,058), Cremona prov., Lombardy, N Italy, on Adda R. and 12 mi. WNW of Cremona; agr. market (cereals, grapes, silkworm cocoons, livestock); mfg. (rayon, vegetable oil).

Pizzo (pē'tsô), town (pop. 7,666), Catanzaro prov., Calabria, S Italy, port on Gulf of Sant'Eufemia, 5 mi. NE of Vibo Valentia; bathing resort. A major tunny fishing center of Italy. Exports fish, citrus fruit, wine, olive oil. Has ruins of 15th-cent. Aragonese castle (now a natl. monument) where Murat was executed in 1815.

Pizzo Camoghè (pē'tsō kämōgā') or **Monte Camoghè** (môn'tĕ), peak (7,324 ft.) in the Alps, S Switzerland, 4 mi. SSE of Bellinzona, near Ital. line.

Pizzo Centrale (chĕnträ'lĕ), peak (9,857 ft.) in Lepontine Alps, S central Switzerland, 4 mi. S of Andermatt.

Pizzoli (pētsô'lē), village (pop. 2,055), Aquila prov., Abruzzi e Molise, S central Italy, 8 mi. NNW of Aquila; mfg. (woolen textiles, fireworks).

Pizzo Rotondo (pĕt'sô rôtôn'dô). **1** Peak (10,483 ft.) in Lepontine Alps, S Switzerland, 7 mi. W of Airolo; highest peak of St. Gotthard. **2** Peak (9,294 ft.) in Rhaetian Alps, SE Switzerland, 10 mi. NE of Biasca.

Plabennec (pläbĕnĕk'), village (pop. 877), Finistère dept., W France, 9 mi. NNE of Brest; furniture mfg. Megalithic monuments.

Placedo Junction (plŭsē'dŭ), village (pop. c.400), Victoria co., S Texas, 13 mi. SE of Victoria, in agr., cattle-raising area; rail junction.

Placencia or **Placencia de las Armas** (plä-thĕn'thyä, dhä läs är'mäs), town (pop. 2,319), Guipúzcoa prov., N Spain, 18 mi. WNW of Tolosa; mfg. of armaments.

Placentia (plŭsĕn'shŭ), town (pop. 538), SE N.F., small port on W coast of Avalon Peninsula, on Placentia Bay, 65 mi. WSW of St. John's; herring, salmon, lobster fishing. First and most important French settlement in N.F. was established here 1622; from here several attacks were made on St. John's, in British hands. After conquest of Quebec (1759) a Royal Navy station was established here. Subsistence farming is carried on in region. Naval base of Argentia is 4 mi. NNW of town.

Placentia, Italy: see PIACENZA, city.

Placentia, city (pop. 1,682), Orange co., S Calif., 8 mi. N of Santa Ana; citrus-fruit groves, oil fields. Health resort, with mineral springs near by. Inc. 1926.

Placentia Bay, inlet (extending 100 mi. NNE inland, 80 mi. wide at entrance) of the Atlantic, SE N.F., bet. Burin Peninsula and Avalon Peninsula. Bay contains several isls.; Merasheen and Long isls. are the largest. On E shore are town of Placentia and U.S. naval base of Argentia. On shores are numerous fishing settlements and fish and lobster canning plants. Deepest and widest bay of N.F., Placentia Bay was subject of Hague Court of International Justice ruling (1910) that territorial waters include the extent of the bay from headland to headland.

Placentia Island, Maine: see LONG ISLAND, plantation.

Placer (plä'sŭr, Sp. plä'sär), town (1939 pop. 4,782; 1948 municipality pop. 9,330), Surigao prov., Philippines, port on NE coast of Mindanao, 13 mi. SE of Surigao; shipping point for surrounding mining area.

Placer (plă'sŭr), county (□ 1,431; pop. 41,649), central and E Calif.; ⊙ Auburn. Narrow strip extending E from Sacramento Valley, across foothills and crest of the Sierra Nevada (here reaching c.9,000 ft.) to L. Tahoe, on Nev. line. Donner Pass is along N boundary. Drained by Bear R., Rubicon R., and Middle Fork of American R. Parts of Tahoe and El Dorado natl. forests are E. Ghost towns like You Bet and Red Dog are reminders of region's rich yields during the gold rush. Winter sports, hunting, fishing, camping in mts. Fruit-growing in foothills and valley (plums, pears, peaches, cherries); also grapes, nuts, olives, some citrus fruit, livestock, poultry, dairy products. Mining and quarrying (clay, placer gold, asbestos, sand and gravel); lumbering (pine, fir, cedar). Formed 1851.

Placer Peak (8,928 ft.), N central N.Mex., in Ortiz Mts., 27 mi. SSW of Santa Fe.

Placerville (plă'sŭrvĭl). **1** City (pop. 3,749), ⊙ El Dorado co., E central Calif., c.40 mi. ENE of Sacramento, in Sierra Nevada foothills, near South Fork of American R.; fruit-shipping center (especially Bartlett pears); lumber milling; limestone quarrying. Gateway to sierra resorts (E). Hq. of El Dorado Natl. Forest. Gold mining in region. Discovery (1848) of gold at near-by Coloma, and soon after also on this site, made settlement one of largest and wealthiest in Calif. in 1850s. Its early inhabitants' celebrated exercise of frontier justice earned it the name "Hangtown." Inc. as town in 1854, as city in 1903. **2** Village (pop. c.50), San Miguel co., SW Colo., on San Miguel R., in NW foothills of San Juan Mts., and 14 mi. WNW of Telluride; alt. c.7,350 ft.; shipping point for cattle and sheep. **3** Village (pop. 17), Boise co., SW Idaho, 25 mi. NNE of Boise; alt. 4,300 ft.; once important gold center.

Placetas (pläsā'täs), city (pop. 19,693), Las Villas prov., central Cuba, on Central Highway, on railroad and 20 mi. ESE of Santa Clara. Trading and processing center in fertile agr. region (tobacco, sugar cane, fruit, cattle). Well built and modern; highest city in Cuba. Gold and asphalt deposits near by.

Plachkovitsa, mountain, Yugoslavia: see PLACKOVICA.

Placid, Lake, N.Y.: see LAKE PLACID.

Placilla or **Placilla de San Fernando** (pläsē'yä dā sän fĕrnän'dō), village (1930 pop. 1,196), Colchagua prov., central Chile, on Tinguiririca R., on railroad, and 8 mi. SW of San Fernando; agr. center (grain, potatoes, peas, fruit, wine, livestock).

Plackovica or **Plachkovitsa** (both: pläch'kôvētsä), Serbo-Croatian *Plačkovica*, mountain, Macedonia, Yugoslavia; bounded (N, E) by Bregalnica R.; heavily forested. Highest peak (5,753 ft.) is 15 mi. E of Stip. Strumica R. rises on SW slope.

Pladda (plă'dŭ), rocky islet (pop. 7), Buteshire, Scotland, at mouth of Firth of Clyde just off S coast of Arran.

Pla de Cabra (plä' dhä kä'vrä), town (pop. 1,684), Tarragona prov., NE Spain, 6 mi. NNE of Valls; cotton milling; sheep raising; agr. trade (olive oil, wine, hazelnuts, cereals).

Pladjoe or **Pladju,** Indonesia: see PLAJU.

Plagwitz (pläk'vĭts), W suburb of Leipzig, Saxony, E central Germany.

Plain, village (pop. 512), Sauk co., S central Wis., 20 mi. SW of Baraboo, in dairy and livestock area.

Plain, Sea of the, Palestine: see DEAD SEA.

Plain City. 1 Village (pop. 1,715), on Madison-Union co. line, central Ohio, 17 mi. WNW of Columbus, and on Darby Creek, in agr. area. Laid out 1818. **2** Town (pop. 829), Weber co., N Utah, 9 mi. NW of Ogden, near Great Salt L.

Plain Dealing, town (pop. 1,321), Bossier parish, NW La., near Ark. line, 27 mi. N of Shreveport, in agr. area (cotton, corn, hay); oil wells; cotton gins, lumber mills. Founded 1888.

Plaine-des-Palmistes (plĕn'-dā-pälmēst'), town and commune (pop. 1,642), E central Réunion isl., on cross-isl. road and 9 mi. SW of Saint-Benoît; hill resort and sugar-cane center.

Plaine-du-Nord (plĕn-dü-nôr'), agr. town (1950 census pop. 562), Nord dept., N Haiti, 6 mi. SW of Cap-Haïtien; tropical fruit.

Plaines-des-Cafres (plĕn'-dā-kä'frŭ), village (pop. 3,054), E central Réunion isl., on cross-isl. road and 11 mi. NNE of Saint-Pierre; summer hill resort for Saint-Pierre.

Plainesti (plŭēnĕsht'), Rum. *Plăinești*, village (pop. 989), Buzau prov., E central Rumania, on railroad and 11 mi. NNE of Ramnicu-Sarat; lumbering center. Sometimes called Targu-Cucului. Suvorov defeated the Turks here (1788).

Plainfaing (plĕfē'), village (pop. 761), Vosges dept., E France, in the Vosges, 9 mi. SSE of Saint-Dié; cotton milling, sawmilling, comb and brush mfg.

Plainfield. 1 Town (pop. 8,071), including Plainfield village (pop. 2,207), Windham co., E Conn., on Quinebaug R. (dammed here) and 15 mi. E of Willimantic; includes MOOSUP village. Agr. (poultry, dairy products); mfg. (textiles, wood products, belts, elastic goods, clothing, furniture) at mfg. villages of Wauregan (wôrē'gŭn) (pop. 1,002) and Central Village. Part of state forest here. Settled c.1690, inc. 1699. **2** Town (pop. 117), Dodge co., S central Ga., 9 mi. NE of Eastman, in agr. area. **3** Village (pop. 1,764), Will co., NE Ill., on Du Page R. (bridged here) and 7 mi. NW of Joliet, in agr. and bituminous-coal area. Settled 1829 on site of an Indian village and a trading post (after 1790); inc. 1867. **4** Town (pop. 2,585), Hendricks co., central Ind., on Whitelick R. and 14 mi. WSW of Indianapolis, in agr. area; lumber, dairy products. A state boys' school is here. **5** Town (pop. 387), Bremer co., NE Iowa, on Cedar R. and 26 mi. NNW of Waterloo; dairy products, feed. Sand pit, limestone quarry near by. **6** Town (pop. 228), Hampshire co., NW Mass., on headstream of Westfield R. and 18 mi. ENE of Pittsfield. **7** Town (pop. 1,011), Sullivan co., W N.H., on the Connecticut and 11 mi. N of Claremont. Includes Meriden village, site of bird sanctuary; 1st bird club in U.S. formed here 1910. **8** City (pop. 42,366), Union co., NE N.J., near Watchung Mts., 15 mi. SW of Newark; mfg. (trucks, printing machinery, concrete products, tools, motors, metal products, concrete mixers). Settled 1684 by Friends, inc. 1869. Here are Green Brook Park, site of Revolutionary fort; Cedar Brook Park, with notable gardens; Friends' meetinghouse (1788); Martine house (1717), home of E. C. Stedman; Drake house (1746), occupied by local historical society and known as Washington's hq. Near by is Washington Rock, now in a state park. **9** Village (pop. 136), Coshocton co., central Ohio, 9 mi. ESE of Coshocton and on Wills Creek. **10** Town (pop. 945), Washington co., central Vt., just E of Montpelier; winter sports. Goddard Col. (founded 1938) is here. Plainfield village (pop. 604) is partly in Marshfield town. **11** Village (pop. 680), Waushara co., central Wis., 21 mi. SE of Wisconsin Rapids, in agr. area (rye, potatoes); dairy products.

Plains. 1 Town (pop. 546), Sumter co., SW central Ga., 10 mi. WSW of Americus. **2** City (pop. 718), Meade co., SW Kansas, 12 mi. W of Meade, in grain area. Corporate name is West Plains. **3** Town (pop. 714), Sanders co., NW Mont., 60 mi. NW of Missoula and on the Clark Fork, near Cabinet Natl. Forest; flour, livestock. **4** Urban township (pop. 12,541), Luzerne co., NE central Pa., on Susquehanna R., in Wyoming Valley, and just NE of Wilkes-Barre. Includes villages of Plains (1940 pop. 8,678, with adjacent Midvale), and Plainsville (1940 pop. 1,431). **5** Village (pop. c.400), ⊙ Yoakum co., NW Texas, on the Llano Estacado, c.60 mi. WSW of Lubbock; trading center for cattle and oil region; gasoline refineries.

Plainsboro, village in Plainsboro township (pop. 1,112), Middlesex co., central N.J., near Millstone R., 12 mi. NE of Trenton; has large dairy farm, with one of world's largest certified-milk plants.

Plainsville, Pa.: see PLAINS.

Plain View, town (pop. 42), Scott co., E Iowa, 14 mi. NW of Davenport.

Plainview. 1 Town (pop. 637), Yell co., W central Ark., 22 mi. SSW of Russellville, near Nimrod Dam. **2** Village (pop. 1,524), Wabasha co., SE Minn., 17 mi. NE of Rochester, in grain, livestock, poultry area; dairy products, canned vegetables. Platted 1857, inc. 1875. **3** City (pop. 1,427), Pierce co., NE Nebr., 30 mi. NNW of Norfolk; dairying; grain, stock, poultry. Inc. 1880. **4** City (pop. 14,044), ⊙ Hale co., NW Texas, on the Llano Estacado, c.40 mi. N of Lubbock; market, shipping, processing center for rich irrigated agr. area (grain, alfalfa, cotton, potatoes, truck, poultry, dairy products); grain elevators, cotton gins, flour, feed, and cottonseed-oil mills, creameries. Seat of Wayland Baptist Col. Has several annual shows and fairs. Founded 1886, inc. 1907.

Plainville. 1 Industrial town (pop. 9,994), Hartford co., central Conn., on Pequabuck R. and 11 mi. SW of Hartford; metal products, radios, tools, ball bearings, electrical equipment, plastics, machinery. State park here. Has several 18th-cent. buildings. Set off from Farmington 1869. **2** Town (pop. 142), Gordon co., NW Ga., 12 mi. NNE of Rome; brick mfg., clay mining. **3** City (pop. 2,082), Rooks co., NW central Kansas, 24 mi. N of Hays; shipping point for wheat and livestock region. Oil wells near by. Settled 1877, inc. 1888. **4** Village (pop. 242), Adams co., W Ill., 16 mi. SE of Quincy, in agr. area. **5** Town (pop. 568), Daviess co., SW Ind., 22 mi. ENE of Vincennes, in agr. area. **6** Town (pop. 2,088), Norfolk co., SE Mass., near R.I. line, 14 mi. NNE of Providence, R.I.; specialty jewelry, metal refining, paper boxes, rugs; dairying. Settled 1661, inc. 1905.

Plainwell, city (pop. 2,767), Allegan co., SW Mich., 11 mi. NNW of Kalamazoo on Kalamazoo R., in onion-growing region; mfg. (paper, office equipment, food products); ships produce. Settled 1836, inc. as city 1934.

Plaisance, village (pop. 2,195), Demerara co., N Br. Guiana, on the coast, on railroad and 5 mi. E of Georgetown, in rice- and sugar-growing region.

Plaisance or **Plaisance-du-Gers** (plāzās'-dü-zhâr'), village (pop. 1,233), Gers dept., SW France, 19 mi. WNW of Mirande; winegrowing, flour milling, horse breeding.

Plaisance, town (1950 census pop. 1,694), Nord dept., N Haiti, in Massif du Nord, 21 mi. SW of Cap-Haïtien; coffee, cacao, bananas. Just S is village and agr. school of Châtard.

Plaisance, Mauritius: see MAHÉBOURG.

Plaistow (plă'stō), town (pop. 2,082), Rockingham co., SE N.H., 19 mi. ENE of Nashua; mfg. (felt products, shoemakers' supplies). Part of Haverhill, Mass. (S), until inc. 1749.

Plaju, Pladju, or **Pladjoe** (all: plä'jōō), suburb of Palembang, SE Sumatra, Indonesia, on Musi R. and 4 mi. E of Palembang; oil-refining center, linked by pipe line with oil fields at Tempino and Bejubang.

Plaka, Greece: see MELOS.

Plake Mountains (plä'kĕ), Serbo-Croatian *Plakenska Planina*, W Macedonia, Yugoslavia; c.10-mi. long N-S; highest point, the Plake (6,557 ft.), is 10 mi. N of Resen.

Plan, Czechoslovakia: see PLANA.

Plana (plä'nä), Czech *Planá*, Ger. *Plan* (plän), town (pop. 2,485), W Bohemia, Czechoslovakia, 30 mi. WNW of Pilsen; rail junction; wheat, barley. Mica deposits near by. Has medieval castle.

Plana or **Velika Plana** (vĕ'lĭkä plä'nä), village (pop. 7,119), N central Serbia, Yugoslavia, 45 mi. SE of Belgrade, near the Morava; rail junction; meat packing.

Planaltina (plŏonŏoltē'nŏo), city (pop. 1,220), SE Goiás, central Brazil, in territory set aside for future federal dist., 95 mi. NE of Anápolis; livestock, mangabeira rubber.

Plancher-Bas (plãshā'-bä'), village (pop. 585), Haute-Saône dept., E France, in Belfort Gap, 8 mi. NW of Belfort, at foot of the Vosges; mfg. of jewelry chains, silk milling.

Plancher-les-Mines (-lā-mēn'), village (pop. 1,840), Haute-Saône dept., E France, in the S Vosges, 10 mi. NNW of Belfort; copper and bronze foundries. Hardware mfg., woodworking.

Planches, Les, Switzerland: see MONTREUX.

Planches-en-Montagne, Les (lā plãsh-ã-mõtä'nyŭ), village (pop. 150), Jura dept., E France, in the central Jura, 19 mi. NNE of Saint-Claude; woodworking.

Planchón (plänchōn'), Andean peak (13,025 ft.) on Argentina-Chile border; 35°14'S. At its foot is a pass (9,350 ft.) on road bet. Malargüe (Argentina) and Curicó (Chile).

Plancoët (plãkôā'), village (pop. 1,521), Côtes-du-Nord dept., W France, on Arguenon R. and 10 mi. WNW of Dinan; distilling. Stone quarries.

Plancy (plãsē'), village (pop. 675), Aube dept., NE central France, on Aube R. and 12 mi. ENE of Romilly-sur-Seine; hosiery mfg.

Plandome (plăn"dōm'), village (pop. 1,102), Nassau co., SE N.Y., on N shore of W Long Isl., on Manhasset Bay, just N of Manhasset. Near by are Plandome Heights (pop. 882) and Plandome Manor (pop. 323).

Plane, village (pop. 2,100, with adjacent Doyle Colony), Tulare co., central Calif.

Planes, Los, Salvador: see LOS PLANES.

Planes de Renderos, Salvador: see LOS PLANES.

Planet Deep. 1 Ocean depth (32,112 ft.) in North Pacific Ocean, off NE Mindanao, in MINDANAO TRENCH. **2** Ocean depth (30,013 ft.) in South Pacific Ocean, off S New Britain.

Planèze (plänĕz'), plateau (□ 115) in Central Massif, S central France, in Cantal dept. bet. Murat and Saint-Flour. Cattle raising, wheat growing. Sometimes called Planèze of Saint-Flour. More generally, the term Planèze identifies a series of basalt tablelands (old lava flows) which surround the volcanic Auvergne Mts.

Planice (plä'nyĭtsĕ), Czech *Plánice*, Ger. *Planitz* (plä'nĭts), town (pop. 1,247), SW Bohemia, Czechoslovakia, 8 mi. E of Klatovy; lumbering.

Planinski Kanal, Yugoslavia: see VELEBIT MOUNTAINS.

Planitz, Czechoslovakia: see PLANICE.

Planitz (plä'nĭts), industrial suburb (1939 pop. 22,513) of Zwickau, Saxony, E central Germany, 3 mi. SSW of city center. Inc. into Zwickau after 1945.

Planken (pläng'kŭn), village, N Liechtenstein, near railroad, 3 mi. N of Vaduz; corn, potatoes, cattle. Founded in 13th cent. by Walsers.

Plankinton, city (pop. 754), ⊙ Aurora co., SE central S.Dak., 23 mi. W of Mitchell; livestock, dairy products, poultry, grain, flour. S.Dak. Training School is here.

Plankstadt (plängk'shtät), village (pop. 6,909), N Baden, Germany, after 1945 in Württemberg-Baden, 1 mi. E of Schwetzingen; asparagus, hops, tobacco.

Plano (plā'nō). **1** City (pop. 2,154), Kendall co., NE Ill., near Fox R., 12 mi. WSW of Aurora; ships grain; mfg. (dairy products, batteries, foundry and bakelite products, plumbing supplies, tin cans). Settled 1835, inc. 1865. **2** Town (pop. 106), Appanoose co., S Iowa, 9 mi. W of Centerville; coal mining. **3** City (pop. 2,126), Collin co., N Texas, 17 mi. NNE of Dallas; trade center in cotton, corn, wheat area; mfg. (clothing, valves, stoves). Founded 1848, inc. as city 1930.

Planta de Guacimal, Costa Rica: see GUACIMAL.

Plantagenet (plăntă'jĭnĭt), village (pop. estimate 600), SE Ont., on South Nation R. and 35 mi. ENE of Ottawa; dairying, mixed farming. Near by are mineral springs.

Plantain Garden River (plăn'tĭn), St. Thomas parish, E Jamaica, rises in S slopes of Blue Mts., flows c.20 mi. E to Jamaica Channel at Holland Bay. In its lower basin are sugar plantations and factories.

Plantain Island, Sierra Leone, in Yawri Bay of Atlantic Ocean, off Shenge. Historically part of the colony; administered under South-Western Prov. of the protectorate. Used in fishing season.

Plantain River, Honduras: see PLÁTANO, RÍO.

Plantation Key, Fla.: see FLORIDA KEYS.

Plantaurel (plãtōrĕl'), mountain range in Ariège dept., S France, part of central Pyrenees foothills, extending c.40 mi. WNW-ESE across dept. parallel to main range; 3 mi. wide; rises to 2,500 ft. Traversed in narrow gorges by Arize and Ariège rivers.

Plant City, city (pop. 9,230), Hillsborough co., W Fla., 20 mi. E of Tampa; shipping and processing (canning, freezing) center for winter strawberries, citrus fruit, and vegetables; also produces feed, molasses, lumber, fertilizer. Has strawberry research station. Settled on site of an Indian village. Inc. 1885.

Plantersville, village (pop. 479), Lee co., NE Miss., 4 mi. SE of Tupelo; truck farming.

Plantsville, Conn.: see SOUTHINGTON.

Plaplaya (pläplī'ä), village, Colón dept., N Honduras, in Mosquitia, on Caribbean Sea, at mouth of Sico R., 17 mi. ENE of Iriona, on coastal bar; coconuts, livestock. Sometimes spelled Paplaya.

Plaquemine (plă'kŭmĭn, plăk'mĭn), town (pop. 5,747), ⊙ Iberville parish, SE central La., 12 mi. SSW of Baton Rouge and on W bank (levee) of the Mississippi (ferry here); machine shops, lumber mills (cypress lumber), sugar refineries, fruit and vegetable canneries, moss gins. Agr. (rice, sugar cane, corn), oil wells, commercial fisheries, timber in region. Inc. 1838. Plaquemine Locks connect Plaquemine-Morgan City Waterway with the Mississippi here. Migratory bird refuge near by.

Plaquemine, Bayou (bī'ō), Iberville parish, SE central La., formerly a distributary of the Mississippi at Plaquemine, whence it flowed SW to Grand R.; its dredged channel is now part of Plaquemine-Morgan City Waterway, connected with the Mississippi at Plaquemine by Plaquemine Locks (55-ft. lift; completed 1909).

Plaquemine Brule, Bayou (brōō'lā), S La., rises in SW St. Landry parish, flows c.75 mi. SW, near Crowley, to Bayou Cannes just above its junction with Bayou Nezpique to form Mermentau R. Navigable for 19 mi. of lower course.

Plaquemine-Morgan City Waterway, S La., connects Mississippi R. (through locks at Plaquemine) with Atchafalaya R. and main Gulf Intracoastal Waterway channel at Morgan City; c.55 mi. long.

Plaquemines (plă'kŭmĭn, plăk'mĭn, -mĭnz), parish (□ 984; pop. 14,239), extreme SE La.; ⊙ Pointe a la Hache. Occupies most of the delta of Mississippi R. below New Orleans; Barataria Bay and Gulf of Mexico are on W and S, Breton Sound and Gulf of Mexico on E. In S, parish is chiefly sea swamps; at tip are isls. separated by the mouths, called "passes," through which the Mississippi enters the Gulf. Migratory waterfowl refuge. Agr. (citrus fruit, rice, sugar cane, truck, lily bulbs). Natural gas, oil, sulphur. Sea-food and vegetable canning, boatbuilding; hunting, fishing, fur trapping. Formed 1807.

Plaridel (plärēdhĕl'). **1** Town (1939 pop. 1,106; 1948 municipality pop. 14,290), Bulacan prov., S central Luzon, Philippines, 22 mi. NNW of Manila; rice growing. **2** Town, Misamis Occidental prov., Philippines: see CALAMBA.

Plasencia (pläsĕn'thyä), city (pop. 15,092), Cáceres prov., W Spain, in Estremadura, situated on hill 42 mi. NE of Cáceres; communications and agr. trade center; ships pepper and olive oil. Mfg. of chocolate, tiles, soap; tanning, cork processing, flour- and sawmilling. Cereals, wine, livestock, and lumber in area. Episcopal see since 12th cent. City is circled by double line of 12th-cent. walls with towers. Has medieval aqueduct and castle, 15th-cent. Gothic cathedral (with later additions), and 16th-cent. Casa de las Bovedas. Near by are remains of Roman town of *Capera*. Modern Plasencia was founded (12th cent.) by Alfonso VIII, after expulsion of Moors from area.

Plasenzuela (pläsĕn-thwā'lä), town (pop. 1,477), Cáceres prov., W Spain, 10 mi. WSW of Trujillo; cereals, olive oil, livestock.

Plashetts, village in parish of Plashetts and Tynehead (pop. 246), W Northumberland, England, on North Tyne R. and 16 mi. N of Haltwhistle; coal mining.

Plaski (plăsh'kē), Serbo-Croatian *Plaški*, village, NW Croatia, Yugoslavia, on railroad and 14 mi. SSE of Ogulin; lumbering. Fortress.

Plassey (plăs'ē), village, Nadia dist., E West Bengal, India, on Bhagirathi R. and 31 mi. NNW of Krishnagar; sugar milling; rice, jute, linseed. Here Robert Clive's decisive victory (1757) over nawab of Bengal resulted, with battle of BUXAR, in English acquisition of Bengal.

Plast (pläst), city (1939 pop. over 10,000), central Chelyabinsk oblast, Russian SFSR, in E foothills of the S Urals, 55 mi. SSW of Chelyabinsk; major gold-mining center; arsenic deposits. Became city in 1940.

Plasterco (plă'stûrkō), industrial village, Washington co., SW Va., near North Fork of Holston R., just SW of Saltville; gypsum mining and processing.

Plastun (plŭstōōn'), coast town (1935 pop. 1,500), E Maritime Territory, Russian SFSR, on Sea of Japan, 250 mi. NNE of Vladivostok; fish canning.

Plastunovskaya, Russian SFSR: see DINSKAYA.

Plasy (plä'sĭ), town (pop. 1,472), W Bohemia, Czechoslovakia, on railroad and 13 mi. N of Pilsen; iron mining.

Plata, La, Bolivia: see SUCRE.

Plata, La, Colombia: see LA PLATA.

Plata, Lago de la (lä'gō dā lä plä'tä), lake (□ 28; alt. 3,087 ft.) in the Andes, NW Comodoro Rivadavia military zone, Argentina, in a bend of the Chile border, just W of L. Fontana (linked by 2-mi. river); c.17 mi. long, 1-3 mi. wide.

Plata, Río de la (rē'ō dā lä plä'tä), or the **River Plate**, great estuary (□ c.13,500) of combined Paraná and Uruguay rivers, bet. Argentina (S and W shore) and Uruguay (N shore). It constitutes the major indentation along E coast of South America, and as the focus of that continent's 2d largest river system (Paraná-Paraguay-Uruguay), it serves as an important route of access to the interior. A drowned river valley, it extends 170 mi. SE to the open Atlantic from a point off Nueva Palmira (Uruguay) at junction of Paraná Bravo (a distributary of Paraná delta) and Uruguay rivers. Max. width at E end, generally considered to be a line connecting Cape San Antonio (Argentina) with Cape Santa María (Uruguay), is c.140 mi. Punta del Este (Uruguay's noted resort) is sometimes considered the easternmost point. Combining the characteristics of a river estuary and of an ocean gulf, the Río de la Plata is a fresh-water body in its narrower NW portion, with salinity increasing beyond a line joining Punta Piedras (Argentina) and Montevideo; its width here is c.60 mi.; the min. width near head of estuary is 25 mi. Although the Río de la Plata carries a tremendous volume of water from a drainage basin of over 1,500,000 sq. mi., it is generally shallow (greatest depth, near open sea, is 65 ft.) and obstructed by sandbanks (largest: Ortis, Playa Honda, Inglés) constantly enlarged by river-transported silt. Continuous dredging of navigation channels is necessary, especially along the approaches to Buenos Aires (for 30-ft. draught) and to the navigable mouths of the Paraná. Principal ports are Buenos Aires and La Plata (Argentina), Montevideo and Colonia (Uruguay). Discovered 1516 by Juan Diaz de Solís, it was explored by Magellan in 1520 and by Sebastian Cabot several years later. First settlement on its banks was made at Buenos Aires by Pedro de Mendoza in 1536. The origin of the name Río de la Plata [Sp.,=river of silver] is attributed to the silver ornaments worn by native Indian pop. at time of discovery; it may also reflect the quest for silver in the Peruvian Andes to which the river provided a route of access. The Viceroyalty of Río de la Plata (established 1776), almost coextensive with present Argentina, was named after it. In Second World War, a naval engagement (Dec., 1939) bet. British and Germans, which led to scuttling of *Graf Spee*, was fought in river near Punta del Este. The name Río de la Plata is sometimes given to the entire river system (Paraná-Paraguay-Uruguay) draining SE central South America.

Plata, Río de la, Puerto Rico: see LA PLATA RIVER.

Plataea (plŭtē'ŭ) or **Plataeae** (plŭtē'ē), anc. town of S Boeotia, Greece, at N foot of the Cithaeron, 8 mi. SSW of Thebes. A faithful ally of Athens after 519 B.C., Plataea fought with Athens at Marathon (490 B.C.). In 479 B.C. the Greeks under Pausanias defeated the Persians under Mardonius and drove them from Greek soil. In memory of the victory festivals were held here every 4 years. It was twice destroyed (431, 373 B.C.) by Thebes. On site is modern village of Plataiai (pop. 999), formerly called Kokla.

Plata Island, La, Ecuador: see LA PLATA ISLAND.

Platani River (plä'tänē), anc. *Halycus*, SW Sicily, rises in several branches joining ESE of Prizzi, flows 70 mi. S, W, and WSW to Mediterranean Sea near Cape Bianco. Eel fishing in lower course.

Plátano, Río (rē'ō plä'tänō) [Sp.,=Plantain River], in Mosquitia region of E Honduras, rises 40 mi. S of Iriona, flows c.50 mi. NE, through plantain area to Caribbean Sea 30 mi. ESE of Iriona.

Plate, River, Argentina and Uruguay: see PLATA, RÍO DE LA.

Platea (plătē'ŭ), agr. borough (pop. 290), Erie co., NW Pa., 18 mi. SW of Erie; planing mill.

Plateado, El, Mexico: see EL PLATEADO.

Plateau, village, Rift Valley prov., W Kenya, on Uasin Gishu Plateau, on railroad and 10 mi. SSE of Eldoret; coffee, tea, wheat, corn.

Plateau Central, France: see MASSIF CENTRAL.

Plateau Heights, village (pop. 1,570, with adjacent Nebbons Hill), Crawford co., NW Pa.

Plateau Mountain (3,855 ft.), Greene co., SE N.Y., in the Catskills, 12 mi. WNW of Saugerties.

Plateau Province (□ 10,423; pop. 540,836), Northern Provinces, central Nigeria; ⊙ Jos. On Bauchi Plateau; savanna with thin soils, occasional wooded valleys. Production of inferior grains (millet, durra); cassava. Major Nigerian tin region, with main centers at Jos, Naraguta, Bukuru.

Platen (plä'tŭn), village (pop. 266), W Luxembourg, 3 mi. NE of Redange; cotton textiles. Agr. village of Bettborn (pop. 115) is contiguous.

Plateros (plätā'rōs), town (pop. 1,635), Zacatecas, N central Mexico, 5 mi. NNE of Fresnillo; cereals, vegetables, maguey, livestock. Silver deposits are near by.

Plathe, Poland: see PLOTY.

Platì (plätē'), village (pop. 3,808), Reggio di Calabria prov., Calabria, S Italy, 12 mi. WSW of Locri; olive oil, wine, cheese.

Platinum, village (pop. 74), SW Alaska, at entrance to Goodnews Bay of Bering Sea, 120 mi. W of Dillingham; 59°1'N 161°47'W; platinum and osmiridium mining; 1st platinum strike made 1927. Air field.

Plato (plä'tō), town (pop. 5,814), Magdalena dept., N Colombia, on Magdalena R. and 85 mi. S of Barranquilla; cattle-raising center.

Plato (plā'tō), village (pop. 263), McLeod co., S Minn., on small lake, c.40 mi. WSW of Minneapolis; dairy products.

Platonovka (plŭtô'nŭfkŭ), village (1939 pop. over 500), central Tambov oblast, Russian SFSR, 20 mi. E of Tambov; rail junction (spur to Rasskazovo); grain.

Platón Sánchez (plätōn' sän'chĕs), town (pop. 2,156), Veracruz, E Mexico, at foot of Sierra Madre Oriental, 11 mi. SW of Tantoyuca; cereals, sugar cane, coffee, fruit.

Platovka, Russian SFSR: see POKROVKA, Chkalov oblast.

Platres, Pano (pä'nō plä'trĕs), summer resort (pop., including adjacent TROODOS, 502), Limassol dist., W central Cyprus, at S foot of Mt. Troodos, 35 mi. SW of Nicosia; alt. c.3,700 ft. Near by are the renowned Troöditissa and Kykko monasteries.

Platt, village (1940 pop. 717), Washtenaw co., SE Mich., 4 mi. SE of Ann Arbor, in farm area.

Platte (plăt). **1** County (□ 414; pop. 14,973), W Mo.; ⊙ Platte City; bounded S and W by Missouri R.; drained by Little Platte R.; agr. region (wheat, corn, oats, tobacco). Formed 1838. **2** County (□ 672; pop. 19,910), E central Nebr.; ⊙ Columbus. Agr. region bounded S by Platte R.; drained by Loup R. Mfg. at Columbus. Grain, livestock, dairy and poultry produce. Formed 1855. **3** County (□ 2,114; pop. 7,925), SE Wyo.; ⊙ Wheatland. Agr. area; watered by Chugwater Creek, N.Platte and Laramie rivers. Sugar beets, grain, livestock, beans. Formed 1911.

Platte, city (pop. 1,069), Charles Mix co., SE S.Dak., 100 mi. SE of Pierre; railroad and trade center for dairying and agr. region; dairy products, flour, cattle feed, corn. Co. fair held annually here. Settled 1882.

Platte Center, village (pop. 422), Platte co., E central Nebr., 10 mi. NW of Columbus and on branch of Platte R.

Platte City, city (pop. 742), ⊙ Platte co., W Mo., on Little Platte R. and 23 mi. NNW of Kansas City; wheat, corn, tobacco.

Plattekill (plă'tŭkĭl"), resort village, Ulster co., SE N.Y., 8 mi. NNW of Newburgh.

Platte Lake (plăt). **1** In Benzie co., NW Mich., 4 mi. N of Beulah, near L. Michigan, in resort area; c.3.5 mi. long, 1.5 mi. wide. Benzie State Park is near by. **2** Largely in Crow Wing co., central Minn., 25 mi. NE of Little Falls; 3 mi. long, 2 mi. wide.

Platten, Czechoslovakia: see HORNI BLATNA.

Plattensee, Hungary: see BALATON, LAKE.

Platte River. 1 In Iowa and Mo.: see LITTLE PLATTE RIVER. **2** In central Minn., rises in Sullivan L., Morrison co., flows 50 mi. SW to Mississippi R. 4 mi. S of Royalton. **3** In Nebr., formed at North Platte city by confluence of NORTH PLATTE RIVER and SOUTH PLATTE RIVER; flows 310 mi. generally E, through agr. area, past Kearney, Grand Island, Columbus, and Fremont, to Missouri R. at Plattsmouth, S of Omaha. Used for irrigation and hydroelectric power; extreme shallowness prevents navigation. Drains □ 90,000. With North Platte R., 990 mi. long. **4** In Grant co., SW Wis., rises c.15 mi. W of Dodgeville, flows c.30 mi. SW to the Mississippi 7 mi. N of Dubuque, Iowa.

Platteville (plăt'vĭl). **1** Town (pop. 570), Weld co., N Colo., on South Platte R. and 30 mi. N of Denver; alt. 4,820 ft. Trade point in irrigated agr. area; dairy, truck, poultry products, sugar beets, livestock, alfalfa. Reconstructed Fort Vasquez, former fur-trading post, is near by. **2** City (pop. 5,751), Grant co., extreme SW Wis., on Little Platte R. (small branch of Platte R.) and 18 mi. NNE of Dubuque, Iowa; trade center for dairying, farming, and lead- and zinc-mining area; mfg. (dairy products, machine-shop products, beer). Seat of Wis. Inst. of Technology and a state teachers col. Wisconsin's early territorial capitol bldg. (1836), now restored in a state park, is near by. Founded 1827, inc. 1876.

Platte Woods, town (pop. 159), Platte co., W Mo.

Plattling (plăt'lĭng), town (pop. 10,713), Lower Bavaria, Germany, on the Isar and 6 mi. SW of Deggendorf; rail junction; glass mfg., metal- and woodworking, brewing. Has Romanesque church with Gothic choir. Chartered before 1320.

Platt National Park (plăt) (912 acres; established 1906), S Okla., adjacent to Sulphur. Wooded, hilly area at NE base of Arbuckle mts.; sulphur, bromide, and fresh-water springs; campgrounds. State veterans' hosp. adjoins park area on S.

Plattsburg. 1 City (pop. 1,655), ⊙ Clinton co., NW Mo., on Little Platte R. and 24 mi. SE of St. Joseph; agr. (corn, wheat, oats). Founded c.1835. **2** City (pop. 17,738), ⊙ Clinton co., extreme NE N.Y., on W shore of L. Champlain, at mouth of Saranac R., 20 mi. NW of Burlington, Vt.; trade center for near-by agr. area and Adirondack resort region to the W. Mfg.: paper and paper products, pulp, lumber, razor blades, dairy products, concrete blocks, machinery, leather goods. Timber. A state teachers col. is here. A Catholic summer school is near by. Military training camps established here during First World War were closed in 1946, and their barracks converted into Champlain Col., a state emergency col. for veterans. Laid out 1784, inc. 1902. In War of 1812, a British sea and land invasion from Canada was repulsed (Sept., 1814) near here by forces under Macdonough and Macomb.

Plattsmouth (plăts'mouth, -mŭth), city (pop. 4,874), ⊙ Cass co., E Nebr., 15 mi. S of Omaha and on Missouri R., near mouth of Platte R.; rail, trade center in grain, dairying region; butter, canned goods, flour, baskets, brooms. Refrigerator cars repaired here. Near-by bluffs along the Missouri contain deposits of clay, sand, and stone suitable for commercial use. Masonic home for aged here. Game refuge just N of city. Founded 1854–55.

Plattsville, village (pop. estimate 700), S Ont., on Nith R. and 14 mi. NE of Woodstock; flax and flour milling, dairying, mixed farming.

Plau (plou), town (pop. 7,969), Mecklenburg, N Germany, on Plau L. at outlet of the Elde, 17 mi. E of Parchim; mfg. of chemicals, refrigerators, bricks; sawmilling. Asparagus market. Tourist resort. Has 13th-cent. church and remains of old castle and town walls.

Plaucheville (plō'shāvĭl), village (pop. 277), Avoyelles parish, E central La., 36 mi. SE of Alexandria; agr.; cotton ginning.

Plaue (plou'ŭ). **1** or **Plaue an der Havel** (än dĕr hä'fŭl), town (pop. 4,679), Brandenburg, E Germany, on N shore of Plaue L., at efflux of the Havel, 6 mi. W of Brandenburg; E terminus of Plaue Canal; optical- and precision-instruments mfg. Popular excursion resort. Has 18th-cent. castle on site of earlier fortress. Site (1713–30) of 1st Prussian porcelain works, subsequently moved to Berlin. **2** Village (pop. 3,929), Saxony, E central Germany, at N foot of the Erzgebirge, 7 mi. E of Chemnitz; cotton milling, hosiery knitting.

Plaue Lake (plou'ŭ), Ger. *Plauer See* (plou'ŭr zā"), lake (□ 2.8), Brandenburg, E Germany, just S of Plaue; irregular in shape; greatest depth 22 ft. Traversed by Havel R., which here connects with the Elbe via 22-mi.-long **Plaue Canal** (built 1743–45; later enlarged to accommodate vessels up to 500 tons).

Plauen (plou'ŭn). **1** or **Plauen im Vogtland** (ĭm fōkt'lănt), city (pop. 84,778), Saxony, E central Germany, at NW foot of the Erzgebirge, on the White Elster and 60 mi. SSW of Leipzig; 50°30'N 12°8'E. Chief town of the Vogtland; rail junction. Textile-milling center (since 15th cent.), with mfg. of wool, cotton, silk, curtains, lace, embroidery; steel products, textile machinery, machine tools, cables, electrical equipment, radios, lamps, musical instruments; tanning. Has 12th-cent. church, 15th-cent. town hall, Hradschin castle (1224). Founded by the Sorbs on important trade route to Bohemia, which was guarded by a Vogt (governor). Region subsequently became known as Vogtland. City became seat of branch of Teutonic Knights in 1224. Later passed to Bohemia; then was dependency of the princes of Reuss. Went to Saxony in 1577. **2** S suburb of Dresden, Saxony, E central Germany; coal mining.

Plauer See, Germany: see PLAU, LAKE; PLAUE LAKE.

Plau Lake (plou), Ger. *Plauer See* (plou'ŭr zā"), lake (□ 15), Mecklenburg, N Germany, just E of Plau; 10 mi. long, 1–5 mi. wide; greatest depth 90 ft., average depth 25 ft. Traversed by Elde R.

Plav (pläf), village (pop. 5,961), E Montenegro, Yugoslavia, 35 mi. ENE of Titograd, near Serbia-Albania borders. Formerly called Plava; long contested by Montenegro and Albania. Situated on **Plav Lake** or **Plav Marsh,** Serbo-Croatian *Plavsko Jezero* or *Plavsko Blato* (□ 1), which gives rise to Lim R.

Plavinas or **Plyavinyas** (plă'vēnyäs), Lettish *Pļaviņas,* Ger. *Stockmannshof,* city (pop. 1,496), S central Latvia, in Vidzeme, on right bank of the Western Dvina and 11 mi. NW of Jekabpils; rail junction; cement mfg., sawmilling.

Plavnica or **Plavnitsa** (both: pläv'nĭtsä), village, S Montenegro, Yugoslavia, on L. Scutari near Moraca R. mouth, 11 mi. SSW of Titograd, in Zeta lowland; terminus of narrow-gauge railway.

Plavsk (pläfsk), city (1938 pop. 8,400), S central Tula oblast, Russian SFSR, 37 mi. SSW of Tula; mfg. of food-processing machines; flour milling. Until c.1928, called Sergiyevskoye. Became city in 1949.

Playa Chiquita (plī'ä chēkē'tä), village (pop. 95), Colón prov., central Panama, on Caribbean Sea, and 4 mi. E of Palenque; cacao, abacá, coconuts, livestock.

Playa de Fajardo (dā fähär'dō), port for Fajardo, NE Puerto Rico, opposite Culebra Isl., 33 mi. ESE of San Juan; ships sugar; fishing. Customhouse. Sometimes Puerto Real.

Playa de Guayanilla, Puerto Rico: see GUAYANILLA.

Playa de Humacao (plī'ä dā ōōmäkou') or **Punta Santiago** (pōōn'tä säntyä'gō), village, E Puerto Rico, port for Humacao (5 mi. WSW; linked by railroad); ships sugar. Beach resort. Small Santiago Isl., on which the School of Tropical Medicine maintains a monkey colony, is 1 mi. off the coast.

Playa del Rey (plī'ŭ dĕl rā'), beach resort and residential community, Los Angeles co., S Calif., part of LOS ANGELES city, on the Pacific, 5 mi. S of Santa Monica. Founded as resort 1903–4; annexed 1911 by Venice (N), 1925 (with Venice) by Los Angeles.

Playa de Ponce (plī'ä dā pōn'sā), port section of Ponce, S Puerto Rico; 2d port of the isl., with fine harbor, shipping sugar cane on large scale. Warehouses, docks, railroad station. Adjoining beaches.

Playa Grande (grän'dā), village (pop. 69) Retalhuleu dept., SW Guatemala, on the Pacific, at mouth of Samalá R., and 13 mi. ESE of Champerico; corn, beans, rice.

Playa Grande or **Central Playa Grande** (sĕnträl'), locality, E Puerto Rico, 6 mi. SW of Isabela Segunda; sugar mill. U.S. weather station.

Playa Verde (vĕr'dā), beach resort, Maldonado dept., S Uruguay, on the Atlantic at mouth of the Río de la Plata, just E of Solís beach, 45 mi. E of Montevideo.

Playa Vicente (vēsĕn'tā), town (pop. 1,721), Veracruz, SE Mexico, in N outliers of Sierra Madre del Sur, 37 mi. S of Cosamaloapan; sugar cane, fruit.

Playgreen Lake (□ 257), central Man., N arm of L. Winnipeg; 62 mi. long, 12 mi. wide. Drains N into Nelson R.

Playón, El, Salvador: see NEJAPA.

Plaza (plă'zŭ), village (pop. 389), Mountrail co., NW central N.Dak., 35 mi. SW of Minot.

Plaza de Almanzor, Spain: see PLAZA DEL MORO ALMANZOR.

Plaza del Moro Almanzor or **Plaza de Almanzor** (plä'thä dhĕl mō'rō älmänthôr'), highest peak (8,504 ft.) of Sierra de Gredos and of central ranges of Spain, 90 mi. E of Madrid. Several passes at N foot. Picturesque L. Gredos on W slopes.

Plaza Huincul (plä'sä wĕngkōōl'), town (1947 pop. 2,522), E central Neuquén natl. territory, Argentina, on railroad and 60 mi. W of Neuquén; oil-producing and stock-raising center. Oil refineries, including large state-owned refinery.

Plazenica, Mala; Plazenica, Velika, mountains, Yugoslavia: see VELIKA PLAZENICA.

Plazuela or **Central Plazuela** (sĕnträl' pläswā'lä), locality, N Puerto Rico, just N of Barceloneta, near the coast; sugar mill.

Plean (plēn), village in St. Ninians parish, E Stirling, Scotland, 5 mi. NW of Falkirk; coal mining.

Pleasant, Lake. 1 In Ariz.: see AGUA FRIA RIVER. **2** In N.Y.: see LAKE PLEASANT.

Pleasant, Mount, N.H.: see PRESIDENTIAL RANGE.

Pleasant Bay. 1 In Washington co., E Maine, branching inlet of the Atlantic, bet. Millbridge and Addison towns; 7 mi. wide, 9 mi. long. **2** In Mass., sheltered inlet of the Atlantic at SE elbow of Cape Cod, bet. Chatham and Orleans.

Pleasant City, village (pop. 511), Guernsey co., E Ohio, 9 mi. SSE of Cambridge, in agr. and coal area.

Pleasant Dale, village (pop. 163), Seward co., SE Nebr., 12 mi. W of Lincoln and on branch of Platte R.

Pleasant Gap, village (pop. 1,312), Centre co., central Pa., 4 mi. S of Bellefonte.

Pleasant Green, town (pop. 24), Cooper co., central Mo., near Missouri and Lamine rivers, 16 mi. ENE of Sedalia.

Pleasant Grove. 1 Town (pop. 1,802), Jefferson co., N central Ala.; SW suburb of Birmingham. Inc. 1933. **2** City (pop. 3,195), Utah co., N central Utah, 10 mi. NNW of Provo, near Utah L. just W of Wasatch Range; alt. 4,621 ft. Fruit-shipping point in livestock and fruit area; canning, flour milling. Gold, silver, lead mines in vicinity. City is served by Provo R. irrigation project. Settled 1849 by Mormons, inc. 1855. Timpanogos Cave Natl. Monument is near by.

Pleasant Hill. 1 Village (pop. 856), Pike co., W Ill., near the Mississippi, 40 mi. WSW of Jacksonville, in agr. area. **2** Village, Ky.: see SHAKERTOWN. **3** Town (pop. 856), Sabine parish, W La., 50 mi. SSE of Shreveport; oil, natural gas. Just N is Old Pleasant Hill, scene of Civil War battle (1864). **4** City (pop. 2,200), Cass co., W Mo., 25 mi. SE of Kansas City; agr.; mfg. (scales, flour). Laid out 1843. **5** Village (pop. 940), Miami co., W Ohio, 9 mi. SW of Piqua, and on Stillwater R., in agr. area; canned foods. **6** Town (pop. 152), Cumberland co., E central Tenn., 9 mi. WNW of Crossville. School for mtn. children here. Tuberculosis sanatorium near by. **7** Village (pop. 4,687, with near-by Lloyd Place and Jericho), Nansemond co., SE Va., a suburb of Suffolk. There are also hamlets called Pleasant Hill in Rockingham and Tazewell counties.

Pleasant Hill Reservoir, Ohio: see PERRYSVILLE.

Pleasant Hills. 1 Village (pop. 5,686), Contra Costa co., W Calif., near Concord. **2** Borough (pop. 3,808), Allegheny co., SW Pa., suburb 7 mi. S of downtown Pittsburgh. Inc. 1947.

Pleasant Hope, town (pop. 174), Polk co., SW central Mo., 16 mi. N of Springfield.
Pleasant Island, SW Pacific: see NAURU.
Pleasant Lake, village (pop. 53), Stearns co., S central Minn., 8 mi. SW of St. Cloud.
Pleasant Mountain (2,007 ft.), SW Maine, in resort area, near Bridgton.
Pleasanton. 1 Town (pop. 2,244), Alameda co., W Calif., 25 mi. ESE of Oakland; dairy products, grapes, horses, cattle; wine making. Co. fairgrounds here. Laid out 1867, inc. 1894. **2** Town (pop. 130), Decatur co., S Iowa, near Mo. line, 11 mi. S of Leon. **3** City (pop. 1,178), Linn co., E Kansas, 22 mi. N of Fort Scott, near Mo. line, in diversified agr. region; flour milling, poultry dressing. Coal, lead, zinc mines in vicinity. Civil War battle took place (1864) on site of city. Laid out 1869, inc. 1870. **4** Village (pop. 188), Buffalo co., S central Nebr., 40 mi. W of Grand Island and on S.Loup R. **5** City (pop. 2,913), Atascosa co., SW Texas, 32 mi. S of San Antonio and on Atascosa R.; trade, shipping center for cattle, truck-farming area, with oil fields; railroad shops. Settled in 1850s, inc. 1928.
Pleasant Plain. 1 Town (pop. 148), Jefferson co., SE Iowa, 11 mi. NE of Fairfield, in agr. area. **2** Village (pop. 164), Warren co., SW Ohio, 24 mi. ENE of downtown Cincinnati.
Pleasant Plains. 1 Town (pop. 153), Independence co., NE central Ark., 15 mi. S of Batesville. **2** Village (pop. 500), Sangamon co., central Ill., 15 mi. WNW of Springfield; agr.; bituminous-coal mines; ships grain. **3** Section of Richmond borough of New York city, SE N.Y., on S Staten Isl.; mfg. (machinery, tools); fishing. Outerbridge Crossing to N.J. is just W.
Pleasant Point, cape, SE Ont., on L. Ontario, on S side of entrance of Adolphus Reach, approach to the Bay of Quinte, 20 mi. WSW of Kingston; lighthouse.
Pleasant Pond, Kennebec co., S Maine, narrow lake (c.5 mi. long) just SW of Gardiner; drains NE into the Kennebec.
Pleasant Ridge. 1 Plantation (pop. 80), Somerset co., central Maine, on the Kennebec just above Bingham; hunting, fishing. **2** City (pop. 3,594), Oakland co., SE Mich., residential suburb just N of Detroit. Detroit Zoological Park is near by. Inc. as village 1919, as city 1928.
Pleasant River. 1 In central Maine, rises in 3 branches in central Piscataquis co., flows c.22 mi. SE to the Piscataquis E of Milo. The Gulf, gorge on W branch, is scenic feature. **2** In Washington co., E Maine, rises in Pleasant L. near W boundary of co.; flows c.25 mi. generally SE to Pleasant Bay below Columbia Falls.
Pleasants, county (□ 130; pop. 6,369), NW W.Va.; ⊙ St. Marys. Bounded NW by Ohio R. (Ohio line), N by Middle Island Creek. Agr. (livestock, tobacco, truck); coal mines, gas and oil wells; timber. Industry at St. Marys. Formed 1851.
Pleasant Unity, village (1940 pop. 732), Westmoreland co., SW central Pa., 5 mi. SE of Greensburg.
Pleasant Valley. 1 Village, Conn.: see BARKHAMSTED. **2** Village, Scott co., E Iowa, on the Mississippi and 8 mi. ENE of Davenport, in onion-growing area. **3** Village (pop. c.500), Dutchess co., SE N.Y., 7 mi. ENE of Poughkeepsie; mfg. (magnesium products, textiles). **4** Village (pop. 1,648), Potter co., N Texas, near Amarillo.
Pleasant View. 1 Village, R.I.: see MISQUAMICUT. **2** or **View,** town (pop. 420), Weber co., N Utah, 6 mi. N of Ogden.
Pleasantville. 1 Town (pop. 893), Marion co., S central Iowa, 24 mi. SE of Des Moines, in bituminous-coal-mining and agr. area; feed mfg. **2** Residential city (pop. 11,938), Atlantic co., SE N.J., 2 mi. W of Atlantic City. Some mfg. (pork products, silk); poultry, fruit, truck. Inc. 1914. **3** Residential village (pop. 4,861), Westchester co., SE N.Y., 7 mi. N of White Plains, in New York city metropolitan area; has large publishing house. Settled 1732, inc. 1897. **4** Village (pop. 618), Fairfield co., central Ohio, 27 mi. ESE of Columbus, in agr. area; grain milling. **5** Borough (pop. 242), Bedford co., S Pa., 12 mi. NNW of Bedford. Post office is Alum Bank. **6** Borough (pop. 704), Venango co., NW Pa., 5 mi. SE of Titusville.
Pleasley (plĕz'lē), town and parish (pop. 2,638), NE Derby, England, 3 mi. NW of Mansfield; coal mining. Has 13th-cent. church.
Pleasureville, Ky.: see SOUTH PLEASUREVILLE.
Pleaux (plō), village (pop. 1,155), Cantal dept., S central France, 11 mi. SW of Mauriac; cheese and footwear mfg.
Plechy, Czechoslovakia: see PLÖCKENSTEIN.
Pleiku (plā'kōō'), town, ⊙ Pleiku prov. (□ 3,600; 1943 pop. 151,200), central Vietnam, in Annam, in Moi Plateaus, 175 mi. SSE of Hue; main town of Kontum Plateau; tea and coffee-growing center; flax, corn, sorghum; cattle raising. Pop. mostly Jarai, one of Moi tribes.
Pleine-Fougères (plĕn-fōōzhâr'), village (pop. 461), Ille-et-Vilaine dept., W France, 21 mi. NW of Fougères; apple orchards.
Pleinfeld (plīn'fĕlt), village (pop. 2,014), Middle Franconia, W central Bavaria, Germany, on the Swabian Rezat and 5 mi. N of Weissenburg; rail junction; mfg. of precision instruments, brewing, flour and lumber milling. Potatoes, cabbage, hops. Limestone quarries in area.
Pleissa (plī'sä), village (pop. 3,445), Saxony, E central Germany, 7 mi. W of Chemnitz; hosiery knitting, sewing-machine mfg.
Pleisse River (plī'sŭ), E central Germany, rises in the Erzgebirge WNW of Reichenbach, flows 56 mi. N, past Werdau, Crimmitschau, Gössnitz, and Altenburg, to the White Elster at Leipzig.
Plekhanovo (plyĭkhä'nŭvŭ), town (1939 pop. over 500), N central Tula oblast, Russian SFSR, 5 mi. NW of Tula; rail junction; metalworks.
Pleknstejn, Czechoslovakia: see PLÖCKENSTEIN.
Plélan-le-Grand (plālã'-lŭ-grã'), village (pop. 829), Ille-et-Vilaine dept., W France, near Forest of Paimpont, 21 mi. WSW of Rennes; sawmilling, cider making.
Plélan-le-Petit (-pŭtē'), village (pop. 290), Côtes-du-Nord dept., W France, 8 mi. W of Dinan; cattle raising.
Plémet (plāmā'), village (pop. 758), Côtes-du-Nord dept., W France, 24 mi. SSE of Saint-Brieuc; refractories. Kaolin quarried near by.
Plencia (plĕn'thyä), town (pop. 1,565), Vizcaya prov., N Spain, on Bay of Biscay, and 11 mi. N of Bilbao. Cereals and truck produce in area. Bathing resort.
Pléneuf (plānûf'), town (pop. 2,551), Côtes-du-Nord dept., W France, near English Channel, 11 mi. ENE of Saint-Brieuc; hosiery mfg. On near-by seashore is resort of Le Val-André with 1.5-mi.-long beach.
Plenita (plä'nētsä), Rum. *Plenița*, town (1948 pop. 6,735), Dolj prov., S Rumania, 30 mi. WSW of Craiova; trade in grain, livestock, animal products; flour milling; mfg. of bricks and tiles.
Plenty, village (pop. 201), W Sask., near Opuntie L. (7 mi. long), 30 mi. NE of Kindersley; wheat.
Plenty, Bay of, inlet of S Pacific, N N.Isl., New Zealand; c.160 mi. E-W; Cape Runaway at NE end; Tauranga harbor on SW shore.
Plentywood, city (pop. 1,862), ⊙ Sheridan co., extreme NE Mont., on Big Muddy Creek and 60 mi. NW of Williston, N.Dak.; shipping point for grain region; coal mines; livestock, dairy and poultry products. Inc. 1912.
Plered (plĕ'rĕd), town (pop. 13,335), W Java, Indonesia, in Preanger region, 25 mi. NW of Bandung; trade center for agr. area (rice, rubber). Also spelled Palered.
Ples (plyĕs), city (1938 pop. 3,400), N Ivanovo oblast, Russian SFSR, on Volga R. and 37 mi. NE of Ivanovo; summer resort.
Pleschen, Poland: see PLESZEW.
Plesetsk (plyĕ'syĭtsk), town (1939 pop. over 10,000), SW Archangel oblast, Russian SFSR, on railroad and 125 mi. S of Archangel; sawmilling center; wood cracking, metalworking.
Pleshchenitsy (plyĭshchĕ'nyĭtsē), town (1948 pop. over 2,000), NW Minsk oblast, Belorussian SSR, 38 mi. NNE of Minsk; agr. products. Also spelled Pleshchanitsy, Pleshchenitsa.
Pleshcheyevo Lake (plyĭshchā'ŭvŭ), one of largest (□ 19) glacial lakes in USSR, in S Yaroslavl oblast, Russian SFSR; picturesque location. Outlet, Nerl R. Scene (1689) of 1st Rus. shipbuilding experiments under Peter the Great. Pereslavl-Zalesski lies on SE shore. Remains of 1st Rus. flotilla are in mus., 2.5 mi. N of city. Lake formerly known as Kleshchino L. or L. Pereyaslavl.
Plesivec (plĕ'shĭvĕts), Slovak *Plešivec*, Hung. *Pelsőc* (pĕl'shûts), village (pop. 2,294), S Slovakia, Czechoslovakia, on Slana (Sajo) R. and 10 mi. SW of Roznava; rail junction; limestone quarries; base for tourist excursions into underground world of SLOVAKIAN KARST.
Pless, Poland: see PSZCZYNA.
Plessa (plĕ'sä), village (pop. 2,939), in former Prussian Saxony prov., central Germany, after 1945 in Saxony-Anhalt, on the Black Elster and 5 mi. E of Elsterwerda; lignite mining. Power station.
Plessis (plĕ'sĭs), resort village, Jefferson co., N N.Y., 5 mi. SE of Alexandria Bay. Lakes near by.
Plessis-Robinson, Le (lŭ plĕsē'-rôbĕsō'), town (pop. 10,118), Seine dept., N central France, a fine residential SSW suburb of Paris, 6 mi. from Notre Dame Cathedral.
Plessisville (plĕ'sēvĭl), village (pop. 3,522), S Que., 24 mi. WNW of Thetford Mines; rayon and linen milling, mfg. of leather, shoes, hosiery, machinery, furniture, maple products; in flax-growing region.
Plessur River (plĕsōōr'), E Switzerland, rises SW of Arosa, flows 16 mi. N and W to the Rhine near Chur, draining Schanfigg valley.
Plestin-les-Grèves (plĕstē'-lā-grĕv'), village (pop. 1,367), Côtes-du-Nord dept., W France, 9 mi. SW of Lannion; dairying; flax growing.
Pleszew (plĕ'shĕf), Ger. *Pleschen* (plĕ'shŭn), town (1946 pop. 8,760), Poznan prov., W central Poland, 16 mi. NW of Kalisz; rail spur terminus; mfg. of machinery, furniture, mirrors; canning, flour milling, sawmilling, tanning, distilling.
Pleszow, Poland: see NOWA HUTA.
Pleternica (plĕ'tĕrnētsä), village, N Croatia, Yugoslavia, on Orljava R. and 14 mi. NW of Slavonski Brod, in Slavonia, in lignite area; rail junction.
Pletipi Lake (plĕtĕpē'), (□ 138), central Que.; 51°45'N 70°7'W; fed and drained by R. aux Outardes; 28 mi. long, 10 mi. wide.
Plettenberg (plĕ'tŭnbĕrk), town (pop. 22,546), in former Prussian prov. of Westphalia, W Germany, after 1945 in North Rhine-Westphalia, 13 mi. SE of Iserlohn; mfg. of screws, rivets, nails, wire; metalworking. Has 14th-cent. church. Chartered bet. 1387–97.
Pleumartin (plûmärtē'), village (pop. 724), Vienne dept., W central France, 12 mi. SE of Châtellerault; sawmilling.
Pleven (plĕ'vĕn), city (pop. 38,997), ⊙ Pleven dist. (formed 1949), N Bulgaria, near Vit R., 85 mi. NE of Sofia; major agr. center and cattle market; mfg. of agr. machinery, steel safes, cement; woolen, cotton, and linen textiles; tanning, flour milling, fruit and vegetable canning, vegetable-oil extracting, wine making. Has school of viticulture, town mus. Once a Thracian settlement; dominated by Romans and Bulgarians; became a commercial town under Turkish rule (15th-19th cent.). During Russo-Turkish War (commemorated by a mausoleum), it was yielded (1877) by Turkish general Osman Pasha after 4-month siege by Russian and Rumanian troops. Also called Plevna. Was ⊙ former Pleven oblast (1934–47).
Plevlje, Yugoslavia: see PLJEVLJA.
Plevna, Bulgaria: see PLEVEN, city.
Plevna, Greece: see PETROUSA.
Plevna (plĕv'nŭ). **1** City (pop. 200), Reno co., S central Kansas, on North Fork Ninnescah R. and 21 mi. WSW of Hutchinson; wheat. **2** Town (pop. 247), Fallon co., E Mont., on branch of O'Fallon Creek and 12 mi. WNW of Baker, in grain and potato region.
Pleyben (plābē'), village (pop. 1,550), Finistère dept., W France, 17 mi. NNE of Quimper; slate quarries. Has 16th-cent. church and fine 17th-cent. calvary in the shape of a triumphal arch.
Pleystein (plī'shtīn), town (pop. 1,758), Upper Palatinate, E Bavaria, Germany, in Bohemian Forest, 11 mi. ESE of Weiden; cut-glass mfg., woodworking. Chartered c.1366. Rose quartz quarried in area.
Plezzo, Yugoslavia: see BOVEC.
Pliassidi, Greece: see PELION.
Pliego (plēā'gō), town (pop. 2,172), Murcia prov., SE Spain, 21 mi. W of Murcia; olive-oil processing, flour milling; truck produce, cereals, wine.
Plieningen (plē'nĭng-ŭn), S suburb of Stuttgart, Germany, 5.5 mi. SSE of city center. Inc. 1942 into Stuttgart.
Plinlimmon or **Plynlimmon** (plĭn-lĭ'mŭn), mountain (2,468 ft.), on border of Cardigan and Montgomery, Wales, 14 mi. ENE of Aberystwyth. Severn, Wye, and Rheidol rivers rise here.
Pliskov (plĭ'skôf), village (pop. 2,016), Kolarovgrad dist., E Bulgaria, in S part of Deliorman upland, 4 mi. WNW of Novi Pazar; grain, truck. Has excavations of 7th-cent. fortified camp of Aboba, ⊙ First Bulgarian Kingdom (679-1018). Bulg. pagans under King Boris converted here to Christianity (866).
Pliskov (plyĭskôf'), agr. town (1926 pop. 4,187), NE Vinnitsa oblast, Ukrainian SSR, 35 mi. ENE of Vinnitsa; sugar beets, wheat.
Plissa (plyē'sŭ), village (1931 pop. 1,200), S central Polotsk oblast, Belorussian SSR, 12 mi. NE of Glubokoye; fruit, rye, flax, potatoes.
Plittersdorf (plĭ'tŭrsdôrf), village (pop. 1,543), S Baden, Germany, near the Rhine (Fr. border; road bridge), 3 mi. NW of Rastatt; customs station; strawberries.
Plitvice Lakes (plēt'vĭtsĕ), Serbo-Croatian *Plitvička Jezera* (-vĭchkä yĕ'zĕrä), W Croatia, Yugoslavia, 65 mi. SSW of Zagreb, near Bosnia border; comprise 16 beautiful lakes (varying up to c.3 mi. in length), set deep among wooded hills and connected by waterfalls (up to c.250 ft. high); give rise to Korana R. Trout fishing. Village of Plitvicka Jezera, on lake 10 mi. E of Vrhovine, is resort.
Pliva River, Yugoslavia: see JAJCE.
Pljesevica (plyĕ'shĕvĭtsä), Serbo-Croatian *Plješevica*, mountain range in Dinaric Alps, Yugoslavia; extends c.25 mi. along Croatia-Bosnia border. Highest points: the Ozeblin (5,435 ft.; 5 mi. WNW of Donji Lapac); Gola Pljesevica (5,409 ft.; 4 mi. NNE of Titova Korenica). Noted for large forests. Also called Pljesivica, Serbo-Croatian *Plješivica*.
Pljesivica, mountain range, Yugoslavia: see PLJESEVICA.
Pljevlja or **Plyevlya** (both: plyĕv'lyä), town (pop. 6,278), N Montenegro, Yugoslavia, on Cotina R. and 65 mi. N of Titograd, near Serbia border, in the Sanjak; trade center (cattle, dairy products). Under Turkish rule (until 1878), in Herzegovina. Also spelled Plevlje and Pljevlje.
Ploaghe (plôä'gĕ), village (pop. 4,426), Sassari prov., NW Sardinia, 11 mi. ESE of Sassari. Near by are Trinità di Saccargia (Romanesque abbey built 1115), 12th-cent. church of San Michele di Salvennero, and a nuraghe (Nuraghe Nieddu).
Ploce, Yugoslavia: see KARDELJEVO.
Plochingen (plô'khĭng-ŭn), town (pop. 7,597), N Württemberg, Germany, after 1945 in Württemberg-Baden, on the Neckar at mouth of Fils R., and 5 mi. ESE of Esslingen; rail junction; mfg. of

machinery, tools, electrical goods, chemicals (artificial resin, gelatine); paper milling, brewing. Head of projected Neckar canalization and of canal to connect river with the Danube at Ulm.

Plock (plôtsk), Rus. *Plotsk* (plôtsk), city (pop. 28,508), Warszawa prov., central Poland, port on the Vistula, on railroad and 60 mi. WNW of Warsaw. Market center for agr. region; mfg. of agr. tools, bricks, vegetable oil, marmalade; fruit canning, distilling, flour milling; airport. Its 12th-cent. cathedral, with tombs of Pol. kings, was damaged in Second World War. City, founded before 10th cent., was a medieval residence of dukes of Masovia. Passed (1793) to Prussia and (1815) to Rus. Poland, when it became ⊙ Plotsk govt.; returned to Poland in 1921. Before Second World War, pop. over 50% Jewish. During war, under administration of East Prussia, called Schröttersburg.

Plöcken Pass (plû′kûn), Ital. *Passo di Monte Croce Carnico*, pass (alt. 4,462 ft.) in Carnic Alps, on Austro-Ital. border, 6 mi. SSW of Kötschach, Austria. Crossed by road bet. Kötschach and Tolmezzo, Italy. Scene of fighting in 1917 campaign during First World War.

Plöckenstein (plû′kûn-shtīn), Czech *Plechý* (plĕ′khē) or *Pleknštejn* (plĕ′kûn-shtān), second-highest peak (4,519 ft.) of the Bohemian Forest, at junction of Austrian, Czechoslovak and German borders, 10 mi. S of Volary.

Ploegsteert (plōōkh′stârt), town (pop. 4,897), West Flanders prov., NW Belgium, near Fr. border, 11 mi. NW of Lille; agr. market (grain, stock). In First World War, it was nicknamed *Plugstreet*; scene of intensive fighting for near-by heights of Hill 60, Mt. Sorel, and Kemmel Hill (just S).

Ploëmeur (plôûmûr′), village (pop. 931), Morbihan dept., W France, 4 mi. WSW of Lorient; important kaolin quarries.

Ploërmel (plôĕrmĕl′), town (pop. 3,130), Morbihan dept., W France, 25 mi. NE of Vannes; commercial center; foundry. Slate quarries near by. Has 16th-cent. Gothic church. Damaged in Second World War.

Ploesti (plô-yĕsht′), Rum. *Ploeşti*, city (1948 pop. 95,632), ⊙ Prahova prov., S central Rumania, in Walachia, 34 mi. NNW of Bucharest; 44°56′N 25°3′E. Chief center of Rumanian petroleum industry. It is a rail hub and has several large refineries, extensive oil-storage installations and oil by-products plants. Six major pipe lines extend to shipping centers, 4 to Giurgiu, 1 to Bucharest, and 1 to Constanta; secondary pipe lines bring in crude from oil fields in vicinity. Abundance of cheap energy has also favored the establishment of other industries. Ploesti manufactures textiles, knitwear, hats, petroleum equipment, hardware, enamelware, paper, cardboard, glass, leather goods, arms, munitions, furniture, rubber, clay products, and printed matter. City area extends to suburbs of Paulesti (NW), Corlatesti (SE), and Tatarani (S). Founded in 16th cent., Ploesti was hq. of Russian army in Russo-Turkish War of 1811. During Second World War, it was the target of repeated Allied bombings, notably in April-August, 1943. Captured by USSR troops in 1944. Sometimes spelled Ploeshti.

Ploeuc (plûk), village (pop. 763), Côtes-du-Nord dept., W France, 11 mi. S of Saint-Brieuc; dairying; horse raising.

Plogastel-Saint-Germain (plôgästĕl′-sē-zhĕrmē′), village (pop. 571), Finistère dept., W France, 8 mi. W of Quimper; cattle raising.

Plöhnen, Poland: see PLONSK.

Plokhino, Russian SFSR: see ULYANOVO.

Plomarion (plômä′rēōn), city (pop. 6,546), on S coast of Lesbos isl., Greece, 12 mi. SW of Mytilene; olive oil, wine, wheat; fisheries. Formerly called Potamos.

Plomb du Cantal, France: see CANTAL, MASSIF DU.

Plombières (plōbyâr′), village, Liége prov., E Belgium, 6 mi. WSW of Aachen, near Ger. border; lead mining.

Plombières-les-Bains (–lā-bē′) or **Plombières**, village (pop. 1,452), Vosges dept., E France, in the SW Vosges, 15 mi. S of Épinal; well-known watering place with radioactive springs. Scene of memorable interview (1858) bet. Napoleon III and Cavour.

Plombières-lès-Dijon (–lā-dēzhō′), W suburb (pop. 1,543) of Dijon, Côte-d'Or dept., E central France, on Ouche R. and Burgundy Canal; cocoa and mustard mfg., truck gardening.

Plomin (plô′mĭn), Ital. *Fianona* (fēänô′nä), village (1936 pop. 381), NW Croatia, Yugoslavia, on Adriatic Sea, 19 mi. SSW of Rijeka (Fiume), in Istria.

Plomo, Nevado del (nävä′dō dĕl plō′mō), Andean peak (19,850 ft.) on Argentina-Chile border, 30 mi. S of Aconcagua peak; 33°7′S.

Plön (plûn), town (pop. 9,332), in Schleswig-Holstein, NW Germany, on an isthmus formed by Plön L. (S) and several small lakes (N), 8 mi. W of Eutin; favorite resort center of the so-called Holsteiner Schweiz [Ger.,=Holsteinian Switzerland], a region noted for its numerous small lakes. Metal- and woodworking. Site of hydrobiological station of Kiel Univ. Castle, built in 17th cent. on site of 12th-cent. fortress, towers over town; here, in 1846, Christian VIII of Denmark published the "Open Letter" regarding succession in Schleswig, which precipitated the war of 1848. Town was chartered 1236.

Plona River (pwô′nä), Pol. *Płona*, Ger. *Plöne* (plû′nù), in Pomerania, after 1945 in NW Poland, rises just N of Barlinek, flows 45 mi. NNW, through L. Miedwie, past Dabie, to Damm L.

Plonge, Lac la (lăk lä plōzh′), lake (□ 64), central Sask., 140 mi. NNW of Prince Albert; 16 mi. long, 10 mi. wide. Drains N into Lac Île-à-Crosse and Churchill R. through Beaver R.

Plön Lake (plûn), Ger. *Plöner See* (plû′nùr zā″), largest lake (□ 12) of Schleswig-Holstein, NW Germany; 6 mi. long, 5 mi. wide; greatest depth c.200 ft., average depth 44 ft.; alt. 71 ft. PLÖN is at N shore.

Plonsk (pwô′nyùsk), Pol. *Płońsk*, town (pop. 7,758), Warszawa prov., E central Poland, on railroad and 40 mi. NW of Warsaw; mfg. of agr. machinery, bricks; sawmilling, brewing, flour milling. Before Second World War, pop. over 50% Jewish. During war, under administration of East Prussia, called Plöhnen.

Ploskosh or **Ploskosh'** (plôs′kùsh), village (1939 pop. over 500), N central Velikiye Luki oblast, Russian SFSR, 23 mi. NW of Toropets; flax.

Ploskoye (plô′skŭyù), village (1939 pop. over 2,000), E Orel oblast, Russian SFSR, 10 mi. NW of Yelets; distilling.

Plotsk, Poland: see PLOCK.

Plottier (plōtyä′), village (pop. estimate 500), E Neuquén natl. territory, Argentina, on railroad, on Limay R. (irrigated area) and 8 mi. W of Neuquén; alfalfa, fruit, grapes, livestock; fishing, wine making, dried-fruit processing.

Ploty (pwô′tĭ), Pol. *Płoty*, Ger. *Plathe* (plä′tù), town (1939 pop. 3,646; 1946 pop. 1,213) in Pomerania, after 1945 in Szczecin prov., NW Poland, on the Rega and 8 mi. SSE of Gryfice; agr. market (grain, sugar beets, potatoes, livestock). Irrigation dam 4 mi. N.

Plouagat (plōōägä′), village (pop. 203), Côtes-du-Nord dept., W France, 7 mi. E of Guingamp, in heart of N Brittany's cider country.

Plouaret (plōōärā′), village (pop. 750), Côtes-du-Nord dept., W France, 8 mi. S of Lannion; dairying. Has 16th-cent. church with Renaissance tower and Gothic porch.

Plouay (plōōĕ′), town (pop. 2,320), Morbihan dept., W France, 12 mi. N of Lorient; agr. market.

Ploubalay (plōōbälĕ′), village (pop. 574), Côtes-du-Nord dept., W France, 10 mi. NNW of Dinan; early potatoes; apple orchards.

Ploudalmézeau (plōōdälmäzō′), village (pop. 1,364), Finistère dept., W France, 13 mi. NNW of Brest; dairying, flour milling.

Ploudiry (plōōdērē′), village (pop. 283), Finistère dept., W France, 16 mi. ENE of Brest; vegetables; dairying.

Plouescat (plōōĕskä′), village (pop. 2,069), Finistère dept., W France, 17 mi. WNW of Morlaix; iodine, bromide mfg.; fruit, vegetable shipping.

Plougastel-Daoulas (plōōgästĕl′-dōōläs′), town (pop. 2,010), Finistère dept., W France, near Brest Roads, 6 mi. E of Brest; truck-gardening center (strawberries, vegetables). Has noted sculptured calvary built 1602–04 after an outbreak of plague, and damaged in Second World War.

Plouguenast (plōōgùnäst′), village (pop. 470), Côtes-du-Nord dept., W France, 16 mi. SSE of Saint-Brieuc; woodworking, flour milling.

Plouha (plōōä′), village (pop. 1,349), Côtes-du-Nord dept., W France, 13 mi. NW of Saint-Brieuc; woodworking. Stone quarries near by. Site of 13th-cent. pilgrimage chapel.

Plouigneau (plōōēnyō′), village (pop. 856), Finistère dept., W France, 6 mi. E of Morlaix; apple orchards.

Ploumanach, France: see PERROS-GUIREC.

Plouzévédé (plōōzāvādā′), village (pop. 496), Finistère dept., W France, 13 mi. W of Morlaix; cattle raising. Near by are ruins of 16th-cent. castle of Kerjean.

Plovdiv (plôv′dĭf), city (pop. 125,440), ⊙ Plovdiv dist. (formed 1949), S central Bulgaria, in Plovdiv Basin, on Maritsa R. and 80 mi. ESE of Sofia; 42°10′N 24°43′E. Second largest city of Bulgaria; major transportation (6 rail lines) and mfg. center with metal, textile, leather, chemical, woodworking, and food-processing (sugar, rice, flour, meat, fruit, vegetables, hops) industries. Mfg. of cigarettes. Major tobacco and livestock-trading center and central market for Plovdiv Basin agr. output. Site of univ., teachers col., technical and commercial schools, theological seminary, theater, natl. library, archaeological mus. Has anc. town walls and gate, Catholic cathedral, old churches and mosques, ruins of Turkish market and baths. Originally Gr. settlement of Eumolpias; became known as stronghold of Peneropolis under Philip II of Macedonia. Successively ⊙ Moesia and Thrace under Roman rule (29 B.C.–A.D. 376); assaulted repeatedly during Barbarian invasions; finally fell to First Bulg. Kingdom. Burned (970) by Kievan Russians and later rebuilt by Byzantines. Invaded by crusaders under Second Bulg. Kingdom; sacked (1364) by Turks. A commercial center under Turkish rule; captured by Russians (1878); proclaimed ⊙ Eastern Rumelia; ceded (1885) to Bulgaria. Of the numerous names carried by Plovdiv throughout its history, the best known are Philippopolis (its charter name; 1st cent. A.D.) Filibe (under Turkish rule), and Plovdiv, used by Bulgarians since 17th cent. and officially assumed after First World War. Was ⊙ former Plovdiv oblast (1934–47).

Plovdiv Basin (□ 1,726; average alt. 650 ft.), central Bulgaria, W part of Thracian Plain, bet. Sredna Gora (N), Rhodope Mts. (S), and basins of Stara Zagora and Khaskovo (E). Drained by Maritsa R. Fertile soils. Extensive agr. (livestock, grain, rice, vineyards, truck, hemp, sugar beets, cotton). Main centers: Plovdiv, Pazardzhik, Parvomai, Chirpan.

Plover (plŭ′vûr), town (pop. 243), Pocahontas co., N central Iowa, 35 mi. NW of Fort Dodge; livestock, grain.

Plover River, central Wis., rises in Langlade co., flows c.50 mi. SSW to Wisconsin R. 2 mi. S of Stevens Point.

Plüderhausen (plü″dùrhou′zùn), village (pop. 3,710), N Württemberg, Germany, after 1945 in Württemberg-Baden, on the Rems and 3 mi. ESE of Schorndorf; mfg. of forks, food processing, leather- and woodworking.

Plum (plōōm), settlement (dist. pop. c.300), New Caledonia, on SW coast, 12 mi. E of Nouméa; agr. products.

Plumas (plōō′mùs), village (pop. estimate 300), S central Man., 20 mi. ENE of Neepawa.

Plumas, county (□ 2,570; pop. 13,519), NE Calif., in the Sierra Nevada; ⊙ Quincy. Mt. Ingalls (8,377 ft.), parts of Plumas and Tahoe natl. forests, and part of Lassen Volcanic Natl. Park (NW) are here. L. Almanor (resorts) and other reservoirs are impounded by power dams. Drained by Feather R., here formed by forks flowing in scenic canyons. Hunting, fishing; hot springs; winter sports. Lumbering (pine, fir, cedar), stock grazing; farming (chiefly hay) and dairying in mtn. basins, largest of which is Sierra Valley (partly in co.). Mining of gold (since 1850), copper, silver; quarrying of sand and gravel. Formed 1854.

Plumas, Las, Argentina: see LAS PLUMAS.

Plumbland, village and parish (pop. 571), W Cumberland, England, 6 mi. NNE of Cockermouth; cattle and sheep raising. Has church of Norman origin.

Plum Branch, town (pop. 158), McCormick co., W S.C., 25 mi. S of Greenwood; lumber.

Plum City, village (pop. 355), Pierce co., W Wis., 35 mi. WSW of Eau Claire; dairying, stock raising.

Plum Coulee (kōōlā′), village (pop. 433), S Man., 55 mi. SW of Winnipeg; mixed farming, grain, stock.

Plum Creek, central Colo., rises in 2 branches in Douglas co., flows generally N, past Castle Rock and Louviers, to S.Platte R. just S of Denver. Length with longest branch, c.40 mi.

Plumerillo, Argentina: see EL PLUMERILLO.

Plumerville or **Plummerville** (both: plŭ′mùrvĭl), town (pop. 550), Conway co., central Ark., 11 mi. WNW of Conway, near Arkansas R.

Plum Island. 1 In NE Mass., sandy island (¼–1 mi. wide) extending c.8 mi. along coast, bet. Plum Isl. R. (bridged) and the Atlantic, from mouth of Merrimack R. (N) to Plum Isl. Sound (arm of Ipswich Bay) at mouth of Ipswich R. (S); summer resort; coastguard station and lighthouse on N end. **2** In SE N.Y., hilly island (c.2½ mi. long) off Orient Point (NE tip of Long Isl.), at N side of entrance to Gardiners Bay; lighthouse (41°10′N 72°13′W). Site of old U.S. Fort Terry. Isl., owned by Suffolk co., is used as recreational area.

Plumlov (plōōm′lôf), town (pop. 1,631), central Moravia, Czechoslovakia, 4 mi. W of Prostejov; barley, oats, sugar beets. Has noted 16th-cent. early baroque castle. Dam just E, on tributary of Morava R.

Plummer. 1 Village (pop. 395), Benewah co., N Idaho, 15 mi. W of St. Maries; trade town in Coeur d'Alene Indian Reservation. **2** Village (pop. 340), Red Lake co., NW Minn., on Clearwater R. and 10 mi. E of Red Lake Falls; dairying.

Plummer Island, Md.: see CABIN JOHN.

Plummerville, Ark.: see PLUMERVILLE.

Plum River, NW Ill., rises in Jo Daviess co., flows c.55 mi. S and SW to the Mississippi at Savanna.

Plumtree, town (pop. 908), Bulawayo prov., SW Southern Rhodesia, in Matabeleland, 55 mi. SW of Bulawayo; alt. 4,561 ft. Railroad station on Bechuanaland Protectorate border; corn; cattle, sheep, goats. Hq. of native commissioner for Bulalima-Mangwe dist. Police post. Secondary school.

Plumtree, village (pop. c.150), Avery co., NW N.C., 8 mi. NNE of Spruce Pine; mica mining.

Plumur, Turkey: see PULUMUR.

Plumville, borough (pop. 452), Indiana co., W central Pa., 12 mi. N of Indiana.

Plunge (plōōng-gä′), Lith. *Plungė*, Rus. *Plungyany*, city (pop. 5,255), W Lithuania, 30 mi. ENE of Memel; flax-processing center (spinning, weaving); mfg. of shoes, bricks; sawmilling. In Rus. Kovno govt. until 1920.

Pluvigner (plüvēnyä'), village (pop. 1,594), Morbihan dept., W France, 18 mi. E of Lorient; sawmilling, horse raising.

Pluzhnoye (plōōzh'nŭyŭ), village (1926 pop. 3,379), NW Kamenets-Podolski oblast, Ukrainian SSR, 21 mi. W of Shepetovka; distilling.

Plyavinyas, Latvia: see PLAVINAS.

Plyevlya, Yugoslavia: see PLJEVLJA.

Plymouth (plĭ'mŭth), county borough (1931 pop. 208,182; 1951 census 208,985) and city, S Devon, England, on PLYMOUTH SOUND, bet. Plym R. and Tamar R., and 37 mi. SW of Exeter; 50°23'N 4°6'W. Consists (since 1914) of contiguous "Three Towns" of Plymouth, Stonehouse (or East Stonehouse), and Devonport. Important maritime center and naval station, with extensive shipbuilding industry, fisheries, dockyards. Exports China-clay, granite, tin, copper, lead. Mfg. (chemicals, ship fixtures, food products, gin). Devonport has engineering col., naval barracks, signal station, hosp., mus. Stonehouse has Royal William Victualling Yard, 16th-cent. artillery tower, old houses. Other landmarks: Marine Biological Laboratories, R.C. cathedral, aquarium, Gothic guildhall, 17th-cent. citadel, library, art gall. Plymouth Hoe, rocky promontory, overlooks the sound. Heavy damage caused by bombing during Second World War, especially in 1941; among other damage, 8 churches and Royal Naval Hosp. were destroyed. Long seafaring history, with associations of Drake, Raleigh, Grenville, the Spanish Armada (rendezvous of anti-Armada fleet), and the Pilgrim Fathers (it was last port touched by the Mayflower before the American voyage). Known as Tamerworth in Anglo-Saxon times, as Sutton in Middle Ages. Plymouth was held by Parliamentarians for 4 years in the Civil War, when the rest of Devon and Cornwall were Royalist.

Plymouth, town (pop. 2,103), ⊙ Montserrat isl., S Leeward Isls., B.W.I., port on W coast, 37 mi. SW of St. John's, Antigua; 16°43'N 62°13'W; on open roadstead in tropical setting. Exports cotton, citrus fruit, vegetable oil, lime juice, sugar cane, cattle. Has near-by hot springs, gypsum and sulphur deposits.

Plymouth, village (pop. 1,180), SW Tobago, B.W.I., 4 mi. NW of Scarborough; coconut growing.

Plymouth. 1 County (□ 863; pop. 23,252), NW Iowa, on S.Dak. line (W; formed here by Big Sioux R.); ⊙ Le Mars. Prairie agr. area (cattle, hogs, poultry, corn, oats, barley) drained by Floyd R. and West Fork Little Sioux R.; sand and gravel pits. Formed 1851. **2** County (□ 664; pop. 189,468), SE Mass.; ⊙ Plymouth. On Massachusetts Bay and Cape Cod Bay (E), Buzzards Bay (S). Its shore communities are popular summer resorts. Some industry, mostly shoe mfg. (especially at Brockton); agr. (cranberries, truck, poultry). Formed 1685.

Plymouth. 1 City (pop. 382), Amador co., central Calif., 35 mi. E of Sacramento, in Sierra Nevada foothills; gold mining; agr. **2** Town (pop. 6,771), Litchfield co., W central Conn., near Naugatuck R., just N of Waterbury. Mfg. (locks, hardware, thermometers, wood and metal products). Includes Terryville (1940 pop. 4,230) and Pequabuck villages. Settled 1728, inc. 1795. **3** Village (pop. c.200), Orange co., central Fla., 15 mi. NW of Orlando, near L. Apopka; large citrus-fruit canneries. **4** Village (pop. 854), Hancock co., W Ill., 35 mi. NE of Quincy, in agr. area (grain; dairy products; livestock, poultry); oil refinery. **5** City (pop. 6,704), ⊙ Marshall co., N Ind., on Yellow R. and 24 mi. S of South Bend; shipping and trading center in agr. area (livestock; dairy products; soybeans, grain). Mfg.: grinding machines, automobile parts, stokers, batteries, butter, emery products. Popular resort lakes near by. The Potawatami Indians had a village on this site. Settled 1834, inc. 1872. **6** Town (pop. 395), Cerro Gordo co., N Iowa, on Shell Rock R. and 8 mi. NE of Mason City; dairy products, feed; sand and gravel pits. **7** Town (pop. 496), Penobscot co., S Maine, 23 mi. WSW of Bangor, in agr. area. **8** Town (pop. 13,608), including Plymouth village (pop. 10,540), ⊙ Plymouth co., SE Mass., on Plymouth Bay and 35 mi. SE of Boston; popular resort, with historic sites and fine beaches. Mfg. (cordage, textiles, hardware), agr. (poultry, dairy products, cranberries). Port of entry. Here was made (1620) 1st permanent white settlement in New England. Most famous of its monuments is Plymouth Rock, since 1880 on its original site; legend has it that on this boulder the Pilgrims stepped when they disembarked from the *Mayflower*. Many 17th-cent. houses; Pilgrim Hall contains many relics. Near site of original village is 80-ft. granite *National Monument to the Forefathers* (1889). Villages in Plymouth include Manomet (măn"ŭmĕt'), North Plymouth, White Horse Beach. Includes most of Myles Standish State Forest (10,910 acres). **9** City (pop. 6,637), Wayne co., SE Mich., 22 mi. W of Detroit and on the River Rouge. Mfg. (auto parts, metal and rubber products, office furniture, typewriters, electrical goods, air rifles, felt products); truck and fruit farming. A co. school for the feeble-minded and a women's prison are near by. Settled 1825; inc. as village 1867, as city 1932. **10** Village (pop. 348), Jefferson co., SE Nebr., 15 mi. NE of Fairbury; grain. **11** Resort town (pop. 3,039), including Plymouth village (pop. 2,107), Grafton co., central N.H., on the Pemigewasset and 18 mi. NNW of Laconia, W of Squam L.; winter sports; mfg. of sports equipment; fruit, poultry, dairy products. Has state's oldest teachers col. (1871). Hawthorne died here. Inc. 1763. **12** Town (pop. 4,486), ⊙ Washington co., E N.C., on navigable Roanoke R. and 28 mi. NE of Washington; food canning, lumber processing, mfg. of paper, boxes; hunting, fishing. Founded late-18th cent.; inc. 1800. **13** Village (pop. 1,510), on Richland-Huron co. line, N central Ohio, 17 mi. NNW of Mansfield; locomotives, machinery, hardware. Settled 1815, inc. 1838. **14** Borough (pop. 13,021), Luzerne co., NE central Pa., 4 mi. W of Wilkes-Barre and on Susquehanna R.; anthracite mines, anthracite by-products. Inc. 1866. **15** Town (pop. 228), Box Elder co., N Utah, 20 mi. NW of Logan, near Malad R.; alt. 4,400 ft.; dry farming, stock raising. **16** Town (pop. 348), Windsor co., S central Vt., 13 mi. SE of Rutland. Birthplace and grave of Calvin Coolidge here; Coolidge State Forest near by. Includes Tyson, resort village on small Echo L. **17** City (pop. 4,543), Sheboygan co., E Wis., on Mullet R. (tributary of Sheboygan R.) and 13 mi. W of Sheboygan, in dairy and grain area; cheese-making center; flour, canned foods, cigars, boxes, foundry products, enamelware. Seat of Wisconsin Cheesemakers' Association and its cheese exchange. Mission House Col. and Theological Seminary is here. Inc. 1877.

Plymouth Bay, SE Mass., inlet of the Atlantic (c.7 mi. long, 4 mi. wide), with entrance bet. Gurnet Point (N) and Rocky Point (S), NW of Cape Cod Bay. Plymouth Harbor is S arm, with PLYMOUTH on its SW shore; Duxbury Bay is N arm, protected from the Atlantic by 5-mi. sandbar with Gurnet Point (lighthouse here) at SE tip (42°00'N 70°36'W).

Plymouth Meeting, village (pop. c.600), Montgomery co., SE Pa., just NE of Conshohocken; mfg. (bricks, magnesia and asbestos products). Has old meetinghouse built 1710–12, rebuilt 1867.

Plymouth Rock, Mass.: see PLYMOUTH.

Plymouth Sound, inlet of the English Channel, bet. Cornwall and Devon, England; 3 mi. long, and 3 mi. wide at mouth. Receives Tamar R. (NW) and Plym R. (NE) through its estuary the Cattewater. Famous roadstead. On it are the "Three Ports" or "Three Towns" (PLYMOUTH, Devonport, Stonehouse). Off the Hoe (promontory on which Plymouth lies) is Drake's Isl. or St. Nicholas's Isl. (fort). The Sound is an important fishing ground and provides deep anchorage for large vessels, protected by breakwaters.

Plympton, town (pop. 697), Plymouth co., SE Mass., 7 mi. W of Plymouth; cranberries. Settled 1662, inc. 1707.

Plympton Erle, England: see PLYMPTON SAINT MAURICE.

Plympton Saint Mary (plĭmp'–), town and parish (pop. 5,077), S Devon, England, 4 mi. ENE of Plymouth; agr. market. Has ruins of Norman priory; 15th-cent. church; and many old houses. Near by are China-clay quarries.

Plympton Saint Maurice (mŏ'rĭs) or **Plympton Erle**, town and parish (pop. 1,075), S Devon, England, adjoining Plympton St. Mary, 4 mi. ENE of Plymouth. Has old grammar school, guildhall, ruins of Norman castle. Sir Joshua Reynolds b. here.

Plymptonville, village (pop. 1,352), Clearfield co., central Pa., near Clearfield.

Plym River (plĭm), Devon, England, rises in Dartmoor Forest, 8 mi. W of Buckfastleigh, flows 16 mi. SW and S to Plymouth Sound at Plymouth; receives Meavy and Tory rivers. Its estuary is called the Cattewater.

Plymstock, residential town and parish (pop. 7,057), S Devon, England, 3 mi. ESE of Plymouth; marble and limestone quarrying. Has 15th-cent. church.

Plynlimmon, Wales: see PLINLIMMON.

Plyussa (plyōō'sŭ), village (1939 pop. over 500), NE Pskov oblast, Russian SFSR, on Plyussa R. and 27 mi. SW of Luga; machine shops.

Plyussa River, W European Russian SFSR, rises NW of Novoselye, flows E, NW past Plyussa and Lady, and N past Chernevo and Slantsy, to Narva R. opposite Narva; 125 mi. long. Navigable (April–Nov.) below Plyussa.

Plzen, Czechoslovakia: see PILSEN.

P.M.S.I., Vietnam: see MOI PLATEAUS.

Pniewy (pŭnyĕ'vĭ), Ger. *Pinne* (pĭ'nŭ), town (pop. 3,195), Poznan prov., W Poland, 30 mi. WNW of Poznan; mfg. of machines, bricks; flour milling, distilling, malt-coffee making; cattle trade.

Pnom Dek or **Phnom Dek** (pŭnôm' dĕk') [Cambodian,=iron mountain], iron-bearing hill in Kompong Thom prov., central Cambodia, 45 mi. N of Kompong Thom. Deposits have been worked by the Kui aborigines.

Pnompenh or **Phnompenh** (nŏm"pĕn', pŭnôm'pĕn'yŭ), city (1948 pop. 110,639), ⊙ Cambodia and ⊙, but independent of, Kandal prov. (□ 1,500; 1948 pop. 528,012), on right bank of the Tonle Sap and Bassac rivers at their junction (QUATRE BRAS) with the Mekong, head of railroad (completed 1942) to Bangkok, and 125 mi. NW of Saigon (linked by highway); airport; 11°33'N 104°51'E. Major river port (accessible to ships of 15-ft. draught) and processing center; rice milling, distilling, brewing, sawmilling; mfg. of textiles, soft drinks; abattoir. Pop. includes Cambodians (40%), Chinese (30%), and Annamese. City includes modern European quarter (N) at foot of the hill Pnom Penh, the commercial (Chinese, Annamese) quarter in center, and the Cambodian quarter (S) surrounding the royal palace (1813), which includes throne room (sacred sword, crown jewels) and royal pagoda. Pnompenh has archaeological museums, royal library, schools for Pali and Buddhist studies. Founded c.1371 by the Khmers, it succeeded (1434) Angkor as the capital, was abandoned several times, and became permanent ⊙ in 1867. Since then, the city has been modernized and expanded through land reclamation.

Po or **P'o**, China: see PO RIVER.

Po (pō), town (pop. c.3,000), S Upper Volta, Fr. West Africa, near Gold Coast border, 80 mi. SSE of Ouagadougou; shea nuts, peanuts, livestock. Customhouse.

Po, river: see PO RIVER.

Poá (pŏŏä'), town (pop. 3,467), SE São Paulo, Brazil, near Tietê R., on railroad and 18 mi. E of São Paulo; truck.

Poai (bŭ'ī'), town, ⊙ Poai co. (pop. 280,563), SW Pingyuan prov., China, 40 mi. WSW of Sinsiang and on railroad; coal-mining center, with main mines at Tsiaotso (E); rice, beans, millet, tea. Called Tsinghwa until 1929. Until 1949 in Honan.

Poarta Alba (pwär'tä-äl'bŭ), Rum. *Poarta Albă*, town (1948 pop. 1,003), Constanta prov., SE Rumania, on the Danube–Black Sea Canal, and 6 mi. ESE of Medgidia. Administrative center of the canal. Former Turkish Alacap.

Poarta de Fier Transilvan, Rumania: see PORTZILE DE FIER.

Poarta Orientala, Rumania: see PORTA ORIENTALIS.

Poás (pwäs), active volcano (8,930 ft.) in the Cordillera Central, central Costa Rica, 12 mi. NW of Heredia (linked by road); 10°10'N 84°14'W. Geyser in its crater is visited by tourists.

Poás, San Pedro de, Costa Rica: see SAN PEDRO, Alajuela prov.

Pobé (pō'bā), town (pop. c.3,900), S Dahomey, Fr. West Africa, rail terminus 35 mi. N of Porto-Novo; palm kernels, corn, cotton, manioc, potatoes, peanuts. Palm oil and peanut research institute. Meteorological station.

Pobeda Peak (pŭbyĕ'dŭ) [Rus.,=victory], highest point (24,406 ft.) in Tien Shan mtn. system and 2d highest (Stalin Peak is higher) in USSR; on China-USSR border, 100 mi. E of the lake Issyk-Kul in Kirghiz SSR; 42°3'N 80°11'E. Discovered 1943, 10 mi. S of the peak KHAN TENGRI.

Pobedino (pŭbyĕ'dyĭnŭ), village (1947 pop. over 500), S Sakhalin, Russian SFSR, in Poronai R. valley, 40 mi. N of Poronaisk; N terminus (1950) of E coast railroad.

Pobedinski or **Pobedinskiy** (pŭbyĕ'dyĭnskē), town (1933 pop. 3,900), W Ryazan oblast, Russian SFSR, 7 mi. S of Skopin, in Moscow Basin; lignite mining.

Pobezovice (pô'byĕzhô"vĭtsĕ), Czech *Poběžovice*, Ger. *Ronsperg* (rôn'spĕrk), village (pop. 875), SW Bohemia, Czechoslovakia, 30 mi. SW of Pilsen, in iron-mining dist.; rail junction.

Pobiedziska (pôbyĕjĕ'skä), Ger. *Pudewitz* (pōō'dŭvĭts), town (1946 pop. 3,615), Poznan prov., W Poland, on railroad and 16 mi. ENE of Poznan; machine mfg., flour milling, sawmilling.

Pobla de Lillet, La (lä pō'vlä dhä lēlyĕt'), town (pop. 1,940), Barcelona prov., NE Spain, 12 mi. NNE of Berga; mfg. (cotton and woolen textiles, cement, chocolate); livestock, lumber, potatoes. Lignite deposits near by.

Pobla de Segur (sāgōōr'), town (pop. 2,332), Lérida prov., NE Spain, on S slopes of central Pyrenees, 7 mi. NE of Tremp, at influx of Flamisell R. into Noguera Pallaresa R., and at N end of Tremp reservoir. Hydroelectric plant near by. Mfg. of cement, liqueurs, soda water; sawmilling. Agr. trade (livestock, cereals, wine, olive oil).

Poblet (pōvlĕt'), famous Cistercian abbey in Catalonia, NE Spain, in Tarragona prov., 4 mi. W of Montblanch. Founded in 12th cent. by counts of Barcelona, it was the burial place of Aragonese kings. Extensive ruins remain; and the Romanesque church, partly destroyed in 19th cent., was rededicated in 1940.

Poblete (pōvlā'tā), town (pop. 544), Ciudad Real prov., S central Spain, 4 mi. SW of Ciudad Real; cereals, vegetables, truck produce, grapes.

Pobo de Dueñas, El (ĕl pō'vō dhā dhwā'nyäs), town (pop. 736), Guadalajara prov., central Spain, 13 mi. E of Molina; flour milling. Iron deposits near by.

Poboktan Mountain (pōbŏk'tŭn) (10,920 ft.), SW Alta., near B.C. border, in Rocky Mts., in Jasper Natl. Park, 50 mi. SE of Jasper.

Pocahontas (pōkŭhŏn'tŭs). **1** County (□ 580; pop. 15,496), N central Iowa; ⊙ Pocahontas. Prairie agr. area (cattle, hogs, poultry, corn, oats, soybeans), with coal deposits in SE. Formed 1851. **2** County (□ 943; pop. 12,480), E W.Va.; ⊙ Marlinton. In the Alleghenies; Allegheny Mtn. extends along E and SE border (Va. line). Includes Droop Mtn. Battlefield and Watoga state parks. Most of co. is in Monongahela Natl. Forest. Drained by Greenbrier, Gauley and short Cranberry rivers and a fork of Cheat R. Agr. (livestock, dairy products, fruit); timber; some mfg. at Marlinton. Formed 1821.

Pocahontas. **1** City (pop. 3,840), ⊙ Randolph co., NE Ark., 32 mi. NNW of Jonesboro and on Black R., in dairy, poultry, cotton, and grain area; mfg. of shoes; cotton ginning, woodworking. **2** Village (pop. 667), Bond co., SW central Ill., 25 mi. WSW of Vandalia, in bituminous-coal-mining and agr. area (corn, wheat, livestock, truck; dairy products). Formerly a stagecoach stop on old Cumberland Road. **3** Town (pop. 1,949); ⊙ Pocahontas co., N central Iowa, 30 mi. WNW of Fort Dodge; ships livestock, grain; mfg. (concrete, feed, fertilizer, dies). Inc. 1892. **4** Town (pop. 130), Cape Girardeau co., SE Mo., near Mississippi R., 8 mi. N of Jackson. **5** Mining town (pop. 2,410), Tazewell co., SW Va., in the Alleghenies, near W.Va. line, 7 mi. NW of BLUEFIELD. A center of Pocahontas bituminous-coal fields; has exhibition coal-mine. Founded 1882; inc. 1884.

Pocasset, Mass.: see BOURNE.

Pocasset Lake (pōkă'sĭt), S Maine, just N of Androscoggin L.; southernmost of 12-mi. chain of ponds in W Kennebec co.; 2 mi. long, 1 mi. wide.

Pocatalico River (pōkŭtă'lĭkō), W W.Va., rises in central Roane co., flows c.75 mi. generally SW to Kanawha R. 8 mi. SSE of Winfield.

Pocatello (pōkŭtĕ'lō), city (pop. 26,131), ⊙ Bannock co., SE Idaho, on Portneuf R., near American Falls Reservoir, and 195 mi. ESE of Boise; alt. 4,464 ft. Second largest city in Idaho. Important railroad-routing center (with repair shops) and wholesale-trade and shipping point for irrigated agr. area; flour milling, brewing, mfg. of overalls, knit goods, superphosphate. Idaho State Col. is here. Game preserve and Fort Hall Indian Reservation (with irrigation project) are near by. Settled 1887–88, inc. as village 1889, as city 1892. Growth followed construction (1887) of railroad repair shops.

Pocatky (pô'chätkĭ), Czech *Počatky,* Ger. *Potschatek,* town (pop. 2,048), SE Bohemia, Czechoslovakia, in Bohemian-Moravian Heights, on railroad and 13 mi. NE of Jindrichuv Hradec; broadcloth mfg.; oats.

Pochayev (pŭchī'ŭf), Pol. *Poczajów* or *Poczajów Nowy* (pôchī'ŏŏf nô'vē), village (1931 pop. 2,320), NW Ternopol oblast, Ukrainian SSR, 11 mi. SW of Kremenets; flour milling, brick mfg. Has 16th-cent. church, 17th-cent. convent with noted shrine. Greek Orthodox religious and pilgrimage center prior to Second World War. Also called Novy Pochayev.

Pochep (pŭchĕp'), city (1926 pop. 13,334), W central Bryansk oblast, Russian SFSR, 45 mi. SW of Bryansk; sawmilling, hemp processing, flour milling, vegetable drying. Chartered 1503.

P'o Chiang, China: see PO RIVER.

Pochinki (pŭchēn'kē), village (1926 pop. 10,832), S Gorki oblast, Russian SFSR, 28 mi. SSE of Lukoyanov; hemp processing; wheat, potatoes. Formerly called Pochinki-Arzamasskiye.

Pochinok (pŭchē'nŭk), city (1948 pop. over 2,000), W central Smolensk oblast, Russian SFSR, 30 mi. SSE of Smolensk; flax processing.

Pöchlarn (pûkh'lärn), town (pop. 2,849), W Lower Austria, on the Danube and 19 mi. W of Sankt Pölten; wheat, rye, cattle.

Pocho, department, Argentina: see SALSACATE.

Pocho, Sierra de (syĕ'rä dā pō'chō), pampean mountain range in W Córdoba prov., Argentina, a W ridge of Sierra de Córdoba; extends c.40 mi. N of Villa Dolores; rises to c.4,800 ft. E is a pampean tableland.

Pochow, China: see POHSIEN.

Pochuta (pōchōō'tä), town (1950 pop. 572), Chimaltenango dept., S central Guatemala, in Pacific piedmont, near Madre Vieja R., 22 mi. SW of Chimaltenango; coffee, sugar cane.

Pochutla (pōchōōt'lä), officially San Pedro Pochutla, town (pop. 2,456), Oaxaca, S Mexico, in Pacific coast lowland, 95 mi. SSE of Oaxaca; coffee-growing center. Petroleum deposits near by. Airfield.

Pocillas (pōsē'yäs), village (pop. 200), Maule prov., S central Chile, 14 mi. SSE of Cauquenes; wheat, potatoes, lentils, wine, sheep; lumbering.

Pocito, Argentina: see ABERASTAIN.

Pocitos (pōsē'tōs), S residential section of Montevideo, S Uruguay; beach resort on the Río de la Plata, with fine hotels and boardwalk.

Pocitos, Salar (sälär'), or **Salar Quirón** (kērōn'), salt desert (□ c.270; alt. c.12,000 ft.) in the puna de Atacama, W Salta prov., Argentina; extends c.35 mi. N-S (5 mi. wide). Contains sodium and borate salts. N is Cerro Pocitos (16,463 ft.).

Pockau (pô'kou), village (pop. 3,669), Saxony, E central Germany, in the Erzgebirge, 5 mi. NE of Marienberg; cotton milling, hosiery knitting.

Pocking (pô'kĭng), village (pop. 3,400), Lower Bavaria, Germany, near Rott R., 13 mi. SSW of Passau; metalworking.

Pocklington, former urban district (1931 pop. 2,640), East Riding, E central Yorkshire, England, 12 mi. E of York; agr. market, with agr.-machinery works. Has church of Norman origin with 15th-cent. tower, and grammar school founded 1514.

Pocoata (pōkwä'tä), town (pop. c.12,100), Potosí dept., W central Bolivia, 12 mi. W of Colquechaca, on Sucre-Oruro road; alt. 11,220 ft.; alpaca, sheep.

Poções (pōōsō'ĭs), city (pop. 2,612), SE Bahia, Brazil, in the Serra do Periperi, 55 mi. SSW of Jiquié; asbestos-mining center; coffee, corn, tobacco, rice, mangabeira rubber. Called Djalma Dutra, 1944–48.

Pocomoke City or **Pocomoke** (pō'kŭmōk), town (pop. 3,191), Worcester co., SE Md., on Delmarva Peninsula 20 mi. S of Salisbury, and on Pocomoke R.; river shipping point in truck-farm and timber area; mfg. (clothing, lumber, flour, feed, fertilizer, metal castings); vegetable canneries, meat-packing and poultry-dressing plants. Founded c.1700.

Pocomoke River, Del. and Md., rises in Great Pocomoke Swamp in S Sussex co., S Del., flows c.65 mi. generally SW, into Md. and past Snow Hill, through Pocomoke State Forest (hunting, fishing, recreation) and past Pocomoke City (head of navigation), to head of **Pocomoke Sound,** an arm (c.15 mi. long, up to 10 mi. wide) of Chesapeake Bay, crossed by Md.-Va. boundary.

Pocona (pōkō'nä), town (pop. c.4,100), Cochabamba dept., central Bolivia, on S slopes of Cordillera de Cochabamba and 15 mi. W of Totora, on Cochabamba–Santa Cruz highway; alt. 8,720 ft.; barley, corn, potatoes.

Poconé (pōōkōōnĕ'), city (pop. 2,135), central Mato Grosso, Brazil, 60 mi. SW of Cuiabá; gold placers, rock crystals. Airfield. Founded 1781.

Pocono Lake (pō'kŭnō), resort village, Monroe co., NE Pa., just E of Pocono L. (c.2.5 mi. long), 17 mi. NW of Stroudsburg, in Pocono Mts. Pocono Lake Preserve (resort) is at W end of lake.

Pocono Manor, resort village, Monroe co., NE Pa., in Pocono Mts., 12 mi. NW of Stroudsburg.

Pocono Mountains, NE Pa., NE-SW range (c.2,000 ft.) in Monroe and Carbon counties, NW of Stroudsburg. Mts. are E escarpment of Pocono plateau (part of Allegheny Plateau), extending W to Wyoming Valley. Scenic summer, winter resort area.

Pocono Pines, resort village, Monroe co., NE Pa., in Pocono Mts., 15 mi. NW of Stroudsburg. Lakes near by.

Pocono Summit, resort village, Monroe co., NE Pa., in Pocono Mts., 13 mi. NW of Stroudsburg. Lakes near by.

Poços de Caldas (pō'sōōs dĭ käl'dŭs) [Port.,=pools of hot springs], city (pop. 13,751), SW Minas Gerais, Brazil, 120 mi. N of São Paulo city; 21°47'S 46°34'W; alt. 3,890 ft. Terminus of rail spur. Noted watering place, with hot sulphur springs and dry, healthful climate. Has many modern hotels, casino, and thermal establishment. Regular air service to Rio de Janeiro and São Paulo. Center of Brazil's leading bauxite-mining dist (mines and beneficiation plant just SW, near São Paulo border). Zirconium mines in area.

Pocotalago (pō″kŭtō'lĭgō), town (pop. 68), Madison co., NE Ga., 17 mi. NNE of Athens.

Pocotopaug Lake (pō'kŭtŭpôg″, –pŏg″), S central Conn., resort lake (c.1.5 mi. long) in East Hampton town, 14 mi. SE of Hartford.

Pocrí (pōkrē'). **1** Village (pop. 1,614), Coclé prov., central Panama, in Pacific lowland, 1 mi. NW of Aguadulce; sugar cane, livestock. **2** Village (pop. 451), Los Santos prov., S central Panama, in Pacific lowland, 8 mi. SE of Las Tablas; sugar cane, coffee, livestock.

Pocsaj (pô'choi), town (pop. 3,433), Bihar co., E Hungary, near Berettyo R., 19 mi. SSE of Debrecen; wheat, corn, cattle.

Poctún, Guatemala: see POPTÚN.

Pocumcus Lake (pōkŭm'kŭs), Washington co., E Maine, in chain bet. Sysladobsis and Grand lakes, 32 mi. W of Calais; 5 mi. long.

Poczajow or **Poczajow Nowy,** Ukrainian SSR: see POCHAYEV.

Podanur, India: see COIMBATORE, city.

Podarades, Greece: see NEA IONIA.

Podbelskaya or **Podbel'skaya** (pŭdbĕl'skĭŭ), village (1939 pop. over 2,000), E Kuibyshev oblast, Russian SFSR, on Greater Kinel R. and 14 mi. WSW of Pokhvistnevo; wheat, sunflowers.

Podberezye, Lithuania: see PABRADE.

Podberezye or **Podberez'ye** (pŭdbĭryĕ'zhyĭ), village (1939 pop. over 500), N Velikiye Luki oblast, Russian SFSR, on Lovat R. and 40 mi. N of Velikiye Luki; flax.

Podborany (pôd'bôrzhänĭ), Czech *Podbořany,* Ger. *Podersam* (pō'dŭrsäm), town (pop. 2,853), W Bohemia, Czechoslovakia, on railroad and 23 mi. E of Carlsbad, in potato- and hop-growing area; kaolin mining.

Podbrezova, Czechoslovakia: see BREZNO.

Podbrodzie, Lithuania: see PABRADE.

Podbuzh (pôd'bōōsh), Pol. *Podbuż,* village (1939 pop. over 500), central Drogobych oblast, Ukrainian SSR, on N slope of East Beskids, 11 mi. W of Drogobych; wheat, rye, oats.

Podchinny or **Podchinnyy** (pŭdchē'nē), town (1948 pop. over 2,000), N Stalingrad oblast, Russian SFSR, 23 mi. SW of Krasnoarmeisk; cotton-milling center. Until 1941 (in German Volga Autonomous SSR), Kratske, Krattske, or Kratzke.

Poddebice (pôdĕbē'tsĕ), Pol *Poddębice,* Rus. *Podembitse* (pŭdyĭmbē'tsĕ), town (pop. 2,937), Lodz prov., central Poland, near Ner R., 23 mi. WNW of Lodz; sawmilling, mfg. of agr. machinery, flour milling; stone quarrying.

Poddorye or **Poddor'ye** (pŭdô'ryĭ), village (1948 pop. over 2,000), SW Novgorod oblast, Russian SFSR, 37 mi. SSW of Staraya Russa; flax.

Podebrady (pô'dyĕbrädĭ), Czech *Poděbrady* or *Lázně Poděbrady* (läz'nyĕ), Ger. *Podiebrad* (pō'dēbrät), town (pop. 10,540), central Bohemia, Czechoslovakia, on Elbe R., on railroad and 15 mi. NNW of Kutna Hora; major health resort with alkaline springs, the discovery of which (1905) made it a spa for treatment of heart diseases. Export of bottled mineral waters. Has Gothic church, 18th-cent. chapel, medical research institute, radio station. Its 16th-cent. Renaissance castle, laid out in 12th cent. as fortress, was birthplace and residence of Hussite King George of Podebrad.

Podejuch, Poland: see PODJUCHY.

Podem (pôdĕm'), village (pop. 2,572), Pleven dist., N Bulgaria, on Vit R. and 9 mi. NNW of Pleven; grain, livestock, truck. Formerly Martvitsa.

Podensac (pôdäsäk'), village (pop. 1,148), Gironde dept., SW France, on left bank of Garonne R. and 17 mi. SE of Bordeaux; white wines; barrelmaking.

Podenzano (pôdĕntsä'nô), village (pop. 801), Piacenza prov., Emilia-Romagna, N central Italy, 7 mi. S of Piacenza; tomato cannery.

Podersam, Czechoslovakia: see PODBORANY.

Podgaitsy or **Podgaysty** (pŭdgī'tsē), Pol. *Podhajce* (pôdhī'tsĕ), city (1931 pop. 5,743), W Ternopol oblast, Ukrainian SSR, 28 mi. SW of Ternopol; rail spur terminus; tanning, flour- and sawmilling, brick mfg. Has old castle and cathedral. Developed as residence of Pol. gentry in 16th cent. Scene of battle (1667) followed by peace treaty bet. Pol. king John III Sobieski and Tatars. Passed to Austria (1772); reverted to Poland (1919); ceded to USSR in 1945.

Podgora (pôd'gôrä), village, S Croatia, Yugoslavia, on Adriatic Sea, 6 mi. SE of Makarska, at SW foot of Biokovo Mts., in Dalmatia; seaside resort.

Podgorica, Yugoslavia: see TITOGRAD.

Podgornoye (pŭdgôr'nŭyŭ). **1** Village (1939 pop. over 500), SE Alma-Ata oblast, Kazakh SSR, 120 mi. E of Alma-Ata; irrigated agr. (wheat, opium, medicinal plants). Pop. largely Uigur. **2** Village (1939 pop. over 500), central Tomsk oblast, Russian SFSR, on Chaya R. and 38 mi. S of Kolpashevo. **3** Village (1926 pop. 5,732), S central Voronezh oblast, Russian SFSR, 17 mi. N of Rossosh; cement works; chalk quarry.

Podgorodnoye (pŭdgŭrôd'nŭyŭ), town (1939 pop. over 10,000), central Dnepropetrovsk oblast, Ukrainian SSR, 8 mi. NNE of Dnepropetrovsk; flour milling.

Podgorski Kanal, Yugoslavia: see VELEBIT MOUNTAINS.

Podgoryany, Ukrainian SSR: see MUKACHEVO.

Podhajce, Ukrainian SSR: see PODGAITSY.

Podhale (pôd-hä'lĕ), highland basin in the Carpathians, Krakow prov., S Poland, near Czechoslovak border, bet. the Beskids (N) and the High Tatra (S). Barren, rocky region, drained by headwaters of Dunajec R. Chief towns: Nowy Targ, Zakopane Gorce mts. and Babia Gora rise N.

Podiebrad, Czechoslovakia: see PODEBRADY.

Podile or **Podili** (pō'dĭlē), village, Nellore dist., NE Madras, India, 30 mi. WNW of Ongole; cattle, millet, cotton.

Po di Levante, Italy: see TARTARO RIVER.

Podivin (pô'dyĭvēn), Czech *Podivín,* village (pop. 2,433), S Moravia, Czechoslovakia, on railroad 5 mi. NNW of Breclav; natural-gas processing, sugar milling.

Podjuchy (pôdyōō'khĭ), Ger. *Podejuch* (pō'dŭyōōkh), town (1939 pop. 7,052; 1946 pop. 511) in Pomerania, after 1945 in Szczecin prov., NW Poland, on E arm of Oder R. estuary and 6 mi SSE of Stettin; rayon milling, cement mfg., fruit processing. Inc. 1935 into Stettin; rechartered 1945.

Podkamen or **Podkamen'** (pŭtkä'mĭnyŭ), Pol. *Podkamień* (pôdkä'myĕnyg), town (1937 estimate pop. 3,040), E Lvov oblast, Ukrainian SSR, 12 mi. SSE of Brody; stone quarrying; brickworks. Has 17th-cent. monastery.

Podkamennaya Tunguska (pŭtkä'myĭnĭŭ tōōn-gōōs'kŭ), village, N Krasnoyarsk Territory, Russian SFSR, on Yenisei R., at mouth of Stony Tunguska R., and 390 mi. NNW of Krasnoyarsk.

Podkamennaya Tunguska River, Russian SFSR: see STONY TUNGUSKA RIVER.

Podkamien, Ukrainian SSR: see PODKAMEN.

Podkarpatska Rus, Ukrainian SSR: see TRANSCARPATHIAN OBLAST.

Podkova, Bulgaria: see MOMCHILGRAD.

Podkumok River (pŭtkōō'mŭk), Stavropol Territory, Russian SFSR, rises on N slope of the central Greater Caucasus, SW of Kislovodsk; flows c.100 mi. NE, past Kislovodsk, Yessentuki, and Pyatigorsk, to Kuma R. below Georgiyevsk.

Podlesnoye (pŭdlyĭsnoi'ŭ), village (1948 pop. over 2,000), central Saratov oblast, Russian SFSR, on left bank of Volga R. and 13 mi. NE of Marks;

metalworks; wheat, sunflowers, fruit. Until 1941 (in German Volga Autonomous SSR), Untervalden or Unterwalden.

Podlipki, Russian SFSR: see KALININGRAD, Molotov oblast.

Podmokly (pôd'môklĭ), Ger. *Bodenbach* (bō'dŭnbäkh), town (pop. 17,558), N Bohemia, Czechoslovakia, in urban area of Decin, on W bank of Elbe R. and 10 mi. NNE of Usti nad Labem; rail junction; customs station near Ger. border; river port, noted for coal export. Mfg. (electrical instruments, cables, machinery, metal articles, soap, edible oils, varnishes, ink), food processing (fish, candy), woodworking.

Podolia (pōdō'lyŭ), Rus. *Podolye*, Pol. *Podole*, region in SW Ukrainian SSR, bet. Dniester and Southern Bug rivers, in center of Volyn-Podolian Upland; drained by the Dniester and Southern Bug and their affluents. Chief cities: Mogilev-Podolski, Kamenets-Podolski, Vinnitsa, Proskurov. Ruled by Kievan Russia from 10th cent., by Tatars (1260–1362), Lithuania and Poland, Turkey (1672–99), Poland again, and by Russia after 1793, when it became a govt. (⊙ Kamenets-Podolski) until 1925. Now included in Kamenets-Podolski and Vinnitsa oblasts. A large Jewish minority, which settled here in the Middle Ages, was severely persecuted in the pogroms of late 19th and early 20th cent. and suffered still worse when area was occupied (1941–43) by Germans in Second World War.

Podolinec (pô'dôlĕnyĕts), Slovak *Podolínec*, Hung. *Podolin* (pô'dôlĭn), village (pop. 1,602), N Slovakia, Czechoslovakia, in E foothills of the High Tatra, on Poprad R., and 18 mi. NE of Poprad; rail terminus; woodworking. Has old castle ruins.

Podolsk or **Podol'sk** (pŭdôlsk'), city (1939 pop. 72,422), S central Moscow oblast, Russian SFSR, on Pakhra R. and 23 mi. S of Moscow. Machine-mfg. center; mfg. of petroleum-refining machinery, sewing machines, electric batteries, cables, boilers; cementworks; ceramics, food processing. Marble and limestone quarries near by. Chartered 1781.

Podolye, Ukrainian SSR: see PODOLIA.

Podor (pôdôr'), town (pop. c.4,000), N Senegal, Fr. West Africa, inland port on Senegal R. (Mauritania border) and 110 mi. ENE of Saint-Louis, 210 mi. NE of Dakar; trading and agr. center in irrigated area. Gums, corn, millet, potatoes, rice, livestock. Fishing. Airfield near by.

Podosinovets (pŭdŭsē'nŭvyĭts), village (1939 pop. over 500), NW Kirov oblast, Russian SFSR, on Yug R. (landing) and 70 mi. SSE of Kotlas; flax processing.

Podporozhye or **Podporozh'ye** (pŭtpŭrô'zhyĭ), town (1939 pop. over 10,000), NE Leningrad oblast, Russian SFSR, on Svir R. and 25 mi. NE of Lodeinoye Pole; hydroelectric station; metalworks, sawmills. During Second World War, a Rus. front-line position (1941–44).

Podravina (pô'drävēnä), region, N Croatia, Yugoslavia, in Slavonia; extends NW-SE along Drava R. and Hung. border. Largest town, OSIJEK. Lumbering, plum growing.

Podravska Slatina, Yugoslavia: see SLATINA.

Podrinje or **Podrinye** (both: pô'drĭnyĕ), plain, Bosnia, Yugoslavia, extends c.30 mi. N–S, partly along right bank of Drina R., S of Loznica; noted for its cattle raising and plum growing. Lead mining near KRUPANJ.

Podsused (pôd'sōōsĕt), village, N Croatia, Yugoslavia, on Sava R., near Krapina R. mouth, and 7 mi. W of Zagreb, on railroad; cement mfg. Terminus of canal to Sisak (begun 1947).

Podtesovo (pŭtyô'sŭvŭ), town (1946 pop. over 500), central Krasnoyarsk Territory, Russian SFSR, on the Yenisei and 15 mi. N of Yeniseisk; lumber milling.

Podujevo or **Poduyevo** (both: pôdōō'yĕvô), village (pop. 2,401), S Serbia, Yugoslavia, 17 mi. ENE of Mitrovica, in the Kosovo.

Podul-Iloaiei (pô'dōōl-ēlwäyā'), village (pop. 3,887), Jassy prov., NE Rumania, 15 mi. WNW of Jassy; rail junction; flour milling.

Podun (pŭdōōn'), village, NW Kemerovo oblast, Russian SFSR, in Kuznetsk Basin, on branch of Trans-Siberian RR and 45 mi. SW of Kemerovo, in agr. area.

Podunajska Nizina, Czechoslovakia and Hungary: see LITTLE ALFÖLD.

Podu-Turcului (pô'dōō-tōōr'kōōlōōē), village (pop. 1,276), Barlad prov., E Rumania, 22 mi. N of Tecuci; mfg. of alcohol; extensive orchards.

Poduyevo, Yugoslavia: see PODUJEVO.

Podvolochisk (pŭdvŭlŭchēsk'), Pol. *Podwołoczyska* (pôdvôwôchĭ'skä), town (1931 pop. 3,895), E Ternopol oblast, Ukrainian SSR, on Zbruch R., opposite Volochisk, and 25 mi. E of Ternopol; grain-trading center; flour milling, distilling, mfg. of bricks and soap. Poland-USSR frontier customs station (1921–39).

Podvoloshnaya, Russian SFSR: see PERVOURALSK.

Podvysoke (pŭdvĭsô'kyĭ), Pol. *Podwysokie*, rail junction in N Stanislav oblast, Ukrainian SSR, 9 mi. ESE of Rogatin.

Podvysokoye (–kŭyŭ), village (1926 pop. 4,514), W Kirovograd oblast, Ukrainian SSR, 23 mi. ESE of Uman; sugar beets.

Podwołoczyska, Ukrainian SSR: see PODVOLOCHISK.

Podwysokie, Ukrainian SSR: see PODVYSOKE.

Podzamek, Poland: see NEUDECK.

Poe, textile-mill village (pop. 3,723, with adjacent Park Place), Greenville co., NW S.C., near Greenville.

Poel (pûl), island (□ 14; pop. 3,504), at mouth of Wismar Bay of the Baltic, N Germany, 4 mi. N of Wismar; 5 mi. long, 4 mi. wide. Kirchdorf, chief commune and seaside resort, is at head of 3-mi.-long bay indenting S coast. Fishing is main occupation. Isl. passed to Sweden in 1648, to Mecklenburg in 1803.

Poelau Laoet, Indonesia: see PULU LAUT.

Poeldijk (pōōl'dīk'), village (pop. 3,216), South Holland prov., W Netherlands, 5 mi. SW of The Hague; a center of Westland agr. area; grape growing (introduced in 17th cent.).

Poeloegoedoe (pōōlōōgōō'dōō), waterfalls in E Du. Guiana, on Marowijne or Maroni R. (Fr. Guiana border), at confluence of Lawa and Tapanahoni rivers, and 40 mi. SE of Dam.

Poeloe Samboe, Indonesia: see SAMBU.

Poenari-Burchi or **Poenarii-Burchi** (pwĕnär'yŭbōōrk'), village (pop. 1,810), Prahova prov., S central Rumania, 11 mi. S of Ploesti.

Poerbolinggo, Indonesia: see PURBOLINGGO.

Poerwakarta, Indonesia: see PURWAKARTA.

Poerwodadi, Indonesia: see PURWODADI.

Poerwokerto, Indonesia: see PURWOKERTO.

Poerworedjo, Indonesia: see PURWOREJO.

Poët, Le (lŭ pōĕt'), village (pop. 198), Hautes-Alpes dept., SE France, 7 mi. NNW of Sisteron. Hydroelectric plant on the Durance near by.

Poeteran, Indonesia: see PUTERAN.

Pogar (pô'gŭr), town (1926 pop. 5,035), S Bryansk oblast, Russian SFSR, 20 mi. E of Starodub; tobacco products.

Poge, Cape, Mass.: see CHAPPAQUIDDICK ISLAND.

Pogegen, Lithuania: see PAGEGIAI.

Poggiardo (pôd-jär'dô), village (pop. 3,932), Lecce prov., Apulia, S Italy, 6 mi. SE of Maglie.

Poggibonsi (pôd-jēbôn'sē), town (pop. 6,443), Siena prov , Tuscany, central Italy, on Elsa R. and 14 mi. NW of Siena. Rail junction; wine-making and -exporting center; glass factories, tanneries, foundry; agr. machinery, soap. Heavily damaged by air bombing (1943–44) in Second World War.

Poggio a Caiano (pôd'jô ä käyä'nô), village (pop. 2,025), Firenze prov., Tuscany, central Italy, 10 mi. WNW of Florence; macaroni factory. Near by is villa (1480–85; damaged 1944) where Francesco de' Medici and his 2d wife, Bianca Capello, died.

Poggio Bustone (bōōstô'nĕ), village (pop. 1,193), Rieti prov., Latium, central Italy, 7 mi. N of Rieti; hosiery.

Poggio Imperiale (ēmpĕrēä'lĕ), village (pop. 3,246), Foggia prov., Apulia, S Italy, 10 mi. N of San Severo.

Poggio-Marinaccio (–mārēnä'chō), village (pop. 136), NE Corsica, 14 mi. NE of Corte; olive-oil mfg. Mineral springs.

Poggiomarino (–märē'nô), town (pop. 6,631), Napoli prov., Campania, S Italy, 6 mi. NE of Torre Annunziata; rail junction; mfg. (soap, fertilizer).

Poggio Mirteto (mērtā'tô), town (pop. 1,544), Rieti prov., Latium, central Italy, 13 mi. SW of Rieti; mfg. (soap, cement, bricks).

Poggio Moiano (môyä'nô), village (pop. 2,005), Rieti prov., Latium, central Italy, 14 mi. S of Rieti; soap mfg.

Poggioreale or **Poggioreale di Sicilia** (pôd″jôrĕä'lĕ dē sēchē'lyä), village (pop. 3,025), Trapani prov., W Sicily, 13 mi. SSE of Alcamo.

Poggioreale Campagna, Free Territory of Trieste: see OPICINA.

Poggio Renatico (pôd'jô rĕnä'tēkô), town (pop. 2,021), Ferrara prov., Emilia-Romagna, N central Italy, near Reno R., 8 mi. SW of Ferrara.

Poggio Rusco (rōō'skô), village (pop. 2,705), Mantova prov., Lombardy, N Italy, 21 mi. SE of Mantua; rail junction; macaroni mfg.

Poggio Sannita (sän-nē'tä), village (pop. 2,402), Campobasso prov., Abruzzi e Molise, S central Italy, 3 mi. SE of Agnone. Formerly Caccavone.

Poglet, Greece: see PAIKON.

Pogoanele (pôgwänā'lĕ), village (pop. 6,032), Buzau prov., SE central Rumania, 17 mi. SE of Buzau; flour milling.

Pogonion, Greece: see DELVINAKION.

Pogoreloye Gorodishche (pŭgŭryĕ'lŭyŭ gŭrŭdyē'-shchĭ), village (1926 pop. 1,379), SW Kalinin oblast, Russian SFSR, 25 mi. ESE of Rzhev; metalworking, flax processing.

Pogorzela (pôgô-zhĕ'lä), town (1946 pop. 1,415), Poznan prov., W Poland, 10 mi. W of Kozmin; cement mfg.

Pogradec (pôgrä'dĕts) or **Pogradeci** (pôgrä'dĕtsē), town (1945 pop. 3,361), SE Albania, on SW shore of L. Ochrida, 21 mi. NNW of Koritsa; commercial center; fruits; distilling, fishing (lake trout). Pop. is largely Moslem. Large hematite deposits (NW; projected steel plant). Under Ital. rule (1939–43) called Perparim or Perparimi [Albanian,=progress].

Pogranichnaya, Manchuria: see SUIFENHO.

Pogrebishchenski or **Pogrebishchenskiy** (pŭgryĭbē'shchĭnskē), town (1926 pop. 9,647), NE Vinnitsa oblast, Ukrainian SSR, on Ros R. and 38 mi. ENE of Vinnitsa; rail junction; sugar refining. Until c.1945, Pogrebishche.

Pogromni Volcano (pŭgrŏm'nē) (6,500 ft.; also given as 7,500 ft.), SW Alaska, on W Unimak Isl., 11 mi. N of Unimak village; 54°34'N 164°42'W. Active.

Po Hai, China: see CHIHLI, GULF OF.

Pohai Strait, China: see CHIHLI, GULF OF.

Pohang (pô'häng'), Jap. *Hoko*, town (1949 pop. 50,681), N.Kyongsang prov., S Korea, fishing port on inlet of Sea of Japan, 65 mi. NNE of Pusan; wine and brandy making. Heavily contested (1950) in Korean war.

Pohangina (pōhăng'gēnŭ), township (pop. 189), ⊙ Pohangina co. (□ 259; pop. 1,258), S N.Isl., New Zealand, 90 mi. NNE of Wellington; agr.

Pohatcong Mountain (pōhăt'kŏng), NW N.J., ridge (alt. c.800 ft.) of the Appalachians extending NE from point E of Phillipsburg to vicinity of Hackettstown; NE part is called Upper Pohatcong Mtn. Agr., dairying region. W of Hackettstown is source of **Pohatcong River,** which flows c.35 mi. SW, along SE foot of the Pohatcongs, to Delaware R. above Riegelsville.

Pohja, Finland: see POJO.

Pohjankuru, Finland: see SKURU.

Pohjois-Pirkkala, Finland: see NOKIA.

Pohorelice (pô'hôrzhĕ"lĭtsĕ), Czech *Pohořelice*, Ger. *Pohrlitz* (pōr'lĭts), village (pop. 2,748), S Moravia, Czechoslovakia, on Jihlava R. and 15 mi. SSW of Brno; rail terminus; agr. center (wine, barley, sugar beets).

Pohorje (pô'hôryĕ), Ger. *Bachergebirge* (bä'khŭrgŭbĭr″gŭ), mountain group in eastern Alps, N Slovenia, Yugoslavia, on right bank of Drava R., E of the Karawanken. Highest peak (5,058 ft.) is 17 mi. SW of Maribor. Marble deposits. Tourist area.

Pohrlitz, Czechoslovakia: see POHORELICE.

Pohsien (bŭ'shyĕn'), town (1922 pop. estimate 80,000), ⊙ Pohsien co. (1936 pop. 595,870), N Anhwei prov., China, near Honan line, 65 mi. N of Fowyang, and on Kwo R.; wheat, cotton, beans, kaoliang, millet; felt mfg. Until 1912, Pochow.

Pohsing (bŭ'shĭng'), town, ⊙ Pohsing co. (pop. 253,238), NW Shantung prov., China, 25 mi. NNE of Changtien and on Siaoching R.; rice center; wheat, cotton, peanuts.

Poiana-Mare (poiä'nä-mä'rĕ), village (pop. 11,431), Dolj prov., S Rumania, 8 mi. SE of Calafat; rail terminus and agr. center. Medicinal plants grown in area. Has agr. school.

Poiana-Rusca Mountains (–rōō'skä), group in SW central Rumania, partly in Banat, partly in Transylvania, extending bet. Mures R. (N), Timis R. (W) and Portzile de Fier pass (S); rise to 4,327 ft.; noted for iron deposits, exploited mainly in E foothills.

Poim (pŭēm'), village (1926 pop. 9,766), W Penza oblast, Russian SFSR, near Vorona R., 10 mi. WNW of Belinski, in grain area; wheat, hemp, legumes; distilling. Peat bogs near by.

Poindimié (pwĕdēmyā'), village (dist. pop. 3,255), New Caledonia, on E coast, 115 mi. NW of Nouméa; agr. products.

Poinsett (poin'sĕt), county (□ 762; pop. 39,311), NE Ark.; ⊙ Harrisburg. Intersected by Crowley's Ridge; drained by St. Francis and L'Anguille rivers. Agr. (cotton, rice, corn, soybeans, alfalfa, truck, livestock; dairy products; hardwood timber. Mfg. at Marked Tree and Lepanto. Country was formed 1838.

Poinsett, Lake, E S.Dak., 20 mi. S of Watertown; 7 mi. long, 3 mi. wide at widest point; 2 small streams flow from it to Big Sioux R.; recreation.

Poinsett State Park (c.1,000 acres), central S.C., just NE of L. Marion, SW of Sumter.

Point Agassiz (ă'gŭsĭz), village (1939 pop. 24), SE Alaska, 8 mi. N of Petersburg, across Frederick Sound; trading center.

Point Arena (ŭrē'nŭ), city (pop. 372), Mendocino co., NW Calif., 40 mi. S of Fort Bragg, on the Pacific; dairy center; livestock (sheep, cattle). Lighthouse at Point Arena, a promontory NW of city.

Point Baker, village (pop. 60), SE Alaska, on NW shore of Prince of Wales Isl., on Sumner Strait, 50 mi. WSW of Wrangell; 56°22'N 133°37'W; fishing.

Point Barrow or **Nuwuk,** Eskimo village (1939 pop. 28), N Alaska, on Point BARROW headland, 9 mi. NW of Barrow; trapping and fishing.

Point Calimere (kăl'ĭmēr), village (pop. 2,877), Tanjore dist., SE Madras, India, projected port on Palk Strait just W of Point Calimere, 33 mi. S of Negapatam; rail terminus (extension from Vedaranniyam, 7 mi. NNE; built 1935). Point Calimere comprises the 2 original villages of Kodiyakadu (or Kodiyakkadu) and Kodiyakkarai (or Kodikkarai).

Point Chautauqua (shŭtô'wŭ), resort village, Chautauqua co., extreme W N.Y., on Chautauqua L., 3 mi. SE of Mayville.

Point Comfort, Texas: see PORT LAVACA.

Point de Galle, Ceylon: see GALLE.

Pointe à Gatineau, Que.: see POINTE GATINEAU.

Pointe a la Hache (point' ŭ lŭ hăsh'), village (pop. c.500), ⊙ Plaquemines parish, extreme SE La., 31 mi. SE of New Orleans, and on E bank of the Mississippi in the delta; sugar cane, rice, fruit. Sea-food canneries; wood products; fur trapping, fishing.

Pointe-à-Pierre (pwănt″-ä-pēâr′), village (pop. 1,413), W Trinidad, B.W.I., landing on the Gulf of Paria, on railroad and 23 mi. SSE of Port of Spain; oil-bunkering port and major refining center (with cracking plants, tanks, laboratories) Its oil-loading jetty is 1½ mi. offshore, linked by pipe lines. In 1808 it was proposed to make the village the capital of Trinidad. Sometimes the name La Carrière (lä kärēâr′), settlement just E with main petroleum installations, is used interchangeably for Pointe-à-Pierre.

Pointe-à-Pitre (pwĕt-ä-pē′trù), city (commune pop. 41,823), SW Grande-Terre, Guadeloupe, on the Petit Cul de Sac, near S entrance of the Rivière Salée, 21 mi. NE of Basse-Terre; 16°15′N 61°32′W. The principal port and commercial center of Guadeloupe, with a harbor flanked by numerous islets, though exposed to occasional hurricanes; 30-ft.-draught vessels can dock alongside. Exports chiefly sugar cane, coffee, cacao, vanilla, rum, bananas, pineapples, and lumber. Fruit canning, sugar milling, distilling, tanning; mfg. of cigarettes, barrels, fruit preserves, musical instruments. A picturesque town with well-built houses, it has cathedral, bishop's palace, courthouse, agr. station. Airfield near by. The Destrellan radio station is in the outskirts. City's name stems from a sailor named Pieters, who brought here (1654) Du. refugees from Brazil.

Pointe au Chien, Bayou (bī′ō point′ ō shēăn′), SE La., flows c.45 mi. SE to L. Raccourci from its source in N Terrebonne parish.

Pointe au Pic (pwĕt ō pēk′), village (pop. 1,083), SE central Que., on the St. Lawrence and 2 mi. SSE of La Malbaie; popular resort.

Pointe Aux Barques (point″ ō bärk′), Huron co., E Mich., resort settlement at the Pointe Aux Barques (N tip of the Thumb), at SE side of entrance to Saginaw Bay, 60 mi. NE of Bay City; lighthouse and coast guard station here.

Pointe aux Trembles (pwĕt ō trā′blù), residential town (pop. 4,314), S Que., on E shore of Montreal Isl., on the St. Lawrence and 11 mi. NNE of Montreal.

Pointe Claire (point klâr′, Fr. pwĕt klâr′), residential town (pop. 4,536), S Que., on S shore of Montreal Isl., on L. St. Louis, 14 mi. SW of Montreal.

Pointe Coupee (point′ kùpā′), parish (□ 564; pop. 21,841), SE central La.; ⊙ New Roads. Bounded E by the Mississippi, N by Red R. distributaries (Old R., Atchafalaya R.), W by Atchafalaya R. Agr. (cotton, sugar cane, corn, sweet and white potatoes, hay); stock raising; fisheries; timber. Some mfg. including processing of farm products. Formed 1805.

Pointe-des-Galets (pwĕt′-dā-gälā′), town and commune (pop. 7,232), an artificial port on Réunion isl., on NW coast, on railroad and 10 mi. WSW of Saint-Denis; isl.'s chief export center. Harbor installations have warehouses and docks. Has hospital and meteorological station. Built on alluvial deposits of the Rivière des Galets (S), it was opened 1886. Locally called Le Port.

Pointe du Bois (point dōōbwä′), village (pop. estimate 250), SE Man., on Winnipeg R. (waterfalls) and 80 mi. ENE of Winnipeg; hydroelectric-power center.

Point Edward, village (pop. 1,363), S Ont., on St. Clair R., at foot of L. Huron; NW suburb of Sarnia, opposite Port Huron, Mich. Docks are part of port of Sarnia.

Pointe Fortune (pwĕt fôrtün′), village (pop. 322), SW Que., on Ottawa R. and 8 mi. SSW of Lachute, on Ont. border; dairying; potatoes.

Pointe Gatineau (pwĕt gätēnō′) or **Gatineau Point** (gă′tĭnō), village (pop. 2,230), SW Que., on Ottawa R., at mouth of Gatineau R., NE suburb of Hull. Also called Pointe à Gatineau.

Pointe-Noire (pwĕt′-nwär′) [Fr.,=black point], town (1950 pop. 21,800), ⊙ Middle Congo territory and Kouilou region (□ 5,790; 1950 pop. 58,400), Fr. Equatorial Africa, on the Atlantic, 240 mi. WSW of Brazzaville; 4°47′S 11°54′E. Main seaport of Fr. Equatorial Africa, terminus of railroad from Brazzaville; also commercial center. Ships chiefly palm products, cotton, hardwoods, copal, rubber, ivory, wax, livestock, lead. Palm-oil milling, sawmilling, woodworking, mfg. of processed foods and soap; fishing; railroad repair shops. Harbor installations (begun 1934, completed after Second World War) include a 2-mi.-long breakwater, liquid-fuels port, and large palm-oil refinery. Customs station. Has the largest airport of Fr. Equatorial Africa, R.C. mission, hosp., military camp and air base. Town area also extends to former port of LOANGO, further N on the coast.

Pointe-Noire, town (commune pop. 7,797), NW Basse-Terre isl., Guadeloupe, minor port 17 mi. NNW of Basse-Terre city; trading; cacao and vanilla growing; alcohol distilling.

Pointe-Percée, France: see BORNES.

Point Fortin (fôr′tĭn), village (pop. 6,127), SW Trinidad, B.W.I., on the Gulf of Paria, 16 mi. WSW of San Fernando; petroleum field with oil refinery and loading pier.

Point Grey, W suburb of Vancouver, SW B.C., on the Strait of Georgia. Site of new bldgs. of Univ. of British Columbia; also agr. col.

Point Harbor, village, Currituck co., NE N.C., 28 mi. SE of Elizabeth City, at confluence of Albemarle, Currituck, Roanoke, and Croatan sounds. Here Wright Memorial Bridge crosses to Kitty Hawk sandspit, 3 mi. E.

Point Hope or **Tigara** (tĭgâ′rù), village (pop. 263), NW Alaska, on Point Hope headland, on Chukchi Sea; 68°20′N 166°45′W. Eskimo settlement; hunting and fishing; formerly important whaling base. Has Episcopal mission; native school; airfield.

Point Independence, Mass.: see WAREHAM.

Point Isabel, Texas: see PORT ISABEL.

Point Judith (jōō′dĭth), promontory and resort village in Narragansett town, Washington co., S R.I., on the coast, SW of Narragansett Bay entrance, 11 mi. SW of Newport. U.S. coast guard station, lighthouse, and Sprague Memorial Park here. Just W is **Point Judith Pond** (c.4 mi. long), sheltered harbor with inlet from the Atlantic. Hard hit by 1938 hurricane.

Point Lake (75 mi. long, 1–14 mi. wide), expansion of Coppermine R., E central Mackenzie Dist., Northwest Territories, ESE of Great Bear L.; 65°N 113°W.

Point Lay, Eskimo village (pop. 75), NW Alaska, on Chukchi Sea, 65 mi. SW of Wainwright; 69°50′N 162°55′W; trapping and fishing settlement; airfield. Coal deposits near by.

Point Marion, borough (pop. 2,197), Fayette co., SW Pa., 50 mi. S of Pittsburgh, near W.Va. line, and on Monongahela R., at mouth of Cheat R.; bituminous coal; glass, metal products, beverages. Laid out 1842.

Point of Air, promontory, Flint, Wales, on Irish Sea at mouth of the Dee, 8 mi. ENE of Rhyl; lighthouse (53°22′N 3°19′W).

Point of Rocks, town (pop. 361), Frederick co., W Md., on the Potomac (bridged here to Va.), at E base of Catoctin Mtn., and 12 mi. SW of Frederick. Marble quarry near by.

Point O'Woods, N.Y.: see FIRE ISLAND.

Point Pedro (pē′drō), town (pop. 3,150), Northern Prov., Ceylon, on NE Jaffna Peninsula, 19 mi. NE of Jaffna, separated by Palk Strait from Point Calimere (40 mi. NW, in SE Madras, India); small seaport; lighthouse. Valvedditturai, another small seaport, is 5 mi. W; also spelled Valvettiturai.

Point Pelee National Park (pē′lē) (□ 6.04), SW Ont., on Point Pelee headland, on L. Erie, 9 mi. SE of Leamington; recreational area with bathing beaches. Established 1918.

Point Pleasant. 1 Town (pop. 101), New Madrid co., extreme SE Mo., on Mississippi R. and 7 mi. E of Portageville. **2** Resort borough (pop. 4,009), Ocean co., E N.J., on the coast, near mouth of Manasquan R., 11 mi. S of Asbury Park; mfg. (boats, cement blocks), fishing, agr. (cranberries, truck, poultry). Settled 1850, inc. 1920. **3** Resort village (1940 pop. 1,122), Monroe co., W N.Y., on Irondequoit Bay of L. Ontario, just E of Rochester. **4** Village, Clermont co., SW Ohio, on Ohio R. and 21 mi. SE of Cincinnati. Here are a replica of Ulysses S. Grant's birthplace, and Grant Memorial State Park. **5** City (pop. 4,596), ⊙ Mason co., W W.Va., on the Ohio, at Kanawha R. mouth, and 35 mi. NNE of Huntington; shipyards, coal mines; mfg. of machinery, iron and carbon products. In battle of Point Pleasant (1774), a large force of Indians was defeated by Andrew Lewis and frontiersmen. Settled around Fort Blair (built 1774).

Point Pleasant Beach, resort borough (pop. 2,900), Ocean co., E N.J., on the coast, at mouth of Manasquan R., just NE of Point Pleasant. Inc. 1886.

Point Reyes Station (rā′ĭs), village (pop. c.150), Marin co., W Calif., at head of Tomales Bay, 17 mi. WNW of San Rafael; dairying. Point REYES is 12 mi. WSW.

Point Roberts, village, Whatcom co., NW Wash., on the Strait of Georgia at tip of Point Roberts peninsula, extending S from British Columbia and separated from Wash. mainland by Boundary Bay (E); resort; salmon fishing. Can be reached overland from U.S. only by going through British Columbia. Point visited and named (1792) by Capt. George Vancouver.

Point Shirley, Mass.: see WINTHROP.

Point Tupper, village (pop. estimate 300), E N.S., SW Cape Breton Isl., on the Strait of Canso opposite Mulgrave. Rail ferry to Mulgrave.

Point Whiteshed, village (pop. 32), S Alaska, on Point Whiteshed, 8 mi. SW of Cordova. Also spelled Whitshed.

Poipet (poi′pĕt′), town, Battambang prov., W Cambodia, on Thailand frontier (military post), 25 mi. W of Sisophon and on railroad, near Aranyaprathet (Thailand).

Poiré-sur-Vie, Le (lù pwärā′-sür-vē′), village (pop. 840), Vendée dept., W France, on Vie R. and 8 mi. NNW of La Roche-sur-Yon; dog breeding; truck gardening.

Poirino (poirē′nô), village (pop. 2,988), Torino prov., Piedmont, NW Italy, 13 mi. SSE of Turin, in grape-growing region; cotton mills.

Poischwitz (poish′vĭts), locality, Saxony, E central Germany, 8 mi. E of Grimma. Armistice signed here (June 4, 1813) bet. Napoleon and the Allies.

Poisevo (pŭēsyĕ′vù), village (1939 pop. over 2,000), E Tatar Autonomous SRR, Russian SFSR, near Ik R., 19 mi. SE of Menzelinsk; grain, livestock.

Poissons (pwäsō′), village (pop. 666), Haute-Marne dept., NE France, 4 mi. ESE of Joinville; woodworking.

Poissy (pwäsē′), town (pop. 11,972), Seine-et-Oise dept., N central France, on left bank of the Seine and 15 mi. WNW of Paris, at W edge of Saint-Germain forest; foundries and metalworks (auto parts, cables, razor blades, padlocks, kitchen ranges); mfg. of ceramics, flourmilling; cattle market. Reformatory. In its 12th-cent. church was held the memorable colloquium (1561) bet. Catholic and Protestant theologians. Poissy suffered some damage in Second World War.

Poitevin, Marais (märĕ′pwätvē′), marshy coastal area of Vendée, Deux-Sèvres and Charente-Maritime depts., W France, on Bay of Biscay N of La Rochelle; c.15 mi. long, 25 mi. wide; traversed by the lower course of Sèvre Niortaise and Vendée rivers. Reclaimed from the sea in 17th cent. by Dutch engineers, it is now a fertile agr. region.

Poitiers (poitērz′, Fr. pwätyā′), anc. *Limonum*, city (pop. 41,279), ⊙ Vienne dept., W central France, on Clain R. and 180 mi. SW of Paris; communication and agr. trade center, goose and swan feather processing, mfg. (chemicals, brushes, hosiery, fruit preserves), metalworking, printing and publishing. Of outstanding architectural interest are a Roman amphitheater and baths; the baptistery of St. John (4th–12th cent.); the churches of Sainte-Radegonde (9th–12th cent.), Saint-Hilaire (11th cent., restored 19th cent.), Saint-Porchaire (12th cent.), and Notre-Dame-la-Grande (11th–12th cent.); the Romanesque-Gothic 12th–14th-cent. cathedral; the courthouse, formerly a royal residence (12th–15th cent.), and numerous late medieval and Renaissance townhouses. Dating from the Pictavi (or Pictones), a Gallic tribe established here in pre-Roman times, Poitiers was christianized when St. Hilary became its 1st bishop (4th cent.). Held by Visigoths until the Frankish victory (507) over Alaric II. In 1st battle of Poitiers (732) probably fought at Moussais-la-Bataille (6 mi. SSW of Châtellerault), Charles Martel stemmed the tide of the invading Saracens. Sharing the history of POITOU, city was twice under English domination (1152–1204, 1360–69). In 2d battle of Poitiers (1356), actually fought at Nouaillé (6 mi. SE of Poitiers), Edward the Black Prince defeated and captured John II of France and his son Philip the Bold of Burgundy. Charles VII founded a univ. here in 1432. In the Wars of Religion city was unsuccessfully besieged (1568) by the Huguenots under Coligny. Poitiers was ⊙ of Poitou prov. until 1790. Named Poictiers during Middle Ages. Suffered some damage in Second World War.

Poitou (poitōō′, Fr. pwätōō′), region and former province of W and W central France; ⊙ Poitiers. Now comprised in Vendée, Deux-Sèvres, and Vienne depts. Generally level region bet. 2 uplands, the Armorican Massif (N) and the Massif Central (SE), linking France's 2 major lowlands, the Paris and Aquitaine basins. Cattle raising and dairying (W), wheat growing (E). Chief towns are Poitiers, Châtellerault, Niort, and La Roche-sur-Yon. Long an invasion route, Poitou fell to the Visigoths (5th cent.) and to the Franks (507). As part of Aquitaine, it passed (1152) to England, but was recovered (1204) by Philip II of France. Reconquered (1356) by Edward the Black Prince, and ceded to England by the Treaty of Brétigny (1360). Du Guesclin won Poitou back for France and Charles VII incorporated it into royal domain after Hundred Years War. During 16th cent. it suffered from Wars of Religion. A Royalist stronghold in French Revolution. Broken up into present depts. in 1790.

Poivre Island (pwä′vrù) (pop. 79), in S Amirantes, outlying dependency of the Seychelles, 165 mi. SW of Mahé Isl.; 5°45′S 53°19′E; coral formation. Copra.

Poix (pwä), village (pop. 1,042), Somme dept., N France, 16 mi. SW of Amiens; road junction. Livestock.

Poix-du-Nord (pwä-dü-nôr′), town (pop. 1,971), Nord dept., N France, 12 mi. SSE of Valenciennes; tulle and chicory mfg.

Pojan or **Pojani,** Albania: see APOLLONIA.

Pojo (pō′hō), town (pop. 1,300), Cochabamba dept., central Bolivia, in E foothills of Cordillera de Cochabamba, on Cochabamba–Santa Cruz highway, 23 mi. E of Totora; coca plantations, corn.

Pojo (pô′yōō), Finnish *Pohja* (pō′yä, pōkh′yä), village (commune pop. 6,507), Uusimaa co., SW Finland, at head of Pojo Bay of Gulf of Finland, 50 mi. W of Helsinki, in metalworking region. Has 14th-cent. church.

Pojoaque (pōwä′kē), pueblo (□ 18.1), Santa Fe co., N central N.Mex. Pojoaque village (1948 pop. 30) is small trading point bet. Sangre de Cristo Mts. and the Rio Grande, 15 mi. NNW of Santa Fe; alt. 5,750 ft. Inhabitants (chiefly Sp. Am.) raise grain and chili.

Pojo Bay, Swedish *Pojoviken* (pô″yōōvē′kùn), inlet (20 mi. long, 1–3 mi. wide) of Gulf of Finland, SW Finland, extends (NE) along E side of Hango peninsula. On bay are Ekenas, Skuru, and Pojo.

Pojorata, Rumania: see FUNDUL-MOLDOVEI.
Pojuca (pŏozhōō'kŭ), city (pop. 2,660), NE Bahia, Brazil, on railroad and 45 mi. NNE of Salvador; lumber, tobacco, sugar.
Pokaakku, Marshall Isls.: see TAONGI.
Pokaran (pō'kŭrŭn), town (pop. 4,328), W Rajasthan, India, 80 mi. NW of Jodhpur, on Thar Desert; rail terminus; exports camels, hides, salt. Camel breeding near by.
Pokatilovka-Karachevka (pŭkŭtyē'lŭfkŭ-kŭrŭchôf'-kŭ), town (1926 pop. 1,598), N central Kharkov oblast, Ukrainian SSR, 6 mi. SSW of Kharkov city center.
Pokegama Lake (pō"kŭgä'mŭ), Itasca co., N central Minn., just SW of Grand Rapids; 13 mi. long, 3 mi. wide. Fishing, boating, and bathing resorts. Has N outlet into Mississippi R. A dam has increased its area to □ 35.
Poke-O-Moonshine Mountain (2,162 ft.), Essex co., NE N.Y., in the Adirondacks, near L. Champlain, 7 mi. S of Keeseville. State camp site here.
Pokesdown, England: see BOURNEMOUTH.
Pokhara (pō'kŭrŭ), town (pop. c.10,000), central Nepal, on right tributary of the Trisuli and 90 mi. WNW of Katmandu; copper mining; barley, rice, millet, vegetables. Important Nepalese military station. Sometimes spelled Pokhra.
Pokhvistnevo (pŭkhvēst'nyĭvŭ), city (1946 pop. over 2,000), E Kuibyshev oblast, Russian SFSR, on Greater Kinel R., on railroad, and 90 mi. ENE of Kuibyshev; petroleum and natural-gas extracting center (pipe lines to Kuibyshev), developed during Second World War. Became town in 1934, city in 1947.
Po Kiang, China: see PO RIVER.
Pokliu Chau, Hong Kong: see LAMMA.
Poklo (bôk'lō'), Mandarin *Polo* (bŭ'lŭ'), town (pop. 18,863), ⊙ Poklo co. (pop. 222,150), E central Kwangtung prov., China, on East R. and 10 mi. NW of Waiyeung; rice trade. Tin mines near by.
Poko (pō'kō), village, Eastern Prov., N Belgian Congo, on Bomokandi R. and 145 mi. ENE of Buta; trading post and cotton center. Gold is mined in vicinity (E). Has Protestant mission.
Pokotu or **Po-k'o-t'u** (bô'kŭ'tōō'), Rus. *Bukhedu* (bŏŏkhŭdōō'), village, N Inner Mongolian Autonomous Region, Manchuria, in the Great Khingan Mts., on Chinese Eastern RR and 110 mi. ESE of Hailar; dairying, oilseed milling. Trades in lumber and furs.
Pokpak (bôk'bäk'), Mandarin *Popai* (bŭ'bī'), town, ⊙ Pokpak co. (pop. 417,756), SE Kwangsi prov., China, on Lim R. and 25 mi. SSW of Watlam; rice, beans. Tin mines near by.
Pokrov (pŭkrôf'), city (1926 pop. 3,249), W Vladimir oblast, Russian SFSR, 11 mi. NE of Orekhovo-Zuyevo; peat works. Chartered 1775.
Pokrovka (–kŭ). **1** Village (1939 pop. over 2,000), central Issyk-Kul oblast, Kirghiz SSR, near SE shore of the Issyk-Kul (lake), 20 mi. WSW of Przhevalsk; wheat; fisheries. **2** Village, Osh oblast, Kirghiz SSR: see LENINSKOYE, Osh oblast. **3** Village (1939 pop. over 2,000), N Talas oblast, Kirghiz SSR, on Talas R. and 15 mi. SE of Dzhambul; tobacco. **4** Village (1926 pop. 2,892), W central Chkalov oblast, Russian SFSR, on Samara R., on railroad (Platovka station) and 50 mi. WNW of Chkalov; metalworking; wheat, livestock. Formerly called Pokrovskoye. **5** Village (1926 pop. 2,872), SW Maritime Territory, Russian SFSR, on Suifun R. and 18 mi. NW of Voroshilov, in agr. area (grain, soybeans, sugar beets, rice); metalworks.
Pokrovo-Marfino (pŭkrô"vŭ-mär'fēnŭ), village (1939 pop. over 500), W Tambov oblast, Russian SFSR, 25 mi. SW of Tambov; wheat, sunflowers.
Pokrovsk (pŭkrôfsk'). **1** City, Saratov oblast, Russian SFSR: see ENGELS. **2** Town (1941 pop. over 500), central Yakut Autonomous SSR, Russian SFSR, on Lena R. and 40 mi. S of Yakutsk, in agr. area. River port; ferry on Yakutsk-Never highway.
Pokrovskaya Bagachka (pŭkrôf'skīŭ bŭgäch'kŭ), village (1939 pop. over 500), central Poltava oblast, Ukrainian SSR, 12 mi. SE of Lubny; sugar beets.
Pokrovski Steklyanny Zavod, Russian SFSR: see SAZONOVO.
Pokrovskoye (pŭkrôf'skŭyŭ). **1** Village, Kalinin oblast, Russian SFSR: see VELIKOOKTYABRSKI. **2** Village (1939 pop. over 500), central Orel oblast, Russian SFSR, 36 mi. SE of Orel; hemp. **3** Village (1926 pop. 7,093), SW Rostov oblast, Russian SFSR, on Mius R. and 15 mi. N of Taganrog; flour mill, metalworks; wheat, sunflowers, livestock. **4** Village (1926 pop. 1,672), S Sverdlovsk oblast, Russian SFSR, near Iset R., 40 mi. SE of Sverdlovsk; wheat, flax, livestock. **5** Village (1926 pop. 8,170), SE Dnepropetrovsk oblast, Ukrainian SSR, on Volchya R. and 40 mi. SSE of Pavlograd; flour milling, metalworking. **6** Village, SW Dnepropetrovsk oblast, Ukrainian SSR: see APOSTOLOVO. **7** Village (1926 pop. 6,786), NW Voroshilovgrad oblast, Ukrainian SSR, 45 mi. NW of Starobelsk; flour milling. Formerly also called Oktyabrskaya. **8** Village, Zaporozhe oblast, Ukrainian SSR: see PRIAZOVSKOYE.
Pokrovsk-Uralski or **Pokrovsk-Ural'skiy** (pŭkrôfsk'-ōōräl'skē), town (1947 pop. over 500), W Sverdlovsk oblast, Russian SFSR, 5 mi. WSW (under jurisdiction) of Severouralsk, on rail spur; magnetite mining. Sawmilling 3 mi. NE, at Boyanovka (1948 pop. over 500; rail spur terminus).
Pokucie, Ukrainian SSR: see POKUTYE.
Pokupje (pô'kōōpyĕ), region in N Croatia, Yugoslavia, extending along middle Kupa R. KARLOVAC is its center.
Pokutye or **Pokut'ye** (pŭkōō'tyĭ), Pol. *Pokucie*, upland in W Ukrainian SSR, bet. E Beskids (S) and Dniester R (N); average alt. 1,000 ft.; drained by Prut R. Scattered lignite deposits. Agr. (grain, sugar beets, tobacco, fruit, truck); hogs. Urban centers: Zabolotov, Snyatyn, Gorodenka.
Pokwan or **Po-kuan** (pŭ'gwän'), town, NE Chekiang prov., China, 20 mi. E of Shaohing and on railroad to Ningpo. Sometimes written Paikwan.
Pola (pōlä'), town (1939 pop. 1,288; 1948 municipality pop. 12,612), on E coast of Mindoro isl., Philippines, near L. Naujan, 24 mi. SE of Calapan; agr. center (rice, copra).
Pola (pô'lŭ), town (1939 pop. over 500), W central Novgorod oblast, Russian SFSR, on Pola R. (head of navigation) and 17 mi. E of Staraya Russa; flax.
Pola, Yugoslavia: see PULA.
Polacca, Ariz.: see WALPI.
Pola de Gordón (pō'lä dhä gôr-dhōn'), town (pop. 790), Leon prov., NW Spain, on Bernesga R. and 18 mi. N of Leon; summer resort. Several coal mines in vicinity (Ciñera basin); also barite mines and limestone quarries.
Pola de Laviana (lävyä'nä), town (pop. 2,643), Oviedo prov., NW Spain, on Nalón R. and 16 mi. SE of Oviedo, in rich iron- and coal-mining area. Dairy products. Mineral springs.
Pola de Lena (lā'nä), town (pop. 2,141), Oviedo prov., NW Spain, on Lena R. and 15 mi. S of Oviedo, in anthracite mining area. Also some copper and mercury mines in vicinity.
Pola de Siero (syā'rō), town (pop. 2,443), Oviedo prov., NW Spain, 9 mi. ENE of Oviedo; tanning, meat processing, champagne and cider distilling; corn, apples, lumber, cattle. Bituminous-coal mines in area.
Polán (pōlän'), village (pop. 2,559), Toledo prov., central Spain, 9 mi. SW of Toledo; cereals, chickpeas, grapes, olives, sheep; olive-oil pressing, cheese making.
Polanco del Yí (pōläng'kō dĕl yē'), village (pop. 300), Florida dept., S central Uruguay, on Yí R., on highway from Sarandí Grande, and 26 mi. ESE of Durazno; grain, livestock.
Poland, Pol. *Polska* (pôl'skä), republic (□ 120,359; 1946 pop. 23,929,757; 1950 pop. 24,976,926; all figures including the former German territory placed 1945 under Pol. administration), E central Europe; ⊙ WARSAW. Borders N on the Baltic and on USSR, W on Germany, S on Czechoslovakia, E on USSR, and NE on Lithuania. Generally a low, rolling plain, partly forested, and studded with numerous small lakes; surface rises toward S and culminates in the Sudetes (5,259 ft. on the Schneekoppe in the Riesengebirge) and the Carpathians (8,212 ft. on Rysy peak in the High Tatra) on Czechoslovak border. Lesser hill ranges in S part of country include Gory Swietokrzyskie and Cracow Jura. Poland is drained towards the Baltic by the Vistula, Oder (Ger. border), Western Bug (USSR border), Narew, San, Warta, Pilica, and Drweca rivers. Canals link major river systems. Large lakes are concentrated in Masurian Lakes region of NE Poland. Low coast line indented by Gulf of Danzig and by Vistula Lagoon. Entire S part of country is rich in mineral resources. Large quantities of coal (one of Poland's principal exports) are mined in SILESIA; Katowice, Beuthen (Bytom), Gleiwitz (Gliwice), Zabrze (Hindenburg), Chorzow, Sosnowiec, Waldenburg (Walbrzych), and Glatz (Klodzko) are chief mining centers. This region also has important iron, lead, and zinc mines; metallurgical industry, with numerous blast furnaces and steel mills, is concentrated here. Oil and natural gas are exploited in Rzeszow prov. (SE); Jaslo and Krosno are production centers and are linked with other industrial regions by natural gas pipe lines. Other minerals worked in Poland include lignite, salt (Wieliczka and Bochnia in Krakow prov., Inowroclaw in Bydgoszcz prov.), copper, tin, manganese, uranium, galena, tetrahedryte, phosphates, and silica sands. Hydroelectric power in S Poland. Over one-half of land is arable; rye, potatoes, oats, barley, wheat, flax, sugar, beets,rapeseed, and hemp are principal crops. Forestry, stock raising, fishing are important. Textile industry is concentrated in Lodz region (cotton-milling center) and in Silesia; heavy mechanical industries (machinery, locomotives, railroad cars, motor vehicles, electrical equipment) are centered on Warsaw, Katowice, Cracow,Breslau (Wroclaw), Gleiwitz, Ratibor (Raciborz), Poznan, Sandomierz, Stettin (Szczecin), and Bydgoszcz. Important glassworks in Silesia (Waldenburg, Szklarska Poreba, Katowice region). Principal ports are Gdynia, Danzig (Gdansk), Stettin, and Elbing (Elblag); fishing centers are Swinemünde (Swinoujscie), Kolberg (Kolobrzeg), and Puck. Odra is terminus of train ferry to Sweden. Other large cities are Czestochowa, Lublin, Radom, Torun, Bialystok, Kielce, Wloclawek, Kalisz, Hirschberg (Jelenia Gora), Grudziadz, Przemysl, Tarnow, Rzeszow, Allenstein (Olsztyn), and Liegnitz (Legnica). Vistula and Oder rivers are major inland-navigation routes; dense rail network serves Silesian industrial dist. Poland is crossed by several important international railroad lines; older E–W lines have served Ger.-Rus. traffic since late 19th cent.; while N–S lines, serving traffic bet. Scandinavia and Czechoslovakia and the Balkans, have gained importance since 1945. Administratively Poland is divided into 17 provs. [Pol. *wojewódzstwa*]: BIALYSTOK, BYDGOSZCZ, GDANSK, KATOWICE, KIELCE, KOSZALIN, KRAKOW, LODZ, LUBLIN, OLSZTYN, OPOLE, POZNAN, RZESZOW, SZCZECIN, WARSZAWA, WROCLAW, and ZIELONA GORA. Warsaw and Lodz cities are independent of their respective provs. Almost entire pop. is Polish-speaking; a vast majority of those affiliated with any creed are Roman Catholics. There are 11 univs., notably those of Warsaw, Lodz, Poznan, Breslau, Cracow, Torun, and Lublin. Authentic Pol. history begins in 9th cent., when Polians [dwellers in the field] obtained hegemony over other Slavic tribes in the country. Their principal dynasty, the Piasts, accepted (966) Christianity; Poznan was earliest ⊙ Poland and Gniezno 1st episcopal see. In wars with Germany, Hungary, Bohemia, Denmark, and Kiev the Piasts expanded their realm greatly, conquering, among other regions, POMERANIA, and in 1025 Boleslaus I took title of king. At death (1138) of Boleslaus III kingdom broke up into independent duchies, but was restored (1320) with accession of Ladislaus I. In meantime Teutonic Knights had gained foothold in then pagan region of N Poland; their power was finally broken by their defeat (1410) at Tannenberg and by subsequent treaties of Torun (1411, 1466), which established Pol. suzerainty over their territory. In 1370 Piast crown passed to Louis I of Hungary and then to his daughter Jadwiga. Jadwiga married Ladislaus Jagiello, duke of Lithuania, took Pol. crown as Ladislaus II in 1386; Jagiello dynasty ruled Poland and Lithuania until 1572. Despite being involved in constant wars, a realm extending from the Baltic to the Black Sea was maintained; arts and sciences flourished and culminated in the figure of Copernicus. King Ladislaus III, after 1440 also king of Hungary, gave Poland prestige of champion of Christianity against the Moslems, though his campaign against Turks ended in his rout and death (1444) in battle of Varna. In Union of Lublin, 1569, Poland absorbed Lithuania. In 1565 the Jesuits introduced the Catholic Reform, which arrested, without coercion, the growth of Protestantism. Bad relations bet. R.C. ruling class and Greek-Orthodox Church in Belorussia and the Ukraine (then parts of Lithuania) involved Poland in frequent wars with Russia. Sigismund III, pushed his claims to Swedish crown, thus starting a long series of Polish-Swedish wars. Reign of John II (1648–68), one of Sigismund's sons, came to be known as the Deluge in Pol. history; Ukrainian Cossacks under Bohdan Chmielnicki rebelled, and in 1655 Charles X of Sweden overran the country, which was also attacked by Tsar Alexis of Russia. Under Treaty of Oliva (1660) Poland lost much territory, and under Treaty of Andrusov (1667) E Ukraine passed to Russia. John III (John Sobieski) briefly restored Pol. prestige, but with his death Poland virtually ceased to be an independent country. In 1697 the elector of Saxony was chosen king as Augustus II. There followed a period of chaotic dynastic conditions. Fearing that the country might fall under complete Rus. domination, Frederick II of Prussia proposed its partition to Catherina II of Russia and Maria Theresa of Austria. In 1772 the 1st partition gave WEST PRUSSIA to Prussia, most of GALICIA to Austria, and Latgale and Belorussia E of Dvina and Dnieper rivers to Russia. A 2d partition (1793) left central section independent, but under Rus. control. Uprising (1794) under Kosciusko led to 3d partition (1795) of the country bet. Prussia, Austria, and Russia; Warsaw, Pol. ⊙ went to Prussia. Under Treaty of Tilsit (1807), Napoleon I created the grand duchy of Warsaw under King Frederick Augustus I of Saxony as a Pol. buffer state; with Napoleon's defeat it disappeared. The Congress of Vienna (1814–15) set up a nominally independent kingdom, in personal union with Russia, while W part of country was awarded to Prussia, and Galicia to Austria. Cracow was made a separate republic (annexed 1846 to Austria after rebellion). General insurrection (1830) in Rus. Poland ended with defeat (1831) of Pol. army at Ostroleka; Pol. constitution was suspended and the kingdom virtually integrated with Russia. While Poles enjoyed some autonomy in Galicia, Prussian part was subjected to increasing Germanization. In First World War Pol. legions under Pilsudski fought with Germany and Austria against Russia; in 1916 Germany and Austria proclaimed independent Pol. kingdom, but when Germany, which occupied the country, retained control over govt., Pilsudski resigned and was imprisoned. Upon armistice, Nov. 11,1918, an independent Poland was established. As constituted under Treaty of Versailles, 1919, country had access to the Baltic through the

POLISH CORRIDOR, and regained Prussian Poland from Germany. Danzig became a free city, and part of Silesia was awarded to Poland after a plebiscite had been held. The Polish-Russian border proposed at the Paris Peace Conference by Lord Curzon and later named the CURZON LINE would have followed the Western Bug R. for c.200 mi. and would have awarded to Russia large parts of the former Poland, inhabited by Belorussians and Ukrainians. Poland, however, insisted on its border of 1772, and in 1920 war with Russia resulted. In Treaty of Riga (1921) Poland secured most of its claims. It also seized (1920) the Vilna region from Lithuania and incorporated (1922) it into Poland after a plebiscite of doubtful validity. After 1922, Poland (□ 150,052; 1931 pop. 32,107,252), remained in constant dispute with Lithuania over Vilna and with Czechoslovakia over CIESZYN (Teschen). Over one-third of pop. consisted of minorities (Germans, Ukrainians, Belorussians, Jews, and Lithuanians) whose inequitable treatment led to eventual disintegration of the country upon outbreak of Second World War. Republican constitution was adopted in 1921; though economic reforms took place, the condition of the peasants remained wretched, while land-owning aristocracy thrived. In 1926 democratic govt. was suspended by military coup d'état that made Pilsudski virtual dictator; from this point onward Poland was ruled by a military clique. With resurgence of Ger. power, Pol. policy swung toward the Axis powers in the 1930s, but in 1939 Poland rejected Ger. demand for return of Danzig, having previously obtained guarantees of help from Great Britain and France in event of Ger. attack. On Sept. 1, 1939, Germany invaded Poland and thus precipitated Second World War; Pol. forces could offer little real resistance, and on Sept. 17 Soviet troops invaded Poland from E. Pol. resistance was quickly crushed, and the country was partitioned bet. Germany and the USSR; a central section, called Government General, was annexed by neither power, but was placed under Ger. rule. After Ger. attack on Russia (1941), all Poland passed under Ger. occupation. This was accompanied by unprecedented savagery against the Jewish pop. (3,113,900 before the war). Jews had settled in Poland from 9th cent. onward and had withstood the persecution of the tsars and, later, the official anti-semitism of the Polish govt. The Germans, sometimes aided by Poles, now proceeded to exterminate Jewish pop. methodically; most notorious among many were the camps at Oswiecim (Auschwitz) and Majdanek. By 1945 only c.100,000 Jews had survived. Many of them sought to emigrate as Polish anti-Semitic outbursts resumed in the wake of the departing Germans. Pol. pop. had in the meantime been reduced to status of slave people and large numbers were deported to work in Ger. war industries. A Pol. underground resistance movement was set up, but political dissension reduced its effectiveness. Poles who fled, especially to the USSR, later formed military units in the Middle East that fought with Allied forces, especially in Italy. At Allied insistence, Pol. govt. in exile, with seat in London, had resumed diplomatic relations with USSR, but broke off relations again after discovery by Germans of bodies of 10,000 Pol. officers allegedly executed by Russians in KATYN forest. In 1944 Soviet forces entered E Poland and under Rus. auspices a left-wing provisional Pol. govt. was set up in Lublin. When Soviet troops reached Praga, suburb of Warsaw on right bank of the Vistula, Pol. resistance forces controlled by Pol. govt. in London rose against the Germans, who crushed the rising while Soviet forces remained inactive. These events, and Rus. demand at Yalta Conference for a Pol. border at the Curzon Line, further deepened rift bet. Pol. govt. in London and Soviet govt. Potsdam Conference (1945) gave Poland a border slightly E of Curzon Line and placed all Ger. territory E of Oder and Lusatian Neisse rivers (with exception of N part of East Prussia, placed under USSR administration) under Pol. administration, pending final settlement by a peace conference; expulsion of Ger. pop. was sanctioned. The region was, however, immediately incorporated as integral Pol. territory. As compared to pre-war Poland, country had ceded 67,936 sq. mi. to USSR and Lithuania, and had gained 39,705 sq. mi. (including former free city of Danzig) from Germany. Border with Czechoslovakia returned to pre-1938 status (Poland had annexed a part of Czech Silesia at time of Ger. annexation of Sudetenland). Govt. on a comparatively broad basis was established in Warsaw after 1945, including members of former Lublin govt., as well as less reactionary elements of former Pol. govt. in London; the latter were, however, soon forced out as Poland came under growing Soviet control, adopted a unicameral parliament, and generally fell in line with the other "peoples' democracies." In 1950 the East German govt. recognized the Oder-Neisse line as Pol.-Ger. boundary.

Poland. 1 Town (pop. 1,503), Androscoggin co., SW Maine, 10 mi. W of Auburn; bottling works, cannery, fibre mill. Includes West Poland on Tripp L. and Poland Spring, summer resort long known for its mineral water (1st inn opened 1797). Maine bldg. of Chicago fair of 1893, rebuilt here, serves as library. Settled c.1768, inc. 1795. **2** Village (pop. 511), Herkimer co., central N.Y., 13 mi. NE of Utica; lumber, wood products. **3** Village (pop. 1,652), Mahoning co., E Ohio, 7 mi. S of downtown Youngstown; dairy products. Settled c.1799.

Poland Spring, Maine: see POLAND.

Polangen, Lithuania: see PALANGA.

Polangui (pōläng'gē), town (1939 pop. 2,685; 1948 municipality pop. 27,623), Albay prov., SE Luzon, Philippines, on railroad and 20 mi. NW of Legaspi; agr. center (abacá, rice, coconuts).

Polanica Zdroj (pôlänē'tsä zdrō͞o'ē), Pol. *Polanica Zdrój*, Ger. *Bad Altheide* (bät″ ält'hīdů), town (1939 pop. 3,947; 1946 pop. 4,832) in Lower Silesia, after 1945 in Wroclaw prov., SW Poland, near Czechoslovak border, at SE foot of Heuscheuer Mts., 7 mi. WSW of Glatz (Klodzko); health resort. Chartered after 1945 and briefly called Puszczykow Zdroj, Pol. *Puszczykow Zdrój*.

Polanow (pôlä'nōōf), Pol. *Polanów*, Ger. *Pollnow* (pôl'nō), town (1939 pop. 3,629; 1946 pop. 1,947) in Pomerania, after 1945 in Koszalin prov., NW Poland, 20 mi. ESE of Köslin (Koszalin); agr. market (grain, sugar beets, potatoes, livestock); sawmilling.

Polaris (pōlă'rĭs), village (pop. 214), Shoshone co., N Idaho, 5 mi. W of Wallace.

Polaris Bay (pōlä'rĭs), wide inlet of Hall Basin, NW Greenland, opposite Lady Franklin Bay, Ellesmere Isl.; 81°25'N 61°15'W. Site (1871–72) of winter quarters of Hall expedition. Northernmost traces of early Eskimo pop. found here.

Pola River (pô'lŭ), W European Russian SFSR, rises in Valdai Hills W of L. Seliger, flows 90 mi. NNW, past Pola (head of navigation), to L. Ilmen, forming a joint delta mouth with Lovat R.

Polathane, Turkey: see AKCAABAT.

Polatli (pôlätlü'), Turkish *Polatlı*, town (1950 pop. 10,332), Ankara prov., Turkey, on railroad and 45 mi. SW of Ankara; agr. center (grain, fruit; mohair goats).

Polavaram, India: see RAJAHMUNDRY.

Polazna (pŭläz'nŭ), village (1926 pop. 1,520), central Molotov oblast, Russian SFSR, on left bank of Kama R. (landing) and 9 mi. S of Dobryanka; truck, livestock. Petroleum deposits. Steel-milling center prior to First World War.

Polczyn Zdroj (pô'ō͝o-chĭn zdrō͞o'ē), Pol. *Polczyn Zdrój*, Ger. *Bad Polzin* (bät″ pôl'tsēn), town (1939 pop. 6,920; 1946 pop. 3,939) in Pomerania, after 1945 in Koszalin prov., NW Poland, 18 mi. SSE of Bialogard; rail junction; health resort with mineral springs; brewing.

Poldhu (pŏl'dū, pŏldū'), village, W Cornwall, England, on Mounts Bay of the Channel and 5 mi. S of Helston, NW of Lizard Point. Marconi's 1st transatlantic transmission of radio signals made from here to Newfoundland in 1901.

Pole Creek Mountain, peak (13,740 ft.) in San Juan Mts., SW Colo., 13 mi. E of Silverton.

Polemidhia or **Kato Polemidhia** (kä'tō pôlĕmē'-dhēä), village (pop. 1,602), Limassol dist., S Cyprus, 40 mi. SW of Nicosia; almonds, carobs; sheep, goats.

Pol-e-Sefid, Iran: see PUL-I-SEFID.

Polesella (pôlĕzĕl'lä), town (pop. 2,828), Rovigo prov., Veneto, N Italy, on Po R. and 8 mi. SSW of Rovigo; mfg. (textile machinery, agr. tools, hemp products).

Polesie (pôlĕ'syĕ), former province (□ 14,218; 1931 pop. 1,133,398) of E Poland, in POLESYE lowland; ⊙ Brzesc nad Bugiem (Brest). Formed 1921 out of Rus. govts.; occupied 1939 by USSR; became part of PINSK and BREST oblasts of Belorussian SSR and VOLYN and ROVNO oblasts of Ukrainian SSR.

Polesine (pôlā'zēnĕ), agricultural district coextensive with Rovigo prov., Veneto, N Italy, extends from Verona prov. E to the Adriatic, bet. Adige and Po rivers. Traversed by Tartaro R. Consists largely of reclaimed plain formerly occupied by marshes and lagoons. Chief crops: sugar beets, hemp, cereals, fruit. Cattle raising.

Polesine Parmense (pärmĕn'sĕ), village (pop. 619), Parma prov., Emilia-Romagna, N central Italy, on Po R. and 9 mi. SSE of Cremona; cutlery mfg.

Polessk (pŭlyĕsk'), city (1939 pop. 6,527), N Kaliningrad oblast, Russian SFSR, port on lower Deima R., near its mouth on Courland Lagoon, and 26 mi. ENE of Kaliningrad; linked by canal with Neman R. delta; lumber milling, mfg. (beverages, cement ware); cattle and horse trade. By treaty signed here (1656), Sweden renounced suzerainty over Prussia. Until 1945, in East Prussia and called Labiau (lä'bēou).

Polesworth, town and parish (pop. 6,466), N Warwick, England, on Anker R. and 3 mi. E of Tamworth; coal mining. Has Norman church, rebuilt in 14th cent.

Polesye or **Poles'ye** (pŭlyĕ'syĭ), oblast (□ 8,400; 1946 pop. estimate 700,000), Belorussian SSR; ⊙ Mozyr. In Polesye lowland (see also PRIPET MARSHES); drained by Pripet R. and its affluents. Largely wooded, swampy region; potatoes, hemp, rubber-bearing plants (*kok-sagyz*), buckwheat grown in drier or drained areas. Salt deposits. Lumbering is important; mills at Mozyr, Lelchitsy, Koptsevichi; peat works (E). Pig raising in potato areas (N, E). Formed 1938.

Polesye or **Poles'ye,** Pol. *Polesie* (pôlĕ'syĕ), swampy wooded lowland in S Belorussian and NW Ukrainian SSRs, largely coextensive with PRIPET MARSHES. Includes former Pol. prov. of POLESIE and Polesye oblast of Belorussian SSR.

Poletayevo (pŭlyĭtī'ŭvŭ), village (1939 pop. over 500), SW Tambov oblast, Russian SFSR, 55 mi. SSW of Tambov; sugar beets.

Polevaya (pŭlyĭvī'ŭ), town (1926 pop. 2,275), N Kharkov oblast, Ukrainian SSR, 5 mi W of Dergachi, in Kharkov metropolitan area; truck, fruit.

Polevskoi or **Polevskoy** (pŭlyĭfskoi'), city (1939 pop. over 20,000), S Sverdlovsk oblast, Russian SFSR, in the central Urals, on small lake, near Chusovaya R., 27 mi. SW of Sverdlovsk, on rail spur. Industrial and mining center, based on magnetite, magnesite, copper, and pyrite deposits; ferrous metallurgy (steel, pig iron, tin plate); chemical processing (pyrite, cryolite), copper refining; marble quarrying. Developed as pyrite-mining center prior to First World War; absorbed copperworks of Gumeshevski Zavod (just S) in 1920s. Until 1928, Polevskoi Zavod; became city in 1942; merged with metallurgical center Severski (4 mi. N; 1939 pop. 7,050) in 1946.

Polezhan (pôlĕzhän'), peak (9,351 ft.) in Pirin Mts., SW Bulgaria, 7 mi. S of Bansko. Also called Mangar-tepe.

Pölfing-Brunn (pûl'fĭng-brō͝on'), village (pop. 1,995), Styria, SE Austria, 11 mi. WSW of Leibnitz; rail junction.

Polgahawela (pōl″gŭhŭvĕl'ŭ), town (pop. 3,517), North Western Prov., Ceylon, 12 mi. SSW of Kurunegala; rail junction; rice, vegetables, coconut palms. Buddhist temple and ruins (3d cent. A.D.) near by.

Polgar (pôl'gär), Hung. *Polgár*, town (pop. 15,167), Szabolcs co., NE Hungary, near the Tisza, 30 mi. WSW of Nyiregyhaza; market center; flour mills. Wheat, corn, potatoes, dairy farming near by.

Polgardi (pôl'gärdē), Hung. *Polgárdi*, town (pop. 4,654), Fejer co., W central Hungary, 11 mi. SSW of Szekesfehervar; distilleries; agr., cattle, sheep.

Polgyo (pŭl'gyō'), Jap. *Bakkyo*, town (1949 pop. 32,882), S.Cholla prov., S Korea, 11 mi. SW of Sunchon; commercial center for agr. area (rice, cotton); paper making, sake brewing.

Poli (pō'lē), village, Benoué region, N central Fr. Cameroons, 60 mi. SSW of Garona; cotton, peanuts, millet; stock raising.

Poli or **P'o-li** (pō'lē'), town (pop. 30,000), ⊙ Poli co. (pop. 120,000), central Sungkiang prov., Manchuria, 65 mi. S of Kiamusze and on railroad; agr. center: barley, rye, kaoliang, millet, corn, soybeans. Coal and gold deposits.

Poliaigos, Greece: see POLYAIGOS.

Poliçan (pôlē'chän) or **Poliçani** (pôlē'chänē), village (1930 pop. 1,536), S Albania, 12 mi. ENE of Argyrokastron, near Gr. line.

Policastro, Gulf of (pôlēkä'strô), inlet of Tyrrhenian Sea, S Italy, bet. Cape Scalea (SE) and Punta degli Infreschi (NW); c.25 mi. long, 15 mi. wide. On its N shore is Policastro Bussentino and port of Sapri.

Policastro Bussentino (bōōs-sĕntē'nô), village (pop. 807), Salerno prov., Campania, S Italy, on N shore of Gulf of Policastro, 17 mi. SE of Vallo della Lucania. Destroyed by Robert Guiscard (1055) and by Turks (1542). Formerly Policastro del Golfo and Policastro Vetere.

Police or **Police nad Metuji** (pô'lĭtsĕ näd' mĕtō͝oyĭ), Czech *Police nad Metuji*, Ger. *Politz* (pō'lĭts), town (pop. 3,146), NE Bohemia, Czechoslovakia, in the Sudetes, on railroad and 10 mi. ENE of Dvur Kralove; popular summer resort and mtn excursion center; linen mfg. Has 13th-cent. church with Gothic portico.

Police (pôlē'tsĕ), Ger. *Pölitz* (pû'lĭts), suburb (1933 pop. 5,465) of Stettin, in Pomerania, after 1945 in Szczecin prov., NW Poland, near Damm L., 8 mi. N of city center; cellulose milling; power station. Synthetic-oil plant destroyed by heavy bombing in Second World War. Inc. 1939 into Stettin.

Policka (pô'lĭchkä), Czech *Polička*, Ger. *Politschka* (pō'lĭchkä), town (pop. 5,600), E Bohemia, Czechoslovakia, in Bohemian-Moravian Heights, on railroad and 31 mi. SE of Pardubice; heavy-munitions mfg.; handmade footwear industry; lumber trade.

Polignac or **Fort Polignac** (pôlĕnyäk'), oasis and military outpost, Saharan Oases territory, SE Algeria, on Fort Flatters-Djanet desert track; 26°29'N 8°18'E.

Polignac, village (pop. 419), Haute-Loire dept., S central France, 2 mi. NW of Le Puy; cereal and vegetable growing. Has ruins of 12th–14th-cent. feudal castle.

Polignano a Mare (pôlēnyä'nô ä mä'rĕ), town (pop. 9,250), Bari prov., Apulia, S Italy, port on the Adriatic, 21 mi. ESE of Bari; fishing; macaroni.

Poligny (pôlēnyē'), town (pop. 3,532), Jura dept., E France, at the foot of the Jura, 13 mi. NE of Lons-le-Saunier; cheese, cereal, and wine market; woodworking, diamond cutting. Salt mines near by. Natl. dairying institute.

Poligyros, Greece: see POLYGYROS.

Polikandros, Greece: see PHOLEGANDROS.

Polikastron, Greece: see POLYKASTRON.
Polikhnitos, Greece: see POLYCHNITOS.
Pol-i-Khomri, Afghanistan: see PUL-I-KHUMRI.
Polikraishte (pôlĭkrä'ēshtĕ), village (pop. 3,934), Gorna Oryakhovitsa dist., N Bulgaria, 5 mi. NW of Gorna Oryakhovitsa; winegrowing, truck, livestock; sugar beets, oil-bearing plants.
Polillo Islands (pōlē'yō, –lyō), group (□ c.295; 1939 pop. 8,084), Quezon prov., Philippines, in Philippine Sea, off E coast of central Luzon; 14°50'N 122°5'E. Comprises Polillo (largest), PATNANONGAN ISLAND, PALASAN ISLAND, JOMALIG ISLAND, and several smaller isls. Fishing, coconut growing. Polillo Isl. (□ 234; 1939 pop. 6,716) is 11 mi. E of central Luzon across Polillo Strait; 30 mi. long, 6–15 mi. wide; rises to 726 ft. in S area. Coal is mined. On W coast of isl. is Polillo town (1939 pop. 1,819), chief town of group.
Polillo Strait, channel bet. E coast of central Luzon and Polillo Isl., Philippines, connecting Lamon Bay (S) with Philippine Sea (N); 35 mi. long, 11–25 mi. wide. Dinahican Point is at SW side of entrance.
Polimlje or **Polimlye** (both: pô'lĭmlyĕ), valley of upper Lim R., in Dinaric Alps, E Montenegro, Yugoslavia, bet. Andrijevica and Plav.
Poliña de Júcar (pōlē'nyä dhä hoo'kär), village (pop. 2,614), Valencia prov., E Spain, on Júcar R. and 5 mi. NE of Alcira, in rice- and orange-growing area; vegetable canning; cereals, peanuts.
Polingmiao (bŭ'lĭng'myou') or **Pailingmiao** (bī'–), town in Suiyuan section of Inner Mongolia, China, 95 mi. NW of Kweisui; Mongolian trading, religious center; trades in furs, wool, tea, silk, cattle.
Polinos, Greece: see POLYAIGOS.
Poliny Osipenko, Imeni (ē'mĭnyē pŭlyē'nŭ ŭsĭp'yĭnkŭ) [Rus.,=named for Polina Osipenko], village (1948 pop. over 500), SW Lower Amur oblast, Khabarovsk Territory, Russian SFSR, on Amgun R. (head of navigation), near mouth of Kerbi R., and 185 mi. WSW of Nikolayevsk, in gold-mining region. Formerly called Kerbi; renamed 1939 for Rus. aviatrix.
Polis (pô'lēs), town (pop. 1,198), Paphos dist., W Cyprus, near the coast, 55 mi. WSW of Nicosia, in agr. region (almonds, carobs, olive oil; sheep, goats). Five mi. WNW are the Baths of Aphrodite (Fontana Amorosa).
Polish Corridor or **Danzig Corridor,** strip of former Ger. territory (20–70 mi. wide) given to Poland under Treaty of Versailles (1919) to provide outlet to the Baltic. Contained lower course of the Vistula, but excluded territory of the Free City of Danzig. It separated East Prussia from the rest of Germany, but provision was made for free Ger. rail and road transit across the corridor; the arrangement caused chronic friction bet. Poland and Germany. Gdynia was developed as chief Pol. port and linked with industrial Katowice region by new N-S railroad. In March, 1939, Germany demanded cession of Danzig and extraterritorial transit route across the corridor. Resulting tension bet. Poland and Germany became acute in summer of 1939 and led (Sept. 1) to world war. Territory was annexed to Germany; returned 1945 to Poland. Until 1939, in Pol. Pomorze prov.; territory inc. in Gdansk prov. after 1945.
Polistena (pôlē'stĕnä), town (pop. 9,690), Reggio di Calabria prov., Calabria, S Italy, 13 mi. ENE of Palmi; olive oil, wine; agr. tools, baskets.
Polist River or **Polist' River** (pŭlyēst'yŭ), W European Russian SFSR, rises N of Loknya, flows 80 mi. N, past Belebelka and Staraya Russa, to Lovat R. just above its delta mouth.
Politotdelski or **Politotdel'skiy** (pŭlyēt"ŭt-dyĕl'skē), town (1939 pop. over 2,000), E Stalino oblast, Ukrainian SSR, in the Donbas, on railroad (Sofino-Brodskaya station) and 2 mi. N of Snezhnoye; coal mines.
Politschka, Czechoslovakia: see POLICKA.
Politz, Czechoslovakia: see POLICE.
Pölitz, Poland: see POLICE.
Polivos, Greece: see POLYAIGOS.
Poliyiros, Greece: see POLYGYROS.
Polizzi Generosa (pôlē'tsē jĕnĕrô'zä), town (pop. 7,149), Palermo prov., N central Sicily, in Madonie Mts. near headwaters of Grande R., 16 mi. S of Cefalù, in cereal-growing, livestock region.
Poljana or **Polyana** (both: pôlyä'nä), village (pop. 5,407), NE Bosnia, Yugoslavia, on Spreca R. and 6 mi. WSW of Tuzla.
Polk (pōk). **1** County (□ 860; pop. 14,182), W Ark.; ⊙ Mena. Bounded W by Okla. line; drained by Ouachita and Saline rivers; situated in the Ouachita Mts. Lumbering, stock raising, agr. (cotton, corn, truck, potatoes, fruit), dairying. Some mfg. at Mena. Contains part of Ouachita Natl. Forest (recreation). Formed 1844. **2** County (□ 1,861; pop. 123,997), central Fla., bounded E by Kissimmee R. and partly N by Withlacoochee R.; ⊙ Bartow. Hilly lake region, swampy in N, drained by Peace R.; includes lakes Hancock, Hamilton, Hatchineha, Weohyakapka, and Crooked. Contains Iron Mt. (325 ft.). Leads state in citrus-fruit growing and canning, and in phosphate mining; raises c.¼ of the citrus fruit and yields more than ⅔ of the phosphate. Also produces truck (especially strawberries), corn, cattle, and poultry. Makes fertilizer and insecticides. Formed 1861. **3** County (□ 312; pop. 30,976), NW Ga. on Ala. line; ⊙ Cedartown. Valley and ridge agr. (cotton, corn, hay, sweet potatoes, fruit, livestock) and textile-mfg. area; sawmilling, iron mining. Formed 1851. **4** County (□ 594; pop. 226,010), central Iowa; ⊙ Des Moines. Prairie agr. area (hogs, cattle, poultry, corn, soybeans, oats) drained by Des Moines, Raccoon, and Skunk rivers and by Beaver Creek. Bituminous-coal deposits mined in S. Contains state park. Formed 1846. **5** County (□ 2,012; pop. 35,900), NW Minn.; ⊙ Crookston. Agr. area bounded W by N.Dak. and Red River of the North and drained by Poplar, Sandhill, and Red Lake rivers. Wheat, small grains, potatoes, dairy products, livestock, poultry. Formed 1858. **6** County (□ 642; pop. 16,062), SW central Mo.; ⊙ Bolivar. In the Ozarks; drained by Pomme de Terre R. and Little Sac R. Corn, wheat, oats, hay; dairy cattle, poultry. Formed 1835. **7** County (□ 433; pop. 8,044), E central Nebr.; ⊙ Osceola. Agr. area bounded N by Platte R.; drained by Big Blue R. Livestock, grain, dairy and poultry produce. Formed 1870. **8** County (□ 234; pop. 11,627), SW N.C., on S.C. line; ⊙ Columbus. Piedmont farm (peaches, cotton, corn, sweet potatoes) and forest area. Formed 1855. **9** County (□ 739; pop. 26,-317), NW Oregon; ⊙ Dallas. Coast Range extends along W border; bounded E by Willamette R. Agr. (fruit, truck, grain, poultry), dairying, lumber milling. Formed 1845. **10** County (□ 436; pop. 14,074), SE Tenn.; ⊙ Benton. Bounded E by N.C., S by Ga.; Unicoi Mts. in NE; drained by Hiwassee R. and Ocoee R. (with 3 TVA dams). Largely included in Cherokee Natl. Forest. In SE is copper-producing region, with mines and smelters. Lumbering (pine, oak), agr. (corn, cotton, hay, soybeans, livestock, dairy products). Formed 1839. **11** County (□ 1,094; pop. 16,194), E Texas; ⊙Livingston. Bounded W and SW by Trinity R., NE by Neches R. Lumbering (pine, hardwoods); oil fields; agr. (cotton, corn, vegetables, pecans, sweet sorghums); livestock (cattle, hogs, poultry); dairying. Minerals (silica, chalk, sandstone). Hunting, fishing. Alabama-Coushatta Indian Reservation is in E. Formed 1846. **12** County (□ 934; pop. 24,944), NW Wis., bounded W by St. Croix R. (on Minn. line); ⊙ Balsam Lake. Has numerous small lakes and part of Interstate Park. Dairying is principal industry. Formed 1853.
Polk. 1 Village (pop. 508), Polk co., E central Nebr., 15 mi. SW of Osceola, near Platte R.; cement products, flour; livestock, poultry produce, grain. **2** Village (pop. 332), Ashland co., N central Ohio, 7 mi. NE of Ashland, in agr. area; makes fireworks. **3** Residential borough (pop. 4,004), Venango co., NW Pa., 5 mi. WSW of Franklin; resort. Settled c.1798, laid out 1839, inc. 1886.
Polk, Camp, La.: see LEESVILLE.
Polk City. 1 Town (pop. 171), Polk co., central Fla., 13 mi. NE of Lakeland. **2** Town (pop. 336), Polk co., central Iowa, near Des Moines R., 14 mi. NNW of Des Moines, in coal-mining, agr. area.
Polkowice (pôlkôvē'tsĕ), Ger. *Polkwitz* (pôlk'vĭts), after 1938 *Heerwegen* (hâr'vāgŭn), town (1939 pop. 1,599; 1946 pop. 646) in Lower Silesia, after 1945 in Zielona Gora prov., W Poland, 20 mi. N of Liegnitz (Legnica); linen, hemp, and jute milling.
Polkton (pōk'tŭn), town (pop. 459), Anson co., S N.C., 7 mi. WNW of Wadesboro; sawmilling.
Polla (pôl'lä), town (pop. 3,930), Salerno prov., Campania, S Italy, on Tanagro R. and 10 mi. NNW of Sala Consilina; woolen mills.
Pollachi (pŏlä'chē), city (pop. 25,198), Coimbatore dist., SW Madras, India, 24 mi. S of Coimbatore; rail junction; trade center E of Palghat Gap; shipping point for products (railway sleepers, tea, coffee, rubber, cinchona, lac) of Anaimalai Hills (S); cotton pressing, peanut-oil extraction. Roman coins of 1st cent. B.C. found here in 1800.
Pollard (pŏ'lŭrd). **1** Trading town (pop. 271), Escambia co., S Ala., 8 mi. SW of Brewton, near Conecuh R. and Fla. line. **2** Town (pop. 165), Clay co., extreme NE Ark., 6 mi. NW of Piggott, near Mo. line.
Pöllau (pŭl'ou), village (pop. 1,703), Styria, SE Austria, 24 mi. NE of Graz; textiles, pottery; summer resort.
Pollensa (pōlyĕn'sä), anc. *Pollentia*, town (pop. 5,722), Majorca, Balearic Isls., 29 mi. NE of Palma. Its port Puerto de Pollensa, a seaplane base, is 3½ mi. NE on Mediterranean Bay of Pollensa. Picturesque town in beautiful setting, with near-by caves. Resort and agr. center, surrounded by vineyards and long known for its wines. Also produces olives, wheat, carobs, vegetables, onions, tubers, and fruit. Has notable churches (Montesión) and ruins of Castell del Rei in vicinity (3 mi. N).
Pollenza (pôl-lĕn'tsä), village (pop. 1,000), Macerata prov., The Marches, central Italy, 6 mi. WSW of Macerata.
Pollino (pôl-lē'nô), highest range (c.10 mi. long) of S Apennines, S Italy, along Basilicata-Calabria border. Rises to 7,451 ft. in Serra Dolcedorme, 7,375 ft. in Monte Pollino, N of Castrovillari.
Pollnow, Poland: see POLANOW.
Polloc Harbor (pōyōk', pōlyōk'), sheltered inlet of Illana Bay, W Mindanao, Philippines, N of Cotabato; Parang is on it.
Pollock (pŏ'lŭk). **1** Town (pop. 421), Grant parish, central La., 15 mi. N of Alexandria, in agr. and lumber area. **2** Town (pop. 395), Campbell co., N S.Dak., 90 mi. WNW of Aberdeen, near Missouri R.; dairy products, livestock, poultry, grain.
Pollocksville, town (pop. 420), Jones co., SE N.C., 12 mi. SW of New Bern and on Trent R.; sawmilling.
Pollokshaws (pŏ"lŭk-shôz'), S industrial suburb (pop. 21,171) of Glasgow, Renfrew, Scotland, on White Cart Water; important textile, textile machinery, and chemical works.
Pollokshields (pŏ"lŭk-shēldz'), SW residential suburb (pop. 28,842) of Glasgow, Lanark, Scotland.
Pollos (pō'lyōs), town (pop. 1,262), Valladolid prov., N central Spain, on Duero (Douro) R. and 26 mi. WSW of Valladolid; cereals, wine, sheep.
Pollutri (pôl-loo'trē), village (pop. 2,301), Chieti prov., Abruzzi e Molise, S central Italy, 6 mi. WNW of Vasto.
Polna (pôl'nä), Czech *Polná*, town (pop. 3,556), SE Bohemia, Czechoslovakia, 10 mi. SSE of Havlickuv Brod; rail terminus; glassmaking. Noted for 14th- and 15th-cent. churches and 18th-cent. baroque church.
Polna (pŭlnä'), village (1939 pop. over 500), NW Pskov oblast, Russian SFSR, 22 mi. SSE of Gdov; dairying.
Polnisch-Ostrau, Czechoslovakia: see SLEZSKA OSTRAVA.
Polo (bŭ'lŭ'). **1** Town, Kwangtung prov., China: see POKLO. **2** Town and oasis (pop. 16,651), N Sinkiang prov., China, 100 mi. NE of Kuldja, near NW shore of lake Ebi Nor and near USSR border; grain, livestock. Tungsten mines near by.
Polo (pō'lō). **1** City (pop. 2,242), Ogle co., N Ill., 32 mi. SW of Rockford; trade center in dairy, livestock, and grain area; creameries, cheese factory, poultry hatchery, nursery. Inc. 1857. **2** City (pop. 549), Caldwell co., NW Mo., 31 mi. SW of Chillicothe.
Polochic River (pōlōchēk'), Alta Verapaz and Izabal depts., central Guatemala, rises E of Tactic, flows 150 mi. E, past Tucurú, Pancajché, and Panzós (head of navigation), to L. Izabal, forming delta S of El Estor. Upper valley used by Verapaz RR. Receives Cahabón R. Carries coffee and lumber.
Polog (pô'lôk), fertile valley in NW Macedonia, Yugoslavia, extending c.25 mi. along upper Vardar R. Consists of upper Polog (S; chief town, GOSTIVAR) and lower Polog (N; chief town, TETOVO).
Pologi (pô'lŭgē), city (1948 pop. over 10,000), E central Zaporozhe oblast, Ukrainian SSR, on Konka R. and 55 mi. SE of Zaporozhe; rail junction; flour mill, metalworks. Kaolin and refractory-clay quarries. Called (c.1928–39) Chubarovka.
Polom (pŭlôm'), village (1926 pop. 491), N Kirov oblast, Russian SFSR, on Vyatka R. and 55 mi. NE of Kirov; grain, flax.
Polonnaruwa (pōlŭn-nŭroo'vŭ), town (pop. 2,312), North Central Prov., Ceylon, 50 mi. SE of Anuradhapura; rice plantations, vegetable gardens. One of anc. ruined cities of Ceylon; became (A.D. 368) a royal residence and (8th cent. A.D.) ⊙ Ceylon, following fall of Anuradhapura to Tamils. Extensive ruins (mostly Buddhist) date mainly from 12th cent.; largely built by Singhalese king, Parakrama Bahu; include large statues of Buddha, stupas, temples, Lotus Bath, and a recently-exposed monastic establishment. Parakrama Samudra (also called Topawewa), anc. irrigation tank (6 mi. long, 3 mi. wide; built 4th cent. A.D.), is just W; formerly much larger. Govt. animal breeding farm 2 mi. SE. Land reclamation project at Parakrama Samudra village, 4 mi. S. Polonnaruwa is sometimes called Topawewa.
Polonnoye (pŭlô'nŭyŭ), city (1926 pop. 16,400), NE Kamenets-Podolski oblast, Ukrainian SSR, 19 mi. E of Shepetovka; ceramic industry; flour mill.
Polonuevo (pōlōnwā'vō), town (pop. 2,681), Atlántico dept., N Colombia, in Caribbean lowlands, 18 mi. SW of Barranquilla; cotton, corn, sugar cane, stock.
Polop (pōlôp'), town (pop. 1,113), Alicante prov., E Spain, 20 mi. ESE of Alcoy; olive-oil processing, flour milling; almonds, fruit. Summer resort.
Polotitlán (pōlōtētlän'), officially Polotitlán de la Ilustración, town (pop. 1,073), Mexico state, central Mexico, 16 mi. SE of San Juan del Río; alt. 7,516 ft.; cereals, livestock.
Polotnyany or **Polotnyanyy** (pŭlŭtnyä'nē), town (1926 pop. 4,082), N central Kaluga oblast, Russian SFSR, 18 mi. NW of Kaluga; limestone works.
Polotsk (pô'lŭtsk), oblast (□ 6,680; 1946 pop. estimate 700,000), N Belorussian SSR; ⊙ Polotsk. In Western Dvina R. basin; swamp and lake area (W). Forested and agr. region; flax (chief crop), grain, fruit; pigs, dairy cattle; orchards near Polotsk. Lumber milling, peat cutting. Rural industry, chiefly flax processing. Industrial center, Polotsk. Formed 1944 out of Vitebsk and Vileika (later called Molodechno) oblasts.
Polotsk, city (1926 pop. 25,826), ⊙ Polotsk oblast, Belorussian SSR, on Western Dvina R., at mouth of short Polota R., and 120 mi. NNE of Minsk; 55°29'N 28°46'E. Transportation and lumber center; junction of 5 rail lines; sawmills, flour mills,

meat-packing plants. Has Peter the Great house mus., 11th-cent. cathedral, city wall (1653). Dates from 9th cent.; became ⊙ principality (10th–13th cent.); flourished as major trading center (pop. c.100,000) under Poles in 14th–16th cent.; passed 1772 to Russia. Scene of battle in Fr. invasion of 1812. During Second World War, held (1941–44) by Germans.

Polovinka (pŭlŭvēn'kŭ). **1** Town, Khabarovsk Territory, Russian SFSR: see UMALTINSKI. **2** City (1939 pop. over 10,000), E central Molotov oblast, Russian SFSR, 9 mi. SSW of Kizel, on railroad; a major mining center in Kizel bituminous-coal basin. Developed in 1928; became city in 1946, absorbing town of Voroshilovski. Renamed Ugleuralsk in 1951.

Polovinnoye (–vē'nŭyŭ), village (1939 pop. 2,551), SE Kurgan oblast, Russian SFSR, near Kazakh SSR border, 40 mi. SSW of Lebyazhye; flour mill, metalworks.

Polovragi, Rumania: see NOVACI.

Polpaico (pōlpī'kō), village (1930 pop. 294), Santiago prov., central Chile, on railroad and 22 mi. NW of Santiago, in agr. area (grain, fruit, livestock); limestone deposits.

Polperro (pŏlpĕ'rō), village, E Cornwall, England, on the Channel, 5 mi. E of Fowey; fishing port, artists' colony.

Pöls (pûls), town (pop. 2,888), Styria, central Austria, 5 mi. NW of Judenburg; lumber, paper mills; cellulose mfg.

Polski Senovets or **Pol'ski Senovets** (pôl'skē sĕnôvĕts'), village (pop. 3,009), Gorna Oryakhovitsa dist., N Bulgaria, 17 mi. NNW of Tirnovo; grain, livestock.

Polski Trambesh or **Pol'ski Trambesh** (trŭmbĕsh'), village (pop. 3,245), Gorna Oryakhovitsa dist., N Bulgaria, on Yantra R. and 20 mi. N of Tirnovo; flour milling; livestock. Formerly Trembesh.

Polson (pōl'sŭn), city (pop. 2,280), ⊙ Lake co., NW Mont., at S end of Flathead L., just NW of Mission Range, 55 mi. N of Missoula; resort; sawmill; dairy products, livestock, fruit. Fish hatchery here. Near by, at issuance of Flathead R. from lake, is Kerr (or Polson) Dam (200 ft. high, 350 ft. long; for power and irrigation; completed 1938). Inc. 1902.

Poltava (pŭltä'vŭ), oblast (□ 13,250; 1946 pop. estimate 2,200,000), central Ukrainian SSR; ⊙ Poltava. In Dnieper Lowland; bounded SW by Dnieper R.; drained by its affluents (Sula, Psel, and Vorskla rivers). Rich agr. region, with sugar beets (NW, center, E), wheat and other grains, pyrethrum, hemp, and mint (W), sunflowers and corn (SE); livestock breeding. Truck produce and orchards near large centers. Rural industry (sugar refining, flour milling) based on agr. products. Mfg. at Poltava, Kremenchug, Lubny, and Zolotonosha. Major rail centers at Grebenkovski, Romodan, and Poltava. Formed 1937.

Poltava, city (1939 pop. 130,305), ⊙ Poltava oblast, Ukrainian SSR, on right bank of Vorskla R. and 180 mi. ESE of Kiev; 49°36'N 34°33'E. Agr. center in rich sugar and wheat region; meat (bacon) packing, flour milling, sunflower-oil extraction; bakery products; clothing mills, machinery works. Agr. and teachers colleges. Has regional historical mus., Shevchenko monument, old monastery. Passed 1667 to Russia. Near by (3 mi. NE) is site of battle of Poltava (1709), which marked defeat of Swedes under Charles XII by Russians under Peter the Great. Homes of Gogol and Korolenko. In Second World War a Rus. air base, held (1941–43) by Germans.

Poltavka (–täf'kŭ). **1** Village, Chelyabinsk oblast, Russian SFSR: see KARTALY. **2** Village (1948 pop. over 2,000), SW Omsk oblast, Russian SFSR, near Kazakh SSR border, 45 mi. SSE of Isil-Kul; metalworks. **3** Village, Nikolayev oblast, Ukrainian SSR: see BASHTANKA.

Poltavskaya, Russian SFSR: see KRASNOARMEISKAYA.

Polton (pōl'tŭn), village, central Midlothian, Scotland, on North Esk R. and 7 mi. SSE of Edinburgh; paper milling, coal mining.

Poltoratsk, Turkmen SSR: see ASHKHABAD, city.

Poltsamaa or **Pyltsamaa**, Est. *Põltsamaa* (pŭlt'sämä), Ger. *Oberpahlen*, city (pop. 2,609), central Estonia, 33 mi. NW of Tartu and on Poltsamaa R. (influx of L. Vortsjarv; 72 mi. long); road hub; agr. market (fodder, livestock).

Polubny (pô'lo͝obnē), Czech *Polubný*, village (pop. 2,890), N Bohemia, Czechoslovakia, in the Isergebirge, on railroad, on Jizera R. and 17 mi. E of Liberec, on Pol. border; glassmaking; lumbering.

Poludino (pŭlo͞o'dyĭnŭ), village (1948 pop. over 2,000), N North Kazakhstan oblast, Kazakh SSR, on Trans-Siberian RR (Yarmy station) and 30 mi. E of Petropavlovsk; cattle; metalworks. Until 1937, Poludeno.

Polunochnoye (pŭlo͞onôch'nē), town (1943 pop. over 500), N Sverdlovsk oblast, Russian SFSR, 13 mi. N (under jurisdiction) of Ivdel; rail spur terminus; manganese mining.

Polur (pō'lo͞or), town (pop. 13,164), North Arcot dist., E central Madras, India, on Cheyyar R. and 28 mi. S of Vellore; trade center for peanuts, sesame, millet, and for products (sandalwood, tanbark, tamarind, nux vomica, hemp narcotics) of Javadi Hills (W).

Polvar River, Iran: see PULVAR RIVER.

Polyaigos or **Poliaigos** (both: pôlē'ägôs), Lat. *Polyaegos* (pŏlē-ē'gŭs), Aegean island (□ 7; pop. 10) in the Cyclades, Greece, off NE Melos isl.; 36°47'N 24°37'E. Also called Polinos or Polivos.

Polyarny or **Polyarnyy** (pŭlyär'nē), city (1939 pop. over 2,000), NW Murmansk oblast, Russian SFSR, on Kola Gulf, on Kola Peninsula, on rail spur from Kola and 20 mi. NNE of Murmansk; ice-free naval base; fisheries, lumber mills. Polar biological station. Founded 1895; administrative center of Kola Peninsula until 1921. Called Aleksandrovsk until 1930s; became city in 1939.

Polybotus, Turkey: see BOLVADIN.

Polychnitos or **Polikhnitos** (both: pôlēkh'nĭtôs), town (pop. 6,667) on S Lesbos isl., Greece, 19 mi. W of Mytilene; olive oil, wines; sulphur springs.

Polygyros or **Poliyiros** (both: pôlē'yĭrôs), town (pop. 4,243), ⊙ Chalcidice nome, Macedonia, Greece, 30 mi. SE of Salonika; trading center for wheat; olive oil; wine; timber. Also spelled Poligyros and Polyghyros.

Polykandros, Greece: see PHOLEGANDROS.

Polykastron or **Polikastron** (both: pôlĭ'kästrôn), town (pop. 4,176), Kilkis nome, Macedonia, Greece, on railroad, on Vardar R. (opposite Axioupolis), and 16 mi. W of Kilkis; cotton, tobacco, silk, rice. Formerly Karasouli, later Maurosouli (Mavrosouli).

Polynesia (pŏlĭnē'zhŭ, –shŭ) [Gr.,=many islands] (□ c.10,000), one of 3 main divisions of Pacific isls., in central and SE Pacific; includes Hawaii, Samoa, Tonga, Tokelau, and Tubuai, Tuamotu, Society, Marquesas, Cook, Ellice, Easter isls. No metal ores, poor mineral resources. Isls. are largely summits of high volcanic mts. Some are low coral isls. Climate is either tropical or subtropical. Inhabitants are mixture of Negroid, Mongoloid, and Caucasian stock. Ethnologically, but not geographically, Polynesia embraces New Zealand, whose Maori inhabitants are of Polynesian stock.

Polzin, Bad, Poland: see POLCZYN ZDROJ.

Poma, La, Argentina: see LA POMA.

Pomabamba, Bolivia: see AZURDUY.

Pomabamba (pōmäbäm'bä), city (pop. 2,568), ⊙ Pomabamba prov. (□ 2,151; pop. 71,392), Ancash dept., W central Peru, on E slopes of Cordillera Blanca, 50 mi. N of Huarás; alt. 10,059 ft. Agr. products (grain, corn, alfalfa). Silver, lead, coal found near by.

Pomacanchi (pōmäkän'chē), town (pop. 2,715), Cuzco dept., S Peru, 45 mi. SSE of Cuzco; corn, beets; mfg. of woolen goods.

Pomacocha (pōmäkō'chä). **1** Town, Amazonas dept., Peru: see FLORIDA. **2** Village (pop. 54), Junín dept., central Peru, in Cordillera Occidental of the Andes, on Yauli R. (dam) and 21 mi. SW of La Oroya; alt. 14,764 ft. Site of reservoir feeding hydroelectric plants at PACHACHACA and LA OROYA.

Pomahuaca (pōmäwä'kä), village (pop. 109), Cajamarca dept., NW Peru, in Cordillera Occidental; near Huancabamba R., 36 mi. WSW of Jaén; wheat, sugar cane, corn; cattle raising.

Pomaia (pômä'yä), village (pop. 371), Pisa prov., Tuscany, central Italy, 15 mi. SE of Leghorn; cementworks.

Pomalca (pōmäl'kä), village (pop. 6,101), Lambayeque dept., NW Peru, on coastal plain, on Lambayeque R. (irrigation), on railroad and 5 mi. E of Chiclayo. Sugar-milling center; alfalfa and carob pastures; cattle raising.

Pomán (pōmän'), village (pop. estimate 1,000), ⊙ Pomán dept. (□ 2,393; pop. 5,811), S Catamarca prov., Argentina, 27 mi. W of Catamarca, on railroad to Andalgalá; limestone processing, cattle raising.

Pomarance (pômärän'chĕ), town (pop. 1,547), Pisa prov., Tuscany, central Italy, 7 mi. S of Volterra, in important salt-mining and boric-acid-producing region; cementworks.

Pomarão (pōomŭrä'ō), village (pop. 318), Beja dist., S Portugal, on the Guadiana just above influx of Chanza R. (Sp. border), and 37 mi. SE of Beja; transshipping point of copper, brought by mining railroad from Mina de São Domingos, onto river barges.

Pomarepe, Cerro de, Chile-Bolivia: see PAYACHATA, NEVADOS DE.

Pomaria (pōmâ'rēŭ), town (pop. 251), Newberry co., NW central S.C., 27 mi. NW of Columbia; lumber. Just E is Parr Shoals hydroelectric dam in Broad R.

Pomarico (pômä'rēkô), town (pop. 5,100), Matera prov., Basilicata, S Italy, 11 mi. SSW of Matera, in cotton-growing, sheep-raising region.

Pomata (pōmä'tä), town (pop. 1,216), Puno dept., SE Peru, on S shore of L. Titicaca and 45 mi. SE of Puno (connected by road); alt. 13,038 ft.; potatoes, quinoa, barley, livestock.

Pomaz (pô'mäz), Hung. *Pomáz*, town (pop. 6,252), Pest-Pilis-Solt-Kiskun co., N central Hungary, 10 mi. N of Budapest; thread mfg. Slovak pop. here; vineyards, poultry raising.

Pomba, city, Brazil: see RIO POMBA.

Pombachi, Tadzhik SSR: see KOMSOMOLABAD.

Pombal (põmbäl'), city (pop. 3,713), W Paraíba, NE Brazil, on railroad and 50 mi. E of Cajàzeiras; cotton, sugar, fruit (pineapples, bananas, pumpkins).

Pombal, town (pop. 2,350), Leiria dist., W central Portugal, on railroad and 16 mi. NE of Leiria; processing of forest products (resins, tar-pitch), sawmilling. Has remains of 11th-cent. castle (residence of the marquês de Pombal after 1777), and a Romanesque church rebuilt from a Moorish mosque.

Pombalinho (põmbŭlē'nyo͞o), village (pop. 1,112), Santarém dist., central Portugal, 10 mi. NE of Santarém; ceramics.

Pomba River (põm'bŭ), SE Minas Gerais, Brazil, rises in the Serra da Mantiqueira near Rio Pomba, flows 85 mi. ESE, past Cataguases, to the Paraíba (left bank) below Santo Antônio de Pádua; followed by railroad.

Pombas (põm'bŭsh), town (pop. 5,831), Cape Verde Isls., on NE shore of Santo Antão Isl., 4 mi. SE of Ribeira Grande; 17°9'N 25'2'W; sugar cane, citrus. Also called Paúl.

Pombetsu, Japan: see HOMBETSU.

Pombos, Ilha dos, Brazil: see ILHA DOS POMBOS.

Pomègues, France: see RATONNEAU.

Pomerania (pŏmŭrā'nēŭ), Ger. *Pommern* (pô'mĕrn), Pol. *Pomorze* (pômô'zhĕ), region of N central Europe, extending along the Baltic Sea from a line W of Stralsund, Germany, to the Vistula R. in Poland and including Rügen isl. From 1919 to 1939 Pomerania was divided among Germany, Poland, and the Free City of Danzig. The German part constituted the Prussian prov. of Pomerania (□ 14,830; 1939 pop. 2,393,844; ⊙ Stettin); the Polish part formed prov. of POMERELIA. After 1945 all the part (□ c.2,800) of former Prussian Pomerania W of the Oder (but excluding Stettin) was inc. into Ger. state of Mecklenburg; the remaining and larger part was transferred to Pol. administration and organized ultimately into the provs. of SZCZECIN (□ 4,869; pop. 307,568; ⊙ Stettin) and KOSZALIN (□ 6,799; pop. 584,999; ⊙ Köslin), with part of it going as Lauenburg (Lebork) dist. (□ 498; pop. 46,305) to Gdansk prov. Minor adjustments of administrative boundaries were made after 1945. Pomerania is a fertile agr. lowland, part of North German Plain. Region is dotted with numerous lakes; drained by Oder, Peene, Uecker, Ina (Ihna), Rega, and Prosnica (Persante) rivers. Coast line deeply indented by Stettin Lagoon, expansion of Oder estuary, separated from the Baltic by Usedom (Uznam) and Wolin (Wollin) isls. Offshore, opposite Stralsund, is Rügen isl. Principal Pomeranian seaports, notably engaged in trade with Scandinavia, are Stralsund and Sassnitz (fishing center) in Germany, and Stettin (major port for Czechoslovak transit traffic) and Odra in Poland. Sassnitz and Odra are termini of train ferries to Sweden. Other important Pomeranian towns are Greifswald, Anklam, Demmin in Germany, and Swinemünde (Swinoujscie), Kolberg (Kolobrzeg), Köslin (Koszalin), Stargard, Szczecinek (Neustettin), and Stolp (Slupsk) in Poland. Numerous seaside resorts and fishing villages line the coast. Stock raising, forestry. Principal crops: rye, potatoes, oats, barley, wheat, sugar beets. Shipbuilding, metallurgy, sugar refining, food processing, paper and pulp milling, woodworking are chief industries. In 10th cent. A.D., at beginning of its recorded history, Pomerania was inhabited by Slavic tribes. Conquered by Poles, it became independent duchy in early 11th cent., but reverted to Pol. control in 12th cent. and was Christianized. Country was split into 2 principalities; duke of W Pomerania became (1181) a prince of the Holy Roman Empire and severed his ties with Poland. E Pomerania, henceforth known as POMERELIA, became independent in 1227 and was to remain an historical and political entity apart from Pomerania. In 16th cent. dukes of Pomerania accepted the Reformation. In Thirty Years War imperial forces under Wallenstein occupied (1628) Pomerania with consent of ruling duke; city of Stralsund, however, resisted with Danish aid and precipitated (1630) Swedish intervention in the war. Under Peace of Westphalia, 1648, country was divided: Hither Pomerania, Ger. *Vorpommern*, in W part of country and including Stettin, Stralsund, and Rügen isl., went to Sweden; Farther Pomerania, Ger. *Hinterpommern*, the E part, including Stargard, went to Brandenburg (after 1701, Prussia). After Northern War Sweden lost (1720) about half of Hither Pomerania to Prussia, but retained Stralsund. Napoleon I overran Swedish Pomerania, but restored it in peace (1809) with Sweden. In Treaty of Kiel (1814) Sweden exchanged Pomerania with Denmark in return for Norway; at Congress of Vienna (1815) Denmark ceded its share of Pomerania to Prussia in return for duchy of Lauenburg. In 1937 Ger. prov. of Grenzmark Posen–West Prussia (□ 2,978; pop. 332,485; ⊙ Schneidemühl), which had been created (1922) from sections of former provs. of Posen and West Prussia remaining in Germany after 1919, was reduced to district status and inc. into Pomerania prov. After Second World War, with the partition of Pomerania, the Ger. pop. of the Pol. section was expelled.

Pomerelia (pŏmĕrē'lyŭ), Ger. *Pommerellen* (pôm"-ŭrĕ'lŭn), Pol. *Pomorze* (pômô'zhĕ), region, N central Europe, after 1945 divided bet. Pol. provs. of GDANSK (□ 4,141; pop. 732,150; ⊙ Danzig) and BYDGOSZCZ (□ 8,106; pop. 1,457,653; ⊙ Bydgoszcz). Undulating lowland region, it borders N on the Baltic and the Gulf of Danzig, and includes Hel Peninsula. In its NW part it includes ethnological region of KASSUBIA. Fishing, agr. (rye, potatoes, oats, wheat), stock raising, are principal occupations. Pomerelia includes port cities of Danzig, Gdynia, and Elbing (Elblag), and industrial cities of Bydgoszcz, Torun, Inowroclaw, and Grudziadz. Until 1227 a part of POMERANIA, it became independent, but was annexed (1295) to Poland. Ceded 1308 to the Teutonic Knights, who incorporated it with their domain in East Prussia. Together with Danzig it was restored (1466) to Poland by Treaty of Torun. With 1st partition (1772) of Poland it passed to Prussia and was constituted into prov. of WEST PRUSSIA. In 1919 W part of Pomerelia came to Poland and was formed into prov. of Pomerelia, Pol. *Pomorze*, (□ 6,335; 1931 pop. 1,080,138; ⊙ Bydgoszcz), constituting the Polish Corridor. Danzig dist. became a free city, while E part of Pomerelia, including Marienburg and Elbing, were inc. with East Prussia. Entire territory was annexed (1939) to Germany. Placed 1945 under Pol. administration, it was inc. into integral Pol. territory and constituted into provs. of Gdansk and Pomorze (renamed Bydgoszcz prov. in 1950). Ger. pop. was expelled.

Pomerol (pômŭrôl'), village (pop. 284), Gironde dept., SW France, 2 mi. NE of Libourne; wine-growing.

Pomeroon River (pŏ"mŭrōōn'), N Br. Guiana, rises at 6°55'N 59°W, flows NE to Charity, where it turns NNW and flows to the Atlantic 18 mi. NW of Charity; 80 mi. long. Drains fertile area where coconuts are grown on large scale. Navigable for c.50 mi. to above Pickersgill.

Pomeroy (pŏ'mŭroi), town (pop. 365), E central Co. Tyrone, Northern Ireland, 9 mi. NW of Dungannon; agr. market (cattle; flax, oats, potatoes).

Pomeroy. **1** Town (pop. 868), Calhoun co., central Iowa, 26 mi. WNW of Fort Dodge, in agr. area. **2** Village (pop. 3,656), ⊙ Meigs co., SE Ohio, on the Ohio and c.40 mi. SW of Marietta; iron and steel foundries; mfg. of chemicals, bromides; coal and salt mines; hardwood timber. Settled in early-19th cent.; inc. 1840. **3** City (pop. 1,775), ⊙ Garfield co., SE Wash., 45 mi. NE of Walla Walla; trade center for agr. area; wheat, livestock, fruit, truck. Settled 1863, inc. 1886.

Pomezia (pômā'tsyä), village, Roma prov., Latium, central Italy, 15 mi. S of Rome. Agr. settlement, established 1939 in conjunction with reclamation of Pontine Marshes.

Pomfret, England: see PONTEFRACT.

Pomfret (pŏm'frĭt, pŭm'–). **1** Town (pop. 2,018), Windham co., NE Conn., on Quinebaug R. and 16 mi. NE of Willimantic; agr., resorts. Pomfret School for boys (1894) here. Includes Abington village, with 1 of state's oldest churches (1751) and public libraries (1793). State parks. Settled before 1700, inc. 1713. **2** Town (pop. 586), Windsor co., E Vt., 24 mi. ENE of Rutland; includes South Pomfret village.

Pomigliano d'Arco (pômēlyä'nô där'kô), town (pop. 11,505), Napoli prov., Campania, S Italy, 8 mi. NE of Naples, in agr. region (fruit, vegetables, grapes).

Pommard (pômär'), village (pop. 846), Côte-d'Or dept., E central France, on SE slope of the Côte d'Or, 2 mi. SW of Beaune; noted Burgundy vineyards.

Pomme de Terre River. **1** (pŭm' dŭ târ") In W Minn., rises in small lake E of Fergus Falls, flows 100 mi. S, past Morris and Appleton, to Minnesota R. at SE end of Marsh L. Used to generate power at Appleton. Passes through Pomme de Terre L. (4 mi. long, 1 mi. wide) in Grant co. **2** (pŭm' dŭ tär", pŭm' lŭ tär") In central Mo.; headwaters rise in Greene and Webster counties, joining S of Bolivar; flows 113 mi. N, through Ozarks, to L. of the Ozarks at its W extremity.

Pommerellen, region, Europe: see POMERELIA.

Pommern, region, Europe: see POMERANIA.

Pommersches Haff, Germany and Poland: see STETTIN LAGOON.

Pomo, island, Yugoslavia: see JABUKA ISLAND.

Pomona (pŭmō'nŭ, pō–) or **Mainland,** island (□ 189, including surrounding small isls.; pop. 13,352), largest of the Orkneys, Scotland, 18 mi. N of mainland of Caithness; 25 mi. long, 17 mi. wide; rises to 881 ft. Coastline is deeply indented by Scapa Bay (SE), inlet of SCAPA FLOW, and by Wide Firth (NE), 5 mi. long. W coast has precipitous cliffs; interior is hilly, with moorland and several large lakes (NW). Valleys are fertile. Chief town is KIRKWALL, ⊙ Orkney co., on Kirkwall Bay, inlet of Wide Firth. Near by are 2 airfields. On SW coast is town of STROMNESS. Other villages are Orphir, on S coast, and Scapa, port for Scapa Flow naval anchorage. At SE extremity is promontory of Rose Ness, site of lighthouse (58°52'N 2°49'W). Many old Norse customs survive on Pomona. There are numerous Pictish remains: mounds, underground dwellings, circles, and standing stones; most famous are MAESHOWE and the Standing Stones of STENNESS. On W coast, 6 mi. N of Stromness, are excavations of Stone Age village of Skara Brae.

Pomona. **1** City (pop. 35,405), Los Angeles co., S Calif., 25 mi. E of Los Angeles, and adjoining Claremont; (seat of Pomona Col.); cans, ships citrus fruit; dairying; mfg. of clay, metal, and paper products; oil refining. Seat of large co. fair and Mt. San Antonio Col. Kellogg horse farm is known for Arabian horses. Founded 1875, inc. 1888. **2** or **Pomona Park,** town (pop. 443), Putnam co., N Fla., 11 mi. SSE of Palatka, on small lake; citrus-fruit packing. **3** City (pop. 453), Franklin co., E Kansas, near Marais des Cygnes R., 10 mi. W of Ottawa, in livestock and grain region. **4** Textile village (1940 pop. 2,093), Guilford co., N central N.C., just W of Greensboro.

Pomoravlje (pômô'rävlyĕ), region, E Serbia, Yugoslavia; extends N-S along Morava R. course. Largely agr. (hemp, flax, sugar beets, corn, potatoes, plums, tobacco, wine); silkworm growing, swine raising. Chief towns: Paracin, Svetozarevo, Pozarevac.

Pomoriye (pômô'rē-ĕ), anc. *Anchialus*, city (pop. 4,721), Burgas dist., E Bulgaria, port on Gulf of Burgas of Black Sea, on rail spur, and 10 mi. ENE of Burgas. Salt-producing and fishing center; wine distilling. Saltworks on Pomoriye L. (□ 2.5), an adjoining salt lagoon (N). Summer resort (mineral springs). Founded (784) by Byzantine empress Irene on site of anc. Roman settlement. A commercial center in Middle Ages; came under Turkish rule (15th–19th cent.), when it was called Ahiolu or Akhiolu. Until 1934, Ankhialo or Anhialo.

Pomoryany (pŭmŭryä'nē), Pol. *Pomorzany* (pômôzhä'nē), town (1931 pop. 4,304), SE Lvov oblast, Ukrainian SSR, on Zolotaya Lipa R. and 11 mi. S of Zolochev; agr. processing (cereals, potatoes). Has old town hall, 14th-cent. castle.

Pomorze, region, Poland: see POMERANIA; POMERELIA.

Pomorze, province, Poland: see BYDGOSZCZ, province.

Pomorze Zachodnie, province, Poland: see SZCZECIN, province.

Pomoshnaya (pô'mŭshnĭŭ), town (1939 pop. over 500), SW Kirovograd oblast, Ukrainian SSR, 28 mi. NE of Pervomaisk, on highway to Uman; rail junction, metalworks. Kaolin quarries.

Pomozdino (pŭmôz'dyĭnŭ), village (1939 pop. over 500), S Komi Autonomous SSR, Russian SFSR, on navigable Vychegda R. and 110 mi. ENE of Syktyvkar; flax; fur trapping. Limestone deposits.

Pompaelo, Spain: see PAMPLONA.

Pompano Beach (pŏm'pŭnō), city (pop. 5,682), Broward co., S Fla., on Atlantic coast, 8 mi. N of Fort Lauderdale; vegetable-packing center. Settled c.1900, inc. 1907.

Pompanoosuc, Vt.: see NORWICH.

Pompéia (pōmpā'ŭ), city (pop. 7,160), W central São Paulo, Brazil, on railroad and 17 mi. WNW of Marília, in pioneer agr. zone; butter processing; cotton, coffee, grain.

Pompeii (pŏmpā'), Ital. *Pompei*, anc. city of Campania, S Italy, whose extensive ruins lie near S foot of Vesuvius and the Bay of Naples, 14 mi. SE of Naples. Damaged by earthquake in A.D. 63; in A.D. 79 it was buried (together with Herculaneum and Stabiae) under beds (c.10-20 ft. thick) of pumice, cinders, and ashes by 1st recorded eruption of Vesuvius. At the time of its destruction, when an estimated 2,000 persons perished (perhaps 10% of the total population), the city was situated on the navigable Sarnus (modern Sarno) which now flows c.½ mi. to the S. Site of the forgotten city was discovered in 1748, and in 1763 systematic excavations were begun. The ruins, since uncovered, were well preserved and constitute a chief source of knowledge of anc. domestic life. Built in the form of an irregular oval, city was c.2 mi. in circumference and enclosed by walls entered by 8 gates. It had numerous lava-paved streets (14–24 ft. wide), terraced one- and two-storied houses, shops, stately mansions richly decorated with murals, mosaics, and sculptures, temples, theaters (one accommodating 5,000 persons), and an amphitheater (at SE end of town) which seated 20,000. Bomb damage in Second World War was widespread but limited in severity. The modern town of Pompei (pop. 5,215) lies just E of the ruins; produces macaroni and packing boxes. Church of Santa Maria del Rosario contains a miraculous image of the Virgin visited annually by thousands of pilgrims.

Pompeiopolis, Turkey: see SOLI.

Pompelle, Fort de la, France: see NOGENT-L'ABBESSE.

Pomperaug River (pŏm'pŭrôg"), W Conn., rises near Bethlehem, flows c.25 mi. S to the Housatonic in Southbury town.

Pompey (pōpā'), town (pop. 3,944), Meurthe-et-Moselle dept., NE France, on the Moselle, at mouth of Meurthe R., on Marne-Rhine Canal and 6 mi. NNW of Nancy; steel milling.

Pompton Lakes, borough (pop. 4,654), Passaic co., NE N.J., near Pompton L. (c.2 mi. long), 9 mi. NW of Paterson; mfg. (explosives, textile products), dairying. Has several pre-Revolutionary houses. Settled 1682 by Dutch, inc. 1895.

Pompton Plains, village (1940 pop. 1,273), Morris co., N N.J., near Pequannock R., 3 mi. S of Pompton Lakes borough, on site of a prehistoric lake.

Pompton River, NE N.J., formed S of Pompton Lakes borough by junction of Ramapo R. (issues from Pompton L.) and Pequannock R.; flows c.8 mi. S to Passaic R.

Pomuch (pōmōōch'), town (pop. 1,724), Campeche, SE Mexico, on NW Yucatan Peninsula, on railroad and 4 mi. SW of Hecelchakán; sugar cane, tobacco, henequen, fruit, livestock.

Ponafidin, Japan: see TORI-SHIMA.

Ponaganset River (pŏnŭgăn'sĭt), N central R.I., small stream rising in W Glocester town, where dam forms Ponaganset Reservoir (c.1.5 mi. long); flows 10 mi. generally SE, through Foster town (where it is dammed to form Barden Reservoir, c.2 mi. long), to W arm of SCITUATE RESERVOIR in Scituate town. Formerly joined Moswansicut R. to form North Branch of Pawtuxet R. in area now flooded by reservoir.

Ponani, India: see PONNANI.

Ponape (pŏ'nŭpä, pō'nä–), volcanic island (□ 129; pop. 5,735), most important of Senyavin Isls., E Caroline Isls., W Pacific, 6°55'N 158°15'E; circular, 13 mi. in diameter. Surrounded by 23 small basalt isls. and 15 coral isls. Has 2 large rivers; highest peak is Mt. Tolocolme (2,579 ft.). Bauxite, iron, iron sulphate. Produces copra, dried bonito, native handicraft. Ruins of anc. stone walls and dikes. In Second World War, isl. was Jap. air base; surrendered after Jap. defeat. Ponape dist. (□ 174; pop. 9,642) includes ANT, KAPINGAMARANGI, KUSAIE, MOKIL, NGATIK, NUKUORO, OROLUK, PAKIN, PINGELAP. Formerly Ascension Isl.

Ponazyrevo (pŭnŭzĭr'yĭvŭ), town (1939 pop. over 500), E Kostroma oblast, Russian SFSR, on railroad and 29 mi. E of Sharya; lumbering.

Ponca (pŏng'kŭ), city (pop. 893), ⊙ Dixon co., NE Nebr., 15 mi. WNW of Sioux City, Iowa, and on Missouri R.; livestock, grain. Near by is state park.

Ponca City, city (pop. 20,180), Kay co., N Okla., c.50 mi. ENE of Enid, near Arkansas R.; trade and mfg. center for oil-producing and agr. (grain, alfalfa), stock-raising, and dairying area. Large oil refineries, grain elevators; mfg. of packed meat, dairy products, flour, feed, steel tanks, metal products, airplanes, clothing, mattresses. Ponca Indian Reservation is c.5 mi. S. L. Ponca (water supply; fishing, boating; 5 mi. long) is 3 mi. NE. Founded 1893 after opening of Cherokee Strip; inc. 1902.

Ponca Creek, S S.Dak. and N Nebr.; rises in Tripp co., S.Dak.; flows c.80 mi. SE to Missouri R. near Niobrara, Nebr.

Ponce (pōn'sä), city (pop. 99,492), S Puerto Rico, 3 mi. from its port section PLAYA DE PONCE, 45 mi. SW of San Juan; 18°1'N 66°37'W. Third largest city of the isl., with rail and road communication to all parts. Commercial and industrial center in fertile agr. region (sugar cane on large scale; also coffee, fruit, cattle); alcohol and rum distilling, sugar refining, brewing, fruit canning, dairying, diamond cutting; mfg. of cotton and rayon textiles, straw hats, needlework, pearl necklaces, candy, shoes. Exports through Playa de Ponce about 40% of Puerto Rico's sugar. Port of entry. Has old colonial mansions, beautiful plazas and gardens, Ponce Fort (1760), cathedral, city hall, theater, airport, and fine residential sections. Sugar mills, ironworks, and a cement plant are in the outskirts. Ponce is seat of a senatorial dist. A U.S. military reservation is SW.

Ponce de Leon (pŏns' dŭ lē'ŭn), village (1940 pop. 562), Holmes co., NW Fla., 17 mi. W of Bonifay. Near by are Ponce de Leon Springs, one of many named for the Spanish explorer.

Ponce de Leon Inlet, NE Fla., break in E coast barrier beach, 13 mi. SSE of Daytona Beach; connects S end of Halifax R. lagoon and N end of Hillsborough R. lagoon with the Atlantic.

Poncé-sur-le-Loir (pŏsā'-sür-lŭ-lwär'), village (pop. 436), Sarthe dept., W France, on the Loir and 27 mi. SE of Le Mans; mfg. of cigarette paper.

Poncha Pass (pŏn'chŭ) (9,010 ft.), central Colo., in N tip of Sangre de Cristo Mts., just W of Salida. Once used by Indians and mountain men; now crossed by highway leading into San Luis Valley.

Poncha Springs, town (pop. 114), Chaffee co., central Colo., on branch of Arkansas R., bet. Sangre de Cristo and Sawatch mts., and 4 mi. W of Salida; alt. 7,500 ft. Hot mineral springs here. Poncha Pass near by.

Ponchatoula (pŏnshŭtōō'lŭ), town (pop. 4,090), Tangipahoa parish, SE La., 45 mi. E of Baton Rouge; ships strawberries, vegetables, poultry; produces crates, lumber, veneer, brick, food products, beverages. Ponchatoula Beach (resort) is on Tangipahoa R. (E). Settled c.1830, inc. c.1860.

Poncin (pōsē'), village (pop. 583), Ain dept., E France, on the Ain and 12 mi. SE of Bourg; basket making, dairying.

Poncitlán (pōnsētlän′), town (pop. 3,120), Jalisco, central Mexico, on Santiago R. and 35 mi. SE of Guadalajara, N of L. Chapala, on railroad; wheat-growing center.

Pondá (pōndä′), town, central Goa dist., Portuguese India, 13 mi. SE of Pangim; market center for rice, cashew nuts, mangoes.

Pond Creek or **Pondcreek,** city (pop. 1,066), Grant co., N Okla., 19 mi. N of Enid, and on Salt Fork of Arkansas R., in wheat-producing area; alfalfa dehydrating; mfg. of flour, toothbrushes, machine-shop products. Settled c.1889.

Pondera (pŏn″dŭrā′), county (□ 1,643; pop. 6,392), N Mont.; ⊙ Conrad. Agr. area drained by L. Frances and branches of Marias R. Grain, sugar beets, livestock. Part of Lewis and Clark Natl. Forest in W. Formed 1919.

Ponderay (pŏn″dŭrā′), town (pop. 248), Bonner co., N Idaho, near L. Pend Oreille, just N of Sandpoint.

Pondharpur, India: see PANDHARPUR.

Pondicherry (pŏn″dĭchĕ′rē), Fr. *Pondichéry* (pōdē-shārē′), chief settlement (after 1947, officially "free city"; □ 112; pop. 222,572) of Fr. India, consisting of several isolated tracts within South Arcot dist., SE Madras, India, on Coromandel Coast of Bay of Bengal, 90 mi. SSW of Madras; divided into 8 communes. Agr.: rice, sugar cane, oilseeds (mainly peanuts), mangoes, millet. Territorial limits established in 1816.

Pondicherry, city (commune pop. 59,835), ⊙ Fr. India and Pondicherry settlement, port on Coromandel Coast, 85 mi. SSW of Madras; terminus of rail branch from Villupuram, 23 mi. W; trade center; exports oilseeds; mfg. of cotton textiles (mills at industrial suburb of Mudaliarpet), rice and oilseed milling. Religious community (*ashram*) of Sri Aurobindo founded here c.1910. Med. col., law school. Public bldgs. mainly in Louis XIV style. Acquired by French in 1674; site was taken 3 times (1761, 1778, 1793) by English in Anglo-Fr. struggle for power in India.

Pond Inlet, trading post (1943 pop. 179), N Baffin Isl., E Franklin Dist., Northwest Territories, on Eclipse Sound, at W entrance of Pond Inlet (40 mi. long), opposite Bylot Isl.; 72°42′N 78°13′W. Radio station, Royal Canadian Mounted Police post. Site of Anglican and R.C. missions.

Pond Island, Sagadahoc co., SW Maine, small lighthouse isl. at mouth of the Kennebec.

Pondoland (pŏn′dōlănd), district (□ 4,000; total pop. 358,648; native pop. 353,669) of the TRANSKEIAN TERRITORIES, E Cape Prov., U. of So. Afr., bounded by Tembuland (S), Griqualand East (W and N), Natal Prov. (NE), and the Indian Ocean (E); center near 31°15′S 29°15′E; ⊙ Port St. Johns. Mealies, citrus fruit, bananas, tobacco are chief products; dairying, stock raising are carried on. Region near Natal Prov. border is forested. Largely a native reserve, dist. joined (1930) area administered by United Transkeian Territories General Council.

Pond River, W Ky., formed 8 mi. SE of Madisonville by junction of headstreams, flows c.50 mi. generally N to Green R. 6 mi. W of Calhoun.

Ponds, Island of (10 mi. long, 9 mi. wide), just off SE Labrador; 53°26′N 55°54′W. At NE extremity is fishing settlement of DOMINO HARBOUR.

Poneloya (pōnäloi′ä), village, León dept., W Nicaragua, 11 mi. SW of León (linked by road); major Pacific seaside resort; bathing beach, hotels.

Ponérihouen (pōnārēwĕn′), village (dist. pop. 1,846), New Caledonia, on E coast, 105 mi. NW of Nouméa; agr. products.

Poneto (pōnē′tō, pōnĕ′tō), town (pop. 244), Wells co., E Ind., 7 mi. SSW of Bluffton, in agr. area.

Ponevezh, Lithuania: see PANEVEZYS.

Ponezhukai or **Ponezhukay** (pŭnyĕzhōōkī′), village (1939 pop. over 2,000), W Adyge Autonomous Oblast, Krasnodar Territory, Russian SFSR, 20 mi. ESE of Krasnodar; flour mill; wheat, sunflowers, tobacco.

Ponfeigh (pŏnfā′), town in Carmichael parish (pop. 1,794), central Lanark, Scotland, on Douglas Water and 4 mi. S of Lanark; coal mining.

Ponferrada (pōmfĕrä′dhä), city (pop. 7,668), Leon prov., NW Spain, on Sil R. and 50 mi. W of Leon; communications center, terminus of mining railroad from Villablino. Metalworking, coal-briquette mfg.; makes also ceramics, candy, soda water; flour mills. Agr. trade (wine, cereals, livestock); lumber. Sulphur springs. Coal and iron mines near by. Has Gothic church, 17th-cent. town hall, remains of castle of Knights Templars.

Pong, Ban, Thailand: see BAN PONG.

Pongaroa (pŏng-gŭrō′ŭ), township (pop. 260), ⊙ Akitio co. (□ 321; pop. 1,005), S N.Isl., New Zealand, 95 mi. NE of Wellington; sheep.

Pongo, Rio, Fr. West Africa: see RIO PONGO.

Pongo de Manseriche, Peru: see MANSERICHE, PONGO DE.

Pongola River (pŏng-gō′lŭ), N Natal, U. of So. Afr., and S Mozambique, rises in Drakensberg range N of Utrecht, flows E through Zululand, then N, crossing into Mozambique (where it is called Maputo R.), to Delagoa Bay 14 mi. SSE of Lourenço Marques; c.350 mi. long. On upper course are irrigation works.

Pong Tamale (pông′ tämä′lā, tŭmä′lē), town, Northern Territories, N central Gold Coast, on road and 18 mi. N of Tamale. Experimental livestock station.

Pongwe (pông′gwā), village, Tanga prov., NE Tanganyika, on railroad and 10 mi. WSW of Tanga; sisal, cotton, copra.

Ponholz (pōn′hôlts), village (pop. 1,651), Upper Palatinate, E central Bavaria, Germany, 10 mi. N of Regensburg; briquette mfg.; lignite mining.

Ponhook Lake (pŏn′hŏŏk) (6 mi. long, 3 mi. wide), W N.S., 16 mi. WSW of Bridgewater. Fed and drained by Medway R. Coal mined near by.

Poniec (pô′nyĕts), Ger. *Punitz* (pōō′nĭts), town (1946 pop. 2,342), Poznan prov., W Poland, 11 mi. SE of Leszno; flour milling, sawmilling; cattle trade.

Poninka (pŭnyĕn′kŭ), town (1926 pop. 2,096), NE Kamenets-Podolski oblast, Ukrainian SSR, 21 mi. E of Shepetovka; paper mill. Until 1930s, spelled Paninka.

Ponino (pŭnyē′nŭ), village (1926 pop. 252), N Udmurt Autonomous SSR, Russian SFSR, 9 mi. NE of Glazov; flax processing.

Ponizovye or **Ponizov'ye** (pŭnyē′zŭvyĭ), village (1939 pop. over 500), W Smolensk oblast, Russian SFSR, on Kasplya R. and 16 mi. W of Demidov; flax processing.

Ponley (pôn′lā′), town, Kompong Chhnang prov., central Cambodia, near S outlet of Tonle Sap, 65 mi. NNW of Pnompenh; trade in dried fish.

Ponnagyun (pōn′näjōōn), village, Akyab dist., Lower Burma, in the Arakan, on Kaladan R. (landing) and 15 mi. NNE of Akyab.

Ponnaiyar River (pŏn-nī′yär), in E Mysore and SE Madras, India, rises on Deccan Plateau SE of Chik Ballapur, flows S and SE past Kaveripatnam and Tirukkoyilur to Coromandel Coast of Bay of Bengal N of Cuddalore; c.250 mi. long. In lower course, linked with Gadilam R. Also called Penner or Southern Penner (sometimes spelled Pennar).

Ponnamaravati (pōn-nŭmŭrä′vŭtē), town (pop. 11,829), Trichinopoly dist., S Madras, India, 20 mi. WSW of Pudukkottai; hand-loom cotton and silk weaving; millet, rice. Also spelled Ponnamaravathy.

Ponnampet or **Ponampet** (pō′nŭmpăt), village (pop. 1,087), S Coorg, India, 24 mi. SSE of Mercara; rice (terrace farming), oranges; coffee estates. Teak and sandalwood plantations (E).

Ponnani (pŏnä′nē), town (pop 17,838), Malabar dist., SW Madras, India, port (mainly coastal trade) on Arabian Sea, at Ponnani R. mouth, 35 mi. SSE of Calicut; ships coir, copra, cashew nuts; sardine-oil extraction; rice milling. Moslem cultural center (mopla religious col.; numerous mosques). Pop. over 80% Moslem. Also spelled Ponani.

Ponnani River, in Malabar dist., SW Madras, India, rises in headstreams in Western Ghats at N side of Palghat Gap, SW of Coimbatore; flows c.100 mi. W past Palghat, Ottappalam, and Shoranur to Arabian Sea at Ponnani. Receives a branch from Anaimalai Hills (S) at point 6 mi. W of Palghat. Also spelled Ponani.

Ponneri (pŏ′nărē), village, Chingleput dist., E Madras, India, 15 mi. NNW of Madras; rice, tamarind.

Ponnuru (pŏnōō′rōō), town (pop., including adjacent rail station of Nidubrolu, 13,370), Guntur dist., NE Madras, India, in Kistna R. delta, 17 mi. SSE of Guntur; rice milling, tanning; tobacco. Also spelled Ponnur or Ponur.

Ponoi or **Ponoy** (pŭnoi′), agr. village (1926 pop. 291), E Murmansk oblast, Russian SFSR, port on short Ponoi R., 10 mi. above its mouth on White Sea, on Kola Peninsula and 245 mi. SE of Murmansk; fisheries.

Ponoka (pŭnō′kŭ), town (pop. 1,468), S central Alta., on Battle R. and 20 mi. NNE of Red Deer; hog-shipping center; lumbering, ranching, mixed farming. Site of prov. mental hosp.

Ponomarevka (pŭnŭmär′yĭfkŭ), village (1926 pop. 3,285), NW Chkalov oblast, Russian SFSR, on Dema R. and 30 mi. SE of Abdulino; metalworking; wheat, livestock.

Ponornitsa (pŭnôr′nyĭtsŭ), town (1926 pop. 5,026), E Chernigov oblast, Ukrainian SSR, 25 mi. SW of Novgorod-Severski; hemp.

Ponorogo (pŏnŭrŏ′gō), town (pop. 21,680), E central Java, Indonesia, 50 mi. ESE of Surakarta, at foot of Willis Mts.; trade center for agr. area (sugar, rice, corn, peanuts); paper mills. Sometimes spelled Panarago.

Ponoy, Russian SFSR: see PONOI.

Pons (pōs), town (pop. 2,679), Charente-Maritime dept., W France, on Seugne R. and 12 mi. SSE of Saintes; road center and agr. market; mfg. (railroad equipment, cement, cheese), brandy distilling, tanning. Stone quarries near by. Has 12th-cent. keep and medieval houses. Protestant stronghold in 16th–17th-cent. dismantled by Louis XIII after fall of La Rochelle. Birthplace of Agrippa d'Aubigné.

Pons (pōns), town (pop. 1,464), Lérida prov., NE Spain, near Segre R., 18 mi. NNW of Cervera; cement works; agr. trade (hogs, olive oil, wine, cereals). Urgel Canal (for irrigation) begins near by.

Ponsacco (pônsäk′kô), town (pop. 2,775), Pisa prov., Tuscany, central Italy, near Era R., 13 mi. ESE of Pisa; wine making, furniture mfg., sawmilling.

Pons Aelii, England: see NEWCASTLE-UPON-TYNE.

Ponson Island (pŏnsōn′) (□ 13; 1948 pop. 8,663), in Camotes Isls., Cebu prov., Visayan Isls., Philippines, in Camotes Sea, just NE of Poro Isl., 13 mi. SSW of MacArthur (Ormoc), Leyte; 7 mi. long, 2 mi. wide. Generally low; rises to 726 ft. Coconut growing, fishing. Isl. is coextensive with Pilar municipality.

Pont-à-Celles (pōtäsĕl′), town (pop. 5,051), Hainaut prov., S central Belgium, on Charleroi Canal, 8 mi. NNW of Charleroi, in coal-mining, steel-milling region.

Pontacq (pōtäk′), village (pop. 1,724), Basses-Pyrénées dept., SW France, 10 mi. WSW of Tarbes; shoe mfg. (chiefly ski boots), horse breeding, winegrowing.

Ponta d' Areia, Brazil: see CARAVELAS.

Ponta Delgada (pōn′tŭ dĕlgä′dŭ), district (□ 325; 1950 pop. 176,707) of E Azores, with SÃO MIGUEL ISLAND and SANTA MARIA ISLAND; ⊙ Ponta Delgada (on São Miguel Isl.).

Ponta Delgada, largest city (pop. 21,048) of the Azores, ⊙ Ponte Delgada dist., on S shore of SÃO MIGUEL ISLAND, 900 mi. W of Lisbon; 37°44′N 25°40′W. Has archipelago's best (artificial) harbor, sheltered by a breakwater almost 1 mi. long, and accommodating ships drawing 32 ft. Also the leading commercial center of the Azores, exporting pineapples, oranges, tea, wine, cereals, vegetables, and dairy produce. Sugar refining, alcohol distilling, tea and chicory processing, mfg. of flour and tobacco products, soap. Trade in whale sperm-oil. Ponta Delgada is a transatlantic port of call, cable station, and seaplane base. Also a winter resort, surrounded by fine gardens and pineapple plantations. Ponta Delgada outgrew Vila Franca do Campo (isl.'s 1st capital) during 15th cent. and became its chief city in 1540. Damaged 1839 by tidal wave. Hq. of U.S. Atlantic fleet in First World War. Important Allied naval base during Second World War.

Ponta de Pedras (pōn′tŭ dĭ pĕ′dräs), city (pop. 1,255), E Pará, Brazil, near SE shore of Marajó isl. in Amazon delta, 28 mi. W of Belém; cattle and horse raising.

Ponta dos Índios (pōn′tŭ dōōs ēn′dyōōs), town, northernmost Amapá territory, N Brazil, on right bank of Oiapoque R. (Fr. Guiana border) near its mouth on the Atlantic, and 80 mi. SSE of Cayenne.

Ponta do Sol (pōn′tŭ dōō sôl′), town, Cape Verde Isls., at northernmost tip of Santo Antão Isl. and of the archipelago, 2 mi. NW of Ribeira Grande; 17°12′N 25°6′W; lighthouse; anchorage.

Ponta do Sol, town (pop. 204), Madeira, on S coast of Madeira isl., 12 mi. W of Funchal; dairying, tanning, flour milling. Winegrowing in region.

Ponta Grossa (grō′sŭ), city (1950 pop. 44,130), SE central Paraná, Brazil, 60 mi. WNW of Curitiba; rail and road center for hog-raising, lumbering, and agr. area, and distribution point for Paraná hinterland; meat packing, lard mfg., coffee and maté processing, sawmilling, and woodworking. Talc quarries. Agr. experiment station.

Pontailler-sur-Saône (pōtäyā′-sür-sōn′), village (pop. 1,042), Côte-d'Or dept., E central France, on the Saône, near junction of Marne-Saône Canal, and 13 mi. SW of Gray; mfg. of explosives. Also called Pontailler.

Pontal (pōntäl′), city (pop. 2,215), N São Paulo, Brazil, 19 mi. NW of Ribeirão Prêto; distilling, pottery mfg., cotton processing.

Pontalina (pōntŭlē′nŭ), city (pop. 1,284), S Goiás, central Brazil, 55 mi. S of Goiânia; livestock. Chromite mining in area.

Pont-à-Marcq (pōtämärk′), village (pop. 933), Nord dept., N France, 8 mi. SSE of Lille; chemicals, textiles.

Pont-à-Mousson (pōtämōōsō′), town (pop. 9,899), Meurthe-et-Moselle dept., NE France, on the Moselle and 16 mi. NNW of Nancy; pig-iron and pipe-founding mills; malt processing. Seat of univ. (1572–1763). Town, in front lines throughout First World War, was seriously damaged. In 1944, Germans shelled it during their withdrawal.

Ponta Porã (pōn′tŭ pōōrã′), former federal territory (□ 39,088; 1945 pop. estimate 101,517), SW Brazil, on Paraguay border. Created as a frontier defense zone in 1943, it was dissolved in 1946, and its area was reincorporated into Mato Grosso. Ponta Porã city was temporary seat of govt.; Maracaju was to become official ⊙.

Ponta Porã, city (pop. 4,480), S Mato Grosso, Brazil, in the Serra de Amambaí, adjoining Pedro Juan Caballero (Paraguay), and 150 mi. SSW of Campo Grande; trading center in cattle-raising and maté-growing area. City is projected terminus of rail spur from Campo Grande which, by 1948, had reached Maracaju. Temporary ⊙ former Ponta Porã territory (1943–46).

Pontardawe (pŏntŭrdou′ē), town in RHYNDWYCLYDACH parish, W Glamorgan, Wales, on Tawe R. and 7 mi. NE of Swansea; tin-plate mfg., coal mining.

Pontardulais (pŏntŭrdĭ′lŭs), town in Dulais parish (pop. 3,161) of Llwchwr urban dist., W Glamorgan Wales, on Loughor R. at mouth of Dulais R., and 7 mi. NNW of Swansea; coal mining, tinplate mfg.; iron foundries, chemical works.

Pontarion (pōtärēō′), village (pop. 506), Creuse dept., central France, on Taurion R. and 12 mi. S of Guéret; hog and cattle raising.

Pontarlier (pōtärlyā′), town (pop. 12,130), Doubs dept., E France, on the upper Doubs and 28 mi. SE of Besançon, near Swiss border; alt. 2,746 ft. Customs station. Liqueur distilleries, sawmills, tanneries, chocolate and cheese factories. Important commerce in lumber and Gruyère cheese. Formerly center of France's absinthe production. Tourist trade and winter sports. Here in 1871 Fr. army made its last stand against Prussians before retreating into Switzerland. Defile of La CLUSE-ET-MIJOUX just S.

Pontassieve (pôntäs-syā′vě), town (pop. 4,108), Firenze prov., Tuscany, central Italy, on the Arno, at mouth of Sieve R., and 9 mi. E of Florence; rail junction; mfg. (agr. machinery, cement, glass, wine, macaroni). Badly damaged by repeated air bombing (1943–44) in Second World War.

Pont-Audemer (pō-ōdmâr′), town (pop. 5,745), Eure dept., NW France, port on the Risle and 21 mi. SE of Le Havre; tanning and leather-trading center; dairying, paper milling, cider distilling. Fresh-water fishing. Heavily damaged in Second World War.

Pontaumur (pōtōmür′), village (pop. 510), Puy-de-Dôme dept., central France, 21 mi. WNW of Clermont-Ferrand; horse breeding; wool spinning.

Pont-Aven (pōtävěn′), village (pop. 1,742), Finistère dept., W France, port at head of Aven R. estuary, 9 mi. W of Quimperlé, sardine fishing; oyster beds. Attracts artists.

Pont-à-Vendin (pōtävādē′), town (pop. 3,084), Pas-de-Calais dept., N France, on Haute-Deûle Canal and 4 mi. NE of Lens; mfg. (Portland cement, chemicals, beer).

Pont-Brulé (pō-brülā′), town, Brabant prov., central Belgium, on Willebroek Canal and 7 mi. N of Brussels; coke plants, chemicals (sulphuric acid, ammonia sulphate).

Pont Canavese (pôn känavā′zě), village (pop. 2,794), Torino prov., Piedmont, NW Italy, on Orco R. and 14 mi. W of Ivrea; cotton mills, dyeworks, tanneries.

Pontcharra (pōshärä′), village (pop. 1,678), Isère dept., SE France, on the Bréda near its influx into the Isère, and 11 mi. SSE of Chambéry, in GRÉSIVAUDAN valley; woodworking, paper milling, tire-cord mfg. Tobacco cultures. Hydroelectric plant in Bréda R. gorge (E). Bayard b. in 13th–15th-cent. castle, 1 mi. S.

Pontchartrain, Lake (pŏn′chůrtrān), SE La., shallow lake (c.41 mi. long, 25 mi. wide, 10–16 ft. deep) just N of New Orleans; crossed by Gulf Intracoastal Waterway route, and joined to the Mississippi at New Orleans by navigation canal. Navigable Pass Manchac links lake's W end with L. Maurepas; at E end, Rigolets and Chef Menteur channels connect it with the Gulf via L. Borgne. Narrow E part is spanned by bridge (10 mi. long, with approaches) bet. New Orleans and Slidell. Receives part of Mississippi R. flood waters via BONNET CARRE FLOODWAY. Fontainebleu State Park and many small resorts are on lake.

Pontchâteau or **Pont-Château** (both: pō-shätō′), village (pop. 1,850), Loire-Inférieure dept., W France, 13 mi. NNE of Saint-Nazaire; rail junction and small commercial center. Gothic castle of La Bretesche and 19th-cent. calvary near by.

Pont-Croix (pō-krwä′), village (pop. 1,804), Finistère dept., W France, 18 mi. WNW of Quimper; food preserving, rug mfg.

Pont-d'Ain (pō-dē′), village (pop. 939), Ain dept., E France, on the Ain and 12 mi. SSE of Bourg, at S tip of Revermont range; dairying; horticulture. Ruins of 15th-cent. castle.

Pont d'Arc, France: see VALLON.

Pont-de-Beauvoisin, Le (lů pō-dů-bōvwäzē′), town (pop. 2,577), SE France, on the Guiers (Isère-Savoie dept. border) and 12 mi. WSW of Chambéry. Mfg. (felt hats, furniture, leather belts). In tobacco-growing area. A 16th-cent. bridge links 2 sections of town.

Pont-de-Chéruy (pō-dů-shārwē′), town (pop. 2,026), Isère dept., SE France, on the Bourbre and 16 mi. E of Lyons; aluminum processing, wiredrawing, rubber mfg.

Pont-de-Claix (–klā′), village (pop. 1,397), Isère dept., SE France, on the Drac, 5 mi. SSW of Grenoble, in Dauphiné Alps; electrochemical works (liquid chlorine, ammonia), paper mill, metalworks. Hydroelectric plant.

Pont-de-la-Deûle (–lä-dûl′), town (pop. 3,175), Nord dept., N France, at junction of Scarpe R. and Haute-Deûle Canal, and 3 mi. N of Douai; coal mines at near-by Flers-en-Escrebieux.

Pont-de-l'Arche (–lärsh′), town (pop. 1,934), Eure dept., NW France, on left bank of braided Seine R. and 10 mi. SSE of Rouen; shoe-mfg. center. Heavily damaged in Second World War. One mi. W are 13th-cent. remains of Bon-Port abbey, founded 1100 by Richard I.

Pont-de-l'Isser (–lēsâr′), village (pop. 1,271), Oran dept., NW Algeria, 14 mi. NNE of Tlemcen; olive and citrus groves. Marble quarry.

Pont-de-Loup (–lōō′), town (pop. 2,767), Hainaut prov., S central Belgium, on Sambre R. and 5 mi. E of Charleroi; coal mining.

Pont-de-Montvert, Le (lů pō-dů-mōvâr′), village (pop. 327), Lozère dept., S France, on S slope of Mont Lozère, on Tarn R. and 8 mi. ENE of Florac; sericulture.

Pont-de-Poitte (pōtpwät′), village (pop. 490), Jura dept., E France, on the Ain and 9 mi. SE of Lons-le-Saunier; makes eyeglasses.

Pont-de-Roide (pō-dů-rwäd′), town (pop. 2,737), Doubs dept., E France, on the Doubs and 9 mi. S of Montbéliard, at foot of Lomont range; metallurgy (foundries; hardware mfg.).

Pont-de-Salars (–sälär′), village (pop. 443), Aveyron dept., S France, on Viaur R. and 9 mi. SE of Rodez; dairying, sheep raising.

Pont-de-Vaux (–vō′), village (pop. 1,529), Ain dept., E France, near the Saône, 10 mi. NNE of Mâcon; agr. market; distilling. Navigation canal (2 mi. long) to Saône R.

Pont-de-Veyle (–vāl′), village (pop. 1,046), Ain dept., E France, 4 mi. SE of Mâcon; ships poultry, vegetables.

Pont d'Inca (pōnt′ dĭng′kä), village (pop. 1,417), Majorca, Balearic Isls., 3 mi. NW of Palma; alcohol and liquor distilling, butter making.

Pont-d'Ouilly (pō-dōōyē′), commune (pop. 1,189), Calvados dept., NW France, on the Orne and 21 mi. S of Caen; hosiery and rubber mfg.

Pont-du-Château (pō-dü-shätō′), town (pop. 2,575), Puy-de-Dôme dept., central France, in Limagne, on Allier R. and 8 mi. E of Clermont-Ferrand; asphalt mining, cement-pipe mfg.

Pont-du-Chéliff (–shālēf′), village (pop. 264), Oran dept., NW Algeria, on the lower Chéliff (bridged here) and 12 mi. NE of Mostaganem; vineyards.

Pont-du-Fahs (–fäs′), town (pop. 1,833), Zaghouan dist., N central Tunisia, on Miliane R., on railroad, and 33 mi. SSW of Tunis; road junction; agr. settlement. Cereal trade. Near by are ruins of Roman *Thuburbo Majus*. Heavy fighting occurred here (Apr.-May, 1943) during Second World War.

Pont du Gard (gär′), Roman aqueduct across Gard R. in Gard dept., S France, 12 mi. NE of Nîmes. Built 19 B.C. to convey waters from springs near Uzès to Nîmes, it consists of 3 tiers of arches and is 900 ft. long and 160 ft. high. It is perfectly preserved. A highway bridge, immediately adjoining the lowest tier, was added in 1743.

Pont-du-Navoy (–nävwä′), village (pop. 236), Jura dept., E France, on the Ain and 12 mi. ENE of Lons-le-Saunier; Gruyère cheese mfg.

Ponte all'Isarco, Italy: see PONTE GARDENA.

Pontéba (pōtābä′), village, Alger dept., N central Algeria, on the Chéliff, on railroad and 4 mi. NE of Orléansville; hydroelectric plant.

Pontebba (pōntěb′bä), town (pop. 2,019), Udine prov., Friuli–Venezia Giulia, NE Italy, near Austrian border, on Fella R. and 16 mi. NE of Tolmezzo; resort (alt. 1,860 ft.); cutlery, agr. tools.

Pontecagnano (pōn″těkänyä′nô), village (pop. 2,989), Salerno prov., Campania, S Italy, 6 mi. ESE of Salerno; sawmill, macaroni and tobacco factories.

Pontecchio Polesine (pôntěk′kyô pôlä′zēně), village (pop. 665), Rovigo prov., Veneto, N Italy, 4 mi. S of Rovigo; hemp mill. Formerly Pontecchio.

Pontecorvo (pōn″těkôr′vô), town (pop. 6,241), Frosinone prov., Latium, S central Italy, on Liri R. and 21 mi. SE of Frosinone. Once part of the PAPAL STATES. Almost completely destroyed by air and artillery bombing (1943–44) in Second World War.

Pontecurone (pôn″těkōōrō′ně), village (pop. 2,983), Alessandria prov., Piedmont, N Italy, 16 mi. ENE of Alessandria.

Ponte da Barca (pōn′tĭ dů bär′ků), town (pop. 874), Viana do Castelo dist., N Portugal, on Lima R. and 18 mi. N of Braga; agr. trade.

Pontedecimo (pôn″tědā′chēmô), town (pop. 7,525), Genova prov., Liguria, N Italy, 6 mi. NNW of Genoa, within Greater Genoa. Industrial and commercial center; flour and textile mills, mfg. (macaroni, biscuits, nitrates, rope); iron- and steelworks. Gypsum quarries near by. Forms N boundary of Greater Genoa.

Ponte dell'Olio (pôn′tě děl-lô′lyô), town (pop. 1,862), Piacenza prov., Emilia-Romagna, N central Italy, on Nure R. and 13 mi. S of Piacenza. Sandstone quarries near by.

Pontedera (pôn″tědä′rä), town (pop. 10,573), Pisa prov., Tuscany, central Italy, on the Arno, at mouth of Era R., and 12 mi. ESE of Pisa. Rail junction; industrial and commercial center; cotton and hemp mills, foundries; mfg. of cement, furniture, mill and agr. machinery, motors, matches, glass, soap, wine, macaroni, briquettes. Badly damaged in Second World War.

Ponte de Sor (pōn′tĭ dĭ sôr′), town (pop. 3,124), Portalegre dist., central Portugal, on railroad and 32 mi. W of Portalegre; cheesemaking center; other mfg. (pottery, fertilizer, soap); cork processing. Airfield.

Ponte di Brenta (pôn′tě dē brěn′tä), village (pop. 2,436), Padova prov., Veneto, N Italy, on Brenta R. and 3 mi. E of Padua; ceramic industry. Heavily damaged (1943–45) in Second World War.

Ponte di Legno (lā′nyô), village (pop. 1,123), Brescia prov., Lombardy, N Italy, in upper Val Camonica, on Oglio R. and 10 mi. NE of Edolo. Noted summer resort (alt. 4,127 ft.) and winter-sports center, at N foot of Adamello group.

Ponte do Lima (pōn′tĭ dōō lē′mů), town (pop. 2,197), Viana do Castelo dist., N Portugal, on Lima R. and 14 mi. ENE of Viana do Castelo; textile milling, pottery mfg. Vineyards, olive groves, chestnut and pine woods in area.

Pontefract (pŏn′tĭfrăkt, pŭm′frĭt), municipal borough (1931 pop. 19,057; 1951 census 23,173), West Riding, S central Yorkshire, England, 13 mi. SE of Leeds; agr. trade center, with some coal mining, mfg. of shoes and making of "Pomfret" licorice cakes. Town grew around great 11th-cent. castle built on site of Saxon fort. Here died Richard II (1400). Castle taken in Pilgrimage of Grace (1536) and besieged four times in Civil War, after which it was dismantled; there are a few remains. Just NW is a race course. The town is sometimes spelled Pomfret.

Ponte Gardena (pôn′tě gärdā′nä), Ger. *Waidbruck*, village (pop. 173), Bolzano prov., Tretino–Alto Adige, N Italy, on Isarco R. and 11 mi. NE of Bolzano. Has one of Italy's chief hydroelectric plants. Formerly Ponte all'Isarco.

Ponte in Valtellina (pôn′tě ēn vältěl-lē′nä), village (pop. 1,925), Sondrio prov., Lombardy, N Italy, near Adda R., 5 mi. E of Sondrio.

Ponteix (pŏntů-ěks′), village (pop. 576), SW Sask., 40 mi. SSE of Swift Current; wheat.

Pontelagoscuro (pōntělägôskōō′rô), town (pop. 3,515), Ferrara prov., Emilia-Romagna, N central Italy, port on Po R., 3 mi. N of Ferrara; mfg. (beet sugar, alcohol, soap, fertilizer). Badly damaged in Second World War.

Pontelandolfo (pôn″těländôl′fô), village (pop. 936), Benevento prov., Campania, S Italy, 12 mi. NNW of Benevento; cement.

Ponte-Leccia, Corsica: see MOROSAGLIA.

Pontelongo (pôn″tělông′gô), village (pop. 2,924), Padova prov., Veneto, N Italy, 14 mi. SSE of Padua; beet-sugar refinery.

Pontelongo, Canale di, Italy: see BACCHIGLIONE RIVER.

Ponte nelle Alpi (pôn′tě něl′lě äl′pē), village (pop. 272), Belluno prov., Veneto, N Italy, on Piave R. and 4 mi. NE of Belluno.

Ponte Nova (pōn′tĭ nô′vů), city (pop. 11,707), SE Minas Gerais, Brazil, on the upper Rio Doce and 75 mi. SE of Belo Horizonte; rail center with spur to Ouro Prêto (40 mi. W); coffee and sugar shipping.

Pont-en-Royans (pōtärwäyä′), village (pop. 820), Isère dept., SE France, in gorge of Bourne R. and 20 mi. SW of Grenoble, in the Pre-Alps; makes electrical equipment, wooden articles. Hydroelectric plant on Bourne R., 2 mi. E.

Ponte-Nuovo (pôn′tě-nwô′vô), hamlet of N central Corsica, on the Golo and 14 mi. NNE of Corte. Here Paoli was definitively defeated by French in 1768.

Pontenure (pôn″těnōō′rě), town (pop. 1,590), Piacenza prov., Emilia-Romagna, N central Italy, 6 mi. SE of Piacenza, near Nure R.; tomato cannery, alcohol distillery.

Ponterwyd (pôntěrwĭd′), agr. village in Cwmrheidol (kōōmrĭ′dôl) parish (pop. 566), NE Cardigan, Wales, on Rheidol R. and 11 mi. E of Aberystwyth. On Rheidol R., 2 mi. SSE, is woolen-milling village of Devil's Bridge.

Ponte San Giovanni (pôn′tě sän jôvän′nē), village (pop. 904), Perugia prov., Umbria, central Italy, near the Tiber, 3 mi. ESE of Perugia; rail junction; macaroni mfg.

Ponte San Pietro (pyā′trô), town (pop. 4,056), Bergamo prov., Lombardy, N Italy, on Brembo R. and 4 mi. W of Bergamo; mfg. of airplane accessories.

Pontesbury, town and parish (pop. 2,833), W central Shropshire, England, 7 mi. SW of Shrewsbury; chemical works; agr. market in dairying region. Church dates from 13th cent.

Pontestura (pôn″těstōō′rä), village (pop. 1,767), Alessandria prov., Piedmont, N Italy, near Po R., 6 mi. W of Casale Monferrato.

Pontet, Le (lů pōtā′), NE suburb (pop. 1,279) of Avignon, Vaucluse dept., SE France, on left arm of Rhone R.; mfg. (paper, pulp, copper sulphate, butane gas).

Pontevedra (pōntāvā′dhrä). **1** Town (1939 pop. 1,837; 1948 municipality pop. 26,329), Capiz prov., N Panay isl., Philippines, 8 mi. SE of Capiz; rice-growing center. **2** Town (1939 pop. 2,022; 1948 municipality pop. 18,060), Negros Occidental prov., W Negros isl., Philippines, on Guimaras Strait, 21 mi. SSW of Bacolod; agr. center (rice, sugar cane).

Pontevedra, province (□ 1,427; pop. 641,763), NW Spain, in Galicia, on the Atlantic; ⊙ Pontevedra. Bounded by Ulla R. (N) and by Portugal (Miño R.; S); mostly hilly, crossed by the Galician Mts.; drained by many short rivers. Deeply indented coast line has many drowned valleys (*rias*), e.g., Arosa, Pontevedra, Vigo. Tin and tungsten mining (Lalín); lignite deposits and granite quarries. Fishing, fish processing, and boatbuilding are chief industries along coast (Vigo is main center; also Bayona, Marín, Pontevedra). Rich pastures (cattle, hogs, horses) and extensive forests (lumbering) cover hills and valleys of interior, favored by abundant rainfall. Inland trade hampered by poor communications. Agr. products: rye, corn, potatoes, fruit, vegetables; vineyards (along coast). Few industries, derived mostly from agr. (dairy products, meat processing, tanning), except for Vigo, which is a growing industrial center.

Pontevedra, city (pop. 14,432), ⊙ Pontevedra prov., NW Spain, in Galicia, seaport amidst green hills at head of Pontevedra Bay, 65 mi. SSW of La Coruña; 42°26'N 8°39'W. Fishing and boatbuilding; sawmilling; mfg. of dairy products, ceramics, candy. Agr. trade (livestock, lumber, fruit, cereals, wine). Has Gothic church of Santa María (16th cent.), 18th-cent. circular church of La Peregrina, ruins of 13th-cent. convent, and episcopal palace (12th-13th cent.); also a Roman bridge and some remains of anc. walls.

Pontevedra Bay, Sp. *Ría de Pontevedra,* inlet of the Atlantic, NW Spain, on W coast of Galicia; 14 mi. long, up to 6 mi. wide. Fishing ports (Pontevedra, Marín, Bueu) and resorts on its shores.

Pontével (pōntĕ'vĕl), town (pop. 1,686), Santarém dist., central Portugal, 10 mi. SW of Santarém, center of important winegrowing region; fruit preserving.

Pont-Évêque (pōtāvĕk'), E suburb (pop. 1,295) of Vienne, Isère dept., SE France; mfg. (felt, cotton padding, slippers), paper milling.

Pontevico (pôntĕvē'kō), town (pop. 4,540), Brescia prov., Lombardy, N Italy, on Oglio R. and 10 mi. N of Cremona; flax and hemp mills, agr.-machinery factory.

Pontevigodarzere (pôn"tĕvēgōdär'tsĕrĕ) or **Vigodarzere,** town (pop. 1,530), Padova prov., Veneto, N Italy, on Brenta R. and 3 mi. N of Padua; mfg. (refrigerators, leather furniture, office supplies). Bombed (1943–45) in Second World War.

Pontgibaud (pōzhēbō'), village (pop. 756), Puy-de-Dôme dept., central France, in the Monts Dôme, on Sioule R. and 12 mi. WNW of Clermont-Ferrand; lead and zinc mining; cheese making. Has 13th-cent. feudal castle.

Pont-Hébert (pō-ābâr'), village (pop. 219), Manche dept., NW France, on the Vire and 4 mi. NNW of Saint-Lô; dairying.

Ponthierry (pōtyĕrē'), village (pop. 1,460), Seine-et-Marne dept., N central France, on left bank of the Seine and 5 mi. W of Melun; mfg. (wallpaper, pharmaceuticals).

Ponthierville (pōtyârvēl'), town, Eastern Prov., E Belgian Congo, on left bank of Lualaba R. and 65 mi. SSE of Stanleyville; terminus of steam navigation and head of railroad which skirts the Stanley Falls to Stanleyville. Also trading and agr. center (palm products, rice, fibers). R.C. mission.

Ponthieu (pōtyû'), old district of N France, now in W Somme dept. Its ⊙ was Abbeville. Apple orchards, pastures.

Pontiac (pŏn'tēăk", Fr. pōtēäk'), county (□ 9,560; pop. 19, 852), SW Que., on Ont. border.

Pontiac. 1 City (pop. 8,990), ⊙ Livingston co., central Ill., on Vermilion R. and 33 mi. NE of Bloomington; trade, shipping, and mfg. center in agr. and bituminous-coal area; stone quarries; corn, oats, soybeans, livestock, poultry, dairy products. Mfg. (farm machinery, shoes, concrete products, auto brakes, candy). A branch of state penitentiary is here. Settled 1833, platted 1837, inc. 1857. **2** Industrial city (pop. 73,681), ⊙ Oakland co., SE Mich., 24 mi. NW of Detroit and on Clinton R., in an area of farms, lakes, and resorts. An automobile-mfg. center; also makes trucks, buses, parts, machinery, rubber products, paint, leather, food products); flour and woolen mills. Has a state hosp. for the mentally ill. Founded by Detroit promoters in 1818; inc. as village 1837, as city 1861. Carriage making, important here in 1880s, prepared the way for rise of automobile mfg. **3** Village, R.I.: see WARWICK.

Pontianak (pôntēūnäk'), town (pop. 45,196), W Borneo, Indonesia, port on S.China Sea at mouth of small stream in Kapuas delta, 400 mi. ESE of Singapore; 0°2'S 109°22'E; trade center for Kapuas basin, shipping timber, copra, rubber, palm oil. Formerly ⊙ sultanate of Pontianak.

Pontian Kechil (pôn"tēän' kŭchēl'), town (pop. 6,132), S Johore, Malaya, minor port on Strait of Malacca, 25 mi. W of Johore Bharu, at mouth of Pontian Kechil R. (Singapore water reservoir in upper reaches); fisheries, coconuts. Sometimes called Pontian.

Ponticelli (pôntēchĕl'lē), town (pop. 12,815), Napoli prov., Campania, S Italy, 3 mi. E of Naples.

Pontigny (pōtēnyē'), village (pop. 405), Yonne dept., on Serein R. and 10 mi. NE of Auxerre; brick and tile mfg. Its noted 12th-cent. abbatial church was damaged in Second World War. Adjoining Cistercian abbey now houses a boarding school.

Pontine Islands (pŏn'tĭn,–tīn) or **Ponza Islands** (pôn'tsä) (□ 4; pop. 7,836), in Tyrrhenian Sea, off central Italy, S of Monte Circeo; part of Latina prov. Volcanic in origin; consist of NE group, including PONZA (main isl.), Palmarola (□ 4; uninhabited), and Zannone (□ 3; pop. 14) isls., and SE group, including VENTOTENE ISLAND and islet of Santo Stefano. Used since anc. times as a place of exile.

Pontine Marshes, plain (□ c.300) in Latina prov., Latium, S central Italy, bet. Tyrrhenian Sea and Apennine hills; extend 30 mi. from Cisterna di Latina (NW) to Terracina (SE); 5–10 mi. wide. Traversed by Appian Way and crossed by drainage canals. Populated and fertile in Volscian and early Roman times; later abandoned because of its unhealthy swamps and malaria. Trajan, Theodoric, and several popes started reclamation works. Under Mussolini a drainage system was completed; large estates were divided and settled by farmers from N Italy. First rural town, Littoria (now Latina), was established 1932, followed by Sabaudia (1934), Pontinia (1935), Aprilia (1937), and Pomezia (1939). Agr. (cereals, sugar beets, fruit, vegetables) and stock raising (cattle, sheep) are carried on. Region badly damaged by fighting in Second World War.

Pontinia (pôntē'nyä), village, Latina prov., Latium, S central Italy, in reclaimed PONTINE MARSHES, 9 mi. SE of Latina. Founded 1935.

Pontivy (pōtēvē'), town (pop. 8,273), Morbihan dept., W France, on Blavet R. (head of navigation) and Brest-Nantes Canal, and 25 mi. NNE of Lorient; commercial center; mfg. (agr. equipment, building materials, chemical fertilizer, beer, biscuits); sawmilling. Old town contains ruins of 15th-cent. castle and Gothic church of Notre-Dame-de-la-Joie. New town built by Napoleon in 1805 as military hq. of Brittany. Known as Napoléonville until 1871.

Pont-l'Abbé (pō-läbā'), town (pop. 5,064), Finistère dept., W France, port on Bay of Biscay, 11 mi. SSW of Quimper; ships and cans early vegetables; mfg. (lace, toys, iodine). Known for elaborate miter-shaped headdress worn by its women.

Pont-l'Évêque (pō-lāvĕk'), town (pop. 1,967), Calvados dept., NW France, on the Touques and 10 mi. N of Lisieux, in dairying region (noted cheese); cider distilling, woodworking. Damaged in Second World War.

Pontlevoy (pōlŭvwä'), village (pop. 1,237), Loir-et-Cher dept., N central France, 14 mi. SSW of Blois; winegrowing. Has Benedictine col., founded 1644, which now houses a preparatory school for boys.

Pontllanfraith, England: see MYNYDDISLWYN.

Pontnewydd, England: see LLANFRECHFA UPPER.

Pontnewynydd, England: see ABERSYCHAN.

Pontoise (pōtwäz'), town (pop. 9,658), Seine-et-Oise dept., N central France, built in amphitheater above right bank of the Oise and 18 mi. NW of Paris; communications and agr. trade center funneling regional produce to Paris; metal works. Has Gothic-Renaissance church of Saint-Maclou. Favorite residence of Capetian kings and old ⊙ Vexin Français. Damaged in Second World War.

Pontonny or **Pontonnyy** (pŭntô'nē), town (1939 pop. over 2,000), central Leningrad oblast, Russian SFSR, on Neva R., at mouth of the Izhora, just SE of Ust-Izhora; shipbuilding, veneering.

Pontoosuc (pŭntōō'sĭk, pŏn–), village (pop. 214), Hancock co., W Ill., on the Mississippi and 14 mi. SSW of Burlington (Iowa), in agr. area.

Pontoosuc Lake, W Mass., in the Berkshires, just N of Pittsfield; c.1.5 mi. long. Park here; swimming.

Pontorson (pōtôrsō'), town (pop. 2,563), Manche dept., NW France, port on the Couësnon (canalized) and 12 mi. SW of Avranches; market. Footwear and clothing mfg., metalworking. Center for tourists visiting Mont-Saint-Michel (6 mi. N).

Pontotoc (pŏn'tŭtŏk", pŏntŭtŏk'). **1** County (□501; pop. 19,994), N Miss.; ⊙ Pontotoc. Drained by Tallahatchie R. tributaries, by Skuna and Yocona rivers, and by small Chiwapa Creek. Agr. (chiefly cotton, corn), dairying. Timber; clay and bauxite deposits. Mfg., including farm-products processing, at Pontotoc. Formed 1836. **2** County (□ 719; pop. 30,875), S central Okla.; ⊙ Ada. Bounded N by Canadian R.; drained by Clear Boggy Creek and Blue R. Agr. (cotton, corn, oats, hay, sorghums, livestock; dairy products). Mfg. at Ada. Oil fields; oil refineries, gasoline plants. Formed 1907.

Pontotoc, city (pop. 1,596), ⊙ Pontotoc co., N Miss., c.60 mi. NNW of Columbus; trade and industrial center for agr. and dairying area; mfg. of clothing, cottonseed and dairy products; lumber mills, cotton gins and compress. Has several notable antebellum houses. Inc. as town in 1837.

Pontremoli (pôntrā'môlē), town (pop. 3,801), Massa e Carrara prov., Tuscany, central Italy, on Magra R. and 18 mi. NNE of Spezia, on La Cisa pass road. Chief center of the Lunigiana; macaroni, cement, tanning. Bishopric. Has cathedral (1503).

Pont-Remy (pō-rŭmē'), village (pop. 1,613), Somme dept., N France, on the Somme and 5 mi. SE of Abbeville; fertilizer and footwear mfg.

Pontresina (pôntrĕsē'nä), Romansh *Puntraschigna* (pōōnträzhē'nyŭ), village (pop. 757), Grisons canton, SE Switzerland, on Bernina R. and 3 mi. E of St. Moritz, at foot of Bernina Alps; summer resort (alt. 5,910 ft.), winter sports center in Upper Engadine.

Pontrieux (pōtrēū'), village (pop. 1,686), Côtes-du-Nord dept., W France, on Trieux R. and 14 mi. ESE of Lannion; cider milling, tanning, carton mfg.

Pont Rouge (pō rōōzh'), village (pop. 1,865), S Que., on Jacques Cartier R. and 23 mi. W of Quebec; dairying, stock raising.

Pont-Rousseau (pō-rōōsō'), S suburb (pop. 15,298) of Nantes, Loire-Inférieure dept., W France, on left bank of Loire R. at influx of the Sèvre Nantaise; hosiery-mfg. center (wool, cotton, rayon). Also building materials, furniture.

Pont-Sainte-Marie (pō-sēt-märē'), N suburb (pop. 1,440) of Troyes, Aube dept., NE central France; mfg. (hosiery, mustard). Damaged in Second World War.

Pont-Sainte-Maxence (–mäksās'), town (pop. 4,162), Oise dept., N France, on left bank of the Oise and 7 mi. N of Senlis; mfg. (leatherette, paper, sandstone pipes, hardware), flour milling. Just E is 14th-cent. abbey of Moncel.

Pont-Saint-Esprit (pō-sētĕsprē'), town (pop. 2,961), Gard dept., S France, on right bank of Rhone R. below influx of the Ardèche, 23 mi. NNW of Avignon; glass-bottle and carton factories. Fruit- and winegrowing. Its 13th-cent. bridge was damaged during Second World War.

Pont-Saint-Martin (–märtē'), village (pop. 1,109), Val d'Aosta region, NW Italy, on Lys R., near confluence with the Dora Baltea, and 10 mi. N of Ivrea, in grape-growing region. Has metallurgy industry (iron, copper), hydroelectric plant. Near by is Roman bridge (100 B.C.). In Second World War, bombed (1945).

Pont-Saint-Pierre (–pyâr'), village (pop. 845), Eure dept., NW France, on the Andelle and 11 mi. SE of Rouen; cotton spinning, leatherworking.

Pont-Saint-Vincent (–vēsā'), town (pop. 2,016), Meurthe-et-Moselle dept., NE France, on the Moselle and Canal de l'Est, opposite Neuves-Maisons, and 7 mi. SSW of Nancy.

Pont-Scorff (pō-skôrf'), village (pop. 941), Morbihan dept., W France, on the Scorff and 6 mi. N of Lorient; makes baking ovens.

Ponts-de-Cé, Les (lā pōd-sā'), town (pop. 3,238), Maine-et-Loire dept., W France, on several isls. in the Loire and 4 mi. SSE of Angers; road center with 7 successive bridges spanning the braided river; copper and bronze foundry; truck farming. Over ¼ of town destroyed in Second World War.

Pont-sur-Seine (pō-sür-sĕn'), village (pop. 690), Aube dept., NE central France, on Seine R. and 5 mi. ENE of Nogent-sur-Seine; furniture mfg.

Pont-sur-Yonne (–yôn'), village (pop. 1,763), Yonne dept., N central France, on Yonne R. and 7 mi. NNW of Sens; brushes, building materials; sawmilling. Has restored 12th-cent. church.

Pontus (pŏn'tŭs), anc. country of NE Asia Minor (present-day Turkey), on the Black Sea. It arose out of a fragment of Alexander the Great's empire, and by 281 B.C. its ruler (Mithridates II) was calling himself king. It grew to power under Mithridates VI (Mithridates the Great), who conquered Asia Minor, controlled the Crimea, and threatened the Romans in Greece. Mithridates was defeated (65 B.C.) by Pompey, and Pharnaces II by Julius Caesar (at Zela, 47 B.C.), and Pontus became part of the Roman prov. of Galatia-Cappadocia. Its cities included Amasia, Trapezus, Neocaesarea, and Zela.

Pontus Euxinus: see BLACK SEA.

Pontvallain (pōvälē'), village (pop. 496), Sarthe dept., W France, 13 mi. ENE of La Flèche; cattle raising.

Pontville, town (pop. 194), SE Tasmania, 13 mi. N of Hobart; sheep center.

Pontyberem or **Pont-y-Berem** (pôntĭbĕ'rĕm), town and parish (pop. 3,201), S central Carmarthen, Wales, 7 mi. N of Llanelly; coal mining.

Pontycymmer (pôntŭkŭ'mŭr), town (pop. 6,113) in Ogmore and Garw urban district, central Glamorgan, Wales, on Garw R. and 7 mi. N of Bridgend; coal mining.

Pontypool (pŏntĕpōōl'), urban district (1931 pop. 6,790; 1951 census 42,683), central Monmouth, England, 8 mi. NNW of Newport; tinplate mfg., coal mining. Iron industry introduced here 1588. Formerly well known for Japan ware (introduced in 17th cent.). Pontypool absorbed (1935) near-by Abersychan and Panteg.

Pontypridd (pôntŭprēdh'), urban district (1931 pop. 42,717; 1951 census 38,622), E Glamorgan, Wales, on Taff R. (1755 single-span bridge), at mouth of Rhondda R., and 11 mi. NW of Cardiff; coal mining, steel milling; mfg. of colliery equipment, electrical equipment, chains, cables; agr. market. Just SE, on Taff R., is town of Treforest, with large trading estate, established in 1930s, designed to attract new light industries to alleviate unemployment in primary industries. There are chemical, pharmaceutical, light metal, rayon, chocolate, and metalworking plants. Just E of Pontypridd, on Taff R., is coal-mining and steel-milling town of Glyntaff (glĭntăf').

Pontyrhyl, Wales: see BETTWS AND PONTYRHYL.

Ponuga (pōnōō'gä), village (pop. 302), Veraguas prov., W central Panama, in Pacific lowland, 18 mi. SSE of Santiago; sugar cane, livestock.

Ponur, India: see PONNURU.

Pony, village (pop. c.200), Madison co., SW Mont., 40 mi. SE of Butte and on branch of Jefferson R., just E of Tobacco Root Mts.; trading point in mining district.

Ponyri (pŭnĭ'rē), village (1926 pop. 1,749), N central Kursk oblast, Russian SFSR, 38 mi. N of Kursk; hemp processing.

Ponza Island (pôn'tsä), main island (□ 2.9; pop. 6,443) of PONTINE ISLANDS, in Tyrrhenian Sea, off central Italy, 20 mi. S of Monte Circeo; 5 mi. long, 1 mi. wide; rises to 781 ft. in S. Chief port, Ponza (pop. 2,787), in S. Agr., fishing. Near by are isls. of Zannone (4 mi. NE) and Palmarola (5 mi. W).

Pool, town and parish (pop. 1,014), West Riding, central Yorkshire, England, on Wharfe R. and 8 mi. NNW of Leeds; paper milling.

Pool, region, Fr. Equatorial Africa: see KINKALA.

Poole, municipal borough (1931 pop. 57,211; 1951 census 82,958), SE Dorset, England, on Poole Harbour, inlet of the Channel, and 5 mi. W of Bournemouth; 50°43'N 2°W; coastal-shipping, naval-supply, and fishing port; commercial seaplane base; clay and pottery shipped from here; tile mfg. Has 15th-cent. Town Cellars (probably used to store wool) and 18th-cent. harbor office. Canute reputedly landed here. Municipal borough includes seaside resort towns of Branksome (NE) and Parkstone (E).

Poole, village (pop. 33), Buffalo co., S central Nebr., 30 mi. W of Grand Island and on S.Loup R.

Poole Harbour, inlet of English Channel, SW Dorset, England, 5 mi. W of Bournemouth; 4 mi. wide, 7 mi. long. Receives Frome and Piddle rivers. One of best harbors on S coast; entrance is sheltered by BROWNSEA ISLAND. On N shore is town of Poole.

Pooler, town (pop. 818), Chatham co., E Ga., 10 mi. WNW of Savannah.

Pooles Island, N Md., low, wooded isl. (c.1½ mi. long, ½ mi. wide) in Chesapeake Bay, 19 mi. E of Baltimore; lighthouse.

Poolesville, town (pop. 161), Montgomery co., central Md., 28 mi. NW of Washington; dairying.

Poon (bō'ôn'), Mandarin *Paoan* (bou'än'), town (pop. 2,360), ⊙ Poon co. (pop. 174,150), S Kwangtung prov., China, on Canton R. estuary, near Hong Kong border, 24 mi. NW of Kowloon; fisheries. Until 1914 called Sinan. Its port of Namtow is just SW.

Poona (pōō'nŭ), district, central Bombay, India, on W edge of Deccan Plateau; ⊙ Poona. Bounded by Bhima R. (SE), Nira R. and Satara North dist. (S); crossed W by Western Ghats. Agr. (millet, rice, wheat, peanuts, sugar cane); grapes, figs, papaya also grown; dairy and agr. farms around Poona city. Handicraft cloth weaving and palm-mat making, gur processing, metalworking. Reservoirs (W) supply important hydroelectric plants in Kolaba dist. Chief towns: Poona, Kirkee, Baramati, Junnar. Anc. Buddhist cave temples near Karli. After expelling Moguls in late-17th cent., Mahrattas dominated area until defeated (early-19th cent.) by British. Original dist. (□ 5,347; 1941 pop. 1,359,408) enlarged by inc. (1949) of part of former Deccan state of Bhor. Pop. 89% Hindu, 5% Moslem, 3% tribal, 2% Christian.

Poona, city (pop. 237,560; including cantonment and suburban areas, 298,001), ⊙ Poona dist., central Bombay, India, on Mutha Mula R. and 75 mi. SE of Bombay; 18°31'N 73°51'E. Major commercial center and military station; rail and road junction; airport; agr. market (grain, cotton, sugar, oilseeds). Cotton milling, carpet weaving, fruit canning, garden-seed farming, mfg. of chemicals, agr. implements, glass, paper, bricks, rubber products, soap, hosiery, biris, gold and silver thread, metalware; ordnance factories, tanneries, motion picture studios, printing presses. Important cultural and educational center (arts, technical, medical, agr., and law cols.; research societies); seat of Poona Univ. (founded 1948; has several affiliated cols. throughout Maharashtra); meteorological station. Summer hq. of Bombay govt. Natl. Acad. (training of military officers) at near-by village of Khadakavasla. In 18th cent., Poona was ⊙ Peshwas and center of Mahratta empire; rise of independent Mahratta dynasties in central India and Br. victories in near-by battles (1817–18) brought its power to an end. It was formerly a favorite residence of Br. administrators, for whose social life in India Poona became something of a byword.

Poonamallee (pōō'nŭmŭlē), town (pop. 18,704), Chingleput dist., E Madras, India, outer suburb of Madras, 12 mi. W of city center; betel farming, hardware mfg. Public health training center.

Poonch, Kashmir: see PUNCH.

Poopó (pōpō'), town (pop. c.4,100), ⊙ Poopó prov., Oruro dept., W Bolivia, in the Altiplano, near NE shore of L. Poopó, 30 mi. SSE of Oruro, and on Oruro-Uyuni RR; alt. 12,168 ft.; sheep.

Poopó, Lake, second largest (□ 970) of Bolivia, in Oruro dept., c.35 mi. S of Oruro; 60 mi. long, 20–30 mi. wide, c.8 ft. deep; alt. 12,106 ft. Receives Desaguadero (outlet of L. Titicaca) and Marquez rivers. Outlet: Lacahahuira R. Large part of water filters into lake bed, creating marshy shores. Panza Isl. in center; Poopó city near NE, Pampa Aullagas town near SW shore. Sometimes called L. Pampa Aullagas.

Poor Fork, city, Ky.: see CUMBERLAND.

Poor Fork, SE Ky., rises in the Cumberlands in E Letcher co., flows c.45 mi. WSW past Cumberland, joining Clover Fork just N of Harlan to form Cumberland R.

Poorman, village (1939 pop. 20), W central Alaska, 45 mi. S of Ruby; placer gold mining.

Pootoo Shan, China: see PUTO SHAN.

Pootung or **P'u-tung** (both: pōō'dōōng'), right-bank industrial suburb of Shanghai, China, on Whangpoo R. The name Pootung is sometimes extended to the entire tidal lowland S of the Yangtze estuary and terminating in Pootung Point or Yangtze Cape (30°53'N 121°53'E) on Yellow Sea.

Popa, Mount (pō'pä), extinct volcano (4,981 ft.), Myingyan dist., Upper Burma, 10 mi. NE of Kyaukpadaung; 20°56'N 95°12'E. Rises 3,000 ft. above surrounding plateau N of Pegu Yoma; crater 1 mi. in diameter. Held in superstitious awe by Burmese. In Second World War, scene of heavy fighting.

Popadiya (pŭpä'dyĕŭ), Polish *Popadja*, peak (5,715 ft.) in Gorgany Mts. of the Carpathians, SW Ukrainian SSR, 20 mi. SW of Pereginsko.

Popai, China: see POKPAK.

Popasnaya (pŭpäs'nīŭ), city (1939 pop. over 10,000), W Voroshilovgrad oblast, Ukrainian SSR, in the Donbas, 40 mi. WNW of Voroshilovgrad; rail junction; metal- and glassworks. Called (c.1935–43) Imeni L. M. Kaganovicha.

Popayán (pōpī'än'), city (pop. 18,292), ⊙ Cauca dept., SW Colombia, on volcanic terrace (1,000 ft. above Cauca R.) at NW foot of Puracé Volcano, on Pan American Highway to Quito (Ecuador), and 235 mi. SW of Bogotá; 2°26'N 76°36'W; alt. 5,774 ft. Rail terminus; cultural, commercial, and processing center in fertile coffeegrowing region; also sugar cane, cacao, tobacco, fique, cereals, fruit, silk, stock. Flour milling, tanning; mfg. of shoes, bricks, fique-fiber bags and mats. Airport. An old colonial city, founded 1536 by Benalcázar, it became a rich aristocratic center of colonial trade and achieved note as the seat of a univ. (founded 1640); since early colonial days it has played an important part in the academic and ecclesiastic life of Colombia. Bishopric. It has fine parks, bldgs. in Andalusian style, cathedral, old monasteries and cloisters, colonial mansions, govt. palace, new natl. palace, museums. The city changed hands several times in War of Independence and rebelled (1876) against central govt.

Pope. **1** County (□ 816; pop. 23,291), N central Ark.; ⊙ Russellville. Bounded S by Arkansas R.; drained by small Illinois Bayou and Big Piney Creek; situated in Ozark region. Diversified farming (fruit, cotton, truck, potatoes, corn, soybeans, livestock, dairy products). Coal mines, natural-gas wells; timber. Formed 1829. **2** County (□ 381; pop. 5,779), extreme SE Ill.; ⊙ Golconda. Bounded SE by Ohio R.; drained by Bay and Lusk creeks, small tributaries of the Ohio. Includes part of Ill. Ozarks, and part of Shawnee Natl. Forest. Predominantly agr. area (fruit, corn, wheat, livestock); wood products; fluorspar mining. Formed 1816. **3** County (□ 681; pop. 12,862), W Minn.; ⊙ Glenwood. Agr. area drained by Chippewa R. and watered by L. Minnewaska and several smaller lakes. Livestock, grain, dairy products, poultry. Formed 1862.

Pope, village (pop. 246), Panola co., NW Miss., 31 mi. NNW of Grenada.

Pope Air Force Base, N.C.: see FAYETTEVILLE.

Pope Creek, NW Ill., rises NE of Galesburg, flows c.50 mi. W to the Mississippi at Keithsburg.

Popejoy (pōp'joi), town (pop. 201), Franklin co., N central Iowa, near Iowa R., 15 mi. SW of Hampton.

Popelnya or **Popel'nya** (pô'pĭlnyŭ), agr. town (1926 pop. 2,334), SE Zhitomir oblast, Ukrainian SSR, 39 mi. SE of Zhitomir; sugar beets; kaolin quarries.

Poperinge (pō'pŭrĭng"ŭ, Fr. pôprēzh'), town (pop. 12,433), West Flanders prov., W Belgium, 7 mi. W of Ypres; market center for hop- and fruitgrowing region. Has 15th-cent. church of St. Bertin. Town nearly destroyed by heavy fighting in First World War. Formerly spelled Poperinghe.

Popesti-Leordeni (pôpĕsht'-lyôrdān'), Rum. *Popeşti-Leordeni*, outer SE rural suburb (1948 pop. 6,052) of Bucharest, S Rumania, near right bank of Dambovita R.; rayon mfg.; dairy farming.

Popham Beach, Maine: see PHIPPSBURG.

Poping or **Po-p'ing** (bŭ'pĭng'), town, ⊙ Poping co. (pop. 169,180), NE Pingyuan prov., China, on main road and 50 mi. W of Tsinan; peanuts, melons, millet. Until 1949 in Shantung prov.

Popintsi (pô'pĭntsē), village (pop. 3,223), Plovdiv dist., W central Bulgaria, at S foot of Sredna Gora, on Luda Yana R. and 7 mi. SSE of Panagyurishte; grain, livestock.

Popitsa (pôpē'tsä), village (pop. 3,696), Vratsa dist., NW Bulgaria, on Skat R. and 2 mi. S of Byala Slatina; livestock, truck, grain.

Pop-Ivan (pôp"-ēvän'), peak (6,647 ft.) in the Chernagora section of the Carpathians, SW Ukrainian SSR, 10 mi. SW of Zhabye. Another peak Pop-Ivan (6,365 ft.) rises in spur of Carpathians on USSR-Rumania border, 25 mi. SW of Zhabye.

Poplar, metropolitan borough (1931 pop. 155,089; 1951 census 73,544) of London, England, on N bank of the Thames, 5 mi. E of Charing Cross; industrial dist., with shipyards, metalworks and docks (East and West India, Milwall). Blackwall Tunnel, under the Thames, links Poplar with Greenwich. The 17th-cent. Church of St. Matthias has oak pillars reputedly made from masts of ships of the Armada. District suffered heavy damage from air raids in 1940–41. In borough is the Isle of Dogs.

Poplar. **1** City (pop. 1,169), ⊙ Roosevelt co., NE Mont., on Missouri R., at mouth of Poplar R., and 70 mi. E of Glasgow; lumber mills; livestock, grain, potatoes. Hq. of Fort Peck Indian Reservation here. Inc. 1916. **2** Village (pop. 489), Douglas co., NW Wis., 16 mi. ESE of Superior; pea canning.

Poplar Bluff, city (pop. 15,064), ⊙ Butler co., SE Mo., in Ozark region, on Black R. and 130 mi. S of St. Louis; agr. trade and shipping center; railroad shops; mfg. (shoes, staves, grain and lumber products); fire-clay, iron mines. Resorts, Clark Natl. Forest, Wappapello Dam near by. Founded 1850.

Poplar Grove. **1** Village (pop. c.300), Phillips co., E Ark., 14 mi. W of Helena, in farm area. **2** Village (pop. 417), Boone co., N Ill., 14 mi. ENE of Rockford, in agr. area. **3** Town, Va.: see PETERSBURG.

Poplar Island, low, wooded isl. (c.2 mi. long, ½ mi. wide), Talbot co., E Md., in Chesapeake Bay at S entrance to Eastern Bay, 17 mi. W of Easton.

Poplar River, Sask. and Mont., rises in S Sask., flows 167 mi. S, past Scobey, NE Mont., to Missouri R. at Poplar.

Poplarville, town (pop. 1,852), ⊙ Pearl River co., SE Miss., 36 mi. SSW of Hattiesburg, in agr. and timber area; pine lumber, tung oil. A jr. col. and a state agr. experiment station are here. Inc. 1883.

Popo Agie River (pōpō' zēŭ, –zhŭ), W central Wyo., rises in 3 forks in S tip of Wind River Range, flows ENE, past Lander and Hudson, joining Wind R. at Riverton to form Bighorn R.; including Middle Fork, c.60 mi. long. Drains productive valley growing fruit and vegetables. Main tributary, Little Popo Agie R. (c.40 mi. long), which joins Popo Agie R. at Hudson.

Popocatepetl (pōpŭkă'tŭpĕtŭl, Sp. pōpōkätā'pĕtŭl) [Aztec,=smoking mountain], dormant volcano (17,887 ft.), central Mexico, on Puebla–Mexico state border, 45 mi. SE of Mexico city, S of Ixtacihuatl; 19°1'N 98°37'W. Second in height only to Pico de Orizaba among Mex. peaks. Has snow-capped symmetrical cone with large crater. Last erupted 1702; still occasionally emits vast clouds of smoke. Large sulphur deposits in crater only partially exploited. Ascent is fairly easy; was probably 1st made in 1519 by one of Cortés' men.

Popof Island (pŏ'pôf) (10 mi. long, 5 mi. wide), Shumagin Isls., SW Alaska, off S coast of Alaska Peninsula, just E of Unga Isl.; 55°19'N 160°24'W; rises to 1,550 ft. Fishing, fish canning, big-game hunting. Sand Point village, E.

Popoli (pô'pôlē), town (pop. 8,282), Pescara prov., Abruzzi e Molise, S central Italy, on Pescara R. and 10 mi. NW of Sulmona; metal foundries; mfg. (fireworks, macaroni). Has 15th-cent. church. Badly damaged by bombing (1944) in Second World War.

Popondetta (pōpŭndĕ'tŭ), village, Territory of Papua, SE New Guinea, 8 mi. N of Higaturu; agr. station; airfield.

Popova (pŭpô'vŭ), town (1948 pop. over 500), S Maritime Territory, Russian SFSR, on W shore of **Popova Island** (in Peter the Great Bay; 4.5 mi. long, 2 mi. wide), 12 mi. SSW of Vladivostok; fish canning.

Popovaca (pô'pôvächä), Serbo-Croatian *Popovača*, village, N Croatia, Yugoslavia, on railroad and 14 mi. ENE of Sisak, in Slavonia.

Popovicheskaya (pŭpô'vēchĭskīŭ), village (1926 pop. 10,715), W Krasnodar Territory, Russian SFSR, 35 mi. NNW of Krasnodar; flour mill, metalworks; wheat, sunflowers, castor beans, ambary and southern hemp; dairying.

Popovka (pŭpôf'kŭ), town (1926 pop. 6,581), N Stalino oblast, Ukrainian SSR, 6 mi. ENE of Krasny Liman.

Popovo (pô'pôvô). **1** City (pop. 6,469), Kolarovgrad dist., NE Bulgaria, near Cherni Lom R., 35 mi. WNW of Kolarovgrad; poultry, grain center; flour milling, sunflower-oil extracting, furniture mfg., tileworks. **2** Village (pop. 3,743), Plovdiv oblast, S central Bulgaria, at N foot of E Rhodope Mts., 12 mi. SSW of Parvomai; tobacco, fruit, truck. Formerly Karadzhilar.

Popovo Plain (pô'pôvô), in Dinaric Alps, S Herzegovina, Yugoslavia, along Trebisnica R. below Trebinje. Fertile land, producing tobacco and corn. Flooded in fall, forming lake 15 mi. long, up to 65 ft. deep.

Poppelsdorf (pô'pŭlsdôrf), S suburb of Bonn, W Germany. Pure-science institutes and agr. col. of Univ. of Bonn located here. Castle (18th cent.) contains zoological and mineralogical collections; large botanical garden.

Poppi (pôp'pē), town (pop. 1,899), Arezzo prov., Tuscany, central Italy, on the Arno and 25 mi. E of Florence; macaroni, soap. Has late 13th-cent. castle of the Guidi family, with a high tower.

Poprad (pô'prät), Hung. *Poprád*, town (pop. 8,123), N Slovakia, Czechoslovakia, on SE slope of the High Tatra, on Poprad R. and 29 mi. NNW of Roznava; rail junction; paper mills, mfg. of agr.

machinery, malt production. Manganese works at Svabovce (shvä'bôftsĕ), Slovak *Švábovce*, 3 mi. SE; ironworks at Zakovce (zhä'kôftsĕ), Slovak *Žakovce*, 5 mi. NE. Former free town, founded in 12th cent. by Saxon immigrants; has 18th-cent. church with old murals, 17th-cent. belfry. Twin town of Velka (vĕl'kä), Slovak *Vel'ka*, Hung. *Felka*, part of Poprad commune, is just NW; has Tatra mus. Summer resort of Ganovce (gä'nôftsĕ), Slovak *Gánovce*, is 2 mi. SE.

Poprad River, N Slovakia, Czechoslovakia, and S Poland, rises in the High Tatra on W slope of Stalin Peak, 7 mi. NW of Stary Smokovec; flows ESE past Poprad, NE past Kezmarok, and NNW for c.20 mi. along Czechoslovak-Pol. border, into Poland, past Piwniczna, to Dunajec R. just SSW of Nowy Sacz; 95 mi. long.

Poptún (pōptōōn') or **Poctún** (pōk–), village (pop. 180), Petén dept., N Guatemala, 45 mi. E of Flores; airfield; chicle-shipping center; agr. (sugar cane, grain).

Populonia (pôpōōlô'nyä), anc. *Pupluna*, village (pop. 72), Livorno prov., Tuscany, central Italy, on small promontory, 5 mi. N of Piombino. An Etruscan seaport; has remains (walls, tombs) of the period and a medieval citadel (badly damaged in Second World War).

Poquonock (pŭkwŏ'nŭk, –nĭk), village (1940 pop. 512) in Windsor town, N Conn., on Farmington R. and 14 mi. N of Hartford.

Poquonock River, SW Conn., rises near Monroe, flows c.15 mi. generally S, past Trumbull, to Long Isl. Sound at Bridgeport; navigable for 1¼ mi. above Bridgeport harbor.

Poquott (pō'kwŏt), village (pop. 136), Suffolk co., SE N.Y., on N shore of Long Isl., on Port Jefferson Harbor, just E of Port Jefferson, in resort, truck-farming, and poultry area.

Porabka (pôrōp'kä), Pol. *Porąbka*, village, Krakow prov., S Poland, 8 mi. N of Zywiec and on Sola R. (hydroelectric station).

Porajärvi, Karelo-Finnish SSR: see POROSOZERO.

Porali River (pōrä'lē), anc. *Arabis*, SE Baluchistan, W Pakistan, rises in hills of central Jhalawan div. of Kalat state, SSW of Khuzdar; flows c.180 mi. S into marsh on shore of Arabian Sea 15 mi. NW of Sonmiani. Drains lowland of central Las Bela; seasonal. In 325 B.C., crossed S of Bela by Alexander the Great. Also spelled Purali.

Porangaba (pôrăng-gä'bŏŏ). **1** Town, Ceará, Brazil: see PARANGABA. **2** City (pop. 1,174), S central São Paulo, Brazil, 28 mi. SW of Botucatu; cotton, coffee, hogs.

Porano (pôrä'nô), village (pop. 718), Terni prov., Umbria, central Italy, 2 mi. S of Orvieto; cement-works.

Porapora, Society Isls.: see BORA-BORA.

Porbandar (pōr'bŭndŭr), town (pop. 48,493), Halar dist., W Saurashtra, India, port on Arabian Sea, on Kathiawar peninsula, 55 mi. WNW of Junagarh. Rail terminus; airport; agr. market (millet, cotton, oilseeds); exports ghee, cotton, cement, salt, building stone; mfg. of matches, hosiery, paint, furniture, ghee; cotton and oilseed milling, shipbuilding, hand-loom weaving, fish curing; cement, engineering, and saltworks. Mahatma Gandhi b. here, 1869. Was ⊙ (1785–1948) former princely state of Porbandar (□ 642; pop. 146,648) of Western India States agency; state established c.16th cent. by Jethwa Rajputs; merged 1948 with Saurashtra.

Porce River (pôr'sä), Antioquia dept., N central Colombia, rises as Medellín R. in Cordillera Central S of Medellín, flows c.150 mi. NNE, past Medellín and Bello, to Nechí R. 6 mi. SSW of Zaragoza. Its alluvial soil is rich in gold. Guadalupe Falls and hydroelectric plant are on a small left affluent.

Porcher Island (pôr'kŭr) (□ 210; 22 mi. long, 18 mi. wide), W B.C., in Hecate Strait, 16 mi. SSW of Prince Rupert, NW of Pitt Isl. S coast is deeply indented. Rises to over 2,000 ft. Villages are Jap Inlet (N), Refuge Bay (NW), and Oona River (E); lumbering.

Porchester, England: see PORTCHESTER.

Porcia (pôr'chä), village (pop. 688), Udine prov., Friuli–Venezia Giulia, NE Italy, 2 mi. W of Pordenone; cotton mill.

Porciúncula (pôrsyōōng'kōōlŏŏ), city (pop. 2,873), NE Rio de Janeiro state, Brazil, on railroad and 17 mi. NNW of Itaperuna; coffeegrowing center.

Porco, province, Bolivia: see UYUNI.

Porco (pôr'kō), village (pop. c.2,100), Potosí dept., W central Bolivia, on E slopes of Cordillera de los Frailes and 22 mi. SW of Potosí, near Río Mulato–Potosí RR; alt. 13,297 ft.; tin- and antimony-mining center. One of 1st silver-mining centers of Inca period.

Porcón (pôrkōn'), village (pop. 2,165), Cajamarca dept., NW Peru, in Cordillera Occidental, 6 mi. NW of Cajamarca; barley, sheep, cattle.

Porcos Island (pôr'kōōs), NE Pará, Brazil, in N distributary of Amazon delta, just NE of Gurupá and NW of Marajó isls. Dissected by river channels.

Porcsalma (pôr'chōlmŏ), town (pop. 3,087), Szatmar-Bereg co., NE Hungary, 15 mi. NW of Satu-Mare, Rumania; grain, beans, tobacco, horses, cattle.

Porcuna (pôrkōō'nä), city (pop. 12,584), Jaén prov., S Spain, in Andalusia, 24 mi. WNW of Jaén; olive-oil production and processing center. Mfg. of furniture, soap, soda water, cheese; flour- and saw-milling, brandy distilling, tanning. Granite quarries. Has ruins of castle of Knights of Calatrava, where Boabdil, last Moorish king, was once imprisoned (15th cent.).

Porcupine, village (pop. estimate 500), E Ont., on Porcupine L., 8 mi. ENE of Timmins; gold and barite mining. Founded 1909 as mining camp, it gives its name to surrounding mining district, which includes famous Dome and Hollinger mines, discovered 1909. In recent years Porcupine has been superseded by near-by South Porcupine.

Porcupine Hills, SW Alta., foothills of Rocky Mts., extend c.30 mi. N–S 40 mi. W of Lethbridge; rise to over 4,000 ft.

Porcupine Mountain, range, W Man., extends 60 mi. along Sask. line W of L. Winnipegosis. Highest point is Hart Mtn. (2,700 ft.), 27 mi. NNW of Swan River.

Porcupine Mountains, Ontonagon co., NW Upper Peninsula, Mich., WSW of Ontonagon, near L. Superior; includes highest point (2,023 ft.) in state. Mining of large copper deposits here began 1951 at White Pine Mine, 15 mi. WSW of Ontonagon.

Porcupine Plain, village (pop. 297), E central Sask., 40 mi. ESE of Tisdale; wheat, dairying.

Porcupine River, N Yukon and NE Alaska, rises in Canada on W slope of Mackenzie Mts. near 65°27'N 139°51'W, flows generally N to 67°30'N 138°25'W, thence WSW into Alaska to Yukon R. at Fort Yukon; 525 mi. long. Passes through fur-trapping and placer gold-mining region. Discovered 1842 by John Bell of Hudson's Bay Co.

Porcupines, The, small isls., Hancock co., S Maine, in Frenchman Bay just E of Bar Harbor; individually known as Long Porcupine, Burnt Porcupine, Sheep Porcupine, and Bald Porcupine isls., and Rum Key.

Pordenone (pôrdĕnô'nĕ), town (pop. 12,179), Udine prov., Friuli–Venezia Giulia, NE Italy, 28 mi. WSW of Udine. Chief industrial center of Friuli; mfg. (automobile chassis, trailers, machinery, furniture, cotton and silk textiles, fertilizer, rope, pottery, jewelry, leather goods). Has palace (1291; remodeled 1927–28), Gothic and Renaissance houses. Cathedral (rebuilt 15th cent.) and picture gall. contain paintings by Pordenone, b. here.

Pordim (pôr'dĭm), village (pop. 3,283), Pleven dist., N Bulgaria, 12 mi. E of Pleven; grain, oil-bearing plants.

Pore (pō'rā), town, ⊙ Casanare intendency (formed 1950), NE Colombia, at E foot of the Cordillera Oriental, 95 mi. ENE of Tunja.

Porec or **Porech** (both: pô'rĕch), Serbo-Croatian *Poreč*, region of W Macedonia, Yugoslavia, extending from Brod Makedonski c.20 mi. N, along Treska R. Sometimes spelled Porece or Poreche, Serbo-Croatian *Poreče*.

Porec, Serbo-Croatian *Poreč*, Ital. *Parenzo* (pärĕn'tsô), village (pop. 4,401), NW Croatia, Yugoslavia, on Adriatic Sea, 30 mi. S of Trieste, in Istria. Has cathedral (535–43) in Byzantine style and bldgs. in Venetian-Gothic and Renaissance styles. Was ⊙ Istria under Austrian rule.

Porechye or **Porech'ye** (pŭryĕ'chyĭ). **1** Pol. *Porzecze*, village (1939 pop. over 500), NW Grodno oblast, Belorussian SSR, 19 mi. NE of Grodno; junction of rail spur to Druskininkai (Lithuania); lumbering. **2** City, Smolensk oblast, Russian SFSR: see DEMIDOV. **3** Village (1926 pop. 146), S Velikiye Luki oblast, Russian SFSR, 17 mi. S of Velikiye Luki; flax.

Porechye-Rybnoye or **Porech'ye-Rybnoye** (–rĭb'nŭyŭ), town (1926 pop. 2,461), SE Yaroslavl oblast, Russian SFSR, near L. Nero, 7 mi. S of Rostov; metalworks.

Poretskoye (pŭryĕt'skŭyŭ), village (1926 pop. 5,517), W Chuvash Autonomous SSR, Russian SFSR, on Sura R. and 26 mi. NNW of Alatyr; wheat, livestock.

Porez (pŭryĕs'), village, E Kirov oblast, Russian SFSR, 45 mi. ENE of Molotovsk; flax, wheat.

Porga (pôr'gä), village, NW Dahomey, Fr. West Africa, near Upper Volta and Fr. Togoland border, on intercolonial road and 55 mi. NNW of Natitingou.

Pori (pō'rē), Swedish *Björneborg* (byûr'nŭbôr"yŭ), city (pop. 41,355), Turku-Pori co., SW Finland, on Kokemäki R. near its mouth on Gulf of Bothnia, 65 mi. W of Tampere; 61°29'N 21°48'E. Seaport, kept ice-free the year round; exports timber products and metals. Lumber, pulp, paper, and cotton mills, nickel and copper refineries, match works, machine shops. Site of radio station. Has mus. Inc. (1365) as Ulvila, moved (1558) to present site. Suffered destructive fires in 16th and 19th cent. Mäntyluoto and Reposaari (NW), on isls. in Gulf of Bothnia, are outports.

Poritsk (pŭrĕtsk'), Pol. *Poryck* (pô'rĭtsk), town (1931 pop. 2,230), SW Volyn oblast, Ukrainian SSR, 15 mi. SSE of Vladimir-Volynski; flour milling, brick mfg. Has old palace. A Lithuanian settlement in 14th cent.; became residence of Pol. gentry. Passed to Russia (1795); reverted to Poland (1921); ceded to USSR in 1945. Pol. historian Thaddeus Czacki b. here (1765).

Po River (pŭ), Chinese *Po Kiang* or *P'o Chiang* (both: jyäng), short stream of N Kiangsi prov., China, formed near Poyang by union of Loan and Chang rivers, flows 5 mi. into Poyang L. at Poyang.

Po River (pō, It. pô), anc. *Padus* and *Eridanus*, longest river (405 mi.) of Italy, with a large drainage basin (□ 28,945), forming bet. the Alps and the Apennines the widest and most fertile plain of the country. Rises at c.6,000 ft. on Monte Viso in Cottian Alps, flows E and NE, past Turin and Chivasso, then generally E, through Piedmont, past Piacenza and Cremona, separating Lombardy and Veneto from Emilia-Romagna, to the Adriatic c.35 mi. S of Venice, emptying into it by many mouths and continually building its large delta farther out into the sea. Navigable for 345 mi. to Casale Monferrato; used extensively for irrigation. Its chief tributaries, Tanaro, Dora Baltea, Ticino, Adda, Oglio, and Mincio rivers, all rise in the Alps; those descending from the Apennines, Trebbia, Taro, Panaro, and Secchia rivers, are mostly much smaller.

Porjus (pôr'yŭs"), village (pop. 1,176), Norrbotten co., N Sweden, on Lule R. and 60 mi. S of Kiruna, within Arctic Circle. Site of major hydroelectric station, supplying power to mines at Kiruna, Gallivare, and Malmberget, and to Lapland railroad (Lulea-Narvik); completed 1914. Near by is new power station at Harspranget.

Porkha, Tibet: see BARKHA.

Porkhov (pôr'khŭf), city (1939 pop. over 10,000), E central Pskov oblast, Russian SFSR, on Shelon R. and 45 mi. E of Pskov; tanning center; flax processing, distilling. Peat works near by. Remains of fortress walls. Founded 1346 as outpost of Novgorod; repeatedly sacked by Lithuanians. During Second World War, held (1941–44) by Germans.

Porkkala (pōrk'kälä), village, Uusimaa co., S Finland, on small Porkkala Peninsula [Porkkala Udd] on Gulf of Finland, 20 mi. SW of Helsinki, opposite Tallinn; 59°59'N 24°26'E. Under the Treaty of Paris (1947), confirming the Russo-Finnish armistice of 1944, the coastal enclave (□ 152; 20 mi. long, 4–10 mi. wide) surrounding Porkkala was leased to USSR as a naval base for 50 years, in exchange for the HANGO peninsula.

Porkonen, Finland: see KITTILÄ.

Porlamar (pôrlämär'), town (pop. 6,426) on Margarita Isl. (SE), Nueva Esparta state, NE Venezuela, 7 mi. S of La Asunción, 45 mi. NW of Carúpano; main trading center of isl., linked by steamer with La Guaira and Orinoco R. Base for pearl and deep-sea fishing (tuna, herring, sardine, Sp. mackerel); fish canneries. Airport.

Porlezza (pôrlā'tsä), village (pop. 1,152), Como prov., Lombardy, N Italy, port at NE end of L. of Lugano, 16 mi. N of Como, in grape-, olive-, and silk-growing region.

Porlock, town and parish (pop. 1,351), W Somerset, England, near Bristol Channel, 5 mi. W of Minehead; agr. market; shoe mfg.; resort. Has 13th-cent. church. Just N, on Bristol Channel, is small fishing port of Porlock Weir.

Pornic (pôrnēk'), town (pop. 2,283), Loire-Inférieure dept., W France, fishing port and bathing resort on Bay of Bourgneuf of the Atlantic, 27 mi. WSW of Nantes. Has a 13th–14th-cent. castle (restored). Scene (1793) of Republican victory over Vendée insurgents.

Pornichet (pôrnēshā'), town (pop. 7,079), Loire-Inférieure dept., W France, on Bay of Biscay and 6 mi. W of Saint-Nazaire; popular bathing resort adjoining La Baule-les-Pins (W). Fishing; oysters.

Poro. **1** Town, La Union prov., Philippines: see SAN FERNANDO. **2** Town on Poro Isl. (Cebu prov.), Philippines: see PORO ISLAND.

Poro Island (pō'rō), largest island (□ 39; 1948 pop. 19,360) of Camotes Isls., Visayan Isls., Philippines, in Camotes Sea, bet. Pacijan and Ponson isls., c.20 mi. W of Leyte; 9 mi. long, 6 mi. wide. Hilly, rising to 1,282 ft. Coconut growing, fishing. On SW coast is Poro town (1939 pop. 1,304; 1948 municipality pop. 12,523).

Poroma (pōrō'mä), town (pop. c.2,140), Chuquisaca dept., W central Bolivia, on Chayanta R. and c.45 mi. NNW of Sucre; wheat, barley, corn, vegetables.

Poronai, Japan: see MIKASA.

Poronai River or **Poronay River** (pŭrŭnī'), Jap. *Horonai-kawa* (hōrōnī'-kä'wŭ), S Sakhalin, Russian SFSR, rises on Mt. Nevelskoi of E range, flows W and S, through central valley, to Terpeniye Gulf of Sea of Okhotsk at Poronaisk; 155 mi. long.

Poronaisk or **Poronaysk** (–nīsk'), city (1940 pop. 27,935), S Sakhalin, Russian SFSR, minor port on Terpeniye Gulf, at mouth of Poronai R., on E coast railroad and 125 mi. SSE of Aleksandrovsk; pulp and paper milling, fish canning; fur-collecting point. Ships coal from near-by Vakhrushev, Gastello, and Leonidovo mines. Developed when reached (1936) by railroad. Under Jap. rule (1905–45), called Shikuka (shĭkōō'kä).

Porongos, Uruguay: see TRINIDAD.

Porongos Lakes (pōrōng'gōs), salt lakes and swamps, NE Córdoba prov., Argentina, just N of the Mar Chiquita, along the lower reaches of the Río Dulce. L. Porongos is a small salt lake on the Dulce.

Poros (pôr'ôs), anc. *Calauria*, island (□ 7.4; 1940 pop. 5,629) in Aegean Sea at mouth of Saronic Gulf and just off E tip of Argolis Peninsula, part of Attica nome, Greece; 5 mi. long, 2 mi. wide. Sheep, goat raising. On S shore lies town and port of Poros (1928 pop. 4,593), a fortified naval station. Remains of temple of Poseidon (NE) are associated with suicide (322 B.C.) of Demosthenes.

Poroshiri-dake (pōrō'shĭrē-dākā) or **Horoshiri-dake** (hōrō'–), peak (6,732 ft.), S Hokkaido, Japan, 30 mi. SW of Obihiro.

Porosozero (pô'rŭsô"zyĭrŭ), Finnish *Porajärvi*, village, SW Karelo-Finnish SSR, on Suna R. and 60 mi. NW of Kondopoga; lumbering. Under Finnish administration, 1918–20.

Poroszlo (pô'rôslō), Hung. *Poroszló*, agr. town (pop. 5,142), Heves co., N Hungary, on Eger R. and 6 mi. WNW of Tiszafüred.

Porozovitsa River, Russian SFSR: see NORTHERN DVINA CANAL.

Porozovo (pŭrô'zŭvŭ), Pol. *Porozów* (pôrô'zŏŏf), village (1937 pop. 2,000), S Grodno oblast, Belorussian SSR, 17 mi. SSW of Volkovysk; agr. processing (flaxseed, grain), cloth mfg.

Porphyrousa, Greece: see KYTHERA.

Porquerolles, Île de (ēl dû pôrkŭrôl'), westernmost of Hyères islands (□ 4.5; pop. c.350) in the Mediterranean off S coast of France (Var dept.), 10 mi. SSE of Hyères. Village and fishing port dominated by 16th-cent. fort. Hotels. Lighthouse. Best reached from Giens Peninsula (3 mi. NW).

Porrentruy (pôrãtrwē'), Ger. *Pruntrut* (prŏŏnt'-rŏŏt), town (pop. 6,121), Bern canton, NW Switzerland, 26 mi. WSW of Basel; watches, knit goods, shoes, metal products, flour; woodworking. Old castle.

Porreras (pôrā'räs), town (pop. 4,620), Majorca, Balearic Isls., on railroad and 20 mi. E of Palma; agr. center (cereals, almonds, grapes, sheep, hogs). Liquor distilling, wine making, meat packing, sawmilling; mfg. of shoes and cement.

Porretta Terme (pôr-rĕt'tä tĕr'mĕ), town (pop. 2,374), Bologna prov., Emilia-Romagna, N central Italy, on Reno R. and 16 mi. NNE of Pistoia, in Etruscan Apennines. Health resort (alt. 1,145 ft.) with hot mineral springs; mfg. (woolen textiles, agr. machinery, shoes, tannic acid, macaroni). Called Bagni della Porretta until c.1931.

Porriño (pôrē'nyō), town (pop. 2,299), Pontevedra prov., NW Spain, 8 mi. SE of Vigo; meat-packing center; tanning, mfg. of ceramics and auto accessories, sawmilling; agr. trade.

Porsang Fjord (pŏr'säng), Nor. *Porsangen Fjord*, inlet (80 mi. long, 5–12 mi. wide) of Barents Sea of Arctic Ocean, Finnmark co., N Norway, 40 mi. E of Hammerfest. Mageroy lies on W side of its mouth.

Porsgrunn (pôrs'grŏŏn), city (pop. 9,003) and port, Telemark co., S Norway, on Skien R. (here called Porsgrunn R.) and 5 mi. SSE of Skien; industrial center, with metallurgical works, shipyards, lumber and ice trade, and mfg. of china and electrical appliances. Founded in 17th cent. Formerly spelled Porsgrund.

Porsuk River (pôrsŏŏk'), W central Turkey, rises 20 mi. W of Afyonkarahisar, flows 175 mi. N and E, past Kutahya and Eskisehir, to Sakarya R. 11 mi. NW of Polatli.

Portachuelo (pōrtächwā'lō), town (pop. c.7,200), ⊙ Gutiérrez (formerly Sara) prov., Santa Cruz dept., central Bolivia, 33 mi. NNW of Santa Cruz; tropical agr. center (sugar cane, rice, cacao).

Port Acres, village (1940 pop. 1,856), Jefferson co., SE Texas; NW suburb of Port Arthur, in industrial area.

Port Adelaide, city (pop. 33,382), SE South Australia, 7 mi. NW of Adelaide and on inlet of Gulf St. Vincent; chief port of state; wool-trading center. Port comprises outer harbor on E shore of gulf and inner harbor (site of city proper) at S end of inlet bet. small peninsula and Torrens Isl. Iron-smelting works; plaster, Portland cement, sulphuric acid. Exports wheat, flour, wool; imports sulphur.

Portadown (pôrtŭdoun'), municipal borough (1937 pop. 12,440; 1951 census 17,202), N Co. Armagh, Northern Ireland, on Bann R. and 25 mi. WSW of Belfast; railroad center; linen milling, food canning, jam making, mfg. of lace, clothing, carpets, rope, fish nets. Town's development dates from 19th cent.

Portaferry (pôr"tŭfĕ'rē), town (pop. 1,746), E Co. Down, Northern Ireland, on E shore of Strangford Lough, near its mouth on the Irish Sea, 8 mi. NE of Downpatrick; fishing port and agr. market (flax, oats).

Portage (pôr'tĭj) or **Portage Junction**, village (pop. 33), S Alaska, 40 mi. SE of Anchorage and on railroad to Seward, at head of Turnagain Arm; junction for Whittier.

Portage (pôr'tĭj). **1** County (□ 504; pop. 63,954), NE Ohio; ⊙ Ravenna. Intersected by Cuyahoga R. and tributaries of the Mahoning. Has many small lakes. Agr. area (dairy products, livestock, fruit, grain, truck); mfg. at Ravenna, Kent, Garrettsville; sand and gravel pits, coal mines. Formed 1807. **2** County (□ 810; pop. 34,858), central Wis.; ⊙ Stevens Point. Intersected by Wisconsin R.; also drained by Plover and small Waupaca rivers. Farming, dairying, and paper making. Formed 1836.

Portage. 1 Village, Maine: see PORTAGE LAKE, town. **2** Village (pop. 1,677), Kalamazoo co., SW Mich., a S suburb of Kalamazoo. **3** Village (pop. 437), Wood co., NW Ohio, on Portage R. and 3 mi. S of Bowling Green; farming; limestone quarrying. **4** Borough (pop. 4,371), Cambria co., SW central Pa., 14 mi. ENE of Johnstown and on Conemaugh R.; silk mills; bituminous coal, timber. **5** Town (pop. 254), Box Elder co., N Utah, 35 mi. NNW of Brigham and on Malad R., near Idaho line; alt. 4,370 ft.; irrigated farming. **6** City (pop. 7,334), ⊙ Columbia co., S central Wis., on both banks of Wisconsin R. and on Portage Canal, and 33 mi. N of Madison, in diversified-farming area; mfg. (shoes, tanks, hosiery, boats, monuments, airplane propellers, beer, dairy products); cannery. Resort. A portage here bet. Wisconsin and Fox rivers was 1st crossed by Louis Jolliet and Father Marquette (1673), and was later used by other early explorers, missionaries, and traders; Portage Canal now follows this route. Site of Fort Winnebago (1828), and the restored Indian Agency house (1832) are here. Zona Gale and Frederick Jackson Turner b. here. Inc. 1854.

Portage des Sioux (pôrtăj' dā sōō, –dĭ sōō), town (pop. 264), St. Charles co., E Mo., 12 mi. NE of St. Charles and on Mississippi R. Settled c.1799 around Sp. fort, at end of a portage bet. Mississippi and Missouri rivers. Negotiations (1815), here, bet. U.S. commissioners and Indian tribes.

Portage du Fort (pôrtäzh' dü fôr'), village (pop. 361), SW Que., on Ottawa R. and 45 mi. WNW of Ottawa; lumbering, dairying; stock.

Portage Island (pôr'tĭj) (3 mi. long, 1 mi. wide), NE N.B., in the Gulf of St. Lawrence, at entrance of Miramichi Bay, 22 mi. ENE of Chatham; 47°10'N 65°2'W. At S end are 2 lighthouses.

Portage Lake, town (pop. 542), Aroostook co., NE Maine, on Portage L. and 23 mi. WNW of Presque Isle, in hunting, fishing region. Includes Portage village.

Portage Lake. 1 In Maine: see FISH RIVER LAKES. **2** In Manistee co., NW Mich., 8 mi. NE of Manistee; c.3 mi. long, c.1 mi. wide. Onekama is on NE shore. Joined to L. Michigan (just W) by dredged canal. **3** In NW Upper Peninsula, Mich.: see KEWEENAW WATERWAY.

Portage Lakes, NE Ohio, S of Akron, group of 7 lakes in 2,250-acre state park; boating, fishing, camping, sports.

Portage la Prairie (pôr"tĭj lŭ prâ'rē), city (pop. 7,620), S Man., near Assiniboine R., 50 mi. W of Winnipeg; wheat center; grain mills, mfg. of agr. machinery and bricks. Has large parks and Indian school. Airport. La Vérendrye here built Fort La Reine, 1738. In fur-trade days it was important as carrying point bet. Assiniboine R. and L. Manitoba. Hudson's Bay Co. post, established there by 1832, moved to site of present city 1870. Post burned 1913.

Portage River, N Ohio, formed in Wood co. by North, Middle, and South branches, flows c.33 mi. NW, past Pemberville, Woodville, and Oakharbor, to L. Erie at Port Clinton. North Branch rises near Leipsic, flows c.40 mi. N. Middle Branch (c.35 mi. long) and South Branch (c.20 mi. long) flow NE and join just before entering main stream.

Portageville (pōr'tĭjvĭl). **1** City (pop. 2,662), New Madrid co., extreme SE Mo., near Mississippi R., 15 mi. SW of New Madrid; cotton, timber processing. Inc. 1903. **2** Resort village, Wyoming co., W N.Y., on Genesee R. and 11 mi. S of Perry, at S entrance to Letchworth State Park.

Port Ahuriri, New Zealand: see NAPIER.

Portaje (pôrtä'hā), village (pop. 1,247), Cáceres prov., W Spain, 32 mi. NNW of Cáceres; sirup mfg., flour milling; cereals.

Portal. 1 Town (pop. 532), Bulloch co., E Ga., 10 mi. WNW of Statesboro. **2** City (pop. 409), Burke co., NW N.Dak., 20 mi. NW of Bowbells and on Can. line. Port of entry.

Port Alberni (ălbûr'nē), city (1941 pop. 4,584; 1946 estimate 6,927), SW B.C., on S central Vancouver Isl., inland port at head of Alberni Canal, 40 mi. W of Nanaimo, 90 mi. NW of Victoria; port of entry; lumbering, fishing center; lumber-shipping port; paper mills. In mining (gold, silver, copper, lead, zinc) region. Alberni is just N.

Portal del Infierno (pôrtäl' dĕl ēnfyĕr'nō), village, Olancho dept., E Honduras, on Patuca R. and 45 mi. ESE of Juticalpa; lumbering. Airfield.

Portalegre (pôrtŏolā'grĭ), city (pop. 639), W Rio Grande do Norte, NE Brazil, on a hill 70 mi. SW of Mossoró; tobacco, sugar. Formerly spelled Porto Alegre.

Portalegre, district (□ 2,358; pop. 186,373), Alto Alentejo prov., E central Portugal; ⊙ Portalegre. Bounded by Spain (E) and Tagus R. (N). Crossed near Sp. border by the Serra de São Mamede. Drained and irrigated by affluents of the Tagus (N) and Guadiana (SE). Chief towns: Portalegre, and former frontier fortresses of Elvas and Campo Maior.

Portalegre, anc. *Ammaia*, city (pop. 12,046), ⊙ Portalegre dist., central Portugal, 100 mi. ENE of Lisbon, on W slope of Serra de São Mamede, near Sp. border; textile-mfg. center (woolens, silk); cork processing and shipping, distilling, footwear mfg. Agr. trade (olive oil, grain, livestock). City has numerous 16th–17th-cent. bldgs., including a cathedral (built 1556 by 1st bishop).

Portales (pûrtă'lĭs, pôr–), city (pop. 8,112), ⊙ Roosevelt co., E N.Mex., on Llano Estacado, near Texas line, 18 mi. SW of Clovis. Trade center in irrigated grazing and agr. area (fruit, truck); food processing (dairy products, canned goods, beverages), cotton gins. Eastern N.Mex. Univ. here. Eastern N. Mex. State Park 7 mi. NE. Founded 1898, inc. 1930.

Portalet, pass, Pyrenees, Spanish name of POURTALET.

Port Alexander, village (1939 pop. 87), SE Alaska, on Chatham Strait, near S tip of Baranof Isl., 60 mi. SSE of Sitka; fishing (cannery at Port Armstrong, 6 mi. N).

Port Alfred, town (pop. 3,243), S central Que., on Ha Ha Bay of the Saguenay, 11 mi. SE of Chicoutimi; lumbering, dairying; resort.

Port Alfred, residential town (pop. 5,961), SE Cape Prov., U. of So. Afr., on Indian Ocean at mouth of Kowie R. (bridge), 80 mi. ENE of Port Elizabeth, 70 mi. SW of East London; popular seaside resort. Airfield. Founded 1825, it was formerly seaport; its harbor is now silted up.

Port Alice, village (pop. estimate 350), SW B.C., on N Vancouver Isl., on an inlet of Quatsino Sound, 27 mi. WSW of Alert Bay; pulp milling; lumber-shipping port.

Porta Littoria, Italy: see THUILE, LA.

Port Allegany (ă'lŭgā"nē, ă"lŭgā'nē), borough (pop. 2,519), McKean co., N Pa., 20 mi. SSE of Olean, N.Y., and on Allegheny R.; glass, bark extracts, toys; tannery. Lumber center in 1830s. Settled c.1816, inc. 1882.

Port Allen, commercial harbor, port of entry, Hanapepe Bay, S Kauai, T.H.; airport near by.

Port Allen, fishing village in Errol parish, SE Perthshire, Scotland, on the Firth of Tay, 9 mi. E of Perth.

Port Allen, town (pop. 3,097), ⊙ West Baton Rouge parish, SE central La., on the Mississippi, opposite Baton Rouge (ferry service); agr. (sugar cane, rice, corn, cotton); sugar and lumber milling. Laid out 1854, inc. 1923.

Port Alma (ăl'mŭ), village, E Queensland, Australia, on SW shore of Keppel Bay, at mouth of Fitzroy R., and 30 mi. SE of Rockhampton; forms outer harbor of port of Rockhampton; coal-loading. Exports wood, hides, cotton.

Port Angeles (ăn'jŭlŭs), city (pop. 11,233), ⊙ Clallam co., NW Wash., on Juan de Fuca Strait and 22 mi. S of Victoria, B.C., 60 mi. NW of Seattle. Seaport and port of entry, on fine harbor sheltered W and N by Ediz Hook, curving sandbar c.3½ mi. long, with lighthouse at tip. Fish, lumber, paper, cellulose, concrete, dairy products; resort center and hq. for Olympic Natl. Park (S). Settled in 1860s.

Port Antonio (ŭntō'nēō, ăn"–), town (pop. 5,482), ⊙ Portland parish, NE Jamaica, 3d largest port of the isl., 27 mi. NE of Kingston (linked by railroad); 18°10'N 76°27'W. Rail terminus, tourist resort, and trading center situated on spacious bay protected by small Navy Isl. Has 2 harbors and is divided into 2 sections, with the residential section, Titchfield, on a promontory. Once a leading banana port, it still ships tropical fruit (coconuts, bananas, cacao). Ice factory, bottling works; mfg. of sweets. Has govt. bldgs., old military barracks.

Porta Orientalis (pôr'tŭ ôrēĕntă'lĭs), Rum. *Poarta Orientală* (pwär'tă ôryĕntä'lŭ), pass (alt. 1,689 ft.) in the Transylvanian Alps, Rumania, 3 mi. S of Teregova; rail and highway corridor. Played important part in various historic invasions bet. Near East and Central Europe. Sometimes called Domasnia Pass.

Port-à-Piment (pôrt-ä-pēmā'), agr. town (1950 census pop. 2,328), Sud dept., SW Haiti, on SW coast of Tiburon Peninsula, 25 mi. W of Les Cayes.

Port Appin, fishing village, N Argyll, Scotland, on Loch Linnhe, 10 mi. NNE of Oban. Ferry to Lismore isl.

Port Aransas (ŭrăn'zŭs), resort town (pop. 551), Nueces co., S Texas, on harbor on Aransas Pass (ship channel) and Intracoastal Waterway, at N end of Mustang Isl., 22 mi. E of Corpus Christi; fishing.

Portarlington (pôrtär'lĭngtŭn), village (pop. 627), S Victoria, Australia, 26 mi. SSW of Melbourne, across Port Phillip Bay; seaside resort.

Portarlington, Gaelic *Cúil an tSúdaire*, town (pop. 2,092), NE Co. Laoighis, Ireland, on Barrow R. and 12 mi. W of Kildare; agr. market (wheat, barley, potatoes, beets); peat-digging center; power plant. Part of it is in Co. Offaly.

Port Armstrong, Alaska: see PORT ALEXANDER.

Port Arthur, city (pop. 24,426), ⊙ Thunder Bay dist., W Ont., on Thunder Bay, on NW shore of L. Superior, 200 mi. NE of Duluth; major grain and iron-shipping center, with large grain elevators, shipyards, drydock, and paper, pulp, and lumber mills; also woodworking, machinery mfg. Center of tourist district. Has technical school and collegiate institute. Just S is its twin city, FORT

WILLIAM. Near-by Kakabaka Falls supply hydro-electric power.

Port Arthur, Chinese *Lüshun* (lü'-shoon'), Jap. *Ryojun* (ryô'joon), Rus. *Port Artur*, city (1947 pop. 27,241), S Manchuria, at S tip of Liaotung peninsula, 23 mi. WSW of Dairen; 38°48'N 121°16'E. A rail terminus and ice-free Yellow Sea port, Port Arthur is a major naval base at entrance to Gulf of Chihli; it has saltworks, and silk-spinning and food-processing industries. Situated on N shore of a landlocked bay accessible through a 1,000-ft.-wide strait, the city consists of the old Chinese town and the modern section, respectively E and W of the rail terminus. An anc. Chinese port, dating at least from Sui dynasty (A.D. 581–618), it was formerly called Tali and Su and received the name Lüshun under the Ming dynasty. It was occupied in 1858 by a British fleet and 1st fortified by the Chinese in 1880s. During Sino-Japanese War, it was briefly held (1894–95) by Japan; and later was leased (1898) by Russia from China. In the Russo-Japanese War, the base was captured in 1905 by the Japanese following a 4-month siege. Subsequently, it was developed as a Jap. naval station within the leased Kwantung territory of which it was the capital until the capital was transferred (1937) to Dairen. After the Second World War, the base became (1945) a joint Soviet-Chinese naval base and hq. of the Port Arthur–Dairen administrative dist. (Chinese *Lü-ta Hsing-cheng Ch'ü*). This dist., the successor to the Jap.-leased territory of Kwantung, consists of the S tip of the Liaotung peninsula (S of c.39°15'N), and includes CHINHSIEN, the free port of DAIREN, and the CHANGSHAN ISLANDS (E).

Port Arthur, town and port (pop. 172), SE Tasmania, on Tasman Peninsula, 32 mi. SE of Hobart; dairy and agr. products, sheep. Site (1834–53) of Australia's principal penal colony.

Port Arthur, city (pop. 57,530), Jefferson co., SE Texas, on Sabine L. and 15 mi. SE of Beaumont; an important deep-water port, on SABINE-NECHES WATERWAY to the Gulf, connecting here with Gulf Intracoastal Waterway; exports much petroleum, also grain, cotton, rice, lumber; port of entry. A major oil-refining center, supplied by fields of Gulf Coast and pipelines from others; has shipyards, railroad shops, brass foundries, chemical plants; also makes steel containers, rubber goods. Seat of Port Arthur Col. Has pleasure pier, on reclaimed land in Sabine L. To NE is high bridge (completed 1938) across Neches R. Founded 1895 as Gulf Coast railroad terminus, in livestock, rice-raising area; ship channel (begun 1897) and the boom following oil discovery near Beaumont (1901) founded its present importance.

Port Arthur Canal, Texas: see SABINE-NECHES WATERWAY.

Portas do Cêrco, Macao: see MACAO.

Port Askaig (pôrtăskāg'), village, NE ISLAY, Hebrides, Scotland.

Port Augusta, town and northernmost port (pop. 4,350) of South Australia, at head of Spencer Gulf, 50 mi. NNW of Port Pirie; 32°30'S 137°46'E. S terminus of Central Australian RR. Exports wool, wheat.

Port au Port (pôr'tō pôr'), peninsula on the Gulf of St. Lawrence, SW N.F., bet. St. George Bay and Port au Port Bay, W of Stephenville; 30 mi. long, up to 10 mi. wide, connected with mainland by narrow isthmus. On N shore of isthmus is fishing settlement of Port au Port (pop. 336), 45 mi. SW of Corner Brook. From N end of peninsula a narrow spit of land projects 15 mi. NE, enclosing Port au Port Bay (18 mi. long, up to 12 mi. wide). At W extremity of peninsula is Cape St. George.

Port-au-Prince (pôrt-ō-prĭns', Fr. pôr-tō-prēs'), city (1950 pop. 142,840, with W suburb of Carrefour; 1950 commune pop. 195,672), ⊙ Haiti and Ouest dept. (□ c.3,000; 1950 pop. 1,094,510), largest town and chief port of the republic, on SE arm of the Gulf of Gonaïves, 150 mi. W of Ciudad Trujillo, 280 mi. E of Kingston (Jamaica); 18°33'N 72°20'W. Commercial and processing center at W end of the fertile Cul-de-Sac plain (sugar cane, cotton). Has a humid, warm climate with little seasonal change; average temp. 81°F.; rains: May–June, Aug.–Oct. Its excellent natural harbor, accommodating vessels of 30 ft. draught, ships about ⅓ of exports and handles bulk of imports. There is air service to Miami, Jamaica, Cuba, Puerto Rico, and the interior. Industries include sugar milling, rum and alcohol distilling, vegetable-oil extracting, rice milling, brewing, tanning; mfg. of shoes and tobacco products. Coastal fishing. Port-au-Prince is an archbishopric and seat of a univ. Among its fine bldgs. are the 18th-cent. cathedral, natl. palace, palace of justice, natl. assembly, Univ. of Haiti, mus., library, and professional schools. City was laid out 1749 by the French, replacing (1770) Cap-Haïtien as capital of old Saint-Domingue colony. It has suffered frequently from earthquakes (especially in 1842), fires, and civil warfare. During U.S. occupation (1915–34), its sanitary conditions were improved. Bicentennial "World Fair" held here in 1949. A highway leads into SE hills to resorts of Pétionville, Kenscoff, and Furcy.

Port Austin, resort village (pop. 724), Huron co., E Mich., c.55 mi. NE of Bay City, on L. Huron.

Port aux Basques (pôrtōbăsk'), town (pop. 879), at SW tip of N.F., on small bay, 310 mi. W of St. John's (connected by rail) and 8 mi. ESE of Cape Ray; 47°35'N 59°10'W. Terminal for mail-ship service across Cabot Strait from North Sydney, N.S. Cod and halibut fishing port, with cold-storage plants and govt. bait depot. During winter months Corner Brook newsprint production is shipped from here. Near by is mink farm. In 1945 Port aux Basques was inc. with near-by CHANNEL as a single municipality.

Port-aux-Français, Indian Ocean: see KERGUELEN ISLANDS.

Port-aux-Poules (pôrtōpool'), village (pop. 600), Oran dept., NW Algeria, on the Gulf of Arzew (Mediterranean Sea), on railroad and 20 mi. SW of Mostaganem; bathing resort; winegrowing.

Porta Westfalica, Germany: see WESER MOUNTAINS.

Portbail (pôrbī'), village (pop. 451), Manche dept., NW France, fishing port on the Channel, on W coast of Cotentin Peninsula, 21 mi. S of Cherbourg; cement-pipe mfg., dairying. Small beach (W).

Port Bannatyne (bă'nŭtĭn), village, Buteshire, Scotland, on E coast of Bute isl., 2 mi. N of Rothesay; fishing port, resort. Near by are remains of 14th-cent. Kames Castle.

Port Barre (pôrt bă'rē), village (pop. 1,066), St. Landry parish, S central La., 8 mi. E of Opelousas; cotton gins; wood products. Oil and natural-gas fields near by.

Port Barrow, village (pop. 1,619, with adjacent Smoke Bend), Ascension parish, SE La., on the Mississippi just N of Donaldsonville.

Port Bell, town, Buganda prov., S Uganda, port on N shore of L. Victoria, 6 mi. ESE of Kampala (linked by rail); cotton, coffee, sugar cane; fishing. Seaplane base.

Port-Bergé (pôr'-bârzhā'), town, Majunga prov., NW Madagascar, on road and 90 mi. ENE of Majunga; trades in cattle, rice, tobacco. Airfield.

Port Blair (blâr), town (pop. 4,111), ⊙ Andaman and Nicobar Isls., India, on SE S.Andaman Isl., 420 mi. SW of Rangoon; 11°41'N 92°46'E. Has fine natural harbor on Andaman Sea; steamer connection with Rangoon, Calcutta (810 mi. NNW), and Madras (840 mi. WNW); airfield; exports timber, matchwood, coconuts, copra. Sawmill, ice plant, bakery; handicraft mfg. (palm mats and baskets, wood products, leather goods, metalware), boat building, fishing. Town has mean temp. of 85°F., with annual rainfall of c.135 in.; meteorological station. Founded 1789 and used for short while by British in effort to suppress piracy; resettled 1856, and made (1858) a penal colony, to which many prisoners were sent after Sepoy Rebellion of 1857, as well as life and long-term convicts. Penal settlement, which comprised town and large surrounding area (□ c.470), was scene of assassination of Lord Mayo (viceroy of India) in 1872. Deportation of prisoners from India ceased after 1921; colony discontinued in 1945. During Second World War, town was used (1942–45) as naval and air base by Japanese and was seat of semi-administration of rebel Indian natl. army.

Port Bolivar (bŏ'lĭvŭr), former port (pop. c.200), Galveston co., S Texas, at tip of Bolivar Peninsula, across mouth of Galveston Bay just NE of Galveston.

Port Borden, town (pop. 512), S P.E.I., on Northumberland Strait, 27 mi. W of Charlottetown; 46°15'N 63°42'W; fishing port, terminal of train ferry from Cape Tormentine, N.B.

Port Bou (bō'), village (pop. 1,664), Gerona prov., NE Spain, 15 mi. NE of Figueras; customs station near Fr. border on railroad from Perpignan to Barcelona; small port on the Mediterranean at foot of the Monts Albères. Fishing; olive oil, wine trade.

Port-Bouet (pôr'-bwā'), Atlantic port, SE Ivory Coast, Fr. West Africa, just opposite ABIDJAN, across Ebrié Lagoon (linked by bridge). Terminus of inland railroad to Bobo-Dioulasso, Upper Volta. Harbor construction begun in 1930s. Sometimes Petit-Bassam.

Port Brabant (brŭbănt', bră'bŭnt), village, NW Mackenzie Dist., Northwest Territories, on Refuge Cove, bay of the Beaufort Sea, 20 mi. ENE of mouth of E channel of Mackenzie R. delta, 100 mi. NE of Aklavik; 69°27'N 133°2'W; Hudson's Bay Co. transport depot and trading post (established 1936); transshipment point from river boats to sea-going ships; radio station. Site of Anglican and R.C. missions. Originally named Tuktoyaktuk, and commonly called Tuk-tuk.

Port-Brillet (pôr-brēyā'), village (pop. 1,179), Mayenne dept., W France, 10 mi. WNW of Laval; iron founding, pottery and hardware mfg.

Port Broughton (brô'tŭn), village and port (pop. 399), S South Australia, near base of Yorke Peninsula, on Spencer Gulf and 29 mi. S of Port Pirie; exports wool, wheat.

Port Burwell. **1** Trading post, W Killinek Isl., SE Franklin Dist., Northwest Territories, on Ungava Bay; 60°25'N 64°49'W; Royal Canadian Mounted Police post. **2** Village (pop. estimate 750), S Ont., on L. Erie, at mouth of Otter Creek, 21 mi. ESE of St. Thomas; fishing and coal port; car ferry to Ashtabula, Ohio.

Port Byron. **1** Village (pop. 1,050), Rock Island co., NW Ill., on the Mississippi and 12 mi. NE of Moline, in agr. area. **2** Village (pop. 1,013), Cayuga co., W central N.Y., in Finger Lakes region, 8 mi. NNW of Auburn; summer resort; some mfg. (feed, food products, plumbers' supplies).

Port Canning, village, 24-Parganas dist., SE West Bengal, India, on river arm of Ganges Delta and 27 mi. SE of Calcutta city center; rail terminus (Canning station); rice milling; trades in rice, pulse, timber. Planned as auxiliary port of Calcutta; now concerned largely with land reclamation in the Sundarbans. Also called Matla. Model land-reclamation project for Sundarbans SE, at Gosaba.

Port Carbon, borough (pop. 3,024), Schuylkill co., E central Pa., 2 mi. NE of Pottsville and on Schuylkill R.; textiles. Laid out 1828, inc. 1852.

Port Carling, resort village (pop. 509), S Ont., in Muskoka lake region, bet. L. Rosseau (N) and L. Muskoka (S), 28 mi. SE of Parry Sound.

Port Caroline, Australia: see KINGSTON.

Port Castries, St. Lucia, B.W.I.: see CASTRIES.

Port Chalmers (chä'mŭrz), borough (pop. 2,165), SE S.Isl., New Zealand, on W shore of Otago Harbour, opposite Otago Peninsula; port for near-by Dunedin. Exports frozen meat, wool.

Port-Chaltin, Belgian Congo: see AKETI.

Port Charlotte, village, W ISLAY, Hebrides, Scotland, on Loch Indaal.

Portchester or **Porchester** (both: pôr'chĭstŭr), town and parish (pop. 2,267), SE Hampshire, England, on Portsmouth Harbour 4 mi. NNW of Portsmouth; agr. market. Has Norman castle, built within walls of Roman settlement of *Portus Castra*, and Norman church of Augustinian abbey. Just S is site of the major Roman coastal fort of *Portus Adurni*. There are many Roman remains.

Port Chester (pôrt' chĕ"stŭr), village (pop. 23,970), Westchester co., SE N.Y., on harbor on N shore of Long Island Sound, at Conn. line, adjacent to Greenwich town, Conn.; residential suburb, in New York city metropolitan area. Mfg.: electric razors, food products, hardware, machinery, furnaces, ranges, clothing, textiles, chemicals, luggage, burial vaults. Inc. 1868.

Port Chicago (shĭkä'gō), village (1940 pop. 1,032), Contra Costa co., W Calif., 8 mi. W of Pittsburg, on S shore of Suisun Bay; industrial port. Hundreds of lives were lost in exposion of ammunition vessels here during Second World War.

Port Chilkoot, Alaska: see CHILKOOT.

Port Cland (klä'), village on W coast of Mahé Isl., Seychelles, port on Indian Ocean opposite Thérèse Isl., 3½ mi. SW of Victoria; copra, essential oils; fisheries. Also spelled Port Gland.

Port Clarence, England: see BILLINGHAM.

Port Clarence, Sp. Guinea: see SANTA ISABEL.

Port Clements, village, W B.C., on E central Graham Isl., on Masset Inlet, 23 mi. S of Massett; lumbering; steamer landing.

Port Clinton. **1** City (pop. 5,541), ⊙ Ottawa co., N Ohio, at mouth of Portage R. on L. Erie, 32 mi. ESE of Toledo, in fruitgrowing area; makes auto parts, boats, gypsum products, canned goods; fisheries. Camp Perry (natl. guard) and Erie Ordnance Depot (at Lacarne) are near by. Founded c.1828. **2** Borough (pop. 451), Schuylkill co., E central Pa., 2 mi. NW of Hamburg and on Schuylkill R. (head of navigation), at mouth of Little Schuylkill R.; clothing mfg.

Port Clyde, Maine: see SAINT GEORGE.

Port Colborne (kōl'bŭrn), town (pop. 6,993), S Ont., on L. Erie, port at S end of Welland Ship Canal, 20 mi. S of St. Catharines; nickel-refining center; iron smelters, cereal mills, grain elevators. Opposite is Humberstone.

Port Conclusion, village, SE Alaska, on Chatham Straight, near S tip of Baranof Isl., 4 mi. SSW of Port Alexander; fishing, cannery.

Port Coquitlam (kōkwĭt'lŭm), city (pop. 1,539), SW B.C., in lower Fraser R. valley, on Coquitlam R. and 15 mi. E of Vancouver; center of truck-gardening and fruitgrowing region; meat packing. Hydroelectric power.

Port Cornwallis (kôrnwŏ'lĭs), village, N.Andaman Isl., on Andaman Sea, 115 mi. NNE of Port Blair; safe anchorage for coastal vessels. Settled by British and used (1791–96) as naval station.

Port-Couvreux, Indian Ocean: see KERGUELEN ISLANDS.

Port Credit, village (pop. 2,160), S Ont., on L. Ontario at mouth of Credit R., 12 mi. SW of Toronto; fruitgrowing, fishing center; oil refining, starch mfg.

Port-Cros, Île de (ēl dü pôr-krō'), one of Hyères islands (□ 2.5) in the Mediterranean off S coast of France (Var dept.), 15 mi. SE of Hyères. Has small harbor and hotel. Pine and cork oak trees. Heights crowned by old forts. Best reached from Salins-d'Hyères. Captured by advance units in Allied invasion (Aug., 1944) of S France.

Port Dalhousie (dălhoo'zē), village (pop. 1,723), S Ont., on L. Ontario, at N end of old Welland Canal, 3 mi. N of St. Catharines, near N terminal of new Welland Ship Canal; port, with coal dock; fruit canning, rubber mfg.; resort.

Port Daniel, village (pop. estimate 750), E Que., SE Gaspé Peninsula, on the Gulf of St. Lawrence, 50 mi. SE of Gaspé; fishing center.
Port Darwin, Australia: see DARWIN.
Port-de-Bouc (pôr-dů-bōōk'), town (pop. 6,013), Bouches-du-Rhône dept., SE France, on Gulf of Fos at W end of outlet (Caronte canal) of Étang de Berre into the Mediterranean, 21 mi. WNW of Marseilles; fishing port at terminus of Arles–Port-de-Bouc Canal; shipbuilding, fertilizer and sulphuric acid mfg., zinc smelting. Saltworks near by. Has 17th-cent. fort.
Port-de-Paix (pôr-dů-pā'), city (1950 census pop. 6,309), ⊙ Nord-Ouest dept. (□ c.1,060; 1950 pop. 168,346), NW Haiti, port on the Atlantic, opposite Tortuga Isl., 40 mi. WNW of Cap-Haïtien; 19°57'N 72°50'W. In agr. region (coffee, bananas, sisal, tobacco, rice, cacao). Its fine harbor ships agr. produce, hides, logwood. Fishing. An old historic site, where Columbus made a landing (Dec. 8, 1492). Fr. filibusters, founding the town in 1665, gained here their 1st foothold after being driven by the British from Tortuga Isl. In Port-de-Paix occurred (1679) 1st revolt of Negro slaves.
Port Deposit, town (pop. 1,139), Cecil co., NE Md., on the Susquehanna and 4 mi. N of Havre de Grace; granite quarrying (since 1808) and shipping; makes fabricated steel products. Jacob Tome Inst., founded here 1889, became Bainbridge Naval Training Station during World War II. Near by are Conowingo Dam and West Nottingham Acad., preparatory school for boys founded 1741. Founded 1812, it was important port in early 19th cent.
Port Desire, Argentina: see PUERTO DESEADO.
Port Dickinson, residential village (pop. 2,199), Broome co., S N.Y., on Chenango R., just N of Binghamton. Inc. 1876.
Port Dickson, town (pop. 3,353), SW Negri Sembilan, Malaya, port on Strait of Malacca, on railroad and 17 mi. SW of Seremban; main port of Negri Sembilan; seaside resort; ships rubber, copra, tin. Weaving handicrafts.
Port Dinorwic, Wales: see LLANDDEINIOLEN.
Port Douglas, village (pop. 122), NE Queensland, Australia, on Trinity Bay and 30 mi. N of Cairns; small sugar port.
Port Dover, village (pop. 1,968), S Ont., on L. Erie, 35 mi. SW of Hamilton; fishing port, hothouse-bldg. center; food canning, sawmilling, cereal-food mfg.
Port Durnford, Ital. Somaliland: see BUR GAO.
Port du Salut, Notre Dame du, France: see ENTRAMMES.
Port Eads (ēdz), village (pop. c.200), Plaquemines parish, extreme SE La., on South Pass (a mouth of the Mississippi) near tip of the delta, c.85 mi. SE of New Orleans; pilot station and hq. for channel-maintenance engineers. Lighthouse here (29°1'N 89°10'W). Marine radio-beacon station near by.
Porte d'Annam, Vietnam: see ANNAM GATE.
Port Edward, village (pop. estimate 250), W B.C., on inlet of Chatham Sound of the Pacific, 7 mi. S of Prince Rupert; rayon milling.
Port Edwards, village (pop. 1,336), Wood co., central Wis., on Wisconsin R. and 4 mi. SSW of Wisconsin Rapids, in timber and dairy region; paper mfg. Inc. 1902.
Port Egmont (ĕg'mŏnt), small settlement of Falkland Isls., on a small isl. just off N West Falkland; 51°22'S 60°4'W. John Byron here took possession (1765) of the Falklands for Britain.
Portel (pôrtĕl'), city (pop. 284), E central Pará, Brazil, on a channel of the Amazon delta and 160 mi. WSW of Belém.
Portel, village (pop. 801), Aude dept., S France, 10 mi. SSW of Narbonne; distilling, winegrowing.
Portel, town (pop. 3,308), Évora dist., S central Portugal, 20 mi. SE of Évora; cork processing, pottery and goat-cheese mfg. A picturesque town.
Portel, Le (lů), SW suburb (pop. 3,397) of Boulogne, Pas-de-Calais dept., N France, fishing port on English Channel; mfg. of fishing vessels and equipment. Site of Lille univ. laboratory of marine zoology. Heavily damaged in Second World War.
Portela (pôrtā'lů), N suburb of Lisbon, central Portugal, near W shore of Lisbon Bay, 4 mi. N of city center. Site of Lisbon's internatl. airport.
Port Elgin (ĕl'gĭn). **1** Village (pop. 681), SE N.B., on Baie Verte of Northumberland Strait, 35 mi. E of Moncton; fishing port (smelt, lobster). **2** Village (pop. 1,395), S Ont., on L. Huron, 25 mi. WSW of Owen Sound; fishing, dairying; mfg. of toilet articles, brushes; resort; tree nurseries.
Port Elizabeth, city (pop. 133,400; including suburbs 147,907), S Cape Prov., U. of So. Afr., on Algoa Bay of the Indian Ocean, 450 mi. E of Cape Town, 430 mi. SW of Durban; 33°58'S 25°37'E. Industrial center and chief seaport of E Cape Prov., with extensive dock facilities; trades in and ships wool, hides, skins, mohair, fruit. Principal imports are automobile parts and rubber; there are important automobile-assembly and tire-mfg. plants; also oil storage installations. Other industries include mfg. of machinery, chemicals, glass, soap, shoes, electric batteries, candy, biscuits; fruit and jam canning, flour milling, woodworking. Fishing port. Features include Fort Frederick (1799), mus., art gallery, and several parks. Chief suburbs are New Brighton, Humewood (Driftsands airport), Walmer, Zwartkops, and Korsten. Founded 1820 by British settlers, city developed rapidly after completion (1873) of railroad to Kimberley. Cape Recife is 7 mi. SE; 30 mi. N is Addo Elephant Natl. Park.
Port Ellen, town in the Hebrides, on SE coast of ISLAY, Argyll, Scotland, 27 mi. NW of Campbeltown; port and seaside resort; whisky distilling. Harbor entrance is marked by lighthouse (55°36'N 6°12'W). Port Ellen airfield is 5 mi. NNW.
Port Elliot, town (pop. 548), SE South Australia, 45 mi. S of Adelaide and on N shore of Encounter Bay; dairying center.
Porteña (pôrtā'nyä), town (pop. estimate 1,500), NE Córdoba prov., Argentina, 30 mi. N of San Francisco; mfg. of agr. implements, dairy products; wheat, flax, oats, livestock.
Port-en-Bessin (pôr-ā-bĕsē'), village (pop. 1,314), Calvados dept., NW France, fishing port on English Channel, 5 mi. NNW of Bayeux. Damaged during Normandy invasion (June, 1944).
Porter, county (□ 425; pop. 40,076), NW Ind.; ⊙ Valparaiso. Bounded N by L. Michigan, S by Kankakee R.; drained by Little Calumet and Grand Calumet rivers. Agr. (corn, grain, hogs, cattle, poultry; dairy products). Mfg. at Valparaiso. Resorts and a state park are in picturesque dunes area along L. Michigan. Formed 1835.
Porter. 1 Town (pop. 1,458), Porter co., NW Ind., near L. Michigan, 13 mi. E of Gary; makes brick. **2** Town (pop. 1,052), Oxford co., W Maine, on the Ossipee and 35 mi. WNW of Portland. Settled c.1781, inc. 1807. **3** Village (pop. 291), Yellow Medicine co., SW Minn., on branch of Yellow Medicine R., near S.Dak. line, and 22 mi. NW of Marshall; dairy products. **4** Town (pop. 562), Wagoner co., E Okla., 11 mi. NW of Muskogee, in agr. area; cotton ginning.
Port'Ercole (pôrtĕr'kôlĕ), village (pop. 562), Grosseto prov., Tuscany, central Italy, port on SE coast of Monte Argentario, 3 mi. S of Orbetello. Badly damaged in Second World War.
Porterdale, town (pop. 3,207), Newton co., N central Ga., 31 mi. ESE of Atlanta and on Yellow R.; mfg. (cordage, yarn). Grew around mills established here in 1868.
Port Erin (ĕr'ĭn), village district (1939 pop. 1,265) on SW coast of Isle of Man, England, 5 mi. W of Castletown; fishing port, seaside resort. Site of Marine Biological Station. Just NW is promontory of Bradda Head (54°6'N 4°48'W).
Port Erroll, Scotland: see CRUDEN.
Porter Springs, resort village, Lumpkin co., N Ga., 7 mi. NNE of Dahlonega, in the Blue Ridge.
Portersville, borough (pop. 294), Butler co., W Pa., 14 mi. WNW of Butler.
Porterville, town (pop. 2,197), SW Cape Prov., U. of So. Afr., 35 mi. NNE of Malmesbury; rail terminus; agr. center (grain, viticulture, tobacco).
Porterville, city (pop. 6,904), Tulare co., S central Calif., at E side of San Joaquin Valley, c.65 mi. SE of Fresno; ships oranges (from foothill thermal belt), deciduous fruit. Region also produces olives, cotton, grain, vegetables, livestock. Hq. for Sequoia Natl. Forest (c.25 mi. NE). Has jr. col. Granite, marble quarries. Founded 1859, inc. 1902.
Portessie, Scotland: see BUCKIE.
Port Essington, village (pop. estimate 250), W B.C., on Skeena R. estuary, 18 mi. SE of Prince Rupert; salmon-canning center. Near by are silver, gold, copper deposits.
Port-Étienne or **Port Étienne** (pôr' ātyĕn'), town (pop. 1,350), W Mauritania, Fr. West Africa, minor Atlantic port on narrow peninsula flanking Lévrier Bay (E), 4 mi. N of La Agüera (Río de Oro), 330 mi. N of Saint-Louis, Senegal; 20°55'N 17°3'W. Cap Blanc, bisected by Mauritania–Río de Oro border, is just S. Base for important coastal fishing grounds. Has fish salting and canning industry. Roadstead can be entered by ships drawing up to 22 ft. Airport, seaplane base.
Portets (pôrtā'), village (pop. 1,486), Gironde dept., SW France, on left bank of Garonne R. and 12 mi. SE of Bordeaux; winegrowing, sawmilling.
Port Everglades, Fla.: see FORT LAUDERDALE.
Port Ewen (ū'ŭn), village (pop. 1,885), Ulster co., SE N.Y., near W bank of the Hudson, just S of Kingston; mfg. (explosives, cloth labels).
Portezuelo (pôrtāswā'lō), village (1930 pop. 548), Ñuble prov., S central Chile, 20 mi. WNW of Chillán; wine, wheat, corn, vegetables, livestock.
Portezuelo, town (pop. 2,154), Jalisco, central Mexico, 16 mi. ENE of Ocotlán; agr. center (grain, beans, oranges, livestock).
Port Fairy, municipality and port (pop. 2,007), SW Victoria, Australia, 150 mi. WSW of Melbourne and on Indian Ocean; rail terminus; exports meat, agr. and dairy products; dairy plant, cheese factory. Formerly Belfast.
Port Florence, Kenya: see KISUMU.
Port-Francqui (pôr-frākē'), town (1946 pop. c.4,000), Kasai prov., central Belgian Congo, on right bank of Kasai R. just above the influx of Sankuru R. and 90 mi. NNW of Luebo. As river port and terminus of railroad from Bukama, it is an important transshipment point for copper ores of Katanga. Has R.C. mission, hosp. for Europeans. Airport. Also known as Ilebo.
Port Frederick, Alaska: see HOONAH.
Port Fuad, Egypt: see PORT SAID.
Port Gamble, lumber-milling and port village (pop. c.500), Kitsap co., W Wash., on Hood Canal near Puget Sound, 20 mi. N of Bremerton.
Port-Gentil (pôr'-zhätēl'), town (1950 pop. 9,300), ⊙ Ogooué-Maritime region (□ 16,600; 1950 pop. 54,500), W Gabon, Fr. Equatorial Africa, 100 mi. SSW of Libreville, on the coast and on an isl. formed by 2 mouths of Ogooué R.; cabotage and lumber port; also whaling and fishing base and cacao outlet. Large lumber mills; mfg. of plywood. Fish processing. Has R.C. mission, airport.
Port Germein, town and port (pop. 262), S South Australia, on Spencer Gulf and 11 mi. N of Port Pirie across Germein Bay; exports wool, wheat.
Port Gibson, town (pop. 2,920), ⊙ Claiborne co., SW Miss., 28 mi. S of Vicksburg, near Bayou Pierre, and the Mississippi; cotton ginning, cottonseed and lumber milling. Near by is Alcorn Agr. and Mechanical Col. Town founded in late-18th cent. A Civil War battle of Vicksburg campaign was fought here.
Port Gland, Seychelles: see PORT CLAND.
Port Glasgow (glăs'gō, glăz'–; glăs'kō), burgh (1931 pop. 19,581; 1951 census 21,612), N Renfrew, Scotland, on the Clyde estuary and 18 mi. WNW of Glasgow; 55°56'N 4°41'W; port, with important shipbuilding yards, iron and brass foundries, and machinery works. Port was founded 1668 as port for Glasgow before the latter became accessible by the deepening of the Clyde. It became burgh in 1775. Just E are remains of 16th-cent. Newark Castle.
Portglenone (pōrtglĕnōn'), town (pop. 514), W Co. Antrim, Northern Ireland, on Bann R. and 8 mi. W of Ballymena; agr. market (cattle; flax, potatoes).
Port Gordon or **Portgordon,** village, NW Banffshire, Scotland, on Moray Firth, 2 mi. WSW of Buckie; salmon-fishing port, built 1874 by duke of Richmond and Gordon.
Port Graham, S Alaska, village (pop. 90), SW Kenai Peninsula, 8 mi. SW of Seldovia; fishing, cannery.
Port Greville (grĕ'vĭl), village (pop. estimate 350), N N.S., on N shore of Minas Channel, 35 mi. SSW of Amherst; fishing port; shipbuilding.
Port-Gueydon (pôr'-gādō'), village (pop. 511), Alger dept., N central Algeria, small port on the Mediterranean, in Great Kabylia, 24 mi. NE of Tizi-Ouzou.
Port Hammond or **Hammond,** village (pop. estimate 700), SW B.C., on Fraser R. and 20 mi. E of Vancouver; lumbering, dairying; fruit, vegetables.
Port Harcourt (här'kůrt), town (pop. 15,201), ⊙ Owerri prov., Eastern Provinces, S Nigeria, on Bonny arm of Niger R. delta and 270 mi. ESE of Lagos; 4°45'N 7°E. Major coaling port and ocean rail terminus. Exports coal from Enugu and Udi, tin from Jos-Bauchi area, palm oil, peanuts, and cacao. Has hosp., airfield. Port, established during First World War and named for Sir William Harcourt, has modern loading facilities.
Port Hardy, village (pop. estimate 200), SW B.C., on N Vancouver Isl., on Queen Charlotte Strait, 27 mi. WNW of Alert Bay; steamer landing; lumbering.
Port Harrison, village, NW Que., on Hudson Bay; 58°28'N 78°7'W; Hudson's Bay Co. trading post.
Port Hastings, village (pop. estimate 300), E N.S., SW Cape Breton Isl., on Canso Strait, 4 mi. NW of Port Hawkesbury; fishing, coal-shipping port.
Port Hawkesbury, town (pop. 1,031), E N.S., SW Cape Breton Isl., on the Strait of Canso, 30 mi. E of Antigonish; fishing port, with cold-storage plants; dairying center. Just S is train-ferry terminal of Point Tupper.
Porthcawl (pôrth-kôl'), urban district (1931 pop. 6,447; 1951 census 9,529), S Glamorgan, Wales, on Bristol Channel, 14 mi. SE of Swansea; coal-shipping port and seaside resort.
Port Hedland, port (pop. 328), N Western Australia, 630 mi. NNE of Geraldton and on Indian Ocean; 20°18'S 118°35'E. Head of railroad to Marble Bar; airport; exports gold. Tantalite mines at near-by Wodgina.
Port Henry, resort village (pop. 1,831), Essex co., NE N.Y., on harbor on L. Champlain, 14 mi. NNW of Ticonderoga, in iron-mining and dairying area; pig-iron foundries. Inc. 1869.
Port Herald, administrative center, Southern Prov., southernmost Nyasaland, on Shire R., on railroad, and 105 mi. S of Zomba; 16°53'S 35°18'E; alt. 120 ft. Customs station on Mozambique border; cotton-growing center; cotton ginning; tobacco, rice, corn. Has agr. experiment station, Marist Fathers mission. Airfield. Coal deposits (W).
Port Herman, Md.: see CHESAPEAKE CITY.
Port Hill, village (pop. estimate 150), W P.E.I., near Malpeque Bay, 14 mi. NW of Summerside; mixed farming, dairying.
Porthill, village, Boundary co., N Idaho, port of entry at British Columbia line, on Kootenai R. and 21 mi. NNW of Bonners Ferry.
Porthleven, fishing port and resort, SW Cornwall, England, on Mounts Bay, 2 mi. SW of Helston.
Port Hobron (hō'brŭn), small bay, N Sitkalidak Isl., S Alaska, on Gulf of Alaska, off SE Kodiak Isl., 50 mi. SW of Kodiak. At head of bay is McCord village, former whaling station.

Port Hood, town (pop. 647), ⊙ Inverness co., E N.S., on SW coast of Cape Breton Isl., on Northumberland Strait, at entrance to George Bay, 20 mi. SW of Inverness; coal mining; coal-shipping port. Seawater seepage has greatly reduced its importance. Just W is Port Hood Isl.

Port Hood Island (2 mi. long, 1 mi. wide), in Northumberland Strait, E N.S., at entrance to George Bay, 2 mi. W of Port Hood, SW Cape Breton Isl.

Port Hope, town (pop. 5,055), ⊙ Durham co., S Ont., on L. Ontario, 60 mi. ENE of Toronto; radium-refining center; food canning, lumbering, metalworking, drug mfg.; resort. Site of Trinity Col., boys' school. Settled 1778.

Port Hope, resort village (pop. 353), Huron co., E Mich., 7 mi. NNW of Harbor Beach, on L. Huron.

Port Hope Simpson, village (pop. 351), SE Labrador, on Alexis R. and 35 mi. WNW of Battle Harbour; 52°31'N 56°18'W; lumbering center.

Port Howe, town (pop. 285), central Bahama Isls., on S shore of Cat Isl., 11 mi. SSE of The Bight; 24°14'N 75°18'W. Cattle and horse raising.

Port Hudson, village, East Baton Rouge parish, SE central La., on E bank of the Mississippi and 16 mi. NNW of Baton Rouge. Strong Confederate fortifications here, besieged (May-July, 1863) by Union troops under Gen. N. P. Banks, surrendered after fall of Vicksburg.

Port Hueneme (wīnē'mē), city (pop. 3,024), Ventura co., S Calif., on dredged harbor near Point Hueneme (lighthouse), 3 mi. S of Oxnard; lemons, walnuts. Formerly Hueneme. Inc. 1948.

Port Huron (hyŏŏ'rŭn), city and port (pop. 35,725), ⊙ St. Clair co., E Mich., c.55 mi. NE of Detroit, at N end of St. Clair R., which here connects L. Huron with L. St. Clair and thence (via Detroit R.) with L. Erie (S). Black R. enters the St. Clair here. Port of entry, connected by bridge and tunnel with Sarnia (Ont.). Lake and rail shipping center; shipyards, railroad shops, grain elevators. Mfg. of copper and brass goods and fittings, other metal products, paper, automobile parts, salt, cement; also makes tools, fishing tackle, clothing, paint. Fisheries. Lake resort. State park and Indian mounds are near by. Has jr. col. Earliest settlement began in 1686 with establishment of Fr. fort. Grew during lumbering era following building (1826) of turnpike to Detroit. After decline of lumbering in 1880s, town turned to sawmilling, papermaking, and shipbuilding and to development of local deposits of salt, oil, and gas. Inc. as village 1849, as city 1857.

Portia (pôr'shŭ), town (pop. 349), Lawrence co., NE Ark., 25 mi. NW of Jonesboro and on Black R., in agr. area.

Port Ibrahim, Egypt: see SUEZ.

Portici (pôr'tēchē), town (pop. 26,049), Napoli prov., Campania, S Italy, port on Bay of Naples, at W foot of Vesuvius, 4 mi. SE of Naples; silk mills, tannery; mfg. (ribbon, furniture, paper). Destroyed in 1631 by eruption of Vesuvius. Royal palace (18th cent.) now houses noted agr. institute.

Portieux (pôrtyû'), village (pop. 867), Vosges dept., E France, on Moselle R. and 13 mi. NNW of Épinal; cotton milling, winegrowing. Large glassworks near by.

Portile de Fier, Rumania: see IRON GATE.

Port Ilicha or **Port Il'icha** (ēlyē'chŭ), town (1948 pop. over 2,000), SE Azerbaijan SSR, on Caspian Sea, on railroad and 8 mi. N of Lenkoran, in subtropical lowland (rice area); fisheries.

Portillo (pōrtē'yō), village (1930 pop. 31), Aconcagua prov., central Chile, on Transandine RR, on Aconcagua R. at S bank of L. Inca, and 35 mi. ESE of San Felipe, on route to Uspallata Pass; alt. 9,450 ft. Mtn. resort; skiing. The famed statue of Cristo Redentor (Christ of the Andes) is near by on Argentina-Chile border, in Uspallata Pass.

Portillo (pôrtē'lyō), town (pop. 1,189), Valladolid prov., N central Spain, 14 mi. SSE of Valladolid; dairy-products mfg.; lumbering; cereals, sugar beets. Has remains of anc. fortifications and castle where Don Alvaro de Luna was imprisoned.

Portillo, Cordón del (kōr-dhōn' dhĕl pōrtē'yō), Andean range in W Mendoza prov., Argentina, W of San Carlos; extends c.35 mi. S from Tupungato peak; rises to over 17,000 ft.

Portillo, Paso del (pä'sō), Andean pass (c.13,500 ft.) on Argentina-Chile border, on road bet. San Juan (Argentina) and Ovalle (Chile); 30°46'S.

Portillo de Toledo (pôrtē'lyō dhā tōlā'dhō), town (pop. 1,889), Toledo prov., central Spain, 18 mi. NW of Toledo; grapes, vegetables, cereals, livestock; brewing, tanning, meat packing.

Portimão (pôrtēmä'ō), city (pop. 9,716), Faro dist., S Portugal, on railroad and 34 mi. WNW of Faro; seaport at head of wide estuary of Portimão R. on the Atlantic (S coast); major fishing and canning center (sardines, tuna); cork industry. Two fortified 15th-cent. castles overlook estuary. Also called Vila Nova de Portimão.

Portis, city (pop. 286), Osborne co., N Kansas, on North Fork Solomon R. and 7 mi. N of Osborne; livestock, grain.

Port Isaac, fishing port, N Cornwall, England, on the Atlantic and 7 mi. WSW of Camelford.

Port Isabel (ĭ'zŭbĕl), city (pop. 2,372), Cameron co., extreme S Texas, on Laguna Madre and 22 mi. NE of Brownsville; deepwater port on Gulf Intracoastal Waterway and ship channel from Gulf of Mexico to Brownsville; ships petroleum, fish. Resort. Oil refining; pipeline terminus. Formerly called Point Isabel. In Mexican War was supply base for Gen. Zachary Taylor. Inc. 1928.

Portishead (pôr'tĭs-hĕd), urban district (1931 pop. 3,909; 1951 census 4,454), N Somerset, England, on Bristol Channel and 8 mi. WNW of Bristol; 51°29'N 2°46'W. Seaport; dock and oil-storage installations; watering resort. Has 15th-cent. church. Tidal rise here is greatest in England.

Port Ivory, SE N.Y., an industrial section of Richmond borough of New York city, on NW Staten Isl.; soap mfg.

Port Jackson, Australia: see JACKSON, PORT.

Port-Jeanne-d'Arc, Indian Ocean: see KERGUELEN ISLANDS.

Port Jefferson. 1 Resort and residential village (pop. 3,296), Suffolk co., SE N.Y., on N shore of Long Isl., on Port Jefferson Harbor (yachting), 19 mi. E of Huntington, in orchard and diversified-farming area; mfg. of film equipment, cement blocks, lace; sand and gravel; boat yards. Ferry connections with Bridgeport, Conn. Port Jefferson Station village (pop. 600), just SE, is terminus of N shore line of Long Isl. RR. **2** Village (pop. 409), Shelby co., W Ohio, 5 mi. NE of Sidney and on Great Miami R.

Port Jefferson Harbor, SE N.Y., inlet (c.2 mi. long) of Long Island Sound, indenting N shore of Long Isl.; Port Jefferson is on its S shore. Setauket Harbor (c.1 mi. long) is W arm.

Port Jefferson Station, N.Y.: see PORT JEFFERSON.

Port-Jérôme, France: see LILLEBONNE.

Port Jervis (jûr'vĭs), resort city (pop. 9,372), Orange co., SE N.Y., on Delaware R. at mouth of Neversink R., near intersection of N.J., N.Y., and Pa. state lines; rail center, with railroad shops; mfg. of textiles, clothing, glass, concrete blocks, silverware, stoves. Settled before 1700, inc. 1907. Grew after opening (1828) of Delaware and Hudson Canal.

Port Jinnah (jĭ'nŭ) or **Chalna Anchorage** (chŭl'nŭ), town, Khulna dist., SW East Bengal, E Pakistan, on Pusur R. and 15 mi. S of Khulna, near village of Chalna. Developed after 1950 as main jute port of E Pakistan.

Port-Joinville (pôr-zhwĕvēl'), village, on ÎLE D'YEU, Vendée dept., W France, 30 mi. NW of Les Sables-d'Olonne; small fishing port and excursion center; horse and sheep raising.

Port Kembla, town and port (pop. 4,960), E New South Wales, Australia, on Pacific Ocean and 45 mi. S of Sydney; coal-loading port for near-by Wollongong; steel mills, copper refineries.

Port Kennedy, Australia: see THURSDAY ISLAND.

Port Kenny, village and port (pop. 166), South Australia, on W Eyre Peninsula, 130 mi. NW of Port Lincoln and on Venus Bay inlet of Anxious Bay; exports sheep.

Port Kent, village, Essex co., NE N.Y., on W shore of L. Champlain, 12 mi. S of Plattsburg. Rail point for resort area; ferry to Burlington, Vt.

Portknockie (pôrtnŏ'kē), burgh (1931 pop. 1,619; 1951 census 1,457), N Banffshire, Scotland, on Moray Firth, 2 mi. NW of Cullen; fishing port.

Port la Joie (pôr lä zhwä'), former French name of CHARLOTTETOWN, P.E.I.

Portland. 1 Town (pop. 2,635), E New South Wales, Australia, 80 mi. WNW of Sydney; coal-mining center; Portland cement. **2** Municipality and port (pop. 3,462), SW Victoria, Australia, on Portland Bay and 185 mi. WSW of Melbourne; rail terminus; outlet for large agr. and livestock area; meat-packing, dairy plants. First settlement (1834) of Victoria. Former sealing, whaling port.

Portland, urban district (1931 pop. 12,019; 1951 census 11,324), S Dorset, England, on the Channel 4 mi. S of Weymouth, and occupying all of the Isle of Portland, rocky peninsula (4½ mi. long, 2 mi. wide) connected with the mainland by narrow Chesil Bank (a shingle ridge). Peninsula slopes S to the Bill of Portland, promontory with lighthouse (49°68'N 2°23'W). Portland Race, a channel, separates the Bill of Portland from the Shambles, a reef 3 mi. offshore. Isl. consists of limestone, quarried for many centuries and supplying building material. At N end of isl. is Portland Castle, built by Henry VIII. Portland Harbour, bet. Portland and Weymouth, is fortified naval anchorage protected by great breakwaters. The convict prison here was converted into a Borstal institution in 1921. Isle of Portland is locale of some of Hardy's novels.

Portland, cape, Iceland: see DYRHOLAEY.

Portland, parish (□ 328.53; pop. 60,712), Surrey co., NE Jamaica; ⊙ Port Antonio. Extends from N slopes of the Blue Mts. to the ocean; watered by the Rio Grande. Its coastline is indented by many fine bays, on which lie its chief towns: Port Antonio, St. Margaret's Bay, Hope Bay, linked by railroad with Kingston. Predominantly agr.: coconuts, bananas, cacao, yams; horses. The region, formerly an important banana center, has suffered from the Panama disease.

Portland. 1 Town (pop. 517), Ashley co., SE Ark., 17 mi. E of Hamburg, in agr. area (cotton). **2** Town (pop. 205), Fremont co., S central Colo., on Arkansas R., just NE of Wet Mts., and 25 mi. WNW of Pueblo, in fruit region; alt. c.5,000 ft.; cement, plaster. **3** Town (pop. 16), Ouray co., SW Colo., 5 mi. NW of Ouray. **4** Town (pop. 5,186), Middlesex co., central Conn., on the Connecticut, here bridged to Middletown; sandstone and feldspar quarries, mfg. (wire, paper and fiber products, metal castings, machinery, fertilizer), tobacco growing. Includes Gildersleeve village, site of early-18th-cent. shipyard. State park, state forest here. Settled c.1690, inc. 1841. **5** City (pop. 7,064), ⊙ Jay co., E Ind., on Salamonie R. and 28 mi. NE of Muncie, in agr. area (livestock; dairy products; soybeans, grain); mfg. (vehicle parts, rubber goods, metal products, clothing, canned goods, silos, brooms, dairy equipment). Natural-gas and oil wells. Settled 1837. Elwood Haynes b. here. **6** Largest city (□ 22; pop. 77,634), in Maine, ⊙ Cumberland co., on peninsula near S end of Casco Bay; 43°43'05"N 70°17'35"W. Includes insular ward of 9 isls. totaling 2,706 acres. First isl. settlement, 1623, followed in 1632 by mainland trading settlement known as Falmouth until Portland set off and inc. as town in 1786. Suffered destruction by Indians in 17th and 18th cent., by English fleet (1775), and by the great fire (1866). State capital, 1820–31; inc. as city 1832. City manager plan adopted 1923. Commercial and shipping center of state; port of entry; excellent harbor (c.8.5 mi. frontage) handles 2,500,000 tons of goods annually; ships general cargoes, grain; receives coal, oil, sulphur, clay, woodpulp. Mfg. (paper, cellulose, and clay products, marine hardware, shoes, furniture, steel, explosives), printing and publishing, fishing, food packing, lumber and petroleum distribution. Gateway to Casco Bay and inland resort areas. Points of interest: municipal auditorium, birthplace and home of Longfellow, Sweat Memorial Art Mus., Portland Society of Natural History and Maine Historical Society museums, Portland Observatory (built 1807). Site of 2 jr. colleges, St. Joseph's Col., Maine General Hosp., state schools for deaf and blind. **7** Village (pop. 2,807), Ionia co., S central Mich., 20 mi. NW of Lansing, at confluence of Lookingglass and Grand rivers. Trade and shipping center for farm area (livestock, grain, corn, beans, celery; dairy products). Mfg. (auto parts, shirts, dog food, flour, feed). Settled 1833, inc. 1869. **8** City (pop. 641), Traill co., E N.Dak., just W of Mayville, near Goose R.; grain elevator, dairy products, potatoes, turkeys. **9** City (pop. 373,628), ⊙ Multnomah co., NW Oregon, on Willamette R. near its mouth on Columbia R., c.110 mi. (river distance) from Pacific Ocean; 45°30'N 122°37'W; alt. 77 ft.; average annual rainfall 39 in.; mean Jan. temp. 39°F, June 67°F. Largest city in Oregon, important industrial and commercial center, fresh-water port (served by ocean-going vessels), and port of entry. Exports lumber, wool, paper, grain, flour, livestock, meat, canned and frozen foods (fruit, vegetables, salmon). Imports copra, burlap, coffee, sugar, and iron and steel products. Lumber, wool, and furniture are important manufactures. Has shipyards, flour and paper mills, canneries, meat-packing plants, creameries, and railroad shops. Seat of Univ. of Portland (R.C.; for men; 1901), Reed Col., Lewis and Clark Col., Cascade Col., Univ. of Oregon medical and dental schools, a col. of law, a school of music, and a jr. col. Marylhurst Col. is near by, at Marylhurst. Has municipal airport (U.S. Air Force base), art mus., and symphony orchestra. Hq. for Mt. Hood Natl. Forest. Annual events: Rose Festival, Pacific International Livestock Exposition, and Winter Sports Carnival. Near-by points of scenic interest may be reached via Columbia River Highway, extending E along river. City laid out 1845 and named for Portland, Maine; inc. 1851. Grew rapidly after founding, serving as supply point (c.1850) during Calif. gold rush and later (1897–1900) during Alaska gold rush. Salmon industry was established here after 1864, railroad arrived 1883, and Lewis and Clark Centennial Exposition took place 1905. Power from BONNEVILLE DAM (completed 1937) was great stimulus to industries. Extensively damaged in May, 1948, when flood waters of Columbia R. inundated low-lying areas of city and destroyed Vanport City, a residential suburb. **10** Borough (pop. 551), Northampton co., E Pa., 7 mi. SE of Stroudsburg and on Delaware R.; lumber, feed, textiles. **11** Town (pop. 1,660), Sumner co., N Tenn., near Ky. line, 32 mi. NNE of Nashville; strawberry-shipping point; crates; flour milling. **12** City (pop. 1,292), San Patricio co., S Texas, on Corpus Christi Bay 10 mi. N of Corpus Christi. Inc. after 1940.

Portland, Cape, NE Tasmania, in Banks Strait, at E end of Ringarooma Bay; 40°44'S 147°55'E.

Portland, Isle of, England: see PORTLAND.

Portland Bay, wide inlet of Indian Ocean, SW Victoria, Australia, bet. Point Danger (W) and Cape Reaumur (E); 24 mi. long E–W, 10 mi. wide N–S. Portland is on W shore.

Portland Bight, Jamaica: see OLD HARBOUR BAY.

Portland Bill, England: see PORTLAND.

Portland Canal, navigable channel bet. extreme SE Alaska and Canada, extending 70 mi. N from Pearse Isl. to Hyder, Alaska, and Stewart, B.C.; 55°–56°N 130°W.

Portland Cays, group of tiny islets off S Jamaica, B.W.I., at SW entrance of Old Harbor Bay, 25 mi. SW of Kingston; 7°43′N 77°5′W.

Portland Head, Maine: see Cottage, Cape.

Portland Inlet, W B.C., near S tip of Alaska panhandle, NE arm (30 mi. long, 4–8 mi. wide) of Dixon Entrance and Chatham Sound; mouth is 26 mi. NNW of Prince Rupert. Contains Pearse, Wales, and Somerville isls. Receives Nass R. at head, and is continued NNE by Portland Canal and NE by Observatory Inlet.

Portland Mountain, Idaho: see Lemhi Range.

Portland Point, cape on Portland Ridge, S Jamaica, at southernmost section of the isl., 30 mi. SW of Kingston; 17°43′N 77°9′W.

Portland Ridge, peninsula of low hills (525 ft.), Clarendon parish, S Jamaica, southernmost part of the isl., 30 mi. SW of Kingston. Has phosphate deposits. Its shore line (□ c.19) was leased as naval base to U.S. in 1940.

Portlandville, resort village, Otsego co., central N.Y., on Goodyear L., 12 mi. S of Cooperstown.

Port Laoighise (lā′ĭsh) or **Maryborough,** town (pop. 3,170), ⊙ Co. Laoighis, Ireland, in central part of co., on tributary of Barrow R. and 38 mi. WSW of Dublin; malting center; also woolen milling, agr.-implement mfg. Slight remains of anc. fort, established in reign of Mary I. There are a military camping ground and mental hosp.

Port Lavaca (lŭvă′kŭ), city (pop. 5,599), ⊙ Calhoun co., S Texas, on Lavaca Bay, 27 mi. SE of Victoria; tourist resort and fishing port on channel to the Gulf Intracoastal Waterway; oil refining, cotton ginning, quick-freezing plants (shrimp, oysters, truck); aluminum plant at near-by Point Comfort. An important 19th-cent. port, founded as La Vaca in 1815; burned by Indians 1846; inc. as city 1909.

Portlaw (pôrtlô′), Gaelic *Portchládhach,* town (pop. 1,010), NE Co. Waterford, Ireland, near Suir R., 6 mi. SE of Carrick-on-Suir; agr. market (cattle raising, dairying, potato growing); tanneries.

Port Leyden (lī′dŭn), village (pop. 841), Lewis co., N central N.Y., on Black R. and 27 mi. N of Rome; wood pulp, clothing.

Port Lincoln, town and port (pop. 3,972), S South Australia, on SW shore of Boston Bay of SE Eyre Peninsula, 165 mi. SW of Port Pirie across Spencer Gulf; 34°43′S 135°51′E. Rail terminus; superphosphate works; graphite, gypsum. Exports wool, wheat, shark-liver oil.

Port Lloyd, Bonin Isls.: see Chichi-jima.

Portlock, village (1939 pop. 31), on S tip of Kenai Peninsula, S Alaska, 15 mi. S of Seldovia; fishing; cannery.

Portlock, town (pop. 3,809), Norfolk co., SE Va., 4 mi. S of Portsmouth. Inc. since 1940.

Port Loko (lō′kō), town (pop. 3,950), Northern Prov., W Sierra Leone, on navigable Port Loko Creek (headstream of Sierra Leone R.) and 38 mi. NE of Freetown; road and trade center; palm oil and kernels, piassava, kola nuts, rice. Has hosp., airfield, 2 mission schools. Hq. Port Loko dist. Sometimes spelled Port Lokko.

Port-Louis (pôr-lwē′), town (pop. 2,905), Morbihan dept., W France, on Bay of Biscay (Blavet R. estuary), 3 mi. S of Lorient; fortified port and bathing resort commanding entrance to Lorient harbor; fish canning, boatbuilding. Named (1598) by Richelieu in honor of Louis XIII. Damaged in Second World War.

Port-Louis (pôr-lwē′), town (commune pop. 2,911), NW Grande-Terre, Guadeloupe, minor port on the Grand Cul de Sac, 14 mi. N of Pointe-à-Pitre, in sugar-growing region; alcohol distilling, sugar milling.

Port Louis (lōō′ĭs, lōō′ē, Fr. pôr lwē′), city (pop. 57,466), ⊙ Mauritius, and its chief sugar-exporting port, on NW coast and on protected deep-water inlet of Indian Ocean; 20°10′S 57°30′E. Center of isl.'s rail network, with work shops at Plaine Lauzun in SW outskirts. Mfg. of cigarettes, matches, coconut oil, soap; sugar-milling, shipbuilding. Corn and manioc mills at Richelieu, 3 mi. SW. Site of govt. house, Mauritius Institute (mus., art gallery, public library), R.C. and Anglican cathedrals, hosp. City is linked by causeway with Fort George Isl., a military reservation (pop. 426) in harbor. Founded 1735 by Mahé de La Bourdonnais, city succeeded Mahébourg as ⊙ Mauritius and developed rapidly until 1860s. Trade declined following opening of Suez Canal.

Port-Lyautey (pôr′-lyōtā′), city (pop. 56,604), Rabat region, NW Fr. Morocco, seaport on Sebou R. 10 mi. above its mouth on the Atlantic, on trunk railroad and 22 mi. NE of Rabat; 34°17′N 6°35′W. Accessible to ships drawing up to 17 ft., it exports grain and other agr. output of fertile Rharb lowland, as well as cork from Mamora Forest (just S). Fish processing, textile milling, mfg. of tobacco products and fertilizer. Formerly called Kénitra, it was renamed (1932) after Marshal Lyautey, on whose orders city had been built up after establishment of Fr. protectorate in Morocco. Its port was opened to shipping in 1913, as a substitute for Mehdia. Its naval air station was a U.S. base 1942–48.

Port Lyttelton, New Zealand: see Lyttelton.

Port MacDonnell, village (pop. 438), extreme SE South Australia, on Discovery Bay of Indian Ocean, 245 mi. SSE of Adelaide; dairy products, livestock.

Port McNicoll, village (pop. 973), S Ont., on Georgian Bay, 22 mi. NW of Orillia; grain-transshipment port, with large elevators.

Port Macquarie (mŭkwŏ′rē), municipality (pop. 2,905), E New South Wales, Australia, at mouth of Hastings R., on small inlet of Pacific Ocean and 120 mi. NE of Newcastle; exports dairy products. Arsenic ore mined near by.

Port Macquarie, New Zealand: see Bluff.

Portmadoc (pôrtmă′dôk), urban district (1931 pop. 3,986; 1951 census 4,060), S Caernarvon, Wales, on inlet of Cardigan Bay of Irish Sea, 16 mi. SSE of Caernarvon; slate-shipping port, agr. market, and beach resort. In urban dist. are granite-quarrying villages of Gest (gĕst) (pop. 625) and Tremadoc (trĕmă′dôk) (pop. 541). T. E. Lawrence b. here. Urban dist. is co-extensive with parish of Ynyscynhaiarn (ŭnĭs-kĭnhī′ärn).

Portmahomack (pôrtmŭhŏ′mŭk), fishing village, NE Ross and Cromarty, Scotland, on Dornoch Firth, 8 mi. ESE of Dornoch. Near by are ruins of 16th-cent. Ballone Castle, and Tarbat Ness promontory.

Port Mahon, Balearic Isls.: see Mahón.

Port Maitland. **1** Village (pop. estimate 500), W N.S., on the Atlantic, 10 mi. N of Yarmouth; dairying center; cod, halibut, haddock fishing. **2** Village (pop. estimate 150), SW Ont., on L. Erie, at mouth of Grand R., 30 mi. SSE of Hamilton; fishing. Car ferry to Ashtabula, Ohio.

Portman, Spain: see Unión, La.

Port Mann, village (pop. estimate 500), SW B.C., 4 mi. E of New Westminster, across lower Fraser R.; gypsum processing.

Port Mansfield, barge port on the Intracoastal Waterway, Willacy co., extreme S Texas, on Red Fish Bay (an inlet of Laguna Madre), 23 mi. E of Raymondville. Dredged basin and channel were opened here in 1949, on site of summer-cottage colony of Red Fish Bay. Ships oil, agr. produce, canned goods.

Port-Margot (pôr-märgō′), town (1950 census pop. 1,586), Nord dept., N Haiti, near the Atlantic, 14 mi. W of Cap-Haïtien; coffee, cacao, fruit.

Port Maria (mŭrī′ŭ), town (pop. 3,167), ⊙ St. Mary parish, N Jamaica, seaport on protected Caribbean inlet, 29 mi. NNW of Kingston; 18°23′N 76°55′W. Trading center and resort; ships bananas. Also produces logwood, coffee, coconuts, pimento, oranges.

Port-Marly, Le (lŭ pôr-märlē′), outer WNW suburb (pop. 1,089) of Paris, Seine-et-Oise dept., N central France, port on left bank of the Seine just above Saint-Germain-en-Laye; metal and chemical works. Golf course.

Port Mathurin, Rodrigues: see Rodrigues.

Port Matilda, borough (pop. 685), Centre co., central Pa., 28 mi. NE of Altoona and on Bald Eagle Creek; sandstone.

Port Mayaca (mŭyă′kŭ), village, Martin co., SE Fla., 37 mi. SW of Fort Pierce, on E shore of L. Okeechobee at entrance (lock here) of St. Lucie Canal.

Port Medway, village (pop. estimate 350), SW N.S., on Medway Harbour, near mouth of Medway R., 10 mi. NE of Liverpool; cod, lobster, halibut, haddock fisheries; pulpwood exports.

Port Melbourne (mĕl′bŭrn), municipality and port (pop. 14,205), S Victoria, Australia, on Hobson's Bay (N arm of Port Phillip Bay), just S of South Melbourne. Principal port of the state; exports wool, dairy products, flour, meat, grain, skins. Mfg. (dehydrated foods, soap).

Port Mellon, village, SW B.C., on inlet of Howe Sound, 25 mi. NW of Vancouver; pulp and paper milling. Opposite is Gambier Isl.

Port Menier (pôr mŭnyā′), village, E Que., on SW Anticosti Isl., on the St. Lawrence, and 70 mi. N of Gaspé; 49°49′N 64°21′W; lumber port.

Port Moller (mō′lŭr), village (pop. 30), SW Alaska, on Alaska Peninsula, at entrance of Port Moller, inlet (20 mi. long) of Bristol Bay of Bering Sea; 56°N 160°31′W; fishing, fish canning.

Port Monmouth (mŏn′mŭth), village (pop. 1,767), Monmouth co., E N.J., on Raritan Bay and 6 mi. E of Keyport; processes fish oil.

Port Moody, city (1941 pop. 1,512; 1946 estimate 2,200), SW B.C., in lower Fraser R. valley, at W end of Burrard Inlet of the Strait of Georgia; 11 mi. E of Vancouver, in lumbering, mixed-farming region; oil refinery.

Port Morant (mŭrănt′), town (pop. 4,438), St. Thomas parish, SE Jamaica, port on Caribbean inlet, 31 mi. ESE of Kingston, in agr. region (bananas, sugar cane, coconuts, vegetables, stock); ships bananas. Morant Point, easternmost cape of the isl., is 10 mi. E.

Port Moresby (môrz′bē), port town (pop. c.1,300), ⊙ Territory of Papua, SE New Guinea, on landlocked Fairfax Harbour; 9°27′S 147°31′E. Exports copper, gold, coffee, rubber. Astrolabe Field (copper, gold, silver) is near by. Harbour discovered 1873 by Capt. John Moresby. In Second World War, site of chief Allied base on New Guinea; Port Moresby was also then the acting capital of the Territory of New Guinea and officially became (1946) temporary capital, replacing Rabaul.

Port Morien (mô′rēŭn), village (pop. estimate 800), NE N.S., N Cape Breton Isl., on Morien Bay, 6 mi. SE of Glace Bay; cod fisheries.

Portnahaven, village, SW Islay, Hebrides, Scotland.

Port Natal, U. of So. Afr.: see Durban.

Port Neches (nĕ′chĭz), city (pop. 5,448), Jefferson co., SE Texas, on Neches R. and 8 mi. SE of Beaumont; port on deep-water channel to Gulf of Mexico; ships oil, asphalt; has huge oil refineries, synthetic-rubber and chemical plants. Inc. 1927; industries developed greatly in Second World War.

Port Nelson, village, N Man., on Hudson Bay, at mouth of Nelson R., 12 mi. W of York Factory; 57°4′N 92°36′W. Hudson's Bay Co. post since 1670; it was proposed terminus of Hudson Bay RR but was abandoned in favor of Churchill in 1927. Now minor port.

Portneuf (pôrt″nŭf′, Fr. pôrnûf′), county (□ 1,440; pop. 38,996), S Que., on the St. Lawrence; ⊙ Cap Santé.

Portneuf or **Notre Dame de Portneuf** (nô′trŭ däm dŭ pôrnûf′), village (pop. 1,015), S central Que., on the St. Lawrence and 32 mi. WSW of Quebec; paper milling, lumbering, tanning, dairying.

Portneuf River (pôrt″nŭf′), SE Idaho, rises in Fort Hall Indian Reservation SE of Blackfoot, flows S, then W and NW, past Pocatello, to American Falls Reservoir; 90 mi. long. Dam in upper course forms Portneuf Reservoir (3.5 mi. long, 1 mi. wide) used for irrigation.

Port Nicholson, New Zealand: see Wellington, city.

Port Nolloth (nŏ′lŭth), town (pop. 1,469), NW Cape Prov., U. of So. Afr., in Namaqualand, on the Atlantic; 29°16′S 16°53′E; seaport for O'Okiep copper-mining region; diamond diggings in dist.

Port Norris, village (pop. 1,735), Cumberland co., S N.J., near mouth of Maurice R., 10 mi. S of Millville; oysters.

Pôrto (pōr′tōō), city (pop. 606), N Piauí, Brazil, on right bank of Parnaíba R. (Maranhão border) and 80 mi. N of Teresina; cotton. Airfield. Called Marruás until 1930s, then João Pessoa until 1944.

Pôrto, district (□ 881; pop. 938,288), Douro Litoral prov., N Portugal; ⊙ Oporto. Bounded by the Atlantic (W), Douro R. (S), Ave R. (N). Chief product: port wine.

Pôrto, city, Portugal: see Oporto.

Porto, Gulf of (pôr′tō), in the Mediterranean, off W coast of Corsica, c.25 mi. N of Ajaccio; 5 mi. wide, 7 mi. deep, bounded (S) by Cape Rosso. Scenic rugged coastline. Calanche di Piana on S shore.

Pôrto Acre (pōr′tōō ä′krĭ), town, SE Acre territory, westernmost Brazil, on Acre R., near Amazonas line, and 33 mi. NNE of Rio Branco. Seat of revolutionary govt. (1900–03) before Acre's incorporation into Brazil.

Pôrto Alegre (pōr′tōō ălā′grĭ). **1** City, Piauí, Brazil: see Luzilândia. **2** City (1950 pop. 381,964), ⊙ Rio Grande do Sul, Brazil, port at N end of the Lagoa dos Patos, on E shore of Guaíba R. estuary, 670 mi. SW of Rio de Janeiro, and 150 mi. NNE of Rio Grande, its outport near the open Atlantic; 30°1′S 51°11′W. One of Brazil's largest cities and its leading commercial and cultural center S of São Paulo. The port, with modern docks accommodating ships which draw 16½ ft., is lined with cold-storage warehouses and processing plants. It is a busy entrepôt for inland water navigation on Jacuí R. (which penetrates fertile agr. hinterland and is used for coal shipments from mines in São Jerônimo area), and on small Sinos, Caí, and Gravataí rivers, which join here to form the Guaíba. Merchandise destined for larger ocean vessels is transshipped at Rio Grande and Pelotas from smaller ships plying the Lagoa dos Patos and Mirim L. Principal exports are preserved meat, animal by-products, manioc meal, hides, wool, cereals, wine, fruit, tobacco, rice, and lumber. Pôrto Alegre is linked by rail with inland city of Santa Maria, thence with São Paulo (NE) and Uruguay (SW). The Gravataí airport is 4 mi. N. City's growing industries are chiefly of the agr.-processing type: they include meat packing, lard refining, tanning, milling of woolen yarn and cloth, brewing; mfg. of soap, candles, macaroni, preserves, wine. Also has metalworks (stoves, furnaces), ship-repair yards, furniture and tobacco factories; and large thermal electric plant. There are publishing houses. Seat of Univ. of Pôrto Alegre and of Catholic Univ. (founded 1948). Pôrto Alegre is a modern, progressive city handsomely laid out, with broad, regular streets, and fine business and govt. bldgs. It owes much of its commercial standing and rapid growth to large-scale German and Italian immigration beginning early in 19th cent. Climate is healthful (average temp. 67°F.; rainfall 30 inches) despite hot summers which are the result of lowland location and distance from the open sea. Founded 1742–43 by immigrants from the Azores. Originally called Pôrto dos Cazaes. Seat of govt. transferred here from Rio Grande and Viamão in 1773. Confirmed as capital of new captain-generalcy in 1808.

Pôrto Alexandre (pōr'tōō ŭlĭshăn'drĭ), town (pop. 2,874), Huíla prov., SW Angola, port on the Atlantic, 50 mi. SSW of Mossâmedes; fishing and fish-processing center. Airfield.

Pôrto Amazonas (pōr'tōō ämŭzō'nŭs), city (pop. 1,577), SE Paraná, Brazil, head of navigation on Iguassú R., on railroad and 40 mi. WSW of Curitiba; sawmilling, coffee and lard processing.

Pôrto Amboim (pōr'tōō ămbōēn'), town (pop. 1,537), Benguela prov., W Angola, small port on the Atlantic, 140 mi. SSE of Luanda; 10°45'S 13°50'E. Terminus of railroad to Gabela (35 mi. ESE) in coffee-growing area. Ships dried and salted fish, coffee, sugar, palm oil, rice. Airfield. Also called Amboim.

Pôrto Amélia (pōr'tōō ŭmĕ'lyŭ), town (1940 pop. c.5,000), Niassa prov., N Mozambique, port on Pemba Bay of Mozambique Channel, 140 mi. N of Mozambique city; 12°58'S 40°32'E. Ships cotton, sisal, coffee. Airfield. Seat of Nyassa Co. territory until 1929 (when company's charter expired); ⊙ Cabo Delgado dist. (□ 30,301; 1950 pop. 497,091).

Porto Azzurro (pôr'tô ätsōō'rô), town (pop. 1,995), port on E coast of Elba isl., Livorno prov., Tuscany, central Italy, 5 mi. SE of Portoferraio; mining and exporting of iron ore. Called Porto Longone until 1949.

Porto Bello, Brazil: see Pôrto Belo.

Portobello (pôr'tōbĕ'lō), township (pop. 375), ⊙ Peninsula co. (□ 40; pop. 2,979), SE S.Isl., New Zealand, on Otago Peninsula, 6 mi. ENE of Dunedin, on E shore of Otago Harbour; summer resort.

Porto Bello, Panama: see Portobelo.

Portobello, suburb (pop. 26,145) 3 mi. E of Edinburgh, Scotland, popular resort on the Firth of Forth, with esplanade, marine gardens, and beaches. Also has electric power station and factories (pottery, bricks, glassware).

Pôrto Belo (pōr'tōō bā'lōō), city (pop. 874), E Santa Catarina, Brazil, small port on the Atlantic, and 30 mi. N of Florianópolis; fish, sugar, rice, bananas, timber. Formerly spelled Porto Bello.

Portobelo (pôrtōbā'lō), **Porto Bello** (pôrtō bĕ'lō), or **Puerto Bello** (pwĕr'tō bĕ'yō), village (pop. 573), Colón prov., central Panama, port on Caribbean Sea, 20 mi. NE of Colón; bananas, abacá, cacao; soap mfg. Founded 1597 on harbor named (1502) Puerto Bello by Columbus, it became a thriving Sp. colonial port, the Caribbean counterpart of Panama city (with which it was joined by a transisthmian highway) for transshipment of riches from Sp. colonies. Sacked repeatedly by English pirates, notably by Henry Morgan in 1668 and by Edward Vernon in 1739. Sir Francis Drake, who died offshore, was buried in the harbor. It declined with building (1848–55) of Panama RR and rise of Colón.

Pôrto Calvo (pōr'tōō käl'vōō), city (pop. 2,134), E Alagoas, NE Brazil, 45 mi. NE of Maceió; sugar, tobacco, cotton.

Porto Ceresio (pôr'tô chĕrā'zyô), village (pop. 784), Varese prov., Lombardy, N Italy, port on L. of Lugano, near Swiss border, 7 mi. NE of Varese. Rail terminus; resort; mfg. (metalware, glue). Granite quarries.

Porto Civitanova (pôr'tô chē"vētänō'vä), town (pop. 8,153), Macerata prov., The Marches, central Italy, port on the Adriatic, near mouth of Chienti R., 14 mi. E of Macerata. Rail junction; bathing resort; shipbuilding, jute milling; mfg. center (railroad cars, machinery, nets, macaroni, soap, shoes).

Port O'Connor, resort, Calhoun co., S Texas, on Matagorda Bay, 19 mi. SE of Port Lavaca; fishing.

Porto Corsini, Italy: see Marina di Ravenna.

Porto Cristo, Balearic Isls.: see Manacor.

Pôrto da Fôlha (pōr'tōō dä fō'lyŭ), city (pop. 2,416), N Sergipe, NE Brazil, near lower São Francisco R., 25 mi. NW of Propriá, in intensive rice-growing region; ships rice, cotton, cereals.

Pôrto de Leixões, Portugal: see Leixões.

Pôrto de Mós (pōr'tōō dĭ môsh'), town (pop. 875), Leiria dist., W central Portugal, 10 mi. S of Leiria; coal mine 6 mi. SSW.

Pôrto de Moz (mōs', mōsh'), city (pop. 544), central Pará, Brazil, landing on right bank of Xingu R. and 260 mi. W of Belém; rubber, cereals.

Pôrto de Pedras (pōr'tōō dĭ pĕ'drŭs), city (pop. 1,827), E Alagoas, NE Brazil, on the Atlantic, and 45 mi. NE of Maceió; ships sugar, cottonseed and coconut oil, and salt (worked near by).

Pôrto do Buriti, Brazil: see Paracatu River.

Pôrto dos Cazaes, Brazil: see Pôrto Alegre.

Porto Edda, Albania: see Sarandë.

Porto Empedocle (pôr'tô ĕmpā'dōklĕ), town (pop. 13,834), Agrigento prov., S Sicily, on Mediterranean Sea, 3 mi. SW of Agrigento. Port for Agrigento; sulphur shipping; sulphur refinery, mfg. (cement, glass); power plant, large warehouses (sulphur, corn). Tunny fishing. Built in 18th cent. with stone from temples of Agrigento, and called Molo di Girgenti. Bombed (1943) in Second World War.

Pôrto Esperança (pōr'tōō ĭspĭrã'sŭ), town (pop. 725), SW Mato Grosso, Brazil, on left bank of Paraguay R. and 45 mi. SSE of Corumbá, in Paraguay flood plain; railroad bridge (under construction in 1946) completes São Paulo–Corumbá rail link. Regular boat service to Corumbá. In Ponta Porã territory, 1943–46.

Porto-Farina (pôrtō-färēnä'), village, Bizerte dist., N Tunisia, on Porto-Farina L. (marshy embayment of Gulf of Tunis), 18 mi. ESE of Bizerte; almonds, potatoes; fisheries, oyster beds. Penitentiary.

Porto-Farina, Cape of, Tunisia: see Sidi Ali el Mekki, Ras.

Pôrto Feliz (pōr'tōō fĭlēs'), city (pop. 5,908), S central São Paulo, Brazil, on Tietê R. and 60 mi. WNW of São Paulo; rail-spur terminus; textile and sugar mills, distilleries. Trades in oranges, cotton, coffee.

Portoferraio (pôr"tôfĕr-rä'yô), chief town (pop. 7,682), port on N coast of Elba isl., Livorno prov., Tuscany, central Italy, 13 mi. SW of Piombino. Has important iron- and steelworks (damaged in Second World War) and a tannery. Exports most of iron mined on isl. In 16th–18th cent. strongly fortified by the Medici. Exiled Napoleon resided in small villa here, while sovereign of Elba (1814–15). Badly damaged by repeated air bombing (1943–44) in Second World War.

Pôrto Ferreira (pōr'tōō fĕrā'rŭ), city (pop. 2,332), E São Paulo, Brazil, head of navigation on Mogi-Guaçu R., on railroad and 10 mi. NNW of Pirassununga; coffee, rice, cattle.

Portofino (pôr"tôfē'nô), village (pop. 743), Genova prov., Liguria, N Italy, port at SE end of promontory of Portofino, 16 mi. SE of Genoa, in olive-growing region; resort; artisan lace industry; fisheries. Near by is monastery of Cervara (1361), where Francis I of France was held prisoner by Emperor Charles V after battle of Pavia (1525). The promontory, a scenic, almost square headland (3 mi. long; 2,001 ft. high in SW) encloses Gulf of Rapallo on W. Much frequented by tourists.

Port of Menteith (mĕntēth'), village and parish (pop. 940), SW Perthshire, Scotland, on Lake of Menteith, 12 mi. W of Dunblane; resort.

Port of Ness, Scotland: see Lewis with Harris.

Pôrto Franco (pōr'tōō frăng'kōō). **1** City (pop. 774), W Maranhão, Brazil, on right bank of Tocantins R. (Goiás border), opposite Tocantinópolis, and 60 mi. N of Carolina; cattle raising; ships hides, babassu nuts. **2** City, Rio Grande do Norte, Brazil: see Areia Branca.

Port of Spain or **Port-of-Spain,** largest city (pop. 92,793) and ⊙ Trinidad and Tobago, Br. crown colony in the West Indies, major port on NW part of isl. of Trinidad, on the Gulf of Paria (Caribbean), c.360 mi. E of Caracas, Venezuela, c.600 mi. SE of San Juan, Puerto Rico; 10°39'N 61°32'W. An important trading and shipping center of the Caribbean, on routes from Europe and U.S. to Venezuela, and serving as entrepôt for the llanos by way of the Orinoco. Strategically placed naval base. Situated on a sheltered harbor, where medium-sized ships berth alongside, it exports the isl.'s agr. products (sugar, cacao, coconuts, rum, bitters) and carries on extensive transshipment business (bauxite) with N coast of South America, principally with the Guianas. From Port of Spain radiate highways and railroads to the interior. It is a clean city, with fine parks, squares, and handsome bldgs. (customhouse, wharves, Royal Victoria Inst., Anglican and R.C. cathedrals, Columbus Monument). The noted Botanic Gardens (established 1818), with Govt. House, adjoin Queen's Park Savannah (N). The international Piarco airport is 12 mi. ESE. Port of Spain occupies site of anc. Indian village Conquerabia. It has been ⊙ Trinidad since 1783, when it replaced St. Joseph. Until 1840 it was ruled by the old colonial body, the *Cabildo.*

Porto Garibaldi (pôr'tô gärēbäl'dē), village (pop. 1,578), Ferrara prov., Emilia-Romagna, N central Italy, on Adriatic Sea, 3 mi. SE of Comacchio. Rail terminus; bathing resort; port for Comacchio; saltworks. Damaged in Second World War. Formerly called Magnavacca.

Pôrto Gouveia (pōr'tōō gōvā'ŭ), village, Cape Verde Isls., on SW shore of São Tiago Isl., 10 mi. W of Praia; anchorage. Oranges, sugar cane.

Pôrto Grande (pōr'tōō grän'dĭ), bay on NW coast of São Vicente Isl., Cape Verde Isls., with the archipelago's best natural harbor; 16°53'N 25°1'W. Mindêlo, a coaling station for transatlantic shipping, is on it.

Porto Grande, E Pakistan: see Chittagong, city.

Portogruaro (pôr"tôgrwä'rô), town (pop. 4,977), Venezia prov., Veneto, N Italy, 16 mi. NE of San Donà di Piave. Agr. center; mfg. (chemicals, textiles). Has Gothic palace (14th–16th cent.) and mus. with antiquities from near-by Concordia Sagittaria.

Pôrto Guaíra (pōr'tōō gwäē'rŭ), village, W Paraná, Brazil, at Paraguay border, on left bank of Paraná R. just above Guaíra Falls, and 100 mi. N of Foz do Iguaçu; downstream end of navigation on the upper Paraná, and N terminus of railroad to Pôrto Mendes (30 mi. S) circumventing Guaíra Falls and Paraná R. gorge. Maté-shipping center. Has modern hotel. Airfield. Also called Guaíra (old spelling, Guahyra or Guayra). At low river stage, Tomás Laranjeira (5 mi. ENE) is maté transshipment point.

Pôrto Henrique (pōr'tōō ĕnrē'kä), village, Sul do Save prov., S Mozambique, 25 mi. SSW of Lourenço Marques; citrus fruit.

Pôrto Inglês (pōr'tōō ēng-glāsh'), town and port, Cape Verde Isls., on SW shore of Maio isl., 25 mi. NE of Praia (on São Tiago Isl.); 15°8'N 23°13'W. Saltworks 1 mi. NW. Anchorage. Occupied by British until end of 18th cent. Also called Nossa Senhora da Luz. Formerly spelled Porto Inglez.

Port Okha, India: see Okha.

Pòrtol (pôr'tōl), village (pop. 1,354), Majorca, Balearic Isls., 7 mi. ENE of Palma; mfg. of pottery, meat products.

Portola (pôrtō'lŭ), city (pop. 2,261), Plumas co., NE Calif., in the Sierra Nevada, 40 mi. NW of Reno, Nev.; railroad division point and trade center for lumbering, stock-raising, and recreational region; winter sports. Inc. 1946.

Porto Lago or **Porto Lagos** (pôr'tô lä'gô, -gôs), village (1928 pop. 196), Xanthe nome, W Thrace, Greece, on inlet (6 mi. wide, 3 mi. long) of Aegean Sea, 15 mi. SE of Xanthe, on isthmus of L. Vistonis; small port with fish hatcheries.

Porto Longone, Italy: see Porto Azzurro.

Portomaggiore (pôr'tô mäd-jô'rĕ), town (pop. 4,164), Ferrara prov., Emilia-Romagna, N central Italy, 13 mi. SE of Ferrara; rail junction; agr. center; tomato cannery, liquor distillery, hemp and flax mills.

Porto Marghera (pôr'tô märgā'rä), port of Venice, Venezia prov., Veneto, N Italy, on mainland shore of Lagoon of Venice, 5 mi. NW of Venice, adjacent to Mestre. Industrial and commercial center; refineries (oil, sulphur), factories (glass, aluminum, furniture, fertilizer), foundries; zinc smelters, shipyards, coke and gas works. Exports food and chemical products, metals, glass, hemp, jute. Imports coal, oil, ores, cereals. Founded in 1919.

Pôrto Martins (pōr'tōō mŭrtēns'), town, central São Paulo, Brazil, head of navigation on Tietê R. and 15 mi. N of Botucatu; rail-spur terminus; asphalt extracting.

Porto Maurizio, Italy: see Imperia.

Pôrto Mendes (pōr'tōō mĕn'dĭs), village, W Paraná, Brazil, on Paraná R. (Paraguay border) and 75 mi. N of Foz do Iguaçu; S terminus of railroad from Pôrto Guaíra, and head of navigation on Paraná R. below Guaíra Falls. Ships maté, lumber.

Pôrto Moniz (pōr'tōō mōōnēzh'), town (pop. 1,037), Madeira, on NW coast of Madeira isl., 21 mi. NW of Funchal; fishing port.

Pôrto Murtinho (pōr'tōō mōōrtē'nyōō), city (pop. 2,273), southwesternmost Mato Grosso, Brazil, port on left bank of Paraguay R. (Paraguay border) and 180 mi. S of Corumbá; 21°43'S 57°53'W. Quebracho-shipping center. Marble quarries near by. In Ponta Porã territory, 1943–46.

Pôrto Nacional (pōr'tōō nŭsyōōnäl'), city (pop. 1,441), N central Goiás, central Brazil, on right bank of Tocantins R. and 220 mi. SSW of Carolina (Maranhão); 10°42'S 48°23'W. Ships rice, corn, sugar, castor beans. Quartz crystals found near by. Airfield. Has large church. Indian tribes in area.

Porto-Novo (pōr'tō-nō'vō), city (pop. c.30,650), ⊙ Dahomey, Fr. West Africa, port on N bank of coastal lagoon, 7 mi. from Gulf of Guinea coast, near Nigeria border, 55 mi. W of Lagos; 6°30'N 2°37'W. Linked by railroad with the port of Cotonou and with Lomé, Fr. Togoland. Administrative and trading center. Principal exports: palm oil, palm kernels, cotton, kapok. Soap mfg. Has governor's residence, agr. school, botanical garden, R.C. and Protestant missions.

Porto Novo (pôr'tō nō'vō), town (pop. 14,175), South Arcot dist., SE Madras, India, port on Coromandel Coast of Bay of Bengal, at mouth of Vellar R., 15 mi. S of Cuddalore; peanuts (kernels, oil cake). Casuarina plantations near by. Was 16th-cent. Port. settlement. English trading center established 1683; decisive English victory here (1781) over Hyder Ali. Sometimes Port Novo.

Portonovo (pôrtōnō'vō), town (pop. 1,226), Pontevedra prov., NW Spain, Atlantic fishing port on Pontevedra Bay, 9 mi. WSW of Pontevedra; fish processing.

Porto Palermo, Albania: see Palermo, Port.

Port Orange, city (pop. 1,201), Volusia co., NE Fla., on Halifax R. lagoon, just S of Daytona Beach; shrimp, oysters; citrus. Established 1861.

Port Orchard, town (pop. 2,320), ⊙ Kitsap co., W central Wash., on an arm of Puget Sound, opposite Bremerton; evergreens, strawberries, clams, dairy products. Settled 1854.

Porto Re, Yugoslavia: see Kraljevica.

Pôrto Real, Brazil: see Iguatama.

Pôrto Real do Colégio (pōr'tōō rĭäl' dōō kōōlĕ'-zhyōō), city (pop. 2,307), E Alagoas, NE Brazil, landing on left bank of São Francisco R., opposite Propriá (Sergipe), and 18 mi. WNW of Penedo. Projected terminus of railroad from Maceió, which by 1949 had reached Palmeira dos Índios and will constitute last link of continuous coastal Natal-Salvador rail line. Ships cotton, cereals, dairy products.

Porto Recanati (pôr'tô rĕkänä'tē), town (pop. 3,561), Macerata prov., The Marches, central Italy, port on the Adriatic, near mouth of Potenza R., 6 mi. ENE of Recanti; bathing resort.

Port Orford, city (pop. 674), Curry co., SW Oregon, on Pacific Ocean and 45 mi. SSW of Coos Bay.

Porto Rico, West Indies: see PUERTO RICO.

Portorose (pôrtōrô'zĕ), Slovenian *Portorož* (pôr'-tôrôzh), village (pop. 390), S Free Territory of Trieste, on Pirano Bay, 2 mi. SE of Pirano; health resort; mineral baths (iodine, bromine); salines (S). Placed 1947 under Yugoslav administration.

Porto San Giorgio (pôr'tô sän jôr'jô), town (pop. 6,793), Ascoli Piceno prov., The Marches, central Italy, port on the Adriatic, 4 mi. ENE of Fermo; rail junction; bathing resort; mfg. (soap, caustic soda, macaroni, agr. tools, bicycles).

Pôrto Santo (pōr'to͞o sän'to͞o), town (pop. 784), Madeira, on SE shore of PÔRTO SANTO ISLAND, 45 mi. NE of Funchal (on Madeira isl). Lime kilns; winegrowing, fishing. Bathing beach. House occupied by Columbus c.1479 still stands. Formerly called Vila Baleira or Vila da Piedade.

Pôrto Santo Island, northernmost (□ 16; 1950 pop. 2,934) of the Madeira isls., in the Atlantic, 30 mi. NE of Madeira; Pôrto Santo (33°4'N 16°20'W), its only town and port, is on SE shore. A low tableland, it rises to 1,660 ft. at the Pico do Facho. It is surrounded by reef islets. Both water and vegetation are scanty. Fruit- and winegrowing, limestone quarrying. Mineral springs; bathing beach. Discovered 1418 for Portugal by João Gonçalves Zarco. Columbus lived here c.1479.

Porto Santo Stefano (pôr'tô sän'tô stä'fänô), town (pop. 6,339), Grosseto prov., Tuscany, central Italy, port on N coast of Monte Argentario, 5 mi. W of Orbetello. Rail terminus; fishing center; bathing resort. Badly damaged in Second World War.

Portoscuso (pôr"tôsko͞o'zô), village (pop. 1,556), Cagliari prov., SW Sardinia, port on Mediterranean Sea and 11 mi. SW of Iglesias; major tunny fisheries, canneries. Porto Vesme (1 mi. SE; rail terminus) is ore-shipping center for lead, zinc, lignite, silver, and other minerals of SW Sardinia to Carloforte for transshipment.

Pôrto Seguro (pōr'to͞o sĭgo͞o'ro͞o). **1** City (pop. 2,117), SE Bahia, Brazil, fishing port on the Atlantic, and 110 mi. S of Ilhéus; ships cacao, lumber. Here, in 1500, Cabral 1st set foot on Braz. soil after sighting Monte PASCOAL, 40 mi. SSW. **2** City, Piauí, Brazil: see GUADALUPE.

Porto-Seguro or **Porto-Segouro** (pôr'tō-sĕgo͞o'rō), village, S Fr. Togoland, small port on Slave Coast of Gulf of Guinea, on a strip of land bet. L. Togo (lagoon) and the sea, on railroad and 18 mi. E of Lomé; palm kernels, copra; fishing.

Porto Spilio, Albania: see SPILË.

Pôrto Tibiriça, Brazil: see PRESIDENTE EPITÁCIO.

Porto Tolle (pôr'tô tôl'lĕ), commune (pop. 16,432), on Po R. delta, Rovigo prov., Veneto, N Italy. Agr. (sugar beets, rice), hunting, and fishing area, traversed by many distributaries and canals. Commune seat is Ca' Tiepolo (pop. 910), 15 mi. SE of Adria; sugar refinery.

Porto Torres (pôr"tô tôr'rĕs), anc. *Turris Libisonis*, town (pop. 6,438), Sassari prov., NW Sardinia, on Gulf of Asinara, at Mannu R. mouth, and 11 mi. NNW of Sassari; seaport of Sassari city; rail terminus; fish canneries (lobster). Iron mines 10 mi. WSW, linked by narrow-gauge line. Has Pisan-Romanesque basilica (11th–13th cent.) of San Gavino, ruins of Temple of Fortune (restored A.D. 247). Originally Carthaginian colony. Also spelled Portotorres.

Pôrto União (pōr'to͞o o͞onyä'ō), city (pop. 3,418), N Santa Catarina, Brazil, on Iguassú R. (Paraná border), opposite União da Vitória, and on São Paulo–Rio Grande do Sul RR (junction for Mafra and Joinvile); ironworking, maté processing; jerked beef. Indian reservation near by. Founded 1769.

Pôrto Valter (pōr'to͞o vältĕr'), town, W Acre territory, westernmost Brazil, on upper Juruá R. and 40 mi. S of Cruzeiro do Sol. Airport. Until 1944, Humaitá. Also spelled Pôrto Walter.

Porto-Vecchio (pôrtō-vĕkēō', It. pôr'tô-vĕk'kyô), village (pop. 1,557), S Corsica, 16 mi. NNE of Bonifacio, sheltered port at head of Gulf of Porto-Vecchio (2 mi. wide, 5 mi. deep) of Tyrrhenian Sea; ships cork and charcoal.

Pôrto Velho (pōr'to͞o vĕ'lyo͞o), city (1950 pop. 10,205), ⊙ Guaporé territory, W Brazil, on the Madeira R. and 460 mi. SW of Manaus; 8°42'S 63°54'W. Head of navigation on the Madeira; and N terminus of Madeira-Mamoré RR, which serves as outlet for rubber shipments from NE Bolivia and Mato Grosso. Also exports lumber, medicinal plants, and oils. Has hosp. Airfield. With completion of railroad (1913), city superseded near-by Alto Madeira (then called Santo Antônio) as regional trade center. After collapse of rubber boom, city and railroad declined in importance. Until formation of Guaporé territory (1943), city was part of Amazonas.

Portovelo (pôrtōvā'lō), gold mines in El Oro prov., S Ecuador, in the Andes, 45 mi. SE of Machala; also copper, silver, lead deposits.

Portovenere (pôr"tôvĕnä'rĕ), anc. *Portus Veneris*, village (pop. 1,163), La Spezia prov., Liguria, N Italy, port at S extremity of promontory forming W boundary of Gulf of Spezia, opposite Palmaria isl., in olive-growing region. Celebrated for its marble. Tunny fishing, mussel beds. Has churches of San Lorenzo (consecrated 1130) and San Pietro (1277), and ruins of medieval castle.

Portoviejo (pôrtōvyä'hō), city (1950 pop. 18,082), ⊙ Manabí prov., W Ecuador, in Pacific lowlands, on right bank of Portoviejo R., on Manta–Santa Ana RR and 90 mi. NNW of Guayaquil, 150 mi. WSW of Quito; 1°2'S 80°25'W. Trading center in lumbering and fertile agr. region (cacao, coffee, sugar cane, cotton, rubber, tagua nuts, balsa wood). Mfg. of Panama hats, baskets, and hammocks; tanning. Bishopric. Founded c.1535 near the coast; removed to its present site in 17th cent.

Portoviejo River, Manabí prov., W Ecuador, rises at SW foot of the Cordillera de Balzar, flows c.65 mi. W and N, past Santa Ana, Portoviejo, and Rocafuerte, to the Pacific 10 mi. SSW of Bahía de Caráquez. Waters a fertile region, producing cacao, sugar cane, rice, coffee, cotton, tagua nuts, rubber, balsa wood.

Porto Viro, Italy: see CONTARINA.

Pôrto Walter, Brazil: see PÔRTO VALTER.

Portpatrick, town and parish (pop. 1,101), W Wigtown, Scotland, on Irish Sea, on the Rhinns of Galloway, 6 mi. SW of Stranraer; small port and seaside resort. It is nearest port to Ireland (21 mi.) and was terminal of mail service to Donaghadee (Northern Ireland) until 1849. The harbor was considerably improved c.1843, but was abandoned in favor of Stranraer. It had brief revival in First World War. Near by are remains of early 16th-cent. Dunskey Castle.

Port Pegasus, small fishing port (pop. 24), on Pegasus Bay, SE Stewart Isl., New Zealand, 30 mi. SW of Oban.

Port Penn, town (1940 pop. 271), New Castle co., E Del., 15 mi. S of Wilmington and on Delaware R. Reedy Isl. is offshore.

Port Penrhyn, Wales: see BANGOR.

Port Perry, village (pop. 1,245), S Ont., on L. Scugog, 40 mi. NE of Toronto; mfg. of shoes and other leather goods; lumbering, dairying.

Port Phillip Bay, large inlet of Bass Strait, S Victoria, Australia, bet. Point Lonsdale (W) and Point Nepean; 30 mi. long N-S, 25 mi. wide E-W. Its N arm, HOBSON'S BAY, is site of Port Melbourne and Williamstown; W arm, CORIO BAY, is site of Geelong. Sometimes called Port Phillip.

Port Pirie (pĕr'ē), city and port (pop. 12,019), S South Australia, at base of Yorke Peninsula, on S inlet of Germein Bay of Spencer Gulf and 125 mi. NNW of Adelaide; 33°10'S 138°1'E. Smelting works for Broken Hill mines (silver, lead). Is 2d largest port of state; exports silver and lead concentrates, wheat. E end of Trans-Australian RR.

Portrack, England: see STOCKTON-ON-TEES.

Port Radium, arctic village, central Mackenzie Dist., Northwest Territories, on Labine Point, small promontory on E shore of Great Bear L.; 66°5'N 118°1'W; pitchblende and uranium mining and milling center; site of govt. radio and meteorological station; Royal Canadian Mounted Police post. Ore is shipped by barge to railhead at Fort McMurray, Alta., thence to refinery at Port Hope, Ont. Pitchblende was discovered here (1929–30); milling plant was established 1933. Mines were closed down 1940, reopened 1942, and taken over by Canadian govt. under a Crown company in 1944. Village formerly called Eldorado.

Port Reading, N.J.: see WOODBRIDGE.

Portreath (-rēth'), fishing port and resort, W Cornwall, England, on the Atlantic and 4 mi. NW of Redruth.

Port Redon (pôr rădō'), town, Quangyen prov., N Vietnam, on inlet of Gulf of Tonkin, 3 mi. NNW of Quangyen; coal-loading port for Uongbi and Maokhe.

Portree (pôrtrē'), town and parish (pop. 2,007), chief town of Isle of SKYE, Inverness, Scotland, on Sound of Raasay, on E coast of isl., 21 mi. NW of Kyle; fishing port, tourist resort.

Port Reitz, Kenya: see MOMBASA.

Port Renfrew (rĕn'fro͞o), village, SW B.C., on S Vancouver Isl., on Port San Juan inlet of Juan de Fuca Strait, 50 mi. W of Victoria; lumber port.

Port Republic. 1 City (pop. 423), Atlantic co., S N.J., 12 mi. NNW of Atlantic City. **2** Village, Rockingham co., NW Va., at junction of North and South rivers to form South Fork of Shenandoah R., 17 mi. NE of Staunton. Here and at Cross Keys (4 mi. NW) was fought last battle (1862) in Shenandoah Valley campaign of Gen. T. J. (Stonewall) Jackson.

Port Richey, city (pop. 376), Pasco co., W central Fla., 27 mi. NW of Tampa, near the Gulf.

Port Richmond, SE N.Y., a section of Richmond borough of New York city, on N shore of Staten Isl., across Kill Van Kull (bridged) from Bayonne, N.J.; trade and mfg. center; makes clothing, dental equipment, asphalt products.

Portrieux, France: see SAINT-QUAY-PORTRIEUX.

Port Robinson, village (pop. estimate 400), S Ont., on Welland Ship Canal and on Welland R., 8 mi. S of St. Catharines; dairying, fruitgrowing.

Port Rowan (rō'ŭn), village (pop. 661), S Ont., on L. Erie, 16 mi. SW of Simcoe; lumbering, dairying; tobacco, fruit, vegetables.

Port Royal, Nova Scotia: see ANNAPOLIS ROYAL.

Port Royal, town (pop. 1,027), ⊙ Port Royal parish, SE Jamaica, on W tip of the Palisadoes peninsula (which encloses Kingston Harbour), 4 mi. SW of Kingston; quarantine station, naval installations. Once one of the most prosperous towns in the West Indies, it was destroyed by 1692 earthquake and partly buried by the sea. Remaining is Fort Charles (begun 1662), where Nelson commanded in 1779. St. Peter's Church was built 1725–26. Port Royal was, in early colonial times, hq. of buccaneers. Port Royal parish (□ c.2) is coextensive with Palisadoes peninsula and is customarily considered part of Kingston parish, though retaining some administrative functions.

Port Royal. 1 Borough (pop. 800), Juniata co., central Pa., 10 mi. SE of Lewistown and on Juniata R.; silk and lumber mills; clothing; agr. **2** Town (pop. 793), Beaufort co., S S.C., on PORT ROYAL ISLAND and 5 mi. S of Beaufort; tourist and fishing center (shrimps), with fine harbor. Ships cotton, phosphate, manganese. Rail terminus. **3** Town (pop. 139), Caroline co., E Va., on the Rappahannock (bridged) and 17 mi. SE of Fredericksburg; cannery, pickle plant.

Port Royal Bay or **Little Sound** (2 mi. long, 1 mi. wide), W Bermuda, 2 mi. SW of Hamilton; opens N on Great Sound. On a spit of land in N is naval base on site leased to U.S. in 1941.

Port-Royal-des-Champs, France: see TRAPPES.

Port Royal Island, Beaufort co., S S.C., one of most important of S.C. SEA ISLANDS, at head of Port Royal Sound, c.30 mi. NE of Savannah, Ga.; c.13 mi. long, 7 mi. wide. Connected to mainland by railway and highway bridges, and by highway bridge to Ladies Isl. (E). Site of BEAUFORT and PORT ROYAL; Burton and Seabrook villages are also on isl. Resort area, with truck farming, fishing (shrimp, oysters, crabs), lumbering. Intracoastal Waterway passes to E and S.

Port Royal Sound, S S.C., inlet of the Atlantic, c.25 mi. NE of Savannah, Ga. At its head is Broad R., a tidal channel which receives Coosawhatchie R.; at its mouth it is flanked S by Hilton Head, N by St. Phillips, isls. Crossed by Intracoastal Waterway.

Portrush (pôrtrŭsh'), urban district (1937 pop. 3,386; 1951 census pop. 4,166), NW Co. Antrim, Northern Ireland, on the coast 5 mi. N of Coleraine; 55°13'N 6°40'W; seaport for Coleraine, salmon-fishing center, and resort, sheltered by promontory of Ramore Head. Offshore are The Skerries. Giant's Causeway is 7 mi. ENE.

Port Said (sīd, säd, säēd'), city (pop., with outlying dists., 178,432), ⊙ Canal Governorate, NE Egypt, on the Mediterranean at entrance to Suez Canal, and 105 mi. NE of Cairo; 31°17'N 32°18'E. Situated on a narrow sand spit bet. L. Manzala and the sea, it is one of the world's great coaling and oiling stations. Also has evaporation works for producing salt, and rice milling, wool spinning, mfg. of chemicals, refrigerants, cigarettes. Rail line to Suez and Cairo. City was founded 1859 by the builders of the canal and named for Said Pasha, then khedive of Egypt. On its outer pier are a lighthouse (174 ft. high) and a massive statue of Ferdinand de Lesseps. Opposite Port Said was built (c.1928) Port Fuad (pop. 3,804), a harbor not yet fully developed.

Port-Sainte-Marie (pôr-sĕt-märē'), village (pop. 996), Lot-et-Garonne dept., SW France, on the Garonne and 11 mi. WNW of Agen, in grape-growing region; fruit and vegetable shipping. Has 15th–16th-cent. houses.

Port Saint Joe, town (pop. 2,752), Gulf co., NW Fla., 32 mi. SE of Panama City; has deepwater harbor on St. Joseph Bay; lumbering and fishing center; paper, paperboard, wood-pulp, and lumber milling. Port of entry. State's 1st constitutional convention met here in 1838. Settled c.1830, inc. 1913.

Port Saint Johns, town (pop. 971), ⊙ Pondoland dist. of the Transkeian Territories, E Cape Prov., U. of So. Afr., on the Indian Ocean, at mouth of Umzimvubu R., 150 mi. SW of Durban, 140 mi. NE of East London; center of agr. area (citrus fruit, bananas, tobacco, mealies); resort. Marble, lime, sulphur worked near by.

Port-Saint-Louis-du-Rhône (pôr-sē-lwē-dü-rōn'), town (pop. 3,817), Bouches-du-Rhône dept., SE France, on left bank of the Grand Rhône near its mouth on Gulf of Lion, 22 mi. SSE of Arles; modern transshipping port (terminus of rail branch to Arles; sea canal, 4 mi. long, to Gulf of Fos) with salt and chemical works.

Port Saint Mary, village district (1939 pop. 1,292), on S coast of Isle of Man, England, 3 mi. W of Castletown; fishing port, resort. Near by is Manx Open Air Mus., with old Manx cottages.

Port-Salut (pôr-sälü'), town (1950 census pop. 900), Sud dept., SW Haiti, on the SW coast of Tiburon Peninsula, 14 mi. SW of Les Cayes; basketmaking.

Port Sandwich, New Hebrides: see MALEKULA.

Port Sanilac (să'nŭlăk), resort village (pop. 247), Sanilac co., E Mich., 31 mi. NW of Port Huron, on L. Huron.

Port San Juan (săn wän'), inlet of Juan de Fuca Strait, in S Vancouver Isl., B.C., 50 mi. W of Victoria, in lumbering area; 4 mi. long. Port Renfrew, lumber port, is on SE shore.

Port San Luis, Calif.: see SAN LUIS OBISPO, city.

Pörtschach am Wörthersee (pûrt'shäkh äm vûrt'-ûrzā), town (pop. 2,732), Carinthia, S Austria, on N shore of the Wörthersee and 8 mi. W of Klagenfurt; resort, spa.

Portsdown, hill range (rising to c.450 ft.), SE Hampshire, England, extending 7 mi. along the coast bet. Fareham and Havant.

Portsea, village (pop. 211), S Victoria, Australia, on S shore of Port Phillip Bay, near E side of entrance, 37 mi. S of Melbourne; seaside resort.

Portsea, a NW district of PORTSMOUTH, Hampshire, England, with great navy yard.

Portsea Island (4 mi. long, 3 mi. wide), on coast of Hampshire, England, bet. Portsmouth and Langston harbors and separated from the mainland by a narrow channel crossed by 4 bridges. PORTSMOUTH is on it.

Port Seton, Scotland: see COCKENZIE AND PORT SETON.

Port Shepstone, town (pop. 2,211), SE Natal, U. of So. Afr., on Indian Ocean at mouth of Umzimkulu R., 70 mi. SSW of Durban; agr. center (sugar, fruit, wattle bark, corn, fibers, poultry); dairying; cement mfg. Near by are limestone quarries and marble deposits.

Port Simpson, village, W B.C., on Tsimpsean Peninsula, on Chatham Sound, 18 mi. N of Prince Rupert; fishing port; lumbering, raspberry growing. Former site of post of Hudson's Bay Co.

Port's Island, islet (900 ft. long, 700 ft. wide) in Great Sound, Bermuda, 2.5 mi. WSW of Hamilton.

Portslade-by-Sea, urban district (1931 pop. 9,527; 1951 census 13,572), S Sussex, England, on the Channel, 3 mi. W of Brighton; small port, with metal, clothing, and soap industries, and flour mills. Has Norman church. Saxon and Roman remains have been found near by.

Portsmouth (pôrts'mŭth), village (pop. 3,135), SE Ont., on L. Ontario, at head of the St. Lawrence; W suburb of Kingston; site of prov. penitentiary and insane asylum.

Portsmouth, town (pop. 1,725), NW Dominica, B.W.I., port on Prince Rupert Bay, 20 mi. NNW of Roseau; limes, cacao, coconuts. Agr. demonstration center.

Portsmouth, county borough (1931 pop. 249,283; 1951 census 233,464) and chief Br. naval base, SE Hampshire, England, on PORTSEA ISLAND, 65 mi. SW of London, at entrance to Portsmouth Harbour on the Spithead; 50°48'N 1°6'W. In E districts of Portsea (pop. 21,339) and Landport are the large naval dockyards. H.M.S. *Victory,* Nelson's flagship at Trafalgar, is preserved here in drydock. The city has 12th-cent. Cathedral of St. Thomas à Becket, containing cenotaph of duke of Buckingham assassinated (1628) in a house formerly called Inn of the Spotted Dog. Dickens' birthplace is now mus. Portsmouth (Latin name *Portus Magnus*) became important naval base during reign of Henry VIII; dockyard regularly established in 1540. Here Charles II and Catherine of Braganza were married. It is birthplace of George Meredith, Walter Besant, Isambard Brunel, and Jonas Hanway. In Second World War the city suffered heavy air raids (1940–41). County borough includes residential dist. and resort of Southsea (S), on the Spithead, with beaches and pier, and residential dists. of Fratton (E; pop. 16,165) and Cosham (N, on mainland; pop. 8,091). Across mouth of the harbor is GOSPORT, connected by bridge.

Portsmouth. 1 Town (pop. 299), Shelby co., W Iowa, on Mosquito Creek and 10 mi. W of Harlan. **2** City (pop. 18,830), Rockingham co., SE N.H., at mouth of Piscataqua R., opposite Kittery, Maine (connected by 2 bridges); 43°5'N, 70°47'W. Only seaport in N.H., handling mainly bulk cargoes; port of entry. Commercial center for agr. and resort region; some mfg. (buttons, tools, gypsum products, shoes, wood products). Lumbering and fishing base established near here at Odiorne's Point in 1623. Granted as Piscataqua township by Plymouth Colony in 1631. Inc. by Mass. as Portsmouth town in 1653; served as provincial ⊙ until Revolution. City inc. 1849. Shipbuilding center and flourishing port in 18th and early 19th cents.; John Paul Jones's *Ranger* built (1777) by Portsmouth shipwrights in Kittery. U.S. (Portsmouth) Naval Base, important submarine-building and repair yard, established (c.1794) on isls. in Piscataqua R. (on Maine side) Treaty of Portsmouth, ending Russo-Japanese War, signed here 1905. *New Hampshire Gazette,* state's 1st newspaper, started here 1756. Noted as summer resort; many fine early houses maintained by antiquarian societies and museums. Points of interest: Old State House (meeting place for Provincial Assembly), Athenaeum (1803), St. John's Church (1807), Warner House (1718), Jackson House (1664), Public Library (1809), Wentworth-Gardiner House (1760), John Paul Jones House (1758). **3** City (pop. 36,798), ⊙ Scioto co., S Ohio, on the Ohio (bridged) at mouth of the Scioto, and 85 mi. ESE of Cincinnati; industrial and railroad center, with railroad shops, steel mills, foundries; mfg. of shoes, stoves, furniture, knit goods, paper products, machinery, refractories. Shawnee State Forest and Roosevelt Game Preserve are near by. Laid out 1803, inc. 1814. **4** Town (pop. 6,578), Newport co., SE R.I., on N Rhode Isl. and 18 mi. SSE of Providence; includes PRUDENCE ISLAND. Residential, resort area; fisheries. Includes BRISTOL FERRY (Mt. Hope Bridge to Bristol here) and South Portsmouth villages. Was 2d white settlement in R.I.; founded by William Coddington, John Clarke, Anne Hutchinson, and associates in 1638; colony's 1st general assembly met here, 1647. British Gen. Richard Prescott captured here, 1777. Scene of battle of Rhode Isl., 1778. **5** Port city (pop. 80,039), in but independent of Norfolk co., SE Va., on Elizabeth R. (bridges) opposite NORFOLK; co. courthouse is here. One of ports on HAMPTON ROADS (U.S. Atlantic Fleet base); seat of Norfolk Navy Yard. Rail terminus and steamship port; ships agr. produce (cotton, tobacco, vegetables), seafood, lumber. Processing industries (seafood, soybeans, cotton, cottonseed, lumber); railroad shops; mfg. of paving materials, fertilizer, knit goods, soap, furniture. Points of interest: navy yard, where ironclad *Merrimac* was built; U.S. naval hosp. (1827–30); Trinity Church (1762); late 18th-cent. houses. Laid out 1750 on site of Indian village; chartered 1758. Used as British landing base in Revolution. In Civil War, navy yard was burned and evacuated (1861) by Federals, and occupied by Confederates; retaken 1862 by Union troops.

Portsmouth Island, Carteret co., E N.C., SW of Ocracoke Isl., bet. Pamlico Sound (NW) and Raleigh Bay (SE); 7 mi. long. Portsmouth, fishing village and resort is on NE end.

Portsoy, burgh (1931 pop. 1,651; 1951 census 1,787), N Banffshire, Scotland, on Moray Firth 6 mi. WNW of Banff; fishing port, resort; noted marble and granite quarries; agr. implement mfg. Just E is 15th-cent. Boyne Castle.

Port Stanley, village (pop. 1,177), S Ont., on L. Erie, 8 mi. S of St. Thomas; fishing port, resort.

Port Stanley, Falkland Isls.: see STANLEY.

Port Stewart, village, NE Queensland, Australia, on SE coast of Cape York Peninsula, at Claremont Point of Princess Charlotte Bay, 240 mi. NW of Cairns; port for gold field at Coen.

Portstewart (pôrtstū'ûrt), urban district (1937 pop. 2,587; 1951 census 3,563), NE Co. Londonderry, Northern Ireland, on the Atlantic, near mouth of Bann R., 4 mi. NNW of Coleraine; fishing port, seaside resort.

Port Sudan (so͞odăn'), city (pop. 47,450), Kassala prov., NE Anglo-Egyptian Sudan, on Red Sea, 250 mi. NE of Atbara and 300 mi. NNE of Kassala; 19°35'N 37°13'E. Chief port of entry into the Sudan, handling 85% of its foreign trade; railhead for rich cotton-growing region (Gezira, Kassala area, Nile valley). Major commercial and shipping center with modern docking facilities; exports cotton and cotton seed, gum arabic, oilseeds, beans, hides and skins, cattle and sheep. Salt pans. Embarkation point for Mecca-bound pilgrims. Airport. Situated on deep bay extending N-S, the town proper (W of harbor) has govt. bldgs., mus., schools, hosps. On bay's E shore are commercial quays, coal and oil depots, customs warehouses, shipping offices. Founded 1906 as a modern harbor to replace SUAKIN, obstructed by rapidly-growing coral reef.

Port Sulphur, village (pop. 1,255, with adjacent Potash), Plaquemines parish, extreme SE La., on W bank (levee) of the Mississippi and 40 mi. SE of New Orleans. Established in 1933 for workers in sulphur mines of marshy L. Grande Ecaille, c.10 mi. SW. Sulphur shipments reach deepwater wharf on the Mississippi here by canal (c.10 mi. long) from mines.

Port Sunlight, town in Bebington municipal borough, on Wirral peninsula, NW Cheshire, England, on Mersey R. opposite Liverpool; "company town," with soap and oleomargarine mfg.

Port-sur-Saône (pôr-sür-sōn'), village (pop. 1,581), Haute-Saône dept., E France, on canalized Saône R. and 7 mi. NW of Vesoul; scale mfg., dairying.

Port Swettenham, town (pop. 11,300), W Selangor, Malaya, port on Strait of Malacca, 23 mi. WSW of Kuala Lumpur (linked by railroad), at mouth of Klang R. One of leading ports of Malaya, accessible to ocean-going vessels via North Klang Strait and sheltered by low mangrove isls. (KLANG ISLAND); ships tin, rubber, copra, pineapples.

Port Sydney, village (pop. 127), S Ont., in Muskoka lake region, on Mary L. (4 mi. long), 14 mi. NNE of Bracebridge; resort.

Port Talbot (tôl'bŭt), municipal borough (1931 pop. 40,678; 1951 census 44,024), W central Glamorgan, Wales, on Swansea Bay of Bristol Channel at mouth of Afon R., 7 mi. ESE of Swansea; 51°35'N 3°47'W; port for Afon valley metallurgical and coal industry, with important steel and tinplate mills; agr. market and seaside resort. Municipal borough includes towns of ABERAVON, CWMAVON, MARGAM.

Port Tampa City (tăm'pŭ), city (pop. 1,497), Hillsborough co., W Fla., 9 mi. SW of Tampa, on peninsula separating Hillsboro and Old Tampa bays. Port Tampa, 2 mi. W on Old Tampa Bay, ships phosphate rock and is a port of entry.

Port Taufiq (toufēk') or **Port Tewfik** (tū'fĭk), port, part of SUEZ, NE Egypt, at head of Gulf of Suez, at entrance to Suez Canal; railhead.

Port Tobacco, village (pop. c.100), Charles co., S Md., on inlet of Potomac R. estuary, 27 mi. S of Washington. Was important Potomac port and co. ⊙ (1658–1895), until its harbor silted up. Near by are 17th- and 18th-cent. manor houses, including "Chandler's Hope" (built 1639; one of oldest Md. houses). Jesuit missionaries visited (1641) the Indian village Potopaco here and acquired land in 1649.

Port Townsend, city (pop. 6,888), ⊙ Jefferson co., NW Wash., port of entry 30 mi. WNW of Everett and on Admiralty Inlet of Puget Sound; ships lumber, woodpulp, coal, fish, grain; processes fish, timber, paper, dairy products. Gateway to Olympic Natl. Park (SW). Near by are Fort Worden, Fort Casey, Fort Flagler. Settled 1851, inc. 1860.

Portugal (pôr'chŭgŭl), anc. *Lusitania* (lūsĭtā'nēŭ, –nyŭ), corporative republic (continental area: □ 34,216; 1950 pop. 7,902,590; with Madeira and Azores: □ 35,409; 1950 pop. 8,490,455), SW Europe; ⊙ LISBON. Occupies W section of Iberian Peninsula along the Atlantic (W and S), being bounded by Spain N and E, bet. c.36°58'–42°9'N and 6°11'–9°30'W. Roughly of rectangular shape, about 360 mi. long, 125 mi. wide. The Atlantic archipelagoes of the AZORES (□ 888; pop. 318,686) and MADEIRA (□ 305; pop. 269,179) form an integral part of the country, which for administrative purposes is divided into 18 districts. The 11 provinces (set up 1936) are derived largely from the 6 historic provinces (ALENTEJO, ALGARVE, BEIRA, ENTRE DOURO E MINHO or Minho, ESTREMADURA, TRÁS-OS-MONTES) still widely in use as regional concepts. Portugal's coast line of c.500 mi. is generally level and sandy, occasionally lined by lagoons, but has rocky bays (*rías*) in NW near Galician border. Some steep offshoots of the Iberian ranges project into the Atlantic, such as Cape ROCA, westernmost point of Europe, and Cape SAINT VINCENT, the southwesternmost point. Portugal's relief is closely connected with that of Spain. Most of the inland and E part is rugged, mountainous country of scenic beauty, deeply incised by rivers. The ridges generally run NE-SW; among the highest are Serra da ESTRÊLA (Malhão, 6,532 ft.), principal mining region, continuing the Sierras de Guadarrama, Gredos, and Gato of Spain. A Portuguese outlier of the Sierra Morena is the Serra de MONCHIQUE near Atlantic S coast. Valleys of the major streams, DOURO RIVER, TAGUS RIVER, and GUADIANA RIVER, widen towards coast. The Tagus, on whose estuary is Lisbon, divides the country into approximately equal parts, of which the more arid S is noted for its earthquakes. Except for the Guadiana, which flows S, these rivers rise in Spain, form part of the international boundary, and flow W to the coast; so does the Minho (Sp. Miño) in N. The climate is generally maritime, equable, and temperate; humid in N half, with heavy rainfall and fogs, increasingly dry towards S. Lisbon's annual mean temp. is c.60°F., rainfall c.60 inches. Trás-os-Montes in NE has a more rigorous mtn. climate, quite cold in winter and occasionally snowbound; it is one of the least developed regions. On the other hand, Algarve, in S, is a subtropical coastal strip, akin in vegetation and climate to North Africa. The wooded slopes of the interior yield Portugal's leading export, cork (more than 75% shipped to U.S.); also timber, naval stores, chestnuts. Wine, economically as important, enjoys high repute. Vineyards are chiefly in the river valleys, foremost along the Douro. OPORTO, with the port LEIXÕES, is at its head, where celebrated port wine is produced in a demarcated area. Sparkling wine comes from Mondego R. area, muscatel from S. There are also fine claret and brandy, and from Madeira comes the fine wine which bears its name. Many of the lower hilly slopes are covered with olive groves, and the flatter uplands, as well as the plains near the coast, are devoted to the growing of cereals—wheat (mainly around BEJA), corn, barley, rye, oats, stringbeans, potatoes, and in warmer, irrigated regions, rice. Mediterranean fruit (almonds, carobs, figs, pomegranates, citrus, some dates) thrive in S, especially in Algarve. The Azores contribute pineapples, artichokes, and winter vegetables. Grain and the wide pasture lands are used to support stock raising. Sheep and hogs are the chief animals bred, although some sections are noted for their horses and cattle (including bulls for the ring). About 60% of the people are engaged in agr., but erosion and varying fertility of the soil, antiquated methods, lack of communications, and social inequities keep the farmers poor. Fisheries and canneries (sardines, tuna), principally based at SETÚBAL and MATOZINHOS, but also at OLHÃO, PORTIMÃO, and VILA REAL, provide another important product for foreign trade. Whale- and cod fishing fleets (to Newfoundland) are maintained. Portugal is quite rich in all kinds of minerals (coals, pyrite, copper, lead, tin, antimony, arsenic, kaolin, sulphur, lithium, titanium, etc.), though little is so far mined, apart from tungsten from Serra da Estrêla (developed during Second World War), pyrites, and cassiterite. Industries are largely con fined to processing (notably wine making) and mfg. of consumer goods. The hydroelectric potential is great, and several large dams have been built. Most of the factories are located at the 2 large port cities, Lisbon and Oporto. These have textile plants (cotton, silk), sugar refineries, shipyards, mfg. of chemicals, glassware. Lisbon, situated on fine sheltered bay, dominates the nation's life and is also a major hub for transatlantic airlines, as are the Azores. COVILHÃ is a center for woolen textiles, BRAGA for silken goods. Chinaware and ceramics at VISTA ALEGRE, VILA NOVA DE GAIA, and Coimbra. ÉVORA (S center) is an inland center. Coimbra has one of Europe's oldest universities (founded 1290). There are also universities at Lisbon and Oporto, both set up in 1911. To the country's great past testify numerous castles, monasteries (Arrábida, ALCOBAÇA, and BATALHA), churches, museums, and archaeological remains. In W is the shrine of Our Lady of FÁTIMA. There are a great many fine resorts, e.g., the beaches of ESTORIL and CASCAIS on so-called Portuguese Riviera adjoining Lisbon; Cintra in coastal hills; and the mtn. resort BUÇACO. The more than 2,000 mi. of railroads, some state owned, include both wide and narrow gauge. A great majority of the Portuguese are R.C., and the people are, in view of their diverse history, remarkably homogeneous in speech and customs. Portugal is among the most backward of European nations; almost half of the population is illiterate. Part of Portugal, bet. Douro and Tagus rivers, was originally settled by the fierce Lusitanians, who resisted the Romans stubbornly in 2d and 1st cent. B.C. Finally subdued by Julius Caesar and Augustus, most of the country was combined with parts of W Spain in prov. of Lusitania. Like rest of Iberian Peninsula, it was overrun by Germanic invaders, followed by the Moors, who defeated (711) the Visigoths. The Algarva flourished then. Portugal was born out of the confusion of Christian reconquest. Ferdinand I of Castile entered Beira and secured possession of the fortress of Viseu and the city of Coimbra by 1064. Henry of Burgundy was made (1095?) count of Coimbra, a title later exchanged for count of Portucalense. His son fought the Moors successfully and declared (1139) himself king as Alfonso I. The year 1140 is generally taken as beginning of Port. history, with Portugal established as independent state. Moors were expelled from Alentejo and Algarve by 1249. Dynastic wars with Castilians continued until ascendance of John I, grand master of order of Aviz, on Port. throne. Thus started Portugal's most glorious period. One of John's sons, Henry the Navigator, instigated exploration of African coast. Madeira and Azores were colonized. Portugal became eventually a leading colonial power. Bartholomew Diaz rounded (1488) the Cape of Good Hope, and Vasco da Gama found (1497–99) road to India; the wealth of the Indies poured back to Portugal. Since the Treaty of Tordessillas (1494) bet. Spain and Portugal virtually divided world into 2 spheres of influence, Brazil, discovered by Pedro Alvares Cabral, became a Port. possession. The empire was flung across the world in Asia, Africa, and America. In 16th cent. Portugal emerged as a prosperous commercial nation, eclipsing the glories of Venice. But the descent was rapid, hastened by King Sebastian's (1557–78) religious and military policies. While Renaissance literature (e.g., Camões' great epic *The Lusiads*) still flourished, the economic and social force was spent. Philip II claimed (1580) Portugal upon disappearance of house of Aviz. Most of the empire was lost to the Dutch. The Sp. yoke was thrown off (1640), and John of Braganza was made king as John IV. No longer a great power, Portugal bound itself (1654) as an ally to England, who became chief customer for port wine. The War of the Spanish Succession (1700–14), absolutism under John V and the dictator Pombal, and the disastrous earthquake of Lisbon (1755) contributed to further decline. Upon the conquest by Napoleon, the royal family fled (1807) to Brazil, establishing Rio de Janeiro as center of the empire. Portugal was rent by the Peninsular War. The king only returned from Brazil in 1820 after a liberal revolution against the regency. John VI accepted (1822) a liberal constitution. Brazil declared its independence under Pedro I (John's elder son) as emperor. Dynastic and civil wars, accompanied by military coups and dictatorships, raged through 19th cent. In 1908 King Charles and his heir were assassinated. Portugal became (1910) a republic, but financial and political chaos continued. It entered First World War on Allied side. Insurrections of both right and left came to an end when Oscar de Fragoso Carmona took over (1926) the government. He was elected (1928) president, while Antonio Oliveira de Salazar emerged as strong man. Through 1933 constitution he inaugurated the *Novo Estado*, a corporative semi-fascist state. The Portuguese govt. was friendly towards Franco in Sp. civil war (1936–39). Portugal maintained neutrality in Second World War (1939–45), when its development as international communications hub made it also a spy center. Naval and air bases were granted (1943) to the Allies in the Azores. After the war Portugal's application for membership in the United Nations was refused. Portugal's colonies (since 1951 known as "overseas provinces") include PORTUGUESE INDIA (GOA, DAMÃO, and DIU isl.), MACAO, and part of TIMOR in Asia; CAPE VERDE ISLANDS in the Atlantic; PORTUGUESE GUINEA, SÃO TOMÉ, and PRÍNCIPE isls., ANGOLA, and MOZAMBIQUE in Africa. Continental Portugal is administratively divided into 18 dists.: AVEIRO, BEJA, BRAGA, BRAGANÇA, CASTELO BRANCO, COIMBRA, ÉVORA, FARO, GUARDA, LEIRA, LISBOA, PORTALEGRE, PÔRTO, SANTARÉM, SETÚBAL, VIANA DO CASTELO, VILA REAL, VISEU; and 11 provs.: ALGARVE, ALTO ALENTEJO, BAIXO ALENTEJO, BEIRA ALTA, BEIRA BAIXA, BEIRA LITORAL, DOURO LITORAL, ESTREMADURA, MINHO, RIBATEJO, TRÁS-OS-MONTES E ALTO DOURO. For further information see also towns, cities, physical features, and the above-mentioned historic provinces.

Portugal Bay, SE inlet of Gulf of Mannar, W Ceylon, bet. Karativu isl. (W) and Ceylon mainland (E), just N of Dutch Bay, at 8°30'N.

Portugalete (pôrtōōgälā'tā), village (pop. c.1,000), Potosí dept., SW Bolivia, at N end of Cordillera de Lípez, c.40 mi. NW of Tupiza; alt. 12,828 ft.; tin mining.

Portugalete, outer NW suburb (pop. 9,092) of Bilbao, Vizcaya prov., N Spain, on left bank of Nervión R. at its mouth on Bilbao Bay (inlet of Bay of Biscay), opposite Las Arenas (transporter bridge). Hog market. Bathing resort.

Portugália (pōōrtōōgä'lyù), town, Malange prov., northeasternmost Angola, in diamond-washing area, 60 mi. S of Tshikapa (Belgian Congo); 7°18'S 20°50'E.

Portuguesa (pôrtōōgā'sä), state (□ 5,870; 1941 pop. 87,151; 1950 census 120,984), W Venezuela; ⊙ Guanare. Except for outliers of Andean spur (W), it consists entirely of llano lowlands drained by secondary tributaries of Orinoco R., including the Portuguesa, Guanare, and Cojedes. Has wet, tropical climate and frequently experiences floods. Contains immense forests with fine timber. Primarily an agr. region, raising cattle and growing cotton; coffee is cultivated in uplands, rice on plains, corn in entire state; other crops are sugar cane, cacao, tobacco, yucca, bananas. Acarigua and Guanare are the commercial centers.

Portuguesa River, W Venezuela, rises in Andean spur SE of Tocuyo (Lara state), flows c.240 mi. SE in llano country through Portuguesa and Cojedes, and along Barinas–Guárico border, past La Unión, to Apure R. 5 mi. NW of San Fernando. Navigable. Cojedes, Pao, and Guanare rivers are its main affluents.

Portuguese East Africa: see MOZAMBIQUE.

Portuguese Guinea (gĭ'nē), Port. *Guiné Portuguesa*, Port. colony (□ 13,948; 1940 pop. 351,089), W Africa, on the Atlantic; ⊙ Bissau. An enclave in Fr. West Africa (Senegal is to N, Fr. Guinea to E and SE), bet. 11°N and 12°40'N, and bet. 13°40'W and 16°45'W. Includes Bijagós Isls. off Geba R. estuary. Has irregular, 100-mi.-long, mangrove-lined coast line. A low, deltaic region, it is traversed by many streams (Geba, Corubal, Cacheu) linked by arms and inlets. Has unhealthful monsoon tropical climate (average yearly temp. 81°F.; small annual range) marked by rainy (May-Nov.) and dry seasons. Yearly rainfall c.80 in. Tropical forest lines lower river courses; park savanna is further inland. Fauna includes elephants, hippopotami, panthers, antelopes, crocodiles. Principal products are almonds, rice, copra, palm oil, palm kernels, peanuts, corn, rubber, kola nuts, millet, beeswax. Cattle and hogs are raised. Rice milling, palm-oil processing, and pottery mfg. are chief industries. Bissau is colony's best port. Others are Bolama (⊙ until 1941), Bafatá, and Bubaque (on Bijagós Isls.). Discovered 1446–47 by Deniz Dias and Nuno Tristão, both in service of Prince Henry the Navigator. Supplied slave trade in 17th-18th cent. British claims on part of territory were set aside (1870) by U.S. President Grant's arbitration award. Administratively separated from Cape Verde Isls. in 1879. Definitive boundaries established by Franco-Port. convention 1886.

Portuguese India, Port. *Índia Portuguesa*, officially *Estado da Índia*, colony (□ 1,538; pop. 624,177) consisting of 3 separate dists.—GOA and DAMÃO (on coast of Bombay state) and DIU, a small isl. off S Kathiawar peninsula; ⊙ Pangim. Acquired in 16th cent., these dists. are all that remain of Port. Indian possessions, which once included trading posts at Calicut, Cochin, and Hooghly. Now under a governor-general, with lieutenant-governors at Damão and Diu, assisted by dist. councils.

Portuguese West Africa: see ANGOLA.

Portumna (pôrtŭm'nù), Gaelic *Port Omna*, town (pop. 924), SE Co. Galway, Ireland, on the Shannon, at N end of Lough Derg, and 13 mi. W of Birr; agr. market (sheep; potatoes, beets). Slight remains of 13th-cent. Dominican convent.

Port Union, village (pop. 641), SE N.F., on N side of entrance of Trinity Bay, 10 mi. S of Bonavista; fishing port.

Portus Adurni, England: see PORTCHESTER.

Portus Cale, Portugal: see OPORTO.

Portus Castra, England: see PORTCHESTER.

Portus Dubris, England: see DOVER.

Portus Hannibalis, Portugal: see ALVOR.

Portus Lemanis, England: see HYTHE, Kent.

Portus Magnus, England: see PORTSMOUTH.

Portus Magonis, Balearic Isls.: see MAHÓN.

Portus Veneris, France: see PORT-VENDRES.

Portus Veneris, Italy: see PORTOVENERE.

Port-Vendres (pôr-vä'drù), anc. *Portus Veneris*, town (pop. 2,689), Pyrénées-Orientales dept., S France, southernmost Fr. port on the Mediterranean, at foot of Monts Albères, 16 mi. SE of Perpignan; dynamite and cork mfg., winegrowing, sardine fishing. Agr. chemistry laboratory. Terminal for passenger lines to Algeria. Harbor heavily damaged in Second World War.

Port Victoria, village and port (pop. 175), S South Australia, on W Yorke Peninsula, 95 mi. SSW of Port Pirie, on SE shore of Port Victoria (inlet of Spencer Gulf); sheltered (W) by Wardang Isl.; exports agr. products.

Port Victoria, village, Nyanza prov., SW Kenya, small port on L. Victoria, 55 mi. WNW of Kisumu, near Uganda border; ships cotton, peanuts, sesame. Fisheries.

Port Victoria, Seychelles: see VICTORIA.

Portville, village (pop. 1,151), Cattaraugus co., W N.Y., on Allegheny R., near Pa. line, and 6 mi. SE of Olean, in oil-producing area; dairy products, grain, potatoes. Inc. 1895.

Port Vladimir (vlŭdyē'mĭr), town (1935 pop. 1,400), NW Murmansk oblast, Russian SFSR, on isl. in Barents Sea, at mouth of Ura Bay, 30 mi. N of Murmansk; fish canning.

Port Vue (pôrt" vū'), borough (pop. 4,756), Allegheny co., SW Pa., on Youghiogheny R. near its mouth on the Monongahela, and just S of McKeesport; mfg. of metal products. Inc. 1892.

Port Wakefield, town and port (pop. 429), S South Australia, at head of Gulf St. Vincent, 55 mi. NNW of Adelaide; exports agr. products.

Port Wallut (pôr wälü'), town, Quangyen prov., N Vietnam, on NE Kebao isl., 35 mi. NE of Hongay; coal-shipping port for isl. mines; oyster culture.

Port Walter, village (1939 pop. 21), SE Alaska, on SE Baranof Isl., 10 mi. N of Port Alexander; fishing; cannery. Sometimes called Big Port Walter.

Port Washington. 1 Residential suburban village (1940 pop. 10,509), Nassau co., SE N.Y., on N shore of W Long Isl., on Manhasset Bay, 7 mi. NNW of Mineola, in estate and agr. area; mfg. (machinery, heating apparatus, buttons, concrete products, boats); sand and gravel quarrying; shellfish. Yachting center. A terminus of Long Isl. R.R. Seat of Vincent Smith School (coeducational). **2** Village (pop. 514), Tuscarawas co., E Ohio, 12 mi. SSW of New Philadelphia and on Tuscarawas R. **3** City (pop. 4,755), ⊙ Ozaukee co., E Wis., on L. Michigan, 24 mi. N of Milwaukee, in dairy and farm area; fishing port; fish processing; mfg. of Diesel engines, tractors, concrete mixers, prefabricated houses, furniture, clothing, beer, canned vegetables. Settled before 1835, inc. 1882.

Port Washington North, residential village (pop. 650), Nassau co., SE N.Y., on NW Long Isl., adjacent to Port Washington.

Port Weld, town (pop. 2,351), NW Perak, Malaya, port on inlet of Strait of Malacca, 8 mi. W of Taiping (linked by rail); fisheries.

Port Weller, village, S Ont., on L. Ontario, port at N end of Welland Ship Canal, 5 mi. N of St. Catharines.

Port Wentworth, village (1940 pop. 1,381), Chatham co., E Ga., NW suburb of Savannah; mfg. of paperboard, felt roofing; sugar refining.

Port William, village (pop. 352), Clinton co., SW Ohio, 24 mi. SE of Dayton.

Port Wing, fishing village, Bayfield co., extreme N Wis., on L. Superior, 32 mi. E of Superior; trade center for cooperative-farm area.

Portwood, industrial suburb (pop. 7,492) in Stockport, NE Cheshire, England; cotton-textile milling, mfg. of leather goods, metal products.

Portzile de Fier (pôr'tsēlĕ dä fyâr') or **Poarta de Fier Transilvan** (pwär'tä, trănsĕl'vän), pass (alt. 2,151 ft.) in SW central Rumania, Transylvania, bet. Poiana-Rusca Mts. and the Transylvanian Alps, 14 mi. SW of Hateg; rail and highway corridor. Janos Hunyadi won a victory over the Turks here in 1442.

Porum (pô'rùm), town (pop. 616), Muskogee co., E Okla., 27 mi. S of Muskogee, in agr. area; cotton ginning.

Porus (pô'rùs), town (pop. 2,400), Manchester parish, central Jamaica, on Kingston–Montego Bay RR and 6 mi. E of Mandeville, in agr. region (tropical fruit and spices).

Porvenir (pôrvänēr'), town (pop. c.1,200), ⊙ Tahuamanu prov., Pando dept., NW Bolivia, on Tahuamanu R. and 15 mi. S of Cobija, on road; rubber.

Porvenir, town (pop. 1,592), ⊙ Tierra del Fuego dept. (□ 19,402; pop. 4,820), Magallanes prov., S Chile, on NW coast of main isl. of Tierra del Fuego, on the Strait of Magellan across from and 25 mi. SE of Punta Arenas; 53°17'S 70°22'W. Minor port and sheep-raising center. Some gold mining is also carried on.

Porvenir, town (pop. 1,000), Paysandú dept., NW Uruguay, on railroad and 15 mi. ESE of Paysandú; agr. colony; vegetables, fruit, grain, cattle.
Porvenir, El, in Latin America: see EL PORVENIR.
Porvoo, Finland: see BORGA.
Poryck, Ukrainian SSR: see PORITSK.
Porz (pôrts), industrial town (pop. 25,908), in former Prussian Rhine Prov., W Germany, after 1945 in North Rhine-Westphalia, on right bank of the Rhine (landing) and 6 mi. SE of Cologne; foundries; mfg. of agr. machinery, armatures, iceboxes, concrete pipes, radios, insulating materials, mirrors, glassware, wooden and fiber floorings.
Porzecze, Belorussian SSR: see PORECHYE.
Porzuna (pôr-thōō'nä), town (pop. 3,443), Ciudad Real prov., S central Spain, 16 mi. NW of Ciudad Real; cereals, grapes, sheep, goats, cattle. Lumbering; dairying, flour milling; mfg. of tiles.
Posada (pôzä'dä), village (pop. 903), Nuoro prov., NE Sardinia, port on Tyrrhenian coast, 30 mi. NE of Nuoro.
Posadas (pōsä'dhäs), city (pop. 36,623), ⊙ Misiones natl. territory and Posadas dept. (□ c.460; pop. estimate 50,000), NE Argentina, in W part of the territory, 180 mi. E of Corrientes, 500 mi. NNE of Buenos Aires; river port on upper Paraná R. (Paraguay border), opposite Encarnación; 27°27'S 55°54'W. Rail terminus and agr. center. Sawmills, meat-packing plants, flour and maté mills, textile factory. Area produces rice, tobacco, corn, maté, fruit; stock raising. Founded 1862 at beginning of war against Paraguay. Has administrative bldgs., natl. col., agr. school.
Posadas, town (pop. 6,990), Córdoba prov., S Spain, on the Guadalquivir and 20 mi. WSW of Córdoba; olive-oil processing, brandy distilling, flour- and sawmilling, soap and straw-hat mfg. Wool trade. Lumbering, stock raising; cereals, fruit, wine, poultry. Silverbearing lead mines near by.
Posavina, region, Yugoslavia: see SAVA RIVER.
Poscaya (pōskī'ä), village, N Salta prov., Argentina, 18 mi. SW of Santa Victoria, in lead- and silver-mining area.
Poschiavino River (pôskyävē'nô), Switzerland and Italy, rises in small lake near Bernina Pass, Switzerland; flows 20 mi. S, past Poschiavo and Brusio, into Italy, to Adda R. 1 mi. SW of Tirano, Italy.
Poschiavo (pôskyä'vô), Ger. *Puschlav* (pōōsh'läf), town (pop. 3,978), Grisons canton, SE Switzerland, on Poschiavino R. and 16 mi. SSE of St. Moritz, near Ital. line; flour. Late-Gothic abbey church, 17th-cent. Protestant church, baroque church, 16th-cent. town hall. **Lake of Poschiavo** (3 mi. long), 2 mi. S, supplies water for Brusio hydroelectric plant. **Val Poschiavo,** a valley, extends along Poschiavino R.
Poseh (bŭ'sŭ'), Mandarin *Paise* (bī'sŭ'), town, ⊙ Poseh co. (pop. 111,414), W Kwangsi prov., China, near Yunnan line, 150 mi. NW of Nanning, and on Yü R. (head of junk navigation); trade center; tobacco processing; indigo, rice, sugar cane, sweet potatoes, beans.
Poseidion, Cape, or **Cape Posidhion** (both: pôsē'dhēôn), Lat. *Posidium*, SW cape of Kassandra prong of Chalcidice peninsula in Greek Macedonia, on Aegean Sea; 39°57'N 23°20'E. Also called Cape Kassandra.
Poseidonia or **Posidhonia** (both: pôsēdhônē'ŭ), village in Loutrakion municipality, Argolis and Corinthia nome, NE Peloponnesus, Greece, port at NW end of Corinth Canal, 2 mi. ENE of Corinth; fisheries.
Poselkovo-Sargatskoye, Russian SFSR: see SARGATSKOYE.
Poselok Severnykh Promyslov Ozera No. 6, Turkmen SSR: see SARTAS.
Posen, Poland: see POZNAN.
Posen (pō'zŭn, pō'sŭn). **1** Village (pop. 1,795), Cook co., NE Ill., S suburb of Chicago. Settled 1893 by Polish immigrants; inc. 1900. **2** Village (pop. 274), Presque Isle co., NE Mich., 12 mi. SSE of Rogers City, in farm area. **3** Village (pop. 172), Howard co., E central Nebr., 9 mi. W of St. Paul. Post office name formerly Farwell.
Posets, Pico (pē'kō pōsĕts'), peak (11,046 ft.) in central Pyrenees, NE Spain (Huesca prov.), 12 mi. W of Pico de Aneto, near Fr. border.
Posevnaya (pŭsyĕv'nīŭ), town (1939 pop. over 2,000), SE Novosibirsk oblast, Russian SFSR, on Turksib RR and 5 mi. NW of Cherepanovo; metalworks, dairying.
Posey (pō'zē), county (□ 414; pop. 19,818), extreme SW Ind.; ⊙ Mount Vernon. Bounded W by Wabash R. (here forming Ill. line), S by Ohio R. (forming Ky. line); drained by Big Creek. Agr. area (grain, hogs, poultry, fruit), with mfg. of machinery, handles, tanks, stoves, cigars, and food products, and meat packing; petroleum fields. Formed 1814.
Poseyville, town (pop. 1,005), Posey co., SW Ind., 18 mi. NW of Evansville, in agr. area; poultry hatchery, meat-packing plant.
Posgam (pōsgäm'), Chinese *Tsehpu* or *Tse-p'u* (both: dzŭ'pōō'), town and oasis (pop. 40,447), SW Sinkiang prov., China, on highway and 15 mi. S of Yarkand, on W edge of Taklamakan Desert; sericulture; agr. products, livestock.
Poshan (bŭ'shän'), town, ⊙ Poshan co. (pop. 215,345), central Shantung prov., China, 45 mi. ESE of Tsinan, in the Tai Mts.; major bauxite- and coal-mining center, on spur of Tsinan-Tsingtao RR; glass, porcelain mfg. Kaolin mines near by.
Poshekhonye-Volodarsk or **Poshekhon'ye-Volodarsk** (pŭshĭkhô'nyĭ-vŭlŭdärsk'), city (1926 pop. 4,304), N Yaroslavl oblast, Russian SFSR, on Rybinsk Reservoir, 33 mi. NNE of Shcherbakov; metalworking, woolen milling, flax processing; handicraft (enamel painting). Chartered 1777.
Poshow (bŭ'shou'), Mandarin *Pai-shou* (bī'shō'), town, ⊙ Poshow co. (pop. 67,670), NE Kwangsi prov., China, 30 mi. WSW of Kweilin; rice, wheat, corn, bananas, oranges. Until 1915 known as Yungning; later (1915–33) called Kuhwa.
Posht Kuh, Iran: see PUSHT KUH.
Posidhion, Cape, Greece: see POSEIDION, CAPE.
Posidhonia, Greece: see POSEIDONIA.
Posidium, Cape, Greece: see POSEIDION, CAPE.
Posillipo or **Posilipo** (pôzē'lēpô), volcanic ridge extending SW from Naples, S Italy; winegrowing. Pierced by tunnels, including one for a railroad and another (Grotto of Posilipo) through which in anc. times passed the road to Puteoli (Pozzuoli). Dotted with villages, including Posillipo, a picturesque suburb of Naples, and many villas. Has remains of Roman villas.
Positano (pôzētä'nô), town (pop. 1,555), Salerno prov., Campania, S Italy, port on Gulf of Salerno, 6 mi. W of Amalfi; bathing resort.
Poso or **Posso** (both: pō'sō), town (pop. 2,875), central Celebes, Indonesia, port on Gulf of Tomini, at mouth of small Poso R., 280 mi. NNE of Macassar; 1°24'S 120°44'E; trade center, shipping ironwood, ebony, rattan, resin, sugar cane.
Poso, Lake, or **Lake Posso** (20 mi. long, 8 mi. wide), central Celebes, Indonesia, 25 mi. SSW of Poso.
Posof (pôsôf'), village (pop. 1,267), Kars prov., NE Turkey, 65 mi. NNW of Kars, near USSR line; barley, potatoes. Formerly Digor.
Posoltega (pōsōltä'gä), town (1950 pop. 912), Chinandega dept., W Nicaragua, on railroad and 10 mi. NW of León; cotton, sesame, corn, sugar cane, fruit. Flourished in colonial period. Just SE is small Posoltega R., fed by hot springs.
Posong (pô'sŭng'), Jap. *Hojo*, town (1946 pop. 16,722), S.Cholla prov., S Korea, 40 mi. E of Mokpo; rail junction; commercial center in agr. area (rice, barley, cotton); makes grass linen.
Posop (pŭsôp'), agr. village (1926 pop. 4,519), SE Mordvinian Autonomous SSR, Russian SFSR, just E of Saransk, across Insar R.; truck.
Posorja (pōsôr'hä), village, Guayas prov., SW Ecuador, beach and fishing resort on the Gulf of Guayaquil, opposite Puná Isl., 45 mi. SW of Guayaquil.
Pospelikha (pŭspyĕ'lyĭkhŭ), village (1939 pop. over 2,000), SW Altai Territory, Russian SFSR, on Turksib RR, on Alei R. and 40 mi. NNE of Rubtsovsk; flour milling.
Possagno (pôs-sä'nyô), village (pop. 929), Treviso prov., Veneto, N Italy, 22 mi. NW of Treviso. Antonio Canova b. here. Has church (1819–30; modeled after Pantheon at Rome) begun by the sculptor and containing his tomb. In Canova's home is a mus. of casts of his works.
Posse (pô'sĭ), city (pop. 772), E Goiás, central Brazil, near Bahia border; 14°8'S 45°57'W. Livestock, cotton, beans.
Possession, La (lä pôsĕsyō'), town (pop. 2,217; commune pop. 5,845), on NW coast of Réunion isl., on railroad and 8 mi. WSW of Saint-Denis; sugar milling, alcohol distilling. Here French took possession of Réunion in 1642.
Possession Islands, group of 9 isls. in W part of Ross Sea, Antarctica, 4 mi. off NE coast of Victoria Land; 72°S 171°10'E. Discovered 1841 by Sir James C. Ross.
Pössneck (pŭs'nĕk''), town (pop. 20,247), Thuringia, central Germany, near Orla R., 16 mi. S of Jena; woodworking, tanning, textile milling, dyeing, printing; mfg. of machine tools, china, chocolate. Has 15th-cent. town hall. Important road center in Middle Ages.
Posso, Indonesia: see Poso.
Possum Kingdom Dam, N central Texas, in Brazos R. 18 mi. WNW of Mineral Wells; 190 ft. high, 2,740 ft. long; completed 1940 for flood control, power, irrigation. Impounds Possum Kingdom L. (□ 32; 730,000 acre-ft. capacity). State park on S shore.
Possum Trot Hollow, Va.: see STONEGA.
Post, city (pop. 3,141), ⊙ Garza co., NW Texas, 40 mi. SE of Lubbock, just below Cap Rock escarpment; shipping point for agr. (cotton, grain) and cattle-ranching region; textile mill. Founded 1907 as balanced agr.-mfg. community.
Postavy (pŭstä'vē), Pol. *Postawy* (pôstä'vē), city (1939 pop. over 3,000), N Molodechno oblast, Belorussian SSR, 70 mi. NE of Vilna; agr. center (grain, flax); brick mfg., brewing. Has old palace with picture gall. Old Pol. military settlement; developed as paper and textile mfg. center in 18th cent.; declined under Rus. rule (1795–1918); reverted (1921) to Poland; ceded to USSR in 1945.
Poste Cortier (pôst' kôrtyā'), Saharan refueling station, Aïn-Sefra territory, S Algeria, on Colomb-Béchar–Gao (Fr. West Africa) auto track across the Tanezrouft; 22°20'N 1°20'E. Lighthouse. Formerly called Bidon V.
Postelberg, Czechoslovakia: see POSTOLOPTRY.
Post Falls, village (pop. 1,069), Kootenai co., N Idaho, on Spokane R., near Wash. line, and 8 mi. WNW of Coeur d'Alene in irrigated agr. area (wheat, apples; dairying). Match plant near by.
Postiglione (pôstēlyô'nĕ), village (pop. 1,539), Salerno prov., Campania, S Italy, 10 mi. ESE of Eboli.
Postiljon Islands, Indonesia: see SABALANA ISLANDS.
Postillion Islands, Indonesia: see SABALANA ISLANDS.
Postmasburg (pōst'mŭsbûrg, Afrik. pôst'mŭsbûrkh), town (pop. 2,105), N central Cape Prov., U. of So. Afr., in Griqualand West, on railroad and 110 mi. WNW of Kimberley, bet. Asbestos Mts. (E) and Langeberg range (W); major manganese-mining center; iron deposits.
Postojna (pô'stoinä), Ital. *Postumia* (pôstōō'mēä), Ger. *Adelsberg* (ä'dŭlsbĕrk), village (pop. 3,651), SW Slovenia, Yugoslavia, on railroad and 23 mi. SSW of Ljubljana. One of best-known caves in the Karst, noted for its great size and for beauty of its stalactites, is here. Has speleological institute (opened 1929) with mus. Until 1947, in Italy.
Postoloptry (pô'stôlôptrĭ), Ger. *Postelberg* (pô'stŭlbĕrk), town (pop. 2,186), NW Bohemia, Czechoslovakia, on Ohre R. and 7 mi. WNW of Zatec, in hop-growing area; rail junction; sugar milling. Castle, cloister ruins.
Postorna (pô'shtôrnä), Czech *Poštorná*, village (pop. 3,146), S Moravia, Czechoslovakia, on railroad, just W of Breclav, on Austrian border; mfg. of sulphuric acid, fertilizers, china, pottery. Inc. into Czechoslovakia in 1919.
Postrervalle (pōsträrvä'yä), town (pop. c.2,300), Santa Cruz dept., central Bolivia, 19 mi. E of Valle Grande; barley, corn, potatoes.
Postumia, Yugoslavia: see POSTOJNA.
Postville, town (pop. 1,343), Allamakee co., NE Iowa, 60 mi. NW of Dubuque; dairy products, packed poultry, feed, fertilizer, concrete. Settled 1841, inc. 1873.
Pöstyen, Czechoslovakia: see PIESTANY.
Posusje or **Posushye** (both: pôsōō'shyĕ), Serbo-Croatian *Posušje*, village, N Herzegovina, Yugoslavia, 26 mi. NW of Mostar, near Dalmatian border. Bauxite deposits near by.
Posuso, Peru: see POZUZO.
Posvol, Lithuania: see PASVALYS.
Posyet or **Pos'yet** (pŭsyĕt'), town (1943 pop. over 500), SW Maritime Territory, Russian SFSR, port on N Posyet Bay, 65 mi. SSW of Vladivostok; rail terminus; fish canning; naval base. Formerly Novgorodsk.
Posyet Bay or **Posyet Gulf,** inlet of Peter the Great Bay of Sea of Japan, SW Maritime Territory, Russian SFSR, near USSR-Korea border; important fishing ground.
Potagannissing Bay, Mich.: see DRUMMOND ISLAND.
Potam (pōtäm'), town (pop. 1,578), Sonora, NW Mexico, in Yaqui R. delta, on railroad and 40 mi. SE of Guaymas; corn, rice, fruit, vegetables.
Potamos, Greece: see PLOMARION.
Potapovo (pŭtä'pŭvŭ), village, SW Taimyr Natl. Okrug, Krasnoyarsk Territory, on Yenisei R. and 50 mi. S of Dudinka; trading post; reindeer farms.
Potaro or **Potaro Landing,** Br. Guiana: see GARRAWAY STREAM.
Potaro River (pōtä'rō), central Br. Guiana, rises in the Guiana Highlands near Brazil border at 5°20'N 59°52'W, flows 110 mi. in a curve SE, NE, and E to Essequibo R. 9 mi. E of Tumatumari. On it, 60 mi. upstream, are the famed KAIETEUR FALLS. Alluvial gold and diamond deposits are found along its course.
Potash, village (pop. 1,255, with adjacent Port Sulphur), Plaquemines parish, SE La., on the Mississippi, 40 mi. S of New Orleans.
Potato Lake. 1 In Hubbard co., Minn.: see ARAGO LAKE. **2** In Itasca co., Minn.: see NORTH STAR LAKE.
Potato Peak (c.10,200 ft.), Mono co., E Calif., 12 mi. N of Mono L.
Potawatomi State Park (pŏtŭwŏ'tŭmē) (1,010 acres), Door co., NE Wis., on Door Peninsula, on wooded bluffs overlooking Sturgeon Bay.
Potchefstroom (pô'chŭfstrōōm''), town (pop. 27,-205), SW Transvaal, U. of So. Afr., on Mooi R., near its mouth on Vaal R., and 65 mi. SW of Johannesburg; alt. 4,433 ft.; agr. market (wheat, corn, lucerne, stock, dairying); grain elevator; malting, sawmilling. Educational center; site of Potchefstroom Univ. Col., affiliated with Univ. of South Africa; theological col.; teachers col.; agr. col.; and govt. experimental farm. Military training center. Airfield. Earliest town and 1st ⊙ Transvaal, it was founded 1838. Pretoria became ⊙ 1860. During Transvaal revolt (1880–81) British garrison here was besieged for 3 months. British troops were stationed here until 1914.
Potcoava or **Potcoava-Falcoeni** (pôt-kwä'vä-fŭlkwān'), Rum. *Potcoava-Fălcoeni*, village (pop. 897), Arges prov., S Rumania, on railroad and 10 mi. E of Slatina.

Poteau (pō'tō), city (pop. 4,776), ⊙ Le Flore co., SE Okla., 25 mi. SSW of Fort Smith (Ark.), and on Poteau R., in agr., lumbering, and resort area; cotton ginning; mfg. of concrete blocks, glass products. Coal mines, gas wells. Small lakes (fishing) near by. The Ouachita Mts. and Ouachita Natl. Forest are c.15 mi. S. Inc. 1898.

Poteau River, in Ark. and Okla., rises in the Ouachita Mts., in Scott co., W Ark., flows W into Okla., where it is joined by the small Fourche Moline, then NNE, past Poteau, Shadypoint, and Panama (Okla.), to Arkansas R. at Fort Smith, Ark.; 128 mi. long. Wister Dam (99 ft. high, 8,700 ft. long, including concrete spillway and earth-fill barrier and dike; completed 1949 by U.S. Army Engineers) is in middle course just S of Wister, Okla.; used for flood control; forms Wister Reservoir (15 mi. long, max. width 1.5 mi.; capacity 430,000 acre-ft.).

Poteca River (pōtā'kä), NW Nicaragua, rises on Teotecacinte peak on Honduras border, flows 40 mi. SE to Coco R. at Poteca village. Claimed by Honduras as its border with Nicaragua.

Poteet (pŭtēt'), city (pop. 2,487), Atascosa co., SW Texas, 26 mi. S of San Antonio; shipping center in truck and strawberry-producing area.

Potel, Lake (pôtĕl') (□ 40), in Dolj prov., S Rumania, W of Corabia; part of swampy region along left bank of the Danube; fishing.

Potengi River (pōōtĕng'gē), Rio Grande do Norte, NE Brazil, flows c.65 mi. E to the Atlantic just below Natal. Intermittent-flowing stream. Receives Jundiaí R. Also called the Rio Grande do Norte. Formerly spelled Potengy.

Potenza (pôtĕn'tsä), province (□ 2,527; pop. 393,-950), BASILICATA, S Italy; ⊙ Potenza. Traversed by the Apennines; well watered by upper courses of Agri, Basento, Bradano, and Sinni rivers. Agr. (cereals, grapes, olives, fruit); stock raising (sheep, goats). Forestry. Has lignite and marble deposits and many mineral springs. Until 1927, when Matera prov. was detached, coextensive with Basilicata. Area increased (c.1947) by addition of area (□ 135) in NE from Matera prov.

Potenza, town (pop. 18,872), ⊙ Basilicata and Potenza prov., S Italy, in the Apennines, near upper Basento R., 55 mi. E of Salerno; 40°38'N 15°48'E. Rail junction; agr. center; macaroni, cheese; lumber; bricks. Bishopric. Has cathedral (rebuilt 18th cent.) and mus. of antiquities. Damaged by several earthquakes; largely rebuilt after that of 1857. Anc. *Potentia,* destroyed by Frederick II and again by Charles of Anjou, lay below present site of town.

Potenza Picena (pēchä'nä), town (pop. 2,145), Macerata prov., The Marches, central Italy, near Potenza R., 10 mi. NE of Macerata; soap mfg.

Potenza River, The Marches, central Italy, rises on Monte Pennino in the Apennines, flows 60 mi. ENE, past Castelraimondo and San Severino Marche, to the Adriatic near Porto Recanati.

Potes (pō'tĕs), town (pop. 1,217), Santander prov., N Spain, on Deva R. and 20 mi. SSE of Llanes, at foot of E slopes of the Picos de Europa; stock raising, lumbering; cereals, potatoes, wine.

Potgietersrust (pôt'khētŭrs-rûst"), town (pop. 5,-698), N Transvaal, U. of So. Afr., near Magalakwin R., at foot of Strydpoort Mts., 35 mi. SW of Pietersburg; tin mining; agr. center (oranges, peaches, cattle). Founded 1855, town was later abandoned because of malaria and hostility of natives; resettled 1870.

Poth (pōth), town (pop. 1,089), Wilson co., S Texas, 34 mi. SE of San Antonio, near San Antonio R.; rail, trade point in agr. area; peanut processing, cottonseed-oil milling, poultry packing.

Poti (pô'tyē), city (1926 pop. 13,137, 1939 pop. 16,000), W Georgian SSR, port on Black Sea, at mouth of Rion R., 35 mi. N of Batum; rail terminus in unhealthy, swampy area (Colchis); exports Chiatura manganese, corn, lumber, wine. Ship repair dock; fish canning, woodworking, light mfg. Center of drainage work in Colchis lowland.

Potidaea (pŏtĭdē'ū, pŏt–), one of leading anc. Gr. cities on Chalcidice peninsula, Macedonia, on isthmus of Kassandra prong, 35 mi. SE of modern Salonika. A Corinthian colony, founded c.600 B.C.; its separation from Athenian League was an immediate cause of Peloponnesian War. It was captured by Athens in 429 after 2-year siege and held until 404. Passed 356 to Philip II of Macedon who razed it. Rebuilt after 316 B.C. by Cassander and named Cassandrea. On its site is modern Gr. village of Nea Potidaia or Nea Potidhaia (pop. 804).

Potigny (pôtēnyē'), town (pop. 2,363), Calvados dept., NW France, 16 mi. SSE of Caen; miners' residences. Iron mines at Soumont (1 mi. N). Large foreign pop.

Potirendaba (pōōtērēndä'bŭ), city (pop. 2,339), NW São Paulo, Brazil, 17 mi. S of São José do Rio Prêto; cotton, corn, coffee. Formerly Potyrendaba.

Poti River (pōōtē'), NE Brazil, rises in several headstreams which join near Crateús (Ceará), enters Piauí state in a gorge of the Serra Grande, flows SW and then NW to the Parnaíba at Teresina. Length, c.200 mi. Not navigable. Formerly spelled Poty.

Potiskum (pōchĕs'kōōm), town (pop. 4,227), Bornu prov., Northern Provinces, NE Nigeria, 180 mi. E of Kano; agr. trade center; cotton, peanuts, cassava, millet; cattle, skins. Diatomite deposits. Airfield. Formerly spelled Putuskum.

Potiyevka (pô'tēŭfkŭ), village (1932 pop. estimate 3,610), E Zhitomir oblast, Ukrainian SSR, 27 mi. NNE of Zhitomir; flax.

Potlatch (pŏt'lăch"), lumbering village (pop. 1,105, with adjacent Onaway), Latah co., N Idaho, on Palouse R. and 15 mi. N of Moscow; one of world's largest lumber mills.

Potlatch River, N Idaho, rises near Bovill, flows c.40 mi. SW to Clearwater R. ENE of Lewiston.

Potlogi (pôtlôj'), village (pop. 3,481), Bucharest prov., S central Rumania, 16 mi. SE of Gaesti. Has 17th-cent. church, remains of 17th-cent. palace.

Poto (pō'tō), village (pop. 247), Puno dept., SE Peru, on the Altiplano, at foot of the Nudo de Apolobamba, 27 mi. SSW of Sandia; alt. 15,213 ft.; gold mining.

Potobamba (pōtōbäm'bä), town (pop. c.3,800), Potosí dept., S central Bolivia, near Pilcomayo R., 18 mi. SSW of Sucre; fruit, vegetables.

Potochi, springs, Peru: see HUANCAVELICA, city.

Potok Zloty, Ukrainian SSR: see ZOLOTOI POTOK.

Potol Point (pōtōl'), northernmost point of Panay isl., Philippines, in Sibuyan Sea, on NW peninsula of isl.; 11°56'N 121°57'E.

Potomac (pŭtō'mŭk). **1** Village (pop. 602), Vermilion co., E Ill., on Middle Fork of Vermilion R. and 13 mi. NW of Danville, in agr. and bituminous-coal area. **2** Residential suburb, Montgomery co., central Md., near the Potomac 13 mi. NW of Washington. Near by are Congressional Country Club (organized 1924), Natl. Women's Country Club, Natl. Capital Horse Show grounds.

Potomac Beach, resort village, Westmoreland co., E Va., on the Potomac and 26 mi. E of Fredericksburg.

Potomac River, E U.S., formed 15 mi. SE of Cumberland, Md., by junction of North and South branches; flows NE and SE along Md.–W.Va. line, cutting gorge through the Blue Ridge at Harpers Ferry, W.Va., and generally SE separating Va. from Md. and Dist. of Columbia, to Chesapeake Bay c.70 mi. SE of Washington; 285 mi. long; mouth of estuary is c.8 mi. wide. Tidal, and navigable for deep drafts, to Washington (c.115 mi. above mouth), where there are several bridges; just upstream are GREAT FALLS OF THE POTOMAC. Small vessels formerly ascended to Cumberland, Md., via old Chesapeake and Ohio Canal. Chief tributary, Shenandoah R. South Branch of the Potomac (c.130 mi. long) rises in Highland co., NW Va.; flows NNE into W.Va., through scenic SMOKE HOLE in the Alleghenies, to junction with North Branch (c.95 mi. long), which rises in W.Va. near W tip of Md. and flows generally NE along W.Va.–Md. line, past Cumberland, Md., thence briefly ESE before joining South Branch. The Potomac is noted for its beauty and its historical associations; Mt. Vernon and other historic shrines and old estates are on its banks near and below Washington.

Potoru (pōtō'rōō), town (pop. 1,021), South-Western Prov., SE Sierra Leone, 19 mi. NE of Pujehun, on road; palm oil and kernels, piassava, rice.

Potosí (pōtōsē'), department (□ 41,297; 1949 pop. estimate 812,900), SW Bolivia; ⊙ Potosí. Bordered by Western Cordillera of the Andes on Chilean frontier (W) and by Argentina (S). Includes Salar de Uyuni (NW). The S Eastern Cordillera of the Andes crosses dept. N-S, separating the Altiplano or high plateau (W; 13-14,500 ft.) from E valleys. The Altiplano is drained by Río Grande de Lípez; E valleys by upper Pilcomayo R. (N) and San Juan and Cotagaita rivers (S). Potato, barley, sheep, and alpaca farming in the Altiplano; corn, fruit, and vegetables in E valleys. One of main mining regions of Bolivia; contains tin-mining centers of Uncía, Llallagua, and Catavi, silver mines of Pulacayo and Huanchaca, and tin mines of Potosí. Saltworks on Salar de Uyuni. Main cities: Potosí, E of Cordillera Real; Uyuni in the Altiplano. La Paz–Villazón RR passes N-S, with branches of Uyuni-Antofagasta (SW) and Río Mulato–Potosí (E).

Potosí, city (1949 pop. estimate 43,700), ⊙ Potosí dept. and Frías (or Cercado) prov., S central Bolivia, on NW slopes of Cerro de Potosí (alt. 15,843 ft.), 260 mi. SE of La Paz and 50 mi. SW of Sucre; 19°35'S 65°45'W. One of highest cities in the world; alt. 13,189 ft. Connected by railroad with Río Mulato and by gasoline rail car with Sucre. Major tin-mining and trade center, with an airport. Site of govt. house, court of justice, cathedral (c.1810), univ., and many colonial-style bldgs., including Casa de la Moneda (mint; built 1572), La Torre de la Compañía (Jesuit's Tower; built in 1590s), Las Cajas Reales (formerly the royal treasury), and about 30 churches. Mines in Cerro de Potosí discovered by Spaniards 1545 and very soon became richest silver mines in world. City officially founded in 1546; pop. rose to 150,000 in 1611 and then declined to 8,000 by 1825. Developed again after 1900s with start of tin mining in Cerro de Potosí, now honeycombed by 5,000 openings. Near by are 30 wall-protected reservoirs constructed by Spaniards for water supply of city and mining plants.

Potosí. 1 Village, Chinandega dept., NW Nicaragua, small port on SW Gulf of Fonseca, 35 mi. NW of Chinandega. **2** Town (1950 pop. 792), Rivas dept., SW Nicaragua, 4 mi. NNW of Rivas; coffee, livestock; dairy products.

Potosí, village, San Miguel dept., E Salvador, 15 mi. NNW of San Miguel, on road; silver mining.

Potosi (pŭtō'sē). **1** City (pop. 2,359), ⊙ Washington co., SE central Mo., in the Ozarks, 55 mi. SW of St. Louis; center of barite-mining area, with zinc, iron, limestone deposits. Lumber, metal, limestone products; shoe factory. Inc. c.1826. **2** Village (pop. 556), Grant co., extreme SW Wis., near the Mississippi and small Grant R., 10 mi. S of Lancaster, in agr. region; brewery.

Potosí, Cerro de, Bolivia: see POTOSÍ, city.

Pototan (pōtō'tän), town (1939 pop. 5,534; 1948 municipality pop. 34,717), Iloilo prov., E Panay isl., Philippines, on railroad and 17 mi. NNE of Iloilo; agr. center (rice, sugar cane).

Potowomut Peninsula, R.I.: see WARWICK.

Potowomut River, R.I.: see HUNT RIVER.

Potralrubio de Guadamajud (pôrtälrōō'vyō dhā gwä-dhämähōōdh'), town (pop. 755), Cuenca prov., E central Spain, 29 mi. WNW of Cuenca; olives, wheat, grapes, livestock; lumbering.

Potrerillo, Cumbre de (kōōm'brā dā pōtrārē'yō), range (20 mi. long) in W Tucumán prov., Argentina; rises to c.8,000 ft.

Potrerillo, Pico (pē'kō), peak (3,205 ft.), Las Villas prov., central Cuba, in the Sierra de Trinidad, 6 mi. N of Trinidad city. At its W slope are scenic Topes de Collantes.

Potrerillos (pōtrārē'yōs), village (pop. estimate 200), N Mendoza prov., Argentina, on railroad, on Mendoza R., at S foot of Sierra de los Paramillos, and 20 mi. WSW of Mendoza. Mtn. resort with thermal springs. Hydroelectric station.

Potrerillos, mining settlement (1930 pop. 8,030), Atacama prov., N Chile, in the Atacama Desert, 75 mi. E of Chañaral; alt. 9,440 ft. Rail terminus; copper-mining and -smelting center.

Potrerillos, town (pop. 831), Cortés dept., NW Honduras, in Sula Valley, on Río Blanco (left affluent of Comayagua R.) and 19 mi. S of San Pedro Sula; rail terminus; major transit point on road to Tegucigalpa; bananas, rice, sugar cane, livestock.

Potrerillos, village (pop. 1,053), Chiriquí prov., W Panama, railhead at S foot of Chiriquí volcano, on David R. and 16 mi. NNW of David; coffee, cacao, livestock.

Potrero, El, Mexico: see EL POTRERO.

Potrero, El, Panama: see EL POTRERO.

Potrero de las Tablas (pōtrā'rō dā läs tä'bläs), village (pop. estimate 200), central Tucumán prov., Argentina, 15 mi. WSW of Tucumán; hydroelectric station.

Potro, Cerro del (sĕ'rō dĕl pō'trō), Andean peak (19,125 ft.) on Argentina-Chile border; 28°22'S.

Potschappel, Germany: see FREITAL.

Potschatek, Czechoslovakia: see POCATKY.

Pötschen Pass (pû'chŭn), in the Salzkammergut, W central Austria, on Styria–Upper Austria border, linking Bad Ischl and Bad Aussee. Road rises to 3,222 ft.

Potsdam (pŏts'dăm, Ger. pôts'däm), residential city (1939 pop. 135,892; 1946 pop. 113,568), ⊙ Brandenburg, E Germany, on the Havel and 17 mi. WSW of Berlin city center. A residence of Prussian kings and later of German emperors, city has, through its history and associations, become a symbol of Prussian militarism. Site of Brandenburg state conservatory; Berlin Univ. observatory (at Neubabelsberg suburb); and astrophysical observatory, on Telegraph Hill, 2 mi. S of city center, at 52°23'N 13°4'E. Textile milling; mfg. of locomotives, precision instruments, phonographs, records, carpets, food products. Center of Ger. moving-picture industry is at suburb of Babelsberg. Among noted features are palace and park of Sans Souci and the New Palace, both built by Frederick the Great; town palace, rebuilt 1745–51; Garrison Church (1731–35), where Frederick William I and Frederick the Great were formerly buried (removed 1945 to Bernterode, Thuringia; reburied 1946 at Marburg); church of St. Nicholas, built 1830–49 by Schinkel; and several other former royal palaces. Though Potsdam was severely damaged in Second World War, these monuments were little damaged. Originally Wendish fishing village. Chartered in 14th cent. Became royal residence under Elector Frederick William, whose Potsdam Edict (1685) encouraged Huguenot settlement in Brandenburg. Under Frederick William I, town became military center. Experienced greatest development during reign of Frederick the Great, when it was virtually capital of Prussia; visitors at Sans Souci included Voltaire, Bach, and other noted contemporaries. After Second World War, scene (July 17–Aug. 2, 1945) of Potsdam Conference among President Truman, Prime Minister Attlee, and Premier Stalin. After 1945, one of Soviet army hq. in Germany. Chief suburb is Babelsberg (E), inc. into Potsdam in early 1940s.

Potsdam. 1 Resort village (pop. 7,491), St. Lawrence co., N N.Y., on Raquette R. and 25 mi. E of Ogdensburg; paper, cheese, lumber, machinery. Agr. (dairy products; potatoes); timber. A state teachers col. and Clarkson Col. of Technology are here. Inc. 1831. 2 Village (pop. 241), Miami co., W Ohio, 16 mi. SW of Piqua. Also called New Lebanon.

Pottangi (pŏt'tŭng-gē), village, Koraput dist., S Orissa, India, 33 mi. SE of Jeypore.

Pottawatomie (pŏtŭwŏ'tŭmē). 1 County (□ 850; pop. 12,344), NE Kansas; ⊙ Westmoreland. Gently rolling to hilly area, bounded S by Kansas R., W by Big Blue R. Livestock, grain. Formed 1856, the year of John Brown's massacre of 5 pro-slavery adherents. 2 County (□ 799; pop. 43,517), central Okla.; ⊙ SHAWNEE. Intersected by North Canadian, Canadian, and Little rivers. Agr. area (corn, cotton, livestock, poultry, truck, pecans, grain; dairy products). Mfg. at Shawnee. Oil and natural-gas wells; gasoline plants. Formed 1891.

Pottawatomie Creek, river in E Kansas, rises in Franklin co. E of Waverly, flows 63 mi. ESE and NE, past Greeley and Lane, to Marais des Cygnes R. at Osawatomie.

Pottawattamie (pŏtŭwŏ'tŭmē), county (□ 946; pop. 69,682), SW Iowa; ⊙ Council Bluffs. Bounded W by Missouri R., which here forms Nebr. line. Prairie agr. area (corn, cattle, hogs), with bituminous-coal deposits. Drained by West and East Nishnabotna rivers, and by Keg, Silver, and Walnut creeks. Includes Lake Manawa State Park. Formed 1847; annexed part of Sarpy co., Nebr., in 1943.

Pottendorf (pô'tŭndôrf), town (pop. 2,821), E Lower Austria, 20 mi. S of Vienna; mfg. (textiles, machinery).

Pottenstein (pô'tŭn-shtīn), town (pop. 2,606), E Lower Austria, on Triesting R., just NW of Berndorf; orchards, vineyards.

Pottenstein, town (pop. 1,482), Upper Franconia, N Bavaria, Germany, in the Franconian Switzerland, on small Püttlach R. and 6 mi. WNW of Pegnitz; brewing, tanning, flour and lumber milling.

Potter. 1 County (□ 1,092; pop. 16,810), N Pa.; ⊙ Coudersport. Agr. and forested region, source of streams draining to Gulf of Mexico by Allegheny R., to Chesapeake Bay by Susquehanna R., and to Gulf of St. Lawrence by Genesee R. Cattle raising, dairying, potatoes; oil and gas wells; mfg. (paper, leather and rubber products, cheese). Formed 1804. 2 County (□ 887; pop. 4,688), N central S.Dak.; ⊙ Gettysburg; irrigated agr. area, bounded W by Missouri R. Dairy products, livestock, corn, wheat, rye, oats, barley. Formed 1873. 3 County (□ 901; pop. 73,366), extreme N Texas, in high plains of the Panhandle; ⊙ AMARILLO. Drained by Canadian R. Wheat and cattle-ranching region. Has helium field producing much of world's supply; also oil and gas wells and pipelines, deposits of clay, caliche, dolomite, gypsum. Agr. (oats, barley, grain sorghums, forage), dairying, hog and poultry raising. Amarillo is commercial and industrial center of Panhandle area. Formed 1876.

Potter. 1 Village (pop. c.300), Atchison co., NE Kansas, on small affluent of Kansas R. and 9 mi. S of Atchison; poultry, apples; dairying. 2 Village (pop. 421), Cheyenne co., W Nebr., 18 mi. W of Sidney and on Lodgepole Creek.

Potter Hill, mill village in Hopkinton and Westerly towns, Washington co., SW R.I., on Pawcatuck R., at Conn. line; woolens.

Potteries, district in the upper Trent valley, Stafford, England, c.9 mi. long (NW–SE), 3 mi. wide. Includes Hanley, Burslem, Tunstall, Fenton, and Longton, which were joined (1910) to STOKE-ON-TRENT. Newcastle-under-Lyme is also in the region. The Potteries is very densely populated and has been a center of china and earthenware making since 16th cent.; Wedgwood, Spode, and Minton are among the famous men who worked here. Most of the raw materials is now brought in from other districts, clay largely from Cornwall and Dorset. Region is also known as the "Five Towns."

Potterne, agr. village and parish (pop. 1,066), central Wiltshire, England, 2 mi. SSW of Devizes. Has 13th-cent. church.

Potters Bar, residential urban district (1951 census 17,163), Middlesex, England, 13 mi. N of London. Just W is village of South Mimms, site of sanitarium.

Potters Fork, Ky.: see CROMONA.

Pottersville. 1 Village, Mass.: see SOMERSET. 2 Resort village, Warren co., E N.Y., in the Adirondacks, at S end of Schroon L., 29 mi. NNW of Glens Falls.

Potter Valley, village (1940 pop. 595), Mendocino co., NW Calif., 12 mi. NE of Ukiah; grapes, fruit.

Potterville, village (pop. 624), Eaton co., S central Mich., 12 mi. SW of Lansing, in stock-raising dist. (sheep, cattle, horses).

Pöttmes (pût'mĕs), village (pop. 2,600), Upper Bavaria, Germany, 17 mi. SE of Donauwörth; peat cutting. Chartered 1324.

Potton, town and parish (pop. 1,955), E Bedford, England, 4 mi. NE of Biggleswade; agr. market, with leather and farm-equipment works. Church dates from 15th cent.

Pottsboro, town (pop. 383), Grayson co., N Texas, 9 mi. N of Sherman, in agr. area.

Potts Camp, town (pop. 432), Marshall co., N Miss. 12 mi. SE of Holly Springs, in Holly Springs Natl. Forest; sawmills.

Pottschach (pôt'shäkh), town (pop. 4,264), SE Lower Austria, 4 mi. WSW of Neunkirchen; wheat, cattle.

Potts Mountain, Va. and W.Va., a ridge of the Alleghenies, extends c.40 mi. NE from Giles co., Va., partly along state line, to Alleghany co., Va.; c.3–4,000 ft. high.

Pottstown, borough (pop. 22,589), Montgomery co., SE Pa., 31 mi. NW of Philadelphia and on Schuylkill R.; mfg. (structural steel, rubber products, dies, cement). Hill School for boys here. First ironworks in Pa. established here, 1716. Settled 1775, inc. 1815.

Pottsville. 1 Town (pop. 224), Pope co., N central Ark., 6 mi. ESE of Russellville, near Arkansas R. 2 City (pop. 23,640), ⊙ Schuylkill co., E central Pa., 27 mi. NW of Reading and on Schuylkill R., in anthracite-mining area. Mfg. (clothing, aluminum and steel products, building materials, paper products, shoes); railroad shops. Seat of Schuylkill Undergraduate Center of Pa. State Col. City grew with advent of extensive anthracite mining, 1824–29. Molly Maguires tried here, 1877. Settled c.1780, laid out c.1816, inc. as borough 1828, as city 1847.

Pottuvil (pŏt'tōōvĭl), village (pop. 1,969), Eastern Prov., Ceylon, near E coast, 58 mi. SSE of Batticaloa. Inhabited by Tamil-speaking Singhalese.

Potucky (pô'tŏŏchkĭ), Czech *Potůčky*, Ger. *Breitenbach* (brī'tŭnbäkh), village (pop. 517), NW Bohemia, Czechoslovakia, in the Erzgebirge, 9 mi. WNW of Jachymov, in uranium-mining region; frontier station on Ger. border opposite Johanngeorgenstadt.

Potwar Plateau (pōt'vär), in Sind-Sagar Doab, N Punjab, W Pakistan; extends from SW offshoots of Punjab Himalayas (N) to Salt Range (S); lies bet. Indus R. (W) and Jhelum R. (E); c.110 mi. long, 40–80 mi. wide, up to 1,500 ft. high. Consists of sandstones and clays with scattered petroleum deposits (wells at Khaur and Balkassar). Chief towns: Rawalpindi, Campbellpur, Chakwal.

Potwin, city (pop. 465), Butler co., SE central Kansas, 23 mi. NE of Wichita, in cattle and grain region; shipping point for gasoline. Oil wells.

Potyrendaba, Brazil: see POTIRENDABA.

Pouancé (pwäsā'), village (pop. 1,933), Maine-et-Loire dept., W France, 9 mi. E of Châteaubriant; road junction. Slate quarries and iron ore deposits in area. Has ruins of 13th–15th-cent. feudal castle of which the walls and 11 towers are still preserved.

Pouce Coupé (pōōs"kōō'pā, kōōpā'), village (pop. 251), E B.C., near Alta. border, 5 mi. SE of Dawson Creek; grain elevators; farming, stock raising.

Poudre d'Or (pōō'drū dôr'), village (pop. 1,404), NE Mauritius, on coast, 3 mi. N of Rivière du Rempart. Sugar milling at Esperance (pop. 906), 2 mi. SW, near Poudre d'Or rail station.

Pouembout (pwĕm'bōōt'), village (dist. pop. 662), New Caledonia, on W coast, 135 mi. NW of Nouméa; agr. products.

Pouëze, La (lä pōōĕz'), village (pop. 781), Maine-et-Loire dept., W France, 14 mi. SSE of Segré; slate quarries.

Poughkeepsie (pŭkĭp'sē), city (pop. 41,023), ⊙ Dutchess co., SE N.Y., on E bank of the Hudson (here crossed by Mid-Hudson Bridge to Highland) and c.65 mi. N of Manhattan; trade center in dairying, farming, resort region. Mfg.: ball bearings, cream separators, business machines, automobile parts, hardware, iron castings, precision instruments, elevators, cabinets, cigars, clothing, buttons, celluloid, pharmaceuticals. Marian Col. and the Oakwood School are here. Vassar Col. is at adjacent Arlington. Annual Intercollegiate Regatta was held here until 1950. Among city's historic sites is Van Kleeck Homestead (1702). A state hosp. for the insane is here. State parks near by. The Federal Constitution was ratified in Poughkeepsie, in 1788. Settled by Dutch in 1687; inc. 1854.

Pougny (pōōnyē'), village (pop. 96), Ain dept., E France, on the Rhone opposite Chancy (Switzerland), 10 mi. WSW of Geneva; hydroelectric plant near by.

Pougues-les-Eaux (pōōg-läzō'), resort (pop. 1,499), Nièvre dept., central France, 6 mi. NNW of Nevers; mineral springs.

Pouillon (pōōyō'), village (pop. 416), Landes dept., SW France, 8 mi. SSW of Dax; dairying, flour milling, poultry raising.

Pouilly or **Pouilly-sur-Loire** (pōōyē'-sür-lwär'), village (pop. 1,308), Nièvre dept., central France, on right bank of Loire R. and 9 mi. S of Cosne; noted for its white wines.

Pouilly-en-Auxois (–änōswä'), agr. village (pop. 851), Côte-d'Or dept., E central France, on Burgundy Canal and 23 mi. WSW of Dijon.

Pouilly-sous-Charlieu (–sōō-shärlyû'), village (pop. 1,469), Loire dept., SE central France, on the Loire and 7 mi. N of Roanne; hosiery mills.

Pouilly-sur-Loire, Nièvre dept., France: see POUILLY.

Poulan (pōōlăn'), city (pop. 750), Worth co., S central Ga., 15 mi. W of Tifton; mfg. (yarn, naval stores).

Pouliguen, Le (lŭ pōōlēgã'), town (pop. 5,148), Loire-Inférieure dept., W France, fishing port and yachting resort on Bay of Biscay, 10 mi. W of Saint-Nazaire; saltworks.

Poulo [island]: for names in Vietnam beginning thus and not found here, see under following part of the name.

Poulo Condore (pōōlō' kŏdôr'), group (□ 40; 1943 pop. 5,200) of 12 islets of volcanic origin in South China Sea, 50 mi. SE of mouths of Mekong R., S Vietnam. Main isl. (10 mi. long, 3 mi. wide) is site of penitentiary. Agr. (tobacco, peanuts, coffee), lumbering, tortoise fishing, collecting of birds nests. Old fort of Fr. India Company.

Poulsbo (pôlz'bō), town (pop. 1,014), Kitsap co., W central Wash., 12 mi. N of Bremerton and on an arm of Puget Sound; fish, timber, agr.

Poulseur (pōōlsûr'), village (pop. 1,559), Liége prov., E central Belgium, on Ourthe R. and 9 mi. S of Liége; stone quarrying.

Poultney (pōlt'nē), town (pop. 2,936), including Poultney village (pop. 1,685), Rutland co., W Vt., on Poultney R. and 15 mi. SW of Rutland; quarry machinery; slate; dairy and maple products. Resorts on L. St. Catharine. Jr. col. here. Settled 1771.

Poultney River, in Vt. and N.Y., rises W of Wallingford in W central Vt., flows NW, past Middletown Springs and Poultney, then SW to L. Champlain near Whitehall; c.40 mi. long.

Poulton-le-Fylde (pōōl'tŭn-lŭ-fīld'), urban district (1931 pop. 3,366; 1951 census 7,672), W Lancashire, England, 3 mi. NE of Blackpool; agr. market for the county's most fertile area (dairy farming, growing of wheat, potatoes, barley, oats).

Poulton with Fearnhead (fûrn'hĕd), parish (pop. 2,141), S Lancashire, England. Includes town of Orford, 2 mi. NNE of Warrington, with leather tanning and mfg. of synthetic fertilizer; and town of Padgate, 2 mi. NE of Warrington, with mfg. of chemicals and paint.

Pound. 1 Town (pop. 1,193), Wise co., SW Va., 11 mi. N of Wise. Inc. since 1940. 2 Village (pop. 354), Marinette co., NE Wis., 20 mi. W of Marinette; trade center for dairying area; makes cheese.

Pound Gap, pass (alt. c.2,300 ft.) in Pine Mtn. of the Cumberlands, on SE Ky.–SW Va. line just SE of Jenkins, Ky. Much used by Indians and pioneers; now traversed by a highway.

Pourri, Mont (mō pōōrē'), Alpine peak (12,428 ft.) in Savoy Alps, Savoie dept., SE France, overlooking Tarentaise valley (N) of upper Isère R., 8 mi. SE of Bourg-Saint-Maurice.

Pourtalet (pōōrtälā'), Sp. *Portalet* (pôrtälā'), pass (5,878 ft.) in central Pyrenees, on Franco-Spanish border, 17 mi. NNE of Jaca (Sp.), at the foot of the Pic du Midi d'Ossau.

Pouso Alegre (pō'zōō ălā'grĭ), city (pop. 11,582), SW Minas Gerais, Brazil, on railroad and 35 mi. NW of Itajubá; mfg. (textiles, hats, matches); agr. trade (coffee, sugar, fruit, wine, cereals).

Pouso Alto (äl'tōō). 1 City, Goiás, Brazil: see PIRACANJUBA. 2 City (pop. 1,458), S Minas Gerais, Brazil, on N slope of the Serra da Mantiqueira, 25 mi. N of Cruzeiro (São Paulo); dairying.

Poussan (pōōsã'), village (pop. 1,404), Hérault dept., S France, 6 mi. N of Sète; winegrowing, bauxite mining.

Pout (pōōt), village, W Senegal, Fr. West Africa, on railroad and 25 mi. E of Dakar, in peanut-growing region.

Poutroye, La, France: see LAPOUTROIE.

Pouyastruc (pōōyästrük'), village (pop. 319), Hautes-Pyrénées dept., SW France, 6 mi. NE of Tarbes; wheat, corn, wine.

Pouzauges (pōōzōzh'), village (pop. 1,847), Vendée dept., W France, 21 mi. N of Fontenay-le-Comte; meat preserving, mfg. of footwear. Has ruins of 13th-cent. castle and keep.

Pouzin, Le (lŭ pōōzē'), village (pop. 1,146), Ardèche dept., S France, on right bank of Rhone and 8 mi. ENE of Privas; macadam and licorice-water mfg., silk weaving.

Povalikha (pŭvŭlyē'khŭ), town (1939 pop. over 2,000), N Altai Territory, Russian SFSR, on railroad and 9 mi. NNE of Barnaul; flour milling.

Povazska Bystrica (pô'väshskä bĭ'strĭtsä), Slovak *Považská Bystrica*, Hung. *Vágbesztercе* (väg'bĕstĕrtsĕ), town (pop. 7,432), W Slovakia, Czechoslovakia, on Vah R., on railroad and 15 mi. SW of Zilina; mfg. of heavy munitions. Popular excursion center among picturesque mountains. Has Gothic church with Renaissance tombstones. Fine castle ruins 2 mi. N.

Povenets (pŭvyĭnyĕts'), town (1926 pop. 2,111), S central Karelo-Finnish SSR, port on Povonets Gulf (70 mi. long, 10 mi. wide) of L. Onega, at S end of White Sea–Baltic Canal, 12 mi. ESE of Medvezhyegorsk; dairying. Founded 1701 under Peter the Great as ironworking center. In Second World War, held (1941–44) by Finns and Germans.

Poverty Bay, inlet of S Pacific, E N.Isl., New Zealand; 6 mi. long, 4 mi. wide; Gisborne on N shore. Here Capt. Cook made 1st landing (1769) in New Zealand.

Poviglio (pôvē'lyô), village (pop. 488), Reggio nell'Emilia prov., Emilia-Romagna, N central Italy, 10 mi. ENE of Parma; mfg. (wine machinery, pumps, plywood).

Povoação (po͞ovwŭsã'ō), town (pop. 1,348), Ponta Delgada dist., E Azores, on SE shore of São Miguel Isl., 23 mi. E of Ponta Delgada; chicory drying, beekeeping; exports oranges.

Póvoa de Lanhoso (pô'vwŭ dĭ lŭnyō'zo͞o), town (pop. 1,079), Braga dist., N Portugal, 7 mi. E of Braga; pottery mfg., lumbering.

Póvoa de Santa Iria (săn'tŭ ērē'ŭ), village (pop. 2,014), Lisboa dist., near head of Tagus estuary, 12 mi. NNE of Lisbon; mfg. (fertilizer, cement, tin cans, fruit preserves).

Póvoa de São Miguel (sã'ō mēgĕl'), village (pop. 1,833), Beja dist., S Portugal, 32 mi. ENE of Beja; grain, olives, figs, sheep.

Póvoa de Varzim (vär'zēn), town (pop. 13,410), Pôrto dist., N Portugal, on Atlantic Ocean, on branch railroad and 17 mi. NNW of Oporto; sardine-fishing port; bathing resort; boat building, fish canning, rope mfg. Also makes biscuits and silk goods.

Póvoa e Meadas (ē mĭä'dŭs), village (pop. 1,751), Portalegre dist., central Portugal, 16 mi. NNW of Portalegre; cork stripping.

Povorino (pŭvô'rēnŭ), town (1926 pop. 10,018), E Voronezh oblast, Russian SFSR, 13 mi. SE of Borisoglebsk; rail junction; meat packing, metalworking.

Povorotny, Cape, or **Cape Povorotnyy** (pŭvŭrôt'nē), SE Maritime Territory, Russian SFSR, on Sea of Japan, 12 mi. SE of Nakhodka; E point of Peter the Great Bay; 42°41'N 133°1'E.

Povrly (pô'vŭrlĭ), village (pop. 1,278), N Bohemia, Czechoslovakia, on Elbe R., on railroad and 5 mi. ENE of Usti nad Labem; major copper works.

Powassan (pōwŏ'sŭn), town (pop. 775), SE central Ont., 17 mi. SSE of North Bay; sawmilling, brick making.

Powazki (pôvä'skē), residential suburb of Warsaw, Warszawa prov., E central Poland, 3 mi. N of city center.

Powderhorn, village (pop. c.100), Gunnison co., SW central Colo., on S branch of Gunnison R., in foothills of San Juan Mts., and 20 mi. SSW of Gunnison; alt. 8,056 ft.; trading point. Mineral hot springs here.

Powder River, county (□ 3,285; pop. 2,693), SE Mont.; ⊙ Broadus. Agr. area bordering on Wyo.; drained by Powder and Little Powder rivers. Livestock. Part of Custer Natl. Forest in W. Formed 1919.

Powder River. 1 In NE Oregon, rises in Elkhorn Ridge S of La Grande, flows N past Baker and North Powder, then ESE to Snake R. (forming Idaho line) S of Wallowa Mts.; c.110 mi. long. A dam (73 ft. high, 390 ft. long; completed 1932), in middle course 17 mi. N of Baker, forms small reservoir, used for irrigation. **2** In Wyo. and Mont., rises in several branches in S foothills of Bighorn Mts., central Wyo.; flows 486 mi. generally N into SE Mont., past Broadus, to Yellowstone R. near Terry. Main tributaries: Little Powder R., in Wyo. and Mont.; Crazy Woman Creek, in Wyo.

Powder River Pass (9,666 ft.), in Bighorn Mts., Washakie co., N Wyo., 13 mi. S of Cloud Peak; crossed by highway.

Powder Springs, city (pop. 619), Cobb co., NW central Ga., 18 mi. WNW of Atlanta.

Powe (pō), city (pop. 95), Stoddard co., SE Mo., near St. Francis R., 8 mi. W of Bernie.

Powell (pow'ŭl). **1** County (□ 173; pop. 6,812), E central Ky.; ⊙ Stanton. Drained by Red R. and several creeks; includes Natural Bridge State Park (near Slade) and part of Cumberland Natl. Forest. Hilly agr. area (livestock, corn, hay, burley tobacco, dairy products); oil wells, bituminous-coal mines, limestone quarries; timber. Formed 1852. **2** County (□ 2,337; pop. 6,301), W central Mont.; ⊙ Deer Lodge. Agr. and mining area, drained by Blackfoot R. Livestock; lead, silver. Parts of Helena Natl. Forest in N and SE, part of Flint Creek Range in SW. Formed 1901.

Powell. 1 Village (pop. 324), Delaware co., central Ohio, 14 mi. NNW of Columbus. Inc. 1947. **2** Town (pop. 3,804), Park co., NW Wyo., near Shoshone R. and Mont. line, 22 mi. NE of Cody; alt. 4,390 ft. Trade center for irrigated agr. region producing sugar beets, sweet-clover seed, potatoes, alfalfa; seed processing. Hq. of Shoshone irrigation project. Gas and oil wells near by; fossil beds in vicinity. Settled 1908, inc. 1910.

Powell, Mount (13,398 ft.), N central Colo., in Gore Range, 35 mi. N of Leadville.

Powell Creek, settlement, central Northern Territory, Australia, 425 mi. SSE of Darwin; sheep.

Powell Island (7 naut. mi. long, 2 naut. mi. wide), South Orkney Isls., E of Coronation Isl., in the South Atlantic; 60°41'S 45°3'W.

Powell Islands, Antarctic region: see SOUTH ORKNEY ISLANDS.

Powell Mountain, NE Tenn. and SW Va., ridge (1,500–3,000 ft.) in Great Appalachian Valley, bet. Powell and Clinch rivers; from Hancock co., Tenn., extends NE into Wise co., Va. In Va., NATURAL TUNNEL through mtn. attracts tourists.

Powell River, town (pop. estimate 5,000), SW B.C., on the Strait of Georgia, at mouth of Powell R., near Powell L., and 80 mi. NW of Vancouver; 49°52'N 124°33'W; pulp and newsprint-milling center and port; lumbering. Hydroelectric power.

Powell River, in Va. and Tenn., rises in Wise co., SW Va.; flows SW past Big Stone Gap, into Tenn., across Hancock co., into Claiborne co., here entering Norris Reservoir, impounded by Norris Dam of Clinch R., into which the Powell formerly emptied. Reservoir extends upstream for 56 mi. of the Powell's 150-mi. length.

Powellsville, town (pop. 250), Bertie co., NE N.C., 5 mi. SSE of Ahoskie; sawmilling.

Powellton (pou'ŭltŭn), village (pop. 1,477), Fayette co., S central W.Va., 25 mi. SE of Charleston, in coal-mining region.

Power, county (□ 1,411; pop. 3,988), SE Idaho; ⊙ American Falls. Stock-raising and agr. area drained by Snake R. and lying partly in Snake River Plain. Wheat, rye, potatoes, sugar beets. American Falls Dam, at American Falls, is used in generation of power and forms irrigation reservoir along N boundary. Part of Fort Hall Indian Reservation is in mtn. region in E. Co. formed 1913.

Power, village (pop. c.100), Teton co., N central Mont., 25 mi. NW of Great Falls; wheat-shipping point.

Powers. 1 Village (pop. 510), Menominee co., SW Upper Peninsula, Mich., 23 mi. WSW of Escanaba and on Cedar R. A tubercular hosp. is here. **2** City (pop. 895), Coos co., SW Oregon, on S.Fork Coquille R. and 21 mi. SSE of Coquille; outfitting point for gold-mines.

Powers Lake, city (pop. 565), Burke co., NW N.Dak., 25 mi. SW of Bowbells.

Powersville, town (pop. 227), Putnam co., N Mo., 17 mi. WNW of Unionville.

Poweshiek (pou-ŭshēk', pou'ŭshēk), county (□ 589; pop. 19,344), central Iowa; ⊙ Montezuma. Rolling prairie agr. area (hogs, cattle, poultry, corn, oats, hay) drained by forks of English R. Bituminous-coal deposits (S,W). Formed 1843.

Powhatan (pou"ŭtăn'), county (□ 268; pop. 5,556), central Va.; ⊙ Powhatan. Bounded N by James R., S by Appomattox R. Agr. (especially tobacco), corn, livestock. Formed 1777.

Powhatan (pou"ŭtăn'). **1** (also pouhă'tŭn) Town (pop. 120), a ⊙ Lawrence co., NE Ark., 28 mi. NW of Jonesboro and on Black R. **2** Village (pop. c.150), ⊙ Powhatan co., central Va., 25 mi. W of Richmond; agr. trade point.

Powhatan Point (pouhă'tŭn), village (pop. 2,135), Belmont co., E Ohio, on the Ohio and 11 mi. SSW of Bellaire, in coal-mining area. Settled 1819, inc. 1895.

Powhattan (pouhă'tŭn), city (pop. 150), Brown co., NE Kansas, 30 mi. NW of Atchison, in corn belt; corn, livestock, poultry. Kickapoo Indian Reservation is just S.

Powidz, Lake (pô'vēts), Pol. *Jezioro Powidzkie* (yĕ-zhô'rô pôvēts'kyĕ) (□ 5), Poznan prov., W central Poland, 16 mi. SE of Gniezno; c.7 mi. long; 132 ft. deep. It was on border of Germany and Russian Poland, 1815–1919. Health resort village of Powidz lies on W shore; flour milling, sawmilling.

Powis, Wales: see WELSHPOOL.

Pownal (pou'nŭl). **1** Town (pop. 752), Cumberland co., SW Maine, 18 mi. NNE of Portland; Bradbury Mtn. State Park here. **2** Town (pop. 1,453), Bennington co., extreme SW Vt., on Hoosic R., just S of Bennington; limestone; dairy products. Seat of Oak Grove Seminary. James Fisk b. here. First settled c.1720, permanently settled after 1760.

Powys, Wales: see WELSHPOOL.

Poxoréu (po͞osho͞orĕ'o͞o), city (pop. 1,662), central Mato Grosso, Brazil, 120 mi. ESE of Cuiabá; diamond washings. Also spelled Poxorêu.

Poya (pôyä'), village (dist. pop. 827), W New Caledonia, 105 mi. NW of Nouméa; livestock, agr. products.

Poyales del Hoyo (poiä'lĕs dhĕl oi'ō), town (pop. 1,479), Ávila prov., central Spain, on S slopes of Sierra de Gredos, 24 mi. NW of Talavera de la Reina; olives, cereals, grapes, tobacco. Olive presses, flour mills; tile mfg.

Poyang or **P'o-yang** (pŭ'yäng'), town (pop. 41,512), ⊙ Poyang co. (pop. 329,805), N Kiangsi prov., China, on E shore of Poyang L., at mouth of short Po R. (formed near by through union of Loan and Chang rivers), 50 mi. ENE of Nanchang; commercial centers; tobacco, cotton, rice, sugar cane. Trades in porcelain. Coal mining, kaolin quarrying. Until 1912 called Jaochow.

Poyang Lake (pō'yäng), Chinese *P'o-yang Hu* (pŭ'yäng'ho͞o'), shallow lake (at low water, □ 1,070), one of largest in China, in N Kiangsi prov., serving as natural overflow reservoir for Yangtze R. (N), with which it is connected by HUKOW Canal. During the summer, the lake receives the flood waters of the Yangtze, rises about 30 ft. and reaches the max. size of 90 mi. (N–S) and 40 mi. (E–W). During the winter, it becomes almost dry. Shores are hilly in N, low and marshy in S. Receives Siu, Kan (main affluent), Kwangsin, and Po rivers. Lake area is gradually decreasing as the result of sedimentation.

Poyarkovo (pŭyär'kŭvŭ), village (1926 pop. 2,617), SE Amur oblast, Russian SFSR, on Amur R. (landing), across from Sünko, on spur of Trans-Siberian RR and 70 mi. SE of Blagoveshchensk, in agr. area (grain, soybeans); metalworks. Cossack village, founded 1858; named for 17th-cent. Rus. explorer.

Poyeh (bŭ'yĕ'), town, ⊙ Poyeh co. (pop. 111,214), W central Hopeh prov., China, 28 mi. S of Paoting; kaoliang, beans, sweet potatoes, peanuts, buckwheat.

Poygan, Lake (poi'gŭn), widening of Wolf R., in Winnebago co., E central Wis., 10 mi. NW of Oshkosh; c.10 mi. long, 3 mi. wide. Its E arm (c.3 mi. long) is called L. Winneconne.

Poynette (poinĕt'), village (pop. 969), Columbia co., S central Wis., on small Rowan Creek and 22 mi. N of Madison; agr.; cannery. State experimental game and fur farm near by.

Poynton with Worth, parish (pop. 3,944), NE Cheshire, England. Includes silk-milling town of Poynton, 4 mi. SSE of Stockport. Coal mining near by.

Poysdorf (pois'dôrf), town (pop. 3,264), NE Lower Austria, 35 mi. NNE of Vienna; rye, corn; wine.

Poza de la Sal (pō'thä dhä lä säl'), town (pop. 1,370), Burgos prov., N Spain, 25 mi. NNE of Burgos; cereals, vegetables, grapes, sheep. Liquor distilling, tanning, plaster mfg.; salt, iron mining.

Pozáldez (pō-thäl'dĕth), town (pop. 1,452), Valladolid prov., N central Spain, 20 mi. SSW of Valladolid; flour milling; sheep, wine.

Pozar or **Pozhar** (pôzhär'), Serbo-Croatian *Požar*, mountain, Macedonia, Yugoslavia, bet. Vardar and Strumica rivers; highest point (3,290 ft.) is 11 mi. WNW of Strumica.

Pozarevac or **Pozharevats** (both: pôzhä'rĕväts), Serbo-Croatian *Požarevac*, Ger. *Passarowitz* (päsä'rôvĭts), town (pop. 16,108), E Serbia, Yugoslavia, 37 mi. ESE of Belgrade, bet. Morava and Mlava rivers, 8 mi. S of its port on the Danube (linked by rail). Rail junction; trade center for grape- and winegrowing region. By a treaty with Austria and Venice, signed here in 1718, Turkey lost the Banat, Muntenia, and N Serbia to Austria, but retained the Peloponnesus.

Pozega or **Pozhega** (pô'zhĕgä). **1** or **Slavonska Pozega** or Slavonska Pozhega (slävôn'skä), Serbo-Croatian *Požega*, Hung. *Pozsega* (pô'zhĕgŏ), anc. *Incerum*, town (pop. 8,854), N Croatia, Yugoslavia, on Orljava R., on railroad and 20 mi. NW of Slavonski Brod, in Slavonia; trade center for winegrowing region. Auriferous gravels, lignite mining near by (SW). Has R.C. monastery and seminary, mus. **2** or **Pozega Uzicka** or **Pozhega Uzhichka** (both: o͞o'zhĭchkä), Serbo-Croatian *Požega Užička*, village (pop. 2,259), W Serbia, Yugoslavia, on railroad and 10 mi. E of Titovo Uzice; apple growing.

Pozharevats, Yugoslavia: see POZAREVAC.

Pozharevo, Bulgaria: see BOZHURISHTE.

Pozharskoye (pŭzhär'skŭyŭ), village (1939 pop. over 500), W Maritime Territory, Russian SFSR, near Trans-Siberian RR (Guberovo station), 27 mi. N of Iman, in agr. area (grain, soybeans, perilla). Prior to 1939, Tikhonovka.

Pozhega, Yugoslavia: see POZEGA.

Pozherevitsy (pŭzhĭryĕ'vĭtsē), village (1939 pop. over 500), SE Pskov oblast, Russian SFSR, 22 mi. SSE of Porkhov; flax.

Pozhva (pôzh'vŭ), town (1926 pop. 2,981), central Molotov oblast, Russian SFSR, on small lake near Kama R. (landing just SE, at Ust-Pozhva), 30 mi. SW of Berezniki; metalworking, machine mfg. Founded 1759; 1st Rus. steamer and locomotive built here, 1817. Formerly called Pozhevski and Pozhevski Zavod.

Pozières (pōzyâr'), village (pop. 289), Somme dept., N France, 4 mi. NE of Albert. Captured by Australians in battle of the Somme (1916). Has Br. First World War military cemetery and monuments.

Poznan (pôz'nän, pōz'-), Pol. *Poznań* (pôz'nänyŭ), Ger. *Posen* (pō'zŭn), province [Pol. *wojewodztwo*] (□ 10,529; pop. 2,085,648), W Poland; ⊙ Poznan. Fertile low and level agr. region, partly forested, with many small lakes; drained by Warta, Notec, and Obra rivers. Principal crops: rye, potatoes, oats, wheat, barley. Stock raising (cattle, pigs) is important. Industry, concentrated in chief cities of Poznan, Kalisz, Gniezno, and Ostrow, include wood- and metalworking, textile milling, food processing, brewing, mfg. of agr. implements, machinery, chemicals, glass, and cement. Boundaries of pre-Second World War prov. (□ 9,256; 1931 pop. 2,106,500) were changed by transfer of territory to Bydgoszcz prov. and from Lodz prov. Before 1919, territory of present-day prov. was divided bet. Prussian Posen (Poznan) prov. (W) and part of Kalish (Kalisz) govt. of Rus. Poland (E). Prov. included (1945–50) present Zielona Gora prov., bordering W on the Oder.

Poznan, Pol. *Poznań*, Ger. *Posen*, industrial city (1946 pop. 267,978; 1950 estimate 327,192), ⊙ Poznan prov., W Poland, port on Warta (Warthe) R. and 175 mi. W of Warsaw; 52°25'N 16°58'E. Major rail junction; trade center (lumber, agr. goods); airport; iron founding; copper, silver, and gold working; mfg. of machinery, agr.

implements, precision instruments, engines, boilers, tools, aircraft, bicycles, automobile bodies, pianos, matches, chemicals, pharmaceuticals, glass, bricks, asphalt, baskets, roofing material, textiles, shoes, tobacco, and food (liqueur, beer, candy, chocolate, cereals). Since 1821, archiepiscopal see of Poznan and Gniezno. Has univ. (founded 1919). Many churches, museums with rich art treasures. Annual international spring fair held since 1922. Field Marshal von Hindenburg b. here. One of oldest Slav towns, developed before coming of Christianity to Poland; in 10th cent. became 1st Pol. episcopal see and a nucleus of the Pol. state. Originally situated on right bank of the Warta, it later shifted to left bank. Poznan had pop. of 30,000 in early-17th cent., when it outgrew its 15-cent. defense walls; later declined. Passed 1793 to Prussia; subsequent history was largely a struggle bet. Germans and Slavs. In grand duchy of Warsaw in 1807; passed 1815 to Prussia as ⊙ newly-created grand duchy of Posen. Reverted to Poland in 1919. During Second World War, when it was annexed to Germany, thousands of Poles were expelled. Was one of farthest targets of British-based aircraft and suffered some damage; its 18th-cent. cathedral largely destroyed.

Pozo Alcón (pō'thō älkōn'), town (pop. 5,583), Jaén prov., S Spain, 17 mi. NW of Baza; olive-oil processing, flour milling, soap mfg. Sheep raising, lumbering; cereals, esparto, potatoes.

Pozo Almonte (pō'sō älmōn'tā), village (pop. 602), Tarapacá prov., N Chile, 25 mi. E of Iquique; rail junction and airport in nitrate-producing area.

Pozo Amargo or **Pozoamargo** (pō"thōämär'gō), town (pop. 820), Cuenca prov., E central Spain, 32 mi. NW of Albacete; cereals, olives, grapes, sheep.

Pozoblanco (pō"thōbläng'kō), city (pop. 13,466), Córdoba prov., S Spain, agr. center 35 mi. N of Córdoba. Mfg. of woolen textiles, soap, tiles, chocolate; olive-oil processing, flour- and sawmilling, tanning. Cereals, vegetables, livestock in area. Silver-bearing lead and copper deposits.

Pozo del Molle (pō'sō dĕl mō'yä), town (pop. 2,114), central Córdoba prov., Argentina, 90 mi. SE of Córdoba; rail junction and agr. center (wheat, flax, corn, livestock).

Pozo del Tigre (tē'grä), town (pop. estimate 1,500), central Formosa natl. territory, Argentina, on railroad and 160 mi. NW of Formosa; trade center for agr. and livestock area.

Pozo Hondo (pō'sō ōn'dō), town (pop. estimate 1,000), W Santiago del Estero prov., Argentina, on railroad and 65 mi. NNW of Santiago del Estero; stock-raising and lumbering center.

Pozohondo (pō"thō-ōn'dō), town (pop. 2,010), Albacete prov., SE central Spain, 19 mi. NW of Hellín; livestock, wine, saffron, esparto.

Pozorrubio (pōsōrōō'byō), town (1939 pop. 2,496; 1948 municipality pop. 21,675), Pangasinan prov., central Luzon, Philippines, near W coast, 15 mi. ENE of Dagupan; agr. center (rice, copra, corn).

Pozorrubio or **Pozorrubio de Santiago** (pō"thō-rōō'vyō, dhä säntyä'gō), town (pop. 1,550), Cuenca prov., E central Spain, 37 mi. ESE of Aranjuez; grain- and winegrowing, sheep raising, lumbering, gypsum quarrying.

Pozos (pō'sōs), officially Villa de Pozos, town (pop. 1,516), San Luis Potosí, N central Mexico, 8 mi. SE of San Luis Potosí; corn, beans, cotton, fruit, stock.

Pozos, Los, Panama: see LOS POZOS.

Pozsega, Yugoslavia: see POZEGA, Croatia.

Pozsony, Czechoslovakia: see BRATISLAVA.

Pozuelo de Alarcón (pō"thwā'lō dhä älärkōn'), town (pop. 2,402), Madrid prov., central Spain, on railroad and 7 mi. W of Madrid; truck produce, grapes, stock. Mfg. of gloves, railroad ties; tanning, sawmilling. Hunting.

Pozuelo de Calatrava (käläträ'vä), town (pop. 2,703), Ciudad Real prov., S central Spain, 7 mi. SE of Ciudad Real; cereals, potatoes, grapes, olives, livestock. Medicinal springs; gypsum quarries, and plaster factories.

Pozuelo de Zarzón (thärth-ōn'), village (pop. 1,284), Cáceres prov., W Spain, 20 mi. NW of Plasencia; olive-oil processing, tanning; cereals, figs, grapes.

Pozuelos, Lake (pōswā'lōs), salt lake (□ 25; alt. 11,000 ft.) in the Puna de Atacama, NW Jujuy prov., Argentina, 5 mi. NW of Rinconada; 8 mi. long, 3 mi. wide. Sometimes called L. Toro.

Pozuelos de Calatrava (pō"thwā'lōs dhä käläträ'vä), town (pop. 998), Ciudad Real prov., S central Spain, 13 mi. WSW of Ciudad Real; grapes, cereals, olives, goats, sheep; lumbering; iron mining.

Pozuzo (pōsōō'sō), village (pop. 132), Huánuco dept., central Peru, in Cordillera Oriental, 48 mi. ESE of Huánuco; sugar cane, coffee, tobacco, fruit, coca. Colony founded 1860 by Bavarians. Also Posuso.

Pozzallo (pôtsäl'lô), town (pop. 9,723), Ragusa prov., SE Sicily, port on Mediterranean Sea, 15 mi. SSE of Ragusa; liquor distilling; soap, lubricating oils; tunny fishing.

Pozzo di Gotto, Sicily: see BARCELLONA POZZO DI GOTTO.

Pozzolo Formigaro (pôtsô'lô fôrmēgä'rô), village (pop. 2,447), Alessandria prov., Piedmont, N Italy, 2 mi. N of Novi Ligure; chemical industry.

Pozzomaggiore (pô"tsômäd-jô'rĕ), village (pop. 4,586), Sassari prov., NW Sardinia, 25 mi. SSE of Sassari.

Pozzuoli (pôtswô'lē), anc. *Puteoli*, town (pop. 24,594), Napoli prov., Campania, S Italy, 8 mi. WSW of Naples, port on Gulf of Pozzuoli, NW inlet (5 mi. long, 4 mi. wide) of Bay of Naples. Iron- and steelworks. Bishopric. Pozzuoli gives its name to pozzuolana, a greyish-brown volcanic ash used for making bldg. cement. A wealthy seaport in Roman times; among its remains (now partly under water) are an amphitheater and the so-called temple of Serapis (a market place). Near by is the SOLFATARA.

Pozzuolo del Friuli (pôtswô'lô dĕl frē'ōōlē), village (pop. 1,780), Udine prov., Friuli-Venezia Giulia, NE Italy, 5 mi. SSW of Udine; mfg. (paper, agr. tools). Has agr. school.

Pra (prä), town (pop. 8,727), Genova prov., Liguria, N Italy, port on Gulf of Genoa and 7 mi. W of Genoa, within Greater Genoa; iron and steel industry; cotton mills.

Prabalingga, Indonesia: see PROBOLINGGO.

Prabatcheanchum (präbät'chĭnchōōm'), town, Takeo prov., S Cambodia, 65 mi. S of Pnompenh, on Vietnam line; rice, pepper. Also called Tamlap.

Prabhas Patan, India: see SOMNATH.

Prabuty (präbōō'tĭ), Ger. *Riesenburg* (rē'zŭnbōōrk), town (1939 pop. 8,051; 1946 pop. 2,298) in East Prussia, after 1945 in Olsztyn prov., NE Poland, 12 mi. E of Marienwerder (Kwidzyn); rail junction; grain and cattle market; sawmilling. Residence (1249–1524) of bishops of Pomerania; chartered 1330. Until 1919, in West Prussia prov.

Praca River or **Pracha River** (both: prä'chä), E Bosnia, Yugoslavia, rises on NE slope of the Jahorina, flows 50 mi. generally E to Drina R. at Ustipraca. Belgrade-Sarajevo RR follows its middle and lower course.

Prachantakham (prächän'tä'käm'), village (1937 pop. 3,583), Prachinburi prov., S Thailand, on Bangkok–Pnompenh RR and 70 mi. ENE of Bangkok.

Pracha River, Yugoslavia: see PRACA RIVER.

Prachatice (prä'khätyĭtsĕ), Ger. *Prachatitz* (prä'khätĭts), town (pop. 3,974), S Bohemia, Czechoslovakia, in Bohemian Forest, on railroad and 22 mi. W of Budweis; mfg. of toys, tools, knit goods. Noted for well-preserved medieval buildings. Health resort of Marketine Lazne (alt. 2,030 ft.) with mineral springs, is just S. Husinec, birthplace of John Huss, is 3 mi. NNE.

Prachinburi (prä'chĭn'bōōrē'), town (1947 pop. 4,394), ⊙ Prachinburi prov. (□ 4,706; 1947 pop. 217,395), S Thailand, port on Bang Pakong R. and Bangkok–Pnompenh RR, 60 mi. ENE of Bangkok, in extensive rice- and sugar-growing region; trading center (hardwoods, charcoal, horns, hides). Also called Pachin or Prachin.

Prachinburi River, Thailand: see BANG PAKONG RIVER.

Prachov Rocks, Czechoslovakia: see BOHEMIAN PARADISE.

Prachuabkhirikhan (prächōō'ŭpkērēkän'), town (1947 pop. 3,076), ⊙ Prachuabkhirikhan prov. (□ 2,422; 1947 pop. 72,343), S Thailand, port on Gulf of Siam, on railroad and 145 mi. SSW of Bangkok, in narrow strip of land bet. Tenasserim Range and sea; trade center and seaside resort; timber and big-game region. Pearl fishing along coast. Tin mining at Ban Krut and Thap Sakae (S).

Prad, Italy: see PRATO ALLO STELVIO.

Praded (prä'dyĕt), Czech *Praděd*, highest mountain (4,888 ft.) of the Jeseniky, W Silesia, Czechoslovakia, 10 mi. S of Jesenik; winter sports. Moravice R. and 2 Opava R. headstreams rise here.

Pradejón (prä-dhähōn'), town (pop. 2,315), Logroño prov., N Spain, 6 mi. WNW of Calahorra; olive-oil processing, canning, flour milling. Wine, vegetables, hemp, livestock in area.

Pradelles (prädĕl'), village (pop. 838), Haute-Loire dept., S central France, in Monts du Velay, near Allier R., 19 mi. S of Le Puy; sawmilling.

Prádena (prä'dhänä), town (pop. 899), Segovia prov., central Spain, on N slopes of the Sierra de Guadarrama, 27 mi. NE of Segovia; grain, potatoes, livestock; flour milling.

Pradera (prädā'rä), town (pop. 3,511), Valle del Cauca dept., W Colombia, in Cauca valley, 18 mi. E of Cali; alt. 3,527 ft. Rail terminus and agr. center (tobacco, sugar cane, coffee, cacao, bananas, corn, cattle).

Prades (präd), town (pop. 4,397), Pyrénées-Orientales dept., S France, in the CONFLENT valley, on Têt R. and 25 mi. WSW of Perpignan; livestock and vegetable market; metallurgical and chemical factories. Blast furnaces at Ria (1 mi. WSW). Iron ore mined in near-by Massif du Canigou.

Prado (prä'dōō), city (pop. 1,410), SE Bahia, Brazil, on the Atlantic, 25 mi. N of Caravelas; cacao, vegetable oils. Iron foundry at Jiquitaia (20 mi. W). Monazite-sand deposits at Cumuruxatiba (17 mi. N).

Prado, Monte (môn'tĕ prä'dô), peak (6,735 ft.) in Etruscan Apennines, N central Italy, 19 mi. NE of Carrara.

Prado Dam, Calif.: see SANTA ANA RIVER.

Prado del Rey (prä'dhō dhĕl rā'), town (pop. 4,827), Cádiz prov., SW Spain, in foothills of the Cordille ra Penibética, 22 mi. W of Ronda, (Málaga prov.) agr. center (olives, cereals, grapes, fruit, vegetables livestock).

Pradoluengo (prä"dhōlwĕng'gō), town (pop. 2,281) Burgos prov., N Spain, on E slopes of the Monte de Oca, near Logroño prov. border, 29 mi. E o Burgos; wool center. Also cereals, timber. Mfg. o dyes, plaster, woolen goods, berets.

Prados (prä'dōōs), city (pop. 1,563), S Minas Ge rais, Brazil, 12 mi. NE of São João del Rei; ti mining; graphite deposits. Also spelled Prado.

Pradum or **Pradumdhani**, Thailand: see PATHUM THANI.

Prae, Thailand: see PHRAE.

Praekestolen, Norway: see GEIRANGER FJORD.

Praeneste, Italy: see PALESTRINA.

Praenestine Way (prē"nĕstĭn'), anc. Roman roa from Rome to Praeneste; 23 mi. long.

Praesidium Julium, Portugal: see SANTARÉM, city

Praesto (prĕs'tû), Dan. *Præstø*, amt (□ 654; 195 pop. 122,955), Denmark, largely on SE Zealand includes Moen, Bogo, and Nyord isls.; ⊙ Praesto Naestved, industrial center. Agr. (grain), dair farming, fisheries.

Praesto, Dan. *Præstø*, city (1950 pop. 1,602), port, ⊙ Praesto amt, Zealand, Denmark, on Praesto Fjor and 42 mi. SSW of Copenhagen; 55°7'N 12°4'E Brewing, perfume mfg.; fishing.

Prag, India: see ALLAHABAD, city.

Praga (prä'gä), industrial and residential suburb o Warsaw, Warszawa prov., E central Poland, o right bank of the Vistula (bridged), NE of cit center. New E-W thoroughfare connects Prag with W outskirts of Warsaw. Captured (1794) b Russians under Suvarov. In 1920, Rus. advanc on Warsaw was halted near by. In Second Worl War, 42% destroyed; toward end of war, Rus advance halted here (Aug.–Oct., 1944) tempo rarily while Warsaw rising was in progress.

Prägarten (prä'gärtŭn), town (pop. 3,647), N Uppe Austria, 11 mi. NE of Linz, N of the Danube earthenware.

Pragel Pass (prä'gŭl) (5,098 ft.), in Glarus Alps, central Switzerland, 10 mi. WSW of Glarus; roa over pass leads from Glarus to Schwyz.

Pragersko (prä'gĕrskô), Ger. *Pragerhof* (prä'gŭr-hōf"), hamlet, NE Slovenia, Yugoslavia, 10 mi. of Maribor; rail junction. Until 1918, in Styria.

Pragjyotishapura, India: see GAUHATI.

Prague (präg, prāg), Czech *Praha* (prä'hä), Ger. *Prag* (präk), city (pop. 922,284), ⊙ Czechoslovakia and Praha prov. (□ 3,756; pop. 2,014,938), in central Bohemia, on Vltava R. (Moldau) and 160 mi NW of Vienna; 50°5'N 14°25'E. Industrial, commercial, and communications center (focal point of 7 main rail lines; air lines), largest city of Czechoslovakia, and a major European cultural center, rich in history. See of R.C. archbishop, primate of Czechoslovakia, of an Orthodox Eastern archbishop, and of the archbishop of the Czechoslovak church. Seat of Constituent National Assembly and Supreme Court. Its major engineering factories and metalworks produce heavy machinery, automobiles, aircraft, rolling stock; mfg. also includes clothing, furniture, leather goods, foodstuffs, chemicals, electrical and radio equipment, paper, tires, beer. It specializes in preparation of smoked meats and its glove-making is 2d in Europe only to France. Czech book publishing is largely concentrated here. Greater Prague (□ 66.5) is divided into 19 administrative districts with the geographical hub at the Old Town (Czech *Staré Město*), on E bank and just above a bend of the Vltava. River port is at HOLESOVICE-BUBNY (NE, on W bank); residential districts lie chiefly on W bank. Oldest sections are VYSEHRAD (c.2 mi. S), on Vysehrad hill, known by the 11th cent., and HRADCANY, on Hradcany hill (W), with its famous castle (dating from 9th cent.), formerly seat of the kings of Bohemia, now presidential residence. Both Vysehrad and Hradcany retain part of medieval fortifications, under protection of which developed the nucleus of the city. The Lesser Town (Czech *Malá Strana*) arose out of a cluster of settlements below Hradcany castle and is connected with E bank by Charles Bridge (14th cent.) most famous of the 12 bridges over the Vltava. Main railroad stations (Wilson, Masaryk, Denis) are located within New Town (Czech *Nové Město*), which is the commercial and business district (to E and SE), traversed by the foremost thoroughfare, Wenceslaus Square. Municipal airport is at Ruzyne. Capital area has been expanded through addition of KARLOVSKE VINOHRADY, workers' suburbs of Nusle (SSE) and Vrsovice (SE), industrial VYSOCANY, Karlin, SMICHOV, HLUBOCEPY, HOSTIVAR, and Liben, and the historical heights of ZIZKOV. Often called "the city of 100 spires," Prague is a treasure-house of the baroque. Outstanding are St. Nicholas church (17th–18th cent.), Loretto and Strahov monasteries, Church of our Lady of Victory (containing world-famous miraculous statuette of Infant Jesus), Clementinum library, Czernin and Waldstein palaces. To Romanesque period belong St. George's Basilica (Hradcany) and St. Martin's chapel (Vysehrad), both of 12th cent. Most remarkable Gothic structures are: 13th-cent. Old Town Hall; 14th-cent. Tyn Cathedral (formerly main Hussite church), with tomb of Tycho Brahe; 15th-cent. Powder Tower (last of 13 gates of Old Town); late-Gothic Bridge Tower at E end of Charles Bridge. Italian Renaissance is represented by "Belvedere," Queen Anne's summer residence (on W bank). Other city landmarks include: the St. Vitus Cathedral (see HRADCANY) with sepulchers of St. Wenceslaus and St. John of Nepomuk; 13th-cent. synagogue in JOSEFOV; 14th-cent. Karlov church; monastery of the Knights of the Cross; Rudolphinum (Artists' House); National Theater; New Town Hall, site of First Defenestration of Prague (1419). Prague has long been a noted central European seat of learning, with Charles Univ. of Prague (dating back to 1348), Technical Univ., Huss Evangelical Faculty, Slovak Univ., military and art academies, numerous state research institutes. There are many museums (notably of Mozart, Smetana, and Dvorak), theaters (in Stavovske Theater Mozart's *Don Giovanni* had its 1st performance), parks, and recreation centers, the latter located mostly on isls. in Vltava R.; huge Masaryk or Strahov Stadium seats 200,000 during Sokol festivals. Following establishment (1232) of the Old Town by German colonists settled here by King Wenceslaus I, Prague became the capital of Bohemia and under Charles IV (1336–78) the 2d largest city in Europe after Paris. From 14th to 17th cent. the emperors resided here as well as in Vienna. The rivalry bet. the Czech and German elements in Prague was a major factor in the reform preached by John Huss; it was with the first defenestration of Prague (1419) that the Hussite Wars began. The city's prosperity suffered in the struggle. A large fire (1541) destroyed a great part of Hradcany and part of Lesser Town. But in late 16th cent. and early 17th cent., under Rudolph II, Prague became a center of science, where Tycho Brahe and Kepler worked. After the Second Defenestration of Prague at Hradcany (1618), and the battle of WHITE MOUNTAIN (1620), execution of Protestant leaders took place on Old Town Square (1621). Swedes occupied (1648) Lesser Town just before the end of Thirty Years War. In the war of Austrian Succession, Prague was captured by the French (1742) and by the Prussians (1744), and in the Seven Years War was bombarded (1757) for two weeks by Frederick II of Prussia. Under Joseph II, the original four towns were united into one magistracy; after adoption of the Constitution of 1860 and treaty of peace between Austria and Prussia, it became the focus of Czech national aspirations and capital of the country at proclamation of Czechoslovak independence in 1918. Its literary, artistic, and musical life flourished bet. the 2 World Wars. Rilke, Kafka, and Karel Capek lived and wrote here. As administrative center of Ger. protectorate of Bohemia-Moravia (1939–45), Prague suffered considerably during Second World War. The Old Town Hall with its famous clock was burned out; 14th-cent. Benedictine monastery of Emmaeus was almost destroyed; but both are being speedily restored. Czech uprising against the Germans on May 5, 1945, was followed by entry of Russian troops on May 7.

Prague (prāg). **1** Village (pop. 396), Saunders co., E Nebr., 35 mi. N of Lincoln and on branch of Platte R. **2** (also prăg) City (pop. 1,546), Lincoln co., central Okla., 17 mi. N of Seminole; trade center for agr. area (cotton, oats, wheat); cotton ginning, cottonseed milling; mfg. of feed, frozen foods, machine-shop products. Settled by Czechs; inc. 1902.

Prahecq (präĕk'), village (pop. 632), Deux-Sèvres dept., W France, 7 mi. SE of Niort; dairying.

Prahova, province, Rumania: see PLOESTI.

Prahova River (prä'khôvä), S central and S Rumania, in Muntenia, rises in E part of the Transylvanian Alps just SW of the Predeal Pass, flows S past Sinaia and SE past Campina to Ialomita R. 27 mi. SE of Ploesti; 80 mi. long. Drains major oil-producing region. Its upper valley, a noted communications corridor, is generally considered the divide bet. the Transylvanian Alps and the Moldavian Carpathians.

Prahovo (prä'hôvô), village, E Serbia, Yugoslavia, port on the Danube (Rum. border) and 5 mi. NNE of Negotin; rail terminus.

Prahran (prŭrăn'), municipality (pop. 59,882), S Victoria, Australia, 3 mi. SE of Melbourne, in metropolitan area; truck gardening; cigarettes.

Prai (prī), town (pop. 5,287), Prov. Wellesley, Penang, NW Malaya, on Penang Channel opposite George Town (ferry service) and on left bank of small Prai R. opposite Butterworth; railroad station of Penang, on direct lines from Singapore and Bangkok (Thonburi); dock installations.

Praia (prä'yŭ), city (pop. 9,364), ⊙ Cape Verde Isls., on S shore of São Tiago Isl., c.400 mi. W of Dakar (Fr. West Africa); 14°55'N 23°31'W; fishing port. Ships oranges, sugar cane, coffee, castor oil. Distilling, fish curing, straw-hat mfg. Airfield just E; seaplane landing 4 mi. W. Cable station; radio transmitter. Has unhealthy climate.

Praia da Graciosa (dä grŭsyô'zŭ), village (pop. 412), Angra do Heroísmo dist., central Azores, on E shore of Graciosa Isl., 3 mi. SE of Santa Cruz; fishing, canning, tile mfg.

Praia da Rocha (rō'shŭ), village (pop. 421), Faro dist., S Portugal, on the Atlantic (S coast), 2 mi. S of Portimão; popular seaside resort. Its rugged shoreline offers interesting rock formations.

Praia da Vitória (vētôr'yŭ), town (pop. 2,029), Angra do Heroísmo dist., central Azores, on E shore of Terceira Isl., 10 mi. NE of Angra do Heroísmo; alcohol distilling, flour milling, mfg. of dairy produce. Fine beach. Repeatedly damaged by earthquakes. Lajes airfield 3 mi. NW.

Praia Grande, Brazil: see NITERÓI.

Praid (prīd), Hung. *Parajd* (pŏ'roit), village (pop. 2,926), Mures prov., central Rumania, 18 mi. NW of Odorhei; rail terminus and salt production center; lumbering, mfg. of bricks and tiles. In Hungary, 1940–45.

Prainha (präē'nyŭ). **1** City (pop. 372), central Pará, Brazil, on left bank of lower Amazon R. and 35 mi. NE of Santarém; rubber, Brazil nuts. **2** City, São Paulo, Brazil: see MIRACATU.

Prairie. **1** County (□ 674; pop. 13,768), E central Ark.; ⊙ Des Arc. Drained by White R. and Bayou des Arc. Agr. (cotton, rice, corn, hay); timber; lumber milling, commercial fishing. Formed 1846. **2** County (□ 1,727; pop. 2,377), E Mont.; ⊙ Terry. Agr. area drained by Yellowstone R. Livestock. Formed 1915.

Prairie, village (pop. 654), Monroe co., E Miss., 7 mi. WSW of Aberdeen.

Prairieburg, town (pop. 210), Linn co., E Iowa, near Buffalo Creek, 22 mi. NE of Cedar Rapids.

Prairie City. **1** Village (pop. 500), McDonough co., W Ill., 15 mi. NE of Macomb, in agr. and bituminous-coal area. **2** Town (pop. 834), Jasper co., central Iowa, 20 mi. E of Des Moines, in coal-mining area; farm equipment, concrete pipes, feed, cereals. **3** City (pop. 822), Grant co., NE central Oregon, 13 mi. ENE of Canyon City and on John Day R.; alt. 3,539 ft.; livestock.

Prairie Creek Redwoods State Park, Humboldt co., NW Calif., tract (c.7,000 acres) of redwood forest, 25 mi. S of Crescent City, near the coast. Cabins, camp sites, recreational facilities.

Prairie Dog Creek, river in NW Kansas and S Nebr., formed by confluence of 2 forks in Decatur co. W of Dresden, flows c.160 mi. ENE, past Norton, into Harlan co. in Nebr., entering Republican R. 6 mi. ESE of Alma.

Prairie Dog Town Fork of Red River, in Texas and Okla., formed in the Panhandle of Texas by junction of intermittent Palo Duro and Tierra Blanca creeks near Canyon, flows c.180 mi. generally ESE, through scenic PALO DURO CANYON, past Childress, and along Okla.-Texas line, joining Salt Fork to form Red R. just S of Elmer, Okla. Sometimes called Prairie Dog Fork.

Prairie du Chien (prâ'rē dŭ shēn'), city (pop. 5,392), ⊙ Crawford co., SW Wis., on Mississippi R. just above influx of the Wisconsin, and 53 mi. S of La Crosse, in agr. area (dairying, grain growing); farm trade center, with mfg. of woolen goods, cement and wood products, tool grinders, fertilizer. City's strategic site on Fox-Wisconsin river route to the Mississippi made it a meeting point for explorers, missionaries, and traders in late-17th cent.; Nicolas Perrot erected Fort St. Nicolas here in 1686; Fr. settlers came c.1781, and an American Fur Company trading post was built here before 1812. In War of 1812, Americans built Fort Shelby (1814), renamed Fort McKay soon after. Fort Crawford (1816; abandoned 1856) was scene of experiments by Dr. William Beaumont. Inc. 1872.

Prairie du Rocher (rō'shā, rŏsh', rō'chŭr), village (pop. 662), Randolph co., SW Ill., near the Mississippi 36 mi. S of East St. Louis; flour, wood products. Settled by French in early-18th-cent. "Mississippi Bubble" enterprise. Old fort (partly restored) is in Fort de Chartres (or Fort Chartres) State Park, just W.

Prairie du Sac (săk'), village (pop. 1,402), Sauk co., S central Wis., on Wisconsin R., adjacent to Sauk City, and 22 mi. NW of Madison, in dairying and farming area (corn, hogs); creamery, cannery, feed mills. Settled 1839, inc. 1885.

Prairie Farm, village (pop. 343), Barron co., NW Wis., 38 mi. NW of Eau Claire; dairying.

Prairie Grove, town (pop. 939), Washington co., NW Ark., 11 mi. WSW of Fayetteville, in the Ozarks; trade center for agr. and timber area. A Civil War battle (Dec. 7, 1862) here resulted in a Confederate retreat.

Prairie Hill, town (pop. 124), Chariton co., N central Mo., near Chariton R., 17 mi. WNW of Moberly.

Prairie Home, town (pop. 208), Cooper co., central Mo., near Missouri R., 14 mi. SE of Boonville.

Prairie Lake, Barron co., NW Wis., 5 mi. SSE of Rice Lake; c.6 mi. long, c.½ mi. wide; connected with 2 smaller lakes (Chetek and Pokegema). Contains several floating isls.

Prairie River, SW Mich., rises in small lakes in SE Branch co. near Ind. line, flows c.45 mi. NW, past Burr Oak and Centerville, to St. Joseph R. 2 mi. S of Three Rivers.

Prairies, Rivière des (rēvyâr' dā prârē'), S Que., branch of Ottawa R., flowing from L. of the Two Mountains 30 mi. NE bet. Montreal Isl. and Jesus Isl. to the St. Lawrence.

Prairie View. **1** City (pop. 192), Phillips co., N Kansas, 14 mi. WNW of Phillipsburg, in corn belt; corn, livestock. **2** Village, Waller co., S Texas, c.45 mi. WNW of Houston; seat of Prairie View Agr. and Mechanical Col.

Prairie Village, city (1951 pop. c.5,350), Johnson co., E Kansas, a suburb of Kansas City. Inc. after 1950.

Praise or **Elkhorn City**, city (pop. 1,349), Pike co., SE Ky., in the Cumberlands near Va. line, on Russell Fork and 12 mi. SE of Pikeville, in bituminous-coal and timber region. Fish hatchery here. Near by are picturesque Breaks of Sandy at N end of Pine Mtn.

Pralboino (prälbôē'nô), village (pop. 2,968), Brescia prov., Lombardy, N Italy, on Mella R. and 13 mi. NE of Cremona.

Pralls Island (prôlz), SE N.Y., small island in Arthur Kill, just W of Staten Isl.; part of Richmond borough of New York city.

Pralognan-la-Vanoise (prälônyä'-lä-vänwäz'), village (pop. 94), Savoie dept., SE France, in Massif de la Vanoise, 12 mi. SE of Moutiers; alt. 4,606. Winter sports.

Pram (präm), town (pop. 1,910), W central Upper Austria, on Pram R. and 20 mi. WNW of Wels; tanning.

Pramaggiore, Monte (môn'tĕ prämäd-jô'rĕ), peak (8,133 ft.) in S Carnic Alps, N Italy, 12 mi. WSW of Ampezzo.

Pramanta or **Pramanda** (both: prä'mŭndŭ), town (pop. 3,021), Ioannina nome, S Epirus, Greece, 13 mi. SE of Ioannina, at N foot of the Tzoumerka; timber, barley; livestock.

Prambachkirchen (präm'bäkhkĭrkhŭn), town (pop. 2,469), central Upper Austria, 18 mi. W of Linz; wheat, cattle.

Prameny, Czechoslovakia: see LAZNE KYNZVART.

Pramollo (prämôl'lô), village (pop. 969), Torino prov., Piedmont, NW Italy, 7 mi. WNW of Pinerolo; graphite mining.

Pram River (präm), NW Upper Austria, rises in Hausruck Mts. W of Haag, flows c.25 mi. NW to the Inn at Schärding.

Prang (präng), town, Northern Territories, central Gold Coast, on Pru R. and 25 mi. SW of Yeji, on road; ferry station; millet, durra, yams.

Prang, town (pop. 13,496), Peshawar dist., central North-West Frontier Prov., W Pakistan, 12 mi. NE of Peshawar, on S outskirts of Charsadda; agr. market (wheat, corn, sugar cane); handicraft weaving of mats, baskets, cloth. Sometimes spelled Parang.

Pranhita River (prän'hĭtŭ), on Hyderabad-Madhya Pradesh border, India, formed by junction of Wardha and Wainganga rivers 14 mi. NE of Sirpur; flows 70 mi. S to Godavari R. 8 mi. ESE of Chinnur.

Prantij, India: see PARANTIJ.

Pra River (prä), S Gold Coast, rises NW of Mpraeso, flows c.150 mi. S, through major agr. area, past Beposo (suspension bridge), to Gulf of Guinea at Shama. Receives Ofin R. (right), Birim R. (left). Not navigable (rapids). Gold placers.

Praschnitz, Poland: see PRZASNYSZ.

Prashka, Poland: see PRASZKA.

Prasias, lake, Greece-Yugoslavia: see DOJRAN, LAKE.

Prasily, Czechoslovakia: see HARTMANICE.

Praskoveya, Russian SFSR: see BUDENNOVSK.

Praslin Island (präzlē') (□ 15; pop. 2,893), one of the Seychelles, in Indian Ocean, 30 mi. NE of Victoria; 4°20'S 55°45'E; 7 mi. long, 5 mi. wide; granite formation. Vanilla and Casuarina cultivation; copra, essential oils; fisheries. Sea coconuts are found here. Hosp. on St. Ann's Bay (SE).

Prasnysh, Poland: see PRZASNYSZ.

Prassberg, Yugoslavia: see MOZIRJE.

Prassonesi, Cape, or **Cape Prassonisi** (präsônē'sē), on small isl. off SW extremity of Rhodes isl., Greece, 90 mi. NE of Cape Sideron (Crete); 35°52'N 27°45'E.

Prasu (prä'sōō), village, Western Prov., S Gold Coast colony, on Pra R. (ferry) and 55 mi. N of Cape Coast, on road; cacao, palm oil and kernels, hardwood.

Praszka (präsh'kä), Rus. *Prashka* (präsh'kŭ), town (pop. 3,013), Lodz prov., S central Poland, on Prosna R. and 12 mi. SSW of Wielun; tanning, flour milling. Until 1939, Pol. frontier station near Ger. border, opposite Gorzow Slaski.

Prata (prä'tŭ). **1** City (pop. 2,970), westernmost Minas Gerais, Brazil, in the Triângulo Mineiro, 40 mi. SW of Uberlândia; road center; cattle raising. Mineral springs. **2** City, Rio Grande do Sul, Brazil: see NOVA PRATA.

Pratabgarh, India: see PARTABGARH, district, town, Uttar Pradesh.

Pratapgarh, India: see PARTABGARH, former princely state.

Prata Sannita (prä'tä sän-nē'tä), village (pop. 1,787), Caserta prov., Campania, S Italy, in the Apennines, 11 mi. S of Isernia; paper mill. Hydroelectric plant near by.

Pratas Island (prä'täs), Chinese *Tungsha* (dŏŏng'-shä') [eastern reef], in S.China Sea, Kwangtung prov., China, 180 mi. S of Swatow; 20°42'N 116°43'E. Radio station; fisheries. Guano deposits. Isl. is situated in W side of circular Pratas coral reef. Vereker Banks are 40 mi. NW of Pratas Isl. Occupied by Japan, 1907–09 and 1939–45.

Prat de Llobregat, El (ĕl prät' dhā lyōbrägät'), outer suburb (pop. 7,723) of Barcelona, Barcelona prov., NE Spain, 6 mi. SW of city center on Llobregat coastal plain; mfg. (rayon, paper); horse breeding, rice growing, truck farming. Has radio station. Airport 2 mi. S.

Prathum Thani, Thailand: see PATHUMTHANI.

Prätigau (prĕ'tēgou), Romansh *Val Pratens* (väl' prä'tŭns), valley of Landquart R., E Switzerland, extending from Klosters to Landquart; pop. German-speaking Protestants.

Prat Island, off coast of Aysén prov., S Chile, N of Wellington Isl.; 48°15'S 75°W; 27 mi. long, 12 mi. wide.

Pratisthan, India: see JHUSI.

Prato or **Prato in Toscana** (prä'tô ēn tôskä'nä), town (pop. 28,646), Firenze prov., Tuscany, central Italy, on Bisenzio R. (right affluent of the Arno) and 10 mi. NW of Florence. Rail junction; large woolen industry dates from 13th cent.; mfg. (textile machinery, refrigerators, furniture, shoes, hosiery, straw hats, brooms, chemicals, soap, macaroni, beer, cotton textiles, hemp products). Bishopric. Cathedral (enlarged 14th cent.) contains frescoes by Filippo Lippi and works by Donatello, Giovanni Pisano, and Andrea della Robbia. Has several fine churches, including Santa Maria delle Carceri (built 1485–92 by G. da San Gallo), 13th-cent. town hall (houses art gall.), and fort. Suffered repeated air bombing in Second World War, with destruction or damage to over 950 houses.

Prato allo Stelvio (prä'tô äl'lô stĕl'vyô), Ger. *Prad,* village (pop. 1,262), Bolzano prov., Trentino-Alto Adige, N Italy, on Stelvio Pass road, 27 mi. WSW of Merano. Resort (alt. 3,002 ft.); packing boxes, balsam sachets. Formerly Prato in Venosta.

Prato in Toscana, Italy: see PRATO.

Pratola (prä'tôlä), village (pop. 1,903), Avellino prov., Campania, S Italy, 6 mi. NE of Avellino; mfg. (irrigation pumps, fireworks).

Pratola Peligna (pĕlē'nyä), town (pop. 9,637), Aquila prov., Abruzzi e Molise, S central Italy, 4 mi. NNW of Sulmona; wine, barrels, wagons, macaroni.

Pratomagno (prä"tōmä'nyô), spur of Etruscan Apennines, Tuscany, central Italy, E of Florence. Extends c.20 mi. N–S within loop formed by upper Arno R., bet. the Casentino (E) and Val d'Arno (W); rises to 5,223 ft. 13 mi. SE of Pontassieve. Served as strongest forward bastion of Ger. Gothic Line (1944) in Second World War.

Pratovecchio (prä"tôvĕk'kyô), town (pop. 1,466), Arezzo prov., Tuscany, central Italy, on the Arno and 22 mi. E of Florence, paper and woolen mills; lignite mining. Damaged in Second World War.

Prats de Llusanés (präts' dhā lūsänās'), town (pop. 1,410), Barcelona prov., NE Spain, 12 mi. SE of Berga; livestock, potatoes, fruit.

Prats-de-Mollo (prä-dŭ-môlō'), village (pop. 1,023), Pyrénées-Orientales dept., S France, in E Pyrenees, at W end of the VALLESPIR, near Sp. border, on Tech R. and 15 mi. WSW of Céret; road and rail terminal; sandal mfg., woodworking.

Pratt, county (□ 729; pop. 12,156), S Kansas; ⊙ Pratt. Gently rolling plain, drained by South Fork Ninnescah R. and Chikaskia R. Grain, livestock. Small gas and oil fields in E. Formed 1879.

Pratt. 1 City (pop. 7,523), ⊙ Pratt co., S Kansas, on South Fork Ninnescah R. and c.75 mi. W of Wichita; trade and shipping center, with railroad repair shops, for wheat area; flour and feed milling. Has jr. col. State fish hatchery near by. Inc. 1884. **2** Town (pop. 457), Kanawha co., W W.Va., 18 mi. SE of Charleston, in coal-mining region.

Pratteln (prä'tŭln), town (pop. 5,142), Basel-Land half-canton, N Switzerland, 5 mi. SE of Basel; chemicals, metal products, tires, foodstuffs; salt mines.

Prattmont, town (pop. 267), Autauga co., central Ala.

Prattsburg, village (pop. 653), Steuben co., W central N.Y., 29 mi. NNW of Corning; canned foods, flour.

Prattsville, resort village, Greene co., SE N.Y., in the Catskills, on Schoharie Reservoir, 29 mi. WNW of Catskill.

Prattville, city (pop. 4,385), ⊙ Autauga co., central Ala., 10 mi. NW of Montgomery; cotton and lumber milling, vegetable canning, cotton-gin mfg. Founded c.1835.

Prausnitz, Poland: see PRUSICE.

Praust, Poland: see PRUSZCZ.

Prauthoy (prōtwä'), agr. village (pop. 418), Haute-Marne dept., NE France, 13 mi. S of Langres.

Pravadia, Bulgaria: see PROVADIYA.

Prävali, Yugoslavia: see PREVALJE.

Pravarapura, Kashmir: see SRINAGAR.

Pravara River (prŭ'vŭrŭ), central Bombay, India, rises in Western Ghats W of Akola, flows 120 mi. E, past Sangamner and Belapur, to Godavari R. 8 mi. NE of Nevasa. Headworks of canal irrigation system 7 mi. E of Sangamner; left (N) canal extends 48 mi. ENE to point 3 mi. NW of Nevasa; right (S) canal extends 33 mi. ESE to point 7 mi. NE of Rahuri.

Pravda (präv'dŭ), town (1947 pop. over 500), S Sakhalin, Russian SFSR, on W coast railroad and 9 mi. SSW of Kholmsk; fisheries. Under Jap. rule (1905–45), called Hirochi.

Pravdino (–dyĭnŭ), village (1939 pop. 118), E Kaliningrad oblast, Russian SFSR, 6 mi. NE of Dobrovolsk; narrow-gauge rail junction. Until 1945, in East Prussia where it was called Grumbkowkeiten (grŏŏmp'kōkī"tŭn) and, later (c.1930–45), Grumbkowfelde (grŏŏmp'kōfĕl"dŭ).

Pravdinsk (präv'dyĭnsk). **1** Town (1939 pop. over 10,000), W Gorki oblast, Russian SFSR, on Volga R. just NW of Balakhna and on railroad; paper-milling center (principally newsprint). **2** City (1939 pop. 4,417), S Kaliningrad oblast, Russian SFSR, on Lyna R. (hydroelectric plant and dam; S) and 27 mi. SE of Kaliningrad; sawmilling; agr.; horse market. Has 14th-cent. town wall and church. Here French defeated Russians on June 14, 1807. Until 1945, in East Prussia and called Friedland (frēt'länt).

Pravdinski or **Pravdinskiy** (–skē), town (1941 pop. over 500), E central Moscow oblast, Russian SFSR, on railroad (Pravda station) and 3 mi. NNE of Pushkino; woodworking center (veneering, furniture mfg.); glassworks.

Pravi or **Pravion,** Greece: see ELEUTHEROUPOLIS.

Pravia (prä'vyä), town (pop. 1,573), Oviedo prov., NW Spain, on Nalón R. and 16 mi. NW of Oviedo; flour milling, dairy-products and candy mfg.; corn, potatoes, lumber, cattle.

Pravishta or **Pravista,** Greece: see ELEUTHEROUPOLIS.

Prawle Point, S extremity of Devon, England, on the Channel, 7 mi. SSE of Kingsbridge; 50°12'N 3°42'W.

Praxedis G. Guerrero (präksā'dēs hā' gĕrā'rō), town (pop. 1,700), Chihuahua, N Mexico, on Rio Grande and 38 mi. SE of Ciudad Juárez; cotton, grain, livestock. Formerly San Ignacio.

Prayag, India: see ALLAHABAD, city.

Prayssac (präsäk'), village (pop. 461), Lot dept., SW France, near the Lot, 13 mi. WNW of Cahors; felt mfg. Truffles, wine, tobacco.

Prayssas (präsäs'), village (pop. 355), Lot-et-Garonne dept., SW France, 8 mi. NW of Agen, in grape-growing area.

Praz, La, France: see FRENEY.

Praz, Les (lā prä'), Alpine village of Haute-Savoie dept., SE France, resort in Chamonix valley, 1.5 mi. NNE of Chamonix; alt. 3,494 ft. Winter sports.

Preanger (präăng'ŭr), region of W Java, Indonesia, extending c.150 mi. E–W, c.60 mi. N–S (from central area to S coast). Generally mountainous with many active and inactive volcanoes, including Gedeh, Salak, and Pangrango. Soil is generally very fertile (tea, rubber, coffee, cinchona, rice, corn, cassava). Textile milling is chief industry. Principal centers: Bandung, Bogor. Formerly area was Du. residency.

Preble (prĕ'bŭl), county (□ 428; pop. 27,081), W Ohio; ⊙ Eaton. Bounded W by Ind. line; drained by small Twin, Seven Mile, and Four Mile creeks and by East Fork of Whitewater R. Includes Fort St. Clair State Park near Eaton. Agr. area (livestock, tobacco, grain, fruit); mfg. at Eaton; limestone quarries; timber; nurseries. Formed 1808.

Preble, village (pop. 5,092), Brown co., E Wis., near Green Bay.

Preble, Fort, Maine: see SOUTH PORTLAND.

Prebuz, Czechoslovakia: see KRASLICE.

Prêcheur (prĕshûr'), town (pop. 935), NW Martinique, at W foot of Mont Pelée, 26 mi. NW of Fort-de-France; minor port; cacao growing; mfg. of lime juice and rum. Heavily damaged by Mont Pelée eruption (1902).

Prechistoye (pryĭchĕ'stŭyŭ). **1** Village (1939 pop. over 500), N Smolensk oblast, Russian SFSR, 33 mi. NNW of Yartsevo; flax. **2** Village (1926 pop. 529), NE Yaroslavl oblast, Russian SFSR, 17 mi. N of Danilov; flax, wheat.

Précigné (prāsēnyā'), village (pop. 986), Sarthe dept., W France, 12 mi. WNW of La Flèche; mfg. of explosives.

Précy-sous-Thil (prāsē'-sōō-tēl'), village (pop. 540), Côte-d'Or dept., E central France, on the Serein and 16 mi. S of Montbard; cattle, sheep.

Predappio (prĕdäp'pyô), town (pop. 1,188), Forlì prov., Emilia-Romagna, N central Italy, on Rabbi R. (branch of Montone R.) and 8 mi. SSW of Forlì; furniture making. Mussolini b. in Dovia, a suburb. Formerly Predappio Nuova.

Predazzo (prĕdä'tsô), town (pop. 3,150), Trento prov., Trentino-Alto Adige, N Italy, on Avisio R. and 18 mi. SE of Bolzano, in Val di Fiemme. Summer resort (alt. 3,327 ft.) and winter-sports center. Has schools for Alpine customs officers and for lacemaking.

Predeal (prĕdyäl'), town (1948 pop. 2,568), Stalin prov., S central Rumania, in the Transylvanian Alps, on Prahova R., on railroad and 12 mi. N of Sinaia; summer and winter-sports resort (alt. 3,608 ft.) just W of the Predeal Pass; also lumbering, stone quarrying. Has meteorological observatory. Yearly ski competitions are held here and at near-by health resort of Timis (Rum. *Timiş*), 2 mi. N.

Predeal Pass (alt. 3,280 ft.), in the Transylvanian Alps, SW central Rumania, E of the Bucegi Mts., 8 mi. N of Sinaia; major rail and highway corridor bet. Walachia and Transylvania. Sometimes called Timis or Tömös pass. Prahova R. rises here just SW.

Predel Pass (prĕ'dĕl) (alt. 3,647 ft.), SW Bulgaria, bet. Pirin and Rila mts., 5 mi. W of Razlog, on highway to Simitli.

Predgornoye (pryĭdgôr'nŭyŭ). **1** Village (1939 pop. over 2,000), NW East Kazakhstan oblast, Kazakh SSR, on railroad and 26 mi. NW of Ust-Kamenogorsk; lead-silver mines. **2** Village (1926 pop. 5,639), S Grozny oblast, Russian SFSR, on Argun R. and 13 mi. SSE of Grozny; corn, wheat, livestock. Lumbering (S). Until 1944, Starye Atagi.

Predil Pass (prĕdēl') (alt. 3,793 ft.), in Julian Alps, on Italo-Yugoslav border, 6 mi. S of Tarvisio, Italy. Crossed by road bet. Tarvisio and Bovec (Yugoslavia).

Predivinsk (pryĭdyē'vĭnsk), town (1933 pop. 5,200), S Krasnoyarsk Territory, Russian SFSR, on Yenisei R. and 70 mi. NNE of Krasnoyarsk; shipbuilding.

Predmosti, Czech *Předmostí* Ger. *Predmost* (pŭrzhĕd' môstyē), village (pop. 1,701), central Moravia, Czechoslovakia, on right bank of Becva R., just NNW of and across from Prerov. Near-by caves are famous as site of extensive paleolithic finds consisting of mammoth bones, stone implements, and human remains.

Preeceville, agr. village (pop. 540), E Sask., on Assiniboine R. and 50 mi. NNW of Yorkton.

Preenkuln, Latvia: see PRIEKULE.

Pré-en-Pail (prā-ā-pī'), village (pop. 1,135), Mayenne dept., W France, at foot of Mont des Avaloirs, 13 mi. W of Alençon; hardware mfg., woodworking.

Preesall, urban district (1931 pop. 2,043; 1951 census 2,231), W Lancashire, England, 2 mi. E of Fleetwood; agr. market for dairy-farming, wheat- and potato-growing region.

Preetz (prāts), town (pop. 11,603), in Schleswig-Holstein, NW Germany, 8 mi. SE of Kiel, on a small lake; mfg. of auto bodies, machinery, tar products, leather goods; meat processing, flour milling, brewing, malting. Former Benedictine nunnery (founded 1226) now houses Protestant sisterhood; has 13th-cent. church.

Pregel River (prā'gŭl), Rus. also *Pregel'* (prĕ'gĭl), formerly in East Prussia, chief river of Kaliningrad oblast, Russian SFSR, formed just below Chernyakhovsk by union of Inster and Angerapp rivers; flows 78 mi. W, past Znamensk and Gvardeisk, to Vistula Lagoon below Kaliningrad. Navigable in entire course, which is partly canalized. Length, including Angerapp headstream, c.180 mi. Receives Lyna R. (left). Canalized Deima R., Ger. *Deime* (dī'mŭ), flows 25 mi. from the Pregel at Gvardeisk to Courland Lagoon below Polessk.

Pregonero (prāgōnā'rō), town (pop. 1,671), Táchira state, W Venezuela, in Andean spur, 37 mi. ENE of San Cristóbal; coffee, grain, cattle.

Pregrada (prĕ'grädä), village (pop. 1,302), N Croatia, Yugoslavia, 25 mi. N of Zagreb, near Slovenia border, in coal area; local trade center. Castle ruins.

Pregradnaya (pryĭgräd'nīŭ), village (1926 pop. 4,431), SW Cherkess Autonomous Oblast, Stavropol Territory, Russian SFSR, on upper Urup R. and 45 mi. SW of Cherkessk; grain, livestock; lumbering. Until 1944, in Karachai Autonomous Oblast.

Preguiça, Cape Verde Isls.: see SÃO NICOLAU ISLAND.

Preignac (prĕnyäk'), village (pop. 1,043), Gironde dept., SW France, on left bank of the Garonne near mouth of Ciron R. and 22 mi. SE of Bordeaux; noted for its sauterne wines; sawmills, tile factory.

Preila or **Preyla** (prā'lä), Ger. *Preil,* seaside resort (1941 pop. 188), W Lithuania, on Courland Spit, 25 mi. S of Memel. In Memel Territory, 1920–39.

Preili or **Preyli** (prā'lē), Lettish *Preiļi,* Ger. *Preli,* city (pop. 1,662), SE Latvia, in Latgale, 30 mi. NNE of Daugavpils, in flax area; tanning, wool processing. In Rus. Vitebsk govt. until 1920.

Preissac (prĕsăk'), village, W Que., near N End of Kewagama L., 15 mi. SW of Amos; molybdenite and bismuth mining.

Prekkak (prĕk'käk'), village, Kompong Cham prov., SE Cambodia, on right bank of Mekong R. and 17 mi. NNE of Kompong Cham; lumber shipping.

Prekmurje (prĕk'mōōryĕ), region, NE Slovenia, Yugoslavia; bounded by Mura R. (S), Austrian frontier (NW), and Hung. frontier (NE). Chief village, MURSKA SOBOTA. Also called Prekomurje and Prekumurje. Until 1920, the region was in Vas co., Hungary.

Preksantek or **Preksandek** (prĕk'sän'tĕk, –dĕk), town, Preyveng prov., S Cambodia, 35 mi. NE of Pnompenh; rice, corn, tobacco; sericulture and fisheries.

Prekule, Latvia: see PRIEKULE.

Prekule, Lithuania: see PRIEKULE.

Prekumurje, region, Yugoslavia: see PREKMURJE.

Prelate, village (pop. 474), SW Sask., near South Saskatchewan R., 45 mi. SSW of Kindersley; wheat.

Preli, Latvia: see PREILI.

Prelog (prĕ'lôk), Hung. *Perlak* (pĕr'lôk), village (pop. 4,209), N Croatia, Yugoslavia, on Drava R. and 13 mi. E of Varazdin, in the Medjumurje; trade center for winegrowing region.

Prelouc (pûrzhĕ'lōch), Czech *Přelouč*, Ger. *Pschelautsch* (pshä'louch), town (pop. 4,228), E Bohemia, Czechoslovakia, on Elbe R., on railroad and 10 mi. W of Pardubice; mfg. of radio parts. Hydroelectric power station. Has 13th-cent. church. Manganese and graphite mined at Chvaletice (khvä'lĕtyĭtsĕ), Ger. *Chwaletitz*, 5 mi. WSW.

Premana (prĕmä'nä), village (pop. 1,365), Como prov., Lombardy, N Italy, 14 mi. NNE of Lecco; cutlery mfg.

Prémeaux (prāmō'), village (pop. 344), Côte-d'Or dept., E central France, on E slope of the Côte d'Or, 8 mi. NE of Beaune; Burgundy wines.

Prémery (prāmûrē'), village (pop. 1,508), Nièvre dept., central France, in Nivernais Hills, 15 mi. NE of Nevers; wood alcohol distilling. Cattle and lumber market. Has 13th–14th-cent. church.

Prëmet or **Prëmeti,** Albania: see PËRMET.

Premiá de Mar (prāmyä' dhä mär'), village (pop. 3,416), Barcelona prov., NE Spain, on the Mediterranean, 12 mi. NE of Barcelona; mfg. (cotton, linen, woolen textiles, soda water), fishing; ships potatoes, wine, hazelnuts, fruit.

Premier, village (pop. estimate 400), NW B.C., on Alaska border, 100 mi. ESE of Wrangell; gold, silver, lead mining.

Premier Group, short range of high peaks of Rocky Mts., SE B.C., 70 mi. W of Jasper, overlooking Fraser R. valley. Highest elevation is Mt. Sir Wilfrid Laurier (11,750 ft.).

Premier Mine, U. of So. Afr.: see CULLINAN.

Premnitz (prĕm'nĭts), town (pop. 6,387), Brandenburg, E Germany, on the Havel and 5 mi. S of Rathenow; rayon milling, chemical mfg.

Prémont, France: see ORELLE.

Premont (prēmŏnt'), town (pop. 2,619), Jim Wells co., S Texas, c.55 mi. SW of Corpus Christi; shipping point in agr. area. At La Gloria (just S) is natural-gas recycling plant. Inc. 1938.

Premuda Island (prĕ'mōōdä), Dalmatian island in Adriatic Sea, W Croatia, Yugoslavia, 35 mi. NW of Zadar; 5 mi. long, less than 1 mi. wide. Chief village, Premuda.

Pren, Yugoslavia: see PRENJ.

Prenai or **Prenay,** Lithuania: see PRIENAI.

Prenj, Pren, or **Pren'** (prĕ'nyŭ), mountain in Dinaric Alps, N Herzegovina, Yugoslavia; c.10 mi. long N–S; bounded on 3 sides by Neretva R. Highest peak (6,895 ft.) is 9 mi. SSW of Konjic.

Prentice, village (pop. 477), Price co., N Wis., 43 mi. W of Rhinelander, in wooded area; dairy and farm products. Has several cooperatives.

Prentiss, county (□ 418; pop. 19,810), NE Miss.; ⊙ Booneville. Drained by East Fork of the Tombigbee and Tuscumbia R. Agr. (cotton, corn, hay); lumbering. Clay deposits. Formed 1870.

Prentiss. 1 Plantation (pop. 315), Penobscot co., E central Maine, 35 mi. SE of Millinocket, in agr., lumbering area. **2** Town (pop. 1,212), ⊙ Jefferson Davis co., S central Miss., 39 mi. WNW of Hattiesburg; cotton, lumber.

Preny, Lithuania: see PRIENAI.

Prenzlau (prĕnts'lou), town (1939 pop. 26,868; 1946 pop. 17,669), Brandenburg, E Germany, on Uecker R., at N end of Lower Uecker L., and 30 mi. WSW of Stettin; sugar refining, iron casting, woolen and paper milling; mfg. of machinery, leather, cigars, margarine. Power station. Heavily bombed in Second World War (destruction c.80%). First mentioned 1183; chartered 1234; passed from Pomerania to Brandenburg in 1250. Scene (Oct., 1806) of French victory over Prussians.

Prenzlauer Berg (prĕnts'lou"ŭr bĕrk"), workers' residential district (1939 pop. 298,025; 1946 pop. 250,960), NE central Berlin, Germany. Mfg. (clothing, food products). After 1945 in Soviet sector.

Preobrazhenskaya, Russian SFSR: see KIKVIDZE.

Preobrazhenskoye, Kirghiz SSR: see TYUP.

Preparis Channels (prĕ'pûrĭs), 2 channels—Preparis North and Preparis South—connecting Bay of Bengal and Andaman Sea, bet. SW Burma and N Andaman Isls., N and S of Preparis Isl. (lies at 14°52'N 93°40'E).

Prerov (pûrzhĕ'rôf), Czech *Přerov*, Ger. *Prerau* (prä'rou), city (pop. 21,041), central Moravia, Czechoslovakia, on left bank of Becva R. and 13 mi. SE of Olomouc; rail junction (railroad workshops); mfg. center (machinery, optical equipment, precision instruments, furniture, woolens, fertilizers, medicine, bags); beer and malt production; sugar refining; large electrical plants. Has botanical gardens. Its 16th-cent. castle (today a mus. with prehistoric collections from Predmosti) was seat of King Matthias Corvinus in 15th cent.

Pré-Saint-Didier (prā-sē-dēdyā'), village (pop. 119), Val d'Aosta region, NW Italy, on Dora Baltea R., at foot of Mont Blanc, and 16 mi. WNW of Aosta; rail terminus. Resort (alt. 3,280 ft.) with baths.

Pré-Saint-Gervais, Le (lŭ prā-sē-zhĕrvā'), town (pop. 14,691), Seine dept., N central France, NE of Paris, 3 mi. from Notre Dame Cathedral, bet. Pantin (N) and Les Lilas (SE); mfg. (bicycle parts, custom jewelry, toys, aluminum furniture, cartons, pharmaceuticals).

Presanella, La (lä prĕsänĕl'lä), glacier-topped N arm of ADAMELLO mtn. group, N Italy, from which it is separated by upper Sarca R. Highest peak, Cima Presanella (11,666 ft.), is 8 mi. ESE of Ponte di Legno.

Presba, Lake, S Europe: see PRESPA, LAKE.

Prescot (prĕ'skŭt), urban district (1931 pop. 9,399; 1951 census 12,474), SW Lancashire, England, 7 mi. E of Liverpool; metalworking; mfg. of electric cables, watches. Site of Liverpool reservoirs. Has 13th-cent. church.

Prescott (prĕ'skŭt), county (□ 494; pop. 25,261), SE Ont., on Ottawa R. and on Que. border; ⊙ L'Orignal.

Prescott, town (pop. 3,223), chief town of Grenville co., SE Ont., on the St. Lawrence, at head of navigation for large lake steamers, and 50 mi. S of Ottawa, opposite Ogdensburg, N.Y.; silk milling, woodworking, distilling; mfg. of hats, tools; grain elevators. Fort Wellington (mus.) was important in War of 1812. At near-by Windmill Point the British in 1814 repulsed the attack, by a large force under James Wilkinson, of the Lacolle mill (now a lighthouse).

Prescott. 1 City (pop. 6,764), ⊙ Yavapai co., central Ariz., 80 mi. NNW of Phoenix; alt. 5,346 ft. Industrial and trade center for mining (gold, silver, copper, lead, zinc), stock-raising and agr. area. Resort center, hq. of Prescott Natl. Forest, site of annual summer rodeo (begun 1888; 1st public rodeo in U.S.) and annual (Aug.) "Smoki" ceremonials. Archaeological and historical museums here. Founded 1864 near Fort Whipple (now a Veterans Administration hosp.); territorial capital 1864–67, 1877–89. **2** City (pop. 3,960), ⊙ Nevada co., SW Ark., c.45 mi. NE of Texarkana; market center for peach-growing region; also cotton, corn. Settled 1873. **3** Town (pop. 372), Adams co., SW Iowa, on East Nodaway R. and 13 mi. W of Creston; feed. **4** City (pop. 283), Linn co., SE Kansas, near Mo. line, 15 mi. N of Fort Scott; agr. **5** Village (pop. 281), Ogemaw co., NE central Mich., 21 mi. WSW of Tawas City. **6** City (pop. 119), Columbia co., NW Oregon, on Columbia R. and 15 mi. NNW of St. Helens. **7** Town (pop. 244), Walla Walla co., SE Wash., 15 mi. N of Walla Walla and on Touchet R., in agr. region. **8** City (pop. 1,005), Pierce co., W Wis., opposite Hastings (Minn.), at confluence of the St. Croix and the Mississippi, in stock-raising and dairying area; boat yards, seed-corn warehouses, dairy plants.

Preservation Inlet, bay of Tasman Sea, Fiordland Natl. Park, SW S.Isl., New Zealand; 35 mi. long, 4 mi. wide; contains several islets. Puysegur Point is at entrance.

Presevo or **Preshevo** (both: prĕ'shĕvô), Serbo-Croatian *Preševo*, village (pop. 9,011), S Serbia, Yugoslavia, on railroad and 22 mi. SSW of Vranje, near Macedonia border, at E foot of Crna Gora.

Presho (prĕ'shō), city (pop. 712), Lyman co., S central S.Dak., 34 mi. SSE of Pierre and on Medicine Creek; trading point for productive wheat area; grain, livestock, poultry, dairy products.

Presicce (prĕzēt'chĕ), town (pop. 5,181), Lecce prov., Apulia, S Italy, 19 mi. SE of Gallipoli; wine, olive oil.

Presidencia de la Plaza (prāsēdĕn'syä dā lä plä'sä), town (1947 pop. 2,285), ⊙ Martínez de Hoz dept. (pop. 26,536), S central Chaco prov., Argentina, on railroad and 65 mi. NW of Resistencia. Cotton-growing, stock-raising, lumbering center; sawmills, cotton gins. Until early 1940s called Presidente de la Plaza.

Presidencia Roque Sáenz Peña (rō'kä sä'ĕns pä'-nyä), city (pop. 23,099), ⊙ Napalpí dept., S central Chaco natl. territory, Argentina, on railroad and 90 mi. WNW of Resistencia; agr. and processing center. Cotton ginning, meat packing; cotton, corn, sunflowers, spurge, tobacco, livestock. Lumbering of quebracho, carob, guaiacum, and guava trees. Airport, seismographic station.

Presidency, former administrative division (□ 16,-402; pop. 12,817,087), S Bengal, Br. India; ⊙ was Calcutta; comprised Calcutta, Jessore, Khulna, Murshidabad, Nadia, and 24-Parganas dists. In 1947 divided bet. West Bengal (India) and East Bengal (E Pakistan).

Presidente Alves (prĭzĕdĕn'tĭ äl'vĭs), city (pop. 1,595), W central São Paulo, Brazil, on railroad and 28 mi. NW of Bauru; coffee and cotton processing.

Presidente Bernardes (bĕrnär'dĭs), city (pop. 3,166), W São Paulo, Brazil, on railroad and 13 mi. WNW of Presidente Prudente, in coffee zone; woodworking, soap mfg., distilling.

Presidente de la Plaza, Argentina: see PRESIDENCIA DE LA PLAZA.

Presidente Dutra (dōō'trŭ), city (pop. 918), central Maranhão, Brazil, 24 mi. NNW of Colinas; cotton, sugar, babassu nuts. Road to Coroatá. Until 1948, called Curador.

Presidente Epitácio (ĭpĕtä'syōō), city (pop. 783), W São Paulo, Brazil, on Paraná R. opposite influx of the Rio Pardo, and 50 mi. WNW of Presidente Prudente; W terminus of railroad serving Sorocabana region. Transshipment point for navigation on Paraná R. Boat landing of Pôrto Tibiriça is 3 mi. SW.

Presidente Hayes (prāsēdĕn'tā ä'yĕs), department (□ 22,579; pop. 14,813), central and W Paraguay, in the Chaco; ⊙ Villa Hayes. Bounded by the Río Verde (N), Paraguay R. (E), and Pilcomayo R. (S and W, Argentina border). Low, marshy grasslands are intersected by sluggish rivers. (e.g., Río Confuso) and swamps. Has humid, almost tropical, climate. Fertile agr. area, in SE near Paraguay R., produces mostly sugar cane; also corn, cotton, alfalfa, tobacco, peanuts. Cattle and horse raising. Alcohol distilleries and sugar refineries at Villa Hayes. The dept., set up 1944 out of Paraguayan Chaco, was named after the Amer. President Rutherford B. Hayes, arbiter in boundary dispute bet. Paraguay and Argentina after War of the Triple Alliance (1865–70).

Presidente Marques, Brazil: see ABUNÃ.

Presidente Olegário (prĭzĕdĕn'tĭ ōōlĭgä'ryōō), city (pop. 1,453), W Minas Gerais, Brazil, 10 mi. NE of Patos de Minas; cattle.

Presidente Penna, Brazil: see RONDÔNIA.

Presidente Prudente (prōōdĕn'tĭ), city (1950 pop. 27,312), W São Paulo, Brazil, on railroad and 300 mi. WNW of São Paulo; commercial and processing center of coffee zone—known as the Sorocabana region—extending over 150 mi. along watershed bet. Peixe (N) and Paranapanema (S) rivers. Produces dairy and flour products, agr. machinery, tile, pottery, beverages. Ships coffee, timber, fruit, corn.

Presidente Roque Sáenz Peña, department, Argentina: see LABOULAYE.

Presidente Vargas. 1 Town, Maranhão, Brazil: see AURIZONA. **2** City, Minas Gerais, Brazil: see ITABIRA. **3** City, Minas Gerais, Brazil: see NOVA ERA.

Presidente Venceslau (vĕnsĭslou'), city (pop. 4,002), W São Paulo, Brazil, on railroad and 34 mi. WNW of Presidente Prudente; sawmilling, coffee and cotton processing, distilling. Formerly spelled Presidente Wenceslau.

Presidential Range, N central N.H., range of the WHITE MOUNTAINS, lying NE of Saco R. and in White Mtn. Natl. Forest. From NE to SW, summits are Mt. Madison (5,363 ft.), Mt. Adams (5,798 ft.), Mt. Jefferson (5,715 ft.), Mt. Clay (5,532 ft.), Mt. WASHINGTON (6,288 ft.; highest peak in state), Mt. Monroe (5,385 ft.), Mt. Franklin (5,004 ft.), Mt. Pleasant (4,761 ft.), Mt. Pierce or Clinton (4,310 ft.), Mt. Jackson (4,052 ft.), and Mt. Webster (3,910 ft.). Small Star L. (alt. 4,900 ft.) lies bet. Mounts Adams and Madison; the 2 Lakes of the Clouds (alt. c.5,000 ft.) lie on slope of Mt. Washington.

Presidio (prûsĭ'dēō, -sē'-), county (□ 3,877; pop. 7,354), extreme W Texas; ⊙ Marfa. Fourth-largest co. in state; in the Big Bend, with Rio Grande (here forming Mex. border) on W and S. High broken plateau (alt. 2,400–7,730 ft.), with mts.: Sierra Vieja (NW), Chinati Mts. (W). Large-scale ranching (cattle, sheep, goats); some irrigated agr. in Rio Grande valley (cotton, grain, truck); silver mines. Scenery attracts tourists; hunting. Formed 1850.

Presidio, Calif., name of 2 U.S. Army posts, at MONTEREY city and at SAN FRANCISCO.

Presidio, village (1940 pop. 1,363), Presidio co., extreme W Texas, on the Rio Grande opposite mouth of Conchos R. and opposite Ojinaga, Mexico, c.60 mi. SW of Marfa; internatl. rail point and port of entry; imports Mex. timber. Shipping point for irrigated agr. (truck, cotton) and ranching area. Sp. mission founded here 1684. Old Fort Leaton (lē'tŭn) (built 1849; restored) is here.

Presidio River (prāsē'dyō), Sinaloa, W Mexico, rises in Sierra Madre Occidental in Durango, flows c.100 mi. SW through fertile coastal lowlands, past Concepción, Siqueros, and Villa Unión, to the Pacific 12 mi. SE of Mazatlán.

Preslav (prĕslăf'), city (pop. 4,114), Kolarovgrad dist., E Bulgaria, 10 mi. SSW of Kolarovgrad; rail terminus; agr. center; wine making; fruit, swine. Has mus., old churches, and ruins of fortress. Founded 821 by Turks; became ⊙ Bulgaria under Bulg. tsar Simeon the Great in 10th cent. Called Yeski Stambolluk or Eski Stambul under Turkish rule (15th–19th cent.). Just S are Preslav Mts., a N outlier of E Balkan Mts.; cut through by Golyama Kamchiya R.

Presnogorkovka or **Presnogor'kovka** (pryĕsnŭgôr'-kŭfkŭ), village (1948 pop. over 2,000), NE Kustanai oblast, Kazakh SSR, 50 mi. S of Lebyazhye; wheat, cattle.

Presnovka (pryĭsnôf'kŭ), village (1948 pop. over 2,000), NW North Kazakhstan oblast, Kazakh SSR, 80 mi. W of Petropavlovsk; cattle; metalworks.

Presov (prĕ'shôf), Slovak *Prešov*, Hung. *Eperjes* (ĕ'pĕryĕs), town (pop. 18,932), ⊙ Presov prov. (□ 3,280; pop. 448,358), E Slovakia, Czechoslovakia, on Torysa R. and 195 mi. NE of Bratislava; 49°N 21°10'E. Rail junction; trading center; specializes in distilling, linen mfg., lace making. Orthodox bishopric. Has 13th-cent. church, 15th-cent. buildings, mementoes of Turkish occupation (16th cent.). Founded in 12th cent.; devastated in 1887 by a great fire. Ruins of Saris (shä'rĭsh), Slovak *Šariš*, castle, important in 15th cent., are 5 mi. NW. Famous milky opals mined at Dubnik (dŏŏb'nyĕk), Slovak *Dubník*, 12 mi. SE.

Presov Mountains, Czechoslovakia: see TOKAJ-EPERJES MOUNTAINS.

Prespa, Lake (prĕ'spä), Albanian *Ligen i Prespës*, Greek *Limni Megale* (or *Megali*) *Prespa*, Serbo-Croatian *Prespansko Jezero*, anc. *Vrygeis*, highest lake (□ 112; alt. 2,798 ft.) in the Balkans, on border of Yugoslavia, Albania, and Greece; 18 mi. long, 8 mi. wide; 177 ft. deep. Located largely in Macedonia (Yugoslavia), it sends a SW inlet into Albania, and, in Greece, is separated by a narrow 1.5-mi.-long sandspit from LITTLE PRESPA LAKE. Important fisheries (mainly carp). Fed by subterranean streams, it is linked by underground channels with L. Ochrida and upper Devoll R. basin. Sometimes spelled Presba.

Presque Isle (prĕsk ēl'), county (□ 654; pop. 11,996), NE Mich.; ⊙ Rogers City. Bounded NE by L. Huron; drained by Black, Rainy, and short Ocqueoc rivers, and by the North Branch of Thunder Bay R. Dairying and agr. area (livestock, potatoes, fruit). Mfg. at Rogers City and Onaway. Limestone quarries, fisheries. Resorts. Fishing in Grand, Long, and Black lakes. Co. has state forests and state parks. Organized 1875.

Presque Isle. 1 (prĕsk īl') City (pop. 9,954), Aroostook co., NE Maine, on Aroostook R. and 40 mi. N of Houlton, near N.B. line. Trade, processing, shipping center for agr. area. (esp. potatoes; oats, hay); mfg. (wood products, farm machinery, fertilizer). State normal school, agr. experiment station, and Aroostook State Park. Site of large U.S. air base (begun 1941) in Second World War. Settled c.1820, inc. 1859, city 1939. **2** (prĕsk ēl') Resort village (pop. c.150), Presque Isle co., NE Mich., 16 mi. N of Alpena, on narrow strip of land separating Grand L. (W) from L. Huron. Lighthouse near by.

Presque Isle (prĕsk īl'), NW Pa., small peninsula (6 mi. long, ⅛–⅜ mi. wide) in L. Erie; encloses Presque Isle Bay, harbor of city of Erie, Pa. Reconstructed blockhouse here, commemorating fort built 1753 by French, is in state park.

Presque Isle River (prĕsk ēl'), W Upper Peninsula, Mich., rises in small lakes at Wis. line, flows c.50 mi. NNW, past Marenisco, to L. Superior in N Gogebic co. Falls and a recreational park are near its mouth.

Presque Isle Stream (prĕsk īl'), Aroostook co., NE Maine, rises N of Houlton, flows c.35 mi. N and E to the Aroostook near Presque Isle.

Presquile River (prĕskīl'), in E Maine and N.B., rises S of Fort Fairfield, flows SSE to St. John R.

Pressana (prĕs-sä'nä), village (pop. 772), Verona prov., Veneto, N Italy, 8 mi. NNE of Legnago; agr. machinery.

Pressath (prĕ'sät), town (pop. 4,744), Upper Palatinate, NE Bavaria, Germany, on small Heidenab R. and 12 mi. NW of Weiden; metal- and woodworking. Chartered before 1317.

Pressbaum (prĕs'boum), town (pop. 4,604), E Lower Austria, 12 mi. W of Vienna; reservoir.

Pressburg, Czechoslovakia: see BRATISLAVA.

Presseck (prĕ'sĕk), village (pop. 1,155), Upper Franconia, NE Bavaria, Germany, in Franconian Forest, 10 mi. NNE of Kulmbach; shoe mfg., woodworking, tanning, weaving.

Pressmen's Home, village, Hawkins co., NE Tenn., 6 mi. NNW of Rogersville; sanatorium, trade school, home for printers here.

Pressnitz, Czechoslovakia: see PRISECNICE.

Prestatyn (prĕstă'tĭn), urban district (1931 pop. 4,512; 1951 census 8,809), Flint, on Irish Sea, 13 mi. NW of Flint; seaside resort at N end of Offa's Dyke. Recent excavations show that it was important glass and pottery center in Roman times.

Prestbury, residential town and parish (pop. 2,154), N central Gloucester, England, 2 mi. NE of Cheltenham. Has church dating from 13th cent. and 16th-cent. mansion.

Prestea (prĕ'stä'ä), town, Western Prov., SW Gold Coast colony, on Ankobra R. and 15 mi. NW of Tarkwa (linked by rail); gold-mining center.

Presteign or **Presteigne** (prĕstēn'), urban district (1931 pop. 1,102; 1951 census 1,257), ⊙ Radnorshire, Wales, in E part of co., on Lugg R. and 20 mi. NW of Hereford; agr. market. Has 15th-cent. church and 17th-cent. half-timbered inn.

Prestice (pûrzhĕ'shtyĭtsĕ), Czech *Přeštice*, Ger. *Pschestitz* (pshĕ'shtĭts), town (pop. 4,199), SW Bohemia, Czechoslovakia, on Uhlava R., on railroad and 12 mi. SSW of Pilsen, in rye- and oat-growing and iron-mining region. Has 10th-cent. church. Near by are 18th-cent. castle ruins.

Presto (prä'stō), town (pop. c.4,000), Chuquisaca dept., S central Bolivia, 20 mi. NW of Zudañez; wheat, corn, vegetables.

Preston, municipality (pop. 46,775), S Victoria, Australia, 5 mi. NNE of Melbourne, in metropolitan area; in agr., sheep region; tannery.

Preston, town (pop. 6,704), S Ont., on Grand R., at mouth of Speed R., and 9 mi. ESE of Kitchener; resort, with sulphur springs; woolen and flour milling, machinery mfg.

Preston (prä'stōn), town (pop. 4,303), Oriente prov., E Cuba, on E shore of Nipe Bay, 40 mi. E of Holguín; sugar-milling center. Ships iron ore.

Preston. 1 County borough (1931 pop. 119,001; 1951 census 119,243), W central Lancashire, England, port on Ribble R. and 28 mi. NW of Manchester; 53°46'N 2°42'W; textile industry (cotton spinning, weaving, and printing); engineering (textile and agr. machinery, electrical equipment); leather tanning; mfg. of shoes, pharmaceuticals, chemicals, asphalt, biscuits, chocolate. Port is accessible to seagoing ships. Site of Lancashire's 1st cotton mill, built 1791 by John Horrocks; birthplace (1732) of Richard Arkwright, inventor of the spinning machine. Scene of foundation of temperance movement. It was capital of the anc. duchy of Lancaster, was sacked by Robert the Bruce in 1323, and suffered in the Civil War and the Jacobite risings of 1715 and 1745. Has Gothic town hall designed by Sir Gilbert Scott and completed in 1867. **2** Suburb, Sussex, England: see BRIGHTON.

Preston, agr. village in Prestonkirk parish, N East Lothian, Scotland, on Tyne R. and 5 mi. W of Dunbar. Has remains of 15th-cent. Preston Tower.

Preston, county (□ 645; pop. 31,399), N W.Va.; ⊙ Kingwood. On Allegheny Plateau; includes part of Laurel Ridge and other mts. Bounded N by Pa., E by Md.; drained by Cheat R. Includes a small part of Monongahela Natl. Forest. Agr. (dairy products, poultry, truck); coal mining; lumbering; limestone quarrying. Formed 1818.

Preston. 1 Town (pop. 1,775), New London co., SE Conn., on Quinebaug R., just E of Norwich; farming, resorts. Seat of Norwich State Hosp. for mental defectives. Settled c.1650, inc. 1687. **2** Town (pop. 260), ⊙ Webster co., W Ga., on Kinchafoonee R. and 17 mi. W of Americus; sawmilling. **3** City (pop. 4,045), ⊙ Franklin co., SE Idaho, on small tributary of Bear R. and 60 mi. SE of Pocatello, near Utah line; alt. 4,714 ft. Commercial center for livestock and irrigated agr. area (sugar beets, peas); beet sugar, dairy products, flour. Settled 1866 by Mormons, platted 1885, inc. 1913. **4** Town (pop. 684), Jackson co., E Iowa, 14 mi. E of Maquoketa; feed milling. **5** City (pop. 307), Pratt co., S Kansas, 13 mi. NE of Pratt, in wheat and grain region, natural gas. **6** Town (pop. 353), Caroline co., E Md., 14 mi. NE of Cambridge, in truck-farm area; canneries. **7** Village (pop. 1,399), ⊙Fillmore co., SE Minn., on branch of Root R., near Iowa line, and 31 mi. SE of Rochester; livestock-shipping point in diversified-farming area; dairy products, flour, poultry. Courthouse built 1863. **8** Town (pop. 109), Hickory co., cen ral Mo., 5 mi. W of Hermitage. **9** Village (pop. 81), Richardson co., extreme SE Nebr., just E of Falls City, near Missouri R. and Kansas line. **10** Village, Pa.: see HAVERFORD.

Preston, Lake, Kingsbury co., E S.Dak.; 5 mi. long, 1 mi. wide; city of Lake Preston at S end.

Preston Brook, England: see PRESTON-ON-THE-HILL.

Prestonhall, Scotland: see CUPAR.

Preston Hollow, Dallas co., N Texas, NW suburb annexed by Dallas, 1945.

Preston-on-the-Hill, parish (pop. 355), N Cheshire, England. Includes village of Preston Brook, on Bridgewater Canal and 5 mi. SSW of Warrington; leather tanning.

Prestonpans (prĕs'tŭnpănz'), burgh (1931 pop. 2,426; 1951 census 2,907), W East Lothian, Scotland, on Firth of Forth, 9 mi. E of Edinburgh; small port with coal mines, breweries, and mfg. of soap, salt, pottery, brick, fireclay; also seaside resort. Salt production was formerly major industry. In 1745 the Young Pretender (Prince Charles Edward) routed English forces under Sir John Cope at battle of Prestonpans.

Preston Peak, Calif.: see SISKIYOU MOUNTAINS.

Prestonsburg, town (pop. 3,585), ⊙ Floyd co., E Ky., in Cumberland foothills, on Levisa Fork and 20 mi. NW of Pikeville, in bituminous-coal-mining and agr. (corn, truck) area; produces artificial dentures, soft drinks; lumber. Has airport. In surrounding mtn. region live many kin to participants in Hatfield-McCoy feud. Settled 1791. Civil War battle of Middle Creek was fought near by, on Jan. 10, 1862; Union forces claimed the victory.

Prestonville, town (pop. 166), Carroll co., N Ky., on the Ohio at mouth of Kentucky R., opposite Carrollton.

Prestwich (prĕst'wĭch), residential municipal borough (1931 pop. 23,881; 1951 census 34,387), SE Lancashire, England, 4 mi. NNW of Manchester; cotton milling. Site of 2 Manchester reservoirs and of county mental hosp. Has 15th-cent. church.

Prestwick, burgh (1931 pop. 8,538; 1951 census 11,386), W Ayrshire, Scotland, on Firth of Clyde, 28 mi. SSW of Glasgow and just NNE of Ayr; seaside resort with well-known golf course. The international airport (55°30'N 4°38'W), 2d largest in Great Britain, was built during Second World War as ferry and transport base for U.S. Air Force; civil airport since 1946. There are aircraft conversion and repair works. Town has 12th-cent. market cross.

Presumpscot River, SW Maine, rises in Sebago L., Cumberland co.; flows c.22 mi. SSE, past Westbrook (water power), then NE and E to the Atlantic at Falmouth.

Prêto, Rio (rē'ŏŏ prä'tŏŏ). **1** River in NW Bahia, Brazil, rises in the Serra Geral de Goiás, flows c.200 mi. ESE to the Rio Grande at 11°25'S 43°48'W. Navigable below São Marcelo. Its headwaters merge along Goiás border with waters of Somno R. draining W to the Tocantins. **2** River in the Serra da Mantiqueira, SE Brazil, flows 90 mi. along Minas Gerais–Rio de Janeiro border to the Paraibuna 10 mi. NW of Três Rios.

Pretoria (prĭtô'rēü), city (pop. 168,058; including suburbs 244,887), administrative ⊙ U. of So. Afr. and ⊙ Transvaal, in S central part of prov., 30 mi. NNE of Johannesburg; 25°45'S 28°12'E; alt. 4,593 ft.; rail center. Govt. offices and diplomatic missions are located here, and Pretoria is residence of cabinet ministers when Parliament is not in session at Cape Town. There are numerous govt. bldgs., including Union Bldg. (1913), designed by Sir Herbert Baker; Palace of Justice (1899); Raadzaal, former govt. office of South African Republic; Government House; Anglican cathedral; the mint; and Voortrekker Monument (1949), on hill overlooking city. Pretoria is noted for its jacaranda-lined streets. Site of Univ. of Pretoria (1930), Univ. of So. Afr., Natl. Zoological Gardens (30 acres), Veterinary Research Foundation (at Onderstepoort, N suburb), New and Old Transvaal museums, Paul Kruger's house and grave, Janse Entomological Mus., Engelenburg Mus., Treaty House, where treaty of Vereeniging (1902) was signed in final form, Natl. Herbarium, Meteorological Research Laboratory, and Radcliffe Observatory of Oxford Univ. (25°47'18"S 28°13'45"E), established here 1938. City's industries include important steelworks (5 mi. W), railroad workshops, cementworks, tanneries; mfg. of chemicals, paint, glassware, pottery, metal products, matches. Near by are iron deposits, granite quarries. Mean temp. ranges from 52.5°F. (July) to 73°F. (Jan.); average annual rainfall 28.28 in. Airport at Zwartkop, 7 mi. SSW. Chief suburbs are Pretoria North (pop. 7,423), 6 mi. N, Hercules (pop. 41,857), 3 mi. NNW, and Ashbury (S). City founded 1855, named in memory of Andries Pretorius. Became ⊙ Transvaal 1860, ⊙ South African Republic 1881. Early in South African War, Winston Churchill was imprisoned in Central Junior High School; he escaped (Dec., 1899) to Mozambique. City surrendered (June 5, 1900) to Lord Roberts. Became administrative ⊙ U. of So. Afr. 1910; made city 1931.

Pretten, Luxembourg: see LINTGEN.

Prettin (prĕtēn'), town (pop. 3,377), in former Prussian Saxony prov., central Germany, after 1945 in Saxony-Anhalt, near the Elbe, 8 mi. NNW of Torgau; metalworking; mfg. of soap, enamelware. Just ESE is 16th-cent. Lichtenberg castle.

Prettingen, Luxembourg: see LINTGEN.

Prettyboy Dam, N Md., in Gunpowder Falls (stream) in N Baltimore co.; 167 ft. high, 845 ft. long; concrete; completed 1933; forms reservoir c.10 mi. long, for water supply to Baltimore.

Pretty Prairie, city (pop. 484), Reno co., S Kansas, 18 mi. SSW of Hutchinson, in wheat area.

Preturo (prĕtōō'rō), village (pop. 530), Aquila prov., Abruzzi e Molise, S central Italy, 6 mi. WNW of Aquila; alcohol distillery.

Pretzsch (prĕch), town (pop. 2,970), in former Prussian Saxony prov., central Germany, after 1945 in Saxony-Anhalt, on the Elbe and 13 mi. SE of Wittenberg; spa; mfg. (musical instruments, pottery). Has 17th-cent. palace.

Preuilly-sur-Claise (prûyē'-sür-klāz'), village (pop. 1,396), Indre-et-Loire dept., W central France, on Claise R. and 18 mi. E of Châtellerault; winegrowing. Has 12th-cent. Romanesque church of Saint-Pierre and ruins of 11th-cent. abbey.

Preussen, Germany: see PRUSSIA.

Preussisch Börnecke (proi'sĭsh bûrn"ĕ'kü), village (pop. 3,363), in former Prussian Saxony prov., central Germany, after 1945 in Saxony-Anhalt, 9 mi. N of Aschersleben; lignite mining; chemical mfg.

Preussisch Eylau, USSR: see BAGRATIONOVSK.

Preussisch Friedland, Poland: see DEBRZNO.

Preussisch Holland, Poland: see PASLEK.

Preussisch Oldendorf (ôl'dündôrf), town (pop. 2,480), in former Prussian prov. of Westphalia, NW Germany, after 1945 in North Rhine-Westphalia, on N slope of Wiehen Mts., 5 mi. W of Lübbecke; grain.

Preussisch Stargard, Poland: see STAROGARD.

Prevalje (prĕ'välyĕ), Ger. *Prävali* (prä'välē), village, N Slovenia, Yugoslavia, on Meza R., on railroad and 35 mi. W of Maribor, near Austrian frontier. Mining of brown coal at LESE (SW), lead and zinc at MEZICA (WSW). Until 1918, in Carinthia.

Preveza (prä'vĕzü), nome (□ 261; pop. 47,692), S Epirus, Greece; ⊙ Preveza. Located on Ionian Sea just N of Gulf of Arta, bet. Acheron and Louros rivers. Agr.: citrus fruit, almonds, wheat, barley; olive oil; wine; sheep and goat raising; fisheries along coast. Main port is Preveza.

Preveza, city (pop. 10,056), ⊙ Preveza nome, S Epirus, Greece, chief port of Epirus, at entrance to Gulf of Arta, 50 mi. S of Ioannina; trading center for olives, citrus fruits; olive oil; almonds, grain, livestock. Developed in Middle Ages, superseding Roman NICOPOLIS, 4 mi. N. Held by Venice until 1797; the French held it in 1798, when it passed to Ali Pasha. Annexed to Greece, 1913. Formerly spelled Prevesa.

Preyla, Lithuania: see PREILA.

Preyli, Latvia: see PREILI.

Preylovea (prālōvā'ä), town, Takeo prov., SW Cambodia, 30 mi. S of Pnompenh; rice, lac. Archaeological remains.

Preynop (prā'nôp'), town, Kampot prov., SW Cambodia, near Gulf of Siam, 13 mi. NE of Ream.

Preyveng (prā'vĕng'), town, ⊙ Preyveng prov. (□ 1,900; 1948 pop. 361,040), S Cambodia, 30 mi. ESE of Pnompenh, in rice- and corn-growing area; sericulture, fishing. R.C. mission.

Priamurye or **Priamur'ye,** USSR: see AMUR RIVER.

Priazovskoye (prēŭzôf'skŭyŭ), village (1926 pop. 5,754), S Zaporozhe oblast, Ukrainian SSR, 15 mi. ESE of Melitopol; metalworks; cotton, wheat. Until c.1935, Pokrovskoye or Pokrovka.

Pribalkhash, Kazakh SSR: see BALKHASH.

Pribenice, castle, Czechoslovakia: see TABOR.

Pribilof Islands (prĭ"bĭlôf'), group of 4 islands (1939 pop. 482) off SW Alaska, in Bering Sea, N of Aleutian Isls., 250 mi. NW of Unalaska, near 56°50'N 170°W. Consists of SAINT PAUL ISLAND, SAINT GEORGE ISLAND, Otter Isl., and Walrus Isl. International seal reserve, isls. are major Alaska furseal breeding ground. The Aleut population engages in hunting seals and white foxes. Visited and named (1786) by Gerasim Pribilof, navigator for Russian fur interests; later Russians brought Aleutian natives to hunt seals. Uncontrolled sealing threatened animals with extinction prior to signing (1911) of North Pacific Sealing Convention (U.S., Great Britain, Russia, Japan), which gave the U.S. the right to enforce its provisions. Japan withdrew from convention, 1941.

Priboj, Priboi, or **Priboy** (all: prē'boi), village (pop. 1,510), W Serbia, Yugoslavia, in the Sanjak, on Lim R. and 25 mi. SW of Titovo Uzice, near Bosnian border; rail terminus.

Pribor (pûrzhē'bôr), Czech *Příbor*, Ger. *Freiberg* (frī'bĕrk), town (pop. 3,958), S central Silesia, Czechoslovakia, on railroad and 15 mi. SSW of Ostrava; makes hats, knit goods. Coal mines in vicinity.

Priboy, Yugoslavia: see PRIBOJ.

Pribram (pûrzhē'bräm), Czech *Příbram*, Ger. *Pibrans* (pē'bränts), town (pop. 9,062), S Bohemia, Czechoslovakia, on railroad and 34 mi. SW of Prague; former gold- and silver-mining center dating from 17th cent. Present silver and lead deep-shaft (down to 3,000 ft.) mining is concentrated at Bohutin (bô'hŏŏtyĭn), 4 mi. SW, and BREZOVE HORY; some zinc, barite, and antimony mining. Mfg. (kitchen utensils, hemp ropes), liquor distilling. Noted mining school, transferred (1945) to Ostrava; mus. Svata Hora pilgrimage center, with 14th-cent. church, is just SE.

Pribyslav (pûrzhĭ'bĭsläf), Czech *Přibyslav*, town (pop. 2,261), E Bohemia, Czechoslovakia, on Sazava R., on railroad and 7 mi. ESE of Havlickuv Brod; lumbering trade. John Zizka died here, 1424.

Price or **Priceville,** village (pop. 2,321), SE Que., on Metis R., near its mouth on the St. Lawrence, 21 mi. NE of Rimouski; lumbering center; hydroelectric station.

Price, county (□ 1,268; pop. 16,344), N Wis.; ⊙ Phillips. Drained by Flambeau and Jump rivers. Contains section of Chequamegon Natl. Forest and several resort lakes. Dairying, lumbering, farming (mostly potatoes). Formed 1879.

Price, city (pop. 6,010), ⊙ Carbon co., central Utah, on Price R. and 100 mi. SE of Salt Lake City; alt. 5,566 ft.; coal-mining center in agr. area (sugar beets, beans, hay) served by near-by irrigation works on Price R. Jr. col. here. Rodeo takes place annually. Growth followed arrival of railroad (in early 1880s) and discovery of coal.

Pricedale, village (pop. 2,357, with adjacent Sandfield), Westmoreland co., SW Pa., 13 mi. S of McKeesport.

Price Island, B.C.: see SWINDLE ISLAND.

Priceland, town (pop. 124), Henry co., W central Mo.

Price River, rises in Wasatch Range NW of Scofield, central Utah, flows 130 mi. generally SE, past Price and through deep canyon, to Green R. 15 mi. NNE of Green River. Scofield Dam (120 ft. high, 575 ft. long; completed 1946), near its source, is used for irrigation.

Price Town, Wales: see NANTYMOEL.

Priceville, Que.: see PRICE.

Prichard (prĭ'chûrd), industrial city (pop. 19,014), N suburb of Mobile, Mobile co., SW Ala.; meat packing, canning; wood and paper products, fertilizer.

Prichsenstadt (prĭk'sŭn-shtät), town (pop. 869), Lower Franconia, NW Bavaria, Germany, 19 mi. E of Würzburg; furniture mfg. Beans, horseradish, cattle; apiculture. Has 17th-cent. town hall. Chartered 1367. Limestone quarry near by.

Prickly Pear Creek, SW central Mont., rises in Jefferson co., flows 32 mi. N, past E. Helena, to L. Helena just W of Missouri R. Drains mining and agr. region. Largest city in valley is Helena.

Prides Crossing, Mass.: see BEVERLY.

Pridmouth, England: see FOWEY.

Priego (prēā'gō), city (pop. 2,655), Cuenca prov., E central Spain, in New Castile, 28 mi. NNW of Cuenca; picturesquely set in fertile Alcarria region, surrounded by pine forests and olive groves. Also raises grapes, cereals, livestock. Potteries; mfg. of woolen goods. Has parochial church with fine steeple. Convent of San Miguel de las Victorias is 1½ mi. E.

Priego de Córdoba (dhā kôr'dhōvä), city (pop. 12,134), Córdoba prov., S Spain, 17 mi. ENE of Lucena; mfg. of woolen and cotton textiles, felt hats, knit goods, soap, chocolate; olive- and peanut-oil processing, flour milling, brandy distilling. Fruit, vegetables, wine in area. Gypsum quarries and saltworks near by.

Priekule or **Prekule** (prā'kŏŏlā), Ger. *Preenkuln*, city (pop. 1,347), W Latvia, in Kurzeme, 23 mi. ESE of Liepaja; rail junction; machine shops, brickworks.

Priekule or **Prekule** (prā'kŏŏlā), Lith. *Priekulė*, Ger. *Prökuls* (prû'kōōls), city (1941 pop. 1,196), W Lithuania, on railroad and 12 mi. SE of Memel. Dates from 16th cent. In Memel Territory, 1920–39.

Prien (prēn), summer resort (pop. 5,683), Upper Bavaria, Germany, near the Chiemsee, on small Prien R. and 10 mi. E of Rosenheim. Has rococo church.

Prienai, Prenai, or **Prenay** (prä'nī), Pol. *Preny*, city (pop. 4,188), S central Lithuania, on left bank of Neman R. and 17 mi. S of Kaunas; lumber-milling center; mfg. (furniture, turpentine, rosin, shoes, vegetable oil, beer). Passed 1795 to Prussia, 1815 to Rus. Poland; in Suvalki govt. until 1920.

Priene (prīē'nē), anc. Ionian town on W coast of Asia Minor (now in Turkey), 10 mi. SW of Soke; notable temple of Athene Polias; ruins excavated 1895–1900.

Prieska (prē'skŭ), town (pop. 3,440), central Cape Prov., U. of So. Afr., on Orange R. (bridge) and 140 mi. WSW of Kimberley; asbestos-mining center; in stock-raising, grain-growing region. Airfield. Near by (E) along Orange R. are large diamond diggings, now mostly exhausted.

Priestholm, Wales: see PUFFIN.

Priest Lake, in mtn. region of N Idaho, 20 mi. NW of Sandpoint, near Wash. line; 24 mi. long, 1–4 mi. wide; center of resort area. Has several small isls. Fed and drained by Priest R.

Priestly Lake, Piscataquis co., N Maine, 66 mi. WSW of Presque Isle, in wilderness recreational area; 3 mi. long.

Priest River, village (pop. 1,592), Bonner co., N Idaho, 20 mi. WSW of Sandpoint and on Pend Oreille R., at mouth of Priest R. (rises in British Columbia and flows 90 mi. S, through Priest L.); woodworking, grain milling. Settled 1889.

Prieto, Cerro (sĕ'rō prēā'tō), peak (9,135 ft.), Guanajuato, central Mexico, in Sierra Madre Occidental, 5 mi. N of Guanajuato.

Prievidza (pryĕ'vĭdzä), Hung. *Privigye* (prĭ'vĭdyĕ), town (pop. 5,650), W central Slovakia, Czechoslovakia, on Nitra R. and 40 mi. NE of Nitra; rail junction; noted for fruit export; mfg. (textiles, chemicals), distilling, woodworking. Has 17th-cent. Piarist monastery, church. Lignite mines SE.

Prigrevica or **Prigrevitsa** (both: prē'grĕvĭtsä), village (pop. 5,077), Vojvodina, NW Serbia, Yugoslavia, 6 mi. S of Sombor, in the Backa. Until 1947, called Prigrevica Sveti Ivan, Hung. *Bácsszentiván*.

Priiskovy or **Priiskovyy** (prĭē'skŭvē), town (1940 pop. over 500), NW Khakass Autonomous Oblast, Krasnoyarsk Territory, Russian SFSR, in the Kuznetsk Ala-Tau, 110 mi. NW of Abakan; gold mines.

Prijedor or **Priyedor** (both: prē'yĕdôr), town (pop. 8,152), NW Bosnia, Yugoslavia, on Sana R., on railroad and 26 mi. NW of Banja Luka, at W foot of the Kozara; wood-pulp mfg.; shipping center for iron ore mined in LJUBIJA area. Coal deposits near by.

Prijepolje or **Priyepolye** (both: prē'yĕpô"lyĕ), village (pop. 2,545), W Serbia, Yugoslavia, on Lim R. and 15 mi. E of Pljevlja, in the Sanjak.

Prikhaby (prēkhä'bē), village (1939 pop. over 500), S Velikiye Luki oblast, Russian SFSR, 22 mi. NNE of Velizh; flax.

Prikumsk, Russian SFSR: see BUDENNOVSK.

Prilep (prē'lĕp), Turkish *Perlepe*, anc. *Heraclea Pelagoniae*, city (pop. 25,996), Macedonia, Yugoslavia, on railroad and 45 mi. S of Skoplje, in Pelagonija valley. Trade center in fruit- and tobacco-growing region; handicraft (homemade carpets). Mica mine near by. Has castle ruins, church and monastery of St. Demetrius (seat of Greek metropolitan). Was temporary ⊙ Serbia (14th cent.) and local rulers who followed him. Formerly called Prilip.

Prilly (prēyē'), town (pop. 3,440), Vaud canton, W Switzerland, NW of and adjacent to Lausanne; metal- and woodworking.

Priluki (prēlōō'kē), city (1926 pop. 28,621), SE Chernigov oblast, Ukrainian SSR, on Udai R. and 75 mi. SE of Chernigov. Agr. center in sugar-beet and tobacco region; tobacco products; flour milling, mfg. (clothing, shoes, furniture). Dates from 12th cent.; passed (1667) to Russia. In Second World War, held (1941–43) by Germans.

Primda (pûrzhĭm'dä), Czech *Přimda*, Ger. *Pfraumberg* (pfroum'bĕrk), village (pop. 217), W Bohemia, Czechoslovakia, 31 mi. W of Pilsen; lumber and mother-of-pearl industries.

Primeira Cruz (prēmā'rŭ krōōz'), town (pop. 1,155), N Maranhão, Brazil, near the Atlantic, 50 mi. E of São Luís; rice, manioc.

Primero, Río (rē'ō prēmā'rō), river, N central Córdoba prov., Argentina, rises in mts. 15 mi. W of Córdoba, flows c.125 mi. E and NE, past Córdoba, Río Primero town, and Santa Rosa, to the Mar Chiquita. At its source a power and irrigation dam forms L. SAN ROQUE; other dams on upper reaches.

Primero de Marzo or **1 de Marzo** (dā mär'sō), town (dist. pop. 6,360), La Cordillera dept., S central Paraguay, 45 mi. ENE of Asunción; tobacco, fruit, cattle.

Primero de Mayo or **1 de Mayo** (mī'ō), town (pop. estimate 1,000), E Entre Ríos prov., Argentina, on railroad and 20 mi. NW of Concepción del Uruguay; wheat, corn, flax, grapes, livestock, poultry.

Primghar (prĭm'gär), town (pop. 1,152), ⊙ O'Brien co., NW Iowa, 24 mi. N of Cherokee, in livestock and grain area. Sand and gravel pits near by.

Primkenau, Poland: see PRZEMKOW.

Primorsk (prēmôrsk'). **1** City (1939 pop. 3,879), W Kaliningrad oblast, Russian SFSR, 20 mi. W of Kaliningrad, on N coast of Vistula Lagoon; fishing port; flour mill, brickworks. Seat (13th–16th cent.) of Samland bishops. By truce signed here (1628), Gustavus Adolphus and the elector of Brandenburg allied in Thirty Years War. Until 1945, in East Prussia and called Fischhausen (fĭsh'houzŭn). **2** City (1948 pop. over 2,000), NW Leningrad oblast, Russian SFSR, port on Gulf of Finland, 22 mi. SSW of Vyborg, on Karelian Isthmus; lumber trade. Paper mill at near-by Krasnoostrovski. First mentioned as port in 1270. Called Koivisto or Koyvisto (koi'vēstŭ), Swedish *Björkö*, while in Finland (until 1940) and, until 1948, in USSR.

Primorskaya, oblast, Russian SFSR: see MARITIME TERRITORY.

Primorski Krai, Russian SFSR: see MARITIME TERRITORY.

Primorsko (prēmôr'skô), village (pop. 1,395), Burgas dist., SE Bulgaria, port on Black Sea, 20 mi. SE of Burgas; charcoal export. Formerly Kyupriya.

Primorsko-Akhtarsk (prēmôr'skŭ-ŭkhtärsk'), city (1926 pop. 11,252), NW Krasnodar Territory, Russian SFSR, port on Sea of Azov, at mouth of Akhtar Liman, 80 mi. NNW of Krasnodar; rail terminus; fishing center; fish processing, metal- and woodworking. Exports grain. Beach resort. Formerly also called Akhtari. Became city in late 1940s.

Primorskoye (–skŭyŭ). **1** Village (1939 pop. under 500), E Crimea, Russian SFSR, on Kerch Peninsula, 15 mi. W of Kerch; metalworks; wheat, sheep raising. Until 1944, Mayak-Salyn. **2** Agr. town (1926 pop. 5,141), S Stalino oblast, Ukrainian SSR, on Kalmius R. and 8 mi. NE of Zhdanov. Until 1946, Sartana.

Primosten (prē'môshtĕn), Serbo-Croatian *Primošten*, Ital. *Cavocesto* (kävôchĕs'tô), village, S Croatia, Yugoslavia, on Adriatic Sea, 10 mi. S of Sibenik, in Dalmatia. Sometimes spelled Primoshten.

Prim Point, cape on S coast of P.E.I., on Northumberland Strait, at E side of Hillsborough Bay entrance, 15 mi. SSE of Charlottetown; 46°3'N 63°2'W; lighthouse.

Primrose. 1 Town (pop. 24), Meriwether co., W Ga., 17 mi. ENE of La Grange; clay mining. **2** Village (pop. 154), Boone co., E central Nebr., 12 miles WSW of Albion and on Cedar R. **3** Village (pop. 2,197, with adjacent Forestville), Schuylkill co., E central Pa., 5 mi. W of Pottsville.

Primrose Lake (□ 181), W Sask. and E Alta., 110 mi. N of Lloydminster; 26 mi. long, 13 mi. wide. Drains into Churchill R. through Beaver R.

Prims River (prĭms), N Saar, rises 3 mi. N of Nonnweiler, flows 30 mi. SW, past Nonnweiler, Schmelz, Nalbach, and Dillingen, to Saar R. just SW of Dillingen. Receives Theel R. (right).

Prince, county (□ 778; pop. 34,490), in NW part of P.E.I.; ⊙ Summerside.

Prince Albert, city (pop. 14,532), central Sask., on North Saskatchewan R. and 80 mi. NNE of Saskatoon; center of lumbering and fur-trapping region, distributing point for N part of prov. Grain elevators, stockyards; industries include tanning, dairying, brewing, wood and sheet-metal working; mfg. of castings; saddlery. Resort, gateway to Prince Albert Natl. Park, 25 mi. NW of city. Site of Anglican and R. C. cathedrals, prov. penitentiary, and St. Albans Ladies' Col.; hq. of Royal Canadian Mounted Police for central and N. Sask. Founded 1866 as Presbyterian mission station to the Cree Indians. Near by is large sanitarium.

Prince Albert, Afrikaans *Prins Albert* (prĭnsäl'bĕrt), town (pop. 2,521), S Cape Prov., U of So. Afr., at S edge of the Great Karroo, on N slope of Swartberg Range, 30 mi. NNW of Oudtshoorn; fruit, viticulture, wheat.

Prince Albert Mountains, Antarctica, extend c.200 naut. mi. along Victoria Land N of McMurdo Sound; center at 75°45′S 161°3′E. Discovered 1841 by Sir James C. Ross.

Prince Albert National Park (□ 1,496), central Sask., 25 mi. NW of Prince Albert, on watershed bet. Saskatchewan and Churchill rivers; 55 mi. long, 47 mi. wide. Has hilly surface, rising to over 2,000 ft. There are numerous lakes; largest are Waskesiu, Crean, and Kingsmere lakes. The many streams are navigable for canoes. On Waskesiu L. is park's principal summer resort. Seaplane-landing facilities. Mostly wooded, park is sanctuary for moose, elk, deer, caribou, bear, and many fur-bearing animals. Established 1927.

Prince Albert Peninsula, NW part of Victoria Isl., SW Franklin Dist., Northwest Territories, separated from Banks Isl. by Prince of Wales Strait; 72°N 115°W; 150 mi. long, 80–150 mi. wide. Rises to c.1,500 ft. on Adventure Mtn. (NW).

Prince Albert Sound, SW Victoria Isl., SW Franklin Dist., Northwest Territories, inlet (170 mi. long, 40 mi. wide) of Amundsen Gulf; 70°30′N 115°W.

Prince Bay, SE N.Y., a section of Richmond borough of New York city, on S Staten Isl.; mfg. (machinery, tools and dies, dental equipment).

Prince Charles Foreland, Nor. *Prins Karls Forland,* island (□ 243) of Spitsbergen group, in Arctic Ocean, off NW West Spitsbergen; 78°12′–78°54′N 10°30′–12°10′E. It is 55 mi. long, 4–8 mi. wide; rises to 3,848 ft. E coast is generally glaciated.

Prince Christian Sound, channel (40 mi. long, 1 mi. wide) of the Atlantic bet. S tip of Greenland mainland (N) and Cape Farewell Archipelago (S). With several small fjords which connect it with SW coast of Greenland, it forms Prince Christian Sound Passage. Near mouth of sound (E), at 60°3′N 43°12′W, is meteorological, radio station.

Prince Edward, county (□ 390; pop. 16,750), SE Ont., on L. Ontario and on Bay of Quinte; ⊙ Picton.

Prince Edward, county (□ 357; pop. 15,398), central Va.; ⊙ Farmville. Rolling agr. area, bounded N by Appomattox R.; drained by Nottoway R. State forests in E. A leading Va. tobacco co.; also hay, corn, grain, livestock, dairy products, some lumbering, lumber milling; mfg. at Farmville. Formed 1753.

Prince Edward Island, province and island (□ 2,184; 1941 pop. 95,047; 1948 estimate 93,000), E Canada, one of the Maritime Provinces; ⊙ Charlottetown. In the Gulf of St. Lawrence, separated from New Brunswick (SW) and Nova Scotia (SE) by Northumberland Strait, 9–30 mi. wide. Isl. is 145 mi. long, up to 35 mi. wide; 45°58′–47°4′N 61°58′–64°25′W. Surface is low and undulating, rising to c.450 ft. There are many short rivers, including Hillsborough, Yorke, Eliot, and Orwell rivers; none are navigable. Coastline is low and deeply indented by Cardigan, Hillsborough, Bedeque, Egmont, Cascumpeque, Malpeque, and Tracadie bays. Climate is maritime; average temp. (Charlottetown) ranges from 15°F. (Feb.) to 65°F. (July); average annual rainfall is 39.9 inches. Land is intensively cultivated; dairying, cattle raising, seed-potato growing are important; meat is packed and exported. Wheat, barley, oats, feed crops, fruit are grown extensively. There are fisheries (lobster, cod, mackerel, herring, smelt) and oyster beds. Lobster and fish canning, packing of dairy products, shipbuilding are carried on. Besides Charlottetown, other towns are Summerside, Souris, Georgetown, Montague, Kensington, Alberton, and Port Borden. Railroad traverses length of isl. There are airports at Charlottetown and Summerside; train ferry links Port Borden with Cape Tormentine on New Brunswick mainland. Isl. was discovered (1534) by Jacques Cartier and described (1603) by Champlain, who established French claim to it, as Île St. Jean (Isle St. John); it retained this name until 1798, when it was renamed for Queen Victoria's father. First settled by Acadians, isl. was occupied by the British in 1758 and annexed to Nova Scotia in 1763; the earl of Selkirk settled Scottish colonists here, 1803. Isl. became separate prov. in 1769, obtained representative govt. in 1851, and joined Canada in 1873.

Prince Edward Island, tiny subantarctic islet in S Indian Ocean, c.1,200 mi. SE of Cape Town, just NE of Marion Isl., with which it forms the Prince Edward Isls.; 46°35′S 38°E. Of circular shape (diameter 5 mi.), it rises to 2,370 ft. Formally annexed by U. of So. Afr. in Dec., 1947. The Prince Edward Isls. were discovered (1772) by Marion du Fresne, who named them Les Îles Froides [cold isls.]. Capt. Cook passed them in 1776.

Prince Frederick, village (pop. c.500), ⊙ Calvert co. (since c.1725), S Md., 31 mi. SSW of Annapolis, in agr. area. Summer-resort area on Chesapeake Bay near by.

Prince Frederick Harbour, Australia: see YORK SOUND.

Prince George, city (pop. 2,027), central B.C., on Fraser R. at mouth of Nechako R., and 300 mi. N of Vancouver; 53°55′N 122°45′W; railroad division point; center of lumbering, mining (gold, silver, lead, zinc), and stock-raising region; distributing point for central and N B.C.; fur trading. Proposed terminal of Alaska railroad. Fur-trading post of Fort George was established here 1807 by Simon Fraser for North West Co.; taken over 1821 by Hudson's Bay Co. Settlement began c.1910 when railroad to Prince Rupert was built through Fort George. Inc. 1915, its name was later changed to Prince George.

Prince George, county (□ 286; pop. 19,679), E Va.; ⊙ Prince George. In tidewater region; bounded NW by Appomattox, N by James rivers; drained by Blackwater and Nottoway rivers. Agr. (peanuts, truck, some tobacco, cotton, grain); poultry, livestock, dairy products. Mfg. at HOPEWELL, in but independent of co. Formed 1702.

Prince George, village, ⊙ Prince George co. (since 1785), E Va., 6 mi. E of Petersburg. Near by is Merchant's Hope Church, built in 1650s.

Prince George Land, Russian SFSR: see GEORGE LAND.

Prince Georges, county (□ 485; pop. 194,182), central Md.; ⊙ Upper Marlboro. Bounded W by Potomac R. (forms Va. line here) and Dist. of Columbia, E and NE by Patuxent R.; drained NW by Anacostia R. Rolling coastal plains, with NW part in the piedmont. Contains many residential suburbs of Washington; agr. portions produce tobacco, truck, dairy products, corn, wheat. Some mfg. (especially machine tools, aircraft parts, radio equipment, chemicals). Includes Univ. of Md. at College Park, Greenbelt (model town), some of the Natl. Capital Parks (W), part of Cedarville State Forest (S), U.S. Dept. of Agr. research center and Patuxent wildlife research refuge near Beltsville, U.S. Bureau of the Census and Navy Hydrographic Office at Suitland, and Andrews Air Force Base, near Camp Springs. Formed 1695.

Prince Gustav Adolph Sea, W Franklin Dist., Northwest Territories, arm (140 mi. long, 60 mi. wide) extending S from the Arctic Ocean bet. North and South Borden isls. (W) and Ellef Ringnes Isl. and the Findlay Isls. (E); 77°–79°N 104°–109°W. Continued S by Byam Martin Channel. Maclean Strait (80 mi. long, 70 mi. wide) is SE arm of the sea. Hazen Strait extends SW.

Prince Harald Coast (hă′rŭld), part of Queen Maud Land, Antarctica, on Indian Ocean, bet. 34° and 39°E. Discovered 1937 by Norwegian expedition.

Prince Leopold Island (10 mi. long, 4 mi. wide), central Franklin Dist., Northwest Territories, in Barrow Strait, off NE Somerset Isl.; 74°N 90°W.

Prince Leopold Mine, Belgian Congo: see KIPUSHI.

Princenhage or **Prinsenhage** (both: prĭn′sŭnhä′-khŭ), town (pop. 6,377), North Brabant prov., SW Netherlands, 2 mi. SW of Breda; mfg. (jams, furniture, fire extinguishers).

Prince of Wales, Cape, W extremity of North American mainland, at W end of Seward Peninsula, NW Alaska, on Bering Strait, 100 mi. NW of Nome and 55 mi. ESE of Cape Dezhnev, Siberia; 65°36′ N 168°4′W.

Prince of Wales Island, SE Alaska, largest isl. (□ 2,231) of Alexander Archipelago, in N Pacific, W of Ketchikan; 54°41′–56°22′N 131°57′–133°40′W; 135 mi. long, 45 mi. wide; rises to 4,000 ft.; has deeply indented coastline; heavily wooded throughout; lumbering, fishing, and canning. Klawak and Craig villages are in W.

Prince of Wales Island, largest island (□ 75) in Torres Strait, 10 mi. N (across Endeavour Strait) of Cape York Peninsula, N Queensland, Australia, at NE tip of entrance to Gulf of Carpentaria; 11 mi. long, 10 mi. wide; rises to 761 ft. Rocky, wooded; pearl shell.

Prince of Wales Island (□ 13,736), S central Franklin Dist., Northwest Territories, in the Arctic Ocean, separated from Victoria Isl. (SW) by McClintock Channel, from Boothia Peninsula (SE) by Franklin Strait, from Somerset Isl. (E) by Peel Sound, from Bathurst Isl. (N) and from Melville Isl. (NW) by Viscount Melville Sound; 71°11′–74°N 96°10′–102°50′W. Isl. is 190 mi. long, 40–130 mi. wide; irregular coastline, generally steep and hilly, is deeply indented by Ommanney Bay (W) and Browne Bay (E). In 1948 the magnetic pole was located in NW part of isl. at 73°N 100°W.

Prince of Wales Island, Malaya: see PENANG.

Prince of Wales Island, Tuamotu Isls.: see AHE.

Prince of Wales Mine, Southern Rhodesia: see BINDURA.

Prince of Wales Strait, SW Franklin Dist., Northwest Territories, arm (200 mi. long, 10–20 mi. wide) of the Arctic Ocean, extending from Viscount Melville Sound (NE) to Amundsen Gulf (SW), separating Banks Isl. and Victoria Isl.; 71°30′–73°30′N 115°–120°W.

Prince Olav Coast (ō′läv), part of Queen Maud Land, Antarctica, on Indian Ocean, bet. 39° and 49°30′E. Discovered 1930 by Hjalmar Riiser-Larsen, Norwegian explorer.

Prince Patrick Island (□ 6,696), Parry Isls., W. Franklin Dist., Northwest Territories, in the Arctic Ocean, separated from Banks Isl. (S) by McClure Strait, from Melville Isl. (E) by Fitzwilliam Strait; 75°43′–77°36′N 115°50′–124°5′W. It is 150 mi. long, 20–50 mi. wide; irregular SE coastline. Center of isl. is plateau over 1,000 ft. high. At Mould Bay (SE ; 76°5′N 119°45′W) is U.S.-Canadian weather station. Isl. was discovered 1853 by Sir Francis McClintock.

Prince Regent Inlet, S Franklin Dist., Northwest Territories, arm (150 mi. long, 40–90 mi. wide) of the Arctic Ocean, bet. Lancaster Sound and Barrow Strait (N) and the Gulf of Boothia (S); 73°N 92°W. Separates Somerset Isl. (W) from Brodeur Peninsula of NW Baffin Isl.

Prince Rupert, city (pop. 6,714), W B.C., on Kaien Isl. in Chatham Sound, on Prince Rupert Harbour, near mouth of Skeena R., 500 mi. NW of Vancouver; 54°20′N 130°18′W; rail terminus, grain-shipping and fishing port (halibut, salmon), with large drydock, fish-processing plants, and a large cellulose factory. The port is ice-free the year round and serves mining, lumbering, and agr. region of central and N B.C.; there are steamship lines to Vancouver, Victoria, and Alaskan ports. Prince Rupert came into existence as a tent town in 1909; inc. 1910. Its growth dates from arrival (1914) of Canadian National RR. N terminus of Caribou Trail, a road completed 1945 from Vancouver.

Prince Rupert Bay, inlet of NW Dominica, B.W.I., 17 mi. NNW of Roseau. Guarded by once strongly fortified hills. Portsmouth is on its NE shore. Site of naval battle (1805), where Rodney defeated the French.

Princesa Isabel (prēnsä′zŭ ēzäbĕl′), city (pop. 2,396), W Paraíba, NE Brazil, on Pernambuco border, 70 mi. SE of Cajàzeiras; cotton, tobacco, livestock. Formerly called Princeza.

Princes Island, Indonesia: see PRINSEN.

Prince's Island, São Tomé e Príncipe: see PRÍNCIPE ISLAND.

Princes Islands, group of 9 small isls. in E end of Sea of Marmara, NW Turkey, just SE of Istanbul and a few miles off Asiatic coast. Comprising Adalar dist. (□ 4.2; pop. 14,053) of Istanbul, they include BUYUK ISLAND, HEYBELI ISLAND, BURGAZ ISLAND, and Kinali Isl. Resort for Istanbul. In Byzantine times they were places of exile.

Princes Risborough (rĭz′bŭrŭ), residential town and parish (pop. 2,827), W central Buckingham, England, 7 mi. S of Aylesbury; agr. market. Has Norman church. Was site of castle of the Black Prince (no remains).

Princess Anne, county (□ 267; pop. 42,277), SE Va.; ⊙ Princess Anne. Low coastal plain; bordered S by N.C., N by Chesapeake Bay, E by the Atlantic; Cape Henry is NE tip. Indented by bays (Lynnhaven, Broad, Back) sheltered by barrier beaches. Crossed by Albemarle and Chesapeake Canal. Agr. (truck, fruit, corn, livestock, poultry, dairy products); fisheries (especially oysters); waterfowl hunting. Includes Virginia Beach (resort), Seashore State Park. Formed 1691.

Princess Anne. 1 Town (pop. 1,407), ⊙ Somerset co. (since 1742), SE Md., on the Eastern Shore, 13 mi. SSW of Salisbury, and on Manokin R.; processing, shipping center for truck-farm area (potatoes, strawberries, tomatoes, beans); canneries, lumber and flour mills, clothing factories. Seat of Md. State Col. (formerly Princess Anne Col.), a division of Univ. of Md. Many old estates in vicinity. Laid out 1733. **2** Village (pop. c.150), ⊙ Princess Anne co. (since 1824), SE Va., 15 mi. SE of Norfolk; truck farming.

Princess Astrid Coast (ă′strĭd, Nor. ä′strē), part of Queen Maud Land, Antarctica, on Indian Ocean, bet. 5° and 20°30′E. Discovered 1931 by Norwegian explorer.

Princess Charlotte Bay, inlet of Coral Sea, NE Queensland, Australia, indenting E coast of Cape York Peninsula at its base, bet. Cape Melville (E) and Claremont Point (W; site of Port Stewart); 38 mi. long, 15 mi. wide; mangrove swamps.

Princess Marie Bay, E Ellesmere Isl., NE Franklin Dist., Northwest Territories, arm (50 mi. long, 8–15 mi. wide) of Kane Basin, on N side of Bache Peninsula; 79°20′N 76°W. It was visited by the *Alert* and *Discovery* of the Nares expedition, 1875–76; by Peary's *Windward* in 1899; and by Shackleton (1935).

Princess Martha Coast (mär′tŭ), part of Queen Maud Land, Antarctica, on Indian Ocean, bet. 5°E and 16°30′W. Discovered 1930 by Hjalmar Riiser-Larsen, Norwegian explorer.

Princess Ragnhild Coast, part of Queen Maud Land, Antarctica, on Indian Ocean, bet. 20°30′ and 34°E. Discovered 1931 by Hjalmar Riiser-Larsen, Norwegian explorer.

Princess Royal Harbour, Australia: see KING GEORGE SOUND.

Princess Royal Island (□ 876; 52 mi. long, 7–26 mi. wide), W B.C., in Hecate Strait, 20 mi. SE of Pitt Isl., and 1 mi. off the mainland; 53°N 129°W. W coast is deeply indented. Rises to 5,500 ft. Lumbering. Surf Inlet village (N) is in gold-mining region; hydroelectric power. On NE coast is Butedale village; fish canning.

Princes Town, village, Western Prov., SW Gold Coast colony, on Gulf of Guinea, 27 mi. WSW of Takoradi; fishing. Here are ruins of castle of Gross-Friedrichsburg, built 1683 by Brandenburgers. Also written Prince's Town.

Princes Town, town (pop. 4,698), W Trinidad, B.W.I., on railroad and 6 mi. E of San Fernando;

trading and sugar-growing center. Formerly a Sp. mission among native Indians. Remarkable small mud volcanoes are near by (SE).

Princeton. **1** Village (pop. estimate 500), S B.C., in Cascade Mts., on Similkameen R. at mouth of Tulameen R., and 45 mi. W of Penticton; alt. 2,098 ft.; coal mining; center of mining (coal, gold, platinum, copper) and lumbering region. **2** Village (pop. estimate 450), S Ont., 12 mi. ENE of Woodstock; dairying, mixed farming.

Princeton. **1** Town (pop. 112), Dallas co., S central Ark., 17 mi. NW of Fordyce. **2** Village (1940 pop. 979), Dade co., S Fla., 22 mi. SW of Miami; packs vegetables, cans fruit. **3** City (pop. 5,765), ⊙ Bureau co., N Ill., 45 mi. N of Peoria, in agr. and bituminous-coal area; mfg. (brick, tile, vinegar, sealing wax); nursery, greenhouses; fruit, livestock, poultry, corn, wheat, oats. Laid out 1833, inc. 1849. It was the home of abolitionist Owen Lovejoy. **4** City (pop. 7,673), ⊙ Gibson co., SW Ind., 27 mi. N of Evansville, in oil and agr. area; oil refining; some mfg. of oil-well supplies, paint brushes, electric clocks, food products; railroad shops. Bituminous-coal mines near by. Settled c.1812, laid out 1814. **5** Town (pop. 495), Scott co., E Iowa, on Mississippi R. and 15 mi. ENE of Davenport. **6** City (pop. 177), Franklin co., E Kansas, 9 mi. S of Ottawa; livestock, grain. **7** City (pop. 5,388), ⊙ Caldwell co., W Ky., 40 mi. E of Paducah; rail junction (shops); trade and industrial center for agr. (burley tobacco, livestock, truck), fluorspar- and coal-mining, stone-quarrying, timber area; mfg. of clothing, harness, saddles, dairy products, concrete blocks; sawmill, tobacco stemmeries; airport. Univ. of Kentucky Col. of Agr. has experiment substation here. Kentucky Reservoir is c.20 mi. SW. Inc. as city after 1930. **8** Town (pop. 865), Washington co., E Maine, near St. Croix R., 15 mi. W of Calais, in lake dist.; wood products. Settled 1815, inc. 1832. **9** Agr. town (pop. 1,032), Worcester co., N central Mass., 13 mi. NNW of Worcester. State park here. Settled 1743, inc. 1771. **10** Village (pop. 2,108), ⊙ Mille Lacs co., E Minn., on Rum R. and c. 45 mi. NNW of Minneapolis; shipping point in agr. area; dairy products, potatoes. Platted 1856, inc. 1877. **11** City (pop. 1,506), ⊙ Mercer co., N Mo., on Weldon R. and 22 mi. N of Trenton; livestock, corn. Settled c.1840, inc. 1853. Calamity Jane b. here. **12** Borough (pop. 12,230), Mercer co., W N.J., on Millstone R. and 10 mi. NE of Trenton, in agr. region. Seat of Princeton Univ.; Inst. for Advanced Study, Princeton Theological Seminary (1812), St. Joseph's Col. (1914), Westminster Choir Col. (1926), and Rockefeller Inst. for Medical Research Settled 1696 by Friends, inc. 1813. Occupied by British, then Americans, in Revolution; monument commemorates victory (Jan. 3, 1777) over British, shortly after battle of Trenton. "Morven" (1701), home of Richard Stockton, was Cornwallis' hq. Continental Congress met (1783) in Nassau Hall of Princeton Univ. William Bainbridge's birthplace is now a public library. Palmer Square, new civic center, has Colonial-style buildings. Paul Robson b. here. **13** Town (pop. 608), Johnston co., central N.C., 10 mi. NW of Goldsboro. **14** Town (1940 pop. 167), Laurens and Greenville counties, NW S.C., 26 mi. SSE of Greenville. **15** Town (pop. 540), Collin co., N Texas, 32 mi. NE of Dallas, in corn, cotton area. **16** City (pop. 8,279), ⊙ Mercer co., S W.Va., 10 mi. NE of Bluefield; trade center for bituminous-coal, timber, agr. area; mfg. of beverages, bricks, tiles, hosiery, handles, foundry products; sawmills, railroad shops. Small L. Shawnee (resort) is NW. Settled 1826. **17** City (pop. 1,371), Green Lake co., central Wis., on Fox R. and 35 mi. W of Fond du Lac, in farm area (dairy products; poultry); poultry hatchery. Settled 1830; inc. as village in 1860, as city in 1920.

Princeton, Mount (14,177 ft.), central Colo., in Collegiate Range of Sawatch Mts., SW of Buena Vista.

Prince Town or **Princetown,** town, SW Devon, England, 7 mi. E of Tavistock in center of Dartmoor, amid prehistoric remains. Site of Dartmoor Prison, built 1806 for Napoleon's soldiers, used 1812 for American sailor captives, and since 1850 prison for Br. convicts.

Princeville, village (pop. 1,145), S Que., 28 mi. W of Thetford Mines; meat packing, mfg. of furniture, plastics; cattle market.

Princeville. **1** Village (pop. 1,113), Peoria co., central Ill., 16 mi. NNW of Peoria, in agr. and bituminous-coal area. **2** Town (pop. 919), Edgecombe co., E central N.C., on Tar R. opposite Tarboro.

Prince William, county (□ 347; pop. 22,612), N Va.; ⊙ Manassas. Bounded E by the Potomac, NE and N by Occoquan Creek and the Bull Run. Agr. (grain, tobacco, fruit, truck), dairying, livestock and poultry raising. Includes Civil War battlefields of Bull Run, marked by Manassas Natl. Battlefield Park; L. Jackson (resort), and Prince William Forest Park (formerly Chopawamsic Recreational Area), a unit (□ 26.8) of Natl. Capital Parks system. Formed 1731.

Prince William Sound, S Alaska, large, irregular inlet of Gulf of Alaska E of Kenai Peninsula, bet. 60° and 61°N and 146° and 148°W. Dotted with isls. Hinchinbrook Island and Montague Island are at its entrance. Valdez (NE) and Cordova (E) are ports. Fishing and mining in surrounding coastal region. Chugach Mts. are N.

Princeza, Brazil: see Princesa Isabel.

Principe Channel (prĭn'sĭpē), strait (50 mi. long, 3 mi. wide) off B.C. coast, bet. Pitt and Banks isls.

Príncipe da Beira, Brazil: see Forte Príncipe da Beira.

Príncipe Island (prēn'sēpĭ), formerly also **Prince's Island,** Portuguese isl. (□ 54; 1950 pop. 4,332) in Gulf of Guinea, c.140 mi. W of Sp. Guinea, forming, with São Tomé Island (90 mi. SSW), Port. colony of São Tomé e Príncipe. Santo António (1°38'N 7°25'E), its chief town, is on E coast. Of volcanic origin, isl. (10 mi. long, 5 mi. wide) is mountainous in S, rising to 3,110 ft. Cacao, coffee, and coconuts are exported.

Principele-Nicolae, Rumania: see Decemvrie 30, 1947.

Principio Furnace (prĭnsĭ'pēō, -ŭ), village, Cecil co., NE Md., 4 mi. NE of Havre de Grace. First important ironworks in the colonies were established near here 1715.

Prineville, city (pop. 3,233), ⊙ Crook co., central Oregon, on Crooked R. near mouth of Ochoco Creek, and 28 mi. NE of Bend, in dairying and livestock area; alt. 2,868 ft.; lumber milling. Hq. of near-by Ochoco Natl. Forest. Settled 1868, laid out 1870, inc. 1880.

Pringle. **1** Borough (pop. 1,727), Luzerne co., NE central Pa., 2 mi. NNW of Wilkes-Barre. Inc. 1914. **2** Town (pop. 193), Custer co., SW S.Dak., 11 mi. S of Custer; trading point for farming and ranching area.

Pringles, department, Argentina: see Cuatro de Junio.

Pringles, city and village, Argentina: see Coronel Pringles.

Prinkipo Island, Turkey: see Buyuk Island.

Prins Albert, U. of So. Afr.: see Prince Albert.

Prinsen (prĭn'sŭn), island (□ c.40), Indonesia, in Sunda Strait opposite Java Head (SW Java); 6°36'S 105°14'E; 12 mi. long, 10 mi. wide; rises to 1,050 ft. Visited by fishermen for trepang and tortoise shell. Also Panaiten and Princes Isl.

Prinsenhage, Netherlands: see Princenhage.

Prins Karls Forland, Spitsbergen: see Prince Charles Foreland.

Prinzapolka or **Prinzapolca** (prēnsäpōl'kä), town (1950 pop. 562), Zelaya dept., E Nicaragua, port on Caribbean Sea, at mouth of Prinzapolka R., 95 mi. NNE of Bluefields; commercial center; bananas, sugar cane, coconuts; lumbering.

Prinzapolka River or **Prinzapolca River,** E Nicaragua, rises on Saslaya peak of Cordillera Isabelia, flows 120 mi. E to Caribbean Sea at Prinzapolka. Has auriferous sands. Navigable for light-draught vessels.

Prinzendorf (prĭn'tsŭndôrf), village (pop. 749), NE Lower Austria, 30 mi. NNE of Vienna; oil well.

Prior, Cape (prēôr'), on Atlantic coast of Galicia, in La Coruña prov., NW Spain, 15 mi. NNE of La Coruña; 43°33'N 8°19'W. Lighthouse.

Prior Lake, village (pop. 536), Scott co., S Minn., 20 mi. SSW of Minneapolis in lake region; dairy products.

Priozersk (prēŭzyôrsk'), city (1944 pop. 3,311), NW Leningrad oblast, Russian SFSR, port on L. Ladoga, at N mouth of Vuoksi R., 50 mi. NE of Vyborg, on Karelian Isthmus; sawmilling, cellulose mfg. Developed around medieval castle (long disputed bet. Swedes and Russians), which was restored after 1887; houses town mus. since 1894. Chartered 1650; called Käkisalmi (kă'kĭsälmē) (Rus. Kyakisalmi), Swedish *Kexholm* (Rus. Keksgolm), while in Finland (until 1940) and, until 1948, in USSR.

Pripet, Maine: see Islesboro.

Pripet Marshes (prĭ'pĕt), forested, swampy area (□33,500) in W European USSR, largely coextensive with Polesye lowland. Extends along Pripet R. and its affluents bet. Brest (W), Mogilev (E), and Kiev (S); forms dense network of rivers, lakes, canals, and marshes. Occasional sandy elevations used for agr. (hemp, flax, potatoes, buckwheat). Generally undeveloped economically; lumbering and associated industries. Drainage of swamps began in 1870s. A natural defense barrier, they were a battlefield in First World War, but were by-passed by the Germans in 1941.

Pripet River, Rus. *Pripyat* or *Pripyat'* (prē'pyŭtyŭ), Pol. *Prypeć* (prĭ'pĕch), in W European USSR, rises SE of Wlodawa (Poland) near Bug R., in Volyn oblast, Ukrainian SSR; flows 500 mi. generally E, through Belorussia, past Pinsk (head of navigation), Turov, Petrikov, Mozyr, and Chernobyl, to Dnieper R. 50 mi. N of Kiev. Navigable along ⅔ of course (chiefly for lumber). Receives Ptich and Sluch (left) and Styr, Goryn, and Uzh (right) rivers. Linked with Bug R. by Dnieper-Bug Canal, with Neman R. by Oginski Canal and Shchara R. Known as Strumen or Strumen', Pol. *Strumień,* in Pinsk section.

Prisecnice (pûrzhē'sĕchnyĭtsĕ), Czech *Přísečnice,* Ger. *Pressnitz* (prĕs'nĭts), town (pop. 788), W Bohemia, Czechoslovakia, 5 mi. ESE of Vejprty, in the Erzgebirge, near Ger. border.

Prishtina, Yugoslavia: see Pristina.

Prislop Pass (prē'slōp) (alt. 4,633 ft.), in NE Rodna Mts., N Rumania, bet. Transylvania and Maramures, c.20 mi. NE of Nasaud; highway corridor. Bistrita R. rises here.

Pristan Lavak or **Pristan' Lavak** (prē'stŭnyŭ lŭväk') [Rus.,=Lavak landing], town (1947 pop. over 500), N Tashauz oblast, Turkmen SSR, port on the Amu Darya and 30 mi. NNW of Tashauz (linked by railroad), on Khiva oasis; cotton-shipping point.

Pristan Przhevalsk or **Pristan' Przheval'sk** (pûrzhĭvälsk'), town (1939 pop. over 500), NE Issyk-Kul oblast, Kirghiz SSR, major port at E end of Issyk-Kul (lake), 7 mi. NW of Przhevalsk; shipbuilding; metalworks. Shipping route to Rybachye.

Pristina or **Prishtina** (both: prē'shtĭnä), Serbo-Croatian *Priština,* town (pop. 19,822), ⊙ Kosovo-Metohija oblast, S Serbia, Yugoslavia, on railroad and 150 mi. S of Belgrade, in Kosovo; handicraft (jewelry). Predominantly Turkish architecture. Temporary ⊙ Serbia (12th cent.; then transferred to Prizren). Under Turkish rule until 1913; in Albania 1941–44. Monastery of Gracanica or Grachanitsa, Serbo-Croatian *Gračanica,* (built 1321) and tomb of Sultan Murad I are near by.

Pritamabad, W Pakistan: see Mohattanagar.

Pritchett, town (pop. 286), Baca co., SE Colo., 13 mi. W of Springfield, in dairying area; alt. 4,810 ft.

Pritzerbe (prĭts'ĕr"bŭ), town (pop. 1,943), Brandenburg, E Germany, on expansion of the Havel and 7 mi. NW of Brandenburg; dairying, stock raising.

Pritzwalk (prĭts'välk), town (pop. 9,416), Brandenburg, E Germany, 20 mi. NE of Wittenberge; woolen milling, brewing, distilling, flour milling. Has late-Gothic church. Former Cistercian monastery of Heiligengrabe (founded 1289, later converted into convent) is 8 mi. E.

Privas (prēvä'), town (pop. 4,000), ⊙ Ardèche dept., S France, on small tributary on the Rhone and 50 mi. S of Saint-Étienne, at foot of the Cévennes; produces glazed marrons. Silk and leather trade. Kieselguhr and iron mines near by.

Priverno (prēvĕr'nô), town (pop. 7,812), Latina prov., Latium, S central Italy, 15 mi. SE of Frosinone; olive oil, wine, dairy products. Has 13th-cent. town hall, medieval houses. Ruins of anc. *Privernum* near by. Called Piperno until 1928.

Privigye, Czechoslovakia: see Prievidza.

Privodino (prēvô'dyĭnŭ), town (1941 pop. over 500), S Archangel oblast, Russian SFSR, on Lesser Northern Dvina R. and 15 mi. SSW of Kotlas; metalworks.

Privokzalny or **Privokzal'nyy** (prēvŭkzäl'nē), town (1940 pop. over 500), W central Sverdlovsk oblast, Russian SFSR, 2 mi. W of Verkhoturye; metalworking. Gold placers near by.

Privolnoye or **Privol'noye** (prēvôl'nŭyŭ). **1** Village (1926 pop. 5,794), N Central Nikolayev oblast, Ukrainian SSR, on Ingul R. and 38 mi. NNE of Nikolayev; metalworks. **2** Town, Voroshilovgrad oblast, Ukrainian SSR: see Privolye.

Privolnyanski or **Privol'nyanskiy** (-nyŭnskē), town (1939 pop. over 500), SW Voroshilovgrad oblast, Ukrainian SSR, in the Donbas, NE of Popasnaya; coal mines.

Privolye or **Privol'ye** (prēvô'lyĭ), town (1939 pop. over 500), W Voroshilovgrad oblast, Ukrainian SSR, in the Donbas, on the Northern Donets and 8 mi. NNW of Lisichansk; coal mines. Also called Privolnoye.

Privolzhsk (prēvôlsh-sk'), city (1939 pop. over 10,000), N Ivanovo oblast, Russian SFSR, near Volga R., 30 mi. NNE of Ivanovo; linen-milling center. Called Yakovlevskoye until 1938, when it became a city.

Privolzhski or **Privolzhskiy** (-skē). **1** Town (1936 pop. estimate 4,500), E Astrakhan oblast, Russian SFSR, port on right bank of the Volga and 4 mi. NNW of Astrakhan; wood- and metalworking; natural-gas extracting; fish processing and preserving. Health resort (mud baths) on small near-by lake. Originally Kalmytski Bazar; renamed (1936) Kanukov; in Kalmyk Autonomous SSR until 1943; renamed Privolzhski in 1944. **2** Town (1939 pop. over 500), central Saratov oblast, Russian SFSR, near Volga R., 5 mi. SSW of Engels; meat packing.

Privolzhskoye (-skŭyŭ), village (1948 pop. over 2,000), S central Saratov oblast, Russian SFSR, on left bank of Volga R. and 29 mi. SSW of Engels; wheat, tobacco, fruit. Until 1941 (in German Volga Autonomous SSR), Kukkus or Kukkuss.

Privolzhye or **Privolzh'ye** (-zhyĭ), village (1926 pop. 2,024), W Kuibyshev oblast, Russian SFSR, on left bank of the Volga (landing) and 22 mi. SSE of Syzran; limestone quarrying; wheat, fruit, cattle, sheep.

Privoz, Czechoslovakia: see Ostrava.

Priyedor, Yugoslavia: see Prijedor.

Priyepolye, Yugoslavia: see Prijepolje.

Prizren (prē'zrĕn), town (pop. 19,839), SW Serbia, Yugoslavia, 38 mi. SW of Pristina, in the Metohija; handicraft (jewelry). Gardening and chestnut-growing in vicinity. Noted for local costumes. Seat of R.C. archbishop and Greek metropolitan.

Numerous old (some ruined) churches and a monastery (burial place of Serbian king Dushan; d. 1355). In Middle Ages, an important trade center and (12th–14th cent.) a royal residence of Serbia. Under Turks, ⊙ Kosovo vilayet. In Albania 1941–44. Temporary ⊙ Kosovo-Metohija oblast briefly after 1945. Formerly also called Prizrend or Prizrendi.

Prizzi (prē'tsē), town (pop. 9,665), Palermo prov., W central Sicily, 10 mi. SE of Corleone, in stock-raising, cereal-growing region; bakeries, macaroni factories.

Prnjavor or **Prnyavor** (both: pûr'nyävôr), village (pop. 2,223), N Bosnia, Yugoslavia, 25 mi. ENE of Banja Luka; local trade center. Mineral springs near by.

Probezhna (prŭbyĕzh'nŭ), Pol. *Probużna* (prôbōozh'nä), village (1931 pop. 3,140), SE Ternopol oblast, Ukrainian SSR, 9 mi. E of Chortkov; flour milling, sunflower-oil extracting.

Probolinggo (prŏbŏolĭng'gō), town (pop. 37,009), E Java, Indonesia, port on Madura Strait, 50 mi. SE of Surabaya; 7°45'S 113°13'E; textile mills, railroad workshops. Exports corn, rubber, coffee. Has large Chinese pop. Also spelled Prabalingga or Perobolinggo.

Probota, Rumania: see DOLHASCA.

Probstzella (prōpst"tsĕ'lä), town (pop. 2,625), Thuringia, central Germany, in Thuringian Forest, 8 mi. S of Saalfeld, 3 mi. N of Ludwigsstadt (Bavaria); china-mfg. center; slate quarrying. After 1945, traffic check point bet. East and West Germany.

Probus (prō'bŭs), village and parish (pop. 1,100), W central Cornwall, England, 5 mi. ENE of Truro; agr. market. Has 15th-cent. church.

Probuzna, Ukrainian SSR: see PROBEZHNA.

Proby Island, Tonga: see NIUAFOO.

Prochowice (prô"khôvē'tsĕ), Ger. *Parchwitz* (pärkh'vĭts), town (1939 pop. 2,797; 1946 pop. 942) in Lower Silesia, after 1945 in Wroclaw prov., SW Poland, on the Katzbach, near its mouth on the Oder, and 10 mi. NE of Liegnitz (Legnica); leather mfg. After 1945, briefly called Parchonice.

Procida (prô'chēdä), anc. *Prochyta*, volcanic island (□ 1.4; pop. 9,452), Napoli prov., S Italy, near NW entrance to Bay of Naples, bet. Ischia isl. and Cape Miseno; 2 mi. long. Agr. (grapes, citrus fruit, potatoes); fishing. Chief town, Procida, on NE coast. Has castle (now a prison). John of Procida was lord of this isl. and took his name from it.

Proconnesus, Turkey: see MARMARA ISLAND.

Procter, village (pop. estimate 250), S B.C., on Kootenay L., 17 mi. NE of Nelson, in lumbering and mining (gold, silver, tungsten) region.

Proctor. **1** Village (pop. 2,693), St. Louis co., NE Minn., just W of Duluth; iron-shipping point; also dairying and truck-farming area. Settled 1893, inc. 1894. Called Proctorknott until 1939. **2** Village (pop. c.300), Comanche co., central Texas, near Leon R., 13 mi. NE of Comanche; rail point in agr., ranching area. **3** Town (pop. 1,917), including Proctor village (pop. 1,813), Rutland co., W central Vt., on Otter Creek, just NW of Rutland. Marble quarrying and finishing center since 19th cent.

Proctorsville, Vt.: see CAVENDISH.

Proctorville (prŏk'tŭrvĭl). **1** Town (pop. 232), Robeson co., S N.C., 10 mi. S of Lumberton. **2** Village (pop. 737), Lawrence co., S Ohio, on the Ohio just E of Chesapeake and opposite Huntington, W.Va.

Prodano, Greece: see PROTE.

Proddatur (prŏ'dŭtōor), city (pop. 26,961), Cuddapah dist., central Madras, India, on Penner R. and 25 mi. NW of Cuddapah; cotton ginning; rice, turmeric; dairy farm. Extensive limestone quarrying near Erraguntla (or Yerraguntla) village, on railroad and 7 mi. S.

Prodhromos (prô'dhrômôs), summer resort (pop. 506), Limassol dist., central Cyprus, in Olympus Mts., 22 mi. NNW of Limassol; alt. c.4,600 ft. Grows grapes, cherries, pears.

Proença-a-Nova (prwän'sänô'vŭ), town (pop. 882), Castelo Branco dist., central Portugal, 24 mi. WSW of Castelo Branco; lumbering in pine, oak, and chesnut forests.

Proença-a-Velha (–vĕ'lyŭ), town (pop. 1,326), Castelo Branco dist., central Portugal, 19 mi. NE of Castelo Branco. Archaeological discoveries made here are exhibited in Lisbon and Castelo Branco museums. Town was important under Romans and Visigoths, was destroyed by Moors, and refounded by Templars in 13th cent.

Profen (prō'fŭn), village (pop. 1,650), in former Prussian Saxony prov., central Germany, after 1945 in Saxony-Anhalt, on the White Elster and 7 mi. NE of Zeitz; lignite mining.

Profile Cliff, Calif.: see YOSEMITE NATIONAL PARK.

Profile Mountain, peak (4,007 ft.) of White Mts., NW N.H., W of Franconia Notch, from which is visible the Old Man of the Mountain (also called Great Stone Face or Profile), a natural stone profile 48 ft. high, on S peak of mtn. Aerial tramway built 1938; ski trails. Also known as Cannon Mtn.

Profintern, Russian SFSR: see DOMBAROVSKI.

Profondéville (prôfōdävēl'), village (pop. 1,534), Namur prov., S central Belgium, on Meuse R. and 6 mi. S of Namur; marble quarrying; apples, plums; tourist resort.

Progorelets (prô'gôrĕlĕts), village (pop. 3,751), Vidin dist., NW Bulgaria, on Tsibritsa R. and 14 mi. SSE of Lom; grain, livestock.

Progreso (prōgrā'sō), village (pop. 283), Northern Dist., Br. Honduras, on lagoon, 9 mi. S of Corozal; corn, sugar cane, coconuts.

Progreso, Guatemala: see EL PROGRESO.

Progreso, city (pop. 6,921), Yoro dept., NW Honduras, in Sula Valley, on Ulúa R. and 37 mi. SW of Tela (linked by rail); trade center in banana area; agr., livestock. A new city, founded in 1920s. Sometimes called El Progreso.

Progreso. **1** Town (pop. 2,121), Coahuila, N Mexico, 45 mi. NE of Monclova; cereals, istle, candelilla wax, cattle. **2** Officially Progreso de Obregón, town (pop. 3,505), Hidalgo, central Mexico, on Tula R. and 30 mi. WNW of Pachuca; rail terminus; agr. center (corn, wheat, beans, potatoes, fruit, livestock). **3** Town, Mexico state, Mexico: see EL PROGRESO INDUSTRIAL. **4** Town (pop. 1,123), Oaxaca, S Mexico, on S slopes of Sierra Madre del Sur, 11 mi. NE of Pochutla; silver and gold mining. **5** City (pop. 11,990), Yucatan, SE Mexico, on offshore bar in Gulf of Mexico, 23 mi. N of Mérida. Railhead; port of entry; seaport. Exports large quantities of sisal hemp, product of great Yucatan henequen-growing industry. Port for Mérida (connected by rail). Airfield.

Progreso, village (pop. 69), Chiriquí prov., W Panama, on railroad and 10 mi. N of Puerto Armuelles, near Costa Rica border; banana center; corn, rice, beans, livestock.

Progreso, town, Canelones dept., S Uruguay, on railroad and 15 mi. N of Montevideo, in wine-growing dist.

Progreso, El, department, Guatemala: see EL PROGRESO.

Progreso de Zaragoza (dā särägō'sä), town (pop. 858), Veracruz, E Mexico, in Sierra Madre Oriental, 29 mi. WSW of Papantla; corn, sugar cane, fruit.

Progreso Industrial, El, Mexico: see EL PROGRESO INDUSTRIAL.

Progress, village (1940 pop. 2,136), Dauphin co., S central Pa., 2 mi. NE of Harrisburg.

Project City, village (pop. 1,078, with adjacent Pinegrove), Shasta co., N Calif., near Shasta L., 8 mi. NE of Redding.

Prokhladny or **Prokhladnyy** (prŭkhläd'nē), city (1932 pop. estimate 13,800), NE Kabardian Autonomous SSR, Russian SFSR, on Malka R., near mouth of the Baksan, and 27 mi. NE of Nalchik; major rail junction; rail workshops, freight yards; machine mfg., brickworking, vegetable-oil pressing. During Second World War, held (1942–43) by Germans.

Prokhorovka, Russian SFSR: see ALEKSANDROVSKI, Kursk oblast.

Prokletije or **Prokletiye**, Albania-Yugoslavia: see NORTH ALBANIAN ALPS.

Prokopyevsk or **Prokop'yevsk** (prŭkôp'yĭfsk), city (1926 pop. 10,717; 1939 pop. 107,227), W Kemerovo oblast, Russian SFSR, on branch of Trans-Siberian RR and 17 mi. NW of Stalinsk; coal-mining center in Kuznetsk Basin. Important suburbs are Usyaty (N; main rail depot), Zenkovo (S), and Yasnaya Polyana (W; founded 1945).

Prokudskoye, Russian SFSR: see CHIK.

Prökuls, Lithuania: see PRIEKULE.

Prokuplje or **Prokuplye** (both: prôkōop'lyĕ), town (pop. 9,842), S central Serbia, Yugoslavia, on Toplica R., on railroad and 16 mi. WSW of Nis.

Proleika, Russian SFSR: see LUGOVAYA PROLEIKA.

Proletari or **Proletariy** (prŭlyĭtä'rē), town (1939 pop. over 2,000), W central Novgorod oblast, Russian SFSR, near L. Ilmen, 17 mi. ESE of Novgorod; glassworking center.

Proletarsk (prŭlyĭtärsk'). **1** Town (1939 pop. over 2,000), central Leninabad oblast, Tadzhik SSR, on railroad and 9 mi. SSW of Leninabad; sericulture; cotton ginning. Rail spur to Sulyukta coal mines. Formerly Dragomirovo. **2** City (1939 pop. over 10,000), W Voroshilovgrad oblast, Ukrainian SSR, in the Donbas, on the Northern Donets, and 3 mi. NNW of Lisichansk; coal mines, glassworks. Formerly called Nesvetevich.

Proletarskaya (–skīŭ), village (1926 pop. 10,480), S Rostov oblast, Russian SFSR, on railroad and 18 mi. NE of Salsk, on the Western Manych (head of navigation; reservoir, locks); metal- and woodworking; dairying, wheat, cotton.

Proletarskaya Pobeda, Russian SFSR: see PIROGOVSKI.

Proletarski or **Proletarskiy** (–skē). **1** Town (1926 pop. 580), SW Kursk oblast, Russian SFSR, on railroad (Gotnya rail junction) and 37 mi. WNW of Belgorod; meat packing, dairying; brickworks. Formerly Gotnya. **2** Town (1926 pop. 1,807), S Moscow oblast, Russian SFSR, on rail spur and 8 mi. N of Serpukhov; woolen-milling center. Until 1928, Proletari. **3** Town (1939 pop. over 500), S Voroshilovgrad oblast, Ukrainian SSR, in the Donbas, on railroad (Kartushino station) and 6 mi. WNW of Rovenki; coal mines.

Prölsdorf (prŭls'dôrf), village (pop. 405), Lower Franconia, N Bavaria, Germany, on small Rauhe Ebrach R. and 12 mi. W of Bamberg; grain, potatoes, hogs.

Prome (prōm), northern dist. (□ 2,953; 1941 pop. 436,714) of Pegu div., Lower Burma, bet. Arakan Yoma and Pegu Yoma, astride Irrawaddy R.; ⊙ Prome. N and NE areas W of Irrawaddy R. are hilly and forested (teak); S and SW areas under rice. Served by Rangoon-Prome RR. Salt wells along Arakan Yoma. Pop. is 90% Burmese.

Prome, town (pop. 28,295), ⊙ Prome dist., Lower Burma, on left bank of Irrawaddy R. and 150 mi. NNW of Rangoon; 18°49'N 95°13'E; head of railroad to Rangoon. Trade center for dry-zone (N) and Irrawaddy delta products; silk textiles, lacquer; placer mining (gold) in Irrawaddy R. Official residences on hill (S). Noted Shwesandaw pagoda. An anc. city, disputed by Mons and Burmese, passed 1757 to Burma under Alaungpaya. Captured by British in 1825 and annexed in 1852. In Second World War recaptured May, 1945, by Br. troops.

Promina (prô'mēnä), mountain in Dinaric Alps, W Croatia, Yugoslavia, in Dalmatia; highest point (3,765 ft.) is 5 mi. N of Drnis. Silveric brown-coal mine at S foot.

Promise City, town (pop. 218), Wayne co., S Iowa, 15 mi. W of Centerville, in coal-mining area.

Promissão (prōmēsä'ō), city (pop. 6,632), NW central São Paulo, Brazil, on railroad and 12 mi. NW of Lins; coffee processing, sawmilling, rum distilling, pottery mfg.

Promontorium Sacrum, Portugal: see SAINT VINCENT, CAPE.

Promontory, monument, Box Elder co., N Utah, 30 mi. WNW of Brigham City, near Great Salt Lake; marks meeting (1869) of E and W branches of 1st continental railroad.

Promontory Point, NW Utah, peninsula extending c.20 mi. S into Great Salt L. from N shore and forming W shore of Bear River Bay. Rises to 7,075 ft. in S. Salt is produced at hamlet in S tip. Railroad cutoff, crossing Great Salt L., passes through peninsula at this point.

Prompton, borough (pop. 197), Wayne co., NE Pa., 4 mi. W of Honesdale and on headstream of Lackawaxen R.

Promyshlennaya (prŭmĭsh'lyĭnŭ), town (1939 pop. over 10,000), NW Kemerovo oblast, Russian SFSR, on branch of Trans-Siberian RR, on Inya R. and 35 mi. SSW of Kemerovo, in Kuznetsk Basin; truck produce; metalworking, sawmilling.

Promysla (prô'mĭslŭ), town (1939 pop. over 500), E Molotov oblast, Russian SFSR, on Koiva R. and 50 mi. ENE (under jurisdiction) of Chusovoi; hematite mining. Charcoal burning, gold placers near by.

Promzino, Russian SFSR: see SURSKOYE.

Pronchishchev Bay (prŭnchē'shchĭf), on E (Laptev Sea) coast of Taimyr Peninsula, Krasnoyarsk Territory, Russian SFSR; 75°40'N 113°10'E. Govt. observation post on shore.

Pronsk (prônsk), village (1926 pop. 1,465), W Ryazan oblast, Russian SFSR, 36 mi. S of Ryazan; grain, hemp. Dates from 12th cent.

Pronya River (prô'nyŭ), E Belorussian SSR, rises SE of Orsha in Smolensk-Moscow Upland, flows c.80 mi. S, past Gorki, to Sozh R. at Slavgorod.

Prophetstown, village (pop. 1,691), Whiteside co., NW Ill., on Rock R. (bridged here) and 31 mi. ENE of Moline; trade and shipping center in agr. area; makes lawn mowers. Settled on site of village of Indian prophet White Cloud; inc. 1859.

Propoisk, Belorussian SSR: see SLAVGOROD, Mogilev.

Propontis, Turkey: see MARMARA, SEA OF.

Propriá (prōprēä'), city (pop. 10,314), N Sergipe, NE Brazil, port on lower São Francisco R. (navigable to the Atlantic), opposite Pôrto Real do Colégio (Alagoas), and 50 mi. NNE of Aracaju; N terminus of railroad from Salvador (Bahia). Ships sugar, rice, cotton, livestock. Rice husking, sugar milling.

Propriano (prôprēä'nô), village (pop. 1,518), SW Corsica, port on Gulf of Valinco of the Mediterranean, serving Sartène (5 mi. SE); mfg. (brier pipestems, cigars, corks, flour products). Spa of Baracci, with sulphurous springs, is 2 mi. NE.

Prosara Mountains (prô'särä), in Dinaric Alps, N Bosnia, Yugoslavia; extend c.10 mi. along Sava R.; highest point (1,191 ft.) is 12 mi. W of Gradiska.

Prosec, Czechoslovakia: see BLANSKO.

Prosecco (prōsĕk'kō), Slovenian *Prosek* (prô'sĕk), town (pop. 1,160), N Free Territory of Trieste, 5 mi. NNW of Trieste; vineyards. Placed 1947 under Anglo-American administration.

Prosek, Free Territory of Trieste: see PROSECCO.

Proserpine (prŏ'sŭrpīn), town (pop. 1,797), E Queensland, Australia, 140 mi. ESE of Townsville; sugar-producing center.

Proskurov (prŭskōo'rŭf), city (1926 pop. 31,989), ⊙ Kamenets-Podolski oblast, Ukrainian SSR, in Podolia, on the Southern Bug and 170 mi. WSW of Kiev; 49°25'N 27°E. Rail junction; machine shops; mfg. of furniture, clothing; food processing (flour, sugar, bakery products). Dates from 15th cent. Passed (1793) to Russia, developing as rail and road center. Pop. 40% Jewish until Second World War, when city was held (1941–43) by Germans.

Prosna River (prôs′nä), W central Poland, rises 7 mi. NE of Olesno, flows 135 mi. NNW, past Wieruszow and Kalisz, to Warta R. 2 mi. SW of Pyzdry.

Prosnica River (prôsh-nē′tsä), Pol. *Prośnica*, Ger. *Persante* (pĕrzän′tů), in Pomerania, after 1945 in NW Poland, rises NW of Szczecinek, flows 102 mi. NW, past Bialogard and Karlino, to the Baltic at Kolberg (Kolobrzeg).

Prosnitsa (prŭsnyē′tsŭ), village, central Kirov oblast, Russian SFSR, near Cheptsa R., on railroad and 20 mi. ESE of Kirov; grain; starch mfg., basket weaving.

Prosotsane or **Prosotsani** (both: prôsôtsä′nē), town (pop. 7,011), Drama nome, Macedonia, Greece, 9 mi. W of Drama; trading center for tobacco, cotton, barley; olive oil. Sometimes spelled Prossotsani; also called Pyrsopolis or Pirsopolis.

Prospect, town (pop. 22,875), SE South Australia, 3 mi. N of Adelaide, in metropolitan area; agr. center.

Prospect, Cayman Isls., B.W.I.: see GRAND CAYMAN.

Prospect. 1 Town (pop. 1,896), New Haven co., SW Conn., just SE of Waterbury; dairy products, poultry. Inc. 1827. **2** Resort town (pop. 392), Waldo co., S Maine, on the Penobscot and 14 mi. NE of Belfast. Site of Fort Knox State Park. **3** Village (pop. 318), Oneida co., central N.Y., on West Canada Creek and 15 mi. N of Utica, in limestone-producing area. **4** Village (pop. 1,031), Marion co., central Ohio, 10 mi. SSW of Marion and on Scioto R.; shipbuilding (tugboats); mfg. of fire engines; dairying. Settled 1832, inc. as village 1876. **5** Residential borough (pop. 726), Butler co., W Pa., 8 mi. WNW of Butler; agr.

Prospect Heights, town (pop. 50), Fremont co., S central Colo., just S of Canon City, near Arkansas R.

Prospect Park. 1 Borough (pop. 5,242), Passaic co., NE N.J., just N of Paterson; mfg. (metal products, textiles, woven labels); dairy products. Inc. 1901. **2** Borough (pop. 5,834), Delaware co., SE Pa., SW suburb of Philadelphia; wire mfg. Inc. 1894.

Prospect Point, N.Y.: see MANHASSET NECK.

Prosper, town (pop. 243), Collin co., N Texas, 31 mi. N of Dallas, in cotton, corn area.

Prosperity, town (pop. 699), Newberry co., NW central S.C., 35 mi. WNW of Columbia.

Prosser (prŏ′sûr). **1** Village (pop. 81), Adams co., S Nebr., 10 mi. NW of Hastings, near Platte R. **2** City (pop. 2,636), ⊙ Benton co., S Wash., at the falls of Yakima R., 30 mi. W of Pasco; dairy products, fruit, flour, livestock. Inc. 1904.

Prossnitz, Czechoslovakia: see PROSTEJOV.

Prossotsani, Greece: see PROSOTSANE.

Prostejov (prô′styĕyôf), Czech *Prostějov*, Ger. *Prossnitz* (prôs′nĭts), city (pop. 31,718), central Moravia, Czechoslovakia, 10 mi. SW of Olomouc; rail junction; clothing-mfg. center; also noted for its agr. processing (malting, brewing, milling); mfg. of textiles, footwear, agr. machinery, ceramics, confectionery. Has 14th-cent. church, 16th-cent. town hall (now a mus.) and castle. Seat of Czechoslovak air navigation acad.

Prosyanaya (prŭsyŭnī′ŭ), town (1939 pop. over 500), SE Dnepropetrovsk oblast, Ukrainian SSR, 6 mi. SE of Chaplino; kaolin and refractory-clay quarries.

Proszowice (prô″shôvē′tsĕ), town (pop. 2,945), Krakow prov., S Poland, 18 mi. NE of Cracow; bricksworks; flour milling. Sulphur deposits W of town.

Prote or **Proti** (both: prô′tē), town (pop. 3,380), Serrai nome, Macedonia, Greece, 26 mi. ESE of Serrai, on slope of Mt. Pangaion; cotton, potatoes, tobacco, beans; under Turkey, called KupKoi.

Prote or **Proti,** uninhabited island (□ 2.9) in Ionian Sea, 1 mi. off SW Peloponnesus, Greece, 6 mi. S of Philiatra; 3 mi. long, 2 mi. wide. Ruins of acropolis. Formerly Prodano.

Protección or **La Protección** (lä prōtĕksyōn′), village (pop. 725), Yoro dept., NW Honduras, in Sula Valley, on Ulúa R. and 26 mi. SW of Tela (linked by rail), in banana zone.

Protection, city (pop. 814), Comanche co., S Kansas, 45 mi. SSE of Dodge City; shipping point for wheat, livestock, and dairy area. Gas wells.

Proti, Greece: see PROTE.

Protivin (prô′tyĭvēn), Czech *Protivín*, village (pop. 2,798), S Bohemia, Czechoslovakia, 8 mi. SSE of Pisek; rail junction; brewing center.

Protivin (prô′tuvĭn, prō′–), town (pop. 283), Howard co., NE Iowa, 10 mi. S of Cresco; feed milling.

Protva River (prôt′vŭ), central European Russian SFSR, rises S of Uvarovka in Smolensk-Moscow Upland, flows c.130 mi. generally SE, past Vereya and Borovsk, to Oka R. 7 mi. WSW of Serpukhov.

Protville (prōvēl′), agr. village, Tunis dist., N Tunisia, on the lower Medjerda, 14 mi. NNW of Tunis; road junction. Ruins of anc. *Utica* are 4 mi. N.

Prouts Neck, SW Maine, peninsula (c.2 mi. long) at mouth of Nonesuch R., 10 mi. SSW of Portland. Prouts Neck village is in SCARBORO town.

Provadiya (prôvä′dēä), city (8,730), Stalin dist., E Bulgaria, on Provadiya R. and 23 mi. W of Stalin; agr. center; cloth milling (linen), wine making. Saltworks 2 mi. S. Has ruins of medieval fortress. Founded by Bulg. tsar Simeon the Great in 10th cent.; later dominated by Byzantines. Became commercial town under Turkish rule (15th-19th cent.), when it was called Pravadi. Sometimes spelled Pravadia or Provadia.

Provadiya River, E Bulgaria, formed by confluence of streams rising in S Deliorman upland; flows SE, past Provadiya, N, and E, through Belovo L., to Stalin L. 2 mi. E of Beloslav; c.45 mi. long.

Provan (prō′vŭn), SE suburb (pop. 41,788) of Glasgow, Lanark, Scotland.

Proven (prû′vŭn), Dan. *Prøven*, whaling and sealing settlement (pop. 275), Upernavik dist., W Greenland, on islet in Baffin Bay, 30 mi. SSE of Upernavik; 72°22′N 55°35′W. Radio station.

Provence (prôvãs′), region and former province of SE France, bounded by the Rhone (W), the Mediterranean (S), and Italy (E); historical ⊙ Aix-en-Provence. Adjoined by Languedoc (W) and Dauphiné (N) regions, it now forms Bouches-du-Rhône, Var, and Basses-Alpes depts., and part of Vaucluse and Alpes-Maritimes depts. Mostly mountainous, it is crossed by the generally arid Provence Alps which extend their southernmost spurs to the Gulf of Lion. In the E, the Maritime Alps along Ital. border form a knot of rugged granite ranges. The rocky, heavily indented coast line bet. Marseilles and Menton is dominated by 2 isolated crystalline mountain blocks, the Monts des Maures and the Estérel. W Provence slopes gently towards the Rhone and includes the latter's delta. Drained by short coastal streams (Roya, Var, Argens, Arc) and by torrential left tributaries of the Rhone (especially the Durance). Fertile Rhone valley noted for its vineyards (Côtes-du-Rhône), orchards, olive and mulberry groves. The eroded hinterland, except for alluvial mtn. valleys, is agr. unproductive. Bauxite mined near Brignoles; ocher quarried near Apt. Livestock raising in the Camargue. Along beautiful Fr. Riviera luxuriant subtropical vegetation alternates with extensive flower fields (especially around Grasse); here tourist industry flourishes; Nice, Cannes, Menton, Antibes, Hyères, and numerous smaller resorts dot Europe's most popular playground. Marseilles, second city of France, carries on most of region's trade. Toulon is chief Fr. naval base. Arles is rich in Roman relics. While the Riviera is reputed for its mild Mediterranean winter climate, W and central Provence suffer from the cold, dry *mistral* (wind descending from the Alps) and severe summer heat. Coastal strip settled c.600 B.C. by Greeks from Asia Minor, and by Phoenician merchants. In 2d cent. B.C. Romans established colonies here, and Provence (the Roman *Provincia*) became oldest of Roman possessions beyond the Alps. A part of Narbonensis under the Empire, it was invaded by Visigoths (5th cent.), Franks (6th cent.) and Arabs (8th cent.); Charles Martel recovered it for the Franks. Roman institutions, however, left a profound impression. Provençal language was standard literary idiom throughout S France in Middle Ages and is still used by some Provençal writers. In 879, Boso, count of Arles, established Kingdom of Cisjurane Burgandy or Provence, which in 933 was united with Transjurane Burgundy to form Kingdom of Arles. Passed under Holy Roman Empire in 1033. Major part, held by house of Aragon, passed (1246) to Angevin dynasty of Naples through marriage. King René left Provence to his nephew, Charles of Maine, who bequeathed it to Louis XI of France. It was formally united with the crown in 1486. Orange was added in 1672. The prov. never included Avignon and the Comtat Venaissin, which were incorporated into France in 1791, nor county of Nice annexed in1860. In recent times large-scale immigration from Italy has taken place. Along Provence coast, bet.Cannes and Hyères, Allies invaded S France (Aug., 1944) during Second World War.

Provence Alps, W offshoots of the Maritime Alps, in SE France. Bounded N by Dauphiné Alps, W by lower Rhone R., S by the Mediterranean. Consists of irregular ranges dissected by valleys of Durance, Var, Argens, and Verdon rivers. Include coastal massifs of Maures and Estérel.

Provenchères-sur-Fave (prôvãshâr′-sür-fäv′), village (pop. 443), Vosges dept., E France, in the Vosges, 6 mi. ENE of Saint-Dié; cotton weaving.

Provencio, El (ĕl prōvĕn′thyō), town (pop. 3,831), Cuenca prov., E central Spain, 45 mi. NW of Albacete; agr. center (saffron, grapes, cereals, goats, sheep). Liquor distilling, sawmilling, dairying, plaster mfg.

Providence or **Providence Plantation,** village (pop. 1,462), Demerara co., N Br. Guiana, on Demerara R., 4 mi. SSW of Georgetown; sugar plantations.

Providence, county (□ 422; pop. 574,973), N R.I., on Conn. and Mass. lines; ⊙ PROVIDENCE, ⊙ R.I., largest city of state and industrial center. Resorts, fisheries, gravel pits, granite quarries, agr. (dairy products, poultry, truck). Includes Scituate, Smith and Sayles, and Pascoag reservoirs; drained by Blackstone (here becoming the Seekonk), Providence, Woonasquatucket, Moshassuck, Branch, and Chepachet rivers. Inc. 1703.

Providence. 1 City (pop. 3,905), Webster co., W Ky., 15 mi. WNW of Madisonville, in bituminous-coal, timber, and agr. (tobacco, corn, hay, livestock) area; flour, feed, and lumber mills; packed meat; plastic articles. **2** City (pop. 248,674), ⊙ R.I. and Providence co., NE R.I., 40 mi. SSW of Boston, on harbor at head of Providence R., here receiving Seekonk and other rivers; 41°50′N 71°25′ W. Largest city of state; port of entry; commercial and industrial center; oil refineries; mfg. (silverware and jewelry, textiles, yarn, petroleum products, textile machinery, tools, hardware, watches, metal and wire products, paper, rubber goods, chemicals, plastics, synthetics, paint, optical goods), textile dyeing and bleaching, printing. Port ships flour, grain, meat, fertilizer, receives cotton, lumber, coal, petroleum, dyewoods, chemicals. Fisheries. Seat of Brown Univ., Providence Col., R.I. Col. of Education, Y.M.C.A. Inst., and R.I. School of Design. Settled on site chosen 1636 by Roger Williams, and named in gratitude for "God's merciful providence"; grew slowly in 17th cent., and suffered in King Philip's War (1675–76). Foreign commerce brought prosperity in 18th cent.; after the Revolution industrial development was rapid. Inc. as city 1831. Silverware and metal-working industry began 1831. Became sole capital of R.I. in 1900 (Newport had been joint capital). In 1901 the legislature began to meet here in new capitol building designed by McKim, Mead, and White. Has several fine libraries, including John Carter Brown Library. Other points of interest: old colony house or old state house (1762); old market house (1773); Stephen Hopkins House (1775); John Brown House (1786); home of one of the Brown brothers, who played leading roles in early growth of city); Sarah Helen Whitman's home; First Baptist Meeting house (1775); capitol, with monuments to Oliver Hazard Perry and Nathanael Greene; Prospect Terrace, with Leo Friedlander's heroic statue of Roger Williams (1939); Roger Williams Park, with mus. of natural history, Benedict Memorial for music, and Betsey Williams Cottage (1773). Much rebuilding followed the 1938 hurricane which inundated center of city. **3** City (pop. 1,055), Cache co., N Utah, just S of Logan; alt. 4,600 ft.; trading point in wheat and fruit area. Limestone quarrying near by. Settled 1859 by Mormons.

Providence, Cape, S Melville Isl., W Franklin Dist., Northwest Territories, on Viscount Melville Sound, at SE end of McClure Strait; 74°24′N 112°30′W.

Providence, La (lä prō″vīdãs′), village (pop. 1,924), S Que., on Yamaska R., W suburb of St. Hyacinthe.

Providence, Lake, La.: see LAKE PROVIDENCE, town.

Providence Bay, village (pop. estimate 350), S central Ont., on S Manitoulin Isl., on L. Huron, 28 mi. SW of Little Current; fishing, lumbering.

Providence Channels, Bahama Isls.: see NORTHWEST PROVIDENCE CHANNEL; NORTHEAST PROVIDENCE CHANNEL.

Providence Forge, village (pop. c.150), New Kent co., E Va., near the Chickahominy, 23 mi. ESE of Richmond; lumber milling. Iron foundry established here in 1770. State game farm near by.

Providence Island, Marshall Isls.: see UJELANG.

Providence Island, outlying dependency (pop. 78) of the Seychelles, near Farquhar Isls., in Indian Ocean, 250 mi. NNW of N tip of Madagascar; 9°13′S 51°2′E; copra; fisheries.

Providence Plantation, Br. Guiana: see PROVIDENCE.

Providence River, E R.I., estuary receiving Seekonk R. and small Woonasquatucket and Moshassuck rivers at Providence; extends 8 mi. S to head of Narragansett Bay; N part is harbor of Providence.

Providencia, Colombia: see OLD PROVIDENCE ISLAND.

Providencia, La, Argentina: see LA PROVIDENCIA.

Providenciales, island, Turks and Caicos Isls.: see BLUE HILLS.

Provideniya (prŭvēdyĕnyēŭ), town (1946 pop. over 500), NE Chukchi Natl. Okrug, Kamchatka oblast, Khabarovsk Territory, Russian SFSR, on Provideniya [Rus.,=providence] Bay of Anadyr Gulf, 275 mi. E of Anadyr; air base and port on Bering Sea; govt. arctic station.

Provident City, village, Colorado co., S Texas, 30 mi. S of Columbus; natural-gasoline plant.

Providentia, Fort, Formosa: see TAINAN.

Province Lake, N.H.: see WAKEFIELD.

Provincetown, town (pop. 3,795), Barnstable co., E Mass., at extreme N tip of Cape Cod, 50 mi. SE of Boston, with good inner harbor on Cape Cod Bay. The Pilgrims landed here 1620—the 250-ft. granite Pilgrim Memorial, erected 1910, is conspicuous in this picturesque village. Permanently settled c.1700, inc. 1727. Fishing was always its staple industry, but whaling, saltmaking, rum-running, and smuggling were also practiced. In 20th cent. town gained fame as a resort favored particularly by artists. The Provincetown Players pioneered in the Little Theater movement. Has summer theater. Port of entry.

Province Wellesley (wĕlz′lē), mainland section (□ 290; pop. 183,616) of PENANG settlement, NW Malaya, on Penang Channel opposite Penang isl.;

main town, Butterworth. Rectangular strip (40 mi. long, 10 mi. wide) enclosed on land side by Kedah, bet. Muda (N) and Krian (S) rivers; rises to 1,787 ft. in the Bukit Mertajam. Agr.: rubber, rice, coconuts. Industry (tin smelting, oil storage) at Butterworth. Served by W coast railroad with spur to Prai railhead. Pop. is 48% Malay, 38% Chinese, 12% Indian. Acquired (1800) by Britain from Kedah and merged with Penang isl. to form Penang, one of the 2 original Straits Settlements.

Proving Ground, Ill.: see SAVANNA.

Provins (prôvē'), town (pop. 7,903), Seine-et-Marne dept., N central France, 30 mi. E of Melun; agr. trade center known for its crimson roses; metalworking, fireclay quarrying. Built by Romans on a rocky height, it grew prosperous in 11th-13th cent. under counts of Champagne and was scene of important fair. The picturesque upper town preserves its 13th-cent. ramparts, a 12th-cent. keep (*tour de César*), and fine church of Saint-Quiriace. Lower town (E; present business dist.) has 12th-16th-cent. church of Saint-Ayoul. Provins suffered from pestilence (1383), English wars, and Wars of Religion. In 1918, it became hq. of Fr. field armies.

Provo (prō'vō), city (pop. 28,937), ⊙ Utah co., N central Utah, on Provo R. and 37 mi. SSE of Salt Lake City, near E shore of Utah L., at base of Wasatch Range; alt. 4,549 ft. Rail, trade, and industrial center for rich agr. and mining area. Mfg. of steel and iron products, bricks, tiles; food processing (dairy products, canned goods, candy). Settled by Mormons 1849, inc. 1851. Grew as agr. trading point. After completion of railroads from Salt Lake City (1873) and Scofield (1878) became shipping center for mining district that now produces silver, lead, copper, and gold. Seat of Brigham Young Univ. and hq. of Uinta Natl. Forest; has state mental hosp. Water supply now supplemented by Provo R. irrigation project. In vicinity are Timpanogos Cave Natl. Monument, state fish and game farm, and, at Geneva (just NW, on Utah L.) a large govt.-constructed steel plant sold (1946) to U.S. Steel Corporation. Near-by peaks in Wasatch Range are Mt. Timpanogos (12,008 ft.), 10 mi. N, and Provo Peak (11,054 ft.), 6 mi. E.

Provo River, rises in Uinta Mts. in N central Utah, flows c.70 mi. generally SW, past Charleston, to Utah L. just W of Provo. A Bureau of Reclamation project (authorized 1936) includes rehabilitation of existing irrigation installations near Utah L. and construction of additional works on Provo R. Deer Creek Dam (235 ft. high, c.1,300 ft. long; completed 1941) forms Deer Creek Reservoir (6.5 mi. long, 1 mi. wide; capacity 152,600 acre-ft.), 14 mi. NE of Provo. Water is also brought to the Provo by 9-mi. canal (built 1930, enlarged 1946), from Weber R. at Oakley to Provo R. near Kamas, and by a diversion tunnel (begun 1940) from fork of Duchesne R. through mtn. divide to headwaters of Provo R. The Salt Lake Aqueduct (⅔ completed in 1948) is designed to carry water 41 mi. from Deer Creek Reservoir to Salt Lake City. The reservoir also supplements domestic water supplies of Salt Lake City, Provo, Orem, Pleasant Grove, Lindon, American Fork, and Lehi.

Provost (prō'vōst), village (pop. 645), E Alta., near Sask. border, 40 mi. SE of Wainwright; grain elevators.

Prowers (prō'ûrz), county (□ 1,626; pop. 14,836), SE Colo.; ⊙ Lamar. Irrigated agr. area, bordering on Kansas; drained by Arkansas R. Livestock, sugar beets, feed grains. Formed 1889.

Proyektnaya (prŭyĕkt'nĭŭ), rail station, W central Kemerovo oblast, Russian SFSR, 8 mi. S of Leninsk-Kuznetski, in Kuznetsk Basin; junction of 2 branches of Trans-Siberian RR.

Prozor (prô'zôr), town (pop. 1,042), S Bosnia, Yugoslavia, 40 mi. W of Sarajevo; handicraft (carpet making). Vineyards near by.

Pruden, mining village (pop. 1,478, with near-by Fonde). Bell co., SE Ky., in the Cumberlands W of Middlesboro, near Tenn. line; bituminous coal.

Prudence Island, in Portsmouth town, SE R.I., in Narragansett Bay, 12 mi. S of Providence; 6 mi. long. Resort area; site of Prudence village. Revolutionary skirmishes fought here, 1776.

Prudentópolis (prōōdĕntô'pōōlēs), city (pop. 1,979), S central Paraná, Brazil, 28 mi. WSW of Ponta Grossa; lard processing, wine making, woodworking, pottery mfg.; maté, rye, sugar cane. Mineral springs, clay quarries near by.

Prudhoe (prŭd'hō, prŭ'dō), urban district (1931 pop. 9,259; 1951 census 9,571), S Northumberland, England, near the Tyne 10 mi. W of Newcastle-upon-Tyne; coal mining. Site of 12th-cent. castle, partly preserved. In urban dist. (W) is coal-mining town of Ettringham.

Prudhoe Island, Australia: see NORTHUMBERLAND ISLANDS.

Prudhoe Land, region, NW Greenland, on Baffin Bay, in N part of Hayes Peninsula; extends c.100 mi. ESE-WNW bet. Inglefield Bay and Etah settlement; 78°N 69°W.

Prud'homme (prōō'dùm), village (pop. 248), central Sask., 35 mi. ENE of Saskatoon; wheat.

Prudnik (prōōd'nēk), Ger. *Neustadt* (noi'shtät), town (1939 pop. 17,339; 1946 pop. 10,866) in Upper Silesia, after 1945 in Opole prov., SW Poland, near Czechoslovak border, at N foot of the Jeseniky, 30 mi. SW of Oppeln (Opole); cotton and linen milling, leather mfg.

Prudon (prüdō'), village (pop. 1,511), Oran dept., NW Algeria, on the Mékerra, on railroad and 6 mi. NE of Sidi-bel-Abbès; truck-gardening, cereal- and winegrowing.

Prudyanka (prōōdyän'kŭ), town (1939 pop. over 500), N Kharkov oblast, Ukrainian SSR, on railroad and 10 mi. N of Dergachi; truck, fruit.

Pruhonice, Czechoslovakia: see UHRINEVES.

Prüm (prüm), town (pop. 2,058), in former Prussian Rhine Prov., W Germany, after 1945 in Rhineland-Palatinate, in the Eifel, 33 mi. NNW of Trier; tanneries.

Pruna (prōō'nä), town (pop. 4,561), Seville prov., SW Spain, in W Cordillera Penibética, near Cádiz prov. border, 4 mi. NE of Olvera; agr. center (cereals, olives, livestock); mfg. of olive oil, dairy products, liquor, soap, plaster. Has mineral springs and gypsum deposits.

Prundul-Bargaului (prōōn'dōōl-bûrgŭ'ōōlōōē), Rum. *Prundul-Bârgăului*, Hung. *Borgóprund* (bôr'gōprōōnt), village (pop. 3,269), Rodna prov., N central Rumania, in W foothills of the Carpathians, 13 mi. NE of Bistrita; rail junction; pulp and paper production. In Hungary, 1940–45.

Prunelli-di-Fiumorbo (It. prōōnĕl'lē-dē-fyōōmôr'bō), village (pop. 199), E Corsica, 22 mi. SSE of Corte; winegrowing. Hot springs near by.

Pruntrut, Switzerland: see PORRENTRUY.

Pru River (prōō), central Gold Coast, rises in Ashanti 33 mi. W of Mampong, flows c.120 mi. NE, along Ashanti-Northern Territories line, past Prang, to Volta R. 3 mi. SE of Yeji. Dries up in dry season (Oct.-March).

Prusa, Turkey: see BURSA, city.

Prushkov, Poland: see PRUSZKOW.

Prusice (prōōsē'tsĕ), Ger. *Prausnitz* (prous'nĭts), town (1939 pop. 2,018; 1946 pop. 505) in Lower Silesia, after 1945 in Wroclaw prov., SW Poland, 18 mi. N of Breslau (Wroclaw); agr. market (grain, flax, potatoes, livestock). Chartered c.1290. After 1945, briefly called Prusnica, Pol. *Prušnica*.

Prusnica, Poland: see PRUSICE.

Prussia (prŭ'shù), Ger. *Preussen* (proi'sùn), former state (□ 113,410; 1939 pop. 41,467,089), the largest and most important of Germany; ⊙ was Berlin. Until Second World War it consisted of 13 provs.: BERLIN, BRANDENBURG, EAST PRUSSIA, HANOVER, HESSE-NASSAU, HOHENZOLLERN, POMERANIA, RHINE PROVINCE, SAXONY, SCHLESWIG-HOLSTEIN, SILESIA (Upper and Lower), and WESTPHALIA. GRENZMARK POSEN-WESTPREUSSEN, as an administrative division [Ger. *Regierungsbezirk*] of Pomerania, was sometimes considered a 14th prov. The dominant state of Germany, Prussia occupied most of the N section of the country, extending from Luxembourg, Belgium, and the Netherlands on the W, to Poland and Lithuania on the E, and from the North Sea, Denmark, and the Baltic on the N, to Main R., Thuringian Forest, and Czechoslovakia on the S. Several small Ger. states (Anhalt, Bremen, Brunswick, Hamburg, Lippe, Oldenburg, Schaumburg-Lippe) formed enclaves in its territory; Hohenzollern was a Prussian exclave in S Germany. The name Prussia applied originally to region (the later East Prussia) inhabited by the Old Prussians, which was conquered in 13th cent. by the Teutonic Knights, who displaced original pop. and secured the territory as fief for their order. In 1466 they ceded Pomerelia (later known as West Prussia) and Ermland to Poland and accepted Polish suzerainty over the rest of their domain. In 1525, Grand Master Albert von Brandenburg secularized the Teutonic Order, assumed the title duke of Prussia (still under Polish suzerainty); from then on duchy was hereditary under a branch of the Brandenburg Hohenzollern dynasty until it passed (1618) to electors of Brandenburg and was finally guaranteed full independence from Polish suzerainty in 1660. Brandenburg formed core of later kingdom of Prussia. During the course of 17th cent., Brandenburg gained a foothold in W Germany (Cleves, Mark, and Ravensberg; 1614); the successful diplomacy of Frederick William, the Great Elector (1640–88), at the Peace of Westphalia (1648) resulted in acquisition of the bishoprics of Halberstadt, Magdeburg, and Minden, and of Farther (i.e., eastern) Pomerania, and he emerged as Germany's most powerful Protestant prince. In 1701 his son had himself crowned king of Prussia as Frederick I; he remained a vassal of the Holy Roman Emperor as elector of Brandenburg, but as king of Prussia (Prussia being outside the imperial boundaries) he was independent of the emperor. Among the Ger. princes only the elector of Saxony rivaled him in power, and only the Hapsburg emperor surpassed him. The next 150 years of Ger. history were dominated by Prussia's successful drive for supremacy in Germany. Frederick William I (1713–40) created and organized the army and bureaucracy with which Frederick the Great (1740–86) fought his wars of acquisition and organized his conquests. Before its brief eclipse during the French Revolutionary Wars and the Napoleonic Wars, Prussia had reached a position as the Continent's leading military power; territorially it had gained most of Silesia and large portions of Poland (including Pomerelia, Poznan, Warsaw, and Danzig). Defeated by the French, Prussia withdrew (1795) from the antirevolutionary coalition and remained neutral until 1806. Its forces were crushed by Napoleon in the twin battles of Jena and Auerstedt (1806); at the Treaty of Tilsit (1807), Prussia lost all lands W of the Elbe, most of its Polish holdings, and became a virtual dependency of France. During that period, however, able men (Stein, Hardenberg, Humboldt) reformed the Prussian govt.; serfdom and nobiliary privileges were abolished, agrarian and other social and economic reforms were introduced, and the groundwork was laid for an exemplary system of universal education. Prussia emerged as a modern and progressive state, whose army in the meantime had been thoroughly reformed by Scharnhorst and Gneisenau. Prussia joined the coalition against France in 1813; its troops under Field Marshal Blücher figured decisively in Napoleon's defeat at Leipzig (1813) and at Waterloo (1815). The kingdom emerged from the Congress of Vienna as one of the leading European states; in addition to recovering all its lost territory, it had gained the entire Rhine Prov. and Westphalia, the N half of Saxony, the remainder of Swedish Pomerania, and a large part of W Poland, including Danzig, Poznan, and Gniezno. With Austria, Prussia headed the German Confederation; it disappointed the hopes of liberal Ger. elements by following Metternich's reactionary policy as member of the Holy Alliance. However, Prussia took the lead in the economic unification of Germany by its leadership in the Zollverein. The 1848 March Revolution was put down with force; Frederick William IV refused the Ger. imperial crown offered him by the Frankfurt Parliament (1848–49). At the Convention of Olmütz (1850), Austria successfully thwarted Prussia's bid for leadership in Germany. In 1862, William I appointed as his chancellor Bismarck, who in 3 deliberately planned wars achieved the expulsion of Austria from Ger. affairs and the hegemony of Prussia over a unified Germany. The settlement after the war of 1864, fought in alliance with Austria against Denmark over Schleswig-Holstein, furnished a pretext for the Austro-Prussian War of 1866, in which Austria and its allies were quickly and decisively defeated; Prussia consequently annexed Hanover, Hesse-Nassau, Schleswig-Holstein, and the free city of Frankfurt. The German Confederation was dissolved, and a Prussian-dominated North German Confederation took its place. In the Franco-Prussian War (1870–71), the North German Confederation defeated France, and in 1871 William I of Prussia was proclaimed emperor of Germany. In its main features, the subsequent history of Prussia coincides with that of GERMANY. Kingdom of Prussia became a republic in 1918, and joined the Weimar Republic. Most of the continental territory lost by Germany through the Treaty of Versailles (1919) was Prussian; and until 1939, East Prussia was separated from Germany by the Polish Corridor. Prussia was dissolved (formally Feb., 1947) after the Second World War by the Allied Control Council for Germany; Prussian lands E of the Oder-Neisse line were placed under Polish administration, with the exception of N East Prussia, which came under Soviet administration. The remaining territories became part of the new Ger. states of Berlin, Brandenburg, HESSE, MECKLENBURG, LOWER SAXONY, NORTH RHINE-WESTPHALIA, RHINELAND-PALATINATE, SAXONY, SAXONY-ANHALT, Schleswig-Holstein, THURINGIA, and WÜRTTEMBERG-HOHENZOLLERN.

Pruszcz or **Pruszcz Gdanski** (prōōshch' gŭdä'nyùskē), Pol. *Pruszcz Gdański*, Ger. *Praust* (proust), town (1946 pop. 2,964), Gdansk prov., N Poland, 7 mi. S of Danzig; rail junction.

Pruszkow (prōōsh'kōōf), Pol. *Pruszków*, Rus. *Prushkov* (prōōsh'kŭf), city (pop. 25,096), Warszawa prov., E central Poland, on railroad and 10 mi. WSW of Warsaw. Industrial center; mfg. of machine tools and molds, automobile accessories, pottery, bricks, chemicals, dyes, coffins, leather goods, clothes, porcelain, faïence, pencils, combs, cosmetics; flour milling.

Prut River (prōōt), USSR and Rumania, rises in the Carpathians at E foot of the Goverla in SW Ukrainian SSR, flows N and ESE past Kolomyya and Chernovtsy, and SSE, forming Rumania-USSR border, past Lipkany, Ungeny, Leovo, and Falciu, to the Danube just above Reni; length, 530 mi. Receives Cheremosh R. (right). Navigable for 70 mi. below Leovo (grain, wine, wool). Formerly also spelled Pruth.

Pruzhany (prōōzhä'nē), Pol. *Prużana* (prōōzhä'nä), city (1931 pop. 8,013), N Brest oblast, Belorussian SSR, on Mukhavets R. and 45 mi. NE of Brest; agr.-processing center (hides, grain, vegetable oils, hops); mfg. of lubricating oil, soap, pottery. Passed (1795) from Poland to Russia; reverted (1921) to Poland; ceded to USSR in 1945.

Pryazha (pryä'zhŭ), village, S Karelo-Finnish SSR, 25 mi. W of Petrozavodsk; grain.

Prydz Bay (prĭdz), inlet (60 mi. long, 175 mi. wide) of Indian Ocean in Antarctica, E of Amery Shelf Ice and off Lars Christensen and Ingrid Christensen Coasts, bet. 73° and 81° E. Discovered 1935 by Klarius Mikkelsen, Norwegian explorer.

Pryor or **Pryor Creek**, city (pop. 2,501), ⊙ Mayes co., NE Okla., c.40 mi. ENE of Tulsa; trade center for agr. area; cotton ginning; mfg. of paper, wood, concrete, and metal products, and of vehicle bodies, mattresses, agr. lime, dairy products. A U.S. agr. experiment station and a state home for children are here. Settled 1872 on site of old trading post (1820).

Prypec River, USSR: see Pripet River.

Przasnysz (pshä'snĭsh), Rus. *Prasnysh* (prä'snĭsh), town (pop. 7,015), Warszawa prov., NE central Poland, 55 mi. N of Warsaw; rail spur terminus; mfg. (cement, rubber goods, flour). During Second World War, under administration of East Prussia, called Praschnitz.

Przedborz (pshĕd'bo͞osh), Pol. *Przedbórz*, Rus. *Przhedborzh* (pûr-zhĕd'bûrsh), town (pop. 3,503), Kielce prov., S central Poland, on Pilica R. and 20 mi. E of Radomsko; flour milling, sawmilling. Before Second World War, pop. 75% Jewish.

Przedecz (pshĕ'dĕch), Rus. *Przhedech* (pûr-zhĕ'-dyĭch), town (pop. 2,424), Bydgoszcz prov., central Poland, 24 mi. SSW of Wloclawek; flour milling, distilling.

Przemkow (pshĕm'ko͞of), Pol. *Przemków*, Ger. *Primkenau* (prĭm'kŭnou), town (1939 pop. 4,860; 1946 pop. 942) in Lower Silesia, after 1945 in Zielona Gora prov., W Poland, 30 mi. NW of Liegnitz (Legnica); agr. market (grain, vegetables, potatoes, livestock). After 1945, briefly called Przemkowo.

Przemsza River (pshĕm'shä), S Poland, formed by junction of Biala Przemsza and Czarna Przemsza rivers just SE of Myslowice; flows 15 mi. S to Vistula R. just N of Oswiecim. Entire course navigable. Until First World War, formed border bet. Austria Hungary and Rus. Poland.

Przemysl (pshĕ'mĭ-shĭl), Pol. *Przemyśl*, city (pop. 36,841), Rzeszow prov., SE Poland, on San R. and 40 mi. SE of Rzeszow, near Ukrainian SSR border. Rail junction; clothing, lumber, chemical, metallurgical, and ceramic industries; distilling, flour milling, tanning, food canning. Castle ruins, city park, 2 museums. Supposedly founded 8th cent.; ruled (981–1340) alternately by Poland and Kiev; became a diocese (1271) of Eastern Orthodox and (1375) of R.C. churches. In Austrian Poland, 1722–1919; former Austrian fortress. Fell to Russians in 1915 and retaken in same year. In 1939–40, when city was split by Ger.-Soviet frontier, section on left bank was called Deutsch Przemysl.

Przemyslany, Ukrainian SSR: see Peremyshlyany.

Przeworsk (pshĕ'vôrsk), town (pop. 8,569), Rzeszow prov., SE Poland, 22 mi. E of Rzeszow; rail junction; flour milling, mfg. of cement products, distilling.

Przhedborzh, Poland: see Przedborz.

Przhedech, Poland: see Przedecz.

Przhevalsk or **Przheval'sk** (pûrzhĭvälsk'), city (1939 pop. 21,173), ⊙ Issyk-Kul oblast, Kirghiz SSR, near SE shore of Issyk-Kul (lake), 190 mi. E of Frunze, on highway from Rybachye; 42°30'N 78°23'E. In wheat area; wines and fruit juices, food processing (flour, sunflower oil), furniture mfg.; machine shops. Its port is Pristan Przhevalsk, 7 mi. NW. Teachers col. Founded 1869. Originally called Karakol; renamed Przhevalsk for Rus. explorer N. M. Przhevalski (who died here, 1888); after1920 again became Karakol and, in 1939, Przhevalsk.

Przhevalsk, Pristan, Kirghiz SSR: see Pristan Przhevalsk.

Psachna or **Psakhna** (both: psäkhnä'), town (pop. 4,309), W central Euboea, Greece, 8 mi. NNE of Chalcis; wheat; wines; livestock raising (sheep, goats). Lignite deposits near by.

Psara (psärä'), anc. *Psyra* (sī'rŭ), Greek Aegean island (□ 16.4; pop. 751), off NW Chios isl. (separated by 11-mi. channel), in Chios nome; 5 mi. long, 4 mi. wide; 38°35'N 25°37'E. Sheep and goat raising; fisheries. Following a revolt against the Turks, the isl. was ravaged (1824) upon its capture by the Turks, and pop. fled to Euboea where it founded the town of Nea Psara [Gr., =new Psara] on site of anc. Eretria. Psara's chief village, on SW shore, is therefore called Palaia Psara [Gr., =old Psara]. Island was known as Ipsara under Turkish rule (until 1913). Kanalis, a naval hero of Gr. war of independence, b. here.

Pschelautsch, Czechoslovakia: see Prelouc.

Pschestitz, Czechoslovakia: see Prestice.

Psebai or **Psebay** (psyĭbī'), village (1939 pop. over 2,000), SE Krasnodar Territory, Russian SFSR, on N slope of the Greater Caucasus, on headstream of Laba R. and 35 mi. S of Labinsk; livestock raising, lumbering. Gypsum quarries near by. Sometimes called Psebaiskaya.

Psedakh, Russian SFSR: see Alanskoye.

Psel River (psyôl), W European USSR, rises E of Oboyan in Central Russian Upland, flows SW, past Oboyan, Sumy, and Gadyach, and S to Dnieper R. near Kremenchug; 435 mi. long. Also spelled Psiol.

Pshish (pshēsh), peak (12,430 ft.) in main range of the W Greater Caucasus, on Russian SFSR–Georgian SSR border, 30 mi. NNE of Sukhumi.

Psiloriti, Mount, Crete: see Ida, Mount.

Psiol River, European USSR: see Psel River.

Psirtskha, Georgian SSR: see Akhali-Afoni.

Pskem River (pskyĕm), SE South Kazakhstan oblast, Kazakh SSR, rises in Pskem Range (outlier of Kirghiz Range) on Kirghiz SSR border, flows c.75 mi. SW, joining Chatkal R. to form Chirchik R.

Pskent (pskyĕnt), village (1926 pop. 7,218), S Tashkent oblast, Uzbek SSR, 30 mi. S of Tashkent; cotton gin, metalworks.

Pskov (pŭskôf', pŭskôf'), oblast (□ 12,240; 1946 pop. estimate 900,000) in NW European Russian SFSR; ⊙ Pskov. In marshy lowland E of lakes Peipus and Pskov (fisheries); drained by Velikaya and Plyussa rivers; clayey soils; humid climate. Important flax-growing region; wheat and potatoes are secondary crops. Rural industries: flax processing, flour milling, distilling, dairying. Some peat digging and limestone quarrying. Lumbering (N); match mfg. at Chernevo. Main centers: Pskov, Porkhov, Pechory, Ostrov, Dno (rail center). Formed 1944 out of Leningrad oblast.

Pskov, city (1939 pop. 59,898), ⊙ Pskov oblast, Russian SFSR, on Velikaya R., 7 mi. SE of L. Pskov, and 160 mi. SW of Leningrad; 57°49'N 28°19'E. Rail and road junction; industrial center; mfg. of flax-processing and agr. machinery; railroad shops, linen and rope mills; tanning, distilling, flour milling, flax processing. Teachers col. Inner walled city (Dormontov Gorod) is site of kremlin (built 12th–16th cent.) with 4-mi.-long walls and towers in Byzantine style, and cathedral with tombs of princes of Pskov. Numerous churches and monasteries (12th–15th cent.), art and archaeological mus. Rail station was scene of abdication (1917) of Nicholas II. Svyatogorski cathedral (14th cent.) lies on Velikaya R., 5 mi. downstream. One of oldest cities of USSR; founded 903 and 1st called Pleskov. Originally outpost of Novgorod; gained independence in 13th cent.; annexed (1510) to Moscow. A flourishing commercial center in Middle Ages, on route from Europe to Asia; lost its importance as a border city after territorial expansion under Peter the Great. Was ⊙ Pskov govt. prior to 1927. Border station on Estonian frontier (1920–40). During Second World War, held (1941–44) and called Pleskau by Germans.

Pskov, Lake, Est. *Pihkva Järv*, S arm of L. Peipus, largely (since 1945) in Pskov oblast of Russian SFSR, but bordering NW on Estonia; 25 mi. long, 10 mi. wide, up to 25 ft. deep. Receives Velikaya R. (SE). Connected by 15-mi.-long strait with L. Peipus, of which it is sometimes considered a part.

Psunj (pso͞o'nyŭ), mountain, N Croatia, Yugoslavia, in Slavonia, in lignite area; highest point (3,228 ft.) is 9 mi. NNW of Nova Gradiska.

Psyra, Greece: see Psara.

Pszczyna (pŭshchĭ'nä), Ger. *Pless* (plĕs), town (pop. 9,731), Katowice prov., S Poland, near the Vistula, 20 mi. S of Katowice; rail junction. Has castle and cloister. Battlefield (1939) near by.

Ptarmigan Peak (tär'mŭgŭn). **1** Peak (13,736 ft.), in Park Range, N central Colo. **2** Peak (12,400 ft.), in Williams River Mts., N central Colo., c.50 mi. W of Denver.

Pteria, Turkey: see Bogazkoy.

Ptich River or **Ptich' River** (pŭtyēch'), central Belorussian SSR, rises W of Minsk in Lithuanian-Belorussian Upland, flows 260 mi. SE and S, past Glussk, to Pripet R. 20 mi. W of Mozyr. Used for logging for 185 mi. above mouth.

Ptolemais or **Ptolemaïs**, Cyrenaica: see Tolmeta.

Ptolemais or **Ptolemaïs** (tŏlŭmā'ĭs), anc. city of Upper Egypt, on left bank of the Nile and 9 mi. S of Sohag. It was a great city of Hellenistic Egypt, but almost nothing remains at the site.

Ptolemais (Gr. ptôlĭmĭs'), Macedonian *Kailar*, town (pop. 7,719), Kozane nome, W Macedonia, Greece, on highway and 16 mi. NNW of Kozane; chief town of Eordaia, in intermontane basin; tobacco, wheat, wine, dairy products. Lignite mines.

Ptolemais or **Ptolemaïs**, Palestine: see Acre.

Ptuj (pto͞o'ē), Ger. *Pettau* (pĕt'ou), anc. *Poetovio*, village (pop. 7,906), NE Slovenia, Yugoslavia, on Drava R., on railroad and 14 mi. SE of Maribor, at S foot of the Slovenske Gorice, in brown-coal area, at W edge of fertile Ptuj Plain. Mfg. (leather, footwear), winegrowing; wine trade. Has anc. relics, notably Orpheus Monument (probably tombstone of Roman decurion) and Roman articles in mus., castle, 14th-cent. church. Until 1918, in Styria.

Púa (po͞o'ä), village (1930 pop. 581), Malleco prov., S central Chile, 45 mi. SE of Angol; rail junction in agr. area (wheat, oats, potatoes, fruit); lumbering.

Pua (po͞o'ŭ), village (1937 pop. 9,271), Nan prov., N Thailand, in valley of Phi Pan Nam Mts. and 30 mi. NNE of Nan; rice, teak; iron deposits.

Puán (pwän), town (pop. 3,222), ⊙ Puán dist. (□ 2,460; pop. 21,488), W Buenos Aires prov., Argentina, at W end of Sierra de Puán (a low-lying hill range), 85 mi. NNW of Bahía Blanca; agr. center (wheat, sheep).

Puan or **P'u-an** (po͞o'än'), town (pop. 2,605), ⊙ Puan co. (pop. 59,453), SW Kweichow prov., China, 120 mi. SW of Kweiyang and on main road to Yunnan; inkstone-quarrying center; rice, wheat, tea, ramie. Coal deposits near by.

Puan (po͞o'än'), Jap. *Fuan*, town (1949 pop. 18,792), N.Cholla prov., S Korea, 17 mi. S of Kunsan across small inlet of Yellow Sea; agr. center (rice, soy beans, cotton).

Publier (püblēā'), village (pop. 93), Haute-Savoie dept., SE France, 3 mi. ENE of Thonon-les-Bains; cigarette-paper factory. Just N, on S shore of L. of Geneva is Amphion, a resort.

Pubnico (pŭb'nĭkō), village (pop. estimate 350), W N.S., at head of Pubnico Harbour (8 mi. long) of the Atlantic, 19 mi. SE of Yarmouth; lobster, halibut, haddock fisheries; lobster packing. Population is of Acadian origin.

Pucalá (po͞okälä'), village (pop. 1,890), Lambayeque dept., NW Peru, on coastal plain, in irrigated area of Lambayeque and Eten rivers, 16 mi. E of Chiclayo; rail terminus; sugar-producing center; sugar and rice milling.

Pucallpa (po͞okäl'pä), town (pop. 2,368), ⊙ Coronel Portillo prov. (formed 1943), Loreto dept., E Peru, landing on Ucayali R. and 105 mi. ENE of Tingo María (linked by highway from Cerro de Pasco and Lima); 8°25'S 74°35'W. Can be reached by 1,000-ton vessels from Iquitos; trades in agr. products (bananas, corn, rice, yucca, tobacco, coffee, coca, cacao, fruit). Airport. Ganso Azul oil field is centered on Agua Caliente, 27 mi. SSW.

Pucara (po͞okä'rä). **1** Town, Potosí dept., W central Bolivia, at confluence of Caine and Chayanta rivers (here forming Río Grande), 42 mi. ESE of San Pedro; corn, orchards. **2** Town (pop. 2,000), Santa Cruz dept., central Bolivia, 16 mi. SSW of Valle Grande, near Río Grande; corn, fruit. Founded 1730.

Pucará (po͞okärä'). **1** Town (pop. 40), Junín dept., central Peru, on E slopes of Cordillera Central, 32 mi. ENE of Tarma; coffee, cacao, sugar cane. **2** Town (pop. 651), Puno dept., SE Peru, on the Altiplano, on Juliaca–Cuzco RR and 60 mi. NNW of Puno, on Ramis R. (here called Pucará); alt. 12,739 ft.; clay quarries; barley, potatoes, stock.

Pucarani (po͞okärä'nē), town (pop. c.21,600), ⊙ Los Andes prov., La Paz dept., W Bolivia, near L. Titicaca, 25 mi. WNW of La Paz; alt. 12,644 ft.; trade center (potatoes, barley, quinoa, sheep). Also Villa Pucarani.

Pucará River, Peru: see Ramis River.

Puchberg or **Puchberg am Schneeberge** (po͞okh'-bĕrk, äm shnā'bĕrgŭ), town (pop. 3,572), SE Lower Austria, 9 mi. WNW of Neunkirchen; resort (alt. 1,909 ft.).

Puchen or **P'u-chen** (po͞o'jŭn'), town, N Kiangsu prov., China, across Yangtze R., on Tientsin-Pukow RR and 5 mi. NW of Nanking.

Pucheng or **P'u-ch'eng** (po͞o'chŭng'). **1** Town (pop. 19,924), ⊙ Pucheng co. (pop. 181,480), N Fukien prov., China, near Chekiang-Kiangsi line, 65 mi. NNE of Kienow; rice, sugar cane, sweet potatoes, wheat, rapeseed. Copper, coal, silver-lead mines near by. **2** Town (pop. 14,631), ⊙ Pucheng co. (pop. 198,639), central Shensi prov., China, 65 mi. NE of Sian; wheat, cotton, corn.

Puchezh (po͞o'chĭsh), city (1926 pop. 5,505), E Ivanovo oblast, Russian SFSR, on Volga R. and 80 mi. E of Ivanovo; linen-milling center; flax processing, clothing mfg., handicrafts (embroidery). Chartered 1745.

Puchi or **P'u-ch'i** (po͞o'chē'), town (pop. 12,050), ⊙ Puchi co. (pop. 131,028), SE Hupeh prov., China, 50 mi. ENE of Yoyang (Hunan prov.) and on Canton-Hankow RR; tea-growing center; hemp. Coal mining.

P'u-chiang, China: see Pukiang.

Puchon River (po͞ochŭn'), Jap. *Fusen-ko*, Korean *Puchon-gang*, S.Hamgyong prov., N Korea, rises in mtn. range 30 mi. N of Hamhung, flows c.60 mi. generally N to Changjin R. near Manchurian border. In upper course are a reservoir (11 mi. long, 3 mi. wide) and major hydroelectric plant feeding industrial Hungnam.

Puchov (po͞o'khôf), Slovak *Púchov*, Hung. *Puhó* (po͞o'hō), town (pop. 4,316), W Slovakia, Czechoslovakia, 20 mi. SW of Zilina; rail junction. Large dam across near-by (E) Vah R.

Puchow. **1** Town, Pingyuan prov., China: see Puhsien. **2** Town, Shansi prov., China: see Yüngtsi.

Puchuncaví (po͞ocho͞ongkävē'), village (1930 pop. 621), Valparaiso prov., central Chile, near the coast, 25 mi. NNE of Valparaiso, in agr. area (grain, fruit, livestock).

Pucioasa (po͞ochwä'sä), town (1948 pop. 4,643), Prahova prov., S central Rumania, in Walachia, in S foothills of the Transylvanian Alps, on Ialomita R., on railroad and 12 mi. N of Targoviste; health resort (alt. 1,480 ft.), with sulphurous springs. Also mfg. of bricks, ceramics, cement; stone and gypsum quarrying. Health resort of Vulcana or Vulcana-Baile (vo͝olkä'nä-bŭ'ēlĕ), with iodine springs, is 3 mi. WSW.

Pucio Point (po͞o'syō), westernmost point of Panay isl., Philippines, in Sulu Sea, on NW peninsula of isl.; 11°46'N 121°50'E.

Puck (po͞otsk), Ger. *Putzig* (po͞o'tsĭkh), town (1946 pop. 3,946), Gdansk prov., N Poland, on Puck Bay, on railroad and 15 mi. NNW of Gdynia. Naval base; airport (seaplanes); fishing port; seaside resort; mfg. of agr. machinery, bricks; fish smoking, flour milling, sawmilling.

Pucka, Mierzeja, Poland: see HEL PENINSULA.

Puckaway, Lake, widening of Fox R., in Green Lake co., central Wis., near Green L., 33 mi. W of Fond du Lac; c.6 mi. long, c.2 mi. wide.

Puck Bay (pōōtsk), Pol. *Zatoka Pucka* (zätô′kä pōōts′kä), Ger. *Putziger Wiek* (pōō′tsĭgûr vēk′), W arm of Gulf of Danzig, N Poland, bet. mainland (W) and Hel Peninsula (NE); c.20 mi. long, up to 10 mi. wide. NW section (up to c.16 ft. deep) is separated from SE section (mostly c.100 ft. deep) by an undersurface formation which is gradually becoming a peninsula. Called Little Sea, Pol. *Male Morze*, by the Kashubs.

Pucklechurch, town and parish (pop. 1,177), SW Gloucester, England, 7 mi. ENE of Bristol; coal mining. Has 13th-cent. church.

Pucón (pōōkōn′), town (pop. 1,720), Cautín prov., S central Chile, tourist center on E shore of L. Villarrica, at N foot of Villarrica Volcano, 45 mi. SE of Temuco; major resort of N Chilean lake dist.; salmon and trout fishing.

Pucusana (pōōkōōsä′nä), village (pop. 335), Lima dept., W central Peru, small port on the Pacific, on highway, and 4 mi. WNW of Chilca; fishing; beach resort. Formerly Puerto Chilca.

Pucyura (pōōkyōō′rä), town (pop. 1,180), Cuzco dept., S central Peru, in high Andean valley, 10 mi. NW of Cuzco; grain, potatoes.

Pudasjärvi (pōō′däsyăr″vē), village (commune pop. 13,064), Oulu co., N central Finland, on small L. Pudas, Finnish *Pudasjärvi*, expansion of Ii R., 50 mi. NE of Oulu; road center, in lumbering region.

Pudde Fjord, Norway: see BERGEN.

Pudem (pōōdyĕm′), village (1948 pop. over 2,000), NW Udmurt Autonomous SSR, Russian SFSR, on railroad and 21 mi. WNW of Glazov; ironworks. Formerly called Pudemski Zavod.

Pudewitz, Poland: see POBIEDZISKA.

Pudino (pōō′dyĭnŭ), village (1948 pop. over 500), SW Tomsk oblast, Russian SFSR, on Chuzik R. (headstream of Parabel R.) and 125 mi. SSW of Narym.

Pudo (pōō′dō), town, Northern Territories, N Gold Coast, near Fr. West Africa frontier, 30 mi. W of Navrongo; shea nuts, millet, durra; cattle, skins. Iron deposits.

Pudozh (pōō′dŭsh), city (1926 pop. 2,194), SE Karelo-Finnish SSR, on Vodla R. (head of navigation) and 70 mi. E of Petrozavodsk, across L. Onega; lumber mill; grain farming, woodworking. Dates from 12th cent.; formerly a trading center.

Pudozhgora (pōōdŭzhgŭrä′), village, SE Karelo-Finnish SSR, on L. Onega, 40 mi. NW of Pudozh; titaniferous iron and vanadium deposits.

Pudsey (pŭd′sē, -zē), municipal borough (1931 pop. 14,761; 1951 census 30,276), West Riding, S central Yorkshire, England, 4 mi. E of Bradford; woolen milling, shoe mfg. Has a Moravian settlement, founded 1746. Absorbed near-by areas in 1937.

Pudukad, India: see TRICHUR.

Pudukkottai (pōōdōōk-kōt′tī), city (pop. 34,188), Trichinopoly dist., S Madras, India, 37 mi. SSE of Trichinopoly; cotton and oilseed milling, mfg. of incense and perfume; tannery. Has col. (affiliated with Madras Univ.). Red ocher and granite quarries near by. Was ⊙ former princely state of Pudukkottai (□ 1,185; pop. 438,348) in Madras States, India; since 1948, state inc. into Trichinopoly dist. State sometimes spelled Pudakotah.

Puduvayal (pōōdōōvŭyŭl′), town (pop. 4,677), Ramnad dist., S Madras, India, 6 mi. ENE of Karaikudi; residence of Chetty merchant community.

Puebla (pwĕ′blä), state (□ 13,126; 1940 pop. 1,294,620; 1950 pop. 1,595,920), central Mexico; ⊙ Puebla. One of Mexico's most densely populated states. It is largely mountainous (average alt. 7,000 ft.), occupying part of the central Mex. plateau. Traversed by the Sierra Madre Oriental in N; the NE tip of state reaches into Gulf lowlands. Across the center extends the volcanic belt, which includes on Puebla's borders 3 highest peaks in Mexico: Pico de ORIZABA (E), POPOCATEPETL and IXTACIHUATL (W). Drained by Ayotac R., upper course of the Balsas. Climate varies with alt.: temperate on plateau, cold in mts., semitropical in lowlands (NE) and valleys (S). Mineral resources include gold, silver, copper (Tetela, Ixtacamaxtitlán, Acatlán); also iron, marble, onyx, sulphur, oil, and coal deposits. Principally an agr. state: main crops are corn, wheat, alfalfa, sugar cane, beans, tobacco, fruit, vegetables, maguey, coffee, cotton, rice, tropical fruit. Stock raising primarily in S. Rural industries: mining, lumbering, flour milling, sugar refining, weaving, maguey processing, distilling; native handicrafts. Processing, ceramic, and textile industries are centered at Puebla, Atlixco, Matamoros, Serdán, Texmelucan, Teziutlán. Tehuacán is a noted health resort. The state contains many archaeological sites of pre-Columbian and pre-Aztec origin; the most famous is the Pyramid of Cholula.

Puebla, officially Puebla de Zaragoza, city (pop. 138,491), ⊙ Puebla, central Mexico, on central plateau, on Inter-American Highway and 65 mi. SE of Mexico city; 19°3′N 98°12′W; alt. c.7,200 ft. Mexico's 4th city and one of its oldest and most picturesque. Important rail and road hub; commercial, industrial, and agr. center (cereals, sugar cane, fruit, vegetables, livestock). Cotton-weaving center, with a number of textile mills in outskirts; mfg. of cement, glazed tiles, pottery, palm-leaf hats; sugar refineries. Onyx quarries. Airfield. Univ. was founded 1537 by Jesuits as Col. of the Holy Ghost. With fine colonial bldgs., Puebla is known as the city of churches; has an outstanding anc. cathedral constructed bet. 1552 and 1649, and a theater (built 1790) claimed to be the oldest on the continent. Famous pre-Columbian pyramid at Cholula, 7 mi. W. Puebla was founded c.1535. It was occupied in turn by U.S. forces during Mexican War (1847) and by the French (1863). Originally called Puebla de los Angeles, it was renamed for Gen. Ignacio Zaragoza, who won a decisive victory over the French (1862).

Puebla, La (lä), town (pop. 10,030), Majorca, Balearic Isls., 24 mi. NE of Palma; agr. center (beans, potatoes, hemp, rice, tobacco, cereals, livestock); flour milling.

Puebla de Alcocer (dhā älkō-thĕr′), town (pop. 3,554), Badajoz prov., W Spain, near the Guadiana, in La Serena region, 70 mi. W of Ciudad Real. Agr. center (cereals, olives, grapes, honey, sheep). Olive-oil pressing, flour milling, tile and pottery mfg. Silver and lead mines near by.

Puebla de Alfindén (älfēndĕn′), village (pop. 1,154), Saragossa prov., NE Spain, 7 mi. E of Saragossa; cereals, livestock.

Puebla de Almenara (älmānä′rä), town (pop. 1,534), Cuenca prov., E central Spain, 19 mi. SE of Tarancón; grain, olives, grapes, livestock. Exports cheese.

Puebla de Almoradiel, La (älmōrädh-yĕl′), town (pop. 5,729), Toledo prov., central Spain, on railroad and 40 mi. SE of Aranjuez; agr. center in upper La Mancha; potatoes, cereals, grapes, livestock. Olive-oil extracting, liquor and cognac distilling; mfg. of scaffolds.

Puebla de Cazalla, La (lä, kä-thä′lyä), town (pop. 8,471), Seville prov., SW Spain, on Carbones R. (affluent of the Guadalquivir), and 38 mi. ESE of Seville; agr. center (olives, potatoes, vegetables, cereals, livestock); apiculture. Mfg. of liquor, shoes, soap, plaster; sawmilling. Has mineral springs.

Puebla de Don Fadrique (dhōn′ fädrē′kä), town (pop. 4,284), Granada prov., S Spain, 40 mi. NE of Baza; flour milling; stock raising, lumbering. Peat, esparto, cereals. Gypsum quarries.

Puebla de Don Rodrigo (rō-dhrē′gō), town (pop. 1,909), Ciudad Real prov., S central Spain, 40 mi. W of Ciudad Real; cereals, vegetables, figs, potatoes, tomatoes, onions, melons, pepper, livestock; flour milling. Lead deposits.

Puebla de Farnáls (färnäls′), village (pop. 1,404), Valencia prov., E Spain, 9 mi. NNE of Valencia; rice, potatoes, melons.

Puebla de Guzmán (gōōth-män′), town (pop. 4,555), Huelva prov., SW Spain, in W Sierra Morena, 30 mi. NW of Huelva; agr. center (wheat, barley, oats, acorns, stock); copper-pyrite mining; lumbering. On near-by hill (W) is church.

Puebla de Híjar (ē′här), village (pop. 1,950), Teruel prov., E Spain, 20 mi. NW of Alcañiz, in irrigated area (sugar beets, fruit, cereals); olive-oil processing, sugar milling.

Puebla de la Calzada (lä käl-thä′dhä), town (pop. 5,672), Badajoz prov., W Spain, 17 mi. E of Badajoz; agr. center (cereals, vegetables, olives, livestock); apiculture, poultry farming. Liquor distilling, sawmilling.

Puebla de la Reina (rā′nä), town (pop. 1,516), Badajoz prov., W Spain, 16 mi. E of Almendralejo; cereals, grapes, olives, livestock.

Puebla del Caramiñal (dhĕl kärämēnyäl′), town (pop. 2,469), La Coruña prov., NW Spain, fishing port on Arosa Bay of the Atlantic, 20 mi. NW of Pontevedra; fish processing, boatbuilding.

Puebla del Duc (dōōk′), town (pop. 1,888), Valencia prov., E Spain, 8 mi. SE of Játiva; brandy and wine distilling; fruit, olive oil. Sulphur springs.

Puebla del Maestre (mäĕ′strā), town (pop. 3,246), Badajoz prov., W Spain, 17 mi. SE of Fuente de Cantos; stock raising; processing of olives and cereals. Lead mines near by.

Puebla de los Infantes, La (dhā lōs ēmfän′tēs), town (pop. 4,601), Seville prov., SW Spain, in the Sierra Morena, 11 mi. NE of Lora del Río; olives, cereals, cork, livestock. Liquor distilling, flour milling, mfg. of meat products.

Puebla del Príncipe (dhĕl prēn′thēpä), town (pop. 1,672), Ciudad Real prov., S central Spain, 28 mi. ESE of Valdepeñas; cereals, grapes, potatoes, livestock; gypsum quarrying; cheese processing.

Puebla del Prior (prēôr′), town (pop. 839), Badajoz prov., W Spain, at NW foot of the Sierra de Hornachos, 13 mi. SE of Almendralejo; cereals, livestock.

Puebla del Río, La (rē′ō), town (pop. 3,339), Seville prov., SW Spain, on the Guadalquivir and 10 mi. SSW of Seville; cereals, licorice, olives, grapes.

Puebla del Salvador (sälvä-dhôr′), town (pop. 763), Cuenca prov., E central Spain, 40 mi. NNE of Albacete; grain, grapes, saffron, sheep, goats. Lumbering; charcoal burning.

Puebla de Montalbán, La (lä, dhā mōntälvän′), town (pop. 6,400), Toledo prov., central Spain, in fertile region near the Tagus, 18 mi. W of Toledo; agr. center (olives, grapes, peaches, apricots, cereals, sheep, goats). Flour milling, liquor distilling, tanning, soap and pottery mfg. Hunting, fishing. Coal mines near by.

Puebla de Obando (ōvän′dō), town (pop. 2,760), Badajoz prov., W Spain, near Cáceres prov. border, 27 mi. NE of Badajoz; produces charcoal.

Puebla de Sanabria (sänäv′ryä), town (pop. 793), Zamora prov., NW Spain, 19 mi. NNE of Bragança (Portugal); flour mills; lumber, livestock, potatoes, cereals. Small lake of San Martín de Castañeda is 6 mi. NW.

Puebla de Sancho Pérez (sän′chō pä′rĕth), town (pop. 3,452), Badajoz prov., W Spain, on railroad and 2 mi. S of Zafra; spa and agr. center (cereals, olives, grapes, stock).

Puebla de Trives (trē′vēs), town (pop. 954), Orense prov., NW Spain, 30 mi. E of Orense; wine, chestnuts, rye, potatoes.

Puebla de Vallbona (väly″bō′nä), town (pop. 4,219), Valencia prov., E Spain, 13 mi. NW of Valencia; flour milling; hog raising; onion shipping; cereals, wine.

Puebla Larga (lär′gä), village (pop. 3,506), Valencia prov., E Spain, 6 mi. SW of Alcira; fertilizer mfg., rice, oranges.

Puebla Nueva, La (lä, nwā′vä), town (pop. 3,081), Toledo prov., central Spain, 9 mi. SE of Talavera de la Reina; cereals, olives, grapes, livestock.

Pueblito, Mexico: see CORREGIDORA.

Pueblo (pwĕ′blō, pūē′blō), county (□ 2,401; pop. 90,188), S central Colo.; ⊙ Pueblo. Industrial and irrigated agr. area, drained by Arkansas R. and Fountain Creek. Mfg. (iron and steel products) at Pueblo; livestock, sugar beets, feed grains. Includes part of San Isabel Natl. Forest. Formed 1861.

Pueblo, city (pop. 63,685), ⊙ Pueblo co., S central Colo., on Arkansas R., at mouth of Fountain Creek, NE of Wet Mts., in foothills of the Rockies and 100 mi. SSE of Denver; 38°15′N 104°37′W; alt. 4,700 ft. Second largest city in Colo.; shipping, trade, and industrial center for large livestock and irrigated agr. area. Metalworks produce steel rails, wire, nails, cables, pipes, cast-iron fittings; smelting, meat packing, oil refining, mfg. (flour, dairy products, bricks, tiles, brooms, tents, awnings, leather goods, plumbing supplies). Site of city used as camping stop in 18th cent.; visited (1806) by Zebulon Pike. Trading post (established 1842; and named Pueblo) was occupied (1846–47) by Mormons. Became Fountain City (1858); later absorbed by Pueblo City, laid out (1860) contiguously. City grew with arrival of railroads (1872 and 1876); inc. as city of Pueblo 1885. Further development followed construction of smelters for reduction of gold, silver, and iron ores from mines in N central Colo. Severe flood (1921) destroyed much of business sec.; Arkansas R. has since been diverted and levees constructed. Has jr. col., state fairgrounds, state hosp. for insane, hq. for San Isabel Natl. Forest, and Army ordnance depot. Points of interest: co. courthouse, Mineral Palace (many-domed structure with large mineral collection). Pueblo Mtn. Park and part of San Isabel Natl. Forest near by.

Pueblo, El, Canary Isls.: see MAZO.

Pueblo Cumarebo (pwĕb′lō kōōmärä′bō), town (pop. 567), Falcón state, NW Venezuela, in Caribbean lowlands, 3 mi. SE of Puerto Cumarebo, 25 mi. E of Coro; petroleum wells; coal deposits. Sometimes Cumarebo.

Pueblo de la Capilla, Uruguay: see SAUCE DEL YÍ.

Pueblo Hundido (ōōndē′dō), village (1930 pop. 954), Atacama prov., N Chile, 38 mi. E of Chañaral and on the Quebrada del Salado; rail junction in copper-mining area.

Pueblo Libre, Peru: see MAGDALENA VIEJA.

Pueblo Navarro, Argentina: see CORONEL BOGADO.

Pueblo Nuevo (nwā′vō). **1** S residential section of Matanzas, Matanzas prov., W Cuba. **2** Town (pop. 1,007), Oriente prov., E Cuba, 32 mi. NW of Santiago de Cuba, in fruit and sugar region.

Pueblo Nuevo. 1 or **Pueblo Nuevo Viñas** (vē′nyäs), town (1950 pop. 1,352), Santa Rosa dept., S Guatemala, in Pacific piedmont, 13 mi. WSW of Cuilapa; alt. 4,430 ft. Coffee-growing center; cattle. **2** Town (1950 pop. 610), Suchitepéquez dept., SW Guatemala, in Pacific piedmont, near Samalá R., 12 mi. NE of Retalhuleu; coffee, sugar cane. Transferred 1944 from Retalhuleu dept.

Pueblo Nuevo, town (pop. 2,531), Guanajuato, central Mexico, on Lerma R. and 11 mi. S of Irapuato; alt. 5,590 ft.; grain, alfalfa, beans, sugar cane, fruit.

Pueblo Nuevo, town (1950 pop. 960), Estelí dept., W Nicaragua, 24 mi. NNW of Estelí; coffee center.

Pueblo Nuevo or **Pueblo Nuevo de las Sabanas** (dā läs säbä′näs), town (pop. 1,447), Panama prov., central Panama, on Trans-Isthmian Highway and 4 mi. NNE of Panama city. Coffee plantations; stock raising.

Pueblo Nuevo. 1 Town (pop. 1,368), Libertad dept., NW Peru, on coastal plain, 17 mi. N of San Pedro, in irrigated rice and cotton area. **2** City, Lima dept., Peru: see CAÑETE. **3** Town (pop. 1,820), Piura dept., NW Peru, on Chira R., near its mouth on the Pacific, and 15 mi. NNE of Paita, in irrigated area; cotton, fruit.

Pueblo Nuevo, E suburb (pop., including section of Ventas, 17,698) of Madrid, central Spain.

Pueblo Nuevo, Uruguay: see Salto, city.

Pueblo Nuevo. **1** Town (pop. 1,588), Falcon state, NW Venezuela, on Paraguaná Peninsula, 40 mi. NNW of Coro; goat grazing. **2** Town (pop. 446), Falcón state, NW Venezuela, 23 mi. SE of Coro.

Pueblo Nuevo Comaltitlán (kōmältētlän'), town (pop. 2,457), Chiapas, S Mexico, in Pacific lowland, 9 mi. NW of Huixtla; cacao, sugar cane, coffee, fruit, stock.

Pueblo Nuevo de las Sabanas, Panama: see Pueblo Nuevo.

Pueblo Nuevo del Mar (dhĕl mär') or **El Cabañal** (ĕl kävänyäl'), NE harbor section of Valencia, E Spain, adjoined S by Villanueva del Grao. Has large bathing establishments.

Pueblo Nuevo Solistahuacán (sōlēstäwäkän'), town (pop. 1,138), Chiapas, S Mexico, in N spur of Sierra Madre, 32 mi. NNE of Tuxtla; alt. 5,446 ft.; cereals, fruit.

Pueblo Nuevo Tiquisate, Guatemala: see Tiquisate.

Pueblo Nuevo Viñas, Guatemala: see Pueblo Nuevo.

Pueblo Olimar, Uruguay: see Santa Clara.

Pueblorrico (pwĕblôrē'kō), town (pop. 1,796), Antioquia dept., NW central Colombia, on E slopes of Cordillera Occidental, 37 mi. SSW of Medellín; alt. 6,371 ft. Coffee, sugar, corn, beans, bananas, yucca, stock.

Puebloviejo (pwĕblōvyā'hō), town (pop. 1,867), Magdalena dept., N Colombia, minor port on Caribbean Sea, and 2 mi. SW of Ciénaga; cotton, corn, fruit.

Puebloviejo, town (1950 pop. 1,206), Los Ríos prov., W central Ecuador, on highway to Guayaquil, on tributary of the Guayas system, and 19 mi. ENE of Vinces; agr. center (cacao, rice, sugar cane, tropical fruit).

Pueblo Viejo, Guatemala: see Villa Canales.

Pueblo Viejo, Mexico: see Villa Cuauhtémoc, Veracruz.

Puelches (pwĕl'chĕs), town (pop. c.250), ⊙ Curacó dept. (pop. 1,475), S La Pampa prov., Argentina, in marshes along Curacó R., 90 mi. SW of General Acha; livestock (sheep, cattle, goats). Sometimes called Cura-Có.

Puelén (pwälĕn'), village (pop. c.200), ⊙ Puelén dept. (pop. 1,219), W La Pampa prov., Argentina, 115 mi. NNE of Neuquén, in agr. area (corn, alfalfa, wine, potatoes, livestock).

Puelo, Lake (pwā'lō) (□ 17; alt. 673 ft.), in the Andes, NW Chubut natl. territory, Argentina, W of L. Epuyén; c.7 mi. long. On W shore is Río Puelo Pass, on Chile line.

Puente (pōōĕn'tē, pū–), unincorporated town (1940 pop. 1,648), Los Angeles co., S Calif., 17 mi. E of downtown Los Angeles; packs walnuts, citrus fruit; also rose growing, poultry and truck farming.

Puente, El, Bolivia: see El Puente.

Puente, El, Spain: see Caldas, Las.

Puente Alto (pwĕn'tä äl'tō), town (1930 pop. 4,083; 1940 pop. 10,145), Santiago prov., central Chile, on Maipo R., on railroad and 12 mi. SSE of Santiago; mfg. and agr. center (grain, fruit, wine, livestock); paper and pulp factories; textiles, chemicals. Hydroelectric plant.

Puenteáreas (pwĕntä-ä'räas), town (pop. 1,595), Pontevedra prov., NW Spain, 12 mi. ESE of Vigo; livestock market; meat processing, tanning, sawmilling. Wine, potatoes, corn in area.

Puente de Génave (pwĕn'tä dhä hā'nävä), town (pop. 1,775), Jaén prov., S Spain, on Guadalimar R. and 24 mi. NE of Villacarrillo; olive-oil processing, flour milling, sandal mfg. Silver-lead and iron mines.

Puente de Ixtla (ē'slä), town (pop. 2,470), Puebla, central Mexico, 22 mi. SSW of Cuernavaca; alt. 2,949 ft.; rice, sugar cane, fruit, vegetables.

Puente del Arzobispo, El (ĕl, dhĕl är-thōvē'spō), town (pop. 1,932), Toledo prov., central Spain, on the Tagus and 21 mi. SW of Talavera de la Reina; cereals, cherries, tubers, garlic, livestock. Olive-oil pressing, meat packing, mfg. of clay products; fishing. Limekilns. Its name stems from an archbishop who had a bridge constructed (1390) here.

Puente del Inca (ēng'kä), village (pop. estimate 80), NW Mendoza prov., Argentina, on Transandine RR, in Mendoza R. valley, at S foot of the Aconcagua, 65 mi. W of Mendoza, on route to Uspallata Pass; alt. 8,920 ft. Health resort with hot springs. Summer and winter sports. Named from natural limestone bridge (130 ft. long, 100 ft. wide) across river.

Puentedeume (pwĕntä-dhĕōō'mä), town (pop. 3,392), La Coruña prov., NW Spain, fishing port on Ares Bay of the Atlantic, 12 mi. ENE of La Coruña; fish processing, tanning; lumber, livestock.

Puente de Vallecas (pwĕn'tä dhä välyä'käs) or **Nueva Numancia** (nwā'vä nōōmän'thyä), SE suburb (pop. 55,707) of Madrid, Madrid prov., central Spain, just NW of Vallecas. Mfg. of tiles, ceramics, cement products, rubber articles, soap, ice, travel goods, meat products; printing.

Puente-Genil (-hānēl'), town (pop. 22,309), Córdoba prov., S Spain, in Andalusia, on Genil R. and 34 mi. S of Córdoba; industrial and agr.-trade center, noted for its special quince sweets and fruit jellies and conserves. Olive-oil processing, wine and brandy distilling, flour- and sawmilling; mfg. also of insecticides, cotton cloth, soap, and tiles. Ships fruit, wine, vinegar, and cereals. Stock raising.

Puente la Reina (lä rā'nä), town (pop. 1,703), Navarre prov., N Spain, on Arga R. and 12 mi. SW of Pamplona, in winegrowing area; mfg. of alcohol, chocolate; flour milling.

Puente Nacional (näsyōnal'), town (pop. 1,386), Santander dept., N central Colombia, in W Cordillera Oriental, on Suárez R., on highway, and 21 mi. NNE of Chiquinquirá; alt. 5,315 ft. Trade center and resort in agr. area (sugar cane, coffee, corn, vegetables, fique fibers, stock). Waterfall near by. Its railroad station is 2 mi. E.

Puente Real (räal'), village, Chinandega dept., W Nicaragua, on the Estero Real (bridged) and 17 mi. NE of Chinandega, on road; sugar cane, corn, rice. Sometimes called El Puente.

Puentes de García Rodríguez (pwĕn'tĕs dhä gärthē'ä rōdhrē'gĕth), town (pop. 1,124), La Coruña prov., NW Spain, 20 mi. ESE of El Ferrol; lumber, livestock. Lignite mines near by.

Puerca, Point (pwĕr'kä), easternmost cape of isl. of Puerto Rico, 7 mi. SE of Fajardo; 18°14'N 65°36'W.

Puerco River (pōōâr'kō), in NW N.Mex. and E Ariz., formed by confluence of 2 forks in mtn. region of McKinley co., N.Mex., flows W, past Gallup, then SW into Apache co., Ariz., passing through Petrified Forest Natl. Monument, to Little Colorado R. just E of Holbrook; 100 mi. long; intermittent in upper course. Also known as Rio Puerco, the name too, of another river in N.Mex.

Puerh, China: see Ningerh.

Puerhtsin, China: see Burchun.

Puers, Belgium: see Puurs.

Puerta, La, Argentina: see La Puerta.

Puerta, La, Venezuela: see La Puerta.

Puerta de Golpe (pwĕr'tä dä gōl'pä), town (pop. 1,597), Pinar del Río prov., W Cuba, on railroad and 9 mi. ENE of Pinar del Río; tobacco, fruit, vegetables.

Puerta de la Laguna (lä lägōō'nä), village, La Libertad dept., W central Salvador, on Inter-American Highway and 4 mi. W of San Salvador; flour-milling center. Also called Puerta La Laguna.

Puerta de Segura, La (lä, sägōō'rä), town (pop. 3,236), Jaén prov., S Spain, 26 mi. NE of Villacarrillo; olive-oil processing, flour milling, mfg. of soap and sandals. Stock raising, lumbering; cereals, fruit, vegetables.

Puerta La Laguna, Salvador: see Puerta de la Laguna.

Puerto, El, or **El Puerto de Santa Maria** (ĕl pwĕr'tō, dhä sän'tä märē'ä), city (pop. 28,262), Cádiz prov., SW Spain, in Andalusia, Atlantic port at mouth of Guadalete R. on Bay of Cádiz, opposite (6 mi. NE of) Cádiz. Main shipping point for sherry from Jerez (8 mi. NE); also a fishing and processing center. Wine, liquor, alcohol, and vinegar distilling; fish canning, tanning, sawmilling. Limekilns, saltworks in vicinity. Situated in agr. region (grapes, cereals, fruit, vegetables, cattle, hogs). Notable bldgs. include parochial church, San Marcos castle, Jesuit col., several *bodegas* (wineries), and one of Spain's largest bull rings.

Puerto Acosta (äkō'stä), town (pop. c.9,100), ⊙ Camacho prov., La Paz dept., W Bolivia, near L. Titicaca, 90 mi. NW of La Paz; alt. 12,631 ft. Trading (alpaca wool) and transportation center, with customs station near Peru border. Until 1908, Huaicho or Huaycho.

Puerto Aguirre, Argentina: see Puerto Iguazú.

Puerto Angel (än'hĕl), village, Oaxaca, S Mexico, minor sheltered port on the Pacific, 6 mi. SW of Pochutla, 100 mi. S of Oaxaca.

Puerto Armuelles (ärmwĕ'yĕs), town (1950 pop. 14,523), Chiriquí prov., W Panama, on Charco Azul Bay, 30 mi. WSW of David, near Costa Rica border. Pacific banana port and railhead. Developed in 1930s to serve new banana-growing region.

Puerto Arroyo Pareja, Argentina: see Arroyo Pareja.

Puerto Asís (äsēs'), village, Putumayo commissary, SW Colombia, landing on Putumayo R., in tropical forest region, and 75 mi. SE of Pasto (connected by road). River boats reach here from the Amazon. Some forest products (rubber, balata gum, fine wood, resins) are gathered.

Puerto Ayacucho (īäkōō'chō), town (1941 pop. 856; 1950 census 2,928), ⊙ Amazonas territory, S Venezuela, landing on Orinoco R. (Colombia border) just below Atures Rapids, and 335 mi. S of Caracas; 5°41'N 68°21'W. Trading post in tropical forest region (rubber, balata). A road here, circumventing both Atures Rapids and Maipures Rapids (further S), leads to Sanariapo, a small river village 33 mi. SSW of Puerto Ayacucho.

Puerto Aysén (īsĕn'), town (pop. 3,767), ⊙ Aysén prov. and coextensive Aysén dept., S Chile, on Aysén R. and 270 mi. S of Puerto Montt, 835 mi. SSW of Santiago, in a region of mts. and fjords; 45°27'S 72°51'W. Inland port; trading, lumbering, and sheep-raising center. Radio station. Its rugged scenery brings it tourist trade. Sometimes called Aysén.

Puerto Ballivián (bäyēvyän'). **1** Port, Beni dept., Bolivia: see Trinidad. **2** Village, La Paz dept., W Bolivia, port on Kaka R., at confluence of its headstreams, and 60 mi. ENE of Sorata.

Puerto Baquerizo (bäkärē'sō) or **Baquerizo Moreno** (mōrā'nō), chief town of Galápagos Isls., on SW tip of San Cristóbal Isl., in the Pacific, c.700 mi. W of Guayaquil, Ecuador; 0°53'S 89°37'W. Port of entry, administrative center, and military base. Fishing. Near by, on the slopes, are raised sugar cane, coffee, yucca, cattle. Formerly Puerto Chico.

Puerto Barrios (bär'yōs), city (1950 pop. 15,659), ⊙ (since 1920) Izabal dept., E Guatemala, on Bay of Amatique, 150 mi. NE of Guatemala city; 15°44'N 88°36'W. Major Caribbean port; chief port of Guatemala; rail terminus of lines from Guatemala city and San Salvador; customhouse, govt. and shipping offices. Exports bananas, chicle, coffee, fruit, wood. Developed in 20th cent. after completion of railroad to Guatemala and expansion of banana plantations in lower Motagua valley.

Puerto Belgrano (bĕlgrä'nō), military port (pop. estimate 1,500), SW Buenos Aires prov., Argentina, on Bahía Blanca (bay), adjoining (W) Punta Alta; training schools, air and seaplane base.

Puerto Bello, Panama: see Portobelo.

Puerto Bello (bĕ'lō), town (1939 pop. 4,719), W Leyte, Philippines, port on Ormoc Bay, 5 mi. WSW of MacArthur (Ormoc); rice-growing center.

Puerto Bermejo (bĕrmā'hō), town (1947 census pop. 2,531), ⊙ Río Bermejo dept. (1947 census pop. 27,036), SE Chaco prov., Argentina, port on Paraguay R. 10 mi. below mouth of Bermejo R., and 45 mi. NE of Resistencia; farming center (cotton, corn, alfalfa); livestock; tannin factory.

Puerto Bermúdez (bĕrmōō'dēs), village (pop. 3), Pasco dept., central Peru, landing on Pichis R. (a headstream of the Pachitea) and 40 mi. EN[illegible] of Oxapampa; coffee, cacao, rubber. Airfield. Formerly terminus and transfer point on road from San Luis de Shuaro.

Puerto Berrío (bĕrē'ō), town (pop. 5,487), Antioquia dept., N central Colombia, inland port on Magdalena R., opposite Puerto Olaya (Santander dept.; on road from Tunja), and 80 mi. ENE of Medellín. Terminus of railroad from Medellín, outlet for almost all Antioquia trade, reached by river ships. Across the Magdalena a highway extends to Bogotá. The area engages in stock raising, lumbering, fishing; agr. products: corn, rice, yucca, bananas, coffee. Limekilns and marble quarries near by.

Puerto Blest (blĕst'), village (pop. estimate 50), SW Río Negro natl. territory, Argentina, on SW shore of L. Nahuel Huapí, at Chile border, 28 mi. W of San Carlos de Bariloche. Tourist resort; customhouse. Cascades near by.

Puerto Bolívar (bōlē'vär), town, El Oro prov., S Ecuador, Pacific port on SE shore of Jambelí Channel serving Machala (2 mi. NE), with which it is connected by railroad; trades in cacao, coffee, rubber. Customhouse; air service.

Puerto Bolognesi (bōlōnyā'sē), hamlet, Cuzco prov., S central Peru, landing at confluence of Mantaro and Apurímac rivers, 50 mi. SSE of Puerto Prado; 11°47'S 74°2'W.

Puerto Boniato (bōnyä'tō), resort village, Oriente prov., E Cuba, in hills 5 mi. N of Santiago de Cuba, with noted view of Santiago de Cuba. Sometimes Puerto de Boniato.

Puerto Borghi, Argentina: see Borghi.

Puerto Caballos, Honduras: see Puerto Cortés.

Puerto Cabello (käbĕ'yō), city (pop. 22,087), Carabobo state, N Venezuela, port on the Caribbean, on Triste Gulf, 20 mi. N of Valencia (linked by railroad and highway), and 75 mi. W of Caracas; 10°28'N 68°1'W. With a fine harbor and with shipyards and drydock, it is Venezuela's 2d port, exporting coffee, cacao, dyewood, hides, copra, copper ores. Industries include meat packing, cotton and flour milling, sawmilling, marble quarrying, soap mfg., cigarette making, fishing. Its old fortifications (partly destroyed 1902) serve as a penitentiary. Along coast near by are mangrove forests and saltworks. Strategically located, and the object of attacks by buccaneers in 16th cent., Puerto Cabello was lost (1812) by Bolívar to royal forces, causing the collapse of republican independence under Miranda. The last of the northern Sp. strongholds, it was recaptured (1823) by Páez.

Puerto Cabezas (käbā'säs), town (1950 pop. 3,571), Zelaya dept., E Nicaragua, major Caribbean port, 140 mi. NNE of Bluefields. Terminus of rail line from banana and lumber dist.; turpentine distilling, sawmilling. Customhouse.

Puerto Caimito (kīmē'tō), village (pop. 200), Panama prov., central Panama, minor port on Gulf of Panama of the Pacific, 4 mi. ESE of La Chorrera; coconuts, oranges; fishing, stock raising.

Puerto Caldas (käl'däs), village (pop. 649), Caldas dept., W central Colombia, landing on Cauca R. and 3 mi. NNW of Cartago; head of navigation of upper Cauca R., terminus of railroad from Manizales; commerce with Buenaventura.

Puerto Cansado (känsä'dhō), village, Southern Protectorate of Morocco, Sp. West Africa, on the Atlantic, 40 mi. NE of Cape Juby.

Puerto Capaz (käpäth'), town (pop. 1,223), Gomara territory, central Sp. Morocco, small fishing port on the Mediterranean, 45 mi. SE of Tetuán.

Puerto Carreño (kärā'nyō), town (pop. 392), ⊙ Vichada commissary, E Colombia, easternmost urban settlement of Colombia, on Orinoco R. at mouth of Meta R. (Venezuela border), and 450 mi. ENE of Bogotá; 6°10'N 67°29'W. Corn, yucca, cattle, gums, resins.

Puerto Casado (käsä'dō), town (dist. pop. 6,757), Boquerón dept., N Paraguay, on Paraguay R., in the Chaco, 85 mi. NNW of Concepción; quebracho, cotton, and cattle center; tannin-extracting plants (founded 1889), sawmills; viticulture experiment station. Ships lumber and tannin. Railroad link with the inland Mennonite settlements (W).

Puerto Casma (käz'mä), town (pop. 319), Ancash dept., W central Peru, Pacific port on Casma Bay (2 mi. wide, 3 mi. long) at mouth of Casma R., 5 mi. WNW of Casma; shipping point for products of dist. (cotton, rice, charcoal).

Puerto Castilla (kästē'yä), town (pop. 1,114), Colón dept., N Honduras, major Caribbean port on S side of Cape Honduras, 6 mi. N of Trujillo, across Trujillo Bay; rail terminus; exports bananas and coconuts. Airfield, radio station. Developed after 1917 to provide well-sheltered port replacing Trujillo.

Puerto Cedeño, Venezuela: see PUERTO PÁEZ, village, Apure state.

Puerto Chacabuco (chäkäbōō'kō), village (1930 pop. 5), Aysén prov., S Chile, on Aysén R. estuary and 6 mi. SW of Puerto Aysén; sheep raising, lumbering.

Puerto Chicama (chēkä'mä), town (pop. 2,274), Libertad dept., NW Peru, Pacific port on Chicama Bay, NE of Chicama Point (7°43'S 79°28'W), 40 mi. NW of Trujillo; rail terminus; shipping point for sugar products; fisheries. Until 1920 called Malabrigo.

Puerto Chico, Ecuador: see PUERTO BAQUERIZO.

Puerto Chilca, Peru: see PUCUSANA.

Puerto Coig, Argentina: see PUERTO COYLE.

Puerto Colombia (kōlōm'byä), town (pop. 4,896), Atlántico dept., N Colombia, minor port on inlet of Caribbean Sea, 10 mi. W of Barranquilla, in agr. region (cotton, corn, sugar cane, stock). Before dredging of Magdalena R. mouth, it served as the ocean port for Barranquilla, with which it was connected by rail. Beach resort. Fisheries. Gold and marble deposits near by.

Puerto Cooper (kō'pĕr), village, Boquerón dept., N central Paraguay, on Paraguay R., in the Chaco, and 33 mi. NW of Concepción; cattle-raising center.

Puerto Cortés (kôrtās'), town (1950 pop. 891), ⊙ Osa canton, Puntarenas prov., S Costa Rica, small Pacific port on lower Diquís R. (navigation head), opposite El Palmar, and 110 mi. SE of Puntarenas; 8°58'N 83°32'W. Exports rice, bananas.

Puerto Cortés, city (pop. 7,955), Cortés dept., NW Honduras, Caribbean banana port on Cortés Bay of Gulf of Honduras, 125 mi. NNW of Tegucigalpa; 15°48'N 87°57'W. Principal Honduran port (1,000-ft. pier); rail terminus (workshops); mfg. center (flour and flour products, banana flour, coconut oil, beverages, soap, leather); dairying. Exports bananas, coconuts, hardwood, flour, coffee. Backed by Alvarado Lagoon (SE); extends c.2 mi. along S shore of Punta Caballos. Founded 1525 at point 3 mi. S (across Cortés Bay); moved (1869) to present site when construction began on railroad to Potrerillos. Called Puerto Caballos until 1869.

Puerto Coyle (koil'), village (pop. estimate 80), SE Santa Cruz natl. territory, Argentina, on Atlantic coast at mouth of Coyle R., and 50 mi. N of Río Gallegos; port and sheep-raising center. Airport. Sometimes Puerto Coig.

Puerto Coyolar or **Coyolar** (koi-ōlär'), Guanacaste prov., NW Costa Rica, port on Tempisque R., at mouth of Bebedero R., and 14 mi. NE of Nicoya; 10°14'N 85°15'W. Trading post.

Puerto Cumarebo (kōōmärā'bō), town (pop. 4,811), Falcón state, NW Venezuela, port on the Caribbean, 23 mi. ENE of Coro, in agr. region (cacao, sugar cane, divi-divi, corn, rice, livestock). Coal and petroleum deposits (at Pueblo Cumarebo) near by. Airfield.

Puerto de Béjar (pwĕr'tō dhā bā'här), village (pop. 1,097), Salamanca prov., W Spain, 4 mi. SW of Béjar; livestock, potatoes, chestnuts, fruit.

Puerto de Cabras (kä'vräs), chief town and port (pop. 1,727) of Fuerteventura, Canary Isls., on isl.'s E coast, 90 mi. ENE of Las Palmas; 28°32'N 13°50'W. Grain, vegetables, fruit; fishing. Limekilns, flour mills. Embroidery mfg.

Puerto de Corral, Chile: see CORRAL.

Puerto de Eten, Peru: see PUERTO ETEN.

Puerto de Hierro (yĕ'rō), port in Sucre state, NE Venezuela, on S shore of Paria Peninsula, on Gulf of Paria, 13 mi. ENE of Güiria; 10°38'N 62°6'W. Transshipment point for iron ore mined at El Pao and other centers in Sierra Imataca (Bolívar state); ore is sent down Orinoco R. from Palua near San Félix. A new port, begun 1941; exports ore to U.S.

Puerto de Iztapa, Guatemala: see IZTAPA.

Puerto de la Concordia, Salvador: see LA CONCORDIA.

Puerto de la Cruz (lä krōōth'), town (pop. 5,134), Tenerife, Canary Isls., 19 mi. WSW of Santa Cruz de Tenerife. Port on isl.'s W shore, exporting produce of immensely fertile Orotava Valley; bananas, tomatoes, potatoes, grapes, tobacco, cochineal. Also has embroidery and textile industry. Botanical garden for exotic plants. Sometimes called Puerto de Orotava.

Puerto de la Cruz, Venezuela: see PUERTO LA CRUZ.

Puerto de la Luz (lōōth'), N port section of Las PALMAS, Grand Canary, Canary Isls.

Puerto del Sauce, Uruguay: see JUAN LACAZE.

Puerto de Nutrias or **Puerto Nutrias** (dā, nōō'trēäs), town (pop. 706), Barinas state, W Venezuela, port on Apure R., just S of Nutrias, and 70 mi. ESE of Barinas, in cattle-raising region; leading shipping point in Barinas.

Puerto de Orotava, Canary Isls.: see PUERTO DE LA CRUZ.

Puerto de San José, Guatemala: see SAN JOSÉ.

Puerto de Santa Cruz (sän'tä krōōth'), town (pop. 1,004), Cáceres prov., W Spain, 10 mi. S of Trujillo; cereals, livestock.

Puerto de Santa María, El, Spain: see PUERTO, EL.

Puerto de San Vicente (sän' vē-thĕn'tā), village (pop. 759), Toledo prov., central Spain, 33 mi. SW of Talavera de la Reina; olives, livestock.

Puerto Deseado (dāsā-ä'dō), town (1947 pop. 3,706), SE Comodoro Rivadavia military zone, Argentina, at mouth of Deseado R. on the Atlantic, 150 mi. SE of Comodoro Rivadavia; 47°45'S 65°53'W. Small Patagonian port at terminus of railroad (extending 175 mi. NW to Colonia Las Heras) serving rich sheep-raising area; exports wool and hides. Meat packing, mfg. of furniture and cider. An old colonial port. Formerly known as Port Desire.

Puerto de Supe (dā sōō'pā), town (pop. 1,373), Lima dept., W central Peru, on the Pacific, 2 mi. WSW of Supe, 4 mi. SSE of Barranca, on Pan American Highway; shipping point for cotton and sugar cane, grown in surrounding area; fisheries.

Puerto Díaz (dē'äs), village, Chontales dept., S Nicaragua, port on NE shore of L. Nicaragua, 14 mi. SW of Juigalpa; grain, vegetables, livestock.

Puerto Domínguez (dōmēng'gēs), village (1930 pop. 152), Cautín prov., S central Chile, on Laguna del Budi and 38 mi. SW of Temuco; tourist resort; fishing. Catholic Indian mission.

Puerto El Triunfo (ĕl trēōōm'fō), town (pop. 428), Usulután dept., SE Salvador, minor Pacific port on Jiquilisco Bay, 5 mi. SSE of Jiquilisco (linked by road); coastal trade; fishing, salt extraction; grain, livestock raising. Town of El Triunfo (pop. 2,060) is road junction on Inter-American Highway, 17 mi. NE of Jiquilisco.

Puerto Escondido (ĕskōndē'dō), town, Oaxaca, S Mexico, minor port on Pacific coast, 50 mi. SSW of Ejutla.

Puerto Esperanza or **La Esperanza** (lä ĕspärän'sä), town (pop. 1,038), Pinar del Río prov., W Cuba, minor port on N coast, 24 mi. N of Pinar del Río; bathing, fishing.

Puerto Estrella (ĕstrē'yä), village, Guajira commissary, N Colombia, on NE Caribbean coast of Guajira peninsula, 85 mi. NE of Uribia. Pearl banks near by.

Puerto Eten (ā'tĕn), town (pop. 2,576), Lambayeque dept., NW Peru, port on the Pacific, just S of ETEN, and 10 mi. S of Chiclayo; railhead; shipping point for sugar, rice, cotton, hides; fisheries. Once the principal port of the dept., replaced since 1922 by Pimentel. Sometimes Puerto de Eten.

Puerto Fermín (fĕrmēn'), town (pop. 2,568), port on Margarita Isl. (NE), Nueva Esparta state, NE Venezuela, on the Caribbean, 6 mi. NNW of La Asunción. Linked by railroad with small Puerto Manzanillo (4 mi. NW). Fishing (pearls, herring, tuna, sharks). Large magnesite mines (SW).

Puerto Fonciere (fōnsyā'rā), village, Concepción dept., N central Paraguay, on Paraguay R. and 75 mi. NW of Concepción, in cattle and quebracho area. Sometimes La Fonciere.

Puerto Frey (frā'), town, Santa Cruz dept., NE Bolivia, port on Paraguá R. and 120 mi. N of San Ignacio; rubber.

Puerto Galera (pwĕr'tō gälä'rä), town (1939 pop. 319; 1948 municipality pop. 3,948), N Mindoro, Philippines, on Verde Isl. Passage, 16 mi. WNW of Calapan.

Puerto Galileo (gälēlā'ō), town (dist. pop. 522), Presidente Hayes dept., central Paraguay, in the Chaco, on Pilcomayo R. (Argentina border) and 20 mi. NW of Asunción, in agr. area (sugar cane, tobacco, corn, alfalfa, livestock).

Puerto Gallegos, Argentina: see RÍO GALLEGOS.

Puerto Galván (gälvän'), SW suburb (pop. estimate 100) and port of Bahía Blanca, SW Buenos Aires prov., Argentina, at mouth of Sauce Chico R., 2 mi. W of Ingeniero White; flour milling, oil refining. Exports agr. products. Sometimes called Galván.

Puerto Grether (grātâr'), village (pop. c.300), Santa Cruz dept., central Bolivia, port on Ichilo R. and 50 mi. WNW of Buena Vista. Formerly Puerto Ichilo.

Puerto Guachalla (gwächä'yä) or **Puerto Sucre** (sōō'krā), village, Santa Cruz dept., E Bolivia, port on L. Cáceres, on Tamengo Canal, at Brazil border, and c.10 mi. SE of Puerto Suárez, in marshy area.

Puerto Guaraní (gwäränē'), town (dist. pop. 2,829), Boquerón dept., N Paraguay, rail terminus on Paraguay R., in the Chaco, and 155 mi. NNW of Concepción; tannin extracting; shipping of quebracho and other hardwood; stock raising.

Puerto Harbertón (ärbĕrtōn') or **Harbertón,** village, S Tierra del Fuego natl. territory, Argentina, on N shore of Beagle Channel and 40 mi. ESE of Ushuaia, in sheep-raising area.

Puerto Heath, village, La Paz dept., NW Bolivia, port on Madre de Dios R., at mouth of Heath R. (Peru-Bolivia border), opposite Puerto Pardo (Peru), and 100 mi. S of Cobija. Formerly also Fortín Puerto Heath.

Puerto Herradura, Chile: see LA HERRADURA.

Puerto Hierro, Venezuela: see PUERTO DE HIERRO.

Puerto Huarmey, Peru: see HUARMEY.

Puerto Ibáñez (ēbä'nyĕs), village (1930 pop. 50), Aysén prov., S Chile, on NW arm of L. Buenos Aires, near Argentina border, 75 mi. SE of Puerto Aysén; sheep raising. Sometimes called Ibáñez.

Puerto Ichilo, Bolivia: see PUERTO GRETHER.

Puerto Iglesias, Costa Rica: see MANZANILLO.

Puerto Iguazú (pwĕr'tō ēgwäsōō') or **Iguazú,** village (pop. c.200), ⊙ Iguazú dept. (pop. 25,422), Misiones natl. territory, Argentina, landing at union of Alto Paraná and Iguassú (Iguazú) rivers (Paraguay-Brazil-Argentina border), 12 mi. NW of Iguassú Falls, 150 mi. NNE of Posadas, and 4 mi. S of Foz do Iguaçu (Brazil). Tourist center for Iguassú Falls. Lumber, maté. Until 1940s, called Puerto Aguirre.

Puerto Inca (ēng'kä), village, Huánuco dept., central Peru, landing on Pachitea R. and 100 mi. NE of Huánuco; lumbering; rubber.

Puerto Ingeniero White, Argentina: see INGENIERO WHITE.

Puerto Jesús (hāsōōs'), village, Guanacaste prov., NW Costa Rica, port on Gulf of Nicoya, 13 mi. ESE of Nicoya (linked by road). Trading center.

Puerto Jiménez (hēmä'nĕs), village (dist. pop. 1,913), Puntarenas prov., S Costa Rica, Pacific port on the Golfo Dulce, on Osa Peninsula, 35 mi. SSE of Puerto Cortés; 8°33'N 83°18'W; rice, bananas, coconuts; pearl fishing. Formerly called Santo Domingo.

Puerto Jobos, Puerto Rico: see JOBOS.

Puerto La Cruz or **Puerto de la Cruz** (dā lä krōōs'), town (pop. 8,164), Anzoátegui state, NE Venezuela, port on the Caribbean, on railroad and 6 mi. NNE of Barcelona; petroleum-shipping center at terminus of oil pipe lines; oil refineries.

Puerto Lagunas, Chile: see CHONOS ARCHIPELAGO.

Puerto La Paloma, Uruguay: see LA PALOMA.

Puerto Lavalle (lävä'yä) or **Lavalle,** town (pop. estimate 1,000), W Corrientes prov., Argentina, port on Paraná R. and 10 mi. NNE of Goya, in rice and citrus-fruit region; also potatoes, cotton, watermelons, peanuts. Sawmills.

Puerto Leguía (lāgē'ä), village, Puno dept., SE Peru, port on Inambari R. and 65 mi. N of Macusani; lumbering; rubber.

Puerto Leguízamo, Colombia: see LEGUÍZAMO.

Puerto Letras (lā'träs) or **Letras,** village, Guanacaste prov., NW Costa Rica, port on Gulf of Nicoya of the Pacific, 11 mi. E of Nicoya; trading center.

Puerto Libertador or **Libertador,** Dominican Republic: see PEPILLO SALCEDO.

Puerto Limón, Costa Rica: see LIMÓN, city.

Puertollano (pwĕrtōlyä'nō), city (pop. 22,099), Ciudad Real prov., S central Spain, in New Castile, on N slopes of the Sierra Morena, on railroad and 22 mi. SSW of Ciudad Real. Mining and metallurgical center. The rich deposits worked include bituminous coal, manganese, iron and copper pyrites. Based on these resources is a chemical industry distilling gasoline, asphalt, ammonium sulphate. Also foundries and limekilns. Region produces cereals, potatoes, olives, livestock. Valdeazogues mercury mines are near by.

Puerto Lobos (lō'bōs), village (pop. estimate 300), NE Chubut natl. territory, Argentina, on San Matías Gulf 55 mi. N of Puerto Madryn; sheep-raising center.

Puerto López (lō'pĕs), village, Meta intendancy, central Colombia, 45 mi. E of Villavicencio; landing on Metica R. (right headstream of the Meta), terminus of highway from Villavicencio; cattle raising. Airfield.

Puerto Madryn or **Madryn** (mä'drĕn), town (1947 pop. 3,299), ⊙ Biedma dept., NE Chubut natl. territory, Argentina, port on the Golfo Nuevo (Atlantic Ocean), 35 mi. N of Rawson; port, rail terminus, farming and trading center. Meat packing, food canning, fishing (mackerel, lobster, shad), alfalfa growing, sheep raising. Beach resort near by. A Welsh settlement, founded 1865.

Puerto Maldonado (mäldōnä'dō), town (pop. 1,087), ⊙ Madre de Dios dept. and Tambopota prov. (□ 40,939; enumerated pop. 3,745, plus estimated 4,000 Indians), SE Peru, landing at junction of Madre de Dios and Tambopata rivers, in Amazon basin, 535 mi. E of Lima; 12°36'S 69°10'W. Rubber-gathering center; cotton, rice, yucca, sugar cane, fruit are also grown in the region, mostly by Japanese, who were introduced as plantation laborers and now form the dominant element. Has cotton gin; wireless station. Town was founded 1903. Gold washing in vicinity.

Puerto Max (mäks′), village, Concepción dept., N central Paraguay, on Paraguay R. and 60 mi. NW of Concepción; quebracho center.

Puerto Melinka, Chile: see GUAITECAS ISLANDS.

Puerto Mensabé, Panama: see MENSABÉ.

Puerto México, Mexico: see COATZACOALCOS.

Puerto Miranda, Ecuador: see NUEVA ROCAFUERTE.

Puerto Monte Carlo, Argentina: see MONTE CARLO.

Puerto Montt (mônt′), city (1940 pop. 21,360; 1949 estimate 18,688), ⊙ Llanquihue prov. and Llanquihue dept. (□ 3,643; 1940 pop. 44,024), S central Chile, at head of Reloncaví Sound, 120 mi. SSE of Valdivia, 575 mi. SSW of Santiago; 41°27′S 72°56′W. It is S terminus of Chile's mainland railways, and a port, resort, and commercial, fishing, and agr. (grain, potatoes, livestock) center. Trades in timber, wheat, wool, leather. Mfg.: fish canning, brewing, tanning, sawmilling; dry docks, machine works. Popular resort at S end of Chilean lake dist., with superb scenery—forested hills, narrow fjords, and snow-capped peaks of the Andes. Starting point for inland waterways through the archipelagoes to the S. Founded 1853, named for President Manuel Montt. It is mainly settled by Germans, to whom it owes its modern features.

Puerto-Moral (pwĕr′tō-mōräl′), town (pop. 313), Huelva prov., SW Spain, in the Sierra Morena, 3 mi. E of Aracena; olives, cork, hogs.

Puerto Morazán or **Morazán** (mōräsän′), town (1950 pop. 892), Chinandega dept., W Nicaragua, port on the Estero Real and 16 mi. NNW of Chinandega (linked by rail); exports grain and dairy products. Formerly called Nacascolo; developed (after 1937) as a port serving coastwise trade of Gulf of Fonseca.

Puerto Morín (mōrēn′), town, Libertad dept., NW Peru, on the Pacific, 10 mi. W of Virú; railhead.

Puerto Murphy, Argentina: see PUERTO RICO.

Puerto Mutis (mōō′tēs), village (pop. 22), Veraguas prov., W central Panama, port (14 mi. S) for Santiago, on Montijo Gulf of the Pacific; sugar cane, livestock.

Puerto Napo, Ecuador: see NAPO.

Puerto Natales (nätä′lĕs), town (pop. 6,475), ⊙ Última Esperanza dept. (□ 19,042; pop. 8,174), Magallanes prov., S Chile, at head of Almirante Montt Gulf, 120 mi. NW of Punta Arenas; 51°44′S 72°30′W. Sheep-raising and meat-packing center; timber, hides. Airport. Base for tourist traffic to majestic Paine Range. Sometimes called Natales.

Puerto Nutrias, Venezuela: see PUERTO DE NUTRIAS.

Puerto Obaldía (ōbäldē′ä), village (pop. 368), San Blas territory, E Panama, port on Caribbean Sea, and 3 mi. W of Colombia border; coastal trade.

Puerto Octay or **Octay** (ōktī′) village (1930 pop. 755), Osorno prov., S central Chile, on N shore of L. Llanquihue, 30 mi. SE of Osorno; tourist resort. Sometimes Puerto Octai.

Puerto Olaya, Colombia: see PUERTO BERRÍO.

Puerto Ospina (ōspē′nä) or **San Miguel** (sän mēgĕl′), village, Putumayo commissary, SW Colombia, landing on Caquetá R. (Ecuador border), at mouth of San Miguel or Sucumbíos R., and 90 mi. SE of Mocoa; forest products (rubber, balata gum, tagua nuts, resins).

Puerto Padre (pä′drā), town (pop. 6,949), Oriente prov., E Cuba, on sheltered Puerto Padre Bay (Atlantic), and 30 mi. NE of Holguín. Sugar port and trading center for fertile, irrigated region (sugar cane, tobacco, fruit, livestock). Sugar mills, tobacco factories, brick- and lumberyards. Near by are the sugar centrals Delicias (2 mi. E) and Chaparra (7 mi. E). Saltworks NE; also asphalt deposits in vicinity.

Puerto Padre Bay, sheltered harbor (c.6 mi. long, 2 mi. wide) on Atlantic coast of E Cuba, Oriente prov., 30 mi. NW of Holguín, linked with ocean by narrows. At its head is the town of Puerto Padre. Adjoining E is Chaparra Bay.

Puerto Páez (pīs′). **1** Town (pop. 701), Apure state, W central Venezuela, landing on Arauca R. and 25 mi. S of San Fernando, in cattle-raising region. **2** or **Puerto Cedeño** (sādā′nyō), village, Apure state, W central Venezuela, at confluence of Meta and Orinoco rivers opposite Puerto Carreño (Colombia), and 115 mi. S of San Fernando, in cattle-raising region. Airfield.

Puerto Pailas, Bolivia: see INGENIERO MONTERO HOYOS.

Puerto Pando (pän′dō), village, La Paz dept., W Bolivia, port on Beni R., at mouth of Kaka R., and 60 mi. SE of Apolo.

Puerto Pardo (pär′dō). **1** Village (pop. 14), Junín dept., central Peru, on Chanchamayo R. (just above confluence with the Paucartambo) and 12 mi. N of San Ramón; coffee, sugar cane. **2** Village (pop. 99), Madre de Dios dept., SE Peru, landing on Madre de Dios R., on Bolivia border opposite Puerto Heath, and 36 mi. ENE of Puerto Maldonado.

Puerto Peleco, Chile: see PELECO.

Puerto Pérez (pä′rĕs), town (pop. c.1,400), La Paz dept., W Bolivia, port on L. Titicaca and 35 mi. WNW of La Paz; alt. 12,542 ft.; potatoes, barley, sheep. Once a flourishing transportation center; declined after rise of Guaqui as main Titicaca port. Called Chililaya before 1900; later also Villa Pérez.

Puerto Pilcomayo or **Pilcomayo** (pēlkōmī′ō), village (pop. estimate 100), E Formosa natl. territory, Argentina, at confluence of Pilcomayo and Paraguay rivers (Paraguay border), 7 mi. S of Asunción. It is port for Clorinda, 7 mi. NW.

Puerto Pilón (pēlōn′), village (pop. 198), Colón prov., central Panama, on Las Minas Bay of Caribbean Sea, 6 mi. E of Colón; bananas, cacao, abacá, livestock. Sometimes called Las Minas.

Puerto Pinasco (pēnä′skō), town (dist. pop. 7,685), Boquerón dept., N central Paraguay, rail terminus on Paraguay R., in the Chaco, and 60 mi. NW of Concepción; trading, lumbering, tannin-extracting, and cattle-raising center; mfg. of soap, shoes; tanneries, sawmills. Large Indian pop.

Puerto Pirámides (pērä′mēdĕs) or **Pirámides,** village (pop. estimate 200), NE Chubut natl. territory, Argentina, port on Valdés Peninsula, 40 mi. NE of Puerto Madryn across Golfo Nuevo; sheep-raising center. Rail line to salt deposits, 15 mi. SE.

Puerto Píritu (pē′rētōō), town (pop. 2,219), Anzoátegui state, NE Venezuela, landing on Orinoco R., adjoined S by Píritu, and 25 mi. WSW of Barcelona; minor port in agr. region (coconuts, cotton, sugar cane, corn, livestock).

Puerto Pizarro (pēsä′rō), town (pop. 528), Tumbes dept., NW Peru, on Tumbes Bay of the Pacific 6 mi. NNE of Tumbes (connected by railroad); port for Tumbes city; fisheries. Pizarro landed here 1527.

Puerto Plata (plä′tä), province (□ 809; 1935 pop. 100,196; 1950 pop. 131,179), N Dominican Republic, on the Atlantic; ⊙ Puerto Plata. Crossed by the Cordillera Central. Fertile agr. region: coffee, cacao, tobacco, sugar cane, rice, corn, tropical fruit. Also much dairying. Puerto Plata city is leading port on N coast. Other centers are Altamira, Imbert, and Luperón. Ruins of Isabela, reputedly 1st town settled by the Spanish in America, are 9 mi. W of Luperón. Prov. was created 1875.

Puerto Plata, officially San Felipe de Puerto Plata, city (1935 pop. 11,722; 1950 pop. 14,419), ⊙ Puerto Plata prov., N Dominican Republic, port 325 mi. E of Santiago de Cuba, and linked by railroad with Santiago 23 mi. S; 19°48′N 70°41′W. The Republic's principal N seaport, serving fertile Cibao region (tobacco, coffee, cacao, rice, sugar cane, bananas, hides, hardwood), it is an exporting, fishing, and processing center. Has chocolate and match industries; mfg. of dairy products, lard, macaroni, essential oils, food preserves, liquor. Has a fine harbor with customhouse, wharves; airfield. The Long Beach resort is just E. Town founded 1503 by Columbus.

Puerto Posada, Panama: see PENONOMÉ.

Puerto Prado (prä′dō), village, Junín dept., central Peru, 70 mi. E of San Ramón, at confluence of Ene and Perené rivers, which here form the Tambo; tropical products (copaiba, sarsaparilla bark, lumber).

Puerto Princesa (pwĕr′tō prēnsä′sä), town (1939 pop. 2,332; 1948 municipality pop. 15,177), ⊙ Palawan prov., on E central coast of Palawan isl., Philippines, c.370 mi. SSW of Manila, on a well-sheltered inlet of Sulu Sea, just S of Honda Bay; 9°45′N 118°44′E. Trade center and inter-isl. shipping port, exporting copra, lumber, rattan. Sawmilling; fishing. Iwahig penal colony is across the harbor.

Puerto Príncipe, Cuba: see CAMAGÜEY.

Puerto Quijarro, Bolivia: see GAIBA, LAKE.

Puerto Real (rāäl′). **1** Village, SW Puerto Rico, on bay of Mona Passage, 8 mi. SSW of Mayagüez. A prosperous port of entry in colonial era, it is now a fishing village. Across the bay are the Cabo Rojo salt mines. **2** Village near SW coast of Vieques Isl., E Puerto Rico, 3 mi. SW of Isabela Segunda; sugar cane, stock. Founded 1816 as a fort. **3** Port for Fajardo, Puerto Rico: see PLAYA DE FAJARDO.

Puerto Real, town (pop. 12,510), Cádiz prov., SW Spain, port on Bay of Cádiz, on railroad and 5 mi. E of Cádiz; beach resort, saltworking and trading center in agr. region (cereals, truck produce, cattle, hogs). Sawmilling, liquor distilling, dairying, tanning; shipyards. Founded in late 15th cent. by Ferdinand and Isabella on site of anc. town.

Puerto Rico (pwĕr′tŭ rē′kō, pwĕr′tō), island and territory (including a few offshore dependent isls.: □ 3,435; land area □ 3,423; 1940 pop. 1,869,255; 1950 pop. 2,210,703) of the U.S., in the West Indies; ⊙ SAN JUAN. Easternmost and smallest isl. of the Greater Antilles, bet. the Atlantic and the Caribbean, separated W from Dominican Republic (Hispaniola isl.) by 75-mi.-wide Mona Passage; Virgin Isls. are just E. Puerto Rico is c.1,400 mi. SE of New York and c.950 mi. ESE of Miami, Fla. Roughly rectangular, isl. is c.100 mi. long, 35 mi. wide, situated bet. 17°55′–18°32′N and 65°35′–67°17′W. Adjacent isls. are Mona Isl. (W), Vieques Isl. and Culebra Isl. (E); many small, mostly uninhabited, islets near its coast. Has pleasant tropical climate with little seasonal changes and tempered by NE trade winds; mean Jan. temp. 74.9°F., July 80°F. Rainfall, scarcer on S and W slopes, averages 60.26 inches annually. Occasional hurricanes are experienced Aug.-Oct. Part of a submarine mtn. range, the isl. is crossed in its entire length by mtn. ranges such as the Cordillera Central (highest peak, Cerro de Punta, 4,400 ft.), Sierra de Luquillo (NE), and Sierra de Cayey (SE). Coastal plain is c.10 mi. wide along N coast, narrower in S where mts. rise abruptly. Numerous small unnavigable rivers, widely used for hydroelectric power and irrigation (especially in S), include the Loíza, La Plata, Manatí, Añasco, Caonillas, and Arecibo. Little-exploited mineral deposits include some gold (mined in early colonial era), high-grade magnetic iron, manganese, galena, gypsum, kaolin, coal, lime, marble, granite. Long an area with a one-crop (sugar) economy, Puerto Rico has also been weighed down by one of the highest pop. densities (646 persons per sq. mi.) in the world. Progress has been made in diversification: coffee (W central), tobacco (in mountainous interior), citrus fruit and pineapples (N and NW); also corn, rice, cacao, coconuts, vanilla (only source on American soil), winter vegetables, cotton, manioc, breadfruit. Some stock raising (plantation oxen, sheep, horses, hogs, mules, cattle, poultry). The coastal lagoons are known for their wild fowl. Large reforestation program in the interior (Caribbean Natl. Forest), where mahogany and other tropical timber thrive. Sugar processing is the main industry, and there are many sugar mills, called *centrales*; also refineries, alcohol and rum distilleries (using molasses). Next rank tobacco processing, and mfg. of cigars and cigarettes, the isl.'s renowned needlework, fruit juices, vegetable oil, straw hats, cotton and leather goods. Most exports are to U.S. Main cities: San Juan (NE), Ponce (S; the isl.'s 3d city), Mayagüez (W), Arecibo (NW), Guayama (SE), Caguas (E center), Río Piedras (NE), Humacao (E), and Aguadilla (NW). Industrialization has made great strides since 1930s, due especially to large hydroelectric projects, such as Carite, Río Blanco, Toro Negro, Garzas, Dos Bocas, Caonillas. Leading port, San Juan, with airport and naval base. Río Piedras, 6 mi. SE, is seat of Univ. of Puerto Rico (founded 1903), whose Col. of Arts and Mechanics is at Mayagüez. The School of Tropical Medicine is at San Juan. San Germán has a polytechnic institute. Puerto Rico is becoming increasingly a winter resort for U.S. tourists, and new luxury hotels are being built. The isl. has an extensive railroad and highway system along the coast and into the interior. Puerto Rico was inhabited in pre-Columbian days by Arawakan Indians who called the isl. Boriquén or Borinquén. Columbus landed here on Nov. 19, 1493, on his 2d voyage, but it was 1st settled by one of his companions, Juan Ponce de León, who returned 15 years later, landing at San Juan harbor and naming it Porto Rico. As the isl.'s 1st governor, he founded Caparra (4 mi. inland), which was abandoned for San Juan in 1521. An Indian uprising was quelled in 1511 and Negro labor was introduced shortly thereafter, while the native pop. was practically wiped out. San Juan soon emerged as one of the most formidable Sp. strongholds in the New World. Puerto Rico was, in early colonial era, frequently subjected to attacks by the British, Dutch, and French. In 1595 Drake made an unsuccessful incursion, and the isl. was held over 5 months in 1598 by George Clifford, earl of Cumberland. The Dutch besieged San Juan in 1625. Movements of independence were started in the 1820s. Slavery continued to exist until 1873. In Feb., 1898, Puerto Rico was finally granted autonomy. A few months later the Spanish-American War broke out, and American troops landed in the same year (Oct. 18, 1898). A treaty ceding Puerto Rico to the U.S. was signed on Dec. 10, 1898. Through the Jones Act (1917), U.S. citizenship was extended to Puerto Ricans, and greater self-government was granted. Since 1948 the governor has been elected by insular vote. It is administratively divided into 7 senatorial dists. and 77 municipalities. Puerto Rico's pop. is about ¾ native-born white and ¼ Negro-mulatto. Though English is an official language, Spanish is spoken predominantly. The U.S. maintains on the strategically important isl. (sometimes referred to as the "Gibraltar of the Caribbean") several military bases. Official name of the isl. was changed from Porto Rico (pōr′tō) to Puerto Rico in 1932.

Puerto Rico, village (pop. estimate 1,000), ⊙ Cainguás dept. (1947 pop. 21,913), W Misiones natl. territory, Argentina, on Paraná R. (Paraguay border) and 70 mi. NE of Posadas; lumbering and farming center (maté, tobacco, citrus fruit, tung); processing of maté, mfg. of honey and lard. Sometimes called Puerto Murphy for Colonia Murphy, an adjoining agr. settlement.

Puerto Rico, town (pop. c.1,000), ⊙ Manuripi prov., Pando dept., NW Bolivia, at confluence of Manuripi and Tahuamanu rivers (here forming Orton R.), 75 mi. ESE of Cobija, on road; port for tropical forest products (rubber, timber, valuable feathers).

Puerto Rico Trench, submarine depression in North Atlantic Ocean, N of Puerto Rico, extending c. 220

mi. E-W. The Brownson Deep (20°N 66°E) was considered the deepest part, with soundings ranging to 27,972 ft., until the discovery (1939) of the Milwaukee Depth (30,246 ft.) at 19°35'N 68°30'W.

Puerto Ruiz (pwĕr'tō rōō-ēs'), village (pop. estimate 400), S Entre Ríos prov., Argentina, rail terminus and port for Gualeguay, on Gualeguay R. and 6 mi. SW of Gualeguay.

Puerto Saavedra (sävā'drä) or **Saavedra**, town (pop. 2,071), Cautín prov., S central Chile, near mouth of Imperial R., 3 mi. inland from the Pacific, 45 mi. W of Temuco; port and beach resort in agr. area (cereals, livestock). The Laguna del Budi, tourist and fishing resort, is 6 mi. SE.

Puerto Salgar (sälgär'), village (pop. 1,767), Cundinamarca dept., central Colombia, landing on Magdalena R., opposite La Dorada, and 18 mi. N of Honda; terminus of rail line from Bogotá to Magdalena valley.

Puerto Samanco (sämäng'kō), village (pop. 327), Ancash dept., W central Peru, Pacific port on Samanco Bay (4 mi. wide, 6 mi. long), and 10 mi. SE of Chimbote; railhead in sugar- and cotton-growing area; fishing center. Puerto Vesique (pwer'tō väsē'kä) (pop. 141) is 1 mi. SSE.

Puerto San Buenaventura, Bolivia: see SAN BUENAVENTURA.

Puerto San José, Guatemala: see SAN JOSÉ.

Puerto San Martín (pwĕr'tō sän' märtēn'), town (pop. estimate 1,000), E central Santa Fe prov., Argentina, port on Paraná R. and 17 mi. NNW of Santa Fe; rail terminus and livestock center (cattle, horses, sheep). Sand deposits; sawmills.

Puerto Santa Cruz, Argentina: see SANTA CRUZ, town.

Puerto Sastre (sä'strā), town (dist. pop. 5,118), Boquerón dept., N central Paraguay, rail terminus on Paraguay R., in the Chaco, and 115 mi. NNW of Concepción; trading and tannin-extracting center; cattle raising, meat packing; iron foundry.

Puerto Sauce, Uruguay: see JUAN LACAZE.

Puerto Serrano (sĕrä'nō), town (pop. 3,649), Cádiz prov., SW Spain, 25 mi. NW of Ronda; almonds, olives, oats, wheat, livestock.

Puerto Siles (sē'lĕs), village (pop. c.300), Beni dept., N Bolivia, on Mamoré R. and 27 mi. NW of San Joaquín; rice, tobacco.

Puerto Soley (sōlā'), village, Guanacaste prov., NW Costa Rica, port on Salinas Bay of the Pacific, 3 mi. W of La Cruz; 11°3'N 85°41'W. Coastal trade bet. Puntarenas and San Juan del Sur.

Puerto Somoza (sōmō'sä), town, Managua dept., SW Nicaragua, Pacific port just NW of Masachapa, 30 mi. SSW of Managua (linked by road). Developed in middle 1940s.

Puerto Suárez (swä'rĕs), town (pop. 3,600), Santa Cruz dept., E Bolivia, 10 mi. W of Corumbá (Brazil), in marshy area. Important port on L. Cáceres and on Corumbá–Santa Cruz RR; exports rubber and coffee; customs station; airport. Connected by Tamengo Canal with Paraguay R. and by road with Santa Cruz.

Puerto Sucre, 1 Town, Beni dept., Bolivia: see GUAYARAMERÍN. **2** Village, Santa Cruz dept., Bolivia: see PUERTO GUACHALLA.

Puerto Sucre (sōō'krā), port for CUMANÁ, Venezuela.

Puerto Tarafa (tärä'fä), N port of NUEVITAS, Camagüey prov., E Cuba.

Puerto Tejada (tāhä'dä), town (pop. 5,566), Cauca dept., SW Colombia, on affluent of Cauca R., on W slopes of Cordillera Central, and 17 mi. SSE of Cali; agr. center (tobacco, cacao, coffee, sugar cane, fique, fruit, stock).

Puerto Thiel (tyĕl'), village, Guanacaste prov., NW Costa Rica, port on Gulf of Nicoya of the Pacific, 20 mi. SE of Nicoya; lumbering. Ships manganese.

Puerto Tirol (tērōl'), town (1947 pop. 3,346), SE Chaco natl. territory, Argentina, on the Río Negro, on railroad and 9 mi. NW of Resistencia; agr. and lumbering center. Sawmills, cotton gins. Cotton, corn, oranges, livestock.

Puerto Todos Santos, Bolivia: see TODOS SANTOS.

Puerto Toledo (tōlā'dō), village (1930 pop. 245), Llanquihue prov., S central Chile, on Maullín R. and 21 mi. W of Puerto Montt; resort in agr. area (wheat, potatoes, livestock); dairying, lumbering. Sometimes called El Salto or Salto.

Puerto Umbría, Colombia: see UMBRÍA.

Puerto Vallarta (väyär'tä), town (pop. 3,150), Jalisco, W Mexico, Pacific port on Banderas Bay S of mouth of Ameca R., 125 mi. W of Guadalajara; only coast outlet of region; banana-growing center. Formerly Las Peñas.

Puerto Varas (vä'räs), town (pop. 4,146), ⊙ Puerto Varas dept. (□ 2,474; pop. 38,799), Llanquihue prov., S central Chile, on S bank of L. Llanquihue, on railroad and 12 mi. N of Puerto Montt; major tourist center of Chilean lake dist., in agr. (wheat, potatoes), dairying, and lumbering area. In a picturesque setting crowned by the volcanoes Osorno and Calbuco, it is the gateway to scenic L. Llanquihue and L. Todos los Santos and, in Argentina, to L. Nahuel Huapí. It was founded 1853.

Puerto Velarde (välär'dā), village, Santa Cruz dept., central Bolivia, 60 mi. NNW of Portachuelo. Abandoned 1929 following flood and change of course of Río Grande.

Puerto Vesique, Peru: see PUERTO SAMANCO.

Puerto Victoria (vēktōr'yä), village (pop. 21), Pasco dept., central Peru, port at confluence of headstreams of the Pachitea, 60 mi. NE of Oxapampa; 9°53'S 74°59'W; cacao, coffee, rubber.

Puerto Viejo (vyā'hō), village, Limón prov., SE Costa Rica, minor port on Caribbean Sea, and 25 mi. SE of Limón; bananas, coconuts; 9°39'N 82°45'W.

Puerto Viejo Lagoon, Mexico: see TAMPICO LAGOON.

Puerto Vilelas (vēlā'läs), town (pop. estimate 1,500), SE Chaco natl. territory, Argentina, on Paraná R., adjoining Barranqueras, and 5 mi. SE of Resistencia; meat packing, cotton ginning, tannin extracting, lead smelting (minerals shipped from Aguilar in Jujuy prov.), mfg. of nonferrous metal products.

Puerto Villamizar (vēyämēsär'), town (pop. 1,442), Norte de Santander dept., N Colombia, in Gulf of Maracaibo lowlands, 5 mi. from Venezuela border, on Zulia R., on railroad and 35 mi. N of Cúcuta. Adjoining N are the Petroléa oil fields of the Barco concession.

Puerto Villazón (vēyäsōn'), village (pop., including near-by El Cafetal, 350), Beni dept., NE Bolivia, port on Guaporé R., just below mouth of the Paraguá, and 150 mi. ESE of Magdalena; rubber.

Puerto Wertheman (wĕr'tāmän), village, Junín dept., central Peru, 14 mi. N of San Ramón, at confluence of Chanchamayo and Paucartambo rivers, which here form the Perené; 10°59'S 75°16'W. Coffee, cacao, sugar cane.

Puerto Wilches (wēl'chĕs), town (pop. 2,055), Santander dept., N central Colombia, landing on Magdalena R. (Bolívar dept. border) and 55 mi. WNW of Bucaramanga (connected by rail); trading and communication center; main outlet for Santander dept. Airport.

Puerto Yessup (yĕ'sōōp), village (pop. 38), Pasco dept., central Peru, landing on Pichis R. (a headstream of the Pachitea) and 40 mi. ENE of Oxapampa; 10°27'S 74°54'W. Coffee, cacao; lumbering. Also Yessup or Yesup.

Puesti (pwĕsht') Rum. *Puești*, village, (pop. 1,926), Barlad prov., E Rumania, 15 mi. NNW of Barlad; viticulture. Includes Puesti-Sat (–sät) and Puesti-Targ (–tûrg), Rum. *Puești-Târg*.

Pueyrredón, Lake (pwārādōn'), freshwater lake (□ 105; alt. 512 ft.) in Patagonian Andes of Chile (Aysén prov.) and Argentina (NW Santa Cruz natl. territory); 47°20'S; c.20 mi. long. Its W part, in Chile, is called L. Cochrane.

Puffin or **Priestholm,** Welsh *Ynys Seiriol* (ŭ'nĭs sī'rēōl), island (58 acres) in Irish Sea, just off E point of Anglesey, Wales, 8 mi. NE of Bangor; 1 mi. long, ¼ mi. wide. Has ruins of early Norman tower. Formerly inhabited by monks.

Puffin Island, islet, E N.F., on N side of Bonavista Bay, just SW of Greenspond; 49°3'N 53°35'W.

Puffin Island, rocky islet (1 mi. long) in the Atlantic, on NW side of St. Finan's Bay, SW Co. Kerry, Ireland, 5 mi. NW of Bolus Head.

Puga (pōō'gä), village, Ladakh dist., SE Kashmir, in Zaskar Range, on left tributary of the Indus and 80 mi. SSE of Leh. Hot springs (174° F); borax workings; sulphur and salt deposits.

Pugachev (pōōgŭchôf'), city (1926 pop. 17,411), E Saratov oblast, Russian SFSR, on Greater Irgiz R. and 120 mi. ENE of Saratov; agr.-processing center; flour and oilseed milling, distilling, metalworking; limestone quarries. Chartered 1835; until early 1920s, called Nikolayevsk.

Pugachevo (–chô'vŭ), village (1947 pop. over 500), S Sakhalin, Russian SFSR, on E coast railroad and 9 mi. S of Vostochny; fishing. Coal mining near by. Under Jap. rule (1905–45), called Maguntanhama (mägoon'tän-hämä').

Puget Island (pū'jĭt) (pop. c.800), Wahkiakum co., SW Wash., agr. isl. (c.5 mi. long) in Columbia R. opposite Cathlamet; herbs, dairy products, fish.

Puget Sound, NW Wash., deepwater inlet of Pacific Ocean extending from Juan de Fuca Strait c.100 mi. S to Olympia. It is navigable for large ships. Admiralty Inlet, entry and northernmost part of the Sound, branches into HOOD CANAL, a W arm; many branches receive streams from Cascade Range. Seattle, Tacoma, and Everett on E shore, and Port Townsend at the entrance, are outlets for a rich industrial and agr. area; the Puget Sound lowland, including the broad trough extending S from Sound, is state's most densely-populated region. The Sound contains a number of isls., largest of which is WHIDBEY ISLAND. Discovered by English voyager in 1787; explored and named by Capt. George Vancouver in 1792.

Puget-sur-Argens (püzhā'-sür-ärzhā'), village (pop. 1,204), Var dept., SE France, at S foot of the Estérel, near Argens R., 3 mi. NW of Fréjus; cork processing, winegrowing.

Puget-Théniers (–tänyā'), village (pop. 940), Alpes-Maritimes dept., SE France, on the Var and 26 mi. NW of Nice, in the Provence Alps; agr. trade. Has Romanesque church.

Puglia, Italy: see APULIA.

Pugu (pōō'gōō), village, Eastern Prov., Tanganyika, on railroad and 10 mi. WSW of Dar es Salaam; sisal, cotton, copra. Kaolin mines.

Pugwash, village (pop. estimate 1,000), N N.S., on Northumberland Strait, at mouth of Pugwash R., 40 mi. NNW of Truro; resort; fisheries.

Puhi (pōō'hē), village (pop. 768), SE **Kauai, T.H.,** near Lihue; sugar plantations.

Puho, Czechoslovakia: see PUCHOV.

Puhos (pōō'hōs), village in Kitee commune (pop. 12,885), Kuopio co., SE Finland, near USSR border, on lake of Saimaa system, 35 mi. S of Joensuu; sawmills, shipyard, machine shop.

Pu-hsi, Manchuria: see PUSI.

Puhsien or **P'u-hsien** (pōō'shyĕn'). **1** Town, ⊙ Puhsien co. (pop. 386,945), central Pingyuan prov., China, on main road, on Yellow R. and 65 mi. ESE of Anyang; cotton weaving; wheat, millet, kaoliang. Called Puchow until 1913. Until 1949 in Shantung prov. **2** Town, ⊙ Puhsien co. (pop. 32,424), SW Shansi prov., China, 40 mi. NW of Linfen; corn, wheat, ramie, beans, medicinal herbs. Coal mining near by.

Pui (pōō'ē), Hung. *Puj* (pōō'ē), village (pop. 879), Hunedoara prov., W central Rumania, on railroad and 26 mi. SSE of Deva; phosphate quarrying.

Puig (pōōch), town (pop. 4,708), Valencia prov., E Spain, near the Mediterranean, 10 mi. NNE of Valencia; pharmaceutical mfg., vegetable canning; truck produce, rice, olive oil. Ruins of Moorish fortress and abbey of Aracristi near by.

Puigcerdá (pōōch-thĕrdhä'), fortified town (pop. 2,428), Gerona prov., NE Spain, 20 mi. NW of Ripoll, in the E Pyrenees, near Segre R.; alt. 3,903 ft. Sp. customs station on trans-Pyrenean RR. Wool and cotton spinning; dairying, lumbering; agr. trade. Has 12th-cent. parochial church (repeatedly restored), and 14th-cent. town hall. Founded in 12th cent. Was ⊙ county of Cerdaña until 17th cent. Suffered much in Fr.–Sp. wars. Near by is artificial lake built in 1310.

Puig de la Coma Pedrosa, Andorra: see COMA PEDROSA, PUIG DE LA.

Puigmal (pwēgmäl', Sp. pōōchmäl'), peak (9,544 ft.) in E Pyrenees on Franco-Spanish border, 10 mi. ESE of Puigcerdá.

Puig Mayor, Balearic Isls.: see TORRELLAS.

Puigpuñent (pōōch-pōōnyĕnt'), town (pop. 832), Majorca, Balearic Isls., 8 mi. NW of Palma; olives, carobs, onions, fruit. Gravel quarries.

Puigreig (pōōch-rĕch'), village (pop. 2,054), Barcelona prov., NE Spain, on the Llobregat and 10 mi. S of Berga; cotton milling; lumbering.

Puigvert de Lérida (pōōch-vĕrt' dhä lā'rē-dhä), village (pop. 1,081), Lérida prov., NE Spain, 8 mi. SE of Lérida, on irrigated Urgel plain (livestock, olive oil, wine, fruit); lumbering.

Puijo (pōō'ēyō), hill (771 ft.), Kuopio co., S central Finland, on L. Kalla, 2 mi. N of Kuopio; tourist and skiing center; noted view.

Puinagua, Canal de (känäl' dā pwēnä'gwä), Loreto dept., E Peru, navigable natural arm of lower Ucayali R. in Amazon basin, extends 85 mi. NE from 6°8'S 75°7'W to 5°12'S 74°7'W.

Puiseaux (pwēzō'), village (pop. 1,851), Loiret dept., N central France, 10 mi. E of Pithiviers; cereal and cattle market.

Puisserguier (pwēsĕrgyā'), town (pop. 2,481), Hérault dept., S France, 9 mi. WNW of Béziers; winegrowing, distilling.

Puj, Rumania: see PUI.

Pujada Bay (pōōhä'dhä), inlet (15 mi. long, 6 mi. wide) of the Pacific in SE Mindanao, Philippines. At mouth is Pajada Isl. (c.2 mi. long); at head is Mati.

Pujato (pōōhä'tō), town (pop. estimate 1,000), S Santa Fe prov., Argentina, 24 mi. WSW of Rosario; agr. center (wheat, flax, alfalfa, cattle, horses, poultry).

Pujehun (pōōjähōōn'), town (pop. 616), South-Western Prov., SE Sierra Leone, on Waanje R. and 40 mi. S of Bo; road and trade center; palm oil and kernels, piassava, rice. Hq. Pujehun dist. Another Pujehun, formerly a gold-mining center, lies 75 mi. N.

Pujerra (pōōhĕ'rä), town (pop. 469), Málaga prov., S Spain, 8 mi. S of Ronda; chestnuts, acorns, livestock; timber; hunting. Thermal springs (Baños de la Corcha) 2 mi. S.

Pujilí (pōōhēlē'), town (1950 pop. 2,149), Cotopaxi prov., N central Ecuador, in the Andes, 7 mi. WSW of Latacunga, in stock-raising and grain-growing region. Hard hit by 1949 earthquake.

Pujols (pü-zhōl'), village (pop. 300), Gironde dept., SW France, in Entre-deux-Mers, 13 mi. SE of Libourne; vineyards.

Pujut, Tanjung, Indonesia: see SAINT NICHOLAS POINT.

Puka, Albania: see PUKË.

Pukaki, Lake (pōōkä'kē) (□ 31), central S.Isl., New Zealand, 55 mi. W of Timaru; 10 mi. long, 2 mi. wide; receives Tasman R. Outlet: Pukaki R., which flows S to Tekapo R.

Pukapuka (pōō'käpōō'kä) or **Danger Island,** atoll (c.1,250 acres; pop. 662), Manihiki group, S Pacific, c.715 mi. NW of Rarotonga; 10°55'S 165°51'E; 3 islets (Pukapuka, Motu Koe, Motu Kavata) joined by reefs; c.3 mi. in diameter. Polynesian inhabitants. Placed 1901 under N.Z. COOK ISLANDS administration. Exports copra, pearl shell. The name Danger Isls. is sometimes given to atoll of which Pukapuka is principal isl.

Pukchong (po͝ok′chŭng′), Jap. *Hokusei*, town (1944 pop. 30,709), S.Hamgyong prov., N Korea, 45 mi. NE of Hungnam; livestock, rice, oats. Has ruins of old castle.

Pukë (po͞o′kŭ) or **Puka** (po͞o′kä), village (1930 pop. 44), N Albania, 20 mi. E of Scutari. Copper and iron deposits near by.

Pukekohe (po͝okŭkoi′), borough (pop. 3,309), ⊙ Franklin co. (□ 551; pop. 15,434), N N.Isl., New Zealand, 25 mi. SSE of Auckland; agr. center; dehydration and dairy plants.

Puket, Thailand: see PHUKET.

Pukhan River, Korea: see HAN RIVER.

Pukhovichi, Belorussian SSR: see MARINA GORKA.

Pukhrayan (po͝okrä′yän), village, Cawnpore dist., central Uttar Pradesh, India, 35 mi. WSW of Cawnpore; gram, wheat, jowar, barley, mustard.

Pukiang or **P'u-chiang** (both: po͞o′jyäng′). **1** Town (pop. 8,335) ⊙ Pukiang co. (pop. 232,086), central Chekiang prov., China, 24 mi. ESE of Kienteh; tung-oil and vegetable-tallow processing, paper-making, cotton weaving; rice, wheat, corn, hams. **2** Town (pop. 27,849), ⊙ Pukiang co. (pop. 112,565), W Szechwan prov., China, 40 mi. SW of Chengtu; rice, wheat, beans, sweet potatoes, millet.

Puko or **P'u-ko** (po͞o′kŭ′), village, ⊙ Puko dist., SE Sikang prov., China, 35 mi. SSE of Sichang; rice, wheat, wax, timber.

Pukow or **P'u-k'ou** (po͞o′kō′), town, N Kiangsu prov., China, on Yangtze R., opposite Nanking (rail ferry); terminus of Tientsin-Pukow RR; major commercial and river-rail transshipment point; wharves, docks, warehouses.

Puksoozero (po͝oksŭô′zyĭrŭ), town (1944 pop. over 500), W Archangel oblast, Russian SFSR, near railroad, 12 mi. SSE of Plesetsk; sawmilling. Developed in early 1940s.

Pukwana (pŭkwä′nŭ), town (pop. 302), Brule co., S central S.Dak., 8 mi. E of Chamberlain; dairy products, livestock, grain.

Pukwei, Manchuria: see TSITSIHAR.

Pul, Caroline Isls.: see PULO ANNA.

Pula (po͞o′lä), village (pop. 2,100), Cagliari prov., S Sardinia, NW of Cape Pula, 15 mi. SW of Cagliari, in olive-growing area; tunny fishing. Ruins of Phoenician-Roman town (Nora) 1 mi. SW.

Pula (po͞o′lä), Ital. *Pola* (pô′lä), city (pop. 22,714), NW Croatia, Yugoslavia, on sheltered bay of Adriatic Sea, 40 mi. SW of Rijeka (Fiume), in S Istria; major seaport (naval harbor, shipyards); rail terminus. Has limestone amphitheater (built at beginning of Roman imperial period), temple of Augustus and Roma (A.D. 2–14), triumphal arch (*Porta Aurea;* c.30 B.C.), mus. with anc. and medieval antiquities. It was already a naval and trading station (*Colonia Pietas Julia*) at the beginning of the Roman imperial period. Passed to Venice in 1148. Austrian naval base (1856–1918) and later capital of Italian prov. of Pola (after 1937, Istria). Heavily damaged during Second World War. Passed to Yugoslavia in 1947. Former Serbo-Croatian name, Pulj.

Pula, Cape, S Sardinia, at W end of Gulf of Cagliari; 38°59′N 9°1′E. Tunny fisheries.

Pulacayo (po͞olăkī′ō), town (pop. c.9,100), Potosí dept., SW Bolivia, on W slopes of Cordillera de Chichas and 10 mi. ENE of Uyuni, on rail branch; alt. 13,156 ft. With near-by HUANCHACA, it is main silver-mining center of Bolivia.

Pulanduta Point (po͞oländo͞o′tä), westernmost point of Masbate isl., Philippines, on Jintotolo Channel; 11°54′N 123°9′E.

Pulangi River (po͞oläng′gē) or **Rio Grande de Mindanao** (rē′ō grän′dā dā mēndänä′ō), Mindanao, Philippines, rises in N Mindanao, flows S to a swampy area N of L. Buluan, then turns sharply NW to Illana Bay of Moro Gulf at Cotabato; c.200 mi. long. Twenty miles above its mouth it splits into 2 arms which surround Cotabato. Drains rich rice-growing area.

Pulantien or **P'u-lan-tien** (po͞o′län′dyĕn′), Jap. *Furanten* (fo͞orän′tĕn′), town (1938 pop. 10,131), southwesternmost Liaotung prov., Manchuria, on Liaotung peninsula, on South Manchuria RR and 40 mi. NE of Dairen, on Fuchow inlet of Gulf of Liaotung; agr. center (peanuts, rice, cotton, vegetables); saltworks. Was in Japanese leased territory of Kwantung (1905–45).

Pulap (po͞o′läp) or **Tamatam** (täm′ätäm′), atoll (pop. 261), Truk dist., E Caroline Isls., W Pacific, 135 mi. W of Truk; 6 mi. long, 4 mi. wide; 3 wooded isls.

Pular, Cerro (sĕ′rō po͞olär′), Andean peak (20,375 ft.), N Chile, near Argentina border; 24°12′S.

Pulaski. 1 (pŭlă′skē, pū–) County (□ 781; pop. 196,685), central Ark.; ⊙ LITTLE ROCK. Intersected by Arkansas R.; drained by small Bayou Meto and Maumelle R. Agr. (cotton, corn, hay, truck, livestock). Mfg. at Little Rock. Bauxite mines, oil and gas wells, stone quarries. Formed 1818. **2** (pūlă′skē) County (□ 254; pop. 8,808), S central Ga.; ⊙ Hawkinsville. Coastal plain area intersected by Ocmulgee R. Agr. (cotton, peanuts, corn, fruit). Formed 1808. **3** (pŭlă′skē) County (□ 204; pop. 13,639), extreme S Ill.; ⊙ Mound City. Bounded S by Ohio R.; drained by Cache R. Agr. area (livestock, wheat, fruit, poultry, cotton, truck; dairy products); lumbering. Wood-products mfg., shipbuilding, flour milling. Formed 1843. **4** (pŭlă′skē) County (□ 433; pop. 12,493), NW Ind.; ⊙ Winamac. Farming and stock-raising area (dairy products; grain, poultry, soybeans). Mfg. at Winamac. Drained by Big Monon Creek and Tippecanoe R. Formed 1835. **5** (pūlă′skē) County (□ 676; pop. 38,452), S. Ky.; ⊙ Somerset. Bounded E by Rockcastle R.; drained by Cumberland R. and small Fishing Creek. Hilly agr. area, partly in Cumberland foothills; burley tobacco, corn, cattle, hogs, poultry, dairy products, lespedeza. Bituminous-coal mines, oil wells, stone quarries, timber. Some mfg. at Somerset. Includes a natl. cemetery and Zollicoffer Memorial Park (both near Somerset), and part of Cumberland Natl. Forest. Formed 1798. **6** (pŭlă′skē,–skī) County (□ 551; pop. 10,392), central Mo.; ⊙ Waynesville. In the Ozarks; drained by Gasconade R. Corn, wheat, fruit, livestock. Part of Mark Twain Natl. Forest here. Formed 1818. **7** (pŭlă′skē, pū–) County (□ 333; pop. 27,758), SW Va.; ⊙ Pulaski. In Great Appalachian Valley, traversed by ridges; drained by New R., here dammed to form Clayton L. Includes part of Jefferson Natl. Forest. Mfg. at Pulaski; agr., stock raising, dairying, lumbering; anthracite, iron, zinc mining. Has mineral springs. Formed 1839.

Pulaski. 1 (pūlă′skē) Town (pop. 234), Candler co., E central Ga., 12 mi. WSW of Statesboro. **2** (pŭlă′skē) Village (pop. 478), Pulaski co., extreme S Ill., 14 mi. N of Cairo, in agr. area. **3** (pūlă′skē) Town (pop. 381), Davis co., SE Iowa, 22 mi. SSE of Ottumwa, in sheep-raising area. **4** (pŭlă′skī,–skē) Village (pop. 2,033), a ⊙ Oswego co., N central N.Y., on Salmon R., near L. Ontario, and 35 mi. N of Syracuse; summer resort; mfg. (boilers, machinery, paper, milk products); gas wells. State park near by. Inc. 1832. **5** (pŭlă′skē) Town (pop. 5,762), ⊙ Giles co., S Tenn., 28 mi. S of Columbia; trade, shipping, and processing center for livestock, cotton, tobacco, truck-farming area; makes shoes, pants, cheese, butter, handles; lumber milling. Timber tracts, phosphate-rock quarries near by. Seat of Martin Col. Tenn. Ku Klux Klan founded here, 1865. Settled 1807; inc. 1819. **6** (pŭlă′skē, pū–) Town (pop. 9,202), ⊙ Pulaski co., SW Va., in the Alleghenies, 13 mi. WSW of Radford; rail junction; trade and industrial center for livestock, lumbering, and dairying area with iron, anthracite-coal, and zinc mines; mfg. of furniture, wood products, chemicals, textiles, structural steel, foundry products, mirrors); flour milling. Claytor L. is E. Inc. 1886. **7** (pŭlă′skē) Village (pop. 1,210), Brown co., NE Wis., 16 mi. NW of Green Bay, in dairying and farming area; canning.

Pulaski, Fort, Ga.: see FORT PULASKI NATIONAL MONUMENT.

Pulau [Malay,=island], for Malayan names beginning thus and not found here: see under following part of the name.

Pulau Laut, Indonesia: see PULU LAUT.

Pulau Sebang (po͞olou′ sŭbäng′), town (pop. 2,478), Settlement of Malacca, SW Malaya, near Tampin rail station, on Negri Sembilan border, 17 mi. N of Malacca, rubber.

Pulau Tikus (tēko͞os′). **1** NW suburb of George Town, Penang isl., NW Malaya. **2** Islet off N coast of Penang isl., guarding N entrance to Penang Channel; lighthouse.

Pulawom, Kashmir: see PULWAMA.

Pulawy (po͞owä′vĭ), Pol. *Puławy*, town (pop. 9,128), Lublin prov., E Poland, port on the Vistula, on railroad and 29 mi. WNW of Lublin; mfg. of cement products; food processing, sawmilling, shipbuilding. Agr. institute. In Rus. Poland (until First World War), called Novaya Aleksandriya. Before Second World War, pop. 50% Jewish.

Pulborough (po͝ol′bŭrŭ), town and parish (pop. 2,020), W Sussex, England, on Arun R. and 12 mi. NW of Worthing; agr. market. The 13th-cent. church has noted brasses.

Pulgan or **Pulgon,** Kirghiz SSR: see FRUNZENSKOYE.

Pulgaon (po͝ol′goun), town (pop. 8,806), Wardha dist., central Madhya Pradesh, India, on Wardha R. and 18 mi. W of Wardha; rail junction; cotton-milling and trade center; oilseed milling; millet, wheat, flax. Building-stone quarries near by.

Pulgar (po͞olgär′), town (pop. 1,216), Toledo prov., central Spain, 13 mi. SSW of Toledo; grain growing, sheep raising, lumbering; cheese processing.

Puli, China: see TASH KURGHAN.

Puli (bo͞o′lē′), Jap. *Hori* (hō′rē), town (1935 pop. 9,580), central Formosa, 22 mi. SE of Taichung, in intermontane basin of central range; coal mining; sugar cane, rice, camphor, lumber. Jihyüeh L. is 7 mi. SSW.

Puliangudi, India: see PULIYANGUDI.

Pulicat (pŭlĭkăt′), town (pop. 3,781), Chingleput dist., E Madras, India, on Coromandel Coast of Bay of Bengal, 25 mi. N of Madras, at S entrance of Pulicat L. (salt pans; prawn fishing); fish processing. Lighthouse just NE, on small isl. Du. settlement (founded 1609); finally ceded to English in 1825.

Pulicat Lake, shallow salt-water lagoon in Nellore and Chingleput dists., E Madras, India; separated from Bay of Bengal (E) by long, narrow Sriharikota isl.; c.30 mi. long, 3–10 mi. wide; prawn fishing; salt pans. Buckingham Canal runs along W edge of Sriharikota isl.; lighthouse near E coast, at site of English settlement of Armagon. Sea entrance S, just N of Pulicat town.

Puligny-Montrachet (pülēnyē′-mōtrăshā′), village (pop. 582), Côte-d'Or dept., E central France, on SE slope of the Côte d'Or, 7 mi. SW of Beaune; noted Burgundy wines.

Pul-i-Khumri or **Pol-i-Khomri** (po͞ol′-ĭ-kho͞omrē′), town (pop. 10,000), Kataghan prov., NE Afghanistan, on Surkhab R. (bridge), on highway and 100 mi. NNW of Kabul; road junction for highways to Mazar-i-Sharif and Khanabad; cotton-milling center (developed in 1940s).

Pulilan (po͞olē′län), town (1939 pop. 1,614; 1948 municipality pop. 16,843), Bulacan prov., S central Luzon, Philippines, 23 mi. NW of Manila; rice growing.

Pulin, Ukrainian SSR: see CHERVONOARMEISK, Zhitomir oblast.

Pul-i-Sefid or **Pol-e-Sefid** (pōl′ĕsĕfēd′), railroad town, Second prov., in E Mazanderan, N Iran, in Elburz mts., 22 mi. S of Shahi.

Pulivendla (po͞olĭvĕnd′lŭ), village, Cuddapah dist., central Madras, India, 40 mi. WSW of Cuddapah; millet, cotton. Limestone quarries, barite workings near by.

Puliyangudi or **Puliangudi** (po͞olĭyŭn′go͞odē), town (pop. 23,695), Tinnevelly dist., S Madras, India, 6 mi. NNE of Tenkasi, in sesame-growing area; cotton weaving.

Pulj, Yugoslavia: see PULA.

Pulkovo (po͞ol′kŭvŭ), village (1939 pop. over 2,000), W Leningrad oblast, Russian SFSR, 10 mi. S of Leningrad. Site of Pulkovo observatory (alt. 256 ft.; 59°46′18″N 30°19′40″E), founded 1839. Acquired (1889) 30-in. refractor, largest of that time. During Second World War, located (1941–44) near Leningrad siege lines; damaged by shelling.

Pullman. 1 Former city, now a part of Chicago, in Cook co., NE Ill. Founded 1880 by G. M. Pullman as experimental model city for workers in his sleeping-car plant; annexed by Chicago in 1889. Scene of famous strike, 1894. **2** City (pop. 12,022), Whitman co., SE Wash., 8 mi. W of Moscow, Idaho, and on South Fork of Palouse R. Wash. State Col. is here. Commercial and shipping center for grain, livestock, and poultry-producing region. Founded 1884, inc. 1888. **3** Town (pop. 210), Ritchie co., W W.Va., 32 mi. W of Clarksburg.

Pullo (po͞o′yō), city (pop. 828), Ayacucho dept., S Peru, in Cordillera Occidental, 15 mi. SSW of Coracora; alt. 10,069 ft. Weaving of native textiles; market for sheep and vicuña wool; livestock.

Pully (pülē′), town (pop. 6,016), Vaud canton, W Switzerland, ESE of and adjacent to Lausanne; metal products, chemicals.

Pulmoddai (po͞olmŏd′dī), village (pop. 1,253), Eastern Prov., Ceylon, on NE coast, 30 mi. NNW of Trincomalee; rice and coconut-palm plantations, vegetable gardens. Ilmenite deposits.

Pulo [Thai spelling of Malay,=island], for Thai names beginning thus: see under following part of the name.

Pulo Anna (po͞o′lō ä′nä) or **Pul** (po͞ol), coral island (pop. 18), Palau dist., W Caroline Isls., W Pacific, 130 mi. WSW of Palau; c.½ mi. long, ¼ mi. wide; wooded.

Pulo Cambing, Portuguese Timor: see ATAURO.

Pulog, Mount (po͞ol′lŏg), peak (9,606 ft.), NW Luzon, Philippines, 24 mi. NE of Baguio; 16°36′N 120°54′E.

Púlpito (po͞ol′pētō), Andean peak (12,834 ft.), Táchira state, W Venezuela, 32 mi. NE of San Cristóbal.

Pulquina (po͞olkē′nä), town (pop. c.400), Santa Cruz, dept., central Bolivia, on Cochabamba-Santa Cruz road and 34 mi. NW of Valle Grande; road junction.

Pulsano (po͞olsä′nô), village (pop. 4,426), Ionio prov., Apulia, S Italy, 9 mi. SE of Taranto.

Pulsatilla, Mount (pŭl″sŭtĭ′lŭ) (10,060 ft.), SW Alta., near B.C. border, in Rocky Mts., in Banff Natl. Park, 23 mi. NW of Banff.

Pulsnitz (po͞ols′nĭts), town (pop. 4,407), Saxony, E central Germany, in Upper Lusatia, 16 mi. NE of Dresden; paper and linen milling, ribbon making, gingerbread baking; mfg. of clothing, ceramics. Power station. Sculptor Rietschel b. here.

Pulteneytown, Scotland: see WICK.

Pultneyville, resort village, Wayne co., W N.Y., on L. Ontario, 23 mi. ENE of Rochester.

Pultusk (po͞o′o͞otŏosk), Pol. *Pułtusk*, town (pop. 8,787), Warzawa prov., E central Poland, port on Narew R. and 33 mi. N of Warsaw; mfg. of agr. machinery, soap, candy; flour milling, distilling. Has old castle, once residence of bishops of Plock. In 1806, French defeated Russians here. In Second World War, under administration of East Prussia, called Ostenburg.

Pulu Laut (po͞olo͞o′ läo͞ot′), **Pulau Laut,** or **Poelau Laoet** (po͞olou′ läo͞ot′), island (□ 796, including near-by SEBUKU; pop. 20,723), Indonesia, just off SE coast of Borneo, in Macassar Strait, 105 mi. E of Banjermasin; 60 mi. long, 20 mi. wide; generally low. Coal mining. Also pepper, rubber. Chief town and port is KOTABARU at N tip of isl. Sometimes called Laut and Laoet.

Pulumur (pülümür') or **Plumur** (plümür'), Turkish *Pülümür* or *Plümür*, village (pop. 1,566), Tunceli prov., E central Turkey, 27 mi. SE of Erzincan; grain.

Puluntohai, China: see BULUN TOKHOI.

Pulupandan (pōō"lōōpän'dän, -pändän'), town (1939 pop. 4,439; 1948 municipality pop. 11,726), Negros Occidental prov., W Negros isl., Philippines, port on Guimaras Strait, 14 mi. SW of Bacolod; ships sugar.

Puluqui Island (pōōlōō'kē) (□ 24; pop. 3,599), Llanquihue prov., S central Chile, in Gulf of Ancud 1 mi. off the coast, opposite Calbuco Isl., 20 mi. SSW of Puerto Montt; 10 mi. long, 2-3 mi. wide; 41°50'S 73°2'W.

Pulu Sambu, Indonesia: see SAMBU.

Pulusuk (pōō'lōōsōōk'), small atoll (pop. 202), Truk dist., E Caroline Isls., W Pacific, c.150 mi. SW of Truk.

Puluwat (pōō'lōōät), atoll (pop. 269), Truk dist., E Caroline Isls., W Pacific, 16 mi. SW of Pulap; 5 low isls.

Pulvar River or **Polvar River** (both: pōlvär'), S central Iran, rises W of Abadeh, flows over 150 mi. SE and SW, cutting through the Zagros ranges, to Kur R. on Marvdasht plain 25 mi. NE of Shiraz. Ruins of Pasargadae and Persepolis are along its course. Isfahan-Shiraz road uses its lower valley.

Pulvermühle, Luxembourg: see LUXEMBOURG, city.

Pulversheim (pülvĕrzĕm', Ger. pōōl'vŏrs-hīm), village (pop. 1,040), Haut-Rhin dept., E France, in Alsace lowland, 7 mi. NNW of Mulhouse; potash mining.

Pulwama (pōōl'vŭnŭ), village, Anantnag dist., SW central Kashmir, in Vale of Kashmir, 15 mi. SSE of Srinagar; rice, corn, oilseeds, wheat. Also called Pulawom.

Pumahuasi (pōōmäwä'sē), village (pop. estimate 1,000), N Jujuy prov., Argentina, on railroad and 14 mi. SSW of La Quiaca; lead-mining center.

Pumanque (pōōmäng'kā), village (1930 pop. 359), Colchagua prov., central Chile, 38 mi. W of San Fernando; grain, fruit, wine, cattle, sheep.

Pumasillo, Cerro (sĕ'rō pōōmäsē'yō), Andean peak (20,492 ft.) in Cuzco dept., S central Peru, in Cordillera Vilcabamba, 75 mi. WNW of Cuzco; 13°11'S 73°1'W.

Pumpherston, village in Mid Calder parish, W Midlothian, Scotland; shale-oil mining and refining.

Puna (pōō'nä) or **Talavera** (tälävä'rä), town (pop. c.8,400), ⊙ Linares prov., Potosí dept., S. central Bolivia, 23 mi. ESE of Potosí on road; tin mining.

Puná Island (pōōnä'), Guayas prov., S Ecuador, at head of Gulf of Guayaquil opposite mouth of Guayas R., flanked by Jambeli and Morro channels; 33 mi. long, c.10 mi. wide. Has fjordlike inlets on E coast. At its NE tip is village of Puná. It is a fishing and hunting resort. Salinas Point, its SW cape, is at 3°3'S 80°16'W.

Punakha or **Punaka** (pōō'nŭkŭ), fortified town [Bhutanese *dzong*], ⊙ Bhutan, on upper Sankosh R. and 105 mi. NE of Darjeeling; residence of maharaja of Bhutan. Main access routes run from India via Buxa Duar and from Gangtok (Sikkim) via Natu La pass. Founded 1577. Largely destroyed by fire in 1832.

Punalur (pōōnŭlōōr'), town (pop. 12,249), S central Travancore, India, 24 mi. NE of Quilon; paper milling, mfg. of textile machinery, plywood, pottery; sawmills.

Punasu or **Peunasoe** (both: pùnä'sōō), island (pop. 840), Indonesia, in Indian Ocean, just off NW tip of Sumatra, 10 mi. WNW of Kutaraja; roughly triangular, 5 mi. wide at base; rises to 1,050 ft. Also called Nasi.

Punata (pōōnä'tä), town (pop. c.20,800), ⊙ Punata prov., Cochabamba dept., central Bolivia, on S slopes of Cordillera de Cochabamba and 25 mi. ESE of Cochabamba, on railroad; alt. 9,000 ft. On highways from Cochabamba to Sucre and to Santa Cruz. Agr. products (wheat, potatoes).

Punawan, India: see GAYA, city.

Punch or **Poonch** (pōōnch), dependency (*jagir*) (□ 1,627; pop. 421,828) of Kashmir, in Jammu prov.; ⊙ Punch. In W Pir Panjal Range; bounded W by Jhelum R. and W Pakistan. Agr. (corn, wheat, rice, pulse, bajra, oilseeds); petroleum, coal, bauxite, and limestone deposits (S). Main town, Punch. W and central area held by Pakistan. Pop. 90% Moslem, 10% Hindu. Prevailing mother tongue, Pahari.

Punch or **Poonch,** town (pop. 8,608), ⊙ Punch jagir, W Kashmir, in Pir Panjal Range, on Punch R. (left tributary of the Jhelum) and 45 mi. SW of Srinagar; trades in grain, ghee. Palace. Heavy fighting here, 1947-48, during India-Pakistan struggle for control.

Punchancha (pōōnchän'chä), town (pop. 313), Loreto dept., NE Peru, just N of Iquitos, on the upper Amazon; experimental station and nursery for rubber plants.

Punchbowl, hill (498 ft.), Honolulu, T.H., has bowl-like extinct crater at summit. Its slopes are heavily populated. In crater is Natl. Cemetery of the Pacific.

Punda Milia (pōōn'dä mēlē'ä), village, Central Prov., S central Kenya, on railroad and 12 mi. S of Fort Hall; coffee, sisal, wheat, corn,

Punganuru (pōōng'gŭnōōrōō), town (pop. 9,610), Chittoor dist., W Madras, India, 37 mi. WNW of Chittoor; peanut milling; large annual cattle fair. Sometimes called Punganur.

Pungarabato, Mexico: see ALTAMIRANO, Guerrero.

Pungesti (pōōn-jĕsht'), Rum. *Pungeşti*, agr. village (pop. 1,309), Jassy prov., E Rumania, 19 mi. WNW of Vaslui.

Pungo-Maká (pōōng'gō-mäkä'), town (pop. c.50,-000), Coquilhatville prov., NW Belgian Congo, on Congo R. and 250 mi. W of Stanleyville; cotton-ginning center; also coffee growing, palm-oil pressing. Large uranium deposits discovered near by. An old tribal capital, 1st reached (1797) by Mungo Park, who described the fabulous wealth of the "Palace of the Black King."

Pungo River (pŭng'gō), E N.C., tidal estuary (c.20 mi. long, 2 mi. wide) of Pamlico Sound; Belhaven is on NW shore. Connected with Alligator R. (NE) by Alligator-Pungo R. Canal, forming part of Intracoastal Waterway.

Pungoteague (pŭng'gŭtēg), village, Accomack co., E Va., on Eastern Shore, 9 mi. SW of Accomac. Old St. George's Church near by.

Pungsan (pōōng'sän'), Jap. *Hozan*, township (1944 pop. 17,453), S.Hamgyong prov., N Korea, 55 mi. WNW of Songjin; lumbering.

Pungue River (pōōng'gwā), in Manica and Sofala prov., central Mozambique, rises at Southern Rhodesia border, flows c.200 mi. SE to Mozambique Channel of Indian Ocean at Beira. Navigable in lower course. Also spelled Pungwe.

Punia (pōōn'yä), village, Eastern Prov., E Belgian Congo, 155 mi. SSE of Stanleyville; tin-mining center; rice processing. Has R.C. mission, hosp. for Europeans.

Punial (pōōn'yŭl), feudatory state (□ 1,600; pop. 8,164) in Gilgit Agency, NW Kashmir; lies astride Gilgit R. in W Karakoram range. Main villages: Gakuch and Sher Qila. Held after 1948 by Pakistan. Inhabitants speak Shina.

Punilla, department, Argentina: see COSQUÍN.

Punilla, Sierra (syĕ'rä pōōnē'yä), subandean mountain range on La Rioja-San Juan prov. border, Argentina, W of Guandacol; extends c.65 mi. N-S; rises to over 15,000 ft.

Puning or **P'u-ning** (pōō'nĭng'), town (pop. 10,711), ⊙ Puning co. (pop. 469,342), E Kwangtung prov., China, 30 mi. WNW of Swatow; rice, wheat, sugar cane. Tin mines near by.

Punitao, Chile: see PANITAO.

Punitaqui (pōōnētä'kē), village (pop. 1,584), Coquimbo prov., N central Chile, 18 mi. SSW of Ovalle; gold-mining center; mercury deposits.

Punitz, Poland: see PONIEC.

Punjab (pŭn"jäb', pŭn'jäb, -jăb) [Sanskrit,=five rivers], a region of NW India and W Pakistan, comprising W half of Indo-Gangetic plain; lies largely bet. Jumna R. (E) and Indus R. (W), and is drained by Sutlej, Beas, Ravi, Chenab, and Jhelum rivers. While the area of the Punjab plain is c.120,000 sq. mi., the combined area of the 3 pre-independence political divisions (Punjab prov., Punjab States, and Punjab Hill States) bearing the name Punjab totaled 148,610 sq. mi., with a 1941 pop. of 35,013,017. Its location bet. NW frontier mtn. passes and plains of anc. Hindustan has given Punjab a major part in Indian history. Excavations at Harappa have uncovered remains of prehistoric Indus Civilization; area around Kurukshetra (battlefield of the Mahabharata) was one of earliest Aryan settlements in India. Alexander the Great penetrated (326 B.C.) as far as the Beas, but the Greeks were later expelled by Chandragupta, founder of Mauryan empire (NW ⊙ was TAXILA). Largely under Kushan rule in 2d cent. A.D.; E section was part of Thanesar kingdom of Harsha in 7th cent. Moslem invasions began with raids of Mahmud of Ghazni in early-11th cent., followed by Mohammed of Ghor (late-12th cent.) and the Slave kings (13th cent.), who established 1st Delhi Sultanate; struggle for power bet. Tughlaks and Mongols marked 14th cent.; Baber's victory over Lodis at PANIPAT (1526) led to foundation of Mogul empire, later consolidated by Akbar. Despite repressions of Aurangzeb, the newly-founded Sikh sect grew into a militant nation and by early-19th cent., under Ranjit Singh, emerged as the dominant power in Punjab, superseding Afghans (who had repulsed Mahrattas at Panipat in 1761) and decadent Mogul empire. Br. influence soon advanced N to the Sutlej; Anglo-Sikh wars (1845-46; 1848-49) resulted in annexation of whole area to Br. India in 1849; Punjab was then created a prov. Although Delhi was center of Sepoy Rebellion of 1857, few outbreaks occurred in rest of newly-conquered prov. North-West Frontier Prov. was created 1901 out of former Punjab territory W of the Indus; area around Delhi was made a separate prov. in 1912. By 1936 all princely states of Punjab, which, previously, had made treaties with British, were grouped into PUNJAB STATES agency under control of govt. of India. Punjab constituted (1937) an autonomous prov. (in 1941: □ 99,089; pop. 24,418,819). In 1947, upon creation of independent dominions of India and Pakistan, it was divided into 2 parts, one part, with a Moslem majority, becoming West Punjab prov. of Pakistan, the other becoming East Punjab prov. of India; both West Punjab and East Punjab were in 1949 renamed simply Punjab by the 2 countries. Mass migrations of Moslems and non-Moslems bet. the 2 areas involved millions of people and caused great social and economic distress. **Punjab** of India is (since 1950) a constituent state (□ 37,428; 1951 pop. 12,638,111) of republic of India; provisional ⊙ SIMLA; permanent ⊙ was begun 1950 at site c.22 mi. N of Ambala. Bounded W by W Pakistan (Punjab and Bahawalpur), S by Rajasthan, E by Jumna R., Uttar Pradesh, Delhi, Himachal Pradesh, and Bilaspur, N by Kashmir and Chamba dist. (Himachal Pradesh), and NW by Ravi R.; NE section extends across Punjab Himalayas to Tibet; surrounds main territory of Patiala and East Punjab States Union and is bordered S and E by detached areas of that state. State is mostly flat alluvial plain, drained by upper courses of Beas and Sutlej rivers and irrigated by extensive systems of Sirhind, Western Jumna, Upper Bari Doab, and Sutlej valley canals. Annual rainfall averages 15-30 in. In the plain wheat, millet, corn, cotton, and gram are chief crops. KANGRA dist. (NE), lying E of Siwalik Range in Punjab Himalayas, consists largely of snow-capped mts. but has several fertile valleys; wheat, corn, barley, potatoes, tea, fruit are cultivated; forests yield bamboo, sal, deodar, pine. Industries include textile mills (chiefly cotton and woolen goods) at Amritsar, Dhariwal, Ludhiana (hosiery center); metalworks at Batala, Amritsar, Ludhiana, Rewari, Jullundur; glassworks at Ambala; paper factories at Abdullapur, Jagadhri; also cotton ginning, flour and sugar milling, oilseed pressing. Handicrafts include woolen carpets, muslin turbans, woodwork (furniture, toys), pottery, copper and brass goods. Cattle raising in Hissar dist. (S); mahseer and trout fishing in N rivers. Grand Trunk Road links Karnal, Ambala, Ludhiana, Jullundur, and Amritsar with Delhi (SE) and Lahore (W). Simla, in small enclave (E) within Himachal Pradesh, is famous hill resort. State contains several historical sites, notably AMRITSAR (Sikh religious center), Kurukshetra, and battlefield of Panipat. Former Punjab states of Loharu, Dujana, and Pataudi merged with state in 1948. Comprises 13 dists.: Ambala, Amritsar, Ferozepore, Gurdaspur, Gurgaon, Hissar, Hoshiarpur, Jullundur, Kangra, Karnal, Ludhiana, Rohtak, and Simla. Chief languages, Punjabi and Western Hindi. **Punjab** of Pakistan is a province (□ 62,987; 1951 pop. 18,814,000) of W Pakistan; ⊙ Lahore. Bounded N by Punjab Himalayas, W by Indus R. and Sulaiman Range, S and SE by Sutlej R.; bordered by North-West Frontier Prov. (N, W), Baluchistan (SW), Bahawalpur (S), Punjab of India (E), and Kashmir (NE). Mostly a broad, flat alluvial plain sloping gradually from NE to SW and drained by Jhelum, Chenab, Ravi, and Sutlej rivers. In NW are POTWAR PLATEAU and SALT RANGE, overlooking desolate THAL region to the S; in SW, bet. Sulaiman Range and Indus R., lies DERAJAT plain. Annual rainfall varies from 20-25 in. in submontane NE section to 5-10 in. in arid SW area (here summer heat is intense). Position of prov. as leading wheat-producing area of Indian subcontinent has been achieved in past century through remarkable irrigation projects which have converted the semi-desert into fertile agr. land. Other crops are gram, millet, cotton, oilseeds, rice, sugar cane; citrus fruit, mangoes, pomegranates, dates cultivated in many places. Sheep and camel raising; mahseer fishing in rivers. Minerals confined to NW section, where large deposits of rock salt, coal, gypsum, and limestone are worked in Salt Range and petroleum drilling is carried on at Balkassar and Khaur on Potwar Plateau (refinery at Rawalpindi). Cotton ginning and rice milling are common; also flour and oilseed milling, metalware mfg., fruit canning. Widespread handicraft mfg.: cloth fabrics, carpets, carved wood and ivory, hosiery, leather goods, metal products, cutlery, pottery. LAHORE is largest city and chief commercial and industrial center (textile mills, metalworks, printing presses, railway workshops); other important cities include Rawalpindi (military station), Multan (textiles), Sialkot (sports goods, surgical instruments), Lyallpur (wheat market), and Gujranwala (metal products); cement works at Wah and Dandot. Grand Trunk Road traverses N part of prov. Large quantities of wheat and other grains exported by rail to Karachi. Foremost educational institution is Punjab Univ. at Lahore; Punjab Agr. Col. is at Lyallpur. Famous archaeological sites at Harappa and Taxila. Comprises 16 dists.: Attock, Dera Ghazi Khan, Gujranwala, Gujrat, Jhang, Jhelum, Lahore, Lyallpur, Mianwali, Montgomery, Multan, Muzaffargarh, Rawalpindi, Shahpur, Sheikhupura, and Sialkot. Chief languages, Punjabi, Lahnda, and Urdu. Sometimes spelled Panjab.

Punjab Hill States, former political agency (□ 11,375; pop. 1,090,644) in the Punjab, India, lying in Punjab Himalayas; hq. were at Simla. Comprised princely states of Tehri (or Tehri Garhwal), Bashahr, Sirmur, Bilaspur, Jubbal, Keonthal, Nalagarh, Kalsia, Baghal, Bhajji, Kumharsain, Tharoch, Balsan, Mailog, Baghat, Dhami, Kuthar, Sangri, Mangal, Kunihar, Bija, and Darkoti. States came under Br. influence in early-19th cent.; most were later known as Simla Hill States or the Hill States. In 1936, constituted as subordinate agency to PUNJAB STATES agency. In 1947–48, Tehri merged with United Provs. (Uttar Pradesh), Bilaspur became centrally administered state, Nalagarh and Kalsia joined Patiala and East Punjab States Union, rest merged with Himachal Pradesh.

Punjab Himalayas (hĭmä'lŭyŭz, hĭmŭlā'ŭz), W subdivision of the HIMALAYAS, in India, Kashmir, and W Pakistan; from bend of Indus R. (NW) extend c.350 mi. ESE, through NE North-West Frontier Prov. (Pakistan), Kashmir, and N India, to Sutlej R. (SE); separated from KARAKORAM mtn. system (N) by the upper Indus. Main range paralleled NE by ZASKAR RANGE, SW by PIR PANJAL and SIWALIK ranges. NANGA PARBAT (26,660 ft.), highest peak, is in NW, with Nunkun (23,410 ft.) in center and Mt. Shilla (23,050 ft.; in Zaskar Range) in SE. Main passes (on important routes) are Zoji La, Burzil, Banihal, and Bara Lacha La. Mts. give rise to Jhelum (in upper course flows through famous Vale of Kashmir, past noted resort of SRINAGAR and through Wular L.), Chenab, Ravi, and Beas rivers, all flowing SW through Punjab plain. Noted hill stations are Murree and Dalhousie. Geological and structural features indicate the trans-Indus extension of Punjab Himalayas into W Gilgit Agency (Kashmir).

Punjab States, former political agency (□ 38,146; pop. 5,503,554) in NW India; hq. were at Lahore. Comprised princely states of Bahawalpur, Khairpur, Patiala, Chamba, Jind, Mandi, Nabha, Kapurthala, Faridkot, Suket, Loharu, Maler Kotla, Dujana, and Pataudi. Constituted in 1921 under central govt. of India; Khairpur included in 1933; PUNJAB HILL STATES became subordinate agency in 1936. In 1947–48, Bahawalpur and Khairpur acceded to Pakistan, Loharu, Dujana, and Pataudi were inc. into dists. of Indian Punjab, Chamba, Mandi, and Suket joined Himachal Pradesh, and rest were merged with Patiala and East Punjab States Union.

Punkudutivu (pŏŏng"kŏŏdŏŏtē'vŏŏ), island (pop. 9,149) in Northern Prov., Ceylon, in S Palk Strait, 10 mi. WSW of Jaffna; 4 mi. long, 3.5 mi. wide. Vegetable gardens (chili, yams), coconut and palmyra palms. Main settlement in S. Ferry to Velanai isl. (N).

Puno (pōō'nō), department (□ 26,140; pop. 646,385), SE Peru, on the altiplano, on Bolivia border; ⊙ Puno. Bounded by Cordillera Occidental (SW) and Cordillera de Vilcanota (W). Its N section extends across Cordillera Oriental. Includes Peruvian section of L. Titicaca. Drained by Coata, Ramis, and Inambari rivers. Grain and livestock (sheep, llamas, alpacas) on the altiplano; coca, tobacco on N slopes of the Andes. Silver mining at Lampa, gold deposits at Poto and Santo Domingo, oil field at Pirin. Main centers: Huancané, Juliaca, Juli. Served by railroads from Arequipa and Cuzco. Puno is an important port on L. Titicaca (connected by steamer with Guaqui, Bolivia).

Puno, city (pop. 15,999), ⊙ Puno dept. and Puno prov. (□ 2,173; pop. 118,060), SE Peru, on NW shore of L. Titicaca, on Puno Bay, 100 mi. ENE of Arequipa, 525 mi. ESE of Lima; 15°50'S 70°1'W; alt. 12,664 ft. Commercial and communication hub of SE Peru, main Peruvian port on L. Titicaca (steamer service to Guaqui, Bolivia), and terminus of rail line from Juliaca; customs station. Joined by rail, highway, and ship with La Paz, Bolivia. Trades in wool, llama and alpaca furs.

Punta, La, Argentina: see LA PUNTA.

Punta, La, Peru: see LA PUNTA.

Punta, Cerro de (sĕ'rō dā pōōn'tä), peak (4,400 ft.), W central Puerto Rico, highest point on the isl., in the Cordillera Central, 3 mi. S of Jayuya; 18°10'N 66°35'W.

Punta Alegre (pōōn'tä älā'grā), town (pop. 2,217), Camagüey prov., E Cuba, on N coast, 22 mi. NW of Morón, in sugar and cattle region. Produces salt and gypsum. Sugar central is just E.

Punta Alta (äl'tä), city (pop. 19,576), ⊙ Coronel L. Rosales dist. (□ 497; pop. 26,352), SW Buenos Aires prov., Argentina, on Bahía Blanca (bay), 15 mi. SE of Bahía Blanca city; railhead and commercial center; mfg.: cement articles, shoes, tiles, dairy products.

Punta Arenas (ärā'näs), city (1940 pop. 29,883; 1949 estimate 24,706), ⊙ MAGALLANES prov. and Magallanes dept. (□ 13,841; 1940 pop. 35,819), S Chile, port on E coast of Brunswick Peninsula, on Strait of Magellan, and 1,350 mi. S of Santiago; 53°9'S 70°53'W. The major city on the strait, it is a sheep-raising, lumbering, commercial, and mfg. center, and a free port trading in wool, mutton, hides, timber. Produces frozen meat, canned fish, beer; has sawmills, tanneries. Coal mining near by (Loreto). Trades also in barley, oats, potatoes, and some fruit. Airport. The southernmost city of the world (only the town of Ushuaia, SE, in Tierra del Fuego, is more southerly), it has a rigorous, healthy climate attracting tourists; reached from Argentina by highway and from S Chile by boat. Has modern bldgs., parks, a theater, and anthropological mus. Founded 1847 to maintain Chile's claim to Strait of Magellan, it flourished as a coaling station for transoceanic ships until opening of Panama Canal. It has since gained importance as exporting center for wool and mutton of S Patagonia. For a time (1927–37) it was called Magallanes.

Punta Arenas, village on NW Vieques Isl., E Puerto Rico, port near westernmost point of the isl., 8 mi. WSW of Isabela Segunda (linked by railroad); sugar loading.

Punta Brava (brä'vä), town (pop. 3,540), Havana prov., W Cuba, on railroad and 12 mi. SW of Havana; tobacco, sugar cane, fruit.

Punta Cardón (kärdōn'), oil refining center, Falcón state, NW Venezuela, on SW shore of Paraguaná peninsula, 30 mi. SW of Pueblo Nuevo.

Punta Chica, Argentina: see VICTORIA, Greater Buenos Aires.

Punta de Bombón (dā bōmbōn'), town (pop. 3,062), Arequipa dept., S Peru, near mouth of Tambo R. (irrigation) on Pacific coast, 55 mi. SSW of Arequipa; agr. center (sugar cane, cotton, rice, corn, alfalfa); cotton ginning.

Punta del Cobre (dĕl kō'brā), village (1930 pop. 586), Atacama prov., N central Chile, on Copiapó R. (irrigation), on railroad and 11 mi. SSE of Copiapó; copper mining; agr. (alfalfa, corn, clover, subtropical fruit, goats).

Punta del Este (ĕ'stā), town (pop. 6,500), Maldonado dept., S Uruguay, on Atlantic promontory at mouth of the Río de la Plata, 4 mi. S of Maldonado, 65 mi. E of Montevideo; 34°58'S 54°58'W. One of the leading and most fashionable beach resorts of Uruguay. Has modern hotels, casino, boardwalk, parks. In the Second World War, near its coast was fought a naval battle (Dec., 1939) bet. British and Germans, which led to scuttling of the *Graf Spee.* Adjoining Punta del Este (E) is a new seaside resort, San Rafael.

Punta Delgada (dĕlgä'dä), village (1930 pop. 223), Magallanes prov., S Chile, on headland in NE Strait of Magellan, 75 mi. NE of Punta Arenas; sheep raising.

Punta de Lobos (dā lō'bōs), village (pop. 270) and cape (21°5'S 70°12'W), Tarapacá prov., N Chile, on Pacific coast, 60 mi. S of Iquique. Salt deposits at the Salar Grande near by.

Punta de Piedras (pyā'dräs), town (pop. 1,912), port on Margarita Isls. (S), Nueva Esparta state, NE Venezuela, on the Caribbean, 19 mi. WSW of La Asunción; fishing (pearls, sardines, herring, sharks).

Punta de Sal (säl'), village, Tumbes dept., NW Peru, landing on the Pacific, at the cape Punta de Sal, 4°S 80°59'W on Pan-American Highway and 32 mi. SW of Zorritos, near Zorritos oil fields; fisheries. Sometimes Punta Sal.

Punta de Vacas (vä'käs), village (pop. estimate 100), NW Mendoza prov., Argentina, on Transandine RR., on Mendoza R. and 55 mi. W of Mendoza, in stock-raising area; alt. 7,855 ft.

Punta Gorda, town (pop. 1,375), ⊙ Toledo dist., S Br. Honduras, port of entry on Gulf of Honduras 100 mi. SW of Belize. Exports sugar cane, bananas, coconuts. Lighthouse, customhouse, and cattle landing (N).

Puntagorda (pōōntägôr'dä), village (pop. 448), Palma, Canary Isls., 14 mi. ENE of Santa Cruz de la Palma; almonds, cereals, figs, wine, poultry, livestock; timber.

Punta Gorda, SE residential suburb of Santiago de Cuba, Oriente prov., E Cuba.

Punta Gorda (pŭn'tŭ gôr'dŭ), city (pop. 1,915), ⊙ Charlotte co., S Fla., on Charlotte Harbor (bridged here), near mouth of Peace R., 23 mi. NW of Fort Myers; resort, and shipping point for fish and vegetables; mfg. of shell novelties. Inc. 1901.

Punta Gorda River, SE Nicaragua, rises in Cordillera de Yolaina, flows c.70 mi. E, through rubber and hardwood forests, to Caribbean Sea at Punta Gorda, 10 mi. SW of Mico Point. Navigable for 25 mi. in lower course.

Punta Icacos, Nicaragua: see CORINTO.

Punta Lara, Argentina: see LA PLATA.

Puntales (pōōntä'lĕs), S section of Cádiz city, Cádiz prov., SW Spain; mfg. of airplanes. Racetrack is just W; and a castle adjoins it E.

Puntallana (pōōntälyä'nä), town (pop. 410), Palma, Canary Isls., 4 mi. NNE of Santa Cruz de la Palma; cereals, potatoes, onions, bananas; flour milling, charcoal burning.

Puntamba (pōōntäm'bŭ), village (pop. 6,675), Ahmadnagar dist., E Bombay, India, on Godavari R. and 45 mi. NNW of Ahmadnagar; trades in gur, millet; sugar milling. Also spelled Puntambe.

Punta Moreno (pōōn'tä mōrā'nō), village (pop. 73), Libertad dept., NW Peru, in Cordillera Occidental, on Chicama R. and 8 mi. SW of Cascas; rail terminus; sugar cane, coffee.

Punta Negra (nä'grä), mining settlement, Antofagasta prov., N Chile, on SE edge of the desert Salar de Punta Negra, on an Andean plateau, 115 mi. NE of Taltal; borax-producing center.

Punta Negra, Salar de (sälär' dā), salt desert area (alt. c.9,500 ft.) in Atacama Desert, Antofagasta prov., N Chile; c.20 mi. long, 5 mi. wide; borax deposits.

Punta Rasa (pŭn'tŭ rä'sŭ), fishing village, Lee co., SW Fla., at mouth of Caloosahatchee R., on San Carlos Bay, 12 mi. SW of Fort Myers; ferry to Sanibel Isl. Sometimes Punta Rassa.

Puntarenas (pōōntärā'näs), largest province (□ 4,300; 1950 pop. 88,168) of Costa Rica, on the Pacific; ⊙ Puntarenas. Situated on Pacific slopes of the main divide, it consists of Puntarenas-Esparta area (NW) and the Diquís R. basin (SE, on Panama border) linked by narrow coastal strip. Includes Osa Peninsula and S part of Nicoya Peninsula. Contains chief banana areas of Costa Rica, with ports of Quepos and Golfito. Rice, beans, corn, fruit. Pearl fishing and coconuts along SE coast. Gold mining (Miramar); salines. Prov. is served by sections of Inter-American Highway and plantation railroads; its chief communications are by sea. Chief centers are Puntarenas, Esparta, Miramar, Buenos Aires, and the ports of Quepos and Golfito.

Puntarenas, city (1950 pop. 13,272), ⊙ Puntarenas prov., W Costa Rica, major Pacific port on Gulf of Nicoya, 50 mi. W of San José (linked by road and railroad); 9°59'N 84°50'W. Principal port of Costa Rica and summer resort, exporting coffee, lumber, tuna. Active coastal trade (rice, corn, livestock). Tuna fishing and processing, shipbuilding, saltmaking, mfg. of tortoise-shell articles, beverages, soap, candles. Situated on 4-mi.-long sandspit (c.600 yards wide), city includes Cocal banana pier (near base of peninsula), the city proper (Pueblo Nuevo) with customhouse, baths, railroad station, resort hotels, and 400 ft. deep-water pier. Toward tip of peninsula is Muellecito, the coastal trade and fishing port, and the residential quarter of El Carmen ending in a lighthouse. Pop. has large Nicaraguan and Chinese elements. Long the sole port of Costa Rica, it declined (19th cent.) following construction of railroad to the Atlantic and rise of Limón. Flourished again briefly after transfer of main banana-growing center to Pacific littoral and until rise of special banana ports of Quepos and Golfito.

Punta Sal, Peru: see PUNTA DE SAL.

Punta Santiago, Puerto Rico: see PLAYA DE HUMACAO.

Puntas de Maciel (pōōn'täs dā mäsyĕl'), village (pop. 300), Florida dept., S central Uruguay, in the Cuchilla Maciel (a N outlier of the Cuchilla Grande Inferior), on railroad and 37 mi. NNW of Florida; grain, linseed, cattle, sheep.

Puntas Negras, Cordón de (kôrdōn' dā pōōn'täs nā'gräs), Andean massif on Chile-Argentina border; 23°45'S 67°40'W; rises to c.22,000 ft.

Punta Zacate Island (pōōn'tä säkä'tä), in Gulf of Fonseca, La Unión dept., E Salvador, at entrance to La Unión Bay, 5 mi. ESE of La Unión; 2 mi. long, 1 mi. wide.

Puntiagudo, Cerro (sĕ'rō pōōntyägōō'dō), or **Cerro Lamas** (lä'mäs), Andean mountain (19,350 ft.) on Argentina-Chile border, 32 mi. WSW of the Cerro Incahuasi; 27°9'S.

Puntiagudo, Cerro, Andean volcanic peak (8,170 ft.), S central Chile, in the lake dist., on SE bank of L. Rupanco, 50 mi. SE of Osorno.

Puntilla, La (lä pōōntē'yä), cape on Pacific coast of Guayas prov., W Ecuador, westernmost point of Santa Elena Peninsula, 80 mi. W of Guayaquil; 2°12'S 81°1'W.

Punucapa (pōōnōōkä'pä), village (1930 pop. 374), Valdivia prov., S central Chile, 6 mi. NNW of Valdivia, in agr. area (cereals, potatoes, fruit, livestock). Manganese deposits near by.

Punxsutawney (pŭngksŭtô'nē), borough (pop. 8,969), Jefferson co., W central Pa., 60 mi. NE of Pittsburgh; bituminous coal; mfg. (metal products, textiles), railroad shops; meat packing; wheat, potatoes. Settled 1772, laid out c.1818, inc. 1850.

Punyü (pōōn'yü'), Mandarin *P'an-yü* (pän'yü'), town (pop. 22,574), ⊙ Punyü co. (pop. 604,054), S Kwangtung prov., China, in Canton R. delta, 14 mi. SE of Canton; cotton milling, embroidering, paper mfg.; sericulture. Punyü was the official name applied 1913–35 to CANTON and 1935–46 to Suntso, Mandarin *Hsin-tsao.* Present Punyü was called Shikiu, Mandarin *Shih-ch'iao,* until it became co. ⊙ in 1946.

Puolanka (pōō'ôläng"kä), Swedish *Puolango* (pōō'ôläng"ō), village (commune pop. 6,726), Oulu co., N central Finland, 60 mi. E of Oulu; kaolin quarries; lumbering.

Pupiales (pōōpyä'lĕs), town (pop. 1,978), Nariño dept., SW Colombia, in the Andes near Ecuador border, 4 mi. NNW of Ipiales; alt. 9,888 ft.; corn, wheat, cacao, coffee, potatoes, fruit, stock.

Puqueldón (pōōkĕldōn'), village (1930 pop. 72), Chiloé prov., S Chile, on N LEMUI ISLAND, off E coast of Chiloé Isl., 10 mi. SE of Castro; potatoes, wheat, livestock; lumbering, fishing.

Puquina (pōōkē'nä), town (pop. 691), Moquegua dept., S Peru, at S foot of Nevado de Pichu Pichu, 28 mi. ESE of Arequipa; alt. 10,105 ft.; grain, livestock raising. Archaeological remains are found near by.

Puquintica, Cerro (sĕ'rō pōōkēntē'kä), Andean mountain (18,897 ft.) on Chile-Bolivia border; 18°45'S 69°W.

Puquio (pōō'kyō), city (pop. 5,561), ⊙ Lucanas prov. (□ 6,818; pop. 74,194), Ayacucho dept., S Peru, in Cordillera Occidental of the Andes, on road from Nazca, and 120 mi. S of Ayacucho; 14°42'S 74°8'W; alt. 12,641 ft. Stock raising (cattle, sheep, llamas); alfalfa, grain.

Puquios (pōō'kyōs), village (1930 pop. 78), Atacama prov., N Chile, on W slopes of the Andes, 30 mi. NE of Copiapó; rail terminus at mtn. pass. Copper mining near by.

Pur (pŏor). **1** Town (pop. 5,532), S central Rajasthan, India, 7 mi. SW of Bhilwara; millet, gram, oilseeds. Garnet and mica deposits near by. **2** Town (pop. 6,664), Muzaffarnagar dist., N Uttar Pradesh, India, 15 mi. NNE of Muzaffarnagar; wheat, gram, sugar cane, oilseeds, corn. Also called Pur Qazi.

Pura, Iran: see IRANSHAHR.

Puracé (pōōräsā'), town (pop. 880), Cauca dept., SW Colombia, at NW foot of Puracé Volcano in Cordillera Central, 11 mi. E of Popayán; base for visits to the volcano. Has old bldgs., San Miguel church. Sulphur mines and waterfalls near by.

Puracé Volcano, active volcano (15,420 ft.) in Cauca dept., SW Colombia, in Cordillera Central, 17 mi. ESE of Popayán. A cone-shaped, snow-capped peak, it emits luminous smoke clouds. Last major eruption, 1869. Sulphur deposits.

Purali River, W Pakistan: see PORALI RIVER.

Purang, Tibet: see TAKLAKOT.

Puranpur (pōō'rŭnpŏor), town (pop. 6,281), Pilibhit dist., N Uttar Pradesh, India, 22 mi. ESE of Pilibhit; road junction; trades in rice, wheat, gram, sugar cane.

Purari River (pōōrä'rē), New Guinea, rises in S slopes of Bismarck range in Territory of New Guinea, flows c.170 mi. S through Papua to Gulf of Papua; c.2 mi. wide at mouth; navigable for c.120 mi.

Purbeck, Isle of (pûr'bĕk), peninsula district of SW Dorset, England, bet. Poole Harbour and the English Channel; c.12 mi. long, 8 mi. wide. Terminates S in St. Alban's Head. There are marble, China-clay, and freestone quarries. Swanage and Corfe Castle are on the peninsula.

Purbolinggo or **Poerbolinggo** (both: pŏorbŏŏlĭng'gŏŏ), town (pop. 16,435), central Java, Indonesia, 70 mi. SE of Cheribon, at foot of Mt. Slamet; trade center for agr. area (rice, rubber, peanuts, corn); textile mills. Also spelled Poerbulinggo.

Purcell (pûrsĕl'). **1** Village, Weld co., N Colo., 15 mi. NNE of Greeley; alt. 5,024 ft. Grain- and cattle-shipping point. **2** City (pop. 334), Jasper co., SW Mo., 12 mi. N of Joplin. **3** City (pop. 3,546), McClain co., central Okla., 32 mi. SSE of Oklahoma City, and on Canadian R. (bridged), in agr. area (cotton, corn, broomcorn, peaches); cotton ginning; mfg. of mattresses, flour, feed.

Purcellville (pûr'sŭlvĭl), town (pop. 945), Loudoun co., N Va., 8 mi. W of Leesburg; processing, shipping point in agr. (apples, wheat, livestock) area; lumber and flour milling.

Purchena (pōōrchä'nä), city (pop. 1,811), Almería prov., S Spain, on Almanzora R. and 24 mi. WSW of Huércal-Overa; flour milling, soap and talcum mfg. Cereals, wine, fruit, sugar beets. Marble quarries. Dominated by castle-crowned hill.

Purdie Islands, Australia: see NUYTS ARCHIPELAGO.

Purdilnagar (pŏor'dĭlnŭgŭr), town (pop. 4,176), Aligarh dist., W Uttar Pradesh, India, 14 mi. ENE of Aligarh; wheat, barley, pearl millet, gram, cotton. Also spelled Purdilpur.

Purdin, town (pop. 255), Linn co., N central Mo., 6 mi. N of Linneus.

Purdon, town (pop. 203), Navarro co., E central Texas, 13 mi. SW of Corsicana, in farm area.

Purdoshki (pōōrdôsh'kē), village (1926 pop. 4,299), NW Mordvinian Autonomous SSR, Russian SFSR, on Moksha R. and 18 mi. NNW of Krasnoslobodsk; grain, potatoes. Peat bogs near by.

Purdy, city (pop. 437), Barry co., SW Mo., in the Ozarks, 7 mi. S of Monett.

Purén (pōōrĕn'), town (pop. 2,711), Malleco prov., S central Chile, 27 mi. SW of Angol; agr. center (cereals, apples, wine, peas, livestock); lumbering, flour milling. Tourist resort.

Purépero (pōōrā'pārō), officially Purépero de Echáiz, town (pop. 7,132), Michoacán, central Mexico, on central plateau, 19 mi. ESE of Zamora; agr. center (corn, sugar cane, tobacco, fruit, stock).

Purfleet, former urban district (1931 pop. 8,511), S Essex, England, on the Thames and 13 mi. E of London; shipbuilding, paper milling. In it is residential area of West Thurrock, with 12th-cent. church. Inc. 1936 in Thurrock.

Purga, Mexico: see MANLIO FABIO ALTAMIRANO.

Purgatoire River (pûr"gŭtwär', pĭ"gŭ–), SE Colo., formed by confluence of North Fork and Middle Fork in Culebra Range of Sangre de Cristo Mts.; flows 186 mi. NE, past Trinidad, to Arkansas R. just E of Las Animas. Below Trinidad, flows in canyon over 100 mi. long. Drains coal-mining and agr. region. Dinosaur foot prints have been found in rock bed of river. The informal spellings Picket Wire and Picketwire are sometimes used.

Purgatory Peak, Colo.: see SANGRE DE CRISTO MOUNTAINS.

Purgi, India: see PARGI.

Puri (pŏor'ē), district (□ 4,002; pop. 1,455,888), E Orissa, India; ⊙ Puri. Bounded E by Bay of Bengal; crossed W by N end of Eastern Ghats; includes most of Chilka L. (S). Rice is chief crop of alluvial plain (E); hill forests (W) yield sal and bamboo. Rice milling, fishing (seerfish, mackerel, sardines, pomfret, hilsa), handicraft cloth weaving, palm-mat making, metalworking. Several sites of historic interest: Bhubaneswar, Puri, Konarak, Dhauli, Khandgiri. Original dist. (□ 2,451); 1941 pop. 1,101,939) enlarged 1949 by inc. of former princely states (were in Orissa States) of Daspalla, Khandpara, Mayagarh, and Ranpur.

Puri, town (pop. 41,055), ⊙ Puri dist., E Orissa, India, a celebrated Hindu pilgrimage center on Bay of Bengal, 45 mi. S of Cuttack. Seaside resort; rail terminus; market center (rice, fish, coconuts, gram); rice milling, handicraft mfg. (cloth, metalware, palm mats, stone idols), fish curing. Has col. Site of famous temple of Jagannath or Juggernaut [Sanskrit,=lord of the world], built in late-12th cent., which stands within sacred enclosure together with many other shrines; its tower, 192-ft. high and elaborately carved, is a well-known landmark. Cult of Jagannath, unattended by any caste distinctions, is one of most popular forms of Vishnuite worship. During annual Car Festival (June-July), image of god is mounted on a huge, unwieldy cart and dragged by thousands of enthusiastic pilgrims through wide main street of town to his summer house c.1 mi. distant. Puri is summer hq. of Orissa govt. Shankaracharya (8th cent. A.D. Vedantic philosopher) founded one of his chief schools here. Coconut farm near by. Sometimes called Jagannath or Jagannathpur.

Purial, Sierra de (syĕ'rä dā pōōryäl'), small range, Oriente prov., E Cuba, near E tip of the isl. and SW of Baracoa, extends c.25 mi. SE from Toa R. to S coast. On its slopes coffee, cacao, bananas, and coconuts are grown. Yields timber.

Purificación (pōōrēfēkäsyōn'), town (pop. 4,196), Tolima dept., W central Colombia, landing on E bank of Magdalena R. and 45 mi. SE of Ibagué; cotton- and cattle-raising center.

Purificación, town (pop. 1,344), Jalisco, W Mexico, in coastal hills, 19 mi. WSW of Autlán; corn, sugar cane, cotton, rice, tobacco, bananas.

Purio (pōōr'yō), village (pop. 487), Los Santos prov., S central Panama, in Pacific lowland, 8 mi. NW of Pedasí; sugar cane, corn, livestock.

Puriscal, Santiago de, Costa Rica: see SANTIAGO.

Purísima or **Purísima del Rincón** (pōōrē'sēmä dĕl rēngkōn'), town (pop. 2,402), Guanajuato, central Mexico, 15 mi. SW of León; alt. 5,659 ft. Rail terminus; cereals, alfalfa, beans, sugar cane, livestock.

Purísima, La, Mexico: see LA PURÍSIMA.

Purísima del Rincón, Mexico: see PURÍSIMA.

Purkersdorf (pōōr'kûrsdôrf), town (pop. 4,696), after 1938 in Penzing dist. of Vienna, Austria; 9 mi. W of city center; vineyards.

Purley, England: see COULSDON AND PURLEY.

Purli, India: see PARLI, Hyderabad state.

Purling, resort village, Greene co., SE N.Y., in the Catskills, 9 mi. NW of Catskill.

Purmamarca (pōōrmämär'kä), village (pop. estimate 500), S central Jujuy prov., Argentina, 35 mi. NW of Jujuy; agr. (alfalfa, tomatoes, wine, livestock), mining (lead, barite).

Purmerend (pûr'mŭrĕnt), town (pop. 6,017), North Holland prov., NW Netherlands, on North Holland Canal (locks), on S edge of Beemster Polder, and 10 mi. N of Amsterdam; mfg. (refrigerators, wood products, tiles, biscuits); cattle, dairy, and fruit market.

Purna (pŏor'nŭ), town (pop. 6,292), Parbhani dist., N Hyderabad state, India, on Purna R. and 17 mi. ESE of Parbhani; rail junction (workshops) in agr. area; cotton ginning.

Purna River. 1 Largely in NW Hyderabad state, India, rises in SW Ajanta Hills E of Chalisgaon, flows SE and S past Purna to Godavari R. 5 mi. S of Purna; 220 mi. long. **2** Mainly in SW Madhya Pradesh, India, rises in central Satpura Range, SW of Betul; flows c.150 mi. S and W, through important cotton-growing valley in Amraoti, Akola, and Buldana dists., to Tapti R. 15 mi. E of Bhusawal (Bombay). **3** In Surat dist., N Bombay, India, rises in NW Western Ghats, flows c.125 mi. W, past Navsari and Jalalpur, to Gulf of Cambay 16 mi. S of Surat.

Purnea (pûr'nēŭ, pŏornē'ŭ), district (□ 4,998; pop. 2,390,105), NE Bihar, India, on Ganges Plain; ⊙ Purnea. Bounded N by Nepal, W by Kosi R., S by the Ganges, SE by Indian Bengal, NE by Pakistan Bengal; drained by Mahananda R. and tributaries of the Ganges. Alluvial soil; rice, jute (major jute area of Bihar), corn, tobacco, oilseeds, wheat, sugar cane. Rice, jute, and rape- and mustard-seed milling, mfg. of hemp narcotics. Main towns: Purnea, Katihar (rail center).

Purnea, town (pop. 19,036), ⊙ Purnea dist., NE Bihar, India, on tributary of Ganges R. and 50 mi. NE of Bhagalpur; trades in jute, corn, tobacco, wheat, sugar cane; rice and jute milling.

Purple Peak (12,900 ft.), W central Colo., in Rocky Mts. in Gunnison co., also known as Slate Peak.

Purranque (pōōräng'kä), village (pop. 2,058), Osorno prov., S central Chile, on railroad and 25 mi. S of Osorno; cereals, livestock; dairying.

Pursat (pŏor'sät'), town (1936 pop. c.20,000), ⊙ Pursat prov. (□ 5,000; 1948 pop. 129,669), E Cambodia, on the Stung Pursat (tributary of the Tonle Sap; navigable at high water) and Pnompenh-Bangkok RR, 100 mi. NW of Pnompenh; commercial center for rice and cardamoms (in near-by Cardamom Mts.); distilling, sericulture, marble quarrying, fishing; trading in hides and horns.

Pursglove, village (1940 pop. 1,063), Monongalia co., N W.Va., 4 mi. NW of Morgantown, in coal-mining region.

Purton, town and parish (pop. 2,547), N Wiltshire, England, 4 mi. WNW of Swindon; agr. market in dairying region. Has 13th-15th-cent. church. Near by are remains of Roman camp.

Purua, Mexico: see ZITÁCUARO.

Puruándiro (pōōrwän'dērō), officially Puruándiro de Calderón, city (pop. 8,643), Michoacán, central Mexico, on central plateau, 40 mi. SSW of Irapuato; alt. 6,204 ft. Agr. center (cereals, vegetables, fruit); flour milling, tanning.

Purulak, Indonesia: see PERLAK.

Purulhá (pōōrōōlä'), town (1950 pop. 806), Baja Verapaz dept., central Guatemala, 12 mi. NNE of Salamá; alt. 5,699 ft. Coffee, sugar cane, grain; livestock.

Purulia (pŏorōōl'yŭ), town (pop. 30,445), ⊙ Manbhum dist., SE Bihar, India, near Kasai R., 135 mi. WNW of Calcutta; rail and road junction; trades in rice, corn, oilseeds, bajra, sugar cane; oilseed milling. Jain temple ruins near by.

Purullena (pōōrōōlyä'nä), town (pop. 1,995), Granada prov., S Spain, 3 mi. WNW of Guadix; cereals, olive oil, wine, sugar beets, hogs, cattle.

Purus River (pōōrōōs'), important right tributary of the Amazon in NW Brazil, rises on E slopes of the Andes in Peru near 11°S 72°W, flows c.2,100 mi. NE, across Acre territory and Amazonas through rubber-growing tropical rain forest, past Bôca do Acre, Lábrea, and Beruri, to the Amazon 100 mi. WSW of Manaus. Sena Madureira on Iaco R. (right tributary of upper Purus R.) is head of navigation. Principal tributary, Acre R. (right).

Purvis, town (pop. 1,270), ⊙ Lamar co., SE Miss., 14 mi. SSW of Hattiesburg, in agr. and pine-timber area.

Purwa (pŏor'vŭ), town (pop. 8,893), Unao dist., central Uttar Pradesh, India, 19 mi. ESE of Unao; shoe and leatherwork mfg.; wheat, barley, rice, gram. Has 3 annual fairs.

Purwakarta or **Poerwakarta** (both: pŏorwŏŏkär'tŏŏ), town (pop. 15,141), W Java, Indonesia, 25 mi. NNW of Bandung, at foot of Preanger highlands; trade center for rice-growing region; railroad workshops.

Purwodadi or **Poerwodadi** (both: pŏorwōdä'dē), town (pop. 10,840), central Java, Indonesia, 35 mi. ESE of Semarang; trade center for agr. area (rice, corn). Has large Chinese pop.

Purwokerto or **Poerwakerto** (–kĕr'tŏŏ), town (pop. 33,266), central Java, Indonesia, 65 mi. SE of Cheribon, at foot of Mt. Slamet; trade center for agr. area (rice, rubber, sugar, peanuts, cassava, coffee, tea, cinchona bark); machine and railroad shops.

Purworejo or **Poerworedjo** (–rā'jō), town (pop. 24,645), S central Java, Indonesia, 25 mi. WNW of Jogjakarta; trade center for agr. area (sugar, rice, peanuts); textile mills, can and drum works.

Puryear (pŭ'rēŭr), town (pop. 430), Henry co., NW Tenn., 10 mi. N of Paris.

Pusa, India: see SAMASTIPUR.

Pusad (pōōsŭd'), town (pop. 11,372), Yeotmal dist., SW Madhya Pradesh, India, on tributary of Penganga R. and 50 mi. SW of Yeotmal; cotton ginning, oilseed milling. Timber (teak) in near-by forests.

Pusan (pōō'sän'), Jap. *Fusan* or *Husan* (both: fōō'sä), city (1949 pop. 473,619), ⊙ S.Kyongsang prov., SE Korea, on Korea Strait, 200 mi. SE of Seoul; 35°6'N 129°3'E; largest port of Korea; railroad and industrial center. Harbor is sheltered by a small isl. There is ferry service to Shimonoseki, Japan (130 mi. SE). It is possible to travel by rail from Pusan to China (via S.Manchurian RR) and to Europe (via Trans-Siberian RR). There are railroad workshops, textile mills, shipyards, ironworks, rubber factories, rice and salt refineries. There is a fishery experiment station. Near by is a hot-springs resort known from anc. times. Pusan exports rice, raw silk, cattle, fish, soybeans. City was invaded 1592 by the Japanese (under Hideyoshi), who had long maintained a trading post here. Port was opened 1876 to the Japanese, and in 1883 to general foreign trade. Was chief U.N. supply and disembarkation port in the Korean war (1950–52).

Puschlav, Switzerland: see POSCHIAVO.

Pushaw Lake (pōō'shô), Penobscot co., SE central Maine, just W of Old Town; 7.5 mi. long.

Pushkar (po͞osh'kŭr), village, N Ajmer state, India, in valley of Aravalli Range, 5 mi. W of Ajmer; local agr. market (millet, corn, wheat, sugar cane); hand-loom weaving, wood carving; trades in cattle. Noted for its very sacred lake and temple dedicated to Brahma, visited annually by numerous pilgrims during large festival fair (Oct.-Nov.).

Pushkin (po͞osh'kĭn), city (1948 pop. over 50,000), central Leningrad oblast, Russian SFSR, 16 mi. S (under jurisdiction) of Leningrad; paper milling, metalworking, clothing and chemical industries. Has palaces of Catherine the Great (construction begun under Elizabeth Petrovna) and of Alexander I (built 1792-96) amid large parks. Agr. col. Pushkin is commemorated here in mus. and literature research institute (in his former lyceum). Founded under Peter the Great as Tsarskoye Selo; became imperial summer residence under Elizabeth and Catherine the Great. Connected with St. Petersburg by 1st Rus. railroad (built 1837). Renamed Detskoye Selo in early 1920s and, in 1937, Pushkin. During Second World War, held (1941–44) by Germans in siege of Leningrad.

Pushkino (–ŭ). **1** Town (1932 pop. estimate 760), SE Azerbaijan SSR, 26 mi. WSW of Salyany; cotton gins, metalworks. **2** City (1939 pop. over 10,000), E central Moscow oblast, Russian SFSR, on Ucha R., near E end of Ucha Reservoir, and 20 mi. NNE of Moscow; woolen-milling center; jute processing; cotton mill, metalworks. Became city in 1925. **3** Village (1948 pop. over 2,000), S central Saratov oblast, Russian SFSR, 40 mi. ESE of Engels; rail junction; metalworks; wheat, cattle. Until 1941 (in German Volga Autonomous SSR), Urbakh or Urbach.

Pushkinskiye Gory (–skēŭ gô'rē), village (1939 pop. over 500), S Pskov oblast, Russian SFSR, on railroad (Trigorskaya station) and 30 mi. SE of Ostrov; flax processing, dairying. Site of former home and tomb of Pushkin. Formerly called Mikhailovskoye.

Pushmataha (po͞oshmŭtä'hä), county (□ 1,423; pop. 12,001), SE Okla.; ⊙ Antlers. Includes part of the Ouchita Mts.; drained by Kiamichi and Little rivers. Agr. (corn, cotton, potatoes, fruit, livestock). Some mfg. at Antlers. Pine and oak timber; lumber milling. Formed 1907.

Pusht Kuh or **Posht Kuh** (both: pōsht'ko͞o'), mountainous region of SW Iran, on extreme W edge of the Zagros system, bet. upper Karkheh R. and Iraq line. Main range is the Kabir Kuh. Tribal Lur pop. engages in sheep raising. Formerly organized as a prov. (⊙ Ilam) of Iran, it forms part (since 1938) of Iran's Fifth Prov. (see Kermanshah).

Pusi or **Pu-hsi** (both: bo͞o'shē'), town, ⊙ Pusi co. (pop. 27,406), W central Heilungkiang prov., Manchuria, on Nonni R. and 90 mi. NNE of Tsitsihar, near Inner Mongolian line.

Pusing (po͞osĭng'), town (pop. 2,501), central Perak, Malaya, 8 mi. SW of Ipoh, on slopes of Kledang Range; tin mining.

Pusnes, Norway: see Tromoy.

Püspökladany (püsh'pûklō"dänyû), Hung. *Püspökladány*, town (pop. 15,204), Hajdu co., E Hungary, 28 mi. SW of Debrecen; rail, market center; flour mills, brickworks. Oldest natural-gas well in Hungary near by.

Püspöknadasd (püsh'pûknädŏzhd), Hung. *Püspöknádasd*, town (pop. 2,480), Baranya co., S Hungary, 15 mi. NE of Pecs; cattle, hogs, plums, nuts.

Pussar River, E Pakistan: see Pusur River.

Pussay (püsā'), village (pop. 1,603), Seine-et-Oise dept., N central France, 9 mi. SW of Étampes; footwear factory.

Pussellawa (po͞osĕl-lä'vŭ), town (pop. 850), Central Prov., Ceylon, in Piduru Ridges, 6 mi. SE of Gampola; extensive tea plantations; rice.

Pustertal (po͞o'stûrtäl), Ital *Pusteria*, Alpine valley bet. Brunico, Italy, and Lienz, Austria; watered by upper Drave and Rienza rivers. Agr. and cattle area; known for its scenic beauties which attract many tourists.

Pustomyty (po͞ostŭmĭ'tē), village (1939 pop. over 500), S Lvov oblast, Ukrainian SSR, 10 mi. SSW of Lvov; grain, livestock.

Pustoshka (po͞o'stŭshkŭ), city (1948 pop. over 2,000), SW Velikiye Luki oblast, Russian SFSR, 40 mi. W of Velikiye Luki; road junction; flax processing, sawmilling, brickworking. During Second World War, held (1941–44) by Germans and severely damaged.

Pustozersk (po͞ostŭzyôrsk', –zyĕrsk'), village, central Nenets Natl. Okrug, Archangel oblast, Russian SFSR, 12 mi. SW of Naryan-Mar and on arm of Pechora R. delta; reindeer raising, fishing.

Pusur River (po͞oso͝or'), Khulna dist., East Bengal, E Pakistan, a distributary of Ganges Delta, leaves Madhumati R. (here called Baleswar) 17 mi. NE of Khulna, flows c.110 mi. generally S, past Port Jinnah or Chalna Anchorage (main jute port of E Pakistan), through the Sundarbans, to Bay of Bengal. Called Atharabanki in upper course. Sometimes spelled Pussar.

Puszczykow Zdroj, Poland: see Polanica Zdroj.

Pusztamerges (po͞os'tŏmärgĕsh), Hung. *Pusztamérges*, town (pop. 2,150), Csongrad co., S Hungary, 21 mi. WNW of Szeged; corn, paprika, dairy.

Pusztaszabolcs (po͞os'tŏsŏbôlch), town (pop. 2,524), Fejer co., central Hungary, 15 mi. E of Szekesfehervar; rail junction; corn, hemp, hogs.

Pusztaszer (po͞os'tŏsĕr), town (pop. 2,078), Csongrad co., S Hungary, 21 mi. N of Szeged; wheat, potatoes, sheep.

Pusztatenyö, Hungary: see Szajol.

Puta (po͞otä'), town (1945 pop. over 500) in Molotov dist. of Greater Baku, Azerbaijan SSR, on railroad and 8 mi. SW of Baku; oil wells (developed 1925).

Putaendo (po͞otĭn'dō), town (pop. 2,666), Aconcagua prov., central Chile, in Andean foothills, 8 mi. N of San Felipe; rail terminus and agr. center (alfalfa, fruit, wine, hemp, livestock). An old colonial town, it had rich gold deposits in 18th cent.

Putah Creek (pū'tŭ), W and central Calif., rises in the Coast Ranges S of Clear L., flows c.85 mi. SE and E to marshes along Sacramento R. W of Sacramento. Site of proposed Monticello Dam of Central Valley project is on upper course.

Putai or **P'u-t'ai** (po͞o'tī'), town, ⊙ Putai co. (pop. 121,731), N Shantung prov., China, 75 mi. NE of Tsinan and on Yellow R.; peanuts, millet. Saltworks near by.

Putai (bo͞o'dī'), Jap. *Hotei* (hō'tā), port (1935 pop. 5,324), W central Formosa, on W coast, 10 mi. NW of Sinying; salt-producing center. Submarine cable runs from here to the Pescadores.

Putanges (pütäzh'), village (pop. 451), Orne dept., NW France, on the Orne and 11 mi. W of Argentan. Scene of fighting (1944) in battle of Argentan-Falaise pocket.

Putao (pŭtou', Burmese po͞o'tŭō) or **Fort Hertz** (hûrts), northernmost post, Myitkyina dist., Kachin State, Upper Burma, near Mali R. and 140 mi. N of Myitkyina, near Assam line; 27°20'N 97°25'E.

Putbus (po͞ot'bo͞os), village (pop. 6,381), in former Prussian Pomerania prov., N Germany, after 1945 in Mecklenburg, on S Rügen isl., near Greifswalder Bodden (a bay of the Baltic), 16 mi. E of Stralsund; agr. market (grain, potatoes, sugar beets, stock); seaside resort. Founded 1810.

Puteaux (pütō'), industrial town (pop. 37,233), Seine dept., N central France, a WNW suburb of Paris, 5.5 mi. from Notre Dame Cathedral, on left bank of the Seine, bet. Courbevoie (NNE) and Suresnes (SSW); metalworking (auto construction), printing, mfg. (rubber articles, perfumes and cosmetics).

Puteoli, Italy: see Pozzuoli.

Puteran or **Poeteran** (both: po͞otŭrän'), island (9 mi. long, 3 mi. wide), Indonesia, in Madura Strait, 6 mi. SE of Madura; generally low. Cattle raising, agr. (corn, cassava). Also called Tarango.

Putfontein (pŭt'fôntān"), town (pop. 2,520), S Transvaal, U. of So. Afr., on Witwatersrand, 7 mi. NE of Benoni; gold mining.

Putien or **P'u-t'ien** (po͞o'tyĕn'), town (pop. 14,123), ⊙ Putien co. (pop. 632,815), SE Fukien prov., China, 45 mi. SSW of Foochow, on Hinghwa Bay of Formosa Strait; litchi nuts, rice, wheat, sugar cane. Chemical industry; food processing, tobacco mfg. Manganese mining. Until 1913 called Hinghwa. The Hinghwa dialect, intermediary bet. N and S Fukienese, is spoken in the area.

Putignano (po͞otēnyä'nō), town (pop. 12,849), Bari prov., Apulia, S Italy, 12 mi. SW of Monopoli; mfg. center (hats, woolen textiles, cutlery, soap, macaroni).

Putila (po͞otyē'lŭ), village (1941 pop. 1,425), W Chernovtsy oblast, Ukrainian SSR, in N Bukovina, in the Carpathians, 45 mi. SW of Chernovtsy; lumbering, woodcarving. A center of the Guzuls. Formerly in Radauti dept. of Rumania; Putila dist. (□ c.300; 1941 pop. 32,958) was ceded (1940), with N Bukovina, to USSR.

Putina (po͞otē'nä), town (pop. 1,208), Puno dept., SE Peru, on the Altiplano, 22 mi. E of Azángaro; potatoes, barley.

Put-in-Bay, village (pop. 191), Ottawa co., N Ohio, on Put-in-Bay harbor of South Bass Isl., in L. Erie, c.35 mi. E of Toledo; tourist resort; has state and Federal fish hatcheries, commercial fisheries. Perry's Victory and International Peace Memorial, a natl. monument (14.3 acres; established 1936), is near here; a granite column 352 ft. high commemorates battle of L. Erie (1813), in which Admiral Perry's U.S. fleet defeated the British, and symbolizes century of peace bet. U.S. and Canada.

Puting or **P'u-ting** (po͞o'dĭng'), town (pop. 6,298), ⊙ Puting co. (pop. 131,329), SW Kweichow prov., China, 10 mi. WNW of Anshun; alt. 4,062 ft.; cotton textiles; rice, wheat, millet. Lead deposits near by. Formerly Tingnan.

P'u-ting-ts'un, Tibet: see Yakalo.

Putivl or **Putivl'** (po͞otyē'vŭl), city (1926 pop. 7,999), central Sumy oblast, Ukrainian SSR, near Seim R., 30 mi. ENE of Konotop; dairying, fruit canning. Pop. mainly Russian. Dates from 12th cent.

Putla (po͞ot'lä), officially Putla de Guerrero, town (pop. 2,394), Oaxaca, S Mexico, on S slopes of Sierre Madre del Sur, 24 mi. SW of Tlaxiaco; alt. 3,970 ft. Cereals, sugar cane, coffee, fruit, vegetables, livestock, timber.

Putlitz (po͞ot'lĭts), town (pop. 2,763), Brandenburg, E Germany, on Stepenitz R. and 14 mi. NE of Perleberg; vegetables, fruit, potatoes, stock. Has remains of anc. castle.

Putna, province, Rumania: see Focsani.

Putna (po͞ot'nä), village (pop. 1,968), Suceava prov., N Rumania, 19 mi. W of Radauti; rail terminus, with important glass- and cementworks; quarrying. Site of famous 15th-cent. monastery built by Stephen the Great and later his burial place; many times looted, destroyed, and restored, notably in 17th and 18th cent. Yearly pilgrimages.

Putnam (pŭt'nŭm). **1** County (□ 803; pop. 23,615), N Fla.; ⊙ Palatka. Lake and swamp area drained by St. Johns R.; includes L. George and part of Crescent L. Agr. (corn, vegetables, peanuts, citrus fruit, poultry, livestock), forestry (lumber, naval stores), fishing, and mining (kaolin, peat, sand). Has resorts. Formed 1849. **2** County (□ 350; pop. 7,731), central Ga.; ⊙ Eatonton. Bounded E by Oconee R.; drained by Little R. Piedmont stock-raising, dairying, farming (cotton, corn, truck, peaches) and sawmilling area. Formed 1807. **3** County (□ 166; pop. 4,746), N central Ill., bounded N and W by the great bend of Illinois R.; ⊙ Hennepin. Agr. (corn, oats, wheat, livestock, poultry; dairy products); bituminous-coal mines; wood products. Includes Senachwine and Sawmill lakes (bayous of the Illinois), with fishing resorts. Formed 1825. **4** County (□ 490; pop. 22,950), W central Ind.; ⊙ Greencastle. Drained by Eel R., Raccoon and Mill creeks. Agr. (grain, livestock, poultry; dairy products). Mfg. at Greencastle. Timber; stone quarries. Formed 1821. **5** County (□ 518; pop. 9,166), N Mo.; ⊙ Unionville. Bounded E by Chariton R. Agr. (corn, wheat, oats), livestock; coal. Formed 1845. **6** County (□ 235; pop. 20,307), SE N.Y., ⊙ Carmel. Bounded W by the Hudson, E by Conn. line; includes part of the Taconic Mts., here meeting the highlands of the Hudson. Hilly summer-resort region, with many lakes (Mahopac, Peekskill, Carmel, Oscawana, Peach), and New York city water-supply reservoirs of Croton R. system. Traversed by Taconic State Parkway. Fahnestock State Park has skiing facilities. Dairying, poultry raising, truck farming. Formed 1812. **7** County (□ 486; pop. 25,248), NW Ohio; ⊙ Ottawa. Intersected by Auglaize and Blanchard rivers. Agr. area (livestock, poultry, grain, sugar beets); mfg. and processing of food and dairy products at Ottawa, Leipsic, Columbus Grove. Clay pits, limestone quarries. Formed 1820. **8** County (□ 408; pop. 29,869), central Tenn.; ⊙ Cookeville. Hilly timber and farm region, on Cumberland Plateau; drained by affluents of Cumberland R. Will include part of Center Hill Reservoir. Agr. (poultry, small grains, tobacco, corn, hay, cattle, hogs); lumbering; coal mining, granite quarrying. Formed 1842. **9** County (□ 349; pop. 21,021), W W.Va.; ⊙ Winfield. Drained by Kanawha and Pocatalico rivers. Bituminous-coal mines; some natural-gas and oil wells; agr. (livestock, fruit, truck, tobacco). Mfg. at Nitro. Formed 1848.

Putnam. 1 Textile city (pop. 8,181) in Putnam town (pop. 9,304), a ⊙ Windham co., NE Conn., on Quinebaug R. and 20 mi. NE of Willimantic. Mfg. (textiles, metal products, paper goods, shoes, hats, thread, optical goods, lumber, chemicals, furniture). Seat of Annhurst Col. Agr. in town (dairy products, poultry, fruit). Has state park. Settled 1693, town set off from Killingly 1855, city inc. 1895. **2** Town (pop. 106), Dewey co., W Okla., 23 mi. N of Clinton, in agr. and stock-raising area. **3** Town (pop. 289), Callahan co., central Texas, 31 mi. E of Abilene; rail point in agr. area (cotton, grain); oil wells.

Putney (pŭt'nē), residential district of Wandsworth, London, England, on S bank of the Thames (here crossed by Putney Bridge), 5 mi. SW of Charing Cross. Bridge is starting point for Oxford and Cambridge boat race. Church of St. Mary dates partly from 14th cent., rebuilt 1836. Thomas Cromwell and Edward Gibbon b. here; Putney residents included William Pitt, Leigh Hunt, and Swinburne. Extensive Putney Heath, formerly resort of highwaymen, was scene of duels bet. Pitt and George Tierney (1798) and bet. Castlereagh and Canning (1809).

Putney, town (pop. 1,019), Windham co., SE Vt., on the Connecticut and 9 mi. N of Brattleboro; paper milling; resorts. Putney School (1935; coeducational) is near Putney village.

Putnok (po͞ot'nôk), town (pop. 4,555), Borsod-Gömör co., NE Hungary, on the Sajo and 8 mi. NE of Ozd; flour mills. Old castle here became fortress in 16th cent.

Putorana Mountains (po͞otŭrä'nŭ), N Krasnoyarsk Territory, Russian SFSR, extend E-W along Taimyr-Evenki natl. okrug border; rise c.5,000 ft.

Puto Shan or **P'u-t'o Shan** (po͞o'tô' shän'), island of Chusan Archipelago, in E.China Sea, off E end of main Chusan isl.; 30°N 122°23'E; 3.5 mi. long, 1 mi. wide; rises to 940 ft. A sacred isl., it has numerous temples and monasteries. Also spelled Pootoo and Putu.

Putre (po͞o'trā), village (pop. 524), Tarapacá prov., N Chile, 55 mi. NE of Arica; llama and alpaca raising.

Putrid Sea, Russian SFSR: see Sivash.

Puttalam (pŏŏt'tŭlŭm) [Tamil *puda*=new; *alam*=salt pans], town (pop. 7,764), ⊙ Puttalam dist. (□ 890; pop., including estate pop., 43,269), North Western Prov., Ceylon, on Puttalam Lagoon, 75 mi. N of Colombo. Rail terminus; fishing. Has major govt. salterns, meteorological observatory. Important port (13th–14th cent.) when visited by Moslem traders; W port of Kandyan kingdom.

Puttalam Lagoon, bet. Kalpitiya Peninsula (W) and Ceylon proper (E), is S extension of Dutch Bay; 17 mi. long (N-S), 7 mi. wide.

Putte (pŭ'tù), agr. village (pop. 6,269), Antwerp prov., N Belgium, at Netherlands border, 10 mi. N of Antwerp. Contiguous with Netherlands village of Putte.

Putte (pû'tù), town (pop. 1,541), North Brabant prov., SW Netherlands, 11 mi. SSE of Bergen op Zoom; frontier post on Belg. border, adjoining Putte (Belgium); egg market; plastics. Also spelled Putten.

Puttelange, Saar: see PÜTTLINGEN.

Putten (pû'tùn). **1** Town, Brabant prov., Netherlands: see PUTTE. **2** Village (pop. 4,330), Gelderland prov., central Netherlands, 15 mi. WNW of Apeldoorn; ceramics. Sanitarium, surrounded by forests, here.

Putten, island, South Holland prov., SW Netherlands, SW of Rotterdam; bounded by the Botlek (NW), Old Maas R. (NE), Spui R. (SE), the Haringvliet (S), Voorne isl. (W); with Voorne isl., forms isl. of Voorne-en-Putten. Chief town, Spijkenisse.

Puttiala, India: see PATIALA, Punjab.

Püttlingen (püt'lĭng-ùn), Fr. *Puttelange* (pütlãzh'), town (pop. 12,689), SW Saar, near Saar R., 6 mi. NW of Saarbrücken; coal mining; tobacco-products mfg.

Puttur (pŏŏ'tŏŏr). **1** Village, Chittoor dist., central Madras, India, 34 mi. NE of Chittoor; rice, millet, oilseeds. Dyewood (red sanders) in near-by forests. **2** Town (pop. 9,563), South Kanara dist., W Madras, India, 25 mi. ESE of Mangalore; rice and oilseed milling. Kaolin-clay pits, granite quarries, teak forests near by. Glazed-pottery mfg. 6 mi. NE, at village of Uppinangadi.

Putú (pōōtōō'), village (1930 pop. 813), Maule prov., central Chile, near the coast, 13 mi. NNE of Constitución; agr. (wheat, potatoes, lentils, wine, sheep). Formerly iron mining.

Putumayo (pōōtōōmī'ō), commissary (□ 10,220; 1938 pop. 15,688, 1950 estimate 15,860), SW Colombia, bordered S by Ecuador and Peru; ⊙ Mocoa. On W are the Andes, on N the Caquetá R., and on S the Putumayo and San Miguel (or Sucumbíos) rivers. Comprising mostly undeveloped, densely forested plains, with tropical, humid climate, the region is populated largely by Indians, who glean from the forests some rubber, balata gum, tagua nuts, resins, fine wood, medicinal plants. Some cattle raising on Andean slopes.

Putumayo River, NW South America, called **Içá** (ēsä') in its lower course in Brazil; rises in the Colombian Andes E of Pasto, flows SE, through tropical rain forests along Colombia-Ecuador and Colombia-Peru border into Brazil, to the Amazon (left bank) at Santo Antônio do Içá; c.1,000 mi. long. Navigable. Main affluent: San Miguel R.

P'u-tung, China: see POOTUNG.

Puturge (pütürgĕ'), Turkish *Pütürge*, village (pop. 2,383), Malatya prov., E central Turkey, 32 mi. ESE of Malatya; wheat, corn. Formerly Imrun.

Putu Shan, China: see PUTO SHAN.

Putuskum, Nigeria: see POTISKUM.

Putyatin, Russian SFSR: see NAZIMOVO.

Putyatino (pōōtyä'tyĭnŭ), village (1926 pop. 4,023), central Ryazan oblast, Russian SFSR, 14 mi. SE of Shilovo; distilling.

Putze or **P'u-tzu** (both: pōō'dzŭ'), Jap. *Bokushi* (bō'kōōshē), town (1935 pop. 10,942), W central Formosa, 12 mi. W of Kiayi; soybeans, sugar cane.

Putzig, Poland: see PUCK, town.

Putziger Nehrung, Poland: see HEL PENINSULA.

Putziger Wiek, Poland: see PUCK BAY.

P'u-tzu, Formosa: see PUTZE.

Puukapele (pōō'kŭpā'lā), peak (3,657 ft.), central Kauai, T.H., on W edge of Waimea Canyon.

Puukolii (pōō'ōōkōlē'ē), village (pop. 688), W Maui, T.H., near Lahaina; sugar cane.

Puu Kukui (pōō'ōō kōōkōō'ē), mountain (5,790 ft.), W Maui, T.H.; dwarfed by Haleakala, but highest peak on W peninsula.

Puunene (pōōnĕ'nĕ), town (1940 pop. 4,456), N Maui, T.H., near Kahului, in sugar-cane area.

Puu Ohia, T.H.: see TANTALUS, MOUNT.

Puurs (pūrs), Fr. *Puers* (püĕrs'), town (pop. 6,090), Antwerp prov., N Belgium, 12 mi. NW of Mechlin; agr. market (vegetables, potatoes). Has 17th-cent. church.

Puu Waawaa (pōō'ōō wä'äwä'ä), peak (3,824 ft.), W Hawaii, T.H., in N Kona dist.

Puxico (pŭk'sĭkō), city (pop. 749), Stoddard co., SE Mo., near St. Francis R., 19 mi. NE of Poplar Bluff; lumber products.

Puy, Le (lù pwē'), town (pop. 18,347), ⊙ Haute-Loire dept., S central France, near the Loire, 36 mi. SW of Saint-Étienne, in the VELAY, of which it was ⊙; commercial and transportation center, noted for its hand- and machine-made lace; vegetable shipping, liqueur mfg. The old town, with noteworthy 11th-12th-cent. cathedral, 11th-cent. baptistry, 14th-cent. church of Saint-Laurent (containing tomb of Du Guesclin), and numerous Gothic bldgs., is clustered around a volcanic rock capped by 50-ft.-high bronze statue of the Virgin Mary. Atop a lesser, needle-shaped, rock is Romanesque church of Saint-Michel d'Aiguilhe; at its foot is 11th-cent. chapel. An episcopal see since 6th cent., Le Puy grew as a major place of pilgrimage and as early center of lace mfg.

Puyallup (pūä'lŭp), city (pop. 10,010), Pierce co., W central Wash., 8 mi. SE of Tacoma and on Puyallup R., in rich agr. valley; berries, bulbs, truck, wood products; canneries. Agr. experiment station here. Settled 1877, inc. 1890.

Puyallup River, W central Wash., rises on W slopes of Mt. Rainier, flows c.45 mi. generally NW, past Puyallup and Tacoma, to Puget Sound near Tacoma. Has hydroelectric plants. Rich valley of lower river produces berries, truck, flower bulbs, hops, poultry, and dairy products.

Puyang or **P'u-yang** (pōō'yäng'), town, ⊙ Puyang co. (pop. 479,784), central Pingyuan prov., China, 65 mi. NE of Sinsiang; road junction; cotton weaving, straw-hat mfg.; wheat, millet, beans. Called Kaichow until 1913. Until 1949 in Hopeh.

Puyango, Ecuador: see ALAMOR.

Puy-de-Dôme (pwē-dù-dōm'), department (□ 3,095; pop. 478,876), in Auvergne and part of Bourbonnais, central France; ⊙ Clermont-Ferrand. Situated wholly within the Massif Central, it consists of the AUVERGNE MTS. (W), the Limagne lowland (center), and the Livradois and Forez massifs (E). Drained by Dordogne (W), Allier (center), and Dore (E) rivers. Agr. (especially fruit growing) in the LIMAGNE. Mts. support cattle and sheep, and a small handicraft industry (lace, cutlery). Dept. has coal mines (near Brassac-les-Mines and St.-Éloy-les-Mines), silverbearing lead and antimony deposits. Lava (for flagstones and chemical industry) is quarried at Volvic. The volcanic Auvergne Mts. with their numerous mineral springs (notably at Mont-Dore, La Bourboule, Royat, and Châtelguyon) attract tourists. Chief towns are Clermont-Ferrand (rubber-mfg. center), Thiers (noted for its cutlery), Riom, Ambert (religious articles), and Issoire.

Puy de Dôme, extinct volcano of the Massif Central, central France, and highest peak (4,806 ft.) of the Monts Dôme group of Auvergne Mts., in Puy-de-Dôme dept., 6 mi. W of Clermont-Ferrand. Has no crater. On its level summit (reached by toll road) are an observatory (built 1876), and the ruins of a temple of Mercury. Here Pascal's experiment confirming Torricelli's theory on air pressure was conducted in 1648.

Puy de Sancy (sãsē'), highest peak (6,187 ft.) of Massif Central, central France, in Monts Dore group of Auvergne Mts., 21 mi. SW of Clermont-Ferrand. Reached by cable car. Here rises Dordogne R. Spa of Mont-Dore on N slope.

Puyehue (pōōyā'wā), village (1930 pop. 17), Osorno prov., S central Chile, on SW shore of L. Puyehue and 30 mi. ESE of Osorno; dairying, lumbering, wood processing (alcohol, acetone, acetate) and charcoal mfg.

Puyehue, Lake (□ 115), Osorno prov., S central Chile, in Chilean lake dist., 30 mi. E of Osorno; 20 mi. long, c.8 mi. wide. On NE shore rises the massif of Puyehue Volcano. On SW shore is Puyehue, on E, Termas de Puyehue, tourist resorts.

Puyehue Volcano, comprises several Andean peaks in Valdivia prov., S central Chile, on NE bank of L. Puyehue, in Chilean lake dist., 55 mi. ENE of Osorno; rises to 7,350 ft.

Puy-Guillaume (pwē gēyōm'), village (pop. 1,823), Puy-de-Dôme dept., central France, in the Limagne, on Dore R. and 8 mi. NNW of Thiers; glass-bottle mfg. (for Vichy water).

Puylaurens (pwēlōrã'), village (pop. 1,151), Tarn dept., S France, 12 mi. WSW of Castres; road center; poultry raising, winegrowing. Its Protestant academy flourished under Pierre Bayle (17th cent.).

Puy-l'Évêque (pwē-lāvĕk'), village (pop. 694), Lot dept., SW France, on the Lot and 15 mi. WNW of Cahors; porcelain factory, vineyards. Iron mined near by.

Puy Mary, France: see CANTAL, MASSIF DU.

Puymirol (pwēmērôl'), village (pop. 342), Lot-et-Garonne dept., SW France, 9 mi. E of Agen; poultry, wheat, fruit.

Puymorens, Col de (kōl dù pwēmôrã'), pass (alt. 6,283 ft.) in central Pyrenees, Pyrénées-Orientales dept., S France, near Andorra border, on road bet. Ax-les-Thermes and Puigcerdá (Spain), 2 mi. S of L'Hospitalet-près-l'Andorre. A railroad tunnel (over 3 mi. long) passes underneath.

Puyo (pōō'yō), town (1950 pop. 1,098), Napo-Pastaza prov., E central Ecuador, on affluent of Pastaza R., on E Andean slopes, 45 mi. ESE of Ambato; trading post serving near-by Mera petroleum field and refinery.

Puyo (pōō'yŭ'), Jap *Fuyo* or *Huyo*, township (1946 pop. 17,202), S.Chungchong prov., S Korea, on Kum R. and 23 mi. NNE of Kunsan; silk cocoons. Has ruins of anc. temples and pagodas. Puyo was ⊙ of a Korean kingdom of 6th–7th cent.

Puyoô (pwēyō'), village (pop. 1,030), Basses-Pyrénées dept., SW France, on the Gave de Pau and 7 mi. WNW of Orthez; railroad junction; distilling, jute spinning.

Puysegur Point (pū'sùgùr), SW S.Isl., New Zealand, 85 mi. W of Invercargill, at entrance to Preservation Inlet; 46°9'S 166°38'E. Lighthouse; site of only settlement (pop. 8) in SW fjord area.

Puzol (pōō-thōl'), town (pop. 4,810), Valencia prov., E Spain, near the Mediterranean, 5 mi. SSW of Sagunto; agr. trade center (rice, truck produce, olive oil); produces jams and marmalades. Has fine palace which belonged to archbishop of Valencia.

Pwela (pwĕ'lä), W state (myosaship) (□ 178; pop. 14,052), Southern Shan State, Upper Burma; ⊙ Pwela, village 20 mi. WNW of Taunggyi.

Pweto (pwĕ'tō), village, Katanga prov., SE Belgian Congo, at NW extremity of L. Mweru at outlet of Luvua R., on Northern Rhodesia border, 175 mi. SSW of Albertville; alt. 3,299 ft. Head of navigation on the lake; customs station and trading post. R.C. and Protestant missions.

Pwinbyu (pwĭn'byōō), village, Minbu dist., Upper Burma, 18 mi. NW of Minbu; road hub.

Pwllheli (pōōl-hĕ'lē), municipal borough (1931 pop. 3,598; 1951 census 3,861), S Caernarvon, Wales, on Lleyn Peninsula, on Cardigan Bay of Irish Channel, 18 mi. SSW of Caernarvon; port, seaside resort, and agr. market, with tanneries.

Pyana River or **P'yana River** (pyä'nŭ), Gorki oblast, Russian SFSR, rises N of Talyzino, flows in hairpin course W, past Gagino, and E, past Pyanski Perevoz and Sergach, to Sura R. below Pilna; 240 mi. long. Limestone and gypsum deposits along banks.

Pyandzh River, USSR and Afghanistan: see PANJ RIVER.

Pyanski Perevoz or **P'yanskiy Perevoz** (pyän"skē pĕrĭvôs'), village (1939 pop. over 500), SE central Gorki oblast, Russian SFSR, on Pyana R. and 32 mi. ENE of Arzamas; hemp milling. Formerly called Pyany Perevoz.

Pyaozero (pyä'ôzyĭrŭ), Finnish *Pääjärvi* (pă'-yărvē), lake (□ 375) in NW Karelo-Finnish SSR, 70 mi. SW of Kandalaksha; 30 mi. long, up to 15 mi. wide; traversed by Kovda R. Numerous isls. Olanga on W shore.

Pyapon (pyä'pōn), district (□ 2,145; 1941 pop. 385,008), Irrawaddy div., Lower Burma; ⊙ Pyapon. Swampy Irrawaddy delta area drained by Pyapon and Bogale delta arms. Rice cultivation, fisheries. Pop. is 80% Burmese, 10% Indian.

Pyapon, town (pop. 12,338), ⊙ Pyapon dist., Lower Burma, on Pyapon R. (arm of Irrawaddy delta) and 45 mi. SW of Rangoon.

Pyarnu, Estonia: see PARNU.

Pyarnu-Yagupi, Estonia: see PARNU-JAGUPI.

Pyasechno, Poland: see PIASECZNO.

Pyasina River (pyä'sēnŭ), Taimyr Natl. Okrug, Krasnoyarsk Territory, Russian SFSR, rises near Norilsk, flows 660 mi. N, through L. Pyasino, to Kara Sea; serves as water route for Norilsk ore.

Pyasino, Lake (–nŭ) (□ 300), Taimyr Natl. Okrug, Krasnoyarsk Territory, Russian SFSR, 40 mi. NE of Dudinka; 40 mi. long; 30 ft. deep. Pyasina R. enters it from S and forms N outlet.

Pyatigorsk (pyŭtyĕgôrsk') [Rus., =five mts.], city (1939 pop. 62,875), S Stavropol Territory, Russian SFSR, in the N Caucasus, at SW foot of Mashuk mtn., on Podkumok R. and 85 mi. SE of Stavropol, on railroad; alt. 1,675 ft. Center of noted health resort area, located amid laccolithic mts. (BESH-TAU, MASHUK, ZMEIKA, ZHELEZNAYA, VERBLYUD). Has sanatoria, hot sulphur springs, mud baths, extensive parks and flower gardens. Metalworking; mfg. of radios, furniture, clothing; food processing (meat, bakery products). Limestone quarries. Has teachers and pharmaceutical colleges, regional and Lermontov museums. A resort since 1780, it developed particularly after 1830s. Lermontov killed here in duel, 1841. Satellite resorts are KISLOVODSK, YESSENTUKI, and ZHELEZNOVODSK. In Second World War, held 1942–43 by Germans.

Pyatikhatki (pyĭtyĕ"khät'kē), city (1939 pop. over 10,000), W Dnepropetrovsk oblast, Ukrainian SSR, 55 mi. W of Dnepropetrovsk. Rail junction in lignite basin; metalworking; chemicals; fire bricks; dairy plant, flour mill. Until 1944, Pyatikhatka.

Pyatt (pī'ŭt), town (pop. 257), Marion co., N Ark., 15 mi. E of Harrison, in the Ozarks.

Pyawbwe (pyôbwĕ'), town (pop. 6,160), Yamethin dist., Upper Burma, on Rangoon-Mandalay RR and 14 mi. N of Yamethin; police post.

Pyaye (pyä'yā), village, Thayetmyo dist., Lower Burma, near right bank of Irrawaddy R., 8 mi. SW of Thayetmyo; natural-gas wells.

Pychas (pĭchäs'), village, S Udmurt Autonomous SSR, Russian SFSR, on railroad and 38 mi. SW of Izhevsk; rye, oats, livestock.

Pydna (pĭd'nŭ), anc. city of Greek Macedonia, on Gulf of Salonika, 25 mi. SW of modern Salonika. Here occurred (168 B.C.) final victory of Romans, under Aemilius Paulus (or Paullus) over Macedonians, under Perseus, putting an end to Macedonian empire. Near by (W) is modern Gr. village of Kitros (1928 pop. 1,629).

Pyengana, village (pop. 124), NE Tasmania, 45 mi. ENE of Launceston; cheese factories.

Pyengyang, Korea: see Pyongyang.

Pyhä, Lake, Finnish *Pyhäjärvi* (pü'hăyăr"vē). **1** Lake (21 mi. long, 1–4 mi. wide), Häme co., SW Finland, extends S from Tampere. Drained W by Kokemä R.; connected N with L. Näsi by Tammer Rapids. **2** Lake (13 mi. long, 2–7 mi. wide), Oulu co., central Finland, 35 mi. W of Iisalmi.

Pyhä Falls, Finland: see Oulu River.

Pyhäjärvi, village (commune pop. 9,231), Oulu co., central Finland, on L. Pyhä, 35 mi. W of Iisalmi; fossil-meal quarrying, lumbering.

Pyhäjoki (pü'hăyō"kē), village (commune pop. 4,818), Oulu co., W Finland, on Gulf of Bothnia, at mouth of Pyhä R., 17 mi. SSW of Raahe, in lumbering, sawmilling region.

Pyhä River, Finnish *Pyhäjoki* (pü'hăyō"kē), W Finland, issues from small L. Pyhä at Pyhäjärvi, flows 100 mi. NW, over numerous rapids, past Oulainen, to Gulf of Bothnia 16 mi. SW of Raahe.

Pyhra (pü'rä), village (pop. 2,103), central Lower Austria, 4 mi. SE of Sankt Pölten; grain, cattle.

Pyhrn Pass (pürn) (3,000 ft.), central Austria, connects valley of the Enns, in Styria, with Krems valley in Upper Austria.

Pyhtää (pü'tă, pükh'tă), Swedish *Pyttis* (pü'tĭs), village (commune pop. 5,472), Kymi co., SE Finland, near Gulf of Finland, 13 mi. W of Kotka; lumber and pulp mills. Has 15th-cent. church.

Pyinbongyi (pyĭnbōn-jē'), village, Pegu dist., Pegu div., central Lower Burma, on Rangoon-Mandalay RR and 60 mi. NNE of Rangoon. Village is at W edge of Moyingyi Reservoir (□ 40), used for irrigation and supplying water for Pegu-Sittang canal.

Pyinmana (pyĭn"mănä'), town (pop. 17,656), Yamethin dist., Upper Burma, 55 mi. NNW of Toungoo, on Rangoon-Mandalay RR; head of railroad to Kyaukpadaung. Extensive teak forests near by; forestry col.

Pykara (pĭkä'rŭ), village, Nilgiri dist., SW Madras, India, on Pykara R. (upper course of the Moyar) and 8 mi. NW of Ootacamund. Pivotal hydroelectric system consists of storage works and power plant (completed 1932) at river falls, 8 mi. NNW, and an additional reservoir, impounded by large Mukurti Dam on Moyar R., 6 mi. SSW of Pykara (completed 1938). The transmission network, linked at Erode with the Mettur system and at Madura with the Papanasam system, powers industries at main receiving station of Coimbatore and in 12 dists. of S Madras. Construction of further works on Moyar River, 8 mi. below falls, begun 1946. Sometimes spelled Paikara.

Pyla, Cape (pē'lä), SE Cyprus, at E end of Larnaca Bay, 13 mi. E of Larnaca. An anc. tower is near its tip.

Pylaia or **Pilaia** (both: pĭlā'ŭ), SE suburb (pop. 3,972) of Salonika, Macedonia, Greece; U.S. agr. col. (S). Formerly called Strepha (Strefa) and Kapoutzedes (Kapoutzidhes).

Pyle, town and parish (pop. 4,947), S Glamorgan, Wales, 6 mi. SE of Port Talbot; agr. market; stone quarries.

Pyli or **Pili** (both: pē'lē) town (pop. 1,968), Kos isl., in the Dodecanese, Greece, 8 mi. WSW of Kos.

Pylos or **Pilos** (pī'lŏs, Gr. pē'lôs), Lat. *Pylus* (pī'lŭs), town (pop. 3,315), Messenia nome, SW Peloponnesus, Greece, at S entrance to Pylos Bay, 23 mi. WSW of Kalamata; fisheries; livestock raising. On N shore of the bay, 4 mi. NW, are ruins of anc. Pylos, said to have been the seat of Nestor. The anc. city declined after the conquest of Messenia by Spartans, who called it *Coryphasium*. In Middle Ages it was renamed Navarino (năvürē'nō); a new town grew on the S shore of the bay. Old Pylos became known as Palaea Navarino [Gr.=old Navarino] or Palaeokastron (Gr.,=old castle], while new Pylos grew as modern Navarino (locally called Neokastron, Gr.=new castle), renamed in late-19th cent., Pylos. It was held by the Turks, 1498–1821, except for brief Venetian inroads (1644–48; 1686–1715). During Gr. war of independence, Turks ruled it again (1825–27) until their defeat in battle of Navarino in Pylos Bay, where a British-French-Russian fleet defeated a Turkish-Egyptian fleet. The bay (4 mi. wide, 2 mi. long; protected by Sphakteria isl.) was also the scene (425 B.C.) of a naval victory by Athens over Sparta.

Pylstaert Island, Tonga: see Ata.

Pyltsama, Estonia: see Poltsamaa.

Pymatuning Creek (pĭmŭtōō'nĭng), in Ohio and Pa., rises in Ashtabula co., Ohio, flows c.27 mi. SSE to Shenango R. just above Sharon, Pa.

Pymatuning Reservoir, lake (16 mi. long, 2½ mi. wide), NW Pa. and NE Ohio, formed (1932) by flood-control dam on Shenango R. 7 mi. NNW of Greenville, Pa. Used also for recreation.

Pymble (pĭm'bŭl), town (pop. 4,631), E New South Wales, Australia, 10 mi. NNW of Sydney; coal-mining center.

Pynacker or **Pynakker,** Netherlands: see Pijnacker.

Pyoktong (pyŭk'tông'), Jap. *Hekido,* township (1944 pop. 11,567), N. Pyongan prov., N Korea, on Yalu R. and 65 mi. NNW of Sinuiju, in agr. and coal-mining area; collection center for textiles.

Pyongan-namdo, Korea: see South Pyongan.

Pyongan-pukdo, Korea: see North Pyongan.

Pyonggang (pyŭng'găng'), Jap. *Heiko,* town (1944 pop. 20,524), Kangwon prov., central Korea, N of 38°N, 60 mi. NNE of Seoul; agr. center (rice, soy beans, wheat, cotton).

Pyongtaek (pyŭng'tăk'), Jap. *Heitaku,* town (1946 pop. 14,420), Kyonggi prov., central Korea, S of 38°N, 40 mi. S of Seoul; rice growing. Gold is mined near by.

Pyongyang (pyŭng'yăng'), Jap. *Heijo* or *Heizyo* (both: hā'jō), city (1944 pop. 342,551), S.Pyongan prov., N Korea, on Taedong R. and 120 mi. NW of Seoul; 39°1'N 125°44'E; cultural and industrial center in coal-mining and agr. area. Situated on a high bluff, Pyongyang was formerly a walled city; has remains of 6 wall gates. There are sugar refineries, chemical plants, machine shops, rayon and cotton mills, briquette yards, breweries, and match factories. Has a univ. (1946). An anc. city, Pyongyang has old Buddhist temples, a mus. with historical relics, and a *Keisang* school (where Korean dancers are trained). Near by are 3 tombs (1st cent. B.C.) containing remarkable murals. According to legend, city was founded in 1122 B.C. by the Chinese sage Ki-tze (Kija). Pyongyang was ravaged by Jap. invasion (1592) led by Hideyoshi, and during Sino-Jap. War (1894) and Russo-Japanese War (1904). After Second World War. it was ⊙ Rus. occupation zone, N of 38th parallel, and, later, ⊙ North Korea. It was heavily damaged in Korean war (1950–51). Formerly spelled Pyengyang, Pingyang, and Phyong-yang.

Pyote (pīōt', pī'ōt), city (1940 pop. 201), Ward co., extreme W Texas, 22 mi. ENE of Pecos; oil-field trading point. Air Force base here.

Pyramid Lake (c.30 mi. long, 5–12 mi. wide), in Pyramid Lake Indian Reservation, W Nev., c.30 mi. NNE of Reno, bet. Lake Range (E) and Pyramid Range (W); remnant of prehistoric L. Lahontan. Fed in S by Truckee R. Discovered 1844 by J. C. Frémont. Anaho Isl. (248 acres) is U.S. bird refuge near E shore.

Pyramid Peak. 1 Mountain (10,020 ft.) in E Calif., in the Sierra Nevada, just SW of L. Tahoe. **2** Mountain (14,000 ft.) in W central Colo., in Elk Mts., 10 mi. SSW of Aspen.

Pyramid Range, W Nev., part of Virginia Mts. in Washoe co., extending N from Truckee R. along W shore of Pyramid L. Rises to 8,340 ft. in S.

Pyramids, Egypt: see Giza, town.

Pyramus River, Turkey: see Ceyhan River.

Pyrbaum (pēr'boum), village (pop. 1,030), Upper Palatinate, central Bavaria, Germany, 8 mi. WNW of Neumarkt; brewing. Has late-Gothic church. Chartered 1527.

Pyrenees (pĭ'rŭnēz), Fr. *Pyrénées* (pērānā'), Sp. *Pirineos* (pērēnā'ōs), anc. *Pyrenaei Montes* or *Pyrene,* folded mtn. chain of SW Europe bet. France and Spain, a formidable barrier bet. the Iberian Peninsula and the European mainland. It extends in an almost straight line c.270 mi. E–W from the Mediterranean (Cape Creuse) to the Atlantic on the Bay of Biscay (Cape Higuer). The Cantabrian Mountains continue W in N Spain. In the Pyrenees along the Fr. side lie (E–W) the depts. of Pyrénées-Orientales (comprising the old county of Roussillon, with Perpignan), of Ariège (comprising the old county of Foix), of Haute-Garonne and Hautes-Pyrénées (a part of Gascony), and of Basses-Pyrénées (roughly coextensive with Béarn, and comprising Fr. Navarre, the Basque regions of Soule and Labourd, and the cities of Bayonne, Pau, and Orthez). On the Sp. side stretch (E–W) the N section of Catalonia (with Gerona and Lérida provs.), N Aragon (with Huesca prov.), Navarre (with Pamplona), and the Basque Provs. Wedged bet. France and Spain in the E central Pyrenees is the small state of Andorra. The Pyrenees consist of one principal latitudinal range, bifurcating for a short distance in the center, where they reach their greatest width (c.80 mi.) and greatest elevation, forming a continuous wall of high snow-capped peaks—most of them above 10,000 ft.—culminating in the Pico de Aneto (11,168 ft.) of the Maladetta Massif. Among other high peaks are Pico del Medio (11,004 ft.), Pico de Maladetta (10,866 ft.), Pico Posets (11,046 ft.), Monte Perdido or Mont Perdu (10,997 ft.) in the Tres Socores, Pic du Midi d'Ossau (9,465 ft.), and Pic de Montcalm (10,105 ft.). In the W, the crest line falls beyond the Pic d'Anie (8,215 ft.) to 3–4,000 ft., while in the E and center it is maintained at 7–9,000 ft., dropping beyond Massif du Canigou (9,137 ft.) abruptly to the Mediterranean coast near the Monts Albères. Less complex and disrupted than most of the major mtn. ranges, the Pyrenees are a clearly defined system, so that subdivisions appear to be somewhat arbitrary. However, a longitudinal division into Eastern, Central, and Western Pyrenees is generally accepted. The Central Pyrenees are identified with the longest (c.160 mi.) most elevated crystalline section of the towering peaks. Its E margin is the Segre River (Cerdaña depression), but its W margin, less easy to define, is sometimes considered the Monte Perdido, sometimes the Pic d'Anie, and sometimes other mts. To these 3 sections correspond more or less the regional Sp. divisions of Catalan, Aragonese, and Navarran Pyrenees. Several separate subranges parallel the main chain, especially on the Sp. side. Of the total area (c.21,380 sq. mi.) of the Pyrenees, ⅔ lie in Spain. They fall more gently towards the Ebro valley than they do on the more picturesque and humid Fr. side. The Franco-Spanish border generally follows the watershed. Among the rivers running N are the Garonne, with its tributary the Ariège, and the Aude, Adour, and Tet rivers, while the S slopes are drained by the Aragon, Gállego, Cinca, and Segre rivers, all flowing to the Ebro. Though the Alps exceed the Pyrenees in altitude, length, and width, the latter are in some respects more forbidding, partly due to their higher average altitude, their greater compactness, and lack of low passes. However, the relative remoteness from Europe's center of activity and the part they played through history as a politico-cultural divide are at least as much responsible for their comparative isolation. Narrow lowland strips on Mediterranean and Atlantic shore permit easy enough communication but have not altogether ruled out the more hazardous mtn. routes. Along the Mediterranean side passes a railroad from Barcelona to Perpignan, while the international rail link Madrid-Hendaye via Irún skirts the W flank. Nevertheless, some low passes occur, the lowest, Le Perthus (915 ft.) in the Eastern Pyrenees, was used by the Romans, and that of Roncesvalles (3,468 ft.), famed in history and literature as scene of Roland's death, was also used in Middle Ages by invaders and pilgrims (to Santiago de Compostela). Other more difficult passes, snowbound through long parts of the year, are (E–W) Somport Pass (5,354 ft.), beneath which runs trans-Pyrenean RR from Saragossa to Pau via Canfranc; Vénasque Pass (8,032 ft.), N of the Maladetta, almost inaccessible; Salou Pass, on projected Lérida–Saint-Girons RR; Col de Puymorens (6,283 ft.), near Andorra border, pierced by over 3-mi-long tunnel of Barcelona–Toulouse RR (Puigcerdá–Ax-les-Thermes); and Col de Perche (5,135 ft.). The Pyrenees owe their present structure—like the Alps, the Caucasus, and Atlas—to the great Tertiary uplift which constitutes the continent's backbone. Like those related systems they possess a paleozoic crystalline core, which becomes exposed in the granite and gneiss masses of the high central crest. The lower sections and subranges consist predominantly of much younger limestone folds. Although quite beautiful in scenic features, the Pyrenees do not, as a rule, present the serrated outline of some of the Alpine massifs. They are also devoid of large glaciers and lakes, as well as of low pleasant valleys, for which the Alps are so famed. But evidence of past glaciation (arrêtes, moraines, U-shaped valleys) is widespread. And a characteristic feature, particularly of the Fr. Pyrenees, are the torrents called *gaves,* often falling in cascades, and the natural amphitheaters known as *cirques,* notably those of Troumouse and the celebrated Cirque de Gavarnie, which rises from its base (5,740 ft.) in terraces another 4,000 ft. and opens into Spain through the Brèche-de-Roland. On the Fr. side also are the best-known resorts, such as Pau, Tarbes, Cauterets, Luchon, Bagnères-de-Bigorre, and a host of spas. On the Atlantic shore, below the Western Pyrenees, are the fashionable resorts of Biarritz and Saint-Jean-de-Luz (France) and San Sebastián (Spain). At N foot of the Central Pyrenees is Lourdes, one of the world's chief places of pilgrimage. The Pyrenees also act as a climatic divide, with most of its steppe-like S side in the rain-shadow. Sheep and goat grazing is here the principal occupation. Rainfall increases markedly towards W, supporting fine pastures. On the well-watered Fr. piedmont thrive cereals, olives, wine, and fruit. There are productive tracts in the Cerdaña (Fr. *Cerdagne*), upper Segre R. valley. Grain is grown in some of the upper valleys, but stock raising predominates in scantily populated mtn. area. The Pyrenees are rich in timber, particularly in the W and N, where there are coniferous forests; there are also oaks and beeches, and, in SE, chestnuts. The snow line runs roughly bet. 5,500 and 6,500 ft. Wild animals include bear, wolf, lynx, wild boar, deer, and chamois. The mineral wealth is limited. There are some iron, zinc, lead, bauxite, and lignite deposits. Marble and gypsum is quarried, and oil deposits are indicated near Saint-Gaudens in France. Of major economic importance is the great hydroelectric potential; partly harnessed, it supplies the Basque and Catalan industries, and, particularly, the metallurgical and chemical plants in Ariège and Garonne valleys of SW France. The population of the Pyrenees is partly of Basque and Bearnese stock, the former retaining their anc. language, which is unrelated to any other tongue spoken in Europe. The high skill reached here by prehistoric man is evidenced by the cave drawings of Aurignac. The Pyrenees were traversed (218 B.C.) from the S by Hannibal. Barbarian hordes (Vandals, Visigoths, etc.) crossed from the N. Through battle of Tours or Poitiers (732) Charles Martel forced Moslem invaders to retreat beyond the Pyrenees. Since the Peace of the Pyrenees (1659)—signed on small Île de Faisans in BIDASSOA RIVER—the Franco-Spanish border has remained unchanged.

Pyrénées, Basses-, France: see BASSES-PYRÉNÉES.

Pyrénées, Hautes-, France: see HAUTES-PYRÉNÉES.

Pyrénées-Orientales (pērānā″zôrēätäl′) [Fr.,=eastern Pyrenees], department (□ 1,600; pop. 228,776) in Roussillon, S France; ⊙ Perpignan. Bounded by Spain (S) and the Gulf of Lion (E). Occupied by the main range and several spurs of E Pyrenees, and by a small coastal plain around Perpignan. The Monts ALBÈRES (SE) drop off abruptly into the Mediterranean. The valley of upper Sègre R. (CERDAGNE), though S of the Pyrenean divide, forms SW part of dept., and is reached from N by 2 passes, Col de PUYMORENS and Col de la PERCHE. Rest of dept. is drained by Tech, Têt, and Agly rivers, all flowing generally E. Only rye and potatoes are grown in rugged uplands. The mountain valleys (VALLESPIR, CONFLENT) have orchards, vineyards, and olive groves. The well-irrigated lowland supports a luxurious sub-tropical vegetation and is known for its Roussillon wines, fruits, and early vegetables. Iron ore is extensively mined on slopes of Massif du CANIGOU. Industries, aside from food-processing, are of minor importance as yet, though rivers have been harnessed for hydroelectric power. Chief towns are Perpignan (regional commercial center), Prades (metallurgy), Rivesaltes (winegrowing), and Port-Vendres (seaport). At Amélie-les-Bains and Le Boulou are baths.

Pyreneos, Serra dos, Brazil: see PIRENEUS, SERRA DOS.

Pyrenópolis, Brazil: see PIRENÓPOLIS.

Pyrgi or **Piryi** (both: pēryē′), town (pop. 2,519), S Chios isl., Greece, 12 mi. SSW of Chios; mastic, wine, olive oil, wheat. Sometimes spelled Pyrghi or Pyrghion.

Pyrgos or **Pirgos** (both: pēr′gôs), city in Letrinoi municipality (pop. 18,943), ⊙ Elis nome, W Peloponnesus, Greece, near mouth of Alpheus R., on railroad, and 40 mi. SSW of Patras. Commercial and industrial center; mfg. of cigarettes, alcoholic beverages. Exports (through its port KATAKOLON) Zante currants, figs, wine, citrus fruit. Sacked 1825 by Turks in Gr. war of independence. Letrinoi municipality is named for anc. city of Letrini, 3 mi. WNW of Pyrgos.

Pyritz, Poland: see PYRZYCE.

Pyrmont, Bad, Germany: see BAD PYRMONT.

Pyrrha (pĭr′ů), anc. city of Lesbos, Greece, on NE shore of Gulf of Kallone.

Pyrsopolis, Greece: see PROSOTSANE.

Pyrzyce (pĭ-zhĭ′tsĕ), Ger. *Pyritz* (pē′rĭts), town (1939 pop. 11,287; 1946 pop 803) in Pomerania, after 1945 in Szczecin prov., NW Poland, 15 mi. SSW of Stargard, in fertile wheat-growing region. Chartered 1263. In Second World War, c.90% destroyed.

Pyshchug (pĭshchōōk′), village (1939 pop. over 500), NE Kostroma oblast, Russian SFSR, 35 mi. N of Sharya, on highway to Kotlas; flax.

Pyshkino-Troitskoye (pĭsh′kĭnů-trô′yĭtskůyů), village (1926 pop. 807), SE Tomsk oblast, Russian SFSR, on Chulym R. and 60 mi. NE of Tomsk, in agr. area; lumbering.

Pyshma (pĭshmä′). **1** Town (1939 pop. over 2,000), S Sverdlovsk oblast, Russian SFSR, on Pyshma R., on Trans-Siberian RR (Oshchepkovo station) and 22 mi. ENE of Kamyshlov; metalworking. **2** City, Sverdlovsk oblast, Russian SFSR: see VERKHNYAYA PYSHMA.

Pyshma River, Sverdlovsk oblast, Russian SFSR, rises in small lake just N or Verkhnyaya Pyshma, flows 390 mi. generally E, past Staro Pyshminsk, Beloyarskoye, Sukhoi Log, Kamyshlov, Pyshma, and Talitsa, to Tura R. 35 mi. E of Tyumen. Has several dams used for industrial water supply.

Pyshminski Zavod, Russian SFSR: see STARO-PYSHMINSK.

Pyskowice (pĭskôvē′tsĕ), Ger. *Peiskretscham* (pīs″-krĕ′chäm), town (pop. 6,771), Katowice prov., S Poland, 8 mi. NNW of Gleiwitz (Gliwice); rail junction in coal-mining region.

Pytalovo (pĭtä′lůvů), Latvian *Abrene* (äbrĕ′nā) (formerly *Jaunlatgale*), city (pop. 1,242), SW Pskov oblast, Russian SFSR, 55 mi. SSW of Pskov; rail junction; grain, flax. In Rus. Pskov govt. until 1920; in Latvian Latgale prov. 1920–45.

Pythion or **Pithion** (both: pē′thēōn), village (pop. 3,222), Hevros nome, W Thrace, Greece, 20 mi. S of Adrianople (Edirne), on Maritsa R. (Turkish line); rail junction and customs station connecting with Turkish rail system.

Pytho, Greece: see DELPHI.

Pyttis, Finland: see PYHTÄÄ.

Pyu (pyōō), town (pop. 7,807), Toungoo dist., Lower Burma, 30 mi. S of Toungoo and on Rangoon-Mandalay RR; at E edge of govt. forest reserves.

Pyuntaza (pyōōntůzä′), town (pop. 6,172), Pegu dist., Lower Burma, on Rangoon-Mandalay RR and 20 mi. NNE of Rangoon, in rice-growing area; railroad shops.

Pyuthan, Nepal: see PIUTHAN.

Pyxaria or **Pixaria** (both: pĭksärēä′), mountain in NE Euboea, Greece, near N coast; rises to 4,405 ft. 17 mi. N of Chalcis.

Pyzdry (pĭz′drĭ), town (1946 pop. 3,868), Poznan prov., W central Poland, on the Warta and 36 mi. ESE of Poznan; rail spur terminus; flour milling. Until 1919, town was located in Rus. Poland, near Ger. frontier.

Q

Qa' Ba Nua, Aden: see KHOREIBA.

Qabr Hud (kä′bůr hōōd′), village, Quaiti state, Eastern Aden Protectorate, 35 mi. ENE of Tarim, in the Wadi Hadhramaut; pilgrimage center.

Qachas Nek (kä′chäz nĕk′), village, ⊙ Qachas Nek dist. (pop. 44,560, with absent laborers 49,326), SE Basutoland, on SE frontier, in the Drakensberg and 90 mi. SE of Maseru. Also spelled Qachasnek or Qacha's Nek.

Qadamgah (kädämgä′), village, Ninth Prov., in Khurasan, NE Iran, 35 mi. SW of Meshed, and on railroad, in agr. area.

Qadas, Israel: see KEDESH.

Qadhima or **Qadimah** (kädhē′mů), town, S central Hejaz, Saudi Arabia, near Red Sea, 60 mi. N of Jidda; dates, vegetables, fruit; goat and sheep raising.

Qadhub (kädhōōb′), village on N coast of Socotra isl., 6 mi. W of Hadibu. British air base is on cape Ras Karma, 2 mi. W.

Qadian (kädyän′), village, Gurdaspur dist., NW Punjab, India, on rail spur and 10 mi. E of Batala; markets wheat, gram, oilseeds; mfg. of electrical appliances, glass, textiles, carpets; oilseed milling, hand-loom weaving; ironworks. Science research institute.

Qadima or **Kadima** (both: kädēmä′), settlement (pop. 260), W Israel, in Plain of Sharon, 5 mi. SE of Natanya; mixed farming, citriculture. Founded 1933.

Qadimah, Saudi Arabia: see QADHIMA.

Qadirabad, India: see JALNA.

Qadmus, El, or **Al-Qadmus** (both: ĕl kädmōōs′), Fr. *Kadmous*, town, Latakia prov., W Syria, 36 mi. SE of Latakia; sericulture, tobacco, cereals.

Qa'en, Iran: see QAIN.

Qaersorssuaq, Greenland: see KAERSORSSUAK.

Qaersut, Greenland: see KAERSUT.

Qaf, Saudi Arabia: see KAF.

Qafl (kä′fůl), **Qafla,** or **Qaflah** (kä′flů), town (pop. 1,000), Hajja prov., N central Yemen, 25 mi. NW of Hajja, in maritime range.

Qafmollë (kyäfmô′lů) or **Qafmolla** (kyäfmô′lä), village (1930 pop. 214), central Albania, 8 mi. ENE of Tirana.

Qaha (kä′hä), village (pop. 6,130), Qalyubiya prov., Lower Egypt, on railroad and 16 mi. N of Cairo; cotton, flax, cereals, fruits.

Qaim, Al (äl kīm′), village, Dulaim prov., W Iraq, on the Euphrates 10 mi. from the Syrian line, and 140 mi. WNW of Ramadi.

Qaimpur (kĭm′pōōr), town (pop. 2,342), Bahawalpur state, W Pakistan, in irrigated tract, 50 mi. NE of Bahawalpur; wheat, cotton, rice, dates. Also spelled Kaimpur.

Qain or **Qa'en** (both: käĕn′), town, Ninth Prov., in Khurasan, NE Iran, in oasis, 60 mi. N of Birjand, and on Zahidan-Meshed road; alt. 4,800 ft. Agr. (opium, barberry, asafetida). Known for its saffron, it also produces rugs and handmade woolen textiles. Former capital of the Qainat, S dist. of Khurasan, it has been largely supplanted by Birjand. Anc. Qain was destroyed and rebuilt by the Timurid Shah Rukh, and later held by the Uzbeks until the coming of Shah Abbas the Great. Sometimes spelled Kain.

Qairwan, Tunisia: see KAIROUAN.

Qais or **Qays** (kīs), Persian *Kish* (kēsh), island (1940 pop. estimate 1,500) in Persian Gulf, off S Iran, 50 mi. W of Lingeh; 26°33′N 54°E; 9 mi. long, 4 mi. wide. Agr., fishing; pearl trade. Was great trade center (11th–14th cent.) in Middle Ages until rise of Hormuz isl.

Qaisar River (kī′sůr), Pashto *Ab-i-Qaisar* (äb′-ĭ–), river in Afghan Turkestan, N Afghanistan, rises in the Band-i-Turkestan (W outlier of the Hindu Kush), flows 150 mi. N, past Maimana and Andkhui, disappearing into the desert N of Andkhui; irrigation.

Qaisumah or **Qaysumah** (kī′sōōmů), settlement in Hasa, Saudi Arabia, 300 mi. NW of Dhahran; 28°26′N 46°2′E. Oil-pumping station on pipe line from Abqaiq to Saida.

Qaiyara or **Qaiyarah** (kīyä′rů), village, Mosul prov., N Iraq, on the Tigris and 40 mi. S of Mosul; oil deposits.

Qala Ahangaran (kŭ′lů ä″hŭng-gůrän′), village, Herat prov., central Afghanistan, on the upper Hari Rud and 165 mi. E of Herat, on mtn. road to Kabul, in W outliers of the Hindu Kush; center of Chakhcharan dist.

Qala Bist (kŭ′lů bēst′), town, Kandahar prov., S Afghanistan, 80 mi. E of Kandahar, and on Helmand R. at mouth of the Arghandab. Also called Bust.

Qalag, El (ĕl kä′lăg), or **Al-Qalaj** (ĕl-kä′lăj), village (pop. 10,205), Qalyubiya prov., Lower Egypt, 11 mi. NE of Cairo; cotton, flax, cereals, fruits.

Qala-i-Jadid, Afghanistan: see SPINBALDAK.

Qala-i-Nau, Afghanistan: see QALA NAU.

Qala-Jadid, Afghanistan: see SPINBALDAK.

Qalamun, El, or **Al-Qalamun** (both: ĕl kälămōōn′), village (pop. 1,590) in Dakhla oasis, S central Egypt, in the Southern Desert prov., 10 mi. S of El Qasr; dates, oranges, wheat, barley.

Qala Nau (kŭ′lů nou′) or **Qala-i-Nau** (–ĭ–), town (pop. 5,500), Herat prov., NW Afghanistan, 70 mi. NE of Herat and on road to Afghan Turkestan; alt. 2,920 ft.; irrigated agr. Pop. is largely Hazara.

Qalandul (kälăn′dōōl), village (pop. 8,008), Asyut prov., Upper Egypt, on W bank of the Nile and 20 mi. SSE of Minya; cereals, dates, sugar cane.

Qala Panja (kŭ′lů pŭn′jů), village, Afghan Badakhshan, NE Afghanistan, in the Wakhan, 115 mi. E of Faizabad, and on the Panj (USSR line) near confluence of Pamir and Wakhan rivers.

Qal'a Salih or **Qal'at Salih** (käl′-ät sä′lē), town, 'Amara prov., SE Iraq, on Tigris R. and 20 mi. SSE of 'Amara; dates, rice, corn, millet, sesame. Also called Shatrat al-'Amara.

Qala Sarkari, Afghanistan: see DARRA-I-SUF.

Qala Shahrak, Afghanistan: see SHAHRAK.

Qal'a Sharqat, Iraq: see SHARQAT.

Qal'at [Arabic,=fort], for names beginning thus and not found here: see under following part of the name.

Qal'at al-Hasa, Jordan: see QAL'AT EL HASA.

Qal'at Dab'a or **Qal'at Dab'aa** (käl-ät′ däb-ä′), village, N central Jordan, on Hejaz RR and 25 mi. SSE of Amman; wheat; camels. Marble deposits.

Qal'at el Hasa or **Qal'at al-Hasa** (both: ĕl hăsä′), village, S central Jordan, on Hejaz RR and 20 mi. E of Tafila, on Wadi el Hasa (affluent of Dead Sea); barley, camel raising. Phosphate deposits.

Qal'at Salih, Iraq: see QAL'A SALIH.

Qalhat, Oman: see KALHAT.

Qallin or **Qalin** (both: kälēn′), town (pop. 6,747; with suburbs, 9,652), Gharbiya prov., Lower Egypt, 6 mi. SW of Kafr el Sheikh; cotton.

Qalyub (käl′yōōb, kälyōōb′), town (pop. 27,080; with suburbs, 31,444), Qalyubiya prov., Lower Egypt, railway junction 9 mi. NNW of Cairo city center; cotton and silk weaving; cotton, flax, cereals, fruits. Sometimes spelled Kaliub.

Qalyubiya or **Qalyubiyah** (kälyōōbē′yů), province (□ 364; pop. 690,156), S Lower Egypt; ⊙ Benha. Bounded S by Cairo Governorate, W by Damietta branch of the Nile, N by Sharqiya prov., E by Arabian Desert. Main industry is cotton ginning. Agr.: cotton, flax, cereals, fruits. Besides Benha, Qalyub is important. Served by rail from Cairo and by Ismailia Canal. Sometimes Kalyubiya.

Qamishliye, El, or **Al-Qamishli** (both: ĕl kä′mĭshlē), Fr. *Kamechlié*, town, Jezire prov., NE Syria, on Turkish border, on railroad, and 45 mi. NE of El Haseke; cereals, rice, sheep. Oil deposits. Also spelled Kameshli.

Qamsar (kämsär′), village, Second Prov., in Kashan, N central Iran, 16 mi. S of Kashan; rose-growing center, known for its rose water. Also spelled Kamsar.

Qanawat, El, Syria: see KANAWAT.

Qanayat, El, or **Al-Qanayat** (both: ĕl känä′yăt), village (pop. 12,385), Sharqiya prov., Lower Egypt, 3 mi. NW of Zagazig; cotton.

Qandahar, Afghanistan: see KANDAHAR.

Qandhar, India: see KANDAHAR.

Qantara, Kantara (kăn′tůrů, kän′tärů), or **Al-Qantarah** (ĕl-kän′tärů), town, Canal Governorate, NE Egypt, on Suez Canal, 27 mi. S of Port Said. Qantara West [Arabic *Qantara Gharb*], on Cairo–Port Said RR, is connected by ferry with Qantara East [Arabic *Qantara Sharq*], rail terminus for Palestine. Two mi. N is an oil depot. The anc. caravan route to Syria crossed at this point. Egyptian and Roman ruins near by.

Qara, in Uigur names, China: see KARA.

Qara (kä′rů), tribal country of S Oman, in Dhofar, extending W of Salala to border of Aden Protectorate; stock raising; collection of frankincense and other gums.

Qara, Al, or **Al-Qarah** (ălkä′rů), town, ⊙ Lower Yafa sultanate, Western Aden Protectorate, 65 mi. NNE of Aden; 13°43′ N 45°17′E.

Qara, El, or **Al-Qarah** (both: ĕl kä′rů), village (pop. 9,686), Qena prov., Upper Egypt, 10 mi. WNW of Nag Hammadi, on Western Oasis RR; airfield; cereals, sugar cane, dates. Sometimes El Kara.

Qara Chai (kärä′ chī′) or **Qara Su** (sōō), river in N central Iran, rises in several branches in Hamadan area, flows over 150 mi. E, past Nubaran and Saveh, to Namak salt lake NE of Qum.

Qara Dagh or **Kara Dagh** (kärä' däg'), mountain range in Azerbaijan, NW Iran, bet. Tabriz and Aras R.; rises to c.10,000 ft.

Qarah, Al-, Aden: see QARA, AL.

Qarajaq Ice Fjord (kä'räyäk), Dan. *Qarajaqs Isfjord,* SE arm (30 mi. long, 4–8 mi. wide) of Umanak Fjord, W Greenland, 10 mi. SE of Umanak; 70°25'N 51°15'W. Contains small Ikerasak Isl. Receives Store Glacier, Dan. *Støre Isbrae,* noted for its rapid rate of flow and of calving.

Qara Su (kärä' sōō'). 1 River in Azerbaijan, NW Iran, rises in area of Ardebil, flows 150 mi. WNW and N to Aras R. (USSR line) 100 mi. ENE of Julfa. 2 River, N central Iran: see QARA CHAI.

Qara Tepe, Afghanistan: see TORGHONDI.

Qarghaliq, China: see KARGHALIK.

Qarn, Al, Aden: see DIS.

Qartaba or **Qartabah** (kär'täbů), Fr. *Kartaba,* village (pop. c.2,500), central Lebanon, 25 mi. NE of Beirut; alt. 3,600 ft.; sericulture, cereals, tobacco, grapes.

Qarun, Birkit, Egypt: see BIRKET KARUN.

Qaryatein, El, or **Al-Qaryatayn** (both: ĕl kär'yätān), Fr. *Kariatein,* town (pop. c.2,500), Homs prov., W Syria, 75 mi. NE of Damascus; health resort; vineyards, apple orchards.

Qasha, Al, or **Al Qasha'** (ăl kä'shů), town, ⊙ Alawi tribal area, Western Aden Protectorate, 45 mi. NNW of Aden; 13°27'N 44°53'E. Sometimes Al Kasha.

Qasim (käsēm'), province of Nejd, Saudi Arabia; ⊙ Anaiza. Consists of group of oases in middle section of the Wadi Rima; main centers are Anaiza and Buraida. Sometimes spelled Kasim.

Qasimiye, Lebanon: see LITANI RIVER.

Qasr [Arabic,=fort or palace], for names beginning thus and not found here: see under following part of the name.

Qasr, El, or **Al-Qasr** (both: ĕl kä'sůr), chief village (pop. 3,459) of Dakhla oasis, Southern Desert prov., S central Egypt, 240 mi. W of Luxor; 25°42'N 28°50'E. Dates, oranges, wheat, barley. Has sulphur springs and remains of an Egyptian temple. Near by (SW) are the ruins of a Roman temple. Sometimes spelled El Kasr.

Qasr, El, or **Al-Qasr.** 1 Village, N central Jordan, on Hejaz RR and 3 mi. S of Amman; barley, camel raising. 2 Village (pop. c.2,000), central Jordan, 10 mi. NNW of Kerak; wheat, barley. Also called Qasr el Rabbah or Qasr er Rabbah.

Qasr el Azraq or **Qasr al-Azraq** (both: kä'sůr ĕl-äz'räk), village, NE Jordan, in desert area 55 mi. ESE of Amman; junction of desert trails; airfield, police post; fruit, sheep, goat raising; fishing in near-by small lakes of Azraq and El Qeisiya (S). Deposits of salt, gypsum.

Qasr er Rabbah, Jordan: see QASR, EL.

Qasr-e-Shirin, Iran: see QASR-I-SHIRIN.

Qasr-i-Shirin or **Qasr-e-Shirin** (both: käs'rĕshērēn'), town, Fifth Prov., in Kermanshah, W Iran, 90 mi. W of Kermanshah, near Khusrawi customs station on Iraq border; trade center for W Iran, on Teheran-Baghdad trade route; grain, dates, rice. Small coal mine. Sassanian ruins near by. Also spelled Kasr-i-Shirin.

Qasrqand, Iran: see NIKSHAHR.

Qassasin, El, or **Al-Qassasin** (both: ĕl käs-sä'sēn), town (pop. 18,610), Sharqiya prov., Lower Egypt, on Ismailia Canal, on Cairo-Ismailia RR, and 24 mi. ENE of Bilbeis. Consists of new town (El Gedida; pop. 10,644) and old town (El Qadima; pop. 7,966).

Qataba, Qa'taba, or **Qa'tabah** (kä'täbů), town (pop. 3,000), Ibb prov., S Yemen, 35 mi. ESE of Ibb, on Aden Protectorate frontier.

Qataghan, Afghanistan: see KATAGHAN.

Qatan, Al, Aden: see QATN, AL.

Qatana (kä'tänů), Fr. *Katana,* village, Damascus prov., SW Syria, 14 mi. WSW of Damascus; fruit, cereals.

Qatar (kä'tär), independent Arab sheikdom (□ 4,000; 1949 pop. 20,000) under British protection, on Persian Gulf (E) coast of Arabian Peninsula; ⊙ Doha. A peninsula extending from the Arabian coast along a 30-mi.-wide base bet. Salwa Bay and the Khor el Odeid, Qatar projects 100 mi. N and reaches a max. width of 50 mi., forming E side of the Gulf of Bahrein. A rocky, pebbly desert on a karstic upland (250 ft. high), Qatar has a very dry climate with 5 inches of annual precipitation. Pop. consists largely of Arab tribes, both sedentary and nomadic, whose chief occupations are pearl fishing and camel breeding. There are a few date groves around the coastal villages, where sedentary pop. is concentrated. Commercial centers are Doha and Waqra. Trade is chiefly with Iran, main exports being dried fish and pearls. Following the granting (1935) of an oil concession, oil was struck in 1939, but commercial production began only after Second World War. Pipe line links producing field of DUKHAN with loading terminal at Umm Said. Under suzerainty of Bahrein prior to 1868, Qatar was occupied by an Ottoman garrison and the Porte controlled the foreign relations of the sheik until the First World War. Since 1916, Britain has exercised a protectorate over Qatar, similar to that over the Trucial Sheikdoms.

Qateibi, Aden: see QUTAIBI.

Qatghan, Afghanistan: see KATAGHAN.

Qatif or **Al Qatif** (ăl kätēf'), town (pop. 20,000) in Hasa, Saudi Arabia, port on Persian Gulf, 15 mi. NNW of Dhahran; site of oil field (discovered 1945); fishing, pearling. Agr.: grain (alfalfa, rice), dates, vegetables, fruit. Local handicrafts. An important Hasa port until development of oil fields, it has been displaced by Dammam. Sometimes spelled Katif.

Qatn, Al, or **Al Qatan** (both: ăl kä'tůn), town (1946 pop. 4,500), Quaiti state, Eastern Aden Protectorate, in the upper Wadi Hadhramaut, 13 mi. SW of Shibam; commercial and agr. center; date groves, orchards. Airport. Also called Hauta, Hautah, or Hawtah.

Qatrana, El, or **Al-Qatranah** (both: ĕl-käträ'nů), village, central Jordan, on Hejaz RR and 20 mi. ENE of Kerak; airfield; grain, camel raising.

Qattara Depression or **Qattarah Depression** (kätä'rů), an arid desert basin (□ 7,500) in the Libyan Desert of N Egypt, beginning 35 mi. S of the coast at Alamein and extending c.170 mi. SW to within 20 mi. of Siwa oasis; 70 mi. wide; lowest point is 440 ft. below sea level. Because of its soft sands it is impassable to vehicles and thus played an important role in Second World War as a natural anchor for the S end of the British defense line at ALAMEIN.

Qattine or **Qattinah** (kät-tē'nů), Fr. *Kattiné,* town, Homs prov., W Syria, on L. Homs, on railroad, and 9 mi. SW of Homs; cereals, fruits.

Qays, Iran: see QAIS.

Qaysumah, Saudi Arabia: see QAISUMAH.

Qazvin, Iran: see KAZVIN.

Qedma or **Kedma** (both: kĕdmä'), settlement (pop. 200), W Israel, in Judaean Plain, 13 mi. S of Rehovot; mixed farming. Founded 1946.

Qeissan, Anglo-Egyptian Sudan: see GEISSAN.

Qena (kĕ'nů, kā'nů) or **Qina** (kĭ'nů), province (□ 705; pop. 1,107,915), Upper Egypt, in Nile valley; ⊙ QENA. Bounded S by Aswan prov., E by Arabian Desert, N by Girga prov., W by Libyan Desert. Pottery making, sugar milling. Agr. (cereals, dates, sugar cane). Main urban centers: Qena, Dishna, LUXOR, ISNA, QUS, NAQADA. Railway, along the Nile, crosses at Nag Hammadi. The prov. is one of the richest in archaeological remains, with ruins at THEBES, Luxor, KARNAK, QURNA, COPTOS. Also spelled Kena and Keneh.

Qena or **Qina,** town (pop. 39,672; with suburbs, 43,037), ⊙ Qena prov., Upper Egypt, on E bank of Nile R. opposite Dendera, on railroad, and 32 mi. NNE of Luxor; 26°10'N 32°43'E. On site of anc. *Caene* or *Caenepolis.* Known for its pottery (water bottles, jars). Agr. (cereals, sugar cane, dates). Road leads ENE through Arabian Desert to Safaga, port on Red Sea. The starting point of routes through the eastern desert, it is thronged with pilgrims during Mecca pilgrimages. Has a temple in good state of preservation. Also spelled Kena and Keneh.

Qeqertaq, Greenland: see KEKERTAK.

Qerrortussoq, Greenland: see KERRORTUSSOK.

Qerveh, Iran: see QURVEH.

Qeshm, Iran: see QISHM.

Qibbuts Mahar, Israel: see GEVARAM.

Qibliya or **Qibliyah** (kĭblē'yů, jĭ–), uninhabited easternmost island (□ 1) of the Kuria Muria group, off SE Oman; 17°31'N 56°23'E; rises to 550 ft. Also spelled Jibliya or Jibliyah.

Qift (kĭft), village (pop. 8,472), Qena prov., Upper Egypt, on E bank of the Nile, on railroad, and 13 mi. SSE of Qena; pottery making; cereals, sugar cane, dates. Site of anc. COPTOS. Also spelled Kift, Quft, and Kuft.

Qila, for Afghan names beginning thus: see under QALA.

Qila Didar Singh, W Pakistan: see KILA DIDAR SINGH.

Qila Saifullah, W Pakistan: see KILLA SAIFULLA.

Qila Sheikhupura, W Pakistan: see SHEIKHUPURA, town.

Qina, Egypt: see QENA.

Qiryat Amal or **Kiryat Amal** (both: kēryät' ämäl'), residential settlement (pop. c.2,000), NW Israel, bet. Zebulun Valley and Plain of Jezreel, 10 mi. SSE of Haifa. Founded 1937.

Qiryat 'Anavim or **Kiryat Anavim** (both: änävēm'), settlement (pop. 400), E Israel, in Judaean Hills, 6 mi. WNW of Jerusalem; dairying, fruitgrowing. Convalescent home. Modern village founded 1920; important Israeli defense and transportation base (1948) during siege of Jerusalem. Near by is site of biblical locality of same name.

Qiryat Benjamin or **Kiryat Benjamin** (both: bĕnyämēn'), residential settlement (pop. 700), NW Israel, in Zebulun Valley, 6 mi. E of Haifa. Founded 1937. Also called Qiryat Binyamin or Kiryat Binyamin.

Qiryat Bialik or **Kiryat Bialik** (both: byä'lēk), residential settlement (pop. 2,500), NW Israel, in Zebulun Valley, near Bay of Acre, 5 mi. E of Haifa. Has immigrants' training school. Founded 1934. Just E is agr. settlement of Kfar Bialik (pop. 220).

Qiryat Binyamin, Israel: see QIRYAT BENJAMIN.

Qiryat Haiyim or **Qiryat Haim** (hä'yēm), residential settlement (pop. 10,000), NW Israel, in Zebulun Valley, near Bay of Acre, on railroad and 5 mi. E of Haifa. Founded 1933. Also spelled Kiryat Haiyim or Kiryat Haim; sometimes spelled Qiryat Hayim or Kiryat Hayim.

Qiryat Haroshet or **Kiryat Haroshet** (härōshĕt'), residential settlement (pop. 260), NW Israel, at NW end of Plain of Jezreel, at SE foot of Mt. Carmel, on Kishon R., on railroad and 10 mi. SE of Haifa. Founded 1935.

Qiryat Motzkin or **Kiryat Motzkin** (mōts'kēn), residential settlement (pop. 4,000), NW Israel, in Zebulun Valley, near Bay of Acre, on railroad and 5 mi. E of Haifa. Founded 1934.

Qiryat Nahum or **Kiryat Nahum** (nähōōm'), residential settlement (pop. 250), NW Israel, in Zebulun Valley, 4 mi. E of Haifa; marmalade mfg. Formerly called Ir Gannim or Ir Ganim.

Qiryat Shaul or **Kiryat Shaul** (shä-ōōl'), settlement (pop. 250), W Israel, in Plain of Sharon, near Mediterranean, 4 mi. NE of Tel Aviv; mixed farming. Founded 1924, abandoned 1929; resettled 1935.

Qiryat Shmuel or **Kiryat Shmuel** (shmōō-ĕl'), residential SW suburb of Jerusalem, E Israel; site of Franciscan convent.

Qishlaq, Iran: see GARMSAR.

Qishm or **Qeshm** (both: kĕ'shům), largest island (1933 pop. estimate 15,000) in Persian Gulf, Eighth Prov., SE Iran, in Strait of Hormuz and separated from Iranian mainland by shallow Clarence Strait; 70 mi. long, 7–20 mi. wide. Fishing, pearling; palm trees, fruit. Salt mining; ferrous-oxide, oil, and sulphur deposits. Main town, Qishm, is at NE tip, 15 mi. S of Bandar Abbas. Isl. had British naval station until 1823. Also spelled Kishm.

Qishn (kĭ'shůn), town, ⊙ mainland section of Mahri sultanate of Qishn and Socotra, port on Arabian Sea, 180 mi. ENE of Mukalla and 220 mi. NW of Socotra isl.; fisheries; frankincense export. Residence of junior Mahri sultan. Airfield.

Qishon River, Israel: see KISHON RIVER.

Qizan (kēzăn') or **Jizan** (jē–), town in Asir, Saudi Arabia, port on Red Sea, 80 mi. S of Abha; 16°54'N. Chief export and shipping center of Asir, sheltered by Farasan Isls.; dhow building; fishing, pearling. Exports grain, sesame, dried fish, dates. Salt pans (S). Sometimes spelled Gizan.

Qizil Ozen, Iran: see QIZIL UZUN.

Qizil Uzun (kĕzĕl' ōōzōōn'), **Qizil Uzen** (üzĕn'), or **Qizil Ozen** (ōzĕn'), longest river of NW Iran, rises in Kurdistan mts. N of Sanandaj, flows 350 mi. E, N, and SE, through deep-cut mtn. gorges of Azerbaijan and Khamseh, joining the Shah Rud at Manjil (in Gilan) to form the SEFID RUD.

Qohpayeh, Iran: see KUHPAYEH.

Qolhak, Iran: see GULHEK.

Qolosna, Egypt: see QULUSNA.

Qom, Iran: see QUM.

Qomul, China: see HAMI.

Qormi (kôr'mē) or **Curmi** (kōōr'mē), town (pop. 14,396), central Malta, 2½ mi. SW of Valletta. Mfg. of bread, macaroni, biscuits. Region grows wheat, potatoes, forage, citrus fruit. Suffered no damage during Second World War. Has several 16th-cent. churches. The Palazzo Stagno (1589), with a walled garden, is built in Maltese style.

Qôrnog, Greenland: see KORNOK.

Qotur, Iran: see QUTUR.

Qsar el Kbir, El, Sp. Morocco: see ALCAZARQUIVIR.

Quabbin Reservoir (kwŏ'bĭn) (□ 39.4), W central Mass., 17 mi. NE of Springfield; completed 1937, inundating sites of Enfield and other small towns. Impounded in Swift R. valley by Winsor Dam (280 ft. high, 2,640 ft. long; completed 1939) and Quabbin Dike; its water flows E to WACHUSETT RESERVOIR through Quabbin Aqueduct (24.6 mi. long); supplies Boston area. Swift R., issuing from S end, flows c.10 mi. S to join Ware R. just above its junction with Quaboag R.

Quaboag River (kwā'bŏg), S central Mass., rises in W Worcester co., flows c.30 mi. SW and W, joining Ware R. to form Chicopee R. in Palmer town.

Quaddick Reservoir (kwŏ'dĭk), extreme NE Conn., lake (c.2.5 mi. long) near Thompson; formed by dam in small Five Mile R. (tributary of Quinebaug R.). Quaddick village near by.

Quadra Island (kwä'drů) (□ 120; 22 mi. long, 1–10 mi. wide), SW B.C., in Discovery Passage, off NE Vancouver Isl., S of Sonora Isl., 23 mi. NNW of Courtenay, opposite Campbell River; gold and copper mining, lumbering. Granite Bay (N) is chief village.

Quadrasais (kwůdrůzīsh'), village (pop. 1,760), Guarda dist., N central Portugal, 20 mi. SE of Guarda; lumber, grain, potatoes.

Quadrath-Ichendorf (kvädrät'-ĭ'khůndôrf), village (pop. 4,078), in former Prussian Rhine Prov., W Germany, after 1945 in North Rhine-Westphalia, near the Erft, 11 mi. W of Cologne; lignite mining.

Quaedmechelen, Belgium: see KWAADMECHELEN.

Quaiti or **Qu'aiti** (kōōī'tē), premier sultanate (1946 pop. 197,500) of Eastern Aden Protectorate, and one of the Hadhramaut states; ⊙ Mukalla. Extends along Gulf of Aden bet. the Wadi Hajr (W) and the mouth of the Wadi Hadhramaut (E) and inland to the Rub' al Khali; includes the Wadi Hadhramaut, except for middle section held by the Kathiri state. Agr. (millet, lucerne, sesame, fruit) in wadies; stock raising on dry plateau. Tobacco (Gheil Ba Wazir) and honey (Wadi Duan) are main export products. Coastal fisheries also yield dried shark and shark fins for export. Lime burning, tanning, cloth weaving and dyeing are chief industries. Transportation is by coastal road, and the 2 ports of Mukalla and Shihr are linked by highways with the Wadi Hadhramaut. The only protectorate state with a well-organized govt., Quaiti sultanate is divided administratively into the 5 provs. of Mukalla, Shihr, Shibam, Hajr, and Duan. A branch of the Yafa, the Quaiti tribe rose to power in early-19th cent. when it challenged Kathiri supremacy in the Hadhramaut. Feuding continued until the conclusion, under British pressure, of the Quaiti-Kathiri agreement (1918; renewed 1939). Protectorate treaty with Britain was concluded in 1888 and closer adviser relations were established in 1937. Sometimes spelled Ka'aiti.

Quakenbrück (kvä'kŭnbrük"), town (pop. 6,917), in former Prussian prov. of Hanover, NW Germany, after 1945 in Lower Saxony, on the Haase (head of navigation) and 27 mi. N of Osnabrück; rail junction; grain, cattle.

Quaker Bridge, village (pop. c.150), Cattaraugus co., W N.Y., in Allegany Indian Reservation, 18 mi. E of Jamestown; dairy products.

Quaker City, village (pop. 655), Guernsey co., E Ohio, 16 mi. ESE of Cambridge, in dairying and fruitgrowing area.

Quaker Hill, Conn.: see WATERFORD.

Quakertown, borough (pop. 5,673), Bucks co., SE Pa., 13 mi. SE of Allentown; clothing, luggage, metal products; agr. Settled c.1700, inc. 1855.

Quakish Lake, Penobscot co., central Maine, just S of Millinocket; c.3 mi. long. West Branch of Penobscot R. flows through.

Qualicum Beach (kwŏ'lĭkŭm), village (pop. estimate 400), SW B.C., on E Vancouver Isl., on Strait of Georgia, 26 mi. WNW of Nanaimo; farming, lumbering; summer resort.

Quamia, Fiji: see NGGAMEA.

Quanah (kwä'nŭ), city (pop. 4,589), ⊙ Hardeman co., N Texas, near Prairie Dog Town Fork of Red R. and 75 mi. WNW of Wichita Falls; trading, processing center for rich irrigated wheat, cotton, cattle area; mfg. (cottonseed oil, dairy products, plaster, wallboard). Annual Texas-Okla. wolf hunt held near by (Sept.). L. Pauline (fishing, hunting), Medicine Mound (Indian relics) are near. Founded 1886, inc. 1887.

Quandary Peak (kwŏn'dŭrē) (14,256 ft.), central Colo., in Park Range, 14 mi. NE of Leadville. Gold, silver, copper, lead, zinc, molybdenum mines in vicinity.

Quangbinh, province, Vietnam: see DONGHOI.

Quangnam, province, Vietnam: see FAIFO.

Quangnam (kwäng'näm'), town, Quangnam prov., central Vietnam, 5 mi. W of Faifo; old Annamese prov. capital; citadel built 1821.

Quangngai (kwäng'ngī'), town, ⊙ Quangngai prov. (□ 1,600; 1943 pop. 549,900), central Vietnam, in former Annam, on railroad and 125 mi. SE of Hue; sugar cane, corn, cinnamon, tobacco. Sugar refining, salt extraction. Graphite deposits near by.

Quangtri (kwäng'trē'), town, ⊙ Quangtri prov. (□ 1,800; 1943 pop. 192,400), central Vietnam, on railroad and 30 mi. NW of Hue, in forested and agr. region; rice, corn, coffee, pepper, tobacco; cattle raising, sericulture. Iron, gold, and silver deposits near by. Early 19th-cent. Annamese citadel.

Quanguyen (kwäng'-ōōyĕn'), town, Caobang prov., N Vietnam, 12 mi. E of Caobang; trading center; pig and poultry raising. Small fort.

Quangyen (kwäng'yĕn'), town (1936 pop. 3,300), ⊙ Quangyen prov. (□ 1,300; 1943 pop. 188,500), N Vietnam, in Tonkin, port on peninsula W of Along Bay, 10 mi. NE of Haiphong; coal-mining center; phosphate processing, zinc smelting; salt and tannin (from mangrove bark) extraction. Quangyen coal basin (60 mi. long, 10 mi. wide), the chief coal-mining region of Vietnam, extends along S slopes of Dongtrieu Hills on Gulf of Tonkin bet. Dongtrieu (W) and Kebao isl. (E). Leading mining centers are Maokhe, Uongbi (served by Port Redon), Hongay, Campha, Kebao isl. with Port Wallut.

Quantico (kwŏn'tĭkō). **1** Village, Wicomico co., SE Md., 8 mi. W of Salisbury, in truck-farm and timber area; lumber mills. **2** Town (pop. 1,240), Prince William co., N Va., on the Potomac and 29 mi. SSW of Washington, D. C. Site of large U.S. Marine Corps base. In the Revolution, a service base for Colonial vessels here. Inc. 1927; reinc. 1934. Prince William Forest Park is near-by recreational area (□ 26.8).

Quantock Hills (kwŏn'tŭk), ridge, W Somerset, England, extends 9 mi. SE from Bristol Channel, E of Watchet; rises to 1,261 ft.

Quapaw (kwô'pô), town (pop. 938), Ottawa co., extreme NE Okla., 18 mi. WSW of Joplin (Mo.), near Kansas and Mo. lines, in zinc- and lead-mining region.

Qu'Appelle (käpĕl'), town (pop. 539), S Sask., 30 mi. ENE of Regina, S of FORT QU'APPELLE. Dairying center, wheat.

Qu'Appelle River, S Sask., rises near the Elbow of South Saskatchewan R., NW of Moose Jaw, flows 270 mi. E, through Buffalo Pound L. (15 mi. long) and Fishing Lakes, past Fort Qu'Appelle, to Assiniboine R. just over the line in Manitoba, 26 mi. NE of Moosomin. Noted for whitefish.

Quaraí (kwŭrăē'), city (pop. 7,726), W Rio Grande do Sul, Brazil, on Quaraí R. (Uruguay border) opposite Artigas, and 55 mi. SW of Alegrete; rail-spur terminus; custom station; airfield. Livestock center; meat and wool processing, mfg. of jerked beef. Amethyst and agate deposits in river valley. Old spelling, Quarahy.

Quaraím, Brazil: see BARRA DO QUARAÍ.

Quaraí River, Sp. *Cuareim* (kwärān'), border stream bet. Brazil and Uruguay, rises in the Cuchilla Negra SW of Rivera, flows c.160 mi. NW, forming international boundary, past Quaraí (Brazil) and Artigas (Uruguay), to Uruguay R. 4 mi. N of Bella Unión (Uruguay) at meeting point of Argentina, Brazil, and Uruguay. Not navigable. Agates and amethysts found in river bed.

Quarante (kärät'), village (pop. 1,635), Hérault dept., S France, 11 mi. N of Narbonne; distilling, bauxite mining.

Quaregnon (kärĕnyō'), town (pop. 18,699), Hainaut prov., SW Belgium, 4 mi. WSW of Mons; coal mining; electric-power station.

Quarnarolo, Quarnaro, Yugoslavia: see KVARNER.

Quarndon, agr. village and parish (pop. 404), S Derby, England, 3 mi. NNW of Derby; medicinal spring.

Quarnero, Quarnerolo, Yugoslavia: see KVARNER.

Quarouble (kärōō'blŭ), town (pop. 2,757), Nord dept., N France, 5 mi. ENE of Valenciennes, near Belg. border; washing-machine mfg.

Quarré-les-Tombes (kärā'-lā-tōb'), village (pop. 406), Yonne dept., N central France, in the Morvan, 9 mi. SSE of Avallon; lumbering.

Quarry Bank, former urban district (1931 pop. 8,100), S Stafford, England, 8 mi. S of Wolverhampton; mfg. (machinery, pottery, glass).

Quarry Heights, military reservation, Balboa dist., S Panama Canal Zone, just W of Panama city.

Quarryville, borough (pop. 1,187), Lancaster co., SE Pa., 12 mi. SE of Lancaster; mfg. (fertilizers, cement blocks); stone quarries. Settled 1791, inc. 1892.

Quarteira (kwŭrtā'rŭ), town (pop. 1,539), Faro dist., S Portugal, on the Atlantic (S coast), 10 mi. WNW of Faro; fishing port and seaside resort; fish canning.

Quarten (kvär'tŭn), town (pop. 2,625), St. Gall canton, E Switzerland, near S shore of L. of Wallenstadt, 4 mi. WSW of Wallenstadt; cotton textiles, chemicals; cementworks.

Quarter Bach, agr. parish (pop. 3,136), E Carmarthen, Wales, 7 mi. ENE of Ammanford. In N of parish is Gareg Lwyd (2,026 ft.), highest point of Carmarthen.

Quartier Militaire (kärtyā' mēlētâr'), village (pop. 1,089), central Mauritius, in central plateau, on railroad and 6 mi. ESE of Moka; road center; sugar milling, alcohol distilling. Administrative hq. of Central Dist.

Quartier-Morin (kärtyā-mōrē'), town (1950 census pop. 604), Nord dept., N Haiti, near the coast, 5 mi. SE of Cap-Haïtien; sugar, fruit.

Quartu Sant'Elena (kwär'tōō säntā'lĕnä), town (pop. 12,104), Cagliari prov., S Sardinia, near Gulf of Cagliari, 4 mi. ENE of Cagliari; distilleries (wine, liquor, beer), paper mills, brickworks, mfg. (motorcycles, bicycles). Exports cereals, wine. Extensive saltworks of Stagno di Quartu are just S.

Quasqueton (kwä'skwĕtŭn), town (pop. 374), Buchanan co., E Iowa, on Wapsipinicon R. and 9 mi. SE of Independence, in agr. area.

Quassapaug Pond (kwŏ'sŭpôg", -pŏg"), SW Conn., resort lake (c.1 mi. long) just W of Middlebury; summer homes; fishing.

Quatá (kwŭtä'), city (pop. 1,951), W São Paulo, Brazil, on railroad and 45 mi. ESE of Presidente Prudente; coffee and rice processing, distilling.

Quatervals, Piz, Switzerland: see PIZ QUATERVALS.

Quatiguá (kwŭtēgwä'), city (pop. 1,337), NE Paraná, Brazil, on railroad and 35 mi. S of Cambará, in coffee- and potato-growing region; sawmilling, rice and coffee processing.

Quatre Bornes (kä'trŭ bôrn'), residential town (pop. 11,100), W central Mauritius, in central plateau, on railroad and 4 mi. NNW of Curepipe; sugar milling (at Trianon mill); site of govt. bag and rope factory (using Mauritius aloe hemp).

Quatre-Bras, Belgium: see GENAPPE.

Quatre Bras (kä'trŭ brä') [Fr.,=four arms], X-shaped river confluence at PNOMPENH, central Cambodia, of TONLE SAP and Mekong rivers, latter dividing into Mekong proper and Bassac R.

Quatsino (kwŏtsē'nō), village, SW B.C., on N Vancouver Isl., port on Quatsino Sound, 30 mi. W of Alert Bay; salmon fishing, pulp milling, lumbering.

Quatsino Sound, inlet of the Pacific in N Vancouver Isl., B.C., 22 mi. W of Alert Bay, in fishing, copper-mining, and lumbering area; 50 mi. long, 1–7 mi. wide. Main arms are Holberg Inlet (N), Neroutsos Inlet (SSE), and Rupert Inlet (E). Settlements at Port Alice and Quatsino.

Quattro Castella (kwät'trô kästĕl'lä), village (pop. 1,401), Reggio nell'Emilia prov., Emilia-Romagna, N central Italy, 9 mi. WSW of Reggio nell'Emilia; macaroni. Has ruins of 4 castles.

Quay (kwā), county (□ 2,883; pop. 13,971), E N. Mex.; ⊙ Tucumcari. Grain and livestock area; watered by Canadian R.; borders on Texas. Formed 1903.

Quay, town (pop. 70), on Pawnee-Payne co. line, N Okla., 13 mi. NNE of Cushing, in agr. area.

Qubba (kōō'bä), Ital. *Gubba*, village, Gojjam prov., NW Ethiopia, near Anglo-Egyptian Sudan border, 50 mi. NW of Wanbera. Gold deposits near by.

Quchan (kōōchän'), town (1940 pop. 21,683), Ninth Prov., in Khurasan, NE Iran, on Atrek R. and 80 mi. NW of Meshed; major trade and road center; grain, opium, nuts; distillery. Frequent earthquakes. Earthquake of 1893 destroyed old Quchan (8 mi. E), and town was rebuilt on present site. Sometimes spelled Kuchan.

Quddaba, El, or **Al-Quddabah** (both: ĕl kōōd-dä'bŭ), village (pop. 5,864), Gharbiya prov., Lower Egypt, on Baguriya Canal, on Rosetta branch of the Nile, and 8 mi. NNW of Kafr el Zaiyat; cotton ginning.

Qudma, Al (ăl kōōdmä'), town, ⊙ Mausatta sheikdom of Upper Yafa, Western Aden Protectorate.

Quds esh-Sherif, El, Palestine: see JERUSALEM.

Quealy (kwā'lē), town (pop. 147), Sweetwater co., SW Wyo., near Bitter Creek, 4 mi. S of Rock Springs.

Queanbeyan (kwĕn'bēŭn), municipality (pop. 5,033), E New South Wales, Australia, 8 mi. ESE of Canberra; mining center (iron, coal, silver-lead).

Queara River, Bolivia: see TUICHI RIVER.

Quebec or **Québec** (kwŭbĕk', kwēbĕk', kŭ-, Fr. kābĕk'), province (land area □ 523,860, total □ 594,860; 1941 pop. 3,331,882; 1948 estimate 3,792,000), E Canada; ⊙ Quebec. Bounded by N.B., Maine, N.H., Vt., N.Y. (S), Ont. (SW and W), James Bay and Hudson Bay (NW), Hudson Strait and Ungava Bay (N), Labrador (NE), and the Gulf of St. Lawrence (SE). Center of population is the St. Lawrence valley (S). In S part of prov. are the Notre Dame Mts., extension of the Appalachian system; N of the St. Lawrence extends the sparsely populated Laurentian Plateau, rising to 3,150 ft. on Mt. Tremblant, with large potential mineral resources. There are plains along James, Hudson, and Ungava bays. GASPÉ PENINSULA (SE) extends into Gulf of St. Lawrence. Prov. is studded with innumerable lakes; the largest are lakes Mistassini, Minto, Clearwater, Bienville, Kaniapiskau, St. John, Payne, and Abitibi (partly in Ont.). Apart from the St. Lawrence, the chief rivers are the Mistassini, Mistassibi, Peribonca, Saguenay, St. Maurice, Gatineau, Lievre, Moisie, Manicouaga, Richelieu, St. Francis, Chaudière, Ottawa rivers flowing into the St. Lawrence; the Harricanaw, Nottaway, Rupert, Fort George, and Great Whale rivers flowing into James and Hudson bays; and the Leaf, Larch, Kaniapiskau, Koksoak, Whale, and George rivers flowing into Ungava Bay. Prov. includes Magdalen Isls., Anticosti, and several smaller isls. in the St. Lawrence, including Montreal and Jesus isls. and Île d'Orléans. S part of prov. is fertile and intensely cultivated, with dairying, stock raising, growing of hay, clover, tobacco, grains, vegetables, fruit, flax. Lumbering is carried on extensively. Mineral resources include the vast iron deposits in UNGAVA (region annexed 1912), gold in Abitibi co. (Rouyn, Noranda), asbestos (Thetford Mines, Asbestos), mica, titanium (lower St. Lawrence valley), copper, zinc, lead, graphite, garnet, magnesite, quartz, feldspar. Granite, limestone, sandstone are quarried. There is some natural gas on Gaspé Peninsula. Arvida is aluminum-production center. Hydroelectric power is extensively available. Industries include metal smelting, paper, pulp, textile milling, mfg. of clothing, shoes, industrial equipment, machinery, electrical appliances, and a wide range of consumer goods and food products. Quebec and Montreal are its great cities, the latter being the largest city of Canada and commercial center and chief summer port of prov. Other cities are Trois Rivières, Sherbrooke, Hull, Sorel, Lévis, Valleyfield, Grand' Mère, Cap de la Madeleine, Arvida, Chicoutimi, Drummondville, Joliette, Thetford Mines, Granby, St. Hyacinthe, St. Jean, Shawinigan Falls, Rivière du Loup. Jacques Cartier landed in Que. in 1534, and in 1608 Champlain founded prov. of New France and city of Quebec. Prov. was captured by the British in 1629, restored to France by Treaty of St. Germain (1632). It suffered from continuous Indian incursions; systematic colonization was not begun until reign of Louis XIV, under administration of Colbert. Prov. was unsuccessfully attacked by the British (1690 and 1711); Wolfe took Quebec city (1759), and Montreal surrendered (1760). Treaty of Paris (1763) formally transferred New France, now called Canada, to Great Britain. Quebec Act (1774) granted 1st constitution. Prov. was invaded by American Revolutionary Army 1775–76. Constitution of 1791 divided Canada into Upper Canada (Ont.) and Lower Canada (Que.). Friction bet. governors and legislatures led to rebellions in 1837 and 1838. Lower Canada was among founding members of the Canadian Confederation (1867) and became prov. of Quebec. More than ¾ of pop. of Quebec is French-Canadian. French *code civil* is basic law of Quebec.

Quebec or Québec, county (□2,745; pop. 202,882), S Que., on the St. Lawrence; ⊙ Beauport.

Quebec or **Québec,** city (pop. 150,757), ⊙ Que. prov., in S part of prov., on the St. Lawrence, at mouth of the small St. Charles R., 150 mi. NE of Montreal; 46°49'N 71°13'W. Built on Cape Diamond, a high cliff rising to 333 ft. above the St. Lawrence, city is divided into Lower Town and Upper Town. French-Canadian cultural center; seaport with extensive wharves, graving docks, grain elevators. Industries include newsprint milling, metalworking, tanning, brewing, mfg. of shoes, clothing, bricks. There is extensive grain and fur trade. Tourist center. Seat of R.C. archbishop and Anglican bishop, with R.C. and Anglican cathedrals; site of Laval Univ. (founded 1852), Grand Seminary, and Jesuit Col. Among notable features are the Citadel, dominating the city, begun 1823, and summer residence of governor general of Canada; the Basilica, begun 1647, largely destroyed by fire 1922, later rebuilt; Chapel of Notre Dame des Victoires (1688); Quebec Seminary (1663); General Hospital (1692), on site of Récollets monastery, founded 1621; Hôtel-Dieu du Précieux-Sang (1639), one of oldest hospitals in North America; Ursuline convent (1639); Kent House (1636), where French commander reputedly signed surrender to the British in 1759; Talon Brewery (1668); Parliament Bldgs.; Provincial Mus.; and mus. of Laval Univ. Battlefield Park is on the Plains of Abraham, overlooking the St. Lawrence, scene (1759) of the battle of Quebec; Wolfe monument. Sections of the old city ramparts also remain. Site of Quebec, then Indian village of Stadacona, was 1st visited (1535) by Jacques Cartier; Champlain founded French colony here 1608. It was taken by the English (1629), returned to France 1632. Quebec became ⊙ royal prov. of New France (1663). English attempts to take it in 1690 and 1711 failed. City was captured (1759) by the British under Wolfe, who defeated Montcalm on the near-by Plains of Abraham. It was formally ceded to Great Britain by Treaty of Paris (1763). American attempts under generals Richard Montgomery and Benedict Arnold to take Quebec (1775) failed. It became ⊙ Lower Canada 1791. Inc. 1832. For short periods after union of Upper and Lower Canada (1841) and before federation (1867) city was ⊙ Canada. Canadian Confederation was founded here 1867. Quebec airport is in SW suburb of Bergerville. SW of city the St. Lawrence is crossed by Quebec Bridge. Opposite city is Lévis (ferry), terminal of many railroad lines serving Quebec. Quebec was scene (Aug., 1943, and Sept., 1944) of important Allied conferences during Second World War.

Quebec West, residential town (pop. 3,619), S. Que., NW suburb of Quebec.

Quebrabasa Rapids (kĕbrăbä'sä), on Zambezi R. in NW Mozambique, 40 mi. above Tete; extend over 70 mi., interrupting navigation bet. Chicoa (upstream) and Tete. Also spelled Cabrabassa, Kebrabassa, Quebrabaça.

Quebrachal, Argentina: see EL QUEBRACHAL.

Quebracho (kābrä'chō), town (pop. 1,000), Paysandú dept., NW Uruguay, near the Arroyo Quebracho Grande (right affluent of the Queguay), on railroad and 28 mi. NNE of Paysandú; local market; wheat, cattle.

Quebracho Coto (kō'tō), village (pop. estimate 500), NW Santiago del Estero prov., Argentina, on Tucumán prov. border, 55 mi. NE of Tucumán; stock-raising center; lumbering.

Quebrachos (–chōs), village, ⊙ Quebrachos dept. (□ 2,185; pop. 14,721), S Santiago del Estero prov., Argentina, at NE slopes of Sierra de Córdoba, 75 mi. SSE of Loreto; agr. center (corn, wheat, alfalfa, goats, cattle). Limekiln.

Quebrada, La, Venezuela: see LA QUEBRADA.

Quebradas, Las, Guatemala: see LAS QUEBRADAS.

Quebradillas (kābrädē'yäs), town (pop. 2,409), NW Puerto Rico, near the Atlantic, 14 mi. W of Arecibo, in irrigated region (sugar cane, fruit, tobacco); mfg. of cigars.

Quebrangulo (kĭbrăng-gōō'lōō), city (pop. 3,528), central Alagoas, NE Brazil, on railroad and 15 mi. NE of Palmeira dos Índios; ships hides, cotton, watermelons. Formerly called Victoria.

Quechee, Vt.: see HARTFORD.

Quechee River, Vt.: see OTTAUQUECHEE RIVER.

Quechisla (kāchē'slä), village (pop. c.1,000), Potosí dept., SW Bolivia, on E slopes of Cordillera de Chichas and c.40 mi. NNW of Tupiza, on road from Atocha; alt. 11,056 ft. Major mining center (tin, antimony, bismuth). Mt. Chorolque (just S) has tin mines.

Quecholac (kāchōläk'), town (pop. 2,015), Puebla, central Mexico, 37 mi. ESE of Puebla; cereals, maguey.

Quechultenango (kāchōōltänäng'gō), town (pop. 1,442), Guerrero, SW Mexico, in Sierra Madre del Sur, 18 mi. SE of Chilpancingo; cereals, fruit, sugar.

Quedlinburg (kvād'lĭnbōōrk), city (pop. 35,142), in former Prussian Saxony prov., central Germany, after 1945 in Saxony-Anhalt, at NE foot of the lower Harz, on the Bode and 30 mi. SW of Magdeburg; 51°47'N 11°10'E. Agr. center (vegetables, sugar beets, flowers); mfg. of railroad cars, machinery, dyes; metalworking. Site of plant-biological research institute; seed nurseries. Overlooked by castle which housed noted convent (founded 936 by Otto I and his mother Mathilda; secularized 1803). Has 11th–12th-cent. church incorporating remains of 10th-cent. structure with graves of Henry I and his wife Mathilda; 9th-cent. chapel; several early-Gothic churches; Gothic town hall; remains of 14th-cent. fortifications. Fortified 922 by Henry I; was member of Hanseatic League (until 1477). Adopted Reformation in 1539. Passed to Brandenburg in 1698. The poet Klopstock and geographer Karl Ritter b. here.

Queen, Cape, SW extremity of Baffin Isl., SE Franklin Dist., Northwest Territories, at W end of Foxe Peninsula, on Foxe Channel; 64°43'N 78°30'W.

Queen Adelaide Islands, Chile: see ADELAIDE ISLANDS.

Queen Alexandra Range, Antarctica, W of Beardmore Glacier at head of Ross Shelf Ice, in 84°S 169°E. Rises to 14,603 ft. in Mt. Kirkpatrick. Discovered 1908 by Sir Ernest Shackleton.

Queen Anne, village (pop. c.300), Queen Annes co., E Md., 12 mi. NNE of Easton and on Tuckahoe Creek, in truck-farm area; vegetable, fruit canneries.

Queen Annes, county (□ 373; pop. 14,579), E Md.; ⊙ Centreville. On the Eastern Shore; bounded E by Del. line, W by Chesapeake Bay. Eastern Bay and a narrow channel (bridged) lie bet. Chesapeake Bay shore and Kent Isl. Tidewater agr. area (vegetables, fruit, dairy products, poultry, wheat, corn); fishing, oystering; several canneries. Includes many historic structures. Formed 1706.

Queen Bess, Mount (10,700 ft.), SW B.C., in Coast Mts., 150 mi. N of Vancouver; 51°16'N 124°31'W.

Queen Charlotte, village (pop. estimate 250), W B.C., on SE Graham Isl., on Skidegate Inlet, 100 mi. SW of Prince Rupert; port, trade center for lumbering, cattle-raising, potato-growing region. Formerly called Queen Charlotte City.

Queen Charlotte Channel (10 mi. long, 2 mi. wide), SW B.C., E entrance of Howe Sound from Strait of Georgia, 10 mi. NW of Vancouver, separating Bowen Isl. (W) from E shore of Howe Sound.

Queen Charlotte Islands, archipelago of c.150 isls. (pop. estimate 1,600), W B.C., in the Pacific, bet. 52°–54°N and 131°–133°W, separated from Alaska (N) by Dixon Entrance, from B.C. mainland (E) by Hecate Strait, and from Vancouver Isl. (S) by Queen Charlotte Sound. Main isls. are GRAHAM ISLAND, MORESBY ISLAND, and KUNGHIT ISLAND. Heavily wooded Queen Charlotte Mts. extend SW from W Graham Isl., form backbone of Moresby Isl., and terminate on Kunghit Isl.; rise to 4,100 ft. on Graham Isl. Haida Indians form bulk of pop.; chief villages are Massett, Queen Charlotte, Skidegate (Graham Isl.) and Sandspit (Moresby Isl.). Lumbering, fishing (halibut, salmon, herring, shellfish), cattle raising are main occupations. Isls. were visited (1774) by Juan Pérez and (1778) by Capt. James Cook; surveyed (1787) by Capt. George Dixon.

Queen Charlotte Sound, bay of the Pacific in B.C., bet. Vancouver Isl. (S) and Queen Charlotte Isls. (N). In the N it merges with Hecate Strait; in S it narrows to **Queen Charlotte Strait** (60 mi. long, 16 mi. wide), separating NE Vancouver Isl. from the mainland. The strait, part of the inland water route to Alaska, is joined to Strait of Georgia via Johnstone Strait and Discovery Passage.

Queen Charlotte Sound, inlet of Cook Strait, NE S.Isl., New Zealand, connected with Cloudy Bay (S) by narrow channel; c.25 mi. long. Arapawa Isl. (c.15 mi. long, 2 mi. wide) is at entrance. Picton is at SW end.

Queen City. 1 City (pop. 554), Schuyler co., N Mo., near Chariton R., 9 mi. S of Lancaster; grain, livestock (dairying). **2** Town (pop. 511), Cass co., NE Texas, 19 mi. SSW of Texarkana.

Queen Mary, Mount (10,600 ft.), SE B.C., near Alta. border, in Rocky Mts., 40 mi. S of Banff.

Queen Mary Coast, part of Antarctica, on Indian Ocean, W of Wilkes Land; extends from Cape Filchner to E of Denman Glacier, bet. 91°52' and 102°E. Discovered by Sir Douglas Mawson in 1911–14 expedition.

Queen Maud Gulf, S Franklin Dist., Northwest Territories, arm (140 mi. long, 50–100 mi. wide) of the Arctic Ocean, on Mackenzie-Keewatin Dist. shore S of Victoria and King William isls. Connected (W) with Dease Strait and Coronation Gulf, N with Victoria Strait, E with Simpson Strait. At W end of gulf is Melbourne Isl.; other isls. in gulf are Jenny Lind Isl. and the Royal Geographical Society Isls. Queen Maud Gulf forms part of Northwest Passage through the Arctic Archipelago.

Queen Maud Land, part of Antarctica, S of Africa, bet. Coats Land and Enderby Land, bet. 16°30'W and 49°30'E. Discovered 1930 by Hjalmar Riiser-Larsen, Norwegian explorer. The area was claimed 1939 by Norway, which made it a dependency in 1949. U.S. does not recognize claims in Antarctica.

Queen Maud Range, Antarctica, extends SE from head of Ross Shelf Ice, near Beardmore Glacier; rises over 13,000 ft. Discovered 1911 by Roald Amundsen, Norwegian explorer.

Queen River or **Queens River,** S R.I., rises in West Greenwich town, flows c.15 mi. S, past Usquepaug village, to Pawcatuck R. near Kenyon. Sometimes called Usquepaug R. below Usquepaug.

Queens. 1 County (□ 1,373; pop. 12,775), S central N.B., intersected by St. John R. and centered on Grand L.; ⊙ Gagetown. **2** County (□ 983; pop. 12,028), SW N.S., on the Atlantic; ⊙ Liverpool. **3** County (□ 765; pop. 41,142), in central part of P.E.I.; ⊙ Charlottetown.

Queen's, county, Ireland: see LAOIGHIS.

Queens, county (□ 108; pop. 1,550,849), SE N.Y., coextensive with QUEENS borough of New York city.

Queens, borough (□ 108; pop. 1,550,849) of NEW YORK city, SE N.Y., on W Long Isl., bet. Brooklyn borough (W) and Nassau co. (E); coextensive with Queens co.; co. courthouses are at JAMAICA and LONG ISLAND CITY. On NW and N, East R. separates Queens from Manhattan and the Bronx; in NE is Little Neck Bay, an inlet of Long Island Sound. In S is Jamaica Bay, protected from the Atlantic by Rockaway Peninsula. Newtown Creek partly separates Brooklyn from W Queens. Connected with Manhattan by Queensboro Bridge, Queens-Midtown Vehicular Tunnel, and rail and subway tunnels; with the Bronx and Manhattan by Triborough Bridge; and with the Bronx by Hell Gate railroad bridge and Bronx-Whitestone Bridge. Has New York municipal airports (LA GUARDIA FIELD, NEW YORK INTERNATIONAL AIRPORT). Transportation facilities include subways, bus and trolley lines, and Long Isl. R.R. Van Wyck expressway (N-S) links Grand Central Parkway system with New York International Airport. Main E-W highways giving access to E Long Isl. include Interboro Parkway, Northern Blvd., Queens Blvd., Hillside Ave., and landscaped Southern, Grand Central, and Whitestone parkways; Cross Island Parkway (N-S) is an important link. Borough's mfg. (mainly consumer commodities for New York metropolitan area) is concentrated in NW in region of Long Island City. Shipping facilities on East R. and Newtown Creek. Mfg. also at ASTORIA and Jamaica. Has huge railroad yards (at Sunnyside and Long Island City), important express terminals. Mainly residential; among its best-known sections are FLUSHING (seat of Queens Col.), Forest Hills (site of West Side Tennis Club), Kew Gardens, Jackson Heights. Recreational areas include beaches of the Rockaway Peninsula (site of Jacob Riis Park), and Forest, Kissena (kŭsē'nŭ), Cunningham, and Alley Pond Parks, as well as Flushing Meadow Park, where New York World's Fair of 1939–40 was held. Jamaica and Aqueduct race tracks and U.S. forts Tilden (on Rockaway Point) and Totten (on Little Neck Bay) are here. Has several large cemeteries. First settled in 1635 by Dutch; old Queens co. (divided 1898 into Queens and Nassau) was established in 1683. British troops held area throughout the Revolution after battle of Long Island (1776). Several 17th- and 18th-cent. bldgs. remain. Became part of New York city in 1898. Greatest growth came with opening of Queensboro Bridge (1909) and railroad tunnel (1910); coming of subways in 1920s and construction of Triborough and Bronx-Whitestone bridges and Queens-Midtown Vehicular Tunnel in 1930s stimulated further expansion.

Queensberry, Scotland: see LOWTHER HILLS.

Queensboro Bridge, New York city, SE N.Y., cantilever bridge across East R. bet. midtown Manhattan and Long Island City dist. of Queens; crosses Welfare Isl. (reached by elevators from the bridge). Including approaches, c.7,450 ft. long; longest span is 1,182 ft. Opened 1909.

Queensborough, municipal borough (1931 pop. 2,941; 1951 census 3,137), on Isle of Sheppey, N Kent, England, on The Swale and 2 mi. S of Sheerness; mfg. of glass, pottery, glue, fertilizer. Has 17th-cent. town hall and some remains of castle of Edward III.

Queensbury, former urban district (1931 pop. 5,761) now in Queensbury and Shelf urban dist. (1951 census 9,067), West Riding, SW Yorkshire, England, 3 mi. N of Halifax; woolen, worsted milling.

Queens Channel, E inlet of Joseph Bonaparte Gulf of Timor Sea, NW Northern Territory, Australia; 15 mi. wide (E-W; across mouth). Merges with estuary of Victoria R.

Queens Channel, Northwest Territories: see WELLINGTON CHANNEL.

Queenscliff, municipality (pop. 2,386), S Victoria, Australia, on W side of entrance to Port Phillip Bay, 35 mi. SSW of Melbourne; seaside resort.

Queensferry or **South Queensferry,** burgh (1931 pop. 1,798; 1951 census 2,486), NE West Lothian, Scotland, on the Firth of Forth, 9 mi. WNW of Edinburgh; small port and agr. market. Modern church incorporates remains of Carmelite priory, founded 1330. Firth of Forth is crossed here to North Queensferry (Fifeshire) by the Forth Bridge, a railroad bridge 150 ft. above high water (c.5,330 ft. long, has 26 cantilever spans), begun 1883, completed 1889. It is among world's longest and most noted bridges. In Second World War, 1st German air raid on British was made against it. Oct., 1939.

Queensferry, Wales: see CONNAH'S QUAY.

Queensland, second largest state (□ 670,500; pop. 1,106,415) of Commonwealth of Australia; bounded E by the Pacific, N by Torres Strait, NW by Gulf of Carpentaria, W by Northern Territory, S by New South Wales, and indented in SW corner by South Australia; comprises whole of NE part of continent E of meridian of 138°E and N of parallel of 29°S, including adjacent isls.; 1,300 mi. long N–S, 900 mi. E–W; chief port and ⊙ BRISBANE. Major part of coastline (3,236 mi. long) is sheltered by the GREAT BARRIER REEF. Great Dividing Range continues from New South Wales border in S to Cape York Peninsula in N, dividing fertile coastal strip from vast interior plains; highest peak in state is Mt. Bartle Frere (5,438 ft.). Principal river is the Fitzroy; relatively small but important rivers are the Brisbane and the Mary. Great Artesian Basin in interior (□ 376,000) provides water supply for vast stock-raising area. Lakes are generally small, shallow. Roughly half of state is in tropical zone, with jungles on Cape York Peninsula (extreme N). Varied climatic regions: 100°–50°F. (N interior), 85°–45°F. (coastal region; cooled by trade winds). Unevenly distributed rainfall, ranging from 5 in. in extreme SW desert area to 160 in. in parts of NE coast. Timber in numerous mtn. ranges: red cedar, oak, walnut, maple, ebony, rose mahogany. Typical Australian fauna includes various monotremes and marsupials; lungfish and barramundi (fossil types) are peculiar to Queensland. Primarily agr. and livestock-raising state. Produces sugar cane (chief crop), cotton, wheat (produced chiefly on Darling Downs), tropical fruits (pineapples, bananas); sheep, cattle. Gold, copper, silver, lead, zinc mined. THURSDAY ISLAND is center of pearling industry. Great Barrier Reef attracts large tourist trade. Principal cities, each having a port, are Brisbane, ROCKHAMPTON, TOWNSVILLE, CAIRNS. Visited 1770 by Capt. Cook. Formerly part of colony of New South Wales; Moreton Bay dist. used (1824–43) as penal settlement. Queensland became (1859) a separate colony; became (1901) a state of Commonwealth of Australia.

Queens-Midtown Tunnel, New York city, SE N.Y., vehicular tunnel under East R. bet. midtown Manhattan and Long Island City dist. of Queens. Twin 2-lane tubes, 3,055 ft. long under the river, 95 ft. below the surface. Built 1936–40.

Queen's Mine, village, Bulawayo prov., SW central Southern Rhodesia, in Matabeleland, on road and 25 mi. NNE of Bulawayo; gold mining.

Queen's Park, town (pop. 1,599), SW Western Australia, SE residential suburb of Perth.

Queens River, R.I.: see QUEEN RIVER.

Queenston, village (pop. estimate 200), S Ont., on Niagara R. and 4 mi. W of Niagara Falls; hydroelectric-power center. Taken by the Americans and retaken by the British, Oct., 1812. Has monument to General Brock, killed here.

Queenstown, village (pop. 1,067), Essequibo co., N Br. Guiana, on the coast, 35 mi. NW of Georgetown, in tropical forest region; rice and coconut plantations; stock raising.

Queenstown, Ireland: see CÓBH.

Queenstown, borough (pop. 854), ⊙ Lake co. (□ 3,872; pop. 1,389), S central S.Isl., New Zealand, 100 mi. N of Invercargill, on N shore of L. Wakatipu; reached by steamer from Kingston. Chief tourist center of S.Isl.; health resort.

Queenstown, town (pop. 3,598), W Tasmania, 95 mi. WSW of Launceston; rail terminus; copper smelting; silver, gold; sawmills. Rich copper mines at near-by Mt. Lyell.

Queenstown, town (pop. 23,600), SE Cape Prov., U. of So. Afr., 100 mi. NW of East London; center of wheat-growing, wool-producing region; dairying, stone quarrying. Seat of local native-affairs council, established 1937, with jurisdiction over Queenstown dist. (□ 1,371; total pop. 50,294; native pop. 37,520), included in Ciskeain General Council. Site of mental hosp. Airport. Founded 1853.

Queenstown, fishing town (pop. 316), Queen Annes co., E Md., on the Eastern Shore 16 mi. NNW of Easton, and on Chester R. estuary; vegetable cannery, oyster-packing plant. Number of 17th-cent. homes in vicinity.

Queens Village, SE N.Y., a residential section of E Queens borough of New York city; some mfg. (wood products, machinery, knit goods).

Queen Victoria Sea, Russian SFSR: see VICTORIA SEA.

Queets River, W Wash., rises in Olympic Natl. Park SE of Mt. Olympus, flows c.60 mi. SW to the Pacific.

Queguay (kāgwī'), village (pop. 350), Paysandú dept., NW Uruguay, near Queguay R., on railroad and 17 mi. NNE of Paysandú; wheat, cattle.

Queguay Island, in Uruguay R. opposite mouth of Queguay R., Paysandú dept., NW Uruguay, 7 mi. NNW of Paysandú, ½ mi. offshore; 32°9'S 58°10'W; 7 mi. long, 1½ mi. wide. Also called Queguay Grande Isl. Queguay Chico Isl. is near.

Queguay River, Paysandú dept., NW Uruguay, rises in the Cuchilla de Haedo NW of Tambores, flows 140 mi. SW and W to the Uruguay opposite Queguay Isl., 25 mi. NNW of Paysandú. Receives the Arroyo Quebracho Grande. Navigable for c.40 mi. above its mouth. Also called Queguay Grande. The Arroyo Queguay Chico rises 20 mi. W of Tambores, flows 55 mi. WSW to the Queguay 15 mi. NNE of Piedras Coloradas.

Quehuy Island or **Quehui Island** (kāwē') (□ 10.5; pop. 1,967), off E coast of Chiloé Isl., S Chile, 15 mi. SE of Castro; 6 mi. long, 3 mi. wide; potatoes, livestock; fishing, lumbering.

Queich River (kvīkh), Rhenish Palatinate, Germany, rises in Hardt Mts., flows 30 mi. E, past Landau, to the Rhine at Germersheim.

Queilén (kālĕn'), village (1930 pop. 453), Chiloé prov., S Chile, on SE coast of Chiloé Isl., 32 mi. SSE of Castro; minor port and fishing center; potatoes, livestock; timber.

Queimada Islands (kāmä'dŭ), islets in the Atlantic, off São Paulo coast, SE Brazil, c.45 mi. SW of Santos, consisting of Little Queimada and Great Queimada (lighthouse).

Queimadas (kāmä'dŭs), city (pop. 1,670), NE Bahia, Brazil, on Itapicuru R., on railroad and 50 mi. SE of Senhor do Bonfim; chromium deposits.

Queis River, Poland: see KWISA RIVER.

Quel (kĕl), town (pop. 2,536), Logroño prov., N Spain, 7 mi. SW of Calahorra; agr. trade center (wine, cereals, vegetables, sheep); mfg. of olive oil, alcohol, brandy, liqueurs, flour.

Quela (kĕ'lŭ), town (pop. 492), Malange prov., N central Angola, 55 mi. ENE of Malange; coffee, corn.

Quelimane, district, Mozambique: see ZAMBÉZIA.

Quelimane (kĕlēmä'nä), town (1940 pop. 4,451), ⊙ Zambézia prov., central Mozambique, seaport on the Rio dos Bons Sinais (estuary of small Cuácua R.), 10 mi. from Mozambique Channel of Indian Ocean, and 200 mi. NE of Beira; 17°52'S 36°54'E. Airfield. Terminus of railroad to Mocuba (70 mi. N). Exports cotton, sisal, copra, tobacco, corn, tea. Has unhealthful climate (mean annual temp. 85°F.; rainfall 56 in., mostly Dec.–March). Visited 1498 by Vasco da Gama. Became town in 1761. Notorious for its slave trade in 18th-19th cent. Formerly sometimes Quilimane or Kilimane.

Quelite or **El Quelite** (ĕl kälē'tä), town (pop. 1,043), Sinaloa, NW Mexico, in coastal lowland, on small Quelite R. and 25 mi. N of Mazatlán; corn, chickpeas, cotton, tobacco, fruit, vegetables; lumbering (dyewood).

Quellón (kĕyōn'), village (1930 pop. 575), Chiloé prov., S Chile, on SE coast of Chiloé Isl., 45 mi. SSE of Castro; potatoes, wheat; fishing, lumbering. Quellón Viejo (1930 pop. 252) is 6 mi. WSW.

Quellyn, Lake, Wales: see LLYN CWELLYN.

Quelpart Island, Korea: see CHEJU ISLAND.

Queltehues or **Los Queltehues** (lōs kĕltä'wĕs), village (1930 pop. 413), Santiago prov., central Chile, on railroad and 35 mi. SE of Santiago, on Maipo R. (hydroelectric plant).

Queluz (kĭlōōzh'). **1** City, Minas Gerais, Brazil: see CONSELHEIRO LAFAIETE. **2** City (pop. 2,115), extreme SE São Paulo, Brazil, on Paraíba R., at foot of the Serra da Mantiqueira, on railroad and 12 mi. ENE of Cruzeiro; sugar milling, distilling, meat packing; agr. (sugar, rice, corn, coffee).

Queluz, town (pop. 3,791), Lisboa dist., central Portugal, on railroad and 6 mi. WNW of Lisbon, in wine- and fruitgrowing region. Has former royal castle.

Quemada or **La Quemada** (lä kämä'dä), ruined Aztec city, N central Mexico, on central plateau, 33 mi. SW of Zacatecas, NE of Villanueva; alt. 6,535 ft. Ruins, of great value to archaeologists, were abandoned long before coming of Spaniards, who discovered them 1535.

Quemado (kämä'dō), city (1940 pop. 314), Maverick co., S Texas, 18 mi. N of Eagle Pass, in irrigated agr. area of Rio Grande valley.

Quemado, Cerro (sĕ'rō kämä'dō), inactive volcano (10,430 ft.), Quezaltenango dept., SW Guatemala, 3 mi. S of Quezaltenango. Active 1785–1818.

Quemado, El, Argentina: see EL QUEMADO.

Quemado de Güines (dā gwē'nĕs), town (pop. 3,276), Las Villas prov., central Cuba, on railroad and 11 mi. W of Sagua la Grande, in cattle-raising and sugar-growing region. Jerked-beef industry. Near by are the centrals of San Ignacio (WSW) and Resolución (NW).

Quemahoning Reservoir (kwĕmŭhō'nĭng), SW Pa., lake (c.3 mi. long) formed by dam in short Quemahoning Creek, 9 mi. S of Johnstown.

Quemas, Las, Chile: see LAS QUEMAS.

Quemchi (kām'chē), village (1930 pop. 481), Chiloé prov., S Chile, on NE coast of Chiloé Isl., opposite Caucahué Isl., in agr. area (potatoes, wheat, livestock); lumbering, fishing.

Quemoy (kĭmoi'), Mandarin *Kinmen* or *Chin-men* (both: jĭn'mŭn'), chief town (pop. 6,078) of Quemoy isl. (pop. 49,485), in Formosa Strait, SE Fukien prov., China, 15 mi. E of Amoy; rice, wheat; kaolin quarrying. Remained Nationalist-held outpost after Communist conquest (1949) of mainland.

Quemú-Quemú (kāmōō'-kāmōō'), town (pop. estimate 1,500), ⊙ Quemú-Quemú dept. (pop. 9,602), NE La Pampa prov., Argentina, 55 mi. NE of Santa Rosa; rail junction, agr. center (wheat, corn, rye, livestock). Salt deposits near by.

Quenac Island (känäk') (□ 7; pop. 1,166), off E coast of Chiloé Isl., S Chile, 20 mi. E of Castro; 4 mi. long. Lumbering, fishing, stock raising.

Quenast (kŭnä'), town (pop. 2,731), Brabant prov., central Belgium, 5 mi. SSW of Hal; porphyry mining.

Quend (kä), village (pop. 189), Somme dept., N France, 16 mi. NNW of Abbeville, in marshy area; resort of Quend-Plage (destroyed in Second World War) is 4 mi. W on the Channel.

Quenemo (kĕnē'mō), city (pop. 391), Osage co., E Kansas, on Marais des Cygnes R. and 33 mi. SSE of Topeka; livestock, grain.

Queniquea (känēkä'ä), town (pop. 848), Táchira state, W Venezuela, 19 mi. NE of San Cristóbal; coffeegrowing.

Quentin, village (1940 pop. 500), Franklin co., SW Miss., 18 mi. WSW of Brookhaven; lumber milling.

Quenu Island (kä'nōō) (780 acres; pop. 178), Llanquihue prov., S central Chile, in Gulf of Ancud NE of Chiloé Isl., 4 mi. S of Calbuco; 41°50'S 73°9'W; fishing.

Quepém (käpĕm'), town (pop. 1,779), S Goa dist., Portuguese India, 24 mi. SSE of Pangim; local market for rice, timber, coconuts.

Quepe River, Chile: see IMPERIAL RIVER.

Queponco, Md.: see NEWARK.

Quepos (kä'pōs), town (pop. 3,130), Puntarenas prov., W Costa Rica, Pacific port 60 mi. SE of Puntarenas; 9°24'N 84°10'W. Second banana port of Costa Rica, linked by rail with Parrita. Has deepwater quay, rail yards, commercial stores. Developed in 1930s, it supplanted (with Golfito) the port of Limón in banana exports.

Que Que (kwä' kwä'), city (pop. 2,070; including suburbs, 5,083), Gwelo prov., central Southern Rhodesia, in Matabeleland, on railroad and 110 mi. SW of Salisbury; alt. 3,999 ft. Industrial and gold-mining center; metalworks, limekilns. Gold mines in suburbs (Chicago-Gaika and Gold and Phoenix mines). Livestock; agr. (tobacco, peanuts, cotton, corn, citrus fruit).

Quequén (käkĕn'), town (pop. 4,627), S Buenos Aires prov., Argentina, port on the Atlantic at mouth of Quequén Grande R. opposite Necochea (joined by suspension bridge). Trades in cattle and grain; mussel fishing; grain elevator. Mus. of fishes and birds. Beach resort.

Quequeña (käkä'nyä), town (pop. 1,268), Arequipa dept., S Peru, at W foot of Pichu Pichu, 13 mi. SSE of Arequipa; alt. 8,235 ft. Alfalfa, potatoes, grain. Silver, copper deposits near by.

Quequén Grande River (käkĕn' grän'dä), S Buenos Aires prov., Argentina, rises c.10 mi. NE of Juárez in L. Quequén (alt. 890 ft.), flows c.100 mi. SE to the Atlantic bet. Necochea and Quequén. Receives the Quequén Chico (left).

Quequén Salado River (sälä'dō), S Buenos Aires prov., Argentina, formed by several arms rising in Sierra Pillahuincó at alt. of c.600 ft., flows 60 mi. S, past Oriente (hydroelectric station), to the Atlantic 13 mi. S of Oriente.

Querceta (kwĕrchä'tä), village (pop. 795), Lucca prov., Tuscany, central Italy, at SW foot of Apuane Alps, 9 mi. SE of Carrara; marble quarrying and processing.

Quercy (kĕrsē'), region and former countship of SW France, now in LOT and Tarn-et-Garonne depts.; chief city, Cahors. Lies chiefly in the CAUSSES, cut by fertile valleys of the Dordogne, Lot, and Aveyron rivers. Sheep raising, fruit- and wine-growing. A fief of the counts of Toulouse, it was ceded to England (1360), reconquered by France (c.1370), and included in Guienne prov. until 1790.

Querecotillo (kärākōtē'yō), town (pop. 3,758), Piura dept., NW Peru, on coastal plain, on irrigated Chira R. and 4 mi. NNE of Sullana; cotton, corn; carob plantations in surroundings.

Queréndaro (kärĕn'därō), officially Queréndaro de Ocampo, town (pop. 4,503), Michoacán, central Mexico, near SE bank of L. Chapala, on railroad and 19 mi. NE of Morelia; alt. 6,010 ft. Cereals, fruit, maguey, livestock.

Querétaro (kärā'tärō), state (□ 4,432; 1940 pop. 244,737; 1950 pop. 282,608), central Mexico; ⊙ Querétaro. Bounded by San Luis Potosí (N and NE), Hidalgo (SE), Mexico state and Michoacán (S), Guanajuato (W). Mountainous region largely on the central plateau, it slopes toward NE; has high, fertile valleys (S and center) and high ranges (W and NW). Climate is semiarid and generally subtropical; tropical in the N and cooler in the sierras. Drained by Moctezuma R., an affluent of the Pachuca, and by Apaseo R. of Lerma R. system. Querétaro is famed for its opals, but has also rich silver, gold, lead, copper, mercury, and antimony deposits, mined at San Juan del Río, Querétaro, and Peñamiller. Main agr. crops: corn, wheat, alfalfa, sugar cane, beans, peas, tobacco, cotton, sweet potatoes, tomatoes, chili; bananas, dates, pineapples, rice in N. Considerable stock raising. The forested sierras abound in fine timber and medicinal plants. Querétaro city is an important textile-milling and tanning center; the opal industry is concentrated at San Juan del Río. Region was habitat of the Chichimec Indians. It was conquered 1531 by the Spanish but not colonized until 1550. Long administered jointly with Guanajuato, until established as a state in 1824.

Querétaro, city (pop. 33,629), ⊙ Querétaro, central Mexico, on central plateau, on affluent of Apaseo R. and 115 mi. SSE of San Luis Potosí, 115 mi. NW of Mexico city; 20°35'N 100°23'W; alt. 5,974 ft. Rail junction; textile-milling, mining (silver, gold, lead, copper), and agr.-processing center (grain, alfalfa, cotton, sugar cane, tobacco, fruit, livestock). One of Mexico's most important centers for mfg. of cotton goods. Airport. Has federal palace, 16th-cent. cathedral, church and monastery of La Cruz, regional mus., theater. Anc. pre-Aztec city, conquered 1531 by Spanish. Called the "City of Independence" because the uprising under leadership of Hidalgo y Costilla was planned here (1810). The forces of Emperor Maximilian surrendered at Querétaro; and Maximilian, together with his generals Miramón and Mejía, was executed (1867) on a hill near by, now the site of a chapel.

Querfurt (kvâr'fŏŏrt), town (pop. 7,976), in former Prussian Saxony prov., central Germany, after 1945 in Saxony-Anhalt, 18 mi. WSW of Halle; sugar refining, lime processing; agr. market (sugar beets, grain, livestock). Overlooked by 12th-cent. castle. Free imperial city until 1495, then passed to Magdeburg archbishopric. Came to Saxony under Peace of Prague (1635); to Prussia in 1815.

Quérigut (kārēgü'), village (pop. 309), Ariège dept., S France, in E Pyrenees, near the Aude, 17 mi. WNW of Prades; potatoes, lumber.

Quero (kä'rō), town, Tungurahua prov., central Ecuador, 12 mi. S of Ambato, in the Andes; agr. center. Hard hit by 1949 earthquake.

Quero, town (pop. 2,581), Toledo prov., central Spain, in lake dist. along upper Gigüela R., on railroad and 8 mi. N of Alcázar de San Juan; cereals, grapes, chick-peas, sheep. Alcohol distilling; gypsum quarrying, magnesium and sodium-sulphate mining.

Querobamba (kārōbäm'bä), town (pop. 1,190), Ayacucho dept., S Peru, on E slopes of Cordillera Occidental, 55 mi. SSE of Ayacucho; corn, wheat, alfalfa, livestock.

Querocotillo (kärōkōtē'yō), town (pop. 580), Cajamarca dept., NW Peru, in Cordillera Occidental, 18 mi. WNW of Cutervo; wheat, corn, tobacco.

Querqueville (kĕrkvēl'), village (pop. 610), Manche dept., NW France, on N shore of Cotentin Peninsula, 4 mi. NW of Cherbourg; small petroleum port inside Cherbourg breakwater; refinery.

Quesada, Guatemala: see QUEZADA.

Quesada (kāsä'dhä), agr. city (pop. 7,711), Jaén prov., S Spain, in the Sierra de Cazorla, 20 mi. SE of Úbeda; olive-oil processing, flour milling, soap mfg. Trades in cereals, fruit, vegetables, lumber. Saltworks.

Quesería (kāsārē'ä), town (pop. 1,552), Colima, W Mexico, in W outliers of Sierra Madre Occidental, 13 mi. NE of Colima; alt. 4,100 ft. Grain, sugar cane, beans, fruit, livestock. Rail station 7 mi. SE.

Quesnel (kûnĕl'), village (pop. 653), S central B.C., on Fraser R. at mouth of Quesnel R., and 70 mi. S of Prince George; dairying, mixed farming, lumbering, plywood mfg. Gold and diatomaceous earth are found in region.

Quesnel Lake (□ 104), E B.C., in Cariboo Mts., 120 mi. SE of Prince George; 60 mi. long, 1–3 mi. wide. Drained NW of Quesnel R. (64 mi. long) into Fraser R. Just S is Horsefly L.

Quesnoy, Le (lù kānwä'), town (pop. 2,834), Nord dept., N France, 9 mi. SE of Valenciennes; market in fruitgrowing area. Has well-preserved 17th-cent. ramparts, scaled by New Zealand troops in Nov., 1918.

Quesnoy-sur-Deûle (kānwä'-sür-dûl'), town (pop. 2,153), Nord dept., N France, on the Deûle (canalized) and 6 mi. NNW of Lille; beet-sugar refining, flax processing, oleomargerine mfg., tanning.

Questa (kwĕ'stù), village (1940 pop. 1,341), Taos co., N N.Mex., on Red R., near its mouth on Rio Grande, in Sangre de Cristo Mts., and 20 mi. N of Taos; alt. 7,461 ft.; agr., livestock. Large molybdenum mine near by. Part of Carson Natl. Forest just E; Latir Peak 9 mi. NE. Settled 1829 as San Antonio del Rio Colorado, named Questa 1884.

Questembert (kĕstābâr'), village (pop. 1,285), Morbihan dept., W France, 14 mi. E of Vannes; tanning. Has 16th-cent. church and calvary.

Quetalco (kātäl'kō), village (1930 pop. 730), Chiloé prov., S Chile, on E coast of Chiloé Isl., 38 mi. SE of Ancud; potatoes, grain, livestock; lumbering.

Quetame (kātä'mä), village (pop. 987), Cundinamarca dept., central Colombia, 25 mi. SE of Bogotá; alt. 5,023 ft.; sugar cane, coffee, fruit, livestock.

Quetena (kātä'nä), village, Potosí dept., SW Bolivia, on Quetena R. (upper course of Río Grande de Lípez) and 60 mi. SW of San Pablo; alt. 13,681 ft.; alpaca.

Quetiquo Provincial Park (kwĕ'tĭkō) (□ 1,720), NW Ont., on Minn. border, 80 mi. W of Fort William; 55 mi. long, 40 mi. wide; wilderness area; contains numerous lakes e.g., Pickerel, Quetiquo, Kawnipi.

Quetrulauquén (kātrōōloukĕn'), village (1930 pop. 991), Llanquihue prov., S central Chile, on Guar Isl. in Reloncaví Sound, 13 mi. S of Puerto Montt; wheat, potatoes, livestock; fishing.

Quetrupillán Volcano (kātrōōpĭyän'), Andean peak (7,740 ft.), Valdivia prov., S central Chile, in Chilean lake dist., 85 mi. NE of Valdivia.

Quetta (kwĕt'tŭ), city (1941 pop. 36,460, including suburbs and cantonment area 64,476; 1951 pop. including these areas, 82,000), ⊙ Baluchistan prov. and Quetta-Pishin dist., W Pakistan, in Central Brahui Range, 370 mi. N of Karachi; 30°13'N 67°E; alt. c.5,500 ft. Important military station and trade (carpets, wool, fruit, leather goods, hides, grain) center; airport. Engineering and motor (trucks, automobiles) transport repair workshops, arsenal, chemical works, distillery; fruit processing, woolen weaving, flour milling, handicrafts (felt goods, embroideries). Near by are dairy farm and large orchards (melons, grapes, pears, apricots, pomegranates, apples); mulberry growing. Col., military staff col. (established 1907). Coal mined in hills (SE). For centuries a strategic site on trade route bet. Kandahar in Afghanistan and lower Indus valley, via Bolan Pass (20 mi. SE); acquired 1876 by British through treaty with khan of Kalat; severely damaged by earthquake in 1935. Locally called Shal or Shalkot.

Quetta-Pishin (–pĭshēn'), dist. (□ 5,310; 1951 pop. 213,000), NE Baluchistan, W Pakistan; ⊙ Quetta. Crossed NE-SW by Toba-Kakar Range and by N spurs of Central Brahui Range (SE); bounded (N, W) by Afghanistan; drained by upper course of the Pishin Lora (seasonal). Agr. (wheat, millet); fruit (chiefly melons, grapes, pomegranates) grown in SE section. Handicrafts (woolen and carpet weaving, felt goods); camel breeding. Chromite (near Khanozai) and coal (SE of Quetta) mined. Held (10th-11th cent.) by Ghaznevid kingdom; annexed 1879 by British. Pop. 72% Moslem, 18% Hindu, 6% Sikh.

Quettehou (kĕt-ōō'), village (pop. 596), Manche dept., NW France, on E coast of Cotentin Peninsula, 15 mi. ESE of Cherbourg; dairying, fishing.

Quettreville-sur-Sienne (kĕtrüvēl'-sür-syĕn'), village (pop. 327), Manche dept., NW France, on the Sienne and 6 mi. S of Coutances; dairying.

Quetzal, El, Guatemala: see EL QUETZAL.

Queue de Tortue, Bayou (bī'ō kwä" dù tôrt'), S La., rises E of Rayne, flows c.40 mi. SW to Mermentau R. just above L. Arthur; partly navigable.

Queue-du-Bois (kû-dü-bwä'), town (pop. 1,865), Liége prov., E Belgium, 4 mi. E of Liége; coal mining.

Queuille (kû'ē), village (pop. 92), Puy-de-Dôme dept., central France, 14 mi. WNW of Riom; 3 hydroelectric plants on Sioule R. Near-by Fades viaduct is one of France's loftiest, 433 ft. above the Sioule.

Quevedo (kāvä'dō), town (1950 pop. 4,146), Los Ríos prov., W central Ecuador, on upper Vinces R. (Guayas system), on highway to Guayaquil, and 40 mi. NNE of Vinces; agr. center (cacao, sugar cane, rice, tropical fruit); rice milling.

Quévy-le-Grand (kāvē-lù-grā'), agr. village (pop. 911), Hainaut prov., SW Belgium, 6 mi. S of Mons; frontier station near Fr. border. Village of Quévy-le-Petit (pop. 851) is just NW.

Queyras (kārä'), high Alpine valley of Guil R., Hautes-Alpes dept., SE France, extending from the Durance near Mont-Dauphin to Ital. border at Monte Viso. Flanked by 100 peaks of Cottian Alps, it is a favorite center for alpinism. Chief resort: Aiguilles.

Quezada (kāsä'dä), town (1950 pop. 1,283), Jutiapa dept., SE Guatemala, in highlands, 10 mi. W of Jutiapa, near Inter-American Highway, corn, beans, livestock. Also spelled Quesada.

Quezalguaque (kāsälgwä'kä), town (1950 pop. 273), León dept., W Nicaragua, on railroad and 6 mi. NNW of León; sesame, corn, sugar cane. Sugar mills of Corcuera and Polvón SW.

Quezaltenango (kāsältänäng'gō), department, (□ 753; 1950 pop. 184,233), SW Guatemala; ⊙ Quezaltenango. In W highlands, sloping S into coastal plain; bounded by Naranjo (SW) and Tilapa (SE) rivers; drained (E) by the Samalá. Includes Santa María, Zunil, and Carro Quemado volcanoes. Mainly agr. (corn, wheat, beans, fodder grasses); livestock in highlands (N); coffee, sugar cane, tropical fruit in coastal plains (SW). Industries (concentrated at the capital) include textile milling (Cantel), flour milling, and making of ceramics. Main centers lie on Inter-American Highway (Quezaltenango, Salcajá, Ostuncalco) and on railroad (Coatepeque).

Quezaltenango, city (1950 pop. 27,782), ⊙ Quezaltenango dept., SW Guatemala, in W highlands, on Inter-American Highway and 70 mi. WNW of Guatemala; 14°49'N 91°30'W; alt. 7,657 ft. Second largest city of Guatemala; commercial and industrial center of W highlands; textile milling (wool, cotton), flour milling, brewing, mfg. (shoes, cigarettes). Industries powered by hydroelectric station at Santa María. Active trade in agr. products (grain, coffee, sugar cane, tropical fruit). Airport at La Esperanza (NW). Situated among volcanoes, the city was destroyed (1902) by an eruption of the Santa María. Although rebuilt in modern fashion, it did not regain its 19th-cent. importance as a quasi-independent commercial center.

Quezaltepeque (kāsältāpā'kä), town (1950 pop. 1,512), Chiquimula dept., E Guatemala, in highlands, 13 mi. SE of Chiquimula; corn, wheat, livestock; mfg. (mats, baskets, fish nets). Colonial church. Extinct volcano Quezaltepeque (3,940 ft.) is 5 mi. E.

Quezaltepeque, city (pop. 7,300), La Libertad dept., W central Salvador, on railroad and 10 mi. NW of San Salvador, N of volcano San Salvador; alt. 1,361 ft. Commercial center in agr. area; sugar cane, coffee, grain, livestock. Just W is hot-spring resort of La Toma (alt. c.5,000 ft.).

Quezon (kä'zŏn", Sp. kä'sōn), province (□ 4,617; 1948 pop. 416,719), central Luzon, Philippines, bounded E by Philippine Sea, S by Tayabas Bay, Mompog Pass, and Ragay Gulf; ⊙ LUCENA. Includes POLILLO ISLANDS and ALABAT ISLAND. The prov. occupies a long, narrow, mountainous area largely on coast, with Bondoc Peninsula projecting S into Sibuyan Sea. Agr. (coconuts, rice), fishing. Until 1946, called Tayabas prov.

Quezon. 1 Town (1939 pop. 8,656) in San Carlos municipality, Negros Occidental prov., Negros isl., Philippines, 28 mi. SE of Bacolod, near Mt. Canlaon; agr. center (sugar cane, rice). **2** Town (1939 pop. 1,550; 1948 municipality pop. 9,452), Nueva Ecija prov., central Luzon, Philippines, 11 mi. WNW of Cabanatuan; rice, corn. **3** Town (1939 pop. 1,377; 1948 municipality pop. 5,346), on S coast of Alabat Isl., Quezon prov., Philippines, 13 mi. SE of Alabat town; fishing.

Quezon City, city (1948 pop. 107,977) in but independent of Rizal prov., S Luzon, Philippines, just E of Manila; principally residential. Officially replaced (July, 1948) Manila as ⊙ Philippines. Area was formerly a private estate.

Quft, Egypt: see QIFT.

Quiaca, La, Argentina: see LA QUIACA.

Quiaios (kyä'yōōsh), village (pop. 1,971), Coimbra dist., N central Portugal, 5 mi. N of Figueira da Foz, just NE of Cape Mondego on the Atlantic, amidst pine-covered dunes.

Quiapo (kyä'pō), fishing village (1930 pop. 418), Arauco prov., S central Chile, on Pacific coast, 13 mi. NNE of Lebu; also grain, vegetables, livestock.

Quibala (kēbä'lä), town (pop. 263), Benguela prov., W Angola, on road and 80 mi. E of Pôrto Amboim; coffee, sisal, corn, beans.

Quibaxi (kēbä'shē), town (pop. 1,783), Congo prov., NW Angola, on road and 100 mi. ENE of Luanda, in coffee-growing region.

Quibdó (kēbdō'), town (pop. 5,278), ⊙ Chocó dept., W Colombia, c.200 mi. WNW of Bogotá, on right bank of Atrato R., which is navigable for ships from the Caribbean; 5°41'N 76°40'W. Platinum- and gold-mining center in forest region (rubber, tagua nuts, coconuts, lumber); liquor distilling. Airport, administrative bldgs. Founded 1654 by Jesuits. Iron and copper deposits are also near by.

Quiberon (kēbrō'), Breton *Kiberen,* town (pop. 3,786), Morbihan dept., W France, at S extremity of Quiberon Peninsula, 21 mi. SW of Vannes; fishing port and watering place; sardine canning. Point of departure for boats to Belle-Île.

Quiberon Bay, in Bay of Biscay E of Quiberon Peninsula, Morbihan dept., W France; 10 mi. wide, 7 mi. long. Scene of naval engagement (1759) in which Br. Admiral Hawke destroyed Fr. invasion fleet.

Quiberon Peninsula, Morbihan dept., W France, projects 7 mi. into Bay of Biscay opposite Belle-Île, c.20 mi. SW of Vannes. At narrowest point (300 yards), 18th-cent. fort of Penthièvre guards access to S tip, site of Quiberon village. Here, in 1795, an invasion force of Royalists was repulsed by Republicans under Gen. Hoche. During Second World War, units of Ger. army sealed off in peninsula by Allied advance held out until May, 1945.

Quibo Island, Panama: see COIBA ISLAND.

Quíbor (kē'bōr), town (pop. 3,511), Lara state, NW Venezuela, on highway, in NE outliers of great Andean spur, and 20 mi. SW of Barquisimeto; agr. center (coffee, sugar cane, cereals, fruit, livestock).

Quichagua, Sierra de (syĕ'rä dä kēchä'gwä), subandean mountain range in W Jujuy prov., Argentina, 20 mi. SE of Rinconada; extends c.25 mi. NE-SW; rises to c.14,000 ft.

Quiché or **El Quiché** (ĕl kēchā'), department (□ 3,234; 1950 pop. 173,516), W central Guatemala; ⊙ Quiché. In highlands (Sierra de Chuacús, Cuchumatanes Mts.), sloping N into lowlands along Mex. border; bounded E by Chixoy R.; drained (S) by Chixoy and Motagua rivers. Agr. (corn, beans, coffee, sugar cane, tobacco, potatoes); livestock raising; lumbering (N). Main centers: Quiché, Chichicastenango.

Quiché or **Santa Cruz del Quiché** (sän'tä krōōs' dĕl), city (1950 pop. 4,200), ⊙ Quiché dept., W central Guatemala, in W highlands, 50 mi. NW of Guatemala; 15°2'N 91°7'W; alt. 6,250 ft. Market center; corn, beans; livestock raising. Ruins of Utatlán, anc. ⊙ of Quiché Indians, are 2 mi. SE.

Quiches (kē'chĕs), town (pop. 515), Ancash dept., W central Peru, on E slopes of Cordillera Occidental, near Marañón R., 30 mi. N of Pomabamba; corn, sugar cane, coffee.

Quickborn (kvĭk'bôrn), village (pop. 7,262), Schleswig-Holstein, NW Germany, 6 mi. NE of Pinneberg; mfg. (autos, machinery, concrete and leather goods). Has 19th-cent. church.

Quicksand, Ky.: see JACKSON.

Quidico (kēdē'kō), village (1930 pop. 253), Arauco prov., S central Chile, on the Pacific, 45 mi. SSE of Lebu; minor port; grain, livestock. Formerly Morla Vicuña.

Quidi Vidi (kĭ"tē vĭ'tē, kwĭ"tů vĭ'tů), SE N.F., N suburb of St. John's; in Second World War, U.S. Army base was established here.

Quiebra Hacha (kyā'brä ä'chä), town (pop. 1,037), Pinar del Río prov., W Cuba, 4 mi. WSW of Mariel; tobacco, sugar cane, livestock.

Quierschied (kvēr'shēt"), town (pop. 9,409), S central Saar, 8 mi. NNE of Saarbrücken; coal mining; textile milling, glass mfg.

Quieto River, Yugoslavia: see MIRNA RIVER.

Quiévrain (kyāvrē'), town (pop. 5,374), Hainaut prov., SW Belgium, 12 mi. WSW of Mons, near Fr. border; coal mining; coke ovens, beet-sugar refining. Customs station.

Quiévrechain (kyāvrůshē'), town (pop. 4,953), Nord dept., N France, on Belg. border, opposite Quiévrain, 7 mi. ENE of Valenciennes; coal mining, steel milling; mining equipment, glass, faïence. Customs station is at Blanc-Misseron, 1 mi. N.

Quiévy (kyāvē'), town (pop. 2,424), Nord dept., N France, 9 mi. E of Cambrai, in sugar-beet dist.; mfg. of handkerchiefs.

Quigua Island (kē'gwä) (□ 9; pop. 1,084), Llanquihue prov., S central Chile, in Gulf of Ancud, 25 mi. SW of Puerto Montt; 41°45'S 73°13'W; wheat, potatoes, livestock.

Quiha (kē'hä), village (pop. 900), Tigre prov., N Ethiopia on road and 5 mi. E of Makale; cereals, livestock.

Quiindy (kēndē', kůĭndů'), town (dist. pop. 15,593), Paraguarí dept., S Paraguay, 55 mi. SE of Asunción; commercial and agr. center (fruit, corn, cotton, livestock); sugar milling. Founded 1773. Also spelled Quyyndy.

Quijarro, Bolivia: see UYUNI.

Quilá (kēlä'), town (pop. 1,199), Sinaloa, Mexico, on San Lorenzo R. and 28 mi. NE of Culiacán; rail junction; agr. center (chick-peas, corn, sugar cane, tomatoes, fruit). Silver mines near by.

Quilacahuín (kēläkäwēn'), village (1930 pop. 180), Osorno prov., S central Chile, 13 mi. NNW of Osorno, in agr. area (wheat, livestock); dairying.

Quilaco (kēlä'kō), village (1930 pop. 355), Bío-Bío prov., S central Chile, on Bío-Bío R., at W foot of the Andes, and 25 mi. SE of Los Angeles; wheat, rye, wine, cattle; lumbering.

Quilalí (kēlälē'), town (1950 pop. 321), Nueva Segovia dept., NW Nicaragua, 35 mi. ESE of Ocotal; cacao, coffee, sugar, livestock. Rubber.

Quilan, Cape (kēlän'), Pacific headland at SW tip of Chiloé Isl., S Chile; 43°16'S 74°27'W.

Quilaquila (kēläkē'lä), town (pop. c.3,200), Chuquisaca dept., S central Bolivia, 15 mi. WSW of Sucre and on Pilcomayo R.; wheat, barley, vegetables.

Quilca (kēl'kä), town (pop. 208), Arequipa dept., S Peru, minor Pacific port at mouth of Vitor R., 20 mi. ESE of Camaná; well-protected harbor in cotton-growing region; also cereals, wine, cattle. Mica, gold, copper, and coal deposits near by.

Quilca River, Peru: see VITOR RIVER.

Quilengues (kēlĕng'gĭsh), town (pop. 472), Huíla prov., W Angola, on road and 70 mi. NNE of Sá da Bandeira; cattle raising.

Quilicura (kēlēkōō'rä), village (1930 pop. 626), Santiago prov., central Chile, 7 mi. NW of Santiago, in agr. area (cereals, fruit, wine, livestock).

Quilimane, Mozambique: see QUELIMANE.

Quilindaña, Cerro (sĕ'rō kēlēndä'nyä), Andean peak (16,000 ft.), Napo-Pastaza prov., E central Ecuador, SE of Cotopaxi volcano, 40 mi. SSE of Quito; 0°47'S 78°20'W.

Quilino or **Villa Quilino** (vē'yä kēlē'nō), town (pop. 2,551), NW Córdoba prov., Argentina, 85 mi. NNW of Córdoba, in irrigated area (grapes, citrus fruit, livestock); glass factory, sawmills; granite quarries.

Quilino, Sierra de (syĕ'rä dā), pampean mountain range in Sierra de Córdoba, NW Córdoba prov., Argentina, extends c.25 mi. NE from Quilino; rises to c.3,000 ft.

Quillabamba (kēyäbäm'bä), town (pop. 1,700), ⊙ La Convención prov. (□ 40,588; enumerated pop. 30,259, plus estimated 10,000 Indians), Cuzco dept., S central Peru, landing on Urubamba R. and 70 mi. NW of Cuzco (linked by highway). Agr. trading center (sugar cane, cotton, rice, coca, coffee, rubber); thermal springs. Adjoining S is Santa Ana (pop. 201).

Quillacollo (kēyäkō'yō), town (pop. c.25,900), ⊙ Quillacollo prov., Cochabamba dept., central Bolivia, on S slopes of Cordillera de Cochabamba, 7 mi. W of Cochabamba city, with which it is connected by tramway; on Oruro-Cochabamba RR; alt. 8,327 ft. Agr. center (wheat, barley, potatoes, corn) and cattle market; distillery.

Quillagua (kēyä'gwä), village (1930 pop. 228), Antofagasta prov., Chile, on Loa R., on railroad and 50 mi. NE of Tocopilla, in irrigated area (wheat, corn, alfalfa). Airport.

Quillan (kēyã'), town (pop. 3,196), Aude dept., S France, on Aude R. and 12 mi. S of Limoux; felt-hat mfg. center.

Quillayute River (kwĭ'lůyōōt), NW Wash., short stream (c.6 mi. long) of Olympic Peninsula, formed by junction of Soleduck and Bogachiel rivers E of Lapush; flows W to Pacific Ocean, where its estuary is harbor of Lapush.

Quillebeuf or **Quillebeuf-sur-Seine** (kēbûf'-sür-sĕn'), village (pop. 936), Eure dept., NW France, on left bank of Seine R. just above its estuary, and 19 mi. E of Le Havre, surrounded by reclaimed marshlands; cattle raising, fishing. Pilot station for Seine R. navigation.

Quilleco (kēyā'kō), village (1930 pop. 835), Bío-Bío prov., S central Chile, on W slopes of the Andes, 19 mi. E of Los Angeles; grain, wine.

Quillen, Lake (kē'yĕn) (□ 11; alt. 3,215 ft.), in the Andes, W Neuquén natl. territory, Argentina, 20 mi. SW of Aluminé; extends c.12 mi. ENE (1–2 mi. wide) from Chile border. Drained by Quillen R., an affluent of Aluminé R.

Quillingok, Alaska: see KWIGILLINGOK.

Quill Lake, village (pop. 322), S central Sask., near the Quill Lakes, 40 mi. ESE of Humboldt; mixed farming, dairying.

Quill Lakes, 2 lakes (□ 236), S central Sask., 90 mi. N of Regina and just N of Wynyard. Larger lake is 19 mi. long, 14 mi. wide; smaller lake, just E, 18 mi. long, 8 mi. wide, drains E into Assiniboine R. through Whitesand R.

Quillón (kēyōn'), village (1930 pop. 891), Ñuble prov., S central Chile, 25 mi. WSW of Chillán; wheat, wine, vegetables, potatoes, livestock.

Quillota (kēyō'tä), town (pop. 17,232), ⊙ Quillota dept. (□ 759; pop. 81,217), Valparaiso prov., central Chile, on Aconcagua R., on railroad and 25 mi. NE of Valparaiso; fruit- and winegrowing center; vegetable and fruit canning, wine making; rayon mills. Lime beds near by.

Quilmes (kēl'mĕs), city (pop. 105,250), ⊙ Quilmes dist. (□ 121; pop. 132,827), in Greater Buenos Aires, Argentina, seaside resort on the Río de la Plata, and 9 mi. SE of Buenos Aires. Also major industrial center: textiles, glass, paper; oil refineries, breweries. Airport, parks, beaches. Here in 1806 landed a Br. expeditionary force under Gen. Beresford which captured Buenos Aires but held it only for short time.

Quilmes, Sierra de, Argentina: see CAJÓN, SIERRA DEL.

Quilon (kwē'lŏn), locally **Kollam** (kŏ'lŭm), known as *Coilum* (koi'lŏŏm) by Marco Polo, SW Travancore, India, port on Malabar Coast of Arabian Sea, 40 mi. NW of Trivandrum, connected by lagoon-canal system with Alleppey and Cochin ports (N). Exports copra, coir, timber, ilmenite, fish, cashew nuts; mfg. of cotton textiles, coir rope and mats, tiles, textile machinery, tin cans, matches, plywood, pencils; processing of ilmenite, monazite, rutile, and zircon; flour, cashew-nut, and tamarind processing. Commercial col. Industrial suburb of Kundara, 8 mi. NE, has ceramic, chemical, and aluminum works.

Quilpie (kwĭl'pē), village (pop. 640), S central Queensland, Australia, 125 mi. WSW of Charleville, in opal-mining area; rail terminus; livestock.

Quilpué (kēlpwā'), town (pop. 9,167), Valparaiso prov., central Chile, on railroad and 11 mi. E of Valparaiso; resort and agr. center (fruit, wine, grain, cattle; horticulture); mfg. of flour products.

Quimbaya (kēmbī'ä), town (pop. 3,427), Caldas dept., W central Colombia, in Cauca valley, on railroad and 15 mi. SW of Pereira; coffeegrowing center.

Quimbele (kēmbĕ'lä), town (pop. 520), Congo prov., NW Angola, near Belgian Congo border, 125 mi. NE of Uíge; manioc, rice, raffia.

Quimby, town (pop. 398), Cherokee co., NW Iowa, on Little Sioux R. and 9 mi. SSW of Cherokee; rendering and feed-milling plants.

Quime (kē'mā), town (pop. c.7,500), La Paz dept., W Bolivia, 6 mi. SSW of Inquisivi; alt. 9,760 ft. Tungsten mining near by.

Quimichis (kēmē'chēs), village (pop. 1,451), Nayarit, W Mexico, in Pacific lowland, on Acaponeta R. and 70 mi. NW of Tepic; corn, sugar cane, tobacco, cotton, tomatoes, bananas. Cooperative settlement.

Quimilí (kēmēlē'), town (1947 pop. 3,581), E central Santiago del Estero prov., Argentina, 115 mi. E of Santiago del Estero; rail junction, stock-raising and lumbering center; sawmills.

Quimistán (kēmēstän'), town (pop. 503), Santa Bárbara dept., NW Honduras, in alluvial Quimistán valley, near Chamelecón R., 25 mi. WSW of San Pedro Sula; livestock center; sawmilling.

Quimixtlán (kēmēslän'), town (pop. 611), Puebla, central Mexico, in Sierra Madre, 30 mi. NE of Serdán; cereals, maguey.

Quimper (kēpâr'), Breton *Kemper*, town (pop. 17,722), ⊙ Finistère dept., W France, port on drowned Odet R. and 32 mi. SSE of Brest; commercial and industrial center famous for its pottery (Quimper or Brittany ware). Mfg. (agr. machinery, cables, tin cans, stoves, hardware, cigarette paper, lace, soap); cider making, fruit and vegetable preserving, sardine canning. Pottery industry concentrated in suburb of Locmaria. Tourists visit 13th–15th-cent. Gothic cathedral, churches of Locmaria (11th cent.) and St. Matthew (16th cent.), and mus. of Breton art. Quimper was medieval ⊙ Cornouaille.

Quimperlé (kēpârlā'), Breton *Kemperle*, town (pop. 7,275), Finistère dept., W France, on small Laïta R. and 27 mi. ESE of Quimper; commercial and industrial center; mfg. (cigarette paper, agr. equipment, tin cans, cider); food preserving, printing. Has restored 11th-cent. Romanesque church.

Quimsa Cruz, Cordillera de, Bolivia: see TRES CRUCES, CORDILLERA DE.

Quinalasag Island (kēnäläsäg') (□ 13; 1939 pop. 652), Camarines Sur prov., Philippines, in Philippine Sea, 26 mi. NW of Rungus Point, SE Luzon; 6 mi. long, 3 mi. wide. Fishing.

Quinamávida (kēnämä'vēdä), village (1930 pop. 334), Linares prov., S central Chile, in Andean foothills, 13 mi. NE of Linares; resort; thermal springs.

Quinault Lake (kwĭnôlt'), W Wash., in Olympic Natl. Forest, 35 mi. N of Hoquiam; c.4 mi. long. Center of Quinault Lake Recreational Area and site of Quinault, resort village. Receives from NE and discharges SW the **Quinault River,** c.75 mi. long, rising SE of Mt. Olympus and flowing SW to Pacific Ocean near Taholah.

Quinchao, department, Chile: see ACHAO.

Quinchao Island (kēnchou') (□ 46; pop. 7,276), off E coast of Chiloé Isl., S Chile, 7 mi. E of Castro; 19 mi. long, 1–8 mi. wide. Village of ACHAO on its E coast. Agr. area (potatoes, wheat, stock); fishing, lumbering.

Quinche (kēn'chä), village, Pichincha prov., N central Ecuador, in the Andes, on Quito-Ibarra RR and 16 mi. ESE of Quito. Its shrine is visited annually by many pilgrims.

Quinches (kēn'chĕs), town (pop. 1,644), Lima dept., W central Peru, in Cordillera Occidental, 15 mi. NW of Yauyos; potatoes, grain, livestock.

Quinchía (kēnchē'ä), town (pop. 2,796), Caldas dept., W central Colombia, in Cauca valley, 23 mi. NW of Manizales; coffeegrowing and coal mining. Salt deposits near by.

Quincy. **1** (kwĭn'sē) Village (pop. 1,330), ⊙ Plumas co., NE Calif., 70 mi. NW of Reno (Nev.), in the Sierra Nevada; lumber milling, copper and gold mining, stock grazing; winter sports. Hq. for Plumas Natl. Forest. **2** (kwĭn'sē) City (pop. 6,505), ⊙ Gadsden co., NW Fla., near Ga. line, 20 mi. WNW of Tallahassee; cigar-mfg. and tobacco-marketing center; also processes fuller's earth from near-by mines, makes boxes and other wood products. Founded c.1825. **3** (kwĭn'sē) City (pop. 41,450), ⊙ Adams co., W Ill., on bluff above the Mississippi (bridged here), c.100 mi. W of Springfield; industrial, trade, and distributing center (air, river, rail, highway) for wide agr. area. Mfg.: pumps, drills, and other machinery; farm machinery, flour, poultry-farm equipment, auto bodies, radio equipment, furniture, wallboard, paper products, clothing, optical goods, pharmaceuticals, insecticides, beverages, feed. Limestone quarries. Quincy Col., a natl. cemetery, and state soldiers' and sailors' home are here. Has co. historical mus. Settled 1822 on site of Indian village; inc. 1839. An important river port in mid-19th cent.; scene of several proslavery-abolitionist struggles. A Lincoln-Douglas debate was held here, 1858. **4** (kwĭn'sē) Town (1940 pop. 46), Adams co., SW Iowa, 4 mi. NW of Corning, in bituminous-coal-mining region. **5** (kwĭn'zē) Mfg. city (pop. 83,835), Norfolk co., E Mass., on Quincy Bay (arm of Boston Bay) and 8 mi. SSE of Boston; granite quarrying (begun 1750), shipbuilding (developed in First World War); machinery, foundry and rubber products, hardware, chemicals, paints, printing, bakery products, beverages, building supplies, soap. First (horse-drawn) railroad in U.S. was built here (1826) to haul granite. Adams Mansion Natl. Historic Site (4 acres; established 1946) preserves home (oldest portion built 1731) of Adams family, 4 generations of whom (including Presidents John and John Quincy Adams, and Charles Francis, Henry, and Brooks Adams) lived here. John and John Quincy Adams are buried in Old Stone Temple. Settled 1625 by Thomas Morton and later known as Merrymount, set off from Braintree 1792, inc. as city 1888. Includes villages of Squantum (naval air station) and Wollaston. **6** (kwĭn'sē) Village (pop. 1,527), Branch co., S Mich., 6 mi. E of Coldwater, in farm area; mfg. (cereal foods, flour, feed, cement); marl and clay deposits. Resort, with small lakes near by. Settled 1833, inc. 1858. **7** (kwĭn'sē) Village (pop. 616), Logan co., W central Ohio, 12 mi. WSW of Bellefontaine, and on Great Miami R., in agr. area. **8** (kwĭn'sē) Town (pop. 804), Grant co., central Wash., 15 mi. SW of Ephrata, in Columbia basin agr. region.

Quincy Adams, Mount (13,560 ft.), on Alaska-B.C. border, in Fairweather Range, 5 mi. E of Mt. Fairweather, 120 mi. WNW of Juneau; 58°54'N 137°27'W.

Quincy Bay, Mass.: see BOSTON BAY.

Quinden (kēn'dĕn), village (pop. 1,518), Cajamarca dept., NW Peru, in Cordillera Occidental, on Pacasmayo–Chilete RR and 12 mi. SW of San Miguel; sugar cane, corn, wheat; cattle raising.

Quindío, Nevado (nävä'dō kēndē'ō), Andean peak (16,900 ft.), W central Colombia, on Caldas Tolima dept. border, in Cordillera Central, just W of Nevado del Tolima, 20 mi. NW of Ibagué; 4°42'N. Historic Quindío Pass (alt. 11,434 ft.), at S foot of the peak, was from colonial times the route over the cordillera here. S of the pass is another pass (10,760 ft.) carrying part of the Pan American Highway (opened 1939) bet. Ibagué and Armenia, linking Bogotá with Buenaventura.

Quinebaug River (kwĭ'nùbôg"), in Mass. and Conn., rises in ponds NW of Sturbridge, Mass.; flows c.80 mi. SE and S, through Conn., past Putnam, Danielson, Plainfield (dam here), and Jewett City, to Shetucket R. just NE of Norwich. On its upper reaches in Mass. are sites of East Brimfield Dam and Westville Dam, both for flood control.

Quines (kē'nĕs), town (pop. estimate 1,000), N San Luis prov., Argentina, at N foot of Sierra de San Luis, on railroad and 80 mi. NNE of San Luis; resort; lumbering and agr. center (alfalfa, corn, wine, livestock). Tin mines near by.

Quingey (kēzhā'), village (pop. 820), Doubs dept., E France, on the Loue and 11 mi. SW of Besançon; silverware mfg.

Quinhagak, Alaska: see KWINHAGAK.

Quinhon (kwē'nyŭn), town (1936 pop. 10,000), ⊙ Binhdinh prov. (□ 2,300; 1943 pop. 780,200), central Vietnam, in Annam, port (opened 1874 to Fr. trade) on South China Sea, on spur of main Saigon-Hanoi RR and 220 mi. SSE of Hue. Coastal and fishing port; salt extraction.

Quinigua, Dominican Republic: see SANTIAGO, city.

Quiniluban Islands (kēnēlōōbän'), small group in N Cuyo Isls., Palawan prov., Philippines.

Quinlan. 1 Town (pop. 107), Woodward co., NW Okla., 19 mi. E of Woodward, in livestock and grain area. **2** City (pop. 599), Hunt co., NE Texas, 16 mi. S of Greenville, in agr. area.

Quinn, town (pop. 214), Pennington co., SW central S.Dak., 55 mi. E of Rapid City.

Quinnesec (kwĭ'nùsĕk"), village (1940 pop. 540), Dickinson co., SW Upper Peninsula, Mich., 4 mi. SE of Iron Mountain, near Menominee R.; mfg. (wood and paper boxes).

Quinnipiac River (kwĭ'nĭpēăk"), Conn., rises near New Britain, flows c.50 mi. generally S, past Southington, Meriden, and Wallingford, to New Haven Harbor at New Haven.

Quinn River, NW Nev., rises in N Humboldt co. near Oregon line, flows c.110 mi. generally SW to disappear in Black Rock Desert. Receives Kings R. NE of Jackson Mts.

Quinsam Lake (kwĭn'sùm), on central Vancouver Isl., SW B.C., 25 mi. SW of Campbell River; iron mining.

Quinsigamond, Lake (kwĭnsĭg'ùmŏnd), central Mass., just E of Worcester; c.7 mi. long. Boat races held here.

Quinta de Tilcoco, Chile: see TILCOCO.

Quintana (kēntä'nù), city, W São Paulo, Brazil, on railroad and 25 mi. WNW of Marília, in pioneer cotton and coffee zone.

Quintana de la Serena (kēntä'nä dhā lä sārā'nä), town (pop. 6,433), Badajoz prov., SW Spain, 6 mi. W of Castuera; agr. center (cereals, vegetables, olives, livestock); tanning, flour milling, mfg. of textile goods. Has granite quarries.

Quintanar de la Orden (kēntänär' dhā lä ôr'dhĕn), town (pop. 9,448), Toledo prov., central Spain, in New Castile, 55 mi. ESE of Toledo; agr., trading, and processing center in upper La Mancha; cereals, anise, saffron, grapes, cumin, sheep. Alcohol, brandy, and vermouth distilling; cheese and meat processing, flour milling, tanning; mfg. of cement articles, woolen goods, hats, shoes, soap, candlesticks. Hydroelectric plant. Historic town which belonged to Santiago order.

Quintanar de la Sierra (syĕ'rä), town (pop. 2,425), Burgos prov., N Spain, 34 mi. WNW of Soria; lumbering, stock raising; hunting. Flour- and sawmills. Fish hatchery.

Quintanar del Rey (dhĕl rā'), town (pop. 4,351), Cuenca prov., E central Spain, 24 mi. N of Albacete; agr. center (cereals, vegetables, olives, almonds, grapes, saffron, stock). Also trades in lumber, pine cones. Alcohol and liquor distilling.

Quintana Redonda (kēntä'nä rādōn'dä), town (pop. 743), Soria prov., N central Spain, on railroad and 12 mi. SW of Soria; grain, potatoes, livestock; stone quarrying, lumbering.

Quintana Roo (rō'), territory (□ 19,630; 1940 pop. 18,752; 1950 pop. 26,996), SE Mexico, on E Yucatan Peninsula, on the Caribbean; ⊙ CHETUMAL. Bordered by states of Yucatan and Campeche (W), by Guatemala (SW), and by Br. Honduras (Río Hondo; S). Tropical lowlands largely covered by jungle, with much rainfall, especially in E. The coast is indented by large bays and dotted by numerous isls. and reefs, the largest being Cozumel Isl. Although the area has great fertility, it is wild and undeveloped; main products are henequen, chicle, cotton, tobacco, coffee, copra, tropical fruit, rubber, dyewood, and hardwood. Sea yields fish, sponge, turtles. Saltworks on Mujeres Isl. Chetumal, on Chetumal Bay, is its main port and trading center. The Spanish made their 1st landing (1517) on Mex. soil at Cape Catoche; but the area, largely populated by Mayas, could not be conquered. Formerly a part of Yucatan; became a territory 1902.

Quintana Roo, town (pop. 693), Yucatan, SE Mexico, 29 mi. NW of Valladolid; henequen, sugar cane.

Quintanilla de Abajo (kēntänē'lyä dhā ävä'hō), town (pop. 1,403), Valladolid prov., N central Spain, on Duero (Douro) R. and 18 mi. ESE of Valladolid; cereals, wine.

Quintanilla del Agua (dhĕl ä'gwä), town (pop. 955), Burgos prov., N Spain, on Arlanza R. and 21 mi. S of Burgos; grapes, cereals, vegetables, truck produce, fruit, sheep.

Quinte, Bay of (kwĭn'tē), arm of L. Ontario, SE Ont., separated from main body of lake by peninsula of Prince Edward co. Including its approach of Adolphus Reach it is 60 mi. long, 1–6 mi. wide. On N shore are Deseronto, Belleville, and Trenton. At head it is separated from L. Ontario by 1-mi.-wide isthmus, cut by Murray Canal. Receives Trent R. at Trenton.

Quinter, city (pop. 741), Gove co., W central Kansas, 32 mi. E of Oakley, in grain and cattle region. State park is N, on Saline R.

Quintero (kēntā'rō), town (pop. 2,047), Valparaiso prov., central Chile, 19 mi. NNE of Valparaiso; rail terminus and beach resort. Naval air base.

Quintin (kētē'), town (pop. 2,229), Côtes-du-Nord dept., W France, 10 mi. SW of Saint-Brieuc; cloth mfg., poultry and cattle raising.

Quinto (kēn'tō), town (pop. 2,170), Saragossa prov., NE Spain, near the Ebro, 25 mi. SE of Saragossa; cement mfg.; cereals, sugar beets, fruit,

Quinto, Río (rē'ō kēn'tō), river, N central Argentina, rises in central San Luis prov. NNE of San Luis city, flows c.175 mi. SE, past Mercedes, into Córdoba prov., where it loses itself in swamps.

Quinton. 1 Village (pop. c.500), Salem co., SW N.J., on Alloway Creek and 3 mi. SE of Salem. Monument marks Revolutionary battle site. **2** Town (pop. 951), Pittsburg co., SE Okla., 26 mi. ENE of McAlester, in agr. and coal-mining region.

Quinwood, town (pop. 838), Greenbrier co., SE W.Va., 22 mi. NNW of Lewisburg.

Quinzano d'Oglio (kwēntsä'nô dô'lyô), town (pop. 4,548), Brescia prov., Lombardy, N Italy, near Oglio R., 12 mi. N of Cremona; hosiery mfg.

Quinze, Lac des (läk dā kĕz'), lake (□ 55), SW Que., 80 mi. N of North Bay; 35 mi. long.

Quinze, Rapide des (räpēd'), torrential stream in W Que., issues from L. des Quinze at Angliers, flows 20 mi. W to L. Timiskaming. Along course are 15 waterfalls. Near Angliers is large barrage and hydroelectric station, supplying Rouyn-Noranda mining region.

Quionga (kyông'gä), Ger. *Kionga*, village, Niassa prov., northernmost Mozambique, on Indian Ocean, bet. mouth of Ruvuma R. (Tanganyika border; just NW) and Cape Delgado (SE); 10°35'S 40°33'E. Formerly part of German East Africa, it passed to Mozambique after First World War.

Quiotepec (kyōtāpĕk'), town (pop. 1,680), Oaxaca, S Mexico, in valley of Sierra Madre del Sur, on railroad and 7 mi. N of Cuicatlán; cereals, sugar cane, tobacco, fruit. Rich archaeological remains near by.

Quiotepec River, Mexico: see TUXTEPEC RIVER.

Quipapá (kēpùpä'), city (pop. 2,357), E Pernambuco, NE Brazil, on railroad and 90 mi. SW of Recife; sugar, coffee, corn.

Quipungo (kēpōōng'gō), town (pop. 987), Huíla prov., SW Angola, on road and 75 mi. E of Sá da Bandeira; cattle raising. Airfield.

Quiquijana (kēkēhä'nä), town (pop. 1,618), Cuzco dept., S Peru, on railroad, on Vilcanota R. and 35 mi. SE of Cuzco; grain, alfalfa, vegetables; mfg. of woolen goods. Coal deposits.

Quiraing or **Quirang** (kwērăng'), mountain (1,779 ft.) near N end of Isle of Skye, Hebrides, Scotland, 16 mi. N of Portree. Its summit is plateau bordered by fantastic basalt formations.

Quirang, Scotland: see QUIRAING.

Quirauk Mountain, Md.: see SOUTH MOUNTAIN.

Quiriego (kēryā'gō), town (pop. 793), Sonora, NW Mexico, on affluent of Mayo R. and 105 mi. ESE of Guaymas; stock raising (cattle, hogs, horses).

Quiriguá (kērēgwä'), village (pop. 450), Izabal dept., E Guatemala, near Motagua R., on railroad and 1 mi. NE of Los Amates, in banana area; hosp. Just NW is village of Quiriguá Viejo [Sp.,=old Quiriguá], site of extensive Maya ruins, discovered 1840.

Quirihue (kērē'wā), town (pop. 3,034), ⊙ Itata dept. (□ 920; pop. 33,932), Ñuble prov., S central Chile, in coastal range 35 mi. NW of Chillán; agr. center (wine, wheat, corn, potatoes, vegetables, sheep); lumbering, flour milling.

Quirimán (kērēmän'), village, Guanacaste prov., NW Costa Rica, on Quirimán R. (right affluent of Nosara R.) and 6 mi. W of Nicoya; grain; stock raising, lumbering.

Quirinal Hill (kwĭ'rĭnùl, kwĭrī'nùl), one of the 7 hills of Rome.

Quirindi (kwŭrĭn'dī), municipality (pop. 2,628), E central New South Wales, Australia, 115 mi. NW of Newcastle; coal-mining and dairying center.

Quirinópolis (kērēnô'pōōlēs), city (pop. 673), S Goiás, central Brazil, 50 mi. SE of Rio Verde; livestock.

Quiriquina Island (kērēkē'nä), at mouth of Concepción Bay of the Pacific, Concepción prov., S central Chile, 10 mi. N of Concepción city; 3 mi. long, 1½ mi. wide.

Quiriquire (kērēkē'rā), town (pop. 3,067), Monagas state, NE Venezuela, 17 mi. N of Maturín; oil wells, linked by pipe line with Caripito. Airfield. Petroleum field was opened 1928.

Quiroga (kērō'gä), town (pop. 3,009), Michoacán, central Mexico, on N shore of L. Pátzcuaro, 25 mi. W of Morelia; resort; fishing and agr. center (corn, fruit, stock).

Quirón, Salar, Argentina: see POCITOS, SALAR.

Quirós (kērōs'), mining area, Oviedo prov., NW Spain, 18 mi. SSW of Oviedo, with coal and iron mines. Chief town, Bárzana (pop. 279).

Quirpon Island (kär'pùn) (□ 4; pop. 162), just off NE extremity of N.F., 20 mi. E of Cape Norman; 51°37'N 55°27'W. Isl. is 4 mi. long, 2 mi. wide, rises to 505 ft. Fishing. A N extremity is Cape Bauld, with lighthouse (51°39'N 55°26'W). On mainland, 2 mi. WSW of isl., is fishing settlement of Quirpon (pop. 145), site of govt. bait depot.

Quirquinchos, Los, Argentina: see LOS QUIRQUINCHOS.

Quirusillas (kērōōsē'yäs), town (pop. c.2,100), Santa Cruz dept., central Bolivia, in E foothills of Cordillera de Cochabamba, 12 mi. S of Samaipata; grain.

Quiruvilca (kērōōvēl'kä), town (pop. 4,018), Libertad dept., NW Peru, in Cordillera Occidental, 13 mi. NW of Santiago de Chuco, 50 mi. ENE of Trujillo; alt. 12,960 ft. Major copper-mining center; mining also at SHOREY (WSW).

Quishuarcancha (kēsh-wärkän'chä), village (pop. 54), Pasco dept., central Peru, in the Nudo de Pasco, 15 mi. NW of Cerro de Pasco; coal deposits.

Quisipicanchi, province, Peru: see URCOS.

Quisiro (kēsē'rō), town (pop. 850), Zulia state, NW Venezuela, in Maracaibo lowlands, 20 mi. NE of Altagracia; corn, coconuts, bananas, goats. Oil wells near by.

Quismondo (kēzmōn'dō), town (pop. 1,821), Toledo prov., central Spain, 24 mi. NW of Toledo; cereals, grapes, vegetables, olives, livestock.

Quisqueya (kēskā'ä), locality, San Pedro de Macorís prov., SE Dominican Republic, 10 mi. NW of San Pedro de Macorís; sugar mill.

Quissac (kwēsäk'), village (pop. 1,400), Gard dept., S France, on the Vidourle and 15 mi. SSW of Alès; cotton-hosiery and cement mfg.

Quissamã (kēsùmä'), town (pop. 1,257), E Rio de Janeiro state, Brazil, 25 mi. SSW of Campos; rail-spur terminus; sugar milling.

Quissanga (kēsäng'gä), village, Niassa prov., N Mozambique, on Mozambique Channel opposite Ibo Isl., 40 mi. N of Pôrto Amélia. Formerly spelled Kissanga.

Quissico (kēsē'kō), village, Sul do Save prov., SE Mozambique, on road and 75 mi. SW of Inhambane; coffee, manioc.

Quissol (kēsōl'), town, Malange prov., N central Angola, on road and 10 mi. SE of Malange, in sugar-growing area.

Quistello (kwēstĕl'lō), village (pop. 2,402), Mantova prov., Lombardy, N Italy, on Secchia R. and 14 mi. SE of Mantua; hydraulic-pump mfg.

Quitandinha, Brazil: see PETRÓPOLIS.

Quitaque (kĭ'tùkwä), city (pop. 647), Briscoe co., NW Texas, 38 mi. ENE of Plainview, just below Cap Rock escarpment (W); cotton, cattle, grain; cotton gins.

Quita Sueño Bank (kētä swā'nyō), coral reef in the Caribbean c.140 mi. off Mosquito Coast of Nicaragua, belonging to Colombia, in SAN ANDRÉS Y PROVIDENCIA intendancy; 14°30'N 81°8'W. Claimed 1919 by U.S.

Quithlook, Alaska: see KWETHLUK.

Quitilipi (kētēlē'pē), town (1947 pop. 3,344), S central Chaco natl. territory, Argentina, on railroad and 16 mi. ESE of Presidencia Roque Sáenz Peña; agr. and lumbering center. Vegetable-oil factory (peanut, spurge, cotton), sawmills, cotton gins. Agr.: cotton, corn, peanuts, spurge, livestock.

Quitman. 1 County (□ 170; pop. 3,015), SW Ga.; ⊙ Georgetown. Bounded W by Ala. line, formed here by Chattahoochee R. Coastal plain agr. (cotton, corn, peanuts, pecans) and sawmilling area. Formed 1858. **2** County (□ 412; pop. 25,885), NW Miss., in rich lowland cotton-growing area; ⊙ Marks. Drained by Coldwater and Tallahatchie rivers. Farm-products and timber processing. Formed 1877.

Quitman. 1 Town (pop. 345), Cleburne co., N central Ark., 24 mi. NNE of Conway, in agr. area. **2** City (pop. 4,769), ⊙ Brooks co., S Ga., 17 mi. WSW of Valdosta; tobacco market and processing center; milling (cotton, lumber, feed), food canning, meat packing. Inc. 1859. **3** Village (pop. 204), Jackson parish, N central La., 38 mi. WSW of Monroe, in agr. and lumbering area; wood products. **4** Town (pop. 1,817), ⊙ Clarke co., E Miss., 23 mi. S of Meridian, and on Chickasawhay R., in agr. and timber area; lumber milling, hosiery mfg. State park near by. **5** Town (pop. 135), Nodaway co., NW Mo., on Nodaway R. and 11 mi. W of Maryville. **6** Village (pop. 927), ⊙ Wood co., NE Texas, 31 mi. NNW of Tyler; trade point in oil, cotton area; oil refining, cotton ginning; nursery stock.

Quitman Mountains, Hudspeth co., extreme W Texas, range extending SSE from point W of Sierra Blanca c.30 mi. to the Rio Grande; highest point, 6,687 ft.

Quito (kē'tō), city (1950 pop. 212,873), ⊙ Ecuador and Pichincha prov., N central Ecuador, high in the Andes, at S foot of Pichincha volcano, on Pan American Highway, on railroad from Guayaquil (170 mi. SW, direct), and 450 mi. SW of Bogotá, Colombia; 0°13'S 78°30'W; alt. c.9,350 ft. Although just S of the equator, it has a temperate, pleasant climate with few seasonal changes, cool nights and almost daily showers; mean temp. 54.6°F. Here converge major roads and natl. and international air lines. The 2d largest city of the country, and its cultural and political metropolis, it is situated in an intramontane hollow, towered over by majestic, snow-capped peaks. The area produces cereals, fruit, sugar cane, vegetables, livestock, and dairy products. It is the principal textile center of Ecuador (cotton, woolen, and silk goods, hosiery, embroidery, lace, carpets). Among its other industries are brewing, ice making, flour milling, tanning; mfg. of leather articles, tagua-nut buttons, furniture, ceramics, cement, gold and silver objects, light-iron products, sisal-fiber goods, soap, chemicals, chocolate. Quito, one of the R.C. centers in the Western Hemisphere, is an archbishopric. Its fine cultural tradition is attested to by its cathedral, the Central Univ., (founded 1787), a natl. library, observatory, Ecuadorian–North American Center of Cultural Relations, natl. mus. of fine arts, the Eloy Alfaro Military Acad., and the oldest art school of the continent (started shortly after the conquest). The picturesque city abounds in beautiful parks, flower gardens, verdant hills, and wide plazas. Its colonial character has been almost entirely retained. Narrow cobbled streets with over-hanging balconies, the ornate architecture of more than 50 old churches with fine sculpture and paintings, and native markets contribute to the local color. The N part of the city contains the modern residential area. The city probably dates back to prehistoric times. Once occupied by the Quitu Indians, it was captured (in 15th cent.) by the Incas, who made it the fortified capital of their "Kingdom of Quito." Benalcázar, a lieutenant of Pizarro, entered Quito (1533) and formally took possession (1534) for the Sp. crown, though the ruined city had to be rebuilt. During the colonial period it became (1563–64) the administrative center of the Quito presidency under the Peruvian viceroyalty; inc. 1721 into Viceroyalty of New Granada. After an unsuccessful revolt in 1809, Quito remained under Sp. control until freed (1822) by Sucre after the victory at near-by Pichincha. Quito then joined Gran Colombia, but proclaimed itself independent (1831). Economically the city has been overshadowed by Guayaquil. It has frequently suffered from earthquakes.

Quitupan (kētōō'pän), town (pop. 1,248), Jalisco, central Mexico, 40 mi. ENE of Guzmán; grain, beans, livestock.

Quivicán (kēvēkän'), town (pop. 3,188), Havana prov., W Cuba, 20 mi. S of Havana; processing and agr. center (sugar cane, yucca, rice, corn); mfg. of cigars, starch. Sugar central near by.

Quivira (kēvē'rä), land in central U.S. sought and found by the Spaniard Coronado in 1541. Exact location unknown, but now often identified with sites of villages of Wichita Indians around Great Bend, Kan. According to Indian tales, Quivira contained fabulous wealth in gold and silver, but Coronado found only rich black soil. The name was finally (and quite erroneously) settled upon Gran Quivira, a natl. monument.

Quixadá (kēshůdä'), city (pop. 5,142), central Ceará, Brazil, on Fortaleza-Crato RR and 90 mi. SSW of Fortaleza; important cattle market in irrigated agr. region (sugar, cotton); dairying, tanning. Airfield. City has noteworthy palace. Cedro dam and reservoir just W.

Quixará (kēshůrä'), city (pop. 1,088), S Ceará, Brazil, 22 mi. NW of Crato; livestock, carnauba.

Quixeramobim (kēshĭrā'mōōbēn), city (pop. 2,425), central Ceará, Brazil, on Fortaleza-Crato RR and 110 mi. SSW of Fortaleza; cattle market; dairying; rutile mining.

Quleita (kōōlā'tů), **Am Quleita** (ăm'), or **Al-Qulaytah** (ăl–), town, Dathina tribal area, Western Aden Protectorate, 55 mi. NE of Shuqra; radio station.

Qulin (kū'lĭn), town (pop. 426), Butler co., SE Mo., in Ozark region, 14 mi. SE of Poplar Bluff.

Qulusna (kōōlōōs'nä), village (pop. 8,349), Minya prov., Upper Egypt, on Ibrahimiya Canal, on railroad, and 3 mi. NE of Samalut; cotton, cereals, sugar cane. Sometimes spelled Qolosna.

Qum (kōōm) or **Qom** (kōm), city (1941 pop. 52,637), Second Prov., N central Iran, 75 mi. SSW of Teheran and on Qum R. (tributary of Zarineh R.); main city of former Qum prov.; road and railroad center at S approaches to Teheran. Cotton spinning, glass and pottery mfg. Agr.: melons, pomegranates, figs, grain, cotton, opium, pistachios, almonds. A Shiite pilgrimage center, visited for the golden-domed shrine of Fatima, sister of the Imam Riza, who is revered at Meshed. Dating from 9th cent. A.D., Qum was sacked by Tamerlane, revived under the Safavid kings (many of whom, including Abbas the Great, are buried here), destroyed 1722 by the Afghans, and developed again in 1930s as a modern transportation hub. Also spelled Kum, Kom, and Ghom. Qum prov. was inc. (1938) into Iran's Second Prov. (see TEHERAN).

Qumbush el Hamra or **Qunbush al-Hamra'** (both: kōōm'bōōsh ĕl häm'rä), village (pop. 8,156), Beni Suef prov., Upper Egypt, 9 mi. SW of Beni Suef; cotton, cereals, sugar cane.

Qumisheh, Iran: see SHAHRIZA.

Qumkhane or **Qumkhanah** (both: kōōmkhă'nů), Fr. *Koumhané*, town, Hama prov., W Syria, on railroad and 4 mi. N of Hama; cotton, cereals, fruit.

Qumul, China: see HAMI.

Qunaytarah, Al-, Syria: see QUNEITRA, EL.

Qunbush al-Hamra', Egypt: see QUMBUSH EL HAMRA.

Qunduz, Afghanistan: see KUNDUZ.

Quneitra, El, or **Al-Qunaytarah** (both: ĕl-kōōnā'trů) Fr. *Kuneitra*, town, Damascus prov., SW Syria, 40 mi. SW of Damascus, near Palestine line; tobacco, olives, fruit, cereals.

Qunfidha or **Al Qunfidhah** (ăl kōōn'fĭdhů), town (pop. 10,000), S Hejaz, Saudi Arabia, small Red Sea port 210 mi. SSE of Jidda; fishing; dates, millet, fruit. Under Turkish rule, was port for Abha in Asir. Sometimes spelled Konfodah and Konfudah.

Quoddy, Maine: see PASSAMAQUODDY BAY.

Quoddy Roads (kwŏ'dē), Washington co., E Maine, strait lying bet. Lubec and Campobello Isl.; joins Passamaquoddy Bay to the Atlantic.

Quogue (kwäg), summer-resort village (pop. 625), Suffolk co., SE N.Y., on S shore of Long Isl., at W end of Shinnecock Bay, 13 mi. W of Southampton, in shore-resort area.

Quoich, Loch (lŏkh koikh'), lake, W Inverness, Scotland, 18 mi. NNW of Fort William; 6 mi. long, 1 mi. wide. Drained by Garry R.

Quoile Quay (koil), small port in E Co. Down, Northern Ireland, on Quoile R. near its mouth on Strangford Lough, 2 mi. NNE of Downpatrick, which it serves.

Quonochontaug (kwŏnůkŏn'tôg), resort village in Charlestown town, Washington co., SW R.I., near the coast, just N of **Quonochontaug Beach,** resort on Block Isl. Sound, near inlet to **Quonochontaug Pond** (c.3 mi. long; bay sheltered by dunes along Block Isl. Sound).

Quonset Point (kwŏn'sĭt), S central R.I., peninsula and village in North Kingstown town, on W shore of Narragansett Bay; site of huge Northeastern Naval Air Station (completed 1941).

Quoram (kōräm'), town (pop. 1,100), Tigre prov., N Ethiopia, near L. Ashangi, 70 mi. S of Makale, in cereal- and coffee-growing region; 12°30'N 39°37'E.

Quorata, Ethiopia: see KORATA.

Quorn, town (pop. 924), S South Australia, 60 mi. N of Port Pirie; rail junction; agr. center; wheat, wool, wine.

Quorndon (kwôrn'–) or **Quorn,** former urban district (1931 pop. 2,604), N Leicester, England, 8 mi. N of Leicester; agr. market. A hunting center, seat of the Quorn Hunt. Has 14th-cent. church.

Quraiyat, Oman: see QURYAT.

Qurayn, Al-, Egypt: see QUREIN, EL.

Qurein, Arabia: see KUWAIT.

Qurein, El, or **Al-Qurayn** (both: ĕl kōōrān'), village (pop. 21,822), Sharqiya prov., Lower Egypt, 14 mi. ENE of Zagazig.

Qurna (kōōr'nů), **El Qurna,** or **Al-Qurnah** (both: ĕl), village (pop. 6,394), Qena prov., Upper Egypt, on W bank of the Nile opposite Luxor. Situated on part of site of anc. THEBES, it has the temple of Seti I, or temple of Qurna, built by Seti I (1300 B.C.) and completed by Ramses II. Here starts the road leading to the Tombs of the Kings (Biban el Muluk), 3 mi. W. W of Qurna lay the Necropolis of Thebes, or City of the Dead, and also a large number of temples. In this area are the Tombs of the Monkeys (Gabbanet el Qurud) to the W, the Tombs of the Queens (Biban el Harim), the temple of Thutmose III, the temple of Thutmose IV, the tomb of Tut-ankh-amen, the Ramesseum, the Colossi of Memnon, and the temple of Merneptah. Sometimes spelled El Kurna.

Qurna, Al, Al-Qurnah (äl), or **Korna** (kôr'nů), village, Basra prov., SE Iraq, in marshy area at the confluence of the Euphrates and the Tigris, 40 mi. NW of Basra; dates.

Qurnet es Sauda, Qurnet el Sauda, or **Qurnat al-Sawda** (all: kōōr'nĕt ĕs-sou'dä), Fr. *Kornet es Saoude*, highest peak (10,131 ft.) of the Lebanon range, N Lebanon, 45 mi. NE of Beirut.

Qurveh or **Qerveh** (kĕrvĕ'), town (1940 pop. 4,636), Fifth Prov., in Kurdistan, W Iran, 45 mi. ESE of Sanandaj and on road to Hamadan; wheat, tobacco.

Quryat (kōōryăt'), town (pop. 3,500), E Oman, port on Gulf of Oman, 30 mi. SE of Muscat, at foot of Eastern Hajar hill country; dates, barley, melons; fisheries. Sometimes spelled Quraiyat.

Qus (kōōs), town (pop. 19,530), Qena prov., Upper Egypt, on E bank of Nile R., on railroad, and 16 mi. NNE of Luxor; produces jams and the confectionery *halvah;* cereals, sugar cane, dates. Site of anc. *Apollonopolis Parva*, an important commercial center in the Middle Ages. Sometimes spelled Kus.

Qusaiba or **Al Qusaybah** (ăl kōōsī'bů), town and oasis, Qasim prov. of Nejd, Saudi Arabia, 50 mi. NW of Buraida; grain, vegetables, fruit; home handicrafts. Sometimes spelled Quseiba.

Qusaiyir, Aden: see QUSEI'AR.

Qusaybah, Al, Saudi Arabia: see QUSAIBA.

Qusaymah, Al-, Egypt: see QUSEIMA, EL.

Qusayr, Al-, Egypt: see KOSSEIR.

Qusayr, Al-, Syria: see QUSEIR, EL.

Qusayyir, Aden: see QUSEI'AR.

Qusei'ar, Qusaiyir, or **Qusayyir** (all: kōōsā'ûr), village, Quaiti state, Eastern Aden Protectorate, on Gulf of Aden, 45 mi. ENE of Shihr, on the cape Ras Qusei'ar.

Quseiba, Saudi Arabia: see QUSAIBA.

Quseima, El, or **Al-Qusaymah** (both: kōōsā'mů), town (1937 pop. 539; 1948 commune pop. 3,088), Sinai prov., NE Egypt, 45 mi. SE of El Arish. Has a school.

Quseir, Egypt: see KOSSEIR.

Quseir, El, or **Al-Qusayr** (both: ĕl-kōōsār'), Fr. *Kousseir*, town, Homs prov., W Syria, on railroad, on the Orontes, and 16 mi. SSW of Homs; cereals, fruits.

Qusiya, El, or **Al-Qusiyah** (both: ĕl kōōsē'yů), town (pop. 16,870), Asyut prov., central Upper Egypt, 8 mi. SSW of Dairut; pottery making, wood and ivory carving; cereals, dates, sugar cane. Sometimes spelled El Kusieh.

Qutaibi, Quteibi, or **Qutaybi** (kōōtā'bē), leading tribal area of RADFAN confederation, Western Aden Protectorate; ⊙ Ath Thumeir. Sheikh concluded protectorate treaty in 1915. Also spelled Qateibi.

Qutaybi, Aden: see QUTAIBI.

Qutayfah, Syria: see QUTEIFE.

Qutb, India: see MAHRAULI.

Qutdligssat, Greenland: see KUTDLIGSSAT.

Quteibi, Aden: see QUTAIBI.

Quteife or **Qutayfah** (both: kōōtā'fů), Fr. *Kouteifé*, village (pop. c.2,500), Damascus prov., SW Syria, 23 mi. NE of Damascus; alt. 3,450 ft.; fruits, olives, cereals.

Quthing (kōō'tĭng), village, ⊙ Quthing dist. (pop. 45,579, with absent laborers 50,764), S Basutoland; S terminus of main N–S road, near Orange R. and 80 mi. SSE of Maseru.

Qutur or **Qotur** (both: kōtōōr'), town, Fourth Prov., in Azerbaijan, NW Iran, on Turkish border, 30 mi. W of Khoi, and on highway. Also spelled Kutur or Kotur.

Quwaysna, Egypt: see QUWEISNA.

Quweira, Jordan: see KUWEIRA.

Quweisna or **Quwaysna** (kōōwās'nä), village (pop. 4,997), Minufiya prov., Lower Egypt, on railroad and 9 mi. E of Shibin el Kom; cereals, cotton, flax.

Quyon (kwē'ŏn, Fr. küyō'), village (pop. 637), SW Que., on Ottawa R. and 25 mi. WNW of Ottawa; lumbering, dairying.

Quyquyó (kēkēō', kůkůō'), town (dist. pop. 7,175), Paraguarí dept., S Paraguay, 80 mi. SE of Asunción; agr. center (sugar cane, fruit, corn, cattle); liquor distilling, tilemaking. Founded 1776. Iron deposits near by.

Quyyndy, Paraguay: see QUIINDY.

Qyteti Stalin, Albania: see KUÇOVË.

R

Raab (räp), town (pop. 2,634), W Upper Austria, 13 mi. SE of Schärding; market center; brewery.

Raab, city, Hungary: see Győr.

Raab River, Hung. *Rába* (rä'bŏ), in Austria and Hungary, rises in Fischbach Alps 8 mi. NW of Weiz (Styria), flows 160 mi. E and NE, past Szentgotthard and Körmend, to the Danube at Győr (Hungary), where it receives the Repce (left).

Raahe (rä'hä), Swedish *Brahestad* (brä"hŭstäd'), city (pop. 4,344), Oulu co., W Finland, on Gulf of Bothnia, 35 mi. SW of Oulu; lumber-shipping port, with shipyards and machine shops. Site of teachers' seminary and commercial col. Has mus. Founded 1649. Lapaluoto, outport, is 3 mi. SW of city, on Gulf of Bothnia; sawmills.

Raakvaag, Norway: see Rakvag.

Raalte (räl'tŭ), town (pop. 3,301), Overijssel prov., E central Netherlands, on Overijssel Canal and 11 mi. NNE of Deventer; cattle market; produces powdered milk, butter, other dairy products.

Raamsdonk (rämz'dŏngk), town (pop. 1,778), North Brabant prov., SW Netherlands, 9 mi. NNE of Breda; leather tanning, shoe mfg.

Raanana or **Ra'anana** (both: rä-änänä'), settlement (pop. 3,500), W Israel, in Plain of Sharon, 9 mi. NE of Tel Aviv; agr. center (mixed farming, citriculture); small industries. Site of large immigrants' reception camp and of Orthodox children's settlement. Founded 1921.

Raas, Indonesia: see Ras.

Raasay (rä'zā), island (□ 28; pop. 354), Inner Hebrides, Inverness, Scotland, off E coast of Skye, from which it is separated by Sound of Raasay (up to 3 mi. wide, narrowing S to 1-mi.-wide Narrows of Raasay). Separated from mainland by Inner Sound, 6–8 mi. wide. Isl. is 13 mi. long, up to 3 mi. wide. Highest elevation is Dun Caan (dŭn kăn') (1,456 ft.), in SE. At S extremity is promontory of Eyre Point, site of lighthouse (57°22'N 6°W). There are iron mines.

Raasepori, Finland: see Raseborg.

Rab, island, Yugoslavia: see Rab Island.

Raba River, Austria and Hungary: see Raab River.

Raba River (rä'bä), Krakow prov., S Poland, rises NNW of Nowy Targ, flows 85 mi. generally NNE, past Rabka, Myslenice, and Dobczyce, to Vistula R. 12 mi. NNE of Bochnia.

Rabastens (räbästä'). **1** or **Rabastens-de-Bigorre** (–dŭ-bēgôr'), village (pop. 879), Hautes-Pyrénées dept., SW France, 11 mi. NNE of Tarbes; irrigated agr.; hog raising. **2** Town (pop. 2,381), Tarn dept., S France, on Tarn R. and 21 mi. NE of Toulouse; furniture mfg., brick and tile works. Winegrowing. Has 13th–14th-cent. church.

Rabat (räbät'), town (pop. 12,503), W central Malta, 6 mi. W of Valletta, adjoining Mdina, the isl.'s anc. capital, in agr. region (grapes, wheat; goats, pigs); mfg. of carts and domestic textiles. Like Mdina, it has many Roman remains, including a partly restored villa, now a mus. There are also extensive catacombs hewn in limestone ridge. Has several cave churches; 15th-cent. St. Bartholomew church; church of St. Agatha (1504); Dominican, Augustinian, and Franciscan monasteries. In the Bingemma Hills (W) is Verdala Palace (1586), the governor's summer residence. Victoria, principal town of Gozo, was formerly called Rabat.

Rabat, city (pop. 161,416), ⊙ Fr. Morocco and Rabat region (□ 7,880; pop. 1,095,200), on the Atlantic at mouth of the Bou Regreg, opposite Salé (footbridge), and 55 mi. NE of Casablanca; 34°2'N 6°50'W. Seat of Fr. resident-general, and principal residence of the sultan of Morocco (whose traditional capitals, prior to Fr. occupation, were Fez and Marrakesh); episcopal see. Overshadowed by Casablanca as an industrial and commercial center, Rabat nevertheless has a modern textile industry; fruits and vegetables are preserved for export. There are flour mills, brickworks, asbestos-processing and fish-cake mfg. plants, and a young movie industry. Rabat is noted for its hand-woven Moroccan rugs. The small port is shallow and has little traffic. Rabat lies on railroad crossing Morocco from Marrakesh (SW) to Oujda (NE); also has excellent highway connections, especially with Casablanca. Airport; short-wave radio transmitter. Mediterranean subtropical climate (yearly average temp. 63°F.; cool winters), with annual rainfall (22 inches) concentrated in fall and winter months. The walled old city on left bank of the Bou Regreg is dominated (N) by Oudaïa *casbah* and adjoining mus. of native art and antiquities. Near the port is city's principal landmark, the massive 12th-cent. Hassane tower (a 180-ft. minaret, similar to Seville's Giralda) next to a ruined mosque. Modern Rabat lies S of the old town. Both the sultan's palace and that of the resident-general are in SE section. Beyond them are the remains of anc. *Chella*, which dates back to Phoenician times. Rabat proper (i.e., the walled town) was founded 12th cent. by Abdu-l-Mumin as a base for his expeditions into Spain. Its present importance, however, dates from establishment of Fr. protectorate in 1912.

Rabat-les-Trois-Seigneurs (räbä'-lā-trwä-sĕnyûr'), village (pop. 327), Ariège dept., S France, in central Pyrenees, 8 mi. SSW of Foix; iron mining.

Rabaul (räboul'), town, NE New Britain, Bismarck Archipelago, SW Pacific, at N corner of Blanche Bay, on Gazelle Peninsula; former ⊙ Territory of New Guinea, supplanted by Port Moresby. Surrounded by extremely active volcanoes; chief crater is Mt. Kombiu (alt. 2,247 ft.), also called The Mother. Extensive botanic gardens. Volcanic eruptions in 1937 ruined much of Rabaul, and Allied bombings in Second World War (when Rabaul was a key Jap. stronghold) added to the destruction.

Rabba (räb'bŭ), **El Rabba**, **Er Rabba**, or **Al-Rabbah** (all: ĕr-räb'bŭ), village (pop. c.2,500), central Jordan, 6 mi. NNE of Kerak, E of Dead Sea; wheat, barley. Site of ruins of biblical Rabbath Moab, later the Gr. Areopolis.

Rabbah, anc. Palestine: see Amman, city.

Rabbath Ammon, Jordan: see Amman, city.

Rabbit Ears Mountain, peak (10,719 ft.) in Rocky Mts., NW Colo., 12 mi. ESE of Steamboat Springs. Rabbit Ears Pass (W) is 9,680 ft. high.

Rabegh, Saudi Arabia: see Rabigh.

Rabenau (rä'bünou), town (pop. 3,790), Saxony, E central Germany, 7 mi. SW of Dresden; mfg. (furniture, electrical appliances).

Rabenstein (rä'bün-shtīn), village (pop. 2,196), central Lower Austria, 12 mi. SSW of Sankt Pölten; summer resort.

Rabenstein. **1** Village (commune pop. 1,363), Lower Bavaria, Germany, in Bohemian Forest, 2.5 mi. NW of Zwiesel; large glassworks at Regenhütte (pop. 603), 2 mi. N. **2** Village (pop. 6,957), Saxony, E central Germany, 5 mi. W of Chemnitz; hosiery, glove, underwear knitting; metalworking.

Rabi, Czechoslovakia: see Susice.

Rabi, Fiji: see Rambi.

Rábida, La (lärä'vē-dhä), monastery, Huelva prov., SW Spain, on mouth of the Río Tinto, across and 3 mi. SE of Huelva, near Palos. Columbus here laid out the plans for his 1st voyage, commemorated by a large monument just S.

Rabigh or **Rabegh** (both: rä'bĭg), city (pop. 7,000), central Hejaz, Saudi Arabia, Red Sea port on the small inlet Sherm Rabigh, 90 mi. N of Jidda; coastal trade; date groves. Barite deposits. Sometimes spelled Rabugh.

Rabinal (räbēnäl'), city (1950 pop. 2,587), Baja Verapaz dept., central Guatemala, in N highlands, 11 mi. W of Salamá; market center; produces mats, pottery, gourds; agr. (rice, corn, beans, fruit). Pop. largely Indian.

Rabin Point (rä'bēn, räbēn'), northernmost point of Leyte, Philippines, in Visayan Sea, opposite Biliran Isl.; 11°34'N 124°18'E.

Rab Island (räp), Ital. *Arbe* (är'bĕ), Dalmatian island (□40) in Adriatic Sea, W Croatia, Yugoslavia; 12 mi. long; northernmost point 35 mi. SSE of Rijeka (Fiume). Tourist area; bathing beaches. Fruit- and winegrowing; bauxite deposits. Chief village, Rab, Ital. *Arbe* (pop. 881), is on W coast, 40 mi. SSE of Rijeka, on small promontory; seaside resort, with 2 small harbors. R.C. bishopric since 10th cent. Village has old walls and palaces, 12th-cent. cathedral, public park.

Râbita, La, Spain: see Albuñol.

Rabka (räp'kä), village, Krakow prov., S Poland, on Raba R., and 10 mi. NNW of Nowy Targ; health resort with salt springs; sawmilling.

Rabkavi (rŭb'kŭvē), town (pop. 6,730), Bijapur dist., S Bombay, India, 50 mi. SW of Bijapur; trade center for cotton, wheat, peanuts; cotton and silk weaving and dyeing, handicraft cloth making.

Rabkob, India: see Dharmjaygarh.

Rabnitz River, Austria and Hungary: see Repce River.

Rabocheostrovsk (rŭbô"chĭŭstrôfsk'), town (1939 pop. over 2,000), E Karelo-Finnish SSR, port of Kem, on isl. in White Sea, at mouth of Kem R., 5 mi. ENE of Kem (linked by rail spur); lumber milling.

Rabotki (rŭbôt'kē), village (1926 pop. 1,518), central Gorki oblast, Russian SFSR, on Volga R. and 30 mi. SE of Gorki; sawmill.

Rabugh, Saudi Arabia: see Rabigh.

Rabun (rā'bŭn), county (□ 369; pop. 7,424), extreme NE Ga., on N.C. and S.C. lines; ⊙ Clayton. In Chattahoochee Natl. Forest and the Blue Ridge, rising here to 4,663 ft. in Rabun Bald (NE); drained by Tallulah R. (dammed; forms lakes Burton and Rabun) and the Little Tennessee. Farm (hay, potatoes, fruit, livestock), lumber, and resort area. Formed 1819.

Rabun Gap, resort village (pop. c.250), Rabun co., extreme NE Ga., 5 mi. N of Clayton, on Little Tennessee R. and in Rabun Gap. highway and railroad pass through Blue Ridge Mts.

Rabun Lake (c.4 mi. long), Rabun co., extreme NE Ga., formed in Tallulah R. by power dam 8 mi. S of Clayton.

Rabupura (rŭbōō'pōōrŭ), town (pop. 5,382), Bulandshahr dist., W Uttar Pradesh, India, 19 mi. SW of Bulandshahr; trades in cattle; wheat, oilseeds, cotton, barley, corn. Founded 11th cent.

Raca (rä'chä), Slovak *Rača*, town (pop. 6,355), W Slovakia, Czechoslovakia, on railroad and 5 mi. N of Bratislava; noted for wine production. Until 1946, called Racistorf, Czech *Račistorf*, Hung. *Récze*.

Raca, Racha, Raca Kragujevacka, or **Racha Kragujevachka** (all: rä'chä, krä'gōōyĕvächkä), Serbo-Croatian *Rača Kragujevačka*, village, central Serbia, Yugoslavia, 15 mi. NNE of Kragujevac.

Racaciuni (rŭkŭchōōn'), Rum. *Răcăciuni*, village (pop. 1,664), Bacau prov., E Rumania, near Siret R., on railroad and 15 mi. SSE of Bacau; lignite mining; alcohol mfg.

Racale (rä'kälĕ), town (pop. 5,415), Lecce prov., Apulia, S Italy, 9 mi. SE of Gallipoli; wine, olive oil.

Racalmas (rä'tsŏlmäsh), Hung. *Rácalmás*, town (pop. 4,129), Fejer co., central Hungary, on the Danube and 17 mi. ESE of Szekesfehervar; river port; corn, wheat, potatoes, poultry.

Racalmuto (räkälmōō'tô), town (pop. 12,679), Agrigento prov., S Sicily, 12 mi. NE of Agrigento. Has 14th-cent. castle. Sulphur, rock salt mines near by.

Racari (rŭkär'yŭ), Rum. *Răcari*, town (pop. 2,519), Bucharest prov., S central Rumania, on railroad and 25 mi. NW of Bucharest; furniture mfg.

Racconigi (räk"kônē'jē), town (pop. 6,552), Cuneo prov., Piedmont, NW Italy, on Maira R. and 21 mi. S of Turin, in sericulture region; raw-silk market; silk and cotton mills, mint distilleries; furniture. Has large royal park and castle.

Raccoon Creek. **1** In W Ind., rises in SW Boone co., flows SW, then turns NW near Rosedale, converging with the Wabash 8 mi. W of Rockville; 75 mi. long. Sometimes called Big Raccoon Creek. **2** In SW N.J., rises SW of Glassboro, flows c.25 mi. generally NW, past Swedesboro, to Delaware R. opposite Chester, Pa. Navigable for c.9 mi. below Swedesboro. **3** In S Ohio, rises in Hocking co., flows c.100 mi. generally S, past Zaleski and Vinton, to the Ohio c.7 mi. S of Gallipolis. **4** In Licking co., central Ohio, W tributary of Licking River; c.25 mi. long.

Raccoon Key, Charleston co., E S.C., coast island, c.30 mi. NE of Charleston, just NE of Bull Bay; c.7 mi. long. Cape Romain lighthouse (now unused) is at E end.

Raccoon River, central Iowa, rises in Buena Vista co., NW Iowa, flows 200 mi. S and SE, past Sac City and Jefferson, to Des Moines R. at Des Moines. South Raccoon R. rises near Guthrie-Audubon co. line, flows c.50 mi. SE, past Guthrie Center, to Raccoon R. near Van Meter. Middle Racoon River rises in NW Carroll co., flows 76 mi. SE, past Carroll City, to South Raccoon R. near Redfield.

Raccourci, Lake (răkōōr'sē), shallow inlet of the Gulf of Mexico, in Lafourche parish, SE La., lying just N of Timbalier Bay, from which it is separated by small isls.; c.7 mi. in diameter; oyster beds, fisheries.

Race, Cape, SE extremity of N.F., at SE end of Avalon Peninsula, 65 mi. SSW of St. John's; 46°40'N 53°5'W.

Race Course, village (pop. 2,970), S central Singapore isl., 5 mi. NW of Singapore; site of Singapore race track.

Race Lake (20 mi. long, 3 mi. wide), SE Ont., 10 mi. SE of Peterborough. Drained E by Trent R.

Raceland. **1** City (pop. 1,001), Greenup co., NE Ky., near left bank of the Ohio, 8 mi. NW of Ashland. Has noted race track; horse-racing center for E Ky. Inc. 1920 as Chinnville; renamed 1930. **2** Village (pop. 2,025), Lafourche parish, SE La., on Bayou Lafourche and 33 mi. SW of New Orleans; sugar refining, shrimp packing and shipping, lumber and feed milling.

Race Point, SE Mass., point on NW side of tip of Cape Cod; has lighthouse (42°4'N 70°15'W).

Racha, Yugoslavia: see Raca.

Rachado, Cape, Malay *Tanjong Tuan* (tän'jōng tōōän'), on Strait of Malacca, Malaya, forming small Malacca enclave in Negri Sembilan state; 2°25'N 101°50'E; lighthouse.

Rachaya, Lebanon: see Rasheiya.

Rachgia (rät'zhä'), town, ⊙ Rachgia prov. (□ 2,600; 1943 pop. 380,600), S Vietnam, in Cochin China, on Rachgia Bay of Gulf of Siam, 120 mi. SW of Saigon. Port of call for local shipping (exports shrimps, fish, honey, wax). Rice-growing center; mat mfg.

Rachin Range (räcl.ēn'), S spur of central Greater Caucasus, in NW Georgian SSR, bet. upper Rion and Kvirila rivers; rises to 7,362 ft.

Rachov, Ukrainian SSR: see Rakhov.

Rachub, Wales: see Bethesda.

Raciaz (rä'chŏs), Pol. *Raciąż*, Rus. *Ratsyonzh* (rŭtsyônsh'), town (pop. 3,704), Warszawa prov., N central Poland, on railroad and 20 mi. ESE of Sierpe; flour and groat milling, tanning.

Raciborz. 1 Town, Koszalin prov., Poland: see OKONEK. 2 Town, Opole prov., Poland: see RATIBOR.

Racine, Que.: see CHUTE SHIPSHAW.

Racine (rŭsēn'), county (□ 337; pop. 109,585), SE Wis.; ⊙ Racine. Bordered E by L. Michigan; drained by Fox and Root rivers. Predominantly farming area (dairy products; livestock, vegetables, corn, oats). Extensive mfg. at Racine and Burlington. Lake resorts. Formed 1836.

Racine. 1 (rāsēn') Village (pop. 536), Meigs co., SE Ohio, on Ohio R. and 7 mi. SE of Pomeroy. 2 (rŭsēn') Industrial city (pop. 71,193), ⊙ Racine co., SE Wis., 24 mi. SSE of Milwaukee, on L. Michigan, at mouth of Root R.; port of entry, with lake harbor. Mfg. of farm machinery, waxes and polishes, paints and varnishes, malted milk, automobile parts, leather and rubber goods, electrical devices, hardware, metal products, clothing, food products; printing. Fisheries; stone quarries. Seat of Dominican Col. Points of interest: the courthouse, containing historical exhibits; public library, with the Hoy bird collection; and Johnson Office Bldg. and Sporer House, designed by Frank Lloyd Wright. Settled 1834, inc. 1848. Improvement of its harbor (c.1844) and coming of railroad brought industrial growth.

Racistorf, Czechoslovakia: see RACA.

Raciu (rŭ'chōō), Rum. *Răciu*, Hung. *Mezőrücs* (mĕ'zûrüch), village (pop. 2,143), Mures prov., central Rumania, on railroad and 13 mi. NW of Targu-Mures; agr. market. In Hungary, 1940–45.

Rackeve (räts'kĕvĕ), Hung. *Ráckeve*, town (pop. 6,701), Pest-Pilis-Solt-Kiskun co., N central Hungary, on Csepel Isl. in the Danube, and 24 mi. S of Budapest; river port, rail terminal; flour mills. Ger. pop. raises wheat, rye, cattle, poultry.

Rackliff Island, Knox co., S Maine, in Penobscot Bay, 3 mi. NE of Tenants Harbor; 1.25 mi. long.

Raco (rä'kō), village, W Tucumán prov., Argentina, 20 mi. NW of Tucumán; road center.

Rada' (rädä'), town (pop. 3,500), Sana prov., S central Yemen, on central plateau, 30 mi. E of Dhamar, in agr. area. Also spelled Reda and Redaa.

Radak Chain, Marshall Isls.: see RATAK CHAIN.

Radaunen See, Poland: see RADUNIA LAKE.

Radauti (rŭdŭōōts'), Rum. *Rădăuţi*, Ger. *Radautz* (rädouts'), town (1948 pop. 14,530), Sucelava prov., N Rumania, in Bukovina, on railroad and 90 mi. NW of Jassy; trading and woodworking center (furniture, Venetian blinds, brushes). Also mfg. of soap, candles, batteries, agr. tools, ribbons, laces; brewing; distilling. Has 14th-cent. church with tombs of 1st voivodes of Moldavia; also 15th-cent. frescoes, regional mus.

Radburn, N.J.: see FAIR LAWN.

Radbuza River (räd'bōōzä), W Bohemia, Czechoslovakia, rises in Bohemian Forest 6 mi. W of Pobezovice, flows E, past Horsovsky Tyn, and NE, past Stod, joining Mze R. at Pilsen to form Berounka R.; c.45 mi. long. Receives Uhlava R. (right).

Radchenskoye (rä'chĭnskŭyŭ), village (1939 pop. over 2,000), S Voronezh oblast, Russian SFSR, 9 mi. S of Boguchar; flour mill.

Radcliffe, municipal borough (1931 pop. 24,675; 1951 census 27,551), SE Lancashire, England, 7 mi. NNW of Manchester; chemical- and paper-mfg. center; coal mining, cotton and rayon milling, metalworking, mfg. of soap, pharmaceuticals, leather goods. Includes town of Black Lane. Has 15th-cent. church and remains of 15th-cent. mansion.

Radcliffe, town (pop. 638), Hardin co., central Iowa, 23 mi. NNE of Ames; livestock, grain.

Radda in Chianti (räd'dä ēn kyän'tē), village (pop. 450), Siena prov., Tuscany, central Italy, 12 mi. N of Siena; wine making.

Raddusa (räd-dōō'zä), village (pop. 4,146), Catania prov., E central Sicily, 16 mi. N of Caltagirone.

Radeberg (rä'dŭbĕrk), town (pop. 16,622), Saxony, E central Germany, 10 mi. NE of Dresden; mfg. of glass, furniture, electrical equipment, paper, hats; metalworking, brewing. Agr. market. Has 16th-cent. palace.

Radebeul (rä'dŭboil), town (pop. 41,207), Saxony, E central Germany, on the Elbe and 4 mi. NNW of Dresden; produces machinery, pharmaceuticals, chemicals, paint, rubber and asbestos products, shoes, glass, furniture, chocolate, musical instruments. Market gardening. Former residence of writer Karl May is now mus. Town extends 6 mi. along the Elbe; includes former communes of Kötzschenbroda, Niederlössnitz, and Oberlössnitz. Includes locality of Madaus, with penicillin mfg.

Radeburg (rä'ŭbōōrk), town (pop. 4,159), Saxony, E central Germany, 12 mi. N of Dresden; mfg. agr. machinery, glass, leather goods); stone quarry.

Radece or **Radece pri Zidanem Mostu** (rä'dĕtsĕ prē zĕ'dänĕm mô'stōō), Slovenian *Radeče*, Ger. *Ratschach* (rä'tshäkh), village, central Slovenia, Yugoslavia, on Sava R., on railroad and 12 mi. SSW of Celje; mfg. of paper and paper products. Until 1918, in Carniola.

Radegast (rä'dŭgäst), town (pop. 3,088), in former Anhalt state, central Germany, after 1945 in Saxony-Anhalt, 10 mi. WNW of Bitterfeld; lignite mining.

Radein, Bad, Yugoslavia: see SLATINA RADENCI.

Radekhov (rŭdyĕ'khŭf), Pol. *Radziechów* (rädzyĕ'-khōōf), city (1931 pop. 5,440), in N Lvov oblast, Ukrainian SSR, 20 mi. SE of Sokal; tanning, sawmilling, agr. processing (cereals, fruit, hops).

Radenci, Yugoslavia: see SLATINA RADENCI.

Radenthein (räd'ŭntīn), town (pop. 4,542), Carinthia, S Austria, 10 mi. E of Spittal; tannery; meteorological station; summer resort. Magnesite, some graphite mined near by.

Radersburg (rā'dûrzbûrg), village (pop. c.150), Broadwater co., SW central Mont., 35 mi. SE of Helena; gold mines.

Radevormwald (rä'dŭfôrmvält'), town (pop. 16,635), in former Prussian Rhine Prov., W Germany, after 1945 in North Rhine-Westphalia, 7 mi. E of Remscheid; mfg. (machinery, hardware, textiles).

Radeyev, Poland: see RADZIEJOW.

Radfan (rädfăn'), hilly tribal area (pop. 36,500) of Western Aden Protectorate, SE of Amiri domain. Its warlike tribesmen, who owe loose allegiance to the Amiri, constitute a confederation of which the QUTAIBI or Quteibi is the most important element.

Radford, W suburb of Nottingham, S Nottinghamshire, England; coal mines, chemical works.

Radford, industrial city (pop. 9,026), in but independent of Montgomery co., SW Va., on New R. and 34 mi. WSW of Roanoke; railroad shops; mfg. of foundry products, textiles, electric irons, boxes, clothing. Seat of Radford Col. Includes former community of East Radford. Claytor L., formed by dam on New R. is SSW; hydroelectric works. Inc. 1885.

Radgona, Austria: see RADKERSBURG.

Radhakishorepur (rädäkĭshō'rāpōōr), village, Tripura, NE India, on Gumti R. (tributary of the Meghna) and 24 mi. SE of Agartala; trades in rice, cotton, tea, mustard, jute. Early 16th-cent. Hindu temple (pilgrimage center). Also called Udaipur or Udaypur.

Radha Kund (rä'dŭ kōōnd'), town (pop. 2,947), Muttra dist., W Uttar Pradesh, India, near Agra Canal and 12 mi. W of Muttra; gram, jowar, wheat, oilseeds, cotton. Cenotaph in honor of noted Jat, Raja Suraj Mal. Pilgrimage center, connected with Krishna legend.

Radhanpur (rä'dŭnpōōr), town (pop. 11,959), Mehsana dist., N Bombay, India, 45 mi. WNW of Mehsana; local trade center for oilseeds, grain, cotton; cotton ginning, oilseed milling, cattle breeding. Was ⊙ former princely state of Radhanpur (□ 1,150; pop. 67,691) of Western India States; state inc. 1949 into Mehsana and Banas Kantha dists., Bombay.

Radhost (räd'hôshtyŭ), Czech *Radhošť*, mountain (4,346 ft.) in the Beskids, NE Moravia, Czechoslovakia, 11 mi. ENE of Valasske Mezirici; resort area with noted skiing terrain. Old chapel on summit. Frenstat pod Radhostem is at N, Roznov pod Radhostem at SW foot.

Radicena, Italy: see TAURIANOVA.

Radicofani (rädēkô'fänē), village (pop. 903), Siena prov., Tuscany, central Italy, 21 mi. NW of Orvieto, E of Monte Amiata, in mercury-mining region.

Radicondoli (rädēkôn'dôlē), village (pop. 758), Siena prov., Tuscany, central Italy, 15 mi. WSW of Siena; cementworks.

Radika River (rä'dēkä), W Macedonia, Yugoslavia, rises c.10 mi. NE of Galicnik, flows c.30 mi. S to the Black Drin 3 mi. S of Debar.

Radimin, Poland: see RADZYMIN.

Radinci, Yugoslavia: see SLATINA RADENCI.

Radishchevo (rŭdyēsh'chĭvŭ), village (1948 pop. over 2,000), S Ulyanovsk oblast, Russian SFSR, 32 mi. SW of Syzran; wheat, sunflowers.

Radisson, town (pop. 324), central Sask., near North Saskatchewan R., 40 mi. NW of Saskatoon; grain elevators.

Raditsa-Krylovka (rŭdyē'tsŭ-krĭlôf'kŭ), town (1939 pop. over 2,000), NE Bryansk oblast, Russian SFSR, 1.5 mi. E of Bezhitsa.

Radium, city (pop. 64), Stafford co., S central Kansas, 14 mi. SSW of Great Bend, in wheat area.

Radiumbad Brambach, Germany: see BRAMBACH.

Radiumbad Oberschlema, Germany: see OBERSCHLEMA.

Radium Hot Springs, resort village, SE B.C., on slope of Rocky Mts., on Columbia R. and 50 mi. SW of Banff; resort, at edge of Kootenay Natl. Park; alt. 3,456 ft.

Radium Springs, resort village, Dougherty co., SW Ga., just S of Albany.

Radja Ampat Islands, Netherlands New Guinea: see RAJA AMPAT ISLANDS.

Radjegwesi, Indonesia: see BOJONEGORO.

Radjou, Syria: see RAJU.

Radkersburg (rät'kŭrsbōōrk), Slovenian *Radgona*, town (pop. 1,907), Styria, SE Austria, on Mur R. (Yugoslav border) opposite Gornja Radgona, 18 mi. NE of Maribor, Yugoslavia; wine.

Radkow (rät'kōōf), Pol. *Radków*, Ger. *Wünschelburg* (vün'shŭlbōōrk), town (1939 pop. 2,556; 1946 pop. 3,238) in Lower Silesia, after 1945 in Wroclaw prov., SW Poland, on Czechoslovak border, at N foot of Heuscheuer Mts., 12 mi. WNW of Glatz (Klodzko); textile milling and knitting. After 1945, briefly called Grodek, Pol. *Gródek*.

Radlett, residential town in parish of Watford Rural (pop. 5,583), SW Hertford, England, 4 mi. NE of Watford; aircraft works. Has 15th-cent. church and grammar school founded 1599.

Radley, agr. village and parish (pop. 1,088), N Berkshire, England, 5 mi. SSE of Oxford; site of Radley Col., a public school. Has 15th-cent. church.

Radmannsdorf, Yugoslavia: see RADOVLJICA.

Radna (räd'nä), Hung. *Máriaradna* (mä'rēŏrŏd"-nŏ), village (pop. 3,424), Arad prov., W Rumania, on Mures R. opposite Lipova, and 18 mi. SE of Arad; rail junction and noted R.C. pilgrimage center, with 16th-cent. Franciscan monastery; granite quarrying.

Radnevo (räd'nĕvô), village (pop. 2,824), Stara Zagora dist., E central Bulgaria, on branch of Sazlika R. and 15 mi. S of Nova Zagora; wheat, barley, livestock; gypsum quarry. Formerly Radne-makhle.

Radnice (räd'nyĭtsĕ), village (pop. 2,067), SW Bohemia, Czechoslovakia, 13 mi. NE of Pilsen; rail terminus; coal mining.

Radnor (răd'nŭr), village, Delaware co., SE Pa., 12 mi. NW of Philadelphia. Gen. Anthony Wayne buried here. Settled c.1685 by Welsh, who built (1715) the extant St. David's Church.

Radnor or **Radnorshire** (răd'nŭr,-shĭr), county (□ 470.5; 1931 pop. 21,323; 1951 census 19,998), central Wales; ⊙ Presteigne. Bounded by Cardigan (W), Montgomery (N), Shropshire and Hereford (E), Brecknock (S). Drained by Wye, Teme, and Lugg rivers. Hilly terrain, rising to 2,166 ft. in Radnor Forest (E). Industries are agr., limestone quarrying, dairying, sheep and cattle raising. Besides Presteigne, other towns are Knighton and Llandrindod Wells (spa). There are remains of anc. castles and camps.

Radnor Forest, wooded mountain range, E Radnor, Wales, extends 15 mi. E-W bet. Llandrindod Wells and Presteign. Highest point, Great Rhos (rōs) (2,166 ft.), 3 mi. NW of New Radnor.

Radnorshire, Wales: see RADNOR.

Radnot, Rumania: see IERNUT.

Radocelo or **Radochelo** (both: rä'dôchĕlô), Serbo-Croatian *Radočelo*, mountain in Dinaric Alps, W Serbia, Yugoslavia; highest point (5,389 ft.) is 20 mi. SSW of Rankovicevo town. Marble quarrying.

Radolfzell (rädôlftsĕl'), town (pop. 8,737), S Baden, Germany, on the Zeller See (a bay of the UNTERSEE), 11 mi. NW of Constance; rail junction; machinery and textile mfg., metal- and woodworking, food processing. Has 15th-cent. church with tomb of St. Radolf. Formerly called Zell.

Radom (rä'dôm), city (1946 census pop. 69,455; 1950 pop. estimate 83,167), Kielce prov., E central Poland, 60 mi. S of Warsaw. Rail junction; center of tanning, munition-mfg., and tobacco-processing industries, linked by pipe line with Jaslo-Krosno natural-gas field. Mfg. of bicycles, wire, nails, machinery, footwear, furniture, beer, bricks; flour milling. One of oldest Pol. towns; believed to have originated as site of local diets; 1st church built 1187. Seat of Pol. diets (14th-16th cent.), a tribunal (1613–1766), and Confederation of Radom (1767) which requested Russia to guarantee Pol. constitution. Passed 1795 to Austria, 1815 to Rus. Poland and was ⊙ Radom govt.; returned 1919 to Poland.

Radom (rā'dŭm), village (pop. 134), Washington co., SW Ill., 16 mi. S of Centralia, in agr. area.

Radomir (rä"dômĕr'), city (pop. 5,778), Sofia dist., W Bulgaria, on Struma R. and 20 mi. SW of Sofia; rail junction; agr. center in Radomir Basin (□ 92; hemp, truck, livestock); porcelain mfg.; apple orchards. Has electrotechnic school.

Radomir (rä'dômĭr), Gr. *Kerkine* or *Kerkini* (both: kĕrkē'nē), highest peak (6,660 ft.) in Belasica mts., on Greek-Bulgarian border, 7 mi. SW of Petrich (Bulgaria). Also called Kalabak.

Radomirtsi (rädômēr'tsē), village (pop. 3,301), Pleven dist., N Bulgaria, 4 mi. NNE of Lukovit; grain, livestock, truck.

Radomsko (rädôm'skô), town (pop. 19,551), Lodz prov., S central Poland, on railroad and 50 mi. S of Lodz; mfg. of furniture, machinery, wire, nails, bricks; sawmilling, brewing, flour milling. In Rus. Poland (until First World War), called Novoradomsk, Pol. *Noworadomsk*.

Radomyshl or **Radomyshl'** (rä'dŭmĭshŭl), city (1926 pop. 12,933), E Zhitomir oblast, Ukrainian SSR, on Teterev R. and 29 mi. NE of Zhitomir; cotton milling, machine mfg. Until 1936, city was called Radomysl.

Radomysl Wielki (rädô'mĭ-shŭl vyĕl'kē), Pol. *Radomyśl Wielki*, town (pop. 942), Rzeszow prov., SE Poland, 34 mi. WNW of Rzeszow; flour milling; brickworks.

Radoshkovichi (rŭdŭshkô'vĕchē), Pol. *Radoszkowice* (rädôshkôvē'tsĕ), town (1931 pop. 2,574), SE Molodechno oblast, Belorussian SSR, 18 mi. SE of Molodechno; concrete-block mfg., tanning, flour milling, dairying. Has ruins of 15th-cent. church. Frontier town (1921–39) on Poland-USSR border.

Radovene or **Rad'ovene** (rä'dyôvĕnĕ), village (pop. 3,531), Pleven dist., N Bulgaria, 5 mi. W of Lovech; grain, livestock, truck.

Radovis or **Radovish** (both: rä'dôvĭsh), Serbo-Croatian *Radoviš*, village (pop. 4,740), Macedonia, Yugoslavia, on Strumica R. and 14 mi. SE of Stip, at S foot of the Plackovica; trade center for tobacco-growing region; handicraft work. Formerly called Radoviste or Radovishte, Serbo-Croatian *Radovište*.

Radovis River, Yugoslavia: see Strumica River.

Radovljica (rädôv'lyĭtsä), Ger. *Radmannsdorf* (rät'mänsdôrf"), village, NW Slovenia, Yugoslavia, on Sava R., on railroad and 25 mi. NW of Ljubljana; local trade center (1st mentioned in 1343); summer resort. Until 1918, in Carniola.

Radoy (räd'ûü), Nor. *Radøy*, island (□ 40; pop. 4,996) in North Sea, Hordaland co., SW Norway, 13 mi. NNW of Bergen; 17 mi. long (NW-SE), 4 mi. wide; flat and wooded; some moors and many lakes; active fishing. At Alverstraumen village (SE tip): fish and meat canning.

Radstadt (rät'shtät), town (pop. 3,614), Salzburg, W central Austria, near the Enns, 12 mi. E of Bischofshofen; copper refinery; resort.

Radstock, England: see Norton Radstock.

Radstock, Cape, S South Australia, on W Eyre Peninsula; forms N end of Anxious Bay; 33°12'S 134°19'E.

Raducaneni (rŭdŏŏkŭnăn'), Rum. *Răducăneni*, village (pop. 2,894), Jassy prov., E Rumania, 31 mi. SE of Jassy; pottery mfg., vegetable growing, stone quarrying.

Radul or **Radul'** (rä'dŏŏl), town (1926 pop. 4,656), NW Chernigov oblast, Ukrainian SSR, on Dnieper R. and 34 mi. NW of Chernigov; peat bogs.

Radun or **Radun'** (rä'dŏŏnyŭ), Pol. *Raduń* (rä'dŏŏnyŭ), village (1931 pop. 1,250), NE Grodno oblast, Belorussian SSR, 17 mi. NW of Lida; flour milling.

Radu-Negru (rä'dōō-nā'grōō), S suburb (1941 pop. 4,235) of Braila, Galati prov., SE Rumania, on Danube R.; grain processing, mfg. (wire, nails, barrels); large lumber yards.

Radunia Lake (rädōō'nyä), Pol. *Jezioro Raduńskie* (yĕ-zhô'rô rädōō'nyŭskyĕ), Ger. *Radaunen See* (rädou'nŭn zā") (□ 4), Gdansk prov., N Poland, SW of Kartuzy; 11 mi. long N-S, ¾ mi. wide; cuts through moraine formation bet. Kartuzy and Koscierzyna; other smaller lakes near by.

Radusa or **Radusha** (both: rä'dōōshä), Serbo-Croatian *Raduša*, village, NW Macedonia, Yugoslavia, in outlier of Sar Mts., on Vardar R. and 12 mi. WNW of Skoplje, near Orasje rail terminus; chromium mine and mill.

Radusa Mountains or **Radusha Mountains,** Serbo-Croatian *Raduša Planina*, in Dinaric Alps, S Bosnia, Yugoslavia; c.5 mi. long (W-E); highest point (6,416 ft.) is 9 mi. WNW of Prozor.

Radviliskis or **Radvilishkis** (both: rädvĭ'lĭsh-kĭs), Lith. *Radviliškis*, Rus. *Radzivilishki*, town (pop. 6,855), N Lithuania, 15 mi. SE of Siauliai; agr. center.

Radville, town (pop. 859), S Sask., 25 mi. WSW of Weyburn; railroad-divisional point; grain elevators, stock.

Radway, village (pop. 179), central Alta., on Namepi Creek, near its mouth on North Saskatchewan R., and 45 mi. NE of Edmonton; wheat, stock.

Radymno (rädĭm'nô), town (pop. 3,436), Rzeszow prov., SE Poland, near San R., 11 mi. N of Przemysl; mfg. of chemicals, ropes.

Radyr (ră'dŭr), agr. village and parish (pop. 1,596), SE Glamorgan, Wales, on Taff R. and 4 mi. NW of Cardiff.

Radziechow, Ukrainian SSR: see Radekhov.

Radziejow (räjĕ'yōōf), Pol. *Radziejów*, Rus. *Radeyev* (rŭdyĕ'yĭf), town (pop. 3,836), Bydgoszcz prov., central Poland, 16 mi. SSE of Inowroclaw; flour milling.

Radzin, Poland: see Radzyn, Lublin prov.

Radzivilov, Ukrainian SSR: see Chervonoarmeisk, Rovno oblast.

Radziwillow, Ukrainian SSR: see Chervonoarmeisk, Rovno oblast.

Radzymin (rädzĭ'mēn), Rus. *Radimin* (rŭdyē'myĭn), town (pop. 4,356), Warszawa prov., E central Poland, 15 mi. NNE of Warsaw; rail junction; brewing, flour milling, brick mfg.

Radzyn (rä'dzĭnyŭ), Pol. *Radzyń*. **1** or **Radzyn Chelminski** (khĕōōmē'nyŭskē), Pol. *Radzyń Chełmiński*, Ger. *Rehden* (rā'dŭn), town (pop. 1,711), Bydgoszcz prov., N Poland, 10 mi. SE of Grudziadz; flour milling. **2** or **Radzyn Podlaski** (pôdlä'skē), Pol. *Radzyń-Podlaski*, Rus. *Radzin* or *Radzin'* (both: rŭdzē'nyŭ), town (pop. 4,694), Lublin prov., E Poland, 37 mi. N of Lublin; mfg. of ceramic products, soap, nonmineral oil; flour milling, sawmilling.

Rae (rā), village (district pop. 767), S Mackenzie Dist., Northwest Territories, on Marian L. 20 mi. long, 4 mi. wide), just N of head of North Arm of Great Slave L., 60 mi. NW of Yellowknife; 62°50'N 116°3'W; fur-trading post; radio station, Royal Canadian Mounted Police post; site of R.C. mission and hosp. Founded 1790 as Fort Providence, at mouth of Yellowknife R., it was moved and renamed 1850. Sometimes Fort Rae.

Rae, Mount (10,576 ft.), SW Alta., near B.C. border, in Misty Range of Rocky Mts., 50 mi. SE of Banff; 50°38'N 114°58'W.

Rae Bareli (rī' bŭrā'lē), district (□ 1,765; pop. 1,064,804), central Uttar Pradesh, India; ⊙ Rae Bareli. On Ganges Plain; bounded S by the Ganges; drained by Sai R. Agr. (rice, wheat, barley, gram, jowar, oilseeds, pearl millet); mango and mahua groves. Main towns: Rae Bareli, Jais, Salon, Dalmau.

Rae Bareli, town (pop. 20,945), ⊙ Rae Bareli dist., central Uttar Pradesh, India, on Sai R. and 45 mi. SSE of Lucknow; rail and road junction; rice, flour, and oilseed milling. Anc. fort, extensive mosques and tombs. Founded by Bhars.

Raeford (rā'fŭrd), town (pop. 2,030), ⊙ Hoke co., S central N.C., 20 mi. WSW of Fayetteville, in agr. area; cotton and rayon mills.

Rae Isthmus (rā), Northwest Territories, land narrows (50 mi. long) at base of Melville Peninsula, bet. head of Committee Bay of the Gulf of Boothia (NNW) and Repulse Bay (SSE); 67°N 86°30'W. At S end of isthmus is Repulse Bay trading post.

Raekot, India: see Raikot.

Raetihi (rī'tĭhē), borough (pop. 1,080), ⊙ Waimarino co. (□ 883; pop. 3,108), W central N.Isl., New Zealand, 70 mi. ESE of New Plymouth; head of rail spur; dairy plant, sawmills.

Raevski Islands (räyĕf'skē), Fr. *Iles Raeffsky*, uninhabited coral group, N Tuamotu Isls., Fr. Oceania, S Pacific; 16°44'S 144°15'W; include Tepoto, Hiti, Tuanaka. Formerly Sea Gull Isls.

Rafa or **Rafah** (both: rä'fä), anc. *Raphia* (rŭfī'ŭ), town (pop. c.1,500) on Palestine-Egypt line, bet. Sinai and the Negev, on the Mediterranean, 19 mi. SW of Gaza, 30 mi. ENE of El Arish, and on Cairo-Haifa RR. Here in 217 B.C. Ptolemy IV defeated Antiochus III. In First World War, site of important Br. military base. The whole region here was occupied by Egypt, 1948.

Rafael (räfäĕl'), village (1930 pop. 361), Concepción prov., S central Chile, on railroad and 20 mi. NE of Concepción, in agr. area (cereals, wine, beans, livestock).

Rafaela (räfäā'lä), city (pop. 23,473), ⊙ Castellanos dept. (□ 2,580; 1947 census 81,463), central Santa Fe prov., Argentina, 50 mi. NW of Santa Fe; rail junction, industrial and agr. center. Mfg.: dairy products, frozen meat, textile goods, cement articles, lime, agr. machinery; sawmills, flour mills, salt refinery. Agr. products: corn, wheat, oats, flax, barley, livestock. Has natl. col., botanical research station. Founded 1881 by Ital. settlers.

Rafael Delgado (räfäĕl' dĕlgä'dō), town (pop. 1,502), Veracruz, E Mexico, in Sierra Madre Oriental, 8 mi. WSW of Córdoba; coffee, fruit.

Rafael J. García (hō'tä gärsē'ä), town (pop. 1,231), Puebla, central Mexico, in Sierra Madre, 27 mi. NE of Serdán; cereals, maguey, fruit, stock. Formerly Chilchotla.

Rafael Lara Grajales (lä'rä grähä'lĕs) or **San Marcos** (sän mär'kōs), town (pop. 1,914), Puebla, central Mexico, 29 mi. NE of Puebla; alt. 7,798 ft.; rail junction; cereals, maguey.

Rafael Lucio (lōō'syō), town (pop. 1,026), Veracruz, E Mexico, in Sierra Madre Oriental, on railroad and 7 mi. NW of Jalapa; coffee, corn.

Rafah, Palestine-Egypt: see Rafa.

Rafaï (räfī'), village, S Ubangi-Shari, Fr. Equatorial Africa, near Bomu R. (Belgian Congo border), 80 mi. ENE of Bangassou; native market and customs station.

Rafal (räfäl'), village (pop. 1,116), Alicante prov., E Spain, 6 mi. ENE of Orihuela; ships hemp, oranges, pepper, potatoes.

Rafalovka (rŭfä'lŭfkŭ), Pol. *Rafałówka* (räfäwōōf'kä), village (1931 pop. 1,320), NW Rovno oblast, Ukrainian SSR, in Pripet Marshes, on Styr R. and 30 mi. W of Sarny; flour milling, sawmilling, woodworking.

Raf'at, Tall, Syria: see Rif'at, Tell.

Rafelbuñol (räfĕlbōōnyōl'), village (pop. 2,575), Valencia prov., E Spain, 9 mi. NNE of Valencia, in rich truck-farming and rice-growing area; olive-oil and meat processing.

Rafelcófer (räfĕlkō'fĕr), village (pop. 1,483), Valencia prov., E Spain, 3 mi. S of Gandía; rice and flour milling; orange groves.

Rafelguaraf (räfĕlgwäräf'), village (pop. 1,357), Valencia prov., E Spain, 6 mi. NE of Játiva; orange groves, rice fields; peanuts, olive oil.

Raffadali (räf-fädä'lē), town (pop. 11,207), Agrigento prov., S Sicily, 7 mi. NNW of Agrigento; agr. products (cereals, olive oil, almonds).

Raffles Bay, inlet of Arafura Sea, bet. Croker Isl. (E) and N shore of Cobourg Peninsula, N Northern Territory, Australia; 12 mi. long, 7 mi. wide; connected with Mountnorris Bay by Bowen Strait. Site of early Br. settlement (1827–29).

Rafha (räf'hŭ), settlement, N Saudi Arabia, at Iraq line, 170 mi. NNE of Hail; 29°35'N 43°35'E. Oil-pumping station on pipe line from Abqaiq to Saida. Formerly called Jumaima.

Raf-Raf (räf-räf'), village, Bizerte dist., N Tunisia, 18 mi. ESE of Bizerte; muscat grapes.

Rafsinjan, Rafsenjan, or **Rafsanjan** (räfsänjän'), town (1942 pop. 14,867), Eighth Prov., in Kerman, SE Iran, 65 mi. W of Kerman and on highway to Yezd; center of rich agr. area, producing grain, cotton, and opium; noted pistachio production. Formerly called Bahramabad.

Rafso, Finland: see Reposaari.

Raft River, in N Utah and S Idaho, rises in Raft River Mts., Utah, flows c.60 mi. generally N, through Cassia co., Idaho, to Snake R. E of L. Walcott.

Raft River Mountains (8–10,000 ft.), in Minidoka Natl. Forest, Box Elder co., NW Utah; extend E–W along Idaho line.

Raftsund (räft'sōōn), strait (1–2 mi. wide) of the North Sea, N Norway, extends 17 mi. SW–NE bet. Austvagoy (Lofoten Isls.) and Hinnoy (Vesteralen group). Overhanging cliffs and high waterfalls are popular tourist attraction.

Raga (rä'gä), village (pop. 600), Bahr el Ghazal prov., S Anglo-Egyptian Sudan, near Fr. Equatorial Africa border, 170 mi. WNW of Wau; road junction.

Ragalla or **Ragala** (rŭgŭl'ŭ), village (pop., including near-by villages, 1,388), Central Prov., Ceylon, in Piduru Ridges, 7 mi. NE of Nuwara Eliya; rail spur terminus; tea-transport center.

Ragan (rā'gŭn), village (pop. 102), Harlan co., S Nebr., 15 mi. N of Alma; grain, livestock, dairy and poultry produce.

Ragang, Mount (rägäng'), active volcano (9,236 ft.), W central Mindanao, Philippines, SE of L. Lanao.

Ragay (rägī'), town (1939 pop. 1,315; 1948 municipality pop. 20,062), Camarines Sur prov., SE Luzon, Philippines, 30 mi. WNW of Naga, near Ragay Gulf; sawmilling.

Ragay Gulf, arm of Sibuyan Sea, SE Luzon, Philippines, separated from Mompog Pass by Bondoc Peninsula, merges SE with Burias Pass; 60 mi. long, 40 mi. wide. Burias Isl. is at entrance.

Ragaz, Switzerland: see Bad Ragaz.

Ragedara (rŭgā'dŭrŭ), village, North Western Prov., Ceylon, 16 mi. NE of Kurunegala; graphite-mining center; coconut palms, vegetables, rice, tobacco.

Ragendorf, Hungary: see Rajka.

Rages, Iran: see Rai.

Ragged Island. 1 In SW Maine, small island in Casco Bay off Phippsburg; the "Elm Island" of Elijah Kellogg's stories. **2** In S Maine; see Matinicus Isle.

Ragged Island and Cays (kāz, kēz), archipelago and district (□ 5; pop. 417), S Bahama Isls., at SE fringe of the Great Bahama Bank, SW of Long Isl., c.175 mi. SE of Nassau, 70 mi. N of Cuba. Consists of Great Ragged Island (or Ragged Isl.) and Little Ragged Isl., and is generally considered to include a chain of small cays stretching c.70 mi. northward. Group sometimes called Jumento Cays.

Ragged Lake, Piscataquis co., central Maine, 32 mi. WNW of Millinocket, SW of Caribou L., to which it is joined by a stream; 6 mi. long, 1.5 mi. wide.

Ragged Mountain, Maine: see Camden Hills.

Raghery, Northern Ireland: see Rathlin.

Raghunathpur (rŭgōōnät'pōōr), town (pop. 8,390), Manbhum dist., SE Bihar, India, on tributary of Damodar R. and 23 mi. NE of Purulia; road center; trades in rice, corn, oilseeds, bajra, sugar cane; silk growing.

Raglan, New Zealand: see Ngaruawahia.

Ragland, town (pop. 1,008), St. Clair co., E Ala., 20 mi. WNW of Anniston, near Coosa R.

Ragnit, Russian SFSR: see Neman.

Ragsdale, village (pop. 1,612, with adjoining Gloriana), Dougherty co., SW Ga.

Raguhn (rä'gōōn), town (pop. 7,523), in former Anhalt state, central Germany, after 1945 in Saxony-Anhalt, on the Mulde and 6 mi. N of Bitterfeld; paper milling, metalworking.

Ragunda (rä'gŭn"dä), village, Jamtland co., N central Sweden, on Indal R. and 30 mi. W of Sollefteа; dairying, lumbering. Has 13th-cent. church. Just SE are Doda Falls (dŭ'dä"), Swedish *Döda Fallet* [=dead falls], noted boulder formation, site of high falls until drained (1796) by landslide which forced Indal R. into new channel.

Ragusa (rägōō'zä), province (□ 582; pop. 223,115), SE Sicily; ⊙ Ragusa. Hilly terrain, rising to 2,500 ft. in N; drained by Irminio and Acate rivers. Agr. (wheat, olives, carob beans, cotton); livestock raising (cattle, sheep). Chief asphalt-mining region of Italy centered at Ragusa and Modica. Prov. formed 1927.

Ragusa, city (pop. 40,480), ⊙ Ragusa prov., SE Sicily, on Irminio R. and 32 mi. SW of Syracuse; 36°56'N 14°44'E. Chief asphalt-mining center of Italy (exports c.2,000,000 tons of asphalt rock annually; estimated reserves of 500,000,000 tons in vicinity). Petroleum refining, stone carving; mfg. (wrought-iron products, cement, cotton and linen textiles, furniture, pianos); agr. products (cheese, wine, olive oil, honey). Site of cathedral, Gothic churches, palaces. Old quarter has town walls and castle of Byzantine period. Near by are necropolises which contained prehistoric weapons and utensils, and Greek tombs (perhaps site of anc. Hybla Heraea).

Ragusa, Yugoslavia: see Dubrovnik.

Ragusavecchia, Yugoslavia: see Cavtat.

Raha (rŭ'hŭ), village, Nowgong dist., central Assam, India, on Kalang R. and 14 mi. SW of Nowgong; rice, jute, rape and mustard.

Raha, Indonesia: see Muna.

Rahad or **Er Rahad** (ĕr rähäd', rä'hăd), town, Kordofan prov., central Anglo-Egyptian Sudan, on railroad and 45 mi. SE of El Obeid; cotton, gum arabic, peanuts, sesame, corn, durra; livestock.

Rahad River, in Ethiopia and Anglo-Egyptian Sudan, rises in highlands W of L. Tana, 30 mi. SW of Chilga, flows over 300 mi. NW to the Blue Nile just N of Wad Medani. Navigable in flood season (late summer).

Rahaeng, Thailand: see TAK.

Rahama (rähä'mä), town, Bauchi prov., Northern Provinces, N central Nigeria, on Bauchi Plateau, 40 mi. NNW of Jos, near railroad (Rahama station is 5 mi. SW, in Zaria prov.); tin mining; cotton, millet, durra.

Raheita (rähä'tä), village, Assab div., SE Eritrea, near Fr. Somaliland border and Bab el Mandeb strait, on Red Sea coast, 30 mi. SE of Assab, in camel-breeding region.

Raheng, Thailand: see TAK.

Rahgird or **Rahgerd** (both: rägĕrd'), town, Second Prov., in Qum, N central Iran, on railroad and 35 mi. SW of Qum. Also spelled Rahjird or Rahjerd.

Rahimatpur (rŭ'hĭmŭtpŏŏr), town (pop. 6,543), Satara North dist., central Bombay, India, 16 mi. SE of Satara; agr. market center (millet, peanuts, wheat, gur); peanut pressing.

Rahimyar Khan (rŭhēm'yŭr khän'), town (pop. 6,239), Bahawalpur state, W Pakistan, on railroad and 105 mi. SW of Bahawalpur; wheat, cotton; cotton ginning and milling, rice husking, hand-loom weaving; glycerine-recovery plant and soap factory. Also written Rahim Yar Khan and Rahim Yarkhan.

Rahjerd or **Rahjird**, Iran: see RAHGIRD.

Rahmaniya, El, Er Rahmaniya, or **Al-Rahmaniyah** (all: ĕr-rämänē'yù), village (pop. 10,894), Beheira prov., NW Lower Egypt, on Rosetta branch of the Nile and 11 mi. NE of Damanhur; cotton, rice, cereals.

Raho, Ukrainian SSR: see RAKHOV.

Rahon (rä'hōn), town (pop. 8,065), Jullundur dist., central Punjab, India, 38 mi. SE of Jullundur; rail terminus; local trade in grain, cotton, sugar; hand-loom weaving, colored-thread spinning.

Rahova, Bulgaria: see ORYAKHOVO.

Rahpar, India: see RAPAR.

Rahuri (rä'hŏŏrē), village (pop. 8,296), Ahmadnagar dist., E Bombay, India, 20 mi. NNW of Ahmadnagar; agr. market; sugar milling, gur mfg.

Rahwali (rä'välē), village, Gujranwala dist., E Punjab, W Pakistan, 6 mi. N of Gujranwala; sugar milling.

Rahway (rô'wā), industrial city (pop. 21,290), Union co., NE N.J., on Rahway R and 10 mi. SW of Newark; mfg. (pharmaceuticals, lubricating oil, chemicals, cereals, dehydrated foods, metal products, books, rubber goods, furniture, vacuum cleaners); truck farms. Drug mfg. is 1 of city's oldest industries. Settled c.1720 from Elizabeth, inc. 1858. British were routed in skirmishes here, 1777. Abraham Clark, b. near by, is buried here.

Rahway River, NE N.J., rises in central Essex co., flows S, past Rahway, then E to Arthur Kill N of Carteret; c.30 mi. long. Receives South Branch (c.10 mi. long) near Rahway.

Rai or **Rai-sur-Rîle** (rā'-sürēl'), village (pop. 662), Orne dept., NW France, 3 mi. SW of Laigle; copper-wire mfg.

Rai, Ray, Rei, Rey (all: rā), or **Shahr Rey** (shä'hŭr), town, Second Prov., in Teheran, N Iran, 6 mi. S of Teheran (linked by narrow-gauge railroad built c.1890) and on railroad to Meshed; cement plant. Excursion suburb and pilgrimage center, visited for golden-domed shrine of Shah Abdul Azim. Identified with the anc. *Rhagae* and the biblical *Rages* of the book of Tobit, Rai was mentioned in the *Avesta* and the Behistun inscriptions of Darius. Alexander the Great passed here in 330 B.C. Later the city was an important center of the Parthian empire. It flourished under Arab rule, was the birthplace of the physican Rhazes and Harun al-Rashid, and the latter's favorite residence. City continued to play an important role under Mahmud of Ghazni, who captured it in 1027, and especially under the Seljuks until 1194. Ruined 1221 by Jenghiz Khan. Extensive excavations have been carried on near the modern town, which is also known as Shah Abdul Azim.

Raiano (räyä'nô), town (pop. 4,083), Aquila prov., Abruzzi e Molise, S central Italy, 7 mi. NW of Sulmona; lye mfg.

Raiatea (rī'ätä'ä), island (□ 92; pop. 4,505), largest of Leeward group, SOCIETY ISLANDS, Fr. Oceania, S Pacific; 16°50'S 151°24'W. Circumference c.30 mi.; volcanic and mountainous; highest peak Mt. Temehani (3,388 ft.). Uturoa is ⊙ and chief port of Leeward Isls.; site of fruit cannery, govt. hosp., and wireless station. Produces copra, tobacco, kapok, oranges, vanilla. Raiatea was anc. seat of learning of Polynesia. Formerly Ulieta.

Raíces, Cordillera de los (kôrdĭyā'rä dā lōs räē'sĕs), Andean range in Malleco prov., S central Chile, 20 mi. E of Curacautín; rises to 6,595 ft. Pierced by a road tunnel bet. Curacautín and Lonquimay, on road to Zapala, Argentina.

Raichikhinsk or **Raychikhinsk** (rī'chĭkhĕnsk), city (1944 pop. over 10,000), SE Amur oblast, Russian SFSR, on spur of Trans-Siberian RR and 85 mi. ESE of Blagoveshchensk; lignite-mining center; power plant. Originally village of Raichikha, it developed in 1930s; became city in 1944, when it incorporated near-by Kivdinski (mining town).

Raichur (rī'chŏŏr), district (□ 6,630; pop. 1,041,959), SW Hyderabad state, India, on Deccan Plateau; ⊙ Raichur. Bordered N by Kistna R., S by Tungabhadra R.; mainly lowland with isolated outcrops. Fertile soil produces millet, cotton, oilseeds (chiefly peanuts), wheat, rice, tobacco. Cotton ginning, oilseed and rice milling, silk weaving; cattle raising. Abandoned gold mines at Hutti reopened in 1949. Main trade centers; Koppal, Raichur. Armies of allied Deccan sultans defeated Vijayanagar forces at battlefield of Talikota (on right bank of the Kistna, 23 mi. S of Talikota village) in 1565. Became part of Hyderabad during state's formation in 18th cent. Pop. 85% Hindu, 12% Moslem, 1% Christian.

Raichur, town (pop. 34,972), ⊙ Raichur dist., SW Hyderabad state, India, 110 mi. SW of Hyderabad; agr. trade center (millet, cotton, wheat, oilseeds); cotton ginning, oilseed and rice milling; ceramics; tannery. Experimental farm. Fort (built c.1300).

Raida, Aden: see REIDAT AL 'ABDUL WADUD.

Raidak River (rī'däk), in Bhutan and India, rises in W Assam Himalayas in NW Bhutan, near the Chomo Lhari; flows S through Bhutan (here called Wong Chu), past Tashi Chho and Marichong, bifurcating just inside India; right arm continues S past Tufanganj to TORSA RIVER SE of Cooch Behar; total length, c.150 mi. In middle course, also called Chin Chu. Left arm (c.25 mi. long) flows S to SANKOSH RIVER. Also spelled Raidhak.

Raidjoea, Indonesia: see SAVU ISLANDS.

Raiford (rā'fürd), town, Union co., N Fla., 29 mi. NNE of Gainesville; corn, vegetables. Florida State Prison near by.

Raifun or **Rayfun** (rā'fōōn), Fr. *Reyfoun*, village (pop. 862), central Lebanon, 12 mi. ENE of Beirut; alt. 3,600 ft.; summer resort; sericulture, tobacco, lemons, fruits.

Raiganj (rī'gŭnj), village, West Dinajpur dist., N West Bengal, India, on tributary of the Mahananda and 50 mi. NW of Balurghat; rice milling; rice, jute, barley, rape and mustard.

Raigarh (rī'gŭr), district (□ 5,121; pop. 849,888), E Madhya Pradesh, India, on W Chota Nagpur Plateau; ⊙ Raigarh. Bordered NW by Surguja dist., NE by Bihar, SE by Orissa; in rugged E highlands (average alt. c.3,000 ft.) of Satpura Range; drained mainly by the Mahanadi and its tributaries. Largely covered with dense sal jungles mixed with bamboo, khair, and myrobalan; lac cultivation. Agr. (rice, oilseeds) in valleys; beekeeping, tussah-silk weaving. Deposits of coal, iron-ore, limestone (quarries near Dharmjaygarh and Sakti), and bauxite; gold placers in mtn. streams. Dist. created in 1948 by merger of former Chhattisgarh States of Jashpur, Raigarh, Sakti, Sarangarh, and Udaipur. Pop. 50% Hindu, 50% tribal.

Raigarh, town (pop. 20,327), ⊙ Raigarh dist., E Madhya Pradesh, India, on tributary of Mahanadi R. and 80 mi. ESE of Bilaspur; jute milling, mfg. (silk, soap, glass bangles). Lac grown in near-by sal forests. Coal and iron-ore deposits near by. Was ⊙ former princely state of Raigarh (□ 1,444; pop. 312,643) of Chhattisgarh States; since 1948, state inc. into Raigarh dist.

Raigorodok or **Raygorodok** (rīgŭrŭdôk'), town (1926 pop. 3,610), N Stalino oblast, Ukrainian SSR, in the Donbas, 7 mi. NE of Slavyansk; chalk quarries. Formerly also Krasny Gorodok.

Raigrod, Poland: see RAJGROD.

Raijua, Indonesia: see SAVU ISLANDS.

Raikoke Island or **Raykoke Island** (rīkô'kyĭ), one of N main Kurile Isls. group, Russian SFSR; separated from Lovushki Isls. (NE) by Kruzenshtern Strait, from Matua Isl. (SE) by Golovnin Strait; 48°18'N 153°15'E; just over 1 mi. in diameter. Truncated volcanic cone rises to 1,808 ft.

Raikot (rī'kōt), town (pop. 13,777), Ludhiana dist., central Punjab, India, 23 mi. SW of Ludhiana; wheat, gram, oilseeds, cotton; hand-loom weaving. Sometimes spelled Raekot.

Raikovo or **Raykovo** (rī'kôvô), village (pop. 2,850), Plovdiv dist., S Bulgaria, in SE Rhodope Mts., on left branch of Arda R. and 4 mi. E of Smolyan; tobacco, rye, potatoes, livestock; mineral springs.

Railroad, borough (pop. 300), York co., S Pa., 14 mi. S of York.

Railton, town (pop. 627), N Tasmania, 38 mi. W of Launceston; rail junction; wheat, dairying center; limestone quarries, cement works.

Raimangal River, India: see JAMUNA RIVER.

Rain (rīn), town (pop. 2,716), Swabia, W central Bavaria, Germany, 6 mi. ESE of Donauwörth; mfg. of precision instruments, weaving, brewing. Has Gothic church. Chartered c.1250.

Rainbach (rīn'bäkh), town (pop. 2,775), NE Upper Austria, 3 mi. N of Freistadt, near Czechoslovak line; rye, potatoes.

Rainbow Bridge National Monument (160 acres; established 1910), S Utah, in Navajo Indian Reservation, bet. Colorado R. and Ariz. line, c.130 mi. NNE of Flagstaff, Ariz. Rainbow Bridge (309 ft. high, c.275 ft. long), rainbow-shaped arch of pink sandstone extending across deep gorge, is largest natural bridge in world.

Rainbow Lake, resort village, Franklin co., NE N.Y., on Rainbow L. (c.3 mi. long), in the Adirondacks, 10 mi. N of Saranac Lake village.

Rainbow Lake, Piscataquis co., central Maine, 19 mi. NW of Millinocket, in hunting, fishing area; 4 mi. long.

Raincy, Le (lù rĕsē'), town (pop. 12,122), Seine-et-Oise dept., N central France, an ENE suburb of Paris, 8 mi. from Notre Dame Cathedral; mfg. (biscuits, furniture, toys, bicycle parts, buttons, filters).

Rainelle (rānĕl'), town (pop. 853), Greenbrier co., SE W.Va., 20 mi. NW of Lewisburg, in agr., lumbering, and coal-mining area; large hardwood lumber mill.

Rainford, urban district (1931 pop. 3,494; 1951 census 4,085), SW Lancashire, England, 4 mi. NW of St. Helens; agr. market.

Rainham. **1** Town and parish (pop. 3,897), SW Essex, England, near the Thames, 12 mi. E of London; chemical- and metalworks (nonferrous metals; tin smelting). Has Norman church. **2** Town, Kent, England: see GILLINGHAM.

Rainhill, residential village and parish (pop. 3,006), SW Lancashire, England, 3 mi. S of St. Helens; truck gardening. Coal mining near by.

Rainier (rùnēr', rā-, rā'nēr). **1** City (pop. 1,285), Columbia co., NW Oregon, on Columbia R. (spanned here by interstate bridge), opposite Longview, Wash., and c.40 mi. NNW of Portland; lumber, flour, canned vegetables. Has salmon and smelt fisheries. Settled 1851, inc. 1885. **2** Town (pop. 331), Thurston co., W Wash., 14 mi. SE of Olympia.

Rainier, Mount, Wash.: see MOUNT RAINIER NATIONAL PARK.

Rains, county (□ 235; pop. 4,266), NE Texas; ⊙ Emory. Prairie in W, woodland in E; drained by Sabine R. (SW boundary). Agr. (cotton, fruit, truck, peanuts, grains); livestock (mainly cattle). Some timber cut; clay deposits. Formed 1870.

Rainsburg, borough (pop. 189), Bedford co., S Pa., 8 mi. S of Bedford.

Rainy Lake (□ c.350), in N Minn. and SW Ont., lying partly in Koochiching and St. Louis counties, Minn.; c.50 mi. long and generally narrow, it lies along Can.– U.S. line for c.35 mi. Fort Frances (Ont.), International Falls (Minn.) are near SW shore. Includes many small isls., peninsulas, and bays, and lies in densely wooded area. It is continuous with Namakan L., SE, and has W outlet in Rainy R., which flows 85 mi. W along Can. line, past International Falls and Baudette, to Lake of the Woods. River is dammed for power at International Falls and used for logging. Lake has numerous fishing and hunting resorts and is used as reservoir.

Rainy River, district (□ 7,276; pop. 19,132), NW Ont., on Minn. border and on Rainy R.; ⊙ Fort Frances.

Rainy River, town (pop. 1,205), NW Ont., on Rainy River (bridge) and 50 mi. W of Fort Frances, on Minn. border; dairying, lumbering, woodworking.

Rainy River. **1** In NE Mich., rises in N Montmorency co., flows c.30 mi. NNW, through forest and farm area, to SE end of Black L. in Presque Isle co. State park at its mouth (camping, bathing). **2** In Minn. and Ont.: see RAINY LAKE.

Raipur (rī'pŏŏr), district (□ 8,205; pop. 1,516,686), E Madhya Pradesh, India, on Deccan Plateau; ⊙ Raipur. Bordered NW by Seonath R.; upper Mahanadi R. valley divides dist. into plains (W) and thickly forested hills (E; rise to over 3,000 ft. in S). Rice, oilseeds (chiefly flax), wheat, and cotton in plains area (canal irrigation). Sal, bamboo, teak, myrobalan in hills (sawmilling, lac cultivation, cattle raising). Sandstone, limestone, and lead deposits. Rice, oilseed, flour, and dal milling, shellac mfg. Pop. 80% Hindu, 18% tribal (mainly Gond), 1% Moslem.

Raipur. **1** Town (pop. 63,465), ⊙ Raipur dist., E Madhya Pradesh, India, 165 mi. E of Nagpur; rail junction (line to Parvatipuram, Madras, completed 1932 as part of Vizagapatam port expansion plan); trade center; rice, oilseed, flour, and dal milling, sawmilling, mfg. of shellac, soap; engineering works. Rajkumar Col. Tuberculosis clinic. Was hq. of former Chhattisgarh States. Experimental farm (rice research, silk growing) is just E. **2** Village, Bankura dist., W West Bengal, India, on Kasai R. and 31 mi. SSW of Bankura; cotton weaving; rice, corn, wheat, sugar cane. Lac growing near by.

Rairakhol (rī'räkōl), village, Sambalpur dist., central Orissa, India, 36 mi. SE of Sambalpur; trades in timber, rice, oilseeds. Formerly called Rampur. Was ⊙ former princely state of Rairakhol (□ 857; pop. 38,185) in Orissa States; state inc. 1949 into Sambalpur dist.

Rairangpur (rī'rŭngpŏŏr), village, Mayurbhanj dist., NE Orissa, India, on railroad and 40 mi. WNW of Baripada; shellac factory.

Raisen (rī'sān), town (pop. 3,886), N Bhopal state, India, 24 mi. ENE of Bhopal; market center (wheat, millet, cloth fabrics). Annual festival fair.

Raisi, Punta (pōōn'tä räē'zē), point on NW coast of Sicily, at E end of Gulf of Castellammare; 38°11'N 13°6'E.

Raisin River, SE Mich., rises SE of Jackson city, flows generally SE c.115 mi. past Clinton, Tecumseh, and Dundee, to L. Erie at Monroe. Raisin R. massacre of Amer. troops occurred (Jan., 1813) at MONROE.

Raiskoye or **Rayskoye** (rī'skŭyŭ), town (1939 pop. over 500), N central Stalino oblast, Ukrainian SSR, in the Donbas, 5 mi. SW of Druzhkovka.

Raismes (rĕm), industrial town (pop. 8,826), Nord dept., N France, 3 mi. NNW of Valenciennes; metallurgical works mfg. railroad rolling stock, mining equipment, chains, and tools. Just N is large forest of Raismes.

Rai-sur-Rîle, France: see RAI.

Raita (rī'tŭ), village, Kushtia dist., W East Bengal, E Pakistan, on the Padma and 17 mi. NW of Kushtia; rail spur terminus; rice, jute, linseed, sugar cane. Until 1947, in Nadia dist. of Br. Bengal prov.

Raivavae (rī'vävä'ä), volcanic island (□ c.6; pop. 748), Tubuai Isls., Fr. Oceania, S Pacific, 100 mi. SE of Tubuai isl. Produces coffee, arrowroot. Chief town is Amaru, site of anc. Polynesian temples. Discovered 1777 by Capt. Cook, annexed 1880 by France. Sometimes called Vavitu.

Raivola, Russian SFSR: see ROSHCHINO.

Raiwind (rī'vĭnd), village, Lahore dist., E Punjab, W Pakistan, 22 mi. S of Lahore; rail junction; cotton ginning; ironworks.

Raja, Mount (rä'jŭ), mountain (7,474 ft.), W Borneo, Indonesia, 100 mi. SE of Sintang; highest peak in Indonesian part of isl.

Raja Ampat Islands (äm'pät), Netherlands New Guinea, just W of Vogelkop peninsula (NW New Guinea), bet. Ceram Sea (S) and the Pacific (N); 1°12'S 129°46'E; WAIGEU and MISOOL are chief isls. Also spelled Radja Ampat.

Rajabhat Khawa (rä'jäbät kä'wŭ), village, Jalpaiguri dist., N West Bengal, India, in Western Duars region, 50 mi. ENE of Jalpaiguri. Rail junction, with spurs to Dalsingpara (16 mi. NW) and Jainti (8 mi. NNE); sawmilling; trades in rice, tea, rape and mustard, tobacco, jute. Formerly called Rajabhatkhoa.

Rajaburi, Thailand: see RATBURI.

Rajagriha, India: see RAJGIR.

Rajah, The, mountain (9,903 ft.), W Alta., near B.C. border, in Rocky Mts., in Jasper Natl. Park 33 mi. NW of Jasper; 53°16'N 118°33'W.

Rajahmundry (rä'jŭmŭndrē), city (pop. 74,564), East Godavari dist., NE Madras, India, on left bank of Godavari R. (rail bridge), at head of delta, and 30 mi. W of Cocanada. Trade center for delta and coastal products (rice, salt) received via DOWLAISWARAM; shipping center for timber (teak, sal) floated down the Godavari from forested hills (N); paper, cotton, and rice milling, mfg. of tiles, crucibles, aluminumware. Has col. Tobacco research institute. A stronghold of Indian powers until taken 1753 by French; ceded to English in 1757. N rail station (bridge) called Godavari. Construction of dam across the Godavari, near Polavaram, 20 mi. NNW, begun 1948 as part of irrigation and hydroelectric project.

Rajaisur, India: see RAJASUR.

Rajakhera (rä"jăkä'rŭ), town (pop. 7,395), E Rajasthan, India, 22 mi. NE of Dholpur; millet, gram.

Rajaldesar (räjŭldä'sŭr), town (pop. 8,310), N Rajasthan, India, 70 mi. E of Bikaner; trades locally in wool and hides.

Rajam, India: see RAZAM.

Rajampet (rä'jŭmpĕt) or **Razampeta** (rä'zŭmpĕtŭ), town (pop. 8,168), Cuddapah dist., central Madras, India, 30 mi. SE of Cuddapah; rice, sugar cane, turmeric. Barite workings near by. Large fruit research station 20 mi. SE, at village of Kodur.

Rajang River (rŭjăng'), largest river of Sarawak, in W Borneo, rises in mts. c.80 mi. E of Bintulu, flows SW, turns generally W, past Kapit and Sarikei, to S.China Sea 45 mi. WSW of Sibu (at confluence of Rajang and small Igan R.); c.350 mi. long. Navigable 80 mi. to Sibu by ocean-going vessels. Large delta. Sometimes spelled Rejang.

Rajanpur (rä'jŭnpŏŏr), town (pop. 5,394), Dera Ghazi Khan dist., SW Punjab, W Pakistan, 70 mi. SSW of Dera Ghazi Khan; market center (grain, cotton, indigo); hand-loom weaving.

Rajaori, dist., Kashmir: see RIASI, dist.

Rajaori (rä'jourē), town (pop. 2,449), Riasi dist., SW Kashmir, in S foothills of Pir Panjal Range, on tributary of the Chenab and 37 mi. NW of Riasi; corn, wheat, rice, oilseeds. Tomb of 19th-cent. raja; residence of former Moslem Rajput rajas of Rajaori. Also spelled Rajauri; also called Rampur, Rampur Rajauri.

Rajapalaiyam or **Rajapalayam** (both: rä"jŭpä'-līyŭm), town (pop. 46,289), Ramnad dist., S Madras, India, 50 mi. SW of Madura; trade center for cotton, sugar, timber; mfg. of surgical cotton goods. Pop. mostly Telugu-speaking Rajus, emigrants from 14th-cent. kingdom of Vijayanagar. Cattle raising in foothills (W); betel farms.

Rajapur (rä'jäpŏŏr). **1** Town (pop. 7,489), Ratnagiri dist., W Bombay, India, 28 mi. SE of Ratnagiri; trades in rice, hemp. Hot springs, sacred to Hindus, near by. Fishing off Rajapur Bay (11 mi. W). **2** Town (pop. 5,249), Banda dist., S Uttar Pradesh, India, on the Jumna and 50 mi. E of Banda; trades in gram, jowar, wheat, oilseeds, rice. Founded by Tulsi Das, author of vernacular version of the Ramayana. Also called Rajpur.

Rajapur, town, SW Nepal, in the Terai, on Kauriala arm of Karnali (Gogra) R. and 70 mi. NNW of Bahraich (India); trades in rice, jute, wheat, barley, buckwheat, sabai grass, vegetables. Connected by road with Indian rail termini at Kauriala Ghat (5 mi. SW) and Katarnian Ghat (7 mi. SSE).

Raja Sansi (rä'jŭ sän'sē), town (pop. 6,033), Amritsar dist., W Punjab, India, 8 mi. NNW of Amritsar; agr. market (wheat, gram, cotton); hand-loom weaving.

Rajasthan (rä'jŭstän) [Sanskrit,=land of princes], constituent state (□ 128,424; 1951 pop. 15,297,979), NW India; ⊙ Jaipur. W half comprises major portion of THAR DESERT, while E section is part of upland region of central India; Chambal R. forms part of E boundary. State is bordered W by W Pakistan (Bahawalpur and Khairpur states and Sind), S by Bombay, SE and E by Madhya Bharat, NE by Uttar Pradesh, N by Punjab (India) and detached S area of Patiala and East Punjab States Union; has large enclave (SE) in Madhya Bharat; surrounds Ajmer (center). Varied topography covers arid sandy wastes (W, N) separated from comparatively fertile E section by ARAVALLI RANGE (general height, 1,500–3,000 ft.), which extends NE–SW through center of state. Drained SW by Luni R., E by Banganga, Banas, Chambal, and Kali Sindh rivers. Annual rainfall in W desert 5–10 in., in E section 20–30 in., in S hills 35–50 in. Predominantly agr. (center, E) and pastoral (N, W); millet, wheat, corn, cotton are cultivated; camels, sheep, goats raised. Leopards, hyenas, and tigers fairly common in hills and E jungles. Few large industries exist, but Bhilwara, Pali, Kotah, Jodhpur, and Kishangarh have cotton mills; cementworks at Lakheri; handicrafts (cotton and woolen fabrics, pottery, metalware, saddlery). Mineral resources include salt (Sambhar L.), sandstone, marble (notably at Makrana), coal (at Palana), mica, and gypsum. Chief cities and trade centers are Jaipur, Jodhpur, Bikaner, Alwar, Kotah, and Udaipur. State contains many interesting historical sites, such as forts of Chitor, Ranthambhor, and Kumbhalgarh, Buddhist ruins at Bairat, anc. Rajput capitals of Amber and Mandor, battlefield of Khanua, and artificial lakes of Dhebar, Raj Samand, and Pichola. Union of Rajasthan was originally formed in March, 1948, by merger of smaller princely states of RAJPUTANA STATES of Kotah, Tonk, Bundi, Banswara, Dungarpur, Partabgarh, Kishangarh, Jhalawar, Shahpura, Kushalgarh, and Lawa; Udaipur joined in April, 1948; Jodhpur, Bikaner, Jaipur, and Jaisalmer were included in March, 1949. Alwar, Bharatpur, Karauli, and Dholpur, which had merged (March, 1948) to form union of Matsya, were inc. into Rajasthan in May, 1949. Former princely state of Sirohi, administered by Bombay govt. during 1949, was partitioned in Jan., 1950, with major portion (N, W) merging with Rajasthan. In 1950, a mutual exchange of small outlying enclaves was effected with Madhya Bharat. State comprises 25 dists.: Alwar, Banswara, Barmer, Bharatpur, Bhilwara, Bikaner, Bundi, Chitor, Churu, Dungarpur, Jaipur, Jaisalmer, Jalor, Jhalawar, Jhunjhunu, Jodhpur, Kotah, Nagaur, Pali, Sawai Madhopur, Sikar, Sirohi, Sri Ganganagar, Tonk, and Udaipur. Chief languages, Rajasthani and Hindi. Pop. 75% Hindu, 12% tribal, 8% Moslem, 2% Jain. Sometimes spelled Rajastan.

Rajasur (rä'jäsŏŏr), town (pop. 5,347), Bidar dist., W central Hyderabad state, India, 33 mi. WSW of Bidar; millet, cotton, oilseeds, rice. Also spelled Rajaisur and Rajeshwar.

Rajauri, Kashmir: see RAJAORI.

Rajbari (räj'bärē), town (pop. 9,048), Faridpur dist., S central East Bengal, E Pakistan, 16 mi. NW of Faridpur; trades in rice, jute, oilseeds, sugar cane.

Rajburi, Thailand: see RATBURI.

Rajec (rä'yĕts), town (pop. 2,753), NW Slovakia, Czechoslovakia, 10 mi. SSW of Zilina; rail terminus. Peat marshes near by. Noted health resort of Rajecke Teplice (rä'yĕtskä tyĕ'plĭtsĕ), Slovak *Rajecké Teplice*, Hung. *Rajecfürdő*, with radioactive thermal springs (84°–102°F.) is c.3 mi. NE, in heavily forested valley (alt. 1,377 ft.).

Rajeshwar, India: see RAJASUR.

Raj Gangpur (räj' gäng'pŏŏr), village, Sundargarh dist., N Orissa, India, 36 mi. E of Sundargarh; mfg. of coir and jute rope.

Rajgarh (räj'gŭr). **1** Town (pop. 7,638), ⊙ Rajgarh dist., central Madhya Bharat, India, 85 mi. NE of Ujjain; agr. market (wheat, millet). Was ⊙ former princely state of Rajgarh (□ 926; pop. 148,609) of Central India agency; since 1948, state merged with Madhya Bharat. **2** Town (pop. 3,524), W Madhya Bharat, India, 2 mi. NW of Sardarpur; local market for cotton, millet, wheat. **3** Town (pop. 12,261), NE Rajasthan, India, 135 mi. ENE of Bikaner; rail junction; market center for millet, gram, wool, hides, cotton; hand-loom weaving, cattle grazing; leather products. **4** Town (pop. 9,165), E Rajasthan, India, 23 mi. S of Alwar; local trade in millet, oilseeds, gram; hand-loom weaving. Built c.1767 by Pratap Singh, founder of Alwar state.

Rajgir (räj'gēr), village, Patna dist., N central Bihar, India, 43 mi. SSE of Patna; rail terminus; rice, gram, oilseeds, barley. In 7th cent. B.C., was 1st ⊙ early Magadha kingdom (⊙ moved to Patna or Pataliputra in 6th cent. B.C.). A residence of Gautama Buddha; site of 1st Buddhist monastery; one of 8 great anc. Buddhist pilgrimage centers. Cave sculpture, Buddhist ruins, and Jain temples in near-by hills. Formerly called Rajagriha.

Rajgrod (rī'grŏŏt), Pol. *Rajgród*, Rus. *Raigrod* or *Raygrod* (both: rī'grŭt), town (pop. 1,683), Bialystok prov., NE Poland, on SE shore of irregularly-shaped Rajgrod L. (6 mi. long N–S), 14 mi. SW of Augustow; cement mfg., flour milling, dairying.

Rajhenburg (rī'hĕnbŏŏrk), Ger. *Reichenburg* (rī'-khŭnbŏŏrk), village, S Slovenia, Yugoslavia, on Sava R., on railroad and 2 mi. N of Krsko; brown-coal mine; cement factory. Until 1918, in Styria.

Rajhrad (rī'hrät), Ger. *Raigern* (rī'gĕrn), village (pop. 2,500), S Moravia, Czechoslovakia, on Svratka R., on railroad and 7 mi. S of Brno; wheat. Has noted 11th-cent. monastery with large library.

Rajinac, peak, Yugoslavia: see VELEBIT MOUNTAINS.

Rajka (roi'kŏ), Ger. *Ragendorf*, town (pop. 3,064), Györ-Moson co., NW Hungary, 29 mi. NW of Györ, on Czechoslovak border; grain, honey; cattle, horses, ducks, geese.

Rajkot (räj'kōt), city (pop. 52,178; including former Br. civil station, 66,353), ⊙ Saurashtra and Madhya Saurashtra dist., India, on Kathiawar peninsula, 125 mi. WSW of Ahmadabad. Rail junction; airport; important commercial and trade (cotton, grain, oilseeds, hides, cloth fabrics, ghee) center; cotton, oilseeds, and flour milling, tanning, wool carding; mfg. of chemicals, matches, soap, perfumes, confectioneries, aerated water; metalworks. Stud farm and dairy near by. Rajkumar Col. (opened 1870). Has some fine public bldgs. Was hq. of former Western India States agency and ⊙ former princely state of Rajkot (□ 284; pop. 117,126) of Western India States agency; state merged 1948 with Saurashtra.

Rajmahal (räj'mŭhäl), town (pop. 4,676), Santal Parganas dist., E Bihar, India, on Ganges Plain, on Ganges R. and 55 mi. ESE of Bhagalpur; rail spur terminus; rice, maize, barley, oilseeds, rape and mustard. Islamic ruins near by. Was ⊙ Bengal under Akbar, and called Agmahal.

Rajmahal Hills, hill range (□ c.1,500), E Bihar, India, SE of Bhagalpur, bet. Dumka (S) and the Ganges (N); rise to 1,861 ft. in center. Coal mines (chiefly in S); bhabar, bamboo, and palms in dispersed forest areas. Habitat of aboriginal tribes (Paharias, Santals).

Rajnagar (räj'nŭgŭr). **1** Town (pop. 3,547), N central Vindhya Pradesh, India, 20 mi. E of Chhatarpur; millet, gram. **2** Village, Birbhum dist., W West Bengal, India, 14 mi. W of Suri; rice, wheat, corn, mango. Was ⊙ Hindu principality until absorbed (early-13th cent.) by Afghans; plundered by Oriyas in 1244. Mosque and palace ruins. Fort ruins 2½ mi. N. Also called Nagar.

Rajnagar, E Pakistan: see MAULAVI BAZAR.

Raj-Nandgaon (räj' nänd'goun), town (pop. 19,039), Drug dist., E central Madhya Pradesh, India, 40 mi. WSW of Raipur; agr.-trade and cotton-textile center; rice and oilseed milling, chemical mfg. Was ⊙ former princely state of Nandgaon, one of Chhattisgarh States.

Raj Nilgiri (räj' nēl'gĭrē), village, Balasore dist., NE Orissa, India, 11 mi. W of Balasore; local trade in rice, sal, bamboo, road metal. Was ⊙ former princely state of Nilgiri. Village formerly called Nilgiri.

Rajpat, India: see KAMATAPUR.

Rajpind Cave, India: see HISUA.

Rajpipla (räj'pēplŭ), town (pop. 15,855), Broach dist., N Bombay, India, 36 mi. ENE of Broach; rail terminus; rice, millet, tobacco; exports teak, blackwood; bobbin mfg. Formerly called Nandod. Was ⊙ former princely state of Rajpipla (□ 1,515; pop. 249,032) in Gujarat States, Bombay; state inc. 1949 into Broach dist.

Rajpur (räj'pŏŏr). **1** Town (pop. 5,732), SW Madhya Bharat, India, 17 mi. SE of Barwani; cotton, millet. Alirajpur, 55 mi. WNW, is known locally as Rajpur. **2** Town, Banda dist., Uttar Pradesh, India: see RAJAPUR. **3** Town (pop. 2,352), Dehra Dun dist., N Uttar Pradesh, India, in W Kumaun Himalaya foothills, 6 mi. NE of Dehra; glass mfg. Quartz and limestone deposits near by. **4** Town (pop. 13,614), 24-Parganas dist., SE West Bengal, India, 11 mi. SSE of Calcutta city center; rice milling; rice, jute, pulse.

Rajpura (räj'pŏŏrŭ), town (pop. 4,735), E Patiala and East Punjab States Union, India, 15 mi. NE of Patiala; rail junction; trades in grain, sugar, spices, cotton; biscuit factory. Refugee settlement for emigrants from W Pakistan.

Rajputana (räj"pŏŏtä'nŭ), name applied to land of Rajput princes (Rajasthan), a region (□ 134,959; pop. 14,253,901) of NW India. In govt. of India (c.1800–1947) official usage, it comprised former RAJPUTANA STATES and prov. of Ajmer-Merwara; it is now roughly equivalent to constituent states of RAJASTHAN and AJMER. Area was (3d cent. B.C.) largely within Asokan empire; partly under Guptas from late-4th to early-6th cent. A.D. Bet. 7th and

13th cent., several Rajput tribes appeared and rose to power, notably the Sesodias (in S parts), Chauhans (center), Kachwahas (NE), and Rathors (SW). Early Moslem invaders included Mahmud of Ghazni (1024), Mohammed Ghori (1193), and Ala-ud-din Khilji (1301–03), but no territorial annexations were firmly held and independence of Rajputs remained intact. In 15th cent., war was waged against Moslem rulers of Malwa. In early-16th cent., Rajput power reached its peak, but after battle of KHANUA (1527) decline set in and country gradually came under Mogul dominion. Fortress of CHITOR was captured 1568 by Akbar, and for next century Moguls exercised control from hq. at Ajmer. Mahrattas, taking advantage of internal feuding in mid-18th cent., held large areas of Rajputana as feudatories, but were forced (1818) to cede control to British, who had made protective treaties with Rajput states. States were subsequently grouped into political agencies (Rajputana States) under a Br. Resident to supervise relations with govt. of India. Ajmer-Merwara made a chief commissioner's prov. in 1871.

Rajputana States, former princely states (□ 132,559; pop. 13,670,208) in Rajputana, India. For administrative purposes all were grouped into political agencies under a Resident, responsible to govt. of India, with hq. at Abu. Eastern Rajputana States agency (originally established in 1869) included Bharatpur, Bundi, Dholpur, Jhalawar, Karauli, and Kotah. Jaipur Residency (originally established in 1887) included Jaipur, Alwar, Kishangarh, Lawa, Shahpura, and Tonk. Mewar and Southern Rajputana States agency (Mewar agency established in 1818; 2 agencies combined in 1931) included Udaipur, Banswara, Dungarpur, Kushalgarh, and Partabgarh; Idar and Vijayanagar were transferred from Western India States agency in early 1940s. Western Rajputana States agency (originally established 1879; revived 1934) included Danta, Jaisalmer, Jodhpur, Palanpur, and Bikaner and Sirohi (last 2 formed temporary Rajputana agency, 1920–42). In 1948–50, Palanpur, Danta, Idar, Vijayanagar, and SE section of Sirohi were inc. into Bombay, while remaining states merged to form union of RAJASTHAN.

Raj Samand (räj sŭmŭnd'), artificial lake in S central Rajasthan, India, 35 mi. NNE of Udaipur; 3½ mi. long (N–S), 1½ mi. wide. Formed by white marble dam, built in 1660s, which extends almost 3 mi. in irregular semicircle around S end; marble pavilions and arches jut out onto water. Seaplane base (E). Village of Kankroli on S shore.

Rajshahi (räj'shähē), district (□ 3,3139) 1951 pop. 2,214,000), W East Bengal, E Pakistan; ⊙ Rajshahi. Bounded S by the Padma (Ganges); drained by Mahananda and Atrai rivers. Alluvial tract; rice, jute, oilseeds, wheat, ganja (centers at Naogaon, Panchupur), sugar cane, corn; hidjal bark (*Barringtonia acutangula*) and sissoo in dispersed jungle area. Central and E section (swamps, marshes) highly malarial. Rajshahi is main industrial center; sugar processing at Gopalpur; jute pressing, rice milling at Atrai; silk-weaving factories (Naogaon, Nator); silk growing (research station near Bagha); fish exported from Chalan Bil. In 12th cent., under Sen kingdom. Present dist. formed 1832. Part of former Br. Bengal prov., India, until inc. 1947 into new Pakistan prov. of East Bengal, following creation of Pakistan; original dist. enlarged by inc. of SE portion (including Nawabganj) of original Malda dist.

Rajshahi, town (pop. 40,778), ⊙ Rajshahi dist., W East Bengal, E Pakistan, on the Padma and 120 mi. WNW of Dacca; road and trade (rice, jute, oilseeds, wheat, sugar cane) center; rice, atta, dal, flour, and sugar milling, soap mfg. Col. Also called Rampur Boalia or Rampur Bauleah.

Raju (räjōō'), Fr. *Radjou*, village, Aleppo prov., NW Syria, near Turkish border, on railroad, and 40 mi. NW of Aleppo; cotton, cereals, oats.

Rajula (rä'jŏōlŭ), town (pop. 7,860), S Saurashtra, India, 70 mi. SW of Bhaunagar; rail spur terminus; local trade in cotton, building stone, grain, timber; hand-loom weaving.

Rajura (räjōō'rŭ). **1** Village (pop. 3,957), Adilabad dist., NE Hyderabad state, India, near Wardha R., 55 mi. E of Adilabad; cotton, rice, oilseeds. Coal, mined just NW, at Wardha R., is shipped via Ballalpur (across river). Sometimes called Rajura Manikgad. **2** Town, Bidar dist., Hyderabad state, India: see AHMADPUR.

Rakahanga (rä'kähäng'ä), atoll (1,000 acres; pop. 318), Manihiki group, S Pacific, c.675 mi. NW of Rarotonga; 10°2'S 161°5'W; 3 mi. long. Discovered 1820 by Russians, became British protectorate 1889, together with MANIHIKI isl. placed 1901 under N.Z. COOK ISLANDS administration. Produces copra. Also known as Reirson.

Rakaia River (räkī'ŭ), E central S.Isl., New Zealand, rises in Southern Alps SW of Arthur's Pass, flows 95 mi. SE, past Highbank (hydroelectric plant), to Canterbury Bight 35 mi. SW of Christchurch.

Rakamaz (rŏ'kŏmŏz), town (pop. 5,497), Szabolcs co., NE Hungary, near the Tisza, 16 mi. NW of Nyiregyhaza; tobacco warehouses, flour mills; wheat, tobacco, potatoes, cattle.

Rakaposhi (räkäpō'shē), peak (c.25,550 ft.) in NW KAILAS-KARAKORAM RANGE of Karakoram mtn. system, Kashmir, 17 mi. SW of Baltit, 12 mi. SE of Chalt.

Rakas Lake or **Rakas Tal** (rä'käs täl'), Tibetan *Landak Tso* (län'däk tsō), sacred lake (□ 140) in W Himalayas, SW Tibet, 80 mi. SE of Gartok; 18 mi. long, 3–13 mi. wide; alt. 14,900 ft. Connected with MANASAROWAR LAKE (E) by 6-mi.-long river Ganga Chu. Sutlej R. (here called Langchen Khambab) rises in N area of lake; Gogra R. (Karnali) rises to SW. Also called Rakshas Tal.

Rakata, Indonesia: see KRAKATOA.

Rake, town (pop. 351), Winnebago co., N Iowa, near Minn. line, 21 mi. NW of Forest City.

Rakek (rä'kĕk), village, SW Slovenia, Yugoslavia, on railroad and 18 mi. SSW of Ljubljana. Large near-by cavern is connected with cave of Postojna. Until 1918, in Carniola.

Rakhmanovskiye Klyuchi (rŭkhmä"nŭfskēŭ klyōōchē'), health resort, E East Kazakhstan oblast, Kazakh SSR, in Altai Mts., on S slope of the peak Belukha, 50 mi. NE of Katon-Karagai; hot springs.

Rakhov (rä'khŭf), Czech *Rachov* (rä'khôf), Hung. *Rahó* (rŏ'hō), town (1941 pop. 12,455), SE Transcarpathian Oblast, Ukrainian SSR, on railroad, on Tissa R. and 45 mi. ESE of Khust; paper milling; iron mining. Mineral springs near by. A town of Austria-Hungary which passed 1920 to Czechoslovakia, 1938 to Hungary, and 1945 to USSR.

Rakhovo, Bulgaria: see ORYAKHOVO.

Rakhshan River (rŭkhshän'), in Makran state, W Baluchistan, W Pakistan, rises in E Siahan Range, flows WSW, past Panjgur, and NW, through W end of Siahan Range, to Mashkel R. near Iran border; c.160 mi. long. Valley noted for date palms.

Rakhya or **Rakh'ya** (rä'khyŭ), town (1945 pop. over 500), N Leningrad oblast, Russian SFSR, 20 mi. NE of Leningrad; peat-working center.

Rakishki, Lithuania: see ROKISKIS.

Rakita (räkē'tä), village (pop. 3,512), Pleven dist., N Bulgaria, 7 mi. NNE of Lukovit; wheat, corn, livestock.

Rakitnitsa River, Bulgaria: see SAZLIKA RIVER.

Rakitno (rŭkēt'nŭ), town (1926 pop. 7,259), central Kiev oblast, Ukrainian SSR, on Ros R. and 18 mi. SE of Belaya Tserkov; dairying, fruit canning. Formerly also called Rakitnoye.

Rakitnoye (-nŭyŭ), village (1926 pop. 9,527), SW Kursk oblast, Russian SFSR, on rail spur and 35 mi. WNW of Belgorod; sugar refinery.

Rakitovo (räkē'tôvô), village (pop. 5,030), Plovdiv dist., SW Bulgaria, in Chepino Basin, 11 mi. W of Peshtera; lumbering, fruit and truck gardening, sheep raising.

Rakityanka (rŭkē'tyŭnkŭ), town (1939 pop. over 500), E central Chkalov oblast, Russian SFSR, in S foothills of the S Urals, 4 mi. NNE (under jurisdiction) of Mednogorsk, in Orsk-Khalilovo industrial dist.; hematite and chromite mining.

Rakiura, New Zealand: see STEWART ISLAND.

Rakka, Syria: see RAQQA.

Rakla (räk'lä), village (pop. 1,284), Stalin dist., E Bulgaria, on Kamchiya R., at confluence of Golyama Kamchiya and Luda Kamchiya rivers, and 10 mi. S of Provadiya; vineyards, livestock; lumbering.

Rakoczifalva (rä'kōtsĭfŏl"vŏ), Hung. *Rákóczifalva*, town (pop. 5,386), Jasz-Nagykun-Szolnok co., E central Hungary, 7 mi. SSE of Szolnok; wheat, cattle, horses.

Rakoniewice (räkônyĕvē'tsĕ), Ger. *Rakwitz* (räk'vĭts), town (1946 pop. 1,607), Poznan prov., W Poland, 33 mi. SW of Poznan; flour milling; grain.

Rakonitz, Czechoslovakia: see RAKOVNIK.

Rakoscsaba (rä'kôsh-chŏbŏ), Hung. *Rákoscsaba*, town (pop. 14,752), Pest-Pilis-Solt-Kiskun co., N central Hungary, 9 mi. E of Budapest; cement-, tile-, brickworks.

Rakoshegy (rä'kôsh-hĕ"dyŭ), Hung. *Rákoshegy*, residential E suburb (pop. 6,888) of Budapest, Pest-Pilis-Solt-Kiskun co., N central Hungary.

Rakoskeresztur (rä'kôsh-kĕ"rĕstōōr), Hung. *Rákoskeresztúr*, town (pop. 11,482), Pest-Pilis-Solt-Kiskun co., N central Hungary, 7 mi. E of Budapest; truck products (eggs, fruit, honey).

Rakospalota (rä'kôsh-pŏ"lôtŏ), Hung. *Rákospalota*, city (pop. 49,000), Pest-Pilis-Solt-Kiskun co., N central Hungary, 6 mi. NNE of Budapest city center. Rail junction; railroad shops; mfg. (chemicals, organs, furniture, textiles, salami, hemp, glass); tanneries.

Rakosszentmihaly (rä'kôsh-sĕntmĭhäē), Hung. *Rákosszentmihály*, NE suburb (pop. 18,329) of Budapest, Pest-Pilis-Solt-Kiskun co., N central Hungary; flax spinning.

Rakov (rä'kŭf), Pol. *Raków* (rä'kōōf), town (1931 pop. 3,481), SE Molodechno oblast, Belorussian SSR, 25 mi. SSE of Molodechno; tanning, flour milling, stone quarrying. Frontier town (1921–39) on Poland-USSR border.

Rakovets (rä'kôvĕts), village (pop. 3,168), Stalin dist., E Bulgaria, on Kamchiya R. and 22 mi. SW of Stalin; grain, livestock; lumbering. Formerly Kopryu-koi.

Rakovica or **Rakovitsa** (both: rä'kôvētsä), village, N central Serbia, Yugoslavia, 5 mi. SSW (suburb) of Belgrade; mfg. center (automobiles, aircraft). Has monastery

Rakovitsa (rä'kôvētsä), village (pop. 3,192), Vidin dist., NW Bulgaria, on E slope of Babin-nos Mts. 9 mi. SSW of Kula; sheep, grain.

Rakovka, Russian SFSR: see SUKHOV VTOROI.

Rakovnik (rä'kôvnyēk), Czech *Rakovník*, Ger. *Rakonitz* (rä'kōnĭts), town (pop. 11,022), W central Bohemia, Czechoslovakia, 30 mi. W of Prague; rail center; mfg. of refractory bricks, beer, soap, candles, edible fats, tiles, pottery, china. Hops growing, bituminous-coal mining in vicinity. Formerly fortified, Rakovnik retains fine churches, Gothic gates, remains of old ghetto, and mus. Once residence of John Huss.

Rakovski, Bulgaria: see DIMITROVGRAD.

Rakow, Belorussian SSR: see RAKOV.

Raksapana Falls, Ceylon: see LAXAPANA FALLS.

Raksha (räk'shŭ), village (1926 pop. 2,637), NE Tambov oblast, Russian SFSR, 11 mi. NW of Morshansk; potatoes.

Rakshas Tal, Tibet: see RAKAS LAKE.

Rakusha (rŭkōō'shŭ), village, N Guryev oblast, Kazakh SSR, on Caspian Sea, 30 mi. S of Dossor, in Emba oil field.

Rakuto-ko, Korea: see NAKTONG RIVER.

Rakvag (rôk'vôg), Nor. *Råkvåg*, village (pop. 275) in Stjorna (Nor. *Stjørna*, formerly *Skjørn*) canton (pop. 2,755), Sor-Trondelag co., central Norway, at head of Stjorn Fjord (a NE arm of Trondheim Fjord), 24 mi. NNW of Trondheim; fishing, lobstering. At Saga (sä'gä) village, 2 mi. S, are canneries. Sometimes spelled Raakvaag.

Rakvere (räk'värā), Ger. *Wesenberg* (vā'zŭnbĕrk"), city (pop. 10,027), N Estonia, on Tallinn-Leningrad RR and 65 mi. E of Tallinn; junction of rail spur to Kunda; mfg. (linen textiles, leather goods, starch, bricks). Has castle ruins. Founded (13th cent.) by Danes; passed in 1346 to Livonian Knights, in 1561 to Sweden; occupied (1710) by Russia.

Rakwana (rŭkvä'nŭ), town (pop. 1,470), Sabaragamuwa Prov., S central Ceylon, in Sabaragamuwa Hill Country, 20 mi. SE of Ratnapura; extensive tea and rubber plantations; vegetables, rice.

Rakwana Hill Country, in E central Sabaragamuwa Hill Country, is just S; rises to over 3,000 ft.; irregular in shape; 10 mi. long (E-W), 5 mi. wide; highest point (4,456 ft.), Gongala peak, is 6.5 mi. SSE of Rakwana.

Rakwitz, Poland: see RAKONIEWICE.

Raleigh (rô'lē, rŏ'lē), county (□ 604; pop. 96,273), S W.Va.; ⊙ BECKLEY. On Allegheny Plateau; bounded E by New R.; drained by Coal and Guyandot rivers. Includes Grandview State Park. Extensive mining of semi-bituminous coal; gas fields; agr. (livestock, fruit, corn, truck, tobacco). Industry at Beckley. Formed 1850.

Raleigh. 1 City (pop. 48), Meriwether co., W Ga., 6 mi. N of Manchester. **2** Village (pop. 262), Saline co., SE Ill., 6 mi. N of Harrisburg, in bituminous-coal-mining and agr. area. **3** Town (pop. 580), ⊙ Smith co., S central Miss., 33 mi. NW of Laurel; trade center in agr. and timber area. Inc. 1935. **4** City (pop. 65,679), ⊙ N.C. and Wake co., 20 mi. SE of Durham, in the piedmont, near geographical center of state; 35°46'N 78°39'W; alt. 363 ft. Cultural, trade, and distribution center; textile, cottonseed-oil, and lumber mills, foundries, printing and publishing plants; tobacco market. Seat of Meredith Col., State Col. of Agr. and Engineering of Univ. of N.C., Shaw Univ. (Negro; coeducational; 1865), St. Augustine's Col. (Negro; coeducational; 1867), 2 jr. colleges (Peace Col., St. Mary's School and Jr. Col.), and state schools for blind and deaf. Birthplace of Andrew Johnson. State park near by. First known as Bloomsbury; selected for site of state capital in 1788; city laid out 1792. The capitol was built 1833–40. **5** Village (pop. 1,164), Raleigh co., S W.Va., 2 mi. SE of Beckley, in coal-mining area.

Raleigh, Fort, N.C.: see ROANOKE ISLAND.

Raleigh Bay, E N.C., arm of the Atlantic bet. Cape Hatteras (NE) and Cape Lookout (SW); c.75 mi. long. Separated from Pamlico Sound by chain of barrier isls.

Raleighvallen (rä'lāgfä'lŭn), waterfalls in central Du. Guiana, on Coppename R. and 110 mi. SW of Paramaribo.

Ralik Chain or **Ralick Chain** (rä'lĭk), W group, Marshall Isls., W central Pacific; comprises 15 atolls (ENIWETOK, BIKINI, RONGELAP, RONGERIK, AILINGINAE, WOTHO, UJELANG, KWAJALEIN, UJAE, LAE, NAMU, AILINGLAPALAP, JALUIT, NAMORIK, EBON) and 3 coral isls. (JABWOT, LIB, KILI). Kwajalein, ⊙ Kwajalein dist., is largest atoll of Marshall Isls. The Ralik Chain is sometimes called Sunset Group.

Ralja or **Ralya** (both: räl'yä), village, N central Serbia, Yugoslavia, on railroad and 18 mi. S of Belgrade; cement plant.

Ralls (rôlz). **1** County (□ 478; pop. 8,686), NE Mo.; ⊙ New London; on Mississippi R.; drained by Salt R. Agr. (wheat, corn, oats), livestock; coal. Formed 1820. **2** Town (pop. 1,779), Crosby co., NW Texas, on Llano Estacado, 28 mi. ENE of Lubbock; a trade and shipping center for agr. area (cotton, wheat, livestock, poultry). Founded 1911, inc. 1921.

Ralos, Los, Argentina: see LOS RALOS.

Ralston. **1** (răl'stŭn) Town (pop. 166), on Carroll-Greene co. line, W central Iowa, 12 mi. E of Carroll; soybean products. **2** (răl'stŭn) Village (pop. 1,300), Douglas co., E Nebr., just SW of Omaha. **3** (rôl'-stŭn) Town (pop. 416), Pawnee co., N Okla., on Arkansas R. and 12 mi. NNE of Pawnee; cotton ginning. **4** (rôl'stŭn) Village (pop. c.750), Lycoming co., N central Pa., 19 mi. N of Williamsport, in bituminous-coal area; makes farm tools. Hunting, fishing near by.

Ralston Creek (rôl'stŭn), N central Colo., rises in Front Range N of Blackhawk, flows c.30 mi. E to Clear Creek just NW of Denver. Ralston Dam (200 ft. high, 1,150 ft. long) is c.10 mi. W of Denver; completed 1938 as unit in city's water-supply system.

Ralya, Yugoslavia: see RALJA.

Rama or **El Rama** (ĕl rä'mä), city (1950 pop. 600), Zelaya dept., E Nicaragua, port (reached by ocean-going vessels) on Escondido R. and 37 mi. WNW of Bluefields; terminus of road from Pacific coast; trade center; bananas, sugar cane, livestock; lumbering.

Rama VI Barrage, Thailand: see THA RUA.

Rama Caída (rä'mä käē'dä), town (pop. estimate 500), central Mendoza prov., Argentina, on railroad, on Diamante R. and 5 mi. SW of San Rafael; wine, alfalfa, fruit, livestock; wine making, dried-fruit processing, dairying.

Ramacca (rämäk'kä), village (pop. 7,031), Catania prov., E central Sicily, 14 mi. NE of Caltagirone; sulphur mining.

Ramachandrapuram (rä"mŭchŭn'drŭpŏŏrŭm). **1** Town (pop. 9,380), East Godavari dist., NE Madras, India, in Godavari R. delta, on rail spur and 15 mi. SW of Cocanada; rice milling; noted handicraft lacework; sugar cane, tobacco, oilseeds. **2** Town (pop. 6,045), Trichinopoly dist., S Madras, India, 9 mi. S of Pudukkottai; hand-loom silk weaving; rice, peanuts.

Ramada, Cordillera de la (kôrdĭyā'rä dā lä rämä'dä), Andean range in SW San Juan prov., Argentina, near Chile border, 40 mi. N of the Aconcagua; rises to c.20,500 ft. at 32°5'S.

Ramada, La, town, Argentina: see LA RAMADA.

Ramada, La, Bolivia: see LA RAMADA.

Ramadi (rämä'dē), town (pop. 92,474), ⊙ Dulaim prov., central Iraq, on the Euphrates and 60 mi. W of Baghdad; dates, corn, millet. Customs office. Here the Turks suffered a serious defeat at the hands of the British in 1917. Also called Rumadiya. SE is L. Habbaniya.

Ramah, Palestine: see RAMALLAH.

Ramah (rā'mŭ), town (pop. 142), El Paso co., E central Colo., 40 mi. NE of Colorado Springs; alt. 6,000 ft.

Ramales de la Victoria (rämä'lĕs dhā lä vēktō'ryä), town (pop. 1,074), Santander prov., N Spain, 22 mi. SE of Santander; cattle and sheep raising, lumbering, trout and salmon fishing; corn, potatoes, chestnuts.

Ramallah (rä'măl-lŭ), town (1946 pop. estimate 5,180) of Palestine, after 1948 in W Jordan, in Judaean Hills, 8 mi. N of Jerusalem. Airfield (SE). Sometimes identified with biblical *Ramah,* Samuel's home.

Ramallo (rämä'yō), town (pop. 5,510), ⊙ Ramallo dist. (□ 357; pop. 19,625), N Buenos Aires prov., Argentina, 15 mi. SE of San Nicolás, on Paraná R.; agr. (wheat, flax, livestock).

Ramandag (rämän'dä), Turkish *Ramandağ,* area in Siirt prov., SE Turkey, S of Besiri, on the Tigris; petroleum discovered 1940.

Ramapo (ră'mŭpō), village (pop. c.300), Rockland co., SE N.Y., in the Ramapos, on Ramapo R., just NW of Suffern; makes railroad equipment.

Ramapo Deep, Pacific Ocean: see JAPAN TRENCH.

Ramapo Mountains, in NE N.J. and SE N.Y., low (c.900–1,200 ft.) forested range of the Appalachians, with many hiking trails; extends SW from region W of Haverstraw, N.Y., to point N of Pompton Lakes, N.J. W of range in N.J. are Wanaque R. and Reservoir. Iron mines (at Ringwood). Range is traversed by **Ramapo River,** rising near Monroe in SE N.Y.; flows c.32 mi. SE, S, and SW, through part of Palisades Interstate Park and past Tuxedo Park, Sloatsburg, and Suffern, N.Y., into N.J., to Pompton L.; issues from S end of lake to join Pequannock R. forming Pompton R. near Pompton Plains.

Ramaquabane (rämäkwäbä'nä), village, Tati dist., NE Bechuanaland Protectorate, near Southern Rhodesia border, 70 mi. WSW of Bulawayo, on railroad; alt. 4,190 ft.

Rama River (rä'mä), in Dinaric Alps, Bosnia and Herzegovina, Yugoslavia; rises at S foot of Radusa Mts. 6 mi. W of Prozor, flows c.20 mi. SE to Neretva R. 3 mi. NNW of Jablanica.

Ramasamudra (rŭmŭsŭ'mŏŏdrŭ) or **Ramasamudram** (–drŭm), town (pop. 5,561), Mysore dist., S Mysore, India, 2 mi. E of Chamarajnagar.

Rama's Bridge, India and Ceylon: see ADAM'S BRIDGE.

Ramassukha, Russian SFSR: see RAMUSIKHA.

Ramatayim (rämätä'yēm), settlement (pop. 2,000), W Israel, in Plain of Sharon, 9 mi. NE of Tel Aviv; mixed farming, citriculture; light industries. Founded 1925. Sometimes spelled Ramataim.

Ramat David (rämät' dävēd'), settlement (pop. 625), NW Israel, in NW part of Plain of Jezreel, 12 mi. SE of Haifa; mixed farming. Founded 1926; comprises 2 settlement groups: Ayanot (äyänōt') (pop. 275) and Hasharon (hăshärōn') (pop. 350).

Ramat Gan (gän'), town (1950 pop. estimate 30,000), W Israel, in Plain of Sharon, 2 mi. E of Tel Aviv; industrial center; metalworking; cotton, woolen, and linen milling; canning of fruit, vegetables, fruit juices, preserves; mfg. of chocolate, electrical equipment, furniture, dyes, tobacco products. Also a vacation resort; has several parks and large stadium. Founded 1921. Near by was Napoleon's hq. during Palestine campaign, 1799.

Ramat Hadar (hädär'), settlement (pop. 230), W Israel, in Plain of Sharon, 3 mi. SE of Herzliya; poultry raising, mixed farming. Founded 1938.

Ramat ha Kovesh or **Ramat Hakovesh** (both: häkōvĕsh'), settlement (pop. 700), W Israel, in Plain of Sharon, 7 mi. NE of Herzliya; citriculture, mixed farming; woodworking, bakery. Founded 1932.

Ramat ha Sharon or **Ramat Hasharon** (both: häshärōn'), settlement (pop. 1,150), W Israel, in Plain of Sharon, 6 mi. NE of Tel Aviv; citriculture, vegetable growing, mixed farming; brickworks. Has large maternity hosp. Founded 1923.

Ramat ha Shofet or **Ramat Hashofet** (both: häshōfĕt'), settlement (pop. 400), NW Israel, in Hills of Ephraim, 15 mi. SSE of Haifa; furniture mfg., woodworking; mixed farming. Founded 1941.

Ramathirtam, India: see VIZIANAGARAM.

Ramat Naftali, Israel: see SHEFER.

Ramat Rahel or **Ramat Rachel** (both: rähĕl', räkhĕl'), residential settlement (pop. 400), E Israel, on Jordan border, in Judaean Hills, just S of Jerusalem; dairying; bakery, laundry. Founded 1921; Arab attacks, 1936–39 and 1947–48.

Ramat Tiomkin (tyōm'kēn), residential settlement (pop. 280), W Israel, in Plain of Sharon, near Mediterranean, just SE of Natanya. Founded 1933.

Ramat Yishai (yēshī') settlement (pop. 150), NW Israel, at NW edge of Plain of Jezreel, 8 mi. W of Nazareth; textile milling, market gardening. Founded 1925, abandoned during Arab riots, 1936, resettled 1943. Formerly called Jeida.

Ramat Yits-haq Ochberg (yēts-häk' ōkh'bĕrg) or **Even Yits-haq Ochberg** (ĕ'vĕn), settlement (pop. 250), NW Israel, in Hills of Ephraim, 7 mi. ESE of Zikhron Yaakov; grain, fruit, stock. Founded 1945. Also spelled Even Yitzhak Ochberg; sometimes called Even Yits-haq or Even Yitzhak.

Ramat Yohanan (yō'hänän'), settlement (pop. 500), NW Israel, in Zebulun Valley, 7 mi. E of Haifa; mixed farming. Scene (April, 1948) of decisive defeat of Syrians by Israeli forces defending Zebulun Valley industrial region.

Ramban (räm'bŭn), village, Doda dist., SW Kashmir, in Pir Panjal foothills, on the Chenab and 23 mi. NNE of Udhampur; corn, wheat, barley, rice.

Rambe, Fiji: see RAMBI.

Ramberg (räm'bĕrk), village (pop. 1,111), Rhenish Palatinate, W Germany, in Hardt Mts., 6 mi. NW of Landau; grain, tobacco. Has ruined castle.

Rambervillers (räbĕrvēlā'), town (pop. 4,632), Vosges dept., E France, on Mortagne R. and 15 mi. NE of Épinal; produces textiles, earthenware, cartons. Metalworks. Has 16th-cent. Renaissance town hall (damaged in Second World War).

Rambha (rŭm'bŭ), village, Ganjam dist., SE Orissa, India, 25 mi. NE of Berhampur, on S shore of Chilka L.; rice milling, chemical mfg.

Rambi, Rambe, or **Rabi** (all: räm'bē), volcanic island (□ 27; pop. 1,048), Fiji, SW Pacific, 4 mi. E of Vanua Levu; 10 mi. long; copra. Formerly Gillett Isl.

Rambla, La (lä räm'blä), city (pop. 7,380), Córdoba prov., S Spain, 20 mi. S of Córdoba; agr. trade center (cereals, wine, aniseed, fruit). Olive-oil processing, brandy distilling, flour milling; mfg. of cotton cloth, pottery, chocolate. Hog raising and horse breeding.

Ramboda (rŭm'bōdŭ), town (pop. 905), Central Prov., Ceylon, in Piduru Ridges, 8 mi. NNW of Nuwara Eliya; extensive tea plantations; rice.

Ramboda Pass, structural depression mainly in Piduru Ridges, extends c.18 mi. NW-SE, bet. Gampola and Nuwara Eliya; traversed by road.

Rambouillet (räbōōyā'), town (pop. 6,531), Seine-et-Oise dept., N central France, 28 mi. SW of Paris; summer resort. Natl. cattle farm. Its 14th-18th-cent. château, where Francis I died (1547) and Charles X signed his abdication (1830), is now official summer residence of presidents of French Republic; splendid park laid out by Le Nôtre. **Forest of Rambouillet** (□ 50), extending NW and SE of town, contains several lakes. Well-stocked in game, it is used for official hunting parties.

Rambukkana (rŭmbŏŏk'kä'nŭ), town (pop., including near-by villages, 2,730), Sabaragamuwa Prov., W central Ceylon, at W foot of Ceylon Hill Country, 17 mi. WNW of Kandy; vegetables, rice.

Ramdas (räm'däs'), town (pop. 5,397), Amritsar dist., W Punjab, India, 23 mi. N of Amritsar; wheat, gram, cotton. Sometimes written Ram Das.

Ramdurg (räm'dōōrg), town (pop. 11,496), Bijapur dist., S Bombay, India, 70 mi. SW of Bijapur; trade center for wheat, cotton, peanuts; cotton ginning, handicraft cloth weaving. A 17th-cent. Mahratta fortress. Was ⊙ former princely state of Ramdurg (□ 166; pop. 40,114) in Deccan States, Bombay; state inc. 1949 into Bijapur, Dharwar, and Belgaum dists.

Ramea Islands (ră'mēŭ), group of 2 isls. (□ 4.5; pop. 520) just off S N.F. Main isl. is Ramea (2 mi. long, 1 mi. wide), 13 mi. ESE of Burgeo; 47°32'N 57°23'W; site of lighthouse. Fishing, salmon canning. Just E is uninhabited Great Isl. (2 mi. long, 1 mi. wide); 47°32'N 57°20'W. Group is surrounded by several islets.

Ramechhap (rä'mächäp), town, E central Nepal, near the Sun Kosi, 55 mi. ESE of Katmandu; rice, corn, wheat, millets, vegetables.

Rame Head, promontory, E Cornwall, England, on the Channel at mouth of Plymouth Sound.

Ramelau, Mount (rämĭlou'), highest peak (9,678 ft.) of Timor, in Portuguese part, near Hato-Lia.

Ramelton or **Rathmelton** (both: rămĕl'tŭn), Gaelic *Ráth Mealltain,* town (pop. 808), NE Co. Donegal, Ireland, on inlet of Lough Swilly, 7 mi. NE of Letterkenny; 55°2'N 7°38'W; seaport, agr. market (cattle, sheep; flax, oats, potatoes).

Ramenskoye (rä'myĭnskŭyŭ), city (1933 pop. 20,100), central Moscow oblast, Russian SFSR, 27 mi. SE of Moscow; cotton milling.

Ramerupt (rämrü'), agr. village (pop. 361), Aube dept., NE central France, on Aube R. and 18 mi. NE of Troyes.

Rameshki (rä'myĭshkē), village (1939 pop. over 500), central Kalinin oblast, Russian SFSR, 25 mi. NE of Likhoslavl; garment mfg.

Rameswaram or **Ramesvaram** (both: rä'măsvŭrŭm), town (pop. 5,774), Ramnad dist., S Madras, India, on N Rameswaram Isl., 90 mi. SE of Madura; fishing center. Hindu pilgrimage center (reputedly founded by Rama) since period of the Ramayana. Present Dravidian temple built c.14th cent.

Rameswaram Island or **Ramesvaram Island,** in Indian Ocean, in Ramnad dist., Madras, India, bet. SE Madras coast and Ceylon, 85 mi. SE of Madura; 16 mi. long, 1–9 mi. wide. Consists of coral reef with long sandstrip (E); separated from mainland by narrow Pamban Channel. Railroad across isl., bet. Pamban and Dhanushkodi, is part of main India-Ceylon rail and steamer route. Pilgrimage center at Rameswaram town (N). Sardine, pearl-oyster, and chank fishing along S and NE coasts. Also called Pamban.

Ramey (rā'mē), borough (pop. 696), Clearfield co., central Pa., 20 mi. N of Altoona.

Ramganga River (räm'gŭng-gŭ). **1** In N Uttar Pradesh, India, rises in Kumaun Himalayas in Garhwal dist., flows generally SSW through Siwalik Range, past Kalagarh, and SSE along Ganges Plain, past Moradabad and Bareilly, to the Ganges opposite Kanauj; c.350 mi. long. As yet little used for irrigation; dam for hydroelectric plant and irrigation project near KALAGARH. **2** In N Uttar Pradesh, India, rises in Kumaun Himalayas in Almora dist., flows c.60 mi. S to Sarda (Kali) River 10 mi. SSE of Pithoragarh. Chief tributary, Sarju R. (right).

Ramganj Mandi (räm'gŭnj mŭn'dē), village, SE Rajasthan, India, 38 mi. SSE of Kotah; agr. market (cotton, oilseeds, wheat, millet); cotton ginning, oilseed milling, hand-loom weaving. Building stone quarried just E.

Ramgarh (räm'gŭr). **1** Town (pop. 3,363), E Rajasthan, India, 13 mi. E of Alwar; millet, gram, oilseeds. **2** Town (pop. 13,202), E central Rajasthan, India, 45 mi. NW of Jaipur; agr. market (millet, wheat, gram); hand-loom weaving. **3** Village, W Rajasthan, India, 39 mi. NW of Jaisalmer, in Thar Desert; local trade in cattle, wool, hides.

Ramgarh, village, Chittagong Hill Tracts dist., SE East Bengal, E Pakistan, on Fenny R. and 37 mi. NW of Rangamati; trades in rice, cotton, oilseeds, tobacco.

Ramgiri, India: see CLOSEPET.

Ram Head, promontory, extreme SE Victoria, Australia, in Tasman Sea, bet. Cape Howe and Cape Everard; 37°47'S 149°28'E. Rises to 378 ft.

Ram Hormuz or **Ram Hormoz** (both: räm' hōrmōz'), town (1940 pop. 17,267), Sixth Prov., in Khuzistan, SW Iran, 55 mi. E of Ahwaz; grain, rice, cotton, onions, garlic. An old town dating from Sassanian dynasty. Also known as Ramuz. Haft Kel oil field is NE.

Ramian (rämēän'), town (1933 pop. estimate 8,000), Second Prov., in Gurgan, NE Iran, 15 mi. S of Gunbad-i-Qawus; cotton, wheat; rugmaking.

Ramid, Tadzhik SSR: see RAMIT.

Ramillies-Offus (rämēyē'-ôfü'), agr. village (pop. 653), Brabant prov., central Belgium, 12 mi. S of Tirlemont. Scene, in War of Spanish Succession, of defeat (1706) of French by Marlborough, commanding British, Dutch, and Danish troops.

Ramim, Israel: see MANARA.

Ramírez or **General Ramírez** (hānärāl' rämē'rĕs), town (pop. estimate 2,000), W Entre Ríos prov., Argentina, on railroad and 35 mi. SE of Paraná; grain, poultry center; flour mills, sawmills.

Ramírez, village (pop. 455), Tamaulipas, NE Mexico, near Rio Grande, on railroad and 19 mi. WNW of Matamoros; cotton, sugar cane, corn, livestock; tanneries. Partly a cooperative farming settlement.

Ramírez, S residental section of Montevideo, S Uruguay; popular beach resort on the Río de la Plata; hotels, casino.

Ramiriquí (rämērēkē'), village (pop. 835), Boyacá dept., central Colombia, in Cordillera Oriental, 9 mi. S of Tunja; alt. 7,693 ft. Cereals, livestock; mfg. (fique bags, woolen goods). Founded 1541 on site of Indian village.

Ram Island, Lincoln co., S Maine, small lighthouse isl. 3.5 mi. SE of Boothbay Harbor.

Ramis River (rä'mēs), Puno dept., SE Peru, rises in Cordillera de Vilcanota in the Andes, flows 110 mi. SE to L. Titicaca 9 mi. WSW of Huancané. The Juliaca–Cuzco RR runs through its valley. Called Pucará R. in upper course.

Ramit (rŭmēt'), village (1939 pop. over 500), NE Stalinabad oblast, Tadzhik SSR, on Kafirnigan R. and 30 mi. ENE of Stalinabad; wheat, cattle. Until c.1935, called Uramir, also spelled Romid and Ramid.

Ramjibanpur (rämjē'bŭnpŏŏr), town (pop. 6,036), Midnapore dist., SW West Bengal, India, 33 mi. NNE of Midnapore; cotton weaving; rice, corn, wheat, sugar cane.

Ramjird or **Ramjerd** (both: rämjĕrd'), town, Seventh Prov., in Fars, S Iran, on Kur R. and 40 mi. N of Shiraz; grain, sugar beets, cotton, rice. Irrigation dam near by.

Ramkola, India: see PADRAUNA.

Ramle or **Ramleh** (both: räm'lĕ), town (1946 pop. estimate 16,380; 1949 pop. estimate 10,592), W Israel, in Judaean Plain, on railroad and 12 mi. SE of Tel Aviv. Largely evacuated by Arab pop., 1948; by 1950 new Jewish immigrants had largely replaced the Arab pop. New industries include mfg. of electric motors. Has 12th-cent. Church of St. John, later converted into mosque; Franciscan convent (founded 1296), Napoleon's hq. (1799) during Palestine campaign, on traditional site of house of Joseph of Arimathea; and 14th-cent. Tower of Ramle. As Rames, town was important during Crusades; after defeat (1102) of Baldwin I by Egyptians, Baldwin IV won victory (1177) over Saladin. Town captured (1187) by Saladin. During 3d Crusade it became (1191) hq. of Richard Coeur de Lion; finally captured (1226) by Baibars.

Ramleh (räm'lă), NE suburb of Alexandria, Egypt, a popular beach resort on the Mediterranean.

Ramlingen mit Ehlershausen (räm'lĭng-ŭn mĭt ā"lŭrs-hou'zŭn), village (pop. 1,261), in former Prussian prov. of Hanover, NW Germany, after 1945 in Lower Saxony, 7 mi. S of Celle; oil wells. Rail station is called Ehlershausen.

Rammelsbach (rä'mŭlsbäkh), village (pop. 1,895), Rhenish Palatinate, W Germany, 2 mi. E of Kusel; grain, potatoes, fruit.

Rammelsberg (–bĕrk), mountain (2,085 ft.), NW Germany, in the upper Harz, just SE of Goslar; highly mineralized (copper, lead, zinc, iron-ore, and sulphur mines). Noted for its rich silver deposits in Middle Ages.

Rammenau (rä'mŭnou), village (pop. 1,888), Saxony, E central Germany, in Upper Lusatia, 3 mi. NW of Bischofswerda. Has 15th-cent. palace. Fichte b. here.

Ramna, E Pakistan: see DACCA, city.

Ramnad (räm'näd), district (□ 4,851; pop. 1,979,643), S Madras, India; ⊙ Ramnad. Bordered E by Palk Strait, SE by Gulf of Mannar, W and NW by Varushanad Hills. Rameswaram Isl. and Adam's Bridge (chain of shoals) stretch E toward Ceylon. Lowland (drained by Vaigai R.) includes black-soil cotton tract (NW to SE). Mainly agr. (cotton, peanuts, grain); palmyra, coconut palms along coasts, rice along rivers, plantain and cardamom in foothills. Cotton ginning and spinning, peanut-oil extraction, rice milling, match mfg., tanning; coir products; chank, pearl-oyster, and sardine fishing off coral-producing isl. of Rameswaram and along coasts (saltworks). Trade centers along traditional pilgrimage route bet. Madura and Rameswaram. Formed 1910 by division of Madura and Tinnevelly dists.

Ramnad, town (pop. 18,152), ⊙ Ramnad dist., S Madras, India, 60 mi. SE of Madura. Was ⊙ kingdom of Ramnad (14th cent.–1801).

Ramnagar (räm'nŭgŭr). **1** Town (pop. 4,520), Bara Banki dist., central Uttar Pradesh, India, 16 mi. NE of Nawabganj; rice, gram, wheat, sugar cane. Sugar processing just W, at Burhwal (rail junction). **2** Village, Bareilly dist., N central Uttar Pradesh, India, 18 mi. W of Bareilly; wheat, rice, gram, sugar cane. Anc. Hindu and Buddhist ruins, coins with inscriptions of 1st–2d. cent. B.C. Was ⊙ anc. Panchala kingdom. Visited by Hsüan-tsang in 7th cent. A.D. Sometimes called Ahichhattra. **3** Town (pop. 12,953), Benares dist., SE Uttar Pradesh, India, on the Ganges and 4 mi. S of Benares city center; glass and rug mfg.; trades in rice, barley, gram, wheat, millet. Was ⊙ former princely state of Benares. Large 18th-cent. fort with palace. **4** Town (pop. 6,216), Naini Tal dist., N Uttar Pradesh, India, on tributary of the Ramganga and 20 mi. W of Naini Tal; rail spur terminus; rice, wheat, oilseeds.

Ramnagar, town (pop. 2,442), Udhampur dist., SW Kashmir, in S Punjab Himalaya foothills, 13 mi. SE of Udhampur; corn, wheat, barley, rice. Former Mian Rajput stronghold; was ⊙ area conferred (early-19th cent.) upon a brother of Gulab Singh by Sikhs.

Ramnagar, town (pop. 5,193), Gujranwala dist., E Punjab, W Pakistan, near Chenab R., 26 mi. NW of Gujranwala; wheat, rice.

Ramnas (räm'nĕs"), Swedish *Ramnäs*, village (pop. 1,072), Vastmanland co., central Sweden, on Kolback R. and 16 mi. NW of Vasteras; rail junction; steel milling, chain mfg.

Ramnes (räm'nās), village and canton (pop. 2,841), Vestfold co., SE Norway, 9 mi. NW of Tonsberg; lumbering, cheese mfg.

Ramnicu-Sarat or **Ramnicul-Sarat** (rûm'nēkōō, –kōōl-sûrät'), Rum. *Râmnicu-Sărat* or *Râmnicul-Sărat*, town (1948 pop. 19,267), Buzau prov., E central Rumania, in Walachia, on railroad and 75 mi. NE of Bucharest; commercial center (grain, wine, livestock, lumber); petroleum refining, flour milling, mfg. of furniture, cotton goods, edible oils. Oil wells in vicinity (E). Has 17th-cent. church, old monastery (now public administration offices). Scene of numerous historic battles. Destroyed by great fire (1854), later rebuilt.

Ramnicu-Valcea or **Ramnicul-Valcea** (–vûl'chä), Rum. *Râmnicu-Vâlcea* or *Râmnicul-Vâlcea*, town (1948 pop. 17,238), ⊙ Valcea prov., S central Rumania, in Walachia, on Olt R., on railroad and 95 mi. NW of Bucharest; trading center (lumber, livestock, animal products, fruit, wines); production of sulphuric acid and copper sulphate, leather and cork goods. Also a summer and winter-sports resort, center of excursions into the picturesque Olt R. country. Has two 16th-cent. churches, restored in 18th cent., 18th-cent. St. Demetrius Church, episcopal residence with 18th- and 19th-cent. bldgs. Orthodox bishopric since 1590.

Ramon or **Ramon'** (rŭmôn'yŭ), town (1948 pop. over 2,000), NW Voronezh oblast, Russian SFSR, on Voronezh R. and 17 mi. NNE of Voronezh; sugar mill.

Ramona (rŭmō'nŭ). **1** Village (pop. 1,158), San Diego co., S Calif., 27 mi. NE of San Diego, in foothills of Coast Ranges; turkeys, fruit, grain. **2** NW suburb (1940 pop. 159) of Colorado Springs, El Paso co., central Colo. **3** City (pop. 190), Marion co., central Kansas, 17 mi. N of Marion; grain, livestock. **4** Town (pop. 583), Washington co., NE Okla., 26 mi. N of Tulsa. **5** Town (pop. 278), Lake co., E S.Dak., 10 mi. NNW of Madison. **6** Village (pop. 2,768), Hidalgo co., S Texas.

Ramones, Los, Mexico: see LOS RAMONES.

Ramón Lista, Argentina: see EL CHORRO.

Ramón M. Castro (rämōn' ā'mä kä'strō), village (pop. estimate 200), central Neuquén natl. territory, Argentina, on railroad and 90 mi. W of Neuquén; stock-raising center; clay quarrying. Sulphur, bauxite, petroleum deposits near by.

Ramón Santana (rämōn' säntä'nä), town (1950 pop. 697), San Pedro de Macorís prov., SE Dominican Republic, 10 mi. NE of San Pedro de Macorís, in sugar-growing region.

Ramor, Lough (lŏkh rŭmôr'), lake (5 mi. long, 1 mi. wide) on the Blackwater, SE Co. Cavan, Ireland, extending S from Virginia.

Ramos (rä'mōs), town (pop. 1,490), San Luis Potosí, N central Mexico, on interior plateau, 20 mi. NW of Salinas; alt. 7,250 ft.; silver mining; corn, wheat, beans.

Ramos Arizpe (ärē'spā), town (pop. 2,766), Coahuila, N Mexico, in Sierra Madre Oriental, 10 mi. N of Saltillo; rail junction in agr. region (corn, beans, alfalfa, istle fibers, candelilla wax, cattle); silver, lead, copper mining.

Ramos Mejía (māhē'ä), industrial city (pop. 28,500) in Greater Buenos Aires, Argentina, 11 mi. W of Buenos Aires; plastics, chemicals, textiles, rubber goods, shoes, electrical appliances; frozen meat, dairy products, canned food.

Ramos River, Durango, NW Mexico, rises in Sierra Madre Occidental 28 mi. W of Durango, flows c.125 mi. N and NE, past Santiago Papasquiaro, joining Río del Oro (or Sestín R.) to form Nazas R. near El Palmito (irrigation dam). Called Santiago R. in upper course.

Ramot ha Shavim or **Ramot Hashavim** (both: rämōt' hăshävēm'), settlement (pop. 500), W Israel, in Plain of Sharon, 2 mi. E of Herzliya; poultry-raising center; mixed farming. Founded 1933.

Ramoutsa (rämōō'tsä), village (pop. c.8,300), Gaberones dist., SE Bechuanaland Protectorate, 70 mi. N of Mafeking, on railroad; hq. of Bamalete tribe. Stock raising.

Rampal (räm'päl), village, Dacca dist., SE East Bengal, E Pakistan, 20 mi. SSE of Dacca; rice, jute. Site of anc. Bikrampur, ⊙ 12th-cent. Sen kingdom; extensive Sen ruins. Noted Sanskrit schools near by.

Rampart, village (1950 pop. 93), central Alaska, on Yukon R. and 85 mi. NW of Fairbanks, just S of Arctic Circle; supply center for placer gold-mining area; trapping and fur trading. Site (1900–25) of agr. experiment station. Airfield. Supply center in Klondike gold rush, when pop. was c.1,500.

Rampart House, village (1939 pop. 14), on Alaska-Yukon border, on Porcupine R. and 130 mi. NE of Fort Yukon; trapping, fishing. Established c.1870 by Hudson's Bay Co.

Rampillon, France: see NANGIS.

Rampur (räm'pŏŏr), former princely state (□ 894; pop. 477,042), N central India; ⊙ was Rampur. Only section of anc. ROHILKHAND kept by Rohillas after their defeat (1774) by nawab of Oudh and English. Joined Gwalior Residency in 1936; inc. 1949 as dist. of Uttar Pradesh.

Rampur, district (□ 894; pop. 477,042), Rohilkhand div., N central Uttar Pradesh, India; ⊙ Rampur. On W Ganges Plain; drained by the Ramganga. Agr. (corn, wheat, rice, gram, millet, sugar cane, barley, cotton, tobacco); mfg. at Rampur. Main centers: Rampur, Tanda, Shahabad, Bilaspur. Was princely state (called Rampur) until 1949.

Rampur. **1** Town, Bombay, India: see SANTRAMPUR. **2** Town (pop. 1,787), E central Himachal Pradesh, India, on Sutlej R. and 37 mi. NE of Simla, on caravan route to Tibet; trades in maize, timber, wool, spices; shawl weaving. Was ⊙ former Punjab Hill state of Bashahr. **3** Village, N Madhya Bharat, India, 12 mi. NW of Guna; sugar milling. **4** Village, Sambalpur dist., NW Orissa, India, 22 mi. N of Sambalpur. Small coal field (worked) near by. **5** Village, Sambalpur dist., central Orissa, India: see RAIRAKHOL. **6** Town (pop. 5,020), Etah dist., W Uttar Pradesh, India, on distributary of Lower Ganges Canal and 30 mi. E of Etah; wheat, pearl millet, barley, corn, jowar, oilseeds. **7** Town (pop. 4,299), Gorakhpur dist., E Uttar Pradesh, India, 30 mi. ESE of Gorakhpur; rice, wheat, barley, oilseeds, sugar cane. **8** City (pop. 89,322), ⊙ Rampur dist., N central Uttar Pradesh, India, near tributary of the Ramganga, 15 mi. ESE of Moradabad; trade center (grains, sugar cane, cotton, tobacco); sugar processing, cotton milling, mfg. of chemicals, electric supplies; distillery. Arabic Col. Library has noted oriental MS. collection. Rohilla fort. Was ⊙ former princely state of Rampur. **9** Town (pop. 6,829), Saharanpur dist., N Uttar Pradesh, India, 12 mi. SSW of Saharanpur; wheat, rice, rape and mustard, gram; mfg. of glass bangles. Jain temple; Moselm saint's tomb (annual mela).

Rampur. **1** or **Rampur Rajauri**, Riasi district, Kashmir: see RAJAORI. **2** Village, Muzaffarabad dist., W Kashmir, in NW Pir Panjal Range, on Jhelum R. and 7 mi. NE of Uri; corn, rice, wheat. Extensive limestone deposits near by. At Buniar, 2 mi. E, is best-preserved of larger Kashmir temples; contains lingams brought from Narbada R.

Rampura (räm'pŏŏrŭ). **1** Town (pop. 9,978), NW Madhya Bharat, India, 36 mi. NE of Mandasor; agr. market (millet, wheat, cotton, corn); cotton ginning, hand-loom weaving. **2** Village, Rajasthan, India: see ALIGARH, village.

Rampur Bauleah or **Rampur Boalia**, E Pakistan: see RAJSHAHI, town.

Rampur Hat (hät'), town (pop. 12,225), Birbhum dist., W West Bengal, India, 26 mi. NNE of Suri; trade center (rice, wheat, gram, corn, sugar cane); silk and cotton weaving, rice milling. Silk growing near by. Also written Rampurhat.

Ramrama Tola (rŭm'rŭmŭ tō'lŭ), village, Balaghat dist., central Madhya Pradesh, India, 17 mi. WNW of Balaghat; rail spur terminus, serving near-by manganese mines.

Ramree Island (răm'rē), Burmese *Yanbye* (yänbyĕ'), in Bay of Bengal, off Arakan coast, Lower Burma, in Kyaukpyu dist., NW of Taungup, separated from mainland (An R. mouth) by mangrove isls. and tidal flats; 50 mi. long, 15 mi. wide. Salt and oil deposits. Main town is Kyaukpyu, at N end; Ramree village is on E coast. Formerly spelled Ramri.

Ramrod Key, Fla.: see FLORIDA KEYS.

Ramsanehighat (rämsŭnā'hēgät), village, Bara Banki dist., central Uttar Pradesh, India, 14 mi. WNW of Rudauli; rice, gram, wheat, oilseeds, corn.

Ramsar (rämsär'), town, First Prov., in W Mazanderan, N Iran, on Caspian Sea, 70 mi. ESE of Resht and 10 mi. NW of Shahsawar; leading seaside and summer resort; mineral springs. Airfield. Formerly called Shakhtsar.

Ramsay (răm'zē), village (pop. 1,466, including near-by Anvil), Gogebic co., W Upper Peninsula, Mich., 2 mi. SE of Bessemer, in iron-mining region. Sometimes Ramsey.

Ramsbottom, urban district (1931 pop. 14,929; 1951 census 14,587), SE Lancashire, England, on Irwell R. and 4 mi. N of Bury; cotton and wool milling, mfg. of paper, soap, pharmaceuticals. Just S is cotton-milling and chemical-mfg. village of Nuttall Lane. In urban dist. are cotton-milling towns of Stubbins and Summerseat.

Ramsbury, agr. village and parish (pop. 1,575), E Wiltshire, England, on Kennet R. and 6 mi. ENE of Marlborough. Has 13th-cent. church.

Ramsdorf (räms'dôrf), town (pop. 1,071), in former Prussian prov. of Westphalia, W Germany, after 1945 in North Rhine-Westphalia, 4 mi. NE of Borken; dairying.

Ramseur (răm'sōōr), town (pop. 1,134), Randolph co., central N.C., on Deep R. and 9 mi. ENE of Asheboro; mfg. of textiles, hosiery, furniture, brooms. Settled c.1850; inc. 1895.

Ramsey. **1** Town and parish (pop. 3,185), NE Essex, England, near Stour R. estuary, 3 mi. W of Harwich; agr. market. **2** Urban district (1931 pop.

5,180; 1951 census 5,772), NE Huntingdon, England, 9 mi. NNE of Huntingdon; agr. market, with agr.-machinery works. Has remains of 10th-cent. Benedictine abbey, now part of Norman Church of St. Thomas à Becket. Property of Cromwell family until after 1670. **3** Town district (1939 pop. 4,240), on NE coast of Isle of Man, England, 12 mi. NNE of Douglas; port and seaside resort, with pier and park.

Ramsey. **1** County (□ 160; pop. 355,332), E Minn.; ⊙ St. Paul. Industrial and residential area crossed in S by Mississippi R. In N are small lake resorts. Formed 1849. **2** County (□ 1,214; pop. 14,373), NE central N.Dak.; ⊙ Devils Lake. Rich agr. area with many lakes; Devils L. is largest. Sheet-metal products, grain, livestock, dairy products, poultry. Formed 1873.

Ramsey. **1** Farming village (pop. 808), Fayette co., S central Ill., 12 mi. N of Vandalia; corn, wheat, dairy products, poultry, livestock. **2** Residential borough (pop. 4,670), Bergen co., NE N.J., 9 mi. N of Paterson; ships dairy products, poultry, fruit, truck; mfg. (neckwear, textile washers). Settled 1846, inc. 1908.

Ramsey Island, in St. George's Channel at N end of St. Bride's Bay, off W Pembroke, Wales, 3 mi. W of St. David's, surrounded by numerous islets and rocks; 2 mi. long, 1 mi. wide. Separated from mainland by Ramsey Sound, 1 mi. wide.

Ramsgate (rămz'gĭt), municipal borough (1931 pop. 33,603; 1951 census 35,748), E Kent, England, on Isle of Thanet, on Channel near The Downs roadstead, 70 mi. ESE of London; popular seaside resort, fishing and yachting port, and important lifeboat station. The harbor is protected by 2 piers, one with promenade. Town is associated with George Eliot, with the Pugins, who built the R.C. Abbey Church, and with Sir Moses Montefiore, who founded the Jewish col. here. In her youth Queen Victoria lived here. In Second World War the town sustained severe air-raid damage. EBBSFLEET is near by.

Ram's Island, Northern Ireland: see NEAGH, LOUGH.

Ramstein (räm'shtīn), village (pop. 3,051), Rhenish Palatinate, W Germany, 3 mi. N of Landstuhl; grain, potatoes.

Ramtek (räm'tāk), town (pop. 9,040), Nagpur dist., central Madhya Pradesh, India, 23 mi. NE of Nagpur, in important manganese-mining area served by rail spur with subsidiary branches, at foot of wooded hill sacred to Rama; extensive betel farms. Several temples on hill's summit (oldest date from 14th cent.) are pilgrimage centers. Large reservoir just E supplies irrigation canals (rice).

Ramtha, Remtha (both: rämthä'), **El Ramtha, Er Ramtha,** or **Al-Ramtha** (all: ĕr-rämthä'), village (pop. c.6,500), N Jordan, 9 mi. E of Irbid; road junction; wheat, barley, olives.

Ramunia, Cape, Malaya: see RUMENIA, CAPE.

Ramuntcho (rämōōn'chō), village (1930 pop. 99), Concepción prov., S central Chile, at tip of a peninsula on the Pacific, 10 mi. W of Concepción; beach resort; fishing; lighthouse.

Ramu River (rä'mōō), NE New Guinea, rises in Kratke Range, drains central Bismarck and SW Finisterre ranges, flows 400 mi. NW to Bismarck Sea; timber on banks. Formerly Ottilien R.

Ramusikha (rŭmōō'sēkhŭ), town (1947 pop. over 500), W central Bryansk oblast, Russian SFSR, 16 mi. W of Pochep; sawmilling. Also Ramassukha.

Ramuz, Iran: see RAM HORMUZ.

Ramvik (räm'vēk"), village (pop. 1,289), Vasternorrland co., NE Sweden, on Angerman R. estuary, near its mouth on Gulf of Bothnia, 13 mi. N of Harnosand; shipbuilding, sawmilling.

Rana (rä'nä), region surrounding Ran Fjord, Nordland co., N central Norway; drained by Rana and Ros rivers; centered at Mo (steelworks, mining). It includes mining region (iron, pyrite, lead, zinc, copper) of Dunderlandsdal, Basmoen, and Korgen, and fishing ports of Nesna and Hemnesberget. Some agr. Formerly called Ranen.

Ranaelv, Norway: see RANA RIVER.

Rana Fjord, Norway: see RAN FJORD.

Ranaghat (rä'nägät), town (pop. 16,488), Nadia dist., E West Bengal, India, near the Hooghly, 16 mi. SSE of Krishnagar; rail junction; trade center (rice, jute, linseed, sugar cane, wheat).

Ranan, Korea: see NANAM.

Ranapur, India: see SADRI.

Rana River (rä'nä), Nor. *Ranaelv* or *Ranelven*, Nordland co., N central Norway, rises in several headstreams on Swedish border E of the Lonsdal, flows c.70 mi. SW through the Dunderlandsdal to Ran Fjord at Mo.

Ranawao (ränä'vou), town (pop. 7,642), W Saurashtra, India, 9 mi. ENE of Porbandar; markets millet, cotton, salt; hand-loom weaving.

Ranbirsinghpura, Kashmir: see NAWANSHAHR.

Rancagua (rängkä'gwä), city (1940 pop. 31,018, 1949 estimate 29,442), ⊙ O'Higgins prov. and Rancagua dept. (□ 1,592; 1940 pop. 97,631), central Chile, in Andean foothills, on Cachapoal R., in the central valley, and 50 mi. S of Santiago; 34°10'S 70°50'W; alt. 1,637 ft. Rail junction, trade and processing center for a large agr. area (cereals, alfalfa, potatoes, fruit, vegetables, cattle); flour mills, fruit and vegetable canneries. Near by is one of Chile's largest copper mines, El Teniente. Bernardo O'Higgins here made (1814) a heroic defense during the war of independence. City was founded 1743 by Manso de Velasco.

Rance (rãs), town (pop. 1,527), Hainaut prov., S Belgium, 20 mi. SSW of Charleroi; marble quarrying and processing.

Rance River. **1** In Côtes-du-Nord dept., W France, rises in the Landes du Méné 1 mi. W of Collinée, flows 60 mi. NE, past Dinan, below which it forms a 13-mi.-long estuary opening on English Channel at Saint-Malo. Navigable for flat-bottom barges to Évran (terminus of Ille-Rance Canal). **2** In Aveyron dept., S France, rises 3 mi. S of Camarès, flows 30 mi. WNW to the Tarn at Aveyron-Tarn dept. line.

Rancharia (rãshŭrē'ŭ), city (pop. 3,174), W São Paulo, Brazil, on railroad and 32 mi. ESE of Presidente Prudente; coffee and rice processing, silk milling.

Ranchería River (rãnchārē'ä), N Colombia, in Magdalena dept. and Guajira commissary, rises on NE slopes of Sierra Nevada de Santa Marta, flows c.125 mi. in large curve E, and NNW, to Caribbean Sea at Ríohacha. Its lower course forms border bet. Magdalena dept. and Guajira commissary. Sometimes called Calancala (kälänkä'lä).

Ranches of Taos (tous) or **Ranchos de Taos** (rän'chōs dä), agr. village (pop. 1,386), Taos co., N N.Mex., on branch of Rio Grande, in Sangre de Cristo Mts., and 4 mi. SSW of Taos; alt. 6,900 ft. Famous for St. Francis of Assisi Mission, adobe church (rebuilt c.1772; 120 ft. long, with 6-ft. wall); has many religious objects, anc. reredos with paintings of saints. Ponce de Leon hot springs, with swimming pools, near by.

Ranchester, town (pop. 251), Sheridan co., N Wyo., on Tongue R., near Mont. line, and 15 mi. NW of Sheridan; rural supply point for Tongue R. valley. Connor Battlefield State Park near by.

Ranchi (rän'chē), district (□ 7,159; pop. 1,675,413), SW Bihar, India, in Chota Nagpur div.; ⊙ Ranchi. On Chota Nagpur Plateau; bounded NE by Subarnarekha R.; drained by Subarnarekha, tributaries of Son, and headstreams of Brahmani rivers. Agr. (rice, corn, oilseeds, cotton, tea, peanuts); sal, kusum, bamboo, and mahua in dispersed forest areas; bauxite deposits in NE. Lac and silk growing, pisciculture; mfg. of shellac, cement, brass utensils. Main towns: Ranchi, Lohardaga, Bundu. Ruins of 18th-cent. Hindu palace near Ranchi.

Ranchi, city (pop., including suburb of Doranda or Dorunda, 62,562), ⊙ Chota Nagpur div. and Ranchi dist., SW Bihar, India, on Chota Nagpur Plateau, on Subarnarekha R. and 70 mi. NW of Jamshedpur; road junction; trade center (rice, corn, oilseeds, cotton, tea, handicrafts); shellac mfg., silk growing; pisciculture. Important lac research institute (experimental growing and mfg.) 3 mi. SE of city center, at Namkum or Namkom. Aluminum workings 34 mi. E, near rail junction of Muri. Large mental hospital, agr. research station 5 mi. N, at Kanke. Ruins of 18th-cent. Hindu palace 39 mi. WSW, at Doisanagar.

Ranchillos (ränchē'yōs), town (pop. estimate 500), central Tucumán prov., Argentina, 13 mi. SE of Tucumán; rail junction; sugar-growing center.

Rancho or **El Rancho** (ĕl rän'chō), village (1921 pop. 946), El Progreso dept., E central Guatemala, on Motagua R. and 5 mi. NE of El Progreso; rail and road junction; corn, beans, livestock.

Rancho Boyeros (rän'chō boiā'rōs), airport, Havana prov., W Cuba, at General Peraza, 9 mi. S of Havana. Sometimes its name is used interchangeably for General Peraza.

Ranchos (rän'chōs), town (pop. 2,472), ⊙ General Paz dist. (□ 462; pop. 9,626), NE Buenos Aires prov., Argentina, 45 mi. SSW of La Plata; agr. center (corn, flax, oats, alfalfa, livestock); flour milling, dairying. Also called General Paz.

Rancho Santa Fe (răn"chō săn"tŭ fā'), village (pop. c.500), San Diego co., S Calif., 21 mi. N of San Diego, near the coast; residential; citrus-fruit, avocado groves.

Rancho Veloz (rän'chō vālōs'), town (pop. 1,834), Las Villas prov., central Cuba, near the coast, on railroad and 20 mi. WNW of Sagua la Grande; sugar cane, fruit, salt. The central of Ramona is 3 mi. SE.

Ranchuelo (ränchwā'lō), town (pop. 4,371), Las Villas prov., central Cuba, 12 mi. WSW of Santa Clara; processing center in well-known tobacco belt. Mfg. of cigars, sweets; meat packing. Near by are centrals of Santa Rosa (E) and Santa María (W).

Ranco, Lake (räng'kō) (□ 200), Valdivia prov., S central Chile, in Chilean lake dist., 25 mi. E of La Unión; 16 mi. long, 13 mi. wide. Surrounded by subandean peaks and forests, it is a noted tourist resort and fishing and lumbering dist. Has a number of isls., among them Guapi Isl. Outlet: Río Bueno (W).

Rancocas Creek (răng-kō'kŭs), Burlington co., SW N.J., rises E of Browns Mills (here forming Mirror L.) flows c.30 mi. W and NW, past Mt. Holly, to the Delaware at Riverside. Navigable c.9 mi. above mouth. South Branch (c.15 mi. long) enters creek W of Mt. Holly.

Rancul, department, Argentina: see PARERA.

Rancul (rängkōōl'), town (pop. estimate 1,500), N La Pampa natl. territory, Argentina, on railroad and 70 mi. NW of General Pico; grain-growing, stock-raising, lumbering center; sawmills. Sometimes called Jardón or Villa Jardón.

Rand, The, U. of So. Afr.: see WITWATERSRAND.

Rand, The, Calif.: see RAND MOUNTAINS.

Randa (rän'dä), peak (1,798 ft.), Majorca, Balearic Isls., 14 mi. E of Palma. The village of Randa (pop. 243) is at its W foot.

Rand Airport, S Transvaal, U. of So. Afr., on Witwatersrand, 3 mi. SW of Germiston, 8 mi. ESE of Johannesburg; 26°15'S 28°9'E.

Randalia, town (pop. 132), Fayette co., NE Iowa, 8 mi. SSW of West Union. Limestone quarries near by.

Randall (răn'dŭl), county (□ 916; pop. 13,774), extreme N Texas; ⊙ Canyon. On high plains of the Panhandle; alt. 3,000–3,800 ft. Cattle and wheat area, producing also grain sorghums, barley, oats, hay, poultry, dairy products. Drained by Tierra Blanca and Palo Duro creeks, here forming Prairie Dog Town Fork of Red R., site of scenic Palo Duro Canyon (state park). Formed 1876.

Randall. **1** Village, Ill.: see EAST GALESBURG. **2** Town (pop. 202), Hamilton co., central Iowa, 18 mi. NNW of Ames. **3** City (pop. 240), Jewell co., N Kansas, on small affluent of Republican R. and 20 mi. WNW of Concordia; grain, livestock. **4** Village (pop. 425), Morrison co., central Minn., on small affluent of Mississippi R. and 10 mi. NW of Little Falls; dairy products.

Randalls Island (194 acres), in New York city, SE N.Y., in East R. at confluence with the Harlem; linked to Manhattan and Queens boroughs by Triborough Bridge. Now a municipal park and sports center, with a large stadium; formerly occupied by city institutions for children.

Randallstown, suburban village (1940 pop. 1,035), Baltimore co., central Md., 11 mi. WNW of downtown Baltimore.

Randalstown (răn'dŭlztoun), town (pop. 1,331), SW Co. Antrim, Northern Ireland, on Main R., near its mouth on Lough Neagh, and 5 mi. WNW of Antrim; agr. market in flax, potato, and cattle region; linen bleaching.

Randan (rãdã'), village (pop. 919), Puy-de-Dôme dept., central France, in the Limagne, 8 mi. SSW of Vichy; mfg. of straw hats, cider making.

Randazzo (rändä'tsō), town (pop. 12,588), Catania prov., NE Sicily, at NW foot of Mt. Etna, near Alcantara R., 27 mi. NNW of Catania; road center; flour mills, distilleries. Point of ascent for Mt. Etna. One of few towns in region to escape eruptions and earthquakes; noted for its medieval houses and churches (particularly Santa Maria, built 1217–39, damaged in Second World War). Largely destroyed by bombing and fighting (1943) in Second World War.

Rander (rän'dār), town (pop. 14,512), Surat dist., N Bombay, India, on Tapti R. and 2 mi. NW of Surat; trades in rice, cotton, millet; cotton ginning, brick mfg., hand-loom weaving. Important port for spices and silks in 16th cent.

Randers (rä'nŭrs), amt (□ 952; 1950 pop. 167,335), Jutland, Denmark; ⊙ Randers. Comprises Djursland peninsula and area bet. Randers Fjord and Mariager Fjord; other cities: Hobro, Grenaa. Highest point, 430 ft. Grain and dairy farming.

Randers, city (1950 pop. 40,098), ⊙ Randers amt, E Jutland, Denmark, port at mouth of Guden R., on Randers Fjord and 22 mi. NNW of Aarhus; 56°28'N 10°2'E. Railroad-car mfg., machine shops, iron foundries, brewing, distilling, meat and dairy processing. City dates from 11th cent.; important commercial center in Middle Ages. Has Gothic church (c.1500).

Randersacker (rän'dŭrsä"kŭr), village (pop. 2,800), Lower Franconia, NW Bavaria, Germany, on the Main (canalized) and 3 mi. SE of Würzburg; textile mfg.; winegrowing.

Randers Fjord (rä'nŭrs), E Jutland, Denmark, inlet (c.15 mi. long) of the Kattegat. At head is Randers city and mouth of Guden R.

Randfontein (ränt'fōntān"), town (pop. 32,523), S Transvaal, U. of So. Afr., on W Witwatersrand, 20 mi. W of Johannesburg; alt. 5,620 ft.; gold-mining center.

Randleman, town (pop. 2,066), Randolph co., central N.C., 18 mi. S of Greensboro and on Deep R.; mfg. of hosiery, lingerie.

Randles, town (pop. 169), Cape Girardeau co., SE Mo., 18 mi. SW of Cape Girardeau.

Randlett, town (pop. 396), Cotton co., S Okla., near Red R., 15 mi. SW of Walters; trade center for farm area.

Rand Mountains, S Calif., range (over 4,000 ft.) in the Mojave Desert, extending c.20 mi. SW from Randsburg. The Rand, a rich mining dist. here, produces silver, tungsten, gold.

Randogne (rãdô'nyŭ), village (pop. 1,136), Valais canton, S Switzerland, 2 mi. NW of Sierre; resort (alt. 4,101 ft.).

Randolph (răn'dŏlf). **1** County (□ 581; pop. 22,513), E Ala., on Ga. line; ⊙ Wedowee. Piedmont region drained by Tallapoosa and Little Tallapoosa rivers. Roanoke is processing center. Cotton, bees, livestock; textiles, quarried products. Formed 1832. **2** County (□ 637; pop. 15,982), NE Ark.; ⊙ Pocahontas. Bounded N by Mo. line; drained by Black, Current, Spring, and Eleven Point rivers. Agr. (grain, cotton, poultry, livestock; dairy products); timber. Formed 1836. **3** County (□ 436; pop. 13,804), SW Ga.; ⊙ Cuthbert. Coastal plain agr. (cotton, corn, peanuts, fruit) and sawmilling area. Formed 1828. **4** County (□ 594; pop. 31,673), SW Ill.; ⊙ Chester. Bounded W and S by Mississippi R.; drained by Kaskaskia R. Agr. (corn, wheat; dairy products; poultry). Mfg. (shoes and leather products, flour, farm machinery, wood products). Bituminous-coal mining; lumbering. Fort Kaskaskia and Fort de Chartres state parks are here. Formed 1795. **5** County (□ 457; pop. 27,141), E Ind., bounded E by Ohio line; ⊙ Winchester. Agr. area (grain, poultry; dairy products; livestock); mfg. at Union City and Winchester; stone quarrying. Drained by Mississinewa and Whitewater rivers and by West Fork of White R. Highest point in Ind. (1,240 ft.) is E of Lynn. Formed 1818. **6** County (□ 484; pop. 22,918), N central Mo.; ⊙ Huntsville. Drained by tributaries of Chariton and Salt rivers. Agr. (corn, wheat, oats); mfg. at Moberly; bituminous coal. Formed 1829. **7** County (□ 801; pop. 50,804), central N.C.; ⊙ Asheboro. Piedmont area, drained by Deep R.; farming (tobacco, hay, corn, wheat, dairy products, poultry), textile mfg., sawmilling. Formed 1779. **8** County (□ 1,036; pop. 30,558), E W.Va., at base of Eastern Panhandle; ⊙ ELKINS. On Allegheny Plateau; traversed N–S by Allegheny Front (E border), Rich Mtn., Cheat Mtn., Shaver's Mtn., and other ridges. Much of co. is within Monongahela Natl. Forest. Drained by Elk and Tygart rivers and headstreams of Cheat R. Agr. (livestock, fruit, tobacco); coal mining; timber; limestone quarries. Mfg., lumber milling, railroad shops at Elkins. Formed 1787.

Randolph. 1 Town (pop. 295), Fremont co., SW Iowa, 12 mi. NW of Shenandoah; livestock, grain. **2** City (pop. 391), Riley co., NE Kansas, on Big Blue R. and 19 mi. NNW of Manhattan, in livestock and grain region; grain milling, poultry packing. **3** Residential town (pop. 1,733), Kennebec co., S Maine, on the Kennebec opposite Gardiner. Inc. 1887. **4** Town (pop. 9,982), Norfolk co., E Mass., 14 mi. S of Boston, 6 mi. N of Brockton; food products, paper boxes, portable buildings, chains. Had large shoe industry in 19th cent. Settled c.1710, set off from Braintree 1793. **5** Village (pop. 259), Dakota co., SE Minn., on Cannon R. and 30 mi. S of St. Paul, in grain, potato, livestock. area. Small reservoir is just E. **6** Village (pop. 243), Pontotoc co., N Miss., 11 mi. WSW of Pontotoc, in agr., dairying, and timber area. **7** City (pop. 1,029), Cedar co., NE Nebr., 25 mi. N of Norfolk; livestock, dairy and poultry produce, grain. Settled 1886, inc. 1887. **8** Resort town (pop. 158), Coos co., N central N.H., on Israel R. and 8 mi. S of Berlin; trail center for Presidential Range. **9** Village (pop. 1,455), Cattaraugus co., W N.Y., 14 mi. ENE of Jamestown; mfg. of feed, flour, furniture, machinery, tin cans; printing. Agr. (dairy products; poultry, grain). Inc. 1867. **10** Town (pop. 562), ⊙ Rich co., N Utah, 35 mi. E of Logan, near Bear R. in livestock and grain area; dairy products; alt. 6,287 ft. **11** Town (pop. 3,499), including Randolph village (pop. 2,223), Orange co., central Vt., 20 mi. SSW of Barre; wood products, machinery, canned corn; dairy products; winter sports. The Morgan horse was 1st bred here. State school of agr. at Randolph Center village. Inc. 1783. **12** Village (pop. 1,350), on Columbia-Dodge co. line, S central Wis., near Beaverdam L., 23 mi. E of Portage, in dairy and livestock region; seed warehouses; mfg. of wood products. Settled 1844, platted 1857, inc. 1870.

Randolph Air Force Base, Texas: see SAN ANTONIO.

Random Island (□ 90; pop. 1,709), just off SE N.F., in arm of Trinity Bay, 30 mi. NW of Carbonear; 20 mi. long, 7 mi. wide; 48°10′N 53°45′W. Rises to 843 ft. Has several fishing settlements. At Snook's Harbour (pop. 66), on NW coast, are brickworks.

Random Lake, village (pop. 679), Sheboygan co., E Wis., on Random L. (resort), 35 mi. N of Milwaukee, in dairy and grain area; cheese, beer, canned vegetables, paper products.

Randon (rădō′), village (pop. 441), Constantine dept., NE Algeria, in coastal lowland, on rail spur and 15 mi. SSE of Bône; extensive vineyards.

Randonnai (rădônā′), village (pop. 312), Orne dept., NW France, 11 mi. NNE of Mortagne; iron founding.

Randsburg, mining village (pop. c.600), Kern co., S central Calif., in Rand Mts., 36 mi. NE of Mojave; silver, tungsten. Airport. Rail point is Searles, c.10 mi. N.

Rands Fjord (räns), lake (□ 52), Opland co., SE Norway, 7 mi. NE of Honefoss; 48 mi. long, 1–4 mi. wide. Drains S via Rand R. into Drammen R.

Randville, village, Dickinson co., N Mich., on the Upper Peninsula, 11 mi. N of Iron Mountain; iron-ore treatment plant.

Randwick, municipality (pop. 100,931), E New South Wales, Australia, 5 mi. SE of Sydney, in metropolitan area. Large race track here.

Ranea (rō′nāō″), Swedish *Råneå*, village (pop. 836), Norrbotten co., N Sweden, near Gulf of Bothnia, 18 mi. N of Lulea; tannery, shoe mfg., brick works.

Ranelagh (ră′nĭlū), former amusement ground in Chelsea, London, England, founded 1742 on estate of earl of Ranelagh, closed 1803 or 1804, when grounds were joined to adjacent Royal Hosp. Ranelagh reached height of fashion in reign of George III.

Ranelagh, village (pop. 619), SE Tasmania, 17 mi. SW of Hobart and on Huon R.; fruit cannery; cattle.

Ranelagh, North, and **South Ranelagh,** S suburbs of Dublin, Co. Dublin, Ireland.

Ranelven, Norway: see RANA RIVER.

Ranem, Norway: see RANHEIM.

Ranen, Norway: see RANA.

Ranenburg, Russian SFSR: see CHAPLYGIN.

Ranen Fjord, Norway: see RAN FJORD.

Ran Fjord (rän), Nor. *Rana Fjord*, inlet of North Sea, Nordland co., N central Norway, extends c.45 mi. NE from Donna isl.; 1–4 mi. wide. On it are Hemnesberget, Basmoen, and Mo. Receives Rana R. Sometimes called Ranen Fjord.

Ranga (răng′gù), village, Tasmania, on W Flinders Isl. of Furneaux Isls. and 3 mi. SE of Whitemark; butter factory.

Rangadih, India: see BALARAMPUR.

Ra Ngae (rä′ ùngă′), village (1937 pop. 3,982), Narathiwat prov., S Thailand, in Malay Peninsula, on railroad and 12 mi. SW of Narathiwat (linked by highway). Locally known as Tanyong Mas or Tanyong Mat.

Rangamati, India: see BERHAMPORE.

Rangamati (răng-gä′mätē), village, ⊙ Chittagong Hill Tracts dist., SE East Bengal, E Pakistan, on Karnaphuli R. and 30 mi. NE of Chittagong; trades in rice, cotton, oilseeds, tobacco; rice milling.

Rangarvalla (räng′gourvät″lä), Icelandic *Rangárvalla*, county [Icelandic *sýsla*] (pop. 2,962), S Iceland; ⊙ Hvolsvollur. Extends bet. coast and Hekla volcano; drained by lower course of Thjorsa R. Sheep and cattle raising, fishing. Thykkvibaer village is market center.

Range, The, Southern Rhodesia: see THE RANGE.

Rangeley (rānj′lē), town (pop. 1,228), Franklin co., W Maine, on Rangeley L. and 28 mi. NNW of Rumford; hq. of hilly, wooded RANGELEY LAKES recreational region. Includes villages of Oquossoc (fish hatchery), Haines Landing (steamboat terminal), and South Rangeley. Settled c.1825, inc. 1855.

Rangeley Lakes, in Maine and N.H., 6 stream-linked lakes at center of large recreational area (hunting, fishing, canoeing, winter sports) at 1,500-ft. alt. Include Rangeley or Oquossoc (ŏkwŏ′sùk), Mooselookmeguntic (mōōs′lŏŏkmĭgŭn′tĭk) (c.13 mi. long), Upper Richardson or Molechunkamunk (mōlŭchŭngk′ŭmŭngk), Lower Richardson, and Cupsuptic lakes in W Maine, and Umbagog L. (ŭmbā′gŏg) on N.H. line (source of Androscoggin R.). Game preserve, fish hatcheries, resorts in area; steamer and seaplane service on lakes.

Rangely (rānj′lē), town (pop. 808), Rio Blanco co., NW Colo., on White R., near Utah line, and 45 mi. W of Meeker; alt. 5,200 ft. Supply point in oil-mining and cattle-grazing area. Growth stimulated by oil boom of 1940s. Founded 1880.

Range Ponds, SW Maine, 3 linked lakes, each c.2 mi. long, in resort area of Androscoggin co., near Poland.

Ranger (rān′jùr). **1** Town (pop. 183), Gordon co., NW Ga., 14 mi. E of Calhoun; sawmilling. **2** City (pop. 3,989), Eastland co., N central Texas, c.80 mi. WSW of Fort Worth; supply center for oil field; oil refining, trade, processing point for agr. area (peanuts, cotton, livestock); mfg. of trailers, clothing. Seat of a jr. col. Founded 1881, inc. 1919; had c.50,000 pop. in boom following oil discovery, 1917.

Rangia (rŭng′gyŭ), village, Kamrup dist., W Assam, India, on tributary of the Brahmaputra and 20 mi. NNW of Gauhati; rail junction; rice, mustard, jute; silk-cloth mfg. Also spelled Rangiya.

Rangiora (răng-gēō′rù), borough (pop. 2,384), ⊙ Rangiora co. (□ 96; pop. 2,883), E S.Isl., New Zealand, 16 mi. N of Christchurch; agr. center; stockyards.

Rangiroa (răng-ērō′ä), atoll (pop. 591), westerly, largest of Tuamotu Isls., Fr. Oceania, S Pacific; 15°3′S 147°45′W; 20 islets surround lagoon 45 mi. long, 15 mi. wide; pearls. Formerly Dean's Isl.

Rangitata River (răng-gĭtä′tù), E central S.Isl., New Zealand, rises in central Southern Alps, flows 75 mi. SE to Canterbury Bight 12 mi. N of Temuka.

Rangitikei, county, New Zealand: see MARTON.

Rangitikei River (răng-gĭtē′kē), S N.Isl., New Zealand, rises in Kaimanawa Mts., flows 115 mi. SW to Cook Strait 25 mi. SE of Wanganui.

Rangitoto Island (răng″gĭtō′tō), uninhabited volcanic island off N N.Isl., New Zealand, at NE entrance to Waitemata Harbour; 5 mi. long. 2 mi. wide; coral causeway to Motutapu Isl.

Rangiya, India: see Rangia.

Rang-Kul or **Rang-Kul′** (rŭn-gù-kōōl′), town (1941 pop. over 500), E Gorno-Badakhshan Autonomous Oblast, Tadzhik SSR, in the Pamir, near Rang-Kul (lake), 30 mi. NE of Murgab; alt. 12,200 ft. Gold mining. Salt deposits near by.

Rangoon (răng-gōōn′), Burmese *Yangon* (yăng′gōn), city (□ 85; 1941 pop. 500,800), ⊙ Burma, Pegu div., and Hanthawaddy dist. and coextensive with Rangoon dist., in Lower Burma, 21 mi. from Andaman Sea, on Rangoon R., here formed by Pegu and Myitmaka rivers; 16°48′N 96°10′E. One of leading ports of SE Asia, Rangoon ranks next to Bombay and Calcutta among the Asian seaports on the Indian Ocean, handling over 80% of Burma's trade. It is the head of railroads to Prome and Mandalay and is connected by navigable Twante and Pegu-Sittang canals with Irrawaddy and Sittang rivers. An international air traffic hub, with airport at Mingaladon, 10 mi. N. Its leading industries (rice- and sawmilling, oil refining) are located in the suburbs of Dalla (across Rangoon R.) and Syriam (across Pegu R.). Aluminum ware, rubber shoes, tobacco (at Kamayut), soap, rope, cornstarch, and matches are also produced. The city proper, laid out in rectangular blocks, is on N (left) bank of Rangoon R. (docks, warehouses). The business quarter extends along the water front from Kemmendine section (W), through Ahlone (lumber yards) and Botataung to Pazundaung (E), and contains govt. buildings, Anglican and R.C. cathedrals, and general hospital. The city is dominated by the imposing 368-ft.-high Shwe Dagon Pagoda (N of business section), one of most venerated in Buddhist world, rising in gilded massiveness on a 168-ft. mound. Traditionally founded 588 B.C., the pagoda is said to contain relics of Buddha and was repeatedly enlarged up to its present size, dating from 1564. It dwarfs the Sule Pagoda, in business section, and Rangoon's numerous monasteries. N of city are Dalhousie Park with Royal Lake, Victoria Memorial Park with zoo, and, on NW outskirts, Victoria Lake with near-by univ. (1920). The Govt. House rises in wooded grounds W of Shwe Dagon Pagoda. Originally a Mon fishing village around the pagoda, Rangoon was won (1755) by the Burmese under Alaungpaya, given its present name, and developed as Burma's chief port. It was briefly held (1824–26) by British in 1st Anglo-Burmese War, annexed 1852 in 2d Anglo-Burmese War, and became (1862) ⊙ Lower Burma and (1886) of all Burma. A municipality since 1874, Rangoon developed as a modern city under Br. rule. In Second World War, it was held 1942–45 by Japanese and badly damaged by bombing.

Rangoon River, marine estuary, Lower Burma, formed at Rangoon by junction of Pegu and Myitmaka (here called Hlaing) rivers, flows 25 mi. SE to Gulf of Martaban of Andaman Sea; access channel for Rangoon, made navigable by dredging for ocean-going vessels. Linked by Twante Canal with Irrawaddy delta.

Rangpo (răng′pô), village, S Sikkim, India, on the Tista and 11.5 mi. SSW of Gangtok, in foothills of W Assam Himalayas; trades in corn, rice, pulse, oranges.

Rangpur, Assam, India: see SIBSAGAR, town.

Rangpur (rŭng′pŏŏr), district (□ 3,606; 1951 pop. 2,931,000), N East Bengal, E Pakistan; ⊙ Rangpur. Bounded N by Cooch Behar dist., E by main course of the Brahmaputra; drained by the Tista. Alluvial plain; rice, jute, tobacco (major tobacco-growing dist. of E Pakistan), oilseeds, sugar cane, wheat, pineapples. Sissoo, mango, and areca palm in dispersed forest area. Railroad workshops at Lalmanir Hat and Saidpur; rice, oilseed, dal, and flour milling, jute pressing. Technical institute at Rangpur. Under successive Kamarupa, Pal, Afghan, and Moslem (15th–16th cent.) kingdoms, and Mogul (16th cent.) empire. Passed to English in 1765; ravaged by dacoits in 18th cent. Part of former Br. Bengal prov., India, until inc. 1947 into new Pakistan prov. of East Bengal.

Rangpur, town (pop. 34,039), ⊙ Rangpur dist., N East Bengal, E Pakistan, near the Tista, 100 mi. NW of Mymensingh; mfg. of bricks, electrical supplies, and cutlery; ivory carving; trades in rice, jute, tobacco, oilseeds. Technical institute.

Rangsang (rängsäng′) or **Medang** (mùdäng′), island (38 mi. long, 10 mi. wide), Indonesia, in Strait of Malacca, off E coast of Sumatra, 50 mi. WSW of Singapore, just NE of Tebingtinggi isl.; 1°N 102°57′E; low and swampy.

Rangsdorf (rängs′dôrf), village (pop. 4,922), Brandenburg, E Germany, on small Rangsdorf L., 15 mi. S of Berlin; ceramics mfg., metalworking.

Rangsum (răng′sōōm′), Chinese *Ch'ia-chiang* (chyä′-jyäng′), after 1913 *Tungpu* or *T'ung-p'u* (both: tōōng′pōō′), town, E Tibet, in Kham prov., near Yangtze R., 80 mi. NE of Chamdo; agr. Copper mining near by.

Ranguevaux (rägùvō′), Ger. *Rangwall* (räng′väl), village (pop. 729), Moselle dept., NE France, 7 mi. SW of Thionville; forges.

Ranheim (rän′hām), village (pop. 2,138) in Strinda canton, Sor-Trondelag co., central Norway, on Trondheim Fjord, on railroad and 5 mi. E of Trondheim; produces bricks, cellulose, paper. Formerly spelled Ranem.

Rani (rä′nē), village, S central Rajasthan, India, 11 mi. N of Bali; millet, oilseeds, cotton, wheat; cotton ginning, oilseed pressing, atta processing, woodworking.

Rania or **Raniyah** (rānē'yŭ), town, Erbil prov., N Iraq, in Kurdistan, near Iran border, 50 mi. E of Erbil; tobacco, fruit, livestock.
Ranibagh, India: see HALDWANI.
Ranibennur (rānē'bān-nŏŏr), town (pop. 16,994), Dharwar dist., S Bombay, India, 70 mi. SSE of Dharwar; cotton ginning, cloth dyeing, handicraft blanket weaving, biri mfg.; trades in grain, betel leaf, chili, oilseeds.
Ranier (rănēr'), village (pop. 227), Koochiching co., N Minn., on Rainy L. and Ont. line, at mouth of Rainy R., just E of International Falls. Port of entry.
Raniganj (rä'nēgŭnj), town (pop. 22,839), Burdwan dist., W West Bengal, India, in Damodar Valley and Raniganj coal field, near the Damodar, 9 mi. ESE of Asansol. A major coal-mining and industrial center; mfg. of chemicals, paper, cement, pottery, silicate, glass, steel products, bricks, tiles, shellac, jewelry; rice, flour, and oilseed milling; general engineering factory, railroad workshops. Was ⊙ dist. until replaced (1906) by Burdwan. Coal-mining centers at Tapasi (3 mi. N), Kaliparhi (7 mi. WNW), Ukhra (8 mi. ENE), and Kajora (4 mi. E) villages.
Ranikhet (rä'nēkāt), cantonment town (pop. 4,894), Almora dist., N Uttar Pradesh, India, 13 mi. WNW of Almora, in E Kumaun Himalaya foothills; alt. c.5,980 ft. Chaubattia cantonment (alt. c.6,940 ft.) is 2 mi. SE. Anc. Hindu temples (some ruined in 18th cent. by Rohillas), tomb ruins, and 11th-cent. inscriptions 10 mi. N, at village of Dwarahat.
Ranipet (rä'nĭpāt), town (pop. 14,270), North Arcot dist., E central Madras, India, on Palar R. and 13 mi. E of Vellore, rail spur terminus; rice and sugar milling, fertilizer (superphosphate) mfg.; orange, mango, and betel farms; cattle market. Formerly also called Ranippettai.
Ranipur (rä'nēpŏŏr), town (pop. 5,211), Jhansi dist., S Uttar Pradesh, India, 4 mi. W of Mau; jowar, oilseeds, wheat, gram.
Ranis (rä'nĭs), town (pop. 2,980), in former Prussian Saxony prov. exclave, central Germany, after 1945 in Thuringia, 9 mi. E of Saalfeld; woodworking; climatic health resort. Towered over by anc. castle, rebuilt 1646.
Raniwari (rănĭvä're), village, SW Rajasthan, India, 40 mi. SSW of Jalor; rail spur terminus.
Raniyah, Iraq: see RANIA.
Rankin (răng'kĭn), county (□ 800; pop. 28,881), central Miss.; ⊙ Brandon. Bounded W and NW by Pearl R.; also drained by Strong R. and tributaries. Agr. (cotton, corn, truck); lumbering. Natural-gas fields (opened in 1930s). Formed 1828.
Rankin. 1 (răng'kĭn, rŏng'kĭn) Village (pop. 737), Vermilion co., E Ill., 25 mi. NNW of Danville; agr. (grain, livestock, poultry; dairy products); timber. 2 (răng'kĭn) Industrial borough (pop. 6,941), Allegheny co., SW Pa., on Monongahela R. just ESE of Pittsburgh; steel. Inc. 1892. 3 (răng'kĭn, răn'-) City (pop. 1,139), ⊙ Upton co., W Texas, 55 mi. S of Midland; trade point for oil-producing and sheep-ranching area.
Rankin's Springs, village (pop. 206), S central New South Wales, Australia, 190 mi. WNW of Canberra; rail terminus, hardwood timber, wheat, sheep.
Rankovicevo or **Rankovichevo** (both: răn'kôvĭchĕvô), Serbo-Croatian *Rankovićevo*. 1 Town (pop. 12,503), central Serbia, Yugoslavia, on Ibar R., just above its mouth, and 75 mi. S of Belgrade. Rail junction; mfg. (railroad cars, aircraft); apple growing. Chromium and magnesite mining (magnesite-brick mfg.), lead smelter near by. Monastery of ZICA SW of town. Until 1949, called Kraljevo or Kralyevo. 2 Village (pop. 5,512), Vojvodina, N Serbia, Yugoslavia, 14 mi. WSW of Vrsac, in the Banat. Until 1947, called Karlovac, Karlovats, Banatski Karlovac, or Banatski Karlovats, Hung. *Nagykárolyfalva.*
Rankweil (rängk'vīl), town (pop. 5,175), Vorarlberg, W Austria, 3 mi. NE of Feldkirch; cotton and paper mills, breweries; hand embroidery. Place of pilgrimage.
Ranlo, village (pop. 2,929, with adjacent Smyre or Smyre Mills), Gaston co., S N.C., 3 mi. E of Gastonia.
Rann, Yugoslavia: see BREZICE.
Ranna (rŭn'nŭ), village (pop. 476), Southern Prov., Ceylon, 8 mi. NE of Tangalla; rice, tomatoes, citronella grass.
Rannoch, Loch (lŏkh ră'nŭkh), lake (9 mi. long, 1 mi. wide; 440 ft. deep), in NW Perthshire, Scotland, 18 mi. WNW of Aberfeldy, at foot of Schiehallion mtn.; drained by Tummel R. and fed by Ericht R. and numerous small streams. It is surrounded by Rannoch Moor, c.30 mi. long and 12 mi. wide.
Rann of Cutch, India: see CUTCH, RANN OF.
Rano (rä'nō), town (pop. 2,637), Kano prov., Northern Provinces, N Nigeria, 30 mi. S of Kano; cotton, peanuts, millet; cattle, skins. Until 19th cent., seat of native emirate.
Ranomena (rānŏŏmĕ'nŭ), village, Fianarantsoa prov., SE Madagascar, 20 mi. W of Vangaindrano; center of native trade.
Ranong (rä'nông'), town (1947 pop. 3,531), ⊙ Ranong prov. (□ 1,381; 1947 pop. 21,488), S Thailand, in Isthmus of Kra, W of Phuket Range, on Pakchan R. estuary opposite Victoria Point (Burma), and 55 mi. SW of Chumphon. Tin-mining center; fisheries. Sometimes spelled Renong.
Ranpur (rän'pŏŏr). 1 Town (pop. 7,265), Ahmadabad dist., N Bombay, India, 75 mi. SW of Ahmadabad; market center for millet, cotton. Founded early-14th cent. by Rajputs. 2 Village, Puri dist., E Orissa, India, 35 mi. WNW of Puri. Was ⊙ former princely state of Ranpur (□ 204; pop. 51,366) in Orissa States, inc. 1949 into Puri dist.
Rănquil (räng'kēl). 1 Village (pop. 308), Arauco prov., S central Chile, near the Pacific, 10 mi. NE of Lebu; grain, leguminous plants, livestock. 2 Village (1930 pop. 76), Concepción prov., S central Chile, 30 mi. ENE of Concepción, in agr. area (cereals, wine, vegetables, livestock).
Ranquitte (rākēt'), town (1950 pop. 728), Nord dept., N central Haiti, in Massif du Nord, 27 mi. SSE of Cap-Haïtien; coffeegrowing.
Ransart (rāsär'), town (pop. 10,160), Hainaut prov., S central Belgium, 4 mi. NNE of Charleroi; coal mining.
Ranshaw, village (pop. 1,477), Northumberland co., E central Pa., 19 mi. NW of Pottsville.
Ranshofen, Austria: see BRAUNAU.
Ransom, county (□ 863; pop. 8,876), SE N.Dak.; ⊙ Lisbon. Rich prairie land drained by Sheyenne R. Livestock raising and farming. Formed 1873.
Ransom. 1 Village (pop. 411), La Salle co., N Ill., 10 mi. E of Streator, in agr. and bituminous-coal area. 2 City (pop. 405), Ness co., W central Kansas, 13 mi. N of Ness City; grain, livestock.
Ransomville, village (1940 pop. 573), Niagara co., W N.Y., near L. Ontario, 13 mi. NE of Niagara Falls city, in fruitgrowing area.
Ranson, industrial town (pop. 1,436), Jefferson co., NE W.Va., in Eastern Panhandle, contiguous to Charles Town (S); brass and iron foundries, apple-processing plants. Inc. 1910.
Rantau, Indonesia: see TEBINGTINGGI.
Rantau (rän"tou'), village (pop. 625), SW Negri Sembilan, Malaya, 9 mi. S of Seremban; rubber, rice; tin mining.
Rantau Panjang (pänjäng'), railroad station, N Kelantan, Malaya, on E coast line and 19 mi. SW of Kota Bharu, on the Sungei Golok (Thailand border stream) opposite Sungei Golok station; Malay customs.
Rantemario, Mount (räntämä'ryō), highest peak (11,286 ft.) of Celebes, Indonesia, at base of SW peninsula, 30 mi. SSW of Palopo.
Ranthambhor (rŭntŭmbōr'), noted Rajput hill fortress, E Rajasthan, India, 4 mi. ENE of Sawai Madhapur. After long siege, captured by Ala-ud-din in 1301; taken 1569 by Akbar.
Rantigny (rātēnyē'), village (pop. 1,123), Oise dept., N France, 11 mi. NW of Senlis, adjoining Liancourt; metalworks (boilers, agr. machinery), sawmills.
Rantomari, Russian SFSR: see YABLOCHNY.
Rantoul. 1 (răn"tōōl') Village (pop. 6,387), Champaign co., E Ill., 14 mi. NNE of Champaign, in agr. area. Inc. 1869. Chanute Air Force Base (shŭnōōt'), the U.S. military air technical school established here in 1917, was greatly expanded in Second World War. 2 (răn'toul") City (pop. 197), Franklin co., E Kansas, near Marais des Cygnes R., 10 mi. ESE of Ottawa, in livestock and grain region.
Rantum-Hörnum (rän'tŏŏm-hûr'nŏŏm), commune (pop. 4,910), in Schleswig-Holstein, NW Germany, on Sylt isl. Hörnum, 10 mi. S of Westerland, is harbor of Sylt isl.; fishing-boat repair shops; lobstering; fish canning. Rantum, 4 mi. S of Westerland, was site of seaplane base.
Rao or **Rao-Poundioum** (rou'-pōōndyōōm'), village, NW Senegal, Fr. West Africa, on railroad to Dakar and 9 mi. SE of Saint-Louis; cheese mfg.
Rao, village, SW central Madhya Bharat, India, 6 mi. SSW of Indore; glassworks. Sanitarium 1 mi. SW. Sometimes spelled Rau.
Raoe, Indonesia: see RAU.
Raon-l'Étape (räō'-lātäp'), town (pop. 5,891), Vosges dept., E France, on the Meurthe and 10 mi. NNW of Saint-Dié; paper mills, sawmills, iron foundries; felt mfg. Partially destroyed, 1914.
Rao-Poundioum, Fr. West Africa: see RAO.
Raoul, Cape, Tasmania: see TASMAN PENINSULA.
Raoul Island, Kermadec Isls: see SUNDAY ISLAND.
Rapa or **Rapa Iti** (rä'pä ē'tē), volcanic island (□ 16; pop. 298), Fr. Oceania, S Pacific, c.325 mi. SE of Raivavae, TUBUAI ISLANDS; 27°35'S 144°25'W; circumference c.25 mi. Mountainous, rising to 2,077 ft. Good harbors. Chief export, copra. Discovered 1791 by Vancouver, annexed 1887 by France. Chief town, Ahurei. Formerly Oparo.
Rapa Iti, Fr. Oceania: see RAPA.
Rapallo (räp-päl'lō), town (pop. 6,766), Genova prov., Liguria, N Italy, port at head of Gulf of Rapallo, 16 mi. ESE of Genoa, in olive-, grape-, and flower-growing region. Celebrated resort of Riviera di Levante. Mfg. (lace, olive oil, wine, candles, Portland cement, bricks, iron alloys); fisheries. Treaties of Rapallo bet. Italy and Yugoslavia (1920) and bet. Russia and Germany (1922) signed here. Gulf of Rapallo, also known as Golfo Tigullio, is an inlet (8 mi. wide at mouth; 2.5 mi. long) on Gulf of Genoa; bounded W by promontory of Portofino.
Rapa Nui Island, Chile: see EASTER ISLAND.
Rapar (rä'pŭr), town (pop. 3,343), E Cutch, India, 65 mi. ENE of Bhuj; market center for salt and wheat. Sometimes spelled Rahpar.
Rapel River (räpĕl'), central Chile, formed by union of Cachapoal R. and Tinguiririca R. 3 mi. WSW of Las Cabras, flows c.45 mi. NW, along Colchagua-Santiago prov. border, to the Pacific 2 mi. N of Navidad; length of Tinguiririca-Rapel, 150 mi. Not navigable.
Raphana (rŭfā'nŭ), anc. city of Palestine, SE of Sea of Galilee; one of the Decapolis.
Raphia, Palestine-Egypt: see RAFA.
Raphoe (rŭfō'), Gaelic *Ráthbhoth*, town (pop. 760), E Co. Donegal, Ireland, 6 mi. NW of Lifford; agr. market (flax, potatoes, oats, cattle, sheep); furniture mfg. The cathedral (built 1702) is on site of monastery founded by St. Columba and converted into cathedral by St. Eunan in 9th cent. Until 1835 it was seat of bishopric.
Rapidan River (răpĭdăn'), Va., rises in the Blue Ridge in Madison co., flows c.90 mi. SE, NE, and E to Rappahannock R. on Stafford-Spotsylvania co. line.
Rapid City, town (pop. 402), SW Man., on Minnedosa R. (rapids) and 20 mi. N of Brandon; dairying.
Rapid City, city (pop. 25,310), ⊙ Pennington co., W S.Dak., 140 mi. W of Pierre, 30 mi. SE of Lead, in Black Hills; 44°5'N 103°15'W; alt. 3,229 ft.; 2d largest city in state. Resort; railway, trade, distribution center for mining and farming region; cement, flour, calcimine, bricks and tiles, meat products; gold, granite; grain, sugar beets. Air Force base near. Points of interest: South Dakota School of Mines and Technology and its mus. of prehistoric fossils, Dinosaur Park, near-by Stratosphere Bowl, from which balloon ascents have been made. Rapid Valley irrigation project is just E. Founded 1876, inc. 1882.
Rapid Creek, rises in Pennington co., SW S.Dak.; flows 86 mi. E, past Rapid City, to South Fork of Cheyenne R. SW of Wasta. Known in upper reaches as Castle Creek, which has Deerfield Dam (built 1947 as unit in Rapid Valley irrigation project) near Wyo. line. Dam is 133 ft. high, 825 ft. long.
Rapides (ră"pēdz'), parish (□ 1,329; pop. 90,648), central La.; ⊙ Alexandria. Bounded NE by Big Saline Bayou and Catahoula L.; drained by Calcasieu and Red rivers. Includes part of Kisatchie Natl. Forest and U.S. army camps Claiborne and Beauregard. Agr. and dairying area; cotton, hay, corn, sugar cane, sweet and white potatoes. Some mfg., including processing of farm products. Formed 1807.
Rapides, Canal des (känäl' dā räpēd'), delta arm of Red R., N Vietnam, connects Red R. at Hanoi with the Song Cau at Sept Pagodes; 40 mi. long.
Rapid Körös River, Hungary and Rumania: see KÖRÖS RIVER.
Rapido River (rä'pēdô), in Frosinone prov., S central Italy, rises in the Apennines 8 mi. E of Atina, flows 20 mi. generally S, past Sant'Elia Fiumerapido and CASSINO, to Liri R. 6 mi. SSE of Cassino. In Second World War divided Ger. and Allied fronts in the winter of 1943–44; scene of heavy fighting. Crossed by Allies in May, 1944.
Rapid River, village (1940 pop. 654), Delta co., S Upper Peninsula, Mich., 13 mi. NNE of Escanaba, at mouth of small Rapid R. on Little Bay De Noc; mfg. of wood products.
Rapids City, village (pop. 487), Rock Island co., NW Ill., on the Mississippi and 10 mi. ENE of Moline, in agr. area.
Rapina or **Ryapina,** Est. *Räpina* (all: ră'pēnä), town (pop. 599), SE Estonia, near L. Pskov, 25 mi. NE of Voru; paper mfg.
Rapla (rä'plä), town (pop. 887), W central Estonia, 30 mi. S of Tallinn; tile works. Rapla rail junction (pop. 107) is 1 mi. SE.
Rapolano (räpôlä'nô), village (pop. 1,109), Siena prov., Tuscany, central Italy, 14 mi. ESE of Siena; mfg. (chemicals, brooms). Hot mineral baths. Travertine quarries and manganese mine near by.
Rapolla (räpôl'lä), village (pop. 3,782), Potenza prov., Basilicata, S Italy, 2 mi. SE of Melfi.
Raponda, Lake, S Vt., resort lake in Wilmington town, 12 mi. W of Brattleboro; c.1.5 mi. long. Formerly Ray Pond.
Raposos (rŭpō'zōōs), town (pop. 4,150), S central Minas Gerais, Brazil, on the Rio das Velhas, on railroad and 8 mi. ESE of Belo Horizonte; gold mining.
Rappahannock (răpŭhă'nŭk), county (□ 267; pop. 6,112), N Va.; ⊙ Washington. In the piedmont; rises (W, NW) to the Blue Ridge; includes part of Shenandoah Natl. Park. Bounded N and NE by Rappahannock R., drained by Thornton R. and short Hughes R. Mainly agr., livestock, corn, wheat, tobacco, hay, apples, truck; dairying. Set off 1833 from Culpeper co.
Rappahannock River, Va., rises in the Blue Ridge E of Front Royal, flows 212 mi. generally SE, past Fredericksburg (head of tidewater and of navigation), to Chesapeake Bay c.20 mi. S of Potomac R. mouth. Rapidan R. is chief tributary. Salem Church Dam (for flood control, power) is 6 mi.

above Fredericksburg. Much Civil War fighting took place along the Rappahannock.

Rappahannock Station, Va.: see REMINGTON.

Rappenau, Bad, Germany: see BAD RAPPENAU.

Rapperswil (rä'pürsvĕl), town (pop. 5,070), St. Gall canton, N Switzerland, on L. of Zurich, 16 mi. SE of Zurich; metalworking, printing; fats, chemicals, leather, paper products. Town hall (15th cent.), castle (14th cent.), R.C. church (15th cent.), monastery (17th cent.). Causeway crosses lake.

Rappoltsweiler, France: see RIBEAUVILLÉ.

Rapri, India: see SIRSAGANJ.

Rapti River (räp'tē), in Nepal and Uttar Pradesh, India, rises in S central Nepal Himalayas N of Piuthan; flows SSE, W parallel to Siwalik Range, and generally SE into India, through rice and sugar-cane area, past Domariaganj, Bansi, and Gorakhpur, to Gogra R. 3 mi. W of Barhaj; c.400 mi. long. Navigable by large boats below Gorakhpur. Another Rapti R., in Nepal, is tributary of Gandak R.

Rapur (rä'pŏŏr), village, Nellore dist., E central Madras, India, 22 mi. W of Gudur; millet, rice, chili; timber, tanbark.

Rapu-Rapu Island (rä"pōō-rä'pōō) (□ 25; 1939 pop. 3,861), Albay prov., Philippines, off SE Luzon, bet. Lagonoy Gulf (N) and Albay Gulf (S), just E of Batan Isl., 23 mi. ENE of Legaspi; 11 mi. long, 3 mi. wide; rises to 1,760 ft. Copper mines. On S coast is Rapu-Rapu town (1939 pop. 1,942). Rapu-Rapu municipality (1948 municipality pop. 14,912) includes adjacent BATAN ISLAND.

Raqqa or **Raqqah** (räk'kŭ), Fr. *Rakka*, town (pop. c.7,500), Euphrates prov., N central Syria, on left bank of Euphrates R. and 100 mi. ESE of Aleppo. In vicinity (S) are oil deposits. The anc. Nicephorium, it was important in early Arab days and was home of Harun ar Rashid.

Raquette Lake (ră'kĭt), resort village, Hamilton co., NE central N.Y., in the Adirondacks, on Raquette L. (c.5 mi. long, ½–3 mi. wide; drained by Raquette R.), c.55 mi. NNE of Utica. Has seaplane port.

Raquette River, N N.Y., issues from Raquette L. in the Adirondacks c.55 mi. NNE of Utica, flows NE, entering and discharging from Long L., then N and NW, widening into irregular Raquette Pond near Tupper Lake village, thence NW, N, and NE, past Potsdam and Massena, to the St. Lawrence 3 mi. W of Hogansburg. Length, c.140 mi.

Raratonga: see RAROTONGA.

Rarden, village (pop. 251), Scioto co., S Ohio, 18 mi. NW of Portsmouth; sawmilling.

Raritan (ră'rĭtŭn), town (pop. 5,131), Somerset co., N central N.J., on Raritan R. (bridged here), just W of Somerville; mfg. (concrete blocks, clothing, wine, metal products); dairying. Inc. 1868.

Raritan Arsenal, N.J.: see METUCHEN.

Raritan Bay, NE N.J. and SE N.Y., W arm of Lower New York Bay, lying S of Staten Isl., N.Y., and W of Point Comfort, Monmouth co., N.J. Arthur Kill joins Newark Bay (N) to dredged deep-water channel in Raritan Bay. Receives from W navigable **Raritan River,** formed W of Raritan by North Branch (c.25 mi. long; rises W of Morristown and flows S) and South Branch (c.50 mi. long; rises in W Morris co. and flows SW, E, and N); flows c.35 mi. generally SE, past Somerville, Bound Brook, and New Brunswick (head of navigation), to Raritan Bay bet. Perth Amboy and South Amboy (here crossed by 2 bridges). Principal freight: coal, refined metals, brick, sand, clay products, manufactured goods. DELAWARE AND RARITAN CANAL (now unused) linked river with the Delaware.

Raroia (rärōē'ä), small atoll (pop. 141), Tuamotu Isls., Fr. Oceania, S Pacific, 16°3'S 142°23'W. Scandinavian ethnologists on Kon-Tiki raft expedition landed here 1947 from Peru. Sometimes called Raroia Reef.

Rarotonga (rärôtông'ä), volcanic isl. (16,500 acres; pop. 5,773), ⊙ COOK ISLANDS, S Pacific; 21°14'S 159°46'W. Largest, most southwesterly of Cook Isls.; c.6 mi. long, 4 mi. wide; rises to 2,110 ft. Discovered 1823 by John Williams, English missionary. Town of Avarua is port and seat of govt. There are 2 harbors; forested hills, coastal lowland; exports fruits, copra. Formerly spelled Raratonga.

Ras [Arabic,=cape], for names beginning thus and not found here: see under following main word.

Ras or **Raas** (both: räs), island (□ 18; 10 mi. long, 3 mi. wide), Indonesia, in Java Sea, at NE side of entrance to Madura Strait, 30 mi. ESE of Madura and just E of Sapudi; generally low. Agr. (corn, sago), fishing.

Rasa (rä'sä), town (pop. 1,088), NE Selangor, Malaya, on railroad and 25 mi. N of Kuala Lumpur, on Selangor R.; tin mining.

Rasa (rä'shä), Serbo-Croatian *Raša*, Ital. *Arsia* (ärs'yä), coal mine, NW Croatia, Yugoslavia, just SW of Labin, in Istria.

Rasafah, Syria: see RISAFE.

Rasa Island (rä'zŭ), islet in the Atlantic, off SE coast of Brazil, guarding entrance to Guanabara Bay, 10 mi. SSE of Rio de Janeiro; lighthouse. Also spelled Raza.

Ras al-'Ayn, Syria: see RAS EL 'AIN.

Ras al Khaima, Ras al Khaimah, or **Ras al-Khaymah** (räs' ăl khī'mŭ), northernmost sheikdom (□ 400; pop. 3,000) of TRUCIAL OMAN, extending 20 mi. along Trucial Coast of Persian Gulf from the isl. Jazirat al Hamra (S) to Sha'm village (N) and across the Oman Promontory to Dibba village on the Gulf of Oman. Largely low desert country along the coast, the dist. rises to the hills of the promontory. The chief town, Ras al Khaima, is on Persian Gulf, 50 mi. NE of Sharja; fishing, pearling; dagger mfg.; date groves. Sheikdom was long a dependency of Sharja; joined trucial league in 1919.

Ras al Mish'ab, Saudi Arabia: see RAS MISHA'AB.

Ras Benas, Egypt: see BENAS, RAS.

Rasberg (räs'bĕrk), village (pop. 2,158), in former Prussian Saxony prov., central Germany, after 1945 in Saxony-Anhalt, just S of Zeitz; mfg. of steel products.

Rasboeni, Rumania: see BALTATESTI.

Rascafría (räskäfrē'ä), town (pop. 907), Madrid prov., central Spain, in the Sierra de Guadarrama, on Lozoya R. and 14 mi. E of Segovia; sawmilling, charcoal burning, paper milling. Has noted Santa María del Paular charterhouse (founded 1390), with great art treasures.

Rascani, Moldavian SSR: see RYSHKANY.

Rasca Point (rä'skä), southernmost cape of Tenerife, Canary Isls., 40 mi. SW of Santa Cruz de Tenerife; 27°59'N 16°40'W.

Raschau (rä'shou), village (pop. 3,955), Saxony, E central Germany, in the Erzgebirge, 7 mi. ESE of Aue, in uranium-mining region; woodworking, enamelware mfg.

Raschkow, Poland: see RASZKOW.

Rascia, Yugoslavia: see NOVI PAZAR.

Ras Dashan (räs' däshän'), highest peak (15,157 ft.) in Ethiopia, in Simen Mts., 75 mi. NE of Gondar; 13°13'N 38°23'E.

Raseborg (rä'sŭbôr"yŭ), Finnish *Raasepori* (rä'-sĕpō"rē), village in Karis commune (pop. 2,967), Uusimaa co., SW Finland, near Pojo Bay of Gulf of Finland, 6 mi. ENE of Ekenas; cattle; dairying. Has remains of 14th-cent. castle.

Raseiniai, Raseinyai, or **Raseynyay** (räsā'nī), Rus. *Rossiyeny*, city (pop. 6,217), W central Lithuania, 45 mi. NW of Kaunas; tanning, shoe mfg., sawmilling, flour milling. Dates from 13th cent.; cultural center (17th–18th cent.) of Samogitia. In Rus. Kovno govt. until 1920.

Ras el 'Ain or **Ras al-'Ayn** (both: räs'ĕl-īn'), Fr. *Ras el Aïn*, town, Jezire prov., NE Syria, on Turkish line opposite CEYLANPINAR, on railroad, and 50 mi. WNW of El Haseke; rice growing. Sulphur deposits near by.

Ras el Barr, Egypt: see DAMIETTA.

Ras-el-Djebel (räs'-ĕl-jĕbĕl'), village, Bizerte dist., N Tunisia, near the Mediterranean, 14 mi. ESE of Bizerte, in fertile agr. region; olive-oil pressing, flour milling.

Ras-el-Hadid, Algeria: see FER, CAP DE.

Ras el Jebel, Oman: see RUUS AL JIBAL.

Ras el Khalig (räs' ĕl khälēg') or **Ra's al-Khalij** (ĕl-khälēj'), village (pop. 6,243), Gharbiya prov., Lower Egypt, on Damietta branch of the Nile, on railroad, and 8 mi. ENE of Shirbin; cotton.

Ras-el-Ma. 1 Village, Constantine dept., Algeria: see JEMMAPES. **2** Village, Oran dept., Algeria: see CRAMPEL.

Ras el Misha'ab, Saudi Arabia: see RAS MISHA'AB.

Ras en Naqura or **Ras en Nakura** (both: räs' ĕn näkōō'rä), Hebrew *Sullam Tsor*, anc. *Scala Tyriorum* (*Ladder of Tyre*), cape on the Mediterranean, on border bet. Israel and Lebanon, 20 mi. NNW of Haifa; 33°6'N 35°6'E.

Raseynyay, Lithuania: see RASEINIAI.

Ras Gharib (räs' gä'rĭb), town (dist. pop. 3,806), E Egypt, on W coast of Gulf of Suez, 115 mi. SSE of Suez; crude-oil production.

Rasgrad, Bulgaria: see RAZGRAD.

Rashad (räshăd'), town, Kordofan prov., central Anglo-Egyptian Sudan, in Nuba Mts., on road and 100 mi. SE of El Obeid; agr. trade center.

Rasheiya (räshā'yä) or **Rashiya** (räshē'yä), Fr. *Rachaya*, village (pop. 3,101), Bekaa prov., central Lebanon, near Syrian border, 31 mi. SE of Beirut, at foot of Mt. Hermon; alt. 4,400 ft.; sericulture, tobacco, cereals. Has old citadel.

Rashid, Egypt: see ROSETTA.

Rashin, Korea: see NAJIN.

Rashiya, Lebanon: see RASHEIYA.

Rashka, Yugoslavia: see RASKA: NOVI PAZAR.

Rashowa-kaikyo, Russian SFSR: see NADEZHDA STRAIT.

Rashowa-to, Russian SFSR: see RASSHUA ISLAND.

Rasht, Iran: see RESHT.

Rashu, Korea: see NAJU.

Rashult (rōs'hŭlt"), Swedish *Råshult*, hamlet, Kronoberg co., S Sweden, on E side of L. Mockel, 5 mi. NNE of Almhult. Linnaeus b. here.

Rasin, Korea: see NAJIN.

Rasinari (rŭshēnär'), Rum. *Răsinari*, Ger. *Städterdorf* (shtĕ'tŭrdôrf"), Hung. *Resinár* (rĕ'shēnär), village (pop. 5,479), Sibiu prov., central Rumania, in Transylvania, on N slopes of the Transylvanian Alps and 8 mi. SW of Sibiu; lumbering and excursion center; mfg. of rugs and cart bodies. Popular subalpine resort of Paltinis (pûltē'nēs), Rum. *Păltinis*, with several sanatoriums and noted ski facilities, is 15 mi. WSW.

Rasina River (rä'sĭnä), S central Serbia, Yugoslavia, rises 17 mi. SSE of Rankovicevo town, flows SE past Brus, and NNE past Krusevac, to Western Morava R. just below Krusevac; c.50 mi. long.

Rasipur (rä'sĭpŏŏr) or **Rasipuram** (–pŏŏrŭm), town (pop. 17,764), Salem dist., S central Madras prov., India, 13 mi. S of Salem; sugar cane, tobacco; cotton and silk weaving; mfg. of brass and bell-metal vessels.

Raska or **Rashka** (both: räsh'kä), Serbo-Croatian *Raška*, village, S Serbia, Yugoslavia, on Ibar R., on railroad and 12 mi. NNE of NOVI PAZAR (the medieval Raska).

Raska River or **Rashka River,** W Serbia, Yugoslavia, rises 10 mi. S of Novi Pazar, flows 25 mi. NNE, past Novi Pazar, to Ibar R. at Raska.

Ras Koh (räs' kō'), hill range (5,000 ft. average height), NW Baluchistan, W Pakistan; extends c.140 mi. NE-SW along border of Chagai dist. and Kharan state; c.20 mi. wide; rises to c.9,860 ft. in Ras Koh peak (center).

Ras Misha'ab, Ras el Misha'ab, or **Ras al Mish'ab** (both: räs' ĕl mĭsh-äb'), settlement in Hasa, Saudi Arabia, on Persian Gulf, at Kuwait–Saudi Arabia neutral zone border, 160 mi. NW of Dhahran; 28°9'N 48°38'E. Safaniya offshore oil field, 12 mi. SE, was discovered in 1950.

Ras Muari, W Pakistan: see MONZE, CAPE.

Rasnov (rŭshnôv'), Rum. *Râşnov*, Ger. *Rosenau* (rō'zŭnou"), Hung. *Barcarozsnyó* (bŏr'kŏrōzh-nyō), village (pop. 5,732), Stalin prov., central Rumania, in NE foothills of Transylvanian Alps, on railroad and 7 mi. SW of Stalin (Brasov); tourist center and climatic resort; mfg. (cloth, knitwear, furniture, toys, chalk, fruit and meat preserves), lumbering, limestone quarrying. Has 14th-cent. churches, remains of noted citadel of Rasnov, 1st built in 13th cent. by the Teutonic Knights. About 30% pop. are Germans.

Raso, Cabo (kä'bōō rä'zōō), headland on the Atlantic, W central Portugal, 19 mi. W of Lisbon, guarding N approaches to Tagus R. estuary; 38°42'N 9°29'W. It is topped by a fort.

Rasocolmo, Cape (räzōkôl'mô), northernmost point of Sicily, on NE coast, at E end of Gulf of Milazzo; 38°18'N 15°31'E.

Raso Island, Cape Verde Isls.: see RAZO ISLAND.

Rasovo (rä'sôvô), village (pop. 3,433), Vidin dist., NW Bulgaria, 8 mi. S of Lom; grain, legumes.

Rasovo (rä'sôvô), village (pop. 6,063), E Montenegro, Yugoslavia, on Lim R. and 2 mi. NE of Bijelo Polje.

Raspberry Island (18 mi. long, 3–8 mi. wide), S Alaska, E of Alaska Peninsula, bet. Afognak and Kodiak isls.; 58°3'N 153°10'W; rises to 1,860 ft. Fishing, fish processing.

Raspberry Strait (20 mi. long, 1–2 mi. wide), S Alaska, bet. Afognak Isl. and Raspberry Isl., connecting Gulf of Alaska and Shelikof Strait.

Raspopeny (rŭspŭpyĕ'nē), Rum. *Răspopeni* (rŭspô-pĕn'), village (1941 pop. 2,393), E central Moldavian SSR, 30 mi. E of Beltsy; flour milling.

Rasquera (räskā'rä), village (pop. 1,411), Tarragona prov., NE Spain, 9 mi. ESE of Gandesa; olive-oil and honey processing; trades in wine, almonds, cereals.

Rasra (rŭs'rŭ), town (pop. 9,865), Ballia dist., E Uttar Pradesh, India, 23 mi. WNW of Ballia; trades in rice, gram, barley, sugar cane, cotton cloth, carbonate of soda.

Rass [Arabic,=cape], for names beginning thus and not found here: see under following main word.

Rass (räs), **Ar Rass,** or **Al Rass** (both: är räs'), town and oasis, Qasim prov. of Nejd, Saudi Arabia, in the Wadi Rima, 35 mi. SW of Anaiza; 25°52'N 43°29'E. Trading center; dates, grain, fruit; stock raising.

Rasses, Les (lā räs'), resort, 1 mi. E of Ste-Croix, Vaud canton, W Switzerland; sports, fine views; alt. 3,870 ft.

Ras Shamra (räs shăm'ră), locality, W Syria, just N of Latakia, near the coast; site of anc. city of UGARIT, excavated after 1930.

Rasshua Island (rŭshōō'ŭ), Jap. *Rashowa-to* (räshō'ä-tō') (□ 25), one of central main Kurile Isls. group, Russian SFSR, separated from Matua Isl. (N) by Nadezhda Strait, from Ushishir Isls. (S) by Sredni Strait; 47°44'N 153°E; 9 mi. long, 4 mi. wide; rises to 3,136 ft.

Ras Siyagha, Jordan: see NEBA, JEBEL.

Rasskazovo (rŭskä'zŭvŭ), city (1926 pop. 25,168), central Tambov oblast, Russian SFSR, 18 mi. ESE of Tambov, on rail spur from Platonovka; woolen-milling center; mfg. of coarse cloths, sheepskin clothing; tannery, distillery. Became city in 1926.

Rastadt, Germany: see RASTATT.

Rastan, Er, El Rastan, or **Al-Rastan** (all: ĕr-rästăn'), Fr. *Rastane*, anc. *Arethusa*, town, Homs prov., W Syria, on railroad, on the Orontes, and 13 mi. N of Homs; cotton, cereals. Site of Roman ruins.

Ras Tanura or **Ras Tanurah** (räs' tănōō'rŭ), town (pop. 6,000) in Hasa, E Saudi Arabia, on Ras Tanura sandspit (12 mi. long), 25 mi. N of Dhahran; major Persian Gulf oil-shipping port, with refinery (built 1943–45), linked with Dhahran, Abqaiq, and Qatif fields. Refinery is connected by pipe lines with marine loading terminal and storage tanks, 6 mi. SE near tip of peninsula.

Rastatt (răsh'tät, räs'tät), town (pop. 13,526), S Baden, Germany, on the Murg at mouth of Oos R., and 14 mi. SW of Karlsruhe; rail junction with bridge across the Rhine (4 mi. W). Railroad workshops; mfg. of railroad cars, machinery, stoves, optical and precision instruments, furniture, textiles. Also paper milling, printing, brewing. Has baroque castle and churches. Of anc. origin, it was destroyed by French (1689) and subsequently rebuilt. In 18th cent., residence of margraves of Baden-Baden. Noted for treaty bet. France and Austria (1714) and series of unsuccessful negotiations bet. France and Germany (1797–99). Fortifications (built 1840) were razed 1892. Second World War damage about 30%. Since Fr. occupation, after 1945, seat of supreme Fr. military tribunal. Sometimes spelled Rastadt.

Rastede (rä'stůdů), village (commune pop. 13,472), in Oldenburg, NW Germany, after 1945 in Lower Saxony, 7 mi. N of Oldenburg city; food processing (fruit juice). Large Benedictine abbey (founded 1121) was converted into castle in 1529.

Rastenberg (rä'stůnběrk), town (pop. 2,954), Thuringia, central Germany, 14 mi. NNE of Weimar; spa.

Rastenburg, Poland: see Ketrzyn.

Rastrick, England: see Brighouse.

Rastrojos (rästrō'hōs), town (pop. 713), Lara state, NW Venezuela, on Acarigua–Barquisimeto highway and 4 mi. SE of Barquisimeto; sugar cane, corn, fruit, stock.

Rastyapino, Russian SFSR: see Dzerzhinsk, Gorki oblast.

Rasu, Monte (môn'tě rä'zōō), highest point (4,130 ft.) in Catena del Goceano, N central Sardinia, 33 mi SE of Sassari.

Rasueros (räswā'rōs), town (pop. 871), Ávila prov., central Spain, 31 mi. E of Salamanca; grain, chickpeas, grapes; limekilns.

Rasul (rŭsōōl'), village, Gujrat dist., NE Punjab, W Pakistan, on Jhelum R. and 31 mi. WNW of Gujrat; small agr. market. Headworks of Lower Jhelum Canal here; site of proposed hydroelectric plant. Engineering school 1 mi. S.

Raszkow (räsh'kōōf), Pol. *Raszków*, Ger. *Raschkow* (räsh'kō), town (1946 pop. 1,375), Poznan prov., W Poland, 6 mi. NNW of Ostrow; orchards.

Raszyn (rä'shĭn), suburb of Warsaw, Warszawa prov., E central Poland, 6 mi. SW of city center; site of major radio transmitter.

Ratabari (rä'täbŭrē), village, Calchar dist., S Assam, India, on tributary of the Kusiyara and 28 mi. SW of Silchar; rice, tea, mustard. Until 1947, in Sylhet dist.

Ratae or **Ratae Coritanorum**, England: see Leicester.

Rataje nad Sazavou (rä'täyě nät' säzävō), Czech *Rataje nad Sazavou*, village (pop. 698), W central Bohemia, Czechoslovakia, on Sazava R. and 16 mi. WSW of Kutna Hora; popular recreation center. Medieval castle.

Ratak Chain (rä'tăk, rä'täk), E group, Marshall Isls., W central Pacific; comprises 14 atolls (Taongi, Bikar, Utirik, Taka, Ailuk, Likiep, Wotje, Erikub, Maloelap, Aur, Majuro, Arno, Mili, Knox Atoll) and 2 coral isls. (Mejit, Jemo); Majuro is ⊙ Majuro dist., which includes part of Ratak Chain. Sometimes called Sunrise Group or Radak Chain.

Ratangarh (rŭtŭn'gŭr), town (pop. 20,961), N Rajasthan, India, 80 mi. E of Bikaner; rail junction; trade center (grain, wool, cattle); hand-loom woolen weaving, pottery making; leather and ivory products.

Ratanpur, India: see Bilaspur, town, Bilaspur dist., Madhya Pradesh.

Ratburi or **Ratchburi** (răt'bŏŏrē'), town (1947 pop. 9,173), ⊙ Ratburi prov. (□ 1,984; 1947 pop. 295,534), S Thailand, on Mae Klong R. and railroad, 50 mi. WSW of Bangkok, in major rice-growing area; coconuts, tobacco, sesame, beans, palm sugar. Tin, lead, antimony and zinc deposits; limestone quarries. Also spelled Rajburi and Rajaburi.

Ratby, town and parish (pop. 2,181), central Leicester, England, 5 mi. W of Leicester; hosiery, shoes. Has 14th-cent. church.

Ratchakhram (răt'chŭkräm'), village (1937 pop. 706), Ayutthaya prov., S Thailand, on Chao Phraya R. at mouth of Lopburi R., 30 mi. N of Bangkok; rice milling.

Ratchburi, Thailand: see Ratburi.

Ratcliff (răt'klĭf), town (pop. 213), Logan co., W Ark., 30 mi. ESE of Fort Smith, near Arkansas R.

Ratece Planica (rä'těchě plä'nētsä), Slovenian *Ratece Planica*, Ger. *Ratschach* (rä'tshäkh), village, NW Slovenia, Yugoslavia, on railroad and 50 mi. NW of Ljubljana, bet. Julian Alps and the Karawanken; winter sport (ski) center.

Ratekau (rä'tükou), village (pop. 9,525), in Schleswig-Holstein, NW Germany, 6 mi. N of Lübeck city center; mfg. of machinery; flour milling. Near by Blücher capitulated to the French (1806). Until 1937 in Oldenburg.

Rath (rät), suburb of Düsseldorf, W Germany, 3.5 mi. NE of city center; mfg. of metal pipes.

Rath (rät), town (pop. 12,785), Hamirpur dist., S Uttar Pradesh, India, 29 mi. NW of Mahoba; saltpeter processing, cotton weaving; trades in gram, jowar, oilseeds, wheat, pearl millet. Has 14th-cent. Moslem tomb, ruins of 18th-cent. Bundela Rajput fort.

Rathangan (ră-thăng'gŭn), Gaelic *Ráth Iomdháin*, town (pop. 456), W Co. Kildare, Ireland, on the Grand Canal and 5 mi. NW of Kildare; agr. market (cattle, horses; potatoes).

Rathbun, town (pop. 229), Appanoose co., S Iowa, 5 mi. N of Centerville, in coal-mining area.

Rathconrath (răthkŏn'rŭth), Gaelic *Ráth Chonnrach*, agr. village (district pop. 317), W Co. Westmeath, Ireland, 9 mi. W of Mullingar; cattle, potatoes.

Rathcormac or **Rathcormack** (răthkôr'mŭk), Gaelic *Ráth Chormaic*, town (pop. 149), E Co. Cork, Ireland, 5 mi. SSW of Fermoy; agr. market (dairying, cattle raising; potatoes, oats, beets).

Rathdowney (răthdou'nē), Gaelic *Ráth Domhnaigh*, town (pop. 786), SW Co. Laoighis, Ireland, 12 mi. ESE of Roscrea; agr. market (wheat, barley, potatoes, beets); breweries.

Rathdrum (răthdrŭm'), Gaelic *Ráth Droma*, town (pop. 1,174), E central Co. Wicklow, Ireland, on Avonmore R. and 9 mi. WSW of Wicklow; agr. market (dairying; cattle, sheep; potatoes); lead mining.

Rathdrum (răth'–), village (pop. 610), Kootenai co., N Idaho, 12 mi. NW of Coeur d'Alene; trading point for irrigated agr. area (wheat, oats, alfalfa). Lead, silver, gold mines near by.

Rathedaung (rä'dhŭdoun), village, Akyab dist., Lower Burma, in the Arakan, on Mayu R. and 25 mi. NNW of Akyab.

Rathen (rä'thŭn), agr. village and parish (pop. 2,399), NE Aberdeen, Scotland, near North Sea, 4 mi. S of Fraserburgh.

Rathenow (rä'tŭnō), city (pop. 27,566), Brandenburg, E Germany, on the Havel and 45 mi. W of Berlin; 52°36'N 12°20'E. Center for important optical- and precision-instruments plants; mfg. of machinery, agr. implements, chemicals, food products; shipbuilding, metalworking. Rail junction. Has church built c.1200, rebuilt in 14th and 16th cent. First mentioned 1216. Chartered 1284. Sacked in Thirty Years War. Scene (June, 1675) of defeat of Swedes by forces of Elector Frederick William. Bombed in Second World War (destruction c.30%).

Rathfarnham (răthfär'nŭm), Gaelic *Ráth Fearnáin*, S suburb (pop. 8,050) of Dublin, Co. Dublin, Ireland.

Rathfriland or **Rathfryland** (răthfrī'lŭnd), town (pop. 1,830), S central Co. Down, Northern Ireland, 8 mi. NE of Newry; iron mining; agr. market (flax, oats).

Rathgar, Ireland: see Rathmines and Rathgar.

Rathkeale (răth-kēl'), Gaelic *Ráth Caola*, town (pop. 1,526), W central Co. Limerick, Ireland, on Deel R. and 16 mi. SW of Limerick; agr. market (grain, potatoes; dairying). Has anc. castle of the Desmonds, later restored, and remains of 13th-cent. Austin abbey.

Rathlin (răth'lĭn), island (3,564 acres; 5 mi. long, up to 3 mi. wide, rising to 449 ft.; pop. 245) off N coast of Co. Antrim, Northern Ireland, 3 mi. NW of Benmore or Fair Head. Main products are grain, fish, kelp; there is a radio station. At NE extremity, Altcarry Head, is lighthouse (55°18'N 6°11'W); W extremity of isl. is Bull Point (55°17'N 6°17'W). In 6th cent. St. Columba founded church here, later destroyed by Danes. There are ruins of castle in which Robert the Bruce reputedly took refuge in 1306 and where incident of spider and web is said to have taken place. Isl. is sometimes called Raghery.

Rathlin O'Birne (răth"lĭn ōbûrn'), islet off SW coast of Co. Donegal, Ireland, at N side of entrance to Donegal Bay; lighthouse (54°40'N 8°50'W).

Ráth Luirc (rô' lōō'ĭrk), town (pop. 1,545), N Co. Cork, Ireland, 15 mi. N of Mallow; rail junction; agr. market (dairying; potatoes, oats). Founded (c.1660) by Roger Boyle and originally named Charleville in honor of Charles II. Boyle mansion was burned 1690 by duke of Berwick.

Rathmelton, Ireland: see Ramelton.

Rathmines and Rathgar (răthmīnz', răthgär'), Gaelic *Ráth Maonais* and *Ráth Garbh*, former urban district, a S suburb (pop. c.45,000) of Dublin, Co. Dublin, Ireland. Rathmines was scene (1649) of Ormonde's defeat by Cromwell.

Rathmore (răthmôr'), Gaelic *Ráth Mhór*, town (pop. 242), E Co. Kerry, Ireland, 12 mi. E of Killarney; agr. market (potatoes, grain; cattle); soap mfg.

Rathmullen or **Rathmullan** (răthmŭ'lŭn), Gaelic *Ráth Maoláin*, town (pop. 396), NE Co. Donegal, Ireland, on W shore of Lough Swilly, 11 mi. NW of Londonderry; 55°5'N 7°31'W; seaport; agr. market (cattle, sheep; flax, oats, potatoes). Has remains of 15th-cent. Carmelite monastery.

Rathnew (răthnū'), Gaelic *Ráth Naoi*, town (pop. 362), E Co. Wicklow, Ireland, near the Irish Sea, 2 mi. WNW of Wicklow; agr. market (dairying; cattle, sheep; potatoes).

Ratho (rä'thō), agr. village and parish (pop. 1,672), NW Midlothian, Scotland, 7 mi. W of Edinburgh. Has noted golf course.

Rathsmannsdorf (räts'mänsdôrf"), village (pop. 1,399), Lower Bavaria, Germany, in Bohemian Forest, 11 mi. WNW of Passau; lignite mining.

Rathven (răth'vŭn), agr. village and parish, NW Banffshire, Scotland, near Moray Firth, 2 mi. E of Buckie.

Rathwell (răth'wŭl), village (pop. estimate 250), S Man., at N end of Pembina Mts., 25 mi. SW of Portage la Prairie; grain, stock.

Ratibor (rä'tĭbôr, Ger. rä'tēbôr) or **Raciborz** (rä-chē'bōōsh), Pol. *Racibórz*, town (1939 pop. 50,004; 1946 pop. 19,605) in Upper Silesia, after 1945 in Opole prov., S Poland, port on the Oder and 40 mi. SSE of Oppeln (Opole). Rail junction; magnetite mining; mfg. of machinery, machine tools, electrodes, electrical goods, fertilizer, soap; food processing (flour products, yeasts, chocolate), linen milling, sugar refining, metalworking, tobacco processing. Chartered 1217; was (1288-1532), ⊙ free imperial principality. Passed 1745 to Prussia; was (1822–1918), ⊙ principality, after 1840 duchy, of Ratibor. Heavily damaged (c.85% destroyed) in Second World War.

Ratingen (rä'tĭng-ŭn), town (pop. 21,683), in former Prussian Rhine Prov., W Germany, after 1945 in North Rhine-Westphalia, 6 mi. NNW of Düsseldorf; mfg. of machinery. Has remains of old walls and towers.

Ratisbon, Germany: see Regensburg.

Ratische Alpen, Switzerland: see Rhaetian Alps.

Ratiskovice (rä'tyěshkôvĭtsě), Czech *Ratíškovice*, village (pop. 2,605), SE Moravia, Czechoslovakia, 5 mi. N of Hodonin; lignite mines, oil wells.

Rat Islands, group of the Aleutians, SW Alaska, SE of Near Isls. and W of Andreanof Isls.; extend c.110 mi. E–W near 51°40'N 177°12'–179°40' E. Largest isls. are Semisopochnoi Island, Amchitka Island, and Kiska Island (scene of action in Second World War). Generally mountainous.

Ratlam (rŭtläm'), town (pop. 44,939), ⊙ Ratlam dist., W Madhya Bharat, India, 65 mi. NW of Indore, on W Malwa plateau; rail junction; trade center (cotton, millet, wheat, cloth fabrics, opium); cotton, silk, and sugar milling, snuff mfg., hand-loom weaving. Was ⊙ former princely state of Ratlam (□ 687; pop. 126,117) of Central India agency; since 1948, state merged with Madhya Bharat. Sometimes spelled Rutlam.

Ratmalana, Ceylon: see Colombo.

Ratmanov Island (rŭtmä'nŭf), largest of Diomede Isls., in Bering Strait, in Chukchi Natl. Okrug, Kamchatka oblast, Khabarovsk Territory, Russian SFSR; 4.5 mi. W of Little Diomede Isl. (Alaska); 3.5 mi. long, 1 mi. wide. Also known as Big Diomede and Imaklit.

Ratnagiri (rŭtnä'gĭrē), district, W Bombay, India; ⊙ Ratnagiri. Bounded W by Arabian Sea, E by Western Ghats, S by Goa; drained by several mtn. streams. Comprises S Konkan, with rocky coast, fertile seaboard (rice, coconuts, mangoes, cashew nuts), and rugged, hilly interior. Rice husking, hand-loom weaving, fishing (mackerel, sardines, catfish, pomfrets), embroidering. Teak and blackwood in S forests. Chromite deposits (S). Small ports of Ratnagiri, Malvan, Vengurla, and Vijayadurg trade in fish, rice, timber, and mangoes; fish curing. Large saltworks near Vengurla. In 16th cent., Portuguese set up trade posts along coast. Small inlets were Mahratta pirate retreats in 18th cent. Original dist. (□ 4,069; 1941 pop. 1,373,466) enlarged by inc. (1949) of former Deccan states of Savantvadi and (part of) Kolhapur. Pop. 93% Hindu, 6% Moslem.

Ratnagiri, town (pop. 17,904), ⊙ Ratnagiri dist., W Bombay, India, port on Arabian Sea, 140 mi. SSE of Bombay, in the Konkan; fish-curing center (sardines, pomfrets, sharks, seerfish); exports firewood, fish, bamboo, rice; tanning, shark-oil extracting. School of Industry. Lighthouse (W). Here Thebaw, last king of Burma, was interned (1886).

Ratnapura (rŭt'nŭpŏŏrŭ) [Singhalese,=city of gems], town (pop. 12,367), ⊙ Sabaragamuwa Prov. and Ratnapura dist. (□ 1,259; pop., including estate pop., 343,552), SW central Ceylon, on the Kalu Ganga and 40 mi. SE of Colombo; major precious and semiprecious stone-mining (including sapphire, ruby, chrysoberyl) center of Ceylon; rubber, tea, rice, areca and coconut palms, vegetables; graphite mining. Meteorological observatory. Noted Buddhist temple near by.

Ratno (rät'nŭ), town (1931 pop. 3,050), N Volyn oblast, Ukrainian SSR, on Pripet R. and 33 mi. NNW of Kovel; tanning, flour milling, brick mfg.

Rato, Formosa: see Lotung.

Ratodero (rŭtōdā'rō), town (pop. 9,925), Larkana dist., NW Sind, W Pakistan, 18 mi. NNE of Larkana; agr. market (rice, millet, wheat, gram); handicraft cloth mfg., palm-mat weaving, rice milling. Also written Rato Dero.

Raton (ră"tōōn', ră'tōōn"), city (pop. 8,241), ⊙ Colfax co., NE N. Mex., near Colo. line, in Raton Mts., 19 mi. S of Trinidad, Colo.; alt. 6,400 ft. Trade center and resort in livestock and mining, (coal, molybdenum) region; flour, cattle feed, wood products. State hosp., home for miners here. Raton Pass is just N; Capulin Natl. Monument 27 mi. ESE. Settled in 1870's on Santa Fe Trail, laid out 1880, inc. 1891.

Raton Mountains, E spur of Sangre de Cristo Mountains in Las Animas co., S Colo., and Colfax co., NE N.Mex. Includes Raton Mesa, just SE of Trinidad, Colo., rising to 9,586 ft. in Fishers Peak. Raton Pass (7,834 ft.), just N of N.Mex. line, carries road and railroad. Coal is mined near Trinidad, Colo., and Raton, N.Mex.

Ratonneau (rätônō'), small island off coast of S France, 3 mi. WSW of harbor of Marseilles, Bouches-du-Rhône dept.; 1.5 mi. long, connected by jetty with Pomègues isl. (.5 mi. S; 1.5 mi. long). Quarantine station. Just W is IF islet.

Raton Pass (7,834 ft.), in Raton Mts., S Colo., just N of N.Mex. line, 12 mi. S of Trinidad. Used by explorers and travelers in 18th and 19th cent.; now crossed by highway and railroad.

Rat Rapids, village, NW Ont., in Patricia dist., at E end of L. St. Joseph, 100 mi. NE of Sioux Lookout; hydroelectric station, supplying Pickle Lake mining region; seaplane landing.

Ratschach, Yugoslavia: see RADECE; RATECE PLANICA.

Ratsyonzh, Poland: see RACIAZ.

Rattelsdorf (rä'tůlsdôrf), village (pop. 1,064), Upper Franconia, N Bavaria, Germany, on Itz R. and 9 mi. N of Bamberg; barley, rye, cattle, hogs.

Rattenberg (rä'tůnběrk), village (pop. 930), Tyrol, W Austria, on the Inn and 25 mi. ENE of Innsbruck. Has old fortress. Mineral springs near by.

Rattlesnake Creek. 1 In S central Kansas, formed by confluence of several headstreams in Kiowa co. NE of Greensburg, flows 122 mi. NE to Arkansas R. 8 mi. W of Sterling. **2** In Ohio: see PAINT CREEK.

Rattlesnake Mountain (1,035 ft.), Cumberland co., SW Maine, in resort area N of Sebago L.

Rattray, Scotland: see BLAIRGOWRIE AND RATTRAY.

Rattray Head (rǎ'trā), promontory on the North Sea, NE Aberdeen, Scotland, 8 mi. NNW of Peterhead; lighthouse (57°37'N 1°49'W).

Rattvik (rět'vēk"), Swedish *Rättvik,* village (pop. 882), Kopparberg co., central Sweden, on E shore of L. Silja, 25 mi. NW of Falun; rail junction; sawmills, chocolate works. Has old church, and mus. It has preserved old customs and traditions, and its quaintness has made it a popular resort. Here Gustavus Vasa (later Gustavus I) made his appeal for support in war for liberation from Danish rule in 1521.

Ratz, Mount (răts) (10,290 ft.), NW B.C., near Alaska border, in Coast Mts., 65 mi. N of Wrangell.

Ratzebuhr, Poland: see OKONEK.

Ratzeburg (rä'tsůbōōrk), town (pop. 12,123), Schleswig-Holstein, NW Germany, 11 mi. SSE of Lübeck, on isl. in and on SE shore of Ratzeburg L.; rail junction; mfg. of machinery, tools, precision instruments, chemicals, shoes, wood and paper products; food processing. Has Romanesque former cathedral. Bishopric established (1154) by Henry the Lion. Residence of Lauenburg dukes from 13th cent. until 1689, when duchy of Lauenburg passed 1st to Hanover, then to Denmark (1815), which ceded it (1864) to Prussia. Inc. 1876 into SCHLESWIG-HOLSTEIN. Territory of bishopric (secularized 1504) went to Mecklenburg in 17th cent.; was for long time possession of Mecklenburg-Strelitz line.

Ratzeburg Lake, Ger. *Ratzeburger See* (rä'tsůbōōr"gůr zā"), lake (□ 6), Schleswig-Holstein, NW Germany, 6 mi. SSE of Lübeck; 7 mi. long, 1 mi. wide; greatest depth 79 ft., average depth 39 ft. Town of Ratzeburg on isl. and on SE shore of lake.

Rau, India: see RAO.

Rau or **Raoe** (both: rou), volcanic island (9 mi. long, 4 mi. wide) of the N Moluccas, Indonesia, just W of Morotai; 2°21'N 128°9'E. Generally hilly, rising to 1,548 ft.; edible birds' nests.

Raub (roub), town (pop. 3,616), W Pahang, Malaya, on road and 45 mi. NNE of Kuala Lumpur; gold-mining center.

Raubling, Germany: see KIRCHDORF.

Rauch (rouch), town (pop. 5,233), ⊙ Rauch dist. (□ 1,667; pop. 14,459), central Buenos Aires prov., Argentina, 40 mi. E of Azul; agr. center (corn, oats, sheep, cattle).

Raucheck (roukh'ěk), highest peak (7,965 ft.) of the TENNENGEBIRGE, in Salzburg, W Austria, NE of Bischofshofen.

Rauco (rou'kō), village (1930 pop. 320), Curicó prov., central Chile, on railroad, on Mataquito R. and 11 mi. W of Curicó; agr. center (grain, chickpeas, beans, wine, livestock).

Raucourt (rōkōōr'), village (pop. 928), Ardennes dept., N France, 7 mi. S of Sedan; metal buckle mfg., brewing.

Raucoux, Belgium: see ROCOUR.

Raudha, Raudah, or **Rawdah** (all: rou'dhů), town and oasis (pop. 2,600), Wahidi sultanate of Balhaf, Eastern Aden Protectorate, 10 mi. NW of Azzan and on the Wadi Meifa'a. Also spelled Rodha.

Raudha, Ar Raudha, or **Al-Rawdah** (both: är rou'dhů), town (pop. 4,000), Sana prov., central Yemen, 3 mi. N of Sana; residential resort in winegrowing area.

Raudian Fields (rô'dyůn), anc. *Campi Raudii,* historic plain in N Italy, probably near Vercelli, where Marius and Catulus defeated the Cimbri in 101 B.C.

Raudnitz an der Elbe, Czechoslovakia: see ROUDNICE NAD LABEM.

Rauenthal (rou'ůntäl), village (pop. 1,274), in former Prussian prov. of Hesse-Nassau, W Germany, after 1945 in Hesse, in the Rheingau, 6 mi. W of Wiesbaden; noted for its wine. Has 15th-cent. church.

Raufarshofn (rů'üvärshü"půn), Icelandic *Raufarshöfn,* village (pop. 342), Thingeyjar co., NE Iceland, on NE side of Melrakkasletta peninsula, at mouth of Thistil Fjord; 66°27'N 15°58'W; fishing.

Rauland (rou'län), village and canton (pop. 1,402), Telemark co., S Norway, on Totak lake, 70 mi. NW of Skien; cattle raising, fishing.

Raulíes Pass (roulē'ěs) (4,400–4,500 ft.), in the Andes, on Argentina-Chile border, at N foot of Monte Tronador, at W end of L. Nahuel Huapí; 41°3'S 71°50'W.

Raul Soares (roul' sōōä'rĭs), city (pop. 4,108), E Minas Gerais, Brazil, on railroad and 35 mi. NE of Ponte Nova; ships coffee, timber. Mica deposits.

Rauma (rou'mä), Swedish *Raumo* (rou'mōō), city (pop. 14,684), Turku-Pori co., SW Finland, on Gulf of Bothnia, 50 mi. NW of Turku; port, shipping timber and cellulose; rail terminus. Shipyards, lumber, pulp, and cellulose mills, tanneries, machine shops; shoe mfg. Noted for its lace since Middle Ages. Old part of city has narrow winding streets, 15th-cent. Franciscan church, and mus. First mentioned 1442. In Crimean War shelled (1855) by British fleet. In late-19th cent. Rauma had Finland's largest fleet of timber-carrying sailing vessels.

Rauma River (rou'mä), W Norway, flows from Lesjaskog L. in the Dovrefjell, Opland co., c.35 mi. NW through the ROMSDAL to Romsdal Fjord bet. Andalsnes and Veblungsnes; rich in salmon; lumber rafts.

Raumo, Finland: see RAUMA.

Raunds (räns), urban district (1931 pop. 3,683; 1951 census 4,616), E Northampton, England, 9 mi. ESE of Kettering; shoe-mfg. center. Has 13th-cent. church.

Raunheim (roun'hīm), village (pop. 3,602), S Hesse, W Germany, in former Starkenburg prov., on left bank of the canalized Main and 12 mi. SW of Frankfurt; leatherworking, tanning.

Raurimu (rourē'mōō), township (pop. 328), ⊙ Kaitieke co. (□ 550; pop. 3,235), W central N.Isl., New Zealand, 65 mi. E of New Plymouth; agr. center; sawmills.

Rauris (rou'rĭs), village (pop. 2,272), Salzburg, W central Austria, on N slope of the Hohe Tauern and 16 mi. SW of Bischofshofen; summer resort. Gold deposits in valley.

Rausand (rou'sän), village in Nesset canton (pop. 2,131), More og Romsdal co., W Norway, port on W shore of Sunndals Fjord, 22 mi. SSE of Kristiansund; iron mine. Formerly called Rodsand, Nor. *Rødsand.*

Rauschen, Russian SFSR: see SVETLOGORSK.

Rauschenberg (rou'shůnběrk), town (pop. 1,800), in former Prussian prov. of Hesse-Nassau, W Germany, after 1945 in Hesse, 8 mi. NE of Marburg; lumber. Has ruins of anc. castle.

Raut, river, Moldavian SSR: see REUT RIVER.

Rautenberg, Russian SFSR: see UZLOVOYE.

Raut River, Moldavian SSR: see REUT RIVER.

Rautu, Russian SFSR: see SOSNOVO.

Rauxel, Germany: see CASTROP-RAUXEL.

Rauza, India: see KHULDABAD.

Rava, Poland: see RAWA MAZOWIECKA.

Ravalgaon, India: see MALEGAON.

Ravalli (rův ǎ'lē), county (□ 2,384; pop. 13,101), W Mont.; ⊙ Hamilton. Agr. region including fertile valley of Bitterroot R.; borders on Idaho. Livestock, sugar beets, grain, fruit. Bitterroot Range in W, part of Bitterroot Natl. Forest, extends N–S. Formed 1893.

Ravanak (růvůnäk'), village (1939 pop. over 500), SE Samarkand oblast, Uzbek SSR, c.7 mi. SE of Samarkand; cotton, fruit.

Ravanica or **Ravanitsa,** monastery, Yugoslavia: see SENJE.

Ravanna (růvě'nů, růvǎ'nů), town (pop. 132), Mercer co., N Mo., near Weldon R., 7 mi. ENE of Princeton.

Ravansar, Iran: see RAWANSAR.

Ravanusa (ravänōō'zä), town (pop. 14,555), Agrigento prov., S Sicily, near Salso R., 12 mi. NNE of Licata; wine, olive oil. Sulphur mines (NE).

Ravar (rävär'), town (1945 pop. 3,000), Eighth Prov., in Kerman, SE Iran, 70 mi. N of Kerman, in Kuh Banan Mts.; fruit, cotton, millet, dairy products: fruit drying, rugmaking.

Ravarino (rävärē'nō), village (pop. 227), Modena prov., Emilia-Romagna, N central Italy, 10 mi. NE of Modena; wine making.

Rava-Russkaya (rä"vů-rōō'skīyů), Pol. *Rawa Ruska* (rä'vä rōō'skä), city (1931 pop. 11,146), NW Lvov oblast, Ukrainian SSR, on left tributary of Bug R. and 30 mi. NNW of Lvov; rail terminus on Pol. border; cement mfg., sawmilling, stone quarrying, agr. processing (fruit, vegetables, cereals). Lignite deposits. Has ruins of old castle. Under Austrian rule (1772–1918); reverted to Poland (1919); ceded to USSR in 1945.

Ravat, Tadzhik SSR: see TAKFAN.

Ravello (rävěl'lō), village (pop. 703), Salerno prov., Campania, S Italy, 1 mi. N of Amalfi. Resort (alt. 1,033 ft.) overlooking Gulf of Salerno. Has Romanesque cathedral (built 1086) and Palazzo dei Ruffoli (begun 11th cent.), one of most anc. palaces in Italy.

Ravelo (räyä'lō). **1** Town (pop. c.4,200), Potosí dept., W central Bolivia, 33 mi. ESE of Colquechaca, on Sucre-Oruro road; sheep, alpaca. Until 1900s, Moromoro. **2** Military post (Fortín Ravelo), Santa Cruz dept., E Bolivia, in the Chaco, 100 mi. S of San José.

Ravels (rä'vůls), town (pop. 3,232), Antwerp prov., N Belgium, 4 mi. NE of Turnhout; Portland cement.

Ravena (růvē'nů), village (pop. 2,006), Albany co., E N.Y., near the Hudson, 12 mi. S of Albany; mfg. (metal products, cider and vinegar, concrete blocks); stone quarrying. Inc. 1914.

Ravenden (rǎ'vůndůn), town (pop. 245), Lawrence co., NE Ark., 15 mi. W of Pocahontas, in agr area.

Ravenden Springs, town (pop. 197), Randolph co., NE Ark., 14 mi. WNW of Pocahontas, in agr. area.

Ravenel (rǎvůněl'), town (pop. 337), Charleston co., S S.C., 17 mi. W of Charleston; rail junction. Formerly Ravenels.

Ravenglass, village in parish of Muncaster (pop. 480), SW Cumberland, England, on Esk R. estuary and 16 mi. SSE of Whitehaven; cattle raising, dairying, granite quarrying. A port since Roman days, it was important in the Middle Ages.

Ravenhead, England: see SAINT HELENS.

Ravenna (růvě'nů, It. rävěn'nä), province (□ 718; pop. 279,127), Emilia-Romagna, N central Italy; ⊙ Ravenna. Borders on the Adriatic; plain covers ⅔ of area, with Etruscan Apennines SW. Watered by Reno, Santerno, Senio, and Lamone rivers. Predominantly agr. (sugar beets, hemp, cereals, fruit). Saltworks at Cervia. Mfg. at Faenza, Lugo.

Ravenna, city (pop. 31,251), ⊙ Ravenna prov., Emilia-Romagna, N central Italy, 43 mi. ESE of Bologna, on plain near the Fiume Uniti (formed by confluence of Montone and Ronco rivers); 44°25'N 12°12'E. Formerly on the Adriatic; now connected with its seaport, Porto Corsini, by 6-mi.-long canal. Rail junction; agr. center; mfg. (wine, macaroni, fertilizer, cement, furniture, metal products, rubber articles). Archbishopric. Famous for its 5th- and 6th-cent. mosaics and for many Roman and Byzantine bldgs. Ornamented with mosaics are the mausoleum of Galla Placidia (5th cent.), octagonal baptistery (once a Roman bath), 6th-cent. churches of Sant'Apollinare Nuovo and Sant'Apollinare in Classe, and especially the Byzantine church of San Vitale. Has tombs of Theodoric and Dante. In Roman times its port, Classis, was station for Roman fleet in the N Adriatic. Made capital (402) of Western empire by Honorius; seat of exarchs (governors of Byzantine Italy) from 6th cent. until it fell to the Lombards in 751. Later ruled by the pope, Da Polenta family (13th–15th cent.), and Venice. Added to Papal States in 1509, passing to Italy in 1860. French defeated (1512) Spanish and papal forces here. Badly damaged by air bombing (1944) in Second World War.

Ravenna. 1 (růvě'nů) Town (pop. 979), Estill co., E central Ky., in Cumberland Natl. Forest, on Kentucky R. and 40 mi. SE of Lexington; lumber milling. Agr., oil wells, timber in region. Inc. 1921. **2** (růvě'nů) Village (pop. 551), Muskegon co., SW Mich., 20 mi. NW of Grand Rapids, in dairying and agr. area; gas wells. **3** (růvě'nů) City (pop. 1,451), Buffalo co., S central Nebr., at junction of Mud Creek and S.Loup R., 30 mi. WNW of Grand Island; flour, feed, dairy produce, grain. Inc. 1886. **4** (rĭvǎ'nů, růvě'nů) City (pop. 9,857), ⊙ Portage co., NE Ohio, 15 mi. ENE of Akron, within Akron metropolitan dist.; rubber goods, yarn, textiles, foundry products, road and hoisting machinery, hardware, furniture, toys, lumber. U.S. arsenal (Ravenna Arsenal) at near-by Apco. Settled 1799, laid out 1808. **5** (rǎvě'nů) Town (pop. 185), Fannin co., NE Texas, 7 mi. NW of Bonham, in agr. area.

Ravensberg (rä'vůnsběrk), former county, NW Germany. It included BIELEFELD. Passed 1346 to county of Berg, and with it to Jülich in 1348. In 1524 it went to duchy of Cleves and, in 1614, to Brandenburg.

Ravensbrück (rä'vůnsbrük), village (pop. 937), Brandenburg, E Germany, just N of Fürstenberg. Site of notorious concentration camp for women under Hitler regime.

Ravensburg (rā'vůnzbûrg, Ger. rä'vůnsbōōrk), town (pop. 23,912), S Württemberg, Germany, after 1945 in Württemberg-Hohenzollern, on the Schussen and 46 mi. SSW of Ulm, 22 mi. NE of Constance; 47°47'N 9°37'E. Mfg. of machinery, chassis, turbines, tools, electrical goods, pharmaceuticals, cosmetics, soap, textiles, furniture, brushes. Food processing (food preserves, dairy products, beer, wine), woodworking, paper milling. Has remains of medieval fortifications; also Gothic churches and town hall. Founded in 12th cent. under protection of ancestral castle (now in ruins) of the Guelphs. Created free imperial city in 13th cent. Flourishing commercial center, also noted for its fine linen, in 15th and 16th cent.

Ravenscrag (rā'vŭnzkrăg"), village (pop. estimate 100), SW Sask., in the Cypress Hills, on Frenchman R. and 35 mi. SE of Maple Creek; alt. 3,127 ft.; coal mining.

Ravenscroft, village (pop. c.600), White co., central Tenn., 10 mi. ENE of Sparta, in coal-mining region.

Ravenshoe, village (pop. 758), NE Queensland, Australia, 55 mi. SSW of Cairns; terminus of spur of Cairns-Charleston RR; sugar-producing center.

Ravensklip (rä'fŭnsklĭp"), town (pop. 3,199), S Transvaal, U. of So. Afr., on Witwatersrand, 2 mi. NW of Benoni; gold mining.

Ravenstein (rä'vŭstīn), town (pop. 4,124), North Brabant prov., E Netherlands, on Maas R. (railroad bridge) and 7 mi. WSW of Nijmegen; mfg. (leather, shoes). Old fortress. Also Ravestein.

Ravensthorpe (rā'vŭnzthôrp"), town (pop. 116), S Western Australia, 210 mi. SSW of Kalgoorlie; head of railroad to Hopetoun; gold-mining center; copper.

Ravensthorpe, England: see DEWSBURY.

Ravenstonedale, village and parish (pop. 838), SE Westmorland, England, 10 mi. S of Appleby; cattle and sheep raising.

Ravenswood, village (pop. 187), E Queensland, Australia, 55 mi. S of Townsville; gold mines. Gold discovered here 1868.

Ravenswood. 1 Town (pop. 498), Marion co., central Ind., N suburb of Indianapolis, on West Fork of White R. **2** Town (pop. 1,175), Jackson co., W W.Va., on the Ohio and 26 mi. SW of Parkersburg, in agr. region (livestock, fruit, tobacco, truck, poultry); dairy products, wood products; gas wells. Chartered 1852.

Ravenwood, town (pop. 319), Nodaway co., NW Mo., on Little Platte R. and 10 mi. E of Maryville; grain, dairy products.

Raver (rä'vär), town (pop. 9,913), East Khandesh dist., NE Bombay, India, 33 mi. NE of Jalgaon; trades in cotton, millet, timber; cotton ginning, handicraft cloth weaving (wearing apparel), gold-thread mfg.

Ravestein, Netherlands: see RAVENSTEIN.

Ravi (rä'vē), village (pop. 953), Grosseto prov., Tuscany, central Italy, 14 mi. NW of Grosseto; iron-pyrites mining.

Ravia (rā'vēü), town (pop. 327), Johnston co., S Okla., 37 mi. S of Ada, near L. Texoma.

Ravières (rävyâr'), village (pop. 1,127), Yonne dept., N central France, on Burgundy Canal and 14 mi. SE of Tonnerre; building materials, limestone flux. Rail junction at Nuits-sous-Ravières (1 mi. W).

Ravika, Greece: see KALLIPHYTON.

Ravilloles (rävēlōl'), village (pop. 248), Jura dept., E France, in the central Jura, 4 mi. NW of Saint-Claude; ivory and horn products.

Ravin, Le, Mauritius: see RIVIÈRE DU REMPART.

Ravinia (rävē'nü), town (pop. 200), Charles Mix co., SE S.Dak., 6 mi. E of Lake Andes.

Ravi River (rä'vē), anc. *Hydraotes,* in NW India and W Pakistan, one of 5 rivers of the Punjab; rises in SE Pir Panjal Range of Punjab Himalayas, c.13 mi. W of Rohtang Pass; flows WNW past Chamba (Himachal Pradesh), and SW along Kashmir-Punjab (India) and India-Pakistan borders, into Pakistan Punjab, past Lahore, to Chenab R. 33 mi. NNE of Multan; total length, c.475 mi. Headworks of Upper Bari Doab Canal at Madhopur; near Balloki, aqueduct carries waters of Upper Chenab Canal across river and into Lower Bari Doab Canal; headworks of Sidhnai Canal 11 mi. WNW of Talamba.

Ravka River, Poland: see RAWKA RIVER.

Ravka Velikaya, peak, Poland: see RAWKA, peak.

Ravna Reka (räv'nä rĕ'kä), village, E central Serbia, Yugoslavia, near Resava R., 15 mi. NE of Cuprija; rail terminus; brown-coal mine.

Ravne, Yugoslavia: see GUSTANJ.

Ravni Kotari (räv'nē kôtä'rē) [Serbo-Croatian,= flat districts], lowland in Dinaric Alps, W Croatia, Yugoslavia, in Dalmatia; extends along Adriatic Sea; bauxite deposits. Benkovac is its trade center.

Ravnina (rŭvnē'nä), state farm settlement, Mary oblast, SE Turkmen SSR, in Kara-Kum desert, on Trans-Caspian RR and 55 mi. NE of Mary; karakul sheep raising.

Ravns Stor (rouns' stôr'), island (2 mi. long, 2 mi. wide), just off SW Greenland, 55 mi. NNW of Frederikshaab; 62°43'N 50°25'W; in season a base of Faroese fishing fleet. Site of radio station and beacon.

Ravvala (rĕv'vō"lä), Swedish *Rävvåla,* village (pop. 827), Kopparberg co., central Sweden, 8 mi. W of Ludvika; iron mining.

Rawalpindi (räwŭlpĭn'dē, rä'vŭlpĭndē), dist. (□2,022; 1951 pop. 872,000), N Punjab, W Pakistan; ⊙ Rawalpindi. Bounded E by Jhelum R.; crossed (N) by W offshoots of Punjab Himalayas; agr. (wheat, millet, maize); horse breeding. Timber forests (N). Famous archaeological site at Taxila.

Rawalpindi, city (1951 pop., including Chaklala and other cantonment areas, 243,000), ⊙ Rawalpindi dist., N Punjab, W Pakistan, on railroad (workshops) and 160 mi. NNW of Lahore. Industrial center; major military station; served by road, rail, and airways; trades in wheat, millet, corn, wool, timber, horses, and piece goods from Kashmir. Has petroleum refinery (oil pipe lines from Attock and Jhelum dists.). Mfg. of chemicals, furniture, electrical apparatus, fruit preserves, tents, sandpaper, buttons, ice, and flour; ordnance factory and arsenal, engineering workshops, steel-rolling mill, gasworks, distillery, brewery, dairy farm. Handicrafts include basket weaving, hosiery mfg., embroidering. Has several colleges. Following Br. occupation of Punjab in 1849, became one of largest cantonments in India.

Rawa Mazowiecka (rä'vä mäzôvyĕts'kä), Rus. *Rava* (rä'vŭ), town (pop. 6,908), Lodz prov., central Poland, on Rawka R. and 23 mi. E of Lodz; brickworks; brewing. Castle ruins.

Rawanduz, Iraq: see RUWANDIZ.

Rawang (räwäng'), town (pop. 3,106), central Selangor, Malaya, on railroad and 15 mi. NW of Kuala Lumpur; tin mining.

Rawansar or **Ravansar** (both: rävänsär'), town, Fifth Prov., in Kermanshah, W Iran, 35 mi. NW of Kermanshah.

Rawa Ruska, Ukrainian SSR: see RAVA-RUSSKAYA.

Rawdah, Aden and Yemen: see RAUDHA.

Rawdah, Al-, Egypt: see RODA, EL.

Rawdon, village (pop. 1,236), S Que., 35 mi. N of Montreal; lumbering, dairying; tobacco, potatoes.

Rawdon, former urban district (1931 pop. 4,574), West Riding, central Yorkshire, England, near Aire R. 5 mi. NE of Bradford; woolen milling; mfg. of pharmaceuticals. Inc. 1937 in Airborough. Near by is a Baptist col.

Rawene (räwē'nē), town (pop. 401), ⊙ Hokianga co. (□ 613; pop. 7,807), N N.Isl., New Zealand, 120 mi. NW of Auckland, on S shore of Hokianga Harbour; woodworking.

Rawicz (rä'vēch), Ger. *Rawitsch* (rä'vĭch), town (pop. 9,063), Poznan prov., W Poland, 36 mi. NNW of Breslau (Wroclaw); rail junction; mfg. of machinery, furniture, cement, paper, roofing material, brushes; marble polishing, tanning, weaving. Until 1939, Pol. frontier station near Ger. border.

Rawil Pass (rä'vēl) (7,980 ft.), in Bernese Alps, SW Switzerland, on border of Bern and Valais cantons, bet. Lenk and Sion. The Rawilhorn (9,542 ft.) rises SSW of pass.

Rawitsch, Poland: see RAWICZ.

Rawka or **Rawka Wielka** (räf'kä vyĕl'kä), Rus. *Ravka Velikaya* (räf'kŭ vyĭlī'kīyŭ), peak (c.4,270 ft.) in the Carpathians, SE Poland, 21 mi. WSW of Turka, Ukrainian SSR, near Poland-Czechoslovakia-USSR border.

Rawka River, Rus. *Ravka,* central Poland, rises 19 mi. E of Lodz, flows E, past Rawa Mazowiecka, and N to Bzura R. 8 mi. ENE of Lowicz; 50 mi. long.

Rawlinna (rô'lĭnü), village (pop. 124), S Western Australia, 230 mi. E of Kalgoorlie, on Trans-Australian RR; some sheep.

Rawlins, county (□ 1,078; pop. 5,728), NW Kansas; ⊙ Atwood. Gently rolling plain area, bordering N on Nebr.; watered by headstreams of Sappa and Beaver creeks. Grain, livestock. Formed 1881.

Rawlins, city (pop. 7,415), ⊙ Carbon co., S Wyo., 90 mi. WNW of Laramie; alt. 6,755 ft. Rail and distribution center for mining and livestock region; railroad shops; mfg. (pistols, soda products). State penitentiary here. Coal mines, oil wells, quarries near by. Founded 1868. Growth followed arrival of railroad.

Rawmarsh, urban district (1931 pop. 18,572; 1951 census 18,793), West Riding, S Yorkshire, England, 2 mi. NNE of Rotherham; coal mines, ironworks, pottery works. On Don R. 2 mi. NE is coal-mining and steel-milling town of Kilnhurst.

Rawson. 1 Town (pop. 2,275), N central Buenos Aires prov., Argentina, 24 mi. E of Chacabuco, in agr. region (grain, livestock; dairying). **2** Village (pop. 2,500), ⊙ Chubut natl. territory and Rawson dept. (pop. 7,837), S Argentina, on Chubut R. estuary (irrigation), on railroad and 680 mi. SW of Buenos Aires, 180 mi. SSW of San Antonio Oeste, on the coast; 43°18'S 65°6'W. Agr. and administrative center. Trades in alfalfa, wheat, fruit, sheep. Fishing and fish canning. Beach resort of Unión is 3 mi. E on the Atlantic. Settled mostly by Welshmen, it was founded 1865 and became ⊙ of territory in 1900. **3** Town (pop. 10,623), ⊙ Rawson dept. (pop. 24,695), S San Juan prov., Argentina, S of San Juan.

Rawson. 1 Village (pop. 32), McKenzie co., W N.Dak., 12 mi. W of Watford City. **2** Village (pop. 407), Hancock co., NW Ohio, c.9 mi. SW of Findlay, in agr. region.

Rawtenstall, municipal borough (1931 pop. 28,587; 1951 census 25,426), E Lancashire, England, on Irwell R. and 6 mi. SSW of Burnley; cotton and woolen milling, carpet weaving; also shoe mfg., electrical engineering. Includes cotton-milling towns: Crawshaw Booth (N), Cloughfold (klŭ'fōld) (E), and WATERFOOT.

Raxalpe (räk'sälpü), Austria, group of Eastern Alps on Lower Austria–Styria border, rising to 6,590 ft. in the Heukuppe; pastures; skiing grounds here reached by suspension railroad. Its springs supply water to Vienna.

Raxaul (rŭk'soul), village, Champaran dist., NW Bihar, India, on Nepal border, 23 mi. N of Motihari; rail junction, with branch to Amlekhganj, Nepal; main customs station for Nepal trade; rice milling. Birganj, Nepalese border town, is 3 mi. N.

Ray, Iran: see RAI.

Ray-, in Rus. names: see RAI-.

Ray, county (□ 574; pop. 15,932), NW Mo.; ⊙ Richmond. Bounded S by Missouri R.; drained by Crooked R. Agr. (corn, wheat, oats, potatoes); coal mines. Formed 1820.

Ray. 1 Village (1940 pop. 594; 1949 estimate 2,000), Pinal co., SE central Ariz., 18 mi. SSW of Miami; copper mining. **2** City (pop. 721), Williams co., NW N.Dak., 25 mi. NE of Williston.

Ray, Cape, promontory at SW extremity of N.F., at entrance of the Gulf of St. Lawrence, 8 mi. WNW of Port aux Basques; 47°37'N 59°22'W; lighthouse, radio-direction finding station.

Raya (rī'ŭ), town (pop. 3,645), Muttra dist., W Uttar Pradesh, India, 8 mi. ENE of Muttra; gram, wheat, jowar, cotton, oilseeds.

Rayachoti (rä'yŭchōtē), town (pop. 8,559), Cuddapah dist., central Madras, India, 30 mi. S of Cuddapah; road center; peanut milling.

Rayadrug (rä'yŭdrōōg), town (pop. 16,033), Bellary dist., NW Madras, India, 32 mi. S of Bellary; rail spur terminus; silk weaving, tanning. Gum arabic, bamboo in near-by forests. Near-by hill fortress has rock-cut Jain sculptures.

Rayagada (rä'yŭgŭdŭ), village, Koraput dist., S Orissa, India, on railroad and 60 mi. ENE of Jeypore; sugar milling. Sometimes spelled Rayaghada.

Rayak, Lebanon: see RIYAQ.

Rayaq, Lebanon: see RIYAQ.

Raychikhinsk, Russian SFSR: see RAICHIKHINSK.

Ray City, town (pop. 576), Berrien co., S Ga., 18 mi. NNE of Valdosta; food canning; mfg. of naval stores.

Raydah, Aden: see REIDAT AL 'ABDUL WADUD.

Rayevskiy or **Rayevskiy** (rī'ŭfskē), town (1926 pop. 6,072), W central Bashkir Autonomous SSR, Russian SFSR, on Dema R. and 11 mi. SSW of Davlekanovo; agr. center (wheat, livestock); meat packing. Formerly Rayevka.

Rayfun, Lebanon: see RAIFUN.

Raygrod, Poland: see RAJGROD.

Rayin (räyēn'), town (1945 pop. 2,900), Eighth Prov., in Kerman, SE Iran, 60 mi. SSE of Kerman; grain, cotton, opium, gums (gum arabic and asafetida), cumin seed; rugmaking, cotton weaving. Wild almonds and pistachios.

Raykoke Island, Russian SFSR: see RAIKOKE ISLAND.

Raykovo, Bulgaria: see RAIKOVO.

Rayland, village (pop. 726), Jefferson co., E Ohio, on the Ohio and 12 mi. SSW of Steubenville, in coal-mining area.

Rayleigh (rā'lē), urban district (1931 pop. 6,256; 1951 census 9,388), S Essex, England, 6 mi. NW of Southend-on-Sea; agr. market, with shoe mfg. Has 15th-cent. church and earthwork remains of Norman castle.

Raylton, Southern Rhodesia: see BULAWAYO, city.

Raymer or **New Raymer,** town (pop. 130), Weld co., NE Colo., 45 mi. ENE of Greeley; alt. 4,779 ft.; small trading point.

Raymond, town (pop. 2,116), S Alta., 18 mi. SE of Lethbridge; beet-sugar refining, mixed farming, honey production. Site of Prov. Agr. Col.

Raymond. 1 Village (pop. 779), Montgomery co., S central Ill., 10 mi. NNE of Litchfield, in agr. and bituminous-coal area; corn, wheat, hay, livestock, dairy products. **2** Resort town (pop. 620), Cumberland co., SW Maine, on Sebago L. and 20 mi. NNW of Portland; fish hatchery. Nathaniel Hawthorne's boyhood home here. **3** Village (pop. 580), Kandiyohi co., SW central Minn., on small affluent of Minnesota R. and 12 mi. SW of Willmar; dairy products. **4** Town (pop. 1,259), a ⊙ Hinds co., W Miss., 14 mi. W of Jackson, in agr. and timber area. Has dist. jr. col. **5** Village (pop. c.100), Sheridan co., NE Mont., port of entry near Sask. line, 7 mi. N of Plentywood. **6** Village (pop. 196), Lancaster co., E Nebr., 10 mi. NNW of Lincoln and on branch of Platte R. **7** Town (pop. 1,428), Rockingham co., SE N.H., 15 mi. ENE of Manchester and on Lamprey R. Settled 1717, inc. 1764. **8** Town (pop. 174), Clark co., E central S.Dak., 10 mi. W of Clark. **9** City (pop. 4,110) and port, Pacific co., SW Wash., 20 mi. SSE of Aberdeen and on Willapa R., near Willapa Bay; lumber, dairy products, oysters. Inc. 1907.

Raymond Terrace, town (pop. 1,369), E New South Wales, Australia, on Hunter R. and 12 mi. NNW of Newcastle; dairying center; hardwood timber.

Raymondville. 1 Town (pop. 175), Texas co., S central Mo., 6 mi. E of Houston. **2** City (pop. 9,136), ⊙ Willacy co., extreme S Texas, c.45 mi. NW of Brownsville; trade, shipping center for irrigated agr. area (citrus, onions, cotton, truck); cattle, some oil; dairy products; cotton-processing plants. Tourist trade. Platted 1904, inc. as city 1921.

Raymore, village (pop. 305), S central Sask., at foot of Touchwood Hills, 30 mi. SW of Wynyard; wheat, stock.

Raymore, town (pop. 208), Cass co., W Mo., 20 mi. S of Kansas City.

Ray Mountains, central Alaska, S extension of Brooks Range, N of Tanana; 150°–152°30′W at 65°45′N; rise to 5,600 ft.

Rayne, Scotland: see OLD RAYNE.

Rayne, town (pop. 6,485), Acadia parish, S La., 6 mi. NE of Crowley, in rice and sugar-cane area; cotton, sweet potatoes, fruit, vegetables, poultry; rice mills, cotton gin; edible-frog industry. Oil wells.

Raynham (rā'nům), town (pop. 2,426), Bristol co., SE Mass., on Taunton R. just NE of Taunton; rivets, boxes; poultry. Ironworks established here 1652. Inc. 1731. Includes East Taunton village.

Raynolds Pass (rě'nůldz) (alt. 6,911 ft.), SW Mont., in Continental Divide, near Idaho line; leads into Henrys L. region of NE Idaho.

Raynor Park, village (pop. 4,311, with adjacent Lidice), Will co., NE Ill., just NW of Joliet.

Rayón (rīōn'). **1** Town (pop. 1,443), Chiapas, S Mexico, in N spur of Sierra Madre, 30 mi. NNE of Tuxtla; cereals, fruit, tobacco, sugar cane. **2** Officially Santa María Rayón, town (pop. 1,354), Mexico state, central Mexico, on railroad and 12 mi. SSE of Toluca; cereals, livestock. **3** City (pop. 2,628), San Luis Potosí, N central Mexico, in Sierra Madre Oriental, 23 mi. ESE of Río Verde; alt. 3,185 ft.; grain, cotton, beans, livestock. **4** Town (pop. 1,241), Sonora, NW Mexico, on San Miguel R. (irrigation) and 50 mi. NNE of Hermosillo; wheat, corn, cotton, fruit. Copper mines near by.

Rayones (rīō'něs), town (pop. 512), Nuevo León, N Mexico, 45 mi. SSE of Monterrey; fruit, livestock.

Rayong (rŭyông'), town (1947 pop. 3,716), ⊙ Rayong prov. (□ 1,452; 1947 pop. 84,197), S Thailand, port on Gulf of Siam, on Chachoengsao-Trat road and 90 mi. SE of Bangkok; rice; fisheries.

Ray Pond, Vt.: see RAPONDA, LAKE.

Raysal (rā'sůl), village (1940 pop. 1,194), McDowell co., S W.Va., on Dry Fork and 13 mi. WSW of Welch, in coal-mining and agr. area.

Raystown Branch, Juniata River, Pa.: see JUNIATA RIVER.

Rayville. 1 Town (pop. 3,138), ⊙ Richland parish, NE La., 21 mi. E of Monroe, near Boeuf R.; agr.; cotton ginning, lumber milling, veneer mfg.; hunting, fishing. **2** Town (pop. 193), Ray co., NW Mo., on Crooked R. and 7 mi. NW of Richmond.

Rayvola, Russian SFSR: see ROSHCHINO.

Raz, Pointe du (pwĕt dü räz'), rocky cape on Atlantic Ocean, in Finistère dept., W France, 26 mi. SSW of Brest; 250 ft. high; 48°2′N 4°44′W. Attracts tourists.

Razam (rŭzŭm'), town (pop. 5,394), Vizagapatam dist., NE Madras, India, 28 mi. NE of Vizianagaram; road center; sugar cane, oilseeds, rice. Also spelled Rajam.

Razampeta, India: see RAJAMPET.

Razan (räzän'), town (1940 pop. 3,195), Fifth Prov., in Hamadan, W Iran, on road and 50 mi. NE of Hamadan; grain, fruit, livestock. Airfield. Sometimes spelled Rizan.

Razdan, Armenian SSR: see ZANGA RIVER.

Razdelnaya or **Razdel'naya** (rŭzdyěl'nīŭ), town (1926 pop. 2,357), SW Odessa oblast, Ukrainian SSR, 40 mi. NW of Odessa; rail junction (workshops); metalworks.

Razdolinsk (rŭzdô'lyĭnsk), town (1939 pop. over 2,000), central Krasnoyarsk Territory, Russian SFSR, 175 mi. NNE of Krasnoyarsk; gold mines.

Razdolnoye or **Razdol'noye** (rŭzdôl'nŭyŭ). **1** Village (1948 pop. over 2,000), NW Crimea, Russian SFSR, near Karkinit Gulf, 40 mi. N of Feodosiya; metalworks; wheat, sheep. Until 1944, Ak-Sheikh. **2** Town (1939 pop. over 2,000), S Maritime Territory, Russian SFSR, on Suifun R. (head of navigation), on Trans-Siberian RR and 28 mi. N of Vladivostok; maral reindeer farms. Former road-river transfer point on Khabarovsk-Vladivostok route.

Razdorskaya (rŭzdôr'skīŭ), village (1926 pop. 2,572), SW central Rostov oblast, Russian SFSR, on right bank of Don R. and 22 mi. ESE of Shakhty; winegrowing center; wheat, sunflowers.

Razelm, Lake (räzĕlm'), anc. *Halmyris*, extensive lagoon (□ 120) of SE Rumania, in Dobruja, c.40 mi. SSE of Tulcea; 20 mi. long, 10 mi. wide. Channel (S) opens on the Black Sea; canal (NE) joins the Sfantu-Gheorghe arm of the Danube delta; another canal (W) links it with L. Babadag. L. Sinoe (sē'nôyĕ) (□ 69.4) and L. Golovita (gōlō'vētsä), Rum. *Golovița* (□ 34.8) are adjacent lagoons to S. Entire area constitutes major fishing grounds, notably for sturgeon and carp; also fish hatcheries. Remains of Roman and pre-Roman settlements abound on W shores.

Razgojna, Razgoina, or **Razgoyna** (all: räz'goinä), village (pop. 5,533), SE central Serbia, Yugoslavia, 7 mi. N of Leskovac.

Razgrad (räz'grät), city (pop. 15,023), Ruse dist., NE Bulgaria, on Beli Lom R. (branch of Rusenski Lom R.) and 34 mi. SE of Ruse; cattle-trading and agr. center for W Deliorman upland; exports grain, legumes, sunflowers, lumber; starch mfg., tanning. Has mus. and 16th-cent. mosque. Under Turkish rule (15th-19th cent.). Sometimes spelled Rasgrad.

Razhdavitsa (rŭzhdä'vētsä), village (pop. 1,163), Sofia dist., W Bulgaria, on Struma R. and 8 mi. NNE of Kyustendil; fruitgrowing center; exports cherries. Has 15th-cent. church.

Razhevo Konare (rŭ'zhĕvô kônä'rĕ), village (pop. 3,781), Plovdiv dist., S central Bulgaria, on Strema R. and 13 mi. NNE of Plovdiv; grain, fruit, truck.

Razina, Imeni Stepana, USSR: see STEPANA RAZINA, IMENI.

Razino (rä'zēnŭ), village (1939 pop. 227), E Kaliningrad oblast, Russian SFSR, 19 mi. NNE of Nesterov, near Sheshupe R. (Lith. border), in marshes; narrow-gauge rail terminus. Until 1945, in East Prussia and called Doristhal (dō'rĭstäl).

Razlog (räzlôk'), city (pop. 6,857), Gorna Dzhumaya dist., SW Bulgaria, in Macedonia, in Razlog valley, bet. Rila and Pirin mts., 20 mi. SE of Gorna Dzhumaya; market center; furniture mfg., sawmilling, coopering; exports lumber. Under Turkish rule and until 1925, called Mekhomiya or Mehomia.

Razo Island (rä'zō) (□ 3), one of Cape Verde Isls., in Windward group, bet. Santa Luzia Isl. (10 mi. NW) and São Nicolau Isl. (10 mi. E), in the Atlantic; 16°38′N 24°36′W; 538 ft. high. Uninhabited and barren. Also spelled Raso.

Razole (räzō'lĕ), town (pop. 5,896), East Godavari dist., NE Madras, India, in Godavari R. delta, 42 mi. SW of Cocanada; rice milling; sugar cane, tobacco, coconuts.

Razorback, mountain (10,667 ft.), SW B.C., in Coast Mts., 170 mi. NNW of Vancouver.

Razvilnoye or **Razvil'noye** (rŭzvēl'nŭyŭ), village (1926 pop. 3,955), S Rostov oblast, Russian SFSR, on railroad and 20 mi. SSW of Salsk; wheat, cotton, sunflowers; livestock.

Razza, Cyrenaica: see LUIGI RAZZA.

Ré, Île de (ēl dů rā'), island (□ 33; pop. 7,908) in Bay of Biscay, part of Charente-Maritime dept., W France; extends WNW-ESE opposite La Rochelle, separated from mainland by the Pertuis Breton (2 mi. wide at narrowest point) and from Île d'Oléron by the Pertuis d'Antioche; 16 mi. long, 3 mi. wide; level and very fertile (early vegetables, potatoes, wine). Has saltworks, oyster beds; active tourist trade. Chief localities are La Flotte and Saint Martin. Formerly sometimes spelled Rhé.

Re, Monte, Yugoslavia: see HRUSICA.

Rea (rē, rā), town (pop. 110), Andrew co., NW Mo., near Little Platte R., 20 mi. N of St. Joseph.

Reach, England: see HEATH AND REACH.

Read, village and parish (pop. 869), NE Lancashire, England, 5 mi. WNW of Burnley; cotton milling.

Read, Fort (rēd), U.S. army base, N Trinidad isl., B.W.I., 15 mi. E of Port of Spain and just E of Arima. Leased to U.S. in 1941.

Reader (rē'důr), town (pop. 79), Ouachita co., S Ark., 20 mi. NW of Camden, near Little Missouri R.

Readfield (rēd'fēld), town (pop. 1,022), Kennebec co., S Maine, 10 mi. NNW of Augusta, in agr., resort, lumbering area; Maine Wesleyan Seminary (1821) is at Kents Hill village.

Reading (rĕ'dĭng), county borough (1931 pop. 97,149; 1951 census 114,176), ⊙ Berkshire, England, in center of co., on the Thames at mouth of Kennet R. and 35 mi. W of London; mfg. of aircraft, agr. machinery, metal products, biscuits, leather, clothing, and pharmaceuticals. There are important seed nurseries. Former Univ. Extension Col., founded 1892, became Reading Univ. in 1926, and has noted departments of agr. and dairying. Notable bldgs. include 15th-cent. grammar school, mus. (containing remains of Roman settlement at SILCHESTER), several old churches, and Royal Berkshire Hosp. Town's history dates from 871, when it was occupied by Danes; it was burned in 1006. There are remains, now surrounded by park, of Benedictine abbey founded 1121 by Henry I, who is buried here. Anc. castle was destroyed by Henry II. In 1643 Reading surrendered to Parliamentarians. Several parliaments were held here. There are many literary associations: Jane Austen attended school here; Oscar Wilde, in prison here, wrote his *Ballad of Reading Gaol;* Chaucer and Bunyan commemorated Reading; and it was the Abrickham of Hardy's *Jude the Obscure.* The first piece of secular music for several voices, *Sumer Is Icumen In,* is reputed to have been composed by Reading monks. In county borough (N, on the Thames) is residential dist. of Caversham (pop. 11,746).

Reading. 1 (rĕ'dĭng) City (pop. 289), Lyon co., E central Kansas, on Marais des Cygnes R. and 15 mi. ENE of Emporia; livestock, grain. **2** (rĕ'dĭng) Town (pop. 14,006), Middlesex co., E Mass., 12 mi. NNW of Boston; mfg. (photographic supplies, stoves, hair brushes, neckwear); dairying, poultry, fruit, truck. Settled 1639, inc. 1644. **3** (rĕ'dĭng) City (pop. 1,125), Hillsdale co., S Mich., 8 mi. SW of Hillsdale, in stock-raising, agr., and lake-resort area. Mfg. (furniture, store fixtures, leather goods). Settled 1840; inc. as village 1873, as city 1934. **4** (rĕ'dĭng) City (pop. 7,836), Hamilton co., extreme SW Ohio, a N suburb of Cincinnati; lithographing; mfg. of chemicals, paperboard containers, grain products. Settled 1795; inc. as village in 1851, as city in 1930. **5** (rĕ'dĭng) City (pop. 109,320), ⊙ Berks co., SE central Pa., c.45 mi. NW of Philadelphia and on Schuylkill R., in fertile agr. area; 40°20′N 75°55′W. Commercial and industrial center. Railroad shops; mfg. (aluminum, steel, and brass products, automobile parts, machinery, optical goods, shoes, bricks, textiles, clothing, drugs, food products). Albright Col. here. City's airport is Air Force base. Early iron industry supplied cannon for Revolution. First settled 1733 by English, later by Germans. Laid out 1748, inc. as borough 1783, as city 1847. **6** (rĕ'dĭng) Town (pop. 470), Windsor co., E Vt., 8 mi. W of Windsor; lumber, chemicals, drugs. Includes Felchville village.

Read Island (5 mi. long, 2 mi. wide), SW Franklin Dist., Northwest Territories, in Dolphin and Union Strait, just off SW Victoria Isl.; 69°12′N 114°30′W; site of trading post and radio station.

Readland (rēd'lůnd), town (pop. 125), Chicot co., extreme SE Ark., 25 mi. SSW of Greenville, Miss., near Mississippi R.

Readlyn (rĕd'lĭn), town (pop. 468), Bremer co., NE Iowa, 14 mi. NNE of Waterloo; dairy products, feed.

Readsboro, town (pop. 847), including Readsboro village (pop. 654), Bennington co., SW Vt., on Deerfield R. and 15 mi. SE of Bennington, in Green Mts. at Mass. line; furniture, wood products. Power plant of near-by Harriman Dam is here. Granted 1764, settled c.1780.

Readstown, village (pop. 541), Vernon co., SW Wis., on Kickapoo R. and 36 mi. SE of La Crosse, in coulee country; cheese, butter, and casein factory; tobacco warehouse.

Reagan (rā'gůn), county (□ 1,133; pop. 3,127), W Texas; ⊙ Big Lake. Broken prairies, at N edge of Edwards Plateau; alt. c.2,500–2,800 ft. Sheep ranching, some cattle; oil, natural-gas wells. Formed 1903.

Reagan, city (1940 pop. 353), Falls co., E central Texas, 31 mi. SE of Waco, in cotton, corn, truck area.

Reagan Dam, Calif.: see PACOIMA.

Real (rē'äl), county (□ 625; pop. 2,479), SW Texas; ⊙ Leakey. On Edwards Plateau, and drained by Nueces and Frio rivers; alt. c.1,500–2,400 ft. Ranching area (goats, sheep, cattle); little agr.; timber (mainly cedar). Hunting, fishing; guest ranches. Frio Canyon is vacation area. Formed 1913.

Real, Cordillera, Bolivia: see ORIENTAL, CORDILLERA.

Real, El, Panama: see EL REAL.

Real, El, Venezuela: see EL REAL.

Real, Rio (rē'ŏŏ rīäl'), coastal stream of NE Brazil, forming Bahia-Sergipe boundary throughout its course (c.100 mi.) to the Atlantic.

Real Campiña (rääl' kämpē'nyä), town (pop. 1,173), Las Villas prov., central Cuba, on railroad and 23 mi. NW of Cienfuegos; sugar-cane growing and stock raising; lumbering.

Real de Catorce, Mexico: see CATORCE.

Real de Gandía (rääl' dhā gändē'ä), village (pop. 1,894), Valencia prov., E Spain, 2 mi. SSW of Gandía, in rich truck-farming dist.; olive oil.

Real de la Jara, El (ĕl rääl' dhā lä hä'rä), town (pop. 3,039), Seville prov., SW Spain, in Sierra Morena, near Badajoz prov. border, 40 mi. NNW of Seville cereals, fruit, timber, livestock.

Real del Monte, Mexico: see MINERAL DEL MONTE.

Real del Oro, Mexico: see EL ORO, Mexico state.

Real del Padre (rääl' dhĕl pä'drā), town (pop. estimate 1,000), central Mendoza prov., Argentina, on railroad, on Atuel R. (irrigation area) and 37 mi. ESE of San Rafael; agr. center (alfalfa, corn, barley, wine, flax, vegetables, fruit, livestock). Dried-fruit processing.

Real de Montroy (rääl' dhā mōntroi'), village (pop. 1,678), Valencia prov., E Spain, 16 mi. SW of Valencia; wine, olive oil, cereals.

Real de San Carlos, Uruguay: see COLONIA, city.

Real de Santa María, El, Panama: see EL REAL.

Real de San Vicente, El (ĕl rääl' dhā sän' vēsĕn'tā), town (pop. 2,038), Toledo prov., central Spain, 13 mi. NE of Talavera de la Reina; cereals, fruit, grapes, livestock; timber. Flour milling. Medicinal waters.

Realejo, El, Nicaragua: see EL REALEJO.

Realejo Alto (räälā'hō äl'tō), town (pop. 2,117), Tenerife, Canary Isls., 21 mi. WSW of Santa Cruz de Tenerife; tobacco, cereals, bananas, grapes, onions, tomatoes, fruit, livestock. Basket mfg.

Realejo Bajo (bä'hō), town (pop. 1,443), Tenerife, Canary Isls., 21 mi. WSW of Santa Cruz de Tenerife; bananas, wheat, tomatoes, potatoes, fruit. Mfg. of embroidery and linen goods.

Realengo (rĭūlĕng'gō), W suburb of Rio de Janeiro, Brazil, in Federal Dist., c.12 mi. from city center. Site of largest low-cost public housing development in Rio area. Has airport and aviation school.

Realicó (räälēkō'), town (pop. estimate 2,000), ⊙ Realicó dept. (pop. 10,577), NE La Pampa prov., Argentina, 50 mi. NW of General Pico; rail junction, agr. center (wheat, corn, flax, rye, livestock); flour milling.

Realitos (rēūlē'tůs), village (1940 pop. 693), Duval co., S Texas, 60 mi. E of Laredo; rail point in cattle-ranching area.

Réalmont (räälmō'), village (pop. 1,801), Tarn dept., S France, near Dadou R., 11 mi. S of Albi; textile milling; lead and zinc mining. Village founded 1270.

Realmonte (rĕälmôn'tĕ), village (pop. 3,627), Agrigento prov., S Sicily, 6 mi. W of Agrigento.

Real Morelos, Mexico: see MORELOS, Chihuahua.

Realp (rā'älp), hamlet (pop. 242), Uri canton, central Switzerland, in Urserental, 5 mi. SW of Andermatt; alt. 5,074 ft.

Réalville (rāälvēl'), village (pop. 410), Tarn-et-Garonne dept., SW France, near the Aveyron, 9 mi. NE of Montauban; flour milling.

Ream (rā'äm), town, Kampot prov., SW Cambodia, deep-water port on Gulf of Siam, and 110 mi. SW of Pnompenh, situated on a small bay; main port (sheltered roadstead) of Cambodia; seaside resort.

Ream, W.Va.: see GARY.

Reamstown, village (1940 pop. 757), Lancaster co., SE central Pa., 14 mi. SW of Reading, in rich tobacco-growing area; makes cigars, clothing.

Reana del Roiale (rĕä'nä dĕl rôyä'lĕ), village (pop. 737), Udine prov., Friuli-Venezia Giulia, NE Italy, 5 mi. N of Udine; alcohol distillery; agr. tools.

Reao (räou'), atoll (pop. 382), S Tuamotu Isls., Fr. Oceania, S Pacific; 18°30'S 136°23'W. Also called Natupe; formerly Clermont-Tonnerre.

Reardan, town (pop. 410), Lincoln co., E Wash., 20 mi. W of Spokane; agr., flour, feed mills.

Rearsby, town and parish (pop. 538), N central Leicester, England, near Wreak R., 8 mi. NE of Leicester; aircraft industry.

Reasi, Kashmir: see RIASI.

Reasnor (rēz'nûr), town (pop. 227), Jasper co., central Iowa, near Skunk R., 30 mi. E of Des Moines, in coal-mining and agr. area.

Reay (rā), agr. village and parish (pop. 719), NW Caithness, Scotland, on the Atlantic, 10 mi. W of Thurso. Seat of head of the Clan Mackay.

Rebais (rùbā'), village (pop. 883), Seine-et-Marne dept., N central France, 18 mi. SE of Meaux; basketmaking.

Rebecca, town (pop. 295), Turner co., S central Ga., 14 mi. WNW of Fitzgerald, near Alapaha R.

Rebecq-Rognon (rùbĕk'-rônyō'), Flemish *Roosbeek* (rōz'bāk), agr. village (pop. 4,069), Brabant prov., central Belgium, 7 mi. SW of Hal.

Rebeval (rĕbĕväl'), village (pop. 1,056), Alger dept., N central Algeria, on the Oued Sebaou and 13 mi. NW of Tizi-Ouzou; tobacco, wine.

Rebiana (rĕbyä'nä), oasis, S Cyrenaica, Libya, 80 mi. W of El Giof, in Libyan Desert. Exports dates to Tibesti Mts. in exchange for sheep.

Rebiba (rĕbēbä'), village, Le Kef dist., W Tunisia, on railroad, near Algerian border, and 31 mi. SW of Le Kef; phosphate mining.

Rebola (rābō'lä), village (pop. 1,074), Fernando Po isl., Sp. Guinea, 3 mi. E of Santa Isabel; cacao, coffee.

Reboly (ryĕ'bùlē), Finnish *Repola*, village (1926 pop. 168), W central Karelo-Finnish SSR, on lake Leksozero, 115 mi. W of Segezha; dairying. Under Finnish administration, 1918–20.

Rebouças (rībō'sùs), city (pop. 1,789), S Paraná, Brazil, on railroad and 90 mi. WSW of Curitiba; sawmilling, grain milling, coffee and maté processing, tanning.

Rebrikha (rĕbrē'khŭ), village (1926 pop. 5,554), N Altai Territory, Russian SFSR, on S.Siberian RR, 60 mi. WSW of Barnaul; metalworks, flour mill.

Rebrovo (rĕbrô'vō), village (pop. 1,627), Sofia dist., W Bulgaria, on W slope of Murgash Mts., in Iskar R. gorge, and 12 mi. N of Sofia; anthracite mining.

Rebstein (rĕp'shtīn), town (pop. 2,126), St. Gall canton, NE Switzerland, 9 mi. E of St. Gall; embroideries, knit goods, foodstuffs.

Rebun-jima (räbōōng'jĭmä) or **Rebun-shima** (–shĭmä), island (□ 26; pop. 8,677), Japan, in Sea of Japan, near NW tip of Hokkaido, in Hokkaido administrative unit; 13 mi. long, 4 mi. wide; mountainous; fishing. Formerly sometimes Rebunshiri.

Recanati (rĕkänä'tē), town (pop. 5,354), Macerata prov., The Marches, central Italy, 9 mi. NE of Macerata; mfg. (harmoniums, agr. machinery, cutlery, furniture, majolica, silk textiles). Bishopric. Has cathedral and house of the poet Leopardi, who was b. here.

Recas (rĕ'käsh), Rum. *Recaş*, Hung. *Temesrékas* (tĕ'mĕsh-rā'kŏsh), village (pop. 4,280), Timisoara prov., W Rumania, on railroad and 14 mi. E of Timisoara; mfg. of bricks and tiles.

Recas (rā'käs), town (pop. 2,050), Toledo prov., central Spain, 30 mi. SW of Madrid; olives, cereals, grapes, truck produce; olive-oil pressing.

Recco (rĕk'kô), town (pop. 2,792), Genova prov., Liguria, N Italy, port on Gulf of Genoa and 11 mi. ESE of Genoa; commercial center; mfg. (clocks, shoes), foundry; tunny fisheries. Resort; starting-point for tour of near-by promontory of Portofino. In Second World War, partly destroyed by air bombing.

Recen (rēsĕn'), town (pop. 53), Summit co., W central Colo., on branch of Blue R., in Rocky Mts., and 8 mi. WSW of Breckenridge; alt. c.10,600 ft. Lead, zinc, silver mines. Fremont Pass near by. Formerly Kokomo (kō'kùmō").

Recey-sur-Ource (rùsā'-sür-ōōrs'), village (pop. 661), Côte-d'Or dept., E central France, on the Ource and 14 mi. ESE of Châtillon-sur-Seine; sheep raising.

Rech (rĕkh), village (pop. 437), in former Prussian Rhine Prov., W Germany, after 1945 in Rhineland-Palatinate, on the Ahr and 3 mi. SW of Ahrweiler; known for its red wine.

Recherche Archipelago or **Archipelago of the Recherche** (rù-shĕrsh'), in Indian Ocean, just off S coast of Western Australia; 33°43'-34°2'S 121°26'-124°4'E. Extends c.120 mi. E-W. Mondrain Isl. (3.3 mi. long, 1.5 mi. wide), largest. Low, sandy; scrub.

Recherche Bay, Tasmania: see CATAMARAN.

Réchicourt-le-Château (rāshēkōōr'-lù-shätō'), Ger. *Rixingen* (rēks'ĭng-ùn), agr. village (pop. 463), Moselle dept., NE France, 11 mi. SW of Sarrebourg.

Rechitsa (ryĕ'chĭtsŭ, ryĭchē'tsŭ), city (1926 pop. 16,559), W Gomel oblast, Belorussian SSR, on Dnieper R. and 27 mi. W of Gomel; road-rail junction; lumbering; mfg. (prefabricated houses, metalware, matches, chemicals); flour milling. Pop. 40% Jewish until Second World War, when city was held (1941–43) by Germans.

Rechlin (rĕkh'lĭn), village (pop. 1,809), Mecklenburg, N Germany, on Müritz L., 14 mi. W of Neustrelitz; jet-aircraft experimental station, established during Second World War.

Rechna Doab (rŭch'nŭ dō'äb), alluvial area in NE Punjab, W Pakistan, bet. Chenab R. (W) and Ravi R. (E). Irrigated by Upper and Lower Chenab canal systems; agr. (wheat, rice). Comprises Sialkot, Gujranwala, Sheikhupura, Lyallpur, and part of Jhang dists.

Rechnitz (rĕkh'nĭts), Hung. *Rohonc* (rô'hônts), town (pop. 3,230), Burgenland, E Austria, 10 mi. NW of Szombathely, Hungary; fruit, vineyards.

Recife (rĭsē'fĭ) [Port.,=reef], city (1950 pop. 522,466), ⊙ Pernambuco, NE Brazil, Atlantic seaport (near easternmost point of Brazilian bulge) and Brazil's 3d-largest city, 1,150 mi. NNE of Rio de Janeiro; 8°3'S 34°51'W. Chief commercial center of the "finger states" of NE Brazil; exports sugar, rum, and molasses—Pernambuco being a leading sugar-growing state—and cotton, lumber and dyewood, fruit (especially pineapples), coconuts, castor beans, caroa fibers, hides, and diatomite (mined near by). Expanding industries include sugar refining, cotton milling, ironworking, pineapple canning, tomato preserving, flour milling; and mfg. of cement, asbestos, paper, roofing, leather goods. City is communications hub with coastwise and overseas shipping, and with rail lines and roads N to João Pessoa and Natal, W to Limoeiro and the interior (*sertão*), and S to Maceió (Alagoas); terminus of transatlantic cables. Ibura airport (U.S. air base in Second World War) is just S. City is built partly on mainland, partly on peninsula, and on isl. in a lagoon (enclosed by reef 50 ft. wide which shelters entire harbor), and is at mouths of small Beberibe and Capiberibe rivers. It is dissected by numerous waterways into separate dists. Best known are São José (commercial and financial dist. on sandy peninsula), Santo Antonio (govt. dist. on Antônio Vaz isl.), and Boa Vista (residential and modern commercial dist. on mainland, with state univ. founded 1945). Noteworthy bldgs. are the 17th-cent. cathedral, the basilica of Our Lady of Carmo, the Dutch fort of Buraco, the govt. palace, and the theater of Santa Isabel. Recife has Rockefeller-financed hosp. facilities, a modern water-supply and sewage-disposal system, and one of Brazil's largest electric plants. Its harbor has recently undergone extensive modernization and accommodates medium-sized vessels. City also contains a Braz. naval station. Recife was port for neighboring Olinda (1st settled in 1530s), and superseded the latter as ⊙ Pernambuco captaincy in 17th cent. Plundered 1595 by English privateer. Occupied (1630–54) by Dutch, and named Mauritzstad, city prospered under enlightened rule of Maurice of Nassau-Siegen. Sometimes called Pernambuco.

Recife, Cape (rùsēf'), S Cape Prov., U. of So. Afr., on Indian Ocean, on W side of entrance of Algoa Bay, 7 mi. SE of Port Elizabeth; 34°2'S 25°42'E; lighthouse, radio beacon.

Recifs Island (rāsēf'), one of the Seychelles, in Indian Ocean, 22 mi. ENE of Victoria; 4°35'S 55°46'E; ½ mi. long, ¼ mi. wide; granite formation.

Recinto (rāsēn'tō), village (1930 pop. 224), Ñuble prov., S central Chile, in Andean foothills, 27 mi. SE of Chillán; rail terminus for the sulphur springs of Termas de Chillán.

Recita, Rumania: see RESITA.

Recke (rĕ'kù), village (pop. 5,883), in former Prussian prov. of Westphalia, NW Germany, after 1945 in North Rhine-Westphalia, 15 mi. NW of Osnabrück; grain.

Reckingen (rĕ'kĭng-ùn), village (pop. 196), S Baden, Germany, at S foot of Black Forest, on the Rhine (Swiss border) and 7 mi. SE of Waldshut; hydroelectric plant.

Recklinghausen (rĕk'lĭng-hou"zùn), city (□ 25; 1950 pop. 104,857), in former Prussian prov. of Westphalia, W Germany, after 1945 in North Rhine-Westphalia, in the Ruhr, extending (S) to Rhine-Herne Canal (port), 13 mi. NW of Dortmund city center; transshipment point; coal-mining center, with coke works and extraction of coal-tar products; foundries. Mfg. of mining machinery and apparatus, pipes, garments, tower clocks, chimes, ceramics. Sawmills, breweries, distilleries. Has Romanesque church; castle. Site of observatory. Chartered 1236. Joined (1316) Hanseatic League. Passed to Prussia in 1815.

Recknitz River (rĕk'nĭts), N Germany, rises just S of Laage, flows c.45 mi. NE and NNW, past Bad Sülze, to an inlet of the Baltic at Damgarten.

Reco (rē'kō), village, W Alta., in Rocky Mts., near E side of Jasper Natl. Park, 40 mi. SSW of Edson; coal mining.

Recoaro Terme (rĕkôä'rô tĕr'mĕ), town (pop. 1,231), Vicenza prov., Veneto, N Italy, in Monti Lessini, 19 mi. NW of Vicenza; health resort (alt. 1,460 ft.) and winter-sports center, noted for its chalybeate baths. Bottling works, machine shops (agr. tools, wine presses). Barite quarries near by. Formerly Recoaro.

Recogne, Belgium: see LIBRAMONT.

Recoleta (rākōlā'tä), village (1930 pop. 309), Coquimbo prov., N central Chile, on railroad and 10 mi. NNE of Ovalle; grain, fruit, livestock. Irrigation dam on affluent of Limarí R.

Recoleta, E residential suburb (pop. 8,421) of Asunción, Paraguay.

Recôncavo (rĭkōng'kùvōō), fertile coastal lowland in E Bahia, Brazil, surrounding Todos os Santos Bay W of Salvador. Occupied by numerous small farmers (mostly descendants of Negro slaves), it grows quantities of sugar cane, tobacco, cotton, and subsistence crops (rice, manioc, beans). Well served by railroads from Salvador and São Roque do Paraguaçu. Bulky products shipped by barge across Todos os Santos Bay to Salvador. Chief towns: Santo Amaro, Cachoeira, Nazaré. In 1939 petroleum and natural gas were discovered just N of Salvador and on Itaparica Isl.

Reconquista (rākōngkē'stä), town (1947 pop. 12,607), ⊙ General Obligado dept. (□ 5,190; 1947 pop. 98,187), NE Santa Fe prov., Argentina, near Paraná R., 175 mi. NNE of Santa Fe; processing center in agr. area; sawmilling, corn milling, tanning, flax processing (fibers, linseed oil). Agr. products: cotton, rice, sunflowers, sugar cane, tobacco, potatoes.

Reconvilier (rùkōvēlyā'), town (pop. 2,245), Bern canton, NW Switzerland, on Birs R. and 7 mi. N of Biel; watches.

Recquignies (rùkēnyē'), village (pop. 1,339), Nord dept., N France, on the Sambre and 3 mi. E of Maubeuge; metalworks.

Recreio (rĭkrā'yōō), city (pop. 2,837), SE Minas Gerais, Brazil, near Rio de Janeiro border, 12 mi. E of Leopoldina; rail junction; coffee and sugar are grown.

Recreo (rĕkrā'ō), town (pop. 2,589), SE Catamarca prov., Argentina, on Córdoba prov. border, 70 mi. SE of Catamarca; road junction; cattle-raising center.

Recreo, El, Nicaragua: see EL RECREO.

Recreo, El, Venezuela: see EL RECREO.

Rector, city (pop. 1,855), Clay co., extreme NE Ark., in St. Francis R. valley, 18 mi. NE of Paragould, in farm area; cotton ginning, sawmilling.

Recuay (rākwī'), city (pop. 1,572), Ancash dept., W central Peru, on Santa R., in the Callejón de Huaylas, and 14 mi. SE of Huarás; alt. 11,043 ft. Mining center (silver, lead, copper).

Reculet, Mont (mō rùkùlā'), rocky summit (5,643 ft.) of the E Jura, in Ain dept., E France, 10 mi. WNW of Geneva, and immediately adjoining the CRÊT DE LA NEIGE.

Reculver (rĭkŭl'vûr), village and parish (pop. 829), NE Kent, England, on Thames estuary, 4 mi. E of Herne Bay; bathing resort. Has some remains of Roman fort of *Regulbium*, and ruins of 14th-cent. church, built on Saxon foundations.

Recz (rĕch), Ger. *Reetz* (rāts), town (1939 pop. 3,648; 1946 pop. 812) in Pomerania, after 1945 in Szczecin prov., NW Poland, on Ina R. and 20 mi. ESE of Stargard; woodworking. After 1945, briefly called Rzeczyca.

Reda or **Redaa,** Yemen: see RADA'.

Rédange (rädäzh'), Ger. *Redingen* (rā'dĭng-ùn), village (pop. 922), Moselle dept., NE France, on Luxembourg border, 3 mi. W of Esch-sur-Alzette; iron mining.

Redange (rädäzh'), village (pop. 823), W Luxembourg, 16 mi. NW of Luxembourg city; market center for agr. area (rye, oats, pulse, potatoes, cattle).

Redang Island (rùdäng'), island (□ 9; pop. 362) in South China Sea, N Trengganu, Malaya, 15 mi. off coast; 5°47'N 103°E.

Red Army Strait, Russian SFSR: see KRASNAYA ARMIYA STRAIT.

Red Bank, borough (pop. 12,743), Monmouth co., E N.J., on Navesink R. estuary and 5 mi. NE of Long Branch; mfg. (clothing, dishwashing machines, boats, soft drinks); nursery products, sand, gravel; fruit, truck. U.S. Fort Monmouth is S. Albert Brisbane helped establish a Fourierist community at near-by Phalanx, 1843. Revolutionary battle of Red Bank was not fought here, but at present NATIONAL PARK, on the Delaware. Inc. 1908.

Redbank Creek, W central Pa., rises in N Jefferson co., flows SW, past Brookville, and W, to Allegheny R. 11 mi. N of Kittaning; c.75 mi. long.

Red Basin, China: see SZECHWAN.
Red Bay, village (pop. 159), S Labrador, on the Strait of Belle Isle, 24 mi. WNW of Cape Norman, N.F.; 51°44'N 56°25'W; fishing port.
Red Bay, town (pop. 1,805), Franklin co., NW Ala., 32 mi. SW of Tuscumbia, at Miss. line; lumber, clothing. Settled 1898, inc. 1908.
Red Bird, town (pop. 411), Wagoner co., E Okla., 16 mi. NW of Muskogee, in agr. area; cotton ginning.
Red Bluff, city (pop. 4,905), ⊙ Tehama co., N Calif., at head of navigation on Sacramento R. and 140 mi. NNW of Sacramento; trading center for livestock and farm area. Inc. 1876.
Red Bluff Lake, extreme W Texas, reservoir (c.8 mi. long; capacity c.300,000 acre-ft.), formed in Pecos R. by Red Bluff Dam c.40 mi. NNW of Pecos; irrigates extensive farm area in Pecos R. valley to SE.
Red Boiling Springs, resort village (1940 pop. 865), Macon co., N Tenn., near Ky. line, 55 mi. NE of Nashville; mineral springs.
Redbourn, town and parish (pop. 2,091), W Hertford, England, on Ver R. and 4 mi. NW of St. Albans; agr. market. Church is partly Norman.
Redbrook, town in parish of Newland (pop. 2,061), W Gloucester, England, on Wye R. and 2 mi. SE of Monmouth; tinplate-rolling mills. Just E is agr. village of Newland, with 13th–14th-cent. church.
Red Bud (rĕd' bŭd"), city (pop. 1,519), Randolph co., SW Ill., 28 mi. SSW of East St. Louis, in agr. area (corn, wheat, truck, livestock); mfg. (wood products, flour, cigars). Inc. 1867.
Redbud, mining village (pop. 3,420, with adjacent Kenvir), Harlan co., SE Ky., in the Cumberlands, 8 mi. E of Harlan; bituminous coal.
Redcar, municipal borough (1931 pop. 20,160; 1951 census 27,512), North Riding, NE Yorkshire, England, on North Sea, 8 mi. NE of Middlesbrough; iron- and steel-milling center; seaside resort, with race course. Just W, on North Sea, is resort town of Coatham, just WSW is steel-milling town of Dormanstown, and 2 mi. W is steel-milling center of Told Point.
Redcastle, Scotland: see KILLEARNAN.
Red Cedar Lake, Barron co., NW Wis., 8 mi. NE of Rice Lake; c.6 mi. long, 1 mi. wide. Drained by Red Cedar R.
Red Cedar River. 1 In S central Mich., rises SW of Howell in Livingston co., flows c.45 mi. NW, past Fowlerville and East Lansing, to Grand R. at Lansing. Sometimes called Cedar R. **2** In Minn. and Iowa: see CEDAR RIVER. **3** In NW Wis., rises in Red Cedar L. (Barron co.), flows c.85 mi. S, past Rice Lake and Menomonie, to Chippewa R. 12 mi. S of Menomonie. Formerly important in lumbering industry.
Redcliff, town (pop. 1,289), SE Alta., near South Saskatchewan R., 6 mi. NW of Medicine Hat; natural-gas production; coal, shale, and clay mining; glass and pottery mfg.; stock raising.
Redcliff, town (pop. 556), Eagle co., W central Colo., on Eagle River, in Gore Range, and 18 mi. N of Leadville; alt. 9,608 ft. Silver, lead, and zinc mines in vicinity. Holy Cross Natl. Monument near by.
Redcliffe, town (pop. 8,871), SE Queensland, Australia, 17 mi. NNE of Brisbane, on Moreton Bay; summer resort. Penal settlement established 1824 near here.
Red Cliffs, town (pop. 3,798), NW Victoria, Australia, 205 mi. ENE of Adelaide; rail junction; dried fruit.
Red Cloud, city (pop. 1,744), ⊙ Webster co., S Nebr., 35 mi. S of Hastings and on Republican R., near Kansas line; flour; livestock, grain, dairy and poultry produce. Inc. 1872.
Redcloud Peak (14,050), SW Colo., in San Juan Mts., 16 mi. NE of Silverton.
Red Creek, village (pop. 617), Wayne co., W N.Y., 17 mi. SW of Oswego; mfg. (canned foods, silos, tanks); agr. (fruit, truck).
Red Creek, SE Miss., rises in S Lamar co., flows c.75 mi. SE to Pascagoula R. in N Jackson co.
Red Cut Heights, village (pop. 2,563), Bowie co., NE Texas.
Red Deer, city (pop. 4,042), S central Alta., on Red Deer R. and 90 mi. S of Edmonton; trade center; oil refining, lumbering, dairying, candy mfg.; grain elevators. Site of prov. training school. Railroad center of Red Deer Junction is 6 mi. N.
Red Deer Lake (14 mi. long, 10 mi. wide), W Man., near Sask. border, 55 mi. S of The Pas and 10 mi. W of N end of L. Winnipegosis. Drains E into L. Winnipegosis by Red Deer R.
Red Deer River, Alta., rises in Rocky Mts. in Banff Natl. Park, flows NE past Red Deer, turns sharply S to Drumheller, thence SE and E, through deep valley, past Empress, where it crosses into Sask., to South Saskatchewan R. 70 mi. NE of Medicine Hat; 385 mi. long.
Reddick. 1 Town (pop. 433), Marion co., N central Fla., 13 mi. NNW of Ocala; truck farming; limestone quarrying. **2** Village (pop. 208), on Livingston-Kankakee co. line, NE central Ill., 20 mi. W of Kankakee, in agr. and bituminous-coal area.
Redding, town in Grangemouth parish, SE Stirling, Scotland, 2 mi. SE of Falkirk; coal mining.
Redding. 1 City (pop. 10,256), ⊙ Shasta co., N Calif., on Sacramento R., near N end of Central Valley, and 170 mi. NNW of Sacramento; Shasta Dam and reservoir are just N. Trade and processing center for lumbering (pine), gold and copper mining, fruitgrowing and farming region; lumber and wood-products mills, metalworking plants, dairies. Gateway to hunting and fishing regions (W, N, and E) of Klamath and Cascade ranges. Lassen Volcanic Natl. Park is c.45 mi. E. Trading center in gold rush days; replaced Shasta as ⊙ Shasta co. in 1887. **2** Residential town (pop. 2,037), Fairfield co., SW Conn., on Saugatuck R. and 13 mi. NW of Bridgeport; includes part of GEORGETOWN village. Library here was gift of Mark Twain, a summer resident. Near-by Putnam Memorial Campground commemorates winter of 1778–79, spent here by Gen. Putnam's Revolutionary troops. Joel Barlow b. here. Settled c. 1711, inc. 1767. **3** Town (pop. 200), Ringgold co., S Iowa, near Mo. line, 31 mi. S of Creston.
Reddish, town in Stockport county borough, on Lancashire-Cheshire line, England, divided into North Reddish and South Reddish; cotton mills, metalworks, chemical works.
Redditch (rĕ'dĭch), urban district (1931 pop. 19,281; 1951 census 29,184), E Worcester, England, on Arrow R. and 12 mi. SSW of Birmingham; needle-mfg. center, producing also leather products, paper, machine tools, bicycles and motorcycles, batteries. Near by are ruins of early-12th-cent. Bordesley Abbey.
Redempção, Brazil: see REDENÇÃO, Ceará.
Reden, Saar: see LANDSWEILER-REDEN.
Redenção (rĭdĕnsä'ō). **1** City (pop. 1,482), N Ceará, Brazil, near railroad, 16 mi. NE of Baturité; sugar, cotton, coffee. Marble deposits. Formerly spelled Redempção. **2** City, São Paulo, Brazil: see REDENÇÃO DA SERRA.
Redenção da Serra (dä sĕ'rŭ), city (pop. 540), SE São Paulo, Brazil, in the Serra do Mar, 15 mi. S of Taubaté; livestock. Until 1944, called Redenção (old spellings, Redemção and Redempção).
Redenfelden, Germany: see KIRCHDORF.
Redenhall, England: see HARLESTON.
Rede River, Northumberland, England, rises on Carter Fell in the Cheviot Hills, flows 21 mi. SE, past Otterburn, to the North Tyne 2 mi. SE of Bellingham. Its picturesque valley is known as Redesdale.
Redesdale, England: see REDE RIVER.
Redeyef (rĕdĕyĕf'), village, Gafsa dist., W Tunisia, near Algerian border, on rail spur and 35 mi. W of Gafsa; Tunisia's leading phosphate-mining center. Sometimes called Redeyef-Mines.
Redfern, municipality (pop. 18,637), E New South Wales, Australia, 2 mi. SSW of Sydney, in metropolitan area; mfg. center (cutlery, shoes, confections, chemicals); brass foundries.
Redfield. 1 Town (pop. 291), Jefferson co., central Ark., 16 mi. NNW of Pine Bluff, near Arkansas R. **2** Town (pop. 892), Dallas co., central Iowa, on Middle Raccoon R. and 30 mi. W of Des Moines; brick and tile plants; soybean products. **3** City (pop. 173), Bourbon co., SE Kansas, 9 mi. W of Fort Scott; dairying, general agr. **4** City (pop. 2,655), ⊙ Spink co., NE central S.Dak., 40 mi. S of Aberdeen; resort, farm trade center; flour, dairy products, grain. Home for aged and school for feeble-minded are here.
Redfield, Mount (4,606 ft.), Essex co., NE N.Y., in the Adirondacks, 2 mi. SW of Mt. Marcy and 13 mi. S of Lake Placid village.
Red Fish Bay, Texas: see PORT MANSFIELD.
Redgorton (rĕdgôr'tŭn), agr. village and parish (pop. 1,677), SE Perthshire, Scotland, near the Tay, 4 mi. NW of Perth.
Redgranite, village (pop. 648), Waushara co., central Wis., on small Willow Creek and 27 mi. W of Oshkosh, in agr. area.
Redhill, village (pop. 202), S South Australia, 27 mi. SSE of Port Pirie; wheat, wool, livestock, fruit, dairy products. Sometimes spelled Red Hill.
Redhill, England: see REIGATE.
Red Hill, borough (pop. 914), Montgomery co., SE Pa., 16 mi. S of Allentown.
Red Hook. 1 Village (pop. 1,225), Dutchess co., SE N.Y., 20 mi. N of Poughkeepsie, in dairying and fruitgrowing area; mfg. (cider, dispensing machines, asbestos). **2** Section of New York city, N.Y.: see SOUTH BROOKLYN.
Redhook Point, E St. Thomas Isl., U.S. Virgin Isls., on Pillsbury Sound, and 5½ mi. E of Charlotte Amalie; 18°20'N 64°51'W.
Red House, village (pop. c.300), Cattaraugus co., W N.Y., in Allegany Indian Reservation, 5 mi. SW of Salamanca. Main entrance to Allegany State Park is here.
Red Indian Lake (□ 70), W central N.F., 5 mi. S of Buchans; 35 mi. long, 3 mi. wide. Receives Lloyds R. (W) and Victoria R. (S); drained by Exploits R. (E). Near N shore is Halfway Mtn. (1,400 ft.).
Redingen, France: see RÉDANGE.
Redington Beach, town (pop. 384), Pinellas co., W Fla., 10 mi. WNW of St. Petersburg.
Redinha (rĭdē'nyŭ), village (pop. 431), Leiria dist., W central Portugal, 23 mi. NNE of Leiria. Site of battle in Peninsular War (1811).
Red Island. 1 Island (□ 9; pop. 322), SE N.F., in Placentia Bay, 10 mi. NW of Argentia; 4 mi. long, 3 mi. wide. Fishing. **2** Island (pop. 69; 1 mi. long), S N.F., 6 mi. ENE of Burgeo; fishing. **3** Islet, SE Que., in the St. Lawrence, opposite mouth of Saguenay R.
Red Island, islet of The Skerries, in the Irish Sea, just N of Skerries town, NE Co. Dublin, Ireland.
Red Jacket. 1 Village, Houghton co., Mich.: see CALUMET. **2** Mining village (pop. 1,575), Mingo co., SW W.Va., 7 mi. ESE of Williamson, in bituminous-coal region.
Redkey or **Red Key,** town (pop. 1,639), Jay co., E Ind., 18 mi. NE of Muncie, in agr. area; canned foods, lumber.
Redkino (ryĕt'kēnŭ), town (1939 pop. over 500), S Kalinin oblast, Russian SFSR, on Volga Reservoir, 20 mi. SE of Kalinin; peat-working center.
Red Lake, village (pop. estimate 1,000), NW Ont., in Patricia dist., on Red L. (30 mi. long, 7 mi. wide), 110 mi. NW of Sioux Lookout; gold mining. Seaplane base, radio station.
Red Lake, county (□ 432; pop. 6,806), NW Minn.; ⊙ Red Lake Falls. Agr. area drained by Red Lake R. Corn, oats, barley, potatoes, dairy products, livestock. Formed 1896.
Redlake, village (pop. c.200), Beltrami co., NW Minn., on S shore of Lower Red L., in Red Lake Indian Reservation, and 28 mi. NNW of Bemidji. Indian school and reservation hq. are here.
Red Lake (□ 430; c.40 mi. long, 25 mi. wide), largely in Red Lake Indian Reservation and Beltrami co., NW Minn., N of Bemidji. Consists of 2 large bodies of water, Upper Red L. (□ 184; 21 mi. long, 10 mi. wide) and Lower Red L. (□ 246; 23 mi. long, 12 mi. wide). Lower Red L. is S of Upper Red L. and connected with it by strait (1–2.5 mi. wide), near W. shore, bet. two peninsulas. Lake was once part of glacial L. Agassiz. Village of Lower Red L. has W outlet in Red Lake R.
Red Lake Falls, city (pop. 1,733), ⊙ Red Lake co., NW Minn., on Red Lake R. and 18 mi. NE of Crookston. Resort; agr. trading point in farming area; dairy products, flour. Established as fur-trading post before 1800, inc. as village 1881, as city 1898.
Red Lake River, principal tributary of Red R. of the North, rises in Lower Red L., NW Minn., flows W to Thief River Falls, then S and W, past Red Lake Falls and Crookston, to Red River of the North at East Grand Forks, on S. Dak. line; 196 mi. long. Chief tributaries are Thief R. and Clearwater R.
Redland, village (1940 pop. 989), Dade co., S Fla., 26 mi. SW of Miami; vegetable packing.
Redlands, city (pop. 18,429), San Bernardino co., S Calif., 60 mi. E of Los Angeles, in San Bernardino Valley; trade and shipping center for large navel-orange-growing area; cans, packs, ships citrus fruit. Seat of Univ. of Redlands. Canyon Crest Park (Smiley Heights), 400-acre garden with many rare plants, is here. Near by is San Bernardino *asistencia* (restored), a branch (established 1830) of San Gabriel Mission. Inc. 1888.
Red Level, town (pop. 656), Covington co., S Ala., 10 mi. NW of Andalusia; lumber.
Red Lion, borough (pop. 5,119), York co., S Pa., 8 mi. SE of York; furniture, cigars. Inc. 1880.
Red Lodge, city (pop. 2,730), ⊙ Carbon co., S Mont., on branch of Clarks Fork of Yellowstone R., NE of Yellowstone Natl. Park, and 55 mi. SW of Billings; resort; dairy products, vegetables, grain; coal mines; beverages. Alt. 5,550 ft. Part of Custer Natl. Forest, in spur of Absaroka Range, is just W. Inc. 1895.
Red Lodge Creek, S Mont., rises in several branches in NE spur of Absaroka Range, flows c.50 mi. NE, past Boyd and Joliet, to the Clark Fork of Yellowstone R. 10 mi. S of Laurel. Drains grain and livestock area.
Redlynch, agr. village and parish (pop. 1,191), SE Wiltshire, England, 7 mi. SE of Salisbury.
Red Main (män), Ger. *Roter Main* (rō'tŭr mīn'), S headstream of the Main, W Germany, rises in the Franconian Jura 4 mi. WSW of Creussen, flows c.35 mi. N and NW, past Bayreuth, to Mainleus, where it joins the WHITE MAIN to form MAIN RIVER.
Redmon, village (pop. 226), Edgar co., E Ill., 8 mi. WNW of Paris, in agr. and bituminous-coal mining area.
Redmond. 1 City (pop. 2,956), Deschutes co., central Oregon, 16 mi. NNE of Bend in irrigated agr. area (clover, alfalfa seed, potatoes); alt. 2,996 ft.; lumber milling, dairying. Inc. 1910. **2** Town (pop. 600), Sevier co., central Utah, 5 mi. N of Salina and on Sevier R.; alt. 5,135 ft.; rock salt. **3** Town (pop. 573), King co., W central Wash., 10 mi. E of Seattle and on Sammamish R.; agr., dairy products, lumber.
Red Mountain, central Ala., ridge (c.1,000 ft.) of Great Appalachian Valley, largely in Jefferson co., extending SW-NE along right bank of Cahaba R., past Bessemer and Birmingham. Coal and iron mining. Statue of Vulcan is on crest of mtn. in Vulcan Park, in SE suburb of Birmingham.
Red Mountain Pass (alt. 11,018 ft.), in San Juan Mts., SW Colo., 6 mi. ESE of Telluride.

Red Mountains, spur of Continental Divide in S part of Yellowstone Natl. Park, NW Wyo., just SW of Yellowstone L. Highest point, Mt. Sheridan (10,385 ft.).

Rednitz River (rād'nĭts), Bavaria, Germany, formed at Georgensgmünd by the FRANCONIAN REZAT and the SWABIAN REZAT, flows 22 mi. N, past Roth and Stein, to Fürth, where it joins PEGNITZ RIVER to form REGNITZ RIVER.

Red Oak. 1 City (pop. 6,526), ⊙ Montgomery co., SW Iowa, on East Nishnabotna R. (hydroelectric plant) and 37 mi. ESE of Council Bluffs; rail junction; mfg. (art calendars, furnaces, feed, concrete and dairy products). Has a jr. col. Inc. 1869. **2** Town (pop. 568), Latimer co., SE Okla., 40 mi. E of McAlester; trade center for farm area; cotton ginning.

Redon (rúdõ'), town (pop. 5,156), Ille-et-Vilaine dept., W France, at junction of the Vilaine with Brest-Nantes Canal, 32 mi. SSW of Rennes; railroad and commercial center; marketing and shipping of dairy products, chestnuts, and food preserves. Mfg. (agr. machinery, furniture, fruit juices). Has a fine Romanesque and Gothic church with 12th-cent. central spire.

Redonda (rúdŏn'dú), islet (□ ½), dependency of Antigua presidency, Leeward Isls., B.W.I., bet. Nevis (NW) and Montserrat (SE), 34 mi. WSW of St. John's, Antigua; 16°55'N 62°19'W. The isolated rock, rising to c.1,000 ft., has phosphate of alumina mines, which were formerly worked.

Redonda Island (rĭdõn'dú), circular rock (alt. 820 ft.) in the Atlantic, off SE coast of Brazil, near entrance to Guanabara Bay, 10 mi. S of Rio de Janeiro.

Redonda Islands (rúdŏn'dú) (□ 108), SW B.C., group of 2 isls. in NE arm of the Strait of Georgia, at entrance of Toba Inlet, 20 mi. NE of Campbell River. W isl. is 14 mi. long, 2–8 mi. wide; E isl. is 10 mi. long, 1–7 mi. wide.

Redondela (rādōndā'lä), town (pop. 3,162), Pontevedra prov., NW Spain, railroad junction and Atlantic port on Vigo Bay, 7 mi. ENE of Vigo; fishing and fish processing, toy mfg., flour milling. Agr. trade (livestock, wine, cereals).

Redondela, La (lä), town (pop. 1,125), Huelva prov., SW Spain, 18 mi. W of Huelva; fruit, tubers, livestock.

Redondo (rĭdŏn'dōō), town (pop. 3,946), Évora dist., S central Portugal, 21 mi. ENE of Évora pottery-mfg. center.

Redondo Beach (rĭdŏn'dō), city (pop. 25,226) and beach resort, Los Angeles co., S Calif., on the coast, 13 mi. S of Santa Monica. Inc. 1892.

Redondo Peak, N.Mex.: see VALLE GRANDE MOUNTAINS.

Redorta, Pizzo (pē'tsō rĕdôr'tä), second highest peak (9,964 ft.) in Bergamasque Alps, Lombardy, N Italy, adjacent to Pizzo di Coca, 9 mi. SE of Sondrio. Has several small glaciers.

Redoubt, Mount (10,198 ft.), active volcano, S Alaska, W of Cook Inlet, 110 mi. WSW of Anchorage; 60°29'N 152°45'W.

Redován (rādōvän'), village (pop. 2,742), Alicante prov., E Spain, 4 mi. NE of Orihuela; hemp growing and processing; olive-oil, vegetables.

Red Peak, Colo.: see GORE RANGE.

Red Range, village (pop. 442), NE New South Wales, Australia, 180 mi. SSW of Brisbane; tin-mining center.

Redriff, London, England: see ROTHERHITHE.

Red River, Annamese *Song Ca* (shông'kä') or *Song Coi* (koi), Chinese *Yüan Kiang* (or *Chiang*) (yüän' jyäng') or *Hung Ho* (hoong' hŭ'), Fr. *Fleuve Rouge* (flûv' rōōzh'), longest river (c.730 mi.) of Tonkin (N Vietnam); rises in China's Yunnan prov. S of the lake Erh Hai at alt. of 6,500 ft., flows SE in deep, narrow gorge, past Yüankiang and Manhao (head of junk navigation), and into Vietnam, past Laokay, Viettri, Sontay, and Hanoi; below Hanoi, its vast delta on the Gulf of Tonkin constitutes the economic heart of N Vietnam. The port of Haiphong is on a N delta arm. Its lower course is followed by Hanoi-Kunming RR. Near Viettri, in a wide valley, it receives its main tributaries, the Black (right) and Clear (left) rivers. An irregular river, subject to floods (high water, June-Oct.), it is contained by dikes in delta. Its red color is the result of large quantities of iron oxide in water.

Red River. 1 Parish (□ 413; pop. 12,113), NW La.; ⊙ Coushatta. Bounded W by Bayou Pierre and Bayou Pierre L., E by Black Lake Bayou; intersected by Red R. Agr. (cotton, corn, hay). Natural gas, oil fields. Cotton ginning, lumber milling. Formed 1848. **2** County (□ 1,033; pop. 21,851), NE Texas; ⊙ Clarksville. Bounded N by Red R. (here the Okla. line), S by Sulphur R. Diversified agr. (cotton, corn, grains, hay, legumes, fruit, truck, pecans); livestock (cattle, horses); some dairying. Lumbering, lumber milling. Mfg., processing at Clarksville. Formed 1836.

Red River, residential town (pop. 346), York co., N S.C., on Catawba R. and 4 mi. NE of Rock Hill.

Red River. 1 In S U.S., southernmost of the large tributaries of the Mississippi, rises on the Llano Estacado of E N.Mex. and N Texas, flows SE and E, across Texas Panhandle and along Texas-Okla. line, across SW Ark. and diagonally across La., to point c.45 mi. NNW of Baton Rouge, La., where it enters 2 distributaries: ATCHAFALAYA RIVER, flowing S to Gulf of Mexico, and Old R., a channel continuing c.7 mi. SE to the Mississippi. Length, c.1,300 mi.; drains □ 91,400. Prairie Dog Town Fork, the main headstream, formed SW of Amarillo in the Panhandle of Texas by intermittent Palo Duro and Tierra Blanca creeks, flows SE to junction with Salt Fork NNW of Vernon, Texas, to form Red R.; soon receiving North Fork, the Red continues E to Fulton, Ark., where it turns and continues S and SE, past Shreveport and Alexandria, La., to head of its distributaries. Principal tributaries: Pease, Sulphur, Wichita, Washita, Little, Kiamichi, Ouachita (Black) rivers, Bodcau and Cypress bayous. Chief unit of Red R. basin development project is multi-purpose DENISON DAM, impounding L. Texoma in Texas and Okla.; dams and reservoirs for flood control, irrigation, and hydroelectric power have been completed or authorized on tributaries, and there is a navigation-improvement project on main stream. Shreveport is head of navigation at medium stages of river; at high water, steamer navigation is possible as far as Ark.-Okla. state line. Semiarid upper basin of the Red yields to rich red-clay farmlands (hence river's name) and, finally, to lowlands with many lakes and bayous in the lower valley. In 1833, work (continued for decades) was begun on clearing the Great Raft, a centuries-old log jam which extended c.160 mi. upstream from near Natchitoches, La., and long prevented extensive navigation. In the Civil War a military and naval expedition (1864) under Gen. N. P. Banks and Admiral Porter attempted to open the route to Texas via the river, but was defeated at Sabine Crossroads, La. **2** or **Red River of the North,** in U.S. and Canada, formed by confluence of Otter Tail and Bois de Sioux rivers at Wahpeton, N.Dak. (opposite Breckenridge, Minn.), flows N past Grand Forks, forming boundary bet. N.Dak. and Minn.; terminates in L. Winnipeg, Manitoba; 533 mi. long. Used for irrigation. Drains Red River Valley (bed of prehistoric L. Agassiz), rich wheat-growing area in N.Dak. and Minn. Navigable in summer to Fargo. Chief tributaries are Sheyenne R., in N.Dak., Red Lake R., in Minn., and Assiniboine R., in Manitoba. **3** E central Ky., rises in E Wolfe co., flows 57 mi. generally W past Clay City, to Kentucky R. 11 mi. SE of Winchester. **4** In S Ky. and N. Tenn., formed in S Logan co., Ky., by confluence of North and South forks; flows 56 mi. WSW to Cumberland R. at Clarksville, Tenn. **5** In N N.Mex., rises near Wheeler Peak in Sangre de Cristo Mts., flows c.40 mi. N and W, past Questa, to Rio Grande 8 mi. N of Arroyo Hondo.

Red River of the North, U.S. and Canada: see RED RIVER.

Red River Pass (alt. 9,852 ft.), N N.Mex., in Sangre de Cristo Mts., 23 mi. NE of Taos.

Red Rock or **Redrock,** town (pop. 253), Noble co., N Okla., 13 mi. NNE of Perry, in agr. area.

Red Rock Lakes, SW Mont., in Beaverhead co., 30 mi. W of Yellowstone Natl. Park, bet. Centennial Mts. (on Idaho line) and Gravelley Range. Lower Red Rock L. (7 mi. long, 3 mi. max. width) is connected to Upper Red Rock Lake (3 mi. long, 2 mi. wide) by Red Rock R., which flows through both lakes. U.S. migratory waterfowl refuge here.

Red Rock River, Mont.: see JEFFERSON RIVER.

Redruth, England: see CAMBORNE-REDRUTH.

Red Sea, anc. *Sinus Arabicus,* Arabic *Al Bahr al Ahmar,* elongated sea (□ 170,000) bet. Asia's Arabian Peninsula and NE Africa (Egypt, Anglo-Egyptian Sudan, Eritrea), in the Great Rift Valley; 1,400 mi. long, up to 220 mi. wide, over 7,000 ft. deep. Connected with Mediterranean Sea by Suez Canal, and with Gulf of Aden of Arabian Sea by the strait Bab el Mandeb. Its 2 N arms, the Gulf of Suez and Gulf of Aqaba, enclose the Sinai peninsula. Situated in a region where evaporation greatly exceeds precipitation, Red Sea water has a surface salinity of 41 per mill and summer temp. exceeding 85°F. Current circulation is conditioned by the prevailing winds, which blow from NNW (May-Sept.) and, in S part, from SSE (Oct.-April). Noted for an extremely hot, humid summer climate. Coral formations abound. The name of the sea is sometimes related to its red-colored algae. The Bible, in recounting the crossing of the Red Sea by the Israelites, probably intended the Gulf of Suez. An important trade route in antiquity, the Red Sea declined following the discovery of the sea route around the Cape of Good Hope. Since the opening (1869) of the Suez Canal, however, it has become one of the world's most active shipping lanes, linking Europe and Asia. It is chiefly important as a transit route, and its ports are minor. They are Suez, at S end of the Suez Canal; Port Sudan, Massawa, and Assab, on W coast; Aqaba, Jidda, and Hodeida, on E coast. Sea contains the Dahlak Archipelago, the Farasan and Kamaran isls. The anc. names Erythraean Sea (*Erythraeum Mare*) and *Rubrum Mare,* sometimes applied to the Red Sea, properly speaking referred to the waters surrounding the Arabian Peninsula: i.e., Red Sea, Arabian Sea, Persian Gulf.

Red Sea Frontier Province, Arabic *Al-Bahr al-Ahmar,* frontier province (settled area □ 24; pop. 22,065) of Egypt, in the Arabian Desert S of Suez, bet. the Nile and the Red Sea; ⊙ Hurghada. Here is the principal mineral wealth of Egypt, the oil and phosphate deposits near SAFAGA, HURGHADA, KOSSEIR.

Red Sea Hills, Egypt and Anglo-Egyptian Sudan: see ETBAI.

Red Slate Mountain (13,152 ft.), E Calif., in the Sierra Nevada, c.25 mi. S of Mono L.

Red Springs, town (pop. 2,245), Robeson co., S N.C., 26 mi. SW of Fayetteville; rayon and lumber mills. Seat of Flora Macdonald Col. Sulphur spring here. Settled c.1775.

Redstone, N.H.: see CONWAY.

Red Tank, town (pop. 1,951), Balboa dist., S Panama Canal Zone, on Miraflores L. (bet. Pedro Miguel and Miraflores Locks), on transisthmian railroad, and 6 mi. NW of Panama city; corn, rice, forage; livestock.

Reducción (rādōōksyōn'), town (pop. estimate 500), N Mendoza prov., Argentina, 28 mi. SE of Mendoza; wine, livestock.

Réduit, Le (lù rādüē'), village (pop. 226), W central Mauritius, in central plateau, on railroad and 1 mi. SSW of Moka; sugar milling. Governor's residence. Has a govt. agr. station.

Redvers (rĕd'vûrs), village (pop. 230), SE Sask., near Man. border, 40 mi. S of Moosomin; mixed farming.

Red Volta River (vŏl'tú), rises in Upper Volta (Fr. W. Africa) NW of Ouagadougou, enters Gold Coast 28 mi. WSW of Bawku, flows c.200 mi. SE and SSE to the White Volta R. 5 mi. NW of Gambaga.

Redwater, village (pop. estimate 150), central Alta., 32 mi. NE of Edmonton; oil production.

Redwater, town (pop. 451), Bowie co., NE Texas, 12 mi. WSW of Texarkana.

Redwater Creek, E Mont., rises in Prairie co., flows c.110 mi. NE, past Circle, to Missouri R. near Poplar.

Red Weisseritz River, Ger. *Rote Weisseritz* (rō'tú vī'sûrĭts), E central Germany, rises in the Erzgebirge just W of Altenberg, flows 20 mi. N, past Dippoldiswalde (irrigation dam), joining Wild Weisseritz R. just above Hainsberg to form the Weisseritz.

Red Willow, county (□ 716; pop. 12,977), S Nebr.; ⊙ McCook. Fertile agr. area bounded S by Kansas; drained by Beaver Creek and Republican R. Dairying; grain, livestock. Formed 1873.

Red Wing. 1 Village, Huerfano co., S Colo., on headstream of Huerfano R., in E foothills of Sangre de Cristo Mts., and 28 mi. WNW of Walsenburg; alt. 7,800 ft.; resort. Dude ranch near by. Blanca Peak 15 mi. SW. **2** City (pop. 10,645), ⊙ Goodhue co., SE Minn., on Mississippi R. near mouth of Cannon R., at NW end of L. Pepin, and 40 mi. SE of St. Paul; trade and industrial center for farming area; dairy products, beverages, flour; mfg. (pottery, sewer pipes, shoes, linseed oil, leather goods, foundry products). Reformatory for boys is here. Prehistoric fossils have been found in vicinity. City settled 1852, inc. 1857. Grew as brickmaking and pottery center.

Redwood, county (□ 874; pop. 22,127), SW Minn.; ⊙ Redwood Falls. Agr. area bounded N by Minnesota R. and drained by Redwood and Cottonwood rivers. Corn, oats, barley, livestock. Sioux Indian reservation is in NE. Co. formed 1862.

Redwood, resort village (pop. c.500), Jefferson co., N N.Y., bet. Mud and Butterfield lakes (fishing), 6 mi. ESE of Alexandria Bay.

Redwood City, city (pop. 25,544) and port, ⊙ San Mateo co., W Calif., c. 25 mi. SSE of San Francisco; connected by deepwater channel with the bay (just E). Residential and mfg. city (tanning, cement and saltmaking, food canning; mfg. of bearings, rubber goods, asbestos products); noted for chrysanthemum growing. In 1850s it was redwood-lumber center. Until 1858, called Embarcadero. Inc. 1868.

Redwood Falls, city (pop. 3,813), ⊙ Redwood co., SW Minn., on Redwood R. near its mouth in Minnesota R. and 35 mi. NW of New Ulm, in grain, stock, and poultry region; resort; shipping point for farm produce and granite from near-by quarries; dairy products, feed. Platted 1865, inc. as village 1875, as city 1891. Adjoining city is Alexander Ramsey State Park, picturesque area with gorges, cliffs, and falls.

Redwood River, rises NE of Pipestone, SW Minn., flows 80 mi. NE and E, past Marshall, to Minnesota R. near Redwood Falls.

Ree, Lough (lŏkh rē'), lake (18 mi. long, 7 mi. wide; 108 ft. deep), Ireland, on the Shannon, bet. cos. Roscommon (W), Longford (NE), and Westmeath (SE). Contains numerous islets. On S shore is Athlone.

Reed, plantation (pop. 351), Aroostook co., E Maine, 30 mi. E of Millinocket, in wilderness recreational area. Includes Wytopitlock (wī"tŭpĭt'lŏk) village.

Reed City, city (pop. 2,241), ⊙ Osceola co., central Mich., 12 mi. N of Big Rapids, near Muskegon R. Livestock, potatoes; dairy products; mfg. (preserved-wood products, foodstuffs, woolen goods); oil refining. Resort (hunting, fishing). Inc. as village 1875, as city 1932.

Reeder, village (pop. 339), Adams co., SW N.Dak., 16 mi. NW of Hettinger.

Reed Lake (□ 78), central Man., 50 mi. E of Flin Flon; 15 mi. long, 10 mi. wide. Drains N into Churchill R.

Reedley, city (pop. 4,135), Fresno co., central Calif., in San Joaquin Valley, 20 mi. SE of Fresno, and on Kings R.; packs, cans, and ships fruit, especially peaches and grapes. Reedley Col. (jr.) is here. Serves as gateway to Kings Canyon Natl. Park (c.30 mi. E). Founded 1889, inc. 1913.

Reeds, town (pop. 136), Jasper co., SW Mo., near Spring R., 9 mi. SE of Carthage.

Reedsburg, city (pop. 4,072), Sauk co., S central Wis., on Baraboo R. and 14 mi. WNW of Baraboo, in timber and agr. area (dairy products; livestock, poultry); mfg. (woolen goods, lumber, canned foods, condensed milk, beer). Inc. 1887.

Reeds Peak (10,011 ft.), SW N.Mex., in Black Range, 35 mi. W of Hot Springs.

Reedsport, city (pop. 2,288), Douglas co., W Oregon, on Umpqua R. near its mouth in the Pacific and c.55 mi. SW of Eugene; lumber, dairy products. Fisheries. Siuslaw Natl. Forest near by. Inc. 1919.

Reeds Spring, town (pop. 313), Stone co., SW Mo., in the Ozarks, near James R., 32 mi. S of Springfield.

Reedsville. 1 Village (pop. 1,238), Mifflin co., central Pa., 5 mi. NW of Lewistown and on Kishacoquillas Creek. **2** Town (pop. 321), Preston co., N W.Va., 10 mi. SE of Morgantown, in agr., coal-mining area. **3** Village (pop. 691), Manitowoc co., E Wis., 15 mi. WNW of Manitowoc, in grain belt; vegetable canning.

Reedville, village (pop. c.1,000), Northumberland co., E Va., on harbor of Chesapeake Bay, at tip of Northern Neck peninsula, 75 mi. SE of Fredericksburg; port of entry; fishing port; menhaden-processing center (oil, fertilizer, animal foods).

Reedy, town (pop. 352), Roane co., W W.Va., 27 mi. S of Parkersburg; flour and lumber mills.

Reedy Island, E Del., in Delaware R. just E of Port Penn; 1½ mi. long. Has U.S. quarantine and detention station; lighthouse.

Reedy River, NW S.C., rises in foothills of the Blue Ridge N of Greenville, flows c.65 mi. SSE, past Greenville, to a N arm of L. Greenwood.

Reefton, township (pop. 1,297), ⊙ Inangahua co. (□ 949; pop. 3,242), W S.Isl., New Zealand, 40 mi. NE of Greymouth; gold, coal mines. School of mines.

Ree Heights (rē), town (pop. 254), Hand co., central S.Dak., 10 mi. W of Miller; dairy products, livestock, poultry, grain.

Reelfoot Lake, extreme NW Tenn., near Mississippi R. and Ky. line, 90 mi. NNE of Memphis; c.20 mi. long, up to 5 mi. wide. Formed 1811–12 by earthquakes, which created a depression filled by inrushing Mississippi R. waters. Lake and surrounding wooded area set aside in 1925 as Reelfoot L. State Fish and Game Preserve; region is known for hunting, fishing.

Reengus, India: see SRI MADHOPUR.

Rees (rās), town (pop. 3,830), in former Prussian Rhine Prov., W Germany, after 1945 in North Rhine-Westphalia, on right bank of the Rhine and 10 mi. WSW of Bocholt. Scene (March, 1945) of Rhine crossing by Canadian troops.

Reese (rēs), village (pop. 632), Tuscola co., E Mich., 13 mi. E of Saginaw, in agr. area.

Reese Air Force Base, Texas: see LUBBOCK.

Reese River, central Nev., rises in S Toiyabe Range, flows c.150 mi. N, bet. Shoshone Mts. and Toiyabe Range, to sink into sands near Battle Mtn.; water used for irrigation.

Reeseville, village (pop. 470), Dodge co., S central Wis., 12 mi. S of Beaver Dam, in dairying region.

Reeve, Lake, long, narrow lagoon (□ 14), SE Victoria, Australia, 125 mi. E of Melbourne; separated from Tasman Sea by sandspit; extends c.35 mi. WSW, parallel with coast, from its opening at L. King.

Reeves, county (□ 2,600; pop. 11,745), extreme W Texas; ⊙ Pecos. Plains area, sloping to Pecos R. (NE boundary) from foothills of Davis Mts. (SW); alt. c.2,500–4,500 ft. Part of Red Bluff reservoir (irrigation, recreation) in N. Cattle, sheep ranching; cotton, hay, melons, truck farming in irrigated sections; some dairying, poultry. Some oil, sulphur production. Formed 1883.

Reeves, town (pop. 106), Allen parish, SW La., 22 mi. NE of Lake Charles city and on tributary of Calcasieu R.

Reevesby Island, Australia: see SIR JOSEPH BANKS ISLANDS.

Reevesville, town (pop. 285), Dorchester co., S central S.C., 25 mi. SSE of Orangeburg.

Refaat, Tell, Syria: see RIF'AT, TELL.

Refahiye (rĕfä'hĭyĕ), village (pop. 922), Erzincan prov., E central Turkey, 40 mi. WNW of Erzincan; grain, vetch.

Reform, town (pop. 1,141), Pickens co., W Ala., 30 mi. NW of Tuscaloosa; lumber.

Reforma or **La Reforma** (lä rāfôr'mä), town (pop. 529), Chiapas, S Mexico, 18 mi. WSW of Villahermosa; cereals, rubber, fruit.

Reforma, La, Guatemala: see LA REFORMA.

Reftele (rĕf'tālů), village (pop. 757), Jonkoping co., S Sweden, 16 mi. W of Varnamo; rail junction; machinery works.

Refugio (rĭfyōō'rēō, rĭfū'rēō), county (□ 771; pop. 10,113), S Texas; ⊙ Refugio. Bounded N by San Antonio R., SW by Aransas R., SE by Copano Bay, NE by San Antonio Bay; drained by Mission R. and Copano Creek. A leading Texas oil-producing co. Ranching (cattle; also sheep); some agr. (mainly cotton; also peanuts, grain sorghums, vegetables, fruit, flax). Oil refineries, pipelines. Formed 1836.

Refugio, town (pop. 4,666), ⊙ Refugio co., S Texas, on Mission R. and 39 mi. SW of Victoria; trade, shipping center for petroleum, cattle, agr. area (cotton, grain); oil refineries; pipelines to Aransas Pass; mfg. of steel tanks. Settled after 1829 around Sp. mission moved here 1795; became pueblo in 1834. Captured (1836) by Mexicans in Texas Revolution and again occupied by Mexicans in 1842.

Refugio Island, Philippines: see SAN CARLOS, Negros Occidental prov.

Regadera, La (lä rāgädā'rä), dam on a mtn. stream in Cundinamarca dept., central Colombia, 15 mi. S of Bogotá; hydroelectric plant.

Regal, village (pop. 64), Kandiyohi co., S central Minn., 22 mi. NNE of Willmar; dairying.

Regalbuto (rĕgälbōō'tô), town (pop. 10,732), Enna prov., E central Sicily, 21 mi. NE of Enna, in cereal- and grape-growing region. Gypsum mines near by.

Regalica River, Poland: see EAST ODER RIVER.

Regal Mountain (13,408 ft.), S Alaska, in Wrangell Mts., 130 mi. NE of Cordova; 61°44'N 142°52'W.

Regan, village (pop. 129), Burleigh co., central N. Dak., 27 mi. NNE of Bismarck.

Regar (ryĕgär'), town (1939 pop. over 500), NW Stalinabad oblast, Tadzhik SSR, on railroad and 30 mi. W of Stalinabad; cotton ginning.

Rega River (rĕ'gä), in Pomerania, after 1945 in NW Poland, rises in lake region NNE of Drawsko, flows N, SW past Swidwin and Lobez, and NW past Ploty, Gryfice, and Trzebiatow, to the Baltic 11 mi. WSW of Kolberg; 118 mi. long.

Regau (rā'gou), town (pop. 3,660), S central Upper Austria, just SE of Vöcklabruck, across Ager R.; wheat, cattle.

Regele-Carol II, Ukrainian SSR: see SUVOROVO.

Regele-Mihai I, Ukrainian SSR: see SUVOROVO.

Regen (rā'gůn), town (pop. 5,319), Lower Bavaria, Germany, in Bohemian Forest, on the Black Regen and 6 mi. SW of Zwiesel; mfg. of precision instruments, organs, matches; brewing. Chartered c.1258.

Regeneração (rĭzhĭnĭrŭsā'õ), city (pop. 1,616), central Piauí, Brazil, 12 mi. E of Amarante; sugar, cotton.

Regenhütte, Germany: see RABENSTEIN.

Regen River (rā'gůn), Bavaria, Germany, formed by BLACK REGEN RIVER and WHITE REGEN RIVER SW of Kötzting, flows 67 mi. W and S, past Cham, to the Danube at Stadtamhof.

Regensburg (rā'gůnzbûrg, Ger. rā'gůnsbŏŏrk), anc. *Castra Regina*, city (1946 pop. 108,604; 1950 pop. 116,997), ⊙ Upper Palatinate, E Bavaria, Germany, port on the Danube (which here reaches its northernmost point), and 65 mi. NNE of Munich; 49°1'N 12°6'E. Communications; industrial and cultural center; head of navigation for vessels over 1,000 tons. Shipbuilding; mfg. of machinery, precision instruments, pencils, soap, tobacco; printing, lime working, brewing, sugar refining. Trades in grain and wood. City has noted religious bldgs. St. Peter's Cathedral, with 10th- and 12th-cent. chapels, was started c.1250 and completed c.1520. St. Jacob's church (12th cent.) has noted carved portal. S wing of former Benedictine abbey St. Emmeran (founded in 7th cent.) was converted into castle in 19th cent.; abbey church has 8th–12th-cent. foundations and tombs of emperors Arnulf and Louis the Child. Former Benedictine nunnery, with 12th-cent. church, is residence of bishops (since 1821). Dominican church is early Gothic. City hall (old part built c.1350 on Romanesque foundations; new part dates from 17th and 18th cent.) was seat (1663–1806) of Imperial Diet. The Porta Praetoria, a Roman gate, was built A.D. 179. City is site of several noted museums, a theological acad., an institute for research in music, an observatory. A Celtic settlement, then a Roman camp, Regensburg became a bishopric in 739. Its capture by Charlemagne in 788 inaugurated 500 years of prosperity. Created free imperial city in 1245; owned considerable territory. Decline began in 15th cent. City suffered through capture and plague in Thirty Years War. Given by Napoleon to Bavaria in 1810, and became ⊙ Upper Palatinate. Occupied by U.S. troops in April, 1945. An airplane-mfg. center until 1945, Regensburg was repeatedly bombed during Second World War. The 11th- and 18th-cent. Old Chapel was damaged; and the mid-12th-cent. stone bridge (Steinerne Brücke), an architectural marvel of the Middle Ages, was blown up. Albrecht Altdorfer and Kepler died here. Sometimes called, in English, Ratisbon (ră'tĭzbŏn, –tĭs–).

Regenstauf (rā'gůn-shtouf), village (pop. 3,969), Upper Palatinate, E Bavaria, Germany, on the Regen and 8 mi. NNE of Regensburg; mfg. (chemicals, metal products, tar paper); whortleberry wine. Limestone quarried in area.

Regent, village (1931 pop. 531), Sierra Leone colony, on Sierra Leone Peninsula, at N foot of Sugar Loaf Mtn., 4 mi. SSE of Freetown.

Regent, village (pop. 405), Hettinger co., SW N. Dak., 10 mi. WNW of Mott and on Cannonball R.

Regente Feijó (rĭzhĕn'tĭ fāzhô'), city (pop. 2,117), W São Paulo, Brazil, on railroad and 9 mi. SE of Presidente Prudente; coffee processing, pottery mfg., sawmilling.

Regenwalde, Poland: see RESKO.

Reger, town (pop. 103), Sullivan co., N Mo., 6 mi. SW of Milan.

Reggan or **Reggane** (rĕgän'), Saharan oasis of the Touat group, in Aïn-Sefra territory, central Algeria, 90 mi. SSE of Adrar; 26°42'N 0°11'E. Junction of trans-Saharan auto tracks from Colomb-Béchar and In-Salah to Gao (Fr. West Africa). Date palms.

Reggello (rĕd'jĕl-lô), village (pop. 814), Firenze prov., Tuscany, central Italy, 15 mi. ESE of Florence, on W slope of the Pratomagno; paper and woolen mills; wine, furniture.

Reggio di Calabria (rĕd'jô dē kälä'brēä), often simply **Reggio Calabria**, province (□ 1,510; pop. 578,262), Calabria, S Italy; ⊙ Reggio di Calabria. On southernmost part of "toe" of Italy; separated from Sicily by Strait of Messina. Has mtn. and hill terrain, culminating in the ASPROMONTE; small plain borders Gulf of Gioia (W). Watered by small rivers. Agr. (citrus fruit, olives, grapes, cereals); stock raising (sheep, goats). Lumbering. Fishing on W coast. Mfg. at Reggio di Calabria, Gioia Tauro, Palmi, Locri. Damaged by many earthquakes, especially those of 1783 and 1908.

Reggio di Calabria, often simply **Reggio Calabria**, anc. *Rhegium*, city (pop. 60,342), ⊙ Reggio di Calabria prov., Calabria, S Italy, port on E coast of Strait of Messina, 7 mi. SE of (opposite) Messina (reached by ferry from near-by Villa San Giovanni); 38°6'N 15°39'E. Produces perfumes and pharmaceuticals from citrus fruit, mfg. (electrical apparatus, furniture, glass, macaroni); foundries; fisheries. Exports citrus fruit, figs, olive oil, wine, raw silk. Archbishopric. Has Greek and Roman remains (baths, theater, town walls), ruined medieval castle, archaeological mus., citrus fruit experimental station. Suffered many earthquakes; rebuilt after those of 1783 and 1908. Founded by Chalcidians and Messenians in 8th cent. B.C.; became a flourishing commercial city. Destroyed (387 B.C.) by Dionysius the Elder; taken by Romans in 270 B.C. In Second World War damaged by air and naval bombing (1943).

Reggiolo (rĕd-jô'lô), town (pop. 2,495), Reggio nell'Emilia prov., Emilia-Romagna, N central Italy, 7 mi. E of Guastalla; wine making.

Reggio nell'Emilia (rĕd'jô nĕlĕmē'lyä), often simply **Reggio Emilia**, province (□ 885; pop. 375,288), Emilia-Romagna, N central Italy; ⊙ Reggio nell'Emilia. Extends from Etruscan Apennines N to Po R.; bet. Enza (W) and Secchia (E) rivers. Plain (N) occupies c.50% of area. Agr. (cereals, fodder, grapes); cattle raising. Wine making and dairying extensively carried on. Mfg. at Reggio nell'Emilia and Guastalla.

Reggio nell'Emilia, often simply **Reggio Emilia**, anc. *Regium Lepidi*, city (pop. 49,069), ⊙ Reggio nell'Emilia prov., N central Italy, 15 mi. WNW of Modena and on small branch of the Po, on the Aemilian Way; 44°42'N 10°38'E. Industrial and agr. center; mfg. (locomotives, automobile chassis, airplane engines, electrical apparatus, cement, bricks, pharmaceuticals, photographic materials, agr. machinery, wine, alcohol, sausage). Bishopric. Has cathedral, church of Madonna della Ghiara (late 16th cent.; fine frescoes), 17th-cent. palace, seminary, technical school, mus., and theater (1825–57). Ariosto and Secchi b. here. A Roman town; became member of Lombard League in Middle Ages; later ruled by Este dukes of Modena until 1859. Bombed (1944) in Second World War.

Reghin (rĕghēn'), Ger. *Sächsisch-Regen* (zĕk'sĭsh-rā'gůn), Hung. *Szászregen* (säs'rĕgĕn), town (1948 pop. 9,599), Mures prov., central Rumania, in Transylvania, on Mures R. and 16 mi. NNE of Targu-Mures; rail junction and trading center, notably in lumber, grain, fruit, hides; woodworking, flour milling, tanning, bast-fiber processing, mfg. of edible oils, alcohol, tiles, bricks. Extensive vineyards and orchards near by. Has 14th-cent. Gothic church, restored. Town was founded in 12th cent. by Saxon colonists. In Hungary, 1940–45.

Regima or **Er-Regima** (ĕr-rĕjē'mä), village (pop. 1,007), W Cyrenaica, Libya, near edge of plateau, on railroad and 16 mi. E of Benghazi; cereals, esparto grass; sheep.

Regina (rĭjī'nů), city (pop. 60,246), ⊙ Saskatchewan, in S part of prov., on Waskana (Wascana) Creek and 350 mi. W of Winnipeg; 50°28'N 104°37'W; alt. 1,885 ft. Principal Sask. wheat, dairy, and poultry market; railroad center, with stockyards, auto-assembly plant, meat-packing, woodworking, printing, and bookbinding plants,

oil refineries; mfg. of shoes, mattresses, dry batteries, castings. Site of Regina Col., Campion Col., Legislative Bldg.; western hq. of Royal Canadian Mounted Police. Has several parks. Founded 1882, Regina became ⊙ Northwest Territories and hq. of North West Mounted Police in 1883. Made ⊙ Sask. when prov. was created, 1905.
Régina (rāzhēnä'), town, ⊙ Approuague commune (pop. 751), N Fr. Guiana, landing on Approuague R. and 45 mi. SSE of Cayenne; sawmills; radio station.
Regina Beach, village (pop. 309), S Sask., on Last Mountain L., 28 mi. NW of Regina; resort.
Regis-Breitingen (rā'gĭs-brī'tĭng-ùn), town (pop. 4,935), Saxony, E central Germany, on Pleisse R. and 4 mi. SW of Borna; lignite mining.
Regisheim, France: see Réguisheim.
Registan (rā'gĭstän″), sandy desert in S Afghanistan, on Baluchistan (Pakistan) border, S of Kandahar; 150 mi. across. Separated from the desert Dasht-i-Margo by Helmand R. (NW). Baluch nomad pop.
Registro (rĭzhē'strōō), city (pop. 1,174), S São Paulo, Brazil, on Ribeira de Iguape R., in humid coastal lowland, and 23 mi. NW of Iguape. Rice, sugar, bananas intensively cultivated by Japanese settlers. Railhead at Juquiá (18 mi. NE).
Registro do Araguaya, Brazil: see Araguaiana.
Regla (rā'glä), city (pop. 23,037), Havana prov., W Cuba, on SE shore of Havana Harbor, opposite Havana (linked by ferry); railhead and industrial center. Has foundries, oil refineries, barite-grinding plant, shipyards, docks, and warehouses; mfg. of shoes, soap, vermicelli, soft drinks. In early 19th cent. it was a great smuggling center.
Reglitz River, Germany and Poland: see East Oder River.
Regniéville, France: see Thiaucourt.
Regnitz River (räg'nĭts), Bavaria, Germany, formed at Fürth by the Pegnitz and the Rednitz, flows 40 mi. N, almost parallel to Ludwig Canal, past Erlangen, Forchheim, and Bamberg, to the Main 3 mi. NW of Bamberg (head of canalized section). Receives the Wiesent (right) and the Aisch (left). Navigable for small vessels.
Regnum, England: see Chichester.
Régny (rānyē'), village (pop. 1,245), Loire dept., SE central France, on the Rhins and 7 mi. ESE of Roanne; mfg. of calico, pencils.
Régoa, Portugal: see Pêso da Régua.
Regöly (rĕ'gûl), town (pop. 2,701), Tolna co., W central Hungary, on Kapos Canal and 22 mi. NW of Szekszard; wheat, barley, vineyards.
Rego Park (rē'gō), SE N.Y., a residential section of Queens borough of New York city.
Reguengo Grande (rĭgāng'gōō grăn'dĭ), agr. village (pop. 1,256), Lisboa dist., central Portugal, 9 mi. SSW of Caldas da Rainha.
Reguengos de Monsaraz (rĭgāng'gōōsh dĭ mōsùräzh'), town (pop. 4,962), Évora dist., S central Portugal, 23 mi. SE of Évora; rail-spur terminus; woodworking, olive-oil and winemaking.
Réguisheim (rāgēzĕm'), Ger. *Regisheim* (rä'gĭshīm), village (pop. 1,256), Haut-Rhin dept., E France, in Alsace lowland, on the Ill and 10 mi. N of Mulhouse; potash mining.
Rehali, India: see Rehli.
Rehania or **Rehana,** Israel: see Rihaniya.
Rehar River, India: see Rihand River.
Rehau (rā'ou, rā'hou), town (pop. 9,207), Upper Franconia, NE Bavaria, Germany, on small Schwesnitz R. and 7 mi. SE of Hof; mfg. of porcelain, shoes, excelsior; weaving, metal- and woodworking, tanning. Kaolin quarried in area.
Rehavia (rĕhäv'yä), residential W suburb of Jerusalem, E Israel. Has bldgs. of Jewish Agency, Jewish National Fund, and Palestine Foundation Fund; Terra Sancta Col. temporarily houses Hebrew Univ., whose bldgs. on Mt. Scopus are surrounded by Arab-controlled territory.
Rehburg (rā'bōōrk), town (pop. 2,874), in former Prussian prov. of Hanover, W Germany, after 1945 in Lower Saxony, 11 mi. S of Nienburg. **Bad Rehburg** (pop. 900), climatic health resort with mineral baths, is 2 mi. S.
Rehden, Poland: see Radzyn, Bydgoszcz prov.
Rehli (rā'lē), village, Saugor dist., N Madhya Pradesh, India, on Sonar R. and 26 mi. SE of Saugor; wheat, oilseeds, millet. Sometimes spelled Rehali.
Rehme (rā'mù), village (pop. 6,122), in former Prussian prov. of Westphalia, NW Germany, after 1945 in North Rhine-Westphalia, on left bank of the Weser, at mouth of Werre R., and 6 mi. SW of Minden.
Rehna (rā'nä), town (pop. 3,519), Mecklenburg, N Germany, 16 mi. ESE of Lübeck; woolen milling, jam making, woodworking. Chartered 1791.
Rehoboth, Palestine: see Rehovot; Ruheiba.
Rehoboth (rĭhō'bùth), town, central South-West Africa, near Tropic of Capricorn, 50 mi. S of Windhoek; alt. 4,546 ft.; center of dist. (□ c.12,420; pop. 16,084) inhabited chiefly by Rehoboth Bastards, tribe of mixed Negro and European origin, who migrated from Cape Colony early in 19th cent. and retain a form of local self-govt. Gold mining began here 1932, ceased after 1941.
Rehoboth. 1 or **Rehoboth Beach,** resort town (pop. 1,794), Sussex co., SE Del., on Atlantic coast 5 mi. SE of Lewes, on Lewes and Rehoboth Canal; canneries; fishing, bathing. Settled c.1675, inc. 1873. **2** Village, Somerset co., SE Md., 23 mi. S of Salisbury and on Pocomoke R. Presbyterian church here was built 1705–6. **3** Town (pop. 3,700), Bristol co., SE Mass., 8 mi. E of Providence, R.I.; enameling. Long called Seekonk or Seeconck; included present town of Seekonk until 1812. Settled 1636, inc. 1645.
Rehoboth Bay, SE Del., lagoon (c.5 mi. long, 3 mi. wide) just S of Rehoboth; joined by channel to Indian River Bay (S); separated from the Atlantic by barrier beach. Lewes and Rehoboth Canal mouth at N end.
Réhon (rāō'), SSW suburb (pop. 3,908) of Longwy, Meurthe-et-Moselle dept., NE France, on Chiers R.; blast furnaces, foundries. Iron mines. Also spelled Rehon.
Rehovot, Rehovoth (both: rĕhōvōt', rĕhō'–), or **Rehoboth** (rĭhō'bùth, –bōth, –bōt), settlement (1950 pop. 15,000), W Israel, in Judaean Plain, on railroad and 13 mi. SSE of Tel Aviv; citrus-growing center; mfg. of pharmaceuticals, glass, breakfast cereals; fruit processing, metalworking, dairying. Site of Weizmann Institutes of Biochemistry, Biophysics, and Technology; Daniel Sieff Research Institute; Agr. Col. of Hebrew Univ.; and citrus-research laboratories. Residence of Chaim Weizmann, 1st President of Israel. Reputed site of biblical city of Rehoboth is Ruheiba.
Rehti (rā'tē), town (pop. 2,189), S Bhopal state, India, 36 mi. S of Bhopal; wheat, oilseeds. Large teak forests (N).
Rehue River, Chile: see Malleco River.
Rei, Iran: see Rai.
Reibell (rābĕl'), village (pop. 2,899), Alger dept., N central Algeria, on the High Plateaus, 50 mi. SW of Boghari; sheep, wool, esparto. Administrative seat of Chellala commune.
Reï-Bouba (rā'-bōō'bä), village, Benoué region, N Fr. Cameroons, on Reï R. (arm of the Benue) and 75 mi. SE of Garoua; peanuts, millet; cattle. Sometimes spelled Rey-Bouba.
Reichenau (rī'khùnou), town (pop. 4,932), SE Lower Austria, on Schwarza R. and 11 mi. W of Neunkirchen, in the Höllental, at SE foot of the Raxalpe; summer resort (alt. 1,597 ft.).
Reichenau, Czechoslovakia: see Rychnov and Rychnov nad Kneznou.
Reichenau, island and commune (□ 1.5; pop. 2,024) in the Untersee (a part of L. of Constance), S Baden, Germany, 4 mi. W of Constance; connected with shore by 1-mi.-long causeway. Winegrowing, fishing. Seat (724–1799) of Benedictine abbey, a missionary and cultural center in Middle Ages.
Reichenau, Poland: see Bogatynia.
Reichenau bei Gablonz, Czechoslovakia: see Rychnov.
Reichenbach (rī'khùnbäkh). **1** Town (pop. 3,158), in former Prussian Lower Silesia prov., E central Germany, after 1945 in Saxony, in Upper Lusatia, 8 mi. W of Görlitz, in lignite-mining region; mfg. (chemicals, paint, optical glass). **2** Town (pop. 34,708), Saxony, E central Germany, at foot of the Erzgebirge, 11 mi. SW of Zwickau; textile-industry center (cotton, wool, silk, rayon, linen, jute; printing, dyeing, carpetmaking); machinery and china mfg. **3** or **Reichenbach an der Fils** (än dĕr fĭls'), village (pop. 4,100), N Württemberg, Germany, after 1945 in Württemberg-Baden, on the Fils and 7 mi. E of Esslingen; grain.
Reichenbach or **Dzierzoniow** (jĕr-zhō'nyōōf), Pol. *Dzierżoniów*, town (1939 pop. 17,253; 1946 pop. 16,646) in Lower Silesia, after 1945 in Wroclaw prov., SW Poland, at NE foot of the Eulengebirge, 30 mi. SSW of Breslau (Wroclaw); cotton milling, metalworking, mfg. of machinery, electrical equipment, radios; grain and cattle market. Gothic church. Austrians were defeated here, 1762, by Prussians under Frederick the Great. Two treaties were signed here. By the 1st (1790), Austria agreed with Prussia to renounce Austrian acquisition of Turkish territory. By the 2d (1813), Austria conditionally agreed to join the coalition against Napoleon. Also Reichenbach im Eulengebirge.
Reichenbach, town (pop. 2,607), Bern canton, SW central Switzerland, on Kander R. and 9 mi. WSW of Interlaken; year-round resort.
Reichenbach, stream in the Bernese Alps, central Switzerland, flowing to the Aar at Meiringen. Noted for the Upper and Lower **Reichenbach Falls;** the former (almost 300 ft. high) is one of the highest in the Alps. The magnificent cascades have now disappeared because of a hydroelectric project. Here Professor Moriarty wrestled to his death.
Reichenbach an der Fils, Germany: see Reichenbach, Württemberg.
Reichenbach im Eulengebirge, Poland: see Reichenbach.
Reichenberg, Czechoslovakia: see Liberec.
Reichenburg, Yugoslavia: see Rajhenburg.
Reichenhall, Bad, Germany: see Bad Reichenhall.
Reichenstein, town, Wroclaw prov., Poland: see Zloty Stok.
Reichenstein Mountains (rī'khùn-shtīn″), Ger. *Reichensteiner Gebirge* (rī'khùn-shtī″nür gùbĭr'gù), Czech *Rychleské Hory* (rĭkh'lĕskā hô'rĭ), Pol. *Góry Złotostockie* (gōō'rĭ zwôtôstôts'kyĕ), range of the Sudetes on Lower Silesia (after 1945, SW Poland) and N Bohemia (Czechoslovakia) border; extend from Glatzer Neisse R. NW of Zloty Stok c.20 mi. SSE; rise to 2,959 ft. 5 mi. SSE of Zloty Stok.
Reichenweier, France: see Riquewihr.
Reichersberg (rī'khùrsbĕrk), village (pop. 1,642), W Upper Austria, on Inn R. and 8 mi. S of Schärding; market center.
Reichertshofen (rī″khùrts-hō'fùn), village (pop. 2,033), Upper Bavaria, Germany, on Paar R. and 8 mi. S of Ingolstadt; metalworking, food processing.
Reichraming (rīkh'rämĭng), town (pop. 2,778), E Upper Austria, on Enns R. and 11 mi. S of Steyr; brass mfg.
Reichshof, Poland: see Rzeszow, city.
Reichshoffen (rĕsh-ôfĕn'), Ger. *Reichshofen* (rīkhs'-hōfùn), town (pop. 2,802), Bas-Rhin dept., E France, 10 mi. NW of Haguenau; metalworking center (cables, springs, rolling stock); cotton and sawmilling. Gives its name to a Fr. attack (1870) in Franco-Prussian War. Obelisk to Fr. dead of that war.
Reichstadt, Czechoslovakia: see Zakupy.
Reichweiler, France: see Richwiller.
Reid, La (lä rīt'), agr. village (pop. 1,342), Liége prov., E Belgium, 16 mi. SE of Liége.
Reidat al 'Abdul Wadud (rā'dù ăl ăbdōōl' wädōōd'), **Raida** or **Raydah** (rā'dù), village and oasis, Quaiti state, Eastern Aden Protectorate, on Gulf of Aden, 50 mi. ENE of Shihr; airfield. Sometimes called Reidat al Quaiti.
Reideburg (rī'dùbōōrk), village (pop. 5,101), in former Prussian Saxony prov., central Germany, after 1945 in Saxony-Anhalt, 3 mi. E of Halle city center.
Reiden (rī'dùn), town (pop. 2,486), Lucerne canton, N Switzerland, near Wigger R., 9 mi. SSE of Olten; metalworking, textiles (cotton, woolen). Former lodge of Knights of Malta.
Reidsville (rēdz'–). **1** City (pop. 1,266), ⊙ Tattnall co., E central Ga., 32 mi. SW of Statesboro, in agr. area (tobacco, cotton, sweet potatoes); sawmilling. State penitentiary near by. Inc. 1838. **2** City (pop. 11,708), Rockingham co., N N.C., 20 mi. NNE of Greensboro; important cigarette-mfg. center and tobacco market; also a port of entry. Settled c.1815; inc. 1873.
Reidville, town (pop. 236), Spartanburg co., NW S.C., 12 mi. SW of Spartanburg.
Reifnig, Yugoslavia: see Ribnica, N Slovenia.
Reigate (rī'gĭt), residential municipal borough (1931 pop. 30,825; 1951 census 42,234), E central Surrey, England, 20 mi. S of London, at edge of North Downs; leatherworking, glass mfg. Near by are sand and stone quarries and deposits of fuller's earth. There are remains of Norman castle, with caves or vaults. The church (partly Norman) has tomb of Lord Howard of Effingham. In municipal borough (E) is residential town of Redhill; some mfg. (leather, chemicals, printing machinery).
Reignier (rĕnyā'), village (pop. 579), Haute-Savoie dept., SE France, near the Arve, 8 mi. SE of Geneva, in Faucigny valley; cheese mfg.
Reijen, Netherlands: see Rijen.
Reikjavik, Iceland: see Reykjavik.
Reilingen (rī'lĭng-ùn), village (pop. 3,653), N Baden, Germany, after 1945 in Württemberg-Baden, on the Kraichbach and 2 mi. SE of Hockenheim; sugar beets, tobacco.
Reillanne (rāyän'), village (pop. 449), Basses-Alpes dept., SE France, 7 mi. WNW of Manosque; winegrowing, footwear mfg., truffle shipping.
Reimannshau, Poland: see Rymanow.
Reims, city, France: see Rheims.
Reims, Montagne de (mōtä'nyù dù rĕs'), wooded tableland in Marne dept., N France, bet. Rheims (N) and Épernay (S); 15 mi. long, 5 mi. wide. Vineyards on its slopes are chief suppliers of champagne industry.
Reina (rā'nä), town (pop. 858), Badajoz prov., W Spain, 5 mi. SE of Llerena; cereals, olives, livestock.
Reina, La, Nicaragua: see San Ramón.
Reina Adelaida, Archipiélago de la, Chile: see Adelaide Islands.
Reinach (rī'näkh). **1** Town (pop. 4,580), Aargau canton, N Switzerland, 8 mi. SE of Aarau; tobacco, flour, metal products; printing. **2** Residential town (pop. 2,813), Basel-Land half-canton, N Switzerland, 4 mi. S of Basel.
Reinbeck (rīn'bĕk), town (pop. 1,460), Grundy co., central Iowa, 18 mi. SW of Waterloo; rail junction; canned corn and asparagus, packed poultry, feed. Inc. 1877.
Reinbek (rīn'bĕk), residential village (pop. 9,465), in Schleswig-Holstein, NW Germany, 10 mi. E of Hamburg city center; metal- and woodworking.
Reindeer Depot, trading post, NW Mackenzie Dist., Northwest Territories, on E channel of Mackenzie R. delta, 50 mi. S of its mouth, 40 mi. NE of Aklavik; 68°43'N 134°7'W; radio station. Field hq. for Reindeer Grazing Reserve (□ 6,600; 170 mi. long, 50 mi. wide), which extends NE and includes Richards Isl. Reserve was established 1935; in 1946 herd numbered c.4,000.
Reindeer Lake (□ 2,444), NE Sask. and NW Man.; 57°N 102°W; alt. 1,150 ft.; 150 mi. long, 30 mi.

wide. Contains numerous isls. Drains S by Reindeer R. into Churchill R.

Reine, Norway: see SORVAGEN.

Reine, La (lä rĕn'), village (pop. 425), W Que., on Ont. border, 50 mi. NNW of Rouyn; gold, copper, zinc mining.

Reineke or **Reyneke** (ryā'nyĭkyĭ), town (1948 pop. over 500), S Maritime Territory, Russian SFSR, on **Reineke Island** (in Peter the Great Bay; 1.5 mi. long and wide), 15 mi. SSW of Vladivostok; fish canning.

Reinerz, Bad, Poland: see DUSZNIKI ZDROJ.

Reinfeld (rīn'fĕlt), town (pop. 6,340), in Schleswig-Holstein, NW Germany, near the Trave, 9 mi. W of Lübeck; mfg. of knäckebröd; flour milling. Fish hatcheries. Chartered 1827. Matthias Claudius b. here.

Reinheim (rīn'hīm), village (pop. 3,665), S Hesse, W Germany, in former Starkenburg prov., on the Gersprenz and 9 mi. ESE of Darmstadt; grain.

Reinheim, village (pop. 714), SE Saar, on Fr. border, on Blies R. and 6 mi. ENE of Sarreguemines; clay quarrying; stock, grain.

Reinickendorf (rī'nĭkŭndôrf"), district (1939 pop. 200,531; 1946 pop. 192,901), NW Berlin, Germany, on the Havel and 6 mi. NW of city center. Mfg. of locomotives, machinery, electrical equipment; light-metal milling. After 1945 in French sector.

Reinosa, Mexico: see REYNOSA.

Reinosa (rānō'sä), city (pop. 8,481), Santander prov., N Spain, in Old Castile, 25 mi. S of Torrelavega; agr. trade center; metalworking (railroad equipment); mfg. of asphalt, glass, ceramics; brewery; dairy and flour products; meat processing. Potatoes, cattle, and lumber in area. Summer resort. Near by rises Ebro R. Lignite and lead mines in vicinity.

Reinovo, Russian SFSR: see DZHALINDA.

Reinsdorf (rīns'dôrf). **1** Village (pop. 7,284), Saxony, E central Germany, 3.5 mi. SE of Zwickau; coal mining. **2** Village (pop. 3,536), in former Prussian Saxony prov., central Germany, after 1945 in Saxony-Anhalt, 3 mi. NW of Wittenberg; cardboard and brick mfg.

Reirson: see RAKAHANGA.

Reisbach (rīs'bäkh), village (pop. 1,657), Lower Bavaria, Germany, on the Great Vils and 22 mi. E of Landshut; grain, cattle. Has 14th–15th-cent. church. Chartered 1470.

Reisdorf (rīs'dôrf), village (pop. 276), E Luxembourg, on Sûre R. and 5 mi. E of Diekirch, near Ger. border; liquor distilling; agr. (nuts, plums, apples).

Reisduoddarhaldde, Norway: see HALTIA, MOUNT, Finland.

Reisen. 1 Town, N.Kyongsang prov., Korea: see YECHON. **2** Town, S.Chungchong prov., Korea: see YESAN.

Reisen, Poland: see RYDZYNA.

Reishahr, Iran: see RISHAHR.

Reishu, Korea: see YOJU.

Reisterstown (rī'stŭrztoun), residential village (1940 pop. 1,577), Baltimore co., N Md., 17 mi. NW of downtown Baltimore, in agr. area; makes radio equipment. Seat of Hannah More Acad. (for girls). Montrose School (a state training school for delinquent girls; chartered 1831) is near by. Settled 1758 by Germans.

Reisui, Japan: see YOSU.

Reitoca (rātō'kä), town (pop. 298), Francisco Morazán dept., S central Honduras, on Reitoca R. (upper course of Nacaome R.) and 10 mi. W of Sabanagrande; corn, livestock.

Reitz (rāts), town (pop. 3,956), E Orange Free State, U. of So. Afr., 30 mi. N of Bethlehem; alt. 5,200 ft.; grain elevator.

Reitzenhain (rī'tsŭnhīn), village (pop. 1,970), Saxony, E central Germany, in the Erzgebirge, 7 mi. SE of Marienberg; frontier station on Czechoslovak border, 11 mi. NW of Chomutov; woodworking.

Rejaf (rĕjăf'), town, Equatoria prov., S Anglo-Egyptian Sudan, on left bank of the Bahr el Jebel (White Nile) and 7 mi. S of Juba (present head of navigation). Until 1928, head of Nile navigation from Khartoum. Formerly in Lado Enclave (leased to Belgian Congo, 1894–1910).

Rejang River, Borneo: see RAJANG RIVER.

Rejmyra (rā'mü"rä), village (pop. 676), Ostergotland co., SE Sweden, 17 mi. NNW of Norrkoping; glass mfg.

Rejowiec or **Rejowiec Lubelski** (rĕyô'vyĕts lŏobĕl'skē), village (commune pop. 8,432), Lublin prov., E Poland; 35 mi. ESE of Lublin; rail junction; cement plant. A smaller Rejowiec (or Rejowiec Poznanski) is in Poznan prov. of W central Poland.

Rejstejn, Czechoslovakia: see KASPERSKE HORY.

Reka (rĕ'kä), Ital. *Timavo* (tēmä'vô), largest of subterranean rivers of the Karst, NW Yugoslavia and Free Territory of Trieste, rises 10 mi. N of Rijeka (Fiume), Yugoslavia, flows c.30 mi. WNW to Skocjan (see DIVACA), disappearing underground and finally emerging near Duino, on Adriatic coast, at Italian-Trieste line.

Reka Devnya (rĕkä' dĕv'nyä), village (pop. 666), Stalin dist., E Bulgaria, on branch of Provadiya R. and 15 mi. W of Stalin; flour milling. Ruins of Roman town of Marcianopolis, founded (1st cent. A.D.) by Emperor Trajan, are just W.

Rekata Bay, Solomon Isls.: see SANTA ISABEL.

Rekingen (rā'kĭng-ŭn), village (pop. 449), Aargau canton, N Switzerland, on the Rhine (Ger. border) and 6 mi. N of Baden; hydroelectric plant.

Rekiniki (ryĕkē'nyĭkē), village (1948 pop. over 500), S Koryak Natl. Okrug, Kamchatka oblast, Khabarovsk Territory, Russian SFSR, on Penzhina Bay, 170 mi. NE of Palana, on isthmus of Kamchatka Peninsula. Coal deposits are SW.

Rekkem (rĕ'kŭm), town (pop. 4,526), West Flanders prov., NW Belgium, on Fr. border, 6 mi. WSW of Courtrai; textile milling.

Relangi (rā'lŭng-gē), town (pop. 9,739), West Godavari dist., NE Madras, India, in Godavari R. delta, 36 mi. E of Ellore; rice and oilseed milling; tobacco, sugar cane.

Relay (rē'lā"), suburban village (pop. c.2,000), Baltimore co., central Md., on Patapsco R. and 8 mi. SW of downtown Baltimore; large distilleries. Patapsco State Park is near.

Relecq-Kerhuon, Le (lŭ rŭlĕk'-kĕrüō), town (pop. 3,419), Finistère dept., W France, on Elorn R. estuary (bridge) and 5 mi. E of Brest; marble quarry. Damaged in Second World War.

Reliance, village (district pop. 94), SE Mackenzie Dist., Northwest Territories, at head of McLeod Bay of Great Slave L.; 62°43'N 109°9'W; trading post; Royal Canadian Mounted Police post.

Reliance. 1 Town (pop. 215), Lyman co., S central S.Dak., 13 mi. E of Kennebec. **2** Village (1940 pop. 710), Sweetwater co., SW Wyo., near Bitter Creek, 5 mi. N of Rock Springs; coal mines.

Religione, Punta (pōōn'tä rĕlējô'nĕ), point on SE coast of Sicily; 36°42'N 14°47'E.

Relizane (rĕlēzän'), town (pop. 19,688), Oran dept., NW Algeria, on the Oued Mina and 28 mi. SE of Mostaganem, in the Tell; important rail junction and trade center of irrigated lowland growing cotton, citrus fruit, apricots, and early vegetables. Olive-oil pressing, brick and cement mfg. Horses, wool, skins, and oriental rugs traded here. Oil deposits located at Tliouanet (8 mi. SW).

Relleu (rĕlyĕ'ōō), town (pop. 1,230), Alicante prov., E Spain, 12 mi. SE of Alcoy; olive-oil processing, flour milling; almonds, fruit.

Rellingen (rĕ'lĭng-ŭn), village (pop. 6,549), in Schleswig-Holstein, NW Germany, adjoining (SE) Pinneberg, in region noted for tree nurseries; mfg. (textiles, leather goods, tobacco products). Residence (1798–1816) of F. L. Schröder.

Rellinghausen (rĕ'lĭng-hou"zŭn), district (since 1910) of ESSEN, W Germany, on the Ruhr and 3 mi. SE of city center. Has 14th–19th-cent. castle.

Reloncaví Sound (rālōngkävē'), inlet of the Pacific in Llanquihue prov., S central Chile, N of Gulf of Ancud. Puluqui Isl. is at its entrance (S), and the port of Puerto Montt is at its head (N). Its numerous inhabited isls. include Maillén and Guar. An arm, Reloncaví Strait, extends inland (E) to receive Petrohué R., outlet for L. Todos los Santos.

Remagen (rā'mä"gŭn), town (pop. 4,954), in former Prussian Rhine Prov., W Germany, after 1945 in Rhineland-Palatinate, on left bank of the Rhine (rail bridge) and 12 mi. SSE of Bonn; rail junction. Here, in March, 1945, Allied (U.S.) troops crossed the Rhine for 1st time in Second World War. Waters of near-by mineral spring are exported as well-known Apollinaris water.

Rémalard (rāmälär'), village (pop. 914), Orne dept., NW France, on the Huisne and 12 mi. SE of Mortagne; cider distilling, stock raising.

Remanso (rĭmä'sōō), city (pop. 3,050), N Bahia, Brazil, near Piauí border, on left bank of São Francisco R. (navigable) and 100 mi. WSW of Juàzeiro; ships maniçoba rubber, carnauba wax, caroa fibers. Has hosp. Airfield.

Remate de Males (rĭmä'tĭ dĭ mä'lĭs), town (pop. 258), W Amazonas, Brazil, on right bank of Javari R. (Peru border), opposite Amelia (Peru), and 40 mi. W of Benjamin Constant. Called Benjamin Constant until 1939.

Rembang (rĕmbäng'), town (pop. 13,791), central Java, Indonesia, port on Java Sea, 100 mi. WNW of Surabaya; 6°42'S 111°22'E; trade center; batik making. Exports petroleum products, teak, rubber, peanuts, rice, cassava.

Rembau (rĕmbou'), village (pop. 755), central Negri Sembilan, Malaya, on W coast railroad and 14 mi. SE of Seremban; rice, timber. Chief town of Rembau, one of the original Negri Sembilan states.

Rembertow (rĕmbĕr'tōōf), Pol. *Rembertów*, town (pop. 13,842), Warszawa prov., E central Poland, 7 mi. E of Warsaw city center; mfg. of munitions, furniture.

Rembrandt, town (pop. 296), Buena Vista co., NW Iowa, 20 mi. ENE of Cherokee; feed.

Remda (rĕm'dä), town (pop. 1,336), Thuringia, central Germany, 6 mi. NW of Rudolstadt; glass mfg. Sometimes called Stadtremda (shtät'rĕm'dä).

Remedios (rāmā'dyōs), town (pop. 1,162), Antioquia dept., NW central Colombia, in Cordillera Central, 40 mi. NW of Puerto Berrío and connected by highway with Zaragoza 35 mi. NNW; alt. 2,525 ft. Gold mining; corn, sugar cane, beans, rice, cacao. Founded 1560.

Remedios or **San Juan de los Remedios** (sän' whän' dā lōs), town (pop. 10,485), Las Villas prov., central Cuba, on railroad and 26 mi. ENE of Santa Clara; trading and processing center in region known for its tobacco; also coffee, sugar cane, fruit. Mfg. of cigars, liquor, sweets, soap, shoes, brooms. Stone quarrying. Near by are the centrals of Adela and San Agustín (S).

Remedios, village (pop. 886), Chiriquí prov., W Panama, in Pacific lowland, on Inter-American Highway and 40 mi. ESE of David. Hardwood lumbering, stock raising.

Remedios de Escalada (dā ĕskälä'dä), industrial city (pop. estimate 30,000) in S Greater Buenos Aires, Argentina, adjoining Lanús, 7 mi. SSW of Buenos Aires; textiles, precision instruments, insecticides, gloves, dairy and food products.

Remenauville, France: see THIAUCOURT.

Remennikovo (ryĭmyĕ'nyĭkŭvŭ), village (1939 pop. over 500), N Stalingrad oblast, Russian SFSR, 23 mi. NW of Kamyshin; wheat, sunflowers. Until 1941 (in German Volga Autonomous SSR), Oberdorf.

Remer (rē'mŭr), resort village (pop. 412), Cass co., N central Minn., 32 mi. E of Walker, in lake and forest area; dairy products. Greater Leech Lake Indian Reservation is near by.

Remerschen (rā'mŭrshĕn), village (pop. 585), extreme SE Luxembourg, 5 mi. S of Remich, near Moselle R. and Saar border; vineyards; plum growing.

Remich (rā'mĭkh), town (pop. 1,716), SE Luxembourg, on Moselle R. and 11 mi. ESE of Luxembourg city, on Ger.-Saar border; vineyards; mfg. (cement, gypsum products); market center for agr. area (wheat, barley, pulse, sugar beets). Suffered considerable destruction (1944–45) in Second World War.

Remicourt (rŭmēkōōr'), town (pop. 1,195), Liége prov., E Belgium, 12 mi. WNW of Liége; mfg. of dairy machinery.

Remington. 1 Town (pop. 1,053), Jasper co., NW Ind., 12 mi. S of Rensselaer, in grain and livestock area. **2** Town (pop. 309), Fauquier co., N Va., on Rappahannock R. and 13 mi. S of Warrenton. Called Rappahannock Station (răpŭhă'nŭk) at time of Civil War; here (Nov., 1863) Union forces won an engagement.

Rémire (rāmēr'), town (commune pop. 539), N Fr. Guiana, on Cayenne Isl., 5 mi. SE of Cayenne; sugar, cacao, coffee, tropical fruit.

Remiremont (rŭmērmō'), town (pop. 8,562), Vosges dept., E France, on upper Moselle R. and 13 mi. SSE of Épinal, in the W Vosges; textile mfg. center. Breweries, metalworks. Until Fr. Revolution site of a noted convent. Abbatial palace now houses town hall (damaged in Second World War).

Remla, Tunisia: see KERKENNAH.

Remmel Dam, Ark.: see OUACHITA RIVER, Ark. and La.

Remolino (rāmōlē'nō), town (pop. 3,465), Magdalena dept., N Colombia, on lower Magdalena R. and 20 mi. S of Barranquilla; cotton-growing center.

Remolinos (rāmōlē'nōs), village (pop. 1,498), Saragossa prov., NE Spain, on Tauste Canal and 20 mi. NW of Saragossa; sugar beets, cereals. Rock-salt mines near by.

Remontnaya, Russian SFSR: see DUBOVSKOYE.

Remontnoye (ryĭmônt'nŭyŭ), village (1926 pop. 5,408), SE Rostov oblast, Russian SFSR, on left headstream of Sal R. and 35 mi. NW of Stepnoi; flour mill; wheat, cotton, livestock.

Remote Mountain (11,000 ft.), SW B.C., in Coast Mts., 190 mi. NW of Vancouver; 51°27'N 125°30'W.

Remouchamps or **Sougné-Remouchamps** (sōōnyā'-rŭmōōshä'), village (pop. 2,269), Liége prov., E Belgium, on Amblève R. and 12 mi. SE of Liége; paving-stone quarrying; tourist resort. Hydroelectric power plant for NONCEVEUX power station. Near by are Château de Montjardin, a modern castle, and caverns created by subterranean stream.

Remoulins (rŭmōōlē'), village (pop. 1,236), Gard dept., S France, on the Gard and 12 mi. NE of Nîmes; road center; sandal mfg., olive-oil pressing; olive and cherry growing. The PONT-DU-GARD is 1.5 mi. NW.

Removka (ryĕ'mŭfkŭ), town (1939 pop. over 500), E Stalino oblast, Ukrainian SSR, in the Donbas, 3 mi. WSW of Snezhnoye; coal mines.

Rempang (rĕmpäng'), island (□ c.75), Riouw Archipelago, Indonesia, just SE of Batam isl., 30 mi. SE of Singapore; 13 mi. long, 7 mi. wide. Timber, pepper, copra, fish.

Remscheid (rĕm'shīt), city (□ 25; 1950 pop. 102,929), in former Prussian Rhine Prov., W Germany, after 1945 in North Rhine-Westphalia, on the Wupper, adjoining Solingen (W) and Wuppertal (N); 51°11'N 7°11'E. Located in ironworking region, it is center of Ger. tool industry: machine and precision tools, cutlery, wrenches, drills; tools for metal, wood, and electrical industry; agr. and gardening implements, crankshafts. Other products: electric steel, machinery, pipes, fittings, locks, measuring instruments, kitchen furnishings, ice skates, roller skates. Textile mfg. (centering at suburbs Lennep and Lüttringhausen): cotton, silk, artificial silk, rayon, worsteds, woollens, knitted goods, ribbons. Bridge across the Wupper (350 ft. above river) connects city with Solingen (W).

Chartered 1808. Second World War damage (about 80%) concentrated in Remscheid proper; suburbs of Lennep and Lüttringhausen (both inc. 1927) escaped major destruction. Remscheid masonry dam (2.5 m. SW) is oldest in Germany (completed 1891).

Remsen. **1** (rĕm'zŭn) Town (pop. 1,280), Plymouth co., NW Iowa, 10 mi. E of Le Mars; livestock, grain. A fire in 1936 destroyed many bldgs. Founded 1839. **2** (rĕm'sŭn) Village (pop. 483), Oneida co., central N.Y., 16 mi. N of Utica, in limestone-producing area. A state park is near by.

Rems River (rĕms), N Württemberg, Germany, rises 4 mi. SW of Aalen, flows 50 mi. generally W, past Schwäbisch Gmünd, to the Neckar 4 mi. ESE of Ludwigsburg.

Remuna (rā'mōōnŭ), village, Balasore dist., NE Orissa, India, 5 mi. WNW of Balasore. Noted Vishnuite temple, visited annually by pilgrims.

Remus (rē'mŭs), village (pop. c.600), Mecosta co., central Mich., 18 mi. W of Mt. Pleasant, in agr. area (livestock, poultry, grain, truck; dairy products.

Rémuzat (rāmüzä'), village (pop. 247), Drôme dept., SE France, in Dauphiné Pre-Alps, 11 mi. ENE of Nyons.

Remy (rā'mē), village (pop. 1,064), St. James parish, SE La., on the Mississippi, 15 mi. ESE of Donaldsonville.

Ren (rān), residential village (pop. 823), Gavleborg co., E Sweden, on Ljusna R., just N of Bollnas.

Rena (rā'nä), village (pop. 845) in Amot (Nor. *Åmot*) canton (pop. 5,231), Hedmark co., E Norway, at foot of the Osterdal, on Glomma R. at mouth of Rena R., on railroad and 25 mi. NNE of Hamar; cardboard and wood-pulp milling.

Rena (rā'nä), town (pop. 326), Badajoz prov., W Spain, 30 mi. ENE of Mérida; cereals, grapes.

Renage (rŭnäzh'), village (pop. 1,466), Isère dept., SE France, in Voiron industrial dist., 15 mi. NW of Grenoble; paper milling, mfg. of edge-tools, agr. equipment, and silk fabrics.

Renaico (rānī'kō), town (pop. 2,224), Malleco prov., S central Chile, 10 mi. NE of Angol; rail junction and agr. center (grain, peas, potatoes, wine, livestock); flour milling.

Renaix (rŭnā'), Flemish *Ronse* (rôn'sŭ), town (pop. 25,959), East Flanders prov., SW central Belgium, 6 mi. S of Oudenaarde; textile center (cotton weaving, artificial silk). Church with 12th–15th cent. crypt.

Renala Khurd (rānä'lŭ kōōrd), village, Montgomery dist., SE Punjab, W Pakistan, 10 mi. NE of Okara, on Lower Bari Doab Canal; local market for wheat, cotton; cotton ginning, fruit farming and canning (citrus, mangoes). Hydroelectric station. Agr. farm 7 mi. ESE.

Rena River (rā'nä), Hedmark co., SE Norway, rises E of Tynset near head of the Osterdal, flows 100 mi. S, through Storsjo, to Glomma R. at Rena.

Renault (rŭnō'), village (pop. 2,113), Oran dept., N Algeria, in the coastal Dahra range, 45 mi. ENE of Mostaganem; cereal- and winegrowing; lumbering.

Renazé (rŭnäzā'), town (pop. 2,332), Mayenne dept., W France, 23 mi. SW of Laval; slate quarry.

Renca (rĕng'kä), village (pop. estimate 500), NE San Luis prov., Argentina, on railroad, 65 mi. NE of San Luis; wheat, flax, alfalfa, livestock. Has old church. San Felipe dam is on Contara R. near by.

Renca, town (pop. 1,534), Santiago prov., central Chile, just NW of Santiago; resort and residential suburb. Fruitgrowing; noted for its strawberries.

Renchen (rĕn'khŭn), village (pop. 2,471), S Baden, Germany, 8 mi. NNE of Offenburg; metal- and woodworking. Tobacco.

Rencontre East (rŏn'kŏntŭr, rŏnkŏn'tŭr), village (pop. 328), SE N.F., at head of Belle Bay, arm of Fortune Bay, 50 mi. NE of Grand Bank; 47°39'N 55°13'W; fishing port; site of largest govt. bait depot in N.F.

Rende (rĕn'dĕ), town (pop. 2,176), Cosenza prov., Calabria, S Italy, 5 mi. NW of Cosenza; licorice, bricks, pottery.

Rendina, Greece: see RENTINA.

Rendina, Gulf of, Greece: see STRYMONIC GULF.

Rendova (rĕndō'vŭ), volcanic island in the New Georgia group, Solomon Isls., SW Pacific, 10 mi. S of New Georgia isl., across Blanche Channel; 15 mi. long, 5 mi. wide.

Rendsburg (rĕnts'bōōrk), town (pop. 35,502), in Schleswig-Holstein, NW Germany, harbor bet. Kiel Canal and Eider R., 18 mi. W of Kiel; rail junction; foundries; shipbuilding; mfg. of cranes, bathtubs, stoves, fertilizer, radios, ceramics, glass products, textiles; woodworking. Canal is here crossed (138 ft. above water) by steel railroad bridge (1.5 mi. long), approached by loop-shaped ramp; total length of structure: 4.6 mi. Rendsburg consists of the old town (on isl. in the Eider), Neuwerk dist. (S), and industrial suburbs (N). Has 13th-cent. church. Chartered 1253. Was fortress from late-17th cent. until 1856.

Rendville, village (pop. 301), Perry co., central Ohio, 9 mi. SE of New Lexington, in coal-mining area.

Renedo (rānā'dhō). **1** Village (pop. 1,169), Santander prov., N Spain, 5 mi. E of Torrelavega; dairy products; cereals, fruit; lumber. **2** Town (pop. 1,133), Valladolid prov., N central Spain, 5 mi. E of Valladolid; cereals, vegetables, wine.

Reneia or **Rinia** (both: rĭnē'ŭ), Lat. *Rhenea* (rēnē'ŭ), Aegean island (□ 5.3; pop. 58), in the Cyclades, Greece, 10 mi. E of Syros isl.; 37°24'N 25°13'E; 5 mi. long, 2 mi. wide; fisheries. Also called Megale [great] Delos as opposed to Mikra [little] Delos or Delos (E).

Renen, Netherlands: see RHENEN.

Renens (rŭnā'), town (pop. 4,587), Vaud canton, W Switzerland, 2 mi. WNW of Lausanne; tiles, chemicals; metal- and woodworking.

Renéville (rŭnāvēl'), village, S Middle Congo territory, Fr. Equatorial Africa, 40 mi. NW of Brazzaville; copper and zinc mining.

Renfrew (rĕn'frōō), county (□ 3,009; pop. 54,720), SE Ont., on Ottawa R. and on Que. border; ⊙ Pembroke.

Renfrew, town (pop. 5,511), SE Ont., on Bonnechère R. and 50 mi. W of Ottawa; woolen milling, woodworking, dairying; mfg. of refrigerators, electrical equipment, machinery, motors, stoves. Iron, mica, and graphite mining near by.

Renfrew or **Renfrewshire** (-shĭr), county (□ 242.9; 1931 pop. 288,586; 1951 census 324,652), SW Scotland, on the Firth of Clyde at mouth of the Clyde; ⊙ Renfrew. Bounded by Ayrshire (S) and Lanark (E). Besides the Clyde, it is drained by Black Cart Water, White Cart Water, and Gryfe rivers. Hilly in W, rising to 1,711 ft., leveling toward E. Stock raising and dairying; coal, oil-shale, and iron mining. Mfg. of thread and shipbuilding are important; other industries include tanning (Bridge of Weir), mfg. of textiles (Paisley, Johnstone), chemicals, sugar refining, and whisky distilling. Besides Renfrew, other towns are major ports of Greenock, Gourock, and Port Glasgow; also Paisley, Barrhead, Johnstone, Bridge of Weir, and Kilmacolm. Port of Glasgow city is in Renfrew. There are several old castles.

Renfrew, burgh (1931 pop. 14,986; 1951 census 17,093), ⊙ Renfrewshire, Scotland, in NE part of co., on the Clyde and 5 mi. WNW of Glasgow. One of the oldest Clyde ports, dating from early 12th cent., it has shipyards and mfg. of boilers, aircraft instruments, soap, paint, cables. Just W is airport for Glasgow. In 1164 Malcolm IV here defeated Somerled, Lord of the Isles. In 1397 Robert III made Renfrew a burgh. The Prince of Wales has held title of baron of Renfrew since 1404. NE sector of burgh is in Lanark.

Renfrow (rĕn'frō), town (pop. 68), Grant co., N Okla., 37 mi. NNE of Enid, in agr. area.

Rengam (rĕng"äm'), town (pop. 1,321), NW Johore, Malaya, on railroad and 40 mi. NW of Johore Bharu; rubber plantations.

Rengat (rĕng"ät'), town (pop. 1,949), E central Sumatra, Indonesia, port on Indragiri R. and 150 mi. ENE of Padang; 0°25'S 102°32'E; rubber-production center. Accessible to small seagoing ships. Also spelled Ringat.

Rengit (rĕng"ĭt'), village (pop. 1,087), SW Johore, Malaya, 18 mi. SE of Bandar Penggaram; coconuts; fisheries.

Rengo (rĕng'gō), town (pop. 6,730), ⊙ Caupolicán dept. (□ 595; pop. 51,502), O'Higgins prov., central Chile, in the central valley, on railroad and 18 mi. SSW of Rancagua; agr. center (beans, corn, oranges, wine, cattle). Meat-processing plants, tanneries, match factory, sawmills.

Renholmen (rān'hōl"mŭn), fishing village (pop. 313), Vasterbotten co., N Sweden, on Gulf of Bothnia, 20 mi. NNE of Skelleftea; dairying.

Reni, India: see TARANAGAR.

Reni (ryĕ'nyē), town (1941 pop. 8,001), SW Izmail oblast, Ukrainian SSR, on the Danube (Rum. border), just below Prut R. mouth, and 11 mi. E of Galati, on railroad; customs station; commercial center; lumber milling, brickworks; grain trade.

Renick (rĕ'nĭk). **1** Town (pop. 157), Randolph co., N central Mo., 5 mi. S of Moberly. **2** or **Falling Springs,** town (pop. 307), Greenbrier co., SE W. Va., on Greenbrier R. and 13 mi. NNE of Lewisburg. Droop Mtn. Battlefield State Park is N.

Renier (rŭnyā'), village (pop. 844), Constantine dept., NE Algeria, on the High Plateaus, 8 mi. SW of Guelma; cereals.

Renigunta, India: see TIRUPATI.

Renishaw, England: see ECKINGTON.

Renk or **Er Renk** (ĕr rĕnk'), town, Upper Nile prov., S central Anglo-Egyptian Sudan, on right bank of the White Nile and 175 mi. NNE of Malakal; cotton, peanuts, sesame, corn, durra; livestock.

Renkum (rĕng'kŭm), town (pop. 8,112), Gelderland prov., central Netherlands, on the Lower Rhine and 8 mi. W of Arnhem; rubber tires, paper products. Sanitarium. Former royal country seat.

Renmark, town (pop. 1,914), SE South Australia, 135 mi. ENE of Adelaide and on Murray R.; citrus-fruit center.

Rennebu (rĕn'nŭbōō), village and canton (pop. 2,702), Sor-Trondelag co., central Norway, on Orkla R. and 29 mi. S of Orkanger. Steatite quarries near by. Tile factory.

Rennell, Cape, N extremity of Somerset Isl., central Franklin Dist., Northwest Territories, on Barrow Strait; 74°11'N 93°15'W.

Rennell Island (rĕ'nŭl), coral island (pop. c.1,500), southernmost of Solomon Isls., SW Pacific, 110 mi. S of Guadalcanal; 11°38'S 160°14'E, c.50 mi. long, 12 mi. wide; coconuts. Polynesian natives.

Rennell Islands, off coast of S Chile, 60 mi. SW of Puerto Natales, NW of Muñoz Gamero Peninsula across Smyth Channel; 52°S 74°W; 43 mi. long, 1–6 mi. wide. Uninhabited.

Rennert (rĕ'nŭrt), town (1940 pop. 194), Robeson co., S N.C., 20 mi. SSW of Fayetteville.

Rennertshofen (rĕ"nŭrts-hō'fŭn), village (pop. 1,129), Swabia, W central Bavaria, Germany, near the Danube, 12 mi. ENE of Donauwörth; wheat, rye, cattle, hogs. Chartered 1332.

Rennes (rĕn), anc. *Condate,* Breton *Roazon,* city (pop. 102,617), ⊙ Ille-et-Vilaine dept., W France, on Vilaine R. at influx of the Ille and 190 mi. WSW of Paris; intellectual center of Brittany, important commercial and transportation hub. Specializes in printing and bookbinding and in the preparation of hides and skins (calf skins); mfg. (shoes, leather goods, pig bristles for brushes, agr. machinery); textile bleaching and dyeing, food processing, dairying. Has a modern cathedral, numerous museums, the 17th-cent. Palais de Justice (seat of prov. States-General under anc. regime), and the town hall, of pure Louis XV style. The 2 latter are the only major structures which survived the 7-day fire of 1720. Rennes was seat of the Redones (a Gallic tribe) and ⊙ duchy of Brittany in the Middle Ages. Its univ. has become a center of Celtic studies and Breton culture. The city was heavily damaged during Second World War.

Rennes-les-Bains (rĕn-lā-bē'), village (pop. 175), Aude dept., S France, in the Corbières, 10 mi. SSE of Limoux; mineral springs. Lumbering.

Renningen (rĕ'nĭng-ŭn), village (pop. 3,466), N Württemberg, Germany, after 1945 in Württemberg-Baden, 11 mi. W of Stuttgart; grain, cattle.

Reno (rē'nō), county (□ 1,255; pop. 54,058), S central Kansas; ⊙ Hutchinson. Wheat-growing region, drained by Arkansas R. and North Fork of Ninnescah R. Oil fields in E. Mfg. and salt refining at Hutchinson. Formed 1872.

Reno. **1** Town (pop. 108), Grady co., SW Ga., 8 mi. SSW of Cairo. **2** City (pop. 32,497), ⊙ Washoe co., W Nev., on Truckee R., near Calif. line, and 25 mi. N of Carson City; 39°31'N 119°48'W; alt. 4,491 ft. Largest city in Nev.; rail, air, commercial, and tourist center in mining and irrigated agr. area served by Truckee storage project on Little Truckee R., Calif. Meat packing, flour milling, and dairying are important industries. Manufactures bricks and tiles, sheet metal and lumber products, beverages; ships wool, potatoes, livestock and ores from near-by gold, silver, copper, and lead mines. Univ. of Nev., mus. and library of state historical society, and state hosp. for insane are here. Has healthful climate and numerous resorts. Rodeo takes place annually. Laid out 1868, with coming of Central Pacific RR; inc. 1903. Grew as trade center for mining and ranching area. Prosperity stimulated by legalizing of gambling (1931) and by state laws permitting easy divorce, for which Reno is famous. L. Tahoe is 20 mi. SSW, bet. Sierra Nevada and Carson Range; Pyramid L. is NE. **3** Village, Venango co., NW central Pa., just W of Oil City; oil refining.

Reno, Fort, Okla.: see EL RENO.

Reno, Lake, Pope co., W Minn., 5 mi. N of Glenwood; 4.5 mi. long, 2 mi. wide.

Renong, Thailand: see RANONG.

Reno River (rā'nô), N central Italy, rises in Etruscan Apennines 8 mi. NW of Pistoia, flows N, past Porretta Terme, Borgo Panigale, and Cento, and ESE, past Argenta, to the Adriatic 13 mi NNE of Ravenna; 131 mi. long. Receives Idice, Sillaro, Santerno, and Senio rivers. Canalized in lower course; used for irrigation.

Renovo (rĭnō'vŭ), borough (pop. 3,751), Clinton co., N central Pa., 21 mi. NW of Lock Haven and on West Branch of Susquehanna R.; railroad shops; bricks; clay, bituminous coal. Laid out 1862, inc. 1866.

Rense, Germany: see RHENS.

Rensselaer (rĕnsŭlēr', rĕn'sŭlŭr), county (□ 665; pop. 132,607), E N.Y.; ⊙ Troy. Bounded W by the Hudson, E by Mass. and Vt. lines; includes part of Taconic Mts. in E. Drained by Hoosic R.; contains Tomhannock Reservoir and small lakes (resorts). Dairying, farming (corn, clover, fruit, potatoes), poultry raising. Troy, Rensselaer are industrial and commercial centers. Includes Bennington Battlefield State Park. Formed 1791.

Rensselaer. **1** (rĕnsŭlēr', rĕn'sŭlŭr) City (pop. 4,072), ⊙ Jasper co., NW Ind., on Iroquois R. and c.45 mi. S of Gary; trade center for livestock and grain area; flour, lumber, dairy products. Settled c.1836, inc. 1897. **2** (rĕn'sŭlŭr, rĕnsŭlēr') Town (pop. 63), Ralls co., NE Mo., 11 mi. WSW of Hannibal. **3** (rĕnsŭlēr', rĕn'sŭlŭr) City (pop. 10,856), Rensselaer co., E N.Y., on the Hudson (bridged), opposite ALBANY, of which it is chief industrial and commercial suburb; mfg. of shirts, textile products, felt, leather goods, chemicals, dyes; railroad shops. Lumber port (part of port of Albany). At 17th-cent. Fort Crailo (now a mus.), British surgeon Richard Shuckburg is said to have written *Yankee Doodle.* Settled in 17th cent.; inc. 1897.

Rensselaer Falls (rĕn'sůlůr), village (pop. 323), St. Lawrence co., N N.Y., on Oswegatchie R. and 11 mi. SE of Ogdensburg, in dairy and poultry area.

Rentería (rĕntärē'ä), town (pop. 8,237), Guipúzcoa prov., N Spain, 4 mi. E of San Sebastián; foundries; paper and textile milling, food processing; mfg. of dyes, perfumes, bakelite articles. Pilgrimage church of Christ of Lezo near by.

Rentiesville, town (pop. 156), McIntosh co., E Okla., 17 mi. SSW of Muskogee, in agr. area.

Rentina or **Rendina** (both: rĕndē'nů), village (pop. 1,790), Karditsa nome, S Thessaly, Greece, at NE foot of the Tymphrestos, 20 mi. S of Karditsa; corn; livestock.

Renton, town in Cardross parish, S Dumbarton, Scotland, on Leven R. and 2 mi. NNW of Dumbarton; textile bleaching and printing. At near-by Dalquharn (dăl-whärn') Tobias Smollett was b.

Renton. 1 Village (pop. 1,014), Allegheny co., W Pa., 16 mi. ENE of downtown Pittsburgh. **2** Mfg. and commercial city (pop. 16,039), King co., W central Wash., on Cedar R. just SSE of Seattle; aircraft mfg.; timber, coal, clay products; poultry, truck. Inc. 1901.

Rentweinsdorf (rĕnt'vīnsdôrf), village (pop. 823), Lower Franconia, N Bavaria, Germany, on small Baunach R. and 13 mi. NNW of Bamberg; brickworks; brewing. Has baroque castle.

Rentwertshausen (rĕnt"vĕrts-hou'zůn), village (pop. 453), Thuringia, central Germany, 8 mi. S of Meiningen, 4 mi. W of Mühlfeld.

Rentz, town (pop. 302), Laurens co., central Ga., 12 mi. SSW of Dublin.

Renville. 1 County (□ 980; pop. 23,954), S Minn.; ⊙ Olivia. Agr. area bounded on S by Minnesota R. Corn, oats, barley, potatoes, livestock. Formed 1855. **2** County (□ 901; pop. 5,405), N N.Dak.; ⊙ Mohall; agr. area drained by Souris R. Diversified farming (dairy products, livestock, poultry, wheat). Formed 1908.

Renville, city (pop. 1,323), Renville co., SW Minn., 17 mi. E of Granite Falls, in grain, livestock, poultry area; dairy products. Settled c.1863.

Renwez (rã'vā'), village (pop. 946), Ardennes dept., N France, at foot of the Ardennes, 8 mi. NW of Mézières; foundry.

Renwick, town (pop. 474), Humboldt co., N central Iowa, near Boone R., 25 mi. NNE of Fort Dodge.

Reocín (rāō-thēn'), village (pop. 916), Santander prov., N Spain, 2 mi. WSW of Torrelavega; zinc mines.

Réole, La (lä rāôl'), town (pop. 3,653), Gironde dept., SW France, on right bank of Garonne R. and 12 mi. WNW of Marmande; livestock-raising center; distilling, fruit preserving. Has 13th-cent. church and 12th–14th-cent. castle and town hall.

Reoti (rā'ōtē), town (pop. 8,340), Ballia dist., E Uttar Pradesh, India, 16 mi. ENE of Ballia; cotton weaving; rice, gram, barley, oilseeds.

Reotipur (rā'ōtēpōōr), town (pop. 12,089), Ghazipur dist., E Uttar Pradesh, India, 8 mi. ESE of Ghazipur; rice, barley, gram, oilseeds, sugar cane.

Repalle (rā'půlē), town (pop. 9,767), Guntur dist., NE Madras, India, in Kistna R. delta, 33 mi. SE of Guntur; rail spur terminus; rice milling; tobacco, coconuts. Casuarina plantations S, on Bay of Bengal.

Repartição, Brazil: see BREJO.

Repce River (răp'tsĕ), Hung. *Répce,* Ger. *Rabnitz* (räp'nĭts), in Austria and NW Hungary, rises in Lower Austria 5 mi. NE of Aspang, flows SE into Hungary NE of Köszeg, then N and E, through the Hansag, to Raab R. at Győr; 100 mi. long. Through a canal it regulates level of Neusiedler L.

Repelen-Baerl (rā'pulůn-bärl'), village (pop. 15,405), in former Prussian Rhine Prov., W Germany, after 1945 in North Rhine-Westphalia, in the Ruhr, on left bank of the Rhine and 4 mi. NNW of Homberg; grain, cattle.

Repelón (rāpālōn'), town (pop. 3,310), Atlántico dept., N Colombia, in Caribbean lowlands, 40 mi. SW of Barranquilla; corn, cotton, sugar, cattle. Petroleum deposits near by.

Repetek (ryĕpĭtyĕk'), desert settlement, central Chardzhou oblast, Turkmen SSR, on Trans-Caspian RR and 40 mi. SW of Chardzhou, in Kara-Kum desert; meteorological and agr.-experiment station.

Repino (ryĕ'pĭnů), town, N Leningrad oblast, Russian SFSR, on Gulf of Finland and 5 mi. SE of Zelenogorsk; seaside resort. Called Kuokkala while in Finland (until 1940) and, until 1948, in USSR. Named for Rus. historical painter I. Y. Repin, who lived here.

Repki (ryĕp'kē), town (1926 pop. 4,100), NW Chernigov oblast, Ukrainian SSR, 23 mi. NNW of Chernigov; grain, flax.

Repola, Karelo-Finnish SSR: see REBOLY.

Reposaari (rĕ'pōsä"rē), Swedish *Räfsö* (răfs'û"), outport of Pori, Turku-Pori co., SW Finland, on small isl. in Gulf of Bothnia, 11 mi. NW of Pori city center.

Reposoir, Chaîne du, France: see BORNES.

Reppel (rĕ'půl), village (pop. 495), Limburg prov., NE Belgium, 11 mi. WNW of Maaseik; arsenic mfg.

Reppen, Poland: see RZEPIN.

Repton, town and parish (pop. 1,518), S Derby, England, 5 mi. NE of Burton-upon-Trent; agr. market. Site of well-known public school founded 1557. Important monastery built here in 7th cent., destroyed by Danes in 9th cent. There are remains of priory founded 1172, including church of St. Wystan with 10th-cent. Saxon crypt.

Repton, town (pop. 364), Conecuh co., S Ala., 17 mi. W of Evergreen.

Republic, county (□ 719; pop. 11,478), N Kansas; ⊙ Belleville. Plains region, bordering N on Nebr.; drained by Republican R. Corn, wheat, livestock. Formed 1868.

Republic. 1 City (pop. 360), Republic co., N Kansas, 12 mi. NW of Belleville, near Republican R. and Nebr. line; corn, wheat, livestock. **2** Village (pop. 1,092), Marquette co., NW Upper Peninsula, Mich., 16 mi. SW of Ishpeming, near Michigamme R. Its abandoned iron mine was one of the richest in Marquette Iron Range. **3** City (pop. 965), Greene co., SW Mo., in the Ozarks, 12 mi. SW of Springfield; dairying; ships apples, strawberries, grapes, tomatoes. **4** Village (pop. 615), Seneca co., N Ohio, 8 mi. E of Tiffin, in livestock and grain area. **5** Village (1940 pop. 2,684), Fayette co., SW Pa., 9 mi. NW of Uniontown; bituminous coal; cement products. **6** City (pop. 895), ⊙ Ferry co., NE Wash., 40 mi. WNW of Colville and on Sanpoil R.; wheat, lumber, lime, poultry; gold mines.

Republican City, village (pop. 580), Harlan co., S Nebr., 5 mi. E of Alma and on Republican R., near Kansas line; grain, livestock, dairy and poultry produce.

Republican River, in S Nebr. and N Kansas; formed by confluence of North Fork, Republican R. and Arikaree R. at Haigler, SW Nebr.; flows E, through Nebr., past McCook, Red Cloud, and Superior, thence SE, through Kansas, joining Smoky Hill R. to form Kansas R. at Junction City; 422 mi. long. River is included in project for flood control and land reclamation in Missouri R. basin. Corps of Engineers began construction of Harlan Co. Dam (1948) on main stream of Republican R., near Alma; Bureau of Reclamation projects on tributaries include dams on South Fork Republican R. (begun 1948), Frenchman Creek (begun 1947), and Medicine Creek (begun 1948).

Republiek (růpůblēk'), village (pop. 20), Surinam dist., N Du. Guiana, on Paramaribo-Dam RR and 23 mi. S of Paramaribo; resort during dry season.

Repulse Bay, inlet of Coral Sea, E Queensland, Australia, bet. Cape Conway (N) and Midge Point; 15 mi. long, 13 mi. wide. Repulse Isls. (small, rocky group) at entrance. Cumberland Isls. near.

Repulse Bay, trading post, S Melville Peninsula, SE Franklin Dist., Northwest Territories, at head of Repulse Bay, inlet (40 mi. long, 19–40 mi. wide) of Foxe Channel; 66°32'N 86°15'W; radio station. Site of R.C. mission.

Repyevka or **Rep'yevka** (rĕ'pyĭfků), village (1926 pop. 2,116), W Voronezh oblast, Russian SFSR, 24 mi. NW of Ostrogozhsk; wheat.

Requa (rĕ'kwů), village (pop. c.200), Del Norte co., NW Calif., at mouth of Klamath R. on the Pacific, 15 mi. SE of Crescent City; sport fishing.

Reque (rā'kā), town (pop. 1,552), Lambayeque dept., NW Peru, on coastal plain, in irrigated Eten R. valley, 6 mi. SSE of Chiclayo; orchards.

Requehua (rākā'wä), town (pop. 1,305), O'Higgins prov., central Chile, on railroad and 27 mi. SW of Rancagua; agr. center (wheat, alfalfa, potatoes, beans, fruit, cattle); flour milling, dairying. Sometimes Requegua.

Requena (rākā'nä), town (pop. 1,774), ⊙ Requena prov. (formed 1943), Loreto dept., NE Peru, landing on right bank of the Ucayali, in Amazon basin, and 115 mi. SW of Iquitos, in tropical forest region. Has Franciscan convent and schools. Airfield.

Requena, city (pop. 8,259), Valencia prov., E Spain, 40 mi. W of Valencia; agr. trade center (olive oil, cereals, truck produce, saffron). Noted for its red wine. Textile mfg. (silk and linen), alcohol and brandy distilling, flour- and sawmilling. Has Gothic church and 15th-cent. houses. Was conquered by the Cid, reconquered by Moors, finally liberated (1219) by Alfonso VIII of Castile.

Reque River, Peru: see ETEN RIVER.

Requínoa (rākē'nōä), town (pop. 1,293), O'Higgins prov., central Chile, on railroad and 8 mi. S of Rancagua, in agr. area (grain, beans, potatoes, wine, cattle).

Réquista (rākēstä'), village (pop. 1,166), Aveyron dept., S France, 21 mi. ENE of Albi; dairying, flour milling.

Rere (rā'rā), village (1930 pop. 620), Concepción prov., S central Chile, 28 mi. SE of Concepción, in agr. area (cereals, vegetables, livestock).

Rerik (rā'rĭk), town (pop. 4,132), Mecklenburg, N Germany, on Mecklenburg Bay of the Baltic, 15 mi. NNW of Wismar; seaside resort. Called Alt Gaarz until 1938, when it inc. seaside resort of Wustrow.

Reriutaba (rĭryōōtä'bů), city (pop. 1,677), W Ceará, Brazil, on Camocim-Crateús RR and 25 mi. SSW of Sobral; cattle, carnauba wax. Until 1944, called Santa Cruz.

Rerrick, parish (pop. 1,228), S Kirkcudbright, Scotland. Includes agr. village of Auchencairn (okh"-ůnkârn'), on Solway Firth, 7 mi. E of Kirkcudbright; bathing resort.

Resaca (rēsä'ků), village (pop. c.150), Gordon co., NW Ga., 13 mi. S of Dalton, on Oostanaula R. Civil War battle in the Atlanta campaign occurred here, May 13–16, 1864.

Resaca de la Palma, Texas: see BROWNSVILLE.

Resadiye (rĕ-shä'dĭyĕ), Turkish *Reşadiye.* **1** Village, Mugla prov., Turkey: see DATCA. **2** Village (pop. 1,545), Tokat prov., N central Turkey, on Kelkit R. and 40 mi. ENE of Tokat; sugar beets, cereals.

Resadiye Peninsula, Turkish *Reşadiye,* SW Turkey, extends 40 mi. into the Aegean bet. isls. of Kos and Rhodes, with Gulf of Kos (Ceramic Gulf) on N; 7 mi. wide. Rises to 3,860 ft. Site of anc. Cnidus is at tip (Cape Krio). Town of Datca (formerly Resadiye) in center.

Résafé, Syria: see RISAFE.

Resan, Yugoslavia: see RESEN.

Resava River (rĕ'sävä), E central Serbia, Yugoslavia, rises 8 mi. S of Zagubica, flows W, through brown-coal-mining area (Ravna Reka), past Despotovac, and ENE, past Svilajnac, to Morava R. just NE of Svilajnac; c.50 mi. long. Resava co. (pop. 38,823; ⊙ Svilajnac) lies along its lower course.

Rescaldina (rĕskäldē'nä), village (pop. 3,062), Milano prov., Lombardy, N Italy, 15 mi. NW of Milan; foundries.

Reschenscheideck, pass bet. Austria and Italy: see RESIA, PASSO DI.

Res-delta, locality, S Mackenzie Dist., Northwest Territories, on S shore of Great Slave L., at mouth of Slave R., 9 mi. NNE of Fort Resolution; 61°17'N 113°35'W; river-lake transshipment point for Yellowknife mining region.

Reseda (rĭsē'dů), suburban section of Los ANGELES city, Los Angeles co., S Calif., in W San Fernando Valley, 9 mi. SW of San Fernando.

Resen (rĕ'sĕn), village (pop. 3,883), Gorna Oryakhovitsa dist., N Bulgaria, on Rositsa R. and 10 mi. NW of Tirnovo; grain, livestock, truck.

Resen (rĕ'sĕn), village (pop. 4,521), W Macedonia, Yugoslavia, N of L. Prespa, 17 mi. WNW of Bitolj; trade center for fruitgrowing (apples, pears) region; pottery making. Roman ruins near by. Formerly called Resan.

Resende (rĭzĕn'dĭ), city (pop. 5,040), W Rio de Janeiro state, Brazil, on Paraíba R. opposite Agulhas Negras (bridge), on railroad and 80 mi. WNW of Rio; dairying, meat and coffee processing, talc pulverizing. Marble quarry near by. Site of new military school. Formerly spelled Rezende.

Resende, town (pop. 457), Viseu dist., N Portugal, on Douro R. and 8 mi. W of Lamego; port wine. Formerly spelled Rezende.

Resende Costa (kō'stů), city (pop. 2,223), S central Minas Gerais, Brazil, 15 mi. N of São João del Rei; alt. 3,600 ft. Dairying. Tin deposits. Formerly spelled Rezende Costa.

Reserva (rĭzĕr'vů), city (pop. 405), central Paraná, Brazil, 50 mi. NW of Ponta Grossa; grain milling, coffee and lard processing, sugar milling. Coal mined at near-by Teresa Cristina.

Reserve. 1 City (pop. 169), Brown co., NE Kansas, near Nebr. line, 9 mi. N of Hiawatha, in corn, dairy, and poultry region. **2** Village (pop. 4,465), St. John the Baptist parish, SE La., on E bank (levee) of the Mississippi and 29 mi. WNW of New Orleans; refining and shipping center for sugar-cane area. **3** Village (pop. c.250), ⊙ Catron co., W N.Mex., on San Francisco R., near Ariz. line, and 70 mi. NNW of Silver City, in Apache Natl. Forest; alt. 5,770 ft.; agr., lumbering. Eagle Peak is 10 mi. E.

Reserve Mines, town (pop. estimate 1,300), NE N.S., on Cape Breton Isl., 4 mi. W of Glace Bay; coal mining.

Reshetikha (ryĭshĕ'tyēkhů), town (1938 pop. 6,965), W Gorki oblast, Russian SFSR, 3 mi. E of Volodary; hemp milling.

Reshetilovka (ryĭshĕ'tyēlŭfků), town (1926 pop. 7,786), central Poltava oblast, Ukrainian SSR, 21 mi. W of Poltava; dairying, flour milling, metalworking; linen and clothing mills.

Reshire, Iran: see RISHAHR.

Reshitsa, Rumania: see RESITA.

Resht (rĕsht) or **Rasht** (räsht), city (1940 pop. 121,625), ⊙ First Prov., N Iran, near Caspian Sea, 150 mi. NW of Teheran, across the Elburz range; 37°15'N 49°35'E. Chief commercial center of former Gilan prov., in subtropical agr. lowland served by Caspian port of Pahlevi; silk-producing center; silk spinning, cocoon breeding; mfg. also of jute sacks, hosiery, matches, glass. Exports silk, glass, poultry. Resht's cobblestone streets and houses with red-clay roofs are unusual for Iran. Flourished in 17th and 18th cent.

Resia, Passo di (päs'sō dē rä'zyä), Ger. *Reschenscheideck* (rĕ"shůn-shī'dĕk) pass (alt. 4,947 ft.) on Austro-Ital. border, just E of Swiss frontier, on watershed bet. Inn and Adige rivers, 33 mi. WNW of Merano (Italy). Forms divide bet. Rhaetian and Ötztal Alps. Crossed by road bet. Malles Venosta (Italy) and Nauders (Austria).

Resicabanya, Rumania: see RESITA.
Resina (rĕzē'nä), town (pop. 26,580), Napoli prov., Campania, S Italy, on Bay of Naples, at W foot of Vesuvius, 5 mi. SE of Naples; tannery, button and glass factories. Bathing resort. Starting point for electric railway ascending Vesuvius. Has fine villas and gardens. Destroyed by eruption of 1631. Occupies site of anc. HERCULANEUM.
Resinar, Rumania: see RASINARI.
Resistencia (räsĕstĕn'syä), city (pop. 51,834), ⊙ Chaco prov., ⊙ Resistencia dept. (pop. 112,886), Argentina, 9 mi. W of Corrientes (across Paraná R.), 480 mi. NNW of Buenos Aires; 27°28'S 58°58'W. Railroad junction; agr., commercial, and mfg. center. Tannin factories, cotton gins, tanneries, lead smelters, sawmills, corn mills, meat-packing plants, vegetable-oil and alcohol distilleries. Trades in cotton, lumber, hides. Agr. products: cotton, corn, fruit, livestock. Lumbering of quebracho and other subtropical woods. City has developed rapidly, and has administrative bldgs., libraries, museums, and institutions of higher learning. Airport. Its ports on the Paraná are near-by Barranqueras and Puerto Vilelas.
Resita (rĕ'shĕtsä), Rum. *Reşiţa*, Hung. *Resicabánya* (rĕ'shĕkŏbä"nyŏ), town (1948 pop. 24,895), Severin prov., SW Rumania, in Banat, in W foothills of the Transylvanian Alps, 22 mi. NNE of Oravita; rail terminus and important metallurgical center. Noted for its integrated steel works (coal and iron mines, coke ovens, blast furnaces, pig iron foundries, rolling mills, machine shops), producing rolling stock, bridge structures, industrial and agr. machinery, electrical appliances, military equipment. Also wood cracking, mfg. of celluloid and casein plastic wares, cabinetmaking. Known in Roman times as a mining center, mostly for precious metals. Local iron and coal deposits were rediscovered in 18th cent. and 1st foundry established (1771) under Maria Theresa. Modern development dates from 1920. Has large Ger. pop. (c.30%). Also sometimes spelled Recita and Reshitsa.
Resiutta (rĕzūt'tä), village (pop. 548), Udine prov., Friuli–Venezia Giulia, NE Italy, on Fella R. and 10 mi. E of Tolmezzo; bituminous schist mining and distilling.
Resko (rĕ'skô), Ger. *Regenwalde* (rā'gŭnväl"dŭ), town (1939 pop. 5,006; 1946 pop. 1,314) in Pomerania, after 1945 in Szczecin prov., NW Poland, on the Rega and 13 mi. SSE of Gryfice; mfg. of agr. machinery, starch; distilling. After 1945, briefly called Lawiczka, Pol. *Ławiczka*.
Resko Dag, Turkey: see CILO DAG.
Reskovec (rĕskô'vĕts) or **Reskoveci** (rĕskô'vĕtsē), village (1930 pop. 199), S central Albania, 12 mi. W of Berat; agr. center in the Myzeqe plain. Also spelled Roskovec (Roskoveci) and Rroskovec (Rroskoveci).
Resolis (rŭsō'lĭs) or **Kirkmichael,** parish (pop. 846), E Ross and Cromarty, Scotland. Agr. village of Resolis is near Cromarty Firth, 3 mi. SW of Invergordon.
Resolute Bay, U.S.–Canadian Arctic weather station, SE Cornwallis Isl., central Franklin Dist., Northwest Territories, on Barrow Strait; 74°42'N 94°34'W.
Resolution Island (□ 1,029), SE Franklin Dist., Northwest Territories, at E entrance of Hudson Strait, off SE Baffin Isl.; 45 mi. long, 10–40 mi. wide. At S extremity is govt. radio direction-finding and meteorological station (61°18'N 64°53'W).
Resolution Island, Fiordland Natl. Park, SW S.Isl., New Zealand, bet. Breaksea and Dusky sounds of Tasman Sea; c. 10 mi. long, 8 mi. wide; has narrow peninsula 9 mi. long; mountainous.
Resolven (rĕzôl'vŭn), town and parish (pop. 4,353), N Glamorgan, Wales, on Neath R. and 6 mi. NE of Neath; coal mining, tinplate mfg.
Resort, resort village, Wayne co., W N.Y., on Sodus Bay of L. Ontario, 35 mi. E of Rochester; sport fishing. Bay here is noted for its lotus beds.
Resplendor (rĭsplĕndôr'), city (pop. 1,631), E Minas Gerais, Brazil, on the Rio Doce, on railroad and 17 mi. NW of Aimorés; mica mining.
Ressaix (rĕsā'), town (pop. 4,564), Hainaut prov., S Belgium, 11 mi. E of Mons; coal mines; coke-mfg. plants.
Ressano Garcia (rĭsä'nōō gŭrsē'ŭ), village, Sul do Save prov., S Mozambique on Komati R. (Transvaal line) opposite Komatipoort, at influx of Crocodile R., and 50 mi. NW of Lourenço Marques. Customs station on Johannesburg-Lourenço Marques RR.
Ressas, Djebel, Tunisia: see LAVERIE, LA.
Ressons-sur-Matz (rĕsõ'-sür-mäts'), village (pop. 924), Oise dept., N France, 10 mi. NNW of Compiègne; dairying, horse raising.
Restauración (rĕstouräsyōn'), town (1950 pop. 557), Libertador prov., NW Dominican Republic, in the Cordillera Central, near Haiti border, 13 mi. S of Dajabón; coffee, corn, fruit.
Rest Haven, town (pop. 147), Gwinnett co., N central Ga., just ENE of Buford.
Resthaven Mountain (10,253 ft.), W Alta., near B.C. border, in Rocky Mts. at N edge of Jasper Natl. Park, 70 mi. NW of Jasper; 53°27'N 119°31'W.
Restigouche (rĕ'stĭgōōsh, rĕstĭgōōsh'), county (□ 3,242; pop. 33,075), N N.B., on Bay of Chaleur and on Que. border; ⊙ Dalhousie.
Restigouche River, NW N.B., rises E of Edmundston, flows in a winding course generally NE to confluence with Matapedia R. 16 mi. W of Campbellton, thence ENE, past Campbellton, to Chaleur Bay at Dalhousie; 130 mi. long. Lower course forms Que.–N.B. border. Tidal estuary, 24 mi. long, is called Escuminac Bay. River is noted for its salmon.
Restín (rĕstēn'), village (pop. 194), Piura dept., NW Peru, on Restín Point (4°18'S 81°16'W), on the Pacific, just S of Cabo Blanco, and 18 mi. N of Talara; oil wells. Petroleum is shipped through Cabo Blanco and LOBITOS.
Restinga Point (răstĭng'gä), southernmost point of Hierro and Canary Isls., 12 mi. SSW of Valverde; 27°37'N 17°57'W. Naos Point is just W.
Reston, village (pop. estimate 400), SW Man., 55 mi. WSW of Brandon, near Sask. border; grain elevators; stock.
Restrepo (rĕstrā'pō), town (pop. 1,349), Meta intendancy, central Colombia, at E foot of Cordillera Oriental, 10 mi. NE of Villavicencio; cattle, coffee; saltworks.
Resulayn, Turkey: see CEYLANPINAR.
Resurreccíon (räsōōrĕksyōn'), town (pop. 2,246), Puebla, central Mexico, at S foot of Malinche volcano, 8 mi. NE of Puebla; cereals, maguey, livestock.
Resurrection, Cape, S Alaska, on SE Kenai Peninsula, 15 mi. S of Seward, at E entrance of Resurrection Bay; 59°32'N 149°17'W.
Resurrection Bay (15 mi. long, 2–7 mi. wide), S Alaska, inlet of Gulf of Alaska, in SE Kenai Peninsula, opening into Blying Sound at 59°56'N 149°23'W. At head of bay is Seward, S terminus of Alaska RR and distribution point for interior Alaska. Named by Baranov, 1792; shipbuilding yard established here 1794 by Russians.
Resuttano (rĕzōōt-tä'nô), village (pop. 4,688), Caltanissetta prov., central Sicily, 13 mi. N of Caltanissetta, in cereal-growing region.
Reszel (rĕ'shĕl), Ger. *Rössel* (rŭ'sŭl), town (1939 pop. 5,058; 1946 pop. 846) in East Prussia, after 1945 in Olsztyn prov., NE Poland, 35 mi. NE of Allenstein (Olsztyn); grain and cattle market; machine mfg. In 14th cent., bishops of Ermland founded castle here; town chartered 1357. In First World War, Hindenburg's hq. during battle of Masurian Lakes (1914–15).
Retalhuleu (rātälōōlĕ'ōō), department (□ 726; 1950 pop. 67,265), SW Guatemala; ⊙ Retalhuleu. On Pacific coast, bounded NW by Tilapa R.; extends from Pacific piedmont (N; site of main centers) to coastal plain (S); drained by the Samalá and other coastal streams. Agr. (coffee, sugar cane, cotton, rice, cacao) on N slopes; corn, beans, livestock raising on coastal plain. Lumbering (hardwoods). Salt extraction along coast. Served by railroad through Retalhuleu city, with branches to San Felipe and Champerico (Pacific port).
Retalhuleu, city (1950 pop. 7,677), ⊙ Retalhuleu dept., SW Guatemala, in Pacific piedmont, on railroad and 23 mi. SSW of Quezaltenango; 14°32'N 91°43'W. Market center in coffee and sugar-cane area; grain, livestock, beekeeping. Has customhouse serving its port of Champerico (linked by rail). Lumbering near by.
Retallack (rĭtă'lĭk), village, SE B.C., 40 mi. N of Nelson; silver, lead, zinc mining.
Retamal (rätämäl'), town (pop. 1,699), Badajoz prov., W Spain, 19 mi. WSW of Castuera; cereals, livestock; flour milling.
Retamito (rätämē'tō), village (pop. estimate 500), S San Juan prov., Argentina, 40 mi. S of San Juan; farming corn, wheat, wine, livestock and stone-quarrying center.
Retavas, Lithuania: see RIETAVAS.
Retezat or **Retezatul** (rĕtyĕzät', –zä'tōōl), picturesque mountain group in W Transylvanian Alps, W central Rumania, Transylvania, c.10 mi. W of Lupeni; rises to 8,236 ft. Numerous glaciated lakes, Alpinism.
Retford, England: see EAST RETFORD.
Rethel (rŭtĕl'), town (pop. 4,482), Ardennes dept., N France, on the Aisne, on Ardennes Canal, and 23 mi. NE of Rheims; agr. trade center (cereals, dairy produce, colza, wool). Tractor factory. Heavily damaged in both world wars. In Middle Ages, seat of a county, later raised to a duchy.
Rethem or **Rethem an der Aller** (rā'tŭm än dĕr ä'lŭr), town (pop. 2,082), in former Prussian prov. of Hanover, NW Germany, after 1945 in Lower Saxony, on the Aller and 10 mi. SW of Walsrode; furniture, flour products, canned goods.
Rethimni, Crete: see RETHYMNE.
Rethimnon, Crete: see RETHYMNON.
Rethondes (rŭtõd'), village (pop. 364), Oise dept., N France, 6 mi. E of Compiègne, in the Forest of Compiègne. Near by, on rail siding 4.5 mi. E of Compiègne, the armistices of 1918 and 1940 were signed.
Rethy, Belgian Congo: see NIOKA.
Réthy, Belgium: see RETIE.
Rethymne or **Rethimni** (both: rĕthĭm'nē), nome (□ 582; pop. 73,056), W central Crete, bet. Mt. Ida (E) and Mt. Leuka (W); ⊙ Rethymnon. Agr.: carobs, almonds, wine, wheat, barley, olive oil; stock raising (sheep, goats, chickens); fisheries. Main port, Rethymnon, is on N shore.
Rethymnon or **Rethimnon** (both: rĕth'ĭmnôn), town (pop. 10,972), ⊙ Rethymne nome, W central Crete, port on Gulf of Almyros, 32 mi. ESE of Canea. Trades in wheat, carobs, almonds, wine, olive oil. Under Venetian rule, one of main strongholds on Crete. Conquered (1645) by the Turks after a short siege. Formerly called Retimo.
Retiche, Alpi, Switzerland and Italy: see RHAETIAN ALPS.
Retie (rā'tē), Fr. *Réthy* (rātē'), town (pop. 4,756), Antwerp prov., NE Belgium, near Netherlands border, 9 mi. SE of Turnhout; agr. market. Church contains noted 16th–18th-cent. statues. Near by is large royal domain.
Retiers (rŭtyā'), village (pop. 1,110), Ille-et-Vilaine dept., W France, 14 mi. N of Chateaubriant; tanning. Megalithic monuments.
Retimo, Crete: see RETHYMNON.
Retinne (rŭtĕn'), town (pop. 2,601), Liége prov., E Belgium, 5 mi. E of Liége; coal mining.
Retiro (rātē'rō). **1** Village (1930 pop. 470), Linares prov., S central Chile on railroad and 17 mi. SW of Linares, in agr. area (wheat, oats, chick-peas, wine). **2** Town (pop. 1,811), Valparaiso prov., central Chile, adjoining Quilpué, 10 mi. E of Valparaiso; fruitgrowing center; also grain, wine, beans, cattle; lumber. Resort.
Retiro, town (pop. 1,590), Antioquia dept., NW central Colombia, in Cordillera Central, 14 mi. SSE of Medellín; alt. 7,303 ft. Salt mining, dairying; agr. products: corn, coffee, potatoes, bananas, yucca. Don Diego waterfalls and grotto near by.
Retournac (rŭtōōrnäk'), village (pop. 1,230), Haute-Loire dept., S central France, on the Loire and 6 mi. NW of Yssingeaux; agr. market; lace-making.
Retovo, Lithuania: see RIETAVAS.
Retsag (rāt'shäg), Hung. *Rétság*, town (pop. 1,974), Nograd-Hont co., N Hungary, 12 mi. SW of Balassagyarmat; rye, potatoes, hogs, sheep.
Retsil, village (pop. 1,538, with Annapolis), Kitsap co., W Wash., on Puget Sound, just NE of Port Orchard.
Retsof (rĕt'sŏf), village, Livingston co., W central N.Y., near Genesee R., 26 mi. SSW of Rochester; large salt mine.
Retszilas, Hungary: see SARSZENTMIKLOS.
Rettenbach, Germany: see MARKT RETTENBACH.
Retuerta de Bullaque (rātwĕr'tä dhä bōōlyä'kä), village (pop. 1,253), Ciudad Real prov., S central Spain, on S slopes of the Montes de Toledo, 40 mi. NW of Ciudad Real; cereals, livestock. Charcoal burning.
Retz (rĕs), 15th-cent. duchy of W France, now comprised in Loire-Inférieure dept. bet. estuary of the Loire (N) and the Bay of Bourgneuf (SW). Former ⊙ Machecoul.
Retzbach (rĕts'bäkh), village (pop. 1,453), Lower Franconia, NW Bavaria, Germany, on the Main (canalized) and 9 mi. NW of Würzburg; potatoes, beets. Sandstone quarries near by.
Retz Stadt (rĕts' shtät") or **Rötz Stadt** (rŭts'), town (pop. 3,399), N Lower Austria, 8 mi. SSW of Znojmo, Czechoslovakia; wine.
Reubens, village (pop. 116), Lewis co., W Idaho, 15 mi. WNW of Nezperce; agr., livestock.
Reudnitz (roit'nĭts), E suburb of Leipzig, Saxony, E central Germany.
Reuilly (rŭyē'), village (pop. 1,301), Indre dept., central France, on Arnon R. and 9 mi. N of Issoudun; noted wines.
Reumén (rĕ-ōōmĕn'), village (1930 pop. 609), Valdivia prov., S central Chile, on railroad and 26 mi. ESE of Valdivia, in agr. area (cereals, potatoes, peas, livestock); lumbering.
Réunion (räünyō'), Fr. island (□ 970; pop. 242,067) of the Mascarene group, in Indian Ocean, an overseas department of France, c.400 mi. E of Madagascar and c.110 mi. SW of Mauritius; 21°S 55°30'E; ⊙ Saint-Denis. It is 50 mi. long, 45 mi. wide. Of volcanic origin, with 2 centers of eruption; the older extinct central massif rises to 10,069 ft. in the Piton des Neiges; the more recent N active volcano (SE) rises to 8,612 ft. The spurs of the central massif are separated by narrow valleys watered by torrential streams. The main NW–SE watershed separates 2 geographic and administrative regions: the humid Windward dist. (pop. 89,899; ⊙ Saint-Denis), exposed to SE trade winds, and the drier Leeward dist. (pop. 152,168; ⊙ Saint-Pierre). In cyclonic zone; disastrous storms in 1829, 1868, 1944, 1945. Rainfall varies bet. 160 in. at Saint-Benoît (windward side) and 28 in. at Saint-Paul (leeward side). Mean summer temp. of 79°F. in tropical coastal lowland; more moderate toward interior uplands (health resorts at Hell-Bourg and Cilaos). Main products are sugar cane (from which rum and industrial alcohol are also made), essential oils (geranium, ilang-ilang, vetiver, citronella), vanilla, tapioca, manioc. Secondary industries: mfg. of chocolate, flour, vegetable oil, cigarettes, canned goods, fiber sacks. Réunion built (1880s) an artificial harbor at Pointe-des-Galets, on coastal railroad linking Saint-Benoît and Saint-Pierre (also connected by cross-isl. high-

way). Pop. is largely Fr. Creole (97%), with minorities of Indians, Chinese, Malagasy, and Kaffirs. Discovered (early 16th cent.) by Portuguese, it remained unsettled until the French took possession in 1642 and named it Bourbon in 1649. Originally administered by Fr. East India Company, it passed to Fr. crown in 1764–67. Renamed Réunion (1793), Bonaparte (1806), again Bourbon (1815), and, finally, Réunion once more (1848). Occupied by British 1810–15. Slavery was abolished 1848. During Second World War, it was captured (1942) by Free French forces. In 1946 it was made an overseas dept. of France. Abd-el-Krim, exiled here 1926, escaped to Egypt 1947.

Reus (rĕ'ōōs), city (pop. 29,480), Tarragona prov., NE Spain, in Catalonia, 8 mi. WNW of Tarragona; industrial, commercial, and communications center. Mfg. of silk and cotton fabrics, knitgoods, agr. machinery, pharmaceuticals, leather goods, soap, ceramics, candy; wine and olive-oil processing, canning (fruit and vegetables). Ships hazelnuts and almonds. Cotton industry introduced by English in 18th cent. Gothic church of St. Peter has high octagonal tower. The painter Fortuny and Gen. Prim were b. here.

Reuss (rois), two former principalities, Thuringia, central Germany. House of Reuss dates from 12th cent. Its complicated genealogical history and numerous territorial subdivisions were finally resolved in 1848 by the emergence of 2 branches—Reuss Older Line, with ⊙ at Greiz, and Reuss Younger Line, with ⊙ at Gera. Both territories were inc. into THURINGIA in 1920.

Reuss River, central Switzerland, formed by 2 headstreams which rise near St. Gotthard and Furka passes, joining SW of Andermatt; flows N, entering L. of Lucerne near Flüelen and emerging at Lucerne, thence N to the Aar at Windisch. Length, 99 mi. Amsteg hydroelectric plant is on it.

Reut, river, Moldavian SSR: see REUT RIVER.

Reutlingen (roit'lĭng-ŭn), city (pop. 36,785; including suburbs 62,869), S Württemberg, Germany, after 1945 in Württemberg-Hohenzollern, at W foot of the Achalm, 20 mi. S of Stuttgart, at N foot of Swabian Jura; 48°30'N 9°13'E. Rail junction; industrial center (especially textiles); other mfg.: textile machinery, machine tools, automobile motors, metal cloth; steel construction. Tanning, paper milling, printing. Church of St. Mary is an outstanding monument of high Gothic. Has 18th-cent. town hall. Site of teachers col., textile school. Free imperial city until 1802. Scene (1377) of Swabian League's decisive victory over Ulrich of Württemberg. Damaged in Second World War. Friedrich List b. here.

Reutov (rŏōtôf'), city (1939 pop. over 10,000), central Moscow oblast, Russian SSR, 10 mi. E of Moscow; rail junction; cotton-milling center. Called Reutovo until 1940, when it became a city.

Reut River (rŏōt'), Rum. *Răut* (rŭ'ōōt), chief right affluent of the Dniester, in Moldavian SSR, rises NW of Tyrnovo, flows c.120 mi. generally SE, past Beltsy, Floreshty, and Orgeyev, to the Dniester opposite Dubossary.

Reutte (roi'tŭ), town (pop. 3,368), Tyrol, W Austria, in Lechtal Alps, on Lech R. and 7 mi. S of Füssen, Germany; cotton mills, breweries.

Reval, Estonia: see TALLINN.

Revard, Mont, France: see AIX-LES-BAINS.

Revaujfalu, Yugoslavia: see NOVO SELO.

Revda (ryĕv'dŭ), city (1933 pop. estimate 18,900), S Sverdlovsk, oblast, Russian SFSR, in the central Urals, on short Revda R. (left tributary of Chusovaya R.) and 25 mi. W of Sverdlovsk; rail junction; major copper-refining center (Sredneuralsk plant), based on DEGTYARKA and local deposits; ferrous metallurgy (based largely on charcoal); mfg. of metalware, ceramics; sawmilling. Developed prior to First World War as iron- and copper-smelting works called Revdinski Zavod.

Revel, Estonia: see TALLINN.

Revel (rûvĕl'), town (pop. 4,155), Haute-Garonne dept., S France, 30 mi. ESE of Toulouse; furniture-mfg. center and agr. market (hogs, poultry). Produces noted peppermint liqueurs and feather quilts. A medieval stronghold built in 1332. Near by is a feeder lake for the Canal du Midi.

Revelganj (rā'vălgŭnj) or **Godna** (gōd'nŭ), town (pop. 10,643), Saran dist., NW Bihar, India, on Ganges Plain, on Gogra R. and 7 mi. W of Chapra; rice, wheat, barley, corn, sugar cane. Sanskrit school.

Revellata, Pointe de la (pwĕt dŭ lä rävĕlätä'), headland of NW Corsica, on the Mediterranean, 2 mi. NW of Calvi; 42°35'N 8°43'E. Lighthouse.

Revello (rĕvĕl'lô), village (pop. 1,049), Cuneo prov., Piedmont, NW Italy, 5 mi. W of Saluzzo; agr. tools.

Revelstoke (rĕ'vŭlstōk), city (pop. 2,106), SE B.C., on Columbia R. at mouth of Illecillewaet R., and 100 mi. E of Kamloops, bet. Selkirk and Monashee mts., at edge of Mt. Revelstoke Natl. Park; alt. 1,496 ft.; railroad division point; distributing center for lumbering and mining (silver, gold, copper, zinc, lead, asbestos, mica) region. Tourist center.

Reventazón, Peru: see BAYOVAR.

Reventazón River (rāvĕntäsōn'), E central Costa Rica, rises on central plateau SE of San José, flows 85 mi., past Turrialba and Peralta, to Caribbean Sea 30 mi. NW of Limón. Sometimes called Parismina R. in lower course, for an important left affluent.

Revere (rā'vĕrĕ), village (pop. 1,960), Mantova prov., Lombardy, N Italy, on Po R. opposite Ostiglia, and 18 mi. ESE of Mantua, in cereal- hemp-, and flax-growing region.

Revere (rŭvēr'). **1** City (pop. 36,763), Suffolk co., E Mass., on Massachusetts Bay and 4 mi. NE of Boston; residential suburb; resort, with popular Revere Beach. Printing, sugar refining, mfg. (optical goods, castings, processed food, lasts, ribbon). Settled c.1630, set off from Chelsea 1871, inc. as city 1914. Includes summer colony of Point of Pines. **2** Village (pop. 198), Redwood co., SW Minn., near Cottonwood R., c.45 mi. WSW of New Ulm; grain. **3** Town (pop. 180), Clark co., extreme NE Mo., near Des Moines R., 6 mi. NNE of Kahoka.

Revermont (rûvĕrmō'), W foothills of the Jura, E France, extending c.45 mi. across Ain and Jura depts., from Pont-d'Ain (S) to Lons-le-Saunier (N), bet. Bresse region (W) and the Ain (E). Average alt. 2,000 ft. Winegrowing, cattle raising.

Reversing Falls, N.B.: see SAINT JOHN; SAINT JOHN RIVER.

Revigny-sur-Ornain (rûvēnyē'-sür-ôrnē'), town (pop. 2,375), Meuse dept., NE France, on Ornain R. and Marne-Rhine Canal, and 9 mi. WNW of Bar-le-Duc; rail junction. Mfg. (clock springs, furniture, saws, tiles). Sacked and burned (1914) by Germans in First World War.

Revillagigedo Channel (rûvĭ'lü-gĭgē'dō, -gĭgē'dō), SE Alaska, in Alexander Archipelago, bet. mainland (E), Revillagigedo Isl. (N), and Duke and Annette isls. (SW); extends c.35 mi. NW from Dixon Entrance; forms part of Inside Passage to Ketchikan.

Revillagigedo Island (□ 1,120), SE Alaska, in Alexander Archipelago, separated from mainland (E) by Behm Canal and from Prince of Wales Isl. (W) by Clarence Strait; center near 55°35'N 131°6'W; 55 mi. long, 30 mi. wide; rises to 4,560 ft. on Mt. Reid (E). Ketchikan town in S; industries are fishing, canning, logging. Visited by Russian, English, and Spanish explorers and named (1793) for Count Revilla Gigedo, viceroy of Mexico (1789–94).

Revillagigedo Islands or **Revilla Gigedo Islands** (rāvē'yä hĕhā'dō), archipelago (□ 320) belonging to Colima, Mexico, in the Pacific, 475 mi. W of Manzanillo. Consist of 3 volcanic isls.: Socorro Isl. (18°20'-19°20'N 110°45'-114°50'W), San Benedicto Isl. (19°20'N 110°48'W), Clarión or Santa Rosa Isl. (18°21'N 114°44'W); and of several smaller adjoining rocks, among them Roca Partida and Roca de la Pasión. Socorro Isl., 24 mi. long and 9 mi. wide, rises to 3,707 ft. Uninhabited; provide good fishing grounds, have some vegetation. Guano deposits.

Revillo (rŭvĭ'lō), town (pop. 249), Grant co., E S.Dak., 15 mi. S of Milbank; dairy products, poultry, grain.

Revin (rûvē'), town (pop. 6,350), Ardennes dept., N France, in the Ardennes, 13 mi. NNW of Mézières, at neck of a Meuse R. meander; metalworks (kitchen ranges, heating apparatus); porcelain plumbing fixtures. Tourists visit the Meuse R. defile (2 mi. SE), with its overhanging cliff walls called *Dames de Meuse.*

Revivim (rĕvēvēm'), agr. settlement (pop. 150), S Israel, in the Negev, 15 mi. S of Beersheba; fish cannery (supplied from Gulf of Aqaba); large water reservoir. On Negev water pipe line. Founded 1943; destroyed during fighting, 1948; rebuilt.

Revuca (rĕ'vōōtsä), Slovak *Revúca*, Hung. *Nagyrőce* (nŏ'dyûrû"tsĕ), town (pop. 1,591), S central Slovakia, Czechoslovakia, in Slovak Ore Mts., on railroad and 50 mi. W of Kosice; iron mining.

Rewa (rā'vŭ), former princely state (□ 12,830; pop. 1,820, 445) of Central India agency; ⊙ was Rewa. Founded c.1400 by Baghela clan of Rajputs; made treaty with British in 1812. In Baghelkhand Agency from 1871 to 1931, when placed in Bundelkhand Agency; in 1933, held direct relations with agent for Central India; in 1948, merged with Vindhya Pradesh. Sometimes spelled Rewah.

Rewa, city (pop. 26,008), ⊙ Vindhya Pradesh and Rewa dist., India, 70 mi. SSW of Allahabad, in Baghelkhand; trade center for grain, timber, building stone; handicraft cloth weaving, wood carving. Was ⊙ former Central India state of Rewa.

Rewa Kantha Agency, India: see GUJARAT STATES.

Rewari (rāvä'rē), town (pop. 30,673), Gurgaon dist., SE Punjab, India, 31 mi. SW of Gurgaon; rail junction; trade center; agr. market (millet, cotton, gram, wheat, oilseeds); mfg. of glue, stationery, copper and brass utensils; handicrafts (cloth weaving, fibre products). Has col.

Rewa River (rā'wä), E Viti Levu, Fiji, SW Pacific, largest river in Fiji, rises in mtn. range near Vatukoula, flows 90 mi. SE to Lauthala Bay near Suva. Navigable by small steamers for 50 mi. from mouth; drains ⅓ of Viti Levu.

Rewey (rōō'ē), village (pop. 252), Iowa co., SW Wis., 8 mi. NNE of Platteville, in dairy and livestock region.

Rexburg, city (pop. 4,253), ⊙ Madison co., E Idaho, on small branch of Teton R., near Snake R., and 25 mi. NE of Idaho Falls; alt. 4,861 ft. Trade center for livestock, poultry, and irrigated agr. area (sugar beets, potatoes); beet sugar, dairy products. Founded 1883 by Mormons. Ricks Col. (Mormon jr. col.; 1888) is here.

Rexford, city (pop. 304), Thomas co., NW Kansas, 17 mi. ENE of Colby, in agr. and cattle area.

Rey, Iran: see RAI.

Rey, Isla del (ēs'lä dĕl rā'), island (□ 15; pop. 660), in Valdivia R. estuary, Valdivia prov., S central Chile, 5 mi. SW of Valdivia; 6 mi. long, 3 mi. wide. Agr. area with several settlements; cereals, potatoes, livestock. Resort.

Rey, Isla del, Panama: see SAN MIGUEL ISLAND.

Rey, Lake, Bolivia: see LIVERPOOL, CURICHE.

Rey-Bouba, Fr. Cameroons: see REÏ-BOUBA.

Reydar Fjord or **Reydhar Fjord** (both: rā'dür, rā'-dhär), Icelandic *Reyðarfjörður* (rā'dhärfyûr"dhür), inlet (20 mi. long, 2–3 mi. wide) of Atlantic, E Iceland; 65°N 13°55'W. Eskifjordur and Budareyri, fishing villages, are on it. Feldspar quarried in region.

Reydon (rā'dŭn), town (pop. 331), Roger Mills co., W Okla., 31 mi. WNW of Elk City, near Texas line, in agr. area.

Reyes (rā'ēs), village (pop. estimate 500), S Jujuy prov., Argentina, on railroad, on the Rio Grande de Jujuy and 5 mi. NW of Jujuy; tourist resort and agr. center (grain, vegetables, livestock). Hot sulphur springs. Hydroelectric station.

Reyes, town (pop. c.1,700), ⊙ General José Ballivián prov., Beni dept., NW Bolivia, on road from Rurrenabaque and 170 mi. WNW of Trinidad; local trade center for tropical agr. products (rice, cacao, coffee).

Reyes. **1** Town, San Luis Potosí, Mexico: see VILLA DE REYES. **2** Town (pop. 245), Veracruz, E Mexico, in Sierra Madre Oriental, 17 mi. SSW of Córdoba; fruit.

Reyes, Los, Mexico: see LOS REYES.

Reyes, Point (rāz), bold promontory on W coast of Calif., at tip of peninsula W of Drakes Bay; lighthouse (294 ft. above sea; established 1870) here. Coast guard station near by.

Reyfoun, Lebanon: see RAIFUN.

Reyhanli (rāhänlŭ'), Turkish *Reyhanlı*, town (pop. 5,512), Hatay prov., S Turkey, 24 mi. ENE of Antioch; grain. Formerly Reyhaniye.

Reykholt (rāk'hôlt"), locality, W Iceland, 40 mi. NE of Reykjavik. Here was home of Snorri Sturluson, author of the *Edda* and the *Heimskringla.*

Reykjanes Peninsula (rā'kyûnĕs"), Icelandic *Reykjanesskaga* (rā'kyänĕs"skä"gä, rā'kä–), SW Iceland, extends WSW from Reykjavik, bet. Faxa Bay (N) and Atlantic (S); 40 mi. long, 10–30 mi. wide. Its tip is Reykjanesta, SW cape (63°48'N 22°44'W) of Iceland. Hilly, it rises to 2,149 ft. at base. W tip widens to 20 mi. At Keflavik is international airport.

Reykjavik (rā'kyûvĭk"), Icelandic *Reykjavík* (rā'-kyävēk", rā'kävēk"), city (pop. 54,707), ⊙ Iceland, in but independent of Gullbringu og Kjosar co., in SW part of Iceland, in Faxa Bay, on N shore of Reykjanes Peninsula; 64°9'N 21°57'W. Chief port, commercial, and fishing center, with fish processing, freezing, and canning plants, cod-liver-oil refinery, shipyards, power station; light industries. International airport at Keflavik (20 mi. WSW). It is a Lutheran bishop's see, and seat of Univ. of Iceland (founded 1911, new bldgs. completed 1940) and Meteorological Institute (1920). A hot-water supply system (completed 1945) uses natural hot springs. Average annual temp. ranges from 30°F. (Jan.) to 52°F. (July); mean annual rainfall 34 inches. Founded 874 as 1st permanent settlement of Iceland. Chartered 1786; made seat of Danish administration 1801; became ⊙ Iceland 1918. Sometimes Reikjavik.

Reyneke, Russian SFSR: see REINEKE.

Reynella (rānĕ'lü), village, SE South Australia, 13 mi. SSW of Adelaide; winery.

Reyno (rē'nō), town (pop. 292), Randolph co., NE Ark., 14 mi. ENE of Pocahontas, near Current R.

Reynolds (rĕ'nŭldz), county (□ 822; pop. 6,918), SE Mo.; ⊙ Centerville. In the Ozarks; drained by Black R. Livestock raising, agr.; pine timber, granite. Part of Clark Natl. Forest here. Formed 1845.

Reynolds. **1** Town (pop. 906), Taylor co., W central Ga., 33 mi. SW of Macon, near Flint R.; textile mfg. **2** Village (pop. 409), on Mercer–Rock Island co. line, NW Ill., 13 mi. SSW of Rock Island, in agr. area. **3** Town (pop. 499), White co., NW central Ind., 24 mi. N of Lafayette, in agr. area. **4** Village (pop. 166), Jefferson co., SE Nebr., 10 mi. SW of Fairbury and on branch of Little Blue R., near Kansas line. **5** City (pop. 335), on Traill–Grand Forks co. line, E N.Dak., 18 mi. S of Grand Forks.

Reynoldsburg (rĕ'nŭldzbûrg), village (pop. 724), Franklin co., central Ohio, 10 mi. E of Columbus, in agr. area; meat products.

Reynoldsville (rĕ'nŭldzvĭl), borough (pop. 3,569), Jefferson co., W central Pa., 11 mi. NNE of Punxsutawney; mfg. (textiles, bricks, caskets); bituminous coal mining; timber. Settled c.1824, laid out 1873.

Reynosa or **Reinosa** (rānō'sä), city (pop. 9,412), Tamaulipas, NE Mexico, on the Rio Grande opposite Hidalgo (Texas), on railroad and 50 mi. WNW of Matamoros; agr. center (cotton, sugar cane, corn, stock); cotton ginning, sawmilling. Oil refinery (E) serves near-by oil fields.

Reyshahr, Iran: see RISHAHR.

Reyville (rāvēl'), village, Sousse dist., E Tunisia, on Gulf of Hammamet, 32 mi. NNW of Sousse; muscat grapes, olives.

Rezaiyeh, Iran: see RIZAIYEH.

Rezat, Germany: see FRANCONIAN REZAT; SWABIAN REZAT.

Rezé (rŭzā'), commune (pop. 16,395), Loire-Inférieure dept., W France, on the Loire opposite Nantes. Contains PONT ROUSSEAU, S industrial suburb of Nantes.

Rezegh, Cyrenaica: see SIDI REZEGH.

Rezekne (rā'zĕknā), Lettish *Rēzekne*, Ger. *Rositten* (rōzĭt'ŭn), Rus. (until 1917) *Rezhitsa* (rā'zhētsä), city (pop. 13,139), E Latvia, in Latgale, 55 mi. NE of Daugavpils; rail and road junction; agr. market (rye, flax); woolen and flax mills; brewing, metalworking. Cultural center of Latgale. Castle ruins. In Rus. Vitebsk govt. until 1920.

Rezende, Brazil: see RESENDE.

Rezende Costa, Brazil: see RESENDE COSTA.

Rezende Mine, Southern Rhodesia: see PENHALONGA.

Rezh (ryĕsh), city (1933 pop. over 10,000), S central Sverdlovsk oblast, Russian SFSR, on Rezh R., on railroad and 47 mi. NE of Sverdlovsk; major nickel-refining center; metalworking; asbestos quarrying; silicate industry. Developed prior to First World War as ironworks called Rezhevski Zavod. Became city in 1943.

Rezhitsa, Latvia: see REZEKNE.

Rezh River, Sverdlovsk oblast, Russian SFSR, rises in the central Urals 15 mi. SE of Nevyansk, flows generally E, past Rezh, and NE, past Koptelovo, joining Neiva R. 20 mi. ENE of Alapayevsk to form Nitsa R.; 110 mi. long.

Rezina (ryĭzē'nŭ), Rum. *Rezina* or *Rezina-Târg* (rĕzē'nä-tûrg'), city (1941 pop. 4,069), E Moldavian SSR, on right bank of Dniester R., opposite Rybnitsa, and 26 mi. NNE of Orgeyev; agr. center; oilseeds, tobacco, wine.

Rezonville (rŭzōvēl'), village (pop. 212), Moselle dept., NE France, 9 mi. WSW of Metz. Near by is the 1870 battlefield of Gravelotte.

Rezova River (rĭzô'vŭ), Turkish *Rezvaya* (rĕzväyä'), in N European Turkey and SE Bulgaria, rises in Istranca (Strandzha) Mts. 10 mi. W of Malko-Tirnovo, flows c.55 mi. E along border to Black Sea 45 mi. SE of Burgas.

Rezsöhaza, Yugoslavia: see KNICANIN.

Rezzato (rĕtsä'tô), village (pop. 3,002), Brescia prov., Lombardy, N Italy, 5 mi. ESE of Brescia; mfg. (textile machinery, cement, hosiery), wine making.

Rha, Russian SFSR: see VOLGA RIVER.

Rhadames, Fezzan: see GHADAMES.

Rhaetia (rē'shŭ), ancient province of the Romans; included modern Grisons canton of Switzerland, part of Tyrol prov. of Austria, and later Vindelicia. Subjugated by Romans in 15 B.C., after a desperate struggle.

Rhaetian Alps (rē'shŭn), Ger. *Rätische Alpen*, Fr. *Alpes Rhétiques*, Ital. *Alpi Retiche*, division of Central Alps along Italo-Swiss and Austro-Swiss border, but principally in Grisons canton (Switzerland); extend from Lepontine Alps at Splügen Pass (WSW) to Ötztal Alps at Passo di Resia (ENE), and Lechtal Alps at the Arlberg (NE), Bounded by Hinterrhein R. (W), by the Valtellina (S), and by the Ortles (E). Crossed SW-NE by ENGADINE valley. Highest peak, Piz Bernina (13,304 ft.) in BERNINA ALPS, S of Pontresina. Other component groups are ALBULA ALPS, the RHÄTIKON, and the SILVRETTA GROUP.

Rhafsaï, Fr. Morocco: see GHAFSAÏ.

Rhagae, Iran: see RAI.

Rhame (rām), village (pop. 340), Bowman co., SW N.Dak., 13 mi. W of Bowman. Gas wells, lignite mines; livestock, poultry, wheat, rye, flax. Highest town (alt. 3,184 ft.) in state.

Rharb or **Gharb** (both: gärb), poorly drained coastal lowland in NW Fr. Morocco, traversed E-W by the meandering Sebou R. A former gulf of the Atlantic, it extends c.50 mi. along the coast NNE of Port-Lyautey, and reaches c.70 mi. inland, beyond Petitjean (site of small petroleum basin). Because of deep alluvial deposits, region is suited to intensive agr. (wheat, tobacco, fruit) and livestock raising.

Rharbi, Tunisia: see KERKENNAH.

Rharsa, Chott el (shôt' ĕl gärsä'), saline lake in SW Tunisia, near Algerian border, forming, together with the larger Chott Djerid (ESE), a continuous depression (former arm of the sea) bet. the Gulf of Gabès and Algeria; 30 mi. long, 10 mi. wide. Slightly below sea level (13–55 ft.). Covered by water only in lowest areas. Extensive salt flats.

Rhat, Fezzan: see GHAT.

Rhätikon (rä'tĭkôn), mountain chain of Rhaetian Alps in Grisons canton of Switzerland, Vorarlberg prov. of Austria, and Liechtenstein; separates Montafon and Prätigau valleys. Scesaplana (shäzäplä'nä), its highest peak (9,736 ft.), is on Austro-Swiss border 9 mi. ENE of Maienfeld, Switzerland.

Rhayader (rī'ŭdûr), town and parish (pop. 927), NW Radnor, Wales, on Wye R. and 7 mi. NW of Llandrindod Wells; agr. market. Near by are reservoirs of Birmingham waterworks.

Rhazir, Lebanon: see GHAZIR.

Rhäzüns (räzüns'), town (pop. 678) and district (pop. 3,559), Grisons canton, E Switzerland, 7 mi. SW of Chur, near the Hinterrhein.

Rhea (rā), county (□ 335; pop. 16,041), E Tenn., ⊙ Dayton. Drained by Tennessee R., impounded (in N) by Watts Bar Reservoir; part of Chickamauga Reservoir (Tennessee R.) in S. Fruitgrowing, agr. (corn, truck, hay, dairy products, livestock), lumbering (hardwoods, pine), bituminous-coal mining. Some industry at Dayton, Spring City. Formed 1807.

Rhea Springs, resort village, Rhea co., E Tenn., 50 mi. NE of Chattanooga; mineral waters. Prehistoric Indian mounds here. Watts Bar Dam and reservoir are near by.

Rheatown (rā'toun), town (pop. 107), Greene co., NE Tenn., 8 mi. ENE of Greeneville.

Rheda (rā'dä), town (pop. 8,383), in former Prussian prov. of Westphalia, NW Germany, after 1945 in North Rhine-Westphalia, on the Ems and 5 mi. SW of Gütersloh; rail junction; pumpernickel; hog raising (ham). Has Renaissance castle.

Rhegium, Italy: see REGGIO DI CALABRIA, city.

Rheidol River (rī'dôl), Cardigan, Wales, rises on Plinlimmon, flows 22 mi. SW, S, and W, past Ponterwyd, to Cardigan Bay of Irish Sea at Aberystwyth.

Rheims or **Reims** (rēmz, Fr. rēs), anc. *Durocortorum*, city (pop. 106,081), Marne dept., N France, on Vesle R., on Aisne-Marne Canal, and 85 mi. ENE of Paris; 49°15'N 4°2'E. Center of France's champagne industry, with fine vineyards on slopes of Montagne de Reims (c.6 mi. S). Famous Merino woolen industry (declining in 19th and early 20th cent.) is being revived by new flannel, velvet, felt and clothing manufactures. Known for its biscuits and gingerbread, Rheims also produces winegrowing equipment, electrical and automotive equipment, wine bottles, chemical fertilizer, textile dyes, and pharmaceuticals. Rheims was a leading city (⊙ of Remi tribe) of Roman Gaul. Clovis I was crowned (496) king of all Franks in its cathedral by St. Remi, bishop of Rheims. Thereafter it became customary for kings of France to be crowned here. Rheims later became an archbishopric. Most celebrated is coronation (1429) of Charles VII in presence of Joan of Arc. Present cathedral (begun 1211, finished a cent. later) is a monument of Fr. Gothic architecture and a national symbol. Shelled by Germans in 1870 and again in First World War when most of its interior, including irreplaceable stained-glass windows, was destroyed. Restored (largely with funds of Rockefeller Foundation), it was reopened in 1938, and escaped further damage in Second World War. Town hall (17th cent.) and 11th-16th-cent. church of St. Remi (both partially destroyed in 1914–18) have been restored in their old style. Rheims has a univ. (founded 1547 by Pope Paul III), mus. of fine arts, and library (built by Carnegie Foundation in 1930). Earliest Fr. newspaper (*Gazette de France*) was first printed here in 1694. Jean Baptiste Colbert, Gobelin brothers, and St. John Baptiste de la Salle b. here. Rheims became France's martyr city during First World War. Taken and sacked by Germans in 1914, it was recaptured after 10 days, and subjected to shelling by Germans (who occupied surrounding heights) until their retreat in 1918. In the process it was virtually leveled. Although it suffered new damages during Second World War, all historical bldgs. were spared. Here, on May 7, 1945, Germany surrendered unconditionally to the Allies.

Rhein, village (pop. 403), E Sask., 16 mi. NE of Yorkton; grain, mixed farming.

Rhein, Ger. name of RHINE RIVER.

Rhein, town, Poland: see RYN.

Rheinau (rī'nou), town (pop. 2,171), Zurich canton, N Switzerland, on the Rhine (Ger. border; bridge) and 4 mi. SSW of Schaffhausen. Has 9th-cent. Benedictine abbey, baroque church.

Rheinbach (rīn'bäkh), town (pop. 3,890), in former Prussian Rhine Prov., W Germany, after 1945 in North Rhine-Westphalia, 10 mi. SW of Bonn. Has late-Gothic church.

Rheinberg (rīn'bĕrk), town (pop. 6,260), in former Prussian Rhine Prov., W Germany, after 1945 in North Rhine-Westphalia, in the Ruhr, near left bank of the Rhine, 6 mi. N of Moers; soda works. Has 15th-cent. town hall.

Rheine (rī'nŭ), town (pop. 32,823), in former Prussian prov. of Westphalia, NW Germany, after 1945 in North Rhine-Westphalia, on the Ems and 25 mi. W of Osnabrück; rail junction; textile center (cotton, linen); machinery mfg. Has Gothic church. Chartered 1327.

Rheineck (rī'nĕk), town (pop. 2,480), St. Gall canton, NE Switzerland, on the Alter Rhein, on Austrian border, and 10 mi. ENE of St. Gall; textiles (mainly silk), knit goods, metal products; woodworking.

Rheinfall (rīn'fäl), **Falls of the Rhine,** or **Schaffhausen Falls** (shäfhou'zŭn), in the upper Rhine R. near Schaffhausen, N Switzerland, bet. NEUHAUSEN (left) and Laufen (right). Among the several cataracts by which, combined, the Rhine descends c.100 ft., are 2 major ones, that on the right bank falling c.50 ft., that on the left bank falling c.65 ft. Despite its small dimensions, the Rheinfall is an impressive, well-known landmark. It is now harnessed for hydroelectric power, particularly utilized by the local aluminum industry.

Rheinfelden (rīn'fĕl"dŭn), town (pop. 7,537), S Baden, Germany, at S foot of Black Forest, on the Rhine (Swiss border; bridge) and 7 mi. SE of Lörrach; hydroelectric plant; aluminum works. Mfg. of silk, chemicals, ceramics; woodworking.

Rheinfelden, town (pop. 3,910), Aargau canton, N Switzerland, on the Rhine (Ger. border; bridge), and 9 mi. E of Basel; tourist center with saline baths. Hydroelectric plant, salt mines; clothes, wooden barrels, beer, tobacco. A free imperial town in Middle Ages. Remains of old walls and towers, town hall with local mus., 15th-cent. church. Has ruins of castle on isl. in the Rhine.

Rheinfels, Germany: see SANKT GOAR.

Rheingau (rīn'gou), region on lower S slope of the Rheingau Mts., W Germany, extending c.15 mi. E of Assmannshausen along right bank of the Rhine; noted for its wines. Main town: Eltville.

Rheingau Mountains, Ger. *Rheingau Gebirge* (gŭbĭr'gŭ), W range of the Taunus, W Germany, rising to 2,034 ft. in the Kalte Herberge. Lower S slope, the Rheingau region, is noted for its wines.

Rheinhausen (rīn'hou"zŭn), town (pop. 42,736), in former Prussian Rhine Prov., W Germany, after 1945 in North Rhine-Westphalia, in the Ruhr, port on left bank of the Rhine, opposite Duisburg; transshipment point. Coal mining, coking; briquettes; iron- and steelworks and rolling mills; steel construction. Mfg. of machinery and apparatus for mining and chemical industry, armatures, measuring instruments, concrete goods, textiles, furniture, barrels; brewing, distilling. Ironworks established here by Friedrich A. Krupp in 1890s. Town was formed 1923 through incorporation of Friemersheim and Hochemmerich; chartered 1934.

Rheinheim (rīn'hīm), village (pop. 338), S Baden, Germany, at S foot of Black Forest, on the Rhine (Swiss border; bridge) and 5 mi. SE of Waldshut; strawberries.

Rhein-Herne-Kanal, Germany: see RHINE-HERNE CANAL.

Rheinhessen, Germany: see RHENISH HESSE.

Rheinisches Schiefergebirge, Germany: see RHENISH SLATE MOUNTAINS.

Rhein Lake, Poland: see RYN, LAKE.

Rheinland, Germany: see RHINELAND.

Rheinland-Pfalz, Germany: see RHINELAND-PALATINATE.

Rheinpfalz, Germany: see RHENISH PALATINATE.

Rheinpreussen, Germany: see RHINE PROVINCE.

Rheinprovinz, Germany: see RHINE PROVINCE.

Rheinquellhorn (rīn'kvĕlhôrn"), peak (10,499 ft.) in Adula group of Lepontine Alps, SE Switzerland, 9 mi. NNE of Biasca.

Rheinsberg (rīns'bĕrk), town (pop. 4,215), Brandenburg, E Germany, on Rhin R., and 12 mi. NNE of Neuruppin, on small lake; mfg. of faïence, chemicals. Has rococo palace, the residence (1736–40) of Frederick the Great as crown prince. Town 1st mentioned 1335.

Rheinstein (rīn'shtīn), picturesque castle, W Germany, on left bank of the Rhine, opposite Assmannshausen. First mentioned in 13th cent.; passed 1348 to electors of Trier. Restored 1825–29 by Prince Frederick of Prussia.

Rheinwald (rīn'vält), valley in Grisons canton, SE Switzerland; extends E of Adula group of Lepontine Alps along upper Hinterrhein R., a headstream of the Rhine.

Rheinwaldhorn, peak (11,173 ft.) in Lepontine Alps, SE Switzerland, 9 mi. NNE of Biasca; highest in Adula group.

Rheinzabern (rīn'tsä"bûrn), village (pop. 2,545), Rhenish Palatinate, W Germany, 10 mi. SE of Landau; grain, tobacco. Roman remains excavated near by.

Rhenea, Greece: see RENEIA.

Rhenen or **Renen** (both: rā'nŭn), town (pop. 5,194), Utrecht prov., central Netherlands, on Lower Rhine R. and 22 mi. ESE of Utrecht, surrounded by high hills. Mfg. (fiber mats, chairs, cigars); stone and limestone quarries; agr. (tobacco, berries, herbs, flower bulbs). Has 14th-cent. church of St. Cunera. Residence (c.1620) of exiled Frederick V, king of Bohemia. Rhenen dates from 1346. Center of town destroyed in Second World War.

Rhenish Hesse (rĕ'nĭsh hĕ'sē, hĕs', rē'nĭsh), Ger. *Rheinhessen* (rīn'hĕ"sŭn), administrative division [Ger. *Regierungsbezirk*] (□ 517; 1946 pop. 349,285; 1950 pop. 382,338) of RHINELAND-PALATINATE, W Germany; ⊙ Mainz. Situated on left bank of a bend in the Rhine (Hessian border), it consists of densely populated, fertile uplands, and is noted for its wine (BINGEN, NIERSTEIN, OPPENHEIM). Historic centers of MAINZ (univ.) and WORMS are seats of industry (chemicals, machinery; leatherworking). Formed in 1816 as the prov. (□ 602; 1939 pop. 459,759) of HESSE-DARMSTADT out of territory lost (1803) by Palatinate and former ecclesiastical state of Mainz. With exception of small right-bank portions, it was placed in 1945 in newly formed state of Rhineland-Palatinate of Fr. occupation zone.

Rhenish Palatinate (pŭlă'tĭnĭt), Ger. *Rheinpfalz* (rīn'pfälts), officially **Palatinate**, Ger. *Pfalz*, administrative division [Ger. *Oberregierungsbezirk*] (□ 2,111; 1950 pop. 1,047,844) of S Rhineland-Palatinate, W Germany; ⊙ Neustadt. Bordered by the Saar (W), France (S), and Württemberg-Baden (E). Mountainous, with exception of Rhine plain (E), it includes Hardt Mountains (center). Drained by Rhine (E border), Lauter, Queich, and Speyer rivers. Fertile region with mild climate; grain, corn, sugar beets, and tobacco grown on Rhine plain; wine, peaches, apricots, and almonds on E slopes and at foot of Hardt Mts.; plums, apples, and pears in N. Ludwigshafen is noted for chemical mfg., Pirmasens for its leather industry (shoes); Neustadt is wine center of area; before Second World War, Frankenthal was site of numerous sugar refineries; there are active textile and tobacco industries (Kaiserslautern, Landau, Speyer). Historically, region formed part of Palatinate of Holy Roman Empire. Formerly in Bavaria, it was included after Second World War in newly formed state of Rhineland-Palatinate in Fr. occupation zone. Frequently also called Bavarian Palatinate, Ger. *Bayrische Pfalz* (bī'rĭshŭ), and Lower Palatinate, Ger. *Niederpfalz* (nē'dŭr–).

Rhenish Prussia, Germany: see Rhine Province.

Rhenish Slate Mountains, Ger. *Rheinisches Schiefergebirge* (rī'nĭ-shŭs shē'fŭrgŭbĭr"gŭ), extensive plateau of W Germany, dissected by the Rhine and its tributaries, and generally located bet. Belgian border (W), Lahn R. (E), Bingen (S), and Bonn (N). Comprises the Eifel (NW), the Hunsrück (SW), the Taunus (SE), the Westerwald (N), and the Rothaargebirge (NE). Consists primarily of folded Devonian slate, and some sandstone.

Rhenok (rā'nôk), village, SE Sikkim, India, 11 mi. SSE of Gangtok, in foothills of W Assam Himalayas; trades in corn, rice, pulse, oranges. Copper mining at Pachikhani, 4 mi. NW.

Rhens (rĕns), village (pop. 2,287), in former Prussian Rhine Prov., W Germany, after 1945 in Rhineland-Palatinate, on left bank of the Rhine and 5 mi. S of Coblenz; mineral spring. Partly surrounded by medieval fortifications. The Königsstuhl [Ger.,=royal throne], a meeting place of the electors of the Holy Roman Empire in 14th cent., is near by. Sometimes spelled Rhense or Rense.

Rhenus, anc. name for Rhine River.

Rhéris, Oued, Fr. Morocco: see Ghéris, Oued.

Rheti, Belgian Congo: see Nioka.

Rhétiques, Alpes, Switzerland: see Rhaetian Alps.

Rheydt (rīt), city (1950 pop. 78,500), in former Prussian Rhine Prov., W Germany, after 1945 in North Rhine-Westphalia, on the Niers and 15 mi. WSW of Düsseldorf; twin city (just S) of München Gladbach; 51°10'N 6°24'E. Rail and industrial center; textile industry (cotton, silk, velvet); mfg.: machinery, cables, chemicals, shoes. Has noted 16th-cent. Renaissance castle. First mentioned 1180. Chartered 1857. United (1929–33) with München Gladbach and Odenkirchen to form Gladbach-Rheydt. Captured by U.S. troops in March, 1945. Second World War destruction about 60%.

Rhin, Fr. name of Rhine River.

Rhin, Bas-; Rhin, Haut-, France: see Bas-Rhin; Haut-Rhin.

Rhin Canal, Germany: see Rhin River.

Rhine (rīn), town (pop. 514), Dodge co., S central Ga., 14 mi. S of Eastman, in agr. area.

Rhinebeck (rīn'bĕk"), village (pop. 1,923), Dutchess co., SE N.Y., across the Hudson from and 5 mi. E of Kingston, with which it is connected by ferry from Rhinecliff village (c.2 mi. W); noted violet-growing center; mfg. (cider, machinery). Settled before 1700, inc. 1834.

Rhine-Herne Canal, Ger. *Rhein-Herne-Kanal* (rīn'-hĕr'nŭ-känäl"), W Germany, a major transportation artery of the Ruhr, connecting Rhine R. at Duisburg with Dortmund-Ems Canal at Henrichenburg (ship elevator; level difference 45.9 ft.); 24 mi. long; 7 locks; navigable for vessels up to 1,250 tons. Built 1907–14.

Rhineland, Ger. *Rheinland* (rīn'länt), region in W Germany, along the Rhine; Cologne is its leading city. Term is frequently used to refer only to former Prussian Rhine Prov., but in its general application also includes Rhenish and SW Hesse, Rhenish Palatinate, and NW Baden. Region was occupied by Allies after First World War; was evacuated by 1930. Treaty of Versailles had provided for complete demilitarization of left-bank territory and of a strip extending 30 mi. (50 km) E of the Rhine. However, in 1936 Hitler began remilitarization and refortification of the Rhineland. The resulting Siegfried Line, a deep and extensive system of fortifications, was penetrated (1944–45) by the Allies in Second World War after heavy fighting.

Rhineland (rīn'lănd"), town (pop. 198), Montgomery co., E central Mo., near Missouri R., 18 mi. S of Montgomery City; agr.

Rhinelander, city (pop. 8,774), ⊙ Oneida co., N Wis., on Wisconsin R. and 47 mi. NNE of Wausau, in dairying and farming area (potatoes, strawberries), and surrounded by forests and numerous lakes; trade center for resort area; paper milling, woodworking. Has mus. with reproduction of early logging camp. City is hq. of Nicolet Natl. Forest.

Rhineland-Palatinate (–pŭlă'tĭnĭt), Ger. *Rheinland-Pfalz* (rīn'länt-pfälts'), state (□ 7,666; 1946 pop. 2,753,656, including displaced persons 2,761,225; 1950 pop. 2,993,652), W Germany; ⊙ Mainz (temporary ⊙ Coblenz). Formed 1945 through union of Rhenish Palatinate, Rhenish Hesse, part of former Prussian prov. of Hesse-Nassau (see Montabaur), and S portion (□ 4,351) of former Prussian Rhine Province, including Coblenz and Trier. Bounded by France (S), the Saar (SW), Luxembourg (W), Belgium (NW), North Rhine-Westphalia (N), Hesse and Württemberg-Baden (E). Situated in Rhenish Slate Mountains (except Rhenish Palatinate); includes the Hunsrück, the Eifel (W), the Westerwald (NE), and Hardt Mts. (S). Drained by scenic Rhine (center), Nahe, Moselle, Ahr (W), Lahn, and Sieg (E) rivers. Intensive winegrowing in valleys of Moselle River and Ahr River (red wine), along the Rhine, in Rhenish Hesse, and on E slopes and at foot of Hardt Mountains; grain, potatoes (except on desolate Eifel plateau); sugar beets and tobacco on Rhine plain of Rhenish Palatinate. Industry is specialized: Ludwigshafen (chemicals), Pirmasens (shoes), Idar-Oberstein (precious- and semiprecious-stone polishing); other mfg. (machinery, textiles) at historic centers of Mainz, Speyer, Trier, and Worms. Tourist city of Coblenz is river-trade hub for Rhine wines. Bad Ems and Bad Kreuznach are noted spas. After capture (winter, 1944–spring, 1945) by Americans, territory was constituted as the state of Rhineland-Palatinate in Fr. occupation zone. Several border adjustments with the Saar were made in 1946–47. Constitution ratified 1947. Joined (1949) German Federal Republic (West German state).

Rhine-Marne Canal, France: see Marne-Rhine Canal.

Rhine Province, Ger. *Rheinprovinz* (rīn'prōvĭnts"), former Prussian province (□ 9,451; 1939 pop. 7,915,830), W Germany; ⊙ was Coblenz. Bounded by Luxembourg and Belgium (W), the Netherlands (NW, N), former Prussian provs. of Westphalia and Hesse-Nassau (E), Hesse (SE), Rhenish Palatinate and France (S). Rhenish Slate Mountains cover S part, lowlands are in N. Drained by the Rhine (major N-S traffic artery), Moselle (SW), Wupper and Ruhr (N) rivers. Until 1801, when all territory W of the Rhine was ceded to France, region was an agglomeration of over 100 independent [i.e. *reichsunmittelbar*] principalities. At Congress of Vienna, whole region (including left-bank area) was given to Prussia and subsequently (1824) constituted into the Rhine Prov., with ⊙ at Coblenz. Treaty of Versailles awarded Eupen, Malmédy, and Moresnet to Belgium, and the Saar became autonomous; the prov. (except Ruhr region) was occupied by Allies. Last Allied occupation troops were withdrawn in 1926; region was remilitarized by Ger. troops in 1936. After capture (1944–45) by British, Canadian, and U.S. troops, prov. was divided: the highly industrialized N portion (including Aachen, Cologne, and Düsseldorf) went to new state of North Rhine-Westphalia in Br. occupation zone; S portion (including Coblenz and Trier) was inc. into new state of Rhineland-Palatinate in Fr. occupation zone. Prov. was also called Rhenish Prussia, Ger. *Rheinpreussen*, or Rhineland.

Rhine-Rhone Canal, France: see Rhone-Rhine Canal.

Rhine River (rīn), Du. *Rijn* (rīn), Fr. *Rhin* (rē), Ger. *Rhein* (rīn), anc. *Rhenus* (rē'nŭs), central and W Europe, major waterway (c.820 mi. long), historically, culturally, and economically one of the world's great streams. A link as well as an area of perpetual dispute among the nations of Western Europe, the Rhine flows from the Alps to the North Sea through one of the continent's most heavily industrialized and populous regions. It passes through or borders on Switzerland, Liechtenstein, Austria, Germany, France, and the Netherlands, and also forms an outlet for Belgium and even for Eastern and Southern Europe (via interconnecting canals). With its longest (c.450 mi.) section in Germany, the Rhine assumes a particular importance in that country, to which it has become something of a national symbol. It is formed 6½ mi. WSW of Chur, in the Grisons, E Switzerland, by the union of 2 small headstreams, the Hinter Rhein and Vorder Rhein, which rise at an alt. of over 7,000 ft. in the Alps. The former has its source in the Adula group (Paradies Glacier) of the Lepontine Alps, while the latter rises in L. Toma in the St. Gotthard group (Oberalp). Turning N in canton of Glarus, the Rhine proper then flows mostly bet. Switzerland on the W and Liechtenstein and Austria (Vorarlberg) on the E before entering L. Constance. In this upper section the river has been partly regulated, retaining lateral channels, such as the Werdenberger Kanal, Rheinthal Binnen Kanal, Vorarlberger Binnen or Inner Kanal; the Alter Rhein (Old Rhine) joins L. Constance farther W near Rheineck. Issuing from the lake's NW extremity at Constance, the Rhine soon widens again into the Untersee as far as Stein, whence it proceeds in a generally westerly course. After passing Schaffhausen, where it descends c.100 ft. at near-by Neuhausen in the famous Rheinfall or Falls of the Rhine (harnessed by hydroelectric plants supplying large aluminum works), it follows the Swiss-German (Baden) border to Basel, head of Rhine navigation. The Thur River, Aar River, and Birs River are the main Alpine affluents above Basel. At this old city the river bends sharply northward while entering the Rhine rift valley or *Graben*. That great, fertile trough (c.175 mi. long N-S, 20 mi. wide) bet. Basel and Mainz is flanked by Hercynian massifs—the Vosges (in Alsace, France) and, in Germany, the Hardt on the W and the Black Forest and Odenwald on the E. The once meandering course here was deepened and canalized in 19th cent. It passes Kehl, known for its strategic bridges across to Strasbourg, which—though actually on paralleling Ill River—now extends its busy port to the Rhine. Just SW of Karlsruhe the river fully enters Ger. territory and continues generally N, past Speyer, the important industrial twin cities Ludwigshafen and Mannheim (where it is joined by Neckar River), the old imperial city of Worms, Mainz (joined by Main River), and the fashionable spa Wiesbaden. From Bingen onward to Bonn the Rhine cuts NW through a steep, c.80-mi.-long gorge, formed by the picturesque defiles of the Rhenish Slate Mountains, which comprise the Eifel and Hunsrück (W) and Taunus, Westerwald, and Rothaargebirge (E). In this narrow valley, the Rhine is particularly famous for its idyllic landscape, its vineyards and superb wine, its romantic castle ruins, its legendary landmarks (such as Lorelei and Drachenfels), and its historic and cultural associations. Most obstacles to navigation were removed. Here the river is plied by many excursion boats. At Coblenz it receives the Moselle River (left)—at confluence is the *Deutsches Eck*, with 121-ft.-high monument to Emperor William I—and, just above, the Lahn River (right), both of whose valleys are also famed for their wine. Above Bonn the Rhine emerges into the lowland, widening to about 3,000 ft. Proceeding farther NW, past the great cities of Cologne, Düsseldorf, Duisburg, and Hamborn, it serves the all-important industrial clusters of the Wupper (Sauerland), and above all, the Ruhr (with Essen, Bochum, Dortmund, Gelsenkirchen, etc.), on its right bank. Just below Emmerich it enters the Netherlands, taking a generally W direction and breaking into the numerous arms of its intricate delta, which turn the alluvial region into a network of waterways mingling with mouths of the Scheldt River and Meuse River (Du. *Maas*). Immediately after crossing the Du. border it splits at Millingen near Nijmegen into the Lower Rhine (Du. *Neder Rijn*) on the right and the Waal River on the left. From the Lower Rhine branches out SE of Arnhem the Ijssel River, which flows 72 mi. N, past Deventer, to the Ijsselmeer (part of what was the Zuider Zee). The Ijssel R., the Lower Rhine (as continued by Lek River), and the Waal R. are the Rhine's 3 principal distributaries, with the Waal—being allotted most of the water (66%)—currently the chief channel. The Lower Rhine forks at Wijk bij Duurstede into the Lek R. and the Crooked Rhine. The latter is continued by the Old Rhine (Du. *Oud Rijn*), once the chief shipping route, linking Utrecht and Leiden with the North Sea at Katwijk aan Zee, but today virtually abandoned. Utrecht's port was, however, saved through construction of crosscutting Merwede Canal, which joins Waal at Gorinchem with the Ijsselmeer at Amsterdam, a major transoceanic port now on North Sea Canal to Ijmuiden. The Lek and the Waal become in their lower courses inextricably interlaced with the Meuse distributaries. The Lek takes the name New Maas below Krimpen aan den Lek (where it receives Noord River), and is joined at Rotterdam—one of Europe's largest ports—by the Old Maas. Beyond Rotterdam extends the major navigation channel (16-mi. long, c.35-ft. deep) New Waterway—called Scheur in upper course—which discharges into the North Sea at Hook of Holland. From Woudrichem, where the Waal and Meuse merge, the Upper Merwede R. continues as the New Merwede R. westward and is joined by the Bergsche Maas River to form the Hollandschdiep of the North Sea, 6 mi. SSE of Dordrecht. The canal systems of Germany, France, Belgium, and the Netherlands and the huge traffic bet. the Rhine-Ruhr industrial basin and Rotterdam make the Rhine commercially the most important river of Europe. Among the intrafluvial canals are the 195-mi.-long Marne-Rhine Canal (built 1841–52); the Rhone-Rhine Canal through the Saône R. (built 1784–1833, now insignificant); the Ludwig Canal, part of projected link bet. the Rhine and Danube via the Main (construction interrupted during Second World War); the Rhine-Herne Canal (built

1907–14); the Dortmund-Ems Canal (built 1892–99, continued farther to Weser River). The later 2 form part of the Mittelland Canal system (Rhine-Weser-Elbe). Principal inland port on the Rhine is Duisburg, handling with adjacent Hamborn in normal times more volume than either Hamburg or Rotterdam. Next rank Mannheim, Cologne, Düsseldorf, Strasbourg, Basel. Seagoing vessels displacing up to 4,000 tons can navigate upstream as far as Cologne, while Basel is reached by 1,200-ton barges. Coal, iron ore, flour, and grain form the bulk of transported goods. The Rhine is regulated throughout its course, and work, especially in upper section above Strasbourg, is still proceeding. It was declared free to international navigation in 1868. By the Treaty of Versailles (1919) an international commission, with its seat at Strasbourg, was set up; it was repudiated by Nazi regime but resumed functioning after the Second World War. In Roman times the Rhine was a fortified boundary of the Empire; traces of Roman civilization are still evident. It has been contested by the major Western powers for more than 1,000 years. Along its banks the Germans and French built their Siegfried and Maginot lines prior to Second World War. The river was crossed by U.S. troops in March, 1945, at Remagen, SE of Bonn.

Rhin Lake, Germany: see Ruppin Lake.

Rhinns of Galloway, Scotland: see Galloway.

Rhino Camp (rī'nō), town, Northern Prov., NW Uganda, small port on the Albert Nile and 35 mi. E of Arua; cotton, coffee, tobacco; fishing.

Rhinocolura, Egypt: see Arish, El.

Rhinow (rē'nō), town (pop. 2,451), Brandenburg, E Germany, on Rhin Canal near its mouth on the Havel, and 10 mi. N of Rathenow; dairying, stock raising. In near-by hills, Otto Lilienthal died in crash (1896) during experimental glider flight.

Rhin River (rēn), E Germany, rises in lake dist. W of Fürstenberg (Mecklenburg), flows S, through Ruppin L., then continues WSW as Rhin Canal to the Havel, 5 mi. W of Rhinow; 65 mi. long. Canalized in late-18th cent. to drain marsh region.

Rhins River (rēs), Rhône and Loire depts., E central France, rises in Monts du Beaujolais 2 mi. SE of Belmont-de-la-Loire, flows 37 mi. S and W, past Régny, to the Loire below Roanne. Sometimes spelled Rheins or Reins.

Rhio Archipelago, Indonesia: see Riouw Archipelago.

Rhion Strait, Greece: see Rion Strait.

Rhir, Cape, Fr. Morocco: see Guir, Cape.

Rhir, Oued (wĕd' rēr'), Saharan wadi in Touggourt territory, E Algeria, giving its name to a string of date-growing oases extending N from Temacine and Touggourt to S edge of the Chott Merouane. Its underground waters, increased by those of the Oued Igharghar, feed artesian wells. Also spelled Rir, R'hir.

Rhisnes (rēn), village (pop. 1,409), Namur prov., S central Belgium, 4 mi. NNW of Namur; chalk quarrying.

Rhiwbryfdir, Wales: see Ffestiniog.

Rhizus, Turkey: see Rize.

Rho (rô), town (pop. 15,081), Milano prov., Lombardy, N Italy, near Olona R., 8 mi. NW of Milan. Rail junction; industrial center; metallurgical, chemical (plastics, celluloid), and textile plants. Has sanctuary designed by Pellegrino Tibaldi.

Rhodanus, France: see Rhone River.

Rhodebay, Greenland: see Rodebay.

Rhode Island, state (land □ 1,058; with inland waters □ 1,214; 1950 pop. 791,896; 1940 pop. 713,346), NE U.S., in New England, bordered N and E by Mass., S by Atlantic Ocean, W by Conn.; 48th in area, 36th in pop.; one of original 13 states, the 13th to ratify (1790) the Constitution; ⊙ Providence. R.I. measures 47 mi. N–S and 40 mi. E–W along its Atlantic front. The dominant physiographic feature is Narragansett basin in the E third of the state, a shallow lowland area of carboniferous sediments, extending into SE Mass. and, in R.I., being partly submerged in Narragansett Bay. The bay (2–12 mi. wide) runs c.30 mi. inland to Providence, where it receives the Blackstone R.; it contains several isls., such as Rhode (on which is Newport), Conanicut, and Prudence. The W ⅔ of the state forms part of the New England upland, rough and hilly, and underlain by old crystalline rocks. Jerimoth Hill (812 ft.), near Conn. line, is state's highest point. The coast line bet. Watch Hill and Point Judith is marked by sand spits and barrier beaches backed by lagoons and salt marshes. Glaciation left many small lakes and morainic deposits throughout the state. Block Island, 10 mi. offshore, is a remnant of the terminal moraine represented by E Long Isl. to the W and Martha's Vineyard to the E. Scituate Reservoir (N center) is largest body of water within the state. R.I. has a humid continental climate—influenced by proximity to the Atlantic and Narragansett Bay—with an annual rainfall of c.45 in. Providence has mean temp. of 29°F. in Jan., 73°F. in July, and 41 in. of rain. The growing season averages 160–175 days. Some 450,000 acres are classified as forest land, in which hardwoods predominate—chestnut, oak, poplar, maple, birch, elm, and, in the SE, scrub oak and pine. Agr. is relatively unimportant. Most of the c.265,000 acres of farm and pasture land is devoted to dairying. Poultry is also raised, notably the Rhode Island Red. Chief crops are hay, potatoes, corn, oats, and fruit (apples, peaches, berries). The best soils are in the Narragansett Bay area, where many truck gardens are found. The bay has several important fishing centers; oysters, lobsters, clams, scallops, flounder, bluefish, herring, and swordfish are caught in quantity. The small mineral output consists mostly of stone, sand, and gravel. Granite is quarried in the SW near Westerly and there are workings of sandstone, quartzite, and greenstone. Coal is found in places in the Narragansett basin but it has a low fuel value. A titaniferous magnetite deposit occurs near Cumberland. R.I. is primarily a mfg. state, with New England characteristics of imported fuel and raw materials, native skilled labor, and high-grade specialty products. Textiles (woolens and worsteds, cotton, silk, and rayon goods) comprise the leading industry, located mainly along Blackstone R. (e.g., at Pawtucket, Woonsocket). Other important items are machinery, fabricated metal products, machine tools, rubber goods, jewelry, silverware, and food products. Providence, the state's largest city and principal industrial center, is also an important port handling foreign and coastwise traffic. Other cities with varied manufactures include Pawtucket, Cranston, Woonsocket, Warwick, Newport, East Providence, Central Falls, West Warwick, and Bristol (yacht building). Several of the rivers furnish hydroelectric power. There are a number of fine summer resorts, including fashionable Newport, Watch Hill, Narragansett Pier, and Block Isl.; fishing and yachting are popular recreations. Narragansett race track is in Pawtucket. Leading educational institutions are Brown Univ. at Providence, R.I. State Col. at Kingston, and the naval war col. and naval training station at Newport; Northeastern Naval Air Station is at Quonset Point. "Little Rhody" is the most densely populated state (748 persons to the sq. mi.) in the U.S. The coast of what is now R.I. was explored by Verrazano in 1524 and Block in 1614. The 1st permanent white settlement in the area was made in 1636 at Providence by Roger Williams, a religious exile from Mass., who purchased the land from the Narragansett Indians. Other fugitives from Mass. settled (1638) on the site of Portsmouth on Aquidneck Isl. (later called Rhode Isl.). Newport was founded 1639, Warwick 1643. Williams secured a parliamentary patent which organized (1647) the 4 towns under one govt., and in 1663 a royal charter was granted incorporating the colony of Rhode Island and Providence Plantations. Religious freedom attracted many settlers, including Quakers and Jews. The hostility of theocratic Conn. and Mass. resulted in protracted boundary disputes and the exclusion of R.I. from the New England Confederation. Peace with the Indians was maintained until the uprising known as King Philip's War (1675–76). Shipbuilding and ocean commerce were early industries, and during the several colonial wars Narragansett Bay was a notorious haven for privateers. Newport flourished as a commercial center, especially from the "triangular trade" in rum, Negro slaves, and molasses with W Africa and the West Indies. The colonists' resentment of Br. trade restrictions culminated in the burning of the revenue cutter *Gaspee* in 1772. The 1st to declare her independence, "the State of Rhode Island and Providence Plantations" (still its full official designation) witnessed little fighting during the Revolution, although Br. troops occupied Newport 1776–79. The 1st successful U.S. cotton mill was established at Pawtucket in 1790. Its prosperous sea trade hurt by the 1807 Embargo Act, R.I. did not fully support the War of 1812, sending delegates to the states' rights convention at Hartford. The Dorr Rebellion in 1842 was instrumental in the adoption (1843) of a new constitution providing for an extension of manhood suffrage. With the growth of the textile and other industries, large numbers of foreign immigrants arrived—at first English and Irish, then French Canadians, and, toward the end of the 19th cent., Poles and Italians. See also articles on the cities, towns, geographic features, and the 5 counties: Bristol, Kent, Newport Providence, Washington.

Rhode Island, island, c.15 mi. long, 1–5 mi. wide, largest in R.I., at entrance to Narragansett Bay from the Atlantic; part of Newport co. Site of Newport, Portsmouth, and Middletown; has resorts, fisheries, agr. Mt. Hope Bridge to mainland at N end. Known to the Indians and early colonials as Aquidneck, it was renamed 1644, and gave its name to the state.

Rhodell (rōdĕl'), town (pop. 829), Raleigh co., S W.Va., 13 mi. SSW of Beckley, in semibituminous-coal region.

Rhoden (rō'dún), town (pop. 1,910), in former Prussian prov. of Hesse-Nassau, W Germany, after 1945 in Hesse, 23 mi. NW of Kassel. Has 17th-cent. castle. Until 1929 in Waldeck principality.

Rhoden, Ausser and Inner, Switzerland: see Appenzell Ausser Rhoden and Appenzell Inner Rhoden.

Rhodes (rōdz), Gr. *Rhodos*, *Rodos*, or *Rodhos* (all: rô'dhûs), Ital. *Rodi* (rō'dē), largest island (□ 542; pop. 55,181) in the Dodecanese, Greece, in Aegean Sea, 12 mi. off Turkey; oriented NE-SW bet. 36°28'N–28°13'E and 35°52'N–27°45'E; 44 mi. long. 20 mi. wide; rises to 3,986 ft. in the Attavyros [Ital. *Attairo*]. Unusually well watered and forested, Rhodes is ⅓ under cultivation, mainly along the coasts. Leading products are barley, tobacco, cotton, figs, olives, wine. Fruit, vegetables, olive oil, and sponges are exported. The leading center is city of Rhodes (at NE end). Good road net; airport at Gadurra. Pop. is largely Greek, Italians constituting about 10%. Colonized c.1000 B.C. by Dorians who formed the 3 city-states of Camirus, Lindus, and Ialysus, members of the Dorian Hexapolis. Rhodes colonists founded (7th cent. B.C.) Gela in Sicily. The isl. retained its independence until the Persian conquest (late 6th cent. B.C.) and joined in the Ionian revolt that led to the Persian Wars. Joined Delian League, 470–411 B.C., but separated during Peloponnesian War. At the same time the original 3 city-states united and founded the federal capital city of Rhodes. After death of Alexander the Great (323 B.C.), Rhodes asserted its independence and entered the period of its greatest prosperity, power, and culture. Its chief source of wealth, the carrying trade, declined, however, in 2d cent. B.C., when Rhodes became an ally of Rome on unfavorable terms and ceased to be a power in the world. Involved in Roman civil wars, it was seized and sacked by Cassius in 43 B.C. The symbol of Rhodes during the height of its greatness was the Colossus of Rhodes (one of the Seven Wonders of the anc. world), which stood in the harbor of the city (see article on the city). The arts and sciences flourished here with the painter Protogenes and the astronomer Hipparchus. Later Rhodes was the seat of a famous school of rhetoric; Julius Caesar studied here, and throughout the early Christian era Rhodes retained a high literary reputation. Rhodes continued under the Byzantine Empire until the capture (1204) of Constantinople by the host of the Fourth Crusade. It then continued under local lords, was held by the Genoese (1248–50), was annexed (1256) by the emperor of Nicaea, and was conquered (c.1282) by the Seljuks. In 1309 it was taken by the Knights Hospitalers, who defended the island against the attacks of the Ottoman sultans for 50 years until its fall to the forces of Suleiman I (1522; final capitulation, Jan. 1, 1523). The island had prospered under the knights but was neglected by the Turks. With the Dodecanese, Rhodes was taken by Italy in 1912 and was ceded by Italy to Greece in 1947.

Rhodes, city (pop. 21,694) at NE tip of Rhodes isl., ⊙ Dodecanese div., Greece, 12 mi. off Turkish coast; 36°28'N 28°13'E. Important trading and mfg. center; trades in tobacco, fruit, grain. Mfg. of cigarettes, brandy, soap, rugs; flour milling, fruit drying, shipbuilding. Seat of Greek metropolitan. The walled medieval city (barred until 1912 to Christians) rises in an amphitheater from main commercial harbor. Amid its narrow winding streets rises the massive 15th-cent. Grand Hospital of the Knights (now archaeological mus.). The adjoining Street of the Knights, with its old hostels, preserves its original 16th-17th-cent. aspect. The modern city (N) has govt. buildings and hotels and to the S extend residential suburbs. Founded 407 B.C. as the capital of the federated Rhodian city-states, Rhodes developed rapidly and surpassed Athens in 4th cent. B.C. as the leading Mediterranean trade center. Its symbol was the Colossus of Rhodes (one of the Seven Wonders of the anc. world), a 100-ft.-high statue of the sun-god Helios, erected 285 B.C. at the entrance to the harbor and destroyed in an earthquake 224 B.C. With Roman expansion, Rhodes declined (2d cent. B.C.) in favor of the new free port of Delos. The modern city was built and fortified by the Knights Hospitalers, who moved their seat here (1309) from Cyprus. The Knights resisted assaults by the Egyptians (1444) and the Turks (1479–80), but yielded to the latter in 1523 and moved their seat to Malta. The armistice ending the Israel War was signed here, 1949.

Rhodes, town (pop. 369), Marshall co., central Iowa, 17 mi. WSW of Marshalltown, in agr. area. Formerly Edenville.

Rhodes, Inner and Outer, Switzerland: see Appenzell Inner Rhoden and Appenzell Ausser Rhoden.

Rhode-Saint-Genèse, Belgium: see Sint-Genesius-Rode.

Rhodesia (rōdē'zhù), region of S Africa, comprising Northern Rhodesia and Southern Rhodesia. It was named 1894 for Cecil Rhodes, the founder of the British South Africa Company, who took the territory for the company in 1888. The company governed from 1890 to 1923, when the present division was effected.

Rhodes Point, Md.: see Smith Island.

Rhodhiss (rō′dĭs), town (pop. 923), Burke and Caldwell counties, W central N.C., on Catawba R. and 5 mi. NW of Hickory; textile mfg. Power dam in Catawba R. here forms Rhodhiss L. (c.15 mi long).

Rhodope (rŏ′dŭpē), Gr. *Rodope*, *Rodopi*, or *Rodhopi* (all: rôdhô′pē), nome (□ 1,013; pop. 106,403), W Thrace, Greece; ⊙ Komotine. Bounded N by Bulgaria (along Rhodope Mts.) and S by Aegean Sea. Main agr. area is Komotine lowland: tobacco, wheat, silk, vegetables. Coastal fisheries. Crossed by Salonika-Adrianople RR. Main centers are Komotine and Sapai.

Rhodope Mountains, Bulg. *Rodopi*, Gr. *Rodope*, *Rodopi*, or *Rodhopi*, Turkish *Despoto Dagh* or *Dospat Dagh*, major mountain system of Balkan Peninsula, SE Europe, in S Bulgaria and NE Greece. Extend generally 180 mi. NW-SE from Struma R. to lower Maritsa R. (Turkish border) bet. Thracian Plain (upper Maritsa Valley; N) and the Aegean Sea (S). It consists of the Rhodope proper, separated by Mesta R. from the PIRIN MOUNTAINS (W), and the RILA MOUNTAINS (NW), which rise in the culminating Stalin Peak (or Musala; 9,596 ft.). The Rhodope proper has a high W section rising to 7,576 ft. in Slav peak and a progressively lower E section, drained by Arda R. The principal passes are Avramov and Dospat (W), Topolov (NE), and Makaz (SE; on Bulgaro-Greek border). An anc. crystalline massif, partly uplifted during Tertiary period, the Rhodope is a major climatic divide bet. the Mediterranean climate of the Aegean and the humid more continental zone of central Bulgaria. Its scattered lead, silver, iron, copper, and zinc deposits were once exploited. The greater part of Bulgaria's forests (largely conifers) are here. In anc. times, the Rhodope formed the Macedonian-Thracian border. In a broader sense, the Rhodope system is sometimes considered to include the SE Yugoslav highlands bet. the Balkan Mts. and the Dinaric Alps, extending along the Vardar-Morava R. axis N to Belgrade.

Rhodos, Greece: see RHODES.

Rhoedestus, Turkey: see TEKIRDAG.

Rhome, town (pop. 461), Wise co., N Texas, 23 mi. NNW of Fort Worth, near West Fork of Trinity R., in agr. area.

Rhondda (rôn′dhù), urban district (1931 pop. 141,346; 1951 census 111,357), central Glamorgan, Wales, on Rhondda R. and 19 mi. NW of Cardiff; coal-mining and steel-milling center. Urban dist. covers greater part of Rhondda valley and includes coal-mining towns of Tonypandy (tônùpăn′dē), scene of 1910 labor riots, Gelli (gĕ′thlē), Ystrad Rhondda (ŭ′strŭd), Pentre (pĕn′trä), Treorky (trēôr′kē), Tynewydd (tĭnē′wĭdh), Treherbert (trĭhûr′bûrt), Trealaw (trēă′lou), Llwynypia (lōōĭnûpē′ù), and Penygraig (pĕnŭgrīg′). Rhondda is still sometimes called Ystradyfodwg (ŭ″strădĭvô′dōōg), name of anc. parish in valley.

Rhondda River, Glamorgan, Wales, rises 4 mi. W of Aberdare, flows 14 mi. SE, past Rhondda, to Taff R. at Pontypridd.

Rhône (rōn), department (□ 1,104; pop. 918,866), in Lyonnais, E central France; ⊙ LYONS. Traversed by the Monts du Lyonnais (S), Monts du Beaujolais (N); bounded by the Saône and Rhone rivers (E). Wine and fruit are grown on slopes of Saône-Rhone valley N and S of Lyons. Rhône is a leading mfg. dept. Its varied industries, which produce silk and rayon textiles, chemicals, durable goods, and processed foods, are heavily concentrated in the Lyons area, bet. Villefranche (N) and Givors (S). Only the textile industries of Tarare (muslins), Cours, and Thizy have resisted the attraction of Lyons. Dept. was formed 1793 from Rhône-et-Loire dept., which in 1790 had replaced Lyonnais prov.

Rhône, Bouches-du-, France: see BOUCHES-DU-RHÔNE.

Rhone Glacier, in the Alps, S central Switzerland, NW of Furka Pass. Source of the Rhone, it descends from Rhone Firn (which extends from the Rhonestock) to hamlet of Gletsch; fed by snows of the Dammastock, Galenstock, and other mts. At its foot is Gletsch village.

Rhone-Marseilles Canal, France: see ARLES–PORT-DE-BOUC-CANAL.

Rhone-Rhine Canal (rōn″-rīn′), Fr. *Canal du Rhône au Rhin* (kănal dü rōn′ ō rē′), in E France, connects the Saône (above Saint-Jean-de-Losne) with the Rhine (at Strasbourg). Ascends the Doubs to Montbéliard area, crosses Belfort Gap, entering Alsatian lowland near Mulhouse. Here one branch swings SE to join the Rhine at Huningue, another parallels the Ill to Strasbourg. Length: 217 mi. Built 1784–1833, it is too narrow and shallow for modern transport.

Rhone River, Fr. *Rhône* (both: rōn), anc. *Rhodanus*, in Switzerland and SE France, 505 mi. long (including 45 mi. flow through L. Geneva). Rises in Rhone glacier at the foot of Furka Pass in upper Valais (Switzerland), flows WSW through narrow flat-bottomed valley bet. Bernese (N) and Pennine (Valaisian; S) Alps, past Brig, Sierre, and Sion, veers NNW near Martigny-Ville, entering L. Geneva 4 mi. SW of Montreux. Leaving lake at Geneva, it enters France near Pougny, beyond which it is forced southward by Jura folds through which it breaks in several narrow gorges (*cluses*), flowing past Bellegarde and Seyssel. S of Belley, it turns NW then W. At Lyons, where it receives the Saône (its chief tributary), it veers S, flowing in a valley bet. the Massif Central (W) and the Fr. Alps (E) past Vienne, Valence, and Avignon, to Arles, beyond which it reaches the Gulf of Lion in a 2-armed delta which consists of the Grand Rhône (E) and Petit Rhône (W) enclosing a deltaic isl., the CAMARGUE. Both these branches being silted, Arles is connected with Marseilles via ARLES–PORT-DE-BOUC CANAL, Étang de BERRE, and ROVE Tunnel. Chief tributaries are the Ain, Saône, Ardèche, Gard (right); the Arve, Fier, Isère, Drôme, and Durance (left), all in France. The Rhone has largest volume of all Fr. rivers, and presents navigation hazards. It is harnessed for hydroelectric power in its upper course in Switzerland and again in France (notably at GÉNISSIAT). An over-all project (navigation, soil conservation, power), patterned on the TVA, was under way in 1950. The lower Rhone valley (below Lyons), with its Mediterranean climate, is covered with excellent vineyards (*Côtes-du-Rhône*), orchards, olive and mulberry groves. It is the principal communication artery bet. N France and the Mediterranean and was the cradle of Provençal culture.

Rhone-Sète Canal (rōn′-sĕt′), in Gard and Hérault depts., S France, connects Beaucaire on the Rhone with Sète on the Étang de Thau, where it meets Canal du MIDI. On it are Saint-Gilles and Aigues-Mortes. Chiefly used for wine shipments. Total length, 61 mi.

Rhonestock (rō′nùshtôk″), peak (11,811 ft.) in the Alps, S central Switzerland, 13 mi. SE of Meiringen; Rhone Firn extends SSW to Rhone Glacier.

Rhön Mountains (rûn), W Germany, extend c.35 mi. along the borders of Bavaria and Hesse; rise to 3,117 ft. in the Wasserkuppe. Main range is the HOHE RHÖN (SE). Noted for harsh climate and heavy rainfall. Of volcanic origin, they still bear numerous traces of extinct volcanoes. Pop. engaged in woodworking and straw weaving.

Rhos, Wales: see COLWYN BAY.

Rhosllanerchrugog (rōs-lă′nĕrkh-rē′gôg), town and parish (pop. 10,690), E Denbigh, Wales, 4 mi. SW of Wrexham; coal mining, brick mfg.

Rhu, Scotland: see ROW.

Rhuddlan (rĭdh′lùn), town and parish (pop. 1,519), Flint, Wales, on Clwyd R. (16th-cent. bridge) and 2 mi. SSE of Rhyl; iron foundries, tanneries. Has 13th-cent. church. In 1284 Edward I here enacted Statute of Rhuddlan, providing for govt. of Wales. There are remains of castle built c.1277 by Edward I; taken and destroyed 1646 by Parliamentarians.

Rhue River or **Rue River** (rü), Cantal dept., S central France, rises in Massif du Cantal near the Puy Mary, flows N then W into the Dordogne 2 mi. below Bort-les-Orgues; 30 mi. long. Powers hydroelectric plant 5 mi. W of Condat and a silk-processing plant near its mouth.

Rhuis Peninsula (rwēs′), Morbihan dept., W France, bet. Gulf of Morbihan (N) and Bay of Biscay (S), c.10 mi. S of Vannes; winegrowing; oyster beds. Small resorts. Also spelled Rhuys, Ruis.

Rhum, Scotland: see RUM.

Rhumel, Oued (wĕd′ rümĕl′), stream of Constantine dept., NE Algeria, rises in the High Plateaus SW of Châteaudun-du-Rhumel, flows NE to CONSTANTINE (where it skirts city in a deep gorge and is harnessed for hydroelectric power), then turns NW and N, and enters the Mediterranean as the Oued el Kebir 45 mi. W of Philippeville. Length, 145 mi. Also spelled Rhummel and Rummel.

Rhumtek, India: see GANGTOK.

Rhyl (rĭl), urban district (1931 pop. 13,485; 1951 census 18,745), Flint, Wales, on Irish Sea at mouth of Clwyd R., 16 mi. WNW of Flint; seaside resort, small port; brick mfg.

Rhymney (rŭm′nē), urban district (1931 pop. 10,506; 1951 census 9,134), W Monmouth, England, on Rhymney R. and 2 mi. W of Tredegar; steel milling, coal mining.

Rhymney River, Wales and England, rises in Brecknock, Wales, 2 mi. NNW of Rhymney, flows 30 mi. SSE, past Rhymney, Abertridwr, Bargoed, and Hengoed, to Bristol Channel 2 mi. E of Cardiff. Forms border bet. Glamorgan and Monmouth.

Rhyndacus River, Turkey: see KIRMASTI RIVER.

Rhyndwyclydach (rĭndwĕklĭ′dăkh), parish (pop. 9,444), W Glamorgan, Wales; coal mining. Includes towns of CLYDACH and PONTARDAWE.

Rhyne, village (pop. 1,159, with near-by Daniels), Lincoln co., W central N.C., near Lincolnton.

Rhyolite (rī′ōlīt), ghost town, Nye co., S Nev., near Calif. line, c.5 mi. W of Beatty; boomed 1905–8 after gold finds.

Rhyolite Mountain (10,731 ft.), peak in Front Range, Teller co., central Colo.

Ria, France: see PRADES.

Riachão (rēăshä′ō), city (pop. 1,204), S Maranhão, Brazil, 60 mi. E of Carolina, in cattle area; hides, cotton, babassu nuts. Manganese deposits near by.

Riachão do Dantas (dōō dăn′tùs), city (pop. 1,509), S Sergipe, NE Brazil, 21 mi. NW of Estância; cotton, sugar, tobacco. Until 1944, called Riachão.

Riacho do Sangue, Brazil: see FRADE.

Riachos (rēä′shōōsh), town (pop. 3,355), Santarém dist., central Portugal, 17 mi. NE of Santarém; alcohol distilling, ceramics mfg.

Riachos Island (rēä′chōs) (□ 5), in Anegada Bay, SW Buenos Aires prov., Argentina, 60 mi. NE of Carmen de Patagones.

Riachuelo (rēächwā′lō), town (pop. estimate 500), NW Corrientes prov., Argentina, on railroad and 10 mi. SSE of Corrientes; agr. (corn, rice, cotton).

Riachuelo (rēùshwā′lōō), city (pop. 2,762), E Sergipe, NE Brazil, 15 mi. NW of Aracaju; has large sugar mill.

Riachuelo (rēächwā′lō), village (1930 pop. 442), Osorno prov., S central Chile, 19 mi. SSW of Osorno, in agr. area (grain, livestock).

Riachuelo River, Argentina: see MATANZAS RIVER.

Riad, Saudi Arabia: see RIYADH.

Riade, Germany: see RITTEBURG.

Riaillé (rēäyā′), village (pop. 572), Loire-Inférieure dept., W France, on Erdre R. and 14 mi. SSE of Châteaubriant; dairying.

Rialto (rēäl′tô), famous bridge of Venice, N Italy, over the Grand Canal, and dist. forming most anc. quarter of the city. Bridge (1588-91) consists of a single marble arch; has arcades lined with shops.

Rialto (rēăl′tō), residential city (pop. 3,156), San Bernardino co., S Calif., just W of San Bernardino, in citrus-fruit area; packing plants. Inc. 1911.

Riana (rĭă′nù), village (pop. 101), N Tasmania, 60 mi. WNW of Launceston; sawmills.

Rianjo (rēän′hō), town (pop. 1,550), La Coruña prov., NW Spain, small port on Arosa Bay of the Atlantic, and 20 mi. SW of Santiago; shellfishing. Lumber, livestock, fruit in area.

Riaño (rēä′nyō), town (pop. 1,827), Leon prov., NW Spain, on Esla R. and 40 mi. NE of Leon; meat processing; livestock, lumber, cereals, potatoes. Coal and antimony mining near by.

Rians (rēä′), village (pop. 760), Var dept., SE France, 16 mi. ENE of Aix-en-Provence; truffles, wine, perfume essences.

Riánsares River (rēän′särĕs), New Castile, central Spain, rises W of Huete in Cuenca prov., flows c.60 mi. SSW, through upper La Mancha, to Gigüela R. 11 mi. E of Madridejos (Toledo prov.).

Riasi or **Reasi** (ryä′sē), district (□ 1,789; pop. 257,903), Jammu prov., SW Kashmir; ⊙ Riasi. In S Punjab Himalayas; drained by Chenab R. Agr. (corn, wheat, rice, oilseeds, pulse, cotton, tea); coal deposits (mines opened c.1941) in central and SE area; iron ore, bauxite, zinc, lead, clay, and limestone deposits in central area. Main towns: Riasi, Rajaori, Katra. Pop. 68% Moslem, 31% Hindu. Prevailing mother tongues, Dogri and Pahari. Renamed (c.1948) Rajaori.

Riasi or **Reasi**, town (pop. 2,822), ⊙ Riasi dist., SW Kashmir, in Siwalik Range, near the Chenab, 24 mi. NNW of Jammu; trades in grain, oilseeds, fruit. Fort.

Riau Archipelago, Indonesia: see RIOUW ARCHIPELAGO.

Riaza (rēä′thä), town (pop. 1,537), Segovia prov., central Spain, on W slopes of the Sierra de Ayllón, on Riaza R. and 40 mi. NE of Segovia; alt. c.3,900 ft. Picturesque mtn. town. Stock raising, grain growing, lumbering, hunting; flour milling, wool-washing, mfg. of woolen goods.

Riaza River, Old Castile, central Spain, rises just S of Riaza in Segovia prov., flows c.70 mi. N and NW to the Douro (Duero) just E of Roa. Used for hydroelectric power.

Ribadavia (rēvädä′vyä), town (pop. 2,880), Orense prov., NW Spain, in Galicia, on Miño R. and 15 mi. WSW of Orense; center of rich winegrowing dist. Linen-cloth mfg., flour- and sawmilling. Cereals, flax, fruit. Ships wine. Has Gothic church of Dominican convent. In 10th cent. it was briefly seat of King García I of Galicia. Hydroelectric plant near by on small Avia R. Tin mines in vicinity are now little exploited.

Ribadeo (rēvä-dhā′ō), town (pop. 3,248), Lugo prov., NW Spain, in Galicia, on Bay of Biscay at mouth of Eo R., 45 mi. NE of Lugo; exports iron ore from Villaodrid mines (direct mining railroad). Fishing and fish processing, boatbuilding, lumbering. Livestock, cereals are raised in the area. Bathing resort.

Ribadesella (rēvä-dhäsĕ′lyä), town (pop. 2,592), Oviedo prov., NW Spain, fishing port on Bay of Biscay at mouth of Sella R., 30 mi. ESE of Gijón; fishing (lobsters, salmon, trout), fish and meat processing, boatbuilding. Popular bathing resort. Coal mine near by.

Ribaflecha or **Ribafrecha** (rēväflā′chä, –frā′–), town (pop. 1,581), Logroño prov., N Spain, 9 mi. SE of Logroño; plaster mfg., flour milling; produces olive oil, wine, cereals, fruit. Gypsum quarries near by.

Ribaforada (rēväfōrä′dhä), town (pop. 1,619), Navarre prov., N Spain, bet. Ebro R. and Imperial Canal, 7 mi. SE of Tudela; vegetable canning, ceramics mfg.; sugar beets, peppers, cereals.

Ribafrecha, Spain: see RIBAFLECHA.

Ribagorza (rēvägôr′thä), historic district of Aragon, now in Huesca prov., NE Spain, in the central Pyrenees, S of Fr. border, bet. Noguera Pallaresa (E) and Cinca (W) rivers. Annexed (11th cent.) by kings of Aragon.

Ribamar (rēbŭmär'), city (pop. 2,231), N Maranhão, Brazil, on NE shore of São Luís Isl., 18 mi. ENE of São Luís; resort on the Atlantic. Until 1944, called São José de Ribamar.

Riba-Riba, Belgian Congo: see LOKANDU.

Ribarroja (rēvärō'hä), town (pop. 4,498), Valencia prov., E Spain, on Turia R. and 11 mi. NW of Valencia; perfume mfg., esparto processing, flour milling. Mineral springs.

Ribarroja de Ebro (dhā ā'vrō), town (pop. 1,511), Tarragona prov., NE Spain, on the Ebro and 14 mi. N of Gandesa; olive-oil processing; agr. trade (wine, almonds, wheat).

Ribarska Banja or **Ribarska Banya** (both: rē'bärskä bä'nyä), village, S central Serbia, Yugoslavia, 14 mi. N of Prokuplje; health resort.

Ribas de Fresser (rē'väs dhā frĕsĕr'), town (pop. 2,189), Gerona prov., NE Spain, on Fresser R. and 19 mi. WNW of Olot, and on S slopes of the E Pyrenees; alt. 3,000 ft. Health resort with mineral springs. Hydroelectric stations near by on Fresser R. Cotton spinning, paper mfg.

Ribas do Rio Pardo (rē'bus dōō rē'ōō pär'dōō), city (pop. 580), S Mato Grosso, Brazil, on the Rio Pardo, on São Paulo–Mato Grosso RR and 55 mi. E of Campo Grande; cattle. Until 1944, called Rio Pardo.

Ribat, W Pakistan: see ROBAT THANA.

Ribatejo (rēbŭtā'zhōō), [Port.,=banks of the Tagus], province (□ 2,794; 1940 pop. 424,063), central Portugal, formed 1936 from old Estremadura prov.; ⊙ Santarém. It contains Santarém dist. and small sections of Lisboa and Portalegre dists. Cities: Santarém, Abrantes, Tomar.

Ribáuè (rēbä'wā), village, Niassa prov., NE Mozambique, near railroad, 65 mi. WNW of Nampula; mica and kaolin deposits; tobacco, beans, rice. Agr. station.

Ribble River, W Yorkshire and central Lancashire, England, rises at Ribblehead in the Pennines in West Riding of Yorkshire, flows 75 mi. SW, past Settle, Clitheroe, and Preston, to the Irish Sea bet. Southport and Saint Anne's-on-the-Sea. Receives Calder R. at Whalley. Navigable below Preston.

Ribbon Fall, Calif.: see YOSEMITE NATIONAL PARK.

Ribchester, village and parish (pop. 1,475), central Lancashire, England, on Ribble R. and 5 mi. NNW of Blackburn; textile industry (cotton, silk, rayon, wool). Has 13th-cent. church with a separate 14th-cent. chapel and 15th-cent. tower; a 17th-cent. bridge over Ribble R. A fortress in Roman times. Remains of a temple of Minerva are visible and excavations have yielded remains of the former fortifications and residential quarters.

Ribe (rē'bŭ), amt (□ 1,184; 1950 pop. 170,448), SW Jutland, Denmark, on North Sea; ⊙ Ribe. It is hilly in the E (highest point, 335 ft.); poor soil. Agr., dairy farming. Esbjerg, chief city.

Ribe, city (1950 pop. 7,219), ⊙ Ribe amt, SW Jutland, Denmark, 4 mi. from the sea, 15 mi. SE of Esbjerg; 55°20'N 8°46'E. Mfg. (textiles, chicory). Has 12th-cent. church. City flourished as port in Middle Ages.

Ribeauvillé (rēbōvēlā'), Ger. *Rappoltsweiler* (rä'pôltsvīlŭr), town (pop. 3,866), Haut-Rhin dept., E France, at E foot of the Vosges, 8 mi. N of Colmar; cotton milling, metalworking, printing. Alsace wine grown in area. Has remains of medieval fortifications. On near-by rocky height are 3 ruined castles.

Ribécourt (rēbākōōr'), village (pop. 1,308), Oise dept., N France, on Oise R. lateral canal and 8 mi. NE of Compiègne; chemical works (fertilizer, glue, gelatine); brush mfg., vegetable canning. Devastated in First World War.

Ribeira (rēbā'rŭ), city (pop. 449), S São Paulo, Brazil, on Ribeira R. (Paraná line) and 95 mi. SW of Itapetininga; sugar milling. In former gold-mining region. Lead, zinc, copper deposits.

Ribeira Brava (brä'vŭ), town (1950 pop. 8,128), Cape Verde Isls., near N São Nicolau Isl., 130 mi. NNW of Praia (on São Tiago Isl.); 16°37'N 24°18'W. Coffee, oranges.

Ribeira Brava, town (pop. 332), Madeira, in a ravine on S coast of Madeira isl., 9 mi. W of Funchal; fishing; flour products; lumbering.

Ribeira da Barca (dä bär'kŭ), village, Cape Verde Isls., on W shore of São Tiago Isl., 23 mi. NW of Praia; anchorage. Oranges, sugar cane.

Ribeira de Iguape River (dĭ ēgwä'pĭ), S São Paulo, Brazil, formed by confluence of RIBEIRA RIVER and Juquiá R. above Registro, flows 40 mi. SSE, through marshy coastal lowland, to the Atlantic at Iguape. Navigable. Japanese agr. colonies in area.

Ribeira de Pena (dĭ pā'nŭ), town, Vila Real dist., N Portugal, near Tâmega R., 16 mi. N of Vila Real; agr. trade.

Ribeira Grande (grăn'dĭ), town (pop. 7,153), Ponta Delgada dist., E Azores, on N shore of São Miguel Isl., 10 mi. NE of Ponta Delgada, amidst tea plantations; 37°49'N 25°32'W. Tea and chicory processing, textile spinning and weaving, sawmilling. Livestock trade. Thermal springs near by.

Ribeira Grande, town (pop. 1,694), Cape Verde Isls., on NE coast of Santo Antão Isl., 180 mi. NW of Praia (on São Tiago Isl.); 17°11'N 25°4'W.

Ribeirão (rēbārā'ō). **1** City, Goiás, Brazil: see GUAPÓ. **2** City (pop. 3,185), E Pernambuco, NE Brazil, 45 mi. SW of Recife; rail junction on Recife-Maceió line, with spurs to Barreiros (SE) and Cortês (W). Ships sugar, manioc, beans.

Ribeirão Bonito (bōōnē'tōō), city (pop. 2,149), central São Paulo, Brazil, on railroad and 19 mi. WSW of São Carlos; mfg. of macaroni, soap, agr. equipment, pottery; corn milling, distilling.

Ribeirão Claro (klä'rōō), city (pop. 2,074), NE Paraná, Brazil, 90 mi. E of Londrina, in coffee- and cotton-growing region; coffee and rice processing, corn milling, mfg. of pottery.

Ribeirão das Lajes (däs lä'zhĭs), stream in coastal range of SW Rio de Janeiro state, Brazil, dammed 5 mi. S of Piraí. Its Fontes hydroelectric plant supplies Rio and Volta Redonda steel mill with electricity.

Ribeirão Prêto (prā'tōō), city (1950 pop. 65,081), São Paulo, Brazil, 175 mi. NNW of São Paulo; important commercial and communication center in coffeegrowing region. Trades in coffee, cotton, cereals, forage crops, sugar. Industrial plants (chiefly agr. processing) include large new cotton mill, distilleries, sawmills, metalworks (agr. machinery, rolling stock), meat-packing plants, breweries. Tobacco products, furniture, building materials are also made. Has business school. Services pioneer agr. settlements of NW São Paulo and stock-raising dist. (N).

Ribeirão Vermelho (vĕrmā'lyōō), town (pop. 2,698), S Minas Gerais, Brazil, 5 mi. NW of Lavras; rail junction.

Ribeira River (rēbā'rŭ), in E Paraná and S São Paulo, Brazil, rises in the Serra Paranapiacaba E of Ponta Grossa, flows ENE, past Ribeira and Eldorado (head of navigation), joining Juquiá R. above Registro to form the Ribeira de Iguape. Length, c.200 mi. Gold, lead, silver, copper, phosphate deposits in valley.

Ribeiro Gonçalves (rēbā'rōō gōsäl'vĭs), city (pop. 815), SW Piauí, Brazil, on right bank of Parnaíba R. and 160 mi. SW of Floriano. Formerly called Estiva.

Ribeirópolis (rēbārō'pōōlēs), city (pop. 2,018), central Sergipe, NE Brazil, 35 mi. NW of Aracaju; cotton, livestock.

Ribemont (rēbmō'), village (pop. 1,520), Aisne dept., N France, on Oise R. and Oise-Sambre Canal, and 8 mi. ESE of Saint-Quentin; weaving, basket making. Condorcet b. here.

Ribera (rēbā'rä), town (pop. 14,483), Agrigento prov., SW Sicily, near Magazzolo R., 10 mi. E of Sciacca; wine, olive oil. Sandstone deposits (SE). Ruins of old castles near by.

Ribérac (rēbārāk'), town (pop. 2,051), Dordogne dept., SW France, near the Dronne, 19 mi. WNW of Périgueux; market center (cattle, hogs, grains); mfg. (pulp, cement pipes).

Ribera del Fresno (rēvā'rā dhĕl frĕ'snō), town (pop. 5,188), Badajoz prov., SW Spain, 13 mi. SE of Almendralejo; agr. center in fertile Tierra de Barros; cereals, olives, grapes, livestock. Liquor distilling.

Riberalta (rēvārāl'tä), city (pop. c.7,200), ⊙ Vaca Diez prov., Beni dept., N Bolivia, port at confluence of Madre de Dios and Beni rivers, 270 mi. NNW of Trinidad; base for navigation lines covering region; airport. Leading rubber-collecting and commercial center of dept. for Brazil nuts, tropical fruits, and Brazilian imports. Banana plantations, corn, rice, sugar cane, and vegetables in surrounding area. Founded 1882 in middle of jungle; rapidly became a leading outpost for rubber collecting.

Ribiers (rēbyā'), agr. village (pop. 292) Hautes-Alpes dept., SE France, near the Buëch, 5 mi. NW of Sisteron; sericulture; lavender-essence distilling.

Rib Lake, resort village (pop. 853), Taylor co., N central Wis., on small Rib L., 37 mi. NW of Wausau; dairy products, lumber, woodwork.

Rib Mountain (1,940 ft.), Marathon co., central Wis., near Wausau; 2d-highest point in state, it is a quartzite outcrop. Summit is a state park. Winter sports.

Ribnica (rēb'nĭtsä). **1** or **Ribnica na Dolenjskem** (nä dô'lĕnskĕm), village, S Slovenia, Yugoslavia, on railroad and 26 mi. S of Ljubljana. Until 1918, in Carniola. **2** or **Ribnica na Pohorju** (nä pô'hôryōō), Ger. *Reifnig* (rīf'nĭk), village, N Slovenia, Yugoslavia, 18 mi. W of Maribor, on N slope of the Pohorje; sports resort; handicraft (woodworking). Until 1918, in Styria.

Ribnitz (rēp'nĭts), town (pop. 10,710), Mecklenburg, N Germany, near mouth of Recknitz R. on the Saaler Bodden (inlet of the Baltic), 18 mi. NE of Rostock; fishing port; shipbuilding, lumbering, jewelry mfg. Has Gothic church and town gate. Site of former monastery (founded 1323; secularized in 16th cent.). Town founded in late-13th cent.

Ribolla (rēbôl'lä), village, Grosseto prov., Tuscany, central Italy, 15 mi. NNW of Grosseto; lignite.

Rib River, central Wis., rises in small Rib L. in Taylor co., flows c.45 mi. SE to Wisconsin R. near Wausau.

Riburg, Switzerland: see RYBURG.

Ricamarie, La (lä rēkämärē'), town (pop. 8,598), Loire dept., SE central France, on the Ondaine and just SSW of Saint-Étienne; coal mining, steel milling, metalworking.

Ricany (ŭrzhē'chänĭ), Czech *Říčany*, Ger. *Ritschan* (rĭt'shän), town (pop. 6,376), E central Bohemia, Czechoslovakia, on railroad and 20 mi. SE of Prague; agr. trade (wheat, sugar beets, potatoes); machinery mfg. Popular excursion center. Has sanatorium for tubercular children.

Riccarton (rĭ'kŭrtŭn), borough (pop. 7,632), E S.Isl., New Zealand; W suburb of Christchurch; orchards, flour mills; horse racing.

Riccarton, industrial town and parish (pop. 8,364), N central Ayrshire, Scotland, S suburb of Kilmarnock, on Irvine R. Parish includes HURLFORD.

Riccia (rēt'chä), town (pop. 8,878), Campobasso prov., Abruzzi e Molise, S central Italy, 11 mi. ESE of Campobasso; woolen mills.

Riccione (rēt-chô'nē), town (pop. 2,229), Forlì prov., Emilia-Romagna, N central Italy, on the Adriatic, 6 mi. SE of Rimini; fashionable bathing resort; mfg. (furniture, shoes, fishing nets, lye).

Rice. 1 County (□ 721; pop. 15,635), central Kansas; ⊙ Lyons. Rolling plain region, drained by Little Arkansas and Arkansas rivers. Wheat, livestock. Oil and gas fields. Formed 1871. **2** County (□ 495; pop. 36,235), SE Minn.; ⊙ Faribault. Agr. area drained by Cannon and Straight rivers and watered by small lakes. Dairy products, livestock, corn, oats, barley. Formed 1858.

Rice. 1 Village (pop. 328), Benton co., central Minn., near Mississippi R., 12 mi. N of St. Cloud; dairy products. **2** City (pop. 396), Navarro co., E central Texas, 10 mi. N of Corsicana, in farm area.

Riceboro, city (pop. 267), Liberty co., SE Ga., 31 mi. SW of Savannah; sawmilling.

Rice Canal, W Pakistan: see SUKKUR BARRAGE.

Rice Lake (20 mi. long, 3 mi. wide), SE Ont., 12 mi. S of Peterborough; drained E by Trent R.

Rice Lake, city (pop. 6,898), Barron co., NW Wis., on small Rice L. and Red Cedar R., and 50 mi. NNW of Eau Claire; commercial center for dairying and cattle-raising area; cheese, wood products, canned vegetables. Has park containing Indian mounds. Near by are lake resorts. City grew as a lumbering town. Inc. 1887.

Rice Lake. 1 Lake in Ill.: see BANNER. **2** Lake in Aitkin co., E central Minn., 15 mi. E of Aitkin; 4 mi. long, 2 mi. wide. Drains into small affluent of Mississippi R. Natl. wildlife refuge is here. Also known as Big Rice L.

Rice Point, cape on S coast of P.E.I., on Northumberland Strait, at W side of Hillsborough Bay entrance, 9 mi. SW of Charlottetown; 48°8'N 63°13'W.

Rices Landing, borough (pop. 796), Greene co., SW Pa., 10 mi. ENE of Waynesburg and on Monongahela R.

Riceville, town (pop. 962), on Howard-Mitchell co. line, NE Iowa, on Wapsipinicon R. and 35 mi. ENE of Mason City; cheese factory, creamery.

Riceys, Les (lā rēsā'), village (pop. 1,163), Aube dept., NE central France, 13 mi. NW of Châtillon-sur-Seine; winegrowing.

Rich (rēsh), village, Meknès region, central Fr. Morocco, on the Oued Ziz, at S foot of the High Atlas, 22 mi. N of Ksar-es-Souk. Alfa and wool trade. Fr. military post since 1916.

Rich, county (□ 1,022; pop. 1,673), N Utah; ⊙ Randolph. Agr. and livestock area bordering on Idaho and Wyo., drained in E by Bear R. Part of Cache Natl. Forest and Wasatch Range in W, S half of Bear L. in N. Formed 1864.

Richard Black Coast, part of Antarctica, at E base of Palmer Peninsula, on Weddell Sea, bet. 70°30' and 75°15'S. Discovered 1940 by U.S. expedition.

Richard City, town (pop. 300), Marion co., S Tenn., on Ala. line near Tennessee R., 23 mi. W of Chattanooga, in farm area; makes cement.

Richard Collinson Inlet, N Victoria Isl., SW Franklin Dist., Northwest Territories, arm (80 mi. long, 15–30 mi. wide) of Viscount Melville Sound; 73°N 113°W.

Richards, town (pop. 190), Vernon co., W Mo., near Marmaton R., 12 mi. WNW of Nevada.

Richards Island (50 mi. long, 6–25 mi. wide), NW Mackenzie Dist., Northwest Territories, in Beaufort Sea of the Arctic Ocean, at mouth of Mackenzie R. delta, 60 mi. N of Aklavik; 69°30'N 134°30'W. Port Brabant is opposite. Isl. forms part of the Reindeer Grazing Reserve, centered on REINDEER DEPOT on mainland.

Richardson, county (□ 548; pop. 16,886), extreme SE Nebr.; ⊙ Falls City. Agr. area bordering on Kansas and Mo.; bounded E by Missouri R.; drained by Nemaha R. Lowest point in Nebr. (840 ft.) in SE Feed, flour; grain, livestock, dairy and poultry produce. Formed 1854.

Richardson, town (pop. 1,289), Dallas co., N Texas, 11 mi. N of Dallas, in cotton, cattle, poultry area.

Richardson, Fort, Texas: see JACKSBORO.

Richardson, Mount. 1 Peak (10,125 ft.), SW Alta., near B.C. border, in Rocky Mts., in Banff Natl. Park, 32 mi. NW of Banff; 51°29'N 116°6'W. **2** Peak (3,885 ft.), E Que., on N side of Gaspé Peninsula, 65 mi. W of Gaspé, in Shickshock Mts.

Richardson Highway, S Alaska, extends 368 mi. bet. Fairbanks (N) and Valdez (S). Connects with Alaska Highway.

Richardson Island, trading post, SW Franklin Dist., Northwest Territories, on islet in Coronation Gulf, off S Victoria Isl.; 65°45'N 118°21'W.

Richardson Mountains, Yukon and Northwest Territories: see ROCKY MOUNTAINS.

Richardson Park, residential village (1940 pop. 1,532), New Castle co., N Del., just SW of Wilmington.

Richardson Sound, Cape May co., S N.J., sheltered inlet of the Atlantic, 7 mi. NE of Cape May city; joined to Grassy Sound (NE) and Jarvis Sound (S) by Intracoastal Waterway channel.

Richardson Springs, health resort, Butte co., N central Calif., in Sierra Nevada foothills, 9 mi. NNE of Chico.

Richard-Toll (rēshär'-tôl'), village, NW Senegal, Fr. West Africa, landing on left bank of the Senegal R. (Mauritania border), 60 mi. ENE of Saint-Louis, in rice- and peanut-growing region; stock raising. Forestry and botanic station. Summer residence of governor general of Fr. West Africa. Sometimes spelled Richard Toll.

Richardton, city (pop. 721), Stark co., W N.Dak., 22 mi. E of Dickinson. Assumption Abbey, which includes a high school and a jr. col., is here.

Richborough, England: see SANDWICH.

Richburg. 1 Village (pop. 514), Allegany co., W N.Y., 14 mi. E of Olean, in oil-producing area. **2** Town (pop. 238), Chester co., N S.C., 12 mi. E of Chester.

Rich Creek, town (pop. 740), Giles co., SW Va., 5 mi. NW of Pearisburg.

Riche, Point (rĭsh), promontory on Gulf of St. Lawrence, NW N.F., on S side of entrance of St. John Bay; 50°43'N 57°27'W; lighthouse.

Richecourt (rēshkōōr'), village (pop. 52), Meuse dept., NE France, 10 mi. E of Saint-Mihiel.

Richelieu (rĭsh'lū, Fr. rēshlyû'), county (□ 221; pop. 23,691), S Que., on the St. Lawrence; ⊙ Sorel.

Richelieu, village (pop. 773), S Que., on Richelieu R., at S end of Chambly Basin, 16 mi. E of Montreal; dairying; vegetables.

Richelieu, village (pop. 1,686), Indre-et-Loire dept., W central France, 11 mi. SSE of Chinon; road center; agr. market; makes meat and fruit preserves. Planned and built by Cardinal de Richelieu, who replaced his paternal home with a château (demolished in 19th cent.).

Richelieu, village (pop. 85), W Mauritius, on railroad and 3 mi. SW of Port Louis; corn and manioc milling, alcohol distilling. Has tobacco research laboratory.

Richelieu River, S Que., issues from N end of L. Champlain near N.Y. line, flows c.75 mi. N, past St. Jean, to the St. Lawrence at Sorel, at head of L. St. Peter; link in waterway connecting the Hudson and the St. Lawrence. Discovered 1609 by Champlain, it was an early route of explorers and military expeditions; later was important in logging.

Richey, town (pop. 595), Dawson co., E Mont., 40 mi. W of Sidney.

Richfield. 1 Village (pop. 429), Lincoln co., S Idaho, 15 mi. NE of Shoshone and on Little Wood R.; alt. 4,280 ft. Trade center in irrigated area. **2** City (pop. 105), ⊙ Morton co., SW Kansas, on North Fork Cimarron R. and 23 mi. WNW of Hugoton; grain. **3** Village (pop. 17,502), S suburb of Minneapolis, Hennepin co., E Minn. **4** Town (pop. 237), Stanly co., S central N.C., 9 mi. NNW of Albemarle. **5** City (pop. 4,212), ⊙ Sevier co., S central Utah, on Sevier R. and 140 mi. S of Salt Lake City; alt. 5,345 ft. Processing center (dairy products, feed, beverages) for agr. and livestock area. Settled 1863 by Mormons. Coal and gypsum mines near by. Sections of Fishlake Natl. Forest E and W. Pavant Mts., are just W. **6** Village (pop. c.200), Washington co., E Wis., 20 mi. NW of Milwaukee, in hilly area; winter sports. Near by is Carmelite church and monastery.

Richfield Springs, village (pop. 1,534), Otsego co., central N.Y., near N end of Canadarago L., 21 mi. SE of Utica, in diversified-farming area; health resort (since early-19th cent.), with sulphur springs. Mfg. of fishing tackle. Inc. 1861, reincorporated 1934.

Richford, town (pop. 2,643), including Richford village (pop. 1,916), Franklin co., N Vt., on Missisquoi R., at Que. line, and 24 mi. NE of St. Albans; port of entry; furniture, maple-sugaring equipment, wood and dairy products; poultry. Settled 1795.

Richha (rĭch'ŭ), town (pop. 1,396), Bareilly dist., N central Uttar Pradesh, India, 23 mi. NNE of Bareilly, rice, wheat, gram, pearl millet, corn.

Richhill (rĭch-hĭl'), town (pop. 298), NE Co. Armagh, Northern Ireland, 5 mi. ENE of Armagh; jam making, furniture mfg.

Rich Hill, city (pop. 1,820), Bates co., W Mo., near Marais des Cygnes R., 12 mi. S of Butler; agr.; coal, timber.

Richibucto (rĭshŭbŭk'tō), village (pop. estimate c.1,000), ⊙ Kent co., E N.B., near mouth of Richibucto R., 40 mi. N of Moncton; fishing port (oysters, smelt); lumber trade.

Richibucto River, E N.B., flows 50 mi. ENE, past Richibucto, to Northumberland Strait 5 mi. ENE of Richibucto.

Richland. 1 County (□ 364; pop. 16,889), SE Ill.; ⊙ Olney. Bounded partly W by Little Wabash R.; drained by small Fox R. and by Bonpas Creek. Agr. (corn, wheat, livestock, apples, poultry); timber. Some mfg. (shoes, dairy and food products, wood and metal products). Formed 1841. **2** Parish (□ 576; pop. 26,672), NE La.; ⊙ Rayville. Bounded W by Bayou La Fourche, intersected by Boeuf R. and many bayous. Large production of natural gas, some oil. Agr. (cotton, corn, oats, hay, sweet potatoes). Cotton processing, lumber milling; hunting, fishing. Formed 1852. **3** County (□ 2,065; pop. 10,366), NE Mont.; ⊙ Sidney. Agr. area bordering on N.Dak.; bounded N by Missouri R.; drained in SE by Yellowstone R. Grain, livestock. Formed 1914. **4** County (□ 1,450; pop. 19,865), extreme SE N.Dak.; ⊙ Wahpeton. Agr. area watered by Sheyenne R. and Wild Rice R. Bois de Sioux R. helps form Red River of the North at Wahpeton. Grain, livestock, dairy. Site of Fort Abercrombie State Park. Formed 1873. **5** County (□ 499; pop. 91,305), N central Ohio; ⊙ MANSFIELD. Drained by forks of Mohican R. Agr. area (livestock, grain, fruit, potatoes, dairy products); mfg. at Mansfield, Shelby, Plymouth; greenhouses; sand and gravel pits. Formed 1813. **6** County (□ 748; pop. 142,565), central S.C.; ⊙ COLUMBIA, capital of the state. In Sand Hills belt; partly bounded SW by Congaree R., E by Wateree R.; parts of L. Murray and Broad R. in W. Cotton, corn, dairy products, poultry, livestock. Columbia is mfg. and trade center. Formed 1785. **7** County (□ 584; pop. 19,245), S central Wis.; ⊙ Richland Center. Bounded S by Wisconsin R.; drained by Pine and Kickapoo rivers. Dairying, stock-raising, lumbering. Formed 1842.

Richland. 1 City (pop. 1,571), Stewart co., SW Ga., 33 mi. SSE of Columbus, in farm and timber area; mfg. (lumber, boxes); peanut shelling. Inc. 1886. **2** Town (pop. 591), Keokuk co., SE Iowa, 24 mi. ENE of Ottumwa, in livestock and grain area. **3** Village (pop. 389), Kalamazoo co., SW Mich., 9 mi. NE of Kalamazoo, in farm area. **4** City (pop. 1,133), Pulaski co., central Mo., in the Ozarks, near Gasconade R., 19 mi. NW of Lebanon; grain, fruit, dairying. Founded c.1870. **5** Village (pop. 141), Colfax co., E Nebr., 8 mi. W of Schuyler, near Platte R. **6** Village (pop. c.500), Atlantic co., S N.J., 11 mi. NE of Millville, in agr. area; poultry. **7** Town (pop. 220), Baker co., NE Oregon, 32 mi. E of Baker and on Powder R.; dairy. **8** Borough (pop. 1,090), Lebanon co., SE central Pa., 9 mi. E of Lebanon. Inc. 1906. **9** Town (pop. 308), Navarro co., E central Texas, 11 mi. S of Corsicana, in farm area. **10** Village (pop. 21,809), Benton co., S Wash., on govt. reservation on Columbia R. and 10 mi. WNW of Pasco. Administrative hq. and residential community (developed 1943–45) for near-by Hanford Works, atomic-energy research and production plant built by U.S. govt. during Second World War on site of former village of Hanford.

Richland Balsam, N.C.: see BALSAM MOUNTAIN.

Richland Center, city (pop. 4,608), ⊙ Richland co., S central Wis., on Pine R. and c.50 mi. WNW of Madison; trade and industrial center for dairying and stock-raising region; dairy products, lumber and wood products, buttons. Has several cooperative enterprises. Settled c.1849, inc. 1887. Frank Lloyd Wright b. here.

Richlands. 1 Town (pop. 877), Onslow co., E N.C., 24 mi. S of Kinston, in farm area; sawmilling. **2** Mining town (pop. 4,648), Tazewell co., SW Va., in the Alleghenies, on Clinch R. and 33 mi. WSW of Bluefield, in bituminous-coal and agr. area; makes brick, caskets; lumber milling, limestone quarrying.

Richland Springs, town (pop. 584), San Saba co., central Texas, 36 mi. S of Brownwood; market point in agr., ranch area (peanuts, cattle, poultry).

Richlandtown, borough (pop. 762), Bucks co., SE Pa., 12 mi. SE of Allentown.

Richlawn, town (pop. 655), Jefferson co., N Ky.

Richmond. 1 Municipality (pop. 3,410), E New South Wales, Australia, 35 mi. NW of Sydney; dairying, fruitgrowing center. **2** Village (pop. 775), central Queensland, Australia, on Flinders R. and 125 mi. E of Cloncurry; livestock. **3** Municipality (pop. 39,390), S Victoria, Australia, E suburb of Melbourne; mfg. center (textiles, dyes, shoes, electrical appliances).

Richmond. 1 County (□ 489; pop. 10,853), NE N.S., in SW part of Cape Breton Isl.; ⊙ Arichat. **2** County (□ 544; pop. 27,493), S Que., on St. Francis R.; ⊙ Richmond.

Richmond. 1 Village (pop. 457), SE Ont., 18 mi. SW of Ottawa; dairying, mixed farming. **2** Town (pop. 3,082), ⊙ Richmond co., S Que., on St. Francis R. and 22 mi. NNW of Sherbrooke; copper, chrome, and steatite mining center; woodworking; in dairying region.

Richmond. 1 Residential municipal borough (1931 pop. 37,797; 1951 census 41,945), N Surrey, England, on the Thames and 8 mi. WSW of London. Was site of Palace of Sheen, residence of Edward III, Richard II, Henry V, Henry VII (who changed the town's name to Richmond), Elizabeth (who died here), and other sovereigns. There is large deer park, established by Charles I. The 18th-cent. Star and Garter Inn, figuring in Scott's works, was torn down in 1919. Richmond is also a holiday resort and market and nursery-garden center, with light industries. In municipal borough is town of KEW. Other residential dists. in borough are Petersham and North Sheen. **2** Municipal borough (1931 pop. 4,769; 1951 census 6,165), North Riding, N Yorkshire, England, on Swale R. and 11 mi. SW of Darlington; paper milling; agr. market. Has ruins of Norman castle built 1071; church of Norman origin with 14th-cent. tower, restored by Sir Gilbert Scott in 1860; and 13th-cent. tower of a Franciscan monastery.

Richmond, village, St. Mary parish, N Jamaica, in uplands, on railroad and 20 mi. NNW of Kingston; fruitgrowing, stock grazing.

Richmond, borough (pop. 1,387), N S.Isl., New Zealand, at S end of Tasman Bay, 6 mi. SW of Nelson; agr. center.

Richmond, town (pop. 414), SE Tasmania, 11 mi. NE of Hobart; dairying center; sheep, wheat, oats.

Richmond, town (pop. 2,202), central Cape Prov., U. of So. Afr., 50 mi. S of De Aar; agr. center (stock, grain, fruit). Airfield.

Richmond. 1 County (□ 325; pop. 108,876), E Ga.; ⊙ Augusta. Bounded NE by S.C. line, formed here by Savannah R. Coastal plain agr. (cotton, truck, fruit, corn, livestock, dairy products), clay mining, and sawmilling area; mfg. at Augusta. Camp Gordon Military Reservation occupies W part. Formed 1777. **2** County (□ 57; pop. 191,555), SE N.Y., coextensive with Richmond borough of New York city, and virtually coextensive with STATEN ISLAND. Formed 1683. **3** County (□ 477; pop. 39,597), S N.C.; ⊙ Rockingham. Bounded S by S.C., W by Pee Dee R. (dammed to form Blewett Falls L. here). Forested sand hills (E) and piedmont (W) region; farming (tobacco, cotton, corn), textile mfg., sawmilling. Formed 1779. **4** County (□ 192; pop. 6,189), E Va.; ⊙ Warsaw. Along S shore (Rappahannock R.) of Northern Neck peninsula. Agr. (truck, tobacco, grain, hay, corn, soybeans); some livestock raising, dairying; extensive fish and shellfish industries; lumbering (pine), sawmilling; vegetable canning. Co. has many historic bldgs., some dating from 18th cent. Formed 1692.

Richmond. 1 City (1940 pop. 23,642; 1950 pop. 99,545), Contra Costa co., W Calif., 10 mi. N of Oakland, on San Francisco Bay; deepwater port (developed by dredging since 1917) and mfg. center, with huge oil refineries, large automobile assembly plant, railroad shops, foundries, canneries. Mfg. also of metal products, chemicals, fish oil and meal, plumbing and building supplies, furniture, physicists' instruments, truck bodies. Has a jr. col. Large shipyards caused pop. influx in Second World War; several shipyard areas were occupied (1947–48) by other industries. Settled with coming of railroad in 1899; inc. 1905; adopted council-manager govt. in 1920. **2** Village (pop. 623), McHenry co., NE Ill., near Wis. line, 25 mi. WNW of Waukegan, in dairying and lake-resort area; mfg. (feed, flour, candy). **3** Industrial city (pop. 39,539), ⊙ Wayne co., E Ind., on East Fork of Whitewater R. and c.65 mi. E of Indianapolis; trade center in farming area; aluminum factory. Mfg. of machine tools, farm implements, automobile parts, drilling machinery, bus bodies, hardware, furniture, caskets, clothing, kitchen equipment, refrigerators, pianos, wire, plastics; hothouse flowers shipped. Earlham Col. is at adjacent Earlham. A tuberculosis sanatorium is here. Settled 1806, inc. 1818. **4** City (pop. 433), Franklin co., E Kansas, 15 mi. S of Ottawa, in livestock and grain region. **5** City (pop. 10,268), ⊙ Madison co., central Ky., 24 mi. SSE of Lexington. Shipping point for agr. area (burley tobacco, livestock, corn), in outer Bluegrass region; mfg. of concrete products, lamps, clothing, soft drinks, dairy products; feed and flour mills, tobacco warehouses; airport. Seat of Eastern Ky. State Col. and U.S. trachoma hosp. Near by are "White Hall" (built 1864 around original house of 1787; home of Gen. Cassius M. Clay), Mt. Zion Church (where Civil War battle of Richmond began on Aug. 30, 1862, and Confederates won their 1st Ky. victory), and the Waco and Bybee potteries (since c.1840). Settled 1784. **6** Town (pop. 2,217), including Richmond village (pop. 1,586), Sagadahoc co., SW Maine, on the Kennebec and 12 mi. N of Bath; wood products, textiles. Named for fort here (1719–54), inc. 1823. **7** Town (pop. 737), Berkshire co., W Mass., in the Berkshires, 7 mi. SW of Pittsfield, near N.Y. line; resort. **8** Village (pop. 2,025), Macomb co., SE Mich., 16 mi. NE of Mt. Clemens, in dairying and grain-growing area; mfg. of plows. Settled 1836, inc. 1879. **9** Resort village (pop. 700), Stearns co., S central Minn., on Sauk R. and 18 mi. SW of St. Cloud, in agr. area; dairy products, concrete blocks, monuments. Granite quarries near by. Small lakes in vicinity. **10** City (pop. 4,299), ⊙ Ray co., NW Mo., near Missouri R., 35 mi. ENE of Kansas City; agr.; mfg. (meal, feed, cement blocks); coal mines. Laid out 1827. **11** Town (pop. 259), Cheshire co., SW N.H., 13 mi. S of Keene; at Mass. line. State fish hatchery here. **12** Borough of New York city, SE N.Y.; coextensive with Richmond co. and virtually coextensive with STATEN ISLAND; also includes small Shooters, Pralls, Meadow, Hoffman, and Swinburne isls. **13** A section of Richmond borough of New York city, SE N.Y., on central Staten Isl., 6 mi. SW of St. George. La Tourette Park is here. **14** Village (pop. 579), Jefferson co., E Ohio, 9 mi. WNW of Steubenville, in agr. area. **15** Village, Lake co., Ohio: see GRAND RIVER. **16** Town (pop. 1,772), Washington co., SW R.I., along Wood R., 26 mi. SSW of Providence; agr., mfg. (textiles, clothing), dairying. Includes Wyoming village and parts of CAROLINA, SHANNOCK, and USQUEPAUG villages. State park. Set off from Charlestown and inc. 1747. **17** Town (pop. 2,030), ⊙ Fort Bend co., S Texas, on Brazos R. and c.25 mi. WSW of Houston, in oil-producing, livestock and agr. area (cotton, truck, corn); cotton ginning, cottonseed-oil milling. Here are graves of Erastus ("Deaf") Smith, Mirabeau B. Lamar. State prison farm near by. Town founded 1822. **18** City (pop. 1,091), Cache co, N Utah, near Idaho line, 13 mi. N of Logan; alt. 4,608 ft. Trade center (dairy plants) for livestock and irrigated agr. area. Settled by Mormons 1859. Naomi Peak (9,980 ft.) is 7 mi. E in Wasatch Range. **19** Town (pop. 1,278), including Richmond village (pop. 731), Chittenden co., NW Vt., on Winooski R. and 12 mi. SE of Burlington; clothing, printing; dairy products; lumber. Has 16-sided church (1812), 1 of 1st U.S. community churches. Settled 1775, formed 1794. **20** City (pop. 230,310), ⊙ Va., in but independent of Henrico and Chesterfield cos., E central Va., on both banks of the James (water power) at the fall line (head of navigation) and c.100 mi. S of Washington. Co. courthouse is here. State's largest city; a cultural, financial, commercial, distribution, and transportation center of the South. Port of entry and seaport at head of dredged deepwater channel; port receives chemicals, coffee, sugar, manufactured goods; ships tobacco, grain, coal, wood products, cotton, paper, fertilizers, iron products. A great tobacco market and tobacco-processing center; mfg. of synthetic textiles, paper, fertilizer, metal goods, foundry products, food products, chemicals, agr. equipment, furniture, clothing; printing and publishing; railroad shops. Richmond's long history began in 1637, when a trading point was established here; town projected by Col. William Byrd in 1733, laid out 1737, and 1st inc. 1742; inc. as city in 1782; became ⊙ Va. in 1779. Arnold pillaged town in 1781. As capital and supply center of the Confederacy during Civil War, city was constant objective of Federal troops; it was threatened (1862) by the Peninsular campaign (when it was saved by the Seven Days Battles fought near by) and again (1864) in the Wilderness campaign; finally fell at end (April, 1865) of Grant's campaign, in which fall of Petersburg opened way to Federal victory. Richmond Natl. Battlefield Park (684.44 acres; established 1944) includes battlefields in and near city. Richmond's points of interest include the neo-classical state capitol (begun 1785), designed by Jefferson and housing Houdon's statue of Washington; Washington Monument (by Thomas Crawford) in Capitol Square; Valentine Mus.; White House of the Confederacy, once the home of Jefferson Davis, and now the Confederate Mus.; Battle Abbey (Confederate Memorial Inst.), with Civil War mementos; St. John's Church (1741), where Patrick Henry made his famous "Give me liberty, or give me death" speech; Poe Foundation (c.1686; oldest bldg. in city); John Marshall's house (1793); home of Robert E. Lee; Virginia Mus. of Fine Arts (1934); Monument Ave., with its statues of Confederate heroes. Belle Isle in the river was once site of a Confederate prison. City is seat of Union Theological Seminary, Richmond Professional Inst. of the Col. of William and Mary, the General Assembly's Training School for Lay Workers (Presbyterian), Va. Union Univ. (for Negroes; Baptist; coeducational; 1685), Medical Col. of Va., and Univ. of Richmond (Baptist; for men and women; 1832). Has natl. cemetery for Civil War dead. In Hollywood cemetery are buried President Monroe, President Tyler, John Randolph, and Jefferson Davis.

Richmond Heights. **1** City (pop. 15,045), St. Louis co., E Mo., near Mississippi R., W of St. Louis. **2** Village (pop. 891), Cuyahoga co., N Ohio, a NE suburb of Cleveland.

Richmond Hill, village (pop. 1,345), S Ont., 14 mi. N of Toronto; truck, grain.

Richmond Hill. **1** Village, Bryan co., SE Ga., 15 mi. SW of Savannah, near Ogeechee R.; mfg. (naval stores). **2** A residential section of central Queens borough of New York city, SE N.Y.; some mfg. (clothing, chemicals; wood, glass, and paper products; machinery, truck bodies). **3** Residential suburb (pop. 2,303) of Burlington, Alamance co., N central N.C.

Richmond Island, SW Maine, in Casco Bay off Cape Elizabeth town; 1 mi. long, ¾ mi. wide. There was a settlement and trading center here early in 17th cent.

Richmond River, NE New South Wales, Australia, rises in McPherson Range, flows SE, past Casino and Coraki, thence NE to the Pacific at Ballina; 163 mi. long. Navigable 70 mi. below Lismore (on N.Arm) by small steamers carrying dairy foods and agr. products, principally sugar cane.

Richmond Valley, SE N.Y., a section of Richmond borough of New York city, on S Staten Isl.

Richmondville, village (pop. 709), Schoharie co., E central N.Y., c.40 mi. W of Albany; makes gloves.

Rich Mountain, E W.Va., name of 2 ridges of the Alleghenies. **1** Ridge (c.3,000 ft.) in W Randolph co.; from Tygart R. bend W of Elkins extends c.25 mi. SSW toward Elk R., here merging into a high plateau; rises to Whitman Knob (3,900 ft.) near S end. Laurel Ridge is its N continuation. On mtn. W of Beverly was fought (July 11, 1861). Civil War battle of Rich Mtn., a Union victory. **2** Ridge (c.3,000 ft. in N; up to 4,335 ft. in S) lying bet. Laurel and Dry forks (headstreams of Black Fork); from S Tucker co. line extends 17 mi. S through Randolph co.

Richrath-Reusrath, Germany: see LANGENFELD.

Rich Square, town (pop. 971), Northampton co., NE N.C., 25 mi. SE of Roanoke Rapids; sawmilling.

Richtenberg (rĭkh'tünbĕrk), town (pop. 2,978), in former Prussian Pomerania prov., N Germany, after 1945 in Mecklenburg, 11 mi. SW of Stralsund; grain, stock, sugar beets, potatoes; dairying.

Richterich (rĭkh'tŭrĭkh), village (pop. 4,527), in former Prussian Rhine Prov., W Germany, after 1945 in North Rhine-Westphalia, near Dutch border, 2.5 mi. N of Aachen; rail junction.

Richterswil (rĭkh'tŭrsvēl), town (pop. 4,554), Zurich canton, N Switzerland, on L. of Zurich and 14 mi. SSE of Zurich; metal and rubber products, silk textiles; woodworking.

Richthofen, Mount, Colo.: see NEVER SUMMER MOUNTAINS.

Richthofen Mountains (rĭkht'hō"fün), N range of the Nan Shan, on Kansu-Tsinghai border, China, N of the lake Koko Nor; mts. rise to 19,000 ft. Named for German explorer Ferdinand Richthofen.

Richton (rĭch'tün), town (pop. 1,158), Perry co., SE Miss., 21 mi. E of Hattiesburg and on Thompsons Creek; lumber milling.

Richton Park, village (pop. 232), Cook co., NE Ill., S suburb of Chicago.

Richview, village (pop. 352), Washington co., SW Ill., 10 mi. S of Centralia, in agr. and bituminous-coal area.

Richville. **1** Village (pop. 141), Otter Tail co., W Minn., 26 mi. NE of Fergus Falls, in lake region; grain, potatoes. **2** Village (pop. 254), St. Lawrence co., N N.Y., on Oswegatchie R. and 20 mi. SSE of Ogdensburg, in dairying area.

Richwiller (rēshvēlâr'), Ger. *Reichweiler* (rīkh'vīlür), village (pop. 989), Haut-Rhin dept., E France, 4 mi. NW of Mulhouse; explosives.

Richwood. **1** Village (pop. 1,866), Union co., central Ohio, 13 mi. SW of Marion, in agr. area; food products, metal products. **2** City (pop. 5,321), Nicholas co., central W.Va., 55 mi. ESE of Charleston, in timber, agr. (livestock, potatoes, fruit, tobacco), and coal region; hardwood lumber milling, limestone quarrying; mfg. of paper and pulp, wood products (especially clothespins). Near by, in the Alleghenies, are Cranberry Glades, 300-acre tract of arctic tundra (alt. 3,400 ft.), noted for flora unusual in W.Va. Inc. as town 1901, as city 1921.

Ricken Pass (rĭ'kün) (2,594 ft.), in the Alps, St. Gall canton, NE Switzerland; road and railway lead from the Toggenburg, over the pass and through Ricken Tunnel (5 mi. long), to E end of L. of Zurich.

Ricketts (rĭ'kĭts), town (pop. 166), Crawford co., W Iowa, 14 mi. WNW of Denison, in agr. area.

Rickling (rĭk'lĭng), village (pop. 2,889), in Schleswig-Holstein, NW Germany, 8 mi. SE of Neumünster; cattle.

Rickmansworth, residential urban district (1931 pop. 10,809; 1951 census 24,518), SW Hertford, England, on Colne R. at mouth of Gade R., 4 mi. SW of Watford; mfg. of rayon, paper, soap, chemicals. The 17th-cent. Basing House was once residence of William Penn. The church has noted 16th-cent. stained glass.

Ricla (rē'klä), town (pop. 2,755), Saragossa prov., NE Spain, on Jalón R. and 17 mi. NE of Calatayud; olive-oil processing; trades in sugar beets, wine, fruit, livestock.

Rico (rē'kō), town (pop. 212), ⊙ Dolores co., SW Colo., on Dolores R., in San Juan Mts., and 30 mi. NNW of Durango; alt. 8,900 ft.; sheep grazing.

Rico, Páramo (pä'rämō rē'kō), Andean peak (13,779 ft.) in Santander dept., N central Colombia, in Cordillera Oriental, 18 mi. NE of Bucaramanga.

Ricobayo (rēkōvī'ō), village (pop. 374), Zamora prov., NW Spain, on Esla R. and 13 mi. W of Zamora. Dam, irrigation reservoir, and hydroelectric plant near by.

Ricote (rēkō'tā), town (pop. 1,646), Murcia prov., SE Spain, near the Segura, 18 mi. NW of Murcia; esparto-rope mfg.; lumbering. Citrus and other fruit, wine, olive oil, cereals.

Ricse (rĭ'chĕ), town (pop. 3,441), Zemplen co., NE Hungary, 15 mi. ESE of Satoraljaujhely; grain, potatoes, plums, nuts, pears; cattle.

Ridder, Kazakh SSR: see LENINOGORSK.

Ridderkerk (rĭ'dŭrkĕrk), town (pop. 4,515), South Holland prov., W Netherlands, on Ijsselmonde isl. and 7 mi. SE of Rotterdam; shipbuilding; fruit and vegetable market, supplying Rotterdam.

Riddings, England: see ALFRETON.

Riddle, town (pop. 634), Douglas co., SW Oregon, 17 mi. S of Roseburg.

Riddlesburg, village (1940 pop. 600), Bedford co., S Pa., on Raystown Branch of Juniata R. and 26 mi. SW of Huntingdon; bituminous coal, coke.

Riddleville, town (pop. 106), Washington co., E central Ga., 10 mi. SE of Sandersville.

Rideau Canal (rēdō', rē'dō), SE Ont., extends 126 mi. SSW-NNE bet. Ottawa R. (at Ottawa) and L. Ontario (at Kingston). Follows course of Rideau R. to Rideau L., summit of canal (alt. 406 ft.), thence that of Cataraqui R. Has 47 locks; built 1826–32.

Rideau Lake (20 mi. long, 4 mi. wide), SE Ont., 45 mi. SW of Ottawa; drained N to the Ottawa by Rideau R. and S to L. Ontario by Cataraqui R.; forms summit level (alt. 406 ft.) of Rideau Canal.

Ridgecrest, village (pop. 2,028), Kern co., S central Calif., c.75 mi. ENE of Bakersfield.

Ridgedale, village (pop. 224), central Sask., on Carrot R. and 23 mi. ENE of Melfort; wheat, stock.

Ridge Farm, village (pop. 905), Vermilion co., E Ill., 15 mi. S of Danville, in agr. and bituminous-coal area; ships grain.

Ridgefield. **1** (rĭj'fēld) Residential town (pop. 4,356), including Ridgefield village (pop. 2,347), Fairfield co., SW Conn., on N.Y. line and 12 mi. NNW of Norwalk; summer resort; agr. (dairy products, poultry). Settled 1708, inc. 1709. Scene of Revolutionary battle (1777). **2** (rĭch'fēld, rĭj'–) Borough (pop. 8,312), Bergen co., NE N.J., 7 mi. N of Jersey City, near Hackensack R.; mfg. (metal products, paints, paper products, chemicals, airplanes). N end of N.J. Turnpike near. Inc. 1892 **3** (rĭj'fēld) Town (pop. 762), Clark co., SW Wash., 14 mi. N of Vancouver and on Columbia R.; lumber, potatoes, strawberries.

Ridgefield Park (rĭch'fēld, rĭj'–), residential village (pop. 11,993), Bergen co., NE N.J., on Hackensack R. just NW of Ridgefield; mfg. (paper products, building blocks, metal products, woodwind reeds, clothing, dental rubber, aquariums). Inc. 1892. N terminus of N.J. Turnpike.

Ridgeland (rĭj'lünd). **1** Village (pop. 526), Madison co., central Miss., 10 mi. NNE of Jackson. **2** Town (pop. 1,078), ⊙ Jasper co., S S.C., 30 mi. NNE of Savannah, Ga., in lumbering, agr., livestock area; wood products, turpentine, beverages. A Gretna Green for citizens of Ga. **3** Village (pop. 273), Dunn co., W Wis., 22 mi. N of Menomonie, in dairying area.

Ridgeley, residential town (pop. 1,754), Mineral co., NE W.Va., in Eastern Panhandle, on North Branch of the Potomac (bridged) opposite Cumberland, Md. Settled 1747; Fort Ohio was established here in 1754.

Ridgely. **1** Town (pop. 834), Caroline co., E Md., 16 mi. NE of Easton; ships truck; vegetable canneries, shirt factory. Univ. of Md. agr. substation here. **2** Town (pop. 1,504), Lake co., extreme NW Tenn., near the Mississippi, 17 mi. NNW of Dyersburg. Reelfoot L. is NNE.

Ridgeside, city (pop. 337), Hamilton co., SE Tenn., E suburb of Chattanooga.

Ridge Spring, town (pop. 598), Saluda co., W S.C., 37 mi. WSW of Columbia; furniture.

Ridgetop, town (pop. 354), on Davidson-Robertson co. line, N Tenn., 16 mi. N of Nashville. Watauga Sanatorium for tubercular patients is here.

Ridgetown, town (pop. 1,944), S Ont., 15 mi. E of Chatham; agr. center (grain, sugar beets, tobacco, fruit, vegetables), with grain elevators, canneries. Has agr. school and experimental farm.

Ridgeview, town (1940 pop. 439), Miami co., N central Ind., just NW of Peru.

Ridgeville. **1** Town (pop. 950), Randolph co., E Ind., on Mississinewa R. and 20 mi. ENE of Muncie, in livestock and grain area; stone quarrying. Settled 1817, inc. 1868. **2** Town (pop. 507), Dorchester co., SE central S.C., 9 mi. NW of Summerville; lumber.

Ridgeway. **1** Town (pop. 307), Winneshiek co., NE Iowa, 10 mi. W of Decorah, in agr. area. **2** City (pop. 560), Harrison co., NW Mo., 10 mi. NE of Bethany. **3** Village (pop. 384), on Hardin-Logan co. line, W central Ohio, 10 mi. S of Kenton. **4** Town (pop. 414), Fairfield co., N central S.C., 22 mi. N of Columbia; lumber. **5** Residential town (pop. 440), Henry co., S Va., near N.C. line, 25 mi. W of Danville, in agr. area; furniture mfg. **6** Village (pop. 410), Iowa co., S Wis., 8 mi. ENE of Dodgeville, in dairy and livestock region.

Ridgewood. **1** Village (pop. 5,586), Will co., NE Ill. **2** Residential village (pop. 17,481), Bergen co., NE N.J., 5 mi. NNE of Paterson; mfg. (steel, oil burners, pumps, building blocks, embroideries, ice cream); nurseries; truck, dairy products. Inc. 1894. **3** A residential section of N Brooklyn and S Queens boroughs of New York city, SE N.Y.; some mfg. (clothing, chemicals, machinery, electrical appliances, leather and paper products, auto parts, trucks, thermometers).

Ridgway (rĭj'wā). **1** Town (pop. 209), Ouray co., SW central Colo., on Uncompahgre R., near San Juan Mts., and 10 mi. NNW of Ouray; alt. 6,770 ft. Railroad div. point with repair shops. **2** Village (pop. 1,148), Gallatin co., SE Ill., c.12 mi. W of junction of Wabash and Ohio rivers and 16 mi. ENE of Harrisburg; agr. (corn, wheat; dairy products; livestock); timber. Inc. 1886. **3** Borough (pop. 6,244), ⊙ Elk co., N central Pa., 36 mi. S of Bradford and on Clarion R.; electrical products, leather, lumber, chemicals; oil and gas wells. Settled 1822, laid out 1833, inc. 1881.

Ridi, Nepal: see RIRI BAZAR.

Riding, East, North, and **West,** administrative divisions of Yorkshire, England. The term derives from a Scandinavian word meaning third. See YORK, county.

Riding Mountain National Park (□ 1,148), SW Man., 10 mi. S of Dauphin; 65 mi. long, 35 mi. wide. Riding Mtn. range rises to 2,200 ft. Contains (S) Clear L. (9 mi. long, 2 mi. wide) and several smaller lakes. Established 1929.

Ridley Park, borough (pop. 4,921), Delaware co., SE Pa., SW suburb of Philadelphia; mfg. of rock-wool insulation. Founded 1870, inc. 1888.

Ridott (rī'dŏt), village (pop. 187), Stephenson co., N Ill., on Pecatonica R. and 7 mi. E of Freeport, in agr. area.

Riduna, Channel Isls.: see ALDERNEY.

Ried or **Ried im Innkreis** (rēt ĭm ĭn'krīs), town (pop. 11,590), W Upper Austria, 25 mi. W of Wels; rail junction; market center for grain and cattle area.

Riedenburg (rē'dunbŏŏrk), village (pop. 2,890), Upper Palatinate, central Bavaria, Germany, on the Altmühl and 19 mi. WSW of Regensburg; brewing. Has mid-16th-cent. castle.

Riederalp, Switzerland: see ALETSCH GLACIER.

Ried im Traunkreise (rēt ēm troun'krīzū), town (pop. 2,347), E central Upper Austria, 9 mi. SSE of Wels; wheat, cattle.

Riedisheim (rēdizĕm', Ger. rē'dĭs-hīm), E suburb (pop. 6,867) of Mulhouse, Haut-Rhin dept., E France, on Rhone-Rhine Canal; mfg. (alcohol, hosiery, tiles).

Riedlhütte, Germany: see SANKT OSWALD.

Riedlingen (rēd'lĭng-un), town (pop. 3,081), S Württemberg, Germany, after 1945 in Württemberg-Hohenzollern, on the Danube and 12 mi. ENE of Sigmaringen; rail junction.

Riegel (rē'gul), village (pop. 1,464), S Baden, Germany, on canalized Dreisam and canalized Elz rivers (where they form Leopold Canal), and 5 mi. NE of Emmendingen; rail junction; brewing.

Riegelsberg (rē'gulsbĕrk), town (pop. 9,414), S Saar, 5 mi. NNW of Saarbrücken; coal mining. Absorbed communes of Güchenbach, Hilschbach, and Überhofen in 1939.

Riegelsville (rē'gulzvĭl). **1** Village (pop. c.500), Warren co., NW N.J., on Delaware R., at mouth of Musconetcong R., and 7 mi. S of Phillipsburg; mfg. (paper, metal products). **2** Residential borough (pop. 871), Bucks co., E Pa., 7 mi. S of Easton and on Delaware R.

Riehen (rē'un), residential town (pop. 7,415), Basel-Stadt half-canton, N Switzerland, 3 mi. NE of Basel, N of the Rhine, on Ger. border.

Rieka, Yugoslavia: see RIJEKA.

Rielasingen (rē'lä"zĭng-un), village (pop. 3,197), S Baden, Germany, on the Aach and 2 mi. S of Singen, near Swiss border; customs station; mfg. (textiles, machinery).

Rienza River (rēĕn'tsä), Ger. *Rienz*, Bolzano prov., N Italy, rises in the Dolomites near Croda Rossa peak, 6 mi. SSW of DOBBIACO; flows N and W, through the Pustertal, past Brunico, and S to Isarco R. at Bressanone; 55 mi. long. Used for hydroelectric power. Receives Aurino R. (right).

Rienzi (rĭn'zē), town (pop. 468), Alcorn co., NE Miss., 12 mi. S of Corinth, in agr. area.

Riesa (rē'zä), town (pop. 34,406), Saxony, E central Germany, harbor on the Elbe, and 25 mi. NW of Dresden; rail junction; steel-milling center; mfg. of tires, glass, chemicals, food products; woolen and flour milling. Power station.

Riesco Island (rē-ĕs'kō) (pop. 503), mountainous island (75 mi. long, 20 mi. wide) in Magallanes prov., S Chile, separated from mainland (N) by Skyring Sound, from Brunswick Peninsula (SE) by Otway Sound. An irregular S peninsula (Córdoba Peninsula) is on the Strait of Magellan. Isl. rises to 5,652 ft. (Cerro Ladrillero). Sparsely populated, it is a sheep-raising and lumbering area with some coal mining at ELENA (NE).

Riese (rēā'zē), village (pop. 1,334), Treviso prov., Veneto, N Italy, 17 mi. WNW of Treviso, in cereal- and grape-growing region. Pope Pius X b. here.

Rieseby (rē'zübē), village (pop. 3,022), in Schleswig-Holstein, NW Germany, 5 mi. N of Eckernförde; food processing. Has late-Romanesque church.

Riesel (rē'sul, rēsĕl'), town (pop. 409), McLennan co., E central Texas, 13 mi. ESE of Waco, in agr. area; cotton ginning, poultry packing, feed milling. Near by is erosion-control experiment station.

Riesenburg, Poland: see PRABUTY.

Riesengebirge (rē'zungubĭr"gu) [Ger., =giant mountains], Czech *Krkonoše* (kŭr'kônô-shĕ), Pol. *Karkonosze* (kärkônô'shĕ), highest range of the Sudetes, along Lower Silesia (after 1945, SW Poland) and N Bohemia, Czechoslovakia, border, bet. upper Jizera (W) and Bobrawa (E) rivers; c.25 mi. long. Highest point (5,259 ft.), the SCHNEEKOPPE, is 12 mi. S of Hirschberg (Jelenia Gora). Lumber and water power are abundant; paper and textile milling, glass blowing are important industries on Pol. and Czech slopes. Noted tourist resorts include Karpacz and Szklarska Poreba (Poland), Spindleruv Mlyn and Johannisbad or JANSKE LAZNE (Czechoslovakia). Bituminous coal mined at Zacler. Elbe R. rises on Bohemian slope of range.

Riesi (rēā'zē), town (pop. 19,190), Caltanissetta prov., S Sicily, 14 mi. S of Caltanissetta; wine, olive oil. Sulphur mines (NW).

Rietavas or **Retavas** (rā'täväs), Rus. *Retovo*, town (1925 pop. 1,720), W Lithuania, 30 mi. E of Memel; sawmilling; flour mill. Dates from 16th cent.; in Rus. Kovno govt. until 1920.

Rietberg (rēt'bĕrk), town (pop. 4,235), in former Prussian prov. of Westphalia, NW Germany, after 1945 in North Rhine-Westphalia, on the Ems and 7 mi. SSE of Gütersloh; pumpernickel; hog raising.

Rietfontein (rēt'fôntān"), town (pop. 2,989), S Transvaal, U. of So. Afr., on Witwatersrand, 6 mi. NW of Germiston; alt. 5,594 ft.; gold mining.

Rietheburg, Germany: see RITTEBURG.

Rieti (rēā'tē), province (□ 1,063; pop. 174,961), Latium, central Italy; ⊙ Rieti. Mtn. terrain, including Sabine Mts.; watered by Velino R. Agr. (cereals, fodder, grapes, olives, potatoes, sugar beets); stock raising (sheep, cattle). Marble quarry at Cottanello. Hydroelectric plant at Cittaducale. Mfg. at Rieti.

Rieti, anc. *Reate*, town (pop. 14,366), ⊙ Rieti prov., Latium, central Italy, on Velino R. and 16 mi. SE of Terni; 42°23'N 12°53'E. Industrial center; woolen, rayon and flour mills, beet-sugar refinery; mfg. (olive oil, wax, soap, furniture, quarry machinery, macaroni). Bishopric. Has cathedral with Romanesque campanile (1252). Badly damaged by bombing (1943–44) in Second World War.

Riet River (rēt), Orange Free State and Cape Prov., U. of So. Afr., rises in SW Orange Free State, NNW of Smithfield, flows c.250 mi. NW, past Koffiefontein, to Vaal R. 55 mi. WSW of Kimberley. Receives Modder R.

Rieumes (rēŭm'), village (pop. 1,184), Haute-Garonne dept., S France, 21 mi. SW of Toulouse; poultry raising, *pâté de foie gras* processing.

Rieupeyroux (rēŭpārōō'), village (pop. 909), Aveyron dept., S France, on Ségala Plateau, 10 mi. ESE of Villefranche-de-Rouergue; furniture mfg.

Rieux (rēŭ'). **1** Agr. village (pop. 694), Haute-Garonne dept., S France, on the Arize and 23 mi. WNW of Pamiers; flour milling. Has a former cathedral (15th cent.). **2** Village (pop. 702), Oise dept., N France, on the Oise and 7 mi. NNW of Senlis; chemical mfg.

Rieux-Minervois (-mēnĕrvwä'), village (pop. 1,719), Aude dept., S France, 13 mi. ENE of Carcassonne; wine-cask mfg., winegrowing. Has 12th-cent. church.

Rievaulx (rē'vōz, rĭ'vŭz) [Rye vale], agr. village and parish (pop. 208), North Riding, N Yorkshire, England, on Rye R. and 15 mi. NW of Malton; stone quarrying. Has ruins of Rievaulx Abbey, a Cistercian monastery founded 1131.

Riez (rēĕz'), village (pop. 1,041), Basses-Alpes dept., SE France, 20 mi. SSW of Digne, on a tableland of Provence Alps; road junction. Lavender essence, olive oil, almonds, truffles, honey, wine. A Gallo-Roman town and former bishopric. Preserves anc. Corinthian columns and a 6th–7th-cent. temple.

Rif, territory, Sp. Morocco: see VILLA SANJURJO.

Rif or **Riff** (rĭf), Arabic *Er Rif*, arc-shaped mountain range of NW Africa, separated from Spain's Cordillera Penibética (of which it is the geological counterpart) by the Strait of Gibraltar. It extends c.180 mi. through central and E Sp. Morocco, from Tangier and Ceuta on the Strait of Gibraltar, to the lower Muluya valley E of Melilla, always hugging Sp. Morocco's Mediterranean coastline. Rises to 8,060 ft. in Tidiguin peak. Several of its highest summits in the central Ketama section are snow-covered during part of the year. There are fine cedar forests on its slopes. Agr. is limited to a few narrow coastal valleys. The Rif contains iron, lead, antimony, and graphite deposits, but only iron (at Beni bu Ifrur) is mined on a large scale for export. Difficult of access, the Rif is inhabited by fiercely independent Berber tribes, who, under the leadership of Abd-el-Krim, successfully revolted against Sp. rule in 1921, and were only subdued in 1926 by a joint French and Sp. military expedition.

Rif'at, Tell, or **Tall Raf'at** (both: tĕl rĭ'fät), Fr. *Tell Refaat*, village, Aleppo prov., NW Syria, near Turkish border, on railroad, and 19 mi. N of Aleppo; cotton, rice.

Riff, mountains, Sp. Morocco: see RIF.

Riffelhorn (rĭ'fulhôrn"), peak (9,615 ft.) in Pennine Alps, S Switzerland, 3 mi. S of Zermatt, overlooking Gorner Glacier; on scenic railway bet. Zermatt and the GORNERGRAT.

Rifle, town (pop. 1,525), Garfield co., W Colo., on Colorado R. and 24 mi. W of Glenwood Springs; alt. 5,332 ft. Trading point in livestock and grain region; sugar beets, potatoes; flour mill, plants for processing of uranium and vanadium. Oil and gas wells in vicinity. Shale-oil experiment station. Near-by Rifle Mtn. Park is scenic area with waterfalls and hydroelectric plant. Inc. 1905.

Rifle River, NE and E Mich., rises in small lakes in Ogemaw co., flows generally SSE c.65 mi., past Omer, to Saginaw Bay; known for its fishing. Its West Branch rises in Ogemaw co., flows c.15 mi. SE, past West Branch city, to main stream.

Rifstangi (rĭf'stäng"gē), cape, N extremity of Iceland, on Greenland Sea, at tip of Melrakkasletta peninsula; 66°32'N 16°13'W. Lighthouse.

Rift Valley: see GREAT RIFT VALLEY.

Rift Valley, province (□ 17,612; pop. 646,177), W central Kenya; ⊙ Nakuru. Occupied by the Great Rift Valley and by escarpments (Nandi, Mau, Aberdare) and plateaus (Uasin Gishu, Kikuyu, Laikipia) along valley's edges. Many extinct volcanoes. Important agr. region (wheat, corn, coffee, tea, pyrethrum, sisal) with European farms and livestock ranches. Kenya-Uganda RR here crosses the Great Rift Valley. Chief centers: Nakuru, Eldoret, Naivasha, Kitale.

Rig, Bandar, Iran: see BANDAR RIG.

Riga (rē'gu), Lettish *Rīga* (rē'gä), city (□ 95; pop. 392,926), ⊙ Latvia, in Vidzeme, on Gulf of Riga, at mouth of the Western Dvina, 520 mi. WNW of Moscow; 56°57'N 24°7'E. Major Baltic port; Latvia's largest city; cultural, political, and industrial center; mfg. (electric railroad cars, bicycles, electrical machinery, telephone and radio equipment, hydroturbines, measuring instruments, superphosphates, glass, wood products, paper, textiles, rubber and leather goods, foodstuffs); shipbuilding. Exports timber, paper, linseed oil, butter, eggs. Has Latvian state univ. (1919), agr. and art academies, teachers col., and conservatory. On right bank of river is old Hansa town (fortified until 1857; now circled by park-lined city moat) with city's principal bldgs., including a castle dating in part from 1515, Renaissance Parliament bldg. (1860s), 13th-cent. cathedral (rebuilt in 16th cent.), 15th-cent. church of St. Peter with 412-ft. steeple, 15th-cent. Hanseatic "Black Heads" house, R.C. church of St. Jacob, guild halls, and natl. opera house. Adjoining old town are modern city sections of Vidzeme (Livonian) suburb (NE), with parks and fine residences, and Latgale or Moscow suburb (SE). Across the river (linked by rail and road bridges) is industrial suburb of Jelgava. Other industrial suburbs extend NE and E to Kis (Kish) and Jugla (Yugla) lakes. Harbor (frozen Dec.-Feb.) includes docks along both banks of the Western Dvina (6-8 mi. from its mouth) and outer ports of MILGRAVIS, BOLDERAJA, and DAUGAVGRIVA. Since 1946, Riga includes noted W beach and resort suburb of RIGAS JURMALA. Founded 1201 on site of native village; became residence of bishops (after 1254, archbishops) of Riga; joined Hanseatic League in 1282 and developed into a major commercial center. Although dominated by the Livonian Knights, the archbishopric of Riga maintained a semi-independent existence and controlled large sections of Livonia until it passed (1561–81) to Poland; passed (1621) to Sweden; occupied (1710) by Russia, to which it was formally ceded in 1721. During 19th cent., it became 2d most important (after St. Petersburg) Baltic port of Russia. During First World War, held (1917–19) by Germans, and again (1941–44) during Second World War. Was ⊙ Vidzeme (1920–40) in independent Latvia.

Riga, Gulf of, Estonian *Riia Laht*, Lettish *Rīgas Jūras Līcis*, Rus. *Rizhskiy Zaliv*, arm of Baltic Sea bordering on Estonia and Latvia; nearly closed off by Estonian Saare isl.; 45-80 mi. wide, 90 mi. long. Its ports, Riga (S) and Parnu (N), lie at mouths of Western Dvina and Parnu rivers. Covered (Jan.–April) by ice; connected by Irbe Strait (W) and Muhu Sound (N) with open Baltic Sea. Contains Estonian isls. of Ruhnu and Kihnu.

Rigachikun (rēgä'shŭkōō), town (pop. 706), Zaria prov., Northern Provinces, N central Nigeria, on railroad and 9 mi. NNE of Kaduna; until construction of railroad, an important road center for transportation of tin ores to coast. Sometimes spelled Rigachikum.

Rigan (rēgän'), village, Eighth Prov., in Kerman, SE Iran, 45 mi. SE of Bam, in irrigated agr. Narmashir dist. (barley, rice, henna, indigo); gum arabic, cumin seed.

Rigas Jurmala or **Rigas Yurmala** (rē'gäs yŏŏr'mälä), Lettish *Rīgas Jūrmala* [=Riga beach], Baltic seaside resort (pop. 7,863) of Latvia, since 1946 within Riga city limits; located W of Riga, on 10-mi.-long pine-clad sand dunes, bet. lower Lielupe R. and Gulf of Riga. Consists of 6 amalgamated resorts (linked to Riga by electric railroad): Bulduri [Ger. *Bilderlingshof*], 10 mi. WNW of Riga city center; Edinburg; Majori or Mayori [Ger. *Majorenhof*]; Dubulti [Ger. *Dubbeln*]; Melluzi or Melluzhi [Ger. *Karlsbad*]; Asari [Ger. *Assern*], 17 mi. W of Riga city center. Sanatoria, rest homes; berry and truck gardens.

Rigaud (rēgō', rē'gō), town (pop. 1,222), S Que., near L. of the Two Mountains, 35 mi. W of Montreal; tanning, lumbering, woodworking, iron casting, silica and granite working; in dairying, apple-growing region. Seat of commercial college and academy.

Rigby, town (pop. estimate 1,000), central Santa Fe prov., Argentina, 38 mi. SW of Santa Fe; agr. center (wheat, flax, corn, alfalfa, livestock); dairying.

Rigby, city (pop. 1,826), ⊙ Jefferson co., E Idaho, 14 mi. NNE of Idaho Falls; alt. 4,949 ft. Shipping point for irrigated farming, dairying area; beet sugar, seed peas. Settled 1884 by Mormons, inc. as village 1903, as city 1915.

Riggins, town (pop. 287), Idaho co., central Idaho, on Salmon R. and 37 mi. SSW of Grangeville.

Righi, Switzerland: see RIGI.

Rigi (rē'gē), mountain in the Alps, N central Switzerland, bet. lakes of Lucerne (S), Zug (N), and Lowerz (E); ascended by rack-and-pinion railways. It commands one of most famous views in the world—a panorama of nearly 180 mi. Several resorts here. Highest peaks from W to E: Rotstock (5,453 ft.), Kulm (5,908 ft.), Schild (5,088 ft.), Dossen (5,539 ft.), Schneidegg (5,463 ft.), Vitznauerstock (4,775 ft.), and Hochfluh (5,586 ft.). Sometimes spelled Righi.

Rignac (rēnyäk'), village (pop. 667), Aveyron dept., S France, 14 mi. WNW of Rodez; plaster mfg., woodworking.

Rignano Garganico (rēnyä'nô gärgä'nēkô), village (pop. 2,353), Foggia prov., Apulia, S Italy, on W slope of Gargano promontory, 11 mi. E of San Severo; cheese making.

Rignano sull'Arno (soolär'nô), village (pop. 1,419), Firenze prov., Tuscany, central Italy, on the Arno and 10 mi. ESE of Florence.

Rigny-Ussé (rēnyē'-üsā'), village (pop. 281), Indre-et-Loire dept., W central France, on Indre R. near its influx into the Loire, 6 mi. NNE of Chinon; mushrooms, truck. Has 16th-cent. château.

Rigo (rē'gō), town, Territory of Papua, SE New Guinea, 35 mi. SE of Port Moresby; mission.

Rigolet (rĭgōlĕt'), settlement (pop. 84), SE Labrador, at head of Hamilton Inlet, at mouth of channel draining L. Melville; 54°11'N 58°25'W. Fishing, lumbering.

Rigolets (rĭ'gùlēz), SE La., navigable waterway (c.8½ mi. long) connecting L. Borgne and L. Pontchartrain, 30 mi. ENE of New Orleans; part of Gulf Intracoastal Waterway system. Old Fort Pike is in memorial park near W end.

Rig-Rig (rēg-rēg'), village, W Chad territory, Fr. Equatorial Africa, near NE shore of L. Chad, 150 mi. WNW of Moussoro, near Fr. West Africa border; customs station and military outpost; livestock, millet, vegetable and fruit raising in near-by oasis.

Riguy, Mount (rē'gē), Dan. *Riguy Bjaerg* (7,824 ft.), SE Greenland, on Blosseville Coast, near Denmark Strait; 69°N 26°10'W. Several glaciers.

Rihand River (rĭhŭnd') or **Rehar River** (rā'hŭr), NE central India, rises on W Chota Nagpur Plateau c.35 mi. SSW of Ambikapur in NE Madhya Pradesh, flows c.190 mi. NNW and NNE through E Vindhya Pradesh and SE Uttar Pradesh to Son R. 12 mi. SSW of Robertsganj. Projected Rihand dam (280 ft. high, 3,000 ft. long) and hydroelectric plant is 15 mi. W of Dudhi (Uttar Pradesh), with subsidiary dam 22 mi. NNW of Dudhi; to provide for irrigation, flood control, navigation, and recreation facilities.

Rihaniya, Rehania (both: rēhänē'ä), or **Rehana** (rĕhänä'), settlement (pop. 250), NW Israel, in Hills of Ephraim, 14 mi. SSW of Haifa; mixed farming. Founded 1944. Sometimes called Ein Haemek or 'Ein Ha'emek (ān' hä-ā'mĕk).

Rii (rē'ē), residential village (pop. 998), Vasternorrland co., NE Sweden, on Indal R., near its mouth on Gulf of Bothnia, 10 mi. NNE of Sundsvall.

Riihimäki (rē'hĭmă"kē), town (pop. 15,681), Häme co., S Finland, 40 mi. N of Helsinki; rail junction; glass-mfg. center; clothing mills.

Rija, Am (ăm'rĭ'jù), or **Al-Rijah** (ărĭ'jù), village, ⊙ Rijai sheikdom, Subeihi tribal area, Western Aden Protectorate, 20 mi. W of Lahej.

Rijai or **Rija'i** (rĭjăē'), petty sheikdom of SUBEIHI tribal area, Western Aden Protectorate; ⊙ Am Rija. Protectorate treaty concluded in 1871. Also spelled Rujai and Rujei.

Rijeka (rĭyĕ'kä), Ital. *Fiume* (fyoo'mä, Eng. fēoo'mē), city (pop. 72,120), ⊙ Rijeka oblast (formed 1949), NW Croatia, Yugoslavia, on Adriatic Sea, 75 mi. WSW of Zagreb, on NE shore of the Kvarner (Gulf of Quarnero), the innermost part of which is called Gulf of Rijeka or Gulf of Fiume; 45°20'N 14°26'E. Major seaport, serving Yugoslavia, Hungary, and Czechoslovakia; terminus of railroads to Zagreb and Ljubljana; shipbuilding, oil refining, wood- and metalworking, mfg. of machines, chemicals, tobacco and leather products; hydroelectric plant. Includes E suburb of Susak, Serbo-Croatian *Sušak* (soo'shäk), a port (exporting chiefly timber) separated from Rijeka proper by small coastal river. Castle of Trsat, Ital. *Tersatto*, stands on hill NE of city center. Near-by pilgrimage church (1453) commemorates site on which the house of the Virgin had allegedly stood (1291–94) before it was borne by angels to LORETO. Situated on site of Roman *Tarsatica*, Fiume was 1st mentioned as *Terra Fluminis Sancti Viti*, Ger. *Sankt Veit am Flaum*, in 13th cent. Passed to Hapsburgs in 1471 and was annexed (1779) to Hungary, where it existed intermittently as a *corpus separatum* (□ 8). Before the First World War it was chief seaport of Hungary. Italy, to which the city had been promised in secret Treaty of London of 1915, claimed it at Paris Peace Conference, but while negotiations still went on Gabriele d'Annunzio at head of an Italian free corps seized Fiume in Sept., 1919. By Treaty of Rapallo (1920) Italy and Yugoslavia agreed to establish a free state of Fiume. However, in 1922, a Fascist coup d'état overthrew the local govt. and Italian troops occupied the city. Tension bet. Yugoslavia and Italy over the Fiume question was somewhat eased by the Treaty of Rome (1924), which left Fiume in Italy—where it became ⊙ Fiume (after 1937, Carnaro) prov. (□ 433; 1936 pop. 109,018) of Venezia Giulia—but awarded its eastern suburb, Susak (Ital. *Porto Barros*), to Yugoslavia. Susak was built up as a leading Yugoslav port. In 1945 Fiume passed under Yugoslav occupation, and in 1947 the Allied peace treaty with Italy formally transferred the city to Yugoslavia. It was reunited with Susak into a single city. From 1700 until the Second World War Fiume was a free port. Damaged heavily in Second World War. Also spelled Rieka.

Rijeka Crnojevica or **Riyeka Tsrnoyevicha** (both: rĭyĕ'kä tsŭr'nôyĕvēchä), Serbo-Croatian *Rijeka Crnojevića*, village, SW Montenegro, Yugoslavia, on Titograd-Cetinje road and 6 mi. ESE of Cetinje, near NW end of L. Scutari. Had a printing press (2d half of 15th cent.), one of 1st in the Balkans.

Rijen or **Reijen** (both: rī'ùn), town (pop. 3,143), North Brabant prov., S Netherlands, 7 mi. WNW of Tilburg; leather tanning, mfg. (shoes, telephone apparatus). Airfield (S). Sometimes spelled Ryen. Village of Gilze (pop. 2,726) is 4 mi. SSE.

Rijkevorsel (rĭk'ùvôrsùl), town (pop. 6,283), Antwerp prov., N Belgium, 8 mi. WNW of Turnhout; brick mfg. Formerly spelled Ryckevorsel.

Rijn, Du. name of RHINE RIVER.

Rijnsburg (rīnz'bûrkh), town (pop. 5,725), South Holland prov., W Netherlands, near the Old Rhine, 3 mi. NW of Leiden; bulb growing, vegetable canning. Residence (1660–63) of Spinoza. Sometimes spelled Rynsburg.

Rijsen, Netherlands: see RIJSSEN.

Rijsenburg or **Rijzenburg** (both: rī'zùnbûrkh), village, Utrecht prov., central Netherlands, 8 mi. ESE of Utrecht. Has Catholic seminary, established 1853. Sometimes spelled Rysenburg.

Rijssel, France: see LILLE.

Rijssen or **Rijsen** (both: rī'sùn), town (pop. 10,805), Overijssel prov., E Netherlands, 7 mi. WSW of Almelo; jute and linen spinning, weaving, and dyeing; bricks, cigars, dairy products. Sometimes spelled Ryssen or Rysen.

Rijswijk or **Ryswick** (rĭz'wĭk, Du. rīs'vĭk), town (pop. 19,963), South Holland prov., W Netherlands, 3 mi. SE of The Hague; mfg. of paint, flour, furniture, hothouse equipment. Site (1697) of treaty of Ryswick, signed by France, the Netherlands, England, Germany, and Spain.

Rijzenburg, Netherlands: see RIJSENBURG.

Rikasikha (rēkä'sēkhŭ), village (1939 pop. over 500), NW Archangel oblast, Russian SFSR, on W arm of Northern Dvina R. delta mouth and 9 mi. W of Archangel; fish canning.

Rikers Island (rī'kùrz) (400 acres), SE N.Y., in East R. bet. the Bronx (of which it is a part) and Queens boroughs of New York city. Site of city penitentiary (1935).

Rikhikesh (rĭkē'kāsh), since 1948 officially **Rishikesh** (rĭshē'–), town (pop. 5,020), Dehra Dun dist., N Uttar Pradesh, India, on the Ganges and 21 mi. SE of Dehra; rail spur terminus; wheat, rice, oilseeds, barley, corn. Pilgrimage center.

Rikord Strait (rĭkôrd'), Jap. *Ketoi-kaikyo* (kĕtoi'-kī'kyō'), central main Kurile Isls. chain, bet. Ushishir Isls. (N) and Ketoi Isl. (S); 16 mi. wide.

Riksgransen (rēks'grĕn"sùn), Swedish *Riksgränsen*, village, Norbotten co., N Sweden, 65 mi. NW of Kiruna, frontier station on Norwegian border, 16 mi. E of Narvik; winter-sports resort.

Rila (rē'lä), village (pop. 4,125), Sofia dist., W Bulgaria, in Rila Mts., on Rila R. and 8 mi. S of Marek; tobacco; wine making, sawmilling. Sometimes called Riloselo.

Rila Mountains (rē'lä), Bulg. *Rila Planina*, NW part of Rhodope Mts., highest range in Bulgaria and in Balkan Peninsula; extend c.50 mi. E–W bet. Thracian Plain and Struma R., c.30 mi. N–S bet. Samokov Basin and Pirin Mts. It may be considered in 4 sections: E Rila Mts. (highest; rise to 9,596 ft. in Stalin Peak (Musala), central Rila Mts. (rise to 8,969 ft. at the Skakavets), NW Rila Mts. (rise to 8,957 ft. at the Malovitsa), and SW Rila Mts. (rise to 8,587 ft. at the Aigidik; separated from Pirin Mts. by Predel Pass). Scattered lead, zinc, and copper deposits. Magnetite (once exploited) in N Rila Mts.; oil shale near Dimitrovo; lignite and marble in central part. Mineral springs in Sapareva-banya, Dimitrovo and Banya. Extensive use of coniferous forests. Cattle and sheep raising in alpine meadows.

Rilán (rēlän'), village (1930 pop. 111), Chiloé prov., S Chile, on E coast of Chiloé Isl., 7 mi. SE of Castro, in agr. area (potatoes, wheat, livestock); fishing, lumbering.

Rila River (rē'lä), W Bulgaria, rises in small alpine lake in NW Rila Mts., flows 33 mi. W, past Rilski Manastir, to Struma R. 4 mi. NNW of Gorna Dzhumaya.

Riley, county (□ 624; pop. 33,405), NE Kansas; ⊙ Manhattan. Level to rolling plain, bounded E by Big Blue R.; drained in S by Kansas R. Livestock, grain. Formed 1855.

Riley. **1** Town (pop. 251), Vigo co., W Ind., 8 mi. SE of Terre Haute; bituminous-coal mines. **2** City (pop. 414), Riley co., NE Kansas, 15 mi. WNW of Manhattan; grain-shipping point in agr. area.

Riley, Fort, Kansas: see JUNCTION CITY.

Rille River, France: see RISLE RIVER.

Rillieux (rēyû'), outer suburb (pop. 1,016) of Lyons Ain dept., E France, 6 mi. NNE of city center; chemicals, construction materials. Truck gardens.

Rillito (rēyē'tō), village, Pima co., S Ariz., 17 mi. NW of Tucson; cementworks.

Rilly-la-Montagne (rēyē'-lä-mōtä'nyù), village (pop. 922), Marne dept., N France, on N slope of the Montagne de Reims, 7 mi. S of Rheims; winegrowing (champagne).

Rilski Manastir (rēl'skē mänästĕr'), monastery (pop. 676), Sofia dist., W Bulgaria, in Rila Mts., on Rila R. and 13 mi. SE of Marek; rail spur terminus; vineyards, livestock. Has library and mus. with 14th-cent. relics. Founded in 9th cent.; became a Greek-Orthodox religious center during Turkish rule (15th–19th cent.). Burned and pillaged several times; finally rebuilt (1833) in Bulg. and Ital. Renaissance style.

Rima (rē'mä), Chinese *Li-ma* (lē'mä'), town, E Tibet, in Kham prov., on Luhit R. and 150 mi. SW of Paan, on Indian border; 28°24'N 97°4'E; trading center. Formerly called Chayü, Ch'a-yü, or Tsa-yü, a name later applied to a town 20 mi. NW of Rima at 28°42'N 96°54'E.

Rima, Wadi, or **Wadi Rummah** (both: wă'dē rĭ'mù), one of chief wadies of Arabian Peninsula, in N Nejd, Saudi Arabia, extends c.300 mi. E–W through Qasim dist.

Rímac (rē'mäk), N industrial section (pop. 57,154) of Lima, Lima dept., W central Peru, across Rímac R., at S foot of San Cristóbal hill. Inc. 1940 into Lima proper.

Rímac River, Lima dept., W central Peru, rises in Cordillera Occidental of the Andes 3 mi. E of Casapalca, flows 80 mi. WSW, past San Mateo, Matucana, Chosica, and Lima, to the Pacific 5 mi. W of Lima. Used for irrigation in lower course. Sometimes called San Mateo R. in its upper course, above confluence with the Santa Eulalia at Chosica.

Ríma River, Nigeria: see KEBBI RIVER.

Rimaszombat, Czechoslovakia: see RIMAVSKA SOBOTA.

Rimatara (rēmätä'rä), volcanic island (pop. 695). Tubuai Isls., Fr. Oceania, S Pacific, 210 mi. WNW of Tubuai; circumference c.20 mi. Discovered 1769 by Capt. Cook, annexed 1889 by France. Edict (1938) excludes non-natives. Sometimes spelled Rimitara.

Rimaucourt (rēmōkoor'), village (pop. 609), Haute-Marne dept., NE France, 13 mi. NE of Chaumont; forges.

Rimavska Sobota (rĭ'mäfskä sô'bôtä), Slovak *Rimavská Sobota*, Hung. *Rimászombat* (rĭ'másōm"-bŏt), town (pop. 6,895), S Slovakia, Czechoslovakia, 47 mi. SE of Banska Bystrica, wheat- and fruitgrowing dist.; rail junction; fruit processing. Held by Hungary, 1938–45.

Rimbey, agr. village (pop. 634), S central Alta., near Gull L., 30 mi. NW of Red Deer.

Rimbo (rĭm'boo"), village (pop. 787), Stockholm co., E Sweden, 12 mi. W of Norrtalje; rail junction; brick mfg. Near by are remains of 16th-cent. castle.

Rimersburg (rī'mùrzbûrg), borough (pop. 1,398), Clarion co., W central Pa., 13 mi. SSW of Clarion; bituminous coal, gas; timber; agr. Settled 1829, laid out 1839, inc. 1853.

Rimini (rē'mēnē), anc. *Ariminum*, city (pop. 31,505), Forlì prov., Emilia-Romagna, N central Italy, port on the Adriatic, 29 mi. SE of Forlì, at mouth of Marecchia R. One of Italy's most frequented bathing resorts. Mfg. (macaroni, shoes, furniture, linen, woolen textiles, soap, pharmaceuticals); shipyards. Bishopric. Has triumphal arch and bridge built by Augustus, 13th-cent. town hall, ruins of Malatesta castle (15th cent.). Church of St. Francis (13th cent.; called Tempio Malatestiano after its renovation, c.1450), one of finest Renaissance bldgs., severely damaged in 1943–44. An Umbrian town, it became a strategic Roman colony at junction of Flaminian and Aemilian ways. Ruled by Malatesta family, 1295–1509, when it passed to the papacy. In Second World War, probably one of Italy's most heavily damaged cities; suffered over 300 bombings, of which 15 were naval.

Rimini (rĭ'mùnē), village (pop. c.50), Lewis and Clark co., W central Mont., 12 mi. SW of Helena; trade point in mining area.

Rimitara, Tubuai Isls.: see RIMATARA.

Rim of the World Drive, Calif.: see SAN BERNARDINO MOUNTAINS.

Rimogne (rēmô'nyù), village (pop. 1,349), Ardennes dept., N France, at foot of the Ardennes, 10 mi. NW of Mézières; enamel plumbing fixtures. Slate quarries.

Rimouski (rĭmoo'skē), county (□ 2,089; pop. 44,233), E Que., on the St. Lawrence and on N.B. border; ⊙ Rimouski.

Rimouski, town (pop. 7,009), ⊙ Rimouski co., E Que., on the St. Lawrence, at mouth of Rimouski R., and 180 mi. NE of Quebec; lumbering, woodworking, butter making, cod-liver-oil refining. Airport. Seat of R.C. bishop; has cathedral, seminary, agr. col. Harbor is sheltered by Île St. Barnabé. A fire in 1950 destroyed much of the town.

Rimouski Est, village (pop. 690), E suburb of Rimouski, E Que., on the St. Lawrence.

Rimpfischhorn (rĭmp'fĭsh-hôrn), peak (13,787 ft.) in Pennine Alps, S Switzerland, 6 mi. E of Zermatt.

Rimske Toplice (rēm'skĕ tô'plĭtsĕ) [Slovenian,= Roman hot baths], Ger. *Römerbad* (rû'mûrbät"), village, central Slovenia, Yugoslavia, on Savinja R., on railroad and 8 mi. WSW of Celje; health resort with radioactive warm springs. Known since Roman times. Until 1918, in Styria.

Rinard (rī'närd), town (pop. 115), Calhoun co., central Iowa, 20 mi. SW of Fort Dodge.

Rincão (rēng-kã'ō), town (pop. 2,936), N central São Paulo, Brazil, near Mogi-Guaçu R., 20 mi. NNE of Araraquara; rail junction; coffee, cotton, grain, sugar cane.

Rincha or **Rintja** (both: rĭn'chŭ), island (18 mi. long, 9 mi. wide), Lesser Sundas, Indonesia, bet. Flores Sea (N) and Sumba Strait (S), just W of Flores; 8°42'S 119°41'E. Fishing.

Rinchenling or **Rinchhen Ling** (rĭn'chĕn lĭng'), Chinese *Jen-chin-li* (rŭn'jĭn'lē'), village, SE Tibet, on left tributary of the Kyi Chu, on Lhasa-Chamdo (China) trade route and 55 mi. ENE of Lhasa.

Rincon (rĭng-kōn'), village, N Bonaire, Du. West Indies, 8 mi. NW of Kralendijk; divi-divi, sisal, goats, sheep.

Rincón (rēngkōn'), town (pop. 1,751), Havana prov., W Cuba, 12 mi. SSW of Havana; rail junction in agr. region (sugar cane, tobacco, cattle). Natl. leprosarium. Shrine.

Rincón or **Rincón de Romos** (dā rō'mōs), city (pop. 4,460), Aguascalientes, N central Mexico, 24 mi. NNW of Aguascalientes; agr. center (grain, beans, wine, fruit, vegetables, livestock). Rail station 2½ mi. SE.

Rincón, town (pop. 1,071), W Puerto Rico, on coast, on railroad and 11 mi. NW of Mayagüez; westernmost settlement of the isl., in fruitgrowing region (mangoes, citrus, breadfruit, plantain, coconuts); mfg. of cigars.

Rincon (rĭng'kŏn"), town (pop. 424), Effingham co., E Ga., 17 mi. NNW of Savannah.

Rincón, Cerro (sĕ'rō rēngkōn'), Andean volcano (18,353 ft.) on Argentina-Chile border, 65 mi. WNW of San Antonio de los Cobres; 24°2'S. The Salina del Rincón, a salt desert (□ 100; alt. 12,100 ft.), is E; 20 mi. long.

Rincón, El, Venezuela: see EL RINCÓN.

Rincón, Lake, fresh-water lake (4 mi. long), Barahona prov., SW Dominican Republic, 7 mi. NW of Barahona city.

Rincona (rĭng-kō'nä), town (pop. 2,151), Málaga prov., S Spain, 12 mi. NNE of Antequera; olive oil, flour. Sometimes called Villanueva or Villanueva de Algaidas, the name of its commune.

Rinconada (rēngkōnä'dä). **1** Village (pop. estimate 500), ⊙ Rinconada dept. (□ 1,520; 1947 pop. 4,871), W Jujuy prov., Argentina, 45 mi. SW of La Quiaca; stock-raising (sheep, donkeys) and mining (lead, tin, zinc) center. **2** Village (pop. estimate 500), S San Juan prov., Argentina, in San Juan R. valley (irrigation area), on railroad and 17 mi. S of San Juan; alfalfa and winegrowing center; wine making. Lime deposits, limekilns.

Rinconada, La (lä), town (pop. 2,043), Seville prov., SW Spain, near left bank of the Guadalquivir, 6 mi. N of Seville; olives, sugar beets, cereals, oranges, vegetables, licorice, livestock. Sugar milling; lumbering.

Rinconada de los Andes (dā lōs än'dēs), village (1930 pop. 1,090), Aconcagua prov., central Chile, 7 mi. SSE of San Felipe, in agr. area (hemp, tobacco, fruit, livestock).

Rinconada de Silva (sēl'vä), town (pop. 1,274), Aconcagua prov., central Chile, in Andean foothills, 10 mi. N of San Felipe; agr. center (fruit, wine, tobacco, hemp, livestock).

Rincón de la Vieja (rēngkōn' dā lä vyā'hä), active volcano (4,928 ft.) in the Cordillera de Guanacaste, NW Costa Rica, 14 mi. NNE of Liberia; sulphur springs.

Rincón del Bonete (dĕl bōnā'tā), major hydroelectric plant and dam, Tacuarembó dept., central Uruguay, on the Río Negro 7 mi. E of Paso de los Toros. It forms (E) large artificial lake on the Río Negro along Tacuarembó-Durazno dept. border. Begun 1937, the completed units of the project supply most of the electric power in Uruguay.

Rincón de Medik (dā mädĕk'), town (pop. 2,275), Yebala territory, NW Sp. Morocco, fishing port on the Mediterranean, on Ceuta-Tetuán RR and 8 mi. NNE of Tetuán; truck farming.

Rincón de Nogoyá (dā nōgoiä'), town (pop. estimate 500), SW Entre Ríos prov., Argentina, 25 mi. SSW of Nogoyá; wheat, flax, alfalfa, livestock.

Rincón de Soto (sō'tō), town (pop. 2,843), Logroño prov., N Spain, 7 mi. SE of Calahorra; canning (fruit and vegetables), wine processing. Potatoes, sugar beets in area.

Rincón de Tamayo (tämī'ō), town (pop. 3,365), Guanajuato, central Mexico, on railroad and 8 mi. SSE of Celaya; cereals, fruit, sugar, alfalfa, tobacco, stock.

Rincón Grande Cascade, Mexico: see ORIZABA.

Rincon Mountains (rĭng'kŏn"), in section of Coronado Natl. Forest, SE Ariz., E of Tucson. MICA MOUNTAIN (8,800 ft.) is highest point. Rincon Peak (8,465 ft.), in S tip of range, is 27 mi. ESE of Tucson. Saguaro Natl. Monument is W.

Rincon Peak (rĭng'kŏn", rĭngkōn') (c.11,600 ft.), N N.Mex., in Sangre de Cristo Mts., 23 mi. ENE of Santa Fe.

Rinderhorn (rĭn'dûrhôrn"), peak (11,343 ft.) in Bernese Alps, S Switzerland, 7 mi. N of Leuk.

Rindge (rĭnj), town (pop. 707), Cheshire co., SW N.H., 18 mi. SE of Keene, on Mass. line, in hilly lake region.

Rindjani, Mount, Indonesia: see RINJANI, MOUNT.

Rindli (rĭnd'lē), village, Bolan subdivision, NE central Baluchistan, W Pakistan, at E end of Bolan Pass, 60 mi. SE of Quetta; wheat; cattle raising.

Rineanna, Ireland: see SHANNON AIRPORT.

Rinfret (rĭn'frĕt, Fr. rēfrĕ'), village, S Que., on North R. and 25 mi. NW of Montreal; mica mining.

Ringarooma (rĭng-gûrōō'mŭ), village (pop. 285), NE Tasmania, 33 mi. ENE of Launceston and on Ringarooma R., in tin-mining area; dairy products, wheat; sawmills.

Ringarooma Bay, inlet of Bass Strait, NE Tasmania; Cape Portland at E end; 15 mi. E–W, 7 mi. N–S. Receives Ringarooma R.

Ringarooma River, NE Tasmania, rises SW of Ringarooma, flows NE, past Ringarooma, Branxholm, Derby, and Gladstone, thence NW to Ringarooma Bay of Bass Strait; 62 mi. long. Tin deposits on banks.

Ringat, Indonesia: see RENGAT.

Ringdom Sankpo, river, Kashmir: see SURU RIVER.

Ringe (rĭng'ŭ), town (pop. 2,291), Svendborg amt, Denmark, on S Fyn isl. and 13 mi. NNW of Svendborg; rail junction; pasteboard, furniture.

Ringebu (rĭng'ŭbōō), village and canton (pop. 5,634), Opland co., S central Norway, in the Gudbrandsdal, on Lagen R., on railroad and 30 mi. NNW of Lillehammer; agr., stock raising. Has stave church (c.1250). Valebru (vô'lŭbrōō) (Nor. *Vålebru*) village (pop. 809) is 3 mi. NNW; sometimes spelled Vaalebru.

Ringelspitz (rĭng'ŭl-shpĭts) or **Piz Bargias** (pēts' bär'jäs), peak (10,666 ft.) in Glarus Alps, E Switzerland, 9 mi. WNW of Chur.

Ringerike (rĭng'ŭrēkŭ), region and administrative district (□ 668; pop. 19,298), Buskerud co., SE Norway, centered at Honefoss; extends bet. Rands Fjord and the lake Sperillen (N) and Tyri Fjord (S); drained by Begna and Rand rivers, which supply power to extensive lumbering and wood-pulp industry.

Ringgold, county (□ 538; pop. 9,528), S Iowa, on Mo. line (S); ⊙ Mount Ayr. Rolling prairie agr. area (hogs, cattle, poultry, corn, oats, wheat) drained by Little Platte and Grand rivers; bituminous-coal deposits. Formed 1847.

Ringgold. 1 Town (pop. 1,192), ⊙ Catoosa co., NW Ga., 13 mi. SE of Chattanooga, Tenn.; textile mfg. Inc. 1847. **2** Village (pop. 1,007), Bienville parish, NW La., 30 mi. ESE of Shreveport, in cotton, lumber, and general-farming area; cotton ginning; mfg. of fertilizer, bricks, tiles, boats; lumber milling. L. Bistineau is W. **3** Village (pop. c.400), Montague co., N Texas, 32 mi. E of Wichita Falls, near Red R.; rail point in farm area.

Ringgold, Fort, Texas: see RIO GRANDE CITY.

Ringgold Isles, small coral group E of Vanua Levu, Fiji, SW Pacific; 16°23'S 179°29'W.

Ringim or **Ringin** (rēn'jŭm), town (pop. 5,274), Kano prov., Northern Provinces, N Nigeria, 45 mi. ENE of Kano, on railroad; cotton, peanuts, durra; cattle, skins.

Ringkobing (rĭng'kûbĭng), Dan. *Ringkøbing,* formerly *Ringkjøbing,* largest amt (□ 1,800; 1950 pop. 186,841) of Denmark, in W Jutland, on North Sea; ⊙ Ringkobing. Terrain mostly flat, with some hilly areas; highest point, 430 ft. Drained by Stor R. and Skern R. Soil sandy and poor in flatlands, clayey in hills; fertile strip in N, along Lim Fjord. Chief cities: Herning, Holstebro. Agr., dairy farming, limestone quarrying.

Ringkobing, Dan. *Ringkøbing,* city (1950 pop. 4,638), ⊙ Ringkobing amt, W Jutland, Denmark, port on Ringkobing Fjord and 75 mi. W of Aarhus; 56°5'N 8°15'E. Iron foundry, cement plant, textile mill; fisheries. City dates from Middle Ages.

Ringkobing Fjord, W Jutland, Denmark, inlet of North Sea; c.20 mi. long, 7 mi. wide; average depth, c.10 ft. Separated from North Sea by Holmslands Klit, a 1-mi.-wide strip. Ringkobing port is on NE shore.

Ringlades or **Ringladhes** (both: rĭn-glä'dhĕs), village (pop. 2,901), S Corfu isl., Greece, 16 mi. SSE of Corfu city; olive oil, wine.

Ring Lake, Swedish *Ringsjön* (rĭng'shûn") (7 mi. long, 1–4 mi. wide), S Sweden, 3 mi. W of Horby; drained NW by Ronne R.

Ringlet (rĭng"lĭt'), township (□ 20; pop. 2,272) of Cameron Highlands, NW Pahang, Malaya, on road and 18 mi. NNE of Tapah (Perak); hill station; experimental farm.

Ringley Road, England: see OUTWOOD.

Ringling. 1 Village (pop. c.150), Meagher co., S central Mont., on branch of Missouri R. and 60 mi. ESE of Helena; wheat-shipping point. **2** Town (pop. 1,092), Jefferson co., S Okla., 26 mi. W of Ardmore, in agr. area (grain, livestock; dairy products); cotton ginning.

Ringmer, agr. village and parish (pop. 1,607), E central Sussex, England, 3 mi. NE of Lewes.

Ringsaker (rĭngs'äkŭr), village and canton (pop. 15,151), Hedmark co., SE Norway, on E shore of L. Mjosa, on railroad and 15 mi. NW of Hamar; lumbering, agr. Has medieval church. Near by are remains of 13th-cent. castle.

Ringsjon, Sweden: see RING LAKE.

Ringsted (rĭng'stĕdh), city (pop. 7,835), Soro amt, Zealand, Denmark, 34 mi. SW of Copenhagen; meat cannery, brewery, furniture factory, machinery plant; rail junction. Site of 11th-cent. Benedictine monastery.

Ringsted (rĭng'stĕd), town (pop. 578), Emmet co., NW Iowa, 18 mi. ESE of Estherville; livestock, grain.

Ringtown, borough (pop. 835), Schuylkill co., E central Pa., 3 mi. NNW of Shenandoah.

Ringus, India: see SRI MADHOPUR.

Ringvaart (rĭng'värt), canal (37 mi. long), North Holland prov., NW Netherlands; forms closed circuit surrounding and draining the Haarlemmermeer. Serves Schiphol, Aalsmeer, Hillegom, Heemstede, Halfweg; navigable along entire length.

Ringvassoy (rĭng'väs-ûĭ), Nor. *Ringvassøy,* island (□ 253; pop. 1,589) in Norwegian Sea, Troms co., N Norway, 10 mi. NNE of Tromso; 22 mi. long (N-S), up to 20 mi. wide; rises to 3,284 ft. Fishing.

Ringwood, municipality (pop. 4,897), S Victoria, Australia, 9 mi. E of Melbourne, in metropolitan area; fruit.

Ringwood, town and parish (pop. 5,887), SW Hampshire, England, on the Avon and 9 mi. NNE of Bournemouth; agr. market, with glove-knitting works and flour mills. Church dates from 13th cent.

Ringwood. 1 Borough (pop. 1,752), Passaic co., N N.J., in Ramapo Mts. near N.Y. line, E of Greenwood L., 15 mi. NNW of Paterson; iron mining (since 1762); produced iron and munitions in Revolution. Ringwood Manor State Park (95 acres) includes historic manor, now a mus. **2** Town (pop. 331), Major co., NW Okla., 20 mi. W of Enid, in agr. area (grain, livestock).

Rinhen, Formosa: see LINYÜAN.

Rinia, Greece: see RENEIA.

Riñihue, Lake (rēnyē'wä) (□ 23), Valdivia prov., S central Chile, in Chilean lake dist., bet. L. Panguipulli and L. Ranco; 13 mi. long, 2–3 mi. wide. Surrounded by forests and subandean peaks, it is a resort at end of rail spur from Los Lagos. Fishing, lumbering.

Rinjani, Mount, or **Mount Rindjani** (both: rĭnjä'nē), highest volcanic peak (12,224 ft.) of Lombok, Indonesia, in N part of isl. An extinct crater contains a lake. Sometimes called Peak of Lombok.

Rinns of Galloway, Scotland: see GALLOWAY.

Rinópolis (rēnô'pōōlēs), city (pop. 1,077), W São Paulo, Brazil, 60 mi. NW of Marília; coffee, cotton, rice, beans.

Rinteln (rĭn'tŭln), town (pop. 9,324), in former Prussian prov. of Hanover, W Germany, after 1945 in Lower Saxony, on left bank of the Weser and 13 mi. NW of Hameln; glassworks. Has 13th-cent. church, 16th-cent. town hall. Was ⊙ medieval county of Schaumburg. Seat of univ. (1621–1809). Belonged to former Prussian prov. of Hesse-Nassau until 1932.

Rintja, Indonesia: see RINCHA.

Rinxent (rēksä'), town (pop. 2,824), Pas-de-Calais dept., N France, 8 mi. NE of Boulogne; marble and stone quarrying.

Rio, Brazil: see RIO DE JANEIRO, city.

Rio (rī'ō), village (pop. 741), Columbia co., S central Wis., 13 mi. SE of Portage, in agr. area (grain, potatoes); lime works.

Río, El (ĕl rē'ō), narrow Atlantic channel (c. 1 mi. wide, 5 mi. long), Canary Isls., bet. Graciosa Isl. (N) and Lanzarote (S). Sheltered anchorage.

Río, El, or **La Ciénaga** (lä syā'nägä), narrow channel on N Yucatan coast (Gulf of Mexico), SE Mexico; extends c.210 mi. W-E from Nimun Point (Yucatan–Campeche border) to Lagartos Lagoon (Yucatan–Quintana Roo border). Separates mainland from narrow bars and peninsulas; joined to sea by small channels. Average width 1 mi.

Río Abajo (rē'ō äbä'hō), town (pop. 5,645), Panama prov., central Panama, in Pacific lowland, on Inter-American Highway and 5 mi. NE of Panama city; coconuts, coffee, livestock.

Rio Acima (rē'ōō äsē'mŭ), town (pop. 1,366), S central Minas Gerais, Brazil, on the Rio das Velhas, on railroad and 16 mi. SE of Belo Horizonte; blast furnaces, ironworks.

Rio Arriba (rē'ō ŭrē'bŭ), county (□ 5,855; pop. 24,997), NW N.Mex.; ⊙ Tierra Amarilla. Livestock-grazing and agr. (grain, chili) region; watered by Rio Chama; borders on Colo. Jicarilla Indian Reservation extends N–S. Natl.-forest areas in E, W, and S; range of Rocky Mts. in NE; Pueblo Indian areas in SE. Formed 1852.

Rio Azul (rē'ŏŏ äzōōl'), city (pop. 1,131), S Paraná, Brazil, on railroad and 60 mi. SW of Ponta Grossa; grain-milling center; linen milling, coffee and maté processing.

Riobamba (rēōbäm'bä), city (1950 pop. 29,611), ⊙ Chimborazo prov., Ecuador, in high Andean basin, on Pan American Highway, on Quito-Guayaquil RR and 100 mi. S of Quito; 1°40'S 78°38'W; alt. c.9,000 ft. Surrounded by a majestic panorama of snow-capped mts. (such as Chimborazo, NW; Tungurahua, NE; Altar, E; and Sangay, SE), it has a cool, temperate climate. Situated in fertile irrigated agr. region (grain, vegetables, potatoes, cattle, sheep), it is a trading and processing center. Mfg. of cotton and woolen goods, carpets, shoes, light-iron products, beer, liquor, butter, cheese. Tagua-nut marketing. Picturesque weekly fairs. Airport. The city has fine churches, parks, and plazas. Dating back to pre-Inca days, it was moved after 1797 earthquake to its present site from Cajabamba (W). Scene of meeting of 1st Ecuadorian Congress.

Río Benito or **Benito** (rē'ō bānē'tō), town (pop. 774), continental Sp. Guinea, on Gulf of Guinea at mouth of the Benito, 20 mi. SSW of Bata; 1°35'N 9°38'E. Exports cabinetwoods, coffee, palm oil. Sawmilling.

Río Bermejo, Argentina: see PUERTO BERMEJO.

Río Blanco (rē'ō bläng'kō). **1** Village (1930 pop. 279), Aconcagua prov., central Chile, in the Andes, on Aconcagua R., on Transandine RR and 25 mi. ESE of San Felipe; mtn. resort. **2** Village (1930 pop. 27), Malleco prov., S central Chile, 75 mi. SE of Angol; alt. 3,645 ft. Health resort with thermal springs. Sometimes Termas de Río Blanco.

Río Blanco, officially Tenango del Río Blanco, town (pop. 9,466), Veracruz, E Mexico, in Sierra Madre Oriental, at SE foot of Pico de Orizaba, on railroad and 3 mi. WSW of Orizaba; cotton-milling center (yarn and cloth); brewery, mfg. of printing presses. Dam and hydroelectric station on Río Blanco near by.

Rio Blanco (rē'ō blăng'kō), county (□ 3,263; pop. 4,719), NW Colo.; ⊙ Meeker. Livestock-grazing region, bordering on Utah; drained by White R. Part of White R. Natl. Forest and Rocky Mts. in E. Has oil field. Formed 1889.

Rio Bonito (rē'ŏŏ bōōnē'tŏŏ). **1** City, Goiás, Brazil: see CAIAPÔNIA. **2** City (pop. 4,492), central Rio de Janeiro state, Brazil, on railroad and 39 mi. ENE of Rio de Janeiro; distilling, match mfg.; agr. (sugar, manioc). **3** City, Santa Catarina, Brazil: see TANGARÁ.

Rio Branco (rē'ŏŏ brăng'kŏŏ), federal territory (□ 82,747; 1940 pop. 12,130; 1950 census 17,623), northernmost Brazil; ⊙ Boa Vista. Bounded by Venezuela (N), Br. Guiana (E), and the Braz. states of Amazonas (W and S) and Pará (SE). Crossed N-S by the Rio Branco, a tributary of the Rio Negro, the territory lies within the tropical rain-forest basin of the Amazon. Extensive stock raising on higher ground (savanna) in Boa Vista area. Diamond, gold, and diatomite deposits in headstreams of the Rio Branco. Territory was carved out of Amazonas in 1943.

Rio Branco. 1 City (1950 pop. 9,592), ⊙ Acre territory, westernmost Brazil, on Acre R., 700 mi. SW of Manaus; 9°59'S 67°52'W. Exports rubber, medicinal plants, Brazil nuts, and timber. Airport. Roads to Sena Madureira and Bolivia border. City's old section (founded 1882 as Empreza) is connected with modern Penápolis by bridge. **2** City, Bahia, Brazil: see PARATINGA. **3** City, Minas Gerais, Brazil: see VISCONDE DO RIO BRANCO. **4** City, Pernambuco, Brazil: see ARCOVERDE.

Río Branco (rē'ō bräng'kō), town (pop. 1,400), Cerro Largo dept., NE Uruguay, on NW edge of the Rincón del Mangrullo, on Yaguarón R. (railroad bridge), opposite Jaguarão (Brazil), and 50 mi. ESE of Melo, on railroad from Treinta y Tres. Trade with Brazil (fruit, grain, cattle, wool). Customhouse; airport. Because of inundations by the river, a higher suburb, La Cuchilla, was built. Named Artigas 1853, renamed Río Branco 1909.

Río Bravo (rē'ō brä'vō), village (pop. 1,085), Suchitepéquez dept., S Guatemala, 14 mi. SE of Mazatenango. Rail junction for Tiquisate banana plantation railroads.

Río Bravo, village (pop. 1,583), Coahuila, N Mexico, 37 mi. SW of Piedras Negras; cereals, cotton, livestock.

Rio Brilhante (rē'ŏŏ brēlyăn'tĭ), city (pop. 1,388), S Mato Grosso, Brazil, 90 mi. S of Campo Grande; cattle, maté. Until 1943, called Entre Rios; and, 1944–48, Caiuás.

Río Bueno (rē'ō bwā'nō), town (pop. 4,852), ⊙ Rio Bueno dept. (□ 2,323; pop. 34,387), Valdivia prov., S central Chile, on the Río Bueno, on railroad and 40 mi. SE of Valdivia, near La Unión; wheat-growing center; also barley, potatoes, peas, livestock. Flour mills, sawmills, tanneries.

Rio Bueno (rē"ō bwĕ'nō), town (pop. 1,027), Trelawny parish, N Jamaica, at mouth of the small Rio Bueno, 12 mi. E of Falmouth; sugar cane, tropical fruit and spices. Has old Fort Dundas (1778).

Rio Caçador, Brazil: see CAÇADOR.

Río Caribe (rē'ō kärē'bā), town (pop. 6,334), Sucre state, NE Venezuela, port on the Caribbean, 9 mi. E or Carúpano, in cacao-growing region. Ships run to Orinoco R. delta and Ciudad Bolívar.

Rio Casca (rē'ŏŏ kä'skŭ), city (pop. 2,870), E Minas Gerais, Brazil, on railroad and 20 mi. NE of Ponte Nova; sugar, coffee, lumber. Pilgrimage center.

Río Ceballos (rē'ō sābä'yōs), town (pop. 4,557), NW central Córdoba prov., Argentina, resort in the hills, 18 mi. NNW of Córdoba; meat packing, tanning, stock raising.

Rio Chama (rē'ō chä'mŭ), river, Colo. and N.Mex., rises near Banded Peak in San Juan Mts., SW Colo.; flows S, into N N.Mex., through El Vado Reservoir and Dam, and SSE to Rio Grande just S of Chamita; c.140 mi. long. Dam (completed 1934) is 175 ft. high, 1,300 ft. long; forms El Vado Reservoir (capacity 200,000 acre-ft.) SW of Tierra Amarilla.

Río Chico. 1 Department, Santa Cruz natl. territory, Argentina: see CAÑADÓN LEÓN. **2** Department, Tucumán prov., Argentina: see AGUILARES.

Río Chico (rē'ō chē'kō), town (pop. 1,686), Miranda state, N Venezuela, on small river 3 mi. inland from the Caribbean, on railroad and 65 mi. ESE of Caracas. Exports coffee, cacao, hides, fruit; mfg. (soap, footwear).

Rio Claro (rē'ŏŏ klä'rŏŏ). **1** City, Rio de Janeiro, Brazil: see ITAVERÁ. **2** City (1950 pop. 35,183), E central São Paulo, Brazil, on railroad, 45 mi. NW of Campinas; industrial center producing silk goods, footwear, cordage, agr. equipment. Tanning, brewing. Trades in coffee, citrus fruit, cereals, livestock, dairy products. Airfield.

Río Claro (rē'ō klä'rō), village (1930 pop. 425), Concepción prov., S central Chile, on railroad and 35 mi. SE of Concepción; wheat, corn, lentils, beans, wine, livestock. Kaolin deposits.

Rio Claro, village (pop. 2,055, including adjoining Lazzari), S central Trinidad, B.W.I., 33 mi. SE of Port of Spain; rail terminus in cacao-growing region.

Río Claro, town (pop. 1,049), Lara state, NW Venezuela, on headstream of Cojedes R. and 11 mi. SSW of Barquisimeto; coffee, sugar cane, corn.

Río Colorado (rē'ō kōlōrä'dō). **1** or **La Adela** (lä ädā'lä), village, ⊙ Caleu-Caleu dept. (pop. 2,024), SE La Pampa prov., Argentina, on left bank of Río Colorado, across from Río Colorado town in Río Negro natl. territory, on railroad and 100 mi. W of Bahía Blanca, in agr. area. **2** Town (1947 pop. 3,279), ⊙ Pichi Mahuida dept., NE Río Negro natl. territory, Argentina, on the Río Colorado and 100 mi. WSW of Bahía Blanca; farming center (irrigated area): alfalfa, potatoes, wine, apples, pears; sheep. Wine making. **3** Town (pop. estimate 1,000), S central Tucumán prov., Argentina, on the Río Colorado and 25 mi. SSW of Tucumán; rail junction and agr. center (sugar cane, corn, potatoes, onions, livestock).

Rio Costilla, N.Mex. and Colo.: see COSTILLA CREEK.

Río Cuarto (rē'ō kwär'tō), city (pop. 49,186), ⊙ Río Cuarto dept. (□ c.7,200; pop. 124,672), SE Córdoba prov., Argentina, on the Río Cuarto and 200 mi. S of Córdoba; rail junction; commercial, industrial, and agr. center. Mfg.: cement products, candy, toys, textile products, food preserves; tanning, meat packing, dairying, flour milling. Rich grain and livestock region; trading in cereals and agr. products. Airport. Bishopric. Has natl. col., law courts, municipal theater, art gall., arsenal and garrison.

Rio das Flores (rē'ŏŏ däs flō'rĭs), city (pop. 562), N Rio de Janeiro state, Brazil, 24 mi. W of Três Rios; dairying; fruit and vegetable growing. Until 1943, called Santa Teresa.

Rio das Pedras (rē'ŏŏ däs pĕ'drŭs), city (pop. 1,473), E central São Paulo, Brazil, on railroad and 8 mi. SSE of Piracicaba; distilling.

Rio de Contas (rē'ŏŏ dĭ kōn'tŭs), city (pop. 1,213), central Bahia, Brazil, on Brumado R. and 60 mi. SSW of Andaraí; gold mined here since colonial times. Rock crystals and semiprecious stones also found in area. Formerly called Minas do Rio de Contas.

Rio de Janeiro (rē'ō dŭ jŭnâ'rō, dā zhŭnâ'rō, Port. rē'ŏŏ dĭ zhŭnā'rŏŏ) [Port.,=river of January], coastal state (□ 16,443; 1940 pop. 1,847,857; 1950 census pop. 2,326,201), SE Brazil; ⊙ Niterói. Its N boundary with Minas Gerais is formed by the Serra da Mantiqueira (NW) and a section of the Paraíba valley (NE); also bounded by São Paulo (WSW) and Espírito Santo (NE), and the Atlantic (S and E). The Federal District (□ 524), containing Rio de Janeiro city, constitutes an enclave bet. Guanabara and Sepetiba bays. The great escarpment (Serra do Mar) traverses state lengthwise, separating coastal lowland (BAIXADA FLUMINENSE) from Paraíba R. valley; the latter runs parallel to the coast as far as its delta (near Campos). Beyond the Paraíba begins the central Brazilian plateau. Climate varies from hot and very humid in poorly drained coastal dists. to temperate and healthful in the zone of the escarpment, noted for its resorts (Petrópolis, Teresópolis, Nova Friburgo). Reclaimed lands around Guanabara Bay supply Rio with fruit (chiefly oranges) and truck. Stock raising and dairying, in addition to localized cultivation of rice and citrus fruit, is carried on in middle Paraíba valley, which in 19th cent. was scene of early coffee boom. The Paraíba delta and lower Pomba R. valley are intensive sugar-growing dists. Rio de Janeiro remains an important coffee-producing state, cultivation being limited to the upper slopes of the Serra do Mar and central plateau. Only important mineral resource are the saltworks along Araruama Lagoon and at Cabo Frio. Industrial development is 2d only to that of São Paulo. Since 1947, Brazil's leading steel mill (Volta Redonda) is in operation in Paraíba valley 60 mi. NW of Rio. The federal capital's large suburbs and satellite cities (including Niterói on E shore of Guanabara Bay) have attracted numerous light consumer industries, as well as cement, textile, chemical, tobacco, and glass factories, and an automobile plant. Sugar mills and alcohol distilleries are concentrated at Campos. Barra do Piraí and Três Rios are important rail junctions for lines to São Paulo and Minas Gerais, respectively. Territory of present state was originally part of São Tomé and São Vicente captaincies. Its history is closely associated with that of Rio de Janeiro city, which in 1834 became a separate administrative unit (neutral *municipio;* later, Federal Dist.). In 1835 Niterói became provincial ⊙ under Brazilian empire; in 1889 it became state ⊙ under federal republic. Bet. 1884 and 1903, seat of state govt. was at Petrópolis.

Rio de Janeiro, colloquially **Rio,** seaport city (1940 pop. 1,519,010; 1950 pop. 2,335,931), ⊙ Brazil, on SW shore of Guanabara Bay, opposite Niterói; 22°55'S 43°10'W. Occupies E part of Federal District (□ 452; including interior waters, □ 524; 1940 pop. 1,764,141; 1950 census 2,413,152); the entire dist. extends 35 mi. W to Sepetiba Bay. Administrative, cultural, commerical, and financial hub of Brazil, and international tourist center famous for the striking beauty of its natural setting. Splendid facilities of a landlocked harbor (including 2 mi. of wharves) enable large vessels to berth near heart of city, and also provide easy transshipment from railroads serving Paraíba valley and interior of São Paulo and Minas Gerais. Rio receives major part of Brazil's imports, is exceeded only by Santos in volume of exports, and is principal clearing point for active coastwise trade. Exports include coffee, minerals from Minas Gerais (iron ore, manganese, rock crystals), jerked and canned meat, cotton, linseed cake, bran, hides, fruit, and lumber. Although it is not Brazil's chief industrial center, Rio produces textiles (including rayon), clothing, glass, electrical and household appliances, chemicals, motors and trucks (natl. motor factory 20 mi. N), rubber tires, tobacco, and leather products for nation-wide distribution. It has machine and railroad shops. For local consumption are made footwear, matches, rope, fats, confectionery, flour products, furniture, and pharmaceuticals. Also processing of coffee, rice, sugar, and imported wheat; and sardine canning. Rio's hot, humid climate (mean temp. 75°F; annual temp. range is small, with Feb. max. in the 90s; yearly rainfall, 44 inches) accounts for popularity of near-by mtn. resorts (Petrópolis, Teresópolis, Nova Friburgo). However, extensive drainage of surrounding fever-breeding areas and urban sanitation work (since beginning of 20th cent.) have made Rio a healthful city. Built on narrow, closed-in lowlands separated from each other by rocky ridges which project into Guanabara Bay, city has had to expand northward into the BAIXADA FLUMINENSE coastal plain, and southward to the crescent-shaped beaches (notably Copacabana, Ipanema, Leblon) festooned from headland to headland along the open Atlantic. Rio's best-known landmarks and tourist attractions are the cone-shaped SUGAR LOAF MOUNTAIN (Pão de Açúcar) overlooking entrance to Guanabara Bay, and jagged CORCOVADO peak (topped by giant statue of Christ) rising abruptly above Botafogo Bay. In the background are Tijuca and Gávea hills partly covered with tropical vegetation, all part of the granitic Carioca range which traverses the Federal Dist. As a result of extensive rebuilding and modernization begun in 1902, under President Rodrigues Alves, broad, uncongested thoroughfares have been laid out. The 108-ft.-wide, tree-lined Avenida Rio Branco, with its multicolored mosaic sidewalks, is central N-S axis, connecting Praça Mauá (square at foot of wharves) with Lapa and Gloria residential dists. On it are the municipal theater (built 1909), natl. library, acad. of fine arts, and the Monroe Palace (which housed Braz. pavilion at St. Louis Exposition of 1904, was later moved to Rio, and is now used by the Senate). The palm-lined Avenida Beira Mar skirts the water front for over 3 mi., and, after circling Botafogo Bay, leads to fashionable Copacabana dist. with its modern apartment houses, places of entertainment, and sparkling beach. Along that avenue are Catete Palace (president's executive office) and Guanabara Palace (presidential residence). Noteworthy also are the Itamarati Palace (now part of Ministry of Foreign Affairs), the sumptuous Tiradentes Palace (completed 1926; houses Chamber of Deputies), and the many public and commercial structures typical of modern Braz. architecture. The ornate Candelaria church, containing tomb of Cabral, serves as Rio's cathedral. The botanical garden (founded 1808 on back slope of the Corcovado, along Rodrigo de Freitas Lagoon) is noted for its fine layout (especially double row of royal palm trees). The Morro do Castelo (hill on which city was originally built) was leveled in 1922; the removed material, used to fill in a portion of Guanabara Bay, now forms a peninsula named Calabouço Point. Here is Santos Dumont airport at edge of city's business dist. Near it are the municipal market and the slips for ferries to NITERÓI, used daily by thousands of commuters. Principal educational institutions are the Univ. of Rio de Janeiro (established 1920; combines numerous faculties), military and naval academies, fine arts acad., and the Colégio Pedro II (a model secondary school). Here also are hq. of nation's scientific institutes; the Oswaldo Cruz Inst. for research in serum therapeutics is in outskirts. Of Rio's many social and entertainment events, none attracts more visitors nor is enjoyed with greater gusto by the *Cariocas* (Rio's citizens) than the yearly pre-Lenten carnival. Guanabara Bay was 1st visited (probably in Jan., 1502) by Portuguese who believed it to be an estuary (whence city's name). In 1555, Villegaignon, for whom a fortified isl. in harbor is named, established a Fr. Huguenot settlement here. He was driven out (1567) by Mem de Sá, governor general of all Port. possessions in New World, who founded city of São Sebastião de Rio de Janeiro. The settlement was sacked by the French, 1710–11. In 1763, seat of viceroyalty was transferred here from Salvador (Bahia). Great prosperity came to city in 18th cent., when it was designated only shipping point for gold from the interior. Its importance was further enhanced in 1808, when Rio became seat of fugitive royal court of Portugal. It became ⊙ Brazilian empire in 1822, and ⊙ federal republic in 1889. In 1834 Rio was administratively detached from Rio de Janeiro prov., and became part of a neutral *municipio*, which in 1891 was renamed Federal District. It is governed by a federal council (1 representative from each state, 10 presidential appointees) headed by a mayor also nominated by the president. Included in the Federal Dist. is a rural zone W of city proper, and most of the isls. in Guanabara Bay, notably Governador (site of Galeão international airport), Paquetá, Cobras, Lage. Rio was the scene of the 1906 Pan-American Congress, and of the Second Inter-American Conference of Foreign Ministers in 1942. The Inter-American Conference for the Maintenance of Continental Peace and Security (1947), which led to the Rio pact, was actually held at Petrópolis. Transfer of seat of federal govt. to a site near the geographical center of Brazil (probably in SE Goiás) was, in 1950, still in blueprint stage.

Rio de Janeiro Bay, Brazil: see GUANABARA BAY.

Río de Jesús (rē'ō dā hāsōōs'), village (pop. 698), Veraguas prov., W central Panama, on the small Río de Jesús and 12 mi. SSW of Santiago; road terminus; sugar cane, corn, rice, livestock.

Río de la Plata, Argentina and Uruguay: see PLATA, RÍO DE LA.

Rio Dell, village (pop. 1,862), Humboldt co., NW Calif., on Eel R. and 20 mi. S of Eureka.

Rio del Rey (rē'ō děl rā'), village (pop. 634), S Br. Cameroons, administered as part of Eastern Provinces of Nigeria, port on Gulf of Guinea, at head of Rio del Rey (navigation channel amid mangrove-swamp isls.), 24 mi. SE of Calabar; fisheries.

Río de Oro (rē'ō dā ō'rō), town (pop. 1,638), Magdalena dept., N Colombia, in Cordillera Oriental, 4 mi. NNW of Ocaña; alt. 5,197 ft.; coffeegrowing.

Río de Oro, colony (□ 71,600; pop. c.24,000) of SPANISH WEST AFRICA, constituting the southern segment of the Saharan coastal region belonging to Spain; ⊙ Villa Cisneros. It has not always been so defined, and the nomenclature of the region has long been confused. The term Río de Oro originally applied to the undefined area of Spanish interest on NW coast of Africa SW of the sultanate of Morocco. The Franco-Spanish treaty of 1900 defined its S (21°20'N) and SE boundaries with Mauritania (Fr. West Africa), but the N boundary of the area of Spanish interest remained vague, a situation only partially rectified by treaties in 1904 (which established the N line at 27°40'N) and in 1912 (which established the S boundary of Fr. Morocco as the Dra wadi or Oued Dra). This left a politically amorphous segment of land S of the Dra and N of 27°40'N, which the Spanish call, casually, the SOUTHERN PROTECTORATE OF MOROCCO or "Zone South of the Dra." In 1934 the area of Spanish interest S of 27°40'N was labeled Spanish Sahara and was divided by lat. 26°N, the area to N being called SAGUIA EL HAMRA and the area to the S continuing to be called Río de Oro. A barren desert tract inhabited by nomadic Berber tribes, Río de Oro has a long coast line extending S from just S of Cape Bojador to Cap BLANC. Offshore trawl fisheries are only source of revenue. Villa Cisneros was settled by Spaniards in 1884.

Río de Oro Bay, narrow inlet of the Atlantic, Río de Oro, Sp. West Africa, bet. Villa Cisneros peninsula (W) and mainland; 20 mi. long, 5–8 mi. wide. Villa Cisneros is on W shore.

Rio do Sul (rē'ōō dōō sōōl'), city (pop. 3,597), E central Santa Catarina, Brazil, on Itajaí Açu R., on railroad and 40 mi. SW of Blumenau, in fertile agr. region; stock raising, dairying, sugar distilling. Founded as Bela Aliança in 1903 by settlers from Blumenau; later called Itajahy (or Itajaí) do Sul.

Río Fenix, Argentina: see LAGO BUENOS AIRES.

Rio Formoso (rē'ōō fôrmō'zōō), city (pop. 1,242), E Pernambuco, NE Brazil, near the Atlantic, 45 mi. SSW of Recife; sugar milling, coconut processing.

Río Frío (rē'ō frē'ō), village (1930 pop. 304), Llanquihue prov., S central Chile, on railroad and 27 mi. NNW of Puerto Montt, in agr. area (wheat, barley, potatoes, livestock); dairying, lumbering.

Ríofrio, town (pop. 689), Ávila prov., central Spain, 7 mi. SSW of Ávila, in fertile agr. region (cereals, forage, potatoes, beans, nuts, livestock); flour milling; stone quarrying.

Rio Frio, village (pop. c.100), Real co., SW Texas, 28 mi. N of Uvalde and on Frio R.; trade point in goat, sheep, cattle ranching area. Scenic Frio Canyon here is vacation area.

Ríofrío de Riaza (dhā ryä'thä), village (pop. 324), Segovia prov., central Spain, on W slopes of the Sierra de Ayllón, 40 mi. NE of Segovia. In midst of pine forest, with beautiful castle built 1751. Lumbering, wood turning, charcoal burning; livestock.

Río Gallegos (rē'ō gäyä'gōs) or **Gallegos,** town (1947 pop. 6,005), ⊙ Santa Cruz natl. territory and Güer Aike dept., S Argentina, port on Gallegos R. estuary (Puerto Gallegos) 10 mi. inland from the Atlantic, and 1,250 mi. SSW of Buenos Aires; 51°37'S 69°13'W. Sheep-raising center. Trading in wool and sheepskins. Processing of frozen meat, tallow. Has airport, administrative bldgs., seismographic station. Site was discovered 1520 by Basco Gallego, member of Magellan's expedition. Road to Punta Arenas, Chile; rail line to El Turbio coal mines.

Río Gato or **El Gato** (rē'ō, ěl, gä'tō), village (1930 pop. 222), Llanquihue prov., S central Chile, 13 mi. W of Puerto Montt; resort in agr. area (grain, flax, livestock); dairying, lumbering.

Ríogordo (rē'ōgôr"dhō), town (pop. 2,685), Málaga prov., S Spain, on the small Río de la Cueva, 15 mi. NNE of Málaga; olives, cereal, raisins; flour milling, olive-oil pressing.

Río Grande (rē'ō grän'dā), village (pop. estimate 1,000), ⊙ San Sebastián dept. (pop. estimate 2,000), E Tierra del Fuego natl. territory, Argentina, port at mouth of the Río Grande on the Atlantic; 53°47'S 67°41'W. Sheep raising, meat packing, wool trading. Airport, seismographic station, hydroelectric plant.

Río Grande, village, Potosí dept., SW Bolivia, in the Altiplano, 40 mi. SW of Uyuni, and on Antofagasta-Uyuni RR; alt. 12,034 ft.; alpaca.

Rio Grande (rē'ōō grän'dĭ), better known as **Rio Grande do Sul** (dōō sōōl'), city (1950 pop. 64,241), S Rio Grande do Sul, Brazil, seaport on the Rio Grande (outlet of Lagoa dos PATOS to Atlantic), on a sandy peninsula 8 mi. from the open sea and 150 mi. SSW of Pôrto Alegre, of which it is the outport; 32°3'S 52°6'W. Linked by rail with Pelotas, the interior, and Uruguay (via Jaguarão); airport. Important commercial and transshipment center serving rich agr. and stock-raising hinterland. Exports meat products (especially jerked beef), hides, lard, tallow, wool and woolens, rice, cereals, and fish. Heat meat-packing and -canning plants, fish and vegetable (chiefly peas, beans) canneries, petroleum refinery, textile mills, breweries; mfg. of cigarettes, footwear, animal by-products, pharmaceuticals. Navigation channel has been deepened and large ships dock alongside. A fine beach with casino is 12 mi. S (linked by rail). A fort was established near by in 1737; settlement moved to present site in 1745. Was ⊙ Rio Grande do Sul until 1763, when seat of govt. was transferred to Viamão, then to Pôrto Alegre. City presents modern appearance. Formerly called São Pedro do Rio Grande do Sul.

Río Grande (rē'ō grän'dā), village, Alajuela prov., W central Costa Rica, on railroad and 3 mi. SE of Atenas (linked by road); potatoes, coffee, beans.

Río Grande, town (pop. 5,111), Zacatecas, N central Mexico, on interior plateau, on railroad and 85 mi. NNW of Zacatecas; agr. center (cereals, sugar cane, tobacco, maguey, stock).

Río Grande or **Barra de Río Grande** (bä'rä dā), village, Zelaya dept., E Nicaragua, minor Caribbean port at mouth of Río Grande, 28 mi. S of Prinzapolka; bananas; lumbering. Police post.

Rio Grande (rē'ō grănd'), former small river in Panama Canal Zone that once drained into Pacific W of Panama City. Now forms part of S section of Panama Canal.

Río Grande (rē'ō grän'dā), town (pop. 2,623), NE Puerto Rico, near the coast, on railroad and 19 mi. ESE of San Juan; sugar and dairy center; mfg. of artificial flowers.

Rio Grande (rē"ō grănd', grăn'dē; rī"ō), county (□ 916; pop. 12,832), S Colo.; ⊙ Del Norte. Irrigated agr. and mining (gold, silver) region, drained by Rio Grande. Livestock, hay, potatoes. Includes part of Rio Grande and San Juan natl. forests and San Juan Mts. Formed 1874.

Rio Grande (rē"ō grănd'), village (pop. 388), Gallia co., S Ohio, 11 mi. WNW of Gallipolis. Seat of Rio Grande Col.

Rio Grande (rē"ō grănd', rē"ō grăn'dē, rī"ō), known in Mexico as **Río Bravo** or **Río Bravo del Norte** (rē'ō brä'vō děl nôr'tā), river c.1,800 mi. long, in SW U.S. and N Mexico. Rises on Continental Divide in San Juan Mts. of SW Colo., flows SE in Colo., then generally S through N.Mex., past Albuquerque, to meeting of N.Mex., Texas, and Mex. boundaries; flows thence generally SE bet. Texas and the Mexican states of Chihuahua, Coahuila, and Tamaulipas, bet. paired border cities of El Paso–Juárez, Laredo–Nuevo Laredo, and Brownsville-Matamoros, to Gulf of Mexico c.22 mi. E of Brownsville. Forms internatl. line for c.1,300 mi. Chief tributaries: Pecos R. in Texas, Conchos R. in Mexico. Drains □ 171,585. BIG BEND NATIONAL PARK includes wild scenic area within river's great bend from SE to NE, S of Alpine, Texas. Used for irrigation of its semi-arid valley since the time of the pueblos, which Coronado found thriving here in 1540. U.S. Bureau of Reclamation Rio Grande project (irrigation, power, flood control; chief units ELEPHANT BUTTE DAM, CABALLO DAM) extends for 200 mi. in S central N.Mex. and extreme W Texas. River also feeds canal networks in Winter Garden region (truck, cotton, citrus) lying E and SE of Eagle Pass, Texas, and in the rich lower valley (often called simply the Rio Grande Valley; known for citrus, truck) extending E from vicinity of Mission to the Gulf. Internatl. projects for irrigation and flood control were authorized by agreement (1945) bet. U.S. and Mexico. River's changes of course gave rise to internatl. controversy (arbitrated unsuccessfully, 1911), over acreage near El Paso. Its irregular flow frequently bares its bed for considerable distances. Although intermittently navigable in lower course, navigation is forbidden by internatl. agreement; port of Brownsville is terminus of a land-cut channel to Gulf of Mexico. River made internatl. boundary by treaty of Guadalupe Hidalgo (1848) at end of Mexican War.

Río Grande, Salina de (sälē'nä dā rē'ō grän'dā), salt desert (□ 85; alt. c.12,000 ft.) in the *puna* of W Salta prov., Argentina, extends c.13 mi. N–S (5 mi. wide) N of the Antofalla group of volcanoes.

Rio Grande City (rē"ō grănd" sĭ'tē), village (pop. 3,992), Starr co., extreme S Texas, c.90 mi. WNW of Brownsville and on the Rio Grande (bridged) opposite Camargo, Mexico. Port of entry and trade, shipping, distribution center for oil, cattle, and irrigated agr. region; cotton ginning, mfg. of clay products. Near by is Fort Ringgold, dating from 1848 and made inactive 1944. Area settled by Spanish, c.1753; town founded 1847 as Rancho Davis.

Rio Grande de Cagayan, Philippines: see CAGAYAN RIVER.

Rio Grande de la Pampanga, Philippines: see PAMPANGA RIVER.

Rio Grande de Mindanao, Philippines: see PULANGI RIVER.

Rio Grande do Norte (rē'ōō grän'dĭ dōō nôr'tĭ), state (□ 20,482; 1940 pop. 768,018; 1950 census 983,572), NE Brazil; ⊙ Natal. Situated on the Atlantic at tip of Brazilian bulge, it is bounded by Ceará (W) and Paraíba (S). Has sandy coastal plain rising in S to Borborema Plateau. Except for E coast, state has semiarid tropical climate, the interior forming part of NE Brazil's drought zone. Drained by intermittent-flowing Apodi, Piranhas, and Potengi rivers. Important mineral resources include country's leading saltworks (at Areia Branca, Mossoró, Macau), gypsum quarries, and large, only partially worked, rare mineral deposits (beryls, diatomite, columbite, tantalite) in Borborema Plateau. Chief agr. products are sugar (in Ceará Mirim valley), carnauba wax, cotton, and livestock (cattle, mules). Railroad tentacles penetrate inland from Natal and Areia Branca, and Natal is N terminus of coastal rail line to Recife. Strategic location near Africa has made Natal important transatlantic air communications center (especially since Second World War). Chief cities are Natal and Mossoró. First European settlement was fort near present site of Natal (founded 1599). Briefly occupied by Dutch in 17th cent. A dependency of Pernambuco in 18th cent., it became a prov. of the Brazilian Empire in 1824, and a state of the federal republic in 1889.

Rio Grande do Sul (sōōl'), southernmost state (□ 103,264; with interior waters □ 109,066; 1940 pop. 3,320,689; 1950 census 4,213,316) of Brazil; ⊙ Pôrto Alegre. Bounded by the Atlantic (E), Santa Catarina state (N), and Argentina (W) and Uruguay (S). The Uruguay R. (with its headstream, the Pelotas) forms most of N and W border. Near S end of the great escarpment (Serra do Mar) NE of Pôrto Alegre, the coastal plain widens and includes numerous lagoons, of which the 2 largest, Lagoa dos Patos and Mirim L., are interconnected through São Gonçalo Canal and communicate with the sea by a channel at Rio Grande. The S escarpment of S Brazil's great basalt tableland crosses N part of state E–W. Just S of it is the fertile Jacuí R. valley, center of intensive agr. Central and S Rio Grande do Sul, with its extensive pastures, merges with the low rolling plateau of Uruguay, and is traversed by several hill ranges near the border. Stock raising is chief source of state's agr. wealth. Rio Grande do Sul leads all others in the number of its sheep, cattle, horses, and hogs, and is therefore Brazil's leading meat-processing state. It is also the nation's breadbasket, and supplies most of Brazil's wine (grown on slopes of the Serra Geral by settlers of Italian descent). Other crops are rice (in Jacuí flood plain), tobacco (chiefly near Santa Cruz do Sul), flax, alfalfa, corn, potatoes, vegetables and table fruit (pears, peaches, grapes). Lumbering and maté gathering in Paraná pine forest (N) and semi-deciduous forests (N of the Jacuí). Climate is humid subtropical, with rainy (May–Sept.) and dry seasons, and cool winters. Principal mineral resource is bituminous coal, mined in São Jerônimo region and shipped down Jacuí R. to Pôrto Alegre and seaports on the Lagoa dos Patos. Beef jerking, meat packing and canning, mfg. of animal by-products, woolwashing and -milling, and agr. processing are state's principal industries, concentrated in Pôrto Alegre, its outports of Pelotas and Rio Grande, and in the cities of the interior—Bagé, Uruguaiana, Livramento. Santa Maria is state's chief rail center, linking Pôrto Alegre with the through-line S to Uruguay and N to São Paulo. Other railroad crossing points to Uruguay are at Jaguarão, Quaraí, and Barra do Quaraí (SW of Uruguaiana). State's prosperity is largely due to progressive agr. methods adopted by German and Italian immigrants (since 1824) and their descendants. Ger. influence remains dominant in Jacuí valley. State's inhabitants are popularly called *gauchos*, in recognition of their traditional ranching economy. First settled along Uruguay R. by Jesuit missionaries in 17th cent. First coastal settlement (near present city of Rio Grande) dates from 1737. A dependency of Rio de Janeiro until 1807, when it became an independent captain-generalcy, with capital (which, until 1763, had been at Rio Grande, later at Viamão) confirmed at Pôrto Alegre. Became prov. of Brazilian Empire in 1822. A separatist revolt lasting 10 years collapsed in 1845. Invaded by Paraguayans in 1865, who briefly occupied Uruguaiana. After establishment of republic, state led unsuccessful revolt (1892–94) against federal govt. Formerly called São Pedro do Rio Grande do Sul.

Rio Grande do Sul, city, Brazil: see RIO GRANDE.

Rio Grande Pyramid (rē″ō grănd′), peak (13,830 ft.) in San Juan Mts., SW Colo., 18 mi. SE of Silverton.

Ríohacha (rē′ō-ä′chä), town (pop. 5,651), Magdalena dept., N Colombia, port on Caribbean Sea, near mouth of Ranchería R., 90 mi. ENE of Santa Marta; 11°33′N 72°55′W. Trading, pearl-fishing, and agr. center (vegetables, livestock, hides, henequen fibers, tagua, divi-divi, rubber); saltworks. Airport, lighthouse, customhouse. Has ship connections with Santa Marta and Curaçao. One of the oldest Sp. towns in Colombia, it was founded 1545, sacked 1596 by Drake. Contains ruins of an old fort. Gold, iron, and coal deposits near by.

Río Hato (rē′ō ä′tō), village (pop. 1,671), Coclé prov., central Panama, in Pacific lowland, on Inter-American Highway, on small Hato R. and 6 mi. ESE of Antón; stock raising; corn, rice, beans. Air base.

Río Hondo or **Villa Río Hondo** (vē′yä rē′ō ōn′dō), town (pop. estimate 1,000), ⊙ Río Hondo dept. (□ 770; 1947 pop. 34,535), W Santiago del Estero prov., Argentina, on the Salí or Río Dulce, at mouth of the short Río Hondo, on Tucumán prov. border, and 45 mi. WNW of Santiago del Estero, in fruitgrowing zone. Warm springs near by.

Río Hondo, town (1950 pop. 814), Zacapa dept., E Guatemala, on Motagua R. and 6 mi. NNW of Zacapa; corn, beans, sugar cane; livestock.

Rio Hondo (rē″ō hŏn′dō), town (pop. 1,125), Cameron co., extreme S Texas, 24 mi. NW of Brownsville and on barge channel joining Gulf Intracoastal Waterway. Shipping point in rich irrigated agr. area of lower Rio Grande valley.

Rio Hondo, river, SE N.Mex., formed just E of Sacramento Mts. in Lincoln co. by confluence of 2 headstreams; flows c.90 mi. E, past Roswell, to Pecos R. 7 mi. E of Roswell.

Río Indio (rē′ō ēn′dyō), village (pop. 126), Colón prov., central Panama, near Caribbean Sea, on Indio R. (small coastal stream) and 8 mi. E of Donoso. Corn, rice, beans, coconuts, livestock.

Rioja (rēō′hä), city (pop. 3,930), ⊙ Rioja prov. (□ 408; enumerated pop. 5,043, plus estimated 2,000 Indians), San Martín dept., N central Peru, in E outliers of the Andes, 11 mi. WSW of Moyobamba, on road from Cajamarca. Straw-hat mfg.

Rioja, La, Argentina: see LA RIOJA.

Rioja, La (lä), region of N Spain, in Old Castile, along right bank of the upper Ebro, and comprising chiefly Logroño prov. and parts of Burgos, Soria, and Álava provs. Of great fertility, it is known for its fine wines. Main industries are wine making, and processing of pepper, tomatoes, fruit. La Rioja has interesting Roman remains. It is named for the small Río Oja, tributary of the Ebro system.

Rioja, Salina, Argentina: see ANTIGUA, SALINA.

Riola (ryō′lä), village (pop. 1,534), Valencia prov. E Spain, on the Júcar and 6 mi. NE of Alcira; rice fields and orange groves.

Río Lagartos (rē′ō lägär′tōs), town (pop. 596), Yucatan, SE Mexico, at entrance to channel leading to Lagartos Lagoon, 30 mi. N of Tizimín; in henequen- and chicle-growing area. Archaeological remains near by.

Rio Largo (rē′ōō lär′gōō), city (pop. 8,762), E Alagoas, NE Brazil, on railroad (junction for Palmeira dos Índios just N) and 13 mi. NW of Maceió, in sugar-cane dist.; sugar and cotton mills.

Riola Sardo (rēō′lä sär′dô), village (pop. 1,538), Cagliari prov., W Sardinia, 7 mi. NNW of Oristano.

Ríolobos (rē′ōlōvōs), village (pop. 1,501), Cáceres prov., W Spain, 14 mi. SW of Plasencia; olive-oil processing; cereals, wine.

Riolo dei Bagni (rēô′lô dā bä′nyē), village (pop. 1,410), Ravenna prov., Emilia-Romagna, N central Italy, on Senio R. and 6 mi. S of Imola; resort, with hot mineral baths; damaged in Second World War.

Riom (rēō′), town (pop. 10,420), Puy-de-Dôme dept., central France, in the Limagne at foot of range of volcanic peaks (Monts Dôme), 8 mi. N of Clermont-Ferrand; mfg. (electric cables, furniture, aluminum ware, ink), fruit preserving (prunes grown in Marsat valley), tanning, printing. Before French Revolution Riom was seat of intendants and chief courts of Auvergne; it has kept its somber 16th-cent. appearance with many houses built of dark lava rock. Scene of unsuccessful trial (Feb.–April, 1942) of French political leaders (including Léon Blum and Édouard Daladier) by Vichy govt. on charges of having plunged France unprepared into Second World War.

Rio Maior (rē′ōō mäyôr′), town (pop. 2,236), Santarém dist., central Portugal, 15 mi. NW of Santarém; coal mines.

Rio Marina (rē′ō märē′nä), town (pop. 2,815), port, on E coast of Elba isl., Livorno prov., Tuscany, central Italy, 5 mi. E of Portoferraio, in island's richest iron-mining region.

Río Martín (märtēn′), town (pop. 4,988), Yebala territory, NW Sp. Morocco, Tetuán's port on the Mediterranean, 6 mi. NE of Tetuán; fish and palm-fiber processing.

Riom-ès-Montagnes (rēō′mĕs-mōtä′nyů), town (pop. 2,015), Cantal dept., S central France, in Auvergne Mts., 16 mi. ENE of Mauriac; cheese-mfg. and shipping center; cattle market. Has 11th–14th-cent. Romanesque church.

Río Mulato (rē′ō mōōlä′tō) or **Río Mulatos** (–tōs), village (pop. c.2,100), Potosí dept., W Bolivia, in the Altiplano, on Mulato (or Murlatos) R. (branch of the Marquez) and 55 mi. N of Uyuni, on Oruro-Uyuni RR; alt. 12,625 ft. Junction point of railroads from Uyuni and Potosí; railroad shops.

Río Muni, W Africa: see SPANISH GUINEA.

Rion, river, Georgian SSR: see RION RIVER.

Rion (rī′ůn), village, Fairfield co., central S.C., 23 mi. NNW of Columbia; granite.

Río Negro (rē′ō nä′grō), national territory (□ 78,220; pop. 134,350), S central Argentina, in N Patagonia and extending from the Andes to the Atlantic; ⊙ Viedma. Bordered by Chubut natl. territory (S), the Río Colorado (N), and the Limay R. (W), it is drained by the Río NEGRO. In W is part of the resort area of L. Nahuel Huapí. Climate is dry and temperate in settled Río Negro valley (N), and more humid in SW lake dist., becoming more severe on arid plateaus (S) and in higher altitudes of the Andes. Predominately stock raising: mainly sheep, but also goats and cattle. Agr. (alfalfa, grain, fruit, wine, sugar beets, tomatoes) in fertile, irrigated valleys of the main rivers and the lake dist. Forests in W. Minerals include gypsum (Río Negro valley), lead (Valcheta, Maquinchao), lime (San Carlos de Bariloche), coal (El Bolsón, Ñorquincó dept., Nahuel Huapí natl. park). Rural industries: lumbering, mining, woolwashing, flour milling, dairying, fruit processing, wine making. Alcohol distilling, food canning, and wine making concentrated at Fuerte General Roca; plaster works at Alejandro Stefenelli. Río Negro natl. territory set up in 1884.

Río Negro, town, Pando dept., N Bolivia, on Abuná R. and c.18 mi. WSW of Manoa, on Brazil border; customs station; rubber.

Rio Negro (rē′ōō nä′grōō), city (pop. 5,326), SE Paraná, Brazil, on the Rio Negro (Santa Catarina border) opposite Mafra, on railroad, and 55 mi. SW of Curitiba; maté and lard processing, grain milling, woodworking, pottery mfg. Clay quarries near by.

Río Negro (rē′ō nä′grō), town (pop. 1,897), ⊙ Río Negro dept. (□ 779; pop. 27,723), Osorno prov., S central Chile, on railroad and 16 mi. S of Osorno; agr. center (grain, livestock); flour milling, dairying, lumbering.

Ríonegro (rē′ōnä′grō). **1** Town (pop. 3,678), Antioquia dept., NW central Colombia, in valley of Cordillera Central, 15 mi. SE of Medellín; alt. 6,955 ft. Trading and agr. center (potatoes, corn, fruit, stock); silver-fox and opossum farming; shoe mfg. Old colonial town. Burned 1819 by patriots. **2** Town (pop, 1,831), Santander dept., N central Colombia, on W slopes of Cordillera Oriental, 10 mi. N of Bucaramanga; coffee center; also rice, corn, sugar cane, tobacco, cacao, livestock; coffee and rice milling. Coal and lime deposits near by.

Río Negro (rē′ō nä′grō), department (□ 3,271; pop. 47,586), W Uruguay; ⊙ Fray Bentos. Bordered S by the Río Negro, W by the Uruguay. The Cuchilla de Haedo crosses dept. NE–SW. Drained by the Arroyo Don Esteban and Arroyo Grande. Produces wheat, corn, grain, cattle, sheep. Only industrial center is Fray Bentos, a port and meat-packing center. Other towns are Young, Nuevo Berlín, Algorta. Served by navigation on the Uruguay and the Río Negro. Dept. was formed 1881.

Río Negro, Cerro de (sĕ′rō dā rē′ō nä′grō), Andean peak (19,815 ft.), N Chile, E of the Salar de Atacama; 23°24′S.

Rionero in Vulture (rēōnā′rô ēn vōōltōō′rě), town (pop. 12,175), Potenza prov., Basilicata, S Italy, 5 mi. S of Melfi. Noted for wine, mineral waters.

Rioni (rēô′nyē), village (1939 pop. over 500), W Georgian SSR, on Rion R., on railroad and 4 mi. S of Kutaisi; rail junction (spur to Kutaisi and Tkibuli); site of Rion hydroelectric station (*Rionges*).

Rio Nido (rē′ō nē′dō), resort village (pop. c.300), Sonoma co., W Calif., on Russian R. and 16 mi. WNW of Santa Rosa.

Rio Novo (rē′ōō nô′vōō). **1** City, Bahia, Brazil: see IPIAÚ. **2** City, Espírito Santo, Brazil: see ITAPOAMA. **3** City (pop. 2,760), S Minas Gerais, Brazil, on railroad and 25 mi. NNE of Juiz de Fora; agr.

Rion River (rēōn′), Georgian *Rioni*, anc. *Phasis*, main stream of W Georgian SSR, rises in the Caucasus on S slope of the Adai-Khokh, near Mamison Pass; flows generally S and W past Oni, S past Kutaisi and Rioni (site of *Rionges* hydroelectric station), and W to Black Sea at Poti, forming swampy delta mouth; 180 mi. long. Lower course passes through COLCHIS lowland. Ossetian Military Road runs through upper valley. Floods suddenly after continuous rains; high water stage, April–July.

Rion Strait (rē′ôn) of Ionian Sea, Greece, joins gulfs of Patras (W) and Corinth (E) bet. capes Andirrion (central Greece, N) and Rion (Peloponnesus, S); 1 mi. wide. Sometimes spelled Rhion; formerly called Strait of Lepanto.

Rio Nunez (rē′ō nōō′nyěth, –nyěz), estuary on coast of Fr. Guinea, Fr. West Africa, 100 mi. NW of Conakry. Near its head is the landing of Victoria, reached by medium-sized vessels.

Rio Paranaíba (rē′ōō pŭrůnäē′bů), city (pop. 1,074), W Minas Gerais, Brazil, at source of Paranaíba R., 45 mi. SSE of Patos de Minas; coffee, cheese, cattle. Formerly spelled Rio Paranahyba.

Rio Pardo (rē′ōō pär′dōō). **1** City, Espírito Santo, Brazil: see IÚNA. **2** City, Mato Grosso, Brazil: see RIBAS DO RIO PARDO. **3** City (pop. 6,365), E central Rio Grande do Sul, Brazil, on navigable Jacuí R. and 70 mi. W of Pôrto Alegre; rail junction (spur to Santa Cruz do Sul); agr. trade center (cereals, rice, tobacco, cattle, hogs); meat processing. Founded as a fort c.1750. Has several 18th-cent. churches.

Rio Pardo de Minas (dĭ mē′nůs), city (pop. 1,206), N Minas Gerais, Brazil, on headstream of the Rio Pardo and 100 mi. NE of Montes Claros. Rose quartz found in area. Until 1944, called Rio Pardo.

Río Piedras (rē′ō pyā′dräs), city (1950 pop. 132,438; 1940 pop. 19,935), N Puerto Rico, on railroad and 6 mi. SE of San Juan; seat of most of Univ. of Puerto Rico (founded 1903), with a fine campus. With the inc. of surrounding areas since 1940, it has become 2d largest city of Puerto Rico. Also a processing and agr. center (sugar cane, tobacco, fruit, cattle); rum distilling, sugar milling, fruit and vegetable canning, dairying; mfg. of cigars, metal products, ceramics. It also has many other educational institutions, an experimental station, psychiatric and tuberculosis hospitals. A near-by reservoir supplies San Juan. Marble deposits in vicinity. Adjoining N is Hato Rey, an industrial and residential suburb.

Rio Piracicaba (rē′ōō pērůsēkä′bů), city (pop. 2,123), E central Minas Gerais, Brazil, on E slope of Serra do Espinhaço, near railroad, 55 mi. E of Belo Horizonte; coffee, beeswax, brandy; beryl deposits. MONLEVADE steel mill is 10 mi. NE.

Rio Pomba (rē′ōō pōm′bů), city (pop. 3,325), S Minas Gerais, Brazil, in the Serra da Mantiqueira, 35 mi. NNE of Juiz de Fora; rail-spur terminus; sugar cane, tobacco, cereals. Deposits of radioactive minerals. Until 1948, called Pomba.

Rio Pongo (rē′ō pông′gō), estuary on coast of Fr. Guinea, Fr. West Africa, 40 mi. NW of Conakry. At its head is the minor port of Boffa.

Rio Prêto (rē′ōō prā′tōō). **1** City, Bahia, Brazil: see IBIPETUBA. **2** City (pop. 1,527), southernmost Minas Gerais, Brazil, on Rio de Janeiro border, 26 mi. N of Barra do Piraí; dairying. **3** City, São Paulo, Brazil: see SÃO JOSÉ DO RIO PRÊTO.

Río Primero, department, Argentina: see SANTA ROSA, Córdoba prov.

Río Primero (rē′ō prēmā′rō), town (pop. estimate 1,500), N central Córdoba prov., Argentina, on the Río Primero and 35 mi. E of Córdoba; rail junction and agr. center (peanuts, wheat, flax, alfalfa, livestock).

Río Puelo Pass (rē'ō pwä'lō) (900 ft.), in the Andes, on Argentina-Chile border, at W shore of L. Puelo; 42°6'S 71°44'W.

Rio Puerco (rē'ō pōōär'kō). **1** River, NW N.Mex., rises near Cuba, flows c.170 mi. S, past Nacimiento Mts. (E) and Sierra Chivato (W), to Rio Grande 22 mi. N of Socorro; intermittent in upper course. San Jose R. is tributary. **2** River in N.Mex. and Ariz.: see PUERCO RIVER.

Rio Real (rē'ōō rïäl'), city (pop. 2,229), NE Bahia, Brazil, near Sergipe border, on railroad and 45 mi. N of Alagoinhas; manioc, corn, beans. Formerly Barração.

Riorges (rēôrzh'), town (pop. 5,267), Loire dept., SE central France, 2 mi. W of Roanne; hosiery-mfg. center; cotton goods, dyes, rayon, perfumes, abrasive paper, glass, pottery.

Ríos, Los, province, Ecuador: see LOS RÍOS.

Rio-Salado (rē'ō-sälä'dō), village (pop. 6,431), Oran dept., NW Algeria, on railroad and 7 mi. NNE of Aïn-Témouchent; winegrowing center; brick mfg., distilling, olive curing.

Rio Saliceto (rē'ō sälēchä'tō), village (pop. 972), Reggio nell'Emilia prov., Emilia-Romagna, N central Italy, 4 mi. WNW of Carpi; elevator mfg.

Río San Juan (rē'ō sän hwän'), village (1950 pop. 734), Samaná prov., N Dominican Republic, on the coast at mouth of small San Juan R., 40 mi. ESE of Puerto Plata; cacao, coffee, tropical fruit.

Río San Juan, department (1950 pop. 8,966), SE Nicaragua; ⊙ San Carlos. Bounded S by Costa Rica (along San Juan R.), E by Caribbean Sea, W by L. Nicaragua. Rice, corn, coconuts; livestock. Formed 1949 out of San Juan del Norte territory and S part of Chantales dept.

Río Seco, Argentina: see VILLA DE MARÍA.

Río Seco (rē'ō sä'kō), village (1930 pop. 421), Magallanes prov., S Chile, on Strait of Magellan, and 5 mi. NNE of Punta Arenas; sheep raising.

Río Seco, Sierra del, Bolivia-Argentina: see ALTO, SIERRA DEL.

Río Segundo, department, Argentina: see VILLA DEL ROSARIO.

Río Segundo (rē'ō sägōōn'dō), town (pop. 4,952), central Córdoba prov., Argentina, on the Río Segundo and 23 mi. SE of Córdoba; rail junction and processing center (vegetable-oil and alcohol distilleries, brewery); peanuts, wheat, corn, alfalfa, stock.

Ríosucio (rē'ōsōō'syō). **1** Town (pop. 5,801), Caldas dept., W central Colombia, on E slopes of Cordillera Occidental, on highway to Medellín, and 27 mi. NNW of Manizales; alt. 5,948 ft. Coffeegrowing center; coal mining. Salt deposits near by. **2** Village (pop. 648), Chocó dept., NW Colombia, river port on Atrato R., at mouth of the Río Sucio, and 125 mi. NNW of Quibdó; rice, bananas, forest products (rubber, lumber).

Río Tercero (rē'ō tĕrsä'rō), town (pop. 9,815), central Córdoba prov., Argentina, on the Río Tercero and 55 mi. S of Córdoba; rail junction and agr. center (cereals, flax, peanuts, sunflowers, livestock).

Río Teuco, Argentina: see EL PINTADO.

Rio Tinto (rē'ōō tēn'tōō), town (1950 pop. 20,352), Paraíba, NE Brazil, on navigable estuary of small Mamanguape R. and 24 mi. NNW of João Pessoa; cotton-milling center.

Rio Tinto, NE suburb of Oporto, Pôrto dist., N Portugal; textile and paper milling, precision metal-working (watchmaking, gold engraving). Here Galicians defeated Moors in 924.

Ríotinto or **Minas de Ríotinto** (mē'näs dhä rē'ōtēntō), town (pop. 2,727), Huelva prov., SW Spain, in Andalusia, in Sierra Morena, near source of the Río Tinto, on railroad and 39 mi. NW of Huelva. Noted for its copper-pyrite mines. The ore is also milled here. Iron and manganese are mined near by. The dist. has been known for its minerals since Phoenician and Roman times, and its copper deposits are considered among the world's largest. The old town of Ríotinto, now NERVA, is 3 mi. ESE. Sometimes spelled Río Tinto and Riotinto.

Rio Tinto, Nev.: see MOUNTAIN CITY.

Río Tocuyo (rē'ō tōkōō'yō), town (pop. 1,014), Lara state, NW Venezuela, on Tocuyo R., in Segovia Highlands, and 45 mi. WNW of Barquisimeto; sugar, corn, cotton, fruit, cattle.

Río Turbio, Argentina: see EL TURBIO.

Rioupéroux, France: see LIVET-ET-GAVET.

Riouw Archipelago or **Riau Archipelago** (both: rēou', rē'ou), island group (□ 2,279; pop. 77,149), Indonesia, off E Sumatra, in S.China Sea, at entrance to Strait of Malacca, and separated from Singapore by Singapore Strait; 0°55'N 104°5'E. Comprises numerous isls., largest being BINTAN. Among other isls. are BATAM, KARIMUN ISLANDS, REMPANG, SUGI, GALANG, CHOMBAL, BULAN. Larger isls. are mountainous; smaller isls. are low-lying and of coral formation. Tin and bauxite are mined chiefly on Bintan. Other products of the group: copra, gambier, pepper, timber, fish. Chief town of group is TANJUNGPINANG on Bintan isl. Group was last seat of Riouw-JOHORE kingdom prior to Du. conquest (late 18th cent.). Also spelled Rhio.

Rio Verde (rē'ōō vĕr'dĭ), city (pop. 4,776), SW Goiás, central Brazil, 125 mi. SW of Goiânia; trade center for livestock, rice, corn, castor beans, tobacco, and sugar. Agr. experiment station.

Río Verde (rē'ō vĕr'dā), city (pop. 8,503), San Luis Potosí, N central Mexico, on interior plateau, on Río Verde and 65 mi. ESE of San Luis Potosí; alt. 3,251 ft. Rail terminus; agr. center (grain, cotton, fruit, livestock).

Rio Vista. 1 (rē'ō vĭ'stů) Town (pop. 1,831), Solano co., central Calif., 30 mi. SSW of Sacramento and on Sacramento R. (bridged); center of reclamation development in low-lying agr. area of Sacramento delta; packs, cans, and ships asparagus and other produce; river port. Natural-gas field near by. Founded 1857, inc. 1894. **2** (rē"ō vĭ'stů) Village (pop. c.400), Johnson co., N central Texas, 8 mi. S of Cleburne, in cotton, truck, dairy area.

Rioz (rēō'), village (pop. 587), Haute-Saône dept., E France, 13 mi. N of Besançon; dairying.

Rip, Mount, Czechoslovakia: see ROUDNICE NAD LABEM.

Ripacandida (rēpäkän'dēdä), town (pop. 4,714), Potenza prov., Basilicata, S Italy, 7 mi. SSE of Melfi; wine, olive oil, cheese.

Ripanj, Ripan, or **Ripan'** (all: rē'pänyů), village (pop. 7,205), N central Serbia, Yugoslavia, 12 mi. SSE of Belgrade; cement mfg.

Riparius (rĭpâ'rēůs), resort village, Warren co., E N.Y., in the Adirondacks, on Hudson R. and 27 mi. NNW of Glens Falls.

Ripatransone (rēpätränsô'nĕ), town (pop. 2,085), Ascoli Piceno prov., The Marches, central Italy, 14 mi. NE of Ascoli Piceno; mfg. (shoes, hardware, soap). Bishopric. Has 14th-cent. palace.

Ripley, village (pop. 391), S Ont., 8 mi. SSE of Kincardine; dairying, mixed farming.

Ripley. 1 Urban district (1931 pop. 13,413; 1951 census 18,194), E Derby, England, 3 mi. S of Alfreton; coal mining, ironworking, hosiery knitting. In urban dist. is coal- and iron-mining town of Butterley and (since 1934) residential town of Heage. **2** Parish, Surrey, England: see SEND AND RIPLEY. **3** Agr. village and parish (pop. 221), West Riding, central Yorkshire, England, near Nidd R. 3 mi. N of Harrogate. Has castle (built 1555; hq. of Cromwell at time of battle of Marston Moor) and 13th–14th-cent. church.

Ripley. 1 County (□ 442; pop. 18,763), SE Ind.; ⊙ Versailles. Drained by small Laughery and Graham creeks. Farming (grain, corn, tobacco), stock raising, dairying. Limestone quarries; timber. Mfg., including farm-products processing, at Batesville and Osgood. Formed 1816. **2** County (□ 639; pop. 11,414), S Mo.; ⊙ Doniphan. In the Ozarks, drained by Current and Little Black rivers. Agr. (cotton, corn, oats), livestock; timber; rock quarries. Part of Clark Natl. Forest here. Formed 1833.

Ripley. 1 Village, Calif.: see PALO VERDE VALLEY. **2** Village (pop. 177), Brown co., W Ill., on La Moine R. (bridged here) and 28 mi. NW of Jacksonville, in agr. and bituminous-coal area. **3** Town (pop. 389), Somerset co., central Maine, 23 mi. NE of Skowhegan, in farming region. **4** Town (pop. 2,383), ⊙ Tippah co., N Miss., 65 mi. ESE of Memphis, Tenn.; shipping center for agr., dairying, and lumbering area; mfg. of insulation, shirts; lumber milling. Blue Mountain Col. is at Blue Mountain (SW). Platted 1835, inc. 1837. **5** Village (pop. 1,229), Chautauqua co., extreme W N.Y., on L. Erie, 24 mi. SW of Dunkirk; mfg. (wood products, corsets, soft drinks); agr. (tomatoes, alfalfa, fruit). Summer resort. **6** Village (pop. 1,792), Brown co., SW Ohio, on the Ohio and 45 mi. SE of Cincinnati: tobacco warehouses, shoe factory Laid out 1812. The Rankin home, once an Underground Railroad station, is a state memorial. **7** Town (pop. 292), Payne co., N central Okla., 12 mi. SE of Stillwater, and on Cimarron R.; grain, livestock, cotton; dairy products. **8** Town (pop. 3,318), ⊙ Lauderdale co., W Tenn., 22 mi. SSW of Dyersburg, in timber and farm area; cotton gins, grist and flour mills; makes baskets, boxes, barrel staves. Open L. (fishing) is near by. Inc. 1838; rechartered 1901. **9** Town (pop. 1,813), ⊙ Jackson co., W W.Va., 33 mi. SSW of Parkersburg, in agr. (livestock, dairy products, poultry, fruit, tobacco), gas-wells, and timber area; lumber milling; poultry hatchery.

Ripogenus Lake (rĭ"pŭjē'nůs), Piscataquis co., N central Maine, 26 mi. NW of Millinocket; 3 mi. long, ½ mi. wide; joined to S end of Chesuncook L. Ripogenus Dam, at SE end, releases waters into West Branch of Penobscot R.

Ripoll (rēpôl'), town (pop. 6,283), Gerona prov., NE Spain, on S slopes of the E Pyrenees, at junction of Fresser R. with Ter R., 15 mi. W of Olot; agr. trade center (livestock, cereals, vegetables, fruit); cotton and woolen milling, machinery and cement mfg., meat processing. Hydroelectric plant on Ter R. Near by is former Benedictine monastery, founded in 9th cent.; its church (9th–16th cent.) was restored and reconsecrated in 19th cent.

Ripollet (rēpôlyĕt'), town (pop. 2,945), Barcelona prov., NE Spain, 8 mi. N of Barcelona, in hemp-growing dist.; brandy mfg., flour milling; wine.

Ripon (rĭ'půn), village (pop. 447), SW Que., 40 mi. NNE of Ottawa; lumbering, dairying, stock raising.

Ripon, municipal borough (1931 pop. 8,591; 1951 census 9,464), West Riding, N central Yorkshire, England, on Ure R. and 22 mi. NW of York; foundries, paint works, tanneries, breweries. Has cathedral, begun in 12th cent., on site of church of a monastery founded c.660 by St. Cuthbert; it was restored by Sir Gilbert Scott in 1872. Also has hosp. built in 12th cent. as home for lepers, and 13th-cent. mayoral residence. In Middle Ages town was famous for its cloth and spur industries.

Ripon. 1 City (pop. 1,550), San Joaquin co., central Calif., near Stanislaus R., 17 mi. SE of Stockton; evaporated milk, wine. Inc. 1945. **2** City (pop. 5,619), Fond du Lac co., E central Wis., on small Silver Creek and 20 mi. WNW of Fond du Lac, in agr. area; mfg. (washing machines, hosiery, gloves, microscope slides, flour, canned foods). Seat of Ripon Col. Settled 1844 as Ceresco by Fourierists; inc. as Ripon in 1858. One of the meetings leading to formation of Republican party was held here in 1854. Carrie Chapman Catt was b. here.

Ripon Falls (rĭ'půn), SE Uganda, on the Victoria Nile at Jinja, just below its outlet from L. Victoria; c.16 ft. high, 900 ft. wide. Discovered 1862 by John Speke, who named them for the then viceroy of India. OWEN FALLS 1.5 mi. downstream.

Riposto (rēpô'stō), town (pop. 8,584), Catania prov., E Sicily, port on Ionian Sea and 17 mi. NNE of Catania, in grape and citrus-fruit region; wine.

Rippey, town (pop. 354), Greene co., central Iowa, 18 mi. WSW of Boone; concrete blocks. Sand and gravel pits near by.

Rippin, Poland: see RYPIN.

Rippoldsau, Bad, Germany: see BAD RIPPOLDSAU.

Ripponden, urban district (1931 pop. 3,059; 1951 census 5,213), West Riding, SW Yorkshire, England, 5 mi. SW of Halifax; cotton and paper milling. Includes cotton-milling village of Soyland.

Rippowam River (rĭ'půwŏm), in N.Y. and SW Conn., rises in N.Y. N of Stamford, Conn.; flows c.20 mi. S, through Conn., to Long Isl. Sound at Stamford; dams form 2 reservoirs.

Ripton, town (pop. 207), Addison co., W central Vt., in Green Mts. just E of Middlebury. Includes Bread Loaf Mtn. (3,823 ft.) and Bread Loaf village, site of Middlebury Col. summer session.

Riquewihr (rēkvēr'), Ger. *Reichenweier* (rīkh'ůnvīůr), village (pop. 1,355), Haut-Rhin dept., E France, at E foot of the Vosges, 2 mi. S of Ribeauvillé; famous Riesling wine grown in area. Numerous old houses and medieval walls attract tourists.

Rir, Oued, Algeria: see RHIR, OUED.

Riri, Korea: see IRI.

Riri Bazar (rĭr'ē bäzär'), town, S Nepal, on the Kali Gandaki and 17 mi. N of Butwal; rice, wheat, vegetables. Considered by Nepalese nearly as sacred as Benares; has noted Vishnuite temple, bathing ghats. Sometimes called Ridi.

Ririe (rĭ'rē), village (pop. 527), Bonneville and Jefferson cos., SE Idaho, 8 mi. ESE of Rigby; alt. 4,965 ft.; grain, dairy.

Risafe or **Rasafah** (both: rĭsä'fů), Fr. *Résafé*, village, Euphrates prov., central Syria, 80 mi. WNW of Deir ez Zor, S of the Euphrates.

Risalpur (rĭsäl'pōōr), town (pop. 9,007), Peshawar dist., central North-West Frontier Prov., W Pakistan, 24 mi. ENE of Peshawar; military station; wheat, corn; poultry farming, handicraft cloth weaving; leather goods. Site of Pakistan Air Force training school (established 1947).

Risan (rē'sän), Ital. *Risano* (rēzä'nô), anc. *Risinum*, village, SW Montenegro, Yugoslavia, on N shore of Bay of Risan (inlet of Gulf of Kotor), 7 mi. NNW of Kotor; seaside resort; woodworking. Allegedly seat of Illyrian Queen Tenta (3d cent. B.C.) and one of oldest Roman settlements on Yugoslav coast. Until 1921, in Dalmatia.

Risan, Bay of, Yugoslavia: see KOTOR, GULF OF.

Risaralda (rēsäräl'dä), town (pop. 2,324), Caldas dept., W central Colombia, in Cauca valley, 18 mi. WNW of Manizales; rice, cacao, bananas, stock. Formerly San Joaquín.

Risby, England: see ROXBY CUM RISBY.

Risca (rĭ'sků), urban district (1931 pop. 16,605; 1951 census 15,131), S Monmouth, England, on Ebbw R. and 5 mi. WNW of Newport; coal mines; iron foundries.

Riscle (rēs'klů), village (pop. 1,645), Gers dept., SW France, on the Adour and 26 mi. WNW of Mirande; has large brick works; canning (*pâté de foie gras*), flour milling.

Risco (rĭ'skō"), town (pop. 495), New Madrid co., extreme SE Mo., near the Mississippi, 8 mi. E of Malden; cotton gin.

Risco, El (ĕl rē'skō), town (pop. 468), Badajoz prov., W Spain, 36 mi. E of Villanueva de la Serena.

Risdon (rĭz'důn), village (pop. 172), SE Tasmania, 2 mi. NE of Hobart across Derwent R. estuary; zinc refinery, superphosphate works. Oldest settlement (1803) of Tasmania; founded as penal colony.

Risen, Korea: see ICHON.

Rishahr, Reishahr, or **Reyshahr** (rā"shä'hůr), town, Seventh Prov., in Fars, S Iran, Persian Gulf port on Bushire peninsula, 5 mi. S of Bushire; serves as deepwater outport of Bushire. A flourishing trade center and Portuguese fort in 16th cent., it was supplanted (18th cent.) by Bushire, which flourished through 19th cent. Shallow harbor conditions in early-20th cent. caused the transfer of most of Bushire's trade to newly developed harbor of Rishahr. Formerly spelled Rishire or Reshire; sometimes called Shahr Rey.

Rishikesh, India: see RIKHIKESH.
Rishire, Iran: see RISHAHR.
Rishiri-shima (rēshērē'shĭmä) or **Rishiri-jima** (-jĭ-mä), island (□ 71; pop. 18,589), Japan, in Sea of Japan, near NW tip of Hokkaido, in Hokkaido administrative unit; roughly circular, 9 mi. in diameter; mountainous, rising to 5,636 ft. in center. Agr., fishing. Sometimes spelled Risiri-sima.
Rishon le Zion or **Rishon le Tsiyon** (both: rēshōn' lĕ tsēyōn'), settlement (1950 pop. estimate 15,000), W Israel, in Judaean Plain, 7 mi. SSW of Tel Aviv; viticulture center; textile milling, brewing, woodworking; mfg. of bricks, irrigation pipes, glass, food products (cheese, olive oil, condiments), razor blades; arts and crafts. Citriculture, tobacco growing. One of earliest modern Jewish settlements in Palestine, founded 1882. Also Rishon-le-Zion.
Rishpon (rēshpōn'), settlement (pop. 275), W Israel, in Plain of Sharon, near Mediterranean, 2 mi. NW of Herzliya; mixed farming. Founded 1936. Near by, on Mediterranean, is site of anc. city of *Arsuf*.
Rishra (rĭsh'rŭ), town (pop., including KONNAGAR, 37,432), Hooghly dist., S central West Bengal, India, on Hooghly R. and 10½ mi. N of Calcutta city center; cotton, jute, and rice milling, chemical mfg. First Indian jute mill established here, 1855. Sometimes called Rishra-Konnagar
Rishtan, Uzbek SSR: see KUIBYSHEVO, Fergana oblast.
Rishton, urban district (1931 pop. 6,633; 1951 census 5,794), central Lancashire, England, 3 mi. ENE of Blackburn; cotton milling.
Rishworth, former urban district (1931 pop. 838), West Riding, SW Yorkshire, England, 5 mi. SW of Halifax; cotton milling. Inc. 1937 in Ripponden.
Risib (rĭsĭb'), village, Quaiti state, Eastern Aden Protectorate, 60 mi. NW of Shihr and on highway to the Wadi Hadhramaut; airfield.
Rising City, village (pop. 374), Butler co., E Nebr., 40 mi. NW of Lincoln and on branch of Big Blue R.
Rising Star, town (pop. 1,289), Eastland co., N central Texas, 25 mi. N of Brownwood; trade, shipping center in oil, fruit, truck area; makes concrete blocks. Settled 1880, inc. 1905.
Rising Sun. 1 Town (pop. 1,930), ⊙ Ohio co., SE Ind., on Ohio R. and 22 mi. SW of Cincinnati, Ohio; shipping point in agr. area (livestock, truck, tobacco); flour, dairy products, furniture. Settled 1812, inc. 1849. **2** Town (pop. 668), Cecil co., NE Md., near Pa. line, 28 mi. W of Wilmington, Del.; trade center for agr. area; canned vegetables, work clothes.
Risingsun, village (pop. 744), Wood co., NW Ohio, 14 mi. ESE of Bowling Green, in agr. area.
Risiri-sima, Japan: see RISHIRI-SHIMA.
Risle River (rēl), Eure dept., NW France, rises N of Courtomer (Orne dept.), flows 75 mi. N, past Laigle, Beaumont-le-Roger, Brionne, and Pont-Audemer (head of navigation) to estuary of Seine R. 7 mi. E of Honfleur. Also spelled Rille.
Risnes, Norway: see TRENGEREID.
Rison (rī'zŭn), town (pop. 953), ⊙ Cleveland co., S central Ark., 21 mi. SSW of Pine Bluff; cotton, corn, hay; cotton ginning, sawmilling
Risor (rē'sûr), Nor. *Risør*, city (pop. 2,729), Aust-Agder co., S Norway, port on the Skagerrak, on a peninsula bet. 2 small fjords, 25 mi. NE of Arendal; shipbuilding; exports timber, wood pulp, lobster, salmon, feldspar, quartz. Formerly Østerrisor.
Ris-Orangis (rēzôrã-zhē'), town (pop. 3,854), Seine-et-Oise dept., N central France, on left bank of the Seine and 4 mi. NNW of Corbeil; mfg. (malt, buttons, hats).
Risosund, Norway: see RISOYSUND.
Risoy, Norway: see HAUGESUND.
Risoyhamn, Norway: see BJORNSKINN.
Risoysund (rēs'ûüsōōn"), Nor. *Risøysund*, strait of the North Sea, N Norway, extends 15 mi. SW–NE bet. Andoy and Hinnoy of the Vesteralen group; 1–3 mi. wide. Has dredged navigation channel. Sometimes spelled Risosund, Nor. *Risøsund*.
Rissa (rĭs'sä), village and canton (pop. 3,182), Sor-Trondelag co., central Norway, 17 mi. NW of Trondheim; agr., lumbering, fishing. Formerly called Rissen. Ruins of Rein monastery (Nor. *Reinskloster*, formerly *Rejnskloster*), a Cistercian nunnery, 4 mi. SE.
Rissen, Norway: see RISSA.
Ristiina (rĭs'tēnä), Swedish *Kristina* (krĭstē'nä), village (commune pop. 6,399), Mikkeli co., SE Finland, on W shore of L. Saimaa, 13 mi. S of Mikkeli; graphite mines. Has remains of 17th-cent. Brahe Castle.
Ristijärvi (rĭs'tĭyăr"vē), village (commune pop. 3,684), Oulu co., E central Finland, on 12-mi.-long L. Ii (ē), Finnish *Iijärvi*, 20 mi. NE of Kajaani; lumbering. Iron deposits in region.
Ristisaari (rĭs'tĭsä"rē), village in Kontiolahti commune (pop. 10,119), Kuopio co., SE Finland, near lake of the Saimaa system, 7 mi. N of Joensuu; lumber-sorting center.
Rita Blanca Creek (rē'tů blăng'ků) or **Mustang Creek,** in NE N.Mex. and extreme N Texas, rises as intermittent stream in N.Mex., flows c.100 mi. generally SE into Texas to Canadian R. 12 mi. SW of Channing. Rita Blanca L. (c.2.5 mi. long; capacity c.12,000 acre-ft.), is formed S of Dalhart by Rita Blanca Dam; irrigation.
Ritchey, town (pop. 137), Newton co., SW Mo., in the Ozarks, 11 mi. ENE of Neosho.
Ritchie, county (□ 452; pop. 12,535), NW W.Va.; ⊙ Harrisville. Drained by North and South forks of Hughes R. Agr. (livestock, dairy products, grain, fruit, tobacco); oil and natural-gas wells. Some industry at Pennsboro. Formed 1843.
Ritchie, Camp, Md.: see SABILLASVILLE.
Ritchie's Archipelago (rĭ'chēz), group of small islands in Andaman Sea, separated from main Andaman Isls. (W) by Diligent Strait. Sometimes called Andaman Archipelago.
Ritenbenk (rē'tůnbĕnk"), Eskimo *Agpat*, settlement (pop. 88), ⊙ Ritenbenk dist. (pop. 1,406), W Greenland, on W shore of Arve Prinsen Isl., on Disko Bay, 65 mi. ENE of Godhavn, in fishing, fowling, hunting region; 69°46'N 51°19'W. Radio station. Founded 1755. Dist. has Kutdligssat lignite mines.
Ritlyab (rētlyäp'), village (1939 pop. over 500), NW Dagestan Autonomous SSR, Russian SFSR, on Aksai R. and 22 mi. SW of Khasavyurt; grain, livestock; lumbering. Until 1944 (in Chechen-Ingush Autonomous SSR), called Sayasan.
Rito Alto Peak (rē"tō ăl'tō) (13,573 ft.), S central Colo., in Sangre de Cristo Mts., bet. Custer and Saguache counties.
Ritom, Lago (lä'gô rētôm'), small dammed lake (alt. 5,990 ft.), Ticino canton, S Switzerland, E of Airolo; supplies Ritom hydroelectric plant (S).
Ritsa-Avadkhara (rētsä'-ŭvůtkhŭrä'), village, NW Abkhaz Autonomous SSR, Georgian SSR, on L. Ritsa (on right affluent of Bzyb R.), 18 mi. NE of Gagry; health resort (mineral springs).
Ritschan, Czechoslovakia: see RICANY.
Ritteburg (rĭ'tůbŏork), village (pop. 408), in former Prussian Saxony prov., central Germany, after 1945 in Saxony-Anhalt, on the Unstrut and 2 mi. SE of Artern. Formerly also called Rietheburg. Near by is reputed site of anc. locality of Riade, where Henry I decisively defeated (933) the Hungarians.
Ritter, Mount (13,156 ft.), Madera co., E Calif., in the Sierra Nevada, 19 mi. SSW of Mono L.
Ritterhude (rĭ"tůrhōō'dů), village (pop. 5,540), in former Prussian prov. of Hanover, NW Germany, after 1945 in Lower Saxony, on the Hamme and 7 mi. N of Bremen; metalworking, sawmilling.
Rittman, village (pop. 3,810), Wayne co., N central Ohio, 14 mi. NE of Wooster, in agr. area (fruit, livestock; dairying); saltmaking, mfg of paper products.
Ritzebüttel, Germany: see CUXHAVEN.
Ritzlihorn (rĭts'lēhôrn"), peak (10,782 ft.) in Bernese Alps, S central Switzerland, 7 mi. SSE of Meiringen.
Ritzville, city (pop. 2,145), ⊙ Adams co., SE Wash., 60 mi. SW of Spokane, in Columbia basin agr. region; wheat, lumber shipping and processing. Settled c.1878, inc. 1906.
Riudoms, Riudôms, or **Ríudôms** (all: rē"ōō-dhōms'), town (pop. 3,638), Tarragona prov., NE Spain, 3 mi. WSW of Reus; soap and wax mfg., olive-oil and honey processing; trades in livestock (sheep, hogs), wine, cereals, fruit.
Riukiu Islands: see RYUKYU ISLANDS.
Riuvenfjell, Norway: see RUVEN MOUNTAINS.
Riva, Dominican Republic: see VILLA RIVAS.
Riva (rē'vä), town (pop. 4,989), Trento prov., Trentino–Alto Adige, N Italy, port at NW extremity of Lago di Garda, 18 mi. SW of Trent; major hydroelectric plant. Has olive-oil refinery, alcohol distillery, paper mill, dyeworks, razor factory. Summer resort. Has castle (12th–15th cent.), Palazzo Pretorio (1370), municipal palace (late 15th cent.) built by Venetians, and churches dating from 1603 and 1720. Belonged to Austria until 1919.
Riva-Bella, France: see OUISTREHAM.
Rivadavia. 1 District, Buenos Aires prov., Argentina: see AMÉRICA. **2** Department, La Rioja prov., Argentina: see MALANZÁN. **3** Department, San Juan prov., Argentina: see MARQUESADO. **4** Department, Santiago del Estero prov., Argentina: see SELVA.
Rivadavia (rēvädä'vyä). **1** Town (pop. estimate 2,000), ⊙ Rivadavia dept. (□ 780; 1947 pop. 28,945), N Mendoza prov., Argentina, on Tunuyán R. (irrigation area), on railroad, and 30 mi. SE of Mendoza; lumbering, agr., mfg. center. Produces wine, alcohol, vegetable oil, flour; sawmills. Agr. products: grapes, fruit, alfalfa, corn, wheat, potatoes. **2** Village (pop. estimate 200), ⊙ Rivadavia dept. (□ 11,115; 1947 pop. 8,637), E Salta prov., Argentina, 120 mi. SE of Orán, in stock-raising area. **3** Town (pop. 4,136), S San Juan prov., Argentina, W of San Juan.
Rivadavia, village (1930 pop. 385), Coquimbo prov., N central Chile, in Andean foothills, on Elqui R. 40 mi. E of La Serena; rail terminus; fruitgrowing.
Rivanna River (rīvă'nů), central Va., formed in Albemarle co. by junction of short Mechum and Moormans rivers (both rising in the Blue Ridge); flows c.50 mi. SE, past Charlottesville, to the James at Columbia. Receives Lynch R. in upper course.
Riva Palacio (rē'vä pälä'syō), town (pop. 708), Chihuahua, N Mexico, in Sierra Madre Occidental, on railroad and 26 mi. WSW of Chihuahua; alt. 6,000 ft.; corn, beans, cattle. Formerly San Andrés.
Rivarolo Canavese (rēvärô'lô känävā'zē), town (pop. 3,836), Torino prov., Piedmont, NW Italy, near Orco R., 18 mi. N of Turin; rail junction; cotton mills, tanneries, vegetable cannery; textile machinery. Has 2 old castles.
Rivarolo Ligure (lē'gōōrē), town (pop. 33,345), Genova prov., Liguria, N Italy, 3 mi. NNW of Genoa, within Greater Genoa; industrial center; soap, refined sugar, olive oil, cotton and woolen textiles, leather goods, railroad car parts, steel, agr. and industrial machinery.
Rivarolo Mantovano (mäntôvä'nô), village (pop. 2,628), Mantova prov., Lombardy, N Italy, 19 mi. WSW of Mantua.
Rivas (rē'väs), department (□ 850; 1950 pop. 45,724), SW Nicaragua; ⊙ Rivas. On isthmus bet. L. Nicaragua and Pacific Ocean; bounded S by Costa Rica; includes Ometepe Isl. Important livestock region; agr. (coffee, cacao, tobacco, sugar cane, sesame, cotton, fruit); dairy products. Industries based on agr.; tanning, sugar milling, coffee and cacao processing, mfg. of rubber goods. Lumbering. Served by Inter-American Highway and by railroad connecting ports of San Jorge (on L. Nicaragua) and San Juan del Sur (on Pacific).
Rivas, city (1950 pop. 4,796), ⊙ Rivas dept., SW Nicaragua, near W shore of L. Nicaragua, on Inter-American Highway, on railroad connecting L. Nicaragua and the Pacific, and 60 mi. SW of Managua. Agr.-processing center in cacao and coffee area; tanning, dairying, mfg. of rubber goods. Founded 1736; originally called Nicaragua. Known for battle (1856) in William Walker war.
Riva Trigoso (rē'vä trēgô'zô), town (pop. 4,171), Genova prov., Liguria, N Italy, 1.5 mi. E of Sestri Levante. Comprises Riva (pop. 3,497), fishing port on Gulf of Genoa, and adjacent Trigoso (pop. 674), industrial center with shipyards, warehouses, chemical plants.
Rive d'Arcano (rē'vĕ därkä'nô), village (pop. 611), Udine prov., Friuli–Venezia Giulia, NE Italy, 11 mi. NW of Udine; agr. tools.
Rive-de-Gier (rēv-dů-zhēā'), town (pop. 13,786), Loire dept., E central France, in the Jarez, on Gier R. and 13 mi. NE of Saint-Étienne; metallurgical center (sheet-metal works, forges, alloy-smelting plants); glassworks; mfg. of refractories, toys; coal mining. A canal (disused) connects the town with the Rhone at Givors.
Rivello (rēvĕl'lô), village (pop. 2,217), Potenza prov., Basilicata, S Italy, 3 mi. S of Lagonegro.
Rivenhall, agr. parish (pop. 2,353), central Essex, England, just N of Witham. Remains of Roman villa found here.
Rivera (rēvā'rä), town (pop. 2,232), W Buenos Aires prov., Argentina, near La Pampa line, 27 mi. W of Carhué; flour mill; wheat, alfalfa, livestock. Jewish colonization center
Rivera (rēvā'rä), department (□ 3,795; pop. 75,464), NE Uruguay; ⊙ Rivera. Bordered by Brazil (NE and NW) and the Río Negro (SE). Drained by Tacuarembó, Cuñapirú, and Yaguarí rivers. Produces grain, vegetables, fruit, tobacco; viticulture; cattle and sheep raising. Gold is found at Cuñapirú and Corrales. Main centers: Rivera, Tranqueras. Dept. was created 1884.
Rivera, city (pop. 30,000), ⊙ Rivera dept., NE Uruguay, in hill range at Brazil border, contiguous with Livramento (Brazil), on railroad and 260 mi. N of Montevideo, 60 mi. NNE of Tacuarembó; 30°54'S 55°32'W. Mfg. of textiles, cigars and cigarettes, mosaics, brooms; trade center for grain, vegetables, fruit, cattle. Viticulture in surrounding region. Customhouse. An adjoining suburb is called Rivera Chica (chē'kä) or Vecinal Rivera (väsēnäl').
Riverbank, city (pop. 2,662), Stanislaus co., central Calif., in San Joaquin Valley, 25 mi. SE of Stockton, and on Stanislaus R., in irrigated farming and fruitgrowing region. Inc. 1922.
River Beaudette, Que : see RIVIÈRE BEAUDETTE.
Riverbend, town (pop. 275), S central Que., on Île d'Alma, on Saguenay R., opposite St. Joseph d'Alma, of which it is suburb.
River Cess, town, Grand Bassa co., S Liberia, port on Atlantic Ocean, at mouth of Cess R., 45 mi. SE of Buchanan; cacao, copra, cassava, rice.
River Clyde, trading post, E Baffin Isl., SE Franklin Dist., Northwest Territories, on River Clyde, inlet (70 mi. long, 7 mi. wide at mouth) of Davis Strait; 70°28'N 68°34'W; radio station. Fur-trading post was established 1923. Sometimes called Clyde. At Cape Christian, 9 mi. NE, is govt. radio and meteorological station.
Riverdale, town (pop. 1,720), St. Catherine parish, central Jamaica, on railroad to Port Antonio and 18 mi. NW of Kingston, in agr. region (citrus fruit, coffee, stock).
Riverdale. 1 Village (pop. c.400), Fresno co., central Calif., in San Joaquin Valley, near Kings R., 13 mi. NW of Hanford; ships fruit, vegetables. **2** Town (pop. 263), Clayton co., N central Ga., 14 mi. S of Atlanta. **3** Residential village (pop. 5,840), Cook co., NE Ill., S suburb of Chicago, on Little Calumet R.; rail center, with a steel plant, truck farms. Settled c.1836, inc. 1892. **4** Town (pop. 5,530), Prince Georges co., central Md., suburb NE of Washington; makes machine tools, aircraft

propellers. Inc. 1920. **5** Village, Mass.: see GLOUCESTER. **6** Village (pop. 134), Buffalo co., S central Nebr., 6 mi. NW of Kearney and on Wood R. **7** Borough (pop. 1,352), Morris co., N N.J., on Pequannock R. and 10 mi. NW of Paterson; sand, gravel. Inc. 1923. **8** A NW residential section of the Bronx borough of New York city, SE N.Y., bet. the Hudson (W) and Van Cortlandt Park (E). Site of Manhattan Col., Col. of Mount St. Vincent, Fieldston School of the Ethical Culture Society. Henry Hudson Memorial here has a statue designed by Karl Bitter. **9** Town (pop. 871), Weber co., N Utah, just S of Ogden.

Riverdale Heights, village (1940 pop. 637), Prince Georges co., central Md., suburb NE of Washington.

River Dragon, Mauritius: see RIVIÈRE DRAGON.

River Edge, borough (pop. 9,204), Bergen co., NE N.J., on Hackensack R. and 6 mi. E of Paterson; makes fireworks. The Zabriskie or Von Steuben house here is pre-Revolutionary; has co. historical society. Inc. 1894.

Rivèrenert (rēvĕrŭnâr'), village (pop. 68), Ariège dept., S France, 5 mi. SE of Saint-Girons; iron mining.

River Falls. 1 Town (pop. 376), Covington co., S Ala., on Conecuh R. (dammed near by) and 5 mi. NW of Andalusia. **2** Hamlet, Greenville co., NW S.C., in the Blue Ridge, 20 mi. N of Greenville, in summer-resort region. **3** City (pop. 3,877), on Pierce-St. Croix co. line, W Wis., on small Kinnikinnic R. (tributary of St. Croix R.) and 24 mi. ESE of St. Paul (Minn.), in dairying and stock-raising area; mfg. (clothing, wood and paper products). Grain elevator, poultry hatcheries. A state teachers col. is here. Settled c.1850, inc. 1875.

River Forest, residential village (pop. 10,823), Cook co., NE Ill., W suburb of Chicago, on Des Plaines R.; some mfg. (metal caps, soap, bakery products); truck, dairy farms. Seat of Concordia Teachers Col. and Rosary Col.; has a mus. of natural history. Settled 1836; named Thatcher in 1862, renamed River Forest in 1872; inc. 1880.

Rivergaro (rēvĕrgä'rō), village (pop. 944), Piacenza prov., Emilia-Romagna, N central Italy, on Trebbia R. and 11 mi. SSW of Piacenza; food cannery.

River Grove, village (pop. 4,839), Cook co., NE Ill., NW suburb of Chicago, on Des Plaines R. Inc. 1888.

Riverhead, village (pop. 4,892), ⊙ Suffolk co., SE N.Y., on Peconic R. near its mouth on Great Peconic Bay of E Long Isl., 21 mi. ENE of Patchogue, in resort and farm area (potatoes, cauliflower); mfg. (fertilizer, bedding, insecticides, food products, concrete blocks and vaults). Fishing, duck hunting. Mus. of Suffolk County Historical Society is here. A large radio receiving station is near by.

River Hebert (hē'bûrt) or **River Hébert** (ābâr'), town (pop. estimate 1,100), N N.S., on Hebert R. (30 mi. long), near its mouth on the Cumberland Basin of Chignecto Bay, 10 mi. SW of Amherst; coal mining.

River Heights, town (pop. 468), Cache co., N Utah, E suburb of Logan.

River Hills, village (pop. 567), Milwaukee co., SE Wis., near Milwaukee R., 9 mi. N of Milwaukee.

Riverhurst, village (pop. 235), S Sask., near South Saskatchewan R., 60 mi. NE of Swift Current; grain elevators.

Riverina (rĭ"vurĭ'nŭ), rural administrative district (□ 26,560; pop. 83,000), S central New South Wales, Australia, bet. Lachlan and Murray rivers. Grassy plains; wool, wheat. Irrigated by Murrumbidgee R.

River John, village (pop. estimate 750), E N.S., near Northumberland Strait, 18 mi. W of Pictou; dairying, mixed farming.

River Jordan, village, SW B.C., on S Vancouver Isl., on Juan de Fuca Strait, near mouth of small Jordan R., 30 mi. W of Victoria; hydroelectric-power plant, supplying Victoria; powder mfg. Sometimes called Jordan River.

River Junction, Fla.: see CHATTAHOOCHEE.

Riverlea, village (pop. 324), Franklin co., central Ohio, just N of Columbus and on Olentangy R. Post office is Worthington.

Rivermines, town (pop. 485), St. Francois co., E Mo., in the St. Francois Mts. near Big R., just S of Flat River; lead mining.

Rivermoor, Mass.: see SCITUATE.

River Oaks, city (pop. 7,097), Tarrant co., N Texas, NW suburb of Fort Worth. Formerly Castleberry. Inc. after 1940.

Rivero Island, Chile: see CHONOS ARCHIPELAGO.

River Plate, Argentina and Uruguay: see PLATA, RÍO DE LA.

River Plaza, village (pop. 1,717, with near-by Fairview), Monmouth co., E N.J., just across Navesink R. from Red Bank.

River Point, village (pop. c.2,000), administrative center of West Warwick town, Kent co., central R.I., on Pawtuxet R. and 10 mi. SW of Providence; textiles, textile soaps.

River Road, village (pop. 4,672, with adjacent South Modesto), Stanislaus co., central Calif., near Modesto.

River Rouge (rōōzh), city (pop. 20,549), Wayne co., SE Mich., adjacent to S Detroit, at mouth of the River Rouge on Detroit R. Mfg. of steel, marine engines, chemicals, paper, gypsum products; shipbuilding and repair, oil refining. Inc. as village 1899, as city 1921. Grew in 1920s with expansion of Ford Motor Company's River Rouge plant at near-by Dearborn.

River Rouge, stream, Mich.: see ROUGE, RIVER.

Rivers, town (pop. 657), SW Man., on Minnedosa R. and 18 mi. NW of Brandon; grain, sand, gravel quarrying.

Riversdale, town (pop. 4,534), S Cape Prov., at foot of Langeberg range, on short Vette R. and 50 mi. W of Mossel Bay; agr. center (stock, dairying, wheat, honey, fruit); lime.

Riverside, residential town (pop. 4,878), S Ont., on Detroit R., near L. St. Clair; E suburb of Windsor, opposite Detroit.

Riverside, county (□ 7,179; pop. 170,046), S Calif.; ⊙ Riverside. Stretches E–W across state, from Colorado R. (Ariz. line) to near the coast. Coastal ranges (including Santa Ana Mts.) in W; San Jacinto and San Bernardino ranges (both over 10,000 ft.) and Little San Bernardino Mts. cross center (NW–SE). E of center is part of COLORADO DESERT, including partially irrigated COACHELLA VALLEY and part of SALTON SEA; part of PALO VERDE VALLEY (irrigated) is in extreme E. Includes JOSHUA TREE NATIONAL MONUMENT, several Indian reservations, sections of Cleveland and San Bernardino natl. forests. Oranges, other citrus fruit (in NW), poultry and eggs, livestock, dairy products, grain, field crops (potatoes, sugar beets, alfalfa, dry beans), dates (Coachella Valley), deciduous fruit, nuts, truck. Working of cement-rock, gypsum, clay, sand, gravel, iron deposits. Large packing and processing industries handle farm produce. Includes desert resorts (notably Palm Springs), mtn. recreational areas, L. Elsinore. Formed 1893.

Riverside. 1 Town (pop. 116), St. Clair co., NE central Ala., on Coosa R. and 22 mi. WSW of Anniston. **2** Residential city (pop. 46,764), ⊙ Riverside co., S Calif., on Santa Ana R. and 50 mi. E of Los Angeles; commercial, packing, and shipping center in citrus-fruit area; tourist resort. Here, in 1873, the navel orange was introduced in Calif.; parent tree is preserved. Seat of a campus (the citrus-fruit experiment station) of Univ. of Calif., and of Sherman Indian Inst., Riverside Col. (jr.), a library service school, and Glenwood Mission Inn. U.S. March Air Force Base (March Field) is near by. In Arlington (city's SW dist.) is La Sierra Col. On near-by Mt. Rubidoux (1,337 ft.) is a huge cross—a memorial to Junípero Serra—where Easter sunrise services have been held since 1908. Founded 1870, inc. 1883. **3** Village, Conn.: see GREENWICH. **4** Town (pop. 395), Colquitt co., S Ga., just W of Moultrie, on Ochlockonee R. **5** Residential village (pop. 9,153), Cook co., NE Ill., W suburb of Chicago, on Des Plaines R. Designed as model suburb by Frederick Law Olmsted and Calvert Vaux; inc. 1875. **6** Town (pop. 631), Washington co., SE Iowa, on English R. and 13 mi. S of Iowa City; processed turkeys, feed. **7** Summer-resort village, Charles co., S Md., on the Potomac estuary c.50 mi. below Washington. **8** Village, Franklin co., Mass.: see GILL. **9** Village, Middlesex co., Mass.: see NEWTON. **10** Village (pop. 1,012, with adjacent Hillside Gardens), Jackson co., S Mich. **11** Village (pop. 7,199), Burlington co., SW N.J., on Delaware R., at mouth of Rancocas Creek, and 11 mi. NE of Camden; mfg. (watch cases, clothing, roller skates, metal products, rugs, paper boxes, textiles, cement, asphalt, boats); printing. **12** Village (pop. 818), Steuben co., S N.Y., just NW of Corning; makes fiber boxes. **13** Village (pop. 370), Montgomery co., W Ohio, just NE of Dayton, on Great Miami R. **14** Borough (pop. 524), Northumberland co., E central Pa., on Susquehanna R. opposite Danville. **15** Village, R.I.: see EAST PROVIDENCE. **16** Village (pop. 8,471, with adjacent City View and Woodside), Greenville co., NW S.C., a suburb of Greenville. **17** Village (pop. c.300), Walker co., E central Texas, on Trinity R. and 11 mi. NE of Huntsville; fuller's earth. **18** Town (pop. 149), Okanogan co., N Wash., 12 mi. N of Okanogan and on Okanogan R. **19** Town (1940 pop. 1,043), Monongalia co., N W.Va., just NW of Morgantown, in coal-mining, gas- and oil-producing region. **20** Town (pop. 50), Carbon co., S Wyo., on Encampment R., just E of the Sierra Madre, and 47 mi. SSE of Rawlins; alt. c.7,200 ft.; rail terminus and small supply point.

Riverside Mills, textile-mill village (pop. 2,397, with adjacent Toxaway), Anderson co., NW S.C., adjacent to Anderson.

Riverton, town (pop. 594), SE South Australia, 55 mi. N of Adelaide; rail junction; wheat, wool, livestock.

Riverton, borough (pop. 893), S S.Isl., New Zealand, 16 mi. W of Invercargill and on Foveaux Strait; summer resort. Small fishing port formerly used by whalers.

Riverton. 1 Village, Conn.: see BARKHAMSTED. **2** Village (pop. 1,450), Sangamon co., central Ill., 6 mi. NE of Springfield, in agr. and bituminous-coal area. Inc. 1873. **3** Town (pop. 472), Fremont co., extreme SW Iowa, on East Nishnabotna R. and 12 mi. WSW of Shenandoah; livestock, grain. **4** Village (pop. 148), Crow Wing co., central Minn., on Mississippi R. and 11 mi. NE of Brainerd. Iron-ore processing. Iron mines near by in Cuyuna iron range. **5** Village (pop. 348), Franklin co., S Nebr., 8 mi. E of Franklin and on Republican R., near Kansas line. **6** Village, N.H.: see JEFFERSON. **7** Residential borough (pop. 2,761), Burlington co., SW N.J., on Delaware R. and 7 mi. NE of Camden; ironworking, agr. (truck, fruit). Inc. 1893. **8** Town (pop. 1,666), Salt Lake co., N central Utah, on Jordan R. and 18 mi. S of Salt Lake City. Inc. after 1940. **9** Town (pop. 4,142), Fremont co., W central Wyo., at junction of Wind and Popo Agie rivers to form Bighorn R., 22 mi. NE of Lander; alt. 4,956 ft. Trade and shipping point for irrigated Wind R. basin; sugar beets, livestock, potatoes, beans, hay. R.C. Indian school near by. Served by Riverton power and land-reclamation project, including Wind R. diversion dam, Bull Lake and Pilot Butte dams, as well as the Pilot Butte power plant.

River View, village (pop. 1,322), Chambers co., E Ala., on Chattahoochee R. (here dammed) and 15 mi. NE of Opelika; cotton goods.

Riverview. 1 Village (pop. 1,432), Wayne co., SE Mich., 13 mi. SSW of downtown Detroit and on Detroit R. **2** Hamlet, Greenville co., NW S.C., in the Blue Ridge, 18 mi. NNW of Greenville, in summer-resort region. **3** Suburb (pop. 14,215) of Hampton, Elizabeth City co., SE Va. There is also a village called Riverview in Wise co.

Rives or **Rives-sur-Fure** (rēv-sür-für'), village (pop. 1,641), Isère dept., SE France, 16 mi. NW of Grenoble, in Voiron industrial dist.; metallurgy (forges, steel mill); paper milling, chestnut-oil processing.

Rives (rēvz). **1** Town, Mo.: see NEW RIVES. **2** Town (pop. 413), Obion co., NW Tenn., 5 mi. S of Union City.

Rivesaltes (rēvzält'), town (pop. 4,894), Pyrénées-Orientales dept., S France, on Agly R. and 5 mi. N of Perpignan; winegrowing and trading center known for its muscatel; olive-oil processing. Marshal Joffre b. here.

Rives-sur-Fure, France: see RIVES.

Rivesville (rēvz'vĭl), town (pop. 1,343), Marion co., N W.Va., near the Monongahela, 4 mi. N of Fairmont, in coal-mining region. Laid out 1837.

Rivet (rēvā'), village (pop. 1,007), Alger dept., N central Algeria, in the Mitidja plain, 15 mi. SE of Algiers; vineyards, Cement mill.

Riviera (rĭvēâ'rŭ), narrow coastal strip bet. southernmost Alpine ranges and the Mediterranean, generally considered to extend c.230 mi. from La Spezia (Italy; E) to Hyères (France; W). Known for its scenic beauty, mild winter climate, and luxuriant subtropical vegetation. Dotted with fashionable resorts, hotels, and villas in a setting of beautiful gardens, it is the major playground of Europe. In addition to olives, wine, and citrus fruit, flowers are widely grown for export and for use in perfume industry (particularly around Grasse, France). Sardine, tunny, anchovy, and lobster fisheries. Panoramic highway and railroad (numerous tunnels) extend full length of the Riviera. Genoa is center of Ital. Riviera (on Gulf of Genoa) and divides it into Riviera di Levante (E; along slopes of Ligurian Appenines), with Rapallo, Portofino, Nervi, and Sestri Levante as principal resorts, and Riviera di Ponente (W), with San Remo, Bordighera, Imperia, and Ventimiglia on S slopes of Ligurian Alps. Fr. Riviera, also known as *Côte d'Azur* (kōt"däzür'), has a more indented coastline and numerous resorts: Nice, Cannes, Menton, Antibes, Juan-les-Pins, Villefranche, and Monte-Carlo (in principality of Monaco). Bet. Nice and Menton, 3 parallel scenic highways (Grande Corniche which rises to 1,600 ft., Moyenne Corniche, and coastal Corniche du Littoral) hug characteristic red cliffs of Maritime Alps. Near W end of the Riviera Allied troops invaded (Aug., 1944) S France in Second World War.

Riviera (rēvyä'rä), district (pop. 5,284) and valley, Ticino canton, S Switzerland, drained by Ticino R. Main town, Biasca.

Riviera (rĭvēr'ŭ), village (pop. c.500), Kleberg co., S Texas, near head of Baffin Bay, 16 mi. S of Kingsville; coast resort.

Riviera Beach (rĭvēr'ŭ). **1** Resort town (pop. 4,065), Palm Beach co., SE Fla., just N of West Palm Beach, on L. Worth (lagoon). Inc. 1922 as Riviera. **2** Summer resort (pop. 1,849), Anne Arundel co., central Md., on Patapsco R. and 11 mi. SE of downtown Baltimore.

Rivière (rēvyâr'), village (pop. 302), Namur prov., S central Belgium, on Meuse R. and 7 mi. N of Dinant; Portland-cement mfg. Just N, on right bank of Meuse R., is municipal sanitarium of town of Namur.

Rivière, La (lä), village (pop. 8,098), SW Réunion isl., on road and 3 mi. NE of Saint-Louis; sugar cane, tobacco, corn, beans.

Rivière à Pierre (ä pyâr'), village (pop. estimate 800), S Que., 50 mi. WNW of Quebec; dairying; pigs, poultry.

Rivière au Renard, Que.: see FOX RIVER.

Rivière Beaudette (bōdĕt′) or **River Beaudette,** village (pop. 202), S Que., near L. St. Francis, 11 mi. WSW of Valleyfield; dairying; pigs, potatoes.
Rivière Blanche, village, Que.: see SAINT ULRIC.
Rivière Bleue or **Saint Joseph de la Rivière Bleue** (sē zhōzĕf′ dü lä rēvyâr′ blü′), village (pop. 1,082), SE Que., on St. Francis R. and 35 mi. SE of Rivière du Loup; dairying, lumbering.
Rivière des Anguilles (däzägē′yü), village (pop. 3,025), S Mauritius, on railroad and 3 mi. NE of Souillac; sugar milling.
Rivière des Lacs, N.Dak.: see DES LACS RIVER.
Rivière Dragon (drägō′) or **River Dragon,** village (pop. 46), S Mauritius, on railroad and 6 mi. NE of Souillac. Sugar milling at Britannia (pop. 955), just S.
Rivière du Loup (dü lōō′), county (□ 723; pop. 34,493), SE Que., on the St. Lawrence; ⊙ Rivière du Loup.
Rivière du Loup, city (pop. 8,713), ⊙ Rivière du Loup co., SE Que., on the St. Lawrence at mouth of R. du Loup, and 110 mi. NE of Quebec; railroad workshops; lumbering, woodworking, dairying, peat digging, stove mfg.; resort. Airport. First visited 1683, it was settled 1833, originally called Fraserville. Opposite, in the St. Lawrence, is the Île aux Lièvres.
Rivière du Moulin (dü mōōlē′), village (pop. 1,561), S central Que., on Saguenay R., at mouth of Rivière du Moulin, E suburb of Chicoutimi.
Rivière du Poste (dü pôst′), village (pop. 733), SE Mauritius, on railroad and 9 mi. WSW of Mahébourg, on the Rivière du Poste (15 mi. long). Sugar cane.
Rivière du Rempart (rāpär′), town (pop. 3,202), N Mauritius, on railroad and 12 mi. ENE of Port Louis; sugar cane. Also called Le Ravin.
Rivière Ouelle (wĕl′), village (pop. estimate 500), SE Que., on the St. Lawrence and 35 mi. SW of Rivière du Loup; dairying, pig raising.
Rivière-Pilote (-pēlôt′), town (pop. 1,629), S Martinique, 14 mi. SE of Fort-de-France; sugar plantations; limekiln.
Rivière Salée (sälā′), narrow strait (4 mi. long, 50–120 yards wide), Guadeloupe, Fr. West Indies, separating Guadeloupe into 2 isls., Basse-Terre (W) and Grande-Terre (E), and linking the bays Grand Cul de Sac (N) and Petit Cul de Sac (S). A tidal channel in mangrove swamps, it is navigable for vessels of light draught; spanned by a bridge. Pointe-à-Pitre is near S entrance.
Rivière-Salée, town (pop. 811), SW Martinique, 7 mi. SE of Fort-de-France; sugar growing and milling; also produces vanilla.
Rivières du Sud, Fr. West Africa: see FRENCH GUINEA.
Rivière Trois Pistoles (trwä pĕstôl′), village (pop. estimate 400), SE Que., on the St. Lawrence and 30 mi. NE of Rivière du Loup; dairying; pigs.
Rivignano (rēvēnyä′nô), village (pop. 2,412), Udine prov., Friuli–Venezia Giulia, NE Italy, 16 mi. SSW of Udine.
Rivoli (rēvôlē′), village (pop. 2,318), Oran dept., NW Algeria, 6 mi. S of Mostaganem; winegrowing.
Rivoli (rē′vôlē), town (pop. 7,573), Torino prov., Piedmont, NW Italy, 8 mi. W of Turin; textile industry. Has 18th-cent. palace (damaged) and many villas. In Second World War, bombed (1943).
Rivoli Veronese (rē′vôlē vĕrōnā′zē), village (pop. 356), Verona prov., Veneto, N Italy, on Adige R. and 13 mi. NW of Verona, in sericulture and livestock region. Scene in 1797 of decisive victory of Napoleon over Austrians.
Rivolta d'Adda (rēvôl′tä däd′dä), town (pop. 4,242), Cremona prov., Lombardy, N Italy, near Adda R., 15 mi. E of Milan.
Rixdorf, Germany: see NEUKÖLLN.
Rixensart (rē′ksüsärt), town (pop. 4,927), Brabant prov., central Belgium, on Asne R. and 13 mi. SE of Brussels; market (dairying, vegetables, poultry).
Rixheim (rēksĕm′, Ger. rĭks′hīm), town (pop. 3,496), Haut-Rhin dept., E France, 3 mi. W. of Mulhouse; mfg. (soap, tiles, wallpaper).
Rixhöft, Cape, Poland: see ROZEWIE, CAPE.
Rixingen, France: see RÉCHICOURT-LE-CHÂTEAU.
Rixton with Glazebrook, parish (pop. 1,069), S Lancashire, England; wheat, potato, and vegetable growing. Includes village of Hollins Green, 6 mi. ENE of Warrington.
Riyadh or **Riyad** (both: rĭyädh′, rĭyäd′), city (pop. 80,000), ⊙ (with Mecca) Saudi Arabia and ⊙ Nejd, in Aridh dist., 480 mi. NE of Mecca, 230 mi. SW of Dhahran (connected by railroad, completed 1951); alt. 2,000 ft.; 24°38′N 46°43′E. Political center of Saudi Arabia and hq. of Wahabi movement, situated in a fertile wadi (oriented N–S); date gardens; fruit, grain; weaving handicrafts; power plant. Has huge palace adjoined by large place of assembly (N). Modern royal residence is in W outskirts. Riyadh's prominence dates from 1818, when it supplanted Deraya as the seat of Wahabism. It was held (1891–1902) by the Rashid family of Hail, but was recaptured by Ibn Saud, who used it as the base for his conquest of most of the Arabian Peninsula, which resulted in the formation of Saudi Arabia. Sometimes spelled Riad.
Riyaq (rĭyäk′) or **Rayaq** (räyäk′), Fr. *Rayak*, town (pop. 947), Bekaa prov., central Lebanon, near Syrian frontier, NE of Zahle, on railroad and 30 mi. E of Beirut; railway junction, with standard-gauge line to Aleppo, narrow-gauge lines to Damascus and Beirut.
Riyeka Tsrnoyevitsa, Yugoslavia: see RIJEKA CRNOJEVICA.
Rizaiyeh, Rezaiyeh, or **Reza'iyeh** (all: rĕzäēyĕ′, rĭ-), town (1940 pop. 45,575), ⊙ Fourth Prov., NW Iran, 75 mi. WSW of Tabriz and 10 mi. from W shore of L. Urima (its lake port is Gelma Khaneh); alt. 4,400 ft.; 37°32′N 45°5′E. Agr. center of W Azerbaijan, in fertile dist. producing grain, fruit, cotton, tobacco, rice; extensive orchards. Rugmaking. Airfield. Center (19th cent.) of Christian missionary activity (Presbyterian, Anglican, R.C.). Reputed birthplace of Zoroaster. Until 1930s called Urmia or Urumiyeh.
Rizaiyeh, Lake, Iran: see URMIA, LAKE.
Rizal (rĭzäl′, Sp. rēsäl′), province (□ 791; 1948 pop. 673,060), S Luzon, Philippines, bounded W by Manila Bay, S by Laguna de Bay (containing TALIM ISLAND, which belongs to the prov.); ⊙ PASIG. Largely a fertile plain drained by the Pasig. There is rugged terrain in E part of prov. Principal products: rice, sugar cane, fruit. Fishing, stock raising. MANILA and QUEZON CITY are in, but independent of, the prov.
Rizal. 1 Town (1939 pop. 2,769; 1948 municipality pop. 16,754), Nueva Ecija prov., central Luzon, Philippines, on Pampanga R. and 17 mi. NE of Cabanatuan; rice-growing center. **2** City (1939 pop. 4,768; 1948 metropolitan area pop. 88,728) in, but independent of, Rizal prov., S Luzon, Philippines, on Manila Bay, just S of Manila; trade center for agr. area (rice, fruit). Just E of city is Fort McKinley, former U.S. army reservation returned to Philippines by pact signed 1947; here is a permanent military cemetery for the dead of Second World War. Formerly Pasay (pä′sī).
Rizan, Iran: see RAZAN.
Rize (rĭzĕ′), prov. (□ 1,415; 1950 pop. 181,084), NE Turkey, on Black Sea; ⊙ Rize. Bordered S by Rize Mts. Zinc, iron, manganese mining. Tea, filberts, olives, corn. Formerly part of a district called Lazistan (majority of the inhabitants were Lazes), part of which passed (with Batum) to Russia in 1878. Rize prov. was formed c.1940 out of a section of Coruh prov.
Rize, anc. *Rhizus*, town (1950 pop. 15,070), ⊙ Rize prov., NE Turkey, Black Sea port 85 mi. NW of Erzurum; citrus, corn, tea. Manganese to S. Rize was formerly ⊙ Coruh prov. before Rize became a separate prov.
Rize Mountains (rĭzĕ′), NE Turkey, S and E of Rize, extend 80 mi. SW-NE bet. Black Sea (NW) and Coruh R. (SE); rise to 12,917 ft. in Kackar Dag. Trebizond Mts. adjoin W. Iron, zinc.
Rizokarpasso (rēzôkär′päsō), village (pop. 4,064), Famagusta dist., NE Cyprus, on Karpas Peninsula, 40 mi. NE of Famagusta; tobacco, wheat, carobs, olives; sheep, cattle, hogs. Noted for its healthful climate.
Rizziconi (rētsē′kônē), village (pop. 3,200), Reggio di Calabria prov., Calabria, S Italy, 7 mi. NE of Palmi, in agr. (fruit, olives), stock-raising region.
Rizzuto, Cape (rētsōō′tô), Calabria, S Italy, at NE end of Gulf of Squillace, 13 mi. S of Crotone; 38°54′N 17°6′E; lighthouse.
Rjukan (ryōō′kän), village (pop. 5,460) in Tinn canton (pop. 8,742), Telemark co., S Norway, on the Mana and 60 mi. NW of Skien; industrial center; mfg. of nitrates, dry ice, and heavy water, with hydroelectric plant at the falls Rjukanfoss (983 ft.). A 10-mi. electric railroad extends E to Mael on Tinn L., meeting a ferry which runs to Tinnoset, terminus of line to Notodden. In Second World War, the heavy-water plant, under German control, was attacked (Feb., 1943) by Norwegian parachutists; put out of action (Nov., 1943) by air bombardment.
Rjuven, Norway: see RUVEN MOUNTAINS.
Roa (rō′ä), town (pop. 2,992), Burgos prov., N Spain, on Douro (Duero) R. and 45 mi. SSW of Burgos, on fertile irrigated plain; cereals, grapes, truck produce, beans, livestock. Lumbering, fishing; flour milling, mfg. of soap and chocolate. Historic town of Roman origin. Has remains of a royal palace (where the Cardinal and Sp. regent Jiménez de Cisneros died), and church with beautiful choir. Suffered during 19th-cent. wars.
Roa Bárcena (rō′ä bär′sänä), town (pop. 1,631), Veracruz, E Mexico, in Sierra Madre Oriental, 9 mi. S of Orizaba; coffee, sugar cane, fruit. Sometimes Tequila.
Roachdale, town (pop. 918), Putnam co., W central Ind., 35 mi. WNW of Indianapolis, in agr. area; dairy products, grain, soybeans.
Road Town, town (pop. 706), ⊙ Br. Virgin Isls., Lesser Antilles, open roadstead on E coast of Tortola isl., 21 mi. ENE of Charlotte Amalie (St. Thomas Isl.), 215 mi. WNW of St. John's (Antigua isl.); 18°26′N 64°32′W. Trading center and only port of entry of the presidency; exports livestock, fish, charcoal, fruit, and vegetables, mainly to St. Thomas Isl. and Puerto Rico. Ships anchor offshore. Has airfield, govt. offices. Agr. station and botanical gardens near by.
Roag, Loch (lŏkh rōg′), large inlet on W coast of Lewis with Harris, Outer Hebrides, Scotland, enclosing Great Bernera isl.; 10 mi. long, 6 mi. wide.
Roan (rō′än), village and canton (pop. 1,906), Sør-Trondelag co., central Norway, on North Sea, 45 mi. N of Trondheim; agr., fishing (cod, herring).
Roan Antelope or **Roan Antelope Mine,** mining township (pop. 15,937), Western Prov., N Northern Rhodesia, just N of Luanshya and 20 mi. SW of Ndola; copper-mining center; smelter. Roan Antelope North (pop. 757), residential, adjoins.
Roan Cliffs, Utah and Colo.: see BOOK CLIFFS.
Roane (rōn). **1** County (□ 379; pop. 31,665), E Tenn.; ⊙ Kingston. In Tennessee R. valley; here Clinch R. enters an arm of Watts Bar Reservoir of the Tennessee. Coal and iron mines, limestone quarries; hardwood lumbering; fruitgrowing, agr. (tobacco, corn, wheat), livestock raising, dairying. Industry at Harriman, Rockwood. Formed 1801. **2** County (□ 486; pop. 18,408), W W.Va.; ⊙ Spencer. Drained by Little Kanawha and Pocatalico rivers and small Sandy Creek. Timber-producing region; agr. (livestock, fruit, tobacco); some mfg. at Spencer. Formed 1856.
Roan High Knob, Tenn. and N.C.: see ROAN MOUNTAIN.
Roan Island (rōn), islet (pop. 61), N Sutherland, Scotland, at mouth of Kyle of Tongue; 1½ mi. long, 1 mi. wide. Rises to 251 ft.
Roan Mountain, on NE Tenn.–W N.C. line, in the Appalachians, 10 mi. SE of Johnson City, Tenn.; its summit, called Roan High Knob, rises to 6,313 ft.
Roann (rōăn′), town (pop. 492), Wabash co., NE central Ind., on Eel R. and 14 mi. NNE of Peru, in agr. area.
Roanne (rōän′), anc. *Rodumna*, city (pop. 40,216), Loire dept., SE central France, on left bank of Loire R. and 40 mi. WNW of Lyons, at S terminus of Loire Lateral Canal; center of important cotton-milling industry extending from Riorges (W) to Tarare (E). In addition to numerous hosiery factories and a rayon plant, Roanne has tanneries, paper and flour mills, and a large arsenal established after First World War. Together with Lyons and Saint-Étienne, it forms the industrial triangle of central France.
Roanoke (rō′ůnōk), county (□ 278; pop. 41,486), SW Va.; ⊙ Salem. In Great Appalachian Valley, traversed by ridges, with mts. in NW and the Blue Ridge (here cut by Roanoke R.) in SE. Includes part of Jefferson Natl. Forest. Traversed by Blue Ridge Parkway and Appalachian Trail. Roanoke city is in but independent of co. Rich agr. and fruitgrowing area; dairying, stock and poultry raising. Mfg. at Salem, Roanoke. Formed 1838.
Roanoke. 1 City (pop. 5,392), Randolph co., E Ala., near Ga. line, 35 mi. N of Opelika; cotton clothing and fabrics, lumber, fertilizer, beverages. Settled c.1835, inc. 1888. **2** Village (pop. 1,368), Woodford co., central Ill., 22 mi. ENE of Peoria, in agr. and bituminous-coal-mining area. Inc. 1874. **3** Town (pop. 905), Huntington co., NE central Ind., on Little R. and 16 mi. SW of Fort Wayne, in agr. area; grain, dairy products; mfg. of electric coils. **4** Town (pop. 65), Randolph and Howard counties, N central Mo., 15 mi. SW of Moberly. **5** City (pop. 511), Denton co., N Texas, 18 mi. NE of Fort Worth, in farm area. **6** City (pop. 91,921), in but independent of Roanoke co., SW Va., on Roanoke R., bet. the Alleghenies and the Blue Ridge (whose crest in just E), and 40 mi. W of Lynchburg. S gateway to Shenandoah Valley; industrial, trade, and railroad center for rich agr., coal, and timber area. Important industries are railroad shops, mfg. of foundry and machine-shop products, structural steel and bridges, viscose rayon yarns, chemicals, building materials; also clothing, textiles, furniture, tin cans, paints; flour milling, lumber millwork. U.S. veterans hosp. near by. Founded 1834 as Big Lick; inc. as town 1874; renamed 1882 with coming of railroad; inc. as city 1884.
Roanoke Island, Dare co., E N.C., bet. Croatan and Roanoke sounds, c.40 mi. N of Cape Hatteras; 12 mi. long, 3 mi. wide. Chief town, Manteo. Explored in 1584 by English navigators sent by Sir Walter Raleigh, who then dispatched unsuccessful colonizing expeditions in 1585 and 1587. Virginia Dare b. here. In 1941, Fort Raleigh Natl. Historic Site (16.45 acres) was established at N end of isl.; excavations have revealed outlines of colonists' fort (to be reconstructed). Since 1937, *The Lost Colony*, a commemorative symphonic drama, has been presented here annually.
Roanoke Rapids, city (pop. 8,156), Halifax co., NE N.C., near Va. line, 37 mi. NNE of Rocky Mount and on Roanoke R.; mfg. center; cotton, pulp, and paper mills. Founded 1893; inc. as city 1931.
Roanoke River, in Va. and N.C., rises in N Montgomery co., SW Va., flows SSW, ENE through the Blue Ridge at Roanoke, thence generally SE, past Altavista, Brookneal, and Clarksville, into NE N.C., past Roanoke Rapids, Weldon, Hamilton (head of 10-ft. navigation channel), and Williamston, and E past Plymouth to head of Albemarle Sound; 410 mi. long. Above Clarksville, where Dan R. enters, the Roanoke was formerly called Staunton R.; Staunton R. State Park (recreational area) is in this region. Buggs Isl. Dam (144 ft.

high, 22,500 ft. long, including dikes) is c.20 mi. below Clarksville; a unit in comprehensive flood-control and hydroelectric power program for river's basin. Chief tributary, Dan R.

Roanoke Sound, E N.C., small body of water E of Roanoke Isl.; joins Albemarle (N), Pamlico (S), sounds.

Roan Plateau, high tableland (7–9,000 ft.) largely in Garfield co., W Colo. Forms E continuation of East Tavaputs Plateau, Utah. Bounded on S by Book Cliffs.

Roaring Fork River, W central Colo., rises W of Mt. Elbert in Sawatch Mts., flows c.70 mi. NW, past Aspen and Carbondale, to Colorado R. at Glenwood Springs. Supplies water, via Twin Lakes tunnel under Sawatch Mts., to Twin Lakes Reservoir.

Roaring Gap, resort town (1940 pop. 24), Alleghany co., NW N.C., 13 mi. NW of Elkin, in the Blue Ridge.

Roaring River, tiny river (c.5 mi. long) in St. Ann parish, N Jamaica, bet. St. Ann's Bay and Ocho Rios; along it are picturesque Roaring River Falls, largest on the isl., used for hydroelectric power.

Roaring Spring, borough (pop. 2,771), Blair co., S central Pa., 12 mi. S of Altoona; paper products; limestone quarrying; agr. Inc. 1888.

Roaring Springs, town (pop. 435), Motley co., NW Texas, just below Cap Rock escarpment, c.50 mi. SW of Childress and on South Pease R.; railway shipping point for Matador (7 mi. N); trade and recreational center, with springs (camping, swimming).

Roaringwater Bay, inlet (12 mi. long, up to 5 mi. wide) on SW coast of Co. Cork, Ireland, N of Clear Isl. On it are ports of Schull and Ballydehob.

Roatán (rōätän'), city (pop. 1,094), ⊙ Bay Islands dept., N Honduras, on S coast of Roatán Isl., 39 mi. NE of La Ceiba; 16°18'N 86°35'W. Fishing center; shipbuilding, canning of fish, fruit, meat; exports coconuts. Ruins of 17th-cent. pirates' fortifications. Sometimes called Coxen Hole.

Roatán Island, largest island (pop. 4,343) in Bay Islands dept., N Honduras, in Caribbean Sea, 30–35 mi. off N coast of Honduras, bet. La Ceiba and Trujillo; 30 mi. long, 2–3 mi. wide; rises to c.900 ft.; well wooded (lumbering). Agr. (coconuts, sugar cane, tropical fruit); livestock. Main centers (on S coast): Roatán, French Harbour, Oak Ridge. Sometimes spelled Ruatán.

Roath, Wales: see CARDIFF.

Roazon, France: see RENNES.

Robat Thana (rōbät' tä'nŭ), village, Chagai dist., NW Baluchistan, W Pakistan, 300 mi. WNW of Nushki, 21 mi. N of Zahidan (Iran). Copper and limestone deposits in near-by hills (S). Sometimes called Ribat.

Robb, village, W Alta., in Rocky Mts., near Jasper Natl. Park, 35 mi. SW of Edson; coal mining.

Robben Island (2 mi. long, 1 mi. wide), SW Cape Prov., U. of So. Afr., at entrance of Table Bay, 6 mi. NNW of Cape Town; military reservation since 1936. Prior to settlement of Table Bay, Indies-bound Dutch vessels deposited mails here, to be picked up by homeward-bound ships. Sheep were introduced 1652; later isl. was prison for native chiefs and subsequently became leper asylum (moved to Pretoria 1931).

Robbins (rŏ'bĭnz). **1** Residential village (pop. 4,766), Cook co., NE Ill., SW suburb of Chicago, in diversified-farming area; an all-Negro community. Inc. 1917. **2** Town (pop. 1,158), Moore co., central N.C., 22 mi. SE of Asheboro; rayon and lumber milling. Pyrophyllite mined near by. Inc. 1935. Formerly Hemp. **3** Village, Barnwell co., W S.C., near Savannah R., 28 mi. SE of Augusta, Ga., in agr. area; rail junction.

Robbinsdale, city (pop. 11,289), Hennepin co., E Minn., NW suburb of Minneapolis; metal appliances. Dairying and truck-farming in vicinity. Platted 1887, inc. as city 1938.

Robbins Island (□ 38), in Bass Strait, 1 mi. off NW coast of Tasmania; 10 mi. long, 7 mi. wide. Mountainous, fertile; dairying. Walker Isl. (3 mi. long) is nearly connected with N end of isl. Sometimes called Robbin Isl.

Robbinston, town (pop. 554), Washington co., E Maine, on St. Croix R. and 13 mi. SSE of Calais; sardines canned.

Robbinsville, resort village (pop. 515), ⊙ Graham co., W N.C., in Nantahala Natl. Forest, 20 mi. NNE of Murphy and on Cheoah R., near L. Santeetlah; sawmilling.

Robbio (rôb'byô), town (pop. 5,117), Pavia prov., Lombardy, N Italy, 7 mi. WNW of Mortara; agr. center; dairy products.

Robe, town (pop. 412), SE South Australia, on Indian Ocean and 165 mi. SSE of Adelaide; dairy products, livestock; summer resort. Fishery (sharks, crayfish).

Robecco d'Oglio (rôbĕk'kô dô'lyô), village (pop. 1,826), Cremona prov., Lombardy, N Italy, on Oglio R. and 9 mi. NNE of Cremona.

Röbel (rû'bŭl), village (pop. 5,443), Mecklenburg, N Germany, on SW shore of Müritz L., 19 mi. W of Neustrelitz; machinery mfg., flour milling; agr. market (grain, potatoes, stock). Has 13th-cent. church.

Robeline (rō'bŭlēn), village (pop. 350), Natchitoches parish, NW central La., 14 mi. SW of Natchitoches, on small Bayou Pedro; cotton, corn.

Roberdel (rŏ'bŭrdĕl") or **Roberdell,** town (pop. 451), Richmond co., S N.C., just NNE of Rockingham; textile mills.

Robe River, Co. Mayo, Ireland, rises 7 mi. E of Claremorris, flows 22 mi. WSW, past Ballinrobe, to Lough Mask.

Robersonville (rŏ'bŭrsŭnvĭl"), town (pop. 1,414), Martin co., E central N.C., 16 mi. NNE of Greenville, in agr. area; tobacco market and processing (stemming) point; sawmilling. Settled 1700s; inc. 1872.

Robert (rôbâr'), town (pop. 1,585), E Martinique, minor port on an Atlantic bay, 9 mi. ENE of Fort-de-France; trading point in sugar-growing region; alcohol and rum distilling, sugar milling. Sometimes called Le Robert.

Roberta, city (pop. 673), Crawford co., central Ga., 22 mi. WSW of Macon; agr. trade center; sawmilling.

Robert English Coast, part of Antarctica, at W base of Palmer Peninsula, bet. 67° and 78°W. Discovered 1940 by Finn Ronne and Carl R. Eklund.

Robert Island, China: see CRESCENT GROUP.

Robert Lee, city (pop. 1,069), ⊙ Coke co., W Texas, 29 mi. N of San Angelo and on Colorado R.; market center for farm and ranch area. Old Fort Chadbourne is 12 mi. NE.

Roberts. 1 County (□ 1,111; pop. 14,929), NE S. Dak., bordering on N.Dak. and Minn.; ⊙ Sisseton. Agr. area watered by numerous lakes and streams, bounded E by Big Stone L. and L. Traverse. Coteau des Prairies runs N–S; Sisseton Indian Reservation extends through much of co. Dairy products, livestock, grain. Formed 1883. **2** County (□ 892; pop. 1,031), extreme N Texas; ⊙ Miami. On high plains of the Panhandle; alt. 2,500–3,000 ft. Cattle-ranching area, producing also wheat, grain sorghums, barley, oats, hay; some sheep and hogs. Drained by Canadian R. and tributaries. Formed 1876.

Roberts. 1 Village (pop. 341), Jefferson co., SE Idaho, 10 mi. WNW of Rigby; alt. 4,773 ft.; trade center in agr. area. **2** Village (pop. 416), Ford co., E Ill., 37 mi. SSW of Kankakee; grain, hay, livestock, poultry. **3** Village (pop. c.200), Carbon co., S Mont., on branch of Clarks Fork of Yellowstone R. and 45 mi. SW of Billings; shipping point in agr. region; grain. **4** Village (pop. 290), St. Croix co., W Wis., 25 mi. E of St. Paul, Minn.

Roberts, Camp, Calif.: see PASO ROBLES.

Robertsbridge, England: see SALEHURST.

Roberts Creek Mountain, Nev.: see ROBERTS MOUNTAINS.

Robertsdale, town (pop. 1,128), Baldwin co., SW Ala., 23 mi. SE of Mobile; vegetable packing, lumber milling, dairying.

Roberts Field, Liberia: see MONROVIA.

Robertsfors (rō'bŭrtsfôrs", –fôsh"), village (pop. 1,262), Vasterbotten co., N Sweden, near Gulf of Bothnia, 30 mi. NE of Umea; mfg. of turbines, machinery, sulphite; pulp milling. Founded 1759.

Robertsganj (rŏb'ŭrtsgŭnj), town (pop. 2,885), Mirzapur dist., SE Uttar Pradesh, India, 45 mi. SE of Mirzapur; rice, gram, barley, wheat, oilseeds.

Roberts Island (12 naut. mi. long, 6 naut. mi. wide), South Shetland Isls., off Palmer Peninsula, Antarctica; 62°25'S 59°30'W.

Roberts Mountain, Wyo.: see WIND RIVER RANGE.

Roberts Mountains, Eureka co., central Nev., SE of Cortez Mts. Rise to 10,125 ft. in Roberts Creek Mtn., 30 mi. NW of Eureka.

Robertson, town (pop. 6,562), SW Cape Prov., U. of So. Afr., near Breede R., 30 mi. ESE of Worcester, at foot of Langeberg range; agr. center (viticulture, fruit drying, dairying, sheep); resort.

Robertson. 1 County (□ 101; pop. 2,881), N Ky.; ⊙ Mt. Olivet. Bounded W and SW by Licking R., N by its North Fork. Gently rolling upland agr. area (dairy products, livestock, poultry, burley tobacco, corn, wheat), in Bluegrass region. Formed 1867. **2** County (□ 474; pop. 27,024), N Tenn.; ⊙ Springfield. Bounded N by Ky.; drained by Red R. and its small affluents Carr Creek and Sulphur Fork. Tobacco and livestock region; some mfg. at Springfield. Formed 1796. **3** County (□ 874; pop. 19,908), E central Texas; ⊙ Franklin. Bounded W by Brazos R., E by Navasota R. Rich diversified agr. area (cotton, corn, legumes, grain, hay, fruit, truck, cattle, hogs, sheep, poultry, dairy products). Oil, natural gas, sand, gravel. Formed 1837.

Robertson Bay, inlet (25 naut. mi. long, 23 naut. mi. wide), Antarctica, bet. capes Barrow and Adare, in Victoria Land; 71°20'S 170°E. Discovered 1841 by Sir James C. Ross.

Robertson Island (10 naut. mi. long, 7 naut. mi. wide), Antarctica, S of Nordenskjöld Coast of Palmer Peninsula, in Weddell Sea; 65°10'S 59°40'W. Discovered 1893 by C. A. Larsen, Norwegian explorer.

Robertsonpet, India: see KOLAR GOLD FIELDS.

Robertsonville, village (pop. 576), S Que., 5 mi. NE of Thetford Mines, in asbestos-mining region.

Robertsport, town, ⊙ Grand Cape Mount co., W Liberia, port on Atlantic Ocean, at outlet of Fisherman L., on Cape Mount and 50 mi. WNW of Monrovia; fishing; cassava, rice. Episcopal mission.

Robertville (rôbârvēl'), village (pop. 1,621), Constantine dept., NE Algeria, on railroad and 14 mi. SSW of Philippeville; olive-oil, flour milling.

Robertville, Belgium: see BARRAGE DE LA WARCHE.

Robert Williams, Angola: see VILA ROBERT WILLIAMS.

Roberval (rŏ'bŭrvŭl, Fr. rôbĕrväl'), town (pop. 3,220), ⊙ Lac St. Jean Ouest co., S central Que., on SW Shore of L. St. John, 130 mi. NW of Quebec, in dairying, potato-growing, salmon-fishing region; furniture mfg.; resort. Airport.

Robeson (rŏ'bŭsŭn), county (□ 944; pop. 87,769), S N.C., on S.C. line; ⊙ Lumberton. Coastal plain tobacco and timber area, drained by Lumber R.; textile and lumber mills. Formed 1786.

Robeson Channel, arm (50 mi. long, 11–18 mi. wide) of the Arctic Ocean, bet. NE Ellesmere Isl. (Canada) and NW Greenland; 82°N 62°W. Connects Lincoln Sea of the Arctic Ocean with Hall Basin (S). Under favorable conditions it is navigable for brief periods during summer months. Channel was explored by the Greely, Peary, Lockwood, Nares, Koch, and Rasmussen expeditions.

Robesonia (rŏbŭsō'nēŭ), borough (pop. 1,590), Berks co., SE central Pa., 11 mi. W of Reading; textiles. Founded 1855.

Robiac (rôbyäk'), village (pop. 587), Gard dept., S France, on the Cèze and 10 mi. N of Alès; coal.

Robik or **Robiku,** Albania: see RRUBIG.

Robinhood, Maine: see GEORGETOWN.

Robin Hood's Bay, inlet of the North Sea in NE Yorkshire, England, 12 mi. NNW of Scarborough. Bounded N by promontory of North Cheek or Ness Point, sheltering fishing village of Robin Hood's Bay.

Robins, town (pop. 272), Linn co., E Iowa, 7 mi. N of Cedar Rapids; livestock, grain.

Robins Air Force Base, Ga.: see MACON, city.

Robins Island, SE N.Y., island (c.2 mi. long) lying bet. Great Peconic and Little Peconic bays, bet. flukes of E Long Isl., 11 mi. E of Riverhead; summer resort.

Robinson. 1 City (pop. 6,407), ⊙ Crawford co., SE Ill., 24 mi. NNW of Vincennes, Ind.; trade and mfg. center in agr. and oil-producing area; mfg. of china, pottery, oil-well equipment, candy, glycerin, caskets; oil refinery. Poultry, livestock, corn, wheat. Inc. 1886. **2** City (pop. 381), Brown co., NE Kansas, on small affluent of Missouri R. and 30 mi. W of St. Joseph, Mo.; corn, poultry, livestock. **3** Village (pop. 166), Kidder co., central N.Dak., 21 mi. N of Steele.

Robinson Island (12 naut. mi. long, 7 naut. mi. wide), Antarctica, 6 naut. mi. E of Cape Northrop, Palmer Peninsula, in Weddell Sea; 67°20'S 63°40'W. Discovered 1928 by Sir Hubert Wilkins.

Robinson Ranges, W central Western Australia, extend 95 mi. E-W, bet. Gascoyne and Murchison rivers; rise to 2,630 ft. (Mt. Fraser).

Robla, La (lä rō'vlä), village (pop. 1,042), Leon prov., NW Spain, on Bernesga R. and 14 mi. N of Leon; tile and ceramic mfg.; lumber, livestock, cereals, potatoes. Coal mines near by.

Roble, El, in Latin America: see EL ROBLE.

Robleda (rōvlā'dhä), village (pop. 1,598), Salamanca prov., W Spain, 15 mi. SSW of Ciudad Rodrigo; flour mills; cereals, livestock, lumber.

Robledillo de Trujillo (rōvlā-dhē'lyō dhā trōōhē'lyō), village (pop. 1,968), Cáceres prov., W Spain, 14 mi. SSW of Trujillo; olive-oil processing; cereals, wine, figs.

Robledo (rōvlā'dhō), town (pop. 1,408), Albacete prov., SE central Spain, 34 mi. SW of Albacete; flour milling; livestock, lumber, saffron.

Robledo de Chavela (dhā chävä'lä), town (pop. 1,219), Madrid prov., central Spain, in Sierra de Guadarrama, 30 mi. W of Madrid; cereals, grapes, livestock. Exports timber, resins.

Robles, department, Argentina: see FERNÁNDEZ.

Robles or **Villa Robles** (vē'yä rō'blĕs), town (pop. estimate 1,000), W central Santiago del Estero prov., Argentina, on left bank of the Río Dulce and 14 mi. SE of Santiago del Estero; agr. center (corn, cotton, alfalfa, livestock). Robles rail station (E).

Robles, Venezuela: see EL PILAR, Nueva Esparta.

Roblin, village (pop. 799), W Man., 60 mi. W of Dauphin, near group of small lakes; grain elevators; tanning, dairying, mixed farming.

Röblitz, Germany: see UNTERWELLENBORN-RÖBLITZ.

Roboré (rōbōrā'), military post (Fortín Roboré) and village (pop. c.2,500), Santa Cruz dept., E Bolivia, 80 mi. ESE of San José, on Corumba–Santa Cruz RR; cattle. Airport; military hq. of E Bolivia.

Robson, Mount (rŏb'sŭn) (12,972 ft.), E B.C., near Alta. border, in Rocky Mts., in Mt. Robson Provincial Park, 50 mi. WNW of Jasper; 53°7'N 119°8'W. Highest peak in the Canadian Rockies.

Robstown, city (pop. 7,278), Nueces co., S Texas, 17 mi. W of Corpus Christi; trade, packing, shipping center for oil-producing and agr. area (truck, cotton, grain); oil refining, cottonseed milling.

Roby, England: see HUYTON WITH ROBY.

Roby (rō'bē), town (pop. 1,051), ⊙ Fisher co., NW central Texas, 20 mi. N of Sweetwater; trading, cotton-ginning point in agr. and cattle-ranching area.

Roca (rō′kù), village (pop. 105), Lancaster co., SE Nebr., 10 mi. S of Lincoln and on branch of Platte R.

Roca, Cape (rō′kù), Port. *Cabo da Roca* (kä′bo͞o dä rô′kù), westernmost point of Portugal and of continental Europe, a headland on the Atlantic, 19 mi. WNW of Lisbon; 38°47′N 9°30′W; lighthouse. The slender granite cliff (c.550 ft. high), named Rock of Lisbon by English sailors, forms W end of the Serra de Sintra.

Roca, La, or **La Roca de la Sierra** (lä rō′kä dhā lä syĕ′rä), town (pop. 2,715), Badajoz prov., W Spain, 22 mi. NE of Badajoz; cereals, olives, grapes, livestock. Limekilns.

Roçadas or **Forte Roçadas** (fôr′tĭ ro͞osä′dùsh), town, Huíla prov., SW Angola, on Cunene R. and 160 mi. SE of Sá da Bandeira. Became ⊙ Cunene dist. (formed 1946).

Roca de la Sierra, La, Spain: see ROCA, LA.

Rocafort (rōkäfôrt′), outer NW suburb (pop. 1,262) of Valencia, Valencia prov., E Spain; silk-textile mfg.; cereals, oranges, grapes.

Rocafuerte (rōkäfwĕr′tä). **1** Town (1950 pop. 2,788), Manabí prov., W Ecuador, in Pacific lowlands, on Portoviejo R., on highway, and 8 mi. N of Portoviejo, in fertile region producing cacao, rice, sugar cane, coffee, cotton, tagua nuts. Mfg. of Panama hats. **2** Former Ecuadorian military post, in Amazon basin, on Napo R. at mouth of the Aguarico, opposite Pantoja (Peru); 0°58′S 75°10′W. Following 1942 border settlement, Rocafuerte was replaced by NUEVA ROCAFUERTE, 20 mi. W.

Rocakong (rôkäkông′), village, Kandal prov., S Cambodia, on the Mekong and 18 mi. NNE of Pnompenh; distillery; corn, tobacco.

Rocamadour (rôkämädo͞or′), village (pop. 177), Lot dept., SW France, in the Causse de Gramat, 12 mi. ENE of Gourdon; cheese making; trade in religious articles. A renowned pilgrimage place built up the side of a sheer cliff. Has well-preserved 12th–15th-cent. ramparts; 12th-cent Basilica of Saint-Sauveur; subterranean crypt of St. Amadour; 15th-cent. church of Notre Dame. The cliff is topped by medieval fortress.

Rocanville (rō′künvĭl), village (pop. 479), SE Sask., near Man. border, 16 mi. N of Moosomin; grain elevators, stock.

Roca Partida Point (rō′kä pärtē′dä), cape in Veracruz, SE Mexico, on Gulf of Campeche, 19 mi. N of San Andrés Tuxtla; 18°43′N 95°10′W.

Rocas (rô′kùs), rocky islets in the South Atlantic, c 140 mi. NE of Cape São Roque on the Brazilian bulge; rise 10 ft. above mean high water; 33°49′29″W 3°51′30″S; lighthouse.

Rocca d'Aspide (rôk′kä dä′spēdĕ) or **Roccadaspide,** town (pop. 3,247), Salerno prov., Campania, S Italy, 15 mi. SSE of Eboli; mfg. (hydraulic pumps, hosiery)

Rocca di Neto (rôk′kä dē nä′tô), village (pop. 2,346), Catanzaro prov., Calabria, S Italy, near Neto R., 10 mi. NW of Crotone; citrus fruit, vegetables.

Rocca di Papa (pä′pä), town (pop. 4,720), Roma prov., Latium, central Italy, in Alban Hills, 6 mi. NW of Velletri; health resort (2,247 ft.); wine making. Damaged in Second World War

Rocca Imperiale (rôk′kä ēmpĕrĕä′lĕ), village (pop. 1,915), Cosenza prov., Calabria, S Italy, near Gulf of Taranto, 29 mi. NNE of Castrovillari.

Roccalbenga (rôk-kälbĕng′gä), village (pop. 749). Grosseto prov., Tuscany, central Italy, 20 mi. E of Grosseto.

Rocca Littorio, Ital. Somaliland: see GALKAYU.

Roccalumera (rôk″kälo͞omä′rä), village (pop. 1,617), Messina prov., NE Sicily, port on Ionian Sea, 17 mi. SSW of Messina.

Roccamonfina (rôk″kämônfē′nä), village (pop. 1,164), Caserta prov., Campania, S Italy, 17 mi. NW of Capua, in extinct volcanic crater. Leucite deposits near by.

Roccapalumba (rôk″käpälo͞om′bä), village (pop. 3,441), Palermo prov., N central Sicily, 13 mi. S of Termini Imerese.

Roccapiemonte (rôk″käpyĕmôn′tĕ), village (pop. 3,168), Salerno prov., Campania, S Italy, 7 mi. NW of Salerno; macaroni mfg.

Rocca Pietore (rôk′kä pyā′tôrĕ), village (pop. 254), Belluno prov., Veneto, N Italy, 11 mi. N of Agordo, in the Dolomites; wrought-iron products.

Roccaraso (rôk″kärä′zô), village (pop. 1,025), Aquila prov., Abruzzi e Molise, S central Italy, in the Apennines, 16 mi. SSE of Sulmona; winter-sports center (alt. 4,055 ft.) Rebuilt after Ger. destruction (1943) in Second World War.

Rocca San Casciano (rôk′kä sän kăshä′nô), village (pop 2,239), Forlì prov , Emilia-Romagna, N central Italy, on Montone R. and 16 mi. S of Faenza; wine making.

Roccasecca (rôk″käsĕk′kä), village (pop. 1,729), Frosinone prov., Latium, S central Italy, 5 mi. NW of Aquino. Overlooked by ruins of castle where St. Thomas Aquinas was b. Louis II defeated Lancelot here 1411.

Roccastrada (rôk″kästrä′dä), town (pop. 2,756), Grosseto prov., Tuscany, central Italy, 17 mi. NNE of Grosseto; agr products (cereals, wine, olive oil). Lignite and copper mines, kaolin and gypsum quarries near by.

Roccella Ionica (rôt-chĕl′lä yô′nēkä), town (pop. 6,972), Reggio di Calabria prov., Calabria, S Italy, fishing port on Ionian Sea, 7 mi. NE of Siderno Marina; olive oil, wine. Has ruined castle.

Rocchetta Sant'Antonio (rôk-kĕt′tä säntäntô′nyô), town (pop. 5,021), Foggia prov., Apulia, S Italy, 9 mi. SSW of Ascoli Satriano, in stock-raising region.

Rocchette, Italy: see PIOVENE ROCCHETTE.

Rocester (rō′stùr), town and parish (pop. 1,113), E Stafford, England, 4 mi. NNE of Uttoxeter; cotton milling. Site of Roman station; has remains of abbey built 1146.

Rocha (rō′chä), department (□ 4,281; pop. 82,814), SE Uruguay, on the Atlantic; ⊙ Rocha. Borders NE on Brazil (L. Mirim); bounded NW by Cebollatí R. A low region with undulating hills, marshes, and large fresh-water lagoons (L. Rocha, L. Castillos, Laguna Negra). Rocha's economy depends primarily on stock raising (sheep, cattle, horses). Trade in wool and hides. The dept. abounds in wildlife, and nutrias are hunted. Peat, marble, and lime deposits are little exploited. Main trading center is Rocha city, served by its Atlantic port La Paloma. The dept. is noted for its remains of colonial Port. fortresses, such as San Miguel and Santa Teresa. Formerly a part of Maldonado dept.

Rocha, city (pop. 25,000), ⊙ Rocha dept., SE Uruguay, on railroad and 105 mi. ENE of Montevideo; 34°29′S 54°22′W. In stock-raising region, it is trading center for wool and hides. Has modern administrative bldgs., airfield. Its port is La Paloma, 16 mi. SE on the Atlantic.

Rocha, Lake, fresh-water lagoon (□ c.45), Rocha dept., SE Uruguay, S of Rocha city. Has intermittent outlet to near-by Atlantic.

Rocha River, Bolivia: see CAINE RIVER.

Rochdale (rŏch′dāl), county borough (1931 pop. 90,263; 1951 census 87,734), SE Lancashire, England, on Roch R. and 10 mi. NNE of Manchester; cotton- and woolen-milling center; mfg. (machinery, chemicals, plastics, pharmaceuticals, asbestos, paper, carpets, electrical equipment). Hq. of Br. cooperative movement, founded here 1844 by a group known as Rochdale Pioneers. John Bright b. here. Rochdale was for many years seat of the Byron family. County borough includes (NNW) town of Shawclough (shô′klŭf), with cotton milling and electrical engineering, and the cotton-milling towns of Castleton (SSW), Smallbridge (NE), and Spotland (SE).

Rochdale. 1 Village, Mass.: see LEICESTER. **2** Village (pop. 1,219), Dutchess co., SE N.Y.

Roche (rōch), town and parish (pop. 1,965), central Cornwall, England, 7 mi. SW of Bodmin; China-clay mining.

Roche or **Roche-les-Beaupré** (rôsh-lā-bōprā′), village (pop. 853), Doubs dept., E France, on Doubs R. and Rhone-Rhine Canal, and 5 mi NE of Besançon; ethyl-alcohol mfg.

Roche, La, or **La Roche-sur-Foron** (lä rôsh′-sür-fôrô′), town (pop. 3,218), Haute-Savoie dept., SE France, in Faucigny valley, 12 mi. SE of Geneva; market, cheese-mfg. center. Has 16th-cent. houses.

Roche-à-Bateau (rōsh-ä-bätō′), village (1950 pop. 502), Sud dept., SW Haiti, on Tiburon Peninsula, 15 mi. W of Les Cayes; basketmaking.

Roche-Bernard, La (–bĕrnär′), agr. village (pop. 1,013), Morbihan dept., W France, on Vilaine R. (bridge) and 13 mi. SW of Redon; road junction; fishing, woodworking.

Rochebrune, Mont (mõ rôshbrün′), summit (6,070 ft.) of Savoy Alps, 3 mi. S of Mégève (aerial tramway). Winter sports.

Rochebrune, Pic de (pēk dù rôshbrün′), peak (10,905 ft.) of Cottian Alps, in Hautes-Alpes dept., SE France, 9 mi. SE of Briançon, just E of Col d'Izoard.

Roche-Canillac, La (lä rôsh-känēyäk′), village (pop. 380), Corrèze dept., S central France, 11 mi. ESE of Tulle; mfg. of photographic materials.

Rochechouart (rôsh-shwär′), town (pop. 2,027), Haute-Vienne dept., W central France, 20 mi. W of Limoges; mfg. (footwear, aluminum paint, vegetable oil) Has 13th–16th-cent. castle.

Rochecorbon (rôshkôrbõ′), village (pop. 1,578), Indre-et-Loire dept., W central France, near Loire R., 3 mi. ENE of Tours; noted wines.

Roche-de-Rame, La (lä rôsh-dù-räm′), village (pop. 205), Hautes-Alpes dept., SE France, on upper Durance R. and 11 mi. SSW of Briançon, in Dauphiné Alps; electrochemical works (magnesium, cyanamide). Fish breeding.

Roche-Derrien, La (lä rôsh-dĕrēē′), agr. village (pop. 988), Côtes-du-Nord dept., W France, 9 mi. E of Lannion; hemp spinning, sawmilling.

Roche-en-Ardenne, La (rôsh-än-ärdĕn′), or **Laroche** (lärōsh′), town (pop. 1,807), Luxembourg prov., SE Belgium, on Ourthe R. and 14 mi. NNW of Bastogne, in the Ardennes; tourist resort; pig market. Ruins of 11th-cent. castle. Les Tombes, a number of prehistoric graves, is 3 mi. S. In Second World War most of town's houses were damaged or destroyed (Battle of the Bulge, 1944–45).

Rochefort (rôshfôr′), town (pop. 3,598), Namur prov., SE central Belgium, 7 mi. SW of Marche; tourist center, with limestone caves; chalk quarrying. Ruins of 13th-cent. castle. Chartered 1285.

Rochefort or **Rochefort-sur-Mer** (–sür-mâr′), town (pop. 22,930), Charente-Maritime dept., W France, on the Charente (10 mi. above its mouth into Bay of Biscay) and 18 mi. SSE of La Rochelle; fishing port, formerly an important naval base; aircraft-engine assembly plant, sawmills (working imported hardwoods); fish processing. Naval arsenal severely damaged in Second World War. Harbor accommodates vessels drawing less than 20 ft. Created (1666) by Colbert and fortified by Vauban, Rochefort lost in importance when Brest became chief Atlantic naval base during First World War. Here Lafayette embarked for his 1st trip to America. Near by Napoleon surrendered himself (1815) to a Br. warship bound for St. Helena. Pierre Loti b. here.

Rochefort-en-Terre (rôshfôr′-ã-târ′), village (pop. 632), Morbihan dept., W France, 19 mi. E of Vannes; slate quarries near by. Picturesque site.

Rochefort-Montagne (–mōtä′nyù), village (pop. 581), Puy-de-Dôme dept., central France, in Auvergne Mts. 15 mi. WSW of Clermont-Ferrand; footwear mfg.; cattle raising.

Rochefort-sur-Mer, France: see ROCHEFORT.

Rochefort-sur-Nenon (–sür-nùnõ′), village (pop. 220), Jura dept., E France, on the Doubs, on Rhone-Rhine Canal, and 4 mi. NE of Dôle; dairying, marble working.

Rochefoucauld, La (lä rôshfo͞okō′), town (pop. 2,347), Charente dept., W France, on the Tardoire and 13 mi. NE of Angoulême; mfg. (woolens, felt, bricks). Has fine castle with 12th-cent. keep and Renaissance spiral staircase.

Roche-la-Molière (rôsh-lä-môlyâr′), town (pop. 4,610), Loire dept., SE central France; 3 mi. W of Saint-Étienne; coal-mining center; mfg. of footwear and ammonia.

Roche-le-Peyroux (rôsh-lù-pāro͞o′), village (pop. 100). Corrèze dept., S central France, on Diège R. near its mouth into the Dordogne and 10 mi. SSE of Ussel; hydroelectric plant. Marèges dam (295 ft. high, 810 ft. long) and one of France's most modern hydroelectric installations supplying power to railroads, on Dordogne R. 2 mi. WSW.

Roche-les-Beaupré, Doubs dept., France: see ROCHE.

Rochelle (rōshĕl′). **1** City (pop. 1,097), Wilcox co., S central Ga., 17 mi. E of Cordele; mfg. (lumber, naval stores). **2** City (pop. 5,449), Ogle co., N Ill., 23 mi. S of Rockford; trade, processing, and shipping center in rich agr. area; mfg. (clothing, canned foods, filters, worsted yarn, Diesel locomotives). Corn, wheat, oats, truck, livestock, poultry, dairy products. Inc. 1869. **3** Village (1940 pop. 1,150), Grant parish, central La., 34 mi. N of Alexandria, and on Little R. just below its formation by junction of Dugdemona R. and Bayou Castor; lumber milling. **4** Village (pop. c.500), McCulloch co., central Texas, 10 mi. NE of Brady; trade point in farm area.

Rochelle, La (lä rôshĕl′), city (pop. 45,864), ⊙ Charente-Maritime dept., W France, on Bay of Biscay opposite Île de Ré, 75 mi. SSE of Nantes. With its outer port of La Pallice (3 mi. W) it is an important terminus for transatlantic shipping, and France's leading fishing port on the Atlantic. Has large chemical industry (superphosphates, acids, pharmaceuticals) based on imports; boat building, fish processing and canning. Other mfg.: plastics, cement, perfumes, jewelry. Railroad yards and workshops. Chief exports: brandy, casein. Picturesque old fishing port in heart of city, the Renaissance town hall, its stately, arcade-lined streets, and remnants of city walls make La Rochelle a tourist center. Only outlying districts and La Pallice damaged in Second World War. Chartered 12th cent., it soon became a leading Fr. seaport. Huguenot stronghold during Wars of Religion, resisted Catholic besiegers for 6 months (1572–73). Fell to Cardinal Richelieu after a 14-month siege (1627–28). Refortified by Vauban. Revocation (1685) of Edict of Nantes by Louis XIV resulted in foundation of New Rochelle, N.Y., by Protestant refugees. City prospered again as trade center with Canada until France lost that colony. La Rochelle has never regained its former importance despite construction (1880s) of modern La Pallice harbor, near by, with facilities for ocean-going vessels unable to reach La Rochelle.

Rochelle Park (rōshĕl′), village in Rochelle Park township (pop. 4,483), Bergen co., NE N.J., on Saddle R. and 5 mi. E of Paterson; mfg. (toys, testing devices, pumps, monuments, chemicals, hypodermic needles).

Rochemaure (rôshmōr′), village (pop. 347), Ardèche dept., S France, on Rhone R. and 3 mi. NW of Montélimar, at foot of Monts du Coiron; has ruins of medieval castle.

Roche Percée (rŏsh pûr′sē), village (pop. estimate 100), SE Sask., on Souris R. and 10 mi. ESE of Estevan, near N.Dak. border; coal mining.

Rocheport (rōsh′pôrt), town (pop. 376), Boone co., central Mo., on Missouri R. and 12 mi. W of Columbia.

Roche-Posay, La (lä rôsh-pōzā′), village (pop. 968), Vienne dept., W central France, on the Creuse and 13 mi. ESE of Châtellerault; spa with mineral springs. Has 12th–14th-cent. tower and ramparts.

Rocheservière (rôsh-sĕrvyâr′), village (pop. 803), Vendée dept., W France, 19 mi. SSE of Nantes; cattle raising.

Roche's Point (rō'chĭz), promontory on E side of entrance to Cork Harbour, SE Co. Cork, Ireland, 5 mi. SE of Cóbh; lighthouse (51°48'N 8°15'W).

Rochester (rŏ'chĭstůr), town (pop. 1,549), N Victoria, Australia, on Campaspe R. and 100 mi. NNW of Melbourne; commercial center for livestock area; cheese factory.

Rochester, village (pop. estimate 200), central Alta., on Tawatinaw R. and 50 mi. N of Edmonton; coal mining, mixed farming; wheat, stock.

Rochester, municipal borough (1931 pop. 31,193; 1951 census 43,899), N Kent, England, on Medway R. estuary just WNW of Chatham; has important aircraft and tractor works. It was site of important Roman settlement of *Durobrivae*. In 604 St. Augustine founded an Episcopal cathedral; in 11th cent. Bishop Gundulf (builder of Tower of London) built a new cathedral, of which there are remains; the present cathedral is a later structure and contains tombs of Bishop Gundulf and St. Paulinus. There are ruins of 12th-cent. castle, built by William de Corbeuil, besieged several times in 13th and 14th cent. A hosp. for lepers founded 1316; Sir John Hawkins established hosp. for mariners (1592). In 1688 James II embarked here in flight to France. Near by is Charles Dickens's home, Gadshill. In municipal borough but across the river are towns of Strood (pop. 5,760) and Frindsbury (pop. 6,835).

Rochester (rŏ'chĕ"stůr, rŏ'chĭstůr). **1** Village (pop. 506), Sangamon co., central Ill., near South Fork of Sangamon R., 6 mi. SE of Springfield, in agr. and bituminous-coal area. **2** City (pop. 4,673), ⊙ Fulton co., N Ind., near L. Manitou (c.2 mi. long) and Tippecanoe R., 24 mi. NNE of Logansport, in agr. area (soybeans, grain); resort; cement products, canned goods, dairy products. Laid out and chartered in 1832. **3** Town (pop. 372), Butler co., W Ky., on Green R., near mouth of Mud R., and 29 mi. WNW of Bowling Green. **4** Town (pop. 1,328), Plymouth co., SE Mass., near head of Buzzards Bay, 9 mi. NE of New Bedford; agr., lumber mills. Settled c.1638, inc. 1686. **5** Village (pop. 4,279), Oakland co., SE Mich., 9 mi. NE of Pontiac and on Clinton R., in diversified farm area; textile and paper milling. The Parke Davis Biological Farm is near by. Settled 1817, inc. 1869. **6** City (pop. 29,885), ⊙ Olmsted co., SE Minn., on branch of Zumbro R. and c.70 mi. SE of St. Paul; commercial center for grain, livestock, poultry area; dairy products, canned vegetables, beverages; mfg. (hosp. supplies, agr. equipment). It is famed as the seat of the Mayo Clinic. Junior col. and state hosp. for insane are here; airport is in outskirts. Settled 1854, inc. 1858. Growth greatly stimulated by establishment of Mayo medical center (1889) by Dr. W. W. Mayo and his sons, Charles and William. Prominent feature of city is Mayo Clinic bldg., 22-story structure completed 1929. There is large transient pop. because of medical center. **7** Industrial city (pop. 13,776), Strafford co., SE N.H., along Cocheco and Salmon Falls rivers just NW of Dover; mfg. (woolens, shoes, wood products, paper, brick); printing. Includes industrial suburbs of Gonic and East Rochester. Town inc. 1722, settled 1728, city inc. 1891. **8** Port and industrial city (pop. 332,488), ⊙ Monroe co., W N.Y., at mouth of Genesee R. (water power) on L. Ontario, 65 mi. ENE of Buffalo, in fruit and truck area. State's 3d-largest city; mfg. center (especially photographic and optical equipment and supplies, clothing, thermometers and other instruments, business machines, chemicals). Also makes furniture, telephone and radio equipment, dental supplies, railway signals, stone products, confectionery, canned foods, flour, gears; printing; meat packing. Port of entry, handling large volume of lake shipping; Barge Canal passes just S of city. Here are the Eastman Kodak, Bausch and Lomb, and Taylor Instrument companies. Seat of Univ. of Rochester, with Eastman School of Music and noted medical center; Rochester Inst. of Technology, Nazareth Col., St. Bernard's Seminary, Colgate-Rochester Divinity School. Philharmonic, Civic, and Eastman orchestras have made city a musical center. Highland Park, with noted lilac gardens, and the many nurseries in city have earned for Rochester the name "Flower City." Points of interest: Ontario Beach and many other parks, Rochester Mus. of Arts and Sciences, Memorial Art Gall., and Rundel Memorial Bldg., with public library and art gall. Permanent settlement by Col. Nathaniel Rochester and others began in 1812; inc. as village in 1817, as city in 1834. Coming of the Erie Canal, and the Civil War and the 2 world wars brought successive periods of industrial expansion. Flour milling was 1st important industry. George Eastman was prominent in the city's growth; Susan B. Anthony lived here; and Frederick Douglass carried on his antislavery work here. **9** Village (pop. 178), Lorain co., N Ohio, 19 mi. SSW of Elyria and on West Branch of Black R. **10** Borough (pop. 7,197), Beaver co., W Pa., on Ohio R., at mouth of Beaver R., and 24 mi. NW of Pittsburgh; abrasives, food products, batteries, boxes, machinery. Shale and sandstone near by. Originally an Indian town; early 19th-cent. river port. Settled 1799, laid out c.1835, inc. 1838. **11** Town (pop. 773), Haskell co., NW central Texas, c.60 mi. N of Abilene; shipping, cotton-ginning point in agr. area (cotton, corn, wheat); cottonseed-oil mill. **12** Resort town (pop. 937), Windsor co., central Vt., on White R. and 27 mi. SW of Barre, in Green Mts.; wood and dairy products, poultry, maple sugar; talc. Winter sports. **13** Village (pop. 333), Racine co., SE Wis., on Fox R. and 26 mi. SW of Milwaukee, in dairy region.

Roche-sur-Foron, La, Haute-Savoie dept., France: see ROCHE, LA.

Roche-sur-Yon, La (lä rôsh-sür-yō'), town (pop. 15,278), ⊙ Vendée dept., W France, on the Yon (tributary of Lay R.) and 38 mi. SSE of Nantes; transportation and agr. trade center; tanning, printing; mfg. of nails and needles; antimony deposits near by. The town was planned and founded 1805 by Napoleon. Named Napoléon-Vendée under the 2 Empires, and Bourbon-Vendée, 1814–48.

Rochette, La (lä rôshĕt'), village (pop. 942), Savoie dept., SE France, on NW slope of Belledonne range (Dauphiné Alps), 12 mi. SE of Chambéry; mfg. (cartons, tanning extracts), silk, sawmilling.

Rochford (rŏch'fůrd), town and parish (pop. 3,009), SE Essex, England, on short Roach R. and 3 mi. N of Southend-on-Sea; agr. market. Has remains of Rochford Hall, residence of Boleyn family and reputed birthplace of Anne Boleyn. Church dates from 15th cent.

Rochlitz (rôkh'lĭts), town (pop. 7,872), Saxony, E central Germany, on the Zwickauer Mulde and 16 mi. NNW of Chemnitz; woolen and rayon milling; mfg. of electrical equipment, shoes, leather, musical instruments, jewelry, cigars. Important porphyry quarries near by. Has 15th-cent. church, 14th-cent. castle. Noted monastery church of Wechselburg is 3 mi. SSW.

Rochlitz an der Iser, Czechoslovakia: see ROKYTNICE NAD JIZEROU.

Roch River (rōch), SE Lancashire, England, rises 2 mi. NNE of Littleborough, flows 12 mi. SW, past Littleborough and Rochdale, to Irwell R. 2 mi. S of Bury.

Rochussen River, Netherlands New Guinea: see MAMBERAMO RIVER.

Rociana (rō-thyä'nä), town (pop. 5,894), Huelva prov., SW Spain, 19 mi. E of Huelva; agr. center (grapes, wheat, corn, barley, tubers, livestock; apiculture); lumbering; alcohol, wine making.

Rociu (rô'chōō), village (pop. 1,340), Arges prov., S central Rumania, 15 mi. SE of Pitesti; orchards.

Rock. 1 County (□ 485; pop. 11,278), extreme SW Minn.; ⊙ Luverne. Agr. area bordering on S.Dak. and Iowa; drained by Rock R. Livestock, corn, oats, barley, potatoes. Formed 1857. **2** County (□ 1,012; pop. 3,026), N Nebr.; ⊙ Bassett; agr. area bounded N by Niobrara R. Livestock, grain. Formed 1888. **3** County (□ 721; pop. 92,778), S Wis., on Ill. line (S); ⊙ Janesville. Drained by Rock and Sugar rivers and Turtle Creek. Rich agr. area (grain, tobacco; dairy products; livestock, poultry). Diversified mfg. (machinery, automobiles, Diesel engines, textiles, fountain pens, and many other products). Winter sports in Beloit area; has resorts near L. Koshkonong. Formed 1836.

Rock, The, village, Australia: see THE ROCK.

Rockabema Lake (rŏk"ūbē'mů), Aroostook co., E central Maine, 26 mi. WNW of Houlton, in hunting, fishing area; 1.5 mi. long.

Rockabill, islet of The Skerries, in the Irish Sea, 5 mi. ENE of Skerries town, NE Co. Dublin, Ireland; lighthouse (53°36'N 6°W).

Rockall (rŏk'ôl), islet in the N Atlantic, c.225 mi. W of the Hebrides; 57°36'N 13°41'W.

Rockaway (rŏ'kůwā). **1** Borough (pop. 3,812), Morris co., N N.J., on Rockaway R. and 17 mi. W of Paterson, on old Morris Canal; mfg. (machinery, metal products, lamps, boxes); dye works; agr., timber. Settled 1739, inc. 1894. **2** City (pop. 1,027), Tillamook co., NW Oregon, on Pacific Ocean and 12 mi. NNW of Tillamook; summer resort. Inc. 1942.

Rockaway Beach. 1 Shore resort (pop. c.250), San Mateo co., W Calif., on the Pacific, 11 mi. S of downtown San Francisco. **2** Section of New York city, N.Y.: see ROCKAWAY PENINSULA.

Rockaway Inlet, SE N.Y., passage connecting Jamaica Bay with the Atlantic, at W tip of Rockaway Peninsula.

Rockaway Peninsula (c.12 mi. long), SE N.Y., extending from (and generally parallel to) S shore of Long Isl., bet. the Atlantic and Jamaica Bay; its W tip (Rockaway Point) marks NE side of entrance to New York Bay. Along Atlantic shore is Rockaway Beach (resorts). Part of Queens borough of New York city; has resort and commuters' communities (Far Rockaway, Rockaway Beach, Rockaway Park, Arverne, Edgemere, Belle Harbor, Neponsit). Site of U.S. Fort Tilden (1917) and Jacob Riis Park (1937). Cross Bay Parkway and a railroad bridge span Jamaica Bay from peninsula to Long Isl., and Marine Parkway Bridge crosses Rockaway Inlet, the passage connecting Jamaica Bay with the Atlantic at tip of peninsula.

Rockaway River, N N.J., rises in NW Morris co., flows c.35 mi. SW, E, and SE, past Dover and Boonton (here dammed to form Parsippany Reservoir), to Passaic R. W of Caldwell.

Rockbridge, county (□ 604; pop. 23,359), W Va.; ⊙ Lexington. At S end of Shenandoah Valley, with mts. in W and NW, the Blue Ridge (here cut by James R.) in E and SE; also drained by North R. Includes part of George Washington Natl. Forest. Scenic mtn. resort area; medicinal springs, NATURAL BRIDGE attract visitors. Livestock raising, dairying, fruitgrowing; mfg. at BUENA VISTA (in but independent of co.). Rock quarrying, lumber milling. Formed 1778.

Rockbridge, village (pop. 243), Greene co., SW central Ill., 25 mi. N of Alton, in agr. and bituminous-coal area.

Rockcastle, county (□ 312; pop. 13,925), central Ky.; ⊙ Mt. Vernon. Bounded SE by Rockcastle R.; drained by Dix R. and several creeks. Hilly agr. area (livestock, grain, burley tobacco); bituminous-coal mines, limestone and sandstone quarries, oil wells; timber. Includes part of Cumberland Natl. Forest and Great Saltpeter Caves (near Mt. Vernon). Formed 1810.

Rockcastle River, SE Ky., formed in N Laurel co. by small headstreams, flows 53 mi. S to Cumberland R. 14 mi. ESE of Burnside.

Rock City, village (pop. 157), Stephenson co., N Ill., 11 mi. NE of Freeport, in agr. area.

Rockcliffe Park, residential village (pop. 1,480), SE Ont., on S shore of Ottawa R., just E of Ottawa.

Rock Creek, village, S B.C., near Wash. border, on Kettle R. and 24 mi. W of Grand Forks; silver, lead, zinc mining.

Rock Creek, village (pop. 604), Ashtabula co., extreme NE Ohio, 14 mi. S of Ashtabula and on small Rock Creek; sawmills.

Rock Creek. 1 In Ill., rises S of Lanark, flows c.45 mi. SSW, past Morrison, to Rock R. below Prophetstown. **2** In Md. and Dist. of Columbia, rises just S of Laytonsville in Montgomery co., Md., flows c.30 mi. S, past Garrett Park, Kensington, and Forest Glen in Md., and through Rock Creek Park and Natl. Zoological Park in Washington, to the Potomac at Georgetown. **3** In SE Wyo., rises in N Medicine Bow Mts., flows 81 mi. NE, past Rock River town, and W to Medicine Bow R. near Medicine Bow.

Rock Creek Butte, highest peak (9,097 ft.) in Elkhorn Ridge, NE Oregon, 14 mi. W of Baker.

Rockdale, municipality (pop. 47,290), E New South Wales, Australia, 7 mi. SW of Sydney, in metropolitan area; mfg. center (shoe factories, brass foundries, knitting mills).

Rockdale, county (□ 128; pop. 8,464), N central Ga.; ⊙ Conyers. Piedmont area drained by Yellow and South rivers. Agr. (cotton, corn, truck, grain, fruit, livestock) and textile mfg. Formed 1870.

Rockdale. 1 Village (pop. 1,393), Will co., NE Ill., on Des Plaines R., just SW of Joliet, in agr. and bituminous-coal area; makes firebrick. Inc. 1903. **2** City (pop. 2,321), Milam co., central Texas, c.50 mi. NE of Austin; market, processing center for cotton, corn, truck, poultry area. Aluminum plant; lignite mine, oil wells; oil refining. Settled 1873, inc. 1874 **3** Village (pop. 161), Dane co., S Wis., on small Koshkonong Creek and 18 mi. ESE of Madison, in dairying and tobacco-growing region.

Rockdale Junction, village (pop. 2,820), Will co., NE Ill., just NW of Joliet.

Rockefeller Plateau, part of Antarctic plateau in W Marie Byrd Land; center at 80°S 135°W. Rises 2,500–4,500 ft. Discovered 1934 by R. E. Byrd.

Röcken (rû'kůn), village (pop. 387), in former Prussian Saxony prov., central Germany, after 1945 in Saxony-Anhalt, 7 mi. ENE of Weissenfels. Nietzsche b. and buried here.

Rockenhausen (rô"kůnhou'zůn), town (pop. 2,450), Rhenish Palatinate, W Germany, 15 mi. SSW of Bad Kreuznach; wine. Lumber milling, tanning; limestone quarrying. Chartered 1332.

Rocker, W suburb of Butte, Silver Bow co., SW Mont.; oil products, mine timbers.

Rockfall, Conn.: see MIDDLEFIELD.

Rock Falls. 1 Industrial city (pop. 7,983), Whiteside co., NW Ill., on Rock R. (bridged here), opposite Sterling; makes farm machinery, builders' hardware. Platted 1837, inc. 1889. **2** Town (pop. 139), Cerro Gordo co., N Iowa, on Shell Rock R. and 7 mi. ENE of Mason City. Sand and gravel pits near by. **3** Village (pop. c.100), Dunn co., W Wis., 12 mi. SW of Eau Claire, in dairying and farming area; canning.

Rock Ferry, England: see BIRKENHEAD.

Rockfish Gap, Va., pass (alt. 1,850 ft.) across the Blue Ridge, just SE of Waynesboro.

Rockfish River, central Va., rises in W Albemarle co., flows c.40 mi. S and SE to James R. 12 mi. E of Lovingston.

Rockford (rŏk'fůrd). **1** Town (pop. 373), ⊙ Coosa co., E central Ala., 35 mi. N of Montgomery; lumber. **2** City (pop. 92,927), ⊙ Winnebago co., N Ill., on both banks of Rock R. (power dam) and c.75 mi. WNW of Chicago; important industrial, shipping, and trade center for wide agr. area; seat of Rockford Col. Mfg.: farm machinery, machine tools, hosiery and knit goods, furniture, airplane and automobile parts, hardware, stone and cement products, air conditioning, electrical and heating equipment, sewing machines, pianos, boxes, paints and varnish, wire goods, leather products. Has large Swedish pop. Indian mounds here. U.S. Camp Grant near by was active in Second World War. Founded 1834 at a stagecoach ford; inc. 1839. **3** Town (pop. 979), Floyd co., N Iowa, on Shell Rock R. at mouth of Lime Creek, and 13 mi. W of Charles City; brick and tile plant. **4** City (pop. 1,937), Kent co., SW Mich., 12 mi. NNE of Grand Rapids and on short Rogue R., in farm area (livestock, potatoes, grain, hay); dairy products; mfg. of leather, shoes, gloves. Resort. Settled 1841; inc. as village 1871, as city 1933. **5** Village (pop. 369), Hennepin and Wright counties, S central Minn., on Crow R. and 25 mi. WNW of Minneapolis; dairy products. **6** Village (pop. 1,112), Mercer co., W Ohio, on St. Marys R. and 10 mi. N of Celina, in agr. region; tomato canneries; limestone quarries. **7** Town (pop. 360), Spokane co., E Wash., near Idaho line, 20 mi. SE of Spokane; wheat, peas, oats, livestock.

Rock Fort, spa and gardens, St. Andrew parish, S Jamaica, in E outskirts of Kingston. Has baths with curative waters. Site of old fort (built 1694). Adjoining is Bournemouth Bath.

Rockglen, village (pop. 278), S Sask., 32 mi. S of Assiniboia, near Mont. border; wheat; in coal-mining region.

Rock Hall, fishing and resort town (pop. 786), Kent co., E Md., 10 mi. SE of Chestertown. Ships oysters, crabs, fish; tomato cannery, shirt factory. Sport fishing.

Rockham (rŏk'hăm, rŏ'kŭm), town (pop. 113), Faulk co., NE central S.Dak., 17 mi. SE of Faulkton; grain market.

Rockhampton, city and port (pop. 34,988), E Queensland, Australia, on Fitzroy R., 49 mi. from its mouth on Keppel Bay, and 325 mi. NNW of Brisbane; 23°24'S 150°31'E, near Tropic of Capricorn. Principal port for livestock and mining regions of central Queensland; rail center. Port of Rockhampton comprises PORT ALMA on coast, and wharves at city itself. Exports wool, gold, coal, copper, hides, meat. Founded 1858 with discovery of gold near by.

Rock Harbor. 1 Village Fla.: see KEY LARGO. **2** Village, Mass.: see ORLEANS. **3** Village, Mich.: see ISLE ROYALE NATIONAL PARK.

Rock Hill. 1 Town (pop. 3,847), St. Louis co., E Mo., near Mississippi R., W of St. Louis. Inc. 1929. **2** City (pop. 24,502), York co., N S.C., near Catawba R., 25 mi. SSW of Charlotte, N.C.; textile-milling center; large rayon plant, cotton, rug, and hosiery mills; wood and concrete products, beverages, chemicals, mattresses. Seat of Winthrop Col. Catawba R. is dammed 6 mi. N (hydroelectric power), forming Catawba L. Catawba Indian Reservation is 10 mi. SE. City settled in mid-19th cent., inc. 1870.

Rockhill or Rockhill Furnace, borough (pop. 567), Huntingdon co., S central Pa., 10 mi. S of Mount Union.

Rockingham (rŏ'kĭng-ŭm), village (pop. 495), SW Western Australia, 15 mi. S of Fremantle; seaside resort.

Rockingham (rŏ'kĭnghăm"). **1** County (□ 691; pop. 70,059), SE N.H., on the coast; ⊙ Exeter. Mfg. (textiles, shoes, wood products), agr., shipping at Portsmouth; resorts on coast and lakes. Drained by Piscataqua, Exeter, and Lamprey rivers (water power). State's 1st settlement made 1623 near Portsmouth. Formed 1769. **2** County (□ 572; pop. 64,816), N N.C., on Va. line; ⊙ Wentworth. Piedmont tobacco and timber area; drained by Dan and Haw rivers; textile mills, cigarette factories, sawmills. Formed 1785. **3** County (□ 869; pop. 35,079), NW Va.; co. courthouse is at HARRISONBURG, in but independent of co. Partly in central Shenandoah Valley; bounded W, NW, N by W.Va.; the Alleghenies are in W and NW, Massanutten Mtn. in E center, Blue Ridge along SE border. Drained by North and South rivers, here joining to form South Fork of the Shenandoah. Scenic areas include part of George Washington Natl. Forest and of Shenandoah Natl. Park; traversed by Skyline Drive and Appalachian Trail; limestone caves attract visitors. Diversified agr. (grain, apples, peaches); a leading poultry co. (especially turkeys); dairying, livestock raising. Mfg. at Harrisonburg. Limestone quarrying; timber. Formed 1778.

Rockingham. 1 Town (pop. 3,356), ⊙ Richmond co., S N.C., 60 mi. ESE of Charlotte, near S.C. line; cotton, woolen, paper, and lumber mills. Settled c.1780; inc. 1887. **2** Town (pop. 5,499), Windham co., SE Vt., on the Connecticut and 20 mi. N of Brattleboro. Includes villages of BELLOWS FALLS and Saxtons River (pop. 715), seat of Vermont Acad., at mouth of small Saxtons R. (c.20 mi. long). Has Congregational church, built 1787. Settled c.1753.

Rockingham Bay, inlet of Coral Sea, E Queensland, Australia, bet. Cape Sandwich of Hinchinbrook Isl. (S) and Dunk Isl. (N); 17 mi. long. 14 mi. wide. Contains small Goold Isl. Cardwell on SW shore.

Rockingham Park, N.H.: see SALEM.

Rock Island, village (pop. 1,395), S Que., 40 mi. SE of Granby, on Vt. border; mfg. of machine tools, clothing, skis; dairying, granite quarrying. Stanstead is near.

Rock Island, county (□ 420; pop. 133,558), NW Ill.; ⊙ ROCK ISLAND, farm-machinery mfg. center. Bounded N and W by the Mississippi and partly E by Rock R.; drained by Rock R. Includes Black Hawk and Campbell's Island state parks and part of a natl. wildlife refuge. Other mfg.; bituminous-coal mines, clay pits; agr. (livestock, corn, wheat, oats, poultry; dairy products.) Formed 1831.

Rock Island. 1 City (pop. 48,710), ⊙ Rock Island co., NW Ill., on the Mississippi (power dam) near mouth of Rock R., adjacent to MOLINE and East Moline and opposite DAVENPORT (Iowa); these 4 cities comprise the Quad-Cities group (cities are joined by several bridges). One of world's leading farm-equipment and -machinery centers. Huge U.S. Rock Island Arsenal (established 1862) is on Rock Isl. in the Mississippi. Distribution, transportation, trade, and insurance center; railroad shops; mfg. of bakery equipment, foundry products, electrical and heating equipment, concrete and wood products, hardware, rubber shoes, clothing. Seat of Augustana Col., Augustana Theological Seminary. Has natl. cemetery. Black Hawk State Park, with mus., is adjacent to city. Founded as Stephenson; renamed Rock Island and inc. 1841. Closely paralleled in its growth by Moline during 1840s and 1850s, when steamboating and lumber-milling became important; 1st railroad bridge across the Mississippi was built here in 1855. Farm-implements industry (founded 1847 at Moline) grew as lumber and steamboat traffic began to vanish from the river after the Civil War. **2** Town (pop. 152), Douglas co., central Wash., 8 mi. SE of Wenatchee and on Columbia R. Rock Island Dam in the river was completed 1931.

Rock Island, island, Wis.: see WASHINGTON ISLAND.

Rocklake or Rock Lake, village (pop. 385), Towner co., N N.Dak., 20 mi. N of Cando, on small Rock L., site of U.S. waterfowl sanctuary.

Rock Lake, Jefferson co., S Wis., 20 mi. E of Madison; c.3 mi. long; outlet to Crawfish R. Town of Lake Mills is on E shore. At bottom of lake are large stone pyramids thought to have been built by prehistoric Indians.

Rockland, town (pop. 2,040), SE Ont., on Ottawa R. and 22 mi. ENE of Ottawa; lumber and flour milling, woodworking. In mica-mining, poultry-raising region.

Rockland, county (□ 178; pop. 89,276), SE N.Y.; ⊙ New City. Bounded E by the Hudson (here widening into Tappan Zee), and SW and S by N.J. line; includes part of the Ramapos. Drained by Hackensack and Ramapo rivers. Has many residential communities of New York city commuters; summer resorts. Farming (truck, fruit), dairying; hothouse flowers and vegetables. Some mfg. at Haverstraw, Nyack, Pearl River, Spring Valley, Suffern. Contains several sections of Palisades Interstate Park, including Bear Mtn. recreational area. Formed 1798.

Rockland. 1 Village (pop. 277), Power co., SE Idaho, 15 mi. S of American Falls; alt. 4,633 ft.; wheat. **2** City (pop. 9,234), ⊙ Knox co., S Maine, on W shore of Penobscot Bay and 35 mi. ESE of Augusta. Resort (with yacht harbor), trade center; fishing place, noted for lobsters; port of entry; quarries and processes limestone, ships lime. Settled c.1770; town inc. 1848 as East Thomaston, city inc. 1854. **3** Town (pop. 8,960), Plymouth co., E Mass., 18 mi. SSE of Boston, ENE of Brockton; mfg. (shoes, abrasives), printing; poultry, dairy. Settled 1673, set off from Abington 1874. **4** Resort village, Sullivan co., SE N.Y., on Beaver Kill and 14 mi. NW of Liberty. Lakes near by. **5** Village (pop. 216), La Crosse co., W Wis., 16 mi. ENE of La Crosse, in dairy and livestock area.

Rockland Lake, resort village, Rockland co., SE N.Y., on Rockland L. (1 mi. long), 3 mi. N of Nyack, near W bank of the Hudson.

Rockledge. 1 City (pop. 1,347), Brevard co., central Fla., on Indian R. lagoon, just S of Cocoa. **2** Borough (pop. 2,261), Montgomery co., SE Pa., 9 mi. NNE of Philadelphia. Settled 1880, inc. 1893.

Rockleigh (rŏk'lē), borough (pop. 110), Bergen co., extreme NE N.J., at N.Y. line, 1 mi. SE of Tappan, N.Y.

Rock Lick, W.Va.: see MINDEN.

Rocklin, town (pop. 1,155), Placer co., central Calif., 20 mi. NE of Sacramento; ships fruit.

Rockmart, city (pop. 3,821), Polk co., NW Ga., 19 mi. SSE of Rome; mfg. (tire fabric, yarn, bedspreads, cement, boxes, lumber); limestone quarrying. Inc. 1872.

Rock Point, summer-resort village, Charles co., S Md., on Wicomico R. near its mouth on the Potomac, and c.45 mi. SSE of Washington; amusement park near by.

Rockport. 1 City (pop. 2,493), ⊙ Spencer co., SW Ind., on Ohio R. and 29 mi. ESE of Evansville, in agr. and oil- and natural gas-producing area; mfg. (brick, tile, concrete blocks, buttons, flour); clay pits. Recreation area at L. Alda (artificial). Lincoln Pioneer Village, a memorial with reconstructed pioneer homes, is here. Settled 1807. **2** Town (pop. 450), Ohio co., W Ky., on Green R. and 31 mi. SSE of Owensboro, in bituminous-coal and agr. area. **3** Resort and fishing town (pop. 1,656), Knox co., S Maine, on Penobscot Bay and just N of Rockland; large lobster-packing plant. Includes villages of Rockville and Glen Cove. Settled 1769, set off from Camden 1891. **4** Town (pop. 4,231), including Rockport village (pop. 2,911), Essex co., NE Mass., on Cape Ann N of Gloucester; summer resort and artists' colony; ships granite. Settled 1690, set off from Gloucester 1840. Includes resort village of Pigeon Cove. **5** City (pop. 1,511), ⊙ Atchison co., NW Mo., near Nishnabotna R., 55 mi. NW of St. Joseph; corn, wheat, livestock. Platted 1851. **6** City (pop. 2,266), ⊙ Aransas co., S Texas, on Aransas Bay 26 mi. NE of Corpus Christi, and on channel to Gulf Intracoastal Waterway; tourist resort (beaches, fishing, duck hunting); fisheries (fish, shrimp, oysters). Carbon black plant. Seat of a state marine laboratory. Founded 1868.

Rock Rapids, city (pop. 2,640), ⊙ Lyon co., extreme NW Iowa, near Minn. line, on Rock R. and c.65 mi. NNE of Sioux City; rail junction; mfg. (feed, concrete blocks, dairy products). Sand and gravel pits near by. Inc. 1886.

Rock River, town (pop. 424), Albany co., SE Wyo., on Rock Creek and 35 mi. NNW of Laramie; alt. 6,705 ft. Trade and shipping center for livestock and oil.

Rock River. 1 In Minn. and Iowa, formed by confluence of 2 forks in Pipestone co., SW Minn., flows generally S, past Luverne, into NW Iowa, past Rock Rapids, to Big Sioux R. 6 mi. N of Hawarden; 100 mi. long. **2** In Wis. and Ill., rises in Fond du Lac co., E Wis., winds S and SW, past Janesville and Beloit, into Ill., thence S and SW, past Rockton, Rockford, Dixon, and Rock Falls, to the Mississippi just below Rock Island city; c.285 mi. long. Extensive power developments. Widens near Koshkonong (Wis.) into L. Koshkonong (c.6 mi. long, c.3 mi. wide).

Rock Sound, town (pop. 735), central Bahama Isls., on inlet of S central Eleuthera Isl., 20 mi. S of Governor's Harbour, 75 mi. ESE of Nassau; 24°55'N 76°12'W. Pineapples, tomatoes.

Rock Springs. 1 Village (pop. 442), Sauk co., S central Wis., on Baraboo R. and 8 mi. W of Baraboo, in dairying region. Until 1947, called Ableman. **2** City (pop. 10,857), Sweetwater co., SW Wyo., on Bitter Creek and 230 mi. WNW of Cheyenne; alt. c.6,270 ft. Trade center in mining and livestock region; hunting and fishing supplies. Coal mines, oil wells near by. Annual event is International Night, with songs and dances by various resident nationalities. City settled in 1860s.

Rocksprings, town (pop. 1,436), ⊙ Edwards co., SW Texas, on Edwards Plateau near headwaters of Colorado and Nueces rivers and c.60 mi. NE of Del Rio; trading center for goat- and sheep-ranching region; important mohair market; tourist center. Settled 1887, inc. 1924; rebuilt after 1927 tornado.

Rockstone, village, Demerara co., N central Br. Guiana, on right bank of Essequibo R. and 29 mi. S of Bartica. A railroad to Wismar (15 mi. E, on the Demerara) circumvents near-by rapids.

Rockton. 1 Village (pop. 1,432), Winnebago co., N Ill., at junction of Rock and Pecatonica rivers (both bridged here), 12 mi. N of Rockford, near Wis. line; agr.; mfg. (boxboard, salt, feed). Inc. 1847. **2** Village, Fairfield co., N central S.C., 25 mi. N of Columbia; granite quarries.

Rockvale, town (pop. 380), Fremont co., S central Colo., near Arkansas R., 30 mi. WNW of Pueblo; alt. 5,260 ft.; coal mining. Part of San Isabel Natl. Forest near by.

Rock Valley, town (pop. 1,581), Sioux co., NW Iowa, near S.Dak. line, on Rock R. and c.50 mi. N of Sioux City; ships sand and gravel; makes concrete blocks, dairy products. Inc. 1888.

Rockville. 1 City (pop. 8,016), ⊙ Tolland co., N central Conn., in Vernon town, on Shenipsit L., at source of Hockanum R. (water power); mfg. (textiles, envelopes, fishline). Chartered 1889. **2** Residential town (pop. 2,467), ⊙ Parke co., W Ind., 23 mi. NNE of Terre Haute, in agr., bituminous-coal, and timber area. A state tuberculosis sanatorium is here. Settled 1823, inc. 1854. **3** Residential town (pop. 6,934), ⊙ Montgomery co. (since 1777), central Md., 15 mi. NNW of Washington, in agr. area (dairy products, grain); airport. Frequently raided by Confederates in Civil War. **4** Village (pop. 288), Stearns co., central Minn., on Sauk R. and 10 mi. SW of St. Cloud; dairy products. Granite quarries here. **5** City (pop. 372), Bates co., W Mo., near Osage R., 16 mi. E of Rich Hill; agr. **6** Village (pop. 164), Sherman co., central Nebr., 13 mi. SSE of Loup City and on Middle Loup R. **7** Village, Dauphin co., S central Pa., 5 mi. N of Harrisburg and on Susquehanna R., here crossed by stone-arch railroad bridge (3,798 ft. long). **8** Village (pop. c.260) in Hopkinton town, Washington co., SW R.I., 4 mi. N of Hopkinton village, near Conn. line, in agr. area; twine mfg. **9** Village, S.C.: see WADMALAW ISLAND.

Rockville Centre, residential village (pop. 22,362) Nassau co., SE N.Y., near S shore of W Long Isl., 8 mi. ESE of Jamaica, in poultry, truck, and dairying area; mfg. of machinery, lighting fixtures, metal and rubber products, stucco products, aircraft parts, screens, weather stripping, organ pipes; lithographing and publishing. Inc. 1870.

Rockwall, county (□ 147; pop. 6,156), NE Texas; ⊙ Rockwall. Smallest Texas co.; drained by East Fork of Trinity R. Agr. (cotton, corn, oats, truck); cattle, poultry, dairy products; some timber. Named for extensive geological formation resembling masonry wall. Formed 1873.

Rockwall, city (pop. 1,501), ⊙ Rockwall co., NE Texas, 21 mi. NE of Dallas, near East Fork of Trinity R.; trade, shipping point in agr. area (cotton, onions); cotton ginning, mfg. of clothing.

Rockwell. 1 Town (pop. 753), Cerro Gordo co., N Iowa, 12 mi. S of Mason City, in agr. area. Limestone quarry near by. **2** Town (pop. 852), Rowan co., W central N.C., 9 mi. SSE of Salisbury; textile mfg.

Rockwell City, city (pop. 2,333), ⊙ Calhoun co., central Iowa, 25 mi. WSW of Fort Dodge; rail junction; dairy products, feed. Has state reformatory for women. State park (N). Inc. 1882.

Rockwood, village (pop. estimate 600), S Ont., 7 mi. NE of Guelph; dairying, mixed farming, limestone quarrying. Site of noted Rockwood Academy.

Rockwood. 1 Village (pop. 175), Randolph co., SW Ill., on the Mississippi and 36 mi. W of Herrin, in agr. area. **2** Resort village (pop. 229), Somerset co., W central Maine, on W shore of Moosehead L., 46 mi. NNE of Bingham; steamer terminal. **3** Village (pop. 1,044), Wayne co., SE Mich., 20 mi. SSW of Detroit, near Huron R., in farm area. Inc. 1926. **4** Borough (pop. 1,237), Somerset co., SW Pa., 7 mi. SW of Somerset and on Casselman R.; bituminous coal; flour, lumber; agr. Laid out 1857, inc. 1885. **5** City (pop. 4,272), Roane co., E Tenn., near Tennessee R., 40 mi. W of Knoxville, in coal, iron, limestone, timber, farm area; mfg. of hosiery, staves, steel alloys; lumbering. Settled c.1816.

Rocky, town (pop. 366), Washita co., W Okla., 26 mi. SSW of Clinton; trade center for diversified farm area; cotton ginning.

Rocky Bottom, summer resort, Pickens co., NW S.C., 27 mi. NW of Greenville, in the Blue Ridge.

Rocky Comfort, town (pop. 230), McDonald co., extreme SW Mo., 18 mi. SE of Neosho.

Rocky Flats, Colo.: see BOULDER, city.

Rockyford, village (pop. 226), S Alta., 25 mi. SW of Drumheller; wheat.

Rocky Ford. 1 City (pop. 4,087), Otero co., SE central Colo., on Arkansas R. and 50 mi. ESE of Pueblo; alt. 4,250 ft. Trade and melon-shipping point in agr. area; mfg. (beet sugar, canned vegetables, dairy products, brooms, pumps, beverages); cantaloupes, livestock, poultry, truck products, flower and vegetable seeds. Melon Day is celebrated annually in Sept. Inc. 1887. **2** Town (pop. 278), Screven co., E Ga., 13 mi. WSW of Sylvania, near Ogeechee R.

Rocky Grove, village (pop. 3,111), Venango co., NW Pa., just NE of Franklin.

Rocky Hill. 1 Town (pop. 5,108), including Rocky Hill village (pop. 2,072), Hartford co., central Conn., on the Connecticut and 7 mi. S of Hartford; agr., mfg. (rayon yarn, chemicals, metal castings). State veterans' home here. Settled 1650, inc. 1843. **2** Borough (pop. 537), Somerset co., central N.J., 12 mi. SW of New Brunswick; makes terra cotta. Washington wrote his farewell address to the army here, 1783.

Rocky Island, China: see AMPHITRITE GROUP.

Rocky Island, islet in Cork Harbour, SE Co. Cork, Ireland, just S of Cóbh; used as magazine.

Rocky Mount. 1 Town (pop. 27), Meriwether co., W Ga., 22 mi. ENE of La Grange. **2** City (pop. 27,697), Nash and Edgecombe counties, E central N.C., 50 mi. ENE of Raleigh and on Tar R. Rail junction (repair shops); one of state's leading bright-leaf-tobacco and cotton markets; mfg. center with tobacco-processing plants, cotton, rayon, cordage, and lumber mills, fertilizer and cottonseed-oil factories. Inc. 1867. **3** or **Rockymount,** town (pop. 1,432), ⊙ Franklin co., S Va., in E foothills of the Blue Ridge, 18 mi. S of Roanoke; tobacco market; mfg. of furniture, textiles, mirrors, wood products; mica mine. Inc. 1873.

Rocky Mountain House, town (pop. 1,017), S central Alta., at foot of Rocky Mts., on North Saskatchewan R., near mouth of Clearwater R., and 50 mi. W of Red Deer; alt. c.3,300 ft.; coal mining, lumbering, grain. Established as North West Co. post in Blackfeet Indian country in 1799, later heavily fortified, it was taken over by Hudson Bay Co., 1821, and remained in operation until 1875. Was sometimes called Blackfoot Post.

Rocky Mountain National Park (□ 395.5; established 1915), N Colo., mainly in Front Range of Rocky Mts. c.50 mi. NW of Denver. Magnificent mtn. area of lofty peaks, glaciers, waterfalls, canyons, many small lakes, and streams (including headstreams of Colorado and Cache la Poudre rivers). FRONT RANGE, extending N–S, is here part of Continental Divide; NEVER SUMMER MOUNTAINS are in NW, MUMMY RANGE in NE. There are 65 named peaks over 10,000 ft.; highest is LONGS PEAK (14,255 ft.), in SE. Other well-known features are Glacier Gorge, near Longs Peak, Moraine Park (E), Tyndall, Andrews, and Taylor glaciers (S), and Rowe Glacier (largest in park), at NE tip of Mummy Range. Trail Ridge Road is scenic route extending from E entrance of park to Grand Lake town (W entrance) and reaching alt. of 12,183 ft. near Continental Divide. Chief highway passes are Milner (10,759 ft.; crossed by Trail Ridge Road) and Fall River 11,797 ft.), both in NW. Alva B. Adams Tunnel passes through park in S. Area is sanctuary for wildlife, including bighorn sheep, deer, and elk, and there are forests of spruce, fir, and pine, and flowering alpine meadows. Lodges, campgrounds, hiking and riding trails, nature museums. Skiing at Hidden Valley, in E, near Trail Ridge Road. Park hq. at town of Estes Park, just E of park boundary.

Rocky Mountains or **Rockies,** major mountain system of W North America, extending over 3,000 mi. from central N.Mex. generally NNW into W Canada and N Alaska, and reaching Bering Strait N of the Arctic Circle. The Rockies rise abruptly from the Great Plains (E), while on W they are bounded by the high plateaus, basins and ranges of the intermountain region. Unlike the Andes, which constitute the entire backbone of South America, the Rockies form but the easternmost belt of the North American cordillera, whose W members are the complex ranges of the Pacific borderland (Sierra Nevada, Cascade Range, Coast Ranges, Coast Mts.). Although the Rocky Mts. proper are generally considered to end on S with the Sangre de Cristo Mts. (N.Mex.), the link bet. the Rockies and their natural S extension in Mexico (Sierra Madre Oriental) can be traced with interruptions through S N.Mex. and W Texas in the Sacramento Mts., Davis Mts., and Santiago Mts. Snow-capped Mt. Elbert (14,431 ft.) and 45 other glaciated peaks reaching above 14,000 ft. are the loftiest summits, all concentrated in the Colorado portion. Highest summit in Canada is Mt. Robson (12,972 ft.). The entire belt is marked by bold, rugged topography, in which stream and ice erosion has carved the features of local relief. A formidable barrier to E–W communications, the Rockies form the CONTINENTAL DIVIDE separating Pacific drainage from Atlantic (Gulf of Mexico) and Arctic drainage. Among the continent's major rivers, the following rise in the Rockies: E of the Continental Divide, the Missouri and its long right tributaries (Yellowstone, Platte) the Arkansas, the Saskatchewan, the headstreams of the MacKenzie (Peace, Athabaska), and the Rio Grande; W of the divide rise the Colorado, Columbia, Fraser, and Yukon. In Colo., W-flowing drainage has recently been diverted to the E slope of the Front Range through Alva B. Adams Tunnel. Geologically, the Rockies consist of an exposed anc. crystalline core (granites, granodiorites, gneisses, schists, quartzites) flanked by thick, upturned layers of Paleozoic and Mesozoic sedimentaries which originally completely covered the uplift. Such tectonic occurrences as faulting, folding, intrusion of igneous masses, and extrusion of lava flows are all associated in the structural features of this complex mtn. mass; up-arching, however, is the most commonly found structure. The major orogeny dates from the Laramide Revolution (Upper Cretaceous and early Tertiary). Active erosion (resulting in the aggrading of the neighboring Great Plains) continued through the Pliocene period, substantially reducing relief and forming interior sedimentary basins. A regional uplift (c.5,000 ft.) at beginning of the Pleistocene, followed by extensive mtn. glaciation and canyon cutting, brought about the present configuration. Topographically, the system may be divided into 4 major sections called the Southern, Middle, Northern, and Arctic Rockies. The Southern Rockies, in N.Mex., Colo., and S Wyo., constitute the highest and most homogeneous section; here 2 major parallel folds, breached to their Pre-Cambrian core, are separated by a series of basins (South Park, Middle Park, North Park, Laramie Plains); in the E are (N–S) the LARAMIE MOUNTAINS, the FRONT RANGE of Colo. (Longs Peak, 14,255 ft.; Pikes Peak, 14,110 ft.), and the SANGRE DE CRISTO MOUNTAINS (Blanca Peak, 14,363 ft.), all rising sheerly 5–8,000 ft. above the high plains and the Colo. piedmont. The MEDICINE BOW RANGE is a NW spur of the Front Range, and extends into Wyo. The W group includes the PARK RANGE and SAWATCH MOUNTAINS, where many of the highest peaks (e.g., Mt. Elbert, 14,431 ft.) are found. S of the Sawatch, in S Colo. and N N.Mex., are the SAN JUAN MOUNTAINS, consisting entirely of lavas and volcanic tuff. Here rises the Rio Grande, whose upper course traverses the fertile San Luis Valley. The Southern Rockies are crossed by 2 railroads, from Denver via Moffat Tunnel, and from Pueblo via the Royal Gorge of the Arkansas R. and Tennessee Pass; the 2 main transcontinental lines by-pass the front ranges on the N (by way of Cheyenne-Laramie) and on the S at Albuquerque. Principal highway passes are Berthoud Pass, Loveland Pass, Tennessee Pass, Monarch Pass. The Lincoln Highway also uses the N by-pass at Cheyenne. The Middle Rockies, separated from the Southern Rockies by the Wyo. basin (a pouch-shaped extension of the Great Plains) are varied in structure, irregular in trend, and do not present a solid front eastward. They lie in NE Utah, NW Wyo., SE Idaho, and SW Idaho. Here are the great horseshoe fold formed by the BIGHORN MOUNTAINS (Cloud Peak, 13,165 ft.), BRIDGER RANGE, and Owl Creek Mts., which (with Absaroka Range) encloses the Bighorn Basin; the folded WIND RIVER RANGE, WYOMING RANGE, SALT RIVER RANGE, and UINTA MOUNTAINS (Kings Peak, 13,498 ft.); the massive tilted blocks of the TETON RANGE (Grand Teton, 13,766 ft.) and WASATCH RANGE (which overlooks the Great Salt Lake section of the Great Basin); and the lava-covered ABSAROKA RANGE and Yellowstone plateau. From this section the Bighorn and Yellowstone rivers drain N to the Missouri, the Snake flows W (partly through Snake R. Plain) to the Columbia, and the Green S to the Colorado. The heavily glaciated Northern Rockies, bounded S and SW by Snake R. Plain and the Columbia plateau and W by the interior plateau of B.C., extend from Mont., Idaho, and NE Wash. almost 1,000 mi. into Canada, where the Continental Divide (along the crest of the Front Ranges usually called the Canadian Rockies) follows the Alta.–B.C. line. These front ranges (including the LEWIS RANGE in Mont.) are great fault blocks thrust eastward over the younger beds of the Great Plains. Separating the ranges from those to the W is a remarkable trough known as the Rocky Mtn. Trench; it extends from W Mont. (S of Flathead L.) NNW to the headwaters of the Yukon, and is occupied in succession by the headstreams of the Kootenai, Columbia, Fraser, Peace, and Liard rivers. W are the roughly parallel PURCELL and SELKIRK ranges, separated by longitudinal grabens (in which the Kootenai, Columbia, and Okanogan rivers form fjord-like lakes). The westernmost members of the Northern Rockies, in Canada, are collectively called the Columbia Mts.; they overlook B.C.'s interior plateaus and extend S to the Columbia R. at Grand Coulee. Among well-known Can. ranges are the Stikine and Cariboo Mts. The southernmost members of the Northern Rockies include the BITTERROOT RANGE (Idaho-Mont. border), and the massive granite CLEARWATER MOUNTAINS and SALMON RIVER MOUNTAINS of central Idaho. The Northern Rockies are crossed by 3 transcontinental railroads in the U.S. and by 2 in Canada. The Arctic Rockies, much of whose area is almost totally unexplored, consist of several discontinuous parallel ranges; the MACKENZIE MOUNTAINS (and their E outliers the FRANKLIN MOUNTAINS) sweep 500 mi. NW across Northwest Territories and Yukon Territory; N of the Mackenzies, the Richardson Mts. (bet. lower Mackenzie R. and the Porcupine R.) reach almost to Mackenzie Bay of Arctic Ocean; and the BROOKS RANGE stretches E–W the full width of N Alaska. The Rocky Mts. contain a wealth of minerals (especially metallics) in various stages of exploitation. Among the most plentiful are gold, silver, lead, zinc, and copper; tungsten, molybdenum, uranium, vanadium, manganese, and radium are also produced, and there are enormous reserves (and some production) of phosphate rock, oil shale, petroleum, and bituminous coal. Principal mining dists. are in Colo. (where many gold camps of the late 19th and early 20th cent. are ghost towns), Mont. (esp. Butte-Anaconda copper dist.), Utah (esp. Park City dist.), Wyo., N.Mex., Idaho (Coeur d'Alene dist.), and B.C. (Trail dist.). Cattle and sheep are grazed in enormous numbers (mainly in U.S. portion) on winter ranges in valleys and plains, on mtn. pastures in the summer; agr. is of less importance, due to the generally high alt. of most of the valleys of the Southern and Middle Rockies, and the high latitude (and consequent short or non-existent growing season) of the lowlands of the Northern Rockies. Hardy crops are produced chiefly in the Southern Rockies; potatoes, wheat, barley, alfalfa, some fruit, and lettuce are grown. Natural vegetation zones begin with grasslands and occasional desert tracts of xerophytic vegetation on the lower slopes, succeeded by a belt of coniferous forest (chiefly yellow pine, spruce, larch, lodgepole and limber pine), which in turn gives way above timberline (c.12,000 ft. in S, c.9,500 ft. in Mont., at level of adjacent plains in N Canada) to the alpine summit vegetation. Difficult terrain for logging and transportation, lack of local markets, and the comparatively low value of much Rocky Mtn. timber have restricted commercial lumbering mainly to N Mont. and N Idaho, although there are logging operations in many scattered areas. In U.S. Rockies, c.¾ of the saw-timber stands are preserved in natl. forests. Native fauna includes the grizzly bear, the bighorn sheep, Rocky Mtn. goat, pronghorn antelope (valleys and plains), mtn. lion (puma), forest caribou. The spectacular scenic beauty of the Rockies, particularly of the glaciated peaks of the N U.S. and S Can. portions, have made the region one of the continent's great vacation lands. In Canada, natl. parks include Jasper, Banff (famed for beauty of L. Louise), Yoho, Kootenay, Waterton Lakes (part of Waterton-Glacier International Peace Park, which incorporates Glacier Natl. Park in U.S.), Glacier, and Mt. Revelstoke natl. parks, and many provincial parks. In U.S. are Yellowstone, Glacier, Grand Teton, and Rocky Mtn. natl. parks and many other recreational regions.

Rocky Point. **1** Village (1940 pop. 538), Suffolk co., SE N.Y., near N shore of Long Isl., 7 mi. E of Port Jefferson, in summer-resort area. **2** Town (1940 pop. 416), Pender co., SE N.C., 14 mi. N of Wilmington; lumber milling. **3** Village, R.I.: see WARWICK.

Rocky Ridge, village (pop. 358), Ottawa co., N Ohio, 19 mi. ESE of Toledo, in agr. area.

Rocky Ripple, town (pop. 528), Marion co., central Ind., N suburb of Indianapolis, on West Fork of White R.

Rocky River, city (pop. 11,237), Cuyahoga co., N Ohio, 8 mi. W of downtown Cleveland, on L. Erie, at mouth of Rocky River; baskets, novelties, metal products, waterproof paper, machinery. Settled 1815, inc. 1903.

Rocky River. **1** In S N.C., rises in S Iredell co., flows c.90 mi. generally ESE to Pee Dee R. 12 mi. N of Wadesboro. **2** In NE Ohio, formed by West and East branches at Olmsted Falls, flows c.10 mi. NNE, through W suburbs of Cleveland, to L. Erie at Rocky River. West Branch rises near Medina, flows c.25 mi. N to junction with East Branch (c.33 mi. long).

Rocky Spruit (sproit), village, Salisbury prov., E central Southern Rhodesia, in Mashonaland, 32 mi. S of Salisbury; tobacco, peanuts, citrus fruit, dairy products. Sometimes spelled Rockey Spruit.

Rocour or **Rocourt** (both: rōkōōr'), agr. village (pop. 2,689), Liége prov., E Belgium, 3 mi. N of Liége. Here the French under Marshal Saxe defeated (1746) duke of Lorraine. Formerly Raucoux.

Rocquencourt (rôkäkōōr'), village (pop. 147), Seine-et-Oise dept., N central France, just NW of Versailles. Military hq. of North Atlantic Treaty Organization was established here, 1951.

Rocroi (rôkrwä'), village (pop. 751), Ardennes dept., N France, in the Ardennes, near Belg. border, 14 mi. NW of Mézières; iron foundries. Fortified by Vauban. Here in 1643 the Great Condé won his greatest victory over Spaniards.

Roc-Saint-André, France: see MALESTROIT.

Roda, Germany: see STADTRODA.

Roda, village (pop. 1,822, with near-by Osaka), Wise co., SW Va., in coal-mining region of the Cumberlands, near Ky. line, 8 mi. NNW of Big Stone Gap.

Roda, El, Er Roda, or **Al-Rawdah** (all: ĕr-rō'dŭ), village (pop. 9,580), Asyut prov., central Upper Egypt, on W bank of the Nile, on railroad, and 21 mi. SSE of Minya; sugar milling, pottery making, wood and ivory carving; cereals, dates, sugar cane.

Roda, La (lä rō'dhä). **1** Town (pop. 10,127), Albacete prov., SE central Spain, in Murcia, 22 mi. NW of Albacete; saffron-production and -shipping center. Mfg. of woolen cloth, knitwear, soap; wine processing, alcohol and brandy distilling, flour- and sawmilling. Chalk and clay quarries. **2** or **La Roda de Andalucía** (dhä ändälōō-thē'ä), town (pop. 4,572), Seville prov., SW Spain, in the Sierra de Yeguas, near Málaga prov. border, 18 mi. E of Osuna; rail junction and agr. center (olives, cereals, livestock). Liquor distilling, flour milling, sulphur refining.

Rodach or **Rodach bei Coburg** (rō'däkh bī kō'bōōrk), town (pop. 3,884), Upper Franconia, N Bavaria, Germany, on the Rodach and 10 mi. NW of Coburg; rail terminus; pottery works, lumber mills. Clay pits near by.

Rodach River. **1** In Germany, rises on Bavarian-Thuringian border, flows 30 mi. SW to the Main just SW of Marktzeuln. **2** In Germany, rises 3 mi. WSW of Hildburghausen (Thuringia), flows c.30 mi. S to the Itz 4 mi. S of Sesslach (Bavaria).

Roda de Andalucía, La, Spain: see RODA, LA, Seville prov.

Roda del Ter (rō'dhä dhĕl tĕr'), town (pop. 2,747), Barcelona prov., NE Spain, on Ter R. and 4 mi. NE of Vich; mfg. of cotton and woolen textiles, sawmilling; sheep, vegetables, fruit.

Roda Island (rō'dŭ) (2 mi. long, ½ mi. wide), in the Nile, N Egypt, part of Cairo, opposite Old Cairo. At S end is the famous Nilometer, used for over a thousand years to measure the water level of the Nile. Has the mosque of Kait Bey, and by tradition is believed to be the spot where the infant Moses was found.

Rodakovo (rŭdä'kuvŭ), town (1926 pop. 1,469), S central Voroshilovgrad oblast, Ukrainian SSR, in the Donbas, 11 mi. W of Voroshilovgrad; rail junction; metalworks.

Rodalben (rōdäl'bun), village (pop. 5,807), Rhenish Palatinate, W Germany, 3 mi. NNE of Pirmasens; rye, potatoes.

Rodange (rōdäzh') town (pop. 3,983), SW Luxembourg, 7 mi. WNW of Esch-sur-Alzette; frontier station on Fr. border; iron mining; steel center (blast furnaces, rolling mills), mfg. (railroad equipment, tar products).

Rodas (rō'däs), town (pop. 3,750), Las Villas prov., central Cuba, on Damují R., on railroad and 37 mi. W of Santa Clara, in agr. region (sugar cane, cattle, honey). Near by (NE) is the central of Parque Alto.

Rodas River, Cuba: see DAMUJÍ RIVER.

Rodaun (rôdoun'), town (pop. 2,768), after 1938 in Liesing dist. of Vienna, Austria, 7 mi. SW of city center; wine.

Rodberg (rû'bărg, rû'băr), Nor. *Rødberg*, village in Nore canton (pop. 2,253), Buskerud co., S Norway, on Lagen R., at head of the Numedal, and 45 mi. W of Honefoss; rail terminus. S of village, Lagen R. falls over 1,150 ft. into Norefjord; major hydroelectric station supplies Oslo and Tonsberg.

Rodborough, town and parish (pop. 3,748), central Gloucester, England, on Frome R. and just SW of Stroud; woolen milling. Church dates from 15th cent.

Rodby (rûdh'bü), Dan. *Rødby*, city (pop. 3,511) with adjacent port, Maribo amt, Denmark, on Lolland isl. and 7 mi. SSW of Maribo; shipbuilding, cement mfg.

Rodding (rû'dhĭng), Dan. *Rødding*, town (pop. 1,486), Haderslev amt, S central Jutland, Denmark, 19 mi. NW of Haderslev; lumber mills.

Rodebay or **Rhodebay** (rōd'bā), fishing and hunting settlement (pop. 124), Jakobshavn dist., W Greenland, on Disko Bay, 8 mi. NNE of Jakobshavn; 69°20'N 51°W. Radio station.

Rodeio (rōōdā'ōō), city (pop. 1,001), E Santa Catarina, Brazil, in Itajaí Açu valley, 20 mi. W of Blumenau, in fertile region of diversified agr. Settled in 19th cent. by Italians and Poles.

Rodekro (rû'dhükrō), Dan. *Rødekro*, town (pop. 1,313), Aabenraa-Sonderborg amt, S Jutland, Denmark, 4 mi. NW of Aabenraa; rail junction; cement and box mfg.

Rödelheim (rû'dulhīm), suburb (pop. 10,229) of Frankfurt, W Germany, on the Nidda and 3 mi. NW of city center.

Roden (rō'dun), town (pop. 1,453), Drenthe prov., N Netherlands, 8 mi. SW of Groningen; cattle market; flax industry.

Rodenbeck (rō'dunbĕk), residential town (pop. 3,024), W Orange Free State, U. of So. Afr., 6 mi. SSE of Bloemfontein.

Rodenberg (rō'dunbĕrk), town (pop. 3,574), in former Prussian prov. of Hanover, W Germany, after 1945 in Lower Saxony, 16 mi. WSW of Hanover. Belonged to former Prussian prov. of Hesse-Nassau until 1932.

Rodenkirchen (rō'dun-kĭr"khun), fishing village (commune pop. 6,554), in Oldenburg, NW Germany, after 1945 in Lower Saxony, near the Weser, 5.5 mi. S of Nordenham; rail junction.

Rodeo (rōdā'ō), town (pop. estimate 500), ⊙ Iglesia dept. (□ c.3,500; 1947 pop. 5,583), N central San Juan prov., Argentina, in irrigated valley, 30 mi. W of Jachal; wine, alfalfa, wheat, livestock (goats, sheep, horses), poultry; sawmills.

Rodeo or **El Rodeo** (ĕl), town (1950 pop. 519), San Marcos dept., SW Guatemala, in Pacific piedmont, on Inter-American Highway and 12 mi. WSW of San Marcos; coffee, sugar, grain, stock.

Rodeo, town (pop. 1,020), Durango, N Mexico, on Nazas R. and 80 mi. N of Durango; corn, cotton, wheat, alfalfa, chick-peas.

Rodeo (rōdā'ō, rō'dēō), village (1940 pop. 1,931), Contra Costa co., W Calif., 8 mi. NE of Richmond, on San Pablo Bay, in industrial area; meat packing.

Rodeo, El, Argentina: see EL RODEO.

Rodeo de la Cruz (rōdā'ō dā lä krōōs'), town (pop. estimate 1,000), N Mendoza prov., Argentina, in Mendoza R. valley (irrigation area), on railroad, and 6 mi. SE of Mendoza, in fruit and wine zone. Wine making, alcohol distilling, fruit processing, sawmilling.

Rodeo del Medio (dĕl mä'dyō), town (pop. estimate 1,000), N Mendoza prov., Argentina, in Mendoza R. valley (irrigation area), on railroad and 12 mi. SE of Mendoza; agr. center (wine, fruit, corn, wheat, goats); wine making, fruit drying.

Rodeos, Los (lōs rō-dhä'ōs), airport, Tenerife, Canary Isls., 13 mi. WSW of Santa Cruz de Tenerife.

Röderau (rû'durou), village (pop. 3,033), Saxony, E central Germany, near the Elbe, 2 mi. NE of Riesa; rail junction.

Roderick Island (□ 91), SW B.C., in SE arm of Hecate Strait; 52°39'N 128°22'W; 20 mi. long, 3–6 mi. wide. Just S is Susan Isl. (□ 14), 8 mi. long, 2–6 mi. wide.

Rodessa (rōdĕ'sŭ), village (1940 pop. 1,605), Caddo parish, extreme NW La., near Texas and Ark. lines, 34 mi. NW of Shreveport; center of Rodessa oil and natural-gas field (discovered 1935).

Rodewisch (rō'duvĭsh), town (pop. 10,985), Saxony, E central Germany, in the Erzgebirge, on Göltzsch R. and 13 mi. ENE of Plauen; woolen and silk milling, knitting, bleaching; felt, underwear mfg.

Rodez (rôdĕz'), anc. *Segodunum* and *Ruthena*, town (pop. 16,366), ⊙ Aveyron dept., S France, bet. Ségala Plateau (S) and Causse du Comtal (N), overlooking Tarn R. and 75 mi. NE of Toulouse; road center and regional agr. market; woolen mfg., copper smelting, furniture making. Commerce in Roquefort cheese, livestock, potatoes. Has 13th–16th-cent. Gothic cathedral and old houses. Episcopal see since 5th cent.; ⊙ former Rouergue countship.

Rodha, Aden: see RAUDHA.

Rodholivos, Greece: see RODOLEIVOS.

Rodhopi, Greece: see RHODOPE.

Rodhos, Greece: see RHODES.

Rodi, Greece: see RHODES.

Rodi Garganico (rô'dē gärgä'nēkô), town (pop. 4,704), Foggia prov., Apulia, S Italy, port on Adriatic Sea, on N shore of Gargano promontory, 15 mi. WNW of Vieste; bathing resort.

Roding (rō'dĭng), village (pop. 4,769), Upper Palatinate, E Bavaria, Germany, in Bohemian Forest, on the Regen and 23 mi. NE of Regensburg; chemicals, textiles. Chartered 1432.

Roding River (rō'dĭng), Essex, England, rises 4 mi. NW of Great Dunmow, flows S and SW, past Ongar, Buckhurst Hill, and Woodford, thence SSE, past East Ham, to the Thames just S of Barking; 30 mi. long.

Rodino (rô'dyēnŭ), village (1926 pop. 5,871), SW Altai Territory, Russian SFSR, near S.Siberian RR, 75 mi. SE of Slavgorod; dairy farming.

Rodionovo-Nesvetaiskoye or **Rodionovo-Nesvetayskoye** (rŭdyēō'nuvŭ-nyĕsvyĭtī'skŭyŭ), village (1926 pop. 2,319), SW Rostov oblast, Russian SFSR, 22 mi. NW of Novocherkassk; metalworks; wheat, sunflowers, livestock. Phosphorite mining near by.

Rodleben (rōt'lā"bun), village (pop. 1,638), in former Anhalt state, central Germany, after 1945 in Saxony-Anhalt, near the Elbe, 5 mi. NNW of Dessau; synthetic-oil plant.

Rodman, town (pop. 123), Palo Alto co., NW Iowa, near West Des Moines R., 10 mi. SE of Emmetsburg.

Rodman's Neck, N.Y.: see PELHAM BAY PARK.

Rodna, province, Rumania: see BISTRITA.

Rodna (rôd'nä), Hung. *Óradna* (ō'rŏdnŏ), village (pop. 4,416), Rodna prov., N central Rumania, in Transylvania, on SE slopes of Rodna Mts., 25 mi. NE of Bistrita; rail terminus and base of excursions into the mts. near by; iron-pyrite mining. Has remains of Gothic church, destroyed by Tatars. A Moldavian mining center in 15th–16th cent. In Hungary, 1940–45. Also called Rodna-Veche.

Rodna Mountains, section of the Carpathians in N Rumania, on border of Transylvania and Maramures; extend E–W for c.25 mi. NW of the Moldavian Carpathians; rise to 6,660 ft. in Pietrosu mtn. Several passes lead from Maramures into Transylvania and from Transylvania into Bukovina.

Rodney, village (pop. 702), S Ont., 28 mi. ENE of Chatham; lumber and flour milling, basket weaving; vegetables, fruit.

Rodney, New Zealand: see WARKWORTH.

Rodney, town (pop. 127), Monona co., W Iowa, near Little Sioux R., 32 mi. SE of Sioux City.

Rodnichek (rŭdnye'chĭk), village (1939 pop. over 500), SW Saratov oblast, Russian SFSR, 13 mi. SW of Balashov; wheat, sunflowers.

Rodniki (rŭdnyĭkē'), city (1926 pop. 15,468), central Ivanovo oblast, Russian SFSR, on rail spur and 30 mi. ENE of Ivanovo; cotton-milling center. Formed (1918) from 5 contiguous mill towns.

Rodnikovski or **Rodnikovskiy** (rŭdnyē'kufskē), village (1939 pop. over 500), NW Aktyubinsk oblast, Kazakh SSR, 25 mi. N of Aktyubinsk; wheat, cattle.

Rodó or **José Enrique Rodó** (hōsā' ĕnrē'kā rōdō'), town (pop. 1,500), Soriano dept., SW Uruguay, in the Cuchilla del Bizcocho, on railroad and 42 mi. SE of Mercedes; wheat, corn, oats, sheep, cattle. Until 1924, called Drable or Drabble, name which is now applied only to its railroad station.

Rodoleivos or **Rodholivos** (both: rôdhôlē'vôs), town (pop. 4,794), Serrai nome, Macedonia, Greece, 26 mi. ESE of Serrai, on slope of Mt. Pangaion; barley, cotton, tobacco. Also spelled Rodolivos.

Rodomum, France: see ROUEN.

Rodoni, Cape (rōdō'nē), Albanian *Kep i Rodonit*, NW Albania, on the Adriatic, at S end of Drin Gulf; 41°35'N 19°27'E; lighthouse.

Rodope or **Rodopi,** Greece: see RHODOPE.

Rodos, Greece: see RHODES.

Rodosto, Turkey: see TEKIRDAG.

Rodovalho (rōōdōōvä'lyōō), village, SE São Paulo, Brazil, on São Paulo–Sorocaba RR and 40 mi. W of São Paulo; has aluminum plant (completed 1944), cement mill.

Rodrigo de Freitas Lagoon (rōōdrē'gōō dĭ frā'tūs), in SW section of Rio de Janeiro city, Brazil, bet. Corcovado peak and the open Atlantic, to which it has an outlet through Leblon residential dist. Near W shore is Rio's botanical garden. Copacabana beach is just E.

Rodrigues or **Rodriguez** (rōdrē'gĕs), volcanic island dependency (□ 40; pop. 11,885) of Mauritius, in Indian Ocean, c.350 mi. ENE of Mauritius; 19°40'S 63°25'E; 9½ mi. long, 4½ mi. wide. One of the Mascarene group. Rises to 1,300 ft. in Mt. Limon; cool, malaria-free climate; frequent cyclones. Agr. (corn, manioc, sweet potatoes, beans, fruit, tobacco), livestock, fish salting. Main town is Port Mathurin (pop. c.600), on N coast. Discovered 1645 by Portuguese; site of Fr. Huguenot colony 1691–93. Occupied by British 1810.

Rodríguez (rōdrē'gĕs). **1** Village (pop. 1,090), Coahuila, N Mexico, 20 mi. N of Monclova; cattle grazing. Coal deposits near by. **2** Village (pop. 1,805), Nuevo León, N Mexico, on Río Salado opposite Anáhuac and 45 mi. SW of Nuevo Laredo, on railroad; in cotton-growing region.

Rodríguez (rōdrē'gĕs), town (pop. 460), San José dept., S Uruguay, on railroad and 10 mi. ESE of San José; cereals, cattle, sheep.

Rodríguez Dam, Mexico: see TIJUANA RIVER.

Rodríguez de Mendoza, province, Peru: see MENDOZA.

Rodsand, Norway: see RAUSAND.

Rodumna, France: see ROANNE.

Roe, village, Monroe co., E central Ark., 6 mi. SW of Clarendon, in farm area. Amateur field trials for bird dogs are held here.

Roebling (rō'blĭng), industrial village (pop. 6,785, with Florence), Burlington co., W N.J., on the Delaware and 7 mi. S of Trenton; founded as "company town" for Roebling steel-cable and wire works.

Roebourne (rō'bûrn), town (pop. 136), NW Western Australia, 380 mi. SW of Broome and on Indian Ocean; 20°47'S 117°9'E. Sheep-raising center; copper, gold, silver, tin, lead.

Roebuck, village, Spartanburg co., NW S.C., just S of Spartanburg; fertilizer, lumber.

Roebuck Bay, inlet of Indian Ocean, N Western Australia, bet. Entrance Point (N; site of Broome) and Cape Villaret (S); 21 mi. long, 11 mi. wide.

Roeland Park, city (1951 pop. c.5,000), Johnson co., E Kansas, a suburb of Kansas City. Inc. after 1950.

Roepat, Indonesia: see RUPAT.

Roermond (rōōr'mōnt), town (pop. 21,215), Limburg prov., SE Netherlands, on Maas R., at mouth of Roer R., and 28 mi. NNE of Maastricht; rail junction; electrochemical industry; mfg. of clothing, linen, bicycles, paints, furniture, wood products, stained glass, church ornaments, organs, flour; fruit, egg, vegetable, and potato market. Has 13th-cent. Romanesque church (*Munsterkerk*), 15th-cent. church (*Sint Kristoffelkerk*). Important medieval trade center. Badly damaged in Second World War.

Roer River (rōōr), Ger. *Rur* (rōōr), in W Germany and SE Netherlands, rises on the Botrange (Belgium), flows c.110 mi. generally N, past Düren and Jülich, enters Netherlands just SSE of Vlodrop, and continues to the Meuse just W of Roermond. Dams in upper course blown up by Germans in Second World War, delaying Allies (Feb., 1945).

Roeselare, Belgium: see ROULERS.

Roeser (rû'zûr), village (pop. 271), S Luxembourg, 5 mi. S of Luxembourg city; grapes, cherry growing.

Roes Welcome Sound, E Keewatin Dist., Northwest Territories, NW arm (180 mi. long, 15–70 mi. wide) of Hudson Bay, bet. Southampton Isl. and mainland; 65°N 88°W. Opens N on Repulse Bay.

Roetgen, Germany: see RÖTGEN.

Rœulx (rû), town (pop. 2,561), Hainaut prov., S Belgium, 8 mi. ENE of Mons; metal industry; agr. and lumber market. Has 15th-cent. castle.

Roeux (rû), village (pop. 700), Pas-de-Calais dept., N France, on canalized Scarpe R. and 6 mi. E of Arras; brewery.

Roff (rôf), city (pop. 623), Pontotoc co., S central Okla., 13 mi. SW of Ada, in agr. area.

Rog or **Kocevski Rog** (kō'chĕfskē rôk'), Slovenian *Kočevski Rog*, peak (3,600 ft.) in Dinaric Alps, S Slovenia, Yugoslavia, 7 mi. ENE of Kocevje.

Rogachev (rŭgŭchôf'), city (1926 pop. 11,226), NW Gomel oblast, Belorussian SSR, on Dnieper R., at mouth of the Drut, and 115 mi. SE of Minsk; sawmills, paper mill; food products, canned milk.

Rogachevo (–chô'vŭ), village (1939 pop. over 500), N Moscow oblast, Russian SFSR, 15 mi. WNW of Dmitrov; dairying. During Second World War, briefly held (1941) by Germans.

Rogagua, Lake (rōgä'gwä), Beni dept., NW Bolivia, c.20 mi. N of Santa Rosa; 21 mi. long, 7 mi. wide. Empties into Beni R. through Río Negro.

Rogaguado, Lake, Bolivia: see ROGOAGUADO, LAKE.

Rogaland (rō'gälän), county [Nor. *fylke*] (□ 3,543; pop. 202,252), SW Norway; ⊙ Stavanger. Lying bet. North Sea coast (W) and the Ruven and Bykle mts. (E), it extends N from Sira R., encompassing Dalane highland, Jaeren lowland, and the mountainous Ryfylke region cut by the many arms of Bokn Fjord. Agr. (grain, vegetables, fruit) flourishes in Jaeren, cattle raising in Ryfylke; fishing along the coast; copper mining on Karmoy. Industrial centers are Egersund, Sandnes, Stavanger, Haugesund, and, on Karmoy, Kopervik and Skudeneshavn; water power is well exploited. Until 1918, co. (then called *amt*) was named Stavanger.

Rogan or **Rogan'** (rŭgän'yŭ), town (1939 pop. over 500), N central Kharkov oblast, Ukrainian SSR, 13 mi. ESE of Kharkov; paper mill, brickworks.

Rogart (rō'gärt), agr. village and parish (pop. 732), SE Sutherland, Scotland, 10 mi. NNW of Dornoch; woolen milling.

Rogasen, Poland: see ROGOZNO.

Rogaska Slatina (rô'gäshkä slä'tēnä), Slovenian *Rogaška Slatina*, Ger. *Rohitsch-Sauerbrunn* (rō'hĭch-zou'ûrbrōōn), village, E Slovenia, Yugoslavia, on railroad and 3 mi. W of Rogatec, near Croatia border, in valley among wooded hills. One of best-known health resorts in Yugoslavia; warm springs. Exports mineral water. Also called Rojc. Until 1918, in Styria.

Rogate, agr. village and parish (pop. 1,098), W Sussex, England, near Rother R., 4 mi. E of Petersfield. Church dates from 12th-cent. Near by are remains of anc. Dureford Abbey.

Rogatec (rô'gätĕch), Ger. *Rohitsch* (rō'hĭch), village, E Slovenia, Yugoslavia, on Sotla R., on railroad and 21 mi. E of Celje, on Croatia border, in brown-coal area; trade center for winegrowing region. Has 2 castles (1 ruined). ROGASKA SLATINA, health resort, is just W.

Rogatica or **Rogatitsa** (both: rô'gätĭtsä), town (pop. 2,003), SE Bosnia, Yugoslavia, 28 mi. E of Sarajevo; center of horse-breeding area; lumber mills. Roman ruins. Formerly called Celebi Pazar or Chelebi Pazar, Serbo-Croatian *Čelebi Pazar*.

Rogatin (rŭgä'tyĭn), Pol. *Rohatyn* (rôhä'tĭn), city (1931 pop. 7,513), N Stanislav oblast, Ukrainian SSR, on Gnilaya Lipa R. and 33 mi. N of Stanislav; chemical industry; cement mfg., grain processing. Gypsum quarried near by. Has old castle. Old Ruthenian settlement, frequently assaulted by Tatars. Passed from Poland to Austria (1772); reverted to Poland (1919); ceded to USSR in 1945.

Roger Mills, county (□ 1,124; pop. 7,395), W Okla.; ⊙ Cheyenne. Bounded W by Texas line, N by Canadian R.; intersected by Washita R. Hilly region of Antelope Hills (c.2,000 ft. alt.) lies in a great bend of the Canadian, in N. Agr. (livestock, wheat, broomcorn, rye, poultry; dairy products). Formed 1891.

Rogers, county (□ 713; pop. 19,532), NE Okla.; ⊙ Claremore. Intersected by Verdigris R., small Bud Creek, and Caney R. Stock raising, agr. (grain, corn, barley, sweet potatoes; dairy products). Mfg. at Claremore. Strip coal mining; oil and natural-gas wells; mineral springs. Formed 1907.

Rogers. **1** City (pop. 4,962), Benton co., extreme NW Ark., 19 mi. N of Fayetteville, in the Ozarks. Market, processing center for dairy, poultry, truck, fruit area; milk cannery; vinegar, silica, and lumber plants; poultry hatchery, nursery. Mtn. resort. Founded 1881. **2** Village (pop. 268), Hennepin co., E Minn., near Mississippi R., 20 mi. NW of Minneapolis; grain, stock, poultry. **3** Village (pop. 113), Colfax co., E Nebr., 7 mi. E of Schuyler and on Platte R. **4** Village (pop. 150), Barnes co., E central N.Dak., 13 mi. NW of Valley City. **5** Village (pop. 297), Columbiana co., E Ohio, 21 mi. S of Youngstown, in agr. and coal area. **6** Town (pop. 948), Bell co., central Texas, 13 mi. SSE of Temple; market point in cotton, corn, grain area; makes soap.

Rogers, Mount (10,525 ft.), SE B.C., in Selkirk Mts., in Glacier Natl. Park, 40 mi. NE of Revelstoke; 51°22'N 117°32'W.

Rogers, Mount, highest point (5,720 ft.) in Va., in spur of Iron Mts., 12 mi. S of Marion.

Rogers City, city (pop. 3,873), ⊙ Presque Isle co., NE Mich., 30 mi. NW of Alpena, on L. Huron, in resort and farm area. Large limestone quarry here ships fluxing stone from near-by port (Calcite). Mfg. (chemicals, cedar products); fisheries. Settled 1869; inc. 1877 as village, 1944 as city.

Rogers Heights, village (1940 pop. 705), Prince Georges co., central Md., suburb ENE of Washington.

Rogers Lake, Calif.: see MUROC.

Rogerstone, town and parish (pop. 4,453), S Monmouth, England, on Ebbw R. and 3 mi. W of Newport; mfg. of light metals; agr. market. Just S is agr. parish of Graig (pop. 1,074).

Rogersville. **1** Town (pop. 531), Lauderdale co., NW Ala., near Wheeler Reservoir (on Tennessee R.), 21 mi. E of Florence. Wheeler Dam is 5 mi. W. **2** Town (pop. 321), Webster co., S central Mo., in the Ozarks, near James R., 14 mi. SE of Springfield; agr. **3** Town (pop. 2,545), ⊙ Hawkins co., NE Tenn., near Holston R., 60 mi. NE of Knoxville; trade center for tobacco, livestock, and timber region; mfg. of cards, labels, hosiery, woodwork; flour milling. Seat of Swift Memorial Jr. Col. Mineral springs near by. Founded 1786.

Roggeveld Escarpment (rô'gŭvĕlt", Afrik. rô"khŭfĕlt'), W Cape Prov., U. of So. Afr., extends 100 mi. NW–SE along SW edge of the Northern Karroo, c.100 mi. NW of Worcester; rises 2–3,000 ft. steeply from the Great Karroo. Komsberg Escarpment is E continuation.

Roggiano Gravina (rôd-jä'nô grävē'nä) or **Rogiano Gravina,** town (pop. 4,230), Cosenza prov., Calabria, S Italy, 14 mi. SSW of Castrovillari; mfg. of agr. machinery.

Roggwil (rôg'vēl), town (pop. 3,025), Bern canton, N Switzerland, 9 mi. SSW of Olten; cotton textiles.

Rogie, Falls of, Scotland: see CONTIN.

Rogliano (rôlyä'nô), village (pop. 1,005), N Corsica, near N tip of Cape Corse peninsula, 20 mi. N of Bastia.

Rogliano, town (pop. 3,925), Cosenza prov., Calabria, S Italy, 9 mi. SSE of Cosenza; olive oil, wine, cheese.

Rognan (rông'nän), village and port (pop. 626) in Saltdal canton (pop. 4,586), Nordland co., N Norway, at head of Saltdal Fjord, at mouth of Salt R., 30 mi. ESE of Bodo; center of Salten region. Agr., lumbering; sawmilling, woodworking. Lonsdal-Rognan section of Trondheim-Bodo RR under construction in 1950.

Rogny (rônyē'), village (pop. 566), Yonne dept., N central France, on Loing R. and Briare Canal, and 13 mi. ENE of Gien; livestock raising.

Rogoaguado, Lake (rōgōägwä'dō) (□ 580), in Beni dept., N Bolivia, c.20 mi. WNW of Exaltación; 25 mi. long, 8 mi. wide. Empties into Arroyo Caimanes (right branch of Yata R.). Also spelled Rogaguado.

Rogovskaya (rŭgôf'skīŭ), village (1926 pop. 12,481), W Krasnodar Territory, Russian SFSR, 12 mi. NW of Timashevskaya; flour mill, metalworks; wheat, sunflowers, sunn hemp.

Rogozen (rô'gôzĕn), village (pop. 3,316), Vratsa dist., NW Bulgaria, 12 mi. WNW of Byala Slatina; grain, legumes, livestock.

Rogozno (rôgôzh'nô), Pol. *Rogoźno*, Ger. *Rogasen* (rōgä'zŭn), town (1946 pop. 5,536), Poznan prov., W Poland, on Welna R. and 24 mi. N of Poznan; rail junction; mfg. of agr. machinery, cement; brewing, sawmilling.

Rogue River, town (pop. 590), Jackson co., SW Oregon, 17 mi. WNW of Medford and on Rogue R.; wood products.

Rogue River. **1** or **Rouge River** (rōōzh), in W central and SW Mich., rises SE of Newaygo in Newaygo co., flows S, E, and again S, past Rockford, to Grand R. just NE of Grand Rapids; c.32 mi. long. **2** In SW Oregon, rises in Cascade Range NE of Medford and NW of Crater L., flows SW, then W through Klamath Mts. and past Grants Pass to the Pacific at Gold Beach; c.200 mi. long. Drains fruitgrowing area (pears, apples, peaches), whose shipping center is Medford.

Rogue River Range, Oregon: see KLAMATH MOUNTAINS.

Roha (rō'hŭ), town (pop. 6,015), Kolaba dist., central Bombay, India, 40 mi. SSE of Bombay; rail terminus; rice market; copper and brass products.

Rohan (rôä'), agr. village (pop. 550), Morbihan dept., W France, on Oust R. and 10 mi. E of Pontivy. Named after a well-known Breton family.

Rohatyn, Ukrainian SSR: see ROGATIN.

Rohia (rôyä'), village, Maktar dist., central Tunisia, 17 mi. SSW of Maktar; esparto, lumber. Phosphate deposits.

Rohilkhand (rō'hĭlkŭnd), division (□ 11,759; pop. 6,673,038), N central Uttar Pradesh, India; ⊙ Bareilly. Comprises Bareilly, Bijnor, Budaun, Moradabad, Rampur (former princely state merged with div. as dist., in 1949), Shahjahanpur, and Pilibhit dists. Anc. area successively invaded by Rajputs, Afghans, Moguls, Pathans, and Mahrattas; ceded 1801 to British.

Rohitsch, Yugoslavia: see ROGATEC.

Rohitsch-Sauerbrunn, Yugoslavia: see ROGASKA SLATINA.

Rohnerville (rō'nûrvĭl), village (pop. 1,500), Humboldt co., NW Calif., 15 mi. S of Eureka.

Rohonc, Austria: see RECHNITZ.

Rohrau (rō'rou), village (pop. 597), E Lower Austria, on Leitha R. and 12 mi. SW of Bratislava, Czechoslovakia. Haydn b. here.

Rohrbach (rōr'bäkh), village (pop. 1,510), N Upper Austria, 22 mi. NW of Linz, near Czechoslovak line; linen mfg.

Rohrbach, town (pop. 4,837), SE Saar, 2.5 mi. E of St. Ingbert; important iron and steel industry.

Rohrbach-lès-Bitche (rôrbäk'-lā-bēch'), Ger. *Rohrbach* (rōr'bäkh), village (pop. 1,312), Moselle dept., NE France, 10 mi. SE of Sarreguemines; woodworking, brick mfg.

Rohrdorf (rōr'dôrf). **1** Village (pop. 1,747), Upper Bavaria, Germany, 4 mi. SSE of Rosenheim; cement mfg., woodworking. **2** Village (pop. 773), S Württemberg, Germany, after 1945 in Württemberg-Hohenzollern, in Black Forest, on the Nagold and 2 mi. NW of Nagold; cotton mfg. Has 15th-cent. castle.

Rohrerstown (rō'rûrztoun), village (1940 pop. 553), Lancaster co., SE Pa., just NW of Lancaster.

Rohri (rō'rē), town (pop. 14,721), Sukkur dist., NE Sind, W Pakistan, on Indus R. (bridged) and 2 mi. E of Sukkur; rail junction (workshops); trade center (grain, ghee, fish, fruit, building stone); silk milling, hand-loom weaving; cement works. Limestone quarried on near-by hills (E, S); small deposits of fuller's earth. Town has relic of prophet Mohammed.

Rohri Canal, irrigation canal of SUKKUR BARRAGE system, central Sind, W Pakistan; from left bank of Indus R. at Sukkur runs c.210 mi. S, through Khairpur state and Nawabshah and Hyderabad dists., to point SE of Tando Muhammad Khan; numerous branches and distributaries; irrigates large area (cotton, millet, wheat, rice).

Röhrnbach (rûrn'bäkh), village (pop. 3,086), Lower Bavaria, Germany, in Bohemian Forest, 12 mi. NNE of Passau; rye, oats, cattle. Granite quarries.

Röhrsdorf (rûrs'dôrf), village (pop. 4,095), Saxony, E central Germany, 5 mi. NW of Chemnitz; hosiery knitting, linen milling, glovemaking.

Rohtak (rō'tŭk), district (□ 2,337; pop. 987,065), SE Punjab, India; ⊙ Rohtak. Bordered E by Jumna R., SE by Delhi state, SW and NW by Patiala and East Punjab States Union. Has enclave in Gurgaon dist. (S). Irrigated (N) by branches of Western Jumna Canal; millet, gram, wheat are main crops. Brine-salt mfg. in SE section. Chief towns: Rohtak, Sonepat, Jhajjar. Original dist. (□ 2,246; pop. 956,399) enlarged 1948 by inc. of former Punjab state of Dujana.

Rohtak, town (pop. 48,148), ⊙ Rohtak dist., SE Punjab, India, 42 mi. NW of New Delhi; road junction; trade center (grain, cotton, oilseeds, cloth fabrics, salt); cotton ginning, glue mfg., hand-loom weaving (muslin turbans). Art and commercial cols., agr. research station.

Rohtang Pass (rōtäng') (alt. 13,050 ft.), in SE Pir Panjal Range of Punjab Himalayas, in Kangra dist., NE Punjab, India, 55 mi. ENE of Dharmsala. Overlooks Kulu valley (S), through which flows upper Beas R.

Rohtas (rō'tŭs), village, Shahabad dist., W Bihar, India, on Son R. and 23 mi. SSW of Sasaram; rail spur terminus. Close by is noted hill fort, taken (1539) from Hindu ruler by Sher Shah; later under Moguls; surrendered to British in 1764; held by rebels for short time during Sepoy Rebellion (1857). Fort area has well-preserved Mogul palace.

Roi, Marshall Isls.: see KWAJALEIN.

Roia River, Maritime Alps: see ROYA RIVER.

Roiet (roi'ĕt'), town (1947 pop. 8,105), ⊙ Roiet prov. (□ 2,439; 1947 pop. 535,662), E Thailand, in Korat Plateau, 100 mi. NW of Ubon; rice, corn, beans, tobacco, cotton; hog and horse raising; sulphur deposits. Also spelled Roi Etch.

Roisel (rwäzĕl'), village (pop. 1,525), Somme dept., N France, 7 mi. ENE of Péronne; copper smelting; elastic fabrics.

Roisin (rwäzē'), agr. village (pop. 1,443), Hainaut prov., SW Belgium, 14 mi. SW of Mons, near Fr. border.

Roitzsch (roich), village (pop. 5,744), in former Prussian Saxony prov., central Germany, after 1945 in Saxony-Anhalt, 4 mi. SW of Bitterfeld; lignite mining.

Rojales (rōhä'lĕs), town (pop. 1,665), Alicante prov., E Spain, on Segura R. and 13 mi. E of Orihuela; flour mills; hemp, wheat, fruit.

Rojas (rō'häs), town (pop. 8,700), ⊙ Rojas dist. (□ 764; pop. 29,727), N Buenos Aires prov., Argentina, 24 mi. SSW of Pergamino; agr. center and rail junction; corn, wheat, flax; stock raising.

Rojhan (rō'jŭn), town (pop. 4,935), Dera Ghazi Khan dist., SW Punjab, W Pakistan, 100 mi. SSW of Dera Ghazi Khan; wheat, rice; handicraft woolen products.

Rojistea (rôzhĕsh'tyä), Rum. *Rojiştea,* village (pop. 1,505), Dolj prov., S Rumania, 18 mi. SSE of Craiova.

Rojo, Cabo (kä'bō rō'hō), headland in Veracruz, E Mexico, on Gulf of Mexico; easternmost point of peninsula separating Tamiahua Lagoon from sea, 55 mi. SE of Tampico; 21°33'N 97°18'W.

Rojo, Cape (rō'hō), on SW coast of Puerto Rico, 19 mi. S of Mayagüez; 17°55'N 67°11'W.

Rokan River (rōkän'), N central Sumatra, Indonesia, rises in Mt. Ophir in Padang Highlands, flows N and NE to Strait of Malacca at Bagansiapiapi; 175 mi. long. Important transportation route, navigable for most of its length.

Rokeby, agr. village and parish (pop. 149), North Riding, N Yorkshire, England, on Tees R. at mouth of Greta R., 14 mi. W of Darlington. Site of Rokeby Park.

Rokel River (rōkĕl') or **Seli River** (sā'lē), N central Sierra Leone, rises in hills on Fr. Guinea border, at 9°45'N; flows SW and S past Bumbuna and Magburaka, and W joining Port Loko Creek (right) to form SIERRA LEONE RIVER 17 mi. SW of Port Loko; length, c.250 mi. Navigable in lower course for canoes. Sometimes called Sierra Leone R.; sometimes spelled Rokell or Rokelle.

Roker, England: see SUNDERLAND.

Rokhati (rŭkhä'tyē), village (1939 pop. over 500), N Stalinabad oblast, Tadzhik SSR, 7 mi. ENE of Stalinabad; wheat.

Rokiskis or **Rokishkis** (rō'kēshkēs), Lith. *Rokiškis,* Rus. *Rakishki,* city (pop. 5,480), NE Lithuania, 37 mi. W of Daugavpils, near Latvian border; woolen-weaving center; lumber products (paper, cardboard, tar, turpentine); flour milling. In Rus. Kovno govt. until 1920.

Rokitnitz im Adlergebirge, Czechoslovakia: see ROKYTNICE V ORLICKYCH HORACH.

Rokitno (rŭkĕt'nŭ), town (1931 pop. 3,990), NE Rovno oblast, Ukrainian SSR, 25 mi. E of Sarny; sawmilling, brick and glassworks.

Rokitzan, Czechoslovakia: see ROKYCANY.

Rokkestad (rôk'kŭstä), village (pop. 2,182; canton pop. 5,562), Ostfold co., SE Norway, on railroad and 13 mi. NE of Sarpsborg; woolen milling, rutile quarrying.

Rokko, Formosa: see LUKANG.

Rokugo (rōkōōgō'), town (pop. 9,436), Akita prefecture, N Honshu, Japan, 7 mi. N of Yokote; commercial center for agr. area (rice, soybeans).

Rokugo Point, Japan: see NAGATE POINT.

Rokupr (rōkōō'pŭr), town (pop. 1,808), Northern Prov., NW Sierra Leone, on Great Scarcies R. and 40 mi. NNE of Freetown. Agr. station for swamp rice development area.

Rokusho, Japan: see NAGAHAMA, Shiga prefecture.

Rokycany (rô'kĭtsänĭ), Ger. *Rokitzan* (rō'kĭtsän), town (pop. 7,848), SW Bohemia, Czechoslovakia, 9 mi. E of Pilsen; rail junction; noted metalworks producing roller bearings, metal furniture, light ammunition; woodworking. Has 18th-cent. church, castle ruins. Fish ponds near by.

Rokytnice nad Jizerou (rô'kĭtnyĭtsĕ näd' yĭzĕrō), Ger. *Rochlitz an der Iser* (rôkh'lĭts än dĕr ē'zŭr), village (pop. 2,670), N Bohemia, Czechoslovakia, at foot of the Riesengebirge, on railroad and 17 mi. ESE of Liberec, near Jizera R.; glassmaking; cotton spinning. Copper formerly mined here.

Rokytnice v Orlickych Horach (vôr'lĭtskēkh hô'räkh), Czech *Rokytnice v Orlických Horách,* Ger. *Rokitnitz im Adlergebirge* (rō"kĕt'nĭts ĭm ä'dlŭrgŭbĭr"gŭ), town (pop. 1,506), E Bohemia, Czechoslovakia, in foothills of the Sudetes, 6 mi. N of Zamberk, near Pol. border; rail terminus; resort.

Roland, village (pop. estimate 500), S Man., 50 mi. SW of Winnipeg; grain elevators, stockyards.

Roland. 1 Town (pop. 687), Story co., central Iowa, 12 mi. NNE of Ames; canned corn and peas, butter. **2** Town (pop. 443), Sequoyah co., E Okla., 6 mi. WNW of Fort Smith, Ark.

Roland, Lake (c.2 mi. long), N Md., water-supply reservoir just N of Baltimore.

Rolândia (rōōlän'dyŭ), city (pop. 3,493), N Paraná, Brazil, on railroad and 12 mi. W of Londrina, in pioneer coffee zone; rice, cotton, beans, potatoes; dairying. Called Caviúna, 1944–48.

Rolandseck, Germany: see OBERWINTER.

Rôlas, islet, São Tomé e Príncipe: see SÃO TOMÉ ISLAND.

Rolava, Czechoslovakia: see KRASLICE.

Roldal (rŭl'däl), Nor. *Røldal,* village and canton (pop. 778), Hordaland co., SW Norway, 19 mi. SSE of Odda; tourist center at N end of the Brattlandsdal, at foot of Breidfonn glacier.

Roldán (rōldän'), town (pop. estimate 1,500), S Santa Fe prov., Argentina, 15 mi. W of Rosario; agr. center (alfalfa, corn, flax, wheat, livestock, poultry); dairying.

Roldanillo (rōldänē'yō), town (pop. 3,183), Valle del Cauca dept., W Colombia, in Cauca valley, 30 mi. SW of Cartago; tobacco-growing center; coffee, sugar cane, cacao, corn, cattle.

Rolesville, town (pop. 288), Wake co., central N.C., 15 mi. NE of Raleigh.

Rolette (rōlĕt'), county (□ 913; pop. 11,102), N N. Dak., bordering on Manitoba; ⊙ Rolla. Prairie, with Turtle Mts. and Turtle Mtn. Indian Reservation in N. Grain, livestock, dairy products, poultry, lumber. Formed 1873.

Rolette, city (pop. 451), Rolette co., N N.Dak., 16 mi. SW of Rolla.

Rolfe, town (pop. 997), Pocahontas co., N central Iowa, 28 mi. NW of Fort Dodge; rail junction; feed mill.

Roliça (rōōlē'sŭ), village, Leiria dist., W central Portugal, 7 mi. SSW of Caldas da Rainha. Here Wellington fought 1st battle of Peninsular War.

Rolla, village (pop. estimate 1,000), E B.C., near Alta. border, near Alaska Highway, 11 mi. NNE of Dawson Creek, 180 mi. NE of Prince George; lumbering, grain, stock.

Rolla (rŏ'lŭ). **1** City (pop. 433), Morton co., extreme SW Kansas, 39 mi. W of Liberal, in grain area. **2** City (pop. 9,354), ⊙ Phelps co., central Mo., in the Ozarks, near Gasconade R., 48 mi. SE of Jefferson City; railroad, farm-trade, educational center; shoe factory; clay, pyrite mines. Univ. of Mo. schools of mines, metallurgy, engineering; state trachoma hosp. Founded c.1856. **3** City (pop. 1,176), ⊙ Rolette co., N N.Dak., 65 mi. NW of Devils Lake, at E end of Turtle Mts. Grain, dairy produce, livestock, poultry. Near Turtle Mtn. Indian Reservation and International Peace Garden. Inc. 1907.

Rollag (rôl'läg), village and canton (pop. 1,546), Buskerud co., SE Norway, on Lagen R., on railroad and 35 mi. WSW of Honefoss; lumbering, stock raising.

Rollán (rōlyän'), town (pop. 1,128), Salamanca prov., W Spain, 13 mi. W of Salamanca; woolen-cloth mfg.; vegetables, cereals.

Rolle (rôl), town (pop. 2,342), Vaud canton, SW Switzerland, on L. Geneva, 15 mi. WSW of Lausanne; metalworking. Has 13th-cent. castle.

Rolleboise, France: see MANTES-GASSICOURT.

Rolleston (rōlz'tŭn), agr. township (pop. 197), E S.Isl., New Zealand, 14 mi. SW of Christchurch; rail junction for line through Southern Alps to Greymouth on W coast.

Rolleville (rōl'vĭl), town (pop. 604), central Bahama Isls., on N Great Exuma Isl., 20 mi. NW of George Town, in stock-raising region (sheep, goats, hogs); 23°41'N 76°W.

Rollingen, Luxembourg: see LAMADELAINE.

Rolling Fork, town (pop. 1,229), ⊙ Sharkey co., W Miss., 38 mi. N of Vicksburg, near Mississippi R.; agr. (cotton, oats, corn); lumber. Indian mounds near by. Settled c.1827.

Rolling Fork, river, central Ky., rises in S Boyle co., flows c.115 mi. W and NW past New Haven, to Salt R. 7 mi. E of Fort Knox.

Rolling Hills, Calif.: see PALOS VERDES ESTATES.

Rollingstone, village (pop. 315), Winona co., SE Minn., near Mississippi R., 10 mi. WNW of Winona; dairy products.

Rollins Dam, Calif.: see BEAR RIVER.

Rollinsford, town (pop. 1,652), Strafford co., SE N.H., on Salmon Falls R., just NE of Dover. Includes Salmon Falls village (pop. 1,290) (textile mills, foundries). In Somersworth until inc. 1849.

Rollinsville, village, Gilpin co., N central Colo., in Front Range, 30 mi. WNW of Denver; alt. c.8,250 ft.; shipping point. Placer mining for gold.

Roma (rō'mŭ), town (pop. 3,894), S central Queensland, Australia, 265 mi. WNW of Brisbane; rail junction; wheat-raising center.

Roma (rō'mä), village, Maseru dist., NW Basutoland, 25 mi. SE of Maseru; R.C. mission and school.

Roma (rō'mŭ) or **Romang** (rōmäng'), island (11 mi. long, 5–9 mi. wide; pop. 1,289), S Moluccas, Indonesia, in Banda Sea, 50 mi. NE of Timor; 7°40'S 127°25'E; copra; fishing.

Roma (rô'mä), province (□ 2,061; pop. 1,562,843), Latium, central Italy, bet. Tyrrhenian Sea and the Apennines; ⊙ Rome. Includes CAMPAGNA DI ROMA, volcanic Alban and Tolfa hills, and crater lakes of Bracciano, Albano, and Nemi. Watered by Aniene R. and the lower Tiber. Agr. (cereals, fodder, grapes, olives, vegetables); livestock raising (sheep, cattle). Winegrowing in Alban Hills. Fishing (Civitavecchia, Anzio). Alum mining (Allumiere, Tolfa). Quarries at Tivoli (travertine) and Subiaco (marble). Hydroelectric plants on Aniene R. Resorts in Alban Hills (Albano Laziale, Frascati, Marino) and on Tyrrhenian Sea (Lido di Roma, Santa Marinella). Mfg. at Rome, Civitavecchia, and Tivoli. Area reduced 1934 to form Latina prov.

Roma (rō'mä), village (pop. 3,100), Libertad dept., NW Peru, on irrigated coastal plain, on Chicama R., on railroad and 5 mi. SW of Ascope; sugar-milling center; distilling.

Roma (rōō'mä"), village (pop. 486), Gotland co., SE Sweden, in central part of Gotland isl., 10 mi. SE of Visby, in agr. region (grain, sugar beets, potatoes, flax); rail junction; sugar refining. Has remains of former Cistercian monastery and church, founded 1164.

Roma or **Roma-Los Saenz** (rō'mŭ-lōsĭnts'), city (pop. 1,576), Starr co., extreme S Texas, on the Rio Grande (bridged) opposite Mier, Mexico, and c.80 mi. SSE of Laredo; port of entry and market point for ranching and agr. area. Inc. 1937.

Romagna (rômä'nyä), historical region, N central Italy, on the Adriatic; now forms E part of EMILIA-ROMAGNA. Within its boundaries, which have varied, are provinces of Forlì and Ravenna, and part of Bologna prov. Center of Byzantine domination (540–751) in Italy, with Ravenna as seat of exarchs. Ruled by papacy from 16th cent. until 1860, with one brief interval (1797–1814) of occupation by French.

Romagnano Sesia (rômänyä'nô sā'zyä), village (pop. 3,985), Novara prov., Piedmont, N Italy, on Sesia R. and 17 mi. NW of Novara, in grape-growing, livestock-raising region; rail junction; mills (cotton, woolen, paper), pottery works.

Romagne-sous-Montfaucon (rômä'nyŭ-sōō-mōfōkō'), village (pop. 403), Meuse dept., NE France, 18 mi. NW of Verdun; dept., NE France, 18 mi. NW of Verdun; sawmilling. Site of Meuse-Argonne American Cemetery, largest U.S. cemetery in Europe of First World War dead (14,240 graves).

Romain, Cape (rōmān'), Charleston co., E S.C., S tip of Cape Isl. (c.5 mi. long), in the Atlantic near coast, 21 mi. S of Georgetown; 33°N 79°24'W. Cape Romain lighthouse (now unused) is at E end of Raccoon Key (just W). Much of surrounding region of low marshy isls. is included in large Cape Romain waterfowl refuge.

Romaine River (rōmān'), E Que., rises on Labrador border at 52°40'N 63°25'W; flows 250 mi. S, through Lac Long (20 mi. long) and Burnt L. (20 mi. long), to the St. Lawrence 10 mi. WNW of Havre St. Pierre, opposite Mingan Isls. There are several rapids. Fishing (trout, muskinonge, pike, carp).

Romainville (rômēvēl'), town (pop. 16,979), Seine dept., N central France, an ENE suburb of Paris, 4.5 mi. from Notre Dame Cathedral, E of Pantin; mfg. (electrical equipment, textiles, jewelry, pharmaceuticals); gypsum quarries.

Roman (rō'män), town (1948 pop. 23,701), Bacau prov., NE Rumania, in Moldavia, on Moldava R. and 180 mi. N of Bucharest; rail junction and mfg. center. Produces wire, tinware, sugar, edible oils, flour, confectionery, dyes, varnishes, soap, glue, bricks, tiles; distilling, tanning. Orthodox bishopric. Has 15th- and 17th-cent. churches. Founded in 14th cent.; burned down by Hung. armies in 1467. Occupied (1944) by USSR troops in the Second World War.

Romana, La, Dominican Republic: see LA ROMANA.

Romanche Deep, ocean depth in Atlantic Ocean, at the equator, in break of Atlantic longitudinal submarine ridge. The original sounding of 24,179 ft. at 18°E was exceeded in 1948 with the discovery of a near-by depth of more than 25,000 ft.

Romanche River (rômăsh'), Hautes-Alpes and Isère depts., SE France, rises in Massif du Pelvoux S of Col du Lautaret, flows 48 mi. generally W, past Le Bourg-d'Oisans, to the Drac below Vizille. Harnessed for hydroelectric power (Chambon Dam; hydroelectric plants in Livet-et-Gavet gorge). Followed by Grenoble-Briançon road (*Route des Alpes*).

Romancoke, Md.: see KENT ISLAND.

Romanèche-Thorins (rômänĕsh'-tôrē'), village (pop. 259), Saône-et-Loire dept., E central France, near Saône R., 9 mi. SSW of Mâcon; vintage wines.

Romanesti, Moldavian SSR: see ROMANOVKA.

Romang (rōmäng′), town (pop. estimate 1,500), NE Santa Fe prov., Argentina, on San Javier R. and 25 mi. SSW of Reconquista; lumbering and farming center (corn, flax, rice, livestock); dairying, tanning, sawmilling.

Romang, Indonesia: see ROMA.

Román Grande Island (rōmän′ grän′dā), in Uruguay R., Río Negro dept., W Uruguay, 5 mi. NNW of Nuevo Berlín, ½ mi. offshore; 32°52′S 58°11′W; 5 mi. long, 1 mi. wide.

Romani, Egypt: see RUMANA, EL.

Romania: see RUMANIA.

Romania, Cape, Malaya: see RUMENIA, CAPE.

Romanija Mountains or **Romaniya Mountains** (both: rômä′nēä), in Dinaric Alps, SE Bosnia, Yugoslavia; extend N–S c.10 mi., partly through Sarajevo coal area. Highest peak (5,343 ft.) is 11 mi. E of Sarajevo.

Roman-Kosh (rŭmän′-kôsh′), highest peak (5,062 ft.) of Crimean Mts., S Crimea, Russian SFSR, 9 mi. SW of Alushta.

Roman Nose, summit (3,140 ft.) of the Alleghenies, Garrett co., extreme W Md., just S of Deep Creek L. and 5 mi. N of Oakland.

Romano, Cape (rō′mūnō), S Fla., S point of sandy island just offshore in the Gulf of Mexico, c.7 mi. S of Collier City; 25°50′N 81°40′W. Ten Thousand Isls. are just E.

Romano, Cayo (kī′ō rōmä′nō), coral island (55 mi. long NW–SE, 10 mi. wide) off N coast of Cuba, in Old Bahama Channel, bet. Cayo Coco (NW) and Cayo Guajaba (SE), 50 mi. N of Camagüey. Salt panning, fishing. Part of Camagüey Archipelago.

Romano d'Ezzelino (rômä′nô dĕtsĕlē′nô), village (pop. 999), Vicenza prov., Veneto, N Italy, 1 mi. NE of Bassano; shoe factory. Marble quarries near by.

Romano di Lombardia (dē lômbärdē′ä), town (pop. 5,971), Bergamo prov., Lombardy, N Italy, near Serio R., 13 mi. SSE of Bergamo; agr. center (cereals, fodder, raw silk); fertilizer mfg.

Romanov, Ukrainian SSR: see DZERZHINSK, Zhitomir oblast.

Romanov-Borisoglebsk, Russian SFSR: see TUTAYEV.

Romanovka (rŭmä′nŭfkŭ). **1** Rum. *Romăneşti* (rômŭnēsht′), town (1941 pop. 1,170), S Moldavian SSR, on Kogalnik R. and 45 mi. S of Kishinev, on Ukrainian SSR border; rail junction (Bessarabskaya station; Rum. *Basarabeasca*); railroad shops. **2** Town (1926 pop. 6,347), W Saratov oblast, Russian SFSR, 22 mi. NW of Balashov; flour-milling center; wheat, sunflowers, fruit.

Romanovo (–nŭvŭ), village (1939 pop. over 2,000), central Altai Territory, Russian SFSR, near S.Siberian RR, 60 mi. W of Aleisk, in agr. area.

Romanovskaya (–nŭfskīŭ), village (1926 pop. 3,169), E Rostov oblast, Russian SFSR, on left bank of Don R. and 35 mi. NW of Zimovniki; flour mill, metalworks; wheat, cotton, vineyards.

Romanovski Khutor, Russian SFSR: see KROPOTKIN, Krasnodar Territory.

Romans, France: see ROMANS-SUR-ISÈRE.

Romans d'Isonzo (rômäns′ dēzōn′tsô), village (pop. 2,052), Gorizia prov., Friuli–Venezia Giulia, NE Italy, near Isonzo R., 9 mi. SW of Gorizia.

Romanshorn (rō′mäns-hôrn), town (pop. 5,862), Thurgau canton, NE Switzerland, port on L. Constance and 9 mi. N of St. Gall; silk textiles, chemicals, clothes, watches, printing.

Romans-sur-Isère (rômä′-sür-ēzâr′), town (pop. 18,865), Drôme dept., SE France, on right bank of Isère R., opposite Bourg-de-Péage, and 11 mi. NE of Valence; tanning and shoe-mfg. center. Chestnut trade. Also makes cartons, mustard, pharmaceuticals; woodworking, vegetable canning, pickling. Here St. Barnard founded an abbey in 837. Fine abbatial church (12th–13th cent.) lost its stained-glass windows in Second World War. Also called Romans.

Romany (rŭmä′nē), town (1939 pop. over 10,000) in Lenin dist. of Greater Baku, Azerbaijan SSR, on central Apsheron Peninsula, 10 mi. NE of Baku; oil wells (developed after 1870s).

Romanzoff Islands, Marshall Isls.: see WOTJE.

Romanzof Mountains (rōmăn′zŏf), range, NE Alaska, in NE Brooks Range, near 69°15′N 144°W; rises to 9,239 ft. on Mt. Michelson.

Romanzov Bay, Japan: see SOYA BAY.

Rombach, France: see ROMBAS.

Rombach, Luxembourg: see MARTELANGE.

Rombakken Fjord, Norway: see OFOT FJORD.

Rombas (rōbäs′), Ger. *Rombach* (rŏm′bäkh), town (pop. 6,186), Moselle dept., NE France, on the Orne and 10 mi. NNW of Metz, in iron-mining dist.; metallurgy (blast furnaces, steel mill); Portland cement mfg.

Romblon (rômblōn′), province (□ 512; 1948 pop. 108,817), Philippines, comprises a group of Visayan Isls. including TABLAS ISLAND (largest), SIBUYAN ISLAND, ROMBLON ISLAND, BANTON ISLAND, SIMARA ISLAND, CARABAO ISLAND, MAESTRE DE CAMPO ISLAND; ⊙ Romblon (on Romblon Isl.). The isls. are generally mountainous and volcanic. Chief products: rice, coconuts.

Romblon Island (□ 32; 1939 pop. 13,106), Romblon prov., Philippines, in Sibuyan Sea, just NW of Sibuyan Isl., separated from Tablas Isl. (W) by Romblon Pass (7 mi. wide); oval-shaped and low-lying, 10 mi. long, 5 mi. wide. Rice, coconuts. Lighthouse at Apunan Point (12°28′N 122°17′E) at S end of isl. On NW coast of isl. is town of Romblon (1939 pop. 3,466; 1948 municipality pop. 12,879), ⊙ prov.

Rombo Islands, Cape Verde Isls.: see SECOS ISLANDS.

Rome, Ital. *Roma* (rō′mä), city (1936 pop. 1,089,996; 1948 pop. estimate 1,613,660), ⊙ Italy and ⊙ Latium and Roma prov.; site of VATICAN CITY, the papal see. Occupies central position on W coast of peninsula; situated on both banks of the Tiber, in the CAMPAGNA DI ROMA, near the Apennines, and 15 mi. inland from Tyrrhenian Sea; 41°54′N 12°30′E. Called the Eternal City, it is one of the richest cities in the world in history and art, and a great cultural, religious, and intellectual center. The climate of Rome, greatly improved since draining of near-by marshes, is noted for its mild winters. Annual mean temp. is 61.5°F. The *tramontana*, a N wind, is often attended by severe storms, while the hot, dry sirocco frequently sweeps up from the S during the summer. Snowfalls and frosts are rare. Rome is intersected by 3 wide meanders of the Tiber, spanned by many bridges. Smaller part of city lies on right bank; contains Vatican City, including St. Peter's Church, modern residential sections, and anc. Trastevere quarter. On left bank is the Piazza Venezia—the "center" of Rome—a large square and the focus of broad avenues, dominated by a huge monument to Victor Emmanuel II and bordered by the Palazzo Venezia, a Renaissance palace. Via dei Fori Imperiali (formerly Via dell'Impero) runs SE, past the Emperors' Fora, the Capitol, and the anc. Forum, to the Colosseum; church of St. Peter in Chains is just N. From the Colosseum Via di San Gregorio (formerly Via dei Trionfi) continues S, past the Arch of Constantine (built A.D. c.315) and Baths of Caracalla (begun A.D. 206), to the Appian Way. Here, as in other outskirts of Rome, are large catacombs. From Piazza Venezia, Via del Mare leads SW to the Tiber and then E, past the basilica of St. Paul without the Walls, the 2d-largest church in Rome, to OSTIA and Lido di Roma, a popular bathing resort on the sea. Central part of city is cut, roughly W to E, by Via Nazionale (called Corso Vittorio Emmanuel bet. Piazza Venezia and the Tiber), continued by a bridge crossing to St. Peter's; another near-by bridge leads to the Castel Sant'Angelo. The busy Via del Corso (formerly Corso Umberto I), chief thoroughfare of Rome, leads N from Piazza Venezia, past Piazza Colonna, to Piazza del Popolo at the gate of the Flaminian Way. E of Piazza del Popolo are Pincian hill, commanding one of finest views of Rome, and Villa Umberto I (formerly Villa Borghese), the largest (245 acres) and most beautiful of the public parks, surrounding a villa (built 1613; art mus.) and bordered N by a zoological garden. In a bend of the Tiber, W of Via del Corso, is the Campo Marzio quarter (Martian Field) containing the Pantheon (now a church), houses of parliament, and most of the medieval bldgs. E of Via del Corso the fashionable Via Condotti leads to Piazza di Spagna; from this square a flight of 132 steps ascends to church of Santa Trinitá dei Monti and Villa Medici. The Quirinal palace (begun 1574), residence of the president of Italy and formerly of the king, is NE of the Piazza Venezia. In SE section of city are Univ. of Rome (founded 1303) and the Lateran bldgs., an exclave of the Vatican including St. John Lateran and Lateran Palace (seat of mus.). Among the countless churches of Rome are 5 patriarchal basilicas: St. Peter's (in Vatican City), St. John Lateran (San Giovanni in Laterno), St. Mary Major (Santa Maria Maggiore), St. Lawrence without the Walls (San Lorenzo fuori le Mura), and St. Paul without the Walls (San Paolo fuori le Mura). With exception of St. Mary Major, the basilicas and other anc. churches occupy sites of martyrs' tombs. Characteristic of the old Roman churches are their fine mosaics (4th–12th cent.) and the use of colored marbles for decoration, introduced in 12th cent. Among the many palaces and villas of Rome, the Farnese Palace (begun 1514) and the Farnesina, a villa built 1508–11, are particularly famous. Others, dating from 17th cent., are those of the great Roman families: the Colonna, Chigi, Torlonia, and Doria. Rome's richest museums and libraries are in the Vatican; others include National, Capitoline, and Torlonia museums, and Borghese, Corsini, Doria, and Colonna collections of paintings. Rome is noted for its beautiful Renaissance and baroque fountains, such as the imposing 18th-cent. Fontana di Trevi. As an educational center the city has, in addition to its univ. and many museums, academies of music (including Accademia di Santa Cecilia, founded 1584) and fine arts, libraries, and colleges of the church. Several foreign nations maintain institutes, among which are the American Acad. (school of fine arts, archaeology, music, and the classics). There are notable athletic stadiums. Rome is the largest city in Italy and as a center of industry and commerce 2d only to Milan. For its art treasures, religious and historic associations, as well as its fine winter climate the city has for centuries attracted a continuous stream of visitors. Tourism is a leading source of income. It has also large printing, publishing, insurance, and motion-picture establishments. Its manufactures include automobile chasses, railroad cars, motorcycles and bicycles, agr. and printing machinery, wood and metal furniture, stoves, silverware, glass, ceramics, statuary, brick, cement, aeronautical accessories, foundry products, pharmaceuticals, soap, chemicals, paint, explosives, fertilizer, plastics, macaroni, wine, and alcohol; also important are artisan products made of metal, leather, cloth, stone, and wood. It is a focus of roads, railroads, and airlines; its port is CIVITAVECCHIA. Anc. Rome was built on E bank of the Tiber on elevations, c.45–275 ft. high, rising from marshy lowlands of the Campagna. The "Seven Hills of Rome" are: the Palatine, roughly in the center; the Capitoline, to NW; the Quirinal, Viminal, Esquiline, Caelian, and Aventine, forming an outlying curve from N to SW. The Pincian is N of the Quirinal, and Martian Field (anc. *Campus Martius*) W of it, in a bend of the Tiber opposite the Vatican. Across the Tiber from the Palatine is the Janiculum, a ridge running N–S. The hills of Rome, freer from malaria than the surrounding plain, were also more easily defensible, had access to the sea, and served as a center for N–S trade. The rise of Rome from an insignificant pastoral settlement to the globe's perhaps most successful empire, supreme as lawgiver and organizer, holding sway over virtually all the then-known world, on which it left a permanent imprint of its material and cultural achievements, is one of history's great epics. Its downfall on the verge of the empire's greatest expansion and splendor still occupies the varied speculations of historians. Rome fell many times, but it recovered just as often. Once it lost its military and imperial glory, it became the religious metropolis of Christendom. When its religious authority was challenged by the Reformation, it triumphed magnificently in the arts over all denominational barriers. Whatever its fortunes throughout almost 3 millenniums, the Eternal City has remained the very symbol of European civilization. Indeed, all the highways of Western heritage lead to Rome. Its humble beginnings are veiled in legend. The traditional story, accepted by Vergil and Livy, tells of the founding of Rome by Romulus in 753 B.C. (hence the dating *ab urbe condita*, or A.U.C., i.e., from the founding of the city). The city most likely originated as a colony of Latin settlers from the Alban Hills, who early came into contact with the neighboring Sabines. In the 8th cent. B.C. the fortified elevation of the Palatine was probably taken by the culturally much more advanced Etruscans (legendary royal house of the Tarquins), who amalgamated the tiny hamlets into a city-state and gave it a hegemony over Latium. About 500 B.C. the Romans ousted their Etruscan rulers and established the Roman Republic, to last for 4 centuries. The govt. was controlled by an oligarchy of the so-called *patricians*, from whom the underprivileged *plebs* gradually wrested equal rights. The administration was headed by a senate and 2 consuls. Under senatorial power Rome began her march to world supremacy. From the 4th and 3d cent. B.C. Roman life came to be greatly influenced by Greek culture, though puritan ideas of old Roman courage and morality were kept alive by such staunch conservatives as the elder Cato. After subduing the Samnites and "pacifying" the inhabitants of Picenum, Umbria, Apulia, Lucania, and Etruria, Rome became master over central Italy. With the return of Pyrrhus—who had won victories at Heraclea (280 B.C.) and Asculum (279 B.C.) in defense of the Greek colonies of S Italy—to Greece, it consolidated its peninsular domain. Coveting the possession of Sicily (a granary of the Old World), Rome clashed with the like ambition of Carthage, which ruled the W Mediterranean. Thus ensued the 3 Punic Wars (264–241, 218–201, 149–146 B.C.), bringing Hannibal to the gates of Rome, but ending through the victories of Scipio Africanus in the Roman dominion over Spain, Sicily, Sardinia, Corsica, N Africa, and the Sea. The E Mediterranean was the next objective. Antiochus of Syria was conquered (190 B.C.) at Magnesia and in 168 B.C. Macedonia became a prov. Opposition of the Greeks, who had formed the Achaean League, was crushed. The Greeks became subject to Rome, while Egypt acknowledged vassalship. A major geographic factor enabling Rome to become a marine power was the central location of the peninsula, reaching through Sicily nearly to the African coast and dividing the Mediterranean into 2 basins. The rapid expansion of Roman dominion had, however, terrible effects at home. Conquered peoples abroad and suppressed classes in the city became more restless. The *plebs* found valiant standard bearers in the Gracchus brothers, who were, however, removed by assassination (133 and 121 B.C.). Jugurtha defied Rome in Numidia for a time, but in 106 B.C. he was defeated by Marius. Marius conquered (112–101 B.C.) also the Cimbri and Teutoni in Transalpine Gaul. A Social War (90–88 B.C.) forced Rome into extending citizenship widely in Italy. Yet, the republic was doomed. The slave revolt, led by Spartacus, was put down mercilessly. Partisans of conservative and liberal factions, generally represented by successful military leaders, assumed ever-increasing influence. Gaining glory and power as proconsuls of outlying provinces, they turned against each other, and plunged the republic into a continuous civil war. Marius's party was destroyed by the conservative Sulla. The latter's reactionary measures were wiped out (70 B.C.) by Pompey, who became virtual lord of Rome. His defeat of Mithridates made Pontus, Syria, and Phoenicia Roman dependencies. Pompey formed (60 B.C.) with Crassus and Julius Caesar the First Triumvirate. After Caesar won (58–51 B.C.) Cisalpine Gaul for Rome, he fell out with Pompey. Through the victory of Phaisala (48 B.C.) Caesar assumed undisputed power over Rome, marking the end of the republic. At the time of Caesar's assassination (44 B.C.) Rome held most of Spain, Gaul, Italy, Illyria, Macedonia, Greece, W Asia Minor, Bithynia, Pontus, Cilicia, Syria, Cyrenaica, Libya, Numidia, Egypt, and Palestine. The age of Caesar meant a high-water mark in Roman culture, and the cosmopolitan Roman—"civis Romanus"—became the ideal of men. Greek letters were fashionable, though Latin poetry of this and a later epoch reached a tone of its own beyond the eclecticism it is so frequently accused of. Typical of the period was Cicero, an urbane lawyer-politician of universal culture. Upon Caesar's death the struggle for power among the available strong men continued. The Second Triumvirate—Octavian (later Augustus), Antony, and Lepidus—brought only a short respite. Final peace was established when Octavian defeated (31 B.C.) Antony and Cleopatra at Actium. Octavian became as Augustus the proper founder of the Roman Imperium. Under him began 200 years of peace, the *Pax Romana*. At this time the empire was at its greatest extent, bounded by Armenia, middle Mesopotamia, the Arabian Desert, Red Sea, Nubia, the Sahara, Atlantic Ocean, Scotland, the Rhine, the Danube, the Black Sea, and the Caucasus. The great system of Roman roads facilitated communication. Augustus died A.D. 14, and was succeeded by his stepson Tiberius. Caligula, who followed, was a cruel tyrant (37–41), and he was succeeded by Claudius I who conquered half of Britain. To the latter's son Nero (54–68) is attributed the great fire (64). This catastrophy and the building programs of the emperors left little of the original city. Most of the people were moved to the right bank of the Tiber. Still standing are parts of the Aurelian Wall. On the Capitoline were the Citadel (*Arx*) and the temple of Jupiter Capitolinus; on the Palatine were the palaces of Augustus and Tiberius; palace of Nero and Trajan's baths were on S slopes of the Esquiline. The Circus Maximus, where the famous chariot races were held, was S of the Palatine. The Forum, extending from the Capitoline almost to the Colosseum, was still the center of the city; NE of it were the Emperors' Fora, with many fine public bldgs., and the Temple of Peace. On Campus Martius were Pompey's theater, the Circus Flaminius, the Pantheon, and baths of Agrippa and Nero. Across the Tiber, Nero's circus occupied the present site of St. Peter's; Hadrian's tomb, now the Castel Sant'Angelo, has survived as a major landmark. Largest of many public baths were those of Caracalla, near the Appian Way. At its height imperial Rome had well over a million inhabitants; it was well policed and maintained a good sanitation system. The rich knew such luxuries as central heating and running water; the poor (c.200,000) were cared for at public expense. At that time Christians made their appearance in Rome and gained a wide following. A barbarous persecution was instigated at Nero's order; among the victims were SS Peter and Paul. Throughout the Roman Empire the Christians expanded steadily for the next centuries. Despite persecution, they penetrated the army and the imperial household. The catacombs of Rome housed not only Christian tombs, but also churches. A brief struggle after Nero's death brought Vespasian (69–79) to the throne, whose son and later successor, Titus, destroyed Jerusalem. Titus was succeeded by his despotic brother Domitian, who ruthlessly persecuted the Christians. The Roman Empire reached a peak under the rule of Trajan (98–117) and Hadrian (117–38), both natives of Spain, symbolizing that Italy was losing its dominant role. The Stoic philosopher-king Marcus Aurelius, who fell in a remote battle against barbaric tribes, marks a dying age. From then on the throne was a gift of the capital soldiery, the *Praetorian* guard. In 3d cent. barbarian invasions increased. Under Diocletian, who made himself emperor, the division of the empire into E and W sections was begun. It was resumed after the death (337) of Constantine I, who moved the capital to Byzantium, renamed Constantinople. By the Edict of Milan (313) Constantine granted universal religious tolerance, thus permitting free worship of Christianity. There was a brief resurgence of paganism under Julian the Apostate. After the death (391) of Theodosius I the empire was permanently divided into East and West. Decline came quickly. Honorius (395–423) made Ravenna the capital of the West. Italy was increasingly ravaged by invaders. Alaric I took Rome in 410, and Gaiseric took it in 455. Attila was kept from sacking it only through the efforts of Pope Leo I. In this general disintegration the popes, originally the bishops of Rome, increased their religious and secular power, which in a certain sense became a competitor and heir of the imperial tradition (see also article on PAPAL STATES). In 476 the last emperor of the West, appropriately named Romulus Augustulus, was deposed by the Goths under Odoacar. The concept of Imperial Rome survived in the East Roman Empire (until fall of Constantinople, 1453) and was revived in the Holy Roman Empire of the Middle Ages, whose 1st protagonist became Charlemagne crowned (800) in Rome. His coronation ended the Byzantine suzerainty over the city. In 846 Rome was sacked by the Arabs. By the 10th cent. the papacy was virtually under control of the noble families of Rome (Orsini, Colonna, etc.). The vigorous Pope Gregory VII reformed abuses, but had to end in exile, Emperor Henry IV having taken Rome in 1083. The Normans under Robert Guiscard sacked the city one year later. In 12th cent. papal authority was challenged by the so-called commune of Rome, such as the one set up (1144–55) by Arnold of Brescia. Eventually a republic under papal patronage was established. During the captivity of the popes at Avignon (1309–77) Rome was in economic ruin and social upheaval. Cola di Rienzi became the champion of the people and tried in vain to revive (1347–54) the anc. Roman institutions, as also envisaged by early Renaissance thinkers and writers (Petrarch, Dante, and, in some respects, Machiavelli). After the Great Schism (1378–1417) a republic was set up once more. With Pope Martin V began (1420) the effective papal dominion of Rome, which more and more increased its temporal power, while patronizing the arts and beautifying the city. The period of the great popes of the Renaissance—Sixtus IV, Innocent VIII, Alexander VI, Julius II, Leo X, Clement VII, and Paul III—made Rome a haven of art and literature. Among the countless artists and architects who served the papal courts were Bramante, Michelangelo, Raphael, Sangallo, and Fontana, doing much to create the cultural attractions of present-day Rome and combining their efforts in the building of St. Peter's. During the Counterreformation Rome continued to prosper and produced fine examples of baroque monuments, initiated by Sixtus V and built by Borromini, Maderna, and notably, Bernini. Bernini created the famous tabernacle in St. Peter's and added the superb collonades that flank the great church. Papal rule terminated briefly when the city came under French control (1798–99, 1808–14) and again during the disorders of 1849. In 1871 Rome, all that remained after 1862 of the Papal States, became capital of Italy. Conflict resulting from papal refusal to recognize loss of city was resolved (1929) by Lateran Treaty, which gave sovereignty over Vatican City to the pope. In Second World War, Rome was taken by U.S. troops on June 4, 1944. An air raid (July, 1943) damaged the basilica of St. Lawrence without the Walls; otherwise Rome remained virtually undamaged by the war. Its suburbs, however, were frequently bombed (1943–44) during the 9 months of Ger. occupation of the city, marked by the massacre of 335 Ital. hostages in the Ardeatine caves. Post-war years witnessed a remarkable economic, artistic, and intellectual revival. Pope Pius XII designated 1950 a Holy Year and Rome received many thousands of pilgrims.

Rome. **1** City (pop. 29,615), ⊙ Floyd co., NW Ga., on Coosa R., formed here by confluence of Etowah and Oostanaula rivers, and c.55 mi. NW of Atlanta. Industrial center; mfg. (rayon yarn, cotton clothing, bedspreads, hosiery, stoves, mining and agr. machinery, furniture, boxes, concrete products, cottonseed oil, feed, fertilizer); meat packing. Shorter Col. here; Berry schools for mtn. children near by. Founded 1834 on site of Cherokee village. Sherman destroyed the city's industrial facilities in 1864. **2** Village (pop. 190), Jefferson co., S Ill., 8 mi. N of Mount Vernon, in agr. area. **3** Town (pop. 134), Henry co., SE Iowa, near Skunk R., 7 mi. W of Mount Pleasant; limestone quarries. Large Indian mound near by. **4** Town (pop. 420), Kennebec co., S Maine, 18 mi. NW of Augusta in Belgrade Lakes recreational area. **5** Town (pop. 189), Sunflower co., NW Miss., 17 mi. SSE of Clarksdale, in cotton-growing area. **6** Industrial city (pop. 41,682), a ⊙ Oneida co., central N.Y., on Mohawk R. and 14 mi. NW of Utica; large copper- and brass-working industry; also mfg. of wire products, machinery, heating and cooling equipment, paints, textiles, clothing, sporting goods; packs fruit, vegetables. Seat of state schools for the deaf and for mental defectives. Jervis Library here was formerly home of J. B. Jervis. Near by are Griffiss Air Force Base and a large state fish hatchery. Laid out on site of Fort Stanwix in c.1786; inc. as village in 1819, as city in 1870. Building of Erie Canal (begun here in 1817) gave impetus to growth. **7** Village, Ohio: see STOUT. **8** Borough (pop. 257), Bradford co., NE Pa., 8 mi. NE of Towanda.

Rome City, resort village, Noble co., NE Ind., on Sylvan L. (c.2 mi. long), 7 mi. NW of Kendallville. "Limberlost," home of G. S. Porter, is near by.

Romeno (rômā'nô), village (pop. 768), Trento prov., Trentino–Alto Adige, N Italy, 13 mi. SW of Bolzano; woolen mill.

Romentino (rômĕntē'nô), village (pop. 3,043), Novara prov., Piedmont, N Italy, 5 mi. E of Novara.

Romeo (rō'mēō). **1** Town (pop. 404), Conejos co., S Colo., in foothills of San Juan Mts., 21 mi. SSW of Alamosa, in San Luis Valley; alt. 8,360 ft. Trading point in grain and potato region. **2** Village (pop. 2,985), Macomb co., SE Mich., 15 mi. NNW of Mt. Clemens; market center for fruitgrowing area; mfg. (cotton textiles, feed). Small game hunting and fishing near by. Inc. 1838.

Romeoville (rō'mēōvĭl"), village (pop. 147), Will co., NE Ill., on Des Plaines R. (bridged here) and 7 mi. N of Joliet, in agr. and bituminous-coal area; oil refinery.

Romeral (rōmäräl'). **1** Mining settlement (1930 pop. 74), Coquimbo prov., N central Chile, 9 mi. SE of Ovalle; high-grade iron-ore deposits. Sometimes El Romeral. **2** Village (1930 pop. 257), Curicó prov., central Chile, 7 mi. NE of Curicó, in agr. area (grain, beans, peas, wine, livestock).

Romeral, El (ĕl), town (pop. 2,518), Toledo prov., central Spain, 24 mi. SSE of Aranjuez; grapes, cereals, olives, saffron, sheep. Olive-oil pressing, gypsum mfg.; limekiln.

Römerbad, Yugoslavia: see RIMSKE TOPLICE.

Römerstadt, Czechoslovakia: see RYMAROV.

Rometan (rŭmyĭtän'), village (1939 pop. over 500), S Bukhara oblast, Uzbek SSR, on Zeravshan R. and 10 mi. N of Bukhara; cotton.

Romford (rŭm'fŭrd), residential municipal borough (1931 pop. 35,918; 1951 census 87,991), SW Essex, England, 12 mi. ENE of London; agr. market, with iron foundries, shoe factories, pharmaceutical works, breweries. It was probably site of Roman settlement of *Durolitum*, and ⊙ Saxon royal lands called "Liberty of Havering-atte-Bower."

Romhany (rôm'hänyŭ), Hung. *Romhány*, town (pop. 2,196), Nograd-Hont co., N Hungary, 10 mi. S of Balassagyarmat; rail terminus; vineyards, potatoes, hogs.

Römhild (rûm'hĭlt"), town (pop. 2,583), Thuringia, central Germany, 13 mi. SSE of Meiningen; gypsum and stone quarrying; woodworking. Has 15th-cent. church, 15th-cent. Glücksburg castle, and medieval town gate. In Middle Ages, seat of counts of Henneberg. Was ⊙ duchy of Saxe-Römhild, 1679–1710; then passed to Saxe-Meiningen. Near by is prehistoric Celtic burial ground.

Romid, Tadzhik SSR: see RAMIT.

Romiley, England: see BREDBURY AND ROMILEY.

Romilly-sur-Andelle (rômēyē'-sür-ädĕl'), village (pop. 1,499), Eure dept., NW France, near the Andelle, 10 mi. SE of Rouen; glass- and metal-works; textile milling.

Romilly-sur-Seine (-sür-sĕn'), town (pop. 12,925), Aube dept., NE central France, near Seine R., 22 mi. NW of Troyes; hosiery center; elastic fabrics, needles; railway shops.

Romita (rōmē'tä), town (pop. 6,159), Guanajuato, central Mexico, on central plateau, 21 mi. SE of León; alt. 5,774 ft. Agr. center (cereals, alfalfa, chick-peas, sugar cane, fruit, vegetables, livestock).

Romney (rŭm'nē), officially **New Romney,** municipal borough (1931 pop. 1,786; 1951 census 2,356), S Kent, England, near the Channel, 12 mi. SW of Folkstone, in Romney Marsh; agr. market. It is one of the CINQUE PORTS, though the sea has receded. Has partly-Norman church and remains of 14th-cent. abbey.

Romney (rŏm'nē), town (pop. 2,059), ⊙ Hampshire co., NE W.Va., in Eastern Panhandle, on South Branch of the Potomac and 40 mi. WSW of Martinsburg; trade center for fruitgrowing and agr. area; flour and lumber mills; beverages; limestone quarries. State schools for deaf and blind here. Ice Mtn., where ice is formed the year around, is E. Founded 1762; one of 2 oldest towns in state.

Romney Marsh (rŭm'nē), tract of drained pasture land along Kent coast, England, NE of Rye and SW of Folkstone, and protected by sea wall dating from Roman times. Romney is chief town. Well known for its breed of sheep.

Romny (rŭmnē'). **1** Village (1939 pop. over 500), SE Amur oblast, Russian SFSR, 80 mi. NE of Blagoveshchensk, in agr. area (wheat, livestock). **2** City (1926 pop. 25,787), SW Sumy oblast, Ukrainian SSR, on Sula R. and 60 mi. WSW of Sumy; flour milling; tobacco products, lumber, clothing, shoes. Petroleum wells near by. Known since 11th cent.

Romo (rŭ'mû), Dan. *Rømø*, island (□ 39; pop. 747) of North Frisian group, Denmark, in North Sea, 4 mi. off SW Jutland; bathing resort. Mostly flat and sandy; cultivated strip in E. In Germany until 1920.

Romodan (rŭmŭdän'), town (1926 pop. 1,157), central Poltava oblast, Ukrainian SSR, 15 mi. E of Lubny; rail junction; sugar refining, chemicals.

Romodanovo (–dŭnô′vŭ), village (1926 pop. 2,021), E central Mordvinian Autonomous SSR, Russian SFSR, on Insar R. and 17 mi. NNE of Saransk; distilling center; grain, potatoes. Krasny Uzel (rail junction) is just E, across Insar R.

Romont (rômõ′), Ger. *Remund* (rā′mo͝ont), town (pop. 2,467), Fribourg canton, W Switzerland, on Glâne R. and affluent of the Sarine, 11 mi. SW of Fribourg; glassware. Medieval walls and towers, 13th-cent. castle, Gothic church.

Romorantin (rômôrãtẽ′), town (pop. 5,991), Loir-et-Cher dept., N central France, on Sauldre R. and 25 mi. SE of Blois; woolen cloth and blanket-mfg. center; produces hosiery, shoes, varnish, tools. Has a 15th-cent. castle, rebuilt by Francis I. The Edict of Romorantin (1560) prohibited the Inquisition in France.

Rompin (rŏm″pĭn′), village (pop. 699), SE Pahang, Malaya, minor fishing port on South China Sea at mouth of minor Rompin R., 45 mi. S of Pekan; rice, coconuts.

Romsdal (rôms′däl, ro͝oms′–), valley (60 mi. long) of Rauma R. (several falls), More og Romsdal co., W Norway; cuts into the Dovrefjell from Andalsnes, at head of Romsdal Fjord, to vicinity of Dombas, near head of the Gudbrandsdal, with which it is connected. Anc. highway bet. W and central and S Norway, valley is traversed by Andalsnes branch (completed 1924) of Dovre RR bet. Oslo and Trondheim. Of the many peaks that rise steeply on both sides of valley, the highest are: Venjetinder (6,549 ft.), 20 mi. SE of Andalsnes; Romsdalshorn (5,961 ft.), 8 mi. SE of Andalsnes; and Trolltinder (5,850 ft.), 16 mi. SSE of Andalsnes. Tourist resorts in valley include Kors, 10 mi. SE of Andalsnes, and Verma (văr′mä), 20 mi. SE of Andalsnes, both in Grytten canton. Until 1918, Romsdal was name of More og Romsdal co. In Second World War, valley was scene of action after British landing (April, 1940) at Andalsnes.

Romsdal Fjord, SE arm (25 mi. long, 2–3 mi. wide) of Molde Fjord of North Sea, More og Romsdal co., W Norway. The valley Romsdal extends SE from head of fjord at Andalsnes. Mouth protected by small Sekken isl.

Romsdalshorn (rôms′däls-hôrn, ro͝oms′–), mountain (5,961 ft.), More og Romsdal co., W Norway, on N side of the Romsdal, 8 mi. SE of Andalsnes.

Romsée (rõsā′), town (pop. 2,981), Liége prov., E Belgium, 4 mi. ESE of Liége; coal mining.

Romsey (rŏm′zē), town (pop. 542), S central Victoria, Australia, 35 mi. NNW of Melbourne; livestock; ham, bacon, dairy foods.

Romsey (rŭm′zē). **1** Suburb, Cambridge, England: see Cambridge, city. **2** Municipal borough (1931 pop. 4,862; 1951 census 6,281), W Hampshire, England, on Test R. and 7 mi. NNW of Southampton; agr. market, with leatherworks and breweries. Church, dating from c.1130, is built over remains of church which was part of Benedictine nunnery founded c.907. Florence Nightingale is buried in neighboring village.

Romsey Extra, agr. parish (pop. 2,118), S Hampshire, England, on Test R. just S of Romsey.

Romulus (rŏ′myŭlŭs), village (1940 pop. 815), Wayne co., SE Mich., 19 mi. SW of Detroit, in dairy-, poultry-, and truck-farm area; foundry.

Ron (rōn), town (pop. 7,686), Dharwar dist., S Bombay, India, 50 mi. ENE of Dharwar; markets cotton, peanuts, wheat, millet; oilseed milling. Has 12th-cent. black stone temples.

Rona (rō′nŭ), island (pop. 16), Inner Hebrides, Inverness, Scotland, N of Raasay, 5 mi. E of NE coast of Skye, from which it is separated by Sound of Raasay; Inner Sound, here 4 mi. wide, separates it from mainland. Isl. is 5 mi. long, 1½ mi. wide; rises to 404 ft. At N extremity is lighthouse (57°37′N 5°52′W).

Roñadoiro, Sierra de (syĕ′rä dhä rōnyä-dhoi′rō), NW spur of the Cantabrian Mts., in Oviedo prov., N Spain; extends c.30 mi. N along Navia R. to Bay of Biscay; rises over 4,100 ft.

Ronaldsvlei (rô″nältsflā′) residential town (pop. 1,380), NE Cape Prov., U. of So. Afr., in Griqualand West, 4 mi. S of Kimberley; site of Kimberley airport; 28°49′S 24°45′E.

Ronan (rō′năn′), town (pop. 1,251), Lake co., NW Mont., near Flathead L. and Flathead R., 45 mi. N of Missoula, in irrigated agr. region; flour, dairy products, grain, sugar beets, seed peas; timber. Settled 1910, inc. 1912.

Ronay (rō′nā), island (pop. 6), Outer Hebrides, Inverness, Scotland, just E of Grimsay and bet. North Uist and Benbecula; 2½ mi. long, 1½ mi. wide; rises to 880 ft.

Ronbibul, Thailand: see Ronphibun.

Roncade (rôngkä′dĕ), village (pop. 1,043), Treviso prov., Veneto, N Italy, 7 mi. SE of Treviso; mfg. (alcohol, fire extinguishers, trailers, hydraulic pumps).

Roncador, Serra do (sĕ′rŭ do͞o rōngkŭdôr′), range in central Mato Grosso, Brazil, in 14°S lat., separates headwaters of Xingu R. (NW) from left tributaries of Araguaia R. Average alt. 1,800 ft.

Roncador Bank (rōngkädôr′), coral reef in the Caribbean c.235 mi. off Mosquito Coast of Nicaragua, belonging to Colombia, in San Andrés y Providencia intendancy; 13°35′N 80°4′W. Claimed 1919 by U.S.

Roncaglia (rôngkä′lyä), village, 4 mi. E of Piacenza, N central Italy. Here medieval Ger. emperors reviewed their forces on their way to Rome.

Roncegno (rônchā′nyô), village (pop. 813), Trento prov., Trentino–Alto Adige, N Italy, in Valsugana, 14 mi. E of Trent. Health resort (alt. 1,657 ft.) with hot mineral springs.

Roncesvalles (rōn″sĕsvä′yĕs), town (pop. 3,904), Tolima dept., W central Colombia, in Cordillera Central, 35 mi. SW of Ibagué; cattle-raising center in agr. area (potatoes, corn, beans); lumbering. Founded 1925.

Roncesvalles (rōn″thĕsvä′lyĕs), Fr. *Roncevaux* (rõs-vō′, Eng. rŏn″sŭvō′), hamlet (pop. 149), Navarre prov., N Spain, in the W Pyrenees, near Fr. border, 22 mi. NE of Pamplona (Spain) and 12 mi. SSW of Saint-Jean-Pied-de-Port (France). Has fortress-like Augustinian convent and 13th-cent. pilgrimage church. The famous **Roncesvalles Pass** or Puerto de Ibañeta (alt. 3,468 ft.), 3 mi. N, is celebrated in history and literature as the scene of Roland's death and of the defeat of rear guard of Charlemagne's army. Pass was long an invasion route and was also used in Middle Ages by pilgrims bound for Santiago de Compostela.

Roncevaux, Spain: see Roncesvalles.

Roncevert (rŏn′sŭvûrt), city (pop. 2,301), Greenbrier co., SE W.Va., on Greenbrier R. and 4 mi. SSW of Lewisburg; trade center for agr. (livestock, fruit, tobacco) and coal-mining area; mfg. of foundry products, dairy products; lumber, flour, and feed mills. Organ Cave, 3 mi. SSE, attracts tourists. Settled c.1800.

Ronchamp (rõshã′), town (pop. 1,864), Haute-Saône dept., E France, at foot of the Vosges, 7 mi. E of Lure; cotton spinning, mfg. of textile machinery, sawmilling. Coal mines near by.

Ronchi dei Legionari (rông′kē dā lĕjōnä′rē), town (pop. 3,692), Gorizia prov., Friuli–Venezia Giulia, NE Italy, 2 mi. NW of Monfalcone. Severely damaged in First World War. From here D'Annunzio headed expedition (1919) to occupy Fiume.

Ronchin or **Ronchin-lez-Lille** (rõshẽ′-lā-lēl′), SE suburb (pop. 8,775) of Lille, Nord dept., N France; metalworking, sugar refining, brewing, mfg. of kitchen ranges, varnishes, dyes, biscuits.

Ronchis (rông′kēs), village (pop. 1,839), Udine prov., Friuli–Venezia Giulia, NE Italy, 2 mi. N of Latisana; alcohol.

Ronciglione (rônchēlyō′nĕ), resort town (pop. 6,261), Viterbo prov., Latium, central Italy, near Lago di Vico, 11 mi. SSE of Viterbo; paper mills, foundries; agr. tools. Has cathedral, castle, and anc. houses.

Roncofreddo (rông″kôfrĕd′dô), village (pop. 504), Forlì prov., Emilia-Romagna, N central Italy, near the Rubicon, 13 mi. W of Rimini; agr. tools.

Roncole (rông′kôlĕ), village (pop. 419), Parma prov., Emilia-Romagna, N central Italy, 16 mi. NW of Parma. Verdi b. here.

Ronco River (rông′kô), N central Italy, rises in Etruscan Apennines 9 mi. E of Dicomano, flows 50 mi. NNE, past Galeata and Meldola, joining Montone R. just S of Ravenna to form the Fiumi Uniti. Called Bidente R. in upper course. Canalized and used for irrigation in lower course.

Ronco Scrivia (skrē′vyä), town (pop. 2,377), Genova prov., Liguria, N Italy, at N end of Giovi Pass railroad tunnel, on Scrivia R. and 14 mi. N of Genoa; rail junction; resort; mfg. (wine, linen, hemp, metal products).

Roncq (rõk), town (pop. 3,177), Nord dept., N France, 3 mi. NNW of Tourcoing; textile industry.

Ronda (rōn′dä), city (pop. 15,813), Málaga prov., S Spain, in Andalusia, in the Sierra de Ronda, on railroad and 40 mi. NNE of Gibraltar, 40 mi. W of Málaga. One of the most colorful Sp. towns, typically Andalusian, it is famous for its picturesque location on 2 hills, separated by the Tajo de Ronda, a deep ravine cut by an affluent of the Guadiaro R. and crossed by several bridges (among them a notable, c.300-ft.-high, 18th-cent. structure). Its healthful climate and architectural attractions (there are many historic relics) make Ronda a popular resort. Also a processing and trading center; exports produce of the region, chiefly olives, grapes, chick-peas, cereals, chestnuts, walnuts, timber, and livestock. Has lumber-, flour-, and sawmills; liquor distilleries, limekiln, tanneries. Also mfg. of soft drinks, tiles, ceramics (majolica), esparto goods, knitwear, soap, plaster. The old town, called San Miguel, is built on S hill; the new town, Mercadillo, on N hill. The former dates back probably to a Roman town, but is chiefly of Moorish character; it has a partly destroyed *alcazaba* (citadel). The new town was founded 1485 by the Catholic Kings after surrender of Ronda. The 16th-cent. poet Vicente Espinel was b. here. An underground stairway leads from Ronda to the river. Five mi. NNW are the remains of Ronda la Vieja, considered to be of Iberian origin, and containing ruins of a Roman theater. The region is sometimes identified with Munda.

Ronda (rŏn′dŭ), town (pop. 545), Wilkes co., NW N.C., on Yadkin R. and 5 mi. WSW of Elkin.

Ronda, Sierra de, or **Serranía de Ronda** (syĕ′rä, sĕrănē′ä, dhä rōn′dä), spur of the Cordillera Penibética, in Andalusia, S Spain, along Málaga-Cádiz prov. border, extends c.40 mi. NW–SE; rises over 5,000 ft. Rich in minerals, such as iron, platinum, antimony, bismuth, gold, coal. The Sierra de Tolox (S), which rises in the Tolox or Torrecilla peak to c.6,300 ft., is sometimes considered part of range. Region is known as a smugglers' hide-out.

Rondane (rôn′nänŭ), mountain range in Opland and Hedmark counties, S central Norway, extends c.50 mi. E–W bet. the upper Gudbrandsdal and the Osterdal; rises to 7,162 ft. in the Rondeslottet (rôn′nŭslôt-tŭ), 60 mi. NNW of Lillehammer. Several small glaciers in N part of range. Sometimes called Rondanefjell.

Ronde (rû′nŭ), Dan. *Rønde*, town (pop. 1,119), Randers amt, E Jutland, Denmark, on Djursland peninsula 20 mi. SE of Randers; dairy products.

Rondebosch (rôn′dŭbŏs), residential town, SW Cape Prov., U. of So. Afr., SSE suburb of Cape Town. Near by is Groote Schuur, formerly residence of Cecil Rhodes, and site of Rhodes Memorial and of Univ. of Cape Town (1916) bldgs.

Ronde Island (rŏnd), islet (pop. 62), S Grenadines, dependency of Grenada, B.W.I., 20 mi. NNE of St. George's; 12°18′N 61°35′W.

Rondo (rŏn′dō), town (pop. 194), Lee co., E Ark., 16 mi. NW of Helena, in agr. area.

Rondônia (rōndō′nyŭ), town, central Guaporé territory, W Brazil, on Cuiabá–Pôrto Velho telegraph line, and 200 mi. SE of Pôrto Velho. Formerly called Presidente Penna.

Rondonópolis (rōndōnô′po͞olēs), town (pop. 82), central Mato Grosso, Brazil, 110 mi. SE of Cuiabá; has airfield. Named after explorer Rondon.

Rondorf (rôn′dôrf), village (pop. 15,753), in former Prussian Rhine Prov., W Germany, after 1945 in North Rhine-Westphalia, 4 mi. S of Cologne.

Rondout Creek (rŏn′dout), SE N.Y., rises in the Catskills in W Ulster co., flows SW, SE, and NE, past Napanoch, Kerhonkson, and Rosendale, to the Hudson at Kingston, where its lower ½ mi. forms Rondout Harbor; c.50 mi. long. Receives small Wallkill R. below Rosendale. Merriman Dam (2,450 ft. long, 200 ft. high; earth-fill) on upper course impounds Rondout Reservoir (8 mi. long; filling begun 1951). From reservoir, to which tunnels extend from Pepacton and Neversink reservoirs, Delaware Aqueduct runs to New York city.

Rondu (rōn′do͞o), village, Ladakh dist., N Kashmir, in Deosai Mts. (alt. c.6,650 ft.), on left bank of the Indus and 34 mi. NW of Skardu; wheat, corn, pulse, fruit trees. Fort. Copper deposits near by. Also called Mendhi.

Ronga (rŭn-gä′), village (1939 pop. over 500), central Mari Autonomous SSR, Russian SFSR, 24 mi. E of Ioshkar-Ola; wheat, rye, oats.

Rongai (rông-gī′), town, Rift Valley prov., W central Kenya, rail junction for Lake Solai and 20 mi. NW of Nakuru; alt. 6,137 ft.; coffee, wheat, corn; dairying.

Rongbuk (rông′bo͝ok), village and lamasery, S Tibet, 35 mi. SSW of Shekar, 16 mi. NNW of Mt. Everest, near N end of 9-mi.-long Rongbuk Glacier rising on Mt. Everest; base for Mt. Everest expeditions.

Ronge, Lac la (läk lä rōzh′), lake (□ 450), central Sask., 140 mi. NNE of Prince Albert; 36 mi. long, 36 mi. wide. Drains NE into Churchill R. Region is rich in minerals.

Rongelap (rông′ĕläp), atoll (□ 3; pop. 95), Ralik Chain, Kwajalein dist., Marshall Isls., W central Pacific, 150 mi. NNW of Kwajalein; c.35 mi. long; 61 islets. Sometimes spelled Rongelab.

Rongerik (rông′ŭrĭk), uninhabited atoll, Ralik Chain, Marshall Isls., W central Pacific, 150 mi. N of Kwajalein; c.30 mi. in circumference; 17 islets. Bikini natives, brought here (1946) by U.S., were moved (1947) to Ujelang, and were settled (1949) on Kili. Sometimes spelled Rongirik.

Roniu, Mount (rōnē′o͞o), highest peak (4,341 ft.) on Taiarapu peninsula, E Tahiti, Society Isls.

Ronkonkoma (rŏngkŏng′kŭmŭ), village (pop. 1,334), Suffolk co., SE N.Y., on central Long Isl., c.2 mi. SSW of Lake Ronkonkoma village and L. Ronkonkoma, in diversified-farming area.

Ronne (rû′nŭ), Dan. *Rønne*, city (1950 pop. 12,696), ⊙Bornholm amt, Denmark, port on W Bornholm isl.; 55°6′N 14°42′E. Granite works, pottery, fisheries. Dates from 12th cent.

Ronne Bay (rŏ′nŭ), broad (c.150 naut. mi. long, 90 naut. mi. wide) SW entrance to George VI Sound, opening off Bellingshausen Sea, bet. Alexander I Isl. and Robert English Coast, in 72°30′S 75°W. Discovered 1940 by Finn Ronne and Carl Eklund, U.S. explorers.

Ronneburg (rô′nŭbo͝ork), town (pop. 9,189), Thuringia, central Germany, 5 mi. E of Gera; woolen milling, synthetic-leather mfg., woodworking. Spa.

Ronneby (rôn′ŭbü″), city (pop. 6,545), Blekinge co., S Sweden, on Ronneby R., Swedish *Ronnebyån* (50 mi. long), near its mouth on the Baltic, 12 mi. WNW of Karlskrona; sugar refining, tanning, enamelware mfg., stone quarrying. Health resort with chalybeate springs. Has 13th-cent. church. Town founded in 13th cent., 1st chartered 1387, rechartered as town 1714, as city 1882.

Ronneby (rŏ'nĭbē), village (pop. 72), Benton co., central Minn., on tributary of Elk R. and 17 mi. ENE of St. Cloud, in grain and livestock area.

Ronnenberg (rô'nŭnbĕrk), village (pop. 3,902), in former Prussian prov. of Hanover, W Germany, after 1945 in Lower Saxony, 5 mi. SW of Hanover city center; rock-salt and potash mining.

Ronne River, Swedish *Rönneå* (rû'nûō"), S Sweden, issues from Ring L., flows 50 mi. NW, past Klippan and Angelholm (head of navigation), to Skalder Bay of the Kattegat 2 mi. NW of Angelholm.

Ronninge (rûn'ĭng-ů), Swedish *Rönninge*, residential village (pop. 1,349), Stockholm co., E Sweden, 3 mi. W of Sodertalje.

Ronnskar (rûn'shâr"), Swedish *Rönnskär*, village, Vasterbotten co., N Sweden, on Gulf of Bothnia, at mouth of Skellefte R., 8 mi. SE of Skelleftea; metal-smelting center, serving mines at Boliden and Kristineberg.

Ronphibun (rôn'pē'bōōn), village (1937 pop. 6,563), Nakhon Sithammarat prov., S Thailand, in Malay Peninsula, 18 mi. SSW of Nakhon Sithammarat, in Sithammarat Range; major tin-mining center. Also spelled Ronpibun, Ronpibul, and Ronbibul.

Ronquillo, El (ĕl rōng-kē'lyō), town (pop. 1,865), Seville prov., SW Spain, 25 mi. NNW of Seville; cereals, oranges, honey, livestock. Lead mining.

Rönsahl (rûn'zäl), village (pop. 1,114), in former Prussian prov. of Westphalia, W Germany, after 1945 in North Rhine-Westphalia, 5 mi. E of Wipperfürth. Kerspe dam and reservoir 1 mi. NW.

Ronsdorf (rôns'dôrf), S section (1925 pop. 15,174) of WUPPERTAL, W Germany, 3.5 mi. S of Barmen; mfg. of tools and ribbons. Inc. (1929) with neighboring towns to form city of Wuppertal.

Ronse, Belgium: see RENAIX.

Ronsperg, Czechoslovakia: see POBEZOVICE.

Ronzan, Korea: see NONSAN.

Roodepoort-Maraisburg (rōō'dŭpōōrt-märä'bûrkh), town (pop. 72,231), S Transvaal, U. of So. Afr., on Witwatersrand, 9 mi. W of Johannesburg; alt. 5,725 ft.; gold-mining and residential center. Sprawling municipality including towns of Roodepoort (W), Florida, and Maraisburg (E).

Roodhouse, city (pop. 2,368), Greene co., W central Ill., 19 mi. SSW of Jacksonville, in agr. area; mfg. of envelopes; railroad shops; bituminous-coal mines. Inc. 1881.

Roodt-sur-Syr (rōt-sür-zēr'), village (pop. 267), SE Luxembourg, on Syre R. and 9 mi. ENE of Luxembourg city; sawmills.

Roof Butte (9,576 ft.), NE Ariz., in Chuska Mts., near N.Mex. line, c.50 mi. WSW of Farmington, N.Mex.

Rooiberg (rōō'ĭbĕrkh), village, W Transvaal, U. of So. Afr., 75 mi. NNW of Pretoria; tin-mining center. Mining believed to have begun here in Phoenician times.

Rooke Island or **Umboi** (ōōm'boi), volcanic island (□ 300), in Morobe dist., Bismarck Archipelago, Territory of New Guinea, SW Pacific, 10 mi. W of New Britain; 27 mi. long, 15 mi. wide; rises to 4,500 ft. Also spelled Rook.

Rooks, county (□ 893; pop. 9,043), N central Kansas; ⊙ Stockton. Rolling prairie region, drained by South Fork Solomon R. Grain (chiefly wheat) and livestock. Scattered oil fields. Formed 1872.

Roopville, town (pop. 202), Carroll co., W Ga., 9 mi. SSW of Carrollton; granite quarrying.

Roorkee (rōōr'kē), town (pop., including cantonment, 27,364), Saharanpur dist., N Uttar Pradesh, India, on tributary of the Ganges and 22 mi. ESE of Saharanpur; textile mfg. Hq. of Ganges Canal workshops; iron foundry. Building Research Inst. (established 1949), Irrigation Research Inst., Thomason Civil Engineering Col. (founded 1847; large library). Also spelled Rurki. Hydroelectric station 7 mi. SSE, at village of Muhammadpur (also spelled Mohammadpur).

Roosbeek (rōz'bāk). **1** Village (pop. 1,112), Brabant prov., central Belgium, near Louvain. **2** or **Rebecq-Rognon** (rŭbĕk'-rônyō'), agr. village (pop. 4,069), Brabant prov., central Belgium, 7 mi. SW of Hal.

Roosebeke, Belgium: see ROZEBEKE.

Roosendaal (rō'zŭndäl), town (pop. 23,900), North Brabant prov., SW Netherlands, 14 mi. WSW of Breda; rail junction (with repair shops); frontier station near Belg. border; cigars, brushes, furniture, copperware, powdered milk; beet-sugar refining, meat packing; tree nurseries. Also spelled Rozendaal.

Roosevelt. 1 County (□ 2,385; pop. 9,580), NE Mont.; ⊙ Poplar. Agr. area bordering N.Dak.; bounded S by Missouri R.; drained by Poplar R. Grain, livestock. Fort Peck Indian Reservation extends throughout most of co. Formed 1919. **2** County (□ 2,455; pop. 16,409), E N.Mex.; ⊙ Portales. Grain and livestock region bordering on Texas. Eastern N.Mex. State Park in NE. Formed 1903.

Roosevelt. 1 Village, Gila co., central Ariz., on Roosevelt Reservoir, 25 mi. NW of Globe; residential community for employees of Roosevelt Dam. Tonto Natl. Monument just SE. **2** Village (pop. 228), Roseau co., NW Minn., near Lake of the Woods, 31 mi. ESE of Roseau, in grain area. **3** Borough (pop. 720), Monmouth co., central N.J., 4 mi. SE of Hightstown. Founded 1933 as Jersey Homesteads, govt.-aided experiment in cooperative agr. and mfg.; sold 1940, later renamed. **4** Residential village (1940 pop. 8,248), Nassau co., SE N.Y., on SW Long Isl., just SE of Hempstead; mfg. (clothing, machinery, cement blocks, textiles, auto accessories, organs). **5** Town (pop. 679), Kiowa co., SW Okla., 13 mi. SSE of Hobart; trading point for farm area; cotton ginning. **6** City (pop. 1,628), Duchesne co., NE Utah, in Uinta R. valley, 110 mi. ESE of Salt Lake City, near Uinta Mts.; alt. 5,100 ft.; trading point for ranching and agr. area served by irrigation works on Lake Fork; dairy products, flour. Settled 1908, inc. 1913. Gilsonite mines in vicinity. Uintah and Ouray Indian Reservation near by.

Roosevelt, Mount (9,500 ft.), N B.C., in Rocky Mts.; 58°27'N 125°20'W.

Roosevelt Dam, central Ariz., on Salt R. and c.55 mi. ENE of Phoenix. Masonry, arch-gravity type (280 ft. high, 1,125 ft. long; completed 1911 by Bureau of Reclamation); 1st major unit of Salt R. irrigation project. Forms Roosevelt Reservoir (23 mi. long, 2 mi. wide; capacity 1,398,000 acre-ft.).

Roosevelt International Bridge, N.Y. and Ont.: see ROOSEVELTOWN, N.Y.

Roosevelt Island, Antarctica, E part of Ross Shelf Ice, 3 mi. S of head of Bay of Whales, in 79°30'S 162°W; 90 naut. mi. long, 40 naut. mi. wide. Discovered 1934 by R. E. Byrd.

Roosevelt Lake, Wash.: see GRAND COULEE DAM.

Rooseveltown, village, St. Lawrence co., N N.Y., 8 mi. ENE of Massena; port of entry. Here is Roosevelt International Bridge (1934) across the St. Lawrence to Cornwall, Ont. Until 1934, called Nyando (nīăn'dō).

Roosevelt Park, city (pop. 1,254), Muskegon co., SW Mich., just SW of Muskegon. Inc. 1946.

Roosevelt River (Port. rōzvĕl'), in Mato Grosso and Amazonas, W Brazil, rises in the Serra dos Parecis (in Guaporé territory) near 12°30'S 60°10'W, flows c.400 mi. N to the Aripuanã near 7°30'S 60°40'W. Called Rio da Dúvida (River of Doubt) until explored by, and named in honor of, Theodore Roosevelt in 1914. Also known as Teodoro or Theodoro R. Lower course of Aripuanã is sometimes also called Roosevelt R.

Roosevelt Roads, U.S. naval reservation in E Puerto Rico, just SE of Ceiba, opposite Vieques Isl., and surrounding the fine harbor of Ensenada Honda. Airfield 2½ mi. SE; Fort Bundy on N shore.

Roost-Warendin (rōst värädē'), town (pop. 2,928), Nord dept., N France, 4 mi. N of Douai; coal-mining center (Escarpelle mines).

Root (rōt), town (pop. 2,001), Lucerne canton, central Switzerland, near Reuss R., 6 mi. NE of Lucerne.

Root, Mount (rōōt) (12,860 ft.), on Alaska-B.C. border, in Fairweather Range, 7 mi. N of Mt. Fairweather; 58°59'N 137°30'W.

Root River. 1 In SE Minn., formed by confluence of North Branch (70 mi. long) and South Branch (50 mi. long) near Lanesboro, flows 60 mi. E, past Rushford and Houston, to Mississippi R. at La Crosse, Wis. **2** In SE Wis., rises in Waukesha co., flows c.35 mi. generally SE, past Greendale, to L. Michigan at Racine.

Roozebeke, Belgium: see ROZEBEKE.

Ropczyce (rôp-chĭ'tsĕ), town (pop. 2,822), Rzeszow prov., SE Poland, 18 mi. W of Rzeszow; brickworks.

Roper, town (pop. 793), Washington co., E N.C., 7 mi. E of Plymouth; sawmilling.

Roper River, NE Northern Territory, Australia, rises in hills NNW of Mataranka, flows 260 mi. E to Limmen Bight of Gulf of Carpentaria. Navigable 100 mi. by small craft.

Ropesville, town (pop. 391), Hockley co., NW Texas, 16 mi. SE of Levelland.

Ropi (rō'pē), mountain (3,084 ft.), Lapland, N Finland, near Swedish and Norwegian borders; 68°50'N 21°36'E.

Ropp (rôp), town (pop. 1,469), Plateau Prov., Northern Provinces, central Nigeria, on Bauchi Plateau, 28 mi. S of Jos; tin-mining center.

Rop-Ruchei, Karelo-Finnish SSR: see SHELTOZERO.

Ropsha (rôp'shŭ), village (1939 pop. over 500), W central Leningrad oblast, Russian SFSR, 8 mi. W of Krasnoye Selo; road center; paper mill, brickworks. Castle (built under Peter the Great) was favorite residence of Elizabeth Petrovna; scene of murder (1762) of Peter III.

Roque (rō'kä), village (pop. 412), Matanzas prov., W Cuba, on the Canal del Roque, on railroad and 21 mi. SE of Cárdenas; sugar cane, fruit.

Roque, Canal del (känäl' dĕl), artificial waterway, Matanzas prov., W Cuba; fed by lagoon SW of Colón, it flows c.30 mi. N to E shore of Cárdenas Bay, joining small San Antonio R. in lower course. Built to prevent flooding during rainy season.

Roquebillière (rôkbēyâr'), village (pop. 926), Alpes-Maritimes dept., SE France, in Vésubie R. valley and 22 mi. N of Nice, in Maritime Alps; sawmilling, olive-oil pressing.

Roque Bluffs (rōk), town (pop. 80), Washington co., E Maine, on Englishman Bay and 7 mi. S of Machias.

Roquebrune (rôkbrün'), Ital. *Roccabruna*, village (pop. 1,397), Alpes-Maritimes dept., SE France, on Fr. Riviera, 11 mi. ENE of Nice, amidst orange and lemon groves. Consists of a single street, the rest being narrow flights of steps. Has ruins of 10th-cent. castle. SE is Cap-Martin, a fashionable resort on headland of same name which commands bays of Menton (NE) and Monte-Carlo (W). In principality of Monaco until 1848.

Roquebrussanne, La (lä rôkbrüsän'), village (pop. 547), Var dept., SE France, 15 mi. N of Toulon; olives, fruits.

Roquecourbe (rôk-kōōrb'), village (pop. 960), Tarn dept., S France, on Agout R. and 5 mi. NNE of Castres; hosiery and furniture mfg.

Roquefavour, France: see ARC RIVER.

Roquefort (rôkfôr'). **1** or **Roquefort-sur-Soulzon** -sür-sōōzō', rŏk'fûrt), village (pop. 1,190), Aveyron dept., S France, at foot of the Causse du Larzac, 9 mi. SSW of Millau; major cheese mfg. and distributing center. **2** Village (pop. 1,208), Landes dept., SW France, on the Douze (headstream of Midouze R.) and 13 mi. NE of Mont-de-Marsan; paper milling, resin extracting.

Roque González de Santa Cruz (rō'kä gōnsä'lĕs dā sän'tä krōōs'), town (dist. pop. 10,706), Paraguarí dept., S Paraguay, 50 mi. SE of Asunción; agr. center (oranges, cattle); oil of petitgrain refining, tanning. Founded 1538. Formerly Tabapy.

Roque Island (rōk), Washington co., E Maine, crescent-shaped isl. in Englishman Bay, 10 mi. SSW of Machias; 3 mi. long.

Roquemaure (rôkmōr'), village (pop. 1,568), Gard dept., S France, on right bank of Rhone R. and 7 mi. N of Avignon; fruit- and winegrowing.

Roque Pérez (rō'kä pā'rĕs), town (pop. 3,618) ⊙ Roque Pérez dist. (□ 607; pop. 11,965), N central Buenos Aires prov., Argentina, on the Río Salado and 20 mi. SW of Lobos; agr. center (flax, grain, livestock); dairying, seed cultivating.

Roque Point, La, Jersey, Channel Isls.: see SAINT CLEMENT.

Roques, Los (lōs rō'kĕs), group of small Caribbean islands and federal dependency of Venezuela, 85 mi. N of Caracas; consist of 2 larger, narrow islets and a great number of smaller ones; 11°43'–12°N 68°35'–66°57'W. Sparsely inhabited; have salt and guano deposits; some sponge fishing.

Roquesteron (rôkĕstûrō'), village (pop. 254), Alpes-Maritimes dept., SE France, 18 mi. NW of Nice; olives.

Roquetas (rōkä'täs), city (pop. 4,084), Tarragona prov., NE Spain, 2 mi. W of Tortosa, and on Ebro lateral canal; mfg. of tower clocks, soap; olive-oil processing; livestock (sheep, goats), vegetables, carob beans.

Roquetas de Mar (dhā mär'), village (pop. 1,626), Almería prov., S Spain, near the Mediterranean, 10 mi. SW of Almería; fishing. Cereals, truck produce, wine grown in the area. Ships grapes. Saltworks.

Roquevaire (rôkvâr'), village (pop. 1,332), Bouches-du-Rhône dept., SE France, 12 mi. ENE of Marseilles, at E foot of Chaîne de l'Étoile; cement-works; mfg. of crating for fruit shipping.

Rora (rû'rä), Nor. *Røra*, village and canton (pop. 942), Nord-Trondelag co., central Norway, on E shore of Trondheim Fjord, on railroad and 7 mi. NNE of Levanger. At Hylla (hül'lä) village, 1 mi. SW, are lime quarries.

Roraas, Norway: see ROROS.

Roraima, Mount (rôrī'mů), peak (9,219 ft.) at junction of Brazil–Br. Guiana–Venezuela boundaries, 275 mi. SE of Ciudad Bolívar, in the Sierra Pacaraima; 5°12'N 60°43'W. Highest point of the Guiana Highlands. A giant table mtn., with a total surface of 26 sq. mi., of which 6 are divided bet. Br. Guiana and Brazil, the rest belonging to Venezuela. First climbed 1884.

Rorkesdrift or **Rorke's Drift** (rôrks"drĭft'), agr. village, Zululand, central Natal, U. of So. Afr., on Buffalo R. and 25 mi. SE of Dundee; mission station. Boundary commission (1878) to settle border dispute bet. Afrikaners and Zulus met here. In Zulu War (1879) it was site of British camp, besieged by Zulu force.

Roros (rû'rōs), Nor. *Røros*, village (pop. 2,556; canton pop. 3,329), Sor-Trondelag co., central Norway, on Glomma R., on railroad and 65 mi. SSE of Trondheim; road junction for Sweden-bound traffic; center for near-by pyrite mines, the most important in Norway. Produces refined copper, wrought iron, exported via Trondheim. Has church (1780), museums. Copper mined since 1644. Formerly spelled Roraas.

Rorschach (rôr'shäkh), town (1950 pop. 11,291), St. Gall, NE Switzerland, 6 mi. NE of St. Gall; an old port and resort on L. Constance; textiles (cotton, artificial silk), aluminum, flour; printing. Has 17th-cent. R.C. church.

Rorschacherberg (rôr'shäkh-ŭrbĕrk"), commune (pop. 2,211), St. Gall canton, NE Switzerland, just S of Rorschach; metal- and woodworking.

Roruks (rōrōōks'), town (pop. 750), Northern Prov., W central Sierra Leone, on railroad and 17 mi. NE of Bauya; palm oil and kernels, piassava, kola nuts. Has mission school.

Rorvik, Norway: see VIKNA ISLANDS.

Ros, lake, Norway: see ROS LAKE.

Ros, river, Norway: see ROS RIVER.

Ros, river, Ukrainian SSR: see ROS RIVER.
Ros, Lake (rôsh), Pol. *Roś*, Ger. *Warshau* (vär′shou) (□ 8.5), in East Prussia, after 1945 in NE Poland, ENE of Pisz; one of Masurian Lakes; 8 mi. long, 1–2 mi. wide; S outlet is Pisa R. (right tributary of Narew R.).
Rosa, India: see SHAHJAHANPUR, city.
Rosa or **Rosaa,** river, Norway: see ROS RIVER.
Rosa, Cape (rô′sä), headland of Constantine dept., NE Algeria, on the Mediterranean, 26 mi. ENE of Bône; 36°57′N 8°15′E. Lighthouse.
Rosa, La, Venezuela: see LA ROSA.
Rosa, Monte, Italy and Switzerland: see MONTE ROSA.
Rosal de la Frontera (rōsäl′ dhā lä frōntä′rä), town (pop. 2,845), Huelva prov., SW Spain, near Port. border, 50 mi. NNW of Huelva; olives, cereals, acorns, cork, peaches, pomegranates, oranges, livestock. Flour milling, olive-oil pressing. Customhouse on highway opposite Vila Verde de Ficalho (Portugal).
Rosales (rōsä′lĕs), town (pop. estimate 1,000), S Córdoba prov., Argentina, 19 mi. E of Laboulaye; grain, livestock; dairying.
Rosales, town (pop. 1,300), Chihuahua, N Mexico, on San Pedro R. and 32 mi. SE of Chihuahua; corn, cotton, beans, sugar cane, cattle. Sometimes Santa Cruz de Rosales.
Rosales, town (1939 pop. 4,119; 1948 municipality pop. 19,851), Pangasinan prov., central Luzon, Philippines, 22 mi. ESE of Dagupan; agr. center (rice, copra, corn). Airfield.
Rosalia (rōzāl′yů), town (pop. 660), Whitman co., SE Wash., 28 mi. S of Spokane; wheat, dairy products.
Rosalie, village (pop. 212), Thurston co., NE Nebr., 12 mi. ESE of Pender, near Missouri R.; grain, livestock.
Rosalie Peak, Colo.: see FRONT RANGE.
Rosalind, village (pop. estimate 100), S central Alta., 23 mi. SE of Camrose; coal mining.
Rosamond, village (pop. c.500), Kern co., S central Calif., in Mojave Desert, 13 mi. S of Mojave; cattle; gold mines near. Rosamond Dry L., a desert playa c.5 mi. in diameter, is E.
Rosamorada (rōsämōrä′dä), town (pop. 1,151), Nayarit, W Mexico, in Pacific lowland, 45 mi. NW of Tepic; corn, tobacco, sugar cane, beans, tomatoes, bananas, cattle.
Rosanna River (rōzä′nä), Tyrol, W Austria, rises near Vorarlberg border, flows 25 mi. N and E, past Sankt Anton, through the Stanzertal, joining Trisanna R., with which it flows (as Sanna R.) 4 mi. E to Inn R. at Landeck.
Rosans (rôzäs′), village (pop. 310), Hautes-Alpes dept., SE France, in Dauphiné Alps, 16 mi. ENE of Nyons; lavender-essence distilling.
Rosario (rōsä′ryō), city (pop. 464,688), ⊙ Rosario dept. (□ 720; 1947 pop. 531,276), SE Santa Fe prov., Argentina, on right bank of Paraná R. and 90 mi. S of Santa Fe, 170 mi. NW of Buenos Aires; 32°57′S 60°38′W. Second city of Argentina, railroad hub, transoceanic port, commercial and industrial center. A great export and import center for the central and northern provs., including the Pampa and Chaco regions, Rosario ships mainly grain, meat, hides, sugar, wool, and quebracho. Its varied industries include sugar refining, flour milling, meat packing, maté processing, brewing, paper milling, tanning, printing, and mfg. of furniture, tools, bricks. There are grain elevators and gasoline storage tanks. Airport. City has administrative bldgs., cathedral (Ital. Renaissance style), theaters, hospitals, Fuentes Palace, a large park, museums, libraries. Its educational institutions include the schools of medicine, law, and economics of the Litoral Univ. The city, founded 1725, developed rapidly after 1859, when Gen. Urquiza declared it the port of the confederation of the upper provs.
Rosário (rōōzä′ryōō). **1** City (pop. 4,080), N Maranhão, Brazil, landing on Itapecuru R. at its mouth on São José Bay of the Atlantic, on São Luís–Teresina RR and 26 mi. S of São Luís; rice, corn, andiroba oil, hides. **2** City, Rio Grande do Sul, Brazil: see ROSÁRIO DO SUL. **3** City, Sergipe, Brazil: see ROSÁRIO DO CATETE.
Rosario or **El Rosario** (ĕl rōsä′ryō), village (1930 pop. 450), Colchagua prov., central Chile, near the coast, 55 mi. NW of San Fernando, in agr. area (grain, potatoes, livestock).
Rosario, town (pop. 2,442), Norte de Santander dept., N Colombia, near Venezuela border, 6 mi. SE of Cúcuta; coffee, cacao, tobacco, stock. Now a natl. shrine, commemorating the congress held here 1821 by patriots, in which the union of New Granada, Ecuador, and Venezuela was confirmed and the name Gran Colombia adopted. The international Bolívar Bridge across Venezuela border (Táchira R.) to San Antonio is 2 mi. E. Sometimes Rosario de Cúcuta.
Rosario, village, Santiago-Zamora prov., SE Ecuador, on E slopes of the Andes, 45 mi. SE of Cuenca, in selva region; alt. 4,659 ft.
Rosario. **1** Village (pop. 305), Northern Territory, Lower California, NW Mexico, near Pacific coast, 140 mi. SSE of Ensenada; some agr. (maguey, livestock). Founded 1774 as Dominican mission. Yaqui Indian colony adjoins. **2** City (pop. 8,323), Sinaloa, NW Mexico, in coastal lowland, on Buluarte R. and 38 mi. SE of Mazatlán, on railroad; silver-mining center; agr. (cotton, sugar cane, fruit, vegetables). **3** Town (pop. 963), Sonora, NW Mexico, 95 mi. E of Guaymas; stock raising (cattle, hogs, horses).
Rosario, town (dist. pop. 6,270), San Pedro dept., central Paraguay, on Paraguay R. and 65 mi. NNE of Asunción; agr. (tobacco, maté, oranges, livestock), processing, and lumbering center; tanneries, distilleries; extraction of oil of petitgrain. Lime quarrying, salt mining.
Rosario. **1** Town (1939 pop. 2,067; 1948 municipality pop. 36,020), Batangas prov., S Luzon, Philippines, 18 mi. SSW of San Pablo; agr. center (rice, sugar cane, corn, coconuts). **2** Town (1939 pop. 1,477; 1948 municipality pop. 12,869), La Union prov., N central Luzon, Philippines, 14 mi. SW of Baguio, near Lingayen Gulf; rice growing.
Rosario (rōsär′yō), town (pop. 8,500), Colonia dept., SW Uruguay, on railroad and 30 mi. ENE of Colonia; agr. products (wheat, corn, milk, butter, cheese).
Rosario, town (pop. 1,958), Zulia state, NW Venezuela, in Maracaibo lowlands, 25 mi. NE of Machiques; sugar, cattle.
Rosario, Canal del (känäl′ dĕl), Caribbean channel (c.2 mi. wide) off S central Cuba, bet. the keys Cayo Rosario (E) and Cayo Cantiles (W); 21°38′N 81°57′W.
Rosario, El (ĕl), village (pop. 1,209), Tenerife, Canary Isls., 7 mi. W of Santa Cruz de Tenerife; cereals, bananas, tomatoes, potatoes, onions, wine, fruit. Also called La Esperanza; El Rosario is name for commune.
Rosario, El, Honduras: see EL ROSARIO.
Rosario, El, Nicaragua: see EL ROSARIO.
Rosario, Peñón del (pānyōn′ dĕl), peak (11,214 ft.), central Mexico, on Tlaxcala–Puebla border, 8 mi. NW of Tlaxco.
Rosario, Sierra del (syĕ′rä dĕl), mountain range, Pinar del Río prov., W Cuba; continuing the Sierra de los Órganos, it extends c.45 mi. ENE. Rises in Pan de Guajaibón to 2,533 ft.
Rosario de Cúcuta, Colombia: see ROSARIO.
Rosario de la Frontera (dā lä frōntä′rä), town (1947 pop. 4,613), ⊙ Rosario de la Frontera dept. (□ 2,200; 1947 pop. 14,248), S Salta prov., Argentina, 75 mi. SSE of Salta; alt. 3,200 ft. Rail junction, health resort (curative thermal waters), lumbering and agr. center (corn, peas, livestock); sawmills, flour mills.
Rosario de Lerma (dā lĕr′mä), town (pop. estimate 1,000), ⊙ Rosario de Lerma dept. (□ 1,730; 1947 pop. 12,111), central Salta prov., Argentina, in Lerma Valley, on railroad and 17 mi. SW of Salta; agr. center (corn, alfalfa, oats, tobacco, livestock). Hydroelectric station on Toro R. Iron deposits near by.
Rosário do Catete (rōōzä′ryōō dōō kŏŏtä′tĭ), city (pop. 1,871), E Sergipe, NE Brazil, on railroad and 15 mi. N of Aracaju; ships sugar, cotton. Mineral springs. Until 1944, called Rosário.
Rosário do Sul (sōōl′), city (pop. 6,733), W central Rio Grande do Sul, Brazil, on railroad and 55 mi. NE of Livramento; meat-packing center (canning, mfg. of jerked beef). Until 1944, called Rosário.
Rosario Island (rōzâ′rēō), Jap. *Nishino-shima* (nē′shĕnō shĭmä), in W Pacific Ocean, W of Bonin Isls.; 27°15′N 140°53′E. Formerly a Jap. possession, it passed after Second World War under U.S. administration.
Rosário Oeste (rōōzä′ryōō wĕ′stĭ), city (pop. 1,584), Mato Grosso, Brazil, on upper Cuiabá R. and 50 mi. NNW of Cuiabá; cattle. Gold placers.
Rosario Point, Nicaragua: see COSIGÜINA PENINSULA.
Rosario Strait (rōzâ′rēō), NW Wash., passage (c.25 mi. long) E of San Juan Isls., linking Georgia Strait (N) to Puget Sound and Juan de Fuca Strait.
Rosario Tala, Rosario de Tala, or **Rosario del Tala** (rōsär′yō dä, dĕl, tä′lä), town (1947 census pop. 10,354), ⊙ Tala dept. (□ 985; 1947 census pop. 30,857), central Entre Ríos prov., Argentina, on railroad and 90 mi. ESE of Paraná; agr. center (corn, flax, wheat, livestock); flour, corn milling.
Rosarno (rōzär′nō), town (pop. 7,793), Reggio di Calabria prov., Calabria, S Italy, 11 mi. NNE of Palmi; agr. center (olives, grapes, citrus fruit). Destroyed by earthquake of 1783.
Rosas (rō′säs), town (pop. 2,644), Gerona prov., NE Spain, 11 mi. E of Figueras, on N shore of Gulf of Rosas. Olive-oil and wine processing, fish salting; lumbering. Has remains of 16th-cent. pentagonal citadel. Fortifications of port, dating from 13th cent., were dismantled by French in 1814.
Rosas, Gulf of, Mediterranean inlet (12 mi. N–S) in Gerona prov., NE Spain, in Catalonia, near Fr. border, 70 mi. NE of Barcelona. Into it flow Fluviá and Ter rivers. On its shores are ports of Rosas (N) and La Escala (SW).
Rosas, Las, Argentina: see LAS ROSAS.
Rosas, Las, Mexico: see LAS ROSAS.
Rosbach (rôs′bäkh), village (pop. 5,853), in former Prussian Rhine Prov., W Germany, after 1945 in North Rhine-Westphalia, on the Sieg and 22 mi. E of Bonn.
Rosbercon, W suburb of New Ross, in SE Co. Kilkenny, Ireland, on Barrow R.
Rosboro (rôs′bûrō), town (pop. 84), Pike co., SW Ark., 30 mi. WSW of Hot Springs.
Roscoe (rŏ′skō). **1** Section of Los Angeles city, Calif.: see SAN FERNANDO VALLEY. **2** Village (pop. 182), Stearns co., central Minn., 25 mi. SW of St. Cloud; dairy products. **3** Town (pop. 128), St. Clair co., W Mo., on Osage R. and 8 mi. SW of Osceola. **4** Resort village (1940 pop. 739), Sullivan co., SE N.Y., in the Catskills, on Beaver Kill and 13 mi. NW of Liberty; mfg. (furniture, wood products, chemicals); stone quarrying. Lakes near by. **5** Village (pop. 720), Coshocton co., central Ohio, on Muskingum R., opposite Coshocton. **6** Borough (pop. 1,396), Washington co., SW Pa., 4 mi. SSE of Charleroi and on Monongahela R.; steel, beer; bituminous coal. Inc. 1892. **7** City (pop. 726), Edmunds co., N S.Dak., 15 mi. W of Ipswich; trade center for farming area; grain elevators; dairy produce, livestock. **8** City (pop. 1,584), Nolan co., W Texas, 6 mi. W of Sweetwater; market point for farm area; railroad shops, grain elevators, cotton gins. Recreation on near-by lakes. Inc. 1907.
Roscoff (rôskôf′), town (pop. 2,262), Finistère dept., W France, port on English Channel, 13 mi. NW of Morlaix; outlet for intensive truck-gardening and dairying dist. of N Brittany with cross-channel trade; fishing. Health resort. Has Flamboyant Gothic church, some 16th-cent. wooden houses and a biological laboratory of the Univ. of Paris.
Roscommon (rŏs-kŏ′mŭn), Gaelic *Ros Comáin*, county (□ 950.8; pop. 72,510), Connacht, W central Ireland; ⊙ Roscommon. Bounded by cos. Galway (S and SW), Mayo (NW), Sligo (N), Leitrim (NE), Longford and Westmeath (E), and Offaly (SE). Drained by the Shannon and Suck rivers and their tributaries. Surface is partly level, with bogs and numerous lakes (including loughs Ree, Allen, Key), becoming hilly in N, where Bralieve Mts. rise to 1,082 ft., Curlew Mts. to 863 ft. Limestone and marble are quarried, coal (Arigna) and iron are mined in N. Raising of cattle, sheep, flax, potatoes main occupation. Trade in farm produce and wool. Besides Roscommon, other towns are Boyle, Castlerea, Elphin, and Ballaghaderreen. Monastic remains at Boyle and on isl. in Lough Key, where *Annals of Lough Cé* were written.
Roscommon, Gaelic *Ros Comáin*, town (pop. 2,038), ⊙ Co. Roscommon, Ireland, in S central part of co., 80 mi. WNW of Dublin; agr. market in cattle, sheep-raising, potato-growing region. Has Dominican priory founded 1257 and remains of castle founded 1268.
Roscommon, county (□ 521; pop. 5,916), N central Mich.; ⊙ Roscommon. Drained by Muskegon R. and branches of Tittabawassee and of Au Sable rivers. Forest area; some farming (livestock, potatoes; dairy products). Resorts; hunting, fishing. Includes Houghton and Higgins lakes, and L. St. Helen; also a state park. Organized 1875.
Roscommon, village (pop. 877), ⊙ Roscommon co., N central Mich., c.45 mi. NE of Cadillac, and on South Branch of Au Sable R. Trade center for resort and farm area. Starting point for Au Sable R. canoe trips. Forest fire experiment station near by. Higgins L. is W.
Roscrea (rŏskrā′), Gaelic *Ros Cré*, town (pop. 3,069), NE Co. Tipperary, Ireland, on Little Brosna R. and 10 mi. SSE of Birr; agr. market and malting center; food canning, bacon and ham curing. Has castle of the Ormondes dating from 1213, and ruins of 7th-cent. priory and of Franciscan friary (1490).
Rosdorf (rôs′dôrf), village (pop. 2,866), in former Prussian prov. of Hanover, W Germany, after 1945 in Lower Saxony, 2 mi. SW of Göttingen; woodworking.
Rose (rô′zĕ), village (pop. 1,783), Cosenza prov., Calabria, S Italy, 8 mi. N of Cosenza.
Rose, Mount, Nev.: see CARSON RANGE.
Roseau (rōzō′), town (pop. 9,752), ⊙ DOMINICA, Windward Isls., B.W.I., on SW coast of the isl., 370 mi. SE of San Juan, Puerto Rico, and 50 mi. NNW of Fort-de-France, Martinique; 15°17′N 61°23′W. Port on open roadstead; exports limes, lime juice, essential oils, tropical vegetables, spices. Picturesquely situated on small Roseau R., it is towered over by some of the highest mts. in the Lesser Antilles, with near-by waterfalls, thermal springs, and scenic plateaus. Has R.C. cathedral (built 1841), St. George's Church, Govt. House, Victoria Memorial Mus., and Botanic Gardens (established 1891). Formerly called Charlotte Town.
Roseau (rō′zō), county (□ 1,676; pop. 14,505), NW Minn.; ⊙ Roseau. Agr. area bounded NE by Lake of the Woods and N by Man., drained by Roseau R. Grain, potatoes, dairy products, livestock; peat deposits. Marshland in N and E. State forest in SE. Co. formed 1894.
Roseau, village (pop. 2,231), ⊙ Roseau co., NW Minn., on Roseau R., near Man. line, and c.55 mi. NNE of Thief River Falls; port of entry and trade and shipping center for agr. area; dairy products, flour.

Roseau River, formed by confluence of 2 forks in marshy area of Roseau co., NW Minn., flows N, past Roseau, then W and NW, into Canada, to Red River of the North in SE Man., 12 mi. N of St. Vincent, Minn.; 140 mi. long.

Roseaux (rōzō'), town (1950 census pop. 442), Sud dept., SW Haiti, on NW coast of Tiburon Peninsula, 8 mi. ESE of Jérémie, in agr. region (sugar cane, coffee).

Rosebank, N suburb of Johannesburg, S Transvaal, U. of So. Afr.

Rosebank, SE N.Y., a section of Richmond borough of New York city, on E Staten Isl., on the Narrows; mfg. of clothing, paints; shipbuilding and repairing. State quarantine station and U.S. Fort Wadsworth are near by.

Rose Belle, village (pop. 2,166), SE Mauritius, on railroad and 7 mi. W of Mahébourg; sugar milling. Administrative hq. for South Dist.

Rosebery (rōz'bürē), village (pop. 1,058), W Tasmania, 85 mi. WSW of Launceston and on Pieman R.; zinc and lead mines.

Roseboro, town (pop. 1,241), Sampson co., S central N.C., 22 mi. ESE of Fayetteville; lumber and cotton mills, brickworks.

Rosebud, village (pop. estimate 100, S Alta., on Rosebud R. and 16 mi. SW of Drumheller; coal.

Rosebud, county (□ 5,032; pop. 6,570), E central Mont.; ⊙ Forsyth. Agr. region drained by Tongue and Yellowstone rivers. Livestock, grain, coal. Tongue R. Indian Reservation in S. Formed 1901.

Rosebud. 1 Town (pop. 254), Gasconade co., E central Mo., 7 mi. NE of Owensville. **2** Village (1940 pop. 641), Todd co., S S.Dak., 80 mi. SSW of Pierre and on branch of South Fork White R.; hq. for Rosebud and Yankton Indian reservations. **3** City (pop. 1,730), Falls co., E central Texas, 35 mi. SSE of Waco; trade, shipping point in cotton, corn, cattle area; feed milling. Settled 1890, inc. 1906.

Roseburg, city (pop. 8,390), ⊙ Douglas co., SW Oregon, on Umpqua R. and 60 mi. SSW of Eugene; rail and trade center, hq. Umpqua Natl. Forest; fruit packing, lumber milling. U.S. veterans' hosp. here. Settled c.1851, inc. 1872.

Rose City, city (pop. 446), Ogemaw co., NE central Mich., c.60 mi. NNW of Bay City, at edge of Huron Natl. Forest.

Rosecrans, Fort, Calif.: see LOMA, POINT.

Rose Creek, village (pop. 314), Mower co., SE Minn., on branch of Cedar R., near Iowa line, and 9 mi. SE of Austin; dairy products.

Rosedale. 1 Town (pop. estimate 1,500), S Alta., on Red Deer R. and 5 mi. SE of Drumheller, in coal- and clay-mining, grain-growing region. **2** Village (pop. estimate 350), S B.C., near Fraser R., 7 mi. E of Chilliwack; lumbering; fruit, hops.

Rosedale. 1 Town (pop. 57), Weld co., NE Colo., near Greeley. **2** Town (pop. 673), Parke co., W Ind., near Raccoon Creek, 14 mi. NNE of Terre Haute, in agr. and bituminous-coal area. **3** Section of KANSAS CITY, Kansas. **4** City (pop. 2,197), a ⊙ Bolivar co., W Miss., on the Mississippi and 31 mi. N of Greenville, in rich agr. area; cotton, cottonseed, and lumber products; ships fish. Inc. as city since 1930. **5** A residential section of SE Queens borough of New York city, SE N.Y. **6** Town (pop. 136), McClain co., central Okla., 12 mi. SE of Purcell, near Canadian R. Inc. 1931.

Roseg Glacier (rō'zĕk), Romansh *Vadret da Roseg* (vädrĕt' dů rōzĕj'), in Bernina Alps, SE Switzerland, descending from Ital. border W of Piz Roseg (12,933 ft.) to Roseg R.

Rose Hall, village (pop. 2,864), Berbice co., NE Br. Guiana, in Atlantic coastland, 12 mi. E of New Amsterdam; sugar, rice plantations.

Rose Hall, village, St. James parish, NW Jamaica, 8 mi. ENE of Montego Bay. Once a flourishing sugar center, with old (18th cent.) palatial houses.

Rosehearty (rōz-här'tē), burgh (1931 pop. 1,079; 1951 census 1,173), N Aberdeen, Scotland, on North Sea, 4 mi. W of Fraserburgh; fishing port. Near by are ruins of Pitsligo Castle (1577).

Rose Hill, residential town (pop. 11,838), W central Mauritius, in central plateau, 5 mi. NNW of Curepipe; rail junction. Contiguous with BEAY BASSIN.

Rose Hill. 1 Village (pop. 128), Jasper co., SE Ill., 21 mi. E of Effingham, in agr. area. **2** Town (pop. 243), Mahaska co., S central Iowa, 21 mi. N of Ottumwa, bet. Skunk and North Skunk rivers, in livestock area. State park is S. Limestone quarries near by. **3** Town (pop. 896), Duplin co., E N.C., 36 mi. S of Goldsboro; sawmilling, mfg. of crates, caskets.

Roseires or **Er Roseires** (ĕr rōsā'rĕs), town, Blue Nile prov., E central Anglo-Egyptian Sudan, near Ethiopian border, on right bank of Blue Nile, on road, and 100 mi. SSE of Singa; head of navigation (June-Dec.) on the Blue Nile; cotton, sesame, corn, durra; gum arabic; livestock.

Rose Island, narrow islet (c.9 mi. long), N central Bahama Isls., just E of E New Providence Isl., 6 mi. ENE of Nassau; tomato growing. Salt ponds.

Rose Island, coral atoll, most easterly isl. of American Samoa, S Pacific, 150 mi. E of Tutuila; claimed 1921 by U.S.

Roseland. 1 Village (pop. 1,552), Sonoma co., W Calif. **2** Town (pop. 984), St. Joseph co., N Ind., N suburb of SouthBend. **3** City (pop. 118), Cherokee co., extreme SE Kansas, 7 mi. N of Columbus, in coal-mining and diversified agr. region. **4** Town (pop. 1,038), Tangipahoa parish, SE La., 45 mi. NE of Baton Rouge; agr.; wood products. Founded 1888, inc. as village 1892, as town 1936. **5** Village (pop. 154), Adams co., S Nebr., 12 mi. SW of Hastings. **6** Borough (pop. 2,019), Essex co., NE N.J., 9 mi. NW of Newark; electronic, photographic equipment. Inc. 1908. **7** Village (pop. 4,296, with adjacent Steel Mill), Richland co., N central Ohio. **8** Mining village, Nelson co., central Va., 26 mi. NNE of Lynchburg; titanium ore.

Rosell (rōsāl'), town (pop. 1,577), Castellón de la Plana prov., E Spain, 14 mi. NW of Vinaroz; olive-oil processing.

Roselle (rōzĕl'). **1** Village (pop. 1,038), Du Page co., NE Ill., WNW of Chicago and 10 mi. ESE of Elgin, in agr. area (grain, poultry; dairy products; truck); nursery. **2** Borough (pop. 17,681), Union co., NE N.J., 3 mi. W of Elizabeth; mfg. (machinery, metal products, restaurant equipment, clothing, leather goods); oil refinery. Early electric street-lighting system installed here by Edison. Abraham Clark b. here. Inc. 1894.

Roselle Park, borough (pop. 11,537), Union co., NE N.J., W of Elizabeth, adjacent to Roselle; mfg. (rugs, machinery, oil burners, surgical equipment, toys, paper products). Inc. 1901.

Rose Lynn, village, SE Alta., 19 mi. SE of Hanna; coal mining.

Rosemarkie (rōzmär'kē), village, SE Ross and Cromarty, Scotland, on Black Isle, on Moray Firth, just NE of Fortrose; seaside resort.

Rosemead (rōz'mēd), unincorporated town (1940 pop. 6,680), Los Angeles co., S Calif., 10 mi. E of downtown Los Angeles, near San Gabriel; truck, citrus fruit, walnuts, rabbits, poultry; residential.

Rosemont, village (1940 pop. 3,101, with adjacent GARRETT HILL), partly in LOWER MERION township, Montgomery co., SE Pa., 9 mi. WNW of Philadelphia; makes auto bodies. Seat of Rosemont Col.

Rosemount, village (pop. 567), Dakota co., SE Minn., near Mississippi R., 15 mi. S of St. Paul, in grain area.

Rosenau, Czechoslovakia: see ROZNAVA.

Rosenau, Rumania: see RASNOV.

Rosenbach (rō'zůnbäkh), village, Carinthia, S Austria, on N slope of the Karawanken and 10 mi. SE of Villach; rail junction. N exit of tunnel through the mountains.

Rosenberg, Czechoslovakia: see RUZOMBEROK.

Rosenberg, Germany: see SULZBACH-ROSENBERG.

Rosenberg. 1 Town, Olsztyn prov., Poland: see SUSZ. **2** Town, Opole prov., Poland: see OLESNO.

Rosenberg (rō'zůnbûrg), city (pop. 6,210), Fort Bend co., S Texas, near Brazos R. and 30 mi. WSW of Houston; market, shipping center in agr. area (cotton, rice, truck); cotton ginning, brick mfg.; oil wells. Founded 1883, inc. 1902.

Rosenburg (rō'zůnbōōrk), village (pop. 488), N Lower Austria, on Kamp R. and 15 mi. N of Krems; paper mill. Castle.

Rosenburg or **Rosenberg,** Czechoslovakia: see ROSMBERK NAD VLTAVOU.

Rosendaël (rōzĕndäĕl'), E suburb (pop. 14,279) of Dunkirk, Nord dept., N France, in irrigated truck-farming dist.; poultry, vegetable, and potato shipping, dairying; metalworking, cod-liver oil mfg. Damaged in Second World War.

Rosendal, Norway: see SUNDE.

Rosendale. 1 Town (pop. 245), Andrew co., NW Mo., on One Hundred and Two R. and 20 mi. N of St. Joseph. **2** Village (pop. 883), Ulster co., SE N.Y., on Rondout Creek and 7 mi. SW of Kingston; mfg. (clothing, cement). Inc. 1890. **3** Village (pop. 388), Fond du Lac co., E central Wis., 10 mi. W of Fond du Lac, in farm area; peony growing.

Roseneath (rōznēth'), agr. village and parish (pop. 2,227), SW Dumbarton, Scotland, on Gare Loch, 3 mi. W of Helensburgh; resort, yachting center. Roseneath Castle is seat of duke of Argyll.

Rosenfeld, village (pop. estimate 200), S Man., 50 mi. SSW of Winnipeg; grain, stock.

Rosenfeld (rō'zůnfĕlt), town (pop. 897), S Württemberg, Germany, after 1945 in Württemberg-Hohenzollern, 6 mi. W of Balingen; cattle.

Rosenfors (rōō"sůnfôrs', -fôsh'). **1** Village (pop. 716), Kalmar co., SE Sweden, on Em R. and 25 mi. W of Oskarshamn; metalworking. Includes Ammenas (ĕ'můnĕs"), Swedish *Ämmenäs,* village. **2** Village, Sodermanland co., Sweden: see SKOGSTORP.

Rosengarten (rō'zůn-gär"tůn), former suburb (pop. 398) of WORMS, Rhenish Hesse, W Germany, on right bank of the Rhine; passed 1945 to Hesse. Frequently mentioned in the Nibelungenlied.

Rosenhayn (rō'zůnhān), village (1940 pop. 685), Cumberland co., SW N.J., 6 mi. NE of Bridgeton.

Rosenheim (rō'zůnhīm), city (1950 pop. 29,645), Upper Bavaria, Germany, on the Inn and 33 mi. SW of Munich; rail junction; saltworks. Mfg. of basic and synthetic chemicals, textiles, precision instruments; metal- and woodworking, lumber and paper milling, brewing. Has 15th-cent. church, rebuilt 1881. Important trade center since early Middle Ages.

Rosenhof, Latvia: see ZILUPE.

Rosenhorn (rō'zůnhôrn"), peak (12,114 ft.) in Bernese Alps, S central Switzerland, 5 mi. E of Grindelwald.

Rosenthal (rō'zůntäl), town (pop. 1,564), in former Prussian prov. of Hesse-Nassau, W Germany, after 1945 in Hesse, 12 mi. NNE of Marburg; grain.

Rose Peak (8,787 ft.), E Ariz., highest in Blue Range, 25 mi. N of Morenci.

Rosepine, village (pop. 334), Vernon parish, W La., 55 mi. SW of Alexandria, near Texas line; cattle, hogs, sheep.

Rosera, India: se RUSERA.

Roseti (rōsāt'), village (pop. 5,673), Ialomita prov., SE Rumania, on left bank of the Borcea arm of the Danube and 6 mi. E of Calarasi; fisheries.

Roseto (rōzē'tō), borough (pop. 1,676), Northampton co., E Pa., just NW of Bangor. Slate quarries near by. Inc. 1910.

Roseto degli Abruzzi (rôzā'tô dĕlyäbrōō'tsē), town (pop. 3,478), Teramo prov., Abruzzi e Molise, S central Italy, on the Adriatic, 16 mi. E of Teramo; bathing resort; sawmill; furniture, ceramics.

Roseto Valfortore (välfôrtô'rē), town (pop. 5,066), Foggia prov., Apulia, S Italy, near right headstream of Fortore R., 11 mi. W of Troia, in stock-raising region.

Rosetown, town (pop. 1,563), SW Sask., 70 mi. SW of Saskatoon; wheat center; grain elevators.

Rosetta (rōzĕ'tů), Arabic *Rashid* (räshĕd'), town (pop. 24,094; with suburbs, 28,698), Beheira prov., Lower Egypt, on the Rosetta (anc. Bolbitinic) mouth of the Nile, 8 mi. upstream, and 35 mi. NE of Alexandria; rice milling, fishing; coastal trade, chiefly in rice, with Alexandria and Damietta. Founded in 9th cent., the town was formerly important as center for East Indies commerce. The Rosetta stone, a basalt slab inscribed by priests of Ptolemy V in hieroglyphic, demotic, and Greek, was found near Fort St. Julien (3 mi. N) by Napoleon's troops in 1799; captured by the British in 1801, it is now in the British Mus. It gave scholars the key to Egyptian hieroglyphic.

Rosettenville, S suburb of Johannesburg, S Transvaal, U. of So. Afr.; gold mining.

Rose Valley, village (pop. 400), SE central Sask., near Ponass L. (12 mi. long, 4 mi. wide), 40 mi. SSE of Tisdale; wheat, dairying.

Rose Valley, borough (pop. 498), Delaware co., SE Pa., 2 mi. SSE of Media.

Roseville (rōz'vĭl). **1** City (pop. 8,723), Placer co., central Calif., in Sacramento Valley, 17 mi. NE of Sacramento; rail center; shipping point for refrigerated fruit; railroad shops. Inc. 1909. **2** Village (pop. 1,080), Warren co., W Ill., 22 mi. SW of Galesburg; trade and shipping center in agr. and bituminous-coal-mining area; corn, wheat, oats, livestock, poultry, dairy products. Inc. 1875. **3** Residential village (pop. 15,816), Macomb co., SE Mich., 13 mi. NNE of downtown Detroit, near L. St. Clair; has sheet metal plant. Inc. 1926. **4** Village (pop. 6,437), Ramsey co., E Minn., NW suburb of St. Paul. Inc. since 1940. **5** Village (pop. 1,808), on Muskingum-Perry co. line, central Ohio, 10 mi. SSW of Zanesville; pottery, chemicals; coal mining. **6** Borough (pop. 126), Tioga co., N Pa., 17 mi. SSW of Elmira, N.Y.

Roseway River, W N.S., issues from small Roseway L., flows 35 mi. S to the Atlantic at Shelburne.

Rosewood, town (pop. 1,548), SE Queensland, Australia, 40 mi. WSW of Brisbane; agr. center (corn, alfalfa, bananas).

Rosewood. 1 Village, Humboldt co., NW Calif., just S of Eureka. **2** Town (pop. 119), Muhlenberg co., W Ky., 27 mi. ENE of Hopkinsville.

Rosewood Heights, village (pop. 1,836), Madison co., SW Ill.

Roseworthy, town (pop. 200), SE South Australia, 29 mi. NNE of Adelaide; rail junction. Roseworthy Agr. Col. (1885).

Roshal or **Roshal'** (rŭshäl'), city (1939 pop. over 10,000), E Moscow oblast, Russian SFSR, on rail spur and 85 mi. E of Moscow; mfg. (gunpowder, explosives). Became city in 1940.

Roshan, Tadzhik SSR: see RUSHAN.

Roshchino (rô'shchĭnŭ), village (1940 pop. over 500), NW Leningrad oblast, Russian SFSR, on Karelian Isthmus, 5 mi. NW of Zelenogorsk; summer resort. Called Raivola or Rayvola while in Finland (until 1940) and, until 1948, in USSR.

Rosheim (rōzĕm', Ger. rōs'hīm), town (pop. 2,639), Bas-Rhin dept., E France, at E foot of the Vosges, 3 mi. SSW of Molsheim; cotton milling, metalworking; winegrowing. Has well-preserved old ramparts and 12th-cent. Romanesque church.

Rosholt. 1 (rŏ'shůlt) Town (pop. 387), Roberts co., extreme NE S.Dak., 21 mi. NE of Sisseton; trade center for rich farming region; dairy products, cattle feed, grain. **2** (rŏ'shōlt) Village (pop. 508), Portage co., central Wis., 15 mi. NE of Stevens Point, in dairying area.

Rosh Pinna or **Rosh Pina** (both: rōsh' pēnä'), settlement (pop. 400), Upper Galilee, NE Israel, 2 mi. E of Safad; grain; dairying. Founded 1882.

Roshtkala (rŭshtkŭlä'), village (1939 pop. over 500), SW Gorno-Badakhshan Autonomous Oblast, Tadzhik SSR, in the Pamir, 24 mi. SE of Khorog.

Rosia, Rumania: see DOBRESTI.
Rosia-Montana (rô'shä-môntä'nü), Rum. *Roşia-Montană*, Hung. *Verespatak* (vĕ'rĕsh-pŏtŏk), anc. *Alburnus Major*, village (pop. 12,861), Cluj prov., central Rumania, in Apuseni Mts., on railroad and 25 mi. NW of Alba-Iulia; gold and silver mining center; also processes lead, copper, zinc, pyrites. Gold mines of the region have been worked since Roman times.
Rosice (rô'sĭtsĕ), Ger. *Rossitz* (rô'sĭts), village (pop. 4,649), S Moravia, Czechoslovakia, on railroad and 10 mi. W of Brno; its extensive bituminous coal deposits supply industrial needs of Brno and feed power station of Oslavany.
Rosiclare (rō'zĕklâr"), city (pop. 2,086), Hardin co., SE Ill., on Ohio R. and 25 mi. SSE of Harrisburg; fluorspar mine. Inc. as village 1874, as city 1932.
Rosier, Cape (rō'zhûr), Hancock co., S Maine, point on E side of Penobscot Bay and 11 mi. SE of Belfast. Cape Rosier village is in Brooksville town.
Rosières (rōzyâr'), village (pop. 1,454), Cher dept., central France, on the Cher and 11 mi. SW of Bourges; foundries.
Rosières-aux-Salines (–ō-sälēn'), village (pop. 1,946), Meurthe-et-Moselle dept., NE France, on Meurthe R. and 8 mi. W of Lunéville; important saltworks.
Rosières-en-Santerre (–ā-sätâr'), town (pop. 1,998), Somme dept., N France, 13 mi. SW of Péronne; hosiery mfg., sugar refining. In front lines throughout First World War, it changed hands twice (1918) in heavy fighting. Also damaged in Second World War.
Rosiers, Cape, E Que., at E end of Gaspé Peninsula, on the Gulf of St. Lawrence, 13 mi. E of Gaspé; 48°51'N 64°12'W; lighthouse.
Rosignano Marittimo (rôzēnyä'nô mërēt'tēmô), town (pop. 2,087), Livorno prov., Tuscany, central Italy, 13 mi. SSE of Leghorn; canned foods.
Rosignano Solvay (sôlvī'), town (pop. 3,922), Livorno prov., Tuscany, central Italy, on coast of Ligurian Sea, 7 mi. NNW of Cecina; chemical industry (sodium carbonate, caustic soda).
Rosignol (rō"sĭgnŏl'), village (pop. 1,204), Berbice co., NE Br. Guiana, on the coast at mouth of Berbice R., opposite New Amsterdam (linked by ferry); terminus of railroad from Georgetown (55 mi. NW); rice, sugar cane, coconuts.
Rosiorii-de-Vede (rôshyôr'yù-dä-vä'dä), Rum. *Roşiorii-de-Vede*, town (1948 pop. 14,905), ⊙ Teleorman prov., S Rumania, in Walachia, 27 mi. NNE of Turnu-Magurele; trading center, rail junction; flour milling, tanning, mfg. of textiles and cheese. Also spelled Rosiori-de-Vede.
Rosita, Mexico: see NUEVA ROSITA.
Rositsa River (rôsē'tsä), N Bulgaria, rises in Kalofer Mts. SW of Gabrovo, flows N, past Sevliyevo, and ENE, to Yantra R. 4 mi. NW of Draganovo; 112 mi. long. Reservoir and dam in upper course.
Rositten, Latvia: see REZEKNE.
Rositz (rō'zĭts), town (pop. 5,698), Thuringia, E central Germany, 4 mi. NW of Altenburg; lignite mining; sugar refining.
Roskilde (rō'skĭldù), city (1950 pop. 26,355), port, Copenhagen amt, E Zealand, Denmark, on Roskilde Fjord and 19 mi. WSW of Copenhagen; 55°39'N 12°5'E. Meat canning, mfg. (spirits, paper, agr. machinery), tanning; fishing. Has cathedral (c.1200; on site of 10th-cent. church) containing tombs of most Danish kings. Until 1443, ⊙ Denmark. Seat of bishop until Reformation in 1536, again since 1923. Treaty bet. Denmark and Sweden signed here, 1658.
Roskilde Fjord, Denmark: see ISE FJORD.
Roskovec or **Roskoveci,** Albania: see RESKOVEC.
Ros Lake (rûs), Nor. *Røsvatn*, Nordland co., N central Norway, 20 mi. S of Mo; □ 73; 22 mi. long, 2–10 mi. wide, 820 ft. deep. Norway's 3d-largest lake; drained N by Ros R.
Roslavl or **Roslavl'** (rô'slŭvŭl, rŭslä'vŭl), city (1926 pop. 25,992), S Smolensk oblast, Russian SFSR, 65 mi. SE of Smolensk; road and rail junction; machine mfg.; hemp mill, oil press; distilling, tanning, brickworking. Dates from 14th cent., chartered 1408 under Lithuania; passed 1667 to Russia. During Second World War, held (1941–43) by Germans.
Roslin (rŏz'lĭn), town in Lasswade parish, central Midlothian, Scotland, 7 mi. S of Edinburgh; coal mining. The fine old chapel dates from 1446.
Roslindale, Mass.: see BOSTON.
Roslyatino (rŭslyä'tyĭnŭ), village (1926 pop. 563), E central Vologda oblast, Russian SFSR, on headstream (Yuza R.) of Unzha R. and 55 mi. ESE of Totma; flax.
Roslyn (rŏz'lĭn). **1** Residential village (pop. 1,612), Nassau co., SE N.Y., on N shore of W Long Isl., at head of Hempstead Harbor, 4 mi. N of Mineola; mfg. (radio parts, machinery, anesthesia and oxygen appliances). "Cedarmere," home of William Cullen Bryant, is here. Inc. 1932. **2** Village, Pa.: see ABINGTON. **3** Town (pop. 222), Day co., NE S.Dak., 11 mi. N of Webster. **4** City (pop. 1,537), Kittitas co., central Wash., 25 mi. NW of Ellensburg; coal mines. Inc. 1889.
Roslyn Estates, residential village (pop. 612), Nassau co., SE N.Y., on N shore of W Long Isl., just SW of Roslyn.
Roslyn Harbor, village (pop. 402), Nassau co., SE N.Y., on W Long Isl., on Hempstead Harbor, S of Glen Cove, in summer-resort area.
Roslyn Heights, residential village (pop. c.4,000), Nassau co., SE N.Y., on N shore of Long Isl., just SW of Roslyn, in summer-resort area.
Rosman (rŏs'mùn), town (pop. 535), Transylvania co., W N.C., 8 mi. SSW of Brevard, near S.C. line; sawmilling, tanning.
Rosmaninhal (rōzh-mùnĕnyäl'), agr. town (pop. 2,970), Castelo Branco dist., central Portugal, near Sp. border, 24 mi. ESE of Castelo Branco. Formerly fortified.
Rosnaes, Denmark: see KALUNDBORG FJORD.
Rosny-sous-Bois (rōnē'-sōō-bwä'), town (pop. 14,153), Seine dept., N central France, an E suburb of Paris, 6 mi. from Notre Dame Cathedral; plaster works; mfg. (bicycles, toys, varnishes).
Rosny-sur-Seine (–sür-sĕn'), village (pop. 1,189), Seine-et-Oise dept., N central France, near left bank of the Seine, 5 mi. W of Mantes-Gassicourt. Has fine 17th-cent. château, park. Sully b. here.
Rosolina (rôzôlē'nä), village (pop. 373), Rovigo prov., Veneto, 9 mi. ENE of Adria.
Rosolini (rôzôlē'nē), town (pop. 12,642), Siracusa prov., SE Sicily, 12 mi. SW of Avola, in cereal-growing, livestock region; cement.
Rosporden (rôspôrdē'), town (pop. 2,320), Finistère dept., W France, on lake formed by Aven R., 13 mi. ESE of Quimper; rail junction; cider making, mfg. (food preserves, furniture, footwear).
Rosport (rōs'pôrt), village (pop. 532), E Luxembourg, on Moselle R. and 4 mi. E of Echternach, on Ger. border; vineyards, mfg. of fruit juices, plum and apple growing.
Rösrath (rûs'rät), village (pop. 10,334), in former Prussian Rhine Prov., W Germany, after 1945 in North Rhine-Westphalia, 10 mi. ESE of Cologne; rail junction.
Ros River, Nor. *Røså* (rûs'ô), Nordland co., N central Norway, rises in Ros L., flows 25 mi. N to arm of Ran Fjord opposite Finneidfjord. Forms several falls; supplies hydroelectric power to Mo steelworks. Sometimes Rosaa or Rossaa, Nor. *Røssâ*.
Ros River or **Ros' River** (rôs), W central Ukrainian SSR, rises SE of Kazatin in Volyn-Podolian Upland, flows c.170 mi. generally E, past Pogrebishchenski, Belaya Tserkov, Boguslav, and Korsun-Shevchenkovski, to Dnieper R. SE of Kanev. Also spelled Ross.
Ross, urban district, Ireland: see NEW ROSS.
Ross, islet in Lough Leane, one of the Lakes of Killarney, Ireland, 3 mi. SW of Killarney. Has anc. castle of the O'Donoghues.
Ross, borough (pop. 446), W S.Isl., New Zealand, 15 mi. SW of Hokitika; rail terminus; gold mines.
Ross, town (pop. 320), E central Tasmania, 45 mi. SSE of Launceston and on Macquarie R.; sheep and agr. (wheat, oats, flax) center; sandstone, silver, lead.
Ross, river, Ukrainian SSR: see ROS RIVER.
Ross, county (□ 687; pop. 54,424), S Ohio; ⊙ CHILLICOTHE. Intersected by Scioto R. and by Paint, Deer, and small Walnut and Salt creeks. Includes MOUND CITY GROUP NATIONAL MONUMENT. Farming (corn, wheat), hog and cattle raising, dairying. Mfg. at Chillicothe. Sand, gravel pits. Formed 1798.
Ross, residential town (pop. 2,179), Marin co., W Calif., just W of San Rafael. Inc. 1908.
Rossaa, Norway: see ROS RIVER.
Ross and Cromarty (krŏ'mùrtē), county (□ 3,089.4; 1931 pop. 62,799; 1951 census 60,503), N Scotland, bet. the Atlantic (W) and Moray Firth and the North Sea (E); ⊙ Dingwall. Bounded N by Sutherland, S by Inverness. Drained by Orrin, Carron, and several other small rivers. Co. includes N part of Lewis with Harris isl. and several other isls. of the Hebrides, which lie off W coast. In SE is Black Isle peninsula. Coastline is irregular and deeply indented by Moray, Cromarty, and Dornoch firths (E), and lochs Broom, Ewe, Gruinard, Torridon, Carron, and others (W). Surface is rugged and mountainous; highest peak is Mam Soul or Mam Sodhail (3,862 ft.); there are many other peaks over 3,000 ft. high. Of the many lakes lochs Maree, Fannich, and Luichart are largest. Fishing and sheep grazing are important; there is little cultivated land. There are whisky distilleries. Besides Dingwall, other towns are Tain, Stornoway, Fortrose, Strathpeffer; Invergordon and Cromarty are naval bases. There are many tourist resorts. Ross and Cromarty were once separate counties, united in 17th cent. by earl of Cromartie.
Rossano (rôs-sä'nô), town (pop. 8,763), Cosenza prov., Calabria, S Italy, in Apennine foothills, near Gulf of Taranto, 29 mi. NE of Cosenza; olive oil, licorice, soap, wine machinery. Archbishopric. Has 10th-cent. Byzantine church.
Rossano Veneto (vä'nĕtô), village (pop. 1,275), Vicenza prov., Veneto, N Italy, 17 mi. NE of Vicenza; silk, woolen, and paper mills.
Rossan Point (rŏ'sùn), promontory, SW Co. Donegal, Ireland, 16 mi. WSW of Ardare; 54°42'N 10°49'W.
Rossbach (rôs'bäkh), village (pop. 2,519), W Bohemia, Czechoslovakia, in the Erzgebirge, 6 mi. N of As; station on Ger. border, opposite Adorf.
Rossbach (rôs'bäkh), village (pop. 2,474), in former Prussian Saxony prov., central Germany, after 1945 in Saxony-Anhalt, 5 mi. NW of Weissenfels, in lignite-mining region. In Seven Years War, Frederick the Great here defeated (1757) the French and imperial forces.
Rossberg, Poland: see BEUTHEN.
Rossberg (rôs'bĕrk), mountain in the Alps, N central Switzerland, S of Zug. Highest peak, Wildspitz (5,196 ft.).
Rossburg (rŏs'bûrg), village (pop. 203), Darke co., W Ohio, 12 mi. N of Greenville.
Rossburn, village (pop. 477), S Man., 40 mi. NE of Brandon, near Riding Mountain Natl. Park; wheat; mixed farming.
Rosscarbery (rŏs"kär'brē), Gaelic *Ros Cairbre*, town (pop. 303), S Co. Cork, Ireland, on the coast 11 mi. E of Skibbereen; small port with timber and coal trade; woolen milling. Has cathedral, rebuilt 1612, and remains of anc. St. Fachnan's Church. E are ruins of commandery of Knights Templars.
Ross Dam, NW Wash., hydroelectric dam in Skagit R., just upstream from Diablo Dam reservoir and c.65 mi. E of Bellingham; 545 ft. high, 1,275 ft. long. Impounds Ruby Reservoir, extending upstream into British Columbia. Dam is owned by city of Seattle.
Ross Dependency (□ 175,000), the part of Antarctica claimed by New Zealand; includes the area bet. 160°E and 150°W, S of 60°S, and comprises the Ross Sea and its isls., VICTORIA LAND (coastal land), and the sector of land approaching the South Pole. Claimed 1887 by Great Britain under Br. Settlements Act (1887), placed 1907 under New Zealand. U.S. does not recognize claims in Antarctica. Site of many expeditions. Little America on Ross Shelf Ice was base for Byrd expeditions.
Rossdorf (rôs'dôrf), village (pop. 5,036), S Hesse, W Germany, in former Starkenburg prov., 4 mi. E of Darmstadt; quarrying.
Rosseau (rŏ'sō), village (pop. 266), S Ont., on L. Rosseau, 20 mi. ESE of Parry Sound, in Muskoka lake region; lumbering; resort.
Rosseau, Lake (12 mi. long, 5 mi. wide), S Ont., in Muskoka lake region, 20 mi. ESE of Parry Sound. Drains into Georgian Bay.
Rössel, Poland: see RESZEL.
Rosselange (rôsùlāzh'), Ger. *Rosslingen* (rôs'lĭng-ùn), town (pop. 3,553), Moselle dept., NE France, on Orne R. and 9 mi. SSW of Thionville; ironworks.
Rossel Island, volcanic island (pop. c.1,100), Louisiade Archipelago, Territory of Papua, SW Pacific, 230 mi. SE of New Guinea; 11°21'S 154°9'E; 20 mi. long, 10 mi. wide; gold. Formerly Yela Isl.
Rossel River (rô'sùl), Fr. *Rosselle* (rôsĕl'), in E France and SW Saar, rises 5 mi. WNW of St. Avold, flows E, past St. Avold, then N, along border bet. France and Saar, past Petite-Rosselle, Grossrosseln, Ludweiler-Warndt, and Geislautern, to Saar R. at Völklingen. Length, 25 mi.
Rosses Point or **Rosses Upper,** Gaelic *Ros Ceite*, town (pop. 254), N Co. Sligo, Ireland, on Drumcliff Bay, 5 mi. WNW of Sligo; seaside resort, with famous golf course.
Rossford, village (pop. 3,963), Wood co., NW Ohio, on Maumee R., just S of Toledo; large plate-glass plant; also mfg. of chemicals, building materials, grain products. Inc. 1939.
Rossie (rä'sē), town (pop. 112), Clay co., NW Iowa, 9 mi. SW of Spencer.
Rossie Island, Scotland: see MONTROSE.
Rossiglione (rôs-sēlyō'nĕ), town (pop. 4,056), Genova prov., Liguria, N Italy, 5 mi. S of Ovada; cotton mills.
Rossignol, Lake (rŏ'sĭg-nyŏl", Fr. rôsēnyôl') (16 mi. long, 10 mi. wide), W N.S., 16 mi. NW of Liverpool, for which it is reservoir. Drained by Mersey R.
Rossington, town and parish (9,547), West Riding, S Yorkshire, England, 4 mi. SE of Doncaster; coal-mining center. Has late-Norman church.
Rossio ao Sul do Tejo (rŏŏsē'ŏŏ ou sōōl dŏŏ tā'zhŏŏ), town (pop. 1,598), Santarém dist., central Portugal, industrial S suburb of Abrantes, on left bank of Tagus R.; rail junction; has cork-processing plants, liquor distilleries, cementworks. Eucalyptus and cork forests in area. Also called Rossio de Abrantes.
Ross Island. 1 Island (39 naut. mi. long, 31 naut. mi. wide), Antarctica, in Weddell Sea just off NE tip of Palmer Peninsula; 64°10'S 57°40'W. Discovered 1903 by Otto Nordenskjöld. Sometimes called James Ross Isl. **2** Island (43 naut. mi. long, 45 naut. mi. wide), Antarctica, in W part of Ross Sea at outer edge of Ross Shelf Ice, just off Victoria Land; 77°30'S 168°E. A volcanic isl. on which are Mt. Erebus (13,202 ft.; active volcano) and Mt. Terror (10,750 ft.).
Ross Island, in central Mergui Archipelago, Lower Burma, in Andaman Sea, 35 mi. WSW of Mergui town; c.45 mi. in circumference.
Rossiter (rŏs'ĭtùr), village (pop. 1,078), Indiana co., W central Pa., 23 mi. NE of Indiana.
Rossitten, Russian SFSR: see RYBACHI.
Rossitz, Czechoslovakia: see ROSICE.
Rossiyeny, Lithuania: see RASEINIAI.

Rosskeen (-kēn'), village, E Ross and Cromarty, Scotland, on Cromarty Firth, 2 mi. WNW of Invergordon.

Rossland, city (pop. 3,657), SE B.C., near Wash. border, in Selkirk Mts., 5 mi. WSW of Trail; alt. 5,150 ft.; fruitgrowing, dairying, ranching center; residential town for Trail mining region (silver, lead, zinc).

Rosslare (rŏs'lâr), Gaelic *Ros Láir*, town (pop. 436), SE Co. Wexford, Ireland, on St. George's Channel, 5 mi. SE of Wexford; seaport for Wexford, and seaside resort; terminal of mail steamers from Fishguard, England.

Rosslau (rôs'lou), town (pop. 17,473), in former Anhalt state, central Germany, after 1945 in Saxony-Anhalt, on the Elbe, opposite mouth of the Mulde, and 4 mi. N of Dessau (with which it was inc., 1935–45); rail junction; shipbuilding, cotton and paper milling; mfg. of chemicals, glass, pottery.

Rossleben (rôs'lā"bün), village (pop. 4,622), in former Prussian Saxony prov., central Germany, after 1945 in Saxony-Anhalt, on the Unstrut and 10 mi. SW of Querfurt; potash mining; woodworking, sugar refining. Site of school founded 1554 in bldgs. of earlier Cistercian convent.

Rosslingen, France: see ROSSELANGE.

Rosslyn, Va.: see ARLINGTON, county.

Rosslyn Farms (rŏz'lĭn), borough (pop. 448), Allegheny co., SW Pa., W suburb of Pittsburgh.

Rossmore, village (pop. 1,833, with adjoining Monaville), Logan co., SW W.Va., 3 mi. S of Logan.

Rossmoyne (rŏsmoin'), village (1940 pop. 1,553), Hamilton co., extreme SW Ohio, 11 mi. NE of downtown Cincinnati; motor vehicles, metal products, furniture.

Rosso (rō'sō), town (pop. c.1,700), SW Mauritania, Fr. West Africa, on Senegal R. and 55 mi. NE of Saint-Louis, Senegal; gum arabic, millet, corn, beans, melons, livestock.

Rosso, Cape (rôs'sô), headland of W Corsica, on the Mediterranean, 24 mi. NNW of Ajaccio. Just N is Gulf of Porto; 42°14'N 8°30'E.

Ross of Mull, Scotland: see MULL.

Ross-on-Wye, urban district (1931 pop. 4,735; 1951 census 5,394), SE Hereford, England, on Wye R. and 11 mi. SE of Hereford; agr. market, with tanning industry. Has 14th-cent. church where John Kyrle, Pope's "Man of Ross," is buried.

Rossony (rô'sůnē), village (1948 pop. over 2,000), N Polotsk oblast, Belorussian SSR, 30 mi. N of Polotsk; dairying, flax processing. Until c.1940, Stanislavovo.

Rossosh or **Rossosh'** (rô'sůsh), city (1926 pop. 16,270), S Voronezh oblast, Russian SFSR, 95 mi. S of Voronezh; agr. center; poultry and meat packing, flour milling, sunflower-oil extraction; metalworks. Teachers col.

Rossport, village (pop. estimate 200), W central Ont., on L. Superior, 80 mi. ENE of Port Arthur; zinc mining.

Ross River, Indian village, S Yukon, on Pelly R. at mouth of Ross River, and 120 mi. NE of Whitehorse; 62°N 132°27'W; fur-trading post.

Ross River, Ukrainian SSR: see ROS RIVER.

Ross Sea, large inlet of Pacific Ocean in Antarctica, bet. Cape Adare (W) and Cape Colbeck (E), N of Ross Shelf Ice (which may be considered its frozen S sector) and E of Victoria Land. Little America is on Bay of Whales, an inlet of Ross Sea. On Ross Isl., in SW part of the sea, is Mt. Erebus, active volcano.

Ross Shelf Ice, extensive area of shelf ice in Antarctica, occupying entire S part of Ross Sea, bet. Marie Byrd Land and Victoria Land, in 80°S 175°W. Its seaward side is a wall of ice c.400 mi. long. In it is Roosevelt Isl. and Little America. Discovered 1841 by Sir James Clark Ross.

Rosston, town (pop. 85), Harper co., NW Okla., 40 mi. NW of Woodward; grain, livestock area.

Rosstrevor, Northern Ireland: see ROSTREVOR.

Rössuln (rûs'ŏŏln"), village (pop. 698), in former Prussian Saxony prov., central Germany, after 1945 in Saxony-Anhalt, 5 mi. ESE of Weissenfels; lignite mining. Includes locality of Köpsen (kûp'sůn), just E, with synthetic-oil plant.

Rossville. 1 City (pop. 3,892), Walker co., NW Ga., on Tenn. line; industrial suburb of Chattanooga, Tenn.; textile mfg. (woolen cloth, yarn, hosiery bedspreads). Chickamauga and Chattanooga National Military Park and Fort Oglethorpe are near by. **2** Village (pop. 1,382), Vermilion co., E Ill., on North Fork of Vermilion R. and 17 mi. N of Danville; vegetable canning, agr. (grain, livestock). Platted 1857, inc. 1872. **3** Town (pop. 739), Clinton co., central Ind., on a fork of Wildcat Creek and 16 mi. E of Lafayette. **4** City (pop. 577), Shawnee co., NE Kansas, on small affluent of Kansas R. and 15 mi. WNW of Topeka; trading point in agr. region (grain, livestock, poultry); dairying. **5** A section of Richmond borough of New York city, SE N.Y., on W Staten Isl., on Arthur Kill; mfg. of pharmaceuticals. **6** Town (pop. 175), Fayette co., SW Tenn., on Wolf R. and 27 mi. E of Memphis.

Rosswein (rôs'vīn), town (pop. 10,675), Saxony, E central Germany, on the Freiberger Mulde and 5 mi. SE of Döbeln; woolen milling, hosiery knitting; mfg. of steel products, machinery, shoes, glass, toys, chemicals.

Rost (rûst), Nor. *Røst*, island (□ 1; pop. 610) in North Sea, Nordland co., N Norway, one of the Lofoten Isls., 65 mi. W of Bodo; fishing, fowling. Rost village is summer resort.

Rostak or **Rostaq,** Afghanistan: see RUSTAK.

Rostak, Rostaq, or **Rustaq** (all: rōstäk'), town, N Oman, in Western Hajar hill country, on N slopes of the Jabal Akhdar, 70 mi. WSW of Muscat; dates, mangoes, plaintains. Hot springs; pre-Islamic castle.

Rostanga (rûs'tông"ä), Swedish *Röstånga*, village (pop. 662), Malmohus co., S Sweden, 20 mi. WSW of Hassleholm; grain, potatoes, sugar beets, sheep.

Rostaq, Oman: see ROSTAK.

Rosthern (rŏs'thûrn, -tûrn), town (pop. 1,218), central Sask., 40 mi. NNE of Saskatoon; site of govt. telephone center; experimental farm, grain elevators, flour mills, dairies.

Rostock (rô'stôk), city (pop. 114,869), Mecklenburg, N Germany, Baltic port 100 mi. ENE of Hamburg, at head of estuary of the Warnow; 54°5'N 12°9'E. Rail junction; seaport and chief point of entry for E Germany's oil supplies, with extensive tank installations and shipyards; outport at WARNEMÜNDE. Mfg. of agr. machinery, chemicals, scales; metalworking, brewing, distilling. Site of univ. (founded 1419), and of Mecklenburg state col. of music. Second World War destruction (about 20%) included 13th-cent. church of St. Mary; univ. library. Has remains of old town walls and gates. Ger. settlement of Rostock founded 1189 on site of anc. Wendish stronghold. Chartered 1218; later became one of the most powerful Baltic members of the Hanseatic League. Field Marshal Blücher b. here. Captured by Soviet troops in May, 1945.

Rostoshi (rŭstô'shē), village (1939 pop. over 2,000), N Voronezh oblast, Russian SFSR, 50 mi. WNW of Borisoglebsk; wheat.

Rostov (rŏ'stŏv, Rus. rŭstôf'), oblast (□ 40,350; 1946 pop. estimate 2,550,000) in S European Russian SFSR; ⊙ Rostov. A typical steppe region (Lower Don region) with fertile black-earth soils, except for brown soils in dry SE; drained by the lower Don and its left affluents, Sal and Western Manysh rivers; continental climate, with hot summers and cold, dry winters. Alluvial meadows along the lower Don. Anthracite deposits of E Donbas, fisheries in Sea of Azov are important resources. Agr. (wheat, sunflowers, melons), livestock (meat, wool); vineyards (Tsimlyanskaya, Razdorskaya); garden crops in Rostov urban area. Industry specializes in mfg. of agr. machinery (Rostov, Morozovsk), locomotives (Novocherkassk), metallurgy (Taganrog, Krasny Sulin), and agr. processing. Main coal-mining centers are Shakhty (large power plant), Novoshakhtinsk, Gukovo, Gundorovka, and, in Bogurayev dist., Koksovy and Sinegorski. Included (until 1924) in Oblast of the Don Cossacks (main pop. element); area again formed (1937) as a separate oblast out of Azov–Black Sea Territory. During Second World War, held (1942–43) by Germans. After 1943, absorbed W section of dissolved Kalmyk Autonomous SSR.

Rostov. 1 or **Rostov-on-Don,** Rus. *Rostov-na-Donu* (-nŭ-dŭnŏŏ'), city (1926 pop. 308,103; 1939 pop. 510,253), ⊙ Rostov oblast, Russian SFSR, port on high right bank of Don R., 25 mi. above its mouth in Sea of Azov, 600 mi. SSE of Moscow; 47°15'N 39°45'E. Major transportation hub on lines bet. Central European USSR, Ukraine, and N Caucasus; industrial center; mfg. of agr. machinery (at Rosselmash, one of largest USSR farm implement plants), concrete mixers, foundry goods (pipes, radiators, armatures), motorcycles, radios, chemicals; auto-assembly plant, sheet-metal rolling mill, locomotive- and car-building shops, shipyards (coastwise vessels). Also produces textiles, shoes and other leather products, enamelware, tobacco, furniture, paper, soap, canned goods, meat, flour products. City consists of Rostov proper (W) and former Armenian suburb of Nakhichevan, which merged c.1926. Rosselmash lies on NE outskirts, within rail belt line circling city. Rostov has state univ., trade schools concerned with agr. implements, construction, and railroads; medical and teachers colleges; mus. of art and antiquity. Rostov (founded originally in 1761 as Rus. fortress in Turkish wars) and Nakhichevan (founded 1780 by Armenian refugees from the Crimea) developed mainly after 1834, when fortress was razed and port established. Throughout 19th cent., Rostov was a major grain-exporting point. A strike center in 1905 revolution; occupied (1917–20) by Ger. and counterrevolutionary troops, prior to establishment of Soviet power. During Second World War, city was much contested as gateway to the Caucasus; held by Germans briefly in 1941 and again (1942–43) in Caucasus campaign; suffered much damage. **2** City (1926 pop. 20,864), SE Yaroslavl oblast, Russian SFSR, on L. Nero, 35 mi. SSW of Yaroslavl; linen milling, metalworking, chicory processing. One of oldest cities of USSR, still maintaining its medieval aspect. Has kremlin with Uspenski cathedral (1214) and former residence of Rostov princes, and other 13th-cent. churches with murals and frescoes. Numerous old monasteries and churches near by. Founded 864; became a leading city of Rostov-Suzdal principality; known as Rostov-Veliki [Rus.,=Rostov the Great]; later also called Rostov-Yaroslavski. Passed 1474 to Moscow.

Rostovtsevo, Uzbek SSR: see KRASNOGVARDEISK, Samarkand oblast.

Rostrenen (rôstrůnã'), village (pop. 2,078), Côtes-du-Nord dept., W France, 24 mi. SSW of Guingamp; road junction, cattle and dairy market; shoe and furniture mfg.

Rostrevor or **Rosstrevor** (rŏstrĕ'vůr), fishing village (district pop. 934), S Co. Down, Northern Ireland, on NE shore of Carlingford Lough, 8 mi. SE of Newry; seaside resort.

Rosu (rôsh), Rum. *Roşu*, outer W rural suburb (1948 pop. 1,431) of Bucharest, Bucharest prov., Rumania, on right bank of Dambovita R.; dairying.

Rosvatn, Norway: see ROS LAKE.

Roswell (rŏz'wůl, -wĕl). **1** Village (pop. 1,029), El Paso co., E central Colo., 2 mi N of Colorado Springs. **2** Town (pop. 2,123), Fulton co., NW central Ga., 18 mi. N of Atlanta, near Chattahoochee R. Settled c.1837, inc. 1854. **3** City (pop. 25,738), ⊙ Chaves co., SE N.Mex., on Rio Hondo, near Pecos R., and 170 mi. SE of Albuquerque. Trade center; resort; wool-shipping point in livestock and irrigated agr. area (cotton, grain, fruit, truck); food processing (meat and dairy products, flour), oil refining, mfg. of cotton gins, cottonseed oil, paints, mattresses. Oil wells and potash mines in vicinity. Settled 1869, inc. 1903. Grew with development of irrigation and oil boom. N.Mex. Military Inst. here. Walker Air Force Base, Bottomless Lakes State Park, and Bitter Lake Migratory Waterfowl Refuge near by. Carlsbad Caverns Natl. Park is c.100 mi. S, Lincoln Natl. Forest W. **4** Village (pop. 267), Tuscarawas co., E Ohio, 5 mi. E of New Philadelphia, in agr. area. **5** Town (pop. 69), Miner co., SE central S.Dak., 8 mi. W of Howard.

Rosyth (rōsīth', rō'sīth), town in Inverkeithing parish, SW Fifeshire, Scotland, on the Firth of Forth, just NW of Inverkeithing; naval base, built 1909, and center of the Grand Fleet in First World War.

Rota (rō'tů, rōtä'), volcanic island (□ 33; pop. 655), Saipan dist., S Marianas Isls., W Pacific, 32 mi. NE of Guam; 11 mi. long, 4 mi. wide; rises to 1,168 ft. Has volcanic base covered with coral limestone; phosphate deposits; sugar plantations. Site of anc. stone columns. Airfield. Formerly Sarpan.

Rota (rō'tä), volcano (2,720 ft.) in Cordillera de los Marabios, W Nicaragua, 11 mi. NE of León.

Rota, town (pop. 9,748), Cádiz prov., SW Spain, minor Atlantic port outside Bay of Cádiz, 6 mi. NNW of Cádiz. Famed for its red (*tintilla*) wine. Trading and fishing center, with fine beaches visited all year round. Fish and vegetable canning, liquor distilling. The ruins of Almadraba castle are 3 mi. NNW.

Rotan (rō'tăn), city (pop. 3,163), Fisher co., NW central Texas, 25 mi. N of Sweetwater; a trade, shipping, processing point for cattle-ranching, oil, agr. region (cotton, grain sorghums, dairy products). Gypsum plant, oil refinery, cotton gins; mfg. of mattresses, cottonseed oil. Inc. 1908.

Rotava (rô'tävä), Ger. *Rothau* (rô'tou), village (pop. 1,232), W Bohemia, Czechoslovakia, in SW foothills of the Erzegebirge, 18 mi. NE of Cheb; rail terminus; tin mines, steel mills.

Rotem (rô'tům), town (pop. 2,273), Limburg prov., NE Belgium, 4 mi. SW of Maaseik; zinc and lead processing. Formerly spelled Rothem.

Rotenburg (rō'tůnbŏŏrk). **1** Town (pop. 11,144), in former Prussian prov. of Hanover, NW Germany, after 1945 in Lower Saxony, 24 mi. E of Bremen; rail junction; mfg. of apparel, furniture, musical instruments, leather goods; metalworking, weaving, dyeing, food processing. **2** or **Rotenburg an der Fulda** (än dĕr fŏŏl'dä), town (pop. 6,307), in former Prussian prov. of Hesse-Nassau, W Germany, after 1945 in Hesse, on the Fulda and 8.5 mi. N of Hersfeld; mfg. (machinery, textiles, leather and wood products). Has 14th–16th-cent. church, 16th-cent. castle.

Rotenfels (rō'tůnfĕls"), village (pop. 2,567), S Baden, Germany, on W slope of Black Forest, on the Murg and 5 mi. SE of Rastatt; woodworking. Has mineral spring.

Roterbaum, Germany: see ROTHERBAUM.

Roter Main, Germany: see RED MAIN.

Roter-Turm, Rumania: see TURNU ROSU PASS.

Rote Weisseritz, Germany: see RED WEISSERITZ RIVER.

Rot-Front, Ukrainian SSR: see DOBROPOLYE, Zaporozhe oblast.

Rötgen (rût'gůn), village (pop. 2,510), in former Prussian Rhine Prov., W Germany, after 1945 in North Rhine-Westphalia, 10 mi. SSE of Aachen, on Belgian border. First Ger. town captured (Sept. 11, 1944) by Allies in Second World War. Sometimes spelled Roetgen.

Roth or **Roth bei Nürnberg** (rōt' bī nürn'bĕrk), town (pop. 8,604), Middle Franconia, W central Bavaria, Germany, on the Rednitz and 11 mi. SSE of Schwabach; rail junction; mfg. of precision instruments, wire, bronze, toys; brewing, printing. Has late-16th-cent. castle. Chartered 1392. Johann Gesner b. here.

Rötha (rû'tä), town (pop. 6,206), Saxony, E central Germany, on Pleisse R. and 10 mi. S of Leipzig, in lignite-mining region; fruitgrowing. Site of Allied hq. during battle of Leipzig (1813).

Rothaargebirge (rōt'här"gůbĭr"gů), mountain range, W Germany, extends c.30 mi. SW of Winterberg; rises to 2,759 ft. in the Kahle Asten (NE). Forested slopes; pastures. Geologically it is considered part of Rhenish Slate Mts.

Rothamsted, England: see HARPENDEN.

Rothau, Czechoslovakia: see ROTAVA.

Rothau (rōtō', Ger. rō'tou), village (pop. 1,607), Bas-Rhin dept., E France, in Bruche R. valley of the E Vosges, and 14 mi. SW of Molsheim; cotton milling.

Roth bei Nürnberg, Germany: see ROTH.

Rothbury, former urban district (1931 pop. 1,255), central Northumberland, England, on Coquet R. and 11 mi. SW of Alnwick; resort and agr. market.

Rothem, Belgium: see ROTEM.

Röthenbach or **Röthenbach an der Pegnitz** (rû'-tůnbäkh än dĕr päg'nĭts), village (pop. 7,953), Middle Franconia, N central Bavaria, Germany, on the Pegnitz and 7 mi. ENE of Nuremberg; lumber milling. Hops, horse-radish, hogs.

Rothenburg (rō'tůnbŏŏrk). **1** or **Rothenburg ob der Tauber** (ôp dĕr tou'bůr), city (1950 pop. 11,223), Middle Franconia, W Bavaria, Germany, on the Tauber and 19 mi. WNW of Ansbach; mfg. of textiles, paper, soap; metal- and woodworking, printing, brewing. Surrounded by 14th–15th-cent. wall, it almost completely retains its medieval appearance. Has many Gothic churches; its Gothic-Renaissance town hall is considered one of most beautiful in S Germany. Created free imperial city in 1172. **2** Town (pop. 2,587) in former Prussian Lower Silesia prov., E Germany, after 1945 in Saxony, in Upper Lusatia, on the Lusatian Neisse and 13 mi. N of Görlitz, in lignite-mining region; china mfg.

Rothenfelde, Bad, Germany: see BAD ROTHENFELDE.

Rothenfels (rō'tůnfĕls"), town (pop. 789), Lower Franconia, NW Bavaria, Germany, on the Main (canalized) and 7 mi. S of Lohr; brewing. Large sandstone quarries in area. On near-by hill (W) are ruins of 16th-cent. castle with Romanesque watchtower.

Rothensee (rō'tůnzā"), N suburb of Magdeburg, Saxony-Anhalt, central Germany, on the Elbe, at E head of Weser-Elbe Canal (ship elevator); power station.

Rotherbaum (rō'tůrboum), university district of Hamburg, NW Germany, on W shore of the Aussenalster, adjoining Sankt Pauli (S), Eimsbüttel (W), and Harvestehude (N) dists.; site of Hamburg Univ. (founded 1919; bldgs. heavily damaged in Second World War), and ethnologic and prehistoric mus. Formerly spelled Roterbaum.

Rotherfield, town and parish (pop. 2,821), NE Sussex, England, 3 mi. ESE of Crowborough; agr. market. Has 14th–15th-cent. church, with Burne-Jones window.

Rotherham (rŏ'dhůrům), county borough (1931 pop. 69,691; 1951 census 82,334), West Riding, S Yorkshire, England, on Don R. and 6 mi. ENE of Sheffield; steel mills, foundries, machine shops; mfg. also of electrical equipment, chemicals, pottery, glass. Coal mines near by. On old bridge (rebuilt) over Don R. is 15th-cent. chantry chapel. Church of All Saints, dating from 15th cent., was rebuilt (1877) by Sir Gilbert Scott. In county borough are, on Don R. (SW), steel-milling center of Templebrough, with remains of a Roman camp; and, just W, steel-milling suburb of Holmes.

Rotherhithe (rŏ'dhůrhīdh") (popularly called Redriff), district of Bermondsey and Deptford metropolitan boroughs, London, England, on S bank of the Thames, 4 mi. E of Charing Cross. Here are the extensive Surrey Commercial Docks. Rotherhithe linked with Wapping by Thames Tunnel, with Stepney by Rotherhithe Tunnel. District heavily bombed 1940–41.

Rother River. 1 In Hampshire and Sussex, England, rises 5 mi. N of Petersfield, flows 40 mi. E, past Midhurst, to Arun R. 7 mi. N of Arundel. **2** In Sussex, England, rises just W of Mayfield, flows E past Salehurst, turning S above Rye, to the Channel 2 mi. SE of Rye; 31 mi. long.

Rothes (rŏ'thĭz, rŏths). **1** Village in Markinch parish, central Fifeshire, Scotland; coal mining, paper milling. **2** Burgh (1931 pop. 1,292; 1951 census 1,211), E Moray, Scotland, on the Spey and 9 mi. SSE of Elgin; agr. market, with whisky distilleries. Near by is anc. Rothes Castle, until 1700 the seat of the Leslies.

Rothesay (rŏth'sē, –sā), residential and resort village (pop. estimate c.500), S N.B., on Kennebecasis Bay, 9 mi. NNE of St. John.

Rothesay, burgh (1931 pop. 9,347; 1951 census 10,145), ⊙ Buteshire, Scotland, on E coast of Bute isl., on Rothesay Bay of the Firth of Clyde, 30 mi. W of Glasgow; fishing port, resort, and yachting center; hq. of Royal Northern Yacht Club and scene of annual regatta. Rothesay Castle was reputedly founded in 11th cent.; extant ruins date mainly from 14th cent. In 1650 Cromwell began destruction of castle; destruction was completed 1685 by earl of Argyll; castle was rebuilt 1871. The prince of Wales has title of duke of Rothesay. Near-by mansion of Mount Stuart, seat of marquis of Bute, dates from 1877.

Rothiemay (rŏ-thĭmā'), agr. village and parish (pop. 926), NE Banffshire, Scotland, on Deveron R. and 4 mi. N of Huntly.

Rothkosteletz, Czechoslovakia: see CERVENY KOSTELETZ.

Rothley (rōth'lē), town and parish (pop. 2,734), central Leicester, England, 5 mi. N of Leicester; hosiery, shoes, lubricating oil. Has Norman church with 15th-cent. tower, and Saxon cross dating from c.800. Near by is Rothley Temple, site of a Knights Templars' preceptory, of which a 13th-cent. chapel remains. Lord Macaulay b. here.

Rothorn (rōt'hôrn), name of several Alpine peaks, Switzerland, notably AROSER ROTHORN, BLÜMLISALP Rothorn, BRIENZER ROTHORN, and ZINALROTHORN.

Rothrist (rōt'rĭst), town (pop. 3,682), Aargau canton, N Switzerland, on Wigger R., near confluence with the Aar, 3 mi. S of Olten; metal products, textiles (cotton, woolen).

Rothsay (rŏth'sē), village (pop. 537), Wilkin co., W Minn., 17 mi. NW of Fergus Falls, in grain and livestock area; dairying.

Rothschild (rŏths'chīld), village (pop. 1,425), Marathon co., central Wis., on Wisconsin R. and 5 mi. S of Wausau; paper products, vanillin, chemicals.

Rothsville (rōts'vĭl), village (1940 pop. 926), Lancaster co., SE Pa., 8 mi. N of Lancaster, in agr. area; makes shirts, cigars.

Rothville (rôth'vĭl), town (pop. 152), Chariton co., N central Mo., 9 mi. S of Brookfield.

Rothwell. 1 Urban district (1931 pop. 4,516; 1951 census 4,617), N central Northampton, England, 4 mi. WNW of Kettering; shoe-mfg. center, producing also clothing and agr. machinery; ironstone quarrying. Has 13th-cent. church and 16th-cent. market house. **2** Urban district (1931 pop. 15,640; 1951 census 24,283), West Riding, S central Yorkshire, England, 4 mi. SE of Leeds; coal mining; mfg. of matches, rope. Near by are stone quarries. Has church of 13th-cent. origin.

Roti (rō'tē), island (□ 467; □ 666, including offshore isls; pop. 59,221), Indonesia, 10 mi. SW of Timor across narrow Roti Strait; 10°43'S 123°5'E; 50 mi. long, 14 mi. wide; generally level. Chief products: rice, corn, ponies. Principal settlement and port is Baa (bä), on N coast.

Rotifunk (rōtēfŏŏngk'), town (pop. 1,800), South-Western Prov., W Sierra Leone, on railroad and 40 mi. ESE of Freetown; trade center; palm oil and kernels, piassava, rice. United Brethren in Christ mission (hosp.).

Rotmistrovka (rôt'mēstrŭfkŭ), village (1926 pop. 4,187), SE Kiev oblast, Ukrainian SSR, 9 mi. SW of Smela; flour mill, metalworks.

Roto, village (pop. 127), central New South Wales, Australia, 245 mi. ESE of Broken Hill; rail junction; sheep.

Rotoava, Tuamotu Isls.: see FAKARAVA.

Rotoiti, Lake (rōtōē'tē). **1** N central N.Isl., New Zealand, 120 mi. SE of Auckland, near L. Rotorua; 10 mi. long, 2 mi. wide, 228 ft. deep; surrounded by hot springs. **2** N S.Isl., New Zealand, 45 mi. SSW of Nelson; 5 mi. long, 2 mi. wide.

Rotomagus, France: see ROUEN.

Rotomahana, Lake, New Zealand: see TARAWERA MOUNTAIN.

Rotonda (rôtôn'dä), village (pop. 1,903), Potenza prov., Basilicata, S Italy, 19 mi. SE of Lagonegro.

Rotondella (rôtôndĕl'lä), town (pop. 4,699), Matera prov., Basilicata, S Italy, 16 mi. S of Pisticci, in agr. (cereals, fruit, cotton), stock-raising region.

Rotondo, Monte (môn'tĕ rôtôn'dô), peak (8,612 ft.) of central Corsica, 8 mi. SW of Corte. Crater-shaped summit is snow-capped.

Rotondo, Pizzo, Switzerland: see PIZZO ROTONDO.

Rotorua (rōtōrŏŏ'ů), borough (pop. 7,512), ⊙ Rotorua co. (□ 989; pop. 7,048), N central N.Isl., New Zealand, 120 mi. SE of Auckland; rail terminus. Largest health resort of Hot Springs Dist.; geysers (Wairoa, largest). Sanatorium on S shore of L. Rotorua. Sulphur, building stone. Rotorua borough is in, but independent of, Rotorua co.

Rotorua, Lake (□ 32), N central N.Isl., New Zealand, 115 mi. SE of Auckland; 7.5 mi. long, 6 mi. wide; surrounded by hot springs. Volcanic Mokoia Isl. is in center, Rotorua sanatorium on S shore.

Rotstock (rōt'shtôk), name of several peaks in the Alps of central Switzerland, notably Uri-Rotstock (9,620 ft.), 6 mi. ENE of Engelberg, and Engelberger Rotstock (9,258 ft.), to the W.

Rottach (rô'täkh), village (pop. 5,770), Upper Bavaria, Germany, in Bavarian Alps, at SE tip of the lake Tegernsee, 10 mi. SE of Bad Tölz; metalworking. Summer resort (alt. 2,395 ft.). Has early-12th-cent. church.

Rottenburg (rô'tůnbŏŏrk). **1** Village (pop. 2,190), Lower Bavaria, Germany, 13 mi. NNW of Landshut; brickworks; brewing. Chartered 1393. **2** Town (pop. 8,311), S Württemberg, Germany, after 1945 in Württemberg-Hohenzollern, on the Neckar and 6 mi. SW of Tübingen; mfg. of watches and screws. Has 15th-cent. cathedral (renovated in 17th cent.); prison on site of former castle. Founded in Middle Ages, it was capital of Austrian (since 1381) county of Hohenberg until both passed to Württemberg in 1805. Created seat of R.C. bishop of Württemberg in 1817; 1st bishop consecrated 1828.

Rottenmann (rô'tůnmän), town (pop. 4,218), Styria, Austria, 28 mi. NNW of Judenburg; ironworks.

Rotten Row, sand track, circling Hyde Park, London, England, for horseback riders.

Rotterdam (rŏ'tůrdăm, Du. rô'tůrdäm), city (pop. 646,248), South Holland prov., W Netherlands, on New Maas R. and 13 mi. SE of The Hague; 51°55'N 4°29'E. Largest port of the Netherlands and major trade center. Main port installations are on left bank of the New Maas, on Ijsselmonde isl., and adjoining suburbs of Hillersluis, Charlois, and Waalhaven (airport). Important petroleum refineries at PERNIS. Port handles greater part of Netherlands' imports and exports, but chiefly owes its importance to being a major transshipping center for overseas traffic to and from Germany. Imports ores, grains, oil, wood, fruit; exports Ruhr coal, oleomargarine, vegetables, dairy products. Shipbuilding (concentrated at Feijenoord, suburb on left bank of the New Maas), petroleum refining (at Pernis), mfg. of chemicals, machinery, metal and food products, clothing. Has fruit markets, stock exchange; hq. of many shipping and trading companies. Rail junction; connected with North Sea by New Maas R., the Scheur, and the New Waterway, with Germany by various branches of the Rhine. Has 15th-cent. Gothic church (*Groote Kerk*), 18th-cent. stock exchange (*Beurs*), Boijmans Mus., univ., technical acad. Several bridges cross the New Maas; vehicular tunnel under it. Contains many examples of modern functional architecture. City lies mainly on right bank of the New Maas, with suburbs to E and W and on opposite river bank. Erasmus, Admiral Piet Hein, and painter Pieter de Hooch b. here. Received its charter from Count William III in 1328, and, while it grew considerably in 16th cent. because of efforts of its Grand Pensionary, Johan van Oldenbarneveldt, it was overshadowed by neighboring Delft and its port of Delfshaven (now a Rotterdam suburb), whence the Pilgrims sailed for America. Separation of the Netherlands and Belgium (1830) transferred much trade from Antwerp to Rotterdam; city experienced its greatest growth in mid-19th cent., especially after port became accessible to largest ocean-going ships following construction of the New Waterway (1866–72). In Second World War, entire center of city destroyed by German bombing (1940) some hours after city had surrendered. Extensive reconstruction and modernization still in progress.

Rotterdam Junction, village (1940 pop. 756), Schenectady co., E N.Y., on Mohawk R., just NW of Schenectady. Near by is Jan Mabie house, one of oldest in Mohawk valley.

Rotthalmünster (rōt'täl"mün'stůr), village (pop. 3,204), Lower Bavaria, Germany, 18 mi. SW of Passau; brewing, woodworking. Chartered c.1343.

Rottingdean, England: see BRIGHTON.

Röttingen (rû'tĭng-ůn), town (pop. 1,915), Lower Franconia, W Bavaria, Germany, 19 mi. S of Würzburg; woodworking; winegrowing. Surrounded by medieval wall; has 13th–14th-cent. church. Chartered 1336.

Rottnest Island (□ 9), in Indian Ocean off Western Australia, 11 mi. NW of Fremantle; 5.5 mi. long, 23 mi. wide; chief tourist resort of state. Salt lakes, many sheltered bays. Formerly penal colony for aborigines.

Rottofreno (rôt-tôfrā'nô), village (pop. 549), Piacenza prov., Emilia-Romagna, N central Italy, 7 mi. W of Piacenza; agr. tools, lye.

Rott River (rôt), Bavaria, Germany, rises 4 mi. ESE of Velden, flows c.70 mi. E of the Inn, 4 mi. ENE of Ruhstorf.

Rottum or **Rottumeroog** (rô'tŭm, –ůrōkh"), uninhabited island (□ 1.5), Groningen prov., N Netherlands, bet. North Sea and the Waddenzee, 6 mi. N of mainland and 10 mi. N of Warffum; 3 mi. long, 1 mi. wide.

Rottumerplaat (rô'tŭmůrplät), uninhabited island, Groningen prov., N Netherlands, bet. North Sea and the Waddenzee, 11 mi. N of Warffum; 2.5 mi. long, 1.5 mi. wide.

Rottweil (rôt'vīl), town (pop. 13,129), S Württemberg, Germany, after 1945 in Württemberg-Hohenzollern, on the Neckar, bet. Black Forest and Swabian Jura, 8 mi. NW of Schwenningen; rail junction; mfg. of artificial silk; metalworking. Has Gothic church, late-Gothic town hall. An anc. settlement, it was chartered in 13th cent. Free imperial city until 1802. Was in close political alliance with the Swiss confederation from 1463 to 18th cent.

Rotuma (rōtŏŏ'mä), volcanic island (□ 18; pop. 2,929), SW Pacific; 12°30'S 177°30'E. Dependency of Br. colony of FIJI; 9 mi. long, c.3 mi. wide; ⊙ Ahau; Motusa, chief town and port. Fertile; exports copra, mats. Surrounded by 8 small isls. (one, Waya, is inhabited). Discovered 1793 by British; annexed 1881. Sometimes called Rotuam; formerly Grenville Isl.

Rötz Stadt, Austria: see RETZ STADT.

Roued, Syria: see RUAD.

Roubaix (rōōbā′), city (pop. 98,834), Nord dept., N France, near Belg. border, 6 mi. NE of Lille; with TOURCOING (its twin city just NNW) it produces 80% of France's woolen textiles (carding, combing, spinning, weaving, dyeing, and finishing; mfg. of clothing, upholstery fabrics, hosiery). Also makes textile machinery, rubber, reinforced concrete, beer, and chocolates. Chief locational factor for wool industry is proximity of vast coal mines in Douai-Valenciennes area. Site of national textile school. Together with suburbs (Wattrelos, Croix, Wasquehal) forms part of important Lille-Roubaix-Tourcoing conurbation (pop. c.600,000). Occupied by Germans in First World War.

Roubaix (rōōbā′), village, Lawrence co., W S.Dak., in Black Hills, 7 mi. SE of Deadwood; alt. 5,392 ft. Gold mine here.

Roubion River (rōōbyō′), in Drôme dept., SE France, rises in the Baronnies above Bourdeaux, flows c.35 mi. W to the Rhone 4 mi. below Montélimar.

Roudnice nad Labem (rōd′nyĭtsĕ näd′ läbĕm), Ger. *Raudnitz an der Elbe* (roud′nĭts än dĕr ĕl′bů), town (pop. 8,683), N central Bohemia, Czechoslovakia, on Elbe R. and 22 mi. NNW of Prague; rail junction; hops trade; machinery mfg. (notably agr. equipment for export). Has medieval castle where Cola di Rienzi was confined (1350) by Emperor Charles IV. Intensive farming of hops and sugar beets in vicinity. Mt. Rip (1,505 ft.), with much-frequented 12th-cent. chapel, is 3 mi. SSE.

Roudny, mountain, Czechoslovakia: see VLASIM.

Rouen (rwã), anc. *Rotomagus*, medieval Latin *Rodomum*, city (pop. 101,187), ⊙ Seine-Inférieure dept., N France, on Lower Seine R. (75 mi. above Le Havre) and 70 mi. NW of Paris; 49°26′N 1°5′E. Functioning as seaport of Paris (it is accessible to ships drawing 25 ft.), it is a prime transshipment point bet. river and seagoing vessels. Important commercial and industrial center known for its textiles (cotton cloth, rayon, felt, rubberized fabrics, woolens). Other mfg.: foundry products, briquettes, chemicals (fertilizer, dyes, pharmaceuticals), leather goods, perfumes, flour products, candied apples. Ship-repair yards, petroleum refineries, and paper mills in suburbs. Port, which clears coal, petroleum, wines, phosphates, timber (imports), and exports ships' stores, textiles, miscellaneous luxury articles from Paris, extends for 7 mi. along both banks of the Seine; includes suburbs of Saint-Étienne-du-Rouvray, SOTTEVILLE-LÈS-ROUEN, Saint-Sever (just opposite city center), Le PETIT-QUEVILLY, Le GRAND-QUEVILLY, and Le PETIT-COURONNE, all on left bank of the Seine. Of pre-Roman origin. Repeatedly raided by Norsemen. Became (10th cent.) ⊙ Normandy and a leading European city. Held (1419–49) by English during Hundred Years War. Joan of Arc was burned here in 1431. Seat of provincial *parlement* (1499–1789). Occupied by Germans, 1870–71. Br. army base in First World War. Archiepiscopal see since 5th cent. Rich in ecclesiastical bldgs. City center and harbor installations very heavily damaged in Second World War. One of the 2 towers of 13th–15th-cent. cathedral of Notre Dame was burned; the other (called Butter Tower, Fr. *Tour de Beurre*) was left intact. The 15th–16th-cent. church of St. Maclou and palace of justice were partially destroyed. Undamaged are church of St. Ouen (begun 14th cent.); the Grosse Horloge (a Renaissance clock tower); and the bldgs. housing the fine arts and wrought ironwork museums. Robert de la Salle, Corneille, Fontenelle, and Flaubert b. here.

Rouergue (rwârg), district and former countship, S France, now occupied by AVEYRON dept.; ⊙ Rodez. A dependency of counts of Toulouse, it passed to Fr. crown in 1271, was in English hands (1360–68), and was joined to Guienne prov. by Henry IV in 1589.

Rouffach (rōōfäk′), village (pop. 1,055), Constantine dept., NE Algeria, 8 mi. W of Constantine; wheat.

Rouffach, Ger. *Rufach* (rōō′fäkh), town (pop. 2,687), Haut-Rhin dept., E France, at E foot of the Vosges, 9 mi. SSW of Colmar in winegrowing area; textile milling (shirts, underwear), mfg. of sulphur wicks, typewriter ribbons, tiles. Coal mines near by. Picturesque old town with 13th–14th-cent. church of Saint-Arbogast.

Rouffaer River (rou′fär), tributary of Mamberamo R., W New Guinea; rises in several branches in N slopes of Nassau Range, flows c.150 mi. generally ENE to junction (c.160 mi. WSW of Hollandia, in marshy area) with Idenburg R. to form the Mamberamo. Lower course sometimes called Willigen R.

Roufias River, Greece: see ALPHEUS RIVER; LADON RIVER.

Rougé (rōō-zhā′), village (pop. 466), Loire-Inférieure dept., W France, 6 mi. NW of Châteaubriant; iron mines.

Rouge, Fleuve, Vietnam: see RED RIVER.

Rouge, River (rōōzh), SE Mich., rises in Oakland co., flows c.30 mi. S and SE, through Dearborn and Detroit, to Detroit R. at River Rouge city. Navigable for deep-draught vessels; principal freight comprises iron ore, limestone, coal, petroleum for industries of Detroit area. Lower River Rouge (c.20 mi. long), Middle River Rouge (c.20 mi. long), Upper River Rouge (c.18 mi. long), all rising in Oakland and Washtenaw counties, join main stream near Dearborn.

Rougemont (rōōzhmõ′), village (pop. 471), S Que., 20 mi. E of Montreal; dairying; vegetables, tobacco, maples.

Rougemont, village (pop. 811), Doubs dept., E France, 13 mi. SE of Vesoul; beer, potatoes, cattle.

Rougemont-le-Château (–lů-shätō′), village (pop. 1,259), Territory of Belfort, E France, 9 mi. NE of Belfort; weaving.

Rouge River, SW Que., rises in Mont Tremblant Park, flows 150 mi. S to Ottawa R. 17 mi. W of Lachute.

Rouge River. 1 W central and SW Mich.: see ROGE RIVER. **2** In SE Mich.: see ROUGE, RIVER.

Rough River, NW Ky., rises in NW Hardin co., flows 136 mi. generally WSW, past Hartford, to Green R. at Livermore.

Rouïba (rōōēbä′), village (pop. 2,341), Alger dept., N central Algeria, in irrigated E section of the Mitidja plain, 13 mi. ESE of Algiers, noted for its sparkling wines; brickworks.

Rouillac (rōōyäk′), village (pop. 843), Charente dept., W France, 13 mi. NW of Angoulême; winegrowing.

Rouïna (rōōēnä′), village (pop. 721), Alger dept., N central Algeria, on the Chéliff, on railroad and 24 mi. WSW of Miliana; cereals. Iron mining.

Roujan (rōōzhã′), village (pop. 1,539), Hérault dept., S France, 12 mi. N of Béziers; winegrowing.

Roulans (rōōlã′), village (pop. 296), Doubs dept., E France, near Doubs R. and Rhone-Rhine Canal, 11 mi. NE of Besançon; dairying.

Rouleau (rōōlō′), town (pop. 445), S Sask., near Moosejaw Creek, 22 mi. SW of Regina; grain elevators, oil depot, lumbering.

Roulers (rōōlârs′), Flemish *Roeselare* (rōō′sůlärů), formerly *Rousselaere*, town (pop. 32,227), West Flanders prov., W Belgium, 10 mi. NW of Courtrai; textile center (linen and jute spinning and weaving; mfg. of other textiles); market center for chicory-growing region. Austrians here defeated (1794) by French under Pichegru and Macdonald. Considerably damaged in First World War.

Roumania: see RUMANIA.

Roumazières (rōōmäzyâr′), village (pop. 106), Charmente dept., W France, 11 mi. SSW of Confolens; rail junction; brick- and tileworks.

Roumelia: see RUMELIA.

Round Bay, summer resort (pop., with adjacent Severna Park, 1,095), Anne Arundel co., central Md., on Severn R. 7 mi. NNW of Annapolis.

Round Hill, village (pop. estimate 200), central Alta., 14 mi. NE of Camrose; coal mining.

Round Hill, town (pop. 403), Loudoun co., N Va., 11 mi. E of Leesburg, in E foothills of the Blue Ridge.

Round Island, one of the Seychelles, in the Mahé group, off NE coast of Mahé Isl., 3¼ mi. E of Victoria; 4°37′S 55°30′E; ⅛ mi. long; ⅛ mi. wide.

Round Island. 1 In N Mich., in the Straits of Mackinac 6 mi. SE of St. Ignace, bet. Mackinac and Bois Blanc isls.; c.2 mi. long, 1 mi. wide. **2** In Jefferson co., N N.Y., one of the Thousand Isls., in the St. Lawrence, near N.Y. shore, just NE of Clayton; c.1 mi. long, ¼ mi. wide. Resort.

Round Lake. 1 Village (pop. 573), Lake co., NE Ill., 12 mi. W of Waukegan, in dairying and lake-resort area. Just N is **Round Lake Beach,** village (pop. 1,892), inc. 1936. Residential **Round Lake Park,** village (pop. 1,836), is just E of Round Lake; inc. 1947. **2** Village (pop. 435), Nobles co., SW Minn., near small lake and Iowa line, 8 mi. SE of Worthington, in agr. area (corn, oats, barley, potatoes). **3** Village, Saratoga co., E N.Y., on small Round L., 11 mi. NNE of Schenectady, in summer-resort and agr. area.

Round Lake, lake, Mich.: see ELK LAKE.

Round Lake Beach, village (pop. 1,892), Lake co., NE Ill., 15 mi. W of Waukegan. Inc. 1936.

Round Lake Park, village (pop. 1,836), Lake co., NE Ill., 15 mi. W of Waukegan. Inc. since 1940.

Round Mountain, The (5,300 ft.), E New South Wales, Australia, on E spur of Great Dividing Range, 170 mi. N of Newcastle.

Round Pond, lake (□ 21), S N.F., 50 mi. SSW of Grand Falls; 7 mi. long, 7 mi. wide; drains into Hermitage Bay.

Round Pond, Maine: see BRISTOL.

Round Rock, town (pop. 1,438), Williamson co., central Texas, 17 mi. N of Austin; market center in rich agr. area (cotton, truck, dairy products); lime kilns, limestone quarries; makes brooms, cheese. In 1878 Sam Bass, famous outlaw, was killed here by Texas Rangers.

Round Top. 1 Resort village, Greene co., SE N.Y., in the Catskills, 9 mi. NW of Catskill. Round Top mtn. is near by. **2** Town (pop. 126), Fayette co., S central Texas, 20 mi. SW of Brenham, in farm area.

Round Top, height, Pa.: see GETTYSBURG.

Roundup, city (pop. 2,856), ⊙ Musselshell co., central Mont., on Musselshell R. and 45 mi. N of Billings; trade center for coal-mining region; flour; livestock, dairy products. Inc. 1909.

Roundway, agr. village and parish (pop. 2,625), central Wiltshire, England, just NNE of Devizes.

Rouphia River, Greece: see ALPHEUS RIVER; LADON RIVER.

Roura (rōōrä′), town (commune pop. 437), N Fr. Guiana, opposite Cayenne Isl., near the coast, 13 mi. S of Cayenne; pepper, coffee, sugar.

Rousay (rou′zē), island (□ 21.5, including EGILSAY and WYRE isls.; pop. 468) of the Orkneys, Scotland, 2 mi. N of Pomona across Eynhallow Sound; 6 mi. long, 5 mi. wide. Generally hilly, rising to 821 ft. W and N coasts are precipitous. A complete Stone Age village was discovered here 1938.

Rouses Point (rou′sĭz), resort village and port of entry (pop. 2,001), Clinton co., extreme NE N.Y., on L. Champlain (bridged to Vt.), near Que. line, 20 mi. N of Plattsburg, in agr. area; makes pharmaceuticals; fisheries. Inc. 1877.

Rouseville (rous′vĭl), borough (pop. 1,009), Venango co., NW central Pa., 2 mi. NNE of Oil City; oil refining; metal products.

Rousies (rōōzē′), E industrial suburb (pop. 3,295) of Maubeuge, Nord dept., N France; mfg. (furnaces, generators, corrugated iron, tiling).

Rousselaere, Belgium: see ROULERS.

Rousses, Les (lā rōōs′), village (pop. 357), Jura dept., E France, near Swiss border, 11 mi. NE of Saint-Claude, in the E Jura; alt. 3,723 ft.; winter-sports resort. Makes eyeglasses, clocks, and wooden chests. At La Cure (2 mi. SSE), on road to Nyon and Geneva, is a customhouse.

Roussillon (rōōsēyõ′), region and former province, S France, on Sp. border, bounded by E Pyrenees (S) and Gulf of Lion (E); ⊙ Perpignan. Roughly coextensive with PYRÉNÉES-ORIENTALES dept. since 1790. Taken from the Arabs by the Franks (8th cent.), it formed a countship which passed, in turn, from the counts of Barcelona, to the kings of Aragon, France, Mallorca, and Spain. Conquered by Louis XIII in 1642, it was annexed to France by Treaty of the Pyrenees (1659).

Roussillon. 1 Village (pop. 921), Isère dept., SE France, near left bank of the Rhone, 11 mi. SSW of Vienne; chemical works; rayon mfg. **2** Village (pop. 307), Vaucluse dept., SE France, 6 mi. WNW of Apt; ocher quarrying.

Routot (rōōtō′), village (pop. 511), Eure dept., NW France, 17 mi. WSW of Rouen; cheese, fruits.

Routt (rout), county (□ 2,330; pop. 8,940), NW Colo.; ⊙ Steamboat Springs. Agr. and coal-mining area bordering on Wyo.; bounded E by Park Range; drained by Yampa R. Livestock, dairy products. Includes parts of Routt and White R. natl. forests. Formed 1877.

Rouville (rōōvēl′), county (□ 243; pop. 15,842), S Que., on Richelieu R.; ⊙ Marieville.

Rouvreux (rōōvrû′), village (pop. 1,141), Liége prov., E Belgium, 11 mi. SSE of Liége, near Amblève R.; paving-stone quarrying.

Roux (rōō), town (pop. 9,777), Hainaut prov., S central Belgium, on Charleroi-Brussels Canal and 3 mi. NW of Charleroi; coal mining; glass, metal, chemical industries.

Rouxville (rōō′vĭl), town (pop. 2,460), SW Orange Free State, U. of So. Afr., near Cape Prov. border, 20 mi. NNE of Aliwal North; alt. 5,071 ft.; stock, grain.

Rouyn (rōō′ĭn, Fr. rōōē′), town (1941 pop. 8,808; 1931 pop. 3,225), W Que., on Osisko L., 140 mi. NNE of North Bay; gold, copper, zinc mining center; lumbering, dairying. Airfield. Inc. 1927. Just N is Noranda.

Rouzerville (rou′zŭrvĭl), village (1940 pop. 785), Franklin co., S Pa., 4 mi. ESE of Waynesboro, near Md. line.

Rovaniemi (rō′vänē″ĕmē), town (pop. 13,721), ⊙ (since 1938) Lapi co., N Finland, on Kemi R., at mouth of Ounas R., 100 mi. N of Oulu, just S of Arctic Circle; 66°31′N 25°44′E; timber-shipping, fur-trading, and winter-sports center. Airfield; terminus of Arctic Highway to Ivalo and Pechenga. Founded 1929. Surrounding region suffered in fighting (1944–45) bet. Finns and Germans.

Rovato (rôvä′tô), town (pop. 5,631), Brescia prov., Lombardy, N Italy, 11 mi. WNW of Brescia. Rail junction; industrial and agr. center; foundries, silk mills, chemical plant (caustic soda, potash), clock and hat factories; dairy products, livestock. Il Moretto (Alessandro Bonvicino) b. here.

Rovdino (rôv′dyĕnŭ), village, SW Archangel oblast, Russian SFSR, on Vaga R. and 43 mi. NNE of Velsk; grain.

Rove, Le (lů rôv′), village (pop. 199), Bouches-du-Rhône dept., SE France, 9 mi. NW of Marseilles. Near-by **Rove Tunnel** (4.5 mi. long, 72 ft. wide) pierces Chaîne de l'Estaque at sea level bet. L'Estaque (SE) and Marignane (NW), linking Marseilles bay with Étang de Berre as section of Rhone-Marseilles canal. Completed 1927.

Rovellasca (rôvĕl-lä′skä), village (pop. 3,095), Como prov., Lombardy, N Italy, 10 mi. S of Como; embroidery mfg.

Rovello Porro (rôvĕl′lô pôr′rô), village (pop. 3,175), Como prov., Lombardy, N Italy, 11 mi. S of Como.

Rovenki or **Roven'ki** (rô′vĭnyŭkē). **1** Village (1926 pop. 10,053), S Voronezh oblast, Russian SFSR, 33 mi. SW of Rossosh; metalworks. **2** City (1939 pop. over 10,000), S Voroshilovgrad oblast, Ukrainian SSR, in the Donbas, 33 mi. S of Voroshilovgrad; coal-mining center; flour milling.

Roverbella (rôvĕrbĕl'lä), village (pop. 1,918), Mantova prov., Lombardy, N Italy, 8 mi. N of Mantua; mfg. (motorcycles, bicycles).
Roveredo, Yugoslavia: see MALINSKA.
Rovereto (rôvĕrā'tô), town (pop. 11,155), Trento prov., Trentino–Alto Adige, N Italy, in Val Lagarina, 13 mi. SSW of Trent. Industrial center; mfg. (railroad equipment, agr. machinery, electrical apparatus, aluminum, furniture, leather goods, pottery, paper, cotton textiles, dyes, insecticides); wine, macaroni, sausage. In suburb of Sacco (pop. 3,144) on the Adige and 1 mi. W, are large tobacco factories. Has 14th-cent. castle (houses war mus.), 17th-cent. church, palace (1772), and monument to Antonio Rosmini-Serbati, who was b. here. Taken by Venice in 15th cent. Before First World War (in which town was captured by Italy), it belonged to the Austrian Tyrol. Formerly Roveredo.
Rovigno d'Istria, Yugoslavia: see ROVINJ.
Rovigo (rôvēgō'), village (pop. 758), Alger dept., N central Algeria, in the Mitidja plain, 17 mi. S of Algiers; vineyards, citrus groves; essential-oil distilling, plaster mfg. Hammam-Mélouane sulphur springs 4 mi. SW.
Rovigo (rôvē'gô), province (□ 697; pop. 336,807), Veneto, N Italy; ⊙ Rovigo. Consists of the POLESINE. Mfg. at Rovigo, Adria, Badia Polesine, and Lendinara.
Rovigo, town (pop. 14,561), ⊙ Rovigo prov., Veneto, N Italy, 37 mi. SW of Venice, in the POLESINE; 45°4'N 11°47'E. Rail junction; agr. center; grain market; beet-sugar and flour mills, mfg. (rope, alcohol, furniture, shoes, hats, and bricks). Experimental station (sugar beets, poultry). Has anc. towered walls, ruins of 10th-cent. castle, Renaissance palace, 17th-cent. cathedral (damage restored) and art. gall. Bombed (1945) in Second World War.
Rovine (rôvē'nĕ), village (pop. 6,861), Arad prov., W Rumania, 12 mi. W of Arad; large cementworks.
Rovinj (rô'vĭnyŭ), Ital. *Rovigno d'Istria* (rôvēn'nyô dē'strēä), town (pop. 9,438), NW Croatia, Yugoslavia, on Adriatic Sea, 17 mi. NNW of Pula, in Istria; seaport; rail terminus. Cathedral contains stone sarcophagus of St. Eufemia. Has biological institute.
Rovira (rōvē'rä), town (pop. 2,715), Tolima dept., W central Colombia, in E foothills of Cordillera Central, 13 mi. S of Ibagué; coffee- and sugar-growing center; bananas, yucca, corn, livestock. Until 1930, Miraflores.
Rovno (rô'vnŭ), oblast (□ 7,950; 1946 pop. estimate 1,200,000), W Ukrainian SSR, in Volhynia; ⊙ Rovno. In lowland extending N into Pripet Marshes; includes N part of Volyn-Podolian Upland; bordered S by Kremenets Hills; drained by Styr, Goryn, and Sluch rivers. Swampy prairie soils (N), loess and black earth (E and S); humid continental climate (short summers). Mineral resources include kaolin (Sarny, Korets), iron ore (Mezhirichi, Kostopol), copper (Mydzk), granite, basalt, phosphorite, lignite. Extensive agr., with grain, potatoes, flax (N); sugar beets, hogs, cattle, truck, fruit, tobacco (E, SE). Industries based on agr. (sugar refining, flour milling, tanning, meat preserving, distilling, vegetable-oil extracting) and timber (sawmilling; mfg. of plywood, prefabricated houses, paper). Iron smelting in Zdolbunov and Kostopol, cement mfg. in Zdolbunov, metalworking in Rovno, light mfg. in Ostrog and Dubno. Oblast is served by main Vilna-Lvov RR with lines crossing at Sarny, Rovno, and Zdolbunov. Formed (1939) out of parts of Pol. Wolyn and Polesie provs., following Soviet occupation of E Poland. Held by Germany (1941–44); ceded to USSR in 1945.
Rovno, Pol. *Równe* (rōōv'nĕ), city (1931 pop. 40,788), ⊙ Rovno oblast, Ukrainian SSR, on Ustye R. (branch of Goryn R.) and 110 mi. NE of Lvov; rail junction (repair shops); mfg. center; metalworking (agr. and milling machinery), woodworking (lumber, turpentine, matches), food processing (cereals, meat, hops, vegetable oils, fruit); leather, paper, and textile industries. Stone quarrying near by. Has ruins of medieval palace. Known as trading center in 13th cent. Passed from Poland to Russia (1793); reverted to Poland (1921); ceded to USSR in 1945. Pop. largely Jewish prior to Second World War.
Rovnoye (rôv'nŭyŭ). **1** Village (1926 pop. 6,222), S Saratov oblast, Russian SFSR, on left bank of Volga R. and 50 mi. S of Saratov; grain-trade center; flour and sawmills, metalworks; wheat, tobacco, fruit. Until 1941 (in German Volga Autonomous SSR), Zelman or Seelman. **2** Village (1926 pop. 12,455), SW Kirovograd oblast, Ukrainian SSR, 29 mi. SW of Kirovograd; metalworks.
Rovuma River, Mozambique and Tanganyika: see RUVUMA RIVER.
Row or **Rhu** (both: rōō), village in Rhu parish (pop. 11,373, including Helensburgh burgh), W Dumbarton, Scotland, on Gare Loch, 2 mi. WNW of Helensburgh; resort.
Rowan. 1 (rou'ŭn) County (□ 290; pop. 12,708), NE Ky.; ⊙ Morehead. Bounded SW by Licking R. Hilly clay-mining and agr. (livestock, grain, burley tobacco) area; sandstone quarries, timber. Some mfg. (especially stone, clay, glass, and wood products). Includes part of Cumberland Natl. Forest. Formed 1856. **2** (rō'ăn") County (□ 517; pop. 75,410), W central N.C.; ⊙ Salisbury. Bounded E by Yadkin R. (power dam forms High Rock L. here), N by small South Yadkin R. Piedmont region; farming (cotton, corn, wheat, hay, dairy products, poultry), textile mfg., granite quarrying, sawmilling. Formed 1753.
Rowan (rō'ŭn), town (pop. 304), Wright co., N central Iowa, near Iowa R., 9 mi. E of Clarion.
Rowandiz, Iraq: see RUWANDIZ.
Rowayton, Conn.: see NORWALK.
Rowe (rō), agr. town (pop. 199), Franklin co., NW Mass., 10 mi. E of North Adams.
Rowena (rōwē'nŭ), village (pop. c.750), Runnels co., W central Texas, 23 mi. NE of San Angelo; trade point in farm area.
Rowes Run (rōz), village (pop. 1,358), Fayette co., SW Pa., 10 mi. NW of Uniontown.
Rowesville (rōz'vĭl), town (pop. 363), Orangeburg co., S central S.C., 9 mi. S of Orangeburg.
Rowhedge, England: see EAST DONYLAND.
Rowland (rō'lŭnd), town (pop. 1,293), Robeson co., S N.C., 17 mi. SW of Lumberton; grain, corn, melons.
Rowlesburg (rōlz'bûrg), town (pop. 1,299), Preston co., N W.Va., on Cheat R. and 17 mi. E of Grafton, in agr. and coal-mining area. Chartered 1858.
Rowley, village (pop. estimate 100), S Alta., 22 mi. N of Drumheller; coal mining.
Rowley (rou'lē). **1** Town (pop. 249), Buchanan co., E Iowa, near Wapsipinicon R., 7 mi. S of Independence; butter. **2** Town (pop. 1,768), Essex co., NE Mass., 6 mi. S of Newburyport. Has fine old houses. Settled 1638, inc. 1639.
Rowley Regis (rō'lē rē'jĭs), municipal borough (1931 pop. 41,235; 1951 census 49,409), S Stafford, England, on Stour R. and 7 mi. W of Birmingham; coal mining, granite quarrying, metalworking, mfg. of pottery. The stone quarried is known as Rowley Rag. In the borough are towns of OLD HILL, TIVIDALE, BLACK HEATH, and CRADLEY HEATH.
Rowne, Poland: see ZLOTY STOK.
Rowne, Ukrainian SSR: see ROVNO, city.
Rowrah, England: see ARLECDON AND FRIZINGTON.
Rowsley or **Great Rowsley** (rōz'lē), agr. village and parish (pop. 273), N central Derby, England, on Derwent R., at mouth of Wye R., 3 mi. ESE of Bakewell; flour milling.
Rox, Lake, Swedish *Roxen* (rôk'sŭn), expansion (14 mi. long, 1–6 mi. wide) of Motala R., SE Sweden, 2 mi. N of Linkoping. Forms part of Gota Canal route.
Roxana (rŏk'să"nŭ), village (pop. 1,911), Madison co., SW Ill., on the Mississippi and 15 mi. N of East St. Louis, within St. Louis metropolitan area; large oil refinery. Inc. 1921.
Roxboro, town (pop. 4,321), ⊙ Person co., N N.C., 27 mi. N of Durham, near Va. line; tobacco market; cotton and lumber mills.
Roxborough, village (pop. 871), NE Tobago, B.W.I., 11 mi. NE of Scarborough.
Roxburgh (rŏks'bûrŭ), borough (pop. 516), S S.Isl., New Zealand, 60 mi. WNW of Dunedin and on Clutha R.; rail terminus; orchards.
Roxburgh or **Roxburghshire** (-shĭr), county (□ 665.6; 1931 pop. 45,788; 1951 census 45,562), SE Scotland, bordering S and SE on England (Cumberland and Northumberland); ⊙ Jedburgh. Bounded by Dumfries (W), Selkirk (NW), Midlothian and Berwick (N). Drained by the Tweed, Teviot, Liddell Water and Jed Water rivers. Surface is generally hilly, cut by wooded valleys. Cheviot Hills form SE border. Sheep grazing is main agr. occupation; main industries are woolen (tweed) milling and mfg. of blankets, flour, and agr. implements. Jedburgh, the ⊙, replaced Roxburgh, razed in 1460 after siege in which James II was killed. Other towns are Kelso, Melrose, and Hawick. There are many relics of border warfare. Melrose has famous abbey. Abbotsford was seat of Sir Walter Scott.
Roxburgh, agr. village and parish (pop. 698), N Roxburghshire, Scotland, on Teviot R. and 3 mi. SW of Kelso. An old town, formerly ⊙ Roxburghshire. Near by are ruins of anc. Roxburgh Castle, on high mound (Marchmond), a former border fortress.
Roxburghshire, Scotland: see ROXBURGH, county.
Roxbury. 1 Resort town (pop. 740), Litchfield co., W Conn., on Shepaug R. and 14 mi. W of Waterbury; agr., dairy products; granite. Iron mined in 18th and 19th cent. Seth Warner (buried at Roxbury Center), Ethan Allen, and Remember Baker lived here. **2** Town (pop. 348), Oxford co., W Maine, on Swift R. and c.8 mi. NNW of Rumford, in agr., resort area. **3** Section of BOSTON, Mass. **4** Town (pop. 117), Cheshire co., SW N.H., just E of Keene, in agr., resort area. **5** Resort village, Delaware co., S N.Y., in the Catskills, on East Branch of Delaware R. and 37 mi. NW of Kingston. John Burroughs' home is near by. **6** Town (pop. 465), Washington co., central Vt., 15 mi. SW of Montpelier; agr., wood products; marble; summer camps. Includes Roxbury State Forest.
Roxby cum Risby, former urban district (1931 pop. 548), Parts of Lindsey, NW Lincolnshire, England. Includes ironstone-quarrying towns of Roxby, 4 mi. NNE of Scunthorpe, with 14th-cent. church, and, just S, Risby.
Roxheim (rôks'hīm), village (pop. 2,703), Rhenish Palatinate, W Germany, on oxbow lake of the Rhine and 3 mi. N of Frankenthal; wine; also sugar beets, tobacco.
Roxie village (pop. 521), Franklin co., SW Miss., 20 mi. E of Natchez.
Roxo, Cape (rō'shō), African headland on Senegal–Port. Guinea border, 170 mi. SSE of Dakar; 12°20'N 16°43'W.
Roxobel (rŏk'sŭbĕl), town (pop. 394), Bertie co., NE N.C., 29 mi. SE of Roanoke Rapids.
Roxton, village (1940 pop. 1,138), Lamar co., NE Texas, 12 mi. SW of Paris; trade center in cotton, corn, hay area.
Roxton Falls, village (pop. 795), SW Que., 20 mi. E of St. Hyacinthe; dairying, fruit and vegetable canning, lumbering, woodworking, furniture mfg.
Roxton Pond or **Sainte Pudentienne** (sĕt pŭdätyĕn'), village (pop. 591), SW Que., 16 mi. SE of St. Hyacinthe; dairying, lumbering, woodworking.
Roy. 1 Village (pop. 1,074), Harding co., NE N.Mex., near Canadian R., 60 mi. NNW of Tucumcari; alt. c.5,900 ft.; grain, beans. Carbon-dioxide fields near by. **2** Town (pop. 3,723), Weber co., N Utah, 5 mi. SW of Ogden, near Great Salt L. Inc. 1937. **3** Town (pop. 263), Pierce co., W central Wash., 18 mi. S of Tacoma; seeds, bulbs, dairy products.
Royal. 1 Town (pop. 495), Clay co., NW Iowa, 9 mi. WSW of Spencer, in livestock and grain area. **2** Village (pop. 157), Antelope co., NE Nebr., 15 mi. NNW of Neligh.
Royal Canal, Ireland, extends 96 mi. bet. Dublin and the Shannon at Termonbarry, serving Cloncurry and Mallingar. Constructed 1789–1802.
Royal Center, town (pop. 876), Cass co., N central Ind., 11 mi. NW of Logansport, in agr. region; lumber, canned foods.
Royal Cotton Mills, N.C.: see ROYALL COTTON MILLS.
Royale, Isle, Mich.: see ISLE ROYALE NATIONAL PARK.
Royale Island (rwäyäl'), rocky islet off coast of Fr. Guiana, one of the Îles du Salut, 28 mi. NNW of Cayenne; lighthouse.
Royal Geographical Society Islands, S Franklin Dist., Northwest Territories, group of 4 small isls. and several islets bet. S end of Victoria Strait and NE side of Queen Maud Gulf, bet. SE Victoria Isl. and SW King William Isl. near 68°50'N 100°15'W.
Royal Gorge (Grand Canyon of the Arkansas), impressive canyon of Arkansas R., S central Colo., extending c.10 mi. WNW from Canon City. Its granite walls (more than 1,000 ft. high) rise abruptly above the river. Crossed by suspension bridge (just W of Canon City) 1,053 ft. above river; main span is 880 ft.; total length 1,260 ft. Cable railway (1,550 ft. long) ascends canyon wall. Railroad along river bank at bottom of canyon is suspended over river by "hanging bridge" at narrowest point in gorge.
Royal Island (c.3½ mi. long), central Bahama Isls., just N of Eleuthera Isl. and W of St. George's Cay, 40 mi. NE of Nassau; 25°32'N 76°50'W. Has fine harbor. Belongs to Spanish Wells dist.
Royalist Island, Caroline Isls.: see KUOP.
Royall Cotton Mills, town (1940 pop. 417), Wake co., central N.C., just NE of Wake Forest; textile mfg. Sometimes Royal Cotton Mills.
Royal Leamington Spa, England: see LEAMINGTON.
Royal Military Canal, England: see HYTHE, Kent.
Royal Oak. 1 City (pop. 46,898), Oakland co., SE Mich., residential suburb just NNW of Detroit; some mfg. (tools, abrasives, paint, mattresses, cushions, scales, building products). The Detroit Zoological Park is here. Settled c.1820; inc. as village 1891, as city 1921. **2** Town (1940 pop. 153), St. Louis co., E Mo., bet. Mississippi and Missouri rivers, W of St. Louis.
Royal River, SW Maine, rises in N central Cumberland co., flows c.25 mi. generally SSE to Casco Bay at Yarmouth.
Royal Society Range, Antarctica, on W shore of Ross Sea, near head of McMurdo Sound; Mt. Lister rises to 13,350 ft. Discovered 1902 by R. F. Scott, Br. explorer.
Royalston, agr. town (pop. 838), Worcester co., N Mass., 21 mi. WNW of Fitchburg.
Royalton. 1 Village (pop. 1,506), Franklin co., S Ill., 7 mi. NW of Herrin, in agr. and bituminous-coal-mining area. Inc. 1907. **2** Village (pop. 500), Morrison co., central Minn., on Platte R. near its mouth in Mississippi R. and 11 mi. SSE of Little Falls, in agr. area; dairy products. **3** Borough (pop. 1,175), Dauphin co., S Pa., on Susquehanna R. just below Middletown, at mouth of Swatara Creek; bricks. **4** Town (pop. 1,331), Windsor co., E central Vt., on White R. and 25 mi. S of Barre, in agr. area; wood and dairy products, maple sugar, poultry, truck. Includes South Royalton village. Raid in 1780 by Indians and Tories is commemorated by a monument.
Royal Tunbridge Wells, England: see TUNBRIDGE WELLS.

Royan (rwäyä'), town (pop. 5,086; 1936 pop. 10,111), Charente-Maritime dept., W France, at the mouth of the Gironde and 21 mi. WSW of Saintes; one of France's most popular seaside resorts, it was 95% destroyed by Allied bombings of besieged German garrison (Jan.–April, 1945).

Roya River (rwäyä'), Ital. *Roia*, rises in Maritime Alps, SE France, at Tenda Pass, flows S past Tende, Saint-Dalmas-de-Tende, entering Italy 2 mi. S of Breil, to the Gulf of Genoa at Ventimiglia; 30 mi. long. Hydroelectric plants. Followed in upper valley by Nice-Turin RR and road.

Royat (rwäyä'), town (pop. 3,420), Puy-de-Dôme dept., central France, on E slope of volcanic Monts Dôme, 2 mi. WSW of Clermont-Ferrand; noted spa with mineral springs (iron, arsenic, carbonic acid) frequented by rheumatic and cardiac patients. Chocolate mfg., diamond cutting. Old village (above spa) has fortified 11th–12th-cent. church. Springs known since Roman times.

Roybon (rwäbõ'), village (pop. 455), Isère dept., SE France, 24 mi. WNW of Grenoble, in the Pre-Alps; sawmilling.

Roy Bridge, agr. village, SE Inverness, Scotland, on Spean R. and 3 mi. E of Spean Bridge, at foot of Ben Nevis, near GLEN ROY. Near by the last clan battle in Scotland was fought in 1688.

Roye (rwä), town (pop. 4,184), Somme dept., N France, on the Avre and 11 mi. ENE of Montdidier; important road junction; sugar-refining center. Slate quarries near by. Leveled in First World War (changed hands 4 times); rebuilt, and again damaged in Second World War.

Royère (rwäyâr'), village (pop. 333), Creuse dept., central France, on Plateau of Gentioux, 15 mi. WSW of Aubusson; livestock raising. Granite quarries.

Royersford, borough (pop. 3,862), Montgomery co., SE Pa., 24 mi. NW of Philadelphia and on Schuylkill R.; metal and glass products, clothing, leather goods; agr. Settled 1839, inc. 1879.

Roy Inks Dam, S central Texas, in Colorado R. 3 mi. below Buchanan Dam and c.10 mi. WSW of Burnet; 1,400 ft. long; for power; completed 1938. Also called Arnold Dam. Impounds Inks L. (capacity c.16,000 acre-ft.); state park on E shore.

Royken (rû'ükûn), Nor. *Røyken*, village (pop. 257; canton pop. 5,923), Buskerud co., SE Norway, on railroad and 6 mi. E of Drammen; market gardening. Canton covers N part of Hurum peninsula, bet. Drammen Fjord and Oslo Fjord; has cement, lime, brick, textile, stonecutting, sawmilling, and dairying industries.

Royo, El (ĕl roi'ō), town (pop. 653), Soria prov., N central Spain, 14 mi. NW of Soria; cereals, vegetables, livestock. Coal deposits.

Royrvik, Norway: see GJERSVIKA.

Royse City (rois), town (pop. 1,266), Rockwall and Collin counties, NE Texas, 30 mi. NE of Dallas; market point in agr. area (cotton, grain, truck). Settled c.1886, inc. 1888.

Royston. 1 Urban district (1931 pop. 3,831; 1951 census 4,663), N Hertford, England, 13 mi. SSW of Cambridge, on Ermine Street (Roman); agr. market, mfg. (farm equipment, fertilizer, cement). Has 13th-cent. church. Was site of 12th-cent. Dominican priory. Roman remains have been found near by. **2** Urban district (1931 pop. 7,166; 1951 census 8,137), West Riding, S Yorkshire, England, 3 mi. NNE of Barnsley; coal mining. Has 13th-cent. church.

Royston, city (pop. 2,039), Franklin, Hart, and Madison cos., NE Ga., 27 mi. NE of Athens; mfg. (clothing, lumber).

Roysville, town, Montserrado co., SW Liberia, on Atlantic Ocean, 18 mi. NW of Monrovia; palm oil and kernels, citrus fruit, coffee. Also spelled Royesville.

Royton, urban district (1931 pop. 16,689; 1951 census 14,772), SE Lancashire, England, near Yorkshire boundary 2 mi. N of Oldham; cotton milling, electrical engineering. Site of anc. Saxon iron forge.

Rozaj, Rozhai, or **Rozhay** (all: rô'zhī), Serbo-Croatian *Rožaj*, village (pop. 6,336), E Montenegro, Yugoslavia, on Ibar R., on Novi Pazar–Berane road and 16 mi. E of Berane, near Serbia border; local trade center.

Rozan (rōō'zhän), Pol. *Różan*, Rus. *Rozhan* (rôzh'-ŭn), town (pop. 1,374), Warszawa prov., E central Poland, on Narew R. and 12 mi. E of Makow Mazowiecki; cement mfg., flour milling, tanning.

Rozana, Belorussian SSR: see RUZHANY.

Rozas de Madrid, Las (läs rō'thäs dhä mädhrē'), village (pop. 860), Madrid prov., central Spain, on railroad and 11 mi. NW of Madrid; cereals, carobs, vegetables, livestock.

Rozas de Puerto Real (pwĕr'tō rääl'), town (pop. 660), Madrid prov., central Spain, 5 mi. SW of San Martín de Valdeiglesias; cereals, grapes, chestnuts, livestock; timber.

Rozay-en-Brie (rōzā'-ā-brē'), village (pop. 1,123), Seine-et-Marne dept., N central France, on the Yères and 17 mi. NE of Melun; agr. market; basketmaking. Has 13th–16th-cent. church. Nearby 14th-cent. castle of Grange-Bléneau (restored 18th cent.) was residence (1802–34) of Lafayette.

Rozdelov (rôz'dyĕlôf), Czech *Rozdělov*, village (pop. 3,631), central Bohemia, Czechoslovakia, 16 mi. WNW of Prague, in urban area of KLADNO.

Rozden or **Rozhden** (rôzh'dĕn), Serbo-Croatian *Rožden*, village, Macedonia, Yugoslavia, near Gr. border, 23 mi. SE of Prilep, in the Marihovo. Abandoned antimony mines near by.

Rozdol (rôz'dŭl), Pol. *Rozdół* (rôz'dōō-ōō), town (1931 pop. 4,212), E Drogobych oblast, Ukrainian SSR, 17 mi. NNE of Stry; agr. processing (cereals, hops), brick mfg. Has old palace and churches.

Rozebeke (rō'zûbäkû), agr. village (pop. 492), East Flanders prov., W central Belgium, 7 mi. E of Oudenaarde. Scene of defeat (1382) of armies of Ghent by French. Formerly spelled Roosebeke or Roozebeke.

Rozel (rōzĕl'), city (pop. 233), Pawnee co., central Kansas, on Pawnee R. and 15 mi. W of Larned; grain, livestock.

Rozendaal, Netherlands: see ROOSENDAAL.

Rozewie, Cape (rôzĕ'vyĕ), Pol. *Przylądek Rozewie* (pshĭlô'dĕk), Ger. *Rixhöft* (rĭks'hûft), Gdansk prov., N Poland, northernmost point of Poland, on Baltic Sea, 9 mi. NNW of Puck; 54°50'N 18°15'E; lighthouse.

Rozhai, Yugoslavia: see ROZAJ.

Rozhan, Poland: see ROZAN.

Rozhden, Yugoslavia: see ROZDEN.

Rozhdestveno (rŭzhdyĕ'stvyĭnŭ), village (1939 pop. over 500), SE Kalinin oblast, Russian SFSR, 22 mi. E of Kalinin; flax. Glassworks (4 mi. E). A Rozhdestveno rail station is 80 mi. SW of Kalinin, 8 mi. S of Rzhev.

Rozhdestvenskaya Khava (–skŭ khä'vŭ), village (1926 pop. 5,434), N central Voronezh oblast, Russian SFSR, 20 mi. E of Voronezh, in agr. area; wheat, potatoes.

Rozhdestvenskoye (–skŭyŭ). **1** Village, E Kostroma oblast, Russian SFSR, on Vetluga R. and 16 mi. S of Sharya; flax. **2** Village, Krasnoyarsk Territory, Russian SFSR: see DZERZHINSKOYE. **3** Village, Kherson oblast, Ukrainian SSR: see SIVASHSKOYE.

Rozhishche (rô'zhĭshchĭ), Pol. *Rożyszcze* (rôzhĭ'shchĕ), town (1931 pop. 4,512), SE central Volyn oblast, Ukrainian SSR, on Styr R. and 12 mi. N of Lutsk; mfg. center (cement, furniture), flour and sawmilling, hatmaking.

Rozhki (rŭshkē'), village (1926 pop. 733), SE Kirov oblast, Russian SFSR, on Vyatka R. and 13 mi. NNW of Malmyzh; machine shops.

Rozhnyatov (rŭzhnyä'tŭf), Pol. *Rozniatów* (rôznyä'-tōōf), town (1931 pop. 3,638), W Stanislav oblast, Ukrainian SSR, at N foot of East Beskids, 25 mi. W of Stanislav; sugar refining, flour and sawmilling. Has old castle.

Rozmberk or **Rozmberk nad Vltavou** (rô'zhŭmbĕrk näd' vŭltävō), Czech *Rožmberk nad Vltavou*, Ger. *Rosenburg* or *Rosenberg* (rō'zŭnbŏŏrk, –bĕrk), village (pop. 348), S Bohemia, Czechoslovakia, in Bohemian Forest, on Vltava R., on railroad and 11 mi. SSE of Cesky Krumlov, near Austrian border; summer resort noted for 13th-cent. castle and church.

Rozmberk, pond, Czechoslovakia: see TREBON.

Rozmital, Czech *Rožmitál* or *Rožmitál pod Tremšínem* (rôzh'mĭtäl pô'trĕmshēnĕm), village (pop. 1,925), S Bohemia, Czechoslovakia, in the Brdy, 8 mi. SW of Pribram; rail terminus; popular summer resort in lake dist. known for fishing.

Roznau, Czechoslovakia: see ROZNOV POD RADHOSTEM.

Roznava (rôzh'nyävä), Slovak *Rožňava*, Ger. *Rosenau* (rō'zŭnou), Hung. *Rozsnyó* (rôzh'nyō), town (pop. 6,644), S Slovakia, Czechoslovakia, in Slovak Ore Mts., on Slana (Sajo) R., on railroad and 33 mi. WSW of Kosice; foundries; antimony works; iron mines; liqueur mfg. Ferruginous springs (E). Seat of R.C. bishopric. Has predominantly Hungarian pop. Vicinity noted for antimony deposits (NE), iron mines at Nadabula (NNW), Drnava (4 mi. ESE), Roznavske Bystre (W), Nizna Slana (7 mi. NW), Vlachov (10 mi. NW). Gombasek limestone quarries are 7 mi. SSW. Krasna Horka castle (3 mi. E) has fine collections of paintings, arms. Roznava was held by Hungary, 1938–45.

Rozniatow, Ukrainian SSR: see ROZHNYATOV.

Roznov pod Radhostem (rôzh'nôf pôd' räd-hôsh-tyĕm), Czech *Rožnov pod Radhoštěm*, Ger. *Roznau* (rōts'nou), town (pop. 3,743), E Moravia, Czechoslovakia, in the Beskids, on Dolni Becva R. and 26 mi. NE of Gottwaldov; rail terminus; health resort (alt. 1,243 ft.) at SW foot of Radhost mtn. Sporting goods and bentwood furniture made here; embroidery. Has sanatorium, open-air mus. of folklore. Formerly known for its whey cure.

Roznow (rôzh'nōōf), Pol. *Rożnów*, village, Krakow prov., S Poland, 10 mi. N of Nowy Sacz and on Dunajec R.; hydroelectric station.

Rozovka (rô'zŭfkŭ), town (1939 pop. over 500), E Zaporozhe oblast, Ukrainian SSR, 45 mi. NNE of Osipenko; flour milling, dairying. Formerly a Ger. settlement called Rozenberg (Rosenberg); later (c.1935–41), Lyuksemburg (Luxemburg).

Rozoy-sur-Serre (rōzwä'-sür-sâr'), village (pop. 1,147), Aisne dept., N France, on Serre R. and 13 mi. SE of Vervins; flour- and sawmilling.

Rozsahegy, Czechoslovakia: see RUZOMBEROK.

Rozsnyo, Czechoslovakia: see ROZNAVA.

Roztoche, Poland and USSR: see ROZTOCZE.

Roztocze (rôstô'chĕ), Rus. *Roztoche* (rŭstô'chĭ), mountain range in SE Poland and W Ukrainian SSR, bet. Krasnik (Poland) and Lvov (Ukrainian SSR); c.100 mi. long NW–SE; rises to over 1,000 ft. Lignite deposits near Zholkev and Rava Russkaya. Also called Tomaszow-Lvov Ridge, Pol. *Grzbiet Tomaszowsko-Lwowski*.

Roztoky (rôs'tôkĭ), village (pop. 3,121), N central Bohemia, Czechoslovakia, on Vltava R., on railroad and 5 mi. NNW of Prague; popular excursion center; explosives mfg.; large penicillin plant.

Rozvazhev (rŭzvä'zhĭf), village (1939 pop. over 2,000), NW Kiev oblast, Ukrainian SSR, 9 mi. W of Ivankov; flax.

Rozwadow (rôzvä'dōōf), Pol. *Rozwadów*, town (pop. 3,436), Rzeszow prov., SE Poland, on San R. and 14 mi. ESE of Sandomierz; rail junction; furniture mfg., sawmilling; tile works.

Rozyszcze, Ukrainian SSR: see ROZHISHCHE.

Rroskovec or **Rroskoveci**, Albania: see RESKOVEC.

Rrubig (rōō'bĕg) or **Rrubigu** (rōō'bĕgōō), village (1930 pop. 110), N Albania, on Fan R. and 7 mi. E of Lesh; copper mining. Also spelled Robik (Robiku), Rubig (Rubigu), or Rubik (Rubiku).

RSFSR: see RUSSIAN SOVIET FEDERATED SOCIALIST REPUBLIC.

Rtanj, Rtan, or **Rtan'** (ŭr'tänyŭ), mountain, E Serbia, Yugoslavia; highest point (5,117 ft.) is 5 mi. SW of Boljevac. High-grade bituminous coal mine on E slope.

Rtishchevo (ŭrtyē'shchĭvŭ), city (1926 pop. 11,409), NW Saratov oblast, Russian SFSR, 105 mi. WNW of Saratov; rail, agr.-processing center (flour and meat products); metal goods. Chartered 1920.

Ruabon (rŭă'bŭn), town and parish (pop. 3,266), SE Denbigh, Wales, 5 mi. SSW of Wrexham; coal mining, steel milling, chemical mfg. Parish church originally founded in 6th cent.

Ruad, Ruwad (rōōwăd'), or **Arwad** (ärwăd'), Fr. *Rouad*, anc. *Aradus*, island, Latakia prov., W Syria, in the Mediterranean Sea, just off Tartus, 30 mi. N of Tripoli, 45 mi. S of Latakia. Was the most northerly of the important Phoenician centers and appears in the Bible as Arvad.

Ruahine Range (rōō"ŭhē'nē), highest range (4–6,000 ft.) of N.Isl., New Zealand, extends 60 mi. S from Kaimanawa Mts. to base of Wellington peninsula; forested slopes.

Ruan, Mont (mõ rüä'), peak (9,998 ft.) in Pennine Alps, SW Switzerland, 8 mi. W of Martigny-Ville.

Ruanda, division, Ruanda-Urundi: see KIGALI.

Ruanda-Urundi (rwän'dä-ōōrōōn'dē, Fr. rwändä'-ōōrōōndē'), United Nations trust territory (□ 20,575; 1949 pop. 3,889,058), E central Africa, administered by Belgium as part of Belgian Congo; ⊙ Usumbura. Ruanda is in N, Urundi in S. Bordered W by Belgian Congo along L. Tanganyika, Ruzizi R., L. Kivu, and the Virunga range; E and S by Tanganyika, partly along Kagera and Malagarasi rivers; N by Uganda. A region of high plateaus (4,500–10,000 ft.) drained by Nyawarongo and Ruvuvu rivers, it is a relatively prosperous pastoral country and one of the most densely populated areas in Africa (193 persons per sq.mi.). Cotton, coffee, tobacco, and sisal are grown by natives; tin, wolfram, and gold are mined. Staple food crops include corn, sweet potatoes, pulse, manioc, plantain, sorghum, ground-nuts, and, in high-lying locations, sesame and wheat. Climate is temperate with alternate wet and dry seasons characterized by frequent dry spells, which sometimes result in famine. Dairying, brick and tile making, mfg. of soap and insecticides. Exports hides, cattle, cotton, native foodstuffs, castor beans, pyrethrum, tin, clay products. Mostly dependent on Indian Ocean ports of Dar es Salaam and Mombasa; roads, lake steamship lines, and airlines connect it with Belgian Congo, Uganda, and Tanganyika; there are no railroads. Native social organization, a kind of feudal society, has 3 ethnic groups: the aristocratic Watusi (guardians of long-horned stock) who arrived from Ethiopia and Egypt c.300 years ago; the peasant Bahutu (90% of pop.) of Bantu stock (mostly originating from Congo basin); and a few aboriginal Batwa, pygmy hunters. Ruanda and Urundi are each ruled by a *mwami* (sultan) supervised by a Belgian resident. Native handicrafts include basketry, pottery, and rugs. Kinyarwanda and Kirundi, 2 Bantu dialects, are spoken. Henry M. Stanley and David Livingstone landed at Usumbura in 1871; Ger. explorers traversed both Ruanda and Urundi (1894–96). During 1899-1917, the territory was part of Ger. East Africa; after First World War it was awarded (1923) to Belgium as a mandate of the League of Nations and became (1946) a United Nations Trust Territory.

Ruapehu (rōō"ŭpä'hōō), dormant volcanic peak (9,175 ft.) in Tongariro Natl. Park, central N.Isl., New Zealand; highest mtn. of N.Isl.; crater lake on summit; skiing.

Ruapuke Island (rōō"ŭpōō'kē), volcanic island in Foveaux Strait, 9 mi. off SE coast of S.Isl., New Zealand; 4.5 mi. long, 2.5 mi. wide; fishing; building stone. Owned by Maoris.

Ruardean (rōōär'dēn), agr. village and parish (pop. 1,225), W Gloucester, England, in Forest of Dean, 13 mi. W of Gloucester. Has Norman church.

Ruashi (rwä'shē), village, Katanga prov., SE Belgian Congo, on railroad and 6 mi. NNW of Elisabethville; copper and cobalt mining.

Ruatán Island, Honduras: see ROATÁN ISLAND.

Rub' al Khali (ro͝ob' ăl khä'lē) [Arabic,=Empty Quarter], great desert (□ 250,000) of S Arabian Peninsula; 750 mi. long, 400 mi. wide. Occupying a structural basin, it consists of the Nafud and Dahana desert types in E and very loose dune land (Arabic *ahqaf*) in extreme W. Relatively unexplored, it was 1st traversed on foot by Bertram Thomas in 1931 from Salala to Doha.

Rubbestadneset (rüb'bŭstänā"sü), village in Bremnes canton (pop. 4,368), Hordaland co., SW Norway, on NE shore of Bomlo isl., 27 mi. N of Haugesund; produces diesel engines.

Rübeland (rü'bülänt), village (pop. 1,413), in former Brunswick exclave, after 1945 in Saxony-Anhalt, central Germany, in the lower Harz, on the Bode and 6 mi. WSW of Blankenburg; paper milling. Noted for near-by Baumannshöhle (W) and Hermannshöhle (S) stalactite caves.

Rubenheim (ro͞o'bŭnhīm), village (pop. 657), SE Saar, near Blies R., 10 mi. SW of Zweibrücken; stock, grain.

Rubeshibe (ro͞obā'shēbā), town (pop. 16,875), E central Hokkaido, Japan, 36 mi. WSW of Abashiri; agr. (soybeans, potatoes, sugar beets); mining (gold, silver). Hot springs near by.

Rubetsu, Russian SFSR: see KUIBYSHEVO, Sakhalin oblast.

Rubezhnoye (ro͞obyĕzh'nŭyŭ), city (1939 pop. over 10,000), W Voroshilovgrad oblast, Ukrainian SSR, in the Donbas, on the Northern Donets and 50 mi. NW of Voroshilovgrad; coal-mining center; glass, paints. Chemical engineering col. Until c.1940, Rubezhnaya.

Rubí (ro͞ovē'), town (pop. 5,687), Barcelona prov., NE Spain, 10 mi. NW of Barcelona; mfg. of cotton, woolen, and silk fabrics, and electrical equipment, knitwear, flour products; flour milling; lumbering. Agr. trade (wine, wheat, olive oil, vegetables).

Rubiana (ro͞ovyä'nä), village (pop. 1,321), Orense prov., NW Spain, 20 mi. WSW of Ponferrada; brandy distilling; cereals, potatoes. Antimony deposits.

Rubicon River (ro͞o'bĭkŏn), Ital. *Rubicone*, N central Italy, rises in foothills of Etruscan Apennines 10 mi. WNW of San Marino, flows 15 mi. NE, past Savignano sul Rubicone and Fiumicino (after which it is sometimes called), to the Adriatic 10 mi. NW of Rimini. Receives Pisciatello R. (left). In Roman times, formed boundary bet. Italy proper and Cisalpine Gaul. Caesar began civil war with Pompey by crossing it, 49 B.C., with his troops.

Rubicon River, E central Calif., rises in Desolation Valley in the Sierra Nevada just SW of L. Tahoe, flows c.60 mi. generally SW, forming part of El Dorado–Placer co. line, to American R. near Auburn.

Rubidoux, Mount, Calif.: see RIVERSIDE, city.

Rubielos de Mora (ro͞ovyā'lōs dhä mō'rä), town (pop. 1,018), Teruel prov., E Spain, 27 mi. SE of Teruel; cereals, olive oil, wine; lumber. Asphalt and coal mines near by.

Rubiera (ro͞obyā'rä), town (pop. 1,732), Reggio nell'Emilia prov., Emilia-Romagna, N central Italy, near Secchia R., 7 mi. W of Modena; mfg. (motors, water pumps).

Rubig or **Rubigu,** Albania: see RRUBIG.

Rubio (ro͞o'byō), town (pop. 5,778), Táchira state, W Venezuela, in Andean spur, near Colombia border, on transandine highway and 10 mi. WSW of San Cristóbal; alt. 2,720 ft. Center for leading coffee region. First Venezuelan oil deposits discovered here 1878. Coal and silver deposits in vicinity.

Rubio, El (ĕl ro͞o'vyō), town (pop. 6,508), Seville prov., SW Spain, on affluent of Genil R. and 10 mi. NE of Osuna; agr. center (olives, cereals, livestock). Mfg. of olive oil, flour, dairy products, plaster. Has Roman inscriptions.

Rubi River, Belgian Congo: see ITIMBIRI RIVER.

Rublevo (ro͞oblyô'vŭ), town (1926 pop. 1,710), central Moscow oblast, Russian SFSR, W suburb of Moscow, on Moskva R. and 5 mi. NW of Kuntsevo; site of Moscow waterworks.

Rubona (ro͞obō'nä), village, central Ruanda-Urundi, in Ruanda, 40 mi. SSW of Kigali; tropical agr. research station.

Rubrum Mare: see RED SEA.

Rubtsovsk (ro͞optsôfsk'), city (1926 pop. 15,904), SW Altai Territory, Russian SFSR, on Alei R., on Turksib RR and 165 mi. SW of Barnaul; agr.-machine mfg. center (tractors, agr. implements, electrical goods); flour milling, dairying. A city since 1927, it was originally an agr.-processing center; industrialized during Second World War.

Ruby, village (pop. 122), W Alaska, on Yukon R. opposite mouth of Melozitna R. and 100 mi. WSW of Tanana; logging, sawmilling, trapping; supply point for placer gold-mining region. Airfield.

Ruby. 1 Village (1940 pop. 842), Santa Cruz co., extreme S Ariz., near Mex. line, 20 mi. WNW of Nogales; alt. 4,335 ft.; mining. **2** Town (pop. 315), Chesterfield co., N S.C., 15 mi. WNW of Cheraw, near N.C. line; cannery.

Ruby Lake, NE Nev., tule marsh lake just E of Ruby Mts.; 13 mi. long, 2 mi. wide. Migratory waterfowl refuge here.

Ruby Mountains, NE Nev., largely in Elko co., SE of Elko, extending c.60 mi. SSW from East Humboldt Range through part of Humboldt Natl. Forest. Rises to 11,400 ft. Ruby L. is just E.

Ruby Range, N extension of Snowcrest Mts. in SW Mont., lies just W of Ruby R.; reaches as far N as Sheridan. Rises to max. alt. of 9,000 ft. in N tip.

Ruby Reservoir, Wash.: see ROSS DAM.

Ruby River, SW Mont., rises in several branches in Gravelly Range, flows 76 mi. generally NNW, bet. Snowcrest Mts. and Tobacco Root Mts., joining Beaverhead R. in Jefferson R. system at Twin Bridges.

Rucar (ro͞o'kŭr), Rum. *Rucăr*, village (pop. 4,339), Arges prov., S central Rumania, on Dambovita R., in the Transylvanian Alps and 8 mi. NE of Campulung; tourist and mtn. excursion center; alt. 2,067 ft. Known for its picturesque folkways and 18th-cent. monastery. Scenic cavern of Dambovicioara (dûm"bôvēchwä'rä) [Rum. *Dâmbovicioara*] is NE.

Rucker, Camp, Ala.: see OZARK.

Ruckersville, town (pop. 74), Elbert co., NE Ga., 6 mi. NE of Elberton.

Ruda (ro͞o'dä), village (pop. 1,267), Udine prov., Friuli–Venezia Giulia, NE Italy, 6 mi. SE of Palmanova; iron sheeting.

Ruda (ro͞o'dä), town (pop. 18,998), Katowice prov., S Poland, 2 mi. E of Hindenburg (Zabrze), in coal-mining region. Inc. after 1946.

Ruda (rü'dä), village (pop. 573), Kalmar co., SE Sweden, near Em R., 18 mi. SW of Oskarshamn; rail junction; mfg. of glass, furniture.

Rudabanya (ro͞o'dŏbänyŏ), Hung. *Rudabánya*, mining town (pop. 2,509), Borsod-Gömör co., NE Hungary, 20 mi. NNW of Miskolc; rail terminus. Iron ore mined near by.

Ruda Pabianicka (ro͞o'dä päbyänēts'kä), S textile-mfg. suburb of Lodz, Poland. Inc. c.1945 into Lodz. Formerly spelled Ruda Pabjanicka.

Rudaria (ro͞odä'ryä), Rum. *Rudăria*, Hung. *Ögerlistye* (ö'gĕrlĕshtyĕ), village (pop. 2,410), Severin prov., SW Rumania, 15 mi. E of Oravita; coal and copper mining.

Rudarpur (ro͞o'dŭrpo͝or), town (pop. 8,385), Gorakhpur dist., E Uttar Pradesh, India, on tributary of the Rapti and 26 mi. SE of Gorakhpur; saltpeter processing; trades in rice, wheat, barley, oilseeds, gram. Noted Hindu temple and anc. ruins near by.

Rudauli (ro͞odou'lē), town (pop. 13,755), Bara Banki dist., central Uttar Pradesh, India, 24 mi. WSW of Fyzabad; hand-loom cotton weaving; trades in rice, gram, wheat, oilseeds, barley. Shrines of 2 noted Moslem saints.

Rudbar (ro͞od'bär), village (pop. over 500), Farah prov., SW Afghanistan, on Helmand R. and 35 mi. ESE of Chahar Burjak, 50 mi. from Baluchistan line, in Afghan Seistan.

Rudbar (ro͞odbär'), town, First Prov., in Gilan, N Iran, 35 mi. SSW of Resht, and on left bank of the Sefid Rud, in Elburz range; olive-growing center; rice, tobacco.

Rudd, town (pop. 398), Floyd co., N Iowa, 15 mi. E of Mason City, in livestock area.

Ruddervoorde (rü'dŭrvōr"dŭ), agr. village (pop. 4,792), West Flanders prov., NW Belgium, 7 mi. S of Bruges.

Ruddington, residential town and parish (pop. 3,064), S Nottingham, England, 4 mi. S of Nottingham; hosiery, lace mfg.

Rudensk (ro͞odyĕnsk'), town (1939 pop. over 500), S Minsk oblast, Belorussian SSR, 25 mi. SE of Minsk; peat bogs.

Rüdersdorf (rü'dŭrsdôrf), town (pop. 10,824), Brandenburg, E Germany, in the low Rüdersdorf Chalk Hills, 18 mi. E of Berlin; limestone-quarrying center (since 13th cent.); mfg. of cement, concrete, phosphates, bricks, wallpaper; flour milling. Sometimes called Rüdersdorf bei Berlin (bī bĕrlēn').

Rüderswil (rü'dŭrsvēl), town (pop. 2,251), Bern canton, W central Switzerland, in the EMMENTAL, 14 mi. E of Bern.

Rud-e-Sar, Iran: see RUD-I-SAR.

Rüdesheim or **Rüdesheim am Rhein** (rü'dŭs-hīm äm rīn'), town (pop. 5,736), in former Prussian prov. of Hesse-Nassau, W Germany, after 1945 in Hesse, in the Rheingau, on right bank of the Rhine (landing) and 16 mi. WSW of Wiesbaden; noted for its white wine. Has Gothic church, 3 castles. First mentioned 864. Rack-and-pinion railway to the Niederwald (W).

Rudgwick, agr. village and parish (pop. 1,273), N Sussex, England, 6 mi. WNW of Horsham. Has 14th-cent. church.

Rudh'a'Mhail, headland, N tip of ISLAY, Hebrides, Scotland.

Rudh Re, promontory on The Minch, W Ross and Cromarty, Scotland, 11 mi. NNW of Gairloch; site of lighthouse (57°53'N 5°52'W).

Rud-i-Sar or **Rud-e-Sar** (ro͞od'ēsär'), town, First Prov., in Gilan, N Iran, small Caspian port 40 mi. E of Resht and 15 mi. E of Lahijan.

Rudki (ro͞otkē'), city (1931 pop. 3,694), N Drogobych Oblast, W Ukrainian SSR, on Vishnya R. and 21 mi. N of Drogobych; agr. processing (grain, potatoes), distilling, brick mfg.

Rudkobing (ro͞odh'kûbĭng), Dan. *Rudkøbing*, city (pop. 4,308) and port, Svendborg amt, Denmark, on W Langeland isl. and 85 mi. SW of Copenhagen; mfg. (machinery, dry goods), meat canning, shipbuilding. Formerly spelled Rudkjobing.

Rudnichny or **Rudnichnyy** (ro͞odnyēch'nē). **1** Town (1939 pop. over 500), W Chelyabinsk oblast, Russian SFSR, in the S Urals, just S of Bakal; rail spur terminus; mining (limonite, brown hematite). Until 1942, Rudnichnoye. **2** Town (1939 pop. over 2,000), NE Kirov oblast, Russian SFSR, on railroad (Fosforitnaya station) and 70 mi. N of Omutninsk; terminus of rail branch from Yar; phosphorite-mining center. **3** Town (1940 pop. over 500), E Molotov oblast, Russian SFSR, adjoining Kizel; bituminous-coal mining. Developed in 1940s. **4** Town (1939 pop. over 2,000), W Sverdlovsk oblast, Russian SFSR, 11 mi. ESE (under jurisdiction) of Karpinsk, on rail spur; magnetite-mining center, supplying Serov metallurgy; copper mining. Developed prior to First World War. Until 1933, Auerbakhovski Rudnik.

Rudnik (ro͞od'nĭk), village (pop. 2,948), Burgas dist., SE Bulgaria, on rail spur and 9 mi. N of Burgas; sheep raising. Lignite mine of Cherno More is near by. Formerly Khodzhamar.

Rudnik (ro͞od'nēk), town (pop. 4,186), Rzeszow prov., SE Poland, on San R., on railroad and 30 mi. NNE of Rzeszow; basket making.

Rudnik (ro͞od'nĭk), mountain (3,713 ft.) in central Serbia, Yugoslavia, 15 mi. WNW of Kragujevac; highest point in the Sumadija. Abandoned lead and zinc mines at Rudnik Kacerski, village, just W of peak.

Rudnik, Lake, Greece: see CHEIMADITIS, LAKE.

Rudnik Imeni Artema, Ukrainian SSR: see ARTEMOVSK, Voroshilovgrad oblast.

Rudnitsa (ro͞odnyē'tsŭ), town (1926 pop. 706), S Vinnitsa oblast, Ukrainian SSR, 55 mi. ESE of Mogilev-Podolski; rail junction.

Rudno (ro͞od'nŭ), town (1939 pop. over 500), W central Lvov oblast, Ukrainian SSR, 6 mi. W of Lvov; wheat, flax; lumbering.

Rudnya (ro͞od'nyŭ). **1** City (1926 pop. 3,554), W Smolensk oblast, Russian SFSR, 38 mi. WNW of Smolensk; dairying center; hemp and flax processing, clothing mfg. Became city in 1926. **2** or Rudnya-Kamyshinskaya (–kŭmĭ'shĭnskĭŭ), village (1926 pop. 3,822), N Stalingrad oblast, Russian SFSR, near Medveditsa R., 37 mi. ESE of Yelan; dairying center; wheat, sunflowers.

Rudok or **Rudog** (ro͞o'dŏk), Chinese *Lo-to-k'o* (lō'-dō'kŭ'), town, W Tibet, in Pangong Range, on Leh-Lhasa trade route, 125 mi. NNW of Gartok; alt. 14,900 ft.

Rudoka (ro͞o'dôkä), highest section of Sar Mts., NW Macedonia, Yugoslavia; extends c.10 mi. N–S, bet. upper Vardar R. and Albanian border. Highest peak (8,863 ft.), the Turcin or Turchin, Serbo-Croatian *Turčin*, is 8 mi. WSW of Tetovo; highest peak of Sar Mts.

Rudolf, Lake (□ c.3,500), NW Kenya, in Great Rift Valley, 250 mi. N of Nairobi; alt. 1,230 ft., depth 240 ft.; 185 mi. long, 35 mi. wide. Receives Omo and Kibish rivers (N) and Turkwell R. (W); has no outlet. N tip extends into Ethiopia. Contains several small volcanic isls. Shrinking rapidly because of high rate of evaporation, it is becoming increasingly saline. Abounds in fish, crocodiles, hippopotamuses. Nile perch (up to 200 lbs.) and fish of similar origin are found in the lake, suggesting its connection with the Nile at one time. Discovered 1888 together with L. Stefanie (NE) by Count Teleki, who named it after the crown prince of Austria. Native name is Basso Narok (dark water). The arid shores of the lake are inhabited by Turkana tribe.

Rudolf Island, northernmost island of Franz Josef Land, Russian SFSR, in Arctic Ocean; 15 mi. long, 10 mi. wide; rises to 905 ft.; 81°45'N 58°30'E. Govt. observation station (established 1932) on Teplitz Bay of W coast, at 81°48'N. Formerly Crown-Prince Rudolf Land; also Rudolph Isl.

Rudolfswerth, Yugoslavia: see NOVO MESTO.

Rudolph Island, Russian SFSR: see RUDOLF ISLAND.

Rudolstadt (ro͞o'dôl-shtät), town (pop. 22,100), Thuringia, central Germany, at NE foot of Thuringian Forest, on the Thuringian Saale and 18 mi. S of Weimar; mfg. of china, glass, machinery, electrical equipment, musical instruments, pharmaceuticals, leather; textile milling, woodworking. Has Heidecksburg palace (rebuilt 1735), now mus.; Ludwigsburg castle (1734); 17th-cent. church. Founded before 800; was seat of Schwarzburg-Rudolstadt line, 1584–1918.

Rudozem, Bulgaria: see SMILYAN.

Rudraprayag, India: see SRINAGAR, Uttar Pradesh.

Rudrur, India: see BODHAN.

Rudy, town (pop. 97), Crawford co., NW Ark., 13 mi. NE of Fort Smith.

Rue (rü), village (pop. 1,677), Somme dept., N France, in marshy area on small Maye R. and 13 mi. NNW of Abbeville; sugar milling. Has Flamboyant 15th–16th-cent. chapel.

Rue, river, France: see RHUE RIVER.

Ruecas River (rwā'käs), Estremadura, W Spain, rises in the Sierra de Guadalupe, flows c.65 mi. SW to the Guadiana 4 mi. W of Medellín.

Rueda (rwā'dhä), town (pop. 2,728), Valladolid prov., N central Spain, 8 mi. NNW of Medina del Campo; cheese processing; cereals, wine, lumber.

Rüeggisberg (rüĕ'gĭsbĕrk), town (pop. 2,257), Bern canton, W central Switzerland, 9 mi. S of Bern; farming.

Rüegsau (rüĕk'sou), town (pop. 2,820), Bern canton, NW central Switzerland, 12 mi. ENE of Bern; cotton textiles, clothes, tobacco, flour; tanning, woodworking.

Rueil-Malmaison (rüā'-mälmāzō'), town (pop. 17,103), Seine-et-Oise dept., N central France, a WNW suburb of Paris, 8 mi. from Notre Dame Cathedral, near left bank of the Seine; mfg. (auto parts, motors, photographic film and equipment, dynamos, pharmaceuticals); distilling, engraving. Château of Malmaison, favorite residence of Napoleon (1800–03) and of Josephine after her divorce (1809–14), contains Napoleonic mus.

Ruelle (rüĕl'), town (pop. 3,833), Charente dept., W France, on the Touvre and 4 mi. ENE of Angoulême; natl. foundries (naval guns); footwear mfg., paper milling. Also called Ruelle-sur-Touvre.

Ruende, Caño (kän'yō rwĕn'dā), side channel of Apure R., W Venezuela, W of San Fernando; 75 mi. long.

Rue River, France: see RHUE RIVER.

Rufaa (rōōfä'-ŭ), town, Blue Nile prov., E central Anglo-Egyptian Sudan, on right bank of the Blue Nile (opposite Hasiheisa) and 80 mi. SE of Khartoum; cotton, wheat, barley, corn, fruits, durra; livestock.

Rufach, France: see ROUFFACH.

Ruffano (rōōf-fä'nô), town (pop. 5,685), Lecce prov., Apulia, S Italy, 16 mi. ESE of Gallipoli; wine, olive oil.

Ruffec (rüfĕk'), town (pop. 3,400), Charente dept., W France, near the Charente, 26 mi. N of Angoulême; road center and agr. market; mfg. (plumbing fixtures, agr. tools, shoes); flour milling, food preserving. Has late-Gothic church of Saint-André with 12th-cent. façade. Medieval fortifications destroyed in French Revolution.

Ruffieux (rüfyû'), village (pop. 180), Savoie dept., SE France, near the Rhone and N end of Lac du Bourget, 20 mi. NNW of Chambéry.

Rufford, extensive parish (pop. 894), central Nottingham, England, 4 mi. E of Mansfield. Site of a number of coal mines. There are remains of 12th-cent. Rufford Abbey.

Rufiji River (rōōfē'jē), E Tanganyika, formed by junction of 2 headstreams (Kilombero, Luwegu) at 8°30'S 37°20'E, flows NE, and, after receiving the Great Ruaha (its chief tributary from SW Tanganyika), flows E to the Indian Ocean opposite Mafia Isl. in a 30-mi.-wide delta. Length, 175 mi. Navigable by small vessels for 60 mi. Cotton grown in lower valley.

Rufina (rōō'fēnä), village (pop. 1,845), Firenze prov., Tuscany, central Italy, on Sieve R. and 12 mi. ENE of Florence; wine making, shoe mfg.

Rufina or **Central Rufina** (rōōfē'nä), locality, S Puerto Rico, 11 mi. W of Ponce, adjoining Guayanilla; sugar mill.

Rufino (rōōfē'nō), town (1947 pop. 10,816), SW Santa Fe prov., Argentina, 150 mi. SW of Rosario; rail junction; commercial, industrial, and agr. center (corn, alfalfa, wheat, flour, livestock). Mfg.: dairy products, oxygen, plastics, paper bags, cement articles, mattresses; flour mills.

Rufisque (rüfēsk'), town (pop. c.30,100), W Senegal, Fr. West Africa, minor Atlantic port at S base of Cape Verde peninsula, on railroad and 10 mi. ENE of Dakar. Peanut-processing center; also tanning, fruit canning, fishing, titanium extracting; mfg. of shoes, cotton yarn and cloth, chocolate, pharmaceuticals. School of fisheries, customhouse; missions.

Rugby, municipal borough (1931 pop. 23,826; 1951 census 45,418), E Warwick, England, on the Avon and 11 mi. E of Coventry; rail and engineering center, producing electrical equipment. Has important post office radio transmitters (at Hillmorton, 2 mi. SE). Noted as site of one of the great English public schools, Rugby School (founded 1567); became well known through its 19th-cent. headmaster, Thomas Arnold, father of the poet Matthew Arnold. The schoolboy classic *Tom Brown's School Days*, by Thomas Hughes, deals with Rugby life. Rugby football originated here in 1823. Rupert Brooke b. in Rugby.

Rugby, city (pop. 2,907), ⊙ Pierce co., N central N.Dak., 60 mi. E of Minot, near geographic center of North America. Dairy products, poultry, grain, livestock. Platted 1885, inc. 1906. Souris Natl. Forest is W.

Rugeley (rōōj'lē), urban district (1931 pop. 5,262; 1951 census 8,525), central Stafford, England, on Trent R. and 8 mi. ESE of Stafford; leather-tanning industry; agr. market. Church dates from 14th cent.

Rügen (rü'gŭn), largest German Baltic island (□ 357.7; pop. 89,306), N Germany, in former Prussian Pomerania prov., after 1945 in Mecklenburg, just NE of Stralsund, separated from mainland by the Bodden and the Greifswalder Bodden (arms of the Baltic). Irregular in shape, isl. is 32 mi. long (N–S), 14–28 mi. wide; greatly indented coast line is low on W side where the sea has made considerable inroads, creating the Jasmund Lake (□ 8.9; salt-water lake). On E shore, sheer chalk cliffs rise to 400 ft. at the Stubbenkammer. Agr. (grain, sugar beets, potatoes, stock) and fisheries provide chief occupations. There are many popular seaside resorts, notably Binz, Sellin, and Putbus. Bergen is chief town; Sassnitz is largest port and terminus of train ferry to Trelleborg, Sweden. Since 1936, isl. is connected (SW) with mainland at Stralsund by Rügen Dam. Originally settled by the Rugieri, then by Slavonic Wends (remains of fortifications, notably at Arkona at N extremity of isl.), Rügen was conquered 1168 by the Danes. Came to Pomerania in 1325. Awarded to Sweden under Treaty of Westphalia (1648). Passed to Prussia 1815. Taken by Soviet troops in May, 1945. Just W are Hiddensee and UMMANZ isls.

Rügen Dam (rü'gŭn), Baltic dike, N Germany, connects Stralsund city with Rügen isl. across the Bodden (strait of the Baltic) via Dänholm islet; 1.6 mi. long. Completed 1936, it carries railroad and road.

Rügenwalde, Poland: see DARLOWO.

Ruger, Fort (rōō'gŭr), on Diamond Head, SE Oahu, T.H., 4 mi. SE of Honolulu, on plateau of extinct crater; U.S. coast artillery post.

Ruggell (rōō'gŭl), village (pop. 605), N Liechtenstein, on the Rhine (Swiss border) and 7 mi. N of Vaduz; corn, potatoes; cattle.

Rugles (rü'glŭ), village (pop. 1,405), Eure dept., NW France, on the Risle and 19 mi. SSE of Bernay; large pin factory.

Rugozero (rōōg'ô"zyĭrŭ), village (1926 pop. 487), central Karelo-Finnish SSR, on rail branch and 50 mi. WNW of Segezha; dairying.

Ruhama (rōōhämä'), settlement (pop. 275), SW Israel, at SW foot of Judaean Hills, at N edge of the Negev, 18 mi. NNW of Beersheba; grain, fruit, vegetables; dairying, poultry. Founded 1913; abandoned and resettled several times; present settlement established 1944.

Ruheiba, Ruheibeh (both: rōōhā'bŭ), or **Khirbet Ruheiba** (khĕrbĕt'), anc. locality, S Palestine, in the Negev, 19 mi. SW of Beersheba; reputed site of biblical city of Rehoboth (rĭhō'bŭth).

Ruhengeri (rōōhĕng-gĕ'rē), village, N Ruanda-Urundi, in Ruanda, near Belgian Congo and Uganda borders, 40 mi. NW of Kigali; alt. 6,100 ft.; center of native trade, transit point and customs station; brick making. There are pyrethrum plantations at Kinigi (kēnē'gē), 5 mi. NNW. Ruhengeri's pop. numbers many Asiatics.

Ruhla (rōō'lä), town (pop. 9,226), Thuringia, central Germany, in Thuringian Forest, 6 mi. SSE of Eisenach; mfg. of machine tools, electrical equipment, cardboard; wood carving (especially pipes), metalworking. Formerly noted for arms and knives.

Ruhland (rōō'länt), town (pop. 4,533), in former Prussian Lower Silesia prov., E central Germany, after 1945 in Saxony, in Upper Lusatia, on the Black Elster and 30 mi. N of Dresden; rail junction; lignite mining; synthetic-oil plant; glass mfg.

Rühle (rü'lŭ), village (commune pop., including Rühlermoor, 1,136), in former Prussian prov. of Hanover, NW Germany, after 1945 in Lower Saxony, on the Ems and 2 mi. SW of Meppen. Oil wells at near-by Rühlermoor.

Rühlertwist (rü'lŭrtvĭst"), village (pop. 634), in former Prussian prov. of Hanover, NW Germany, after 1945 in Lower Saxony, c.10 mi. SW of Meppen; oil wells.

Ruhnu or **Rukhnu** (rōōkh'nōō), Swedish *Runö*, Baltic island (□ 4; pop. 282) of Estonia, in center of Gulf of Riga, 60 mi. SW of Parnu; 3 mi. long, 1.5 mi. wide. Has 17th-cent. wooden church; lighthouse. Swedish pop.; agr., sealing.

Ruhpolding (rōō'pôl"dĭng), village (pop. 5,512), Upper Bavaria, Germany, in Salzburg Alps, on small Weisse Traun R. and 7 mi. S of Traunstein; rail terminus; textile mfg., lumber milling, woodworking. Summer resort (alt. 2,265 ft.).

Ruhr (rōōr), major coal-mining and industrial region (□ c.2,000; pop. estimate 4,000,000), W Germany, in Westphalia and former Rhine Prov. of Prussia, after 1945 in North Rhine-Westphalia, bet. Dutch border (W) and Hamm (E), Ruhr R. (S) and Lippe R. (N); in a wider sense it includes (S) the industrial belt E and W of Düsseldorf. Intensive coal mining and steel production, supplemented by mfg. of chemicals, constitute basic industries. From Duisburg, the Ruhr harbor on the Rhine, to Dortmund, the region is one continuous urbanized dist. (including Bochum, Essen, Gelsenkirchen, Oberhausen, and Recklinghausen), traversed by a web of railroad and trolley lines. Rhine-Herne (via the Rhine) and Dortmund-Ems canals connect region with Dutch coast and N German seaports, respectively; Datteln is important canal junction. Möhne reservoir (at Günne) constitutes major water and power supply of the Ruhr. Rapid industrial development began in 19th cent., when Krupp and Thyssen concerns started large-scale coal mining and built their steel plants. Occupied 1923–25 by France and Belgium in reparations dispute. Devastated by Allied air attacks in Second World War. In March–April, 1945, a large concentration of German forces was sealed off in the "Ruhr pocket" by the Allies and eventually surrendered. The disposition of the Ruhr after the war and the status of ownership and operation of its mines and industries were major factors of disagreement among the Allies. In 1949 a temporary disposition of the Ruhr was made by the establishment of an international authority for the Ruhr, with the participation of France, England, the U.S., Belgium, the Netherlands, and Luxembourg, and (after Nov., 1949) the West German Federal Republic; hq. at Düsseldorf, with full economic control.

Ruhrort (rōōr'ôrt), industrial district (since 1905) of DUISBURG, on N bank of Ruhr R. at its mouth on the Rhine, and 2 mi. NW of city center, at head of Rhine-Herne Canal. Coal port of the Ruhr; extensive harbor installations on all 3 waterways. Blast furnaces, steel mills.

Ruhr River (rōōr), W Germany, rises just N of Winterberg, flows 145 mi. W, past Witten (head of navigation), Essen, and Mülheim, to the Rhine at Duisburg. Receives the Lenne R. (left), Möhne R. (right). Forms S border of Ruhr industrial region.

Ruhstorf (rōōs'tôrf), village (pop. 2,047), Lower Bavaria, Germany, on Rott R. and 10 mi. SSW of Passau; mfg. of precision instruments, metal- and woodworking.

Ruhuhu River (rōōhōō'hōō), S Tanganyika, rises S of Njombe, flows 100 mi. SE and SW to L. Nyasa just S of Manda. Major coal deposits near mouth.

Rui Barbosa (rōōē' bŭrbô'zŭ), city (pop. 2,845), E central Bahia, Brazil, 100 mi. WNW of Cachoeira; coffee, manioc, cattle. Formerly spelled Ruy Barbosa.

Ruidera (rwē-dhä'rä), village (pop. 493), Ciudad Real prov., S central Spain, 55 mi. E of Ciudad Real. Has gunpowder factory. Near by are the Lagunas de Ruidera, several lakes, from which the Alto Guadiana rises. In vicinity are Montesinos caverns, believed by Don Quixote to lead to earth's center.

Ruidoso (rōō"ēdō'sō), town (pop. 806), Lincoln co., S central N.Mex., 18 mi. SW of Lincoln.

Ruien (rû'yŭn), town (pop. 2,199), East Flanders prov., SW central Belgium, on Scheldt R. and 7 mi. SW of Oudenaarde; textile industry. Formerly spelled Ruyen.

Rui Mountains or **Ruy Mountains** (rōō'ē), W Bulgaria and E Yugoslavia, extend c.20 mi. E–W along border; rise to 5,679 ft. at Rui peak, 4 mi. NW of Trin (Bulgaria). Lead, silver, and copper deposits (once exploited).

Ruindi (rwĕn'dē), village, Kivu prov., E Belgian Congo, on Ruindi R. (S tributary of L. Edward), and 120 mi. NNE of Costermansville; tourist center in Albert Natl. Park.

Ruindi River or **Rwindi River,** E Belgian Congo, rises on NW slopes of the Virunga range 17 mi. WSW of Rutshuru, flows c.60 mi. N to L. Edward, 50 mi. SW of Katwe. Its lower course is in Albert Natl. Park.

Ruinen (roi'nŭn), town (pop. 843), Drenthe prov., N Netherlands, 9 mi. ENE of Meppel; cattle market; food canning, dairying.

Ruinerwold (roi'nŭrvōlt), village (pop. 848), Drenthe prov., N central Netherlands, on the Smildervaart just ENE of Meppel; cattle raising; agr.

Ruines (rwēn), village (pop. 310), Cantal dept., S central France, in Montagnes de la Margeride, 7 mi. ESE of Saint-Flour; woodworking. Garabit viaduct (400 ft. high, 1,853 ft. long) spans gorge of the Truyère, 3 mi. SW.

Ruinette (rwēnĕt'), peak (12,726 ft.) in Pennine Alps, S Switzerland, 11 mi. SE of Bagnes.

Ruiru (rōōē'rōō), town (pop. c.1,000), S central Kenya, on railroad and 15 mi. NNE of Nairobi; major coffee center; coffee research station.

Ruisbroek (rois'brōōk), town (pop. 5,309), Brabant prov., central Belgium, on Charleroi-Brussels Canal and 5 mi. SW of Brussels; mfg. (safety glass, electric motors, soda). Formerly Ruysbroeck.

Ruiselede (roi'sŭlādŭ), village (pop. 5,556), West Flanders prov., W Belgium, 4 mi. NE of Tielt; agr., lumbering. Site of radio station with beams to America and Belgian Congo. Formerly spelled Ruysselede.

Ruislip Northwood (rī'slĭp), residential urban district (1931 pop. 16,042; 1951 census 68,274), Middlesex, England, 14 mi. WNW of London. Has 13th-cent. church. In urban dist. are N residential areas of Northwood, with pharmaceutical works, and Eastcote. Near by are a large park, and a reservoir.

Ruivo, Pico (pē'vōō rwē'kōō), highest peak (6,106 ft.) of Madeira, 8 mi. N of Funchal. Climbed from Santana (on N slope).

Ruiz, spa, Colombia: see TERMALES.

Ruiz (rōōēs'), town (pop. 3,431), Nayarit, W Mexico, on San Pedro R., on Pacific coastal plain, on railroad and 35 mi. NNW of Tepic; agr. center (corn, sugar cane, tobacco, cotton, tomatoes, bananas).

Ruiz, Nevado del (nävä'dō dĕl), Andean volcanic peak (17,720 ft.), W central Colombia, on Caldas-Tolima dept. border, in Cordillera Central, 20 mi. SE of Manizales; 4°53'N. On its slopes coffee is grown. At NW foot are the thermal springs of Termales or Ruiz. Some sulphur deposits.

Ruiz de los Llanos, Argentina: see TALA, village.

Rujai, Aden: see RIJAI.

Rujan (rŏŏjăn′), airport, Eastern Aden Protectorate, in Quaiti state, 15 mi. ENE of Mukalla.

Rujei, Aden: see RIJAI.

Rujen or **Ruyen** (both: rōō′yĕn), peak (c.7,390 ft.) in Osogov Mts., on Yugoslav-Bulgarian border, 12 mi. SW of Kyustendil, Bulgaria.

Rujiena or **Ruyena** (rōō′yĕnä), Lettish *Rūjiena*, Ger. *Rujen*, city (pop. 4,337), N Latvia, in Vidzeme, 25 mi. N of Valmiera; rail junction; wool processing, sawmilling.

Rukhlovo, Russian SFSR: see SKOVORODINO.

Rukhnu, Estonia: see RUHNU.

Ruki River (rōō′kē), W Belgian Congo, formed at Ingende by union of Momboyo and Busira rivers, flows c.100 mi. WNW to Congo R. at Coquilhatville. Navigable for steamboats along entire course.

Rukopol or **Rukopol'** (rŏŏkô′pŭl), village (1939 pop. over 500), E central Saratov oblast, Russian SFSR, on railroad and 14 mi. SSW of Pugachev; oil-shale shipping point for Gorny mine (10 mi. SW; connected by rail spur); metalworks.

Rukwa, Lake (rōō′kwä), SW Tanganyika, E of L. Tanganyika and NW of Mbeya; 90 mi. long, 10 mi. wide; alt. 2,602 ft. No outlet. Crocodiles, hippopotamuses. Ufipa Plateau rises to 6,000 ft. in a steep escarpment along W shore.

Rule, town (pop. 1,251), Haskell co., NW central Texas, c.50 mi. N of Abilene; trade, shipping center in agr. area (cotton, corn); oil wells, cotton compress, cottonseed-oil mills. Inc. 1909.

Ruleville, town (pop. 1,521), Sunflower co., W Miss., 25 mi. WNW of Greenwood, near Sunflower R.; trade center in cotton-growing area; cotton compress, lumber mill. Vocational school for Negroes near by. Laid out 1898.

Rulles, Belgium: see MARBEHAN.

Rullion Green, Scotland: see PENTLAND HILLS.

Rully (rülē′), village (pop. 962), Saône-et-Loire dept., E central France, 8 mi. NW of Chalon-sur-Saône; Burgundy wines.

Rulo, village (pop. 639), Richardson co., extreme SE Nebr., 9 mi. E of Falls City and on Missouri R., near Kansas line.

Rülzheim (rülts′hīm), village (pop. 3,828), Rhenish Palatinate, W Germany, 9 mi. ESE of Landau; grain, tobacco, sugar beets.

Rum or **Rhum** (rōōm), island (pop. 32), Inner Hebrides, Inverness, Scotland, 8 mi. W of Point of Sleat (on Skye); 8 mi. long, 9 mi. wide. Mountainous (rises to 2,659 ft. in Askival mtn., SE) and has extensive deer forest.

Rum, Sultanate of, Turkey: see KONYA, city.

Ruma, village (pop. 107), Randolph co., SW Ill., 33 mi. SSE of East St. Louis, in agr. area.

Ruma (rōō′mä), village (pop. 14,049), Vojvodina, N Serbia, Yugoslavia, 16 mi. S of Novi Sad, in the Srem; rail junction. Inhabited by Germans before Second World War.

Rumadiya, Iraq: see RAMADI.

Rumaitha or **Rumaythah** (rōōmī′thŭ), town, Diwaniya prov., central Iraq, on the Hilla (a branch of the Euphrates) and 40 mi. SE of Diwaniya; rice, dates.

Rumana, El, Er Rumana, or **Al-Rumanah** (all: ĕr rōōmă′nŭ), village, Sinai prov., NE Egypt, near the coast, on Cairo-Haifa RR and 30 mi. SE of Port Said. Sometimes Rumani and Romani. Fighting bet. British and Turks, 1916.

Rumangabu(rōōmäng-gä′bōō), village, Kivu prov., E Belgian Congo, at NW foot of Mt. Mikeno, 15 mi. SW of Rutshuru; tourist center and administrative hq. of Albert Natl. Park.

Rumani, Egypt: see RUMANA, EL.

Rumania (rōōmā′nēŭ), **Romania** (rō–), or **Roumania** (rōō–), Rumanian *România* (rômŭ′nyä), republic (□ 91,700; pop. 15,872,624), SE Europe, on the Black Sea, in NE Balkan Peninsula; ⊙ BUCHAREST. Bounded N and E by Ukrainian and Moldavian republics (along Prut R.) of the USSR; Hungary is NW, Yugoslavia SW; in S it is separated from Bulgaria by the lower Danube, which also forms part of its frontier with Yugoslavia and falls in a wide, marshy delta into the Black Sea. Rumania is located bet. 43°37′–48°16′N and 20°16′–29°43′E. Though administratively divided into 28 provs., its 7 old historic regions are more familiar and more useful concepts. MOLDAVIA and WALACHIA (E and S) were merged in mid-19th cent. to form the original state. They constitute together with the S BUKOVINA (N) and N DOBRUJA (SE) the main lowland sections beyond the Carpathian ranges. In the center is the elevated plateau (1,000–1,600 ft.) of TRANSYLVANIA, a mountain fortress fringed by rugged ridges of the Moldavian Carpathians (E), the APUSENI MOUNTAINS (W), and the scenic TRANSYLVANIAN ALPS (S; rise in the Negos Peak, 8,361 ft., to country's highest elevation). CRISANA-MARAMURES region (NW) on the Carpathians' W slopes opens to the ALFÖLD plain of Hungary. The small BANAT plain in SW is contiguous with its Hungarian and Yugoslav sections in the Tisza valley. Of its many rivers only the Danube and its affluent the Prut are navigable. The Danube is indeed a major artery for national and international commerce, bound to achieve even greater importance when the DANUBE–BLACK SEA CANAL from CERNAVODA to NAVODARI (at Cape Midia) above CONSTANTA is completed. Constanta is still the principal ocean port, shipping mostly oil. But inland Danube ports like GALATI and BRAILA, which load wheat, and GIURGIU, foremost outlet for the PLOESTI oil fields, handle more trade. Other rivers, chiefly used for logging of the great forest resources (conifers, oaks, beeches) of the mts.—about 25% of the entire area—possess a high, yet little exploited hydroelectric potential. Among these streams are MURES RIVER, SOMES RIVER, OLT RIVER, SIRET RIVER, JIU RIVER—all tributary to the Danube. Some cut deeply through the mts. which are also incised by comparatively low passes, such as TURNU ROSU PASS and PREDEAL PASS on Walachia-Transylvania railroads. The climate of Rumania is, in spite of its frontage on the Black Sea, of the rigorous continental type. Severe droughts frequently occur during the hot summer months; winters are cold and windy. Bucharest has a Jan. mean of 9.2°F. and a July mean of 72.9°F. Rainfall varies bet. 17 and 30 inches. Most of Rumania's soil is very fertile, rendering it one of the continent's most important granaries, though the yield is still limited by antiquated methods and climatic hazards. About 80% of the people depend on agr. for their livelihood. Largest crop is corn, grown for home consumption, while wheat is largely exported. Other crops include oats, barley, rye, sugar beets, hemp, flax, soybeans, sunflowers, tobacco, leguminous plants, potatoes, forage. There are extensive vineyards and deciduous fruit orchards. Apiculture and, particularly, sericulture are widespread. Stockraising (sheep, cattle, buffaloes, hogs, horses) ranks next to agr. The Transylvanian plateau as well as the plains provide fine pasturelands. Fish, especially in the Danube, is plentiful. For its diverse mineral resources Rumania ranks among the continent's richest countries, but the income derived from them is not commensurate with their potential value. By far the most important mineral product is petroleum, drilled principally in Prahova Valley around Ploesti, a refining and industrial center from which 4 pipe lines lead to Giurgiu and one each to Bucharest and Constanta. Near Ploesti are the additional oilfields of Dambovita, CAMPINA, MIZAL, and BUZAU. The latter 2 also have refineries. Other petroleum sources are near BACAU and in Oltenia (W Walachia). The natural gas (methane) deposits of Transylvania (SARMAS, SARMASEL, TARNAVENI) is increasingly used in industry; pipe line from Sarmasel to TURDA. Coal is mined in Jiu R. valley, particularly at PETROSANI, PETRILA, and LUPENI. On the iron resources of Transylvania, Banat, and Crisana-Maramures are based the foundries and steel works of ORAVITA, RESITA, and STEIERDORFANINA, and the recently enlarged metallurgical combines of HUNEDOARA and BAIA MARE. Precious metals occur in the Muntii Metalici of the Apuseni Mts. Other minerals include copper (TULCEA hills of Dobruja), manganese, lead, zinc, pyrite, bauxite, kaolin, sulphur. Salt is extracted near Bacau, TARGU-OCNA, and SIGHET. Rumania abounds in spas (e.g., VATRA DORNEI, GOVORA, BAILE HERCULANE). Her resorts are renowned for their picturesque setting; among them are SINAIA, PREDEAL, CALIMANESTI, OLANESTI. Fine beaches adjoin Constanta on the Black Sea: MAMAIA, EFORIE, CARMEN-SYLVA. Textile milling and food processing (flour milling, wine making, sugar refining, canning, etc.) lead among industries. Vehicles and machinery still have to be largely imported. However, the principal inland centers, such as CLUJ, SIBIU, JASSY, STALIN (formerly Brasov), FAGARAS, CRAIOVA, TIMISOARA, ARAD, and ORADEA, now turn out varied consumer goods, rolling stock, appliances, explosives, fertilizers, and chemicals. Bucharest has major railroad shops and mfg. of newsprint, plastics, pharmaceuticals, aircraft, radios, glass, etc. This city, among the largest and most cosmopolitan of SE Europe, dominates the nation's commercial, political, and cultural life. It has one of the country's 4 universities. The others are at Jassy, Cluj, and Timisoara. Railroads link Rumania with all the neighboring countries. The railroads (5,962 mi. at close of Second World War), as well as merchant shipping and air lines, are state owned. Ethnologically, Rumania is one of the most complex of nations. Its heterogeneity is responsible for frequent territorial fluctuations and interior conflicts. In some sections Rumanians are actually in the minority. In Transylvania the German and, particularly, Hungarian elements are strong. There are also Szekely Magyar, Turkish, Jewish, Bulgar, Macedonian, Tatar, and Gypsy minorities. Chief religious body is the Orthodox Eastern Church, which in 1948 absorbed the Greek Catholics (Uniates), once 10% of the people. About 8% are R.C. The Rumanians themselves represent a blend of the various racial strains, though they speak a Latin language—with strong Slavic admixture—and trace back their origin to the settlers of the Roman prov. DACIA (2d and 3d cent. A.D.), which roughly corresponded to present-day Rumania. After the Mongol invaders withdrew in the 13th cent., the history of the Rumanian people became in essence that of the 2 Rumanian principalities—Moldavia and Walachia—and of Transylvania. The last was for most of the time a Hungarian dependency. Under Michael the Brave of Walachia (end of 16th cent.) Moldavia, Walachia, and Transylvania were briefly united. From then on the Ottoman Empire virtually controlled the 2 former regions, while the Magyars ruled over Transylvania. As an outcome of the Russo-Turkish War (1828–29) the 2 principalities became Russian protectorates, nominally within the Ottoman Empire. The Crimean War brought (1854) the evacuation of the Russian troops, who were replaced by a neutral Austrian occupation force. The Congress of Paris (1856) established Moldavia and Walachia as principalities under Turkish suzerainty and awarded S Bessarabia to Moldavia. The principalities were joined (1861) under the name of Rumania, headed by Alexander John Cuza as prince. He was deposed in 1866, replaced by Carol of the house of Hohenzollern-Sigmaringen. At the Congress of Berlin (1878) Rumania gained full independence but had to restore S Bessarabia to Russia and accepted Dobruja instead. The ensuing history was one of violence and turmoil, caused largely by the discontent of the impoverished peasants, political corruption, and continuous foreign interference. In Second Balkan War (1913) Rumania gained the S Dobruja from Bulgaria. After initial neutrality in the First World War, it sided (1916) with the Allies. Though overrun by Austro-German forces, Rumania was eventually liberated and acquired Bessarabia from Russia; Bukovina from Austria; Transylvania, Crisana-Maramures, and part of the Banat from Hungary. The acquisitions, approximately doubling Rumania's territory, were confirmed by treaties of Saint-Germain (1919) and Trianon (1920). Ethnic frictions, half-hearted agrarian reforms, and dynastic confusions increased. Rumania entered the Little Entente (1921) and the Balkan Entente (1934). King Carol, who had renounced the throne in favor of his son Michael, returned in 1930. Rumania grew closer to the Axis powers, and Carol assumed dictatorial powers in 1938. He collided, however, with other fascist groups, of which the Iron Guard was the most notorious. With the signing, however, of the German-Soviet pact of June, 1940, Rumania was powerless to resist Russian demands for Bessarabia and N Bukovina; Rumania also ceded S Dobruja to Bulgaria, and the Banat, Crisana-Maramures, and part of Transylvania to Hungary. Michael returned to the throne and German troops occupied the country. The dictator Ion Antonescu declared war on Russia early in 1941. Despite initial successes, Rumania had to surrender to Russia in 1944, and reentered the war on Allied side after ousting Antonescu. Peace treaty was signed 1947 at Paris. Rumania recovered all its pre-war territory except Bessarabia, N Bukovina, and S Dobruja. Politically and economically, it became a satellite of Russia. A communist-led coalition govt. came into power in 1945, the king abdicated in 1947, and by 1948 Rumania's constitution was modeled after the Soviets. Industries, banking, transport, and national resources were nationalized, with the USSR holding the major share of control over the chief industries, notably petroleum. Industrialization was speeded up. In 1950 the administrative organization was altered to comprise the following 28 provs.: Arad, Arges, Bacau, Baia-Mare, Barlad, Bihor, Botosani, Bucharest, Buzau, Cluj, Constanta, Dolj, Galati, Gorj, Hunedoara, Ialomita, Jassy, Mures, Prahova, Putna, Rodna, Severin, Sibiu, Stalin, Suceava, Teleorman, Timisoara, Valcea. For further information see individual entries on regions, cities, towns, and physical features.

Rumaythah, Iraq: see RUMAITHA.

Rumbek (rōōm′bĕk), town (pop. 1,200), Bahr el Ghazal prov., S Anglo-Egyptian Sudan, at S edge of the Sudd swamps, on road and 130 mi. SE of Wau; agr. trade.

Rumbeke (rŭm′bākŭ), town (pop. 7,724), West Flanders prov., W Belgium, just ESE of Roulers; textiles; market center for tobacco-growing area. Has 14th-cent. Gothic church.

Rumburk (rōōm′bōōrk), Ger. *Rumburg* (rōōm′-bōōrk), town (pop. 6,759), N Bohemia, Czechoslovakia, 30 mi. NE of Usti nad Labem, near Ger. border; rail junction; produces linen, cotton, and woolen textiles, carpeting. Has 16th-cent. church, Capuchin abbey.

Rum Cay (kā, kē), island (9½ mi. long, 5 mi. wide) and district (□ 29; pop. 219), central Bahama Isls., bet. Long Isl. (W) and San Salvador or Watling Isl. (NE), 185 mi. SE of Nassau; 23°40′N 74°55′W. Main industry is salt panning; also produces sisal and coconuts. Second isl. visited by Columbus, who landed here on Oct. 15, 1492, naming it Santa María de la Concepción, a name later applied to an islet, Conception Isl., 15 mi. NW.

Rumelange (rümŭlăzh′), town (pop. 4,072), S Luxembourg, 3 mi. SE of Esch-sur-Alzette, at Fr. border; iron and ocher mining; mfg. (steel products, railroad and electrical equipment, fertilizer, plastics, malt and chicory products).

Rumelia (rōōmē′lyŭ), name used to designate possessions of Ottoman Empire in Balkan Peninsula, including Thrace, Macedonia, and Albania. Its NE part was set up in 1878 as Bulgaria (under nominal Turkish suzerainty) and the autonomous prov. of EASTERN RUMELIA. Sometimes spelled Roumelia.

Rumenia, Cape, or **Cape Ramunia,** SE extremity of Malay Peninsula, E of Singapore; 1°22'N 104°15'E. Sometimes spelled Romania.

Rumes (rüm), agr. village (pop. 1,917), Hainaut prov., SW Belgium, 5 mi. SW of Tournai, near Fr. line.

Rumford. **1** Town (pop. 9,954), including Rumford Falls village (pop. 7,888), Oxford co., W Maine, c.40 mi. NW of Augusta, at falls of the Androscoggin (water power), at influx of Swift R.; paper mills; winter sports. Settled 1774, inc. 1800. **2** Village, R.I.: see EAST PROVIDENCE.

Rumichaca (rōōmēchä'kä), natural bridge across small Carchi R. on Colombia-Ecuador border, in the Andes, 3 mi. N of Tulcán. Across it passes the Pan American Highway (Bogotá-Quito).

Rumigny (rümēnyē'), agr. village (pop. 486), Ardennes dept., N France, 16 mi. E of Vervins.

Rumija or **Rumiya** (both: rōō'mēä), mountain in Dinaric Alps, S Montenegro, Yugoslavia, on isthmus bet. the Adriatic and L. Scutari; highest point (5,225 ft.) is 5 mi. E of Bar.

Rumilly (rümēyē'), town (pop. 3,592), Haute-Savoie dept., SE France, on Chéran R. and 9 mi. WSW of Annecy, in Savoy Pre-Alps; dairying center (mfg. of condensed and powdered milk, cheese); tanning, mfg. of clothing. Also called Rumilly-Albanais.

Rumiñahui, Cerro (sĕ'rō rōōmēnyä'wē), extinct Andean volcano (15,482 ft.), Pichincha prov., N central Ecuador, NW of Cotopaxi volcano, 25 mi. S of Quito. It is a twin peak.

Rumisapa (rōōmēsä'pä), town (pop. 531), San Martín dept., N central Peru, in E Andean outliers, 3 mi. SE of Lamas; sugar, coca, cotton, rice.

Rumiya, mountain, Yugoslavia: see RUMIJA.

Rummah, Wadi, Arabia: see RIMA, WADI.

Rumman, El, Er Rumman, or **Al-Rumman** (all: ĕr-rōōm-măn'), agr. village (pop. c.150), N central Jordan, near Wadi Zerqa', 16 mi. NNW of Amman.

Rummel, Oued, Algeria: see RHUMEL, OUED.

Rummelsburg (rōō'mŏŏlsbŏŏrk), industrial section of Lichtenberg dist., E Berlin, Germany, on the Spree and 4 mi. ESE of city center. Site of major power station and of extensive railroad switchyards. Mfg. of air brakes. After 1945 in Soviet sector.

Rummelsburg, Poland: see MIASTKO.

Rumney, residential town and parish (pop. 3,348), S Monmouth, England, 3 mi. NE of Cardiff.

Rumney, town (pop. 859), Grafton co., central N.H., on Baker R. and 6 mi. NW of Plymouth; partly in White Mtn. Natl. Forest. Winter sports.

Rumoi (rōōmō'ē), city (1940 pop. 20,341; 1947 pop. 30,057), W Hokkaido, Japan, fishing port on Sea of Japan, 38 mi. WNW of Asahigawa; agr. and lumbering center. Coal mined near by.

Rumonge (rōōmông'gä), village, W Ruanda-Urundi, in Urundi, on NE shore of L. Tanganyika, 50 mi. SW of Kitega; steamboat landing; large palm groves, trade in palm oil. First R.C. mission of Ruanda-Urundi was founded here in 1879.

Rumpst, Belgium: see RUMST.

Rum River, rises in Mille Lacs L., central Minn., flows S, past Milaca and Princeton, then E, to Cambridge, and S to Mississippi R. at Anoka; 160 mi. long. Was important route for explorers and fur traders.

Rumsey, village (pop. 98), S Alta., 27 mi. NNW of Drumheller; wheat, mixed farming.

Rumsey (rŭm'sē), town (pop. 301), McLean co., W Ky., on Green R. (bridged) and 19 mi. NE of Madisonville.

Rumson, resort borough (pop. 4,044), Monmouth co., E N.J., bet. Navesink R. and Shrewsbury R. estuaries, near the Atlantic, 4 mi. ENE of Red Bank; estate center; boating. Settled c.1700, inc. 1907.

Rumst (rŭmst), town (pop. 5,575), Antwerp prov., N Belgium, at confluence of Nèthe R. and Dyle R. (here forming Rupel R.), 9 mi. S of Antwerp; site of Antwerp waterworks; brick mfg. Formerly spelled Rumpst.

Rumtek, India: see GANGTOK.

Rumula, village, NE Queensland, Australia, 35 mi. NW of Cairns; rail terminus; sugar cane.

Rumuruti (rōōmōōrōō'tē), town (pop. c.800), W central Kenya, on Laikipia Plateau E of Great Rift Valley, on road and 50 mi. NNE of Nakuru; 0°16'N 36°32'E; wheat, corn, livestock.

Rumyantsevo (rōōmyän'tsyĭvŭ). **1** Town (1939 pop. over 2,000), central Stalino oblast, Ukrainian SSR, in the Donbas, on railroad (Trudovaya station) and 3 mi. N of Gorlovka; coal mines. Terminus of kerosene pipe line from Grozny. **2** Town, Ulyanovsk oblast, Russian SFSR: see LENINA, IMENI V. I.

Runanga (rōōnăng'gŭ), borough (pop. 1,798), W S.Isl., New Zealand, 6 mi. N of Greymouth; coal mines. School of mines.

Runaway, Cape, NE N.Isl., New Zealand, at NE end of Bay of Plenty; 37°32'S 178°E.

Runaway Bay, town (pop. 1,150), St. Ann parish, N Jamaica, 8 mi. W of St. Ann's Bay; minor seaport and resort. Here the last Sp. governor embarked on his flight from Jamaica. At Dry Harbour, 5 mi. W, Columbus made his 1st landing in Jamaica (1494), taking possession of the isl. for Spain.

Runcorn, urban district (1931 pop. 18,127; 1951 census 23,933), N Cheshire, England, on Mersey R. and on Manchester Ship Canal, at mouth of Bridgewater Canal, 11 mi. ESE of Liverpool; shipbuilding, metalworking, leather-tanning center; mfg. of chemicals, pharmaceuticals. Linked with Widnes in Lancashire by bridge across the Manchester Ship Canal and Mersey R. Near by, remains of a medieval priory. Was site of fortification of Æthelflæd in 916. Town has given its name to the stone found in near-by quarries. Town developed after construction of Bridgewater Canal in 18th cent.

Ründeroth (rün'dûrōt), village (pop. 6,725), in former Prussian Rhine Prov., W Germany, after 1945 in North Rhine-Westphalia, 5 mi. SW of Gummersbach; foundries; iron mining.

Rundle Passage, Chile: see GUAYANECO ISLANDS.

Rundvik (rŭnd'vēk"), village (pop. 1,381), Västerbotten co., N Sweden, on small inlet of Gulf of Bothnia, 35 mi. SW of Umea; wallboard works, sawmills.

Runge (rŭng'ē), town (pop. 1,055), Karnes co., S Texas, c.60 mi. SE of San Antonio, near San Antonio R.; trade point in cotton, corn area; cotton gins, hatchery. Settled 1884, inc. 1913.

Rungu (rōōng'gōō), village, Eastern Prov., NE Belgian Congo, on Bomokandi R. and 210 mi. ENE of Buta, in cotton, palm, and coffee area. Noted for its Dominican mission trade school for natives.

Rungue (rōōng'gā), village (1930 pop. 220), Santiago prov., central Chile, on railroad and 33 mi. NW of Santiago; copper mining.

Rungus Point (rōōng'gōōs), SE Luzon, Philippines, at tip of peninsula forming N shore of Lagonoy Gulf, opposite Catanduanes isl. across Maqueda Channel; 13°42'N 123°58'E.

Rungwe, Mount (rōōng'gwä), volcanic peak (9,713 ft.), Southern Highlands prov., S Tanganyika, 20 mi. SE of Mbeya, N of L. Nyasa.

Runkel (rōōng'kŭl), town (pop. 1,721), in former Prussian prov. of Hesse-Nassau, W Germany, after 1945 in Hesse, on the Lahn and 4 mi. E of Limburg. Has 15th-cent. bridge; and ruined ancestral castle of house of Wied.

Runnells (rŭ'nŭlz), town (pop. 307), Polk co., central Iowa, near Des Moines R., 14 mi. ESE of Des Moines, in coal-mining and agr. area.

Runnels (rŭ'nŭlz), county (□ 1,060; pop. 16,771), W central Texas; ⊙ Ballinger. Drained by Colorado R. and tributaries (including Elm Creek, with flood-control reservoir). A leading Texas agr. co.: cotton, grains, grain sorghums, peanuts, truck, pecans; extensive dairying, poultry and livestock raising (cattle, sheep); wool marketed. Oil wells. Formed 1858.

Runnemede (rŭ'nĭmēd), residential borough (pop. 4,217), Camden co., SW N.J., 7 mi. SSE of Camden, near Big Timber Creek. Settled 1683 by Friends as New Hope, inc. 1926.

Runn of Cutch, India: see CUTCH, RANN OF.

Runnymede or **Runnimede,** England: see EGHAM.

Runo, Estonia: see RUHNU.

Ruokolahti (rōō'ôkōlä"tē, -läkh"tē), Swedish *Ruokolaks* (rōō'ôkōläks"), village (commune pop. 8,227), Kymi co., SE Finland, near USSR border, on E shore of L. Saimaa, 30 mi. ENE of Lappeenranta; center of lumbering region.

Ruoms (rüôm'), village (pop. 977), Ardèche dept., S France, on the Ardèche and 12 mi. S of Aubenas; breweries.

Ruoppoja, Karelo-Finnish SSR: see SHELTOZERO.

Ruo River (rōō'ō), on Mozambique-Nyasaland border, rises in Mlanje Mts. NE of Mlanje, Nyasaland, flows 70 mi. W and S, along international border, to Shire R. at Chiromo.

Ruoti (rōōō'tē), village (pop. 3,152), Potenza prov., Basilicata, S Italy, 9 mi. NW of Potenza, in agr. region (grapes, olives, cereals).

Rupanco (rōōpäng'kō), village (1930 pop. 398), Osorno prov., S central Chile, on NE shore of L. Rupanco, in Chilean lake dist., 50 mi. SE of Osorno; lumbering, dairying. Thermal springs.

Rupanco, Lake (□ 90), Osorno prov., S central Chile, in Chilean lake dist., 27 mi. SE of Osorno; 25 mi. long, c.4 mi. wide. Surrounded by forests. Cerro Puntiagudo rises on SE shore. Tourist resort; lumbering.

Rupanyup (rŭpăn'yŭp), town (pop. 603), W central Victoria, Australia, 150 mi. NW of Melbourne; flour mill.

Rupar (rōō'pŭr), town (pop. 10,385), Ambala dist., E Punjab, India, on Sutlej R. and 42 mi. NNW of Ambala; rail terminus; market center for grain, spices, salt, cotton, potatoes; hand-loom weaving; iron products. Col. Headworks of Sirhind Canal system just N. Scene of meeting (1831) bet. Ranjit Singh and Lord William Bentinck, which redefined spheres of Sikh and Br. influence, established by treaty of 1809.

Rupat or **Roepat** (both: rōōpät'), island, Indonesia, in Strait of Malacca, just off E coast of Sumatra across 3-mi.-wide channel, opposite Malacca; 1°55'N 101°35'E; roughly circular, 30 mi. in diameter; low, swampy.

Rupea (rōō'pyä), Hung. *Kőhalom* (kû'hōlôm), village (pop. 2,781), Stalin prov., central Rumania, on railroad and 22 mi. SE of Sighisoara; summer resort with sulphurous springs; woodworking, mfg. of peasant headcloths. Has remains of 13th-cent. fortress and castle, 14th-cent. church.

Rupelmonde (rü'pŭlmōndŭ), town (pop. 3,539), East Flanders prov., N Belgium, on Scheldt R., opposite mouth of Rupel R., and 8 mi. SW of Antwerp; brickworks. The cartographer Mercator b. here. Fortified town in Middle Ages.

Rupel Pass (rōō'pĕl), strategic defile in Struma R. valley, E Macedonia, Greece, near Bulg. border, 7 mi. N of Siderokastron. German invasion route in 1941. Named for village of Kleidi or Klidhi (formerly known as Rupel).

Rupel River (rü'pŭl), N Belgium, formed at Rumpst by confluence of Nèthe R. and Dyle R.; flows 7.5 mi. WNW, past Boom, to Scheldt R. 7.5 mi. SW of Antwerp, opposite Rupelmonde. Joined by Willebroek Canal just SW of Niel.

Rupert. **1** Village (pop. 4,490), Yuba co., N central Calif., near Marysville. **2** City (pop. 3,098), ⊙ Minidoka co., S Idaho, near Snake R., 8 mi. NE of Burley; alt. 4,200 ft. Shipping center for farm produce (potatoes, sugar beets, peas, beans, alfalfa, wheat) and livestock grown on Minidoka irrigation project (on Snake R.); dairying, alfalfa milling. Laid out (1905) as model city by govt. engineers, inc. as village 1906, as city 1917. **3** Town (pop. 713), Bennington co., SW Vt., on N.Y. line, 28 mi. N of Bennington; patent medicines, lumber, wood products. An early mint made coins here, at East Rupert, for independent State of Vermont in the 1780s. **4** Town (pop. 952), Greenbrier co., SE W.Va., 17 mi. NW of Lewisburg.

Rupert House, village, NW Que., on James Bay of Hudson Bay, near mouth of Rupert R.; 51°30'N 78°46'W. Oldest post of Hudson's Bay Co., it was established 1668; subsequently alternated bet. French and British possession, until restored to British possession by Treaty of Utrecht, 1713.

Rupert River, W Que., issues from L. Mistassini, flows 380 mi. W, through Nemiscau L., past Rupert House, to James Bay 3 mi. W of Rupert House.

Ruphia River, Greece: see ALPHEUS RIVER; LADON RIVER.

Rupin Grande, Free Territory of Trieste: see MONRUPINO.

Rupnagar (rōōp'nŭgŭr), town (pop. 2,836), central Rajasthan, India, 15 mi. N of Kishangarh; millet.

Rupnarayan River (rōōpnärä'yŭn), in Bihar and West Bengal, India, rises in E foothills of Chota Nagpur Plateau, NE of Purulia; flows SE, past Bankura and Bishnupur, and SSE, past Arambagh and Tamluk, to Hooghly R. 9 mi. W of Diamond Harbour; 150 mi. long. In upper course, called Dhalkisor; in middle course, bet. Bankura and Arambagh, called Dwarkeswar.

Rupperswil (rōōp'ŭrsvēl), village (pop. 1,697), Aargau canton, N Switzerland, near Aar R., 4 mi. E of Aarau; hydroelectric plant; metal products, cotton textiles, sugar.

Ruppert Coast (rōō'pŭrt), part of Marie Byrd Land, Antarctica, W of Hobbs Coast and backed by Edsel Ford Ranges, bet. 76°S 147°W and 75°45'S 140°30'W. Discovered 1934 by R. E. Byrd.

Ruppin Lake (rōōpēn'), Ger. *Ruppiner See* (rōōpē'-nŭr zā"), narrow lake (□ 3.3), E Germany, extends 8 mi. S of Alt Ruppin; c.1 mi. wide, greatest depth 79 ft., average depth 39 ft. Traversed by Rhin R. Neuruppin is on W shore. Sometimes called Rhin L.

Rupsa (rōōp'sŭ), village, Balasore dist., NE Orissa, India, 11 mi. NNE of Balasore; rail junction; rice milling.

Rupt de Mad Creek (rüdmäd'), in Meuse and Meurthe-et-Moselle depts., NE France, rises in the Côtes de Meuse 5 mi. NE of Commercy, flows c.25 mi. NE, past Thiaucourt, to the Moselle N of Pagny-sur-Moselle. Figured in battle of Saint-Mihiel (1918) in First World War.

Rupununi (rōō"pōōnōō'nē), district (□ 37,380; pop. 4,703), S Br. Guiana, bordering S and SW on Brazil, E on Du. Guiana; ⊙ Lethem. A mountainous region of the Guiana Highlands, watered by Essequibo, Rupununi, New, and Courantyne rivers. A gold-bearing region of dense tropical forests; cattle raised on W savannas. The Rupununi cattle trail leads from Dadanawa across the Essequibo at Kurupukari to Takama on the lower Berbice. Rupununi dist. forms part of S Essequibo and Berbice counties.

Rupununi River, S Br. Guiana, rises in the Guiana Highlands on Brazil border at 1°52'N 59°36'W, flows c.250 mi. N and E, past Dadanawa, and through a cattle-raising and gold-bearing savanna region, to Essequibo R. at 4°3'N 58°34'W. Numerous cataracts and falls.

Rur, Germany and Netherlands: see ROER RIVER.

Rural Retreat, town (pop. 478), Wythe co., SW Va., 10 mi. WSW of Wytheville; cabbage.

Rural Valley, borough (pop. 857), Armstrong co., W central Pa., 11 mi. E of Kittanning; bituminous coal, gas; planing mill; agr.

Rurki, India: see ROORKEE.

Rurrenabaque (rōōrānäbä'kā), town (pop. c.1,700), Beni dept., NW Bolivia, port on Beni R. and 17 mi. SW of Reyes, opposite San Buenaventura (W);

trade and transfer point; terminus of projected La Paz–Beni RR. Airport.

Rurutu (rōōrōō'tōō), volcanic island (pop. 1,174), Tubuai Isls., Fr. Oceania, S Pacific, 80 mi. NW of Tubuai isl.; 22°30'S 151°20'W; 5 mi. long, 3 mi. wide. Edict (1938) excludes non-natives. Copra, vanilla, arrowroot produced. Chief village is Moerai. Discovered 1769 by Capt. Cook, annexed 1889 by France. Formerly Oheteroa.

Ruruwei (rōōrōōwā'), town, Kano prov., Northern Provinces, N Nigeria, 40 mi. SSE of Tudun Wada; tin-mining center; wolfram mining; cassava, millet, durra.

Rus (rōōs), town (pop. 3,335), Jaén prov., S Spain, 5 mi. NW of Úbeda; olive-oil processing, flour milling. Hog raising; cereals, onions. Gypsum, limestone quarries.

Rusaddir, N Africa: see MELILLA.

Rusambo (rōōsäm'bō), village, Salisbury prov., NE Southern Rhodesia, in Mashonaland, 45 mi. ENE of Mount Darwin (linked by road); mica mining.

Rusanda, Banja, Yugoslavia: see MELENCI.

Rusanovo (rōōsä'nŭvŭ), settlement on S coast of S isl. of Novaya Zemlya, Russian SFSR; 70°35'N 56°20'E. Trading post.

Rusape or **Rusapi** (rōōsä'pē), town (pop. 1,567), Umtali prov., E Southern Rhodesia, in Mashonaland, on railroad and 85 mi. SE of Salisbury; alt. 4,616 ft. Tobacco, corn; livestock. Corundum mining. Hq. Makoni dist.

Rusayfah, Al, Jordan: see RUSEIFA, EL.

Rusca-Montana (rōōs'kä-môntä'nä), Rum. *Rusca-Montană*, Hung. *Ruszkabánya* (rōōs'kŏbä"nyŏ), village (pop. 1,504), Severin prov., W Rumania, in the Poiana-Rusca Mts., 16 mi. NE of Caransebes; coal-mining center; mfg. of agr. tools.

Rüschegg (rü'shĕk), town (pop. 2,062), Bern canton, W central Switzerland, 11 mi. S of Bern; farming.

Ruschuk, Bulgaria: see RUSE, city.

Ruse (rōō'sĕ), city (pop. 53,420), ⊙ Ruse dist. (formed 1949), NE Bulgaria, port and rail junction on right bank of the Danube (Rum. border) opposite Giurgiu (ferry) and 150 mi. NE of Sofia. Major commercial and mfg. center, with metal, textile, leather, and food-processing (sugar, flour, meat, fruit) industries; petroleum refining, ceramics, mfg. of furniture, soap, tobacco, cigarettes. Winegrowing and truck gardening near by. Has Polytechnical Inst., schools of flour milling and of metal- and woodworking, mus., theater, old churches and mosques, ruins of fortresses. Founded as Roman town of Prista; destroyed (7th cent.) by the Barbarians; rebuilt on present site of Cherven (15 mi. S; pop. 2,032); burned (1594) by the Walachians. In 17th cent. developed (on its original site), under Turkish rule, as port of Ruschuk or Rustchuk (properly Rushchuk). Subjected to several Rus. assaults in 19th cent.; finally captured (1877) and ceded to Bulgaria. Was ⊙ former Ruse oblast (1934–47). Sometimes spelled Russe.

Ruse (rōō'sĕ, rōō'shĕ), Slovenian *Ruše*, Ger. *Maria Rast* (mä'rēä räst'), village, NE Slovenia, Yugoslavia, on Drava R., on railroad and 6 mi. W of Maribor; chemical industry, powered by hydroelectric plant at Fala. Summer resort. Roman ruins. Until 1918, in Styria.

Ruseifa, El, Er Ruseifa, or **Al-Rusayfah** (all: ĕr-rōōsā'fü), village (pop. c.500), N central Jordan, on Hejaz RR and 7 mi. NE of Amman; phosphate deposits.

Rusein, Piz, Switzerland: see TÖDI.

Rusenski Lom River (rōō'sĕnskē lôm'), NE Bulgaria, formed 10 mi. S of Ruse by confluence of Beli Lom R. (rising c.7 mi. S of Razgrad) and Cherni Lom R. (rising c.8 mi. W of Targovishte); flows c.15 mi. N to the Danube just W of Ruse.

Rusera (rōōsä'rŭ), town (pop. 10,154), Darghanga dist., N Bihar, India, on Borhi Gandak R. and 30 mi. SSE of Darghanga; trades in rice, corn, wheat, sugar cane, barley. Also spelled Rosera.

Rush, Gaelic *Ros Eó*, town (pop. 1,747), NE Co. Dublin, Ireland, on the Irish Sea, 15 mi. NNE of Dublin; fishing port.

Rush. 1 County (□ 409; pop. 19,799), E central Ind.; ⊙ Rushville. Drained by Big Blue R. and Flatrock Creek. Grain, corn, livestock, poultry; stone quarrying. Mfg. at Carthage and Rushville. Formed 1821. **2** County (□ 724; pop. 7,231), central Kansas; ⊙ La Crosse. Agr. region, watered by Walnut Creek. Wheat, livestock. Oil, gas fields in E. Formed 1874.

Rushan (rōōshän'), village (1939 pop. over 500), W Gorno-Badakhshan Autonomous Oblast, Tadzhik SSR, in the Pamir, on Panj R., near mouth of the Bartang, and 30 mi. N of Khorog; wheat, cattle. Until c.1935, Kalai-Vamar; also spelled Roshan.

Rush City, resort village (pop. 1,175), Chisago co., E Minn., bet. St. Croix R. and Rush L., 50 mi. N of St. Paul, in agr. region; dairy products, flour. Settled before 1873.

Rush Creek, S Okla., rises near Rush Springs in Grady co., flows c.50 mi. E, through Garvin co., to Washita R. just S of Pauls Valley.

Rushden (rŭsh'dun, rŭzh'–), urban district (1931 pop. 14,248; 1951 census 16,321), E Northampton, England, 4 mi. E of Wellingborough; leather and shoe-mfg. center; also produces electrical equipment, soap, detergents, wax polish. Has 14th-cent. church.

Rushford. 1 City (pop. 1,270), Fillmore co., SE Minn., on Root R. and 26 mi. W of LaCrosse, Wis.; trade and shipping center for agr. area; dairy products, beverages, feed. Settled before 1854. **2** Village (pop. 612), Fillmore co., SE Minn., adjacent to Rushford city. **3** Village (pop. c.500), Allegany co., W N.Y., 23 mi. NNE of Olean; maple syrup, dairy products, apples.

Rushford, Lake, N.Y.: see CANEADEA.

Rush Hill, town (pop. 127), Audrain co., NE central Mo., near West Fork of Cuivre R., 9 mi. E of Mexico.

Rushikulya River (rōōshĭkōōl'yŭ), SE Orissa, India, rises in Eastern Ghats 25 mi. WNW of Sorada, flows c.115 mi. SE, past Sorada and Aska, to Bay of Bengal at Ganjam village. Irrigation canal (headworks 7 mi. NE of Aska) serves region bet. Russellkonde (N) and Berhampur area (S).

Rush Lake. 1 In Chisago co., E Minn., near Wis. line, c.50 mi. N of St. Paul. E arm is 4.5 mi. long, W arm 3.5 mi. long; average width 1 mi. Rush City is near by. **2** In Otter Tail co., W Minn., near Otter Tail L., 38 mi. NE of Fergus Falls; □ 8; 5 mi. long, max. width 3 mi. Fishing, bathing, boating resorts. Fed and drained by Otter Tail R. **3** In Cavalier co., NE N.Dak., near Can. line; 5 mi. long. It is slowly receding. **4** In Winnebago co., E central Wis., 12 mi. SW of Oshkosh, in resort region; c.5 mi. long, c.3 mi. wide.

Rushmore, village (pop. 368), Nobles co., SW Minn., near Iowa line, 11 mi. W of Worthington, in grain, livestock, poultry area; ice cream plant.

Rushmore, Mount, S.Dak.: see MOUNT RUSHMORE NATIONAL MEMORIAL.

Rusholme (rŭ'shŭm, rŭsh'hōm), S suburb of Manchester, SE Lancashire, England; cotton and engineering industries.

Rush Springs, town (pop. 1,402), Grady co., central Okla., 18 mi. S of Chickasha, and on small Rush Creek; market and shipping center; watermelons, tomatoes, cotton.

Rushsylvania, village (pop. 563), Logan co., W central Ohio, 8 mi. NE of Bellefontaine and on small Rush Creek. Limestone quarry near by.

Rushton Spencer, village and parish (pop. 375), N Stafford, England, 7 mi. S of Macclesfield; mfg. of chemicals. Has 14th-cent. wooden church.

Rushville. 1 City (pop. 2,682), ⊙ Schuyler co., W Ill., 24 mi. SSE of Macomb; trade center in agr. and bituminous-coal-mining area; livestock, corn, wheat, fruit, poultry, dairy products; meat-packing plant, bottling works. Founded 1825, inc. 1839. Lincoln pleaded cases and made a campaign speech here. **2** City (pop. 6,761), ⊙ Rush co., E central Ind., on Flatrock Creek and 40 mi. ESE of Indianapolis; trade center in agr. area (livestock, grain); lumber, furniture, machinery, flour, packed meat, canned goods, gloves. Stone quarry. Settled 1821. **3** Town (pop. 319), Buchanan co., NW Mo., near Missouri R., 15 mi. SW of St. Joseph; agr., livestock, poultry. **4** City (pop. 1,266), ⊙ Sheridan co., NW Nebr., 30 mi. ESE of Chadron; flour; livestock, dairy and poultry produce, grain. Founded c.1885; inc. as city 1932. **5** Village (pop. 465), on Ontario-Yates co. line, W central N.Y., 15 mi. SW of Geneva, in Finger Lakes region; canned foods, flour. **6** Village (pop. 252), Fairfield co., central Ohio, 10 mi. ENE of Lancaster and on small Rush Creek.

Rushworth, town (pop. 1,260), N central Victoria, Australia, 85 mi. N of Melbourne; rail junction; commercial center in livestock area.

Rusicade, Algeria: see PHILIPPEVILLE.

Rusk. 1 County (□ 944; pop. 42,348), E Texas; ⊙ Henderson. Rolling wooded area (extensive lumbering), drained by Sabine and Angelina rivers and Attoyac Bayou. A leading Texas petroleum co., with NW and W parts in rich East Texas oil field; also natural gas. Agr. (cotton, corn, truck, fruit, peanuts, forage crops), dairying; beef cattle, poultry. Clay, iron, lignite deposits. Mfg., oil refining, lumber and produce processing at Henderson, Overton. Formed 1843. **2** County (□ 910; pop. 16,790), N Wis.; ⊙ Ladysmith. Drained by Chippewa and Flambeau rivers. Largely wooded, with many resort lakes. Dairying, lumbering, stock raising. Formed 1901.

Rusk, town (pop. 6,598), ⊙ Cherokee co., E Texas, 40 mi. S of Tyler, in truck-farming, dairying, lumbering, oil area; ships produce; woodworking, cheese making, canning. Seat of a state mental hosp. Iron smelter near by. Settled 1846, inc. 1858.

Ruski Krstur (rōō'skē kŭr'stōōr), Hung. *Bácskeresztúr* (bäch'kĕrĕstōōr), village (pop. 5,771), Vojvodina, NW Serbia, Yugoslavia, on Novi Sad-Mali Stepar Canal and 14 mi. SE of Sombor, in the Backa; Rus. agr. settlement.

Ruskin, village (pop. estimate 200), SW B.C., on Fraser R. at mouth of Stave R., and 7 mi. WNW of Mission; hydroelectric power station; lumbering.

Ruskin. 1 Village (1940 pop. 983), Hillsborough co., W Fla., 18 mi. S of Tampa, near Tampa Bay; ships vegetables (especially tomatoes) and citrus fruit. **2** Village (pop. 214), Nuckolls co., S Nebr., 12 mi. ESE of Nelson, near Kansas line; livestock, grain.

Ruskington, town and parish (pop. 1,246), Parts of Kesteven, central Lincolnshire, England, 3 mi. NNE of Sleaford; agr. market, with agr.-machinery- and brickworks.

Rusne (rōōsnā'), Lith. *Rusnė*, Ger. *Russ* (rōōs), city (1941 pop. 2,454), W Lithuania, on Neman R. delta, 30 mi. SSE of Memel; fishing center; sawmill. In Memel Territory, 1920–39.

Ruso, village (pop. 37), McLean co., central N.Dak., 33 mi. SSE of Minot.

Rusovce (rō'sôftsĕ), Hung. *Oroszvár* (ô'rôsvär), town (1941 pop. 1,708), SW Slovakia, Czechoslovakia, on railroad, near right bank of the Danube, and 6 mi. SSE of Bratislava; transferred from Hungary by peace treaty of 1947.

Ruspoli, Lake, Ethiopia: see CHAMO, LAKE.

Russ, Lithuania: see RUSNE.

Russas (rōō'sŭs), city (pop. 3,519), NE Ceará, Brazil, on Jaguaribe R. and 32 mi. SSW of Aracati; cotton, carnauba wax, cattle. Gypsum deposits. Formerly called São Bernardo das Russas.

Russe, Bulgaria: see RUSE, city.

Russell, town (pop. estimate 500), S Mendoza prov., Argentina, on railroad and 8 mi. SSE of Mendoza; wine making, alcohol distilling.

Russell, county (□ 407; pop. 17,448), SE Ont., on Ottawa R. and on Que. border; ⊙ L'Orignal.

Russell, town (pop. 885), SW Man., 60 mi. WSW of Dauphin; grain elevators; dairying.

Russell, town (pop. 441), N N.Isl., New Zealand, 115 mi. NNW of Auckland and on S shore of Bay of Isls. Small oyster port; summer resort. Deep-sea fishing. Manganese. Oldest Br. settlement (1829) of New Zealand.

Russell, village (1931 pop. 212), Sierra Leone Colony, on Sierra Leone Peninsula, on N Yawri Bay coast of the Atlantic, 7 mi. S of Waterloo; cassava, corn.

Russell. 1 County (□ 639; pop. 40,364), E Ala.; ⊙ Seale and Phenix City. Coastal plain, bounded on E by Chattahoochee R. and Ga. Cotton, peanuts, corn, poultry; textiles. Formed 1832. **2** County (□ 897; pop. 13,406), central Kansas; ⊙ Russell. Sloping to gently rolling plain, drained by Saline and Smoky Hill rivers. Livestock, wheat. Oil fields. Formed 1872. **3** County (□ 282; pop. 13,717), S Ky.; ⊙ Jamestown. Drained by Cumberland R. and Russell Creek. Hilly agr. area in Cumberland foothills; corn, livestock, burley tobacco. Formed 1825. **4** County (□ 483; pop. 26,818), SW Va.; ⊙ Lebanon. In the Alleghenies; Clinch Mtn. along SE boundary; drained by Clinch R. Includes part of Jefferson Natl. Forest. Hilly livestock (cattle, sheep) and agr. (tobacco, grain, clover, fruit) area; dairying. Mining of bituminous coal, some lead and zinc. Formed 1786.

Russell. 1 Town (pop. 241), White co., central Ark., 15 mi. ENE of Searcy, in agr. area. **2** City (pop. 129), Barrow co., NE central Ga., just SE of Winder. **3** Town (pop. 566), Lucas co., S Iowa, near source of Cedar Creek, 6 mi. ESE of Chariton, in coal-mining and stock-raising area. **4** City (pop. 6,483), ⊙ Russell co., central Kansas, c.65 mi. W of Salina, bet. Saline and Smoky Hill rivers, in oil-producing and agr. area; oil refining, flour milling. Inc. 1872. **5** Town (pop. 1,681), Greenup co., NE Ky., on left bank (levee) of Ohio R. (bridged) opposite Ironton, Ohio, and 6 mi. NW of Ashland; railroad yards and shops, creosoting plant; airport. **6** Town (pop. 1,298), Hampden co., SW Mass., on Westfield R. and 16 mi. WNW of Springfield. Settled 1782, inc. 1792. Includes village of Woronoco (wŏrŭnō'kō) (paper milling). **7** Village (pop. 508), Lyon co., SW Minn., on Redwood R. and 12 mi. SW of Marshall; dairy products. **8** Resort village, St. Lawrence co., N N.Y., on Grass R. and 25 mi. SE of Ogdensburg. **9** Village (pop. 51), Bottineau co., N N.Dak., 23 mi. WSW of Bottineau.

Russell, Mount (11,500 ft.), S central Alaska, in Alaska Range, at SW corner of Mt. McKinley Natl. Park, 130 mi. NW of Anchorage; 62°48'N 151°56'W.

Russell, Mount (14,190 ft.), E Calif., in the Sierra Nevada, just N of Mt. Whitney, on E boundary of Sequoia Natl. Park.

Russell Creek, S Ky., rises in W Russell co., flows c.70 mi. generally NW, past Columbia, to Green R. 2 mi. S of Greensburg.

Russell Fiord, Alaska: see DISENCHANTMENT BAY.

Russell Fork, stream, in SW Va. and E Ky., rises in E Dickenson co., Va.; flows c.50 mi. generally NW, past Haysi, into Pike co., Ky., to Levisa Fork (a branch of the Big Sandy) 7 mi. SE of Pikeville. At state line are scenic Breaks of Sandy, a 5-mi. stretch of river's gorge at N end of Pine Mtn.; here the stream, descending 350 ft. in a series of falls and rapids, has cut an inner gorge (Grand Canyon of Kentucky) c.150 ft. deep; river has also carved sandstone pinnacles, notably the Towers (c.1,600 ft. high), in Dickenson co., Va.

Russell Gardens, suburban residential village (pop. 912), Nassau co., SE N.Y., on NW Long Isl., near Great Neck village.

Russell Island (40 mi. long, 7 mi. wide), central Franklin Dist., Northwest Territories, in Barrow Strait, off N Prince of Wales Isl.; 73° 55'N 99'W.

Russell Islands, small volcanic group, Solomon Isls., SW Pacific, 30 mi. NW of Guadalcanal; comprise 2 isls. and several islets. Largest isl. is Pavuvu (c.10 mi. long, 5 mi. wide); Banika (c.6 mi. long, 1 mi. wide) is 2d largest. Produce copra. In Second World War, group was occupied 1942 by the Japanese; taken 1943, without opposition, by U.S. forces.

Russellkonda (rŭs'ŭlkōndŭ), town (pop. 7,227), Ganjam dist., SE Orissa, India, 45 mi. NNW of Berhampur; local trade in timber, hides, rice, sugar cane; sawmills. Formerly called Goomsur or Gumsur.

Russell Point, E extremity of Banks Isl., SW Franklin Dist., Northwest Territories, at junction of McClure Strait and Viscount Melville Sound, at N end of Prince of Wales Strait; 73°30'N 115°W.

Russells Point or **Russell Point,** resort village (pop. 909), Logan co., W central Ohio, on Great Miami R. at its source in Indian L., and 9 mi. NW of Bellefontaine.

Russell Springs. 1 City (pop. 161), ⊙ Logan co., W Kansas, on Smoky Hill R. and 23 mi. SW of Oakley; grain, livestock. **2** Town (pop. 1,125), Russell co., S Ky., in Cumberland foothills, 26 mi. W of Somerset; resort (alt. c.1,000 ft.), with mineral springs. Inc. 1936.

Russellville. 1 City (pop. 6,012), ⊙ Franklin co., NW Ala., 20 mi. S of Florence; grain mills, cotton gins, stone quarries. Iron mines in vicinity. Settled c.1815. **2** City (pop. 8,166), ⊙ Pope co., N central Ark., c.60 mi. NW of Little Rock, near Arkansas R. Market and shipping center for diversified-farming area (fruit, truck, cotton, potatoes, corn, alfalfa, livestock; dairy products). Coal mining, cotton processing, sawmilling. Natural gas. Has Ark. Polytechnic Col. and hq. of Ozark Natl. Forest. Settled 1835, inc. 1870. **3** Village (pop. 207), Lawrence co., SE Ill., on the Wabash (ferry here) and 10 mi. NE of Lawrenceville, in agr., oil, and natural-gas area. **4** Town (pop. 361), Putnam co., W central Ind., 36 mi. NE of Terre Haute, in grain, poultry, and livestock area. **5** City (pop. 4,529), ⊙ Logan co., S Ky., 27 mi. WSW of Bowling Green, in agr. (dark tobacco, corn, dairy products, livestock, poultry), coal- and asphalt-mining, stone-quarrying, timber area. Mfg. of clothing, dairy products, beverages, candy, tobacco products, wood products, venetian blinds, agr. lime; flour and feed mills; horse abattoir. Founded as Big Boiling Spring c.1790; inc. 1798. Advocates of state sovereignty passed Act of Secession here in 1861, declaring Ky. a Confederate state. **6** Town (pop. 336), Cole co., central Mo., 15 mi. WSW of Jefferson City. **7** Village (pop. 438), Brown co., SW Ohio, 6 mi. E of Georgetown, in agr. area.

Rüsselsheim (rü'sŭls-hīm), town (pop. 16,682), S Hesse, W Germany, in former Starkenburg prov., on left bank of the canalized Main and 13 mi. NW of Darmstadt; mfg. (cars, bicycles, iceboxes).

Russelton, village (pop. 1,670), Allegheny co., W Pa., 15 mi. NE of downtown Pittsburgh.

Russey, Le (lü rüsā'), village (pop. 785), Doubs dept., E France, near Swiss border, 6 mi. NW of La Chaux-de-Fonds; Gruyère cheese, watches. Hydroelectric plant on Doubs 5 mi. E.

Russi (rōōs'sē), town (pop. 3,064), Ravenna prov., Emilia-Romagna, N central Italy, 9 mi. WSW of Ravenna; rail junction; vinegar, artificial fruit and flowers.

Russia, Rus. *Rossiya* (rŭsē'ŭ), originally *Rus* or *Rus'*, name commonly applied to the Soviet Union, though it applies in a more precise historic sense to the former Russian Empire (whose ⊙ was St. Petersburg), and in a more precise modern sense only to the RUSSIAN SOVIET FEDERATED SOCIALIST REPUBLIC, chief member of the Soviet Union, where Russian is the language of the majority. This article treats briefly with the growth of Russia until the Russian Revolution of 1917; for the geography and economy, and for the history after that date, see the article on UNION OF SOVIET SOCIALIST REPUBLICS. The name Russia was 1st applied (10th cent.) to the Kievan state or Kievan Russia, a loose confederation of E Slav (Russian) tribes under the leadership of the Varangians (Normans). At the decline (12th cent.) of Kiev, political supremacy over the Russians, then divided into separate principalities, passed to the Rostov-Suzdal principality (NE), which later became the Vladimir grand duchy. Following the Mongol-Tatar raids (1237–40), which resulted in the establishment of the Golden Horde on Russia's SE margins, the leadership of the Russians passed (early 14th cent.) to Moscow. Moscow's ruler, Dmitri Donskoi, captured Vladimir (1364), won a decisive victory over the Golden Horde at Kulikovo (1380), and thus established the power of the Grand Duchy of Moscow. The Muscovite state expanded and under Ivan III (reign 1462–1505) absorbed the last Russian principalities and Novgorod and began to be called the Russian state, with Ivan IV (the Terrible) the 1st to assume the title tsar, in 1547. During the 16th cent. the Tatar khanates of Kazan (1552) and Astrakhan (1556) were conquered and the conquest of Siberia was begun (1581–82) by the Cossack Yermak. By 1640 the Cossacks had reached the shores of the Pacific. In wars with Poland, Russia won the left-bank Ukraine in 17th cent., and under Peter I (the Great) secured a foothold on the Baltic Sea in the Northern War (1700–21), founding St. Petersburg, the "window on Europe," in 1703. Under Catherine II (the Great), Russia expanded through the 3 successive partitions of Poland (1772, 1793, 1795) and, having defeated the Turks, reached the northern shore of the Black Sea. Finland (1809), Bessarabia (1812), and Poland (Grand Duchy of Warsaw; 1815) were added to the Russian Empire under Alexander I, and the conquest of the Caucasus, begun in 1801, was completed (1878) with the annexation of Kars. In the mid-19th cent., Russia began a series of campaigns in Central Asia that won W Turkestan by the 1880s. In 1858–60 the Amur and Ussuri areas were annexed from China; Alaska was sold to the U.S. in 1867. In the scramble for rights in China, Russia secured Manchuria railroad rights and the Kwantung lease (1898) but lost them, as well as S Sakhalin (annexed 1875) in the Russo-Japanese War (1904–05). Russia fought in the First World War on the side of the Allies until the Russian Revolution (1917), which culminated (1922) in the formation of the USSR. Administratively, the pre-revolutionary Russian Empire was divided at the time of the 1897 census into European Russia (consisting of 50 govts.), Russian Poland (10 govts.), Finland (8 govts.), the Caucasus (11 govts. and oblasts), Siberia (9 govts.), Central Asia (9 govts.). The govts. were generally subdivided into uyezds, and these, in turn, into volosts.

Russian Central Asia: see CENTRAL ASIA.

Russian Island, Rus. *Ostrov Russki* (ô'strŭf rōō'skē), island in Peter the Great Bay of Sea of Japan, Russian SFSR, just S of Muravyev-Amurski Peninsula (separated by Eastern Bosphorus strait); under jurisdiction of Vladivostok; 8 mi. long, 8 mi. wide. Agr. (grain, soybeans). Fisheries. Fjordlike Novik Bay, which penetrates N section of isl., is site of naval and military installations.

Russian Mission, village (pop. 55), W Alaska, on Yukon R. and 70 mi. NNE of Bethel; 61°47'N 161°20'W. Supply center; mink farming, gold mining. On Yukon steamer line. Site of mother church of Russian missions, now closed and decaying.

Russian River, W Calif., rises in Mendocino co., flows c.100 mi. S, past Ukiah and Healdsburg, then SW, through redwood groves, to the Pacific 20 mi. W of Santa Rosa. Along its lower course are many resorts.

Russian Soviet Federated Socialist Republic, commonly abbreviated RSFSR, largest and most populous constituent republic (□ 6,501,500, with coastal seas □ 6,533,600; 1947 pop. estimate 111,000,000; in Europe, □ 1,578,700, pop. 91,500,000; in Asia, □ 4,922,800, pop. 19,500,000) of the USSR; ⊙ Moscow (*Moskva*). Constitutes 76% of the area of the USSR and 58% of the pop. Borders on seas of Arctic Ocean (N), seas of the Pacific (E), China, Mongolia, and Kazakhstan (S), Azerbaijan and Georgia (SW), Ukraine, Belorussia, the Baltic republics, Finland, and Karelia (W). Extends 5,000 mi. from Baltic Sea (W) to the Pacific (E), 1,500–2,500 mi. from Arctic Ocean (N) to the Caucasus, Caspian Sea, Altai and Sayan mts., and Amur R. (S). Of the USSR latitudinal soil and vegetation zones, it includes the entire tundra and taiga belts, nearly the entire wooded steppe, the N black-earth steppes, and only isolated sections of the semi-desert, desert, and subtropical zones. Its dominant relief features are (W to E) the East European (Russian) Lowland, the Urals, W.Siberian Plain, and Central Siberian Plateau drained by Volga, Ob, Yenisei, Lena, and Amur rivers. Pop. consists of Russians (74%), Ukrainians (8%), Belorussians, Tatars, Jews, Mordvinians, Chuvash, Bashkirs, Udmurts, and numerous other ethnic groups. Administratively, areas with a predominant Rus. pop. are constituted as oblasts [variously translated as region, district, province, etc.] and territories [Rus. *krai* or *kray*], while non-Russian nationalities are constituted as autonomous republics, autonomous oblasts, and natl. okrugs [also variously translated], in accordance with their importance. In early 1950, the Russian SFSR administered directly 48 oblasts, 6 territories, 12 autonomous republics and Tuva Autonomous Oblast. Other oblasts, autonomous oblasts, and nat. okrugs are included in the primary territories or oblasts. These first-order administrative divisions can be grouped into physico-economic regions: Central Industrial Region (oblasts of MOSCOW, VLADIMIR, IVANOVO, YAROSLAVL, KOSTROMA, RYAZAN, TULA); Central Black-Earth Region (oblasts of OREL, KURSK, VORONEZH, TAMBOV); European West (oblasts of BRYANSK, KALUGA, SMOLENSK, KALININ, VELIKIYE LUKI); European Northwest (oblasts of PSKOV, LENINGRAD, NOVGOROD); European North (oblasts of MURMANSK, ARCHANGEL, VOLOGDA, and KOMI AUTONOMOUS SSR); KALININGRAD oblast; upper (wooded) Volga Region (GORKI and KIROV oblasts, MARI AUTONOMOUS SSR); middle (wooded-steppe) Volga Region (oblasts of ULYANOVSK, PENZA, and KUIBYSHEV; CHUVASH, TATAR, and MORDVINIAN Autonomous SSRs); lower (steppe) Volga Region (oblasts of SARATOV, STALINGRAD, ASTRAKHAN); the CRIMEA; the Lower Don and Northern Caucasus (ROSTOV and GROZNY oblasts, KRASNODAR and STAVROPOL territories, KABARDIAN, NORTH OSSETIAN, and DAGESTAN Autonomous SSRs); the Urals (oblasts of MOLOTOV; SVERDLOVSK, CHELYABINSK, and CHKALOV, UDMURT and BASHKIR Autonomous SSRs); Western Siberia (oblasts of KURGAN, TYUMEN, OMSK, NOVOSIBIRSK, TOMSK, and KEMEROVO, and ALTAI Territory); Eastern Siberia (KRASNOYARSK Territory, IRKUTSK and CHITA oblasts, BURYAT-MONGOL and YAKUT Autonomous SSRs, and TUVA Autonomous Oblast); the Far East (MARITIME and KHABAROVSK territories, SAKHALIN and AMUR oblasts). There are extensive mineral resources of coal (Kuznetsk, Moscow, Pechora, and Bureya basins), petroleum (Grozny, Maikop, Second Baku, Sakhalin), iron ore (Kursk magnetic anomaly, Kerch, Bakal, Komarovo, Zigazinski), nonferrous and rare metals (Urals, Siberia), apatite (Khibiny Mts.), phosphorite, salt, potash, Glauber's salt, chromite, pyrite, timber, and hydroelectric reserves. Principal industries are machine mfg., nonferrous and high-grade steel metallurgy, mfg. of chemicals, textiles, leather goods, fish and lumber products. Agr.: wheat (central Black-Earth Region), rye, barley, oats, corn (N Caucasus), millet (dry steppes), buckwheat (European West), rice (N Caucasus, Khanka Plain), potatoes, flax, hemp, sunflowers, sugar beets. Dairy farming (Vologda, Baraba Steppe), beef-cattle, hog, sheep, and reindeer raising are principal pastoral occupations. Transportation relies on a dense railroad network in European Russian SFSR and on Trans-Siberian RR in the Asiatic part, on river and canal navigation (mainly Volga, Kama and Oka rivers, Mariinsk, White Sea–Baltic, and northern Dvina canal systems), and coastwise shipping (including the Arctic Sea route). Principal urban centers are Moscow, Leningrad, Gorki, Novosibirsk, Sverdlovsk, Kuibyshev, Omsk, Kazan, Rostov. Proclaimed 1917; joined (1922) Ukrainian and Belorussian SSRs and Transcaucasian SFSR to form the USSR. During Second World War, W European section was occupied (1941–43) by Germans. While the term Russia is sometimes applied to the RSFSR, it more commonly refers to the Russian Empire prior to 1917 and to the USSR since 1917.

Russian Turkestan: see TURKESTAN.

Russkaya Gavan or **Russkaya Gavan'** (rōō'skŭ gä'vŭnyŭ) [Rus., = Russian harbor), settlement and bay on W coast of N isl. of Novaya Zemlya, Russian SFSR; 76°12'N 62°30'E. Govt. observation station; trading post.

Russkaya Polyana (pŭlyä'nŭ), village (1939 pop. over 500), S Omsk oblast, Russian SFSR, near Kazakh SSR border, 85 mi. S of Omsk, in agr. area.

Russki Brod or **Russkiy Brod** (rōō'skē brôt"), village (1939 pop. over 500), central Orel oblast, Russian SFSR, 15 mi. NW of Livny; potatoes.

Russki Island, Russian SFSR: see NORDENSKJÖLD ARCHIPELAGO.

Russki Kameshkir or **Russkiy Kameshkir** (kŭmyĭshkēr'), village (1932 pop. estimate 7,900), SE Penza oblast, Russian SFSR, 28 mi. SW of Kuznetsk, in grain area; sunflowers, legumes. Also called Kameshkir Russki. Mordovski [Rus., = Mordvinian] Kameshkir, village (1939 pop. over 500), is 6 mi. NNE.

Rust (rōōst), Hung. *Ruszt* (rōōst), town (pop. 1,653), Burgenland, E Austria, 8 mi. ESE of Eisenstadt and on Neusiedler L.; excellent wine.

Rustak or **Rustaq** (rōōstäk'), town (pop. 10,000), Afghan Badakhshan, NE Afghanistan, 40 mi. W of Faizabad; grain, fruit. Also spelled Rostak or Rostaq.

Rustaq, Oman: see ROSTAK.

Rustavi (rōōstä'vē), city (1948 pop. over 10,000; planned pop. 50,000), SE Georgian SSR, on Kura R., on railroad and 20 mi. SSE of Tiflis; metallurgical center (pig iron, ingot and rolled steel products, tubing); power plant. Bridge connects residential section (on right bank) and industrial sites (on left bank). Developed after 1943, on basis of coal from Tkibuli and Tkvarcheli, and Dashkesan iron ore; became city in 1948. It is near site of anc. town of Rustavi, destroyed 1400 by Tamerlane and birthplace (13th cent.) of Rustaveli, Georgia's natl. poet.

Rustburg, village (pop. c.350), ⊙ Campbell co., SW central Va., 9 mi. SSE of Lynchburg.

Rustchuk, Bulgaria: see RUSE, city.

Rustenburg (rŭ'stŭnbûrg, Afrikaans rŭ'stŭnbûrkh"), town (pop. 11,549), SW Transvaal, U. of So. Afr., 60 mi. WNW of Johannesburg, at foot of Magaliesberg mts.; mining (chrome, platinum) and agr. center (fruit, tobacco, cotton); tobacco processing, fruit packing, marmalade making. A gold field discovered 1923 near by has not yet been exploited. Nickel mines at Vlakfontein, 30 mi. NW. The Union's chief iron mines are in the district N of Rustenburg extending to the Thabazimbi area.

Rust en Werk (rûst' ĕn vĕrk'), village (pop. 541), Commewijne dist., N Du. Guiana, on Commewijne R., opposite Nieuw Amsterdam, and 8 mi. NE of Paramaribo; sugar cane, coffee, rice.

Rustico (rŭ'stĭkō), fishing port, N P.E.I., on small Rustico Bay of the Gulf of St. Lawrence, 15 mi. NW of Charlottetown; 1st settled by Acadians 1710.

Ruston (rŭ'stŭn). **1** Town (pop. 10,372), ⊙ Lincoln parish, N La., 31 mi. W of Monroe; commercial center for dairying and agr. area (cotton, corn, tomatoes, potatoes, peanuts, fruit); mfg. of powdered milk, cottonseed products, beverages, brick, candy; lumber milling. Natural gas. Seat of La. Polytechnic Inst. Town established c.1884 on railroad. **2** Town (pop. 838), Pierce co., W central Wash., on Puget Sound, near Tacoma; a copper smelter is here.

Rüstringen (rüs'trĭng-ŭn), N section of Wilhelmshaven, NW Germany. Formed 1911 through union of Bant, Heppens, and Neuende. Inc. (1933; pop. 48,562) into Wilhelmshaven.

Ruswil (rōōs'vēl), town (pop. 4,528), Lucerne canton, central Switzerland, 14 mi. W of Lucerne; farming.

Ruszkabanya, Rumania: see Rusca-Montana.

Ruszt, Austria: see Rust.

Rutaka, Russian SFSR: see Aniva.

Rutana (rōōtä'nä), village, S Ruanda-Urundi, in Urundi, near Tanganyika border, 34 mi. S of Kitega; customs station, native cattle market; mfg. of bricks and tiles, lime kilns.

Rutba or **Rutbah** (rōōt'bŭ), desert outpost, W Iraq, on the Wadi Hauran and 230 mi. W of Baghdad. Airfield. It is a supply station on the Baghdad-Damascus road. The Kirkuk-Haifa oil pipe line passes just N.

Rutbo, Sweden: see Skogsbo.

Rutchenkovo (rōōchĭn-kô'vŭ), SW suburb (1939 pop. over 10,000) of Stalino, Stalino oblast, Ukrainian SSR; rail junction; coal mines, coking plant.

Rute (rōō'tā), town (pop. 13,155), Córdoba prov., S Spain, in Andalusia, 9 mi. SE of Lucena; liqueur (anisette, cognac, gin) production and shipping. Mfg. of knitwear, cotton cloth, soap, glass, chocolate; olive-oil processing, flour milling. Cereals, truck produce, lumber, and livestock in area. Clay, stone, and gypsum quarries near by.

Rütenbrock (rü'tŭnbrôk), village (pop. 1,306), in former Prussian prov. of Hanover, NW Germany, after 1945 in Lower Saxony, at junction of Süd-Nord and Haren-Rütenbrock canals, 13 mi. NW of Meppen, on Dutch border.

Ruth. 1 Village (pop. 1,244), White Pine co., E Nev., 5 mi. W of Ely in Egan Range; alt. c.7,200 ft.; copper mining (large open pit). **2** Town (pop. 324), Rutherford co., W N.C., just N of Rutherfordton; lumber milling. Called Hampton until 1939.

Rüthen (rü'tŭn), town (pop. 3,489), in former Prussian prov. of Westphalia, W Germany, after 1945 in North Rhine-Westphalia, near the Möhne, 13 mi. SSE of Lippstadt; grain.

Ruthenia (rōōthē'nēŭ), Latinized form of the word Russia. Term was used in Middle Ages when princes of Galich briefly assumed the title kings of Ruthenia. In modern times, term Ruthenians was used in Austro-Hungarian Monarchy to designate Ukrainian population of the NE Carpathians, divided among Hungary, Austrian Poland (i.e., Galicia), and Bukovina. After 1918 the name Ruthenia was applied to the easternmost prov. of Czechoslovakia; it went also under various modifications of the name, was annexed for a time by Hungary, and finally was included in USSR. See the article on Transcarpathian Oblast.

Rutherford (rŭ'dhŭrfŭrd). **1** County (□ 566; pop. 46,356), S N.C., on S.C. line; ⊙ Rutherfordton. Piedmont agr. (cotton, corn, sweet potatoes) and timber area; drained by Broad R. Textile and lumber mills; resorts. Formed 1779. **2** County (□ 630; pop. 40,696), central Tenn.; ⊙ Murfreesboro. In central basin; drained by Stones R. Includes Stones River Natl. Military Park. Agr. (corn, hay, wheat, cotton), livestock raising, dairying; lumbering. Mfg. at Murfreesboro. Formed 1803.

Rutherford. 1 (rŭ'dhŭrfŭrd) Village (pop. c.325), Napa co., W Calif., in Napa R. valley, 4 mi. SE of St. Helena; wineries. **2** (rŭ'thŭrfŭrd) Residential suburban borough (pop. 17,411), Bergen co., NE N.J., near Passaic R. just SE of Passaic; dye works; mfg. (metal products, machines, clothing, awnings, asphalt, asbestos). Fairleigh Dickinson Col. here. Has pre-Revolutionary houses. Laid out 1862, inc. 1881. **3** (rŭ'dhŭrfŭrd) Town (pop. 994), Gibson co., NW Tenn., on headstream (South Fork) of the Obion and 10 mi. N of Trenton; shipping center for farm area; makes jackets.

Rutherford Island, Maine: see South Bristol.

Rutherfordton (rŭ'dhŭrfŭrtŭn), town (pop. 3,146), ⊙ Rutherford co., W N.C., 36 mi. SE of Asheville; cotton and lumber mills. Diversified agr., timber in region. Founded 1779; inc. 1841.

Rutherglen (rŭ'dhŭrglĕn), town (pop. 1,410), N Victoria, Australia, near New South Wales border, 145 mi. NNE of Melbourne; chief wine center of state. Agr. experiment station. Tin mines in vicinity.

Rutherglen (rŭ'dhŭrglĕn), burgh (1931 pop. 25,157; 1951 census 24,225), NW Lanark, Scotland, on the Clyde and 3 mi. SE of Glasgow; steel-milling center, with coal mines, chemical, dye, paper, and biscuit works, and shipyards. Has remains of anc. church in which truce bet. England and Scotland was signed (1297), resulting in betrayal of Wallace. Anc. castle, taken (1313) by Bruce and burned (1568) by Murray, was destroyed in 18th cent. In 1679 the Covenanters here published the Declaration and Testament which preceded battles of Drumclog and Bothwell Brig. Rutherglen became royal burgh in 1126 and was a leading Clyde port for some time.

Ruthin (rōō'dhĭn, rĭth'ĭn), municipal borough (1931 pop. 2,912; 1951 census 3,599), central Denbigh, Wales, on Clwyd R. and 7 mi. SE of Denbigh; agr. market. There are ruins of 13th–14th-cent. castle, dismantled (1646) by Parliamentarians; part of grounds now occupied by large mansion. Church dates from 1308. Other notable bldgs.: 13th-cent. cloisters, Elizabethan Christ's Hosp., grammar school. Municipal borough includes districts of Llanfwrog (lănvōō'rôg) (pop. 1,019) and Llanrhydd (lănrēdh') (pop. 793).

Ruthton (rōōth'tŭn), resort village (pop. 534), Pipestone co., SW Minn., on headstream of Redwood R. and 17 mi. NE of Pipestone, in grain, livestock area; dairy products.

Ruthven, Inverness, Scotland: see Kingussie.

Ruthven (rōōth'vŭn), town (pop. 868), Palo Alto co., NW Iowa, 13 mi. E of Spencer, in livestock and grain area; summer resort near state park.

Ruthwell (rŭdh'wŭl), village and parish (pop. 646), S Dumfries, Scotland, near Solway Firth, 9 mi. SE of Dumfries. Parish church contains anc. Ruthwell Cross, with writing in Runic characters. Just SW are ruins of Comlongon Castle.

Rüti (rü'tē), town (pop. 5,818), Zurich canton, N Switzerland, 16 mi. ESE of Zurich; metalworking, silk textiles.

Rutigliano (rōōtēlyä'nô), town (pop. 10,016), Bari prov., Apulia, S Italy, 6 mi. SW of Mola di Bari; ceramics, macaroni.

Rutlam, India: see Ratlam.

Rutland or **Rutlandshire** (–shĭr), county (□ 152; 1931 pop. 17,401; 1951 census 20,510), E central England; ⊙ Oakham. Bounded by Leicester (W), Lincoln (N and E), Northampton (S). Drained by Witham R. and Welland R. Agr. country, with ironstone quarrying, and leather and hosiery industry. Town of Uppingham has noted public school. Rutland is smallest co. of England, though the administrative co. of London is smaller.

Rutland, county (□ 929; pop. 45,905), SW Vt., partly bounded W by L. Champlain and rising to Green Mts. in E; ⊙ Rutland. Marble and slate quarrying and finishing; agr. (dairying, fruit, poultry); mfg. (wood products, textiles, scales, tools, quarry machinery); lumber; maple sugar. Mtn. and lake resorts, winter sports. Includes part of Green Mtn. Natl. Forest and Killington Peak. Drained by Otter Creek and Castleton, Poultney, and Clarendon rivers. Organized 1781.

Rutland. 1 Village (pop. 486), La Salle co., central Ill., 23 mi. S of La Salle, in agr. and bituminous-coal area. **2** Town (pop. 225), Humboldt co., N central Iowa, on Des Moines R. and 19 mi. NNW of Fort Dodge. Limestone quarries, sand pits near by. **3** Town (pop. 3,056), including Rutland village (pop. 1,629), Worcester co., central Mass., 10 mi. NW of Worcester; dairying, truck, poultry. Has several tuberculosis sanitariums. Settled 1716, inc. 1722. **4** Village (pop. 309), Sargent co., SE N.Dak., 7 mi. ESE of Forman. **5** Village (pop. 554), Meigs co., SE Ohio, 5 mi. W of Pomeroy, in coal-mining area. **6** City (pop. 17,659), ⊙ Rutland co., W central Vt., bet. Green Mts. (E) and the Taconics, on Otter Creek and 53 mi. N of Bennington. Rutland town (pop. 1,416; chartered 1761), surrounding the city, includes Center Rutland village (marble cutting). City, second largest in Vt., has varied industries (marble, scales, machinery, tools, metal products, lumber, cement products, clothing, printing, food processing); railroad center; winter sports, especially at Pico Peak (NE). Has a jr. col. Two Revolutionary forts were here, and there was early strife over land grants made by N.H. and N.Y. Marble quarrying flourished after 1845. Points of interest: public library, new Federal bldg., R.C. Church of Christ the King. John Deere b. here. Settled 1770, village inc. 1847, city inc. 1893.

Rutland Island, one of Andaman Isls., in Bay of Bengal; southernmost isl. of Great Andaman group; 11 mi. long N–S, 2–7 mi. wide.

Rutland Island, islet (1 mi. long) off W coast of Co. Donegal, Ireland, just E of Aran Isl.

Rutlandshire, England: see Rutland.

Rutledge (rŭt'lĭj). **1** Town (pop. 370), Crenshaw co., S Ala., 20 mi. WSW of Troy, near Patsaliga Creek. **2** Town (pop. 482), Morgan co., N central Ga., 27 mi. SSW of Athens; mfg. (clothing, fertilizer). State park near by. **3** Village (pop. 163), Pine co., E Minn., on Kettle R. and c.50 mi. SW of Duluth, in grain and livestock area. **4** Town (pop. 217), Scotland co., NE Mo., near North Fabius R., 11 mi. SSE of Memphis. **5** Borough (pop. 919), Delaware co., SE Pa., 10 mi. WSW of Philadelphia. **6** Village (pop. c.500), ⊙ Grainger co., E Tenn., 30 mi. NE of Knoxville, in timber and farm area; cotton hosiery; lumber milling. Marble quarrying near by.

Rütli (rüt'lē) or **Grütli** (grüt'lē), meadow on W shore of L. of Uri, central Switzerland, 6 mi. NNW of Altdorf. Here, according to legend, representatives of Uri, Schwyz, and Unterwalden met in 1307 to swear the Rütli Oath, on which Swiss freedom was founded.

Rutongo (rōōtông'gō), village, N Ruanda-Urundi, in Ruanda, 12 mi. N of Kigali; center of tin-mining area. Gold is also mined in vicinity.

Rutshuru (rōōchōō'rōō), town, Kivu prov., E Belgian Congo, on right bank of Rutshuru R. and 50 mi. NNE of Costermansville, near Uganda border; alt. 4,248 ft. Trading and tourist center in coffee-plantation area; customs station. Airfield. One of main bases for ascensions of the Virunga volcanoes and excursions to Albert Natl. Park; formerly ⊙ Kivu dist. Noted R.C. mission of Tongres-Sainte-Marie (tō'grŭ-sĕt-märē'), also known as Lulenga (lōōlĕng'gä), is 7 mi. SSW.

Rutshuru River, in SW Uganda and E Belgian Congo, rises in Uganda just across the border c.30 mi. ESE of town of Rutshuru, flows c.75 mi. in a curve W and N to L. Edward 40 mi. SW of Katwe. Most of its course is in Albert Natl. Park. Rutshuru plain, with swamps and hot springs, is known for its abundance of animal life.

Rüttenscheidt (rü'tŭn-shīt), industrial district (since 1901) of Essen, W Germany, 1.5 mi. S of city center; coal mining.

Rutul (rōōtōōl'), village (1932 pop. estimate 1,770), S Dagestan Autonomous SSR, Russian SFSR, in the E Greater Caucasus, on Samur R. and 15 mi. WNW of Akhty; grain, livestock. Dist. inhabited by Rutul mtn. tribe.

Rutupiae, England: see Sandwich.

Ruus al Jibal (rōō-ōōs' ăl jĭbăl'), district exclave of Oman sultanate, on Strait of Hormuz, at tip of Oman Promontory, separating Persian Gulf and Gulf of Oman; main town, Khasab. A mountainous region with rocky, deeply indented coast, terminating in Cape Masandam; separated from rest of Oman sultanate by Kalba and Fujaira sheikdoms of Trucial Oman. Pop. (tribal Arabs with Persian admixture) engages in pearling, fishing, date cultivation. Sometimes spelled Ras el Jebel.

Ruven Mountains (rōō'vŭn), Nor. *Ruven*, *Rjuven*, or *Riuvenfjell*, in Vest-Agder and Aust-Agder counties, S Norway, extend from Bykle Mts. S to the valleys of the Sira and Kvina; rise to 4,527 ft. in the peak Urdalsknud, 65 mi. NNE of Flekkefjord.

Ruvo del Monte (rōō'vô dĕl môn'tĕ), village (pop. 2,614), Potenza prov., Basilicata, S Italy, 12 mi. SSW of Melfi.

Ruvo di Puglia (dē pōō'lyä), anc. *Rubi*, town (pop. 24,748), Bari prov., Apulia, S Italy, 5 mi. SE of Corato. Agr. center (cereals, vegetables, almonds, olive oil, wine); pottery mfg. Bishopric. Has 13th-cent. cathedral and collection of fine Apulian vases unearthed near by.

Ruvu (rōō'vōō), town, Eastern Prov., Tanganyika, on Ruvu (Kingani) R. and 40 mi. W of Dar es Salaam, on railroad; sisal, cotton, rice.

Ruvubu River, Ruanda-Urundi: see Ruvuvu River.

Ruvuma River (rōōvōō'mä), Port. *Rovuma*, in E Africa, rises in N Mozambique highlands E of L. Nyasa, flows N then E, forming most of Tanganyika-Mozambique border, to the Indian Ocean just N of Cape Delgado. Length, 450 mi. Navigable for small craft in lower course. Receives the Lugenda (right).

Ruvu River. 1 In E Tanganyika: see Kingani River. **2** In NE Tanganyika: see Pangani River.

Ruvuvu River (rōōvōō'vōō), Ruanda-Urundi, rises in several branches E of Usumbura, flows NNE, joining the Nyawarongo at Tanganyika border to form Kagera River. Length, with the Luvironza, over 300 mi. The Luvironza, its longest headstream, is considered the remotest source of the Nile. Also spelled Ruvubu.

Ruwad, Syria: see Ruad.

Ruwandiz (rōōwän'dĭz) or **Rawanduz** (räwän'dōōz), town, Erbil prov., N Iraq, in Kurdistan, 40 mi. NE of Erbil; tobacco, livestock, grapes, oranges. Sometimes spelled Rowandiz.

Ruwanwella (rōōvŭn'vĕlŭ), village, Sabaragamuwa Prov., SW central Ceylon, on the Kelani Ganga and 28 mi. ENE of Colombo; road junction; rubber, vegetables, coconut and areca palms, rice. Dutch fort ruins. Scene of early-19th-cent. struggles bet. English and king of Kandy.

Ruwe (rōō'wā), village, Katanga prov., SE Belgian Congo, near railroad, 5 mi. NE of Kolwezi; copper- and gold-mining center; palladium-platinum metals also occur here.

Ruwenzori (rōōwĕnzō'rē), mountain group, E central Africa, on Belgian Congo–Uganda border, bet. L. Edward (S) and L. Albert (N); c.75 mi. long, 40 mi. wide. Of its 6 snow-capped masses, Mt. Stanley, the highest, rises to 16,795 ft. in Mt. Margherita and to 16,750 ft. in Mt. Alexandra. W part of the range is within Albert Natl. Park. Unlike other leading African heights, it is not of volcanic nature but mostly of crystalline rock. Has extensive glaciers (snow line, 14,500 ft.) and several glacial lakes. Dense equatorial forests are at the base of range, and several vegetation zones succeed each other in alt. Ruwenzori was 1st discovered (1889) by Henry Stanley and Emin Pasha and became the object of various attempts at ascent (1891–1906). Duke of Abruzzi's expedition finally reached summit (1906) from Uganda side. Belgian expedition (1932) thoroughly explored the massif. Present-day ascents are usually made from Mutwanga camp. The range is commonly identified with the fabulous "Mountains of the Moon," supposed by the ancients to be the source of the Nile.

Ruyen, Belgium: see RUIEN.

Ruyen, peak, Bulgaria and Yugoslavia: see RUJEN.

Ruyena, Latvia: see RUJIENA.

Ruyigi (rōōyē'gē), village, E Ruanda-Urundi, in Urundi, near Tanganyika border, 22 mi. E of Kitega; customs station and trading post; coffee, cattle, mfg. of bricks and tiles.

Ruy Mountains, Bulgaria and Yugoslavia: see RUI MOUNTAINS.

Ruysbroeck, Belgium: see RUISBROEK.

Ruysselede, Belgium: see RUISELEDE.

Ruza (rōō'zŭ), city (1926 pop. 2,822), W Moscow oblast, Russian SFSR, on Ruza R. (left tributary of Moskva R.; c.50 mi. long) and 55 mi. W of Moscow; mills (woodworking, clothing). Chartered 1328.

Ruzayevka (rōōzī'ŭfkŭ). **1** Village (1948 pop. over 2,000), SW Kokchetav oblast, Kazakh SSR, 105 mi. WSW of Kokchetav; sheep. **2** City (1939 pop. over 10,000), S Mordvinian Autonomous SSR, Russian SFSR, on Insar R. and 14 mi. SW of Saransk; rail junction; major metalworking center; flour milling, brick mfg. Became city in 1937.

Ruzhany (rōōzhä'nē), Pol. *Różana* (rōōzhä'nä), town (1931 pop. 3,986), N Brest oblast, Belorussian SSR, 13 mi. NE of Kossovo; tanning, textile mfg., flour milling, sawmilling.

Ruzhichna (rōō'zhĭchnŭ), village (1926 pop. 2,768), central Kamenets-Podolski oblast, Ukrainian SSR, 3 mi. S of Proskurov.

Ruzhin (rōō'zhĭn), village (1926 pop. 4,643), SE Zhitomir oblast, Ukrainian SSR, 30 mi. ESE of Berdichev; metalworks.

Ruzhino, Russian SFSR: see LESOZAVODSK.

Ruzhitsa (rōōzhē'tsä), village (pop. 1,109), Kolarovgrad dist., NE Bulgaria, in N Deliorman upland, 14 mi. N of Novi Pazar; rail junction; sheep raising, lumbering. Formerly Gyuller.

Ruzizi River (rōōzē'zē), S outlet of L. Kivu in E central Africa, along Belgian Congo–Ruanda-Urundi border. Issues just E of Costermansville and flows c.100 mi. SSE and S to L. Tanganyika 15 mi. NE of Uvira. Upper course is cut by numerous rapids; hydroelectric power plant supplying energy to Costermansville and vicinity is just below its exit from L. Kivu. Lower Ruzizi plain is noted as hunting grounds.

Ruzomberok (rōō'zhômbĕrôk), Slovak *Ružomberok*, Ger. *Rosenberg* (rō'zŭnbĕrk), Hung. *Rózsahegy* (rō'zhōhĕ"dyŭ), town (pop. 15,437), N Slovakia, Czechoslovakia, on Vah R. and 28 mi. SSE of Zilina; rail junction; mfg. center (textiles, paper, cellulose, matches); also known for cheese production. Still retains part of old fortifications, 16th-cent. church with huge bronze bell. Has mus. with valuable ethnographic collections. Several peasant communities near by are noted for their picturesque regional folkways. Health resort of Korythnica (alt. 2,792 ft.) is 13 mi. S, on E slope of the Low Tatra.

Ruzyne (rōō'zĭnyĕ), Czech *Ruzyně*, village (pop. 4,469), W central Bohemia, Czechoslovakia, on railroad and 5 mi. W of Prague; site of municipal airport for Prague.

Rwamagana (rwämägä'nä), village, E Ruanda-Urundi, in Ruanda, 40 mi. E of Kigali; center of native trade; cattle raising. R.C. mission.

Rwaza (rwä'zä), village, N Ruanda-Urundi, in Ruanda, 42 mi. NW of Kigali; cigar making. R.C. mission and trade schools.

Rwindi River, Belgian Congo: see RUINDI RIVER.

Ry, Denmark: see RYE.

Ryakhovo (ryä'khôvô), village (pop. 3,599), Ruse dist., NE Bulgaria, on the Danube (landing) and 17 mi. NE of Ruse; sugar beets, sunflowers, vineyards.

Ryan. **1** Town (pop. 362), Delaware co., E Iowa, 28 mi. NNE of Cedar Rapids, in livestock area. **2** City (pop. 1,019), Jefferson co., S Okla., 30 mi. ENE of Wichita Falls (Texas), and on Beaver Creek near its mouth on Red R., in agr. area (cotton, grain, corn); cotton ginning. Oil wells. Founded 1892.

Ryan, Loch (lŏkh rī'ŭn), narrow, sheltered inlet of Irish Sea, W Wigtown, Scotland, washing NE shore of the Rhinns of Galloway; extends 9 mi. N–S from S entrance of Firth of Clyde and is c.1½ mi. wide. At S end is seaport of Stranraer. It figures in Scottish literature as Lochryan.

Ryan Peak, Idaho: see PIONEER MOUNTAINS.

Ryans Slough (slōō), village (pop. 1,727), Humboldt co., NW Calif.

Ryapina, Estonia: see RAPINA.

Ryazan or **Ryazan'** (ryŭzän'yŭ), oblast (□ 18,200; 1946 pop. estimate 2,100,000) in central European Russian SFSR; ⊙ Ryazan. In Oka-Don river lowland; includes forested, swampy Meshchera region (N of Oka R.) and black-earth wooded steppe (S). Lumbering, peat working (N), dairy farming (along Oka R.), and agr. (S) are chief economic activities. Easternmost part of Moscow lignite basin reaches area of Skopin. Basic crops: wheat, rye, oats (S), potatoes (N); sugar beets, rubber-bearing plants, tobacco (S), hemp (E) also raised; poultry farms, apiaries. Industry (flour milling, distilling, starch, molasses) based on agr.; sawmilling (N); machine mfg. (Ryazan). Trade oriented toward Moscow. Formed 1937 out of Moscow oblast.

Ryazan or **Ryazan'**, city (1939 pop. 95,358), ⊙ Ryazan oblast, Russian SFSR, near Oka R., 115 mi. SE of Moscow; 54°38'N 39°45'E. Industrial and agr. center; mfg. (agr. machines, cash registers, light bulbs, shoes, clothing); agr. industries include flour milling, fruit canning, distilling; tanning, woodworking. Site of castle of Prince Oleg, former seat of archbishop, now one of best regional museums of USSR; kremlin wall (erected 1208) surrounds former monasteries of 15th and 17th cent. Teachers and agr. colleges. Ryazan was originally founded (1095) 30 mi. SE, near SPASSK-RYAZANSKI. Old Ryazan was destroyed (1237) by Tatars, and seat of Ryazan principality was moved to present site, then called Pereyaslavl-Ryazanski. Principality annexed (1520) to Moscow. City renamed Ryazan and reconstructed (1778). Scene of pogroms (1905). Was ⊙ Ryazan govt. until 1929.

Ryazanskaya (–skīŭ), village (1926 pop. 6,512), central Krasnodar Territory, Russian SFSR, 30 mi. E of Krasnodar; flour mill, metalworks; wheat, sunflowers, tobacco.

Ryazantsevo (–tsyĭvŭ), village (1926 pop. 162), SE Yaroslavl oblast, Russian SFSR, 13 mi. ESE of Pereslavl-Zalesski; wheat.

Ryazhsk (ryäsh-sk), city (1938 pop. c.20,000), SW central Ryazan oblast, Russian SFSR, 65 mi. SSE of Ryazan; rail junction (Novo-RYAZHSK); agr. center (flour, tobacco, fruit). Chartered 1502.

Rybachi or **Rybachiy** (rĭbä'chē), town (1939 pop. 691), N Kaliningrad oblast, Russian SFSR, fishing port and summer resort on lagoon side of Courland Spit, 20 mi. NE of Zelenogradsk. Glider school established here, 1924. Bird sanctuary. Until 1945, in East Prussia and called Rossitten (rŏsĭt'tŭn).

Rybachi Peninsula or **Rybachiy Peninsula** [Rus.,= fisherman], at NW end of Kola Peninsula, Russian SFSR, bet. Barents Sea and Motovka Gulf; 35 mi. long, 15 mi. wide; connected with mainland by 1-mi.-wide isthmus. Main fishing settlements are Tsyp-Navolok (NE) and Vaida-Guba, Finnish *Vaitolahti* (NW). W coast belonged (1920–40) to Finland.

Rybachye or **Rybach'ye** (–chyĭ), town (1945 pop. estimate 5,000), NW Issyk-Kul oblast, Kirghiz SSR, port at W end of Issyk-Kul (lake), 80 mi. ESE of Frunze (linked by road and railroad) in arid, windy location. Major transportation center at junction of rail, highway, and steamer routes; grain elevator, oil tanks; meat packing; fisheries.

Rybare (rĭ'bärzhĕ), Czech *Rybáře*, town (pop. 4,264), W Bohemia, Czechoslovakia, 31 mi. NW of Pilsen, in urban area of Carlsbad; large porcelain factories.

Rybatskoye (rĭbät'skŭyŭ), town (1939 pop. over 2,000), central Leningrad oblast, Russian SFSR, on Neva R. and 10 mi. SE of Leningrad; sawmilling center; lumber port.

Rybinsk, city, Russian SFSR: see SHCHERBAKOV.

Rybinskoye (rĭ'bĭnskŭyŭ), village (1948 pop. over 500), SE Krasnoyarsk Territory, Russian SFSR, 45 mi. SW of Kansk, in lignite-mining region.

Rybinsk Reservoir (rĭ'bĭnsk), Rus. *Rybinskoye Vodokhranilishche*, largest (□ 1,800) artificial lake of USSR, in N central European Russian SFSR, on upper Volga R., in Yaroslavl, Vologda, and Kalinin oblasts; 80 mi. long N–S (bet. its major ports, Cherepovets and Shcherbakov), 35 mi. wide; fisheries. Formed (1941) bet. Volga R. and its left affluents, the Mologa and Sheksna, with completion of dam and hydroelectric station at Shcherbakov. Filling of reservoir flooded low alluvial plain, including Mologa city. Receives Sheksna R. (N; part of Mariinsk canal system) and Mologa R. (NW; part of Tikhvin canal system). Also called Rybinsk Sea, Rus. *Rybinskoye More*.

Rybkino (rĭp'kēnŭ), village (1948 pop. over 2,000), S Mordvinian Autonomous SSR, Russian SFSR, on Moksha R. and 13 mi. S of Krasnoslobodsk; grain, hemp, potatoes. Phosphorite deposits near.

Rybnaya Sloboda (rĭb'nīŭ slŭbŭdä'), village (1948 pop. over 2,000), central Tatar Autonomous SSR, Russian SFSR, port on Kama R. and 45 mi. ESE of Kazan; handicrafts (silver jewelry).

Rybnik (rĭb'nēk), city (pop. 23,052), Katowice prov., S Poland, 23 mi. WSW of Katowice. Rail junction; industrial center; mfg. of machinery, bricks, furniture; flour milling, brewing, sawmilling, tanning; coal mining. Salt deposits near by. Has cloister. Originally a fish (carp) hatchery, established c.1100; passed from Germany to Poland in 1921.

Rybnitsa (rĭb'nyĭtsŭ), city (1926 pop. 9,371), E Moldavian SSR, on left bank of Dniester R., opposite Rezina, on railroad and 50 mi. NNE of Kishinev; cement and sugar-milling center; limestone works; dairying, fruit canning, flour milling.

Rybnovsk (rĭb'nŭfsk), village (1948 pop. over 2,000), N Sakhalin, Russian SFSR, on Tatar Strait, 50 mi. WSW of Okha; fisheries.

Rybnoye (–nŭyŭ), town (1926 pop. 1,561), NW Ryazan oblast, Russian SFSR, 11 mi. NW of Ryazan; flour mill; truck produce.

Ryburg or **Riburg** (both: rē'bŏŏrk), hamlet, Aargau canton, N Switzerland, near the Rhine, 11 mi. E of Basel; salt mining. Ryburg-Schwörstadt hydroelectric plant here.

Rychlebske Hory, Czechoslovakia: see REICHENSTEIN MOUNTAINS.

Rychnov (rĭkh'nôf), Ger. *Reichenau* or *Reichenau bei Gablonz* (rī'khŭnou bī gä'blônts), village (pop. 1,848), N Bohemia, Czechoslovakia, on railroad and 7 mi. SSE of Liberec; glassmaking.

Rychnov nad Kneznou (nät' knyĕzhnō), Czech *Rychnov nad Kněžnou*, Ger. *Reichenau*, town (pop. 5,069), E Bohemia, Czechoslovakia, in foothills of the Adlergebirge, on railroad and 29 mi. ESE of Hradec Kralove; summer resort; textile mfg. Has 17th-cent. castle, 13th- and 16th-cent. churches.

Rychvald (rĭkh'vält), village (pop. 6,021), NE Silesia, Czechoslovakia, on railroad and 5 mi. NE of Ostrava; coal- and iron-mining center.

Rychwal (rĭkh'väō), Pol. *Rychwał*, Rus. *Rykhval* (rĭkh'vŭl), town (pop. 1,563), Poznan prov., W central Poland, 10 mi. SSW of Konin; flour milling.

Rychwald, Poland: see BOGATYNIA.

Ryckevorsel, Belgium: see RIJKEVORSEL.

Rycon Mine, Northwest Territories: see YELLOWKNIFE.

Rycroft (rī'krŏft), village (pop. 272), W Alta., near B.C. border, 40 mi. N of Grande Prairie; tanning, lumbering, mixed farming, wheat.

Rydalmere, Australia: see ERMINGTON AND RYDALMERE.

Rydal Mount (rī'dŭl), locality in W Westmorland, England, just NW of Ambleside, on the small lake of Rydal Water and within parish (pop. 503) of Rydal and Loughrigg. Residence of Wordsworth from 1817 until his death in 1850.

Ryd (rüd), village (pop. 742), Kronoberg co., S Sweden, on Morrum R. and 22 mi. NNW of Karlshamn; health resort with mineral springs; glass mfg.

Ryde (rīd), municipality (pop. 36,418), E New South Wales, Australia, on N shore of Parramatta R. and 8 mi. WNW of Sydney, in metropolitan area; shipyards, brickyards, potteries.

Ryde, municipal borough (1931 pop. 10,520; 1951 census 20,084), on N coast of Isle of Wight, Hampshire, England, on the Spithead, 6 mi. SW of Portsmouth; seaside resort; beaches, pier. Scene of annual regatta. Near by is a Cistercian abbey founded 1131. Includes (since 1932) St. Helens-town.

Ryder, village (pop. 330), Ward co., central N.Dak., 28 mi. SW of Minot; dairy products, wheat, flax, barley.

Rydzyna (rĭdzĭ'nä), Ger. *Reisen* (rī'zŭn), town (pop. 1,727), Poznan prov., W Poland, 6 mi. SE of Leszno; cattle trade. Old castle.

Rye or **Ry** (rü), town (pop. 1,389), Skanderborg amt, E Jutland, Denmark, 7 mi. NW of Skanderborg; wood products.

Rye (rī), municipal borough (1931 pop. 3,947; 1951 census 4,511), E Sussex, England, on Rother R., 2 mi. from its mouth on a small bay of the Channel, and 10 mi. NE of Hastings; agr. market and fishing port; tourist resort, frequented by artists. It is one of the "ancient towns" added to the CINQUE PORTS under Henry III. Until the sea receded in early 19th cent. it was an important trade center and a smugglers' hideout. Has medieval church, Ypres Tower (c.1160), remains of anc. Augustinian friary, and school (1636; scene of Thackeray's *Denis Duval*). John Fletcher b. here. For some years Henry James lived in Rye.

Rye. **1** Town (pop. 166), Pueblo co., S Colo., just E of Wet Mts., 30 mi. SW of Pueblo; alt. 6,725 ft. Farming town and resort. **2** Resort town (pop. 1,982), Rockingham co., SE N.H., on coast S of Portsmouth; includes villages of Rye, Rye Beach (seat of Atlantic Air Acad. for boys), Rye North Beach. First settled (1623) at Odiorne's Point by David Thomson; earliest settlement in N.H. Set off from New Castle 1726. **3** City (pop. 11,721), Westchester co., SE N.Y., on N shore of Long Island Sound, just SW of Port Chester; residential suburb, in New York city metropolitan area. Boatbuilding; yachting. Rye Beach is bathing and amusement resort. Settled 1660; inc. as village in 1904, as city in 1942.

Ryegate. **1** Town (pop. 339), ⊙ Golden Valley co., S central Mont., on Musselshell R. and 50 mi. NW of Billings; livestock, dairy and poultry products, grain, turkeys. **2** Town (pop. 996), Caledonia co., NE Vt., on the Connecticut and 20 mi. E of Barre; granite, paper. Includes villages of South Ryegate (1940 pop. 346) and East Ryegate (paper milling, winter sports). Chartered 1763, settled 1773.

Ryen, Netherlands: see RIJEN.

Rye Patch Dam, Nev.: see HUMBOLDT RIVER.

Ryes (rē), village (pop. 283), Calvados dept., NW France, near Channel coast, 4 mi. NE of Bayeux.

In Second World War, occupied (June 6, 1944) by Br. troops in Normandy invasion.

Ryfylke (rü'fülkü), mountainous region in NE Rogaland co., SW Norway, indented by NE and E branches of Bokn Fjord; rises to 5,000 ft. (NE). It borders E on Ruven and Bykle mts. Fishing, lumbering. Has well-developed hydroelectric plants. Tourist traffic and winter sports centered in the Brattlandsdal. Chief villages: Sand, Suldalsosen, Sauda.

Rygene, Norway: see RYKENE.

Rygnestad (rüng'nüstä), village in Valle canton, Aust-Agder co., S Norway, on Otra R. and 75 mi. N of Kristiansand.

Ryhope (rī'ŭp), town and parish (pop. 9,856), NE Durham, England, on coast 3 mi. S of Sunderland; coal mining.

Rykene (rük'nü), village (pop. 229) in Oyestad (Nor. *Øyestad*, formerly *Øjestad*) canton (pop. 4,559), Aust-Agder co., S Norway, 6 mi. SW of Arendal; wood-pulp factory. Hydroelectric station at waterfall on Nid R., 1 mi. W. Also spelled Rygene.

Rykhval, Poland: see RYCHWAL.

Rykovo, Ukrainian SSR: see YENAKIYEVO.

Rykovskoye, Russian SFSR: see KIROVSKOYE, Sakhalin oblast.

Ryley, village (pop. 338), central Alta., near Beaverhill L., 25 mi. NE of Camrose; rail junction; coal mining, mixed farming, dairying.

Ryllshyttan, Sweden: see DALA-FYNNHYTTAN.

Rylsk or **Ryl'sk** (rĭlsk), city (1926 pop. 11,011), W Kursk oblast, Russian SFSR, on Seim R. and 65 mi. WSW of Kursk; flour milling, meat packing, distilling, sugar refining. Chalk quarries near by. Dates from 9th cent.; chartered 1152; became ⊙ principality (12th–13th cent.); passed 1503 to Moscow.

Rylstone (rĭl'stōn), village (pop. 740), E central New South Wales, Australia, 105 mi. NW of Sydney; coal-mining center; marble.

Rymanow (rĭmä'nōōf), Pol. *Rymanów*, town (pop. 2,407), Rzeszow prov., SE Poland, 32 mi. S of Rzeszow; health resort with hot baths; mfg. of photographic articles. Petroleum wells near by. In Second World War, under Ger. rule, called Reimannshau.

Rymarov (rē'märzhôf), Czech *Rýmařov*, Ger. *Römerstadt* (rû'mŭrshtät), town (pop. 4,230), N Moravia, Czechoslovakia, in the Jeseniky, on Moravice R. and 23 mi. N of Olomouc, in fertile agr. area (barley, wheat, oats); rail terminus; major lead works; textile mfg. (silk, cotton, linen); production of liqueurs. The 14th-cent. castle of Sovinec, several times unsuccessfully besieged by Swedes, is 6 mi. S.

Ryn (rĭn), Ger. *Rhein* (rīn), town (1939 pop. 2,429; 1946 pop. 642) in East Prussia, after 1945 in Olsztyn prov., NE Poland, in Masurian Lakes region, on L. Ryn, 12 mi. SE of Ketrzyn; grain and cattle market.

Ryn, Lake (rĭn), Pol. *Jezioro Ryńskie* (yĕ-zhô'rô rĭ'nyŭskyĕ), Ger. *Rhein* (rīn) (□ 8), in East Prussia, after 1945 in NE Poland, S of Ryn; one of Masurian Lakes; 12 mi. long; drains S into L. Sniardwy.

Rynsburg, Netherlands: see RIJNSBURG.

Ryojun, Manchuria: see PORT ARTHUR.

Ryotsu (rēō'tsōō) or **Ryozu** (rēō'zōō), town (pop. 8,892) on E Sado Isl., Niigata prefecture, Japan, on Sea of Japan, 40 mi. WNW of Niigata, off N Honshu; fishing center. Winter outer port for Niigata; exports oil, charcoal, lumber. Formerly called Ebisu (also spelled Yebisu).

Rypin (rĭ'pēn), town (pop. 7,350), Bydgoszcz prov., N central Poland, 33 mi. E of Torun; rail junction; mfg. (cement, ceramic products, caps), flour and groat milling. During Second World War, under Ger. rule, called Rippin.

Rysen, Netherlands: see RIJSSEN.

Rysenburg, Netherlands: see RIJSENBURG.

Ryshkany (rĭshkä'nē), Rum. *Râşcani* (rûshkän'), town (1941 pop. 1,239), N Moldavian SSR, 20 mi. NW of Beltsy; agr. market; corn, wheat, sugar beets.

Ryssel, France: see LILLE.

Ryssen, Netherlands: see RIJSSEN.

Ryswick, Netherlands: see RIJSWIJK.

Rysy (rĭ'sĭ), peak (8,212 ft.) in the High Tatra, on Pol.-Czechoslovak border, 10 mi. SE of Zakopane, Poland; highest peak in Poland.

Ryton (rī'tŭn), urban district (1931 pop. 14,204; 1951 census 13,779), N Durham, England, on Tyne R. and 6 mi. W of Newcastle-upon-Tyne; coal-mining center, with iron foundries.

Ryton-on-Dunsmore, town and parish (pop. 697), central Warwick, England, on Avon R. and 4 mi. SE of Coventry; automobile factory.

Ryugampo, Korea: see YONGAMPO.

Ryugasaki (rūgä'-sä'kē), town (pop. 14,206), Ibaraki prefecture, central Honshu, Japan, 21 mi. NNE of Chiba, in rice-growing area; market town; also mfg. (textiles, noodles).

Ryuge (rū'gā), town (pop. 20,634), Osaka prefecture, S Honshu, Japan, just SE of Osaka, in agr. area (rice, wheat, market produce); poultry.

Ryujin (rū'jēn), village (pop. 1,930), Wakayama prefecture, S Honshu, Japan, on S central Kii Peninsula, 19 mi. NNE of Tanabe; hot-springs resort; lumbering.

Ryukyu Islands (rū'kū), Jap. *Ryukyu-retto* or *Nansei-shoto* [=southwest group], archipelago (□ 1,803; 1950 pop. 917,400), between Formosa and Kyushu; form 650-mi. chain separating E.China Sea (W) from Philippine Sea (E). Comprise 3 groups: AMAMI-GUNTO (N), OKINAWA ISLANDS (central), SAKISHIMA ISLANDS (S). Larger isls. are volcanic and mountainous, smaller are coralline and relatively flat. Climate is semi-tropical; mean annual temp. 70°F., rainfall 84 in.; frequent typhoons. Fauna: poisonous snakes, wild boars, deer, black rabbits. S isls. have camphor, banyan, and banana trees; Jap. cedars and pines on N isls. Principal agr. products are sugar cane and sweet potatoes. Produce Panama hats and textiles. Inhabitants are said to be related to the Ainus, and speak a language very different from standard Japanese. An independent kingdom in anc. times, the group was first invaded in 7th cent. by Chinese, who began exacting tribute in 14th cent. After invasion (17th cent.) led by Jap. prince of Satsuma, kingdom paid tribute to both China and Japan. China relinquished her claims in a treaty (1874) with Japan; group was inc. 1879 in Jap. empire. OKINAWA isl. was the scene (1945) of a crucial battle of Second World War. After the war, Amami-gunto (formerly part of Kagoshima prefecture) and Okinawa and Sakishima Isls. (formerly constituting Okinawa prefecture) were placed (Aug., 1945) under U.S. military governor with hq. at Naha on Okinawa; in 1951 a native civil govt. was installed. Formerly sometimes spelled Liukiu, Liu-ch'iu, Lu-chu, Loo-choo, and Riukiu.

Ryutan, Formosa: see LUNGTAN.

Ryvingen (rü'vĭngün), small island in the Skagerrak, Vest-Agder co., S Norway, 4 mi. SSE of Mandal; lighthouse.

Rzeczyca, Poland: see RECZ.

Rzepin (zhĕ'pēn), Ger. *Reppen* (rĕ'pün), town (1939 pop. 6,442; 1946 pop. 1,543) in Brandenburg, after 1945 in Zielona Gora prov., W Poland, 8 mi. E of Frankfurt, near E Germany border. Frontier station on main Berlin-Warsaw line; rail junction; metal- and woodworking, distilling, printing. Founded c.1330. In Second World War, c.85% destroyed.

Rzeszow (zhĕ'shōōf), Pol. *Rzeszów*, province [Pol. *województwo*] (□ 7,210; pop. 1,535,400), SE Poland; ⊙ Rzeszow. Borders E on USSR, S on Czechoslovakia. Slopes from the W Beskids (S) toward Vistula valley; drained by Vistula, San, and Wislok rivers. S part of prov. is rich in oil; gas pipe lines link Krosno and Jaslo oil fields with other Pol. industrial centers. Lumbering, metalworking, textile milling, chemicals mfg. are leading industries. Chief crops are rye, oats, potatoes, wheat, flax, hemp; livestock. Principal cities: Przemysl, Rzeszow, Jaroslaw, Krosno. Prov. created 1945; includes part of pre-Second World War Krakow prov. and W part of former Lwow (Lvov) prov. (E part transferred to USSR). Before First World War, territory formed part of Austro-Hungarian Galicia. In 1951 the prov. acquired Ustrzyki Dolne area (□ 185) from Ukrainian SSR.

Rzeszow, Pol. *Rzeszów*, city (pop. 29,407), ⊙ Rzeszow prov., SE Poland, on Wislok R. and 90 mi. E of Cracow. Rail junction; mfg. of aircraft engines, agr. machinery, cement products; sawmilling; brickworks, foundries. Manganese ore deposits, insulator mfg. in vicinity. Passed 1772 to Austria; returned 1919 to Poland. In Second World War, under Ger. rule, called Reichshof.

Rzhaksa (ŭrzhäk'sŭ), village (1939 pop. over 2,000), SE Tambov oblast, Russian SFSR, 45 mi. SE of Tambov; metalworks.

Rzhava, Russian SFSR: see MARINO, Kursk oblast.

Rzhev (ŭrzhĕf'), city (1939 pop. 54,081), SW Kalinin oblast, Russian SFSR, on Volga R. and 70 mi. SW of Kalinin; rail junction; hemp spinning, oil pressing, distilling, mfg. (agr. machines, cardboard), sawmilling, woodworking. Mus. of natural history and of archaeology. Dates from 1216; became trading point on Novgorod-Kiev route. Passed (early 15th cent.) to Moscow. Center of Old Believers in 18th cent. During Second World War, held (1941–43) by Germans.

Rzhishchev (ŭrzhē'shchĭf), town (1926 pop. 8,535), E central Kiev oblast, Ukrainian SSR, on Dnieper R. (landing) and 40 mi. SE of Kiev; metalworking, food processing.

S

Saa (sä), village, Nyong et Sanaga region, central Fr. Cameroons, 40 mi. NNW of Yaoundé, in palm region.

Saada, Yemen: see SADA.

Saadabad or **Sa'adabad** (sä-äd"äbäd'), royal summer residence of Iran, 9 mi. N of Teheran, just S of Darband, at S foot of Elburz mts. The 1937 pact bet. Iran, Afghanistan, Turkey, and Iraq was signed here.

Saal (zäl), village (pop. 3,180), Lower Bavaria, Germany, on the Danube and 3 mi. SE of Kelheim; carbide mfg. Limestone quarrying in area.

Saalach (zä'läkh), river, W Austria and S Germany; rises in the Gaisstein of Kitzbühel Alps; flows E and N, through Salzburg, Austria, and across part of Bavaria, Germany, to the river Salzach 3.5 mi. NNW of Salzburg. Length, 60 mi.

Saalbach (zäl'bäkh), village (pop. 1,287), Salzburg, W central Austria, on river Saalach and 12 mi. ESE of Kitzbühel; winter sports resort (alt. 3,290 ft.).

Saalbach, river in N Baden, Germany, rises just NE of Maulbronn, flows 30 mi. NW, past Bruchsal, to an arm of the Rhine at Philippsburg.

Saalburg (zäl'bōōrk), town (pop. 1,246), Thuringia, central Germany, on reservoir of Bleilochsperre dam, 7 mi. SW of Schleiz, in fruitgrowing region; climatic health resort. Has remains of medieval town walls, 16th-cent. town gate. Towered over by 13th-cent. church.

Saale, Germany: see SAALE RIVER.

Saaler Bodden, Germany: see DARSS.

Saale River (zä'lü). **1** or **Franconian Saale** (frăngkō'nēŭn), Ger. *Fränkische Saale* (frĕng'kĭ-shü), river in W Germany, rises on Bavarian-Thuringian border, flows 84 mi. W, S, and SW, past Bad Neustadt and Bad Kissingen, to the Main at Gemünden. **2** or **Saxonian Saale** (săksō'nēŭn), Ger. *Sächsische Saale* (zĕk'sĭ-shü), central Germany, rises in the Fichtelgebirge, flows in picturesque course 265 mi. generally N, past Hof, Saalfeld, Rudolstadt, Jena, Naumburg (head of navigation), Weissenfels, Merseburg, Halle, Bernburg, and Nienburg, to the Elbe 18 mi. SE of Magdeburg. Chief tributaries: the White Elster (right); Ilm, Unstrut, and Bode rivers (left). Major dams (with large reservoirs) are the Bleilochsperre and the Hohenwartetalsperre. Called Thuringian Saale (thyōōrĭn'jün), Ger. *Thüringer Saale* (tü'rĭng-ür), in Thuringia.

Saales (säl), village (pop. 767), Bas-Rhin dept., E France, near crest of central Vosges Mts., 8 mi. NE of Saint-Dié, on Saint-Dié–Molsheim RR, at head of Bruche R. valley; resort. Saales pass (alt. 1,821 ft.) is 1 mi. W.

Saaletalsperre, Germany: see BLEILOCHSPERRE.

Saalfeld (zäl'fĕlt), town (pop. 26,387), Thuringia, central Germany, on NE slope of Thuringian Forest, on the Thuringian Saale and 25 mi. S of Weimar, in iron-mining and slate-quarrying region; rail junction; mfg. of machine tools, electrical equipment, dyes, paper, chocolate; textile milling, metal- and woodworking, tanning. Power station. Has 14th-cent. church; 16th-cent. town hall; mus., housed in former Franciscan monastery (13th cent.); Hoher Schwarm castle, built after 1280. Was ⊙ duchy of Saxe-Saalfeld, 1680–1735. Passed to duchy of Saxe-Meiningen in 1826. Silver-mining center in 16th cent.

Saalfelden or **Saalfelden am Steinernen Meer** (zäl'fĕldün äm shtīn'ŭrnŭn mār'), town (pop. 7,954), Salzburg, W central Austria, at W foot of Steinernes Meer, in Salzburg Alps, 28 mi. SSW of Salzburg; leather goods, brewery; resort.

Saanen (zä'nün), Fr. *Gessenay* (zhĕsnā'), town (pop. 4,650), Bern canton, SW central Switzerland, on Saane R. and 17 mi. ENE of Montreux; cheeses, cotton textiles. Medieval church.

Saane River (zä'nü) or **Sarine River** (särēn'), W Switzerland, rises near the Diablerets, flows 80 mi. N, past Fribourg, to the Aar 9 mi. W of Bern. Hauterive and Oelberg hydroelectric plants are on the river.

Saanich Inlet (să'nĭch), SW B.C., arm of Strait of Georgia, SE Vancouver Isl., 10 mi. NW of Victoria. Entered from Stuart Channel.

Saar, Czechoslovakia: see ZDAR.

Saar (zär) or **Saar Territory**, Fr. *Sarre* (sär), territory (1948 □ 988; 1946 pop. 851,615; 1948 pop. 904,040), bet. France (W, SW) and Germany (SE, E, N); ⊙ Saarbrücken. A region of low, partly wooded hills, it is drained by Saar R. and some small tributaries, including Blies, Prims, Sulz, and Rossel rivers. Its great importance lies in vast coal resources, on which important iron and steel industry is based. Iron ore is imported from Lorraine. Other major industries are the mfg. of glass, ceramics, pottery. Agr. is on small scale (stock, grain, potatoes); production does not cover local food requirements. Some viticulture near Perl (NW). There is an extensive rail network; Saar R. is canalized bet. Völklingen and Sarreguemines, whence Sarre Coal Canal connects it with Rhine-Rhône Canal. Chief cities are Neunkirchen, Saarlouis, Homburg, Völklingen, Dillingen, St. Ingbert, St. Wendel, Dudweiler, Sulzbach, and Merzig. Saar territory possessed little historic unity before 20th cent. Until ceded (1797) to France, it was divided among Palatine duchy of Saar-Zweibrücken, county of Saarbrücken, and France, which held Saarlouis and adjacent region. Under Treaty of Paris (1815), SE part of Saar passed to Bavaria (i.e., Rhenish or Bavarian Palatinate), the remainder to Prussia. By Treaty of Versailles (1919), autonomous Saar Territory was created, to be administered by France under League of Nations supervision, pending plebiscite as to future status. In the plebiscite (1935), pop. voted for return to Germany, where it was organized as Saarland prov. Toward close of Second World War, the Saar was scene of heavy land fighting; greater part of pop. had been evacuated in 1944. Taken by U.S. troops (winter, 1944–spring, 1945); came under Fr. military govt. in July, 1945. Referendum (Oct., 1947) favored economic union with France; on Jan. 1, 1948, customs union with France was completed. Has autonomous govt. under Fr. high commissioner. Several border adjustments were made bet. Germany and the Saar (1946–47).

Saaralben, France: see SARRALBE.

Saarbrücken (zär″brü′kŭn), Fr. *Sarrebruck* (särübrük′), city (pop. 89,700), ⊙ Saar, in S part of territory, on Saar R., at mouth of Sulz R., and 100 mi. SW of Frankfurt; 49°14′N 7°W. Rail center and frontier station opposite Forbach, France; industrial center in major coal-mining region. Railroad shops; mfg. of steel products, machinery, clothing, paper, soap, salt, candy, flour products, cigarettes; breweries. Among noted features are Old Bridge (16th cent.; later rebuilt), Castle Church (15th cent.), town hall (1750), baroque Ludwigskirche (1762–75). Sections (inc. into city in 1909) include Malstatt-Burbach (NW), Sankt Johann (SE) with remains of Roman castle, and Sankt Arnual (E) with airport. In Roman times a Saar crossing, later site of castle of Frankish kings, city was chartered 1321; was capital of counts of Nassau-Saarbrücken from 1381 until occupied by French in 1793, except for Fr. interregnum of 1648–97. In Napoleonic era it was armaments center, on Napoleon's road from Paris to Mainz. Passed to Prussia in 1815. Became ⊙ Saar in 1919. During Second World War, city was shelled (1939) and later heavily bombed. Captured by U.S. troops in March, 1945, after heavy fighting in adjacent Siegfried Line sector.

Saarburg, France: see SARREBOURG.

Saarburg (zär′bo͝ork), town (pop. 3,928), in former Prussian Rhine Prov., W Germany, after 1945 in Rhineland-Palatinate, on the Saar and 10 mi. SW of Trier, 6 mi. E of Luxembourg line. Has ruined former castle of electors of Trier. Was temporarily (1946–47) in the Saar.

Saare (sä′rā), **Saaremaa,** or **Sarema** (both: sä′rĕmä), Rus. *Ezel* (ā′zĕl), Swedish *Ösel* (û′zŭl), largest island (□ 1,046; pop. c.50,000) of Estonia, in Baltic Sea, across entrance to Gulf of Riga, S of Hiiumaa isl. (separated by Soela Sound), 13 mi. off Estonian mainland. Irregular in shape; 55 mi. long, 25 mi. wide; terminates (SW) in 20-mi.-long Sorve Peninsula (separated by Irbe Strait from Latvia). Level terrain; sandy glacial soils on limestone base (tuff quarries). Dairy farming, hogs, sheep; small grain, potatoes; fishing. Connected by 3-mi. causeway with Muhu isl. (NE). Kuressaare, on S coast, is main town and port; also a health resort (mud baths). Isl. passed from Livonian Knights to Denmark in 1560, to Sweden in 1645; occupied (1710) by Russia.

Saargemünd, France: see SARREGUEMINES.

Saarijärvi (sä′rĭyăr″vē), village (commune pop. 11,517), Vaasa co., S central Finland, in lake region, 35 mi. NNW of Jyväskylä; road center; tourist resort. In lumbering region. Residence (1823–25), of Finnish natl. poet Runeberg.

Saar in Mähren, Czechoslovakia: see ZDAR.

Saarlouis (zär″lo͞o′ē), Fr. *Sarrelouis* (särŭlwē′), city (pop. 26,088), W Saar, near Fr. border, on Saar R. and 12 mi. NW of Saarbrücken; steel industry; woodworking, tobacco processing, brewing; mfg. of ceramics, glass, paper products, chemicals. Electric power station. Situated in coal-mining region. Founded 1680 by French, named Sarrelouis for Louis XIV. Major fortress built (1680–85) by Vauban. Town became ⊙ Fr. Sarre prov. after 1680. During French Revolution, it was for some time called *Sarrelibre*. In Napoleonic era, site of important arms works. Ceded to Prussia in 1815. During League of Nations administration, was seat of international court of justice for Saar Territory. Called Saarlautern (zär″lou′tŭrn), 1936–45. Marshal Ney b. here. Just NE is industrial suburb of Fraulautern.

Saar River (zär), Fr. *Sarre* (sär), in France, Saar, and Germany; rises in 2 headstreams near Le Donon summit of the Vosges, flows N through Moselle and Bas-Rhin depts. of NE France, past Sarrebourg, Sarre-Union, and Sarreguemines, where it enters the Saar; it flows along border bet. France and Saar to Saarbrücken, thence NW, past Völklingen, Saarlouis, and Merzig; it enters Germany 8 mi. SSE of Saarburg, flows N, past Saarburg, to Moselle R. at Konz, 5 mi. SW of Trier. Length 150 mi. Paralleled in France by a coal-shipping canal (Canal des Houillères de la Sarre); canalized and navigable bet. Sarreguemines and Völklingen. Receives Blies, Sulz, Rossel, Prims, Nied rivers.

Saar Territory: see SAAR.

Saarunion, France: see SARRE-UNION.

Saarwellingen (zär″vĕ′lĭng-ŭn), town (pop. 5,708), W Saar, 4 mi. NW of Saarlouis; explosives-mfg. center; woodworking.

Saastal (zäs′täl), valley of Saaservisp R. (a headstream of the Visp) in Valais canton, S Switzerland; resort area extending E of the Mischabelhörner to S of Visp. Main resort villages: Saas-Almagel (alt. 5,508 ft.), Saas-Fee (alt. 5,900 ft.), and Saas-Grund (alt. 5,124 ft.).

Saatly (sŭät′lē), town (1926 pop. 1,213), E Azerbaijan SSR, on Aras R. and 7 mi. SW of Sabirabad, on railroad; cotton gins, metalworks.

Saavedra, district, Argentina: see PIGÜÉ.

Saavedra (sävā′drä). **1** N residential section of Buenos Aires, Argentina. **2** Town (pop. 2,100), SW Buenos Aires prov., Argentina, at S foot of Sierra de Curumalán, 10 mi. SSE of Pigüé; grain, sheep, cattle; dairying.

Saavedra, Chile: see PUERTO SAAVEDRA.

Saaz, Czechoslovakia: see ZATEC.

Saba (sä′bä), islet (□ 5; 1948 pop. estimate 1,100), Du. West Indies, in NW Leeward Isls., belonging to Du. Antilles (formerly Curaçao territory), 16 mi. NW of St. Eustatius, 30 mi. NW of St. Kitts; 17°38′N 63°14′W. Principal settlement, Bottom. Actually a single volcanic cone (rising to 2,851 ft.), in whose extinct crater the people live. Contains steep cliffs, and has no sheltered anchorage. Considerable rainfall and luxuriant vegetation. While potatoes and yams are produced for local consumption, the male inhabitants are fishermen, known as boatbuilders; women make lacework for export. The isl. trades mostly through St. Thomas and St. Kitts. It was occupied by Dutch in 1st half of 17th cent. Though its relatively large proportion of white pop. is of Du. origin, English is spoken throughout.

Saba, Ukrainian SSR: see SHABO.

Saba, Yemen: see SHEBA.

Sabac or **Shabats** (both: shä′bäts), Serbo-Croatian *Šabac*, town (pop. 18,238), W Serbia, Yugoslavia, port on Sava R. and 40 mi. W of Belgrade. Rail terminus; trade center (plums, fish), fishing. Economic center of region bet. Sava and Drina rivers, including MACVA co.

Sabadell (sävädăl′), city (pop. 45,931), Barcelona prov., NE Spain, in Catalonia, 12 mi. NNW of Barcelona; a leading center of the textile industry (wool and cotton), dating from 13th cent. Mfg. includes knit goods, chemical fertilizers, dyes, textile machinery, precision tools, diesel engines, electrical equipment, transmission belts, leather goods, paper, soap, and liqueurs; sawmilling. Wheat- and winegrowing in area.

Sabae (säbä′ā), town (pop. 6,132), Fukui prefecture, central Honshu, Japan, 3 mi. NNE of Takebu; silk and rayon textiles, pottery; tea processing.

Sabak (sŭ′bäk′), village (pop. 1,608), NW Selangor, Malaya, on Bernam R. (Perak line) and 17 mi. S of Telok Anson; rice, coconuts.

Sabalan, Iran: see SAVALAN.

Sabalana Islands (sŭbŭlä′nŭ) or **Postillion Islands,** Du. *Postiljon*, group of islets, Indonesia, in Flores Sea, bet. SW peninsula of Celebes and Sumbawa; 6°51′S 118°40′E; largest isl. is Sabalana (2 mi. long). Coconut growing.

Sabalgarh (sŭbŭl′gŭr), town (pop. 4,824), NE Madhya Bharat, India, 47 mi. W of Lashkar; gram, millet; wood carving and lacquering. Forest lies S (big game preserve).

Sábana, La, Argentina: see LA SÁBANA.

Sabana Archipelago (säbä′nä), group of keys off Las Villas prov., N central Cuba, forming S fringe of Nicholas Channel; extend c.60 mi. WNW–ESE.

Sabana Arriba (ärē′bä), town (pop. 4,367), Táchira state, W Venezuela, suburb of San Cristóbal; coffeegrowing.

Sabana de la Mar (dā lä mär′), town (1950 pop. 2,780), Seibo prov., E Dominican Republic, port on S shore of Samaná Bay, 31 mi. NW of Seibo, in agr. region (coffee, cacao, fruit, cattle).

Sabana de Mendoza (mĕndō′sä), town (pop. 1,598), Trujillo state, W Venezuela, on La Ceiba–Valera RR and 23 mi. WNW of Trujillo; sugar-cane center.

Sabanagrande (–grän′dā), town (pop. 2,385), Atlántico dept., N Colombia, in Caribbean lowlands, on Magdalena R. and 13 mi. SSW of Barranquilla; cotton, corn, cattle; tanning.

Sabana Grande, town (1950 pop. 1,000), Trujillo prov., S Dominican Republic, on the coast, 20 mi. SW of Ciudad Trujillo, in agr. region (rice, coffee, fruit, sugar cane).

Sabanagrande, town (pop. 1,678), Francisco Morazán dept., S central Honduras, on road and 19 mi. SSW of Tegucigalpa; market center; dairying; sugar cane, rice, corn, beans. A gold- and silver-mining center in Sp. colonial times.

Sabanagrande, village, Managua dept., SW Nicaragua, on railroad and 8 mi. ESE of Managua, in livestock area; coffee, corn, beans.

Sabana Grande, village (pop. 280), Los Santos prov., S central Panama, in Pacific lowland, 7 mi. SE of Los Santos; bananas, sugar cane, livestock.

Sabana Grande, town (pop. 4,867), SW Puerto Rico, at foot of Cordillera Central, 15 mi. ESE of Mayagüez; rail terminus and processing center in sugar- and coffeegrowing region; mfg. of cigars, liquor, alcohol, needlework.

Sabana Grande. 1 City, Federal Dist., Venezuela: see EL RECREO. **2** Town (pop. 1,909), Trujillo state, W Venezuela, in Maracaibo lowlands, 25 mi. W of Trujillo; sugar cane, cattle.

Sabanalarga (–lär′gä). **1** Village (pop. 764), Antioquia dept., NW central Colombia, in Cauca valley, 20 mi. N of Antioquia; coffee, corn, beans, sugar cane, yucca, livestock. **2** Town (pop. 11,432), Atlántico dept., N Colombia, in Caribbean lowlands, 27 mi. SSW of Barranquilla; commercial and agr. center (cotton, corn, sugar cane, livestock); tanning.

Sabana Libre (säbä′nä lē′brā), town (pop. 831), Trujillo state, W Venezuela, in Andean spur, 3 mi. NW of Valera; coffee, sugar cane, corn.

Sabandía (säbändē′ä), town (pop. 869), Arequipa dept., S Peru, at S foot of El Misti volcano, 4 mi. SSE of Arequipa, in agr. region (alfalfa, potatoes, wheat, corn); resort, with thermal springs. Copper deposits near by.

Sabaneta (säbänā′tä), town (pop. 522), Barinas state, W Venezuela, in llanos, 21 mi. ENE of Barinas; cattle.

Sabaneta Larga (lär′gä), town (pop. 6,598), Zulia state, NW Venezuela, in Maracaibo lowlands, 31 mi. WNW of Maracaibo; oil wells.

Sabang (sŭbäng′), town (pop. 6,855) on E coast of We Isl., Indonesia, on Andaman Sea, 280 mi. NW of Medan; 5°54′N 95°19′E; free port and coaling station; important transit port for NW Sumatra. Has airport, radio station, lighthouse. In Second World War, Sabang was Jap. fuel-supply center.

Sabanilla (säbänē′yä) or **Juan Gualberto Gómez** (hwän′ gwälbĕr′tō gō′mĕs), town (pop. 1,944), Matanzas prov., W Cuba, on railroad and 13 mi. S of Matanzas; sugar cane, rice, beans, fruit. Sometimes Sabanilla del Encomendador.

Sabanilla, town (pop. 216), Chiapas, S Mexico, 16 mi. NE of Simojovel; fruit.

Sabanilla del Encomendador, Cuba: see SABANILLA.

Sabanozu (shäbä′nŭzü), Turkish *Şabanözü*, village (pop. 1,583), Cankiri prov., N central Turkey, 19 mi. WSW of Cankiri; grain, mohair goats.

Sabará (sŭbŭrä′), city (pop. 7,588), S central Minas Gerais, Brazil, on the Rio das Velhas and 8 mi. ENE of Belo Horizonte; important rail junction and metallurgical center (blast and open-hearth furnaces, steel-rolling mill, refractory-brick plant), using Itabira iron ore and charcoal. Serves as feeder for larger Monlevade steel mill (45 mi. E). Gold- and silverworking. Founded as a gold-mining center in 1711. Has fine churches (decorated by Aleijadinho), colonial houses with wrought-iron balconies, and cobblestone streets.

Sabaragamuwa Hill Country (sŭbŭrŭgä′mo͞ovŭ), S extension of Ceylon Hill Country, SW Ceylon; consists of parallel ridges extending c.50 mi. NW–SE; c.25 mi. wide. Highest point (4,465 ft.) is Gongala peak, in RAKWANA HILL COUNTRY. Contains precious and semi-precious stone and graphite mines, iron-ore deposits.

Sabaragamuwa Province, administrative division (□ 1,893; pop., including estate pop., 746,109), SW central Ceylon; ⊙ Ratnapura. E area is in Ceylon Hill Country; extension called Sabaragamuwa Hill Country in S; bounded E by the Walawe Ganga. Agr. (tea, rubber, rice, areca and coconut palms, vegetables, cardamom). Has major precious and semi-precious stone mines (centers at Ratnapura and Pelmadulla) of Ceylon; graphite mines near Kegalla, Ratnapura, Kendangomuwa; iron-ore deposits near Balangoda. Created 1889.

Sabari River (sä′bŭrē), mainly in SW Orissa and SE Madhya Pradesh, India, rises in N Eastern Ghats 30 mi. S of Jeypore, flows c.260 mi. NW and generally SSW, past Konta, to Godavari R. 25 mi. W of Bhadrachalam, on Hyderabad-Madras border. Receives Machkund R. (here called Sileru) opposite Konta. In upper course, called Kolab.

Sabar Kantha (sŭb′ŭr kän′tŭ), district, N Bombay, India; ⊙ Himatnagar. Bounded W by Sabarmati R., NE by S offshoots of Aravalli Range, S by Kaira dist. Agr. (cotton, millet, wheat, oilseeds, sugar cane); hand-loom weaving; sandstone, kaolin, and pottery-clay deposits worked. Main towns: Modasa, Himatnagar, Idar, Parantij. Formed 1949 by merger of several former Western India states, including Vijayanagar, most of Idar, and detached NE parts of Ahmadabad dist. **Sabar Kantha Agency** (□ 4,273; pop. 457,813), subdivision of Western India States agency, comprised princely states of Vav, Tharad, Thara, and numerous petty states; since 1949 inc. into Sabar Kantha and Banas Kantha dists.

Sabarmati (sä′bŭrmŭtē), village (pop. 7,703), Ahmadabad dist., N Bombay, India, on Sabarmati R. and 5 mi. N of Ahmadabad; rail junction; flour milling, cotton ginning.

Sabarmati River, in S Rajasthan and N Bombay, India, rises in several headstreams in S Aravalli Range, W of Udaipur; flows c.250 mi. S, across Gujarat plain, past Ahmadabad, to head of Gulf of Cambay 15 mi. W of Cambay.

Sabastiya, Palestine: see SAMARIA, city.

Sabathu (sŭbä'tōō), town (pop. 2,181), E Patiala and East Punjab States Union, India, cantonment 14 mi. SW of Simla; hand-loom weaving. Sometimes spelled Subathu.

Sabatia (säbätē'ä), village, Rift Valley prov., W Kenya, on railroad and 10 mi. SSE of Eldama Ravine; alt. 7,248 ft.; coffee, tea, wheat, corn. Views of Great Rift Valley (E).

Sabattus, Maine: see WEBSTER.

Sabaudia (säbou'dyä), village (pop. 659), Latina prov., Latium, S central Italy, in PONTINE MARSHES, on narrow coastal lagoon (Lago di Sabaudia; 4 mi. long), 12 mi. W of Terracina; wheat growing. Founded 1934.

Sabaya (säbī'ä), village (pop. c.2,500), Oruro dept., W Bolivia, in the Altiplano, on Sabaya R. (affluent of Salar de Coipasa) and 110 mi. SW of Oruro; alt. 12,365 ft.; potatoes, alpaca.

Sabaya, Serranía de (sĕrānē'ä dā), spur of Western Cordillera of the Andes, Oruro dept., W Bolivia; extends 30 mi. E from Isluga Volcano to Sabaya village; separates Sabaya R. (N) and Salar de Coipaza (S). Also called Tata Sabaya.

Sabazan (säbäzä'), village (pop. 56), Gers dept., SW France, 22 mi. NW of Mirande; Armagnac brandy mfg.

Sabbathday Lake, Maine: see NEW GLOUCESTER.

Sabbath Day Point, resort, Warren co., E N.Y., on W shore of L. George, 13 mi. S of Ticonderoga.

Sabbioncello, Yugoslavia: see OREBIC; PELJESAC.

Sabbioneta (säb-byōnä'tä), village (pop. 1,071), Mantova prov., Lombardy, N Italy, 18 mi. SW of Mantua; agr. center; mfg. (silk, furniture), tanning.

Sabden, residential village and parish (pop. 1,521), E Lancashire, England, 5 mi. NW of Burnley; textile printing, truck gardening.

Sabderat (säbdĕrät'), village (pop. 60), Agordat div., W Eritrea, on Anglo-Egyptian Sudan border, 17 mi. E of Kassala (road); customs station; date palms.

Sabero (sävā'rō), town (pop. 1,385), Leon prov., NW Spain, near Esla R., 28 mi. NE of Leon; cereals, vegetables, fruit; lumbering, stock raising. Coal mines and iron deposits near by.

Sabetha (sŭbē'thŭ), city (pop. 2,173), Nemaha co., NE Kansas, near Nebr. line, c.55 mi. N of Topeka; trading center for livestock and grain region; dairying. Small L. Sabetha, 5 mi. W, is used for water supply. Inc. 1874.

Sabie (sä'bē), village (pop. 2,140), E Transvaal, U. of So. Afr., on Sabie R. and 20 mi. E of Lydenburg; gold mining, lumbering, wattle growing. Gateway to Kruger Natl. Park.

Sabile (sä'bēlā), Ger. *Zabeln,* city (pop. 1,817), NW Latvia, in Kurzeme, 14 mi. S of Talsi; match mfg.

Sabillasville (sŭbĭ'lŭzvĭl), resort village, Frederick co., N Md., in the Blue Ridge near Pa. line, 20 mi. N of Frederick. Has state tuberculosis sanatorium. Near by are Catoctin Recreational Demonstration area (S) and U.S. Camp Ritchie (W), where the army began constructing underground installations in 1951.

Sabin, village (pop. 211), Clay co., W Minn., 10 mi. SE of Fargo, N.Dak., in Red R. valley; grain.

Sabina (sŭbī'nŭ), village (pop. 1,696), Clinton co., SW Ohio, 11 mi. ENE of Wilmington; trade center for farm area (corn, grain); makes tools, pumps, cement products, canned goods.

Sabinal (săb'ĭnăl'), town (pop. 1,974), Uvalde co., SW Texas, near Sabinal R., 21 mi. ENE of Uvalde; trade, shipping point in cattle, sheep, goat, and farm area; mohair, wool. Settled before 1870, inc. 1906.

Sabinal, Cayo (kī'ō säbēnäl'), coral island (25 mi. NW–SE, c.6 mi. wide) off NE Cuba, at entrance of Old Bahama Channel, SE of Cayo Guajaba, just N of Nuevitas, and linked with main isl. by tidal marshes. Charcoal burning.

Sabinal River (săb'ĭnăl'), S central Texas, rises in springs on Edwards Plateau, flows c.55 mi. generally S, through Sabinal Canyon and past Sabinal, to Frio R. 15 mi. NE of Batesville.

Sabiñánigo (sävēnyä'nēgō), village (commune pop. 1,768), Huesca prov., NE Spain, on Gállego R. and 10 mi. ESE of Jaca; aluminum processing (near-by bauxite mines); chemical works (ammonia, calcium carbide, potassium).

Sabinas (säbē'näs), town (pop. 6,825), Coahuila, N Mexico, 160 mi. NW of Monterrey, 23 mi. E of Múzquiz; rail junction and shipping center for rich coal-mining area; has coke ovens and other industries.

Sabinas Hidalgo (ēdäl'gō), town (pop. 6,912), Nuevo León, N Mexico, on Inter-American Highway and 60 mi. N of Monterrey; mining center (silver, lead, gold); cereals, cactus fibers, stock.

Sabinas River, Coahuila, N Mexico, rises on NE slopes of Sierra del Carmen, flows c.100 mi. SE, past San Juan de Sabinas and San Felipe, to Don Martín Dam 23 mi. NE of Progreso; from there usually called Río Salado, it flows to Rio Grande near Guerrero. Don Martín Dam irrigates large cotton-growing area in Coahuila and Nuevo León.

Sabine (săbēn'). **1** Parish (□ 1,029; pop. 20,880), W La.; ⊙ Many. Bounded W by Sabine R., here forming Texas line; drained by tributaries of the Sabine. Agr. (cotton, corn, hay, peanuts). Natural gas; oil fields; timber. Formed 1843. **2** County (□ 567; pop. 8,568), E Texas; ⊙ Hemphill. Bounded E by Sabine R. (here the La. line); most of co. is in Sabine Natl. Forest. Lumbering, lumber milling are chief industries; also agr. (cotton, corn, sweet potatoes, truck, fruit), livestock (cattle, hogs, poultry), dairying. Hunting, fishing. Formed 1836.

Sabine, village, Texas: see SABINE PASS, village.

Sabine, Cape (să'bĭn), E Ellesmere Isl., NE Franklin Dist., Northwest Territories, on Smith Sound; 78°43'N 74°20'W; 4 mi. NW is cave which was hq. of Greely expedition in 1884; 18 members of expedition died here.

Sabine, Mount (sā'bēn, -bīn), peak (9,859 ft.) of Admiralty Range, Victoria Land, Antarctica; 72°5'S 169°10'E. Discovered 1841 by Sir James C. Ross.

Sabine Crossroads, La.: see MANSFIELD.

Sabine Lake, Texas and La.: see SABINE RIVER.

Sabine Mountains (sŭbēn'), Ital. *Monti Sabini,* range of the Apennines, central Italy, bet. Turano R. (E) and the lower Tiber (W), NE of Rome; c.40 mi. long N–S. Chief peak, Monte Pellecchia (4,488 ft.)

Sabine-Neches Waterway (săbēn' nĕ'chĭs), SE Texas, system of deepwater channels leading N from Gulf of Mexico through Sabine Pass, thence through 2 land cuts on W side of shallow Sabine L.—Port Arthur Canal (c.7 mi. long) to Port Arthur, and Sabine-Neches Canal (c.12 mi. long) from Port Arthur to channels entering Sabine and Neches rivers at N end of lake. Sabine R. arm continues to Orange, connecting just below Orange with Lake Charles Canal to Lake Charles city, La. Neches R. arm extends to Beaumont, Texas. System tidal throughout; followed in part by Gulf Intracoastal Waterway. Section connecting Beaumont and Port Arthur sometimes called Beaumont–Port Arthur Canal.

Sabine Pass (săbēn'), village (1940 pop. 567), Jefferson co., SE Texas, 28 mi. SE of Beaumont; oil port on W shore of Sabine Pass (deepwater channel). On April 8, 1863, at near-by Sabine (now a port of entry), a small Confederate force repulsed a Federal invasion in battle of Sabine Pass; park, monument mark site.

Sabine Pass, waterway, La. and Texas: see SABINE RIVER.

Sabine River (săbēn'), in Texas and La., rises in NE Texas, flows SE to Logansport, La., whence it is the state line, then generally S, widening to form shallow Sabine L. (c.17 mi. long, 7 mi. wide) below Orange, Texas; enters Gulf of Mexico through Sabine Pass (c.7 mi. long), 15 mi. SSE of Port Arthur, Texas; length, 578 mi. Sabine L. receives Neches R. in NW. Deep-water channel from head of Sabine L. to Orange is an arm of SABINE-NECHES WATERWAY system to the Gulf, and is joined near its head by Lake Charles Canal to Lake Charles city, La.; followed by Gulf Intracoastal Waterway.

Sabinio, Mount (säbē'nyō, säbēnē'ō), extinct volcano (c.11,500 ft.), part of the Virunga range, in E central Africa, NE of L. Kivu and 17 mi. SSE of Rutshuru; 1°23'S 29°36'E. Its summit has been adopted by international treaties to mark junction of Belgian Congo, Ruanda-Urundi, and Uganda borders.

Sabino, Mexico: see EL SABINO.

Sabinópolis (sŭbēnô'pōōlēs), city (pop. 1,416), central Minas Gerais, Brazil, 40 mi. SE of Diamantina; semiprecious stones (especially tourmalines) found here.

Sabinosa (sävēnō'sä), village (pop. 229), Hierro, Canary Isls., 11 mi. SW of Valverde; fruitgrowing; cheese processing.

Sabinov (sä'bĭnôf), Hung. *Kisszeben* (kĭsh'sĕbĕn), town (pop. 3,909), NE Slovakia, Czechoslovakia, on Torysa R., on railroad and 10 mi. NW of Presov, in fruitgrowing area.

Sabiote (sävyō'tā), town (pop. 7,191), Jaén prov., S Spain, 6 mi. NE of Úbeda; olive-oil processing, footwear mfg. Stock raising; beans, wheat, wine.

Sabirabad (sŭbērŭbät'), city (1932 pop. estimate 2,480), E Azerbaijan SSR, on Kura R., at mouth of Aras R., and 75 mi. WSW of Baku; cotton-ginning center. Formerly Petropavlovka.

Sabi River (sä'bē), Port. *Save,* in SE Africa, rises 50 mi. S of Salisbury (Southern Rhodesia), flows SE and S to Mozambique border, then E to Mozambique Channel of Indian Ocean at Mambone. Length, c.400 mi.; navigable for light craft in lower 100 mi.

Sabkha or **Sabkhah** (săb'khŭ), village, Euphrates prov., N Syria, on right bank of Euphrates R. and 60 mi. NW of Deir ez Zor. Oil deposits near by.

Sable, Cape, S extremity of Nova Scotia, on an islet just S of CAPE SABLE ISLAND, from which it is separated by tidal flat, off SW N.S.; 43°23'N 65°37'W; lighthouse.

Sable, Cape, southernmost extremity of the U.S. mainland, in Monroe co., S Fla.; it is a swampy, mangrove-covered peninsula (c.20 mi. long, 5–10 mi. wide) bet. Florida (S) and Whitewater (N) bays. East Cape, its southernmost point, is at 25°7'N 81°5'W.

Sable Island (30 mi. long, 2 mi. wide), in the Atlantic off SE N.S., 110 mi. SSE of Canso; 43°56'–44°2'N 59°38'–60°8'W. It is the visible part of an extensive sand shoal, a major hazard to navigation. There are lighthouses at E and W extremities; latter has radio beacon. Causeway to mainland.

Sables-d'Olonne, Les (lā sä'blŭ-dôlôn'), town (pop. 17,013), Vendée dept., W France, port on Bay of Biscay, 21 mi. SW of La Roche-sur-Yon; noted bathing resort; sardine, anchovy, and tuna fishing and marketing center; boat building; oyster beds, saltworks.

Sablé-sur-Sarthe (säblā'-sür-särt'), town (pop. 5,412), Sarthe dept., W France, on Sarthe R. and 15 mi. NW of La Flèche; anthracite-mining center; foundries and metalworks; meat canning, chicory mfg., marble working. Grain and cattle market.

Sablino, Russian SFSR: see ULYANOVKA, Leningrad oblast.

Sablon, Pointe du (pwēt dü säblõ'), rounded sandy headland of Bouches-du-Rhône dept., SE France, on Gulf of Lion, 22 mi. S of Arles, formed by alluvial deposits of Rhone delta. Encloses several lagoons of the Camargue. 43°22'N 4°33'E.

Sablya (sä'blyŭ), peak (5,407 ft.) in N Urals, Russian SFSR, W of main divide; 64°45'N.

Saboeiro (sŭbōō-ā'rōō), city (pop. 685), S Ceará, Brazil, on upper Jaguaribe R. and 50 mi. WSW of Iguatu; cattle, maniçoba rubber. Airstrip.

Saboga Island (säbō'gä), one of Pearl Islands of Gulf of Panama, Panama prov., Panama, 40 mi. SE of Panama city; 2 mi. long, 1 mi. wide. Pearl fisheries; pineapple plantations. Village of Saboga (pop. 184) is on NE shore.

Sabóia (sŭbô'yŭ), village (pop. 1,566), Beja dist., S Portugal, on railroad, on Mira R., and 50 mi. SW of Beja; grain, cork, livestock; pottery.

Sabôr River (sŭbôr'), in Bragança dist., N Portugal, rises near Bragança, flows c.65 mi. SSW to the Douro near Tôrre de Moncorvo.

Sabotsy, Madagascar: see ANJIRO.

Saboyá (säboiä'), town (pop. 489), Boyacá dept., central Colombia, 5 mi. NNE of Chiquinquirá, in the Cordillera Oriental at foot of the Peña de Saboyá (13,133 ft.).

Sabratha (să'brŭtŭ), town, W Tripolitania, Libya, on Mediterranean coast, 40 mi. WSW of Tripoli, on highway and railroad; tunny fishing. Ital. agr. settlement (dates, grapes, olives, cereals; livestock) established here 1922. Has archaeological mus. Near by are extensive Roman ruins (temples, theater, amphitheater, basilicas) of anc. Sabratha or Sabrata founded by Phoenicians.

Sabraton (să'brŭtŏn), town (1940 pop. 1,810), Monongalia co., N W.Va., just SE of Morgantown, in coal-mining, gas, and oil region; mfg. of sheet steel, tin plate, glass products.

Sabres (sä'brŭ), village (pop. 804), Landes dept., SW France, 21 mi. NW of Mont-de-Marsan; woodworking, flour milling, extracting of resinous products.

Sabrina, Wales and England: see SEVERN RIVER.

Sabrina Coast (sŭbrī'nŭ), part of Wilkes Land, Antarctica, on Indian Ocean, on the Arctic Circle bet. 115° and 117°E. Sighted 1839 by John Balleny, rediscovered 1931 by Sir Douglas Mawson.

Sabrosa (sŭbrō'zŭ), town (pop. 1,347), Vila Real dist., N Portugal, 9 mi. ESE of Vila Real; port wine. Magellan b. here.

Sabtang Island (säbtäng') (□ 13; 1948 pop. 1,656), Batanes prov., Batan Isls., N Philippines, N of Luzon, in Luzon Strait, just SW of Batan Isl.; 6 mi. long, 3 mi. wide; rice, corn.

Sabugal (sŭbōōgäl'), town (pop. 2,287), Guarda dist., N central Portugal, on upper Côa R. and 16 mi. SE of Guarda; agr. trade (livestock, grain, lumber). Has remains of 13th-cent. castle.

Sabugi, Brazil: see SANTA LUZIA, Paraíba.

Sabula (sŭbū'lŭ), town (pop. 888), Jackson co., E Iowa, on the Mississippi (bridged here) and c.40 mi. SE of Dubuque, in livestock and grain area.

Sabunchi (sŭbōōnchē'), town (1939 pop. over 2,000) in Lenin dist. of Greater Baku, Azerbaijan SSR, on central Apsheron Peninsula, 7 mi. NE of Baku, on electric railroad; oil wells (developed after 1870s).

Saburovo (sŭbōō'rŭvŭ), town (1939 pop. over 500), central Moscow oblast, Russian SFSR, on Moskva R., on railroad (Moskvorechye station) and 3 mi. SW of Lyublino; nonferrous ore refinery.

Saby, Russian SFSR: see BOGATYE SABY.

Sabya, As Sabya, or **Al-Sabya** (both: ăs să'byŭ), chief town of Tihama section of Asir, Saudi Arabia, 60 mi. S of Abha. Was seat of Idrisi dynasty (late-19th cent. to 1925). Its port is Qizan (W).

Sabzal Kot, W Pakistan: see KOT SABZAL.

Sabzawar, Afghanistan: see SHINDAND.

Sabzawar or **Sabzevar** (both: säbzävär'), town (1941 pop. 28,151), Ninth Prov., in Khurasan, NE Iran, 120 mi. W of Meshed and on road to Teheran; cotton-growing center; opium, cumin seed, wheat. Cotton ginning, rice and flour milling; handmade woolen textiles, rugs. Airfield. Ruined by Mongols and reconstructed by the Safavid kings (16th–17th cent.).

Sabzawaran or **Sabzavaran** (both: säbzävärän'), town (1942 pop. 4,350), Eighth Prov., in Kerman, SE Iran, on Halil R. and 120 mi. SSE of Kerman; dates, cotton, rice, tobacco; rugmaking. Charcoal burning in near-by tamarisk woods. Formerly called Jiroft.

Sac (sôk), county (□ 578; pop. 17,518), W Iowa; ⊙ Sac City. Prairie agr. area (cattle, hogs, corn, oats, alfalfa) drained by Raccoon and Boyer rivers. Gravel pits, coal deposits. Formed 1851.
Saca, Ethiopia: see SAKA.
Sacaba (säkä'bä), city (pop. c.19,000), ⊙ Chaparé prov., Cochabamba dept., central Bolivia, on S slopes of Cordillera de Cochabamba, on Rocha R. and 8 mi. E of Cochabamba, on Cochabamba–Todos Santos road; alt. 8,530 ft.; agr. (corn, wheat, potatoes), orchards.
Sacaca (säkä'kä), town (pop. c.9,500), ⊙ Alonso de Ibáñez prov., Potosí dept., W central Bolivia, on E slopes of Cordillera de Azanaques and 45 mi. E of Oruro; alt. 11,483 ft.; wheat, potatoes.
Sacagawea, Mount, Wyo.: see WIND RIVER RANGE.
Sacajaewea Peak (să"kŭjŭwē'ŭ) (10,033 ft.), NE Oregon, in Wallowa Mts., near Wallowa L., c.40 mi. E of La Grande. Sometimes spelled Sacajawea.
Sacalum (säkäloom'), town (pop. 1,371), Yucatan, SE Mexico, 33 mi. S of Mérida; henequen, sugar, fruit, timber.
Sacanche (säkän'chä), town (pop. 672), San Martín dept., N central Peru, on affluent of Huallaga R. and 10 mi. SSE of Saposoa; coca, sugar, rice.
Sacandaga or **Sacandaga Park** (săkŭndä'gŭ, –dô'gŭ), resort village, Fulton co., E central N.Y., on NW arm (bridged) of Sacandaga Reservoir, opposite Northville.
Sacandaga Lake, Hamilton co., E central N.Y., in the Adirondacks, just W of L. Pleasant (joined by a stream) and 2 mi. W of Speculator; c.2 mi. in diameter. Source of a headstream of Sacandaga R.
Sacandaga Park, N.Y.: see SACANDAGA.
Sacandaga River, NE N.Y., formed in the Adirondacks S of Wells by East Branch (c.35 mi. long) and West Branch (c.25 mi. long); flows c.12 mi. S to Sacandaga Reservoir (□ c.250; c.27 mi. long), which is impounded by dam at Conklingville, thence c.7 mi. E to the Hudson opposite Lake Luzerne village.
Sacapulas (säkäpoo'läs), town (1950 pop. 1,000), Quiché dept., W central Guatemala, on upper Chixoy R. and 20 mi. NNE of Quiché; alt. 4,035 ft. Market center; silversmithing, salt production; sugar cane, fruit. Has 16th-cent. colonial church.
Sacarambu (sŭkŭrŭmb'), Rum. *Săcărâmbu,* Hung. *Nagyág* (nŏ'dyäk), village (pop. 723), Hunedoara prov., W central Rumania, 9 mi. NE of Deva; gold, silver and cobalt processing.
Sacarita del Tapiche (säkärē'tä dĕl täpē'chä), town (pop. 932), Loreto dept., NE Peru, on Tapiche R. and 12 mi. S of Requena, in forest region.
Sá Carvalho (sä' kŭrvä'lyoo), village, E central Minas Gerais, Brazil, on Piracicaba R., on Rio Doce valley RR and 18 mi. NE of Nova Era. New hydroelectric power plant for Coronel Fabriciano steel mill (15 mi. NE).
Sacatepéquez (säkätäpā'kĕs), department (□ 180; 1950 pop. 58,595), S central Guatemala; ⊙ ANTIGUA. In central highlands; drained (S) by Guacalate R.; includes AGUA (SE) and FUEGO (SW) volcanoes. Mainly agr. (corn, coffee, black beans, fodder grasses); cattle and hog raising. Home industries produce pottery, metalware, cotton textiles. Main centers: Antigua, Sumpango, Ciudad Vieja, Santa María.
Sacaton (säkŭtōn'), village (1940 pop. 584), Pinal co., central Ariz., 32 mi. SE of Phoenix. Hq. for Gila River, Fort McDowell, Maricopa, and Salt River Indian reservations.
Sacavém (sŭkŭvān'), town (pop. 4,870), Lisboa dist., central Portugal, on W shore of Tagus estuary (Lisbon Bay), 6 mi. NNE of Lisbon center; industrial center (mfg. of chemical fertilizer, soap, pottery). Has 16th-cent. Franciscan convent. Portela airport is just SW.
Saccarello, Monte (môn'tĕ säk-kärĕl'lô), or **Cima Saccarello** (chē'mä), peak (alt. 7,218 ft.) in Ligurian Alps, on Fr.-Ital. border, 6 mi. SE of Tende. Tanaro R. rises on N slopes. Until 1947, border lay 6 mi. S.
Sac City (sôk), city (pop. 3,170), ⊙ Sac co., W Iowa, on Raccoon R. and c.40 mi. W of Fort Dodge; agr. trade and processing center; canned foods (corn, peas), popcorn, feed. Sand and gravel pits near by. Indian mounds in vicinity. Inc. 1856.
Saccolongo (säk"kōlôn'gô), village (pop. 196), Padova prov., Veneto, N Italy, 6 mi. W of Padova; textile machinery.
Sacco River (säk'kô), in Latium, S central Italy, rises in the Apennines 8 mi. WSW of Subiaco, flows 54 mi. ESE, past Ceccano, to Liri R. 2 mi. S of Ceprano.
Sacedón (sä-thādhōn'), town (pop. 1,933), Guadalajara prov., central Spain, near the Tagus, 25 mi. ESE of Guadalajara; processing and agr. center (grapes, olives, cereals, honey, wax, sheep); flour milling, woolwashing; mfg. of chocolate, plaster, woolen goods. The veronica is said to have appeared here. La Isabela spa is 3 mi. SSE.
Saceruela (sä-thārwā'lä), town (pop. 1,014), Ciudad Real prov., S central Spain, 40 mi. W of Ciudad Real; cereals, tubers, chick-peas, livestock.
Sachem Head, Conn.: see GUILFORD.
Sachin (sŭch'ēn), town (pop. 1,316), Surat dist., N Bombay, India, 8 mi. SSE of Surat; cotton, millet, sugar cane; cotton ginning, hand-loom weaving. Was ⊙ former princely state of Sachin (□ 49; pop. 26,231) in Gujarat States, Bombay; state inc. 1949 into Surat dist.
Sachkhere (sŭchkhĕ'ryĭ), town (1926 pop. 2,757), N Georgian SSR, on Kvirila R. and 35 mi. ENE of Kutaisi; rail terminus; vineyards. Formerly also spelled Sachkheri.
Sachon (sä'chŭn'), Jap. *Shisen,* town (1946 pop. 14,585), S.Kyongsang prov., S Korea, 8 mi. S of Chinju; fishing and salt-collection center.
Sachsa, Bad, Germany: see BAD SACHSA.
Sachseln (zäk'sŭln), town (pop. 2,117), Obwalden half-canton, central Switzerland, on L. of Sarnen, 2 mi. S of Sarnen; summer resort; woodworking. Has 17th-cent. church.
Sachsen, province and state, Germany: see SAXONY.
Sachsen-, former duchies, Germany: see SAXE-ALTENBURG, SAXE-COBURG, SAXE-COBURG-GOTHA, SAXE-GOTHA, SAXE-MEININGEN, SAXE-WEIMAR, SAXE-WEIMAR-EISENACH.
Sachsen-Anhalt, state, Germany: see SAXONY-ANHALT.
Sachsenberg (zäk'sŭnbĕrk), town (pop. 1,236), in former Prussian prov. of Hesse-Nassau, W Germany, after 1945 in Hesse, 11 mi. SSW of Korbach; lumber. Until 1929 in former Waldeck principality.
Sachsenberg-Georgenthal (–gäôr'gŭntäl), village (pop. 5,179), Saxony, E central Germany, in the Erzgebirge, 18 mi. ESE of Plauen, near Czechoslovak border; cotton milling, musical-instruments mfg.
Sachsenhagen (zäk"sŭnhä'gŭn), town (pop. 1,806), in former Prussian prov. of Hanover, W Germany, after 1945 in Lower Saxony, near Weser-Elbe Canal, 20 mi. W of Hanover. Belonged to former Prussian prov. of Hesse-Nassau until 1932.
Sachsenhausen (–hou'zŭn). **1** Village (pop. 3,397), Brandenburg, E Germany, on the Havel and 2 mi. N of Oranienburg. Site of former concentration camp. **2** S district (pop. 45,625) of Frankfurt, Hesse, W Germany, on left bank of the canalized Main. Bldg. of noted Städel art institute was destroyed in Second World War; valuable collection is preserved. Fruitgrowing in S outskirts. **3** Town (pop. 1,879), in former Prussian prov. of Hesse-Nassau, W Germany, after 1945 in Hesse, 6 mi. ESE of Korbach. Until 1929 in former Waldeck principality.
Sachsenland, Rumania: see SAXONLAND.
Sächsische Saale, Germany: see SAALE RIVER.
Sächsische Schweiz, Germany: see SAXONIAN SWITZERLAND.
Sächsisch-Regen, Rumania: see REGHIN.
Sacile (säche'lĕ), town (pop. 4,021), Udine prov., Friuli–Venezia Giulia, NE Italy, on Livenza R. and 7 mi. W of Pordenone; mfg. (silk textiles, agr. machinery, alcohol, brushes, chemicals). Has cathedral (rebuilt 15th cent.) with paintings by Jacopo Bassano and palaces frescoed by Pordenone. Scene of fighting in First World War.
Sackets Harbor, village (pop. 1,247), Jefferson co., N N.Y., on Black River Bay and Sackets Harbor (inlets of L. Ontario), 11 mi. W of Watertown; summer resort. Settled c.1801, inc. 1814. Was a naval base and scene of a battle in War of 1812. Zebulon Pike is buried here.
Säckingen (zĕ'kĭng-ŭn), town (pop. 6,519), S Baden, Germany, at S foot of Black Forest, on the Rhine (Swiss border) and 14 mi. ESE of Lörrach; mfg. of silk, cotton, ceramics, chemicals, watches; woodworking. Has 16th-cent. bridge. The 17th–18th-cent. castle figures in Scheffel's noted epic, *The Trumpeter of Säckingen.*
Sackville, town (pop. 2,489), SE N.B., near head of Chignecto Bay (part of Bay of Fundy), 24 mi. SE of Moncton; mfg. of stoves, machinery, leather goods, paper boxes, plastics; woodworking, printing; strawberry market. Site of Mt. Allison Univ. and of large radio transmitter. Town founded 1760, inc. 1903. Surrounding Tantramar Marshes were dyked-in and reclaimed by early Fr. settlers.
Saco. **1** (sô'kō) City (pop. 10,324), York co., SW Maine, at falls of the Saco (water power) opposite Biddeford, near the coast, 14 mi. SW of Portland; residential, industrial (textiles, textile machinery, shoes, wood products). Seat of 1st legislative and judicial "court" in Maine, held 1636. Thornton Acad. here. Settled 1631, inc. 1867. **2** (sä'kō) Town (pop. 539), Phillips co., N Mont., on branch of Milk R. and 25 mi. ENE of Malta, in irrigated region; shipping point for livestock and farm products; sugar beets, grain.
Sacol Island (säkōl') (□ 17; 1939 pop. 2,478), Zamboanga prov., Philippines, included in Zamboanga city, off E coast of tip of Zamboanga Peninsula, SW Mindanao.
Saco River (sô'kō), in W N.H. and S Maine, rises in White Mts. of N.H. at c.1,900 ft. near Crawford Notch, flows c.105 mi. SE to the Atlantic 5 mi. below Saco and Biddeford, Maine (head of navigation), where falls furnish water power. Hydroelectric dam, completed 1949 at Union Falls, c.8 mi. above Saco and Biddeford, backs up 6-mi. lake.
Sacramenia (säkrämā'nyä), town (pop. 1,193), Segovia prov., central Spain, 38 mi. NNE of Segovia; cereals, beans, potatoes, sugar beets.
Sacramento (sŭkrŭmĕn'too). **1** City (pop. 4,042), W Minas Gerais, Brazil, near the Rio Grande (São Paulo) and near railroad, 32 mi. ESE of Uberaba. Noted for its cheese. Extensive limestone caves near by. **2** Town, Pará, Brazil: see ITATUPÃ.
Sacramento (säkrämĕn'tō), town (pop. 1,711), Coahuila, N Mexico, in E outliers of Sierra Madre Oriental, 23 mi. WNW of Monclova; cattle grazing.
Sacramento (săkrŭmĕn'tō), county (□ 985; pop. 277,140), central Calif.; ⊙ Sacramento. At heart of Central Valley; bounded W by Sacramento R., which is joined in SW by San Joaquin R.; also crossed by American and Cosumnes rivers. Rich agr. area: fruit (pears, grapes, peaches, apricots, prunes, citrus fruit), nuts, and olives; vegetables, especially asparagus, grown in diked lands of rivers, delta; also cattle, poultry, dairy products, sugar beets, grain, beans, alfalfa, hops, corn, sorghums. Sacramento is processing, packing, river and rail shipping, and mfg. center for wide region; many towns have packing houses, canneries. A leading Calif. co. in natural-gas production, gold dredging (American R.); also produces sand and gravel, stone, silver. Formed 1850.
Sacramento. **1** City (pop. 137,572), ⊙ Calif. and Sacramento co., central Calif., 75 mi. NE of San Francisco, midway bet. the coast and the Sierra Nevada, and on left bank of Sacramento R. (here joined by the American) at head of 10-ft. channel; 38°35'N 121°29'W; alt. c.30 ft. River and rail shipping, distribution, wholesale and retail trade center for wide agr., lumbering, mining, and recreational region of the Sacramento Valley and N Calif. One of state's chief processing centers, with packing and freezing plants and canneries for vegetables, fruit, meat, and poultry; sugar refineries; flour, rice, lumber, and feed mills; dairies. Also huge railroad shops; mfg. of metal products (tin cans, iron and steel); printing. Points of interest include the Roman Corinthian state capitol (1860) in Capitol Park; memorial auditorium; state library, with Calif. historical collections; Crocker Art Gal., with many works of great masters; Sutter's Fort (1840; restored), with a mus. containing Indian and pioneer relics; Sacramento Col. (jr.); state fairgrounds. Near by are U.S. air force bases: Mather Field (mă'thŭr) (E) and McClellan Field (NE). Sacramento was founded in 1848 at settlement of New Helvetia, begun in 1839 by John Sutter on his land grant from Mexico; became state capital (1854) after discovery of gold (1848) by James W. Marshall at Sutter's Mill near COLOMA. Grew as supply point for gold rush miners, then for mines of the Mother Lode; became terminus of 1st Calif. railroad (a short line to Folsom) in 1856, of the Pony Express in 1860, and of 1st transcontinental railroad (Central Pacific RR) in 1869. **2** Town (pop. 378), McLean co., W Ky., 15 mi. ENE of Madisonville, in agr., coal, and timber area.
Sacramento, Pampa del, Peru: see PAMPA DEL SACRAMENTO.
Sacramento Mountains, in N.Mex. and Texas, extend generally N–S bet. Pecos R. and Rio Grande from Ancho, S central N.Mex., into Culberson co., W Texas; include JICARILLA MOUNTAINS, SIERRA BLANCA, and GUADALUPE MOUNTAINS. Sometimes defined as part of S Rocky Mts. Lincoln Natl. Forest and Mescalero Indian Reservation are in N half, in N.Mex. Highest peak is Sierra Blanca (12,003 ft.), 33 mi. NNE of Alamogordo, N.Mex.
Sacramento Pass, Nev.: see SNAKE RANGE.
Sacramento River, largest in Calif., rises in Klamath Mts. in S Siskiyou co., flows 382 mi. S, through N section (Sacramento Valley) of great Central Valley, to Suisun Bay (E arm of San Francisco Bay), which it enters just after joining the San Joaquin in their joint delta. Principal tributaries enter from E: Pit and McCloud rivers, from Cascade Range; Feather and American rivers, from the Sierra Nevada. From W come short streams, including Cache and Putah creeks. Drains □ 27,100. Sacramento, 67 mi. upstream at head of 10-ft. navigation channel, is principal city and port on river. Once normally navigable beyond Red Bluff (256 mi. upstream), river now carries small steamers that far only during high water. The Sacramento gives its name to the Sacramento Valley, N section (c.200 mi. long N–S) of Central Valley, bet. Coast Ranges and Klamath Mts. (W), Cascade Range and the Sierra Nevada (E). A major unit of CENTRAL VALLEY project (one of whose purposes is to supply Sacramento R. water to San Joaquin Valley to S) is great SHASTA DAM in the upper Sacramento; with Keswick Dam (159 ft. high, 1,046 ft. long), just downstream, it regulates river for navigation, flood control, power and irrigation. The valley (and the MOTHER LODE country in foothills to E) saw the great gold strike of 1848; many of its cities sprang up in the gold rush.
Sacramento Valley, Calif.: see SACRAMENTO RIVER; CENTRAL VALLEY.
Sacratif, Cape (säkrätēf'), on the Mediterranean, in Granada prov., S Spain, 5 mi. SE of Motril; 36°41'N 3°27'W. Lighthouse.
Sacrau, Poland: see SAKRAU.
Sacré Coeur Saguenay (sä'krā kûr sägŭnā') or **Sacré Coeur de Jésus** (dŭ zhäzü'), village (pop.

242), SE Que., near Saguenay R., 8 mi. NNW of Tadoussac, in mica-mining region; dairying, lumbering. Airfield.

Sacred Heart, village (pop. 745), Renville co., SW Minn., near Minnesota R., 10 mi. E of Granite Falls, in grain, livestock, poultry area; dairy products.

Sacrificios, Isla de los (ēslä dā lōs säkrēfē'syōs), small island in Gulf of Mexico, 3 mi. SE of Veracruz, Mexico; alleged place of Aztec human sacrifices.

Sac River (sôk), SW Mo.; headwaters rise in Lawrence and Greene counties, joining near Greenfield; flows 107 mi. N, through the Ozarks, to Osage R. just below Osceola.

Sacsahuamán, Peru: see CUZCO, city.

Sacueni (sŭkwän'), Rum. *Săcueni*, Hung. *Székelyhid* (sā'kāhēt), village (pop. 5,915), Bihor prov., W Rumania, near Hung. border, 21 mi. NNE of Oradea; rail junction; noted for wine production; mfg. of cardboard and pottery. Former medieval fortress. In Hungary, 1940–45.

Sacul (sä'kōōl'), Hung. *Szákul* (sä'kōōl), village (1,288), Severin prov., W Rumania, on Timis R., on railroad and 11 mi. SE of Lugoj; flour milling; mfg. of edible oils.

Sacupana, Caño (kä'nyō säkōōpä'nä), E arm of Orinoco R. delta, Delta Amacuro territory, NE Venezuela; branches off from the main arm, the Río Grande, flows c.75 mi. NE to the Atlantic.

Sada (sä'dhä), town (pop. 2,001), La Coruña prov., NW Spain, fishing port on Ares Bay of the Atlantic, 7 mi. E of La Coruña; sardine fishing and processing, boatbuilding, flour- and sawmilling.

Sada, Saada, Sa'da, or **Sa'dah** (sä'dŭ), town (pop. 4,000), ⊙ Sada prov. (pop. 280,000), N Yemen, 110 mi. NNW of Sana, near Asir border; center of N Yemen and original seat of the Yemen Imams, from c.900 until shift of residence to Sana in 17th cent.

Sádaba (sä'dhävä), town (pop. 2,555), Saragossa prov., N Spain, 23 mi. NE of Tudela; agr. center (sugar beets, cereals). Terminus of branch railroad from Gallur. Irrigation reservoir near by.

Sadabad (sŭdä'bäd), town (pop. 4,526), Muttra dist., W Uttar Pradesh, India, 22 mi. ESE of Muttra; cotton, gram, jowar, wheat, oilseeds.

Sá da Bandeira (sä' dä bändā'rŭ), town (pop. 8,521), ⊙ Huíla prov., SW Angola, 160 mi. S of Benguela, near W edge of central plateau; 14°55'S 13°30'E. Inland terminus of railroad from Mossâmedes (90 mi. WSW). Agr. trade center in upland region (4–6,000 ft.) of European settlement. Ships hides and skins, dairy produce, rice, flour. Agr. processing, tanning. Airfield. Formerly called Lubango.

Sadagura, Ukrainian SSR: see SADGORA.

Sa'dah, Yemen: see SADA.

Sadamitsu (sädä'mĭtsōō), town (pop. 7,009), Tokushima prefecture, E central Shikoku, Japan, 28 mi. W of Tokushima; tobacco-growing center; rice, wheat, raw silk.

Sadani (sädä'nē), town, Eastern Prov., Tanganyika, minor fishing port on Zanzibar Channel of Indian Ocean, at mouth of Wami R., 30 mi. NNW of Bagamoyo; ships cotton, sisal, copra. Caravan terminus in 19th cent.

Sada Point (sä'dä), Jap. *Sada-misaki*, westernmost point of Shikoku, Japan, at tip of long narrow peninsula in Ehime prefecture, in Hoyo Strait; 33°20'N 132°1'E; lighthouse.

Sadaseopet (sŭdä'sāōpāt) or **Sadasivpet** (sŭdä'-sĭvpāt), town (pop. 8,158), Medak dist., central Hyderabad state, India, 40 mi. NW of Hyderabad; rice milling.

Saddleback, mountain (2,847 ft.) in the Cumbrians, S central Cumberland, England, 5 mi. NE of Keswick. Also called Blencathara.

Saddleback Mountain. 1 Peak (4,116 ft.) in Franklin co., W Maine, 5 mi. E of Rangeley L. **2** Peak (4,530 ft.) of the Adirondacks, Essex co., NE N.Y., 2½ mi. ENE of Mt. Marcy and 11 mi. SSE of Lake Placid village. **3** Peak (3,623 ft.) of the Adirondacks, Essex co., NE N.Y., 16 mi. E of Lake Placid village.

Saddle Ball, Mass.: see GREYLOCK, MOUNT.

Saddlebunch Key, Fla.: see FLORIDA KEYS.

Saddlehead, promontory on the Atlantic, NW extremity of Achill Isl., W Co. Mayo, Ireland, 54°N 10°12'W.

Saddle Islands, northeasternmost group of Chusan Archipelago, in E. China Sea, Kiangsu prov., China, NE of Parker Isls. Largest and northernmost is North Saddle Isl., 2 mi. long, 1 mi. wide; 30°52'N 122°40'E; lighthouse.

Saddle Peak, highest point (2,400 ft.) in Andaman Islands, on N.Andaman Isl., 105 mi. NNE of Port Blair; 13°10'N 93°1'E.

Saddle River, borough (pop. 1,003), Bergen co., NE N.J., on small Saddle R. and 8 mi. NNE of Paterson; paper products.

Saddle River, in SE N.Y. and NE N.J., rises in small streams in Rockland co., SE N.Y., near N.J. line; flows c.25 mi. S to Passaic R. opposite Passaic, N.J.

Saddle Rock, residential village (pop. 33), Nassau co., SE N.Y., on Little Neck Bay, near Great Neck village.

Saddleworth, village (pop. 394), SE South Australia, 60 mi. N of Adelaide; wheat, wool, livestock, dairy products.

Saddleworth, urban district (1931 pop. 12,574; 1951 census 16,762), West Riding, SW Yorkshire, England, 11 mi. SW of Huddersfield; cotton and woolen milling; mfg. of carpets, paper, textile machinery. In urban dist. are cotton- and woolen-milling towns of Delph, Dobcross, Greenfield, and Uppermill.

Sadec (sädĕk'), town, ⊙ Sadec prov. (□ 600; 1943 pop. 260,600), S Vietnam, in Cochin China, on right bank of Mekong R., 70 mi. SW of Saigon; river port, trading and agr. center (rice, corn, vegetables, fruit); sawmills, brickworks. A former Khmer dist., annexed (18th cent.) by Annamese.

Sadgora (sŭdgô'rŭ), Rum. *Sadagura* (sädägōō'rä), village (1941 pop. 2,415), central Chernovtsy oblast, Ukrainian SSR, in N Bukovina, 4 mi. N of Chernovtsy, across Prut R.; agr. center; flour, dairy products, alcohol.

Sadhaura (sä'dourŭ), town (pop. 8,815), Ambala dist., E Punjab, India, 25 mi. E of Ambala; trades in grain, cotton, timber; cotton ginning, flour milling.

Sadieville (sā'dēvĭl), town (pop. 355), Scott co., N Ky., on Eagle Creek and 25 mi. N of Lexington, in Bluegrass agr. region.

Sadina (sä'dēnä), village (pop. 4,266), Kolarovgrad dist., NE Bulgaria, 9 mi. NNE of Popovo; wheat, corn, livestock.

Sadiya (sŭd'yŭ), former frontier tract (□ 20,034; pop. estimate c.300,000; pop. was 60,118 in the 3,309 sq. mi. which was covered by the 1941 census), NE Assam, India; ⊙ was Sadiya. Divided (1950) into ABOR HILLS and MISHMI HILLS tribal dists. and TIRAP frontier tract. Bounded N by Assam Himalayas and China (border undefined), W by Subansiri R., E by Burma (border undefined); mainly mountainous area (Mishmi Hills, N and NE of Sadiya; Abor Hills, N and NW of Pasighat); alluvial soil in S central area; drained by Brahmaputra (called Dihang in Sadiya), Dibang, Luhit, and Subansiri rivers. Agr. (rice, tea, rape and mustard, sugar cane); tea processing, sawmilling. Figured in 16th-cent. struggles of Ahom (Shan) kingdom. Pop. 30% Hindu, 66% Animist tribes (including Abors and Mishmis).

Sadiya, town (pop. 2,056), NE frontier tract of Assam, India, in Brahmaputra valley, on Luhit R. and 53 mi. ENE of Dibrugarh; rice, tea, rape and mustard, sugar cane. Copper temple. Rail station is Saikhoa Ghat. Figured in 16th-cent. struggles of Ahom (Shan) kingdom. Extensive fort ruins near by. Town is ⊙ Mishmi Hills tribal dist.

Sadki (sŭtkē'), village, NW Chkalov oblast, Russian SFSR, on Lesser Kinel R. and 15 mi. SSW of Buguruslan; natural-gas extracting (pipe line to Buguruslan); petroleum and asphalt deposits. Developed in Second World War.

Sadohara, Japan: see SADOWARA.

Sado Island (sä'dō), Jap. *Sado-shima* (□ 330; 1940 pop. 109,016; 1947 pop. 124,250), Niigata prefecture, Japan, in Sea of Japan, 30 mi. W of Niigata, off N Honshu; 35 mi. long, 12 mi. wide. Generally mountainous, with central plain producing rice, wheat, soybeans, potatoes. Cattle raising, lumbering, fishing. Gold and silver mined on W coast. Known as place of exile in feudal times; Emperor Juntoku exiled here by Kamakura shogun. Chief centers: AIKAWA, RYOTSU (outer port for Niigata).

Sadon (sŭdōn') or **Fort Harrison,** village, Myitkyina dist., Kachin State, Upper Burma, near China border 30 mi. E of Myitkyina, on road to Tengchung (Yunnan prov.).

Sadon (sŭdôn'), town (1939 pop. over 2,000), S North Ossetian Autonomous SSR, Russian SFSR, in the central Greater Caucasus, 36 mi. WSW of Dzaudzhikau; lead-zinc-silver mines, connected by cableway with MIZUR mill, 5 mi. E.

Sado River (sä'dōō), S Portugal, rises near Ourique (Beja dist.), flows 110 mi. N, past Alcácer do Sal (head of sea-going navigation), to the Atlantic at Setúbal, forming a wide, indented estuary (marshy near its head; saltworks) which a sand bar shelters from the open sea, except for inlet SW of Setúbal.

Sadorus (sŭdō'rŭs), village (pop. 388), Champaign co., E Ill., on Sangamon R. and 11 mi. SSW of Champaign, in agr. area.

Sadova (sä'dôvä), Czech *Sadová*, Ger. *Sadowa* (zädō'vä), village, S Bohemia, Czechoslovakia, on railroad and 8 mi. NW of Hradec Kralove. Famous battle of Sadowa or Königgrätz (1866), culminating in total defeat of Austrians by Prussians, was fought near by, on hilly grounds to SE.

Sadovets (sä'dôvĕts), village (pop. 5,096), Pleven dist., N Bulgaria, on Vit R. and 11 mi. NE of Lovech; flour milling; livestock, legumes, oil-bearing plants.

Sadovo (sä'dôvô), village (pop. 2,088), Plovdiv dist., S central Bulgaria, 10 mi. E of Plovdiv; cotton, rice, sugar beets, truck. Has agr. school and experimental station. Formerly Cheshnegir.

Sadovoye (sŭdô'vŭyŭ). **1** Village (1939 pop. over 500), W Astrakhan oblast, Russian SFSR, 40 mi. N of Stepnoi; cattle, horse raising; wheat, mustard. Until 1944 (in Kalmyk Autonomous SSR), Kegulta. **2** Village (1939 pop. over 2,000), S Stalingrad oblast, Russian SFSR, on E slope of Yergeni Hills, 65 mi. S of Stalingrad; wheat, mustard; cattle raising.

Sadovoye, Pervoye (pyĕr'vŭyŭ), or **Sadovoye 1,** village (1939 pop. over 2,000), N central Voronezh oblast, Russian SFSR, 55 mi. ESE of Voronezh; sugar mill.

Sadowa, Czechoslovakia: see SADOVA.

Sadowara (sädō'wärŭ) or **Sadohara** (–härŭ), town (pop. 6,364), Miyazaki prefecture, E Kyushu, Japan, 9 mi. N of Miyazaki; rice, raw silk.

Sadowa Wisznia, Ukrainian SSR: see SUDOVAYA VISHNYA.

Sadra (sä'drŭ), town (pop. 2,314), Sabar Kantha dist., N Bombay, India, on Sabarmati R. and 23 mi. SW of Himatnagar; local agr. market (millet, wheat). Also called Sadra Bazar.

Sadras, India: see TIRUKKALIKKUNRAM.

Sadri (sä'drē), town (pop. 8,701), S central Rajasthan, India, 10 mi. E of Bali; markets millet, wheat, barley. At Ranapur, 5 mi. SSE, in foothills of Aravalli Range, is noted 15th-cent. Jain temple of intricate design.

Sadska (sät'skä), Czech *Sadská*, village (pop. 3,047), E central Bohemia, Czechoslovakia, on railroad, 5 mi. SW of Nymburk; goose breeding; feather production. Health resort, with springs and peat baths.

Saebovik, Norway: see HALSNOY.

Saeby (sĕ'bü), city (pop. 3,153) and port, Hjorring amt, N Jutland, Denmark, on the Kattegat and 22 mi. SE of Hjorring; seafaring; machinery mfg., meat packing, fishing.

Saegerstown (sā'gŭrztoun), borough (pop. 836), Crawford co., NW Pa., 5 mi. N of Meadville and on French Creek.

Saei, Formosa: see TSOYING.

Saeki (sää'kē), city (1940 pop. 32,505; 1947 pop. 38,891), Oita prefecture, E Kyushu, Japan, on inlet of Hoyo Strait, 28 mi. NNE of Nobeoka; timber-producing center (cedar, pine). Fishery. Sometimes spelled Saiki.

Sa el Hagar (säl'-hä'gär), **Sa el Hajar,** or **Sa al-Hajar** (both: säl-hä'jär), village (pop. 8,776), Gharbiya prov., Lower Egypt, on Rosetta branch of the Nile and 10 mi. NNW of Kafr el Zaiyat; cotton. On site of anc. SAÏS.

Saelices (säēlē'thēs), town (pop. 2,090), Cuenca prov., E central Spain, on Madrid-Valencia highway, and 32 mi. WSW of Cuenca; grain-growing and flour-milling center. Hydroelectric plant; thermal springs. Near by is the Cabeza de Griego (hill), of great archaeological interest because of its Roman remains and traces of an anc. city.

Sáenz Peña (sä'ĕns pā'nyä), residential city (pop. estimate 25,000) in W Greater Buenos Aires, Argentina, adjoining Santos Lugares.

Saetabis, Spain: see JÁTIVA.

Saetersdal, Norway: see SETESDAL.

Saeul (zoil), village (pop. 295), W Luxembourg, 10 mi. NW of Luxembourg city; sawmills, lumbering. Village of Schwebach (pop. 48) is 2 mi. NNW.

Saevareid (säv'är-äd), village in Strandvik canton, Hordaland co., SW Norway, on Bjorna Fjord (an inlet of North Sea), 21 mi. SE of Bergen; paper mfg.

Safad or **Safed** (both: sä'fŭd), Hebrew *Tsfat* or *Tsefat* (both: tsfät), town (1946 pop. estimate 12,600; 1949 pop. estimate 4,000), N Israel, Upper Galilee, at foot of Mt. Canaan, 30 mi. ENE of Haifa; alt. 2,897 ft.; tourist resort. Has anc. Ari Synagogue and remains of medieval Crusaders' castle. Mentioned by Josephus Flavius, town later became Jewish cultural center and, in 16th cent., important seat of Cabalistic learning; still considered as one of 4 Jewish holy cities in Palestine. First Hebrew book in Palestine printed from movable type here 1577. Suffered heavy earthquake destruction 1837. Formerly predominantly Arab town, captured by Israeli forces, May, 1948.

Safaga (säfä'gŭ) or **Safajah** (–jŭ), town (pop. 809), E Egypt, on the Red Sea, 85 mi. ENE of Qena (connected by road); port protected by Safaga Isl. Ships phosphate production of mines at near-by Umm Huweitat. Because of its sheltered location it rivals Kosseir as chief Egyptian Red Sea port.

Safakulevo (sŭfŭkōō'lyĭvŭ), village (1939 pop. over 2,000), W Kurgan oblast, Russian SFSR, 15 mi. SSW of Shchuchye; metalworks, dairy plant.

Safaniya or **Safaniyah** (säfănē'yŭ), offshore oil field, in Hasa, Saudi Arabia, in Persian Gulf off cape Ras Safaniya, 12 mi. SE of Ras Misha'ab; 28°2'N 48°46'E. Discovered 1950.

Safara (sŭfä'rŭ), village (pop. 1,899), Beja dist., S Portugal, 13 mi. E of Moura; grain, sheep.

Safaraliyev (sŭfŭrä'lyĕŭf), village, W Azerbaijan SSR, 6 mi. N of Kirovabad, in winegrowing and cotton dist.

Safarikovo (shä'färĭ"kôvô), Slovak *Šafárikovo*, town (pop. 3,180), S Slovakia, Czechoslovakia, on railroad, on Slana (Sajo) R. and 60 mi. SE of Banska Bystrica. Vineyards in vicinity. Until 1949, known as Tornala, Slovak *Tornal'a*, Hung. *Tornalja*.

Safdar Jang, airport, India: see DELHI, city.

Safed, Israel: see SAFAD.

Safed Koh or **Safid Koh** (sŭfăd' kō') [Persian,= white mountains]. **1** W outlier of the Hindu Kush, one of the Firoz Koh ranges, in NW Afghanistan, extending c.100 mi. along left (S) watershed of the Hari Rud bet. 63° and 65°E; rises to c.10,000 ft. 11 mi. NW of Shahrak. The name Safed Koh is sometimes applied to the E section of the Paropamisus Mts., N of the Hari Rud. Also spelled Sefid Koh or Sefid Kuh. 2 Pashto *Spin Ghar* [=white mountains] Range on Afghanistan-Pakistan border, extending 100 mi. W from Peshawar to Logar valley S of Kabul, and forming S watershed of Kabul R.; rises to 15,620 ft. in the Sikaram. Khyber Pass is at its E end, Paiwar Pass at W end.

Safe Harbor, village, Lancaster co., SE Pa., 9 mi. SW of Lancaster. Safe Harbor Dam (5,000 ft. long; 106 ft. high; completed 1932) in Susquehanna R. here, produces hydroelectric power in conjunction with small Holtwood Dam c.8 mi. downstream.

Safety Harbor, city (pop. 894), Pinellas co., W Fla., 15 mi. W of Tampa, at head of Old Tampa Bay; health resort with mineral springs; bottling works.

Safety Valve Entrance, S Fla., chief passage through the Florida Keys bet. Biscayne Bay and the Atlantic, 10 mi. S of Miami Beach.

Saff, El, Es Saff, or **Al-Saff** (all: ĕs-säf'), village (pop. 6,816), Giza prov., Upper Egypt, on E bank of the Nile and 35 mi. S of Cairo; wool weaving, mfg. of bricks, clay tubing; corn, cotton, sugar.

Saffelaere, Belgium: see ZAFFELARE.

Saffi, Fr. Morocco: see SAFI.

Saffle (sĕf'lü), Swedish *Säffle*, town (pop. 7,930), Varmland co., W Sweden, on By R. near its mouth on L. Vaner, 25 mi. SW of Karlstad; paper, pulp, and rayon milling, metalworking. Just ESE is hamlet of Kyrkerud (chür"kürüd'), where Tegnér was born.

Safford, town (pop. 3,756), ⊙ Graham co., SE Ariz., on Gila R. and 85 mi. NE of Tucson, in agr. area (livestock, grain, poultry, cotton); trade center, hq. for Crook Natl. Forest. Pinaleno Mts. are SW, Gila Mts. N. Founded 1872, inc. 1901.

Saffron Walden, municipal borough (1931 pop. 5,930; 1951 census 6,825), NW Essex, England, near Gam R., 11 mi. NNE of Bishop's Stortford, 50 mi. NNE of London; agr. market. The 15th-cent. church of St. Mary has tomb of Lord Audley, chancellor of Henry VIII. There are a notable mus. and remains of 12th-cent. castle. Town is named for saffron crocus grown here from time of Edward III until 18th cent. Roman remains have been found here.

Saffuriya, Israel: see TSIPORI.

Safi (säfē'), city (pop. 50,845), Marrakesh region, W Fr. Morocco, port on the Atlantic, 85 mi. NW of Marrakesh (for which it is the chief outlet) and 125 mi. SW of Casablanca; 32°18'N 9°14'W. Morocco's leading fishing port and a ranking sardine-canning center. Linked by rail with Louis Gentil (phosphate mine, 40 mi. E) and beyond it with Benguérir (junction with trunk railroad), Safi has also become a phosphate port (1st shipments in 1936). The artificial harbor accommodates ships drawing 28 ft. at all tides. Besides fish-processing plants, there are jute and linen mill, boat-building yards, plaster works, and fiber plant. Pottery mfg. is chief handicraft industry. Airfield. Saltworks at Zima L. (35 mi. ESE). The massive citadel (*Kechla*) is the principal remnant of Port. occupation (1508–41). City's rapid expansion dates from the 1930s. Formerly spelled Saffi or Asfi.

Safi, El, Es Safi, or **Al-Safi** (all: ĕs-sä'fē), village (pop. c.5,000), S central Jordan, near mouth of Wadi el Hasa on Dead Sea, 15 mi. SW of Kerak; 909 ft. below sea level. Alluvial deposits of bitumen, salts, potash.

Safid Koh, Afghanistan: see SAFED KOH.

Safidon (sŭfē'dōn), town (pop. 7,807), S central Patiala and East Punjab States Union, India, 22 mi. ENE of Jind, on branch of Western Jumna Canal; agr. market (millet, gram, wheat, sugar).

Safiertal (zä'fērtäl"), valley of Rabiusa R. (affluent of lower Plessur R.), Grisons, E Switzerland.

Safipur (sŭfē'po͝or), town (pop. 6,920), Unao dist., central Uttar Pradesh, India, 16 mi. NNW of Unao; wheat, barley, rice, gram, oilseeds. Tombs of Moslem saints. Sometimes called Saipur.

Safirah, Syria: see SFIRA.

Safita (sä'fētä), town, Latakia prov., W Syria, near Lebanese border, 30 mi. NE of Tripoli; sericulture, cereals. Built on site of old castle.

Safonovka (sŭfô'nŭfkŭ), village, SE Tula oblast, Russian SFSR, 11 mi. N of Yefremov; distilling.

Safonovo (–nŭvŭ), town (1939 pop. over 2,000), central Smolensk oblast, Russian SFSR, on railroad (Dorogobuzh station) and 14 mi. N of Dorogobuzh; rail junction; building materials.

Safranbolu (säfrän'bôlo͞o), village (pop. 5,164), Zonguldak prov., N Turkey, near Arac R., 45 mi. ESE of Zonguldak; coal mines; grain, hemp, sugar beets, dye plants.

Saf-Saf, Oued (wĕd' säf-säf'), stream of Constantine dept., NE Algeria, rises in the Constantine Mts., flows c.50 mi. N to the Mediterranean just E of Philippeville. Zardézas Dam (115 ft. high; 4 mi. SE of El-Arrouch) irrigates lower valley and supplies water for Philippeville.

Safsafa or **Safsafah** (säf'säfü), Fr. *Safsafé*, town, Latakia prov., W Syria, near Lebanese border, 20 mi. NE of Tripoli; sericulture, cereals.

Saft el Khammar or **Saft al-Khammar** (both: säft' ĕl khăm'mär), village (pop. 8,549), Minya prov., Upper Egypt, 6 mi. SW of Minya; cotton, cereals, sugar.

Saft Rashin (säft rä'shēn), village (pop. 8,530), Beni Suef prov., N Upper Egypt, 13 mi. SW of Beni Suef; cotton, cereals, sugar cane.

Saft Turab (säft' to͞oräb'), village (pop. 9,566), Gharbiya prov., Lower Egypt, on railroad and 6 mi. SSW of El Mahalla el Kubra; cotton.

Safwa or **Safwah** (säf'wü), town in Hasa, Saudi Arabia, 10 mi. NNW of Qatif; fisheries. Agr. oasis irrigated by fresh-water springs; model farming project (dates, vegetables, fruit).

Saga (sä'gä), prefecture [Jap. *ken*] (□ 946; 1940 pop. 701,517; 1947 pop. 917,797), NW Kyushu, Japan; ⊙ Saga. Bounded N by Genkai Sea, S by the Ariakeno-umi. Chief port, KARATSU. Comprises part of hilly Hizen Peninsula; drained by many small streams. Coal fields in NW; hot springs at Takeo and Ureshino in SW. Known primarily for fine porcelain ware produced at ARITA and IMARI. Cotton mills and ironworks at Saga. Widespread production of rice, sweet potatoes, raw silk; extensive cultivation of mulberry trees (for feeding silkworms) and tallow trees (*sapium sebiferum*).

Saga. 1 Town (pop. 6,315), Kochi prefecture, SW Shikoku, Japan, on Tosa Bay, 42 mi. SW of Kochi; lumber, rice, raw silk; stock raising. Sometimes called Tosa-saga. **2** City (1940 pop. 50,406; 1947 pop. 64,978), ⊙ Saga prefecture, NW Kyushu, Japan, on E Hizen Peninsula, 35 mi. ENE of Sasebo; 33°15'N 130°18'E. Rail junction; mfg. center; cotton mills, ironworks. Produces camphor, rice. Coal-distributing center. Formerly ⊙ feudal prov. of Hizen.

Saga, Norway: see RAKVAG.

Sagadahoc (săg"ŭdühŏk'), county (□ 257; pop. 20,911), SW Maine; ⊙ Bath (shipbuilding center, on the navigable Kennebec). First English colony in New England planted at Fort St. George (now Popham Beach) in 1607. Mfg. (paper and pulp, textiles, hardware, wood products, building supplies), feldspar mining and milling, fishing; agr.; dairying. Summer colonies on coast and isls. Androscoggin R. joins the Kennebec at Merrymeeting Bay, noted for duck hunting. Formed 1854.

Sagae (sägä'ā), town (pop. 14,748), Yamagata prefecture, N Honshu, Japan, 9 mi. NNW of Yamagata; rice, raw silk, market produce; sake brewing.

Sagaing (sŭgĭng'), northern division (□ 39,008; 1941 pop. 1,895,050), of Upper Burma; ⊙ Sagaing. Bounded W by Indian states of Assam and Manipur, NE by Kachin State, and E by Shan State; it is drained by Irrawaddy R. (in Katha, Shwebo, and Sagaing dists.), by Chindwin R. (in Upper Chindwin and Lower Chindwin dists.), and includes the Naga Hills dist. (on Assam border; N). Agr.: rice, cotton, sesame, vegetables, opium. Pop. is 75% Burmese, 5% Thai. Main cities are Sagaing, Shwebo, and Monywa.

Sagaing, southernmost district (□ 1,870; 1941 pop. 387,270) of Sagaing div., Upper Burma; ⊙ Sagaing. Astride Irrawaddy R. just above Chindwin R. mouth, in dry zone (yearly rainfall 31 in.). Irrigated agr.: rice, cotton, sesame. Salt (brine) extraction along Irrawaddy R. Served by railroads from Mandalay and by Irrawaddy steamers. Pop. is nearly entirely Burmese.

Sagaing, town (pop. 14,127), ⊙ Sagaing div. and dist., Upper Burma, on railroad and 10 mi. SW of Mandalay, across Irrawaddy R. (rail bridge) opposite ruined Ava; trade center; cotton, sesame, salt, fruit. In 14th cent., ⊙ petty Shan kingdom; dominated (16th cent.) by Pegu; was briefly (18th cent.) ⊙ Burma.

Sagallo (sägäl'lō), village, Fr. Somaliland, on N shore of Gulf of Tadjoura, 13 mi. SW of Tadjoura; small fishing port; formerly had flourishing caravan trade.

Sagami (sä"gä'mē), former province in central Honshu, Japan; now part of Shizuoka and Kanagawa prefectures.

Sagami Bay, Japan: see SAGAMI SEA.

Sagamihara (sägämē'härü), town (pop. 73,217), Kanagawa prefecture, central Honshu, Japan, 15 mi. WNW of Yokohama, in forested area; mulberry and rice fields; raw-silk production. Formed in early 1940s by combining former towns of Kami-mizo (1940 pop. 5,533) and Ono (1940 pop. 10,242).

Sagami Sea (sägä'mē), Jap. *Sagami-nada*, inlet of Philippine Sea, central Honshu, Japan, bet. Izu Peninsula (W) and Miura Peninsula (E); connected with Tokyo Bay by Uraga Strait; 60 mi. long, 40 mi. wide. O-shima (northernmost of isl. group Izu-shichito) is at entrance. N section is called Sagami Bay (formerly sometimes called Odawara Bay). Atami is on W shore, Kamakura on NE shore.

Sagamore (să'gümôr). **1** Village, Mass.: see BOURNE. **2** Village (pop. 1,128), Armstrong co., W Pa., 15 mi. ESE of Kittanning.

Sagamore Hills, former village, Summit co., N Ohio, just SE of Cleveland. Inc. 1931, disincorporated 1947.

Sagan (zä'gän) or **Zagan** (zhä'gänyü), Pol. *Żagań*, town (1939 pop. 22,770; 1946 pop. 4,359) in Lower Silesia, after 1945 in Zielona Gora prov., W Poland, on Bobrawa R. and 35 mi. NNE of Görlitz; rail junction; textile (cotton, woolen, linen) milling, lignite mining, glass mfg., kaolin quarrying. Heavily damaged in Second World War. Has late-Gothic church of former Franciscan monastery, palace built 1629 by Wallenstein. Founded in 12th cent.; was (1274–1472) ⊙ independent principality. Property of Wallenstein, 1628–35; purchased (1786) by dukes of Courland; passed (1844) to dukes of Talleyrand and Sagan. Pol. name sometimes spelled *Żegań* (zhĕ'gänyü).

Sagana (sägä'nä), village, Central Prov., S central Kenya, on railroad and 5 mi. NNE of Fort Hall; coffee, sisal, wheat, corn.

Saganaga Lake (săgünä'gü), in NE Minn. and W Ont., in chain of lakes on Can. line; lies partly in Cook co., Minn., c.40 mi. NW of Grand Marais; c.15 mi. long, max. width 5 mi. Has deeply indented shore line and several small isls. Minn. section of lake is in Superior Natl. Forest. Surrounding countryside is resort and vacation area.

Saganeiti (sägänä'tē), town (pop. 2,000), Adi Caieh div., central Eritrea, 25 mi. SE of Asmara; alt. c.7,230 ft.; road junction. Agr. trade center founded by Italians.

Sagani Lagoon, Ukraine: see SHAGANY LAGOON.

Saganoseki (sägä'-nō'sākē), town (pop. 16,480), Oita prefecture, E Kyushu, Japan, on SE shore of Beppu Bay, 16 mi. E of Oita; metal-refining center (gold, silver, tin). Fish canneries.

Sagan River, Ethiopia: see GALANA SAGAN.

Sagaponack (săgüpŏ'nük), resort village, Suffolk co., SE N.Y., on S peninsula of E Long Isl., just ESE of Bridgehampton. Sagaponack L. (c.1½ mi. long) is near by.

Sagar, district, India: see SAUGOR.

Sagar (sä'gŭr). **1** Town (pop. 7,513), Shimoga dist., NW Mysore, India, on railroad and 40 mi. WNW of Shimoga; trades in rice, sandalwood, betel nuts; tile mfg. (kaolin deposits near by); handicrafts (wickerwork, lacquerware, sandalwood carving). Also spelled Sagara. Famous Gersoppa Falls are 16 mi. WNW. **2** Town, Madhya Pradesh, India: see SAUGOR.

Sagara (sä"gä'rä), town (pop. 14,938), Shizuoka prefecture, central Honshu, Japan, on SW shore of Suruga Bay, 23 mi. SSW of Shizuoka, in agr. area (tea, rice); cotton textiles. Building-stone quarries; fishery.

Sagar-Chaga (sŭgär"-chŭgä'), village, central Mary oblast, Turkmen SSR, on Murgab oasis, 12 mi. NW of Mary; cotton.

Sagard (zä'gärt), village (pop. 3,707), in former Prussian Pomerania prov., N Germany, after 1945 in Mecklenburg, on E Rügen isl., near an inlet of the Baltic, 9 mi. NE of Bergen; grain, potatoes, sugar beets, stock. Site of largest prehistoric grave found on Rügen.

Sagaredzho (sŭgŭryĕ'jü), village (1926 pop. 5,625), E Georgian SSR, on railroad and 25 mi. E of Tiflis; vineyards.

Sagar Island (sä'gŭr), westernmost island of Ganges Delta, India, in 24-Parganas dist., in Bay of Bengal, 51 mi. SSW of Calcutta; 18 mi. long, 1–7 mi. wide; separated from mainland (E) by arm of the Hooghly; bounded W by Hooghly R. mouth. Subject to severe cyclones. Hindu pilgrimage center (noted bathing festival), large annual fair. Lighthouse on SW shore.

Sagauli (sŭgou'lē), village, Chamaparan dist., NW Bihar, India, 15 mi. NW of Motihari; rail junction; rice, wheat, barley, corn, oilseeds. Treaty signed here, 1816, bet. English and Nepalese, ended 2d Gurkha War. Formerly spelled Segowlie.

Sagavanirktok River (săgüvünürk'tŏk), NE Alaska, rises on N slope of Brooks Range near 68°35'N 147°W, flows c.180 mi. NNW to Beaufort Sea at 70°13'N 147°50'W.

Sagay (sägī'), town (1939 pop. 3,977; 1948 municipality pop. 67,152), Negros Occidental prov., N Negros isl., Philippines, on Visayan Sea, 37 mi. NE of Bacolod; sawmilling.

Sage, Mount (1,781 ft.), W Tortola isl., Br. Virgin Isls., just W of Road Town.

Sagerton (să'gürtün), village (1940 pop. 906), Haskell co., W central Texas, c.45 mi. N of Abilene; rail point in cotton, cattle area.

Sageville, town (pop. 118), Dubuque co., E Iowa, near Mississippi R., just N of Dubuque.

Saghalien or **Saghalin,** Russian SFSR: see SAKHALIN.

Sag Harbor, resort village (pop. 2,373), Suffolk co., SE N.Y., on SE peninsula of Long Isl., on Sag Harbor (inlet of Gardiners Bay), 9 mi. NE of Southampton; mfg. (machinery, metal products, aircraft parts). An important 19th-cent. whaling port. The *Long Island Herald* (1791) was Long Isl.'s 1st local paper. The Whalers' Church and Whalers' Mus., noted for their architecture, are among its historic bldgs. Settled 1720–30, inc. 1846. Had 1st customhouse in N.Y.

Saghghiz, Iran: see SAQQIZ.

Saghiada, Greece: see SAGIADA.

Saghiz, Iran: see SAQQIZ.

Sagho, Djebel (jĕ'bĕl sägō'), mtn. massif of S Fr. Morocco, forming NE extension of the Anti-Atlas range beyond the upper Oued Dra; rises to 8,400 ft. Linked to S spur of the High Atlas near Boumalne. Region was among the last to be pacified by French, 1933–34. Also spelled Djebel Sarho.

Sagiada or **Sayiadha** (both: sāyä'dhů), village (pop. 485), Thesprotia nome, S Epirus, Greece, on inlet of Strait of Corfu, near Albanian line, 7 mi. WNW of Philiates, which it serves as port. Also spelled Saghiada.

Saginaw (să'gĭnô), county (□ 812; pop. 153,515), E central Mich.; ⊙ Saginaw. Drained by Saginaw R. and its affluents; by Cass, Flint, Shiawassee, Bad, and Tittabawassee rivers; and by small Mistequay Creek. Agr. (sugar beets, beans, truck, grain, corn, livestock, poultry; dairy products). Mfg. at Saginaw. Oil fields, salt deposits, coal mines. State game area in co. Organized 1835.

Saginaw. 1 City (pop. 92,918), ⊙ Saginaw co., E central Mich., 31 mi. NNW of Flint, and on both banks of navigable Saginaw R. c.20 mi. above its mouth on Saginaw Bay (N). Port of entry. Fourth largest city in state; and market, industrial, and processing center for bean, sugar-beet, and grain region, with oil wells, salt and coal deposits. Mfg. of auto parts, machinery, foundry and machine-shop products, tools, construction materials, furniture, paper, graphite, and wood products, leather goods, tents, awnings, chemicals, flour, feed, canned goods. Salt processing, oil refining. Indian trails and villages were located here and in surrounding area. Here Lewis Cass negotiated the treaty with the Indians (1819) which ceded much of Mich. territory to U.S. The city's large lumber industry, following upon an era of fur trade, declined in 1890s. Settled c.1816, inc. as city 1857. **2** Town (pop. 561), Tarrant co., N Texas, just N of Fort Worth.

Saginaw Bay, E Mich., a SW arm of L. Huron, extends c.60 mi. SW from its mouth bet. Au Sable Point (NW) and Pointe Aux Barques (SE); 15–25 mi. wide. Bay City, its chief port, is at its head, near mouth of Saginaw R. Resorts; commercial fishing.

Saginaw River, E Mich., formed by confluence of Shiawassee and Tittabawassee rivers just SW of Saginaw, flows NNE, through Saginaw and Bay City (both ports), to SW end of Saginaw Bay just below Bay City; c.22 mi. long; entirely navigable.

Sagiz (sŭgēs'), oil town (1948 pop. over 2,000), N Guryev oblast, Kazakh SSR, 13 mi. E of Dossor, in Emba oil fields.

Sagliano Micca, Italy: see ANDORNO MICCA.

Sagmyra (sōg'mü"rä), Swedish *Sågmyra*, village (pop. 1,054), Kopparberg co., central Sweden, 13 mi. NW of Falun; woolen and lumber milling.

Sagona Island (sůgō'nů), islet, SE N.F., on NW side of Fortune Bay, 20 mi. N of Grand Bank.

Sagone, Gulf of (sägōnā', It. sägô'nĕ), in the Mediterranean, off W coast of Corsica, c.10 mi. N of Ajaccio; 11 mi. wide, 8 mi. deep, bounded (S) by Cap de Feno.

Sagor, Yugoslavia: see ZAGORJE.

Sagra, La (lä sä'grä), region in Toledo prov., New Castile, central Spain, a high plain of the central plateau on right bank of the Tagus and S of Madrid prov. Illescas is its center, though the region is sometimes considered to include Talavera de la Reina. Watered by Alberche R. Chiefly a grain-growing region.

Sagrado (sägrä'dô), village (pop. 1,169), Gorizia prov., Friuli-Venezia Giulia, NE Italy, on Isonzo R. and 8 mi. SW of Gorizia; mfg. (furniture, chains).

Sagres (sä'grĭsh), village (pop. 826), Faro dist., S Portugal, on Sagres Point, 3 mi. SE of Cape St. Vincent; fishing. Near by Prince Henry the Navigator established (c.1420) a school for navigators and an observatory.

Sagres Point, headland on the Atlantic, near SW tip of Portugal, 3 mi. SE of Cape Saint Vincent; 36°58'N 8°57'W; lighthouse. Sagres village is here.

Sagri, India: see JIANPUR.

Sagthali (säg'tŭlē), village, S Rajasthan, India, 14 mi. SSE of Partabgarh; millet, corn, wheat.

Sagu (sůgōō'), town (pop. 4,207), Minbu dist., Upper Burma, 7 mi. NW of Minbu.

Saguache (sůwŏch'), county (□ 3,144; pop. 5,664), S central Colo.; ⊙ Saguache. Irrigated agr. area, including part of fertile San Luis Valley in E. Livestock, hay, potatoes. Includes ranges of Rocky Mts. and parts of Gunnison, Rio Grande, Cochetopa, and San Isabel natl. forests. Part of Great Sand Dunes Natl. Monument in SE. Formed 1867.

Saguache, town (pop. 1,024), ⊙ Saguache co., S central Colo., on Saguache Creek, in S foothills of Sawatch Mts., W of Sangre de Cristo Mts., and 32 mi. SSW of Salida; alt. 7,800 ft. Trading point in livestock region. Gold, silver, copper, and lead mines in vicinity. Founded 1866, inc. 1891.

Saguache Creek, SW Colo., rises in San Juan Mts., flows c.75 mi. NE and SE, past Saguache, to San Luis Creek in N part of SAN LUIS VALLEY. At Saguache stream divides into parallel channels which rejoin just above San Luis Creek. Streams flow jointly 4 mi. S to irrigation canal leading into San Luis L., 8 mi. SE of confluence. Other irrigation canals connect Saguache Creek with headwaters of Rio Grande.

Sagua de Tánamo (sä'gwä dā tä'nämō), town (pop. 2,864), Oriente prov., E Cuba, on Sagua de Tánamo R. and 29 mi. E of Mayarí, in agr. region (tobacco, coconuts, bananas).

Sagua de Tánamo River, Oriente prov., E Cuba, rises at S foot of the Sierra del Cristal, flows 40 mi. N, past Sagua de Tánamo, to N coast just E of Tánamo Bay. Navigable in lower reaches for small boats.

Sagua la Grande (lä grän'dā), city (pop. 24,044), Las Villas prov., central Cuba, on Sagua la Grande R. and 28 mi. NNW of Santa Clara, 10 mi. SSW of its port Isabela de Sagua; rail junction and trading center in sugar-cane region. Has alcohol distillery, foundries, railroad shops, lumberyards. Mfg. of caustic soda. Sugar centrals in outskirts.

Sagua la Grande River, Las Villas prov., central Cuba, rises S of Santa Clara, flows c.75 mi. N, past Santo Domingo and Sagua la Grande, to Nicholas Channel at Isabela de Sagua. Navigable 15 mi. upstream for small vessels. The Sagua la Chica, rising near the Sagua la Grande, empties into ocean 25 mi. SE of Isabela de Sagua.

Saguaro National Monument (sůgwä'rō, sůwä'rō) (□ 83.8; established 1933), SE Ariz., 20 mi. E of Tucson. Mtn. and desert area, with extensive stands of saguaro, a giant cactus (up to 50 ft.) with edible fruits, native to arid regions of SW U.S. and NW Mexico; its blossom is Ariz. state flower.

Saguenay (să'gůnā, –nē, Fr. sägůnā'), county (□ 315,176; pop. 29,419), SE Que., extending N from the St. Lawrence and lower course of Saguenay R.; ⊙ Tadoussac.

Saguenay River, S central Que., issues from L. St. John by Grande Décharge (hydroelectric station) and Petite Décharge, 2 short channels enclosing Île d'Alma; flows 110 mi. ESE, past St. Joseph d'Alma, Chute à Caron (falls; hydroelectric station), Arvida, Chicoutimi, and Tadoussac, to the St. Lawrence just SE of Tadoussac. ESE of Chicoutimi is the inlet HA HA BAY. Below Ha Ha Bay, river flows bet. steep high banks, rising to over 1,500 ft. at Eternity and Trinity capes. On its upper tributaries are important hydroelectric power centers. Saguenay R. is navigable below Chicoutimi and is major lumber-transport route. It is a popular fishing and canoeing stream; steamer excursions.

Saguia el Hamra (säg'yä ĕl äm'rä) or **Saguia Hamra,** territory (□ c.32,000; pop. 13,000) of SPANISH WEST AFRICA, constituting the middle segment of the Saharan coastal region belonging to Spain; ⊙ Aiun. Lat. 27°40'N marks its N boundary with the so-called Southern Protectorate of Morocco, and lat. 26°N marks its S boundary with RÍO DE ORO. Saguia el Hamra and Río de Oro are grouped, for administrative purposes, as a region called Spanish Sahara. Drained E-W by the Saguia el Hamra (principal wadi of Sp. West Africa, c.280 mi. long), it consists of barren desert region. Agr. (barley, corn) limited to irrigated patches. Offshore fisheries. By treaty of 1904, France granted Spain "liberty of action" in this zone. Also spelled Saguiet el Hamra, Sekia el Hamra.

Sagunto (sägōōn'tō), formerly **Murviedro** (mōōr-vyä'dhrō), anc. *Saguntum*, city (pop. 10,352), Valencia prov., E Spain, near the Mediterranean, 16 mi. NNE of Valencia; mfg. of hardware, tiles, citric acid; vegetable canning, olive-oil processing, flour milling. Its seaport (pop. 9,146; 2.5 mi. SSE), terminus of mining railroad from Ojos Negros iron mines, is a metallurgical center (iron and steel foundries); exports minerals, wine, oranges. On ridge S of city (site of anc. town) are well-preserved remains of Roman theater and of fortifications of medieval Castillo de San Fernando and of Moorish citadel; N of city are ruins of Roman circus and bridge. Also has Gothic parochial church and several medieval houses. Flourishing Iberian town, later a Greek settlement; as an ally of Rome, was besieged and captured (219–218 B.C.) by Carthaginians under Hannibal after heroic resistance; conquered by Romans (214 B.C.). Taken by Moors (8th cent.); reconquered by Christians (13th cent.). Restoration of Bourbon dynasty proclaimed here (1874). Called Murviedro by Arabs, a name it retained until 1877.

Sagvag (säg'vôg), Nor. *Sagvåg*, village in Stord canton, Hordaland co., SW Norway, port on SW shore of Stord isl., on North Sea, 24 mi. NNE of Haugesund; boatbuilding, canning; exports wood pulp and pyrite from Litlabo.

Sagwara (säg'värŭ), town (pop. 6,200), S Rajasthan, India, 22 mi. SE of Dungarpur; market center for maize, rice, millet, barley.

Sahaganj, India: see HOOGHLY, town.

Sahagún (sägōōn'), town (pop. 4,308), Bolívar dept., N Colombia, in savannas, 33 mi. NE of Montería; stock raising.

Sahagún, town (pop. 3,606), Leon prov., NW Spain, 33 mi. ESE of Leon; agr. trade center (cereals, vegetables, grapes, livestock); brandy distilling, flour milling, textile mfg.; lumbering. Has ruined Benedictine abbey, a center of Castilian culture from 10th to 15th cent.; abbey's church contains tomb of Alfonso VI.

Saham (sähäm'), town (pop. 3,800), Batina dist., N Oman, port on Gulf of Oman, 16 mi. SE of Sohar; coastal trade; fishing; date cultivation.

Sahand (sähänd'), volcanic cone (12,140 ft.) in Azerbaijan, NW Iran, 30 mi. SSE of Tabriz and E of L. Urmia; snow-capped; mineral springs.

Sahanpur (sŭhän'pōōr), town (pop. 3,732), Bijnor dist., N Uttar Pradesh, India, just NW of Najibabad; sugar refining; rice, wheat, gram, barley, sugar cane. Also called Girdawa Sahanpur.

Sahara (sůhä'rů) [Arabic,=the desert] or, often, **Sahara Desert,** vast arid region (estimated over □ 3,000,000) of N Africa, the largest desert on earth. Extends W-E across the continent from the Atlantic (17°W) to the Red Sea (36°E), although the Nile valley (32°E) is sometimes considered its E border. It is c.1,200 mi. wide (17°N–34°N), its S limit being an ill-defined transition zone (steppe vegetation) merging with the SUDAN; in N it is bounded by the folded ranges of the ATLAS MOUNTAINS in Morocco, Algeria, and Tunisia, and by the Mediterranean which it reaches in Libya and in Egypt. Its E portion in Libya and Egypt is known as the LIBYAN DESERT; the narrow strip bet. the Nile and the Red Sea is called the ARABIAN DESERT in Egypt, and, in Anglo-Egyptian Sudan, the NUBIAN DESERT. The Sahara forms but the W portion of an enormous arid belt which extends eastward into Asia, crossing the desert of Arabia and the great Syrian Desert in Syria, Jordan, Arabia, and Iraq, the tableland of Iran, the Kara-Kum and Kyzyl-Kum of Turkestan, the Taklamakan of Sinkiang, and the Gobi of Mongolia. The aridity of the Sahara is due to its latitude in the zone of the NE trade winds (whose moisture-holding capacity increases as they sweep toward the equator) and to its location along the SE edge of the high-pressure area which hovers permanently over the Atlantic near the Azores and deflects cyclonic disturbances from N Africa. Rainfall is everywhere below 10 in. per year (except in isolated uplands) and occurs with great irregularity, so that records of no precipitation whatsoever during several consecutive years exist at several stations. When it does rain, downpours are violent and of short duration, turning dry wadis into raging torrents. Because of low atmospheric humidity and the rapid radiation of surface heat, the diurnal temperature range is extreme, as much as 100 degrees of Fahrenheit at times. Daytime summer temperatures are very high, a reading of 136°F. having been recorded at Azizia, Libya. Torrid, dust-laden winds originating in the Sahara influence the climate of adjoining regions and are known under such names as sirocco, simoom, khamsin, and harmattan. Physiographically, the Sahara may be described as a series of low and moderately elevated tablelands, above which rise several isolated volcanic masses: the AHAGGAR MOUNTAINS (9,850 ft.) in Algeria, the Aïr (5,900 ft.) in Fr. West Africa, and the TIBESTI MASSIF in Fr. Equatorial Africa and Libya, where the Emi Koussi volcano (highest in the Sahara) rises to 11,204 ft. There are several local depressions, the largest of which, along the Sahara's N edge in Algeria and Tunisia, is filled by saline lakes (Chott Melrhir, 60 ft. below sea level; Chott Djerid). Wind is the desert's most active agent in erosion. Typical landforms are: the *erg* (e.g., Great Western Erg and Great Eastern Erg in Algeria, Libyan Erg along Egypt-Cyrenaica border), with its stretches of high shifting sand dunes; the *hammada* (e.g., Hammada el Hamra in S Tripolitania) or denuded rock platform; and the *reg* or gravel-covered surface. Aside from the 2 major rivers (Nile and Niger) which cross but the edges of the Sahara, there are no permanent streams, although the size of existing wadis appears to prove that drainage had been more abundant during Pleistocene times. Several streams, rising on S slope of the High Atlas in Morocco and of the Saharan Atlas in Algeria, water a string of oases before losing themselves in the desert's great ergs. The Oued Igharghar can be traced northward from the Ahaggar to the depression of the shotts. Vegetation, outside of the oases, is sparse and xerophytic; short scrub grasses, locally known as *ashab*, are widespread immediately after a downpour; acacias and tamarisks are found at higher elevations. The date-palm which marks an oasis supplies the region's principal export item; the Deglet Nur dates (grown especially in the Algerian oases of Biskra, Touggourt, Ouargla, and El-Oued) are in greatest demand. Cereals, vegetables, and Mediterranean fruit are also grown in well-watered oases. Salt is mined (especially at Bilma in Fr. West Africa), and coal is exploited at Kenadsa (Algeria) at foot of the Saharan Atlas. In anc. times the inhabitants of the desert were predominantly Sudanese Negroes. After the introduction of the camel, probably in early Christian era, Berbers and, later, Arabs gradually drove back the Negroes or employed them as laborers in the oases. The Tibesti, inhabited by the Tibus or Tibbus, is one of the few regions still dominated by Negroid tribes. The white pop. extended the oases by tapping underground waters and introduced date-palm cultivation. Outstanding among the nomad groups are the Berber Tuaregs (especially in the Ahaggar). Among the Sahara's principal groups of oases are Kharga, Dakhla, Farafra, Bahariya, and Siwa in the WESTERN DESERT of Egypt; Jarabub, Kufra, and the FEZZAN oases in Libya; Biskra, Touggourt, Ouargla, MZAB,

Touat, Gourara, Tidikelt, and the Ahaggar oases in Algeria; and the Tafilelt in Morocco. The W part of the Sahara, in Mauritania and Sp. West Africa, is almost without oases down to the Atlantic coast, here washed by the cold Canaries Current. Although N Africa's Mediterranean shores have long been dominated by foreign powers, most of the Sahara was not penetrated by Europeans until 19th cent. René Caillié (Caillé) was one of the earliest explorers to cross it and to return (c.1828). He was followed by Barth, Nachtigal, Duveyrier, and de Foucauld. The Algerian section of the Sahara was systematically explored after 1880 (Flatters, Foureau, Lamy), and effective military occupation was completed by 1910. Italian penetration of the Libyan Sahara took place in 1930s. Trans-Saharan trade (especially bet. Timbuktu and Algerian-Moroccan coastal areas), which had flourished in 16th cent., was severely curtailed in 19th cent. by suppression of slave trade. Today the desert is crossed by several trunk auto and caravan tracks, with spurs connecting the principal oases. In the French Sahara, 2 main routes link Colomb-Béchar, Djelfa, and Touggourt (all termini of rail lines from the Algerian coast at Sahara's N edge) with Gao (Fr. West Africa) on the great bend of the Niger; one passes Reggan and crosses the Tanezrouft, the other touches In-Salah and traverses the Ahaggar. Near the Atlantic coast, SW Fr. Morocco is linked with Mauritania by a route circumventing Sp. West Africa. In Libya, Tripoli and Misurata on the Mediterranean have roads to the Fezzan across the Gebel es-Soda; the Kufra oases are connected with the Cyrenaica coast (N), and by a tenuous route with Fort-Lamy, Fr. Equatorial Africa (SSW). The Egyptian oases are reached from the Nile valley. Although construction of a trans-Saharan railroad has been contemplated for 100 years, only the N section (Nemours to Colomb-Béchar, and slightly beyond) of a line projected to the Niger had been completed in 1947, when work was suspended. For political and administrative data about the Sahara region, see articles on ALGERIA, MOROCCO, TUNISIA, SPANISH WEST AFRICA, FRENCH WEST AFRICA, FRENCH EQUATORIAL AFRICA, LIBYA, EGYPT, and ANGLO-EGYPTIAN SUDAN.

Saharan Oases, Fr. *Oasis Sahariennes* (wäzĕs' säăryĕn'), military territory (□ 411,776; 1948 pop. 61,686) of S Algeria, largest of the Southern Territories in the Sahara; ⊙ Ouargla. Bounded by the Fezzan (E) and by Fr. West Africa (S). Includes large portion of the Great Eastern Erg (NE), and of the Tademaït Plateau (W); the Ahaggar Mts. (S center); and the Tassili plateaus (E and S). Chief oases are Ouargla, the Tidikelt group (In-Salah, Aoulef), and the Ahaggar oases of Tamanrasset and Silet. Territory is traversed (N-S) by trans-Saharan auto track from Touggourt to Zinder (Fr. West Africa). In 1945, the Fezzan region of Ghat-Serdèles was administratively attached to the Saharan Oases territory.

Saharanpur (sŭhä'rŭnpŏŏr), district (□ 2,134; pop. 1,179,643), N Uttar Pradesh, India; ⊙ Saharanpur. In Ganges-Jumna Doab; bounded N by Siwalik Range, W by the Punjab. Agr. (wheat, rice, rape and mustard, gram, sugar cane, corn, barley, cotton); a leading sugar-processing dist. of India. Main centers: Saharanpur, HARDWAR, Deoband, Roorkee.

Saharanpur, city (pop. 108,263), ⊙ Saharanpur dist., N Uttar Pradesh, India, 90 mi. NNE of Delhi. Rail and road junction; trade center (wheat, rice, rape and mustard, gram, sugar cane, corn, barley); sugar processing, cotton ginning, mfg. of cigarettes, hosiery, cotton cloth; railroad workshops, large paper mill. Central Fruit Research Inst. Govt. botanical gardens. Civil aviation training center; remount depot. Founded c.1340.

Sahara Village, village (pop. 1,636), Davis co., N Utah, c.20 mi. N of Salt Lake City, near Layton.

Sahaspur (sŭhŭs'pŏŏr), town (pop. 7,626), Bijnor dist., N Uttar Pradesh, India, near the Ramganga, 34 mi. SE of Bijnor; hand-loom cotton weaving; rice, wheat, gram, sugar cane. Serai. Also called Sahaspur-khas.

Sahaswan (sŭhŭs'vän), town (pop. 20,443), Budaun dist., central Uttar Pradesh, India, 23 mi. W of Budaun; perfume mfg.; wheat, pearl millet, mustard, barley, gram. Also spelled Sahsawan.

Sahatwar (sŭhŭt'vär), town (pop. 8,502), Ballia dist., E Uttar Pradesh, India, 12 mi. NE of Ballia; trades in rice, gram, barley, oilseeds, sugar cane, cotton. Sometimes called Mahatwar.

Sahawar (sŭhä'vŭr), town (pop. 6,993), Etah dist., W Uttar Pradesh, India, 12 mi. E of Kasganj; wheat, pearl millet, barley, corn, jowar, oilseeds. Founded 12th cent. A.D.

Sahdol (sŭdōl'), town (pop. 6,753), ⊙ Sahdol dist., SE Vindhya Pradesh, India, 85 mi. S of Rewa; local market for millet, gram, building stone. Coal mined near by.

Sahel (sähĕl'), name given to various Mediterranean coastal strips in Tunisia and Algeria. Most frequently it designates a region (c.80 mi. long, 10–25 mi. wide) along E coast of Tunisia bet. the Gulf of Hammamet (N) and the Gulf of Gabès (S). Chief city is Sousse. Noted for its olive trees. The hilly dist. flanking Algiers (Algeria) is also called Sahel.

Sahel, Oued, Algeria: see SOUMMAM, OUED.

Saheth Maheth, India: see SET MAHET.

Sahibganj (sä'hibgŭnj), town (pop. 20,742), Santal Parganas dist., E Bihar, India, on Ganges Plain, on Ganges R. and 43 mi. E of Bhagalpur; trade center (rice, corn barley, oilseeds, bhabar); cattle market.

Sahiwal (sä'hĭväl), town (pop. 8,090), Shahpur dist., central Punjab, W Pakistan, 22 mi. SW of Sargodha; local market for wheat, millet, cotton, ghee; hand-loom weaving, lacquer work.

Sahlis, Germany: see KOHREN-SAHLIS.

Sahmaw (sŭhmô'), village, Myitkyina dist., Kachin State, Upper Burma, on railroad and 40 mi. WSW of Myitkyina; sugar milling.

Sahneh (sänĕ'), town, Fifth Prov., in Kermanshah, W Iran, 38 mi. ENE of Kermanshah and on road to Hamadan; grain, opium.

Sahovci or **Shakhovichi** (shä'hôvĭchē, –khô–), Serbo-Croatian *Šahovići*, village, NE Montenegro, Yugoslavia, 6 mi. NW of Bijelo Polje, near Serbia border.

Sahpau (sä'pou), town (pop. 3,850), Muttra dist., W Uttar Pradesh, India, 28 mi. ESE of Muttra; cotton, gram, jowar, wheat, oilseeds.

Sahra' al-Janubiyah, Al-, Egypt: see SOUTHERN DESERT.

Sahsawan, India: see SAHASWAN.

Sahuaripa (säwärē'pä), city (pop. 3,195), Sonora, NW Mexico, on Sahuaripa R. (affluent of the Yaqui) and 105 mi. E of Hermosillo; mining center (molybdenum, tungsten, silver, gold, lead, copper) in rich iron dist.; stock raising.

Sahuayo or **Sahuayo de Porfirio Díaz** (säwī'ō dā pôrfēr'yō dē'äs), town (pop. 10,465), Michoacán, central Mexico, on central plateau, near S shore of L. Chapala, 60 mi. SE of Guadalajara; agr. center (cereals, sugar cane, tobacco, beans, fruit, stock); flour milling.

Sahy (shä'hĭ), Slovak *Šahy*, Hung. *Ipolyság* (ĭ'poishäg), town (pop. 4,019), S Slovakia, Czechoslovakia, on Ipel R. and 45 mi. SSW of Banska Bystrica, in wheat-growing area; rail junction.

Sahyadri, mts., India: see Western GHATS.

Sahyun (säyōōn'), Fr. *Sihiyoun* or *Sahyoun*, village, Latakia prov., NW Syria, 16 mi. E of Latakia; sericulture, cotton, tobacco, cereals. Here is a castle built by Crusaders on site of Byzantine fort.

Saibai (sī'bī), island (pop. 426), in Torres Strait, 90 mi. N of Cape York Peninsula, Queensland, Australia, just off S coast of New Guinea; 15 mi. long, 5 mi. wide; low, swampy; fishing.

Saiburi (sī'bŏŏrē'), village (1937 pop. 4,118), Pattani prov., S Thailand, minor South China Sea port on E coast of Malay Peninsula, 30 mi. SE of Pattani, at mouth of small Saiburi R.; rice; coconuts. Local name, Taluban.

Said or **Sa'id** (säĕd'), town and oasis (pop. 800), Wahidi sultanate of Balhaf, Eastern Aden Protectorate, 12 mi. ESE of Azzan and on the Wadi Meifa'a.

Saïda (sīdä'), town (pop. 13,292), Oran dept., NW Algeria, on S slopes of the Tell Atlas at fringe of the High Plateaus (steppe country), on railroad to the interior (terminus, Colomb-Béchar) and 40 mi. S of Mascara; Algeria's leading sheep market; wine-growing, truck gardening; distilling, flour milling, cement mfg. Just S, ruins of Abd-el-Kader's fortress.

Saida or **Sayida** (both: sī'dä, sīdä'), Fr. *Saïda*, anc. *Sidon* (sī'dŭn) or *Zidon* (zī'–), town (pop. 17,739), ⊙ South Lebanon prov., Lebanon, on the Mediterranean 25 mi. SSW of Beirut; 33°33'N 35°25'E. Fishing port, agr. trade center, and oil-transshipment center. Handles apples, citrus fruit, bananas, sugar cane, cotton, cereals, almonds, apricots; sericulture. It has huge storage tanks for petroleum received here via a large oil pipe line opened 1950 from Abqaiq in Saudi Arabia. Sidon was the most anc. city of Phoenicia, older than Tyre, which it colonized and which eventually eclipsed it late in 2d millenium B.C. It was long an important port and commercial center, and was known for its purple dyes and glassware (glass-blowing is said to have been invented here). It was destroyed many times during the centuries in which it was the object of numerous conquests, falling successively to the Assyrians, Babylonians, Persians, Seleucids, Romans, Byzantines, Crusaders, Arabs (1249), French (1253), Mongols (1261), and Arabs (1291). By then in complete ruin, it became a small provincial town. It is often mentioned in the Bible. There are excavations of Phoenician ruins.

Saidabad, Iran: see SIRJAN.

Saida-Guba or **Sayda-Guba** (sī"dŭ-gōōbä') [Rus.,= Saida bay], town (1939 pop. over 2,000), NW Murmansk oblast, Russian SFSR, on Small Saida Bay of Kola Gulf, 20 mi. N of Murmansk; fish canning.

Saidaiji (sīdī'jē), town (pop. 14,501), Okayama prefecture, SW Honshu, Japan, 5 mi. E of Okayama; rail terminus; commercial center for agr. area (rice, wheat); cotton textiles, yarn, sake. Has race tracks.

Saïda Mountains (sīdä'), southern range of the Tell Atlas, Oran dept., NW Algeria, overlooking the High Plateaus (S), and extending c.70 mi. from Saïda (SW) to Tiaret (NE). Rises to 3,950 ft. Heavily forested.

Saidapet (sī'dŭpĕt), city (pop. 41,347), ⊙ Chingleput dist., E Madras, India; contiguous suburb of Madras, 5 mi. SW of city center; includes several dispersed residential areas and public parks. Has Teachers Col. (affiliated with Madras Univ.), YMCA Col. of Physical Education. In SE area, called Guindy, are noted King Inst. of Preventive Medicine (major bacteriological laboratory; mfg. of vaccine and serum), Col. of Engineering (includes telecommunication), Col. of Technology (chemical engineering, leather and textile technology), Govt. House (residence of Madras govt. officials), and Guindy Race Course.

Saideli, Turkey: see KADINHANI.

Saïdia (sīdyä'), village, Oujda region, northeasternmost Fr. Morocco, on Algerian border, 20 mi. W of Nemours; Fr. Morocco's only port on the Mediterranean (no harbor installations); bathing resort; ships early fruits and vegetables, wine.

Saidnaya or **Saydanaya** (both: sīdnä'yä), Fr. *Seyd Naya*, village (pop. c.2,500), Damascus prov., SW Syria, 13 mi. NNE of Damascus; alt. 4,640 ft.; summer resort; olives. Site of old convent (6th cent. A.D.). Pop. mostly Greek Catholic and Eastern Orthodox.

Saidpur (sīd'pŏŏr), town (pop. 6,059), Ghazipur dist., E Uttar Pradesh, India, on the Ganges and 23 mi. WSW of Ghazipur; trades in rice, barley, gram, oilseeds, cotton, hides. Important Gupta inscriptions, including inscribed red sandstone pillar of a Magadha king, 4 mi. ENE, at Bhitri village.

Saidpur, town (pop., including rail settlement, 19,516), Rangpur dist., N East Bengal, E Pakistan, 22 mi. W of Rangpur; large rail workshops; rice and oilseed milling, jute pressing; trades in rice, jute, tobacco, oilseeds, sugar cane.

Saidu (sī'dōō), village, ⊙ Swat state, N North-West Frontier Prov., W Pakistan, near Swat R., 65 mi. NE of Peshawar; local market for grain, ghee. Also called Saidu Sharif.

Saifganj, India: see KATIHAR.

Saigawa, Japan: see SAIKAWA.

Saighan or **Sayghan** (sīgän'), village, Kabul prov., E Afghanistan, at N foot of the Hindu Kush, 95 mi. NW of Kabul, and on Saighan R. (left tributary of the Surkhab); sulphur deposits.

Saignes (sĕ'nyü), village (pop. 460), Cantal dept., S central France, in Auvergne Mts., 10 mi. NNE of Mauriac; cheese mfg., sawmilling.

Saigo (sīgō'), chief town (pop. 6,862) of isl. group Oki-gunto, Shimane prefecture, Japan, port on SE coast of Dogo; fishing center; fish canneries. Exports raw silk, lumber, charcoal.

Saigon (sīgôn'), city (1936 pop. 110,577), ⊙ Vietnam and of Cochin China (now South Vietnam), on right bank of Saigon R. at mouth of the Chinese Arroyo, 50 mi. (by river) from South China Sea; 10°47'N 106°42'E. Administrative, shipping, and industrial center, linked by railroad with Hanoi (N Vietnam), Mytho, and Locninh; and connected with Mekong delta canal network; airport. Since 1932 combined with CHOLON in a separate administrative unit (1943 pop. 492,200; 1948 pop. 1,179,000), constituting the greatest industrial urban complex of Vietnam. Shipyards (naval base and arsenal); food processing (rice, sugar, oilseeds), brewing and distilling, mfg. of rubber goods, leather, cotton textiles, tobacco products. Saigon ships rice (largely milled in Cholon), corn, dried fish, copra, and rubber. Although an important port with large export and import trade, it is not used extensively as a port of call on main maritime routes owing to its inland position. Unlike Cholon, Saigon is of typically European aspect, laid out in rectilinear fashion with wide, tree-lined avenues and parks, known for their beauty throughout the East; has modern govt. palace, Romanesque cathedral, city hall, art mus., botanical and zoological gardens. The administrative section of the city, on higher ground, is adjoined by the commercial riverside quarters. The maritime quarter (docks, shipping offices) is in S suburb of Khanhhoi, across the Chinese Arroyo. Annamese section extends W of city toward Cholon. An anc. Khmer settlement, Saigon passed (17th cent.) to Annamese, was first visited (1789) by Fr. mission. Captured 1859 by the French, Saigon was unsuccessfully besieged (1861) by the Annamese and formally ceded to France in 1863. A small village at the time of Fr. conquest, the city has been built since 19th cent., in part through marsh reclamation. It was ⊙ Union of Indochina from 1887 until its transfer to Hanoi in 1902, and ⊙ Cochin China until the formation of Vietnam after the Second World War.

Saigon River, S Vietnam, rises on Cambodia border W of Locninh, flows S and SSE c.140 mi., past Thudaumot (54 ft. deep at high tide) and Saigon, forming a common delta with Dongnai R. on South China Sea. At Saigon, it receives the Chinese Arroyo.

Saihut, Aden: see SEIHUT.

Saijo (sījō′). **1** City (1940 pop. 33,667; 1947 pop. 44,840), Ehime prefecture, N Shikoku, Japan, 24 mi. ENE of Matsuyama; mfg. center in rice-growing area; cotton textiles, paper. Has agr. school. Starting point for ascent of Mt. Ishizuchi. Also called Iyo-saijo. Includes (since early 1940s) former town of Himi. **2** Town (pop. 15,888), Hiroshima prefecture, SW Honshu, Japan, 17 mi. E of Hiroshima; commercial center in agr. area (persimmons, mushrooms); sake brewing, rice milling, mfg. of agr. implements. **3** Town (pop. 9,476), Hiroshima prefecture, SW Honshu, Japan, 55 mi. NE of Hiroshima; agr., stock raising.

Saikawa (sī′käwä) or **Saigawa** (–gäwä), town (pop. 9,546), Fukuoka prefecture, N Kyushu, Japan, 19 mi. S of Moji; rice, wheat, barley, raw silk.

Saikhoa Ghat (sīkō′ŭ gät′), village, NE frontier tract of Assam, India, 5 mi. SW of Sadiya, across Luhit R.; rail terminus; rice, tea, rape and mustard, sugar cane. Track leads ESE, through Chaukan Pass on India-Burma border, to Putao area of Upper Burma.

Saiki, Japan: see SAEKI.

Saikyo, Japan: see KYOTO, city.

Sailana (sīlä′nŭ), town (pop. 5,337), W Madhya Bharat, India, 12 mi. NW of Ratlam, at foot of N offshoot of Vindhya Range; markets millet, corn, wheat; agr. farm. Was ⊙ former princely state of Sailana (□ 300; pop. 40,228) of Central India agency, in scattered areas around Ratlam; since 1948, state merged with Madhya Bharat.

Saillagouse (säyägōōz′), agr. village (pop. 377), Pyrénées-Orientales dept., S France, in Cerdagne, on Sègre R. and 6 mi. ENE of Puigcerdá (Spain); grazing.

Saillans (säyäs′), village (pop. 910), Drôme dept., SE France, on the Drôme and 9 mi. SW of Die; vineyards; fruit and vegetable shipping.

Saillant, Le, France: see ALLASSAC.

Saillat (säyä′), village (pop. 548), Haute-Vienne dept., W central France, on the Vienne and 4 mi. WSW of St.-Junien; mfg. (tanning extracts, wrapping paper). Also called Saillat-sur-Vienne.

Sailor Springs, village (pop. 259), Clay co., S central Ill., 15 mi. W of Olney, in agr., oil, and natural-gas area.

Sail Rock, Caribbean islet, U.S. Virgin Isls., halfway bet. Culebra Isl. (W) and St. Thomas Isl. (E) in Virgin Passage; 18°17′N 65°6′W.

Sail-sous-Couzan (sī-sōō-kōōzä′), village (pop. 890), Loire dept., SE central France, on the Lignon and 10 mi. NNW of Montbrison; mineral springs; velvet weaving. Hydroelectric plant.

Sailu (sī′lōō), town (pop. 9,564), Parbhani dist., NW Hyderabad state, India, WNW of Parbhani; agr. market (chiefly cotton, millet, wheat, peanuts); cotton ginning.

Sailyugem Range or **Saylyugem Range** (sĭl′yōōgĕm), in the Altai Mts., on USSR-Mongolia border, extends NE from the mtn. knot Tabun Bogdo; rises to 13,927 ft.

Saimaa, Swedish *Saima* (both: sī′mä), lake system (□ 1,699), SE Finland, near USSR border, extends c.180 mi. bet. Lappeenranta (S) and Iisalmi (N), comprising c.120 connecting lakes, dotted with numerous isls. (total □ 656). L. Saimaa (S), largest (□ 502) of the system, drains SE into L. Ladoga through Vuoksi R.; the Saimaa Canal connects it with Gulf of Finland. Industrial and commercial centers on system are Lappeenranta, Lauritsala (N end of Saimaa Canal to Gulf of Finland), Mikkeli, Savonlinna, Varkaus, Kuopio, and Joensuu. Many small canals facilitate lake shipping. In major lumbering and timber-industry region, system is important route for lumber rafts and lake freighters. System is also called Great Saimaa, Finnish *Iso Saimaa* (ĭ′sō).

Saimaa Canal, Finnish *Saimaan kanava* (sī′män kä′nävä), Swedish *Saima kanal*, Russian *Saimenski Kanal*, SE Finland and Leningrad oblast, RSFSR, extends 36 mi. (length of artificial waterway, 20 mi.) from L. Saimaa at Lauritsala to inlet of Gulf of Finland 7 mi. N of Vyborg. Canal overcomes difference in height of 249 ft. with aid of 9 locks. Completed 1856; important timber-shipping route.

Saimbeyli (sīmbālē′), village (pop. 1,143), Seyhan prov., S Turkey, 55 mi. SE of Kayseri; grain, legumes, potatoes. Formerly Hacin.

Saimenski Kanal, USSR and Finland: see SAIMAA CANAL.

Sain Alto (sīn′ äl′tō), town (pop. 2,372), Zacatecas, N central Mexico, on interior plateau, 27 mi. SW of Río Grande; alt. 6,860 ft.; mercury mining.

Sainam (sī′näm′), Mandarin *Hsi-nan* (shē′nän′), town, S Kwangtung prov., China, on a North R. branch of Canton R. delta, on railroad and 5 mi. ESE of Samshui; industrial center; machinery mfg., silk milling.

Saincaize (sĕkāz′), village (pop. 45), Nièvre dept., central France, on Allier R. near its mouth into the Loire, and 6 mi. SW of Nevers; railroad junction. Near by, Loire Lateral Canal crosses Allier R. on aqueduct.

Saindon, Que.: see SAYABEC.

Sainei, Korea: see CHAERYONG.

Sainghin-en-Weppes (sĕgē′-ā-vĕp′), town (pop. 3,471), Nord dept., N France, 8 mi. SW of Lille; dairying center in sugar-beet area.

Saining, China: see WATNAM.

Sain Qaleh, Iran: see SHAHIN DEZH.

Sains-du-Nord (sē-dü-nôr′), town (pop. 2,157), Nord dept., N France, 4 mi. SE of Avesnes; wool spinning, paper milling, mfg. of jute bags and milk sugar.

Sains-en-Gohelle (sĕz″ä-gôĕl′), town (pop. 4,097), Pas-de-Calais dept., N France, 6 mi. SSE of Béthune; coal mines.

Sain Shanda or **Sayn Shanda** (sīn′ shän′dä), town, ⊙ East Gobi aimak, SE Mongolian People's Republic, 260 mi. SE of Ulan Bator, near highway to Kalgan; food processing; coal mining.

Sains-Richaumont (sē-rēshōmō′), village (pop. 989), Aisne dept., N France, 9 mi. W of Vervins; wool weaving.

Saint Abb's Head, promontory on North Sea, E Berwick, Scotland, at E end of Lammermuir Hills, 12 mi. NNW of Berwick-on-Tweed; lighthouse (55°55′N 2°8′W). Just SSE is small seaside resort and fishing village of Saint Abb's.

Saint-Acheul (sĕtäshûl′), locality near Amilus, Somme dept., N France. Paleolithic remains found here gave name to the Acheulian period of the Lower Paleolithic.

Saint-Affrique (sĕtäfrēk′), town (pop. 5,231), Aveyron dept., S France, 14 mi. SW of Millau; mfg. of gloves, woolens, chemicals; tanning. Roquefort cheese trade.

Saint Agapit or **Saint Agapitville** (sĕtägäpēt′, sĕtägäpĕt′vĭl), village (pop. 592), S Que., 20 mi. SW of Quebec; dairying, lumbering, pig raising.

Saint Agatha (sānt ă′gŭthŭ, sĕntügät′), town (pop. 1,512), Aroostook co., N Maine, 7 mi. S of Madawaska and on Long L.; fishing resort. In Frenchville until inc., 1899.

Saint-Agnant or **Saint-Agnant-les-Marais** (sĕtänyä′-lā-märĕ′), village (pop. 231), Charente-Maritime dept., W France, 5 mi. S of Rochefort; dairying.

Saint Agnes, town and parish (pop. 3,379), W Cornwall, England, on the Atlantic and 8 mi. NW of Truro; fishing port and agr. market; former tin-mining center. Just W is promontory of St. Agnes Head, with lighthouse (50°19′N 5°14′W), at foot of St. Agnes Beacon, a hill (629 ft.).

Saint Agnes, island (433 acres; pop. 78), southernmost of the SCILLY ISLANDS, Cornwall, England, 3 mi. SW of St. Mary's; 49°53′N 6°20′W. Has prehistoric stone ruins.

Saint-Agrève (sĕtägrĕv′), village (pop. 1,400), Ardèche dept., S France, in the Monts du Vivarais, 16 mi. SE of Yssingeaux; alt. 3,445 ft. Road center and summer resort. Powdered-milk mfg.

Saint-Aignan or **Saint-Aignan-sur-Cher** (sĕtĕnyä′-sür-shâr′), village (pop. 1,842), Loir-et-Cher dept., N central France, on the Cher and 18 mi. WSW of Romorantin; winegrowing, mfg. (hosiery, baskets, leather goods, vegetable oil). Has Renaissance château and ruins of a feudal castle.

Saint-Aignan-sur-Roë (–sür-rō′), village (pop. 481), Mayenne dept., W France, 14 mi. NE of Châteaubriant; woodworking, cider milling.

Saint-Aimé (sĕtämā′), village (pop. 1,553), Oran dept., N Algeria, near the Chéliff, 20 mi. NE of Relizane; cereals, livestock.

Saint Alban (ôl′bŭn, Fr. sĕtälbä′), village (pop. 616), S Que., on Ste. Anne R., and 34 mi. NE of Trois Rivières; dairying; cattle, pigs, poultry.

Saint-Alban-Leysse (sĕtälbä′-lās′), commune (pop. 1,678), Savoie dept., SE France, 3 mi. ENE of Chambéry; paper milling. Until 1946, Saint-Alban.

Saint Albans (sŭnt ôl′bŭnz), residential municipal borough (1931 pop. 28,624; 1951 census 44,106) and city, S central Hertford, England, on hill above Ver R., 20 mi. NNW of London. Site of the Roman *Verulamium* and of Benedictine abbey founded 793 by King Offa of Mercia in honor of Alban, martyred here A.D. 303. Notable chroniclers of the abbey included Roger of Wendover, Matthew Paris, William Rishanger, and Thomas Walsingham. Church was rebuilt 1077 by Abbot Paul of Caen, using Roman materials; restored 1871–85 by Sir Gilbert Scott and Lord Grimthorpe; became cathedral in 1877. It is a fine example of Norman architecture and has the longest Gothic nave in the world. A grammar school was attached to abbey from 10th cent. to the Dissolution; refounded by Edward VI. Church of St. Michael (10th-cent.) contains memorial to Francis Bacon, Viscount St. Albans, who lived near by. The town was successively a British, Roman, and Danish stronghold. In Wars of the Roses Yorkists defeated Lancastrians here in 1455 and captured Henry VI; in 1461 Lancastrians were victorious and Henry VI was freed. Site of one of the Eleanor Crosses is marked by fountain. The Fighting Cock, old inn, is one of oldest inhabited houses in England. Extensive excavations have been made of the old Roman town. St. Albans makes hosiery, shoes, pharmaceuticals, electrical equipment.

Saint Albans (sānt ôl′bŭnz). **1** Town (pop. 1,035), Somerset co., central Maine, 8 mi. N of Pittsfield and on Big Indian L.; agr.; wood products. Settled 1800, inc. 1813. **2** A residential section of E Queens borough of New York city, SE N.Y.; some mfg. (neckwear, handbags, wood products). **3** City (pop. 8,552), ⊙ Franklin co., NW Vt., 24 mi. N of Burlington. Saint Albans town (pop. 1,908), on St. Albans Bay of L. Champlain, surrounds city, which is resort, railroad, and mfg. center and a port of entry. Produces metal, wood, and paper products; granite, lime; feed, maple and dairy products, poultry, canned foods. Town chartered 1763, organized 1788; St. Albans city inc. as village 1859, as city 1897. Smugglers' base in early 19th cent.; scene of Confederate bank raid from Canada in 1864; gathering point (1866) for Fenians planning invasion of Canada. Became railroad center, 1850. Seat of Bellows Free Acad. **4** City (pop. 9,870), Kanawha co., W W.Va., on the Kanawha, at Coal R. mouth, and 11 mi. W of Charleston, in bituminous-coal, gas, oil, timber, and agr. (tobacco, dairy products, poultry) area; mfg. of machine-shop products. Battle of Scary Creek (1861) was fought near by. Settled c.1790 on site of Fort Tackett.

Saint Alban's Head or **Saint Aldhelm's Head,** promontory, SW Dorset, England, on S coast of Isle of Purbeck and 5 mi. WSW of Swanage; 50°35′N 2°10′W. Has ruins of Norman chapel.

Saint-Alban-sur-Limagnole (sĕtälbä′-sür-lēmänyôl′), village (pop. 688), Lozère dept., S France, on W slope of Montagnes de la Margeride, 19 mi. NNW of Mende; pottery mfg.

Saint Albert, town (pop. 804), central Alta., on Sturgeon R. and 7 mi. NW of Edmonton; coal mining; grain, dairying.

Saint Aldhelm's Head, England: see SAINT ALBAN'S HEAD.

Saint Alexandre de Kamouraska (sĕtälĕksä′drù dù kämōōräskä′) or **Saint Alexandre,** village (pop. estimate 1,000), SE Que., near the St. Lawrence, 12 mi. SSW of Rivière du Loup; dairying, pig raising.

Saint Alexandre d'Iberville (dēbĕrvēl′), village (pop. 265), S Que., 8 mi. SE of St. Jean; dairying.

Saint Alexis de la Grande Baie, Que.: see GRANDE BAIE.

Saint Alexis de Montcalm (sĕtälĕksēs′ dù mōkälm′) or **Saint Alexis,** village (pop. 426), S Que., 30 mi. N of Montreal; lumbering, dairying; tobacco, potatoes.

Saint Alexis des Monts (dā mō′), village (pop. estimate 750), S Que., on R. du Loup and 30 mi. WNW of Trois Rivières; dairying, pig raising.

Saint-Alvère (sĕtälvâr′), village (pop. 400), Dordogne dept., SW France, 17 mi. ENE of Bergerac; dairying, food preserving.

Saint-Amand, Belgium: see SINT-AMANDS.

Saint-Amand or **Saint-Amand-les-Eaux** (sĕtämä′-lāzō′), town (pop. 10,037), Nord dept., N France, on Scarpe R. (canalized) and 8 mi. NW of Valenciennes, near Belg. border; industrial center with renowned faïence works, large hosiery mills, ironworks (cables, chains, anchors), and plumbing-fixture factories. Thermal establishment for rheumatic ailments is 2.5 mi. E on edge of large forest.

Saint-Amand-de-Vendôme (–dù-vädōm′), village (pop. 612), Loir-et-Cher dept., N central France, 8 mi. SSW of Vendôme; small grains, vegetables.

Saint-Amand-en-Puisaye (–ä-pwēzā′), village (pop. 866), Nièvre dept., central France, 11 mi. NE of Cosne; decorative pottery, parquetry mfg.

Saint-Amand-les-Eaux, Nord dept., France: see SAINT-AMAND.

Saint-Amand-Montrond (–mōtrō′), town (pop. 9,831), Cher dept., central France, on Cher R. and Berry Canal, 25 mi. SSE of Bourges; road and market center; mfg. (linen goods, liqueurs, footwear, cement and organic fats); railroad shops in suburban Orval (W). Well-preserved 13th–15th-cent. Cistercian cloister of Noirlac abbey, and extensive Roman ruins near by. Sometimes spelled Saint-Amand-Mont-Rond.

Saint-Amans or **Saint-Amans-la-Lozère** (sĕtämä′-lä-lōzâr′), village (pop. 185), Lozère dept., S France, 10 mi. NNW of Mende; sheep raising.

Saint-Amans-des-Cots (–dā-kō′), village (pop. 534), Aveyron dept., S France, on Viadène Plateau, 20 mi. SE of Aurillac; sheep raising, cheese making.

Saint-Amans-la-Lozère, France: see SAINT-AMANS.

Saint-Amans-Soult (–sōōlt′), village (pop. 864), Tarn dept., S France, on N slope of the Montagne Noire, on Thoré R. and 15 mi. SE of Castres; brick- and tileworks. Marshall Soult b. here. Formerly called Labastide-Saint-Amans.

Saint-Amant-de-Boixe (sĕtämä′-dù-bwäks′), village (pop. 450), Charente dept., W France, 10 mi. N of Angoulême. Has a 12th-cent. Romanesque church and 12th–15th-cent. cloister.

Saint-Amant-Roche-Savine (–rôsh-sävēn′), agr. village (pop. 360), Puy-de-Dôme dept., central France, in Massif du Livradois, 6 mi. WNW of Ambert; silverbearing lead mines near by.

Saint-Amant-Tallende (–tälăd′), village (pop. 885), Puy-de-Dôme dept., central France, 8 mi. S of Clermont-Ferrand; paper milling.

Saint-Amarin (sĕtämärē′), Ger. *Sankt Amarin* (zängkt′ä′märēn), village (pop. 1,570), Haut-Rhin dept., E France, in the S Vosges, 6 mi. NW of Thann; textile bleaching, envelope mfg.

Saint Ambroise de Chicoutimi (sĕtäbrwäz′ dù shēkōō′tēmē′), village (pop. 458), S central Que., on R. des Aulnets and 15 mi. NW of Chicoutimi; lumbering, dairying.

Saint-Ambroix (sĕtäbrwä′), town (pop. 2,460), Gard dept., S France, on the Cèze and 11 mi. NNE of Alès; asphalt mining, distilling, biscuit mfg., silk spinning.

Saint-Amè (sĕtāmā'), commune (pop. 1,235), Vosges dept., E France, in W Vosges, on Moselotte R. and 4 mi. E of Remiremont; cotton milling; granite quarries.

Saint-Amour (sĕtämōōr'), village (pop. 1,615), Jura dept., E France, in the Revermont, 15 mi. SSE of Louhans; ironworking; marble quarrying.

Saint-André, Belgium: see SINT-ANDRIES.

Saint-André (sĕtädrā'), N residential suburb (pop. 6,083) of Lille, Nord dept., N France; mfg. (dyes, lubricants, malt), meat processing.

Saint-André, town (pop. 10,152; commune pop. 43,108), NE Réunion isl., on railroad and 14 mi. ESE of Saint-Denis; agr. processing (sugar, alcohol, vanilla).

Saint-André, Cape, headland, W coast of Madagascar, 100 mi. WSW of Majunga; 16°12'S 44°25'E. Is closest point (250 mi.) to the African coast across Mozambique Channel.

Saint-André-de-Cubzac (–dŭ-kübzäk'), village (pop. 1,950), Gironde dept., SW France, near Dordogne R., 12 mi. NNE of Bordeaux; road center; winegrowing, cattle raising.

Saint André de Kamouraska (kämōōrä'skä) or **Andréville** (ăndrā'vĭl), village (pop. 564), SE Que., on the St. Lawrence and 15 mi. SW of Rivière du Loup; dairying, pig raising.

Saint-André-de-l'Eure (–lûr'), village (pop. 1,542), Eure dept., NW France, 10 mi. SE of Évreux; baby carriage mfg., dairying, distilling.

Saint-André-de-Sangonis (–sāgōnē'), town (pop. 2,120), Hérault dept., S France, near Hérault R., 11 mi. SE of Lodève; winegrowing, distilling.

Saint-André-de-Valborgne (–välbôr'nyü), village (pop. 393), Gard dept., S France, near the Mont Aigoual in the Cévennes, 12 mi. NNE of Le Vigan; iron mine at L'Estréchure (6 mi. ESE).

Saint-André-les-Alpes (–lāzälp'), village (pop. 590), Basses-Alpes dept., SE France, on the Verdon and 16 mi. SE of Digne, in Provence Alps; lavender distilling, fruitgrowing.

Saint-André-les-Vergers (–lā-vĕrzhā'), S suburb (pop. 4,423) of Troyes, Aube dept., NE central France; hosiery mills.

Saint Andrew, agr. village and parish (1931 pop. 1,800), Guernsey, Channel Isls., 2 mi. SW of St. Peter Port. Post office is St. Andrew's.

Saint Andrew, parish (□ 181.30; pop. 128,146), Surrey co., E Jamaica; ⊙ Half Way Tree. Lies just N of Kingston and includes W section of the Blue Mts. In the parish are the Hope agr. school, botanical garden, and research station, with Mona reservoir adjoining S. Main agr. products: mangoes, cacao, peas, beans, sugar cane, coffee, cattle, and dairy goods. Cigar and cigarette mfg. at Half Way Tree.

Saint Andrew, county (□ 282.74; pop. 23,285), E Trinidad, B.W.I., bordering on the Atlantic. Forms, together with St. David, Nariva, and Mayaro, the administrative dist. of Eastern Counties.

Saint Andrew Auckland (ô'klŭnd) or **South Church,** town and parish (pop. 5,401), central Durham, England, just SE of Bishop Auckland; coal mining. Has 13th-cent. church.

Saint Andrew Bay, Bay co., NW Fla., irregular arm of the Gulf of Mexico, with which it is connected by narrow channel (c.5 mi. long) bet. barrier beaches; c.35 mi. long E–W, bay has 3 arms (East, West, and North bays). Chief port: Panama City. Linked by Gulf Intracoastal Waterway to Apalachicola Bay (SE), Choctawhatchee Bay (NW). Sometimes Saint Andrews.

Saint Andrew Channel, arm (22 mi. long, 3 mi. wide) of Great Bras d'Or, NE N.S., in Cape Breton Isl., opening on the Atlantic. Forms SE side of Boularderie Isl.

Saint Andrews, town (pop. 1,167), ⊙ Charlotte co., SW N.B., on headland in Passamaquoddy Bay 50 mi. WSW of St. John, just E of Maine border; fishing and golfing resort; cod, haddock, pollock, herring fisheries; lobster market. Formerly important lumber-shipping port, trading with Great Britain and the West Indies. Atlantic Biological Station is 2 mi. N.

Saint Andrew's, Guernsey, Channel Isls.: see SAINT ANDREW.

Saint Andrews, burgh (1931 pop. 8,269; 1951 census 9,459), E Fifeshire, Scotland, on St. Andrews Bay of North Sea, 9 mi. E of Cupar, 10 mi. SE of Dundee; agr. market and resort, with famous golf course. Here is the Royal and Ancient Golf Club (founded 1754), which establishes rules for the game. Town was seat of an archbishopric by 10th cent., the cathedral (in ruins) was founded in 1160, and castle (ruins) was begun in 1200 as episcopal residence. St. Andrews Univ., the oldest in Scotland, was founded 1411; includes United Col. of St. Salvator and St. Leonard, St. Mary Col., and University Col. (at Dundee). Town Church dates from 1412. Martyr's Monument commemorates burning for heresy of Protestant reformers George Wishart, Patrick Hamilton, and others.

Saint Andrews East, village (pop. estimate 800), S Que., on North R., near its mouth on Ottawa R., and 7 mi. S of Lachute; dairying.

Saint Andrews Island, Sp. *San Andrés* (sän ändrās'), island (pop. 4,261), in Caribbean Sea 115 mi. off Mosquito Coast of Nicaragua, belonging to Colombia as part of SAN ANDRÉS Y PROVIDENCIA intendancy; 12°30'N 81°42'W; 7 mi. long, ¾–1½ mi. wide. A coral reef, rising to c.340 ft., like the group of neighboring isls. it is inhabited by Protestant English-speaking Negroes. The town San Andrés (pop. 1,143), ⊙ San Andrés y Providencia intendancy, is in its S part. Main products are coconuts, oranges, guano, which it exports; some deep-sea fishing.

Saint Andrew's Island, Gambia: see FORT JAMES ISLAND.

Saint Andrew's Major, agr. village and parish (pop. 2,854), SE Glamorgan, Wales, 4 mi. SW of Cardiff.

Saint Anicet (sĕtänēsā'), village (pop. estimate 300), S Que., on the St. Lawrence and 15 mi. SW of Valleyfield; dairying; cattle, pigs.

Saint Ann, parish (□ 481; pop. 96,193), Middlesex co., central and N Jamaica; ⊙ St. Ann's Bay. The 2d largest parish of the isl., with narrow, indented coastal strip and picturesque uplands (Dry Harbour Mts., Mt. Diablo), noted for its limestone caves. Rich in agr. products: limes, corn, oranges, pimento, coffee, ginger, sweet potatoes, yams, annatto, coconuts; cattle, horses, hogs. Trading centers are St. Ann's Bay, Brown's Town, and Ocho Rios. This region is noted for historical associations. At Dry Harbour, Columbus made his 1st landing (May 4, 1494), taking possession of the isl. for Spain. Seville or Sevilla Nueva, founded 1509 upon orders of his son Diego, was 1st ⊙ Jamaica.

Saint Ann, town (pop. 4,557), St. Louis co., E Mo., near St. Louis. Inc. since 1940.

Saint Ann, Cape, W extremity of Sherbro Isl., Sierra Leone, on the Atlantic and 65 mi. SSE of Freetown; 7°34'N 12°58'W.

Saint Anna's Church, Ceylon: see KALPITIYA, village.

Saint Ann Bay, inlet (extends 12 mi. SW inland, 4 mi. wide at entrance) of the Atlantic, NE Nova Scotia, on NE Cape Breton Isl., 15 mi. W of North Sydney. On E side of entrance is Cape Dauphin (46°21'N 60°25'W). SW part of bay is called St. Ann's Harbour.

Saint Anne, town, ⊙ ALDERNEY, Channel Isls., in center of isl. Has Norman church.

Saint Anne, village (pop. 1,403), Kankakee co., NE Ill., 11 mi. SE of Kankakee, in agr. area; brick, tile; dairy products, canned foods. Founded by French settlers in 1852; inc. 1872.

Saint Anne Island (500 acres; pop. 40), one of the Seychelles, in the Mahé group, off NE coast of Mahé Isl., 3 mi. ENE of Victoria; 4°36'S 55°30'E; 1½ mi. long, 1 mi. wide. Separated from Round and Moyenne Isls. (S) by St. Anne Channel. Copra, fisheries.

Saint Anne's-on-the-Sea, England: see LYTHAM SAINT ANNE'S.

Saint Ann's, village (pop. 3,680), NW Trinidad, B.W.I., just N of Port of Spain, in cacao region.

Saint Ann's Bay, town (pop. 3,133), ⊙ St. Ann parish, N Jamaica, Caribbean port 40 mi. NW of Kingston; 18°26'N 77°13'W. Principal products (fruit, pimento, coffee, dyewood, coconuts) exported through its unprotected harbor; vessels anchor offshore. Mfg. of essential oils. Also bathing and fishing resort. Just W is the now defunct Seville or Sevilla Nueva, the 1st ⊙ Jamaica, founded upon orders of Diego Columbus in 1509. The site of St. Ann's Bay had been named Santa Gloria by Columbus on his 2d voyage (1494). Fort, built 1777, is now a slaughterhouse.

Saint Ann's Head, promontory on the Atlantic, at entrance to MILFORD HAVEN inlet, S Pembroke, Wales, 7 mi. WSW of Milford Haven town; lighthouse (51°40'N 5°10'W).

Saint Anselme (sĕtāsĕlm'), village (pop. 510), SE Que., on Etchemin R. and 18 mi. SE of Quebec; dairying, pig raising.

Saint Ansgar, town (pop. 981), Mitchell co., N Iowa, near Cedar R., 20 mi. NE of Mason City; crushed rock, agr. limestone; feed. Sand and gravel pits near by.

Saint-Anthème (sĕtātĕm'), agr. village (pop. 805), Puy-de-Dôme dept., central France, in Monts du Forez, 9 mi. E of Ambert.

Saint Anthony, town (pop. 946), NE N.F., on small inlet near N side of Hare Bay; 51°22'N 55°35'W; fishing port, with cold-storage plants; lumbering, mink farming. Site of hosp. established by Grenfell mission.

Saint Anthony. 1 City (pop. 2,695), ⊙ Fremont co., E Idaho, on Henrys Fork, in valley of Snake R., and 40 mi. NE of Idaho Falls; alt. 4,965 ft. Shipping and flour-milling point in irrigated agr. area (seed peas, potatoes, grain, livestock); hq. Targhee Natl. Forest. State industrial school here. Crystal Falls Cave (with frozen river and waterfall) is 24 mi. NNW. Founded 1890 near site of Fort Henry (fur-trading post; 1810), inc. as city 1905. **2** Town (pop. 175), Marshall co., central Iowa, 15 mi. WNW of Marshalltown. **3** Village (pop. 1,406), Hennepin co., E Minn., NE suburb of Minneapolis. **4** Village (pop. 66), Stearns co., central Minn., 23 mi. WNW of St. Cloud, in grain and livestock area.

Saint Anthony, Falls of, Minn.: see MINNEAPOLIS.

Saint Anthony-in-Roseland, agr. village and parish (pop. 100), SW Cornwall, England, on inlet of Carrick Roads and 3 mi. E of Falmouth. Has 13th-cent. church. Just SW, on Falmouth Bay of the Channel, is lighthouse (50°8'N 5°1'W) marking entrance to Carrick Roads.

Saint Antoine (sĕtātwăn'), village (pop. estimate 300), S Que., on the St. Lawrence and 20 mi. SW of Quebec; dairying; pigs, cattle.

Saint-Antoine, village (pop. 344), Isère dept., SE France, 6 mi. WNW of Saint-Marcellin. Its ruined abbey (founded 1095) has 12th–15th-cent. church.

Saint Antoine sur Richelieu (sĕtātwăn' sür rĕshlyû'), village (pop. estimate 500), S Que., on Richelieu R. and 16 mi. NW of St. Hyacinthe; dairying.

Saint-Antonin (sĕtātônē'), village (pop. 1,266), Tarn-et-Garonne dept., SW France, in gorge of Aveyron R. and 22 mi. ENE of Montauban; small tourist resort; cementworks, hosiery mill; plum growing. Has a restored 12th-cent. town hall.

Saint-Arnaud (sĕtärnō'), town (pop. 10,506), Constantine dept., NE Algeria, on railroad and 15 mi. E of Sétif; agr. center (wheat, barley, livestock) settled by Europeans in late-19th cent. Djemila, with its Roman remains, is 12 mi. N.

Saint Arnaud (sānt är'nō), municipality (pop. 2,900), central Victoria, Australia, 125 mi. NW of Melbourne; commercial center for agr. region; flour mill. Gold-mining in vicinity.

Saint Asaph (sŭnt ă'sŭf), town and parish (pop. 1,845), Flint, Wales, on Clwyd R. and Elwy R., 5 mi. SSE of Rhyl; agr. market. Has 14th-cent. cathedral, restored by Sir Gilbert Scott, with collection of early Bibles and other religious books. Town probably became seat of bishopric c.560. The anc. monastery of Llanelwy here was renamed to honor Asaph, a 6th-cent. abbot; traditionally he is called a bishop. Morgan, translator of Bible into Welsh, was bishop here. In 1920 bishop of St. Asaph became Anglican archbishop for Wales.

Saint-Astier (sĕtāstyā'), village (pop. 1,585), Dordogne dept., SW France, on Isle R. and 10 mi. WSW of Périgueux; mfg. (Portland cement, tile flooring, furniture). Has a domed 12th-cent. church, with 16th-cent. alterations.

Saint-Auban (sĕtōbā'). **1** Village (pop. 103), Alpes-Maritimes dept., SE France, in Provence Alps, 16 mi. NW of Grasse. **2** Village, Basses-Alpes dept., France: see CHÂTEAU-ARNOUX.

Saint Aubert (sĕtōbâr'), village (pop. estimate 550), SE Que., on Trois Saumons R. and 3 mi. SE of St. Jean Port Joli; dairying, lumbering, pig raising.

Saint Aubin (sŭnt ō'bĭn, ô'–), fishing village in St. Brelade parish, Jersey, Channel Isls., on St. Aubin Bay, on S coast of isl. Lighthouse (49°11'N 2°9'W).

Saint-Aubin-d'Aubigné (sĕtōbē'-dōbēnyā'), village (pop. 511), Ille-et-Vilaine dept., W France, 11 mi. NNE of Rennes; slaked-lime mfg.

Saint-Aubin-du-Cormier (–dü-kôrmyā'), village (pop. 994), Ille-et-Vilaine dept., W France, 11 mi. SW of Fougères; mfg. (hosiery, footwear). Scene of a battle (1488) in which Charles VIII dealt a deathblow to Brittany's independence.

Saint-Aubin-lès-Elbeuf (–lāzĕlbûf'), N suburb (pop. 4,718) of Elbeuf, Seine-Inférieure dept., N France, on Seine R.; pencil mfg., wool, cotton, and paper milling.

Saint-Aubin-sur-Mer (–sür-mâr'), village (pop. 1,498), Calvados dept., NW France, resort on English Channel, 11 mi. N of Caen; oysters. Heavily damaged in Allied Normandy invasion (June 6, 1944) in Second World War.

Saint Augustin (sĕtōgüstē'), village (pop. 348), S Que., 20 mi. WNW of Montreal; dairying; vegetables.

Saint-Augustin Bay or **Saint Augustine Bay,** inlet of Mozambique Channel on SW coast of Madagascar; c.15 mi. wide, 8 mi. long; 23°30'S 43°40'E. Also known as Tuléar Bay, for the port of Tuléar, on N shore. Receives Onilahy R.

Saint Augustine, village (pop. 1,274), NW Trinidad, B.W.I., 8 mi. E of Port of Spain, in sugar-growing region. Seat of Imperial Col. of Tropical Agr. (established 1921) with research station.

Saint Augustine (sānt" ô'gŭstēn). **1** City (pop. 13,555), ⊙ St. Johns co., NE Fla., 37 mi. SSE of Jacksonville, on peninsula bet. Matanzas (E) and small San Sebastian (W) rivers and partly sheltered from the Atlantic by Anastasia Isl. (N end connected with city by bridge); port of entry. Popular year-round resort; shrimping and shipping center. Railroad shops; some mfg. of cigars, food products, lumber, boats, cement. Truck farming in area. The oldest city in U.S., it was founded 1565 by Pedro Menéndez de Avilés, on site of Indian village, near Ponce de Leon's landing place (1513). Town was burned by the English buccaneers Sir Francis Drake (1586) and Capt. John Davis (1665); attacked by South Carolinians (1702–3), and by Oglethorpe in 1740. Passed to England in 1763, becoming a haven for Tories in the American Revolution; returned to Spain in 1783; and was ceded to U.S. in 1821. An important post during the Seminole War, city was occupied by Federal troops in Civil War. Here is Castillo de San Marcos (kăstē'ō dŭ săn mär'kŭs), oldest masonry fort in the country, built 1672–1756; called Fort St. Mark during British occupation and Fort Marion after

1825; made natl. monument (18 acres) in 1924, and renamed Castillo de San Marcos in 1942. FORT MATANZAS NATIONAL MONUMENT is 15 mi. SSE, at S entrance to Matanzas R. Other points of interest: the old schoolhouse said to be "oldest house" in U.S. and believed to be built in late-16th cent.; the slave market; the cathedral (1793–97; partly restored); and several other old bldgs., the libraries, and Flagler Memorial Church. Since 1937, the Carnegie Institution has been restoring historic sites and landmarks. **2** Village (pop. 198), Knox co., NW central Ill., 15 mi. S of Galesburg, in agr. and coal area.

Saint Augustine Bay, Madagascar: see SAINT-AUGUSTIN BAY.

Saint Augustine Island, Ellice Isls.: see NANUMEA.

Saint-Aulaye (sĕtōlā'), village (pop. 508), Dordogne dept., SW France, on the Dronne and 11 mi. WSW of Ribérac; mfg. of refractory products; winegrowing (for cognac).

Saint Austell (sŭntô'stŭl), urban district (1931 pop. 8,295; 1951 census 23,634), S central Cornwall, England, near St. Austell Bay of the Channel and 10 mi. SSW of Bodmin; kaolin-mining and shipping center; paper milling, woodworking, mfg. of storage batteries. Cornish China clay was 1st discovered here c.1755 by Sir Thomas Cookworthy. Has 13th-cent. church. Near by is Carclaze tin mine, said to have been worked since Phoenician times.

Saint-Avertin (sĕtävĕrtē'), village (pop 1,481), Indre-et-Loire dept., W central France, on Cher R. and 2 mi. SSE of Tours; noted wines; tanning extracts. Has 11th–15th-cent. church.

Saint-Avold (sĕtävôld'), Ger. *Sankt Avold* (zängkt ä'fôlt), town (pop. 4,214), Moselle dept., NE France, 10 mi. SW of Forbach, near Saar border; road center in coal-mining dist. Mfg. (kitchen stoves, work clothing), beekeeping. Military hosp. Miners' residences at near-by Cité Jeanne-d'Arc (pop. 2,015). Forest of Saint-Avold (just N) extends to Saar border. U.S. military cemetery (Second World War) here.

Saint-Avre (sĕtä'vrü), village (pop. 120), Savoie dept., SE France, in Alpine Maurienne valley, on Arc R. and 5 mi. NNW of Saint-Jean-de-Maurienne; electro-chemical works (calcium carbide).

Saint Barbe Islands (sē bärb') or **Horse Islands,** group of 2 isls. at entrance of White Bay, NE N.F.; 50°13'N 55°50'W. Eastern Isl. (□ 6; pop. 30), 20 mi. NW of Cape St. John, is 4 mi. long, 2 mi. wide; rises to 550 ft. Western Isl. (3 mi. long), 2 mi. W, rises to 500 ft.

Saint Barnabé Nord (sē bärnäbā' nôr'), village (pop. estimate 500), S Que., 16 mi. W of Trois Rivières; dairying, pig raising.

Saint Barthélémi (sē bärtālāmē'), village (pop. estimate 1,000), S Que., 11 mi. N of Sorel; dairying; grain, potatoes.

Saint-Barthélemy (sē-bärtālümē') or **Saint Bartholomew,** island (□ 9.5; pop. 2,231), dependency of Guadeloupe, Fr. West Indies, in Leeward Isls., 12 mi. SE of St. Martin, 125 mi. NW of Guadeloupe. Principal town is Gustavia, at 17°54'N 62°52'W. Mountainous and of irregular shape, 11 mi. long (W–E), up to 2½ mi. wide; rises to 990 ft. While of little economic importance, it produces some cotton, tropical fruit, livestock. Fishing, salt panning, mfg. of fiber hats. Has small lead and zinc deposits. Settled by the French, the isl. was ceded to Sweden (1784) but was returned to France by 1877 treaty.

Saint-Barthélemy-d'Anjou (–dãzhōō'), village (pop. 451), Maine-et-Loire dept., W France, 3 mi. E of Angers; slate quarrying, winegrowing.

Saint-Barthélemy-le-Plain (–lü-plē'), village (pop. 109), Ardèche dept., S France, on the Doux and 4 mi. WSW of Tournon; zinc mining. Hydroelectric plant. Until 1939, Saint-Barthélemy-le-Plein.

Saint Bartholomew, Guadeloupe: see SAINT-BARTHÉLEMY.

Saint Bartholomew, Lake of, Germany: see KÖNIGSSEE.

Saint-Béat (sē-bāä'), village (pop. 588), Haute-Garonne dept., S France, on Garonne R., near Sp. border, and 10 mi. NNE of Luchon; electrometallurgy. Noted marble quarries near by.

Saint-Beauzély (sē-bōzālē'), village (pop. 355), Aveyron dept., S France, on E slope of Lévézou range, 7 mi. NW of Millau; leather-glove mfg.

Saint Bees (sŭnt bēz'), village and parish (pop. 1,028), SW Cumberland, England, on Irish Sea 4 mi. S of Whitehaven; dairy farming. Has 12th-cent. Norman church, formerly part of nunnery said to have been founded in 7th cent. by St. Bee (or St. Bega); school founded in 16th cent. St. Bees Head, a promontory and lighthouse on Solway Firth, is 2 mi. NW.

Saint-Bel (sē-bĕl'), village (pop. 960), Rhône dept., E central France, 12 mi. WNW of Lyons; hat-making. Pyrite mines near by.

Saint Benedict, hamlet, Marion co., NW Oregon, 14 mi. NE of Salem, in fruitgrowing region; canning. Mt. Angel Seminary (R.C.; 1883) is here.

Saint Benedict, Mount, hill (c.800 ft.), NW Trinidad, B.W.I., 6 mi. E of Port of Spain. Tourist site known for its view. Benedictine monastery on summit.

Saint-Benin-d'Azy (sē-bünē'-däzē'), village (pop. 457), Nièvre dept., central France, 11 mi. E of Nevers; stud farm.

Saint Benoît (sē bünwä'), village (pop. 355), S Que., 25 mi. W of Montreal; dairying, vegetable growing.

Saint-Benoît, town (pop. 8,175; commune pop. 10,566) on NE coast of Réunion isl., 20 mi. SE of Saint-Denis; linked with Saint-Pierre by coastal railroad and cross-isl. road; agr. processing (sugar, alcohol, tapioca, vanilla).

Saint-Benoît-du-Sault (sē-bünwä'-dü-sō'), village (pop. 768), Indre dept., central France, 21 mi. SE of Le Blanc; cattle, cereals. Has 11th-cent. church.

Saint Benoît Joseph Labre, Que.: see AMQUI.

Saint-Benoît-sur-Loire (–sür-lwär'), village (pop. 508), Loiret dept., N central France, on right bank of the Loire and 20 mi. ESE of Orléans. Its celebrated Romanesque abbatial church (11th cent.) contains remains of St. Benedict.

Saint Bernard (sānt bûrnärd'), parish (□ 510; pop. 11,087), extreme SE La.; ⊙ St. Bernard. Just SE of New Orleans, and bounded N by L. Borgne, E by Chandeleur Sound, S by Breton Sound, W by the Mississippi. Industrial communities near New Orleans have sugar refineries, oil refineries, stockyards, automobile assembly plants, diversified mfg. Agr. (truck, dairy products, livestock); hunting, fishing. Formed 1807.

Saint Bernard. **1** Village (pop. c.400), ⊙ St. Bernard parish, extreme SE La., 15 mi. SE of New Orleans, near E bank of the Mississippi. **2** City (pop. 7,066), Hamilton co., extreme SW Ohio, within but politically independent of Cincinnati; soap, fertilizer, motor vehicles, wooden containers. Settled 1794; inc. as village in 1878, as city in 1912.

Saint Bernard Pass, Alps: see GREAT SAINT BERNARD PASS (Italo-Swiss border); LITTLE SAINT BERNARD PASS (Fr.-Ital. border).

Saint-Béron (sē-bārõ'), village (pop. 377), Savoie dept., SE France, near the Guiers, 10 mi. SW of Chambéry; electro-metallurgy.

Saint-Bertrand or **Saint-Bertrand-de-Comminges** (sē-bĕrtrã-dù-kômēzh'), anc. *Lugdunum Convenarum*, village (pop. 243), Haute-Garonne dept., S France, near the Garonne, 10 mi. WSW of Saint-Gaudens; has noteworthy Romanesque and Gothic cathedral of Notre Dame and a Romanesque cloister. Founded 72 B.C. by Iberians.

Saint Blazey, town and parish (pop. 3,267), S Cornwall, England, 4 mi. ENE of St. Austell; agr. market; China-clay mining.

Saint-Blin (sē-blē'), agr. village (pop. 325), Haute-Marne dept., NE France, 15 mi. SW of Neufchâteau; horse breeding.

Saint-Bon, Savoie dept., France: see SAINT-BON-TARENTAISE.

Saint Bonaventure (bō"nŭvĕn'chür, Fr. sē bônävãtür'), village (pop. estimate 500), S Que., 22 mi. ESE of Sorel; dairying, pig raising.

Saint Bonaventure, N.Y.: see ALLEGANY, village.

Saint Boniface (bō'nĭfās), city (pop. 21,613), SE Man., on E bank of Red R. (bridges), opposite Winnipeg; oil refining; paper, lumber, and flour milling; mfg. of tar, cereal foods, bricks, wire, paint, furniture; grain elevators, breweries, sheet-metal works. Seat of R.C. archbishop; site of noted cathedral and of St. Boniface Col. (R.C.), founded as mission school 1818. La Vérendrye established Fort Rouge near by in 1738.

Saint Boniface de Shawinigan (bō'nĭfās dù shùwĭ'nĭgùn, sē bônēfäs') or **Boniface,** village (pop. 563), S Que., on branch of Yamachiche R. and 6 mi. SW of Shawinigan Falls; dairying, cattle.

Saint Bonifacius (sānt" bŏnĭfā'shùs), village (pop. 438), Hennepin co., E Minn., near L. Minnetonka, 24 mi. W of Minneapolis; grain, potatoes, livestock.

Saint-Bonnet or **Saint-Bonnet-en-Champsaur** (sē-bünā'-ã-shãzōr'), village (pop. 822), Hautes-Alpes dept., SE France, on the Drac and 9 mi. N of Gap; market. Mineral springs.

Saint-Bonnet-de-Joux (–dù-zhōō'), village (pop. 532), Saône-et-Loire dept., E central France, in the Monts du Charollais, 9 mi. ENE of Charolles; cattle.

Saint-Bonnet-le-Château (–lù-shätō'), village (pop. 1,905), Loire dept., SE central France, in Monts du Forez, 13 mi. S of Montbrison; handicraft textile industry; woodworking, mfg. of small-arms parts. Has 15th–16th-cent. houses and an old church.

Saint-Bon-Tarentaise (sē-bō-tärätĕz'), village (pop. 159), Savoie dept., SE France, in Massif de la Vanoise, 6 mi. SE of Moutiers; alt. 3,600 ft. Alpine winter-sports resort. Until 1941, called Saint-Bon.

Saint Boswells, agr. village and parish (pop. 952), N Roxburgh, Scotland, on the Tweed and 4 mi. ESE of Melrose; resort. Sometimes called Lessuden. Just E is DRYBURGH ABBEY.

Saint Brandon Islands, in Indian Ocean: see CARGADOS CARAJOS SHOALS.

Saint Brelade (sŭnt brùlād'), Fr. *Sainte-Brelade* (sĕnt-brùlād'), fishing village and parish (1945 pop. 2,368), Jersey, Channel Isls., on St. Brelade Bay, on SW coast of isl., 5 mi. W of St. Helier. Has 12th-cent. church. Post office is St. Brelade's Bay.

Saint-Brévin-les-Pins (sē-brāvē'-lā-pē'), town (pop. 5,019), Loire-Inférieure dept., W France, on Bay of Biscay at mouth of the Loire, 3 mi. SE of Saint-Nazaire; well-known summer resort with attractive beach at Saint-Brévin-l'Océan.

Saint-Briac-sur-Mer (sē-brēäk'-sür-mâr'), village (pop. 552), Ille-et-Vilaine dept., W France, on English Channel, 7 mi. WSW of Saint-Malo; fishing port and small watering place. Until 1939, Saint-Briac.

Saint-Brice-en-Coglès (sē-brēs'-ã-kôglĕs'), village (pop. 1,197), Ille-et-Vilaine dept., W France, 8 mi. WNW of Fougères; wooden shoes. Granite quarries near by.

Saint Bride, Mount (10,875 ft.), SW Alta., near B.C. border, in Rocky Mts., in Banff Natl. Park, 30 mi. NW of Banff; 51°32'N 115°58'W.

Saint Brides Bay, inlet (8 mi. wide) of the Atlantic, W Pembroke, Wales, extends 9 mi. bet. Skomer Isl. and Ramsey Isl.

Saint Bride's Major, agr. village and parish (pop. 1,051), S Glamorgan, Wales, 3 mi. S of Bridgend. Church contains 13th-cent. altar tomb. Near by is Ogmore Castle (Norman).

Saint Bride's Minor, town and parish (pop. 2,464), S central Glamorgan, Wales, 3 mi. NNE of Bridgend; agr. market; brickworks.

Saint-Brieuc (sē-brēû'), town (pop. 28,596), ⊙ Côtes-du-Nord dept., W France, on small river Gouët near its mouth on English Channel, and 55 mi. NW of Rennes; commercial center; metal founding and rolling; mfg. (explosives, brushes, hosiery, furniture, rubber articles, pharmaceuticals, fertilizer). Fisheries at Le Légué (just N), the town's seaport. Named after a Welsh missionary (c.6th cent.) who founded a monastery here. Episcopal see since 9th cent. Has 13th–15th-cent. cathedral (recently restored), and many old houses.

Saint-Brieuc, Bay of, on English Channel, Côtes-du-Nord dept., W France; 15 mi. wide, 8 mi. long. Saint-Brieuc is near its head. Numerous beaches and resorts along shore.

Saint Bruno (Fr. sē brünō'), village (pop. 491), S central Que., 6 mi. S of St. Joseph d'Alma; dairying, pig raising.

Saint Budeaux (sŭnt bŭ'dùks), agr. village and parish (pop. 1,819), SW Devon, England, 4 mi. NW of Plymouth. Line of forts around village forms part of old Plymouth defense system. Its commander, Sir Ferdinando Gorges, was 1st governor of Maine.

Saint Buryan (sŭnt bŭr'ēùn, bĕ'rēùn), agr. village and parish (pop. 1,145), W Cornwall, England, 5 mi. SW of Penzance. Has 15th-cent. church.

Saint-Calais (sē-kälĕ'), town (pop. 2,760), Sarthe dept., W France, 17 mi. WNW of Vendôme; agr. trade center; textile milling, vegetable and fruit preserving. Has 14th–16th-cent. church and ruins of 11th-cent. feudal castle.

Saint Canut (sē känü'), village (pop. estimate 200), S Que., on North R. and 27 mi. WNW of Montreal; quartz mining.

Saint Casimir (sē käzēmēr'), village (pop. 1,307), S Que., on Ste. Anne R. and 23 mi. NE of Trois Rivières; lumbering, mfg. of agr. implements; dairying; cattle, pigs, poultry.

Saint Casimir Est (ĕst'), village (pop. 544), S Que., on Ste. Anne R. and 23 mi. NE of Trois Rivières, opposite St. Casimir; dairying; cattle, pigs.

Saint-Cast (sē-kä'), village (pop. 206), Côtes-du-Nord dept., W France, on headland extending into English Channel, 16 mi. NW of Dinan; popular seaside resort.

Saint Catharine, Lake, W Vt., 15 mi. SW of Rutland; 5 mi. long; resorts.

Saint Catharines, city (pop. 30,275), ⊙ Lincoln co., S Ont., near L. Ontario, S of Toronto, NW of Niagara Falls, 25 mi. NW of Buffalo, N.Y., and on Welland Ship Canal; center of important fruit-growing region (apples, plums, peaches, berries, grapes); textile and paper milling, fruit and vegetable canning; jam, fruit-juice, wine making; silk milling and dyeing, woolen milling; mfg. of agr. implements, hardware, tools, motors, carpets, clothing, electrical equipment, metal and food products. Known for its mild equable climate, it is also a resort, with mineral springs and tuberculosis sanitarium. Site of Ridley Col., business col., and other educational institutions; scene of annual Canadian rowing regatta. Just SE is suburb of Meritton. Church of England mission was established (1792) on site of present city.

Saint Catherine, parish (□ 483.27; pop. 121,032), Middlesex co., central and S Jamaica, W of Kingston; ⊙ Spanish Town. Largest parish of the isl. Watered by Cobre R., widely used for irrigation. Along the river lie some of the principal settlements, such as Spanish Town, Bog Walk, Linstead, linked by railroad to Port Antonio. The region produces: annatto, breadfruit, coffee, cassava, cacao, mangoes, bananas, sugar cane, citrus fruit, honey, livestock, dairy products. Spanish Town, former ⊙ Jamaica, is the isl.'s leading communication center. There is a new milk-condensing plant at Bog Walk. Along S shore line, bases were leased, in 1940, by Great Britain to the U.S. for 99 years, in the bases-for-destroyers agreement.

Saint Catherine, Mount (2,749 ft.), N Grenada, B.W.I., highest elevation of the isl., 8 mi. NE of St. George's.

Saint Catherines Island, one of the Sea Isls., in Liberty co., SE Ga., just off the coast, bet. Ossabaw and Sapelo isls.; c.10 mi. long, 2–4 mi. wide. Small St. Catherines Sound at N end.

Saint Catherine's Point, northernmost point of Bermuda, on St. George's Isl.; 32°23'N 64°40'W.
Saint Catherine's Point, S tip of Isle of Wight, Hampshire, England, on the Channel, 9 mi. S of Newport. Site of lighthouse (50°34'N 1°18'W).
Saint Célestin (sē sălĕstē'), village (pop. 350), S Que., 12 mi. SSE of Trois Rivières; dairying, pig raising.
Saint-Céré (sē-sărā'), town (pop. 2,457), Lot dept., SW France, 19 mi. NNW of Figeac; produces fruit juices, embroidery and leather articles; fruit and vegetable shipping. A 16th-cent. Renaissance castle is near by.
Saint-Cergue (sē-sârg'), village (pop. 346), Vaud canton, W Switzerland, 17 mi. N of Geneva; resort (alt. 3,421 ft.) at foot of the Dôle. Fr. frontier station at La Cure (4 mi. WNW).
Saint-Cernin (sē-sĕrnē'), village (pop. 561), Cantal dept., S central France, on W slope of Massif du Cantal, 9 mi. N of Aurillac; cattle, cheese; sawmills.
Saint Césaire (sē săzâr'), village (pop. 1,209), S Que., on Yamaska R. and 30 mi. E of Montreal; woodworking, food canning; agr. (dairying; vegetables, tobacco).
Saint-Chamas (sē-shămä'), town (pop. 2,648), Bouches-du-Rhône dept., SE France, port at NW tip of Étang de Berre, 25 mi. NW of Marseilles; natl. gunpowder plant, olive-oil mfg. Roman bridge near by with triumphal arch at each end.
Saint-Chamond (sē-shămō'), town (pop. 14,546), Loire dept., SE central France, in the Jarez on Gier R. and 6.5 mi. ENE of Saint-Étienne; metallurgical and textile center; steel milling, metalworking, mfg. of elastic fabrics, laces, braids, and ribbons; tanning.
Saint-Chaptes (sē-shăpt'), agr. village (pop. 697), Gard dept., S France, near the Gard, 10 mi. NNW of Nîmes.
Saint-Charles (sē-shărl'), village (pop. 868), Constantine dept., NE Algeria, on the Oued Saf-Saf and 9 mi. S of Philippeville; rail junction (spur to Bône); winegrowing.
Saint Charles. 1 Village (pop. estimate 500), S Man., on Assiniboine R. and 8 mi. WSW of Winnipeg; grain, stock. **2** Village (pop. estimate 200), S Que., on Richelieu R. and 14 mi. WNW of St. Hyacinthe; dairying, pig raising. A center of the Lower Canada Rebellion (1837); the Confederation of the Six Counties was proclaimed here Oct., 1837. Subsequently British troops here defeated the insurgents and burned the village, which was later rebuilt.
Saint Charles. 1 Parish (□ 304; pop. 13,363), SE La.; ⊙ Hahnville. Bounded N by L. Pontchartrain, SE by Salvador and Cataouatche lakes, SW by Bayou Des Allemands; intersected by the Mississippi. Agr. (truck, rice, sugar cane, corn). Oil and natural-gas production and refining; other mfg. Formed 1807. **2** County (□ 561; pop. 29,834), E Mo.; ⊙ St. Charles. Bounded E by Mississippi R., S by Missouri R., which enters the Mississippi here. Rich agr. region (corn, oats, wheat, hay, potatoes); coal deposits; mfg. centered at St. Charles. One of Missouri's 5 original counties. Formed 1812.
Saint Charles. 1 Town (pop. 313), Arkansas co., E central Ark., 25 mi. ESE of Stuttgart and on White R. (ferry); commercial fishing. Has important natl. wildlife refuge. **2** Town (1940 pop. 65), Coweta co., W Ga., 7 mi. S of Newnan. **3** Village (pop. 363), Bear Lake co., SE Idaho, 8 mi. S of Paris on NW shore of Bear L.; alt. 5,985 ft.; agr., dairying. **4** Industrial city (pop. 6,709), Kane co., NE Ill., on Fox R. (bridged here) and 33 mi. W of Chicago, in agr. area (dairy products; livestock); mfg. (kitchen cabinets, metal products, hardware, musical instruments, amplifying and photoelectric equipment, fiber products). State game preserve here. Near by is the state school for boys. Founded 1834, inc. 1839. **5** Town (pop. 319), Madison co., S central Iowa, 23 mi. SSW of Des Moines. **6** Mining town (pop. 534), Hopkins co., W Ky., 11 mi. SSW of Madisonville; bituminous coal. **7** Village (pop. 1,469), Saginaw co., E central Mich., 13 mi. SW of Saginaw; bituminous coal mines. **8** City (pop. 1,548), Winona co., SE Minn., 20 mi. E of Rochester, in grain, livestock, and poultry area. Platted 1854, inc. 1870. Whitewater State Park near by. **9** City (pop. 14,314), ⊙ St. Charles co., E Mo., 15 mi. NW of St. Louis and on left bank of Missouri R. Agr. center (wheat, corn, oats); mfg. (steel dies, railroad coaches, foundry products, oil engines, shoes); lumber yards. Sand, gravel, coal deposits. Sacred Heart Convent, Lindenwood Col. here; state park near by. First permanent white settlement on Missouri R.; was trading post and starting point on westward Boone's Lick Trail; temporary (1821–26) ⊙ Mo. Settled by French traders 1769, inc. 1809, became city 1849. **10** Town (pop. 550), Lee county, extreme SW Va., in the Cumberlands near Ky. line, 16 mi. WSW of Big Stone Gap; bituminous-coal mining.
Saint Charles, Cape, at E extremity of Labrador, at N end of Strait of Belle Isle, 22 mi. NW of Misery Point, Belle Isle; 52°13'N 55°40'W. Site of fishing settlement of Cape Charles (pop. 90).
Saint Charles Bay, Texas: see ARANSAS BAY.
Saint Charles de Bellechasse (sē shărl dů bĕlshăs'), village (pop. 752), S Que., 14 mi. ESE of Quebec; lumbering, dairying, fruitgrowing; mfg. of maple products.
Saint Charles de Caplan (kăplă'), village (pop. estimate 500), E Que., S Gaspé Peninsula, on Chaleur Bay, 33 mi. E of Dalhousie; fishing port.
Saint Charles des Grondines, Que.: see GRONDINES.
Saint-Chély-d'Apcher (sē-shālē'-dăpshâr'), town (pop. 2,761), Lozère dept., S France, 18 mi. SSE of Saint-Flour; road center. Electrometallurgical factory; furniture mfg. Feldspar quarried near by.
Saint-Chély-d'Aubrac (–dōbrăk'), village (pop. 332), Aveyron dept., S France, on W slope of Monts d'Aubrac, 24 mi. NE of Rodez; sheep and cattle raising.
Saint-Chinian (sē-shēnyă'), village (pop. 1,996), Hérault dept., S France, 15 mi. WNW of Béziers; bauxite and copper mines. Olive-oil pressing, winegrowing.
Saint-Christophe-en-Bazelle (sē-krēstôf'-ă-băzĕl'), village (pop. 277), Indre dept., central France, 21 mi. NW of Issoudun; sheep, cereals.
Saint-Christophe-en-Oisans (–wăză'), village (pop. 37), Isère dept., SE France, in the Massif du Pelvoux, Dauphiné Alps, 10 mi. SE of Le Bourg-d'Oisans. La Bérarde (6 mi. ESE; alt. 5,700 ft.), at head of steep summer road, is gateway for Écrins-Pelvoux natl. park (□ 40). Rugged alpinism.
Saint-Christophe Island, Indian Ocean: see JUAN DE NOVA ISLAND.
Saint Christopher, island, Leeward Isls., B.W.I.: see SAINT KITTS.
Saint Christopher-Nevis, presidency, Leeward Isls., B.W.I.: see SAINT KITTS-NEVIS.
Saint Chrysostôme (krĭsŏ'stům, Fr. sē krēsôstōm'), village (pop. 656), S Que., 22 mi. ESE of Valleyfield; dairying.
Saint-Ciers-sur-Gironde (sē-syâr-sür-zhĕrōd'), village (pop. 1,064), Gironde dept., SW France, 32 mi. N of Bordeaux; fish and grain market.
Saint-Cirq-Lapopie (sē-sĕrk' lăpôpē'), village (pop. 93), Lot dept., SW France, on the Lot and 7 mi. E of Cahors; woodworking. Has 13th–16th-cent. castle.
Saint Clair. 1 County (□ 641; pop. 26,687), NE central Ala.; ⊙ Pell City. Hilly area bounded E by Coosa R. Cotton, livestock; coal mining. Deposits of iron ore, limestone. Formed 1818. **2** County (□ 670; pop. 205,995), SW Ill.; ⊙ Belleville. Bounded NW by Mississippi R.; also drained by Kaskaskia R. and Silver Creek. Includes part of St. Louis metropolitan area; highly industrialized in section centered at EAST SAINT LOUIS. Railroad, river shipping; bituminous coal, clay, sand, oil, limestone; timber; agr. (corn, wheat; dairy products; poultry, livestock). Includes Cahokia Mounds State Park. Formed 1790. **3** County (□ 740; pop. 91,599), E Mich.; ⊙ Port Huron. Bounded E by L. Huron and St. Clair R., S by L. St. Clair; drained by Belle and Black rivers, and by short Mill Creek. Stock raising and agr. (grain, sugar beets, truck); dairy products. Mfg. at Port Huron and Marysville. Salt mines; fisheries. Resorts. Organized 1821. **4** County (□ 699; pop. 10,482), W Mo.; ⊙ Osceola. Drained by Osage and Sac rivers. Agr. (corn, hay), livestock; coal. Formed 1841.
Saint Clair. 1 City (pop. 4,098), St. Clair co., E Mich., 11 mi. SSW of Port Huron, on St. Clair R.; salt processing, mfg. of chemicals, auto parts. Laid out 1818; inc. as village 1850, as city 1858. Officially, according to the U.S. Postal Guide, the name of the city is always abbreviated, St. Clair. **2** Village (pop. 324), Blue Earth co., S Minn., on Le Sueur R. and 9 mi. SE of Mankato; dairy products. **3** Town (pop. 1,779), Franklin co., E central Mo., bet. Bourbeuse and Meramec rivers, 45 mi. WSW of St. Louis; mfg. (shoes, staves); coal, lead, zinc, barite mines. State park and forest near by. Settled 1840s. **4** Borough (pop. 5,856), Schuylkill co., E central Pa., 3 mi. N of Pottsville; anthracite; textiles. Laid out 1831, inc. 1850.
Saint Clair, Lake (□ 21), W central Tasmania, 75 mi. NW of Hobart, at E foot of Mt. Olympus (4,680 ft.), in mountainous, forested region reserved as natl. park; 9 mi. long, 3 mi. wide. Source of Derwent R.
Saint Clair, Lake, bet. S Ont. and SE Mich., just NE of Detroit; □ 460; 26 mi. long N–S, 24 mi. wide. Joined to L. Huron (N) by St. Clair R. and to L. Erie (S) by Detroit R., it carries much Great Lakes shipping. Grosse Pointe and other Detroit suburbs are on its shores. Isls. in delta (NE) of St. Clair R. have summer colonies. Anchor Bay, N arm of lake, indents Macomb and St. Clair counties, Mich.
Saint-Clair-de-Halouze (sē-klâr-dů-ălōōz'), village (pop. 158), Orne dept., NW France, 6 mi. N of Domfront; iron mining.
Saint-Clair-de-la-Tour (–lä-tōōr'), village (pop. 500), Isère dept., SE France, on the Bourbre and 2 mi. ENE of La Tour-du-Pin; linen and silk milling.
Saint Clair River (sānt" klâr'), bet. SE Mich. and S Ont., outlet of L. Huron, flows c.40 mi. S, bet. Port Huron (Mich.) and Sarnia (Ont.), which are linked by bridge and tunnel, and past Marysville and Marine City (Mich.), to L. St. Clair, from which Detroit R. flows to L. Erie; forms international line. At its mouth is a delta (St. Clair Flats) containing a number of isls. (resorts), largest of which are Walpole (Ont.) and Harsens (Mich.).
Saint Clair Shores, residential village (pop. 19,823), Macomb co., SE Mich., 12 mi. NE of downtown Detroit, and on L. St. Clair. Inc. 1925. Officially, according to the U.S. Postal Guide, the name is always abbreviated, St. Clair.
Saint-Clair-sur-Epte (sē-klâr-sür-ĕpt'), village (pop. 376), Seine-et-Oise dept., N central France, 12 mi. ESE of Les Andelys. A treaty signed here in 911 gave Rollo of Normandy the Vexin Norman and left the Vexin Français to the crown.
Saint-Clair-sur-l'Elle (–lĕl'), village (pop. 202), Manche dept., NW France, 6 mi. NNE of Saint-Lô; cattle.
Saint Clairsville (sānt" klârz'–). **1** Village (pop. 3,040), ⊙ Belmont co., E Ohio, near Ohio R., 10 mi. W of Wheeling, W.Va.; trade center for coal-mining and dairying area; oil and gas wells. Laid out 1801. **2** Agr. borough (pop. 127), Bedford co., S Pa., 9 mi. N of Bedford.
Saint-Clar (sē-klär'), village (pop. 651), Gers dept., SW France, 19 mi. NNE of Auch; wheat, corn, cattle.
Saint-Claud (sē-klō'), village (pop. 522), Charente dept., W France, 13 mi. SW of Confolens; cattle raising. Also called Saint-Claud-sur-le-Son.
Saint-Claude (sē-klōd'), town (pop. 9,865), Jura dept., EFrance, 19 mi. NW of Geneva, in scenic gorge above Bienne R., in the Jura; produces brier pipes, carved and inlaid toys and ornaments, fountain pens, rulers, cigarette holders, etc., collectively known as *articles de Saint-Claude*, which are worked in plastics, shells, horn, and ivory. Diamond and gem cutting, wood turning. Primarily an artisan industry, it is also carried on in neighboring villages of Ravilloles, Saint-Lupicin, Lavans-lès-Saint-Claude, and Molinges. Its 14th–18th-cent. cathedral with beautiful 15th-cent. choir stalls is sole relic of an abbey founded in 5th cent. The monks of Saint-Claude held the land under mortmain and, despite Voltaire's polemics, kept their peasants in complete servitude until 1789.
Saint-Claude (sē-klōd'), town (commune pop. 7,065), S Basse-Terre isl., Guadeloupe, 2 mi. NE of Basse-Terre city; coffee, cacao, bananas, honey; mfg. of alcohol. Also a health resort, with adjoining Matouba thermal springs.
Saint Clears (klârz), town and parish (pop. 893), SW Carmarthen, Wales, on Taf R. and 9 mi. WSW of Carmarthen; agr. market; cheese making. Church (13th cent.) was formerly part of Cluniac priory.
Saint Cleer, village and parish (pop. 1,516), E Cornwall, England, 2 mi. N of Liskeard. Prehistoric remains near by.
Saint Clement, fishing village and parish (1945 pop. 3,367), Jersey, Channel Isls., on SE coast of isl., 3 mi. E of St. Helier; site of lighthouse (49°10'N 2°3'W). Just ESE is La Roque Point, SE extremity of isl. (49°10'N 2°2'W).
Saint-Clément (sē-klămă'), village (pop. 795), Meurthe-et-Moselle dept., NE France, near the Meurthe, 6 mi. SE of Lunéville; faïence mfg.
Saint Clements Island, Md.: see BLAKISTON ISLAND.
Saint Clet (sē klā'), village (pop. 287), S Que., 8 mi. NW of Valleyfield; dairying; pigs, potatoes.
Saint-Cloud (sē-klōō'), village (pop. 3,838), Oran dept., NW Algeria, on railroad and 13 mi. NE of Oran; winegrowing center.
Saint-Cloud, town (pop. 17,101), Seine-et-Oise dept., N central France, a W residential suburb of Paris, 6 mi. from Notre Dame Cathedral, on height overlooking left bank of Seine R., opposite Boulogne-Billancourt; ceramics and metalworks. Its name derives from St. Clodoald (6th cent.), who built a monastery here. The palace of Saint-Cloud, built 1572 and destroyed by fire in siege of Paris (1870), was a residence of Napoleon I (who was declared emperor here by the senate in 1804), Charles X, and Napoleon III. Its beautifully laid-out park (area 970 acres) extends S to Sèvres.
Saint Cloud (sānt kloud'). **1** City (pop. 3,001), Osceola co., central Fla., 22 mi. SSE of Orlando, near East Tohopekaliga L.; trade center for cattle area. Settled in 1880s. **2** City (pop. 28,410), Benton, Sherburne, and Stearns counties, ⊙ Stearns co., central Minn., on Mississippi R. at mouth of Sauk R. and c.60 mi. NW of Minneapolis; trade and industrial center for grain, livestock, and poultry area; dairy products, canned vegetables, beverages; mfg. (wood and foundry products). Near-by quarries are source of fine-grain granite, and city is known for granite-finishing works and monuments. Has state teachers col., state reformatory, U.S. veterans' hosp., and orphans' home. Settled 1853, platted 1855, inc. as village 1857, as city 1868. Grew with development of quarries. **3** Village (pop. 408), Fond du Lac co., E Wis., near Sheboygan R., 14 mi. ENE of Fond du Lac, in dairying and mixed farming region.

Saint Coeur de Marie, Que.: see DÉLISLE.
Saint Columbans (kŭlŭm'bŭnz), village, Sarpy co., E Nebr., 15 mi. S of Omaha and on Missouri R. St. Columbans Seminary is here.
Saint Columb Major (sŭnt kŏ'lŭm, –kŭ'lŭm), town and parish (pop. 3,051), central Cornwall, England, 6 mi. E of Newquay; agr. market. Has 14th-cent. church.
Saint Columb Minor, village (pop. 1,728), central Cornwall, England, 2 mi. E of Newquay; tourist resort. Has 13th–14th-cent. church.
Saint Côme, Que.: see LINIÈRE.
Saint Croix (sānt" kroi'), county (□ 736; pop. 25,905), W Wis.; ⊙ Hudson. Bounded W by St. Croix R.; drained by Eau Galle R.; has several small lakes. Primarily a dairying and stock-raising area, with some mfg. of wood products. Formed 1840.
Saint Croix, Lake, Minn., Wis.: see SAINT CROIX RIVER.
Saint Croix Falls, resort village (pop. 1,065), Polk co., NW Wis., on St. Croix R., opposite Taylors Falls (Minn.), and 40 mi. NE of St. Paul, in dairying and farming area; has large trout hatchery. Hydroelectric plant supplies power to St. Paul and Minneapolis. INTERSTATE PARK is here. Settled 1837, an early lumbering center. Inc. 1888.
Saint Croix Island, Washington co., E Maine, islet (c.7 acres) in St. Croix R. 6 mi. NW of St. Andrews, N.B., and below Calais, Maine; has lighthouse (45°8'N 67°8'W). First settlement in Acadia made here (1604) by de Monts and Champlain; abandoned 1605 because of scurvy, settlement was moved to Port Royal (see ANNAPOLIS ROYAL). In dispute bet. U.S. and Britain, isl. was assigned (1798) to U.S. Originally St. Croix Isl., name was officially Dochet (dō-shā') or Dochet's Isl. for many years. In 1949, establishment of a natl. monument here was authorized.
Saint Croix Island (sānt" kroi'), largest island and a municipality (□ 81.93; pop. 12,096) of U.S. Virgin Isls., West Indies, 40 mi. S of St. Thomas and St. John isls., from which it is separated by a Caribbean deep, 90 mi. ESE of San Juan, Puerto Rico; ⊙ Christiansted. It is 23 mi. long W–E, up to 6 mi. wide, bet. 17°40'–17°47'N and 64°33'–64°53'W. Rises in Mt. Eagle to 1,165 ft. Bet. the rugged hills lies a fertile limestone plain—once occupied by large sugar estates—with Negro villages and 2 urban centers, Christiansted and Frederiksted. The climate, though healthful, is somewhat warmer than St. Thomas. Rainy season Aug.–Dec. Northeast trade winds blow most of the year, and hurricanes occur occasionally. Once called the "Garden of the Danish West Indies," its agr. is now reduced. Sugar growing has been largely replaced by cattle raising. Main industries whose products are exported: sugar milling, alcohol and rum distilling, meat packing. St. Croix, originally inhabited by Carib Indians, was discovered 1493 by Columbus on his 2d voyage. Here was reportedly fought the 1st pitched battle in America bet. the natives and Sp. invaders. The isl. was depopulated within 50 years. In 17th cent., St. Croix was in turn occupied, and partly settled, by the Dutch, French, Spanish, and English. For several years it was held by the Knights of Malta (1651–65). Purchased by Denmark in 1733. Temporary Br. occupations, 1801 and 1807–14. Several severe slave riots occurred in 19th cent. Isl. was bought by the U.S. in 1917. The original name, Santa Cruz, bestowed by Columbus, is sometimes used. The pop. is predominantly colored. English is the prevailing language, but Spanish, Danish, French, and a Creole patois are also spoken.
Saint Croix River. 1 In E Maine and SW N.B., rises in Chiputneticook Lakes, Maine; flows c.75 mi. S and E, forming international boundary, to Passamaquoddy Bay. Head of navigation is Calais; lumber is chief freight. **2** In Wis. and Minn., rises in lake region in Douglas co., NW Wis., flows 164 mi. SW and S, through L. St. Croix (natural widening of river, extending 24 mi. S from Stillwater, Minn.) and enters Mississippi R. at Prescott, Wis. Forms Wis.–Minn. boundary through greater part of its course. INTERSTATE PARK (on both sides of river, at Taylors Falls, Minn., and St. Croix Falls, Wis.) includes scenic gorge known as the Dalles of the St. Croix. Hydroelectric plant at St. Croix Falls supplies power for St. Paul and Minneapolis. River was important shipping route in early lumbering days.
Saint Croix Stream, Aroostook co., E Maine, rises in St. Croix L., flows c.20 mi. NW to the Aroostook.
Saint Cuthbert, village (pop. estimate 500), S Que., 9 mi. NNW of Sorel; dairying; stock, poultry.
Saint Cuthbert Without, parish (pop. 1,959), N central Cumberland, England. Includes village of Carleton, 3 mi. SE of Carlisle, with dairy farming, sawmilling.
Saint Cyprian Bay (sānt sĭp'rēŭn), Sp. *Bahía de San Cipriano* (bäē'ä dā sän sēpryä'nō), along coast of Río de Oro, Sp. West Africa, c.100 mi. SSW of Villa Cisneros. Uninhabited desert shore.
Saint-Cyprien (sē-sēprēē'), village (pop. 1,347), Dordogne dept., SW France, near Dordogne R., 8 mi. W of Sarlat; Portland cement plant; fruit, vegetable, and tobacco growing.
Saint-Cyprien, village, Tunis dist., N Tunisia, 11 mi. WSW of Tunis; winegrowing.
Saint-Cyr or **Saint-Cyr-sur-Loire** (sē-sēr'-sür-lwär'), NW suburb (pop. 4,532) of Tours, Indre-et-Loire dept., W central France, on right bank of Loire R.; mfg. (minium of lead, buttons), sawmilling. Balzac, Béranger, and Anatole France lived here.
Saint Cyrille de Wendover (sē sērēl' dù wĕn'dōvür), village (pop. 723), S Que., 5 mi. NE of Drummondville; dairying; cattle, pigs.
Saint-Cyr-l'École (sē-sēr-lākôl'), town (pop. 4,288), Seine-et-Oise dept., N central France, 3 mi. W of Versailles. Here in 1684 was founded a famous school for daughters of impoverished noblemen. Its buildings later housed the famous military academy established 1808 by Napoleon I; completely destroyed in 1944. After Second World War school was temporarily transferred to Coëtquidam, Morbihan dept.
Saint-Cyr-sur-Loire, France: see SAINT-CYR.
Saint-Cyr-sur-Mer (–sūr-mâr'), village (pop. 689), Var dept., SE France, near La Ciotat bay of the Mediterranean, 12 mi. WNW of Toulon; winegrowing.
Saint Cyrus, agr. village and parish (pop. 1,173), SE Kincardine, Scotland, on North Sea, 5 mi. SSE of Laurencekirk. Near by are remains of 15th-cent. "The Kaim of Mathers" castle.
Saint-Dalmas-de-Tende (sē-dälmä'-dù-tād'), Ital. *San Dalmazzo di Tenda* (sän dälmä'tsō dē tĕn'dä), village (1936 pop. 697), Alpes-Maritimes dept., SE France, in Roya R. valley of Maritime Alps, 30 mi. NE of Nice and 7 mi. S of Tenda Pass (Ital. border); resort amidst chestnut groves. Hydroelectric plants power zinc smelters (ore mined at La Miniera 4 mi. W). Part of Italy until 1947.
Saint David, county (□ 78.95; pop. 5,037), NE Trinidad, B.W.I., bordering on the Caribbean (N) and the Atlantic (W). Forms, together with St. Andrew, Nariva, and Mayaro, the administrative dist. of Eastern Counties.
Saint David. 1 Village (pop. 812), Fulton co., W central Ill., 4 mi. S of Canton, in agr. and bituminous-coal area. **2** Village, Maine: see MADAWASKA.
Saint David d'Yamaska (dā'vĭd dyùmä'skù, Fr. sē dävēd'), village (pop. estimate 800), S Que., on small tributary of Yamaska R. and 14 mi. ESE of Sorel; dairying, pig raising.
Saint David's, town and small seaport in Dalgety parish (pop. 1,481), SW Fifeshire, Scotland, on the Firth of Forth, 2 mi. ESE of Inverkeithing. Just W is agr. village of Donibristle, with 12th-cent. Dalgety parish church and remains of anc. Donibristle Castle.
Saint David's, anc. *Menevia,* town and parish (pop. 1,580), W Pembroke, Wales, 14 mi. WNW of Haverfordwest; agr. market. Its famous 12th-cent. cathedral is one of largest and finest in Wales. There are remains of anc. walls which enclosed monastic bldgs., and ruins of 14th-cent. palace of Bishop Gower. Town was for centuries an important place of pilgrimage. Near by is SAINT DAVID'S HEAD.
Saint David's Head, Welsh *Penmaen Dewi* (pĕnmīn'dū'ē), promontory, W Pembroke, Wales, on the Atlantic at entrance to St. George's Channel, 3 mi. NW of St. David's; 51°54'N 5°19'W; westernmost point of Wales.
Saint David's Island (3½ mi. long, ¾ mi. wide), NE Bermuda, bet. St. George's Harbour and Castle Harbour, 8 mi. E of Hamilton, 1 mi. S of St. George. Leased (1941) to the U.S. for 99 years as naval base and airfield. Causeways join it with neighboring isls. Area of the isl. has been increased by fill after becoming a U.S. base.
Saint Day, England: see GWENNAP.
Saint Denis (sē dùnē'), village (pop. 727), S Que., on Richelieu R. and 15 mi. NW of St. Hyacinthe; dairying, lumbering.
Saint-Denis, industrial city (pop. 68,595), Seine dept., N central France, a N suburb of Paris, 6 mi. from Notre Dame Cathedral, on right bank of Seine R.; metalworks (auto and truck chassis, motors, machine tools, boilers); mfg. of chemicals, pharmaceuticals, glass, pianos; tanning, liqueur distilling. Its early Gothic Basilica (12th–13th cent.), restored after Fr. Revolution, contains tombs of many kings of France. Outstanding are the tombs of Francis I, by Delorme, and Henry II, by Pilon. Louis XVI and Marie Antoinette are buried in the crypt. City grew around a Benedictine abbey founded (626) by Dagobert I at the tomb of St. Denis, patron saint of France. The abbey, rebuilt in 18th cent. and now a school for the daughters of Legion of Honor members, played important role in Fr. medieval history. Here Abelard became a monk. City was called Franciade during French Revolution.
Saint-Denis, town (pop. 25,332; commune pop. 36,096), ⊙ Réunion isl. and of Windward dist., on N coast, on railroad and 10 mi. ENE of Pointe-des-Galets, its port; 20°52'S 55°27'E. Administrative and commercial center; agr. processing (sugar, tapioca, vanilla, cacao); food canning, cigarette mfg. Has a cathedral, govt. and missionary primary and secondary schools, colonial garden with museum, broadcasting station.
Saint-Denis-du-Sig (sē-dùnē'-dü-sēg'), town (pop. 13,220), Oran dept., NW Algeria, 28 mi. SE of Oran; commercial center of irrigated Sig lowland (extending N to the Gulf of Arzew), which grows cereals, citrus fruit, cotton, and truck; vegetable canning, olive curing, oil pressing. Kieselguhr quarries in area. Cheurfas Dam (89 ft. high), on Oued Mékerra 12 mi. above town, stores water for irrigation. Town has large Spanish pop.
Saint-Denis-lès-Martel (–lā-märtĕl') or **Saint-Denis-près-Martel** (–prā–), village (pop. 220), Lot dept., SW France, on Dordogne R. and 16 mi. SSE of Brive-la-Gaillarde; railroad center, hog market. Site of last Gallic oppidum.
Saint-Denis-lez-Gembloux (–lā-zhäblōō'), village (pop. 743), Namur prov., S central Belgium, 6 mi. NNW of Namur; iron mining. Village of Bovesse (pop. 495) is 1 mi. S.
Saint Dennis, town and parish (pop. 2,359), central Cornwall, England, 5 mi. NW of St. Austell; China-clay mining center. Church dates from 14th cent.
Saint-Didier-en-Velay (sē-dēdyā'-ā-vùlā'), village (pop. 1,562), Haute-Loire dept., S central France, 11 mi. SSW of Saint-Étienne; mfg. of cartons, paper products, silk ribbons, cotton textiles. Formerly called Saint-Didier-la-Séauve.
Saint-Dié (sē-dyā'), town (pop. 11,423), Vosges dept., E France, on Meurthe R. and 25 mi. ENE of Épinal, in the Vosges; rail center (2 lines across the Vosges to Strasbourg and Sélestat); produces hosiery, men's clothing, prefabricated houses, baby carriages, mirrors; printing, metalworking. Its 7th-cent. monastery later became a well-known chapter of noble canons and an episcopal see. Here in 1507 was printed the *Cosmographiae Introductio,* a geographic work mentioning America for first time. During First World War Saint-Dié was in German hands for brief period in 1914, and in 1917–18 was E anchor of American lines. In 1944, in Second World War, retreating German army dynamited its Romanesque and Gothic cathedral, destroyed 75% of town (including part of 14th–16th-cent. cloisters), and massacred or deported large part of pop. It fell to the Allies in Nov., 1944. Jules Ferry b. here.
Saint-Dier or **Saint-Dier-d'Auvergne** (sē-dyâr'-dōvâr'nyù), village (pop. 351), Puy-de-Dôme dept., central France, in Massif du Livradois, 13 mi. SSW of Thiers; woodworking.
Saint-Dizier (sē-dēzyā'), town (pop. 15,936), Haute-Marne dept., NE France, port on Marne-Saône Canal, on Marne R., and 35 mi. SE of Châlons-sur-Marne; metallurgical and transportation center; iron and bronze foundries, forges, casting and stamping works; large brewery; mfg. (bldg. materials for public works, tools, hardware, household articles). Important iron and lumber trade.
Saint Dogmells or **Saint Dogmaels** (both: sŭnt dŏg'mŭlz), agr. village in Saint Dogmells Rural parish (pop. 1,076), NE Pembroke, Wales, on Teifi R. estuary, just W of Cardigan. Has ruins of 12th-cent. abbey.
Saint Dominique (sē dômēnēk'), village (pop. 381), SW Que., 6 mi. SE of St. Hyacinthe; dairying; cattle, pigs.
Saint Donat de Montcalm (sē dônä' dù mōkälm'), village (pop. estimate 750), S Que., in the Laurentians, on L. Archambault (alt. 1,281 ft.), 20 mi. NNE of Ste. Agathe des Monts; dairying; skiing resort.
Saint-Donat-sur-l'Herbasse (–sūr-lĕrbäs'), village (pop. 1,468), Drôme dept., SE France, 14 mi. NNE of Valence; footwear mfg., silk milling; wine.
Sainte Adèle (sĕtädĕl'), village (pop. estimate 700), SW Que., in the Laurentians, 10 mi. SE of Ste. Agathe des Monts; dairying; skiing resort.
Sainte-Adresse (sĕtädrĕs'), WNW suburb (pop. 4,285) of Le Havre, Seine-Inférieure dept., N France, on English Channel, just SE of Cape La Hève; bathing resort partially destroyed in Second World War. Seat of Belg. government during First World War.
Sainte Agathe (sĕtägät'), village (pop. 310), S Que., 30 mi. SSW of Quebec; dairying, lumbering; pigs.
Sainte Agathe des Monts (dā mō'), town (pop. 3,308), S Que., in the Laurentians, on North R. and 50 mi. NW of Montreal; alt. 1,205 ft.; furniture mfg., butter making; popular skiing resort. Inc. 1915. Near by are small L. Brulé (S) and L. des Sables (N).
Sainte Agnès de Charlevoix (sĕtänyĕs' dù shärlvwä'), village (pop. estimate 1,500), SE central Que., 6 mi. NW of La Malbaie; dairying, lumbering center; mica mining.
Sainte Angèle de Laval (sĕtä-zhĕl' dù läväl') or **Laval,** village (pop. 419), S Que., on the St. Lawrence, opposite Trois Rivières (ferry); dairying.
Sainte Angèle de Rimouski (dù rēmōōskē') or **Sainte Angèle de Mérici** (dù mārēsē'), village (pop. 584), E Que., on Mitis R. and 20 mi. ENE of Rimouski; dairying, pig raising.
Sainte-Anne (sĕt-än'), town (commune pop. 13,675), S Grande-Terre, Guadeloupe, 9 mi. E of Pointe-à-Pitre, in sugar-growing region; rum distilling.
Sainte-Anne, town (pop. 600), SE Martinique, 17 mi. SE of Fort-de-France; sugar-cane growing, distilling.

Sainte-Anne, village (pop. 2,391), on NE coast of Réunion isl., 3 mi. SSE of Saint-Benoît; vanilla processing.

Sainte Anne, Cape, headland on Atlantic coast of NW Mauritania, Fr. West Africa, 30 mi. ESE of Port-Étienne; 20°41′N 16°41′W.

Sainte-Anne-d'Auray (sĕtän'-dōrā'), town (pop. 2,510), Morbihan dept., W France, 4 mi. NE of Auray. Here is the famous basilica of St. Anne d'Auray, built in Renaissance style in 19th cent. The yearly pilgrimage, dating back to 1623 when St. Anne appeared to a peasant, takes place on July 26.

Sainte Anne de Beaupré (sŭnt ăn' dŭ bōprā', Fr. sĕtän'), village (pop. 1,783), S Que., on the St. Lawrence and 20 mi. NE of Quebec, opposite Île d'Orléans. Seat of a famous shrine established 1620 by sailors who had been shipwrecked. A chapel was built 1658 and a large church 1876. Burned in 1922, the church was magnificently rebuilt. It is one of Canada's foremost pilgrimage resorts.

Sainte Anne de Bellevue (ăn dŭ bĕl'vū, Fr. sĕtän' dŭ bĕlvü'), residential town (pop. 3,006), S Que., at SW end of Montreal Isl., bet. L. St. Louis and L. of the Two Mountains, 20 mi. WSW of Montreal; lumbering, printing. Seat of Macdonald Col., branch of McGill Univ.

Sainte Anne de Chicoutimi (ăn' dŭ chĭkōō'tĭmē, Fr. sĕtän'dŭ shēkōōtēmē'), village (pop. 1,540), S central Que., on Saguenay R., opposite Chicoutimi; lumbering, dairying.

Sainte Anne de la Pérade (ăn' dŭ lä pärād', sĕtän') or **La Pérade,** village (pop. 1,014), S Que., on Ste. Anne R., near its mouth on the St. Lawrence, and 23 mi. NE of Trois Rivières; dairying, lumbering.

Sainte Anne de la Pocatière (ăn' dŭlä pôkätyâr', Fr. sĕtän'), village (pop. estimate 300), SE Que., on the St. Lawrence and 40 mi. SE of Rivière du Loup, in dairying, wheat- and flax-growing region; furniture mfg., woodworking. Has agr. col., experimental farm, and acad.

Sainte Anne de Portneuf, Que.: see HAMILTON COVE.

Sainte Anne des Chênes (ăn' dā shān', Fr. sĕtän' dā shĕn'), village (pop. estimate 800), SE Man., on Seine R. 27 mi. SE of Winnipeg; grain, dairying.

Sainte Anne des Monts (ăn' dā mō', Fr. sĕtän'), village (pop. estimate 1,000), ⊙ Gaspé West co., E Que., on the St. Lawrence, on N side of Gaspé Peninsula, 50 mi. ENE of Matane; dairying, lumbering.

Sainte Anne River (ăn', Fr. sĕtän'). **1** In S Que., rises in S part of Laurentides Provincial Park, flows 90 mi. SW, past St. Raymond and St. Casimir, to the St. Lawrence at Ste. Anne de la Pérade. **2** In S Que., rises in SE part of Laurentides Provincial Park, flows 60 mi. SW to the St. Lawrence 3 mi. NE of St. Anne de Beaupré.

Sainte-Barbe-du-Tlélat (sĕt-bärb'-dü-tlālät'), village (pop. 2,489), Oran dept., NW Algeria, 15 mi. SE of Oran; rail and road junction; wine, olives; horse raising.

Sainte-Baume, France: see SAINT-MAXIMIN-LA-SAINTE-BAUME.

Sainte-Catherine-de-Fierbois (sĕt-kätrēn'-dŭ-fyĕrbwä'), village (pop. 226), Indre-et-Loire dept., W central France, 19 mi. E of Chinon; its Flamboyant church built on site of a chapel founded (732) by Charles Martel.

Sainte-Clotilde (sĕt'-klôtēld'), village (pop. 6,649), N Réunion isl., 1 mi. E of Saint-Denis; sugar mill.

Sainte-Colombe-sur-l'Hers (sĕt-kôlômb'-sür-lâr'), village (pop. 570), Aude dept., S France, on Hers R. and 15 mi. SW of Limoux; comb mfg.

Sainte-Croix, Belgium: see SINT-KRUIS.

Sainte Croix (kroi', Fr. sĕt krwä'), village (pop. 841), ⊙ Lotbinière co., S Que., on the St. Lawrence and 28 mi. WSW of Quebec; lumbering, dairying, pig raising.

Sainte-Croix (sĕt-krwä'), village (pop. 261), Ariège dept., S France, 10 mi. N of Saint-Girons; flour milling, winegrowing. Also called Sainte-Croix-de-Volvestre.

Sainte-Croix, town (pop. 6,048), Vaud canton, W Switzerland, 7 mi. WNW of Yverdon, 3 mi. E of Fr. border; radios, phonographs, motion pictures, watches; woodworking. Les Rasses is E.

Sainte-Croix-aux-Mines (sĕt-krwäzō-mēn'), Ger. *Sankt Kreuz* (zängkt kroits'), village (pop. 1,606), Haut-Rhin dept., E France, in the Vosges, 2 mi. NE of Sainte-Marie-aux-Mines; cotton milling, carton mfg.

Sainte-Croix-de-Volvestre, France: SAINTE-CROIX.

Sainte-Croix-du-Mont (sĕt-krwä'-dü-mō'), village (pop. 840), Gironde dept., SW France, on right bank of the Gironde and 22 mi. SE of Bordeaux; sauterne wines.

Sainte Dorothée (sĕt dôrôtā'), village (pop. estimate 500), S Que., at W extremity of Jesus Isl., on L. of the Two Mountains, 15 mi. W of Montreal; truck gardening, dairying, fruitgrowing.

Saint Edward, village (pop. 917), Boone co., E central Nebr., 10 mi. SE of Albion and on Beaver Creek; livestock, poultry produce, grain.

Sainte-Énimie (sĕtänēmē'), village (pop. 317), Lozère dept., S France, bet. Causse de Sauveterre (N) and Causse Méjan (S), in the Tarn gorge, 9 mi. WNW of Florac; winegrowing.

Sainte Famille (sĕt fämē'), village (pop. estimate 300), S Que., on NW shore of Île d'Orléans, on the St. Lawrence and 16 mi. NE of Quebec; dairying; vegetables, fruit. Founded 1661, it has church built 1742.

Sainte-Florine (sĕt-flôrēn'), town (pop. 2,125), Haute-Loire dept., S central France, near the Allier, 8 mi. NNW of Brioude; coal-mining center; lacemaking.

Sainte-Foy-la-Grande (sĕt-fwä-lä-grăd'), town (pop. 3,170), Gironde dept., SW France, on the Dordogne and 23 mi. ESE of Libourne; wine-trading center; early-vegetable and tobacco growing, cement mfg., woodworking. Protestant stronghold in 16th cent. Geographer Élisée Reclus b. here.

Sainte-Foy-l'Argentière (–lär-zhätyâr'), village (pop. 1,105), Rhône dept., E central France, on SE slopes of the Monts du Beaujolais, 17 mi. WSW of Lyons; brick- and tileworks; porcelain, perfume.

Sainte-Foy-lès-Lyon (–lā-lēō'), SW residential suburb (pop. 3,265) of Lyons, Rhône dept., E central France, on right bank of Saône R., near its mouth on the Rhone.

Sainte Genevieve (sănt" jĕ'nŭvēv), county (□ 500; pop. 11,237), E Mo.; ⊙ Ste. Genevieve. On Mississippi R. (NE). Agr. region (corn, wheat, hay), livestock; lime, marble quarries, copper deposits. Part of Clark Natl. Forest here. Formed 1812.

Sainte Genevieve, city (pop. 3,992), ⊙ Ste. Genevieve co., E Mo., on Mississippi R. and 45 mi. S of St. Louis; trade center for farm area; clothing, lime products; marble quarries near by. Founded c.1735, it was earliest permanent white settlement in Missouri; important port in steamboat days.

Sainte Geneviève de Pierrefonds (sĕt zhŭnŭvyĕv' dŭ pyĕrfō'), village (pop. 489), S Que., on W shore of Montreal Isl., on R. des Prairies, opposite Bizard Isl., 15 mi. WSW of Montreal; market gardening, dairying; resort.

Sainte-Geneviève-des-Bois (–dā-bwä'), residential town (pop. 10,229), Seine-et-Oise dept., N central France, 15 mi. S of Paris.

Sainte-Geneviève-sur-Argence (–sür-ärzhäs'), village (pop. 566), Aveyron dept., S France, on Viadène Plateau, 18 mi. ESE of Aurillac; cheese making, sawmilling.

Sainte Hélène de Bagot (sĕt ālĕn' dŭ bägō'), village (pop. 235), S Que., 14 mi. NE of St. Hyacinthe; dairying, stock raising.

Sainte Hénédine (sĕt änādēn'), village (pop. estimate 500), ⊙ Dorchester co., S Que., 20 mi. SE of Quebec; dairying.

Sainte-Hermine (sĕt ĕrmēn'), village (pop. 1,133), Vendée dept., W France, 13 mi. WNW of Fontenay-le-Comte; cattle raising.

Sainte Irénée (sĕt ērānā'), village (pop. estimate 500), SE central Que., on the St. Lawrence and 7 mi. SSW of La Malbaie; lumbering, dairying; resort.

Sainte Julie de Verchères (sĕt zhülē' dŭ vĕrshâr'), village (pop. estimate 400), S Que., 15 mi. NE of Montreal; dairying, pig raising.

Sainte Julienne (sĕt zhülyĕn'), village (pop. estimate 750), ⊙ Montcalm co., S Que., 32 mi. N of Montreal; lumbering, dairying; tobacco, potatoes.

Sainte-Juliette (sĕt-zhülyĕt'), village, Sfax dist., E Tunisia, on railroad and 17 mi. N of Sfax; olive groves.

Sainte Justine, Que.: see LANGEVIN.

Saint Elias, Cape (sănt" ŭlī'ŭs), S Alaska, S extremity of Kayak Isl., 30 mi. S of Katalla; 59°48′N 144°36′W. Named 1741 by Bering.

Saint Elias, Mount (18,008 ft.), on Yukon-Alaska border, in St. Elias Mts., 200 mi. W of Whitehorse, 70 mi. NW of Yakutat, on S edge of Seward Glacier; 60°17′N 140°55′W. First seen July 16, 1741, by Vitus Bering. First climbed 1897 by the duke of the Abruzzi.

Saint Elias, Mount, Greece: see HAGIOS ELIAS; OCHE.

Saint Elias Mountains, section of the Coast Ranges, SW Yukon and SE Alaska, extending c.200 mi. NW–SE; continued NW by Wrangell Mts. and W by Waxell Ridge, Chugach Mts., and Kenai Mts. Highest peak is Mt. LOGAN (19,850 ft.), 2d highest mtn. of North America; other important peaks are mts. St. Elias (18,008 ft.), Lucania (17,150 ft.), King (17,130 ft.), Steele (16,439 ft.), Bona (16,420 ft.), Wood (15,880 ft.), Vancouver (15,696 ft.), Hubbard (14,950 ft.). Valleys bet. the peaks are filled by extensive glaciers which extend from Mt. St. Elias to Alsek R. (SE) and to Bering Glacier (W), forming world's largest glacier system apart from Polar ice caps; includes Malaspina, Hubbard, and Seward glaciers.

Saint-Élie (sĕtālē'), town, ⊙ Centre dist. (pop. 634), Inini territory, N Fr. Guiana, on affluent of Sinnamary R. and 65 mi. W of Cayenne; gold placers.

Sainte-Livrade-sur-Lot (sĕt-lēvräd'-sür-lôt'), village (pop. 1,797), Lot-et-Garonne dept., SW France, on the Lot and 6 mi. W of Villeneuve-sur-Lot; prune and plume market; mfg. of butchers' equipment; fruit and vegetable preserving.

Saint Elizabeth, parish (□ 474.44; pop. 100,182), Cornwall co., SW Jamaica; ⊙ Black River. Watered by Black R., largest and only navigable river of the isl. Has fertile plains: cassava, corn, peas and beans, pimento, ginger, annatto, tobacco, cacao, coffee, fruit. Considerable stock raising (goat, sheep, hogs, cattle, horses). Logwood is exported through Black River. The govt. here runs a sisal plantation and factory for relief of unemployment. Traversed by Kingston–Montego Bay RR.

Saint Elizabeth, town (pop. 59), Miller co., central Mo., 21 mi. SSW of Jefferson City.

Saint Elmo. 1 Town (1940 pop. 8), Chaffee co., W central Colo., on branch of Arkansas R., in Sawatch Mts., and 22 mi. NW of Salida; alt. 10,051 ft. Mt. Shavano 7 mi. SE. **2** City (pop. 1,716), Fayette co., S central Ill., 14 mi. ENE of Vandalia, in oil-producing and agr. area (corn, wheat; dairy products; poultry); railroad shops, oil refineries, brickyards. Settled 1830, inc. 1903.

Saint-Éloy-les-Mines (sĕtālwä'-lā-mēn'), town (pop. 5,307), Puy-de-Dôme dept., central France, in Combrailles, on Bouble R. and 17 mi. SE of Montluçon; coal-mining center for Montluçon-Commentry industrial dist.

Sainte-Luce (sĕt-lüs'), town (pop. 623), S Martinique, 13 mi. SE of Fort-de-France, in sugar-growing region; distilling.

Sainte Madeleine (sĕt mädlĕn'), village (pop. 450), S Que., 8 mi. WSW of St. Hyacinthe; dairying.

Sainte Madeleine (sĭnt mă'dŭlĭn), village (pop. 1,878), W Trinidad, B.W.I., on railroad and 3 mi. E of San Fernando. Has large sugar mill, said to be largest in Br. colonial empire; also rum distilling and sawmilling.

Sainte Marguerite (sĕt märgŭrēt') or **Lac Masson** (lăk măsō', Fr. läk mäsō'), village (pop. estimate 750), SW Que., in the Laurentians, on small L. Masson (alt. 1,102 ft.), 11 mi. E of Ste. Agathe des Monts; dairying; skiing center.

Sainte-Marguerite, island, France: see LÉRINS, ÎLES DE.

Sainte-Marguerite-Lafigère (sĕt-märgŭrēt'-läfēzhâr'), village (pop. 270), Ardèche dept., S France, on the Chassezac, 24 mi. E of Mende; lead mining.

Sainte Marie or **Sainte Marie Beauce** (mŭrē' bōs, Fr. sĕt märē' bōs'), village (pop. 1,736), S Que., on Chaudière R. and 28 mi. SSE of Quebec; textile knitting, dairying, woodworking; mfg. of leather, shoes, furniture.

Sainte-Marie (sĕt-märē'), town (pop. 1,944), E Martinique, 13 mi. NNE of Fort-de-France; cacao, pineapples; fruit canning; limekiln.

Sainte-Marie, town (pop. 6,014; commune pop. 8,853), on N coast of Réunion isl., on railroad and 6 mi. E of Saint-Denis; sugar milling, perfume distilling.

Sainte Marie or **Saint Marie** (sănt" mŭrē'), village (pop. 352), Jasper co., SE Ill., 13 mi. N of Olney, in agr. area (livestock, poultry, redtop seed, fruit).

Sainte-Marie, Cape, or **Cape Saint Mary,** S tip of Madagascar, 125 mi. WSW of Fort-Dauphin; 25°35′S 45°5′E.

Sainte-Marie-aux-Mines (sĕt-märē'-ō-mēn'), Ger. *Markirch* (mär'kĭrkh), town (pop. 6,096), Haut-Rhin dept., E France, near crest of the Vosges, 14 mi. NW of Colmar, on Sélestat–Saint-Dié RR; wool- and cotton-milling center; textile bleaching and dyeing, metal founding. Arsenic mined near by. Until 18th cent. silver and lead mined in area. Saint-Marie-aux-Mines pass (alt. 2,560 ft.) across crest of the Vosges is 2 mi. W.

Sainte Marie Beauce, Que.: see SAINTE MARIE.

Sainte Marie du Castel, Guernsey, Channel Isls.: see SAINT MARY DE CASTRO.

Sainte-Marie-du-Zit (sĕt-märē'-dü-zēt'), agr. village, Zaghouan dist., NE Tunisia, 27 mi. SSE of Tunis.

Sainte-Marie Island or **Sainte-Marie-de-Madagascar Island** (sĕt'-märē'-dŭ-mädägäskär') (□ 77; 1948 pop. 9,200), in Indian Ocean just off E coast of Madagascar and part of Tamatave prov.; 35 mi. long, 5 mi. wide; 16°55′S 49°52′E. Clove growing and processing; vanilla, essential oils. Small port and main town of Ambodifototra (ämbōō"dēfōōtōō'trŭ), also known as Sainte-Marie, is on W shore. The isl., sometimes called Nosy-Boraha, was claimed by France in 18th cent. Attached to Madagascar, 1896.

Sainte Marthe (sĕt märt'), village (pop. 257), SW Que., 14 mi. NW of Valleyfield; dairying; potatoes.

Sainte Martine (sĕt märtēn'), village (pop. estimate 600), ⊙ Châteauguay co., S Que., on Châteauguay R. and 20 mi. SSW of Montreal; dairying.

Sainte-Maure (sĕt-mōr'), village (pop. 1,902), Indre-et-Loire dept., W central France, 18 mi. ESE of Chinon; road and market center; winegrowing, fertilizer mfg. Has a 12th-cent. church with 11th–12th-cent. crypts. Numerous megalithic monuments near by.

Sainte-Maxime (sĕt-mäksēm'), village (pop. 1,779), Var dept., SE France, on N shore of Gulf of Saint-Tropez, 2 mi. N of Saint-Tropez, at foot of Monts des Maures; fishing port and Fr. Riviera resort amidst luxuriant flora; winegrowing. Here Allies landed unopposed (Aug., 1944) in Second World War. Also called Sainte-Maxime-sur-Mer.

Sainte-Menehould (sĕt-mŭnōō', –ōōld'), town (pop. 3,086), Marne dept., N France, on the Aisne and 22 mi. WSW of Verdun, on SW slope of the Argonne; rail junction; tanning. Was medieval fortress.

Sacked by Germans in 1914; later Fr. hq. for Argonne front. Heavily damaged in Second World War. Has First World War military cemetery.

Sainte-Mère-Église (sẽt-mâr-āglēz′), village (pop. 712), Manche dept., NW France, on Cotentin Peninsula, 21 mi. SE of Cherbourg; cattle raising. First Fr. village liberated in Second World War by American airborne troops who landed here (June 6, 1944) prior to Allied assault upon Normandy beaches.

Saint Émilien, Que.: see DESBIENS.

Saint-Émilion (sĕtāmēlyõ′), village (pop. 766), Gironde dept., SW France, 4 mi. ESE of Libourne; noted winegrowing center. Has anc. church hewn out of cliff by disciples of St. Emilion (8th cent.); 12th-cent. collegiate church; castle built 1225 by Louis VIII; 13th-cent. belfry; and ruins of 15th-cent. Franciscan convent.

Saint Endellion (sŭnt ĕndĕl′yŭn), agr. village and parish (pop. 1,090), central Cornwall, England, 9 mi. NW of Bodmin. Has 15th-cent. church.

Saint Enoder, town and parish (pop. 1,607), central Cornwall, England, 9 mi. NE of Truro; agr. market. Has 15th-cent. church.

Saint-Énogat, France: see DINARD.

Sainte-Odile, Mont (mõ sĕtōdēl′), Ger. *Odilienberg* (ōdē′lyŭnbĕrk), summit (c.2,500 ft.) of the E Vosges, Bas-Rhin dept., E France, 8 mi. SSW of Molsheim. Site of convent of St. Odile, a well-known pilgrimage place. Splendid panorama over Alsatian lowland.

Sainte Pétronille (sẽt pātrônē′) or **Beaulieu** (bōlyû′), village (pop. 442), S Que., at SW end of Île d'Orléans, on the St. Lawrence and 5 mi. NE of Quebec; dairying; fruit, vegetables.

Saint Éphrem de Beauce (sĕtāfrĕm′ dů bōs′), village (pop. 485), S Que., 14 mi. SW of Beauceville; dairying.

Sainte Pudentienne, Que.: see ROXTON POND.

Sainte Rose (sĕt rōz′), town (pop. 2,292), ⊙ Île Jésus co., S Que., on N shore of Jesus Isl., on Milles Îles R. and 12 mi. NW of Montreal; dairying.

Sainte-Rose, town (commune pop. 13,955), N Basse-Terre, Guadeloupe, minor port 13 mi. WNW of Pointe-à-Pitre; sugar milling, distilling.

Sainte-Rose, town and commune (pop. 2,588), on E coast of Réunion isl., 27 mi. SE of Saint-Denis, amid filao woods; agr. processing (sugar, vanilla), food canning.

Sainte Rose de Lima (sĕt rōz′ dů lēmä′) or **Templeton,** village (pop. 949), SW Que., near Ottawa R., 8 mi. NE of Hull; mica, silica mining.

Sainte Rose du Lac (rōz′ dū lăk′, Fr. sĕt rōz dü läk′), village (pop. 539), SW Man., 24 mi. ESE of Dauphin; wheat; mixed farming.

Saint Erth (sŭnt ûrth), agr. village and parish (pop. 1,085), W Cornwall, England, 4 mi. SE of St. Ives. Has 15th-cent. church.

Saintes (sĕt), anc. *Mediolanum,* town (pop. 20,711), Charente-Maritime dept., W France, on the Charente and 38 mi. WNW of Angoulême; road and railroad center (yards); foundries, machine shops (rolling stock, agr. equipment), distilling, food preserving, mfg. (shoes, hosiery, soap, pottery). Has a Roman amphitheater (1st cent. A.D.), still in use; triumphal arch of Germanicus (A.D. 21); 12th–15th-cent. Romanesque church of Saint-Eutrope; 11th–12th-cent. abbatial church of Sainte-Marie-des-Dames; and a noteworthy archaeological mus. Chief town of the Santones in Gallo-Roman times, it became ⊙ of county, later prov., of Saintonge, and for a short time (1790–1810) of Charente-Inférieure dept. Suffered extensive damage during Second World War.

Saintes, Les (lā sĕt′), or **Îles des Saintes** (ēl dā), archipelago (□ 5.5; pop. 2,358), Guadeloupe dept., Fr. West Indies, 10 mi. SSE of Basse-Terre, Guadeloupe; 15°50′N 61°35′W. The group consists of numerous rocks and 11 islets, among them TERRE-DE-BAS, TERRE-DE-HAUT, and Grand Îlet. Of volcanic origin, the isls. rise to c.1,000 ft. Have an exceptionally healthful climate, but are of little economic importance. Main activity of their Breton inhabitants is fishing, stock raising, and charcoal burning. Some sugar and coffee is grown. Isls. are famous for the Saintes naval battle (1782), in which Rodney defeated De Grasse in these waters.

Sainte-Savine (sĕt-sävēn′), W suburb (pop. 9,874) of Troyes, Aube dept., NE central France; hosiery center.

Sainte Scholastique (sĕt skôlästēk′), village (pop. 775), ⊙ Deux Montagnes co., S Que., 25 mi. WNW of Montreal; dairying; vegetables. Scene of 2 battles in 1837 revolt.

Sainte-Sévère-sur-Indre (sĕt-sāvâr′-sür-ē′drů), village (pop. 715), Indre dept., central France, on Indre R. and 8 mi. SSE of La Châtre; grain, cattle.

Sainte-Sigolène (sĕt-sēgōlĕn′), town (pop. 2,126), Haute-Loire dept., S central France, 9 mi. NE of Yssingeaux; mfg. of silk goods and elastic fabrics.

Saintes-Maries-de-la-Mer (sĕt-märē′-dů-lä-mâr′), village (pop. 765), Bouches-du-Rhône dept., SE France, on Gulf of Lion just E of mouth of the Petit Rhône, 18 mi. SSW of Arles, in the Camargue; fishing port. Has fortified Romanesque church. Attracts pilgrims, especially gypsies. Also written Les Saintes-Maries-de-la-Mer.

Saint-Esprit (sĕtĕsprē′), town (pop. 1,917), S Martinique, 10 mi. ESE of Fort-de-France; bananas, coffee, sugar. Sometimes Le Saint-Esprit.

Saint-Estèphe (sĕtĕstĕf′), village (pop. 354), Gironde dept., SW France, near W shore of the Gironde, 30 mi. NNW of Bordeaux; produces fine Médoc red wines.

Sainte-Suzanne (sĕt-süzän′). **1** W suburb (pop. 1,153) of Montbéliard, Doubs dept., E France; steel milling, clock making. **2** Village (pop. 460), Mayenne dept., W France, 19 mi. E of Laval; hosiery mfg.; quartzite quarries. Remains of 9th-cent. feudal fortifications.

Sainte-Suzanne, agr. town (1950 census pop. 383), Nord dept., N Haiti, on the Plaine du Nord, 15 mi. SE of Cap-Haïtien; coffee.

Sainte-Suzanne, town and commune (pop. 7,393), on N coast of Réunion isl., on railroad and 10 mi. E of Saint-Denis; sugar milling; vanilla and tapioca processing.

Sainte Thècle (sĕt tĕ′klů), village (pop. 904), S Que., 16 mi. NE of Grand' Mère; dairying; lumber.

Sainte Thérèse, Île (ēl sĕt tārĕz′), island (3 mi. long, 1 mi. wide), S Que., in the St. Lawrence, at N end of Montreal Isl.

Sainte Thérèse de Blainville (dů blĕvēl′), town (pop. 4,659), S Que., 16 mi. NNW of Montreal; mfg. of furniture, pianos, plywood, clothing, agr. machinery; dairying.

Saint-Étienne (sĕtātyĕn′). **1** or **Saint-Étienne-les-Orgues** (–lāzôrg′), village (pop. 427), Basses-Alpes dept., SE France, on S slope of Montagne de Lure, 13 mi. SW of Sisteron; lumbering, lavender distilling. **2** City (pop. 156,315), ⊙ Loire dept., SE central France, on the Furens and 31 mi. SW of Lyons; 45°26′N 4°24′E. Leading industrial center in coal-mining basin. Its metallurgical plants include blast furnaces, iron foundries, smelters, forges, and steel-rolling mills. Among its output of heavy durable goods are machines (agr., textile, electrical), automotive supplies, and armaments. Also important are the silk and rayon mills which produce ribbons, trimmings, and elastic fabrics. The city is known for its firearms, including mass-produced military rifles and custom-made hunting weapons and revolvers (the latter traditionally of superior craftsmanship). There also are glassworks, breweries, tanneries, flour mills, and large printing shops. The importance of Saint-Étienne is enhanced by its location at SW end of heavily industrialized JAREZ region, and near steel-milling towns of Firminy, Unieux, Le Chambon-Feugerolles, and La Ricamarie. In spite of its large size, Saint-Étienne is strung out along one central thoroughfare, with factories, residential dists., and railroad stations hugging the slopes of the Furens R. valley. Although its coal deposits have been known since 12th cent., the city did not grow until the development of artisan ribbon weaving in 15th cent. It received its major impetus during the Industrial Revolution. Together with Lyons and Roanne it now constitutes the industrial triangle of central France. Saint-Étienne was damaged during Second World War. **3** Town, Vosges dept., France: see SAINT-ÉTIENNE-LÈS-REMIREMONT.

Saint-Étienne-Cantalès (sĕtātyĕn′-kätälĕs′), village (pop. 184), Cantal dept., S central France, on the Cère and 11 mi. W of Aurillac; dam and new hydroelectric plant.

Saint-Étienne-de-Baïgorry (–dů-bīgôrē′), village (pop. 508), Basses-Pyrénées dept., SW France, in W Pyrenees, near Sp. border, on headstream of Nive R. and 23 mi. SSE of Bayonne; ophite quarries. Hydroelectric plant at Banca (3 mi. S). Basque pop.

Saint-Étienne-de-Lugdarès (–lügdärĕs′), village ((pop. 185), Ardèche dept., S France, 21 mi. W of Aubenas; barite quarrying, sheep raising.

Saint-Étienne-de-Montluc (–mōlük′), village (pop. 1,056), Loire-Inférieure dept., W France, 12 mi. WNW of Nantes; dairying, flour milling.

Saint-Étienne-de-Saint-Geoirs (–sē-zhwär′), village (pop. 807), Isère dept., SE France, 21 mi. NW of Grenoble in agr. lowland; silk and velvet mfg.

Saint Étienne des Grès (dā grĕ′), village (pop. estimate 500), S Que., on St. Maurice R. and 14 mi. NW of Trois Rivières; dairying; pigs, potatoes.

Saint-Étienne-de-Tinée (–dů-tēnā′), village (pop. 882), Alpes-Maritimes dept., SE France, in upper Tinée valley and 17 mi. SE of Barcelonnette, in Maritime Alps, near Ital. border; alt. 3,743 ft. Resort; winter sports.

Saint-Étienne-du-Rouvray (–dü-rōōvrā′), town (pop. 8,419), Seine-Inférieure dept., N France, on left bank of the Seine and 4 mi. S of Rouen; metalworks, paper mill, cider distillery. Damaged in Second World War.

Saint-Étienne-en-Dévoluy (–ā-dāvôlwē′), village (pop. 95), Hautes-Alpes dept., SE France, in Dévoluy range, 11 mi. NW of Gap; alt. 4,157 ft.

Saint-Étienne-les-Orgues, Basses-Alpes dept., France: see SAINT-ÉTIENNE.

Saint-Étienne-lès-Remiremont (–lā-růmĕrůmō′), NE suburb (pop. 1,984) of Remiremont, Vosges dept., E France, on the Moselle; cotton milling. Until 1937 called Saint-Étienne.

Sainte-Tulle (sĕt-tül′), village (pop. 913), Basses-Alpes dept., SE France, in Durance valley, 4 mi. S of Manosque; important hydroelectric plant on Durance R. (SE).

Saint-Eugène (sĕtûzhĕn′), town (pop. 10,474), Alger dept., N central Algeria, a residential NW suburb of Algiers, on the Mediterranean; cement mfg., olive-oil pressing. Insane asylum.

Saint Eustache (sĕtûstäsh′), village (pop. 1,564), S Que., on L. of the Two Mountains 15 mi. W of Montreal; dairying; vegetable canning; resort.

Saint Eustache sur le Lac (sür lů läk′), village (pop. 1,472), S Que., on L. of the Two Mountains, 15 mi. W of Montreal; dairying; resort.

Saint Eustatius (sānt″ ūstā′shůs), Du. *Sint Eustatius,* islet (□ 7.7; 1948 pop. c.950), Du. West Indies, in NW Leeward Isls., belonging to Du. Antilles (formerly Curaçao territory), 8 mi. NW of St. Kitts; principal settlement, Oranjestad, at 17°29′N 62°58′W. Has humid trade-wind climate; subject to earthquakes and hurricanes. It consists of 2 volcanoes (highest point 1,978 ft.) with intervening valley, where yams, corn, and sea-island cotton are grown. Some stock raising (cattle, sheep, goats). Taken by the Dutch in 1632, it frequently changed hands. In 18th cent. it became one of the leading trading centers of the West Indies, prospering during American Revolution as supply base for the colonies, but it has declined steadily after Br. occupation (1781). English is generally spoken. The isl. is sometimes called Statia.

Saint Évariste Station (sĕtāvärēst′), village (pop. 627), S Que., 27 mi. N of Megantic; dairying, lumbering.

Saint-Fargeau (sĕ′-fär-zhō′), village (pop. 1,489), Yonne dept., N central France, on Loing R. and 17 mi. NNE of Cosne; wood- and metalworking. Has 13th-cent. castle.

Saint Faustin Station (sĕ fōstĕ′), village (pop. 375), S Que., in the Laurentians, 11 mi. NW of Ste. Agathe des Monts; alt. 1,254 ft.; dairying; ski resort.

Saint Félicien (sĕ fālēsyĕ′), village (pop. 1,603), S central Que., on Ashuapmuchuan R., near its mouth on L. St. John, 15 mi. NW of Roberval; dairying center, lumbering. Near by are the Salmon Falls (20 ft. high).

Saint-Félicien, village (pop. 458), Ardèche dept., S France, 10 mi. W of Tournon; dairying.

Saint-Félix-de-Pallières, France: see LASALLE.

Saint Félix de Valois (sĕ fālēks′ dů välwä′), village (pop. 1,130), S Que., 10 mi. N of Joliette; dairying, lumbering; tobacco, potatoes, poultry.

Saint Ferdinand (sĕ fĕrdēnä′) or **Bernierville** (bĕr′-nyāvĭl), village (pop. 1,638), S Que., on L. William (4 mi. long), 15 mi. W of Thetford Mines; dairying; cattle, pigs.

Saint Ferdinand, Mo.: see FLORISSANT.

Saintfield, town (pop. 1,383), NE Co. Down, Northern Ireland, 10 mi. SE of Belfast; linen milling; agr. market (flax, oats). In 1798 it was scene of engagement bet. the United Irishmen and the Yeomanry.

Saint Fillans, Scotland: see EARN, LOCH.

Saint Finan's Bay (sŭnt fī′nŭnz), inlet (5 mi. long, 4 mi. wide) of the Atlantic, SW Co. Kerry, Ireland, bet. Puffin Isl. (NW) and Bolus Head (SE).

Saint-Firmin or **Saint-Firmin-en-Valgodemard** (sĕ-fĕrmĕ′ā-välgôdmär′), village (pop. 371), Hautes-Alpes dept., SE France, 16 mi. N of Gap in Dauphiné Alps; dairying, woolen milling. Hydroelectric plant near by.

Saint Flavien (sĕ flävyĕ′), village (pop. 507), S Que., 25 mi. SW of Quebec; dairying, lumbering, pig raising.

Saint-Florent (sĕ-flôrā′), Ital. *San Fiorenzo,* village (pop. 1,080), N Corsica, port on Saint-Florent gulf of the Mediterranean, 7 mi. W of Bastia, at W base of Cape Corse peninsula; lobster fishing. Founded 15th cent.

Saint-Florent or **Saint-Florent-sur-Auzonnet** (–sür-ōzōnā′), village (pop. 270), Gard dept., S France, 8 mi. N of Alès; iron and coal mines.

Saint-Florentin (sĕ-flôrātĕ′), town (pop. 2,603), Yonne dept., N central France, on Armançon R. and Burgundy Canal, and 16 mi. NNE of Auxerre; road and market center; boiler works; building materials. Unfinished Renaissance church damaged, 1944, in Second World War.

Saint-Florent-le-Vieil (sĕ-flôrā′-lů-vyā′), village (pop. 878), Maine-et-Loire dept., W France, on Loire R. and 23 mi. WSW of Angers; mfg. of leather goods; winegrowing. Has ruins of a 4th-cent. abbey founded by St. Florent and sacked by Normans in 875, and well-known for the role it played in the Vendée war; it contains the tombs of 2 Vendéan leaders.

Saint-Florent-sur-Auzonnet, Gard dept., France: see SAINT-FLORENT.

Saint-Florent-sur-Cher (–sür-shâr′), town (pop. 4,232), Cher dept., central France, on Cher R. and 10 mi. SW of Bourges; precision metalworks (hardware, automobile and heating equipment); mfg. of wheelbarrows and household implements.

Saint-Flour (sĕ-flōōr′), town (pop. 4,576), Cantal dept., S central France, on the Planèze, 32 mi. ENE of Aurillac; alt. 2,890 ft.; tourist center; hosiery mfg., tanning, flour milling. Seat of a bishop. Has 15th-cent. cathedral, a Renaissance Consular mansion, steep narrow streets and remains of medieval ramparts. Its commercial importance declined due to poor communications.

Saint-Fons (sē-fō'), S suburb (pop. 10,592) of Lyons, Rhône dept., E central France, near left bank of the Rhone; chemical-mfg. center with large fertilizer production.

Saint Francis, county (□ 636; pop. 36,841), E Ark.; ⊙ Forrest City. Intersected by Crowley's Ridge; drained by St. Francis and L'Anguille rivers. Agr. (fruit, cotton, corn, sweet potatoes, rice). Mfg. at Forrest City and Hughes. Timber; sand, gravel. Formed 1827.

Saint Francis. 1 Town (pop. 292), Clay co., extreme NE Ark., 6 mi. NE of Piggott and on St. Francis R., near Mo. line. **2** City (pop. 1,892), ⊙ Cheyenne co., NW Kansas, on South Fork Republican R. and 30 mi. N of Goodland; trade and shipping center in agr. area; grain milling. Founded 1885, inc. 1903. **3** Plantation (pop. 1,384), Aroostook co., N Maine, on St. John R., opposite mouth of St. Francis R., and 16 mi. WSW of Fort Kent; wood products, lumber. **4** Town (pop. 241), Todd co., S S.Dak., 90 mi. SSW of Pierre. **5** Village (1940 pop. 662), Milwaukee co., SE Wis., near L. Michigan, just S of Milwaukee.

Saint Francis, Cape, promontory, SE N.F., on Avalon Peninsula, on E side of entrance to Conception Bay, 18 mi. NNW of St. John's; 47°49'N 52°47'W.

Saint Francis, Cape, S Cape Prov., U. of So. Afr., on Indian Ocean, 45 mi. WSW of Port Elizabeth, on W side of entrance of St. Francis Bay; 34°12'S 24°52'E.

Saint Francis, Isles of, Australia: see NUYTS ARCHIPELAGO.

Saint Francis, Lake, or **Lake Saint François** (frãswä'). **1** Expansion (□ 85) of the St. Lawrence, S Que. and SE Ont., extends 30 mi. bet. Cornwall (SW) and Valleyfield (NE); 5 mi. wide. Rapids (NE) of the St. Lawrence are bypassed by Beauharnois and Soulanges canals, connecting L. St. Francis and L. St. Louis. **2** Lake (□ 13), S Que., 20 mi. NW of Megantic; 14 mi. long, 3 mi. wide. Drained by St. Francis R.

Saint Francis Bay (15 mi. long, 35 mi. wide at mouth), S Cape Prov., U. of So. Afr., inlet of the Indian Ocean, 15 mi. W of Port Elizabeth; receives Gamtoos R. On W side of entrance is Cape St. Francis.

Saint Francis Mountains, Mo.: see SAINT FRANCOIS MOUNTAINS.

Saint Francis River. 1 In S Que., issues from L. St. Francis, 30 mi. NW of Megantic, flows SW, through L. Aylmer, past East Angus, to Lennoxville, thence flows NW, past Sherbrooke, Richmond, Drummondville, and Pierreville, to L. St. Peter (part of the St. Lawrence) 12 mi. ENE of Sorel; 150 mi. long. **2** In E Que., flows c.60 mi. SE to St. John R., forming boundary bet. Que. and extreme N Maine.

Saint Francis River, in SE Mo. and NE Ark., rises in St. Francois Mts. in headstreams joining in St. Francois co., Mo.; flows c.470 mi. irregularly S, forming part of Mo.-Ark. boundary, to Mississippi R. above Helena, Ark. Impounded by Wappapello Dam in Wayne co., Mo.

Saint Francisville. 1 City (pop. 1,117), Lawrence co., SE Ill., on the Wabash (ferry here) and 9 mi. S of Lawrenceville, in agr., oil, and natural-gas area. Inc. 1843. **2** Town (pop. 936), ⊙ West Feliciana parish, SE central La., 26 mi. NW of Baton Rouge and on the Mississippi; agr. (cotton, sweet and white potatoes); sweet-potato canning, cotton ginning, feed and lumber milling. Fine ante-bellum houses in vicinity.

Saint-François (sē-frãswä'), town (commune pop. 5,709), SE Grande-Terre, Guadeloupe, 17 mi. E of Pointe-à-Pitre, in agr. region (sugar cane, cotton); sugar mill.

Saint Francois (sānt" frăn'sĭs), county (□ 457; pop. 35,276), E Mo.; ⊙ Farmington. Partly in St. Francois Mts.; drained by Big R. and St. Francis R. Agr. (corn, wheat, hay), livestock, mining (lead, zinc, cobalt, nickel, limestone). Part of Clark Natl. Forest here. Formed 1821.

Saint François, Lake, Canada: see SAINT FRANCIS, LAKE.

Saint François du Lac (sē frãswä' dü läk'), village (pop. 673), S Que., on St. Francis R. opposite Pierreville, and 14 mi. E of Sorel; dairying, pig raising. Mineral springs near by.

Saint François Island, Seychelles: see ALPHONSE ISLAND.

Saint Francois Mountains (sānt" frăn'sĭs), SE Mo., mountain group rising above Ozark plateau, bet. Flat River (N) and Piedmont (S); Taum Sauk Mtn. (1,772 ft.), W of Ironton, is highest point in range and in Mo. An outcrop of igneous rocks, mts. are center of mining region yielding iron, lead (especially in Flat River dist.), barite, zinc, manganese, cobalt, nickel, granite, and limestone. Sometimes spelled St. Francis.

Saint Frédéric (sē frādārĕk'), village (pop. estimate 400), S Que., 40 mi. SSE of Quebec; lumbering, dairying; cattle, pigs.

Saint Froid Lake, Maine: see FISH RIVER LAKES.

Saint-Fulgent (sē-fülzhã'), village (pop. 628), Vendée dept., W France, 17 mi. NE of La Roche-sur-Yon; cattle raising.

Saint Gabriel de Brandon (gä'brēŭl dŭ brăn'dŭn, Fr. sē gäbrēĕl'), village (pop. 1,632), S Que., on L. Maskinonge, 22 mi. NW of Sorel; lumber; dairying.

Saint Gall (sānt gôl'), Fr. *Saint-Gall* (sēgäl'), Ger. *Sankt Gallen* (zängkt gä'lŭn), canton (□ 777; 1950 pop. 308,483), NE Switzerland, borders N on L. Constance, E on the Rhine; ⊙ St. Gall. It surrounds half-cantons of Appenzell Inner Rhoden and Appenzell Ausser Rhoden. In N and E are meadowland, valleys, some cultivated fields, and orchards; mountainous S has some pastureland. Several resorts are situated on the Rhine, near L. of Wallenstadt, and at the source of the Thur. Well-developed textile industry, principally of silk, embroidery, and cotton goods. Became a canton in 1803. Pop. German speaking and both Catholic (majority) and Protestant.

Saint Gall, Fr. *Saint-Gall,* Ger. *Sankt Gallen,* town (1950 pop. 67,865), ⊙ St. Gall, NE Switzerland. Originally an abbey, the town became a free imperial city in 1311 and allied itself with the Swiss Confederation in 1454. Seat of a bishopric since 1846. Protestant and Catholic pop., equally divided. Embroideries, cotton textiles, knit goods, chemicals, fats, chocolate, beer, biscuits, canned goods produced; metal- and woodworking, printing. Modern suburbs, which extend to SE and NW, surround medieval *Altstadt.* Abbey of St. Gall (founded 8th cent. on 7th-cent. site; 17th–18th-cent. bldgs.) contains cantonal offices and clerical residences. Baroque abbey church, and abbey library with valuable incunabula and MSS, are here. There are a school of economics, industrial mus., historical and ethnological mus.

Saint-Galmier (sē-gälmyā'), village (pop. 1,830), Loire dept., SE central France, in Forez Plain, 12 mi. E of Montbrison; well-known mineral springs. At Veauche (vōsh), on the Loire 2 mi. SW, are glass- and cementworks.

Saint-Gaudens (sē-gōdā'), town (pop. 6,916), Haute-Garonne dept., S France, near the Garonne, 50 mi. SW of Toulouse; woolen mills, breweries, distilleries. Paper mills near by. Has mutilated 11th–12th-cent. Romanesque church. Natural gas tapped in area is piped to Bordeaux and Toulouse.

Saint-Gaultier (sē-gōtyā'), town (pop. 2,062), Indre dept., central France, on Creuse R. and 18 mi. SW of Châteauroux; limestone and chalk quarrying and processing.

Saint Gédéon (sē zhādāõ'), village (pop. 696), S central Que., on E shore of L. St. John, 8 mi. SE of St. Joseph d'Alma; dairying, pig raising.

Saint-Genest-Lerpt (sē-zhünĕ'-lĕrpt'), town (pop. 2,504), Loire dept., SE central France, 3 mi. W of Saint-Étienne; coal-miners' residences; hosiery.

Saint-Genest-Malifaux (–mälēfō'), village (pop. 711), Loire dept., SE central France, on SW slope of Mont Pilat, 7 mi. S of Saint-Étienne; silk milling.

Saint-Gengoux-le-National (sē-zhãgōō'-lù-näsyōnäl), village (pop. 957), Saône-et-Loire dept., E central France, 15 mi. SW of Chalon-sur-Saône; winegrowing.

Saint-Geniez-d'Olt (sē-zhünyā-dôlt'), village (pop. 1,983), Aveyron dept., S France, on the Lot and 21 mi. ENE of Rodez; woolen mfg. Strawberry growing and shipping. Silver-bearing lead mines near by.

Saint-Genis-de-Saintonge (sē-zhünē'-dù-sētōzh'), village (pop. 608), Charente-Maritime dept., W France, 7 mi. WNW of Jonzac; brandy distilling, dairying.

Saint-Genis-Laval (läväl'), outer suburb (pop. 3,445) of Lyons, Rhône dept., E central France, 5 mi. SSW of city center; mfg. of velvets and woolens; distilling.

Saint-Genix-sur-Guiers (sē-zhünē'-sür-gyâr'), village (pop. 947), Savoie dept., SE France, on Guiers R. near its influx into the Rhone, and 14 mi. W of Chambéry; makes surgical trusses, silk hose.

Saint-Genou (sē-zhünōō'), village (pop. 1,031), Indre dept., central France, on the Indre and 19 mi. NW of Châteauroux; pottery mfg., cattle and hog raising. Has fine Romanesque church originally part of an abbey (founded 9th cent.).

Saint-Geoire-en-Valdaine (sē-zhwär'-ã-väldĕn'), village (pop. 484), Isère dept., SE France, 12 mi. SE of La Tour-du-Pin; silk spinning, sawmilling.

Saint George, village (pop. 1,249), S Queensland, Australia, on Balonne R. and 180 mi. SE of Charleville; wheat, cattle.

Saint George, town (1949 pop. estimate c.1,500) on St. George's Isl., Bermuda, 9 mi. NE of Hamilton, on St. George's Harbour (1.5 mi. long, 1 mi. wide). Has mus., St. Peter's Church (built 1713). Founded 1612 and ⊙ Bermuda until replaced (1815) by Hamilton. It was long the isl.'s chief port, and in American Civil War was hq. for Confederate blockade runners.

Saint George. 1 Town (pop. 1,169), SW N.B., on Magaguadavic R. estuary, 5 mi. E of its mouth on Passamaquoddy Bay, and 40 mi. WSW of St. John; fishing port (sardines, herring, quahaug, pollock); ships pulp and lumber. Has pulp mills, hydroelectric station. Near by are airport and granite quarries. L. Utopia is 4 mi. NE. **2** Village (pop. estimate 500), S Ont., 8 mi. N of Brantford; sawmilling, dairying, mixed farming.

Saint George, E suburb (pop. 47,162) of Bristol, SW Gloucester, England; leather, shoe, metal, and glass industries.

Saint George, town, Grenada, B.W.I.: see SAINT GEORGE'S.

Saint George, Rumanian *Sfantu-Gheorghe* (sfŭn'tōō-gyôr'ge), S arm of the Danube delta (Mouths of the Danube) in Dobruja, E Rumania. Formed above Tulcea, it meanders c.70 mi. ESE to the Black Sea at Sfantu-Gheorghe, enclosing with Sulina arm (N) St. George Isl. Sometimes called St. Georges.

Saint George, county (□ 354.68; pop. 137,947, exclusive of Port of Spain and Arima), NW Trinidad, B.W.I., bordering on the Caribbean and the Gulf of Paria.

Saint George. 1 City (pop. 251), Pottawatomie co., NE Kansas, on Kansas R. and 8 mi. E of Manhattan; livestock, grain. **2** Town (pop. 1,482), Knox co., S Maine, on peninsula S of Rockland; includes villages of St. George, Port Clyde, and Tenants Harbor. Fishing, resorts, granite quarries. Area was visited 1605, trading post c.1630. Fort St. George (1809) fell to British in War of 1812. **3** Town (pop. 642), St. Louis co., E Mo. **4** Village, ⊙Richmond co., SE N.Y., and seat of borough hall of Richmond borough of New York city, on NE STATEN ISLAND, 5 mi. SSW of tip of Manhattan; terminus of ferries to Manhattan and Brooklyn and isl.'s chief business and transportation center. Here are hq. and mus. of Staten Isl. Inst. of Arts and Sciences. Fort Hill was site of British-held fort in the Revolution. **5** Town (pop. 1,938), ⊙ Dorchester co., S central S.C., 45 mi. NW of Charleston; trading center for agr. area (lumber, grain products, cotton, livestock). Settled 1788. Methodist campgrounds near by. **6** Resort city (pop. 4,562), ⊙ Washington co., SW Utah, on Virgin R., and c.50 mi. SW of Cedar City, near Ariz. line; trade and tourist center in diversified-farming area. Gold, copper, iron mines near by. Seat of Dixie Jr. Col., Mormon temple (completed 1877), and Mormon tabernacle (completed 1871). Settled in 1860s as cotton center. Dixie Natl. Forest is N, Zion Natl. Park c.30 mi. ENE. **7** Town (pop. 117), Chittenden co., NW Vt., 8 mi. SE of Burlington.

Saint George, Cape, E New South Wales, Australia, SW projection of small peninsula forming S shore of Jervis Bay; 35°12'S 150°43'E.

Saint George, Cape, promontory on the Gulf of St. Lawrence, SW N.F., at W end of Port au Port peninsula, on N side of entrance to St. George Bay, 70 mi. SW of Corner Brook; 48°28'N 59°18'W; lighthouse.

Saint George, Cape, Fla.: see SAINT GEORGE ISLAND.

Saint George, Gulf of, Argentina: see SAN JORGE, GULF OF.

Saint George, Point, promontory on NW coast of Calif., just NW of Crescent City; site of govt. radio station. Lighthouse just offshore.

Saint George Bay (60 mi. long, 40 mi. wide at mouth), SW N.F.; 48°N 59°W. Entrance is bet. Cape Anguille (S) and Cape St. George (N); N shore is bounded by Port au Port Peninsula. Anguille Mts. extend along SE shore. There are several fishing settlements, including St. George's and Stephenville.

Saint George Channel, Bismarck Archipelago, SW Pacific, bet. New Ireland (N) and New Britain (S); 20 mi. wide.

Saint George Fjord, inlet (60 mi. long, 3–7 mi. wide) of Lincoln Sea of Arctic Ocean, N Greenland; 81°55'N 53°30'W. Receives Steensby Glacier.

Saint George Island (12 mi. long, 2–7 mi. wide; pop. 188), Pribilof Isls., SW Alaska, in Bering Sea; 56°35'N 169°36'W; rises to 1,012 ft. The natives hunt fur-seals (under license from U.S. Bureau of Fisheries) and foxes. St. George village is in N.

Saint George Island. 1 In NW Fla., narrow wooded barrier island (c.20 mi. long) in the Gulf of Mexico S and SE of Apalachicola, bet. Dog (NE) and St. Vincent (W) isls.; partly shelters Apalachicola Bay and St. George Sound. Formerly c.30 mi. long; W end, including Cape St. George (lighthouse at 29°35'N 85°3'E), was detached when a storm cut a channel (New Inlet). **2** In S Md., island (c.3 mi. long, 1 mi. wide) in the Potomac near mouth of St. Marys R., 14 mi. SE of Leonardtown; bridge to left bank. Fishing, oystering; also a summer resort.

Saint George Lake, Waldo co., S Maine, in 5,310-acre Lake St. George State Park, 13 mi. WSW of Belfast; 2 mi. long.

Saint George River, S Maine, rises in S Waldo co., flows c.30 mi. SE and S to Thomaston, where it becomes 12-mi. inlet (.5–1 mi. wide) opening into Muscongus Bay bet. St. George and Cushing.

Saint-Georges or **Saint-Georges-sur-Meuse** (sē-zhôrzh-sür-mûz'), town (pop. 5,796), Liége prov., E Belgium, near Meuse R., 10 mi. WSW of Liége, in steel-milling, metalworking region.

Saint George's, parish (1939 pop. 2,664), NE Bermuda. Includes all isls. E and S of Castle Harbour and the SE part of Bermuda Isl. called Tucker's Town.

Saint George's, village (pop. 670), SW N.F., on SE side of St. George Bay, 9 mi. SE of Stephenville; fishing port; mink and fox farming.

Saint Georges, Que.: see SAINT GEORGES DE CHAMPLAIN.

Saint-Georges (sẽ-zhôrzh′), village (pop. 540), Vienne dept., W central France, near Clain R., 7 mi. NNE of Poitiers; winegrowing. Also called Saint-Georges-les-Baillargeaux.

Saint-Georges or **Saint-Georges-de-l'Oyapock** (sẽ-zhôrzh′-dů-lôyäpôk′), town, ⊙ Oyapock or Oyapoc commune (pop. 1,244), NE Fr. Guiana, landing on Oyapock R. (Brazil border) and 85 mi. SE of Cayenne. Radio station, customhouse.

Saint George's or **Saint George,** town (pop. 5,772), ⊙ GRENADA and WINDWARD ISLANDS colonies, B.W.I., port on SW coast of Grenada isl., 90 mi. N of Port of Spain, Trinidad, and 175 mi. SSW of Fort-de-France, Martinique; 12°3′N 61°45′W. Its deep, landlocked harbor is one of the most beautiful in the West Indies; ships cacao, nutmeg, mace. Rum distilling, sugar milling. Has public bldgs., St. George's Church, botanic station, Govt. House, and old Fort George in SW. Founded as a Fr. settlement in 1650.

Saint Georges, town (1940 pop. 339), New Castle co., N central Del., 14 mi. S of Wilmington and on Chesapeake and Delaware Canal (bridged here).

Saint George's Cay (kā, kē), islet, central Bahama Isls., just N of Eleuthera Isl., 50 mi. NE of Nassau; 25°34′N 76°45′W. On it is Spanish Wells village. Produces tomatoes, coconuts, pineapples; fishing. The British here defeated (1798) the Spanish, marking end of Sp. claims in Br. Honduras.

Saint George's Channel, sea arm (c.100 mi. long, 50–95 mi. wide) linking the Atlantic and the Irish Sea, separating SE Ireland from Wales.

Saint Georges de Beauce (sẽ zhôrzh dů bōs′) or **Saint Georges Est** (ĕst′), village (pop. 1,945), S Que., on Chaudière R. and 55 mi. SE of Quebec; rayon, woolen-milling center; shoe mfg., dairying.

Saint Georges de Champlain (shãplẽ′) or **Saint Georges,** village (pop. 753), S Que., on St. Maurice R., opposite Grand'Mère; dairying, lumbering.

Saint-Georges-de-l'Oyapock, Fr. Guiana: see SAINT-GEORGES.

Saint-Georges-des-Groseillers (–dā-grōzāyā′), commune (pop. 2,283), Orne dept., NW France, 2 mi. N of Flers; cider distilling.

Saint-Georges-du-Vièvre (–dü-vyĕ′vrů), agr. village (pop. 379), Eure dept., NW France, 11 mi. N of Bernay.

Saint-Georges-en-Couzan (–ã-kōōzã′), village (pop. 262), Loire dept., SE central France, in Monts du Forez, on the Lignon and 9 mi. NW of Montbrison; handicraft textile industry.

Saint Georges Est, Que.: see SAINT GEORGES DE BEAUCE.

Saint George's Island (3 mi. long, ¼–1 mi. wide), one of principal islands of Bermuda, in NE part of the isl. group, 7 mi. ENE of Hamilton. Tourist center, with numerous fine beaches. Town and port of St. George is on S shore. Linked by road and rail with the other isls.

Saint George's Island, Port. *São Jorge* (sã′ō zhôr′zhů), island (□ c.1) of Goa dist., Portuguese India, in Arabian Sea, 10 mi. SSW of Pangim. The term St. George Isls. was formerly used to include other smaller isls. lying bet. here and Mormugão port, 3 mi. NNE.

Saint George Sound (c.25 mi. long, 5 mi. wide), arm of the Gulf of Mexico in Franklin co., NW Fla., partly sheltered by St. George and Dog isls.; communicates with Apalachicola Bay (SW). W part is traversed by Gulf Intracoastal Waterway.

Saint-Georges-sur-Loire (sẽ-zhôrzh-sür-lwär′), village (pop. 821), Maine-et-Loire dept., W France, near Loire R., 11 mi. WSW of Angers; winegrowing, truck gardening. Renaissance Castle of Serrant near by.

Saint-Gérard (sẽ-zhärär′), village (pop. 1,636), Namur prov., S central Belgium, 10 mi. SSW of Namur; marble quarrying; agr.

Saint-Germain (sẽ-zhĕrmẽ′). **1** Village (pop. 961), Hauge-Saône dept., E France, 3 mi. NNE of Lure; cotton milling. **2** or **Saint-Germain-du-Belair** (–dübĕlâr′), village (pop. 324), Lot dept., SW France, 14 mi. N of Cahors; hogs, nuts.

Saint-Germain (sẽ-zhĕrmẽ′), town (pop. 2,196), Tunis dist., N Tunisia, on S shore of Gulf of Tunis, 8 mi. ESE of Tunis; summer resort; casino.

Saint-Germain-de-Calberte (sẽ-zhĕrmẽ′-dů-kälbârt′), village (pop. 254), Lozère dept., S France, in the Cévennes, 13 mi. SE of Florac; fruitgrowing. Antimony mining at Le Collet-de-Dèze, 5 mi. ENE.

Saint Germain de Grantham (grăn′thům) or **Saint Joseph de Grantham** (sẽ zhōzĕf′), town (pop. 5,559), S Que., 24 mi. NE of St. Hyacinthe, in dairying, stock-raising (cattle, pigs) region.

Saint-Germain-des-Fossés (–dā-fôsā′), town (pop. 3,339), Allier dept., central France, in Limagne, near the Allier, 5 mi. N of Vichy; important railroad center; mfg. of vegetable oil, fruit preserving.

Saint-Germain-des-Prés (–prā′), one of oldest churches in Paris, France, in the Faubourg Saint-Germain near left bank of the Seine. Dating from 11th cent., it belonged to a powerful Benedictine abbey founded in 6th cent.

Saint-Germain-du-Belair, France: see SAINT-GERMAIN.

Saint-Germain-du-Bois (–dü-bwä′), agr. village (pop. 1,039), Saône-et-Loire dept., E central France, 9 mi. N of Louhans; pottery.

Saint-Germain-du-Plain (–plẽ′), agr. village (pop. 378), Saône-et-Loire dept., E central France, near Saône R., 8 mi. SE of Chalon-sur-Saône.

Saint-Germain-du-Teil (–tā′), village (pop. 318), Lozère dept., S France, near Lot R., 16 mi. W of Mende.

Saint-Germain-en-Laye (–ã-lā′), town (pop. 20,028), Seine-et-Oise dept., N central France, an excursion center and outer WNW suburb of Paris, 12 mi. from Notre Dame Cathedral, on left bank of the Seine; metalworking (precision instruments), mfg. (chocolate, ink), distilling. A beautiful terrace (1.5 mi. long; laid out by Le Nôtre in 1670s) overlooks the Seine and its bordering villas from atop a ridge. At its S end is a pavilion (only remnant of 16th-cent. Château Neuf in which Louis XIV was born) where peace treaty with Austria was signed in 1919. The handsome Renaissance château, a major royal residence from Francis I to Louis XIII, now houses natl. mus. of antiquities. Forest of Saint-Germain (□ 15), just N, occupies area within large Seine R. bend. Debussy b. in Saint-Germain.

Saint-Germain-Laval (sẽ-zhĕrmẽ′-läväl′), village (pop. 1,129), Loire dept., SE central France, at N end of Forez Plain, 15 mi. SSW of Roanne; mfg. of work clothes; fruit and vegetable shipping.

Saint-Germain-Lembron (–lãbrõ′), village (pop. 1,313), Puy-de-Dôme dept., central France, 6 mi. S of Issoire; mfg. of paints and dyes.

Saint-Germain-les-Belles (–lā-bĕl′), village (pop. 775), Haute-Vienne dept., W central France, in Monts du Limousin, 18 mi. SE of Limoges; cider. Also called Saint-Germain-les-Belles-Filles.

Saint-Germain-l'Herm (–lârm′), village (pop. 502), Puy-de-Dôme dept., central France, resort in Massif du Livradois, 12 mi. SW of Ambert.

Saint Germans, town and parish (pop. 1,964), E Cornwall, England, 8 mi. SE of Liskeard; agr. market; stone quarrying. Seat of Cornish bishops in 10th and 11th cent. Has Norman church.

Saint-Gervais or **Saint-Gervais-sur-Mare** (sẽ-zhĕrvā′-sür-mär′), village (pop. 808), Hérault dept., S France, in the Monts de l'Espinouse, 15 mi. WSW of Lodève; hard- and soft-coal mining.

Saint-Gervais-d'Auvergne (–dōvâr′nyů), village (pop. 1,083), Puy-de-Dôme dept., central France, in Combrailles, 17 mi. NW of Riom; woodworking, horse breeding. Part of Saint-Éloy-les-Mines coal field. Formerly called Saint-Gervais.

Saint-Gervais-les-Bains (–lā-bẽ′), commune (pop. 3,574), Haute-Savoie dept., SE France, at influx of small Bon-Nant R. into the Arve, and 8 mi. WSW of Chamonix. Consists of Le Fayet (alt. 1,903 ft.; spa and transfer point on railroad to Chamonix) and of Saint-Gervais (alt. 2,657 ft.; 1 mi. S of Le Fayet), a popular tourist and health resort. Numerous hotels. Winter sports. Aerial tramway to Mont d'Arbois; rack-and-pinion railway to Col de Voza and Bionnassay glacier.

Saint-Gervais-sur-Mare, France: see SAINT-GERVAIS.

Saint-Géry (sẽ-zhārē′), village (pop. 190), Lot dept., SW France, on the Lot and 7 mi. E of Cahors; wine, truffles.

Saint-Ghislain (sẽ-zhēzlẽ′), town (pop. 3,198), Hainaut prov., SW Belgium, on Haine R. and 6 mi. W of Mons; ceramics; glass-blowing center.

Saint-Gildas, Pointe de (pwẽt dů sẽ-zhēldä′), headland on Bay of Biscay, in Loire-Inférieure dept., W France, bet. Loire R. estuary (N) and Bay of Bourgneuf (S); 47°8′N 2°15′W.

Saint-Gildas-de-Rhuis (sẽ-zhēldä′-dů-rüēs′), village (pop. 302), Morbihan dept., W France, resort on Quiberon Bay (Atlantic Ocean), 11 mi. S of Vannes. Has 11th-cent. Romanesque church.

Saint-Gildas-des-Bois (–dā-bwä′), village (pop. 540), Loire-Inférieure dept., W France, 19 mi. NNE of Saint-Nazaire; dairy products. Has 13th–15th-cent. church of Benedictine abbey founded 1025.

Saint-Gilles (sẽ-zhēl′), Flemish *Sint-Gillis* (sĭnt-khĭ′lĭs), SW suburb (pop. 61,984) of Brussels, Brabant prov., central Belgium; mfg. (clothing, leather, shoes, chemicals, metals, wood products, pottery, food products).

Saint-Gilles. 1 or **Saint-Gilles-du-Gard** (–dü-gär′), town (pop. 4,421), Gard dept., S France, on Rhone-Sète Canal and 10 mi. W of Arlès, near the Petit-Rhone; distilling, wine and wheat growing. Has medieval church. **2** Village (pop. 133), Manche dept., NW France, 4 mi. WSW of Saint-Lô. Captured by Americans (July, 1944) in Saint-Lô offensive.

Saint-Gilles-les-Bains (–lā-bẽ′), village (pop. 1,423), on W coast of Réunion isl., on railroad and 4 mi. SW of Saint-Paul; seaside resort.

Saint-Gilles-lez-Termonde (–tĕrmõd′), Flemish *Sint-Gillis-bij-Dendermonde* (sĭnt-khĭ′lĭs-bī-dĕn′-důrmōndů), town (pop. 9,808), East Flanders prov., W Belgium, just SE of Dendermonde; textile industry.

Saint-Gilles-sur-Vie (–sür-vē′), town (pop. 2,006), Vendée dept., W France, on Bay of Biscay at mouth of Vie R. opposite Croix-de-Vie and 16 mi. NNW of Les Sables-d'Olonne; bathing; fishing.

Saint-Gilles-Waas, Flemish *Sint-Gillis-Waas* (both: –väs″), town (pop. 5,723), East Flanders prov., N Belgium, 4 mi. N of St-Nicolas; textiles; market.

Saint-Gingolph (sẽ-zhẽgôlf′), village on Fr.-Swiss border and on S shore of L. Geneva, 5 mi. SSW of Vevey, consisting of Fr. section in Haute-Savoie dept. (pop. 425) and Swiss section in Valais canton (commune pop. 700). Summer resort.

Saint-Girons (sẽ-zhērõ′), town (pop. 5,812), Ariège dept., S France, at foot of central Pyrenees, on Salat R. and 45 mi. SSW of Toulouse; commercial center (livestock, agr. produce); paper milling, cheese and fertilizer mfg. Iron mines, whetstone and marble quarries near by.

Saint-Gobain (sẽ-gôbẽ′), village (pop. 1,476), Aisne dept., N France, on a wooded tableland (Saint-Gobain Forest), 11 mi. WNW of Laon; its well-known mirror and optical glass factory was established in 1685. Important defensive bastion held by Germans until Oct., 1918, in First World War.

Saint-Gond, Marshes of (sẽ-gõ′), in Marne dept., N France, near W edge of Champagne badlands, 17 mi. SSW of Épernay; 10 mi. long, 3 mi. wide. Here Foch defeated Von Bülow in 1st battle of the Marne (1914).

Saint Gotthard, Hungary: see SZENTGOTTHARD.

Saint Gotthard (sānt gŏ′thůrd), Ger. *Sankt Gotthard* (zängkt gôt′härt), Fr. *Saint-Gothard* (sẽ-gôtär′), Ital. *San Gottardo* (sän gōt-tär′dô), mountain group in Lepontine Alps, S central Switzerland, culminating in the Pizzo Rotondo (10,483 ft.). St. Gotthard Road (fine views) leads through the mts.; bet. Göschenen (2 mi. N of Andermatt) and Andermatt it runs through the Schöllenen (a mtn. defile), crosses Reuss R. by DEVIL'S BRIDGE, and passes through Urner Loch (a cave); bet. Andermatt and Airolo it crosses **Saint Gotthard Pass** (6,929 ft.), originally made accessible in the Middle Ages. St. Gotthard Hospice (14th cent.) and a meteorological station are in the pass. Mts. are also crossed by St. Gotthard Railway (constructed 1872–82), which passes through **Saint Gotthard Tunnel** (9.3 mi. long; max. alt 3,786 ft.; 2d longest among Alpine tunnels); it leads from Göschenen to Airolo.

Saint Gowan's Head, promontory at W end of Carmarthen Bay, Pembroke, Wales, 5 mi. SSW of Pembroke; 51°36′N 4°55′N.

Saint-Gratien (sẽ-grätyẽ′), town (pop. 6,100), Seine-et-Oise dept., N central France, an outer NNW suburb of Paris, on W shore of Enghien L., 8 mi. from Notre Dame Cathedral; mfg. (diesel engines, plumbing equipment).

Saint-Guénolé (sẽ-gänôlā′), town (pop. 2,555), Finistère dept., W France, fishing port and bathing resort on Bay of Biscay, 16 mi. SW of Quimper.

Saint Guillaume d'Upton (sẽ gēyōm′ dŭp′tůn), village (pop. 769), S Que., 20 mi. NE of St. Hyacinthe; dairying, pig raising.

Saint-Haon-le-Châtel (sẽtã′-lů-shätĕl′), village (pop. 209), Loire dept., SE central France, on E slope of Montagnes de la Madeleine, 8 mi. WNW of Roanne; winegrowing. Has medieval forts.

Saint-Héand (sẽ-āã′), village (pop. 800), Loire dept., SE central France, in Monts du Lyonnais, 6 mi. N of Saint-Étienne; mfg. of optical instruments.

Saint Helen, Lake, Roscommon co., N central Mich., 12 mi. NW of West Branch, in forest area; c.4 mi. long, 1½ mi. wide; resort; fishing. Source of South Branch of Au Sable R.

Saint Helena (sānt hĕlē′nů), British island (□ 47; pop. 4,748) in S Atlantic Ocean, c.1,200 mi. W of the nearest African coast, 700 mi. SE of Ascension Isl., and 1,695 mi. NW of Cape Town, at about 15°56′S 5°42′W; ⊙ Jamestown, its chief port. It is a Br. crown colony and includes the dependencies of: ASCENSION ISLAND (since 1922), and TRISTAN DA CUNHA ISLAND, GOUGH ISLAND, NIGHTINGALE ISLAND, and INACCESSIBLE ISLANDS (all since 1938). St. Helena isl. is 10.5 mi. long, 6.5 mi. wide. Of volcanic origin and mountainous, it rises in Mt. Actaeon to 2,685 ft. The rugged slopes are cut by deep ravines and gushing brooks. A few plains in N. Though in the tropics, it has a pleasant climate, tempered by SE trade winds. Jamestown has an annual mean temp. of c.70°F., with little seasonal change. Rainfall c.8 in. on the coast, increases up to 40 in. in the uplands. The people are mostly farmers. Principal commercial crop is New Zealand flax (introduced 1874), accounting for more than 90% of all exports. Fibers are treated at 6 mills which also make rope and twine. Lily bulbs are exported. Small-scale fishing. Some lace and embroidery are made. Isl.'s pop. is of mixed European, Asiatic, and African origin. English is spoken throughout. It was uninhabited when 1st sighted (1502) by Portuguese. The Dutch annexed it (1633) but did not occupy it. It was seized in 1633 by the Br. East India Co., in Jan., 1673, by the Dutch, and finally in May, 1673, by the British. The East India Co. held it until 1834, when it passed to the Crown. It is best known as the place of exile of Napoleon, who was kept under guard by the British at Longwood from 1815 until his death in 1821. His body was removed to France in 1840. St. Helena also served as confinement of Zulu Chief Denizula (1890–97), a sultan of Zanzibar, and other colonial rebels. In 1900 Boer prisoners of war were sent here. The isl. is linked by cable with Tristan da Cunha and overseas countries.

Saint Helena (lē'nů, hůlē'nů), parish (□ 420; pop. 9,013), SE La.; ⊙ Greensburg. Bounded W by Amite R., N by Miss. line; intersected by Tickfaw R. Agr. (cotton, corn, sweet potatoes, strawberries); lumber. Formed 1810.

Saint Helena. 1 (hůlē'nů) City (pop. 2,297), Napa co., W Calif., on Napa R. and 17 mi. NNW of Napa; center of chief winegrowing dist. of Napa R. valley. Sanitarium in vicinity. Near by, at Angwin, is Pacific Union Col. Inc. 1876. 2 (hĕ'lůnů) Industrial suburb, Baltimore co., central Md., 5 mi. ESE of downtown Baltimore; makes chemicals. 3 (hůlē'nů) Village (pop. 77), Cedar co., NE Nebr., 10 mi. below Yankton, S.Dak., on Missouri R.

Saint Helena, Mount (hůlē'nů), extinct volcanic peak (4,343 ft.), W Calif., at meeting of Napa, Lake, and Sonoma co. lines, 7 mi. N of Calistoga. Robert Louis Stevenson Monument marks site where he lived in 1880.

Saint Helena Bay (5 mi. long, 15 mi. wide at mouth), SW Cape Prov., U. of So. Afr., inlet of Atlantic, 15 mi. NE of Saldanha. Receives Great Berg R.

Saint Helena Island, in Moreton Bay, SE Queensland, Australia, 8 mi. E of Brisbane R. mouth; 3 mi. long, 1.5 mi. wide; penal settlement.

Saint Helena Island (hĕ'lůnů), Beaufort co., S S.C., one of largest of SEA ISLANDS, bet. St. Helena Sound and Port Royal Sound, 30 mi. NE of Savannah, Ga.; c.15 mi. long, 3–5 mi. wide. Connected by highway to Ladies Isl. (W), and thence to Port Royal Isl. and mainland; also bridged to Hunting Isl. (E). Diversified agr. area. "Frogmore" and other antebellum plantations and old Fort Fremont (near S end) are here. Isl. discovered and named by Sp. explorers in early 16th cent. Chiefly populated by Gullah-speaking Negroes, descendants of slaves on isl. cotton plantations abandoned by owners in face of Union invasion early in Civil War. Penn Normal, Industrial, and Agr. School, founded here by Northerners in 1862, is one of 1st schools of its kind established for Southern Negroes.

Saint Helena Sound, S S.C., coastal inlet (7.5 mi. wide) E of Beaufort, bet. Edisto Isl. and Hunting Isl. Receives Combahee and other rivers; Coosaw R. connects its N end with Broad R. channel (W). Crossed by Intracoastal Waterway.

Saint Helen Auckland (ô'klůnd), town and parish (pop. 1,373), central Durham, England, 2 mi. SW of Bishop Auckland; coal.

Saint Helen Island, islet, S Que., in the St. Lawrence opposite Montreal. It became crown property 1812 and for many years was British garrison.

Saint Helens. 1 County borough (1931 pop. 106,789; 1951 census 110,276), SW Lancashire, England, 10 mi. ENE of Liverpool; 53°27'N 2°44'W; glass-mfg. center; also mfg. of chemicals for textile industry, soap, pharmaceuticals; metallurgy, antimony refining, locomotive building, coal mining. On site of cemetery are ruins of 15th-cent. abbey. In county borough are coal-mining villages of Thatto Heath (SW), Sutton Heath (S), Sutton Oak (SE), and Ravenhead (SW). 2 Former urban district (1931 pop. 5,501), near E coast of Isle of Wight, England, on the Spithead, 3 mi. SE of Ryde; seaside resort, with beach; agr. market. Inc. 1932 in Ryde. 3 Village, Yorkshire, England: see HOYLAND NETHER.

Saint Helen's, village (pop. 713), NE Tasmania, 55 mi. E of Launceston and on George Bay (8 mi. long, 4 mi. wide) of Tasman Sea; summer resort (deep-sea fishing); tin mining; sawmill. Also spelled St. Helens.

Saint Helens, city (pop. 4,711), ⊙ Columbia co., NW Oregon, on the Columbia (here forming Wash. line) and 25 mi. N of Portland; river port; mfg. (paper, lumber); salmon fisheries. Founded 1847–48, inc. 1889.

Saint Helens, Mount (9,671 ft.), SW Wash., volcanic peak in Cascade Range, 35 mi. E of Kelso.

Saint Helier (sůnt hĕl'yůr), Fr. *Saint-Hélier* (sētālyā'), town and parish (1945 pop. 19,398), ⊙ Jersey, Channel Isls., on S coast of isl., on E shore of St. Aubin Bay; 49°10'N 2°6'W; port, trade center, and resort. Has 14th-cent. church, mus., art gall., Victoria Col. (1852), and observatory. Royal Square was scene of battle (1781) in which French unsuccessfully tried to regain Jersey. Port is protected by Elizabeth Castle (1551–86), on adjacent islet, and by Fort Regent. On near-by rock are remains of reputed hermitage of St. Helier or St. Helerius. Post office name of town is St. Heliers.

Saint Henri (sētārē'). 1 SW suburb of Montreal, S Que. 2 Village (pop. 481), S Que., on Etchemin R. and 12 mi. SE of Quebec; dairying.

Saint Henry, village (pop. 715), Mercer co., W Ohio, 10 mi. SSW of Celina; lumber milling.

Sainthia (sĭnt'yů), town (pop. 7,584), Birbhum dist., W West Bengal, India, on Mor R. and 10 mi. ENE of Suri; trade center (rice, gram, sugar cane, wheat); rice and oilseed milling, cotton weaving. Rice milling 8 mi. S, at Ahmadpur.

Saint Hilaire (sētēlâr'), village (pop. 686), S Que., on Richelieu R. and 16 mi. E of Montreal; sugar refining, fruit canning, dairying; fruit, vegetables, tobacco.

Saint-Hilaire. 1 Village (pop. 632), Aude dept., S France, in the Corbières, 5 mi. NE of Limoux; cereal- and winegrowing. Has fine 12th-cent. abbatial church. 2 or **Saint-Hilaire-de-Ville-franche** (–dů-vēlfrăsh'), village (pop. 345), Charente-Maritime dept., W France, 9 mi. NNE of Saintes; brandy distilling, dairying. 3 or **Saint-Hilaire-du-Touvet** (–dü-tōōvā'), village (pop. 98), Isère dept., SE France, in E Grande Chartreuse massif overlooking Grésivaudan valley, 11 mi. NE of Grenoble; alt. c.3,000 ft. Large sanatoriums.

Saint Hilaire (sānt″ hĭlâr'), village (pop. 276), Pennington co., NW Minn., on Red Lake R. and 7 mi. S of Thief River Falls; dairy products.

Saint-Hilaire-des-Loges (sētēlâr-dā-lôzh'), village (pop. 411), Vendée dept., W France, 7 mi. E of Fontenay-le-Comte; truck gardening, cattle raising.

Saint-Hilaire-de-Villefranche, France: see SAINT-HILAIRE, Charente-Maritime dept.

Saint-Hilaire-du-Harcouët (–dü-ärkōōā'), town (pop. 2,542), Manche dept., NW France, near the Sélune, 15 mi. SE of Avranches; wool spinning, hosiery mfg., cider distilling, dairying. Damaged in Second World War.

Saint-Hilaire-du-Touvet, France: see SAINT-HILAIRE, Isère dept.

Saint-Hilaire-en-Woëvre (–ã-vôĕ'vrů), village (pop. 63), Meuse dept., NE France, 16 mi. E of Verdun.

Saint-Hilaire-lez-Cambrai (–lā-kābrā'), town (pop. 2,007), Nord dept., N France, 8 mi. E of Cambrai, in sugar-beet dist.; cambric mfg.

Saint-Hilaire-Saint-Florent (–sē-flôrã'), NW suburb (pop. 2,202) of Saumur, Maine-et-Loire dept., W France; well-known winegrowing center, with wine cellars excavated in the hillside. Preserves remains of a 12th-cent. abbey.

Saint Hilarion (sētēlärēō'), village (pop. estimate 400), SE central Que., 10 mi. NE of Baie St. Paul; lumbering, dairying, silver-fox breeding.

Saint Hilary (sůnt hĭ'lůrē), village and parish (pop. 658), W Cornwall, England, 5 mi. E of Penzance; tin mining. Has 13th-cent. church.

Saint-Hippolyte (sētēpôlēt'). 1 Village (pop. 733), Doubs dept., E France, on Doubs R. and 13 mi. S of Montbéliard, in the N Jura; forges; tanning. Painter Jacques Courtois b. here. 2 Ger. *Sankt Pilt* (zängkt pĭlt'), village (pop. 1,125), Haut-Rhin dept., E France, at E foot of the Vosges, 4 mi. NE of Ribeauvillé; winegrowing, soap mfg. On a rocky height (c.2,500 ft.) 2 mi. NW is the restored fortress of Haut-Koenigsbourg.

Saint-Hippolyte-du-Fort (–dü-fôr'), town (pop. 2,371), Gard dept., S France, at foot of the Cévennes, 15 mi. SW of Alès; silk and cotton hosiery mfg., woodworking. Cement works near by.

Saint-Honorat, island, France: see LÉRINS, ÎLES DE.

Saint-Honoré or **Saint-Honoré-les-Bains** (sētônôrā'-lā-bē'), village (pop. 942), Nièvre dept., central France, in the Morvan, 12 mi. SSW of Château-Chinon; hot springs.

Saint-Hubert (sētübâr'), town (pop. 3,099), Luxembourg prov., SE central Belgium, 17 mi. W of Bastogne in the Ardennes; tourist resort; pig market. Has 7th-cent. Benedictine abbey, 16th-cent. church with tomb of St. Hubert. Several 18th-cent. abbey bldgs. are used as a reformatory.

Saint Hugues (sē üg'), village (pop. 452), S Que., near Yamaska R., 12 mi. NNE of St. Hyacinthe; lumbering, dairying; cattle, pigs.

Saint Hyacinthe (hī'ůsĭnth, Fr. sētēäsēt'), county (□ 278; pop. 31,645), S Que., on Yamaska R.; ⊙ St. Hyacinthe.

Saint Hyacinthe, city (pop. 17,798), ⊙ St. Hyacinthe co., S Que., on Yamaska R. and 30 mi. ENE of Montreal; hosiery-mfg. center; cotton, silk milling and knitting, mfg. of clothing, shoes, paper products, machinery, organs, furniture. Has R.C. cathedral, a seminary, and St. Maurice Col. Inc. as town 1849, as city 1857.

Saint Ignace (sānt ĭg'nůs), city (pop. 2,946), ⊙ Mackinac co., SE Upper Peninsula, Mich., on the Straits of Mackinac, opposite Mackinaw City (S); resort and fishing center, with ferry and freight docks; Mackinac Isl. is just E. Agr. (potatoes, fruit, truck); dairy products. Has a state park. The grave of Father Marquette is in St. Ignace. Its early history is that of MACKINAC region. Inc. as village in 1882, as city in 1883.

Saint Ignace, Isle (ĭg'nůs) (17 mi. long, 7 mi. wide), W Ont., in L. Superior, at entrance of Nipigon Bay, 60 mi. ENE of Port Arthur. Rises to over 1,000 ft. Just E is Simpson Isl.

Saint Ignatius (ĭgnā'shůs), town (pop. 781), Lake co., W Mont., near Flathead R., 30 mi. N of Missoula; sawmill; livestock, dairy products. R.C. mission school, church, and hosp. here. Inc. 1938.

Saint-Imier (sētēmyā'), town (pop. 5,716), Bern canton, W Switzerland, on Schüss R. and 11 mi. NNW of Neuchâtel, in long, narrow valley of the Jura; watches, beer, flour. Has 12th-cent. church.

Saintines (sētēn'), village (pop. 578), Oise dept., N France, at SW edge of Forest of Compiègne, 8 mi. SSW of Compiègne; match factory; marble works.

Saint-Ingbert, Saar: see SANKT INGBERT.

Saint Inigoes (sānt″ ĭ'nĭgōz), hamlet, St. Marys co., S Md., near the Potomac, 17 mi. SE of Leonardtown. Near by is "Cross Manor" (built 1643), one of oldest Md. houses.

Saint Ishmael, agr. village and parish (pop. 1,470), S Carmarthen, Wales, on Towy R. estuary and 3 mi. WNW of Kidwelly. Near by are traces of village of Halkin, submerged in 1606.

Saint Isidore (ĭ'zůdôr, Fr. sētēzēdôr'), village (pop. 548), SE Que., 18 mi. SSE of Quebec; dairying, lumbering, pig raising.

Saint Issells, Wales: see SAUNDERSFOOT.

Saint Ive (sůnt ēv'), agr. village and parish (pop. 1,250), E Cornwall, England, 4 mi. ENE of Liskeard. Has 12th-cent. hostel, built by Knights Templars, and 15th-cent. church.

Saint Ives (sůnt īvz'). 1 Municipal borough (1931 pop. 6,687; 1951 census 9,037), W Cornwall, England, on St. Ives Bay (4 mi. wide) of the Atlantic, 7 mi. NE of Penzance; fishing port, tourist resort; well-known artists' colony. Has 15th-cent. St. Ia's church. Sloop Inn is artists' residence. 2 Municipal borough (1931 pop. 2,664; 1951 census 3,077), E Huntingdon, England, on Ouse R. and 5 mi. E of Huntingdon; agr. market, with agr.-machinery works. Has 15th-cent. church and 15th-cent. bridge. There is a statue of Oliver Cromwell, who lived here c.1635.

Saint Jacob, village (pop. 478), Madison co., SW Ill., 22 mi. ENE of East St. Louis; dairying.

Saint Jacob on the Birs, Switzerland: see SANKT JAKOB AN DER BIRS.

Saint Jacobs, village (pop. estimate 500), S Ont., on Conestogo R. and 7 mi. NNW of Kitchener; sawmilling, grist milling, dairying, mixed farming.

Saint Jacques (sē zhäk'), village (pop. 1,634), S Que., 30 mi. N of Montreal; tobacco growing and processing, dairying.

Saint-Jacut-de-la-Mer (sē-zhäkü'-dů-lä-mâr'), village (pop. 1,010), Côtes-du-Nord dept., W France, on narrow headland extending into English Channel, 12 mi. NW of Dinan; popular seaside resort.

Saint-James (sē-zhäm'), village (pop. 1,485), Manche dept., NW France, 12 mi. S of Avranches; wool spinning, dairying.

Saint James, parish (□ 240.61; pop. 63,542), Cornwall co., NW Jamaica; ⊙ Montego Bay. Largely hilly, it has fertile valleys along its small rivers, where bananas are principally grown. Produces also sugar cane, honey, and goats. Montego Bay, 3d largest city of the isl., is the leading port, trading and processing center in the W, ranking also highly as seaside resort (Doctor's Cave). Other centers are: Montpelier, Cambridge, Catadupa, and Anchovy, all along Kingston–Montego Bay RR.

Saint James, parish (□ 249; pop. 15,334), SE central La.; ⊙ Convent. Intersected by the Mississippi. Agr. (sugar cane, rice, corn, hay, truck, perique tobacco). Sugar and rice milling, moss ginning. Oil and natural-gas fields. Formed 1807.

Saint James. 1 Village, Mich.: see BEAVER ISLAND. 2 City (pop. 3,861), ⊙ Watonwan co., S Minn., 34 mi. WSW of Mankato; shipping and food-processing center for farming area; dairy and poultry products, beverages; cement blocks. Platted 1870, inc. as village 1871, as city 1899. 3 City (pop. 1,811), Phelps co., central Mo., in the Ozarks, 10 mi. ENE of Rolla; ships agr. products; lumber mills, clothing, wine. State Federal soldiers' home here. Founded c.1857. 4 Residential village (pop. 1,390), Suffolk co., SE N.Y., near N shore of Long Isl., 14 mi. E of Huntington, in diversified-agr. and summer-resort area; nurseries.

Saint James, Cape, W B.C., S extremity of Kunghit Isl. and of the Queen Charlotte Isls.; 51°56'N 131°1'W; lighthouse.

Saint James City, Fla.: see PINE ISLAND.

Saint James Islands, group (225.29 acres), U.S. Virgin Isls., just off E tip of St. Thomas Isl., on Pillsbury Sound, 8 mi. ESE of Charlotte Amalie; 18°18'N 64°49'W.

Saint James's Palace, in Westminster, LONDON, England.

Saint Jean (sē zhã'), county (□ 205; pop. 20,584), S Que., on Richelieu R.; ⊙ St. Jean.

Saint Jean or **Saint Johns,** city (pop. 13,646), ⊙ St. Jean co., S Que., on Richelieu R. and 20 mi. SE of Montreal; silk and paper milling, food canning, mfg. of hosiery, clothing, felt, matches, sewing machines, cables, storage batteries. Has Dawson Col. and Col. de St. Jean sur Richelieu. Terminus of 1st Canadian railroad (1836), built from Laprairie. Site of fort, built 1666, rebuilt 1749; British here checked Montgomery's advance (1775); supply base for Carleton and Burgoyne. A center of 1837 revolt.

Saint-Jean, Jersey, Channel Isls.: see SAINT JOHN.

Saint-Jean or **Saint-Jean-du-Sud** (sē-zhã'-dü-süd'), agr. town (1950 census pop. 272), Sud dept., SW Haiti, on SW coast of Tiburon Peninsula, 9 mi. SW of Les Cayes; basketmaking.

Saint Jean Baptiste (sē zhã băptēst'), village (pop. estimate 1,200), S Man., on Red R. and 45 mi. SSW of Winnipeg; grain, stock.

Saint-Jean-Bonnefonds (–bônfõ'), town (pop. 2,038), Loire dept., SE central France, in Monts du Lyonnais, 3 mi. ENE of Saint-Étienne; iron foundries.

Saint-Jean-Brévelay (–brāvlā'), agr. village (pop. 490), Morbihan dept., W France, 13 mi. N of Vannes.

Saint-Jean-Cap-Ferrat (–käp-fĕrä'), village (pop. 1,158), Alpes-Maritimes dept., SE France, 3 mi.

E of Nice, on E shore of Cape Ferrat peninsula; fishing port and health resort of Fr. Riviera. Rocky Cape Ferrat (lighthouse) is at S tip of peninsula (2 mi. long; naval meteorological station) linked with mainland by narrow isthmus bet. Villefranche (W) and Beaulieu-sur-Mer (E).

Saint Jean d'Acre, Israel: see ACRE.

Saint-Jean-d'Angély (–dãzhälē'), town (pop. 6,436), Charente-Maritime dept., W France, on the Boutonne and 15 mi. NNE of Saintes. Commercial center; cognac distilling, jute milling, mfg. (footwear, vegetable oils, casein, biscuits). Has 15th-cent. clock tower and a Renaissance fountain. Protestant stronghold in 16th cent.; captured by Louis XIII after a siege (1621).

Saint Jean de Boischatel, Que.: see SAINT JEAN D'ORLÉANS.

Saint-Jean-de-Bournay (–dŭ-bōōrnā'), village (pop. 1,502), Isère dept., SE France, 13 mi. E of Vienne; silk spinning, embroidering; furniture, soap mfg.

Saint-Jean-de-Braye (–brā'), E suburban commune (pop. 3,577) of Orléans, Loiret dept., N central France, on right bank of the Loire; fruit preserving, metalworking. Chemicals, wines.

Saint-Jean-de-Daye (–dā'), village (pop. 282), Manche dept., NW France, 8 mi. N of Saint-Lô. Captured (1944) by Americans who landed at Omaha Beach in Normandy invasion.

Saint-Jean-de-Losne (–lōn'), village (pop. 1,159), Côte-d'Or dept., E central France, port on Saône R. at junction of the Burgundy Canal, 18 mi. SE of Dijon; mfg. of iron and cement pipes.

Saint-Jean-de-Luz (–lüz'), town (pop. 8,848), Basses-Pyrénées dept., SW France, on Bay of Biscay, 12 mi. SW of Bayonne; fishing port and popular bathing resort; fish canning, chocolate mfg. A prosperous commercial center in Middle Ages; its Basque fishermen were 1st to exploit the Newfoundland codfish banks in 1520. Here Louis XIV was married to Marie Thérèse of Austria (1660).

Saint-Jean-de-Maruéjols-et-Avejan (–märwäzhôl'-ā-ävü-zhã'), village (pop. 557), Gard dept., S France, near the Cèze, 14 mi. NE of Alès; important asphalt mines.

Saint Jean de Matha (mätä'), village (pop. estimate 1,000), S Que., near L'Assomption R., 16 mi. NNW of Joliette; dairying; potatoes, poultry.

Saint-Jean-de-Maurienne (–mōryĕn'), town (pop. 3,663), Savoie dept., SE France, on the Arc at influx of small Arvan R. and 28 mi. SE of Chambéry; industrial center and old ⊙ of Alpine MAURIENNE valley, bet. Massif de la Vanoise (Savoy Alps; E) and Grandes Rousses (Dauphiné Alps; SW), on road to Mont Cenis pass; makes aluminum, electrodes for Saint-Michel steel mill, slaked lime and plaster. Slate and red marble quarried near by. Episcopal see with 15th-cent. cathedral.

Saint-Jean-de-Monts (–mõ'), village (pop., 1,866), Vendée dept., W France, near Bay of Biscay, 25 mi. NNW of Les Sables-d'Olonne; bathing resort with 15-mi.-long beach and pine forests; poultry raising, fishing.

Saint-Jean-des-Vignes (–dā-vē'nyŭ), N suburb (pop. 2,776) of Chalon-sur-Saône, Saône-et-Loire dept., E central France; hosiery mfg., truck gardening.

Saint Jean d'Orléans (sē zhã dôrlāã') or **Saint Jean de Boischatel** (dŭ bwäshätĕl'), village (pop. 882), S Que., on SE shore of Île d'Orléans, on the St. Lawrence and 16 mi. ENE of Quebec; dairying; vegetables, fruit.

Saint-Jean-du-Falga (–dü-fälgä'), village (pop. 50), Ariège dept., S France, on the Ariège and 2 mi. S of Pamiers; pharmaceuticals.

Saint-Jean-du-Gard (–gär'), village (pop. 1,592), Gard dept., S France, in the Cévennes, on the Gardon d'Anduze and 10 mi. WSW of Alès; silk spinning, lumbering.

Saint-Jean-du-Sud, Haiti: see SAINT-JEAN.

Saint-Jean-en-Royans (–ã-rwäyã'), village (pop. 1,862), Drôme dept., SE France, in the Vercors, 20 mi. NE of Valence; woodworking, dairying. Damaged in Second World War. Excursions into Forest of Lente (□ 25), 5 mi. S.

Saint-Jean-Pied-de-Port (sē-zhã-pyā-dŭ-pôr'), village (pop. 1,303), Basses-Pyrénées dept., SW France, in W Pyrenees, on Nive R. and 26 mi. SSE of Bayonne; dairying, chocolate mfg., apple- and winegrowing. Has citadel and ramparts built by Vauban. During Middle Ages it was N terminal of much traveled road to Spain via Roncesvalles pass (11 mi. SSW). Passed to France in 1589 and became ⊙ French Navarre. Named Donajouna in Basque.

Saint Jean Port Joli (pôr zhôlē'), village (pop. estimate 1,000), ⊙ L'Islet co., SE Que., on the St. Lawrence and 50 mi. ENE of Quebec; wood-carving center; furniture mfg., dairying. Founded 1721.

Saint-Jean-Soleymieux (–sôlāmyû'), village (pop. 238), Loire dept., SE central France, in Monts du Forez, 7 mi. S of Montbrison; cattle, potatoes; cheesemaking.

Saint-Jeoire (sē-zhwär'), village (pop. 677), Haute-Savoie dept., SE France, in Chablais, 16 mi. ESE of Geneva; produces ferro-alloys, calcium carbide.

Saint Jérôme (jŭrōm', Fr. sē zhārōm'). **1** Village, Chicoutimi co., Que.: see METABETCHOUAN. **2** Town (pop. 11,329), ⊙ Terrebonne co., S Que., on North R. and 30 mi. NW of Montreal; woolen knitting, paper milling, woodworking, mfg. of shoes, furniture, plastics, rubber products. Scene of annual passion play. Inc. 1881.

Saint Jérôme de Matane, Que.: see MATANE.

Saint Jo, city (pop. 1,147), Montague co., N Texas, c.55 mi. E of Wichita Falls; trade, shipping point in ranch, farm area (hay, truck, poultry); feed mfg.; oil wells. Settled c.1870 on old California Trail.

Saint Joe. **1** Town (pop. 187), Searcy co., N Ark., 21 mi. SE of Harrison, in the Ozarks. **2** Town (pop. 479), De Kalb co., NE Ind., on St. Joseph R. and 21 mi. NE of Fort Wayne, in agr. area; pickles, feed, flour.

Saint Joe River, N Idaho, rises near Mont. line in N half of Bitterroot Range, flows c.130 mi. generally W, past St. Maries, where it receives St. Maries R., to S tip of Coeur d'Alene L. Passes through rugged canyon and has many small falls. Used for logging in lower course. Navigable for 32 mi. above mouth.

Saint John, Antigua, B.W.I.: see SAINT JOHN'S.

Saint John, county (□ 611; pop. 68,827), S N.B., on the Bay of Fundy; ⊙ St. John.

Saint John, city (pop. 51,741), ⊙ St. John co., largest town of New Brunswick, in S part of prov., on the Bay of Fundy, at mouth of St. John R.; 45°17'N 66°3'W; commercial and mfg. center and major port, with one of the world's largest dry docks. Ice-free the year round, the port has shipyards and ship connections with the major European and American ports, especially with the West Indies and South America. With large grain elevators and with the spacious terminal yards of the Canadian Pacific and Canadian Natl. RRs, it is the outlet for N.B.'s lumbering, agr., and mining industries. Large quantities of lumber are shipped. Mfg. of cotton goods, sugar, pulp, wood products, metal products, canned fish. Fishing, especially for salmon, is important. Features of city are the court house, R.C. cathedral, New Brunswick Mus., Fort Howe (1778), Horticultural Gardens; law faculty of Univ. of N.B. is here. Noted phenomenon are the Reversing Falls Rapids of St. John R.; strong tides of Bay of Fundy cause part of river to reverse its flow at high tide. The site of St. John was visited 1604 by Champlain; Charles de la Tour established fort here, 1631–35. It was involved in Anglo-French struggle for Acadia, finally becoming Br. possession after being taken by Anglo-American force in 1758. Thousands of United Empire Loyalists landed here after the Revolutionary War and established (1783) the place as Parr Town; in 1785 it became 1st inc. city in Canada and was renamed St. John. Benedict Arnold lived here, 1786–91. Half of city was destroyed by fire in 1877. In 1912 it became 1st Canadian city to adopt commission form of local govt. There is an airport. Limestone, diatomite, iron are mined in region. Near by is Lepreau Game Refuge.

Saint John, Fr. *Saint-Jean* (sē-zhã'), agr. village and parish (1945 pop. 1,230), Jersey, Channel Isls., on N coast, 5 mi. N of St. Helier. Post Office is St. John's Church.

Saint John. **1** Town (pop. 684), Lake co., extreme NW Ind., 12 mi. SSW of Gary. **2** City (pop. 1,735), ⊙ Stafford co., S central Kansas, 42 mi. W of Hutchinson, near Rattlesnake Creek; trade center for wheat area. Oil wells near by. Platted 1879, inc. 1885. **3** Plantation (pop. 569), Aroostook co., N Maine, on St. John R. and 12 mi. ESE of Fort Kent. **4** Town, Mo.: see SAINT JOHNS. **5** Village (pop. 451), Rolette co., N N.Dak., 6 mi. NW of Rolla; port of entry. **6** Town (pop. 542), Whitman co., SE Wash., 17 mi. NW of Colfax, in agr. region; ships wheat.

Saint John, Cape, E N.F., bet. White Bay (N) and Notre Dame Bay (S); 49°58'N 55°29' W.

Saint John, Lake. **1** Lake (4 mi. long, 3 mi. wide), SE N.F., on Terra Nova R., 40 mi. S of Gander. **2** Lake (□ 375), S central Que., c.110 mi. NNW of Quebec, W of Chicoutimi; 28 mi. long, 18 mi. wide. Fed by Ashuapmuchuan, Mistassini, and Peribonca rivers, drained by Saguenay R. Riparian towns are Roberval, Chambord, and Metabetchouan. Saguenay R. leaves lake by Grande Décharge (hydroelectric station) and Petite Décharge, channels enclosing Île d'Alma.

Saint John, Lake, Concordia parish, E central La., oxbow lake formed by a cutoff of the Mississippi, 7 mi. NE of Ferriday; c.7 mi. long. Fishing.

Saint John Bay, shallow inlet (10 mi. long, 25 mi. wide at entrance) of Gulf of St. Lawrence, W N.F., bet. Ferolle Point (N) and Point Riche (S); 50°55'N 57°10'W; contains several isls., largest of which is St. John Isl.

Saint John Island (□ 9; inhabited in fishing season only), W N.F., in St. John Bay, 10 mi. NE of Point Riche; 50°49'N 57°15'W.

Saint John Island, Mandarin *Shangchwan* or *Shangch'uan* (shäng'chwän') (□ 44), in S.China Sea, Kwangtung prov., China, 55 mi. SW of Macao; 21°40'N 112°45'E; 14 mi. long, 1–5 mi. wide. Fisheries. Main village is Shangtsunsamchow, on N coast. Opened to Portuguese in 1550. St. Francis Xavier died here in 1552. Sometimes spelled Changchuen and Sancian.

Saint John Island, Egypt: see SAINT JOHN'S ISLAND.

Saint John Island, island (□ 19.2; pop. 747), U.S. Virgin Isls., just E of St. Thomas Isl. across Pillsbury Sound, and SW of Tortola (Br. Virgin Isls.), 80 mi. E of San Juan, Puerto Rico; ⊙ Cruz Bay. It is 9 mi. long (W–E), 5 mi. wide, bet. 18°18'–18°22'N and 64°39'–64°48'W. Its irregular coastline has excellent harbors. Rises in Bordeaux Mtn. to 1,277 ft. Its agr. has declined to subsistence crops, though vegetables and fruit grow well. Major industries are cattle raising, and gathering of bay leaves, which are processed at Charlotte Amalie (St. Thomas Isl.). Discovered 1493 by Columbus on his 2d voyage, taken 1684 by Denmark, though not settled before 1716. Then mainly devoted to sugar-cane planting, worked by Negro slaves, who revolted in 1773. Served as hide-out for buccaneers. Since it was ceded 1917 to the U.S., it forms a municipality together with St. Thomas. The pop. is predominantly Negro. Isl. preserves its unspoiled beauty, and has excellent beaches, fishing, and wildlife.

Saint John River, in New Brunswick and Maine, rises in N Somerset co., Maine, flows NE and E past Edmundston, N.B., forming 75-mi. section of international line almost to Grand Falls, where it turns S in N.B., flows past Woodstock, and turns E, past Fredericton, and finally S into the Bay of Fundy at St. John; 400 mi. long. At St. John are the famous Reversing Falls, caused by strong Bay of Fundy tides, which force the river to reverse its flow at high tide. At Grand Falls the river falls 75 ft. in an impressive cataract. Chief tributaries are St. Francis, Madawaska, Aroostook, Tobique, Nashwaak, and Oromocto rivers. St. John R. is navigable for vessels up to 120 tons to Fredericton (85 mi.), for smaller ships to Woodstock (65 mi. farther). It was formerly an important logging-transportation route, declining in importance after First World War, but logging is still important on its tributaries. River was named by de Monts and Champlain, who discovered its mouth on day of St. John the Baptist, 1604.

Saint John River, central Liberia, rises SW of Ganta on Fr. Guinea border, flows c.125 mi. SW to the Atlantic at Upper Buchanan, 2 mi. NNW of Buchanan.

Saint John's, city (pop. 10,965), ⊙ Antigua presidency and Leeward Isls. colony, B.W.I., port on sheltered bay of NW Antigua isl., 285 mi. ESE of San Juan (Puerto Rico); 17°6'N 61°50'W. Trading and processing center (sugar, rum, cotton). Larger vessels anchor outside the shallow harbor. City is on Miami-Trinidad air route. Picturesquely situated on a gentle slope, it is also a resort. Has dockyards, customhouse, cathedral, Govt. House, botanic station. Flanked by old fortifications: Fort James (N), Goat Hill Fort (S). Sugar *central* in outskirts. Coolidge airfield opened 1946. Fort James is adjoined by a popular bathing beach. City is sometimes called St. John.

Saint John's, city (pop. 56,709), ⊙ Newfoundland, in SE part of isl., on NW coast of Avalon Peninsula, on Freshwater Bay; 47°34'N 52°43'W. Largest city in N.F., it is a seaport, with fine harbor, and the commercial center of the isl. Center for the great N.F. fishing fleet (cod, seal, herring), with fish-freezing, filleting, smoking, canning, and storage plants. Industries also include mfg. of clothing, hardware, fishing equipment, paint, shoes, furniture, oleomargarine, soap, marine engines, cans; shipbuilding, tanning, brewing, tobacco processing, fish-oil refining. Near by are mink and fox farms; dairying, poultry raising, vegetable growing are carried on. Shipping lines connect St. John's with U.S., Canadian, and British ports; there is railroad connection with W coast of isl. Picturesquely located on hills, backed by hills up to 600 ft. high, St. John's has R.C. and Anglican cathedrals, denominational colleges, and an Athenaeum. Average temp. ranges bet. 25°F (Jan.) and 57°F. (July); average annual rainfall is 60 inches. Sir Humphrey Gilbert landed here in 1583 and took possession of N.F.; later a fishing settlement was established here by men from Devon. Several times taken or attacked by the French, it was finally retaken by the British in 1762. Fire almost wholly destroyed city in 1816, 1846, and 1892. In Second World War, Fort Pepperell, U.S. Army base, was established on N edge of town at Quidi Vidi, Canadian air base was built at Torbay, 7 mi. NNW of St. John's.

Saint Johns, city, Que.: see SAINT JEAN.

Saint Johns, county (□ 609; pop. 24,998), NE Fla., bounded by St. Johns R. (W) and the Atlantic (E); ⊙ St. Augustine. Lowland area, partly swampy, with Anastasia Isl. (barrier beach) and Matanzas R. (lagoon). Agr. (corn, potatoes, vegetables, poultry; dairy products), fishing, and some forestry (naval stores, lumber). Formed 1821.

Saint Johns. **1** Town (pop. 1,469), ⊙ Apache co., E Ariz., on left bank of Little Colorado R. and c.80 mi. SW of Gallup, N.Mex., in livestock and grain area; alt. 5,650 ft. Inc. since 1940. Small dam forms reservoir here. **2** Village (pop. 275), Perry co., SW Ill., just N of Du Quoin, in agr. and bituminous-coal-mining area. **3** City (pop. 4,954), ⊙ Clinton co., S central Mich., 19 mi. N of Lansing, in farm area (livestock, peppermint, beans, fruit); mfg. (farm implements, castings, trailers). Inc. as village 1857, as city 1904. **4** or **Saint John,** town (pop. 2,499), St. Louis co., E Mo. Inc. since 1940.

Saint Johnsbury, town (pop. 9,292), including Saint Johnsbury village (pop. 7,370), ⊙ Caledonia co., NE Vt., on Passumpsic and Moose rivers and 29 mi. NE of Montpelier. It is known for its maple sugar. Other mfg.: scales, tools, machinery, wood products, feed, granite; dairy products. Winter sports. Points of interest: St. Johnsbury Acad. (1842), Mus. of Natural Hist., athenaeum and art gall., war monument by Larkin G. Mead. Settled 1786.

Saint John's Church, Jersey, Channel Isls.: see SAINT JOHN.

Saint John's Island or **Saint John Island,** Arabic *Zebirget* (zĕbĭr'găt), *Zibirjat* (zĭbĭr'jăt), or *Zeberged* (zĕbĕr'găd), SE Egypt, in the Red Sea 30 mi. SE of Ras Benas; beryl deposits.

Saint John's Island, Malay *Sakijang Bendera,* island (pop. 1,661) off S Singapore isl., in Singapore Strait; 1°13'N 103°51'E; 1 mi. long. Site of Singapore quarantine station.

Saint John's Point, Northern Ireland: see DUNDRUM BAY.

Saint Johns River. 1 In Calif.: see KAWEAH RIVER. **2** In E and NE Fla., rises at alt. of less than 20 ft. in swamps of Brevard co. c.13 mi. SW of Melbourne (on Atlantic coast), flows N, forming 8 lakes (including Harney, Monroe, and George), to Jacksonville, then turns E, emptying into the Atlantic; 285 mi. long. It receives many streams, notably the Oklawaha; and drains swampy area. Lower course, above L. George, is an estuary. Dredged 200 mi. to N end of L. Harney (head of steamboat navigation); channel deepest (30 ft.) from Jacksonville to the sea. Forms part of Intracoastal Waterway from Palatka (86 mi. upstream) to the Atlantic.

Saint Johnstoun, Scotland: see PERTH, burgh.

Saint Johnsville, village (pop. 2,210), Montgomery co., E central N.Y., on Mohawk R. and the Barge Canal, and 28 mi. ESE of Utica; textile milling; mfg. of handles, shoes, clothing, gloves. Settled c.1775, inc. 1868.

Saint John's Wood, residential district of St. Marylebone metropolitan borough, London, England, N of the Thames, 3 mi. NW of Charing Cross, bordering on Regent's Park. Lord's Cricket Ground is hq. of the Marylebone Cricket Club, authority for rules of the game. District was once popular artists' residence.

Saint John the Baptist, parish (□ 225; pop. 14,861), SE La.; ⊙ Edgard. Bounded N by L. Maurepas and Pass Manchac, E by L. Pontchartrain, S partly by L. Des Allemands; intersected by the Mississippi. Agr. (sugar cane, corn, truck, hay, rice). Natural gas, oil. Sugar refining. Formed 1807.

Saint Jones River, E central Del., rises in Kent co. in Silver L., flows c.25 mi. E and SE, past Dover (head of navigation), to Delaware Bay just N of Bowers. Fishing, bird hunting in marshes along lower course.

Saint Jorge de Lidde, Palestine: see LYDDA.

Saint-Jorioz (sē-zhôrēōz'), village (pop. 100), Haute-Savoie dept., SE France, on W shore of L. of Annecy, 5 mi. SSE of Annecy; resort; cheese mfg.

Saint Joseph, village (pop. estimate 500), SE N.B., on Memramcook R. and 14 mi. SE of Moncton; site of St. Joseph's Univ., founded 1864.

Saint Joseph, village (pop. 1,511), W Dominica, B.W.I., 6 mi. NNW of Roseau; cacao, coconuts, limes.

Saint-Joseph (sē-zhōzĕf'), town (pop. 1,006), central Martinique, 5 mi. NNW of Fort-de-France; agr. center (sugar cane, bananas, pineapples, cacao, coffee, vanilla).

Saint-Joseph (sē-zhōzĕf'), town (pop. 5,467; commune pop. 13,815), on S coast of Réunion isl., 10 mi. ESE of Saint-Pierre; sugar milling; vanilla. Has home for the aged.

Saint Joseph, town (pop. 2,582), NW Trinidad, B.W.I., on railroad and 6 mi. E of Port of Spain, in cacao-growing region. Has anc. colonial church. Founded as San José de Oruña (1577–84), it is the oldest town of the isl., of which it was capital until 1783. Sir Walter Raleigh destroyed it in 1595. At adjoining Valsayn, site of govt. stock farm, the last Sp. governor signed treaty of capitulation (Feb. 18, 1797). The St. Augustine Imperial Col. of Tropical Agr. is just E.

Saint Joseph. 1 County (□ 467; pop. 205,058), N Ind., bounded N by Mich. line; ⊙ SOUTH BEND. Agr. (dairy products; corn, grain, fruit, mint, livestock, truck). Diversified mfg. at South Bend. Lake resorts. Drained by St. Joseph, Yellow, and Kankakee rivers. Formed 1830. **2** County (□ 508; pop. 35,071), SW Mich.; ⊙ Centerville. Bounded S by Ind. line; drained by St. Joseph R. and its affluents. Stock raising and agr. (grain, potatoes, corn, mint, truck, poultry); dairy products. Mfg. at Sturgis, Three Rivers, and White Pigeon. Small lakes (resorts). Formed and organized 1829.

Saint Joseph. 1 Village (pop. 941), Champaign co., E Ill., 10 mi. E of Champaign, in agr. area; corn, wheat, soybeans. **2** Town (pop. 1,218), ⊙ Tensas parish, E La., near the Mississippi, 36 mi. SW of Vicksburg (Miss.), in cotton-growing area; cotton gins; cottonseed products; cypress timber. State agr. experiment station is here. Fine ante-bellum houses near by. **3** City (pop. 10,223), ⊙ Berrien co., extreme SW Mich., on St. Joseph R. at its mouth on L. Michigan, opposite Benton Harbor. Resort (beaches; mineral springs); port and market center for fruitgrowing area. With Benton Harbor, holds annual Blossom Festival. Mfg. (clothing, rubber goods, paper and dairy products, machinery, electrical equipment, auto parts, metal products); fisheries. Indian villages, a Jesuit mission, Fort Miami (Fr. trading fort, founded 1679 by Robert Cavelier, sieur de la Salle), and a fur-trading post were here before permanent settlement began in c.1830. Inc. as village 1836, as city 1891. **4** Village (pop. 1,246), Stearns co., central Minn., near Mississippi R., 7 mi. W of St. Cloud in farming area; dairy products. St. Benedict Col. is here. **5** City (pop. 78,588), ⊙ Buchanan co., NW Mo., on left bank of Missouri R. and 50 mi. NNW of Kansas City; rail center; port of entry; important midwest grain and livestock center. Has large meat-packing houses, grain-processing (especially flour) industries; mfg. (lumber products, structural steel, hog-cholera serum, chemicals, beverages). Here are homes of Eugene Field and Jesse James, pony express stables (E terminus of pony express after 1860), state hosp., jr. col. On site of trading post founded 1826; laid out c.1843. Often called St. Joe.

Saint Joseph, Lake (□ 187), NW Ont., in Patricia dist., 70 mi. NE of Sioux Lookout; 52 mi. long, 12 mi. wide; alt. 1,218 ft. Drained by Albany R. into James Bay.

Saint Joseph, Lake, Tensas parish, E La., oxbow lake formed by a cutoff of the Mississippi, extends 14 mi. N from Newellton; fishing.

Saint Joseph Bay, arm (c.13 mi. long, 3–6 mi. wide) of the Gulf of Mexico, in Gulf co., NW Fla.; sheltered S and W from Gulf by a sandspit extending 4 mi. W from the mainland to Cape San Blas and thence 17 mi. N to St. Joseph Point. The bay, 20–35 ft. deep, forms an excellent harbor for Port St. Joe.

Saint Joseph d'Alma (dăl'mŭ, Fr. sē zhōzĕf'), town (pop. 6,449), ⊙ Lac St. Jean Est co., S central Que., on Saguenay R., near L. St. John, and 130 mi. NW of Quebec; wool carding, lumbering, mfg. of paper products, bricks. Inc. 1924.

Saint Joseph de Beauce (dŭ bōs', Fr. sē zhōzĕf'), village (pop. 1,892), S Que., on Chaudière R. and 40 mi. SSE of Quebec; lumbering, dairying, marble quarrying; mfg. of shoes, furniture, powdered milk.

Saint Joseph de Grantham, Que.: see SAINT GERMAIN DE GRANTHAM.

Saint Joseph de la Rive (dŭ lä rēv'), village (pop. 316), SE central Que., on the St. Lawrence and 6 mi. E of Baie St. Paul, opposite Île aux Coudres; dairying; vegetables. Hydroelectric station.

Saint Joseph de la Rivière Bleue, Que.: see RIVIÈRE BLEUE.

Saint-Joseph-de-Pelichy, Belgian Congo: see BOBANDANA.

Saint Joseph de Sorel (dŭ sûrĕl', Fr. sē zhōzĕf' dŭ sôrĕl'), village (pop. 2,207), S Que., on the St. Lawrence, at mouth of Richelieu R. opposite Sorel; dairying, fruitgrowing.

Saint Joseph Island (20 mi. long, 12 mi. wide), central Ont., at W extremity of North Channel, in NW L. Huron, 18 mi. SE of Sault Ste. Marie.

Saint Joseph Island (Fr. sē zhōzĕf'), rocky islet off coast of Fr. Guiana, one of the Îles du Salut, 27 mi. NNW of Cayenne.

Saint Joseph Island, in central Amirantes, outlying dependency of the Seychelles, 155 mi. WSW of Mahé Isl.; 5°26'S 53°22'E; 4 mi. long, 4 mi. wide; coral formation. Copra.

Saint Joseph Island, S Texas, barrier isl. c.23 mi. long, 1–5 mi. wide, bet. Aransas Bay and Gulf of Mexico. Separated by Aransas Pass from Mustang Isl. (SW), by a narrow channel from Matagorda Isl. (NE).

Saint Joseph River. 1 In Ind. and Mich., rises near Hillsdale, S Mich., flows 1st NW, then generally W and SW, past Elkhart and South Bend, Ind., then NW to L. Michigan bet. Benton Harbor and St. Joseph, Mich.; c.210 mi. long. Power dam on river near Union City, Mich. **2** In Mich., Ohio, and Ind.; rises in Hillsdale co., S Mich., near source of NW-flowing St. Joseph R. of Mich. and Ind.; flows SE into Williams co. in NW Ohio, thence SW, past Montpelier and Edgerton (Ohio) and through De Kalb and Allen counties (Ind.), joining St. Marys R. to form the Maumee at Fort Wayne; c.100 mi. long.

Saint-Josse-ten-Noode (sē-zhôs-tŭ-nō'dŭ), Flemish *Sint-Joost-ten-Node* (sĭnt-yōst'-tĭn-nō'dŭ), E suburb (pop. 27,968) of Brussels, Brabant prov., central Belgium; mfg. (textiles, clothing, chemicals, metal products).

Saint-Jouin-de-Marnes (sē-zhwē-dŭ-märn'), village (pop. 662), Deux-Sèvres dept., W France, 11 mi. SW of Loudon. Its 11th-12th-cent. church is built on site of a Benedictine abbey founded 4th cent.

Saint Jovite (sē zhôvēt'), village (pop. 1,059), S Que., in the Laurentians, 16 mi. WNW of Ste. Agathe des Monts; dairying; ski resort.

Saint-Juéry (sē-zhwārē'), town (pop. 3,100), Tarn dept., S France, 4 mi. ENE of Albi; foundry (agr. machinery, tools) and hydroelectric plant on falls of Tarn R.

Saint Julian's, town (pop. 9,122), E Malta, summer resort on St. Julian's Bay, 1½ mi. NW of Valletta. Has Bronze Age and megalithic remains; parish church (1580, enlarged 1682). Near by is large palace. Town was bombed in Second World War.

Saint-Julien (sē-zhülyē'). **1** or **Saint-Julien-sur-le-Suran** (–sür-lŭ-sürā'), village (pop. 298), Jura dept., E France, in the Revermont, 14 mi. NE of Bourg; winegrowing. **2** or **Saint-Julien-lès-Metz** (–lā-mĕs'), NNE suburb (pop. 1,789) of Metz, Moselle dept., NE France, on right bank of the Moselle; tanning.

Saint Julien, village (pop. 1,646), E Mauritius, on road and 6 mi. SW of Flacq; sugar cane.

Saint-Julien-aux-Bois (sē-zhülyē'-ō-bwä'), village (pop. 211), Corrèze dept., S central France, 11 mi. WSW of Mauriac.

Saint-Julien-Beychevelle (–bāshvĕl'), village (pop. 309), Gironde dept., SW France, on W shore of the Gironde and 23 mi. NNW of Bordeaux; its vineyards produce outstanding Médoc red wines. Also called Saint-Julien.

Saint-Julien-Chapteuil (–shäptû'yē), village (pop. 923), Haute-Loire dept., S central France, 9 mi. E of Le Puy; lacemaking. Stone quarries near by.

Saint-Julien-de-Maurienne (–dŭ-mōryĕn'), village (pop. 424), Savoie dept., SE France, in Alpine Maurienne valley, 3 mi. SE of Saint-Jean-de-Maurienne; slate quarrying.

Saint-Julien-de-Valgalgues (–välgälg'), village (pop. 512), Gard dept., S France, 4 mi. N of Alès; pyrite mining.

Saint-Julien-de-Vouvantes (–vōōvät'), village (pop. 392), Loire-Inférieure dept., W France, 8 mi. SE of Châteaubriant; butter mfg.

Saint-Julien-du-Sault (–dü-sō'), village (pop. 1,402), Yonne dept., N central France, near Yonne R., 12 mi. S of Sens; mfg. (razors, towlines), tanning, cider distilling.

Saint-Julien-en-Genevois (–ã-zhŭnŭvwä'), village (pop. 1,244), Haute-Savoie dept., SE France, custom station on Swiss border, 5 mi. SSW of Geneva; cheese mfg.

Saint-Julien-en-Jarez (–zhärā'), town (pop. 3,511), Loire dept., SE central France, in the Jarez on Gier R. and 7 mi. ENE of Saint-Étienne; iron foundry; mfg. of elastic fabrics, braids and laces, work gloves.

Saint-Julien-Lars (–lär'), village (pop. 593), Vienne dept., W central France, 8 mi. E of Poitiers; dairying, winegrowing. Also spelled Saint-Julien-l'Ars.

Saint-Julien-lès-Metz, France: see SAINT-JULIEN.

Saint-Julien-les-Villas (–lā-vē-lä'), S residential suburb (pop. 2,979) of Troyes, Aube dept., NE central France.

Saint-Julien-Molin-Molette (–mōlē'-mōlĕt'), village (pop. 1,117), Loire dept., SE central France, 14 mi. SE of Saint-Étienne; silk reeling and spinning; mfg. of crosses.

Saint-Julien-sur-le-Suran, France: see SAINT-JULIEN, Jura dept.

Saint-Junien (sē zhünyē'), town (pop. 8,103), Haute-Vienne dept., W central France, on Vienne R. and 18 mi. WNW of Limoges; industrial center, with glove factories and paper mills; wool washing and spinning; mfg. of industrial glue and dyes, slippers, furniture. Its Romanesque church contains tomb of St. Junien. The Vienne is spanned by 13th-cent. bridge.

Saint Just or **Saint Just-in-Penwith** (pĕn'wĭth), urban district (1931 pop. 4,359; 1951 census 4,122), W Cornwall, England, near the Atlantic (Cape Cornwall), 7 mi. W of Penzance; China-clay and tin-mining center. Site of Ding Dong mine, one of oldest in England. Has 15th-cent. church, with one of earliest Christian tombs in England. Near by is anc. amphitheater, called St. Just Round, scene of early miracle plays. In urban dist. (2 mi. N) is tin-mining village of Pendeen.

Saint-Just-en-Chausée (sē-zhüst-ã-shōsā'), town (pop. 2,777), Oise dept., N France, 17 mi. ENE of Beauvais; road and rail junction; mfg. of sugar, hosiery, agr. equipment; tanning (for glove mfg.).

Saint-Just-en-Chevalet (–shŭvälā'), village (pop. 798), Loire dept., SE central France, bet. Bois Noirs and Montagnes de la Madeleine, 14 mi. SW of Roanne; mfg. of cotton goods, velvet weaving.

Saint-Just-la-Pendue (–lä-pädü'), village (pop. 887), Loire dept., SE central France, in Monts du Beaujolais, 13 mi. SE of Roanne; weaving of cotton upholstery.

Saint-Just-Malmont (–mälmō'), village (pop. 1,266), Haute-Loire dept., S central France, 8 mi. SSW of Saint-Étienne; mfg. of silk and cotton textiles.

Saint-Just-Sauvage (–sōväzh'), village (pop. 706), Marne dept., N France, 4 mi. NE of Romilly-sur-Seine; hosiery.

Saint-Just-sur-Loire (–sür-lwär'), town (pop. 2,158), Loire dept., SE central France, at S end of Forez Plain, on the Loire and 7 mi. NW of Saint-Étienne; glass factory; mfg. of hunting rifles, hardware; printing, textile dyeing.

Saint Keverne, agr. village and parish (pop. 1,631), SW Cornwall, England, 8 mi. S of Falmouth. Has 14th-cent. church. Just E is Manacle Point, promontory on the Channel. Offshore are Manacle Rocks, dangerous reefs.

Saint Kilda, municipality (pop. 58,318), S Victoria, Australia, on SE shore of Hobson's Bay, 4 mi. S of Melbourne, in metropolitan area; seaside resort.

Saint Kilda, borough (pop. 7,353), SE S.Isl., New Zealand; residential suburb of Dunedin.

Saint Kilda, westernmost island of the Outer Hebrides, Inverness, Scotland, 42 mi. WNW of North Uist; 57°49'N 8°36'W; 3 mi. long, 2 mi. wide; rises to 1,372 ft. in NE. Has precipitous cliffs, with a landing place in S. Site of radio station. In 1930 pop. of 36 was removed to Argyllshire at own request; isl. is now bird sanctuary. It has been property of the Macleods for many centuries. It is sometimes called Hirta (hûr'tŭ), its Gaelic name.

Saint Kitts or **Saint Christopher,** island (□ 68; pop. 29,818), St. Kitts-Nevis presidency, Leeward Isls., B.W.I.; ⊙ Basseterre. Oval-shaped (18 mi. long, up to 5 mi. wide), volcanic isl. bet. St.Eustatius (NW) and Nevis (SE), c.200 mi. ESE of Puerto Rico. Traversed by rugged mts. rising to the cone of Mt. Misery (3,711 ft.). In SE it narrows inte an isthmus, which expands into a knob whero there are salt ponds. Equable, tropical climate; mean temp. 79°F.; annual rainfall 55 inches. The fertile lower slopes and valleys yield sugar cane; also sea-island cotton and coconuts and other tropical fruit, which, as well as refined sugar and molasses, are exported through Basseterre, the leading port and processing center. Higher slopes are used for pasturage. St. Kitts, called Liamuiga (=fertile isl.), by the Caribs, was reputedly discovered 1493 by Columbus and was the 1st to be settled (1623) by the British under Sir Thomas Warner; it is often referred to as the "mother isl." of the Br. West Indies. Fr. settlers led by Esnambuc were admitted (1625), and the isl. was partitioned. Later frequently disputed, it was entirely ceded to Great Britain in 1713 (Peace of Utrecht), and, after further troubles, finally restored to Britain in 1783 (Treaty of Versailles).

Saint Kitts-Nevis or **Saint Christopher-Nevis** (-nē'vĭs), presidency (□ 153; pop. 46,243) of Leeward Isls. colony, B.W.I.; ⊙ Basseterre. Consists of Saint Kitts and NEVIS, and dependencies of ANGUILLA and SOMBRERO.

Saint-Lager (sē-läzhā'), village (pop. 225), Rhône dept., E central France, 9 mi. N of Villefranche; winegrowing.

Saint Lambert (lăm'bûrt, Fr. sē lãbâr'), residential city (pop. 6,417), S Que., on the St. Lawrence opposite Montreal (railroad bridges).

Saint Landry (lăn'drē), parish (□ 930; pop. 78,476), S central La.; ⊙ Opelousas. Bounded E by Atchafalaya R.; drained by Bayou Teche and other bayous. Fertile agr. area: cotton, corn, sugar cane, truck, pecans, rice, sweet potatoes, hay. Processing and shipping of farm products and lumber. Oil and natural-gas fields. Formed 1807.

Saint Laurent (sē lōrā'). **1** Village (pop. estimate 300), S Man., on L. Manitoba, 50 mi. NW of Winnipeg; resort; fishing. **2** Residential town (pop. 6,242), S Que., on Montreal Isl., W suburb of Montreal.

Saint-Laurent, Jersey, Channel Isls.: see SAINT LAWRENCE.

Saint-Laurent (sē-lōrā'). **1** or **Saint-Laurent-lès-Mâcon** (-lā-mäkō'), village (pop. 1,913), Ain dept., E France, on left bank of Saône R. opposite Mâcon; produces rennet; furniture and bicycle-part mfg. **2** or **Saint-Laurent-sur-Mer** (-sür-mâr'), village (pop. 139), Calvados dept., NW France, near the Channel, 10 mi. NW of Bayeux. Just N Americans landed (Omaha Beach; June 6, 1944) in Normandy invasion. U.S. military cemetery (Second World War) here. **3** Village, Gironde dept., France: see SAINT-LAURENT-ET-BENON. **4** or **Saint-Laurent-de-Neste** (-dù-nĕst'), village (pop. 575), Hautes-Pyrénées dept., SW France, on Neste R. and 13 mi. W of Saint-Gaudens; livestock and poultry raising, winegrowing. **5** or **Saint Laurent-du-Jura** (-dü-zhürä'), village (pop. 698), Jura dept., E France, in the central Jura, 14 mi. NNE of Sainte-Claude; alt. 3,000 ft. Makes toys and cheese. Grazing. Destroyed by fire in 1867.

Saint-Laurent or **Saint-Laurent-du-Maroni** (-dü-märōnē'), town (commune pop. 2,095), NW Fr. Guiana, port on Maroni R., opposite Albina (Du. Guiana), and 125 mi. WNW of Cayenne. Former hq. of penal settlement (liquidation begun 1946). Sawmills, shipyard. Radio station, customhouse.

Saint-Laurent-Blangy (sē-lōrā'-blāzhē'), N industrial suburb (pop. 2,979) of Arras, Pas-de-Calais dept., N France, on the Scarpe; mfg. (chemical fertilizer, lead cables, clocks, hosiery, vegetable oils, malt).

Saint-Laurent-de-Cerdans (-dù-sĕrdã'), village (pop. 1,687), Pyrénées-Orientales dept., S France, in E Pyrenees, near Sp. border, 10 mi. SW of Céret; sandal mfg., sawmilling.

Saint-Laurent-de-Chamousset (-shämōōsā'), village (pop. 685), Rhône dept., E central France, on S slope of Monts du Beaujolais, 17 mi. W of Lyons; cattle, sheep.

Saint-Laurent-de-la-Salanque (-lä-sälãk'), town (pop. 2,981), Pyrénées-Orientales dept., S France, near the coast, on Agly R. and 7 mi. NE of Perpignan, in winegrowing area; distilling, fruit and vegetable shipping, sulphur refining. Fishing port of Le Barcarès (pop. 331) is 2 mi. ENE.

Saint-Laurent-de-Médoc, France: see SAINT-LAURENT-ET-BENON.

Saint-Laurent-de-Neste, France: see SAINT-LAURENT, Hautes-Pyrénées dept.

Saint-Laurent-d'Olt (-dôlt'), village (pop. 255), Aveyron dept., S France, on the Lot and 20 mi. WSW of Mende; strawberries; woodworking. Copper deposits near by.

Saint-Laurent-du-Jura, France: see SAINT-LAURENT, Jura dept.

Saint-Laurent-du-Maroni, Fr. Guiana: see SAINT-LAURENT.

Saint-Laurent-du-Pape (-dü-päp'), village (pop. 570), Ardèche dept., S France, on the Érieux and 10 mi. SW of Valence; peach growing and shipping.

Saint-Laurent-du-Pont (-pō'), village (pop. 1,214), Isère dept., SE France, on N slopes of Grande Chartreuse, 14 mi. N of Grenoble; mfg. of steel busks, files, graters.

Saint-Laurent-du-Var (-vär'), town (pop. 2,837), Alpes-Maritimes dept., SE France, on the Var near its mouth into the Mediterranean, and 5 mi. WSW of Nice, on Fr. Riviera; roses.

Saint-Laurent-et-Benon (-ā-bùnō') or **Saint-Laurent-Médoc** (mādôk'), village (pop. 750), Gironde dept., SW France, in Médoc, 24 mi. NNW of Bordeaux; brick- and tileworks, sawmills. Extensive vineyards. Also called Saint-Laurent and Saint-Laurent-de-Médoc.

Saint-Laurent-le-Minier (-lù-mēnyā'), village (pop. 273), Gard dept., S France, in the Cévennes, 5 mi. SSE of Le Vigan; silk spinning. Zinc mines near by.

Saint-Laurent-lès-Mâcon, France: see SAINT-LAURENT, Ain dept.

Saint-Laurent-Médoc, France: see SAINT-LAURENT-ET-BENON.

Saint-Laurent-sur-Gorre (-sür-gôr'), village (pop. 491), Haute-Vienne dept., W central France, 8 mi. SSE of St-Junien; brush mfg.

Saint-Laurent-sur-Mer, France: see SAINT-LAURENT, Calvados dept.

Saint Lawrence, village (pop. 264), E Queensland, Australia, on Broad Sound and 95 mi. NW of Rockhampton; cotton.

Saint Lawrence, SE residential suburb of Bridgetown, SW Barbados, B.W.I.

Saint Lawrence or **Great Saint Lawrence,** town (pop. 1,241), SE N.F., on SW shore of Placentia Bay, on Burin Peninsula, 22 mi. ESE of Grand Bank; fluorspar-mining center. Just NE is Little St. Lawrence, site of hydroelectric station.

Saint Lawrence, Fr. *Saint-Laurent* (sē-lōrā'), agr. village and parish (1945 pop. 2,247), Jersey, Channel Isls., 3 mi. NW of St. Helier. Has 13th-cent. church.

Saint Lawrence, county (□ 2,772; pop. 98,897), N N.Y.; ⊙ Canton. Bounded NW by the St. Lawrence; drained by St. Regis, Indian, Grass, Oswegatchie, and Raquette rivers. Plains area along the St. Lawrence; rises to the Adirondacks in SE. A leading U.S. dairying co.; also farming, maple-sugar production. Lead, zinc, pyrite mines; limestone, talc deposits. Diversified mfg. Resorts on the St. Lawrence and on Black and Cranberry lakes. Formed 1802.

Saint Lawrence. 1 Borough (pop. 810), Berks co., SE central Pa., 3 mi. ESE of Reading. **2** Town (pop. 261), Hand co., central S.Dak., 3 mi. E of Miller; trade center for dairying region.

Saint Lawrence, Cape, N extremity of Cape Breton Isl., NE N.S., on Gulf of St. Lawrence, 65 mi. NNW of Sydney; 47°3'N 60°35'W.

Saint Lawrence, Gulf of, E Canada, bay (□ 100,000) of the Atlantic, at mouth of the St. Lawrence, bet. Quebec (N), Gaspé Peninsula and New Brunswick (W), Nova Scotia (S), and Newfoundland (E); extends c.500 mi. N-S, 250 mi. E-W. Contains Anticosti Isl., Prince Edward Isl., Magdalen Isls., and numerous small isls. on N shore. Chaleur Bay is W arm, on S side of Gaspé Peninsula. Strait of Belle Isle (NE), Cabot Strait (E), and narrow Strait of Canso (bet. Nova Scotia peninsula and Cape Breton Isl.) lead to the Atlantic. Gulf is important fishing ground. Fogs are frequent; navigation season from mid-April to early Dec.; at other times gulf is covered with large drifting sheets of ice.

Saint Lawrence Island (90 mi. long, 8–22 mi. wide), W Alaska, in Bering Sea, near entrance of Norton Sound; 63°25'N 168°42'–171°36'W; rises to 2,070 ft. (N). Of volcanic origin; treeless, snow-covered more than half the year; covered with tundra vegetation. Centers of Eskimo pop. are Savoonga (N) and Gambell (NW). Principal activities are whaling and fox trapping. Primitive Eskimo society here is of interest to anthropologists. Discovered by Vitus Bering on St. Lawrence's Day, 1728.

Saint Lawrence Islands National Park, Ont.: see THOUSAND ISLANDS.

Saint Lawrence River, North America, one of principal rivers of the continent and chief outlet of the Great Lakes, which it links to Gulf of St. Lawrence to form waterway c.2,350 mi. long from W end of L. Superior to the Atlantic. The St. Lawrence proper issues from NE end of L. Ontario, flows 744 mi. NE to its mouth on the Gulf of St. Lawrence N of Cape Gaspé. Below L. Ontario, river forms c.114 mi. of international line bet. N N.Y. and SE Ont.; in this section lie the scenic THOUSAND ISLANDS, bet. Kingston and Brockville, Ont., and the International Rapids section (c.48 mi. long) below Ogdensburg, N.Y.; below rapids, widens into L. St. Francis, then passes into S Que. and widens again into L. St. Louis at mouth of Ottawa R., and descends through Lachine Rapids to Montreal, which is head of navigation for ocean-going vessels. Bet. Sorel and Trois Rivières is L. St. Peter, a widened section c.28 mi. long; below Quebec river is tidal, and increases gradually in width to c.90 mi. at its mouth. Canals around rapids make entire river navigable for vessels of limited drafts. Principal tributaries from S are the Richelieu (navigable link with L. Champlain and the Hudson) and the St. Francis; from the N come the Ottawa, the St. Maurice, and the Saguenay. Principal cities on its banks are Ogdensburg,N.Y.; Kingston, Brockville, and Cornwall, Ont.; and Montreal, Sorel, Trois Rivières, and Quebec city in Que. Its many bridges include Thousand Islands International Bridge (1938) bet. Collins Landing, N.Y., and Ivy Lea, Ont.; Roosevelt International Bridge (1934) bet. Cornwall, Ont., and Rooseveltown, N.Y.; Quebec Bridge (1917) near Quebec, and Victoria Bridge (remodeled 1898) and Jacques Cartier Harbour Bridge (1930) at Montreal. The heavily forested St. Lawrence valley has many lumbering and paper-milling centers. River is an important source of hydroelectric power. Agreements bet. U.S. and Canada govern navigation and power distribution in international section. The St. Lawrence was visited (1534) and ascended (1535) by Jacques Cartier; 1st settlement on its banks made at Quebec by Champlain, 1608. System was long an important route for fur traders, explorers, and missionaries. Fr. possession of valley continued until end of French and Indian war (1763), when Canada was surrendered to the British; after U.S. independence, the British continued to hold trading posts in W region until after War of 1812. Since then, international arbitration has settled all issues arising from use of river system. The proposed international St. Lawrence seaway and power project, which would produce additional hydroelectric power and give ocean-going vessels access to Great Lakes ports, has long been under discussion.

Saint-Léger (sē-lā-zhā'), Alpine village (pop. 32), Savoie dept., SE France, on the Arc and 12 mi. NNW of Saint-Jean-de-Maurienne; electro-metallurgy.

Saint-Léger-des-Vignes (sē-lā-zhā"-dā-vē'nyù), N suburb (pop. 1,547) of Decize, Nièvre dept., central France, on right bank of the Loire at mouth of Arnon R. and at junction of Nivernais Canal; rubber and plaster factories. Winegrowing.

Saint-Léger-sous-Beuvray (-sōō-bûvrā'), village (pop. 382), Saône-et-Loire dept., E central France, 9 mi. WSW of Autun. On near-by Mont Beuvray was anc. BIBRACTE.

Saint-Léger-sur-Dheune (-sür-dûn'), village (pop. 1,365), Saône-et-Loire dept., E central France, on Dheune R. and Canal du Centre, 11 mi. WNW of Chalon-sur-Saône; brick and tile works.

Saint Leo. 1 Town (pop. 261), Pasco co., W central Fla., 29 mi. NE of Tampa. Benedictine abbey here. **2** Village (pop. 128), Yellow Medicine co., SW Minn., 26 mi. WSW of Granite Falls.

Saint Leon, town (pop. 288), Dearborn co., SE Ind., 29 mi. E of Greensburg, in agr. area.

Saint-Léonard, Belgium: see SINT-LENAARTS.

Saint Leonard, town (pop. 1,095), NW N.B., on St. John R. and 24 mi. SE of Edmundston, on Maine border; potato-growing region.

Saint Léonard d'Aston (dă'stŭn, Fr. sē lãōnär'), village (pop. 569), S Que., on Nicolet R. and 14 mi. SE of Nicolet; dairying, lumbering.

Saint-Léonard-de-Noblat (sē-lãōnär"-dù-nôblä'), town (pop. 3,185), Haute-Vienne dept., W central France, near Vienne R., 11 mi. E of Limoges; industrial center (paper milling, mfg. of porcelain and plastics). Wolfram mined near by. Has 11th–13th-cent. Romanesque church. Gay-Lussac b. here.

Saint Léonard de Port Maurice (pôr mōrēs'), town (pop. 518), S Que., on Montreal Isl., N suburb of Montreal.

Saint-Léonard-des-Bois (-dā-bwä'), village (pop. 147), Sarthe dept., W France, on Sarthe R. and 9 mi. SW of Alençon; tourist resort in the Alpes Mancelles.

Saint Leonards, England: see HASTINGS.

Saint Leonards, town (pop. 1,260), NE central Tasmania, 5 mi. SE of Launceston and on N.Esk R.; meat-packing plants.

Saint-Leu (sē-lû'), village (pop. 518), Oran dept., NW Algeria, on Gulf of Arzew, 22 mi. NE of Oran; winegrowing. Near-by are Roman ruins of *Portus Magnus*.

Saint-Leu, town (pop. 4,720; commune pop. 12,152), on W coast of Réunion isl., on railroad and 16 mi. NW of Saint-Pierre; sugar milling, alcohol mfg.

Saint-Leu-la-Forêt (–lä-fôrĕ′), town (pop. 6,607), Seine-et-Oise dept., N central France, 7 mi. ESE of Pontoise, at SW edge of Forest of Montmorency, adjoining Taverny (NW); resort; mfg. (watch cases, fountain pens, radio sets); mica processing. Its church contains tombs of several members of Bonaparte family. Formerly called Saint-Leu-Taverny.

Saint Liboire (sĕ lēbwär′), village (pop. 464), ⊙ Bagot co., S Que., 9 mi. ENE of St. Hyacinthe; dairying; cattle, pigs.

Saint Libory (sānt″ lĭ′bùrē), village (pop. 324), St. Clair co., SW Ill., 28 mi. SE of East St. Louis, in agr. area.

Saint Lin, Que.: see LAURENTIDES, town.

Saint-Lizier (sē-lēzyā′), anc. *Lugdunum Consoranorum,* N industrial suburb (pop. 562) of Saint-Girons, Ariège dept., S France, on the Salat; paper mills, chemical factory. Dairying, whetstone mfg., sawmilling. Asylum in former episcopal palace. Has a 12th–14th cent. church and a fine Romanesque cloister. Was a leading city of Roman Novempopulana.

Saint-Lô (sē-lō′), town (1946 pop. 5,190; 1936 pop. 10,009), ⊙ Manche dept., NW France, on the Vire and 34 mi. WSW of Caen; road center in hedgerow country (apple orchards); cider distilling, meat preserving, horse breeding. Pillaged by Norsemen (889), by Geoffrey Plantagenet (1141), by Edward III of England (1346), and by Huguenots (16th cent.). Partially destroyed during Normandy campaign of Second World War, during which it served as jumping-off point for American offensive (July, 1944) to break out of initial landing area.

Saint-Lô-d'Ourville (sē-lō-dōōrvēl′), village (pop. 99), Manche dept., NW France, near W coast of Cotentin Peninsula, 21 mi. S of Cherbourg. Here Americans cut off last Ger. escape route from Cherbourg area in Normandy campaign (June, 1944) of Second World War.

Saint-Lon-les-Mines (sē-lō′-lā-mēn′), village (pop. 105), Landes dept., SW France, 7 mi. SSW of Dax; lignite mining.

Saint-Loubès (sē-lōōbā′), village (pop. 755), Gironde dept., SW France, near the Dordogne, 9 mi. NE of Bordeaux; winegrowing. Petroleum refinery at Cavernes (1.5 mi. N of Dordogne R.) damaged during Second World War.

Saint-Louis (sē-lwē′), village (pop. 1,260), Oran dept., NW Algeria, 13 mi. E of Oran; winegrowing.

Saint-Louis (sē-lwē′), Ger. *Sankt Ludwig* (zängkt lōōd′vĭkh), town (pop. 6,209), Haut-Rhin dept., E France, near the Rhine, 3 mi. NNW of Basel; customs station on Mulhouse-Basel RR; industrial center mfg. cotton fabrics, hosiery, electrical equipment (especially furnaces), chemicals, plumbing, aluminum products, and liqueurs.

Saint-Louis (sē-lwē′), city (pop. c.62,900, of which c.3,150 are Europeans), ⊙ Senegal and Mauritania overseas territories, Fr. West Africa, Atlantic port 110 mi. NE of Dakar, linked by rail; 16°2′N 16°30′W. Largely built on small Saint-Louis isl. in Senegal R. estuary. Railhead and commercial center, shipping products of region (peanuts, kapok, gums, sisal, hides, skins). Fisheries; printing, mfg. of textile goods. Well-equipped port serves also as terminal for inland shipping route to Podor and Kayes. Airport. Bridges join city center with other isls., such as Sor, where the railroad station is. Probably the 1st permanent Fr. settlement on West African coast, Saint-Louis was built (c.1658) as a fort by a Fr. trading company on Sor isl. Prospered through slave trade. It was ⊙ Fr. West Africa from 1895 to 1902, when it was replaced by Dakar.

Saint-Louis (sē-lwē′), town (commune pop. 7,199), W Marie-Galante isl., Guadeloupe, 27 mi. E of Basse-Terre, in sugar region; distilling.

Saint-Louis (sē-lwē′), town (pop. 9,778; commune pop. 23,936), on SW coast of Réunion isl., on railroad and 6 mi. NW of Saint-Pierre; agr. processing (sugar, alcohol, tobacco, fibre). Sugar mill at Le Gol, in NW outskirts.

Saint Louis (sānt″ lōō′ĭs). **1** County (□ 6,281; pop. 206,062), NE Minn.; ⊙ Duluth. Extensively watered area served by St. Louis R. and Little Fork R.; bounded N, along Ont. line, by Rainy L., Namakan L., and Lac La Croix; SE by L. Superior. Vermilion iron range, in NE, and Mesabi iron range, extending E–W through central area, have immensely productive mines. Other activities are dairying and potato raising. Chief lakes are Burntside, in NE, Trout and Vermilion, in N, and Pelican and Kabetogama, in NW. State forests and Superior Natl. Forest extend throughout N half of region; part of Fond du Lac Indian Reservation is in S. Formed 1855. **2** County (□ 497; pop. 406,-349), E Mo.; ⊙ Clayton. Bounded by Mississippi R. (E), Missouri R. (NW), and Meramec R. (SE, SW). Agr. (corn, wheat, hay, potatoes), horticulture; dairy, lime, lumber products. Formed 1877.

Saint Louis (sānt″ lōō′ĭs). **1** City (pop. 3,347), Gratiot co., central Mich., 34 mi. W of Saginaw and on Pine R., in oil-bearing and agr. area (livestock, poultry, grain, sugar beets; dairy products). Oil and beet-sugar refining; mfg. of flour, salt, chemicals; poultry hatcheries. Clay deposits; mineral springs (health resort). Settled 1849, inc. as city 1891. **2** City (□ 65; 1940 pop. 816,048; 1950 pop. 856,796), independent of any co., E Mo., on right bank (levees) of Mississippi R. (here crossed by 5 bridges), c.10 mi. below influx of the Missouri and 265 mi. SW of Chicago; 38°37′N 90°15′W. Largest city of state, 8th largest in U.S., and strategically located at crossroads of transcontinental and N–S routes, St. Louis is a major transportation center served by 25 railroads, river shipping lines, airlines, and a network of highways; commercial, financial, and industrial center for wide region, it has wholesale and distributing trade reaching far into S and SW U.S. Port of entry. One of world's largest raw-fur markets, and an important market for livestock, grain, wool, and lumber. Among large industries are food processing (notably meat packing), brewing (has one of world's largest breweries), and distilling, and mfg. of chemicals, drugs, shoes, clothing, machinery, airplanes, automobiles, railroad cars, stoves, hardware, boxes and other wood products, brick, terra cotta, and products of iron, steel, petroleum, coal, rubber, tobacco, and stone; printing, publishing. Extensive industrial suburbs center on East St. Louis (Ill.), across the Mississippi. Port of St. Louis (part of city's 19-mi. frontage on river) handles cargoes of oil, coal, sulphur, grain, cement, sugar, farm products, and manufactured goods (including paper, chemicals, automobiles). City is seat of St. Louis Univ., Washington Univ., Concordia Theological Seminary, Kenrick Seminary, 2 teachers colleges, and schools of pharmacy and music. Has a fine symphony orchestra (one of oldest in U.S.) and a noted art mus. Seat of R.C. and Episcopal cathedrals. Points of interest: Eads Bridge (1869–74), world's 1st steel-truss span; Forest Park (1,380 acres), in which are large open-air theater (annual summer opera season), city's art mus., Jefferson Memorial Bldg., built during La. Purchase Exposition of 1904 and now housing Mo. Historical Society, and zoological gardens; Mo. Botanical Garden (Shaw's Garden); Municipal Plaza, surrounded by civic bldgs., including large municipal auditorium; Aloe Plaza (in front of Union Station), with Carl Milles' fountain "Meeting of the Waters"; Eugene Field's house, now a mus.; Jefferson Natl. Expansion Memorial (82.58 acres; designated a natl. historic site in 1935 to commemorate territorial expansion of U.S.), in which are preserved old courthouse (1839–62), containing monument hq. and a historical mus., the old cathedral (1834), oldest church in city, and the Rock House, built 1818 as fur warehouse. Has Air Force and naval air fields. In S outskirts of city is Jefferson Barracks (established 1826), with a natl. cemetery; in NW outskirts is Lambert-St. Louis Municipal Airport. Residential suburbs lie to N, W, and S. City's site was chosen in 1763 by Pierre Laclede for a fur-trading post; founded 1764 by Auguste Chouteau, it was named for Louis IX of France, the patron saint of Louis XV. Although transferred to Spain (1770), later retroceded to France, then sold with other lands of Louisiana Purchase (1803) to U.S., settlement retained predominantly French pop. and customs well into 19th cent.; by 1850, many Germans, whose cultural and industrial contributions have been large, had arrived. As gateway city to the West, it was market and supply point for fur traders and the later mountain men, and for explorers, notably the Lewis and Clark expedition. Town was inc. in 1808, but did not grow rapidly until after War of 1812, when flatboat immigrants arrived; became a city in 1823, and grew (1st steamer docked here 1817) as one of greatest U.S. river ports. Heyday of steamboats continued for some time after railroads came in mid-19th cent., and only faded under the blockade of the South and increased railroad and towboat competition after Civil War. City was a base of Federal operations and was Unionist in sympathy during war, to which its flourishing industries supplied vast quantities of goods. Later, industries were given further stimulus by opening (1874) of Eads Bridge, which gave access to Ill. industrial sites and coal supplies. St. Louis celebrated a century of growth and confirmed its position as one of nation's great cities with the La. Purchase Exposition ("St. Louis Fair") of 1904. Extensive civic improvement program was begun in 1920s. **3** Town (pop. 290), Pottawatomie co., central Okla., 18 mi. S of Shawnee, in agr. area.

Saint Louis, Lake (lōō′ē, Fr. sē lwē′), expansion (□ 57) of the St. Lawrence, S Que., 8 mi. SW of Montreal; 18 mi. long, up to 7 mi. wide, bounded N by Montreal Isl. Receives Ottawa R. (W) through 2 channels on either side of Perrot Isl., and Châteauguay R. (S).

Saint Louis Bay (sānt″ lōō′ĭs). **1** In Minn.: see SAINT LOUIS RIVER. **2** In S Miss., inlet of Mississippi Sound, c.10 mi. W of Gulfport; c.5 mi. long N–S, c.6 mi. wide. Its mouth is bridged. Bay St. Louis is on W shore.

Saint Louis de Courville, Que.: see COURVILLE.

Saint Louis de Kent (Fr. sē lwē dù), agr. village (pop. estimate c.500), E N.B., on Kouchibouguac R. and 7 mi. NW of Richibucto, in Acadian district; peat.

Saint-Louis-du-Nord (sē-lwē-dü-nôr′), agr. town (1950 census pop. 3,073), Nord-Ouest dept., N Haiti, minor port on the Atlantic, 8 mi. E of Port-de-Paix, in rice-growing region.

Saint-Louis-du-Sud (–süd′), town (1950 census pop. 1,403), Sud dept., SW Haiti, on Tiburon Peninsula, on the Caribbean, 7 mi. NE of Les Cayes; bananas, sugar cane.

Saint-Louis-lès-Bitche (sē-lwē-lā-bēch′), village (pop. 811), Moselle dept., NE France, in the N Vosges, 16 mi. SE of Sarreguemines; crystal works.

Saint Louis Park (sānt lōō″ĭs pärk′), village (pop. 22,644), SW suburb of Minneapolis, Hennepin co., E Minn.; ice cream; tools, dental supplies. Settled 1853, inc. 1896. Mus. of co. historical society is here.

Saint Louis River (sānt″ lōō′ĭs), rises in small lake in St. Louis co., NE Minn., flows SW, through Mesabi iron range, to Floodwood, then SE and E to L. Superior at Duluth; 160 mi. long; largely navigable. Its estuary (called St. Louis Bay) is c.1 mi. wide and forms part of the harbor for the twin ports of Duluth and Superior. Drains part of Superior Natl. Forest in upper course, passes through picturesque gorge in Jay Cooke State Park, just W of Duluth. Dammed for power just E of Carlton. Important tributaries are Cloquet and Whiteface rivers.

Saint Louisville (lōō′ĭsvĭl), village (pop. 336), Licking co., central Ohio, 7 mi. N of Newark, and on North Fork of Licking R., in agr. area.

Saint-Loup-de-Naud (sē-lōō-dù-nō′), village (pop. 218), Seine-et-Marne dept., N central France, 4 mi. WSW of Provins; mfg. (electrical equipment, vaseline). Its 12th-cent. church has beautifully sculptured portal.

Saint-Loup-sur-Semouse (sē-lōō-sür-sùmōōz′), town (pop. 2,605), Haute-Saône dept., E France, 19 mi. NNE of Vesoul; furniture mfg. center. Also produces footwear and lace.

Saint-Loup-sur-Thouet (–tōōā′), village (pop. 668), Deux-Sèvres dept., W France, on the Thouet and 10 mi. NNE of Parthenay; dairying. Has 17th-cent. castle.

Saint Lucas, town (pop. 158), Fayette co., NE Iowa, 10 mi. NW of West Union, in agr. area.

Saint Lucia (sĭnt lōō′shù), island constituting a Br. colony (□ 233.29; pop. 70,113), part of the Windward Isls. colony, SE West Indies; ⊙ Castries. Separated from Martinique (N) by 20-mi.-wide St. Lucia Channel and from St. Vincent (S) by 25-mi.-wide St. Vincent Passage; situated in 13°43′–14°7′N at about 61°W. The climate, influenced by NE trade winds, is healthful, temp. varying bet. 70° and 90°F.; rainfall range 70–160 inches. Roughly oval-shaped, but broader in S, 28 mi. long N–S, up to 12 mi. wide. The rugged, mountainous isl. is traversed by a volcanic range, rising in the Morne Gimie to 3,145 ft. There are many fertile valleys and a few coastal plains, watered by numerous streams. The interior is still largely covered by virgin forest of fine tropical timber. Among noted landmarks of the picturesque isl. are the mineral springs and *solfataras* near Soufrière, and the pyramidical cones of The Pitons twin peaks. While sugar cane is the isl.'s chief product, it also exports molasses, rum, lime, lime juice and lime oil, coconuts, copra, cacao, spices, bananas, mangoes, bay oil, bay rum, and cotton. Sugar milling, lime-oil extracting, rum and bay-rum distilling, cotton ginning. Main trading center and port is Castries, with one of the finest harbors in the West Indies, and long an important coaling station, now largely replaced by Colón. The isl., called Hewanorra by the aboriginal Carib Indians, was reputedly discovered 1502 by Columbus on his 4th voyage. Early Du. and English settlements met with little success. Though included into the grant made (1627) to the earl of Carlisle, it was 1st colonized by the French, who signed (1660) a treaty with the fierce natives. St. Lucia was held by the British from 1663 to 1667, its possession being disputed constantly thereafter by the 2 powers until 1803, when the British gained permanent control. Though it forms a part of the Windward Isls. colony, it has an administration and legislative council of its own. Military and naval bases were leased (1940) for 99 years to the U.S. at Vieux Fort (S) and Gros Islet (N). The pop. is predominantly Negro, and generally speaks a Fr. patois. A large group of the population is of East Indian stock.

Saint Lucia Channel, SE West Indies, c.20 mi. wide bet. Martinique (N) and St. Lucia (S).

Saint Lucie (sānt″ lōō′sē), county (□ 588; pop. 20,180), SE Fla., on the Atlantic (E); ⊙ Fort Pierce. Largely a swampy lowland area, with towns along coast; bordered E by a barrier beach enclosing Indian R. lagoon. Citrus-fruit and truck region, with some fishing, cattle and poultry raising. Formed 1905.

Saint Lucie Canal, Martin co., SE Fla., extends c.30 mi. ENE from L. Okeechobee at Port Mayaca to St. Lucie R. near Stuart; has 2 locks and is crossed by bridges. Part of OKEECHOBEE WATERWAY.

Saint Lucie Inlet, SE Fla., narrow passage through barrier beach, 5 mi. ESE of Stuart, connects mouth of St. Lucie R. (E end of Okeechobee Waterway) and S end of Indian R. lagoon (part of Intracoastal Waterway) with the Atlantic.

Saint-Lucien (sē-lüsyē'), village (pop. 1,801), Oran dept., NW Algeria, 18 mi. SE of Oran; wine, cereals.
Saint Lucie River (sānt" lōō'sē), SE Fla., rises in swamp c.10 mi. WSW of Fort Pierce, flows E and S c.35 mi. into the Atlantic through St. Lucie Inlet at S end of Indian R. lagoon. Its lower course, an estuary, receives the St. Lucie Canal near Stuart and forms E end of Okeechobee Waterway.
Saint Ludger (sůnt lŭ'jůr), village (pop. 255), S Que., on Chaudière R. and 15 mi. NE of Megantic; dairying, lumbering.
Saint-Lunaire (sē-lünâr'), village (pop. 775), Ille-et-Vilaine dept., W France, on English Channel and 4 mi. WSW of Saint-Malo; small but well-known bathing resort near a rocky headland. Damaged in Second World War.
Saint-Lupicin (sē-lüpēsē'), village (pop. 983), Jura dept., E France, in the central Jura, 4 mi. W of Saint-Claude; makes plastic articles (fountain pens, pencils, pipe stems).
Saint-Lys (sē-lēs'), village (pop. 535), Haute-Garonne dept., S France, 15 mi. WSW of Toulouse; horse and mule raising, potato shipping.
Saint-Macaire (sē-mäkâr'), village (pop. 1,451), Gironde dept., SW France, on right bank of Garonne R. and 25 mi. SE of Bordeaux, in wine- and fruitgrowing area. Stone quarries near by. Has 13th-cent. gateway, 12th-13th-cent. church.
Saint-Macaire-en-Mauges (-ā-mōzh'), town (pop. 2,166), Maine-et-Loire dept., W France, 7 mi. NW of Cholet; shoe mfg. Until 1939, Saint-Macaire.
Saint Magnus Bay, inlet on W coast of MAINLAND isl., Shetlands, Scotland. Papa Stour isl. at mouth.
Saint-Maixent-l'École (sē-mĕksā'-lākôl'), town (pop. 4,825), Deux-Sèvres dept., W France, on the Sèvre Niortaise and 14 mi. ENE of Niort; road center; shoe factories. Has 12th–15th-cent. church on site of anc. abbey destroyed (16th cent.) by Huguenots. Castle occupied by an infantry training school.
Saint Malo (sē mälō'), village (pop. estimate 500), S Man., on Rat R. and 40 mi. S of Winnipeg; dairying; grain.
Saint-Malo, town (pop. 10,873), Ille-et-Vilaine dept., W France, port on English Channel at mouth of the Rance and 40 mi. NNW of Rennes; together with SAINT-SERVAN (S) and PARAMÉ (E), it constitutes a popular resort area; active seaport with passenger and freight service to England. Constructs and equips deep-sea fishing vessels. Other mfg.: hosiery, morocco leather, cider, vegetable preserves. Town proper is on a rocky peninsula and consists of 17th- and 18th-cent. houses, narrow winding streets, the Renaissance church of Saint-Vincent (all heavily damaged during Second World War), a 15th-cent. castle and continuous ramparts (which escaped destruction). Connected with the mainland by a narrow isthmus, on N shore of which is beach. Off the peninsula are several rocky isls., one of which contains the grave of Chateaubriand. Founded by Welsh abbots in 6th cent., Saint-Malo became hq. of corsairs who attacked Br. shipping during 16th and 17th cent. Hard hit in the Second World War when, in addition to Allied bombings, it was set afire by the Germans in 1944. Saint-Malo is the birthplace of many well-known Frenchmen, including Cartier, Chateaubriand, and Lamennais.
Saint-Malo, Gulf of (sůnt mä'lō, Fr. sē mälō'), on English Channel, off N coast of Brittany, W France; 60 mi. wide, c.20 mi. long, extending from Bréhat isl. off Côtes-du-Nord dept. to W coast of the Cotentin Peninsula (Manche dept.). It includes the Bay of Saint-Brieuc and the Bay of Mont-Saint-Michel. Its shore is dotted with numerous bathing resorts (Saint-Cast, Saint-Jacut-de-la-Mer, Saint-Lunaire, Dinard, Saint-Malo, Paramé, Cancale, Granville).
Saint-Malo-de-la-Lande (sē-mälō'-dü-lä-lãd'), village (pop. 80), Manche dept., NW France, 5 mi. WNW of Coutances; cheese mfg.
Saint-Mamert-du-Gard (sē-mämâr'-dü-gär'), village (pop. 380), Gard dept., S France, in the Garrigues, 9 mi. WNW of Nîmes; winegrowing.
Saint-Mamet-la-Salvetat (sē-mämā'-lä-sälvtä'), village (pop. 450), Cantal dept., S central France, 8 mi. SW of Aurillac; tanning, cheese mfg., cider distilling.
Saint-Mammès (sē-mämĕs'), village (pop. 1,500), Seine-et-Marne dept., N central France, 5 mi. ESE of Fontainebleau; river port at junction of the Seine and Loing Canal (locks).
Saint-Mandé (sē-mãdā'), town (pop. 22,279), Seine dept., N central France, residential E suburb of Paris, 4 mi. from Notre Dame Cathedral, just S of Vincennes; mfg. (optical equipment, cycles, paper bags); sand quarries for glass mfg.
Saint-Mandrier Peninsula (sē-mãdrēā'), in Var dept., SE France, guarding entrance to Toulon roadstead; 3 mi. long; connected by isthmus with Cape Sicié peninsula (W). Terminates in Cape Cépet (E). Dotted with coastal defenses.
Saint-Marc (sē-märk'), part of Brest, Finistère dept., W France, until 1945 a separate commune; chemical and dyeworks; distilling.
Saint-Marc, town (1950 census pop. 10,485), Artibonite dept., W Haiti, port on Gulf of Gonaïves, 45 mi. NW of Port-au-Prince (linked by railroad). Together with Gonaïves (23 mi. N), it is outlet for fertile Artibonite Plain, shipping cotton, coffee, bananas, precious wood. Cotton and rice milling, vegetable-oil extracting; mfg. of soap and lard. Sisal plantations in vicinity.
Saint Marc des Carrières (dā kărēâr'), village (pop. 2,118), S Que., 33 mi. NE of Trois Rivières; limestone quarrying, lumbering, dairying.
Saint-Marcel (sē-märsĕl'). **1** Village (pop. 773), Aude dept., S France, on Aude R. and 5 mi. NW of Narbonne; winegrowing. **2** E suburb (pop. 2,794) of Chalon-sur-Saône, Saône-et-Loire dept., E central France; ships early vegetables and poultry. **3** Village (pop. 146), Savoie dept., SE France, in Tarentaise valley, on the Isère and 3 mi. NNE of Moutiers; electrochemical works (chlorine, ammonia).
Saint-Marcel-lès-Annonay (-lāzänônā'), village (pop. 345), Ardèche dept., S France, 4 mi. NW of Annonay; paper mill.
Saint-Marcellin (sē-märslē'), town (pop. 3,703), Isère dept., SE France, near the Isère, 20 mi. WSW of Grenoble; goat-cheese-mfg. center; also makes electrical equipment, shoes, barrels, tool handles, ebonite. Abbey of Saint-Antoine is 6 mi. WNW.
Saint-Marcet (sē-märsĕ'), village (pop. 58), Haute-Garonne dept., SW France, 6 mi. NW of Saint-Gaudens; oil and natural-gas wells.
Saint-Marcouf (sē-märkōōf'), village (pop. 279), Manche dept., NW France, on E coast of Cotentin Peninsula, 19 mi. SE of Cherbourg. Here (Utah Beach) Americans landed June 6, 1944, in Normandy invasion during Second World War.
Saint-Marcouf Islands, in English Channel, 5 mi. off E coast of Cotentin Peninsula, part of Manche dept., NW France, 24 mi. SE of Cherbourg. Comprise 2 islets, Île du Large (lighthouse) and Île de Terre.
Saint-Mard, Belgium: see VIRTON.
Saint-Margaret's-at-Cliffe, town and parish (pop. 1,267), E Kent, England, on the Channel, 4 mi. NE of Dover; seaside resort on St. Margaret's Bay. Has Norman church.
Saint Margaret's Bay, town (pop. 1,320), Portland parish, E Jamaica on N coast, on railroad and 5 mi. WNW of Port Antonio, in fruitgrowing region (bananas, coconuts, cacao).
Saint Margaret's Hope, Scotland: see FORTH RIVER.
Saint Margaret's Island, Wales: see CALDY.
Saint Marie, Ill.: see SAINTE MARIE.
Saint Maries (mā'rēz), city (pop. 2,220), ⊙ Benewah co., N Idaho, SE of Coeur d'Alene L., at confluence of St. Joe and St. Maries rivers, 45 mi. SE of Spokane, Wash.; lumber town. Hq. St. Joe Natl. Forest. Has steamboat connections. Named for mission founded here (1842) by Father De Smet. Settled 1888, inc. 1902.
Saint Maries River, N Idaho, rises in SW corner of Shoshone co., flows c.50 mi. NW to St. Joe R. at St. Maries.
Saint Marks. **1** Fishing town (pop. 391), Wakulla co., NW Fla., 20 mi. SSE of Tallahassee, near mouth of St. Marks R. (c.30 mi. long; receives Wakulla R. here) on Apalachee Bay. Natl. wildlife refuge near by. **2** Town (pop. 43), Meriwether co., W Ga., 13 mi. NE of La Grange.
Saint-Mars-la-Brière (sē-mär-lä-brēâr') village (pop. 425), Sarthe dept., W France, 9 mi. ENE of Le Mans; mfg. (cigarette paper, office supplies).
Saint-Mars-la-Jaille (-zhī'), village (pop. 961), Loire-Inférieure dept., W France, on Erdre R. and 16 mi. SE of Châteaubriant; fertilizer mfg.
Saint Martin (Fr. sē märtē'), village (pop. estimate 750), S Que., on Jesus Isl., 8 mi. WNW of Montreal; dairying, truck gardening.
Saint Martin. **1** Agr. village and parish (1931 pop. 3,678), on E coast of Guernsey, Channel Isls., 2 mi. S of St. Peter Port. Has partly-Norman church. Post office name St. Martin's. **2** Agr. village and parish (1945 pop. 1,757), Jersey, Channel Isls., 4 mi. NE of St. Helier. Has 13th-cent. church and 14th-cent. manor house.
Saint-Martin or **Saint-Martin-de-Ré** (sē-märtē'-dů-rā'), village (pop. 1,083), Charente-Maritime dept., W France, small port on N shore of Île de Ré, 11 mi. WNW of La Rochelle; bathing resort; vegetables, winegrowing. Has a 12th–15th-cent. church and a 17th-cent. citadel (built by Vauban) now used as penitentiary.
Saint Martin, Fr. *Saint-Martin* (sē-märtē'), Du. *Sint Maarten* (sĭnt mär'tůn), island (□ 32.8; 1948 pop. estimate 8,500), in NW Leeward Isls., West Indies, bet. Anguilla (N) and Saint-Barthélemy (S); 18°5'N 63°5'W. Has tropical, trade-wind climate. Roughly triangular in shape, hilly (rising to 1,168 ft.), it provides good harbors and has several lagoons yielding salt. The isl. is divided politically into 2 almost equal sections: the N belonging to France and constituting a dependency (□ 19.7; pop. 6,786) of Guadeloupe; and the S belonging to the Netherlands and constituting a part (□ 13.1; 1948 pop. estimate 1,600) of the Du. Antilles (formerly Curaçao territory). Principal Fr. settlement is Marigot, principal Du. settlement Philipsburg. Both sections raise some cotton, sugar cane tropical fruit, and cattle, but salt worked by the Dutch is the chief export. St. Martin was peacefully divided (1648) bet. the Dutch and French. The predominantly Negro pop. speaks English.
Saint Martin (sānt" mär'tĭn), parish (□ 738; pop. 26,353), S La.; ⊙ St. Martinville. Divided into 2 sections, separated by part of Iberia parish; traversed by Atchafalaya and Grand rivers and Bayou Teche; contains several lakes. Agr. (sugar cane, cotton, corn, hay, truck, condiment pepper, sweet potatoes, rice); natural gas, oil; fur trapping; lumbering. Processing of farm products and lumber. Includes Longfellow-Evangeline Memorial State Park. Formed 1807.
Saint Martin. **1** Village (pop. 195), Stearns co., central Minn., on Sauk R. and 25 mi. WSW of St. Cloud; grain, potatoes, livestock. **2** Village (pop. 129), Brown co., SW Ohio, 15 mi. W of Hillsboro.
Saint Martin Bay, SE Upper Peninsula, Mich., inlet of L. Huron lying N of Mackinac Isl. and bounded N by Mackinac co., E by peninsula terminating at St. Martin Point; c.7 mi. long, 5 mi. wide. Small St. Martin Isls. are in bay. Receives Carp R.
Saint-Martin-Boulogne (sē-märtē'-bōōlô'nyů), E suburb (pop. 4,138), Pas-de-Calais dept., N France, in intensive truck-farming dist. Damaged in Second World War.
Saint-Martin-d'Auxigny (-dōsēnyē'), village (pop. 758), Cher dept., central France, 8 mi. N of Bourges, in fruit-growing dist. (apples, pears, cherries, peaches, nuts); dairying.
Saint-Martin-de-Crau (-dů-krō'), village (pop. 707), Bouches-du-Rhône dept., SE France, in the Crau, 9 mi. ESE of Arles; dynamite factory.
Saint-Martin-de-la-Porte (-lä-pôrt'), village (pop. 276), Savoie dept., SE France, in Alpine Maurienne valley, on Arc R. and 6 mi. SE of Saint-Jean-de-Maurienne; cementworks. Aluminum mill at Calypso, 1 mi. S.
Saint-Martin-de-Londres (-lō'drů), village (pop. 566), Hérault dept., S France, 15 mi. NW of Montpellier; alcohol and essential-oil distilling.
Saint-Martin-de-Ré, France: see SAINT MARTIN.
Saint-Martin-des-Champs (-dā-shā'), W suburb (pop. 2,061) of Morlaix, Finistère dept., W France; paper milling, meat preserving.
Saint-Martin-de-Seignanx (-dů-sĕnyā') village (pop. 361), Landes dept., SW France, 6 mi. NE of Bayonne; wine, corn.
Saint-Martin-d'Estréaux (-dĕstrāō'), village (pop. 552), Loire dept., E central France, on N slope of Montagnes de la Madeleine, 17 mi. NW of Roanne; hosiery mfg.
Saint-Martin-de-Valamas (-dů-välämäs'), village (pop. 1,007), Ardèche dept., S France, on Érieux R. and 18 mi. NW of Privas, in the Monts du Vivarais; silk throwing and spinning, jewelry mfg.
Saint-Martin-de-Valgalgues (-välgälg'), N suburb (pop. 772) of Alès, Gard dept., S France; coal and pyrite mines; blast furnaces, foundries. Slaked-lime mfg.
Saint-Martin-d'Uriage (-dürēäzh'), village (pop. 232), Isère dept., SE France, in Belledonne range, 6 mi. ESE of Grenoble. Just S is Alpine spa of Uriage (alt. 1,358 ft.), with mineral springs.
Saint-Martin-en-Bresse (-ā-brĕs'), agr. village (pop. 369), Saône-et-Loire dept., E central France, 10 mi. ENE of Chalon-sur-Saône.
Saint-Martin-en-Coailleux (-kōāyû'), town (pop. 2,503), Loire dept., SE central France, 6.5 mi. ENE of Saint-Étienne; cable factory; produces elastic fabrics.
Saint-Martin-la-Plaine (-lä-plān'), village (pop. 871), Loire dept., E central France, in Jarez, 12 mi. NE of Saint-Étienne; forges; sheet-iron milling, hardware mfg.
Saint Martins, village (pop. estimate c.500), S N.B., on the Bay of Fundy, 26 mi. ENE of St. John; cod fishing. Manganese deposits near by.
Saint Martin's, Guernsey and Jersey, Channel Isls.: see SAINT MARTIN.
Saint Martin's, town and parish (pop. 1,945), N Shropshire, England, 4 mi. NNE of Oswestry; coal mining. Has 13th–15th-cent. church.
Saint Martin's, island (682 acres; pop. 134), Cornwall, England, one of SCILLY ISLANDS, 3 mi. NNE of St. Mary's isl. Has tower (38 ft. high) built 1637.
Saint-Martin-Vésubie (sē-märtē'-vāzübē'), village (pop. 1,354), Alpes-Maritimes dept., SE France, near head of scenic Vésubie valley in Maritime Alps, 26 mi. N of Nice, near Ital. border; alt. 3,173 ft. Summer resort; also winter sports.
Saint Martinville, town (pop. 4,614), ⊙ St. Martin parish, S La., on navigable Bayou Teche and 45 mi. SW of Baton Rouge, in agr. area; produces condiments, syrup, wine, sugar; cotton gins, machine shops, sawmill; commercial fisheries; oil wells. Settled c.1760, it was a resort during steamboat era. Supposedly the site of the Evangeline romance, commemorated by Longfellow-Evangeline Memorial State Park (just N).
Saint-Martory (sē-märtôrē'), village (pop. 999), Haute-Garonne dept., S France, on the Garonne and 11 mi. E of Saint-Gaudens; paper mills.
Saint Mary, parish (□ 254.04; pop. 90,902), Middlesex co., N Jamaica; ⊙ Port Maria. Situated bet. Portland (E) and St. Ann (W) parishes. Watered by Wag Water R. Several bays along coast, with ports of Port Maria, Annotto Bay, and Oraca-

bessa—ports mainly shipping bananas. Other products include coconuts, cacao, coffee, citrus fruit, vegetables, breadfruit, pimento, annatto, stock, logwood. Crossed by Kingston–Port Antonio RR.

Saint Mary, parish (□ 605; pop. 35,848), S La.; ⊙ Franklin. On the Gulf Coast, and bounded W and S by West Cote Blanche, East Cote Blanche, and Atchafalaya bays, and NE by Grand L. (widening of Atchafalaya R.); crossed by Gulf Intracoastal Waterway; drained by Atchafalaya R. and Bayou Teche. Agr. (sugar cane, rice, corn, hay, truck). Natural gas, oil; fisheries. Sea-food canning, lumbering; sport fishing, hunting. Includes Belle Isle and Cote Blanche Isl. (salt domes), and Chitimacha Indian Reservation. Formed 1811.

Saint Mary, village, Ky.: see LEBANON.

Saint Mary, Cape. 1 Promontory, SE N.F., on SE side of entrance of Placentia Bay, at SW extremity of Avalon Peninsula, 33 mi. SSW of Argentia; 46°50′N 54°12′W; lighthouse. **2** W extremity of N.S. mainland, at entrance to St. Mary Bay, 18 mi. NNW of Yarmouth; 44°5′N 66°13′W; lighthouse.

Saint Mary, Cape, on W coast of Africa, on S shore of Gambia R. estuary, in Gambia colony; 13°29′N 16°40′W. Site of town of Bakau, 7 mi. WNW of Bathurst.

Saint Mary, Cape, Madagascar: see SAINTE-MARIE, CAPE.

Saint Mary Bay, inlet (35 mi. long, 4–12 mi. wide) of the Atlantic, W N.S., 5 mi. SE of Digby. NW shore of bay is formed by Digby Neck, Long Isl., and Brier Isl. On mainland shore is Weymouth.

Saint Mary Bourne, agr. village and parish (pop. 1,123), NW Hampshire, England, 5 mi. NE of Andover. Has 12th-cent. church.

Saint Mary Church, village of S Devon, England, on Babbacombe Bay, near Torquay; tourist resort.

Saint Mary Cray, town and parish (pop. 2,155), NW Kent, England, on Cray R. just N of Orpington; paper milling; produces electrical equipment and asphalt. Has 14th-cent. church.

Saint Mary de Castro (dů kă′strō), Fr. *Sainte-Marie-du-Castel* (sĕt-märē′-dü-kästĕl′), **Catel,** or **Castel,** agr. village and parish (1931 pop. 3,210), Guernsey, Channel Isls., 2 mi. W of St. Peter Port. Reputed site of anc. "Castel du Grand Sarazin." Early Bronze Age statue found here.

Saint Mary Lake, Mont.: see GLACIER NATIONAL PARK.

Saint Marylebone, London, England: see MARYLEBONE, SAINT.

Saint Mary-of-the-Woods, Ind.: see TERRE HAUTE.

Saint Mary River. 1 In NW Mont. and SW Alta., rises on Mt. Jackson, NW Mont., flows c.150 mi. NE, through St. Mary lakes, crossing into Alta. just E of Carway, to Oldman R. 6 mi. SW of Lethbridge. **2** In E N.S., rises in 2 branches in Cobequid Mts.: East R. St. Mary rises 7 mi. S of New Glasgow, flows 50 mi. ESE; West R. St. Mary rises 20 mi. SW of New Glasgow, flows 50 mi. E; branches unite 10 mi. NNW of Sherbrooke, whence St. Mary R. flows 25 mi. SSE, past Sherbrooke, to the Atlantic 10 mi. SE of Sherbrooke.

Saint Mary's, municipality (pop. 5,370), E New South Wales, Australia, 27 mi. WNW of Sydney, in metropolitan area; coal-mining center. Sometimes spelled Saint Marys.

Saint Mary's, village (pop. 426), SE N.F., on E side of St. Mary's Bay, 60 mi. SW of St. John's; fishing port with govt. bait depot and radio station; lumbering.

Saint Marys, town (pop. 3,635), S Ont., on North Thames R. and 11 mi. SW of Stratford; woodworking, dairying, lumbering, cement making.

Saint Mary's, island (1,611 acres; pop. 1,196), Cornwall, England, largest of SCILLY ISLANDS; just SE of Tresco; 2 mi. wide, 2 mi. long. Chief town, Hugh Town. Flower growing; tourist resort. Has hosp., light (49°55′N 6°19′W), and 16th-cent. castle.

Saint Mary's, town (pop. 746), E Tasmania, 55 mi. ESE of Launceston; rail terminus; coal-mining and agr. center; cheese factories. Also spelled St. Marys.

Saint Marys, county (□ 367; pop. 29,111), S Md.; ⊙ Leonardtown. Tidewater peninsula, bounded NE by Patuxent R., E by Chesapeake Bay, S by the Potomac (forms Va. line here); S tip is Point Lookout. Tidewater agr. area (chiefly tobacco), with some lumbering and commercial fishing; SE portion, suffering from soil erosion, is sparsely settled and little cultivated. Small resorts; fishing, hunting, water sports. Includes Patuxent Naval Air Test Center at Cedar Point. As first (March, 1634) region of settlement in Md., co. contains many points of historic interest (notably St. Marys City), and much of its land is still held under original patents of the Lords Baltimore. Formed 1637, it is oldest Md. co.

Saint Marys. 1 City (pop. 1,348), Camden co., extreme SE Ga., 30 mi. S of Brunswick and on St. Marys R. (forms Fla. line here), near the Atlantic; paper milling, shrimp canning. Inc. 1802. **2** Town (pop. 89), Warren co., S central Iowa, 20 mi. SSW of Des Moines, in agr., coal area. **3** City (pop. 1,201), Pottawatomie co., NE Kansas, on Kansas R. and 23 mi. WNW of Topeka, in livestock and grain area. Laid out as town in 1866, inc. as city in 1869. Here is St. Mary's Col. (divinity school of St. Louis Univ.), outgrowth of R.C. mission (established 1848) to Potawatomi Indians. **4** City (pop. 635), Ste. Genevieve co., E Mo., near Mississippi R., 9 mi. SE of Ste. Genevieve; grain mills. **5** City (pop. 6,208), Auglaize co., W Ohio, 19 mi. SW of Lima, and on St. Marys R., near Grand L.; lake resort. Mfg.: food products, rubber goods, furniture, paperboard containers, cigars, blankets, iron and steel foundry products. State fish hatchery. **6** Borough (pop. 7,846), Elk co., N central Pa., 36 mi. S of Bradford; carbon and clay products, electrical equipment, beer; bituminous coal; potatoes, dairying. Settled 1842 by German Catholics, laid out 1844, inc. 1848. **7** City (pop. 2,196), ⊙ Pleasants co., NW W.Va., on the Ohio and 21 mi. NE of Parkersburg, in agr., coal, and natural-gas area; glass making, petroleum and natural-gas processing. Training school for mentally defective children near by. Settled c.1850.

Saint Marys, Lake, Ohio: see GRAND LAKE.

Saint Mary's Bay, inlet (40 mi. long, 25 mi. wide at entrance) of the Atlantic, SE N.F., on S coast of Avalon Peninsula, 50 mi. SW of St. John's; 46°55′N 53°45′W. Contains Colinet Isls. On shore are several fishing settlements and fish-canning plants.

Saint Marys City, historic village, St. Marys co., S Md., on St. Marys R. and 14 mi. ESE of Leonardtown. It was 1st town settled (1634) in Md.; Leonard Calvert's colonists took over small Piscataway Indian village here and built Fort St. George. In 1676, town became provincial ⊙; after capital's removal to Annapolis in 1694, and removal of co. seat to Leonardtown in 1710, town declined rapidly. Seat of St. Marys Female Seminary and Jr. Col. Has reproduction of 1st statehouse (1676), built 1934 as tercentenary memorial.

Saint Mary's Island or **Island of Saint Mary,** low, partly swampy sandbank (2,500 acres) in Gambia R. estuary (here 2½ mi. wide), Gambia colony, off Kombo mainland; 3½ mi. long, 1 mi. wide; 13°27′N 16°35′W. BATHURST occupies E half. Connected with mainland (W) by road bridge spanning narrow creek. Originally called Banjol; ceded 1816 to British and renamed St. Mary's.

Saint Mary's Loch (lŏkh), lake in W Selkirk, Scotland, 14 mi. WSW of Selkirk; at foot of Moffat Hills; 3 mi. long, ½ mi. wide. Outlet (NE): Yarrow Water. Connected (S) with small Loch of the Lowes. On S shore is Tibbie Shiels Inn; tourist resort. Lake is described in Scott's *Marmion.*

Saint Marys Locks, Mich.: see SAULT SAINTE MARIE CANALS.

Saint Mary's Park, SE N.Y., a residential section of S Bronx borough of New York city.

Saint Mary's Peak, Australia: see FLINDERS RANGES.

Saint Marys River. 1 In SE Ga. and NE Fla., rises in Okefenokee Swamp, Charlton co., Ga., flows S, E, and N in a great bend, then E to the Atlantic bet. Cumberland (Ga.) and Amelia (Fla.) isls.; 180 mi. long. Lower course tidal for 80 mi. and dredged; mouth crossed by Intracoastal Waterway. Forms part of Ga.-Fla. boundary. **2** In S Md., rises in SE St. Marys co., flows c.22 mi. SE, past Saint Marys City, to the Potomac c.8 mi. above its mouth. Its estuary (c.2 mi. wide at mouth) is a deepwater anchorage. **3** In central Ont. and NE Mich., issues from SE end (Whitefish Bay) of L. Superior, flows E to twin cities of Sault Sainte Marie (Ont. and Mich.), where SAULT SAINTE MARIE CANALS (Soo Canals) by-pass its rapids (19-ft. drop), then flows SE to NW end of L. Huron, which it enters through Detour Passage W of Drummond Isl. It is c.63 mi. long; forms part of international boundary. Widens into NICOLET, GEORGE, and MUNUSCONG lakes. SUGAR and NEEBISH isls. are in river. As sole water link bet. L. Superior and the lower Great Lakes, river is one of world's busiest waterways; during navigation season (6–7 months), it carries world's greatest annual tonnage of cargoes, chiefly iron ore and grain; other important cargoes are coal, limestone, lumber, oil, and copper. Hydroelectric plants at Sault Sainte Marie rapids. **4** In W Ohio and E Ind., rises in Auglaize co., Ohio, flows c.100 mi. NW, past St. Marys, Mendon, Rockford, and Willshire (Ohio) into Ind., past Decatur, to Fort Wayne, where it joins St. Joseph R. to form the Maumee.

Saint-Mathieu (sĕ-mätyû′), village (pop. 415), Haute-Vienne dept., W central France, 8 mi. SSW of Rochechouart; cider; wire mfg.

Saint-Mathieu, Pointe de (pwĕt dů), headland on the Atlantic, Finistère dept., W France, 14 mi. WSW of Brest, protecting N entrance to Brest Roads; 48°20′N 4°47′W.

Saint-Mathurin (sĕ-mätürē′), village (pop. 563), Maine-et-Loire dept., W France, on Loire R. and 12 mi. ESE of Angers; vegetables, flowers.

Saint Matthew Island (22 mi. long, 1–3 mi. wide), W Alaska, in Bering Sea, 170 mi. WNW of Nunivak Isl.; 60°22′N 172°25′W. Rocky and uninhabited, isl. is game sanctuary; rises to 1,500 ft.

Saint Matthews. 1 Village (1940 pop. 5,449), Jefferson co., N Ky., 9 mi. E of downtown Louisville; ships potatoes. **2** Town (pop. 2,351), ⊙ Calhoun co., central S.C., 13 mi. NNE of Orangeburg, in agr. area (cotton, truck, livestock); lumber, fertilizer, beverages. Settled in early 18th cent.

Saint Matthew's Island, in S Mergui Archipelago, Lower Burma, in Andaman Sea, 20 mi. W of Victoria Point; 10°N 98°10′E; 20 mi. long, 8 mi. wide; rises to 2,500 ft.

Saint Matthias Islands, Bismarck Archipelago: see MUSSAU.

Saint-Maur (sĕ-mōr′), village (pop. 594), Oran dept., NW Algeria, at foot of Tessala Mts., 20 mi. S of Oran; wheat growing.

Saint-Maur-des-Fossés (-dā-fōsā′), city (pop. 55,079), Seine dept., N central France, an ESE suburb of Paris, 8 mi. from Notre Dame Cathedral, within Marne R. bend; mfg. (flour products, hosiery, toys, fountain pens, furniture, morocco leather, electrical equipment, perfumes). Here in 1465 a treaty was signed by Louis XI and other members of the League of the Common Weal.

Saint Maurice (Fr. sĕ mōrēs′), county (□ 1,820; pop. 80,352), S Que., extends NW from the St. Lawrence; ⊙ Yamachiche.

Saint-Maurice (sĕ-mōrēs′), town (pop. 9,231), Seine dept., N central France, a SE suburb of Paris, 4 mi. from Notre Dame Cathedral, on right bank of the Marne just above its influx into the Seine, at S edge of Bois de Vincennes; mfg. of electric cables; flour milling. Site of large insane asylum commonly known as Charenton.

Saint-Maurice, town (pop. 2,699), Valais canton, SW Switzerland, on the Rhone and 17 mi. W of Sion; anc. Celtic *Agaunum*, later named after St. Maurice, a 4th-cent. martyr. Augustinian abbey (established 515), here, is oldest convent in Switzerland; its church was built in 17th cent. on site of an earlier (4th cent.); fine collection of antiquities. Aluminum is produced.

Saint-Maurice-de-Beynost (sĕ-mōrēs′-dů-bānō′), village (pop. 664), Ain dept., E France, 11 mi. NE of Lyons; rayon factory; truck gardens.

Saint Maurice River, Que., rises in central part of prov. on St. Lawrence–Hudson Bay watershed, flows 325 mi. SE and S, through Gouin Reservoir and several small lakes, past La Tuque, Grand'-Mère, and Shawinigan Falls, to the St. Lawrence at Trois Rivières. Main tributaries are Ribbon, Vermilion, Croche, and Bostonnais. Navigable below La Tuque. There are falls at La Tuque, Grand'Mère, and Shawinigan Falls.

Saint-Max (sĕ-mäks′), NE residential suburb (pop. 5,182) of Nancy, Meurthe-et-Moselle dept., NE France, on the Meurthe.

Saint-Maximin-la-Sainte-Baume (sĕ-mäksēmĕ′-lä-sĕt-bōm′), town (pop. 1,998), Var dept., SE France, in Lower Provence Alps, 23 mi. N of Toulon; road junction. Has fine provençal Gothic 13th–16th-cent. church containing tomb of St. Madeleine, and 14th–15th-cent. bldgs. of a once famous Dominican monastery. Grotto of Sainte-Baume (where St. Madeleine lived in penitence), a pilgrimage center, is 9 mi. SSW in Sainte-Baume range (c.3,000 ft. high), and 20 mi. E of Marseilles.

Saint-Médard-en-Jalles (sĕ-mädär′-ā-zhäl′), town (pop. 2,519), Gironde dept., SW France, on edge of the Landes, 8 mi. NW of Bordeaux. During Second World War its important powder works were blown up, damaging the town.

Saint-Méen-le-Grand (sĕ-mäã′-lů-grã′), village (pop. 1,777), Ille-et-Vilaine dept., W France, 24 mi. WNW of Rennes; dairying, leatherworking. Has 12th-13th-cent. remains of an abbey, founded c.600. Also Saint-Méen.

Saint Meinrad (mīn′rǔd), village, Spencer co., SW Ind., on small Anderson R. and 15 mi. N of Tell City. Seat of a Benedictine abbey and seminary.

Saint-Même or **Saint-Même-les-Carrières** (sĕ-mĕm′-lā-kärēâr′), village (pop. 772), Charente dept., W France, 8 mi. ESE of Cognac; noted brandy distilleries.

Saint Mewan, town and parish (pop. 1,442), central Cornwall, England, just WSW of St. Austell; China-clay mining. Has 15th-cent. church.

Saint Michael, village (pop. 157), W Alaska, on St. Michael Isl. (12 mi. long, 5–8 mi. wide), just off SE shore of Norton Sound, 110 mi. NE of mouth of Yukon R., 120 mi. SE of Nome; 63°29′N 162°1′W; trade and supply center; transshipment port for Yukon R. steamers, now declined in importance. Has territorial school; radio station. Established 1831 by Wrangel as trading post of Russian America Co.

Saint Michael, village (pop. estimate 200), central Alta., 40 mi. ENE of Edmonton; mixed farming, dairying.

Saint Michael, Finland: see MIKKELI.

Saint Michael. 1 Village (pop. 487), Wright co., E Minn., on Crow R. and 26 mi. NW of Minneapolis; dairy products. **2** Village (pop. 1,829), Cambria co., central Pa., 8 mi. E of Johnstown.

Saint Michael Island, Azores: see SÃO MIGUEL ISLAND.

Saint Michaels, town (pop. 1,470), Talbot co., E Md., on the Eastern Shore, 17 mi. NNW of Cambridge, on narrow neck bet. Miles R. and inlet of Choptank R.; oyster-dredging and fishing center; summer resort, with yachting. Many early clipper ships were built here.

Saint Michael's Bay, inlet (25 mi. long, 7 mi. wide at entrance) of the Atlantic, SE Labrador; 52°45′N 56°W. In entrance is Square Isl.

Saint Michael's Mount, island (21 acres; pop. 71), SW Cornwall, England, in Mounts Bay of the Channel, just off Marazion; 1 mi. in circumference; rises to over 200 ft. St. Aubyn's Castle (built on site of anc. priory), at summit, contains St. Michael's Chair (ruin of old lighthouse). Isl. became monastic fortress in 1047. At low tide it is connected with mainland by causeway.

Saint Michel, Que.: see CÔTE SAINT MICHEL.

Saint-Michel (sē-mēshĕl'). **1** Town (pop. 3,955), Aisne dept., N France, near Belg. border, 3 mi. E of Hirson; mfg. (stoves and kitchen ranges, shoes). **2** or **Saint-Michel-de-Maurienne** (–dù-mōrēĕn'), town (pop. 2,174), Savoie dept., SE France, in Alpine Maurienne valley, on Arc R. and 8 mi. SE of Saint-Jean-de-Maurienne; large high-grade steel (electric furnaces) and aluminum works. Explosives mfg., rice milling. Junction for Col du Galibier road. Damaged in Second World War.

Saint-Michel, Bay of, on English Channel, off NW France, indenting SW corner of Normandy and extending from Pointe du Grouin (W) to Carolles (NE); 13 mi. wide, 10 mi. long. Shallow and sandy SE part is uncovered at low tide. Contains MONT-SAINT MICHEL and Tombelaine isls. Receives Couësnon, Sée, and Sélune rivers. Chief port: Cancale. Also called Bay of Mont-Saint-Michel.

Saint-Michel, Mont-, France: see MONT-SAINT-MICHEL.

Saint Michel de Bellechasse (sē mēshĕl' dù bĕlshäs'), village (pop. estimate 700), S Que., on the St. Lawrence, opposite Île d'Orléans, 16 mi. ENE of Quebec; lumbering, dairying, pig raising.

Saint-Michel-de-l'Atalaye (–lätälā'), town (1950 census pop. 2,328), in Artibonite dept., N central Haiti, in Massif du Nord, 24 mi. ESE of Gonaïves, cotton- and tobacco-growing center. Sometimes called Saint-Michel-du-Nord.

Saint-Michel-de-Maurienne, France: see SAINT-MICHEL, Savoie dept.

Saint-Michel-du-Nord, Haiti: see SAINT-MICHEL-DE-L'ATALAYE.

Saint-Michel-du-Sud (–dü-süd'), village, Sud dept., SW Haiti, 34 mi. WSW of Léogane; coffeegrowing.

Saint-Michel-en-l'Herm (–ā-lârm'), village (pop. 1,707), Vendée dept., W France, in the Marais Poitevin, 22 mi. WSW of Fontenay-le-Comte; truck gardening. Remains of abbey founded 682.

Saint-Michel-lez-Bruges, Belgium: see SINT-MICHIELS.

Saint Michels, Finland: see MIKKELI.

Saint-Mihiel (sē-mēyĕl'), town (pop. 4,134), Meuse dept., NE France, on right bank of the Meuse (canalized) and 9 mi. NNW of Commercy; copper foundry; mfg. (furniture, eye-glasses, malt). Has 13th-18th-cent. Flamboyant church of Saint-Étienne (containing *Entombment* by Ligier Richier), and 17th–18th-cent. bldgs. of Benedictine abbey (founded 709). Captured by Germans in Sept., 1914, it formed tip of a German-held salient (which cut the vital Verdun-Toul-Nancy rail link) until victorious American attack of Sept., 1918. Atop near-by Montsec is Saint-Mihiel American Memorial. Saint-Mihiel American Cemetery is at Thiaucourt (15 mi. ENE).

Saint Moïse (sē mōēz'), village (pop. 836), E Que., at base of Gaspé Peninsula, 25 mi. SW of Matane; lumbering, dairying.

Saint Monance, formerly **Saint Monan's** (both: (mō'nùns), burgh (1931 pop. 1,819; 1951 census 1,517), E Fifeshire, Scotland, on the Firth of Forth, 3 mi. NE of Elie; fishing port and resort frequented by artists. Has church built c.1362 by David II.

Saint Moritz (sänt mùrĭts'), Fr. *Saint-Moritz* (sē-môrēts'), Ger. *Sankt Moritz* (zängkt mō'rĭts), Romansh *San Murezzan* (sùn' mo͞orĕts'ùn), town (pop. 2,418), Grisons canton, SE Switzerland, on Inn R. and on L. of St. Moritz, in Upper ENGADINE, surrounded by magnificent peaks; winter and summer resort. Known as early as the 15th cent., and originally noted for its curative mineral springs, it developed into one of the world's greatest winter sports centers (several Olympic winter games have been held here). Town consists of St. Moritz-Dorf (6,080 ft.), with the Leaning Tower of a Romanesque church, Seganti (art) and Engadine (historical) museums; and St. Moritz-Bad (5,824 ft.), with mineral baths. Includes resort hamlet of Campfèr.

Saint Moritz, Lake of, Ger. *Sankt Moritzersee* (zängkt″ mō'rĭtsùrzā″), Grisons canton, SE Switzerland; less than □ 1, alt. 5,869 ft. St. Moritz is on W shore.

Saint-Nabord (sē-näbôr'), commune (pop. 1,830), Vosges dept., E France, on the Moselle and 2 mi. N of Remiremont; textile and paper milling.

Saint-Nazaire (sē-näzâr'), town (1946 pop. 4,408; 1936 pop. 37,710), Loire-Inférieure dept., W France, seaport at mouth of Loire R. and 30 mi. WNW of Nantes; metallurgical center, with France's largest shipbuilding yards (Penhoët Basin). Smelting of imported alloys, mfg. of chemical fertilizer. As outport of Nantes, it is accessible to largest vessels and has important transshipment trade. Harbor enlarged and modernized in First World War to receive British and American expeditionary forces. After 1940, chief Ger. submarine base on the Atlantic. Almost completely destroyed by Allied bombing (1941–44). Surrounded by Allied armies Aug., 1944; surrendered May, 1945. Shipyards again in operation 1948.

Saint Nazianz (sānt″ nä'zēänts), village (pop. c.500), Manitowoc co., E Wis., 14 mi. WSW of Manitowoc. Seat of Salvatorian Seminary (R.C.). Settled 1854 by colony of German Christian communists.

Saint-Nectaire (sē-nĕktâr'), village (pop. 385), Puy-de-Dôme dept., central France, in Monts Dore, 14 mi. SSW of Clermont-Ferrand; noted spa with mineral springs for kidney diseases. Old village (Saint-Nectaire-le-Haut) has fine 12th-cent. Romanesque church.

Saint Neot (sùnt nēt'), agr. village and parish (pop. 1,009), E Cornwall, England, on Fowey R. and 5 mi. NW of Liskeard.

Saint Neots (sùnt nēts', nē'ùts), urban district (1931 pop. 4,314; 1951 census 4,697), S Huntingdon, England, on Ouse R. and 8 mi. SSW of Huntingdon; agr. market, with iron foundries and paper mills. Has fine 15th-cent. church and bridge dating from 14th cent. Site of abbey founded by St. Neot, reputed brother or relative of King Alfred. The 1st modern paper machine was built here 1799. In urban dist. (S) is Eynesbury (pop. 1,296).

Saint Nicholas Island, Cape Verde Isls.: see SÃO NICOLAU ISLAND.

Saint Nicholas Point, Indonesian *Tanjung Pujut* (tänjo͝ong' po͝ojo͝ot'), Du. *Sint Nicolaas Punt* (sĭnt″ nē'kōläs po͝ont'), on Java Sea, NW Java, Indonesia, on NE side of entrance to Sunda Strait; 5°53'S 106°2'E. In Second World War, naval action (Feb., 1942) offshore in battle of Java Sea.

Saint-Nicolas (sē-nēkōlä'), Flemish *Sint-Niklaas* (sĭnt-nĭ'kläs). **1** Town (pop. 44,612), East Flanders prov., N Belgium, 12 mi. WSW of Antwerp; textile center (wool, artificial silk), carpet weaving, mfg. of drainage pipes. Trade center for the rich agr. area Pays de Waas. Has 16th–17th-cent. church, local mus. **2** Town (pop. 9,274), Liége prov., E Belgium, 2 mi. W of Liége; coal mining. Has 11th-cent. Romanesque chapel. Grape-growing center until 18th cent.

Saint-Nicolas or **Saint-Nicolas-de-Port** (–dù-pôr'), town (pop. 4,617), Meurthe-et-Moselle dept., NE France, on Meurthe R. and Marne-Rhine Canal and 7 mi. SE of Nancy; breweries, textile mill. Salt mines near by. Its 15th–16th-cent. Flamboyant church heavily damaged in 1940. Sometimes called Saint-Nicolas-du-Port.

Saint Nicolas, Cape (sē nēkôlä'), NW Haiti, on Windward Passage, 2½ mi. SW of Môle-Saint-Nicolas; 19°48'N 73°25'W.

Saint-Nicolas-d'Aliermont (sē-nēkōlä'-dälyĕrmō'), town (pop. 2,339), Seine-Inférieure dept., N France, 7 mi. SE of Dieppe; clock-mfg. center.

Saint-Nicolas-de-la-Grave (–dù-lä-gräv'), village (pop. 749), Tarn-et-Garonne dept., SW France, near the Garonne, 5 mi. WNW of Castelsarrasin; cereals, cattle, poultry.

Saint-Nicolas-de-Port, Meurthe-et-Moselle dept., France: see SAINT-NICOLAS.

Saint-Nicolas-de-Redon (–dù-rùdō'), village (pop. 846), Loire-Inférieure dept., W France, on Brest-Nantes Canal and 1 mi. ESE of Redon; sawmilling, fertilizer mfg.

Saint-Nicolas-du-Pélem (–dü-pālĕm'), village (pop. 946, Côtes-du-Nord dept., W France, 17 mi. S of Guingamp; dairying, cider milling. Near-by gorge of Blavet R. attracts tourists.

Saint-Nicolas-près-Granville (–prĕ-grävĕl'), village (pop. 1,343), Manche dept., NW France, on the Channel, 2 mi. E of Granville; fertilizer mfg.

Saint Ninians (sùnt nĭ'nēùnz), industrial suburb and parish (pop. 14,757), NE Stirlingshire, Scotland, just S of Stirling. Parish includes BANNOCKBURN.

Saint Norbert (Fr. sē nôrbâr'), village (pop. estimate 800), S Man., on Red R. and 10 mi. S of Winnipeg; farming; grain, stock; honey processing. Site of Trappist monastery of Notre Dame des Prairies.

Saint Octave (sētôktäv'), village (pop. estimate 500), E Que., near the St. Lawrence, 23 mi. NE of Rimouski; lumbering, dairying.

Saint Olaf, town (pop. 158), Clayton co., NE Iowa, 6 mi. N of Elkader, in agr. and dairying region; feed milling.

Saint-Omer (sētōmâr'), town (pop. 15,785), Pas-de-Calais dept., N France, on canalized Aa R. and 22 mi. SE of Calais; commercial and industrial center in polder-like intensive truck-farming region (locally called *lègres*); foundries, Portland cement- and brickworks, sugar mills, breweries, hosiery and lingerie factories. Vegetable and fruit shipping. Important paper industry in near-by lower Aa valley (Lumbres, Wizernes, Blendecques). Glass and crystal-works in suburban Arques. Rich in medieval art and architecture. Its fine Gothic basilica (formerly cathedral) of Notre Dame (13th–14th cent.) was slightly damaged in Second World War. Underwent many sieges before being annexed to France in 1677 by Louis XIV. Br. general hq., 1914–16, in First World War. Heavily bombed in Second World War.

Saint Omer (sùnt ō'mùr), village (pop. 43), N S.Isl., New Zealand, 8 mi. NNE of Picton and on Pelorus Sound; tourist center; sheep.

Saintonge (sētōzh'), region and former province, W France, on Bay of Biscay N of Gironde estuary, now forming most of Charente-Maritime, and part of Charente and Deux-Sèvres depts.; historical ⊙ Saintes. Chiefly agr. (cattle raising, dairying, winegrowing), it is noted for its cognac distilleries. Saltworks and oyster beds in coastal area. Occupied by Santones in Roman times; later became subfief of Aquitaine. After its reconquest from the English, Saintonge became part (1372) of Fr. royal domain.

Saint Osyth (sùnt ō'sĭth), agr. village and parish (pop. 1,463), E Essex, England, 4 mi. E of Clacton-on-Sea. Site of 12th-cent. remains of anc. St. Osyth's Priory, scene of murder (c.870) of East Saxon queen Osyth by Danes.

Saint Ouen (sùnt wän', Fr. sēto͞oā'), agr. village and parish (1945 pop. 1,537), Jersey, Channel Isls., near St. Ouen Bay, 6 mi. WNW of St. Helier. Has 13th-cent. church and fortified manor house dating from 13th cent. Post office name, St. Ouen's.

Saint-Ouen (sēto͞oā'). **1** City (pop. 45,360), Seine dept., N central France, just N of Paris, 4 mi. from Notre Dame Cathedral, N of Montmartre; center of electrical industry; automobile construction; machine-tool mfg., liqueur distilling. In its castle (since dismantled) Louis XVIII signed (1814) declaration of Saint-Ouen. Also called Saint-Ouen-sur-Seine. **2** Town (pop. 2,465), Somme dept., N France, 13 mi. NW of Amiens; furniture mfg.

Saint-Ouen-l'Aumône (–lōmōn'), town (pop. 3,700), Seine-et-Oise dept., N central France, on left bank of Oise R., opposite Pontoise; rail center (workshops); mfg. of chemicals. Its Oise R. port damaged in Second World War.

Saint Ours (sēto͞or'), town (pop. 600), S Que., on Richelieu R. and 12 mi. S of Sorel; shoe mfg., woodworking, flour milling; market in dairying region.

Saint-Ours, village (pop. 207), Puy-de-Dôme dept., central France, in Auvergne Mts., 10 mi. WNW of Clermont-Ferrand; electrolytic copper smelting.

Saint Pacôme (sē päkōm'), village (pop. 1,254), SE Que., near the St. Lawrence, 35 mi. SSW of Rivière du Loup; dairying, lumbering, pig raising.

Saint-Pair-sur-Mer (sē-pâr-sür-mâr'), village (pop. 1,586), Manche dept., NW France, bathing resort on the Channel, 2 mi. SE of Granville.

Saint-Palais (sē-pälā'), village (pop. 1,389), Basses-Pyrénées dept., SW France, 17 mi. SW of Orthez; horse and poultry raising, dairying.

Saint Pancras (sùnt păng'krùs), metropolitan borough (1931 pop. 198,133; 1951 census 138,364) of London, England, N of the Thames, 2 mi. N of Charing Cross. Borough includes part of BLOOMSBURY, and Euston and St. Pancras stations, important railroad termini for N England and Scotland. It is named for 4th-cent. Roman boy martyr, popular in medieval England.

Saint-Pardoux-la-Rivière (sē-pärdo͞o'-lä-rēvyâr'), village (pop. 861), Dordogne dept., SW France, on the Dronne and 5 mi. ESE of Nontron; mfg. (edge-tools, copper ware), tanning.

Saint Paris, village (pop. 1,422), Champaign co., W central Ohio, 11 mi. W of Urbana; honey, grain. Settled 1813.

Saint Pascal (sē päskäl'), village (pop. 1,265), ⊙ Kamouraska co., SE Que., near the St. Lawrence, 25 mi. SSW of Rivière du Loup; dairying, lumbering, pig raising.

Saint-Paterne (sē-pätârn'), agr. village (pop. 108), Sarthe dept., W France, near Sarthe R., 2 mi. SE of Alençon.

Saint Patrick, county (□ 260.80; pop. 69,170), SW Trinidad, B.W.I., bordering on the Gulf of Paria (N) and the Serpent's Mouth (S).

Saint Patrick Channel, arm (20 mi. long, up to 4 mi. wide) of Great Bras d'Or, NE N.S., in central part of Cape Breton Isl. On N side of entrance is village of Baddeck.

Saint Patrick's Island, islet of The Skerries, in the Irish Sea, just E of Skerries town, NE Co. Dublin, Ireland.

Saint Paul or **Saint Paul de Métis** (Fr. sē pôl dù mātē'), town (pop. 1,187), E Alta., near small Upper Therien L., 50 mi. NNW of Vermilion; grain elevators, fruit canning, lumbering, dairying; mfg. of chemicals, castings.

Saint-Paul (sē-pôl'). **1** or **Saint-Paul-sur-Ubaye** (–sür-übī'), Alpine village (pop. 84), Basses-Alpes dept., SE France in upper Ubaye valley, near Ital. border, 10 mi. NNE of Barcelonnette, just SE of Col de Vars; alt. 4,823 ft. **2** or **Saint-Paul-de-Fenouillet** (–dù-fùno͞oyā'), town (pop. 2,004), Pyrénées-Orientales dept., S France, on Agly R. and 14 mi. NNE of Prades; produces biscuits, plaster, soap; woodworking, winegrowing. Iron mines near by. Gorge of Galamus (3 mi. N) attracts tourists.

Saint-Paul, town (pop. 4,770; commune pop. 25,959), on NW coast of Réunion isl., on railroad and 15 mi. SW of Saint-Denis; agr. processing (sugar, alcohol, rum, vanilla); grain. Original settlement and port for Réunion. Near by (SW) is beach resort of Saint-Gilles-les-Bains.

Saint Paul. 1 Town (pop. 136), Madison co., NW Ark., 26 mi. SE of Fayetteville, in the Ozarks. **2** Town (pop. 669), on Decatur-Shelby co. line, SE central Ind., 11 mi. SE of Shelbyville, in agr. area. 3 Town (pop. 113), Lee co., SE Iowa, 28 mi. NNW of Keokuk, in livestock area. 4 City (pop. 783), Neosho co., SE Kansas, on Neosho R. and 14 mi. NNE of Parsons; shipping point for stock-raising and general-farming area. Gas wells near by. 5 City (pop. 311,349), ⊙ Minn. and Ramsey co., E Minn., on high bluffs overlooking Mississippi R. at mouth of Minnesota R., adjacent to Minneapolis, and c.350 mi. NW of Chicago; 44°56′N 93°05′W; alt. 703 ft. Second largest city in state, port of entry, and commercial, industrial, and transportation center served by several air lines and numerous railroads. Chief industries are meat packing and dairy products. Produces canned goods, beverages, and ice cream, and has large assembly plant of Ford Motor Co. Manufactures refrigeration and dental equipment, hoists and derricks, clothing, paint, and paper and foundry products. Printing and publishing are important and long-established activities; *Pioneer Press*, dating back to 1849, is one of oldest newspapers in the Middle West. Earliest settlement took place in early 1800s in vicinity of MENDOTA fur-trading post and Fort Snelling. Traders, lumbermen, and settlers made their homes here, and in 1841 it was named St. Paul, after the church erected here by Father Lucian Galtier. Location at head of navigation on Mississippi R. was important factor in early development. Became territorial capital 1849, was inc. as city 1854, made state capital 1858, when Minn. was admitted to Union. Grew as trade and supply point for settlers and immigrants from E, including group of Irish Catholics led by Bishop Ireland. In 1870s, became center of railroad empire of James J. Hill. St. Paul and Minneapolis, the Twin Cities, are the metropolis of vast agr. area. Residential area has wide streets and numerous parks, 2 largest of which, Como and Phalen, have lakes and recreation facilities. Points of interest are Cathedral of St. Paul (R.C.; begun 1906, dedicated 1915), capitol (completed 1904, designed by Cass Gilbert), state historical society building (with mus. and library), St. Paul Inst. (with science collections), and 19-story building (City Hall and Ramsey Co. Courthouse), completed 1932, which houses legal chambers and peace memorial designed by Carl Milles. Institutions of education are Hamline Univ. (Methodist), Macalester Col. (Presbyterian), Col. of St. Thomas (R.C.), and St. Paul School of Art. Agr. branch of state univ. and state fairgrounds are in St. Paul part of the Midway, district that includes sections of both St. Paul and Minneapolis. Robert Street Bridge (built 1926, 1,920 ft. long) is one of several bridges across Mississippi R. State fish hatchery and Holman Airport are in outskirts. Fort Snelling, historic military outpost completed 1823 and now used as military training camp, is just SW. 6 City (pop. 1,676), ⊙ Howard co., E central Nebr., 20 mi. N of Grand Island, near confluence of N.Loup and Middle Loup rivers; trade and shipping center for agr. area; flour; grain, livestock, dairy and poultry products. Founded 1871. 7 City (pop. 226), Marion co., NW Oregon, 18 mi. N of Salem. 8 Town (pop. 1,014), Wise co., SW Va., on Clinch R. and 17 mi. E of Norton in agr. and coal area; rail junction.

Saint Paul, Cape, SE Gold Coast, on Gulf of Guinea, 23 mi. E of Ada; 5°47′N 0°56′E; lighthouse.

Saint-Paul-Cap-de-Joux (sē-pôl-käp-dů-zhōō′), village (pop. 603), Tarn dept., S France; on Agout R. 14 mi. WNW of Castres; lingerie mfg. Limekilns.

Saint-Paul-de-Fenouillet, France: see SAINT-PAUL.

Saint Paul de Métis, Alta.: see SAINT PAUL.

Saint Paul du Nord (dü nôr′), village (pop. estimate 250), E Que., on the St. Lawrence and 30 mi. WNW of Rimouski; lumbering center.

Saint-Paul-en-Jarez (-ā-zhärā′), village (pop. 1,196), Loire dept., E central France, in the Jarez, 9 mi. ENE of Saint-Étienne; mfg. of pencils, lighters.

Saint-Paulien (sē-pôlyē′), anc. *Revessco*, village (pop. 900), Haute-Loire dept., S central France, in Monts du Velay, 7 mi. NNW of Le Puy; lacemaking; brickworks. Ancient ⊙ of the Vellaves, a Gallic tribe, and, until 6th cent., seat of bishops of Velay.

Saint Paulin (sē pôlē′), village (pop. 752), S Que., 23 mi. W of Trois Rivières; dairying, pig raising.

Saint Paul Island (14 mi. long, 2–8 mi. wide; pop. 359), Pribilof Isls., SW Alaska, in Bering Sea; 57°11′N 170°16′W; rises to 665 ft. Fox and fur-seal hunting. St. Paul village in S.

Saint Paul Island (3 mi. long, 1 mi. wide), in Cabot Strait, bet. the Atlantic and the Gulf of St. Lawrence, off NE N.S., 16 mi. NE of Cape North, Cape Breton Isl.; 47°12′N 60°9′W.

Saint Paul Island, outlying dependency (□ 3) of Madagascar, in S of Indian Ocean, c.2,800 mi. off SE coast of Africa, 1,000 mi. NE of Kerguelen Isls. and S of Amsterdam Isl., 38°43′S 77°31′E; 3 mi. long, 1½ mi. wide. A broken volcanic crater invaded by sea, it rises to 1,618 ft.; numerous thermal springs. Insular waters abound with langoustes, seals, fish. Discovered in 16th cent.; temporarily settled (18th cent.) by fishermen from Réunion; claimed by France 1843. A langouste-canning plant functioned here, 1908–39.

Saint-Paul-lès-Dax, France: see DAX.

Saint-Paul-Lizonne, France: see VERTEILLAC.

Saint Paul Park, village (pop. 2,438), Washington co., E Minn., on Mississippi R. just SE of St. Paul, in grain, potato, livestock area; oil refinery.

Saint Paul River, W central Liberia, rises in 2 branches on Fr. Guinea border, flows c.125 mi. SW, past White Plains (head of navigation), to the Atlantic 4 mi. N of Monrovia, forming 2 arms which enclose Bushrod Isl., site of port of Monrovia and modern cold-storage plant. River was bridged 1949 for rail and road traffic to Bomi Hills.

Saint Paul Rocks, Port. *Rochedos São Paulo*, uninhabited rocky islets in the Atlantic, c.600 mi. NE of Natal, Brazil. Braz. possession; 0°23′N 29°23′W. Sometimes called St. Peter and St. Paul.

Saint Pauls, town (pop. 2,251), Robeson co., S N.C., 18 mi. S of Fayetteville; textile and lumber mills.

Saint Paul's Bay, village (parish pop. 3,440), NE Malta, seaside resort and fishing port on St. Paul's Bay. Its Old Church of St. Paul (16th cent.) was bombed during Second World War. Among fortifications of the bay is the large Wignacourt Tower (1610). A megalithic temple is near by. Here and at tiny Selmun Isl., St. Paul is believed to have been shipwrecked.

Saint Paul's Cray, residential town and parish (pop. 2,172), NW Kent, England, on Cray R. just N of Orpington; paper milling. Has 13th-cent. church.

Saint Pauls Harbor, Alaska: see KODIAK.

Saint-Paul-sur-Ubaye, France: see SAINT-PAUL, Basses-Alpes dept.

Saint-Paul-Trois-Châteaux (sē-pôl-trwä-shätō′), village (pop. 751), Drôme dept., SE France, 15 mi. NNW of Orange; quarries. Has former cathedral (12th-cent. Romanesque).

Saint-Pé or **Saint-Pé-de-Bigorre** (sē-pā′-dů-bēgôr′), village (pop. 1,034), Hautes-Pyrénées dept., SW France, on Gave de Pau R. and 7 mi. NNW of Argelès-Gazost; woodworking, biscuit mfg.

Saint-Péray (sē-pārā′), village (pop. 1,725), Ardèche dept., S France, near Rhone R., 3 mi. WNW of Valence; known for its sparkling wines.

Saint-Perdoux (sē-pĕrdōō′), village (pop. 16), Lot dept., SW France, 5 mi. N of Figeac; coal mining.

Saint-Père-en-Retz (sē-pâr-ā-rĕs′), village (pop. 856), Loire-Inférieure dept., W France, 9 mi. ESE of Saint-Nazaire; dairying.

Saint Peter, Fr. *Saint-Pierre* (sē-pyâr′), agr. village and parish (1945 pop. 1,891), Jersey, Channel Isls., 4 mi. NW of St. Helier. Site of Jersey airport. Post office name St. Peter's.

Saint Peter. 1 Village (pop. 354), Fayette co., S central Ill., 15 mi. ESE of Vandalia, in agr. area. **2** City (pop. 7,754), ⊙ Nicollet co., S Minn., on Minnesota R. and 11 mi. N of Mankato; trade and mfg. center for grain, livestock, and poultry area; dairy products, beverages, overalls, tiles, cement blocks. Settled 1853, inc. 1865. Gustavus Adolphus Col. and state hosp. are here. Near by is Traverse des Sioux State Park, on site of which treaty was signed (1851) with Sioux Indians.

Saint Peter, Lake (□ 130), S Que., expansion of the St. Lawrence, extending 30 mi. ENE from Sorel almost to Trois Rivières; 9 mi. wide. Receives St. Francis, Yamaska, Nicolet, and several smaller rivers. At SW end of lake are several isls.

Saint Peter, Point, cape at E end of Gaspé Peninsula, E Que., on the Gulf of St. Lawrence, on S side of Gaspé Bay, 20 mi. SE of Gaspé; 48°37′N 64°10′W; lighthouse.

Saint Peter-in-the-Wood or **Saint-Pierre-du-Bois** (sē-pyâr′-dü-bwä′), agr. village and parish (1931 pop. 1,653), Guernsey, Channel Isls., 4 mi. WSW of St. Peter Port.

Saint Peter Island, largest of Nuyts Archipelago, in Denial Bay of Great Australian Bight, 2 mi. off S coast of South Australia; 8 mi. long, 4 mi. wide; tapers (NE) to long, sandy point. Grassy hills; geese, petrels.

Saint Peter Port, Fr. *Saint-Pierre* (sē-pyâr′), town and parish (1931 pop. 16,720), ⊙ Guernsey, Channel Isls., on E coast of isl.; 49°27′N 2°32′W; has shallow, protected port, shipping dairy products, vegetables, fruit, flowers. Castle Cornet dates from 13th cent. In suburb of Hauteville is Hauteville House, long-time residence of Victor Hugo. Church of St. Peter dates from 14th cent. Elizabeth Col., boys' school, was founded 1563.

Saint Peters. 1 Municipality (pop. 12,404), E New South Wales, Australia, 4 mi. SW of Sydney, in metropolitan area; mfg. (shoes, furniture), brass foundries. **2** E residential suburb (pop. 12,522) of Adelaide, SE South Australia.

Saint Peters. 1 Village (pop. estimate 800), E N.S., S Cape Breton Isl., on canal (bridge) linking Bras d'Or L. and the Atlantic, 23 mi. E of Port Hawkesbury; fishing port. In early 17th cent. it was fishing and trading station, later a fort. **2** or **Saint Peters Bay,** village (pop. estimate 400), NE P.E.I., at head of St. Peters Bay of the Gulf of St. Lawrence, 30 mi. ENE of Charlottetown; cod, lobster, hake fisheries.

Saint Peter's, England: see BROADSTAIRS.

Saint Peters, Japan: see TORI-SHIMA.

Saint Peters, town (pop. 377), St. Charles co., E Mo., 7 mi. W of St. Charles.

Saint Peters Bay, P.E.I.: see SAINT PETERS.

Saint Petersburg, Russia: see LENINGRAD, city.

Saint Petersburg. 1 City (pop. 96,738), Pinellas co., W Fla., 18 mi. SW of Tampa, at S end of Pinellas peninsula; port of entry on Tampa Bay, spanned here by Gandy Bridge to Tampa area. Popular winter resort, called the "Sunshine City" for its annual average of 360 sunny days. Mfg. (fishing tackle, preserves, millwork, concrete products, shell novelties). Places of interest include the yacht basin, municipal pier, historical mus., an alligator basin, and large shell mounds on site of an Indian village. City has a jr. col., a U.S. coast guard base. It is the winter training ground of big-league baseball teams. Near by is a U.S. veterans hospital. First settled in mid-19th cent.; but city's real founder was John C. Williams, who came c.1876. Railroad arrived in late 1880s. St. Petersburg was inc. 1903. **2** Borough (pop. 451), Clarion co., W central Pa., 18 mi. S of Oil City.

Saint Petersburg Beach, town (pop. 722), Pinellas co., W Fla., near St. Petersburg.

Saint Peter's Island, islet in the Atlantic, E N.S., off S Cape Breton Isl., 7 mi. SE of St. Peters.

Saint Peters Island, islet at entrance of Hillsborough Bay, S P.E.I., 8 mi. SSW of Charlottetown; 46°7′N 63°11′W; lighthouse.

Saint-Philbert-de-Grand-Lieu (sē-fēlbâr′-dů-grãlyû′), village (pop. 1,001), Loire-Inférieure dept., W France, near L. of Grand-Lieu, 12 mi. SSW of Nantes; cheese, ducks. Has church containing 9th-cent. tomb of St. Philibert (founder of abbey of Jumièges in Normandy), and parts of a Carolingian nave.

Saint Philip, Fort, La.: see TRIUMPH.

Saint-Philippe (sē-fēlēp′), town (pop. 1,065; commune pop. 2,355), on SE coast of Réunion isl., on road and 18 mi. ESE of Saint-Pierre; vanilla processing; sugar cane.

Saint Phillips Island, Beaufort co., S S.C., one of Sea Isls., NE of entrance to Port Royal Sound; 6 mi. long.

Saint Pie (sē pē′), village (pop. 1,009), S Que., on tributary of Yamaska R. and 9 mi. SSE of St. Hyacinthe; woodworking, dairying; cattle, pigs.

Saint Pie de Guire (sē pē dů gēr′), village (pop. estimate 250), ⊙ Yamaska co., S Que., near St. Francis R., 18 mi. ESE of Sorel; dairying, pig raising.

Saint Pierre, Que., near Montreal: see VILLE SAINT PIERRE.

Saint-Pierre. 1 Guernsey, Channel Isls.: see SAINT PETER PORT. **2** Jersey, Channel Isls. see SAINT PETER.

Saint-Pierre or **Saint-Pierre-d'Oléron** (sē-pyâr-dôlārō′), village (pop. 1,186), Charente-Maritime dept., W France, in center of Île d'Oléron, 16 mi. W of Rochefort; vegetables; winegrowing, distilling; saltworks.

Saint-Pierre, town (pop. 4,847; commune pop. 6,218), NW Martinique, minor port on the Caribbean, 11 mi. NW of Fort-de-France, in sugar-growing region; rum distilling. Has customhouse, mus., and geological research laboratory. Founded 1635 by Fr. settlers under Esnambuc, it was the leading commercial center of the isl. until completely destroyed by eruption (May 8, 1902) of Mont PELÉE. Of the flourishing city's inhabitants (c.28,000), only one person survived. Many tourists now visit the ruins.

Saint Pierre, village (pop.285), W central Mauritius, in central plateau, on railroad and 5 mi. SSE of Port Louis; sugar milling, alcohol distilling.

Saint-Pierre, chief town (pop. 13,539; commune pop. 22,379) of S Réunion isl., ⊙ Leeward dist., fishing port on S coast, 31 mi. S of Saint-Denis. Linked with Saint-Benoît by coastal railroad and cross-isl. road. Agr. processing (sugar, rum, vanilla); food canning; tanning. Geranium plantations. R.C. and Seventh Day Adventist missions, maternity hospital, orphanage. Formerly a whaling supply port.

Saint Pierre (sānt pēâr′, Fr. sē pyâr′), town, ⊙ SAINT PIERRE AND MIQUELON territory, on E shore of tiny Saint Pierre isl. (□ c.10; 1946 pop. 3,636), c.180 mi. WSW of St. John's, Newfoundland (from which it is separated by c.15-mi.-wide channel); 46°46′N 56°11′W. An important cod-fishing station (canning and salting); connected by cable with American mainland and Europe. Due to tempering influence of the Gulf Stream, its fine port is free of ice throughout the year. Town retains old Fr. colonial and Norman atmosphere, but was badly damaged by 1939 fire. Saint Pierre isl. has 7 islet dependencies: Grand Colombier and Petit Colombier just NE; Île aux MARINS (E); Île aux Pigeons; Île aux Vainqueurs (Lazaret); Île aux Moules; and Île aux Massacres. Ownership of Île Verte (lighthouse) is shared with the British.

Saint-Pierre, Île (ēl sē-pyâr′), Ger. *Sankt Peters Insel* (zängkt pā′tůrs ĭn′zůl), highest point of peninsula jutting out into L. Biel, W Switzerland, 7 mi. SW of Biel; an isl. until 1875; once a residence of Rousseau. Former priory here.

Saint Pierre and Miquelon (sānt pēâr′, mĭ′kůlŏn), Fr. *Saint-Pierre-et-Miquelon* (sē-pyâr′-ā-mēkůlō′), Fr. territory and archipelago (□ 93; 1946 pop. 4,354); ⊙ Saint Pierre. Just off S Newfoundland (separated by c.15-mi.-wide channel), it consists of the isls. of SAINT PIERRE (SE) and MIQUELON (W). To Saint Pierre belong several tiny islet dependencies, among them Île aux MARINS. The archipelago is situated bet. 46°45'–47°7'N and 56°5'–56°25'W. Entire economy depends on cod fishing, for which town of Saint Pierre is an important base, near the Grand Banks. Fish salting, drying, and canning are principal industries. There is some silver-fox breeding; seal skins are also exported. Practically all consumer goods have to be imported, since the rocky isls. support only an evergreen scrub vegetation. On Miquelon are slate and ocher deposits. Saint Pierre is connected by cable with the mainland. Shipping service to Sydney and Halifax; airline to Sydney. Due to tempering influence of the Gulf Stream, the port of Saint Pierre is free of ice throughout the year. The climate is typically maritime, with heavy fogs. Isl.'s inhabitants are mostly of Norman French descent and are strongly R.C. The last residual of France's once-vast colonial empire in North America (outside the West Indies), the archipelago was known to Breton and Basque fishermen as early as 16th cent., but permanent settlement developed after the expulsion of the French from Acadia in 1763. The group was taken by the British several times during 18th cent. and early 19th cent., but has been in continuous Fr. possession since 1814 (Treaty of Paris). Saint Pierre profited greatly through bootlegging trade during prohibition in U.S. In Second World War, after the fall of France, the territory came under the authority of the Vichy govt. In Dec., 1941, a Free French naval force captured the isls., but the old regime was restored upon U.S. pressure. Group became (1946) a territory within the French Union and is represented in the parliamentary bodies of France.

Saint-Pierre-d'Albigny (sē-pyâr-dälbēnyē'), village (pop. 906), Savoie dept., SE France, in Isère R. valley, at S foot of the Bauges, 11 mi. E of Chambéry; red wines. Medieval castle of Miolans overlooks valley 2 mi. NE.

Saint-Pierre-d'Allevard (–dälvär'), village (pop. 805), Isère dept., SE France, 2 mi. SW of Allevard, in Belledonne range of Dauphiné Alps; iron mines supply Allevard electrometallurgical works.

Saint-Pierre-de-Boeuf (–dů-bûf'), village (pop. 718), Loire dept., SE central France, on the Rhone and 18 mi. ESE of Saint-Étienne; crepe de Chine weaving.

Saint-Pierre-de-Chartreuse (–shärtrůz'), village (pop. 167), Isère dept., SE France, in Grande Chartreuse, 11 mi. NNE of Grenoble; alt. c.2,900 ft. Winter-sports resort. Celebrated monastery of La Grande Chartreuse is 2 mi. NW.

Saint-Pierre-de-Chignac (–shēnyäk'), village (pop. 279), Dordogne dept., SW France, 7 mi. SE of Périgueux; fruits, vegetables.

Saint-Pierre-des-Corps (–dā-kôr'), SE suburb (pop. 6,595) of Tours, Indre-et-Loire dept., W central France; important railroad center with freight yards and repair shops; mfg. of chemical fertilizer.

Saint-Pierre-d'Oléron, France: see SAINT-PIERRE.

Saint Pierre d'Orléans (dôrlāā'), village (pop. estimate 400), S Que., on NW shore of the Île d'Orléans, on the St. Lawrence and 10 mi. NE of Quebec; dairying; vegetables, poultry.

Saint Pierre du Bois, Guernsey, Channel Isls.: see SAINT PETER-IN-THE-WOOD.

Saint-Pierre-du-Regard (–dü-růgär'), village (pop. 361), Orne dept., NW France, just S of Condé-sur-Noireau (Calvados dept.); hosiery and chocolate factories.

Saint-Pierre-Église (–āglēz'), village (pop. 1,120), Manche dept., NW France, near NE extremity of Cotentin Peninsula, 10 mi. ENE of Cherbourg; dairying. Abbé de Saint-Pierre b. here.

Saint-Pierre-en-Port (–ā-pôr'), village (pop. 1,037), Seine-Inférieure dept., N France, resort on English Channel, 6 mi. NE of Fécamp; fishing. Les Grandes-Dalles (1 mi. NE) has small beach and sanatorium.

Saint-Pierre-et-Miquelon, Fr. territory: see SAINT PIERRE AND MIQUELON.

Saint Pierre Island, outlying dependency (pop. 84) of the Seychelles, near Farquhar Isls., in Indian Ocean, 200 mi. NNE of N tip of Madagascar; 9°19'S 50°43'E; guano.

Saint Pierre-Jolys (sē pyâr-zhôlē'), village (pop. estimate 1,000), SE Man., on Joubert Creek and 30 mi. SSE of Winnipeg; dairying; grain.

Saint-Pierre-la-Palud (–lä-pälü'), village (pop. 238), Rhône dept., E central France, 11 mi. W of Lyons; copper and pyrite mines.

Saint-Pierre-le-Moûtier (–lů-mōōtyā'), village (pop. 1,472), Nièvre dept., central France, 14 mi. S of Nevers; parquetry mfg., kaolin quarrying. Has 12th-cent. church. Fortified in Middle Ages, it was captured from the English by Joan of Arc.

Saint-Pierre-lès-Elbeuf (–lāzĕlbûf'), outer SE suburb (pop. 3,149) of Elbeuf, Seine-Inférieure dept., N France; woolen and asbestos mills; chemicals and brick mfg.

Saint-Pierre-Montlimart, France: see MONTREVAULT.

Saint-Pierre-Quilbignon (–kēlbēnyō'), W dist. of city of Brest, Finistère dept., W France, a separate commune until 1945; flour milling, woodworking.

Saint-Pierre-sur-Dives (–sür-dēv'), town (pop. 2,635), Orne dept., NW France, on the Dives and 19 mi. SE of Caen; market center in dairying and apple-growing area. Its 12th–14th-cent. church and 13th-cent.-covered market bldg. damaged in Second World War.

Saint-Pierreville (sē-pyĕrvēl'), village (pop. 387), Ardèche dept., S France, 8 mi. NW of Privas; sericulture.

Saint-Point, Lake of (sē-pwē'), Doubs dept., E France, largest (4 mi. long, ½ mi. wide) in the Fr. Jura, c.5 mi. SSW of Pontarlier; alt. 2,780 ft. Traversed S–N by Doubs R. Village of Malbuisson on E shore.

Saint-Pois (sē-pwä'), village (pop. 311), Manche dept., NW France, in Normandy Hills, 10 mi. SW of Vire; woodworking, granite quarrying.

Saint-Pol or **Saint-Pol-sur-Ternoise** (sē-pôl-sür-tĕrnwäz'), town (pop. 4,189), Pas-de-Calais dept., N France, 20 mi. WNW of Arras; rail junction and agr. trade center (cereals, tobacco, livestock). Clothing mfg. Briefly occupied by Germans (1914); shelled in 1918; damaged in Second World War.

Saint-Pol-de-Léon (–dů-lāō'), Breton *Kastell Paol*, town (pop. 5,095), Finistère dept., W France, near English Channel, 11 mi. NW of Morlaix; market center of truck-farming region (exports to England); horse breeding, mfg. (clothing, footwear). Feldspar quarries near by. Noted for its many spires. Chief bldgs. are the Norman Gothic cathedral (13th–14th cent.) and the 14th–15th cent. Kreisker chapel.

Saint-Pol-sur-Mer (–sür-mâr'), W suburb (pop. 10,341) of Dunkirk, Nord dept., N France; petroleum refining, dairying, truck farming. Damaged in Second World War during evacuation (1940) and siege (1944–45) of Dunkirk.

Saint-Pol-sur-Ternoise, Pas-de-Calais dept., France: see SAINT-POL.

Saint Polycarpe (sē pôlēkärp'), village (pop. 464), S Que., 10 mi. WNW of Valleyfield; dairying; pigs, potatoes.

Saint-Pons (sē-pō'), town (pop. 2,045), Hérault dept., S France, in the Monts de l'Espinouse, 25 mi. WNW of Béziers; road center; tanning, textile milling. Marble quarries near by. Has restored 12th-cent. fortified church. Episcopal see 1318–1790. Formerly Saint-Pons-de-Thomières.

Saint-Porchaire (sē-pôrshâr'), village (pop. 530), Charente-Maritime dept., W France, 9 mi. NW of Saintes; wheat and winegrowing (cognac). Has 12th–13th-cent. church.

Saint-Pourçain-sur-Sioule (sē-pōōrsē'-sür-syōōl'), town (pop. 3,050), Allier dept., central France, on the Sioule and 14 mi. NNW of Vichy; known for its wines since 13th cent. Agr. market; mfg. (fertilizer, malt). Has 14th-cent. abbatial church.

Saint-Priest (sē-prēēst'), town (pop. 3,846), Isère dept., SE France, 7 mi. SE of Lyons; silk spinning.

Saint-Priest-en-Jarez (sē-prēēst'-ā-zhärā'), town (pop. 2,161), Loire dept., SE central France, on the Furens and 3 mi. N of Saint-Étienne; produces parts for Saint-Étienne bicycle industry; mfg. of chocolate, cartons.

Saint Prime (sē prēm'), village (pop. 441), S central Que., on W shore of L. St. John, at mouth of Ashuapmuchuan R., 8 mi. NE of Roberval; dairying, pig raising.

Saint-Privat (sē-prēvä'). **1** Village (pop. 728), Corrèze dept., S central France, 13 mi. WSW of Mauriac; woodworking. **2** or **Saint-Privat-la-Montagne** (–lä-mōtä'nyů), village (pop. 859), Moselle dept., NE France, 8 mi. NW of Metz. Here, in 1870, French lost a battle (also known as battle of Gravelotte) which led to Ger. capture of Metz in Franco-Prussian War.

Saint-Prix (sē-prē'), village (pop. 93), Saône-et-Loire dept., E central France, in the Monts du Morvan, 11 mi. W of Autun; manganese mining.

Saint-Quay, France: see SAINT-QUAY-PORTRIEUX.

Saint-Quay-Portrieux (sē-kā-pôrtrēû'), commune (pop. 4,121), Côtes-du-Nord dept., W France, on English Channel, 10 mi. NNW of Saint-Brieuc. Saint-Quay (pop. 1,290) is a bathing resort, Portrieux a fishing village.

Saint-Quentin (sānt-kwĕn'tĭn, Fr. sē-kātē'), anc. *Augusta Veromanduorum*, city (pop. 46,876), Aisne dept., N France, on Somme R. and Saint-Quentin Canal, and 80 mi. NE of Paris; textile mills (lace curtains, gauze, percale, flannels, and muslin) and metalworks (sugar-distilling machinery, furnaces); other mfg. (sugar, chemicals, beer, brushes, rubber, bricks). Has large 12th–15th-cent. collegiate church of St. Quentin; a Flamboyant townhall (slightly damaged in Second World War); and the La Tour mus. with pastels by Maurice Quentin de La Tour, b. here. Of Roman origin; ⊙ of medieval Vermandois county. Captured by Spaniards in 1557, by Prussians in 1871. Occupied by Germans in First World War until Oct., 1918, it was systematically burned and pillaged by them. In battle of Saint-Quentin (March, 1918), British line was pierced bet. Saint-Quentin and La Fère.

Saint-Quentin Canal (58 mi. long), in Aisne and Nord depts., N France, connects Oise R. (near Chauny) with the Escaut (at Cambrai) and with canalized Somme R. (at Saint-Simon). Passes Saint-Quentin. Large coal and metal shipments. S part sometimes called Crozat Canal. Scene of heavy fighting in First World War, especially near tunnel (4 mi. long) at Bellicourt.

Saint-Rambert or **Saint-Rambert-en-Bugey** (sē-rābâr'-ā-büzhā'), town (pop. 2,035), Ain dept., E France, in gorge of the Albarine and 16 mi. SW of Nantua, in the S Jura; silk-waste milling, distilling, carton mfg.

Saint-Rambert-d'Albon (–dälbō'), town (pop. 2,610), Drôme dept., SE France, on left bank of Rhone R. and 17 mi. SSW of Vienne; rail junction; fruit-shipping center. Silk milling, tanning, candle mfg.

Saint-Rambert-en-Bugey, Ain dept., France: see SAINT-RAMBERT.

Saint-Rambert-l'Île-Barbe (–lēl-bärb'), N suburb (pop. 3,119) of Lyons, Rhône dept., E central France, on the Saône.

Saint-Rambert-sur-Loire (–sür-lwär'), village (pop. 1,510), Loire dept., SE central France, at S end of Forez Plain, near Loire R., 8 mi. NW of Saint-Étienne; mfg. of elastic fabrics; vegetable growing and shipping. Has an 11th–12th-cent. Romanesque church and old houses.

Saint Raphael (Fr. sē räfäĕl'), village (pop. 712), ⊙ Bellechasse co., S Que., 22 mi. E of Quebec; lumbering, dairying.

Saint-Raphaël (sē-räfäĕl'), town (pop. 6,642), Var dept., SE France, port on the Mediterranean, at SW foot of the Estérel 15 mi. SW of Cannes, near mouth of Argens R.; noted resort of Fr. Riviera, with sheltered beaches; flower- and winegrowing. Porphyry quarrying. Its small port replaces that of Fréjus (2 mi. WNW) built by Romans and now silted. Here Bonaparte landed (1799) on his return from Egypt. In Second World War, Ger. opposition to Allied landings caused assault to be shifted to Agay beaches (5 mi. E). Fashionable Vallescure resort annex is 2 mi. N amidst pinewoods.

Saint-Raphaël, town (1950 census pop. 1,463), Nord dept., N central Haiti, in Massif du Nord, 23 mi. S of Cap-Haïtien; coffee.

Saint Raymond (Fr. sē rāmō'), village (pop. 2,157), S Que., on Ste. Anne R. and 30 mi. W of Quebec; paper milling, lumbering, brick mfg., dairying.

Saint Rédempteur (sē rādāmptûr'), residential village (pop. 680), S Que., on Chaudière R., opposite Charny and 9 mi. SW of Quebec.

Saint Régis (rē'jĭs, Fr. sē rā-zhēs'), village, S Que., on the St. Lawrence, at mouth of St. Regis R., opposite Cornwall, on N.Y. border; formerly important Iroquois village, it still has predominantly Indian population.

Saint Regis (rē'jĭs), village (pop. c.300), Mineral co., W Mont., on the Clark Fork and 60 mi. WNW of Missoula; supply point in logging region.

Saint Regis Falls, village (1940 pop. 1,005), Franklin co., N N.Y., on St. Regis R. and 18 mi. SW of Malone, in agr. area.

Saint Regis River, N N.Y., rises in the Adirondacks in region NW of Saranac Lake village, flows generally NW and N, past St. Regis Falls, to the St. Lawrence just N of Hogansburg; c.80 mi. long. Receives West Branch (c.65 mi. long) near Brasher Falls; East Branch (c.35 mi. long) joins above St. Regis Falls. River's headstreams drain Upper St. Regis L. (c.2 mi. long, ½–1½ mi. wide), Lower St. Regis L. (1¼ mi. long, ½ mi. wide), St. Regis Pond (c.2 mi. long), and other Adirondack lakes.

Saint Rémi (sē rāmē'), village (pop. 1,431), S Que., 16 mi. S of Montreal, in dairying, vegetable-growing region; lumbering, food canning.

Saint Rémi d'Amherst (dăm'hûrst, ä'mürst), village (pop. estimate 800), S Que., 23 mi. WSW of Ste. Agathe des Monts; quartz mining, dairying, poultry raising.

Saint Rémi de Tingwick (dů tĭng'wĭk), village (pop. estimate 500), S Que., 9 mi. NE of Asbestos; asbestos mining.

Saint-Rémy (sē-rāmē'). **1** or **Saint-Rémy-de-Provence** (–dů-prôvās'), town (pop. 3,942), Bouches-du-Rhône dept., SE France, at N foot of the Alpines, 12 mi. NE of Arles; seed-growing (for vegetables, forage crops, and flowers) and shipping center. Near-by ruins of Roman *Glanum*, including splendid triumphal arch and mausoleum (1st cent. A.D.), adjoin 12th-cent. priory of St. Paul. **2** Village (pop. 646), Calvados dept., NW France, in Normandy Hills, on the Orne and 18 mi. SSW of Caen; iron mines. Bandage mfg.

Saint-Rémy-en-Bouzemont (–ā-bōōzmō'), agr. village (pop. 493), Marne dept., N France, near the Marne, 7 mi. SSE of Vitry-le-François.

Saint-Rémy-lès-Chevreuse (–lā-shĕvrûz'), village (pop. 1,764), Seine-et-Oise dept., N central France, resort on Yvette R. and 7 mi. SSW of Versailles.

Saint-Rémy-sur-Avre (–sür-ä'vrů), village (pop. 999), Eure-et-Loir dept., NW central France, on the Avre and 6 mi. W of Dreux; cotton milling.

Saint-Rémy-sur-Durolle (–dürôl'), village (pop. 1,242), Puy-de-Dôme dept., central France, 3 mi. NE of Thiers; cutlery-mfg. center (especially surgical instruments).

Saint-Renan (sē-rünā'), town (pop. 2,546), Finistère dept., W France, 7 mi. NNW of Brest; cider mills, truck gardens.

Saint-Rhémy (sē-rāmē'), village (pop. 35), Val d'Aosta region, NW Italy, on Great St. Bernard road, 3 mi. SSE of the pass.

Saint-Riquier (sẽ-rēkyā'), village (pop. 992), Somme dept., N France, 6 mi. ENE of Abbeville; dairying, sugar-beet processing. Site of noted Benedictine abbey (founded 7th cent.; burned 1487; rebuilt 16th–18th cent.) with richly adorned Gothic church (mainly 16th cent.).

Saint-Romain-de-Colbosc (sẽ-rômẽ'-dů-kôlbōs'), town (pop. 2,067), Seine-Inférieure dept., N France, 11 mi. ENE of Le Havre; agr. market.

Saint-Romain-le-Puy (–lů-pwē'), village (pop. 606), Loire dept., SE central France, in Forez Plain at foot of Monts du Forez, 5 mi. SE of Montbrison; bottles and ships mineral waters; shirt mfg.

Saint-Rome-de-Tarn (sẽ-rôm-dů-tärn'), village (pop. 673), Aveyron dept., S France, on the Tarn and 9 mi. WSW of Millau; glove mfg., fruit- and wine-growing. Hydroelectric plants at Saint-Victor-et-Melvieu (3 mi. W) and Le Truel (6 mi. W).

Saint Romuald (sẽ rômwäld'), village (pop. estimate 4,500), ⊙ Lévis co., S Que., on the St. Lawrence and 5 mi. SSW of Quebec; textile milling, lumbering. Site of Trappist monastery.

Saint Rosa, village (pop. 69), Stearns co., central Minn., 12 mi. E of Sauk Centre.

Saint Rose, coal-mining village, NE N.S., W Cape Breton Isl., on Gulf of St. Lawrence, 10 mi. NE of Inverness.

Saint-Saëns (sẽ-sã'), town (pop. 2,041), Seine-Inférieure dept., N France, 18 mi. NNE of Rouen; sawmilling, shirt mfg. N is Forest of Eawy (□ 25).

Saint Sampson, town and parish (1931 pop. 5,333), Guernsey, Channel Isls., on E coast of isl., 3 mi. NNE of St. Peter Port; small port in granite-quarrying region. Near by are ruins of medieval Ivy Castle or Château d'Orgueil. Post office name St. Sampson's.

Saint-Saulge (sẽ-sōzh'), village (pop. 888), Nièvre dept., central France, in the Nivernais Hills, 19 mi. NE of Nevers; livestock trade.

Saint-Saulve (sẽ-sōv'), NE suburb (pop. 3,170) of Valenciennes, Nord dept., N France; metalworks; chicory, soap.

Saint-Sauveur, Jersey, Channel Isls.: see SAINT SAVIOUR.

Saint-Sauveur or **Saint-Sauveur-en-Puisaye** (sẽ-sōvûr'-ã-pwēzā'), village (pop. 959), Yonne dept., N central France, on Loing R. and 21 mi. SW of Auxerre; sandstone-pipe mfg.; cattle raising.

Saint Sauveur des Monts (dā mõ'), village (pop. 595), SW Que., in the Laurentians, 40 mi. NW of Montreal; dairying; skiing resort.

Saint-Sauveur-des-Pourcils (–po͞orsē'), village (pop. 250), Gard dept., S France, near the Causse Noir, 11 mi. NW of Le Vigan; lead mines.

Saint-Sauveur-en-Puisaye, France: see SAINT-SAUVEUR.

Saint-Sauveur-Lendelin (–lãdlẽ'), village (pop. 443), Manche dept., NW France, 6 mi. N of Coutances; livestock, apple orchards.

Saint-Sauveur-les-Bains, France: see LUZ.

Saint-Sauveur-le-Vicomte (–lů-vēkōt'), village (pop. 662), Manche dept., NW France, 18 mi. SSE of Cherbourg; dairying, distilling, sawmilling. Captured (June, 1944) by American troops driving across Cotentin Peninsula. Its 12th-cent. castle was damaged.

Saint-Sauveur-sur-Tinée (–sür-tēnā'), village (pop. 532), Alpes-Maritimes dept., SE France, in Tinée valley of Maritime Alps, 28 mi. NNW of Nice, near Ital. border.

Saint-Savin (sẽ-sävẽ'). **1** Village (pop. 476), Gironde dept., SW France, 22 mi. NNE of Bordeaux; wine, cattle. **2** Village (pop. 1,060), Vienne dept., W central France, on Gartempe R. and 24 mi. E of Poitiers. Has abbey founded 811 by Charlemagne, and 11th-cent. church with 300-ft. spire and life-size mural paintings. Also called Saint-Savin-sur-Gartempe.

Saint-Savinien (sẽ-sävēnyẽ'), village (pop. 1,057), Charente-Maritime dept., W France, on Charente R. and 14 mi. ESE of Rochefort; large stone quarries; distilling.

Saint Saviour. 1 Agr. village and parish (1931 pop. 1,230), Guernsey, Channel Isls., 4 mi. WSW of St. Peter Port. Post office name St. Saviour's. **2** Fr. *Saint-Sauveur* (sẽ-sōvûr'), agr. village and parish (1945 pop. 5,066), Jersey, Channel Isls., 2 mi. NE of St. Helier. Lily Langtry b. at rectory here.

Saint-Sébastien (sẽ'-säbästyẽ'), headland, N Madagascar, on Mozambique Channel, 39 mi. SW of Diégo-Suarez; 12°23'S 48°40'E.

Saint Sébastien de Beauce (dů bōs'), village (pop. 226), SE Que., 15 mi. NNW of Megantic; dairying, lumbering.

Saint-Seine-l'Abbaye (sẽ-sĕn-läbā'), agr. village (pop. 351), Côte-d'Or dept., E central France, at S end of Plateau of Langres, 14 mi. NW of Dijon; has 13th–15th-cent. Gothic church, once part of Benedictine abbey (founded 6th cent.). Seine R. rises 5 mi. NW.

Saint Serf's Island, Scotland: see LEVEN, LOCH.

Saint-Sernin-sur-Rance (sẽ-sĕrnẽ'-sür-rãs'), village (pop. 667), Aveyron dept., S France, 23 mi. E of Albi; wheat, rye, cattle.

Saint-Servais (sẽ-sĕrvā'), town (pop. 8,633), Namur prov., S central Belgium, 1 mi. NW of Namur; paper mills.

Saint-Servan or **Saint-Servan-sur-Mer** (sẽ-sĕrvã'-sür-mâr'), town (pop. 10,815), Ille-et-Vilaine dept., W France, port on English Channel at mouth of Rance R. and 1 mi. SSE of Saint-Malo; together with SAINT-MALO and PARAMÉ it forms an important tourist resort area. Passenger and freight service to England and to Dinard (2 mi. W). Imports lumber, coal. Fishing; mfg. (cables, fishing boats, cider, biscuits. Has 18th-cent. church of Saint-Croix and noted 14th-cent. tower (Tour Solidor) which commands Rance estuary. Both were damaged in Second World War.

Saint-Sever (sẽ-sůvâr'), town (pop. 2,022), Landes dept., SW France, on Adour R. and 10 mi. SSW of Mont-de-Marsan; market center (hogs, horses, geese); meat processing. Has restored 10th–12th-cent. Romanesque church.

Saint-Sever-Calvados (–kälvädōs'), village (pop. 978), Calvados dept., NW France, 7 mi. W of Vire; cider distilling, sawmilling. Granite quarries near by. Damaged in Second World War.

Saint Siméon (sẽ sēmāõ'), village (pop. 858), SE central Que., on the St. Lawrence and 18 mi. NE of La Malbaie; lumbering, dairying, vegetables; resort.

Saint-Simon (sẽ-sēmõ'), agr. village (pop. 328), Aisne dept., N France, at junction of Somme and Saint-Quentin canals, 9 mi. SE of Saint-Quentin. Was property of Duc de Saint-Simon.

Saint Simon de Bagot (sẽ sēmõ' dů bägō'), village (pop. estimate 450), S Que., near Yamaska R., 9 mi. NE of St. Hyacinthe; dairying, pig raising.

Saint Simon de Rimouski (rĭmo͞o'skē), village (pop. estimate 550), SE Que., on the St. Lawrence and 40 mi. NE of Rivière du Loup; dairying, lumbering, pig raising.

Saint Simons Island (sī'můnz) (pop. 1,706), one of the Sea Isls., in Glynn co., SE Ga., just off the coast, at mouth of Altamaha R.; c.13 mi. long, 3–7 mi. wide. At S end is resort village of St. Simons Island, connected by causeway to Brunswick, 7 mi. W on the mainland, and small St. Simons Sound, with dredged deepwater channel. On W coast of isl. is Fort Frederica Natl. Monument (74.5 acres; established 1945), including ruins of English fort built (1736–54) by Oglethorpe; near-by Battle of Bloody Marsh (1742; won by English) was decisive engagement in struggle with Spain for control of what is now SE U.S.

Saint's Island, islet in S part of Lough Derg, S Co. Donegal, Ireland, 5 mi. NNW of Pettigo and just N of Station Isl. Site of remains of monastery founded by St. Daveog, disciple of St. Patrick; destroyed 1632.

Saint Stanislas de Champlain (sẽ stänēsläs' dů shăplē') or **Deux Rivières** (dû rēvyâr'), village (pop. 642), S Que., on Batiscan R. and 15 mi. E of Grand'Mère; dairying, lumbering.

Saint Stephen, town (pop. 3,306), SW N.B., on St. Croix R. (international bridge) opposite Calais, Maine, and 60 mi. W of St. John; cotton milling; mfg. of shoes, soap, chemicals, food products, confectionery. Formerly a lumbering center and lumber-shipping port. Laid out by United Empire Loyalists after Revolutionary War; inc. 1871. Nickel is mined near by.

Saint Stephen or **Saint Stephens,** town (pop. 1,341), Berkeley co., E S.C., 37 mi. W of Georgetown; lumber, bricks.

Saint Stephen in Brannel, town and parish (pop. 4,801), central Cornwall, England, 4 mi. W of St. Austell; China-clay mining center. Has 15th-cent. church.

Saint Stephens, agr. village in extensive parish of Saint Stephen (pop. 3,149), S central Hertford, England, just SSW of St. Albans.

Saint Stephens. 1 Hamlet, Washington co., SW Ala., on the Tombigbee and c.60 mi. N of Mobile. Here, in settlement on site of a Sp. fort (built 1789) and a trading post (1803), the 1st territorial legislature of Ala. met in 1818. **2** Village (pop. 234), Stearns co., central Minn., near Mississippi R., 10 mi. NNW of St. Cloud; grain, livestock.

Saint-Sulpice or **Saint-Sulpice-la-Pointe** (sẽ-sülpēs'-läpwẽt'), town (pop. 2,088), Tarn dept., S France, on Agout R. near its mouth on the Tarn, and 17 mi. NE of Toulouse; rail junction. Mfg. of saddlebows, brushes, metal furniture, hardware.

Saint-Sulpice-Laurière (–lōrēâr'), village (pop. 1,600), Haute-Vienne dept., W central France, 18 mi. NNE of Limoges; rail junction (Paris-Toulouse and Lyons-Bordeaux lines). Gold deposits near by.

Saint-Sulpice-les-Champs (–lā-shã'), village (pop. 157), Creuse dept., central France, 7 mi. WNW of Aubusson; sheep and cattle raising.

Saint-Sulpice-les-Feuilles (–fû'ē), village (pop. 618), Haute-Vienne dept., W central France, 20 mi. NE of Bellac; brewing, hardware mfg.

Saint Sylvestre (sẽ sēlvĕ'strů), village (pop. 295), S Que., 30 mi. S of Quebec; dairying; cattle, pigs.

Saint-Sylvestre, village (pop. 78), Haute-Vienne dept., W central France, in the Monts d'Ambazac, 13 mi. NNE of Limoges; uranium ore deposits discovered here in 1949.

Saint-Symphorien (sẽ-sẽfôrēẽ'), town (pop. 1,242), Hainaut prov., SW Belgium, 3 mi. ESE of Mons; synthetic fertilizer.

Saint-Symphorien. 1 Village (pop. 1,171), Gironde dept., SW France, in the Landes, 29 mi. S of Bordeaux; woodworking, mfg. of resinous products. **2** N suburb (pop. 5,413) of Tours, Indre-et-Loire dept., W central France, residential dist. on right bank of Loire R.

Saint-Symphorien-de-Lay (–dů-lā'), village (pop. 856), Loire dept., SE central France, 9 mi. SE of Roanne; mfg. of hosiery, agr. machinery. Quarrying of road-building materials.

Saint-Symphorien-de-Marmagne (–märmä'nyů), village (pop. 207), Saône-et-Loire dept., E central France, 5 mi. NW of Le Creusot; uranium mining.

Saint-Symphorien-d'Ozon (–dôzõ'), village (pop. 1,327), Isère dept., SE France, 9 mi. S of Lyons; footwear mfg.; water-cress cultivation.

Saint-Symphorien-sur-Coise (–sür-kwäz'), town (pop. 2,178), Rhône dept., E central France, bet. Monts du Beaujolais (N) and Monts du Lyonnais (S), 14 mi. NNE of Saint-Étienne; sausage mfg.

Saint Tammany (sānt" tă'můnē), parish (□ 908; pop. 26,988), SE La.; ⊙ Covington. Bounded S by L. Pontchartrain, E by Pearl R. (here forming Miss. line); drained by the Bogue Chitto, Bogue Falia, and Tchefuncta R. Resorts on lakes. Agr. (cotton, corn, hay, sugar cane, sweet potatoes, strawberries); stock raising. Mfg., including boatbuilding; hunting, fishing. Formed 1810.

Saint Teath (sůnt tĕth'), village and parish (pop. 1,893), central Cornwall, England, 9 mi. N of Bodmin. Has 15th-cent. church.

Saint-Thégonnec (sẽ-tāgônĕk'), village (pop. 641), Finistère dept., W France, 7 mi. WSW of Morlaix. Noted ossuary chapel (1676), calvary (1610), and Renaissance church with fine wood carvings.

Saint Thomas, city (pop. 17,132), ⊙ Elgin co., S Ont., near L. Erie, 110 mi. WSW of Toronto; railroad workshops, foundries, lumber mills; printing, meat packing, mfg. of shoes, dairy products, brushes. Center of fruitgrowing district. Founded 1810. Has Alma Col. (jr. col.).

Saint Thomas, parish (□ 300.17; pop. 60,693), Surrey co., E Jamaica; ⊙ Morant Bay. Situated in E end of the isl., S of the Blue Mts. Crossed by Plantain Garden R. Predominantly agr.: bananas, coconuts, copra, sugar cane, coffee, mangoes, peas and beans, honey, livestock. Morant Bay and Port Morant are its main trading and shipping points. Bowden, served by narrow-gauge railroad, is banana port. Bath has thermal springs.

Saint Thomas. 1 City (pop. 566), Pembina co., NE N.Dak., 13 mi. N of Grafton. **2** Village (pop. c.400), Franklin co., S Pa., 7 mi. W of Chambersburg. Near-by caves attract tourists.

Saint Thomas, city and harbor, U.S. Virgin Isls.: see CHARLOTTE AMALIE.

Saint Thomas Island, São Tomé e Príncipe: see SÃO TOMÉ ISLAND.

Saint Thomas Island, second largest island (□ 27.12; pop. 13,811) of U.S. Virgin Isls., 40 mi. E of Puerto Rico, 2½ mi. W of St. John Isl. across Pillsbury Sound, 150 mi. NW of St. Kitts; ⊙ CHARLOTTE AMALIE. The rugged, indented isl., of volcanic origin, is 12 mi. long (W–E), 1–3 mi. wide, extends bet. 18°18'–18°23'N and 64°50'–65°3'W; rises to 1,550 ft. Has a healthful, pleasant climate, particularly during winter when trade winds blow. Its area, little cultivated, is now mostly given over to cattle raising. More than ¾ of the pop. live in Charlotte Amalie, chief port and center of the U.S. territory. Rum and bay-rum distilling are chief industries, but tourist trade is becoming of increasing importance. Originally inhabited by Caribs and Arawaks, St. Thomas was discovered 1493 by Columbus on his 2d voyage. First unsuccessful attempts at colonization were made by the Dutch (1657) and the Danes (1666). The latter settled permanently at St. Thomas Harbor in 1672. The isl. was for some time controlled by a Danish company, but returned to the crown in 1755, when Charlotte Amalie was declared a free port. The English held it 1801–02 and 1807–15. Slavery was abolished in 1848. It became a U.S. possession in 1917. It forms, together with St. John, one municipality. The pop. is predominantly Negro, who speak a kind of English dialect. There is also a considerable minority of French-Norman settlers. U.S. maintained a base here during Second World War.

Saint Thomas Mount, cantonment (pop., including cantonment area of Pallavaram, 9,317), Chingleput dist., E Madras, India; suburb of Madras, 7 mi. SW of city center; parade ground. Named for near-by hill traditionally associated with martyrdom of the apostle Thomas. Site of Nestorian monastery from early-9th cent. A.D. until Portuguese built R.C. church here in 1547; a Franciscan convent is near the church. Minambakkam (airport for Madras city) is just SW. St. Thomé is the name of an early-16th-cent. Port. settlement within present city limits of Madras.

Saint Thomas-ye-Vale (sůnt tŏ'můs ĭn dhů vāl'), interior valley in E central Jamaica, along upper Cobre R., c.20 mi. NW of Kingston. Tropical fruit grown extensively. Main towns: Linstead, Bog Walk, and Ewarton, linked by railroad.

Saint Thomé, India: see MADRAS, city.

Saint Timothée (sẽ tēmôtā'), village (pop. 716), S Que., on the St. Lawrence and 5 mi. NE of

Valleyfield; tanning, linen milling, dairying; arms mfg. Hydroelectric station.

Saint Tite (sē tēt'), town (pop. 2,385), S Que., 10 mi. NE of Grand'Mère; mfg. of shoes, gloves; lumbering, dairying.

Saint-Trivier-de-Courtes (sē-trēvyā'-dù-ko͞ort'),village (pop. 490), Ain dept., E France, 16 mi. NE of Mâcon; poultry market; dairying.

Saint-Trivier-sur-Moignans (–sür-mwänyā'), agr. village (pop. 416), Ain dept., E France, 10 mi. NE of Villefranche; woodworking.

Saint-Trojan-les-Bains (sē-trôzhā'-lā-bē'), village (pop. 934), Charente-Maritime dept., W France, on S end on Île d' Oléron, 14 mi. SW of Rochefort; bathing resort; oyster- and mussel-beds.

Saint-Trond (sē-trõ'), Flemish *Sint-Truiden* (sĭnt-troi'dùn), town (pop. 19,236), Limburg prov., NE Belgium, 11 mi. SSW of Hasselt; rail junction; sugar refining, liquor distilling, brewing, tobacco mfg.; market center for fruitgrowing area (apples, cherries, plums). Has 13th-cent. Beguinage church, 15th-cent. church of Notre Dame, town hall with 17th-cent. belfry. Abbey founded here (655) by St. Trudo. Town conquered by Charles the Bold in 15th cent.

Saint-Tropez (sē-trôpā'), town (pop. 3,171), Var dept., SE France, on S shore of Gulf of Saint-Tropez, 37 mi. ENE of Toulon; fishing port and popular resort on Fr. Riviera. Mfg. of cables and torpedoes. Heavily damaged during Allied landings (Aug., 1944) in Second World War.

Saint-Tropez, Gulf of, deep embayment of the Mediterranean, off Var dept., SE France, surrounded by abrupt spurs of Monts des Maures; 3 mi. wide, 6 mi. deep. Saint-Tropez is on S shore. Bounded (SE) by Cape of Saint-Tropez. Sometimes called Gulf of Grimaud. Here Allies landed (Aug., 1944) in S France invasion in Second World War.

Saint Ubald (sētübäld'), village (pop. 448), S Que., 22 mi. NE of Grand'Mère; dairying; stock, poultry.

Saint Ulric (sētülrēk') or **Rivière Blanche** (rēvyâr' blãsh'), village (pop. 898), E Que., on the St. Lawrence, and 9 mi. WSW of Matane; lumbering, dairying, fishing.

Saint Urbain de Charlevoix (sētürbē' dù shärlvwä'), village (pop. estimate 700), SE central Que., 19 mi. ESE of La Malbaie; titanium mining, dairying, lumbering.

Saint-Uze (sētüz'), village (pop. 1,353), Drôme dept., SE France, near left bank of the Rhone, 18 mi. N of Valence; porcelain mfg., metalworking.

Saint-Vaast (sē-väst'), town (pop. 3,223), Hainaut prov., SW Belgium, 9 mi. E of Mons; coal mining.

Saint-Vaast-la-Hougue (–lä-o͞og'), town (pop. 2,087), Manche dept., NW France, fishing port and resort on E coast of Cotentin Peninsula, 16 mi. ESE of Cherbourg; livestock, oysters. Fort La Hougue, built by Vauban (17th cent.) on what was then an isl., is 1 mi. S. Tatihou isl. (formerly fortified) is 1 mi. E. Here, in 1692, a Fr. fleet under Tourville was defeated by superior English and Dutch forces in battle of La Hougue (sometimes La Hogue).

Saint-Valéry-en-Caux (sē-välārē'-ã-kō'), town (pop. 2,268), Seine-Inférieure dept., N France, on English Channel, 17 mi. WSW of Dieppe; fishing port and bathing resort amidst chalk cliffs. Heavily damaged, 1940, in Second World War.

Saint-Valéry-sur-Somme (–sür-sôm'), town (pop. 2,647), Somme dept., N France, port on sandy Somme R. estuary, 11 mi. NW of Abbeville, at seaward end of Somme R. navigation canal. Lower town, called La Ferté, is bathing resort (heavily damaged in Second World War). Upper town has part of medieval fortifications and ruins of 13th-cent. abbey.

Saint-Vallier (sē-välyā'). **1** or **Saint-Vallier-de-Thiey** (–dù-tyā'), village (pop. 271), Alpes-Maritimes dept., SE France, in Provence Alps, 5 mi. NW of Grasse. **2** Town (pop. 3,379), Drôme dept., SE France, on left bank of the Rhone and 18 mi. NNW of Valence; mfg. (cartons, porcelain, wooden wheels), silk milling. Fruit- and winegrowing. Sometimes called Saint-Vallier-sur-Rhône.

Saint-Varent (sē-värã'), village (pop. 934), Deux-Sèvres dept., W France, 17 mi. N of Parthenay; dairying, casein mfg., winegrowing.

Saint-Vaury (sē-vōrē'), village (pop. 549), Creuse dept., central France, 6 mi. WNW of Guéret; sheep and cattle raising.

Saint-Véran (sē-vārã'), village (pop. 316), Hautes-Alpes dept., SE France, in Cottian Alps, resort near Ital. border, 18 mi. SE of Briançon; highest Alpine village (6,693 ft.). Cheese mfg.

Saint Victor de Beauce (Fr. sē vēktôr' dù bōs') or **Saint Victor de Tring,** village (pop. 466), S Que., 20 mi. ENE of Thetford Mines; dairying, pig raising.

Saint-Victor-de-Cessieu (sē-vēktôr'-dù-sēsyû'), village (pop. 127), Isère dept., SE France, 3 mi. SW of La Tour-du-Pin; paper milling.

Saint Victor de Tring, Que.: see SAINT VICTOR DE BEAUCE.

Saint-Victoret (sē-vēktôrā'), village (pop. 1,524), Bouches-du-Rhône dept., SE France, near E shore of Étang de Berre, 12 mi. NW of Marseilles. Mfg. of electric heaters and broomcorn processing at Pas-des-Lanciers (2 mi. SE).

Saint-Victor-et-Melvieu, France: see SAINT-ROME-DE-TARN.

Saint-Victor-la-Coste (sē-vēktôr'-lä-kôst'), village (pop. 563), Gard dept., S France, 12 mi. NW of Avignon; lignite mining, slaked-lime mfg.

Saint-Victor-sur-Rhins (–sür-rēs'), village (pop. 559), Loire dept., SE central France, in Monts du Beaujolais, 10 mi. ESE of Roanne; rayon and cotton textiles.

Saint-Victurnien (sē-vēktürnyē'), village (pop. 566), Haute-Vienne dept., W central France, on the Vienne and 5 mi. E of St-Junien; paper milling. Has 12th–15th-cent. church.

Saint Vigeans, Scotland: see ARBROATH.

Saint-Vincent (sē-vēsã'), village (pop. 754), Val d'Aosta region, NW Italy, near Dora Baltea R., 16 mi. E of Aosta; marble quarries. Health resort, with baths.

Saint Vincent, village (pop. 272), Kittson co., extreme NW Minn., on Red River of the North, near Man. line, and 19 mi. NW of Hallock, in grain and potato area.

Saint Vincent, island (□ 133; pop. 57,168), central Windward Isls., B.W.I., 27 mi. S of St. Lucia and just N of the GRENADINES; ⊙ Kingstown. Of volcanic origin, it has a backbone of densely forested, rugged mts., rising in the now-dormant SOUFRIÈRE volcano to 4,048 ft. The main range branches off, forming picturesque valleys and fertile level tracts watered by numerous rivers. Healthful climate, with a dry season Jan.–April; mean temp. about 80°F.; annual rainfall 102 inches. Hurricanes and earthquake shocks occur occasionally. The isl.'s mainstays are arrowroot (starch), sea-island cotton, coconuts, cassava, and sugar cane, which are processed (rum, molasses, vegetable oil) in local plants and exported through Kingstown. The Hairoun ("home of the blessed") of the aboriginal Indians, it is popularly considered to have been discovered by Columbus in 1498. The native Caribs retained possession of it until 1627, when St. Vincent was included in the grant to the earl of Carlisle. Like most of the Lesser Antilles, it was constantly disputed by England and France, though here the natives put up a spirited resistance. By a treaty (1773) the Caribs were allotted a dist., but rebelled again in 1795, making common cause with the French. Most of them (5,080) were deported 2 years later to Roatán Isl. off Honduras. Portuguese and East Indian laborers were introduced during 19th cent. The pop. is now predominantly Negro with some admixture of Carib. The isl. was subjected in 1898 to a disastrous earthquake, and in 1902 to the eruption of the Soufrière. St. Vincent isl. forms the larger section of **Saint Vincent** colony (□ 150.3; pop. 61,647), which includes most of the Grenadines (Bequia, Mustique, Cannouan, Mayreau, and Union isls.), in S Lesser Antilles, just N of Grenada colony, and extending bet. 12°35' and 13°23'N. Though belonging to the Br. colony of the Windward Isls., St. Vincent has a local govt. and legislative council of its own.

Saint-Vincent, Cape (Fr. sē'-vēsã'), headland, SW Madagascar, on Mozambique Channel, 5 mi. SW of Morombe; 21°56'S 43°15'E.

Saint Vincent, Cape, Port. *Cabo de São Vicente* (kä'bo͞o dĭ sã'ō vēsān'tĭ), anc. *Promontorium Sacrum,* SW extremity of Portugal and of continental Europe, a headland on the Atlantic 60 mi. W of Faro; 37°1'N 9°W. Lighthouse atop 175-ft. cliff is built within walls of a 16th-cent. monastery. Ruins of Prince Henry the Navigator's 15th-cent. town (including possibly his school for navigators and observatory) are near by. Several naval battles have been fought off cape.

Saint Vincent, Gulf, large inlet of Indian Ocean, South Australia, bet. Yorke Peninsula (W) and mainland (E); connected with Indian Ocean by Investigator Strait (SW) and Backstairs Passage (SE); 90 mi. long, 45 mi. wide. Port Adelaide on E shore. Salt beds.

Saint Vincent de Paul (sē vēsã' dù pôl'), village (pop. estimate 1,500), S Que., on S shore of Jesus Isl., on R. des Prairies, and 12 mi. NW of Montreal; truck gardening, dairying. Site of hydroelectric station and penitentiary.

Saint-Vincent-de-Tyrosse (–tērôs'), village (pop. 1,699), Landes dept., SW France, 13 mi. WSW of Dax; shoe and felt-slipper factories.

Saint Vincent Island, Cape Verde Isls.: see SÃO VICENTE ISLAND.

Saint Vincent Island (9 mi. long, 4½ mi. wide), barrier island in the Gulf of Mexico, off Franklin co., NW Fla., W of St. George Isl. and 7 mi. SW of Apalachicola. Shelters St. Vincent Sound (c.2 mi. wide), which communicates with Apalachicola Bay (E). Isl., and sound, sometimes spelled St. Vincents.

Saint Vincent Island, Windward Isls., B.W.I.: see SAINT VINCENT.

Saint Vincent Passage, channel, SE West Indies, c.25 mi. wide bet. St. Lucia and St. Vincent.

Saint Vincent Sound, Fla.: see SAINT VINCENT ISLAND.

Saint-Vit (sē-vē'), village (pop. 1,080), Doubs dept., E France, near Doubs R. and Rhone-Rhine Canal, 11 mi. WSW of Besançon; cattle shipping.

Saint-Vith (sē-vēt'), Ger. *Sankt-Vith* (zängkt-fēt'), village (pop. 2,195), Liége prov., E Belgium, in N Ardennes, 11 mi. SSE of Malmédy; market center. Part of area belonging to Germany prior to First World War; awarded to Belgium in 1919. A key road center in Battle of the Bulge (1944–45) in Second World War.

Saint-Vivien-de-Médoc (sē-vēvyē'-dù-mādôk'), village (pop. 340), Gironde dept., SW France, in N Médoc, 45 mi. NNW of Bordeaux; turpentine mfg., horse raising.

Saint Vrain Creek, N Colo., rises in 2 branches in N Front Range, near Mt. Audubon; flows 68 mi. E and NE, past Lyons and Longmont, to South Platte R. 5 mi. S of Milliken.

Saint Walburg (wăl'bûrg), village (pop. 464), W Sask., 70 mi. NNW of North Battleford; grain.

Saint-Wandrille-Rançon (sē-vādrē'-rāsō'), commune (pop. 980), Seine-Inférieure dept., N France, near right bank of Seine R., 16 mi. WNW of Rouen. Its Benedictine abbey (founded 7th cent.; reoccupied 1931), with ruined 13th–14th-cent. church, damaged in Second World War.

Saint-Wendel, Saar: see SANKT WENDEL.

Saint Woollos, residential town and parish (pop. 4,758), S Monmouth, England, just SW of Newport.

Saint-Yorre (sē-yôr'), town (pop. 2,145), Allier dept., central France, on the Allier and 4 mi. SSE of Vichy; mineral springs; bottling and shipping of Vichy water.

Saint-Yrieix-la-Perche (sētērēā'-lä-pârsh'), town (pop. 3,707), Haute-Vienne dept., W central France, in Monts du Limousin, 21 mi. S of Limoges; chief kaolin-quarrying center of France, supplying porcelain factories of Limoges and Sèvres since mid-18th cent. Gold mined at Coussac-Bonneval (5 mi. W); antimony at Les Biards (5 mi. SSE). Has a 12th–13th-cent. church. Also called Saint-Yrieix.

Saint-Zacharie (sē-zäkärē'), village (pop. 1,310), Var dept., SE France, 18 mi. ENE of Marseilles; mfg. of enameled tiles.

Saint Zotique (sē zôtēk'), village (pop. 214), S Que., on L. St. Francis, 7 mi. W of Valleyfield; dairying; pigs, potatoes.

Saio (sä'yō), town (pop. 8,000), Wallaga prov., W central Ethiopia, on road and 55 mi. WNW of Gore; 8°32'N 34°48'E; alt. 5,974 ft. Trade center (coffee, hides, beeswax, cotton goods, salt); mills (flour, lumber). Town consists of commercial (Saio) and adjacent administrative section (Dembidollo). Airfield.

Saipan (sī'păn, sīpän'), volcanic island (□ 47; pop. 4,945), largest, most important of former Jap. mandated MARIANAS ISLANDS, W Pacific, 150 mi. NNE of Guam; 13 mi. long, 5.5 mi. wide; composed of madrepore limestone. U.S. trusteeship (1947) under U.N. Mt. Tapotchau, extinct volcano, is highest peak (1,554 ft.). Magicienne (Laulau) Bay in SE. Sugar, coffee, copra plantations. Manganese, phosphate deposits. In Second World War, isl. (site of Jap. air base) was taken in June–July, 1944, by U.S. forces after a fierce and bloody batte. U.S. naval base at Tanapag Harbor in NW. Isely Field (formerly Aslito Field) is largest of 3 airfields. Garapan (former ⊙ Jap. mandated Marianas Isls.), on W coast, is ⊙ Saipan dist. of U.S. trust territory. Saipan dist. (□ 154; pop. 5,636) includes AGRIHAN, AGUIJAN, ALAMAGAN, ANATAHAN, ASUNCION, GUGUAN, MAUG, MEDINILLA, PAGAN, PAJAROS, ROTA, SAIPAN, SARIGAN, TINIAN. Formerly spelled Saypan.

Saipur, India: see SAFIPUR.

Saipurú (sīpo͞oro͞o'), village (pop. c.300), Santa Cruz dept., SE Bolivia, in Serranía de Charagua, on W edge of the Chaco and 30 mi. ENE of Lagunillas; oil fields 5 mi. S. Former mission.

Sairam or **Sayram** (sīräm'), village (1926 pop. 12,791), S South Kazakhstan oblast, Russian SFSR, 7 mi. E of Chimkent; cotton, orchards.

Sairam Nor or **Sayram Nuur** (both: sīräm' nōr'), lake in NW Sinkiang prov., China, 50 mi. N of Kuldja, near USSR border, S of the Dzungarian Ala-Tau.

Sairang (sī'räng), village, Lushai Hills dist., S Assam, India, on tributary of Barak (Surma) R. and 6 mi. NW of Aijal; orange-growing center; rice, cotton.

Sai River (sī), central Uttar Pradesh, India, rises on Ganges Plain, 15 mi. SE of Shalijahanpur; flows c.280 mi. SE, past Hasanganj, Rae Bareli, and Bela, to Gumti R. 8 mi. SE of Jaunpur.

Sairma (sīērmä'), village (1939 pop. under 500), SW Georgian SSR, in Adzhar-Imeretian Range, 12 mi. SSW of Mayakovski; mtn. resort; mineral springs.

Sairt, Turkey: see SIIRT.

Sair Usu or **Sayr Usa** (sīr' o͞o'sù), village, Middle Gobi aimak, S central Mongolian People's Republic, 50 mi. SE of Mandal Gobi; 44°48'N 106°54'E. Formerly a junction of trade routes from Pailingmiao (China).

Saïs (sā'ĭs), anc. city of Lower Egypt, whose site is 55 mi. SE of Alexandria and on Rosetta branch of the Nile, at Sa el Hagir. Anciently on the Canopic branch of the Nile, it was capital of Lower Egypt during the XXVI dynasty (663–525 B.C.), its kings ruling Egypt for c.150 years, until the Persian invasion under Cambyses.

Saishu, Korea: see CHEJU.

Saison River (sāzõ'), in Basses-Pyrénées dept., SW France, rises in W Pyrenees near Sp. border, flows 45 mi. NNW, through the heart of the Basque country, past Tardets-Sorholus and Mauléon-Licharre, to the Gave d'Oloron below Sauveterre.

Saissac (sāsäk'), village (pop. 550), Aude dept., S France, on SW slope of Montagne Noire, 11 mi. ENE of Castelnaudary; grazing, potato growing.

Saisyu-to, Korea: see CHEJU ISLAND.

Saitama (sī'tämŏ), prefecture [Jap. *ken*] (□ 1,468; 1940 pop. 1,608,039; 1947 pop. 2,100,453), central Honshu, Japan, N of Greater Tokyo; ⊙ URAWA. Largely a fertile plain growing rice, wheat, potatoes. Extensive production of raw silk. Mfg. of textiles, *tabi* (a kind of sock); woodworking. Principal centers: KAWAGOE, KAWAGUCHI, KUMAGAYA, OMIYA.

Saitta (sī'tä), summer resort (pop., including adjacent Moniatis, 345), Limassol dist., S central Cyprus, c.25 mi. SW of Nicosia; alt. c.2,200 ft. Has experimental fruit station and vineyard.

Saiun, Aden: see SEIYUN.

Saiwun, Aden: see SEIYUN.

Saizaki (sī'zäkē), town (pop. 6,913), Hiroshima prefecture, SW Honshu, Japan, just SW of Mihara; commercial center for agr. area (rice, corn, tobacco, citrus fruit); makes insect powder.

Sajama (sähä'mä), village (pop. c.1,000), Oruro dept., W Bolivia, at W foot of Sajama peak, 125 mi. W of Oruro and on Sajama R. (branch of the Lauca); alt. 13,920 ft.; customs station near Chilean border.

Sajama, highest peak (21,390 ft.) in Western Cordillera of the Bolivian Andes, in its N section (Cordillera de Pacajes y Carangas), Oruro dept., W Bolivia, 120 mi. W of Oruro, in spur 10 mi. E of main range.

Saji (sä'jē), town (pop. 3,321), Hyogo prefecture, S Honshu, Japan, 8 mi. SW of Fukuchiyama; rice, raw silk.

Sajo River (shŏ'yō), Hung. *Sajó*, Slovak *Slaná* (slä'nä), S Slovakia, Czechoslovakia, and NE Hungary, rises on NE slope of Stolica mtn. of Slovak Ore Mts., 18 mi. NW of Roznava; flows c.60 mi. S, past Dobsina and Roznava, and SE, across Hung. border, past Miskolc, to Tisza R. c.20 mi. SW of Tokaj; total length, c.125 mi. Navigable in lower part for small boats. Lignite outcrops mined in its valley at Miskolc and Sajoszentpeter. Main tributary, Hernad R.

Sajoszentpeter (shŏ'yōsĕntpā"tĕr), Hung. *Sajószentpéter*, town (pop. 7,321), Borsod-Gömör co., NE Hungary, on Sajo R. and 9 mi. N of Miskolc; glass mfg. Lignite mine near by.

Saka (sä'kä), Ital. *Saca*, town, Kaffa prov., SW Ethiopia, 40 mi. NNE of Jimma. Chief center of the Enarea dist.; coffee growing.

Saka (sä'kä), town, S Tibet, in E Kailas Range, on main Leh-Lhasa trade route and 225 mi. W of Shigatse; alt. 15,140 ft.

Sakado (sä"kä'dō), town (pop. 7,750), Saitama prefecture, central Honshu, Japan, 6 mi. NW of Kawagoe; spinning; rice, wheat, sweet potatoes, raw silk.

Sakaehama, Russian SFSR: see STARODUBSKOYE.

Sakai (säkī'). **1** Town (pop. 7,741), Gumma prefecture, central Honshu, Japan, 5 mi. SE of Isezaki; raw silk, textiles. **2** Town (pop. 7,341), Ibaraki prefecture, central Honshu, Japan, on Tone R. and 8 mi. SE of Koga; rice, silk cocoons; textiles. **3** City (1940 pop. 182,147; 1947 pop. 194,048), Osaka prefecture, S Honshu, Japan, on Osaka Bay, just S of Osaka, at mouth of short Yamato R.; industrial center (chemical plants, machine shops, cutlery and aluminum-ware factories, hosiery mills). Agr. and aviation schools. An important port in anc. times, it declined when mouth of Yamato R. became filled with silt, and now accommodates small craft only. Includes (since early 1940s) former towns of Hamadera (1940 pop. 18,823) and Otori (1940 pop. 7,061). **4** Town (pop. 8,660), Tottori prefecture, S Honshu, Japan, port on inlet of Sea of Japan, 11 mi. ENE of Matsue across lagoon Naka-no-umi; rice, raw silk. Exports fish.

Sakaide (säkī'dā), city (1940 pop. 31,030; 1947 pop. 40,311), Kagawa prefecture, N Shikoku, Japan, on Hiuchi Sea, 11 mi. W of Takamatsu; mfg. center in agr. area (rice, wheat, fruit); cotton textiles, soy sauce, sake, salt. Fishery. Exports cotton thread, machinery, sugar.

Sakaka or **Sakakah** (säkä'kŭ), village and outlying oasis of Jauf, Hejaz, northernmost Saudi Arabia, 25 mi. NE of Jauf.

Sakaki (sä"kä'kē), town (pop. 6,879), Nagano prefecture, central Honshu, Japan, 6 mi. NW of Ueda, in agr. area (rice, wheat, raw silk).

Sakal (sä'käl), village, NW Senegal, Fr. West Africa, on railroad and 20 mi. SE of Saint-Louis; peanut growing, stock raising.

Sakalapie (sä'klŭpē), town, Central Prov., N central Liberia, 20 mi. SSE of Ganta; palm oil and kernels, kola nuts. Kaolin deposits near by. Sometimes spelled Sakripie.

Sakalespur, India: see SAKLESHPUR.

Sakami Lake (säkämē') (55 mi. long, 20 mi. wide), NW Que., bet. Fort George R. (N) and Eastmain R. (S); 53°N 76°45'W; alt. 640 ft.

Sakamoto (säkä'mōtō), town (pop. 2,918), Gumma prefecture, central Honshu, Japan, 10 mi. NW of Tomioka; rice. Hot springs.

Sakania (säkän'yä), village, Katanga prov., SE Belgian Congo, on railroad and 100 mi. SE of Elisabethville; customs and quarantine station near Northern Rhodesia border; cattle raising. Has R.C. mission and is seat of vicar apostolic.

Sakanmaw (sŭkän'mô), village, Kyaukpyu dist., Lower Burma, in the Arakan, on An R. (head of navigation) and 35 mi. NE of Kyaukpyu.

Sakano (sä"kä'nō), town (pop. 8,654), Tokushima prefecture, E Shikoku, Japan, on Kii Channel, 7 mi. SE of Tokushima; agr. center (rice, wheat); raw silk.

Sakanoichi (säkä'-nō'ĭchē), town (pop. 15,244), Oita prefecture, E Kyushu, Japan, on S shore of Beppu Bay, 8 mi. E of Oita; mfg. center in rice-growing area (earthenware, drain pipes, tiles).

Sakar (sŭkär'), village, E Chardzhou oblast, Turkmen SSR, 15 mi. SE of Chardzhou; cotton.

Sakaraha (säkärä'hŭ), village, Tuléar prov., SW Madagascar, on highway and 50 mi. NE of Tuléar; cattle market; also beans, corn.

Sakar Balkan Mountains, Bulgaria: see LISA MOUNTAINS.

Sakari (sä"kä'rē), town (pop. 4,366), Iwate prefecture, N Honshu, Japan, 16 mi. SW of Kamaishi; sake, soy sauce.

Sakar Mountains (sä'kär), SE Bulgaria, extend 30 mi. NW-SE bet. Maritsa and Tundzha rivers N of their confluence; rise to 2,152 ft. Prehistoric and anc. relics found.

Sakarya River (säkäryä'), anc. *Sangarius*, important river (490 mi. long) of Asia Minor, in W central Turkey; rises 18 mi. NNE of Afyonkarahisar and forms several huge bends, flowing E, N, W, and N, past Seyitgazi, Osmaneli, Geyve, and Adapazari, to Black Sea at Karasu, c.85 mi. E of the Bosporus. Receives Porsuk and Goksu rivers (left), Ankara, Kirmir, and Aladag rivers (right).

Sakashita (säkä'shĭtä). **1** Town (pop. 5,457), Aichi prefecture, central Honshu, Japan, 6 mi. NW of Seto; lignite mining. **2** Town (pop. 6,310), Gifu prefecture, central Honshu, Japan, 17 mi. WNW of Iida; raw-silk center; poultry raising; paper milling.

Sakata (sä"kä'tä), city (1940 pop. 31,958; 1947 pop. 49,526), Yamagata prefecture, N Honshu, Japan, port on Sea of Japan, at mouth of Mogami R., 53 mi. NW of Yamagata; commercial center for agr. area; mfg. (lacquer ware, soy sauce), metalworking. Exports rice, lumber.

Sakawa (sä"kä'wä), town (pop. 7,260), Kochi prefecture, S Shikoku, Japan, 15 mi. WSW of Kochi; metalworking; coral ornaments; sake brewing. Limestone quarry near by.

Sakchi, India: see JAMSHEDPUR.

Sakchu (säk'chōō'), Jap. *Sakushu*, township (1944 pop. 13,568), N Pyongan prov., N Korea, on Yalu R. and 40 mi. NE of Sinuiju; gold mining, agr. (soy beans, millet, potatoes, tobacco).

Sake (sä'kā), village, Kivu prov., E Belgian Congo, on NW shore of L. Kivu, 34 mi. N of Costermansville; agr. (coffee, bananas) and trading center. Protestant mission. Prior to 1938 eruption of Nyamlagira volcano, which closed Sake Bay, Sake was a steamboat landing and main point of access to region NW of L. Kivu.

Sakesar (sŭkā'sŭr), village, Shahpur dist., W central Punjab, W Pakistan, 55 mi. NW of Sargodha; hill resort (sanitarium); highest point (c.4,992 ft.) of Salt Range.

Sakété (säkĕ'tā), town (pop. c.11,800), S Dahomey, Fr. West Africa, 15 mi. N of Porto-Novo; trading and agr. center; palm kernels, palm oil, corn, cotton, manioc, potatoes, peanuts. Agr. station.

Sakhalin, town, Manchuria: see AIGUN.

Sakhalin (să'kŭlēn", săkŭlēn', Rus. sŭkhŭlyēn'), Jap. *Karafuto* (kärä'fōōtō), elongated island (□ 29,700; 1948 pop. estimate 500,000) off E coast of Siberian Russian SFSR, bet. Tatar Strait and Sea of Japan (W) and Sea of Okhotsk (E); extends S from 54°25'N (Cape Yelizaveta) to 45°53'N (Cape Crillon); separated from Hokkaido, Japan, by La Pérouse Strait; 560 mi. long, 17–140 mi. wide. Has 2 parallel mtn. ranges (rising to 6,604 ft. at Mt. Nevelskoi in E range), separated by a central valley watered by Tym and Poronai rivers; Severe climate, with annual mean temp. near freezing and annual rainfall of 20–25 in. Largely forested. Agr. in central valley and S portion (Susunai Valley) of isl.; grain (rye, oats, barley), potatoes, vegetables, and, in S, beans, sugar beets, some wheat and rice. Industry based on coal (Aleksandrovsk, Uglegorsk, Gornozavodsk, Sinegorsk), oil (Okha), and, in S, on paper and pulp milling and fish canning. Railroads (S) and highways (N) are, together with coastwise shipping, chief transportation routes. Pop. and main urban centers concentrated along coast: Aleksandrovsk and Okha (N); Uglegorks, Kholmsk, and Korsakov (S); Dolinsk and Yuzhno-Sakhalinsk (in Susunai Valley). Pop. largely Russian. Indigenous pop. includes c.4,000 Ainu and Nivkhi (Gilyaks) in S, Evenki (Tungus) and Nanai (Orochon) in N. Jap pop. largely repatriated from S Sakhalin after Second World War. First visited (1644) by Rus. explorer Poyarkov; assumed to be a peninsula until early-19th cent.; colonized by Japanese (late-18th cent.) and by Russians, who established 1st military post at Korsakov in 1853. It was under joint Russo-Japanese control (formalized 1854) until it passed entirely to Russia in 1875, when Japan obtained the Kuriles in exchange; developed as a tsarist place of exile. By treaty of Portsmouth (1905), Japan obtained S half of Sakhalin (S of 50°N), called Karafuto (□ 13,000; 1940 pop. 398,838). N Sakhalin was temporarily (1920–25) occupied by Japan and in 1932 became an oblast within Far Eastern (after 1938, Khabarovsk) Territory. Following Soviet occupation (1945) of Karafuto and the Kuriles, these areas were joined to N Sakhalin and constituted (1947) as a separate oblast (□ 35,400, including Kurile Isls.) of Russian SFSR. Formerly spelled Saghalien or Saghalin.

Sakhalin-Ula, town, Manchuria: see AIGUN.

Sakhalin Ula, river, China and USSR: see AMUR RIVER.

Sakhnovshchina (sŭkhnôf'shchĭnŭ), town (1926 pop. 3,155), SW Kharkov oblast, Ukrainian SSR, 25 mi. NW of Lozovaya; flour-milling center; dairying.

Sakhtsar, Iran: see RAMSAR.

Saki (sä'kē), town (1938 pop. 7,987), W Crimea, Russian SFSR, on railroad and 12 mi. ESE of Yevpatoriya; health resort on Saki salt lake (noted mud baths); chemical works (salt, bromide, magnesium chloride).

Sakiai, Shakyai or **Shakyay** (shäkyī'), Lith. *Šakiai*, Ger. *Schaken*, Pol. *Szaki*, Rus. *Shaki*, city (pop. 2,577), SW Lithuania, 35 mi. WNW of Kaunas; mfg. of textiles, chemicals, vegetable oil; sawmilling, flour milling. Dates from 14th cent.; passed 1795 to Prussia, 1815 to Rus. Poland; in Suvalki govt. until 1920.

Sakiet-Sidi-Youssef (säkyĕt'-sē'dē-yōōsĕf'), village, Le Kef dist., W Tunisia, on Algerian border, 20 mi. W of Le Kef; zinc mining. Customhouse.

Sakinohama (säkē'-nō'hämŭ), town (pop. 4,153), Kochi prefecture, SE Shikoku, Japan, on Philippine Sea, 40 mi. ESE of Kochi; rice, silk; fishing.

Sakir, peak, W Pakistan: see TOBA-KAKAR RANGE.

Saki-shima (säkē'shĭmä), island (□ 4; pop. 3,426), Hiroshima prefecture, Japan, in Hiuchi Sea (central section of Inland Sea), just S of Mihara on SW Honshu; 3 mi. long, 1.5 mi. wide; mountainous. Produces sweet potatoes, radishes, chrysanthemums (for making insecticide), corn. Fishing.

Sakishima Islands (säkē'shĭmä), Jap. *Sakishima-gunto*, S group (□ 343; 1950 pop. 118,585) of RYUKYU ISLANDS, between East China Sea (W) and Philippine Sea (E), 70 mi. E of Formosa; 24°27'–24°46'N 122°58'–125°20'E. Its 150-mi. chain includes volcanic isls. of ISHIGAKI-SHIMA (largest), MIYAKO-JIMA, IRIOMOTE-JIMA, IRABU-SHIMA, YONAGUNI-SHIMA, TARAMA-JIMA, SENKAKU-GUNTO, and scattered coral islets. Mountainous and fertile. Principal product, sugar cane. Coal mining on Iriomote-jima. Produces sake, dried tuna, pottery. Formerly called Majicoshima. Chief town, Ishigaki. Group is sometimes divided into 2 subgroups, YAEYAMA-GUNTO and MIYAKO-GUNTO.

Sakit (sŭkēt'), town (pop. 2,278), Etah dist., W Uttar Pradesh, India, 11 mi. SE of Etah; wheat, pearl millet, barley, corn, jowar, oilseeds.

Sakiz, Iran: see SAQQIZ.

Sakiz-Adasi, Greece: see CHIOS.

Sakkara, Saqqara, or **Saqqarah** (säk-kä'rŭ), village (pop. 8,230), Giza prov., Upper Egypt, 3 mi. W of the Nile, 15 mi. S of Cairo. The Necropolis of Sakkara contains sepulchral monuments of many periods of Egyptian history, the oldest mummy (over 6,000 years old) and the oldest dated papyrus (VI dynasty). The famous pyramids of Sakkara (built by V dynasty kings) are less than half the height of the Great Pyramid at Giza; of limestone and of poor core construction, they are now in complete ruin. Near by are the wonderful tombs of the Sacred Bulls.

Sakkiz, Iran: see SAQQIZ.

Sakleshpur (sŭklāsh'pŏŏr), town (pop. 3,620), Hassan dist., W Mysore, India, on Hemavati R. and 22 mi. WSW of Hassan; coffee curing; rice, sugar cane. Coffee, tea, and cardamom estates in near-by slopes of Western Ghats. Also spelled Saklaspur or Sakalespur.

Sakmara or **Sakmarskoye** (sŭkmä'rŭ, –mär'skŭyŭ), village (1926 pop. 3,458), central Chkalov oblast, Russian SFSR, on Sakmara R. and 17 mi. NE of Chkalov, near railroad; mfg. of building materials, metalworking; wheat, livestock.

Sakmara River, SE European Russian SFSR, rises in the S Urals SW of Askarovo, flows S, through forested valley rich in gold, copper, and asbestos, past Yuldybayevo, and generally W, through wheat and livestock region, past Kuvandyk, Saraktash, and Sakmara to Ural R. just W of Chkalov; 440 mi. long. Navigable below Saraktash. Receives Zilair, Greater Ik, and Silmysh rivers (right).

Sakoa (säkōō'ŭ), small stream, Tuléar prov., SW Madagascar, rises 15 mi. SE of Betioky, flows c.25 mi. to Savazy R., a right tributary of the Onilahy. Sakoa basin is the main source of coal in Madagascar and is being connected by a railroad with port of Soalara.

Sakoi (sŭkoi'), S state (myosaship) (□ 82; pop. 2,272), Southern Shan State, Upper Burma; ⊙ Sakoi, village on the Nam Pilu and 20 mi. NNW of Loikaw. Hilly country E and W of Nam Pilu valley.

Sakoli (sä'kōlē), village, Bhandara dist., central Madhya Pradesh, India, 23 mi. ESE of Bhandara; rice milling; wheat, oilseeds. Corundum deposits in forested hills (SE).

Sakonnakhon (säkôn'näkôn'), town (1947 pop. 5,975), ⊙ Sakonnakhon prov. (□ 3,963; 1947 pop. 273,262), NE Thailand, in Korat Plateau, 85 mi. E of Udon (linked by road and projected railroad); airport; agr. center (rice, cattle, cotton, tobacco). Also spelled Sakolnagor and Sakolnakon.

Sakonnet (sukŏ'nĭt), resort village in Little Compton town, Newport co., SE R.I., 6 mi. ESE of Newport and on **Sakonnet Point**, peninsula on Atlantic coast E of mouth of **Sakonnet River**, arm of Narragansett Bay extending c.14 mi. N-S from the Atlantic to Mt. Hope Bay, E of Rhode Isl.

Sakoshi (säkō'shē), town (pop. 5,720), Hyogo prefecture, S Honshu, Japan, on Harima Sea, 16 mi. WSW of Himeji; agr. (rice, wheat, sweet potatoes); fishing. Small copper mine.

Sakota (sä'kōtä), town (pop. 4,500), Wallo prov., NE Ethiopia, near Tsellari R., 65 mi. SW of Makale; 12°38'N 39°4'E. Trade center (salt, honey, beeswax, coffee, mules); cotton weaving. Has churches and a mosque. Sometimes Sokota.

Sakrand (sŭk'rŭnd), village, Nawabshah dist., central Sind, W Pakistan, 10 mi. SW of Nawabshah; rail junction; wheat, millet, tobacco, gram. Agr. col., cotton research station, seed depot (fruit, vegetables).

Sakrau or **Sacrau** (both: zä'krou) or **Zakrzow** (zäk'-zhōōf), Pol. *Zakrzów*, commune (1939 pop. 3,142; 1946 pop. 3,518) in Lower Silesia, after 1945 in Wroclaw prov., SW Poland, 6 mi. NE of Breslau (Wroclaw). Graves of Vandal kings, dating from 4th cent. B.C., excavated here.

Sakri (sŭk'rē), village (pop. 2,250), West Khandesh dist., N Bombay, India, 32 mi. WNW of Dhulia; local market for cotton, millet, peanuts.

Sakripie, Liberia: see SAKALAPIE.

Sak River, U. of So. Afr.: see ZAK RIVER.

Saksagan River or **Saksagan' River** (sŭksŭgän'yŭ), Dnepropetrovsk oblast, Ukrainian SSR, rises near Verkhovtsevo, flows c.60 mi. SW to Ingulets R. at Krivoi Rog. Traverses rich iron-mining dist. in lower course.

Saksak Dag (shäk-shäk' dä), Turkish *Şakşak Dağ*, peak (10,335 ft.), E central Turkey, 25 mi. S of Erzurum.

Saksaulski or **Saksaul'skiy** (sŭksŭōōl'skē), town (1948 pop. over 2,000), NW Kzyl-Orda oblast, Kazakh SSR, on Trans-Caspian RR and 30 mi. NW of Aralsk; metalworks.

Sakskobing (säk'skûbĭng), Dan. *Sakskøbing*, city (pop. 2,473) and port, Maribo amt, Denmark, on Lolland isl., at head of Sakskobing Fjord, and 5 mi. ENE of Maribo; sugar refining, mfg. of agr. machinery. Formerly spelled Sakskjobing.

Sakti (sŭk'tē), town (pop. 4,187), Raigarh dist., E Madhya Pradesh, India, 30 mi. WNW of Raigarh; tussah-silk weaving; rice, oilseeds. Limestone quarries near by. Was ⊙ former princely state of Sakti (□ 137; pop. 54,517), one of Chhattisgarh States, since 1948, inc. into Raigarh dist.

Saku (sä'kōō), town (pop. 293), NW Estonia, 9 mi. S of Tallinn; brewery.

Sakumi, Japan: see KATAYAMAZU.

Sakura (sä"kōō'rä), town (pop. 12,368), Chiba prefecture, central Honshu, Japan, 10 mi. NE of Chiba; rail junction; commercial center for agr. area.

Sakurai (säkōō'rī'). **1** Town (pop. 9,656), Ehime prefecture, N Shikoku, Japan, on Hiuchi Sea, 3 mi. SE of Imabari; commercial center for agr. area (rice, wheat, barley); raw silk. Sometimes called Iyo-sakurai. **2** Town (pop. 16,786), Nara prefecture, S Honshu, Japan, 12 mi. S of Nara; rail junction; lumbering center. Buddhist temple (7th cent.) near by. **3** Town (pop. 22,483), Toyama prefecture, central Honshu, Japan, on E shore of Toyama Bay, 19 mi. NE of Toyama, in agr. area (rice, watermelons); sake, textiles. Formed in late 1930s by combining former town of Mikkaichi and several villages.

Sakura-jima (säkōō'rä'-jĭmä), peninsula (□ 30; pop. 13,506), NW projection of Osumi Peninsula, Kagoshima prefecture, S Kyushu, Japan, opposite Kagoshima; 7 mi. E-W, 5 mi. N-S. Has 3 volcanic cones; highest (Kita-dake) rises to 3,668 ft. Hot springs. Fertile coast produces citrus fruit, loquats, giant radishes. An island until 1914, when lava from a volcanic eruption, which damaged Kagoshima, filled the narrow channel separating it from Osumi Peninsula.

Sakushu, Korea: see SAKCHU.

Sakuyama (säkōō'yämŭ), town (pop. 5,308), Tochigi prefecture, central Honshu, Japan, 18 mi. NNE of Utsunomiya; rice growing.

Sakya (sä'kyä), lamasery, S Tibet, on tributary of the Brahmaputra, on main Katmandu-Lhasa trade route and 55 mi. SW of Shigatse. In 1270, the abbot of Sakya traveled to China and converted Kublai Khan to Lamaism; returned to found Sakya dynasty (1270–1340) and to become 1st priest-king of Tibet.

Sal (säl), northeasternmost island (□83; 1940 pop. 1,142; 1950 pop. 1,784) of the Cape Verde Isls., in Windward group, 25 mi. N of Boa Vista Isl., in the Atlantic. Santa Maria (16°36'N 22°55'W), its chief town, is on S coast. Isl. is 18 mi. long, 2–7 mi. wide, and the least mountainous of the archipelago, rising to 1,332 ft. in isolated Monte Grande (near N shore). Saltworks near Santa Maria and Pedra Lume. Espargo international airport for trans-Atlantic flights was inaugurated 1949.

Sal, Punta (pōōn'tä säl'), rocky cape of N Honduras, on Caribbean Sea, 14 mi. NW of Tela; 15°52'N 87°37'W.

Sal, Punta de, Peru: see PUNTA DE SAL.

Sala (shä'lyä), Slovak *Sal'a*, town (pop. 4,397), SW Slovakia, Czechoslovakia, on Vah R. and 15 mi. SW of Nitra; agr. center (wheat, barley, sugar beets); vineyards.

Sala or **Sala di Caserta** (sä'lä dē käzĕr'tä), village, Caserta prov., Campania, S Italy, 1 mi. N of Caserta; silk-milling center.

Sala (sä'lä"), city (pop. 8,488), Vastmanland co., central Sweden, 20 mi. N of Vasteras; rail junction; machinery, concrete, brick, and lime works. Has 17th-cent. church, 18th-cent. town hall, and mus. Chartered 1624, it was formerly silver-, lead-, and zinc-mining center (mines now abandoned), and scene of important annual trade fairs.

Sala Baganza (sä'lä bägän'tsä), village (pop. 1,519), Parma prov., Emilia-Romagna, N central Italy, 7 mi. SSW of Parma; sausage, canned tomatoes.

Salaberry de Valleyfield, Que.: see VALLEYFIELD.

Salaca River or **Salatsa River** (sä'lätsä), Ger. *Salis*, in N Latvia, N outlet of Burtnieki L., flows 58 mi. generally W, past Mazsalaca, to Gulf of Riga at Salacgriva.

Salacgriva or **Salatsgriva** (sä'lätsgrē"vä) Lettish *Salacgrīva*, Ger. *Salismünde*, city (pop. 921), N Latvia, in Vidzeme, on Gulf of Riga, 55 mi. NNE of Riga, at mouth of Salaca R., in forest marshes.

Salach (zä'läkh), village (pop. 4,763), N Württemberg, Germany, after 1945 in Württemberg-Baden, on the Fils and 4 mi. E of Göppingen; grain, cattle.

Sa-la-ch'i, China: see SARATSI.

Salacia Imperatoria, Portugal: see ALCÁCER DO SAL.

Sala Consilina (sä'lä kônsēlē'nä), town (pop. 6,228), Salerno prov., Campania, S Italy, near Tanagro R., 20 mi. SW of Potenza. Agr. trade center (grapes, olives, vegetables, cereals); macaroni, electric products.

Salada, Laguna (lägōō'nä sälä'dä), salt lake (□ c.250), N Lower California, NW Mexico, 18 mi. SW of Mexicali, bet. Sierra Juárez (W) and Sierra de los Cocopás (E); c.25 mi. long, c.6 mi. wide. Size varies widely, depending on overflow of Colorado R.

Salada Beach, Calif.: see SHARP PARK.

Saladas (sälä'däs), town (pop. 3,835), ⊙ Saladas dept. (□ c.800; pop. 21,918), W Corrientes prov., Argentina, on railroad and 55 mi. SSE of Corrientes; agr. center (alfalfa, rice, manioc, cotton, tobacco, oranges, livestock); tanning.

Saladillo (säläde'yō). **1** Town (pop. 8,631), ⊙ Saladillo dist. (□ 1,054; pop. 26,641), central Buenos Aires prov., Argentina, near the Río Saladillo, 105 mi. SW of Buenos Aires; rail junction; agr. center (alfalfa, sunflowers, grain, flax, cattle, sheep); tanning, dairying, flour milling. Has natl. col. **2** Village, San Luis prov., Argentina: see VILLA SALADILLO.

Saladillo, Río (rē'ō säläde'yō). **1** River, central Buenos Aires prov., Argentina, rises near General Lamadrid, flows c.200 mi. NE to the Río Salado 15 mi. SW of Monte. Its upper course is called the Villamanca. **2** River, Córdoba prov., Argentina: see CUARTO, Río. **3** River, N Argentina, in Tucumán, Santiago del Estero, and Córdoba provs.: see DULCE, Río. **4** River, Santa Fe prov., Argentina, rises 38 mi. N of Vera, flows c.200 mi. S, through several swamps and lakes, and through the bayou L. Guadalupe, to the Paraná NE of Santa Fe. Called Caraguatay R. in upper course.

Salado (sälä'dō), village (pop. 113), Atlántida dept., N Honduras, minor port on Caribbean Sea, at mouth of small Río Salado 14 mi. W of La Ceiba; rail terminus; coconuts, plantains, corn, beans. Also called Barra Salado.

Salado (sŭlā'dō), village (pop. c.400), Bell co., central Texas, 15 mi. SW of Temple; trade point in farm area.

Salado, El, Mexico: see EL SALADO.

Salado, Quebrada del (kābrä'dä dĕl sälä'dō), river in Atacama prov., N Chile, rises in S Atacama Desert, flows c.115 mi. S and W, past Llanta and Pueblo Hundido, to the Pacific at Chañaral.

Salado, Río (rē'ō). **1** River, Buenos Aires prov., E Argentina, rises at alt. of 130 ft. in L. Chañar on Santa Fe prov. border 14 mi. NW of General Arenales, flows 400 mi. SE, past Junín, Roque Pérez, and General Belgrano, to Samborombón Bay 25 mi. SSW of Punta Piedras. Has meandering course, often flooded. Feeds large irrigation system in lower course. Receives the Arroyo de las Flores. **2** River, in Catamarca and La Rioja provs., W Argentina: see COLORADO, Río. **3** River, part of a central Argentine river system (sometimes called the Desaguadero) which forms a broad 600-mi.-long basin from the Andes of N La Rioja prov. southward across N Patagonia to the Río Colorado in S La Pampa natl. territory. Rises as the Bermejo in W La Rioja prov., flows c.250 mi. S to the HUANACACHE lakes 75 mi. SE of San Juan, continues S along Mendoza-San Luis prov. border as the Desaguadero to the swamps S of L. Bebedero, whence, as the Río Salado, it flows S into La Pampa in a marshy area, turning SE and sometimes reaching the Río Colorado 150 mi. W of Bahía Blanca. Its lower course, below Limay Mahuida, is often called the Chadileufú, and, below Puelches, the Curacó. Total length, 750 mi. Receives the Atuel, Diamante, and Tunuyán rivers. **4** or **Río Salado del Norte** (dĕl nôr'tā), river, N central Argentina, rises in the Andes in branches NW and SW of Salta, flows 1,250 mi. SE across provs. of Salta, Santiago del Estero, and Santa Fe to the Paraná at Santa Fe. Formed by confluence of TORO RIVER and GUACHIPAS RIVER just E of Coronel Moldes, 35 mi. S of Salta, it flows thence E and S for 150 mi. as the Pasaje (päsä'hä) or Juramento (hōōrämĕn'tō) to a swampy area in NW Santiago del Estero prov., where it takes the name Río Salado.

Salado, Río. 1 River, N Mexico, continuation of Sabinas R. from Don Martín Dam on Coahuila-Nuevo León border; flows c.110 mi. SE, partly along Nuevo León-Tamaulipas border, past Guerrero, to the Rio Grande opposite Zapata, Texas. Used to irrigate cotton-growing area. **2** River, Colima, W Mexico, rises at S foot of Colima volcano, flows c.40 mi. SSE to Tuxpan R.; used for irrigation.

Salado del Norte, Río, Argentina: see SALADO, Río.

Salaga (sä'lŭgŭ), town (pop. 3,111), Northern Territories, central Gold Coast, 60 mi. SSE of Tamale; road junction; shea nuts, durra, yams. Hq. Gonja dist.

Salagasta (sälägä'stä), village, N Mendoza prov., Argentina, in SE of Sierra de los Paramillos, 17 mi. NW of Mendoza; coal-mining center.

Salahiya, Iraq: see KIFRI.

Salahkai Mesa (säläkī') (c.7–8,000 ft.), tableland in Navajo Indian Reservation, NE Ariz., c.75 mi. NE of Winslow.

Salair (sŭlŭēr'), city (1938 pop. estimate 21,500), W Kemerovo oblast, Russian SFSR, on Salair Ridge, 25 mi. SW of Belovo (linked by railroad); lead-zinc mines, barite deposits. City since 1941.

Salair Ridge, SW Siberian Russian SFSR, along borders of Altai Territory and Kemerovo oblast; extends c.200 mi. N from Biya R., bet. Ob and Tom rivers; rises to 2,000 ft. Rich in iron, silver, lead, zinc. Crossed by S.Siberian RR.

Salajar, Indonesia: see SALAYAR.

Salak, Mount (sŭläk'), volcanic peak (7,254 ft.), W Java, Indonesia, in Preanger region, 8 mi. SSW of Bogor.

Salak North, village (pop. 411), N central Perak, Malaya, on railroad and 7 mi. NE of Kuala Kangsar; tin mining.

Salak South, town (pop. 742), central Selangor, Malaya, 3 mi. S of Kuala Lumpur; tin mining.

Salala or **Salalah** (sä'lälä), town, Central Prov., central Liberia, 55 mi. NE of Monrovia, on road; palm oil and kernels, cassava, rice.

Salala or **Salalah** (sälä'lŭ), chief town of Dhofar dist., S Oman, port on Arabian Sea, 700 mi. ENE of Aden; 17°N 54°6'E. Trading center, shipping frankincense from the Jabal Samhan; cotton, wheat, tobacco, sugar cane, melons. Airfield.

Salamá (sälämä'), city (1950 pop. 2,648), ⊙ Baja Verapaz dept., central Guatemala, in N highlands, on Salamá R. (right affluent of the Chixoy) and 37 mi. NNE of Guatemala; 15°6'N 90°16'W; alt. 3,018 ft. Market center in agr. area; coffee, sugar cane, olives; livestock.

Salamá, town (pop. 947), Olancho dept., central Honduras, on Telica R. (left affluent of Guayape R.) and 26 mi. NW of Juticalpa; commercial center in agr. area.

Salamanca (sălŭmăng'kŭ, Sp. sälämäng'kä), town (pop.2,819), Coquimbo prov., N central Chile, on railroad, on Choapa R. and 16 mi. SE of Illapel; rail terminus, trade and agr. center (grain, fruit, cattle). Copper and gold deposits near by. Old colonial town.

Salamanca, city (pop. 11,985), Guanajuato, central Mexico, on central plateau, on Lerma R. and 30 mi. S of Guanajuato; alt. 5,590 ft. Rail junction; agr. center (wheat, corn, alfalfa, cotton, sugar cane, fruit, stock); flour mills, tanneries; oil refining, mfg. of cotton goods, chemicals, ceramics.

Salamanca, town (pop. 1,092), Arequipa dept., S Peru, at W foot of the Nudo Coropuna, 23 mi. NW of Chuquibamba; cereals, potatoes. Gold mines near by.

Salamanca, town (1939 pop. 5,402), Negros Occidental prov., NE Negros isl., Philippines, on Tañon Strait, 40 mi. ENE of Bacolod; agr. center (rice, sugar cane).

Salamanca, province (□ 4,754; pop. 390,468), W Spain, in Leon; ⊙ Salamanca. Bounded by Portugal (W and NW) and by crest of the Sierra de Gata (S); consists of tableland (N) and mountainous region(S; Sierra de Gata, Peña de Francia). Drained by Duero or Douro R. (Port. border; NW) and its tributaries (Tormes, Agueda). Some tungsten and lead mining. Essentially agr.: cereals, vegetables, wine, olive oil, fruit, flax; lumbering and stock raising (cattle, sheep, hogs). Industries derived from agr. (flour milling, dairy-products mfg., meat processing, tanning); other products include woolen textiles (Béjar), linen, tiles, beer. Wool trade. Primitive agr. methods and poor communications hamper development. Prov. crossed by 2 railroads from Salamanca to Portugal (Lisbon and Oporto). Chief cities: Salamanca, Béjar, Ciudad Rodrigo.

Salamanca, city (pop. 71,725), ⊙ Salamanca prov., W Spain, in Leon, on Tormes R. and 110 mi. WNW of Madrid; 40°58'N 5°40'W. Communications and agr. trade center (cereals, wine, livestock, hides). Chemical works (fertilizers, sulphuric acid, industrial products), tanneries, brewery, flour and sawmills; mfg. of cement pipes, furniture, jewelry, brandy and liqueur, chocolate, processed meat, flour products. Granite quarries near by. Seat of bishop and of famous univ., Salamanca is one of the most notable historic and artistic cities of Spain. It has narrow, tortuous streets and numerous beautiful bldgs.; and in center of city is arcaded Plaza Mayor, one of finest squares in Spain, with town hall by Churriguera. On height above river—spanned here by Roman bridge still retaining 15 of its original arches—stands the old (12th-cent.) cathedral adjoined by imposing new (16th–18th cent.) cathedral, both with fine cloisters and countless works of art. Near by are univ. palace and episcopal palace (15th cent.). Bet. plaza and cathedrals are Casa de las Conchas (1514; named for shells adorning façade), Casa de la Salina (16th cent.), and Torre de Clavero, a typical Castilian tower of 15th cent. Among numerous other notable bldgs. are: 16th-cent. church and convent of St. Stephen, Romanesque church of St. Martin (12th cent.), former Jesuit col. (16th cent.), and impressive Monterrey mansion (1540). The old city was taken (222 B.C.) by Hannibal; later in 3d cent. B.C. occupied by the Romans, then by the Visigoths (6th cent. A.D.) and Moors (8th cent.); reconquered from the Moors by the Christians in late 11th cent. The univ., founded in early 13th cent. by Alfonso IX of Leon, soon became one of the greatest in Europe; in late Middle Ages and throughout Renaissance it was the center of cultural and religious life of Spain, reaching its zenith in 16th cent., after which it declined with the city. City partly demolished in 1811 by French; scene of battle won 1812 by Wellington against French. In the Sp. civil war, it was capital for a time in 1937–38 of the Nationalists.

Salamanca, city (pop. 8,861), Cattaraugus co., W N.Y., on Allegheny R. and 10 mi. NW of Olean; trade and mfg. center, in Allegany Indian Reservation. Allegany State Park is just S. Furniture, dairy products, machinery, textiles, wood products, aircraft parts; printing. Settled in 1860s; inc. 1913 as city.

Salamanca Island (sälämäng'kä), on Caribbean coast of Magdalena dept., N Colombia, narrow alluvial bar across mouth of the lagoon Ciénaga Grande de Santa Marta, 20 mi. SSW of Santa Marta; 30 mi. long.

Salamat, region, Fr. Equatorial Africa: see AM-TIMAN.

Salamat, Bahr, Fr. Equatorial Africa: see BAHR SALAMAT.

Salamaua (sälämou'ä, sälŭmou'), town, Morobe dist., NE New Guinea, on narrow isthmus of Bayern Bay in Huon Gulf and 160 mi. N of Port Moresby; founded 1927 to serve air transport lines into gold fields. In Second World War, site of Jap. air base (established 1942) taken 1943 by Allied forces.

Salamazet, Madagascar: see TAMATAVE, town.

Salambô, Tunisia: see SALAMMBÔ.

Salambria River, Greece: see PENEUS RIVER.

Salamina (sälämē'nä). **1** Town (pop. 6,183), Caldas dept., W central Colombia, in Cordillera Central, 23 mi. N of Manizales; alt. 5,978 ft. Coffee and cattle center; tobacco, sugar cane, wheat, potatoes; sericulture, dairying, flour milling; mfg. of soap, paraffin candles. **2** Town (pop. 2,424), Magdalena dept., N Colombia, on lower Magdalena R. and 33 mi. S of Barranquilla; corn, cotton.

Salamis (să'lŭmĭs), ruined city in Famagusta dist., E Cyprus, on Famagusta Bay, 6 mi. N of Famagusta. Its harbor is now silted up. Probably of Mycenaean origin, it was, according to legend, founded by Teucer, native of the Gr. isl. of Salamis, after the Trojan War. A Gr. stronghold, it revolted several times against Persia in 4th cent. B.C. Site of decisive naval victory won (306 B.C.) by Demetrius Poliorcetes over Ptolemy I of Egypt. Salamis was visited by St. Paul and St. Barnabas. The latter's tomb is located at near-by (1 mi. W) Apostolos Varnavas monastery. Town was damaged by earthquakes and rebuilt (4th cent. A.D.) by Constantine II and name *Constantia*. Decayed after Arab invasion 647–48. Ruins include a large Roman forum and aqueduct.

Salamis (să'lŭmĭs, sälämēs'), island (□ 39; 1940 pop. 17,312) in Saronic Gulf of Aegean Sea, off Bay of Eleusis, N of Aegina, in Attica nome, E central Greece, 1 mi. off mainland; 9 mi. long, 8 mi. wide. Wheat, olive oil, wine, fisheries. On Bay of Salamis (W), which nearly bisects isl., is town and port of Salamis (1928 pop. 7,757), 15 mi. W of Athens; 37°59'N 23°28'E. Naval base of Arapis (1928 pop. 4,049) is on channel bet. isl. and mainland, where in 480 B.C. the Greeks under Themistocles gained a decisive naval victory over the Persians under Xerxes. An early possession of Aegina, Salamis was (c.600 B.C.) under the control of Megara, and was later taken by Athens. It was formerly called Koulouri or Kuluri.

Salamiyah, Syria: see SELEMIYA.

Salammbô (sälämbō'), village, N Tunisia, on Gulf of Tunis, 9 mi. NE of Tunis, near Carthage; oceanographic station. Also spelled Salambô.

Salamonia (să'lŭmō"nē), town (pop. 181), Jay co., E Ind., on Salamonie R. and 30 mi. ENE of Muncie, in agr. area.

Salamonie River (să'lŭmō"nē), E and NE central Ind., rises near Salamonia in E Jay co., flows 82 mi. NW, past Portland and Montpelier, to the Wabash opposite Largo.

Salamvria River, Greece: see PENEUS RIVER.

Salana (sä'lŭnŭ), village, Nowgong dist., central Assam, India, 18 mi. ENE of Nowgong; rice, jute, rape and mustard.

Salandra (sälän'drä), village (pop. 3,160), Matera prov., Basilicata, S Italy, near Cavone R. (here called the Salandrella), 18 mi. SW of Matera; olive oil, wine.

Salang, Ujong, Thailand: see PHUKET, island.

Salangen (säl'ängŭn), fishing village and canton (pop. 2,885), Troms co., N Norway, at head of Asta Fjord of Norwegian Sea, 30 mi. NNE of Narvik. Near-by iron deposits not worked at present.

Salango Island (säläng'gō), small islet off Pacific coast of Manabí prov., W Ecuador, 80 mi. WNW of Guayaquil; 1°36'S 80°53'W.

Salanpur, India: see KULTI.

Salaparuta (säläpäroo'tä), village (pop. 3,036), Trapani prov., W Sicily, 14 mi. S of Alcamo; macaroni. Limestone deposits near by.

Salar (sälär'), town (pop. 2,759), Granada prov., S Spain, 5 mi. ESE of Loja; agr. trade center (cereals, olive oil, sugar beets, wine).

Salara (sälä'rä), village (pop. 603), Rovigo prov., Veneto, N Italy, near Po R., 14 mi. NW of Ferrara.

Salard (sŭlärd'), Rum. *Sălard*, Hung. *Szalárd* (sŏ'-lärt), village (pop. 3,003), Bihor prov., W Rumania, on Berettyo R. and 12 mi. NNE of Oradea; sawmilling. In Hungary, 1940–45.

Salares (sälä'rĕs), town (pop. 539), Málaga prov., S Spain, on coastal hills, 24 mi. ENE of Málaga; grapes, olives, oranges, livestock.

Salas (sä'läs), town (pop. 840), Lambayeque dept., NW Peru, in W foothills of Cordillera Occidental, 35 mi. NE of Lambayeque; corn, sugar cane, vegetables; cattle raising.

Salas, town (pop. 997), Oviedo prov., NW Spain, 21 mi. WNW of Oviedo; meat processing; lumbering; cereals, fruit, livestock. Iron and copper mines near by.

Salas or **Salash** (both: sä'läsh), Serbo-Croatian *Salaš*, village, E Serbia, Yugoslavia, 13 mi. SW of Negotin.

Salas de los Barrios (sä'läs dhā lōs bä'ryōs), town (pop. 1,086), Leon prov., NW Spain, 3 mi. SE of Ponferrada; wine, vegetables, fruit.

Salas de los Infantes (ĭmfän'tĕs), city (pop. 1,679), Burgos prov., N Spain, on Arlanza R., on Burgos-Soria RR and highway, and 30 mi. SE of Burgos, on irrigated plain (*La Campiña*); cereals, chickpeas, beans, livestock. Lumbering, fishing. Flour milling; mfg. of chocolate, cotton goods, meat products, naval stores. Historic city. Urns of the 7 infants of Lara housed in Santa María church were transferred (1924) to Burgos cathedral. Near by is the Siete Salas palace; San Pedro de Arlanza monastery; and the noted Santo Domingo de Silos monastery (8 mi. SE), an anc. Benedictine convent dating back to 6th cent., and containing a beautiful cloister.

Salatau (sŭlŭtou'), outlier of the E Greater Caucasus, in N central Dagestan Autonomous SSR, Russian SFSR, bet. Andi Range and Sulak R. gorge; c.10 mi. long E-W; rises to over 7,000 ft.

Salatiga (sŭlŭtē'gŭ), town (pop. 24,274), central Java, Indonesia, 35 mi. NNE of Jogjakarta, at foot of Mt. Merbabu; alt. 1,916 ft.; trade center for agr. area (rice, corn, rubber, cassava, coffee, cacao, cinchona bark).

Salat River (sälä'), Ariège and Haute-Garonne depts., S France, rises in central Pyrenees on Sp. border, flows 47 mi. NNW, past Oust, Saint-Girons, and Salies, to the Garonne below Saint-Martory.

Salatsa River, Latvia: see SALACA RIVER.

Salatsgriva, Latvia: see SALACGRIVA.

Salaverry (sälävĕ'rē), town (pop. 3,403), Libertad dept., NW Peru, pacific port on Salaverry Bay, on Pan American Highway and 8 mi. SSE of Trujillo; rail terminus. Shipping point for products of dist. (coca, sugar, cotton, rice); fisheries.

Salavina (sälävē'nä), village (pop. estimate 500), ⊙ Salavina dept. (□ 1,086; 1947 census 12,098), S Santiago del Estero prov., Argentina, on W bank of the Río Dulce and 60 mi. SE of Loreto; corn, wheat, alfalfa, livestock; flour milling.

Salawa, India: see KHATAULI.

Salawati (sŭlŭwä'tē), island (pop. 1,689), Netherlands New Guinea, W of Vogelkop peninsula (NW New Guinea); roughly circular, 30 mi. in diameter. Generally level with mountainous NW area rising to 2,900 ft. Produces sago, copra. Also called Salawat.

Salay (sälī'), town (1939 pop. 3,291; 1948 municipality pop. 13,194), Misamis Oriental prov., N Mindanao, Philippines, on Macajalar Bay, 28 mi. NNE of Cagayan; agr. center (corn, coconuts).

Salaya (sŭlä'yŭ), town (pop. 6,522), W Saurashtra, India, near Gulf of Cutch, 32 mi. WSW of Jamnagar; rail spur terminus; markets cotton, grain, oilseeds, salt; oilseed pressing.

Salayar or **Salajar** (both: sŭlŭyär'), island (□ 259; pop. 59,937), Indonesia, 10 mi. S of SW peninsula of Celebes isl. across narrow Salayar Strait; 6°5'S 120°30'E; long, narrow, 50 mi. long, 8 mi. wide; generally mountainous. Fishing, salt production. Chief agr. products: coconuts, pepper, corn. On W coast are principal centers, Benteng (chief port) and Padang. Also spelled Saleijer.

Sala y Gómez Island (sä'lä ē gō'mĕs), in the South Pacific, belonging to Valparaiso prov., Chile, 2,100 mi. W of Chile, c.250 mi. ENE of Easter Isl.; 26°28'S 105°28'W. An arid uninhabited islet of volcanic origin, 3,900 ft. long, 500 ft. wide.

Salazar (säläsär'), town (pop. 3,017), Norte de Santander dept., N Colombia, 22 mi. WSW of Cúcuta; coffee, cacao, corn, livestock. Coal mines near by.

Salazie (säläzē'), town (pop. 2,553; commune pop. 6,147), N central Réunion isl., on road and 8 mi. SW of Saint-André, in Salazie cirque of the central massif; furniture mfg. Also called Petit-Sable and Hell-Ville. Health resort of Hell-Bourg is SSW.

Salbani, India: see CHANDRAKONA.

Salbris (sälbrē'), town (pop. 3,395), Loir-et-Cher dept., N central France, in Sologne, on Sauldre R. and 15 mi. ENE of Romorantin; sheep market; mfg. (cotton goods, brooms, cement pipes, gingerbread).

Salcajá (sälkähä'), town (1950 pop. 3,259), Quezaltenango dept., SW Guatemala, on Samalá R. and 5 mi. NE of Quezaltenango, on Inter-American Highway; alt. 7,641 ft.; distilling; corn, wheat, fodder grasses, livestock.

Salcantay, Cerro (sĕ'rō sälkäntī'), Andean peak (20,551 ft.) in Cuzco dept., S central Peru, in Cordillera Vilcabamba, 45 mi. WNW of Cuzco; 13°18'S 72°35'W.

Salcedo (sälsā'dō), town (1950 pop. 4,622), Espaillat prov., N Dominican Republic, on railroad and 6 mi. E of Moca; agr. center (cacao, coffee, corn).

Salcedo, Ecuador: see SAN MIGUEL, Cotopaxi prov.

Salces or **Salses** (both: säls), village (pop. 1,512), Pyrénées-Orientales dept., S France, near Salces L. (a lagoon on Gulf of Lion) and 9 mi. N of Perpignan; winegrowing. Has 15th-cent. fortified castle restored in 17th cent.

Salcia (säl'chä), agr. village (pop. 1,291), Teleorman prov., S Rumania, on railroad and 14 mi. NNE of Turnu-Magurele.

Salcombe (sôl'kŭm, sŏl'–), urban district (1931 pop. 2,384; 1951 census 2,576), S Devon, England, on inlet of the Channel and 4 mi. S of Kingsbridge; seaside resort and fishing port; agr. market. Has ruins of Norman castle. There are tropical gardens.

Salda, Lake (säldä') (□ 14), SW Turkey, 35 mi. SE of Denizli; 6 mi. long, 5 mi. wide.

Saldae, Algeria: see BOUGIE.

Saldán (säldän'), town (pop. estimate 500), NW central Córdoba prov., Argentina, 11 mi. NW of Córdoba; health resort (mineral waters); lime quarries, cement factories, liquor distillery.

Saldaña (säldä'nyä), town (pop. 1,803), Palencia prov., N central Spain, on Carrión R. and 37 mi. NNW of Palencia; brewery, flour mills; livestock, cereals, flax.

Saldanha (säldä'nyŭ), village (pop. 2,069), SW Cape Prov., U of So. Afr., on Saldanha Bay, 70 mi. NNW of Cape Town; rail terminus; production of salt, potassium salts, bromine from sea water; oyster fishing. Site of So. Afr. naval training base; naval base in Second World War. Sometimes called Hoedjes Bay. Phosphates mined in region; near-by Donkergat whaling station closed 1938.

Saldanha Bay (17 mi. long, 1–7 mi. wide), SE Cape Prov., U. of So. Afr., inlet of the Atlantic, 60 mi. NNW of Cape Town. Sheltered bay with 5-mi.-wide entrance, it served as naval base in Second World War. First entered by English ships, 1591; later became Dutch, then British whaling base.

Saldé (säl'dā), village, N Senegal, Fr. West Africa, on left bank of Senegal R. (Mauritania border) and 75 mi. ESE of Podor; gums, millet.

Saldus (säl'dōōs), Ger. *Frauenburg*, city (pop. 4,410), SW Latvia, in Kurzeme, 55 mi. E of Liepaja; mfg. center; agr. market; agr. machines, woolens, rope, leather goods, matches, beer.

Sale (sāl), municipality (pop. 5,119), S Victoria, Australia, 115 mi. E of Melbourne; grain and livestock center; flour and woolen mills, dairy plants; ham, bacon. Principal town of GIPPSLAND.

Sale (sŭlē'), village, Magwe dist., Upper Burma, on left bank of Irrawaddy R. (landing) and 7 mi. SW of Chauk; lacquer-ware mfg.

Sale (sāl), residential municipal borough (1931 pop. 28,071; 1951 census 43,167), N Cheshire, England, near Mersey R. 5 mi. SSW of Manchester; mfg. of biscuits; truck gardening.

Sale (sä'lĕ), village (pop. 2,394), Alessandria prov., Piedmont, N Italy, 11 mi. NE of Alessandria.

Salé (sälā'), Arabic *Sla*, city (pop. 57,188), Rabat region, NW Fr. Morocco, on the Atlantic at mouth of the Bou Regreg, opposite RABAT (footbridge), of which it is a N suburb; flour milling, cork processing (from Mamora Forest, just NE), fish canning, palm-fiber and esparto working. Native artisans make Moroccan carpets and pottery. Rabat-Salé airport is E. Founded in 11th cent., Salé soon was leading commercial port along Morocco's W coast. Coveted by successive Berber rulers, it became (17th cent.) a quasi-independent republic and a haven for pirates, who came to be called Sallee rovers.

Salebabu or **Salebaboe** (both: sùlùbä'bōō), island (□ 60; pop. 4,475), Talaud Isls., Indonesia, just SW of Karakelong; 3°55'N 126°42'E; 17 mi. long, 4 mi. wide; hilly, forested. Timber, copra, sage, nutmeg; fishing.

Sale City, town (pop. 289), Mitchell co., SW Ga., 12 mi. E of Camilla, in agr. area.

Salée, Rivière, Guadeloupe: see RIVIÈRE SALÉE.

Salegard, Russian SFSR: see SALEKHARD.

Salehabad, Iran: see ANDIMISHK.

Salehurst, town and parish (pop. 1,991), E Sussex, England, on Rother R. and 5 mi. N of Battle; agr. market. Has 13th–14th-cent. church and remains of 14th-cent. Bodiam Castle. Just S is village of Robertsbridge, with fragments of anc. Cistercian abbey.

Saleijer, Indonesia: see SALAYAR.

Saleilles (sälā'), village (pop. 348), Pyrénées-Orientales dept., S France, 4 mi. SE of Perpignan; noted vineyards.

Salekhard (sŭlyĭkhärt'), city (1937 pop. estimate 8,800), ⊙ Yamal-Nenets Natl. Okrug, Tyumen oblast, Russian SFSR, on Arctic Circle, on lower Ob R. and 650 mi. N of Tyumen; sawmilling, fish canning, ship repair. Agr. experimental station. Founded 1595 as Obdorsk; renamed (c.1930) and spelled Salegard until 1938.

Salem (sä'lŭm), district (□ 7,073; pop. 2,869,226), S Madras, India; ⊙ Salem. Bordered NW by S Eastern Ghats, W and SW by Cauvery R. Upland (N) and lowland (S) are drained by Ponnaiyar, Vellar, and affluents of Cauvery rivers. Kanjamalai, Pachaimalai, Kollaimalai, and Kalrayan hills (outliers of S Eastern Ghats) have extensively mined magnetite, magnesite, and chromite deposits (ores shipped from Salem Junction). Steatite, limestone, corundum, bauxite, mica also mined. Chalk Hills are a major source of India's magnesite. Shevaroy Hills (sandalwood, Casuarina) have extensive coffee plantations (factories). Rice, millet, peanuts, castor beans (wide cultivation), sesame, cotton, tobacco, sugar cane; mango groves, mulberry farms. Cauvery-Mettur hydroelectric and irrigation system (main works: Mettur Dam; Stanley Reservoir) furnishes power to industrial center of METTUR and cotton-milling center of Salem. Other chief towns: Dharmapuri, Hosur, Tiruchengodu.

Salem, city (pop. 129,702), ⊙ Salem dist., S central Madras, India, on affluent of the Cauvery and 170 mi. SW of Madras; rail and road junction; cotton-milling center (mills powered by Mettur hydroelectric plant) in agr. area (mangoes, castor beans, peanuts, sesame); silk weaving. Municipal Col. Salem Junction (or Suramangalam) is 3 mi. WNW; terminus of rail branch to Mettur Dam; shipping center for magnesite and chromite mines of Chalk Hills (N) and magnetite, magnesite, and chromite mines of Kanjamalai hill (SW). Corundum and steatite also mined near by.

Salem, Palestine: see JERUSALEM.

Salem (sā'lùm), county (□ 350; pop. 49,508), SW N.J., bounded W by Delaware R.; ⊙ Salem. Mfg. (chemicals and allied products, glass, canned foods), dairying, agr. (truck, poultry, fruit); large marl deposits. Includes Parvin State Park. Drained by Maurice and Salem rivers and Oldmans, Alloway, and Stow creeks. Formed 1681.

Salem. 1 Town (pop. 687), ⊙ Fulton co., N Ark., c.40 mi. NNW of Batesville, near Mo. line; ships livestock, poultry, cotton, feed. **2** Town (pop. 618), New London co., SE Conn., 12 mi. NW of New London; agr.; summer homes. Part of Gardner L. here. **3** City (pop. 6,159), ⊙ Marion co., S central Ill., 12 mi. NE of Centralia; mfg. of clothing, paint, shoes; lumber milling; railroad shops. Bituminous-coal mines, oil wells; timber. Agr. (fruit, corn, wheat; dairy products; livestock). William Jennings Bryan was b. here. Inc. 1837. **4** Residential city (pop. 3,271), ⊙ Washington co., S Ind., on Blue R. and 27 mi. SE of Bedford; trade center for agr. area; mfg. (furniture, wood products, work clothes, rock wool, lumber); limestone quarries; timber. Settled c.1800; inc. as town 1815, as city 1933. John Hay b. here. **5** Town (pop. 473), Henry co., SE Iowa, 8 mi. SSW of Mount Pleasant, in livestock and grain area. **6** Village (pop. 67), Franklin co., W central Maine, on branch of Carrabassett R. and 17 mi. NW of Farmington. **7** Village, Dorchester co., E Md., 12 mi. ESE of Cambridge; vegetable canneries. **8** City (pop. 41,880), a ⊙ Essex co., NE Mass., 15 mi. NE of Boston; mfg. (textiles, electrical supplies, shoes, machinery). Port of entry. Settled 1626 from Cape Ann. Early history was darkened by witchcraft trials of 1692. A leading port from colonial times to mid-19th cent., its harbor is today silted up. Salem Maritime Natl. Historic Site (8.6 acres; established 1938) preserves waterfront area, including 18th-cent. wharves, Custom House (1819), Derby House (1761–62), Rum Shop (c.-1800), and Hawkes House (c.1780), in commemoration of early maritime greatness of New England. Other points of interest are Nathaniel Hawthorne's birthplace (17th cent.); the House of the Seven Gables; Essex Inst. (fine library and historical collection), and Peabody Mus. (marine collection). Inc. as city 1876. **9** Town (pop. 253), Daviess co., NW Mo., near Grand R., 32 mi. NW of Chillicothe. **10** City (pop. 3,611), ⊙ Dent co., SE central Mo., in the Ozarks, 75 mi. SE of Jefferson City; alt. 1,182 ft. Agr.; mfg. (clothing, cheese, lumber); iron mines. State park near by. Inc. 1860. **11** Village (pop. 341), Richardson co., SE Nebr., 7 mi. W of Falls City and on Nemaha R., near Kansas line. **12** Town (pop. 4,805), Rockingham co., SE N.H., just W of Haverhill, Mass. Site of Rockingham Park race track. Shoe factories at Salem Depot village (pop. 1,637). Inc. 1750. **13** City (pop. 9,050), ⊙ Salem co., SW N.J., on Salem R., c.3 mi. above its mouth on the Delaware, and 16 mi. NW of Bridgeton; market center for agr. region; glass-making center, mfg. (linoleum, canned foods, canning machinery). Noted for its colonial buildings. Salem Oak (30 ft. in circumference, 80 ft. high) stands in Friends' burial ground. Settled 1675 by Friends, inc. 1858. **14** Village (pop. 1,067), Washington co., E N.Y., near Vt. line, 24 mi. ENE of Saratoga Springs; mfg. of clothing, gloves, feed, paper products; lumber milling; slate quarrying. Small lakes (resorts) near by. Settled 1764, inc. 1803. **15** City (pop. 12,754), Columbiana co., E Ohio, 18 mi. SW of Youngstown; blast furnaces, steel mills; mfg. of metal stampings, machinery, washing machines, dairy products, furnaces, chinaware; coal mining. Laid out 1806 by Society of Friends. **16** City (pop. 43,140), ⊙ Oregon and Marion co., in Marion and Polk counties, NW Oregon, on Willamette R. and c.50 mi. (river distance) SSW of Portland; 44°56'N 123°02'W; alt. 159 ft.; second-largest city in state. Processing, mfg. center for livestock, agr. area (fruit, grain, flax, hops); canned fruit and vegetables, meat products, lumber, paper, wool, linen. Seat of Willamette Univ., state fairgrounds, and other state institutions: schools for deaf, blind, and feeble-minded, hosp. for insane, tuberculosis hosp., industrial school for girls, and penitentiary. City founded 1841 by missionary group led by Jason Lee, inc. 1857. Became ⊙ Oregon Territory 1851, state ⊙ 1859, when Oregon was admitted to U.S. Capitol bldg. (1939) replaced earlier structure destroyed (1935) by fire. **17** City (pop. 1,119), ⊙ McCook co., SE S.Dak., 35 mi. WNW of Sioux Falls; trade and distribution center; grain, poultry, dairy products, livestock. Settled 1880, inc. 1885. **18** Town (pop. 781), Utah co., central Utah, 3 mi. E of Payson; alt. 4,600 ft. **19** Town (pop. 6,823), ⊙ Roanoke co., SW Va., on Roanoke R. and 6 mi. W of Roanoke; mfg. of textiles, cigarette machinery, elevators, locks, drugs, brick, packed meat, leather, canned foods, flour. Roanoke Col. (1842) here. U.S. veterans hosp. near by. Dixie Caverns (SW) attract tourists. Laid out 1802; inc. 1806. **20** City (pop. 2,578), Harrison co., N W.Va., 12 mi. W of Clarksburg, in agr., coal, gas, oil, and timber region; oil refineries, glass factories. Seat of Salem Col. and a state industrial home for girls. Settled 1790.

Salemburg, town (pop. 435), Sampson co., S central N.C., 22 mi. ESE of Fayetteville. Seat of Pineland Jr. Col. and Edwards Military Inst.

Salem Church, battlefield, Va.: see CHANCELLORSVILLE.

Salem Church Dam, Va.: see RAPPAHANNOCK RIVER.

Salem Heights, village (pop. 2,351), Marion co., NW Oregon, a suburb of Salem.

Salemi (sälā'mē), anc. *Halycyae*, town (pop. 12,348), Trapani prov., W Sicily, 21 mi. SE of Trapani; olive oil. Sandstone deposits near by. Relics of Christian basilica (3d–6th cent.), ruins of Norman castle.

Salem River, SW N.J., rises in E Salem co., flows c.30 mi. W and S, past Woodstown and Salem (head of navigation), to Delaware R. near Salem.

Salen, village on MULL, Hebrides, Scotland.

Salento (sälĕn'tō), town (pop. 1,723), Caldas dept., W central Colombia, in Cordillera Central, at W foot of Nevado del Tolima, 15 mi. SE of Pereira; alt. 6,217 ft. Coffeegrowing; flour milling; sericulture. Gold mines near by.

Salernes (sälârn'), village (pop. 1,478), Var dept., SE France, in Provence Alps, 12 mi. W of Draguignan; mfg. of enameled tiles; wine and olive trade.

Salerno (sùlûr'nō, It. sälĕr'nô), province (□ 1,900; pop. 705,277), Campania, S Italy, bordering on Tyrrhenian Sea; ⊙ Salerno. Traversed by the Apennines; predominantly (75%) mtn. and hilly terrain. Chief lowland is coastal plain S of Salerno. Watered by Sele and Tanagro rivers. Agr. (cereals, grapes, olives, fruit, vegetables, tobacco, potatoes); livestock raising. Fishing. Marble quarries at Buccino. Hydroelectric plants (Pertosa, Ariano). Resorts along coast (Amalfi, Positano, Ravello). Chief industries are tomato canning and macaroni mfg. (Nocera Inferiore, Salerno), textiles (Angri, Cava de' Tirreni, Sarno), paper mills (Amalfi, Maiori).

Salerno, anc. *Salernum*, city (pop. 41,925), ⊙ Salerno prov., Campania, S Italy, port on Gulf of Salerno, 30 mi. SE of Naples; 40°40'N 14°45'E. Rail junction; industrial and commercial center; macaroni factories, tomato canneries, tanneries, flour, cotton, and lumber mills; shipbuilding, alcohol distilling; ceramics, machinery (agr., cannery), soap, glass. Exports olive oil, wine, fruit. Archbishopric. Has 9th-cent. cathedral with 11th-cent. bronze doors and anc. mosaics. Its famous medical school, where Latin, Greek, Arabic, and Jewish influences were merged, originated in 9th cent., reached its peak in 12th cent., and was closed in 1817. A Roman colony, it became (6th cent.) part of duchy of Benevento. In 9th cent. seat of independent principality which fell to Normans in 1076. In Second World War, modern (S) end of town was badly damaged in fierce battle (Sept. 9–16, 1943) bet. Allied landing forces and Germans on the beaches around Salerno.

Salerno, Gulf of, S Italy, inlet of Tyrrhenian Sea; separated from Bay of Naples by peninsula of Sorrento, bet. Punta della Campanella (NW) and Punta Licosa (SE); c.40 mi. long, 25 mi. wide. Receives Sele R. On its N shore are SALERNO and Amalfi.

Salers (sälâr'), village (pop. 527), Cantal dept., S central France, on NW slope of Massif du Cantal, 9 mi. SE of Mauriac; cattle-raising center. Has 15th–16th-cent. Gothic church.

Salesi, Greece: see AULON.

Salesópolis (sùlĭzô'pōōlēs), city (pop. 933), E São Paulo, Brazil, 50 mi. E of São Paulo; meat packing. Formerly Sallesópolis.

Salesville, village (pop. 187), Guernsey co., E Ohio, 14 mi. ESE of Cambridge, in coal-mining area.

Salette, Notre-Dame-de-la-, France: see CORPS.

Salève, Mont (mõ sälĕv'), isolated limestone range (3,000–4,500 ft.) in Haute-Savoie dept., SE France, extending c.10 mi. from Cruseilles (SSW) to Annemasse (NNE) and overlooking Geneva (4 mi. NW). Resorts of Monnetier and Les Treize-Arbres (alt. 3,880) reached by funicular railway and new crest road. Fine view of Mont Blanc and Jura mts.

Salford (sŏl'fùrd, sôl'–), county borough (1931 pop. 223,438; 1951 census 178,036), SE Lancashire, England, on Manchester Ship Canal, just W of Manchester across the Irwell; textile center (cotton spinning, weaving, bleaching, and printing; mfg. of textile machinery, textile chemicals, aniline dyes, sewing cotton); steel production; mfg. of shoes, automobile tires, soap, paint, plastics; electrical engineering. Site of world's 1st free municipal library. In county borough (S) is industrial area of TRAFFORD PARK.

Salgado (sŭlgä'dōō), city (pop. 1,322), E Sergipe, NE Brazil, on railroad and 15 mi. N of Estância; sugar and cotton growing. Mineral springs.

Salgan (sŭlgän'), village (1939 pop. over 2,000), SE Gorki oblast, Russian SFSR, 20 mi. S of Sergach; hemp, wheat.

Salgar (sälgär'). **1** Town (pop. 2,092), Antioquia dept., NW central Colombia, on E slopes of Cordillera Occidental, 36 mi. SW of Medellín; alt. 4,370 ft. Coffee and livestock center (cattle, horses, hogs). Founded 1880. **2** Village, Bolívar dept., N Colombia, on Caribbean coast, 10 mi. W of Barranquilla, on a rail spur.

Salgir River (sŭlgēr'), longest river of Crimea, Russian SFSR, rises in the Chatyr-Dag 7 mi. NW of Alushta, flows NW past Simferopol, and NE past Nizhnegorski, to Sivash lagoon 30 mi. E of Dzhankoi; c.100 mi. long. Lower course dries up in summer months.

Salgotarjan (shŏl'gōtŏryän), Hung. *Salgótarján*, city (pop. 20,318), Nograd-Hont co., N Hungary, on branch of Zagyva R. and 53 mi. NE of Budapest. One of Hungary's important mining, industrial centers; steel, iron mills, mfg. (machines, glass, shoes); distilleries. Extensive coal, lignite mining in area.

Salgueiro (sŭlgā'rōō), city (pop. 1,626), W Pernambuco, NE Brazil, 60 mi. SSE of Crato (Ceará); cotton, corn, livestock.

Salhiya, El, Es Salhiya, or **Al-Salihiyah** (all: ĕs-sälhē'yù), village (pop. 8,190), Sharqiya prov., Lower Egypt, terminus of Zagazig railway and 12 mi. ENE of Faqus; cotton.

Salhus (säl'hōōs), village (pop. 966) in Asane canton (pop. 5,087), Hordaland co., SW Norway, on Oster Fjord, 8 mi. NNW of Bergen; produces knit goods. At Eidsvag (āts'vôg) (Nor. *Eidsvåg*) village (pop. 483), 5 mi. SSE: woolen milling, mfg. of barrels and cigars.

Salice Salentina (sä'lēchĕ sälĕntē'nä), town (pop. 5,131), Lecce prov., Apulia, S Italy, 11 mi. WNW of Lecce; olive oil, wine.

Salida. 1 (sùlē'dù) Village (pop. 1,300), Stanislaus co., central Calif., in San Joaquin Valley, 6 mi. NW of Modesto; wine making; ships fruit, hay, grain. **2** (sùlī'dù) City (pop. 4,553), Chaffee co., central

Colo., on Arkansas R., bet. Sangre de Cristo and Sawatch mts., and 80 mi. WNW of Pueblo; alt. 7,050 ft. Resort, trade center, and railroad div. point in grain, mineral, and livestock region; dairy, truck, and poultry products; creosoting plant, granite and sheet-metal works. Repair shops and hosp. maintained by railroad. Fluorspar mines in vicinity. Near by are hot springs and part of Cochetopa Natl. Forest, for which city is hq. Founded by railroad c.1880, inc. 1891.

Saliente Point (sälyĕn'tā), Pacific cape, Coquimbo prov., N central Chile, 13 mi. SW of La Serena; 30°1'S 71°27'W.

Salies (sälē'). **1** or **Salies-de-Béarn** (–dü-bāär'), town (pop. 2,847), Basses-Pyrénées dept., SW France, 8 mi. W of Orthez; health resort (salt springs); saltworks, shoe factories. **2** or **Salies-du-Salat** (–dü-sälä'), village (pop. 1,332), Haute-Garonne dept., S France, on Salat R. 12 mi. E of Saint-Gaudens; resort. Saltworks, ophite quarries.

Salif (sălĕf'), village, Hodeida prov., W Yemen, minor Red Sea port, opposite main Kamaran Isl., 40 mi. NNW of Hodeida; rock-salt deposits.

Salignac (sälēnyäk'), village (pop. 461), Dordogne dept., SW France, 8 mi. NE of Sarlat; meat-canning (*pâté de foie gras* and truffles); kaolin quarries near by.

Salignière, La, France: see LIVET-ET-GAVET.

Saligrama (sälĭgrä'mŭ), town (pop. 4,923), Mysore dist., SW Mysore, India, 33 mi. NW of Mysore; tobacco, rice, millet.

Salihiyah, Al-, Egypt: see SALHIYA, EL.

Salihiye (să"lĭhē'yü, sä"–), **Qal'at es Salihiye, Qal'at el Salihiye,** or **Qal'at al-Salihiyah** (kä'lăt ĕs-sälĭhē'yü), village, Euphrates prov., E Syria, on right bank of Euphrates R. and 50 mi. SE of Deir ez Zor. Site of anc. city of DURA or Dura-Europus, where important excavations have been made.

Salihli (sä'lēlē"), town (1950 pop. 13,261), Manisa prov., W Turkey, on railroad, on Gediz R., 39 mi. ESE of Manisa; raisins, valonia, wheat, barley, sugar beets, cotton, tobacco.

Salima (sälē'mä), village, Central Prov., Nyasaland, near L. Nyasa, 50 mi. ESE of Lilongwe; resort (lake-shore hotels); rail terminus of Nyasaland Railways; tobacco, corn; livestock.

Salin (sŭlĭn'), town (pop. 6,654), Minbu dist., Upper Burma, 30 mi. NNW of Minbu; trade center; lake fisheries. Near by is Salin R. (short right tributary of Irrawaddy R.) used for irrigation of N Minbu dist.

Salín, Cerro (sĕ'rō sälēn'), Andean volcano (19,880 ft.) on Argentina-Chile border; 24°18'S.

Salina (sälē'nä), anc. *Didyme*, second largest island (□ 10; pop. 3,541) of Lipari Isls., in Tyrrhenian Sea off NE Sicily, 30 mi. NNW of Milazzo; 4 mi. long, 3 mi. wide. Separated from Lipari (SE) by channel 3 mi. wide. Consists of 2 extinct volcanoes; higher rises to 3,156 ft. Exports malmsey wine, raisins, figs, olives. Chief port, Santa Marina Salina (pop. 908), on E coast.

Salina (sülī'nü). **1** Hamlet, Boulder co., N Colo., on branch of Boulder Creek, in E foothills of Front Range, and 6 mi. WNW of Boulder; alt. c.6,500 ft.; gold mining. **2** City (pop. 26,176), ⊙ Saline co., central Kansas, on Smoky Hill R., near mouth of Saline R., and 75 mi. NNW of Wichita; trade and distribution center for winter-wheat and livestock area; grain storage. Flour milling, dairying; mfg. of farm implements, cement, canvas, bricks and tiles, foundry products. Kansas Wesleyan Univ., Marymount Col., and a military school are here. Near-by air force base was active in Second World War. Platted 1858, inc. 1870. Growth stimulated by arrival of railroad (1867). **3** Town (pop. 905), Mayes co., NE Okla., 9 mi. E of Pryor, near Neosho R. Settled on site of the 1st Okla. trading post, founded in early 19th cent. by Jean Pierre Chouteau. **4** City (pop. 1,789), Sevier co., central Utah, on Sevier R. and 18 mi. NE of Richfield, near Wasatch Plateau; alt. 5,147 ft.; shipping point for livestock, coal, salt, and farm produce. Settled 1864, abandoned during Indian troubles (1866), resettled 1871.

Salina Cruz (sälē'nä krōōs'), city (pop. 4,614), Oaxaca, S Mexico, on Pacific coast, 12 mi. S of Tehuantepec; rail terminus; minor port; fishing, lumber milling, fruitgrowing. Linked by oil pipe line with Minatitlán.

Salina Grande (sälē'nä grän'dā) or **Salina de Hidalgo** (dā ēdäl'gō), salt desert (□ 170) in W La Pampa natl. territory, Argentina, 25 mi. W of Puelén; extends c.18 mi. W–E, 12 mi. wide. Sodium and calcium salts.

Salinas, province, Bolivia: see ENTRE RÍOS.

Salinas (sälē'näs), town (pop. c.1,000), Tarija dept., S Bolivia, on Salinas R. (left affluent of Tarija R.) and 20 mi. S of Entre Ríos; corn, sheep.

Salinas (sŭlē'nŭs). **1** City (pop. 2,613), NE Minas Gerais, Brazil, on left tributary of Jequitinhonha R. and 40 mi. N of Araçuaí; semi-precious stones (aquamarines, topazes, tourmalines). **2** City, Pará, Brazil: see SALINÓPOLIS.

Salinas (sälē'näs), town (1950 pop. 2,868), Guayas prov., W Ecuador, Pacific port on S Santa Elena Bay, on arid Santa Elena Peninsula, and 75 mi. W of Guayaquil (connected by rail, highway, air line); major seaside resort, international cable station, port of call for steamers. Salt, sulphur, and petroleum (at La Libertad; E) are worked near by.

Salinas, city (pop. 4,255), San Luis Potosí, N central Mexico, on interior plateau, on railroad and 55 mi. NW of San Luis Potosí; alt. 6,886 ft. Salt- and cinnabar-mining center. Sometimes Salinas del Peñón Blanco or Peñón Blanco. Railroad station (Peñón Blanco) 11 mi. SW.

Salinas, town (pop. 4,367), S Puerto Rico, near the coast (adjoining is the port Playa Salinas), 12 mi. W of Guayama; sugar-milling and -trading center; produces also coconuts, cattle, and salt. Airport just W. Many caves with Indian relics in vicinity.

Salinas (sŭlē'nŭs), city (pop. 13,917), ⊙ Monterey co., W Calif., c.45 mi. S of San Jose, in N Salinas R. valley; market and shipping center for livestock and irrigated farming (especially lettuce) area; beet-sugar refining. Rubber is produced from guayule plant, grown here. Seat of Hartnell Col. (jr.). EAST SALINAS adjoins. U.S. Fort Ord is W. Holds annual rodeo. Settled 1856, inc. 1874.

Salinas, Cape (sälē'näs), southernmost point of Majorca, Balearic Isls., 30 mi. SE of Palma; 39°16'N 3°4'E.

Salinas, Laguna de (lägōō'nä dā), salt lake (5 mi. long, 1–3 mi. wide), Arequipa dept., S Peru, at N foot of Nevado de Pichu Pichu, 25 mi. E of Arequipa; alt. 13,993 ft. Borax works.

Salinas Bay, NE inlet of Papagayo Gulf of the Pacific, on Nicaragua–Costa Rica border; 3 mi. wide, 7 mi. long. Puerto Soley is on E shore. Coal deposits (N).

Salinas de Garci Mendoza (dā gärsē' mĕndō'sä), town (pop. c.1,900), ⊙ Ladislao Cabrera prov., Oruro dept., W Bolivia, in the Altiplano, at E end of Cordillera de Llica, on N shore of Salar de Uyuni and 120 mi. SSW of Oruro; alt. 12,730 ft.; saltworks. Saltpeter and sulphur deposits near by.

Salinas Grandes (grän'dĕs). **1** Salt desert (□ 3,200), N Argentina, largely in NW Córdoba and SW Santiago del Estero provs., extends c.180 mi. NE–SW, W of the Sierra de Córdoba. The Córdoba-Tucumán RR embankment cuts it in half. Has sodium and potassium salts. **2** Salt desert (□ 200; alt. c.12,000 ft.), in the puna de Atacama, Jujuy and Salta provs., N Argentina; c.45 mi. long. Contains sodium, borate, and aluminum salts.

Salinas Peak (sŭlē'nŭs) (9,040 ft), in San Andres Mts., SW N.Mex., c.45 mi. NW of Alamogordo.

Salinas Point or **Lachay Point** (läché'), cape on Pacific coast of Lima dept., W Peru, 13 mi. S of Huacho; 11°18'S 77°39'W.

Salinas River, Guatemala: see CHIXOY RIVER.

Salinas River (sälē'näs), N Mexico, rises in Coahuila in Sierra Madre Oriental near Saltillo, flows c.150 mi. N and E, past Hidalgo, Carmen, Salinas Victoria, Ciénga de Flores, and General Zuazua (all in Nuevo León), to Pesquería R. 5 mi. E of Pesquería Chica.

Salinas River (sŭlē'nŭs), W Calif., rises in the Coast Ranges E of San Luis Obispo, flows c.150 mi. NW (partly underground), bet. Santa Lucia (W) and Gabilan and Diablo (E) ranges, and past Paso Robles and King City, to Monterey Bay 10 mi. NE of Monterey. The alluvial Salinas valley (6–10 mi. wide; c.100 mi. long from river's mouth) is a major Calif. truck-producing area (especially of lettuce); also sugar beets, beans, alfalfa, grain, flower seed; cattle grazing.

Salinas Victoria (sälē'näs vēktōr'yä), town (pop. 2,303), Nuevo León, N Mexico, on Salinas R., on railroad, and 20 mi. N of Monterrey; mining (silver, lead) and agr. center (cotton, corn, sugar cane, livestock).

Salin-de-Giraud (sälē'-dü-zhērō'), town (pop. 3,203), Bouches-du-Rhône dept., SE France, in the Camargue, near right bank of the Grand Rhône, 19 mi. SSE of Arles; chemical plants based on large saltworks just S.

Salindres (sälē'drü), town (pop. 2,252), Gard dept., S France, 5 mi. NE of Alès; electrochemical and aluminum works.

Saline (să'lĭn), agr. village and parish (pop. 1,510), SW Fifeshire, Scotland, 5 mi. NW of Dunfermline.

Saline (sülēn'). **1** County (□ 726; pop. 23,816), central Ark.; ⊙ Benton. Drained by Saline R. and its tributaries. Agr. (cotton, truck, corn, livestock). Bauxite mining and processing; gravel and clay pits; timber. Industries at Bauxite, Benton. Formed 1835. **2** County (□ 384; pop. 33,420), SE Ill.; ⊙ Harrisburg. Agr. (corn, wheat, fruit, livestock; dairy products). Extensive bituminous-coal fields. Mfg. (wood products, brick, flour). S portion lies in Ill. Ozarks. Drained by Saline R.; includes part of Shawnee Natl. Forest. Formed 1847. **3** County (□ 720; pop. 33,409), central Kansas; ⊙ Salina. Rolling plain region, intersected by Smoky Hill, Saline, and Solomon rivers. Winter wheat, other grains, livestock. Formed 1859. **4** County (□ 759; pop. 26,694), central Mo.; ⊙ Marshall. Bounded N and E by Missouri R.; drained by Blackwater R. Agr. (corn, wheat, oats), cattle, hogs; dairy products; mfg. at Marshall. Formed 1829. **5** County (□ 575; pop. 14,046), SE Nebr.; ⊙ Wilber. Farming region drained by Big Blue R. Flour; livestock, grain, dairy and poultry produce. Formed 1867.

Saline. **1** Village (pop. 357), Bienville parish, NW La., 50 mi. ESE of Shreveport, and on Saline Bayou, in truck-farming region. **2** City (pop. 1,533), Washtenaw co., SE Mich., 8 mi. SSW of Ann Arbor, in diversified farm area; mfg. (auto parts, handles); soybean-oil milling. Cooperative Saline Valley Farms near by. Settled 1824, inc. as city 1931.

Saline, La (lä sälēn'), village (pop. 5,001), near W coast of Réunion isl., on road and 5 mi. S of Saint-Paul; sugar milling.

Saline Bayou (sülēn' bī'ō), NW La., rises in N Bienville parish, flows S to Saline L. (c.6 mi. long) in game preserve, thence SSW to Red R. 7 mi. E of Natchitoches; c.65 mi. long.

Saline Lake. **1** In Avoyelles and La Salle parishes, E central La., widening of BIG SALINE BAYOU. **2** In Natchitoches parish, NW La., widening of SALINE BAYOU.

Saline River. **1** In S central Ark., rises in the Ouachita Mts. W of Little Rock, flows c.300 mi. SSE to Ouachita R. 10 mi. W of Crossett; navigable for shallow drafts for c.140 mi. above mouth. **2** In SE Ill., formed near Equality by confluence of South Fork (c.50 mi. long) and North Fork (c.50 mi. long); flows c.25 mi. generally SE to Ohio R. 9 mi. below Shawneetown. Middle Fork (c.30 mi. long) enters South Fork c.7 mi. W of Equality. **3** In Kansas, formed by confluence of 2 headstreams near Oakley, NW Kansas, flows 342 mi. E, past Sylvan Grove and Lincoln, to Smoky Hill R. 6 mi. E of Salina.

Salines, Les (lā sälēn'), village, Le Kef dist., N central Tunisia, 16 mi. SE of Le Kef; rail junction; lead and zinc mines near by.

Salines, Pointe des (pwĕt dā sälēn'), headland, SE Martinique, 19 mi. SE of Fort-de-France; 14°24'N 60°53'W.

Salineville (sülēn'vĭl), village (pop. 2,018), Columbiana co., E Ohio, 13 mi. W of East Liverpool, in coal-mining area. Confederate raiders, under Gen. John Morgan, were captured near here in 1863.

Salingyi (sŭlĭn'jē"), village, Lower Chindwin dist., Upper Burma, 10 mi. SSW of Monywa; road center.

Salinópolis (sŭlēnô'pōōlĭs), city (pop. 1,833), E Pará, Brazil, on the Atlantic, 95 mi. NE of Belém; pilot station for Amazon shipping, and health resort; ships cattle, cacao, Brazil nuts; mfg. of ceramics. Until 1944, Salinas.

Salins-d'Hyères, France: see HYÈRES.

Salins-les-Bains (sälē'-lā-bē'), town (pop. 3,576), Jura dept., E France, in the Jura, 21 mi. SSW of Besançon; well-known spa with brine wells. Lumber and wine trade. Produces crockery, plaster, and honey. Saltworks. Dismantled fortification on surrounding heights.

Salí River, Argentina: see DULCE, RÍO.

Salis, river, Latvia: see SALACA RIVER.

Salisburg, Latvia: see MAZSALACA.

Salisbury (sôlz'–), village (pop. 2,496), SE South Australia, 12 mi. N of Adelaide; rail junction; wheat; supply center for rocket base at Woomera.

Salisbury, village (pop. estimate c.350), SE N.B., on Petitcodiac R. and 14 mi. WSW of Moncton; dairying, fur farming.

Salisbury (sôlz'brē) or **New Sarum** (sâr'ŭm), municipal borough (1931 pop. 26,460; 1951 census 32,910), ⊙ Wiltshire, England, in SE part of co., on the Avon, at mouth of the Wylye, and 20 mi. NW of Southampton; agr. market. The great cathedral, a splendid example of Early English architecture, with tallest spire in England (404 ft.), was begun in 1220, when bishopric was transferred from OLD SARUM, some of the materials being brought from the razed cathedral there. Other noted bldgs.: 13th-cent. palace of the bishops, several 13th-cent. churches, 15th-cent. Audley House, 14th-cent. King's House, library containing copy of Magna Carta, and 2 museums. City is laid out in regular squares or "checkers." It is Thomas Hardy's *Melchester*.

Salisbury, province (□ 40,842; pop. c.635,000), N Southern Rhodesia; ⊙ Salisbury. Bounded NW by Northern Rhodesia (along Zambezi R.), N by Mozambique. Lies largely in middle veld (2–4,000 ft.); a ridge of high veld (4–6,000 ft.), on which main centers (Gatooma, Eiffel Flats, Hartley, Salisbury, Marandellas) are located, is followed by Bulawayo-Salisbury and Salisbury-Beira railroads. Chief crops: tobacco (especially near Salisbury), peanuts, corn, wheat, citrus fruit; livestock raising, dairying. Region is noted for its mines: gold (mined at Bindura, Shamva, and in Hartley and Lomagundi dists.), mica (Miami, Rusambo), asbestos (Mount Darwin), chrome (Umvukwe Range). European pop. (1946), 36,530, concentrated in high veld.

Salisbury, city (pop. 53,211; including suburbs 69,101), ⊙ Southern Rhodesia and Salisbury prov., in Mashonaland, on small Makabusi R. and 230 mi. NE of Bulawayo; alt. 4,831 ft.; 17°50'S 31°3'E. Administrative, industrial, and tobacco center; linked by rail with Beira (Mozambique) and Bulawayo, and with mining areas of Bindura and Shamva (gold) and Umvukwe Range (chrome). Tobacco curing, grading, and packing. Produces bacon, flour, butter, biscuits, clothing, soap, candles, fertilizer, beer. City receives its water from Cleveland Dam (on Makabusi R.) and from Prince

Edward Dam (on the upper Hunyani). Has Anglican and R.C. cathedrals, numerous churches, St. George's Col. and other secondary schools, Queen Victoria Memorial Library and Mus. Principal suburbs: Ardbennie and Parktown (SW), Meyrick Park, Highlands, and Borrowdale (NE). Founded 1890 and named for Lord Salisbury; became a municipality in 1897; reached 1899 by railroad from Beira. Mean annual temp. 65°F. average yearly rainfall 32 in. European pop. (1946), including suburbs, was 21,295.

Salisbury (sôlz'bĕ"rē, –bůrē). **1** Resort town (pop. 3,132), Litchfield co., NW Conn., in Taconic Mts., on N.Y. and Mass. lines, and 20 mi. NW of Torrington; patent medicines, cutlery, handles; agr. (dairy products, poultry). Includes villages of LAKEVILLE on L. Wononskopomuc, Salisbury (with Salisbury school for boys, 1901), Taconic (tůkŏn'ĭk), Ore Hill, and Lime Rock. Bear Mtn., state's highest peak, and Twin Lakes, resort on small Twin Lakes, here. Settled c.1720, inc. 1741. Old iron mines and forges made Revolutionary munitions here. **2** City (pop. 15,141), ⊙ Wicomico co. (since 1867), SE Md., c.55 mi. S of Dover, Del., at head of navigation on Wicomico R.; water, rail, and trade center for wide area of the Eastern Shore; a center for poultry-raising industry; truck farms, timber tracts in region. Mfg. (clothing, machine tools, gasoline pumps, boats, bricks, fertilizer); food-processing plants. Hunting near by. Seat of a state teachers col. and Eastern Shore Branch Inst. (tuberculosis). Near by are Wicomico State Game Farm, a race track, and some fine mansions. Occupied (1861) by Federal troops in Civil War. Laid out 1732, inc. 1887. **3** Town (pop. 2,695), Essex co., extreme NE Mass., on coast, 4 mi. N of Newburyport, at mouth of Merrimack R. State park on coast. Settled 1638, inc. 1640. Includes resort village of Salisbury Beach (post office, Cushing). **4** City (pop. 1,676), Chariton co., N central Mo., near Missouri R., 19 mi. W of Moberly; grain, flour, feed; coal. Settled 1877, inc. 1891. **5** Town (pop. 423), Merrimack co., S central N.H., 15 mi. NNW of Concord; agr. **6** City (pop. 20,102), ⊙ Rowan co., W central N.C., 32 mi. SSW of Winston-Salem, near High Rock L.; mfg. center (cotton yarn, clothing, lumber, rubber hose); railroad shops. Granite quarries near by. Salisbury Natl. Cemetery, with graves of Union soldiers who died in a Confederate prison, is here. Seat of Catawba Col. and Livingstone Col. Settled 1751; inc. 1753. **7** Borough (pop. 865), Somerset co., SW Pa., 18 mi. S of Somerset and on Casselman R., near Md. line; bituminous coal. **8** (also sälz'–) Town (pop. 573), Addison co., W Vt., on L. Dunmore and 8 mi. S of Middlebury, in Green Mts.; resorts, state fish hatchery.

Salisbury, Lake, Uganda: see KYOGA, LAKE.

Salisbury Beach, Mass.: see SALISBURY.

Salisbury Island (□ 490), SE Franklin Dist., Northwest Territories, at W entrance of Hudson Strait, off SW Baffin Isl., E of Nottingham Isl; 63°30'N 77°W; 32 mi. long, 12 mi. wide.

Salisbury Island, in central Franz Josef Land, Russian SFSR; 50 mi. long, 10 mi. wide; 81°N 55–57°E.

Salisbury Mills (sôlz'bĕ"rē, –bůrē), resort village, Orange co., SE N.Y., 7 mi. SW of Newburgh, in dairying area; paper mfg. Ski jumping.

Salisbury Plain, undulating chalk plateau (□ 300), S Wiltshire, England, N of Salisbury; largely used as pasture for sheep. Military camps and training grounds occupy most of N part. There are many anc. monuments, notably STONEHENGE.

Salismünde, Latvia: see SALACGRIVA.

Salis River, Latvia: see SALACA RIVER.

Saliste (sälēsht'yĕ), Rum. *Salişte*, Hung. *Szelistye* (sĕ'lĕshtyĕ), village (pop. 3,087), Sibiu prov., central Rumania, in N foothills of the Transylvanian Alps, on railroad and 11 mi. W of Sibiu; noted for its colorful folklore and handicrafts; bell foundry.

Salitral (sälĕträl'), village (dist. pop. 1,605), San José prov., central Costa Rica, on central plateau, 1 mi. S of Santa Ana; mineral springs; bottling industry.

Salitral or **San Andrés de Salitral** (sän' ändrās' dā), town (pop. 397), Piura dept., NW Peru, on W slopes of Cordillera Occidental, on upper Piura R. and 32 mi. SE of Chulucanas; sugar cane, alfalfa; cattle raising.

Salix (sā'lĭks), town (pop. 337), Woodbury co., W Iowa, 15 mi. SSE of Sioux City, in agr. area.

Salkehatchie River, S.C.: see COMBAHEE RIVER.

Salkhad (säl'khăd), town, Jebel ed Druz prov., S Syria, near Jordan border, in the mts. 17 mi. SSE of Es Suweida; cereals; alt. 4,460 ft.

Salkhia (sälk'yŭ), N suburb of Howrah, Howrah dist., S West Bengal, India, on Hooghly R. and 1.5 mi. NNE of Howrah, 2 mi. N of Calcutta city center; jute and cotton milling, chemical mfg.; tanneries. Also spelled Salkia. Sometimes called Howrah Salkia.

Salkine, Syria: see SALQIN.

Salla (säl'lä), agr. village (commune pop. 8,558), Lapi co., NE Finland, 65 mi. ENE of Rovaniemi; reindeer raising. Formerly called Kursu, it was renamed (1940) when original Salla village, 30 mi. ENE, was transferred to Karelo-Finnish SFSR and renamed KUOLAYARVI (Kuolajärvi); its pop. was evacuated here.

Salladasburg (să'lŭdůzbûrg), borough (pop. 250), Lycoming co., N central Pa., 10 mi. WNW of Williamsport.

Sallal (säläl'), military outpost and oasis, W Chad territory, Fr. Equatorial Africa, on the Bahr el Ghazal, 95 mi. NE of Moussoro.

Sallanches (sälăsh'), town (pop. 2,622), Haute-Savoie dept., SE France, on the Arve and 25 mi. ENE of Annecy, in Faucigny valley; wool spinning, metalworking, chocolate mfg. Resort. Burned in 1840, it was rebuilt on a regular plan.

Sallaumines (sälōmēn'), ESE suburb (pop. 13,102) of Lens, Pas-de-Calais dept., N France, in coal-mining dist.

Salle, La (lä säl'), Alpine village (pop. 145), Hautes-Alpes dept., SE France, on Guisane R. and 5 mi. NW of Briançon, at E foot of Massif du Pelvoux; hosiery mfg., graphite mining.

Sallee, Fr. Morocco: see SALÉ.

Sallent (sälyĕnt'), town (pop. 5,930), Barcelona prov., NE Spain, on Llobregat R. and 9 mi. NNE of Manresa; cotton milling; mfg. of dyes, brandy, flour products; lumbering. Wine, wheat in area. Potash deposits near by.

Sallent de Gállego (dhā gä'lyāgō), village (pop. 551), Huesca prov., NE Spain, in the central Pyrenees, on Gállego R. and 18 mi. NE of Jaca. Customs station on Pourtalet road.

Salles-Curan (säl-kürā'), village (pop. 547), Aveyron dept., S France, 15 mi. SE of Rodez; basket-making, sheep raising.

Salles-la-Source (–lä-sōōrs'), village (pop. 377), Aveyron dept., S France, 7 mi. NNW of Rodez; blanket mfg. Iron ore deposits near by.

Sallesópolis, Brazil: see SALESÓPOLIS.

Salles-sur-l'Hers (–sür-lâr'), agr. village (pop. 405), Aude dept., S France, 9 mi. W of Castelnaudary; stock raising.

Salley, town (pop. 407), Aiken co., W central S.C., 32 mi. SSW of Columbia.

Salling (sä'lĭng), peninsula of Viborg amt, NW Jutland, Denmark, extending W into Lim Fjord. Sallingsund (2 mi. wide) runs bet. W coast and Mos isl.; Hvalpsund and Skive Fjord along E coast.

Salliqueló (säyēkälō'), town (pop. 3,852), W Buenos Aires prov., Argentina, 33 mi. NNW of Carhué; grain, livestock; dairying (cheese, casein).

Sallis (să'lĭs), village (pop. 228), Attala co., central Miss., 11 mi. W of Kosciusko.

Sallisaw (să'lĭsô), city (pop. 2,885), ⊙ Sequoyah co., E Okla., 22 mi. W of Fort Smith (Ark.), in hilly region; center of farm area (cotton, corn, potatoes); cotton ginning, creosoting; mfg. of cottonseed oil, canned foods, fishing tackle. Coal mines, salt deposits near by. Site of Short Mtn. Reservoir in Arkansas R. is S. Founded c.1886.

Sallom (sä'lŏm), village, Kassala prov., NE Anglo-Egyptian Sudan, 18 mi. SSW of Port Sudan; rail junction for Suakin.

Sallum, Egypt: see SALUM.

Sallyana (sŭl-lyä'nŭ), town, SW Nepal, in Mahabharat Lekh range, 170 mi. NNE of Bahraich (India); corn, millet, vegetables, rice, buckwheat, fruit. Nepalese military station. Absorbed by Gurkhas in late-18th cent. Also spelled Salyana.

Salma, Jabal, Saudi Arabia: see SHAMMAR, JEBEL.

Salmas, Iran: see SHAHPUR.

Salmerón (sälmārōn'), town (pop. 977), Guadalajara prov., central Spain, 36 mi. E of Guadalajara; olives, wheat, fruit, sheep, cattle. Lumbering; olive-oil pressing.

Salmi (säl'mē), town (1948 pop. over 500), SW Karelo-Finnish SSR, on L. Ladoga, on railroad and 45 mi. SE of Sortavala. In Finland until 1940.

Salmiyarvi (säl'mēyär"vē), Finnish *Salmijärvi* (säl'mĭyär"vē), agr. village (1939 pop. under 500), W Murmansk oblast, Russian SFSR, on Arctic highway and 25 mi. WSW of Pechenga, on Paz R. (Norwegian border). NIKEL mines are 5 mi. SE, across small lake. In Finland until 1944.

Salmo (săl'mō), village (pop. estimate 300), S B.C., on Salmo R. at mouth of Beaver Creek, and 20 mi. S of Nelson; tungsten mining.

Salmon, Indian village, E Alaska, near Yukon border on upper Black R. and 75 mi. E of Fort Yukon; fishing, trapping.

Salmon, city (pop. 2,648), ⊙ Lemhi co., E Idaho, at confluence of Salmon and Lemhi rivers, 160 mi. NE of Boise; alt. 4,003 ft. Distributing center for gold-mining, stock-raising, agr. area; dairy products. Ships cobalt ore from Forney (SW). U.S. fish hatchery. Hq. Salmon Natl. Forest are here. Founded (1867) as Salmon City after discovery of gold here (1866); dropped "City" 1869.

Salmon Arm, city (pop. 836), S B.C., on Salmon Arm of Shuswap L., 30 mi. N of Vernon; dairying, lumbering, fruitgrowing; resort.

Salmon Arm, ENE arm (14 mi. long, 1–2 mi. wide) of Seechelt Inlet, SW B.C., 35 mi. NW of Vancouver; in lumbering area. Receives small Clowham R. at head (shingle mill at mouth).

Salmon Creek, NW suburb (pop. 33) of Juneau, SE Alaska.

Salmon Dam, Idaho: see SALMON FALLS CREEK.

Salmon Falls, N.H.: see ROLLINSFORD.

Salmon Falls Creek, rises in Elko co., NE Nev., flows 100 mi. N, into Twin Falls co., S Idaho, entering Snake R. 10 mi. NNW of Buhl. Salmon Dam (230 ft. high, 480 ft. long), in Idaho 15 mi. N of Nev. line, forms Salmon Creek Reservoir (11 mi. long, 1 mi. wide), used for irrigation.

Salmon Falls River, in Maine and N.H., rises in N.H. near Great East Pond, flows SSE, forming c.28 mi. of state line, joining Cocheco R. to form Piscataqua R. at Dover, N.H.; furnishes water power at Salmon Falls and Somersworth, N.H., and Berwick, Maine.

Salmon Mountains, Calif.: see KLAMATH MOUNTAINS.

Salmon River. **1** In E central Conn., rises near Hebron, flows c.18 mi. SW, through summer-resort area, to the Connecticut near East Haddam; power dam near Leesville village. **2** In central Idaho, rises in Sawtooth and Salmon River mts., flows generally NNE, past Salmon, where it receives Lemhi R., then W and N to Snake R. 38 mi. SSE of Lewiston; c.425 mi. long. There is large salmon run. Salmon River Canyon (1 mi. deep, 10 mi. wide in places; explored 1935) is impressive gorge formed by river in lower course. Chief tributaries are South Fork (rising in Sawtooth Mts. E of Cascade, flowing c.70 mi. N to main stream in S part of Idaho co.) and Middle Fork, rising in Sawtooth Mts. E of Deadwood Reservoir, and flowing c.100 mi. NNE, through deep canyon, to main stream near Yellowjacket Mts. Lower course of Middle Fork is in primitive area that extends S from main stream and lies in natl. forest area of Valley and Idaho counties. **3** In N.Y. and Que., rises in lakes in E Franklin co., NE N.Y., flows c.45 mi. NNW, past Malone (water power) and Fort Covington, to the St. Lawrence in Que., 10 mi. E of Cornwall, Ont. **4** In N and central N.Y., rises in Lewis co., flows c.30 mi. generally W to L. Ontario 4 mi. below Pulaski. Dam 5 mi. NE of Altmar impounds Salmon Reservoir (c.7 mi. long).

Salmon River Mountains, in E Idaho, occupies parts of Custer, Lemhi, Valley, and Idaho counties, and bounded on S, E, and N by Salmon R. Includes sections of Challis and Salmon natl. forests and much of Salmon R. primitive area. Chief peaks: Bald Mtn. (10,314 ft.), Twin Peaks (10,328 ft.). N extension of range is Yellowjacket Mts.

Salmon-Trinity Alps, Calif.: see KLAMATH MOUNTAINS.

Salmoral (sälmōräl'), town (pop. 1,321), Salamanca prov., W Spain, 26 mi. SE of Salamanca; cereals, wine, vegetables.

Salmünster (zäl'mün"stůr), town (pop. 2,509), in former Prussian prov. of Hesse-Nassau, W Germany, after 1945 in Hesse, on the Kinzig and 9 mi. SW of Schlüchtern; lumber milling.

Salmydessus, Turkey: see MIDYE.

Salo (sä'lō), town (pop. 8,982), Turku-Pori co., SW Finland, at head of 30-mi.-long inlet of Gulf of Bothnia, 30 mi. E of Turku; sugar refinery, machine shops.

Salò (sälô'), town (pop. 4,258), Brescia prov., Lombardy, N Italy, port on W shore of Lago di Garda, 15 mi. ENE of Brescia, in olive and citrus fruit region; resort. Produces lemon liqueur, wine, olive oil, linen textiles, wrought-copper souvenirs. Has church begun 1453.

Salobelyak (sŭlŭbĭlyăk'), village (1926 pop. 305), S Kirov oblast, Russian SFSR, 32 mi. NNE of Ioshkar-Ola; flax processing.

Salobreña (sälōvrā'nyä), town (pop. 4,415), Granada prov., S Spain, on the Mediterranean, 4 mi. W of Motril; sugar mills, brandy distilleries. Agr. trade (sugar cane, raisins, cereals, vegetables). Has ruined Moorish castle.

Salobro, Brazil: see CANAVIEIRAS.

Salom (sälōm'), town (pop. 677), Yaracuy state, N Venezuela, in coastal range, 33 mi. W of Valencia; sugar cane, corn, coffee, cacao, livestock.

Salomon Islands, coral atoll (□ 2; pop. 215) of Chagos Archipelago in Indian Ocean, a dependency of Mauritius; 5°20'S 72°15'E. Encloses lagoon, 5 mi. long, 3 mi. wide. Main settlement is on Île Boddam (SW). Coconut plantations.

Salon or **Salon-de-Provence** (sälō'-dů-prôvăs'), town (pop. 10,625), Bouches-du-Rhône dept., SE France, 28 mi. NNW of Marseilles; commercial and agr.-processing center with numerous oil presses and soap factories. Coffee roasting, candy mfg. Has 14th-cent. Gothic church of Saint-Laurent (containing tomb of Nostradamus); 17th-cent. belfry and town hall, and 13th–14th-cent. castle of archbishops of Arles. Just E begins the irrigated, olive-growing Crau lowland.

Salon (sŭlōn'), town (pop. 5,751), Rae Bareli dist., central Uttar Pradesh, India, 20 mi. SE of Rae Bareli; rice, grains, gram, oilseeds.

Salona, Greece: see AMPHISSA.

Salona, Yugoslavia: see SOLIN.

Salon-de-Provence, France: see SALON.

Salonga River (sälông'gä), W Belgian Congo, formed by 2 headstreams 45 mi. WSW of Bokwankusu, flows c.210 mi. NW to Busira R. 60 mi. E of Ingende. Navigable for 70 mi. from Watsi-Kengo downstream.

Salonika, Salonica (both: sŭlō'nĭků), or **Saloniki** (sälônē'kē), Gr. *Thessalonike* or *Thessaloniki* (both:

thĕsŭlônē'kē), nome (□ 1,897; 1940 pop. 502,887), Macedonia, Greece; ⊙ Salonika. Located on Gulf of Salonika of Aegean Sea, it is bordered SW by Olympus and Pieria mts., and extends E across base of Chalcidice peninsula (past lakes Koroneia and Volve) to the Strymonic Gulf. Drained by lower Aliakmon, Loudias, and Vardar (Axios) rivers. Agr. (in Salonika and Katerine lowlands): wheat, cotton, wine, silk. Industry and trade are focussed on Salonika. The nome is divided into 2 sections, Salonika (pop. 425,855) and Pieria (pop. 77,032).

Salonika, Salonica, or **Saloniki,** Gr. *Thessalonike* or *Thessaloniki,* Macedonian *Solun,* anc. *Therma,* later *Thessalonica* (thĕsŭlō'nīkŭ), city (1951 pop. 216,138), ⊙ Greek Macedonia and Salonika nome, Greece, port at head of Gulf of Salonika, 190 mi. NNW of Athens, at base of Chalcidice peninsula and just W of Vardar R. mouths; 40°38'N 22°56'E. Second largest city of Greece and, next to the Athens-Piraeus dist., the leading economic center, Salonika is the natural outlet of Macedonia, connected by the Vardar-Morava axis with the middle Danube reaches. An important communications hub, it connected by rail with Sofia, Adrianople, and Istanbul (E), with Skoplje and Belgrade (N), and with Athens (S). Its airport is at Therme (Sedes). Its advantageous geographical position has been reduced considerably, however, by international frontier barriers across its hinterland. Its industries include textile mills (producing cotton, woolen, and silk goods), foundries, shipyards, and flour mills; tobacco, cigarettes, leather, soap, and beer are also produced. The port, opened 1901 and repeatedly modernized, exports chiefly tobacco, manganese and chrome ores, and hides. Bet. the 2 world wars, it included a free port with a separate Yugoslav section. Presenting a picturesque appearance, Salonika rises from the waterfront (where the 15th-cent. White Tower is a noted landmark) to a height crowned by a 15th-cent. Venetian citadel (now a prison). The city proper, surrounded in part by white turreted Byzantine walls, is traversed by the Roman Via Egnatia, which passes through Vardar Gate (NW; destroyed 1867) and Kalamaria Gate (SE; remains of 4th-cent. triumphal arch). The seat of a Gr. metropolitan, Salonika has numerous Byzantine churches dating from 5th and 6th cents. (converted into mosques under Turkish rule), the chief of which are St. Sophia (built along the lines of its Istanbul namesake), with fine mosaics, St. George, originally a Roman rotunda, and the 6th-cent. St. Demetrius (completely destroyed by fire in 1917; later rebuilt). Salonika is the seat of a univ. (1925). The city is surrounded by industrial suburbs and adjoined SE by the Kalamaria residential quarter, with exposition grounds. Originally called Therma for near-by hot springs, the city was refounded 315 B.C. by Cassander, king of Macedon, who named it for its wife, Thessalonica. Situated on the important Roman Via Egnatia linking Dyrrhachium (Durazzo) and Constantinople, Salonika flourished greatly (after 146 B.C.) as ⊙ Roman prov. of Macedonia, and under Byzantium was 2d only to Constantinople. To the infant church here St. Paul addressed his 2 epistles to the Thessalonians. The massacre (A.D. 390) of the rebellious citizens of Salonika by order of Theodosius I led to the emperor's temporary excommunication. The city was occupied 904 by the Saracens and 1185 by the Normans of Sicily. For the duration (1204–61) of the Latin Empire of Constantinople, the kingdom of Thessalonica, comprising N central and NE Greece, was its largest fief. It was given by Baldwin I to his rival, Boniface, marquis of Montferrat, but was seized 1222 by the despot of Epirus, and 1246 by the Greek emperors of Nicaea, who in 1261 restored it to the Byzantine Empire. Conquered by Sultan Murad I in 1387, Salonika was returned 1405 to the Byzantines, was briefly held (1423–1430) by Venice until it was again conquered by the Turks under Sultan Murad II and became known as Selanik. The city's Jewish colony, of importance since early times, was greatly increased in late 15th and early 16th cents. by influx of Sephardic Jews from Spain. The Jewish element (20% of total pop.) was the largest single Ladino (Dzhudezmo)-speaking community in the Mediterranean area until its liquidation by the Germans during Second World War. The birthplace (1881) of Kemal Ataturk, founder of modern Turkey, Salonika became the hq. of the Young Turk revolution (1908). It passed from Turkish rule to Greece as a result of the Balkan Wars (1912–13). During First World War, the Allies landed here (1915), using the city as a base for the Salonika campaigns, which culminated (1918) in the defeat of the German and Bulg. divisions in the Balkans. The city suffered considerable damage during Second World War, when it was held (1941–44) by the Germans.

Salonika, Gulf of, arm of Aegean Sea in NE Greece, bet. Thessaly and Macedonia (W) and Chalcidice peninsula (E); 70 mi. long, 30–50 mi. wide. Receives Aliakmon, Loudias, and Vardar (Axios) rivers (N) and Peneus R. (W). The name Gulf of Salonika [Gr. *Kolpos Thessalonikes* (*Thessalonikis*)] is often restricted to the northernmost inlet (10 mi. long, 5 mi. wide) on which lies Salonika, while the greater part of the inlet is known as Thermaic Gulf (thûrmā'ĭk) [Gr. *Thermaikos Kolpos*; Lat. *Thermaicus Sinus*], for Therma, the anc. name of Salonika.

Salonta (sä'lôntä), Hung. *Nagyszalonta* (nŏ'dyŭsŏ"-lôntŏ), town (1948 pop. 15,251), Bihor prov., W Rumania, in Crisana, 22 mi. SW of Oradea; rail junction near Hung. border; mfg. (knitwear, edible oils, flour, canned vegetables). Has remains of 17th-cent. Turkish fortress. In Hungary, 1940–45.

Salop, England: see SHROPSHIRE.

Salorino (sälōrē'nō), village (pop. 2,479), Cáceres prov., W Spain, 34 mi. W of Cáceres; produces cereals.

Salorno (sälôr'nô), Ger. *Salurn,* village (pop. 1,910), Bolzano prov., Trentino–Alto Adige, N Italy, near the Adige, 19 mi. SSW of Bolzano.

Salor River (sälōr'), Cáceres prov., W Spain, rises near Montánchez, flows 78 mi. NW to the Tagus at Port. border, 10 mi. SW of Alcántara.

Salou, Cape (sä'lō), rocky promontory of Tarragona prov., NE Spain, on the Mediterranean, 6 mi. SW of Tarragona; 41°3'N 4°51'E. Lighthouse.

Saloum River (sälōōm'), W Senegal, Fr. West Africa, flows c.150 mi. W, past Kaffrine and Kaolack, to Foundiougne, where it forms a wide tidal delta stretching c.35 mi. S to Br. Gambia. Navigable upstream to Kaolack. Sometimes spelled Salum.

Salpi (säl'pē), former lagoon (□ 14), Foggia prov., S Italy, 25 mi. ESE of Foggia; now drained; forms part of extensive saltworks of Margherita di Savoia. On its W banks are ruins of anc. Salapia.

Salpo (säl'pō), town (pop. 1,580), Libertad dept., NW Peru, in Cordillera Occidental, 9 mi. SSW of Otusco, 29 mi. ENE of Trujillo; alt. 13,483 ft. Gold- and silver-mining center, connected with SAMNE concentrating plant (5 mi. WNW) by aerial cableway. Mining also at Milluachaqui.

Salqin (sălkēn'), Fr. *Salkine,* village, Aleppo prov., NW Syria, near Turkish border, 40 mi. W of Aleppo; cereals, tobacco.

Sal-Rei (säl'-rā), town, Cape Verde Isls., on NW shore of Boa Vista Isl., 95 mi. NNE of Praia (on São Tiago Isl.); 16°11'N 22°57'W. Saltworks.

Sal River (säl), SE Rostov oblast, Russian SFSR, rises in 2 main headstreams W of Stepnoi in Yergeni Hills, joining near Zavetnoye; flows generally W, through steppe, past Dubovskoye, to Don R. just W of Semikarakorskaya. Length (including the Dzhuryuk-Sal, its main headstream), over 400 mi.

Salsacate (sälsäkä'tā), village (pop. estimate 700), ⊙ Pocho dept. (□ c.1,100; pop. 7,923), W Córdoba prov., Argentina, 55 mi. W of Córdoba; stock-raising center.

Salsadella (sälsä-dhĕ'lyä), town (pop. 1,353), Castellón de la Plana prov., E Spain, 15 mi. WSW of Vinaroz; produces olive oil.

Salses, France: see SALCES.

Salsette Island (sălsĕt'), in Arabian Sea, off Bombay, India; separated from mainland by Ulhas R. (N), Thana Creek and Bombay Harbour (E). 28 mi. long (N–S), up to 15 mi. wide (N). Part of Thana dist. and its ⊙, Thana, lie on N portion of isl.; larger S section includes Bombay Suburban dist.; city of Bombay is on S peninsula, sometimes called Bombay Isl., but now joined to Salsette Isl. by drainage and reclamation projects. Tidal creeks and marshes on W and SE coasts. Rice is main crop; fishing, salt panning, hand-loom weaving. Chief towns: Bandra, Kurla, Thana, Ghatkopar, Andheri. Has 3 artificial lakes (center), which supply Bombay city with water. Noted Kanheri cave-temples are 4 mi. SE of Borivli. Occupied 16th-17th cent. by Portuguese; annexed 1782 by British.

Salsigne (sälsē'nyü), village (pop. 545), Aude dept., S France, 8 mi. N of Carcassonne; important arsenic and gold mine.

Salsipuedes Grande, Arroyo (äroi'ō sälsēpwā'dĕs grän'dā), river on Tacuarembó-Paysandú dept. border, N central Uruguay, rises in the Cuchilla de Haedo NW of Piedra Sola, flows 75 mi. S to the Río Negro 8 mi. W of Paso de los Toros.

Salsk or **Sal'sk** (sälsk), city (1939 pop. over 10,000), S Rostov oblast, Russian SFSR, 100 mi. SE of Rostov; rail junction; agr. center; processes local products (wheat, cotton), sawmilling; metalworks, foundry. Horse breeding near by. Formerly called Torgovy.

Salsomaggiore (säl"sômäd-jô'rĕ), town (pop. 7,751), Parma prov., Emilia-Romagna, N central Italy, 17 mi. W of Parma, in Apennine foothills; rail spur terminus; resort (alt. 525 ft.) with hot mineral springs. Has petroleum refinery, liquor factory, pharmaceutical, dye and varnish works. Oil wells near by.

Salso River (säl'sō). **1** In central Sicily, rises in Madonie Mts. N of Petralia Sottana, flows 70 mi. S to Mediterranean Sea at Licata; used for hydroelectric power. Also called Imera Meridionale, anc. *Himera Meridionalis.* **2** In E central Sicily, rises in Madonie Mts. SE of Gangi, flows 36 mi. SE, past Nicosia and Agira, to Simeto R. just SW of Adrano.

Salt, river: see SALT RIVER.

Salt (sălt), **El Salt, Es Salt,** or **Al-Salt** (all: ĕs-sălt'), town (pop. c.12,000), N central Jordan, on main Amman-Jerusalem road and 13 mi. WNW of Amman, 25 mi. NE of N end of Dead Sea; alt. 2,610 ft.; trade center, producing sumac and raisins; vineyards, distilleries. Kaolin quarries.

Salt (sält), town (pop. 4,687, including adjacent San Antonio), Gerona prov., NE Spain, on Ter R. and 2 mi. WSW of Gerona, in irrigated agr. area (cereals, vegetables); cotton milling.

Salta (säl'tä), province (□ 59,757; pop. 290,826), NW Argentina, in the Andes; ⊙ Salta. Borders Chile and Bolivia. The Andes slope E through the dry *puna* region to the Chaco plains. Has fertile valleys. Drained by Bermejo, Juramento or Pasaje, Guachipas, and Calchaquí rivers. There are large salt deserts in W. Climate varies from dry cold of the highlands to warm, humid Mediterranean climate of the inhabited valleys. Among its rich mineral resources are sodium and borax (deserts of Rincón, Arizaro, Pocitos), lead and silver (Poscaya), iron (Rosario de Lerma), copper (San Antonio de los Cobres), lime (La Merced), nickel and cobalt (Santa Victoria), oil (Tartagal, Vespucio, Orán). Agr. in irrigated area of its main rivers: corn, alfalfa, sugar cane, oats, rice, potatoes, tobacco, fruit, livestock. Rural industries: lumbering, milling, dairying, mining, oil drilling. Urban industries: cement works (Campo Santo, Salta), sugar refineries (El Tabacal, Campo Santo, Orán), oil refineries (Embarcación); tobacco processing (Chicoana), wine making (Cafayate), and vegetable-oil refining, meat packing, tanning, flour milling at Salta. Major resorts: Chicoana, Salta, Rosario de la Frontera, El Galpón. San Antonio de los Cobres and Pastos Grandes depts. were inc. in the prov. in 1943, when Los Andes territory was dissolved.

Salta, city (pop. 66,785), ⊙ Salta prov. and Salta dept. (□ 668; 1947 census 75,600), NW Argentina, on a headstream of the Río Salado, in irrigated Lerma Valley, on the new Transandine RR of the North (opened 1948 to Antofagasta, Chile), and 775 mi. NW of Buenos Aires, 140 mi. N of Tucumán; 24°48'S 65°26'W; alt. 3,893 ft. Commercial and trade center for an extensive farming, lumbering, stock-raising, and mining area. Meat packing, vegetable-oil refining, tanning, flour milling, cement making. Agr. products: alfalfa, corn, wheat, sugar, tobacco, grapes; cattle and sheep raising. Trading in tobacco, hides, lumber, and livestock. Oil, silver, lead, copper, marble, and lime deposits near by. An old colonial city, it has administrative bldgs., a cathedral, several churches, bishop's palace, a theater, and institutions of higher learning. Near-by thermal springs make it something of a resort. Founded 1582. Here Gen. Belgrano defeated the Sp. royalists in 1813.

Saltabarranca (säl'täbäräng'kä), town (pop. 919), Veracruz, SE Mexico, in Sotavento region, 23 mi. WNW of San Andrés Tuxtla; fruit, cattle.

Saltair, village, Salt Lake co., N Utah, 12 mi. W of Salt Lake City, on Great Salt L.; bathing resort (water here c.25% salt).

Saltaire, England: see SHIPLEY.

Saltaire, N.Y.: see FIRE ISLAND.

Saltara (sältä'rä), village (pop. 577), Pesaro e Urbino prov., The Marches, central Italy, 9 mi. SW of Fano; wine.

Saltash (sôl'tăsh), municipal borough (1931 pop. 3,603; 1951 census 7,924), SE Cornwall, England, on Tamar R. (crossed by 2,240-ft. railroad bridge) and 4 mi. NW of Plymouth; agr. market. Has Norman church.

Saltburn-by-the-Sea, former urban district (1931 pop. 3,911) now in Saltburn and Marske-by-the-Sea urban dist. (1951 census 8,428), North Riding, NE Yorkshire, England, on North Sea 4 mi. ESE of Redcar; seaside resort. Near by are iron mines.

Salt Cay (kā), islet (□ 4; pop. 420), Turks and Caicos Isls., dependency of Jamaica, 7 mi. SW of Grand Turk isl.; 21°20'N 71°12'W. Salt panning.

Saltcoats, town (pop. 445), SE Sask., on small Anderson L., 18 mi. SE of Yorkton; grain elevators, lumbering.

Saltcoats, burgh (1931 pop. 10,173; 1951 census 13,108), N Ayrshire, Scotland, on Firth of Clyde, 13 mi. NW of Ayr; 55°39'N 4°48'W; port and seaside resort. Saltworks were established here by James V in 16th cent.; town was formerly noted shipbuilding and salt-production center.

Salt Creek. 1 In central Ill., rises in McLean co., flows c.100 mi. SW and W to Sangamon R. 8 mi. N of Petersburg. **2** In S central Ind., rises in Brown co. in small streams joining SE of Bloomington, then flows c.45 mi. SW and S to East Fork of White R. 3 mi. SW of Bedford. **3** In SE Nebr., rises in Lancaster co., flows 88 mi. NE, through Lincoln, to Platte R. near Ashland. **4** In central Wyo., rises in Natrona co., flows c.50 mi. N, past Midwest, through Salt Creek oil field, to Powder R. 16 mi. E of Kaycee.

Salt Creek Pass, Oregon: see CASCADE RANGE.

Saltdal, canton, Norway: see ROGNAN.

Saltdal Fjord, Norway: see SALT FJORD.

Saltdalselv, Norway: see SALT RIVER.

Saltee Islands (sôl'tē), group of islets in St. George's Channel, off Crossfarnoge Point, S Co. Wexford, Ireland. Great Saltee Isl. (215 acres; 1 mi. long;

rises to 186 ft.), 3 mi. S of Crossfarnoge Point, was hiding place of leaders of 1798 insurrection. Little Saltee Isl. (93 acres) is 2 mi. S of Crossfarnoge Point. Lightships are near by.

Saltelv, Norway: see SALT RIVER.

Salten (säl'tůn), region and administrative district (□ 6,143; pop. 63,875), central Nordland co., N central Norway, bet. Swedish border (E), North Sea (W), Salt Fjord (S), and Ofot Fjord (N); rises to c.5,600 ft. Coast indented by numerous fjords, including Tys Fjord. S part drained by Salt R. Bodo and Rognan are centers of pop. Mining (iron, pyrites), marble quarrying, fishing.

Salteras (sältä'räs), town (pop. 1,753), Seville prov., SW Spain, 7 mi. W of Seville; grain- and wine-growing, stock raising; olive-oil processing.

Saltese (sŏltēz'), village (pop. c.150), Mineral co., W Mont., 80 mi. NW of Missoula and on branch of the Clark Fork, near Idaho line; supply point for near-by gold and silver mines.

Salt Fjord (sôlt, Nor. sält), inlet (40 mi. long) of North Sea, Nordland co., N Norway, just S of Bodo; 5 mi. wide at mouth, up to 1,180 ft. deep. Narrows (8 mi. SE of Bodo) to SALTSTRAUM sound, then extends E and SE—here called Skjerstad Fjord, which forms several arms, including Saltdal Fjord (Rognan village at head). Sometimes called Salten Fjord.

Salt Fork of Arkansas River (ärkăn'zůs, är'kůnsô") or **Salt Fork,** in S Kansas and N Okla., formed by confluence of several headstreams in Comanche co. in S Kansas, flows SE into Okla. to Alva, then E, past Pond Creek city, to Arkansas R. 7 mi. S of Ponca City; 192 mi. long; not navigable. Great Salt Plains Dam (68.5 ft. high, 5,700 ft. long; completed 1948 by U.S. Army Engineers) is in stream 12 mi. E of Cherokee, Okla.; used for flood control; forms Great Salt Plains Reservoir (capacity 259,000 acre-ft.) in salt-encrusted plains area. Part of reservoir serves as wildlife refuge. Agr. and stock raising are leading activities in river basin. Gas and oil fields are in E.

Salt Fork of Brazos River, Texas: see BRAZOS RIVER.

Salt Fork of Red River, in N Texas and SW Okla., rises in intermittent streams in Armstrong and Donley counties, Texas, and flows c.140 mi. SE, across SW Okla., to join Prairie Dog Town Fork to form Red R. just S of Elmer, Okla.

Saltholm (sält'hôlm), island (□ 6.1; pop. 16), Denmark, in the Oresund, just E of Amager isl.; divides the Oresund into Drogden (W) and Flinterenden (E) straits; 5 mi. long.

Saltillo (sältē'yō). **1** City (pop. 49,430), ⊙ Coahuila, N Mexico, on plateau of Sierra Madre Oriental, 45 mi. SW of Monterrey, 430 mi. NNW of Mexico city; 25°25'N 101°W; alt. 5,213 ft. Rail junction; resort; agr. (cotton, grain, cattle), mfg., and mining center. Silver, lead, gold, copper, zinc, iron, and coal mines in vicinity. Cotton and rayon mills; mfg. of clothing, flour, shoes, kitchen utensils, ceramics, pencils, cottonseed oil, forest products (resin, turpentine, candelilla wax). Famous for woolen serapes. Founded in late 16th cent. Captured by U.S. forces during Mexican War. Decisive battle fought at BUENA VISTA near by. **2** Town (pop. 707), Puebla, central Mexico, 24 mi. NE of Serdán; cereals, maguey, livestock. Sometimes Lafragua.

Saltillo. 1 (sôltĭ'lō) Town (pop. 122), Washington co., S Ind., 37 mi. NW of New Albany, in agr. area. **2** (säl'tĭ"lů) Town (pop. 501), Lee co., NE Miss., 8 mi. N of Tupelo; mfg. of pencils. **3** (sôltĭ'lō) Borough (pop. 435), Huntingdon co., S central Pa., 13 mi. SSW of Mount Union.

Salt Island, islet, Br. Virgin Isls., 6 mi. E of Tortola isl., bet. Peter Isl. (W) and Cooper Isl. (E); 18°22'N 64°30'W. Has salt ponds.

Salt Key, Bahama Isls.: see CAY SAL.

Salt Lake (□ 900), NW Western Australia, near Shark Bay, 300 mi. NNW of Geraldton; 65 mi. long, 25 mi. wide; usually dry.

Salt Lake, county (□ 764; pop. 274,895), N central Utah; ⊙ Salt Lake City, the state capital. Tableland area drained by Jordan R.; bounded NW by Great Salt L. Wasatch Range is in E. Mfg. at Salt Lake City. Copper, lead, silver, zinc, gold; livestock, alfalfa, sugar beets, grain, fruit, truck. Formed 1850.

Salt Lake, The (□ 25), NW New South Wales, Australia, 135 mi. NNE of Broken Hill; 6 mi. long, 5 mi. wide; shallow.

Salt Lake City, city (pop. 182,121), ⊙ Utah and Salt Lake co., N Utah, on Jordan R., near SE end of Great Salt L., at foot of Wasatch Range, and 375 mi. WNW of Denver; 40°46'N 111°53'W; alt. c.4,300 ft. Largest city in state; distribution, commercial, transportation, and cultural center. Mfg. of steel, petroleum, and iron products, coke, textiles; food processing (dairy, meat, and bakery products, canned goods, candy); oil refining; printing and publishing, saltmaking. Has stockyards and smelters (for reduction of ores from near-by copper, silver, lead, zinc, coal, and iron mines); ships farm produce of rich irrigated area. Founded 1847 by Brigham Young as Mormon capital, inc. 1851, called Great Salt Lake City until 1868. From its founding was leading city of Utah. Served as territorial capital until 1896, when it became state capital. Was agr. trade center and outfitting point on Calif. gold-rush route and for many years center of dispute bet. Mormon Church and U.S. govt. Growth stimulated by construction of rail line (1869–70) from Salt Lake City to transcontinental line at Ogden and by establishment of other rail connections in 1870s and early 1880s. Now an important transcontinental communications center, with large municipal airport and numerous rail, highway, and airline connections. Points of interest: Mormon temple (built 1853–93), Tabernacle (completed 1867), state capitol (completed 1915; has art collection and mus. of pioneer relics), grave of Brigham Young, the "Lion House" (now used as social center; once occupied by some of Brigham Young's wives), art center, and Fort Douglas (military reservation in outskirts; founded 1862 as Camp Douglas by Gen. P. E. Connor). Seat of Univ. of Utah, Col. of St. Mary-of-the-Wasatch, Westminster Jr. Col., and McCune School of Music and Art. There are veterans' hosp., state prison, and numerous parks and monuments.

Saltley, E industrial suburb (pop. 39,930) of Birmingham, NW Warwick, England.

Salt Lick, town (pop. 488), Bath co., NE Ky., near Licking R. and Cumberland Natl. Forest, 36 mi. ESE of Paris; lumber, flour.

Saltney, town in East Saltney parish (pop. 2,642), Flint, Wales, on the Dee and 2 mi. SW of Chester; railroad shops, iron foundries, mfg. of chemicals.

Salto (säl'tō), town (pop. 8,020), ⊙ Salto dist. (□ 622; pop. 29,084), N Buenos Aires prov., Argentina, on the Salto R. (right branch of the Arrecifes) and 45 mi. SE of Pergamino; commercial and agr. center (corn, wheat, livestock); rail junction. Sometimes called Marcelino Ugarte. Fossil remains of prehistoric animals have been found near by.

Salto (säl'tōō), city (pop. 8,108), S São Paulo, Brazil, on Tietê R., on railroad and 45 mi. NW of São Paulo; cotton milling, paper mfg. Trades in sugar, grain, grapes.

Salto (säl'tō). **1** Village, Llanquihue prov., Chile: see PUERTO TOLEDO. **2** or **El Salto** (ĕl), village (1930 pop. 597), Santiago prov., central Chile, just N of Santiago; resort; copper mining (1930 mine pop. 38).

Salto or **El Salto,** village (pop. 900), Escuintla dept., S Guatemala, on Michatoya R. and 2 mi. E of Escuintla; sugar-milling center.

Salto, department (□ 4,866; pop. 100,840), NW Uruguay; ⊙ Salto. Bordered by Argentina (W, across Uruguay R.) and Daymán R. (S). Drained by Arapey R. Livestock (cattle, sheep, horses); agr. products (grain, grapes, vegetables, fruit). Industry concentrated at Salto; other centers: Constitución, Belén, Lavalleja. Steamer service on the Uruguay. Dept. was formed 1837.

Salto, city (pop. 44,000), ⊙ Salto dept., NW Uruguay, on Uruguay R., opposite Concordia (Argentina), on railroad and 250 mi. NW of Montevideo, 70 mi. N of Paysandú; 31°23'S 57°58'W. Third largest city of Uruguay, important river port (reached by small ocean-going vessels), and railroad junction, with airport, it is in cattle- and sheep-raising area. Industrial center: meat packing and salting, flour milling; mfg. of beverages, chemicals, pharmaceuticals; wickerwork plants, shipyards. Center of orange and tangerine orchards, vineyards, apiaries. Trade in agr. products (vegetables, grain). Bishopric. Has library, theaters, agr. school, customhouse. Although Salto is sometimes said to have been established 1756 as a military post, it is more often thought to have been founded 1817. It developed after Uruguay became independent a decade later. A newly risen suburb (NW) is called Pueblo Nuevo. In 1946 the Argentinian and Uruguayan govts. agreed to start a joint hydroelectric development at Salto Grande rapids, just N.

Salto, El, Mexico: see EL SALTO.

Salto da Divisa (säl'tōō dä dēvē'zů), city (pop. 1,085), northeasternmost Minas Gerais, Brazil, on Bahia border, downstream end of navigability on middle Jequitinhonha R., and 70 mi. WSW of Canavieiras (Bahia). Salto Grande falls (140 ft. high) are here.

Salto de Agua (säl'tō dä ä'gwä), town (pop. 680), Chiapas, S Mexico, on affluent of Grijalva R., in Gulf lowland, 45 mi. SE of Villahermosa; fruit.

Salto de las Rosas (läs rō'säs), town (pop. estimate 500), central Mendoza prov., Argentina, in Atuel R. valley (irrigation area), on railroad and 10 mi. SE of San Rafael; agr. center (wine, grain, potatoes, fruit, livestock); fruit drying, nutria breeding.

Salto Grande (säl'tō grän'dä), cataracts in Uruguay R., on Argentina (Entre Ríos)-Uruguay border just N of Salto, extending for several miles. Site of a joint hydroelectric development, upon which Argentina and Uruguay agreed in 1946.

Salto Grande (säl'tōō grän'dĭ), city (pop. 1,565), W São Paulo, Brazil, on Paranapanema R. (Paraná line), on railroad and 10 mi. NW of Ourinhos; brandy distilling, pottery mfg.; coffee, rice, corn.

Salto Grande, falls, Minas Gerais and Bahia, Brazil: see SALTO DA DIVISA.

Salton Sea (sôl'tůn), S Calif., shallow saline lake (c.30 mi. long, 10 mi. wide; surface c.240 ft. below sea level), c.80 mi. NE of San Diego, in center of arid trough which continues SE as IMPERIAL VALLEY, NW as COACHELLA VALLEY. Until 1905, this area was a salt-covered depression (Salton Sink, c.280 ft. below sea level), part of prehistoric floor of Gulf of California, subject to periodic natural flooding (most recently in 1891) by Colorado R.; in 1905–07, the Colorado broke through an irrigation gap in its levee in Imperial Valley and filled the basin over an area of c.450 sq. mi. and to max. depth of 67 ft. Evaporation reduced lake's area to point where surplus water from irrigation ditches (much of it discharged through drainage channels called New and Alamo rivers) now prevents further rapid recession. Waterfowl refuge on S shore.

Saltonstall, Lake (sôl'tůnstôl), S Conn., in East Haven and Branford towns, just E of New Haven; c.3 mi. long; fishing.

Saltoro Range, Kashmir: see KAILAS-KARAKORAM RANGE.

Saltpond, town, Western Prov., S Gold Coast colony, port on Gulf of Guinea, 15 mi. ENE of Cape Coast; fishing center; coconuts, cassava, corn. Exports cacao. A Br. trade station in 19th cent. Just W is old Du. fort of Kormantyn or Cormantyn (built 1631).

Salt Range, hill system in NW Punjab, W Pakistan; from E Jhelum dist. extends c.200 mi. W and NW to Indus R. opposite Kalabagh; rises again on W bank, curving S to meet NE offshoot of Sulaiman Range; c.10–15 mi. wide. Forms S limit of Potwar Plateau; overlooks N Thal region and Jhelum valley (S). Highest point (c.4,992 ft.) at hill resort of Sakesar. Derives name from its extensive rock salt deposits (works near Khewra, Nurpur, Warcha, Kalabagh); coal mining, limestone quarrying. Small saline lakes (center, E).

Salt River (sôlt, Nor. sält), Nor. *Saltelv* or *Saltdalselv*, Nordland co., N Norway, rises on Swedish border 30 mi. SSW of Sulitjelma, flows c.35 mi. NW and N to Saltdal Fjord (arm of Salt Fjord) at Rognan.

Salt River. 1 In S central Ariz., formed in plateau region of E Ariz. by confluence of Black R. and White R. c.40 mi. NE of Globe, flows 200 mi. generally W, past Sierra Ancha and Mazatzal Mts., to Gila R. 15 mi. WSW of Phoenix. Was used for irrigation centuries ago by Indians and in 19th cent. by early settlers. Valley is now served by Salt R. irrigation project, 1st major undertaking in U.S. reclamation program. Important dams built on river as units in project are ROOSEVELT DAM, HORSE MESA DAM, MORMON FLAT DAM, STEWART MOUNTAIN DAM, and Granite Reef Dam (small, concrete weir, completed 1908, c.25 mi. ENE of Phoenix). Cave Creek Dam (109 ft. high, 1,648 ft. long; completed 1923; used for flood control) is on small, intermittent tributary and N of Phoenix. BARTLETT DAM is on Verde R., chief tributary of Salt R. Water is distributed through more than 1,000 mi. of irrigation canals; cotton, alfalfa, fruit, and truck products are raised. Favorable climate makes river valley popular as resort area. Chief cities are Phoenix, Tempe, Mesa, and Glendale. **2** In N Ky., rises W of Danville, flows N, generally W past Taylorsville and Shepherdsville (head of navigation), and N to Ohio R. at West Point; 125 mi. long. Main tributaries: Rolling Fork (and its tributary Beech Fork), Floyds Fork. **3** In NE Mo., rises in Schuyler co., flows c.200 mi. SE and E to Mississippi R. above Louisiana. **4** In W Wyo. and SE Idaho, rises in several branches on state line, flows c.40 mi. N, along W foot of Salt River Range, Wyo., to Snake R. in Idaho. Drains part of Star Valley, rich grain and dairy region (c. 50 mi. long, 5–7 mi. wide) in Wyo. and Idaho.

Salt River Mountains, S central Ariz., bet. Gila and Salt rivers, S of Phoenix; rise to 2,612 ft. in W tip. Include Phoenix South Mountain Park. Gold is mined in park.

Salt River Range, in Rocky Mts. of W Wyo., just E of Idaho line; extends c.70 mi. N–S bet. Salt R. and Greys R. Prominent peaks: Virginia Peak (10,143 ft.), Man Peak (10,327 ft.), Mt. Wagner (10,745 ft.). Range includes part of Bridger Natl. Forest.

Saltrou (sältrōō'), agr. town (1950 census pop. 1,113), Ouest dept., S Haiti, minor port on the Caribbean, 28 mi. SE of Port-au-Prince; coffee, cacao, construction wood.

Saltsburg, borough (pop. 1,156), Indiana co., SW Pa., 28 mi. E of Pittsburgh and on Kiskiminetas R., at junction of Conemaugh R. and Loyalhanna Creek. Bituminous coal; agr. Laid out 1817, inc. 1838.

Salt Sea, Palestine: see DEAD SEA.

Saltsjobaden (sält'shů"bä"důn), Swedish *Saltsjöbaden*, town (pop. 3,750), Stockholm co., E Sweden, on small fjord of the Baltic, opposite Varmdo isl., 9 mi. ESE of Stockholm city center; 59°16'N 18°18'E. Popular seaside resort. Site of Stockholm observatory.

Saltspring Island, largest (□ 70) of Gulf Isls., B.C., in Strait of Georgia just off SE Vancouver Isl., 7 mi. E of Duncan, 25 mi. N of Victoria; 16 mi. long, 2–7 mi. wide. Lumbering, dairying, poultry raising, sheep raising, fruitgrowing. Chief settlements: Ganges on E central shore, Fulford Harbour on SE shore. Formerly Admiral Isl.

Salt Springs Dam, Calif.: see Mokelumne River.

Saltstraum (sält′stroum), narrow tidal sound bet. Salt Fjord and Skjerstad Fjord, Nordland co., N Norway, 7 mi. ESE of Bodo; 2 mi. long, 490 ft. wide at narrowest point. At high tide, whirlpools are created by onrushing sea. Also called Saltstrom, Nor. *Saltstrøm*.

Salt Sulphur Springs, village, Monroe co., SE W. Va., in the Alleghenies, 21 mi. SW of White Sulphur Springs. A health resort (5 mineral springs) since 1820s.

Saltvik, Sweden: see Vansbro.

Saltville, town (pop. 2,678), Smyth and Washington cos., SW Va., in Holston R. valley, near North Fork of the Holston R., 14 mi. W of Marion; salt wells, large chemical works (alkalies). Saltmaking began in 1788; saltworks destroyed by Federal forces in 1864, but re-established later. Inc. 1894.

Saltykovka (sŭltĭkôf′kŭ), village (1939 pop. over 500), NW Saratov oblast, Russian SFSR, 15 mi. SE of Rtishchevo; flour milling; wheat, fruit.

Saltykovo (–kô′vŭ), village (1926 pop. 3,343), NW Penza oblast, Russian SFSR, on railroad and 10 mi. NNW of Zemetchino, in sugar-beet area. Pashkovo, village (1939 pop. over 500), is 5 mi. NW; sawmilling.

Saluafata (sä″lōōäfä′tä), American naval station and harbor, NE coast of Upolu, Western Samoa.

Salud, La, Cuba: see La Salud.

Saluda (sulōō′dŭ), county (□ 442; pop. 15,924), W central S.C.; ⊙ Saluda. Bounded N by Saluda R. and L. Murray; includes part of Sumter Natl. Forest. Sparsely settled agr. area (cotton, timber); some mfg. (textiles, lumber). Formed 1895.

Saluda. 1 Resort city (pop. 547), Polk co., W N.C., 8 mi. SE of Hendersonville, in the Blue Ridge foothills. **2** Town (pop. 1,594). ⊙ Saluda co., W central S.C., 45 mi. W of Columbia, in agr. area; lumber, textiles. **3** Village, ⊙ Middlesex co., E Va., near the Rappahannock, 12 mi. ENE of West Point.

Saluda River, W central S.C., rises in the Blue Ridge near N.C. line in 2 forks (North Saluda R. and South Saluda R.), joining 10 mi. NW of Greenville; flows SE, across the piedmont, past Pelzer, joining Broad R. at Columbia to form Congaree River; length from junction of its forks, c.145 mi. Dammed above Columbia by huge earthen Saluda (or Dreher Shoals) (drēr) Dam (208 ft. high, 7,838 ft. long; built 1930; used for hydroelectric power) to form L. Murray. E of Greenwood, earthen Buzzard Roost Dam (85 ft. high, 2,400 ft. long; completed 1940; used for hydroelectric power) forms L. Greenwood.

Saluggia (sälōōd′jä), village (pop. 2,258), Vercelli prov., Piedmont, N Italy, near Dora Baltea R., 21 mi. WSW of Vercelli.

Salum, Sallum, Solum, Sollum (all: sŭlōōm′), or **Al-Salum** (ĕs-sälōōm′), Mediterranean port (pop. 1,011), Western Desert prov., NW Egypt, at the Libyan frontier 280 mi. W of Alexandria. In Second World War, an important strategic objective in the 1941–42 Western Desert campaign, changing hands several times.

Salumbar (sŭlōōm′bŭr), town (pop. 5,257), S Rajasthan, India, 37 mi. SE of Udaipur, 6 mi. S of Dhebar L.; agr. (corn, millet, barley).

Salum River, Fr. West Africa: see Saloum River.

Salur (sä′lōōr), town (pop. 20,574), Vizagapatam dist., NE Madras, India, 31 mi. NNW of Vizianagaram; rail spur terminus; trades in produce (sal, teak, bamboo, tanning bark, lac) of Eastern Ghats (W); sugar cane, oilseeds, rice. Graphite deposits near by.

Salurn, Italy: see Salorno.

Salut, Îles du (ēl dü sälü′), archipelago c.8 mi. off coast of Fr. Guiana, 28 mi. NNW of Cayenne; 5°17′N 52°35′W. Consists of 3 rocky islets: Devils Island and Royale and St. Joseph isls.

Saluzzo (sälōō′tsô), town (pop. 10,433), Cuneo prov., Piedmont, NW Italy, at E foot of Cottian Alps, near Po R., 31 mi. SSW of Turin; rail junction. A major chestnut market of Italy; textiles, food products, furniture, cement. Bishopric. Consists of lower town with Gothic cathedral (built 1491–1501; interior modernized), and upper town with medieval castle (restored 1826; now a prison) and 15th-cent. Renaissance house (mus.). Capital of marquisate, 1175 until mid-16th cent.

Salvacañete (sälväkänyā′tā), town (pop. 738), Cuenca prov., E central Spain, in the Serranía de Cuenca, 27 mi. SW of Teruel; cereals, beans, sugar beets, potatoes, livestock. Lumbering; flour milling. Hydroelectric plant.

Salvada (sŭlvä′dŭ), village (pop. 2,173), Beja dist., S Portugal, 7 mi. SE of Beja; grain, olives, sheep, goats.

Salvador (săl′vŭdôr, Sp. sälvädhōr′) or **El Salvador,** smallest, but most densely populated republic (□ 13,176; 1950 pop. 1,858,656) of Central America; ⊙ San Salvador. Has c.170-mi. coast line along the Pacific, but, unlike the other Central American nations, has no Atlantic coast. It is bounded on W, partly along Río de la Paz, by Guatemala, N, NE, and E by Honduras. With Honduras and Nicaragua (SE) it shares frontage on Gulf of Fonseca. The country is crossed E–W by 2 roughly parallel volcanic ranges which rise to 7,825 ft. in the Santa Ana. Other more or less extinct volcanoes are San Salvador (6,400 ft.), San Miguel (7,064 ft.), and San Vicente (7,132 ft.). The most active, Izalco (6,184 ft.), near Sonsonate, arose in 18th cent. and has become a beacon for Pacific mariners. Earthquakes cause frequent havoc. Bet. the ranges stretches a low plateau (c.2,000 ft.), upon whose fertile soil are the principal cities and cultivated areas. N of the volcanic crests lies the wide Lempa River valley, a region of tropical savannas flanked by the highlands of Honduras. The Lempa R., rising in Guatemala and emptying into the Pacific, is by far the largest stream, though of little value for navigation. There are a number of picturesque lakes, such as L. Ilopango and L. Coatepeque, tourist resorts near the capital. The largest, L. Guija, lies on Guatemalan border. The climate, varying with altitude, is tropical in the lowlands, somewhat more temperate in the intermontane basin. Rainy period May-Oct. San Salvador (2,238 ft.) has an average annual temp. of 75°F.; rainfall about 70 in. While Salvador is reputed to be rich in minerals, only small-scale silver and gold mining is carried on. Copper, lead, iron, mercury, and coal deposits occur. Intensively cultivated, Salvador is essentially a one-crop country, coffee—mostly of the "mild" variety—furnishing 80% of all exports; but corn, the staple food, covers more acreage. Other agr. yields, chiefly grown for domestic consumption, are sugar (there are quite a few refineries), grain, rice, beans, sesame, tobacco, cotton, henequen, limes, indigo (once the mainstay), cacao. The forests, especially near NW coast, yield the so-called Peruvian balsam, on which Salvador has a virtual monopoly. The savannas afford excellent pasturage for cattle. Small consumer industries have attained some measure of self-sufficiency; mfg. of cigars and cigarettes, liquor, furniture, hats, textiles, and yarns. Coffee bags made of henequen are exported. Salvador's foreign trade is principally with the U.S., which takes 80% of the exports and furnishes 75% of imports (cotton, hardware, flour, chemicals, machinery). Communications are of a relatively high standard. Most goods are shipped through Puerto Barrios, Guatemalan port on the Atlantic, and Cotuco, the port of La Unión on Fonseca Bay. Other ports are Acajutla and La Libertad. The country is traversed by the International Railways of Central America (Puerto Barrios–Cotuco). A rail line also links San Salvador and Santa Ana with Acajutla. Through the capital runs the Inter-American Highway, which crosses the Lempa R. at Cuscatlán suspension bridge. Next to San Salvador (also seat of a univ.), leading cities are Santa Ana, the 2d-largest city, San Miguel, San Vicente, Ahuachapán, Sonsonate, and Nueva San Salvador (Santa Tecla). The bulk of the country's people (c.80%) are mestizo or ladino; almost 20% are Indian. Less than 1%, the landowning and politically prominent upper class, are of pure Sp. descent. Illiteracy exceeds 50%. The overwhelming majority are R.C. Conquered by the Spanish under Pedro de Alvarado, Salvador belonged throughout colonial period to captaincy general of Guatemala. The declaration of independence from Spain in 1821 led to a brief period under Iturbide's empire. Was part (1823–38) of Central American Federation, of which San Salvador became (1831) capital. Its political history has been full of revolutions and coups d'état down to most recent times. Salvador's phenomenal increase in pop. was due to the development of coffee-growing in 2d half of 19th cent. For further information see separate articles on cities, towns: physical features, and the following 14 depts., Ahuachapán, Cabañas, Chalatenango, Cuscatlán, La Libertad, La Paz, La Unión, Morazán, San Miguel, Santa Ana, San Salvador, San Vicente, Usulután.

Salvador (săl′vŭdôr, Port. sŭlvŭdôr′), formerly **Bahia** or **São Salvador,** city (1950 pop. 395,993), ⊙ Bahia, E Brazil, Atlantic port commanding entrance to Todos os Santos Bay, 750 mi. NNE of Rio de Janeiro; 13°S 38°31′W at Cape Santo Antônio (S extremity of city; lighthouse). Fourth largest city of Brazil. Commercial hub of fertile agr. coastal plain (Recôncavo) and of SE Bahia cacao dist.; terminus of railroads from Aracaju (Sergipe) and Juàzeiro (end of navigation on São Francisco R.); noted cultural center. Exports tobacco, sugar, cacao, textiles, hides, carnauba wax, vegetable fibers, cabinet wood, and industrial diamonds. Chief industries are sugar refining, distilling, cotton milling, cacao processing, flour milling, fruit preserving, shipbuilding; and mfg. of tobacco products, furniture, footwear, soft drinks. Petroleum and natural-gas wells recently drilled in N suburbs (Lobato, Candeias) and on Itaparica Isl. City has mean annual temp. of 78° F.; annual rainfall, 52 in. Laid out on a tongue of land bet. the open Atlantic (E) and Todos os Santos Bay (W), city consists of 2 sections, the lower and the upper town, connected by electric elevators and inclined-plane railways, one of which (Lacerda, with reinforced concrete shaft 234 ft. high) has become Salvador's landmark. The older, crowded lower part is the harbor and market dist. and contains merchandise exchange, modern cacao institute, and tobacco institute. Upper town (alt. 200–275 ft.) is administrative and residential section. Here are colonial and modern govt. bldgs. (including Rio Branco palace on site of original fort), shopping dist., numerous open squares, cathedral, pseudoclassical monastery of São Bento, and many 17th-to-18th-cent. baroque churches. Several well-preserved forts (mostly 17th cent.) surround city. Salvador has univ. (faculties of medicine, law, engineering, fine arts). Bishopric since 1551; archbishopric since 1676; seat of Braz. primate for over 200 years. City was founded in 1549 as São Salvador da Bahia de Todos os Santos by Tomé de Souza after earlier settlement (1534) had been wiped out by Indians. It was capital of Port. possessions in Brazil until seat of govt. was shifted to Rio de Janeiro in 1763. Captured (1624) by Dutch; recaptured (1625), and thereafter successfully defended by Portuguese. Became prosperous center of colonization and trade with growth of sugar plantations and influx of large number of Negro slaves, who have left an indelible imprint upon city's cultural development and present pop. Salvador became provincial ⊙ in 1823, and state ⊙ after declaration of republic in 1889.

Salvador (sŭlvŭdôr′), agr. village (pop. 1,433), Castelo Branco dist., central Portugal, near Sp. border, 29 mi. NE of Castelo Branco; livestock; oak and chestnut forests.

Salvador, Lake (săl′vŭdôr), SE La., shallow lake (c.12 mi. long, 6 mi. wide), 10 mi. SW of New Orleans; receives Bayou Des Allemands in SW. Joined by other waterways to L. Cataouatche and the Mississippi (N), and to the Gulf Intracoastal Waterway, passing near lake on E and SE.

Salvage Head (sălvăj′), cape, SE N.F., on NW side of Trinity Bay, 2 mi. SE of Trinity; 48°22′N 53°22′W.

Salvage Islands, Madeira: see Selvagens.

Salvagnac (sälvänyäk′), agr. village (pop. 405), Tarn dept., S France, 18 mi. ESE of Montauban.

Salvaleón (sälväläōn′), town (pop. 3,529), Badajoz prov., W Spain, 27 mi. SSE of Badajoz; olives, cork, acorns, grapes, sheep, hogs.

Salvan (sälvā′), village (pop. 1,017), Valais canton, SW Switzerland, 3 mi. W of Martigny-Ville; resort (alt. 3,060 ft.). Vernayaz hydroelectric plant is NE.

Salvaterra de Magos (sŭlvŭtĕ′rŭ dĭ mä′gōōsh), town (pop. 3,269), Santarém dist., central Portugal, near left bank of the lower Tagus, 15 mi. SW of Santarém; agr. trade center; alcohol distilling. Formerly a royal summer residence, it has several old palaces and summer mansions.

Salvaterra do Extremo (dōō ĭshtrā′mōō), village (pop. 1,676), Castelo Branco dist., central Portugal, on Sp. border, 32 mi. ENE of Castelo Branco; grain, corn, livestock, cork. Has mineral springs and old fortifications.

Salvatierra (sälvätyĕ′rä), city (pop. 8,341), Guanajuato, central Mexico, on Lerma R. and 23 mi. SSW of Celaya, on railroad; alt. 5,735 ft. Agr. center (cereals, sugar cane, alfalfa, cotton, fruit, livestock); mfg. of cotton goods; lumber works. Founded 1643.

Salvatierra, town (pop. 1,831), Álava prov., N Spain, 14 mi. E of Vitoria; mfg. of ceramics, paints and varnishes, candles; tanning, sawmilling; livestock market. Has 2 Gothic churches.

Salvatierra de los Barros (dhā lōs bä′rōs), town (pop. 3,842), Badajoz prov., W Spain, 31 mi. SE of Badajoz; pottery center. Trades in cork, olives, grapes, livestock. Wine making. Mineral springs near by.

Salvatierra de Santiago (säntyä′gō), town (pop. 1,620), Cáceres prov., W Spain, 14 mi. SW of Trujillo; olive-oil processing; cereals, wine.

Salvetat, La (lä sälvŭtä′). **1** or **La Salvetat-Peyralès** (–pärälā′), village (pop. 357), Aveyron dept., S France, 12 mi. SE of Villefranche-de-Rouergue; dairying, wheat growing. **2** or **La Salvetat-sur-Agout** (sür-ägōō′), village (pop. 650), Hérault dept., S France, bet. Monts de Lacaune (N) and Monts de l'Espinouse (S), on Agout R. and 23 mi. E of Castres; textile and flour milling.

Salviac (sälvyäk′), village (pop. 480), Lot dept., SW France, 7 mi. SW of Gourdon; truffles, poultry; woodworking.

Salwa (săl′wŭ), village in Hasa, Saudi Arabia, at base of Qatar peninsula, 70 mi. SE of Oqair, at S end of Salwa Bay (S inlet of Gulf of Bahrein).

Salwarpe River, Worcester, England, rises just W of Bromsgrove, flows 14 mi. S and SW, past Droitwich, to Severn R. 3 mi. N of Worcester.

Salwat, Ceylon: see Chilaw.

Salween (săl″wēn′, săl′wēn), northernmost district (□ 2,577; 1941 pop. 56,878) of Tenasserim div., Lower Burma; ⊙ Papun. Located on right bank of Salween R. (Thailand frontier), in S Karenni Hills; drained by Yunzalin R.; forested. Pop. is 85% Karen, 7% Thai.

Salween River, Chinese *Lu Chiang* (lōō′ jyäng′) or *Nu Chiang* (nōō), Tibetan *Chiama Ngu Chu* (chyä′-mä′ ŭngōō′ chōō′), one of the great rivers of SE

Asia; 1,750 mi. long. Rises at 32°N 94°E in the Tanglha Range of E Tibet, flows SE in deep gorges paralleling Mekong and Yangtze rivers, and S through Yunnan prov. into Burma. Here it cuts a gorge through the Shan plateau and the Karenni hills, and enters the Gulf of Martaban of Andaman Sea at Moulmein, forming a common mouth with Gyaing and Ataran rivers of the Tenasserim. Obstructed by rapids, the Salween is navigable only below Kamamaung, 74 mi. above mouth. In lower course it forms short section of Burma-Thailand line. A considerable obstacle to transportation, it is crossed by the Burma Road and by road ferries at Kunlong and Takaw in Burma's Shan State. Sometimes spelled Salwin.

Salyana, Nepal: see SALLYANA.

Salyany or **Sal'yany** (sŭlyä'nē), city (1938 pop. estimate 12,689), SE Azerbaijan SSR, on Kura R., near mouth, on railroad and 65 mi. SW of Baku; cotton ginning; center of fishing industry in Kura R. delta.

Salyany Steppe, Azerbaijan SSR: see KURA LOWLAND.

Salyersville (săl'yŭrzvĭl), town (pop. 1,174), ⊙ Magoffin co., E Ky., on Licking R. and 36 mi. N of Hazard, in the Cumberlands. Farms, coal mines, and oil wells in region. Settled as Adamsville; renamed 1860.

Salyuzi, Russian SFSR: see KOTELNIKOVO, Leningrad oblast.

Salza (zäl'tsä), town (pop. 5,963), in former Prussian Saxony prov., central Germany, after 1945 in Thuringia, at S foot of the lower Harz, 2 mi. NW of Nordhausen.

Salzach (zäl'tsäkh), principal river of Salzburg, W central Austria; rises in the Hohe Tauern of Eastern Alps; flows E into central Salzburg, then N, past Bischofshofen, Hallein, and Salzburg, forming part of Austro-Ger. border N of Salzburg to Inn R. 6 mi. SW of Braunau; length, 130 mi. Receives the Saalach N of Salzburg.

Salza River (zäl'tsä), Styria, central Austria, rises E of Mariazell, flows c.70 mi. W to Enns R. N of Landl; timber floating.

Salzberg, Poland: see BOCHNIA.

Salzbergen (zälts'bĕr"gŭn), village (pop. 2,067), in former Prussian prov. of Hanover, NW Germany, after 1945 in Lower Saxony, on left bank of the Ems and 5 mi. NW of Rheine; rail junction; mfg. of synthetic oil.

Salzbrunn, Bad, Poland: see SZCZAWNO ZDROJ.

Salzburg (sôlz'bûrg, Ger. zälts'bŏŏrk), autonomous prov. [*Bundesland*] (□ 2,762; 1951 pop. 324,117), W central Austria, bordering Carinthia (S), Tyrol (S, W), Germany (W), Upper Austria (N, E), and Styria (E); ⊙ Salzburg. Mtn. region: Hohe Tauern (S); E portion of Salzburg Alps (center); part of Niedere Tauern (E), bordering the Salzkammergut. The Salzach drains it. Active tourist trade in numerous Alpine resorts. Area long known for its production of salt. Mining: salt (Hallein), copper (Mitterberg), iron ore (Werfen); deposits of precious stones and gold on N slope of the Hohe Tauern. Cattle on mtn. pastures; horses in the Pinzgau; some agr. (wheat, rye) and fruit in NE. Industry centers at Salzburg and Hallein (chemicals, metallurgy). In early times inhabited by Celts; conquered by Romans and became part of prov. of Noricum; governed by archbishops of Salzburg in Middle Ages; passed to Grand Duke Ferdinand of Tuscany in 1802, to Austria 1805, becoming a crownland in the 1840s. Placed (1945) in U.S. occupation zone.

Salzburg, anc. *Juvavum*, city (1951 pop. 100,096), ⊙ Salzburg prov., Austria, near Ger. line, 160 mi. WSW of Vienna; picturesquely situated on both banks of the Salzach, at foot of the Hohensalzburg, a medieval (1077) fortress. Rail, industrial, tourist center; airport; metal industry; mfg. of textiles, chemicals; breweries; trade in food products. For 1,000 years was seat of autocratic archbishops of Salzburg; secularized in 1802. Univ. (founded 1623) was closed in 1810 except for its theological seminary. Places of interest: 17th-cent. cathedral, Carolino-Augusteum Mus., 13th-cent. Franciscan church, 7th-cent. Benedictine abbey, memorial to Mozart (who was b. here), theological seminary, old Capuchin monastery. Has important annual music festival. Became hq. of U.S. occupation zone in 1945.

Salzburg, Rumania: see OCNA-SIBIU.

Salzburg Alps, division of the Eastern Alps along Austro-Ger. border S of Salzburg; centered on the Königssee dist. of Upper Bavaria and surrounded by short, high ranges (Hagengebirge, Übergossene Alm, Steinernes Meer). W outliers (Kaisergebirge) reach Inn R. valley at Kufstein. Highest peaks, Hochkönig (9,639 ft.) in Austria, Watzmann (8,901 ft.) in Germany. Chief resorts: Berchtesgaden, Reichenhall.

Salzderhelden (zälts'dŭrhĕl'dŭn), village (pop. 1,676), in former Prussian prov. of Hanover, W Germany, after 1945 in Lower Saxony, on the Leine and 2 mi. SE of Einbeck; saltworks; resort with saline baths.

Salzdetfurth, Bad, Germany: see BAD SALZDETFURTH.

Salzelmen, Bad, Germany: see SCHÖNEBECK.

Salzgitter, Germany: see WATENSTEDT-SALZGITTER.

Salzgrub, Rumania: see COJOCNA.

Salzig, Bad, Germany: see BAD SALZIG.

Salzkammergut (zälts'kä"mŭrgōōt"), beautiful lake and mtn. area of Eastern Alps in Upper Austria, Styria, and Salzburg, Austria. Long known for its production of salt before becoming popular resort area. Mtns. include the Dachstein, Totes Gebirge, and Höllengebirge; among its lakes are Attersee, L. Traun, Sankt Wolfgangsee, L. of Hallstatt, Mondsee. Bad Ischl is its center; other towns are Gmunden, Hallstatt, Bad Aussee.

Salzkotten (zälts'kô"tŭn), town (pop. 5,839), in former Prussian prov. of Westphalia, NW Germany, after 1945 in North Rhine-Westphalia, 7 mi. WSW of Paderborn; mfg. of machinery. Resort with saline springs and baths.

Salzschlirf, Bad, Germany: see BAD SALZSCHLIRF.

Salzuflen, Bad, Germany: see BAD SALZUFLEN.

Salzungen, Bad, Germany: see BAD SALZUNGEN.

Salzwedel (zälts'vā"dŭl), city (pop. 24,564), in former Prussian Saxony prov., central Germany, after 1945 in Saxony-Anhalt, 50 mi. NNW of Magdeburg, 8 mi. E of Nienbergen; 52°51'N 11°9'E. Rail hub; rock-salt mining center; sugar refining, chemical mfg. Noted for its pastry. Has 13th- and 15th-cent. churches; and remains of castle founded c.780 by Charlemagne. First mentioned 1112. Albert the Bear from here conquered (1134) Brandenburg. Chartered 1247; joined Hanseatic League in mid-13th cent.

Sama (säm'ä'), Mandarin *Sanya* (sän'yä'), town S Hainan, Kwangtung prov., China, on Sama Bay, 20 mi. ESE of Aihsien, and on coastal railway. Airport. Developed by Japanese as part of Yülin military base.

Sama (sä'mä), village, S Fr. Sudan, Fr. West Africa, on the Niger and 38 mi. ENE of Ségou; sisal.

Sama (sä'mŭ), village (1939 pop. over 500), N Sverdlovsk oblast, Russian SFSR, on Sosva R. and 40 mi. NNW of Serov, on rail spur; center of hematite-mining region supplying Serov metallurgy. Formerly called Samski Rudnik.

Samac or **Shamats** (both: shä'mäts). **1** or **Bosanski Samac** or **Bosanski Shamats** (bô'sänskē), Serbo-Croatian *Bosanski Šamac*, village (pop. 2,251), N Bosnia, Yugoslavia, on Sava R. opposite Slavonski Samac (Croatia), at Bosna R. mouth, on railroad and 80 mi. N of Sarajevo; center of plum-growing region. Founded in 1863. **2** or **Slavonski Samac** or **Slavonski Shamats** (slävôn'skē), Serbo-Croatian *Slavonski Šamac*, village, N Croatia, Yugoslavia, on Sava R. (Bosnia border) 22 mi. E of Slavonski Brod, in Slavonia. Terminus of railroad to Osijek. Bosanski Samac lies across the Sava.

Samacá (sämäkä'), town (pop. 710), Boyacá dept., central Colombia, in Cordillera Oriental, 10 mi. WSW of Tunja, on railroad from Bogotá; alt. 8,743 ft. Cotton and wool spinning. Site of 1st Colombian cotton mill. Iron deposits near by. Waterfall and artificial lake in vicinity.

Sama de Langreo (sä'mä dhä läng-grā'ō), town (pop. 5,991), Oviedo prov., NW Spain, on Nalón R. and 10 mi. SE of Oviedo; important center of coal-mining basin of Langreo; iron foundries.

Samaden (zämä'dŭn), Romansh *Samedan* (sä'mĕdŭn), village (pop. 1,427), Grisons canton, SE Switzerland, on Inn R. and 2 mi. NE of St. Moritz; summer and winter health resort (alt. 5,665 ft.) in Upper Engadine. Late-Gothic church.

Samadun (sămă'dōōn), village (pop. 10,359), Minufiya prov., Lower Egypt, on railroad and 3 mi. NNW of Ashmun; cereals, cotton, flax.

Samagaltai or **Samagaltay** (sŭmŭgŭltī'), village, S Tuva Autonomous Oblast, Russian SFSR, 75 mi. SSE of Kyzyl, in Tannu-Ola Range, on Kyzyl-Uliassutai road, near Tes R.

Sama Grande (sä'mä grän'dā), village (pop. 366), Tacna dept., S Peru, landing on Sama R. (irrigation) and 25 mi. NW of Tacna; wine, fruit, sugar.

Samaguri (sä'măgōōrē), village, Nowgong dist., central Assam, India, on Kalang R. and 10 mi. ENE of Nowgong; rice, jute, rape and mustard.

Samahil (sämäēl'), town (pop. 786), Yucatan, SE Mexico, 18 mi. WSW of Mérida; henequen.

Sama'il, Wadi (wă'dē sămă'ĭl), intermittent coastal stream of Oman, entering Gulf of Oman at Sib, 25 mi. W of Muscat. Its valley (chief town, Sarur) is a populous date-growing dist. Upper course separates Western and Eastern Hajar hill country. Also spelled Sema'il.

Sama'inah, Al-, Egypt: see SAMA'NA, EL.

Samaipata (sämīpä'tä), town (pop. c.4,200), ⊙ Florida prov., Santa Cruz dept., central Bolivia, in E foothills of Cordillera de Cochabamba, on Cochabamba–Santa Cruz road and 55 mi. SW of Santa Cruz; oil deposits. Founded 1620. Ruins of pre-Inca civilization near by.

Samakh, Israel: see TSEMAH.

Samakof or **Samakov**, Turkey: see DEMIRKOY.

Samakov, Bulgaria: see SAMOKOV.

Samal (sä'mäl), town (1939 pop. 4,679; 1948 municipality pop. 6,995), Bataan prov., S Luzon, Philippines, on E Bataan Peninsula, on Manila Bay, 32 mi. WNW of Manila; sugar cane, rice.

Samal, Turkey: see SENJIRLI.

Samalá River (sämälä'), SW Guatemala, rises W of San Francisco (Totonicapán dept.), flows c.75 mi. SSW, past Salcajá, Cantel, Zunil (power station), Santa María (power station), and San Felipe, to the Pacific at Playa Grande. Not navigable.

Samales Group (sämä'lās) (□ c.50), Sulu prov., Philippines, NE isl. group of the Sulu Archipelago, E of Jolo and S of Basilan. Coextensive with Tungkil municipal dist. (1948 pop. 3,673). Isls. include Tongquil, Simisa, Balanguingui.

Samal Island (sä'mäl) (□ 96; 1948 pop. 20,334), Davao prov., S central Mindanao, Philippines, in Davao Gulf just off Davao; 21 mi. long. Chief town, Peñaplata. Abacá, coconuts.

Samalkot (sä'mŭlkōt), town (pop. 22,349), East Godavari dist., NE Madras, India, 8 mi. NW of Cocanada; port and sugar-processing center on irrigation canal; rail junction (spur to Cocanada); rice milling, mfg. of crucibles, tiles, fertilizer, confectionery; distillery. Has agr. research station (sugar cane, rice, sunn hemp; beekeeping), coconut plantations. Sugar milling 10 mi. N, at village of Kirlampudi.

Samalut or **Samallut** (sămă'lōōt), town (pop. 10,873; with suburbs, 12,471), Minya prov., Upper Egypt, on W bank of the Nile, on Ibrahimiya Canal, on railroad, and 15 mi. NNW of Minya; woolen and sugar milling; cotton, cereals, sugar cane. Cotton-ginning center of Ma'saret (Ma'sarit) Samulut (pop. 9,791; with suburbs, 12,494) is just N.

Samán, El, Venezuela: see EL SAMÁN.

Samaná (sämänä'), town (pop. 1,747), Caldas dept., W central Colombia, in Magdalena valley, 20 mi. WNW of La Dorada; alt. 4,921 ft.; rice, corn, bananas, yucca. Gold deposits near by.

Samaná, province (□ 840; 1935 pop. 41,910; 1950 pop. 82,977), NE Dominican Republic, on the Atlantic; ⊙ Samaná. Consists of little-settled Samaná Peninsula and fertile E section of Cibao valley. Watered by Yuna R. Main products: cacao, coconuts, coffee, rice, tobacco, corn, beeswax, cattle, tropical hardwood. Fishing along the coast. Sánchez, at head of sheltered Samaná Bay, is linked by railroad with Santiago. Other trading and agr. centers are Samaná, Matanzas, Julia Molina, Cabrera. Formed 1908 from part of Seibo.

Samaná or **Santa Bárbara de Samaná** (sän'tä bär'bärä dā–), town (1935 pop. 1,638; 1950 pop. 2,477), ⊙ Samaná prov., NE Dominican Republic, port on S coast of Samaná Peninsula, on Samaná Bay, 60 mi. NE of Ciudad Trujillo; 19°13'N 69°20'W. Trades in precious wood, cacao, coconuts, rice. Tanning. Airfield; beach resort. Founded 1756 by settlers from Canary Isls., followed by Amer. Negroes in 1825.

Samana (sä'mänŭ), town (pop. 14,912), E central Patiala and East Punjab States Union, India, 17 mi. SW of Patiala; local agr. market (millet, wheat, cotton); wood carving.

Samaná, Cape (sämänä'), headland, NE Dominican Republic, easternmost point of Samaná Peninsula, 14 mi. NE of Samaná; 19°18'N 69°8'W.

Sama'na, El, Es Sama'na, or **Al-Sama'inah** (ĕl-, ĕs-sămă'nŭ), village (pop. 8,748), Sharqiya prov., Lower Egypt, on railroad and 5 mi. NE of Faqus; cotton.

Samaná Bay (sämänä'), Atlantic inlet on NE coast of Dominican Republic, bounded N by Samaná Peninsula. Deep, well-protected bay, c.30 mi. long (W-E), 10 mi. wide. Sánchez is at its head, Samaná on N shore. Into it flows Yuna R. Tourist and fishing site. Discovered by Columbus on his 1st voyage.

Samana Island (sŭmă'nŭ, sämänä') or **Atwood Cay** (kā, kē), islet (10 mi. long, up to 2 mi. wide), SE Bahama Isls., 22 mi. NE of Acklins Isl.; 23°5'N 73°45'W. Produces cascarilla bark.

Samanaliya, Ceylon: see ADAM'S PEAK.

Samaná Peninsula (sämänä'), on NE coast of Dominican Republic, bet. Samaná Bay (S) and Escocesa Bay (NW); 30 mi. long from Sánchez, at its base, to Cape Samaná; c.6 mi. wide. On its coast are grown cacao, coffee, and coconuts. Rich in tropical hardwood. Samaná on S shore.

Samanco, Puerto, Peru: see PUERTO SAMANCO.

Samaniego (sämänyā'gō), town (pop. 3,205), Nariño dept., SW Colombia, on affluent of Patía R., in S Cordillera Occidental, and 23 mi. WNW of Pasto; alt. 5,036 ft. Agr. center (cereals, coffee, cacao, potatoes, sugar cane, fruit, forest products, livestock). Gold mines near by.

Samanli Mountains (sämänlŭ'), Turkish *Samanlı*, NW Turkey, extend 70 mi. W from Geyve into Sea of Marmara, bet. Gulf of Izmit (N) and Gulf of Gemlik and L. Iznik (S); rise to 5,270 ft. Lignite and chromium in W; iron and copper in E.

Samannud or **Samanud** (both: sămănōōd'), town (pop. 19,795), Gharbiya prov., Lower Egypt, on Damietta branch of the Nile, on railroad, and 5 mi. E of El Mahalla el Kubra; noted for pottery making. Near by mounds mark site of anc. SEBENNYTOS, which flourished under the Sebennite kings (4th cent. B.C.). Also spelled Semenud.

Samar (sămăr'), town (pop. c.550), N Jordan, 9 mi. NNW of Irbid; grain, olives.

Samar (sä'mär), island (□ 5,050; 1939 pop. 470,678), Visayan Isls., 3d largest of the Philippines, bet. Samar Sea (W) and Philippine Sea (E), separated from Luzon by San Bernardino Strait, and from Leyte isl. by narrow San Juanico Strait and by

Leyte Gulf; 11°1'–12°35'N 124°15'–125°45'E. It is c.100 mi. long, 25–60 mi. wide. Mountainous, rising to 2,789 ft. in central area. Lumbering, agr. (rice, coconuts, hemp, corn), iron mining (at Hernani). Samar province (□ 5,309; 1948 pop. 757,212) includes Samar isl. and offshore isls.: HOMONHON ISLAND, CALICOAN ISLAND, MANICANI ISLAND, DARAM ISLAND, BUAD ISLAND, SANTO NIÑO ISLAND, ALMAGRO ISLAND, DALUPIRI ISLAND, LAOANG ISLAND, BATAG ISLAND, BIRI ISLAND; ⊙ CATBALOGAN.

Samara, city, Russian SFSR: see KUIBYSHEV, city, Kuibyshev oblast.

Samara Bend (sŭmâ'rŭ, Rus. sŭmä'rŭ), Rus. *Samarskaya Luka*, noted region (□ 390) within oxbow of middle Volga R. course, in W Kuibyshev oblast, Russian SFSR; consists of forested ZHIGULI MOUNTAINS and tilled lowland on the Volga, W of Kuibyshev city. Mining and quarrying (petroleum, asphalt, dolomite, limestone); agr. processing; orchards, truck. Main center is oil boom-town of Zhigulevsk. Site of ZHIGULEVSK, with hydroelectric station of KUIBYSHEV DAM.

Samarai (sämŭrī'), port town, Papua, SW Pacific, on small isl (59 acres), also called Samarai, 2 mi. SE of New Guinea; 2d most important commercial center of Territory of Papua; exports copra, pearls, pearl shell.

Samara River (sŭmâ'rŭ, Rus. sŭmä'rŭ). **1** In SE European Russian SFSR, rises in Obshchi Syrt foothills of the S Urals 15 mi. NW of Pavlovka (Chkalov oblast); flows 365 mi. generally WNW, past Perevolotskoye, Novo-Sergiyevka, Sorochinsk, Buzuluk, Borskoye, and Pavlovka (Kuibyshev oblast), to the Volga at Kuibyshev. Navigable in lower course. Receives Tok and Greater Kinel (right) and Buzuluk (left) rivers. **2** In E Ukrainian SSR, rises in W Donets Ridge W of Druzhkovka, flows 215 mi. W in S-shaped course, past Novo-Moskovsk, to Dnieper R. near Dnepropetrovsk. Receives Volchya R. (left). Navigable for 25 mi. above mouth.

Samarate (sämärä'tĕ), village (pop. 2,711), Varese prov., Lombardy, N Italy, 2 mi. S of Gallarate; mfg. (cotton textiles, silk shawls, lamps, machinery).

Samaria (sŭmâ'rēŭ), hilly region, W Jordan, extends c.35 mi. N-S bet. Judaea (Ramallah region) and S edge of Plain of Jezreel; bounded by Plain of Sharon (W) and Jordan valley (E). Rises to 3,084 ft. in Mt. Ebal, just NE of Nablus, chief town of the region. In anc. times a division of Palestine.

Samaria, anc. city of Palestine, on whose site is village of Sebastye or Sabastiya (both: sĕbăst'yŭ), after 1948 in W Jordan, 6 mi. NW of Nablus (Shechem), and on railroad in Samarian Hills. The biblical city of Samaria (named for Shemer, who owned the land) was built in early 9th cent. by King Omri as ⊙ northern kingdom of Israel. Scene of the wickedness of Omri's son Ahab and Ahab's wife Jezebel, Samaria was considered a place of iniquity by the Hebrew prophets. In the expansion of Assyria, it fell in 722 B.C. to Shalmaneser V and perhaps to Sargon II. Taken 331 B.C. by Alexander the Great. Destroyed 120 B.C. by Hyrcanus and rebuilt by Herod the Great, who called it Sebaste. Here Philip preached and the incident of Simon Magus occurred. According to tradition, John the Baptist is buried here. The Samaritans took their name from the city. Has remains of 12th-cent. Crusaders' church. Excavations, begun 1909, have yielded remains of Israelite palace with noted collection of ivories, of city walls dating from c.800 B.C., and of anc. temples.

Samarinda (sŭmŭrĭn'dŭ), town (pop. 11,086), E Borneo, Indonesia, port on the Mahakam, near its delta, 260 mi. NE of Banjermasin; 0°30'S 117°10'E; trade center, shipping coal, timber, rattan, reptile skins, gutta-percha, rubber. Near by are coal mines and oil fields (connected to Balikpapan refineries by pipe line).

Sama River (sä'mä), Tacna dept., S Peru, rises in Cordillera Occidental near Cuzco dept. border, flows c.80 mi. SW to the Pacific 45 mi. NW of Arica. Irrigation. Navigable for small craft.

Samarkand (sămŭrkănd', sä'–, Rus. sŭmŭrkänt'), oblast (□ 12,300; 1946 pop. estimate 900,000), E Uzbek SSR; ⊙ Samarkand. Drained by Zeravshan R. (S; Samarkand oasis), with ranges Nura-Tau and Ak-Tau in N. Extensive cotton growing, sericulture, and orchards in Zeravshan valley; elsewhere, dry farming (wheat) and goat and karakul-sheep raising. Industry (cotton ginning, wine making, food processing) at Samarkand, Katta-Kurgan, and Dzhizak. Molybdenum and tungsten mining at Lyangar. Trans-Caspian RR passes E-W. Pop. chiefly Uzbeks; some Russians and Tadzhiks. Formed 1938. An earlier and larger Samarkand oblast (including part of present Tadzhik SSR) had been abolished in 1926.

Samarkand. 1 City, Karaganda oblast, Kazakh SSR: see TEMIR-TAU, city. **2** Second-largest city (1939 pop. 134,346) of Uzbek SSR, ⊙ Samarkand oblast, near Zeravshan R., on Trans-Caspian RR and 170 mi. SW of Tashkent; 39°38'N 66°58'E. Cotton-ginning and silk-milling center; clothing and shoe mfg., wine and tea production, food canning. City consists of a new Rus. section (W; developed after 1868) and an old quarter (E), centered on the Registan (main square), which is site of many architecturally famous bldgs. decorated with characteristic carvings, majolica work, and mosaics, including Tamerlane's mausoleum (1404) and the main mosque (Bibi-Khan; 1399–1404). On N outskirts are mosque and mausoleum of Shakh Zinda (14th–15th cent.). Has Uzbek state univ., agr., medical, and teachers colleges, regional mus., institute of tropical medicine. Oldest city of Central Asia; anc. site of Afrosiab (ruins just N of Samarkand), which dates from 3d to 4th millennium B.C. Present site known to Greeks as Maracanda; conquered (329 B.C.) by Alexander the Great; subsequently seat of Arab culture (to 9th cent.); destroyed (1220) by Jenghiz Khan. Flourished (1370–1405) as capital (pop. c.150,000) of empire of Tamerlane, who decorated city with sumptuous mosques, gardens, and palaces. Later ruled by Uzbeks (1499) and by emirs of Bukhara (after 1784). Samarkand fell (1868) to Russians. Was ⊙ Uzbek SSR from 1925 to 1930; succeeded by Tashkent.

Samarobriva, France: see AMIENS.

Samarovo (sŭmä'rŭvŭ), village (1948 pop. over 2,000), S Khanty-Mansi Natl. Okrug, Tyumen' oblast, Russian SFSR, on Irtysh R., near its confluence with the Ob, and just S of Khanty-Mansisk; sawmilling, fish canning. Founded in 16th cent.

Samarra (sämä'rä), town, Baghdad prov., N central Iraq, on left bank of the Tigris and 70 mi. NNW of Baghdad. The ruins of the great anc. city of Samarra extend 20 mi. along the river. The old city was ⊙ Abbasid caliphs from 836 to 876. The 17th-cent. mosque with its golden dome is sacred to the Shiite sect of Moslems. There are also remains of the Great Mosque (built 847).

Samar Sea (sä'mär), Philippines, bet. Luzon (N), Samar (E), Leyte (S), Masbate (W); opens W on Visayan Sea, leads N via San Bernardino Strait to Philippine Sea.

Samarskaya Luka, Russian SFSR: see SAMARA BEND.

Samarskoye (sŭmär'skŭyŭ). **1** Village (1926 pop. 2,211), W East Kazakhstan oblast, Kazakh SSR, 70 mi. SSE of Ust-Kamenogorsk; cattle. Gold mining near by. **2** Village (1926 pop. 6,003), SW Rostov oblast, Russian SFSR, on railroad, on Kagalnik R. and 20 mi. S of Rostov; flour mill, metalworks; grain, truck produce, livestock.

Samasata, W Pakistan: see BAHAWALPUR, town.

Samassi (sämäs'sē), village (pop. 3,379), Cagliari prov., S Sardinia, near bend of Flumini Mannu R., 21 mi. NNW of Cagliari.

Samassi River, Sardinia: see FLUMINI MANNU RIVER.

Samastipur (sŭmä'stĭpo͝or), town (pop. 13,293), Darbhanga dist., N Bihar prov., India, on Burhi Gandak R. and 20 mi. SSE of Darbhanga; rail junction (workshops); road center; trades in rice, corn, wheat, barley, sugar cane. Agr. col. at Pusa, 13 mi. NW; Imperial Agr. Research Inst. moved to Delhi.

Samata, El, Es Samata, or **Al-Samata** (all: ĕs-sămätä'), village (pop. 7,655), Girga prov., central Upper Egypt, on W bank of the Nile and 2 mi. S of El Balyana; cotton, cereals, dates, sugar cane.

Samatan (sämätã'), village (pop. 1,089), Gers dept., SW France, on the Save and 20 mi. SE of Auch; corn, wheat, fruits.

Samatiguila (sämätēgē'lä), town (pop. 3,200), NW Ivory Coast, Fr. West Africa, 20 mi. N of Odienné; millet, rice, corn, yams; sheep, goats.

Samawa or **Samawah** (sämä'wŭ), town, Diwaniya prov., SE central Iraq, on railroad and 50 mi. SSE of Diwaniya, on the Euphrates near where the Hilla and Hindiya branches reunite; agr. (rice, dates) and trade center, on Baghdad-Basra RR.

Samayac (sämīäk'), town (1950 pop. 2,987), Suchitepéquez dept., SW Guatemala, in Pacific piedmont, 4.5 mi. NE of Mazatenango; coffee, sugar cane, grain; livestock.

Samayapuram, India: see MANNACHCHANALLUR.

Samba (säm'bŭ), town (pop. 3,287), Jammu dist., SW Kashmir, 19 mi. SE of Jammu; wheat, rice, bajra, corn, barley.

Sambaina (sämbä'nŭ), village, Tananarive prov., central Madagascar, near railroad, 18 mi. NNE of Antsirabe; bituminous schists and lignite. Apple orchards in vicinity.

Sambalpur (sŭm'bŭlpo͝or), district (□ c.5,000; pop. c.1,000,000), W Orissa, India; ⊙ Sambalpur. Bordered W by Madhya Pradesh; drained by Mahanadi R. Open, undulating country (W); forested hill ranges (E). Rice is chief crop; oilseeds, lac, tobacco, myrobalans also grown. Biri mfg.; handicrafts (cotton and silk cloth, metalware). Trade centers: Sambalpur, Jharsuguda. In 1949, the original dist. (□ 5,419; 1941 pop. 1,182,622) was altered by inc. of former princely states of Bamra, Rairakhol, and part of Sonepur, and by transfer of its S subdivision (□ 829; pop. 196,500) to newly-created Kalahandi dist.

Sambalpur. 1 Village, Bastar dist., S Madhya Pradesh, India, 30 mi. W of Kanker, in dense forest area (sal, bamboo, myrobalan; lac cultivation). Also called Sambalpur-Kanker or Bhanupratappur. **2** Town (pop. 17,079), ⊙ Sambalpur dist., NW Orissa, India, on Mahanadi R. and 140 mi. WNW of Cuttack; rail terminus; trade center (rice, oilseeds, timber, hides); rice and flour milling, biri and soap mfg., handicraft cloth weaving; metal products. Col. Has sacred Vishnuite temple. Was hq. of Orissa States. Dam (3 mi. long, 145 ft. high) under construction across Mahanadi R., is 7 mi. NW, near Hirakud; flood control, irrigation canals, 2 hydroelectric plants planned.

Sambas (sämbäs'), town, W Borneo, Indonesia, 30 mi. N of Pamangkat; mining center (diamonds, gold).

Sambava (sämbä'vŭ), town, Tamatave prov., NE Madagascar, small port on E coast, 145 mi. SSE of Diégo-Suarez; vanilla, cloves, coffee.

Sambhal (sŭm'bŭl), city (pop. 53,887), Moradabad dist., N central Uttar Pradesh, India, 22 mi. SW of Moradabad; road junction; sugar refining; trades in wheat, rice, pearl millet, sugar cane, hides. Mosque reputedly built by Babar. Important post under Afghans and early Moguls. Noted 18th-cent. Pindari leader, Amir Khan, b. here.

Sambhar (säm'bŭr) or **Sambhar Lake,** town (pop. 14,112), E central Rajasthan, India, 39 mi. W of Jaipur, on Sambhar L.; salt is important industry (evaporation pans lie N and W); also hosiery mfg., hand-loom weaving.

Sambhar Lake, shallow depression in E central Rajasthan, India, 37 mi. W of Jaipur; fed largely by seasonal drainage from Aravalli Range (W); 19 mi. long, 3–6 mi. wide when full. Famous for its brine-salt deposits; evaporation pans and refining works, chiefly near Sambhar on E shore. Worked since 16th cent.

Sambiase (sämbyä'zĕ), town (pop. 11,055), Catanzaro prov., Calabria, S Italy, 2 mi. W of Nicastro; wine, olive oil. Hot sulphur baths near by.

Sambirano (sämbērä'no͞o), fertile natural region, NW Madagascar, embracing coastal plain, Nossi-Bé Isl., and W slopes of Tsaratanana Massif. Humid, tropical climate. Lower reaches produce spices, essential oils, sugar cane, copra, bananas, cacao; also raphia processing, tapioca mfg., rum distilling. Forests, extensive pastures in highlands.

Samboan (sämbō'än, sämbōän'), town (1939 pop. 1,846; 1948 municipality pop. 11,050), S Cebu isl., Philippines, 10 mi. E of Tanjay across Tañon Strait; agr. center (corn, coconuts).

Samboe, Indonesia: see SAMBU.

Sambongi (säm'bōng'gē). **1** Town, Aomori prefecture, Japan: see SANBONGI. **2** Town (pop. 6,982), Miyagi prefecture, N Honshu, Japan, 3 mi. SSW of Furukawa; rice, wheat, silk cocoons.

Sambonifacio, Italy: see SAN BONIFACIO.

Sambonmatsu (säm'bōm'mätso͞o), town (pop. 5,926), Kagawa prefecture, NE Shikoku, Japan, on Harima Sea, 19 mi. NW of Tokushima, in agr. and poultry-raising area; medicine, sake, soy sauce, cotton thread. Sometimes spelled Sanbonmatsu.

Sambor (sämbôr'). **1** Village, Kompong Thom prov., central Cambodia, on the Stung Sen and 15 mi. NE of Kompong Thom; ruins of anc. Khmer ⊙ of Isanapura (7th cent.). **2** Town, Kratie prov., E Cambodia, port on left bank of Mekong R. (head of navigation below Sambor rapids) and 20 mi. N of Kratie; lumber-shipping center; hides, horns. There are Khmer ruins of the 7th-cent. city of Sambhupura.

Sambor (säm'bŭr), city (1931 pop. 22,111), central Drogobych oblast, Ukrainian SSR, in Dniester R. valley, 18 mi. NW of Drogobych; rail junction; agr. processing (grain, potatoes), textile mfg., sawmilling; iron foundry (scattered ore deposits near by). Technical schools. Has old churches, town hall. Old Pol. town, often assaulted by Tatars (14th–15th cent.); destroyed (early 18th cent.) during Polish-Swedish War; passed to Austria in 1772. Developed as trade center; reverted to Poland in 1919; ceded to USSR in 1945.

Samborombón Bay (sämbōrōmbōn'), on the Río de la Plata, NE Buenos Aires prov., Argentina, 100 mi. SE of Buenos Aires; 60 mi. wide bet. Punta Piedras (N) and N head of Cape San Antonio (S), 25 mi. long. Receives the Río Salado and Samborombón R. Has low, irrigated shore. Fisheries.

Samborombón River, E Buenos Aires prov., Argentina, rises near Coronel Brandsen, flows c.80 mi. SE, past Coronel Brandsen, to Samborombón Bay 25 mi. SSW of Punta Piedras.

Samborondón (sämbōrōndōn'), village, Guayas prov., W central Ecuador, landing on Guayas R. and 21 mi. NNE of Guayaquil, in agr. region (cacao, tropical fruit, rice, cotton); rice milling.

Sambre-Oise Canal, France: see OISE-SAMBRE CANAL.

Sambre River (sã'brŭ), N France and SE Belgium, rises near Le Nouvion (Aisne dept.), is paralleled in upper course by Oise-Sambre Canal, flows NE across Nord dept., past Landrecies (head of canalization), Maubeuge, Jeumont (Belg. border), Thuin, Charleroi (junction with Charleroi-Brussels Canal), Châtelet, and Auvelais, to the Meuse at Namur; 120 mi. long. Traverses important Franco-Belgian coal basin and industrial dist. Scene of Br. victory, 1918, in last days of First World War.

Sambrial (sŭmbrēäl'), town (pop. 4,320), Sialkot dist., E Punjab, W Pakistan, 11 mi. W of Sialkot; wheat. Sometimes spelled Sambarial.

Sambro, Cape (săm'brō), on Sambro Harbour, small inlet of the Atlantic, S N.S., 12 mi. S of Halifax; 44°28'N 63°36'W.

Sambu or **Samboe** (säm'bōō), small island of Riouw Archipelago, Indonesia, on Singapore Strait, 1°10'N 103°54'E; seaplane base. Also called Pulu Sambu or Poeloe Samboe.

Sambuca di Sicilia (sämbōō'kä dē sēchē'lyä), town (pop. 7,828), Agrigento prov., W Sicily, 18 mi. E of Castelvetrano; agr. center (cereals, wine, olive oil).

Sambuca Pistoiese (pēstôyā'zē), village (pop. 184). Pistoia prov., Tuscany, central Italy, 12 mi. NNE of Pistoia, in agr. and livestock region.

Samburg, town (pop. 378), Obion co., extreme NW Tenn., on Reelfoot L., 22 mi. N of Dyersburg; outfitting point for hunters, fishermen.

Sambú River (sämbōō'), E Panama, rises in Aspavé Highlands near Colombia border, flows 45 mi. NW to Garachiné Bay of the Pacific. Its basin is inhabited by Choco Indians.

Samburu (sämbōō'rōō), town, Coast Prov., SE Kenya, on railroad and 33 mi. NW of Mombasa; copra, sisal, coffee, bananas.

Samchok (säm'chŭk'), Jap. *Sanchoku,* town (1949 pop. 26,153), Kangwon prov., central Korea, S of 38°N, coal-loading port on Sea of Japan, 85 mi. SE of Chunchon; major coal-mining center; fertilizer.

Samchonpo (säm'chŭn'pô'), Jap. *Sansenho* or *Sanzenpo,* town (1949 pop. 34,294), S.Kyongsang prov., S Korea, on Korea Strait, 18 mi. S of Chinju; fishing port; fish processing.

Samdari (sŭndä'rē), village, W central Rajasthan, India, 45 mi. SW of Jodhpur; rail junction (spur to Raniwari).

Samdi Dag (sämdē' dä), Turkish *Samdi Dağ,* peak (12,503 ft.), SE Turkey, in Hakari Mts., 15 mi. W of Semdinli.

Samding, Tibet: see NAGARTSE.

Same or **Sami** (both: sä'mē), town (pop. 1,065) on E coast of Cephalonia, Greece, on small Same Bay, 10 mi. NE of Argostoli; trade center. Steamer service to Ithaca. Anc. Same (just SE) flourished as one of the 4 cities of Cephalonia under Macedon. Sometimes called Samos.

Same (sä'mä), town, Tanga prov., NE Tanganyika, on railroad and 120 mi. NW of Tanga, at foot of Pare Mts.; hardwood.

Same (sä'mē), town, Portuguese Timor, in central Timor, 31 mi. SSE of Dili; rubber, copra.

Samedan, Switzerland: see SAMADEN.

Samehalli, India: see SWAMIHALLI.

Samer (sämâr'), town (pop. 1,959), Pas-de-Calais dept., N France, 9 mi. SE of Boulogne; mfg. (pencils, fertilizer, porcelain).

Samgora or **Samkhora** (sŭmgô'rŭ, –khô'–), dry steppe (□ c.140) in E Georgian SSR, just E of Tiflis. Site of irrigation scheme.

Samgorodok (säm"gŭrŭdôk'), village (1926 pop. 4,221), N Vinnitsa oblast, Ukrainian SSR, 25 mi. NE of Vinnitsa; metalworks; kaolin.

Samhan, Jabal (jă'băl sămhän'), hill country of Dhofar dist., Oman, extending along Arabian Sea and separated from coast by 20-mi.-wide Dhofar plain; rises to 5,506 ft. NE of Murbat. Frankincense is exported via Salala.

Samhka (säm'kä"), SW state (sawbwaship) (□ 314; pop. 12,907), Southern Shan State, Upper Burma; ⊙ Samhka, village on the Nam Pilu and 45 mi. S of Taunggyi. Nam Pilu valley (W) and mtn. range (E). Sometimes spelled Samka.

Sam Houston, Fort, Texas: see SAN ANTONIO.

Sami, Greece: see SAME.

Sami (sŭm'ē), town (pop. 3,919), Mehsana dist., N Bombay, India, 55 mi. WNW of Mehsana; agr. market; cotton ginning.

Samina River (zämē'nä), Liechtenstein, rises at N foot of Naafkopf near Austro-Swiss border, flows c.14 mi. NNW and NNE to Ill R. at Frastanz (Austria).

Samiopoula (sämēôpōō'lŭ), Greek Aegean island (less than □ 1; pop. 11), just off S shore of Samos isl.; 37°38'N 26°48'E.

Sami Rock, Ceylon: see TRINCOMALEE.

Samirum or **Semirom** (both: sämērōm'), town (1945 pop. estimate 5,000), Seventh Prov., in Fars, S central Iran, 80 mi. SSE of Isfahan and on road to Shiraz; center of agr. dist.; grain, fruit, opium, cotton; rugmaking. Sometimes called Yezd-i-Khast.

Samka, Burma: see SAMHKA.

Samkhora, Georgian SSR: see SAMGORA.

Samland (zäm'länt), peninsular region of former East Prussia, on the Baltic, bet. Courland and Vistula lagoons; rises to 361 ft. Agr.; amber extraction (Yantarny). Conquered 1255 by Teutonic Knights; ceded to Prussia in 1525.

Samlesbury (sămz'–, sämz'–), village and parish (pop. 1,060), W central Lancashire, England, on Ribble R. and 3 mi. E of Preston; paper milling; agr. market.

Sammamish Lake (sŭmă'mĭsh), W central Wash., resort lake (c.8 mi. long) 10 mi. E of Seattle; drained by **Sammamish River,** flowing c.15 mi. N and W to N end of L. Washington.

Sammichele di Bari (säm-mēkā'lĕ dē bä'rē), town (pop. 6,699), Bari prov., Apulia, S Italy, 17 mi. SSE of Bari; olive oil, wine.

Samnan (sämnän') or **Semnan** (sĕm–), town (1941 pop. 23,078), Second Prov., N Iran, on road and on railroad to Meshed, and 110 mi. E of Teheran, at S foot of Elburz mts.; alt. 3,738 ft. Airfield. Chief trade center of former Samnan prov.; tobacco, cotton, pistachios; cotton spinning, rugmaking. Iron (N) and sulphur (S) mining near by. Samnan prov., which included Damghan, was bounded E by Shahrud, S by Yezd, W by Kashan and Teheran, and N by Mazanderan and Gurgan; it was inc. (1938) into Iran's Second Prov. (see TEHERAN).

Samnanger, Norway: see TYSSE.

Samnangjin (säm'näng'jēn'), Jap. *Sanroshin,* township (1946 pop. 18,982), S.Kyongsang prov., S Korea, on Naktong R. and 21 mi. NW of Pusan; rail junction; fruitgrowing (pears, apples, peaches).

Samnaun (zämnoun'), easternmost commune (pop. 405) of Lower Engadine, Grisons canton, E Switzerland, 11 mi. NNE of Schuls, in Samnaun Valley. Samnaunerjoch, a pass (8,350 ft.), leads W into Austria.

Samne (säm'nä), village, Libertad dept., NW Peru, in Cordillera Occidental, 5 mi. WNW of Salpo, in mining region (silver, copper); alt. c.5,000 ft. Hydroelectric and concentrating plants.

Samneua (säm'nŭ'ä), town, ⊙ Houaphan prov. (□ 6,300; 1947 pop. 78,000), N Laos, 120 mi. ESE of Hanoi. Benzoin-producing center, rice, corn, cotton, lac, indigo; cattle raising. Sulphur springs.

Samni (sŭm'nē), village, Broach dist., N Bombay, India, 12 mi. NNW of Broach; rail junction; market center (millet, wheat); cotton ginning.

Samoa (sŭmō'ŭ, sämō'ä), island group, S Pacific, 2,570 naut. mi. NE of Sydney; 13°26'–14°22'S 168°10'–172°48'W. Consists of 10 principal inhabited isls. and several uninhabited islets extending in 350-mi. chain. Volcanic and mountainous, with highest peak (6,094 ft.) on Savaii. Temp. ranges from 90°F. (Dec.–Feb.) to 75°F. (Aug.); annual rainfall, 190 in.; rainy season, Dec.-March; group in hurricane zone. There are fern, coconut, hardwood, and rubber trees; isls. also produce taro, breadfruit, cacao, pineapples, oranges, bananas, and yams. Chief export is copra. Very little fauna: birds, rats, and some snakes. Discovered 1722 by Dutch. Part of group, comprising SAVAII, UPOLU, APOLIMA, MANONO, and 4 uninhabited isls., formerly belonged (1899–1914) to Germany; these isls., placed in 1920 under N.Z. mandate, and in 1947 under U.N. trusteeship to New Zealand, comprise the **Territory of Western Samoa** (□ c.1,135; 1945 pop. 68,197). Apia, ⊙ and chief port, and Saluafata (U.S. naval station) are on Upolu. Rest of isls., belonging to U.S. and known as **American Samoa** (□ 76; 1950 pop. 18,602), consist of TUTUILA, AUNUU, 3 isls. in MANUA group, SWAINS ISLAND, and uninhabited ROSE ISLAND. Pagopago on Tutuila, the only port, was ceded to the U.S. as a naval station in 1872 and was long hq. of U.S. naval command which governed all of American Samoa; in July, 1951, the isls. passed to civilian (Dept. of Interior) control. Polynesian natives own nearly all land; local govt. is by *matai* (chiefs). Feleti (F. D. Barstow Memorial) School trains sons of chiefs. Formerly Navigators' Islands.

Samoa (sŭmō'ŭ), mill village (1940 pop. 509), Humboldt co., NW Calif., on Sandspit just across Humboldt Bay from Eureka; site of large redwood mill.

Samo Alto (sä'mō äl'tō), village (1930 pop. 259), Coquimbo prov., N central Chile, 20 mi. NE of Ovalle; agr. center (wheat, corn, fruit, livestock).

Samobor (sä'môbôr), village (pop. 4,153), N Croatia, Yugoslavia, 12 mi. W of Zagreb; rail terminus; mineral baths. Copper mine; iron-ore deposits.

Samod (sŭmōd'), town (pop. 2,693), NE Rajasthan, India, 18 mi. N of Jaipur; bobbin mfg.

Samoded (sŭmŭdyĕt'), town (1938 pop. 3,500), W Archangel oblast, Russian SFSR, on railroad (Permilovo station) and 65 mi. S of Archangel; sawmilling.

Samoé (sämōā'), village, SE Fr. Guinea, Fr. West Africa, near Liberia border, 4 mi. N of N'zérékoré. R.C. mission.

Samoëns (sämwēs'), village (pop. 513), Haute-Savoie dept., SE France, near the Giffre, 15 mi. E of Bonneville, in Savoy Pre-Alps; cold sulphur springs; sawmilling, cheese mfg.

Samogitia (sămōjĭsh'yŭ, –ēŭ), historical region of W Lithuania, N of Neman R. Main towns: Raseiniai, Telsiai. In Middle Ages, inhabited by a Lith. tribe, the Samogitians or Zhmud; area ceded (1411) by Teutonic Knights to Lithuania-Poland.

Samoilovka or **Samoylovka** (sŭmoi'lŭfkŭ), village (1926 pop. 10,881), SW Saratov oblast, Russian SFSR, 35 mi. SE of Balashov; flour milling, metalworking; wheat, sunflowers.

Samokov (sä'môkôf), city (pop. 12,784), Sofia dist., W Bulgaria, on Iskar R. and 27 mi. SSE of Sofia; agr. center in Samokov Basin (□ 70; livestock, rye, oats, flax); textile (woolen, linen) mfg.; dairying, hog raising. Fruitgrowing (plums, apples) near by. Has old churches, monasteries, and bldgs. in Bulg. Renaissance architecture. Flourished as iron-mining, metal-handicraft, and stock-trading center under Turkish rule (15th–19th cent.). Sometimes spelled Samakov.

Samon River (sŭmōn'), central Upper Burma, rises in E edge of Shan plateau, near Yamethin; meanders c.110 mi. N to Myitnge R. SW of Mandalay.

Samora Correia (sŭmô'rŭ kōōrā'ŭ), town (pop. 2,336), Santarém dist., central Portugal, 22 mi. NE of Lisbon.

Samorin (shä'môrēn), Slovak *Šamorín,* Ger. *Sommerein* (zô'mŭrīn), Hung. *Somorja* (shô'môryŏ), town (pop. 3,834), SW Slovakia, Czechoslovakia, 12 mi. SE of Bratislava, on Great Schütt isl., in rich agr. region (wheat, sugar beets, barley); rail terminus; flour milling.

Samos. 1 Town, Cephalonia isl., Greece: see SAME. **2** Town, Samos isl., Greece: see TEGANION.

Samos (sā'mŏs), Greek Aegean island (□ 194; pop. 56,273), off Mycale peninsula of Turkey (separated by 1-mi.-wide Samos Channel); 37°45'N 26°45'E. Forms with Icaria and the Phournoi isl. group a nome (□ 322; pop. 69,138) of Aegean Isls. division of Greece; ⊙ Limen Vatheos. Situated on S side of Gulf of Kusadasi, Samos is 27 mi. long and 12 mi. wide; it is mountainous in W (Kerketeus, 4,703 ft.) and has fertile plains in E and S. Agr.: wine, tobacco, olive oil, citrus fruit, carobs, cotton, honey. Tobacco and tanning industry. The chief centers are Vathy, its port Limen Vatheos, and Neon Karlovasi. Colonized (c.11th cent. B.C.) by Ionian Greeks, Samos flourished as one of the 12 Ionian centers of Asia Minor and reached its greatest splendor as a commercial and maritime power and as a center of culture under the tyrant Polycrates (6th cent. B.C.). Anacreon and Aesop lived on Samos; Pythagoras was b. here. Subjected to the Persians under Darius, Samos joined the Ionian revolt, regained its independence after the battle of Mycale (479 B.C.) and joined the Delian League. It seceded in 441 B.C., but was reduced by Athens. Eclipsed by Rhodes in the Hellenistic period (when it produced the astronomer Conon). In Middle Ages, Samos passed 1204 from Byzantium to Latin Empire of Constantinople, was held (14th cent.) by Genoese, and finally passed 1550 to Turks. During Gr. war of independence, Samos held off Turkish attacks, but remained (after 1832) under Ottoman rule as a semi-independent isl., ruled by a Christian prince, until its annexation (1913) to Greece. It was called Susam-Adasi under Turkish rule.

Samosata, Turkey: see SAMSAT.

Samos Channel, arm of Aegean Sea, separating Samos isl. and Mycale peninsula of Turkey; 1 mi. wide at narrowest point.

Samoset (să'mŭsĕt"), village (pop. 1,617), Manatee co., SW Fla., 2 mi. SE of Bradenton; quarrying (dolomite, limestone).

Samosir, Indonesia: see TOBA, LAKE.

Samothrace (să'mōthrās"), Gr. *Samothrake* or *Samothraki* (both: sämōthrä'kē), Greek island (□ 71; 1940 pop. 3,993) in NE Aegean Sea, off Maritsa R. mouth, 28 mi. SSW of Alexandroupolis and 15 mi. NW of Turkish isl. of Imbros; belongs to Hevros nome, Thrace. Of oval shape, 13 mi. long, 7 mi. wide, rises to 5,249 ft. in Mt. Phengari (Fengari), highest in Aegean isls., from which Poseidon, in the *Iliad,* surveys the plain of Troy. Agr.: olives, grain; beekeeping, goat raising; sponge fisheries, sulphur springs (on N coast). Town of Samothrace or Khora (1928 pop. 2,055) is near NW coast. In Gr. mythology, the home of Dardanus, founder of Troy (and sometimes known as anc. Dardania), Samothrace was in anc. times a Pelasgian center of worship of the Cabiri; ruins of a Cyclopean temple dating from 6th cent. B.C. The famous winged Nike (Victory) of Samothrace, erected in 306 B.C. to commemorate a Gr. naval victory at Cyprus over the Egyptians and discovered here 1863, is now in the Louvre in Paris. Samothrace was the first stop in St. Paul's Macedonian itinerary. Known as Semadrek, Semedrek, or Semenderek under Turkish rule. Ceded to Greece, 1913.

Samothrake or **Samothraki. 1** Island in the Ionian Sea, in Corfu nome, Greece: see MATHRAKE. **2** Island in the Aegean Sea, in Hevros nome, Greece: see SAMOTHRACE.

Samotschin, Poland: see SZAMOCIN.

Samouco (sŭmō'kōō), village (pop. 1,060), Setúbal dist., S central Portugal, 6 mi. E of Lisbon; grain, rice, wine.

Samovit, Bulgaria: see SOMOVIT.

Samovodeni (sämôvô'dĕnē), village (pop. 3,820), Gorna Oryakhovitsa dist., N Bulgaria, on Yantra R. and 5 mi. NNW of Tirnovo; winegrowing, truck, sugar beets, livestock.

Samoylovka, Russian SFSR: see SAMOILOVKA.

Samozero, Karelo-Finnish SSR: see SYAMOZERO.

Sampacho (sämpä'chō), town (pop. 3,277), SW Córdoba prov., Argentina, 30 mi. SW of Río Cuarto; rail junction and agr. center (flax, alfalfa, cereals, livestock); stone quarries.

Sampang (sämpäng'), town (pop. 12,673), S Madura, Indonesia, on Madura Strait, 35 mi. E of Surabaya; trade center for agr. area (tobacco, rice, corn, peanuts).

Sampanmangio Point (sŭmpăng"măng'yō), northernmost point of Borneo, in S.China Sea, at NW side of entrance to Marudu Bay; 7°2'N 116°44'E. Kudat is on NW shore. Sometimes spelled Sempang Mangayau.

Sampedor (sämpā′dhōr′), town (pop. 1,761), Barcelona prov., NE Spain, 5 mi. N of Manresa; cotton milling; trades in wine and wheat.

Sampeire (sämpā′rĕ), town (pop. 639), Cuneo prov., Piedmont, NW Italy, in Cottian Alps, on Varaita R., and 16 mi. WSW of Saluzzo; hydroelectric plant. Formerly Sampeyre.

Samper de Calanda (sämpĕr′ dhä kälän′dä), town (pop. 2,319), Teruel prov., E Spain, 17 mi. NW of Alcañiz; button mfg., olive-oil processing, flour milling; sugar beets.

Sampeyre, Italy: see SAMPEIRE.

Sampgaon (sŭmp′goun), village, Belgaum dist., S Bombay, India, 17 mi. ESE of Belgaum; rice, millet, cotton, spices.

Sampierdarena, Italy: see SAN PIER D'ARENA.

Sampit (sämpĕt′), town, SW Borneo, Indonesia, 135 mi. WNW of Banjermasin; large sawmill.

Sampit River (săm′pĭt), SE S.C., rises in swampy region of W Georgetown co., flows c.25 mi. E to Winyah Bay at Georgetown; navigable.

Sampson, county (□ 963; pop. 49,780), S central N.C.; ⊙ Clinton. Bounded W by South R.; drained by Black R. Coastal plain agr. (tobacco, corn, cotton) and timber (pine, gum) area. Formed 1784.

Sampson, village, Seneca co., W central N.Y., on E shore of Seneca L., 12 mi. S of Geneva. Air force base and training center here, which had been built 1942 as a naval training station, functioned for a time after 1946 as Sampson Col., a state emergency col. for veterans of Second World War.

Sampués (sämpwās′), town (pop. 3,677), Bolívar dept., N Colombia, in Caribbean lowlands, 9 mi. S of Sincelejo; sugar cane, tobacco, coffee, cattle.

Sampur (säm′pŏŏr), village (1948 pop. over 2,000), central Tambov oblast, Russian SFSR, on Tsna R. and 28 mi. SSE of Tambov; wheat.

Sampwe (säm′pwä), village, Katanga prov., SE Belgian Congo, 115 mi. NNE of Jadotville; center for native trade. Benedictine mission.

Samrah, Turkey: see MAZIDAGI.

Samre (säm′rä), town (pop. 2,500), Tigre prov., N Ethiopia, 28 mi. SW of Makale; trade center (cereals, honey, beeswax, cotton, salt).

Samsa Bay (säm′sä), Mandarin *Sansha* (sän′shä), ramified inlet of E.China Sea, in NE Fukien prov., China, 40 mi. NE of Foochow; contains Santu isl. with former treaty port of Santuao.

Samsat (sämsät′), anc. *Samosata* (sŭmŏ′sŭtŭ), village (pop. 640), Malatya prov., S Turkey, on the Euphrates and 28 mi. NNW of Urfa (anc. Edessa). There are ruins of the anc. city, which was an important city of Syria; was ⊙ of anc. kingdom of Commagene (3d cent. B.C.) and later (1st cent. A.D.) of Roman prov. Lucian b. here.

Samshui (säm′swā′), Mandarin *Sanshui* (sän′shwā), town, ⊙ Samshui co. (pop. 155,766), S Kwangtung prov., China, in NW part of Canton R. delta, at junction of North and West rivers, 25 mi. W of Canton (linked by railroad); trade center; exports paper, matting, hemp bags, fans, firecrackers. Opened to foreign trade in 1897.

Samski Rudnik, Russian SFSR: see SAMA.

Samso (säm′sû), Dan. *Samsø*, island (□ 43.1; pop. 7,100), Denmark, in the Kattegat, bet. Jutland and Zealand; separated from Zealand by Samso Belt; 15 mi. long; agr. Main town, Tranebjaerg.

Samso Belt, Dan. *Samso Bælt*, Denmark, strait (c.10 mi. wide) bet. Samso isl. (W) and Zealand (E); joins Great Belt (S) and Kattegat (N).

Samson, town (pop. 2,204), Geneva co., SE Ala., 12 mi. NW of Geneva, near Fla. line and Pea R.; lumber, peanuts. Settled 1895, inc. 1906. Conecuh Natl. Forest is W.

Samson (shäm′shŭn′), village, Thanhhoa prov., N central Vietnam, seaside resort on Gulf of Tonkin, 10 mi. SE of Thanhhoa.

Samsonovo (sŭmsô′nŭvŭ), town, SE Chardzhou oblast, Turkmen, SSR, on railroad, on the Amu Darya and 3 mi. NNE of Kerki, across the river.

Samsonville, resort village, Ulster co., SE N.Y., in the Catskills, 15 mi. W of Kingston. High Point mtn. is just N.

Sam's Point, N.Y.: see SHAWANGUNK MOUNTAIN.

Samsun (säm′sōōn, sämsōōn′), province (□ 3,626; 1950 pop. 475,953), N Turkey, on Black Sea; ⊙ Samsun. Bordered S by Canik Mts. Drained by lower Kizil Irmak and Yesil Irmak. Agr. area, known for its tobacco; also spelt, corn, beans, flax, walnuts, apples; wool. Well forested (spruce 40%, pine 10%). Formerly Canik (Janik).

Samsun, anc. *Amisus*, city (1950 pop. 43,937), ⊙ Samsun prov., N Turkey, Black Sea tobacco port, on railroad, 110 mi. NNW of Sivas; 41°15′N 36°20′E. Tobacco factory processes local crop; market and exchange for grain and legumes. The anc. Amisus, founded 6th cent. B.C. by Greek colonists, became an important city of Pontus and was much favored under the Roman Empire. In Middle Ages, held at various times by the Byzantines, the Seljuks, the Genoese, and the empire of Trebizond before falling (14th cent.) to the Ottoman Turks.

Samsun Dag, Turkey: see MYCALE, MOUNT.

Samter, Poland: see SZAMOTULY.

Samthar (sŭm′tŭr), town (pop. 8,196), S Uttar Pradesh, India, 33 mi. NE of Jhansi, near Betwa canal; local agr. market (millet, gram, wheat). Was ⊙ former princely state of Samthar (□ 189; pop. 38,279) of Central India agency; in 1948, state merged with Vindhya Pradesh; in 1950, transferred to Uttar Pradesh.

Samt-i-Junubi, Afghanistan: see SOUTHERN PROVINCE.

Samt-i-Mashriqi, Afghanistan: see EASTERN PROVINCE.

Samt-i-Shimali (sŭmt′-ĭ-shĭmä′lē) [Pashto,=N district], valley region of Kabul prov., E Afghanistan, extending N from Kabul toward Ghorband R., along E foot of Paghman Mts.; 40 mi. long, 10 mi. wide. Reached from Kabul via Khairkhana Pass (S). Rich agr. area (fruit, wine); grape and raisin export. Main centers are Jabal-us-Siraj, Charikar (administrative hq.), and Istalif. Sometimes called Koh-i-Daman.

Samtredia (sŭmtrĕ′dyēŭ), city (1926 pop. 13,682), W Georgian SSR, in Mingrelia, near Rion R., on railroad and 20 mi. WSW of Kutaisi, in Colchis lowland; junction of rail branch to Batum; silk-spinning center; produces silk, tea, jams; metalworks, sawmills. Exports silk cocoons. Model poultry farm near by. Until 1936, Samtredi.

Samud-, in Thailand names: see SAMUT-.

Samuhi (sämōō′ē), town (pop. estimate 500), S Chaco natl. territory, Argentina, on railroad and 50 mi. S of Presidencia Roque Sáenz Peña; agr. center (cotton, corn, spurge, peanuts; tannin factories, cotton gins, sawmills.

Samui, Ko (kô′ sŭmōō′ē), island (□ 105; 1937 pop. 18,980) in Gulf of Siam, Suratthani prov., S Thailand, 45 mi. ENE of Surat Thani; roughly 12 mi. square; rises to 2,086 ft.; coconut plantations; lead deposits. Village of Ko Samui (1937 pop. 2,455) is on W coast.

Samukawa (sämōō′käwŭ), town (pop. 11,005), Kanagawa prefecture, central Honshu, Japan, 4 mi. NE of Hiratsuka; agr. (rice, wheat, sweet potatoes, soybeans); raw silk.

Samukh (sŭmōōkh′), former village, W central Azerbaijan SSR, 21 mi. NNE of Kirovabad, bet. Kura and Iora rivers, near their confluence. Flooded (1950) by filling of Mingechaur Reservoir.

Samundri (sŭmōōn′drē), village, Lyallpur dist., E central Punjab, W Pakistan, 25 mi. SSW of Lyallpur; wheat, millet, cotton; hand-loom weaving.

Samur-Divichi Canal (sŭmōōr′-dyĭvē′chē), in NE Azerbaijan SSR, leads from lower Samur R. on Dagestan border 147 mi. SE, along Caspian coastal plain, past Divichi, to Apsheron Peninsula. Irrigates orchards, vineyards, olive groves. Built in 2 sections: to Divichi (1940) and to Apsheron Peninsula (late 1940s).

Samur River, in S Dagestan Autonomous SSR, Russian SFSR, rises on the Dyulty-Dag (outlier of the E Greater Caucasus), flows SE, through deep gorges, past Akhty, and NE, past Magaramkent, to Caspian Sea, forming delta mouth SE of Derbent; c.130 mi. long. Used extensively for irrigation in lower course, where it forms Dagestan-Azerbaijan border. Connected by Samur-Divichi Canal with Apsheron Peninsula.

Samus or **Samus'** (sä′mōōs), town (1939 pop. 5,000), SE Tomsk oblast, Russian SFSR, on Tom R. and 22 mi. NNW of Tomsk; shipbuilding.

Samutprakan (sŭmōōt′ prä′kän′), town (1947 pop. 11,633), ⊙ Samutprakan prov. (□ 349; 1947 pop. 164,227), S Thailand, port on Gulf of Siam at mouth (left bank) of Chao Phraya R. (naval forts), 15 mi. SSE of Bangkok (linked by interurban electric railroad); rice, fisheries. Local name, Paknam. Also spelled Samudprakar.

Samutsakhon (sŭmōōt′sä′kôn′), town (1947 pop. 20,316), ⊙ Samutsakhon prov. (□ 342; 1947 pop. 112,052), S Thailand, port on Gulf of Siam at mouth of Tha Chin R., on interurban electric railroad and 20 mi. SW of Bangkok, in fertile rice-growing area; rice milling, fisheries. Local name, Tha Chin or Tachin. Also spelled Samudsagor and Samudsakon.

Samutsongkhram (sŭmōōt′sông′kräm′), town (1947 pop. 9,332), ⊙ Samutsongkhram prov. (□ 155; 1947 pop. 125,328), S Thailand, port on Gulf of Siam at mouth of Mae Klong R., 40 mi. SW of Bangkok (linked by interurban electric railroad); coconuts, rice, fisheries. Local name, Mae Klong (or Meklong). Also spelled Samudsonggram.

Samye (säm′yĕ), Chinese *Sang-yüan Ssu* (säng′-yüän′ sŭ′), lamasery, SE Tibet, near the Brahmaputra, 36 mi. SE of Lhasa; residence of Tibetan oracle; oldest (founded 8th cent. A.D.) of large Tibetan lamaseries.

San, Egypt: see SAN EL HAGAR.

San (sän), town (pop. c.6,900), S Fr. Sudan, Fr. West Africa, near right bank of Bani R. (Niger affluent) and 215 mi. ENE of Bamako; market and agr. center (peanuts, shea nuts, kapok, cotton, corn, rice, millet, manioc, potatoes, sesame, tobacco; livestock). Kapok and cotton ginning. Lime kiln. Protestant mission.

San, Se (sä′ sän′), river in NE Cambodia, formed by several small streams in Annamese Cordillera near Kontum at alt. of c.1,600 ft., flows SSW c.200 mi., past Voeune Sai, to Cambodian plain; shortly after receiving the Srepok, it flows into the Se Khong just above Stungtreng.

Saña (sä′nyä), town (pop. 1,589), Lambayeque dept., NW Peru, on coastal plain, on Saña R. and 20 mi. ESE of Chiclayo, on railroad from Puerto Eten; lime deposits; orchards. Also Zaña.

Sana, Sanaa, San'a, or **San'a'** (all: sänä′, sän-ä′), city (pop. 28,000), ⊙ Yemen and Sana prov. (pop. 960,000), on high plateau, 90 mi. NE of port of Hodeida (linked by motor road), at W foot of the Jabal Nuqum; alt. 7,750 ft.; 15°22′N 44°12′E. Extending 2½ mi. E–W, Sana consists of 2 sections in the form of an irregular figure "8", at whose junction are the Imam's palace grounds. The E section, or the Arab city proper, is the administrative and commercial city. It is overlooked (E) by the citadel and contains the Great Mosque with its small kaaba and Turkish-style mosques, such as the Mahdi Abbas and the Bakiliye, dating from 16th cent. The W section, or Bir al Azab, is a residential garden city, dating from the 2d Turkish occupation (1872–1918) and containing (SW) the Jewish quarter (largely evacuated by emigration to Israel in late 1940s). Sana has handicraft industries (jewelry, gold- and silverwork; weaving, cutting of semiprecious stones), and contains univ. and other centers of learning. Situated on site of the anc. fortress of Ghumdan (1st cent. A.D.), Sana succeeded (4th cent. A.D.) Zafar as the political center of Yemen until the coming of Islam. In 17th cent., following the 1st Turkish occupation, it succeeded Sada as the seat of the Rassite dynasty. Occupied by the Turks again 1872–1918.

Sanabu (sănăbōō′), village (pop. 11,873), Asyut prov., central Upper Egypt, 5 mi. SSW of Dairut; pottery making, wood and ivory carving; cereals, dates, sugar cane.

San Adrián (sän ädhrēän′), town (pop. 2,619), Navarre prov., N Spain, 24 mi. SSE of Estella, and on the Ebro near influx of the Ega; agr. trade center (wine, truck, cereals, cattle); vegetable canning (especially asparagus), meat processing, flour milling. Gypsum quarries near by.

San Adrián de Besós (dā bāsōs′), outer suburb (pop. 6,557) of Barcelona, NE Spain, near Besós R., 4 mi. NNE of city center; foundry; cotton milling; mfg. of paper, disinfectants, glass, phonographs; truck farming (strawberries).

Sanafa (sănăfă′), village (pop. 7,529), Daqahliya prov., Lower Egypt, 18 mi. NW of Zagazig; cotton, cereals.

Sanafir Island (sănăfēr′), in Red Sea, at entrance to Gulf of Aqaba, N Hejaz, Saudi Arabia, 3 mi. E of Tiran Isl.; 4 mi. long, 3 mi. wide.

Sanaga-Maritime (sänägä′-märētēm′), administrative region (□ 5,675; 1950 pop. 159,700), SW Fr. Cameroons, on Gulf of Guinea; ⊙ Edéa. Drained by lower Sanaga and Nyong rivers. Principal products are palm oil and kernels, rubber, cacao, hardwoods, exported through Douala via Douala-Yaoundé railroad, which traverses this territory. Titanium deposits near Edéa.

Sanaga River, large tributary of Gulf of Guinea in central and W Fr. Cameroons, formed by Lom R. and another headstream c.90 mi. NW of Batouri, flows c.325 mi. WSW, past Nanga-Eboko and Edéa, to the Atlantic 30 mi. S of Douala. Its lower course is navigable for c.50 mi. (up to Edéa) and is connected by side-streams with Nyong R. and Cameroons R. Rapids in middle course. Receives M'Bam R. (right).

Sanagasta, Argentina: see VILLA BUSTOS.

San Agustín (sän′ ägōōstēn′). **1** Town (pop. estimate 1,000), ⊙ Calamuchita dept. (□ c.2,000; pop. 27,088), W Córdoba prov., Argentina, 40 mi. S of Córdoba; stock-raising dist. **2** Town (pop. estimate 1,000), ⊙ Valle Fértil dept. (□ c.2,000; 1947 census 3,697), E San Juan prov., Argentina, at SE foot of Sierra de Valle Fértil, 90 mi. NE of San Juan; fruitgrowing, stock raising. Mica mines. Also called Valle Fértil. **3** Village (pop. estimate 1,000), E central Santa Fe prov., Argentina, 10 mi. WSW of Santa Fe, in grain and livestock area.

San Agustín, town (pop. 1,538), Huila dept., S central Colombia, in Cordillera Central, on upper Magdalena R. and 16 mi. W of Pitalito; alt. 5,544 ft. Rice, cotton, cacao, coffee, stock. Noted for its vast archaeological remains (monolithic statues, temples) whose origins are unknown.

San Agustín or **San Agustín Acasaguastlán** (äkäsägwäslän′), town (1950 pop. 2,503), El Progreso dept., E central Guatemala, near Motagua R., 8 mi. NE of El Progreso; market center; corn, wheat, sugar cane. Mayan remains near by. Pop. is largely Indian.

San Agustin, Cape (sän ägōōstēn′), tip of SE peninsula of Mindanao, Philippines, at entrance to Davao Gulf; 6°16′N 126°11′E.

San Agustín Tlaxiaca, Mexico: see TLAXIACA.

Sanahcat (sänäkät′), town (pop. 733), Yucatan, SE Mexico, 29 mi. SE of Mérida; henequen.

Sanain, Armenian SSR: see ALAVERDI.

Sanak (să′năk), village (1939 pop. 39), NW Sanak Isl., SW Alaska, E of Unimak Isl., 45 mi. SSW of King Cove; cod fishing and canning, fur trapping.

Sanak Island (13 mi. long, 4 mi. wide), Aleutian Isls., SW Alaska, 30 mi. SE of Unimak Isl.; 54°26′N 162°40′W; rises to 1,740 ft. Devoid of bushes and trees. Cod fishing, fish processing, fox farming; beef cattle. Surrounded by several small isls., it is largest of Sanak Isls. group.

San Alberto, department, Argentina: see SAN PEDRO, Córdoba prov.

San Alberto, town, Argentina: see EL ARAÑADO.

San Albino, Nicaragua: see EL JÍCARO.

San Alejo (sän älä'hō), city (pop. 4,563), La Unión dept., E Salvador, 16 mi. NW of La Unión; stone-cutting; agr., livestock raising.

San al-Hajar, Egypt: see SAN EL HAGAR.

Sanamayn, Al-, Syria: see SANAMEIN, ES.

San Ambrosio Island (sän' ämbrō'syō) (□ c.1), in the South Pacific, c.600 mi. W of Chile, to which it belongs; 26°21'S 79°54'W. Barren, uninhabited isl., rising to 1,570 ft. With San Félix Isl., 12 mi. WNW, it was discovered 1574 by Sp. navigator Juan Fernández.

Sanamein, Es, El Sanamein, or **Al-Sanamayn** (all: ĕs-sänämän'), town, Hauran prov., SW Syria, 31 mi. SSW of Damascus; cereals, wheat.

Sanana (sünä'nü), island (35 mi. long, 10 mi. wide; pop. 12,933), Sula Isls., N Moluccas, Indonesia, in Molucca Sea, just S of Mangole; 2°10'S 125°55'E; mountainous. Agr. (coconuts, corn, sago), fishing. Sanana on NE coast is chief town of Sula Isls. Sometimes called Sula Besi.

Sanand (sä'nŭnd), town (pop. 8,733), Ahmadabad dist., N Bombay, India, 13 mi. WSW of Ahmadabad; millet, cotton, wheat, peanuts; handicraft cloth weaving.

Sanandaj (sänändäj'), town (1940 pop. 29,711), Fifth Prov., W Iran, on road and 70 mi. N of Kermanshah; main town of Iranian Kurdistan; wheat, tobacco; sheep raising; handmade rugs, fine woodwork. Formerly known as Sinneh.

Sanandita (sänändē'tä), village (pop. c.2,100), Tarija dept., SE Bolivia, in Serranía de Aguaragüe, 29 mi. S of Villa Montes, on road; important oil center. Sanandita oil fields and refinery 4 mi. W.

San Andreas (săn ăn'drās), village (pop. 1,263), ⊙ Calaveras co., central Calif., 38 mi. NE of Stockton; gold mining; cement making. Rail point is Valley Springs (8 mi. W).

San Andreas Fault or **San Andreas Rift,** W Calif., a fault zone in earth's surface, extending from the Pacific at Point Arena for more than 500 mi. SE.

San Andrés (sän ändrās'). **1** Town (pop. estimate 5,000) in Greater Buenos Aires, Argentina, adjoining San Martín, 10 mi. NW of Buenos Aires; food preserves, silk fabrics. **2** Town (pop. estimate 500), central Tucumán prov., Argentina, on railroad and 5 mi. S of Tucumán; sugar-refining center.

San Andrés. 1 Town (pop. c.1,000), Beni dept., NE Bolivia, in the llanos, 27 mi. SE of Trinidad; cattle. **2** or **San Andrés de Machaca** (dā mächä'kä), town (pop. 4,100), La Paz dept., W Bolivia, in the Altiplano, near Peru border, 26 mi. SSW of Guaqui; potatoes, barley, sheep.

San Andrés, town (pop. 249), Palma, Canary Isls., 8 mi. N of Santa Cruz de la Palma; sugar cane, onions, potatoes, bananas, tomatoes; timber; sheep, goats.

San Andrés. 1 Town, San Andrés y Providencia intendancy, Colombia: see SAINT ANDREWS ISLAND. **2** Town (pop. 2,282), Santander dept., N central Colombia, in Cordillera Oriental, 28 mi. SE of Bucaramanga; alt. 5,269 ft. Coffee, sugar cane, wheat, corn, potatoes, cattle, sheep, hogs. Waterfalls near by.

San Andrés, village, Chimborazo prov., central Ecuador, in the Andes, 7 mi. NW of Riobamba, in henequen-growing area. Damaged by 1949 earthquake.

San Andrés. 1 Town (1950 pop. 999), Petén dept., N Guatemala, on W shore of L. Petén and 3 mi. NNW of Flores; sugar cane, grain, livestock. **2** or **San Andrés Villa Seca** (vē'yä sä'kä), town (1950 pop. 644), Retalhuleu dept., SW Guatemala, in Pacific piedmont, on railroad and 7 mi. ENE of Retalhuleu; coffee, sugar cane, cacao, cotton, grain; livestock. **3** or **San Andrés Semetabaj** (sāmātäbäkh') town (1950 pop. 770), Sololá dept., SW central Guatemala, on Inter-American Highway and 5 mi. ESE of Sololá; alt. 6,384 ft.; vegetables, grain, beans. **4** or **San Andrés Xecul** (säkōōl'), town (1950 pop. 2,700), Totonicapán dept., W central Guatemala, 8 mi. W of Totonicapán; alt. 6,880 ft.; corn, wheat, beans.

San Andrés. 1 Officially San Andrés Totoltepec, town (pop. 1,012), Federal Dist., central Mexico, 12 mi. S of Mexico city; cereals, fruit, livestock. **2** Town, Jalisco, Mexico: see MARIANO ESCOBEDO. **3** or **San Andrés Cuexcontitlán** (kwĕskōntētlän'), town (pop. 3,390), Mexico state, central Mexico, 9 mi. SSE of Toluca; agr. center (cereals, livestock). **4** or **San Andrés Cholula** (chōlōō'lä), town (pop. 1,884), Puebla, central Mexico, 6 mi. W of Puebla; cereals, fruit, livestock.

San Andrés, town (pop. 1,288), Ica dept., SW Peru, on the Pacific, 1 mi. SW of Pisco; fish canning.

San Andrés Chiautla, Mexico: see CHIAUTLA, Mexico state.

San Andrés Cholula, Mexico: see SAN ANDRÉS, Puebla.

San Andrés Cuexcontitlán, Mexico: see SAN ANDRÉS, Mexico state.

San Andrés de Giles (dā hē'lĕs), town (pop. 5,573), ⊙ San Andrés de Giles dist. (□ 437; pop. 15,334), N Buenos Aires prov., Argentina, 20 mi. WNW of Luján, in agr. area (wheat, flax, corn, cattle, sheep).

San Andrés del Congosto (dĕl kōng-gō'stō), village (pop. 376), Guadalajara prov., central Spain, on affluent of the Henares (Bornaba R.; crossed by Roman bridge), and 27 mi. NNE of Guadalajara, in irrigated region (wheat, grapes, beans, olives); flour milling, plaster mfg.

San Andrés de Llevaneras (dā lyävänä'räs), village (pop. 1,520), Barcelona prov., NE Spain, 3 mi. NE of Mataró; knit-goods mfg.; produces wine, fruit, cereals. Summer resort.

San Andrés de Machaca, Bolivia: see SAN ANDRÉS.

San Andrés de Palomar (pälōmär'), N section of Barcelona, Barcelona prov., NE Spain.

San Andrés de Salitral, Peru: see SALITRAL.

San Andrés de Sotavento (sōtävĕn'tō), town (pop. 1,959), Bolívar dept., N Colombia, in Caribbean lowlands, 15 mi. SSW of Sincelejo; corn, sugar cane, tobacco, stock.

San Andrés Island, Colombia: see SAINT ANDREWS ISLAND.

San Andrés Itzapa, Guatemala: see ITZAPA.

San Andrés Jaltenco, Mexico: see JALTENCO.

San Andres Mountains (săn ŭndrās'), S N.Mex., in Socorro and Dona Ana counties, paralleling Rio Grande; extend N from San Augustin Mts. to Sierra Oscura. Highest point, Salinas Peak (9,040 ft.), in N. White Sands Natl. Monument is just E.

San Andrés Semetabaj, Guatemala: see SAN ANDRÉS.

San Andrés Tuxtla (tōōst'lä), city (pop. 10,154), Veracruz, SE Mexico, at S foot of Tuxtla Volcano, 80 mi. SE of Veracruz. Rail terminus; agr. center (fruit, high-grade tobacco). Airfield. Formerly Los Tuxtlas.

San Andrés Villa Seca, Guatemala: see SAN ANDRÉS.

San Andrés Xecul, Guatemala: see SAN ANDRÉS.

San Andrés y Providencia (ē prōvēdhĕn'syä), intendancy (□ 21; 1938 pop. 6,528; 1950 estimate 6,600), of Colombia, comprising 2 small isls. and 7 groups of coral reefs and cays in the Caribbean c.125–200 mi. off the Mosquito Coast of Nicaragua, bet. 12°–16°N and 78°–82°W; ⊙ San Andrés, on SAINT ANDREWS ISLAND, the largest isl.; OLD PROVIDENCE ISLAND is 55 mi. NNE of St. Andrews. Reefs include (N-S) Serranilla Bank, Bajo Nuevo, Serrana Bank, Quita Sueño Bank, Roncador Bank, Courtown Cays, and Albuquerque Cays. The group produces coconuts mainly; also some corn, sugar cane, cotton, oranges, bananas, yucca, stock. Deep-sea fishing. The banks have deposits of guano, of poor quality. The isls. are populated by Protestant English-speaking Negroes. Coconuts, copra, and oranges are exported. In 1919 the U.S. claimed Quita Sueño, Serrana, and Roncador, under an 1856 act of Congress dealing with unoccupied guano isls.

San Angel, Mexico: see VILLA OBREGÓN, Federal Dist.

San Angelo (săn ăn'jūlō), city (pop. 52,093), ⊙ Tom Green co., W Texas, c.180 mi. NW of Austin, at junction of North and Middle Concho rivers to form Concho R.; an important wool and mohair market; trade, shipping, and processing center for large ranching (sheep, goats, cattle) and irrigated farm area (cotton, grains, dairy products, poultry); oil fields near. Cotton ginning, cottonseed-oil milling, oil refining, meat packing, dairying; mfg. of leather goods, clay and concrete products, agr. machinery, foundry and sheet-metal products. Seat of a jr. col. Fish hatcheries here. Goodfellow Air Force Base near. L. Nasworthy (náz'wûrdhē, năz'–) (municipal reservoir) is just SW. Annual stock shows. Founded near old Fort Concho (kŏn'chō) (bldgs. now house a mus.) on cattle and stage routes; laid out 1869, inc. 1889. Grew after coming of railroad, 1888.

San Anselmo (săn ănsĕl'mō), residential town (pop. 9,188), Marin co., W Calif., 16 mi. N of San Francisco and adjacent to San Rafael (E). San Francisco Theological seminary is here. Inc. 1907.

San Antero (sän äntä'rō), town (pop. 4,355), Bolívar dept., N Colombia, in Caribbean lowlands, near the coast, 10 mi. NNE of Lorica; corn, rice, sugar, fruit, livestock.

San Antonio, department, Argentina: see SAN ANTONIO OESTE.

San Antonio (sän äntō'nyō). **1** or **San Antonio de la Paz** (dā lä päs'), village (pop. estimate 500), ⊙ La Paz dept. (□ 1,655; pop. 12,690), SE Catamarca prov., Argentina, on Córdoba prov. boundary, 55 mi. SE of Catamarca, on Tucumán-Córdoba RR; stock raising (cattle, goats, mules). **2** Village, ⊙ San Antonio dept. (□ 243; 1947 pop. 2,200), SE Jujuy prov., Argentina, 12 mi. S of Jujuy, in agr. area (corn, sugar cane, livestock).

San Antonio. 1 Village (pop. 1,100), Beni dept., NE Bolivia, in the llanos, 20 mi. ESE of Trinidad; cattle. **2** or **San Antonio de Lora** (dā lō'rä), village, Beni dept., NE Bolivia, on Mamoré R. just above Secure R. mouth and 26 mi. SSW of Trinidad, in the llanos; cattle. **3** Village, Cochabamba dept., central Bolivia, on Chaparé R. and 6 mi. NNE of Todos Santos, in tropical lowlands; sugar cane, rice. Another San Antonio lies 17 mi. WSW of Todos Santos. **4** or **San Antonio de Esmoraca** (dā ĕsmōrä'kä), village, Potosí dept., SW Bolivia, in Cordillera de Lípez, on a headstream of San Juan R. and 20 mi. SSE of San Pablo; alpaca.

San Antonio, village (pop. 1,099), Toledo dist., Br. Honduras, 18 mi. NNW of Punta Gorda; sugar cane, timber. Road terminus near Maya Mts.

San Antonio. 1 Town (1930 pop. 5,994; 1940 pop. 11,859), ⊙ San Antonio dept. (□ 775; pop. 40,475), Santiago prov., central Chile, on the Pacific, on railroad and 55 mi. WSW of Santiago, 37 mi. S of Valparaiso; 33°35'S 71°39'W. Port, popular beach resort, trading and mfg. center. Exports fruit, wine, wheat, barley, copper; imports coal. With a small but well-protected harbor and a rail line to Santiago, it is an outlet for the fertile central valley. Has chemical industry, hydroelectric plant. **2** Nitrate-mining settlement (pop. 16), Tarapacá prov., N Chile, on railroad and 12 mi. E of Pisagua.

San Antonio, town (pop. 2,028), Tolima dept., W central Colombia, in Cordillera Central, 40 mi. SSW of Ibagué; alt. 4,892 ft.; sugar cane, coffee, corn, potatoes, livestock.

San Antonio. 1 Village (pop. 6,102), Guanacaste prov., NW Costa Rica, 4 mi. NNE of Nicoya; livestock, plantains, coffee. **2** or **San Antonio de Belén** (dā bĕlĕn'), town (1950 pop. 569), Heredia prov., central Costa Rica, on central plateau, on railroad and 5 mi. WSW of Heredia. Agr. (onions, tomatoes); apiculture; rice milling. Owes its development to location on road and railroad to Puntarenas.

San Antonio or **Central San Antonio** (sĕnträl'), sugar-mill village (pop. 2,366), Oriente prov., E Cuba, 8 mi. E of Guantánamo. Also Río Seco.

San Antonio, village, Pichincha prov., N central Ecuador, in the Andes, near the equator, 16 mi. NNE of Quito; manganese deposits.

San Antonio. 1 or **San Antonio Aguas Calientes** (ä'gwäs kälyĕn'tĕs), town (1950 pop. 2,195), Sacatepéquez dept., S central Guatemala, 4 mi. WSW of Antigua; alt. 4,741 ft.; huipil weaving; coffee, sugar cane, grain. **2** or **San Antonio Sacatepéquez** (säkätāpā'kĕs), town (1950 pop. 684), San Marcos dept., SW Guatemala, near headwaters of Naranjo R., on Inter-American Highway and 5 mi. E of San Marcos; alt. 7,875 ft. Market center; coffee, grain; lumbering. **3** or **San Antonio Palopó** (pälōpō'), town (1950 pop. 992), Sololá dept., SW central Guatemala, on E shore of L. Atitlán and 7 mi. SE of Sololá; alt. 5,200 ft. Reed-mat weaving; coffee, grain; lumbering. **4** or **San Antonio Suchitepéquez** (sōōchētāpā'kĕs), town (1950 pop. 2,204), Suchitepéquez dept., SW Guatemala, in Pacific piedmont, near Nahualate R., 6 mi. E of Mazatenango; rail terminus; coffee, cacao, grain; livestock.

San Antonio. 1 Town, Comayagua dept., Honduras: see VILLA DE SAN ANTONIO. **2** or **San Antonio de Cortés** (dā kōrtās'), town (pop. 974), Cortés dept., W central Honduras, in hills S of Ulúa R., 26 mi. SSW of San Pedro Sula; coffee, wheat, corn, livestock. Until early 1930s called Talpetate.

San Antonio, town (pop. 971), Southern Territory, Lower California, NW Mexico, 30 mi. SE of La Paz; silver, lead, gold mining.

San Antonio or **Ingenio San Antonio** (ĕnhä'nyō), village, Chinandega dept., W Nicaragua, 3 mi. SSW of Chichigalpa; served by sugar-cane-plantation railroad; major sugar-milling center; sawmilling, woodworking, metalworks.

San Antonio, town (dist. pop. 5,857), Central dept., S Paraguay, on Paraguay R. (Argentina border) and 11 mi. SSE of Asunción; meat packing; soap factory.

San Antonio. 1 Village, Cajamarca dept., Peru: see SAN JUAN. **2** Town (pop. 985), San Martín dept., N central Peru, 6 mi. NNW of Tarapoto; sugar cane, coffee, cotton.

San Antonio (săn" ăntō'nēō, Sp. sän äntō'nyō). **1** Town (1939 pop. 1,310; 1948 municipality pop. 16,518), Nueva Ecija prov., central Luzon, Philippines, on Pampanga R. and 6 mi. E of San Fernando; rice, corn. **2** Town (1939 pop. 6,025; 1948 municipality pop. 8,381), Zambales prov., central Luzon, Philippines, near W coast, 65 mi. WNW of Manila; rice-growing center.

San Antonio, Gerona prov., Spain: see SALT.

San Antonio, Sp. Guinea: see ANNOBÓN.

San Antonio. 1 (săn ăntō'nēō) City (pop. 286), Pasco co., W central Fla., 27 mi. NE of Tampa. **2** (săn ăntō'nyü, –nēō) Village (pop. c.400), Socorro co., W central N.Mex., on Rio Grande, just SE of Magdalena Mts., and 10 mi. S of Socorro, in irrigated alfalfa region; alt. 4,500 ft. Trading point for ranches. Nogal Canyon (300–1,000 ft. deep) near by. Natl. wildlife refuge just S. **3** (săn ăntō'nyü, –nēō) City (1940 pop. 253,854; 1950 pop. 408,442), ⊙ Bexar co., S central Texas, on San Antonio R. (here formed by headstreams) and 190 mi. W of Houston. Third-largest city in state, and one of its chief commercial centers; port of entry, with a foreign trade zone (free port) opened in 1950; transportation (rail, air, highway) and distribution center. Ships cattle, wool, mohair, cotton, truck, fruit, pecans from wide area. Large oil-refining, meat-packing, ironworking and food-processing industries; also pecan shelling, brewing, and mfg. of clay products, clothing, batteries, cement, furniture; railroad shops. Tourists are attracted by city's mild climate (average temp. 68.9 °F.), by exotic atmosphere contributed by large Mex. pop., and by Alamo and old missions. San Jose Mission (established 1720) was largely restored in 1930s and designated as natl. historic site (4.1 acres) in 1941; includes granary, mill, fine cloisters, and church with elaborate baroque carvings. U.S. Fort Sam Houston (established 1865), with Brooke Army Medical center, is in city; Brooks, Kelly, Randolph, and Lackland Air Force bases, among largest military airfields in U.S., are near by. City is see of R.C. archbishop and Protestant Episcopal bishop. Seat of Trinity Univ., Univ. of San Antonio, San Antonio Col., St. Mary's Univ., Our Lady of the Lake Col., and Incarnate Word Col. Early the most important Texas settlement under Sp. and Mex. rule, it was founded 1718 as mission of San Antonio de Valero and presidio of San Antonio de Béjar (or Béxar). Near by were established missions of San José (1720), Concepción (1721), San Francisco de la Espada (1721), and San Juan Capistrano (1731), all adjoining town of San Fernando (now central part of city), which was founded in 1731. In Texas Revolution, Texans under Ben Milam took city in Dec., 1835; its heroic defenders were massacred (March, 1836) in the Alamo, whose remaining section, once the chapel of Mission San Antonio, is now one of best-known U.S. historic shrines. In 1842, city was taken and held briefly by Mex. invaders. Became roaring "cow town" in the trail-driving period following Civil War; coming of railroad in 1877 made it a cattle-shipping center.

San Antonio (sän äntō'nyō). **1** Town (pop. 1,200), Canelones dept., S Uruguay, 12 mi. ENE of Canelones; wheat, corn, livestock. **2** Town (pop. 3,000), Salto dept., NW Uruguay, on railroad and 12 mi. ENE of Salto; cereals, vegetables, fruit; vineyards.

San Antonio. 1 or **San Antonio de Maturín** (dā mätōōrēn'), town (pop. 1,539), Monagas state, NE Venezuela, in coastal range, 40 mi. SE of Cumaná; coffee plantations. **2** Town (pop. 4,943), Táchira state, W Venezuela, in Andean spur, on Colombia border, on transandine highway and 15 mi. WNW of San Cristóbal; coffeegrowing center. The international Bolívar Bridge crosses Táchira R. to Colombia. **3** Town (pop. 504), Zulia state, NW Venezuela, on S shore of L. Maracaibo, 10 mi. SW of Bobures; sugar cane.

San Antonio, Cape, E Buenos Aires prov., Argentina, at mouth of the Río de la Plata (on S side), the southernmost point of Samborombón Bay. Lat. 30°19'S; 150 mi. SE of Buenos Aires. Sometimes the N tip of Cape San Antonio headland is called Punta Norte and its S tip Punta Sur.

San Antonio, Cape, western extremity of Cuba, Pinar del Río prov., on Guanahacabibes Peninsula, facing Yucatan Peninsula, 190 mi. SW of Havana; 21°52'N 84°57'W. Lighthouse.

San Antonio, Cape, on the Mediterranean, in Alicante prov., E Spain, 53 mi. NE of Alicante; 38°48'N 0°13'E. Lighthouse.

San Antonio, Sierra, Bolivia-Argentina: see ALTO, SIERRA DEL.

San Antonio Abad (ävädh'), town (pop. 2,360), Iviza, Balearic Isls., port (linked with Barcelona) on fine sheltered bay (Puerto Magno), 7 mi. NW of Iviza city; olives, cereals, fruit, grapes. Flour milling.

San Antonio Abad, N suburb (pop. 5,846) of Cartagena, Murcia prov., E Spain; iron foundries; flour products.

San Antonio Aguas Calientes, Guatemala: see SAN ANTONIO.

San Antonio Bay (săn ăntō'nyū, -nēō), S Texas, 27 mi. SSE of Victoria, an inlet sheltered from Gulf of Mexico by Matagorda Isl.; c.19 mi. long NW-SE, c.19 mi. wide. A NW arm is called Hynes Bay. Receives Guadalupe R. in N. Joined by Gulf Intracoastal Waterway to Aransas Bay (SW) and to Espiritu Santo Bay and thence to Matagorda Bay (NE).

San Antonio de Areco (sän äntō'nyō dā ärä'kō), town (pop. 7,359), ⊙ San Antonio dist. (□ 331; pop. 13,668), N Buenos Aires prov., Argentina, 30 mi. WNW of Luján, in agr. area (grain, cattle, sheep).

San Antonio de Belén, Costa Rica: see SAN ANTONIO, Heredia prov.

San Antonio de Cabezas, Cuba: see CABEZAS.

San Antonio de Cortés, Honduras: see SAN ANTONIO, Cortés dept.

San Antonio de Esmoraca, Bolivia: see SAN ANTONIO, Potosí dept.

San Antonio de Lacamaca, Peru: see SAN JUAN, Cajamarca dept.

San Antonio de la Paz, Argentina: see SAN ANTONIO, Catamarca prov.

San Antonio de las Vegas (läs vā'gäs), town (pop. 1,473), Havana prov., W Cuba, on railroad and 10 mi. S of Havana; dairying, sugar growing.

San Antonio de las Vueltas, Cuba: see VUELTAS.

San Antonio del Golfo (dĕl gōl'fō), town (pop. 1,286), Sucre state, NE Venezuela, on SE shore of Gulf of Cariaco, 25 mi. E of Cumaná; coconuts, rice.

San Antonio de Lípez (lē'pēs), village, Potosí dept., SW Bolivia, in the Cordillera de Lípez, 19 mi. SW of San Pablo; alpaca.

San Antonio de Litin (lē'tēn), town (pop. estimate 1,000), E Córdoba prov., Argentina, 35 mi. NE of Villa María; wheat, flax, livestock. Formerly Capilla San Antonio.

San Antonio del Norte, Honduras: see EL NORTE.

San Antonio de Lora, Bolivia: see SAN ANTONIO, Beni dept.

San Antonio de los Baños (lōs bä'nyōs), city (pop. 16,512), Havana prov., W Cuba, on small San Antonio de los Baños R., on railroad and 19 mi. SSW of Havana; popular health resort with thermal springs. Also produces high-quality tobacco, pineapples, sugar cane. Mfg. of cigars, yeast, underwear. Has military airport. Sugar central near by.

San Antonio de los Cobres (kō'brĕs), village (pop. estimate 500), ⊙ San Antonio de los Cobres dept. (□ 8,200; 1947 census pop. 4,254), W Salta prov., Argentina, in the Puna de Atacama, on Transandine RR and 75 mi. NW of Salta; alt. 12,000 ft. Mining center (bismuth, copper, sulphur); sulphur refining. Hydroelectric station. Until 1943 in Los Andes natl. territory.

San Antonio del Parapetí, Bolivia: see SAN FRANCISCO DEL PARAPETÍ.

San Antonio del Río Blanco (dĕl rē'ō bläng'kō), town (pop. 1,767), Havana prov., W Cuba, 2½ mi. NE of Jaruco; sugar cane, fruit. Also called San Antonio de Río Blanco or San Antonio de Río Blanco del Norte.

San Antonio del Tule, Mexico: see EL TULE.

San Antonio de Maturín, Venezuela: see SAN ANTONIO, Monagas state.

San Antonio de Oriente (dā ōryĕn'tā), town (pop. 263), Francisco Morazán dept., S central Honduras, 12 mi. ESE of Tegucigalpa; grain, livestock; tanning, pottery making. A major silver-mining center in colonial times.

San Antonio de Padua (päd'wä), town (pop. 3,025), NE Buenos Aires prov., Argentina, 2 mi. E of Merlo; agr. center (grain, flax, livestock; dairying). Has Franciscan seminary.

San Antonio de Padua, Mission, Calif.: see JOLON.

San Antonio de Río Blanco, Cuba: see SAN ANTONIO DEL RÍO BLANCO.

San Antonio Guazú River, Argentina-Brazil: see SANTO ANTÔNIO RIVER.

San Antonio Huista (wē'stä), town (1950 pop. 1,689), Huehuetenango dept., W Guatemala, on W slopes of Cuchumatanes Mts., 31 mi. NW of Huehuetenango; alt. 5,315 ft. Mfg. (palm hats, rope); corn, sugar cane, coffee, bananas.

San Antonio la Isla, Mexico: see LA ISLA.

San Antonio Oeste (sän äntō'nyō wĕ'stä), town (1947 pop. 3,883), ⊙ San Antonio dept., E Río Negro natl. territory, Argentina, Atlantic port on a sheltered bay of San Matías Gulf, 100 mi. W of Viedma; stock raising (sheep, cattle), fishing (sardines, cod). Linked with the Río Negro by canal.

San Antonio Palopó, Guatemala: see SAN ANTONIO.

San Antonio Peak (săn ăntō'nēō) or **Mount San Antonio** (10,080 ft.), S Calif., highest point in San Gabriel Mts., 23 mi. NW of San Bernardino. Popularly called Old Baldy or Mt. Baldy.

San Antonio River (săn ăntō'nyū, -nēō), Texas, rises in springs in San Antonio city, flows c.195 mi. SE to Guadalupe R. just above its mouth on San Antonio Bay. Receives Medina R. and Cibolo Creek.

San Antonio Sacatepéquez, Guatemala: see SAN ANTONIO.

San Antonio Suchitepéquez, Guatemala: see SAN ANTONIO.

San Antonio Tecomitl, Mexico: see TECOMITL.

Sanarate (sänärä'tā), town (1950 pop. 2,990), El Progreso dept., E central Guatemala, in highlands, on railroad and 9 mi. WSW of El Progreso; market center; corn, beans, sugar cane, livestock.

Sanare (sänä'rā), town (pop. 2,251), Lara state, NW Venezuela, in N Andean spur, 32 mi. SW of Barquisimeto; alt. 4,455 ft.; agr. center (coffee, wheat, fruit, vegetables, stock).

Sanariapo (sänäryä'pō), village, Amazonas territory, S Venezuela, landing on Orinoco R. (Colombia border) and 33 mi. SSW of Puerto Ayacucho (connected by road circumventing Maipures and Atures Rapids, major obstacles to navigation on upper Orinoco R.).

Saña River (sä'nyä), Lambayeque dept., NW Peru, rises on W slopes of Cordillera Occidental 5 mi. NE of Niepos (Cajamarca dept.), flows 60 mi. W and SW, through major sugar-cane region, past Cayaltí and Saña, to the Pacific 14 mi. SE of Puerto Eten. Feeds numerous irrigation channels in lower course. Also spelled Zaña.

Sana River (sä'nä), NW Bosnia, Yugoslavia, rises 16 mi. W of Jajce, flows c.100 mi. N, past Kljuc, Sanski Most, and Prijedor, to Una R. at Novi. Railroad follows its lower course.

Sanary-sur-Mer (sänärē'-sür-mâr'), town (pop. 2,718), Var dept., SE France, on the Mediterranean, 7 mi. W of Toulon, on W shore of Cape Sicié peninsula; resort damaged in Second World War.

San Atenógenes (sän ätänō'hĕnĕs), town (pop. 1,224), Durango, N Mexico, 40 mi. E of Durango; grain, cotton, sugar cane, vegetables, livestock.

Sanatorium, Texas: see CARLSBAD.

San Augustin, Plains of (săn ôgŭstēn'), W N.Mex., playa basin in Catron and Socorro counties, just below SE edge of Colorado Plateau; 75 mi. long (NE-SW), 15-20 mi. wide; alt. c.6,900 ft.

San Augustine (săn ô'gŭstēn), county (□ 612; pop. 8,837), E Texas; ⊙ San Augustine. Bounded W by Attoyac Bayou, SW by Angelina R. Includes part of Angelina Natl. Forest. Lumbering (pine, hardwoods) is important. Agr. (cotton, corn, sweet potatoes, truck, fruit), beef cattle. Hunting, fishing. Formed 1836.

San Augustine, town (pop. 2,510), ⊙ San Augustine co., E Texas, on small Ayish Bayou and 32 mi. ESE of Nacogdoches; center of pine-lumbering area. Region was site of a Sp. mission (1716-19; 1721-73); a fort here (1756-73) protected Sp.-Fr. border. Settled 1818 by Anglo-Americans.

San Augustin Mountains (săn ôgŭstēn'), S N.Mex., E of the Rio Grande; form link bet. Organ Mts. (S) and San Andres Mts. (N). Highest point, San Augustin Peak (7,030 ft.). San Augustin Pass is just S.

San Augustin Pass (săn ôgŭstēn') (alt. 5,719 ft.), S N.Mex., 15 mi. NE of Las Cruces, bet. Organ Mts. and San Augustin Mts. Crossed by highway.

Sanaur (sŭnour'), town (pop. 8,426), E Patiala and East Punjab States Union, India, 3 mi. ESE of Patiala; agr. market (wheat, millet, gram).

Sanawad (sănä'vŭd), town (pop. 7,974), SW Madhya Bharat, India, 39 mi. SSE of Indore; local cotton market (ginning).

Sanawar (sŭnä'vär), town (pop. 757), E Patiala and East Punjab States Union, India, 15 mi. SW of Simla; hill resort; has tuberculosis sanatorium.

San Bartolo (sän bärtō'lō). **1** Village, Durango, Mexico: see GENERAL SIMÓN BOLÍVAR. **2** Officially San Bartolo Tutotepec, town (pop. 1,418), Hidalgo, central Mexico, 40 mi. ENE of Pachuca; cereals, sugar cane, coffee, tobacco, fruit. **3** Officially San Bartolo del Llano, town (pop. 2,374), Mexico state, central Mexico, 40 mi. WNW of Mexico city; cereals, fruit, livestock. **4** Town, Michoacán, Mexico: see ALVARO OBREGÓN.

San Bartolo Coyotepec, Mexico: see COYOTEPEC, Oaxaca.

San Bartolo Cuautlalpan, Mexico: see CUAUTLALPAN.

San Bartolomé or **San Bartolomé de Lanzarote** (sän' bärtōlōmā' dā län-thärō'tā), village (pop. 1,870), Lanzarote, Canary Isls., 4 mi. NW of Arrecife, in agr. region (cereals, grapes, white and sweet potatoes, melons, onions, tomatoes; goats). Flour milling.

San Bartolomé or **San Bartolomé Milpas Altas** (mēl'päs äl'täs), town (1950 pop. 901), Sacatepéquez dept., S central Guatemala, on Inter-American Highway and 4 mi. NE of Antigua; alt. 7,005 ft.; corn, beans, fruit.

San Bartolomé, Mexico: see VENUSTIANO CARRANZA, Chiapas.

San Bartolomé de Lanzarote, Canary Isls.: see SAN BARTOLOMÉ.

San Bartolomé de las Abiertas (dā läs ävyĕr'täs), village (pop. 1,520), Toledo prov., central Spain, 14 mi. SE of Talavera de la Reina; cereals, olives, grapes, livestock.

San Bartolomé de la Torre (lä tô'rā), town (pop. 2,031), Huelva prov., SW Spain, 15 mi. NW of Huelva, in agr. region (cereals, olives, grapes, oranges, figs, acorns, cork); stock raising. Olive-oil extracting, flour- and sawmilling.

San Bartolomé del Pino (dĕl pē'nō), town (pop. 1,213), Querétaro, central Mexico, 34 mi. SE of Querétaro; grain, alfalfa, sugar, vegetables, stock.

San Bartolomé de Pinares (dā pēnä'rĕs), town (pop. 1,341), Ávila prov., central Spain, 10 mi. SE of Ávila; cereals, grapes, livestock; meat processing.

San Bartolomé de Tirajana (tērähä'nä), town (pop. 1,021), Grand Canary, Canary Isls., 15 mi. SSW of Las Palmas; almonds, corn, wheat, tomatoes, potatoes, bananas, tobacco; cattle, sheep, hogs.

San Bartolomé Milpas Altas, Guatemala: see SAN BARTOLOMÉ.

San Bartolomeo in Bosco (sän bärtôlômā'ō ēn bôs'kō), village (pop. 887), Ferrara prov., Emilia-Romagna, N central Italy, 1 mi. SE of Ferrara; canned fruit.

San Bartolomeo in Galdo (gäl'dô), town (pop. 10,434), Benevento prov., Campania, S Italy, 23 mi. NNE of Benevento; cement, wine, olive oil.

San Bartolo Morelos, Mexico: see MORELOS, Mexico state.

San Bartolo Naucalpan, Mexico: see NAUCALPAN.

San Basile (sän bäzē'lĕ), village (pop. 2,023), Cosenza prov., Calabria, S Italy, 2 mi. W of Castrovillari; wine, olive oil, cheese.

San Baudilio de Llobregat (sän bou-dhē'lyō dā lyōvrägät'), town (pop. 9,857), Barcelona prov., NE Spain, on Llobregat R., on coastal plain, and 8 mi. SW of Barcelona; cotton and silk spinning; mfg. of rayon, dyes, soda water; sawmilling. Winegrowing and truck farming in area.

San Bautista (sän boutē'stä), town (pop. 1,500), Canelones dept., S Uruguay, on railroad (Cazot station) and 30 mi. NNE of Montevideo.

San Beise, Mongolia: see CHOIBALSAN, city.

San Benedetto, Sardinia: see IGLESIAS.

San Benedetto del Tronto (sän bĕnĕdĕt'tô dĕl trôn'tô), town (pop. 12,337), Ascoli Piceno prov., The Marches, central Italy, port on the Adriatic,

17 mi. ENE of Ascoli Piceno. Fishing center; bathing resort; (cotton and hemp mills, cement works, box factory; agr. machinery, furniture, sausage. Exports citrus fruit. Damaged in Second World War by bombing (1943–44).

San Benedetto Po (pô'), village (pop. 1,840), Mantova prov., Lombardy, N Italy, near Po R., 11 mi. SE of Mantua; flour and lumber mills, alcohol distillery. Has ruins of anc. Benedictine abbey.

San Benedicto Island, Mexico: see REVILLAGIGEDO ISLANDS.

San Benigno Canavese (sän bĕnē'nyô känävä'sĕ), village (pop. 2,111), Torino prov., Piedmont, NW Italy, near Orco R., 12 mi. NNE of Turin. Has abbey (now a Salesian institution) founded 1006.

San Benito (sän bānē'tō), town (pop. c.4,700), Cochabamba dept., central Bolivia, in Cordillera de Cochabamba, on road and 60 mi. NW of Punata; wheat, potatoes.

San Benito, town (1950 pop. 1,349), Petén dept., N Guatemala, on S shore of L. Petén, just SW of Flores; sugar cane, grain, livestock. Terminus of road from Cobán.

San Benito (săn bůnē'tō), county (□ 1,396; pop. 14,370), W Calif.; ⊙ Hollister. San Benito R. flows through southernmost part (locally called San Benito valley) of Santa Clara Valley, bet. Santa Cruz Mts. and Gabilan Range (W) and Diablo Range (E). San Benito Mtn. (5,258 ft.) in Diablo Range is c.20 mi. NNW of Coalinga. PINNACLES NATIONAL MONUMENT is in co. San Juan Bautista has mission (1797). Fruit (apricots, prunes, pears, grapes, apples), nuts, livestock, sugar beets, truck, garden seed, grain. Co. leads Calif. in quicksilver production; also granite, sand, gravel, cement. Formed 1874.

San Benito, city (pop. 13,271), Cameron co., extreme S Texas, in lower Rio Grande valley 18 mi. NW of Brownsville; important processing, shipping center for irrigated citrus, truck, cotton region; canneries, creameries, cotton gins; tourist trade. State fish hatchery near by.

San Benito Mountain, Calif.: see DIABLO RANGE.

San Benito River, W Calif., rises in Diablo Range in S San Benito co., flows c.70 mi. NW, bet. Gabilan (W) and Diablo (E) ranges, to Pajaro R. W of Hollister; drains S part (locally called San Benito Valley) of Santa Clara Valley.

San Bernardino (sän bĕrnär-dhē'nō), town (1950 pop. 1,217), Suchitepéquez dept., SW Guatemala, in Pacific piedmont, 3 mi. ENE of Mazatenango; coffee, grain, livestock.

San Bernardino, town (dist. pop. 5,145), La Cordillera dept., S central Paraguay, on E shore of L. Ypacaraí and 23 mi. E of Asunción. Paraguay's main pleasure and health resort, in agr. area (maté, oranges, tobacco, stock). Tanning, distilling. Originally a Ger. colony, founded 1881. La Gruta (4 mi. away in the hills), with chapel of Our Lady of Lourdes, is a popular tourist site.

San Bernardino (sän' bĕrnärdē'nô), summer resort (alt. 5,270 ft.), Grisons canton, SE Switzerland, on Moësa R. and 20 mi. NNE of Bellinzona, in Valle Mesolcina, near Ital. border; winter sports center. Road leads N to San Bernardino Pass.

San Bernardino (săn bûrnůrdē'nō), county (□ 20,131; pop. 281,642), S Calif.; ⊙ San Bernardino. Largest co. in U.S. The SW corner (San Bernardino Valley), which lies S and W of San Gabriel Mts. and San Bernardino Mts. (both over 11,000 ft.), is agr. area, and has most of co.'s pop. To N and NE of mts. (crossed by Cajon Pass) is MOJAVE DESERT, into which sinks Mojave R.; to E, bounded by Nev. and Ariz. line (Calif.-Ariz. line formed in part by Colorado R.), is part of COLORADO DESERT. About 75% of co. is publicly owned lands: San Bernardino Natl. Forest, JOSHUA TREE NATIONAL MONUMENT, DEATH VALLEY NATIONAL MONUMENT, state parks, Indian and military reservations. Mtn. summer and winter resorts (notably Arrowhead and Big Bear lakes). In San Bernardino Valley and adjacent foothill belt are produced citrus and other fruit, nuts, poultry, rabbits, dairy products, truck. In desert are cattle ranches, some agr. (at irrigated oases—Victorville, Barstow, Needles), and mines and quarries (potash, borax, iron, cement rock, copper, sand, gravel, gold, talc, bentonite, clay, lead, manganese, zinc). Large steel plant (at Fontana); mineral-processing industries; extensive packing, processing, shipping of farm products. Formed 1853.

San Bernardino, city (pop. 63,058), ⊙ San Bernardino co., S Calif., in fertile San Bernardino Valley, at foot of San Bernardino and San Gabriel mts., near S end of Cajon Pass, c.55 mi. E of Los Angeles; railroad center (with repair shops); citrus-fruit packing, trade, and commercial center for wide region. Mfg. of food products, wine, cement, metal products; printing. Gateway to scenic mtn.-resort region, with lakes (notably Arrowhead, Big Bear), and spectacular Rim of the World Drive (5–7,000 ft. alt.) in the San Bernardino Mts. Seat of a jr. col. and Norton Air Force Base. Holds annual natl. orange show (Feb.). Arrowhead Hot Springs (health resort) is just N. Hq. for San Bernardino Natl. Forest. Laid out 1853 by Mormons (arrived 1851); inc. 1854.

San Bernardino Island (sän bĕrnär-dhē'nō), islet at seaward entrance to San Bernardino Strait, Philippines, 9 mi. E of Bulusan, Luzon; lighthouse; 12°45'N 124°17'E.

San Bernardino Mountains (săn bûrnůrdē'nō), S Calif., extend c.55 mi. SE from Cajon Pass at E end of San Gabriel Mts. to San Gorgonio Pass at N end of San Jacinto Mts. San Bernardino Mtn. (10,630 ft.) is 22 mi. E of San Bernardino; Mt. San Gorgonio (11,485 ft.), highest point in S Calif., is 27 mi. E of San Bernardino. Much of range included in San Bernardino Natl. Forest. Arrowhead, Big Bear lakes are resort centers. Rim of the World Drive is a 45-mi. loop highway over scenic mile-high route.

San Bernardino Pass (sän' bûrnůrdē'nō), Ger. *Sankt Bernhardin Pass* (zängkt' bĕrnhärdēn'), Ital. *Passo di San Bernardino* (pä'sô dē sän' bĕrnärdē'nô) (alt. 6,770 ft.), in Lepontine Alps, Grisons canton, SE Switzerland; possibly used since prehistoric times. Road over pass connects valleys of Hinterrhein and Möesa rivers. Hamlet of San Bernardino is S.

San Bernardino Strait, Philippines, bet. SE tip of Luzon and NW tip of Samar, leading from Philippine Sea to the inland waters via Ticao Pass or Visayan Sea; chief sea route to Manila and through the Philippines to Asia. Scene of a naval battle (Oct. 24–25, 1944), part of the action corollary to the battle of LEYTE GULF, in which the Jap. fleet was defeated.

San Bernardino Valley, Calif.: see SAN BERNARDINO, county.

San Bernardo (sän bĕrnär'dhō), city (1940 pop. 20,673; 1949 estimate 27,115), ⊙ San Bernardo dept. (□ 87; 1940 pop. 35,456), Santiago prov., central Chile, 11 mi. S of Santiago; rail junction, agr. center (wheat, fruit, wine, tobacco, livestock), and mfg. city (chemical industry, railroad shops, mfg. of iron, steel products). Also health resort.

San Bernardo, town (pop. 1,109), Cundinamarca dept., central Colombia, in Cordillera Central, 37 mi. SW of Bogotá; resort in agr. region (coffee, sugar cane, fruit). The natural bridge of Icononzo, with hieroglyphic inscriptions, is near by.

San Bernardo, town (pop. 903), Durango, N Mexico, on affluent of Nazas R. and 65 mi. N of Santiago Papasquiaro; fluor spar and antimony mining.

San Bernardo de Díaz, Argentina: see CORONEL MOLDES, Salta prov.

San Bernardo Point, Caribbean headland on coast of Bolívar dept., N Colombia, at N edge of Gulf of Morrosquillo, 50 mi. SSW of Cartagena; 9°43'N 75°42'W. Just W are the small San Bernardo Isls.

San Bernard River (săn bûrnärd'), S Texas, rises in N Colorado co., flows c.120 mi. generally SSE to Gulf of Mexico 7 mi. SW of Freeport.

San Blas, San Blas de los Sauces, or **Los Sauces** (sän bläs', dā, lōs sou'sĕs), village (pop. estimate 600), ⊙ Pelagio B. Luna dept. (□ 620; 1947 census 3,847), N La Rioja prov., Argentina, at N foot of Sierra de Velasco, 70 mi. NNW of La Rioja; stock raising (goats, sheep, cattle).

San Blas. 1 Town (pop. 752), Nayarit, W Mexico, minor port on the Pacific, on narrow ocean inlet, S of mouth of Santiago R., 23 mi. W of Tepic; 21°32'N 105°19'W. Corn, tobacco, coffee, cotton, bananas. Once important shipping point, especially in viceregal times, when it had pop. of c.30,000. Harbor has gradually silted up. **2** Town (pop. 1,747), Sinaloa, NW Mexico, on Río del Fuerte and 22 mi. S of El Fuerte; rail junction; sugar cane, corn, chick-peas, tomatoes, fruit.

San Blas, territory [Sp., *comarca*] (□ c.1,000; 1950 pop. 17,926) of E Panama; ⊙ El Porvenir. Extends in narrow strip along Caribbean coast to Colombia border (E); includes offshore Mulatas Isls. Pop. is largely Kuna Indian. Agr. (plantains, yams, coconuts); fisheries. Forming E portion of Colón prov., the territory is centrally administered.

San Blas, Cape (săn blăs'), Gulf co., NW Fla., on Gulf of Mexico, 12 mi. SW of Port St. Joe, at SW point of sandspit enclosing SAINT JOSEPH BAY; lighthouse (29°40'N 82°21'W).

San Blas, Cordillera de (kôrdīyā'rä dā sän bläs'), section of continental divide in E Panama, separated from Caribbean Sea by narrow coastal plain; rises to c.3,600 ft. Part of Serranía del Darién.

San Blas Bay, Argentina: see ANEGADA BAY.

San Blas Bay or **San Blas Gulf** (sän bläs'), inlet of Caribbean Sea in E central Panama, 60 mi. ENE of Colón, S of San Blas Peninsula (7 mi. long, 1.5 mi. wide) which terminates in Cape San Blas (9°34'N 78°58'W). The inlet (6 mi. wide, 10 mi. long) has port of Mandinga on its W shore.

San Blas de los Sauces, Argentina: see SAN BLAS.

San Blas Islands, Panama: see MULATAS ISLANDS.

Sanbongi (sämbōng'gē) or **Sambongi,** town (pop. 18,530), Aomori prefecture, N Honshu, Japan, 17 mi. WNW of Hachinohe; commercial center for rice-growing, horse-breeding area.

San Bonifacio (sän bônēfä'chô) or **Sambonifacio,** town (pop. 4,693), Verona prov., Veneto, N Italy, on Chiampo R. and 14 mi. E of Verona; beet-sugar refinery, furniture and button factories.

Sanbonmatsu, Japan: see SAMBONMATSU.

San Borja (sän bôr'hä), town (pop. c.1,900), Beni dept., NW Bolivia, 50 mi. SE of Reyes; rice, cacao, coffee. Airport.

Sanborn, county (□ 571; pop. 5,142), SE central S.Dak.; ⊙ Woonsocket; agr. area watered by James R. Dairy produce, livestock, poultry, grain. Formed 1883.

Sanborn. 1 Town (pop. 1,337), O'Brien co., NW Iowa, 60 mi. NE of Sioux City; railroad shops; dairy and concrete products. Founded 1878, inc. 1880. **2** Village (pop. 613), Redwood co., SW Minn., on Cottonwood R. and 34 mi. WSW of New Ulm, in grain, livestock, and poultry area; dairy products. **3** Village (pop. 324), Barnes co., E central N.Dak., 10 mi. W of Valley City.

Sanbornton (săn'bôrntůn), town (pop. 755), Belknap co., central N.H., bet. Winnisquam L. and Pemigewasset R., 7 mi. SW of Laconia.

San Bruno (săn brōō'nō), city (pop. 12,478), San Mateo co., W Calif., suburb c.10 mi. S of downtown San Francisco; ships poultry, truck. San Francisco municipal airport and Tanforan (tăn'fůrăn) race track are near by. Inc. 1914.

San Buenaventura (sän bwānävĕntōō'rä), town (pop. c.600), ⊙ Iturralde prov. (created 1938), La Paz dept., NW Bolivia, port on Beni R., opposite Rurrenabaque, and 145 mi. NNE of La Paz; rice, cacao, sugar cane. Also called San Buena Ventura and Puerto San Buenaventura.

San Buenaventura, town (pop. 513), Francisco Morazán dept., S central Honduras, on road and 14 mi. S of Tegucigalpa; alt. 4,108 ft.; grain, livestock.

San Buenaventura. 1 Town, Chihuahua, Mexico: see BUENAVENTURA. **2** Town (pop. 3,541), Coahuila, N Mexico, 15 mi. NW of Monclova; agr. center (corn, wheat, fruit, cattle, sheep). **3** Town (pop. 1,934), Mexico state, central Mexico, 8 mi. SW of Toluca; cereals, livestock; dairying.

San Buenaventura, Calif.: see VENTURA, city.

San Camilo (sän' kämē'lō), village, ⊙ Bermejo dept. (pop. 3,448), Formosa territory, Argentina, on Bermejo R., opposite El Pintado; corn, cotton, livestock.

San Candido (sän kän'dēdô), Ger. *Innichen,* town (pop. 1,571), Bolzano prov., Trentino–Alto Adige, N Italy, near Austrian border, 3 mi. E of Dobbiaco. Resort (alt. 3,850 ft.); tannery. Has Romanesque collegiate church (13th cent.; restored).

San Canziano, Yugoslavia: see DIVACA.

San Carlos (sän kär'lōs). **1** Village (pop. estimate 500), NE Corrientes prov., Argentina, 27 mi. S of Posadas; agr. and livestock center; maté and tung plantations. **2** Town (pop. estimate 1,500), ⊙ San Carlos dept. (□ 4,590; 1947 census pop. 14,272), central Mendoza prov., Argentina, 65 mi. SSW of Mendoza; rail terminus, health resort, and agr. center in irrigated area (wine, alfalfa, grain, fruit, vegetables, livestock). Dairying and lumbering. Sulphur springs. **3** Village (pop. estimate 500), ⊙ San Carlos dept. (□ 1,830; 1947 pop. 5,678), S Salta prov., Argentina, in irrigated Calchaquí valley, 85 mi. SSW of Salta; agr. center (alfalfa, wine, wheat, livestock); limeworks.

San Carlos, village (pop. 1,724), Iviza, Balearic Isls., 12 mi. NE of Iviza city; almonds, olives, cereals, fruit, livestock; flour milling. Unused lead mine.

San Carlos, town (pop. c.2,200), Santa Cruz dept., central Bolivia, 7 mi. NW of Buena Vista; sugar cane, rice. Founded as mission in 18th cent.

San Carlos, town (pop. 9,411), ⊙ San Carlos dept. (□ 1,252; pop. 50,236), Ñuble prov., S central Chile, in the central valley, on railroad and 14 mi. NNE of Chillán; agr. center (wheat, corn, rye, potatoes, vegetables, wine, cattle). Sawmills, tanneries, dairy plants.

San Carlos (săn kär'lŏs), small port on NW coast of East Falkland Isl., near N entrance of Falkland Sound; 51°27'S 59°W.

San Carlos (sän kär'lōs), town (1950 pop. 1,238), ⊙ Río San Juan dept., S Nicaragua, port on SE L. Nicaragua, at efflux of San Juan R., and 80 mi. SE of Juigalpa, near Costa Rica border; lumbering; livestock. Served as fort against pirates in colonial times. Partly destroyed by fire (1948).

San Carlos, village (pop. 378), Panama prov., central Panama, on Gulf of Panama of the Pacific, on Inter-American Highway and 40 mi. SW of Panama city; oranges and grapefruit, livestock.

San Carlos, town (dist. pop. 1,038), Concepción dept., N central Paraguay, on Apa R. (Brazil border) and 85 mi. N of Concepción, in stock-raising and lumbering area.

San Carlos, town (pop. 309), Amazonas dept., N Peru, in E Andean foothills, 20 mi. N of Chachapoyas, in agr. region (coffee, cotton, coca, sugar, cattle); mfg. of textile goods; distilling. Former ⊙ Bongará prov.

San Carlos. 1 Town (1939 pop. 10,899; 1948 municipality pop. 92,250), Negros Occidental prov., E Negros isl., Philippines, 35 mi. ESE of Bacolod; port on Tañon Strait, opposite small Refugio Isl. (răfōō'hyō) (3½ mi. long, ½ mi. wide); 1939 pop. 1,861). Connected by ferry with Toledo, Cebu isl. Sugar milling, sawmilling. Exports sugar, tobacco. **2** Town (1939 pop. 5,835; 1948 municipality pop. 61,671), Pangasinan prov., central Luzon, Philippines, on railroad and 8 mi. S of Dagupan; agr. center (rice, copra, corn).

San Carlos, town (pop. 1,002), on SW coast of Fernando Po isl., Sp. Guinea, 25 mi. SSW of Santa Isabel; 3°27'N 8°33'E. Ships cacao, bananas, coffee, palm oil, kola and coconuts.

San Carlos (săn kär'lōs). **1** Village (pop. c.100), Gila co., SE central Ariz., on San Carlos R., in San Carlos Indian Reservation, and 20 mi. E of Globe; hq. and trading point for reservation. Indian school here. San Carlos Reservoir is 10 mi. S. **2** Residential city (pop. 14,371), San Mateo co., W Calif., 20 mi. SSE of downtown San Francisco and on the bay; flower growing and shipping. Inc. 1925.

San Carlos (sän kär'lōs), town (pop. 10,700), Maldonado dept., S Uruguay, on railroad and 8 mi. N of Maldonado. Trades in agr. produce (grain, livestock). Has impressive old cathedral. Airfield. Founded 1762–63.

San Carlos. 1 or **San Carlos de Río Negro** (dā rē'ō nāg'rō), town (pop. 468), Amazonas territory, S Venezuela, landing on Río Negro and 260 mi. S of Puerto Ayacucho, in tropical forest (rubber, balata); 1°55'N 67°4'W. **2** Town (1941 pop. 3,761; 1950 census 7,174), ⊙ Cojedes state, N Venezuela, on Tirgua (or San Carlos) R., on Acarigua–Valencia highway and 130 mi. WSW of Caracas; 9°40'N 68°36'W. In agr. region (corn, sugar cane, yucca, rice, cattle); rice milling, dairying, sawmilling. Airfield. Founded 1678 by Capuchin monks. Formerly ⊙ Falcón state, of which Cojedes and Portuguesa states once formed part. **3** Town (pop. 569), Zulia state, NW Venezuela, on SE tip of San Carlos Isl. in S Gulf of Venezuela, 23 mi. N of Maracaibo; fishing. **4** or **San Carlos del Zulia** (děl sōō'lyä), town (pop. 4,258), Zulia state, NW Venezuela, landing on Escalante R. and 60 mi. WNW of Mérida. Transships agr. products (cacao, coffee); sugar-cane growing, cattle raising.

San Carlos Alzatate, Guatemala: see ALZATATE.

San Carlos Bay, Fla.: see CALOOSAHATCHEE RIVER.

San Carlos Borromeo Mission, Calif.: see CARMEL.

San Carlos Centro (sän kär'lōs sěn'trō), town (pop. estimate 2,500), E central Santa Fe prov., Argentina, 25 mi. WSW of Santa Fe; agr. center (wheat, flax, alfalfa, corn, livestock, poultry); dairying.

San Carlos de Bariloche (sän kär'lōs dā bärēlō'chā), town (1947 pop. 6,362), ⊙ Bariloche dept., SW Río Negro natl. territory, Argentina, on S shore of L. Nahuel Huapí and 225 mi. SW of Neuquén. Rail terminus. Main summer and winter resort in Argentine lake dist.; numerous hotels. Skiing on slopes of near-by peaks Otto and López. Funicular railway to Cerro Catedral. Also lumbering, limequarrying, salmon-breeding center. Has mus. of Patagonia, customhouse, seismographic station, airport. Settled 1905 by Swiss immigrants, it resembles an Alpine village. Near by is an atomic-energy research plant.

San Carlos de la Rápita (lä rä'pētä), city (pop. 7,065), Tarragona prov., NE Spain, in Catalonia, port on Puerto de los Alfaques bay of the Mediterranean, near S edge of Ebro R. delta (rice growing), 14 mi. SSE of Tortosa. Ships rice, oranges, and salt (worked on sandspit across bay); fishing; sawmilling. Cereals, olive oil, fruit, vegetables. Canal to Amposta.

San Carlos del Valle (děl vä'lyā), town (pop. 1,754), Ciudad Real prov., S central Spain, 37 mi. E of Ciudad Real; olives, cereals, grapes.

San Carlos del Zulia, Venezuela: see SAN CARLOS.

San Carlos de Río Negro, Venezuela: see SAN CARLOS, Amazonas territory.

San Carlos Island (sän kär'lōs), Zulia state, NW Venezuela, on SW shore of Gulf of Venezuela at N gate of Tablazo Bay, separated from mainland by small river, 23 mi. N of Maracaibo; 18 mi. long NW–SE, up to 4 mi. wide. Toas Isl. is off SE tip.

San Carlos Reservoir, Ariz.: see COOLIDGE DAM.

San Carlos River, Bolivia: see SAN RAFAEL RIVER.

San Carlos River (sän kär'lōs), Alajuela prov., N Costa Rica, rises in Aguacate Mts. 10 mi. NW of San Ramón, flows 70 mi. NNE, past Muelle de San Carlos (head of navigation), to San Juan R. 35 mi. ENE of San Juan del Norte. Navigable in lower and middle course. Receives Arenal R. (left).

San Carlos River (săn kär'lōs), formed by confluence of 2 forks near Gila Mts., SE Ariz., flows c.40 mi. W and S, past San Carlos village, to San Carlos Reservoir (in Gila R.). Drains San Carlos Indian Reservation.

San Carlos River, Venezuela: see TIRGUA RIVER.

San Carlos Sija, Guatemala: see SIJA.

San Casciano in Val di Pesa (sän käshä'nô ēn väl dē pā'zä), town (pop. 2,343), Firenze prov., Tuscany, central Italy, near Pesa R., 8 mi. SW of Florence; wine making. Has 14th-cent. church.

San Casimiro (sän käsēmē'rō), town (pop. 2,046), Aragua state, N Venezuela, 35 mi. SSW of Caracas; coffee, cacao, corn, sugar.

San Cataldo (sän kätäl'dô), town (pop. 15,863), Caltanissetta prov., central Sicily, 4 mi. W of Caltanissetta. Rich sulphur mines (S).

San Cayetano (sän kīētä'nō), town (pop. 4,156), S Buenos Aires prov., Argentina, 50 mi. WNW of Necochea; grain and livestock center.

San Cebrián de Mudá (sän thāvrēän' dā mōōdhä'), mining village (pop. 412), Palencia prov., N central Spain, on S slopes of Cantabrian Mts., 48 mi. SW of Santander. Anthracite and bituminous mines.

Sancellas (sän-thě'lyäs), town (pop. 1,695), Majorca, Balearic Isls., 14 mi. ENE of Palma; cereals, almonds, apricots, wine, livestock. Lumbering; hunting; shoe mfg.

San Celoní (sän thālōnē'), town (pop. 4,749), Barcelona prov., NE Spain, 8 mi. NNW of Arenys de Mar; cork processing, sawmilling; mfg. of cotton fabrics, cement, electrical equipment, dairy products; cattle, cereals, hazelnuts.

Sancergues (säsârg'), village (pop. 575), Cher dept., central France, 16 mi. NW of Nevers; woodworking, cattle raising; iron deposits near by. Has church with Romanesque choir, 13th-cent. nave.

Sancerre (säsâr'), village (pop. 1,565), Cher dept., central France, on hill overlooking Loire valley, 26 mi. NE of Bourges; center of renowned winegrowing dist.; large printshops. Has winding streets, 15th–16th-cent. houses and the 15th-cent. Tour des Fiefs. Long a Huguenot stronghold, it capitulated after 8-month siege in 1573, and was economically ruined by the Wars of Religion.

Sancerrois Hills (säsěrwä'), Cher dept., central France, extend c.25 mi. WSW–ENE bet. Saint-Martin d'Auxigny and Sancerre, rising to 1,420 ft. SE of Henrichemont. Well-known Sancerre vineyards on E slopes adjoining Loire valley.

San Cesario di Lecce (sän chězä'rēô dē lět'chě), town (pop. 5,541), Lecce prov., Apulia, S Italy, 3 mi. S of Lecce, in cereal- and tobacco-growing region; wine, alcohol, olive oil. Has 17th-cent. palace.

San Cesario sul Panaro (sōōl pänä'rô), village (pop. 1,088), Modena prov., Emilia-Romagna, N central Italy, near Panaro R., 8 mi. SE of Modena; paper mills. Has Romanesque church.

Sancha or **San-ch'a** (sän'chä'), Jap. *Sansa* (sän'sä), village (1935 pop. 2,485), NW Formosa, 10 mi. S of Miaoli and on railroad; oolong and black tea; stock raising; sericulture.

Sanchakow, Manchuria: see TUNGNING.

Sanchan, Manchuria: see KOSHAN.

Sánchez (sän'chěs), town (1950 pop. 3,135), Samaná prov., E Dominican Republic, port at head of Samaná Bay, near mouth of Yuna R., 18 mi. W of Samaná; rail terminus, trading and shipping point for E section of fertile Cibao region (cacao, rice, coffee, tobacco, beeswax, timber, cattle). Railroad shops, sawmills; airfield. Also bathing and fishing. Vessels anchor offshore.

Sánchez (sän'chěs), village, Río Negro dept., W Uruguay, 35 mi. ENE of Fray Bentos; grain, wheat, cattle, sheep.

Sanchi (sän'chē), village, N Bhopal state, India, 26 mi. NE of Bhopal, near Betwa R., on E side of flat-topped sandstone hill rising c.300 ft. above surrounding country, on which stands famous group of Buddhist monuments, the best preserved in India. Most noteworthy is the Great Stupa, probably begun by Asoka in mid-3d cent. B.C. and later enlarged by stone casings (2d–1st cent. B.C.); has terraced balustrade and outer railing with 4 gateways (1st cent. B.C.); c.120 ft. in diameter at base (including balustrade), c.54 ft. high. Detailed carvings on gateways depict many scenes from Buddha's life. Other notable remains include smaller stupas, structural chaitya hall (c.7th cent. A.D.), stump of Asokan pillar with inscription, and several monasteries (4th–11th cent. A.D.). Although not connected with life of Buddha, Sanchi was important Buddhist center from 3d cent. B.C. to 12th cent. A.D. Extensive excavations and restoration carried out, 1912–19. Small mus. (built 1919) has sculptures, inscriptions, and other fragments.

San-chiang, China: see SANKIANG.

Sanchidrián (sänchēdhryän'), town (pop. 1,007), Ávila prov., central Spain, 17 mi. NNE of Ávila; grain, grapes, vegetables, fruit, livestock; flour milling, tile mfg.

San Chirico Raparo (sän kē'rēkô räpä'rô), village (pop. 2,715), Potenza prov., Basilicata, S Italy, 12 mi. ESE of Moliterno; wine making.

Sanchis y Miláns del Bosch, El (ěl sän'chēs ē mēläns' děl bōsch'), outer industrial suburb (pop. 6,578) of Barcelona, NE Spain, near Besós R., 6 mi. NNW of city center.

Sanchoku, Korea: see SAMCHOK.

Sanchonuño (sänchōnōō'nyō), town (pop. 959), Segovia prov., central Spain, 28 mi. NNW of Segovia; cereals, grapes, livestock; timber, resins. Chicory drying.

Sanchursk (sŭnchōōrsk'), town (1948 pop. over 2,000), SW Kirov oblast, Russian SFSR, on Greater Kokshaga R. and 32 mi. NW of Ioshkar-Ola; food processing. Until 1918, Tsarevo-sanchursk.

Sancian Island, China: see SAINT JOHN ISLAND.

San Cipirello (sän chēpērěl'lô), village (pop. 4,524), Palermo prov., NW Sicily, adjacent to San Giuseppe Iato, 15 mi. SW of Palermo, in grape- and cereal-growing region, macaroni. Also written Sancipirello.

San Cipriano, Bahía de, Río de Oro: see SAINT CYPRIAN BAY.

San Clemente (sän kläměn'tā), town (pop. 1,749), Talca prov., central Chile, on railroad and 13 mi. SE of Talca; agr. center (grain, wine, beans, livestock); dairying, flour milling.

San Clemente, town (pop. 5,715), Cuenca prov., E central Spain, in La Mancha region of New Castile, 40 mi. NW of Albacete; trades in agr. produce (saffron, potatoes, grapes, fruit, livestock). Flour milling, cheese making; mfg. of plaster, rubber stockings. Historic town was old ⊙ upper La Mancha. Preserves several fine bldgs., such as consistory, collegiate church (formerly of Knights Templars), Jesuit col., Inquisition palace.

San Clemente (săn klĭměn'tē), residential city (pop. 2,008), Orange co., S Calif., on the Pacific, 26 mi. SSE of Santa Ana. Founded in 1920s as real-estate development restricted to Spanish-type architecture. State park (beach) adjacent.

San Clemente, Cerro, Chile: see SAN VALENTÍN, CERRO.

San Clemente de Llobregat (dā lyōvrägät'), village (pop. 1,203), Barcelona prov., NE Spain, 10 mi. WSW of Barcelona; red-lead processing. Grows perfume plants.

San Clemente Island, Calif.: see SANTA BARBARA ISLANDS.

Sancoins (säkwē'), town (pop. 2,949), Cher dept., central France, on Aubois R. and Berry Canal, and 16 mi. SW of Nevers; cattle-fattening and agr. trade center; brick- and tileworks; mfg. of rubber goods.

San Colombano al Lambro (sän kôlômbä'nô äl läm'brô), town (pop. 5,428), Milano prov., Lombardy, N Italy, on Lambro R. and 9 mi. S of Lodi; agr. center. Noted for its mineral waters.

Sancos (säng'kōs), town (pop. 1,290), Ayacucho dept., S Peru, on W slopes of Cordillera Occidental, 30 mi. SSE of Puquio; alt. 7,821 ft.; wheat, corn, alfalfa, livestock.

San Cosme (sän kōz'mā), village (pop. estimate 1,000), ⊙ San Cosme dept. (□ c.200; pop. 9,011), NW Corrientes prov., Argentina, 20 mi. ENE of Corrientes; rail terminus and agr. center (alfalfa, sugar cane, cotton, livestock); sugar refining.

San Cosme, town (dist. pop. 3,755), Itapúa dept., SE Paraguay, on the Paraná and 28 mi. W of Encarnación; maté, fruit, livestock; lumbering. Old Jesuit mission.

San Cristóbal (sän krēstō'bäl), town (pop. estimate 4,000), ⊙ San Cristóbal dept. (□ 5,700; 1947 census 69,454), central Santa Fe prov., Argentina, 95 mi. NNW of Santa Fe; rail junction (with workshops); commercial and agr. center (flax, wheat, corn, livestock); dairying. Airport.

San Cristóbal, town, Potosí dept., SW Bolivia, near Río Grande de Lípez and 55 mi. SSW of Uyuni; alt. 14,304 ft.; alpaca, quinoa.

San Cristóbal, town (pop. 3,346), Pinar del Río prov., W Cuba, on small San Cristóbal R., on Central Highway and on railroad, and 45 mi. ENE of Pinar del Río; agr. and processing center (tobacco, sugar, coffee, fruit, cattle); apiculture.

San Cristóbal, city (1935 pop. 4,479; 1950 pop. 9,668), ⊙ Trujillo prov., S Dominican Republic, 5 mi. from the Caribbean, on highway, and 15 mi. WSW of Ciudad Trujillo; trading center in fertile agr. region (rice, coffee, potatoes, tubers, sugar cane, fruit, livestock). Attractive modern city with Palace of Justice, historical mus., arsenal (mfg. of small arms and munitions), agr. school. Founded by Sp. settlers in 1575, when gold was discovered. The 1st constitution of Dominican Republic was signed here in 1844. Trujillo b. here.

San Cristóbal, village, San Cristóbal Isl., Galápagos Isls., Ecuador, inland just E of Puerto Baquerizo; sugar-cane growing and milling.

San Cristóbal. 1 or **San Cristóbal Verapaz** (värāpäs'), town (1950 pop. 2,842), Alta Verapaz dept., central Guatemala, in N highlands, 7 mi. SW of Cobán, on small L. San Cristóbal; alt. 4,530 ft.; market center; coffee, sugar cane, livestock; tanning, mfg. (leather goods, shoes). **2** or **San Cristóbal Acasaguastlán** (äkäsägwäslän'), town (1950 pop. 293), El Progreso dept., E central Guatemala, on Motagua R. and 11 mi. ENE of El Progreso; corn, beans, livestock. Has old colonial church. Sometimes called Acasaguastlán. **3** or **San Cristóbal Frontera** (frōntā'rä), village (1940 pop. 289), Jutiapa dept., SE Guatemala, in highlands, 16 mi. SE of Jutiapa, on Salvador border; customs station on Inter-American Highway. **4** or **San Cristóbal Totonicapán** (tōtōnēkäpän'), town (1950 pop. 5,300), Totonicapán dept., W central Guatemala, on Samalá R. and 5 mi. W of Totonicapán, on Inter-American Highway; alt. 7,874 ft. Market and textile (silk and woolen cloth) center; flour milling; wheat, corn, beans. Has colonial church, built by Franciscan friars.

San Cristóbal, volcano, Nicaragua: see EL VIEJO.

San Cristobal (săn krĭ'stŭbôl), volcanic island, Solomon Isls., SW Pacific, 40 mi. SE of Guadalcanal; c.80 mi. long, 25 mi. wide; copra. Sometimes spelled San Cristoval.

San Cristóbal (sän krēstō'bäl), city (1941 pop. 31,447; 1950 census 56,073), ⊙ Táchira state, W Venezuela, in Andean uplands at SW end of Sierra Nevada de Mérida, on transandine highway and 21 mi. ESE of Cúcuta (Colombia), 385 mi. WNW of Caracas; 7°46'N 72°15'W; alt. 2,705 ft. Commercial center in coffee country (also growing cacao, corn, wheat, cotton, sugar cane; cattle); outlet for W llanos. Has tanneries, cigarette factories, liquor distilleries, cement plant, asphalt mine. Iron and coal deposits near by. Bishopric. Founded 1561. Heavily damaged in 1875 earthquake. Santo Domingo airport is 17 mi. SE.

San Cristóbal Acasaguastlán, Guatemala: see SAN CRISTÓBAL.

San Cristóbal de Entreviñas (sän krēstō'bäl dā ĕntrāvē'nyäs), village (pop. 1,569), Zamora prov., NW Spain, 4 mi. NE of Benavente; cereals, vegetables, wine; lumbering, sheep raising.

San Cristóbal de las Casas (läs kä'säs) or **Ciudad de las Casas** (syōō-dhädh'), city (pop. 11,768), Chiapas, S Mexico, in Sierra de Hueytepec, 32 mi. E of Tuxtla; alt. c.7,000 ft. Processing, trading, and agr. center (cereals, fruit, sugar cane, livestock); tanning, alcohol and liquor distilling, flour milling, fruit canning, lumbering, mfg. of native footwear. Famous for silver saddles. Airfield. Has theater, institute of arts and sciences, cathedral, church of Santo Domingo (begun 1547). Founded c.1530 as Ciudad Real. Later named for Bartolomé de las Casas, protector of Indians and 1st bishop of diocese. Was state capital until 1891.

San Cristóbal Frontera, Guatemala: see SAN CRISTÓBAL.

San Cristóbal Huichochitlán, Mexico: see SAN CRISTÓBAL.

San Cristóbal Island or **Chatham Island** (chă'tŭm) (□ 195; 1950 pop. 802), E Galápagos Isls., Ecuador, in the Pacific, c.600 mi. W of Ecuador coast; PUERTO BAQUERIZO, its port, is at 0°53'S 89°37'W. A volcanic isl. (26 mi. long), it rises to 4,490 ft. The most populated and productive isl. of the archipelago, it grows sugar cane, coffee, yucca; there is cattle raising, fishing. Lime quarries. Puerto Baquerizo, administrative center of the Galápagos, is also a military base. San Cristóbal village has a sugar mill.

San Cristóbal Totonicapán, Guatemala: see SAN CRISTÓBAL.

San Cristóbal Verapaz, Guatemala: see SAN CRISTÓBAL.

San Cristoval, Solomon Isls.: see SAN CRISTOBAL.

Sancta Maria (săngk'tŭ mŭrē'ŭ), mission station, Barotse prov., W Northern Rhodesia, on Zambezi R. and 60 mi. N of Mongu; fishing; corn, millet; hardwood.

Sancti Spíritu (sängk'tē spē'rētōō), town (pop. estimate 2,000), SW Santa Fe prov., Argentina, 25 mi. SW of Venado Tuerto; agr. center (wheat, flax, alfalfa, corn, potatoes, livestock); meat packing, dairying.

Sancti-Spíritus (–tōōs), city (pop. 28,262), Las Villas prov., central Cuba, on Central Highway, on railroad and 45 mi. SE of Santa Clara, 20 mi. N of its port Tunas de Zaza. Trading and processing center in fertile agr. region (sugar cane, tobacco, cattle). Dairying, tanning, lumbering; mfg. of straw hats, pottery, cigars, condensed milk, jerked beef. The old city (founded 1514) preserves its colonial atmosphere—streets are crooked, there are fine churches and plazas. Bartolomé de las Casas here advocated (1516) tolerant treatment of the Indians. In early times frequently subjected to pirate attacks. Gold, copper, and asphalt deposits near by.

Sancti Spíritus. 1 Town (pop. 846), Badajoz prov., W Spain, 34 mi. E of Villanueva de la Serena; cereals, olives, wool, livestock; mfg. of tiles. **2** Village (pop. 1,637), Salamanca prov., W Spain, 10 mi. NE of Ciudad Rodrigo; potatoes, cereals.

Sancti-Spíritus, Sierra de (syĕ'rä dā), small mountain range, Las Villas prov., central Cuba, 7 mi. SW of Sancti-Spíritus city; 10 mi. long NW-SE; rises to 2,785 ft. (Loma de Banao). Yields tropical timber.

Sanctórum (sängktō'rōōm), town (pop. 1,043), Tlaxcala, central Mexico, 20 mi. NW of Tlaxcala; maguey, grain, livestock.

San Cugat del Vallés (sän kōōgät' dĕl välyās'), town (pop. 4,950), Barcelona prov., NE Spain, 8 mi. NW of Barcelona; mfg. of woolen and cotton fabrics, leather goods, rugs, furniture; sawmilling. Wine, cereals, fruit. Lead deposits. Has Romanesque convent-church with cloisters.

Sancy, Puy de, France: see PUY DE SANCY.

Sand (sän), village (pop. 519; canton pop. 1,136), Rogaland co., SW Norway, on Sand Fjord, at mouth of Suldal R., 35 mi. E of Haugesun in the Ryfylke; tannery, box and barrel factory.

Sanda (sän'dä), town (pop. 8,357), Hyogo prefecture, S Honshu, Japan, 15 mi. NNE of Kobe; rail junction in agr. area (rice, wheat); sake, raw silk, pottery. Agr. and forestry schools.

Sanda (săn'dŭ), island (pop. 14), S Argyll, Scotland, in North Channel at mouth of Kilbrannan Sound, 2 mi. S of Kintyre peninsula; c.1 mi. long; rises to 405 ft. At S end is lighthouse (55°16'N 5°34'W).

Sandabast (săn'däbäst"), village (pop. 8,294), Gharbiya prov., Lower Egypt, on Damietta branch of the Nile and 1 mi. SSE of Zifta; cotton.

Sandafa el Far or **Sandafa al-Far** (both: săn'dăfā ĕl făr'), village (pop. 7,495), Minya prov., Upper Egypt, on the Bahr Yusuf and 9 mi. WNW of Beni Mazar; cotton, cereals, sugar cane.

Sandakan (sŭndŭkän'), largest town (1951 pop. 14,045, with environs) of Br. North Borneo, port on Sandakan Harbour (inlet of Sulu Sea, 20 mi. long, 3–10 mi. wide), 140 mi. E of Jesselton; 5°50'N 118°5'E; ⊙ East Coast residency; trade center for rubber-producing and lumbering area. Sawmills, fisheries. Virtually destroyed in Second World War. Until June, 1947, town was ⊙ Br. North Borneo; succeeded by Jesselton.

Sandal, England: see WAKEFIELD.

San Dalmazio (sän dälmä'tsyô), village (pop. 311), Pisa prov., Tuscany, central Italy, 10 mi. S of Volterra; copper mining.

San Dalmazzo di Tenda, France: see SAINT-DALMAS-DE-TENDE.

Sandalwood Island, Fiji: see VANUA LEVU.

Sandalwood Island, Indonesia: see SUMBA.

Sandalwood Strait, Indonesia: see SUMBA STRAIT.

San Damiano d'Asti (sän dämyä'nô dä'stē), village (pop. 2,309), Asti prov., Piedmont, NW Italy, 8 mi. SW of Asti, in grape- and peach-growing region; clothing, wood, food industries.

San Damián Texoloc, Mexico: see TEXOLOC.

Sandane, Norway: see VEREIDE.

San Daniele del Carso, Yugoslavia: see STANJEL NA KRASU.

San Daniele del Friuli (sän dänyā'lĕ dĕl frē'ōōlē), town (pop. 5,218), Udine prov., Friuli–Venezia Giulia, NE Italy, near Tagliamento R., 12 mi. NW of Udine; shoes, sausage, awnings. Has library (founded 1464) with 11th–16th-cent. MSS, and cathedral containing altarpiece by Pordenone.

Sandanski (sändän'skē), city (pop. 7,422), Gorna Dzhumaya dist., SW Bulgaria, in Macedonia, in Struma R. valley, 32 mi. SSE of Gorna Dzhumaya; agr. center (tobacco, cotton, wine, opium). Has thermal springs and baths. Called Sveti Vrach until 1949.

Sandar, Norway: see SANDEFJORD.

Sandau (zän'dou), town (pop. 1,632), in former Prussian Saxony prov., central Germany, after 1945 in Saxony-Anhalt, on the Elbe and 15 mi. NE of Stendal; brick mfg. Has late-Romanesque church.

Sanday (săn'dā). **1** Island (pop. 20), Inner Hebrides, Inverness, Scotland, 2 mi. NW of Rum, just off SE coast of Canna; 2 mi. long, 1 mi. wide. **2** Island (□ 21.4, including NORTH RONALDSAY isl.; pop. 1,160) of the Orkneys, Scotland, 2 mi. E of Eday and 3 mi. N of Stronsay; 13 mi. long, 5 mi. wide; rises to 216 ft. Consists of 3 long peninsulas joined in center; NE peninsulas form excellent harbor of Otters Wick. On Start Point (E) is lighthouse (59°17'N 2°23'W). Farming and fishing are main occupations. Has prehistoric remains.

Sandbach (săn'băch), urban district (1931 pop. 6,411; 1951 census 9,250), S central Cheshire, England, 5 mi. NE of Crewe; salt mining, motor-vehicle construction, soap mfg. Site of 2 well-known Saxon crosses. Near by, 16th-cent. church.

Sandbank, village, E Argyll, Scotland, on Holy Loch, 3 mi. N of Dunoon; resort. S is resort village of Ardnadam.

Sandborn, town (pop. 572), Knox co., SW Ind., 24 mi. NE of Vincennes, in agr. and bituminous-coal area.

Sandcoulee (sănd"kōōlē'), coal-mining village, Cascade co., W central Mont., 8 mi. SE of Great Falls.

Sanddola (săn'dŭlä), Nor. *Sanddøla*, river in Nord-Trondelag co., central Norway, rises in lake near Swedish border E of Grong, flows 45 mi. W to Nams R. at Grong.

Sande (săn'nŭ), village (pop. 524; canton pop. 4,447), Vestfold co., SE Norway, on Oslo Fjord, on railroad and 10 mi. S of Drammen; tannery, machine shop, dairy products.

Sandefjord (săn'nŭfyōr), city (pop. 6,302), Vestfold co., SE Norway, port at head of a 6-mi. fjord near mouth of Oslo Fjord, on railroad and 12 mi. SSW of Tonsberg; shipping and fishing center, with a large whaling fleet. Has whale-oil refineries, shipyards, machinery and chemical works; and mfg. of shoes, tar, tobacco products. Formerly known for its mineral springs. Town dates from 14th cent. Just ENE is GOKSTAD, where anc. Viking ship was excavated. Sandar canton (pop. 17,454), which surrounds city, engages in fishing and whaling, and has machine shops, tannery, flour mill, fish- and vegetable-oil factory.

Sandeid (săn'ād), village and canton (pop. 774), Rogaland co., SW Norway, at head of 13-mi.-long Sandeid Fjord (a N arm of Bokn Fjord), 22 mi. ENE of Haugesund; agr., lumbering. Formerly spelled Sandejd.

San Demetrio Corone (sän dĕmā'trēô kôrô'nĕ), village (pop. 2,362), Cosenza prov., Calabria, S Italy, 20 mi. NNE of Cosenza, in stock-raising, fruit-growing region.

Sandene, Norway: see VEREIDE.

Sanderay, Scotland: see SANDRAY.

Sanderey, Du. Guiana: see ZANDERIJ.

Sanders, county (□ 2,811; pop. 6,983), NW Mont.; ⊙ Thompson Falls. Agr. region bordering on Idaho; drained by the Clark Fork and Flathead R. Livestock, grain, dairy products. Cabinet Mts. and Cabinet Natl. Forest in NW. Formed 1905.

Sanders, town (pop. 206), Carroll co., N Ky., on Eagle Creek and 13 mi. E of Carrollton.

Sandersdorf (zän'dŭrsdôrf), village (pop. 7,499), in former Prussian Saxony prov., central Germany, after 1945 in Saxony-Anhalt, 2 mi. WNW of Bitterfeld; lignite mining; chemical mfg.

Sandersleben (zän'dŭrslā"bŭn), town (pop. 4,385), in former Anhalt state, central Germany, after 1945 in Saxony-Anhalt, on the Wipper and 11 mi. SW of Bernburg; rail junction; machinery mfg., metalworking.

Sanderson, village (pop. 2,047), ⊙ Terrell co., extreme W Texas, near the Rio Grande, on Del Rio–El Paso highway and c.75 mi. ESE of Alpine; shipping, trading point for sheep, goat, cattle ranching region; railroad shops, airport.

Sanderson's Hope, Greenland: see KAERSORSSUAK.

Sanderstead, England: see COULSDON AND PURLEY.

Sandersville. 1 City (pop. 4,480), ⊙ Washington co., E central Ga., c.50 mi. ENE of Macon; trade and processing center; vegetable canning, cotton, lumber, and paper milling; kaolin mining. Founded 1796, inc. 1812. **2** Town (pop. 681), Jones co., SE Miss., 9 mi. NE of Laurel; oil refinery.

Sandesund, Norway: see SARPSBORG.

Sandfield, village (pop. 2,357, with adjacent Pricedale), Westmoreland co., SW Pa., 13 mi. S of McKeesport.

Sand Fjord (sän), NE branch of Bokn Fjord, Rogaland co., SW Norway, extends 15 mi. NE to village of Sand, where it branches into 12-mi. Sauda Fjord (N) and 14-mi. Hyle Fjord (NE).

Sandfly (sănd'flī), village (pop. 371), SE Tasmania, 10 mi. SW of Hobart; coal mines.

Sandford-on-Thames (săn'fŭrd, tĕmz'), village and parish (pop. 426), S Oxfordshire, England, on the Thames and 3 mi. SSE of Oxford; paper mills. Site of Templars' preceptory, founded 1274.

Sandgate (sănd'gāt, –gĭt), town (pop. 12,057), SE Queensland, Australia, on Moreton Bay, 10 mi. NNE of Brisbane; seaside resort.

Sandgate, former urban district (1931 pop. 2,190), SE Kent, England, on the Channel 2 mi. W of Folkestone; seaside resort and coastguard station. Has remains of castle built by Henry VIII. Was site of Shorncliffe Camp, major military training area in First World War.

Sandgate, town (pop. 158), Bennington co., SW Vt., on N.Y. line, 20 mi. N of Bennington.

Sandgerdi or **Sandgerdhi** (sänt'gĕr"dhē), Icelandic *Sandgerði*, fishing village (pop. 420), Gullbringu og Kjosar co., SW Iceland, on W shore of Reykjanes Peninsula, 25 mi. WSW of Reykjavik.

Sandhausen (zänt'hou"zŭn), village (pop. 6,219), N Baden, Germany, after 1945 in Württemberg-Baden, 4 mi. NNW of Wiesloch; mfg. of cigars and cigarettes; paper milling.

Sandhaven, fishing village in Pitsligo parish, N Aberdeen, Scotland, on North Sea, 2 mi. W of Fraserburgh. Site of ruins of 17th-cent. Pittulie Castle.

Sandhem (sänd'hām"), village (pop. 605), Skaraborg co., S Sweden, 15 mi. SE of Falkoping; peat digging, metalworking.

Sandhill River, rises in small lake in Polk co., NW Minn., flows 80 mi. W, past Winger and Fertile, to Red R. near Climax. Canalized in lower course.

Sandhills, village, Mass.: see SCITUATE.

Sandhills or **Sand Hills,** SE U.S., belt (20–40 mi. wide) of sandy, low (to c.500 ft. alt.) hills extending along inner border of the coastal plain, from central Ga. on SW, across S.C. to central N.C. on NE. Native vegetation is mainly pine, oak; cotton and peaches are grown, and several areas (esp. Southern Pines and Pinehurst, N.C., Aiken and Camden, S.C.) are noted winter resorts, with generally mild and sunny winter climate.

Sandhurst, Australia: see BENDIGO.

Sandhurst, residential town and parish (pop. 3,702), SE Berkshire, England, on Blackwater R. and 10 mi. SE of Reading, N of Aldershot. Royal Military Col., here, was founded at Great Marlow in 1802.

Sandi (sŭn'dē), town (pop. 7,416), Hardoi dist., central Uttar Pradesh, India, on tributary of the Ramganga and 13 mi. SW of Hardoi; rail spur terminus; mfg. of blankets and cotton cloth; trades in wheat, gram, barley, millet, oilseeds.

Sandia (sän'dyä), city (pop. 1,720), ⊙ Sandia prov. (□ 5,864; pop. 37,211), Puno dept., SE Peru, on N slopes of Cordillera Oriental of the Andes, 110 mi. NNE of Puno; alt. 6,666 ft. Coca, tobacco, corn.

Sandia (sănde'ŭ). **1** Pueblo (□ 35.8), Sandoval and Bernalillo counties, central N.Mex. Sandia village (1948 pop. 141) is on E bank of the Rio Grande and 12 mi. N of Albuquerque in irrigated region; alt. c.5,000 ft. Annual fiesta and dance June 13 honors Our Lady of Sorrows. U.S. Indian school and ruins of 17th-cent. mission and monastery are here. Present village settled c.1740. Sandia Mts. are just E. **2** Village (pop. c.300), Jim Wells co., S Texas, 32 mi. WNW of Corpus Christi, near Nueces R.; trade, shipping point in area producing oil, natural gas, dairy products, truck.

Sandia Base, N.Mex.: see ALBUQUERQUE.

Sandiacre, town and parish (pop. 4,513), SE Derby, England, on Erewash R. and 6 mi. WSW of Nottingham; cotton and silk milling; lace mfg. Church dates from 14th cent.

Sandia Mountains (sănde'ŭ), central N.Mex., E of the Rio Grande, NE of Albuquerque; largely within part of Cibola Natl. Forest. Prominent points: South Sandia Peak (9,900 ft.); Sandia Peak (10,695 ft.), highest point in range.

San Diego (săn dēā'gō), county (□ 4,258; 1940 pop. 289,348; 1950 pop. 556,808), S Calif., bounded W by the Pacific, S by Mexico border; ⊙ San Diego.

Rolling coastal plain (W), mts. (center), COLORADO DESERT (E). Cuyamaca Peak (6,515 ft.) is 35 mi. ENE of San Diego; Mt. Palomar (astronomical observatory) is 45 mi. NNE of San Diego. Includes part of Cleveland Natl. Forest. Cabrillo Natl. Monument is near San Diego; Anza Desert State Park is in E. Drained by Santa Margarita, San Luis Rey, Sweetwater, Otay, and San Diego rivers and Cottonwood Creek. Many Indian reservations. Cattle ranching and agr. in valleys and on coastal plain; citrus fruit, truck, avocados, lima beans, hay, grain, grapes, olives, apples, walnuts; flower and bulb growing, poultry raising, dairying. Mfg. (especially aircraft) in San Diego metropolitan area; processing industries in smaller towns. Ocean fisheries (from San Diego) are important. Coast and mtn. resorts, hot springs, sport fishing, scenery attract vacationers; equable coast climate has made it winter-resort area. Quarrying and mining (sand, gravel, clay, salt, magnesia, gem stones). Formed 1850.

San Diego. 1 City (□ 105.8; 1940 pop. 203,341; 1950 pop. 334,387), ⊙ San Diego co., S Calif., on E shore of San Diego Bay, c.15 mi. from Mexico border and 110 mi. SSE of Los Angeles; 32°43'N 117°10'W; alt. varies from sea level to c.820 ft. Long a residential and year-round resort city (beaches; sport fishing), noted for mild climate (most equable in U.S.) of cool (67°F.) summers and temperate (55°F.) winters, San Diego has had huge pop. increase in recent years, stimulated by growing industries (especially aircraft mfg.), and activity of military and naval installations. Has one of best natural harbors in U.S.; port's chief commerce is inbound (coastwise and foreign), but it also ships canned fish, agr. produce (it is water outlet for Imperial Valley), minerals, and manufactured goods; receives petroleum, steel, lumber, and raw materials. Port of entry. Leading U.S. tuna port, whose fishing fleet supplies 6 canneries here. Served by transcontinental rail, bus, air lines. Major U.S. naval base: naval air station at North Isl. (tip of Coronado peninsula across the bay); also has marine base, naval and marine training schools, naval hosp., army and coast guard installations, and a large municipal airport (Lindbergh Field). Processing industries handle fish (more than ½ of U.S. tuna), meat, fruit, vegetables, and dairy products; also brewing, sugar refining, boatbuilding, and mfg. of building materials. Seat of San Diego State Col. (coeducational; 1897); Army and Navy Acad.; a jr. col. Balboa Park (1,400 acres) contains permanent bldgs. erected for Panama-California International Exposition (1915–16) and for California Pacific International Exposition (1935–36); park has museums, art galleries, zoological and botanical gardens, an open-air pavilion with one of world's largest organs. Other points of interest: Old Town, city's oldest dist., with adobe bldgs. dating from early-19th cent.; restored Mission San Diego de Alcalá; Presidio Hill; Serra Mus.; Cabrillo Natl. Monument, on Point LOMA; the community of CORONADO, across bay; and outlying residential and resort communities within San Diego city limits (LA JOLLA, Pacific Beach, Mission Beach, Point Loma, Encanto, Ocean Beach). First permanent white settlement in Calif.; Cabrillo entered bay in 1542, and site was visited 1602 by Vizcaíno. Junípero Serra here established 1st of Calif. missions—San Diego de Alcalá—in 1769. Settlement was organized as a pueblo in 1834 and inc. as a city in 1850, after coming of U.S. rule. **2** City (pop. 4,397), ⊙ Duval co., S Texas, 10 mi. W of Alice; a rail, trade center for area producing oil, natural gas, salt, cattle, corn. Inc. 1935.

San Diego (sän dyā'gō), town (pop. 894), Carabobo state, N Venezuela, 5 mi. NNE of Valencia; cotton, sugar cane, corn, fruit, livestock.

San Diego, Cape (sän dyā'gō), easternmost point of main isl. of Tierra del Fuego, Argentina, on the South Atlantic, at N entrance of LeMaire Strait; 54°40'S 65°7'W.

San Diego Bay (săn dēā'gō), S Calif., landlocked natural harbor (12 mi. long, 1–3 mi. wide) of San Diego city, sheltered from the Pacific by overlapping peninsulas (Point Loma, N; Coronado Beach culminating at North Isl., S).

San Diego de Alejandría (sän dyā'gō dā älähändrē'ä), town (pop. 1,257), Jalisco, central Mexico, near Guanajuato border, 22 mi. SW of León; grain, beans, stock.

San Diego de la Unión (lä ōōnyōn'), city (pop. 2,416), Guanajuato, central Mexico, 23 mi. E of Doctor Hernández Alvarez; alt. 6,499 ft.; corn, wheat, sugar cane, vegetables, stock.

San Diego de los Baños (lōs bä'nyōs), town (pop. 702), Pinar del Río prov., W Cuba, resort at S foot of Sierra del Rosario, 26 mi. NE of Pinar del Río. Sulphurous springs.

San Diego del Valle (dĕl vä'yä), town (pop. 1,071), Las Villas prov., central Cuba, on railroad and 12 mi. NW of Santa Clara; sugar cane, tobacco, cattle.

San Diego Islands (săn dēā'gō), 2 islets off NW Trinidad, B.W.I., in the Gulf of Paria, 6 mi. N of Port of Spain. Consists of Carrera Isl. (E), a convict depot, and Cronstadt Isl. (W), a bathing resort.

San Diego River (sän dyā'gō) or **Caiguanabo River** (kīgwänä'bō), Pinar del Río prov., W Cuba, rises in the Sierra del Rosario, flows c.40 mi. S to the Gulf of Batabanó.

San Diego River (săn dēā'gō), San Diego co., S Calif., rises c.25 mi. E of Escondido, flows 52 mi. SW to Mission Bay at San Diego. On upper course is El Capitan Dam (ĕl kăpĭtăn') (270 ft. high, 1,200 ft. long; completed 1935; for water supply). On San Vicente Creek (săn vĭsĕn'tē), a short tributary, is San Vicente Dam (199 ft. high, 980 ft. long; completed 1943; for water supply).

Sandikli (sändŭklŭ'), Turkish *Sandıklı*, town (pop. 7,937), Afyonkarahisar prov., W central Turkey, on railroad and 25 mi. SW of Afyonkarahisar, in opium-poppy growing area; also wheat, barley, chick-peas. Sometimes spelled Sandukli.

Sandila (sŭndē'lŭ), town (pop. 17,526), Hardoi dist., central Uttar Pradesh, India, 30 mi. NW of Lucknow; hand-loom cotton-weaving center; silk weaving; trades in wheat, gram, barley, sugar cane, betel leaves, ghee, firewood. Has 16th-cent. Moslem building with tomb.

San Dimas (sän dē'mäs), town (pop. 749), Durango, N Mexico, on W slopes of Sierra Madre Occidental, 80 mi. W of Durango; alt. 2,953 ft.; silver, gold, lead, copper mining.

San Dimas (săn dē'mŭs), unincorporated town (pop. 1,840), Los Angeles co., S Calif., at base of San Gabriel Mts., 5 mi. NW of Pomona; citrus-fruit groves; nurseries. Seat of Voorhis School for Boys.

Sand in Taufers, Italy: see CAMPO TURES.

San Dionisio (sän dyōnē'syō), town (1950 pop. 459), Matagalpa dept., W central Nicaragua, 17 mi. SSE of Matagalpa; sugar cane, corn, beans, rice, plantains.

Sandisfield, rural town (pop. 437), Berkshire co., SW Mass., in the Berkshires, 24 mi. SSE of Pittsfield, near Conn. line; dairying, maple sugar, cheese. West Branch of Farmington R. skirts township on E. Includes state forests, villages of Montville, New Boston, West New Boston, South Sandisfield.

Sand Lake, village (pop. 394), Kent co., SW Mich., 24 mi. NNE of Grand Rapids; trade center for lake-resort region.

Sand Lake, lake, Minn.: see WABATAWANGANG LAKE.

Sand Mountain, dissected plateau (c.1,500 ft.), largely in De Kalb co., NE Ala., and partly in Dade co., extreme NW Ga.; extends 80 mi. SW from Walden Ridge, near Chattanooga, Tenn., parallel to Lookout Mtn.; part of Cumberland Plateau.

Sandnes (sän'nās). **1** Village, Nordland co., Norway: see SULITJELMA, village. **2** Town (pop. 4,184), Rogaland co., SW Norway, port at head of Gands Fjord (a branch of Bokn Fjord), on railroad and 8 mi. S of Stavanger; industrial center of Jaeren region. Produces galvanized-metal products, bicycles, boat equipment, construction materials (bricks, stone, road material), furniture, clothing, ceramics; exports food products.

Sandnessjoen (sän'nās-shûûn), Nor. *Sandnessjøen*, village (pop. 1,577) in Stamnes canton (pop. 2,392), Nordland co., N central Norway, at N tip of Alsten Isl., 20 mi. NW of Mosjoen; fish canning, woodworking, peat digging; ocean-traffic center for N Norway and the Lofoten and Vesteralen groups. Formerly spelled Sannessjoen, Nor. *Sannessjøen*.

Sando (sä'nû), Dan. *Sandø*, Faeroese *Sandoy*, island (□ 43; pop. 1,590) of the S Faeroe Isls. Terrain is flatter than on most of Faeroes, but only a few sq. mi. are cultivated; fishing, sheep raising.

Sandoa (sändō'ä), town, Katanga prov., S Belgian Congo, on Lulua R. and 345 mi. WNW of Elisabethville, near Angola border; trading center in cotton and coffee area; customs station. Has R.C. and Protestant missions; hosp. for Europeans.

Sandokedal, Norway: see SANNIDAL.

Sandomierz (sändô'myĕsh), Rus. *Sandomir* (sŭndŭmēr'), town (pop. 8,357), Kielce prov., SE Poland, port on left bank of the Vistula and 50 mi. ESE of Kielce, near railroad (station across the Vistula). Linked by pipe line with Jaslo-Krosno natural-gas field; mfg. of rubber products, knit goods, tiles, bricks, flour. Airport. Has many churches, town hall, 14th-cent. castle (now jail) and R.C. cathedral. First known in 1002; became (1139) ⊙ a duchy; then lay W of its present location, but after Tatar invasion (13th cent.) was moved eastward and surrounded by walls (only a gate now remains). Synod (1570) here united all Pol. Protestants. Although attacked by Tatars, Lithuanians, and Swedes and often destroyed, it was (16th cent.) noted for its beauty and was an administrative, commercial, and cultural center. Passed (1795) to Austria and (1815) to Rus. Poland; returned to Poland in 1919.

Sandominic (sûndō'mēnēk), Rum. *Sândominic*, Hung. *Csíkszentdomokos* (chēk'sĕntdô"môkôsh), village (pop. 6,706), Stalin prov., E central Rumania, in Transylvania, on Olt R., in W foothills of the Moldavian Carpathians, 15 mi. N of Mercurea-Ciuc; copper mining and smelting, woodworking, limestone quarrying. In Hungary, 1940–45. Copper is also mined at near-by Balan, 4 mi. NE.

Sandon, village (pop. estimate 100), S B.C., in Selkirk Mts., 30 mi. N of Nelson; silver, lead, zinc mining.

Sandonà (sändōnä'), town (pop. 3,382), Nariño dept., SW Colombia, at NW foot of Galeras Volcano, in S Cordillera Central, 14 mi. WNW of Pasto; alt. 4,391 ft. Cereals, coffee, cacao, sugar cane, potatoes, livestock.

San Donaci (sän dô'nächē), village (pop. 3,821), Brindisi prov., Apulia, S Italy, 13 mi. S of Brindisi; wine, olive oil.

San Donà di Piave (sän dônä' dē pyä'vĕ), town (pop. 8,379), Venezia prov., Veneto, N Italy, on Piave R. and 17 mi. NE of Venice; mfg. (agr. machinery, automobile chassis, jute products, macaroni). Has cathedral. Rebuilt after ruin in First World War.

San-Donato, Russian SFSR: see NIZHNI TAGIL.

San Donato di Lecce (sän dônä'tô dē lĕt'chĕ), village (pop. 2,818), Lecce prov., Apulia, S Italy, 6 mi. S of Lecce.

San Donato in Poggio (ēn pôd'jô), village (pop. 605), Firenze prov., Tuscany, central Italy, near Pesa R., 17 mi. S of Florence; wine making.

San Donato Val di Comino (väl dē kômē'nô), village (pop. 3,032), Frosinone prov., Latium, S central Italy, 11 mi. E of Sora.

Sandorfalva (shän'dôrfŏlvŏ), Hung. *Sándorfalva*, town (pop. 5,964), Csongrad co., S Hungary, 8 mi. N of Szeged; founded after 1879 innundation of Tisza R.; agr.

San Dorligo della Valle (sän dôrlē'go dĕl-lä väl'lä), Slovenian *Dolina* (dô'lēnä), village (pop. 902), N Free Territory of Trieste, 5 mi. SE of Trieste, near Yugoslav line. Pop. is Slovenian. Placed 1947 under Anglo-American administration.

Sandoval (săndō'vŭl), county (□ c.3,710; pop. 12,438), NW central N.Mex.; ⊙ Bernalillo. Stock-grazing and agr. (grain, chili) area; drained by Rio Grande. Part of Santa Fe Natl. Forest and Bandelier Natl. Monument in NE, part of Jicarilla Indian Reservation in NW, ranges of Rocky Mts. in N. Pueblo Indian area in SE. Formed 1903. Part of co. (□ c.100) was used to form (1949) part of Los Alamos co.

Sandoval, village (pop. 1,531), Marion co., S central Ill., 6 mi. N of Centralia, in oil-producing, bituminous-coal-mining, and agr. area. Inc. 1859.

Sandovo (sän'dŭvŭ), village (1926 pop. 495), NE Kalinin oblast, Russian SFSR, 50 mi. N of Bezhetsk; flax processing.

Sandoway (săn'dŭwā), Burmese *Thandwe* (thän-dwĕ'), southern district (□ 4,150; 1941 pop. 139,747) of Arakan div., Lower Burma; ⊙ Sandoway. Bet. Bay of Bengal and Arakan Yoma; drained by Sandoway R. Forested hills inland, rice fields on coastal plains. Yearly rainfall 200 in. Pop. is 90% Burmese, 7% Chin.

Sandoway, town (pop. 4,070), ⊙ Sandoway dist., Lower Burma, in the Arakan, at mouth of minor Sandoway R., 150 mi. SE of Akyab. Coastal trade with Ramree Isl. and Akyab. Sanskrit stone inscriptions (8th cent.) near by.

Sandown, former urban district (1931 pop. 6,168) now in urban dist. of Sandown-Shanklin (1951 census 12,693), E coast of Isle of Wight, England, on Sandown Bay of the Channel, 7 mi. ESE of Newport; seaside resort, with beaches and pier.

Sandown, town (pop. 315), Rockingham co., SE N.H., on Exeter R. and 15 mi. ESE of Manchester. Early meetinghouse (1773–74) is one of the state's finest.

Sandown Park, England: see ESHER.

Sandoy (sän'ûü), Nor. *Sandøy*, island (□5; pop. 525) in North Sea, More og Romsdal co., W Norway, one of the Sor Isls., 27 mi. SW of Alesund; 3 mi. long, 2 mi. wide. Fishing and cattle raising. Cannery at Sandshamn village (E) in Sande canton (pop. 2,738).

Sand Point, village (pop. 107), on E Popof Isl., Shumagin Isls., SW Alaska; 55°19'N 160°32'W; fishing, fish canning; supply point for fishermen and big-game hunters.

Sandpoint, resort city (pop. 4,265), ⊙ Bonner co., N Idaho, on NW shore of Pend Oreille L. (here spanned by 2-mi. bridge), 60 mi. NE of Spokane, Wash. Rail, highway center; lumber milling, dairying. Has steamboat connections. Laid out 1898, inc. 1900.

Sand Point, Wash.: see SEATTLE.

Sandras Dag (sändräs' dä), Turkish *Sandras Dağ*, peak (7,526 ft.), SW Turkey, in Mentese Mts., 12 mi. NE of Koycegiz.

Sandray or **Sanderay** (săn'drā), island, Outer Hebrides, Inverness, Scotland, 4 mi. S of Barra; 1½ mi. long, 1½ mi. wide. Consists of single gneiss hill rising to 678 ft.

Sandrigo (sändrē'gô), town (pop. 2,376), Vicenza prov., Veneto, N Italy, 8 mi. NNE of Vicenza; mfg. (celluloid, packing boxes, automatic pencils, fountain pens).

Sandringham (săn'drĭng-ŭm), residential municipality (pop. 26,435), S Victoria, Australia, on NE shore of Port Phillip Bay, 11 mi. SSE of Melbourne, in metropolitan area; rail terminus; truck gardens.

Sandringham, royal estate and parish (pop. 174), NW Norfolk, England, 7 mi. NE of King's Lynn. Has old church, rebuilt in 16th cent. Sandringham House with its 7,000-acre estate was purchased by Edward VII, then Prince of Wales, in 1861. George V died here in 1936.

Sandshamn, Norway: see SANDOY.

Sand Shoal Inlet, Va.: see COBB ISLAND.

Sands Key, Fla.: see FLORIDA KEYS.

Sandslan (sänts'lōn"), Swedish *Sandslån*, village (pop. 658), Vasternorrland co., NE Sweden, on Angerman R. estuary, 25 mi. N of Harnosand; site of largest Swedish timber-sorting installation.

Sandspit, village, W B.C., on NE Moresby Isl., on Skidegate Inlet, 11 mi. E of Queen Charlotte; lumbering; cattle, sheep; steamer landing.

Sandspitze (zänt'shpĭtsů), highest peak (9,391 ft.) of Gailtal Alps, S Austria, 6 mi. SSE of Lienz, in Lienz Dolomites group.

Sands Point, residential village (pop. 860), Nassau co., SE N.Y., on N shore of Long Isl., on Manhasset Neck, c.4 mi. NNW of Roslyn, in summer-resort area. Sands Point promontory (lighthouse) is at tip of Manhasset Neck, NW of village.

Sand Springs, city (pop. 6,994), Tulsa co., NE Okla., on Arkansas R. and 7 mi. WSW of Tulsa; industrial suburb (textiles, petroleum products, glass jars, tanks, iron fixtures, lawn furniture, pet foods, boxes, peanut products, concrete blocks). Oil and natural-gas wells. Founded 1907 as site of a widows' and orphans' home; platted 1911.

Sandston, village (pop. 3,902, with near-by Seven Pines), Henrico co., E central Va., 8 mi. E of Richmond.

Sandstone, village (pop. 1,097), Pine co., E Minn., on Kettle R. and c.60 mi. SW of Duluth, in agr. area; dairy and concrete products. Sandstone quarries near by. Settled 1885, when quarries were opened. Small lakes and resorts in vicinity.

Sand Tank Mountains, Maricopa co., S Ariz., SE of Gila Bend; rise to c.4,000 ft.

Sandtorg, Norway: see GAUSVIK.

Sandukli, Turkey: see SANDIKLI.

Sandur (sän'tür) or **Hellisandur** (hĕt'lĭsän"tür), village (pop. 344), Snaefellsnes co., W Iceland, NW Snaefellsnes peninsula, on Breidi Fjord; 64°55'N 23°53'W; cod fisheries.

Sandur (sŭndŏŏr'), town (pop. 5,529), Bellary dist., NW Madras, India, 26 mi. WSW of Bellary; betel farming; distillery. Important manganese mines (S); ore shipped from Swamihalli, 8 mi. SSE. Hematite deposits in surrounding hills. Was ⊙ former princely state of Sandur (□ 158; pop. 15,814) in Madras States, India; since 1949, state inc. into Bellary dist.

Sandusky (sündŭ'skē, săn–), county (□ 410; pop. 46,114), N Ohio; ⊙ Fremont. Bounded NE by Sandusky Bay of L. Erie; intersected by Sandusky and Portage rivers and small Muddy and Green creeks. Has state park with home and tomb of Rutherford B. Hayes. Agr. (grain, fruit, truck, sugar beets); mfg. at Fremont and Clyde; limestone quarries. Formed 1820.

Sandusky. 1 City (pop. 1,819), ⊙ Sanilac co., E Mich., 37 mi. NW of Port Huron, in farm area (livestock, poultry, grain); mfg. (steel bridges, drainage pipes, machinery). Inc. as village 1885, as city 1905. **2** City (pop. 29,375), ⊙ Erie co., N Ohio, c.50 mi. W of Cleveland, on harbor in Sandusky Bay of L. Erie; industrial and resort city; shipping point for coal; port of entry. Mfg. of paper products, communications equipment, electrical appliances, clay products, crayons, fertilizer, machinery, boats, novelties. Fisheries; wineries; limestone quarries. Seat of state soldiers' home. Near by are Blue Hole Spring (6 mi. W), Crystal Rock Caves, the Marblehead Peninsula, Cedar Point (summer resort), and many small isls. Laid out 1817 as Portland; known as Sandusky after 1844.

Sandusky Bay, N Ohio, landlocked arm of L. Erie at mouth of Sandusky R.; c.18 mi. long, 5 mi. wide. Sandusky is on harbor near its mouth. Marblehead Peninsula shelters bay on N, and small Cedar Point peninsula (site of Cedar Point, summer resort) extends from SE shore partly across its mouth.

Sandusky River, N Ohio, rises near Bucyrus in Crawford co., flows W to Upper Sandusky, thence N, past Tiffin and Fremont, to Sandusky Bay of L. Erie; c.120 mi. long.

Sandvig, Denmark: see ALLINGE-SANDVIG.

Sandvika (sän'vē"kä), village (pop. 1,752) in Baerum canton, Akershus co., SE Norway, at head of Oslo Fjord, on railroad and 9 mi. WSW of Oslo; mfg. of chemicals, electrical appliances, linoleum, paper. Has large hosp.

Sandviken (sänd'vē"kün), city (1950 pop. 18,784), Gavleborg co., E Sweden, on N shore of Stor L., 13 mi. WSW of Gavle; iron-, steel-milling center; machinery works, stone quarries. Founded 1862; inc. 1943 as city.

Sandwich, SW suburb of Windsor, S Ont., on Detroit R., opposite Detroit; 1st settled by the French and called L'Assomption, it received influx of Br. inhabitants of Detroit in 1796. Merged with Windsor 1935. Seat of Assumption Col.

Sandwich (săn'wĭch), municipal borough (1931 pop. 3,287; 1951 census 4,142), E Kent, England, near the Channel, on Stour R., and 12 mi. E of Canterbury; resort with tanning and cereal-food industry. Most anc. of the CINQUE PORTS, it was chief naval and military port of England under Henry VII; the harbor is now silted up. Has anc. walls with Fisher Gate (1384) and Barbican Gate (1539). St. Bartholomew's Hosp. dates from 12th cent. St. Clement's church has fine Norman tower. The suburb of Richborough, 2 mi. N, was Caesar's chief Br. port (*Rutupiae*); there are extensive Roman remains. In First World War Sandwich was one of chief supply ports for British Expeditionary Force, with train ferry to Calais.

Sandwich. 1 City (pop. 3,027), De Kalb co., N Ill., 17 mi. WSW of Aurora; mfg. (farm machinery, auto trailers, overalls); corn, oats, wheat, livestock, dairy products, poultry. Inc. 1859. **2** Town (pop. 2,418), including Sandwich village (pop. 1,007), Barnstable co., SE Mass., on Cape Cod Bay, at base of Cape, 11 mi. WNW of Barnstable; summer resort; agr. (cranberries). State game farms, fish hatcheries, forest preserves here. Famous for glass made 1825–88; local mus. has glass collection. Hoxie House dates partly from 1637. Settled 1636, one of earliest settlements on Cape; inc. 1639. Includes villages of East Sandwich, Forestdale. **3** Resort town (pop. 615), Carroll co., E central N.H., on Squam L. and 19 mi. NNE of Laconia; handicraft products, lumber, dairy products, poultry. Includes part of White Mtn. Natl. Forest.

Sandwich, Cape, Australia: see HINCHINBROOK ISLAND.

Sandwich Bay, inlet (30 mi. long, 10 mi. wide at entrance), SE Labrador; 53°40'N 57°15'W. In entrance are Huntington Isl. and Earl Isl. On shore are several lumbering settlements, largest of which is Cartwright (pop. 183).

Sandwich Islands, old name for HAWAIIAN ISLANDS.

Sandwich Range, E central N.H., range of White Mts. NE of Plymouth and W of Conway. Principal peaks: Sandwich Mtn. (3,993 ft.), Mt. Whiteface (3,985 ft.), Mt. Passaconaway (4,060 ft.), and Mt. Chocorua (3,475 ft.).

Sandwip Island (sŭndvēp'), easternmost island of Ganges Delta, Noakhali dist., SE East Bengal, E Pakistan, in Bay of Bengal, 18 mi. WNW of Chittagong; 25 mi. long, 3–9 mi. wide; separated from Chittagong dist. (E) by Sandwip Channel (E arm of Meghna R. delta mouth; 7–13 mi. wide, c.30 mi. long) and from Hatia Isl. (W) by Hatia R. Sandwip village is near W shore. Steamer service with mainland. Isl. subject to severe cyclones. Was 17th-cent. Port. and Arakanese pirate stronghold. Became part of Noakhali dist. in 1822.

Sandy, urban district (1931 pop. 3,140; 1951 census 3,667), E central Bedford, England, on Ivel R. and 3 mi. NW of Biggleswade; agr. market. Has 14th-cent. church.

Sandy. 1 City (pop. 1,003), Clackamas co., NW Oregon, 20 mi. ESE of Portland; resort; lumber. Mt. Hood is 27 mi. E. **2** Village (pop. 1,866), Clearfield co., central Pa., near Du Bois. **3** or

Sandy City, city (pop. 2,095), Salt Lake co., N central Utah, 10 mi. S of Salt Lake City, near Jordan R., just W of Wasatch Range; alt. 4,451 ft. Manufactures rock wool from slag. Settled 1871. Was ore-shipping and smelting center in late 19th cent. Little Cottonwood Canyon is near-by recreational area.

Sandy Bay, town (pop. 1,050), Hanover parish, NW Jamaica, on coast; seaside resort, 12 mi. W of Montego Bay; bananas, rice, yams.

Sandy Bay, village (pop. 923), N St. Vincent, B.W.I., 15 mi. N of Kingstown, on lower slopes of the Soufrière; arrowroot growing. A Carib settlement, it was removed, because of floods, to adjoining site (1947).

Sandy Cape, Australia: see FRASER ISLAND.

Sandy Creek, village (pop. 708), Oswego co., N central N.Y., near L. Ontario, 25 mi. NE of Oswego; gas and oil wells; dairying. Summer resort.

Sandy Creek, SW central Wyo., rises in S tip of Wind River Range, flows c.90 mi. generally S to Green R. 22 mi. SSW of Eden. Dam 13 mi. NNE of Eden creates Eden Valley Reservoir, unit in irrigation project.

Sandycroft, town in West Saltney parish (pop. 4,221), Flint, Wales, on the Dee and 5 mi. W of Chester; steel milling, chemical mfg.

Sandy Falls, waterfalls (34 ft. high), NE Ont., on Mattagami R. and 6 mi. NW of Timmins; hydroelectric station.

Sandy Hook. 1 Village, Conn.: see NEWTOWN. **2** or **Martinsburg**, town (pop. 238), ⊙ Elliott co., NE Ky., 40 mi. SW of Ashland, in mtn. timber and agr. (tobacco, corn, hay) area; sawmill. Cumberland Natl. Forest is near by. **3** Town (pop. 57), Moniteau co., central Mo., on Missouri R. and 11 mi. NE of California.

Sandy Hook, Monmouth co., NE N.J., narrow sandy peninsula bet. Sandy Hook Bay (W) and the Atlantic; extends c.5 mi. N toward New York City; marks S side of entrance to Lower New York Bay. Peninsula is govt. reservation, with Fort Hancock at tip. Sandy Hook Lighthouse (85 ft. high; built 1763) is oldest now in use in U.S. Hudson explored Sandy Hook in 1609; British held it in Revolution.

Sandy Hook Bay, NE N.J., triangular S arm of Lower New York Bay, off N shore of Monmouth co.; protected from the Atlantic by Sandy Hook peninsula (E); ½–4 mi. wide, c.5 mi. long. Passage at S end connects with Navesink R. and Shrewsbury R. estuaries.

Sandykachi (sündē"kŭchē'), town (1948 pop. over 500), S Mary oblast, Turkmen SSR, 80 mi. SE of Mary, on Murgab R. and Kushka RR; irrigated farming.

Sandy Lake. 1 Lake (□ 49), W central N.F., just NE of Grand L. (with which it is connected), 40 mi. ENE of Corner Brook; 15 mi. long, 5 mi. wide. **2** Lake (□ 270), NW Ont., in Patricia dist., near Man. border; 53°N 93°W; 48 mi. long, 8 mi. wide. Drained E by Severn R.

Sandy Lake, borough (pop. 767), Mercer co., NW Pa., 8 mi. W of Polk; dairy products; lumber, flour; oil wells.

Sandy Lake, Aitkin co., central Minn., 26 mi. NE of Aitkin in state forest; 6 mi. long, max. width 4 mi. Fishing resorts. Dam on NE outlet controls flow into Mississippi R. Sometimes called Big Sandy L. Used as reservoir. Since construction of dam it covers □ 17; □ 8 in natural state.

Sandymount, SE suburb of Dublin, Co. Dublin, Ireland, on Dublin Bay. W. B. Yeats b. here.

Sandy Point, town (pop. 382), N Bahama Isls., on SW shore of Great Abaco Isl., on Northwest Providence Channel, 65 mi. N of Nassau; 26°2'N 77°24'W.

Sandy Point, town (pop. 2,681), NW St. Kitts, B.W.I., 8 mi. WNW of Basseterre, in agr. region (sugar cane, sea-island cotton, fruit).

Sandy Point, point of land, Anne Arundel co., central Md., on Chesapeake Bay at S side of entrance to Magothy R., 7 mi. ENE of Annapolis. Here are a state park, the W terminus of Chesapeake Bay Bridge, and a lighthouse. Near by is Whitehall (built c.1765), one of Md.'s most beautiful plantation houses.

Sandy Ridge, Va.: see CUMBERLAND PLATEAU.

Sandy River, plantation (pop. 55), Franklin co., W Maine, at E end of Rangeley L., 24 mi. N of Rumford; Sandy R. rises here. Organized 1905.

Sandy River. 1 In W Maine, rises in Franklin co., near Rangeley L.; flows c.60 mi. generally SE, past Farmington, then NE to the Kennebec above Norridgewock. **2** In NW Oregon, rises in glaciers of Mt. Hood, flows c.50 mi. generally NW to Columbia R. 14 mi. E of Portland.

Sandy's, parish (1939 pop. 3,660), W Bermuda, including W tip of Bermuda Isl., and Somerset and Ireland isls.

Sandyville, town (pop. 92), Warren co., S central Iowa, 19 mi. SE of Des Moines, in agr. area.

San Eduardo (sän ādwär'dō), town (pop. estimate 2,000), S Santa Fe prov., Argentina, 11 mi. SE of Venado Tuerto; agr. center (wheat, flax, corn, alfalfa, livestock).

San el Hagar (sän' ĕl hä'gär) or **San al-Hajar** (hä'jär), village (pop. 3,065), Sharqiya prov., Lower Egypt, on the Bahr Saft and 17 mi. NNE of Faqus, c.30 mi. (across L. Manzala) SW of Port Said. A lagoon San el Hagar is 7 mi. NE. Site of anc. TANIS. Sometimes called simply San.

San Elizario (săn ĕlĭzâ'rēō, –ză'–), village (1940 pop. 1,285), El Paso co., extreme W Texas, 13 mi. SE of El Paso and on the Rio Grande, in irrigated farm area. One of oldest communities in Texas, founded in early 1680's as a presidio town; scene of Salt War violence (1877) and one-time ⊙ El Paso co. Here is noted chapel (*Capilla de San Elizario*), 4th chapel bldg. on site.

San Emigdio Mountains (săn ĭmĭ'dēō), S central Calif., short range (c.4–7,000 ft.), part of S wall of San Joaquin Valley, linking Temblor Range (NW) with Tehachapi Mts. (E).

San Estanislao (sän ĕstänēslou'), town (pop. 4,770), Bolívar dept., N Colombia, on Canal del Dique and 27 mi. E of Cartagena; sugar cane, corn, rice, stock.

San Estanislao, town (dist. pop. 11,178), San Pedro dept., central Paraguay, 90 mi. NE of Asunción; trading center in livestock and maté area. Limestone deposits near by.

San Esteban (sän ĕstā'vän), town (pop. 358), Olancho dept., E central Honduras, on Sico R. and 45 mi. NNE of Juticalpa; agr., livestock.

San Esteban, village (pop. 1,787), Oviedo prov., NW Spain, 21 mi. W of Gijón; coal-shipping port on Bay of Biscay; fishing and fish processing, boatbuilding, mfg. of barium hydroxide.

San Esteban de Gormaz (dā gôrmäth'), town (pop. 1,957), Soria prov., N central Spain, on Duero (Douro) R. (crossed by old bridge), on railroad to Valladolid and 26 mi. ESE of Aranda de Duero. Picturesquely situated at foot of hill, on which is an imposing castle. In agr. region (cereals, vegetables, potatoes, livestock). Lime quarrying; flour milling, tanning, soap and tile mfg.; fishing. Was heavily disputed during Moorish wars. Mozarabic watchtowers in vicinity.

San Esteban de la Sierra (lä syĕ'rä), town (pop. 1,279), Salamanca prov., W Spain, 11 mi. NW of Béjar; junction of 2 rail lines from Portugal (Lisbon and Oporto). Olive-oil and wine processing.

San Esteban de Litera (lētā'rä), town (pop. 1,491), Huesca prov., NE Spain, 14 mi. SE of Barbastro; brewery; agr. trade (olive oil, wine, grain, fruit).

San Esteban de los Patos (lōs pä'tōs), town (pop. 213), Ávila prov., central Spain, 7 mi. NE of Ávila; copper mining; grain growing and stock raising.

San Esteban del Valle (dĕl vä'lyā), town (pop. 1,884), Ávila prov., central Spain, in the Sierra de Gredos, 29 mi. SSW of Ávila; olives, chestnuts, grapes, livestock; apiculture. Four milling, olive-oil pressing.

San Estevan (săn ĕstā′vŭn), village (pop. 282), Northern Dist., Br. Honduras, on New R. and 5 mi. NNE of Orange Walk; sugar cane, corn, timber.
San Eugenio, Uruguay: see ARTIGAS, city, Artigas dept.
San Fabián or **San Fabián de Aliço** (sän fäbyän′ dā älē′kō), village (1930 pop. 690), Ñuble prov., S central Chile, on Ñuble R. and 30 mi. E of Chillán; health resort; grain, fruit, cattle, timber.
San Fabian (săn″ fā′bēŭn, Sp. sän fäbyän′), town (1939 pop. 1,671); 1948 municipality pop. 23,997), Pangasinan prov., central Luzon, Philippines, on railroad and 7 mi. NE of Dagupan; port on small inlet of Lingayen Gulf; agr. center (rice, copra, corn).
San Fabián de Alico, Chile: see SAN FABIÁN.
San Fele (sän fā′lĕ), village (pop. 1,751), Potenza prov., Basilicata, S Italy, 19 mi. NW of Potenza.
San Felice a Cancello (sän fĕlē′chĕ ä känchĕl′lō) town (pop. 4,670), Caserta prov., Campania, S Italy, 9 mi. ESE of Caserta.
San Felice Circeo (chērchā′ō), village (pop. 2,381), Latina prov., Latium, S central Italy, on Monte Circeo, 10 mi. WSW of Terracina. Near by are anc. ruins and walls.
San Felices de los Gállegos (sän fālē′thĕs dā lōs gä′lyägōs), town (pop. 1,561), Salamanca prov., W Spain, 20 mi. NNW of Ciudad Rodrigo; olive-oil processing; wine, cereals, livestock.
San Felice sul Panaro (sōōl pänä′rō), town (pop. 2,167), Modena prov., Emilia-Romagna, N central Italy, 18 mi. NE of Modena; rail junction; agr. center; macaroni, dairy products. Has Este castle, built 1340.
San Felipe (sän fālē′pā), town (pop. 13,168), ⊙ Aconcagua prov. and San Felipe dept. (□ 809; pop. 49,305), central Chile, in Andean foothills (alt. 2,085 ft.), on Aconcagua R. and 50 mi. N of Santiago, on Transandine RR; 32°45′S 70°44′W. Rail junction, commercial and agr. center (hemp, tobacco, fruit, wine, livestock). Tanning, fruit packing, hemp processing. Silver, copper, and gold mining. Old colonial town, founded 1740. Played an important part during war of independence. Sometimes San Felipe de Aconcagua or Aconcagua.
San Felipe, town (pop. 1,107), Havana prov., W Cuba, 20 mi. S of Havana; rail junction; sugar cane, vegetables, cattle.
San Felipe. 1 Village (1940 pop. 66), Izabal dept., E Guatemala, on NE shore of L. Izabal, at outlet of Río Dulce, 27 mi. WSW of Puerto Barrios; bananas, coconuts, grain. A 17th-cent. fort guarded L. Izabal against pirate inroads. **2** Town (1950 pop. 2,378), Retalhuleu dept., SW Guatemala, in Pacific piedmont, on Samalá R. and 9 mi. NE of Retalhuleu; rail terminus; market center; fruit, coffee, sugar cane, grain.
San Felipe. 1 Mining settlement (pop. 1,584), Coahuila, N Mexico, in Sabinas coal district, 10 mi. SE of Sabinas; rail terminus. **2** City, Guanajuato, Mexico: see DOCTOR HERNÁNDEZ ALVAREZ. **3** Officially San Felipe del Progreso, town (pop. 717), Mexico state, central Mexico, 55 mi. WNW of Mexico city; cereals, livestock. **4** Officially San Felipe Santiago, town (pop. 2,693), Mexico state, central Mexico, 33 mi. WNW of Mexico city; cereals, livestock. **5** Town (pop. 1,837), Nayarit, W Mexico, in Pacific lowland, near Acaponeta R., 70 mi. NW of Tepic; corn, sugar cane, tobacco, vegetables, fruit, cattle. **6** or **San Felipe de Jesús** (dā hā sōōs′), town (pop. 400), Sonora, NW Mexico, 80 mi. SE of Nogales; livestock, wheat. **7** Town (pop. 287), Yucatan, SE Mexico, on bar offshore, 30 mi. NNW of Tizimín; henequen-growing dist.
San Felipe, town (1939 pop. 4,033; 1948 municipality pop. 7,781), Zambales prov., central Luzon, Philippines, near W coast, just N of San Narciso, 45 mi. SW of Tarlac; rice-growing center.
San Felipe. 1 (săn fúlē′pē) Pueblo (□ 67.8), Sandoval co., N central N.Mex. San Felipe village (1948 pop. 787) is on W bank of the Rio Grande and 33 mi. SW of Santa Fe. Ceremonial dances take place in May and Dec. Settled c.1700. **2** (săn fĕ′lĭpē) Town (pop. 296), Austin co., S Texas, on Brazos R. and c.45 mi. W of Houston. Founded 1823 as hq. of Steven F. Austin's colony. Conventions (1832, 1833, 1835) held here before and during Texas Revolution; burned 1836, later rebuilt. A state park and monument here commemorate Austin and town's history. Also called San Felipe de Austin.
San Felipe (sän fālē′pā), city (1941 pop. 11,067; 1950 census 13,178), ⊙ Yaracuy state, N Venezuela, on slopes of coastal range, on Barquisimeto–Puerto Cabello highway and 125 mi. W of Caracas, 50 mi. WNW of Valencia; 10°20′N 68°44′W. Rail terminus and trading center in lumbering and agr. region (cacao, coffee, cotton, sugar cane, rice, fruit, cattle, hides); sugar milling, liquor distilling. Copper deposits near by.
San Felipe, Cayos de (kī′ōs dā), group of keys (c.20 mi. long) off coast of SW Cuba, 19 mi. NW of Isle of Pines, 30 mi. S of Pinar del Río.
San Felipe Bay, shallow inlet of Gulf of California, in NE Lower California, NW Mexico, 120 mi. SSE of Mexicali; 10 mi. long, c.3 mi. wide. Pure salt deposits.
San Felipe de Aconcagua, Chile: see SAN FELIPE.
San Felipe de Colavi, Bolivia: see COLAVI.
San Felipe de Jesús, Mexico: see SAN FELIPE, Sonora.
San Felipe del Progreso, Mexico: see SAN FELIPE, Mexico state.
San Felipe de Vichayal, Peru: see VICHAYAL.
San Felipe Ixtacuixtla, Mexico: see IXTACUIXTLA.
San Felipe Orizatlán, Mexico: see ORIZATLÁN.
San Felipe Tepatlán, Mexico: see TEPATLÁN.
San Felíu de Codinas (sän fālē′ōō dā kō-dhē′näs), town (pop. 2,290), 20 mi. N of Barcelona; cotton and silk milling, olive-oil processing; agr. trade. Summer resort. Sanctuary of San Miguel del Fay is 3 mi. NW.
San Felíu de Guixols (gē-shôls′), city (pop. 7,169), Gerona prov., NE Spain, port on the Mediterranean, 17 mi. SE of Gerona. Cork processing and exporting, lumbering, fish salting; agr. trade. Of 10th-cent. monastery, only gate is left. Important port since 12th cent. Popular bathing resort.
San Felíu de Llobregat (lyōvrāgät′), city (pop. 6,355), Barcelona prov., NE Spain, on irrigation canal near Llobregat R., and 7 mi. W of Barcelona; a center of the metallurgical industry; mfg. of cotton and silk fabrics, velvets, dyes, glue, rubber. Grows flowers, wine, fruit.
San Felíu de Torelló, Spain: see TORELLÓ.
San Félix (sän fā′lēks), village (pop. 876), Chiriquí prov., W Panama, in Pacific lowland, 3 mi. N of Las Lajas, near Inter-American Highway; lumbering, stock raising. Partly Indian pop.
San Félix, town (pop. 1,324), Bolívar state, E Venezuela, port on right bank of Orinoco R., near mouth of Caroní R., and 60 mi. ENE of Ciudad Bolívar; trading point in cattle-raising region. Iron deposits are S, at El Pao. Ore transshipment port of Palua is near by.
San Félix Island, in the South Pacific, 600 mi. W of Chile, to which it belongs; 26°17′S 80°7′W; 3 mi. long, c.1 mi. wide; rises to 600 ft. Arid, uninhabited islet. At its SE tip is islet of Gonzalez. Small SAN AMBROSIO ISLAND is 12 mi. ESE. San Félix was discovered 1574 by Sp. navigator Juan Fernández.
San Ferdinando (sän fĕrdēnän′dō), village (pop. 3,608), Reggio di Calabria prov., Calabria, S Italy, fishing port on Gulf of Gioia, 3 mi. W of Rosarno.
San Fermín (sän fĕrmēn′), village, La Paz dept., NW Bolivia, on Tambopata R. and 60 mi. NW of Apolo, on Peru border.
San Fernando (sän fĕrnän′dō), city (pop. 27,990), ⊙ San Fernando dist. (□ 9; pop. 47,618), in Greater Buenos Aires, Argentina, on the Río de la Plata and 16 mi. NW of Buenos Aires; cattle-raising and mfg. center; dairy products, canned fish, cider, furniture, buttons, footwear, brushes, mirrors, paper products; sawmills, sand quarries.
San Fernando, village (pop. 193), Formentera, Balearic Isls., 12 mi. S of Iviza; flour milling. Saltworks near by.
San Fernando. 1 E suburb (pop. 1,257) of San Felipe, Aconcagua prov., central Chile. **2** Town (pop. 14,419), ⊙ Colchagua prov. and San Fernando dept. (□ 1,200; pop. 58,142), central Chile, on Tinguiririca R., in the central valley, on railroad and 80 mi. S of Santiago; 34°36′S 70°59′W. Agr. center (grain, wine, fruit, peas, potatoes, livestock). Mfg. (food preserves, cigarettes, shoes, flour, leather). Trades also in sulphur. Founded 1742, the town retains its colonial character.
San Fernando. 1 Town, Chiapas, Mexico: see VILLA ALLENDE. **2** Town (pop. 1,471), Tamaulipas, NE Mexico, on San Fernando R., on Gulf plain, and 85 mi. SSW of Matamoros; cereals, sugar, cattle.
San Fernando, town (1950 pop. 328), Nueva Segovia dept., NW Nicaragua, 10 mi. ENE of Ocotal; mfg. of sweets; lime making; livestock.
San Fernando (săn″ fúrnăn′dō, Sp. sän fĕrnän′dō). **1** Town (1939 pop. 2,458; 1948 municipality pop. 16,132), central Cebu isl., Philippines, on railroad and 16 mi. SW of Cebu city, on Bohol Strait; agr. center (corn, coconuts). **2** Town (1939 pop. 2,803; 1948 municipality pop. 28,742), ⊙ La Union prov., N central Luzon, Philippines, on W coast of isl., at E side of entrance to Lingayen Gulf, 23 mi. NW of Baguio; 16°37′N 120°18′E. Northernmost rail terminus; port for inter-isl. shipping; trade center for rice-growing area. Also called Poro. **3** Town (1939 pop. 2,456; 1948 municipality pop. 17,417), on E coast of Ticao Isl., Masbate prov., Philippines, 12 mi. NE of Masbate town; agr. center (rice, coconuts). **4** Town (1939 pop. 3,981; 1948 municipality pop. 39,549), ⊙ Pampanga prov., central Luzon, Philippines, 35 mi. NW of Manila; 15°1′N 120°41′E. Rail center; sugar milling, cotton ginning. Sometimes called Santo Rosario (sän′tō rōsär′yō). **5** Village, Romblon prov., Philippines: see SIBUYAN ISLAND.
San Fernando, city (pop. 32,300), Cádiz prov., SW Spain, in Andalusia, Atlantic port on León or San Fernando Isl., on Bay of Cádiz, 7 mi. SE of Cádiz. A city of great maritime tradition, with Carraca arsenal (2 mi. N), pantheon to illustrious navigators, naval acad., and workshops; observatory. Surrounded by salt marshes; saltworking is its chief industry. Also fishing, fish canning, flour milling, liquor distilling, lime and sand quarrying. Among agr. products of the region are grapes, cereals, almonds, olives, cattle, hogs. In its theater met (1810) the Cortes. Formerly Isla de León.
San Fernando (săn″ fúrnăn′dō), city (pop. 28,842), SW Trinidad, B.W.I., port on the Gulf of Paria opposite Venezuela, 27 mi. S of Port of Spain (linked by rail); 10°39′N 61°31′W. Second city of the colony, trading center for rich petroleum region; has large sugar *central* and is surrounded by sugar estates; also lumber industry. Has Carnegie Free Library, Teachers Training Col. New housing developments in outskirts. Originally a private land grant (1786); inc. 1846.
San Fernando (săn fúrnăn′dō), city (pop. 12,992), Los Angeles co., S Calif., 20 mi. NW of downtown Los Angeles, in N SAN FERNANDO VALLEY; packs and processes citrus and other fruit, truck; oil wells and refineries. San Fernando Reservoir (just NW) is S terminus of Los Angeles Aqueduct. Near by are a U.S. veterans' hosp., and San Fernando (or San Fernando Rey de España) Mission, established 1797. Valley 1st entered in 1769 by white men; town settled, and mission founded, by Spaniards; city inc. 1911. Gold was produced for a time after 1842. Much of surrounding area was annexed (1915) by Los Angeles city.
San Fernando or **San Fernando de Apure** (sän fĕrnän′dō dā äpōō′rā), city (1941 pop. 8,761; 1950 census 13,377), ⊙ Apure state, W central Venezuela, port on S bank of Apure R., near mouth of Portuguesa R., and 185 mi. S of Caracas, 265 mi. W of Ciudad Bolívar; 7°53′N 67°28′W. Port of call for steamers on Orinoco and Apure rivers. Trading center in cattle country; deals in livestock, alligator hides, egret feathers; has meat-canning plant. Airport. Next to Ciudad Bolívar, it is leading town of Venezuelan llanos. Founded 1789 by Capuchin missionaries.
San Fernando de Atabapo (sän fĕrnän′dō dā ätäbä′pō), town (pop. 143), Amazonas territory, S Venezuela, port on Orinoco R. at influx of Guaviare and Atabapo rivers, on Colombia border, and 115 mi. S of Puerto Ayacucho, in tropical forest region (rubber, balata, vanilla); 4°3′N 67°42′W. Its fine location on major navigable rivers provides communication with Brazil, Colombia, N Venezuela.
San Fernando de Camarones (kämärō′nĕs), town (pop. 2,176), Las Villas prov., central Cuba, 24 mi. WSW of Santa Clara; sugar cane, fruit, livestock. Near by (NW) is the sugar central Hormiguero.
San Fernando de Catamarca, Argentina: see CATAMARCA, city.
San Fernando de Henares (ānä′rĕs), town (pop. 1,957), Madrid prov., central Spain, 8 mi. E of Madrid, and on Madrid-Saragossa RR; olives, grapes, cereals, fruit, stock. Was royal residence during rule of Ferdinand IV; the large palace is now a factory.
San Fernando di Puglia (sän fĕrnän′dō dē pōō′lyä), town (pop. 11,484), Foggia prov., Apulia, S Italy, near Ofanto R., 9 mi. ENE of Cerignola; agr. center (olives, grapes, almonds, wheat).
San Fernando Island, Spain: see LEÓN ISLAND.
San Fernando Point (sän fĕrnän′dō), La Union prov., N central Luzon, Philippines, at tip of small peninsula on W coast of isl., at E side of entrance to Lingayen Gulf; 16°37′N 120°16′E.
San Fernando Reservoir, Calif.: see OWENS RIVER.
San Fernando River, Argentina: see BELÉN RIVER.
San Fernando River (sän fĕrnän′dō), Tamaulipas, NE Mexico, rises as Conchos R. on E slopes of Sierra Madre Oriental SW of Linares (Nuevo León); flows c.175 mi. E, past Méndez and San Fernando, to Laguna Madre, lagoon on Gulf of Mexico. Forms cascades in upper course. Navigable on small scale at mouth.
San Fernando Valley (săn fúrnăn′dō), Los Angeles co., S Calif., fertile basin (□ c.260) NW of downtown Los Angeles, and walled by Santa Monica Mts. (S), Simi Hills (sēmē′) (W), Santa Susana Mts. (N), San Gabriel Mts. (NE and E); communicates with Los Angeles basin via Cahuenga Pass (S) to Hollywood, and by valley (SE) of Los Angeles R. Irrigated small farms, orchards, and poultry ranches are mingled with residential suburbs; San Fernando (in N) is chief independent city. Although much of the valley was annexed (1915) by LOS ANGELES city, after construction here of terminal reservoir of Los Angeles Aqueduct, many communities, though officially part of Los Angeles, retain their individuality: among them are North Hollywood, Sherman Oaks, Woodland Hills, Tarzana, Encino, VAN NUYS (seat of municipal govt. branch offices), Canoga Park, Chatsworth, Pacoima, Reseda, Roscoe, Sepulveda (sĭpŭl′vúdú), Sunland, Sylmar, Tujunga, Northridge.
Sanfins do Douro (sãnfēnsh′ dōō dō′rōō), village (pop. 1,861), Vila Real dist., N Portugal, 12 mi. E of Vila Real; winegrowing; olives, figs, almonds.
Sanford, town (pop. estimate 1,500), S Santa Fe prov., Argentina, 40 mi. WSW of Rosario; agr. center (wheat, corn, flax, alfalfa); grain elevator.
Sanford (săn′fúrd). **1** Town (pop. 666), Conejos co., S Colo., on Conejos R., E of San Juan Mts., and 14 mi. S of Alamosa, in San Luis Valley; alt. 7,560 ft.; truck farming. **2** City (pop. 11,935), ⊙ Seminole co., E central Fla., 19 mi. NE of Orlando, on L. Monroe; chief celery marketing center of Fla., with

many packing houses; also ships citrus fruit; makes concrete products. Resort. Founded 1871 on site of Mellonville, established 1837 near a fort. **3** Industrial town (pop. 15,177), including Sanford village (pop. 11,094), York co., SW Maine, c.35 mi. SW of Portland and on Mousam R.; textiles (since mid-18th cent.), wood products, shoes. Nasson Col. is at Springvale village (pop. 2,745). Inc. 1768. **4** Town (pop. 10,103), ⊙ Lee co., central N.C., 37 mi. SW of Raleigh; trade center, tobacco market; cotton and lumber mills, brick, tile, and pottery plants; foundries. Inc. 1889. Annexed adjacent Jonesboro in 1947.

Sanford, Mount (16,208 ft.), S Alaska, highest peak of Wrangell Mts., 100 mi. NE of Valdez; 62°14′N 144°8′W; 1st climbed 1938.

Sanford Lake, Essex co., NE N.Y., in the Adirondacks, c.55 mi. NNW of Glens Falls; c.3 mi. long; resort. Titanium mining. Drains S through outlet to a headstream of the Hudson.

San Francique, Trinidad, B.W.I.: see ERIN.

San Francisco (sän fränsē′skō). **1** City (pop. 23,933), ⊙ San Justo dept. (□ c.5,500; pop. 117,041), E Córdoba prov., Argentina, 125 mi. E of Córdoba; rail center; commercial, industrial, and agr. activities. Mfg.: linseed oil, batteries, leather goods, shoes, brushes, agr. implements, dairy products, frozen meat, liquor. Grain and flax growing, stock raising. **2** Town (pop. estimate 1,500), ⊙ Ayacucho dept. (□ 3,240; 1947 pop. 19,301), N San Luis prov., Argentina, resort at foot of Sierra de San Luis, 50 mi. NNE of San Luis; stock raising; mining (gold, lime); sawmills. **3** Town, Santa Fe prov., Argentina: see SAN FRANCISCO DE SANTA FE.

San Francisco, village (pop. c.1,000), Beni dept., N central Bolivia, in the llanos, 27 mi. SSE of San Ignacio; cattle.

San Francisco, village, Putumayo commissary, SW Colombia, on headstream of Putumayo R., in the Andes, and 28 mi. E of Pasto (connected by road); alt. 7,380 ft.; cattle raising.

San Francisco. 1 Town (1950 pop. 808), Petén dept., N Guatemala, 9 mi. SSW of Flores: lumbering, agr. Formerly called Chachaclún. **2** or **San Francisco Zapotitlán** (säpōtētlän′), town (1950 pop. 1,024), Suchitepéquez dept., SW Guatemala, in Pacific piedmont, 4 mi. NNW of Mazatenango; coffee, sugar cane, grain. **3** or **San Francisco El Alto** (ĕl äl′tō), town (1950 pop, 4,514), Totonicapán dept., W central Guatemala, on Samalá R. and 6 mi. WNW of Totonicapán; alt. 8,812 ft.; market; wool weaving; livestock; corn, wheat, beans.

San Francisco. 1 or **San Francisco de Cuajiniquilapa** (dā kwähēnēkēlä′pä), town (1950 pop. 649), Chinandega dept., W Nicaragua, 12 mi. NNE of Somotillo; corn, beans. **2** Village, Chontales dept., S Nicaragua, 55 mi. SE of Juigalpa; livestock; lumbering.

San Francisco or **San Francisco de la Montaña** (dā lä mōntä′nyä), village (pop. 748), Veraguas prov., W central Panama, on Santa María R., in plateau region, and 13 mi. NNW of Santiago; coffee center; gold, lead, and zinc mines.

San Francisco, Philippines: see PACIJAN ISLAND.

San Francisco, city (pop. 3,189), ⊙ Morazán dept., E Salvador, on Río Grande de San Miguel and 15 mi. NNE of San Miguel, on branch of Inter-American Highway; alt. 3,110 ft.; 13°41′N 88°6′W. Trading center in agr. and livestock area. Silver and gold mining near by. Called Gotera until 1887.

San Francisco (săn frŭnsĭ′skō), city coextensive with San Francisco co. (□ 44.6, land only; 1940 pop. 634,636; 1950 pop. 775,357), W Calif., on Pacific coast, c.350 mi. NW of Los Angeles; 37°47′N 122°26′W. Occupies narrow, hilly tip of San Francisco–San Mateo peninsula, bounded W by Pacific Ocean, N by the GOLDEN GATE (bridged to Marin co.), E by SAN FRANCISCO BAY (one of world's best harbors; bridged to E bay-shore cities). State's 2d-largest city (after Los Angeles) and 11th-largest in U.S., financial center of the West, great cosmopolitan seaport, and commercial and distribution center for vast hinterland of inland Calif. and the Pacific coast. Key city of metropolitan web around San Francisco Bay: Oakland, Berkeley, Alameda, across bay to E; Richmond, Vallejo, Benicia, Martinez, Pittsburg, to NE along N bay and its tributaries; San Rafael, Mill Valley, Sausalito, in Marin co. to N; and chain of suburbs extending S down the peninsula—South San Francisco, San Bruno, Burlingame, San Mateo, Redwood City, Menlo Park, Palo Alto. Port's annual water-borne commerce (part of it handled by neighboring cities) is generally highest in value among Pacific coast ports, and is exceeded in volume only by Los Angeles. Imports coffee, tea, copra, cacao, spices, raw sugar, tropical fruit (especially Hawaiian pineapple), Manila hemp, newsprint, burlap, tung oil, fish, rubber, silk, cotton, lumber, wool, fertilizer; exports oil, precious metals, iron and steel products, cereals, canned and dried fruit, canned fish, hops, cotton, rice. Port of entry since 1849. Served by foreign and domestic shipping lines, transcontinental and Pacific coast railroads, domestic and transpacific airlines, and N–S and E–W highways (transcontinental Lincoln Highway ends here). Seat of a U.S. mint. In the bay industrial dist. (San Francisco, plus parts of Alameda, Contra Costa, Marin, and San Mateo counties), refining of oil (brought by pipe lines) leads in value; also important are shipbuilding, canning and processing of fruit and vegetables, sugar refining, printing and publishing, steel milling and finishing of iron and steel products (especially tin cans), mfg. of machinery (electrical, agr., mining, industrial, and construction), lumber milling, automobile assembling, meat slaughtering and packing, coffee roasting, spice grinding; and mfg. of chemicals (paints, oils, soaps, fertilizer), rubber goods, textiles, paper, furniture, leather, cement and clay products, clothing, baked goods, beer. Except for shipyards, foundries, railroad shops, and wire, pipe, and cement plants, most of industries located within San Francisco handle food products and other consumer goods. State-owned port of San Francisco (served by 66-mi. belt-line railroad) stretches for 3 mi. along water front (the Embarcadero) of peninsula's NE shore; includes a foreign trade zone (free port) opened in 1948. Passenger and freight piers (17½ mi. of berth space) extend on both sides of old Ferry Bldg. (1903), a beloved landmark which was one of world's busiest passenger terminals before completion of transbay bridges. From the Embarcadero, Market St., the city's main thoroughfare, angles sharply off to SW as far as Twin Peaks (in city's center), where tunnels carry traffic to residential dists. beyond. Along Market St. and in downtown dist. to N are the financial center (Montgomery St.); city's finest hotels, apartments, and shops, theaters; the Civic Center (City Hall; Civic Auditorium, presented to city by Panama-Pacific Exposition; Opera House, only municipally owned opera in U.S., where city's symphony orchestra also performs; U.S. courthouse, seat of U.S. Circuit Court of Appeals; the public library; and the Veterans' Bldg., which includes an auditorium and an art mus.); and the famed Chinatown (largest Chinese settlement outside the Orient). In NE section are Telegraph Hill, topped by Coit Memorial Tower (1933; 210 ft. high); Nob Hill, on which millionaires' homes once stood; and Russian Hill. The "Latin Quarter," home of many artists and of colonies of people speaking Italian, French, Portuguese, and Spanish, centers on Telegraph Hill; near by is site (then on water front) of old Barbary Coast, defunct since 1917 but famous in 1890s for its flourishing wickedness. Fisherman's Wharf, at W end of Embarcadero, is home port for picturesque fishing fleet and is known for its sea-food restaurants. Along N water front (E–W) are Aquatic Park (casino; bathing, fishing, boating); U.S. Fort Mason, with army transport docks; Marina Park, along bay to N of Marina residential dist.; municipal yacht harbor (breakwater); and the Presidio. The last mentioned, a U.S. military reservation of 1,480 acres, lies along S shore of Golden Gate and includes S anchorage (at Fort Point) of Golden Gate Bridge; a fortified post since 1776, it now includes Fort Winfield Scott (hq. for harbor defenses), the army's huge Letterman General Hosp. and a natl. military cemetery. Beyond, along NW tip of peninsula and on W (ocean) shore, are James D. Phelan Beach State Park (popularly, China Beach); Lincoln Park, with replica of Palace of Legion of Honor; Land's End and Point Lobos, rugged promontories; U.S. Fort Miley; picturesque Seal Rocks offshore (habitat of seal herds), overlooked by the old Cliff House and Sutro Heights; Ocean Beach (bathing); and W end of Golden Gate Park, which is one of finest in U.S., created from once-barren sand dunes, stretching 4½ mi. E to city's center. Farther S along ocean are Fleishhacker pool, playgrounds, and zoo; in city's SW corner are U.S. Fort Funston and L. Merced (formerly water supply). Dist. to W and SW of Twin Peaks is residential. In E, S of Market St., are Rincon Hill (W approach to bridge to Oakland) and densely populated Mission Dist., taking its name from well-preserved Mission Dolores (built 1782). Beyond, along bay, are industrial plants, railroads, shipyards, and Hunter's Point, site of huge navy yards. In S, San Bruno Mts. (c.1,400 ft.; pierced by tunnels) separate city from suburbs to S. San Francisco is seat of the medical, dental, nursing, pharmacological, law, and medical-research schools of Univ. of Calif.; the Univ. of San Francisco (R.C.; for men); San Francisco Col. for Women (R.C.); school of medicine of Stanford Univ.; San Francisco State Col. (coeducational); Golden Gate Col. (coeducational); 2 jr. colleges; and of Grace Cathedral (Episcopal), and St. Mary's Cathedral (R.C.). City officially includes Farallon Isls., 26 mi. off the Golden Gate. Water supply is brought from the Sierra Nevada by 156-mi. Hetch Hetchy Aqueduct. San Francisco was founded in 1776, when a Spanish presidio and a mission (San Francisco de Asís, now Mission Dolores) were established at location chosen by Juan Bautista de Anza; village (by then known as Yerba Buena), a port for Orient-bound vessels, was taken (1846) for U.S. in Mexican War by Commodore John D. Sloat. Became officially San Francisco in 1847; inc. 1850. Co. included present San Mateo co. until 1856. At discovery (1848) of gold in Calif., city had pop. of c.800; 2 years later, it had c.25,000 souls and was chief gateway to mines for newcomers from the world over. Period of lawlessness during gold rush saw rise of the Barbary Coast and the organization of the Vigilantes to fight crime and corruption. Overland links with the East came with the Pony Express (1860), and Union Pacific RR (1869). Disastrous earthquake (April 18, 1906), followed by even more destructive fire, leveled much of city, but rebuilding was rapid; by 1910, pop. was c.417,000. In 1915, city celebrated opening of Panama Canal with Panama-Pacific Exposition. Communications bet. cities of the region were improved by opening (1907) of rail tunnels through hills to S; and by opening of SAN FRANCISCO-OAKLAND BAY BRIDGE in 1936, and of GOLDEN GATE BRIDGE in 1937. Golden Gate International Exposition (1939–40) was held on man-made Treasure Isl. Conference that drafted the United Nations Charter met in San Francisco in 1945. Peace treaty with Japan signed here in 1951. The individuality for which San Francisco is almost legendary derives from such things as its fogs, its cool, even climate (mean Jan. temp. 50° F., July 59° F., Sept. 62° F.; average rainfall 22 inches, mainly Oct.–May); its many hills (highest is Mt. Davidson, 938 ft., near Twin Peaks); busy water front, unique cable cars, fine shops and restaurants (many of foreign cuisine), street flower stands, magnificent Golden Gate Park, and the soaring bridges; and from the international flavor contributed by its communities of foreign descent, and the interest in art, music, letters, and the theater which has made it one of the cultural capitals of the nation. "Frisco," the city's nickname, though used affectionately by visitors, is often deplored by residents.

San Francisco (sän fränsē′skō). **1** Town (pop. 895), Lara state, NW Venezuela, in Segovia Highlands, 19 mi. WNW of Carora; corn, goats. **2** Town (pop. 715), Zulia state, NW Venezuela, on NW shore of L. Maracaibo; oil wells.

San Francisco, Cape (sän fränsē′skō), on Pacific coast of Esmeraldas prov., NW Ecuador, 37 mi. SW of Esmeraldas; 0°39′N 80°8′W.

San Francisco, Cerro (sĕ′rō sän fränsē′skō), Andean volcano (19,750 ft.) on Argentina-Chile border; 26°54′S. San Francisco Pass is at its NW slope.

San Francisco Bay (săn frŭnsĭ′skō), W Calif., large landlocked bay (c.50 mi. long, 3–12 mi. wide) occupying part of great depression (continued S by Santa Clara Valley) parallel to coast; its entrance from the Pacific is through the GOLDEN GATE (bridged in 1937), a strait bet. tips of 2 peninsulas; San Francisco is on S peninsula. One of world's best-sheltered harbors, bay has depths reaching 100 ft.; 50-ft. dredged channel crosses bar off Golden Gate. Bay's N part (San Pablo Bay) communicates via Carquinez Strait with Suisun Bay (E), into which pour combined Sacramento and San Joaquin rivers, both navigable for considerable distances. The E shore, linked 1936 with San Francisco by SAN FRANCISCO–OAKLAND BAY BRIDGE, is lined with industrial and residential cities (Alameda, Oakland, Berkeley, Richmond, Albany, Emeryville). On secondary bays and Carquinez Strait are industrial Vallejo, Benicia, Martinez, Pittsburg. Dumbarton Bridge was constructed in 1927 across narrow S end of bay, near Palo Alto; San Mateo Toll Bridge near San Mateo was built in 1929. Bay was entered by Sir Francis Drake in 1579, sighted by Gaspar de Portolá in 1769, and entered by Juan Manuel Ayala in 1775. YERBA BUENA ISLAND, ANGEL ISLAND, TREASURE ISLAND, and ALCATRAZ are here.

San Francisco de Asís (sän fränsē′skō dā äsēs′), town (pop. 1,334), Aragua state, N Venezuela, near E shore of L. Valencia, 13 mi. SSE of Maracay; coffee, cacao, sugar, corn, cattle.

San Francisco de Asís, Calif.: see SAN FRANCISCO.

San Francisco de Borja (bôr′hä), town (pop. 1,103), Chihuahua, N Mexico, in Sierra Madre Occidental, on San Pedro R. and 65 mi. SW of Chihuahua; grain, cotton, cattle.

San Francisco de Conchos (kōn′chōs), town (pop. 554), Chihuahua, N Mexico, on Conchos R., on railroad and 13 mi. SW of Camargo; corn, cotton, beans, tobacco, cattle; timber.

San Francisco de Cuajiniquilapa, Nicaragua: see SAN FRANCISCO, Chinandega dept.

San Francisco de la Caleta (lä kälā′tä), town (pop. 1,278), Panama prov., central Panama, on Bay of Panama of the Pacific, and 2 mi. NE of Panama city; coconuts, livestock; fishing.

San Francisco de la Montaña, Panama: see SAN FRANCISCO.

San Francisco de la Paz (päs′), town (pop. 796), Olancho dept., central Honduras, 15 mi. N of Juticalpa; coffee, tobacco, sugar cane; livestock. Cigar mfg., tanning in Guacoca (gwäkō′kä) (pop. 70), 8 mi. ESE. Sugar milling in El Regadillo (ĕl rägä-dhē′yō), 2 mi. ENE.

San Francisco del Carnicero (dĕl kärnēsä′rō), village (1950 pop. 942), Managua dept., SW Nicaragua, port on N shore of L. Managua, 23 mi. N of Managua; livestock and grain trade; hogs, poultry.

San Francisco del Chañar (dĕl chänyär′), village (pop. estimate 700), ⊙ Sobremonte dept. (□ c.2,200; pop. 5,683), N Córdoba prov., Argentina, 115 mi. NNE of Córdoba; grain, livestock. Manganese deposits near by. Leper colony.

San Francisco de Limache (dä lē mä'chä), town (pop. 6,322), Valparaiso prov., central Chile, on railroad and 21 mi. ENE of Valparaiso, adjoining Limache (SE); fruit- and winegrowing center; also grain, vegetables, livestock.

San Francisco del Oro (dĕl ō'rō), town (pop. 10,809), Chihuahua, N Mexico, in E outliers of Sierra Madre Occidental, 12 mi. SW of Hidalgo del Parral; mining center (silver, gold, lead, copper, zinc).

San Francisco de los Adame, Mexico: see Luis Moya.

San Francisco del Parapetí (päräpätē'), village (pop. c.700), Santa Cruz dept., SE Bolivia, on Parapetí R. and 45 mi. ESE of Lagunillas; sugar cane, fruit, vegetables. Franciscan mission until 1913. San Antonio del Parapetí (pop. c.1,500) is 2 mi. SW.

San Francisco del Rincón (rēnkōn'), city (pop. 12,015), Guanajuato, central Mexico, on central plateau, 14 mi. SW of León, alt. 5,646 ft. Rail terminus; agr. center (grain, sugar cane, fruit, vegetables, stock); flour mills; chicle, straw hats.

San Francisco de Macaira (dā mäkī'rä), town (pop. 957), Guárico state, N central Venezuela, on S slopes of coastal range, 60 mi. SE of Caracas; coffee, cattle.

San Francisco de Macorís (mäkōrēs'), city (1935 pop. 10,100; 1950 pop. 16,152), ⊙ Duarte prov., E central Dominican Republic, in fertile La Vega Real valley, on affluent of Camú R. and 32 mi. ESE of Santiago, 60 mi. NNW of Ciudad Trujillo; 19°18'N 70°15'W. Rail terminus, processing and trading center for rich agr. region (cacao, coffee, fruit, rice, hides, beeswax). Founded 1777.

San Francisco de Mostazal (mōstäsäl'), town (pop. 2,070), O'Higgins prov., central Chile, in the central valley, on railroad and 14 mi. N of Rancagua. Agr. center (wheat, alfalfa, potatoes, beans, fruit, cattle); flour milling, dairying.

San Francisco de Paula (sän frän-thē'skō dä pou'lä), village (pop. 663), Iviza, Balearic Isls., 3 mi. SW of Iviza city; winegrowing. Saltworks near by.

San Francisco de Paula (sän' fränsē'skō), town (pop. 2,860), Havana prov., W Cuba, 6 mi. SE of Havana; dairying, sugar growing.

San Francisco de Santa Fe (sän'tä fā'), town (pop. estimate 1,000), SW Santa Fe prov., Argentina, 14 mi. NW of Venado Tuerto; grain and livestock center. Formerly called San Francisco de Venado Tuerto; sometimes San Francisco.

San Francisco de Selva, Chile: see Copiapó.

San Francisco de Solano, Mission, Calif.: see Sonoma, city.

San Francisco de Venado Tuerto, Argentina: see San Francisco de Santa Fe.

San Francisco de Yare (yä'rā), town (pop. 973), Miranda state, N Venezuela, on Tuy R., on railroad and 25 mi. SSE of Caracas; coffee, cacao, sugar cane, corn.

San Francisco de Yojoa (yōhō'ä), town (pop. 554), Cortés dept., W central Honduras, N of L. Yojoa, 33 mi. S of San Pedro Sula; bananas, rice, corn, livestock.

San Francisco El Alto, Guatemala: see San Francisco.

San Francisco Javier (sän frän-thē'skō hävyĕr'), village (pop. 256), Formentera, Balearic Isls., 14 mi. S of Iviza; saltworks; flour milling; wine.

San Francisco–Oakland Bay Bridge (săn frŭnsĭ'skō), W Calif., suspension-cantilever bridge over San Francisco Bay, from San Francisco (Rincon Hill) to Oakland; begun May, 1933, and opened Nov. 12, 1936. A double-decker structure (upper level: 6 passenger-automobile lanes; lower level: 3 truck lanes and 2 sets of interurban car tracks). Over-all length is 8¼ mi. From San Francisco side, 2 suspension bridges, each with a main span of 2,310 ft. and 2 smaller spans of 1,160 ft. each, lead 2 mi. to Yerba Buena Isl., halfway across the bay; a tunnel (76 ft. wide, 58 ft. high, and 540 ft. long) leads through the isl. to a cantilever bridge (1,400 ft. long) and to 5 small spans which meet the Oakland approach.

San Francisco Pass (sän fränsē'skō), (15,505 ft.), in the Andes, on Argentina-Chile border, at NW foot of Cerro San Francisco, on road bet. Fiambalá (Argentina) and Copiapó (Chile); 26°53'S 68°15'W.

San Francisco Peaks (săn frŭnsĭ'skō), N Ariz., an eroded volcano c.10 mi. N of Flagstaff. Humphreys Peak (12,655 ft.; highest in state), Agassiz Peak (12,340 ft.), and Fremont Peak (11,940 ft.) are on its rim.

San Francisco River (sän fränsē'skō), in Jujuy and Salta provs., Argentina, formed by confluence of the Río Grande de Jujuy and Lavayén R. 9 mi. ENE of San Pedro, flows c.100 mi. NNE in fertile irrigated valley to Bermejo R. 5 mi. SE of Embarcación.

San Francisco River (săn frŭnsĭ'skō), in E Ariz. and W N.Mex., rises in S part of Apache co., Ariz., flows E into N.Mex., then S and W, re-entering Ariz. in Greenlee co. and joining Gila R. 7 mi. SW of Clifton; c.160 mi. long.

San Francisco Solano Point (sän fränsē'skō sōlä'nō), headland on Pacific coast of Chocó dept., W Colombia, 70 mi. NW of Quibdó; 6°18'N 77°28'W. Sometimes Solano Point.

San Francisco Zapotitlán, Guatemala: see San Francisco.

San Fratello (sän frätĕl'lō), town (pop. 7,665), Messina prov., N Sicily, 15 mi. NE of Mistretta, in cereal, citrus-fruit region; cheese. Has govt. mule-breeding station.

San Fructuoso de Bages (sän frōōktwō'sō dā bä'hĕs), village (pop. 1,283), Barcelona prov., NE Spain, 3 mi. NE of Manresa; cotton milling, alcohol distilling. Has 10th-cent. monastery.

Sanga (säng'gä), village, Leopoldville prov., W Belgian Congo, on Inkisi R., near rapids, and 140 mi. NE of Boma; 2 hydroelectric power plants supply energy to both Leopoldville and Brazzaville.

San Gabriel (sän gäbrē-ĕl'), village (1930 pop. 107), Santiago prov., central Chile, on railroad, on Maipo R., in the Andes, and 34 mi. SE of Santiago; health resort.

San Gabriel, town (1950 pop. 6,382), Carchi, N Ecuador, in the Andes, on branch of Pan-American Highway, and 17 mi. SSW of Tulcán. Agr. center (cereals, potatoes, sugar cane, coffee, cattle, sheep). Mfg. of native woolen rugs and ponchos.

San Gabriel, town (1950 pop. 457), Suchitepéquez dept., SW Guatemala, in Pacific piedmont, 2 mi. S of Mazatenango; coffee, cacao, grain, fodder grasses.

San Gabriel, Jalisco, Mexico: see Venustiano Carranza.

San Gabriel (săn gā'brēŭl), residential city (pop. 20,343), Los Angeles co., S Calif., 9 mi. E of downtown Los Angeles. San Gabriel (or San Gabriel, Arcángel) Mission, founded 1771, contains rare paintings and relics. Inc. 1913.

San Gabriel Chilac, Mexico: see Chilac.

San Gabriel Island (sän gäbrē-ĕl'), small rocky islet in the Río de la Plata, off coast of Colonia dept., SW Uruguay, 3 mi. W of Colonia city, opposite Buenos Aires.

San Gabriel Mountains (săn gā'brēŭl), S Calif., E–W range rising bet. the Mojave Desert on N and the Los Angeles basin and part of San Fernando Valley on S; extends c.60 mi. E, from E end (Newhall Pass) of Santa Susana Mts. N of San Fernando, to Cajon Pass at NW end of San Bernardino Mts. San Antonio Peak (Old Baldy), 10,080 ft. in alt., is highest point. Range also includes Mt. Wilson (astronomical observatory), just NE of Pasadena; and twin peaks of North Baldy (9,131 ft.) and Mt. Baden-Powell (bā'dŭn-pō'ŭl) (9,389 ft.; formerly also called North Baldy), c.65 mi. NE of Los Angeles. S foothills, in Los Angeles and San Bernardino counties, are productive citrus-fruit belt, with a chain of residential and agr. communities.

San Gabriel River. 1 In S Calif., intermittent stream formed in San Gabriel Mts. NE of Los Angeles by 3 forks, flows c.75 mi. SSW from their junction, spreading in a broad wash at base of the mts., to Alamitos Bay just E of Long Beach. Subject to torrential floods, it has extensive control works (levees, dams): on West Fork is San Gabriel No. 2 Dam (290 ft. high, 620 ft. long; completed 1935); on upper main stream are San Gabriel No. 1 Dam (381 ft. high, 1,540 ft. long; completed 1938) and Morris Dam (328 ft. high, 780 ft. long; completed 1934; water-supply reservoir for Pasadena). On lower course is Santa Fe flood-control basin, formed by Santa Fe Dam (92 ft. high, c.2,400 ft. long). **2** In central Texas, formed at Georgetown by North and South forks rising in Burnet co., flows c.50 mi. generally E to Little R. 6 mi. S of Cameron.

Sangachelling, India: see Namchi.

Sanga Cho (säng'gä chō'), Chinese *Sang-ang* (säng'-äng'), after 1913 *Komai* or *K'o-mai* (kŭ'mī') or *Komo* or *K'o-mo* (kŭ'mō'), town [Tibetan *dzong*], E Tibet, in Kham prov., 120 mi. SW of Paan, and on upper Zayul (Luhit) R.; stock raising; iron deposits.

Sangalkam (säng-gälkäm'), village, W Senegal, Fr. West Africa, at base of Cape Verde peninsula, 15 mi. ENE of Dakar; sisal, peanuts; dairying.

Sangallán Island (säng-gäyän'), SW Peru, 3 mi. off coast of Ica dept., opposite Paracas Peninsula, 17 mi. WSW of Pisco; 13°51'S 76°27'W; 2 mi. wide, 3 mi. long. Large guano deposits.

Sangamankanda, promontory, Ceylon: see Komari.

Sangamner (săng'gŭmnăr), town (pop., including suburban area, 18,730), Ahmadnagar dist., central Bombay, India, on Pravara R. and 50 mi. NW of Ahmadnagar; trade center for cotton and silk yarn, millet, salt, rice; handicraft cloth weaving, biri mfg., vegetable farming. Headworks of Pravara R. canal irrigation system 7 mi. E.

Sangamon (săng'gùmùn), county (□ 880; pop. 131,484), central Ill., in the Corn Belt; ⊙ Springfield. Agr. (corn, wheat, oats, soybeans, livestock, poultry; dairy products). Bituminous-coal mining; limestone, clay, oil, sand, gravel deposits. Mfg. at Springfield. Drained by Sangamon R. and its South Fork; and by Spring, and small Brush and Sugar creeks. Includes artificial L. Springfield (water supply and resort). Formed 1821.

Sangamon River, central Ill., formed by headstreams in NW Champaign co., flows SW to Decatur, where dam impounds L. Decatur, thence W and NW to Illinois R. N of Beardstown; c.250 mi. long. Receives South Fork (c.65 mi. long) E of Springfield.

Sanganer, India: see Jaipur, city.

Sang-ang, Tibet: see Sanga Cho.

Sangar (sŭn-gär'), town (1939 pop. over 2,000), central Yakut Autonomous SSR, Russian SFSR, on Lena R. and 135 mi. NNW of Yakutsk; coal-mining center.

Sangarará (säng-gärärä'), town (pop. 2,108), Cuzco dept., S Peru, in the Andes, 40 mi. SE of Cuzco; alt. 12,355 ft. Grain, potatoes; mfg. of woolen goods.

Sangareddipet (sŭng-gŭrā'dĭpāt) or **Sangareddi,** town (pop. 6,927), ⊙ Medak dist., central Hyderabad state, India, near Manjra R., 31 mi. NW of Hyderabad; rice, sugar cane, oilseeds. Experimental farm. Paint and enamel factory 18 mi. SE, at Lingampalli. Sometimes spelled Sangareddy.

Sangarius River, Turkey: see Sakarya River.

Sanga River or **Sangha River** (säng-gä'), W Ubangi-Shari and central Middle Congo territories, Fr. Equatorial Africa, formed by 2 headstreams at Nola, flows 140 mi. S, partly along Fr. Cameroons border, to Ouesso, thence 225 mi. SSE and, near its mouth, SW to Congo R. at Mossaka. Navigable year around for steamboats below Ouesso, and intermittently up to Nola. Its lower swampy course splits into several mouths and is connected by divergent streams with Likouala-aux-herbes, Likouala-Mossaka, and Ubangi rivers. Palm products are shipped on it.

Sanga Sanga Island (säng-ä' säng-ä') (7 mi. long; 1939 pop. 1,485), in Tawitawi Group, Sulu prov., Philippines, in Sulu Archipelago, just off SW tip of Tawitawi Isl.

Sangatte (sãgät'), village (pop. 559), Pas-de-Calais dept., N France, on Strait of Dover, 5 mi. W of Calais; bathing resort heavily damaged in Second World War.

San Gavino Monreale (sän gävē'nô mônrĕä'lĕ), village (pop. 5,061), Cagliari prov., W central Sardinia, 29 mi. NNW of Cagliari; rail junction; smelter (lead, silver).

Sangay Volcano (säng-gī'), Andean peak (17,454 ft.), Santiago-Zamora prov., E central Ecuador, 30 mi. SE of Riobamba; 2°S 78°20'W. Snow-capped volcano of great activity.

Sangchih (säng'jŭ'), town, ⊙ Sangchih co. (pop. 140,847), NW Hunan prov., China, near Hupeh line, on branch of Li R. and 60 mi. NNW of Yüanling; rice, wheat, cotton. Lead-zinc and copper mining near by.

Sangeang (sŭng-ääng'), volcanic island (9 mi. in diameter), Indonesia, in Flores Sea, just off NE coast of Sumbawa; 8°12'S 119°4'E; rises to 6,344 ft.; fishing.

San Genaro (sän hänä'rō), town (pop. estimate 1,500), S central Santa Fe prov., Argentina, 55 mi. NW of Rosario; agr. center (corn, flax, wheat, livestock); grain elevators.

Sangeorgiul-de-Padure (sŭnjôr'jōōl-dä-pŭ'dōōrĕ), Rum. *Sângeorgiul-de-Pădure*, Hung. *Erdőszentgyörgy* (ĕr'dŭsĕntdyûr"dyû), village (pop. 3,514), Mures prov., central Rumania, on railroad and 23 mi. NW of Odorhei; mfg. of vinegar. In Hungary, 1940–45.

Sanger (săng'ŭr). **1** City (pop. 6,400), Fresno co., central Calif., in San Joaquin Valley, near Kings R., 13 mi. E of Fresno; ships grapes, raisins; lumber milling, wine making. Inc. 1911. **2** Town (pop. 1,170), Denton co., N Texas, c.45 mi. N of Fort Worth; farm trade center; hatchery, cottonseed-oil mill, cotton gins.

Sangerberg, Czechoslovakia: see Lazne Kynzvart.

Sangerei, Moldavian SSR: see Synzhereya.

Sangerhausen (zäng"ŭrhou'zŭn), town (pop. 16,220), in former Prussian Saxony prov., central Germany, after 1945 in Saxony-Anhalt, at SE foot of the lower Harz, in the Goldene Aue, 30 mi. W of Halle; copper-slate mining; woodworking; mfg. of bicycles, machinery, toys, food products. Rose-growing center. Has 11th-cent. church, and Rosarium.

San Germán (sän' hĕrmän'), town (pop. 3,713), Oriente prov., E Cuba, on railroad and 20 mi. SSE of Holguín; sugar-milling center.

San Germán, town (pop. 8,872), SW Puerto Rico, on Guanajibo R. and 10 mi. SE of Mayagüez, in agr. region (sugar cane, coffee, tobacco); rail junction and processing center; mfg. of needlework. An old Sp. settlement selected by Columbus' son Diego, with one of America's oldest churches (built 1511), Porta Coeli, partly in ruins. Adjoining the town (W) is the Polytechnic Inst. (founded 1912). San Germán is the birthplace of St. Rose of Lima, 1st Amer. saint.

San Germano Vercellese (sän jĕrmä'nô vĕrchĕllä'zĕ), village (pop. 2,408), Vercelli prov., Piedmont, N Italy, near Cavour Canal, 9 mi. WNW of Vercelli.

San Gerónimo, Argentina: see San Jerónimo Sud.

San Gerónimo, Peru: see San Jerónimo.

San Geronimo de Taos, N.Mex.: see Taos, village.

San Gerónimo de Tunán, Peru: see San Jerónimo, Junín dept.

San Gerónimo Island (sän hārō'nēmō), in Paraná R., NE Santa Fe prov., Argentina, near Reconquista; 17 mi. long, c.5 mi. wide.

Sangerville (săng'gŭrvĭl), town (pop. 1,161), Piscataquis co., central Maine, on the Piscataquis and just W of Dover-Foxcroft; agr.; textile mills. Settled 1801, inc. 1814.

Sang-e-Sar, Iran: see SANG-I-SAR.
Sangha, region, Fr. Equatorial Africa: see OUESSO.
Sangha (säng'hä), village, S Fr. Sudan, Fr. West Africa, 55 mi. E of Mopti, in agr. region (rice, millet, stock). Noted for its view of surrounding cliffs and cascades.
Sangha River, Fr. Equatorial Africa: see SANGA RIVER.
Sangi, Indonesia: see SANGI ISLANDS.
Sangiang (sŭng-ēäng'), Du. *Dwars-in-den-Weg* (dwärs'-ĭn-dŭ-vā'), volcanic islet (□ 2.8; 3 mi. long), Indonesia, in Sunda Strait bet. Java and Sumatra, 9 mi. W of Merak; 5°58'S 105°52'E.
Sangi Islands or **Sangihe Islands** (säng'ē), volcanic group (□ 314; pop. 134,904), Indonesia, bet. Celebes Sea (W) and Molucca Passage (E), 30 mi. NNE of Celebes; 3°N 125°30'E. Comprise isls. of Sangi (largest isl.), SIAU, TAHULANDANG, BIARO, and several islets. Mountainous, forested (ebony, rattan, coconuts). Agr. (sago, nutmeg), fishing, copra production. Sometimes spelled Sangir. Largest isl., Sangi or Sangihe (□ 217; pop. 79,537), is c.120 mi. N of NE tip of Celebes; 3°33'N 125°32'E; 30 mi. long, 10 mi. wide. Mountainous, it rises to 6,002 ft. at Mt. Awu. On W coast is Tahuna or Tahoena (both: täōō'nŭ), chief town and port of group, exporting timber, nutmeg, copra.
San Gil (sän hēl'), town (pop. 7,811), Santander dept., N central Colombia, in W Cordillera Oriental, on Pan-American Highway and 40 mi. S of Bucaramanga; alt. 3,592 ft. Processing and agr. center (sugar cane, coffee, tobacco, corn, fique, vegetables, livestock); mfg. of fique bags, cordage; tanning, corn and coffee milling. Archaeological remains have been found near by.
San Gil Mountains, Guatemala: see MICO, SIERRA DEL.
San Gimignano (sän jēmēnyä'nô), town (pop. 3,426), Siena prov., Tuscany, central Italy, 18 mi. SW of Siena; alcohol distilling, ironworking. Noted for its medieval aspect. Its town walls, palaces, and famous 13 towers remain much as they were in 13th and 14th cent. Frescoes by Benozzo Gozzoli in 12th-cent. collegiate church (war damage restored) and church of St. Augustine (1280–98). In Second World War damaged by air bombing and artillery fire.
San Ginés de Vilasar (sän hēnās' dā vēläsär'), town (pop. 3,169), Barcelona prov., NE Spain, 5 mi. WSW of Mataró; textile center (cotton and silk). Wine, strawberries, oranges in area.
San Ginesio (sän jēnā'zyô), village (pop. 1,187), Macerata prov., The Marches, central Italy, 15 mi. SSW of Macerata; mfg. (soap, hosiery).
San Giorgio a Cremano (sän jôr'jô ä krĕmä'nô), town (pop. 12,298), Napoli prov., Campania, S Italy, at W foot of Mt. Vesuvius, 4 mi. W of Naples; tomato canning.
San Giorgio Canavese (känävā'zĕ), village (pop. 1,880), Torino prov., Piedmont, NW Italy, 10 mi. SSW of Ivrea.
San Giorgio della Richinvelda (dĕl-lä rēkēnvĕl'dä), village (pop. 726), Udine prov., Friuli–Venezia Giulia, NE Italy, 17 mi. W of Udine, near Tagliamento R.; mfg. (soap, alcohol, iron chests).
San Giorgio di Lomellina (dē lômĕl-lē'nä), village (pop. 2,189), Pavia prov., Lombardy, 6 mi. SSE of Mortara; silk mill.
San Giorgio di Nogaro (nôgä'rô), town (pop. 4,047), Udine prov., Friuli–Venezia Giulia, NE Italy, 16 mi. S of Udine; rail junction.
San Giorgio di Piano (pyä'nô), town (pop. 2,291), Bologna prov., Emilia-Romagna, N central Italy, 10 mi. N of Bologna; hemp mill.
San Giorgio Ionico (yô'nēkô), town (pop. 5,380), Ionio prov., Apulia, S Italy, 8 mi. E of Taranto; olive oil, wine, cheese; cereals, tobacco.
San Giorgio la Molara (lä môlä'rä), village (pop. 3,136), Benevento prov., Campania, S Italy, 12 mi. NNE of Benevento.
San Giorgio Lucano (lōōkä'nô), village (pop. 2,554), Matera prov., Basilicata, S Italy, 10 mi. SW of Tursi, in stock-raising region; wine, olive oil.
San Giorgio Maggiore (mäd-jô'rĕ), one of islands forming S quarter of Venice, N Italy.
San Giorgio Morgeto (môrjā'tô), village (pop. 4,126), Reggio di Calabria prov., Calabria, S Italy, 14 mi. ENE of Palmi; wine, olive oil.
San Giorgio Piacentino (pyächĕntē'nô), village (pop. 1,049), Piacenza prov., Emilia-Romagna, N central Italy, near Nure R., 7 mi. SSE of Piacenza; canned tomatoes, sausage.
San Giorgio su Legnano (sōō lĕnyä'nô), town (pop. 3,941), Milano prov., Lombardy, N Italy, 1 mi. S of Legnano; foundries.
San Giovanni, Sardinia: see IGLESIAS.
San Giovanni, Yugoslavia: see BRAC ISLAND.
San Giovanni alla Vena (sän jôvän'nē äl-lä vā'nä), village (pop. 1,303), Pisa prov., Tuscany, central Italy, on the Arno and 9 mi. E of Pisa; toy mfg.
San Giovanni a Teduccio (ä tĕdōōt'chô), SE suburb (pop. 30,188) of Naples, S Italy; shipyards, foundry; food canning, mfg. of cannery machinery.
San Giovanni Bianco (byäng'kô), village (pop. 1,063), Bergamo prov., Lombardy, N Italy, on Brembo R. and 13 mi. N of Bergamo; barite mining.
San Giovanni di Medua, Albania: see SHËNGJIN.
San Giovanni Gemini (jā'mēnē), village (pop. 5,239), Agrigento prov., central Sicily, adjacent to Cammarata, 22 mi. N of Agrigento. Rock salt mines near by.
San Giovanni Incarico (ēnkä'rēkô), village (pop. 1,603), Frosinone prov., Latium, S central Italy, near Liri R., 15 mi. SE of Frosinone. Oil deposits near by.
San Giovanni in Fiore (ēn fyô'rĕ), town (pop. 13,460), Cosenza prov., Calabria, S Italy, on Neto R., near mouth of Arvo R., and 25 mi. E of Cosenza. Resort (alt. 3,307 ft.); chief center in La Sila mts.; woolen and lumber mills, woodcarving, dairying. Orichella hydroelectric plant is 5 mi. SSE, on Ampollino R.
San Giovanni in Persiceto (pĕrsēchā'tô), town (pop. 5,321), Bologna prov., Emilia-Romagna, N central Italy, 12 mi. NW of Bologna; rail junction; mfg. (agr. machinery, metal furniture, ribbon, hemp products).
San Giovanni Lupatoto (lōōpätô'tô), town (pop. 5,314), Verona prov., Veneto, N Italy, near Adige R., 4 mi. SSE of Verona; mfg. (chemicals, furniture); tannery.
San Giovanni Rotondo (rôtôn'dô), town (pop. 12,920), Foggia prov., Apulia, S Italy, on S slope of Gargano promontory, 19 mi. NNE of Foggia. Agr. center (wheat, olives, grapes, walnuts, sheep). Bauxite mines near by.
San Giovanni Suergiu (swĕr'jū), village (pop. 525), Cagliari prov., SW Sardinia, adjacent to Palmas Suergiu; lignite cracking (synthetic carbide, oil, coke), barite processing.
San Giovanni Valdarno (väldär'nô), town (pop. 8,386), Arezzo prov., Tuscany, central Italy, on the Arno and 20 mi. SE of Florence, in lignite-mining region. Mfg. center; cotton textiles, hosiery, pottery, glass; foundry. Has 15th-cent. church (damaged 1944) with a terra cotta by G. della Robbia. Masaccio b. here. Damaged by air bombing in Second World War.
Sangir Islands, Indonesia: see SANGI ISLANDS.
Sang-i-Sar or **Sang-e-Sar** (both: säng'gĕsär'), village, Second Prov., in Samnan, N Iran, in Elburz mts., 12 mi. N of Semnan; grain, cotton; sheep raising.
San Giuliano, Monte, Sicily: see ERICE.
San Giuliano Terme (sän jūlyä'nô tĕr'mĕ), town (pop. 1,353), Pisa prov., Tuscany, central Italy, at W foot of Monte Pisano, 4 mi. NE of Pisa; cotton mill, lamp factory. Health resort with mineral springs. Stone quarries and gravel pits near by. Formerly Bagni San Giuliano.
San Giulio (sän jū'lyô), rocky islet (pop. 197), in L. of Orta, Novara prov., Piedmont, N Italy, opposite Orta Novarese. Has seminary, anc. basilica of San Giulio (built 4th cent.; reconstructed several times since) containing tomb of St. Julius.
San Giuseppe di Cairo (sän jūsĕp'pĕ dē kī'rô), village (pop. 375), Savona prov., Liguria, NW Italy, on Bormida di Spigno R. and 11 mi. WNW of Savona; rail junction. Large storage center (coal, cotton, steel) for Savona (linked by 10¾-mi. aerial railway; longest in Europe). Produces coke and coal-tar products.
San Giuseppe Iato (yä'tô), town (pop. 8,840), Palermo prov., NW Sicily, adjacent to San Cipirello, 14 mi. SW of Palermo, in cereal-growing region; wine. Also spelled San Giuseppe Jato.
San Giuseppe Vesuviano (vĕzōōvyä'nô), town (pop. 6,099), Napoli prov., Campania, S Italy, at E foot of Vesuvius, 6 mi. NNE of Torre Annunziata; macaroni and sausage factories, cotton mill, alcohol distillery.
San Giustino (sän jūstē'nô), village (pop. 858), Perugia prov., Umbria, central Italy, 2 mi. SE of Sansepolcro; mfg. of agr. tools.
San Giusto Canavese (sän jūs'tô känävā'zĕ), village (pop. 2,200), Torino prov., Piedmont, NW Italy, 18 mi. NNE of Turin.
Sangju (säng'jōō'), Jap. *Shoshu*, town (1949 pop. 43,760), N.Kyongsang prov., S Korea, 43 mi. NW of Taegu; commercial center for rice-growing and mining area (graphite, gold, silver).
Sangkan River, Chinese *Sangkan Ho* (säng'gän' hŭ'), Chahar prov., China, rises near Shansi line in area of Shohsien, flows over 100 mi. ENE, joining Yang R. near Cholu to form Yungting R.
Sangkapura, Indonesia: see BAWEAN.
Sangla (säng'glŭ) or **Sangla Hill,** town (pop. 5,721), Sheikhupura dist., E central Punjab, W Pakistan, 35 mi. W of Sheikhupura; rail junction; wheat, cotton, millet; cotton ginning.
Sanglang (säng"läng'), village, Perlis, NW Malaya, minor port on Strait of Malacca, 12 mi. S of Kangar, at Kedah line; fisheries.
Sangley Point, Philippines: see CAVITE, city.
Sangli (säng'glē), town (pop., including W suburb of Sanglivadi, across Kistna R., 37,756), ⊙ Satara South dist., S Bombay, India, on Kistna R. and 185 mi. SSE of Bombay. Rail terminus; trade center; agr. market (cotton, grain, peanuts, sugar); cotton and oilseed milling, hand-loom weaving, coffee curing, mfg. of agr. implements, peanut decorticators, dairy products, rope, ice. Engineering col. Was ⊙ former princely state of Saugli (□ 1,146; pop. 293,381) in Deccan States, Bombay; state inc. 1949 into Dharwar, Belgaum, Satara South, Satara North, Sholapur, and Bijapur dists., Bombay.
Sangmélima (sängmĕlē'mä), village, N'Tem region, S central Fr. Cameroons, 55 mi. E of Ebolowa; coffee plantations.
Sangnga Chöling, India: see NAMCHI.
Sangod (sŭngōd'), town (pop. 5,726), SE Rajasthan, India, 33 mi. SE of Kotah; wheat, millet, oilseeds.
Sangola (säng'gōlŭ), town (pop. 5,818), Sholapur dist., central Bombay, India, 50 mi. WSW of Sholapur; trade center for millet, cotton, peanuts.
Sangolquí (säng-gōlkē'), town (1950 pop. 3,082), Pichincha prov., N central Ecuador, in the Andes, on Guaillabamba R. and 8 mi. SSE of Quito, in the fertile Chillos Valley; processing and agr. center (cereals, potatoes, tobacco, stock); textile milling; mfg. of tobacco products and brooms. Severely damaged (1938) by tectonic disturbances caused by underground water.
San Gorgonio, Mount (săn gôrgō'nēō), peak (11,485 ft.) of San Bernardino Mts., highest point in S Calif., c.80 mi. E of Los Angeles.
San Gorgonio Pass (alt. 2,804 ft.), S Calif., rail and highway pass 15 mi. ESE of San Bernardino, connecting N end of Coachella Valley with San Bernardino Valley. Mt. San Gorgonio (in San Bernardino Mts.) is N, Mt. San Jacinto (San Jacinto Mts.) is S. Broad floor of pass (3–4 mi. wide) is orchard region.
Sangorodok (sän"gŭrŭdôk'), agr. town (1939 pop. over 500), NE Komi Autonomous SSR, Russian SFSR, on Usa R. (head of May–Oct. navigation) and 32 mi. S of Vorkuta; trading post. Until construction of N. Pechora RR (1940), it was river port for Vorkuta coal (rail link). Until c.1945, called Ust-Vorkuta.
San Gottardo, Switzerland: see SAINT GOTTHARD.
Sangpiling, China: see TINGSIANG, Sikang prov.
Sangre, Sierra de (syĕ'rä dā säng'grā), range in the Patagonian Andes, NW Santa Cruz natl. territory, Argentina, extends c.30 mi. N–S along Chile border, N and E of L. San Martín; rises to c.7,000 ft.
Sangre de Cristo Mountains (săng'grē dŭ krĭ'stō), southernmost range of Rocky Mts., and extension of the Front Range; extend c.220 mi. SSE and S, bet. the Great Plains (E) and the San Luis Valley and upper course of the Rio Grande (W), from Salida, S central Colo., into Santa Fe co., N central N.Mex.; include extensive natl.-forest area. Part of range in Alamosa, Huerfano, and Costilla counties, Colo., is known as SIERRA BLANCA (highest part of the system, rising to 14,363 ft. in Blanca Peak). Other peaks in Colo.: Horn Peak (13,400 ft.), Trinchera Peak (trĭnchâ'rŭ) (13,540 ft.), Purgatory Peak (13,719 ft.), KIT CARSON PEAK (14,100 ft.), HUMBOLDT PEAK (14,044 ft.), the CRESTONE peaks (highest 14,291 ft.). WHEELER PEAK (13,151 ft.), in N.Mex., is highest point in the state, though one of the TRUCHAS peaks was formerly thought to be higher. The part of the range bet. La Veta Pass, Colo., and N.Mex. line is sometimes referred to as Culebra Range, which rises to 14,069 ft. in CULEBRA PEAK. Coal mines near Trinidad, Colo.; lead, zinc, coal, gold, and silver mines near Santa Fe, N.Mex. S tip of range drained by headwaters of Pecos R.
San Gregorio (sän grägōr'yō), town (pop. 2,000), S Santa Fe prov., Argentina, 40 mi. S of Venado Tuerto; agr. center (wheat, flax, barley, corn, cattle, hogs).
San Gregorio. 1 Village (1930 pop. 145), Magallanes prov., S Chile, on shore of Strait of Magellan, and 45 mi. NE of Punta Arenas; sheep raising. **2** Village (1930 pop. 269), Ñuble prov., S central Chile, 27 mi. NE of Chillán, in agr. area (grain, wine, vegetables, potatoes, livestock).
San Gregorio, Nicaragua: see SANTO DOMINGO.
San Gregorio (sän grägōr'yō), town (pop. 2,850), Tacuarembó dept., central Uruguay, on large artificial lake formed by the Río Negro, and 65 mi. SSE of Tacuarembó; road junction; agr. products (vegetables, grain); cattle raising.
San Gregorio Atlapulco, Mexico: see ATLAPULCO.
San Gregorio Atzompa, Mexico: see ATZOMPA.
San Gregorio Magno (sän grĕgô'rēô mä'nyô), town (pop. 4,847), Salerno prov., Campania, S Italy, 2 mi. NE of Buccino.
Sangre Grande (săng'grē grăn'dē), town (pop. 3,762), N Trinidad, B.W.I., 27 mi. ESE of Port of Spain; rail terminus and market center for cacao-growing region. Prospered after opening (1941) of U.S. army base Fort Read, just W. The railroad station is called Cunapo, adjoining NW.
Sangri (säng'grē), former princely state (□ 21; pop. 3,839) of Punjab Hill States, India, NE of Simla. Since 1948, merged with Himachal Pradesh.
Sangro River (säng'grô), S central Italy, rises in the Apennines 15 mi. SW of Sulmona, flows 73 mi. SW and NE, past Castel di Sangro and Villa Santa Maria, to the Adriatic 8 mi. E of Lanciano.
Sangrur (sŭng-grōōr'), town (pop. 17,132), ⊙ Sangrur dist., central Patiala and East Punjab States Union, India, 34 mi. WSW of Patiala; trades in millet, corn, gram, ghee, vegetable oils; hand-loom weaving, handicrafts (leather goods, furniture). Has col. Was ⊙ former Punjab state of Jind.
Sang Sang, Nicaragua: see SANSANG.

Sangudo (săn-gōō'dō), village (pop. 236), central Alta., on Pembina R. and 65 mi. WNW of Edmonton; mixed farming, lumbering.

Sanguém (säng-gĕm'), town (pop. 3,186), central Goa dist., Portuguese India, in foothills of Western Ghats, 28 mi. SE of Pangim; manganese mining. Timber in near-by forests. Also called Cotarli.

Sangüesa (säng-gwā'sä), city (pop. 3,587), Navarre prov., N Spain, on Aragon R. and 25 mi. SE of Pamplona; terminus of branch railroad from Pamplona. Agr. trade center (wine, wheat, truck produce); flour- and sawmilling. Has medieval castle of kings of Navarre, Romanesque church, and several Renaissance mansions. Was Navarre's stronghold in wars with Aragon.

San Guillermo (sän gēyĕr'mō), town (pop. estimate 1,000), W central Santa Fe prov., Argentina, on railroad and 40 mi. W of San Cristóbal; agr. (wheat, flax, alfalfa, livestock); dairying.

Sanguin, Liberia: see SANGWIN.

Sanguinetto (säng-gwēnĕt'tō), village (pop. 1,532), Verona prov., Veneto, N Italy, 8 mi. W of Legnago; beet-sugar refinery.

Sangu River (sŭng'gōō), in SE East Bengal, E Pakistan, rises in S Chittagong Hills, on E Pakistan-Burma border; flows N, past Bandarban, and W to Bay of Bengal 15 mi. S of Chittagong; 120 mi. long.

Sangvor (sŭn-gvôr'), village (1939 pop. over 500), S Garm oblast, Tadzhik SSR, on N slope of Darvaza Range, on Obi-Khingou R. and 50 mi. SE of Garm; gold mining.

Sangwin (săng'gwĭn), town, Sinoe co., SE Liberia, on Atlantic Ocean, at mouth of Sangwin R. (70 mi. long), and 25 mi. WNW of Greenville; palm oil and kernels, cassava, rice. Mission station. Also spelled Sanguin.

Sang-yüan Ssu, Tibet: see SAMYE.

San Hilario Sacalm (sän ēlä'ryō säkälm'), town (pop. 1,562), Gerona prov., NE Spain, 17 mi. SW of Gerona; health resort, noted since 18th cent. for its mineral springs; agr. trade center; sawmilling.

Sanhing, China: see SUNHING.

San Hipólito de Voltregá (sän ēpō'lētō dā vōltrāgä'), town (pop. 1,947), Barcelona prov., NE Spain, 6 mi. NNW of Vich; cotton-yarn mfg.; cereals, potatoes, vegetables.

Sanho (sän'hŭ'). **1** Town, ⊙ Sanho co. (pop. 239,057), N Hopeh prov., China, 35 mi. E of Peking; wheat, kaoliang, millet, corn. **2** Town, Kweichow prov., China: see SANTU.

San-hsia, Formosa: see SANSIA.

Sanhsing, China: see SUNHING.

San-hui, China: see SANHWEI.

Sanhur (sän'hōōr), **Sanhur el Qibliya,** or **Sanhur al-Qibliyah** (both: ĕl kĭblē'yü), village (pop. 12,061), Faiyum prov., Upper Egypt, 8 mi. NNW of Faiyum; cotton, cereals, sugar cane, dates. Sometimes spelled Senhur.

Sanhur el Medina or **Sanhur al-Madinah** (both: ĕl mĕdē'nü), village (pop. 12,795), Gharbiya prov., Lower Egypt, on railroad and 5 mi. ESE of Disuq; cotton.

Sanhut el Birak or **Sanhut al-Birak** (both: săn'hōōt ĕl bĭräk'), village (pop. 7,439), Sharqiya prov., Lower Egypt, 10 mi. ENE of Benha; cotton.

Sanhwei or **San-hui** (both: sän'hwā'), town, NE central Szechwan prov., China, 15 mi. NE of Chühsien and on right bank of Chü R.; river port.

Sanibel Island (să'nĭbŭl), SW Fla., narrow barrier island (c.12 mi. long) in Gulf of Mexico, c.20 mi. SW of Fort Myers; partly shelters San Carlos Bay and Pine Island Sound. Lighthouse and Sanibel village at SE end. Ferry connections with Punta Rasa.

Sanica or **Sanitsa** (both: sä'nĭtsä), village (pop. 6,048), NW Bosnia, Yugoslavia, 9 mi. NW of Kljuc.

San Ignacio (sän ēgnä'syō), town (pop. estimate 1,500), ⊙ San Ignacio dept. (□ c.700; 1947 pop. 29,191), S Misiones natl. territory, Argentina, near Paraná R., 25 mi. ENE of Posadas, in agr. area (maté, corn, rice, citrus fruit, tobacco). Agr. research station. An old (early 17th cent.) Jesuit settlement, it attracts visitors because of its ruins which include a baroque church.

San Ignacio. 1 Town (pop. c.4,700), ⊙ Moxos prov., Beni dept., N central Bolivia, in the llanos, c.50 mi. W of Trinidad; cattle, cotton. Airport. **2** Town (pop. c.4,200), ⊙ Velasco prov., Santa Cruz dept., E Bolivia, 170 mi. NE of Santa Cruz; rubber business center. Airport. Founded 1748 as Jesuit mission.

San Ignacio, town (pop. 1,180), Ñuble prov., S central Chile, 15 mi. SSE of Chillán; agr. center (wheat, corn, wine, lentils, potatoes, livestock); lumbering.

San Ignacio, Costa Rica: see ACOSTA.

San Ignacio. 1 Town, Chihuahua, Mexico: see PRAXEDIS G. GUERRERO. **2** Village (pop. 1,169), Coahuila, N Mexico, on Nazas R., in Laguna Dist., and 23 mi. ENE of Torreón; cotton, cereals, wine, vegetables. Cooperative settlement. **3** Town (pop. 1,914), Sinaloa, NW Mexico, in W outliers of Sierra Madre Occidental, on Piaxtla R. and 50 mi. N of Mazatlán; gold and silver mining; lumbering.

San Ignacio, town (dist. pop. 7,943), Misiones dept., S Paraguay, 120 mi. SSE of Asunción; agr. center (maté, rice, oranges, cattle); lumbering, rice and maté milling. Anc. Jesuit mission, founded 1609.

San Ignacio, village (pop. 175), Cajamarca dept., NW Peru, in Cordillera Occidental, near Peru-Ecuador border, 41 mi. NNW of Jaén; alt. 4,344 ft. Wheat, corn, potatoes, cattle.

San Ignacio de Acosta, Costa Rica: see ACOSTA.

San Ignacio Island (□ 19), islet just off coast of Sinaloa, NW Mexico, in Gulf of California, 20 mi. SW of Los Mochis; 15 mi. long, c.1½ mi. wide; alluvial.

Sanikatta, India: see GOKARN.

Sanilac (să'nŭlăk), county (□ 961; pop. 30,837), E Mich.; ⊙ Sandusky. Bounded E by L. Huron; drained by Black and Cass rivers. Agr. (beans, sugar beets, fruit, grain, livestock; dairy products). Mfg. at Sandusky. Fisheries. Resorts. Organized 1849.

San Ildefonso (sän ēldāfōn'sō). **1** Town (pop. 1,046), Hidalgo, central Mexico, 40 mi. WSW of Pachuca; cereals, vegetables, fruit, cotton. **2** Town (pop. 1,615), Mexico state, central Mexico, 17 mi. NW of Mexico city; hydroelectric station. **3** Town (pop. 1,342), Querétaro, central Mexico, 40 mi. SE of Querétaro; grain, sugar cane, beans, alfalfa, livestock.

San Ildefonso (săn ĭl"dŭfŏn'sō, Sp. sän ēldāfōn'sō), town (1939 pop. 1,442; 1948 municipality pop. 18,288), Bulacan prov., S central Luzon, Philippines, 33 mi. N of Manila, near railroad; rice, corn.

San Ildefonso or **La Granja** (lä grän'hä), town (pop. 1,717), Segovia prov., central Spain, in Old Castile, in the Sierra de Guadarrama at foot of the Peñalara, 38 mi. NW of Madrid; alt. 3,907 ft. Henry IV here built a hunting lodge in 1450. Famed as royal summer residence, founded (1719) by Philip V. It was designed to rival Versailles. Has beautiful palace, collegiate church, 18th-cent. gardens and fountains. Here took place major events in modern Sp. history, such as abdication (1724) of Philip V, signing of Treaty of San Ildefonso (1796) by Spain and France with England, revocation (1832) of Pragmatic Sanction by Ferdinand VII. The Queen Regent Christina accepted (1836) here the liberal Cádiz constitution. The palace was partly destroyed by 1918 fire. Mfg. of crystal articles.

San Ildefonso (săn ĭldŭfŏn'sō), pueblo (□ 40.2), Santa Fe co., N central N.Mex. San Ildefonso village (1948 pop. 174) is on E bank of the Rio Grande and 17 mi. NW of Santa Fe in irrigated region; alt. c.5,500 ft. Inhabitants raise grain, chili, and vegetables. Known for excellence of pottery and painting. Fiesta in Jan. includes ceremonial dances. Present settlement established c.1700.

San Ildefonso Hueyotlipan, Mexico: see HUEYOTLIPAN, Tlaxcala.

San Ildefonso Ixtahuacán, Guatemala: see IXTAHUACÁN.

San Ildefonso Peninsula, Quezon prov., central Luzon, Philippines, in Philippine Sea, on E coast of isl., forms E shore of Casiguran Sound; 25 mi. long, 1–5 mi. wide. Mountainous, rising to 2,120 ft. Casiguran town is at base of peninsula; Cape San Ildefonso (16°1'N 121°59'E) is at S tip.

Sanine, Lebanon: see SANNIN, JEBEL.

Sanish (să'nĭsh), village (pop. 507), Mountrail co., NW central N.Dak., 24 mi. SSW of Stanley and on Missouri R. Resort; fisheries, coal mining, timber, livestock, vegetables. Adjoining is VERENDRYE NATIONAL MONUMENT. Fort Berthold Indian Reservation is near by.

San Isidro (sän ēsē'dhrō). **1** City (pop. 25,070), ⊙ San Isidro dist. (□ 20; pop. 91,770), in N Greater Buenos Aires, Argentina, on the Río de la Plata and 13 mi. NW of Buenos Aires; residential and mfg. center. Frozen meat, dairy products, tires, paper, ceramics, candles, novelties, leather goods. Resort for fishing, yachting, swimming, racing. Has natl. col., theaters, history mus. **2** Village (pop. estimate 1,000), ⊙ Valle Viejo dept. (□ 444; pop. 6,289), SE Catamarca prov., Argentina, on the Río del Valle and 4 mi. NE of Catamarca; agr. center (grain, cotton, wine, livestock). San Isidro with adjoining Dolores (N) is sometimes called Valle Viejo.

San Isidro. 1 Town (1950 pop. 336), Heredia prov., central Costa Rica, on central plateau, 5 mi. NE of Heredia; coffee, potatoes, livestock. Has Gothic church. **2** or **San Isidro de Coronado** (dā kōrōnä'dō), town (pop. 735), San José prov., central Costa Rica, on central plateau, 5 mi. NE of San José; summer resort for San José. Trading center in livestock and dairying area; coffee, vegetables, grain; abattoir. Milk and butter exports. Has school colony for handicapped children. **3** Town, San José prov., Costa Rica: see UREÑA.

San Isidro, town (pop. 994), Choluteca dept., S Honduras, c.10 mi. ENE of Pespire; reed weaving; corn, beans, livestock.

San Isidro, town (1950 pop. 1,385), Matagalpa dept., W central Nicaragua, 24 mi. W of Matagalpa, on Inter-American Highway; corn, poultry.

San Isidro, S residential section (pop. 8,778) of Lima, Lima dept., W central Peru, just N of Miraflores. Inc. 1940 into Lima proper. Remains of anc. pre-Columbian city near by.

San Isidro. 1 Town (1939 pop. 7,200; 1948 municipality pop. 31,243), NW Leyte, Philippines, on Visayan Sea, 45 mi. WNW of Tacloban; agr. center (rice, coconuts). **2** Town (1939 pop. 2,192; 1948 municipality pop. 13,191), Nueva Ecija prov., central Luzon, Philippines, 32 mi. NNW of Manila; rice, corn.

San Isidro, town (pop. 798), Cabañas dept., N central Salvador, 7 mi. WSW of Sensuntepeque; grain, livestock; gold mining.

San Isidro de Coronado, Costa Rica: see SAN ISIDRO, San José prov.

San Isidro de las Cuevas, Mexico: see VILLA MATAMOROS, Chihuahua.

San Isidro de Zaragoza, Mexico: see ZARAGOZA, VERACRUZ.

Sanitary and Ship Canal, NE Ill., federally operated navigable waterway and drainage canal (c.30 mi. long) linking South Branch of Chicago R. in Chicago with Des Plaines R. (locks) at Lockport; part of ILLINOIS WATERWAY. Opened 1900 as Chicago Drainage Canal, later improved and renamed. Carries the reversed flow of Chicago R., which disposes of city's treated sewage; and replaces old Illinois and Michigan Canal, part of whose course it parallels, as a shipping artery.

Sanitsa, Yugoslavia: see SANICA.

Sanivarsante (sŭnĭvär'sŭntā) or **Shanivarsante** (shŭ–), village (pop. 756), N Coorg, India, 23 mi. NNE of Mercara; sandalwood, rice (terraces).

San Jacinto (sän häsēn'tō), village (pop. estimate 500), central Buenos Aires prov., Argentina, 7 mi. SW of Olavarría; cement-milling center.

San Jacinto, town (pop. 5,891), Bolívar dept., N Colombia, 50 mi. SE of Cartagena; agr. center (coffee, tobacco, corn, livestock).

San Jacinto, village (pop. 2,091), Ancash dept., W central Peru, in W foothills of Cordillera Negra of the Andes, on railroad and 15 mi. ENE of Puerto Samanco, 22 mi. ESE of Chimbote; major sugar- and cotton-producing center (irrigation); sugar milling, cotton ginning.

San Jacinto, town (1939 pop. 3,686; 1948 municipality pop. 20,208), on E coast of Ticao Isl., Masbate prov., Philippines, 15 mi. NE of Masbate town; agr. center (rice, coconuts).

San Jacinto, extinct volcano (3,855 ft.), central Salvador, just SE of San Salvador.

San Jacinto (săn jŭsĭn'tŭ), county (□ 619; pop. 7,172), E Texas; ⊙ Coldspring. Bounded N and E by Trinity R., and drained by headstreams of San Jacinto R. Most of co. is in Sam Houston Natl. Forest. Lumbering (including pulpwood) is chief industry; also agr. (corn, cotton, legumes, truck); livestock (cattle, hogs). Oil wells. Hunting, fishing. Formed 1869.

San Jacinto (săn jŭsĭn'tō, yŭ–, hŭ–), city (pop. 1,778), Riverside co., S Calif., c.25 mi. SE of Riverside, at base of Mt. San Jacinto; fruitgrowing. With near-by Hemet, holds annual Ramona Pageant. Soboba Hot Springs and Gilman Hot Springs (health resorts) and Soboba Indian Reservation are near by. Inc. 1888.

San Jacinto (săn jŭsĭn'tŭ), battlefield, Harris co., S Texas, c.16 mi. E of Houston, bet. Houston Ship Channel (Buffalo Bayou) and San Jacinto R. San Jacinto State Park here (c.400 acres), with monument 570 ft. high, marks site of battle of San Jacinto (April, 1836), in which Gen. Sam Houston's Texan troops defeated Mexicans under Santa Anna and won Texas' independence. Historical mus.; picnic grounds.

San Jacinto (sän häsēn'tō), town, Canelones dept., S Uruguay, on highway, and 30 mi. NE of Montevideo; grain, flax, livestock.

San Jacinto, Fort, Texas: see GALVESTON.

San Jacinto, Mount, Calif.: see SAN JACINTO MOUNTAINS.

San Jacinto Bay, Texas: see GALVESTON BAY.

San Jacinto Mountains (săn jŭsĭn'tō, yŭ–, hŭ–), Riverside co., S Calif., range extending c.30 mi. SSE from San Gorgonio Pass (separating range from the San Bernardinos) to N end of Santa Rosa Mts. At N end is Mt. San Jacinto or San Jacinto Peak (10,805 ft.); at peak's E base is Palm Springs. Mount San Jacinto State Park (c.13,000 acres) has trails, camp sites (at Idyllwild, a resort c.20 mi. E of Hemet), tracts of desert and timberland.

San Jacinto River (săn jŭsĭn'tŭ), SE Texas, formed in NE Harris co. by junction of West Fork (c.80 mi. long) and East Fork (c.65 mi. long; often called San Jacinto R. for entire length); flows c.50 mi. generally S to San Jacinto Bay, a NW arm of Galveston Bay. Near mouth, receives Buffalo Bayou from W; lower river and Buffalo Bayou are followed to Houston by deep-water HOUSTON SHIP CHANNEL. SAN JACINTO battlefield is on river near Houston.

San Jaime, Argentina: see JUAN B. ARRUABARRENA.

Sanjak, region, Yugoslavia: see NOVI PAZAR.

Sanjarpur (sŭn'jŭrpōōr), town (pop. 1,727), Bahawalpur state, W Pakistan, 23 mi. SW of Rahimyar Khan.

San Javier (sän'hävyĕr'). **1** Town (pop. estimate 1,500), ⊙ San Javier dept. (1947 pop. 40,343), S Misiones natl. territory, Argentina, on Uruguay R. (Brazil border) and 60 mi. SE of Posadas; agr. (maté, corn, citrus fruit, tobacco); maté processing, lumbering. Has ruins of old Jesuit settlement. **2** Town (pop. estimate 1,000), ⊙ San Javier dept. (□ 2,610; 1947 pop. 18,930), E central Santa Fe prov., Argentina, on right bank of San Javier R. and 85 mi. NNE of Santa Fe; grain and livestock center; lumbering.

San Javier, town (pop. c.5,500), Santa Cruz dept., E Bolivia, 40 mi. W of Concepción; rubber. Founded as Jesuit mission.

San Javier or **San Javier de Loncomilla** (dā lōng-kōmē'yä), town (pop. 5,183), ⊙ Loncomilla dept. (□ 338; pop. 30,884), Linares prov., S central Chile, on Loncomilla R., in the central valley, and 19 mi. NNW of Linares; agr. center (cereals, vegetables, wine); flour milling.

San Javier, town (pop. 1,204), Murcia prov., SE Spain, near the Mar Menor, 17 mi. NNE of Cartagena; olive-oil processing; fishing. Cereals, almonds, wine. Military airport 5 mi. S.

San Javier, village, Río Negro dept., W Uruguay, on Uruguay R. and 33 mi. NNE of Fray Bentos; Rus. colony; agr. products (wheat, grain); cattle.

San Javier de Loncomilla, Chile: see SAN JAVIER.

San Javier River (sän hävyĕr'), E Santa Fe prov., Argentina, rises 25 mi. N of Reconquista, flows c.200 mi. S, past Romang, San Javier, Helvecia, and Cayasta, to a right arm of Paraná R. (which it parallels) 30 mi. NE of Santa Fe.

Sanjawi (sŭnjä'vē), village, Loralai dist., NE Baluchistan, W Pakistan, 17 mi. SW of Loralai; rice, barley; mat making. Sometimes spelled Sinjawi.

Sanjeli (sŭnjā'lē), village, Panch Mahals dist., N Bombay, India, 30 mi. NE of Godhra; local agr. market. Was ⊙ former princely state of Sanjeli, in Gujarat States, Bombay; state inc. 1949 into Panch Mahals dist.

San Jerónimo, dept., Argentina: see CORONDA.

San Jerónimo, town, Argentina: see SAN JERÓNIMO SUD.

San Jerónimo (sän hārō'nēmō), town (pop. 1,694), Antioquia dept., NW central Colombia, on W slopes of Cordillera Central, near Cauca R., on highway, and 17 mi. NW of Medellín; alt. 2,690 ft. Rice-growing center; coffee, sugar cane, corn, yucca, tropical fruit.

San Jerónimo, town (1950 pop. 953), Baja Verapaz dept., central Guatemala, in N highlands, 6 mi. SE of Salamá; market center; coffee, sugar cane, grain; livestock raising; alcohol distilling. Wine-producing center in 17th cent.

San Jerónimo, town (pop. 1,052), Copán dept., W Honduras, in Sierra del Gallinero, 14 mi. NNW of Santa Rosa; tobacco, coffee, sugar cane.

San Jerónimo, peak (over 7,000 ft.) in main Andean divide of Honduras, 6 mi. SSW of La Encarnación. Here Sierra Merendón system branches off (N).

San Jerónimo, officially San Jerónimo de Juárez, town (pop. 2,654), Guerrero, SW Mexico, in Pacific lowland, 40 mi. WNW of Acapulco; rice, sugar cane, fruit, livestock.

San Jerónimo. 1 Town (pop. 890), Apurímac dept., S central Peru, in the Andes, 1½ mi. ESE of Andahuaylas; wheat, potatoes. Gold, silver, copper, coal, and marble deposits. Sometimes San Gerónimo. 2 Town (pop. 2,310), Cuzco dept., S central Peru, in high Andean valley, on railroad and 7 mi. ESE of Cuzco. Sand and gypsum quarries; grain, alfalfa, fruit. Sometimes San Gerónimo. 3 or **San Jerónimo de Tunán** (dā tōōnän'), town (pop. 3,025), Junín dept., central Peru, on Mantaro R. and 9 mi. N of Huancayo (connected by railroad); alfalfa, quinoa; sheep raising. Also San Gerónimo.

San Jerónimo, village (pop. estimate 500), Santa Ana dept., NW Salvador, on railroad and 7 mi. W of Metapán; customs station on Guatemala border.

San Jerónimo, Serranía de (sĕränē'ä dā sän hārō'nēmō), N spur of the Cordillera Occidental, in Antioquia and Bolívar depts., NW Colombia; extends c.100 mi. N from the Paramillo massif.

San Jerónimo Caleras (kälā'räs), town (pop. 1,632), Puebla, central Mexico, near Tlaxcala border, 6 mi. NNW of Puebla; cereals, maguey, stock.

San Jerónimo de Tunán, Peru: see SAN JERÓNIMO, Junín dept.

San Jerónimo Ixtepec, Mexico: see IXTEPEC, Oaxaca.

San Jerónimo Norte (nôr'tā), town (pop. estimate 1,500), central Santa Fe prov., Argentina, 23 mi. WNW of Santa Fe; grain and livestock center; dairying, tanning.

San Jerónimo Sud (sōōdh') or **San Jerónimo,** town (pop. estimate 1,500), S Santa Fe prov., Argentina, 22 mi. WNW of Rosario; agr. center (alfalfa, wheat, corn, flax, fruit, hogs, cattle); dairying. Sometimes spelled San Gerónimo.

San Jerónimo Taviche, Mexico: see TAVICHE.

San Jerónimo Tecuanipan, Mexico: see TECUANIPAN.

San Jerónimo Xayacatlán (sīäkätlän'), town (pop. 1,556), Puebla, central Mexico, 7 mi. ENE of Acatlán; agr. center (corn, rice, fruit, livestock). Xayacatlán, or Xayacatlán de Bravo, is 3 mi. W.

Sanjo (sän'jō'), city (1940 pop. 36,541; 1947 pop. 45,238), Niigata prefecture, central Honshu, Japan, on Shinano R. and 22 mi. SSW of Niigata; commercial center for agr. area; mfg. (dyes, cotton textiles, cutlery), metalworking. Sometimes spelled Sanzyo.

San Joaquín (hwäkēn'), town (pop. c.2,100), ⊙ Mamoré prov., Beni dept., NE Bolivia, on Machupo R. and 110 mi. N of Trinidad; cattle. Airport.

San Joaquín, town (1950 pop. 320), ⊙ Flores canton, Heredia prov., central Costa Rica, on central plateau, on Inter-American Highway, on railroad and 2 mi. W of Heredia; coffee, sugar cane, tobacco, grain. Has granite church amid gardens.

San Joaquín, town (dist. pop. 4,228), Caaguazú dept., S central Paraguay, 40 mi. NE of Coronel Oviedo; oranges, livestock; processing of oil of petitgrain. Founded 1746.

San Joaquin (săn" wäkēn', Sp. sän hwäkēn'), town (1939 pop. 2,420; 1948 municipality pop. 22,255), Iloilo prov., SW Panay isl., Philippines, on Panay Gulf, 30 mi. WSW of Iloilo; agr. center (rice, sugar cane).

San Joaquin (săn wäkēn'), county (□ 1,410; pop. 200,750), central Calif.; ⊙ STOCKTON. Level San Joaquin Valley country, touching Coast Ranges (Diablo Range) in SW and foothills of Sierra Nevada in E; marshy delta (partly reclaimed) of San Joaquin R. in W. Also watered by Mokelumne, Stanislaus, and Calaveras rivers. Rich irrigated agr. region; grapes, asparagus, tomatoes, celery, and other truck, cherries, nuts, rice, grain alfalfa, corn, sugar beets, dairy products, cattle, hogs, sheep, poultry. Extensive packing and processing industries (wineries, canneries, beet-sugar refineries); Stockton is inland seaport and a mfg. center. Sand, gravel, and clay quarrying; gold dredging; natural-gas wells. Formed 1850.

San Joaquin, city (pop. 632), Fresno co., central Calif., near San Joaquin R., 25 mi. W of Fresno; grain, cotton, alfalfa, flax.

San Joaquín (sän hwäkēn'). 1 Town (pop. 731), Anzoátegui state, NE Venezuela, 27 mi. ESE of Aragua de Barcelona; cotton, sugar cane, cattle. San Joaquín oil field is near by 7 mi. W. 2 Town (pop. 1,820), Carabobo state, N Venezuela, near N shore of L. Valencia, 16 mi. ENE of Valencia; cotton, sugar cane, corn, cacao, fruit, cattle.

San Joaquin River (săn wäkēn'), central Calif., master stream of S part (San Joaquin Valley) of the Central Valley; it is formed by forks uniting in the Sierra Nevada SW of Mono L., flows SW and W, past Friant and Firebaugh, then NNW, past Stockton (head of deep-draught navigation), and through isl. maze of Sacramento–San Joaquin delta, to join the Sacramento just above Suisun Bay; 317 mi. long. Receives from the Sierra Nevada the Chowchilla, Merced, Tuolumne, Stanislaus, Fresno, Calaveras, and Mokelumne rivers. Dams on San Joaquin headwaters impound FLORENCE, SHAVER, and HUNTINGTON lakes. River gives name to San Joaquin Valley (250 mi. long N–S), the S part of Central Valley, and extending bet. Coast Ranges (W) and the Sierra Nevada; Kings and Kern rivers, independent of San Joaquin R. system, enter S end of valley. This fertile, extensively irrigated basin is one of richest farm regions in U.S. The CENTRAL VALLEY project (of which FRIANT DAM on the San Joaquin is a major unit) contemplates increased irrigation and flood control. Valley's chief centers are Bakersfield (S; rich oil region), Stockton (N), and Modesto, Merced, and Fresno.

San Joaquin Valley, Calif.: see CENTRAL VALLEY; SAN JOAQUIN RIVER.

San Jon (săn hōn'), village (pop. 362), Quay co., E N.Mex., 23 mi. ESE of Tucumcari, near Texas line; alt. c.4,200 ft. Trading point in ranching area.

San Jorge (sän hôr'hā), town (pop. estimate 3,500), W central Santa Fe prov., Argentina, 70 mi. WSW of Santa Fe; flour, wheat, flax, livestock; flax processing, flour milling.

San Jorge, village (pop. 250), Iviza, Balearic Isls., 2 mi. SW of Iviza city; almond growing.

San Jorge, town (1950 pop. 968), Rivas dept., SW Nicaragua, port on L. Nicaragua, 3 mi. ENE of Rivas; rail terminus; plantains, livestock; pottery making.

San Jorge, town (pop. 1,112), Castellón de la Plana prov., E Spain, 7 mi. NW of Vinaroz; olive-oil processing; beans, wine, cereals.

San Jorge, Gulf of (sän hôr'hä), broad inlet of the Atlantic in Comodoro Rivadavia military zone, Argentina, bet. Cabo Dos Bahías (N) and Cabo Tres Puntas (S); 145 mi. N-S, 100 mi. W-E. Port of Comodoro Rivadavia on W shore. Also called Gulf of St. George.

San Jorge, Gulf of, on the Mediterranean coast of Tarragona prov., NE Spain, on N side of Ebro R. delta. Fishing port of Amettla is on it. At SE end is Cape Tortosa.

San Jorge River (sän hôr'hä), Bolívar dept., N Colombia, rises at N foot of the Paramillo in the Cordillera Occidental of Antioquia, flows c.200 mi. NNE, through Bolívar savannas, to the Brazo de Loba (a left arm of the Magdalena), 8 mi. S of Magangué. Not navigable. Along its course is a rich cattle country.

San José (sän hōsā'). 1 Town (pop. estimate 500), E Catamarca prov., Argentina, on Cajón R. and 7 mi. S of Santa María; cattle-raising center. 2 City (1947 pop. 15,932), N Mendoza prov., Argentina, E suburb of Mendoza; mfg. center; wine making, food canning, meat packing, tanning, textile milling, lumbering. 3 Village (pop. estimate 1,000), S Misiones natl. territory, Argentina, on railroad and 27 mi. SSE of Posadas; farming center (maté, citrus fruit, sugar cane, rice, corn); lumbering, maté processing.

San José, village (pop. 99, commune pop. 5,985), Iviza, Balearic Isls., at N foot of the Atalayasa, 7 mi. W of Iviza, city in agr. region (carobs, vegetables, grapes, almonds, cereals, olives, figs, apricots, livestock). Charcoal burning, sawmilling.

San José. 1 Village, Oruro dept., Bolivia: see ORURO, city. 2 or **San José de Chiquitos** (dā chēkē'tōs), town (pop. c.2,600), ⊙ Chiquitos prov., Santa Cruz dept., E Bolivia, 160 mi. E of Santa Cruz, on N edge of the Chaco, on Corumbá–Santa Cruz RR; airport; cattle, sugar cane, grain. Founded 1699 as mission, with remains of old buildings extant. 3 or **San José de Uchupiamomas** (dā ōōchōōpyämō'mäs), village, La Paz dept., NW Bolivia, on Tuichi R. and 37 mi. NW of San Buenaventura; oil deposits.

San José, Canary Isls.: see BREÑA BAJA.

San José. 1 Village (1930 pop. 150), Santiago prov., central Chile, on railroad and 35 mi. SW of Santiago; agr. center (grain, fruit, potatoes, livestock). 2 or **San José de Maipo** (dā mī'pō), town (pop. 1,269), Santiago prov., central Chile, on Maipo R., on railroad, and 22 mi. SE of Santiago, in the Andes, in agr. area (grain, fruit, livestock). Health resort. Formerly a mining area for silver deposits discovered in late 18th cent.

San José, province (□ 1,900; 1950 pop. 281,822) of W central Costa Rica; ⊙ San José. Situated largely on Pacific slopes, it is bordered E by the Cordillera de Talamanca, and extends N across central plateau to La Palma saddle of the Central Cordillera. Separated from Pacific coast by narrow strip of Puntarenas prov., it is drained by Tárcoles and upper General rivers. It has temperate climate in highlands and tropical conditions in Pacific lowlands. Agr.: coffee (mainly on central plateau around San José city), sugar cane, vegetables, fruit, flowers. Pop. and transportation routes (Inter-American Highway, rail lines) are concentrated on central plateau, site of main centers: San José, Guadalupe, Aserrí, Acosta, Escazú, Villa Colón, and Santiago.

San José, city (1950 pop. 86,909), ⊙ Costa Rica and San José prov., on central plateau, on Inter-American Highway, on railroad and 50 mi. E of its Pacific port Puntarenas; alt. 3,838 ft.; 9°56'N 84°4'W. Industrial and commercial center; mfg. of cacao and chocolate products, flour, beer, wines, canned goods, cotton goods, perfumes, furniture. Situated in rich coffee region, it is linked by rail with Limón (on Caribbean Sea) and Puntarenas (on the Pacific). Located bet. Torres (N) and María Aguilar (S) rivers (tributaries of the Tárcoles), San José is laid out in checkerboard fashion, with central thoroughfares meeting in govt. and business center of city. Here are chief public bldgs.: natl. congress (1855), municipal palace (1937), mus., library, theater, post office, and (facing Parque Central) the cathedral. Near E outskirts of city are Parque Nacional (with monument to Central American republics) and Parque Bolívar (zoo). La Sabana, a large, flat expanse W of city, has airport and natl. stadium, connected with city center by the Paseo Colón, a fine residential street. Developed in early 18th cent. and, because of favorable location, rapidly overtook older colonial centers of Cartago, Heredia, and Alajuela.

San José, town (1950 pop. 2,218), Bolívar prov., central Ecuador, in Andean valley of Chimbo R., 5 mi. SSW of Guaranda; cereals, sugar cane, fruit, tobacco, coffee. Also called Chimbo.

San José. 1 or **Puerto San José** (pwĕr'tō), town (1950 pop. 2,683), Escuintla dept., S Guatemala, principal Guatemalan port on the Pacific, 26 mi. S of Escuintla; 13°55'N 90°49'W; rail terminus; ships coffee, sugar, lumber. Tropical tourist resort. Also called Puerto de San José. 2 or **San José del Golfo** (dĕl gōl'fō), town (1950 pop. 493), Guatemala dept., S central Guatemala, 12 mi. NE of Guatemala; alt. 4,701 ft.; corn, black beans, livestock. 3 or **San José Pinula** (pēnōō'lä), town (1950 pop. 1,847), Guatemala dept., S central Guatemala, on Inter-American Highway and 9 mi. SE of Guatemala; alt. 5,610 ft.; corn, black beans, livestock.

San José or **San José de Copán** (dā kōpän'), town (pop. 1,339), Copán dept., W Honduras, 8 mi. NE of Santa Rosa, in tobacco area.

San José or **San José de los Remates** (dā lōs rämä'tēs), town (1950 pop. 508), Boaco dept., central Nicaragua, 14 mi. WNW of Boaco; agr. center (corn, rice, beans, sugar cane, coffee); livestock.

San José, town (dist. pop. 12,240), Caaguazú dept., S central Paraguay, 60 mi. ESE of Asunción; agr. center (sugar cane, tobacco, fruit, livestock); sugar refining, liquor distilling. Founded 1781.

San José. 1 Town (pop. 1,553), Lambayeque dept., NW Peru, minor port on the Pacific, 6 mi. SW of Lambayeque; shipyard; fisheries; tourist resort. Rice is grown in vicinity. 2 Town (pop. 580), Libertad dept., NW Peru, on coastal plain, on railroad and 6 mi. NE of San Pedro, in irrigated Jequetepeque R. valley; rice, cotton.

San Jose (sän hōsä'). 1 Town, Antique prov., Philippines: see SAN JOSE DE BUENAVISTA. 2 Town, Bulacan prov., Philippines: see BULACAN, town.

3 Town (1939 pop. 1,586; 1948 municipality pop. 12,788), Camarines Sur prov., SE Luzon, Philippines, near Lagonoy Gulf, 23 mi. ENE of Naga; agr. center (rice, abacá, corn). 4 Town (1939 pop. 1,111; 1948 municipality pop. 12,443), SW Mindoro isl., Philippines, on Mangarin Bay (mäng"gärēn') (small inlet of Mindoro Strait), 75 mi. SSW of Calapan; agr. center; sugar milling. Just E is its port Mangarin (1939 pop. 863), shipping sugar to Manila. 5 Town (1939 pop. 5,504) in Victorias municipality, Negros Occidental prov., NW Negros isl., Philippines, 18 mi. NE of Bacolod; agr. center (rice, sugar cane). 6 Town (1939 pop. 5,904; 1948 municipality pop. 33,017), Nueva Ecija prov., central Luzon, Philippines, 20 mi. N of Cabanatuan; rail terminus; agr. center (rice, corn). 7 Town, Pampanga prov., Philippines: see SANTA RITA.

San José or **Central San José** (sĕnträl'), locality, NE Puerto Rico, SW of Río Piedras; sugar mill.

San Jose. 1 (sănúzā', săn hōzā') City (pop. 95,280), ⊙ Santa Clara co., W Calif., c.40 mi. SE of San Francisco, in rich fruitgrowing Santa Clara Valley; one of world's largest canning and dried-fruit packing centers. The 1st pueblo (city) founded in Calif. (1777), it was meeting place of 1st state legislature (1849) and capital in 1849–51. Seat of San Jose State Col. To N (at Mission San Jose) is Mission San Jose de Guadalupe (1797). Inc. 1850. Willow Glen annexed 1936. 2 (săn jōz') Village (pop. 562), on Logan-Mason co. line, central Ill., 18 mi. S of Pekin, in agr. area; ships seeds.

San José (săn' hōsā'), department (□ 2,688; pop. 97,687), S Uruguay, on the Río de la Plata; ⊙ San José. Bounded E by Santa Lucía R. and watered by San José R. A purely stock-raising (cattle, sheep) and agr. region (wheat, corn, flax, fruit). Flour mills at city of San José. The dept. is traversed by the Montevideo-Mercedes RR. It was set up 1816, then comprising a much larger territory. Florida dept. was separated in 1856 and Flores in 1885.

San José, city (pop. 30,000), ⊙ San José dept., S Uruguay, on right bank of San José R., on railroad and 50 mi. NW of Montevideo; trading center for rich stock-raising (cattle, sheep) and agr. region (cereals, flax, fruit); flour milling. Noted for its fine church, modern administrative bldgs., theater, and monument to Artigas. Founded 1783 by settlers from Spain. Proclaimed provisional capital during patriot uprising (1825). Sometimes called San José de Mayo.

San José or **San José de Río Chico** (dā rē'ō chē'kō), town (pop. 1,797), Miranda state, N Venezuela, SW suburb of Río Chico, on railroad and 65 mi. ESE of Caracas; cacao, fruit.

San José Acatempa (äkätĕm'pä), town (1950 pop. 1,724), Jutiapa dept., SE Guatemala, in highlands, on Inter-American Highway and 14 mi. W of Jutiapa; alt. 4,619 ft.; corn, beans, livestock. Formerly called Azacualpa.

San José Acateno, Mexico: see ACATENO.

San José Atlán (ätlän'), town (pop. 1,575), Hidalgo, central Mexico, on railroad and 65 mi. WNW of Pachuca; corn, beans, maguey, livestock.

San José Colinas, Honduras: see COLINAS.

San José de Amacuro (dā ämäkōō'rō), village (pop. c.1,000), Delta Amacuro territory, NE Venezuela, at mouth of Amacuro R. on Boca Grande (main mouth of Orinoco R. delta), and 115 mi. ESE of Tucupita; 8°32'N 60°28'W; corn, fruit. Capuchin mission for Indians.

San José de Areocuar (ärā-ōkwär'), town (pop. 2,276), Sucre state, NE Venezuela, 7 mi. SW of Carúpano; cacao, sugar cane, corn, tobacco.

San Jose de Buenavista (bwānävē'stä), town (1939 pop. 4,722; 1948 municipality pop. 34,639), ⊙ ANTIQUE prov., W Panay isl., Philippines, on Cuyo East Pass, 40 mi. WNW of Iloilo; rice-growing and copper-mining center. Exports copper, copra, rice, sugar. Sometimes called simply San Jose.

San José de Chiquitos, Bolivia: see SAN JOSÉ, Santa Cruz dept.

San José de Copán, Honduras: see SAN JOSÉ.

San José de Cúcuta, Colombia: see CÚCUTA.

San José de Feliciano (fälēsyä'nō), town (1947 pop. 7,187), ⊙ Feliciano dept. (□ 1,170; 1947 pop. 17,000), N Entre Ríos prov., Argentina, on railroad and 80 mi. NNW of Concordia, in lumbering and agr. area (corn, alfalfa, livestock); corn mill. Founded 1573.

San José de Guadalupe, Mission, Calif.: see MISSION SAN JOSE.

San José de la Esquina (lä ĕskē'nä), town (pop. estimate 2,000), SW Santa Fe prov., Argentina, on Carcaraña R. and 65 mi. WSW of Rosario; agr. center (corn, flax, wheat, potatoes, sunflowers, livestock); flour milling.

San José de la Isla or **José de la Isla** (ē'slä), town (pop. 1,902), Zacatecas, N central Mexico, on interior plateau, 23 mi. SSE of Zacatecas; alt. 7,293 ft. Silver mining; corn, beans, maguey, livestock.

San José de la Mariquina (märēkē'nä), town (pop. 1,516), Valdivia prov., S central Chile, on Cruces R. and 35 mi. NE of Valdivia; resort and agr. center (wheat, barley, potatoes, peas, livestock). Flour milling, dairying, lumbering. Coal deposits near by. Apostolic mission.

San José de las Lajas (läs lä'häs), town (pop. 7,797), Havana prov., W Cuba, 17 mi. SE of Havana; rail junction and commercial center in dairying and sugar-growing region. Has thermal springs. The Cotilla Caves are near by.

San José de las Matas (mä'täs), town (1950 pop. 1,487), Santiago prov., N central Dominican Republic, 17 mi. SW of Santiago; tobacco, chick-peas. Lumbering and gold washing in vicinity.

San José del Boquerón (dĕl bōkärōn'), village (pop. estimate 200), N Santiago del Estero prov., Argentina, on left bank of the Río Salado and 85 mi. NE of Pozo Hondo, in lumbering area (quebracho); plant nurseries.

San José del Cabo (kä'bō), town (pop. 2,553), Southern Territory, Lower California, NW Mexico, near SE tip of peninsula, 85 mi. SSE of La Paz; sugar cane, maguey, oranges, palms.

San José del Golfo, Guatemala dept., Guatemala: see SAN JOSÉ.

San José del Guaviare (gwävyä'rā), village, Vaupés commissary, S central Colombia, on Guaviare R. (Meta intendancy border), in region of tropical forests; 2°35'N 72°38'W. Forest products (rubber, balata gum). Airfield.

San José de los Molinos (dā lōs mōlē'nōs), town (pop. 1,221), Ica dept., SW Peru, in Ica R. valley, on road, and 10 mi. NNE of Ica; cotton, grapes.

San José de los Ramos (rä'mōs), town (pop. 1,462), Matanzas prov., W Cuba, on railroad and 33 mi. ESE of Cárdenas; sugar cane, fruit.

San José de los Remates, Nicaragua: see SAN JOSÉ.

San José del Rincón (dĕl rēngkōn'), village (pop. estimate 1,000), E central Sante Fe prov., Argentina, on arm of Paraná R. and 8 mi. NE of Santa Fe, in agr. area (corn, oranges, watermelons, livestock).

San José de Mayo, Uruguay: see SAN JOSÉ, city.

San José de Metán (dā mätän'), town (1947 pop. 6,907), ⊙ Metán dept. (□ 2,380; 1947 pop. 18,485), S central Salta prov., Argentina, 55 mi. SE of Salta; rail junction (Metán station) and agr. center (corn, rice, alfalfa, flax, cotton, livestock); lime works; soda factories.

San José de Ocoa (ōkō'ä), town (1950 pop. 3,970), Trujillo Valdez prov., S Dominican Republic, in the Sierra de Ocoa, on Ocoa R. and 21 mi. NW of Baní; tobacco-growing center. Coal deposits near.

San José de Oruña, Trinidad, B.W.I.: see SAINT JOSEPH.

San José de Río Chico, Venezuela: see SAN JOSÉ.

San José de Sisa or **Sisa** (sē'sä), town (pop. 1,812), San Martín dept., N central Peru, in E outliers of the Andes, on affluent of Huallaga R. and 45 mi. SSE of Moyobamba, on road; sugar cane, cotton, tobacco, rice, coffee.

San José de Surco, Peru: see BARRANCO.

San José de Uchupiamomas, Bolivia: see SAN JOSÉ, La Paz dept.

San José Guayabal, Salvador: see GUAYABAL.

San José Gulf (sän hōsā'), NE Chubut natl. territory, Argentina, sheltered inlet of San Matías Gulf, bordered E and S by Valdés Peninsula; 27 mi. W–E, 14 mi. N–S.

San José Island (□ 83), in Gulf of California, off SE coast of Lower California, NW Mexico, 50 mi. NNW of La Paz; 20 mi. long, 3–7 mi. wide; rises to c.2,000 ft. Of volcanic origin; barren, uninhabited.

San José Island, one of the Pearl Islands, in Gulf of Panama of the Pacific, Panama prov., Panama, 7 mi. W of San Miguel Isl.; 8 mi. long, 4 mi. wide.

San José Ixtapa, Mexico: see IXTAPA, Puebla.

San José Miahuatlán or **Miahuatlán** (myäwätlän'), town (pop. 2,915), Puebla, central Mexico, 13 mi. SSE of Tehuacán; alt. 3,674 ft.; agr. center (corn, sugar cane, fruit, stock).

San José Nanacamilpa, Mexico: see NANACAMILPA.

San José Poaquil (pwäkĕl'), town (1950 pop. 3,728), Chimaltenango dept., S central Guatemala, 15 mi. NNW of Chimaltenango; alt. 6,500 ft.; grain, black beans.

San José Purua, Mexico: see ZITÁCUARO.

San Jose River (săn hōzā'), W N.Mex., rises in 2 forks in Zuni Mts., flows c.90 mi. ESE, past Bluewater, Grants, and Laguna, to Rio Puerco 20 mi. NW of Belen. Dam on headstream, 8 mi. WNW of Bluewater, forms Bluewater Reservoir (4 mi. long, 1 mi. wide).

San José River (sän hōsā'), S Uruguay, rises in W Cuchilla Grande Inferior S of Trinidad, flows c.75 mi. SSE, past San José, to Santa Lucía R. 8 mi. ENE of Libertad. Not navigable.

San José Volcano (sän hōsā'), Andean peak (19,130 ft.) on Argentina-Chile border, 80 mi. S of the Aconcagua; 33°48'S.

San Juan (sän hwän'), province (□ 34,910; pop. 261,229), W Argentina; ⊙ San Juan. Bordered W by the Andes; on the Chile line. Largely mountainous, with fertile irrigated valleys (San Juan, Bermejo rivers). Has dry, Mediterranean climate in its inhabited valleys. Among its little-exploited mineral resources are: lime (Jachal, Rinconada, Carpintería, Pampa del Chañar), coal (Jachal, Sierra del Pie de Palo, Sierra de la Huerta), iron, manganese, and aluminum (Barreales), lead and silver (Sierra del Tontal, Sierra de la Huerta), mica (Sierra de Valle Fértil), asbestos and graphite (Sierra del Pie de Palo). Also copper, molybdenum, tungsten. Agr. activity in irrigated subandean valleys: wine, wheat, corn, alfalfa, fruit, olives, apples; apiculture; stock raising (sheep, cattle, horses, goats). Lumbering, mining, wine making, flour milling, alcohol distilling, meat packing, dairying, brewing, food canning. La Laja is known for its warm springs.

San Juan, city (pop. 81,747), ⊙ San Juan prov. and San Juan dept., W Argentina, on San Juan R. (irrigation area) and 600 mi. NW of Buenos Aires, 100 mi. N of Mendoza; 31°32'S 68°33'W; alt. 2,100 ft. Rail, industrial, and commercial center for an agr. area known for viticulture. Local trade with Chile. Deals in wine, alcohol, frozen meat, dairy products, cider, dried fruit, canned food, beer, machinery, cement articles, timber. Dam and hydroelectric plant near by. An old colonial city, preserving early Sp. style, it has administrative bldgs., historical mus., Sarmiento Library (in Sarmiento's birthplace), natl. col., Cuyo Univ. (mining faculty), agr. school, seismographic station. City was founded 1562, when area belonged to Chile. A stronghold against Indian tribes, formerly called San Juan de la Frontera. The Argentinian liberal statesman and author Sarmiento b. here 1811. San Juan was severely damaged (1944) by an earthquake. Bishopric since 1834; archbishopric since 1934.

San Juan, town (pop. 2,017), Majorca, Balearic Isls., 20 mi. E of Palma; cereals, grapes, onions, garlic, fruit, hogs. Cement milling. The San Juan thermal springs are in S part of isl., 24 mi. SE of Palma.

San Juan, village (pop. c.1,000), Santa Cruz dept., E Bolivia, at W end of the Serranía de Sunsas, 50 mi. E of San José; tropical agr. products (rice, sugar cane); livestock.

San Juan or **San Juan de Tibás** (dā tēbäs'), town (pop. 1,783), San José prov., central Costa Rica, on central plateau, 2 mi. N of San José; trading center in coffee area; flowers, vegetables.

San Juan, officially San Juan de la Maguana, city (1935 pop. 3,699; 1950 pop. 10,093), ⊙ Benefactor prov., W Dominican Republic, in San Juan Valley, on affluent of the Yaque del Sur, on highway, and 90 mi. WNW of Ciudad Trujillo; 18°48'N 71°15'W. Agr. center (rice, coffee, corn, fruit, tubers). Airfield. Founded 1504, became ⊙ prov. in 1938.

San Juan. 1 or **San Juan Sacatepéquez** (säkätāpā'kĕs), market town (1950 pop. 3,431), Guatemala dept., S central Guatemala, 10 mi. NW of Guatemala; alt. 5,814 ft. Agr. center (corn, coffee, sugar cane); textile weaving; livestock. Flower gardens. Zinc and lead mining near by. 2 or **San Juan La Laguna** (lä lägōō'nä), town (1950 pop. 741), Sololá dept., SW central Guatemala, on W shore of L. Atitlán, 7.5 mi. SW of Sololá; alt. 4,500 ft.; corn, wheat, beans.

San Juan, town (pop. 111), Intibucá dept., W Honduras, on San Juan R. (right headstream of Guarajambala R.) and 19 mi. NW of La Esperanza; tanning, footwear mfg.; livestock.

San Juan or **San Juan de las Huertas** (dā läs wĕr'täs), town (pop. 2,713), Mexico state, central Mexico, 8 mi. WSW of Toluca; cereals, stock.

San Juan. 1 or **San Juan de Telpaneca** (dā tĕlpänā'kä), village, Madríz dept., NW Nicaragua, 12 mi. E of Telpaneca; coffee, cacao; hardwood. 2 or **San Juan de Oriente,** or **San Juan de los Platos** (dā ōryĕn'tä; -dā lōs plä'tōs), town (1950 pop. 606), Masaya dept., SW Nicaragua, on road and 5 mi. SSE of Masaya; grain. Noted for mfg. of clay articles, mainly tableware [Sp.=*platos*].

San Juan, mine, Nicaragua: see LA LIBERTAD.

San Juan. 1 or **San Juan de Lacamaca** (dā läkämä'kä), village (pop. 1,246), Cajamarca dept., NW Peru, in Cordillera Occidental, near Llaucán R., 3 mi. NNW of Bambamarca; barley, corn, potatoes. San Antonio or San Antonio de Lacamaca (pop. 1,214) is just WSW. 2 or **San Juan de la Virgen** (dā lä vēr'hĕn), town (pop. 412), Tumbes dept., NW Peru, on coastal plain, on Tumbes R. and 4 mi. SSE of Tumbes; cotton, tobacco.

San Juan (săn" wän', Sp. sän hwän'). 1 Town (1939 pop. 1,635; 1948 municipality pop. 28,642), Batangas prov., S Luzon, Philippines, near Tayabas Bay, 18 mi. SSE of San Pablo; agr. center (rice, sugar cane, corn, coconuts). 2 Town, Pampanga prov., Philippines: see APALIT. 3 Town, Rizal prov., Philippines: see MORONG. 4 Town (1939 pop. 5,028) in Hinatuan municipality, Surigao prov., E Mindanao, Philippines, copra port on Philippine Sea, 45 mi. S of Tandag. Sawmill near by.

San Juan, city (1950 pop. 224,767; 1940 pop. 167,247), ⊙ Puerto Rico, on NE coast, a major port of the West Indies, c.1,000 mi. ESE of Havana; 18°28'N 66°9'W. With its old section situated on 2 rocky islets guarding a fine, almost landlocked harbor, and linked by bridges with the mainland, San Juan is the trading, shipping, cultural, banking, and processing center of Puerto Rico. From it radiate rail, road, and air communications to all parts of the isl. International airport; port of entry; seat of senatorial dist. Also a resort esteemed for its healthy, tropical climate (mean temp. 78°F.) relieved by NE trade winds, and famed for its fine cultural tradition. San Juan's modern harbor installations handle about

55% of all Puerto Rico's trade, shipping mostly sugar cane, tobacco, coffee, and fruit to the U.S. Among its industries are: sugar milling and refining, alcohol and rum distilling, brewing, bottling, cigar and cigarette making; mfg. of needlework, buttons, pharmaceuticals, metal products, cement, clothing. The old, formerly walled city, with its narrow streets and many plazas, keeps its Sp. character, and has many well-preserved historic bldgs. such as the high battlements of El Morro (begun 1539) commanding the entrance to San Juan Bay, San Cristóbal castle (1631), and La Fortaleza (begun 1529), now Governor's Palace. Other noteworthy bldgs. include Casa Blanca (built 1523), the old Sp. cathedral (started 1542, reconstructed 1802) with tomb of Juan Ponce de León, the San Francisco church, arsenal, Federal bldg., School of Tropical Medicine, and part of Univ. of Puerto Rico. Site of city was visited 1508 by Juan Ponce de León, who called the bay Puerto Rico (Sp.,= rich port). After the abandonment of 1st Eur. settlement at CAPARRA, Juan Ponce de León founded San Juan as Puerto Rico (1521). Fortified, the city was, during early colonial era, the most formidable Sp. stronghold in the New World. Frequently subjected to Br., Du., and Fr. assaults, it was unsuccessfully attacked by Drake and Hawkins in 1595, held in 1598 by George Clifford, earl of Cumberland, and besieged by the Dutch in 1625. Uprising against Sp. administration in 1885. San Juan was bombarded by the U.S. fleet during Spanish-American War (1898). The city's main residential section is Santurce, just S on the mainland, adjoined W by Isla Grande, U.S. air base. In the vicinity are fine resort beaches such as Condado, Isla Verde, and Boca de Cangrejos (known for its submarine gardens).

San Juan (sănʺ wänʹ), village (pop. 6,534), NW Trinidad, B.W.I., on railroad and 5 mi. E of San Fernando; market town (sugar cane, coconuts).

San Juan (săn wänʹ). **1** County (□ 392; pop. 1,471), SW Colo.; ⊙ Silverton. Mining and livestock-grazing region, drained by Animas R. Lead, silver, gold, copper, zinc. San Juan Mts. and San Juan Natl. Forest throughout. Formed 1876. **2** County (□ 5,515; pop. 18,292), extreme NW N.Mex.; ⊙ Aztec. Agr. and livestock-grazing area; drained by Chaco and San Juan rivers. Fruit, grain, vegetables raised in San Juan valley; oil and natural gas fields near Shiprock (NW); Indian artifacts produced by Navajo Indians on reservation in W. Chaco Canyon Natl. Monument in SE, Aztec Ruins Natl. Monument in NE, Chuska Mts. in SW. NW boundary is only point in U.S. common to 4 states (Ariz., Colo., Utah, N.Mex.). Formed 1887. **3** County (□ 7,884; pop. 5,315), SE Utah; ⊙ Monticello. Mtn. and plateau area bordering on Colo. and Ariz., bounded on W by Colorado R., crossed in S by San Juan R. Includes part of Navajo Indian Reservation in S. Abajo Mts. are W of Monticello, La Sal Mts. in NE, both lying in sections of La Sal Natl. Forest. Natural Bridges Natl. Monument is W of Blanding; Rainbow Bridge Natl. Monument is in SW; part of Hovenweep Natl. Monument is in SE. Hay, grain, sheep, and cattle are raised in irrigated region near Blanding. Co. formed 1880. SE tip is only point in U.S. common to 4 states (Ariz., N.Mex., Colo., Utah). **4** County (□ 172; pop. 3,245), NW Wash., on British Columbia line; ⊙ Friday Harbor. It includes the main isls. (San Juan, Lopez, and Orcas are largest) of the SAN JUAN ISLANDS, an archipelago SW of Bellingham, at N end of Puget Sound. Lime, salmon, truck; resorts, recreational areas. Formed 1873.

San Juan (săn wänʹ). **1** Town, Calif.: see SAN JUAN BAUTISTA. **2** Pueblo (□ 19.1), Rio Arriba co., N N.Mex. San Juan village (1948 pop. 788) is on E bank of the Rio Grande and 26 mi. NNW of Santa Fe; alt. c.5,600 ft. Sangre de Cristo Mts. are E. Chief festival, June, honors John the Baptist. First permanent Sp. settlement in N.Mex. made here 1598 by Juan de Oñate, on site of Indian village. Popé, medicine man of San Juan, led Pueblo revolt of 1680. **3** City (pop. 3,413), Hidalgo co., extreme S Texas, 5 mi. E of McAllen, in lower Rio Grande valley; trade, shipping center in irrigated fruit, truck, cotton area; cotton ginning; mfg. (fruit-packing equipment, foundry products).

San Juan or **San Juan de los Cayos** (sän hwänʹ dā lōs kīʹōs), town (pop. 646), Falcón state, NW Venezuela, minor port on the Caribbean, 26 mi. NNW of Tucacas; fishing.

San Juan, Cape, or **Cabezas de San Juan** (kābāʹsäs dā), headland on NE coast of Puerto Rico, 34 mi. ESE of San Juan; 18°23′N 65°37′W.

San Juan, Cape, headland of continental Sp. Guinea, on Gulf of Guinea, 33 mi. SSW of Río Benito. Forms N end of Corisco Bay; 1°10′N 9°23′E.

San Juan, Cape, easternmost point of Staten Isl., off Tierra del Fuego, in the South Atlantic; 54°42′S 63°43′W.

San Juan, Sierra de (syĕʹrä dā sän hwänʹ), low range, Las Villas prov., central Cuba, W of the Sierra de Trinidad; 12 mi. long E–W; rises in the Pico San Juan to 3,793 ft.

San Juan Alotenango, Guatemala: see ALOTENANGO.

San Juan Atenco, Mexico: see ATENCO, Puebla.

San Juan Atzompa, Mexico: see ATZOMPA, Puebla.

San Juan Bautista (boutēʹstä), village (pop. 1,479), Iviza, Balearic Isls., 12 mi. NNE of Iviza city; almonds, carobs, grapes, livestock; timber. Charcoal burning. Lead deposits.

San Juan Bautista, village, Chile: see JUAN FERNÁNDEZ ISLANDS.

San Juan Bautista, Mexico: see VILLAHERMOSA.

San Juan Bautista (sän hwänʹ boutēʹstä), town (dist. pop. 9,232), ⊙ Misiones dept., S Paraguay, 100 mi. SSE of Asunción; 26°37′S 57°6′W; trading and stock-raising center; maté.

San Juan Bautista (săn wänʹ bôtēʹstŭ) or **San Juan,** town (pop. 1,031), San Benito co., W Calif., 8 mi. W of Hollister. Has many historical bldgs., including Mission San Juan Bautista (1797), largest in Calif., still in use as church. Orchards; cement plant; granite quarry. Rail point: Sargent, 5 mi. N.

San Juan Bautista, Uruguay: see SANTA LUCÍA.

San Juan Bautista, town (pop. 454), on Margarita Isl., Nueva Esparta state, NE Venezuela, 5 mi. W of La Asunción; sugar cane, corn, fruit.

San Juan Bautista del Téul, Mexico: see TÉUL DE GONZÁLEZ ORTEGA.

San Juan Bautista de Ñeembucú (dā nyāĕmbōō-kōōʹ), town (dist. pop. 2,848), Ñeembucú dept., S Paraguay, 35 mi. NE of Pilar; agr. center (oranges, corn, cotton, cattle). Sometimes San Juan de Ñeembucú.

San Juan Capistrano (săn wänʹ kăpĭsträʹnō, kă–), village (1940 pop. 724), Orange co., S Calif., 20 mi. SE of Santa Ana, near the coast. Grew up around Mission San Juan Capistrano (extant), established by Junípero Serra in 1776 and completed in 1806. The Capistrano swallows are said to return every March 19.

San Juan Chamelco, Guatemala: see CHAMELCO.

San Juancito (sän hwänsēʹtō), town (pop. 6,305), in Central Dist., Francisco Morazán dept., S central Honduras, on road and 12 mi. NE of Tegucigalpa; alt. 4,035 ft. Silver- and gold-mining center.

San Juan Comalapa, Guatemala: see COMALAPA.

San Juan Cosalá (sän hwänʹ kōsäläʹ), town (pop. 1,009), Jalisco, central Mexico, on NW shore of L. Chapala, 25 mi. S of Guadalajara; beans, grain, fruit, stock.

San Juan Cotzal, Guatemala: see COTZAL.

San Juan de Alcaraz, Spain: see FÁBRICAS DE SAN JUAN DE ALCARAZ.

San Juan de Alicante (dā älēkänʹtā), town (pop. 2,048), Alicante prov., E Spain, near the Mediterranean, 4 mi. NNE of Alicante; mfg. of folding tables, cigarette paper; olive-oil processing. Almonds, figs, cereals.

San Juan de Aznalfarache (äthnälʺfäräʹchā), town (pop. 3,813), Seville prov., SW Spain, 2 mi. SW of Seville (linked by rail and tramway); popular picnic resort in agr. region (cereals, olives, apples, oranges, livestock). Mfg. of fertilizer, liquor, ceramics. Arboretum. Its wharves on the Guadalquivir load iron and copper ore from Cala mines (Huelva prov.). On a hill lies an anc. castle with fine parochial church.

San Juan de César (sāʹsär), town (pop. 2,235), Magdalena dept., N Colombia, at E foot of Sierra Nevada de Santa Marta, 55 mi. S of Ríohacha; corn, coffee, stock.

San Juan de Ciénaga, Colombia: see CIÉNAGA.

San Juan de Corrientes, Argentina: see CORRIENTES, city.

San Juan de Flores (flōʹrĕs), town (pop. 1,054), Francisco Morazán dept., S central Honduras, on Choluteca R. and 16 mi. NE of Tegucigalpa on road; market center; grain, sugar cane, livestock.

San Juan de Guadalupe (gwädälōōʹpā), town (pop. 2,641), Durango, N Mexico, near Zacatecas border, 75 mi. SE of Torreón; silver, lead, copper, gold mining.

San Juan de Lacamaca, Peru: see SAN JUAN, Cajamarca dept.

San Juan de la Costa (lä kōʹstä), village (1930 pop. 105), Osorno prov., S central Chile, 18 mi. WNW of Osorno; grain, livestock; lumbering.

San Juan de la Frontera, Argentina: see SAN JUAN, city.

San Juan de la Maguana, Dominican Republic: see SAN JUAN.

San Juan de la Nava (dā lä näʹvä), town (pop. 1,181), Ávila prov., central Spain, 12 mi. S of Ávila; grain, vegetables; lumber.

San Juan de la Punta, Mexico: see CUITLÁHUAC.

San Juan de la Rambla (rämʹblä), town (pop. 579), Tenerife, Canary Isls., 25 mi. WSW of Santa Cruz de Tenerife; corn, potatoes, grapes, onions, bananas, tomatoes, cereals, livestock; timber. Fishing.

San Juan de las Abadesas (läs ävä-dhāʹsäs), town (pop. 2,048), Gerona prov., NE Spain, on S slopes of the E Pyrenees, on Ter R. and 11 mi. WNW of Olot; cotton spinning, cement mfg.; agr. trade. Coal mines near by. Has former monastery (founded 9th cent.), 12th-cent. church with 15th-cent. Gothic cloister.

San Juan de las Huertas, Mexico: see SAN JUAN.

San Juan de la Vega (vāʹgä), town (pop. 2,167), Guanajuato, central Mexico, on railroad and 8 mi. NNE of Celaya; cereals, alfalfa, sugar, fruit, vegetables, stock.

San Juan de la Virgen, Peru: see SAN JUAN, Tumbes dept.

San Juan de Lima Point (dā lēʹmä), cape on Pacific coast of Michoacán, W Mexico, 6 mi. SSE of mouth of Tuxpan R.; 18°37′N 103°49′W.

San Juan de Limay, Nicaragua: see LIMAY.

San Juan del Monte (sän hwänʺ dĕl mōnʹtā), town (1939 pop. 6,219; 1948 municipality pop. 31,493), Rizal prov., S Luzon, Philippines, just E of Manila; agr. center (rice, fruit).

San Juan del Norte, territory, Nicaragua: see RÍO SAN JUAN.

San Juan del Norte (nôrʹtā), town (1950 pop. 307), Río San Juan dept., SE Nicaragua, on Caribbean Sea, at mouth of navigable San Juan R., 75 mi. S of Bluefields. Commercial center; exports hides, rubber, bananas, coconuts, mahogany, tortoise shell. Has govt. buildings, customhouse. Formerly called Greytown. Was occupied (1848) by the British to secure control of the MOSQUITO COAST and to check U.S. efforts to build an interoceanic canal; this led to Clayton-Bulwer treaty of 1850. Became thriving E terminus of a transisthmian transport company during the California gold rush. In 1854 it was bombarded by a U.S. warship in retaliation for insults to the U.S. minister and damage to U.S. property in Nicaragua. Port was important in filibustering activities of William Walker.

San Juan de los Cayos, Venezuela: see SAN JUAN.

San Juan de los Lagos (dā lōs läʹgōs), city (pop. 5,792), Jalisco, central Mexico, 45 mi. S of Aguascalientes; corn-growing center; wheat, beans, livestock.

San Juan de los Morros (môʹrōs), town (1941 pop. 6,120; 1950 census 13,580), ⊙ Guárico state, N central Venezuela, in S outliers of coastal range, 50 mi. SW of Caracas; 9°55′N 67°21′W. Trading center; health resort, with warm sulphur springs. Natural gas (helium, argon, neon, krypton) deposits. Since 1934, capital of state, succeeding Calabozo.

San Juan de los Platos, Nicaragua: see SAN JUAN, Masaya dept.

San Juan de los Remedios, Cuba: see REMEDIOS.

San Juan de los Yeras (yāʹräs), town (pop. 3,489), Las Villas prov., central Cuba, on railroad and 10 mi. SW of Santa Clara; sugar cane, tobacco, fruit, livestock; mfg. of cigars. The sugar central Pastora is SE.

San Juan del Piray (dĕl pērīʹ), town (pop. c.2,580), Chuquisaca dept., SE Bolivia, on Piray R. (headstream of the Parapetí) and 34 mi. SSW of Monteagudo; corn, sugar cane, fruit.

San Juan del Puerto (pwĕrʹtō), town (pop. 3,624), Huelva prov., SW Spain, rail junction near the Río Tinto, 7 mi. ENE of Huelva; cereals, grapes, hogs; fishing; sawmilling, alcohol distilling, mfg. of cotton goods. Near by is the Bermejal dam and hydroelectric plant.

San Juan del Río (rēʹō). **1** Town (pop. 1,956), Durango, N Mexico, on affluent of Nazas R. and 55 mi. NNE of Durango; alt. 5,630 ft.; grain, cotton, fruit; silver and lead deposits. **2** City (pop. 6,694), Querétaro, central Mexico, on central plateau, on railroad and 79 mi. SE of Querétaro; alt. 6,243 ft. Famous for its opals, mined at nearby La Trinidad, it is also a mining (silver, lead, copper) and agr. center (corn, wheat, sugar cane, beans, alfalfa, fruit, livestock).

San Juan del Sur (sōōrʹ), town (1950 pop. 1,019), Rivas dept., SW Nicaragua, port on the Pacific, 14 mi. S of Rivas; terminus of rail line from Rivas; seaside resort; coffee, livestock. Exports lumber, coffee, sugar. Has cable station, lighthouse. During California gold rush it was Pacific terminus of transisthmian traffic route.

San Juan de Mezquital, Mexico: see JUAN ALDAMA.

San Juan de Micay River (dā mēkīʹ), Cauca dept., SW Colombia, rises in Cordillera Occidental W of Popayán, flows c.100 mi. N and W to the Pacific at 3°N. Along its course are alluvial gold and platinum deposits.

San Juan de Mozarrifar (dā mō-thärēfärʹ), outer suburb (pop. 4,681) of Saragossa, Saragossa prov., NE Spain, 4 mi. NNE of city center.

San Juan de Murra, Nicaragua: see MURRA.

San Juan de Najasa River, Cuba: see NAJASA RIVER.

San Juan de Ñeembucú, Paraguay: see SAN JUAN BAUTISTA DE ÑEEMBUCÚ.

San Juan de Oriente, Nicaragua: see SAN JUAN, Masaya dept.

San Juan de Payara (dā pīäʹrä), town (pop. 294), Apure state, W central Venezuela, in llanos 21 mi. SSW of San Fernando, in cattle region.

San Juan de Ríoseco (rēʺōsāʹkō), town (pop. 1,545), Cundinamarca dept., central Colombia, on W slopes of Cordillera Oriental, above Magdalena R., 40 mi. WNW of Bogotá; alt. 4,275 ft. Sugar-producing center.

San Juan de Sabinas (säbēʹnäs), town (pop. 785), Coahuila, N Mexico, on railroad and 10 mi. NW of Sabinas; coal mining.

San Juan de Salvamento (sälvämĕnʹtō), village, small port on E coast of Staten Isl., E Tierra del Fuego natl. territory, Argentina; 54°47′S 63°50′W.

San Juan Despí (däspēʹ), village (pop. 1,809), Barcelona prov., NE Spain, 6 mi. WSW of Barcelona; truck farming; wine, corn, fruit.

San Juan de Telpaneca, Nicaragua: see SAN JUAN, Madríz dept.
San Juan de Tibás, Costa Rica: see SAN JUAN.
San Juan de Ulúa, Mexico: see VERACRUZ, city.
San Juan de Vera, Argentina: see CORRIENTES, city.
San Juan de Vilasar (dä vēläsär'), town (pop. 3,434), Barcelona prov., NE Spain, on the Mediterranean, 4 mi. SW of Mataró, in winegrowing area; cotton milling, soap mfg.; ships hazelnuts, oranges. Summer resort.
San Juan Evangelista (ävänhälē'stä), town (pop. 2,528), Veracruz, SE Mexico, on Isthmus of Tehuantepec, on San Juan R. and 16 mi. WSW of Acayucan; fruit, livestock. Sometimes Santana Rodríguez.
San Juan Hill (săn wän', Sp. sän hwän'), Oriente prov., E Cuba, just E of Santiago de Cuba; scene (July, 1898) of battle in Spanish-American War in which Theodore Roosevelt and his Rough Riders took part. Now site of a public park.
San Juanico Strait (sän hwänē'kō), narrow channel (25 mi. long, less than ½ mi. wide in some places), Philippines, separating Samar from Leyte; Tacloban (Leyte) is at S end. Leads from Leyte Gulf to Samar Sea.
San Juan Islands (săn wän'), NW Wash., archipelago of 172 isls. at N end of Puget Sound, bounded E by Rosario Strait and W by Haro Strait; international line passes W and N of main group (San Juan, Orcas and Lopez isls.), which form San Juan co. Discovered and named (c.1790) by the Spanish. Awarded to U.S. (1872) after settlement of San Juan boundary dispute with Great Britain. An oceanographic laboratory is at FRIDAY HARBOR.
San Juanito, town, Mexico: see ANTONIO ESCOBEDO.
San Juanito Island, Mexico: see TRES MARÍAS ISLANDS.
San Juan Ixtayopan (sän hwän' ēstīō'pän"), town (pop. 1,913), Federal Dist., central Mexico, 16 mi. SE of Mexico city; cereals, fruit, livestock.
San Juan La Laguna, Guatemala: see SAN JUAN.
San Juan Mixtepec, Mexico: see MIXTEPEC.
San Juan Mountains (săn wän'), range of Rocky Mts., SW Colo. and N N.Mex., lying W of San Luis Valley, S of Gunnison R.; extend SSE toward Rio Chama, N.Mex. Prominent points: HANDIES PEAK (14,013 ft.), SUNSHINE PEAK (14,018 ft.), WETTERHORN PEAK (14,020 ft.), REDCLOUD PEAK (14,050 ft.), Mt. EOLUS (14,079 ft.), WINDOM PEAK (14,091 ft.), Mt. SNEFFELS (14,143 ft.), SAN LUIS PEAK (14,149 ft.), UNCOMPAHGRE PEAK (14,306 ft.). Range includes much of San Juan Natl. Forest; drained by branches of San Juan R. and headwaters of Rio Grande. Wolf Creek Pass (10,850 ft.), bet. Mineral and Archuleta counties, is crossed by highway. Cumbres Pass (10,025 ft.; near N.Mex. line) was used by Sp. explorers in 16th and 17th centuries and is also crossed by highway. Range is of volcanic origin; gold, silver, lead, copper mined in vicinity of Silverton, Ouray, and Telluride.
San Juan Nepomuceno (näpōmōōsā'nō), town (pop. 4,124), Bolívar dept., N Colombia, 45 mi. SE of Cartagena; agr. center (corn, tobacco, sugar cane, livestock).
San Juan Nepomuceno, town (dist. pop. 12,407), Caazapá dept., S Paraguay, 125 mi. SE of Asunción, 37 mi. SE of Villarrica; lumber, fruit, livestock.
San Juan Nonualco (nōnwäl'kō), city (pop. 6,309), La Paz dept., S Salvador, on road and 3 mi. W of Zacatecoluca; agr., livestock raising.
San Juan Opico, Salvador: see OPICO.
San Juan Ostuncalco, Guatemala: see OSTUNCALCO.
San Juan Parangaricutiro, Mexico: see PARANGARICUTIRO.
San Juan River (sän hwän'), S San Juan prov., Argentina, formed by union of Castaño R. and the Río de los Patos 6 mi. N of Calingasta, flows c.150 mi. E and S, past Ullún, San Juan, Angaco Sud, and Villa Independencia, to HUANACACHE lakes at Mendoza prov. border. Waters a fertile irrigated valley (wine, sugar cane, fruit, grain). Used for hydroelectric power.
San Juan River, SW Bolivia, rises on E slopes of Cordillera de Lípez in 2 branches which join on Bolivia-Argentina border 35 mi. SE of San Pablo; flows 170 mi. generally E, past Suipacha, and N, joining Cotagaita R. just SE of Villa Abecia to form PILAYA RIVER. Receives Tupiza R. (left). Known also as Río Grande de San Juan in upper course and as Talina R. in middle course.
San Juan River. 1 In Chocó dept., W Colombia, rises in Cordillera Occidental at Caldas dept. border, flows c.200 mi. SW, past Tadó and Istmina, to the Pacific in wide delta at border of Valle del Cauca dept. Navigable almost its entire length. Along its course are rich gold- and platinum-placer mines. **2** On Colombia-Ecuador border, rises in the Andes at W foot of the Nevado de Chiles, flows c.50 mi. NW along international line to Mira R.
San Juan River, Matanzas prov., W Cuba, flows c.20 mi. to Matanzas Bay at Matanzas.
San Juan River. 1 N Mexico, formed in Nuevo León NE of Montemorelos by several headstreams rising in Sierra Madre Oriental; flows c.75 mi. N and NE, past China, General Bravo, Doctor Coss, and Los Aldamas, into Tamaulipas, and past Camargo, to Rio Grande 2 mi. SE of Rio Grande City, Texas. Receives Pesquería R. Used for irrigation. **2** In Veracruz, SE Mexico, rises at foot of Zempoaltépetl (Oaxaca), flows c.160 mi. NE and NW, past San Juan Evangelista, to PAPALOÁPAM RIVER at Tlacotalpan. Navigable for shallow-draft vessels.
San Juan River, outlet of L. Nicaragua on Nicaragua–Costa Rica border, issues from SE end of lake at San Carlos, flows 120 mi. ESE through tropical forest, past El Castillo, to the Caribbean at San Juan del Norte. Shallow-draught navigation is hampered by rapids of Toro (4 mi. WNW of El Castillo), El Castillo, and Machuca (10 mi. SE of El Castillo). Receives San Carlos and Sarapiquí rivers (right). Near its mouth it forms 3 main arms: the minor Juanillo (N), the San Juan proper, and the Río COLORADO (S). The San Juan was to be canalized as part of the projected Nicaragua Canal route.
San Juan River or **Chincha River** (chēn'chä), Ica dept., SW Peru, rises in the Cordillera Occidental NNW of Castrovirreyna, flows 80 mi. SW, past Chincha Alta and Chincha Baja, to the Pacific near Tambo de Mora. Irrigates, in middle and lower course, major cotton-producing region.
San Juan River (săn wän'), in SW Colo., NW N.Mex., and SE Utah, rises in several branches in San Juan Mts., NE of Pagosa Springs, Colo.; flows SW into NW N.Mex., past Farmington, thence NW into Utah, and W to Colorado R. near Rainbow Bridge Natl. Monument, SE Utah; c.400 mi. long. Not navigable. Irrigates areas in Colo., N.Mex., and Utah. Tributaries: Los Pinos, Animas, La Plata, and Mancos rivers. Fruit, vegetables, and grain grown in N.Mex. area of river valley.
San Juan River (sän hwän'), in Sucre and Monagas states, NE Venezuela, rises in coastal range SW of Carúpano, flows c.75 mi. SE to Gulf of Paria; good navigability. Receives Guarapiche R. Tankers call at oil terminal Caripito, on its right bank.
San Juan Sacatepéquez, Guatemala: see SAN JUAN.
San Juan Tecuaco, Guatemala: see TECUACO.
San Juan Teotihuacán, Mexico: see TEOTIHUACÁN.
San Juan Tepa (tā'pä), town (pop. 1,431), Hidalgo, central Mexico, 23 mi. NW of Pachuca; corn, maguey, stock.
San Juan Totolac, Mexico: see TOTOLAC.
San Juan Valley, W Dominican Republic, bet. the Cordillera Central (N) and Sierra de Neiba (S), extends c.50 mi. E from Haiti border to the Yaque del Sur. Bananas, chick-peas, rice, corn, coffee, sugar cane are grown. Main centers: San Juan, Las Matas, and Elías Piña.
San Juan Valley, Calif.: see SANTA CLARA VALLEY.
San Juan y Martínez (sän hwän' ē märtē'nēs), town (pop. 4,124), Pinar del Río prov., W Cuba, on railroad and 12 mi. SW of Pinar del Río; tobacco-growing center in rich Vuelta Abajo region. Tobacco experiment station.
San Juan Zitlaltepec, Mexico: see ZITLALTEPEC, Mexico state.
San Julián (sän hōōlyän'), town (1947 pop. 3,193), ⊙ Magallanes dept., E Santa Cruz natl. territory, Argentina, port on San Julián Bay (sheltered inlet of the Atlantic), 60 mi. NE of Santa Cruz, sheep-raising and fishing (sardines, mackerel) center. Tanning, meat packing. Kaolin deposits. Airport.
San Julián, town (pop. 1,806), Jalisco, central Mexico, in Sierra Madre Occidental, 18 mi. SE of San Juan de los Lagos; corn, beans, livestock.
San Julián, town (pop. 2,058), Sonsonate dept., SW Salvador, 12 mi. ESE of Sonsonate; balsam extraction; grain, livestock.
San Julián de Loria (dä lōr'yä), village (pop. c.700), Andorra, near Sp. border, on the Valira and 4 mi. SSW of Andorra la Vella; tobacco processing. Sandal and woolen mfg. Hotels. Sometimes called San Julia de Loria.
San Justo, department, Argentina: see SAN FRANCISCO, Córdoba prov.
San Justo (sän hōō'stō). **1** City (pop. 3,630, with suburbs, c.10,000), ⊙ Matanza dist. (□ 127; pop. 99,888), in Greater Buenos Aires, Argentina, 11 mi. WSW of Buenos Aires; stock-raising and mfg. center. Plows, automobile accessories, rubber goods, paper. Alfalfa and grain growing. Has old church dating from 1735. **2** Town (pop. estimate 3,000), ⊙ San Justo dept. (□ 2,150; 1947 pop. 33,995), central Santa Fe prov., Argentina, 55 mi. N of Santa Fe; rail junction, commercial and agr. center (flax, corn, sunflowers, sheep, horses, hogs); makes flax fibers, dairy products.
San Justo de la Vega (dä lä vä'gä), village (pop. 1,171), Leon prov., NW Spain, 2 mi. E of Astorga; mfg. (cotton cloth, candy); lumbering, stock raising; cereals, sugar beets, flax.
San Justo Desvérn (dĕsvĕrn'), outer suburb (pop. 2,494) of Barcelona, NE Spain, 5 mi. W of city center; mfg. (cement, ceramics, tiles); hazelnut shipping; wine, almonds, fruit.
Sankamankandimunai, promontory, Ceylon: see KOMARI.
San Kamphaeng Range (sän' käm'păng'), SE Thailand, at SW edge of Korat Plateau, bet. Dong Phaya Yen Range (N) and Dangrek Range (E); rises to 2,000 ft.; densely forested.
Sankapura, Indonesia: see BAWEAN.
Sankaranayinarkoil (sŭng"kŭrŭnīnärkō'ĭl) or **Sankaranayinarkovil** (–kō'vĭl), town (pop. 16,923), Tinnevelly dist., S Madras, India, 22 mi. NE of Tenkasi, in sesame-growing area; bell-metal industry. Becomes seasonal cattle-trade center during temple pilgrimage festival. Also spelled Sankaranayinarkovyil and Sankaranainarkoil.
Sankaridrug (sŭng'kŭrĭdrōōg), village, Salem dist., S central Madras, India, 25 mi. SW of Salem; road center. Isolated peak (2,343 ft.) just W; limestone workings.
Sankaty Head, Mass.: see NANTUCKET ISLAND.
Sankertown, borough (pop. 865), Cambria co., SW central Pa., just N of Cresson.
Sankeshvar (sŭngkā'shvŭr), village, Mehsana dist., N Bombay, India, 38 mi. WSW of Mehsana; cotton ginning. Jain pilgrimage center.
Sankeshwar (sŭngkā'shvŭr), village (pop. 11,172), Belgaum dist., S Bombay, India, 28 mi. N of Belgaum; local trade center for millet, chili, tobacco, rice. Also spelled Sankeshvar.
Sankheda (sŭnkē'dŭ), town (pop. 5,867), Baroda dist., N Bombay, India, 25 mi. ESE of Baroda; market center for cotton, millet, rice; calico printing and dyeing, wood carving, lacquer work.
Sankheda Mewas, India: see GUJARAT STATES.
Sankh River (sŭngk), SW Bihar and N Orissa, India, rises on Chota Nagpur Plateau c.35 mi. WSW of Lohardaga, flows 135 mi. SSE, joining South Koel R. 14 mi. E of Raj Gangpur to form Brahmani R.
Sankiang or **San-chiang** (both: sän'jyäng'), former province (□ 34,910; 1940 pop. 1,415,633) of NE Manchukuo, on lower Sungari R.; ⊙ was Kiamusze. Formed 1934 out of old Heilungkiang and Kirin provs., it became part of Hokiang prov. in 1946 and of Sungkiang prov. in 1949.
Sankiang or **San-chiang,** town, ⊙ Sankiang co. (pop. 147,546), N Kwangsi prov., China, 50 mi. NW of Kweilin, near Kweichow-Hunan line; timber, rice, wheat. The name Sankiang (until 1914, Hwaiyüan) was formerly applied to Tanchow, 30 mi. SSW. Present Sankiang was then known as Kuyi.
Sankieh, China: see KIASHAN.
Sankioh, China: see SANTU.
Sankisa, India: see FARRUKHABAD, city.
Sankosh River (sŭngkōsh'), in Bhutan and India, rises in W Assam Himalayas near the Chomo Lhari, on undefined Tibet-Bhutan border; flows SSE through Bhutan (here called Mo Chu), past Gasa, Punakha, and Wangdu Phodrang, SSW, and S along Assam–West Bengal border, receiving left arm of Raidak R.; combined stream (here called Gangadhar R.) flows S past Golakganj to the Brahmaputra 9 mi. W of Dhubri; total length, c.200 mi.
San Kosi River, Nepal: see SUN KOSI RIVER.
Sankpo, river, Kashmir: see SURU RIVER.
Sankt Aegyd (or **Ägyd**) or **Sankt Aegyd am Neuwalde** (zängkt ā'güt, äm noi'väldŭ), town (pop. 3,192), S Lower Austria, on Traisen R. and 24 mi. S of Sankt Pölten; mfg. (machinery, wire).
Sankt Amarin, France: see SAINT-AMARIN.
Sankt Andreasberg (ändrā'äsbĕrk), town (pop. 4,799), in former Prussian prov. of Hanover, W Germany, after 1945 in Lower Saxony, in the upper Harz, 8 mi. NW of Herzberg; rail terminus; noted for its canary birds; woodworking, sawmilling. Climatic health resort (alt. 1,900–2,065 ft.); winter sports. Was mining (iron, lead, silver, copper) center from 16th to early-20th cent. Chartered 1535.
Sankt Anton am Arlberg (än'tōn äm ärl'bĕrk), village (pop. 1,651), Tyrol, W Austria, on Rosanna R. and 14 mi. W of Landeck, in Arlberg region; well-known ski center (alt. 4,277 ft.) and health resort. E entrance to ARLBERG TUNNEL.
Sankt Arnual (är'nōōäl"), E section (since 1909) of Saarbrücken, S Saar, on Saar R.; site of Saarbrücken airport. Has 13th-cent. abbey church, with tombs of counts of Nassau-Saarbrücken.
Sankt Avold, France: see SAINT-AVOLD.
Sankt Blasien (blā'zyŭn), village (pop. 2,578), S Baden, Germany, in Black Forest, 10 mi. WNW of Waldshut; cotton mfg. Well-known climatic health resort (alt. 2,526 ft.), with tuberculosis sanatoriums. Site (945–1805) of noted Benedictine abbey; bldgs. now house Jesuit acad.
Sankt Florian or **Sankt Florian am Inn** (flō'rēän, äm ĭn'), town (pop. 2,719), W Upper Austria, on Inn R., just SE of Schärding. Has 8th-cent. Augustinian abbey, with large library.
Sankt Gallen, Switzerland: see SAINT GALL.
Sankt Gallenkirch (gäl'ŭnkĭrkh), village (pop. 1,740), Vorarlberg, W Austria, on Ill R. and 11 mi. SE of Bludenz; tourist resort (alt. 2,900 ft.).
Sankt Georgen (gäōr'gŭn). **1** Town (pop. 2,488), Carinthia, S Austria, 9 mi. SSE of Wolfsberg; wheat, rye, cattle, fruit. **2** or **Sankt Georgen am Längsee** (äm lĕng'zā), town (pop. 3,375), Carinthia, S Austria, on small Längsee and 12 mi. NNE of Klagenfurt; summer resort. Imposing fortress of Hochosterwitz (with 14 towers) is 2 mi. S. **3** or **Sankt Georgen an der Gusen** (än dĕr gōō'zŭn), town (pop. 1,678), NE Upper Austria, 6 mi. E of Linz, N of the Danube; wheat, cattle. **4** or **Sankt Georgen im Attergau** (ĕm ät'ŭrgou), town (pop. 2,551), SW Upper Austria, in the Salzkammergut, 14 mi. W of Gmunden; wheat, cattle, fruit.

Sankt Georgen (gäôr'gůn), town (pop. 5,865), S Baden, Germany, in Black Forest, 8 mi. NW of Villingen; watch industry; machinery and machine-tool mfg. Climatic health resort and winter-sports center (alt. 2,827 ft.). Has former Benedictine abbey (late 11th cent.–1806).

Sankt Georgen, Yugoslavia: see DJURDJEVAC.

Sankt Gilgen (gĭl'gůn), town (pop. 3,208), Salzburg, W central Austria, on N shore of Sankt Wolfgangsee and 15 mi. ESE of Salzburg, in the Salzkammergut; summer resort.

Sankt Goar (gōär'), town (pop. 1,816), in former Prussian Rhine Prov., W Germany, after 1945 in Rhineland-Palatinate, on left bank of the Rhine (landing) and 8 mi. SE of Boppard; wine. Has Romanesque-Gothic church. Ruined 13th-cent. fortress Rheinfels [Ger.,=Rhine rock], destroyed by French in 1797, towers above town. Sankt Goar was main town of Lower County of Katzenelnbogen, passing with it to HESSE in 1479. County was part of independent (1567–83) Hessen-Rheinfels, which was subsequently divided bet. HESSE-DARMSTADT and HESSE-KASSEL.

Sankt Goarshausen (gōärs"hou'zůn), town (pop. 1,902), in former Prussian prov. of Hesse-Nassau, W Germany, after 1945 in Rhineland-Palatinate, on right bank of the Rhine and 11 mi. SSE of Oberlahnstein; wine. Just S is the Lorelei.

Sankt Gotthard, Switzerland: see SAINT GOTTHARD.

Sankt Ingbert (ĭng'bĕrt), Fr. *Saint-Ingbert* (sĕtĕbĕr'), city (pop. 22,996), S central Saar, 7 mi. ENE of Saarbrücken; coal-mining, and steel-industry center; cotton milling, woodworking, brewing; mfg. of chemicals, window glass, leather and tobacco products. First foundry established here in 1732. Sankt Ingbert dist. formed part (1815–1919) of Rhenish Palatinate.

Sankt Jakob an der Birs (yä'kôp än dĕr bĭrs') or **Saint Jacob on the Birs,** SE suburb of Basel, N Switzerland. Known for heroic resistance here, in 1444, of Swiss against Armagnacs.

Sankt Joachimsthal, Czechoslovakia: see JACHYMOV.

Sankt Johann (yōhän'). **1** or **Sankt Johann im Pongau** (ĭm pōn'gou), town (pop. 6,008), Salzburg, W central Austria, on the Salzach and 4 mi. S of Bischofshofen; cattle market; leather goods, brewery; resort. Scenic gorge is 3 mi. N. **2** or **Sankt Johann im Saggauthale** (ĕm zäg'outälů), village (pop. 2,453), Styria, SE Austria, 25 mi. S of Graz; vineyards, poultry. **3** or **Sankt Johann in Tirol** (ĭn tĕrōl'), town (pop. 4,314), Tyrol, W Austria, 6 mi. NNE of Kitzbühel; summer resort with mineral springs. Black-marble quarry near by.

Sankt Johann (yōhän'), SE industrial section (since 1909) of Saarbrücken, S Saar, on Saar R. Has remains of Roman castle.

Sankt Kreuz, France: see SAINTE-CROIX-AUX-MINES.

Sankt Lambrecht (läm'prĕkht), village (pop. 1,786), Styria, S central Austria, 18 mi. WSW of Judenburg; explosives.

Sankt Leon (lā'ôn), village (pop. 3,164), N Baden, Germany, after 1945 in Württemberg-Baden, on the Kraichbach and 5 mi. WSW of Wiesloch; mfg. of cigars and cigarettes.

Sankt Leonhard (lā'ōnhärt). **1** Village, Carinthia, Austria: see BAD SANKT LEONHARD IM LAVANTTALE. **2** or **Sankt Leonhard im Pitztal** (ĭm pĭts'-täl), village (pop. 988), Tyrol, W Austria, in the Pitztal, valley of Ötztal Alps, 13 mi. SSE of Imst; cattle. Until 1935, called Pitzthal.

Sankt Ludwig, France: see SAINT-LOUIS.

Sankt Marein, Yugoslavia: see SMARJE.

Sankt Margarethen im Lavantthale (märgärā'tůn ĕm läf'änt-tälů), town (pop. 2,495), Carinthia, S Austria, 2 mi. WNW of Wolfsberg.

Sankt Margrethen (mär'grĕtůn), town (pop. 3,162), St. Gall canton, NE Switzerland, on the Alter Rhein, on Austrian border, and 12 mi. ENE of St. Gall; embroideries, chemicals, metal- and woodworking; sulphur baths.

Sankt Marien (märē'ůn), town (pop. 2,854), E central Upper Austria, 10 mi. S of Linz; potatoes, fruit.

Sankt Martin (mär'tēn), village (pop. 1,943), Rhenish Palatinate, W Germany, on E slope of Hardt Mts., 4 mi. SSW of Neustadt; wine.

Sankt Martin im Mühlkreise (mär'tēn ĭm mül'-krīzů), town (pop. 2,132), N central Upper Austria, near left bank of the Danube, 13 mi. NW of Linz; rye, vineyards.

Sankt Mauritz (mou'rĭts), E suburb (pop. 5,823) of Münster, NW Germany.

Sankt Michael (mĭ'khäĕl), town (pop. 2,348), Salzburg, W central Austria, on Mur R. and 22 mi. N of Spittal; leather goods.

Sankt Michael in Obersteiermark (ĭn ōbůrshtī'-ůrmärk), town (pop. 3,477), Styria, SE central Austria, on Mur R. and 4 mi. SW of Leoben; rail junction. Graphite and magnesite mined near by.

Sankt Michaelsdonn (mĭ'khäĕls"dôn'), village (pop. 3,558), in Schleswig-Holstein, NW Germany, 8 mi. S of Meldorf, in the S Dithmarschen; rail junction; sugar refining, distilling; sawmilling.

Sankt Michel, Finland: see MIKKELI.

Sankt Moritz, Switzerland: see SAINT MORITZ.

Sankt Oswald (ôs'vält), town (pop. 2,211), NE Upper Austria, 4 mi. E of Freistadt near Czechoslovak border; rye, potatoes.

Sankt Oswald, village (commune pop. 2,818), Lower Bavaria, Germany, in Bohemian Forest, 12 mi. SE of Zwiesel; brewing. Glassworks at Riedlhütte (pop. 785), 2 mi. NW.

Sankt Pauli (pou'lē), district of Hamburg, NW Germany, on right bank of the Norderelbe, adjoining city center (E), Altona (W) and Rotherbaum (N) dists., and with pier (1906–10) on which Hamburg's inter-harbor traffic centers; site of the Reeperbahn, well-known amusement center. Has marine acad. (founded 1749), institute of tropical diseases. Heavily damaged in Second World War. Noted tunnel under the Norderelbe (here 33 ft. deep, 1,312 ft. wide), completed 1911, connects Hamburg with shipyards on Steinwärder isl. and free-port area.

Sankt Peter (pā'tůr). **1** Village (pop. 1,511), S Baden, Germany, in Black Forest, 8 mi. E of Freiburg; climatic health resort (alt. 2,362 ft.). Former Benedictine abbey (founded 1083; since 1842, theological seminary) has baroque church. **2** or **Sankt Peter-Ording** (–ôrdĭng), commune (pop. 3,885), in Schleswig-Holstein, NW Germany, on Eiderstedt peninsula, 20 mi. SW of Husum; popular North Sea resort (especially for children). Includes village of Sankt Peter, Nordseebad Sankt Peter, and small fishing village of Ording.

Sankt Peter-Freienstein (pā'tůr frī'ůnshtīn), village (pop. 1,860), Styria, SE central Austria, 3 mi. NW of Leoben; dairy farming.

Sankt Peters Insel, Switzerland: see SAINT-PIERRE, ÎLE.

Sankt Pilt, Haut-Rhin dept., France: see SAINT-HIPPOLYTE.

Sankt Pölten (pûl'tůn), city (1951 pop. 40,338), Lower Austria, on Traisen R. and 30 mi. W of Vienna; rail center; hydroelectric plant; mfg. (textiles, machinery). Bishopric; abbey church (11th cent.; rebuilt 18th cent.).

Sankt Stefan (shtā'fän). **1** Town (pop. 3,605), Carinthia, S Austria, on Lavant R. and 2 mi. S of Wolfsberg. Lignite mined near by. **2** Village (pop. 2,123), Styria, SE central Austria, near Mur R., 7 mi. SW of Leoben; vineyards, cattle.

Sankt Tönis (tû'nĭs), village (pop. 10,392), in former Prussian Rhine Prov., W Germany, after 1945 in North Rhine-Westphalia, 3 mi. W of Krefeld; cattle.

Sankt Ulrich (ŏŏl'rĭkh), village (pop. 219), NE Lower Austria, 35 mi. NE of Vienna, near Neusiedl an der Zaya; oil.

Sankt Ulrich, Italy: see ORTISEI.

Sankt Ulrich bei Steyr (bī shtīr'), village (pop. 2,027), E Upper Austria, on Enns R., just S of Steyr; truck farming.

Sankt Valentin (fäl'ĕntēn), town (pop. 6,803), W Lower Austria, 4 mi. SE of Enns; rail junction; grain, cattle.

Sankt Veit (fīt'). **1** Town (pop. 2,128), Salzburg, W central Austria, near the Salzach, 6 mi. SSW of Bischofshofen; summer resort (alt. 2,575 ft.). **2** or **Sankt Veit an der Glan** (än dĕr glän'), town (pop. 8,855), Carinthia, S Austria, on Glan R. and 10 mi. N of Klagenfurt; rail junction; textiles; summer resort. Was ⊙ Carinthia until 16th cent. Has 14th-cent. church, city hall (1468), mus. **3** or **Sankt Veit an der Gölsen** (än dĕr gûl'zůn), town (pop. 3,553), central Lower Austria, 11 mi. SSE of Sankt Pölten; grain, cattle.

Sankt-Vith, Belgium: see SAINT-VITH.

Sankt Wendel (vĕn'důl), Fr. *Saint-Wendel* (sē-vĕndĕl'), city (pop. 9,408), NE Saar, near Ger. border, on Blies R. and 20 mi. NNE of Saarbrücken; rail junction; railroad workshops; mfg. of leather and tobacco products; brewing. Has 14th-cent. church. Town 1st mentioned in 7th cent.

Sankt Wolfgang (vôlf'gäng), town (pop. 2,640), S Upper Austria, in the Salzkammergut, on E shore of Sankt Wolfgangsee and 8 mi. W of Bad Ischl; well-known resort (alt. 1,800 ft.). Gothic church with beautiful carved altar. Cogwheel railroad to the Schafberg (N), 5,580 ft. high.

Sankt Wolfgangsee (vôlf'gängsā") or **Wolfgangsee,** lake (□ 5.09) in Salzburg, W central Austria, at W foot of the Schafberg, 15 mi. E of Salzburg; 7 mi. long, c.1 mi. wide, average depth 375 ft., alt. 1,768 ft. Also called Abersee. Site of tourist resorts (Sankt Gilgen, Sankt Wolfgang, Strobl).

Sankuru, district, Belgian Congo: see LUSAMBO.

Sankuru River (săngkōō'rōō), main tributary of the Kasai in central Belgian Congo. Rises as Lubilash R. in Katanga highlands 55 mi. NE of Malonga, flows 285 mi. N and NW to a point 15 mi. S of Tshilenge, where it becomes the Sankuru R. and flows N, forming rapids, W past Lusambo, and again N and W to Kasai R. opposite Basongo; total length c.750 mi. Sankuru R. is navigable for 365 mi. below Pania Mutombo. Receives Bushimaie R. There are 2 large hydroelectric power plants on Lubilash R. at Tshala.

Sankyo, Formosa: see SANSIA.

San Lázaro (sän lä'särō), town (dist. pop. 935), Concepción dept., N central Paraguay, at confluence of Apa and Paraguay rivers (Brazil border), 100 mi. NW of Concepción, in cattle-raising and lumbering area.

San Lázaro, town (pop. 749), Trujillo state, W Venezuela, in Andean spur, 8 mi. SSW of Trujillo; coffee, fruit, corn.

San Lazzaro (sän lätsä'rô), islet in Lagoon of Venice, N Italy, 2 mi. SE of Venice; famous for its Armenian monastery.

San Lazzaro Parmense (pärmĕn'sĕ), SE suburb (pop. 717) of Parma, in Emilia-Romagna, N central Italy; dairy machinery, canned tomatoes, paper.

San Leandro (săn lēăn'drō), city (pop. 27,542), Alameda co., W Calif., S suburb of Oakland. Annual flower show and cherry festival celebrate area's produce. Dairying, canning, automobile assembling; mfg. of tractors, engines, office machines. L. Chabot (shăbō') (2½ mi. long) is near by. Inc. 1872; was ⊙ Alameda co., 1855–72.

San Leonardo (sän lāōnär'dhō), town (1939 pop. 2,761; 1948 municipality pop. 15,385), Nueva Ecija prov., central Luzon, Philippines, 9 mi. S of Cabanatuan; rice-growing center.

San Leonardo, town (pop. 1,165), Soria prov., N central Spain, on railroad and 32 mi. W of Soria; cereals, tubers, vegetables, livestock; lumbering; flour milling.

San Leucio (sän lā'ōōchō), village (pop. 583), Caserta prov., Campania, S Italy, 3 mi. NW of Caserta; silk mills.

Sanlisanchen, Manchuria: see MINGSHUI.

San Lorenzo (sän lōrĕn'sō). **1** Town (pop. estimate 700), NE Corrientes prov., Argentina, on railroad and 50 mi. SSE of Corrientes; cattle and horse center. **2** Town (1947 pop. 11,270), ⊙ San Lorenzo dept. (□ 785; 1947 pop. 56,530), S Santa Fe prov., Argentina, port on Paraná R. and 15 mi. NNW of Rosario; rail junction, commercial and agr. center (corn, flax, wheat, potatoes, watermelons, sunflowers). Has grain elevator, vegetable-oil mill, state gasoline refinery. Fisheries.

San Lorenzo (sän lōrĕn'thō), village (pop. 1,607), Iviza, Balearic Isls., 8 mi. NNE of Iviza city; fruit, livestock.

San Lorenzo (sän lōrĕn'sō). **1** Town (pop. c.1,500), Beni dept., N central Bolivia, in the llanos, c.35 mi. SSW of San Ignacio; cattle. **2** Village, Beni dept., NE Bolivia, in the llanos, 20 mi. SE of Trinidad; cattle. **3** Village, Pando dept., N Bolivia, on Beni R. and 80 mi. SW of Riberalta; rubber. **4** Town (pop. c.3,200), ⊙ Méndez prov., Tarija dept., SE Bolivia, on Tarija R. and 7 mi. N of Tarija, on road; vineyards, fruit.

San Lorenzo (sän lōrĕn'thō), village (pop. 785), Grand Canary, Canary Isls., 4 mi. SW of Las Palmas, in fertile irrigated region; bananas, tomatoes, potatoes, barley, wheat; timber; goats, sheep, cattle. Flour milling.

San Lorenzo (sän lōrĕn'sō). **1** Village (1930 pop. 985), Aconcagua prov., central Chile, on Ligua R. and 15 mi. E of La Ligua; kaolin quarrying. **2** Village (1930 pop. 584), Bío-Bío prov., S central Chile, at W foot of the Andes, 40 mi. E of Los Angeles; health resort with thermal springs.

San Lorenzo, village, Esmeraldas prov., N Ecuador, on small Pacific inlet of the Ancón de Sardinas (bay) and 60 mi. ENE of Esmeraldas, in tropical forest region (balsa wood, rubber, mangrove, tagua nuts, bananas, coco). Projected terminus of railroad from Ibarra.

San Lorenzo, town (1950 pop. 697), Suchitepéquez dept., SW Guatemala, in Pacific piedmont, 4 mi. SSW of Mazatenango; grain; livestock raising.

San Lorenzo, town (pop. 2,723), Valle dept., S Honduras, Pacific port on San Lorenzo Bay of Gulf of Fonseca, on spur of Inter-American Highway and 8 mi. SSE of Nacaome; brickworks; saltworking. Airport. Launch service to port of Amapala on Tigre Isl.

San Lorenzo. 1 Town, Chihuahua, Mexico: see DOCTOR BELISARIO DOMÍNGUEZ. **2** or **San Lorenzo Tepaltitlán** (tāpältētlän'), town (pop. 2,222), Mexico state, central Mexico, 3 mi. NE of Toluca; cereals, stock; dairying. **3** Town, Veracruz, Mexico: see YANGA.

San Lorenzo, town (1950 pop. 447), Boaco dept., S central Nicaragua, 8 mi. S of Boaco; coffee; livestock.

San Lorenzo or **San Lorenzo del Campo Grande** (dĕl käm'pō grän'dā), city (dist. pop. 12,377), Central dept., S Paraguay, 9 mi. E of Asunción; rail terminus and mfg. center; soap works, vegetable-oil plants, sugar refineries, rice mills, lumber mills, tanneries. Founded 1775.

San Lorenzo, town (pop. 143), Madre de Dios dept., SE Peru, on Tahuamanu R. and 38 mi. SSE of Iñapari, in rubber region.

San Lorenzo, town (pop. 6,745), E Puerto Rico, in outliers of the Cordillera Central, 22 mi. SSE of San Juan; tobacco and sugar center; tobacco stripping, mfg. of cigars.

San Lorenzo, town (pop. 762), Ahuachapán dept., W Salvador, port on Río de la Paz (Guatemala border) and 4 mi. NNW of Atiquizaya; grain, livestock. Beach resort.

San Lorenzo (săn lůrĕn'zō), village (pop. c.500), Alameda co., W Calif., bet. San Leandro (NW) and Hayward; fruit, vegetable, and flower growing.

San Lorenzo (sän lōrĕn'sō). **1** Town (pop. 889), Falcón state, NW Venezuela, in Caribbean lowlands, 21 mi. NNW of Tucacas; tropical forests (hardwood, divi-divi). Petroleum deposits near by. **2** Town (pop. 681), Sucre state, NE Venezuela, in coastal range, adjoining Cumanacoa, 23 mi. SE of

Cumaná; sugar cane, cacao, coffee. 3 Landing, Zulia state, NW Venezuela, on L. Maracaibo (E), 10 mi. W of Mene Grande (connected by railroad and pipe line), and 70 mi. SE of Maracaibo; ships petroleum.

San Lorenzo, Cape, on Pacific coast of Manabí prov., W Ecuador, 15 mi. WSW of Manta; 1°3'S 80°56'W. The village of San Lorenzo is near by.

San Lorenzo, Cerro (sĕ'rō), Patagonian peak (12,140 ft.) in the Andes, on Argentina-Chile border, 47°35'S. Also called Cerro Cochrane.

San Lorenzo, Cerro de (thĕ'rō dā sän lōrĕn'thō), peak (7,556 ft.), Logroño prov., N Spain, in Old Castile, in the Sierra de la Demanda (Cordillera Ibérica), 30 mi. WSW of Logroño.

San Lorenzo de Calatrava (dā käläträ'vä), town (pop. 1,106), Ciudad Real prov., S central Spain, 34 mi. S of Ciudad Real; cereals, olives, cork, honey, livestock; timber. Copper, lead, silver-bearing lead mines.

San Lorenzo de Descardazar (dĕskär-dhä-thär'), town (pop. 2,369), Majorca, Balearic Isls., 34 mi. E of Palma; almonds, grapes, figs, carobs, wheat, sheep, hogs. Flour milling, cement mfg.

San Lorenzo de la Frontera, Paraguay: see ÑEMBY.

San Lorenzo de la Parrilla (lä pärē'lyä), town (pop. 3,108), Cuenca prov., E central Spain, 19 mi. SW of Cuenca; agr. center (cereals, grapes, saffron, sheep). Lumbering. Flour milling; mfg. of dairy products, chocolate, biscuits, plaster.

San Lorenzo del Campo Grande, Paraguay: see SAN LORENZO.

San Lorenzo del Escorial (dĕl ĕskōryäl'), town (pop. 6,276), Madrid prov., central Spain, in New Castile, summer resort on E slopes of the Sierra de Guadarrama, adjoined S by ESCORIAL monastery and palace, 26 mi. WNW of Madrid. Region produces potatoes, vegetables, and cattle. Lumbering. Mfg. of soft drinks, sweets, dairy products. Has several religious colleges. Hydroelectric plant. Formerly called Escorial de Arriba, it is sometimes just called Escorial, a name now officially applied to the lower-lying, near-by town (SE), which was formerly called Escorial de Abajo.

San Lorenzo de Quinti (sän lōrĕn'sō dā kēn'tē), town (pop. 1,358), Lima dept., W central Peru, on Mala R., just opposite Huarochirí, and 55 mi. ESE of Lima; vegetables, grain, livestock.

San Lorenzo di Sebato (sän lôrĕn'tsō dē sĕbä'tō), village (pop. 478), Bolzano prov., Trentino-Alto Adige, N Italy, on Rienza R. and 2 mi. SW of Brunico; hydroelectric plant. Formerly San Lorenzo in Pusteria.

San Lorenzo Huitzizilapan, Mexico: see HUITZIZILAPAN.

San Lorenzo in Campo (sän lôrĕn'tsô ēn käm'pô), village (pop. 1,244), Pesaro e Urbino prov., The Marches, central Italy, 9 mi. SE of Fossombrone.

San Lorenzo in Pusteria, Italy: see SAN LORENZO DI SEBATO.

San Lorenzo Island (sän lōrĕn'sō), small Pacific islet (5 mi. long, 1 mi. wide; alt. 1,220 ft.), Lima dept., W central Peru, 5 mi. off Callao, the harbor of which it guards. Has an arsenal and submarine base. Small Frontón Isl., adjoining SE, has a penal settlement.

San Lorenzo Nuovo (sän lôrĕn'tsô nwô'vô), village (pop. 1,675), Viterbo prov., Latium, central Italy, near L. Bolsena, 11 mi. WSW of Orvieto; hosiery.

San Lorenzo River (sän lōrĕn'sō), NW Mexico; formed in Durango by headstreams (c.75 mi. long) rising in Sierra Madre Occidental, flows 72 mi. WSW into Sinaloa, past Santa Cruz and Quilá, to Gulf of California at its mouth on the Pacific.

San Lorenzo River (săn lùrĕn'zō), W Calif., rises in N Santa Cruz co., flows c.25 mi. S, through Santa Cruz Mts., to Monterey Bay at Santa Cruz; agr. in valley.

San Lorenzo Savall (sän lōrĕn'thō säväl'), town (pop. 1,425), Barcelona prov., NE Spain, 8 mi. NNW of Sabadell, in winegrowing area; cotton milling.

San Lorenzo Tepaltitlán, Mexico: see SAN LORENZO.

San Lorenzo Tezonco (sän lōrĕn'so täsōng'kō), town (pop. 1,934), Federal Dist., central Mexico, 12 mi. SSE of Mexico city; cereals, fruit, livestock.

Sanlúcar de Barrameda (sänlōō'kär dā bärämä'-dhä), city (pop. 28,446), Cádiz prov., SW Spain, in Andalusia, Atlantic port at mouth of the Guadalquivir, 17 mi. N of Cádiz. Popular bathing resort with fine beaches; and important wine-shipping center, through its port Bonanza (2 mi. N). Surrounded by vineyards, chiefly on dunes, it produces famed manzanilla wine. Also grain, vegetables, truck, fruit; fishing; flour- and sawmilling, alcohol distilling. Has mineral springs. An old maritime city with many notable bldgs., such as palace of dukes of Montpensier containing art treasures, a medieval castle, 16th-cent. St. George Hosp. (built for English seamen), and Santo Domingo parochial church. Of Roman origin, Sanlúcar flourished after discovery of the New World when all ships passed it to sail upstream to Seville. From here Columbus embarked on his 3d voyage (1498) and Magellan sailed on his voyage around the world (1519). Espíritu Santo castle is 2 mi. W.

Sanlúcar de Guadiana (gwädh-yä'nä), agr. town (pop. 1,021), Huelva prov., SW Spain, on Port. border opposite Alcoutim, on navigable Guadiana R. and 18 mi. N of Ayamonte; almonds, cereals, livestock.

Sanlúcar la Mayor (lä mïôr'), city (pop. 5,114), Seville prov., SW Spain, in fertile valley, on railroad and 11 mi. W of Seville; processing (olive oil) and agr. center (olives, cereals, grapes, livestock). Has churches in Mozarabic style.

San Lucas (sän lōō'käs), town (pop. c.7,700), Chuquisaca dept., S Bolivia, on Sucre-Tarija road and 38 mi. N of Camargo; barley, potatoes.

San Lucas. 1 or **San Lucas Sacatepéquez** (säkätāpā'kĕs), town (1950 pop. 931), Sacatepéquez dept., S central Guatemala, on Inter-American Highway and 5 mi. ENE of Antigua; alt. 8,924 ft.; grain, beans, fruit. **2** or **San Lucas Tolimán** (tōlē-män'), town (1950 pop. 2,329), Sololá dept., SW central Guatemala, on SE shore of L. Atitlán, 5 mi. ENE of town of Atitlán; alt. 4,000 ft.; coffee, sugar cane. Ascent of Atitlán and Tolimán volcanoes (SW) starts here.

San Lucas, town (pop. 1,047), El Paraíso dept., S Honduras, 15 mi. SSW of Yuscarán; grain, beans.

San Lucas. 1 Town, Chiapas, Mexico: see EL ZAPOTAL. **2** or **Cabo de San Lucas** (kä'bō dā), town (pop. 611), Southern Territory, Lower California, NW Mexico, at S tip of peninsula, 90 mi. SSE of La Paz; cattle raising, sugar-cane growing; fish canning. Lead deposits near by. Cape San Lucas, at W gate of Gulf of California, is 2 mi. S. **3** Town (pop. 1,495), Michoacán, central Mexico, 8 mi. SE of Huetamo; sugar cane, coffee, cereals, fruit.

San Lucas, town (1950 pop. 387), Madríz dept., NW Nicaragua, 6 mi. SSW of Somoto; corn; livestock.

San Lucas, Cape, S extremity of Lower California, Mexico, at entrance to Gulf of California; 22°52'N 109°53'W.

San Lucas Island, in Gulf of Nicoya of Pacific Ocean, W central Costa Rica, in Puntarenas prov., 4 mi. W of Puntarenas; 2 mi. long, 1.5 mi. wide. Penal colony.

San Lucas Sacatepéquez, Guatemala: see SAN LUCAS.

San Lucas Tolimán, Guatemala: see SAN LUCAS.

San Lucido (sän lōō'chēdō), village (pop. 2,576), Cosenza prov., Calabria, S Italy, on Tyrrhenian Sea, 12 mi. W of Cosenza, in fruitgrowing, stock-raising region.

San Luis (sän lwēs'), province (□ 28,520; pop. 165,546), W central Argentina, ⊙ San Luis. Bordered W by Desaguadero and Salado rivers; drained by the Río Quinto. A salt desert is in N, Sierra de Comechingones in NE, Sierra de San Luis in N. Has dry, temperate climate. Its extensive mineral resources include tin (Quines), silver, lead, zinc (Sierra de San Luis), tungsten (El Morro, Concarán, Los Cóndores), gold (San Francisco, Las Carolinas, Cañada Honda), copper, nickel, sulphur, mica (Trapiche), gypsum (Alto Pencoso), lime (San Francisco), granite, onyx (La Toma, San Luis), salt (Balde). Large areas, mainly S, covered by forests (carob, quebracho). Agr. activity restricted to irrigated basins of Conlara R. (NE) and the Río Quinto (center): rye, corn, alfalfa, wheat, fruit, and wine prominent only in N. Some stock raising (goats, cattle, sheep). Rural industries: mining, lumbering, charcoal burning, flour milling, wine making. Woodworking, food industries, tanneries concentrated in Mercedes and San Luis. Resorts: Trapiche, San Francisco. Together with Mendoza and San Juan provs., it belonged to Chile until 1776, when it formed with those provs. the Cuyo region, which was dissolved in 1820. Became a prov. in 1832.

San Luis, city (pop. 26,152), ⊙ San Luis prov. and San Luis dept. (□ 8,280; 1947 pop. 38,613), W central Argentina, at S foot of Sierra de San Luis, on railroad and 400 mi. WNW of Buenos Aires, 150 mi. ESE of Mendoza; 33°17'S 66°20'W; alt. 2,428 ft. Trading, lumbering, and farming center. Mfg.: sawmills, flour mills, plaster factories. Onyx and diorite quarries. Agr.: grain, wine, livestock; apiculture. Potrero de Funes irrigation dam and hydroelectric station near by. An old colonial city, it has administrative bldgs., govt. palace, church of Santo Domingo, branch of Cuyo Univ., natl. col., theaters, seismographic station. Founded 1596 by Martín de Loyola, governor of Chile. Formerly called San Luis de la Punta.

San Luis, town (pop. 1,322), Minorca, Balearic Isls., 2 mi. S of Mahón; winegrowing, stock raising; flour milling.

San Luis. 1 Village, Pando dept., NW Bolivia, 17 mi. SE of Cobija, on road; rice, coffee. **2** Town, Tarija dept., Bolivia: see ENTRE RÍOS.

San Luis. 1 Town (pop. 9,873), Oriente prov., E Cuba, 12 mi. N of Santiago de Cuba; rail junction, processing and trading center (sugar cane, coffee, fruit); coffee roasting. Manganese deposits. Sugar centrals are near by. **2** Town (pop. 1,751), Pinar del Río prov., W Cuba, on railroad and 10 mi. SSW of Pinar del Río; tobacco-growing center.

San Luis, town (1950 pop. 563), Petén dept., N Guatemala, 55 mi. SSE of Flores; lumbering, agr.

San Luis. 1 or **San Luis Mextepec** (mĕstäpĕk'), town (pop. 2,288), Mexico state, central Mexico, 6 mi. W of Toluca; cereals, livestock. **2** or **San Luis Río Colorado** (rē'ō kōlōrä'dhō), town (pop. 558), Sonora, NW Mexico, on affluent of lower Sonora R. (irrigation area), in lowlands of Gulf of California, and 35 mi. SW of Hermosillo; citrus fruit, wheat, corn, rice, beans.

San Luis, town (pop. 1,702), Lima dept., W central Peru, on irrigated coastal plain, on Cañete-Cerro Azul highway, and 2 mi. NW of Cañete. Sugar growing and milling in surrounding area.

San Luis, town (1939 pop. 1,503; 1948 municipality pop. 9,472), Pampanga prov., central Luzon, Philippines, on Pampanga R. and 6 mi. E of San Fernando; agr. (sugar cane, rice), fishing.

San Luis. 1 (săn lōō'ĭs, lōō'ē) Village, Yuma co., SW Ariz., port of entry at Mex. line, 17 mi. SW of Yuma. **2** (săn lōō'ĭs) Village (pop. 1,239), ⊙ Costilla co., S Colo., in W foothills of Sangre de Cristo Mts., on E slope of San Luis Valley, 30 mi. SE of Alamosa; alt. c.8,000 ft.; truck farming. Sanchez Reservoir near by.

San Luis (sän lwēs'), town (pop. 981), Falcón state, NW Venezuela, 20 mi. S of Coro; coffee, cacao.

San Luis, Lake, Bolivia: see ITONAMAS, LAKE.

San Luis, Point (săn lōō'ĭs), SW Calif., headland 10 mi. SW of San Luis Obispo; protects San Luis Obispo Bay on W. Lighthouse.

San Luis, Sierra de (syĕ'rä dā sän lwēs'), range in N San Luis prov., Argentina, SW spur of Sierra de Córdoba, extends c.65 mi. SSW from Luján to San Luis; rises to c.6,500 ft. It is drained by the Río Quinto (S), Conlara R. (SE), and Pampa de las Salinas (NW). Silver, zinc, lead deposits.

San Luis, Sierra de, range in Falcón state, NW Venezuela, S of Coro, N outlier of great Andean spur; c.35 mi. long; rises over 3,500 ft.

San Luis Acatlán (äkätlän'), town (pop. 2,570), Guerrero, SW Mexico, in Pacific lowland, 65 mi. E of Acapulco; sugar cane, coffee, cotton, fruit, livestock.

San Luis Creek (săn lōō'ĭs), S Colo., rises in NE Saguache co., bet. Sawatch and Sangre de Cristo mts.; flows c.50 mi. S, past Villagrove and Mineral Hot Springs, to join Saguache Creek in N part of SAN LUIS VALLEY. Streams flow jointly 4 mi. S to irrigation canal leading into San Luis L., 8 mi. SE of confluence.

San Luis de la Paz (sän lwēs" dā lä päs'), city (pop. 4,821), Guanajuato, Mexico, in Sierra Madre Occidental, 50 mi. ENE of Guanajuato; alt. 6,627 ft. Rail junction; agr. center (cereals, sugar cane, wine, oranges, vegetables, stock); alcohol distilling, wine and liquor making.

San Luis del Cordero (dĕl kôr-dhā'rō), town (pop. 1,352), Durango, NW Mexico, on interior plateau, 55 mi. W of Torreón; alt. 4,921 ft.; corn, wheat, chick peas, stock.

San Luis del Palmar (dĕl pälmär'), town (pop. 2,483), ⊙ San Luis del Palmar dept. (□ c.900; pop. 18,070), NW Corrientes prov., Argentina, 17 mi. E of Corrientes, on Corrientes-General Paz RR; agr. center (corn, cotton, tobacco, sugar cane, watermelons, oranges, livestock).

San Luis de Shuaro (dā shwä'rō), village (pop. 8), Junín dept., central Peru, on Paucartambo R. and 16 mi. N of San Ramón; terminus of road to Chanchamayo valley; coffee, cacao, sugar cane.

San Luis Jilotepeque, Guatemala: see JILOTEPEQUE.

San Luis Mextepec, Mexico: see SAN LUIS, Mexico state.

San Luis Obispo (săn lōō'ĭs ōbĭ'spō, ŭbĭ'spō), county (□ 3,326; pop. 51,417), SW Calif., on the Pacific; ⊙ San Luis Obispo. Santa Lucia Range in NW, Temblor and La Panza ranges in E. Drained by Salinas R. and Santa Maria R. Cattle and wheat ranching; growing of hay, truck, fruit, nuts; dairying, poultry raising; flower and vegetable seed grown near coast. Oil and natural-gas field; Port San Luis ships oil. Clay, sand, gravel quarrying; chromite, quicksilver mining. Coast resorts (Pismo Beach, Morro Bay); mineral springs at Paso Robles. Old missions at San Miguel, San Luis Obispo. Formed 1850.

San Luis Obispo, city (pop. 14,180), ⊙ San Luis Obispo co., SW Calif., near the coast, c.80 mi. NW of Santa Barbara; 8 mi. S is San Luis Obispo Bay, with oil port and port of entry (Port San Luis) which ships petroleum (mainly in coastwise vessels), brought from oil fields by pipeline. City is railroad division point, and center for dairying and truck-farming region; mfg. of clay products, fertilizer. Site of San Luis Obispo de Tolosa Mission (founded 1772; still in use as church), Calif. State Polytechnic Col., and a jr. col. Inc. 1856.

San Luis Peak (14,149 ft.), SW Colo., in San Juan Mts., 9 mi. N of Creede.

San Luis Potosí (sän lwēs' pōtōsē'), state (□ 24,417; 1940 pop. 678,779; 1950 pop. 855,336), N central Mexico; ⊙ San Luis Potosí. Bounded by Nuevo León and Tamaulipas (NE), Zacatecas (W), Guanajuato and Queretaro (S), Veracruz (E). A mountainous region (average alt. c.6,000 ft.), it is traversed by Sierra Madre Oriental (NW-SE), and includes broken ranges and extensive plateaus which continue the large central plateau. Mostly desert in N; a small SE section, in fertile Gulf lowlands, is irrigated by Moctezuma and Santa María rivers (Pánuco system). Climate is cool in mts., temperate and arid on plateaus, humid and semi-tropical in lowlands. Primarily a mining state, known for its silver deposits since early colonial days. Main silver mines are in Catorce dist and Cerro de San Pedro; there also gold, lead, copper, zinc, antimony and arsenic are mined. Other mining centers: Matehuala, San Luis Potosí, Ramos, Guadalcázar, Cedral. Cinnebar at Santa María del Río, manganese at Santo Domingo, salt at Salinas (Peñón Blanco). Petroleum near Veracruz border. Some of the forested sierras are rich in fine cabinet and construction timber. Agr. crops in the uplands are wheat, corn, beans, cotton; maguey also in arid N sections. The fertile lowlands (E) produce some coffee, tobacco, sugar cane, rice, corn, alfalfa, chick-peas, chili, tomatoes, peppers, tropical fruit; and provide good pastures for cattle. Stock raising (hides, tallow, wool) on considerable scale on the plateaus.

San Luis Potosí, city (pop. 77,161), ⊙ San Luis Potosí, N central Mexico, on the interior plateau, on a small plain amid mts., 200 mi. W of Tampico, 225 mi. NW of Mexico city; 22°10′N 100°58′W; alt. 6,158 ft. Rail junction; commercial, metallurgical, and agr. center (cereals, cotton, tobacco, fruit, maguey); silver, lead, and gold mining. Foundries, smelters, arsenic refineries, railroad shops, cordage factories, flour and textile mills, tanneries, brewery. Exports minerals, opals, fiber products, hides. Airport. Old colonial town, with parks and fine bldgs., govt. palace, baroque cathedral and other interesting churches, theater. Founded in late 16th cent.

San Luis Reservoir, Calif.: see CENTRAL VALLEY.

San Luis Rey (săn lōō′ĭs rā′), village (pop. c.375), San Diego co., S Calif., near the coast, 4 mi. NE of Oceanside. Mission San Luis Rey or San Luis Rey de Francia (established 1798; restored) is here.

San Luis Rey River, SW Calif., formed by headstreams S of Mt. Palomar in N San Diego co., flows NW, then SW, to the Pacific at Oceanside; c.65 mi. long. Dam impounds L. Henshaw (Henshaw Reservoir), c.6 mi. long, in upper course. Lower valley is rich agr. area.

San Luis Río Colorado, Mexico: see SAN LUIS, Sonora.

San Luis Soyatlán (soiätlän′), town (pop. 1,829), Jalisco, central Mexico, on S shore of L. Chapala, 33 mi. S of Guadalajara; grain, beans, fruit, stock.

San Luis Valley (săn lōō′ĭs), in S Colo. and N N.Mex., irrigated area (125 mi. long, average width 50 mi.; alt. 7,500–8,000 ft.), extending S from Saguache co., through Alamosa and Conejos counties (Colo.), into Taos co. (N.Mex.). Bounded E by Sangre de Cristo Mts., N by Sawatch Mts., W by San Juan Mts.; watered by Saguache and San Luis creeks in N and by Rio Grande, which flows S through middle of valley. Once formed bottom of extensive lake; now used for agr. (potatoes, grain, vegetables). Farm resettlement project S of Alamosa. Chief valley towns: Monte Vista and Alamosa, Colo.

Sanluri (sänlōō′rē), village (pop. 5,284), Cagliari prov., S central Sardinia, near Flumini Mannu R., 26 mi. NNW of Cagliari, in grape- and almond-growing area. Agr. settlement of Stabilimento Vittorio Emmanuele (□ 6; completed 1919) is on drained land 3 mi. SW.

San Manuel (sän mänwĕl′), town (pop. 1,670), Oriente prov., E Cuba, 28 mi. NW of Holguín; sugar cane, livestock.

San Manuel, town (pop. 516), Cortés dept. NW Honduras, in Sula Valley, near Ulúa R., 4 mi. ESE of Villanueva, in banana zone.

San Manuel, town (1939 pop. 4,527; 1948 municipality pop. 15,376), Pangasinan prov., central Luzon, Philippines, 22 mi. E of Dagupan; agr. center (rice, copra, corn).

San Manuel Chaparrón, Guatemala: see CHAPARRÓN.

San Marcelino (sän märsälē′nō), town (1939 pop. 4,111; 1948 municipality pop. 10,316), Zambales prov., central Luzon, Philippines, 60 mi. WNW of Manila; rice-growing center.

San Marcello Pistoiese (sän märchĕl′lō pēstôyä′zē), village (pop. 1,239), Pistoia prov., Tuscany, central Italy, in Etruscan Apennines, 11 mi. NW of Pistoia. Summer resort (alt. 2,044 ft.); foundry, ribbon factory.

San Marco, Cape (sän mär′kô), point on W coast of Sardinia, at N end of Gulf of Oristano; 39°51′N 8°26′E. Fisheries (tunny, coral). Site of Phoenician town (Tharros) in N; ruined abbey, necropolis near by.

San Marco, Cape, point on SW coast of Sicily, W of Sciacca; 37°29′N 13°1′E; coral fisheries.

San Marco Argentano (sän mär′kô ärjĕntä′nô), town (pop. 2,427), Cosenza prov., Calabria, S Italy, 20 mi. NNW of Cosenza, in fruit-growing, livestock-raising, lumbering region. Bishopric.

San Marco dei Cavoti (dā kävô′tē), village (pop. 3,110), Benevento prov., Campania, S Italy, 14 mi. NNE of Benevento.

San Marco in Lamis (ēn lä′mēs), town (pop. 19,505), Foggia prov., Apulia, S Italy, on W slope of Gargano promontory, 13 mi. E of San Severo; agr. center (wheat, olive oil, almonds, sheep); toy mfg. Marble quarries near by.

San Marco la Catola (lä kä′tôlä), village (pop. 3,556), Foggia prov., Apulia, S Italy, 17 mi. W of Lucera.

San Marcos (sän mär′kōs), town (pop. 2,482), Bolívar dept., N Colombia, in savannas along San Jorge R., 50 mi. ESE of Montería; cattle-raising center. Airport.

San Marcos or **San Marcos de Tarrazú** (dā täräsōō′), town (pop. 202), San José prov., S central Costa Rica, on upper reaches of Parrita R. and 19 mi. SSE of San José; commercial center; coffee, sugar cane, livestock; sawmilling.

San Marcos, department (□ 1,464; 1950 pop. 230,987), SW Guatemala; ⊙ San Marcos. On Mex. border; in W highlands, sloping S to coastal plain, with short Pacific coast. Includes Tacaná and Tajumulco volcanoes. Drained by Suchiate R. (on SW border) and Naranjo R. (in S). Mainly agr.: coffee, rice, corn, bananas, sugar cane, in coastal plain; corn, beans, wheat, and livestock (mainly sheep) in highlands. Industries include textile milling (woolen and cotton) and salt-working. Main centers: San Marcos and San Pedro (on Inter-American Highway), Ayutla (rail terminus on Mex. border), and Ocós (Pacific port).

San Marcos. 1 City (1950 pop. 4,700), ⊙ San Marcos dept., SW Guatemala, in W highlands, on Inter-American Highway and 20 mi. WNW of Quezaltenango; 14°58′N 91°48′W; alt. 8,136 ft. Important market center in coffee zone; corn, wheat, vegetables. Has airport, radio station, and notable govt. building. With adjoining (E) San Pedro, sometimes called La Unión (lä ōōnyōn′). **2** or **San Marcos La Laguna** (lä lägōō′nä), town (1950 pop. 506), Sololá dept., SW central Guatemala, on NW shore of L. Atitlán, 5 mi. SW of Sololá; alt. 5,400 ft.; fruit, grain.

San Marcos. 1 or **San Marcos de Colón** (dā kōlōn′), city (pop. 2,289), Choluteca dept., S Honduras, on Inter-American Highway, on Coco R. and 28 mi. ENE of Choluteca, near Nicaragua border; commercial center in agr. area (coffee, sugar cane, henequen, livestock); beverages, bricks; tanning, dairying. Airfield. Dates from early 19th cent. **2** Town (pop. 1,207), Ocotepeque dept., W Honduras, on upper Jicatuyo R. and 18 mi. E of Nueva Ocotepeque; trade center; flour milling; wheat, corn, coffee. **3** Town (pop. 1,052), Santa Bárbara dept., W Honduras, on Chamelecón R. and 28 mi. SW of San Pedro Sula; livestock, corn, beans.

San Marcos. 1 Town (pop. 1,690), Guerrero, SW Mexico, in Pacific lowland, 35 mi. E of Acapulco; rice, sugar cane, coffee, fruit, cotton, livestock. **2** Town (pop. 2,085), Hidalgo, central Mexico, on Tula R., on railroad and 40 mi. WSW of Pachuca; agr. (cereals, sugar cane, cotton, fruit, livestock). **3** Town (pop. 1,572), Jalisco, W Mexico, 18 mi. NNW of Ameca; rail terminus; grain, sugar cane, beans, alfalfa, livestock. **4** or **San Marcos Tlazalpan** (tläsäl′pän), town (pop. 2,665), Mexico state, central Mexico, 40 mi. NW of Mexico city; cereals, maguey, fruit, livestock. **5** Town, Puebla, Mexico: see RAFAEL LARA GRAJALES.

San Marcos, town (1950 pop. 2,435), Carazo dept., SW Nicaragua, on railroad and 4 mi. NNW of Jinotepe, at road crossing; center of coffee zone; processing plants.

San Marcos. 1 Town (pop. 593), Ancash dept., W central Peru, at SE foot of Cordillera Blanca, 12 mi. S of Huari; alt. 9,728 ft. Thermal springs in agr. region (barley, corn, potatoes). **2** City (pop. 908), Cajamarca dept., NW Peru, in Cordillera Occidental, 27 mi. ESE of Cajamarca; barley, potatoes.

San Marcos or **San Marcos Lempa** (lĕm′pä), village (pop. estimate 300), Usulután dept., SE Salvador, port on Lempa R. (rail and road bridges) and 18 mi. WNW of Usulután; grain, livestock.

San Marcos (săn mär′kŭs), city (pop. 9,980), ⊙ Hays co., S central Texas, 30 mi. SSW of Austin and on San Marcos R., in agr., ranching area; resort, with springs near by (source of San Marcos R.). Mfg. of blankets, livestock remedies, clothing, building materials; grain, cottonseed-oil milling, cotton ginning. Cottonseed-breeding farm near; U.S. fish hatchery. Seat of Southwest Texas State Teacher's Col. and an Air Force base. Settled 1845, inc. 1877.

San Marcos de Colón, Honduras: see SAN MARCOS, Choluteca dept.

San Marcos de Tarrazú, Costa Rica: see SAN MARCOS.

San Marcos Island (□ 12; pop. 189), Lower California, NW Mexico, in Gulf of California, 10 mi. SE of Santa Rosalía; 6 mi. long, c.2 mi. wide. Gypsum deposits.

San Marcos La Laguna, Guatemala: see SAN MARCOS.

San Marcos Lempa, Salvador: see SAN MARCOS.

San Marcos River (săn mär′kŭs), S central Texas, rises near San Marcos city in huge San Marcos Springs, flows c.90 mi. generally SE, past Luling, to Guadalupe R. just W of Gonzales. Power plants; recreational areas. Receives Blanco R. in upper course.

San Marcos Sierra or **San Marcos Sierras** (sän mär′kōs syĕ′rä, syĕ′räs), town (pop. estimate 1,000), NW Córdoba prov., Argentina, 50 mi. NNW of Córdoba; grain, citrus fruit, wine, livestock; flour milling.

San Marcos Sud (sōōdh′), town (pop. 2,051), E Córdoba prov., Argentina, 50 mi. ESE of Villa María; wheat, flax, corn, oats, alfalfa; livestock.

San Marcos Tlazalpan, Mexico: see SAN MARCOS, Mexico state.

San Marino (săn mŭrē′nō, Ital. sän märē′nô), old independent republic (□ 23; pop. 13,948), in the Apennines, near Adriatic coast, SW of Rimini, E Italy; ⊙ San Marino. Agr. (corn, grapes, fruit), stock raising (cattle, pigs), and issuing of postage stamps for collectors are main sources of revenue. Governed by 2 regents and a general council. Traditionally founded in 4th cent. by St. Marinus, a Christian Dalmatian stonecutter fleeing religious persecution; has maintained its independence with only a few interruptions. San Marino (pop. 1,850), its capital, is built on precipitous Mt. Titano and connected with Rimini, 11 mi. away, by road and railroad. Has 14th-cent. church, cathedral (containing tomb of St. Marinus), and pinnacled walls. A bust of Lincoln, who in 1861 accepted honorary citizenship of San Marino, was unveiled here in 1937.

San Marino, residential city (pop. 11,230), Los Angeles co., S Calif., suburb just SE of Pasadena. Seat of Henry E. Huntington Library and Art Gall., which contains largest collection of incunabula in America, fine collections of rare legal documents, Americana and literary manuscripts; and art treasures which include Gainsborough's *Blue Boy* and Thomas Lawrence's *Pinkie*.

San Martín. 1 Department, Corrientes prov., Argentina: see LA CRUZ. **2** Department, La Rioja prov., Argentina: see ULAPES. **3** Department, San Juan prov., Argentina: see ANGACO SUD. **4** Department, Santa Fe prov., Argentina: see SASTRE. **5** Department, Santiago del Estero prov., Argentina: see TABOADA.

San Martín (sän märtēn). **1** or **General San Martín** (hānäräl′), city (pop. estimate 40,000), ⊙ San Martín (or General San Martín) dist. (□ 38; pop. 270,615), in NW Greater Buenos Aires, Argentina; major industrial center; linseed oil, lubricants, cotton goods, dairy products, frozen meat, liquor, rubber and cement articles, textile machinery, cigarettes, needles, toys, chocolate, candles, paper. Site of battle of Monte Caseros (1852), in which Gen. Urquiza defeated the dictator Rosas. **2** Town, Corrientes prov., Argentina: see YAPEYÚ. **3** or **General San Martín,** town (pop. estimate 3,000), ⊙ San Martín dept. (□ 555; 1947 census pop. 41,263), N Mendoza prov., Argentina, in Mendoza R. valley (irrigation area), 25 mi. SE of Mendoza; farming, lumbering, and mfg. center. Meat packing, fruit canning, wine making, sawmilling. Agr. products: wine, alfalfa, corn, fruit. Founded 1823. **4** Village (pop. estimate 700), ⊙ San Martín dept., (□ 995; 1947 census pop. 10,560), NE San Luis prov., Argentina, 70 mi. NNE of San Luis; mining (bismuth, tungsten, vanadium deposits) and farming center (alfalfa, corn, livestock).

San Martín, town (pop. 1,276), Meta intendancy, central Colombia, in llano lowlands, at E foot of Cordillera Oriental, 32 mi. S of Villavicencio. Gold placer mines; coffee, cattle. Airfield.

San Martín. 1 or **San Martín Sacatepéquez** (säkätāpā′kĕs), town (1950 pop. 1,267), Quezaltenango dept., SW Guatemala, 8 mi. WSW of Quezaltenango; alt. 7,798 ft.; coffee, sugar cane, grain. **2** or **San Martín Zapotitlán** (säpōtētlän′), town (1950 pop. 332), Retalhuleu dept., SW Guatemala, in Pacific piedmont, on Samalá R. and 7 mi. NE of Retalhuleu; coffee, sugar cane, grain.

San Martín. 1 Officially San Martín de las Pirámides, town (pop. 2,243), Mexico state, central Mexico, 27 mi. NE of Mexico city; cereals, maguey, livestock. **2** Officially San Martín Chalchicuautla, town (pop. 2,157), San Luis Potosí, E Mexico, in fertile Gulf plain, 55 mi. SW of Pánuco; agr. center (tobacco, sugar cane, coffee, rice, fruit, livestock).

San Martín, department (□ 17,452; enumerated pop. 100,913, plus estimated 20,000 Indians), N central Peru; ⊙ Moyobamba. Sloping eastward to Amazon basin, it is traversed by E Andean ridges. Watered by Huallaga R., an affluent of the Marañón. Has a generally humid, tropical climate. Predominantly agr. in the settled fertile valleys, it produces sugar cane, coca, rice, corn, cacao, coffee, tobacco, yucca, fruit. The virgin forests yield rubber, balata, vanilla, and fine timber. Among its little-exploited mineral deposits are gold, salt, gypsum, petroleum, lignite, lime. Main industries: mfg. of straw hats, distilling of alcohol and liquor, centered at Moyobamba and Tarapoto. Formerly a part of Loreto dept., San Martín dept. was set up 1906.

San Martín, city and province, Peru: see TARAPOTO.

Sanmartin (sûn-mûr′tēn), Rum. *Sânmartin*, Hung. *Csíkszentmárton* (chēk′sĕntmär′tôn), village (pop. 1,508), Stalin prov., E central Rumania, on W slopes of the Moldavian Carpathians, 9 mi. SE of Mercurea-Ciuc; lumbering, flour milling, stone quarrying. In Hungary, 1940–45.

San Martín, city (pop. 2,662), San Salvador dept., central Salvador, on railroad and 9 mi. ENE of San Salvador, N of L. Ilopango; mfg. (mats, baskets, rope); agr. (coffee, grain). Became city in 1946.

San Martín, Cape, on the Mediterranean, in Alicante prov., E Spain, 51 mi. NE of Alicante; 38°45'N 0°15'E.

San Martín, Lake, fresh-water lake (□ 390; alt. 935 ft.) in Patagonian Andes of Argentina and Chile, 20 mi. N of Cerro Fitz Roy; extends c.60 mi. NW–SE in many branches across Chile-Argentina frontier at about 49°S; bordered by Sierra de Sangre (N).

San Martín Atexcal, Mexico: see ATEXCAL.

San Martín de Bolaños (sän märtēn' dā bōlä'nyōs), town (pop. 883), Jalisco, W Mexico, on Bolaños R. and 70 mi. NW of Guadalajara; grain, stock.

San Martín de las Escobas (läs ĕskō'bäs), town (pop. estimate 1,000), S central Santa Fe prov., Argentina, 55 mi. WSW of Santa Fe; agr. center (wheat, alfalfa, flax, livestock); dairying. Adjoining, NE, is its railway station Avena.

San Martín de las Flores (flō'rĕs), town (pop. 2,414), Jalisco, central Mexico, 7 mi. SE of Guadalajara; grain, peanuts, sugar cane, stock.

San Martín de la Vega (lä vā'gä), town (pop. 2,232), Madrid prov., central Spain, on Jarama R. and 16 mi. SSE of Madrid; cereals, grapes, sugar beets, livestock. Chemical works. Mineral springs.

San Martín de Loba (dā lō'bä), town (pop. 1,634), Bolívar dept., N Colombia, on the Brazo de Loba (a left arm of the Magdalena) and 6 mi. SW of El Banco; corn, fruit, livestock.

San Martín de los Andes (lōs än'dĕs), town (1947 census pop. 2,359), ⊙ Lacar dept. (1947 pop. 5,822), SW Neuquén natl. territory, Argentina, on E bank of L. Lacar in Argentina lake dist., 115 mi. SW of Zapala. Resort; stock-raising center; flour milling. Hydroelectric plants near by.

San Martín de los Cansecos (känsä'kōs), town (pop. 473), Oaxaca, S Mexico, in Sierra Madre del Sur, on railroad and 28 mi. S of Oaxaca; alt. 4,980 ft.; silver and gold deposits.

San Martín del Río (dĕl rē'ō), village (pop. 1,012), Teruel prov., E Spain, 4 mi. SSE of Daroca; wine, fruit, sugar beets.

San Martín de Montalbán (dā mōntälvän'), town (pop. 1,694), Toledo prov., central Spain, 21 mi. SW of Toledo; cereals, olives, grapes, livestock. Flour milling; granite, kaolin, and clay quarrying. Has ruins of medieval castle.

San Martín de Provensals (prōvĕnsäls'), industrial N section of Barcelona, NE Spain.

San Martín de Pusa (pōō'sä), town (pop. 1,882), Toledo prov., central Spain, 17 mi. SE of Talavera de la Reina; cereals, olives, grapes, sheep; olive-oil pressing.

San Martín de Trevejo (trāvā'hō), town (pop. 1,638), Cáceres prov., W Spain, 30 mi. SW of Ciudad Rodrigo; olive-oil center.

San Martín de Unx (ōōnsh'), town (pop. 1,480), Navarre prov., N Spain, 7 mi. E of Tafalla; olive-oil processing, sawmilling; wine.

San Martín de Valdeiglesias (väl"dhāēglā'syās), town (pop. 4,278), Madrid prov., central Spain, in New Castile, near Alberche R., 38 mi. W of Madrid, in fertile region (grapes, olives, vegetables, fruit, livestock). Known for its table wines. Alcohol and liquor distilling, olive-oil pressing, soap mfg. Originated from Cistercian abbey; the monks left many hermitages in vicinity.

San Martín Hidalgo (ē-dhäl'gō), town (pop. 3,662), Jalisco, W Mexico, 12 mi. SE of Ameca; rail terminus; agr. center (sugar cane, corn, beans, chick-peas, alfalfa, stock).

San Martín Jilotepeque (hēlōtāpā'kā), town (1950 pop. 2,132), Chimaltenango dept., S central Guatemala, 12 mi. N of Chimaltenango; alt. 5,900 ft.; market center (grain, beans, sugar cane, cattle); cotton weaving, jug making. Thermal springs (iron sulphate).

San Martino, Yugoslavia: see BRAC ISLAND.

San Martino Buon Albergo (sän märtē'nō bwôn älbĕr'gô), village (pop. 1,528), Verona prov., Veneto, N Italy, 5 mi. E of Verona, in hay-growing region; foundry; wine, olive oil.

San Martino di Lupari (dē lōō'pärē), town (pop. 3,134), Padova prov., Veneto, N Italy, 16 mi. N of Padua, in cereal-growing, cattle-raising region; insecticide mfg.

San Martino in Rio (ēn rē'ô), village (pop. 1,786), Reggio nell'Emilia prov., Emilia-Romagna, N central Italy, 8 mi. ENE of Reggio nell'Emilia; wine making.

San Martino Valle Caudina (väl'lĕ koudē'nä), village (pop. 3,353), Avellino prov., Campania, S Italy, 10 mi. NW of Avellino.

San Martín River (sän märtēn'), Santa Cruz and Beni depts., NE Bolivia; rises near Santa Rosa de la Roca; flows c.250 mi. N, NNW, and W, through the Curiche Liverpool, to Río Blanco. Navigable in lower course for c.100 mi. Upper course also called Paraíso R.; lower course, below the Curiche Liverpool, is also called Baures R.

San Martín Sacatepéquez, Guatemala: see SAN MARTÍN.

San Martín Texmelucan, Mexico: see TEXMELUCAN.

San Martín Tuxtla Volcano, Mexico: see TUXTLA VOLCANO.

San Martín Xaltocan, Mexico: see XALTOCAN.

San Martín Zapotitlán, Guatemala: see SAN MARTÍN.

San Marzano di San Giuseppe (sän märtsä'nô dē sän jūsĕp'pĕ), town (pop. 4,369), Ionio prov., Apulia, S Italy, 14 mi. E of Taranto; agr. center; wine, olive oil; figs, cereals.

San Marzano sul Sarno (sōōl sär'nô), town (pop. 4,507), Salerno prov., Campania, S Italy, 3 mi. NW of Nocera Inferiore, in agr. region (cereals, fruit, vegetables).

San Mateo (sän mätā'ō), village (pop. 898), Iviza, Balearic Isls., 7 mi. N of Iviza city; cereals, fruit.

San Mateo (sän mutā'ō), village, SW B.C., on SW Vancouver Isl., on Barkley Sound, near mouth of Alberni Canal, 23 mi. SSW of Port Alberni; fishing port; fish packing.

San Mateo, Canary Isls.: see VEGA DE SAN MATEO.

San Mateo (sän mätā'ō), town (pop. 495), Alajuela prov., W central Costa Rica, on Tárcoles plain, on road from Orotina, and 21 mi. WSW of Alajuela; important agr. and mining center. Rice, corn, beans, tobacco, fruit; lumbering. Gold mining in Aguacate hills (N).

San Mateo, town (1950 pop. 848), Quezaltenango dept., SW Guatemala, on Inter-American Highway and 5 mi. WNW of Quezaltenango; alt. 8,400 ft. corn, wheat, fodder grasses, livestock.

San Mateo or **San Mateo Atzacatipan** (ätsäkätē'-pän), town (pop. 4,348), Mexico state, central Mexico, 2 mi. NW of Toluca; agr. center (cereals, stock); dairying.

San Mateo, town (pop. 1,243), Lima dept., W central Peru, on upper Rímac R. (here sometimes called San Mateo R.) and 55 mi. ENE of Lima (connected by railroad); grain, potatoes, livestock; medicinal springs.

San Mateo, town (1948 municipality pop. 6,811), Quezon prov., S central Luzon, Philippines, 10 mi. NE of Manila.

San Mateo, town (pop. 2,927), Castellón de la Plana prov., E Spain, 13 mi. W of Vinaroz; olive-oil processing; mfg. of colored tiles, soap, chocolate. Wine and cereals in area.

San Mateo (săn mutā'ō), county (□ 454; pop. 235,659), W Calif.; ⊙ Redwood City. On San Francisco-San Mateo peninsula; includes many suburbs of San Francisco (industrial South San Francisco; residential San Mateo, Burlingame, Hillsborough, San Bruno, Atherton, Menlo Park). Redwood City (residential, industrial) is a port. Santa Cruz Mts. divide low-lying suburban area along San Francisco Bay in E from rugged Pacific coast, indented by bays (notably Half Moon Bay). Coastal valleys of W produce a large part of U.S. artichoke crop. In E, flower growing, truck, hog, and dairy farms, and nurseries are important. Cement mfg. (from oyster shell); salt evaporating; extraction of magnesium from sea water; quarrying of stone, sand, gravel. Redwood timber in mts. Formed 1856 from San Francisco co.

San Mateo. 1 Residential city (1940 pop. 19,403; 1950 pop. 41,782), San Mateo co., W Calif., 15 mi. S of downtown San Francisco; flower and truck growing. Has a jr. col. San Francisco Bay is here crossed to Hayward (E) by San Mateo Toll Bridge (7 mi. long over water; completed 1929). Bay Meadows race track is near by. Laid out 1863, inc. 1894. **2** Village, Valencia co., W N.Mex., 60 mi. WNW of Albuquerque, just N of San Mateo Mts.; alt. c.7,300 ft. Trading point in sheep region. Ruins of Pueblo Alto, part of Cibola Natl. Forest near by.

San Mateo (sän mätā'ō). **1** Town (pop. 950), Anzoátegui state, NE Venezuela, on El Tigre–Barcelona highway and 29 mi. SSE of Barcelona, on oil pipe line; cotton, cacao, sugar, cattle. **2** Town (pop. 2,203), Aragua state, N Venezuela, on small Aragua R., on railroad and highway, and 13 mi. ESE of Maracay; coffee, cacao, corn, sugar cane, fruit. Has history mus. and the shrine of the Virgin of Belén.

San Mateo, Cape (sän mätā'ō), on Pacific coast of Manabí prov., W Ecuador, 7 mi. W of Manta; 0°57'S 80°49'W.

San Mateo Atenco, Mexico: see ATENCO **1**.

San Mateo Atzacatipan, Mexico: see SAN MATEO.

San Mateo de Gállego (dā gä'lyāgō), village (pop. 1,620), Saragossa prov., NE Spain, on Gállego R. and 14 mi. NNE of Saragossa; sugar beets, cereals, potatoes, fruit, livestock.

San Mateo Ixtatán (ēkstätän'), town (1950 pop. 1,954), Huehuetenango dept., W Guatemala, in N Cuchumatanes Mts., 35 mi. N of Huehuetenango; alt. 8,540 ft. Produces salt, wool; wheat.

San Mateo Mountains (săn mutā'ō). **1** In W central N.Mex., in Socorro co., W of the Rio Grande. Chief peaks: San Mateo Peak and Vicks Peak, both over 11,000 ft. **2** In NW N.Mex., in Valencia co., just N of San Jose R. Highest at Mt. Taylor (11,389 ft.). NE extension of range is Sierra Chivato (sēē'rù chēvä'tō), sometimes known as Cebolleta Mts. (sābōyĕ'tù), which rise to c.9,300 ft. Ranges lie within part of Cibola Natl. Forest.

San Mateo Peak (over 11,000 ft.), in San Mateo Mts., SW central N.Mex., c.45 mi. SW of Socorro.

San Mateo Point, promontory, San Diego co., S Calif., 18 mi. NNW of Oceanside.

San Mateo Texcalyacac, Mexico: see TEXCALYACAC.

San Matías (sän mätē'äs), village (pop. c.2,400), Santa Cruz dept., E Bolivia, 190 mi. NE of San José, near Brazil border; customs station; cattle.

San Matías Gulf, Argentina, inlet of S Atlantic Ocean, in Patagonia, indenting Río Negro natl. territory and bordered by Chubut; c.80 mi. wide (W–E), c.65 mi. long (N–S). Port of San Antonio Oeste is on N coast.

San Mauro Castelverde (sän mou'rô kästĕlvĕr'dĕ), village (pop. 4,088), Palermo prov., N Sicily, in Madonie Mts., 14 mi. SE of Cefalù.

San Mauro Forte (fôr'tĕ), village (pop. 3,074), Matera prov., Basilicata, S Italy, 11 mi. SE of Tricarico; wine, olive oil, cheese.

Sanmen (sän'mŭn'), town (pop. 4,193), ⊙ Sanmen co. (pop. 154,670), E Chekiang prov., China, 55 mi. S of Ningpo, on S shore of Sanmen Bay; fisheries, saltworks. Called Kienkangtang until 1940, when co. seat was moved here from Nantien, on isl. 25 mi. E.

Sanmen Bay, inlet of E.China Sea, in Chekiang prov., China, 40 mi. S of Ningpo; entered through N deepwater channel leading past Shihpu.

San Michele (sän mēkā'lĕ), island in Venice lagoon, bet. isls. of Venice and Murano, N Italy. Cemetery of Venice since 1813. Formerly site of convent; has Renaissance church (1469–78) and chapel (1527–43).

San Michele all'Adige (sän mēkā'lĕ äl-lä'dējĕ), village (pop. 719), Trento prov., Trentino-Alto Adige, N Italy, on Adige R. and 8 mi. N of Trento; wine making.

San Michele del Quarto (dĕl kwär'tô), village (pop. 284), Venezia prov., Veneto, N Italy, on Sile R. and 10 mi. N of Venice; agr. machinery.

San Michele di Ganzaria (dē gänzärē'ä), village (pop. 4,294), Catania prov., S Sicily, 6 mi. WNW of Caltagirone.

San Michele Salentino (sälĕntē'nô), village (pop. 3,022), Brindisi prov., Apulia, S Italy, 16 mi. W of Brindisi; wine, olive oil.

San Miguel (sän mēgĕl'). **1** City (pop. 15,812), ⊙ General Sarmiento dist. (□ 80; pop. 47,469), NE Buenos Aires prov., Argentina, 18 mi. WNW of Buenos Aires; cattle raising and dairying. Observatory. **2** Village (pop. estimate 500), ⊙ San Miguel dept. (□ c.1,200; pop. 7,661), N Corrientes prov., Argentina, 85 mi. SE of Corrientes; agr. center (corn, cotton, sugar cane, livestock).

San Miguel, village (pop. 1,735), Iviza, Balearic Isls., 11 mi. N of Iviza city; cereals, fruit, livestock; flour milling.

San Miguel, town (pop. c.3,600), Santa Cruz dept., E Bolivia, 22 mi. S of San Ignacio, on road; cattle. Founded 1745 as Jesuit mission.

San Miguel, town (pop. 1,191), Tenerife, Canary Isls., 35 mi. SW of Santa Cruz de Tenerife; tomatoes, cereals, potatoes, fruit, grapes. Cheese processing, embroidery mfg.

San Miguel, village, Colombia: see PUERTO OSPINA.

San Miguel or **San Miguel de Sarapiquí** (dā säräpēkē'), village, Heredia prov., N Costa Rica, 20 mi. NNW of Heredia and on Sarapiquí R.; bananas, fodder crops, livestock.

San Miguel. 1 Town (1950 pop. 1,707), Bolívar prov., central Ecuador, in Chimbo valley of the Andes, 8 mi. SSW of Guaranda; alt. 8,100 ft. Agr. center (cereals, potatoes, sugar cane, fruit, tobacco, coffee). **2** or **Salcedo,** or **San Miguel de Salcedo** (dā sälsä'dō), town (1950 pop. 2,594), Cotopaxi prov., N Ecuador, on Pan American Highway, on Quito-Guayaquil RR and 9 mi. S of Latacunga; trading center in agr. region (cereals, cattle). Severely damaged in 1949 earthquake.

San Miguel. 1 or **San Miguel el Alto** (ĕl äl'tō), town (pop. 5,442), Jalisco, central Mexico, 17 mi. SSW of San Juan de los Lagos; alt. 6,093; agr. center (corn, wheat, beans, fruit, livestock). **2** or **San Miguel Totomaloya** (tōtōmäloi'ä), town (pop. 1,696), Mexico state, central Mexico, 7 mi. SSE of Sultepec; sugar cane, fruit, coffee. **3** Town, Sinaloa, Mexico: see SAN MIGUEL ZAPOTITLÁN.

San Miguel, village (pop. 1,249) on N shore of San Miguel Isl., Panama, in Gulf of Panama of the Pacific, 50 mi. SE of Panama city. Important pearl-fishing center; tourist resort.

San Miguel, town (dist. pop. 6,202), Misiones dept., S Paraguay, 12 mi. NE of San Juan Bautista; cattle-raising center. Near by are iron (magnetite), copper pyrites, talc and ocher deposits.

San Miguel. 1 City (pop. 775), ⊙ La Mar prov. (□ 2,560; enumerated pop. 42,376, plus estimated 10,000 Indians), Ayacucho dept., S central Peru, on San Miguel R. (a left affluent of the Pampas), on road, and 22 mi. NE of Ayacucho; alt. 10,170 ft. Grain, coca, coffee, potatoes. **2** or **San Miguel de Pallaques** (dā päyä'kĕs), city (pop. 1,925), Cajamarca dept., NW Peru, in Cordillera Occidental, 25 mi. WNW of Cajamarca; sugar cane, coffee. **3** SW residential section (pop. 3,961) of Lima, Lima dept., W central Peru, beach resort on the Pacific just W of Magdalena Vieja. Inc. 1940 into Lima proper. **4** Town (pop. 831), San Martín dept., N central Peru, on Mayo R. and 4 mi. W of Lamas; sugar cane, tobacco, coca, rice.

San Miguel. 1 Town (1939 pop. 1,637; 1948 municipality pop. 38,093), Bulacan prov., S central Luzon, Philippines, 38 mi. N of Manila, and on Manila-Cabanatuan RR; agr. center (rice, sugar cane, corn). Iron is mined near by. **2** Town (1939 pop. 2,662) in Concepcion municipality, Tarlac prov., central Luzon, Philippines, just N of Concepcion; sugar milling.

San Miguel, dept. (□ 1,344; 1950 pop. 170,157), E Salvador, on the Pacific; ⊙ San Miguel. Bounded N by Honduras, NW by Lempa R.; largely mountainous (volcanoes San Miguel and Chinameca); includes Jucuarán coastal range barring access to its rocky coast. Drained by Río Grande de San Miguel, which receives waters of L. Olomega. Major grain-growing region; also henequen, cotton, sugar cane, coffee. Stock raising and dairying (butter, cheese) are important. Main centers, San Miguel and Chinameca, are served by railroad and Inter-American Highway. Formed 1875.

San Miguel, city (1950 pop. 26,831), ⊙ San Miguel dept., E Salvador, on railroad and Inter-American Highway, at foot of volcano San Miguel, on Río Grande de San Miguel, 70 mi. ESE of San Salvador; alt. 348 ft.; 13°29'N 88°11'W. Largest city of E Salvador; commercial and industrial (cotton, henequen) center; cotton and cottonseed milling, vegetable-oil pressing, mfg. of rope, pottery, mats, musical instruments, jewelry, leather goods, drugs. Agr. (grain, henequen, coffee, cotton, sugar cane). Has cathedral, many old churches and monasteries, parks, and old Sp. residences. Founded 1530. Formerly an important indigo-trading center.

San Miguel, active volcano (7,064 ft.) in San Miguel dept., E Salvador, 7 mi. SW of San Miguel. Its large fuming crater tops a perfect cone.

San Miguel (săn mēgĕl'). **1** County (□ 1,283; pop. 2,693), SW Colo.; ⊙ Telluride. Mining and livestock-grazing region, drained by Dolores and San Miguel rivers. Gold, silver, lead. Includes part of San Miguel Mts. in SE, and of Montezuma and Uncompahgre natl. forests. Formed 1883. **2** County (□ 4,749; pop. 26,512), NE N.Mex.; ⊙ Las Vegas. Agr. area watered E by Canadian R., W by Pecos R. Grain, livestock; gold. Part of Santa Fe Natl. Forest and Sangre de Cristo Mts. in W; Conchas Reservoir in E. Formed 1862.

San Miguel, village (pop. c.500), San Luis Obispo co., SW Calif., 9 mi. N of Paso Robles. Well-preserved Mission San Miguel Arcángel (founded 1797) is in use as church.

San Miguel (sän mēgĕl'), fort in Rocha dept., SE Uruguay, near Brazil border, just E of Diez y Ocho de Julio, 10 mi. WNW of Chuy. Built 1735 by the Portuguese, it was taken 1763 by the Spanish; partly destroyed.

San Miguel, town (pop. 688), Lara state, NW Venezuela, 22 mi. SW of Barquisimeto; coffee, cacao, cattle.

San Miguel Acatán (äkätän'), town (1950 pop. 1,180), Huehuetenango dept., W Guatemala, on W slope of Cuchumatanes Mts., 29 mi. NNW of Huehuetenango; alt. 6,020 ft.; flour, hats, rope. Lead mining near by.

San Miguel Arcángel (ärkän'hĕl), town (pop. 1,812), Mexico state, central Mexico, 30 mi. SW of Mexico city; cereals, livestock.

San Miguel Bay (sän mēgĕl'), inlet of Philippine Sea, SE Luzon, Philippines, bet. Camarines Norte prov. (NW) and Camarines Sur prov. (S and E); 25 mi. long, 10–18 mi. wide. At entrance are many isls., including Butauanan and Canimo isls.

San Miguel Canoa, Mexico: see CANOA.

San Miguel Chicaj (chēkäkh'), town (1950 pop. 666), Baja Verapaz dept., central Guatemala, in N highlands, 4 mi. W of Salamá; alt. 3,600 ft. Market center; sugar cane, grain, livestock. Pop. largely Indian.

San Miguel Cozumel, Mexico: see COZUMEL.

San Miguel de Allende (dā äyĕn'dā) or **Allende,** city (pop. 9,030), Guanajuato, central Mexico, on central plateau, on railroad and 33 mi. ESE of Guanajuato; alt. 6,397 ft. Agr. center (beans, cereals, sugar cane, fruit, livestock); flour and textile (cotton) milling, tanning. Founded 1542. Birthplace of revolutionary hero Ignacio Allende.

San Miguel de Bulí, Chile: see BULÍ.

San Miguel de Cauri, Peru: see CAURI.

San Miguel de Horcasitas, Mexico: see HORCASITAS.

San Miguel de Huachi, Bolivia: see HUACHI.

San Miguel de la Palma, Canary Isls.: see PALMA, island.

San Miguel de la Ribera (dā lä rēvā'rä), town (pop. 1,027), Zamora prov., NW Spain, 15 mi. SSE of Zamora; cereals, wine.

San Miguel del Arroyo (dĕl äroi'ō), town (pop. 1,286), Valladolid prov., N central Spain, 15 mi. SE of Valladolid; cereals, chicory, wine.

San Miguel del Monte, Argentina: see MONTE.

San Miguel de los Baños (dā lōs bä'nyōs) or **San Miguel,** spa (pop. 173), Matanzas prov., W Cuba, 20 mi. SE of Matanzas. Resort in hilly country, with sulphurous springs.

San Miguel del Padrón (dĕl pädrōn'), town (pop. 3,513), Havana prov., W Cuba, 5 mi. SE of Havana; dairying, sugar growing.

San Miguel del Valle (dĕl vä'lyä), village (pop. 1,115), Zamora prov., NW Spain, 10 mi. ENE of Benavente; cereals, wine, livestock.

San Miguel de Mezquital, Mexico: see MIGUEL AZUZA.

San Miguel de Pallaques, Peru: see SAN MIGUEL, Cajamarca dept.

San Miguel de Piura, Peru: see PIURA, city.

San Miguel de Salcedo, Ecuador: see SAN MIGUEL, Cotopaxi prov.

San Miguel de Salinas (dā sälē'näs), village (pop. 1,462), Alicante prov., E Spain, 12 mi. SE of Orihuela; olive-oil processing. Saltworks and gypsum quarries near by.

San Miguel de Sarapiquí, Costa Rica: see SAN MIGUEL.

San Miguel de Serrezuela (sĕrā-thwā'lä), town (pop. 953), Ávila prov., central Spain, 28 mi. SE of Salamanca; cereals, forage, livestock. Medicinal springs.

San Miguel de Tucumán, Argentina: see TUCUMÁN, city.

San Miguel de Valero (välā'rō), town (pop. 1,077), Salamanca prov., W Spain, 13 mi. NW of Béjar; wine, chestnuts.

San Miguel Dueñas, Guatemala: see DUEÑAS.

San Miguel el Alto, Mexico: see SAN MIGUEL, Jalisco.

San Miguel Gulf (sän mēgĕl'), E section of Gulf of Panama of the Pacific, E Panama, at mouth of TUIRA RIVER; 10 mi. long, 10 mi. wide.

San Miguel Island or **El Rey Island** (ĕl rā'), Sp. *Isla del Rey*, largest of the Pearl Islands, in Gulf of Panama, Panama prov., E Panama, 50 mi. SE of Panama city; 17 mi. long, 8 mi. wide. Pearl fisheries; coconuts, pineapples. Main center is San Miguel on N coast.

San Miguel Island (□ 8; 1939 pop. 2,452), Albay prov., Philippines, in Lagonoy Gulf, just off SE coast of Luzon, adjacent to Cagraray Isl. (SE), 5 mi. E of Tabaco; 6 mi. long, 2 mi. wide; rises to 298 ft. Fishing. Isl. is included in Tabaco municipality.

San Miguel Island, Calif.: see SANTA BARBARA ISLANDS.

San Miguelito (mēgālē'tō), village, Pando dept., NW Bolivia, on Manuripi R. and 65 mi. SW of Puerto Rico; rubber.

San Miguelito, town (1950 pop. 604), Río San Juan dept., S Nicaragua, port on SE shore of L. Nicaragua, 65 mi. SE of Juigalpa; livestock; lumbering.

San Miguel Ixtahuacán (sän mēgĕl' ēkstäwäkän'), town (1950 pop. 234), San Marcos dept., SW Guatemala, in the Sierra Madre, 20 mi. N of San Marcos; alt. 6,700 ft.; corn, wheat, livestock.

San Miguel Mountain, N.Mex.: see NACIMIENTO MOUNTAINS.

San Miguel Mountains (săn mēgĕl'), SW Colo., W spur of San Juan Mts. Highest points: Dolores Peak (13,502 ft.), Mt. WILSON (14,250 ft.).

San Miguel Octopan (sän mēgĕl' ōktō'pän), town (pop. 1,796), Guanajuato, Mexico, on Laja R. 5 mi. NE of Celaya; cereals, sugar cane, vegetables, potatoes, fruit.

San Miguel Petapa (pātä'pä), town (1950 pop. 1,376), Guatemala dept., S central Guatemala, 10 mi. SSW of Guatemala, near N shore of L. Amatitlán; alt. 3,806 ft.; coffee, sugar cane, fodder grasses; livestock.

San Miguel River (sän mēgĕl'), Santa Cruz and Beni depts., NE Bolivia; rises in L. CONCEPCIÓN, flows 340 mi. NNW, past Santa Rosa del Palmar and San Pablo, to L. ITONAMAS. Middle course forms part of Santa Cruz-Beni border.

San Miguel River or **Sucumbíos River** (sōōkōōmbē'ōs), in Colombia and Ecuador, rises at SE foot of Cerro Pax, flows c.120 mi. ESE, mostly along international line, to Putumayo R. at Puerto Ospina.

San Miguel River, in Sonora, NW Mexico, rises SW of Cananea in outliers of Sierra Madre Occidental, flows c.130 mi. S, past Rayón, to Sonora R. 7 mi. NE of Hermosillo. Gold and silver deposits along course.

San Miguel River (săn mēgĕl'), SW Colo., rises in San Juan Mts. S of Telluride, flows c.90 mi. NW, past Vanadium and Placerville, to Dolores R. near Utah line.

San Miguel Tlaxcaltepec (sän mēgĕl' tläskältäpĕk'), town (pop. 1,509), Querétaro, Mexico, 38 mi. SSE of Querétaro; grain, alfalfa, beans, livestock.

San Miguel Totolapan (tōtōlä'pän), town (pop. 2,224), Guerrero, SW Mexico, on the Río de las Balsas and 23 mi. SE of Altamirano; cereals, sugar cane, fruit; silver, gold, lead, and copper mining.

San Miguel Totomaloya, Mexico: see SAN MIGUEL, Mexico state.

San Miguel Tucurú, Guatemala: see TUCURÚ.

San Miguel Uspantán, Guatemala: see USPANTÁN.

San Miguel Zapotitlán (säpōtētlän') or **San Miguel,** town (pop. 1,367), Sinaloa, NW Mexico, in Gulf of California lowland, on Río del Fuerte and 13 mi. N of Los Mochis; sugar cane, tomatoes, chick-peas, fruit.

San Millán de la Cogolla (sän mēlyän' dā lä kōgō'lyä), town (pop. 527), Logroño prov., N Spain, 24 mi. WSW of Logroño. Noted for its 2 medieval Benedictine monasteries, Yuso (11th cent., rebuilt 16th-17th; Gothic cloisters), and Suso (10th cent.).

San Miniatello (sän mēnyätĕl'lô), village (pop.837), Firenze prov., Tuscany, central Italy, on Arno R. and 12 mi. W of Florence; pottery making.

San Miniato (sän mēnyä'tô), town (pop. 3,082), Pisa prov., Tuscany, central Italy, 21 mi. WSW of Florence. Tannery center; mfg. (canned foods, glass, hosiery, ribbon). Bishopric. Has 12th-cent. cathedral and 16th-cent. palace, both damaged in Second World War, and church of San Domenico (1330) with a work by G. della Robbia. A residence of Frederick II.

San Muñoz (sän mōōnyōth'), town (pop. 1,029), Salamanca prov., W Spain, 28 mi. WSW of Salamanca; wool trade; cereals, vegetables, sheep.

San Narciso (sän närsē'sō). **1** Town (1939 pop. 1,068; 1948 municipality pop. 7,006), Quezon prov., S Luzon, Philippines, on E Bondoc peninsula, on Ragay Gulf, 70 mi. ESE of Lucena; fishing, agr. (coconuts, rice). **2** Town (1939 pop. 6,338; 1948 municipality pop. 14,085), Zambales prov., central Luzon, Philippines, 65 mi. WNW of Manila, near S.China Sea; trade center for rice-growing area.

Sanna River, Austria: see ROSANNA RIVER; TRISANNA RIVER.

Sannazzaro de' Burgondi (sän-nätsä'rô dĕ bōōrgôn'dē), town (pop. 3,199), Pavia prov., Lombardy, N Italy, near Po R., 14 mi. WSW of Pavia; agr. center; silk mill.

Sannessjoen, Norway: see SANDNESSJOEN.

Sanni (sŭn'nē), village, Kalat state, central Baluchistan, W Pakistan, at E foot of Central Brahui Range, 32 mi. SW of Sibi, on Kachhi plain. Sulphur-ore and gypsum deposits in near-by hills.

Sannicandro di Bari (sän-nēkän'drô dē bä'rē), town (pop. 8,261), Bari prov., Apulia, S Italy, 9 mi. SSW of Bari; olive oil, wine, soap.

Sannicandro Garganico (gärgä'nēkô) or **San Nicandro Garganico,** town (pop. 14,314), Foggia prov., Apulia, S Italy, on Gargano promontory, 15 mi. NNE of San Severo. Agr. trade center (sheep, cereals, olives, grapes, almonds).

Sannicola (sän-nēkô'lä), village (pop. 4,114), Lecce prov., Apulia, S Italy, 6 mi. ENE of Gallipoli.

San-Nicolao (sän-nēkôlou'), village (pop. 510), E Corsica, 22 mi. S of Bastia, near Tyrrhenian Sea; lime growing.

San Nicolás (sän nēkōläs'), city (pop. 24,829), ⊙ San Nicolás dist. (□ 252; pop. 42,427), N Buenos Aires prov., Argentina, port on Paraná R. and 37 mi. SE of Rosario; rail junction in agr. area (cattle, sheep, fruit); mfg. of ceramics (cement products, tiles), textiles, chemicals. Ships frozen meat, wool, hides. Has historical mus. and library. Founded 1748. Sometimes San Nicolás de los Arroyos.

San Nicolás, village (pop. 1,429), Grand Canary, Canary Isls., 24 mi. WSW of Las Palmas; cereals, tomatoes, cochineal, bananas, honey, livestock; charcoal.

San Nicolás, village (1930 pop. 226), Ñuble prov., S central Chile, 13 mi. NW of Chillán, in lumbering and agr. area (grain, wine, fruit, livestock).

San Nicolás, town (pop. 4,907), Havana prov., W Cuba, on railroad and 38 mi. SE of Havana; agr. center (sugar, rice, tomatoes). Sugar milling at adjoining (SE) central Gómez Mena. Fishing, hunting at near-by lagoons.

San Nicolás. 1 Town (pop. 1,840), Copán dept., W Honduras, 15 mi. NNE of Santa Rosa, in tobacco area; cigar mfg., pottery making; sugar cane. **2** Town (pop. 1,992), Santa Bárbara dept., W Honduras, 5 mi. W of Santa Bárbara, across Ulúa R.; palm-hat mfg.; sugar cane, tobacco, corn, hogs.

San Nicolás. 1 Officially San Nicolás de Agustinos, village (pop. 2,440), Guanajuato, central Mexico, near Lerma R. (irrigation area), 23 mi. SW of Celaya; rice, corn, sugar cane, alfalfa, vegetables, fruit. Cooperative settlement. **2** Town, Nuevo León, Mexico: see HIDALGO. **3** Town (pop. 298), Tamaulipas, NE Mexico, in E outliers of Sierra Madre Oriental, 50 mi. ESE of Linares; gold, silver, lead, copper mining.

San Nicolás. 1 City, Amazonas dept., Peru: see MENDOZA. **2** Village (pop. 9), Ica dept., SW Peru, on San Nicolás Bay (2 mi. long, 12 mi. wide) of the Pacific, 45 mi. SW of Nazca; fisheries. **3** Village (pop. 1,968), Lima dept., W central Peru, on coastal plain, on railroad and 5 mi. SE of Barranca; cotton-growing center.

San Nicolas. 1 Town (1939 pop. 9,438; 1948 municipality pop. 15,567), Ilocos Norte prov., NW Luzon, Philippines, just S of Laoag; rice-growing center. **2** Town (1939 pop. 3,469; 1948 municipality pop. 18,218), Pangasinan prov., central Luzon, Philippines, 25 mi. SSE of Baguio; agr. center (rice, copra, corn).

San Nicolás de Agustinos, Mexico: see SAN NICOLÁS, Guanajuato.

San Nicolás de Buenos Aires (dā bwā'nōs ī'rĕs), town (pop. 2,100), Puebla, central Mexico, 45 mi. ENE of Puebla; cereals, maguey. Malpaís or San Nicolás Malpaís until 1941.

San Nicolás de Carretas, Mexico: see GRAN MORELOS.

San Nicolás de Ibarra (ēbä'rä), town (pop. 1,041), Jalisco, central Mexico, on N shore of L. Chapala, 28 mi. SE of Guadalajara; grain, vegetables, stock.

San Nicolás de los Arroyos, Argentina: see SAN NICOLÁS.

San Nicolás de los Garzas (lōs gär'säs), town (pop. 3,038), Nuevo León, N Mexico, 6 mi. N of Monterrey; chick-peas, barley, corn, stock.

San Nicolás de los Ranchos (rän'chōs), town (pop. 2,449), Puebla, central Mexico, 18 mi. E of Puebla; corn, wheat, maguey.

San Nicolás del Puerto (dĕl pwĕr'tō), town (pop. 1,159), Seville prov., SW Spain, in Sierra Morena, on railroad to Seville and 7 mi. NE of Cazalla de la Sierra, in agr. region (cereals, cork, acorns, fruit, livestock). Lead and coal mines. At El Cerro del Hierro, 3 mi. SE, are iron mines; linked by rail.

San Nicolas Island, Calif.: see SANTA BARBARA ISLANDS.

San Nicolás Malpaís, Mexico: see SAN NICOLÁS DE BUENOS AIRES.

San Nicolás Tolentino (tōlĕntē'nō), town (pop. 415), San Luis Potosí, N central Mexico, 27 mi. ENE of San Luis Potosí; grain, beans, stock.

San Nicolás Totolapan (tōtōlä'pän), town (pop. 2,048), Federal Dist., central Mexico, 12 mi. SSW of Mexico city; cereals, fruit, livestock.

Sannicolaul-Mare (sûn-nēkôloul'-mä'rĕ), Rum. *Sânnicolaul-Mare*, town (1948 pop. 9,789), Timisoara prov., W Rumania, in Banat, on railroad and 36 mi. NW of Timisoara; trading center (grain, livestock); tanning, mfg. of bricks and tiles. Has agr. school, castle-mus. Large Ger. pop.

San Nicolò, Sicily: see CATANIA, city.

Sannidal (sän'nĕdäl), village and canton (pop. 2,542), Telemark co., SE Norway, on Toke R. and 4 mi. NW of Kragero. Near by are lumber mills and hydroelectric plant. Formerly Sandokedal.

Sannikov Island (sä'nyĭkŭf), mythical island in Arctic Ocean, N of New Siberian Isls., Russian SFSR. Although it may have existed once and was reported (1810) in 79°N 145°E by Rus. explorer Sannikov, its existence was disproven by subsequent expeditions.

Sannikovo (–kŭvŭ), village, NE Altai Territory, Russian SFSR, 5 mi. SE of Barnaul, in agr. area.

Sannikov Strait, joins Laptev and E.Siberian seas of Arctic Ocean at 74°30'N lat.; separates Anjou and Lyakhov groups of NEW SIBERIAN ISLANDS, Russian SFSR; 30 mi. wide.

Sannin, Jebel, or **Jabal Sannin** (both: jĕ'bĕl sännēn'), Fr. *Sanine* (sänēn'), mountain (c.8,500 ft.), Lebanon range, N Lebanon, 22 mi. ENE of Beirut. Iron mines on W slopes.

Sanniya, Hor (hōr' sän-nē'yŭ), lake (c.70 mi. long, 10 mi. wide), SE Iraq, just W of the Tigris, in a swampy area.

Sannohe (sän-nō'ā), town (pop. 7,219), Aomori prefecture, N Honshu, Japan, 16 mi. SW of Hachinohe; commercial center for agr. and livestock area.

Sannois (sänwä'), town (pop. 12,243), Seine-et-Oise dept., N central France, an outer NNW suburb of Paris, 9 mi. from Notre Dame Cathedral; rail junction; metalworks; mfg. (precision instruments, furniture).

Sann River, Yugoslavia: see SAVINJA RIVER.

Sanntal Alpen, Yugoslavia: see SAVINJA ALPS.

Sano (sä'nō). **1** Town (pop. 3,854) on Awaji-shima, Hyogo prefecture, Japan, on Osaka Bay, 9 mi. NNE of Sumoto; fishing port. **2** Town (pop. 31,530), Osaka prefecture, S Honshu, Japan, on Osaka Bay, 4 mi. SW of Kaizuka; cotton-textile center; mfg. of electric insulators. **3** City (1940 pop. 17,873; 1947 pop. 55,302), Tochigi prefecture, central Honshu, Japan, 25 mi. SW of Utsunomiya; mfg. (textiles, clothing, umbrellas), flour milling. Includes (since early 1940s) former towns of Horigome (1940 pop. 3,545) and Inubushi (1940 pop. 6,029), and several villages.

Sanoghie (sä'nōgē), town, Central Prov., W central Liberia, near St. Paul R., 18 mi. N of Salala; palm oil and kernels, cotton, cassava, rice.

Sanok (sä'nôk), town (pop. 11,176), Rzeszow prov., SE Poland, on San R., on railroad and 34 mi. S of Rzeszow; mfg. (rolling stock, bicycles, storage batteries, rubber footwear, cement products), flour milling, sawmilling; brickworks. Natural-gas wells near by; gas pipe line to Sanok. Manganese ore deposits in vicinity.

Sanokwele, Liberia: see SANOQUELLI.

San Onofre (sän ōnō'frā), town (pop. 2,937), Bolívar dept., N Colombia, in Caribbean lowlands, 50 mi. S of Cartagena; corn, rice, sugar cane, fruit, stock.

San Onofre (săn ŭnō'frē), coast village, San Diego co., S Calif., near San Mateo Point, 17 mi. NNW of Oceanside.

Sanoquelli (sä"nōkwĕ'lē), town, Central Prov., N Liberia, 22 mi. NE of Ganta, near Fr. Guinea border; palm oil and kernels, kola nuts; cattle raising. Kaolin and iron deposits. Mission station. Road to Monrovia. Sometimes spelled Sanokwele or Saniquellie.

San Pablo (sän pä'blō). **1** Village, E Tierra del Fuego natl. territory, Argentina, on the Atlantic at Cape San Pablo (54°17'S 66°40'W), 55 mi. SE of Río Grande. **2** Town (pop. estimate 700), central Tucumán prov., Argentina, 7 mi. SW of Tucumán; sugar-refining and stock-raising center.

San Pablo. 1 Village, Pando dept., N Bolivia, on left bank of Madre de Dios R. and 14 mi. W of Riberalta; rubber. **2** Town (pop. c.400), ⊙ Sud Lípez or Sur Lípez prov., Potosí dept., SW Bolivia, 85 mi. S of Uyuni; alt. 14,370 ft.; alpaca. **3** Village (pop. c.1,100), Santa Cruz dept., E central Bolivia, on San Miguel R. and 85 mi. WNW of Concepción; cotton growing. Mission.

San Pablo, village (1930 pop. 968), Osorno prov., S central Chile, 13 mi. NNE of Osorno; grain growing, stock raising, dairying, lumbering.

San Pablo. 1 or **San Pablo de Tarrazú** (dā täräsōō'), village (dist. pop. 3,191), San José prov., S Costa Rica, on upper reaches of Parrita R., on road, and 3 mi. NW of San Marcos; coffee, livestock; lumbering. **2** or **San Pablo de Turrubares** (dā tōōrōōbä'rĕs), town (dist. pop. 1,446), San José prov., W central Costa Rica, in Tárcoles R. valley, 25 mi. WSW of San José; commercial center; grain, rice, beans; lumbering.

San Pablo, village, Imbabura prov., N Ecuador, in the Andes, near L. San Pablo, 10 mi. SSW of Ibarra; tourist resort; fishing, hunting; mfg. of straw hats, woolen and cotton goods. Colorful native settlement.

San Pablo. 1 Town (1950 pop. 590), San Marcos dept., SW Guatemala, in Pacific piedmont, on Inter-American Highway and 14 mi. WSW of San Marcos; coffee, sugar cane, grain. **2** or **San Pablo La Laguna** (lä lägōō'nä), town (1950 pop. 1,136), Sololá dept., SW central Guatemala, on NW shore of L. Atitlán, 5.5 mi. SW of Sololá; alt. 4,000 ft.; center of local henequen industry; hammocks, netting. **3** or **San Pablo Jocopilas** (hōkōpē'läs), town (1950 pop. 615), Suchitepéquez dept., SW Guatemala, in Pacific piedmont, 5 mi. NE of Mazatenango; coffee, sugar cane; livestock.

San Pablo. 1 Town, Chiapas, Mexico: see CHALCHIHUITÁN. **2** or **San Pablo Autopan** (outō'pän), town (pop. 5,533), Mexico state, central Mexico, 4 mi. N of Toluca; agr. center (cereals, livestock); dairying. **3** or **San Pablo de las Tunas** (dā läs tōō'näs), town (pop. 1,137), Puebla, central Mexico, 33 mi. ESE of Puebla; cereals, maguey, fruit.

San Pablo. 1 Town (pop. 1,619), Cajamarca dept., NW Peru, in Cordillera Occidental, 20 mi. W of Cajamarca; sugar cane, wheat, corn. **2** or **Cacha** (kä'chä), town (pop. 1,392), Cuzco dept., S Peru, on Vilcanota R., on railroad and 7 mi. NW of Sicuani; grain, potatoes; flour milling.

San Pablo, city (1939 pop. 15,393; 1948 metropolitan area pop. 50,435) in but independent of Laguna prov., S Luzon, Philippines, on railroad and 45 mi. SSE of Manila, surrounded by volcanic mts.; 14°4'N 121°19'E. Trade center for agr. area (rice, coconuts, sugar cane).

San Pablo. 1 E suburb (pop. 3,979) of Seville, SW Spain. Airport. **2** Village (pop. 2,717), Toledo prov., central Spain, in the Montes de Toledo, 28 mi. SW of Toledo; cereals, fruit, livestock; apiculture. Flour milling, lumbering, dairying, charcoal burning. Limekiln; marble quarry.

San Pablo (săn pă'blō), city (pop. 14,476), Contra Costa co., W Calif., just N of Richmond, near San Pablo Bay; lumber, metal products, plumbing supplies, paint; fish-processing plants.

San Pablo (sän pä'blō), town (pop. 1,014), Yaracuy state, N Venezuela, 10 mi. SW of San Felipe; coffee, sugar cane, corn, livestock.

San Pablo, Lake (c.1½ mi. wide), in the high Andes, Imbabura prov., N Ecuador, 2 mi. E of Otavalo; popular tourist resort in magnificent setting.

San Pablo Autopan, Mexico: see SAN PABLO, Mexico state.

San Pablo Balleza or **Balleza** (bäyä'sä), town (pop. 964), Chihuahua, N Mexico, on Balleza R. and 40 mi. W of Hidalgo del Parral; gold and silver mining.

San Pablo Bay (săn pă'blō), N portion of SAN FRANCISCO BAY, W Calif., connected to Suisun Bay (E) by Carquinez Strait. Mare Isl. (navy yard) is in bay at VALLEJO.

San Pablo de las Tunas, Mexico: see SAN PABLO, Puebla.

San Pablo del Monte, Mexico: see VILLA VICENTE GUERRERO.

San Pablo de Tarrazú, Costa Rica: see SAN PABLO.

San Pablo de Tiquina, Bolivia: see TIQUINA.

San Pablo de Turrubares, Costa Rica: see SAN PABLO.

San Pablo Jocopilas, Guatemala: see SAN PABLO.

San Pablo La Laguna, Guatemala: see SAN PABLO.

San Pablo Oxtotepec (ōstōtäpĕk'), town (pop. 2,167), Federal Dist., central Mexico, 18 mi. SSE of Mexico city; cereals, fruit, vegetables, livestock.

San Pablo River (sän pä'blō), SW Panama, rises in the Serranía de Tabasará 10 mi. WNW of Santa Fe, flows 50 mi. S, past Cañazas, San Pablo, and Soná, to Montijo Gulf of the Pacific, 10 mi. WSW of Puerto Mutis. Navigable for 10-ft. draught 11 mi. upstream from mouth.

San Pancrazio Parmense (sän pängkrä'tsyô pärmĕn'sĕ), village (pop. 636), Parma prov., Emilia-Romagna, N central Italy, 3 mi. WNW of Parma; canned tomatoes.

San Pancrazio Salentino (sälĕntē'nô), town (pop. 5,273), Brindisi prov., Apulia, S Italy, 16 mi. SSW of Brindisi; agr. center (wine, olive oil, cheese, wool, cereals).

San Pantaleo, Sicily: see STAGNONE ISLANDS.

San Pascual, Philippines: see BURIAS ISLAND.

San Pasqual (săn păskwôl'), hamlet, San Diego co., S Calif., 7 mi. E of Escondido. Near by a monument and state park mark San Pasqual battlefield, where an engagement of Mexican War was fought (Dec., 1846) bet. Gen. Stephen W. Kearny and Andrés Pico.

San Patricio (sän pätrē'syō), town (dist. pop. 2,706), Misiones dept., S Paraguay, 30 mi. SE of San Juan Bautista, in cattle-raising and maté-growing area.

San Patricio (săn pŭtrĭ'shēō), county (□ 689; pop. 35,842), S Texas; ⊙ Sinton. Bounded E by Aransas Bay (sheltered from Gulf of Mexico by St. Joseph and Mustang isls.), S by Nueces R., Nueces and Corpus Christi bays, N by Aransas R. A leading Texas oil and natural-gas producing co.; also petroleum and gas processing. Aransas Pass is deep-water port. Agr. (cotton, grain sorghums, corn, truck, peanuts, fruit), livestock. Resort area (beaches, fishing). Includes part of L. Corpus Christi (in W). Formed 1836.

San Pedro, department, Argentina: see MONTE CARLO.

San Pedro (sän pā'dhrō). **1** Town (pop. 9,786), ⊙ San Pedro dist. (□ 474; pop. 32,767), N Buenos Aires prov., Argentina, 95 mi. NW of Buenos Aires, on Paraná R., in fruit-growing area (apples, cherries, pears, plums, citrus fruit). **2** Town (pop. estimate 500), ⊙ San Alberto dept. (□ c.1,500; pop. 19,785), W Córdoba prov., Argentina, on the Río de los Sauces, opposite Villa Dolores, and 75 mi. SW of Córdoba; alfalfa, corn, oats, wine, livestock. Dam and hydroelectric station (completed 1944) near by. **3** or **San Pedro de Jujuy** (dā hōō-hwē'), town (1947 pop. 6,331), ⊙ San Pedro dept. (□ 870; 1947 pop. 23,656), SE Jujuy prov., Argentina, on railroad, on the Río Grande de Jujuy and 32 mi. E of Jujuy; mfg., lumbering, and agr. center (sugar cane, rice, corn, vegetables, livestock). Sugar refineries, alcohol distillery, tanneries, corn mills. Hydroelectric station. **4** Village (pop. estimate 1,000), ⊙ Guasayán dept. (□ c.1,100; 1947 pop. 8,807), E Santiago del Estero prov., Argentina, on railroad and 60 mi. WSW of Santiago del Estero; stock-raising (goats, cattle) and lumbering center; sawmills. Sulphur springs near by.

San Pedro. 1 Town (pop. c.1,000), Beni dept., NE Bolivia, in the llanos, 29 mi. N of Trinidad; cattle. **2** Village, Pando dept., N Bolivia, on Orton R. and 20 mi. WNW of Riberalta; rubber. **3** or **San Pedro de Buena Vista** (dā bwä'nä vē'stä), town (pop. c.8,000), ⊙ Charcas prov., Potosí dept., W central Bolivia, on San Pedro R. (branch of the Chayanta) and 95 mi. N of Potosí; wheat, potatoes, *oca*.

San Pedro (săn' pā'drō), village on Ambergris Cay, Belize dist., Br. Honduras, 37 mi. NNE of Belize. Coconut plantations.

San Pedro (sän pā'dhrō). **1** Village (1930 pop. 107), Antofagasta prov., N Chile, oasis on railroad, on affluent of Loa R., at SW foot of San Pedro Volcano, and 45 mi. NE of Calama; alt. 10,575 ft. Fruitgrowing; llama and alpaca raising. **2** Village (1930 pop. 305), Santiago prov., central Chile, 20 mi. SW of Melipilla, in agr. area (grain, fruit, livestock).

San Pedro. 1 or **San Pedro de Poás** (dā pwäs'), village (1950 pop. 708), Alajuela prov., central Costa Rica, on central plateau, at S foot of Poás volcano, 6 mi. NW of Alajuela; pineapples, manioc. **2** or **San Pedro de Montes de Oca** (mōn'tĕs dā ō'kä), town (1950 pop. 6,413), San José prov., Costa Rica, on central plateau, just E of San José (tramway connection); coffee, truck produce. **3** or **San Pedro de Turrubares** (tōōrōōbä'rĕs), village (pop. 1,153), San José prov., W central Costa Rica, in Tárcoles R. valley, 2 mi. S of San Pablo; corn, beans, rice, sugar cane, fruit; lumbering.

San Pedro, village, SW Ivory Coast, Fr. West Africa, minor landing on Gulf of Guinea (Atlantic), 35 mi. WSW of Sassandra; lumbering, fishing.

San Pedro. 1 or **San Pedro Sacatepéquez** (säkätäpā'kĕs), market town (1950 pop. 2,710), Guatemala dept., S central Guatemala, 9 mi. WNW of Guatemala; alt. 6,890 ft.; tile making, textiles; corn, black beans. **2** or **San Pedro Pinula** (pēnōō'lä), town (1950 pop. 1,843), Jalapa dept., E central Guatemala, in highlands, 9 mi. E of Jalapa; alt. 3,330 ft.; corn, beans. **3** or **San Pedro Sacatepéquez** (säkätäpā'kĕs), city (1950 pop. 5,949), San Marcos dept., SW Guatemala, on Naranjo R., on Inter-American Highway, just E of SAN MARCOS; alt. 8,136 ft. Market center; grain, fodder grasses, livestock. Govt. textile school. **4** or **San Pedro La Laguna** (lä lägōō'nä), town (1950 pop. 2,583), Sololá dept., SW central Guatemala, on W shore of L. Atitlán, at N foot of volcano San Pedro, and 5 mi. NW of Atitlán; alt. 5,269 ft.; fisheries; grain, beans.

San Pedro, inactive volcano (9,921 ft.), SW central Guatemala, near L. Atitlán, 2 mi. S of San Pedro.

San Pedro or **San Pedro de Copán** (dā kōpän'), town (pop. 650), Copán dept., W Honduras, 9 mi. SSW of Santa Rosa, in tobacco area; cigar mfg.; sugar cane, livestock.

San Pedro. 1 or **San Pedro Atocpan** (ätōk'pän), town (pop. 1,700), Federal Dist., central Mexico, 17 mi. SSE of Mexico city; cereals, fruit, livestock. **2** Officially San Pedro los Baños, town (pop. 2,550), Mexico state, central Mexico, on Lerma R. and 45 mi. WNW of Mexico city; cereals, fruit, livestock. **3** Town, San Luis Potosí, Mexico: see CERRO DE SAN PEDRO. **4** Town (pop. 1,119), Sonora, NW Mexico, on Río Mayo (irrigation), near Gulf of California, and 100 mi. SE of Guaymas; chick-peas, rice, corn, fruit, livestock.

San Pedro or **San Pedro de Potrero Grande** (dā pōtrā'rō grän'dā), town (1950 pop. 260), Chinandega dept., W Nicaragua, 2 mi. SE of Villanueva; corn, beans, rice.

San Pedro, department (□ 7,723; pop. 59,244), central Paraguay; ⊙ San Pedro. Bordered W by Paraguay R., N by Ypané R., and drained by the Jejuí-guazú. Largely low forested areas with marshlands (SW) and some outliers of central Brazilian plateau (E). Has humid, subtropical climate. Produces mostly maté; also oranges, livestock, lumber. Processing centered at San Pedro, Rosario, Itacurubí del Rosario, Antequera. Lime quarrying at San Estanislao and Rosario.

San Pedro, town (dist. pop. 11,483), ⊙ San Pedro dept., central Paraguay, near Jejuí-guazú and Paraguay rivers, 90 mi. NNE of Asunción; 24°4'S 57°10'W. Trading center in maté-growing and lumbering area. Livestock, oranges. Sawmills.

San Pedro. 1 Town (pop. 1,166), Ayacucho dept., S Peru, in Cordillera Occidental, 6 mi. SSE of Puquio; grain, corn, alfalfa, livestock. **2** Town (pop. 880), Cuzco dept., S Peru, on Vilcanota R., on railroad and 10 mi. NW of Sicuani; grain, potatoes; mfg. of woolen goods. **3** or **San Pedro de Lloc** (dä yōk'), city (pop. 5,286), ⊙ Pacasmayo prov. (□ 1,000; pop. 44,101), Libertad dept., NW Peru, on coastal plain, on railroad and 5 mi. ESE of its port Pacasmayo, 60 mi. NW of Trujillo, on Pan American Highway. Rice milling, weaving of native textiles; local trading in agr. products (rice, sugar, cotton, corn, fodder). Horse raising near by. Sugar milling at Cavour, just NE, on railroad.

San Pedro or **San Pedro Perulapán** (pärōōläpän'), city (pop. 957), Cuscatlán dept., central Salvador, 7 mi. WNW of Cojutepeque; mat weaving, rope making; grain, coffee, sugar cane.

San Pedro. 1 (săn pē'drō, pä'drō) Extreme S section (pop. c.40,000) of Los ANGELES city, S Calif., on Los ANGELES HARBOR and San Pedro Bay, adjacent to Wilmington and 22 mi. S of downtown Los Angeles; handles much of harbor's commerce (mainly exports), and has shipyards, dry docks, fish canneries, oil refineries. On Point Fermin are U.S. Fort MacArthur and a park. Cabrillo Beach (park; bathing, amusements) is near tip of point. Laid out 1882 on San Pedro Bay, it early became a port, despite bay's shallowness and exposed position; inc. as city in 1888; in 1909, it was annexed (together with Wilmington) by Los Angeles city and development of modern harbor was begun. **2** (săn pä'drō) Village (pop. 8,127), Nueces co., S Texas.

San Pedro (sän pä'drō). **1** Town (pop. 710), Lara state, NW Venezuela, 22 mi. S of Carora; coffee, sugar, cereals, livestock. **2** Town (pop. 575), Miranda state, N Venezuela, 4 mi. WNW of Los Teques; coffee, sugar cane, cacao. **3** Town (pop. 2,198), Nueva Esparta state, NE Venezuela, on Coche Isl. (W), 15 mi. SW of Porlamar (Margarita Isl.); saltworks; fishing.

San Pedro, Point, Calif.: see PEDRO VALLEY.

San Pedro Ahuacatlán (äwäkätlän'), town (pop. 1,029), Querétaro, central Mexico, 38 mi. SE of Querétaro; grain, alfalfa, potatoes, beans, sugar cane, stock.

San Pedro Alcántara (älkän'tärä), village (pop. 1,161), Málaga prov., S Spain, near Mediterranean coast, 32 mi. NE of Gibraltar; sugar cane, grapes, oranges, olives, cork. Just SW is the sugar refinery San Pedro Alcántara (pop. 391).

San Pedro Apulco or **Apulco** (äpōōl'kō), town (pop. 764), Zacatecas, N central Mexico, 40 mi. SW of Aguascalientes; grain, fruit, vegetables, livestock.

San Pedro Arriba (ärē'bä), town (pop. 2,073), Mexico state, central Mexico, 28 mi. W of Mexico city; cereals, stock.

San Pedro Ayampuc (īämpōōk'), town (1950 pop. 2,782), Guatemala dept., S central Guatemala, 10 mi. NNE of Guatemala; alt. 3,999 ft.; sugar cane. Founded 1549.

San Pedro Bay (săn" pē'drō, Sp. sän pä'drō), inlet (12 mi. wide, 15 mi. long) of Leyte Gulf, Philippines, bet. Samar and Leyte; San Juanico Strait leads off it (N) at Tacloban.

San Pedro Bay (săn pē'drō, pä'drō), Los Angeles co., S Calif., broad bay sheltered on W by Palos Verdes Hills and Point Fermin. On its shores are San Pedro, Wilmington, and Long Beach—on man-made Los Angeles and Long Beach harbors.

San Pedro Carchá, Guatemala: see CARCHÁ.

San Pedro Caro, Mexico: see VENUSTIANO CARRANZA, Michoacán.

San Pedro Channel (săn pē'drō, pä'drō), off S Calif., passage (c.20 mi. wide) bet. Santa Catalina Isl. and S Los Angeles co. (San Pedro dist.); Santa Monica Bay is NW, Gulf of Santa Catalina to SE. Often called Catalina Channel.

San Pedro de Atacama (sän pä'dhrō dā ätäkä'mä), village (1930 pop. 325), Antofagasta, Chile, oasis in Puna de Atacama, near N edge of the Salar de Atacama, 55 mi. SE of Calama; corn- and fruit-growing.

San Pedro de Buena Vista, Bolivia: see SAN PEDRO, Potosí dept.

San Pedro de Ceque (thā'kä), village (pop. 1,264), Zamora prov., NW Spain, 22 mi. WNW of Benavente; cereals, flax, wine.

San Pedro de Colalao (dā kōlälä'ō), town (pop. estimate 1,000), NW Tucumán prov., Argentina, 45 mi. NNW of Tucumán; agr. center (corn, alfalfa, livestock); lumbering.

San Pedro de Copán, Honduras: see SAN PEDRO.

San Pedro de Durazno, Uruguay: see DURAZNO, city.

San Pedro de Jujuy, Argentina: see SAN PEDRO, Jujuy prov.

San Pedro de la Cueva (dā lä kwā'vä), town (pop. 1,127), Sonora, NW Mexico, in W outliers of Sierra Madre Occidental, 60 mi. NNE of Hermosillo; corn, wheat, stock. Sometimes Cuevas.

San Pedro de las Colonias (läs kōlō'nyäs), city (pop. 15,713), Coahuila, N Mexico, in Laguna Dist., 33 mi. NE of Torreón; rail junction; agr. center (cotton, cereals, grapes, fruit, vegetables); cotton ginning, flour milling, vegetable-oil distilling, tanning.

San Pedro de Latarce (lätär'thā), town (pop. 1,553), Valladolid prov., N central Spain, 18 mi. SW of Medina de Ríoseco; flour mills; cereals, wine.

San Pedro del Cotorro, Cuba: see COTORRO.

San Pedro del Gallo (dĕl gä'yō), town (pop. 1,703), Durango, N Mexico, 55 mi. W of Torreón; alt. 5,577 ft.; silver, gold, lead, copper mining.

San Pedro de Lloc, Peru: see SAN PEDRO, Libertad dept.

San Pedro de los Incas (dā lōs ēng'käs), town (pop. 783), Tumbes dept., NW Peru, on coastal plain, on Pan American Highway and 3 mi. SW of Tumbes; road junction; charcoal burning. Also Corrales.

San Pedro de Lóvago (lō'vägō), town (1950 pop. 509), Chontales dept., S Nicaragua, 22 mi. ENE of Juigalpa; sugar cane, grain.

San Pedro del Paraná (dĕl päränä'), town (dist. pop. 15,845), Itapúa dept., S Paraguay, 45 mi. NW of Encarnación; lumber, maté, livestock; sawmills. Founded 1789.

San Pedro del Pinatar (pēnätär'), town (pop. 1,034), Murcia prov., SE Spain, 21 mi. SE of Murcia, near Mar Menor of the Mediterranean; olive-oil processing; fishing; pepper and wine. Saltworks near by. Bathing beaches on the coast.

San Pedro de Macorís (dā mäkōrēs'), province (□ 520; 1935 pop. 69,166; 1950 pop. 64,214), SE Dominican Republic, on the Caribbean; ⊙ San Pedro de Macorís. Its fertile tropical lowlands are the Republic's main sugar-growing region. Produces also cattle, tropical fruit, timber. San Pedro de Macorís city is a leading sugar port and processing center. Prov. was set up 1908.

San Pedro de Macorís, city (1935 pop. 18,617; 1950 pop. 19,994), ⊙ San Pedro de Macorís prov., SE Dominican Republic, port on the Caribbean, at mouth of Higuamo R., 38 mi. E of Ciudad Trujillo; 18°27'N 69°17'W. Leading sugar center, surrounded by cane fields, and one of the largest exporting ports of the Republic (sugar, molasses). Other products include cattle, timber, beeswax. Sugar milling, alcohol distilling, tanning, corn milling; mfg. of clothing, candles, soap. International airport.

San Pedro de Mérida (mā'rēdhä), town (pop. 855), Badajoz prov., W Spain, near the Guadalete, 9 mi. E of Mérida; olives, sheep; charcoal burning.

San Pedro de Montes de Oca, Costa Rica: see SAN PEDRO, San José prov.

San Pedro de Poás, Costa Rica: see SAN PEDRO, Alajuela prov.

San Pedro de Potrero Grande, Nicaragua: see SAN PEDRO.

San Pedro de Ribas (rē'väs), village (pop. 1,299), Barcelona prov., NE Spain, 4 mi. NE of Villanueva y Geltrú, in winegrowing area; lumbering; livestock, cereals, hazelnuts.

San Pedro de Riudevitlles (rē"ōō-dhävēt'lyĕs), town (pop. 1,469), Barcelona prov., NE Spain, 10 mi. SSE of Igualada, in winegrowing area; paper-mfg. center; also makes woolens, dyes.

San Pedro de Tiquina, Bolivia: see TIQUINA.

San Pedro de Torelló (tōrĕlyō'), town (pop. 1,310), Barcelona prov., NE Spain, 10 mi. NNE of Vich; woodturning, toy mfg.; cereals, apples, potatoes, livestock.

San Pedro de Turrubares, Costa Rica: see SAN PEDRO, San José prov.

San Pedro de Tutule, Honduras: see TUTULE.

San Pedro Hills, Calif.: see PALOS VERDES HILLS.

San Pedro Island (sän pä'dhrō) (□ 24; pop. 67), off coast of SE Chiloé Isl., S Chile, 60 mi. S of Castro; 43°22'S; 8 mi. long, c.4 mi. wide; rises to 3,200 ft.

San Pedro Lagunillas (lägōōnē'yäs), town (pop. 1,337), Nayarit, W Mexico, 28 mi. SSE of Tepic; corn, beans, sugar cane, cattle.

San Pedro La Laguna, Guatemala: see SAN PEDRO, town.

San Pedro los Baños, Mexico: see SAN PEDRO, Mexico state.

San Pedro Manrique (mänrē'kä), town (pop. 954), Soria prov., N central Spain, 23 mi. NE of Soria; cereals, potatoes, vegetables, livestock; flour milling. Has sulphur springs.

San Pedro Mártir, Guatemala: see PALÍN.

San Pedro Mártir, Sierra (syĕ'rä, mär'tēr), central range of Lower California, NW Mexico, c.90 mi. long. Mostly barren; rich in minerals (copper, silver, gold, lead); has some fertile, flat valleys. Rises to 10,063 ft. in Cerro La Encantada, 31°N.

San Pedro Masahuat (mäsäwät'), city (pop. 2,691), La Paz dept., S central Salvador, in coastal range, near Jiboa R., 11 mi. NW of Zacatecoluca; mfg. (palm hats, mats); grain, coffee.

San Pedro Necta (nĕk'tä), town (1950 pop. 875), Huehuetenango dept., W Guatemala, on W slopes of Cuchumatanes Mts., 24 mi. WNW of Huehuetenango; alt. 4,950 ft.; sugar cane, corn, wheat.

San Pedro Nonualco (nōnwäl'kō), city (pop. 5,033), La Paz dept., S central Salvador, 4 mi. NNW of Zacatecoluca, at SW foot of volcano San Vincente; grain, coffee.

San Pedro Ocampo, Mexico: see MELCHOR OCAMPO, Zacatecas.

San Pedro Perulapán, Salvador: see SAN PEDRO.

San Pedro Piedra Gorda (pyā'dhrä gôr'dhä), town (pop. 2,542), Zacatecas, N central Mexico, on interior plateau, 26 mi. SE of Zacatecas; alt. 6,847 ft.; gold, silver, lead, copper mining.

San Pedro Pinula, Guatemala: see SAN PEDRO, town.

San Pedro Remate, Mexico: see BELLA VISTA.

San Pedro River, Chile: see CALLE-CALLE RIVER.

San Pedro River (sän pä'dhrō), Camagüey prov., E Cuba, formed just S of Camagüey, flows c.55 mi. SW and W to the Caribbean.

San Pedro River. 1 In Petén dept. (N Guatemala), and Tabasco (Mexico), rises N of L. Petén, flows 200 mi. W and NW, to the Usumacinta SE of Balancán (Tabasco). Navigable for 90 mi. in lower course. **2** In W Mexico, rises in Sierra Madre Occidental 45 mi. ENE of Durango, flows S, past Nombre de Dios and Mezquital, into Nayarit, then W, past Tuxpan, to coastal lagoons which drain into the Pacific; c.250 mi. long. Sometimes called Tuxpan R. Its upper course is called Mezquital R. in Durango. **3** or **Aguascalientes River** (ägwäskälyĕn'tĕs), N central Mexico, rises 15 mi. S of Zacatecas, flows c.180 mi. S and SW, across Aguascalientes state (there extensively used for irrigation), and into Jalisco to Santiago (Lerma) R. 6 mi. NE of Guadalajara. Called Río Verde or Río Verde Grande de Belén in Jalisco.

San Pedro River (săn pā'drō, pē'drō), N Mexico and S Ariz., intermittent stream rising in Sonora (state), Mexico; flows c.170 mi. N, past Benson, to Gila R. near Hayden, Ariz.

San Pedro Sacatepéquez, Guatemala dept., Guatemala: see SAN PEDRO, town.

San Pedro Soloma, Guatemala: see SOLOMA.

San Pedro Sula (sän pä'dhrō sōō'lä), city (pop. 22,116), ⊙ Cortés dept., NW Honduras, on railroad and 24 mi. SSW of Puerto Cortés, in Sula Valley; 15°28'N 88°2'W. Major commercial and mfg. center in banana and sugar-cane zone; flour and flour products, beer, soft drinks, dairy products, soap, candles, cigarettes, furniture; meat packing, sugar milling, tanning, sawmilling. Distributing center for W and NW Honduras; major air-traffic hub. Has col., govt. hosp., parks, modern residences. Founded 1536 at point just E of present site, where it was moved in 17th cent.

San Pedro Tenango (tänäng'gō), town (pop. 1,109), Guanajuato, central Mexico, 13 mi. E of Celaya; grain, alfalfa, fruit, vegetables, stock.

San Pedro Tesistán (täsēstän'), town (pop. 1,160), Jalisco, central Mexico, on W shore of L. Chapala, 32 mi. S of Guadalajara; beans, grain, fruit, stock.

San Pedro Tlaquepaque, Mexico: see TLAQUEPAQUE.

San Pedro Valley, Calif.: see PEDRO VALLEY.

San Pedro Volcano (sän pä'dhrō). **1** Andean peak (19,585 ft.) in Antofagasta prov., N Chile, near Bolivian border; 21°53'S. **2** Andean peak, Linares prov., Chile: see YEGUAS VOLCANO.

San Pedro Yepocapa, Guatemala; see YEPOCAPA.

San Pedro y San Pablo River (sän pä'dhrō ē sän pä'blō), in SE Mexico, delta arm of lower Usumacinta R.; branches off 12 mi. NNW of Jonuta in Tabasco, flows c.40 mi. NW to Gulf of Campeche 15 mi. NE of Alvaro Obregón.

San Pedro Zacapa, Honduras: see ZACAPA.

San Pelayo (sän pälī'ō), town (pop. 1,684), Bolívar dept., N Colombia, in savannas near Sinú R., 14 mi. N of Montería; rice, livestock.

San Pellegrino (sän pĕl-lĕgrē'nô), village (pop. 1,917), Bergamo prov., Lombardy, N Italy, on Brembo R. and 10 mi. N of Bergamo; mineral spa and health resort, with thermal alkaline springs (80.6°F.). Jute mills.

Sanpete (sănpēt'), county (□ 1,597; pop. 13,891), central Utah; ⊙ Manti. Mtn. area crossed N–S by Wasatch Plateau, watered by Sevier and San Pitch rivers. Includes irrigated Sanpete Valley (extending N–S) and Manti Natl. Forest in E. Livestock, hay, sugar beets, fruit, truck; rock salt, gypsum. Formed 1850.

Sanpete Valley, Sanpete co., central Utah, just W of Wasatch Plateau, along San Pitch R. Sanpete irrigation project (completed 1939) brings water to the valley from headstream of San Rafael R. Alfalfa, hay, grain, vegetables, fruit; sheep and turkey raising. Principal cities: Mt. Pleasant, Ephraim, Fairview, Moroni, Spring City.

San Pier d'Arena (sän pyĕr' dārä'nä), W suburb (pop. 57,216) of Genoa, Genova prov., Liguria, N Italy; rail junction; industrial center; mfg. (locomotives, marine engines, tools, nitrates, refined sugar, flour, jute products, rope). Its shipyards built 1st Italian locomotive, 1854. Has villas, 16th-cent. palaces. Also spelled Sampierdarena.

San Pier Niceto (sän pyĕr' nēchä'tô), village (pop. 4,117), Messina prov., NE Sicily, in Peloritani Mts., 11 mi. WSW of Messina.

San Piero Patti (sän pyā'rô pät'tē), village (pop. 3,312), Messina prov., NE Sicily, 6 mi. S of Patti.

San Pietro, Yugoslavia: see BRAC ISLAND.

San Pietro a Patierno (sän pyā'trô ä pätyĕr'nô), town (pop. 8,391), Napoli prov., Campania, S Italy, 3 mi. N of Naples; glass mfg.

San Pietro del Carso, Yugoslavia: see SENT PETER NA KRASU.

San Pietro in Casale (ēn käzä'lē), town (pop. 1,655), Bologna prov., Emilia-Romagna, N central Italy, 14 mi. N of Bologna; hemp mill.

San Pietro in Gu (gōō), village (pop. 798), Padova prov., Veneto, N Italy, 8 mi. NE of Vicenza; textile machinery factory.

San Pietro in Lama (lä'mä), village (pop. 3,618), Lecce prov., Apulia, S Italy, 4 mi. SSW of Lecce.

San Pietro Island, anc. *Accipitrum Insula* (□ 20; pop. 8,030), in Mediterranean Sea, 4 mi. off SW Sardinia, in Cagliari prov.; 6 mi. long, 5 mi. wide; rises to 692 ft. Major tunny fisheries off NE end; extensive saltworks, orchards, vineyards in E, manganese-ocher-jasper mines in W. Chief port, CARLOFORTE.

San Pietro Vernotico (vĕrnô'tēkô), town (pop. 9,038), Brindisi prov., Apulia, S Italy, 11 mi. SSE of Brindisi; wine, alcohol, olive oil.

San Pitch River, central Utah, rises in Wasatch Range N of Fairview, flows c.70 mi. SSW, through SANPETE VALLEY, to Sevier R. 7 mi. SSW of Gunnison. Dammed for irrigation 6 mi. SW of Manti.

Sanpoil River (săn'poil, sănpoil'), NE Wash., rises in Colville Natl. Forest, flows c.70 mi. S, past Republic and through Colville Indian Reservation, to Columbia R. c.20 mi. above Grand Coulee Dam.

San Pol de Mar (sän pôl' dämär'), town (pop. 1,528), Barcelona prov., NE Spain, on the Mediterranean, 4 mi. NE of Arenys de Mar; mfg. (knit-goods, cotton fabrics, sailcloth); salted fish; wine, oranges.

Sanquelim (săngkä'lĭm), town, N Goa dist., Portuguese India, 11 mi. ENE of Pangim; rice, timber.

San Quentin (săn kwĕn'tĭn), village (pop. c.325), Marin co., W Calif., on a small peninsula on San Francisco Bay, just SE of San Rafael; ferry to Richmond (E). State prison is here.

Sanquhar (săng'kŭr), burgh (1931 pop. 1,753; 1951 census 2,381), NW Dumfries, Scotland, on Nith R. and 25 mi. NW of Dumfries; coal mines, iron foundries, brickworks; agr. market. Monument marks site of cross to which "Sanquhar Declarations" were affixed by Convenanters in 1680 and 1685. Village of Eliock, 2 mi. SSE, is site of ruined castle, reputed birthplace of "Admirable Crichton."

San Quintin (sän kēntēn'), town (1939 pop. 3,594; 1948 municipality pop. 15,330), Pangasinan prov., central Luzon, Philippines, 33 mi. SSE of Baguio; rail terminus; agr. center (rice, copra, corn).

San Quintín de Mediona (sän kēntēn' dā mā-dyō'nä), town (pop. 1,344), Barcelona prov., NE Spain, 9 mi. SSE of Igualada, in winegrowing area; mfg. (cotton fabrics, cream of tartar, cigarette paper, alcohol).

San Quirico or **San Quirico Vernio** (sän kwē'rēkô vĕr'nyô), village (pop. 848), Firenze prov., Tuscany, central Italy, 12 mi. N of Prato; cotton and woolen mills.

San Quírico de Besora (sän kē'rēkō dā bäsō'rä), village (pop. 2,306), Barcelona prov., NE Spain, on Ter R. and 12 mi. N of Vich; cotton spinning, carbide processing, lumbering; livestock; alfalfa. Mineral springs.

San Quirico d'Orcia (sän kwē'rēkô dôr'chä), village (pop. 1,045), Siena prov., Tuscany, central Italy, 23 mi. SE of Siena; agr. tools. Has late 12th-cent. collegiate church.

San Quirico Vernio, Italy: see SAN QUIRICO.

San Rafael (sän räfäĕl'). **1** City (pop. 28,245), ⊙ San Rafael dept. (□ 28,110; 1947 pop. 109,209), central Mendoza prov., Argentina, on left bank of Diamante R. (irrigation area), on railroad and 125 mi. SSE of Mendoza; farming, mining, and mfg. center. Wine making, meat packing, fruit drying and canning, dairying, oil distilling. Agr. products: wine, fruit, potatoes, grain. Onyx, travertine, and asphalt mines; oil wells. Has natl. col., theaters. Founded 1901. **2** Town (pop. estimate 300), central Tucumán prov., Argentina, on railroad and 13 mi. SW of Tucumán; sugar-growing and lumbering center.

San Rafael, village (pop. 1,382), Iviza, Balearic Isls., 2 mi. N of Iviza city; fruitgrowing, stock raising.

San Rafael, town (pop. c.1,000), Santa Cruz dept., E Bolivia, c.35 mi. SE of San Ignacio; cattle. Jesuit mission in 18th cent.

San Rafael. 1 or **San Rafael de Guatuso** (dā gwätōō'sō), village, Alajuela prov., N Costa Rica, in tropical Guatuso Lowland, on the Río Frío and 28 mi. SSW of San Carlos; stock raising, lumbering; cacao, ipecac root. **2** or **San Rafael de Ojo de Agua** (dā ō'hō dā ä'gwä), village (dist. pop. 2,695), Alajuela prov., central Costa Rica, on central plateau, on railroad and 3 mi. S of Alajuela; important summer resort; park, baths. Local fresh-water springs supply port of Puntarenas. Sometimes called Ojo de Agua. **3** or **San Rafael de Oreamuno** (dā ōräämōō'nō), town (pop. 895), Cartago prov., central Costa Rica, 1 mi. NE of Cartago; brewery; potatoes, corn, fruit, fodder crops. **4** Town (1950 pop. 288), Heredia prov., central Costa Rica, on central plateau, 2 mi. NE of Heredia; coffee, corn, fodder crops; lumbering, stock raising.

San Rafael, province (□ 788; 1935 pop. 27,068; 1950 pop. 33,255), W Dominican Republic, on Haiti border; ⊙ Elías Piña. Bounded by the Cordillera Central (N) and Sierra de Neiba (S); watered by Artibonito R. Agr. region: corn, rice, cotton, coffee, sugar cane, fruit; also goats, hides, timber. Prov. was set up 1942.

San Rafael. 1 or **San Rafael Pie de la Cuesta** (pyā' dā lä kwĕ'stä), town (1950 pop. 915), San Marcos dept., SW Guatemala, in Pacific piedmont, on Inter-American Highway and 8 mi. WSW of San Marcos; coffee, sugar cane, grain. **2** or **San Rafael Las Flores** (läs flō'rĕs), town (1950 pop. 1,144), Santa Rosa dept., S Guatemala, in highlands, 15 mi. NNE of Cuilapa; alt. 4,500 ft.; corn, fodder grasses, livestock.

San Rafael, town (pop. 5,150), Mexico state, central Mexico, at NW foot of Ixtacihuatl, 30 mi. SE of Mexico city; rail terminus; paper-milling center.

San Rafael, Paraguay: see JUAN DE MENA.

San Rafael, town (1939 pop. 1,360; 1948 municipality pop. 14,632), Bulacan prov., S central Luzon, Philippines, 24 mi. N of Manila; rice, corn.

San Rafael or **San Rafael Cedros** (sā'dhrōs), town (pop. 1,589), Cuscatlán dept., central Salvador, on railroad and Inter-American Highway, 3 mi. E of Cojutepeque; grain, sugar cane.

San Rafael, village (pop. 1,265), Segovia prov., central Spain, resort on S slopes of the Sierra de Guadarrama, 16 mi. SSW of Segovia.

San Rafael (săn rūfĕl'). **1** Residential city (pop. 13,848), ⊙ Marin co., W Calif., on San Francisco Bay, 15 mi. N of San Francisco. Has replica (1949) of Mission San Rafael Arcángel (established 1817). Seat of Dominican Col. of San Rafael, a military acad., and Tamalpais School for boys. Hamilton Air Force Base is c.5 mi. N. Mfg.: furnaces, gloves, aluminum goods. Inc. 1874. **2** Agr. village (pop. c.200), Valencia co., W N.Mex., near San Jose R., just SE of Zuni Mts., 70 mi. W of Albuquerque; alt. 6,509 ft. Perpetual Ice Caves and Cibola Natl. Forest near by.

San Rafael (sän räfäĕl'), beach resort, Maldonado dept., S Uruguay, on the Atlantic at mouth of the Río de la Plata, just E of Punta del Este.

San Rafael. 1 Town (pop. 238), Mérida state, W Venezuela, on transandine highway, on upper Chama R., at W foot of Pico Mucuñuque, and 22 mi. NE of Mérida; alt. 10,302 ft. Highest urban settlement in Venezuela. Emerald mining near by. **2** or **El Moján** (ĕl mōhän'), town (pop. 2,221), Zulia state, NW Venezuela, on Tablazo Bay, in Maracaibo lowlands, opposite Toas Isl., 25 mi. NNW of Maracaibo; oil wells.

San Rafael, Lake (sän räfäĕl'), fjord (9 mi. long) in Aysén prov., S Chile, 115 mi. SW of Puerto Aysén, bet. mainland and Taitao Peninsula. With the San Rafael Glacier flowing into it from the W slope of Cerro San Valentín, it is one of Chile's most magnificent sights.

San Rafael Cedros, Salvador: see SAN RAFAEL.

San Rafael de Atamaica (sän räfäĕl' dā ätämī'kä), town (pop. 280), Apure state, W central Venezuela, in llanos, 26 mi. S of San Fernando, in cattle region.

San Rafael de Carvajal or **Carvajal** (kärvähäl'), town (pop. 771), Trujillo state, W Venezuela, opposite Valera across Motatán R.; sugar cane, cacao, coffee, grain.

San Rafael de Guatuso, Costa Rica: see SAN RAFAEL, Alajuela prov.

San Rafael del Norte (dĕl nôr'tä), town (1950 pop. 810), Jinotega dept., W Nicaragua, 13 mi. NW of Jinotega; alt. 3,350 ft. Agr. center (sugar cane, wheat); mfg. (flour, turpentine); livestock.

San Rafael del Sur (sōōr'), town (1950 pop. 1,973), Managua dept., SW Nicaragua, on road and 24 mi. SSW of Managua; grain, livestock; cement mfg., limestone quarrying. Petroleum deposits.

San Rafael del Yuma (yōō'mä), village (1950 pop. 365), La Altagracia prov., SE Dominican Republic, on small Yuma R. and 36 mi. SE of Seibo, in fruit and cattle region. Formerly Yuma.

San Rafael de Ojo de Agua, Costa Rica: see SAN RAFAEL, Alajuela prov.

San Rafael de Oreamuno, Costa Rica: see SAN RAFAEL, Cartago prov.

San Rafael de Orituco (dā ōrētōō'kō), town (pop. 621), Guárico state, N central Venezuela, 3 mi. SSW of Altagracia de Orituco; corn, coffee, stock.

San Rafael Las Flores, Guatemala: see SAN RAFAEL.

San Rafael Mountains (săn rūfĕl'). **1** In Santa Barbara co., SW Calif., one of the Coast Ranges, beginning at Cuyama R. at SE end of Santa Lucia Range, and curving c.50 mi. SE to merge with other ranges near Santa Barbara–Ventura co. line. San Rafael Mtn. (6,596 ft.) is 22 mi. NNW of Santa Barbara; Big Pine Mtn. (6,490 ft.) is 20 mi. N of Santa Barbara. **2** In E central Utah, W of San Rafael R.; uranium, vanadium deposits. San Rafael Knob (7,934 ft.) is highest point.

San Rafael Pie de la Cuesta, Guatemala: see SAN RAFAEL.

San Rafael River (sän räfäĕl'), E Bolivia, rises in Serranía de Santiago c.25 mi. S of San Juan, flows 90 mi. ESE, joining Tucavaca R. c.3 mi. S of Tucavaca to form the OTUQUIS. In its lower course also called San Carlos, in its middle course Aguas Calientes.

San Rafael River (săn rūfĕl'), E central Utah, formed by confluence of headstreams SE of Castle Dale, flows c.90 mi. generally SE, past San Rafael Mts., to Green R. 15 mi. S of Green River city. Headwaters are tapped by 2 diversion tunnels passing through Wasatch Plateau and used to supplement irrigation in SANPETE VALLEY.

San Raimundo (sän rīmōōn'dō), market town 1950 pop. 1,243), Guatemala dept., S central Guatemala, 12 mi. NNW of Guatemala; alt. 6,000 ft.; pottery (jugs) and textiles; sugar cane, corn, black beans. Founded late 16th-cent. Sometimes spelled San Raymundo.

San Ramón (sän rämōn'), town (pop. c.1,100), Beni dept., NE Bolivia, port on Machupo R. and 18 mi. SSE of San Joaquín; cattle.

San Ramón, city (pop. 3,747), Alajuela prov., W central Costa Rica, on central plateau, on Inter-American Highway and 19 mi. WNW of Alajuela; commercial center; coffee processing, woodworking. Agr.: coffee, corn, beans, potatoes, tobacco, sugar cane, fodder crops, livestock. Founded in 1880s.

San Ramón, town (1950 pop. 579), Matagalpa dept., central Nicaragua, 7 mi. E of Matagalpa; coffee, rice, corn, wheat, beans, sugar cane. Gold-mining center for near-by La Reina mine.

San Ramón, town (pop. 1,275), Junín dept., central Peru, on Chanchamayo R. (formed here by confluence of 3 headstreams) and 33 mi. NE of Tarma, on edge of forests (lumbering); fruit, coffee, cacao, sugar cane. Airport (hydroplane service to Iquitos).

San Ramón (sän rämōn'), town (pop. 6,000), Canelones dept., S Uruguay, on Santa Lucía R., on railroad and 45 mi. NNE of Montevideo, in agr. region (grain, cattle, sheep).

San Raymundo, Guatemala: see SAN RAIMUNDO.

San Remigio (sän rĕmē'hyō), town (1939 pop. 1,992; 1948 municipality pop. 20,645), N Cebu isl., Philippines, 55 mi. N of Cebu city, on E side of entrance to Tañon Strait; agr. center (corn, coconuts).

San Remo (sän rā'mô), city (pop. 23,963), Imperia prov., Liguria, NW Italy, port on Gulf of Genoa and 27 mi. ENE of Nice, in flower- and olive-growing region. Chief winter resort (mean winter temp. 51°F.) of Riviera di Ponente. Comprises an old, upper town and, along the shore, a modern city with fine hotels, numerous villas, scenic promenades, and gardens. Has 12th-cent. Romanesque church of San Siro, 15th-cent. Palazzo Boreo d'Olmo, and a Genoese fort (now a prison). Market for flowers (roses, geraniums, violets), wine, olive oil. Conference of San Remo held here in April, 1920. In Second World War, modern city severely damaged and palace ruined.

San River (sän), SE Poland, rises at Uzhok Pass in Beshchady Mts., flows NNW past Lesko and Sanok, N, E past Przemysl, and NW past Jaroslaw and Nisko, to Vistula R. 5 mi. NE of Sandomierz; 247 mi. long. Navigable in lower course, below Jaroslaw; in upper course forms Poland–Ukrainian SSR border. Main tributaries: Wisznia, Lubaczowka, Tanen (right), and Wislok (left) rivers.

San Román, Peru: see JULIACA.

San Román (sän rōmän'), town (pop. 898), Toledo prov., central Spain, 8 mi. NNE of Talavera de la Reina; cereals, grapes, olives, livestock.

San Román, Cape (sän rōmän'), Falcón state, NW Venezuela, northernmost tip of Paraguaná Peninsula, on the Caribbean at entrance to Gulf of Venezuela, 19 mi. NNW of Pueblo Nuevo; 12°12'N 70°1'W.

San Román de Hornija (dā ôrnē'hä), town (pop. 1,246), Valladolid prov., N central Spain, 6 mi. SE of Toro; cereals, wine.

San Romano (sän rômä'nô), village (pop. 748), Pisa prov., Tuscany, central Italy, on the Arno and 18 mi. E of Pisa; shoe factories, alcohol distillery.

San Roque (sän rō'kä), town (pop. 2,501), ⊙ San Roque dept. (□ c.1,000; pop. 16,736), W Corrientes prov., Argentina, on railroad and 60 mi. NW of Mercedes; agr. center (cotton, rice, tobacco, corn, livestock).

San Roque, town (pop. 2,373); Antioquia dept., N central Colombia, on E slopes of Cordillera Central, 40 mi. NE of Medellín; alt. 4,826 ft. Lumbering, gold mining, stock raising; agr. products: sugar cane, coffee, rice, yucca, corn.

San Roque, Philippines: see CAVITE, city.

San Roque. 1 S suburb (pop. 6,422) of Badajoz, Badajoz prov., W Spain. **2** City (pop. 5,932), Cádiz prov., SW Spain, in Andalusia, near Algeciras Bay, 5 mi. NNW of Gibraltar and 55 mi. ESE of Cádiz; cork and cereals; also fruit, vegetables, livestock: liquor. A strategically placed modern city at foot of S spur of the Cordillera Penibética. It was resettled (1704) on site of anc. city by Sp. refugees from Gibraltar.

San Roque, Lake, artificial lake (5 mi. long) in NW central Córdoba prov., Argentina, 16 mi. W of Córdoba, in the Sierra Chica; formed by damming the headstreams of the Río Primero, which drains it. The dam, built 1866, was long the largest of its kind in South America; it supplies hydroelectric power and irrigates the agr. area near Córdoba. Yachting and fishing resort.

San Rosendo (sän rōsĕn'dō), town (pop. 3,315), Concepción prov., S central Chile, on Bío-Bío R. at mouth of Laja R., and 37 mi. SE of Concepción; rail junction in agr. area (cereals, vegetables, potatoes, livestock); flour milling.

Sanroshin, Korea see SAMNANGJIN.

Sansa, Formosa: see SANCHA.

San Saba (săn sä'bŭ, să'bŭ), county (□ 1,122; pop. 8,666), central Texas; ⊙ San Saba. On NE Edwards Plateau; bounded N and E by Colorado R., with part of L. Buchanan in SE; drained by San Saba R. and Brady Creek. Ranching, agr.: cattle, sheep, goats (wool, mohair shipped), poultry; pecans, peanuts, grain sorghums, corn, oats, fruit, truck, barley, some cotton. Hunting, fishing. Formed 1856.

San Saba, town (pop. 3,400), ⊙ San Saba co., central Texas, on Edwards Plateau c.40 mi. SE of Brownwood and on San Saba R.; market, trade, shipping center for livestock, agr. area; ships pecans, melons, sheep, wool, cattle, mohair, turkeys. Tourist trade; hunting, fishing near by. Settled c.1846.

San Saba River, W central Texas, rises on Edwards Plateau W of Menard, flows c.110 mi. generally ENE to the Colorado 8 mi. NE of San Saba.

San Salvador (săn″ săl'vŭdôr, Sp. sän sälvä-dhôr'), town (pop. estimate 3,000), E Entre Ríos prov., Argentina, 32 mi. SW of Concordia; rail junction and agr. center (rice, wheat, oats, flax, peanuts, livestock, poultry). Surrounded by agr. settlements.

San Salvador. 1 Town (pop. 366), Hidalgo, central Mexico, 23 mi. NW of Pachuca; corn, maguey, livestock. **2** Town, Zacatecas, Mexico: see EL SALVADOR.

San Salvador, village, Concepción dept., N central Paraguay, on Paraguay R. and 50 mi. NW of Concepción, in livestock and lumber area; meat-packing plant.

San Salvador, dept. (□ 790; 1950 pop. 299,250), central Salvador; ⊙ San Salvador. Bounded N by Lempa R.; reaches S nearly to the Pacific; crossed E-W by coastal range. Contains E slopes of volcano San Salvador and W part of L. Ilopango. Agr. (coffee, sugar cane, grain), livestock and poultry raising. Mfg. concentrated at San Salvador and suburbs, center of rail and road network. Formed 1859.

San Salvador, city (1950 pop. 160,380), ⊙ Salvador and San Salvador dept., at foot of volcano San Salvador, on Inter-American Highway and railroad, 110 mi. SE of Guatemala city; alt. 2,238 ft.; 13°42'N 89°13'W. Major commercial and mfg. center, connected by road with its port of La Libertad and by rail with ports of La Unión, Acajutla, and Puerto Barrios, Caribbean port of Guatemala. Rail stations are in NE part of city and airport at Ilopango (5 mi. E). Mfg. of cotton and silk textiles, coffee bags, sweets, cigarettes, cigars, flour, alcohol, soap and candles; woodworking, distilling, meat packing. Laid out in rectangular fashion, San Salvador centers on Parque Barrios, site of Natl. Palace (W), cathedral (N; destroyed by fire 1951) and Natl. Univ., (NW). Adjoining (E) is Parque Dueñas with statue to Liberty and (N) Parque Morazán with Natl. Theater and treasury. San Salvador is site of natl. library, academy of sciences and fine arts, astronomical observatory, has natl. stadium (built in 1930s; SW) and parade ground of Campo de Marte (NW) with race track. Founded 1525 at present site, the original settlement was temporarily transferred (1528–39) to La Bermuda (S of Suchitoto), and was made city in 1546. Was ⊙ Central American Union (1831–39) and ⊙ Salvador since 1840. Has suffered considerably from earthquakes (latest in 1917) and from floods (last in 1934). Its principal suburbs are Mejicanos (N), Soyapango (E), and Villa Delgado (NE).

San Salvador, dormant volcano (6,400 ft.), La Libertad dept., W central Salvador, 7 mi. WNW of San Salvador (linked by road). Its crater (5 mi. in circumference), filled by lake prior to 1917 earthquake), and with secondary cone (E), has been made a natl. park. Quezaltepeque is at N, Nueva San Salvador at S foot.

San Salvador, Cuchilla (kōōchē'yä sän sälvä-dhôr'), hill range on Soriano-Colonia dept. border, SW Uruguay, continuation of the Cuchilla Grande Inferior, extends from Cardona 40 mi. W to area of Nueva Palmira; rises to 590 ft.

San Salvador de Breda, Spain: see BREDA.

San Salvador el Seco, Mexico: see EL SECO.

San Salvador el Verde, Mexico: see EL VERDE, Puebla.

San Salvador Island (săn″ săl'vŭdôr), **Watling Island** (wŏt'lĭng), or **Watlings Island,** island (13 mi. long, c.5 mi. wide) and district (□ 60; pop. 693), central Bahama Isls., ESE of Cat Isl. and NNE of Rum Cay, 200 mi. ESE of Nassau; 24°N 74°30'W. On this isl. (which the native Indians called Guanahani), Columbus made his 1st landfall in the New World, on Oct. 12, 1492. It was long thought that the San Salvador of Columbus was CAT ISLAND, to NW.

San Salvador Island, Galápagos: see SANTIAGO ISLAND.

San Salvador River (sän sälvä-dhôr'), Soriano dept., SW Uruguay, rises at junction of the *cuchillas* of Bizcocho and San Salvador NW of Cardona, flows 83 mi. WNW, past Dolores, to the Uruguay 6 mi. SW of Soriano. Navigable to Dolores.

San Salvatore Monferrato (sän sälvätô'rĕ mônfĕrrä'tô), village (pop. 2,832), Alessandria prov., Piedmont, N Italy, 6 mi. NNW of Alessandria.

San Salvatore Telesino (tĕlĕzē'nô), village (pop. 1,892), Benevento prov., Campania, S Italy, 14 mi. NE of Caserta; wine making.

Sansanding (sänsändĭng'), village, S Fr. Sudan, Fr. West Africa, on left bank of the Niger and 150 mi. ENE of Bamako. Large irrigation dam (completed 1946) across Niger here. Cotton, rice.

Sansané-Haoussa (sänsä'nā-hou'sä), village, SW Niger territory, Fr. West Africa, on the Niger and 40 mi. NW of Niamey; millet, peanuts; livestock.

Sansang (säng-säng'), village, Cabo Gracias a Dios territory, Zelaya dept., N Nicaragua, on Coco R. (at end of its middle-course rapids) and 100 mi. WSW of Cabo Gracias a Dios; gold deposits. Head of navigation on lower Coco R. Sometimes spelled Sang Sang.

Sansanné-Mango (sänsä'nā-mäng'gō) or **Mango,** town, N Fr. Togoland, on Oti R. and 100 mi. NNW of Sokodé, on intercolonial route; peanuts, kapok; shea nuts and butter; livestock raising.

Sansapor, Cape (săn'sŭpôr", sŭnsŭpôr'), on Vogelkop peninsula, NW New Guinea; 0°28'S 132°6'E. In Second World War U.S. troops landed here July, 1944.

Sansare (sänsä'rā), town (1950 pop. 1,123), El Progreso dept., E central Guatemala, in highlands, 7 mi. SSW of El Progreso; corn, beans, sugar cane, livestock.

San Saturnino de Noya (sän sätōōrnē'nō dā noi'ä), Catalan *Sant Sadurní de Noya* (sänt sä-dhōōrnē' dā noi'ä), town (pop. 3,428), Barcelona prov., NE Spain, 7 mi. NE of Villafranca del Panadés; wine-production center (especially champagne); mfg. of paper, hemp rope; cotton spinning, meat processing, flour- and sawmilling.

San Sebastián, department, Argentina: see RÍO GRANDE.

San Sebastián (sän sävästyän'), village, NE Tierra del Fuego natl. territory, Argentina, on San Sebastián Bay (inlet of the Atlantic), 45 mi. NW of Río Grande; sheep raising and gold washing.

San Sebastián or **San Sebastián de la Gomera** (dā lä gomä'rä), town (pop. 2,856), chief port and town of Gomera, Canary Isls., 60 mi. SW of Santa Cruz de Tenerife; 28°6'N 17°5'W. Exports bananas, tomatoes, potatoes. Fishing; flour milling, wine making, meat packing. Columbus landed (1492) here on his 1st voyage.

San Sebastián, town (1950 pop. 2,438), Retalhuleu dept., SW Guatemala, in Pacific piedmont, on railroad and 2 mi. NE of Retalhuleu; coffee, sugar cane, grain, cacao; livestock; lumbering.

San Sebastián, town (pop. 632), Lempira dept., W Honduras, on E slopes of Sierra de Celaque, 15 mi. SW of Gracias; coffee, wheat.

San Sebastián. 1 Town (pop. 1,272), Hidalgo, central Mexico, on railroad and 22 mi. ESE of San Juan del Río; corn, beans, maguey, livestock. **2** Town (pop. 706), Jalisco, W Mexico, in coastal foothills, 22 mi. NNW of Mascota; sugar cane, cotton, tobacco, fruit, chili. **3** Town, Jalisco, Mexico, near Guzmán: see GÓMEZ FARÍAS. **4** Town (pop. 1,851), Mexico state, central Mexico, 35 mi. NW of Mexico city; grain, maguey, fruit, livestock.

San Sebastián, town (pop. 1,987), Cuzco dept., S central Peru, in high Andean valley, on railroad and 3 mi. ESE of Cuzco; corn, fruit, stock. Mineral springs.

San Sebastián, town (pop. 5,206), W Puerto Rico, on Culebrinas R. and 13 mi. NE of Mayagüez; coffee center; mfg. of cigars, raw sugar, fruit products.

San Sebastián. 1 Village (pop. estimate 1,200), La Unión dept., E Salvador, on branch of Inter-American Highway and 3 mi. W of Santa Rosa; gold and silver mining. **2** City (pop. 3,784), San Vicente dept., central Salvador, 7 mi. NNW of San Vicente; cotton-milling center; sugar milling, indigo processing.

San Sebastián, city (pop. 89,276), ⊙ Guipúzcoa prov., N Spain, in the Basque Provs., port on Bay of Biscay at mouth of Urumea R., 220 mi. NNE of Madrid, and 10 mi. from the Fr. line; 43°20'N 1°59'W. Picturesquely situated on peninsula (terminating in rocky Mt. Urgull, crowned by castle) and extending W along beautiful Concha Bay, it is the most fashionable sea-bathing resort in Spain, formerly the summer residence of the royal family. Industries include metalworking (motors), boatbuilding, rubber processing; mfg. of electrical equipment (phonographs, records), chemicals (pharmaceuticals, perfumes, printing inks), cement, glass, tiles, knitwear, flour products; brewery, tobacco factory. Constitution square was scene of famous bullfights. Alameda avenue (crossing the peninsula) separates the old from new town. SW from the fine Casino there are parks and promenades with fine villas, and resorts lining Concha Bay beach to Miramar palace (19th cent.), former royal residence. City was burned (1813) by English and Portuguese; played important role in Carlist Wars (19th cent.).

San Sebastián, town (pop. 1,770), Aragua state, N Venezuela, 45 mi. SSW of Caracas; coffee, cacao, corn, sugar cane. Shrine to the Virgin of Charity.

San Sebastián Bay, inlet of the South Atlantic in NE Tierra del Fuego natl. territory, Argentina, bet. Punta de Arenas (N) and Cape San Sebastián (S); c.18 mi. N-S, 13 mi. W-E. Small settlement of San Sebastián is on its W shore.

San Sebastián de la Gomera, Canary Isls.: see SAN SEBASTIÁN.

San Sebastián de los Ballesteros (dā lōs bälyĕstā'rōs), town (pop. 1,466), Córdoba prov., S Spain, 17 mi. SSW of Córdoba; olive-oil processing, soap mfg.; cereals, livestock.

San Sebastián de los Reyes (rā'ĕs), village (pop. 1,315), Madrid prov., central Spain, 9 mi. N of Madrid; grain, wine.

San Sebastián de Yalí, Nicaragua: see YALÍ.

San Sebastiano al Vesuvio (sän sĕbästyä'nō äl vĕzōō'vyō), town (pop. 1,652), Napoli prov., Campania, S Italy, on NW slope of Vesuvius, 5 mi. E of Naples. Destroyed by eruption in 1944.

San Secondo Parmense (sän sĕkôn'dô pärmĕn'sĕ), town (pop. 1,911), Parma prov., Emilia-Romagna, N central Italy, near Taro R., 10 mi. NNW of Parma; canned tomatoes.

Sansenho, Korea: see SAMCHONPO.

Sansepolcro (both: sän″sĕpôl'krô) or **San Sepolcro,** town (pop. 6,006), Arezzo prov., Tuscany, central Italy, near the Tiber, 15 mi. ENE of Arezzo; macaroni, liquor, pottery; woodworking. Has cathedral (12th–14th cent., remodeled), and town hall with picture gall. containing works by Luca Signorelli and Piero della Francesca (*Resurrection*), who was b. here. Formerly also called Borgo San Sepolcro.

San Severino Marche (sän sĕvĕrē'nô mär'kĕ), town (pop. 3,975), Macerata prov., The Marches, central Italy, on Potenza R. and 15 mi. WSW of Macerata; cement works, foundry, caustic-soda factory. Bishopric. Has 13th-cent. cathedral with a Madonna by Pinturicchio.

San Severino Rota, Italy: see MERCATO SAN SEVERINO.

San Severo (sän sĕvā'rô), town (pop. 37,159), Foggia prov., Apulia, S Italy, 18 mi. NNW of Foggia. Rail junction; wine, liquor, olive oil, macaroni; mfg. stearine, leather goods, bicycles, cement). Bishopric.

Sansha Bay, China: see SAMSA BAY.

Sanshui. 1 Town, Kwangtung prov., China: see SAMSHUI. **2** Town, Shensi prov., China: see SÜNYI.

Sansia or **San-hsia** (both: sän'shyä'), Jap. *Sankyo* (säng'kyō), village (1935 pop. 1,900), N Formosa, 7 mi. SW of Taipei; coal mining.

San Silvestre de Guzmán (sän sĕlvĕ'strā dā gōōthmän'), town (pop. 1,021), Huelva prov., SW Spain, 24 mi. WNW of Huelva; cereals, honey, acorns, livestock.

San Simeon (săn sĭ'mēŭn), village, San Luis Obispo co., SW Calif., on Pacific Ocean, 30 mi. W of Paso Robles. William Randolph Hearst estate here.

San Simon (sän sēmōn'), town (1939 pop. 1,628; 1948 municipality pop. 9,607), Pampanga prov., central Luzon, Philippines, on Pampanga R. and 6 mi. ESE of San Fernando; agr. (sugar cane, rice), fishing.

San Simon Creek (săn sĭmōn'), SW N.Mex. and SE Ariz., intermittent stream rising in SW N.Mex. and flowing c.80 mi. NW to Gila R. at Solomonsville.

San Simón de Guerrero (sän sēmōn' dā gĕrā'rō), town (pop. 1,696), Mexico state, central Mexico, 33 mi. SW of Toluca; sugar cane, coffee, fruit, stock.

Sansing, Manchuria: see ILAN.

Sanski Most (sän'skē môst), village (pop. 3,427), NW Bosnia, Yugoslavia, on Sana R., on railroad and 26 mi. W of Banja Luka; sulphur springs. Prehistoric relics here. Coal deposits in vicinity.

Sansom Park Village, town (pop. 1,611), Tarrant co., N Texas. Inc. since 1940.

Sanson (săn'sŭn), township (pop. 313), ⊙ Manawatu co. (□ 265; pop. 6,245), S N.Isl., New Zealand, 75 mi. NNE of Wellington; agr. center.

San Sperate (sän spĕrä'tē) or **Santo Sperato** (sän'tô spĕrä'tô), village (pop. 2,861), Cagliari prov., S Sardinia, 11 mi. NNW of Cagliari, in orange- and herb-growing area.

Sans Souci (săn sōō'sē). **1** Town, Mich.: see HARSENS ISLAND. **2** Residential village (pop. 9,337, with adjacent Union Bleachery village), Greenville co., NW S.C., a suburb of Greenville.

San Stefano (săn stĕ'fŭnō, sän stā'fänō), Turkish *Yeşilköy* (yĕ-shĭlkû'ē), village (pop. 6,448), Istanbul prov., Turkey in Europe, on Sea of Marmara, 8 mi. WSW of Istanbul. Treaty bet. Russia and Turkey signed here March 3, 1878. Airport.

Sans Toucher, Mont (mõ sä tōōshā'), dormant volcano (4,855 ft.), Guadeloupe, Fr. West Indies, 7 mi. NNE of Basse-Terre city, just N of the Soufrière.

Sansui (sän'swā'), town (pop. 4,337), ⊙ Sansui co. (pop. 67,435), E Kweichow prov., China, 14 mi. SE of Chenyüan, near Hunan line; embroideries; tobacco, rice, millet. Until 1913 called Angshui; and 1926–31, Lingshan.

Sant, India: see SUNTH.

Santa (sän'tä), village (pop. 1,134), Br. Cameroons, administered as part of Eastern Provinces of Nigeria, 7 mi. S of Bamenda, in Bamenda hills; customs station on Fr. Cameroons border; durra, millet, stock raising.

Santa, province, Peru: see CHIMBOTE.

Santa (sän'tä), town (pop. 1,089), Ancash dept., W central Peru, on coastal plain, near mouth of Santa R., on Pan American Highway and 65 mi. SSE of Trujillo, in sugar- and cotton-producing area. Salt mining near by.

Santa, El, Es Santa, or **Al-Santah** (all: ĕs-săn'tŭ), village (pop. 4,054), Gharbiya prov., Lower Egypt, on Bahr Shibin, on railroad, and 8 mi. ESE of Tanta; cotton.

Santa Adélia (sätädĕl'yŭ), city (pop. 2,232), N central São Paulo, Brazil, on railroad and 12 mi. SE of Catanduva; mfg. of macaroni, soap, furniture; coffee, sugar.

Santa Águeda, Spain: see MONDRAGÓN.

Santa Amalia (sän'tä ämä'lyä), town (pop. 3,511), Badajoz prov., W Spain, 19 mi. ENE of Mérida; agr. center (cereals, olives, honey, grapes, livestock); flour- and sawmilling.

Santa Ana (sän'tä ä'nä). **1** Town (pop. 500), E Jujuy prov., Argentina, 55 mi. NNE of Jujuy; stock-raising center (sheep, cattle). **2** Town (pop. estimate 1,500), S Misiones natl. territory, Argentina, 20 mi. E of Posadas, in agr. area (maté, citrus fruit, corn, peanuts); corn milling, maté processing. **3** Town (pop. estimate 500), SW Tucumán prov., Argentina, 55 mi. SSW of Tucumán; rail junction and agr. center (sugar cane, alfalfa, livestock); sugar refining. Meteorological station.

Santa Ana. 1 Town (pop. c.5,700), ⊙ Yacuma prov., Beni dept., N Bolivia, port on Yacuma R. and c.90 mi. NW of Trinidad, in the llanos; cattle. Airport. **2** Village, La Paz dept., W Bolivia, on Beni R., opposite Suapi, and 60 mi. N of Chulumani; quina. Site of mission. **3** Town (pop. c.1,100), Santa Cruz dept., E Bolivia, 25 mi. SE of San Ignacio; cattle. **4** Town (pop. 1,900), Tarija dept., S Bolivia, 7 mi. E of Tarija; road center; vineyards; fruit, grain, livestock.

Santa Ana, town (pop. 2,407), Magdalena dept., N Colombia, on the Brazo Seco de Mompós (a right arm of the Magdalena) and 11 mi. NW of Mompós; yucca, tobacco, cattle, tagua.

Santa Ana, town (pop. 361), San José prov., central Costa Rica, on central plateau, 7 mi. W of San José; summer resort; agr. (sugar cane, onions, beans, rice); mfg. of brooms. Salitral mineral springs, S.

Santa Ana, town (pop. 420), Matanzas prov., W Cuba, 8 mi. S of Matanzas; sugar cane, livestock.

Santa Ana, town (1950 pop. 3,976), Manabí prov., W Ecuador, in lowlands, on Portoviejo R. and 12 mi. S of Portoviejo; rail terminus of line to Manta, 27 mi. NW, on the Pacific. Mfg. of Panama hats. The fertile region produces cacao, coffee, rice, sugar cane, cotton, tagua nuts.

Santa Ana. 1 Officially Santa Ana Tlacotenco, town (pop. 1,895), Federal Dist., central Mexico, 19 mi. SE of Mexico city; cereals, fruit, livestock. **2** Officially Santa Ana Hueytlalpan, town (pop.1 ,632), Hidalgo, central Mexico, 28 mi. ENE of Pachuca; maguey, corn, livestock. **3** or **Santa Ana Tlapaltitlán** (tläpältētlän'), town (pop. 3,312), Mexico state, central Mexico, on railroad and 2 mi. SE of Toluca; agr. center (cereals, livestock); dairying. **4.** Town, Michoacán, Mexico: see ISAAC ARRIAGA. **5** City (pop. 3,057), Sonora, NW Mexico, on Magdalena R. (irrigation), on railroad and 55 mi. SSW of Nogales; agr. center (wheat, corn, cotton, fruit, livestock).

Santa Ana, Peru: see QUILLABAMBA.

Santa Ana, dept. (□ 1,374; 1950 pop. 202,131), W Salvador; ⊙ Santa Ana. Bounded W and N by Guatemala, N by Honduras, E by Lempa R.; hilly on N border and in S (Santa Ana volcano); slopes E to Lempa R. valley. Contains lakes Güija and Coatepeque. Mainly agr. (coffee, sugar cane, grain), livestock raising. Iron and copper mines, limestone quarries near Metapán. Inter-American Highway and rail lines join at Santa Ana. Other centers: Chalchuapa, Coatepeque, Metapán. Formed 1855.

Santa Ana, city (1950 pop. 51,676), ⊙ Santa Ana dept., W Salvador, on Inter-American Highway and 32 mi. NW of San Salvador; alt. 2,123 ft.; 13°59'N 89°34'W. Second largest city of Salvador; major coffee center in rich agr. area (sugar, grain); rail junction (Santa Lucía and Occidente stations); coffee processing, sugar milling, brewing, mfg. of cotton textiles, footwear, furniture. Has Sp. Gothic cathedral and El Calvario church. Noteworthy buildings: city hall, natl. theater, art school, garrisoned fortress. Known as Santa Ana since 1708. Became ⊙ dept. in 1855.

Santa Ana, highest volcano (7,825 ft.) of Salvador, in Santa Ana dept., 10 mi. SSW of Santa Ana. L. Coatepeque is at E foot.

Santa Ana (săn'tŭ ă'nŭ), city (pop. 45,533), ⊙ Orange co., S Calif., at base of Santa Ana Mts., on Santa Ana R. and 15 mi. E of Long Beach; cans, packs, processes, and ships agr. products (citrus and deciduous fruit, sugar beets, peppers, pimentos, nuts). Oil fields near by. Seat of a jr. col. Founded 1869, inc. 1886.

Santa Ana, pueblo (□ 29.9), Sandoval co., central N.Mex. Santa Ana village (1948 pop. 294) is on Jemez Creek and 24 mi. N of Albuquerque; alt. c.5,300 ft. Agr. is chief means of livelihood. Church of Santa Ana de Alamillo dates from 1692.

Santa Ana (sän'tä ä'nä). **1** Town (pop. 674), Anzoátegui state, NE Venezuela, 15 mi. SE of Aragua de Barcelona; cotton, sugar cane, cattle. Oil wells near by. **2** Town (pop. 1,301), on Margarita Isl., Nueva Esparta state, NE Venezuela, 5 mi. NW of La Asunción; sugar cane, cotton, corn, yucca, tropical fruit. **3** Town (pop. 1,850), Táchira state, W Venezuela, in Andean spur, on highway and 9 mi. SSW of San Cristóbal; coffee, grain, cattle. **4** Town (pop. 1,120), Trujillo state, W Venezuela, in Andean spur, 13 mi. NE of Trujillo, in agr. region (coffee, wheat, corn, potatoes); alt. 5,252 ft. Meeting here (Dec. 27,1820) of Bolívar with Sp. general Morillo is commemorated by a monument.

Santa Ana, Cuchilla de (kōōchē'yä dā sän'tä ä'nä), Port. *Coxilha de Santana* (kōōshē'lyŭ dĭ sãntä'nŭ), hill range on Uruguay-Brazil border, extending c.75 mi. SE from Rivera (Uruguay) and Livramento (Brazil); rises to 1,000 ft. A NW extension entirely in Rio Grande do Sul (Brazil) parallels the border for c.100 mi. to Uruguay R.

Santa Ana Chiautempan, Mexico: see CHIAUTEMPAN.

Santa Ana de Pusa (sän'tä ä'nä dā pōō'sä), village (pop. 1,250), Toledo prov., central Spain, 16 mi. SSE of Talavera de la Reina; olives, cereals, forage, hogs, sheep; olive-oil extracting, flour milling.

Santa Ana do Livramento, Brazil: see LIVRAMENTO, Rio Grande do Sul.

Santa Ana Island (săntä'nŭ), in the Atlantic near coast of Maranhão, NE Brazil, at NE end of São José Bay, 50 mi. NE of São Luís. Lighthouse.

Santa Ana la Real (sän'tä ä'nä lä rääl'), town (pop. 566), Huelva prov., SW Spain, in the Sierra Morena, 9 mi. W of Aracena; fruit, cork, olives, chestnuts, livestock; timber.

Santa Ana Maya (mī'ä), town (pop. 2,608), Michoacán, central Mexico, on N shore of L. Cuitzeo, 23 mi. NNE of Morelia; cereals, fruit, stock; fishing.

Santa Ana Mixtán (mēstän'), town (pop. 396), Escuintla dept., S Guatemala, in coastal plain, on Coyolate R. and 37 mi. SW of Escuintla; livestock raising.

Santa Ana Mountains (săn'tŭ ă'nŭ), S Calif., range running c.25 mi. SW from Santa Ana R., along Orange-Riverside co. line. Santiago Peak (säntēä'gō) (5,696 ft.), 20 mi. E of Santa Ana, is highest point.

Santa Ana Nextlalpan, Mexico: see NEXTLALPAN.

Santa Ana River, SW Calif., intermittent stream rising in San Bernardino Mts. E of San Bernardino, flows c.90 mi. generally SW, past Riverside and Santa Ana, to the Pacific just NW of Newport Beach. Prado Dam (prā'dō), an earth-fill flood-control dam (106 ft. high, 2,280 ft. long), was completed 1941 near Corona.

Santa Ana Tepetitlán (täpätētlän'), town (pop. 1,822), Jalisco, central Mexico, 12 mi. WSW of Guadalajara; grain, fruit, vegetables, sugar cane, stock.

Santa Ana Tlapaltitlán, Mexico: see SANTA ANA, Mexico state.

Santa Anita (sän'tä änē'tä), town (pop. estimate 1,000), E central Entre Ríos prov., Argentina, 40 mi. NW of Concepción del Uruguay; agr. center (wheat, flax, sunflowers, livestock).

Santa Anita. 1 Town (pop. 1,841), Federal Dist., central Mexico, SE suburb of Mexico city; cereals, livestock. **2** Town (pop. 2,522), Jalisco, central Mexico, 12 mi. SW of Guadalajara; corn, wheat, beans, peanuts, sugar cane.

Santa Anita, Calif.: see ARCADIA.

Santa Anna (săn'tŭ ă'nŭ), town (pop. 1,605), Coleman co., central Texas, at foot of Santa Anna Mtn. (2,000 ft.), 19 mi. W of Brownwood; farm market, processing point; glass mfg. (silica pits here). Small lakes (fishing) to NE.

Santa Anna Bay, Curaçao, Du. West Indies: see SINT ANNA BAY.

Santa Anna do Livramento, Brazil: see LIVRAMENTO, Rio Grande do Sul.

Santa Anna Mountain, Texas: see SANTA ANNA.

Santa Apolonia (sän'tä äpōlō'nyä), town (1950 pop. 406), Chimaltenango dept., S central Guatemala, on branch of Inter-American Highway and 3 mi. NE of Tecpán; alt. 7,280 ft.; corn, wheat, black beans.

Santa Bárbara, department, Argentina: see SANTA CLARA, Jujuy prov.

Santa Barbara (sän'tŭ bär'bŭrŭ). **1** City (pop. 2,738), S central Minas Gerais, Brazil, in the Serra do Espinhaço, on railroad and 35 mi. E of Belo Horizonte; marble and lignite deposits. Steel mill at BARÃO DE COCAIS (formerly Morro Grande), 6 mi. WNW. **2** City, São Paulo, Brazil: see SANTA BÁRBARA D' OESTE.

Santa Bárbara (sän'tä bär'bärä), town (pop. 2,292), Bío-Bío prov., S central Chile, on Bío-Bío R. and 23 mi. SE of Los Angeles; agr. center (wheat, rye, wine). Silver, gold, and copper deposits near by.

Santa Bárbara, town (pop. 3,120), Antioquia dept., NW central Colombia, in Cauca valley, 27 mi. S of Medellín; alt. 6,027 ft. Agr. center (corn, sugar cane, yucca, potatoes, rice, oranges, tropical fruit, cattle). Iron ores are mined near by and shipped to Medellín.

Santa Bárbara, town (1950 pop. 875), Heredia prov., central Costa Rica, on central plateau, 4 mi. NW of Heredia; coffee, sugar cane, grain.

Santa Barbara (săn'tŭ bär'brŭ, -bŭrŭ), village, S Curaçao, Du. West Indies, 6 mi. E of Willemstad; phosphate deposits. Linked by cableway with New Port on coast, whence phosphates are shipped.

Santa Bárbara (sän'tä bär'bärä), town (1950 pop. 470), Suchitepéquez dept., SW Guatemala, in Pacific piedmont, 20 mi. ESE of Mazatenango; coffee, sugar cane, grain; livestock; lumbering.

Santa Bárbara, department (□ 2,864; 1950 pop. 106,036), W Honduras, on Guatemala border; ⊙ Santa Bárbara. Largely mountainous; includes sierras de la Grita, de Colinas, and de Atima; drained by Chamelecón, Jicatuyo, and Ulúa rivers. Includes W shore of L. Yojoa. Largely agr.: coffee (Colinas, Trinidad, Naranjito), sugar cane, tobacco, corn, and beans; livestock (Quimistán); lumbering. Chief industry is mfg. of harvest and palm hats; mat weaving, ropemaking. Main centers (oriented toward San Pedro Sula): Santa Bárbara, Naranjito, Colinas, Trinidad. Formed 1825.

Santa Bárbara, city (pop. 2,684), ⊙ Santa Barbara dept., W Honduras, near Ulúa R., on road and 45 mi. SSW of San Pedro Sula; 14°52'N 88°17'W. Commercial center in agr. area; mfg. of harvest and palm hats; livestock raising, sugar cane. Has col., airfield. Founded 1761 by settlers from Gracias.

Santa Bárbara, city (pop. 13,902), Chihuahua, N Mexico, in E outliers of Sierra Madre Occidental, 13 mi. SW of Hidalgo del Parral; alt. 6,348 ft. Silver, gold, copper, lead, and zinc mining. Rich mineral deposits known since early colonial days.

Santa Barbara (săn'tŭ bär'bŭrŭ, Sp. sän'tä bär'bärä). **1** Town (1939 pop. 4,335; 1948 municipality pop. 21,951), Iloilo prov., SE Panay isl., Philippines, 9 mi. NNW of Iloilo; rice-growing center. **2** Town (1939 pop. 1,080; 1948 municipality pop. 19,570), Pangasinan prov., central Luzon, Philippines, 6 mi. SE of Dagupan, near Lingayen Gulf; agr. center (rice, copra, corn).

Santa Bárbara (sän'tä bär'bärä), town (pop. 3,842), Tarragona prov., NE Spain, 7 mi. S of Tortosa; olive-oil processing, mfg. of soap and lye; livestock, cereals, wine, fruit.

Santa Barbara (săn'tŭ bär'brŭ, -bŭrŭ), county (□ 2,745; pop. 98,220), SW Calif.; ⊙ Santa Barbara. On coast (here trending E-W) along Santa Barbara Channel; includes several of SANTA BARBARA ISLANDS. Point Conception and Point Arguello are W. From coastal plain (agr.) rise the Santa Ynez Mts. (c.2–4,000 ft.) and San Rafael Mts. (over 6,500 ft.). Drained by intermittent Cuyama, Sisquoc, Santa Maria, and Santa Ynez rivers. Includes part of Los Padres Natl. Forest; U.S. Camp Cooke; Santa Ynez, La Purisima Concepcion, and Santa Barbara missions. Diversified agr.; LOMPOC is seed-growing center; also sugar beets, truck, citrus and deciduous fruit, nuts, beans, alfalfa; beef-cattle grazing, some dairying. Site of proposed reclamation project using waters of Santa Ynez R. Oil and natural-gas fields (Santa Maria and Summerland dists.); diatomite mining (a leading co. in Calif.); asphalt, clay also produced. Formed 1850.

Santa Barbara, residential and resort city (pop. 44,913), ⊙ Santa Barbara co., SW Calif., on Santa Barbara Channel, at base of Santa Ynez Mts., c.85 mi. WNW of Los Angeles; a beautiful city, known for its Mediterranean setting, mild climate (average July temp. 66°F.; Jan. average, 53°F.), and the subtropical luxuriance of its flowers and fruit. Region produces cattle, citrus fruit, field crops, petroleum. An old city, founded 1782 and inc. 1850. Santa Barbara Mission, established 1786 (present bldg. completed 1820) is Western hq. for Franciscan order. Many bldgs. (including noted co. courthouse) in Spanish architectural style. Seat of a branch (formerly Santa Barbara Col.) of Univ. of Calif., a jr. col., an art mus., and a mus. of natural history. Has fine beach, pier (fishing), yacht and fishing-boat harbor. Annual 3-day fiesta celebrates city's history.

Santa Bárbara (sän'tä bär'bärä). **1** Town (pop. 743), Barinas state, W Venezuela, in Andean foothills, 55 mi. SW of Barinas; livestock. Airfield. **2** Town (pop. 1,383), Monagas state, NE Venezuela, 30 mi. WSW of Maturín; petroleum wells, linked by pipe line with Puerto La Cruz. Airfield. Lignite deposits near by. **3** Village, Zulia state, NW Venezuela, in Maracaibo lowlands, on Escalante R. and just SE of San Carlos; rail terminus; milk-drying plant.

Santa Bârbara, Sierra de (syĕ'rä dä sän'tä bär'bärä), subandean mountain range in SE Jujuy prov., Argentina, E of Santa Clara; extends c.45 mi. N–S; rises to c.5,000 ft. Covered by subtropical forests.

Santa Barbara Channel, strait (c.20–30 mi. wide, c.70 mi. long) bet. coast of S Calif. (here trending almost E-W) and Santa Barbara Isls.; U.S. navy speed-testing course; popular for yachting, fishing.

Santa Bârbara de Casa (dä kä'sä), town (pop. 2,413), Huelva prov., SW Spain, in the Sierra Morena, 40 mi. NNW of Huelva; cereals, olives; grapes, cork, wax, wool, livestock.

Santa Bârbara de Samaná, Dominican Republic: see SAMANÁ, town.

Santa Bârbara d' Oeste (sän'tủ bär'bủrủ dwĕ'stĭ), city (pop. 3,247), E central São Paulo, Brazil, on railroad and 25 mi. WNW of Campinas; silk and cotton weaving, mfg. of agr. machinery, distilling, sugar milling. Until 1944, Santa Bárbara.

Santa Bârbara do Rio Pardo (dōō rē'ōō pär'dōō), city (pop. 532), W central São Paulo, Brazil, 40 mi. E of Ourinhos; tobacco, coffee, sugar, cattle.

Santa Barbara Islands (săn'tủ bär'brủ, –bủrủ), chain of 8 rugged islands and many islets, extending c.150 mi. along S Calif. coast from Point Conception (N) to San Diego (S). N group (Santa Barbara group) is separated from mainland by Santa Barbara Channel (c.20–30 mi. wide); includes San Miguel (săn mĭgĕl'), c.8 mi. long, reputed burial place (1543) of Cabrillo, its discoverer; Santa Rosa, 17 mi. long; Santa Cruz (săn'tủ krōōz'), 23 mi. long; and small Anacapa (ănủkă'pủ). S chain (Santa Catalina group), separated from coast by San Pedro Channel and Gulf of Santa Catalina, includes (W–E) San Nicolas (săn nĭ'kủlủs) or San Nicholas, c.9 mi. long, site of an airfield; Santa Barbara, c.1½ mi. long; SANTA CATALINA (Catalina), c.22 mi. long, noted resort and site of Avalon city. About 20 mi. S of Santa Catalina is San Clemente (săn klĭmĕn'tē), c.21 mi. long, with 2 military airfields. Channel Islands Natl. Monument (land only, c.1,120 acres; land and water, □ 41.9) was established in 1938 on Santa Barbara Isl. and Anacapa Isl.; sea-lion herds, notable bird and plant life; fossils of marine invertebrates and Pleistocene elephants have been found. Only Santa Cruz and Catalina are wooded; most of isls. support sheep ranches, and several have large sea caves. Name of Channel Isls. is sometimes applied to N group, sometimes to both groups, and sometimes includes Coronado Isls. (S) of Mexico.

Santa Branca (sän'tủ brăng'kủ), city (pop. 1,050), SE São Paulo, Brazil, on Paraíba R. and 45 mi. ENE of São Paulo; distilling; sugar, oranges, manioc, cotton.

Santa Brígida (sän'tä brē'hē-dhä), town (pop. 799, with suburbs 7,829), Grand Canary, Canary Isls., 7 mi. SW of Las Palmas; potatoes, cereals, chickpeas, tubers, tomatoes, beets, fruit, wine, honey, and livestock. Flour milling, wine making. Inland resort.

Santacara (säntäkä'rä), town (pop. 1,246), Navarre prov., N Spain, on Aragon R. and 14 mi. SE of Tafalla; cereals, wine, sugar beets.

Santa Catalina (sän'tä kätälē'nä). **1** Village (pop. estimate 500), W Córdoba prov., Argentina, at W foot of the Sierra Chica, 38 mi. N of Córdoba; tourist resort and stock-raising center. Has bldgs. of Jesuit mission founded 1622; cloisters and church were completed 1767. **2** Town (pop. estimate 300), ⊙ Santa Catalina dept. (□ 2,540; 1947 pop. 3,293), NW Jujuy prov., Argentina, near Bolivia border, at N foot of Sierra de Santa Catalina, 30 mi. WNW of La Quiaca; stock-raising center (sheep, llamas, donkeys).

Santa Catalina or **Santa Catalina Palopó** (pälōpō'), town (pop. 477), Sololá dept., SW central Guatemala, on N shore of L. Atitlán, 4.5 mi. SE of Sololá; alt. 5,184 ft.; reed-mat weaving; fishing, crabbing.

Santa Catalina, town (pop. 482), Loreto dept., E central Peru, near San Martín dept. border, 60 mi. NW of Contamana; bananas, yucca.

Santa Catalina (sän'tä kätälē'nä), town (pop. 700), Soriano dept., SW Uruguay, in the Cuchilla del Bizcocho, on railroad and 48 mi. SE of Mercedes; shipping point for agr. products (wheat, corn, oats), sheep, cattle.

Santa Catalina, town (pop. 213), Barinas state, W Venezuela, landing on Apure R. and 30 mi. ESE of Puerto de Nutrias, in stock-raising region.

Santa Catalina, Gulf of (săn'tủ kătủlē'nủ), S Calif., reach of the Pacific lying bet. San Clemente Isl. and the coast N of San Diego; communicates via San Pedro Channel with Santa Monica Bay to NW.

Santa Catalina, Sierra de (syĕ'rä dä sän'tä kätälē'nä), range in NW Jujuy prov., Argentina, W of Rinconada, near Bolivia line; extends c. 70 mi. NNE-SSW; rises to c.15,000 ft.

Santa Catalina Island (sän'tä kätälē'nä), islet in the Caribbean 145 mi. off Mosquito Coast of Nicaragua, just N of OLD PROVIDENCE ISLAND.

Santa Catalina Island (săn'tủ kătủlē'nủ) or **Catalina Island**, one of the Santa Barbara Isls., in Pacific Ocean off S Calif. coast, 24 mi. SSW of Los Angeles Harbor; part of Los Angeles co.; popular resort. Isl. (22 mi. long) is almost split by isthmus in NW, and rises to over 2,000 ft.; partly wooded, partly chaparral-covered. AVALON, on SE shore of Avalon Bay, is center of resort activities; steamer, air connections with Wilmington. Offshore sport fishing (including tuna, swordfish); seal herds, flying-fish schools, and submarine gardens are other attractions. Wild mtn. goats, hogs are hunted in interior. Isl. discovered in 1542 by Cabrillo, named by Vizcaíno in 1602; was mainly developed as resort after purchase (1919) by William Wrigley.

Santa Catalina Mountains, Pima co., SE Ariz., N of Tucson, in section of Coronado Natl. Forest; Mt. LEMMON (9,185 ft.) is highest point.

Santa Catalina Palopó, Guatemala: see SANTA CATALINA.

Santa Catarina (săn'tủ kủtủrē'nủ), coastal state (□ 36,435; 1940 pop. 1,178,340; 1950 census pop. 1,578,159), S Brazil; ⊙ Florianópolis. Bounded by Argentina (W); and by Paraná (N) and Rio Grande do Sul (S). Its long Atlantic coastline includes the offshore isls. of Santa Catarina and São Francisco. Just W of a narrow coastal lowland—which widens only W of Joinvile and Blumenau, and includes the fertile valley of Itajaí Açu R.—rises the great escarpment Serra do Mar, which here has several spurs, known collectively as Serra Geral, reaching inland. Central and W Santa Catarina is a rolling, sparsely settled tableland, dissected by tributaries of the Iguassú and Uruguay rivers, which form state's N and S borders, respectively. Climate is temperate, except along coast, where it is subtropical. Freezing temperatures are known in upland areas. The corn-hog economy predominates throughout state. Diversified agr. (cereals, potatoes, tobacco, European-type fruit and vegetables, manioc, rice), winegrowing, and dairying are practiced along modern methods by small farmers in settlements at foot of the Serra do Mar (especially in Itajaí Açu valley W of Blumenau). Bananas and rice are grown near coast. Coal mined at Araranguá, Criciúma, Urussanga, and Lauro Müller, is beneficiated at Tubarao, then taken to Laguna and Imbituba for shipment to Rio de Janeiro steel mill (Volta Redonda). Chief industries are textile milling, sawmilling, maté and meat processing, brewing, distilling. Chief cities are Florianópolis, Blumenau (which ships its agr. output through port of Itajaí), Joinvile and its port of São Francisco do Sul. First settled by pioneers from São Paulo in 1660s. In 19th cent. it was settled by numerous immigrants from Germany (who founded Blumenau in 1850), Italy, and E Europe, to whom state owes much of its agr. prosperity. Ger. culture remains in evidence in many areas, especially near Blumenau. Chapecó *municipio* (westernmost Santa Catarina) became part of Iguaçu territory in 1943, but was restored to the state of Santa Catarina in 1946. Formerly Santa Catharina.

Santa Catarina (sän'tä kätärē'nä). **1** or **Santa Catarina Pinula** (pēnōō'lä), town (1950 pop. 1,159), Guatemala dept., S central Guatemala, 5 mi. SSE of Guatemala; alt. 5,499 ft.; corn, livestock. Sometimes called Santa Catalina. **2** or **Santa Catarina Mita** (mē'tä), town (1950 pop. 2,324), Jutiapa dept., SE Guatemala, in highlands, on Ostúa R. (inlet of L. Güija) and 15 mi. NE of Jutiapa; corn, beans, livestock. **3** or **Santa Catarina Barahona** (bäräō'nä), town (1950 pop. 815), Sacatepéquez dept., S central Guatemala, at NE foot of volcano Acatenango, 5 mi. WSW of Antigua; alt. 4,741 ft.; coffee, sugar cane, grain. **4** or **Ixtahuacán** or **Santa Catarina Ixtahuacán** (ēkstäwäkän'), town (1950 pop. 776), Sololá dept., SW central Guatemala, on Nahualate R. and 9 mi. W of Sololá; corn, beans. Sometimes called Santa Catalina.

Santa Catarina. 1 Town (pop. 252), Guanajuato, central Mexico, 30 mi. ESE of San Luis de la Paz; alt. 6,116 ft.; tin mining. **2** Town (pop. 1,067), Nuevo León, N Mexico, in foothills of Sierra Madre Oriental, 10 mi. W of Monterrey; silver, lead, iron, copper, zinc mining.

Santa Catarina Barahona, Sacatepéquez dept., Guatemala: see SANTA CATARINA.

Santa Catarina Island (săn'tủ kủtủrē'nủ), in the Atlantic, just off S coast of Brazil, forming part of Santa Catarina state; 33 mi. long, up to 10 mi. wide. At FLORIANÓPOLIS (on W shore) it is linked with mainland by steel bridge. Rises to c.1,000 ft. in narrow central mtn. range. Sparsely settled outside of capital.

Santa Catarina Ixtahuacán, Sololá dept., Guatemala: see SANTA CATARINA.

Santa Catarina Mita, Guatemala: see SANTA CATARINA.

Santa Catarina Pinula, Guatemala dept., Guatemala: see SANTA CATARINA.

Santa Caterina Villarmosa (sän'tä kätĕrē'nä vēllärmô'zä), town (pop. 8,919), Caltanissetta prov., central Sicily, 7 mi. NNW of Caltanissetta. Sulphur and rock salt mines near by.

Santa Catharina, state, Brazil: see SANTA CATARINA.

Santa Cecília (săn'tủ sủsē'lyủ), village, SW Rio de Janeiro state, Brazil, on Paraíba R. (dam) and 2 mi. SW of Barra do Piraí. Water from Santa Cecília reservoir (1,158 ft.) is pumped via 2-mi. Santa Cecília tunnel and canal into SANTANA reservoir (1,191 ft.) as part of the Paraíba-Paraí diversion project.

Santa Cecilia, Mexico: see TLALNEPANTLA, Mexico state.

Santa Clara (sän'tä klä'rä). **1** Town (pop. estimate 300), ⊙ Santa Bárbara dept. (□ 1,880; 1947 census 6,823), SE Jujuy prov., Argentina, at W foot of the Sierra de Santa Bárbara, 40 mi. E of Jujuy; lumbering and stock-raising center; sawmilling, sugar refining. **2** Town, Santa Fe prov., Argentina: see SANTA CLARA DE BUENA VISTA.

Santa Clara, province, Cuba: see LAS VILLAS.

Santa Clara, city (pop. 53,981), ⊙ Las Villas prov., central Cuba, on interior elevated plain, on Central Highway and 160 mi. ESE of Havana; 22°24'N 79°57'W. One of Cuba's leading railroad and communications centers, important for its trade in sugar cane, tobacco, coffee, and cattle, and for its mining industry (asphalt, iron, manganese, copper, gold deposits). Mfg. of cigars, soft drinks, jerked beef, furniture; tanning, distilling. Several sugar centrals are in outskirts. Among the fine bldgs. of the old colonial but progressive city are the city hall, Charity Theater, and several churches. Has an airfield. City occupies site of anc. Indian Cubanacan, taken by Columbus for residence of Kublai Khan. It is sometimes called Villa Clara.

Santa Clara or **Santa Clara La Laguna** (lä lägōō'na), town (1950 pop. 1,263), Sololá dept., SW central Guatemala, near W end of L. Atitlán, 8 mi. WSW of Sololá; alt. 6,234 ft.; basket weaving; corn, wheat, beans.

Santa Clara, inactive volcano (9,186 ft.), SW central Guatemala, near L. Atitlán, 4 mi. SW of San Pedro.

Santa Clara. 1 Town (pop. 1,623), Durango, N Mexico, on affluent of Aguanaval R. and 90 mi. ENE of Durango; grain, cotton, vegetables, livestock. **2** Town, Michoacán, Mexico: see VILLA ESCALANTE.

Santa Clara, volcano (4,512 ft.) in Cordillera de los Marabios, W Nicaragua, 12 mi. ENE of Chinandega.

Santa Clara (sän'tủ klä'rủ), town (pop. 2,205), Coimbra dist., N central Portugal, on left bank of Mondego R. opposite Coimbra. Has 17th-cent. convent (containing tomb of St. Isabel). Inés de Castro was murdered (1355) at the Quinta das Lágrimas.

Santa Clara (săn'tủ klă'rủ, klâ'rủ), county (□ 1,305; pop. 290,547), W Calif.; ⊙ SAN JOSE. Includes N part of rich fruitgrowing SANTA CLARA VALLEY, extending SE from San Francisco Bay bet. Diablo Range (E; includes Mt. HAMILTON) and Santa Cruz Mts. (W). Drained by Coyote Creek and short Guadalupe Creek. Besides fruit, co. produces truck, general farm crops, livestock, poultry, dairy products, flowers, and seed. Has one of world's largest cement plants; also mfg. of magnesium, agr. machinery, canning and packing equipment, chemicals, printing. Working of cement, clay, sand and gravel, quicksilver deposits. PALO ALTO, Santa Clara are educational centers. Formed 1850.

Santa Clara, pueblo (□ 71.5), in Rio Arriba, Sandoval, and Santa Fe counties, N N.Mex. Santa Clara village (1948 pop. 579) is on W bank of the Rio Grande and 21 mi. NNW of Santa Fe; alt. c.5,600 ft. Pueblo Indians produce highly regarded black pottery. Feast day, Santa Clara de Assisi, Aug. 12; accompanied by ceremonial dances. Village settled c.1700. Near by are Puyé ruins, remains of 15th-cent. Tewa pueblo that included cliff dwellings, kivas, and 4 terraced community houses on mesa top. Pictographs and pottery remains have been found.

Santa Clara. 1 City (pop. 11,702), Santa Clara co., W Calif., adjoining San Jose; fruit canneries and packing houses, lumber mill. Seat of Univ. of Santa Clara. Restored Santa Clara de Asís Mission (founded 1777) is now chapel of the univ. Inc. 1866. **2** Town (pop. 319), Washington co., SW Utah, 4 mi. NW of St. George and on Santa Clara R. (a 30-mi. stream which joins Virgin R. near St. George); orchards.

Santa Clara, Olimar, or **Santa Clara del Olimar** (sän'tä klä'rä dĕl ōlēmär'), town, Treinta y Tres dept., NE Uruguay, in the Cuchilla Grande Principal, on railroad and 55 mi. SW of Melo, on Cerro Largo dept. line. Local trade center (wheat, corn, oats); cattle and sheep raising. Military post. Also called Pueblo Olimar.

Santa Clara Bay (sän'tä klä'rä), inlet (15 mi. long, 4 mi. wide), NW Cuba, Matanzas prov., 15 mi. E of Cárdenas and flanked N by the Cayos de las Cinco Leguas.

Santa Clara de Buena Vista (sän'tä klä'rä dä bwā'nä vē'stä), town (pop. estimate 1,500), central Santa Fe prov., Argentina, on railroad and 36 mi. WSW of Santa Fé; agr. center (wheat, flax, livestock, poultry); dairying.

Santa Clara del Olimar, Uruguay: see SANTA CLARA.

Santa Clara Island, Chile: see JUAN FERNÁNDEZ ISLANDS.

Santa Clara Island (sän'tä klä'rä) or **El Muerto Island** (ĕl mwĕr'tō), small islet off Pacific coast of Guayas prov., SW Ecuador, in Gulf of Guayaquil, 13 mi. SW of Puná Isl.; 3°10'S 80°25'W; site of lighthouse.

Santa Clara La Laguna, Guatemala: see SANTA CLARA, town.

Santa Clara River, Mexico: see CARMEN RIVER.

Santa Clara River (săn'tů klă'rů, klâ'rů), in Los Angeles and Ventura counties, S Calif., rises on N slope of San Gabriel Mts. N of Los Angeles, flows c.65 mi. W and SW, past Fillmore and Santa Paula, to the Pacific 3 mi. S of Ventura; flow is intermittent. Its wide delta plain is chief agr. area of Ventura co.; upper valley has citrus-fruit groves, oil and gas fields. There is also a SANTA CLARA VALLEY S of San Francisco.

Santa Clara Valley, in Santa Clara and San Benito counties, W Calif., S extension of San Francisco Bay depression; stretches c.75 mi. SE from bay shore, bet. Santa Cruz Mts. and Gabilan Range (W) and Diablo Range (E), to point where ranges meet; 15 mi. wide in N. Drained by Coyote Creek and short Guadalupe Creek in N; S of Gilroy, where Pajaro R. valley breaks mtn. barrier to W, valley's S section is given local names (San Juan Valley, San Benito Valley). Fertile irrigated agr. region, almost entirely given to fruitgrowing (since 1850s); prunes, apricots, peaches, almonds, cherries, apples, pears. SAN JOSE is chief canning, drying, shipping center. Santa Clara valley of Ventura and Los Angeles counties is drained by SANTA CLARA RIVER.

Santa Claus, village, Spencer co., SW Ind., 38 mi. ENE of Evansville. Its post office annually postmarks and remails tons of Christmas letters and parcels.

Santa Coloma de Farnés (sän'tä kōlō'mä dā färnās'), city (pop. 3,348), Gerona prov., NE Spain, 12 mi. SW of Gerona; cork processing; trades in lumber and agr. products (livestock, wine, olive oil, nuts). Has ruins of 12th-cent. castle.

Santa Coloma de Gramanet (grämänĕt'), outer suburb (pop. 3,992) of Barcelona, NE Spain, on Besós R. and 6 mi. NNE of city center. Has metallurgical industry. Also cotton-cloth mfg. and printing, tanning; produces aniline dyes, bicycles and accessories, cigarette paper, leather goods.

Santa Coloma de Queralt (kārält'), town (pop. 2,866), Tarragona prov., NE Spain, 16 mi. NE of Montblanch; mfg. (cotton and woolen fabrics, cement, champagne); sheep raising. Trades in cereals, fruit, forage. Has 13th-cent. parochial church and a Romanesque church.

Santa Comba Dão (sãn'tů kõm'bů dã'ō), town (pop. 1,875), Viseu dist., N Portugal, 21 mi. NW of Coimbra; railroad junction (spur to Viseu); sawmilling, resin extracting; agr. trade (wine, olives, rye).

Santa Cristina (sän'tä krēstē'nä), village (pop. 293), Bolzano prov., Trentino–Alto Adige, N Italy, in Val Gardena, 18 mi. ENE of Bolzano; resort (alt. 4,685 ft.); toymaking center.

Santa Cristina de la Polvorosa (sän'tä krēstē'nä dā lä pôlvōrō'sä), village (pop. 1,192), Zamora prov., W Spain, on Órbigo R. and 2 mi. W of Benavente; cereals, vegetables, cattle, sheep.

Santa Croce (sän'tä krô'chĕ), village (pop. 654), Aquila prov., Abruzzi e Molise, S central Italy, on Liri R. and 6 mi. S of Avezzano; paper mills.

Santa Croce, Cape, point on E coast of Sicily, NE of Augusta; 37°15'N 15°16'E.

Santa Croce, Lago di (lä'gô dē), lake (□ c.2) in Belluno prov., Veneto, N Italy, 6 mi. ESE of Belluno; 2.5 mi. long, 1 mi. wide, 115 ft. deep. Dammed at N end and linked by canal with Piave R. Piave–Santa Croce system (begun 1920) supplies water to 5 hydroelectric plants in vicinity of lake.

Santa Croce Camerina (kämĕrē'nä), village (pop. 6,308), Ragusa prov., SE Sicily, 13 mi. SW of Ragusa. Ruins of Camarina (Syracusan colony founded 598 B.C., destroyed 258 B.C.), including walls, small temple, necropolises, are 4 mi. NW.

Santa Croce del Sannio (dĕl sän'nyô), village (pop. 1,728), Benevento prov., Campania, S Italy, 13 mi. SSE of Campobasso.

Santa Croce di Magliano (dē mälyä'nô), town (pop. 5,291), Campobasso prov., Abruzzi e Molise, S central Italy, 7 mi. SE of Larino.

Santa Croce sull'Arno (sōōlär'nô), town (pop. 3,482), Pisa prov., Tuscany, central Italy, on the Arno and 18 mi. E of Pisa; tannery center; shoes, glue, cutlery, liquor.

Santa Cruz (sän'tä krōōs'), national territory (□ 77,843; pop. 24,582), in S Patagonia, Argentina; ⊙ Río Gallegos. Southernmost area of continental Argentina, bet. the Deseado R. (N) and the Strait of Magellan (S) and bounded by the Andes and the Atlantic. Drained by the Río Chico, and Santa Cruz, Coyle, and Gallegos rivers. Among its large lakes are San Martín, Viedma, and Argentino, in a resort area of natl. parks. Has dry, cold climate; S parts are more humid. Among its mineral resources are kaolin (San Julián), platinum (Cabo Vírgenes), coal (El Turbio, El Calafate), iron, manganese, salt (El Turbio). Predominately a sheep-raising area, with some agr. activity in river valleys: alfalfa, potatoes, grain. Mining, woolwashing, some lumbering and flour milling. Meat-packing plants at Río Gallegos, Santa Cruz, San Julián, Comandante Luis Piedrabuena. Trading in wool and hides. The Atlantic coast and Andean lakes offer rich fishing grounds. With the definite establishment in 1946 of Comodoro Rivadavia military zone, the territory lost part of its northern area.

Santa Cruz or **Puerto Santa Cruz** (pwĕr'tō), town (pop. estimate 1,500), ⊙ Corpen Aike dept. (pop. estimate 3,000), E Santa Cruz natl. territory, Argentina, on Santa Cruz R. estuary 10 mi. inland from the Atlantic, and 120 mi. NNE of Río Gallegos; 50°1'S 68°32'W. Port and center for sheep raising, fishing, wool trading and shipping; meat-packing plant. Meteorological station, airport. Monolith commemorates Commodore Py, who raised here in 1878 the Argentinian flag. The bay was discovered May 3, 1520, by Magellan. Town is former ⊙ Santa Cruz natl. territory.

Santa Cruz (sän'tů krōōzh'). **1** or **Santa Cruz da Graciosa** (dä grŭsyô'zŭ), town (pop. 944), Angra do Heroísmo dist., central Azores, on N shore of GRACIOSA ISLAND, 50 mi. NW of Angra do Heroísmo (on Terceira Isl.); 39°5'N 28°1'W. Fishing port (whaling). Trade in cereals, wine, livestock. Thermal springs. Founded 1485. **2** or **Santa Cruz das Flores** (däs flō'rĭsh), town (pop. 1,741), Horta dist., W Azores, on E shore of FLORES ISLAND, 150 mi. WNW of Horta (on Faial Isl.); 39°27'N 31°9'W. Whaling, dairying. Meteorological observatory.

Santa Cruz (sän'tä krōōs'), department (□ 143,570; 1949 pop. estimate 409,800), E Bolivia; ⊙ Santa Cruz. Bordered by Paraguay (S) and Brazil (E). Consists mainly of extensive tropical areas along Brazilian border, covered partly by marshy lakes; includes foothills of Cordillera de Cochabamba (W) and part of Bolivian Chaco (S). Drained by Río Grande, Piray, San Miguel, San Martín, and Paraguá rivers, of which only short sections are navigable. Bolivia's main production area for sugar cane, rice, tobacco, cotton; large quantities of rubber from trees located in dense tropical forests (N); extensive cattle raising. Oil in Cordillera de Charagua (SW) at petroleum fields of Camiri, Saipurú, and Guariri. Dept. served by road net centered on Santa Cruz. Main centers: Santa Cruz, San José, Puerto Suárez.

Santa Cruz. 1 Village, Pando dept., NW Bolivia, on Acre R. and 10 mi. W of Cobija, on Brazil border; rubber. **2** or **Santa Cruz de la Sierra** (dā lä syĕ'rä), city (1949 pop. estimate 36,400), ⊙ Santa Cruz dept. and Andrés Ibáñez (or Cercado) prov., central Bolivia, in tropical lowlands, 330 mi. ESE of La Paz and 195 mi. E of Cochabamba; 17°48'S 63°11'W; alt. 1,575 ft. Important trade center for subtropical and tropical agr. products (sugar cane, rice, coffee, tobacco) and general merchandise; produces alcohol, cigars, leather, chocolates; sugar refining. Connected by roads with Cochabamba, Sucre, Villa Montes, and Puerto Suárez (Brazil border); junction of projected railroads from Cochabamba, Corumbá (Brazil), and Yacuiba (Argentina border); airport. Site of govt. palace, city hall, cathedral, univ., bacteriological institute; bishopric. City founded in 1560 by Ñuflo de Chávez at site of present San José de Chiquitos; because of Indian attacks, it was moved c.1595 to present location on banks of Piray R. and called Santa Cruz de la Sierra. One of earliest revolutionary centers, declaring itself independent in 1811; recaptured temporarily by Spaniards.

Santa Cruz (sän'tů krōōzh'). **1** City, Ceará, Brazil: see RERIUTABA. **2** City, Espírito Santo, Brazil: see ARACRUZ. **3** City, Goiás, Brazil: see PIRES DO RIO. **4** City (pop. 2,705), E Rio Grande do Norte, NE Brazil, 65 mi. SW of Natal; cotton and cattle shipping. Gypsum quarries. **5** City, Rio Grande do Sul, Brazil: see SANTA CRUZ DO SUL.

Santa Cruz (sän'tä krōōs'), town (pop. 2,132), ⊙ Santa Cruz dept. (□ 2,056; pop. 73,106), Colchagua prov., central Chile, in the central valley, 23 mi. WSW of San Fernando; agr. center (grain, potatoes, fruit, livestock); flour milling, dairying.

Santa Cruz. 1 Village (pop. 3,012), Cartago prov., central Costa Rica, on SE slopes of Turrialba volcano, 5 mi. NW of Turrialba; corn, sugar cane, livestock. **2** Town (dist. pop. 7,201), Guanacaste prov., NW Costa Rica, 13 mi. NW of Nicoya; agr. (rice, corn, beans) and livestock center.

Santa Cruz. 1 or **Santa Cruz Naranjo** (närän'hō), town (1950 pop. 1,276), Santa Rosa dept., S Guatemala, in Pacific piedmont, 8 mi. NW of Cuilapa; alt. 3,500 ft.; corn, beans, cattle. **2** or **Santa Cruz La Laguna** (lä lägōō'nä), town (1950 pop. 300), Sololá dept., SW central Guatemala, on N shore of L. Atitlán and 3 mi. SW of Sololá; alt. 4,000 ft.; grain, beans.

Santa Cruz (săn"tů krōōz'), village, Bombay Suburban dist., W Bombay, India, 10 mi. N of Bombay city center; mfg. of matches, batteries. Cantonment is just SE, military airport 2 mi. NE, civil airport (for Bombay city) 1 mi. NW.

Santa Cruz (săn"tů krōōz'), town (pop. 2,200), St. Elizabeth parish, SW Jamaica, 29 mi. W of May Pen, in agr. region (corn, spices, livestock).

Santa Cruz (sãn'tů krōōzh'), town (pop. 609), Madeira, on E coast of Madeira isl., 7 mi. NE of Funchal; fishing port; alcohol distilling, dairying, lumbering, beekeeping.

Santa Cruz (sän'tä krōōs'). **1** City, Guanajuato, Mexico: see JUVENTINO ROSAS. **2** or **Santa Cruz Ayotusco** (īōtōō'skō), town (pop. 1,693), Mexico state, central Mexico, 14 mi. W of Mexico city; cereals, livestock. **3** Town (pop. 757), Sonora, NW Mexico, on railroad and 23 mi. ESE of Nogales; stock raising; beans, wheat. **4** Officially Santa Cruz Tlaxcala, town (pop. 1,939), Tlaxcala, central Mexico, on railroad and 6 mi. NE of Tlaxcala; corn, wheat, alfalfa, maguey, livestock.

Santa Cruz, Fr. Morocco: see AGADIR.

Santa Cruz (sän'tä krōōs'). **1** Town (pop. 1,512), Cajamarca dept., NW Peru, in Cordillera Occidental, 25 mi. WNW of Hualgayoc; barley. **2** Town (pop. 352), Loreto dept., N central Peru, landing on Huallaga R. and 30 mi. NE of Yurimaguas; bananas, yucca.

Santa Cruz (săn"tů krōōz', Sp. sän'tä krōōs'). **1** Town, Bulacan prov., Philippines: see ANGAT. **2** Town (1939 pop. 1,841); 1948 municipality pop. 54,772), Davao prov., SE Mindanao, Philippines, on the coast, 65 mi. E of Davao; abacá, coconuts. **3** Town (1939 pop. 2,734; 1948 municipality pop. 13,799), Ilocos Sur prov., N Luzon, Philippines, 36 mi. SSE of Vigan, near W coast; rice-growing center. **4** Town (1939 pop. 1,330; 1948 municipality pop. 22,534), ⊙ LAGUNA prov., S Luzon, Philippines, on Laguna de Bay, on railroad and 16 mi. NNE of San Pablo; trade center for agr. area (rice, sugar cane, coconuts). **5** Town (1939 pop. 4,450; 1948 municipality pop. 27,430), on N coast of Marinduque isl., Philippines, port on inlet of Mompog Pass, 13 mi. ENE of Boac; iron-mining and agr. center (coconuts, rice, abacá). **6** Town (1939 pop. 5,387) in Tanjay municipality, Negros Oriental prov., SE Negros isl., Philippines, near Tañon Strait, 3 mi. NW of Tanjay; agr. center (corn, coconuts, sugar cane). **7** Town (1939 pop. 1,334; 1948 municipality pop. 14,613), Zambales prov., central Luzon, Philippines, port on S.China Sea, near Dasol Bay, 50 mi. WNW of Tarlac; ships chrome ore mined at Lucapon (1939 pop. 776), 5 mi. SSE.

Santa Cruz (sän'tä krōōth'), old SE section of SEVILLE, S Spain.

Santa Cruz (săn'tů krōōz'). **1** County (□ 1,246; pop. 9,344), S Ariz., on Mex. line; ⊙ Nogales. Patagonia Mts. are in S, Santa Rita Mts. in N. Irrigated farming area along Santa Cruz R. Tumacacori Natl. Monument is in W. Coronado Natl. Forest extends throughout most of co. Mining (lead, zinc, silver, copper), agr. (livestock, alfalfa, cotton). Formed 1899. **2** County (□ 439; pop. 66,534), W Calif.; ⊙ Santa Cruz. At base of San Francisco–San Mateo peninsula, in Santa Cruz Mts.; bounded W by Pacific Ocean and Monterey Bay, S by Pajaro R. Also drained by San Lorenzo R. and short Soquel Creek. Pajaro R. valley is noted for apples (shipped from Watsonville); co. also produces lettuce, vegetables, berries, nuts, sugar beets, dry beans, hay, dairy products, poultry, eggs, livestock. Farm-products packing and processing industries, tanning, cement mfg.; fisheries; lumbering (redwood); cement, clay, gravel, limestone quarrying. Contains beach, mtn. resorts; Big Basin Redwoods State Park. Formed 1850.

Santa Cruz. 1 City (pop. 21,970), ⊙ Santa Cruz co., W Calif., c.60 mi. S of San Francisco, at mouth of San Lorenzo R. on Monterey Bay; beach resort; yachting, deep-sea fishing. Big Basin Redwoods State Park (in Santa Cruz Mts.) near by. Commercial fishing, fish canning; mfg. of cement, poultry and dairy equipment, redwood novelties. Truck, fruit, poultry farms, nurseries in vicinity. Settled on site of Santa Cruz Mission (founded 1791; replica extant), and of Branciforte colony (founded 1797). Inc. 1866. **2** Village (pop. c.500), Santa Fe co., N N.Mex., bet. Rio Grande and Sangre de Cristo Mts., in Santa Clara Pueblo land grant, 21 mi. NNW of Santa Fe; alt. c.5,700 ft.; fruit, grain, chili. Sp. Mission is massive church (1733) containing treasures of Sp.-Mex. religious painting and sculpture. Santa Cruz day (May 3) is celebrated with presentation of play in which Christians recover Cross from Moors. Village settled by Sp. colonists who came (1598) with Juan de Oñate.

Santa Cruz (sän'tä krōōs'). **1** Town (pop. 1,956), Aragua state, N Venezuela, in L. Valencia basin, on Aragua R. and 7 mi. SE of Maracay; coffee, cacao, sugar cane, corn, cattle. **2** Town (pop. 844), Falcón state, NW Venezuela, 9 mi. N of Churuguara; sugar, coffee, cacao, corn. **3** Town (pop. 1,839), Mérida state, W Venezuela, in Andean spur, on transandine highway and 36 mi. WSW of Mérida; sugar cane, coffee, grain, cacao, vegetables. **4** or **Santa Cruz del Zulia** (dĕl sōō'lyä), town (pop. 674), Zulia state, NW Venezuela, in Maracaibo lowlands, on affluent of Escalante R. and 7 mi. SSW of San Carlos; sugar cane, cacao, cattle.

Santa Cruz, island, U.S. Virgin Isls.: see SAINT CROIX ISLAND.

Santa Cruz, Sierra de (syĕ'rä dā sän'tä krōōs'), range in Alta Verapaz and Izabal depts., E Guatemala; E extension of Sierra de Chamá, bet. area of Cahabón (W) and Bay of Amatique (E); forms divide bet. Sarstoon R. (N) and L. Izabal–Río Dulce (S). Rises to over 3,000 ft.

Santa Cruz Acalpixca (sän'tä krōōs' äkälpē'skä), town (pop. 1,971), Federal Dist., central Mexico, 14 mi. S of Mexico city, adjoining Xochimilco; cereals, fruit, livestock.

Santa Cruz Atizapán, Mexico: see ATIZAPÁN.

Santa Cruz Ayotusco, Mexico: see SANTA CRUZ.

Santa Cruz Balanyá, Guatemala: see BALANYÁ.
Santa Cruz Barillas, Guatemala: see BARILLAS.
Santa Cruz Cabrália (sän'tŏŏ krōōzh' kŏŏbrä'lyŏŏ), city (pop. 588), SE Bahia, Brazil, on the Atlantic, and 10 mi. N of Pôrto Seguro. On near-by Coroa Vermelha islet, Cabral celebrated 1st mass on Brazilian soil in 1500.
Santa Cruz Chinautla, Guatemala: see CHINAUTLA.
Santa Cruz da Graciosa, Azores: see SANTA CRUZ.
Santa Cruz das Flores, Azores: see SANTA CRUZ.
Santa Cruz das Palmeiras (sän'tŏŏ krōōzh' däs pŏŏlmä'rŏŏs), city (pop. 2,743), E São Paulo, Brazil, on railroad and 55 mi. SE of Ribeirao Prêto; coffee, sugar cane, grain, cattle. Until 1944, Palmeiras.
Santa Cruz de Bravo, Mexico: see FELIPE CARRILLO PUERTO.
Santa Cruz de Campezo (sän'tä krōōth' dā kämpä'thō), town (pop. 1,021), Álava prov., N Spain, on Ega R. and 20 mi. SE of Vitoria; wood turning, tanning. Livestock market.
Santa Cruz de Galeana, Mexico: see JUVENTINO ROSAS.
Santa Cruz de la Palma (lä päl'mä), city (pop. 8,802), chief town and principal port of Palma isl., Canary Isls., on fine bay of isl.'s E shore, 90 mi. W of Santa Cruz de Tenerife; 28°40'N 17°45'W. Ships bananas, tobacco, cochineal, tomatoes, cereals, wine. Fishing. Sawmilling, flour milling, meat packing, tobacco processing; mfg. of shoes, embroidery, chocolate, ice, tobacco goods. Limekilns. Airfield near by.
Santa Cruz de las Flores (sän'tä krōōs' dā läs flō'rĕs), town (pop. 1,407), Jalisco, central Mexico, 18 mi. SW of Guadalajara; wheat, corn, beans, fruit, stock.
Santa Cruz de la Sierra, Bolivia: see SANTA CRUZ, city.
Santa Cruz de la Sierra (sän'tä krōōth' dā lä syĕ'rä), town (pop. 1,120), Cáceres prov., W Spain, 9 mi. S of Trujillo; cereals, olive oil, flax.
Santa Cruz de la Soledad (sän'tä krōōs' dā lä sōlā-dhädh'), town (pop. 1,081), Jalisco, central Mexico, on L. Chapala and 28 mi. SE of Guadalajara, on railroad; grain, vegetables, fruit.
Santa Cruz de la Zarza (sän'tä krōōth' dā lä thär'thä), town (pop. 5,788), Toledo prov., central Spain, on railroad and 40 mi. SE of Madrid; cereals, grapes, olives, livestock. Olive-oil pressing, liquor distilling, plaster and tile mfg.; lumbering.
Santa Cruz del Norte (sän'tä krōōs' dĕl nôr'tä), town (pop. 2,728), Havana prov., W Cuba, on the Gulf of Mexico, on railroad and 27 mi. E of Havana; sugar milling and refining, distilling, sunflower-oil pressing. Airfield. The sugar central Hershey is 2 mi. SSW.
Santa Cruz de los Cáñamos (sän'tä krōōth' dā lōs kä'nyämōs), town (pop. 1,001), Ciudad Real prov., S central Spain, 29 mi. ESE of Valdepeñas; cereals, grapes, potatoes, livestock.
Santa Cruz del Quiché, Guatemala: see QUICHÉ, city.
Santa Cruz del Retamar (dĕl rātämär'), town (pop. 1,867), Toledo prov., central Spain, 37 mi. SW of Madrid; grapes, cereals, livestock. Flour milling, charcoal burning, tile mfg.
Santa Cruz del Seibo, Dominican Republic: see SEIBO, city.
Santa Cruz del Sur (sän'tä krōōs' dĕl sōōr'), town (pop. 2,571), Camagüey prov., E Cuba, minor port on the Caribbean, 45 mi. S of Camagüey; fishing, fish-canning, and lumbering center. Ships mainly timber (mahogany, cedar). In agr. region (sugar cane, oranges, cattle, beeswax, honey). Sugar centrals are near by. Destroyed by 1932 hurricane, it was rebuilt just N of its former site.
Santa Cruz del Valle (sän'tä krōōth' dĕl vä'lyä), town (pop. 972), Ávila prov., central Spain, in the Sierra de Gredos, 31 mi. SW of Ávila; olives, fruit, grapes, livestock; olive-oil pressing, resin mfg.; lumbering.
Santa Cruz de Moya (dā moi'ä), village (pop. 1,295), Cuenca prov., E central Spain, near Turia R., 28 mi. SSW of Teruel; saffron, grapes, fruit, stock. Gypsum quarrying, salt mining.
Santa Cruz de Mudela (mōō-dhā'lä), town (pop. 8,781), Ciudad Real prov., S central Spain, in New Castile, on highway to Jaén, and 10 mi. SSW of Valdepeñas; agr. center on La Mancha plain (olives, grapes, cereals, sheep, goats). Olive-oil pressing, alcohol distilling, flour milling, dairying; mfg. of knives and spoons, soap, tiles. Airfield near by.
Santa Cruz de Rosales, Mexico: see ROSALES.
Santa Cruz de Tenerife (dā tĕnĕrē'fā), province (pop. 359,770), CANARY ISLANDS, Spain; ⊙ Santa Cruz de Tenerife. Includes the 4 major western isls. of the archipelago: TENERIFE, GOMERA, PALMA, and HIERRO. Prov. was set up in 1927. Two variant official figures for its area are □ 1,239 and □ 1,329.
Santa Cruz de Tenerife, city (pop. 53,726, with suburbs 72,358), ⊙ Tenerife isl. and Santa Cruz de Tenerife prov., Canary Isls., Spain, Atlantic port on isl.'s NE coast, 55 mi. WNW of Las Palmas and 850 mi. SW of Cádiz; 28°28'N 16°15'W. Active trading center with magnificent harbor serving transoceanic shipping and exporting isl.'s produce, such as tomatoes, onions, winter vegetables, potatoes, bananas, tobacco. Industries are few. From the city radiate roads to other parts of the isl., and there is a tramway via La Laguna to Tacoronte. A handsome white city of almost oriental character, it has many distinguished bldgs., among them San Cristóbal castle, Concepción parochial church, monument to Our Lady of Candelaria built of Carrara marble by Canova. There are several institutions of higher learning. Its spendid scenery and mild subtropical climate have made it a favorite tourist resort.
Santa Cruz de Yojoa (sän'tä krōōs' dā yōhō'ä), town (pop. 690), Cortés dept., W central Honduras, NE of L. Yojoa, 36 mi. SSE of San Pedro Sula; coffee, fruit, grain, livestock.
Santa Cruz do Rio Pardo (sän'tŏŏ krōōzh' dŏŏ rē'ŏŏ pär'dŏŏ), city (pop. 6,235), W central São Paulo, Brazil, 15 mi. ENE of Ourinhos; rail-spur terminus; cotton ginning, coffee processing, corn and rice milling, distilling, cheese mfg.
Santa Cruz do Sul (dŏŏ sōōl'), city (pop. 9,489), E central Rio Grande do Sul, Brazil, 80 mi. WNW of Pôrto Alegre; terminus of rail spur from Rio Pardo. Tobacco-growing center. Iron founding, mfg. of chemicals. Airfield. Until 1944, called Santa Cruz.
Santa Cruz Island, Galápagos: see CHAVES ISLAND.
Santa Cruz Island (sän'tä krōōs') (□ 6), in Gulf of California, 13 mi. off SE coast of Lower California, NW Mexico, 85 mi. NNW of La Paz; 4 mi. long, 1½ mi. wide; rises to c.1,500 ft.
Santa Cruz Island, Calif.: see SANTA BARBARA ISLANDS.
Santa Cruz Islands (săn"tŭ krōōz'), small volcanic group (□ 370; pop. c.5,000), Solomon Isls., SW Pacific, c.300 naut. mi. E of Guadalcanal; 10°45'S 165°55'E. Comprise NDENI (largest isl.), UTUPUA, VANIKORO, and many smaller islets; kauri pine. Polynesian natives known for canoe building. In Second World War, naval battle of Santa Cruz, won 1942 by U.S., thwarted Jap. relief of Guadalcanal.
Santa Cruz La Laguna, Guatemala: see SANTA CRUZ.
Santa Cruz Mountains (săn'tŭ krōōz'), W Calif., one of the Coast Ranges, extending c.70 mi. NW from Pajaro R. at N end of Gabilan Range, along W side of Santa Clara Valley, and up San Francisco–San Mateo peninsula to N San Mateo co.; highest (3,806 ft.) in S.
Santa Cruz Muluá, Guatemala: see MULUÁ.
Santa Cruz Naranjo, Guatemala: see SANTA CRUZ.
Santa Cruz River (sän'tä krōōs'), Patagonian stream in central Santa Cruz natl. territory, Argentina, rises in L. Argentino, flows 150 mi. E, past Comandante Luis Piedrabuena and Santa Cruz, to the Atlantic. Not navigable. At its estuary it receives the Río Chico.
Santa Cruz River (săn'tŭ krōōz'), in Ariz. and Mexico, rises in Patagonia and Huachuca Mts., S Ariz., flows S into Sonora, NW Mexico, then N, re-entering Ariz. near Nogales and continuing N to Tucson, where it turns NW toward Casa Grande. Stream is intermittent, sometimes flowing to Gila R. Used for irrigation in Pima co.
Santa Cruz Tepexpan, Mexico: see TEPEXPAN.
Santadi (säntä'dē), village (pop. 910), Cagliari prov., SW Sardinia, 23 mi. SW of Cagliari. Barite mine near by.
Santa Ecilda, Uruguay: see ECILDA PAULLIER.
Santa Elena (sän'tä ālā'nä), town (1947 pop. 7,545), NW Entre Ríos prov., Argentina, port on Paraná R. and 15 mi. SSW of La Paz; stock-raising and meat-packing center.
Santa Elena, town (pop. c.6,120), Chuquisaca dept., S Bolivia, on Santa Elena R. (right affluent of the Pilcomayo) and 27 mi. ENE of Camargo; vineyards, grain.
Santa Elena, town (1950 pop. 2,764), Guayas prov., W Ecuador, on arid Santa Elena Peninsula, near Santa Elena Bay, on Guayaquil-Salinas railroad and 70 mi. W of Guayaquil; center of petroleum-drilling and salt-mining dist. Oil refining. Near by are also sulphur, platinum, and gold deposits.
Santa Elena. 1 Town, Sonora, Mexico: see BANAMICHI. **2** Town (pop. 1,234), Yucatan, SE Mexico, 6 mi. SW of Ticul; henequen, fruit, timber.
Santa Elena, town (dist. pop. 5,449), La Cordillera dept., S central Paraguay, 55 mi. E of Asunción, in agr. area (fruit, tobacco, cattle); distilling of oil of petitgrain.
Santa Elena, village (pop. 36), Libertad dept., NW Peru, on the Pacific, 3 mi. SSW of Pacasmayo; beach resort.
Santa Elena, city (pop. 5,603), Usulután dept., SE Salvador, 3 mi. NE of Usulután; coffee, grain.
Santa Elena, mining town (pop. 1,569), Jaén prov., S Spain, in rich lead-mining dist., 6 mi. NE of La Carolina.
Santa Elena, village, Bolívar state, SE Venezuela, in Guiana Highlands, near Brazil border, 50 mi. SW of Mt. Roraima; diamond fields. Airport.
Santa Elena Bay, SE inlet of Papagayo Gulf of the Pacific, in NW Costa Rica, just N of Santa Elena Peninsula; 5 mi. wide, 5 mi. long. Abounds in turtles.
Santa Elena Bay, inlet of the Pacific in Guayas prov., W Ecuador, N of Santa Elena Peninsula, W of Guayaquil; port and beach resort of Salinas is on its SW shore.
Santa Elena Canyon, Texas: see BIG BEND NATIONAL PARK.
Santa Elena de Jamúz (dā hämōōth'), village (pop. 1,384), Leon prov., NW Spain, 16 mi. SE of Astorga; cereals, vegetables, wine.
Santa Elena Island, in Bay Islands dept., N Honduras, in Caribbean Sea, just E of Roatán Isl.; 1 mi. long, ½ mi. wide. Sometimes called Helena Isl.
Santa Elena Peninsula, on Pacific Ocean, in NW Costa Rica, bet. Papagayo Gulf (N) and Culebra Gulf (S); 15 mi. long, 8 mi. wide at base. Terminates in Cape Santa Elena (10°54'N 85°58'W), westernmost point of Costa Rican mainland.
Santa Elena Peninsula, Guayas prov., W Ecuador, bet. Santa Elena Bay (N) and Gulf of Guayaquil (S), on the Pacific, W of Guayaquil (connected by railroad). Its westernmost point, La Puntilla, is at 2°12'S 81°1'W. An arid region with petroleum wells and refineries (at La Libertad, Salinas, Ancón), and salt mines; also has sulphur, platinum, and gold deposits. Salinas is a popular seaside resort.
Santa Elena River, W central Bolivia, rises in Cordillera de Cochabamba 45 mi. NNW of Cochabamba, flows c.90 mi. NNW, past Covendo, joining Bopi R. at Huachi to form BENI RIVER. Receives Cotacajes and Altamachi rivers. Formerly also called Altamachi.
Santaella (säntäĕ'lyä), town (pop. 2,923), Córdoba prov., S Spain, 11 mi. WNW of Aguilar; olive-oil processing, flour milling; cereals, livestock. Mineral springs.
Santa Ernestina (sän'tä ĕrnĕstē'nä), village, Rivera dept., NE Uruguay, 45 mi. SSE of Rivera; gold placers.
Santa Eufemia (sän'tä ĕŏŏfā'myä), town (pop. 2,557), Córdoba prov., S Spain, in the Sierra Morena, 16 mi. NNW of Pozoblanco; olive oil, cereals, vegetables, honey; lumbering, sheep raising. Limestone quarries. Tungsten, coal, antimony deposits in area.
Santa Eugenia (sän'tä ĕŏŏhā'nyä), town (pop. 805), Majorca, Balearic Isls., on railroad and 11 mi. ENE of Palma; cereals, almonds, grapes, sheep, hogs.
Santa Eugenia or **Santa Eugenia de Ribeira** (dā rēvā'rä), city (pop. 3,569), La Coruña prov., NW Spain, fishing port on Ares Bay of the Atlantic, 32 mi. SW of Santiago; fish processing and shipping, boatbuilding; lumber, livestock.
Santa Eulalia, Mexico: see AQUILES SERDÁN.
Santa Eulalia (sän'tä ĕŏŏlä'lyä), town (pop. 203), Lima dept., W central Peru, on Santa Eulalia R. and 15 mi. NNE of Lima. Water reservoir and hydroelectric plant (serving Lima) near by.
Santa Eulália (sän'tŭ ĕŏŏlä'lyŭ), village (pop. 2,424), Portalegre dist., central Portugal, on railroad and 22 mi. SSE of Portalegre; grain, olives, beans, livestock. Cork-oak forests.
Santa Eulalia or **Santa Eulalia del Campo** (sän'tä ĕŏŏlä'lyä dĕl käm'pō), village (pop. 2,681), Teruel prov., E Spain, on Jiloca R. and 19 mi. NNW of Teruel; sugar mill; cereals, sheep.
Santa Eulalia del Río (rē'ō), town (pop. 2,660), Iviza, Balearic Isls., at mouth of small Santa Eulalia R., 8 mi. NE of Iviza city; almonds, vegetables, olives, cereals, potatoes, fruit, carobs, livestock.
Santa Eulalia de Provenzana (dā prōvĕn-thä'nä), industrial suburb (pop. 10,689) of Barcelona, NE Spain, 3 mi. WSW of city center; chemical works (fertilizers, dyes, lubricants, vaseline); steel milling, olive-oil and vinegar processing, sugar refining, cotton and hemp milling; mfg. of liqueurs, cement, linen.
Santa Eulalia River, Lima dept., W central Peru, rises on Junín dept. border, flows c.35 mi. SW to Rímac R. at Chosica. Used for hydroelectric power, supplying Lima.
Santa Fe (sän'tä fā'), province (□ 51,127; pop. 1,702,975), NE central Argentina; ⊙ Santa Fe. Bordered E by Paraná R., it is drained by the Salado, San Javier, and Carcaraña. Has a warm, moist climate. It includes part of the Chaco (N) and the pampas (S), and is well irrigated. Mainly agr.: corn, wheat, flax, alfalfa (center and S); cotton (N); sugar (NE); potatoes and other vegetables (S); grapes (SE). Extensive stock raising: cattle, hogs, goats, horses. Few mineral deposits. Fisheries on the Paraná; game hunting in N forests. Rural industries: flour milling, dairying, cotton ginning, lumbering, flax processing. Major industries: meat packing (Rosario, Santa Fe, Venado Tuerto), canning (Rafaela), sugar refining (Tacuarendí, Las Toscas, Rosario), gasoline distilling (San Lorenzo), paper milling (Andino, Juan Ortíz), quebracho extracting (Tartagal, Rosario), plant-oil pressing (Avellaneda), agr. implements (Maggiolo, Angélica); also glass, dairy, tobacco, beer, pharmaceutical industries concentrated in Santa Fe and Rosario. Its major ports on the Paraná are Santa Fe and Rosario (2d largest town of Argentina), where ocean-going vessels load the agr. produce of N provinces.
Santa Fe, city (pop. 168,011), ⊙ Santa Fe prov. and Santa Fe dept. (□ 1,150; 1947 pop. 206,263), E central Argentina, inland port at mouth of the Río Salado (which here enters the bayou L. Guadalupe), linked by short canal with Paraná R.,

240 mi. NW of Buenos Aires, 12 mi. WNW of Paraná (across Paraná R.); 31°38'S 60°43'W. Rail, shipping, commercial, industrial, and agr. center. Mfg. and trade involve: flour, dairy products, frozen meat, quebracho extracts, tobacco products, flax fibers, paper, lumber, hides, vinegar, ceramics, lime, leather. It is an outlet for the grain-growing and stock-raising area of the E Pampa. It has a univ. and other educational institutions, administrative bldgs., La Merced church (Jesuit), San Francisco church (built 1680), art gall., and theaters, all grouped around 2 large plazas. Santa Fe, founded 1573 by Juan de Garay and named Santa Fe de Vera Cruz, played a prominent part in Argentinian history as center of Jesuit missions, an outpost against Indians, and seat of the constitutional assembly of the republic in 1853.

Santa Fe, village (1930 pop. 108), Bío-Bío prov., S central Chile, 13 mi. W of Los Angeles; rail junction in agr. area (wheat, rye, wine).

Santa Fe, town (pop. 1,098), Isle of Pines, SW Cuba, 10 mi. SSE of Nueva Gerona; resort with mineral springs.

Santa Fe, locality, San Pedro de Macorís prov., SE Dominican Republic, 3 mi. NE of San Pedro de Macorís city; sugar mill.

Santa Fe, town (pop. 3,585), Federal Dist., central Mexico, W suburb of Mexico city (connected by tramway); powder plant.

Santa Fe, village (pop. 390), Veraguas prov., W central Panama, on Santa María R. and 25 mi. NNE of Santiago; road terminus; gold mining center; lumbering.

Santafé (säntäfä'), city (pop. 7,940), Granada prov., S Spain, 7 mi. W of Granada, on fertile plain watered by Genil R. and producing sugar beets, cereals, truck, tobacco. Sawmilling, olive-pressing, brandy distilling, meat processing. Has notable town hall and parochial church. Founded (1491) by the Catholic Kings, while they were besieging Granada, the surrender of which was signed here a few months later. Scene of Queen Isabella's agreement (1492) with Columbus regarding his 1st voyage to New World.

Santa Fe (săn'tů fā", săn'tů fā'), county (□ c.1,930; pop. 38,153), N central N.Mex.; ⊙ Santa Fe. Livestock-grazing and agr. (grain, chili) area; drained NW by the Rio Grande. Mining (lead, zinc, coal, gold, silver) in vicinity of Santa Fe. Includes part of Santa Fe Natl. Forest and Sangre de Cristo Mts. Pueblo Indian area in N, part of Bandelier Natl. Monument in NW. Formed 1852. Part of co. (□ 13) was used to form (1949) part of Los Alamos co.

Santa Fe. 1 Town (pop. 83), Monroe co., NE central Mo., on South Fork of Salt R. and 12 mi. SE of Paris. **2** City (pop. 27,998), ⊙ N.Mex. and Santa Fe co., N central N.Mex., c.290 mi. SSW of Denver, Colo., 55 mi. NE of Albuquerque, in Sangre de Cristo Mts., bet. Pecos R. and the Rio Grande; 35°41'N 105°56'W; alt. 6,954 ft. Second largest city in state; health resort; tourist center; shipping point for Indian handicraft articles, minerals, livestock, fruit, potatoes. Grain and livestock raised in vicinity; lead, zinc, coal, gold, and silver are mined. Became capital of N.Mex. in 1912, when state was organized, but has been seat of govt. virtually since it was founded (c.1609) by Spaniards on site of anc. Indian village. Was early outpost for R.C. missionaries and, for more than 200 years, colonial commercial center. Seized by Pueblo Indians in revolt of 1680 and held until 1692, when Diego de Vargas restored Sp. rule. Trade with U.S. began on Santa Fe Trail shortly after Mex. independence from Spain (1821). In 1846 city was surrendered without resistance to U.S. troops under Gen. S.W. Kearny. In 1851 became capital of Territory of N.Mex. (created 1850 out of surrounding area) and in 1875 see of archbishopric. Railroad reached Lamy (the station for Santa Fe), 16 mi. S, in 1879, and there is now freight spur from Santa Fe to main line of Atchison, Topeka, and Santa Fe RR. Long a center of Roman Catholicism in North America, Santa Fe has several outstanding churches, including San Miguel Mission (c.1636) and Cathedral of St. Francis (built 1869 on site of monastery constructed in 1622). State school for deaf, St. Michael's Col., 2 Indian schools (U.S. and R.C.), regional hq. of Natl. Park Service, and state penitentiary are here. Annual fiesta celebrates reconquest of Sp. N.Mex. (1692–96) by Spaniards under De Vargas. Points of interest are state capitol, state-owned art gallery, laboratory of anthropology. Palace of the Governors, built of adobe and more than 300 years old, has been occupied by Sp., Indian, Mex., and American governors; now houses state mus., state historical society, and school for archaeological research. Several pueblos are in vicinity, part of Bandelier Natl. Monument is 18 mi. W, Santa Fe Natl. Forest is just E. **3** City (pop. 8), Stephens co., S Okla., 16 mi. ESE of Duncan, in agr. area.

Santa Fe Dam, Calif.: see SAN GABRIEL RIVER.

Santa Fe de Bogotá, Colombia: see BOGOTÁ.

Santa Fe del Río (săn'tä fā' děl rē'ō), town (pop. 1,521), Michoacán, central Mexico, on Lerma R. and 16 mi. SE of La Piedad; alt. 5,492 ft.; cereals, stock.

Santa Fe Island or **Barrington Island** (□ 7.5), Galápagos Isls., Ecuador, in the Pacific, 30 mi. W of Puerto Baquerizo (San Cristóbal Isl.); 0°50'S 90°5'W.

Santa Fe Lake (săn'tů fā') (c.5 mi. long), N Fla., on Alachua-Bradford co. line, 15 mi. ENE of Gainesville; source of Santa Fe R.

Santa Fe River, N Fla., rises in Santa Fe L. on Alachua-Bradford co. line, flows c.65 mi. generally W to Suwannee R. 6 mi. SE of Branford. Receives outlets of several small lakes.

Santa Fe Springs, unincorporated town (pop. c.2,000), Los Angeles co., S Calif., 13 mi. SE of downtown Los Angeles, in industrial dist.; oil wells, refineries.

Santa Fe Trail, central and SW U.S., historic route used by explorers and traders from early 19th cent. until coming of railroad (1880) to Santa Fe, N.Mex.; from vicinity of Westport and Independence, Mo., it led W and SW across present Kansas, Okla., N Texas, and N.Mex. to Santa Fe, whence the old Spanish trail continued to W coast. An alternate route for the portion W of present Dodge City, Kansas led across present SE Colo. to Bent's Fort, then SW across Raton Pass (N.Mex.) to Santa Fe.

Santa Filomena (săn'tů fēlōōmä'nů), city (pop. 650), SW Piauí, Brazil, on upper Parnaíba R. (Maranhão border), opposite Alto Parnaíba; 9°6'S 45°56'W. Cattle, hides. Formerly spelled Santa Philomena.

Santa Fiora (sän'tä fyô'rä), village (pop. 1,645), Grosseto prov., Tuscany, central Italy, near Monte Amiata, 6 mi. SW of Abbadia San Salvatore, in mercury-mining region.

Sant'Agata Bolognese (säntä'gätä bôlônyā'zē), town (pop. 1,542), Bologna prov., Emilia-Romagna, N central Italy, 10 mi. E of Modena; mfg. of agr. tools.

Sant'Agata de'Goti (dĕgô'tē), town (pop. 3,312), Benevento prov., Campania, S Italy, 9 mi. WNW of Caserta, in agr. region (cereals, grapes, olives). Has medieval walls and castle.

Sant'Agata di Militello (dē mēlētĕl'lô), village (pop. 5,826), Messina prov., N Sicily, on Tyrrhenian Sea and 18 mi. NE of Mistretta; macaroni; agr. market (olives, grapes, citrus fruit).

Sant'Agata di Puglia (pōō'lyä), town (pop. 6,946), Foggia prov., Apulia, S Italy, 12 mi. SW of Ascoli Satriano; macaroni mfg.

Sant'Agata Feltria (fĕl'trēä), village (pop. 805), Pesaro e Urbino prov., The Marches, central Italy, 24 mi. WNW of Urbino; wood, wool, cheese, fruit.

Santa Gertrudis (sän'tä hĕrtrōō'dhēs), village (pop. 1,315), Iviza, Balearic Isls., 6 mi. N of Iviza city; almonds, olives, cereals, fruit, livestock.

Sant'Agostino (säntägôstē'nô), town (pop. 1,139), Ferrara prov., Emilia-Romagna, N central Italy, near Reno R., 12 mi. WSW of Ferrara; foundry, hemp mill, machinery factory.

Santahar (sŭn'tŭhŭr), village, Bogra dist., N central East Bengal, E Pakistan, 24 mi. W of Bogra; rail junction (workshops); rice milling; rice, jute, rape and mustard.

Santa Helena (săntälä'nů), city (pop. 191), N Maranhão, Brazil, head of navigation on Turiaçu R. and 80 mi. WNW of São Luís. Gold mines near.

Santai or **San-t'ai** (sän'tī'), town (pop. 24,312), ⊙ Santai co. (pop. 878,998), NW central Szechwan prov., China, 65 mi. ENE of Chengtu and on Fow R.; cotton textiles; indigo processing; rice, sweet potatoes, sugar cane, wheat, beans. Until 1913 called Tungchwan.

Santa Ignacia (sän'tä ēgnä'syä), town (1939 pop. 1,420; 1948 municipality pop. 14,061), Tarlac prov., central Luzon, Philippines, 13 mi. NW of Tarlac; coconuts, rice, sugar cane.

Santa Ignez, Brazil: see SANTA INÊS.

Santa Inés (sän'tä ēnās'), village (pop. 732), Iviza, Balearic Isls., 8 mi. NW of Iviza city; cereals, fruit, stock.

Santa Inês (sän'tů ēnās'), city (pop. 2,859), E Bahia, Brazil, on railroad and 55 mi. WSW of Nazaré; coffee, sugar, livestock. Formerly Santa Ignez.

Santa Ines, Calif.: see SANTA YNEZ.

Santa Inés (sän'tä ēnās'), town (pop. 901), Anzoátegui state, NE Venezuela, 28 mi. SE of Barcelona; cotton, coffee, sugar cane, cacao.

Santa Inés Ahuatempan, Mexico: see AHUATEMPAN.

Santa Inés Island (sän'tä ēnās'), large, desolate, mountainous island (75 mi. long, 50 mi. wide) of Tierra del Fuego, Chile, W of Brunswick Peninsula, bet. the Pacific and Strait of Magellan.

Santa Inés Zacatelco, Mexico: see ZACATELCO.

Santa Inez, Calif.: see SANTA YNEZ.

Santa Isabel (sän'tä ēsäbĕl'). **1** Village (pop. c.400), ⊙ Chalileo dept. (pop. 2,413), NW La Pampa prov., Argentina, on Atuel R. near its junction with the Río Salado, in stock-raising area. **2** Town (pop. estimate 500), S Santa Fe prov., Argentina, 20 mi. SE of Venado Tuerto; rail terminus and agr. center (corn, wheat, flax, vegetables, poultry).

Santa Isabel (săn'tēzäbĕl'). **1** Town, Amazonas, Brazil: see TAPURUQUÁ. **2** City, Pará, Brazil: see JOÃO COELHO. **3** City (pop. 1,145), SE São Paulo, Brazil, 30 mi. NE of São Paulo; jute milling (burlap bags); sugar cane, grain.

Santa Isabel (sän'tä ēsäbĕl'), town (pop. 1,830), Tolima dept., W central Colombia, at E foot of Nevado del Tolima in Cordillera Central, 22 mi. NE of Ibagué; alt. 7,556 ft. Lumbering and coffee-growing; yucca, bananas, livestock. Gold and silver mines near by.

Santa Isabel, archipelago, Cuba: see COLORADOS, Los.

Santa Isabel, town (1950 pop. 1,186), Azuay prov., S Ecuador, in the Andes, 36 mi. SW of Cuenca; corn, cattle, sheep.

Santa Isabel. 1 Town, Chihuahua, Mexico: see GENERAL TRÍAS. **2** or **Santa Isabel Cholula** (chōlōō'lä), town (pop. 591), Puebla, central Mexico, on railroad and 13 mi. WSW of Puebla; cereals, livestock.

Santa Isabel, village (pop. 366), Colón prov., central Panama, on Caribbean Sea, and 11 mi. ESE of Palenque; cacao, coconuts, abacá, corn, livestock.

Santa Isabel, town (pop. 4,117), S Puerto Rico, near the coast, 14 mi. ESE of Ponce, in sugar-growing region. Airport just E.

Santa Isabel or **Ysabel** (săn'tů ĭ'zůbĕl), volcanic island (□ 1,800; pop. c.5,000), Solomon Isls., SW Pacific, 50 mi. NW of Guadalcanal; 130 mi. long, 20 mi. wide; copra. In Second World War, isl. was occupied 1942 by Japanese; Rekata Bay in NW was Jap. base taken 1943 by U.S. forces.

Santa Isabel (sän'tä ēsäbĕl'), town (pop. 9,280), ⊙ Sp. Guinea, chief port on Fernando Po isl. (N coast), 150 mi. NNW of Bata (continental Sp. Guinea) and c.30 mi. S of Br. Cameroons coast; 3°46'N 8°46'W. Cacao-shipping center. Other exports are coffee, palm oil, bananas, kola nuts, coconuts, cabinetwoods. Airfield. Has humid tropical climate (annual mean temp. 82°F.), rainfall of 60–80 in. Town is laid out on modern, rectangular pattern. Chief buildings are governor's palace, cathedral, hosp., and R.C. mission. Founded 1820s by English as Clarencetown or Port Clarence.

Santa Isabel, Uruguay: see PASO DE LOS TOROS.

Santa Isabel, Nevado de (nävä'dhō dā sän'tä ēsäbĕl'), Andean volcanic peak (16,730 ft.), W central Colombia, on Caldas-Tolima dept. border, in Cordillera Central, 21 mi. SSE of Manizales.

Santa Isabel Cholula, Mexico: see SANTA ISABEL.

Santa Isabel de las Lajas, Cuba: see LAJAS.

Santa Isabel Peak, volcano and highest peak (9,350 or 9,449 ft.) of Fernando Po isl., Sp. Guinea, 12 mi. S of Santa Isabel. Its fertile slopes grow cacao. Called Clarence Peak by British in 19th cent.

Santa Isabel River, Guatemala: see PASIÓN RIVER.

Santa Isabel Tetlatlahuca, Mexico: see TETLATLAHUCA.

Santa Island (1 mi. wide, 2 mi. long), 2 mi. off Pacific coast of Ancash dept., W central Peru, 5 mi. SW of Santa; 9°2'S 78°41'W; guano deposits.

Santa Juana (sän'tä hwä'nä), town (pop. 1,310), Concepción prov., S central Chile, on Bío-Bío R. and 25 mi. S of Concepción; coal-mining and agr. center (cereals, wine, vegetables).

Santa Juana or **Central Santa Juana** (sĕnträl'), locality, E Puerto Rico, NE of Caguas; sugar mill.

Santa Leopoldina (săn'tů lĭōōpōōldē'nů), city (pop. 1,240), central Espírito Santo, Brazil, head of navigation on Santa Maria R. and 18 mi. NW of Vitória. Agr. colony, settled chiefly by Swiss, producing coffee, oranges, bananas, sugar, potatoes, corn. Until 1944, called Cachoeiro de Santa Leopoldina.

Santal Parganas (sŭntäl' pŭr'gŭnŭs), district (□ 5,480; pop. 2,234,497), E Bihar, India; ⊙ Dumka. Bounded N and NE by Ganges R.; drained by tributaries of the Ganges; irrigated by MOR RIVER. Chota Nagpur foothills in SW, with Rajmahal Hills (bhabar, bamboo, palms) extending N across Ganges Plain to the Ganges. Alluvial soil along the Ganges (rice, corn, barley, oilseeds, cotton, rape and mustard); shellac mfg. Coal mining near Deoghar. Main towns: Deoghar (pilgrimage center), Sahibganj (cattle market).

Santalpur (sän'tŭlpōōr), village, Mehsana dist., N Bombay, India, 27 mi. WSW of Radhanpur; salt panning.

Santa Luce (sän'tä lōō'chĕ), village (pop. 513), Pisa prov., Tuscany, central Italy, 14 mi. ESE of Leghorn; cement works. Alabaster quarries near.

Santa Lucía (sän'tä lōōsē'ä). **1** Town (pop. 2,989), ⊙ Lavalle dept. (□ c.550; pop. 30,443), W Corrientes prov., Argentina, on Santa Lucía R. near its mouth on the Paraná, on railroad and 13 mi. NE of Goya; rice, corn, cotton, tobacco, citrus fruit. **2** Town (1947 census pop. 3,857), ⊙ Santa Lucía dept. (□ 20; 1947 pop. 15,434), S San Juan prov., Argentina, E suburb of San Juan; winegrowing; sawmills, alcohol and wine distilleries, food canneries, flour mills. **3** Town (pop. estimate 1,000), central Tucumán prov., Argentina, 27 mi. SW of Tucumán; rail terminus and sugar-refining center; stock raising; sawmills.

Santa Lucía, town (pop. c.2,600), Potosí dept., W central Bolivia, 7 mi. W of Potosí; truck, grain, livestock.

Santa Lucía (sän'tä lōō-thē'ä), village (pop. 980), Grand Canary, Canary Isls., 15 mi. W of Las Palmas; fruit, corn, tobacco, potatoes, wheat, olives, almonds, barley; flour milling.

Santa Lucía (sän′tä lōōsē′ä), town (pop. 1,969), Oriente prov., E Cuba, near N coast inlet, on railroad and 9 mi. ESE of Gibara; sugar milling.

Santa Lucía. 1 or **Santa Lucía Cotzumalguapa** (kōtsōōmälgwä′pä), town (1950 pop. 3,550), Escuintla dept., S Guatemala, in Pacific piedmont, on railroad and 15 mi. W of Escuintla; road center; sugar cane, coffee, grain; livestock. Sawmilling near by. Sugar mill at El Baúl (N). **2** or **Santa Lucía Milpas Altas** (mēl′päs äl′täs), town (1950 pop. 471), Sacatepéquez dept., S central Guatemala, 3 mi. E of Antigua; alt. 6,293 ft.; grain, beans, fruit. **3** or **Santa Lucía Utatlán** (ōōtätlän′), town (1950 pop. 634), Sololá dept., SW central Guatemala, 5 mi. W of Sololá; alt. 8,199 ft.; corn, beans. Colonial church.

Santa Lucía, town (pop. 519), Francisco Morazán dept., S central Honduras, 6 mi. E of Tegucigalpa; alt. 4,760 ft.; grain; dairying. A gold-mining center in colonial times.

Santa Lucía, town (1950 pop. 410), Boaco dept., central Nicaragua, 7 mi. WNW of Boaco; coffee, corn, rice.

Santa Lucía, village (pop. 308), Puno dept., SE Peru, on the Altiplano, on railroad and 34 mi. WSW of Juliaca; alt. 13,251 ft. The Berenguela copper and silver mines are c.6 mi. N.

Santa Lucia (sän′tä lōōsē′ä). **1** Town (1939 pop. 2,090; 1948 municipality pop. 10,021), Ilocos Sur prov., N Luzon, Philippines, 31 mi. SSE of Vigan, near W coast; rice-growing center. **2** Town, Pampanga prov., Philippines: see SEXMOAN.

Santa Lucía, Salvador: see SANTA ANA, city.

Santa Lucía (sän′tä lōō-thē′ä), E suburb (pop. 6,104) of Cartagena, Murcia prov., SE Spain; lead smelting, manganese processing, glass and pottery mfg. Mineral springs.

Santa Lucía (sän′tä lōōsē′ä), town (pop. 15,000), Canelones dept., S Uruguay, on Santa Lucía R., on railroad and 10 mi. NW of Canelones; resort in agr. region (grain, fruit, stock). The water works supplying Montevideo are near by. Sometimes called San Juan Bautista.

Santa Lucía, town (pop. 2,735), Miranda state, N Venezuela on SE slopes of coastal range, on Caracas–Ocumare RR and 22 mi. SE of Caracas; agr. center (coffee, sugar cane, cacao, corn).

Santa Lucía, Cape (sän′tä lōōsē′ä), W headland of Cambridge Isl., off W coast of Patagonia, Chile; 51°35′S 75°19′W.

Santa Lucía Chico, Arroyo (äroi′ō sän′tä lōōsē′ä chē′kō), river, Florida dept., S central Uruguay, rises in the Cuchilla Grande Inferior 2 mi. W of Cerro Colorado, flows 70 mi. SW and S, past Florida, to Santa Lucía R. 7 mi. NNE of Santa Lucía.

Santa Lucía Cotzumalguapa, Guatemala: see SANTA LUCÍA.

Santa Lucia del Mela (sän′tä lōōchē′ä dĕl mā′lä), village (pop. 6,151), Messina prov., NE Sicily, on N slope of Peloritani Mts. and 6 mi. SSE of Milazzo; soap mfg.

Santa Lucia di Piave (dē pyä′vĕ), village (pop. 1,409), Treviso prov., Veneto, N Italy, 14 mi. NNE of Treviso; cotton mill.

Santa-Lucia-di-Tallano (sän′tä-lōōchē′ä-dē-täl-lä′nô), village (pop. 940), S Corsica, 7 mi. NE of Sartène; olive-oil mfg.; winegrowing.

Santa Lucía Milpas Altas, Guatemala: see SANTA LUCÍA.

Santa Lucia Range (săn′tu̇ lōōsē′u̇), in Monterey and San Luis Obispo counties, W Calif., one of the Coast Ranges, extends c.140 mi. SE from S shore of Carmel Bay to Cuyama R. at N end of San Rafael Mts. For c.60 mi. in N, it rises steeply from the Pacific; S part is bordered by coastal strip. Range is W wall of Salinas valley. Junipero Serra Peak (hŭnĭ′pûrō sĕ′rū) (5,844 ft.), 17 mi. W of King City, is highest point. Mt. Carmel (kärmĕl′) (4,430 ft.) is 15 mi. SSE of Carmel.

Santa Lucía River (sän′tä lōōsē′ä), S Uruguay, rises NE of Minas (Lavalleja dept.), flows c.125 mi. W and S, past San Ramón and Santa Lucía, along Florida–Canelones and San José–Canelones dept. borders, to the Río de la Plata just W of Montevideo at Santiago Vázquez, where it is crossed by a large bridge.

Santa Lucía Utatlán, Sololá dept., Guatemala: see SANTA LUCÍA.

Santa Luisa (sän′tä lwē′sä), mining settlement (1930 pop. 3,085), Antofagasta prov., N Chile, on railroad and 28 mi. NE of Taltal; nitrate mining.

Santaluz (săntu̇lōōzh′), city (pop. 1,893), NE Bahia, Brazil, on railroad and 90 mi. NW of Alagoinhas; sisal shipping. Chromite mine; cadmium deposits. Until 1944, called Santa Luzia.

Santa Luzia (săn′tu̇ lōōzē′u̇). **1** City, Bahia, Brazil: see SANTALUZ. **2** City, Goiás, Brazil: see LUZIÂNIA. **3** City (pop. 3,544), S central Minas Gerais, Brazil, on the Rio das Velhas and 10 mi. NNE of Belo Horizonte; textile milling, cinnabar mining. **4** City (pop. 1,997), central Paraíba, NE Brazil, on Borborema Plateau, 27 mi. NE of Patos; important bismuth deposits found here in 1942; also has tungsten, beryl, and vanadium deposits. Formerly called Santa Luzia do Sabugy; and, 1944–48, Sabugi.

Santa Luzia, village (pop. 150), Faro dist., S Portugal, on the Atlantic (S coast), just S of Tavira; bathing resort; fisheries.

Santa Luzia do Itanhi (dōō ētūnyē′), city (pop. 730), S Sergipe, NE Brazil, 5 mi. S of Estância. Called Inajaroba, 1944–48.

Santa Luzia do Norte (dōō nôr′tĭ), town (pop. 1,213), E Alagoas, NE Brazil, on a lagoon 6 mi. NW of Maceió; textile and sugar milling.

Santa Luzia Island (□ 14), one of Cape Verde Isls., in Windward group, bet. São Vicente Isl. (5 mi. NW) and São Nicolau Isl. (18 mi. ESE), in the Atlantic; 8 mi. long, up to 3 mi. wide; 16°45′N 24°45′W. Uninhabited, barren. Rises to 1,296 ft.

Santa Magdalena de Pulpis (sän′tä mägdälä′nä dā pōōl′pēs), village (pop. 1,036), Castellón de la Plana prov., E Spain, 12 mi. SW of Vinaroz; olive-oil processing; wine, almonds. Stone quarries.

Santa Margarita (sän′tä märgärē′tä), town (pop. 3,787), Majorca, Balearic Isls., 25 mi. ENE of Palma; agr. center (cereals, fruit, almonds, grapes, vegetables, hogs); lumbering. Alcohol distilling, flour milling, wine making, apricot-purée mfg.

Santa Margarita (săn′tu̇ märgu̇rē′tu̇), village (pop. c.725), San Luis Obispo co., SW Calif., 9 mi. N of San Luis Obispo; ships cattle.

Santa Margarita Island (sän′tä märgärē′tä) (□ 85), off Pacific coast of Lower California, NW Mexico, sheltering Magdalena Bay, 90 mi. WNW of La Paz; 24 mi. long NW–SE, 2–5 mi. wide. Uninhabited, barren; rises to 1,858 ft. Magnesite deposits. Sometimes Margarita Isl.

Santa Margarita River (săn′tu̇ märgu̇rē′tu̇), S Calif., rises in SW Riverside co., flows c.50 mi. SW to the Pacific near Oceanside; flow is intermittent.

Santa Margherita di Belice (sän′tä märgĕrē′tä dē bĕlē′chĕ), town (pop. 7,629), Agrigento prov., W Sicily, 13 mi. E of Castelvetrano; cereals, wine, olive oil.

Santa Margherita Ligure (lē′gōōrĕ), town (pop. 6,518), Genova prov., Liguria, N Italy, port on Gulf of Rapallo and 15 mi. ESE of Genoa, in olive- and vegetable-growing region; fisheries (coral, tunny); mfg. (rope, lace). Winter resort, bathing place.

Santa María, department, Argentina: see ALTA GRACIA.

Santa María (sän′tä märē′ä), town (pop. 2,028), ⊙ Santa María dept. (□ 2,712; pop. 12,208), E Catamarca prov., Argentina, 65 mi. NNE of Andalgalá, on Cajón or Santa María R., near Tucumán prov. border; agr. center (fruit, tomatoes, pepper, nuts, cattle). Mining near by.

Santa Maria, Azores: see SANTA MARIA ISLAND.

Santa María, town (pop. 3,236), Majorca, Balearic Isls., on railroad and 8 mi. NE of Palma; agr. center (olives, almonds, carobs, grapes, figs, tubers, cereals, livestock). Mfg. of ceramics, cotton goods, meat products. Near by are Sou Pou caverns.

Santa Maria (săn′tu̇ mu̇rē′u̇). **1** City, Bahia, Brazil: see SANTA MARIA DA VITÓRIA. **2** City (1950 pop. 45,907), Rio Grande do Sul, Brazil, 150 mi. W of Pôrto Alegre, near head of fertile Jacuí valley, at foot of the Serra Geral; important rail center with extensive trade in livestock, alfalfa, rice, wine, fruit, maté, coal, and timber. Has railroad shops, breweries, tanneries, meat-processing plants. Airfield. One of state's most progressive cities, with faculty of pharmacy (established 1931). Formerly also called Santa Maria da Bôca (old spelling, Bocca) do Monte.

Santa Maria (săn′tu̇ mu̇rē′u̇), town, Cape Verde Isls., port on S coast of SAL isl., 125 mi. NNE of Praia (on São Tiago Isl.); 16°36′N 22°55′W. Saltworks 1 mi. N.

Santa María (sän′tä märē′ä), town (pop. 1,401), Aconcagua prov., central Chile, in Andean foothills, 5 mi. E of San Felipe; agr. center (hemp, tobacco, fruit, wine, livestock).

Santa María or **Santa María de Dota** (dā dō′tä), town (pop. 139), San José prov., S central Costa Rica, in W spur of Cordillera de Talamanca, 22 mi. SSE of San José; coffee, corn, beans, livestock; lumbering.

Santa María. 1 or **Santa María de Jesús** (dā hāsōōs′), village (1940 pop. 716), Quezaltenango dept., SW Guatemala, on Samalá R. (power station) and 8 mi. S of Quezaltenango, at SE foot of volcano Santa María; alt. c.5,000 ft. **2** or **Santa María de Jesús,** town (1950 pop. 4,229), Sacatepéquez dept., S central Guatemala, at N foot of Agua volcano, 5 mi. SE of Antigua; alt. 8,596 ft.; cotton weaving; vegetables, corn, beans. Ascent of the Agua starts here. **3** or **Santa María Chiquimula** (chēkēmōō′lä), town (1950 pop. 1,414), Totonicapán dept., W central Guatemala, 8 mi. NNE of Totonicapán; alt. 6,601 ft.; market center; corn, wheat, beans.

Santa María, active volcano (12,362 ft.), Quezaltenango dept., SW Guatemala, 6 mi. SSW of Quezaltenango. Its eruption of 1902 destroyed Quezaltenango. Active last in 1929. Santa María village at SE foot.

Santa María or **Santa María Ajoloapan** (ähōlwä′pän), town (pop. 2,639), Mexico state, central Mexico, 37 mi. N of Mexico city; cereals, maguey, livestock.

Santa María, town (1950 pop. 153), Nueva Segovia dept., NW Nicaragua, 16 mi. NW of Ocotal; sugar cane, livestock.

Santa María, village (pop. 543), Herrera prov., S central Panama, on branch of Inter-American Highway, in Santa María R. valley, and 18 mi. NW of Chitré; corn, rice, beans, livestock.

Santa María, town (dist. pop. 4,451), Misiones dept., S Paraguay, 15 mi. SE of San Juan Bautista; cattle raising. Founded near by in 1592, moved to its present site in 1669. Has noted Jesuit relics. Sometimes Santa María de Fe.

Santa Maria (săn′tu̇ mu̇rē′u̇, Sp. sän′tä märē′ä). **1** Town (1939 pop. 2,174; 1948 municipality pop. 17,509), Bulacan prov., S central Luzon, Philippines, 15 mi. N of Manila; rice-growing center. **2** Town (1939 pop. 2,324; 1948 municipality pop. 13,637), Ilocos Sur prov., N Luzon, Philippines, 11 mi. SSE of Vigan, near W coast; rice-growing center.

Santa Maria (săn′tu̇ mu̇rē′u̇). **1** City (pop. 10,440), Santa Barbara co., SW Calif., 25 mi. SSE of San Luis Obispo and on Santa Maria R.; trade and shipping center for Santa Maria valley (flower seed, bulbs, vegetables, grain, beans, sugar beets). Oil refining; oil fields near by. Seat of co. fair and a jr. col. Inc. 1905. **2** Village (pop. c.100), Cameron co., extreme S Texas, 25 mi. WNW of Brownsville; rail point in irrigated agr. area.

Santa María, Uruguay: see PIRARAJÁ.

Santa María (sän′tä märē′ä), town (pop. 806), Sucre state, NE Venezuela, in coastal range, 37 mi. SW of Carúpano; coffee, tobacco.

Santa Maria, Cape (săn′tu̇ mu̇rē′u̇), low headland on the Atlantic, the southernmost point of Portugal just SE of Faro; 36°58′N 7°53′W; lighthouse. It lies at S tip of sandy isls. extending along this section of coast.

Santa María, Cape, on coast of Rocha dept., SE Uruguay, just S of La Paloma; 34°40′S 54°9′W. Frequently considered to mark mouth of the Río de la Plata on the Atlantic.

Santa María, Cayo (kī′ō sän′tä märē′ä), narrow key (8 mi. long), off N Cuba, 26 mi. ESE of Caibarién.

Santa María, Lake (□ 30), in Chihuahua, N Mexico, 60 mi. SW of Ciudad Juárez (U.S. border); 15 mi. long, 2–4 mi. wide. Receives Santa María R.

Santa María Ajoloapan, Mexico: see SANTA MARÍA.

Santa Maria a Monte (sän′tä märē′ä ä môn′tĕ), village (pop. 1,032), Pisa prov., Tuscany, central Italy, 15 mi. E of Pisa.

Santa María Atarasquillo, Mexico: see ATARASQUILLO.

Santa Maria a Vico (vē′kô), town (pop. 6,544), Caserta prov., Campania, S Italy, 8 mi. ESE of Caserta; macaroni.

Santa Maria Capua Vetere (kä′pwä vā′tĕrĕ), town (pop. 21,916), Caserta prov., Campania, S Italy, 3 mi. SE of Capua; rail junction; foundries, sausage factories, food cannery, silk and paper mills. Has large agr. trade (grapes, olives, fruit, livestock). Occupies site of anc. CAPUA.

Santa María Chiquimula, Guatemala: see SANTA MARÍA, town.

Santa Maria da Bôca do Monte, Brazil: see SANTA MARIA, Rio Grande do Sul.

Santa Maria da Vitória (săn′tu̇ mu̇rē′u̇ dä vētô′ryu̇), city (pop. 1,685), W Bahia, Brazil, head of navigation on Corrente R. (left tributary of the Sao Francisco) and 65 mi. WSW of Bom Jesus da Lapa; sugar, hides, wool, lumber. Until 1944, called Santa Maria.

Santa María de Dota, Costa Rica: see SANTA MARÍA.

Santa María de Huerta (dā wĕr′tä), town (pop. 1,327), Soria prov., N central Spain, on Madrid-Barcelona RR and 37 mi. SSE of Soria. Noted for its monastery (founded 1179) with refectory, declared a natl. monument, and for the former palace of duke of Cerralbo, now a religious col. Region produces wheat, sugar beets.

Santa María de Ipire (sän′tä märē′ä dä ēpē′rā), town (pop. 1,357), Guárico state, N central Venezuela, in llanos, 37 mi. S of Zaraza; cattle raising.

Santa María de Jesús, Guatemala: see SANTA MARÍA, town.

Santa María del Berrocal (dĕl bĕrōkäl′), town (pop. 1,330), Ávila prov., central Spain, 35 mi. SSE of Salamanca; flour milling, mfg. of textile goods.

Santa María del Campo (käm′pō), town (pop. 1,303), Burgos prov., N Spain, 20 mi. SE of Burgos; grain- and winegrowing, sheep raising. Has a noted 16th-cent. tower and 13th–15th-cent. Gothic church.

Santa María del Campo Rus (rōōs′), town (pop. 2,179), Cuenca prov., E central Spain, 38 mi. SSW of Cuenca; grain- and winegrowing, stock raising.

Santa María del Monte (mōn′tä). **1** Town (pop. 2,884), Mexico state, central Mexico, 11 mi. W of Toluca; cereals, livestock. **2** Town (pop. 1,406), Puebla, E Mexico, in Sierra Madre, 13 mi. NE of Tehuacán; alt. 8,399 ft.; cereals, sugar cane, livestock. Sometimes Vicente Guerrero.

Santa María del Oro (dĕl ō′rō). **1** Town, Durango, Mexico: see EL ORO. **2** Town (pop. 1,023), Nayarit, W Mexico, near Pacific coast, 20 mi. SSE of Tepic; corn, beans, sugar cane, cattle, hogs. Silver deposits near by.

Santa María de los Ángeles (dā lōs än′hĕlĕs), town (pop. 1,445), Jalisco, W Mexico, on N affluent of Santiago R. and 4 mi. N of Colotlán; alt. 5,797 ft.; grain, vegetables, stock.

Santa María de los Llanos (dä lōs lyä'nōs), town (pop. 1,029), Cuenca prov., E central Spain, 7 mi. SW of Belmonte; cereals, grapes, livestock. Mineral springs.

Santa María del Páramo (dĕl pä'rämō), town (pop. 1,759), Leon prov., NW Spain, 20 mi. SW of Leon; tanning, flour milling, brandy distilling; cereals, beans, wine, fruit.

Santa María del Pirarajá, Uruguay: see PIRARAJÁ.

Santa María del Río (dĕl rē'ō), city (pop. 2,816), San Luis Potosí, N central Mexico, in Sierra Madre Oriental, 30 mi. SE of San Luis Potosí; alt. 5,587 ft. Agr. center (grain, cotton, fruit, stock). Cinnabar deposits.

Santa María del Rosario (rōsär'yō), town (pop. 1,581), Havana prov., W Cuba, 8 mi. SE of Havana; dairying, sugar growing. Has asphalt deposits and mineral springs. Noted for its richly decorated church.

Santa María del Tule (dĕl tōō'lā), town (pop. 1,109), Oaxaca, S Mexico, in Sierra Madre del Sur, 6 mi. E of Oaxaca; cereals, fruit, sugar cane. Famous for its great cypress tree (*Taxodium distilium*), considered to be oldest living thing on earth, c.160 ft. in height and in circumference; estimated to be 4,000–5,000 years old; was worshipped by Zapotecs as god of growth.

Santa María del Valle (vä'yä), town (pop. 1,129), Huánuco dept., central Peru, in Cordillera Central, on Huallaga R. and 7 mi. NE of Huánuco, on a highway to Tingo María; coca, coffee, cacao; cattle raising.

Santa María de Nieva, Spain: see SANTA MARÍA LA REAL DE NIEVA.

Santa María de Otáez, Mexico: see OTÁEZ.

Santa Maria di Leuca, Cape (dē lā'ōōkä), SE extremity of Italy, on "heel" of Ital. peninsula, at NE entrance to Gulf of Taranto; 39°48'N 18°23'E; lighthouse. Punta Ristola (39°47'18"N) lies 1 mi. WSW.

Santa Maria di Licodia (lēkō'dyä), village (pop. 4,920), Catania prov., E Sicily, on SW slope of Mt. Etna, 13 mi. NW of Catania, in orange-growing region.

Santa Maria do Araguaia, Brazil: see ARAGUACEMA.

Santa Maria do Suassuí or **Santa Maria do Suaçuí** (both: sän'tü mürē'ü dōō swüswē'), city (pop. 1,659), E central Minas Gerais, Brazil, 75 mi. E of Diamantina; mica and rock-crystal deposits.

Santa María Falls, Argentina and Brazil: see IGUASSÚ FALLS.

Santa Maria Island, easternmost island (□ 37; 1950 pop. 11,786) of Azores, in the Atlantic, forming, together with São Miguel Isl. (50 mi. N), the archipelago's E group; Vila do Pôrto (36°56'N 25°9'W), the isl.'s only port, is on SW shore. Santa Maria is the only isl. of the Azores without volcanic features. It is 10 mi. long, 5 mi. wide; rises to 1,936 ft. at the double-peaked Pico Alto. Wine and vegetable growing; cattle raising; earthenware mfg. Near W coast, N of Vila do Pôrto, is Santa Maria airport, an important stop for transatlantic flights, and an Allied air base since Second World War. Gonçalo Velho Cabral visited the isl. in 1432, thus confirming the existence of the archipelago. Administratively, part of Ponta Delgada dist.

Santa María Island (sän'tä märē'ä) (□ 12), 5 mi. off coast of Arauco prov., S central Chile, at entrance to Arauco Gulf, 27 mi. SW of Concepción; 37°S 73°30'W. Cattle and sheep raising.

Santa María Island, Galápagos: see FLOREANA ISLAND.

Santa María Ixhuatán, Guatemala: see IXHUATÁN.

Santa Maria la Longa (lä lông'gä), village (pop. 911), Udine prov., Friuli-Venezia Giulia, NE Italy, 9 mi. SSE of Udine; alcohol distillery.

Santa María la Real de Nieva (lä räāl' dā nyā'vä) or **Santa María de Nieva,** town (pop. 932), Segovia prov., central Spain, 18 mi. WNW of Segovia; cereals, carobs, grapes, chickpeas, sheep. Has noted 15th-cent. church, with magnificent portal and beautiful cloister.

Santa Maria Madalena (sän'tü mürē'ü müdülā'nü), city (pop. 1,095), E central Rio de Janeiro state, Brazil, on railroad and 45 mi. WSW of Campos, in coffeegrowing region; distilling, dairying.

Santa María Moyotzingo, Mexico: see MOYOTZINGO.

Santa Maria Nuova (sän'tä märē'ä nwô'vä), village (pop. 1,162), Ancona prov., The Marches, central Italy, 4 mi. SE of Iesi; woolen mills.

Santa María River (sän'tä märē'ä) or **Cajón River** (kähōn'), NW Argentina, a headstream of the Río Salado, joining the Calchaquí in S Salta prov. 10 mi. E of Cafayate to form GUACHIPAS RIVER.

Santa Maria River (sän'tü mürē'ü), central Espírito Santo, Brazil, flows c.50 mi. SE to Espírito Santo Bay of the Atlantic at Vitória. Navigable below Santa Leopoldina.

Santa María River (sän'tä märē'ä). **1** In Chihuahua, N Mexico, rises in Sierra Madre Occidental NE of Ciudad Guerrero, flows c.200 mi. N, past Bachíniva, Namiquipa, Buenaventura, and Galeana, to L. Santa María 70 mi. SW of Ciudad Juárez. Often dry. **2** River, N central and E Mexico, rises in Sierra Madre Oriental S of San Luis Potosí near Guanajuato border, flows c.200 mi. E, past Villa de Reyes and Santa María del Río, along San Luis Potosí–Querétaro border, to join Moctezuma R. in forming Pánuco R. in fertile La Huasteca plains 50 mi. SW of Tampico. Used for irrigation. Called Tamuin R. (täm'wēn) in lower course. Receives Río Verde.

Santa María River, SW Panama, rises in the Serranía de Tabasará 4 mi. NW of Santa Fe, flows SE c.55 mi., past Santa Fe and San Francisco, to Parita Gulf of the Pacific, 8 mi. NNW of Chitra. Navigable for small vessels to San Francisco.

Santa Maria River (săn'tü mürē'ü). **1** In W central Ariz., intermittent headstream which rises in mountain region W of Prescott and flows c.50 mi. SW to point near S tip of Hualpai Mts., where it joins Big Sandy R. to form Bill Williams R. **2** In SW Calif., formed by intermittent headstreams in NW Santa Barbara co., flows c.30 mi. NW and W to the Pacific 11 mi. W of Santa Maria. Its valley (c.30 mi. long; up to 10 mi. wide) is oil-producing, seed-growing, and farming region; Santa Maria is chief center.

Santa-Maria-Siché (sän'tä-märē'ä-sē-shā'), village (pop. 607), central Corsica, 13 mi. ESE of Ajaccio.

Santa María Visitación, Guatemala: see VISITACIÓN.

Santa Marina del Rey (sän'tä märē'nä dĕl rā'), town (pop. 1,194), Leon prov., NW Spain, 11 mi. ENE of Astorga; lumber, livestock, cereals, wine.

Santa Marinella (sän'tä märēnĕl'lä), town (pop. 1,852), Roma prov., Latium, central Italy, on Tyrrhenian Sea, 5 mi. SE of Civitavecchia; resort.

Santa Marta (sän'tä mär'tä), city (pop. 25,113), ⊙ Magdalena dept., N Colombia, port on Caribbean Sea, at NW foot of Sierra Nevada de Santa Marta, 40 mi. NE of Barranquilla, 450 mi. N of Bogotá; 11°15'N 74°13'W. Shipping, trading, fishing, and banana-growing center, connected S by railroad with Ciénaga and Fundación. Its banana-shipping industry is the most important on the continent. Also has fish canneries, brick- and tileworks, ice plants, distilleries. Exports, besides bananas, coffee and hides. The see of a bishop, it has a cathedral (once tomb of Bolívar); and also Fort San Fernando, ruins of Santo Domingo monastery, modern United Fruit Company hosp. One of the oldest cities in South America, founded 1525 by Rodrigo de Bastidas. Looted by Drake (1596) and other freebooters. During War of Independence it sided with the royalists, was captured briefly (1813) by Cartagena, and was finally captured 1821. On the near-by estate San Pedro Alejandrino (3 mi. SE), Simón Bolívar died.

Santa Marta or **Santa Marta de los Barros** (dā lōs bä'rōs), town (pop. 5,101), Badajoz prov., W Spain, 26 mi. SE of Badajoz; mining (silver-bearing lead) and agr. center (cereals, olives, grapes, livestock).

Santa Marta, Sierra Nevada de (syĕ'rä nävä'dhä dā sän'tä mär'tä), Andean massif in Magdalena dept., N Colombia, E of Barranquilla, rises abruptly from Caribbean coast as steep volcanic formation, separated from Cordillera Oriental (E) by César R. depression; rises pyramidally to snow-covered Pico Cristóbal Colón (18,950 ft.), highest in Colombia. The region is little developed and mostly inhabited by primitive Aruac Indian tribes.

Santa Marta de los Barros, Spain: see SANTA MARTA.

Santa Marta de Ortigueira, Spain: see ORTIGUEIRA.

Santa Marta de Penaguião (sän'tü mär'tü dĭ pĭnügyä'ō), town, Vila Real dist., N Portugal, on Corgo R. and 6 mi. SSW of Vila Real, in heart of port-wine-growing region.

Santa Marta Grande, Cape (sän'tü mär'tü grän'dĭ), headland on the Atlantic, Santa Catarina, S Brazil, 10 mi. S of Laguna; 28°38'S 48°51'W.

Santa Maura, Greece: see LEUKAS.

Sant'Ambrogio di Valpolicella (säntämbrô'jô dē välpôlēchĕl'lä), village (pop. 1,343), Verona prov., Veneto, N Italy, at SW foot of Monti Lessini, 10 mi. NW of Verona; marble quarries.

Santa Mônica (sän'tä mō'nēkä), town (pop. 1,306), Hidalgo, central Mexico, on railroad and 14 mi. SE of Pachuca; corn, maguey, livestock.

Santa Monica (săn'tü mŏ'nĭkü), residential city (pop. 71,595), Los Angeles co., S Calif., suburb 15 mi. W of downtown Los Angeles, on Santa Monica Bay, with Santa Monica Mts. in background; resort, with yacht harbor, piers, beaches; has amusement zone (in Ocean Park section, S). Site of large aircraft factory and airport. Mfg. of tile and other clay products, tools, cosmetics, plastics. Santa Monica City Col. (jr.) is here. Ranch (186 acres) and home of Will Rogers are in a state park. Laid out 1875; inc. as town 1886, as city 1902.

Santa Mônica Ario, Mexico: see ARIO, Michoacán.

Santa Monica Mountains (c.1–3,000 ft.), S Calif., an E-W range c.40 mi. long; mts. closely parallel N shore of Santa Monica Bay from Oxnard E to Santa Monica, where they continue inland to Los Angeles R. valley, which connects Los Angeles basin (S of range) with San Fernando Valley (N).

Santana (säntä'nü). **1** City (pop. 2,446), W Bahia, Brazil, 90 mi. SE of Barreiras; sugar, manioc; nitrates. Formerly called Sant' Anna dos Brejos. **2** City, Ceará, Brazil: see LICANIA. **3** City, Goiás, Brazil: see URUAÇU. **4** Village, SW Rio de Janeiro state, Brazil, on Piraí R. (dam) and 3 mi. S of Barra da Piraí. Its reservoir (alt. 1,191 ft.) receives water pumped from Santa Cecília reservoir (alt. 1,158 ft.) and itself feeds the Forçacava hydroelectric plants via VIGÁRIO tunnel.

Santana, town (pop. 4,468), Madeira, near N coast of Madeira isl., 11 mi. N of Funchal; alt. 1,367 ft. Resort. Alcohol distilling. Sugar cane and sweet potatoes grown in area. Pico Ruivo (6,106 ft.) ascended from here.

Santana, village (pop. 1,049), Coimbra dist., N central Portugal, 8 mi. NE of Figueira da Foz; pinewoods; wine and oranges.

Santana, Coxilha de, Brazil and Uruguay: see SANTA ANA, CUCHILLA DE.

Santana de Parnaíba (dĭ pŭrnäē'bü), city (pop. 906), SE São Paulo, Brazil, on Tietê R. and 18 mi. NW of São Paulo; brewing, distilling. Until 1944, Parnaíba.

Santana do Ipanema (dōō ēpünā'mü), city (pop. 2,270), W Alagoas, NE Brazil, 40 mi. W of Palmeira dos Índios; cotton, hides, cattle, cheese, castor beans. Handicraft lacemaking. Formerly spelled Sant' Anna do Ipanema.

Sant' Ana do Livramento, Brazil: see LIVRAMENTO, Rio Grande do Sul.

Santana do Matos (mä'tōōs), city (pop. 954), central Rio Grande do Norte, NE Brazil, 95 mi. W of Natal; cattle-raising center; carnauba wax. Asbestos and marble deposits. Formerly spelled Sant' Anna do Mattos.

Santana do Paranaíba, Brazil: see PARANAÍBA.

Santana Rodríguez, Mexico: see SAN JUAN EVANGELISTA.

Sant'Anastasia (säntänästä'syä), town (pop. 7,760), Napoli prov., Campania, S Italy, at N foot of Vesuvius, 7 mi. ENE of Naples; mfg. (rope, copper cooking utensils).

Santander (säntändĕr'), department (□ 12,382; 1938 pop. 615,710; 1950 estimate 756,420), N central Colombia; ⊙ Bucaramanga. Bounded W by Magdalena R., watered by Sogamoso and Suárez rivers. Apart from the Magdalena lowlands, it consists of spurs of the Cordillera Oriental, with high, fertile valleys. Climate varies from the heat and humidity of the plains to the coolness of the high cordilleras; heaviest rains, Sept.-Nov. Among its main resources are the rich petroleum fields around Barrancabermeja, and there is gold mining in Bucaramanga vicinity. Agr. is of prime importance, especially coffee, cacao, tobacco, sugar cane crops; also rice, corn, wheat, silk, cotton, bananas, fique. Considerable stock raising. Forested mtn. slopes yield cinchona, rubber, balsam, fine wood. Processing and textile industries are centered at Bucaramanga, Socorro, Piedecuesta, and San Gil. Barrancabermeja has important petroleum-refining plants and is the starting point of oil pipe line to Cartagena on the Caribbean.

Santander, town (pop. 4,421), Cauca dept., SW Colombia, on Popayán-Manizales highway, on slopes of Cordillera Central, 30 mi. S of Cali; alt. 3,658 ft. Rail terminus, road and agr. center (cacao, sugar cane, tobacco, coffee, fique, quinine, stock). Founded 1543. Copper, gold, and platinum mines near by.

Santander (săntăndâr', săntăn'dür, Sp. säntändĕr'), mountainous coastal province (□ 2,044; pop. 393,710), N Spain, in Old Castile, bordering the Bay of Biscay; ⊙ Santander. Covered by the Cantabrian Mts. reaching highest peaks in the Picos de Europa bet. Santander and Oviedo provs. Drained by short, swift rivers—Miera, Besaya, Deva—forming deep, green valleys; Ebro R. rises in S near Reinosa. High, rocky coast with several good harbors (Santander, Santoña, Castro Urdiales, Laredo). Favored by abundant rainfall, mtn. region of interior has extensive forests and excellent pastures (cattle raising, dairy products); along coast, chief occupations are fishing, fish processing, and boatbuilding. Iron, zinc, and some lead mines; rock-salt and limestone quarries. Agr. products: corn, potatoes, vegetables, apples, wine. Metallurgical industries, including iron and steel (Santander, Los Corrales de Buelna); other processing: dairy products, chemicals, leather, textiles, perfumes. Exports minerals, fish, and dairy products. Chief cities: Santander, Torrelavega, Reinosa, Castro Urdiales, Santoña.

Santander, city (pop. 84,971), ⊙ Santander prov., N Spain, seaport finely situated on sheltered inlet of Bay of Biscay circled by hills, 215 mi. N of Madrid; 43°28'N 3°49'W. Chief city and sea outlet of Old Castile, and a popular resort. Exports minerals, wheat, wool, and wine; has active fishing industry. Iron and steel mills, shipyards; mfg. of tubes, cables, machinery, tools; lead and zinc processing; oil refinery and chemical works (plastic materials, acetic acid, ammonium sulphate, tobacco factory, breweries, tanneries; makes also cement, perfumes, ceramics, cotton and linen cloth. Episcopal see. Consists of old town (on hill), with crooked streets and site of Gothic cathedral (13th cent.; restored) and modern town hall (with library and mus.); and new town (along bay), with fine promenade and modern bldgs. The excellent harbor has huge warehouses and numerous piers. Avenue following crest of hills behind city has many villas and gardens. Just NE on Bay of Biscay is resort of El Sardinero with fine bathing beaches. City is sometimes identified with Roman colony of *Portus Blendium*. In spite of its geographic position beyond Cantabrian Mts., it has had close historical and commercial ties with Castile since Middle Ages. Was sacked by France (1808). Commercial area, practically destroyed by fire (1941), is being rebuilt.

Santander Jiménez, Mexico: see JIMÉNEZ, Tamaulipas.

Santander Norte, department, Colombia: see NORTE DE SANTANDER.

Santander River, Mexico: see SOTO LA MARINA RIVER.

Sant'Andrea, island, Yugoslavia: see SVETI ANDRIJA, ISLAND OF.

Sant'Andrea Apostolo dello Ionio (säntändrā'ä äpô'stôlô dĕl-lô yô'nyô), town (pop. 5,170), Catanzaro prov., Calabria, S Italy, near Gulf of Squillace, 20 mi. S of Catanzaro; wine, olive oil.

Sant'Angelo, Sicily: see LICATA.

Sant'Angelo, Monte (môn'tĕ säntän'jĕlô), highest point (4,734 ft.) in mts. around Bay of Naples, at SW base of peninsula of Sorrento, Italy, 4 mi. SSE of Castellammare di Stabia.

Sant'Angelo de' Lombardi (dĕlômbär'dē), town (pop. 1,964), Avellino prov., Campania, S Italy, 20 mi. E of Avellino; bell foundry.

Sant'Angelo in Vado (ēn vä'dô), town (pop. 1,922), Pesaro e Urbino prov., The Marches, central Italy, on Metauro R. and 12 mi. WSW of Urbino; woolen mill. Bishopric.

Sant'Angelo Lodigiano (lôdējä'nô), town (pop. 7,707), Milano prov., Lombardy, N Italy, on Lambro R. and 7 mi. SW of Lodi. Agr. center; dairy industry, mfg. (dairy machinery, tank cars), foundry. Has medieval Visconti castle (gutted by fire in 1911).

Santanilla Islands, Honduras: see SWAN ISLANDS.

Santa Ninfa (sän'tä nēn'fä), village (pop. 6,494), Trapani prov., W Sicily, 15 mi. SSW of Alcamo, in olive-growing, livestock region.

Sant' Anna, Brazil: see LICANIA.

Sant' Anna do Livramento, Brazil: see LIVRAMENTO, Rio Grande do Sul.

Sant' Anna dos Brejos, Brazil: see SANTANA, Bahia.

Santanoni Peak (săn'tùnō"nē) (4,621 ft.), Essex co., NE N.Y., a summit of the Adirondacks, 11 mi. W of Mt. Marcy and 16 mi. SW of Lake Placid village.

Santanópole (sāntùnô'pōōlĭ), city (pop. 1,442), S Ceará, Brazil, on N slope of Serra do Araripe, 24 mi. W of Crato; sugar, cotton, tobacco, livestock. Formerly called Sant' Anna do Cariry.

Sant'Antimo (säntän'tēmô), town (pop. 11,713), Napoli prov., Campania, S Italy, 2 mi. SSE of Aversa.

Sant'Antioco (säntäntē'ôkô), town (pop. 6,774) and port on NE Sant'Antioco Isl., just off SW Sardinia; linked by rail (across chain of small islands) with mainland; fisheries (coral, tunny); wine. On site of Phoenician city (Sulci); has Phoenician-Roman necropolis, Christian catacombs.

Sant'Antioco Island (□ 42; pop. 9,353), in Mediterranean Sea, 1 mi. off SW Sardinia, in Cagliari prov.; volcanic, rocky; 11 mi. long, 6 mi. wide; rises to 889 ft. Linked by rail with mainland. Major fisheries in NE (tunny, coral, sea mussels, oysters); saltworks (NW); palm weaving (mats, rope, brooms); vineyards, herbs. Chief port, SANT'ANTIOCO. Phoenician-Roman ruins in NE.

Sant'Antonio Abate (säntäntô'nyô äbä'tĕ), village (pop. 2,221), Napoli prov., Campania, S Italy, 2 mi. SW of Angri; food canning.

Santany (säntänyē'), town (pop. 3,757), Majorca, Balearic Isls., rail terminus 39 mi. SE of Palma; agr. center (almonds, cereals, carobs, truck produce, livestock). Lime quarrying; meat packing.

Santaokow or **San-tao-kou** (sän'dou'gō'), village, SE Kirin prov., Manchuria, on rail spur and 35 mi. SW of Yenki, near Tumen R. (Korea line); coal mining.

Santa Olalla (sän'tä ōlä'lyä), town (pop. 2,291), Toledo prov., central Spain, 25 mi. NW of Toledo; cereals, vegetables, olives, grapes, sheep; olive-oil pressing, dairying. Hydroelectric plant.

Santa Olalla del Cala (dĕl kä'lä), town (pop. 3,545), Huelva prov., SW Spain, in Sierra Morena, near Seville prov. border, on railroad and 18 mi. E of Aracena; agr. center (cereals, olives, cork, timber, livestock; agriculture). Sawmilling, flour milling. The Tauler iron mines are 3 mi. NW.

Santa Panagia, Cape (sän'tä pänäjē'ä), point on SE coast of Sicily, N of Syracuse; 37°7'N 15°18'E. Major tunny fisheries (W).

Santa Paula (săn'tù pô'lù), city (pop. 11,049), Ventura co., S Calif., near the coast, on Santa Clara R. and 13 mi. ENE of Ventura; oil-producing center, with refineries; packs, ships citrus fruit. Near by is lemon orchard reputed to be world's largest. Laid out 1875, inc. 1902.

Santa Perpetua de Moguda (sän'tä pĕrpĕ'twä dā mōgōō'dhä), village (pop. 1,901), Barcelona prov., NE Spain, 2 mi. E of Sabadell; brandy mfg. Livestock, wine, cereals, hemp in area.

Santa Philomena, Brazil: see SANTA FILOMENA.

Santa Pola (sän'tä pō'lä), town (pop. 5,325), Alicante prov., E Spain, port on the Mediterranean, 11 mi. SSW of Alicante; boatbuilding, sail mfg., brandy distilling; rice, wine, cereals, fruit. Bathing beaches. Elche lagoon 3 mi. WSW. Saltworks. Iberian and Roman relics found near by.

Santa Pola, Cape, on the Mediterranean, in Alicante prov., E Spain, 10 mi. SSW of Alicante; 38°14'N 0°28'W. Lighthouse.

Santaquin (săntùkēn'), city (pop. 1,214), Utah co., central Utah, 19 mi. SSW of Provo, in livestock and agr. area irrigated by water from Utah L. (NW) and Strawberry R. Settled 1851 by Mormons. Inc. 1931.

Santa Quitéria (sän'tù kētĕ'ryù). **1** City (pop. 1,367), N central Ceará, Brazil, 45 mi. S of Sobral; cotton, cattle. Kaolin deposits. Airfield. **2** City, Maranhão, Brazil: see SANTA QUITÉRIA DO MARANHAO.

Santa Quitéria do Maranhão (dōō mùrùnyä'ō), city (pop. 1,067), NE Maranhão, Brazil, on left bank of Parnaíba R. (Piauí line) and 60 mi. SW of Parnaíba; hides, cotton, carnauba wax. Until 1944, Santa Quitéria; and, 1944–48, Bacuri.

Santar (săntär'), village (pop. 1,042), Viseu dist., N central Portugal, 6 mi. S of Viseu; winegrowing.

Sant'Arcangelo (säntärkän'jĕlô), town (pop. 5,418), Potenza prov., Basilicata, S Italy, near Agri R., 38 mi. SE of Potenza, in cereal- and fruitgrowing region.

Sant'Arcangelo di Romagna (dē rômä'nyä), town (pop. 3,011), Forlì prov., Emilia-Romagna, N central Italy, 6 mi. W of Rimini; paper and lumber mills. Has a Malatesta castle.

Santarém (săntärĕm'). **1** City, Bahia, Brazil: see ITUBERÁ. **2** City (pop. 7,527), W Pará, Brazil, on right bank of the Tapajós at its influx into the Amazon, and 430 mi. W of Belém. State's 2d largest city, port of call for Amazon steamers and hydroplane landing. Commercial center with guarana trade and handicraft industries. Ships rubber, cacao, cotton, jute, sugar, vanilla, fish. Founded 1661 as Jesuit mission and Port. fort. Here settled many Confederate veterans after U.S. Civil War.

Santarém, district (□ 2,583; pop. 421,996), central Portugal, almost coextensive with Ribatejo prov.; ⊙ Santarém. Traversed NE-SW by lower Tagus R., whose alluvial valley, except for marshy mouth on Lisbon Bay, is one of Portugal's richest agr. areas. Chief towns are Santarém, Abrantes, Tomar, Aleirim, and Torres Novas.

Santarém, anc. *Scalabis*, later *Praesidium Julium*, city (pop. 11,785), ⊙ Santarém dist. and Ribatejo prov., central Portugal, above right bank of lower Tagus R. and 45 mi. NE of Lisbon; commercial center of one of Portugal's richest agr. regions, with trade in olive oil, wine, fruit, grain, and cork. River port. Mfg. of chemical fertilizer, alcohol distilling. Important since Roman times because of its strategic location along approaches to Lisbon, it was a Moorish stronghold 715–1093. The upper town has a Jesuit seminary (built 1676); a Franciscan convent (1240; now used as barracks); and several old churches, including one, rebuilt 13th cent. from a mosque, which contains municipal mus. The railroad station is in Ribeira dist. along waterfront.

Santaren Channel (săntùrĕn'), strait (c.125 mi. long) in the West Indies, S of Florida, bet. Cay Sal Bank (W) and Great Bahama Bank (E), linking the Straits of Florida (N) with Old Bahama Channel (S) off N Cuba.

Santa Rita (sän'tù rē'tù). **1** City (pop. 10,805), E Paraíba, NE Brazil, on right bank of Paraíba R., on railroad and 8 mi. W of João Pessoa; cotton and sugar milling, alcohol distilling. Ships fruit, agave fibers, and vegetables. Airfield. **2** City, São Paulo, Brazil: see SANTA RITA DO PASSA QUATRO.

Santa Rita (sän'tä rē'tä). **1** Town (pop. 475), Copán dept., W Honduras, 5 mi. ENE of Copán; tobacco, grain. **2** Town (pop. 1,293), Santa Bárbara dept., W Honduras, near Ulúa R., 10 mi. SSW of Santa Bárbara; mfg. of harvest hats; rice, corn, coffee, tobacco.

Santa Rita, Mexico: see VILLA HIDALGO, Zacatecas.

Santa Rita (sän'tä rē'tä). **1** Village, Batangas prov., Philippines: see BATANGAS, town. **2** Town (1939 pop. 1,451; 1948 municipality pop. 12,684), Pampanga prov., central Luzon, Philippines, 5 mi. WSW of San Fernando; sugar cane, rice. Sometimes San Jose.

Santa Rita (săn'tù rē'tù), village (pop. 2,135), Grant co., SW N.Mex., in foothills of Pinos Altos Mts., 12 mi. E of Silver City; alt. c.6,400 ft. Large open-pit copper mines here. Santa Rita Mine, once worked by Sp. convict labor, was rediscovered 1800. Molybdenum also mined. Black Peak is 9 mi. NW, Gila Natl. Forest just N.

Santa Rita (sän'tä rē'tä), town (pop. 3,513), Zulia state, NW Venezuela, landing on narrows of L. Maracaibo, 9 mi. SE of Maracaibo; agr. center (coconuts, corn, beans, bananas, cotton) in goat-grazing region.

Santa Rita de Catuna, Argentina: see CATUNA.

Santa Rita do Araguaia, Brazil: see GUIRATINGA.

Santa Rita do Jacutinga (sän'tù rē'tù dōō zhùkōō-tēng'gù), city (pop. 1,393), S Minas Gerais, Brazil, in the Serra da Mantiqueira, on Rio de Janeiro border, 26 mi. NW of Barra do Piraí; rail junction.

Santa Rita do Paranaíba, Brazil: see ITUMBIARA.

Santa Rita do Passa Quatro (sän'tù rē'tù dōō pä'sù kwä'trōō), city (pop. 3,636), E São Paulo, Brazil, on railroad and 40 mi. SSE of Ribeirão Prêto; sugar milling, distilling; citriculture, viticulture; coffee. Until 1944, Santa Rita.

Santa Rita do Rio Prêto, Brazil: see IBIPETUBA.

Santa Rita do Sapucaí (sän'tù rē'tù dōō sùpōōkäē'), city (pop. 5,184), SW Minas Gerais, Brazil, on N slope of the Serra da Mantiqueira, on railroad and 18 mi. NW of Itajubá; agr. trade center (coffee, tobacco, cattle); dairying. Formerly spelled Santa Rita do Sapucahy.

Santa Rita do Weil (sän"tù rē'tù dōō wāl'). town (pop. 208), W Amazonas, Brazil, on left bank of the Amazon and 20 mi. W of São Paulo de Olivença. Until 1939, Boa Vista.

Santa Rita Mountains (săn'tù rē'tù), Santa Cruz co., SE Ariz., N of Nogales; Mt. WRIGHTSON (9,432 ft.) is highest point. Range is in section of Coronado Natl. Forest. Large amounts of gold have been mined.

Santa River (sän'tä), Ancash dept., W central Peru, rises in Cordillera Occidental of the Andes 9 mi. WNW of Chiquián, flows NNW, through the Callejón de HUAYLAS, past Huarás, Carhuás, and Yungay, and below Huallanca turns W to the Pacific 2 mi. NW of Santa; 200 mi. long. Feeds irrigation system in lower course, forming one of Peru's main sugar-producing areas. Just above Huallanca and below the Callejón de Huaylas, where the Santa falls through a narrow gorge (Canyón de Perote), is a govt. hydroelectric development (including a dam, pressure tunnel, and transmission line) designed to turn Chimbote, with its fine natural harbor, into a major port and steel-milling center, drawing on the rich iron and coal resources along Santa R. and its affluents.

Santa Rosa, department, Argentina: see BAÑADO DE OVANTA.

Santa Rosa (sän'tä rō'sä). **1** Town (pop. 2,960), ⊙ Río Primero dept. (□ c.2,200; pop. 45,485), N central Córdoba prov., Argentina, on the Río Primero and 55 mi. ENE of Córdoba; wheat, flax, corn, alfalfa, livestock; dairying. **2** Town (1947 pop. 14,643), ⊙ La Pampa natl. territory and Santa Rosa dept. (1947 pop. 18,294), central Argentina, on railroad and 350 mi. WSW of Buenos Aires, 180 mi. NW of Bahía Blanca; 36°32'S 64°21'W. Rail junction, agr. center. Meat packing, dairying, flour milling. Trade in grain (rye, wheat, barley, corn) and livestock. Has govt. houses, natl. col., history mus., theater. Founded 1892. Sometimes called Santa Rosa de Toay. **3** Village (pop. estimate 1,000), ⊙ Santa Rosa dept. (□ 3,330; 1947 pop. 12,069), N Mendoza prov., Argentina, on Tunuyán R. (irrigation area), on railroad and 45 mi. SE of Mendoza; agr. center (wine, fruit, potatoes; grazing). Wine making, food canning. **4** Town (pop. estimate 1,200), ⊙ Junín dept. (□ 1,135; 1947 pop. 12,646), NE San Luis prov., Argentina, on Conlara R., on railroad and 90 mi. NE of San Luis; farming and lumbering center. Alfalfa, corn, wine, livestock; sawmills. Irrigation dam near by. **5** or **Santa Rosa de Calchines** (kälchē'nĕs), town (pop. estimate 1,000), E central Santa Fe prov., Argentina, on arm of Paraná R. and 27 mi. NE of Santa Fe; agr. (peanuts, flax, oats, livestock; citrus nurseries).

Santa Rosa. 1 Village (pop. c.2,100), Beni dept., NW Bolivia, near Yacuma R., 35 mi. ENE of Reyes, in the llanos; rice, sugar cane; sugar milling. **2** Town (pop. c.300), ⊙ Abuná prov., Pando dept., N Bolivia, on Abuná R. and 95 mi. ENE of Cobija; road junction; rubber collecting. **3** Town (pop. c.1,800), Santa Cruz dept., central Bolivia, 20 mi. NW of Portachuelo; sugar cane, cattle.

Santa Rosa (sän'tù rō'zù). **1** City (pop. 1,532), NW Rio Grande do Sul, Brazil, on W slope of Serra Geral, 30 mi. NNW of Santo Ângelo; rail-spur terminus; livestock, corn, maté, tobacco. Airfield. Sometimes called Santa Rosa das Missões. **2** City, São Paulo, Brazil: see SANTA ROSA DE VITERBO.

Santa Rosa. 1 or **Santa Rosa de Osos** (sän'tä rō'sä dā ō'sōs), town (pop. 4,133), Antioquia dept., NW central Colombia, in Cordillera Central, 30 mi. NNE of Medellín; alt. 8,661 ft. Gold-mining and stock-raising (cattle, hogs) center; potatoes, corn, sugar cane, coffee, yucca, fruit. **2** Town (pop. 2,111), Bolívar dept., N Colombia, 12 mi. E of Cartagena; corn, livestock. **3** or **Santa Rosa de Viterbo** (dā vētĕr'bō), town (pop. 2,119), Boyacá dept., central Colombia, in Cordillera Oriental, on Pan American Highway and 35 mi. NE of Tunja; alt. 8,267 ft. Potatoes, wheat, fruit, livestock. Colonial bldgs. Founded 1690. Copper deposits near by.

Santa Rosa, town (1950 pop. 4,672), El Oro prov., S Ecuador, on small navigable Santa Rosa R. and 13 mi. S of Machala (connected by railroad); trades in cacao, coffee, tobacco, cinchona, wax, lumber, copper, gold. Tanning.

Santa Rosa, department (□ 1,141; 1950 pop. 108,437), S Guatemala; ⊙ Cuilapa. On the Pacific; in Pacific piedmont, sloping S to coastal plain; drained by Esclavos R. In it are L. Ayarza and volcanoes Tecuamburro and Jumaitepeque. Rich agr. region: coffee, sugar cane, sesame, rice in low areas; corn, beans in highlands. Large cattle herds raised on fodder grasses. Main centers: Cuilapa (on Inter-American Highway), Chiquimulilla, Guazacapán. Chiquimulilla Canal serves coastal trade (fish, salt).

Santa Rosa or **Santa Rosa de Lima** (dä lē'mä), town (1950 pop. 742), Santa Rosa dept., S Guatemala, in Pacific piedmont, on Esclavos R. and 8 mi. N of Cuilapa; coffee, sugar cane, grain, cattle. Dept. capital until 1871.

Santa Rosa or **Santa Rosa de Copán** (dä kōpän'), city (pop. 7,972), ⊙ Copán dept., W Honduras, 115 mi. WNW of Tegucigalpa; 14°45'N 88°50'W; alt. 3,806 ft. Chief commercial center of W Honduras, in tobacco area; cigar mfg., coffee, rice, and sugar milling, mat weaving. Antimony mining near by. Has hosp., col.; bishopric. Airfield. Dates from 18th cent.; called Los Llanos until 1843.

Santa Rosa. **1** Town (pop. 2,586), Mexico state, central Mexico, 5 mi. S of El Oro; silver mining; stock raising. **2** or **Santa Rosa de Jáuregui** (dä hou'rägē), town (pop. 2,166), Querétaro, central Mexico, on affluent of Apaseo R. and 12 mi. NNW of Querétaro; alt. 6,594 ft. Agr. center (corn, wheat, beans, alfalfa, sugar, fruit, livestock). **3** City, Veracruz, Mexico: see MENDOZA.

Santa Rosa or **Santa Rosa del Peñón** (dĕl pänyōn'), town (1950 pop. 303), León dept., W Nicaragua, 40 mi. NE of León, in mining area (copper, gypsum); corn, beans.

Santa Rosa, village (pop. 83), Colón prov., central Panama, on Canal Zone border, on Chagres R. and 19 mi. SE of Colón; bananas, abacá, cacao.

Santa Rosa, town (dist. pop. 5,006), Misiones dept., S Paraguay, 25 mi. SE of San Juan Bautista; agr. center (maté, fruit, sugar cane, cattle); alcohol and liquor distilling. Has old Jesuit church, mostly destroyed by fire (1883). Founded 1697.

Santa Rosa. **1** Village (pop. 951), Lambayeque dept., NW Peru, minor port on the Pacific, 8 mi. SW of Chiclayo; fisheries. **2** Town (pop. 1,767), Puno dept., SE Peru, on the Altiplano, on Pucará R., on railroad and 21 mi. NW of Ayaviri; alt. 12,802 ft. Grain, quinoa, potatoes, livestock.

Santa Rosa (săn'tŭ rō'zŭ, Sp. sän'tä rō'sä). **1** Town (1939 pop. 2,615; 1948 municipality pop. 17,259), Laguna prov., S Luzon, Philippines, 22 mi. SSE of Manila, on Laguna de Bay; agr. center (rice, coconuts, sugar). **2** Town (1939 pop. 2,151; 1948 municipality pop. 11,764), Nueva Ecija prov., central Luzon, Philippines, on Pampanga R., on railroad and 5 mi. SSW of Cabanatuan.

Santa Rosa or **Santa Rosa de Lima** (dä lē'mä), city (pop. 3,353), La Unión dept., E Salvador, on branch of Inter-American Highway and 21 mi. NE of San Miguel; livestock-raising center. Founded in 18th cent. Gold and silver mining at San Sebastián, 3 mi. W.

Santa Rosa (săn'tŭ rō'zŭ), county (□ 1,204; pop. 18,554), NW Fla., bet. Ga. line (N) and Gulf of Mexico (S), and bounded W by Escambia R.; ⊙ Milton. Includes part of Pensacola Bay and Santa Rosa Sound in S. Rolling agr. area (corn, peanuts, cotton, vegetables, livestock), drained by Blackwater and Yellow rivers; also forestry (lumber, naval stores). Formed 1842.

Santa Rosa. **1** City (pop. 17,902), ⊙ Sonoma co., W Calif., 50 mi. N of San Francisco; trade, processing, and shipping center for rich fruitgrowing region (including Sonoma Valley, to SE); wine making, fruit canning and drying, meat and egg packing, brewing; mfg. of shoes, chemicals, brass products. Seat of a jr. col. Home and gardens of Luther Burbank, who conducted his experiments here, are preserved. A petrified forest, Armstrong Redwoods State Park (17 mi. WNW), and Old Fort Ross (30 mi. WNW) are near by. Inc. 1868. **2** Town (1940 pop. 141), De Kalb co., NW Mo., near Grand R., 36 mi. NE of St. Joseph. **3** Village (pop. 2,199), ⊙ Guadalupe co., E central N.Mex., on Pecos R. and 55 mi. WSW of Tucumcari; alt. 4,615 ft. Shipping point for wool and livestock; trade center; grain, beans, fruit. Copper mines and deposit of asphalt rock in vicinity. Billy the Kid mus. and U.S. fish hatchery near by. Settled c.1865. **4** Town (pop. 400), Cameron co., extreme S Texas, 34 mi. NW of Brownsville; rail point in irrigated agr. area.

Santa Rosa (sän'tä rō'sä). **1** Town, Artigas dept., Uruguay: see BELLA UNIÓN. **2** Town (pop. 2,000), Canelones dept., S Uruguay, on railroad and 25 mi. NNE of Montevideo; grain trade.

Santa Rosa. **1** Town (pop. 569), Anzoátegui state, NE Venezuela, 45 mi. SE of Barcelona; cotton, corn, cattle. Santa Rosa oil field is S. **2** Town (pop. 479), Barinas state, W Venezuela, in llanos, 37 mi. ESE of Barinas; cattle. **3** Town (pop. 809), Lara state, NW Venezuela, on transandine highway, on upper Cojedes (or Barquisimeto) R. and 3 mi. E of Barquisimeto.

Santa Rosa das Missões, Brazil: see SANTA ROSA, Rio Grande do Sul.

Santa Rosa de Aguán, Honduras: see AGUÁN.

Santa Rosa de Cabal (sän'tä rō'sä dä käbäl'), town (pop. 9,329), Caldas dept., W central Colombia, on W slopes of Cordillera Central, on highway and railroad, and 16 mi. SSW of Manizales; commercial center in agr. region (coffee, stock); sericulture. Silver, gold, mercury mines near by.

Santa Rosa de Calchines, Argentina: see SANTA ROSA.

Santa Rosa de Copán, Honduras: see SANTA ROSA.

Santa Rosa de Jáuregui, Mexico: see SANTA ROSA, Querétaro.

Santa Rosa de la Mina (dä lä mē'nä), town (pop. c.400), Santa Cruz dept., E Bolivia, 45 mi. SW of Concepción; cattle.

Santa Rosa de la Roca (dä lä rō'kä), village (pop. c.1,500), Santa Cruz dept., E Bolivia, 40 mi. NW of San Ignacio; rubber.

Santa Rosa de Leales (dä lā-ä'lĕs), town (pop. estimate 1,000), central Tucumán prov., Argentina, on railroad and 22 mi. S of Tucumán; agr. center (sugar cane, corn, oats, livestock).

Santa Rosa de Lima, Guatemala: see SANTA ROSA.

Santa Rosa de Lima, Salvador: see SANTA ROSA.

Santa Rosa de los Andes, Chile: see LOS ANDES.

Santa Rosa del Palmar (dĕl pälmär'), town (pop. c.1,100), Santa Cruz dept., E Bolivia, on San Miguel R. and 50 mi. SW of Concepción; cattle.

Santa Rosa del Peñón, Nicaragua: see SANTA ROSA.

Santa Rosa de Osos, Colombia: see SANTA ROSA, Antioquia dept.

Santa Rosa de Pastos Grandes (dä pä'stōs grän'dĕs), village, ⊙ Pastos Grandes dept. (□ c.8,100; pop. estimate 3,000), W Salta prov., Argentina, in arid *puna* area, 85 mi. WNW of Salta; alt. 12,900 ft. Salt mining.

Santa Rosa de Sucumbíos (sōōkōōmbē'ōs), village (1950 pop. 210), Napo-Pastaza prov., N Ecuador, on Colombia border, 50 mi. SE of Tulcán. Seat of Carmelite mission. Sometimes Sucumbíos.

Santa Rosa de Toay, Argentina: see SANTA ROSA, La Pampa natl. territory.

Santa Rosa de Viterbo (săn'tŭ rō'zŭ dĭ vētĕr'bōō), city (pop. 1,795), NE São Paulo, Brazil, on railroad and 34 mi. SE of Ribeirão Prêto; corn, coffee, sugar cane, beans, grain. Until 1944, called Santa Rosa; and, 1944–48, Icaturama.

Santa Rosa de Viterbo, Colombia: see SANTA ROSA, Boyacá dept.

Santa Rosa Island, Mexico: see REVILLAGIGEDO ISLANDS.

Santa Rosa Island (săn'tŭ rō'zŭ). **1** In Calif.: see SANTA BARBARA ISLANDS. **2** In NW Fla., narrow barrier beach on Gulf of Mexico, extends c.50 mi. parallel to the coast, sheltering Santa Rosa Sound (N) and almost enclosing Choctawhatchee (E) and Pensacola (W) bays. Connected by several bridges with the mainland. Fort Pickens (completed 1834), at W end of isl., was held by Union forces during the Civil War.

Santa Rosalía (sän'tä rōsälē'ä), town (pop. 5,451), Southern Territory, Lower California, NW Mexico, 95 mi. SW of Guaymas across Gulf of California; 27°20'N 112°16'W. Copper-mining and -smelting center; fruitgrowing (dates, figs). Gypsum deposits near by.

Santa Rosa Mountains (săn'tŭ rō'zŭ), S Calif., range along W side of Coachella Valley, extends c.30 mi. SE from S end of San Jacinto Mts.; rises to 8,716 ft. at Toro Peak, 22 mi. S of Palm Springs.

Santa Rosa Range, N Nev., in NE Humboldt co., near Oregon line, N of Humboldt R. Rises to 9,400 ft. in Spring Peak and 9,600 ft. in Santa Rosa Peak, highest point in range, c.40 mi. N of Winnemucca. N half is in Humboldt Natl. Forest. Gold is mined.

Santa Rosa Sound, lagoon in NW Fla., sheltered from the Gulf of Mexico by Santa Rosa Isl. (S); opens into Choctawhatchee (E) and Pensacola (W) bays; c.35 mi. long, up to 2 mi. wide. Forms part of Gulf Intracoastal Waterway.

Sant'Arsenio (säntärsä'nyō), village (pop. 3,535), Salerno prov., Campania, S Italy, near Tanagro R., 8 mi. NNW of Sala Consilina.

Santa Severina (sän'tä sĕvĕrē'nä), town (pop. 1,762), Catanzaro prov., Calabria, S Italy, near Neto R., 12 mi. WNW of Crotone, in citrus-fruit and livestock region. Archbishopric. Has restored Byzantine baptistery, 11th-cent. Norman castle. Damaged by earthquakes, especially in 1783.

Santa Sofia (sän'tä sôfē'ä), village (pop. 2,170), Forlì prov., Emilia-Romagna, N central Italy, on Ronco R. and 20 mi. SSW of Forlì; silk mills.

Santa Susana Mountains (săn'tŭ sōōză'nŭ), S Calif., short E-W range (to c.3,750 ft. alt.) lying W of San Gabriel Mts., from which it is separated by Newhall Pass, and bet. San Fernando Valley (S) and valley of Santa Clara R. (N).

Santa Tecla, Salvador: see NUEVA SAN SALVADOR.

Santa Tecla (sän'tä tā'klä), SW suburb (pop. 1,287) of Vigo, Pontevedra prov., NW Spain; fish processing, boatbuilding, flour- and sawmilling.

Santa Teresa (sän'tä tārā'sä), town (pop. estimate 2,000), S Santa Fe prov., Argentina, 35 mi. S of Rosario; rail junction in agr. area (corn, potatoes, flax, wheat, vegetables, livestock); grain elevators.

Santa Teresa (săn'tŭ tĭrē'zŭ). **1** City (pop. 872), central Espírito Santo, Brazil, 30 mi. NW of Vitória; coffee hulling. Formerly spelled Santa Thereza. **2** City, Rio de Janeiro, Brazil: see RIO DAS FLORES.

Santa Teresa (sän'tä tārā'sä), town (1950 pop. 2,057), Carazo dept., SW Nicaragua, on Inter-American Highway and 5 mi. SE of Jinotepe, in sugar-cane zone.

Santa Teresa, spa just W of Ávila, Old Castile, central Spain.

Santa Teresa, town (pop. 2,127), Miranda state, N Venezuela, on Tuy R., on railroad and 25 mi. SE of Caracas; coffee, cacao, sugar cane, corn.

Santa Teresa, Fort, Rocha dept., SE Uruguay, on the Atlantic 18 mi. SSW of Chuy. Built in 18th cent. by the Portuguese, it was frequently disputed by Spanish and Portuguese. A massive structure (c.650 yards in circumference), surrounded by a large park, it has been restored and is a natl. monument.

Santa Teresa di Riva (sän'tä tĕrā'zä dē rē'vä), village (pop. 3,189), Messina prov., NE Sicily, port on Ionian Sea, 19 mi. SSW of Messina; chemical industry.

Santa Teresa Gallura (gäl-lōō'rä), village (pop. 1,566), Sassari prov., NE Sardinia, on Strait of Bonifacio and 50 mi. NE of Sassari; port for crossing to Bonifacio (Corsica).

Santa Thereza, Brazil: see SANTA TERESA, Espírito Santo.

Santa Úrsula (sän'tä ōōr'sōōlä), village (pop. 736), Tenerife, Canary Isls., 12 mi. WSW of Santa Cruz de Tenerife; cereals, truck, bananas, grapes.

Santa Úrsula, residential town (pop. 2,006), Federal Dist., central Mexico, 7 mi. S of Mexico city.

Santa Venera or **Santa Vennera** (sän'tä vĕ'nĕrä), town (pop. 4,535), E Malta, NW residential suburb of Hamrun, 2 mi. W of Valletta. Has large warehouses. During Second World War its monuments were little damaged, except for Wignacourt Aqueduct (1610–15). Among noteworthy bldgs. are the parish church (1647) with adjoining monastery, Vilhena Palace (1730), now residence of the lieutenant governor, and San Giuseppe Palace.

Santa Victoria (sän'tä vēktō'ryä), town (pop. estimate 300), ⊙ Santa Victoria dept. (□ 1,525; 1947 census 6,708), N Salta prov., Argentina, on Santa Victoria R., at SE foot of Sierra Santa Victoria, and 60 mi. NNW of Orán, near Bolivia line. Lead, nickel, and cobalt deposits in mts. near by.

Santa Victoria, Sierra (syĕ'rä), subandean mountain range on Jujuy-Salta prov. border, NW Argentina, W of Santa Victoria; extends c.40 mi. N-S, forming W watershed of upper Bermejo R.; rises to c.15,000 ft. Nickel and cobalt deposits.

Santa Vitória do Palmar (săn'tŭ vētô'ryŭ dōō pŭlmär'), city (pop. 5,702), S Rio Grande do Sul, Brazil, on low, sandy strip bet. the Atlantic (E) and Mirim L. (W), 125 mi. SSW of Rio Grande; southernmost city of Brazil, near Uruguay border; 33°30'S 53°21'W. Livestock center; trades in wool, lard, cereals, fruit. Airfield. Formerly spelled Santa Victoria do Palmar.

Santa Vittoria in Matenano (sän'tä vēt-tô'rēä ēn mätĕnä'nô), village (pop. 671), Ascoli Piceno prov., The Marches, central Italy, 11 mi. NNW of Ascoli Piceno; cementworks.

Santa Ynez (săn'tŭ ēnĕz'), village (1940 pop. 526), Santa Barbara co., SW Calif., near Santa Ynez R., 25 mi. WNW of Santa Barbara. Site of Mission Santa Ynez (established 1804), still in use as a church. Also spelled Santa Inez, Santa Ines.

Santa Ynez Mountains, S Calif., E-W coastal range (c.2–4,000 ft.) bordering the Pacific (Santa Barbara Channel) for c.75 mi. bet. Point Arguello (W) and Ventura R. (E). Santa Ynez R. and Lompoc Valley are along N base.

Santa Ynez River, SW Calif., rises in SE Santa Barbara co., flows c.75 mi. W, along N base of Santa Ynez Mts. and through Lompoc Valley, to the Pacific 10 mi. WNW of Lompoc. Flow is intermittent. Reservoir formed by Gibraltar Dam (185 ft. high, 1,100 ft. long; completed 1920) supplies water to Santa Barbara city. Cachuma Dam (kŭ-chōō'mŭ) and reservoir have been planned as a U.S. Bureau of Reclamation project.

Santee (săn'tē"), town (pop. 107), Orangeburg co., S central S.C., near L. Marion, 21 mi. E of Orangeburg.

Santee River, E S.C., with its tributaries is most important river system in state; formed 30 mi. SE of Columbia by junction of WATEREE RIVER and CONGAREE RIVER; flows 143 mi. SE, entering the Atlantic by 2 mouths (North Santee R. and South Santee R.), c.15 mi. S of Georgetown. Navigable. With its principal headstream (rising in N.C.), it forms Catawba-Wateree-Santee Watercourse, 438 mi. long. The Santee is center of a huge hydroelectric and navigation development (built 1939–42). Santee Dam (concrete; 45 ft. high, 7.8 mi. long, including earth fill wings; completed 1941; for power, navigation, flood control), 15 mi. S of Manning, forms L. Marion or Santee Reservoir, extending 40 mi. upstream to the Wateree-Congaree confluence. A 5-mi. canal by-passes dam (S) and diverts water to L. Moultrie, a reservoir formed by Pinopolis Dam (78 ft. high, 2.1 mi. long) on near-by Cooper R., which flows S to Charleston Harbor at Charleston. (Cooper R. had been joined to Santee R. by a navigation canal, built 1792–1800.) At Pinopolis Dam is large hydroelectric plant of Moncks Corner.

Santeetlah, Lake (săn"tĕt'lŭ), irregularly-shaped reservoir, W N.C., c.40 mi. S of Knoxville, Tenn., and just SW of Great Smoky Mts. Natl. Park; 5 mi. long, 1 mi. wide. Formed by Santeetlah Dam

(200 ft. high, 1,150 ft. long; completed 1928; used for power) in Cheoah R. Boating and fishing.

Sant'Egidio alla Vibrata (säntĕjē'dyô äl-lä vēbrä'tä), village (pop. 1,050), Teramo prov., Abruzzi e Molise, S central Italy, 12 mi. N of Teramo; macaroni mfg.

Sant'Elia a Pianisi (säntĕlē'ä ä pyänē'zē), town (pop. 4,336), Campobasso prov., Abruzzi e Molise, S central Italy, 12 mi. ENE of Campobasso; metalworking, soap mfg.

Sant'Elia Fiumerapido (fū"mĕrä'pēdô), village (pop. 1,723), Frosinone prov., Latium, S central Italy, on Rapido R. and 18 mi. SE of Sora; paper and woolen mills.

San Telmo Point (sän tĕl'mō), cape on Pacific coast of Michoacán, W Mexico, 40 mi. SSW of Coalcomán; 18°20'N 103°31'W.

Sant'Elpidio a Mare (säntĕlpē'dyô ä mä'rĕ), town (pop. 2,505), Ascoli Piceno prov., The Marches, central Italy, 5 mi. NNW of Fermo; mfg. (shoes soap, macaroni).

Santena (sän'tĕnä), village (pop. 2,040), Torino prov., Piedmont, NW Italy, 9 mi. SSE of Turin, in peach-growing region. Has château with grave of Cavour.

Santenay (sãtùnā'), village (pop. 928), Côte-d'Or dept., E central France, on S slope of the Côte d'Or, near Canal du Centre, 10 mi. SW of Beaune; Burgundy wines. Mineral springs.

Santeramo in Colle (säntä'rämô ēn kôl'lĕ), town (pop. 16,589), Bari prov., Apulia, S Italy, 11 mi. E of Altamura; agr. trade; cereals, wool, wine, cheese.

Santerno River (säntĕr'nô), N central Italy, rises in Etruscan Apennines near La Futa pass, flows 61 mi. NE, past Firenzuola and Imola, to Reno R. 6 mi. NW of Alfonsine.

Santerre (sãtâr'), old district and low tableland of N France, now included in SE Somme dept., bet. the Somme (N) and the Avre (SW). Chief towns: Péronne and Montdidier. Knitting and weaving. Devastated (1918) in First World War.

Sant'Eufemia, Gulf of (säntĕōōfā'myä), an inlet of Tyrrhenian Sea, Calabria, S Italy, bet. Cape Suvero (NE) and Cape Cozzo (SW); 19 mi. long, 8 mi. wide. Chief port, Pizzo.

Sant'Eufemia d'Aspromonte (däsprômôn'tĕ), town (pop. 5,238), Reggio di Calabria prov., Calabria, S Italy, on N slope of the Aspromonte, 16 mi. NE of Reggio di Calabria, in agr. (olives, fruit), lumbering, livestock-raising region. Rebuilt after earthquake of 1908.

Santhià (säntēä'), village (pop. 4,075), Vercelli prov., Piedmont, N Italy, 12 mi. WNW of Vercelli, in irrigated region (cereals, rice); rail junction.

Santiago (säntyä'gō), town (pop. c.1,700), Santa Cruz dept., E Bolivia, in Serranía de Santiago, 85 mi. ESE of San José, on road; coffee. Also Santiago de Chiquitos.

Santiago (sãntyä'gōō), city (pop. 8,205), W central Rio Grande do Sul, Brazil, on W slope of the Serra Geral, on railroad and 75 mi. NW of Santa Maria; cattle- and horse-raising center; meat processing. Airfield. Until 1938, called Santiago do Boqueirão.

Santiago (săntēä'gō, Sp. säntyä'gō), province (□ 6,727; 1940 pop. 1,268,505, 1949 estimate 1,839-768), central Chile, bet. the Andes and the Pacific; ⊙ Santiago, capital of Chile. Watered by Maipo and Mapocho rivers, it includes N part of the fertile central valley and high Andean peaks (e.g., Tupungato, San José and Maipo volcanoes) on Argentine border. Has temperate climate, with generally warm days and cool nights, of little seasonal change. Produces: grain, alfalfa, clover, potatoes, peas, peaches, apples, oranges; its wine is famous. Livestock: cattle, sheep; leads in horse breeding. Mineral wealth includes: copper (Las Condes, Naltagua), gypsum (upper Maipo valley); also lead, manganese, silver, gold, lime, marble, salt. Rural industries: mining, flour milling, distilling, tanning, lumbering. Mfg. concentrated at Santiago, San Bernardo, Puente Alto, and San Antonio. Major resorts: San Antonio, Cartagena (W), Colina (N), San Gabriel, Lo Valdés (E). One of the original 8 Chilean provs., it was set up 1826.

Santiago, city (1930 pop. 696,231; 1940 pop. 952,075; 1949 estimate 1,161,633), ⊙ Chile, Santiago prov., and Santiago dept. (□ 4,026; 1940 pop. 1,068,676), central Chile, on broad plain at foot of the Andes (whose snow-capped peaks form a magnificent background), on the canalized Mapocho R. and 60 mi. SE of its port Valparaiso; 33°27'S 70°39'W; alt.1,705 ft. The 4th largest city of South America in one of the world's healthiest climates (warm days, cool nights almost the year round), it dominates Chilean commercial, industrial, and cultural life. Leads as trading and distributing center for the fertile central valley (cereals, wine, fruit, vegetables, livestock), with head offices of natl. and international banks, corporations, import and export firms, and retail houses. Responsible for more than 50% of Chile's industrial output, it is a center for textiles (cotton, silk, and rayon fabrics, hosiery, clothing), leather goods, chemicals (including plastics, explosives, paints, varnishes, pharmaceuticals, cosmetics), paper and printed products, glassware, metal products (iron and steel parts, machinery, electrical appliances), rubber, tobacco; food processing, brewing, meat packing, flour milling, distilling, tanning. Hydroelectric power station. Also important rail and road center, linked by the longitudinal rail line with the famous Transandine RR to Argentina. Its airport is at Los Cerrillos (on SW outskirts). While some architectural elements of the colonial era remain, the atmosphere of Santiago is largely modern, with neoclassical govt. edifices, modern functional office bldgs., sumptuous homes, and fine plazas and parks. Here is the country's foremost school of higher learning, the natl. univ. (successor to Univ. of San Felipe founded by royal decree of 1738), and other cultural institutions: Catholic Univ.; art, military, and aviation academies; municipal theater, historical mus., art gall., natl. library. Its principal artery is the wide Alameda Bernardo O'Higgins, formerly called Las Delicias, which traverses the whole city and, together with Mapocho R. (N), carves off the main business and administrative section. There, in the center, is the historic Plaza de Armas with adjoining cathedral (completed 1619 but often rebuilt) and archbishop's palace, city hall, and post office. On Plaza Libertad near by is the Government House, usually called La Moneda, where the president resides. Among its many parks are those on Cerro Santa Lucía, in the heart of the city which it overlooks, and on Cerro Cristóbal (N), reached by funicular railway. The latter has a 72-ft.-high statue of the Virgin at its summit; on a near-by peak is an observatory. The city was founded Feb. 12, 1541, as Santiago de Nueva Estremadura by Pedro de Valdivia, but in Sept. of that year it was almost completely wiped out by the Araucanian Indians; an earthquake leveled it in 1647, and the torrential Mapocho R. —now regulated—frequently caused severe damage. The city's development has, however, been steady. It was occupied (1817) by San Martín and declared (1818) capital of Chilean Republic. The fifth Pan-American Conference was held here in 1923.

Santiago or **Santiago de Puriscal** (dā pōōrēskäl'), town (pop. 468), San José prov., W central Costa Rica, in NW outlier of Cordillera de Talamanca, 17 mi. WSW of San José; rice, tobacco, beans, corn. Sometimes called Puriscal.

Santiago, Cuba: see SANTIAGO DE CUBA, city.

Santiago, province (□ 1,367; 1935 pop. 195,023; 1950 pop. 262,232), N and NW central Dominican Republic; ⊙ Santiago or Santiago de los Caballeros. An interior prov. in the most fertile and populous region (Cibao) of the Republic, intersected by the Yaque del Norte; bounded by the Cordillera Setentrional (N) and Cordillera Central (S). Main crops: tobacco, cacao, coffee, rice, corn, vegetables, tropical fruit, cattle. Much lumbering and gold washing. Railroad from Sánchez. Prov. was set up 1845.

Santiago or **Santiago de los Caballeros** (dā lōs käbäyä'rōs), city (1935 pop. 34,175; 1950 pop. 56,192), ⊙ Santiago prov., N Dominican Republic, on the Yaque del Norte, in fertile Cibao valley, on railroad, and 23 mi. S of its port Puerto Plata, 85 mi. NW of Ciudad Trujillo; 19°28'N 70'42'W. The 2d largest city of the Republic, with fine scenery and healthful climate, it is the most important trading, distributing, and processing center for the N, where tobacco, rice, cacao, coffee, beeswax, cattle, and hides are produced extensively. Among its industries are cigar and cigarette making, coffee and rice milling, tanning, liquor and alcohol distilling, dairying; mfg. of pharmaceuticals, furniture, straw hats, pottery, hammocks, baskets. Large starch factory at near-by Quinigua (1935 pop. 1,846). An anc. colonial city, Santiago has notable bldgs., such as San Luis fort, a cathedral and other churches, municipal palace. Airfield. Founded c.1500 by Bartholomew Columbus; rebuilt near the original site after 1564 earthquake. Here was fought the decisive battle of Dominican struggle for independence (March 30, 1844).

Santiago. 1 or **Santiago Sacatepéquez** (säkätäpā'kĕs), town (1950 pop. 3,452), Sacatepéquez dept., S central Guatemala, 5 mi. NE of Guatemala; alt. 7,316 ft.; grain, beans, fruit. **2** Town, Sololá dept., Guatemala: see ATITLÁN, town.

Santiago. 1 Officially Santiago de Anaya, town (pop. 1,049), Hidalgo, central Mexico, 23 mi. NW of Pachuca; corn, maguey, livestock. **2** Officially Santiago Tezontlale, town (pop. 1,770), Hidalgo, central Mexico, on central plateau, 23 mi. WNW of Pachuca; corn, beans, fruit, livestock. **3** Officially Santiago Tulantepec, town (pop. 1,742), Hidalgo, central Mexico, on railroad and 26 mi. SE of Pachuca; grain, maguey, livestock. **4** Town (pop. 746), Southern Territory, Lower California, NW Mexico, in valley 60 mi. SE of La Paz; sugar cane and fruit (coconuts, dates, figs, grapes). **5** or **Santiago Oxtempan** (ōstĕm'pän), town (pop. 2,151), Mexico state, central Mexico, 3 mi. SE of El Oro; silver mining. **6** Town (pop. 1,804), Nuevo León, N Mexico, in foothills of Sierra Madre Oriental, on Inter-American Highway and 20 mi. SE of Monterrey; fruit, chick-peas, grain, livestock.

Santiago, active volcano (1,800 ft.), SW Nicaragua, just W of Masaya volcano. Last active in 1903.

Santiago, town (1950 pop. 13,028), ⊙ Veraguas prov., W central Panama, in Pacific lowland, on Inter-American Highway and 110 mi. SW of Panama city. Its port is Puerto Mutis. Commercial center; woodworking. Gold deposits near by. Has normal school. Flourished in colonial times as ⊙ old Veraguas prov., covering entire W section of isthmus.

Santiago, town (dist. pop. 7,894), Misiones dept., S Paraguay, 55 mi. WNW of Encarnación; agr. center (maté, fruit, cattle). Anc. Jesuit mission founded in 17th cent.

Santiago or **Santiago de Compostela** (dā kōmpōstā'lä), anc. *Campus Stellae*, city (pop. 30,127), La Coruña prov., NW Spain, road center on height circled by hills, 34 mi. SSW of La Coruña; cultural capital of Galicia and Spain's most celebrated pilgrimage resort, with numerous religious bldgs. and a marked medieval aspect. Its great feature is the imposing cathedral of St. James (built 11th-13th cent. on site of earlier chapel), one of the finest examples in Spain of early Romanesque style (although the exterior was restored in 16th-18th cent.) The cathedral contains the relics of St. James, whose tomb is said to be beneath the high altar. Notable are the 12th-cent. sculptured Gothic vestibule (*Pórtico de la Gloria*) and the fine plateresque cloisters. The huge Hospital Real is a pilgrims' hospice built 1501–10 by Ferdinand and Isabella. Other noteworthy bldgs. include several medieval churches and convents, the church of St. Martin (16th-17th cent.), and the archbishop's palace. City is seat of archbishop and of univ. (founded 17th cent.); also has pontifical univ. and other religious schools. The state univ. is housed in the Colegio Fonseca (1525). Has 18th-cent. palace. City, originating in 9th cent. around chapel built by Alfonso II of Asturias on site of tomb of St. James, was destroyed by the Moors in 997. Throughout the Middle Ages it was one of the most frequented pilgrimage places and religious centers in Europe, reached by the road across Roncesvalles Pass in the Pyrenees and through Asturias. Besides its tourist industry and mfg. of religious articles, Santiago has considerable trade and also makes shoes, distilled spirits, flour, furniture, linen, soap.

Santiago, Cape, S Luzon, Philippines, at tip of peninsula on W side of Balayan Bay; 13°46'N 120°39'E.

Santiago, Cerro, Panama: see TABASARÁ, SERRANÍA DE.

Santiago, Serranía de (sĕränē'ä dā säntyä'gō), range in Santa Cruz dept., E Bolivia; watershed bet. Tucavaca (N) and San Rafael (S) rivers, extending 80 mi. NW-SE; rises to 4,675 ft. at Cerro Chochis. Santiago town in center.

Santiago Atitlán, Guatemala: see ATITLÁN, town.

Santiago Cuilápan, Mexico: see CUILÁPAN.

Santiago de Calatrava (säntyä'gō dā käläträ'vä), town (pop. 2,748), Jaén prov., S Spain, 20 mi. W of Jaén; olive oil, cereals.

Santiago de Cao (kä'ō), town (pop. 957), Libertad dept., NW Peru, on coastal plain, in irrigated Chicama R. valley, 18 mi. NW of Trujillo; sugar.

Santiago de Carbajo (kärvä'hō), village (pop. 2,443), Cáceres prov., W Spain, 21 mi. SE of Castelo Branco (Portugal); olive oil, cereals.

Santiago de Chiquitos, Bolivia: see SANTIAGO.

Santiago de Chocorvos (chōkôr'vōs), town (pop. 1,127), Huancavelica dept., S central Peru, in Cordillera Occidental, 45 mi. SSE of Castrovirreyna; corn, barley, livestock.

Santiago de Chuco (chōō'kō), city (pop. 4,127), ⊙ Santiago de Chuco prov. (□ 1,382; pop. 51,140), Libertad dept., NW Peru, in Cordillera Occidental of the Andes, 60 mi. E of Trujillo; alt. 10,220 ft. Local trade center for barley, corn. Sheep raising.

Santiago de Compostela, Spain: see SANTIAGO.

Santiago de Cuba, province, Cuba: see ORIENTE.

Santiago de Cuba (kōō'bä), city (pop. 118,266), ⊙ Oriente prov., E Cuba, 2d largest city of the isl. and major Caribbean port, on landlocked inlet (5 mi. long, c.1½ mi. wide), 460 mi. ESE of Havana, 240 mi. WNW of Port-au-Prince, Haiti; 20°1'N 75°49'W. Railhead, E terminus of the Central Highway, and important outlet for rich agr. and mining region; exports sugar cane, tobacco, fruit, hides, beeswax, honey, lumber, iron, manganese, copper. Also an industrial center: sugar milling, distilling, tanning, sawmilling; mfg. of cigars, preserves, rum, soap, matches, bricks, tiles, perfumes; foundries, machine shops. The picturesque, historic city nestles in an amphitheater of mts. and attracts—in spite of its tropical climate (mean annual temp. c.85°F.)—many tourists. Just E rises famed San Juan Hill. Old Morro Castle is S at the harbor's entrance. Among its fine bldgs. are the isl.'s oldest cathedral (rebuilt in Florentine style), where Diego de Velázquez is buried; the Govt. Palace; a univ.; Convent of San Francisco. Has the San Pedrito airport. Narrow streets contrast with wide promenades and parks. Santiago de Cuba was founded by Velázquez on W shore of the bay in 1514. It was for some time, in early colonial era, ⊙ Cuba. Several times the city was sacked by Fr. and English buccaneers, and it was a center of smuggling for the British West Indies. It was the scene of the chief military operations of the Spanish-American War in Cuba; the Sp. fleet under Cervera y Topete was completely destroyed (1898) in Santiago harbor by U.S. forces. Formerly exceedingly unhealthful; yellow fever was stamped out after Spanish-American War. Water is now supplied from the Charco Mono dam. Residential sections Punta Gorda and Ciudmar (SE). Manganese deposits near by. The city is commonly called Santiago.

Santiago de Huata (wä'tä), town (pop. c.11,740), La Paz dept., W Bolivia, port on L. Titicaca, on Achacachi Peninsula and 8 mi. W of Achacachi; barley, potatoes, sheep. Formerly Huata.

Santiago de la Espada (lä ěspä'dhä) town (pop. 2,367), Jaén prov., S Spain, 30 mi. E of Villacarrillo; wool spinning; olive oil, cereals, livestock.

Santiago de la Puebla (pwě'blä), town (pop. 1,439), Salamanca prov., W Spain, 23 mi. SE of Salamanca; cereals, wine, livestock.

Santiago de las Vegas (läs vā'gäs), town (pop. 9,385), Havana prov., W Cuba, on railroad and 10 mi. S of Havana; processing and agr. center (tobacco, sugar cane, citrus fruit, potatoes); mfg. of cigars, shoes, paint, pottery; tanning. Has agr. station.

Santiago del Campo (děl käm'pō), village (pop. 1,631), Cáceres prov., W Spain, 11 mi. N of Cáceres; flour mills; livestock, cereals.

Santiago del Estero (ěstā'rō), province (□ 56,243; pop. 479,473), N Argentina; ⊙ Santiago del Estero. Bordered W by outliers of the mts. of Catamarca and Tucumán provs., it slopes E to the pampas and is intersected (NW-SE) by the Río Dulce and Río Salado. Includes N part of Salinas Grandes (SW). Has subtropical climate. Among small mineral resources (mainly in the Sierra de Guasayán) are manganese, lime, quartzite and granite, salt, petroleum. Most of prov. is covered by forests (quebracho, carob, guaiacum, oak), its main source of income. Agr.: grain (mostly SE and E); fruit, including grapes (center); cotton (NW), flax (SE). Stock raising: cattle and sheep (center and SE), goats and mules (center and W). Fishing in the Río Hondo and Río Dulce. Rural industries: lumbering, flour milling, cotton ginning, dairying, charcoal burning. Urban industries: cementmaking (Frías), manganese mining (Ojo de Agua dept.), textile milling, lumbering, tannin extracting, and tanning concentrated in Santiago del Estero. Major resorts: Termas del Río Hondo (curative waters) and Santiago del Estero. Prov. was established 1820, being separated from Tucumán prov.

Santiago del Estero, city (pop. 63,491), ⊙ Santiago del Estero prov. and Santiago del Estero dept. (□ c.750; 1947 pop. 82,766), N central Argentina, on right bank of the Río Dulce, on railroad and 575 mi. NW of Buenos Aires, 90 mi. SE of Tucumán; 27°47'S 64°15'W. Agr., commercial, and lumbering center. Mfg.: flour and sawmills, dairy plants, tanneries, textile mills. Trading in cotton and livestock. Sand quarries near by. It is visited by tourists in the spring. An old colonial city, founded 1553, it has administrative bldgs., institutions of higher learning, art gall., historical mus., theater, Gothic church of San Francisco Solano.

Santiago de los Caballeros, Dominican Republic: see SANTIAGO, city.

Santiago del Teide (děl tā'dä), town (pop. 238), Tenerife, Canary Isls., 38 mi. WSW of Santa Cruz de Tenerife; almonds, cereals, fruit, grapes, potatoes, tomatoes, bananas, cochineal. Basketmaking.

Santiago de Machaca (mächä'kä), town (pop. c.3,300), La Paz dept., W Bolivia, in the Altiplano, 55 mi. WNW of Corocoro, near Peru border; alpaca and sheep raising; barley, potatoes.

Santiago de María (märē'ä), city (pop. 6,879), Usulután dept., E Salvador, on SE slope of volcano Tecapa, 9 mi. NNW of Usulután; coffee, sugar cane, honey.

Santiago de Puriscal, Costa Rica: see SANTIAGO.

Santiago de Surco, Peru: see SURCO.

Santiago do Boqueirão, Brazil: see SANTIAGO.

Santiago do Cacém (säntyä'gōō dōō kŭsān'), town (pop. 2,903), Setúbal dist., S central Portugal, on railroad and 38 mi. SSE of Setúbal; major cork-producing center; cheese and pottery mfg.

Santiago Island, Cape Verde Isls.: see SÃO TIAGO ISLAND.

Santiago Island (săntēä'gō, Sp. säntyä'gō), **San Salvador Island** (sän sälvädôr'), or **James Island** (□ 203), central Galápagos Isls., Ecuador, in the Pacific, 80 mi. WNW of Puerto Baquerizo (San Cristóbal Isl.). Volcanic in origin, it is 25 mi. long and rises to 1,700 ft. at 0°15'S 90°45'W. Maguey growing.

Santiago Island (□ 8; 5 mi. long, 3 mi. wide; 1939 pop. 3,922), Pangasinan prov., Philippines, at W side of entrance to Lingayen Gulf, just off N tip of Cape Bolinao peninsula of central Luzon; rice.

Santiago Island, small islet off E Puerto Rico, 1 mi. off Playa de Humacao. The School of Tropical Medicine here maintains a monkey colony.

Santiago Ixcuintla (säntyä'gō ēskwēn'tlä), city (pop. 7,322), Nayarit, W Mexico, on Pacific coastal plain, on lower Santiago R. and 30 mi. NW of Tepic; processing and agr. center (corn, tobacco, beans, tomatoes, bananas); mfg. (tobacco products, soap, vegetable oil, steel furniture). Gold placers near by.

Santiago Maravatío, Mexico: see MARAVATÍO, Guanajuato.

Santiago Mexquititlán or **Mexquititlán** (měskētētlän'), town (pop. 1,688), Querétaro, central Mexico, 40 mi. SE of Querétaro; corn, wheat, alfalfa, beans, fruit, stock.

Santiago Miahuatlán (myäwätlän'), town (pop. 2,756), Puebla, central Mexico, on railroad and 7 mi. NW of Tehuacán; agr. center (corn, rice, sugar cane, fruit, livestock). Sometimes Miahuatlán.

Santiago Mountains (săntēä'gō), extreme W Texas, in the Big Bend, extend c.35 mi. SE from region SE of Alpine to NW end of Sierra del Carmen; partly in Big Bend Natl. Park. Highest point is Santiago Peak (6,521 ft.).

Santiago Nonualco (säntyä'gō nōnwäl'kō), city (pop. 3,971), La Paz dept., S Salvador, 7 mi. W of Zacatecoluca; coffee, sisal; palm products; livestock raising.

Santiago Oxtempan, Mexico: see SANTIAGO, Mexico state.

Santiago Papasquiaro (päpäskyä'rō), city (pop. 3,204), Durango, N Mexico, on E slope of Sierra Madre Occidental, on Ramos R. and 85 mi. NW of Durango, on railroad; alt. 5,643 ft. Silver, gold, lead, and copper mining; grain, alfalfa, chick-peas, livestock.

Santiago Peak. 1 In Calif.: see SANTA ANA MOUNTAINS. **2** In Texas: see SANTIAGO MOUNTAINS.

Santiago River, in Imbabura and Esmeraldas provs., N Ecuador, rises in the Andes at W foot of the Yanaurcu, flows c.100 mi. NW, through forested tropical lowlands, past Concepción, to the Pacific 15 mi. W of San Lorenzo in wide estuary. Main tributary is navigable Cayapas R. Gold washing.

Santiago River, in Ecuador and Peru, formed by Paute R. and Zamora R. in Santiago–Zamora prov. (Ecuador) at c.3°S, flows c.150 mi. S to Marañón R. at W end of Pongo de Manseriche.

Santiago River. 1 In Durango, Mexico: see RAMOS RIVER. **2** or **Río Grande de Santiago** (rē'ō grän'dā dā), Jalisco, W Mexico, continuation of LERMA RIVER; issues from L. Chapala at Ocotlán, Jalisco, flows c.275 mi. NW, past Juanacatlán (waterfalls) in Jalisco, and Yago and Santiago Ixcuintla in lowlands of Nayarit, to the Pacific 10 mi. NW of San Blas. Used for irrigation and water power; not navigable. Among its many affluents are Juchipila and Bolaños rivers.

Santiago River, Salvador: see BARRA DE SANTIAGO.

Santiago Rodríguez (säntyä'gō rōdrē'gěs), town (1950 pop. 1,483), Monte Cristi prov., NW Dominican Republic, in Cordillera Central, 32 mi. SE of Monte Cristi; principal products are tobacco, beeswax, fine wood, hides. Until 1936, Sabaneta.

Santiago Sacatepéquez, Guatemala: see SANTIAGO.

Santiago Temple (säntyä'gō těm'plā), town (pop. estimate 1,200), central Córdoba prov., Argentina, 45 mi. E of Córdoba; wheat, flax, corn, livestock; distilling.

Santiago Tepalcatlálpam (tāpälkätläl'päm), town (pop. 2,163), Federal Dist., central Mexico, 14 mi. S of Mexico city; cereals, vegetables, fruit, stock.

Santiago Texcaltitlán, Mexico: see TEXCALTITLÁN.

Santiago Tuxtla (tōō'slä), town (pop. 5,392), Veracruz, SE Mexico, at SE foot of Tuxtla Volcano, 6 mi. WNW of San Andrés Tuxtla; agr. center (tobacco, coffee, sugar cane, fruit, livestock). Airfield.

Santiago Vázquez (vä'skěs), town, Montevideo dept., S Uruguay, resort on the Río de la Plata at mouth of Santa Lucía R. (crossed by large bridge), 13 mi. WNW of Montevideo (linked by railroad). Boating, fishing.

Santiago Yeché (yāchā'), town (pop. 2,524), Mexico state, central Mexico, 37 mi. NW of Mexico city; cereals, stock.

Santiago-Zamora (–sämō'rä), province (□ 18,358; 1950 enumerated pop. 17,664, excluding non-tabulated Indians), SE Ecuador; ⊙ Macas. On Peru border (E and S); bounded by the Andes (W), including the Sangay Volcano. Intersected by tributaries of the Amazon, it is almost entirely covered by virgin forests or selvas. Has humid tropical climate. Of its minerals, only gold has been exploited (at Méndez). Its forests yield rubber, balata, tagua nuts, vanilla, drugs, fine timber. Wild beasts are hunted for their furs. On the Andean slopes there is cattle grazing, and some coffee, cacao, corn, and tropical fruit are grown. Most towns and villages are missionary settlements among the backward Jívaro Indians, who are known for their practice of shrinking human skulls. The prov. was formed 1925 from the old prov. of Oriente. The Ecuador boundaries with Peru were established (1942) at the Rio de Janeiro Conference.

Santiaguillo, Laguna de (lägōō'nä dā säntyägē'yō), lake in Durango, N Mexico, on interior plateau, at E foot of Sierra Madre Occidental, 45 mi. N of Durango; 30 mi. long, 1–5 mi. wide; alt. 6,400 ft.

Santiam Pass (săn'tēăm") (4,817 ft.), W central Oregon, in Cascade Range, bet. Linn and Jefferson counties, c.60 mi. SE of Salem. Crossed by highway. Skiing facilities near by.

Santiam River, W Oregon, formed near Jefferson by North Santiam R. (c.90 mi. long) and South Santiam R. (c.60 mi. long), which rise in Cascade Range; flows c.10 mi. W to Willamette R. below Albany. Site of Detroit Dam (448 ft. high, 1,580 ft. long; for flood control) is on the North Santiam.

Santibáñez de Béjar (säntēvä'nyěth dā bā'här), village (pop. 2,067), Salamanca prov., W Spain, 14 mi. NE of Béjar; vegetables, livestock, lumber.

Santibáñez el Bajo (ěl bä'hō), village (pop. 1,452), Cáceres prov., W Spain, 10 mi. NW of Plasencia; olive-oil processing; cereals, livestock.

Santiesteban, Bolivia: see MONTERO.

Santigron (säntēgrôn'), village, Saramacca dist., N Du. Guiana, on Saramacca R. and 16 mi. SW of Paramaribo; Bush Negro settlement.

Sant'Ilario d'Enza (säntēlä'rēō děn'tsä), town (pop. 1,356), Reggio nell'Emilia prov., Emilia-Romagna, N central Italy, near Enza R., 6 mi. ESE of Parma; mfg. of electrical apparatus.

Santillana (säntēlyä'nä), town (pop. 669), Santander prov., N Spain, 2.5 mi. NW of Torrelavega; corn, lumber, cattle. Has collegiate church (9th cent.; rebuilt 12th–13th) with cloisters. Altamira Cave is 1 mi. SW.

Santillana, reservoir, Madrid prov., central Spain, just E of Manzanares el Real, and formed by head-streams of Manzanares R. 22 mi. NNW of Madrid. Has a hydroelectric plant, and is adjoined by medieval Santillana castle.

San Timoteo (sän tēmōtā'ō), town (pop. 3,880), Zulia state, NW Venezuela, on E shore of L. Maracaibo, just N of San Lorenzo, 70 mi. SE of Maracaibo; oil wells.

Santiniketan (sŭntĭnĭkä'tŭn) or **Shantiniketan** (shŭn–), village, Birbhum dist., W West Bengal, India, 1 mi. NNW of Bolpur. Seat of Visva Bharati, univ. founded 1922 by Rabindranath Tagore to develop closer understanding bet. diverse cultures of the East and concord bet. the East and West; includes separate cols. for fine arts and crafts, Chinese studies, music and dancing, research in Asian languages, and general studies. At adjacent settlement of Sriniketan is another of its cols., devoted to rural reconstruction and revival of anc. handicraft and arts; many outstanding Indian painters, including Abanindranath Tagore, studied here. Begun 1901 as children's school.

Santiponce (säntēpōn'thā), town (pop. 2,568), Seville prov., SW Spain, 4 mi. NW of Seville (linked by rail), in agr. region (barley, corn, wheat, livestock). Has notable 14th-cent. San Isidoro del Campo monastery (badly damaged in 1936). Just NW are the ruins of ITALICA.

Santipur (sän'tĭpŏŏr), town (pop. 29,892), Nadia dist., E West Bengal, India, near Hooghly R., 12 mi. SSW of Krishnagar; major hand-loom cotton-weaving center; pottery mfg.; trades in rice, jute, linseed, sugar cane. Former hand-woven muslin center. Sacred bathing ghats on river.

Santi Quaranta, Albania: see SARANDË.

Säntis or **Sentis** (both: zěn'tĭs), peak (8,217 ft.) in Alpstein mtn. of the Alps, NE Switzerland, 6 mi. SSW of Appenzell. Meteorological observatory.

Santísima Trinidad, Paraguay: see TRINIDAD, suburb of Asunción.

Santistebán del Puerto (säntēstävän' děl pwěr'tō), town (pop. 6,727), Jaén prov., S Spain, 20 mi. NE of Úbeda; olive-oil production and processing center. Mfg. of footwear, soap, plaster; flour- and sawmilling. Cereals, fruit, livestock. Dominated by ruins of Moorish castle.

Santiuste de San Juan Bautista (säntyōō'stā dā sän hwän' boutē'stä), town (pop. 1,200), Segovia prov., central Spain, 28 mi. NW of Segovia; grain, grapes, chick-peas, livestock; flour milling.

Santiváñez (säntēvä'nyěs), town (pop. c.3,900), Cochabamba dept., central Bolivia, on S outliers of Cordillera de Cochabamba and 11 mi. N of Capinota; alt. 8,825 ft.; wheat, corn, potatoes; livestock. Until 1900s, Caraza.

Sant Martí de Maldá (sänt märtē' dā mäldä'), town (pop. 1,025), Lérida prov., NE Spain, 14 mi. SW of Cervera; olive-oil processing; sheep raising; cereals, wine.

Santo or **El Santo** (ěl sän'tō), town (pop. 1,807), Las Villas prov., central Cuba, near N coast, 18 mi. NW of Caibarién; sugar cane, fruit.

Santo, New Hebrides: see ESPIRITU SANTO.

Santo, Tadzhik SSR: see KIM.

Santo Agostinho, Cape (săn'tōō ägōōstē'nyōō), headland on Atlantic coast of Pernambuco, NE Brazil, 20 mi. SSW of Recife; 8°21'S 34°54'W. Lighthouse. Also called São Agostinho.

Santo Aleixo (săn'tōō ālā'shōō), town (pop. 4,190), central Rio de Janeiro state, Brazil, 8 mi. SE of Petrópolis.

Santo Aleixo, village (pop. 2,630), Beja dist., S Portugal, 18 mi. ESE of Moura, near Sp. border; the noted *Serra de Aires* wine is grown in area.

Santo Amaro (săn'tōō ämä'rōō). **1** City (pop. 10,929), E Bahia, Brazil, near N shore of Todos os Santos Bay, on railroad and 35 mi. NNW of Salvador; industrial center with sugar mills, distilleries, tobacco factories, and iron foundry. **2** City, Rio Grande do Sul, Brazil: see GENERAL CÂMARA. **3** Southernmost section of São Paulo city, in São Paulo state, SE Brazil, 7 mi. from city center; residential dist. Here is dam—at N end of reservoir supplying city with light and power.

Santo Amaro da Imperatriz (dä ēmpĭrŭtrēz'), town (pop. 988), E Santa Catarina, Brazil, 15 mi. SW of Florianópolis; watering place with hot springs. Until 1944, called Santo Amaro; and, 1944–48, Cambirela.

Santo Amaro das Brotas (däs brô'tŭs), city (pop. 1,597), E Sergipe, NE Brazil, 10 mi. N of Aracaju; sugar milling. Until 1944, called Santo Amaro.

Santo Amaro Island, near SE coast of Brazil, just off Santos (São Paulo), whose harbor it shelters from the open Atlantic; separated from mainland (N) and São Vicente Isl. (W) by narrow Bertioga channel; 15 mi. long, up to 8 mi. wide. GUARUJÁ, its port and resort, is linked by rail with Santos.

Santo Anastácio (săn'tōō änŭstä'syōō), city (pop. 4,007), W São Paulo, Brazil, on railroad and 20 mi. WNW of Presidente Prudente; sawmilling, distilling; coffee, cotton, grain, cattle raising.

Santo André (săn'tōō ändrĕ'), city (1950 pop. 98,313), São Paulo, Brazil, SE suburb of São Paulo, 10 mi. from city center, and on São Paulo–Santos RR. Important industrial center producing copper, brass, and aluminum articles, and agr. machinery, electrical motors, machine tools, armaments. Also has fertilizer factory (using apatite from Jacupiranga), agr.-processing plants, sawmills; mfg. of toys, mattresses, footwear, cement, tiles. Airfield.

Santo Ângelo (săn'tōō ä'zhĭlōō), city (pop. 7,792), NW Rio Grande do Sul, Brazil, on Ijuí R., on railroad and 50 mi. NW of Cruz Alta; center of agr. colony (cereals, livestock). Airfield. Founded as a Jesuit mission.

Santo Antão Island (săn'tōō äntä'ō), northwesternmost island (□ 301; 1940 pop. 35,930; 1950 pop. 27,805) of the Cape Verde Isls., in the Windward group, 8 mi. NW of neighboring São Vicente Isl., in the Atlantic. Ribeira Grande (17°11'N 25°4'W), its chief town, is on NE shore. Isl. is 25 mi. long, 12–15 mi. wide. Of volcanic origin, it rises to 6,493 ft. in the Tope da Corôa. Although only ½ isl. is cultivated, it produces coffee, oranges, sugar cane, tobacco, castor beans, and cinchona. Horses, sheep, and cattle are raised. Tarrafal Bay on SW shore is best anchorage.

Santo Antônio (săn'tōō äntō'nyōō). **1** Village, Guaporé territory, Brazil: see ALTO MADEIRA. **2** City, Mato Grosso, Brazil: see SANTO ANTÔNIO DO LEVERGER. **3** City (pop. 1,428), E Rio Grande do Norte, NE Brazil, 37 mi. SSW of Natal; cotton, carnauba, cheese. Called Padre Miguelinho, 1944–48. **4** City (pop. 1,412), E Rio Grande do Sul, Brazil, 35 mi. ENE of Pôrto Alegre; honey, brandy, sugar, rice. Until 1938, called Santo Antônio da Patrulha.

Santo Antônio (săn'tōō äntō'nyōō), town, São Tomé e Príncipe, on E coast of Príncipe Isl., 100 mi. NNE of São Tomé; 1°38'N 7°25'E. Ships cacao, coffee, coconuts.

Santo Antônio, Cape, Brazil: see SALVADOR.

Santo Antônio da Alegria (äntō'nyōō dä älĭgrē'ŭ), city (pop. 1,115), NE São Paulo, Brazil, at Minas Gerais border, 40 mi. ENE of Ribeirão Prêto; grain, coffee, fruit, sugar cane, cattle.

Santo Antônio da Cachoeira, Brazil: see ITAGUATINS.

Santo Antônio da Patrulha, Brazil: see SANTO ANTÔNIO, Rio Grande do Sul.

Santo Antônio da Platina (dä plŭtē'nŭ), city (pop. 3,499), NE Paraná, Brazil, 70 mi. E of Londrina; rice, coffee, and lard processing; mfg. of pottery and furniture; corn, hog raising.

Santo Antônio da Serra (äntô'nyōō dä sĕ'rŭ), village, Madeira, in E part of Madeira isl., 13 mi. NE of Funchal; alt. 2,310 ft. Summer resort amidst pine woods; golf course. Agr. experiment station. Wickerwork. Also called Santo da Serra.

Santo Antônio de Balsas, Brazil: see BALSAS.

Santo Antônio de Jesus (äntō'nyōō dĭ zhä'zōōs), city (pop. 8,518), E Bahia, Brazil, on railroad and 50 mi. W of Salvador; manganese-mining center; ships tobacco, coffee, sugar.

Santo Antônio de Pádua (pä'dwŭ), city (pop. 3,360), NE Rio de Janeiro state, Brazil, on Pomba R., on railroad and 35 mi. ESE of Cataguases (Minas Gerais); coffee and rice processing, meat jerking.

Santo Antônio do Içá (dōō ēsä'), town (pop. 319), W Amazonas, Brazil, steamer and hydroplane landing on left bank of the Amazon at influx of Içá R., and 80 mi. ENE of São Paulo de Olivença. Missionary settlement.

Santo Antônio do Leverger (lĭvĭrzhĕr'), city (pop. 964), central Mato Grosso, Brazil, on Cuiabá R. (navigable) and 20 mi. S of Cuiabá; sugar, alcohol, cattle. Until 1939, Santo Antônio do Rio Abaixo; 1939–43, Santo Antônio; 1944–48, Leverger.

Santo Antônio do Monte (mōn'tĭ), city (pop. 2,516), S central Minas Gerais, Brazil, on railroad and 25 mi. W of Divinópolis, ships dairy produce, cereals, tanning bark.

Santo Antônio do Rio Abaixo, Brazil: see SANTO ANTÔNIO DO LEVERGER.

Santo Antônio do Zaire (äntō'nyōō dōō zī'rĭ), town (pop. 528), ⊙ Zaire dist. (□ c.2,340; pop. 45,198), Congo prov., northwesternmost Angola, at mouth of Congo R., 200 mi. NNW of Luanda, and diagonally opposite Banana (Belgian Congo); 6°7'S 12°18'W. Fishing port. Trade in palm oil and kernels, oilseeds. R.C. mission. Airfield. Also called Sazaire.

Santo Antonio e Almas, Brazil: see BEQUIMÃO.

Santo Antônio River (äntō'nyōō), Sp. *San Antonio Guazú*, on Argentina-Brazil border, rises at SE foot of the Sierra de la Victoria, flows c.50 mi. NNW to Iguassú R. 40 mi. E of Puerto Iguazú (Argentina).

Santo Cerro (sän'tō sĕ'rō), village and hill, La Vega prov., central Dominican Republic, 4 mi. N of La Vega city. Site of 16th-cent. church and shrine of Our Lady of Las Mercedes, where Columbus fought a battle against the Indians and the Virgin appeared to him.

Santo Corazón (sän'tō kōräsōn'), village (pop. c.350), Santa Cruz dept., E Bolivia, 90 mi. NW of Puerto Suárez; road center.

Santo Domingo (săn'tŭ dŭmĭng'gō, Sp. sän'tō dōmēng'gō), former Spanish colony on HISPANIOLA, West Indies, now the DOMINICAN REPUBLIC.

Santo Domingo, Canary Isls.: see GARAFÍA.

Santo Domingo, resort village, Santiago prov., central Chile, on the Pacific at mouth of Maipo R., opposite Tejas Verdes, 55 mi. WSW of Santiago.

Santo Domingo, town (pop. 2,263), Antioquia dept., NW central Colombia, in Cordillera Central, 32 mi. NE of Medellín; alt. 6,463 ft.; coffee, corn, beans, bananas, potatoes, cattle.

Santo Domingo. 1 City (1950 pop. 2,165), Heredia prov., central Costa Rica, on central plateau, on railroad and 3 mi. NNW of San José; coffee center; cereals, livestock. Founded 1710; a wheat-growing center in colonial times. **2** Village, Puntarenas prov., Costa Rica: see PUERTO JIMÉNEZ.

Santo Domingo, town (pop. 3,888), Las Villas prov., central Cuba, on Sagua la Grande R., on railroad and 20 mi. WNW of Santa Clara; agr. center (sugar cane, tobacco, corn, fruit, vegetables, cattle). The sugar central Washington is 4 mi. W.

Santo Domingo, district (□ 548; 1935 pop. 116,992; 1950 pop. 241,228), S Dominican Republic, on the Caribbean; ⊙ Ciudad Trujillo. A narrow coastal strip where sugar cane and tropical fruit are grown and cattle raised. Boca Chica, 19 mi. E, is a beach resort with sugar refinery. Fishing along the coast. It was set up as a natl. dist. in 1935 out of former Santo Domingo prov.

Santo Domingo, city, Dominican Republic: see CIUDAD TRUJILLO.

Santo Domingo or **Santo Domingo Suchitepéquez** (sän'tō dōmēng'gō sōōchētäpā'kĕs), town (1950 pop. 1,347), Suchitepéquez dept., SW Guatemala, in Pacific piedmont, 5 mi. SSE of Mazatenango; coffee, sugar cane, grain; livestock; lumbering.

Santo Domingo. 1 Officially Santo Domingo de Guzmán, town (pop. 2,164), Mexico state, central Mexico, on Lerma R. and 40 mi. WNW of Mexico city; cereals, fruit, livestock. **2** Town (pop. 554), San Luis Potosí, N central Mexico, on interior plateau, 95 mi. NW of San Luis Potosí; alt. 6,466 ft.; manganese mining. **3** Town, Veracruz, Mexico: see FILOMENA MATA.

Santo Domingo, town (1950 pop. 3,110), Chontales dept., S Nicaragua, 30 mi. NE of Juigalpa; sugar cane, citrus fruit. Gold- and silver-mining center since 1880s. El Jabalí (S) and San Gregorio (N) mines obtain hydroelectric power from plant at falls on Siquia R.

Santo Domingo, village (pop. 1,109), Los Santos prov., S central Panama, in Pacific lowland, 15 mi. SE of Las Tablas; sugar cane, corn, beans, yucca, livestock.

Santo Domingo, village, Puno dept., SE Peru, on Inambari R. and 34 mi. NNW of Sandia; alt. 6,540 ft.; gold mining.

Santo Domingo. 1 Town (1939 pop. 2,859; 1948 municipality pop. 11,082), Ilocos Sur prov., N Luzon, Philippines, 5 mi. NNE of Vigan, near W coast; rice-growing center. **2** Town (1939 pop. 3,506; 1948 municipality pop. 12,730), Nueva Ecija prov., central Luzon, Philippines, 9 mi. NW of Cabanatuan; agr. center (rice, corn).

Santo Domingo (săn"tŭ dōmĭng'gō), pueblo (□ 103.5), Sandoval co., central N.Mex. Santo Domingo village (1950 pop. 1,169) is on E bank of the Rio Grande and 26 mi. SW of Sante Fe; alt. c.5,200 ft. Agr., pottery making. Green-corn dance takes place on St. Dominic's day (Aug. 4). Present village founded c.1700.

Santo Domingo (sän'tō dōmēng'gō), village (pop. under 500), Táchira state, W Venezuela, in Andean outliers, 17 mi. SE of San Cristóbal. Airport.

Santo Domingo, Sierra de (syĕ'rä dā), range in Mérida state, W Venezuela, NE section of Andean spur Sierra Nevada de Mérida, along left bank of upper Chama R., 20 mi. ENE of Mérida; rises to 15,328 ft. in Pico MUCUÑUQUE.

Santo Domingo Cay (sän"tō dōmĭng"gō kā', kē', săn"tŭ dŭmĭng'gō), islet, S Bahama Isls., on S fringe of Columbus Bank, 40 mi. N of Cuba, 32 mi. S of Great Ragged Isl.; 21°42'N 75°46'W.

Santo Domingo de la Calzada (sän'tō dōmēng'gō dā lä käl-thä'dhä), city (pop. 4,592), Logroño prov., N Spain, 26 mi. W of Logroño; tanning, flour- and sawmilling; mfg. of woolen fabrics, soap, tiles. Agr. trade (wine, cereals, potatoes, sugar beets). Has a 12th-cent. cathedral with Gothic cloisters (16th cent.) and baroque tower, a 16th-cent. Franciscan convent, and fine old mansions; partly surrounded by 14th-cent. walls. Resort.

Santo Domingo de los Colorados (lōs kōlōrä'dhōs), village, Pichincha prov., N central Ecuador, at W slopes of the Andes, 45 mi. W of Quito; communication center connected by roads with Quito, Esmeraldas, and Bahía de Caráquez (on the Pacific). Cotton, balsa wood, rubber, stock; mfg. of charcoal. Near by is the Santo Domingo settlement of aboriginal Indians, of interest to tourists and anthropologists.

Santo Domingo de Moya (moi'ä), village (pop. 794), Cuenca prov., E central Spain, 32 mi. SSW of Teruel; cereals, fruit, grapes, truck, saffron, livestock. Has ruins of old castle. Sometimes Moya.

Santo Domingo de Silos (sē'lōs), town (pop. 534), Burgos prov., N Spain, 31 mi. SE of Burgos; cereals, fruit, livestock; timber. Known for its monastery (founded by Benedictines in 6th cent.) with beautiful cloister.

Santo Domingo de Soriano, Uruguay: see SORIANO, town.

Santo Domingo Island, West Indies: see HISPANIOLA.

Santo Domingo Nancinta, Guatemala: see NANCINTA.

Santo Domingo River (sän'tō dōmēng'gō), W Venezuela, rises in the Andes at NW foot of Pico Mucuñuque, flows c.125 mi. SE in Barinas state, past Barinas, to Apure R. 17 mi. W of Puerto de Nutrias. Navigable for small craft.

Santo Domingo Teojomulco, Mexico: see TEOJOMULCO.

Santo Domingo Xenacoj, Guatemala: see XENACOJ.

Santo Inácio (sän' tōō ēnä'syōō), city (pop. 643), W central Bahia, Brazil, in the Serra do Açuruá, 35 mi. ESE of Barra; center of diamond- and gold-mining region; ships caroa fibers, carnauba wax. Formerly called Gamelleira do Assuruá, then Assuruá until 1939.

Santolea (säntōlā'ä), town (pop. 365), Teruel prov., E Spain, on Guadalope R. and 24 mi. SSW of Alcañiz. Irrigation reservoir near by. Coal mines.

Santomischel, Poland: see ZANIEMYSL.

Santoña (säntō'nyä), town (pop. 10,781), Santander prov., N Spain, in Old Castile, 17 mi. E of Santander, important fishing port on inlet of S shore of small peninsula in Bay of Biscay; fish processing (anchovies, tuna, salmon) and shipping, boatbuilding, lumbering. Of anc. origin, town was strongly fortified. Has 13th-cent. Gothic church, convent of St. Sebastian, and penitentiary. Fine bathing beaches.

Santo Niño Island (sän'tō nē'nyō) (□ 8; 1939 pop. 2,505), Samar prov., Philippines, in Samar Sea, bet. Masbate and Samar isls.; 11°54'N 124°26'E; 3 mi. in diameter. Hilly, rising to 1,150 ft. Coconut growing.

Santo-Pietro-di-Tenda (sän'tô-pyĕ'trô-dē-tĕn'dä), village (pop. 550), N Corsica, 11 mi. SW of Bastia; olive-oil and candle mfg.

Santo Pipó (sän'tō pēpō'), town (pop. estimate 1,000), S Misiones natl. territory, Argentina, 40 mi. NE of Posadas; agr. center (corn, maté, citrus fruit); maté processing, ceramics mfg.

Santorcaz (säntōrkäth'), town (pop. 636), Madrid prov., central Spain, 24 mi. E of Madrid; cereals, grapes, olives; wine making, olive-oil pressing.

Santorin or **Santorini,** Greece: see THERA.

Santo Rosario, Philippines: see SAN FERNANDO, Pampanga prov.

Santorso (säntōr'sō), village (pop. 415), Vicenza prov., Veneto, N Italy, 2 mi. NE of Schio; agr. tools, cutlery. Kaolin quarries near by.

Santos (săn'tōōs), city (1950 pop. 201,739), SE São Paulo, Brazil, 33 mi. SE of São Paulo, whose port it is; state's 2d largest city, situated on coastal São Vicente Isl., which is separated from mainland (N) and Santo Amaro Isl. (E) by a tidal channel (sometimes called Santos R.) here widening into a landlocked bay; 23°56'S 46°21'W. World's leading coffee port and principal outlet for interior of São Paulo (Brazil's wealthiest and most populous state), it exceeds Rio de Janeiro (210 mi. NE) in volume of exports. Santos also ships sugar, alcohol, citrus fruit, bananas, cotton, hides, and meat. Imports include machinery, semifinished goods, and wheat. The modern harbor, with over 3 mi. of concrete, rodent-proof docks, accommodates up to 50 steamers. All quays are served by railroad tracks. Coffee bags are loaded in a continuous operation by mechanical conveyers directly from warehouses which line the water front. City is linked with São Paulo by a double-track railroad (which ascends the precipitous, 2,600-ft. coastal escarpment by means of cables) and by a modern 4-lane highway. Another rail line (recently completed) crosses the Serra do Mar farther W, to Sorocaba. Coffee (grading, storing, transshipping, and trading) dominates all activities in Santos, and its fragrance is omnipresent. Flour milling, shark-liver oil processing, and distilling are of secondary importance. City has a humid, subtropical climate (mean temp. 72°F., average rainfall 80 in.), which, together with the low, marshy site, impeded the eradication of yellow fever until beginning of 20th cent. At the hub of the crowded commercial dist. is the dignified Coffee Exchange, which controls the city's economic pulse. It is overlooked by steep, 700-ft.-high Monteserrat, a hill (ascended by funicular railway) topped by a shrine and a meteorological observatory. The rest of the city is laid out along regular lines, but is rather unattractive. Two thoroughfares connect the harbor area and airport with residential dists. and beaches on S shore of isl. Gonzaga beach has the largest hotels and a famous orchidarium. Guarujá (5 mi. from city center on

Santo Amaro Isl.) is one of Brazil's finest playgrounds and beach resorts. Other seashore places on mainland (SW) are reached via São Vicente, through miles of banana plantations. The great Cubatão hydroelectric installation serving São Paulo and Santos is 6 mi. NW at foot of the Serra do Mar. Santos was settled 1543–46, after the Portuguese had established their 1st post on São Paulo coast in 1532. Captured by English privateers in 1591. Replaced São Vicente as chief seaport after São Paulo became capital of captaincy in 1681. Santos owes its prosperity to the extension of coffee cultivation into the interior of São Paulo in 19th cent., and to the completion (1867) of the railroad across the coastal escarpment, a major feat of engineering. Extension of railroad across Mato Grosso (1914) and into Bolivia (under construction) is steadily increasing city's potential hinterland.

Santos, Los, Panama: see Los SANTOS.

Santos, Los (lōs sän'tōs). **1** or **Los Santos de Maimona** (dā mīmō'nä), town (pop. 8,045), Badajoz prov., SW Spain, in Estremadura, on Mérida-Seville RR and 35 mi. SE of Badajoz. Processing and agr. center on fertile Tierra de Barros plain (cereals, vegetables, grapes, olives, livestock); alcohol and liquor distilling, flour milling, vegetable canning, olive-oil pressing; mfg. of soap, bags, tiles, caramels. Lumbering. **2** Town (pop. 1,766), Salamanca prov., W Spain, 11 mi. N of Béjar; cereals, vegetables, livestock.

Santos de la Humosa, Los (lōs sän'tōs dā lä o͞omō'sä), town (pop. 972), Madrid prov., central Spain, 23 mi. E of Madrid; olives, grain, grapes.

Santos de Maimona, Los, Spain: see SANTOS, LOS, Badajoz prov.

Santos Dumont (sän'to͝os do͞omōnt'), city (pop. 11,385), S Minas Gerais, Brazil, in the Serra da Mantiqueira, on Belo Horizonte–Rio de Janeiro highway and 25 mi. NNW of Juiz de Fora; alt. 2,750 ft. Rail junction. Noted cheese-mfg. center, important also as exporter of other dairy products; mfg. of calcium carbide. Santos Dumont, the Braz. aviation pioneer, was b. here. Called Palmyra until 1930s.

Santos Lugares (sän'tōs lo͞ogä'rĕs), town (pop. estimate 8,000), in W Greater Buenos Aires, Argentina; mfg. center (food preserves, sweets, plaster, wire netting); railroad shops.

Santo Sperato, Sardinia: see SAN SPERATE.

Santo Stefano Belbo (sän'tô stā'fänô bĕl'bô), village (pop. 1,227), Cuneo prov., Piedmont, NW Italy, on Belbo R. and 10 mi. E of Alba; wine.

Santo Stefano d'Aveto (dä'vĕtô), village (pop. 394), Genova prov., Liguria, N Italy, near Monte Maggiorasca, 17 mi. NNE of Chiavari; resort (alt. 3,337 ft.).

Santo Stefano di Camastra (dē kämä'strä), town (pop. 5,785), Messina prov., N Sicily, port on Tyrrhenian Sea, 6 mi. N of Mistretta; wine, olive oil.

Santo Stefano di Magra (dē mä'grä), village (pop. 1,575), La Spezia prov., Liguria, N Italy, near Magra R., 7 mi. NE of Spezia; rail junction; bricks, paving stones. Marble deposits near by.

Santo Stefano Quisquina (kwēskwē'nä), town (pop 6,084), Agrigento prov., W central Sicily, near head of Magazzolo R., 22 mi. NNW of Agrigento; cereals, almonds, meat and dairy products.

Santo Stino di Livenza (sän'tô stē'nô dē lēvĕn'tsä), village (pop. 1,738), Venezia prov., Veneto, N Italy, on Livenza R. and 10 mi. SE of Oderzo.

Santo Tirso (sän'to͝o tēr'so͝o), town (pop. 2,675), Pôrto dist., N Portugal, on Ave R. and 14 mi. NNE of Oporto; textile milling; agr. trade. Has 14th–17th-cent. Benedictine monastery, now partially occupied by agr. school. Warm springs near by.

Santo Tomás (sän'tō tōmäs'), town (pop. 3,489), Atlántico dept., N Colombia, in Caribbean lowlands, near Magdalena R., 20 mi. S of Barranquilla; cotton, corn, sugar cane, stock.

Santo Tomás, village (pop. 200), Izabal dept., E Guatemala, minor Caribbean port on Santo Tomás Bay (inlet of Bay of Amatique), across from Puerto Barrios; fisheries; coastal trade.

Santo Tomás, inactive volcano (9,793 ft.), SW Guatemala, on Quezaltenango-Retalhuleu-Suchitepéquez dept. border, 10 mi. SSE of Quezaltenango. Hot-spring resorts of Aguas Amargas and Fuentes Georginas on N slope.

Santo Tomás. 1 Village (pop. 170), Northern Territory, Lower California, NW Mexico, in irrigated valley 23 mi. SE of Ensenada; fruitgrowing (grapes, olives, peaches, figs, quinces). **2** Officially Santo Tomás de los Plátanos, town (pop. 571), Mexico state, central Mexico, on Michoacán border, 40 mi. WSW of Toluca; sugar cane, fruit, corn.

Santo Tomás. 1 Town (1950 pop. 401), Chinandega dept., W Nicaragua, on Honduras border, 10 mi. N of Somotillo; sugar cane, rice, corn. Another Santo Tomás (village) is near Pacific coast, 19 mi. NW of Chinandega. **2** Town (1950 pop. 762), Chontales dept., S Nicaragua, on road and 29 mi. E of Juigalpa; grain, sugar cane, livestock.

Santo Tomás. 1 Town (pop. 1,015), Amazonas dept., N Peru, in E Andean range, 25 mi. S of Chachapoyas; sugar, fruit; gold washing. **2** Town (pop. 974), ⊙ Chumbivilcas prov. (□ 3,395; pop. 50,498), Cuzco dept., S Peru, in high valley of Cordillera Occidental, 75 mi. SSW of Cuzco; alt. 12,000 ft. Grain, livestock; gold washing; mfg. (woolen goods, hats).

Santo Tomas, town (1939 pop. 1,326; 1948 municipality pop. 17,022), Batangas prov., S Luzon, Philippines, on railroad and 13 mi. WNW of San Pablo; rice, sugar cane, corn, coconuts.

Santo Tomás, town (pop. 3,107), San Salvador dept., S central Salvador, 6 mi. SE of San Salvador, in coastal range; agr. center; sugar cane. Pop. largely Indian.

Santo Tomás Chichicastenango, Guatemala: see CHICHICASTENANGO.

Santo Tomás La Unión (lä o͞onyōn'), town (1950 pop. 735), Suchitepéquez dept., SW Guatemala, in Pacific piedmont, 10 mi. NE of Mazatenango; coffee, grain, tobacco; livestock. Transferred 1944 from Quezaltenango dept.

Santo Tomé (sän'tō tōmā'). **1** Town (pop. 9,688), ⊙ Santo Tomé dept. (□ c.3,000; pop. 22,550), E Corrientes prov., Argentina, port on Uruguay R. (Brazil border), on railroad and 80 mi. SSW of Posadas; agr. center (rice, corn, jute, citrus fruit, maté, livestock). Has natl. col. **2** Town (pop. estimate 2,000), E central Santa Fe prov., Argentina, 4 mi. SW of Santa Fe; rail junction in agr. area (corn, potatoes, vegetables, livestock); vegetable-oil factories.

Santo Tomé, town (pop. 2,298), Jaén prov., S Spain, 6 mi. SSW of Villacarrillo; olive-oil processing, flour milling; horse breeding; cereals.

Santovenia (säntōvā'nyä), village (pop. 1,056), Zamora prov., NW Spain, 9 mi. S of Benavente; cereals, wine, livestock.

Santrampur (sŭn'trŭmpo͝or), town (pop. 3,988), Panch Mahals dist., N Bombay, India, 34 mi. NNE of Godhra; market center for corn, oilseeds, ghee, hides; hand-loom weaving, palm-mat making. Forests (teak, bamboo) near by. Was ⊙ former Gujarat state of Sunth. Also called Rampur.

Sant Sadurní de Noya, Spain: see SAN SATURNINO DE NOYA.

Santu (sän'do͞o'), town (pop. 2,718), ⊙ Santu co. (pop. 60,532), SE Kweichow prov., China, 90 mi. SE of Kweiyang and on upper Liu R. (head of junk navigation); rice, wheat, millet. Mercury mines, and iron, antimony, lead deposits near by. Formerly Sankioh; and later, until 1942, Sanho.

Santuao (sän'do͞o'ou'), town (1931 pop. 9,000), NE Fukien prov., China, port on Santu isl. in Samsa Bay, 25 mi. SW of Siapu; porcelain mfg. (kaolin quarrying near by); fisheries. Opened to foreign trade in 1899 as treaty port, serving Siapu (former Funing); formerly had large tea trade.

Santuario (säntwär'yō). **1** Town (pop. 2,303), Antioquia dept., NW central Colombia, in Cordillera Central, 22 mi. ESE of Medellín; alt. 7,058 ft.; corn, potatoes, livestock. **2** Town (pop. 3,215), Caldas dept., W central Colombia, in Cauca valley, 32 mi. W of Manizales; coffeegrowing; sericulture.

Santuario, town (pop. 1,124), Hidalgo, central Mexico, 45 mi. NE of Pachuca; corn, beans, maguey, stock.

Santuit, Mass.: see BARNSTABLE, town.

Santu Lussurgiu (sän'to͞o lo͞os-so͞or'jo͞o), village (pop. 4,264), Cagliari prov., W Sardinia, on Monte Ferru and 17 mi. N of Oristano; chestnuts.

Santurce (säntōōr'sā), S residential section of San Juan, NE Puerto Rico, on mainland; also rum and alcohol distilling, mfg. of clothing; dye works. Modern housing developments.

Santurce (säntōōr'thā), NW suburb (pop. 7,023) and outer port of Bilbao, Vizcaya prov., N Spain, at head of Bilbao Bay (inlet of Bay of Biscay), just inside W breakwater; iron-ore shipping; fishing. Oil refinery.

San Ubaldo (sän o͞obäl'dō), village, Chontales dept., S Nicaragua, port on E shore of L. Nicaragua, 12 mi. WSW of Acoyapa; grain, sugar cane.

Sanuki (sä"no͞o'kē), former province in NE Shikoku, Japan; now Kagawa prefecture.

Sanuki, town (pop. 5,011), Chiba prefecture, central Honshu, Japan, on W Chiba Peninsula, 9 mi. SSW of Kisarazu; agr.; summer resort.

Sanuma (sä"no͞o'mä), town (pop. 8,776), Miyagi prefecture, N Honshu, Japan, 19 mi. NNW of Ishinomaki; rice, wheat, raw silk, sheep.

San Urbano (sän o͞orbä'nō), town (pop. estimate 2,500), ⊙ General López dept. (□ 4,415; 1947 census 146,366), S Sante Fe prov., Argentina, near a lake, 70 mi. SW of Rosario; rail junction, fishing and agr. center (corn, wheat, flax, livestock). Beach resort near by. Formerly called Melincué.

San Valentín, Cerro (sĕ'rō sän välĕntēn'), or **Cerro San Clemente** (klāmĕn'tā), peak (13,313 ft.), Aysén prov., S Chile, 90 mi. SSW of Puerto Aysén, in vast area of snow-covered peaks and glaciers. San Rafael Glacier is on its W slope.

San Valentino in Abruzzo Citeriore (sän välĕntē'nô ēn äbro͞ot'tsô chētĕrēô'rē), town (pop. 1,495), Pescara prov., Abruzzi e Molise, S central Italy, 13 mi. SW of Chieti; cement mfg., asphalt processing. Has Romanesque church (12th–13th cent.). Asphalt mines near by.

San Valentino Torio (tô'rēô), village (pop. 2,998), Salerno prov., Campania, S Italy, 2 mi. SSW of Sarno, in agr. region (cereals, fruit, vegetables).

San Venanzo (sän vĕnän'tsô), village (pop. 380), Terni prov., Umbria, central Italy, 13 mi. NE of Orvieto; agr. tools.

San Vendemiano (vĕndĕmyä'nô), commune (pop. 4,828) and village, Treviso prov., Veneto, N Italy, 6 mi. S of Vittorio Veneto, in cereal- and grape-growing region; rail junction; brush mfg.

San Vero Milis (sän vā'rô mē'lēs), village (pop. 2,090), Cagliari prov., W Sardinia, 7 mi. N of Oristano.

Sanvic (sävēk'), NW suburb (pop. 17,307) of Le Havre, Seine-Inférieure dept., N France. Damaged in Second World War.

San Vicente (sän vēsĕn'tā), town (pop. 2,170), ⊙ San Vicente dist. (□ 282; pop. 7,994), NE Buenos Aires prov., Argentina, 27 mi. S of Buenos Aires; cattle raising, nutria breeding.

San Vicente (sän vē-thĕn'tā), village (pop. 570), Iviza, Balearic Isls., 13 mi. NE of Iviza city; cereals, fruit, livestock.

San Vicente (sän vēsĕn'tä). **1** Town (pop. 1,022), Concepción prov., S central Chile, just W of Talcahuano, on the Pacific; seaside resort on small San Vicente Bay. A modern steel mill was built (late 1940s) on sandy Huachipato beach just S. **2** or **San Vicente de Tagua-Tagua** (dātä'wä-tä'wä), town (pop. 4,264), ⊙ San Vicente dept. (□ 305; pop. 32,492), O'Higgins prov., central Chile, on railroad and 28 mi. SW of Rancagua; agr. center (alfalfa, wheat, beans, fruit, wine, cattle); flour milling, dairying.

San Vicente. 1 Officially San Vicente del Caguán, village, Caquetá commissary, S Colombia, on Caguán R. and 70 mi. NE of Florencia; forest products (rubber, balata gum, resins). **2** or **San Vicente de Chucurí** (dā cho͞oko͞orē'), town (pop. 2,602), Santander dept., N central Colombia, 27 mi. SW of Bucaramanga; coffee, cacao, tobacco, sugar cane, rice, fruit, cattle, hogs; coffee and rice milling, tanning, soapmaking.

San Vicente or **San Vicente de Moravia** (dāmōrä'vyä), town (pop. 2,081), San José prov., central Costa Rica, on central plateau, 3 mi. NE of San José, in coffee area; grain, truck produce.

San Vicente, spa, Pinar del Río prov., W Cuba, 5 mi. N of Viñales; sulphurous springs.

San Vicente, village, Guayas prov., W Ecuador, at base of Santa Elena Peninsula, on railroad and highway, and 60 mi. W of Guayaquil; spa with hot sulphur springs.

San Vicente or **San Vicente Pacaya** (päkī'ä), town (1950 pop. 1,929), Escuintla dept., S Guatemala, in Pacific piedmont, at E foot of volcano Pacaya, 12 mi. ENE of Escuintla; alt. 5,052 ft.; coffee, corn, wheat. Ascent of the volcano starts here. Formerly also called San Vicente Mártir.

San Vicente, Mexico: see SAN VICENTE TANCUAYALAB.

San Vicente, Peru: see CAÑETE.

San Vicente or **Central San Vicente** (sĕnträl'), locality, N Puerto Rico, on railroad and 1½ mi. NE of Vega Baja; sugar mill.

San Vicente, dept. (□ 883; 1950 pop. 87,423), S central Salvador, on Pacific Ocean; ⊙ San Vicente. Mountainous (San Vicente volcano) in NW, sloping toward Lempa R. (E border) and coast (S). Agr. (sugar cane, coffee, manioc, fruit, grain), Lumbering in Pacific coastal plain. Cotton milling (San Sebastián), sugar production. Crossed by railroad and Inter-American Highway. Main centers: San Vicente, San Sebastián. Formed 1835.

San Vicente, city (1950 pop. 10,945), ⊙ San Vicente dept., S Salvador, on railroad, on spur of Inter-American Highway, and 27 mi. ESE of San Salvador, at NE foot of volcano San Vicente; alt. 1,381 ft.; 13°38'N 88°48'W. Commercial and industrial center; sugar milling, mfg. (textiles, footwear, hats); agr. (grain, sugar cane, coffee). Has noted clock tower in central park; annual fair. Founded 1635; ⊙ Salvador (1832–39); seat (1854–59) of natl. univ. Suffered in 1936 earthquake.

San Vicente, extinct volcano (7,132 ft.), on San Vicente–La Paz dept. border, S central Salvador, 4.5 mi. SW of San Vicente.

San Vicente, Cape, E tip of main isl. of Tierra del Fuego, Argentina, on the South Atlantic, 5 mi. NW of Cape San Diego; 54°38'S 65°15'W.

San Vicente Coyotepec, Mexico: see COYOTEPEC, Puebla.

San Vicente Creek and **San Vicente Dam,** Calif.: see SAN DIEGO RIVER.

San Vicente de Alcántara (sän vē-thĕn'tā dā älkän'tärä), town (pop. 8,321), Badajoz prov., W Spain, near Cáceres prov. border, 35 mi. NNW of Badajoz; agr. center (cereals, grapes, olives, chestnuts, fruit, cork, livestock). Tanning, flour milling, olive-oil pressing, mfg. of cork products. Has mineral springs.

San Vicente de Baracaldo, Spain: see BARACALDO.

San Vicente de Cañete, Peru: see CAÑETE.

San Vicente de Castellet (kästĕlyĕt'), village (pop. 3,570), Barcelona prov., NE Spain, on Llobregat R. and 4 mi. SSE of Manresa; cotton milling; mfg. of paper, rope; lumbering.

San Vicente de Castillos, Uruguay: see CASTILLOS.

San Vicente de Chucurí, Colombia: see SAN VICENTE, Santander dept.

San Vicente de la Barquera (dā lä bärkā'rä), town (pop. 1,558), Santander prov., N Spain, fishing port on Bay of Biscay, 18 mi. ESE of Llanes; fish processing and shipping, boatbuilding, lumbering. Apples, chestnuts, cattle in area. Dominated by hill crowned by ruins of anc. fort. Has church (13th–16th cent.) and remains of medieval walls.

San Vicente de la Sonsierra (sŏnsyĕ'rä), town (pop. 1,760), Logroño prov., N Spain, near the Ebro, 17 mi. WNW of Logroño, in winegrowing area; also cereals, sheep.

San Vicente del Raspeig (dĕl räspĕch'), town (pop. 3,663), Alicante prov., E Spain, 4 mi. N of Alicante; cement and soap mfg.; agr. trade (cereals, almonds, vegetables, wine). Clay quarries and ocher mines.

San Vicente dels Horts (dĕls ôrts'), outer W suburb (pop. 2,819), of Barcelona, Barcelona prov., NE Spain, on Llobregat R.; cotton milling, aluminum processing, cement mfg. Starting point of irrigation canal watering c.30 sq. mi.

San Vicente de Moravia, Costa Rica: see SAN VICENTE.

San Vicente de Tagua-Tagua, Chile: see SAN VICENTE, O'Higgins prov.

San Vicente Mártir, Guatemala: see SAN VICENTE.

San Vicente Pacaya, Guatemala: see SAN VICENTE.

San Vicente Tancuayalab (sän vēsĕn'tā täng-kwīäläb') or **San Vicente,** town (pop. 762), San Luis Potosí, E Mexico, in fertile Gulf plain, near Moctezuma R., 35 mi. SW of Pánuco; corn, sugar cane, tobacco, cotton, rice, fruit, stock.

San Vicenzo (sän vēchĕn'tsô), village (pop. 2,319), Livorno prov., Tuscany, central Italy, on Ligurian Sea, 15 mi. S of Cecina; bathing resort; quartz mining.

Sanvignes-les-Mines (sāvē'nyü-lā-mēn'), village (pop. 378), Saône-et-Loire dept., E central France, 11 mi. SW of Le Creusot; coal mining.

San Vito (sän vē'tô), village (pop. 4,521), Cagliari prov., SE Sardinia, near Flumendosa R., 28 mi. NE of Cagliari. Lead-zinc-silver mine near by. Sometimes called San Vito Sardo.

San Vito, Cape, NW extremity of Sicily, at W end of Gulf of Castellammare; 38°11'N 12°44'E. Site of **San Vito lo Capo,** village (pop. 2,481) and port, 16 mi. NE of Trapani, in citrus-fruit area; tunny fishing.

San Vito al Tagliamento (äl tälyämĕn'tô), town (pop. 4,135), Udine prov., Friuli–Venezia Giulia, NE Italy, near Tagliamento R., 21 mi. SW of Udine; rail junction; alcohol distilleries, paper mill. Has cheese-making school.

San Vito Chietino (kyĕtē'nô), village (pop. 1,996), Chieti prov., Abruzzi e Molise, S central Italy, on Adriatic coast, 4 mi. SSE of Ortona; fishing center.

San Vito dei Normanni (dā nôrmän'nē), town (pop. 13,441), Brindisi prov., Apulia, S Italy, 13 mi. W of Brindisi; agr. trade center (wine, olive oil, figs, almonds, wheat).

San Vito Romano (rômä'nô), town (pop. 4,201), Roma prov., Latium, central Italy, 11 mi. ESE of Tivoli; mfg. (agr. machinery, explosives, pumps).

San Vito sullo Ionio (sōōlô yô'nyô), village (pop. 3,611), Catanzaro prov., Calabria, S Italy, 17 mi. SSW of Catanzaro; cereal-, fruitgrowing region.

San Vittore Olona (sän vēt-tô'rĕ ôlô'nä), town (pop. 3,679), Milano prov., Lombardy, N Italy, near Olona R., 5 mi. SE of Busto Arsizio; shoe mfg. center; foundries.

San Xavier del Bac, Ariz.: see TUCSON.

Sanya, China: see SAMA.

Sanya Juu (sä'nyä jōō'), village, Northern Prov., Tanganyika, on road and 17 mi. W of Moshi; coffee, corn, vegetables; cattle, sheep, goats.

Sanyati River (sänyä'tē), in N Southern Rhodesia, formed 55 mi. W of Sinoia by union of UMFULI RIVER and UMNIATI RIVER; flows 100 mi. NNW to Zambezi R. above Kariba Gorge, 40 mi. S of Chirundu.

Sanyen, China: see WUCHENG, Sikang prov.

San Ygnacio (săn ĭgnä'sēō), village (1940 pop. 758), Zapata co., extreme S Texas, on the Rio Grande and 33 mi. S of Laredo; trade center in ranch area. Settled in 18th cent.; near by are ruins of old fort.

San Ysidro (săn ēsē'drō), village (pop. 2,381), San Diego co., extreme S Calif., 15 mi. SSE of San Diego, in agr. area; port of entry on Mexico border just N of Tijuana.

Sanyüan (sän'yüän'). **1** Town (pop. 3,769), ⊙ Sanyüan co. (pop. 34,829), W central Fukien prov., China, on Sha R. and 45 mi. SW of Nanping; rice, sweet potatoes, sugar cane. **2** Town (pop. 27,882), ⊙ Sanyüan co. (pop. 100,030), S central Shensi prov., China, 25 mi. N of Sian and on railroad; commercial center; cotton weaving; medicinal herbs, millet.

Sanza (sän'zä), town (pop. 2,604), Salerno prov., Campania, S Italy, 15 mi. E of Vallo di Lucania.

Sanza Pombo (sän'zä pōm'bō), town (pop. 269), Congo prov., NW Angola, 80 mi. NE of Uíge; rice, raffia, rubber.

Sanzoles (sän-thō'lĕs), town (pop. 1,234), Zamora Prov., NW Spain, 11 mi. SE of Zamora; wine, fruit.

Sanzyo, Japan: see SANJO.

São Bartolomeu de Messines (sã'ō bŭrtōōlōōmĕ'-ōō dĭ mĭsē'nĭsh), village (pop. 1,227), Faro dist., S Portugal, at W end of the Serra do Caldeirão, on railroad and 25 mi. NW of Faro; cork processing; marble and grindstone quarries.

São Benedito (bĭnĭdē'tōō). **1** City (pop. 2,256), NW Ceará, Brazil, in the Serra Grande, near Piauí border, 40 mi. SW of Sobral; sugar, tobacco, manioc. Marble deposits. Airfield. Formerly São Benedicto. **2** Town, Maranhão, Brazil: see CURURUZU. **3** City, Piauí, Brazil: see BENEDITINOS.

São Bento (bĕn'tōō). **1** City (pop. 4,654), N Maranhão, Brazil, near W shore of São Marcos Bay, 32 mi. WSW of São Luís; agr.-trade and -processing center in sugar-, cotton-, and cereal-growing region; cheese mfg., cattle raising. **2** City, Santa Catarina, Brazil: see SÃO BENTO DO SUL.

São Bento do Sapucaí (dōō sŭpōōkäē'), city (pop. 1,792), SE São Paulo, Brazil, in the Serra da Mantiqueira, on Minas Gerais border, 25 mi. NNW of Taubaté; dairying; sugar, rice. Formerly spelled São Bento do Sapucahy.

São Bento do Sul (sōōl'), city (pop. 1,779), NE Santa Catarina, Brazil, resort in the Serra do Mar, near Paraná border, on railroad and 35 mi. W of Joinvile; textile milling, dairying, fruit preserving. Founded late 19th cent. by Ger. settlers. Until 1944, called São Bento; and, 1944–48, Serra Alta.

São Bento do Una (dōō'nŭ), city (pop. 2,233), E central Pernambuco, NE Brazil, 25 mi. N of Garanhuns; cotton, cereals, cattle. Until 1944, called São Bento.

São Bernardo (bĕrnär'dōō). **1** City (pop. 749), NE Maranhão, Brazil, near left bank of Parnaíba R. (Piauí border), 40 mi. SW of Parnaíba; rice, tobacco. **2** City, São Paulo, Brazil: see SÃO BERNARDO DO CAMPO.

São Bernardo das Russas, Brazil: see RUSSAS.

São Bernardo do Campo (dōō kăm'pōō), city (1950 pop. 20,075), SE São Paulo, Brazil, outer SSE suburb of São Paulo city, adjoining Santo André (N), and in truck-gardening dist. Mfg. (chemicals, fabrics, ceramics).

São Borja (bôr'zhŭ), city (pop. 8,690), W Rio Grande do Sul, Brazil, on Uruguay R. (Argentine border) and 7 mi. SSE of Santo Tomé (Argentina), 100 mi. NE of Uruguaiana; rail terminus and livestock center; cereals, flax, rice, tobacco. Airfield. Settled 1808 by Portuguese on site of Indian village. Getúlio Vargas b. here.

São Brás (bräs'), city (pop. 1,244), E Alagoas, NE Brazil, landing on left bank of lower São Francisco R. and 24 mi. NW of Penedo. Formerly São Braz.

São Braz de Alportel (brăzh' dĭ älpôrtĕl'), town (pop. 1,450), Faro dist., S Portugal, 10 mi. NNE of Faro; cork processing, gunpowder mfg., sailmaking; figs, almonds, carobs, oranges are products of region. Basket weaving is a home industry. Also spelled São Brás de Alportel; sometimes called Alportel.

São Caetano de Odivelas (dōōdēvĕ'lŭs), city (pop. 1,012), E Pará, Brazil, near mouth of Pará R. on the Atlantic, 60 mi. NNW of Belém; lumber, medicinal plants. Formerly spelled São Caetano de Odivellas.

São Caetano do Sul (kītä'nōō dōō sōōl'), SE industrial suburb (1950 census pop. 55,797) of São Paulo city, São Paulo, Brazil, 6 mi. from city center, and on railroad to Santos; has large automobile assembly plant, sheet-metal works, leather and glass factories; mfg. of refrigerators, batteries.

São Caitano (kītä'nōō), city (pop. 2,811), E Pernambuco, NE Brazil, on railroad and 10 mi. W of Caruaru; cotton, manioc, cattle.

São Carlos (kär'lōōs), city (1950 pop. 31,539), E São Paulo, Brazil, 55 mi. S of Ribeirão Prêto; rail junction; commercial and agr.-processing center; cotton milling, meat packing, brewing, distilling; ships coffee, sugar, corn, potatoes, grain, fruit, livestock. Has fine cathedral. Formerly São Carlos do Pinhal.

São Cristóvão (krēstô'vã̃ō), city (pop. 4,133), E Sergipe, NE Brazil, port (coastwise shipping) near mouth of Vasa Barris R., on railroad and 12 mi. SW of Aracaju; sugar milling, distilling. Has 17th-cent. monastery of São Francisco. Was provincial ⊙ until 1855. Formerly spelled São Christovão.

São Domingos (sã'ō dōōmēng'gōōsh), city (pop. 666), E Goiás, central Brazil, near Bahia border; 13°32'S 46°18'W; timber, meat, dairy products.

São Domingos, village, NW Port. Guinea, near Fr. Senegal border, on arm of Cacheu R. and 55 mi. NW of Bissau; copra, peanuts, rice, palm oil, palm kernels.

São Domingos, Mina de, Portugal: see MINA DE SÃO DOMINGOS.

São Domingos, Serra de, Brazil: see GERAL DE GOIÁS, SERRA.

São Domingos da Boa Vista, Brazil: see CAPIM.

São Domingos do Capim, Brazil: see CAPIM.

São Domingos do Prata (dōō prä'tŭ), city (pop. 1,265), E central Minas Gerais, Brazil, near the Rio Doce, 60 mi. E of Belo Horizonte; nickel and mica deposits.

São Felipe, Brazil: see EIRUNEPÉ; IÇANA.

São Félix (sã'ō fĕ'lēs), city (pop. 6,559), E Bahia, Brazil, port on Paraguaçu R. near its mouth on Todos os Santos Bay, and 40 mi. NW of Salvador; noted cigar-mfg. center; also ships tobacco leaves. Connected by railroad bridge (1,200 ft. long) with Cachoeira (opposite bank). Formerly called São Félix do Paraguassú.

São Fidélis (fēdĕ'lēs), city (pop. 3,243), E Rio de Janeiro state, Brazil, on lower Paraíba R., on railroad and 28 mi. WNW of Campos; alcohol distilling, cotton ginning; agr. (sugar, coffee, rice, fruit). Graphite and mica deposits.

São Filipe (fēlē'pā), city (1950 pop. 5,223), Cape Verde Isls., on W Fogo isl., 70 mi. W of Praia (on São Tiago Isl.); 14°53'N 24°41'W. Agr. processing (coffee, oranges, tobacco, castor oil).

São Francisco (frăsē'skōō). **1** City, Bahia, Brazil: see SÃO FRANCISCO DO CONDE. **2** City, Ceará, Brazil: see ITAPAGÉ. **3** City, Maranhão, Brazil: see SÃO FRANCISCO DO MARANHÃO. **4** City (pop. 2,390), N Minas Gerais, Brazil, landing on right bank of São Francisco R. and 90 mi. NW of Montes Claros; ships cotton, sugar, cattle. **5** City, Santa Catarina, Brazil: see SÃO FRANCISCO DO SUL. **6** City, Sergipe, Brazil: see PARAPITINGA.

São Francisco de Assis (dĭ äsēs'), city (pop. 2,509), W central Rio Grande do Sul, Brazil, near Ibicuí R., 40 mi. ENE of Alegrete; stock raising, brandy distilling; corn, rice, timber.

São Francisco de Paula (pou'lŭ), city (pop. 1,971), NE Rio Grande do Sul, Brazil, in the Serra do Mar, 65 mi. NE of Pôrto Alegre; alt. 3,000 ft. Winegrowing; maté, fruit, lumber.

São Francisco do Conde (dōō kōn'dĭ), city (pop. 1,442), E Bahia, Brazil, fishing port on N shore of Todos os Santos Bay, 25 mi. NNW of Salvador; sugar, tobacco. Settled early in 16th cent. Has convent of São Francisco (1618). Until 1944, called São Francisco.

São Francisco do Maranhão (mŭrŭnyä'ō), city (pop. 569), E Maranhão, Brazil, on left bank of Paraíba R. (Piauí border), opposite Amarante, and 80 mi. S of Teresina; babassu nuts, cotton, rice. Until 1944, called São Francisco; and, 1944–48, Iguaratinga.

São Francisco do Sul (sōōl'), city (pop. 10,192), NE Santa Catarina, Brazil, Atlantic port on NW shore of São Francisco isl. (20 mi. long, 12 mi. wide) facing mainland across 1-mi.-wide tidal channel, and 12 mi. ENE of Joinvile (for which it is the port). Rail terminus; important pine-lumber shipping center; sawmilling, meat processing, fish canning. Manganese deposits near by. Settled c.1660 by pioneers from São Paulo. Received German, Swiss, and Scandinavian immigrants after 1850. Until 1944, called São Francisco. Isl. linked by railroad trestle with mainland at Araquari.

São Francisco River, E Brazil, forms with its tributaries the country's third largest drainage basin (after Amazon and Paraná-Paraguay systems). Length, 1,800 mi. Rises in the Serra da Canastra (SW Minas Gerais), flows NNE across central plateau of Minas Gerais and Bahia, swings NE through semiarid hinterland (*sertão*) of NW Bahia, then turns ESE, forming Pernambuco-Bahia and Alagoas-Sergipe borders, and enters the Atlantic at 10°30'S 36°25'W, 60 mi. NE of Aracaju. With its principal navigable affluents (Paracatu, Carinhanha, Corrente, Rio Grande—left; Rio das Velhas—right), it constitutes chief route of access to interior of E Brazil. Regular navigation in middle course (850 mi.) bet. Pirapora (Minas Gerais) and Juàzeiro (Bahia), both rail termini. In lower course, navigation is interrupted for over 200 mi. by rapids and by the PAULO AFONSO FALLS; bet. Petrolândia (Pernambuco) and Piranhas (Alagoas), this stretch is circumvented by a railroad. Diamond washings in headwaters. Cotton plantations along valley. A development project, patterned on TVA and based on the harnessing of hydroelectric power, was begun in 1949 to further agr. settlement in the drought zone and industrialization in NE states of Pernambuco, Alagoas, Sergipe, and Bahia.

São Gabriel (sã'ō gŭbrē-ĕl'). **1** City, Amazonas, Brazil: see UAUPÉS. **2** City (pop. 12,288), W central Rio Grande do Sul, Brazil, on railroad and 55 mi. SW of Santa Maria; livestock center (slaughtering, meat packing, mfg. of jerked beef). Marble deposits. Limekilns in vicinity. Airfield.

São Gonçalo (gōsä'lōō). **1** City, Bahia, Brazil: see SÃO GONÇALO DOS CAMPOS. **2** City, Ceará, Brazil: see ANACETABA. **3** City, Pernambuco, Brazil: see ARARIPINA. **4** City (1950 pop. 20,856), S Rio de Janeiro, Brazil, near Guanabara Bay, 7 mi. NE of Niterói; citrus-growing center; chemical works (caustic soda, hydrochloric acid), match factory. Metallurgical plant (steel furnaces, rolling and sheet mills) at Neves (just W). Large cement mill at Guaxindiba (just E). **5** Town, Rio Grande do Norte, Brazil: see FELIPE CAMARÃO.

São Gonçalo Canal, natural channel, SE Rio Grande do Sul, Brazil, linking Mirim L. and Lagoa dos Patos, thus forming Mirim L.'s only outlet to the sea; 45 mi. long. Port of Pelotas is on it, 6 mi. from its influx into Lagoa dos Patos. Navigable. Receives Piratini R.

São Gonçalo do Sapucaí (dōō sŭpōōkäē'), city (pop. 3,789), S Minas Gerais, Brazil, in N spur of the Serra da Mantiqueira, 35 mi. N of Itajubá; rail-spur terminus; agr. trade (cattle, dairy products). Gold placers; manganese and iron deposits. Formerly spelled São Gonçalo do Sapucahy.

São Gonçalo dos Campos (dōōs kăm'pōōs), city (pop. 3,145), E Bahia, Brazil, on rail spur, and 17

mi. NNE of Cachoeira; ships tobacco leaves. Until 1944, called São Gonçalo.
São Gotardo (gōōtär'dōō), city (pop. 2,214), W Minas Gerais, Brazil, in the Serra da Canastra, 50 mi. SE of Patos de Minas; alt. 3,600 ft. Dairying. Formerly spelled São Gothardo.
Sao Hill (sou), town, Southern Highlands prov., S Tanganyika, on road and 50 mi. SW of Iringa; tobacco, wheat, corn; livestock.
São Jerônimo (sã'õ zhĭrō'nĕmōō). **1** City, Paraná, Brazil: see ARAÍPORANGA. **2** City (pop. 2,416), E Rio Grande do Sul, Brazil, on Jacuí R. opposite Bom Jesus do Triunfo, at mouth of Taquari R., and 30 mi. W of Pôrto Alegre; important coal-mining center, with mines at Arroio dos Ratos (8 mi. S), Butiá (20 mi. SW), and Leão. Coal is taken by rail to Jacuí R. loading points, thence by barge to Pôrto Alegre and its outports (Pelotas, Rio Grande). Founded in late 18th cent. Has 2 old churches. Formerly spelled São Jeronymo.
São Jerônimo, Serra de (sĕ'rŭ dĭ), range of central Brazilian plateau, in E Mato Grosso, separating drainage of Araguaia R. (E) and tributaries of Paraguay R. (W). Rises to 2,300 ft. Old spelling, São Jeronymo.
São João Baptista de Ajudá (bäptē'stŭ dĭ äzhōōdä'), Portuguese fort and tiny enclave in OUIDAH, S Dahomey, Fr. West Africa; founded 1788, it is a dependency of São Tomé e Principe.
São João da Barra (zhwã'õ dä bä'rŭ), city (pop. 2,137), NE Rio de Janeiro state, Brazil, at mouth of Paraíba R. on the Atlantic, 18 mi. ENE of Campos; rail terminus; sugar, fish, dairy products.
São João da Boa Vista (dä bō'ŭ vē'stŭ), city (pop. 12,071), E São Paulo, Brazil, on railroad and 65 mi. NNE of Campinas. Mfg. of textiles, hats, furniture, flour products; meat packing and storing. Ships coffee, potatoes, cotton, corn, beans, alcohol, livestock. Airfield. Águas da Prata (6 mi. NE) is a noted spa. Brazil's principal zirconium mine is at Cascata (11 mi. NE) on Minas Gerais border.
São João da Bocaina, Brazil: see BOCÂINA.
São João da Chapada (shŭpä'dŭ), town (pop. 1,076), central Minas Gerais, Brazil, in the Serra do Espinhaço, 12 mi. NW of Diamantina; diamond mining.
São João da Foz (dä fôzh'), W suburb of Oporto, Pôrto dist., N. Portugal, at mouth of Douro R. on the Atlantic where sand bar renders navigation hazardous; bathing resort. A 17th-cent. fort guards entrance to Oporto harbor.
São João da Madeira (mŭdā'rŭ), town (pop. 988), Aveiro dist., N central Portugal, 20 mi. NNE of Aveiro; hat-mfg. center (felt hats, berets); also makes footwear, rubber goods, pencils, candles, and brooms.
São João da Pesqueira (pĭshkā'rŭ), town (pop. 1,744), Viseu dist., N central Portugal; near Douro R., 22 mi. E of Lamego; port wine, figs, almonds, olives, oranges.
São João de Camaquã, Brazil: see CAMAQUÃ.
São João de Côrtes (dĭ kôr'tĭs), town (pop. 484), N Maranhão, Brazil, on Cumã Bay of the Atlantic, 30 mi. NW of São Luís.
São João del Rei (dĕl rā'), city (1950 pop. 25,228), S Minas Gerais, Brazil, on railroad, 90 mi. SSW of Belo Horizonte; alt. 2,900 ft. Center of manganese-mining region. Gold and tin deposits. Industries include cotton milling and tanning. Ships coffee, sugar, tobacco, dairy products. Founded at end of 17th cent.; 1st large gold mine opened 1831. Noted for fine 18th-cent. churches (sculptured portals) and for colonial bridges across the small Rio das Mortes. Formerly São João d' El Rey.
São João de Meriti (dĭ mĭrĕtē'), NW suburb (1950 pop. 44,146) of Rio de Janeiro, Brazil, 10 mi. NW of city center. Until 1944, called Meriti (Merity).
São João de Montenegro, Brazil: see MONTENEGRO.
São João de Uruburetama, Brazil: see URUBURETAMA.
São João do Araguaia (dōō ärŭgwī'ŭ), town (pop. 184), SE Pará, Brazil, on left bank of Araguaia R. at its influx into the Tocantins, and 260 mi. S of Belém, on Maranhão-Goiás border; projected terminus of unfinished railroad from Tucuruí, and downstream end of navigation on upper Tocantins R. Diamonds found in area.
São João do Campo (kãm'pōō), village (pop. 1,160), Coimbra dist., N central Portugal, 5 mi. WNW of Coimbra; olives, grain, wine.
São João do Cariri (kŭrērē'), town (pop. 530), central Paraíba, NE Brazil, on Borborema Plateau, 45 mi. WSW of Campina Grande; cotton, corn, livestock. Graphite deposits.
São João do Muqui, Brazil: see MUQUI.
São João do Piauí (pyou-ē'), city (pop. 1,252), S Piauí, Brazil, on upper Piauí R. and 120 mi. SSE of Floriano; cattle raising; carnauba wax.
São João do Rio Peixe, Brazil: see ANTENOR NAVARRO.
São João dos Patos (dōōs pä'tōōs), city (pop. 1,352), E Maranhão, Brazil, 120 mi. SSW of Caxias, in the Serra do Valentim; cattle raising; babassu nuts, resins, cereals.
São João do Triunfo (dōō trēōōm'fōō), city (pop. 727), S Paraná, Brazil, 65 mi. WSW of Curitiba; sawmills; maté, grain.
São João Evangelista (ĭvãzhĭlē'stŭ), city (pop. 1,820), central Minas Gerais, Brazil, 50 mi. ESE of Diamantina; coffee, honey.
São João Nepomuceno (nĭpōōmōōsā'nōō), city (pop. 5,879), S Minas Gerais, Brazil, on railroad and 26 mi. NE of Juiz de Fora; textile milling, shoe mfg.; ships coffee, sugar, butter. Has mica and recently discovered bauxite deposits.
São Joaquim (zhwäkēm'). **1** City (pop. 1,667), S Santa Catarina, Brazil, in the Serra Geral, 80 mi. W of Laguna; alt. 4,450 ft. Dairying center; fruit- and cereal-growing. Formerly also called São Joaquim da Costa da Serra. **2** City, São Paulo, Brazil: see SÃO JOAQUIM DA BARRA.
São Joaquim da Barra (dä bä'rŭ), city (pop. 4,379), NE São Paulo, Brazil, on railroad and 40 mi. N of Ribeirão Prêto; distilling, cheese processing; coffee, sugar, cattle. Until 1944, São Joaquim.
São Joaquim da Costa da Serra, Brazil: see SÃO JOAQUIM, Santa Catarina.
São Joaquim do Monte (dōō mõn'tĭ), city (pop. 1,821), E Pernambuco, NE Brazil, 15 mi. SE of Caruaru; cotton. Called São Joaquim until 1944; called Camaratuba, 1944–48.
São Jorge, island, Portuguese India: see SAINT GEORGE'S ISLAND.
São Jorge dos Ilhéos, Brazil: see ILHÉUS.
São Jorge Island (zhôr'zhĭ), volcanic island (□ 92; 1950 pop. 16,378) of central Azores, in Atlantic, 30 mi. WSW of Terceira Isl.; Velas (38°41'N 28°13'W), near isl.'s W tip, is chief town. Cigar-shaped (33 mi. long, up to 4 mi. wide), isl. is traversed by a narrow volcanic range (culminating in Pico da Esperança, 3,497 ft.); steep cliffs along N coast. Agr.: cereals, wine; livestock raising, dairying; fishing. Administratively part of Angra do Heroísmo dist.
São José (zhōōzĕ'), city (pop. 2,585), E Santa Catarina, Brazil, on the Atlantic, opposite Santa Catarina Isl., 3 mi. W of Florianópolis (linked by large steel bridge); grows rice, tapioca, bananas. First Germans to settle in state established a colony at near-by São Pedro de Alcântara in 1828.
São José Bay, inlet of the Atlantic off NE Brazil, bet. mainland of Maranhão (E) and São Luís Isl. (W); c.50 mi. long. Near its head (S) it receives Itapecuru R.
São José da Lagoa, Brazil: see NOVA ERA.
São José da Laje (dä lä'zhĭ), city (pop. 4,368), E Alagoas, NE Brazil, on railroad and 45 mi. NNW of Maceió; ships sugar, coffee, cotton, alcohol. Large sugar refinery near by.
São José de Mipibu (dĭ mēpēbōō'), city (pop. 2,297), E Rio Grande do Norte, NE Brazil, on railroad and 18 mi. S of Natal; cotton and sugar growing.
São José de Piranhas, Brazil: see JATOBÁ, Paraíba.
São José de Ribamar, Brazil: see RIBAMAR.
São José do Calçado (dōō kŭlsä'dōō), city (pop. 1,515), S Espírito Santo, Brazil, near Rio de Janeiro state border, 36 mi. WSW of Cachoeiro de Itapemirim; coffee.
São José do Campestre (kãmpĕ'strĭ), city (pop. 1,398), E Rio Grande do Norte, NE Brazil, 50 mi. SW of Natal. Until 1944, called Campestre.
São José do Egito (dōōzhĕ'tōō), city (pop. 1,567), central Pernambuco, NE Brazil, 30 mi. S of Patos (Paraíba); sugar, cotton, goats.
São José do Norte (dōō nôr'tĭ), city (pop. 1,019), SE Rio Grande do Sul, Brazil, near S tip of sandy peninsula separating the Lagoa dos Patos from the Atlantic, on the Rio Grande (outlet of Lagoa dos Patos) opposite Rio Grande city; fish drying and salting, beef jerking.
São José do Rio Negro, Brazil: see MANAUS.
São José do Rio Pardo (rē'ōō pär'dōō), city (pop. 8,436), NE São Paulo, Brazil, on the Rio Pardo, near Minas Gerais border, on railroad and 65 mi. SE of Ribeirão Prêto; agr.-processing center (flour and dairy products, jerked beef, soap). Trades in coffee, rice, livestock, timber.
São José do Rio Prêto (prā'tōō), city (1950 pop. 37,717), N São Paulo, Brazil, on railroad, 100 mi. W of Ribeirão Prêto. Distributing and processing center of pioneer agr. region extending NW toward Paraná R. Has important livestock trade. Produces butter, cheese, sausages, leather; cotton ginning, manioc and rice milling, coffee roasting. Has school of pharmacy and dentistry. Until 1944, called Rio Prêto.
São José dos Campos (dōōs kãm'pōōs), city (1950 pop. 26,287), SE São Paulo, Brazil, in Paraíba valley, on railroad, 55 mi. NE of São Paulo; textile milling, distilling, pottery mfg. Trades in poultry, dairy products, rice, fruit. New aviation center (school, assembly plant) here. Manganese deposits near by. Founded as Jesuit mission.
São José dos Cocais, Brazil: see NOSSA SENHORA DO LIVRAMENTO.
São José dos Matões, Brazil: see PARNARAMA.
São José dos Pinhais (pēnyĭs'), city (pop. 1,628), SE Paraná, Brazil, on Iguassú R. and 8 mi. SSE of Curitiba; sawmilling center; mfg. of furniture, barrels, pottery; grain milling.
São José do Tocantins, Brazil: see NIQUELÂNDIA.
São Leopoldo (sã'õ lĭōōpōl'dōō), city (pop. 13,876), E Rio Grande do Sul, Brazil, on Sinos R. and 20 mi. N of Pôrto Alegre; rail junction; iron smelting, tanning, mfg. of matches and aluminum ware. Rice and tobacco grown in area. Has Jesuit and Protestant seminaries. First German settlement (1824) in S Brazil.
São Lourenço (lōrãn'sōō). **1** City (pop. 7,247), S Minas Gerais, Brazil, on N slope of the Serra da Mantiqueira, on the Rio Verde and 32 mi. N of Cruzeiro (São Paulo; linked by rail); alt. 2,850 ft. Fashionable resort and spa (therapeutic mineral waters) with fine hotels. Air service to Rio de Janeiro in tourist season (Sept.–May). **2** City, Rio Grande do Sul, Brazil: see SÃO LOURENÇO DO SUL.
São Lourenço da Mata (dä mä'tŭ), city (pop. 3,315), E Pernambuco, NE Brazil, on Capiberibe R. and 14 mi. NW of Recife; sugar growing and milling. Until 1944, called São Lourenço.
São Lourenço do Sul (dōō sōōl'), city (pop. 4,125), SE Rio Grande do Sul, Brazil, on W shore of the Lagoa dos Patos and 35 mi. NE of Pelotas; rice, oats, barley, fruit, tobacco. Until 1944, called São Lourenço.
São Lourenço Point, easternmost headland of Madeira isl., 15 mi. ENE of Funchal. Just offshore is Fora islet with lighthouse (32°43'N 16°39'W).
São Lourenço River, S central Mato Grosso, Brazil, rises near Poxoréu, flows c.300 mi. SW through Paraguay flood plain to Paraguay R. 80 mi. N of Corumbá. Receives (left) the Pequiri and (right) the Cuiabá, the latter sometimes giving its name to lower course. Navigable.
São Luís (lwēs'), city (1950 pop. 81,432), ⊙ Maranhão, N Brazil, on São Luís Isl., 300 mi. ESE of Belém; 3°30'S 44°18'W. Commercial and industrial center at N terminus of São Luís–Teresina RR and at mouths of navigable Mearim and Itapecuru rivers, with sheltered port on São Marcos Bay. Ships babassu oil, castor beans, balsam, hides and skins, lumber, and produce of a fertile agr. hinterland (cotton, sugar, rice, grain). Important cotton-milling center. Other industries: sugar refining, distilling, babassu and cacao processing, fruit preserving, mfg. of hammocks and margarine. Airport. City has kept much of its Port. colonial character. Outstanding bldgs. are the fort, the govt. palace, the 17th-cent. cathedral (one of largest in Brazil) restored in 19th cent., the monastery of Santo Antonio, and the church of Our Lady of Carmo. City has schools of law, pharmacy, agr., fine arts, and a historical and geographical institute. A noted cultural center, São Luís has been called "the Athens of Brazil." Birthplace of many leading Braz. writers and poets. Founded 1612 by a French military expedition and named in honor of Louis XIII. Captured (1615) by Portuguese under Captain Jeronimo de Albuquerque. In 1682 a commercial company was formed having a crown monopoly on region's foreign trade. Despite a local rebellion, monopoly was not removed until 1780. City was formerly known as São Luiz do Maranhão or, in short, as Maranhão.
São Luís do Paraitinga (dōō pŭrĭtēng'gŭ), city (pop. 1,164), SE São Paulo, Brazil, in the Serra do Mar, 22 mi. SE of Taubaté; sugar milling, distilling. Formerly spelled São Luiz do Parahytinga.
São Luís do Quitunde (kētōōn'dĭ), city (pop. 2,646), E Alagoas, NE Brazil, near the Atlantic, 24 mi. NNE of Maceió; sugar growing, alcohol distilling.
São Luís Gonzaga (gõzä'gŭ). **1** City, Maranhão, Brazil: see IPIXUNA. **2** City (pop. 6,020), W Rio Grande do Sul, Brazil, on W slope of the Serra Geral, 70 mi. WNW of Cruz Alta. Agr. colony (rice, tobacco, fruit, sugar); stock raising. Airfield. Founded by Jesuits. Formerly São Luiz Gonzaga.
São Luís Island, N Maranhão, Brazil, bet. bays of São Marcos (W) and São José (E), and separated from mainland (S) by narrow Mosquitos channel; 35 mi. long, 20 mi. wide. On its NW shore is city of São Luís, on E shore, Ribamar. At Estiva (16 mi. S of São Luís), the São Luís–Teresina RR crosses channel to mainland.
São Luiz de Cáceres, Brazil: see CÁCERES.
São Luiz do Maranhão, Brazil: see SÃO LUÍS.
São Luiz Gonzaga, Brazil: see SÃO LUÍS GONZAGA, Rio Grande do Sul.
São Mamede, Serra de (sĕ'rŭ dĭ sã'õ mŭmā'dĭ), range in E central Portugal, near Sp. border, extending c.25 mi. SE from Castelo de Vide; rises to 3,363 ft. Portalegre is on W slope. Pine, chestnut, and cork-oak forest.
São Mamede de Infesta (dĭ ēnfĕ'stŭ), N suburb (pop. 7,388) of Oporto, Pôrto dist., N Portugal. Oporto airport near by. Also called Infesta.
São Mamede de Riba Tua (rē'bŭ tōō'ŭ), village (pop. 1,232), Vila Real dist., N Portugal, on Tua R. and 17 mi. ESE of Vila Real; winegrowing.
São Manuel (mänwĕl'). **1** City, Minas Gerais, Brazil: see EUGENÓPOLIS. **2** City (pop. 5,911), central São Paulo, Brazil, on railroad and 60 mi. W of Piracicaba; produces sugar, alcohol, macaroni products, tile, pottery, beverages; corn milling. Coffee trade. Formerly spelled São Manoel.
São Manuel do Mutum, Brazil: see MUTUM.
São Manuel River, right headstream of the Tapajós, in N Mato Grosso, Brazil, rises near 14°45'S 54°45'W on Amazon-Paraguay river divide, flows c.700 mi. NNW, forming Mato Grosso–Pará border for c.200 mi. before joining Juruena R. at Pará–Amazonas–Mato Grosso frontier, where joint streams form TAPAJÓS RIVER. Interrupted by

falls and rapids. Also called Teles Pires R. (old spelling, Telles Pires), or Rio das Três Barras. Its upper course is sometimes known as Paranatinga R. Formerly spelled São Manoel.

São Marcelo (mŭrsä'lōō), village, NW Bahia, Brazil, head of navigation on the Rio Prêto and 150 mi. W of Barra.

São Marcos Bay (mär'kōōsh), inlet of the Atlantic off NE Brazil, bet. mainland of Maranhão (W) and São Luís Isl.; c.60 mi. long, up to 10 mi. wide. On it is city of São Luís. Its head (S) is formed by estuary of Mearim R.

São Marcos da Serra (dŭ sĕ'rŭ), village (pop. 648), Faro dist., S Portugal, in the Serra de Monchique, on railroad, and 12 mi. NNE of Silves; health resort (ferruginous springs); figs, almonds, olives, cork.

São Martinho do Pôrto (mŭrtē'nyōō dōō pôr'tōō), town (pop. 1,301), Leiria dist., W central Portugal, on the Atlantic, on railroad and 8 mi. N of Caldas da Rainha; bathing resort and fishing port (lobsters) on sheltered bay.

São Mateus (mätĕ'ōōs). **1** City, Ceará, Brazil: see JUCÁS. **2** City (pop. 2,738), N Espírito Santo, Brazil, 120 mi. NNE of Vitória; head of navigation on São Mateus R. and E terminus of railroad to Nova Venécia; coffee, oranges, bananas, manioc. Airfield. Formerly spelled São Matheus. **3** City, Paraná, Brazil: see SÃO MATEUS DO SUL.

São Mateus do Sul (dōō sōōl'), city (pop. 2,207), S Paraná, Brazil, on Iguassú R. and 75 mi. WSW of Curitiba; furniture mfg.; coffee, maté, and grain processing; tanning. Until 1943, called São Mateus (old spelling, São Matheus).

São Mateus River, N Espírito Santo, Brazil, rises in the Serra dos Aimorés, flows E, past São Mateus, to the Atlantic at Conceição da Barra. Length, including N headstream which originates near Teófilo Otoni (Minas Gerais), c.180 mi. Interrupted by rapids.

São Matheus. 1 City, Ceará, Brazil: see JUCÁS. **2** City, Espírito Santo, Brazil: see SÃO MATEUS. **3** City, Paraná, Brazil: see SÃO MATEUS DO SUL.

São Miguel (mĕgĕl'). **1** City, Bahia, Brazil: see SÃO MIGUEL DAS MATAS. **2** City (pop. 882), SW Rio Grande do Norte, NE Brazil, near Ceará border, 110 mi. SW of Mossoró; cotton, cereals.

São Miguel Arcanjo (ärkä'zhōō), city (pop. 1,350), S São Paulo, Brazil, 20 mi. S of Itapetininga; tobacco, cotton, tung, cattle.

São Miguel das Matas (däs mä'tŭs), city (pop. 1,109), E Bahia, Brazil, 38 mi. W of Nazaré; rail junction (spur to Amargosa); sugar- and coffee-growing. Until 1944, São Miguel.

São Miguel de Acha (dĭ ä'shŭ), village (pop. 1,807), Castelo Branco dist., central Portugal, 16 mi. NNE of Castelo Branco; grain, corn, horse beans, livestock; oak and chestnut woods.

São Miguel de Jucurutu, Brazil: see JUCURUTU.

São Miguel do Guamá, Brazil: see GUAMÁ.

São Miguel do Rio Torto (dōō rē'ōō tôr'tōō), town (pop. 1,689), Santarém dist., central Portugal, near left bank of Tagus R., 3 mi. SSW of Abrantes; cork-processing center; knitwear, flour products, soap.

São Miguel dos Campos (dōōs käm'pōōs), city (pop. 3,847), Alagoas, NE Brazil, 23 mi. SW of Maceió; ships sugar and lumber. Textile milling.

São Miguel do Tapuio (dōō tŭpwē'ōō), city (pop. 430), E central Piauí, Brazil, on W slope of Serra Grande, 40 mi. SW of Crateús (Ceará).

São Miguel Island or **Saint Michael Island**, largest (□ 288; 1950 pop. 164,836) of the Azores, in the Atlantic, forming, together with Santa Maria Isl. (50 mi. S), the archipelago's E group; PONTA DELGADA (37°44'N 25°40'W), its chief city and port, is on S coast, c.900 mi. W of Lisbon. Isl. is 40 mi. long, up to 9 mi. wide, and consists of 2 mountainous volcanic sections separated by a central lowland. Rises to 3,625 ft. in the Pico da Vara near E coast. Its rugged shoreline has no natural harbors. Of great fertility, isl. grows pineapples, oranges, tea, wine, tobacco, cereals, potatoes. Livestock is raised for meat and dairy produce. Mild climate and isl.'s impressive volcanic features attract winter tourists. Chief resorts are Furnas (thermal springs) and Sete Cidades (in a huge crater). Principal towns are Ponta Delgada, Ribeira Grande, and Vila Franca do Campo (isl.'s 1st capital). Devastated by 12 major earthquakes and eruptions since 15th cent. (last in 1880). Administratively, São Miguel is part of Ponta Delgada dist.

São Miguel Paulista (poulē'stŭ), E suburb of São Paulo city, São Paulo, SE Brazil, on left bank of Tietê R. and 12 mi. from city center; has large chemical works.

Saona Island (sou'nä) (15 mi. long, 2–3 mi. wide), just off SE Dominican Republic, 20 mi. SE of La Romana.

Saonara (säônä'rä), village (pop. 506), Padova prov., Veneto, N Italy, 6 mi. SE of Padua; machinery (agr., wine); nurseries (fruit, ornamental plants and trees).

Saône, Haute-, France: see HAUTE-SAÔNE.

Saône-et-Loire (sōn-ā-lwär'), department (□ 3,331; pop. 506,749), in Burgundy, E central France; ⊙ Mâcon. Bounded by foothills of the Jura (E), Loire R. (SW), and the Monts du Morvan (NE). Crossed N-S by the Saône, its tributaries (Doubs, Seille, Dheune, Grosne) draining most of dept.; Arroux and Bourbince rivers flow SW to the Loire; 2 drainage basins divided by the Monts du Beaujolais (S) and Monts du Charollais (center). A region of great agr. diversification and fertility, it grows cereals, hemp, colza, potatoes, and various vegetables. Noted for its red wines (in Mâcon area), high-grade cattle (in Charolais), and poultry (in Bresse). Important coal mines at Montceau-les-Mines and Blanzy supply Le Creusot industries with fuel. Bituminous schists mined at Épinac-les-Mines are worked at Autun. Along the Canal du Centre (which traverses dept. from Digoin on the Loire to Chalon-sur-Saône) are numerous plants mfg. refractories. Chief towns and centers of dept.'s varied industrial output are Chalon-sur-Saône (leading agr. market; machine shops), Mâcon (wine-trading center), Le Creusot (large railroad-engine and armament plants), and Autun (oil products, dyes).

Saoner (sou'nār), town (pop. 8,520), Nagpur dist., central Madhya Pradesh, India, on railroad and 20 mi. NW of Nagpur; cotton ginning; millet, wheat, oilseeds. Rail spur serves manganese mines bet. here and Khapa, 5 mi. NE.

Saône River (sōn), anc. *Arar*, E central France, rises 14 mi. SW of Épinal (Vosges dept.), flows 268 mi. SSW, past Gray, Chalon-sur-Saône, Mâcon, and Villefranche, to the Rhone at Lyons. Receives Ognon, Doubs, Seille rivers (left), and Tille, Ouche, Dheune rivers (right). Its valley, lined with Burgundy vineyards below Chalon-sur-Saône, is chief communications artery bet. Paris and Marseilles. Navigable almost from its source (canalized upper course), it is connected to the Moselle by Canal de l'EST, to the Marne by MARNE-SAÔNE CANAL, to the Yonne by BURGUNDY CANAL, and to the Loire by Canal du CENTRE.

São Nicolau Island (sä'ō nēkōōlou') or **Saint Nicholas Island** (□ 132; 1940 pop. 14,827; 1950 pop. 10,311), one of Cape Verde Isls., in Windward group, near center of archipelago, bet. Santa Luzia Isl. (18 mi. WNW) and Boa Vista Isl. (75 mi. ESE), in the Atlantic; Ribeira Brava (16°37'N 24°18'W), its chief town, is near N shore. Of irregular shape, isl. is 28 mi. long, 2–14 mi. wide. Of volcanic origin and very mountainous, it rises to 4,278 ft. at Monte Gordo. Preguiça, on S shore, is only safe landing. Less than ½ isl. is cultivated (coffee, oranges, beans, corn). Horse raising. One of 1st isls. in group to be settled in 15th cent.

São Paulo (sä'ō pou'lōō), state (□ 95,453; 1940 pop. 7,180,316; 1950 census 9,242,610), SE Brazil; ⊙ Sao Paulo. Brazil's most populous and leading agr. and industrial state. Bounded by Rio de Janeiro (E), Minas Gerais (NE and N), Mato Grosso (W), Paraná (S), and the Atlantic (SE). A narrow coastal strip (widening only in the Ribeira de Iguape lowland—S) with several offshore isls. (São Sebastião, Santo Amaro, São Vicente) is skirted by the Serra do Mar (great escarpment), which forms an effective barrier (2,600–2,900 ft. high) bet. the seashore and the interior. The evenly rolling upland W of the escarpment contains a series of low mts., lesser crystalline ranges, and an interior depression (W of Sorocaba and Campinas). Farther W, a diabase cuesta marks the edge of the Paraná plateau, which slopes gently to Paraná R. (Mato Grosso line). Under topographic control, all major streams (some of which rise near the coast) drain westward in generally parallel courses; among them are the Paranapanema (forming Paraná border), Peixe, Aguapeí, Tietê, and Rio Grande (Minas Gerais border). Only the Paraíba, which drains extreme SE part of São Paulo, flows NE into Rio de Janeiro state. While the coastal strip, with its heavy rainfall (reaching 150 inches along face of great escarpment), has humid, subtropical climate, the interior is drier (50–60 inches), cooler (mean temp. 64°F.), and more bracing because of greater diurnal and seasonal range. Although many areas in the state are suitable for agr. and stock raising, the diabase *terra roxa* [Port.,=purple soil] along the watersheds and E edge of the Paraná plateau is exceptionally fertile. Here grows half of Brazil's coffee, the country's chief export crop. Its cultivation, from 19th cent. and beginning in the Paraíba valley, has swept like a steam roller across São Paulo, exhausting soils in SE part of state; it is now most intensively grown in virgin soils of the W watersheds and in Ribeirão Prêto region. Cotton has become the great boom crop since the coffee crisis in 1930s. São Paulo now grows about ⅔ of the nation's output—in the Sorocaba area and in the pioneer dists. (especially Marília) of the W. Sugar cane is cultivated near Piracicaba, truck farming is concentrated around São Paulo city, and bananas are grown on São Vicente Isl. and on mainland opposite Santos. Oranges (near Campinas and in W) are São Paulo's newest important crop. Corn, manioc, beans, temperate-zone vegetables, tobacco, rice (especially in the Paraíba and Ribeira de Iguape valleys), alfalfa, castor seeds, mint, and tung nuts are also successfully grown in a statewide trend toward agr. diversification. Dairy cattle are raised in densely populated SE part of state where former coffee plantations (*fazendas*) have depleted soil fertility. Beef cattle and hogs are shipped to São Paulo slaughterhouses from N and W. Greatest agr. development is foreseen for small-farm pioneer settlements expanding toward the Paraná along railroads of penetration. Construction of Brazil's densest rail net (especially in coffee regions) and of good highways has greatly facilitated São Paulo's industrialization and the regional interchange of products. While many of the larger towns—Campinas, Sorocaba, Ribeirão Prêto—have textile and agr.-processing plants, the bulk of the state's diversified manufactures is concentrated in São Paulo city. Industries use hydroelectric power generated in the great Cubatão plant at foot of the Serra do Mar and in smaller plants located along falls of the Paraná's tributaries. Collecting, packing, and shipping of São Paulo's chief crops are the principal activities of numerous smaller towns (Bauru, Marília, São José do Rio Prêto, Araçatuba, Botucatu, Araraquara, Presidente Prudente). Santos, Brazil's chief export center and the world's leading coffee port, is reached by rail from São Paulo and Sorocaba across the great escarpment. Other main lines link São Paulo with Rio de Janeiro via the Paraíba valley (largest city, Taubaté), and with the capitals of the southern states. One rail line crosses the Paraná and traverses S Mato Grosso to Corumbá and on to Bolivia; another, extending SW from Ourinhos, taps the agr. colonies of N Paraná. São Paulo was 1st settled by Portuguese who landed (1532) at São Vicente. A captaincy, covering all of Brazil S of Rio de Janeiro, was organized in 1534. From São Paulo, pioneers, adventurers and prospectors (*bandeirantes*) penetrated the W hinterland, advancing along the valleys of Paraná R. tributaries. In 1681, ⊙ was transferred from São Vicente to São Paulo city. Immigration, encouraged by coffee-plantation owners and sponsored by state govt., brought 3,000,000 people (Italians, Spaniards, Portuguese, Germans, Slavs, and, since 1908, Japanese) to São Paulo in 19th and early part of 20th cent. São Paulo became in 1822 a prov. of Brazilian Empire, and in 1889 a state of federal republic.

São Paulo. 1 City (1940 pop. 1,258,482; 1950 pop. 2,041,716; 1950 urban dist. pop. 2,227,512), ⊙ São Paulo state, SE Brazil, 33 mi. NW of Santos (its port on the Atlantic), 220 mi. WSW of Rio de Janeiro, and on a plateau (c.2,700 ft. high) dissected by winding Tietê R. and separated from the coast by the great escarpment (Serra do Mar); 23°33'S 46°39'W. Brazil's ranking industrial center; one of the world's most dynamic and rapidly growing cities (1920 pop. 579,000); commercial, financial, and cultural metropolis of the nation's wealthiest agr. state. Its diversified industries, unparalleled elsewhere in South America, include the production of capital equipment (textile, electrical, and specialized machinery; finished steel and wire products, rolling stock), and of such consumer goods as textiles (4 rayon, and numerous cotton, silk, wool, and jute mills), automobiles, trucks (assembled here from imported parts), tires, pianos, radios, sanitary supplies, glass, pottery, china- and enamelware, household fixtures and utensils (aluminum, copper, brass), office and metal furniture, cutlery, pens, pencils, and matches. Mfg. of footwear and hosiery is especially important. Among the chief processing industries are meat packing, flour milling; mfg. of dairy products, corn starch, glucose, vegetable oils, beverages; and food canning. Cement plants serve the booming building industry, and chemical works produce fertilizer, dyes, pharmaceuticals. Heavier industries are concentrated in the suburbs lining the Tietê R. and the São Paulo–Santos RR (Santo André, Utinga, São Caetano, Osasco) and in the low-lying dists. of the city proper (Braz, Lapa, Moóca). Industries are powered mainly by electricity which originates in the CUBATÃO and Tietê valley hydroelectric works. Although the state is served by Brazil's densest rail net, only 4 lines (from Santos, Rio de Janeiro and the Paraíba valley, Sorocaba, Campinas) lead into the capital city. Nevertheless, due to its size and economic importance, São Paulo is a hub for communications and a huge entrepôt for the interior's agr. output (coffee, cotton, corn, rice, citrus fruit, livestock, dairy produce, vegetables). Roads out of São Paulo are good, especially the modern, 4-lane highway across the Serra do Mar to Santos. The municipal airport (Congonhas) is just N of Tietê R. The urban pattern of São Paulo resembles that of most U.S. metropolises. At the heart of the city is the Triângulo (comparable to Chicago's Loop) with its modern skyscrapers which house banks and business firms. From here, avenues radiate in all directions, but not according to any simple plan. Surrounding the central business section (which has spread beyond the congested Triângulo) is an area of run-down residences, while the newer residential dists. (Jardim Europa, Jardim América, Cantareira, Brooklyn) occupy the ridges on the outskirts. Expansion during the coffee boom preceding 1930, and again since Second World War, has been southward toward Santo Amaro (which has been incorporated into São Paulo), where the huge reservoirs of the Cubatão hydroelectric project provide an attractive setting. Principal points of interest in the city are the govt. palace; the palaces of agr., finance, and industry; the state univ. (notably the faculty of medicine and school of public health completed in 1931 with the aid of a Rockefeller Foundation grant); Mackenzie Inst. (established 1871 by U.S. Methodist missionaries); the Catholic Univ.; the state police training school (founded 1910); the grandiose Luz railroad station with adjoining park; the modern, 22-story public library; the municipal theater; and the stadium seating 70,000. The centrally located Parque Anhangabaú is bridged by a viaduct (Viaduto do Chá) connecting the Praça do Patriarca in the Triângulo with the fashionable Barão de Itapetininga shopping street. Avenida São Joao is São Paulo's "Broadway." About 6 mi. SW of city center is the well-known Butantan Inst. ("snake farm"), where serums against snake bites are prepared. The Ypiranga or Paulista Mus. of Ethnography, History, and Natural History is 5 mi. SE of the Triângulo. An elaborate monument in the surrounding park commemorates the place where Dom Pedro I proclaimed Brazil's independence from Portugal in 1822. Although the Tropic of Capricorn passes through São Paulo's N outskirts, the climate is decidedly temperate and invigorating; mean annual temp. is 65°F. (Jan., 71°F.; July, 58°F.); sizable diurnal range because of alt.; average yearly precipitation, 58 inches (max. in Jan.–Feb.). Health conditions have been improved and flood damage reduced as a result of the draining and regulating of the Tietê river bed. City was founded in 1554 on site of Indian village of Piratininga by Jesuits who crossed the coastal escarpment from São Vicente. From here, adventurous *bandeirantes* (i.e., flagbearers) penetrated the interior during 17th and 18th cent. in search of gold and diamonds. In 1681, seat of the captaincy was transferred here from São Vicente, but the city long remained a backward frontier community (1883 pop. 35,000). Its meteoric growth after 1885 coincided with the extension of coffee cultivation throughout São Paulo, and with the ensuing large-scale immigration of Europeans (principally Italians) and Japanese (since 1908) under state sponsorship. With coffee as Brazil's chief export product, city became the funnel through which the crop was shipped to Santos on the only railroad (completed (1867) across the Serra do Mar. Much of the city's subsequent commercial and industrial leadership stems from the business acumen and spirit of enterprise characteristic of the *paulista* pop. **2** City, Sergipe, Brazil: see FREI PAULO.

São Paulo de Loanda, Angola: see LUANDA.

São Paulo de Olivença (dōōlĕvĕn'sù), city (pop. 1,039), W Amazonas, Brazil, steamer and hydroplane landing on right bank of the Amazon, and 600 mi. W of Manaus, 80 mi. NE of Leticia (Colombia); rubber, cacao, manioc. Missionary town.

São Paulo do Potengi (pōōtĕng'gē), city (pop. 676), E Rio Grande do Norte, NE Brazil, 38 mi. WSW of Natal.

São Pedro (pā'drōō). **1** City, Ceará, Brazil: see CARIRIAÇU. **2** City, Maranhão, Brazil: see PINDARÉ MIRIM. **3** City, Rio Grande do Sul, Brazil: see SÃO PEDRO DO SUL. **4** City (pop. 3,583), E central São Paulo, Brazil, near Piracicaba R., 20 mi. NW of Piracicaba; rail-spur terminus; resort with mineral springs. Agr. trade.

São Pedro da Aldeia (dä äldä'ù), city (pop. 1,051), S Rio de Janeiro state, Brazil, on N shore of Araruama Lagoon, and 6 mi. NW of Cabo Frio City; saltworks. Founded 1617 by Jesuits. Has ruins of convent.

São Pedro de Alcântara, Brazil: see SÃO JOSÉ.

São Pedro de Mallet, Brazil: see MALÉ.

São Pedro do Cariry, Brazil: see CARIRIAÇU.

São Pedro do Piauí (dōō pyou-ē'), city (pop. 1,179), central Piauí, Brazil, 55 mi. S of Teresina; cattle, hides, cotton, babassu nuts. Formerly São Pedro.

São Pedro do Rio Grande do Sul, Brazil: see RIO GRANDE DO SUL, state; RIO GRANDE, city.

São Pedro do Sul (dōō sōōl'), city (pop. 2,306), W central Rio Grande do Sul, Brazil, on SW slope of the Serra Geral, 22 mi. W of Santa Maria; livestock. Until 1944, called São Pedro.

São Pedro do Sul, town (pop. 1,854), Viseu dist., N central Portugal, on Vouga R. and 9 mi. NW of Viseu; frequented spa (radioactive hot sulphur springs) known since Roman times. The baths are 2 mi. SW.

São Pedro do Turvo (tōōr'vōō), city (pop. 985), W central São Paulo, Brazil, 17 mi. NNE of Ourinhos; distilling; coffee, cotton, sugar cane.

São Raimundo das Mangabeiras (rīmōōn'dōō däs māng-gùbā'rùs), town (pop. 1,316), S central Maranhão, Brazil, 50 mi. NE of Balsas, in cattle-raising area.

São Raimundo Nonato (nōōnä'tōō), city (pop. 1,869), S Piauí, Brazil, on upper Piauí R. and 60 mi. NW of Remanso (Bahia); cattle; nitrate deposits. Formerly spelled São Raymundo Nonato.

São Raymundo Nonato, Brazil: see SÃO RAIMUNDO NONATO.

Saori (säō'rē), town (pop. 11,851), Aichi prefecture, central Honshu, Japan, 10 mi. W of Nagoya; agr. center (rice and mulberry fields); cotton textiles.

São Romão (rōōmä'ō), city (pop. 962), N Minas Gerais, Brazil, landing on left bank of upper São Francisco R. and 90 mi. WNW of Montes Claros; irrigation agr. (cotton).

São Romão, village (pop. 1,814), Guarda dist., N central Portugal, in Serra da Estrêla, 26 mi. WSW of Guarda; wool spinning, cheese mfg. Excursion center.

São Roque (rô'kĭ). **1** Town, Bahia, Brazil: see SÃO ROQUE DO PARAGUAÇU. **2** City (pop. 5,367), S São Paulo, Brazil, on railroad and 30 mi. W of São Paulo; cotton weaving, paper milling, wine making; viticulture; coffee, cotton. Black-marble deposits.

São Roque, Cape, headland of NE Brazil, on the Atlantic, in Rio Grande do Norte state, 20 mi. N of Natal; 5°29'S 35°13'W. Lighthouse. Frequently considered Brazil's and South America's easternmost point, but Cabo Branco (7°9'S 34°47'W), SE of João Pessoa (Paraíba), is farther E.

São Roque do Paraguaçu (dōō pŭrŭgwŭsōō'), town (pop. 716), E Bahia, Brazil, at mouth of Paraguaçu R. on Todos os Santos Bay, 25 mi. NW of Salvador; terminus of railroad to Amargosa and Jiquié. Until 1944, called São Roque.

São Roque do Pico (pē'kōō), town (pop. 654), Horta dist., central Azores, on N coast of Pico Isl., 17 mi. E of Horta (on Faial Isl.); alcohol distilling, dairying; whaling, sperm-oil processing.

São Salvador or **São Salvador do Congo** (sã'ō sŭlvŭdōr' dōō kōng'gōō), town (pop. 2,965), Congo prov., NW Angola, 70 mi. SE of Matadi (Belgian Congo); 6°22'S 14°17'E. Almonds, sesame, manioc. Airfield. Jesuit mission. Was ⊙ native kingdom of Congo 16th–18th cent.

São Salvador, Brazil: see SALVADOR.

São Sebastião (sĭbŭstyã'ō). **1** City, Bahia, Brazil: see SÃO SEBASTIÃO DO PASSÉ. **2** Town, Rio Grande do Norte, Brazil: see SEBASTIANÓPOLIS. **3** City (pop. 1,633), SE São Paulo, Brazil, seaport 60 mi. ENE of Santos, on the coast and protected by São Sebastião Isl. across a narrow channel; agr. (manioc, corn, grain, bananas).

São Sebastião da Boa Vista (dä bō'ù vē'stù), city (pop. 390), E Pará, Brazil, on S shore of Marajó isl. in Amazon delta, 70 mi. WSW of Belém; cattle, horses.

São Sebastião da Grama (grä'mù), city (pop. 1,615), E São Paulo, Brazil, 18 mi. ENE of Casa Branca; coffee. Until 1948 called Grama.

São Sebastião do Alto (dōō äl'tōō), city (pop. 415), NE Rio de Janeiro state, Brazil, in the Serra do Mar, 35 mi. NE of Nova Friburgo; coffee, corn, tobacco.

São Sebastião do Caí, Brazil: see CAÍ.

São Sebastião do Paraíso (pŭrŭē'zōō), city (pop. 9,663), SW Minas Gerais, Brazil, near São Paulo border, 55 mi. NE of Ribeirão Prêto; rail junction (spur to Passos); agr. trade center (coffee, tobacco, cattle). Mineral springs.

São Sebastião do Passé (pùsĕ'), city (pop. 1,791), E Bahia, Brazil, 30 mi. N of Salvador; sugar. Until 1944, called São Sebastião.

São Sebastião Island (□ 130; 18 mi. long), on SE coast of Brazil, off port of São Sebastião in São Paulo state, and separated from the mainland by a channel 2–4 mi. wide. Rises to 4,524 ft. in S. ILHABELA, on NW coast, is its port. Lighthouse at SE tip (Punta do Boi). Several rocky islets (Vitória, Buzios) off its E shore.

São Sepé (sĭpĕ'), city (pop. 1,865), S central Rio Grande do Sul, Brazil, 35 mi. SSE of Santa Maria; rice, tobacco; cattle raising; asbestos.

São Simão (sēmã'ō), city (pop. 3,831), NE São Paulo, Brazil, 22 mi. SSE of Ribeirão Prêto; rail junction; sugar milling; coffee, sugar, grain.

São Thiago Island, Cape Verde Isls.: see SÃO TIAGO ISLAND.

São Thomé, Brazil: see SÃO TOMÉ.

São Thomé Island, São Tomé e Príncipe: see SÃO TOMÉ ISLAND.

São Tiago (sã'ō tyä'gōō), village, Cape Verde Isls., on E shore of São Tiago Isl., 15 mi. N of Praia; anchorage in Pedra Badejo bay; fishing.

São Tiago Island or **Santiago Island** (säntyä'gōō), largest and most populous isl. (□ 383; 1940 pop. 77,192; 1950 pop. 58,907) of Cape Verde Isls., in Leeward group, bet. Maio (15 mi. NE) and Fogo (35 mi. WSW) isls., in the Atlantic, c.400 mi. W of Cape Verde (Fr. West Africa). Praia (14°55'N 23°31'W), the archipelago's capital, is on S shore. Isl. is 33 mi. long, up to 18 mi. wide. Mountainous throughout, it rises to 4,567 ft. in Antónia Peak. Coast is rocky and fronted by reefs. About ½ isl. is cultivated; coffee, oranges, sugar cane, and castor beans are export crops. Formerly São Thiago.

São Tomé (tōōmĕ'), city (pop. 887), central Rio Grande do Norte, NE Brazil, on upper Potengi R. and 60 mi. W of Natal; cattle. Formerly spelled São Thomé.

São Tomé, town (pop. 5,607), ⊙ São Tomé e Príncipe, on NE coast of São Tomé Isl., on Ana de Chaves Bay; 0°20'N 6°43'E; port linked by rail with cacao and coffee plantations.

São Tomé Cape, headland on the Atlantic in Rio de Janeiro state, Brazil, formed by deltaic sediments of the Paraíba R. 25 mi. SE of Campos; 22°1'S 40°59'W.

São Tomé e Príncipe (ē prēn'sēpĭ), Port. colony (□ 372; 1950 pop. 60,159) in the Gulf of Guinea off Fr. Equatorial Africa, consisting of SÃO TOMÉ ISLAND and PRÍNCIPE ISLAND; ⊙ São Tomé. Discovered 1470–71 by Portuguese. Occupied by Dutch 1641–1740. Formerly spelled São Thomé e Príncipe.

São Tomé Island or **Saint Thomas Island,** Portuguese island (□ 319; pop. 55,827) in Gulf of Guinea, 150 mi. NW of Cape Lopez (Gabon, Fr. Equatorial Africa), forming, with Príncipe Isl. (90 mi. NNE), Port. colony of São Tomé e Príncipe; ⊙ São Tomé (0°20'N 6°43'E). Of volcanic origin, it rises in Pico de São Tomé to 6,640 ft. Coast is steep and rocky. Has humid tropical climate (equator passes through Rôlas islet off S coast), with long rainy season (Oct.-June; yearly rainfall 40–100 in., increasing with alt.). Heavy tropical vegetation. Principal exports: cacao (chief crop), coffee, palm oil, kola nuts, cinchona bark, copra. Fish canning, palm-oil processing, soap mfg. are only industries. São Tomé (town on NE coast), with good harbor on Ana de Chaves Bay, is linked by rail with Trindade in the interior; rail extension southward is under construction. Discovered 1470–71 by Portuguese. Formerly spelled São Thomé.

Saouaf (säwäf'), village, Zaghouan dist., NE central Tunisia, 11 mi. S of Zaghouan and 38 mi. S of Tunis; lignite mining and processing for chemical industry; glassworks.

Saoula (soulä'), village (pop. 602), Alger dept., N central Algeria, 5 mi. SSW of Algiers; distillery.

Saoura, Oued (wĕd' sourä'), Saharan wadi in Aïn-Sefra territory, W Algeria, skirting the Great Western Erg (E), and watering a string of oases, among which are Béni-Abbès and Adrar.

São Vicente (sã'ō vēsĕn'tĭ). **1** City, Goiás, Brazil: see ARAGUATINS. **2** City, Rio Grande do Sul, Brazil: see GENERAL VARGAS. **3** City (1950 pop. 28,581), SE São Paulo, Brazil, on São Vicente Isl., 4 mi. WSW of Santos; banana-growing and -processing center; glass mfg., tanning. Beach. Linked by road and railroad with mainland, from which it is separated by narrow tidal channel. First Port. settlement (1532) on São Paulo coast. In 16th-17th cent. was ⊙ São Vicente captain-generalcy. Seat of govt. was transferred to São Paulo in 1681.

São Vicente, town (pop. 1,406), Madeira, on N coast of Madeira isl., 14 mi. NW of Funchal; distilling, dairying; cereal- and winegrowing. Road to S coast across rugged interior.

São Vicente, Cabo de, Portugal: see SAINT VINCENT, CAPE.

São Vicente Ferrer (fĕrĕr'), city (pop. 1,040), N Maranhão, Brazil, near W shore of São Marcos Bay, 30 mi. SW of São Luís; cotton, sugar.

São Vicente Island, off SE coast of Brazil, separated from mainland of São Paulo by tidal channels, and sheltered (E and S) from the open Atlantic by Santo Amaro Isl.; 8 mi. long, 4 mi. wide. Ports of SANTOS (on N shore) and SÃO VICENTE (W shore) linked by railroad and road with mainland. A leading banana-growing center.

São Vicente Island or **Saint Vincent Island** (□ 88; 1940 pop. 15,867; 1950 pop. 18,907), one of Cape Verde Isls., in the Windward group, bet. Santo Antão Isl. (8 mi. NW) and Santa Luzia Isl. (5 mi. SE), in the Atlantic; Mindêlo (16°53'N 25°W), its chief town and port, is on NW shore. Isl. is 15 mi. long, 8 mi. wide. Of volcanic origin, it rises to 2,539 ft. at Monte Verde. Generally barren, isl. grows only subsistence crops (corn, beans, potatoes). Pop. is engaged in fishing and coal mining. Pôrto Grande, a bay on NW shore (Mindêlo is on it), is a coaling station for transatlantic shipping. Cable station.

Sapahaqui (säpä-ä'kē), town (pop. c.3,700), La Paz dept., W Bolivia, on Caracato R. (branch of the Luribay) and 32 mi. SSE of La Paz; alt. 10,663 ft.; vineyards, orchards. Hot springs of Urmiri are 2 mi. S.

Sapai or **Sapaioi,** Kavala nome, Macedonia, Greece: see CHRYSOUPOLIS.

Sapai or **Sappai** (both: sä'pĕ), town (pop. 6,203), Rhodope nome, W Thrace, Greece, on highway and 17 mi. ESE of Komotine; trading center for tobacco, wheat, barley, cotton; sheep, cattle. Sometimes spelled Sappe.

Sapaleri, Cerro, Andean peak: see ZAPALERI, CERRO.

Sapallanga (säpäyäng'gä), town (pop. 2,708), Junín dept., central Peru, in Cordillera Central, on road, and 5 mi. SE of Huancayo; wheat, corn, sheep.

Sapanca, Lake (sä'pänjä") (□ 16), NW Turkey, 12 mi. ESE of Izmit; 10 mi. long, 3 mi. wide; alt. 100 ft. Connected with Sakarya R.

Sapangbato (säpängbä'tō), town (1939 pop. 5,335) in Angeles municipality, Pampanga prov., central Luzon, Philippines, 50 mi. NW of Manila, and on short spur of Manila–San Fernando RR; agr. center (sugar cane, rice). Near by are Fort Stotsenburg and Clark Field, U.S. bases.

Sapareva-banya (säpä'rĕvä-bä'nyä), village (pop. 2,956), Sofia dist., W Bulgaria, on N slope of Rila Mts., on Dzherman R. and 8 mi. ENE of Marek; major health resort; thermal springs; vineyards, fruit. Has 13th-cent. church. Formerly Gornabanya. Saparevo (pop. 2,731), just NE, is at SW end of Klisura Pass (alt. 3,359 ft.), on highway to Samokov (E).

Saparua or **Saparoea** (both: sŭpŭrōō'ŭ), island (□ 73; pop. 23,204), Uliaser Isls., Indonesia, in Banda Sea, just E of Haruku and 5 mi. S of SW coast of Ceram across narrow Ceram Strait; 3°33'S 128°38'E; generally flat; 12 mi. long, 2–8 mi. wide, deeply indented in central part. Coconuts, cloves, sago. Also called Honimoa.

Sapcote, town and parish (pop. 862), SW Leicester, England, 4 mi. E of Hinckley; hosiery knitting; stone quarrying. Has 14th-cent. church.

Sapé (säpě'). **1** Town, Bahia, Brazil: see SAPEAÇU. **2** City (pop. 4,739), E Paraíba, NE Brazil, on railroad and 22 mi. W of João Pessoa; cotton, sugar, manioc, bananas, pineapples, oranges, mangoes.

Sapeaçu (sŭpĭă'sōō), town (pop. 1,022), E Bahia, Brazil, on railroad and 13 mi. ENE of Castro Alves; manganese deposits. Until 1944, Sapé.

Sapele (säpä'lā), town (pop. 4,143), Warri prov., Western Provinces, S Nigeria, port on Benin R., at head of navigation (ferry), and 28 mi. N of Warri; sawmilling center (hardwood); large plywood plant (completed 1948); rubber, palm oil and kernels, cacao, kola nuts.

Sapello (sŭpă'ō), hamlet, San Miguel co., N central N.Mex., in Sangre de Cristo Mts., 13 mi. N of Las Vegas; alt. c.6,900 ft. Small trading point in wheat and alfalfa area.

Sapelo Island (să'pŭlō), one of the Sea Isls., in McIntosh co., SE Ga., just off the coast, bet. St. Catherines and St. Simons isls.; c.10 mi. long, 5 mi. wide. Small Sapelo Sound at N end.

Saphane Dag (shäp-hänĕ' dä), Turkish *Şaphane Dağ*, peak (6,959 ft.), W Turkey, 6 mi. WNW of Gediz.

Sapientza (säpēĕn'dzŭ), island (□ 3.4; pop. 7), Oinousai Isls., in Ionian Sea off SW Peloponnesus, Greece, 2 mi. S of Methone; 5 mi. long, 1–2 mi. wide; fishing, sheep raising.

Sapinero (săpĭnē'rō), village (pop. c.70), Gunnison co., W central Colo., on Gunnison R., just N of San Juan Mts., and 21 mi. WSW of Gunnison; alt. 7,245 ft.; resort. Black Canyon of the Gunnison begins here.

Sapo, Serranía de (sĕrănē'ä dā sä'pō), mountain range of E Panama, extends c.60 mi. (NW–SE) along Pacific coast from Garachiné Bay to Aspavé Highlands on Colombia border; rises to 4,265 ft. in Sapo peak, 8 mi. S of Garachiné.

Sapoá (säpwä'), village, Rivas dept., SW Nicaragua, on SW shore of L. Nicaragua, at mouth of short Sapoá R., and 20 mi. SE of Rivas, on Inter-American Highway; livestock.

Sapoedi, Indonesia: see SAPUDI.

Saposoa (säpōsō'ä), city (pop. 3,457), ⊙ Huallaga prov. (□ 4,839; enumerated pop. 12,521, plus estimated 2,000 Indians), San Martín dept., N central Peru, on affluent of Huallaga R. (Amazon basin), in E outliers of the Andes, and 65 mi. S of Moyobamba (linked by road); 6°57'S 76°48'W. Reached by canoe from its landing Tingo de Saposoa on the Huallaga 16 mi. SE. Situated in fertile agr. region (tobacco, cotton, sugar cane, cacao, coffee); some cattle raising; alcohol and liquor distilling.

Sapotra (sŭpō'trŭ), town (pop. 1,976), E Rajasthan, India, 22 mi. SW of Karauli; millet, gram.

Sapozhok (sŭpŭzhôk'), town (1926 pop. 9,042), S central Ryazan oblast, Russian SFSR, 30 mi. NE of Ryazhsk; agr. implements; wheat, tobacco.

Sappa Creek, river in NW Kansas and S Nebr., formed by confluence of North Fork (90 mi. long) and South Fork (70 mi. long) near Oberlin in Kansas, flows 100 mi. ENE into Furnas co. in Nebr., to Beaver Creek 10 mi. E of Beaver City.

Sappada (säp-pä'dä), village (pop. 1,325), Belluno prov., Veneto, N Italy, on Piave R. and 37 mi. NE of Belluno; resort (alt. 3,993 ft.); sawmill.

Sappai or **Sappe,** Greece: see SAPAI.

Sappemeer (să'pŭmār), town (pop. 4,565), Groningen prov., NE Netherlands, on the Winschoter Diep and 10 mi. ESE of Groningen; mfg. (agr. machinery, yeast, spirits). Railroad station is Hoogezand-Sappemeer.

Sapphar, Yemen: see ZAFAR, JABAL.

Sapphire, village, Transylvania co., W N.C., in resort region of the Blue Ridge, c.20 mi. SW of Brevard; near by is small Sapphire L.

Sapphire Mountains, range of Rocky Mts. in W Mont., rise just S of the Clark Fork; extend S bet. Flint Creek and Bitterroot R. to Anaconda Range. Elevations of 7–9,000 ft. Deposits of silver, sapphires, and phosphates. Skalkaho Pass (skăl'kŭhō) (c.7,250 ft.) is 20 mi. E of Hamilton.

Sapporo (säp-pō'rō), city (1940 pop. 206,103; 1947 pop. 259,602), ⊙ Hokkaido, Japan, at base of SW peninsula, 100 mi. NNE of Hakodate; 43°3'N 141°21'E. Cultural and mfg. center; condensed milk, hemp cloth, processed soybeans, rubber goods. Seat of Hokkaido Imperial Univ. (1918). Has botanical gardens with alpine flora; ski slopes in suburbs. Popular Josankei hot springs are 11 mi. SW of city. City planned 1871, with wide streets. Includes (since early 1940s) former town of Maruyama (1940 pop. 16,724). Formerly sometimes spelled Satsporo.

Sapri (sä'prē), town (pop. 3,985), Salerno prov., Campania, S Italy, port on Gulf of Policastro, 23 mi. S of Sala Consilina. Bathing resort; agr. (grapes, olives, citrus fruit, vegetables), fishing.

Sapt Gandaki River, Nepal: see GANDAK RIVER.

Sapt Kosi River, Nepal: see KOSI RIVER.

Sapucaí or **Sapucay** (säpōōkäē'), town (dist. pop. 6,768), Paraguarí dept., S Paraguay, on railroad and 55 mi. ESE of Asunción; railroad shops; agr. center (fruit, corn, cattle); ocher processing.

Sapucaia (sŭpōōkī'ŭ), city (pop. 1,343), N Rio de Janeiro state, Brazil, on Paraíba R. (Minas Gerais border), on railroad and 20 mi. ENE of Três Rios; dairying, coffeegrowing.

Sapucaí-Guaçu River (sŭpōōkäē'-gwŭsōō'), SW Minas Gerais, Brazil, rises in the Serra da Mantiqueira near São Bento do Sapucaí (São Paulo), flows c.200 mi. N in a winding course to the Rio Grande (left bank) 35 mi. E of Passos. Navigable in stretches bet. rapids. Receives (right) the Rio Verde. Formerly spelled Sapucahy-Guassú.

Sapudi or **Sapoedi** (both: sŭpōō'dē), island (□ 61), Indonesia, in Java Sea, 13 mi. E of Madura across Sapudi Strait (connecting Madura Strait with Java Sea). Sapudi census div. (□ 94; pop. 63,534) includes adjacent islets. Sapudi is 10 mi. long, 7 mi. wide, and generally low. Cattle raising, fishing, agr. (corn, cassava). Madurese inhabitants.

Sapulpa (sŭpŭl'pŭ), city (pop. 13,031), Creek co., central Okla., 12 mi. SSW of Tulsa; trade, distribution, and mfg. center for agr., stock-raising, and oil-producing region; mfg. of glass, clay products, gasoline, packed meat, clothing, dairy and other food products, oil-field equipment, tanks; cotton ginning. Ships cattle. Oil and gas wells near by. Has a U.S. school for Indians. Inc. 1898.

Sapurara (sŭpōōrä'rŭ), village, W Amazonas, Brazil, port of entry (steamer and hydroplane landing) on right bank of the Amazon, at Peru-Colombia border, and 3 mi. SSE of Leticia (Colombia); 4°20'S 69°55'W. Lignite deposits. Formerly Tabatinga.

Saqqara, Egypt: see SAKKARA.

Saqqiz or **Saqqez** (both: säk-kēz'), town (1940 pop. 10,479), Fifth Prov., in Kurdistan, W Iran, on road and 75 mi. NW of Sanandaj; tobacco, wheat, gums; sheep raising. Also spelled Sakiz (Sakkiz) and Saghiz (Saghghiz).

Saquarema (sŭkwŭrā'mŭ), city (pop. 871), S Rio de Janeiro state, Brazil, picturesque old fishing port on a bar bet. the Atlantic (S) and a tidal lagoon (of same name), 40 mi. E of Niterói.

Saquisilí (säkēsēlē'), town (1950 pop. 3,217), Cotopaxi, N central Ecuador, in the Andes, 8 mi. NW of Latacunga; grain growing, dairying.

Sar, mountains, Yugoslavia: see SAR MOUNTAINS.

Sara, Bolivia: see PORTACHUELO.

Sara (sä'rŭ), village, Pabna dist., W East Bengal, E Pakistan, on the Padma (Ganges) and 15 mi. WNW of Pabna; trades in rice, jute, rape and mustard. Rail bridge across the Padma 3 mi. S, at Paksey.

Sara (sä'rä), town (1939 pop. 2,598; 1948 municipality pop. 16,042), Iloilo prov., E Panay isl., Philippines, 28 mi. SE of Capiz; agr. center (rice, corn). Manganese is mined near by.

Sara (sŭră'), village (1926 pop. 2,327), E central Chkalov oblast, Russian SFSR, on railroad and 15 mi. ENE of Mednogorsk, in Orsk-Khalilovo industrial dist.; metalworking. Terminus of projected rail line from Magnitogorsk. Formerly called Petropavlovskoye.

Sara, mountains, Yugoslavia: see SAR MOUNTAINS.

Sara, Bahr, Fr. Equatorial Africa: see BAHR SARA.

Sarab (säräb'), town (1941 pop. 29,712), Third Prov., in Azerbaijan, NW Iran, 75 mi. E of Tabriz, and on road to Ardebil, at S foot of the Savalan; grain, fruit; sheep raising; rugmaking.

Sarabat River, Turkey: see GEDIZ RIVER.

Saraburi (sŭră'bōōrē'), town (1947 pop. 7,112), ⊙ Saraburi prov. (□ 1,182; 1947 pop. 203,562), S Thailand, on Pa Sak R., on railroad, and 60 mi. NNE of Bangkok, in rice-growing area; cattle trading. Local name, Pak Phrieo (Pak Preo or Pakpriew). Sometimes spelled Sraburi.

Saracena (säräch̄ā'nä), village (pop. 2,994), Cosenza prov., Calabria, S Italy, 4 mi. SW of Castrovillari, in olive- and grape-growing region.

Sarafand (să'răfănd), village, W Israel, in Judaean Plain, 9 mi. SE of Tel Aviv; military center with extensive army installations.

Saragosa (să'rŭgō'sŭ), village (pop. c.200), Reeves co., extreme W Texas, 28 mi. S of Pecos, near NE base of Davis Mts.; market point in irrigated agr. area (cotton, hay, melons).

Saragossa (sărŭgō'sŭ), Sp. *Zaragoza* (thärägō'thä), province (□ 6,615; pop. 595,095), NE Spain, in Aragon; ⊙ Saragossa. Bounded N by crest of the W Pyrenees (Fr. border), which slope to dry, barren Ebro plain containing some fertile valleys and oases; S occupied by spurs of central plateau. Drained by the Ebro and its tributaries, (the Gállego, Huerva, and Jalón). Along Ebro banks are the Imperial and Tauste irrigation canals. Climate characterized by extremes of temp. and scarcity of rainfall. Lignite mines, iron and manganese deposits, marble and limestone quarries. Essentially agr.: sugar beets (leading producer in Spain), cereals, wine, olive oil, hemp; stock raising (especially sheep). Industrial and commercial development (mostly connected with agr. and concentrated in Saragossa city) hampered by poor communications. Chief towns: Saragossa, Calatayud, Tarazona, Caspe.

Saragossa, Sp. *Zaragoza*, anc. *Caesarea Augusta* or *Caesaraugusta*, city (pop. 205,833, with suburbs 238,601), ⊙ Saragossa prov. and chief town of Aragon, NE Spain, on right bank of the Ebro (spanned by 15th-cent. arched stone bridge and 2 modern bridges) at influx of Gállego and Huerva rivers, and 160 mi. W of Barcelona, 175 mi. NE of Madrid; 41°39'N 0°54'W. Major communications, trading, and mfg. hub for the entire region, linked by rail with Madrid, Valencia, Barcelona, and via trans-Pyrenean railroad with France. Situated in a fertile, irrigated oasis (*huerta*) of an otherwise arid hinterland, growing grapes, sugar beets, cereals, and fruit. Among its industrial plants are sugar refineries, metalworks, brewery, chemical works; and textile, paper, and cement mills. Mfg. of electrical equipment, agr. machinery, glassware, furniture, and flour products. Renowned cultural center, with a univ. (confirmed 1474), school of industrial art, priests' seminary, provincial mus., theater, military acad. (reopened 1942). Archbishopric. The anc. city bears splendid witness to Sp. history and art. Its most outstanding edifices are the 2 cathedrals; the older Gothic-Mudejar La Seo (begun in 12th cent.); and the sumptuous, baroque El Pilar or Our Lady of the Pillar (containing murals by Goya), built in 17th cent. and named for a sacred pillar on which the Virgin is said to have appeared to St. James. Equally impressive is 13th-cent. San Pablo church, crowned by an octagonal turret. Moorish influence is also displayed in San Miguel and Santa María churches. Other fine bldgs. include the Mozarabic castle of Aljafería (once residence of Aragonese kings, it served also as palace of the Inquisition; now used as barracks); the Lonja or Exchange (completed 1551) with Gothic and Renaissance features; the Audiencia (court of appeal), former palace of the counts of Luna; the archbishop's palace; and many mansions. The more modern sections are intersected by beautiful boulevards, parks, and squares. Founded as a Celtiberian town, Saragossa became a Roman military colony under Augustus. Successively occupied (5th cent.) by the Suevi and Visigoths, then taken (714) by the Moors, under whom it later (10th-11th cent.) flourished as capital of an emirate until Alfonso I captured it (1118) after a 9-month siege. It then became ⊙ Aragon (12th cent.–2d half of 15th cent.), but decayed after the union of Aragon with Castile under the Catholic Kings, Ferdinand and Isabella. During War of Spanish Succession, the English here defeated (1710) the French. Saragossa achieved fame through its heroic part in the Peninsular War; under the leadership of Palofax it resisted 2 Fr. sieges, but had finally to yield (Feb., 1809). In the struggle, tens of thousands perished, and many historic bldgs. were damaged. With the defenders fought the "Maid of Saragossa," immortalized by Byron's *Childe Harold*. Early in the Sp. civil war, Saragossa came (1936) under the control of the Nationalists.

Saraguay (särägā'), village (pop. 263), S Que., on NW shore of Montreal Isl., on R. des Prairies, opposite Jesus Isl., 10 mi. W of Montreal; market gardening, dairying.

Saragur, India: see SARGUR.

Saraguro or **Zaraguro** (both: särägōō'rō), town (1950 pop. 1,334), Loja, S Ecuador, in Andean valley, on Pan-American Highway and 29 mi. N of Loja; alt. 8,241 ft. Agr. center (cereals, potatoes, livestock).

Sarah Anne Island, name erroneously given to isl. long thought to exist in the central Pacific, near Line Isls. In 1937 it was established that no such isl. existed.

Sarahsville, village (pop. 170), Noble co., E Ohio, 16 mi. SSE of Cambridge, in agr. area.

Sarai or **Sarai-Batu** (sŭrī'bŭtōō'), former city in SE European Russia, on the Akhtuba (arm of lower Volga) and 65 mi. NNW of modern Astrakhan. Was 13th-cent. ⊙ Golden Horde. In 14th cent., the hq. were moved to another Sarai (or Sarai-Berke), 45 mi. E of modern Stalingrad.

Sarai (sŭrī'), village (1926 pop. 5,698), S Ryazan oblast, Russian SFSR, 40 mi. E of Ryazhsk; hemp processing.

Sarai Akil (sŭrī' ä'kĭl), town (pop. 4,685), Allahabad dist., SE Uttar Pradesh, India, 20 mi. WSW of Allahabad; rice, gram, wheat, barley, oilseeds. Also spelled Sarai-Aqil.

Sarai-Batu, USSR: see SARAI.

Sarai-Berke, USSR: see SARAI.

Sarai Ekdil, India: see EKDIL.

Sarai-Kamar, Tadzhik SSR: see KIROVABAD, Stalinabad oblast.

Saraikela or **Seraikela** (both: sŭrīkā'lŭ), town (pop. 6,105), Singhbhum dist., S Bihar, India, on tributary of the Subarnarekha and 18 mi. WSW of Jamshedpur; rice, oilseeds, corn, jowar. Copper and iron-ore deposits near by; asbestos quarries (SE). Limestone quarries for Jamshedpur iron- and steelworks 6 mi. N, at Sini village. Town was ⊙ former princely state of Saraikela or Seraikela (□ 446; pop. 154,844) in Orissa States; state merged 1948 with Singhbhum dist., Bihar.

Sarai Mir (sŭrī' mēr), town (pop. 3,764), Azamgarh dist., E Uttar Pradesh, India, 17 mi. WSW of Azamgarh; rice, barley, wheat, sugar cane.

Saraj (sŭrăj′), SE subdivision of Kangra dist., NE Punjab, India; crossed by E Punjab Himalayas (average height, 8,000 ft.); bordered W, S, and E by Himachal Pradesh, N by Kulu subdivision.

Sarajevo or **Sarayevo** (both: să″rüyā′vō, –jā′vō; Serbo-Croatian să′räyĕvô), largest city (pop. 118,158) and ⊙ Bosnia and Herzegovina and Sarajevo oblast (formed 1949), central Yugoslavia, 125 mi. SW of Belgrade, on Miljacka R., at E edge of a wide valley bet. the Trebevic (S) and the Ozren (N); 43°51′N 18°26′E. Economic and cultural center of Bosnia; rail center; handicraft (gold, silver work); mfg. of carpets, tobacco, beer, leather, Oriental jewelry, machine tools; lumbering. Seat of Orthodox Eastern metropolitan, R.C. archbishop, and head of Moslem church in Yugoslavia. Consists of hilly oriental section (E) and occidental section in valley (W). Has numerous mosques, acad. of commerce, school of applied arts, medical school, Moslem seminary, music conservatory, theater, and one of richest Yugoslav museums. Some old fortifications and an oriental market (*Bas-Carsija*) remain. Dates from 14th cent.; originally called Vrh-Bosna. Fell (1429) to Turks, who called it Bosna-Sarai. Succeeded (1851) Travnik as ⊙ Bosnia. Scene of assassination (June 28, 1914) of Archduke Francis Ferdinand, which precipitated the First World War; after the war, Sarajevo passed to Yugoslavia. Sometimes spelled Serajevo or Serayevo. Resorts of Ilidza and Pale near by. Sarajevo coal area extends N of city, bet. Usora and Drina rivers; mines at Zenica, Kakanj, and Breza.

Sarakhs (sărăkhs′), town (1936 pop. estimate 12,500), Ninth Prov., in Khurasan, northeasternmost Iran, 85 mi. ENE of Meshed, and on Tedzhen R. (USSR border), opposite Serakhs; grain, cotton, opium; hides, wool, meat.

Saraktash (sŭrŭktăsh′), town (1939 pop. over 2,000), N Chkalov oblast, Russian SFSR, in S foothills of the S Urals, on Sakmara R., opposite mouth of Greater Ik R., and 50 mi. ENE of Chkalov, on railroad; metalworking. Petroleum and asphalt deposits.

Sarala (sŭrŭlä′), town (1939 pop. over 10,000), N Khakass Autonomous Oblast, Krasnoyarsk Territory, Russian SFSR, 115 mi. NW of Abakan; gold mines; power plant.

Saramabila (sărămăbē′lä), village, Kivu prov., E Belgian Congo, 70 mi. NE of Kasongo; gold mining.

Saramacca, district, Du. Guiana: see GRONINGEN.

Saramacca Point (sărămä′kä), on Atlantic coast of N Du. Guiana, at Saramacca R. mouth, 50 mi. W of Paramaribo; 5°53′N 55°58′W.

Saramaccapolder (–pôl″dŭr), village (pop. 4,032), Surinam dist., N Du. Guiana, 3 mi. W of Paramaribo; rice, coffee, sugar, fruit.

Saramacca River, Du. Guiana, rises in outliers of the Guiana Highlands at c.4°N, flows N through tropical forests, and W of Paramaribo turns W to the Atlantic near mouth of Coppename R., 50 mi. W of Paramaribo; c.250 mi. long. Many rapids and falls on upper course; lower course navigable c.70 mi. for medium-sized vessels. Rice, sugar cane, and tropical fruit are grown along its lower reaches. Has important gold deposits. Saramacca Canal links it with Surinam R. just S of Paramaribo.

Saramati (sŭrä″mŭtē′), highest peak (12,553 ft.) of Patkai Range, on Burma-India frontier; 25°44′N 95°03′E; a symmetrical cone known for its beauty.

Saramenha (sŭrŭmä′nyŭ), SW suburb of Ouro Prêto, SE central Minas Gerais, Brazil, on railroad; has aluminum plant now producing sulphuric acid, copper sulphates, ferromanganese.

Saramin, Syria: see SERMIN.

Saramon (sărămō′), village (pop. 495), Gers dept., SW France, on the Gimone and 12 mi. SE of Auch; poultry, cattle, fruits. Cementworks near by.

Saran (sărä′), outer N suburb (pop. 2,094) of Orléans, Loiret dept., N central France; airport.

Saran (să′rŭn), district (□ 2,669; pop. 2,860,537), NW Bihar, India, in Tirhut div.; ⊙ Chapra. On Ganges Plain; bounded E by Gandak, SW by Gogra, S by Ganges rivers; drained by tributaries of the Ganges. Alluvial soil; rice, wheat, corn, barley, cotton, linseed, sugar cane; mango groves. Rice, sugar, oilseed milling, saltpeter processing; pottery and brasswork. Main towns: Chapra, Siwan. Annual Hindu bathing festival and fair at Sonpur. Rajendra Prasad, 1st president of Republic of India, was b. in Saran dist.

Saran, Kazakh SSR: see KARAGANDA, city.

Sarana (sŭrä′nŭ), town (1939 pop. over 2,000), SW Sverdlovsk oblast, Russian SFSR, on Ufa R. and 11 mi. S of Krasnoufimsk, near railroad (Saraninski Zavod station); mfg. (transportation equipment, milk separators, ceramics). Until 1933, called Nizhne-Saraninski or Nizhnyaya Sarana.

Saranac (să′rŭnăk), village (pop. 885), Ionia co., S central Mich., 24 mi. E of Grand Rapids and on Grand R., in farm area (livestock, grain; dairy products).

Saranac Lake, village (pop. 6,913, on Essex-Franklin co. line, NE N.Y., on small Flower L. in the Adirondacks, just NE of Lower Saranac L. and 8 mi. NW of Lake Placid; alt. 1,534 ft. Noted health and year-round resort. Mfg. (clothing, wood products); agr. (dairy products; truck, potatoes); timber. A tuberculosis sanatorium (1884) and a research laboratory (1894) were established here by Edward L. Trudeau. Robert Louis Stevenson, whose *Master of Ballantrae* describes the region, was a patient here (1887–88). The Will Rogers Memorial Sanatorium (1930) is here. Settled c.1819, inc. 1892.

Saranac Lakes, NE N.Y., 3 resort lakes in the Adirondacks, W of Saranac Lake village and c.50 mi. SW of Plattsburg. Upper Saranac L. (□ c.8; c.8 mi. long), Middle Saranac L. (□ c.2½; c.2 mi. long), and Lower Saranac L. (□ c.3½; c.5 mi. long) are linked by **Saranac River,** which issues from Lower Saranac L., flows c.50 mi. NE, past Saranac Lake village and through resort region of the Adirondacks, to L. Champlain at Plattsburg.

Saranap (să′rŭnăp), village (pop. 2,362), Contra Costa co., W Calif., 25 mi. E of Berkeley.

Saranda (sărăn′dä), town, Central Prov., central Tanganyika, on railroad and 10 mi. ENE of Manyoni; cotton, peanuts; gum arabic, beeswax; livestock.

Sarandaporos River. 1 Epirus, Greece: see SARANTAPOROS RIVER. **2** Thessaly, Greece: see TITARESIOS RIVER.

Sarandapotamos, Greece: see CEPHISUS RIVER.

Sarandë (särän′dŭ) or **Saranda** (–dä), Ital. *Santi Quaranta* and (1939–43) *Porto Edda*, town (1945 pop. 1,643), S Albania, port on Ionian Sea at N entrance to Channel of Corfu, 50 mi. SE of Valona; commercial center with natural harbor serving S Albania; flour mill. Naval base. Byzantine church ruins near by. The anc. Onchesmus, it was the port of anc. Fenice. Became bishopric in 5th cent. The modern port developed as Ital. naval station during First World War.

Sarandí (säränd̄ē′), town (pop. estimate 25,000) in E Greater Buenos Aires, Argentina, adjoining Avellaneda, 4 mi. SSE of Buenos Aires; industrial center; asphalt processing, vegetable- and fish-oil refining, tanning; textiles, enamel, varnish, soap, chemicals, boxes, dairy and food products.

Sarandi (sŭrăndē′), city (pop. 1,498), W Rio Grande do Sul, Brazil, in the Coxilha de Santana, near Uruguay border, 28 mi. WNW of Livramento; corn, wheat. Formerly spelled Sarandy.

Sarandí (säränd̄ē′). **1** Town, Florida dept., Uruguay: see SARANDÍ GRANDE. **2** or **Sarandí de Navarro** (dā nävä′rō), village (pop. 630), Río Negro dept., W Uruguay, 24 mi. WNW of Paso de los Toros; grain, cattle, sheep.

Sarandí del Yí (dĕl yē′), town (pop. 5,600), Durazno dept., central Uruguay, on Yí R. (bridge), on railroad and 65 mi. NNE of Florida, on highway from Montevideo; commercial center; cattle and sheep raising. Military post.

Sarandí Grande (grän′dā) or **Villa Sarandí** (vē′yä), town (pop. 5,000), Florida dept., S central Uruguay, in the Cuchilla Grande Inferior, on railroad and 28 mi. NNW of Florida; road junction; agr. center (wheat, corn, oats, linseed, livestock). Also called Sarandí.

Sarangani Bay (säräng-gä′nē), inlet of Celebes Sea in S Mindanao, Philippines; 20 mi. long, 10 mi. wide.

Sarangani Island (□ 14; 1939 pop. 849), Davao prov., Philippines, just off S tip of Mindanao, across Sarangani Strait (7 mi. wide). Chief town, Tumanao or Tomanao. With Bulit Isl. (just W) and offshore islets, it comprises the Sarangani Isls. Sulphur deposits.

Sarangarh (sä′rŭng-gŭr), town (pop. 8,045), Raigarh dist., E Madhya Pradesh, India, 30 mi. SW of Raigarh; tussah-silk weaving; rice, oilseeds. Lac cultivation in sal forests (S). Was ⊙ former princely state of Sarangarh (□ 540; pop. 140,785) of Chhattisgarh States, India; since 1948, state inc. into Raigarh dist.

Sarangpur (sä′rŭngpŏŏr), town (pop. 7,095), central Madhya Bharat, India, on Kali Sindh R. and 15 mi. NE of Shajapur; local market for wheat, millet, cotton; sugar milling, hand-loom weaving. An old site, with many Hindu and Jain ruins; important in 15th and 16th cent. under Moslems.

Saranovo, Bulgaria: see SEPTEMVRI.

Saran-Paul or **Saran-Paul′** (sŭrän′-pŭŏŏl′), village, NW Khanty-Mansi Natl. Okrug, Tyumen oblast, Russian SFSR, on E slope of the N Urals, 125 mi. WNW of Berezovo; trading post. Mtn. crystal and platinum mined near by.

Saransk (sŭränsk′), city (1926 pop. 15,431; 1939 pop. 41,211), ⊙ Mordvinian Autonomous SSR, Russian SFSR, on left bank of Insar R., on railroad and 320 mi. ESE of Moscow; 54°12′N 45°11′E. Agr.-processing center (hemp, bast fiber, meat, tobacco, potatoes, dairy products); mfg. (agr. machinery, electrical equipment, clothing, furniture, bricks), canning. Has teachers col., regional research institute, mus., theater. Founded 1641 as Rus. stronghold; assaulted by Cossack rebels under Stenka Razin in 1670. Developed in 1920s as cultural center of Mordvinians; became ⊙ Mordvinian Autonomous Oblast in 1930 and ⊙ Mordvinian Autonomous SSR in 1934.

Sarantaporos River or **Sarandaporos River** (both: särŭndä′pôrôs). **1** In S Epirus, Greece, rises in the Voion, near Albanian line, flows 31 mi. SW to Aoos R. on Albanian border 9 mi. W of Konitsa. **2** In Thessaly, Greece: see TITARESIOS RIVER.

Sarantapotamos, Greece: see CEPHISUS RIVER.

Sarany (sŭrä′nē), town (1940 pop. over 500), E Molotov oblast, Russian SFSR, 45 mi. ENE (under jurisdiction) of Chusovoi, near railroad (Biser station); chromite-mining center.

Sara-Ostrov (sŭrä′-ô″strŭf) [Rus.,=Sara island], town (1939 pop. over 2,000), SE Azerbaijan SSR, on S section of former Sara Isl. (since c.1945 a peninsula), on Caspian Sea and 7 mi. NNE of Lenkoran; fisheries.

Sarapiquí or **Muelle de Sarapiquí** (mwĕ′yä dā säräpēkē′), village, Heredia prov., N Costa Rica, on Sarapiquí R. and 36 mi. NNE of Heredia; bananas, fodder crops, livestock. Terminus of road from San José, an important traffic artery in middle 19th cent.

Sarapiquí River, Heredia prov., N Costa Rica, rises on slopes of the volcano Barba, flows 55 mi. NNE, past San Miguel and Sarapiquí (head of navigation), to San Juan R. 20 mi. SW of San Juan del Norte. Was chief route (in 19th cent.) from central plateau to the Caribbean.

Sarapuí (sŭrŭpwē′), city (pop. 688), S central São Paulo, Brazil, 15 mi. ESE of Itapetininga; cotton, corn.

Sarapul (sŭrä′pŏŏl), city (1938 pop. estimate 42,000), SE Udmurt Autonomous SSR, Russian SFSR, port on right bank of Kama R., on railroad and 33 mi. SE of Izhevsk; tanning, shoe-mfg. center; food processing (flour, meat, butter), distilling, woodworking, sawmilling. Has mus. and theater. Founded in 16th cent. as Rus. stronghold on trade route to Siberia; chartered 1663; assaulted by peasant rebels under Yemelyan Pugachev in 1774.

Sarapulka (–kŭ), town (1947 pop. over 500), S Sverdlovsk oblast, Russian SFSR, 10 mi. ESE of Berezovski; lumbering, peat digging.

Saraqab, Syria: see SERAQAB.

Sarare (sărä′rā), town (pop. 1,076), Lara state, NW Venezuela, on Acarigua-Barquisimeto highway and 23 mi. SSE of Barquisimeto; sugar cane, cacao, corn, fruit, stock.

Sarare River, Apure state, W Venezuela, rises in Colombia near international line E of Pamplona in Cordillera Oriental, flows c.150 mi. E, past Guadualito, joining Uribante R. 4 mi. NNE of Guadualito to form Apure R.

Saraskand (säräskänd′), town (1940 pop. 7,450), Fourth Prov., in Azerbaijan, NW Iran, on road and 35 mi. W of Mianeh; center of Hashtrud agr. area (grain growing; sheep raising), at E foot of Sahand massif.

Sarasota (sărŭsō′tŭ), county (□ 586; pop. 28,827), SW Fla., on Gulf of Mexico (W); ⊙ Sarasota. Lowland area, drained by Myakka R.; coastal section bordered by barrier beaches and Sarasota Bay. Truck farming; also citrus-fruit growing, fishing, cattle raising, and quarrying (coquina, dolomite, limestone). Tourist region. Formed 1921.

Sarasota, city (pop. 18,896), ⊙ Sarasota co., SW Fla., c.45 mi. S of Tampa, on shallow Sarasota Bay, a lagoon (c.20 mi. long, ½–3 mi. wide) connected with Tampa Bay (N) and Gulf of Mexico (W); winter resort; packing and shipping center for vegetables (especially celery) and citrus fruit; fishing; mfg. of feed, concrete and wood products. Holds colorful Sara de Soto Pageant annually. The winter hq. of the Ringling Brothers'-Barnum and Bailey Circus, and the John and Mable Ringling Mus. of Art (largest art gall. in the state) are here. Settled c.1884 by Scotch. Myakka River State Park and State Forest are 15 mi. SE.

Saraspur, India: see AHMADABAD, city.

Saraswati River (sŭrŭs′vŭtē), N Bombay, India, rises in S offshoot of Aravalli Range E of Palanpur; flows c.105 mi. generally SW, past Sidhpur and Patan, into Little Rann of Cutch 20 mi. SSW of Radhanpur. A holy stream, visited by Hindu pilgrims.

Sarata (sŭrä′tŭ), Rum. *Sărata* (sŭrä′tä), village (1930 pop. 2,661; 1941 pop. 294), central Izmail oblast, Ukrainian SSR, on railroad and 35 mi. WSW of Belgorod-Dnestrovski. Founded, after 1812, as Ger. agr. colony; Ger. pop. repatriated in 1940.

Sarata-Monteoru (sŭrä′tä-môntyô′rōō), Rum. *Sărata-Monteoru*, village (pop. 763), Buzau prov., SE central Rumania, 10 mi. W of Buzau; health and summer resort with cold and warm mineral springs. Oil production in recent years.

Saratice (shä′rätyĭtsĕ), Czech *Šaratice*, village (pop. 1,076), S Moravia, Czechoslovakia, 10 mi. SE of Brno; mineral springs; exports medicinal bitter waters.

Saratoga (sărŭtō′gŭ), county (□ 814; pop. 74,869), E N.Y.; ⊙ Ballston Spa. Partly in the S Adirondacks; bounded E by the Hudson, S by Mohawk R. Includes Saratoga Natl. Historical Park, SARATOGA SPRINGS (noted spa), Saratoga L., and part of Sacandaga Reservoir. Dairying, farming (corn, hay), poultry and stock raising. Mfg. at Ballston Spa, Corinth, Mechanicville, Schuylerville, South Glens Falls, Saratoga Springs, Waterford. Formed 1791.

Saratoga. 1 Town (pop. 110), Howard co., SW Ark., 19 mi. WNW of Hope. **2** Residential village (pop. 1,329), Santa Clara co., W Calif., 9 mi. SW of San Jose, in foothills of Santa Cruz Mts.; orchards. Holds annual Blossom Festival. **3** Town (pop. 333), Randolph co., E Ind., 25 mi. E of Muncie, in agr. area. **4** City, N.Y.: see SARATOGA SPRINGS. **5** Town (pop. 366), Wilson co., E central N.C., 9 mi. SE of Wilson. Inc. 1939. **6** Town (pop. 926), Carbon co., S Wyo., on N.Platte R., near the Sierra Madre, and 33 mi. SE of Rawlins; alt. 6,790 ft. Supply point for hunters, fishermen, and ranchers; livestock, grain, timber. Hot mineral springs near by set aside as state reserve for treatment of rheumatic illnesses.

Saratoga Lake (□ c.7), Saratoga co., E N.Y., 23 mi N of Albany and just SE of Saratoga Springs; c.5 mi. long. Drains through outlet from its N end to the Hudson (E).

Saratoga Place, village (pop. 1,314), Nansemond co., SE Va., near Suffolk.

Saratoga Springs, city (pop. 15,473), Saratoga co., E N.Y., near Saratoga L., 30 mi. N of Albany; noted health and pleasure resort, with mineral springs, state-owned spa (1935) containing curative baths, and the Simon Baruch Research Inst. The springs' waters are bottled and shipped. Horse racing, one of city's main attractions, was begun after 1850. Also mfg. of chemicals, clothing, textiles, paper products, gloves, machinery. Seat of Skidmore Col. and St. Faith's School for girls. The large estate "Yaddo" is a retreat for artists and authors. Inc. as village in 1826, as city in 1915. Most fashionable resort of North America in 19th cent. Often called simply Saratoga. State tree nursery near by. Saratoga Natl. Historical Park (□ 3.3; established 1948; mus., replicas of blockhouse and other bldgs.) is 9 mi. SE; includes important parts of battlefields of Saratoga campaign, where colonial troops under Gen. Horatio Gates defeated Burgoyne (Sept. 19 and Oct. 7, 1777) in 2 battles that marked turning point of the Revolution and led to alliance of France with colonists.

Saratok (sŏŏrätôk'), town (pop. 1,962), S Sarawak, in W Borneo, 70 mi. E of Kuching; rice, sago, stock.

Saratov (sŭrä'tŭf), oblast (□ 39,500; 1946 pop. estimate 2,400,000) in SE European Russian SFSR; ⊙ Saratov. Drained by lower Volga (center), Khoper and Medveditsa (W), and Irgiz (E) rivers. Consists of hilly (Volga Hills) right-bank section of the Volga and drier, lower, left-bank section extending to the Obshchi Syrt (E). Dry steppe climate; black-earth to brown soils. Mineral resources: natural gas (Saratov), phosphorite (along Volga R.), limestone rock (Volsk), oil shale (Gorny, Ozinki). An important agr. region, with wheat, rye, oats, potatoes, sunflowers on right-bank wooded steppe; hard-grained wheat as main crop in drought-ridden left-bank section; tobacco and mustard seed (near Engels), melons and other garden crops in Volga R. valley. Beef cattle; meat packing plant at Privolzhski. Agr. processing is main industry, with centers at Balashov, Rtishchevo, Atkarsk, Petrovsk, and Pugachev. Mfg. (machines, chemicals, textiles) in Saratov-Engels area; cement works at Volsk. Volga R. and railroad crossing it at Saratov are chief transportation routes. Projected irrigation and tree-shelter belts to improve agr. in left-bank area of the Volga. Originally contained within Saratov govt.; area was part of Lower Volga Territory (1928–34); then separated as a territory containing German Volga Autonomous SSR until 1936, when it became an oblast. In 1941, it absorbed N section of dissolved German Volga Autonomous SSR.

Saratov, city (1939 pop. 375,860; 1946 pop. estimate 450,000), ⊙ Saratov oblast, Russian SFSR, port on high right bank of Volga R. and 200 mi. SW of Kuibyshev, 460 mi. SE of Moscow; 51°30'N 46°E. Major industrial and natural-gas-producing center (linked since 1946 by pipe line to Moscow); mfg. of agr. machines (tractors, combines) and gear-milling machines, locomotive tenders, ballbearings, instruments, electric drills, gas equipment, small metal products, chemicals, cotton textiles, leather goods, soap; agr. processing (flour, oilseeds), oil refining, lumber milling, shipbuilding. Major transfer point for petroleum and timber (shipped along Volga R.). Univ. (1919), institutes for road construction and agr. mechanization, conservatory, agr., medical, and teachers colleges. Has archaeological and ethnographic museums and museums dedicated to Radishchev and Chernyshevski (b. here). Laid out in checkerboard fashion in its central section, Saratov extends from Sokolov mtn. (on N limits; frequent landslides) c.10 mi. S, past lumber mills, to oil port and refinery at the Volga rail bridge leading to Engels. During Second World War, following discovery of natural gas at Yelshanka and Kurdyum (8 and 12 mi. NW of city center), Saratov expanded NW along the railroad to include new gas sites within its city limits. Founded originally (1590) as a Rus. fortress on left Volga R. bank; held (1670) by Stenka Razin; moved (1674) to present site; chartered in 1780. In 19th cent., developed as a major grain-trade center and transfer point for Baku oil shipments. During civil war, successfully defended (1918–19) by Soviet troops. Its greatest industrial development dates from 1930s and Second World War. In 1943, city was placed under direct jurisdiction of Russian SFSR govt. Was ⊙ Saratov govt. until 1928 and Lower Volga Territory (1928–34).

Saratovskaya Manufaktura, Russian SFSR: see KRASNY TEKSTILSHCHIK.

Saratsi (särätsē'), Chinese *Sa-la-ch'i* (sä'lä'chē'), town (pop. 22,737), ⊙ Saratsi co. (pop. 138,637), central Suiyuan prov., China, on railroad and 20 mi. E of Paotow, near Yellow R.; agr. center for extensive irrigation area (S), developed in 1930s; cattle raising; wheat, oats, licorice. Coal mining (N).

Sarauli, India: see SIRAULI.

Saraurcu, Cerro (sĕ'rō särä-ōōr'kōō), Andean peak (15,341 ft.) in Napo-Pastaza prov., N Ecuador, 40 mi. E of Quito; 0°7'S 77°55'W.

Saravane (sä'rä'wän'), town, ⊙ Saravane prov. (□ 8,300; 1947 pop. 120,000), S Laos, on the Se Done and 55 mi. NE of Pakse.

Saravia (sărä'vyä), town (1939 pop. 3,628; 1948 municipality pop. 19,204), Negros Occidental prov., NW Negros isl., Philippines, 14 mi. N of Bacolod; agr. center (rice, sugar cane).

Sarawak (sŏŏrä'wäk), British crown colony (□ 47,071; pop. 546,385), NW Borneo, bounded W by S.China Sea, NE by Br. North Borneo, S by Indonesian Borneo; 0°50'–5°N 109°40'–115°30'E; ⊙ KUCHING. Colony consists of long coastal strip, 450 mi. long, 40–120 mi. wide. Coastal areas are low-lying and swampy; interior (near boundaries of Indonesian Borneo) is forested and mountainous, rising to 7,798 ft. at Mt. Mulu. Drained by numerous rivers, largest being Rajang R. Warm, humid climate with mean daily temp. of 85°F. Rainfall ranges from 100 in. in coastal areas to 200 in. in interior; NE monsoon (Oct.–March). Malaria is prevalent. Predominantly agr., the colony produces rice, sago, pepper. Rubber is a major product; lumbering and fishing are important. Stock raising and mining (gold, silver) are on a small scale. There are important oil fields at Miri. Coal mining ceased in 1932. Principal exports are oil, rubber, sago flour, jelutong or jungle rubber (*Dyera costulata*), pepper. Pop. consists of culturally diverse Malayan groups including the Dyaks, some of whom practice headhunting in interior. Roughly 25% of pop. is Chinese. Chief centers: Kuching, MIRI, SIBU, SIMANGGANG, LUTONG (oil-refining center). Sarawak was dependency of Brunei until 1841 when it was ceded to James Brooke for his aid in suppressing rebellion in 1840. Brooke ruled as raja over his domain which was originally small but which was gradually enlarged (1841–1905). Recognized 1888 by Britain as independent state, Sarawak became Br. protectorate. During Second World War it was occupied 1941–45 by the Japanese. The raja, Sir Charles Vyner Brooke (3d in line), resumed rule briefly in 1946, ceding country (July, 1946) to Britain. Sometimes Serawak.

Sarawaket, Mount, New Guinea: see FINISTERRE RANGE.

Sarawak River, S Sarawak, in W Borneo, formed by 2 branches rising in highlands S of Kuching near border of Indonesian Borneo, flows generally NE past Kuching to S.China Sea; navigable 22 mi. by ocean-going vessels to Kuching.

Sarawan (sŭrŭvän'), N division (□ 4,986; pop. 28,270) of Kalat state, central Baluchistan, W Pakistan; hq. at Mastung. Crossed N–S by Central Brahui Range; mountainous region, with several peaks 7–10,000 ft. high. Chief crops: wheat, millet, tobacco. Hand-loom carpet weaving, embroidering; livestock raising. Coal mined in NE section. Kalat and Mastung are trade centers. Pop. 97% Moslem.

Saray (särī'). **1** Village (pop. 3,486), Tekirdag prov., Turkey in Europe, on Ergene R. and 38 mi. NE of Tekirdag; wheat, rye, flax, sugar beets. Also spelled Serai, Sarai. **2** Village, Van prov., Turkey: see OZALP.

Saraya (särä'yä), village, SE Senegal, Fr. West Africa, 30 mi. NE of Kédougou; shea-nut butter, kapok, beeswax; livestock.

Sarayevo, Yugoslavia: see SARAJEVO.

Saraykoy (särīkû'ē), Turkish *Sarayköy,* village (pop. 4,458), Denizli prov., SW Turkey, on railroad, on Buyuk Menderes R., and 14 mi. NW of Denizli; lignite, chromium; cotton, barley.

Sarbaz (sărbäz'), town, Eighth Prov., in Baluchistan, SE Iran, 100 mi. NNE of Chahbahar; wheat, corn.

Sarbhang (sär'băng), village, S Bhutan, on small Saralbhanga R. and 55 mi. SSE of Punakha, on trade route from Kokrajhar (Assam); local trade center (rice, oranges, potatoes, mustard, salt). Annual fair. Pop. Nepalese.

Sarbinowo, Poland: see ZORNDORF.

Sarbisheh (särbēshĕ'), village, Ninth Prov., in Khurasan, E Iran, 40 mi. SE of Birjand and on Meshed-Zahidan highway; rug weaving. Uzbek watchtower near by.

Sarbogard (shär'bôgärd), Hung. *Sárbogárd,* town (pop. 7,076), Fejer co., W central Hungary, 23 mi. SSE of Szekesfehervar; rail junction; market center in agr. (wheat, corn, rye), dairy area.

Sarca River, Italy: see MINCIO RIVER.

Sarcedo (särchā'dô), village (pop. 709), Vicenza prov., Veneto, N Italy, 2 mi. E of Thiene; foundry, woolen mill.

Sarcelles (särsĕl'), town (pop. 6,222), Seine-et-Oise dept., N central France, N suburb of Paris, 10 mi. from Notre Dame Cathedral; mfg. (paints, pharmaceuticals, plastics).

Sarchí Norte (särchē' nôr'tä), village (1950 pop. 245), Alajuela prov., W central Costa Rica, 2 mi. NW of Grecia; tapioca milling, saddle making; coffee, sugar cane, beans, corn.

Sarcoxie (särkŏk'sē), city (pop. 1,042), Jasper co., SW Mo., near Spring R., 21 mi. E of Joplin; ships strawberries. Laid out 1834.

Sardanyola (särdänyō'lä), town (pop. 3,210), Barcelona prov., NE Spain, 8 mi. N of Barcelona; mfg. of soap, knit goods, insulating materials, cement pipes, windmills; produces sparkling wine.

Sardão, Cape (sŏrdä'ō), on SW coast of Portugal, 10 mi. W of Odemira; 37°36'N 8°49'W.

Sardar, Azerbaijan SSR: see KARYAGINO.

Sardara (sär'därä), village (pop. 3,541), Cagliari prov., W central Sardinia, 23 mi. SSE of Oristano; health resort (thermal baths 2 mi. W); mineral springs; bottling and munition works. Site of San Gregorio (13th-cent. church). Nuraghe near by.

Sarda River (sär'dŭ), in Nepal and N India, formed by junction of 2 headstreams 45 mi. SSE of Milam, India, on Nepal border; flows SSE (as Kali R.) along India-Nepal border, bet. Kumaun and Nepal Himalayas, becoming Sarda R. below Ramganga R. (right tributary) mouth, thence S across Siwalik Range and the Terai, SE into India, along Ganges Plain, and SSE to Gogra R. 20 mi. SW of Bahraich; total length, c.310 mi. Also called Chauka in lower course. **Sarda Canal** leaves right bank of river near BANBASSA, India (headworks; hydroelectric plant); irrigates large area of Uttar Pradesh N and S of Lucknow via numerous distributaries; opened 1928.

Sardarpur (sŭrdär'pŏŏr), town (pop. 2,381), W Madhya Bharat, India, on upper Mahi R. and 21 mi. WNW of Dhar; local trade in grain, cotton, timber; distillery.

Sardarshahr (sŭrdär'shŭhŭr), town (pop. 26,048), N Rajasthan, India, 75 mi. ENE of Bikaner, on Thar Desert; rail spur terminus; exports wool, cattle, leather goods; hand-loom weaving, pottery making; handicraft jewelry.

Sardasht (särdäsht'), town, Fourth Prov., in Azerbaijan, NW Iran, in Kurd country, 40 mi. SSW of Mehabad, near the Little Zab, 10 mi. E of Iraq border; sheep raising; grain, tobacco, grapes.

Sardegna, Sardinia: see SARDINIA.

Sardes, Asia Minor: see SARDIS.

Sardhana (sŭr'dŭnŭ), town (pop. 12,607), Meerut dist., NW Uttar Pradesh, India, on Upper Ganges Canal and 12 mi. NNW of Meerut; trades in wheat, millet, sugar cane, oilseeds, cotton. Noted as residence of Begum Sumru, a Kashmiri dancing girl who became wife of Luxemburg adventurer Walter Reinhardt (Sumru); former palace now orphanage and school. Hydroelectric station 10 mi. S, at village of Bhola.

Sardica, Bulgaria: see SOFIA.

Sardinal (särdēnäl'), village (dist. pop. 3,207), Guanacaste prov., NW Costa Rica, in Pacific coastal hills, 8 mi. NW of Filadelfia; sugar cane, stock.

Sardinas, Ancón de, or **Sardinas Bay** (ängkōn' dā särdē'näs), bay of the Pacific on Ecuador-Colombia coast, S of Mangles Point. Receives Mataje R., which forms the international boundary on a forested coastal plain.

Sardinata (särdēnä'tä), town (pop. 1,291), Norte de Santander dept., N Colombia, on cableway from Gamarra (Magdalena R.) to Cúcuta, and 25 mi. NW of Cúcuta; coffee, cacao, fique fibers. Mineral springs.

Sardinero, El (ĕl sär-dhēnä'rō), popular beach resort just NE of Santander, Santander prov., N Spain, on Bay of Biscay.

Sardinia (särdĭ'nēŭ, -nyŭ), Ital. *Sardegna* (särdā'nyä), second largest island (□ 9,196; pop. 1,005,249) in Mediterranean Sea; forms with some neighboring small isls., chiefly Sant'Antioco, San Pietro, Asinara, Maddalena, and Caprera, an autonomous region (□ 9,302; pop. 1,034,206) of Italy; ⊙ Cagliari. Separated from Corsica by Strait of Bonifacio (7.5 mi. wide), 160 mi. WSW of Rome. Situated bet. 38°51'N (Cape Teulada) and 41°15'N (Point Falcone), and bet. 8°10'E (Cape Caccia) and 9°49'E (Cape Comino); 166 mi. long, 89 mi. wide. Comprises 3 provs.: SASSARI (N), NUORO (central), Cagliari (S). Mountainous terrain, including (N) ranges of Catena del Marghine, Catena del Goceano, and Monti di Alà, extending SW–NE; in E center Monti del GENNARGENTU rises to 6,016 ft.; CAMPIDANO lowland in SW. Drained by Tirso, Flumini Mannu, and Flumendosa rivers. Hot, dry summers, moderate winters, strong N winds (summer and spring), and light rainfall (annual average 28 in.) ranging from 16 to 24 in. in lowlands to over 40 in. in highest mts. Malaria has long hampered development of isl., as did feudalism (abolished 1835). Forests, once covering 20% of area, reduced to 5% (cork in NE; evergreen oaks, chestnuts in E center). Leads Italy in production of cork. One of country's foremost mining regions (around IGLESIAS), producing zinc, lead, lignite, manganese, iron, antimony, molybdenum, copper, barite, kaolin, anthracite, talc, and steatite. Salt extraction near Cagliari and Carloforte. Has large pasture area (51.5%) and leads Italy in sheep and goat raising. Habitat of Mouflon sheep. Mixed agr. (cultivable area 28.6%) chiefly in Campidano lowland; cereals, grapes, olives, almonds, herbs, citrus fruit. Fisheries (tunny, lobster, coral, sea mussels, oysters) in SW (off San Pietro and Sant'Antioco isls.), W, and N. Mfg. concentrated at Cagliari, Iglesias, Carloforte, Tempio Pausania, Alghero, Olbia, and Macomer. Hydroelectric power plants at lakes Tirso and Coghinas. Chief ports: Cagliari (trade), Olbia (passenger service to mainland), and Carloforte (ore shipping). Exports salt, ores, wine, cereals, lignite; imports coal. Main railroad runs from Cagliari to Olbia, branching off at Chilivani for Sassari and Porto Torres and at Decimomannu for Iglesias. Earliest Sardinians, the prehistoric nuraghi-builders, are unknown (nuraghi zone from Sassari S to Oristano). Phoenicians were first civilized settlers (at Cagliari, Sant'Antioco). Carthaginians then gained control, followed by Romans (238 B.C.). Suffered Saracen invasions (8th–11th cent.), followed by long wars (11th–14th cent.) bet. Pisa and Genoa for supremacy over isl. After 1720 formed, under House of Savoy, part of kingdom of Sardinia, which included Savoy, Piedmont, and Nice, with Liguria added in 1814; after the wars of the Risorgimento, included most of Italy. Its king, Victor Emmanuel II, was proclaimed king of Italy in 1861. Under republican constitution (1947) received administrative autonomy.

Sardinia. 1 Village (pop. c.500), Erie co., W N.Y., on Cattaraugus Creek and 30 mi. SE of Buffalo; canned foods, dairy products; poultry, potatoes. 2 Village (pop. 699), Brown co., SW Ohio, 17 mi. SW of Hillsboro and on small White Oak Creek; lumber, veneer.

Sardis (sär'dĭs) or **Sardes** (–dēz), anc. ⊙ Lydia, W Asia Minor, in present-day Turkey, 35 mi. ENE of Smyrna, at foot of Mt. Tmolus, near Pactolus R. It was guarded by an almost impregnable rock citadel, but was taken by the Persians and later by the Romans. An early seat of Christianity, one of the "Seven Churches in Asia." Destroyed by Tamerlane. Important Hittite inscriptions have been found here.

Sardis, village (pop. estimate 500), SW B.C., in lower Fraser valley, on Chilliwack R., and 3 mi. S of Chilliwack; dairying; stock, fruit, hops, tobacco. Site of Coqualettza Indian tuberculosis hosp.

Sardis. 1 Town (pop. 695), Burke co., E Ga., 17 mi. SE of Waynesboro; sawmilling. 2 Town (pop. 176), Mason co., NE Ky., 12 mi. SW of Maysville, in outer Bluegrass agr. region. 3 Town (pop. 1,913), a ⊙ Panola co., NW Miss., c.50 mi. S of Memphis, Tenn.; trade center for agr., dairying, poultry, and timber area; cotton gins, lumber mills, creamery. Sardis Dam and Reservoir are E. Founded 1836. 4 Town (pop. 299), Henderson co., W Tenn., 32 mi. ESE of Jackson.

Sardis Dam, Miss.: see TALLAHATCHIE RIVER.

Sardis Reservoir, Miss.: see TALLAHATCHIE RIVER.

Sârdlok or **Sârdloq** (both: sär'lôk), fishing settlement (pop. 120), Julianehaab dist., SW Greenland, on the Atlantic, at mouth of Igaliko Fjord, 12 mi. S of Julianehaab; 60°32'N 45°59'W. Radio station.

Sardo (sär'dō), village (pop. 460), Wallo prov., NE Ethiopia, on Dessye-Assab road and 55 mi. NW of L. Abbé; 11°41'N 44°12'E. Chief center of AUSSA dist.

Sardoal (sŭrdwäl'), town (pop. 1,156), Santarém dist., central Portugal, 5 mi. NNE of Abrantes; agr. market; pottery mfg.

Sarema, Estonia: see SAARE.

Sarentino (särĕntē'nō), Ger. *Sarnthein,* village (pop. 777), Bolzano prov., Trentino–Alto Adige, N Italy, 10 mi. N of Bolzano; woolen blankets. Resort (alt. 3,153 ft.). Has 13th-cent. castle, church with 15th-cent. frescoes.

Sar-e-Pol, Iran: see SAR-I-PUL.

Sarepta, Syria: see ZAREPHATH.

Sarepta, Russian SFSR: see KRASNOARMEISK, Stalingrad oblast.

Sarez Lake (sŭryĕs'), Gorno-Badakhshan Autonomous Oblast, Tadzhik SSR, in the Pamir, 80 mi. NE of Khorog: 30 mi. long; alt. 10,500 ft. Murgab R. enters lake (E), leaves it (W) as BARTANG RIVER. Formed (1911) by landslide which destroyed Usoi village and blocked Murgab R.

Sarezzo (sărĕ'tsō), village (pop. 1,965), Brescia prov., Lombardy, N Italy, on Mella R. and 8 mi. N of Brescia; agr.-machinery factories, foundry.

Sarfanguak, Sarfánguak, or **Sarfánguaq** (all: säkhfäng'wäk), fishing settlement (pop. 149), Holsteinsborg dist., SW Greenland, at E end of Sarfanguak Isl. (17 mi. long, 3 mi. wide), on Ikertok Fjord, 35-mi. inlet of Davis Strait, 20 mi. E of Holsteinsborg; 66°53'N 52°54'W. Radio station.

Sargans (zärgäns'), town (pop. 1,878) and district (pop. 23,881), St. Gall canton, E Switzerland, 7 mi. SE of Wallenstadt.

Sargasso Sea (särgă'sō), part of North Atlantic Ocean, bet. 20° and 40°N, and 35° and 75°W, extending from the West Indies to the Azores. A large tract of relatively still water in midst of the clockwise ocean circulation, the Sargasso Sea is named for the prevalent sargasso weed (gulfweed).

Sargatskoye (sŭrgät'skŭyŭ), village (1948 pop. over 2,000), central Omsk oblast, Russian SFSR, on Irtysh R. and 40 mi. N of Omsk; dairy farming. Formerly Poselkovo-Sargatskoye.

Sargeant, village (pop. 121), Mower co., SE Minn., 13 mi. NE of Austin, in grain and livestock area.

Sargent, county (□ 855; pop. 7,616), SE N.Dak.; ⊙ Forman. Agr. area drained by Wild Rice R. Formed 1883.

Sargent. 1 Town, Calif.: see SAN JUAN BAUTISTA. 2 Village (pop. 818), Custer co., central Nebr., 20 mi. NE of Broken Bow and on Middle Loup R.; shipping point for grain and livestock region.

Sargentville, Maine: see SEDGWICK.

Sargodha (sŭrgō'dŭ), town (pop. 36,420), ⊙ Shahpur dist., central Punjab, W Pakistan, in Chaj Doab, on branch of Lower Jhelum Canal and 105 mi. WNW of Lahore. Rail junction (workshops); commercial center; trades in cotton, wheat, oilseeds, millet; cotton ginning, oilseed milling, rice husking, mfg. of flour, dal, soap, aerated water; engineering workshops, steel-rolling mill. Has col. Dairy and agr. farms and citrus orchards near by. Developed since early 1900s as hq. of Lower Jhelum Canal colony.

Sargur (sŭr'gōōr), town (pop. 3,033), Mysore dist., SW Mysore, India, on Kabbani R. and 25 mi. SW of Mysore; rice, millet, tobacco. Sometimes spelled Saragur.

Sarho, Djebel, Fr. Morocco: see SAGHO, DJEBEL.

Sari (särē'), town (1941 pop. 23,990), Second Prov., in E Mazanderan, N Iran, on Tajan R. (short Caspian coastal stream) and 20 mi. E of Babul, and on road and railroad from Teheran across Elburz mts.; rice, oranges, sugar cane. It was ⊙ Mazanderan until replaced by Babul in 19th cent.

Saria (sŭrē'ŭ), Aegean island (□ 8.2; pop. 20) in the Dodecanese, Greece, off N tip of Karpathos; 35°51'N 27°14'E; 4 mi. long, 2 mi. wide.

Sariaya (säryä'yä), town (1939 pop. 4,591; 1948 municipality pop. 29,904), Quezon prov., central Luzon, Philippines, 16 mi. ESE of San Pablo; agr. center (coconuts, rice).

Sáric (sä'rēk), town (pop. 340), Sonora, NW Mexico, 30 mi. SW of Nogales; wheat, corn, livestock.

Sarid (särēd'), settlement (pop. 500), NW Israel, in NW part of Plain of Jezreel, 5 mi. SW of Nazareth; mixed farming. School serves surrounding region. Modern settlement founded 1926 on site of biblical locality of same name.

Sarigan (särēgän') or **Sariguan** (särēgwän'), volcanic island (□2), N Marianas Isls., W Pacific, c.100 mi. N of Saipan; 2 mi. long; rises to 1,801 ft. Extinct volcano; feldspar basalt, limestone.

Sarikamis or **Sarikamish** (both: särŭ'kämŭsh"), Turkish *Sarıkamış,* town (pop. 10,513), Kars prov., NE Turkey, on railroad and 33 mi. SW of Kars; wheat, barley. Long disputed bet. Russians and Turks, it passed to Russian Armenia in 1878, scene of battle in 1914, reverted to Turkey by treaty of 1921.

Sarikei (sŭrēkā'), town (pop. 1,870), S Sarawak, in W Borneo, on Rajang R. and 25 mi. SW of Sibu; rubber, sago, rice; stock raising, fishing.

Sarikol Range or **Sarykol Range** (sŭrĭkōl', –kôl'), on China-USSR border, forming E edge of the Pamir; rises over 15,000 ft. The Muztagh Ata Range parallels it on the E.

Sarila (sŭrē'lŭ), village, Hamirpur dist., S Uttar Pradesh, India, 32 mi. WSW of Hamirpur. Was ⊙ former petty state of Sarila (□ 35; pop. 7,250) of Central India agency; in 1948, state merged with Vindhya Pradesh; in 1950, inc. into Hamirpur dist. of Uttar Pradesh.

Sarina (sŭrī'nŭ), town (pop. 1,729), E Queensland, Australia, 155 mi. NNW of Rockhampton; sugar-producing center.

Sariñena (särēnyā'nä), town (pop. 2,639), Huesca prov., NE Spain, on Alcanadre R. and 27 mi. SE of Huesca, in winegrowing dist.; flour milling; mfg. of sausages, soap. Olive oil, sugar beets, esparto in area. Monastery of Sigęs (founded in 12th cent.), with Gothic mural paintings in chapter house, is 9 mi. S.

Sarine River, Switzerland: see SAANE RIVER.

Sar-i-Pul (sŭr'-ĭ-pōōl'), town (pop. 10,000), Mazar-i-Sharif prov., N Afghanistan, 75 mi. WSW of Mazar-i-Sharif and on Sar-i-Pul R. (irrigation). Sar-i-Pul R. rises in the Band-i-Turkestan, flows 150 mi. N, disappearing into the desert N of Shibarghan.

Sar-i-Pul or **Sar-e-Pol** (both: sär'ĕpōl'), village, Fifth Prov., in Kermanshah, W Iran, 70 mi. W of Kermanshah, and on road to Qasr-i-Shirin, near Iraq border; junction for Ilam and Mehran. Sometimes called Sar-i-Pul Zahab, and simply Sarpol.

Saris, Czechoslovakia: see PRESOV.

Sarisap (shä'rĭ-shäp), Hung. *Sárisáp,* town (pop. 3,831), Komarom-Esztergom co., N Hungary, 9 mi. SSW of Esztergom; vineyards, wheat, corn, dairy farming.

Sarisbury (särz'–, sârz'–), town and parish (pop. 4,338), S Hampshire, England, near Hamble R. 5 mi. ESE of Southampton; agr. market; brickworks.

Sari Shaban, Greece: see CHRYSOUPOLIS.

Sarishabari, E Pakistan: see JAMALPUR.

Sarita (sŭrē'tŭ), village (pop. c.200), ⊙ Kenedy co., extreme S Texas, 21 mi. S of Kingsville; rail point in cattle-ranching area.

Sariwon (sä'rē'wŭn'), Jap. *Shariin* or *Syariin,* town (1944 pop. 42,957), Hwanghae prov., central Korea, N of 38°N, 35 mi. S of Pyongyang; rail junction; commercial center for agr. and mining area (coal, iron). Silk reeling, flour milling, cotton ginning. Damaged in fighting, 1951.

Sariyer (särŭyĕr'), Turkish *Sarıyer,* town (pop. 25,540), Turkey in Europe, on Bosporus 12 mi. NNE of Istanbul, included in Istanbul metropolitan area; commercial and residential suburb.

Sariz (särŭz'), Turkish *Sarız,* village (pop. 522), Kayseri prov., central Turkey, 55 mi. ESE of Kayseri; grain, legumes. Formerly Koyyeri, Turkish *Köyyeri.*

Sarjapur (sŭr'jäpoor), town (pop. 3,240), Bangalore dist., E Mysore, India, 15 mi. SE of Bangalore, in silk-growing area; training center for hand-loom weaving.

Sarju River (sŭr'jōō). 1 In Almora dist., Uttar Pradesh, India, right tributary of Ramganga R. 2 In Nepal and India, left tributary of Gogra R.; in Nepal, also called Babai.

Sark (särk), Fr. *Sercq* (sârk), island (1,274 acres; 1951 pop. 560), one of Channel Isls., 7 mi. E of Guernsey; 3½ mi. long, 2 mi. wide. Consists of 2 portions, Great Sark (N) and Little Sark (S), connected by natural isthmus (316 ft. high), the Coupée. Chief village, Creux (krû), is on E coast; interior is reached through series of tunnels from the landing at Creux. On E coast is lighthouse (49°26'N 2°20'W). Local govt. is a sort of survival of the feudal system.

Sarkad (shŏr'kŏd), town (pop. 12,633), Bihar co., E Hungary, 16 mi. ENE of Bekescsaba; market center; sugar refinery.

Sarkadkeresztur (shŏr'kŏtkĕ"rĕstōōr), Hung. *Sarkadkeresztúr,* town (pop. 2,624), Bihar co., E Hungary, 5 mi. N of Sarkad; cattle, hogs.

Sarkak or **Sarqaq** (both: säkh'käk), fishing and hunting settlement (pop. 207), Ritenbenk dist., W Greenland, on SE shore of Nugssuak peninsula, on the Vaigat, 20 mi. NW of Ritenbenk; 70°1'N 51°56'W.

Sarkand (sŭrkänt'), village (1948 pop. over 2,000), E Taldy-Kurgan oblast, Kazakh SSR, in the Dzungarian Ala-Tau, 80 mi. NE of Taldy-Kurgan; irrigated agr. (wheat); sheep.

Sarkany, Rumania: see SERCAIA.

Sarkikaraagac (shärkē'kärăch"), Turkish *Şarkikaraağaç,* village (pop. 3,305), Isparta prov., W central Turkey, near N end of L. Beysehir, 50 mi. NE of Isparta; wheat, barley, rye; opium.

Sarkisla (shärkŭshlä'), Turkish *Şarkışla,* village (pop. 3,731), Sivas prov., central Turkey, on railroad and 45 mi. SW of Sivas; wheat, potatoes, onions.

Sarkoy (shärkû'ē), Turkish *Şarköy,* village (pop. 3,567), Tekirdag prov., Turkey in Europe, on Sea of Marmara, 33 mi. SW of Tekirdag, in hilly, unproductive dist.; wheat, tobacco. Lignite in area. Sometimes spelled Sharkoy, Shar Keui.

Sark River, Dumfries, Scotland, rises 6 mi. SW of Langholm, flows 11 mi. S to head of Solway Firth 2 mi. SSW of Gretna Green. Lower course forms boundary bet. England and Scotland.

Sarlat (särlä'), town (pop. 3,748), Dordogne dept., SW France, 24 mi. SW of Brive-la-Gaillarde; meat-canning center (*pâté de foie gras* and truffles); distilling, mfg. (tin cans, edge tools). Trade in tobacco and green walnuts. Has medieval cathedral and numerous 14th–16th-cent. houses.

Sarleinsbach (zär'līnsbäkh), town (pop. 2,222), N Upper Austria, 20 mi. E of Passau, Germany, N of the Danube; summer resort (alt. 1,805 ft.).

Sarles, village (pop. 285), Cavalier and Towner counties, N N.Dak., 31 mi. WNW of Langdon; dairy products, livestock, grain. Port of entry.

Sarmakovo (sŭrmä'kŭvŭ), village (1926 pop. 4,046), NW Kabardian Autonomous SSR, Russian SFSR, on Malka R. and 27 mi. NW of Nalchik; potatoes, grain, livestock.

Sarmany (sŭrmä'nē), village (1939 pop. over 2,000), E Tatar Autonomous SSR, Russian SFSR, on Menzelya R. (left tributary of Ik R.) and 38 mi. SW of Menzelinsk; grain, livestock. Distilling near by. Also called Sarmanovo.

Sarmas or **Sarmasu** (sŭrmäsh'), Rum. *Sărmaş* or *Sărmaşu,* Hung. *Nagysármás* (nŏ'dyŭ-shär"mäsh), village (pop. 3,126), Cluj prov., W central Rumania, on railroad and 28 mi. E of Cluj; methane production. Methane is also produced at near-by Sarmasel (sŭrmŭshĕl'), Rum. *Sărmăşel,* Hung. *Kissármás* (kēsh'shärmäsh), which supplies natural gas by pipe line to Turda.

Sarmatia (särmā'shŭ), anc. district occupied by the Sarmatians (Latin *Sarmatae*) about the lower Don R. from 3d cent. B.C. through 2d cent. A.D. The term is vague and is also used for the territory into which the people were later driven by German pressure, along the Danube and across the Carpathians.

Sarmato (sär'mätō), village (pop. 1,552), Piacenza prov., Emilia-Romagna, N central Italy, 10 mi. W of Piacenza.

Sarmellek (shär'mĕl-lāk), Hung. *Sármellék*, town (pop. 2,342), Zala co., W Hungary, 17 mi. SE of Zalaegerszeg; vineyards, rye, corn; dairy farming.

Sarmiento, for Argentine names not found here: see under General Sarmiento.

Sarmiento (särmyĕn'tō). **1** Department, San Juan prov., Argentina: see Media Agua. **2** Department, Santiago del Estero prov., Argentina: see Garza.

Sarmiento. 1 or **Colonia Sarmiento** (kōlō'nyä), town (1947 census pop. 2,075), central Comodoro Rivadavia military zone, Argentina, bet. lakes Musters (W) and Colhué Huapí (E), on railroad and 80 mi. WNW of Comodoro Rivadavia; farming center in Senguerr valley irrigation area (alfalfa, fruit, sheep). **2** Town (pop. estimate 1,500), central Santa Fe prov., Argentina, 45 mi. NW of Santa Fe; grain and livestock center; dairying. Formerly called Ingeniero Boasi.

Sarmiento, Lake (□ 35), Magallanes prov., S Chile, 50 mi. S of L. Argentino, at S foot of Paine Range; 16 mi. long, 1–4 mi. wide; resort area.

Sarmiento, Mount, peak (7,500 ft.) in W part of main isl. of Tierra del Fuego, Chile, overlooking Gabriel Channel; 54°27'S 70°51'W.

Sarmine, Syria: see Sermin.

Sarmizegetuza (särmēzägätōō'zä), Hung. *Várhely* (vär'hā), village (pop. 975), Hunedoara prov., W central Rumania, in the Transylvanian Alps, on railroad and 25 mi. SSW of Deva; lumbering center. Extensive excavations here since 1944 uncovered large amphitheater, forum, and palace; it is believed to be the site of ancient ⊙ of Roman Dacia. Has archaeological mus. Also spelled Sarmisegetusa and Sarmizegetusa.

Sar Mountains or **Shar Mountains** (both: shär), Serbo-Croatian *Šar Planina*, or **Sara** or **Shara** (shä'rä), Serbo-Croatian *Šara*, mountain group, SW Yugoslavia, forming with the Pindus (S) the so-called Sar-Pindus system, a continuation of the Dinaric Alps. Located bet. the Metohija (N), Lepenac R. (NE), upper Vardar R. (E, S), and Albania (W); c.50 mi. long (NE–SW). Highest peak, the Turcin (8,863 ft.), is in the Rudoka. Chromium mines at Radusa and Gorance, and near the Ljuboten and the Jezerska Cesma. Noted for production of cheese.

Sarmousakli or **Sarmusakli**, Greece: see Pentapolis.

Sarna (sĕr'nä"), Swedish *Särna*, village (pop. 1,314), Kopparberg co., W Sweden, on upper East Dal R. and 110 mi. NW of Falun, near Norwegian border; winter-sports resort; stock raising, dairying. Has old church, folk mus.

Sarnano (särnä'nō), village (pop. 1,048), Macerata prov., The Marches, central Italy, 12 mi. S of Tolentino; metalworking machinery. Resort (alt. 1,768 ft.) with mineral waters.

Sarnath (sär'nät), anc. *Isipattana*, archaeological site, Benares dist., SE Uttar Pradesh, India, 4 mi. N of Benares city center. Mus. of Buddhist relics. One of 8 great places of Buddhist pilgrimage in anc. times. Site of Deer Park, where Buddha 1st preached after enlightenment at Buddh Gaya. Buddhist remains include an Asokan pillar, 6 monasteries dating from Kushan period, and a stupa. During Gupta period, center of a noted school of sculpture, including 1st cent. A.D. Bodhisattva image. Destroyed 12th cent. A.D. by an Afghan, Mohammud Ghori. Singhalese monastery contains body relics (considered to be authentic) of Buddha.

Sarne, Poland: see Sarnowa.

Sarnen (zär'nŭn), town (pop. 5,591), ⊙ Obwalden half-canton, central Switzerland, on the Sarner Aa, on L. of Sarnen, and 11 mi. SSW of Lucerne; tourist center; woodworking. Town hall (1729–32), local mus., cantonal library, church (1739–42).

Sarnen, Lake of, Ger. *Sarnersee* (zär'nŭrzā"), Obwalden half-canton, central Switzerland; 4 mi. long, □ 3; numerous fish.

Sarner Aa (zär'nŭr ä'), river of Unterwalden canton, central Switzerland, emerges from L. of Sarnen near Sarnen, flows 6 mi. NNE to L. of Lucerne near Alpnach.

Sarnersee, Switzerland: see Sarnen, Lake of.

Sarnia (sär'nēŭ), city (pop. 18,734), ⊙ Lambton co., S Ont., on St. Clair R., at foot of L. Huron, opposite Port Huron, Mich., and 55 mi. NE of Detroit; major coal, lumber, and grain transshipment port, with 2-mi.-long waterfront and extensive anchorages in St. Clair R. and L. Huron. Oil-refining center, serving surrounding oil fields. There are steel, lumber, and flour mills, grain elevators, machinery works, foundries. Bridge and tunnel link city with Port Huron. Founded 1833 as The Rapids, it was named (1836) Port Sarnia by Sir John Colborne, a former governor of Guernsey, which was called *Sarnia* by the Romans. Name changed to Sarnia, 1886.

Sarnia, Channel Isls.: see Guernsey.

Sarnico (sär'nēkō), village (pop. 2,410), Bergamo prov., Lombardy, N Italy, port on SW shore of Lago d'Iseo, at efflux of Oglio R., 14 mi. ESE of Bergamo. Rail terminus; silk industry, varnish works, whetstone factory; fisheries.

Sarno (sär'nō), town (pop. 14,811), Salerno prov., Campania, S Italy, near headwaters of Sarno R., 12 mi. NW of Salerno. Rail junction; agr. (cereals, fruit, wine, olive oil) and textile (hemp and cotton mills) center. Mineral springs (baths).

Sarno River (sär'nō), anc. *Sarnus*, in Campania, S Italy, rises at foot of S Apennines near Sarno, flows 10 mi. SW, past Scafati and the ruins of Pompeii, to Bay of Naples 2 mi. SSE of Torre Annunziata.

Sarnowa (särnō'vä), Ger. *Sarne* (zär'nŭ), town (1946 pop. 1,381), Poznan prov., W Poland, 3 mi. ENE of Rawicz; flour milling; cattle and horse trade.

Sarnthein, Italy: see Sarentino.

Sarny (sär'nē), city (1931 pop. 7,587), N Rovno oblast, Ukrainian SSR, on Sluch R. and 50 mi. NNE of Rovno; rail junction; flour and sawmilling, tanning, soap mfg.; stone quarrying. Kaolin deposits near by. Passed from Poland to Russia (1793); reverted to Poland (1921); ceded to USSR in 1945.

Sarobi (särōbē'), village, Kabul prov., E Afghanistan, on Kabul R. and 32 mi. E of Kabul. Site of projected hydroelectric station.

Sarola (sä'rōlŭ), village, SE Rajasthan, India, 55 mi. SE of Kotah; millet, oilseeds. Tobacco farm near by.

Saroma, Lake (särō'mä), Jap. *Saroma-ko*, lagoon (□ 58), E Hokkaido, Japan, 15 mi. NW of Abashiri; separated from Sea of Okhotsk by narrow sand spit with 2 openings; 16 mi. long, 5 mi. wide. Sometimes called Saruma.

Sarona, Palestine: see Hakirya.

Saronic Gulf (sŭrŏ'nĭk) or **Gulf of Aegina** (ējī'nŭ), anc. *Saronicus Sinus*, inlet of Aegean Sea, central Greece, bet. capes Sounion (NE) and Skylaion (SW), separates Attica (NE) from Peloponnesus (SW); 50 mi. long, 30 mi. wide. Connected by Corinth Canal (W) with Gulf of Corinth. Contains isls. of Salamis, Aegina, and Angistri. Its main ports are Piraeus (port of Athens), Eleusis, and Megara.

Saronno (särôn'nō), town (pop. 15,782), Varese prov., Lombardy, N Italy, 13 mi. NNW of Milan. Rail junction; industrial center; silk, cotton, paper, and flour mills; mfg. (textile machinery, glass, glue, liquor). Has sanctuary begun 1498.

Saronville (sâ'rŭnvĭl"), village (pop. 87), Clay co., S Nebr., 23 mi. E of Hastings.

Saros, Gulf of (sä'rôs), anc. *Sinus Melas*, inlet of Aegean Sea, Turkey in Europe, bordering E on Gallipoli Peninsula; 22 mi. wide, 37 mi. long.

Sarospatak (shä'rôsh-pŏtŏk), Hung. *Sárospatak*, town (pop. 13,213), Zemplen co., NE Hungary, on Bodrog R. and 26 mi. NNW of Nyiregyhaza; wineries, flour mills, brickworks. Calvinist acad. founded 1530; law school added in 18th cent.; library has 1308–1848 MSS. Fortress, now in ruins, dates from 13th cent.; Windischgrätz castle, from 19th cent.

Sarova (sä'rŭvŭ), town (1939 pop. over 500), NW Mordvinian Autonomous SSR, Russian SFSR, 21 mi. NNE of Temnikov, on rail spur from Shatki (Gorki oblast). Refractory-clay deposits near by. Formerly called Sarov.

Sarpa Lakes (sär'pŭ), chain of small lakes in SE Stalingrad oblast, Russian SFSR, along E foot of Yergeni Hills; extend c.100 mi. NNW–SSE, bet. the Volga at Krasnoarmeisk (S suburb of Stalingrad) and Caspian Lowland. Connected, in spring, by Sarpa R. flowing N to the Volga. Reached (1942) by Germans during Stalingrad drive. Stalingrad Dam project (begun 1951) uses the lake depression as irrigation reservoir for NW Caspian lowland.

Sarpan, Marianas Isls.: see Rota.

Sarpol, Iran: see Sar-i-Pul.

Sarpsborg (särps'bôr), city (pop. 12,943), Ostfold co., SE Norway, on Glomma R. (72-ft. falls) and 45 mi. SSE of Oslo; rail junction and paper-milling center, with cellulose and staple-fiber mills, and woodworking, chemical, and hydroelectric plants; also mfg. of condensed milk, electrical equipment. Largest paper mills are in SE suburb of Borregard or Borregaard (Nor. *Borregård*). Founded by St. Olaf, who established fortress here in 1016, Sarpsborg was meeting place of the Borgarthing, anc. law body. City was destroyed 1567 by Swedes, rebuilt 1838. Sandesund village, just W, is head of Glomma R. navigation and port for Sarpsborg. Surrounding Borge canton (pop. 6,176) has important lumbering industry and includes Vedsten (väd'stān) village (pop. 306), where Amundsen was b. Hafslund (häfs'lōōn), ESE suburb (pop. 709) of Sarpsborg, has ferroalloy and carbide works.

Sarpy, county (□ 230; pop. 15,693), E Nebr.; ⊙ Papillion. Agr. region bounded E by Missouri R. and Iowa, W and S by Platte R. Feed, livestock, grain, fruit, dairy and poultry produce. Formed 1857; lost territory (1943) to Pottawatamie co., Iowa.

Sarqaq, Greenland: see Sarkak.

Sarqardlit Island, Greenland: see Manermiut.

Sarrail, Mount (10,400 ft.), SW Alta., near B.C. border, in Rocky Mts., 45 mi. SSE of Banff; 50°35'N 115°10'W.

Sarralbe (säräb'), Ger. *Saaralben* (zä'rälbŭn), town (pop. 2,311), Moselle dept., NE France, on Saar R. and 8 mi. SSW of Sarreguemines; cement mfg. Important saltworks in area.

Sarraméa (särämā-ä'), village (dist. pop. 366), W central New Caledonia, 60 mi. NW of Nouméa; agr. products.

Sarrancolin (säräkôlē'), village (pop. 836), Hautes-Pyrénées dept., SW France, on the Neste and 13 mi. SE of Bagnères-de-Bigorre; mfg. of aluminum, abrasives. Marble quarries near by.

Sarrans, France: see Brommat.

Sarrat (särät'), town (1939 pop. 2,928; 1948 municipality pop. 14,345), Ilocos Norte prov., NW Luzon, Philippines, 5 mi. SW of Laoag; rice-growing center.

Sarre: see Saar.

Sarre, La (lä sär'), village (pop. 2,167), W Que., 40 mi. NNW of Rouyn; gold and copper mining, lumbering, pulpwood milling, dairying.

Sarreal (särääl'), town (pop. 1,560), Tarragona prov., NE Spain, 6 mi. NE of Montblanch; cement mfg., wine and olive-oil processing; agr. trade (cereals, vegetables, almonds).

Sarrebourg (särbōōr'), Ger. *Saarburg* (zär'bōōrk), town (pop. 7,013), Moselle dept., NE France, on the Saar and 28 mi. ENE of Lunéville; communications center near W end of Saverne Gap, and garrison town; mfg. (glass, clock springs, hardware, furniture), brewing, printing. Has natl. cemetery of prisoners of war who died in Germany.

Sarrebruck, Saar: see Saarbrücken.

Sarreguemines (särgŭmēn'), Ger. *Saargemünd* (zär'gŭmünt), town (pop. 12,876), Moselle dept., NE France, port on Saar R. (at influx of the Blies) and 9 mi. SSE of Saarbrücken; communications center on Saar border; mfg. (porcelain, cement, chemicals, strongboxes), tanning, copper and bronze smelting. Damaged in Second World War.

Sarrelouis, Saar: see Saarlouis.

Sarretudvari (shär'rātōōdvōrē), Hung. *Sárrétudvari*, town (pop. 4,805), Bihar co., E Hungary, 14 mi. ESE of Karcag; near-by swamps have been drained.

Sarre-Union (sär-ünyō'), Ger. *Saarunion* (zär'-ōōnyôn'), town (pop. 2,532), Bas-Rhin dept., E France, on the Saar and 14 mi. N of Sarrebourg; road center; mfg. (hats, chemical fertilizer, metal furniture).

Sarria (sä'ryä), town (pop. 2,916), Lugo prov., NW Spain, in Galicia, agr. trade center 18 mi. SSE of Lugo; meat processing; mfg. of dairy and flour products, linen, candy. Ships chestnuts, potatoes, vegetables. Mineral springs. Near by is Benedictine monastery of Samos (founded in 6th cent.).

Sarriá (säryä'), W section of Barcelona, NE Spain. Near by (W) is ruined Gothic Pedralbes convent, founded in 1327.

Sarrión (säryōn'), village (pop. 1,711), Teruel prov., E Spain, 20 mi. SE of Teruel; cereals, wine, saffron; lumber.

Sars (särs), town (1948 pop. over 2,000), SE Molotov oblast, Russian SFSR, 3 mi. NW of Chad; glassworking. Until 1939, Sarsinski Zavod.

Sarsawa (sŭrsä'vŭ), town (pop. 3,202), Saharanpur dist., N Uttar Pradesh, India, 10 mi. WNW of Saharanpur; wheat, rice, rape and mustard, gram, sugar cane. Important under early Moguls.

Sarsina (sär'sēnä), town (pop. 939), Forlì prov., Emilia-Romagna, N central Italy, near Savio R., 16 mi. SSW of Cesena. Bishopric. Has mus. with antiquities from near-by Roman necropolis. In Second World War, semi-destroyed and pop. decimated by German reprisals.

Sarsinski Zavod, Russian SFSR: see Sars.

Sars-la-Buissière, Belgium: see Fontaine-Valmont.

Sars-Poteries (sär-pôtŭrē'), village (pop. 1,740), Nord dept., N France, 5 mi. NE of Avesnes; pottery and glass mfg.

Sarstedt (zär'shtĕt), town (pop. 8,551), in former Prussian prov. of Hanover, NW Germany, after 1945 in Lower Saxony, on Innerste R., near its mouth on the Leine, and 7 mi. NW of Hildesheim; mfg. (chemicals, canned goods, flour products).

Sarstein (zär'shtīn), Alpine peak (6,483 ft.) of the Salzkammergut, in S Upper Austria near Styria line, overlooking L. of Hallstatt (SW). Excellent view. Pötschen Pass on N slope.

Sarstoon River (särstōōn'), Sp. *Sarstún*, on Guatemala–Br. Honduras border, rises in Alta Verapaz dept. N of Cahabón, flows 75 mi. E along frontier to Bay of Amatique at Guatemalan village of Sarstoon (1921 pop. 36), 25 mi. WNW of Puerto Barrios. Navigable for 25 mi. below rapids of Gracias a Dios for rubber and lumber shipments.

Sarszentmiklos (shär'sĕntmĭklōsh), Hung. *Sárszentmiklós*, town (pop. 3,054), Fejer co., W central Hungary, 25 mi. SSE of Szekesfehervar; agr. Rail junction at near-by Retszilas.

Sartaguda (särtägōō'dhä), town (pop. 1,295), Navarre prov., N Spain, on the Ebro and 7 mi. NW of Calahorra; sugar beets, pepper, potatoes, wine.

Sartana, Ukrainian SSR: see Primorskoye, Stalino oblast.

Sartas (sŭrtäs'), town (1939 pop. over 500), NW Ashkhabad oblast, Turkmen SSR, on W shore of Kara-Bogaz-Gol Gulf, 115 mi. N of Krasnovodsk; Glauber's salt extracted. Railroad crosses isthmus to Bek-Dash, Caspian Sea salt port, 13 mi. SW of Sartas. Also known as Poselok Severnykh Promyslov Ozera No. 6 [Rus.,=settlement No. 6 of N shore works].

Sarteano (särtĕä'nō), village (pop. 1,635), Siena prov., Tuscany, central Italy, 8 mi. SSE of Montepulciano; paper mill.

Sartell, village (pop. 662), Benton and Stearns counties, central Minn., on Mississippi R. just N of St. Cloud, in grain and livestock area. Paper plant here.

Sartène (särtĕn'), town (pop. 3,917), S Corsica, 24 mi. SSE of Ajaccio; trades in hides, skins, lumber, olive oil and wines through its seaport, PROPRIANO, 5 mi. NW. Preserves medieval appearance. Here vendetta has survived most obstinately.

Sarteneja (särtĕnä'hä), village (pop. 359), Northern Dist., Br. Honduras, on Chetumal Bay of Caribbean Sea, 17 mi. E of Corozal; coconuts; fisheries.

Sarthe (särt), department (□ 2,411; pop. 412,214), in Maine, W France; ⊙ Le Mans. Generally level region with low hilly ranges in N and NW; drained by the Sarthe and its tributaries (Huisne and Loir). Chiefly agr., leading France in hemp cultivation; also grows potatoes, cereals, apples, and pears; raises Percheron draft horses, cattle, and poultry. Anthracite mines near Sablé-sur-Sarthe; marble quarries. Chief industry is paper milling (Bessé-sur-Braye, La Flèche, Le Lude), followed by hemp processing and metalworking (Le Mans, Sablé-sur-Sarthe). Principal towns are Le Mans, La Flèche, Sablé-sur-Sarthe, and La Ferté-Bernard.

Sarthe River, Sarthe and Maine-et-Loire dept., W France, rises in Perche hills 8 mi. N of Mortagne (Orne dept.), flows 175 mi. S and SW, past Alençon, Le Mans (head of navigation), Sablé-sur-Sarthe, and Châteauneuf-sur-Sarthe, joining the Mayenne above Angers to form MAINE RIVER. Receives the Huisne and the Loir (left).

Sartilly (särtēyē'), village (pop. 569), Manche dept., NW France, 7 mi. NW of Avranches; furniture mfg. Agr. school.

Sartirana Lomellina (särtērä'nä lômĕl-lē'nä), village (pop. 2,647), Pavia prov., Lombardy, N Italy, near confluence of Sesia R. with the Po, 10 mi. SSW of Mortara.

Sartlan, Lake (sŭrtlän') (□ 104), SW Novosibirsk oblast, Russian SFSR, 20 mi. S of Barabinsk, in Baraba Steppe; 17 mi. long, 11 mi. wide; well stocked with fish.

Sartoroy, Norway: see STORE SOTRA.

Sartrouville (särtrōōvēl'), town (pop. 17,494), Seine-et-Oise dept., N central France, an outer NW suburb of Paris, 10 mi. from Notre Dame Cathedral, on right bank of the Seine, opposite Maisons-Laffitte; aircraft factory.

Saruhan, Turkey: see MANISA, province.

Saruhashi (särōō'hāshē), town (pop. 6,681), Yamanashi prefecture, central Honshu, Japan, 23 mi. E of Kofu; raw silk.

Sarum, New, England: see SALISBURY.

Sarum, Old, England: see OLD SARUM.

Saruma, Lake, Japan: see SAROMA, LAKE.

Sarumilla, Peru: see ZARUMILLA.

Saruq (särōōk'), village, First Prov., in Arak, W central Iran, 26 mi. NNW of Arak; wheat, grapes, melons. Noted for its rugs.

Sarur (särōōr'), town, Eastern Hajar dist., Oman, 35 mi. SW of Muscat; chief center of fertile Sama'il (Sema'il) valley irrigated by the Wadi Sama'il; date-growing center; cotton; orchards; cloth weaving.

Sarus River, Turkey: see SEYHAN RIVER.

Sarvar (shär'vär), Hung. *Sárvár*, town (pop. 11,678), Vas co., W Hungary, on Gyöngyös R. and 14 mi. E of Szombathely; rail junction; mfg. (sugar, wool, artificial silk), metal-, brickworks; agr., dairy farming near by.

Sarviz River (shär'vĭz), Hung. *Sárvíz*, W central Hungary; formed by confluence of Sed and Gaja rivers W of Szekesfehervar; flows 60 mi. SE to the Danube near Szekszard. Drainage canal (Malom Canal) parallels its upper course.

Sarwar (sŭrvär'), town (pop. 4,054), E central Rajasthan, India, 37 mi. SSE of Kishangarh; local market (millet, barley, gram, cotton). Garnet and mica deposits worked near by.

Sary-Adyr (sŭrē"-ŭdĭr'), village, NE Akmolinsk oblast, Kazakh SSR, 95 mi. NE of Akmolinsk; extensive coal deposits.

Saryagach (sŭrē"ŭgäch'), village (1939 pop. over 2,000), S South Kazakhstan oblast, Kazakh SSR, on Trans-Caspian RR (Kzyl-Tu station) and 10 mi. NW of Tashkent; cotton-ginning center.

Sary-Assiya (–äsē'ŭ), village (1926 pop. 1,627), NE Surkhan-Darya oblast, Uzbek SSR, on railroad and 90 mi. NNE of Termez; cotton; metalworks.

Sarych, Cape (sŭrĭch'), southernmost point of Crimea, Russian SFSR, on Black Sea, 11 mi. SE of Balaklava; 44°23'N 33°47'E.

Sary-Chashma (sŭrē"-chŭshmä'), village (1939 pop. over 500), SE Kulyab oblast, Tadzhik SSR, near Panj R., c.20 mi. SE of Kulyab; wheat, fruit.

Sarychev Peak, Russian SFSR: see MATUA ISLAND.

Saryeksan Dag (shäryĕk-shän' dä), Turkish *Şaryeksan Dağ*, peak (8,402 ft.), E central Turkey, in the Taurus Mts., 15 mi. ESE of Palu.

Saryg-Bulun (sŭrĭk"-bōōlōōn'), village, S Tuva Autonomous Oblast, Russian SFSR, 90 mi. SSE of Kyzyl, on Kyzyl-Uliassutai road, on Tes R.

Saryg-Sep (–syĕp'), village, E central Tuva Autonomous Oblast, Russian SFSR, on the Lesser Yenisei and 50 mi. ESE of Kyzyl.

Sary-Ishik-Otrau (sŭrē'-ēshĭk'-ŭtrou'), sandy desert in Taldy-Kurgan and Alma-Ata oblasts, Kazakh SSR, in the Dzhety-Su, S of L. Balkhash (fisheries), bet. Ili and Kara-Tal rivers; sheep.

Sary-Khosor (–khŭsôr'), village (1939 pop. over 500), N Kulyab oblast, Tadzhik SSR, 40 mi. N of Kulyab; wheat, walnut woods, sheep.

Sarykol Range, China and USSR: see SARIKOL RANGE.

Sary-Su (sŭrē"-sōō'), river in central Kazakh SSR, rises in several branches in Kazakh Hills, flows 465 mi. SW, along W edge of the Bet-Pak-Dala, to a small lake, Tele-Kul, 60 mi. NE of Kzyl-Orda; pastures in lower course. Formerly drained into the Syr Darya.

Sary-Uzek (–ōōzyĕk'), town (1942 pop. over 500), S Taldy-Kurgan oblast, Kazakh SSR, in the Dzungarian Ala-Tau, on Turksib RR and 50 mi. SSW of Taldy-Kurgan; highway (E) to China-USSR border. Also spelled Sary-Ozek.

Sarzana (särtsä'nä), town (pop. 4,645), La Spezia prov., Liguria, N Italy, near Magra R., 7 mi. E of Spezia; rail junction. Industrial and commercial center: glass, bricks, paving stones; wine, grain, olive oil, canned foods. Bishopric since 1202 (transferred here from near-by LUNA). Has white-marble cathedral (1355–1477; roof damaged in Second World War), 13th-cent. Pisan castle (altered 1488, 1496; now a prison), remains of 15th-cent. town walls. Pope Nicholas V b. here. On near-by hill is 10th-cent. fortress of Sarzanello (damaged in Second World War).

Sarzeau (särzō'), village (pop. 819), Morbihan dept., W France, on Rhuis Peninsula, 9 mi. S of Vannes; oyster beds. Le Sage b. here. Just SE is ruined 13th-15th-cent. castle of Sucinio, anc. residence of dukes of Brittany.

Sasa (sä'sä) or **Saza** (sä'zä), town (pop. 17,255), Nagasaki prefecture, NW Kyushu, Japan, on W Hizen Peninsula, 7 mi. NW of Sasebo; agr. center (rice, wheat, sweet potatoes).

Sasabe (sŭsä'bē), village, Pima co., S Ariz., port of entry at Mex. line, 35 mi. WNW of Nogales.

Sasagawa (säsä'gäwŭ) or **Sasakawa** (–käwŭ), town (pop. 5,939), Chiba prefecture, central Honshu, Japan, on Tone R. and 12 mi. NW of Choshi; rice, poultry, raw silk.

Sasaguri (säsä'gōōrē), town (pop. 5,861), Fukuoka prefecture, N Kyushu, Japan, 7 mi. E of Fukuoka; rice, wheat; coal.

Sasaima (säsī'mä), village (pop. 797), Cundinamarca dept., central Colombia, in Cordillera Oriental, 33 mi. NW of Bogotá; alt. 4,019 ft.; sericulture. The silk is exported to the U.S.

Sasakawa, Japan: see SASAGAWA.

Sasakwa (sŭsä'kwŭ), town (pop. 365), Seminole co., central Okla., 13 mi. S of Wewoka, in agr. area.

Sasamón (säsämōn'), town (pop. 1,046), Burgos prov., N Spain, 18 mi. WNW of Burgos; grain- and winegrowing, stock raising.

Sasape (säsä'pā), village (pop. 1,813), Lambayeque dept., NW Peru, on coastal plain, in irrigated Leche R. valley, 13 mi. N of Lambayeque; rice, corn, cotton.

Sasaram (sŭs'ŭräm), town (pop. 27,201), Shahabad dist., W Bihar, India, on tributary of the Ganges and 60 mi. SW of Arrah; rail junction; trades in rice, wheat, gram, oilseeds, barley; carpet and pottery mfg. Tomb of Sher Shah, Afghan emperor of Delhi, here. Cement mfg. 20 mi. SSW, at Banjari.

Sasayama (säsä'yämŭ), town (pop. 8,167), Hyogo prefecture, S Honshu, Japan, 31 mi. WNW of Kyoto; rail terminus; agr. center (rice, wheat, mushrooms, bamboo shoots); raw silk, charcoal, paper and pottery making.

Sasbach (zäs'bäkh), village (pop. 1,991), S Baden, Germany, 4.5 mi. SW of Bühl; lumber milling. Has monument to Marshal Turenne, who was killed in battle here (1675).

Sasca-Montana (sä'skä-môntä'nŭ), Rum. *Sasca Montană*, Hung. *Szászkabánya* (sä'skōbä'nyŏ), village (pop. 1,027), Severin prov., SW Rumania, 11 mi. SSE of Oravita; iron mining; saltworks.

Saschiz (säskēz'), Hung. *Szászkézd* (säs'kāzd), village (pop. 2,126), Sibiu prov., central Rumania, 13 mi. ESE of Sighisoara. Has old fortified church.

Sasd (shäzhd), Hung. *Sásd*, town (pop. 2,154), Baranya co., S Hungary, 17 mi. SE of Kaposvar; potatoes, nuts, hogs.

Sasebo (säsā'bō), city and naval port (1940 pop. 205,989; 1947 pop. 175,233), Nagasaki prefecture, W Kyushu, Japan, on NW Hizen Peninsula, 30 mi. NNW of Nagasaki, on Sasebo harbor (3.5 mi. long, 1 mi. wide; inlet of E.China Sea), near mouth of Omura Bay; 33°10'N 129°43'E. Naval base. Coal mines near by. Includes Ainoura (since 1938) and Haiki (since early 1940s). Heavily bombed in Second World War.

Saseno (sä'sĕnō), Albanian *Sazan* (sä'zän) or *Sazani* (sä'zänē), fortified island (□ 2.2) of Albania, in Strait of Otranto, off Bay of Valona and 3 mi. NNW Cape Linguetta; 2.5 mi. long, 1.5 mi. wide; rises to 1,086 ft. The anc. Sason, it was occupied (1914; confirmed 1920) by Italians, who developed isl. as major naval base guarding entrance to the Adriatic. Returned to Albania by Treaty of Paris (1947).

Sashalom (shŏsh-hŏlôm), E residential suburb (pop. 14,219) of Budapest, Pest-Pilis-Solt-Kiskun co., N central Hungary; mfg. (gymnastic apparatus, felt hats, candy).

Sashiki (sä'shĭkē), town (pop. 11,430), Kumamoto prefecture, W Kyushu, Japan, on Yatsushiro Bay, 36 mi. SSW of Kumamoto; commercial center; rice, charcoal. Fishing.

Sasic Lagoon, Ukrainian SSR: see SASYK LAGOON.

Saskatchewan (săskă'chŭwŏn"), province (land area □ 237,975, total □ 251,700; 1946 pop. 832,688; 1948 estimate 854,000), W central Canada, one of the Prairie Provinces; ⊙ Regina. Bounded by Mackenzie Dist. (N), Alta. (W), Mont. and N.Dak. (S), and Man. (E). S part of prov. is undulating prairie country, generally over 1,500 ft. high, rising to over 4,500 ft. in the Cypress Hills near Alta. border. Several elevated regions in S center rise to over 2,000 ft. and comprise the Touchwood and Beaver hills and Moose Mtn. N part of prov. is forested and is partly on edge of the Laurentian Plateau. Prov. is drained by the Saskatchewan, Beaver, Churchill, Qu'Appelle, and Assiniboine rivers. There are numerous lakes (N); largest are lakes Athabaska, Reindeer, Cree, Wollaston, Churchill, Peter Pond, Methy, Snake, Lac la Ronge, Doré, and Deschambault. Temperature ranges are from 10°F. (SW) to –23°F. (NE) in January; from 67°F. (S) to 57°F. (N) in July. Average annual rainfall ranges from 7–20 inches (W) to 10–26 inches (E). Minerals include important lignite coal deposits near U.S. boundary; gold and copper are found in NE; pitchblende working has begun in L. Athabaska region. Sodium sulphate and magnesium sulphate are produced extensively; oil and natural gas are exploited near Lloydminster, on Alta. border. Brick and pottery clay are also worked. Wheat is chief crop in S part of prov., ranching country begins in SW. S central Sask. is grain-growing, mixed-farming, and dairying country. N of Prince Albert important timber stands are worked. Besides Regina, other cities are Moose Jaw, North Battleford, Prince Albert, Swift Current, Weyburn, and Yorkton. Important towns are Assiniboine, Estevan, Humboldt, Indian Head, Kamsack, Maple Creek, Melfort, Melville, and Nipawin. Of early importance to the fur trade, territory of present prov. was 1st visited by white men at end of 17th cent.; in middle of 18th cent. several French trading posts were established, followed by Hudson's Bay Co. and North West Co. posts. Hudson's Bay Co. territories were acquired (c.1870) by the Dominion and became part of the Northwest Territories. Arrival of Canadian Pacific RR (1882) and later completion of the Soo Line from the United States resulted in heavy influx of settlers. Region was scene of Riel's Rebellion in 1884. Sask. became prov. of Canada in 1905. Its population has shown marked increases and decreases: 1911 pop. 492,432; 1921 pop. 757,510; 1931 pop. 921,785; 1941 pop. 895,992.

Saskatchewan, Mount (10,964 ft.), SW Alta., in Rocky Mts., in Banff Natl. Park, 70 mi. SE of Jasper, overlooking North Saskatchewan R.

Saskatchewan River, Canada, is formed in Sask 30 mi. E of Prince Albert by confluence of 2 great streams, the North Saskatchewan and the South Saskatchewan, which rise in Rocky Mts. of W Alta. and drain the great plains of Alta. and Sask. The North Saskatchewan rises in Columbia Icefield at foot of Mt. Saskatchewan, flows generally E in a rapid and winding course, past Rocky Mountain House and Edmonton (Alta.) and North Battleford and Prince Albert (Sask.); 760 mi. long; navigable for barges below Rocky Mountain House, and for small steamers below Edmonton, during 2 summer months; chief tributaries are Clearwater, Brazeau, Vermilion and Battle rivers. The South Saskatchewan is formed by confluence of Bow and Oldman rivers in S Alta., flows E past Medicine Hat, then NE and into Sask. (where it receives Red Deer R.) and E once more, turning N in S Sask. to flow past Saskatoon to its junction with the North Saskatchewan E of Prince Albert; length 550 mi. (with Bow R., 865 mi.). From junction of these 2 streams the Saskatchewan flows 340 mi. E, past Nipawin and into Manitoba, past The Pas, and through Cedar L. to L. Winnipeg; length to the head of Bow R., 1,205 mi. In fur-trading days it was chief artery to the western plains and to mtn. region beyond; many trading posts were on it.

Saskatoon (săskŭtōōn'), city (pop. 46,028), S central Sask., on South Saskatchewan R. (5 bridges) and 150 mi. NW of Regina; distributing center for large farming region; grain elevators, stockyards, breweries, cereal-food plants, tractorworks, metal and woodworking plants, meat-packing plants; mfg. of machinery, chemicals, soap, powdered eggs. Site of Univ. of Sask., agr. col., experimental farm, tree nurseries, and Dominion Forestry Station. Site was laid out 1883; reached by railroad 1890. Its development was rapid after inc. as city in 1906; 1911 pop. 12,004; 1921 pop. 25,739; 1931 pop. 43,291.

Saskylakh (sŭskĭläkh'), village (1948 pop. over 500), NW Yakut Autonomous SSR, Russian SFSR, on Anabar R. (head of navigation) and 140 mi. SE of Nordvik; reindeer raising, hunting.

Saslaya (säslī'ä), highest peak (6,500 ft.) of Nicaragua, in E Cordillera Isabelia, 35 mi. SW of Bonanza.

Sasni (säs'nē), town (pop. 4,265), Aligarh dist., W Uttar Pradesh, India, 12 mi. S of Aligarh; glass mfg.; wheat, barley, pearl millet, gram.

Sason (sä'sōn), village, Sambalpur dist., NW Orissa, India, on railroad and 8 mi. NE of Sambalpur; rice milling.

Sason, Turkey: see SASUN.

Sasov (sä'sûf), Pol. *Sasów* (sä'sōōf), town (1931 pop. 3,112), SE Lvov oblast, Ukrainian SSR, 5 mi. NNE of Zolochev; paper mfg., flour milling; stone quarrying. Founded 1615; site of defeat (1649) of Tatars. Noted delftware-mfg. center under Austrian rule (1772–1919). Reverted to Poland (1919); ceded to USSR in 1945.

Sasovo (sä'sùvŭ), city (1939 pop. 16,000), E Ryazan oblast, Russian SFSR, on Tsna R. and 90 mi. ESE of Ryazan; textile milling, metalworking, flour milling.

Sasow, Ukrainian SSR: see SASOV.

Saspamco, village (1940 pop. 597), Wilson co., S Texas, near San Antonio R., 17 mi. SE of San Antonio; tile mfg.

Sassabaneh (sä'säbänä), village, Harar prov., SE Ethiopia, in the Ogaden, bet. Fafan and Jerer rivers, on road and 22 mi. SE of Dagahbur; nomadic stock raising (camels, sheep). Occupied by Italians (1936) in Italo-Ethiopian War and by British (1941) in Second World War.

Sassafras, mining village (pop. 1,333, with near-by Wiscoal). Knott co., E Ky., 8 mi. ESE of Hazard; bituminous coal.

Sassafras Mountain (3,560 ft.), NW S.C., highest point in S.C., in the Blue Ridge NW of Greenville, near N.C. line.

Sassafras River, NE Md., on the Eastern Shore; rises just over Del. line in New Castle co., flows c.20 mi. W through Md., forming Cecil-Kent co. line, to Chesapeake Bay at Betterton; navigable to Fredericktown.

Sassandra (sùsăn'drù), town (pop. c.4,200), SW Ivory Coast, Fr. West Africa, minor Atlantic (Gulf of Guinea) port, at mouth of Sassandra R., 145 mi. W of Abidjan. Ships cacao, coffee, rubber, kola nuts, dried and fresh bananas, palm kernels, hardwood. Fishing (lobster, shrimps). Sawmilling. Airfield. Customhouse. R.C. and Protestant missions. Vegetable-oil institute in vicinity (SW).

Sassandra River, W Ivory Coast, Fr. West Africa, rises in uplands near Upper Volta border, flows c.350 mi. S and SSE to Gulf of Guinea at Sassandra. Navigation impeded by rapids.

Sassano (säs-sä'nô), village (pop. 2,614), Salerno prov., Campania, S Italy, 5 mi. SSW of Sala Consilina.

Sassari (säs'särē), province (□ 2,903; pop. 302,362), N Sardinia; ⊙ Sassari. Mtn. terrain (granitic in NE, volcanic in NW), rising to 4,468 ft. at Monte Limbara; drained by Coghinas R. and 3 Mannu rivers; average elev. 984 ft. Cork forests in NE. Deposits of iron (NW), lead and zinc at Argentiera-Nurra, copper and cadmium near Alghero; granite quarries (NE), white marble (NW). Livestock raising (sheep, goats, cattle, pigs) in NW and about Tempio Pausania. Agr. (18% of area) mainly in NW (barley, corn, olives, potherbs, tobacco); potatoes and oats in NE; also fruit (pears) S of L. Coghinas; vineyards. Fisheries (lobster, tunny, coral) in NE and NW. Industry concentrated at Sassari, Tempio Pausania, and Alghero. Served by main N-S rail line, forking at Chilivani, to chief ports of Olbia, Porto Torres, and Alghero. Numerous nuraghi S of Sassari.

Sassari, city (pop. 44,130), ⊙ Sassari prov., N Sardinia, 110 mi. NNW of Cagliari; 40°43'N 8°33'E. Rail junction; agr. center; cheese, olive oil, macaroni, agr. machinery, furniture, clothing, leather goods, glass, pottery, toys, pharmaceuticals, soap. Archbishopric. Has cathedral of San Nicola, several palaces, and university (founded 1677) with archaeological mus. Its port is Porto Torres, 11 mi. NNW, on Gulf of Asinara. Important in Middle Ages.

Sassenage (säsùnäzh'), village (pop. 1,130), Isère dept., SE France, near the Isère, 4 mi. WNW of Grenoble; perfume and slaked-lime mfg. Goat raising (for cheese) in area.

Sassenheim (sä'sùnhīm), town (pop. 7,171), South Holland prov., W Netherlands, 5 mi. N of Leiden, at E foot of North Sea dunes; bulb and flower growing (hothouses); mfg. (crates, boxes, window frames). Ruins of 11th-cent. Teilingen castle.

Sasser, town (pop. 371), Terrell co., SW Ga., 14 mi. NW of Albany, in agr. area.

Sassetot-le-Mauconduit (sästō'-lù-mōkōdwē'), village (pop. 642), Seine-Inférieure dept., N France, 8 mi. NE of Fécamp. Beach resort of Les Petites-Dalles is 1.5 mi. N.

Sassière, Lac de la, France: see TIGNES.

Sassmacken, Latvia: see VALDEMARPILS.

Sassnitz (zäs'nĭts), town (pop. 6,841), in former Prussian Pomerania prov., N Germany, after 1945 in Mecklenburg, on E Rügen isl., on the Baltic, 25 mi. NE of Stralsund. Fishing and canning center; terminus (since 1909) of ferry train to Trelleborg, Sweden. Seaside resort. Near by are large chalk quarries. Port established here in 1896; developed after 1945 as center of Mecklenburg sea fisheries.

Sassoferrato (säs"sôfĕr-rä'tô), town (pop. 2,070), Ancona prov., The Marches, central Italy, 7 mi. NNW of Fabriano; mfg. (cement, shoes, macaroni). Has church with a Madonna by G. Salvi, surnamed Sassoferrato, who was b. here. Near by are ruins of anc. Sentinum, where Romans gained decisive victory (295 B.C.) over allied Samnites and Gauls.

Sasso Pisano (säs'sō pēsä'nô), village (pop. 568), Pisa prov., Tuscany, central Italy, 13 mi. SSW of Volterra. Has *soffioni* used to produce boric acid and electricity.

Sass Town (săs), town, Sinoe co., SE Liberia, minor port on Atlantic Ocean, 50 mi. ESE of Greenville; copra, cassava, rice; cattle raising. Sometimes spelled Soss Town.

Sassuolo (säs-swô'lô), town (pop. 5,499), Modena prov., Emilia-Romagna, N central Italy, near Secchia R., 10 mi. SW of Modena; wine and liquor distilleries, tannery, cork factory, pottery works; agr. machinery, sausage. Has Este palace, transformed 1634 from anc. castle.

Sástago (sä'stägō), town (pop. 2,627), Saragossa prov., NE Spain, on the Ebro and 17 mi. WNW of Caspe; calcium-carbide mfg.; agr. trade (cereals, olive oil, wine, sheep).

Sastin (shäsh'tyĭn), Slovak *Šaštín*, Hung. *Sasvár* (shŏsh'vär), village (pop. 2,438), W Slovakia, Czechoslovakia, on railroad and 14 mi. SE of Breclav; pilgrimage center with picturesque castle remains.

Sastre (sä'strā), town (pop. estimate 2,500), ⊙ San Martín dept. (□ c.1,900; 1947 pop. 50,644), W central Santa Fe prov., Argentina, 65 mi. W of Santa Fe; rail junction and farming center (wheat, flax, barley, alfalfa, livestock; plant nursery). Produces harvesters, dairy products.

Sas-Tyube (säs"-tyōōbyĕ'), town (1945 pop. over 500), SE South Kazakhstan oblast, Kazakh SSR, on Turksib RR and 25 mi. NE of Chimkent. Also spelled Sas-Tobe.

Sasun (sä'sōōn), village (pop. 1,144), Siirt prov., SE Turkey, 40 mi. NW of Siirt; grain. Sometimes spelled Sason. Formerly Kabilcoz.

Sasun Dag, Turkish *Sasun Dağ*, peak (9,735 ft.), E central Turkey, in Bitlis Mts., 8 mi. E of Sasun. Sometimes called Malato Dag.

Sasvad (sä'svŭd), town (pop. 5,745), Poona dist., central Bombay, India, 15 mi. SE of Poona; market center for millet, gur, peanuts. Sometimes spelled Saswad.

Sas van Gent (säs' fän khĕnt'), town (pop. 3,512), Zeeland prov., SW Netherlands, on Flanders mainland and 8 mi. S of Terneuzen, on Ghent-Terneuzen Canal, at Belg. border; sugar refining; starch, glucose, flour, glass mirrors, chemicals, dyes, textiles.

Sasyk-Kul or **Sasyk-Kul'** (sŭsĭk"-kōōl'), salt lake (□ 180) along border of Semipalatinsk and Taldy-Kurgan oblasts, Kazakh SSR, just NW of the Ala-Kul, 65 mi. E of E end of L. Balkhash; swampy shores.

Sasyk Lagoon (sŭsĭk'), Rum. *Sasic* (säsēk'), or **Kunduk Lagoon** (kōōndōōk'), Rum. *Cunduc* (kōōndōōk'), Black Sea coastal lagoon, SE Izmail oblast, Ukrainian SSR, N of Danube R. delta, 15 mi. NE of Kiliya; separated from sea by narrow sandspit; 20 mi. long, 8 mi. wide. Receives Kogalnik R. (N) at Tatarbunary.

Sasykoli (sŭsĭkô'lyē), village (1926 pop. 4,837), NE Astrakhan oblast, Russian SFSR, on Akhtuba R. and 95 mi. NNW of Astrakhan; fruit, cotton, wheat; cattle, sheep. Formerly Sasykolskoye.

Sata, Cape (sä'tä), Jap. *Sata-misaki*, southernmost point of Kyushu, Japan, on S Osumi Peninsula; forms NW side of entrance to Osumi Strait; 31°N 130°40'E; lighthouse.

Satadougou (sätädōō'gōō), village, SW Fr. Sudan, Fr. West Africa, on Falémé R. (Senegal border) and 120 mi. S of Kayes; gold placers. Meteorological station, dispensary.

Satahip, Thailand: see SATTAHIP.

Satak, Turkey: see CATAK.

Satalia, Turkey: see ANTALYA, city.

Satana (sŭtä'nŭ), village (pop. 6,652), Nasik dist., central Bombay, India, 50 mi. NE of Nasik; local market for cotton, gur, wheat; handicraft cloth weaving, oilseed milling.

Satanger, Indonesia: see TENGA ISLANDS.

Satankulam, India: see SATTANKULAM.

Satanov (sŭtŭnôf'), town (1926 pop. 4,056), W Kamenets-Podolski oblast, Ukrainian SSR, on Zbruch R. and 40 mi. NNW of Kamenets-Podolski; sugar refining.

Satanta (sùtăn'tù), city (pop. 667), Haskell co., SW Kansas, 26 mi. N of Liberal, in grain area; grain milling; mining and refining of volcanic ash. Gas wells near by.

Satara (sätä'rŭ), former district (□ 4,891; pop. 1,327,249), Bombay, India; ⊙ was Satara. A center of Mahratta power in 18th and early-19th cent. Inc. 1949 into newly-created dists. of Satara North and Satara South.

Satara, town (pop., including suburban area, 36,405), ⊙ Satara North dist., central Bombay, India, 115 mi. SE of Bombay; road and trade center; agr. market (grain, millet); oilseed milling, hand-loom weaving, mfg. of biris, plastics, metal products. Mus. with many Mahratta documents and relics; industrial school. At Satara Road (8 mi. NE, on railway) is large engineering works (mfg. of combustion engines, machine tools, agr. and textile machinery). In 18th cent., Satara was residence of Mahratta titular kings, while peshwas ruled confederacy from Poona.

Satara North, district (created 1949), S central Bombay, India, on W edge of Deccan Plateau; ⊙ Satara. Bounded N by Nira R., S by Satara South dist.; W section crossed N-S by Western Ghats. Agr. (millet, rice, wheat, peanuts); strawberries and garden vegetables (NW). Chief towns: Satara, Karad, Phaltan. Mahabaleshwar is noted health resort. Formed 1949 by merger of N part of former Satara dist. and former Deccan states of Phaltan and (parts of) Aundh, Sangli, Jamkhandi, Akalkot, and Bhor.

Satara Road, India: see SATARA, town.

Satara South, district (created 1949), S Bombay, India, on W Deccan Plateau; ⊙ Sangli. Bordered W by Western Ghats, N by Satara North dist.; drained (W) by Kistna R. Agr. (millet, peanuts, tobacco, sugar cane, cotton); handicraft cloth weaving. Chief towns: Sangli, Miraj, Urun Islampur, Tasgaon, Kurandvad. Formed 1949 by merger of parts of former Deccan states of Sangli, Jath, Aundh, Kurandvad Senior, Miraj Senior, Miraj Junior, and Kolhapur and S part of former Satara dist.

Satartia (sùtär'shēù), village (pop. 105), Yazoo co., W central Miss., 15 mi. SSW of Yazoo City and on Yazoo R.

Satawal (sä'tùwäl), coral island (pop. 216), Yap dist., W Caroline Isls., W Pacific, 39 mi. E of Lamotrek; c.1 mi. long, ½ mi. wide; coconut palms, fresh-water pond. Formerly Satuwal.

Satawan (sä'täwän), atoll, (pop. 1,262), Nomoi Isls., Truk dist., E Caroline Isls., W Pacific, 150 mi. SSE of Truk; 5°24'N 153°36'W; 17 mi. long, 7 mi. wide; 60 low islets, of which 4 are inhabited. In Second World War, site of Jap. air base.

Satengar, Indonesia: see TENGA ISLANDS.

Sater (sä'tùr), Swedish *Säter*, city (pop. 2,202), Kopparberg co., central Sweden, near Dal R., 19 mi. SSE of Falun; cotton, lumber, and flour mills. In iron- and copper-mining region. Founded by Gustavus Adolphus; chartered 1642. Its economic importance has grown rapidly in recent times.

Saterland, Germany: see SCHARREL.

Satevó (sätävō'), town (pop. 300), Chihuahua, N Mexico, in E outliers of Sierra Madre Occidental, and 50 mi. S of Chihuahua; alt. 4,488 ft.; grain, tobacco, beans, cattle.

Satgaon (sät'goun), village, Hooghly dist., S central West Bengal, India, 6 mi. NW of Hooghly. A 15th-cent. mosque ruin and tombs mark former town that was mercantile ⊙ lower Bengal; flourished for 1,500 years. Declined in 16th cent., when course of Hooghly R. moved away from town.

Saticoy (sä'tĭkoi), village (pop. 2,216), Ventura co., S Calif., on Santa Clara R. and 6 mi. SW of Santa Paula. Citrus fruit; mineral springs near by.

Satilla River (sùtĭ'lù), SE Ga., c.200 mi. long, rises near Fitzgerald, flows generally E, past Woodbine, to the Atlantic 10 mi. S of Brunswick; lower course dredged. Receives Little Satilla River (c.70 mi. long) 8 mi. NE of Nahunta.

Satillieu (sätēyû'), village (pop. 1,166), Ardèche dept., S France, in the Monts du Vivarais, 7 mi. SSW of Annonay; silk milling.

Satipo (sätē'pō), town (pop. 232), Junín dept., central Peru, on Satipo R. (a right affluent of the Perené) and 29 mi. N of Andamarca; cacao, copaiba, rubber, sawmilling.

Satirlar, Turkey: see YESILOVA.

Satka (sät'kŭ), city (1926 pop. 12,656; 1939 pop. 29,000), W Chelyabinsk oblast, Russian SFSR, in the S Urals, 26 mi. ESE of Zlatoust, on rail spur; magnesite-mining center; metallurgy; fireproof-brick mfg., sawmilling, charcoal burning. Founded 1756 as ironworking settlement; became city in 1937. Formerly called Satkinski Zavod.

Satkhira (sät'kĭrŭ), town (pop. 14,769), Khulna dist., SW East Bengal, E Pakistan, 31 mi. WSW of Khulna; rice, jute, oilseeds.

Satkinski Zavod, Russian SFSR: see SATKA.

Satmar, Rumania: see SATU-MARE, city.

Satna (sŭt'nŭ), town (pop. 11,575), ⊙ Satna dist., central Vindhya Pradesh, India, 28 mi. W of Rewa; trade center (wheat, oilseeds, rice, ghee, cloth fabrics); flour and oilseed milling, hand-loom weaving; limestone works. Near by is village of Bharhut, where remains of 2d-cent. B.C. Buddhist stupa were discovered in 1873; railing and gateway (both elaborately sculptured) removed to Indian Mus. in Calcutta in 1876.

Satool, Thailand: see SATUN.

Satoraljaujhely (shä'tôrôlyô-ōōĭhĕl), Hung. *Sátoraljaújhely*, city (pop. 18,427), Zemplen co., NE Hungary, at NE foot of the Hegyalja, 44 mi. NE of Miskolc, on Czechoslovak frontier; rail, market center. Petroleum refining, mfg. (furniture, tobacco, candles); tanneries, distilleries, flour mills. Vineyards, grain, potatoes. Formerly sometimes called Ujhely.

Sator Mountains or **Shator Mountains** (both: shä'tôr), Serbo-Croatian *Šator Planina*, in Dinaric Alps, W Bosnia, Yugoslavia; highest peak, Veliki Sator (6,140 ft.), is 11 mi. E of Bosansko Grahovo.

Satoura, Japan: see MUYA.

Satpura Range (sät'po͝orü), line of hills in central India, S of Narbada R., forming N limit of Deccan Plateau; extends almost 600 mi. generally ENE from point c.50 mi. E of Broach, along Bombay–Madhya Bharat border and across Madhya Pradesh, to junction with Vindhya Range on plateau (alt. c.3,400 ft.) of Amarkantak; 30–80 mi. wide. Average height, 2,000–2,500 ft.; rises to 4,429 ft. in peak near Pachmarhi (center). Gives rise to Wainganga, Pench, and Wardha rivers, which empty via Godavari R. into Bay of Bengal, and Tapti R., which flows W to Gulf of Cambay, skirting S foothills of range. Crossed by Khandwa-Bhusawal, Hoshangabad-Nagpur, and Jubbulpore-Nagpur rail lines. Satpuras form rough boundary bet. Aryan N India and the Dravidian Deccan region.

Satriano (sätrēä'nô), village (pop. 3,519), Catanzaro prov., Calabria, S Italy, 18 mi. SSW of Catanzaro, in cereal- and fruitgrowing region.

Satrikh (sŭt'rĭk), town (pop. 4,633), Bara Banki dist., central Uttar Pradesh, India, 5 mi. S of Nawabganj; rice, gram, wheat, oilseeds, sugar cane.

Satrunjaya, hill, India: see PALITANA, town.

Satrup (zä'tro͞op), village (pop. 2,167), in Schleswig-Holstein, NW Germany, 9 mi. SE of Flensburg, in the Angeln; flour milling, meat processing. Has Romanesque church.

Satsop River, W Wash., formed NE of Montesano by West Fork (c.45 mi. long) and East Fork (c.40 mi. long) rising in S part of Olympic Natl. Forest; flows c.6 mi. S from junction of forks to Chehalis R.

Satsporo, Japan: see SAPPORO.

Satsuma (sätso͞o'mä), former province in S Kyushu, Japan; now part of Kagoshima prefecture.

Satsuma (sătso͞o'mŭ), village (1940 pop. 749), Mobile co., SW Ala., 12 mi. N of Mobile, near Mobile R.; naval stores.

Satsuma Peninsula, Jap. *Satsuma-hanto,* in Kagoshima prefecture, SW Kyushu, Japan, bet. E. China Sea (W) and Kagoshima (E); 35 mi. N-S, 25 mi. E-W. Hilly, fertile; hot springs. Subtropical vegetation; bamboo, bananas, tobacco, sugar cane. Gold and silver mines. Extensive horse breeding. Area is known for fine porcelain, called Satsuma ware. Kagoshima on E coast. Site of major part of former feudal prov. of Satsuma.

Sattahip (sät'tŭhēp'), village (1937 pop. 4,478), Chonburi prov., S Thailand, minor port on Gulf of Siam, 50 mi. S of Chonburi. Also Satahip.

Sattanapalle, India: see SATTENAPALLE.

Sattankulam or **Satankulam** (both: sät"tänko͞olŭm'), town (pop. 8,688), Tinnevelly dist., S Madras, India, 26 mi. SE of Tinnevelly; jaggery and other palmyra products.

Satte (sät'tä), town (pop. 8,796), Saitama prefecture, central Honshu, Japan, 13 mi. NNE of Omiya; textiles, raw silk; rice, wheat.

Sattenapalle (sŭ'tĕnŭpŭl"ĕ), town (pop. 9,579), Guntur dist., NE Madras, India, on rail spur and 21 mi. WNW of Guntur; cotton ginning, dairy farming. Diamond mines of 16th–17th cent. N, along Kistna R.; celebrated Koh-i-noor diamond reputedly found 23 mi. NNW, near Kollur village. Formerly spelled Sattanapalle.

Satthwa (sät'thwä), village, Magwe dist., Upper Burma, on Pyinmana-Kyaukpadaung RR and 40 mi. NE of Allanmyo.

Sattur (sät'to͝or), town (pop. 9,831), Ramnad dist., S Madras, India, 40 mi. SSW of Madura; match-mfg. and cotton trade center; sesame-oil extraction.

Satul, Thailand: see SATUN.

Satulung (sätŏolo͞ong'), Ger. *Langendorf* (läng'ŭndôrf"), Hung. *Hosszúfalu* (hôsh'so͞ofŏ"lo͞o), village (pop. 6,237), Stalin prov., central Rumania, in SE foothills of the Carpathians, 7 mi. SE of Stalin (Brasov); climatic resort. Has church with fine murals. Large Hung. pop.

Satu-Mare (sä'to͞o-mä'rĕ), Hung. *Szatmárnémeti* (sŏt'märnä"mĕtē) or *Szatmár,* city (1948 pop. 46,519), Baia-Mare prov., NW Rumania, in Crisana-Maramures, near Hung. border, on Somes R., and 285 mi. NW of Bucharest; 47°48'N 22°53'E. Rail junction; commercial and agr. center (truck gardening, orchards). Mfg. of textiles, knit goods, machinery, refrigerators, furniture, explosives, arms, toys, cement and clay products, wax articles, dyes, inks, straw hats, chocolate, liquor, yeast, corks; tanning; oil refining. Exports grain, livestock, lumber, wine, and fruit. R.C. bishopric. City is also known as bathing resort. Has an old palace, 3 cathedrals, Vincentian monastery. Two-thirds of pop. are Magyars. Peace of Szatmar (1711) signed after Hung. revolt against Austria, guaranteed religious freedom and maintenance of Hung. liberties. In Hungary, 1940–45.

Satun (sŭto͞on'), town (1947 pop. 2,545), ⊙ Satun prov. (□ 807; 1947 pop. 46,514), S Thailand, on W coast of Malay Peninsula, port on Strait of Malacca, 55 mi. SW of Songkhla, near Malaya border; rice, rubber, and coconut plantations; tin mining near by. Part of Kedah until 1821. Also spelled Satul and Satool.

Saturna Island (□ 11), SW B.C., Gulf Isls., in Strait of Georgia, 30 mi. S of Vancouver; 7 mi. long, 1–3 mi. wide; lumbering, farming. Just E is Wash. boundary line.

Saturnino M. Laspiur (säto͞ornē'nō ā'mā läspyo͞or'), town (pop. estimate 1,500), E Córdoba prov., Argentina, 30 mi. SW of San Francisco; cattle raising, dairying.

Satut or **Sâtut** (both: sä'to͞ot), fishing and hunting settlement (pop. 179), Umanak dist., W Greenland, on islet in Umanak Fjord, 15 mi. NE of Umanak; 70°48'N 51°37'W. Radio station.

Satuwal, Caroline Isls.: see SATAWAL.

Satyamangalam (sŭtyŭmŭng'gŭlŭm), town (pop. 8,981), Coimbatore dist., SW Madras, India, on Bhavani R. and 40 mi. NNE of Coimbatore, on trade route to Mysore; road center in tobacco area; sandalwood, teak, lac. Noted 10th–16th cent. temple ruins near by. Irrigation works 10 mi. WSW, near Moyar R. mouth.

Sauce (sou'sā), town (pop. 3,352), ⊙ Sauce dept. (□ c.950; pop. 9,981), S Corrientes prov., Argentina, 75 mi. SW of Mercedes; livestock and agr. center.

Sauce, town (pop. 709), San Martín dept., N central Peru, in E outliers of the Andes, 18 mi. SE of Tarapoto; sugar cane, cotton, coca.

Sauce. 1 Town (pop. 2,500), Canelones dept., S Uruguay, on railroad and 18 mi. NNE of Montevideo, in agr. area (grain, fruit, stock). **2** Town, Colonia dept., Uruguay: see JUAN LACAZE.

Sauce, El, Nicaragua: see EL SAUCE.

Sauce, Lake, fresh-water lagoon (c.6 mi. long, 4 mi. wide), Maldonado dept., S Uruguay, 5 mi. NW of Maldonado; short outlet channel to the Río de la Plata.

Sauce Chico River (sou'sā chē'kō), SW Buenos Aires prov., Argentina, rises at alt. of 1,300 ft. 15 mi. SE of Saavedra, flows c.70 mi. SW and SE, past Tornquist, to the Bahía Blanca (bay) W of Bahía Blanca city.

Sauce Corto, Arroyo (ăroi'ō sou'sā kôr'tō), river in W Buenos Aires prov., Argentina, rises at alt. of 1,300 ft. 15 mi. NE of Tornquist, flows c.75 mi. N, losing itself in marshes near L. Alsina, 37 mi. ENE of Guaminí.

Sauce del Yí (sou'sā dĕl yē'), town (pop. 1,200), Florida dept., S central Uruguay, in the Cuchilla Grande Inferior, on railroad and 8 mi. S of Sarandí del Yí; flour milling; wheat, corn, cattle, sheep. Until 1924, Pueblo de la Capilla.

Sauce Grande River (sou'sā grän'dā), S Buenos Aires prov., Argentina, rises in Sierra de la Ventana at alt. of 1,500 ft. 15 mi. E of Tornquist, flows c.100 mi. S to Atlantic Ocean 22 mi. SSE of Coronel Dorrego.

Saucejo, El (ĕl sou-thā'hō), town (pop. 5,153), Seville prov., SW Spain, in SW outliers of the Sierra de Yeguas, 11 mi. S of Osuna; agr. center (olives, olive oil, cereals, flour, livestock; timber); dairy products, soap, plaster.

Sauces, Bolivia: see MONTEAGUDO.

Sauces, Los, Argentina: see LOS SAUCES.

Sauces, Los (lōs sou'thĕs), city (pop. 1,999), Palma, Canary Isls., adjoined S by San Andrés, 8 mi. N of Santa Cruz de la Palma; sugar cane, onions, cereals, potatoes, bananas, tomatoes, livestock. Lumbering; embroidery mfg.

Sauces, Los, Chile: see LOS SAUCES.

Sauces, Río de los (rē'ō dā lōs sou'sĕs), river in W Córdoba prov., Argentina, rises in S Sierra Grande W of the Cerro Gigante, flows S, past Villa Dolores and San Pedro, losing itself near San Luis prov. border, 15 mi. W of San Pedro; c.65 mi. long. Near San Pedro a dam furnishes hydroelectric power.

Sauchar Point, Scotland: see ELIE AND EARLSFERRY.

Sauchie (sŏkh'ē), village in Alloa parish, Clackmannan, Scotland; coal mining.

Saucillo (sousē'yō), town (pop. 3,826), Chihuahua, N Mexico, on Conchos R. (irrigation area) and 65 mi. SE of Chihuahua, on railroad; alt. 3,953 ft. Mining (silver, gold, lead) and agr. center (corn, cotton, beans, tobacco, livestock).

Sauda (sou'dä), village (pop. 3,299; canton pop. 5,202), Rogaland co., SW Norway, at head of Sauda Fjord (a branch of Sand Fjord), 40 mi. ENE of Haugesund, in the Ryfylke; metallurgical center, producing iron alloys and iron products. A zinc-mining center in 1880s. During Second World War, Saudasjoen (Nor. *Saudasjøen*) village (pop. 687), 3 mi. W, was site of alumina plant.

Sauda River (sou'dä), Nor. *Saudavasdrag,* Rogaland co., SW Norway, rises in lakes N of Sauda and flows S to Sauda Fjord. NE of Sauda are 3 falls, sites of hydroelectric stations.

Saudarkrokur or **Saudharkrokur** (sû'üdhourkrō"-kür), Icelandic *Sauðárkrókur,* city (pop. 1,003), ⊙ and in but independent of Skagafjardar co., N Iceland, at head of Skaga Fjord, 130 mi. NE of Reykjavik; 65°45'N 19°40'W; fishing port.

Saudasjoen, Norway: see SAUDA.

Saúde (säo͞o'dĭ). **1** City (pop. 1,517), N central Bahia, Brazil, on railroad and 35 mi. SSW of Senhor do Bonfim; chromium and manganese deposits; gold and rock-crystal extracting. **2** Town, Minas Gerais, Brazil: see PERDIGÃO. **3** City, Minas Gerais, Brazil: see DOM SILVÉRIO.

Saudharkrokur, Iceland: see SAUDARKROKUR.

Saudi Arabia or **Sa'udi Arabia** (säo͞o'dē ŭrā'bēü), Arabic *Al-'Arabiyah as-Sa'udiyah,* kingdom (□ 600,000; 1947 pop. estimate 6,000,000) of SW Asia, occupying most of ARABIAN PENINSULA; ⊙ Riyadh and Mecca. It is bounded N by Jordan, Iraq, Kuwait, and 2 neutral zones, E by the Persian Gulf, W by the Red Sea, and S by Yemen and the great S desert Rub' al Khali, which separates Saudi Arabia from Aden Protectorate, Oman, Trucial Oman, and Qatar along undetermined frontiers. Kingdom occupies the Arabian platform, uptilted in the Hejaz and Asir highlands (up to 9,000 ft.) along the Red Sea coast, and gradually sloping as a desert-steppe plateau (average alt. 2,500–3,500 ft.) E to the Persian Gulf. Its low-latitude desert climate restricts agr. to the ASIR highlands and to oases strung along the wadies (Sirhan, Rima, Hanifa, Dawasir). In addition to anc. oases, such as Medina, Hofuf, and Qatif, there are also modern agr. projects (KHARJ). Basic economy remains agr. and pastoral. Dates constitute the staple crop, while grain (wheat, barley, millet), fruit, and vegetables are also grown. Bedouin tribes raise camels, sheep, and goats, yielding hides, wool, and ghee for export. There are local industries (tanning, weaving, pottery making, soap mfg., jewelry- and metalwork). Pearling and fishing are of some importance along the coast. Apart from gold mined at Mahd Dhahab, mineral exploitation is dominated by the young and powerful oil industry in HASA along the Persian Gulf. Here the main production centers at Dhahran, Abqaiq, Qatif, and Ain Dar, with refinery and loading terminal at Ras Tanura, have put Saudi Arabia in 5th place among the world's oil nations. Country's Arab pop. is predominantly Sunni Moslem, with many adherents of the Wahabi movement. The leading towns are the religious centers of Mecca and Medina in Hejaz, to whose pilgrim trade Saudi Arabia traditionally owed most of its natl. income. These cities, still barred to unbelievers, are served by the summer resort of Taif and the main Red Sea port of Jidda (seat of foreign legations), as well as by the lesser harbors of Wejh, Yenbo, and Rabigh. In Asir, Abha and Sabya are the chief towns; and in inland, Nejd, Riyadh, and Hail. In the Persian Gulf region of Hasa, the anc. Hofuf surpasses the modern oil towns in size, but its old port of Oqair has been superseded by the deepwater harbor of Dammam. Although most transportation continues to be by sea and camel caravan, motor tracks link the country's main centers. The Hejaz railway (completed 1908) is in disuse within Saudi Arabia, but a line (completed 1951) links Dammam and Riyadh via Abqaiq, Hofuf, and Haradh. There are airfields at Dhahran (a major international air hub and U.S. base), Riyadh, and Jidda. The last-mentioned remains the chief port of entry of the kingdom, accounting for most of the imports and the overseas pilgrim arrivals, and engaging (with Mecca) in most of the commercial activity. Aside from oil, which is shipped from Ras Tanura terminal and via pipe line (completed 1950) from Abqaiq to Saida (Lebanon), Saudi Arabia exports gold concentrates to U.S. and charcoal, hides, skins, and sea shells to the Red Sea countries of the Sudan, Eritrea, and Aden. A political unit of relatively recent origin, Saudi Arabia had its beginning in the Wahabi reform movement (18th cent.) of Islam, which was revived in mid-19th cent. under the protection of the Saudi tribe of Nejd. Crushed in 1818 by an Egyptian punitive expedition, the Wahabi movement revived in mid-19th cent., but was reduced now (1880s) by the Rashid dynasty of Jebel Shammar. In 20th cent., it was under Ibn Saud, descendant of the early Wahabi rulers, that the movement became once more the driving political power in Arabia, culminating in the creation of the Saudi Arabian state. Ibn Saud, then in exile in Kuwait, embarked upon his conquest at the turn of the century. He rewon the old Wahabi capital of Riyadh in 1902 and defeated the Rashids in 1906. By 1910, he had reconquered all Nejd proper ranging from Qasim (N) to the Wadi Dawasir (S). Ibn Saud annexed (1913) Hasa from the Turks on the eve of the First World War, and during the war was recognized (1916) by the British as emir of Nejd. Following the defeat of the Turks, Ibn Saud resumed his drive, adding Abha and upland Asir (1920), Jebel Shammar (1921), and Jauf (1922). The stage was set for the conquest of the kingdom of Hejaz, ruled since 1916 by Husein ibn Ali, sherif of Mecca. Hejaz fell to the Saudi forces in 1924–25 and Ibn Saud was proclaimed king of Hejaz in 1926, having already changed his title to king of Nejd in 1921. The new ruler of Nejd and Hejaz was recognized by Britain in 1927, and the united kingdom of Saudi Arabia was proclaimed in 1932. In the following year, oil concessions were granted in Hasa to a U.S. company. Difficulties in Asir resulted in a brief war with Yemen, settled by the Taif treaty of 1934. Oil was struck in 1936 and 1938 in the Dammam field; and during the Second World War, commercial production began. Saudi Arabia maintained its neutrality until nearly the end of the war, but was one of the original members of the United Nations and joined the Arab League in 1945. Great expansion in oil production after the war led to the construction of the pipe line from Abqaiq to Saida, of the Dammam-Riyadh railroad, and other improvements in the economy. The country remains, however, a nearly absolute monarchy with patriarchal rule exercised by the king, Ibn Saud, and his sons under Moslem Sharia law. Although the unity of Saudi Arabia was proclaimed in 1932, the kingdom retains provisionally its dual character. It falls into the 2 major divisions or viceroyalties of Nejd and dependencies (⊙ Riyadh) and Hejaz (⊙ Mecca), each with separate administrations.

Sauer, river, Luxembourg: see Sûre River.

Sauerbrunn or **Bad Sauerbrunn** (bät' zou'ûrbrŏŏn), village (pop. 1,779), Burgenland, E Austria, 5 mi. ESE of Wiener Neustadt; mineral springs.

Sauerland (zou'ûrlänt"), region in Westphalia, NW Germany, on right bank of the Rhine, bet. Ruhr R. (N) and Sieg R. (S). The densely forested hills of its Rothaargebirge form part of the Rhenish Slate Mts. Has heavy rainfall. While there is little agr., the region has old established industries (textiles, ironworks) depending on near-by Ruhr coalfields. Chief center is the conurbation of Wuppertal, adjoined by Solingen (SW) and Remscheid (S), known for their mfg. of cutlery.

Sauer River (sōär', Ger. zou'ûr), Bas-Rhin dept., E France, rises in the N Vosges just across Ger. border, 10 mi. E of Bitche, flows c.40 mi. SE, past Woerth, through Forest of Haguenau, to the Rhine below Seltz. In battle area during Franco-Prussian War and Second World War.

Sauer River, Luxembourg: see Sûre River.

Sauersack, Czechoslovakia: see Kraslice.

Sauerstownship (sou'ûrz–), suburb (pop. 626) of Bulawayo, Southern Rhodesia, 3 mi. NNE of Bulawayo station. Has preparatory school. Also called Sauer's Township.

Saugatuck (sô'gûtŭk"). **1** Village, Conn.: see Westport. **2** Village (pop. 770), Allegan co., SW Mich., 20 mi. NW of Allegan, on L. Michigan at mouth of Kalamazoo R. Art colony, with summer art school; resort. Area contains large sand dunes.

Saugatuck River, SW Conn., rises S of Danbury, flows c.30 mi. SE and S to Long Isl. Sound, forming harbor of Westport.

Saugeen Peninsula (sô'gēn'), S Ont., extends 60 mi. NNW into L. Huron from Owen Sound toward Manitoulin Isl., forming SW side of Georgian Bay.

Saugeen River, S Ont., rises in several branches S of Owen Sound; main headstreams (North and South Saugeen rivers) unite 15 mi. SSE of Southampton to form Saugeen R., which flows N to L. Huron at Southampton; c.100 mi. long.

Saugerties (sô'gûrtēz), village (pop. 3,907), Ulster co., SE N.Y., at foot of the Catskills, on Esopus Creek near its mouth on the Hudson, and 11 mi. N of Kingston; summer resort. Mfg. (paper, clothing, machinery, canvas, leather goods, brick, cement); limestone, flagstone quarries. Inc. 1831.

Saugor (sô'gûr, sä'gŭr), Hindi *Sagar* [=lake], district (□ 6,761; pop. 939,068), N Madhya Pradesh, India; ⊙ Saugor. Bordered SW by Bhopal state, W by Madhya Bharat, N by Uttar Pradesh and Vindhya Pradesh; S escarpment of central Vindhya Range in SE; undulating plains, drained mainly by Sonar R. Wheat, millet, oilseeds in alluvial river valleys; mahua, pipal, tamarind; mango groves. Teak, bamboo, sunn hemp, and ebony in dispersed forested hills. Oilseed milling, sawmilling, mfg. of essential oil (*rosha* or Andropogon) and sunn-hemp products (mats, cordage); cattle raising, ghee processing; sandstone quarrying. Damoh and Saugor are agr. trade centers. Dist. enlarged in early 1930s by merger of former dist. of Damoh (E). Pop. 83% Hindu, 9% tribal (mainly Gond), 5% Moslem, 3% Jain.

Saugor, town (pop., including cantonment, 63,933), ⊙ Saugor dist., N Madhya Pradesh, India, on small lake, 90 mi. NW of Jubbulpore; road and agr. trade center (wheat, oilseeds, cotton); oilseed milling, ghee processing, sawmilling; railway-engineering works; experimental farm (sericulture). Saugor Univ. (founded 1946), industrial school, school of horsemanship. Sandstone quarries and asbestos deposits near by.

Saugstad, Mount (sŭg'städ) (10,000 ft.), W B.C., in Coast Mts., 50 mi. E of Ocean Falls, S of Tweedsmuir Park; 52°15'N 126°31'W.

Saugues (sōg), village (pop. 1,387), Haute-Loire dept., S central France, in Montagnes de la Margeride, 18 mi. WSW of Le Puy; livestock, wool, lumber trade; mfg. of lace, woolens.

Saugus (sô'gŭs), residential town (pop. 17,162), Essex co., NE Mass., 8 mi. N of Boston; mfg. (oil burners, air-conditioning apparatus, dies, metal stampings, turbine ventilators, other metal products). Saugus ironworks (1645) were 1st to succeed in the colonies. Settled before 1637, set off from Lynn 1815. Includes villages of Cliftondale, East Saugus.

Saujbulagh, Iran: see Mehabad.

Saujon (sōzhō'), town (pop. 2,619), Charente-Maritime dept., W France, on the Seudre and 14 mi. WSW of Saintes; road and railroad junction; paper milling. Has hydrotherapeutic establishments.

Sauk (sôk), county (□ 840; pop. 38,120), S central Wis.; ⊙ Baraboo. Bounded NE and S by Wisconsin R.; drained by Baraboo R. and tributaries of the Wisconsin. Dairying, stock raising, lumbering; some mfg. Has several lake resorts; Devils Lake State Park is here, in Baraboo Range (E). Formed 1840.

Sauk Centre, city (pop. 3,140), Stearns co., central Minn., on Sauk R., at S end of Sauk L., and c.40 mi. WNW of St. Cloud. Resort; trading point in grain and livestock area; dairy products, beverages. State industrial school for girls is here. City was birthplace of Sinclair Lewis, who used it as setting for *Main Street*. Settled 1856, platted 1863, inc. as village 1876, as city 1889.

Sauk City, village (pop. 1,755), Sauk co., S central Wis., on Wisconsin R., adjoining Prairie du Sac, and 21 mi. NW of Madison, in timber, dairying, and farming area (corn, peas, oats, hogs); farm trade center, with mfg. (wood products, dairy products, canned foods). Resort. Founded 1838, inc. 1854. Haraszthy de Mokcsa settled here in 1840, and other liberal European refugees followed.

Sauk Lake, Stearns and Todd counties, central Minn., at Sauk Centre; 7 mi. long, ½ mi. wide. Fed and drained in S by Sauk R. Fishing and bathing resorts.

Sauk Rapids, village (pop. 3,410), Benton co., central Minn., on E bank of Mississippi R., opposite St. Cloud, at mouth of Sauk R., in agr. area; dairy products, flour. Granite quarries near by. Platted 1851, inc. 1881.

Sauk River. **1** Rises in lake region of Pope co., W Minn., flows E, through S end of Sauk L., in Sauk Centre, then SE and ENE to Mississippi R. at St. Cloud; 100 mi. long. Drains small lakes in Stearns co. **2** In NW Wash., rises in Cascade Range SW of Glacier Peak, flows c.45 mi. NW to Skagit R. c.10 mi. above Concrete.

Sauk-Sai or **Sauk-Say** (sŭŏŏk"-sī'), river in N Tadzhik SSR, in the Pamir, on S slope of Trans-Alai Range; flows c.30 mi. SW to the Muk-Su; gold placers.

Saukville (sôk'–), village (pop. 699), Ozaukee co., E Wis., on Milwaukee R. and 23 mi. N of Milwaukee, in dairy and farm area; ornamental ironwork.

Sauland (sou'län), village in Hjartdal canton (pop. 2,066), Telemark co., S Norway, 38 mi. NW of Skien, in lumber and livestock area; flour- and sawmills, woolen mills. Tuddal, 10 mi. NNW, is site of a sanatorium.

Sauldre River (sō'drù), in Cher and Loir-et-Cher depts., central France, formed by Grande Sauldre and Petite Sauldre both rising in Sancerrois Hills near Henrichemont; flows 100 mi. generally W across the Sologne, past Salbris and Romorantin, to the Cher below Selles-sur-Cher. Sections of river are canalized.

Saulgau (zoul'gou), town (pop. 6,617), S Württemberg, Germany, after 1945 in Württemberg-Hohenzollern, 14 mi. WSW of Biberach; mfg. of agr. machinery, woodworking. Has Gothic church. First mentioned 819. Chartered 1239. Was Austrian, 1299–1803.

Saulges (sōzh), village (pop. 106), Mayenne dept., W France, 17 mi. SE of Laval. Its caverns were anciently inhabited. The Grotte Rochefort has stalagmites and stalactites.

Saulieu (sōlyû'), town (pop. 2,579), Côte-d'Or dept., E central France, on NE slopes of the Monts du Morvan, 23 mi. N of Autun; road center. Furniture mfg., tanning, vegetable shipping. Has 12th-cent. Romanesque abbatial church of Saint-Andoche.

Saulnes (sōn), town (pop. 2,360), Meurthe-et-Moselle dept., NE France, on Luxembourg border, 3 mi. NE of Longwy; customhouse. Pig-iron mfg. center of Longwy metallurgical dist. Iron mines.

Saulsbury, town (pop. 143), Hardeman co., SW Tenn., 50 mi. E of Memphis, in cotton, corn, livestock area.

Sault (sō), village (pop. 718), Vaucluse dept., SE France, 18 mi. ENE of Carpentras; road junction; lavender distilling.

Sault au Mouton (sōō' ō mōōtō'), village (pop. estimate 700), E Que., on the St. Lawrence, at mouth of Sault au Mouton R., and 35 mi. WNW of Rimouski; lumbering center.

Sault au Récollet (rākōlā'), N suburb of Montreal (pop. estimate 2,500), S Que., on NW Montreal Isl., on R. des Prairies.

Sault-Brénaz (sō-brānä'), village (pop. 608), Ain dept., E France, on the Rhone and 15 mi. NW of Belley; marble quarrying.

Sault Sainte Marie (sōō' sānt mûrē'), city (pop. 25,794), ⊙ Algoma dist., S central Ont., on N shore of St. Marys R., which connects L. Huron and L. Superior, opposite Sault Ste Marie, Mich. (connected by railroad bridge, ferry), 300 mi. N of Detroit. Rapids are by-passed by Sault Sainte Marie Canals on Mich. and Ont. sides of river. Port, with ore docks, steel, pulp, paper, and lumber mills, foundries, railroad shops, smelting and chemical works, breweries. Tourist center; gateway to hunting, fishing resorts in region of woods and lakes. The long history of this region (called "the Soo") around the rapids is closely related to that of Sault Sainte Marie, Mich. The 2 cities were linked (1887) by railroad bridge.

Sault Sainte Marie, city (pop. 17,912), ⊙ Chippewa co., E Upper Peninsula, Mich., 300 mi. N of Detroit, opposite Sault Sainte Marie, Ont. (connected by railroad bridge and ferry), and on St. Marys R. (connecting lakes Huron and Superior). Sault Sainte Marie Canals circumvent river's rapids here. Port of entry. Mfg. (carbide, leather, foundry products, lumber, woolens, beer, food products); hydroelectric plants. Resort, with hunting and fishing in region. Coast Guard hq. here. Forestry substation of Mich. State Col. is near by. Points of interest: the huge locks in the ship canals; site of Father Marquette's mission; house of J. R. Schoolcraft; house of fur trader John Johnston; the library, with mus. containing historic documents. This region of U.S. and Canada, often called "the Soo," was visited by Étienne Brulé in 1618, followed by Jean Nicolet in 1634. The rapids were named Sault Sainte Marie (after the river) by Isaac Jogues and Charles Raymbault in 1641. Father Marquette established a mission in 1668. In 18th and 19th cent., a succession of Fr. and Br. fur-trading posts were built at this strategic portage around the rapids. Region passed to U.S. under Treaty of Paris (1783). After negotiation of an Indian treaty by Lewis Cass here in 1820, U.S. Fort Brady was built; it continued in use until end of Second World War. First canal and lock to permit continuous boat travel from L. Superior to lower Great Lakes were constructed c.1799 by North West Company and destroyed by Americans in War of 1812. Canal (since modernized) was built on Mich. side in 1855; the Ont. canal was constructed in 1895. An international railroad bridge linking the 2 cities was built in 1887, and replaced in 1913. The Mich. community was inc. as village 1879, as city 1887.

Sault Sainte Marie Canals, popularly the **Soo Canals**, bet. Upper Peninsula, N Mich., and S central Ont.; 2 parallel, toll-free, govt.-operated ship canals by-passing rapids (19-ft. drop) in Saint Marys River, at twin cities of Sault Sainte Marie (Mich. and Ont.); annual cargo volume (generally over 100,000,000 tons) is world's greatest. Canal on Mich. side is 1.6 mi. long, has 2 channels, each with 2 locks, completed bet. 1881 and 1919; 2 of them, each 1,350 ft. long and 80 ft. wide, are among largest in world. Canadian canal (opened 1895) is c.1.4 mi. long and has 1 lock; there are large docks at E end. First canal and lock in Soo region were built (on present Ont. side) in 1799 and destroyed in War of 1812. Present U.S. installations are outgrowth of those built in 1853–55.

Saulx (sō), agr. village (pop. 471), Haute-Saône dept., E France, 8 mi. NE of Vesoul.

Saulx River, Meuse and Marne depts., NE France, rises SSE of Montiers-sur-Saulx, flows c.50 mi. NW to the Marne just below Vitry-le-François. Paralleled by Marne-Rhine Canal below Sermaize-les-Bains. Receives the Ornain (right).

Saulxures-sur-Moselotte (sōzür'-sür-mōzùlôt'), village (pop. 1,427), Vosges dept., E France, on Moselotte R. and 10 mi. ESE of Remiremont in the Vosges; cotton milling. Granite quarries near by.

Saulzais-le-Potier (sōzā'-lù-pôtyā'), village (pop. 345), Cher dept., central France, 9 mi. S of Saint-Amand-Montrond; cattle raising.

Saumane (sōmän'), village (pop. 117), Gard dept., S France, in the Cévennes, 12 mi. NE of Le Vigan; silk spinning.

Saumâtre, Étang (ātā' sōmä'trù), lake (□ c.65) SE Haiti, bordering on Dominican Republic, 18 mi. E of Port-au-Prince, on fertile Cul-de-Sac plain; 18 mi. long, up to 6 mi. wide.

Saumlaki, Indonesia: see Tanimbar Islands.

Saumur (sōmür'), town (pop. 14,885), Maine-et-Loire dept., W France, on a tongue of land bet. the Loire and the Thouet and on an isl. in the Loire, 27 mi. SE of Angers; commercial and railroad center; noted for its sparkling white wines; glass, paper, carton, and leather industry; mfg. of religious articles (mainly rosaries); distilling, fruit and vegetable (mushrooms) preserving, sugar refining. Has 11th–12th-cent. church of Notre-Dame-de-Nantilly containing fine 15th–17th-cent. tapestries; the castle (now an arsenal), founded by Fulk Nerra (10th cent.) and rebuilt several times, showing the transition from feudal to Renaissance architecture; and the well-known cavalry school established in 1768. Under Henry IV, Saumur became a center of Protestantism in France, but the revocation of the Edict of Nantes brought ruin to the town, driving the skilled Huguenot pop. overseas. In 1793 the Vendée army defeated the Republicans near by and captured the town. During the Second World War ⅓ of Saumur was destroyed.

Saundatti (soun'dŭt-tē), town (pop. 8,730), Belgaum dist., S Bombay, India, 40 mi. ESE of Belgaum; local market center (wheat, millet, cotton, peanuts); cotton ginning. Hindu shrine on Yellamma Hill, 3 mi. SE, is noted place of pilgrimage; annual fair. Sometimes spelled Soundatti.

Saunders (sôn'dûrz, sän'–), county (□ 756; pop. 16,923), E Nebr.; ⊙ Wahoo. Farm area bounded E and N by Platte R. Feed, grain, livestock, dairy and poultry produce. Formed 1867.

Saunders, Cape (sôn'dûrz), SE S.Isl., New Zealand, on Otago Peninsula E of Portobello; 45°53'S 170°45'E.

Saundersfoot, town in Saint Issells parish (pop. 2,040), SE Pembroke, Wales, on Carmarthen Bay

of Bristol Channel, 3 mi. N of Tenby; fishing port; coal mining.
Saunderstown, R.I.: see NORTH KINGSTOWN.
Saundersville, Mass.: see GRAFTON.
Saunemin (sô'nûmĭn″), village (pop. 338), Livingston co., E central Ill., 11 mi. E of Pontiac, in agr. and bituminous-coal area.
Saunk, India: see SONKH.
Saunshi (soun'shē), town (pop. 4,048), Dharwar dist., S Bombay, India, 26 mi. SE of Dharwar; small cotton market.
Sauqira, Ras, Ras Sauqirah, or **Ras Sawqirah** (all: räs' sou'kĭrû), cape of SE Oman coast, on Arabian Sea; 18°8′N 56°36′E; limestone cliff. **Sauqira Bay,** 100-mi.-wide inlet of Arabian Sea, extends from Ras Sauqira NE to Ras Madraka. Also spelled Sauqra and Sauqrah.
Sauquoit (sûkwoit'), village (pop. 1,227), Oneida co., central N.Y., 7 mi. S of Utica.
Sauran (sŏŏrän'), village, central South Kazakhstan oblast, Kazakh SSR, on Trans-Caspian RR and 25 mi. NW of Turkestan; cotton, cattle.
Saurashtra (sourāsh'trû), constituent state (□ 21,062; 1951 pop. 4,136,005), W India; ⊙ Rajkot. Comprises major portion of KATHIAWAR peninsula; bounded W and S by Arabian Sea, SE by Gulf of Cambay, E by Bombay, N by Little Rann of Cutch, NW by Gulf of Cutch; surrounds detached areas of Amreli dist. (Bombay). Mostly an undulating plain with low hill ranges—notably GIR region (S)—and central tableland, where majority of streams rise; Girnar hill (S central) is highest point (3,666 ft.). Annual rainfall averages 20–30 in.; irrigation by storage tanks and wells. State predominantly agr. (millet, cotton, oilseeds, wheat, sugar cane, coconuts); also fishing (pomfrets, mackerel, Bombay duck), cattle raising, salt panning, cotton and oilseed processing; limestone and sandstone quarried in some places. Main commercial centers are Bhaunagar, Jamnagar, Rajkot, Junagarh, Porbandar, Morvi, and Gondal. From several small ports cotton, ghee, oilseeds, building stone, and salt are exported. Area well served by rail- and airways. Has several sites of historic and religious importance, notably at Palitana, Somnath, Girnar, Vala, and Thangadh. State created 1948 by merger of former princely states of WESTERN INDIA STATES of Bhaunagar, Dhrangadhra, Dhrol, Gondal, Jafarabad, Limbdi, Morvi, Navanagar, Palitana, Porbandar, Rajkot, Wadhwan, Wankaner, and those of WESTERN KATHIAWAR AGENCY and EASTERN KATHIAWAR AGENCY; Junagarh inc. in 1949. Comprises 5 dists.: Madhya Saurashtra, Halar, Gohilwad, Sorath, Zalawad. Pop. 84% Hindu, 11% Moslem, 4% Jain. Chief language, Gujarati. Sometimes spelled Surashtra.
Saurimo, Angola: see VILA HENRIQUE DE CARVALHO.
Sau River, Yugoslavia: see SAVA RIVER.
Saur Range (sŏŏr'), northernmost outlier of the Tien Shan system on China-USSR border, 70 mi. SE of L. Zaisan; rises to 12,300 ft. Coal and oil-shale deposits along Kenderlyk R. on W slopes.
Sausal (sousäl'), village (pop. 2,935), Libertad dept., NW Peru, in W foothills of Cordillera Occidental, in irrigated Chicama R. valley, 11 mi. NE of Chicama, on railroad; sugar-milling center; distilling; cattle raising.
Sausalito (sôsûlē'tù), city (pop. 4,828), Marin co., W Calif., residential suburb of San Francisco, on San Francisco Bay, near N end of Golden Gate Bridge; fishing, yachting resort. Alcohol distilling; mfg. of furniture, clay products. Large shipyards built here in Second World War. U.S. forts Barry and Baker overlook bay. Inc. 1893 as town, 1935 as city.
Sausar (sou'sŭr), town (pop. 6,313), Chhindwara dist., central Madhya Pradesh, India, on railroad and 30 mi. SSW of Chhindwara; cotton ginning; wheat, rice, oilseeds. Rail spur serves manganese mines 5 mi. N, near village of Kachchhiahana. Marble quarries, sawmills near by.
Sauternes (sōtârn'), village (pop. 112), Gironde dept., SW France, 24 mi. SSE of Bordeaux, near Langon; known for its outstanding white wines (Château-Yquem).
Sautet Dam (sōtā'), Isère dept., SE France, on upper Drac R. and 2 mi. W of Corps, 27 mi. SSE of Grenoble; 443 ft. high, 263 ft. wide at crest. Hydroelectric plant.
Sauteurs (sōtûr', sōtŏŏr'), town (pop. 875), N Grenada, B.W.I., 13 mi. NE of St. George's; coconuts, cacao. Scene of Carib massacre by French (1650). Near by is the crater lake Antoine.
Sautour (sōtŏŏr'), village (pop. 301), Namur prov., S Belgium, 2 mi. SSE of Philippeville; marble quarrying.
Sauve (sōv), village (pop. 1,062), Gard dept., S France, on the Vidourle and 14 mi. SSW of Alès; hosiery, farm tools.
Sauveterre (sōvtâr'). **1** or **Sauveterre-d'Aveyron** (–dävärō'), village (pop. 433), Aveyron dept., S France, on Ségala Plateau, 15 mi. SW of Rodez; wheat, cattle. **2** or **Sauveterre-de-Béarn** (–dù bäär'), village (pop. 696), Basses-Pyrénées dept., SW France, on the Gave d'Oloron and 10 mi. SW of Orthez; mfg. of tannic extracts, meat canning.
Sauveterre, Causse de, France: see CAUSSES.
Sauveterre-de-Guyenne (–dù-gēyĕn'), village (pop. 695), Gironde dept., SW France, in Entre-deux-Mers, 17 mi. SSE of Libourne; road center; wheat, tomatoes. Cementworks near by. Medieval stronghold.
Sauveterre-la-Lémance (–lä-lāmãs'), village (pop. 314), Lot-et-Garonne dept., SW France, 20 mi. NE of Villeneuve-sur-Lot; limekilns; mfg. of gloves and pit props.
Sauviat-sur-Vige (sōvyä'-sür-vēzh'), village (pop. 584), Haute-Vienne dept., W central France, 8 mi. NE of Saint-Léonard-de-Noblat; porcelain.
Sauxillanges (sōksēyãzh'), village (pop. 813), Puy-de-Dôme dept., central France, 6 mi. E of Issoire; lace mfg.
Sauzal (sou-thäl'), village (pop. 503), Tenerife, Canary Isls., 9 mi. W of Santa Cruz de Tenerife; cereals, grapes, bananas, tomatoes, onions.
Sauzal (sousäl'). **1** Village (1930 pop. 445), Maule prov., S central Chile, 22 mi. NE of Cauquenes; grain, potatoes, lentils, wine, sheep; lumbering. **2** Village, O'Higgins prov., Chile: see EL SAUZAL.
Sauzé-Vaussais (sōzā'-vōsā'), village (pop. 1,050), Deux-Sèvres dept., W France, 30 mi. ESE of Niort; rope mfg., dairying.
Savá (sävä'), village (pop. 827), Colón dept., N Honduras, on Aguán R. and 32 mi. SW of Trujillo; rail junction; trade center in banana area.
Sava (sä'vä), town (pop. 12,141), Ionio prov., Apulia, S Italy, 18 mi. ESE of Taranto; agr. center (grapes, olives, cereals, figs, almonds).
Sava, river, Yugoslavia: see SAVA RIVER.
Sava Bohinjka River (sä'vä bô'hĭn-kä), Ger. *Wocheiner Sau* (vô'khĭnûr zou'), NW Slovenia, Yugoslavia, rises in Julian Alps on S slope of the Triglav, flows S, through Bohinj L., forming Savica Fall (c.200 ft. high) just W of lake, and ENE, joining Sava Dolinka R. just NW of Radovljica to form SAVA RIVER; 25 mi. long. Known as Savica R., Ger. *Savitza*, in upper course, above lake.
Sava Dolinka River (sä'vä dô'lĭn-kä), Ger. *Wurzner Sau* (vŏŏrts'nûr zou'), NW Slovenia, Yugoslavia, rises in the Karawanken near Italo-Austrian border, flows 30 mi. ESE, past Kranska Gora (hydroelectric plant), Mojstrana, and Jesenice, joining Sava Bohinjka R. just NW of Radovljica to form SAVA RIVER. Receives Zavrsnica R. (left).
Savage. 1 Village (pop. 1,238), Howard co., central Md., at confluence of Middle and Little Patuxent rivers and 16 mi. SW of Baltimore; mfg. of Christmas ornaments, store fixtures. **2** Village (pop. 389), Scott co., S Minn., on Minnesota R. and 14 mi. S of Minneapolis; corn, oats, barley, potatoes, livestock, poultry. **3** Village (pop. c.250), Richland co., NE Mont., 20 mi. SSW of Sidney and on Yellowstone R., near N.Dak. line; shipping point for grain and sugar beets.
Savage Dam, Calif.: see OTAY RIVER.
Savage Island: see NIUE.
Savage River, NW Md., rises in Garrett co., just S of Pa. line, flows SW and SE to North Branch of the Potomac at Luke; c.25 mi. long. Savage R. Dam (175 ft. high; begun 1939) is c.5 mi. above mouth.
Savage's Station, locality, Henrico co., E central Va., c.8 mi. E of Richmond. Here was fought (June 29, 1862) one of Seven Days Battles.
Savaii (sävī'ē), volcanic island (□ 703; pop. 18,654), Western SAMOA, under N.Z. mandate. Largest, most westerly isl. of Samoa; mountainous; highest peak Mauga Silisili (6,094 ft.); many craters with forested slopes. Tuasivi is hq. of resident commissioner. Formerly Chatham Isl.
Savajbolagh, Iran: see MEHABAD.
Savalan (sävälän') or **Sabalan** (säbä–), volcanic cone (15,592 ft.) in Azerbaijan, NW Iran, 70 mi. E of Tabriz; snow-capped throughout year. Barren, rocky; has warm springs.
Savalgi (sŭv'ŭlgē), town (pop. 3,470), Bijapur dist., S Bombay, India, 27 mi. SW of Bijapur; millet, cotton, wheat.
Savalou (sävä'lōō), town (pop. c.3,800), central Dahomey, Fr. West Africa, 100 mi. NNW of Porto-Novo. Grows cotton, shea nuts, peanuts, castor beans, corn, millet. Cotton ginning. R.C. mission.
Savan. 1 Rail station, Bihar, India: see SIWAN. **2** Town, Bombay, India: see SAVANUR.
Savana Island (sùvă'nù), islet (173.3 acres), U.S. Virgin Isls., in Virgin Passage, 2 mi. off W tip of St. Thomas Isl.; 18°20′N 65°5′W.
Savanat, Iran: see ISTAHBANAT.
Savanette (sävänĕt'), town (1950 pop. 642), Ouest dept., E Haiti, near Dominican Republic border, 35 mi. NE of Port-au-Prince; coffee, timber, cattle.
Savankalok, Thailand: see SAWANKHALOK.
Savanna (sùvă'nù). **1** City (pop. 5,058), Carroll co., NW Ill., on the Mississippi (bridged here) at mouth of Plum R., and 16 mi. N of Clinton, Iowa; trade and shipping center in rich agr. area (corn, oats, wheat, livestock, poultry; dairy products; railroad shops. At Proving Ground (8 mi. NW, on the Mississippi) is U.S. Army's Savanna Ordnance Depot. Mississippi Palisades State Park (c.800 acres) is just N on cliffs above river. Settled 1828, inc. 1874. **2** Village, Pittsburg co., SE Okla., 9 mi. SSW of McAlester, in coal-mining region; cotton ginning, grain milling.
Savannah (sùvă'nù). **1** City (pop. 119,638), ⊙ Chatham co., SE Ga., on Savannah R. 17 mi. from its mouth on the Atlantic, and 125 mi. NNE of Jacksonville, Fla.; 32°4′N 81°7′W. Georgia's oldest and 2d largest city, it is a port of entry and an important industrial and shipping center with a good harbor. It is one of the world's largest naval-stores markets, and besides its huge paper and pulp mill, sugar refinery, and shipyards, it has plants mfg. sulphuric acid, cottonseed oil, fertilizer; asphalt, gypsum, and concrete products; canned fruits, vegetables, and sea food; trucks, trailers, castings, and other metal products. Its mild climate makes it a popular winter resort. Seat of Christ Episcopal Church (1838), R.C. co-cathedral of St. John the Baptist (1876), Telfair Acad. of Arts and Sciences, Ga. Historical Society, Ga. State Col. (Negro; 1891), Armstrong Col. (1935), and fine ante-bellum houses. Fort Pulaski Natl. Monument, Fort Screven, U.S. Army post, and Hunter Air Force Base near by. City was founded 1733 by James Oglethorpe; inc. 1789. Became seat of government of Royal Prov., 1754. Captured 1778 by British in American Revolutionary War and held until 1782. State capital, 1782–85. Growth of trade, especially after the Revolutionary War and War of 1812, made Savannah a commercial center. The 1st steamship (*The Savannah*) to cross the Atlantic sailed from here to Liverpool, 1819. In the Civil War city fell to the Federals 1864, when Sherman completed his march to the sea. **2** City (pop. 2,332), ⊙ Andrew co., NW Mo., near Missouri R., 12 mi. N of St. Joseph; agr. (corn, oats, wheat); ships stock, poultry, truck products. Laid out 1842. **3** Village (pop. 582), Wayne co., W N.Y., 14 mi. NW of Auburn; canning. **4** Village (pop. 407), Ashland co., N central Ohio, 7 mi. NNW of Ashland, in agr. area. **5** Town (pop. 1,698), ⊙ Hardin co., SW Tenn., on the Tennessee and 40 mi. SE of Jackson, in rough timber and farm area; makes shoes, handles, buttons; cotton gins, sawmills, marble and limestone quarries. Pickwick Landing Dam and Shiloh Natl. Military Park are near by.
Savannah Beach, resort town (pop. 1,036), Chatham co., E Ga., 15 mi. E of Savannah and on Tybee Isl. near Cockspur Isl. (site of Fort Pulaski Natl. Monument). Locally called Tybee.
Savannah River, 314 mi. long, forming the Ga.-S.C. line from its source, the confluence of the Tugaloo and Seneca rivers, 8 mi. NE of Hartwell, Ga., to the Atlantic; flows SE, past Augusta (head of shallow-draft navigation; 212 mi. upstream) and Savannah (17 mi. upstream) to the Atlantic. Receives Broad and Little rivers and Brier Creek in Ga. Savannah Harbor (deep-draft navigation), which includes lower 22 mi. of river, is crossed by Intracoastal Waterway just below Savannah. River is used for hydroelectric power; 2 dams are near Augusta and the CLARK HILL DAM is 22 mi. above Augusta. Along river in Aiken and Barnwell counties, S.C., is U.S. Atomic Energy Commission's Savannah R. Plant (202,000 acres; begun 1951), for production of hydrogen-bomb materials.
Savannakhet (säwän-näkĕt'), town, ⊙ Savannakhet prov. (□ 8,400; 1947 pop. 194,000), central Laos, port on left bank of Mekong R. (Thailand line) opposite Mukdahan and on highway from Dongha (central Vietnam). Sericulture. Seno airfield is 20 mi. NE.
Savanna-la-Mar (sùvă'nù-lù-mär'), town (pop. 4,046), ⊙ Westmoreland parish, SW Jamaica, port 90 mi. WNW of Kingston; 18°13′N 78°8′W. Trading center on open bay; exports sugar, coffee, cacao, ginger, annatto, pimento, dyewood, rum. Ice factory; mfg. of aerated water. Frequently damaged by hurricanes.
Savant Lake (25 mi. long, 5 mi. wide), NW Ont., in Patricia dist., 60 mi. ENE of Sioux Lookout; alt. 1,306 ft. Drains N into Albany R.
Savantvadi (sä″vûntvä'dē), town (pop. 10,024), Ratnagiri dist., S Bombay, India, 85 mi. SSE of Ratnagiri, in the Konkan; trades in rice, coconuts, betel nuts, tobacco, timber (teak, blackwood in near-by forests); wood carving, biri mfg., embroidering, palm-mat weaving. Has col. Sometimes called Vadi. Was ⊙ former princely state of Savantvadi (□ 937; pop. 252,050) in Deccan States, Bombay; state inc. 1949 into Ratnagiri dist.; also spelled Sawantwadi.
Savanur (sŭv'ŭnŏŏr), town (pop. 12,628), Dharwar dist., S Bombay, India, 40 mi. SSE of Dharwar; trade center for cotton, millet, gur, betel leaf; cotton ginning, hand-loom weaving, oilseed pressing. Sometimes called Savan. Was ⊙ former princely state of Savanur (□ 70; pop. 22,440) in Deccan States, Bombay; state inc. 1949 into Dharwar dist.
Savargalok, Thailand: see SAWANKHALOK.
Sava River (sä'vä) or **Save River** (sä'vĕ), Ger. *Sau* (zou), Hung. *Száva* (sä'vŏ), anc. *Savus*, N Yugoslavia, a large tributary of the Danube and longest river entirely in Yugoslavia; length 583 mi. Formed by junction of 2 headstreams, the SAVA DOLINKA and the SAVA BOHINJKA just NW of Radovljica; flows generally ESE, through Slovenia, Croatia, and Serbia, past Kranj, Zagreb, Sisak, Gradiska, Slavonski Brod, Samac, Brcko, Mitrovica, and

Sabac, to the Danube at Belgrade. Receives Krka, Kupa, Una, Vrbas, Bosna, and Drina rivers. Its basin includes nearly half of Yugoslavia. The Sava forms NE limits of Dinaric Alps; partly constitutes Croatia-Bosnia frontier and S border of Slavonia and the Srem. Navigable for freight vessels below Sisak, for passenger vessels below mouth of the Drina at Mitrovica; above Sisak, used only for barks and rafts; potentially navigable below Zagreb. Marsh draining, 1947–51; fishing. Posavina is region along the lower Sava.

Savar Kundla, India: see KUNDLA.

Savarsin (sŭvûr'shĕn), Rum. *Săvârşin,* Hung. *Soborsin* (sô'bôrshĕn), village (pop. 1,358), Arad prov., W Rumania, on railroad and 45 mi. ESE of Arad.

Savasse (sävăs'), village (pop. 811), Drôme dept., SE France, 4 mi. NNE of Montélimar, near left bank of the Rhone; winegrowing. Cementworks at near-by L'Homme-d'Armes.

Savda (säv'dŭ), town (pop. 10,809), East Khandesh dist., NE Bombay, India, 23 mi. ENE of Jalgaon; market center for cotton, millet, linseed, wheat, cattle; cotton ginning, handicraft cloth weaving. Sometimes spelled Sawda.

Savé (sä'vā), town (pop. c.5,100), S central Dahomey, Fr. West Africa, on railroad and 100 mi. N of Porto-Novo. Head of road to Niger territory. Native trade; region produces cotton, shea nuts, castor beans, peanuts, corn, millet. R.C. and Protestant missions.

Savedalen (sā'vŭdä"lŭn), Swedish *Sävedalen,* residential village (pop. 5,075), Goteborg och Bohus co., SW Sweden, on Save R. and 4 mi. ENE of Goteborg; electrical and mechanical works.

Saveh (sävĕ'), town (1941 pop. 15,365), First Prov., W central Iran, 80 mi. WSW of Teheran and on the Qara Chai; agr. center of former Saveh prov.; known for its pomegranates and melons, wheat and cotton. An anc. town, ruined (13th cent.) by Mongols who also destroyed its valuable library. Archaeological excavations near by. Saveh prov. was inc. (1938) into Iran's First Prov. (see GILAN).

Savelli (sävĕl'lē), town (pop. 3,394), Catanzaro prov., Calabria, S Italy, in La Sila mts., 6 mi. NE of San Giovanni in Fiore, in stock-raising, fruit-growing, lumbering region. Health resort (alt. 3,327 ft.).

Savelugu (sävĕlōō'gōō), town, Northern Territories, N central Gold Coast, 13 mi. N of Tamale; shea nuts, cotton, durra, yams; cattle, skins.

Savelyevka, Russian SFSR: see GORNY.

Savenay (sävŭnā'), village (pop. 2,246), Loire-Inférieure dept., W France, 13 mi. ENE of Saint-Nazaire; rail junction; dairying, sawmilling. Scene of decisive battle (1793), in which Gen. Kléber defeated the insurgent army of the Vendée.

Saveni (sŭvăn'), Rum. *Săveni,* town (1948 pop. 6,470), Botosani prov., NE Rumania, in Moldavia, 20 mi. E of Dorohoi; trading center for grain, livestock products.

Savenstein, Yugoslavia: see SEVNICA.

Saventhem, Belgium: see ZAVENTEM.

Saverdun (sävĕrdŭ'), village (pop. 1,837), Ariège dept., S France, on Ariège R. and 8 mi. N of Pamiers; livestock market; hosiery mfg., dairying. Was stronghold of old countship of Foix, and bulwark of Protestantism.

Save River (säv), Haute-Garonne and Gers depts., SW France, rises in Lannemezan Plateau, flows 90 mi. NE, past Lombez and L'Isle-Jourdain, to the Garonne just below Grenade-sur-Garonne. Its valley is lined with orchards.

Save River, Southern Rhodesia and Mozambique: see SABI RIVER.

Save River, Swedish *Säveån* (sĕ'vŭōn"), SW Sweden rises NW of Boras, flows in wide arc NW to L. Mjor at Alingsas, thence flows SW to Gota R. at Goteborg; 70 mi. long.

Save River, Yugoslavia: see SAVA RIVER.

Saverne (sävârn'), Ger. *Zabern* (tsä'bŭrn), town (pop. 8,218), Bas-Rhin dept., E France, on the Zorn and Marne-Rhine Canal (locks), and 21 mi. NW of Strasbourg, just E of Saverne Gap; metalworking center (agr. machinery, tools, alarm clocks, office and distilling equipment, steel furniture, scales, and barbed wire); grindstone quarrying, optical glass mfg., woodworking. Has 18th-cent. castle (now barracks) and old houses.

Saverne Gap, lowest pass (1,086 ft.) of the N Vosges, E France, on Moselle–Bas-Rhin dept. border, bet. Sarrebourg and Saverne. Consists in part of narrow gorge (c.8 mi. long) of Zorn R., just W of Saverne, followed by Marne-Rhine Canal, road, and railroad; 5 mi. E of Sarrebourg, canal and railroad cross crest of the Vosges in tunnel (1.5 mi. long). A strategic gateway to Rhine lowland, it was captured (Nov., 1944) by Americans sweeping to Ger. border in Second World War.

Saviano (sävyä'nô), town (pop. 3,834), Napoli prov., Campania, S Italy, 1 mi. SW of Nola.

Savica River, Yugoslavia: see SAVA BOHINJKA RIVER.

Savièse (sävyĕz'), town (pop. 2,887), Valais canton, SW Switzerland, 1 mi. N of Sion; farming.

Savigliano (sävēlyä'nô), town (pop. 9,244), Cuneo prov., Piedmont, NW Italy, on Maira R. and 30 mi. S of Turin; rail junction; metalworking center; railroad shops; silk mills, perfume industry.

Savignac-Lédrier (sävēnyäk'-lādrēā'), village (pop. 73), Dordogne dept., SW France, on the Auvézère and 21 mi. NW of Brive-la-Gaillarde; paper mill.

Savignac-les-Églises (–lāzāglēz'), village (pop. 263), Dordogne dept., SW France, on Isle R. and 11 mi. NE of Périgueux; grains, walnuts.

Savignano di Puglia (sävēnyä'nô dē pōō'lyä), village (pop. 3,353), Avellino prov., Campania, S Italy, 7 mi. NNE of Ariano Irpino; furniture mfg.

Savignano sul Panaro (sōōl pänä'rô), village (pop. 377), Modena prov., Emilia-Romagna, N central Italy, on Panaro R. 1 mi. E of Vignola; paper mill.

Savignano sul Rubicone (sōōl rōōbēkō'nĕ), town (pop. 2,966), Forlì prov., Emilia-Romagna, N central Italy, on the Rubicon and 9 mi. WNW of Rimini, on the Aemilian Way; tannery. Roman bridge destroyed (1944) by retreating Germans.

Savignone (sävēnyō'nĕ), village (pop. 686), Genova prov., Liguria, N Italy, NE of Giovi Pass, 11 mi. N of Genoa; cotton mills; health resort.

Savigny-lès-Beaune (sävēnyē"-lā-bōn'), village (pop. 975), Côte-d'Or dept., E central France, on E slope of the Côte d'Or, 3 mi. NNW of Beaune; noted Burgundy wines.

Savigny-sur-Braye (–sür-brā'), village (pop. 1,115), Loir-et-Cher dept., N central France, 13 mi. WNW of Vendôme; horse and cattle raising.

Savigny-sur-Orge (–sür-ôrzh'), town (pop. 14,508), Seine-et-Oise dept., N central France, near left bank of the Seine, 13 mi. S of Paris; metalworking, tanning, fertilizer mfg.

Saviñan (sävē'nyän), village (pop. 1,650), Saragossa prov., NE Spain, on Jalón R. and 8 mi. NE of Calatayud, in fruit-, wine-, and flower-growing region; olive-oil processing, sawmilling.

Savines (sävēn'), village (pop. 770), Hautes-Alpes dept., SE France, on the Durance and 16 mi. E of Gap; cotton spinning.

Savinja Alps (sä'vĭnyä) or **Kamnik Mountains** (käm'nĭk), Slovenian *Savinjske Alpe* or *Kamniške Planine,* Ger. *Sanntal Alpen* or *Steiner Alpen,* spur of main Karawanken range in N Slovenia, Yugoslavia, extending c.15 mi. SE from Austrian border at Loibl Pass. Highest peak, Grintavec, Ger. *Grintouz* (8,390 ft.). Tourist area.

Savinja River, Ger. *Sann* (zän'), N Slovenia, Yugoslavia, rises in Savinja Alps 6 mi. NE of the Grintavec, flows SE, through brown-coal region, past Mozirje and Celje, and S, past Lasko and Rimske Toplice, to Sava R. at Zidani Most; c.60 mi. long. Several hydroelectric plants on river and its tributaries. Hops grown in Savinja Valley, Slovenian *Savinjska Dolina,* which extends from Celje c.10 mi. upstream.

Savino (sä'vēnŭ), town (1948 pop. over 2,000), S Ivanovo oblast, Russian SFSR, 19 mi. SSW of Shuya; cotton textiles, clothing.

Savintsy (sä'vēntsē), village (1926 pop. 6,320), E Kharkov oblast, Ukrainian SSR, on the Northern Donets and 18 mi. NW of Izyum; metalworks.

Savio (sä'vēō), village in Tuusula commune (pop. 16,079), Uusimaa co., S Finland, 15 mi. NNE of Helsinki; rubber and brickworks.

Savio River (sä'vyô), N central Italy, rises in Etruscan Apennines on Monte Fumaiolo, 5 mi. SE of Bagno di Romagna; flows 50 mi. NE, past Sarsina, Mercato Saraceno, and Cesena, to the Adriatic 4 mi. N of Cervia.

Savitri River, India: see MAHAD.

Savitza River, Yugoslavia: see SAVA BOHINJKA RIVER.

Savli (säv'lē), town (pop. 5,955), Baroda dist., N Bombay, India, 16 mi. N of Baroda; local trade in cotton, oilseeds, grain, cattle; rice milling. Stone (for road building) quarried near by.

Savnik or **Shavnik** (both: shäv'nĭk), Serbo-Croatian *Šavnik,* town (pop. 3,550), N central Montenegro, Yugoslavia, on Piva R., on Pljevlja-Niksic road and 36 mi. NNW of Titograd; local trade center. Dates from 1860. The Durmitor rises 12 mi. NNW of town.

Savoie (sävwä'), department (□ 2,389; pop. 235,939), in Savoy, SE France; ⊙ Chambéry. Bounded by Italy (E), by the Rhone (NW). A mountainous region lying almost wholly within Savoy Alps (Massif de la Vanoise, Bauges, Beaufortin) which merges with Graian Alps in E. Agr. (tobacco and winegrowing, dairying, beekeeping) and pop. concentrated in deep Alpine valleys of the Isère (TARENTAISE, Combe de Savoie) and of the Arc (Maurienne), where numerous hydroelectric plants power aluminum, steel, and chemical industries. Principal resort area is Lac du Bourget, with spa of Aix-les-Bains catering to foreign tourists. Two important passes (Little Saint Bernard, Mont Cenis) lead into Po valley of Italy. Dept. formed 1860 after Fr. annexation of Savoy. As a result of 1947 treaty with Italy, 2 small areas around Little St. Bernard Pass and Mont Cenis were added to Savoie dept.

Savoie, Combe de, France: see COMBE DE SAVOIE.

Savoie, Haute-, France: see HAUTE-SAVOIE.

Savo Island (sä'vō, sä'vô), volcanic island, Solomon Isls., SW Pacific, 10 mi. N of Guadalcanal; 5 mi. long, 2 mi. wide. In Second World War, naval battle of Savo Isl. resulted (1942) in costly defeat for U.S. forces.

Savona (sävō'nä), province (□ 597; pop. 219,108), Liguria, NW Italy; ⊙ Savona. Comprises central RIVIERA di Ponente, enclosed by Ligurian Alps and Apennines; drained by Arroscia and upper Bormida rivers. Forests cover 62% of area. Agr. (fruit, vegetables, flowers, olives, grapes), with horticulture predominating (center at Albenga); livestock raising (sheep, goats); fishing. Limestone quarries. Industry at Savona, Vado Ligure, Varazze. Resorts (Albenga, Alassio, Varazze) on the Riviera. Formed 1927 from Genova prov.

Savona, anc. *Savo,* city (pop. 57,354), ⊙ Savona prov., Liguria, NW Italy, port on Gulf of Genoa and 24 mi. SW of Genoa; 44°19'N 8°29'E. A main trade center and port of Italy, serving as S outlet for Piedmont; rail junction. Exports staves, chestnuts, dynamite, pottery, glassware; imports coke, coal, iron, petroleum; large warehouses at SAN GIUSEPPE DI CAIRO. Chief industrial and commercial center of Riviera di Ponente; iron- and steelworks, mfg. (aluminum, pottery, bricks, glass), tanneries, wine distilleries, sulphur refineries; shipyards; railroad shops. Bishopric. Has cathedral (1589–1604), mus. with art gall., theater (1853; dedicated to Gabriello Chiabrera, b. here). During Middle Ages, waged long and unsuccessful rivalry with Genoa. Famous in Renaissance for its majolica. Became ⊙ prov. 1927. In Second World War, heavily bombed (1942–44).

Savona (sŭvō'nŭ), village (pop. 869), Steuben co., S N.Y., on Cohocton R. and 12 mi. NW of Corning; flour, lumber milling.

Savonburg (să'vŭnbûrg, să–), city (pop. 155), Allen co., SE Kansas, 17 mi. ENE of Chanute; livestock, grain.

Savonlinna (sä'vōnlĭn"nä), Swedish *Nyslott* (nü'-slŏt"), city (pop. 10,995), Mikkeli co., SE Finland, on isl. (bridges) in narrows bet. lakes of the Saimaa system, 55 mi. E of Mikkeli; lake port, with shipyards, machine shops, lumber and plywood mills. Tourist center. Has Olav Castle (1475), until 1812 of strategic importance in Russo-Swedish wars.

Savonnières-en-Perthois (sävônyâr'-ā-pĕrtwä'), village (pop. 547), Meuse dept., NE France, 9 mi. ESE of Saint-Dizier; building and cutting-stone quarries.

Savoonga (sŭvōōn'gŭ), Eskimo village (pop. 249), on N St. Lawrence Isl., W Alaska, in Bering Sea, 40 mi. E of Gambell; whaling, fox trapping, reindeer herding. Cooperative store.

Savoy (sŭvoi'), district of W central London, England, bet. the Strand and N bank of the Thames (S), adjoining The Adelphi. It includes the Savoy Hotel, Savoy Theater (where Gilbert and Sullivan operettas were 1st performed), and Savoy Chapel, made royal chapel by George III and, according to tradition, scene of Chaucer's marriage. Chapel (completed 1511) is sole remaining part of Savoy Palace, built c.1245 by Peter of Savoy; scene of imprisonment of King John of France (who died here 1364); burned (1381) in Wat Tyler's rebellion. In 1661 the Savoy Conference of Puritans and bishops was held in the district. Since First World War many new office bldgs. have been erected here.

Savoy (sŭvoi'), Fr. *Savoie* (sävwä'), Alpine region of SE France, now administratively divided into 2 depts., Haute-Savoie (N; ⊙ Annecy) and Savoie (S; ⊙ Chambéry, historical seat of early dukes of Savoy). Bounded by Italy (E), Switzerland (NE), L. Geneva (N), and Rhone R. (W). Physically, it lies chiefly in Savoy Alps, which merge with Mont Blanc massif and Graian Alps along Alpine crest (E). Savoy contains Mont Blanc (highest peak of the Alps), and commands access to important passes (Little Saint Bernard, Mont Cenis) to Po valley. Cattle raising and dairying are chief agr. pursuits. Numerous hydroelectric plants, especially in Maurienne and Tarentaise valleys, power aluminum, steel, chemical industries. Principal tourist centers and health resorts are Chamonix, Aix-les-Bains, Évian-les-Bains, and Annecy. Settled by the Allobroges when Caesar conquered region for Rome, Savoy was part of 1st and 2d kingdoms of Burgundy, and, after 933, that of Arles. Divided into several fiefs under 1st counts of Savoy (11th cent.), it became a duchy under Amadeus VIII. Bet. 1475 and 1601, it lost Lower Valais, Geneva, and Vaud to Switzerland, Gex, Bresse, and Bugey to France. In 1720, Victor Amadeus II became king of Sardinia, making Savoy part of that state. Annexed (1792) by France; returned (1815) to Sardinia. In 1860, Savoy (mostly Fr. speaking) was again ceded to France, which annexed it after a plebiscite, creating present depts.

Savoy. 1 Town (pop. 291), Berkshire co., NW Mass., 15 mi. NE of Pittsfield. Savoy Mtn. State Forest is just N, in Hoosac Range. **2** Town (pop. 314), Fannin co., NE Texas, 11 mi. W of Bonham, in agr. area.

Savoy Alps, Fr. *Alpes de Savoie,* NW offshoots of Graian Alps, in SE France. Bounded N by L. Geneva, W by the middle Rhone, S by the Arc and Isère valleys. Rises to 12,668 ft. at the Grande-Casse (in Massif de la Vanoise), and includes the Beaufortin, Bauges, Bornes, and Chablais mtn. districts. The MONT BLANC group (just E on Fr.-Ital. border) is sometimes considered part of Savoy Alps.

Savoyeux (sävwäyû'), village (pop. 252), Haute-Saône dept., E France, on Saône R. and 10 mi. NE of Gray; paper mill.

Savran or **Savran'** (säv'rŭnyŭ), village (1926 pop. 8,243), N Odessa oblast, Ukrainian SSR, 34 mi. W of Pervomaisk; metalworks.

Savsat (shävshät'), Turkish *Şavşat*, village (pop. 537), Coruh prov., NE Turkey, 34 mi. ENE of Artvin; maize, wheat. Also called Yenikoy.

Savsjo (säv'shû"), Swedish *Savsjö*, village (pop. 2,403), Jonkoping co., S Sweden, 17 mi. S of Nassjo; rail junction; metalworking, furniture mfg. Site of large tuberculosis sanitarium.

Savu Islands or **Sawoe Islands** (both: sä'vōō), small group (pop. 33,622), Lesser Sundas, Indonesia, in Savu Sea, 100 mi. W of Timor; 10°31'S 121°52'E. Comprise Savu (□ 160; pop. 29,450; 23 mi. long, 10 mi. wide), Raijua or Raidjoea (both: rījōō'ü) (□ 14; pop. 4,172; 8 mi. long, 3 mi. wide), and several islets. Group is generally low. Pony raising, agr. (copra, corn, cotton), trepang fishing.

Savur (sävōōr'), village (pop. 2,803), Mardin prov., SE Turkey, 19 mi. NNE of Mardin; barley, wheat, lentils.

Savu Sea or **Sawoe Sea** (both: sä'vōō), part of Indian Ocean, Indonesia, bounded W by Sumba isl., N by Flores isl., E by Timor isl., connected with Banda Sea by Ombai Strait; c.170 mi. wide. Contains Savu Isls.

Savuto River (sävōō'tô), in Calabria, S Italy, rises in La Sila mts. near Lago Ampollino, 19 mi. N of Catanzaro; flows 35 mi. W and SW to Tyrrhenian Sea 3 mi. W of Nocera Tirinese. Forms part of Catanzaro-Cosenza prov. boundary.

Savvino (sä'vēnŭ), town (1926 pop. 2,046), central Moscow oblast, Russian SFSR, on rail spur and 15 mi. E of Moscow; cotton mill.

Saw (sô), village, Pakokku dist., Upper Burma, 45 mi. WNW of Seikpyu, on road to Kanpetlet (S Chin Hills).

Sawahlunto or **Sawahloento** (both: sŭwälōōn'tō), town (pop. 15,146), W Sumatra, Indonesia, in Padang Highlands, 35 mi. ENE of Padang; mining center in Ombilin coal fields. Connected by railroad with coal-landing port of Padang.

Sawai Madhopur (sŭvī' mä'dōpōōr), town (pop. 8,392), ⊙ Sawai Madhopur dist., E Rajasthan, India, 75 mi. SSE of Jaipur; trades in millet, wheat, gram, metalware; food processing, handicrafts (copper and brass vessels, lacquered woodwork). Rail junction 2 mi. N.

Sawane (sä"wä'nä), town (pop. 3,875) on Sado Isl., Niigata prefecture, Japan, on W coast, 3 mi. SE of Aikawa; rice, silk cocoons. Gold, silver, copper mined.

Sawankhalok (sŭwän'kŭlôk'), town (1937 pop. 5,205), Sukhothai prov., N Thailand, 20 mi. N of Sukhothai, on spur of Bangkok-Chiangmai RR, and on Yom R. (head of navigation); pottery making; cotton plantations. Founded c.1800 on present site, 10 mi. S of a former Thai capital of Sukhothai period (14th cent.). Also spelled Savankalok and Savangalok.

Sawantwadi, India: see SAVANTVADI, former princely state.

Sawara (sä"wä'rä), town (pop. 23,460), Chiba prefecture, central Honshu, Japan, port on Tone R. and 22 mi. NW of Choshi; agr. center (rice, wheat); raw silk, poultry. Near by is anc. Shinto shrine.

Sawatch Mountains (sŭwŏch'), range of Rocky Mts. in central Colo., extending c.100 mi. S from Eagle R. to Saguache town; bounded E by Arkansas R., W by Elk Mts. Prominent peaks: OURAY PEAK (13,955 ft.), Mt. of the Holy Cross (13,986 ft.), Grizzly Mtn. (14,020 ft.), Shavano Peak (14,179 ft.), Mt. ANTERO (14,245 ft.), LA PLATA PEAK (14,342 ft.), Mt. MASSIVE (14,418 ft.), Mt. ELBERT (14,431 ft.; highest point in Colo.). Part of range just N of St. Elmo, is known as Collegiate Range; includes Mt. YALE (14,172 ft.), Mt. PRINCETON (14,177 ft.), and Mt. HARVARD (14,399 ft.). Independence Pass (12,095 ft.), near Mt. Massive, is crossed by highway, as is Hagerman Pass (11,495 ft.), bet. Lake and Pitkin counties. MONARCH PASS (11,312 ft.) is W of Salida and crossed by highway. Marshall Pass (10,846 ft.) is SW of Salida and serves railroad. Range is penetrated 10 mi. W of Leadville by Busk-Ivanhoe Tunnel (9,394 ft. long), constructed as railroad tunnel (1890) and now used by state highway. Twin Lakes Tunnel, near Twin Lakes village, is unit in water-diversion project.

Sawbridgeworth (sô'brĭjwûrth, săps'wûrth), residential urban district (1931 pop. 2,604; 1951 census 3,692), E Hertford, England, 10 mi. E of Hertford. Has 14th–15th-cent. church.

Sawda, India: see SAVDA.

Sawel, highest peak (2,240 ft.) of Sperrin Mts., on Londonderry-Tyrone border, Northern Ireland.

Sawmill Bay, S Alaska, small inlet on E side of Evans Isl., Prince William Sound, 4 mi. W of Latouche; 60°3'N 148°2'W; site of fish wharves; supply point for fishing in Prince William Sound.

Sawmill Bay, locality, central Mackenzie Dist., Northwest Territories, on E shore of Great Bear L., 35 mi. SW of Port Radium; 65°44'N 118°55'W; U.S.-Canadian Arctic weather station.

Sawmill Lake, N Ill., bayou lake (c.2½ mi. long) of Illinois R. along its left bank, c.7 mi. S of Hennepin.

Sawmills, village, Bulawayo prov., W Southern Rhodesia, in Matabeleland, on Umguza R., on railroad and 55 mi. NW of Bulawayo; sawmilling (teak).

Sawoe Islands, Sawoe Sea, Indonesia: see SAVU ISLANDS, SAVU SEA.

Sawqirah, Ras, Oman: see SAUQIRA, RAS.

Sawston, town and parish (pop. 1,684), S Cambridge, England, on Cam R. and 6 mi. SSE of Cambridge; leather, paper, and color-film industries. Site of England's 1st village col., opened 1930. Has 14th-cent. church. Refuge of Mary Tudor.

Sawtelle (sôtĕl'), old name for section of W Los ANGELES city, S Calif., adjoining Santa Monica (W); often called (with adjacent dists.) West Los Angeles. Site of U.S. veterans' home and hosp.

Sawtooth Mountains, in S central Idaho, NE of Boise, at head of Salmon R. and of its Middle Fork and South Fork. Include parts of Sawtooth, Challis, Payette, and Boise natl. forests. Prominent point is CASTLE PEAK (11,820 ft.). Sawtooth Range (rising to 10,704 ft.) is largely in Elmore co., in S part of system. Deposits of gold, silver, lead, zinc, and copper.

Sawyer, county (□ 1,273; pop. 10,323), N Wis.; ⊙ Hayward. Drained by Chippewa R. Generally forested area, with many lakes, the largest being L. Chippewa. Dairying, lumbering, farming (potatoes). Contains Lac Court Oreilles Indian Reservation, Ojibwa State Roadside Park, and part of Chequamegon Natl. Forest. Formed 1883.

Sawyer. 1 City (pop. 223), Pratt co., S Kansas, 11 mi. SSE of Pratt, in wheat region. **2** Village (pop. 264), Ward co., central N.Dak., 15 mi. SE of Minot and on Souris R.

Sawyer Island, S Maine, in Sheepscot R., just W of Boothbay, to which it is bridged; c.¾ mi. in diameter.

Sawyerville, village (pop. 621), S Que., on Eaton R., a tributary of St. Francis R. and 17 mi. ESE of Sherbrooke; dairying, stock raising.

Sawyerville, village (pop. 390), Macoupin co., SW central Ill., 24 mi. ENE of Alton, in agr. and bituminous-coal area.

Sax (säsh), town (pop. 3,376), Alicante prov., E Spain, 25 mi. NW of Alicante; mfg. of shoes, toys, furniture; olive-oil processing; lumbering, stock raising; wine, cereals, fruit. Porphyry quarries.

Saxapahaw (săk"sŭpŭhô', săk"sŭpô'), village (1940 pop. 555), Alamance co., N central N.C., 23 mi. WSW of Durham and on Haw R.; textile mfg.

Saxe-Altenburg (săks'-ăl'tŭnbûrg), Ger. *Sachsen-Altenburg* (zäk'sŭn-äl'tŭnbōōrk), former duchy, Thuringia, central Germany; ⊙ was Altenburg. Was separate duchy ruled by Ernestine branch of house of Wettin (1603–72), then passed to Saxe-Gotha. From 1826 until 1918 it was again separate duchy under a collateral line. Was inc. 1920 into THURINGIA.

Saxe-Coburg (–kō'bûrg), Ger. *Sachsen-Coburg* (zäk'sŭn-kō'bōōrk), former duchy, Thuringia, central Germany. A possession of Ernestine branch of house of Wettin, it was ruled by Saxe-Gotha line (1679–99) and then by Saxe-Saalfeld line (which, until 1826, also ruled duchy of Saalfeld) until 1918. In 1826, Ernestine lands were redivided; Saalfeld passed to Saxe-Meiningen; Ernest III of Saxe-Coburg received duchy of Gotha and assumed title Ernest I, duke of **Saxe-Coburg-Gotha** (–gō'thŭ, –gō'tŭ). His brother Leopold became, in 1831, King Leopold I of Belgium; his younger son was Prince Albert, consort of Queen Victoria of England. In 1918, duke of Saxe-Coburg-Gotha abdicated; in 1920, COBURG was inc. into Bavaria, Gotha into THURINGIA.

Saxe-Gotha (–gō'thŭ, –gō'tŭ), Ger. *Sachsen-Gotha* (zäk'sŭn-gō'tä), former duchy, Thuringia, central Germany. A possession of Ernestine branch of house of Wettin, it passed to Saxe-Weimar in 16th cent. Upon death (1605) of Duke John of Weimar, his territories were divided; one of his younger sons, Ernest the Pious, received Saxe-Gotha, Coburg, Meiningen, and Saalfeld, and inherited (1672) SAXE-ALTENBURG. After Ernest's death in 1679, his holdings were divided among his 7 sons; the eldest, Frederick I, received Gotha and Altenburg. In 1826, Gotha came to duke of Saxe-Coburg, who consequently ruled as duke of SAXE-COBURG-GOTHA until 1918. Saxe-Altenburg was ruled (1826–1918) as independent duchy by a collateral line.

Saxe-Meiningen (–mī'nĭng-ŭn), Ger. *Sachsen-Meiningen* (zäk'sŭn-mī'nĭng-ŭn), former duchy, Thuringia, central Germany; ⊙ was Meiningen. A possession of Ernestine branch of house of Wettin, it became independent duchy in 17th cent. under one of the sons of Ernest the Pious of SAXE-GOTHA. At redivision (1826) of Ernestine lands, Saxe-Meiningen received Saalfeld from Saxe-Coburg (which was compensated with Gotha), and Hildburghausen. Last duke abdicated in 1918; in 1920, Saxe-Meiningen was inc. into THURINGIA.

Saxe-Saalfeld, former duchy, Germany: see SAXE-COBURG.

Saxe-Weimar (–vī'mär), Ger. *Sachsen-Weimar* (zäk'sŭn-vī'mär), former grand duchy, Thuringia, Germany; ⊙ was Weimar. Remained with Ernestine branch after redivision of Wettin lands in 1547. Shortly thereafter, Ernestine lands were divided into duchies of Weimar, Gotha (see SAXE-GOTHA), Coburg (see SAXE-COBURG), Altenburg, and Eisenach. After the failure of several lines, and repeated redivisions of the Ernestine lands, duchy of Weimar in 1741 was united with duchy of Eisenach (including Jena) and was thenceforth known as **Saxe-Weimar-Eisenach** (–ī'zŭnäkh). The prolonged residence of Goethe in Weimar made city an intellectual center of Europe. Raised to grand duchy at Congress of Vienna (1815); last grand duke resigned in 1918. Saxe-Weimar-Eisenach was inc. into THURINGIA in 1920.

Saxis, fishing village (1940 pop. 589), Accomack co., E Va., on Saxis Isl. in Chesapeake Bay (separated from shore by marshes), 13 mi. SW of Pocomoke City, Md.

Saxlingham Nethergate, agr. village and parish (pop. 569), SE Norfolk, England, 7 mi. S of Norwich; flour milling. Has 13th-cent. church with Saxon foundations and medieval glass.

Saxman, fishing village (pop. 76), SE Alaska, on S coast of Revillagigedo Isl., 2 mi. SE of Ketchikan.

Saxmundham (săksmŭn'dŭm), urban district (1931 pop. 1,260; 1951 census 1,438), E Suffolk, England, 18 mi. NE of Ipswich; agr. market; mfg. (agr. implements, shoes). Church rebuilt in 14th cent.

Saxon (säksō'), town (pop. 2,194), Valais canton, SW Switzerland, near the Rhone, 11 mi. WSW of Sion; farming, canning. Ruined castle; iodine spring.

Saxon. 1 Village (pop. 3,088), Spartanburg co., NW S.C., just W of Spartanburg; textile milling. **2** Village, Iron co., N Wis., 23 mi. ESE of Ashland; railroad junction; trade center in submarginal farm area.

Saxonburg, borough (pop. 602), Butler co., W Pa., 9 mi. SSE of Butler.

Saxonian Saale, Germany: see SAALE RIVER.

Saxonian Switzerland (săksō'nēŭn), Ger. *Sächsische Schweiz* (zĕk'sĭ-shŭ shvīts'), properly called *Elbsandsteingebirge* (ĕlp'zänt'shtīn"gŭbĭr"gŭ), E central Germany, plateau astride the Elbe (scenic gorge), SE of Dresden, extends c.20 mi. along Czechoslovak border bet. the Erzgebirge (W) and Lusatian Mts. (E). Consists of deeply dissected sandstone rising to craggy cliffs (BASTEI). Noted tourist area: Bad Schandau, Königstein, Wehlen.

Saxonland, Ger. *Sachsenland* (zäk'sŭnlänt), name given to S part of Transylvania, Rumania, which was settled in 12th cent. and after by Saxon immigrants from Germany.

Saxonville, Mass.: see FRAMINGHAM.

Saxony (săk'sŭnē), Ger. *Sachsen* (zäk'sŭn), state (□ 6,561; pop. 5,558,566), E central Germany; ⊙ DRESDEN. Bordered by Thuringia (W), Bavaria (SW), Czechoslovakia (S), Polish-administered Germany (E), Brandenburg and Saxony-Anhalt (N). Almost completely situated in the Erzgebirge (S) and its foothills. Drained by Elbe (major N-S traffic artery), Mulde, Spree, and White Elster rivers. Highly industrialized region with widespread textile mfg.: cotton and wool milling in W part of state (ZWICKAU); cloth weaving is concentrated E of the Elbe, linen and jute milling in SE (ZITTAU); textile knitting is centered at CHEMNITZ. Major industrial centers are AUE, Chemnitz, CRIMMITSCHAU, Dresden (precision and optical instruments), GLAUCHAU, GÖRLITZ (railroad cars), MEERANE, MEISSEN (porcelain), PLAUEN (textile machinery), and RIESA (steel). Metal- and woodworking in mtn. regions. LEIPZIG is leading commercial hub. Coal mining around Zwickau and Dresden (FREITAL); extensive lignite deposits S of Leipzig (BORNA) and in E and NE; nonferrous metals mined in the ERZGEBIRGE. Univ. at Leipzig. The original land of the Saxons on German soil extended far beyond the present boundaries of the state and included roughly the present state of Lower Saxony. Conquered (8th cent.) by Charlmagne and inc. into his empire. First duchy of Saxony, one of German stem duchies, was created in 9th cent. Duke Henry I was elected German king in 919; his son, Emperor Otto I, bestowed duchy on a Saxon nobleman, whose descendants ruled until 1106. Duchy subsequently passed to the Guelphs. After Henry the Lion lost all his fiefs in 1180, stem duchy was broken up into numerous fiefs, out of which most central and NW German states eventually developed (Brunswick, Hanover, Holstein, Lippe, Oldenburg, Westphalia). Bernard of Anhalt, a younger son of Albert the Bear of Brandenburg, received ducal title of Saxony and became founder of Ascanian line of Saxon dukes. Besides ANHALT, Bernard received Lauenburg and region around Wittenberg, on the Elbe. After 1260, these widely separated territories continued under separate Ascanian branches as the duchies of Saxe-Lauenburg and Saxe-Wittenberg. Duke of latter was raised to permanent rank of elector by Golden Bull of 1356; duchy became known as Electoral Saxony. The Ascanian line became extinct in 1422; margrave Frederick the Warlike of Meissen (of the powerful house of Wettin) added (1423) Electoral Saxony to his territories (already comprising larger parts of Thuringia and Lower Lusatia), and became (1425) Elector Frederick I. In 1485, Wettin lands were partitioned into Saxony of the Ernestine line, including Electoral Saxony with Wittenberg and most of the Thuringian lands, and into Saxony of the Albertine line (or ducal Saxony), including the Meissen territories with Dresden and Leipzig. In early 16th cent., the Ernestine line actively supported Luther; Elector John Frederick I, a leader of the Schmalkaldic League, was defeated by Emperor Charles V at battle of Mühlberg (1547). By the Capitulation of WITTENBERG, in same year, John Frederick was deprived of the electorate, and the Ernestine line retained only the several duchies of THURINGIA. Electoral title passed to Albertine line, which retained it until 1806. In Thirty Years War, Saxony changed sides repeatedly; while allied with Sweden it obtained Upper and Lower Lusatia at the Peace of Prague (1635); later in the same year, it sided with the Imperials and was devastated by the Swedes. At Peace of Westphalia, however, Elector John George emerged as one of Germany's most powerful Protestant princes, being 2d only to the elector of Brandenburg. From 1697 until 1763, the electors of Saxony were also kings of Poland. The old rivalry bet. Saxony and Brandenburg (after 1701 the kingdom of Prussia) and the electors' traditional policy of shifting sides led to several invasions of Saxony in the 18th cent. and to a loss of its prestige among Ger. princes. However, the 18th cent. marked the apex of Saxon culture: Augustus II and Augustus III were lavish patrons of art and learning and beautified their capital, Dresden; Leipzig was a center of Ger. literature (Lessing, Schiller) and music (Bach). Saxony sided with France in Napoleonic Wars; in 1806 its elector became King Fredrick Augustus I of Saxony, and his failure to change sides and join the Allies cost him about half his kingdom at Congress of Vienna (1814–15). Saxony thus lost Lower LUSATIA, E part of Upper Lusatia, and its entire N territory (including Wittenberg and Merseburg), all to Prussia. In 1816 most of this territory, together with some Prussian dists., was constituted into Prussian province (□ 9,753; 1939 pop. 3,616,635) of Saxony (see following article). After fighting in Austro-Prussian War on losing side, Saxony was forced to join (1866) North German Confederation; from 1871 until abdication (1918) of King Frederick Augustus III, it was member of German Empire. As the state of Saxony (□ 5,789; 1939 pop. 5,231,739), it joined Weimar Republic. After Second World War, state was reconstituted in Soviet occupation zone; lost small area E of Lusatian Neisse but gained part of former Prussian Lower Silesia prov. Saxony became (1949) one of the states of the German Democratic Republic (East German state).

Saxony, Ger. *Sachsen,* former Prussian province (□ 9,753; 1939 pop. 3,616,635), central Germany; ⊙ was Magdeburg. Bordered by Saxony state (S), Thuringia (SW), Brunswick (W), and former Prussian provs. of Hanover (NW) and Brandenburg (E); Anhalt formed almost complete enclave. Prov. was constituted in 1816 from N portion of kingdom of Saxony and several other Prussian holdings. Was briefly divided (1944–45) into separate Halle-Merseburg (S) and Magdeburg (N) provs. After 1945 it was inc. into newly formed state of SAXONY-ANHALT, losing several exclaves to Thuringia.

Saxony-Anhalt (săk'sunē-ăn'hält), Ger. *Sachsen-Anhalt* (zäk'sůn-än'hält), state (□ 9,515; 1946 pop. 4,160,539), central Germany; ⊙ HALLE. Formed after 1945 through incorporation of former state of ANHALT and former Prussian SAXONY prov. Bordered by Brandenburg (E), Saxony (S), Thuringia (SW), and Lower Saxony (W and N). Major portion of state is situated in N German lowlands, S is hilly; includes (W) the lower HARZ. Drained by Elbe and Saxonian Saale rivers. Sugar beets, grain, vegetables, and oil seeds grown in fertile N; QUEDLINBURG is horticultural, NAUMBURG is wine-growing center. Highly industrialized S portion is rich in mineral resources: copper-slate mining in MANSFELD region; potash mined around STASSFURT; Halle, MERSEBURG, and WEISSENFELS are located in one of Germany's richest lignite fields. DESSAU, HALBERSTADT, and MAGDEBURG are also industrial centers (chemicals, machinery). Luther was b. at EISLEBEN; WITTENBERG is the cradle of the Reformation. At TORGAU, on the Elbe, 1st contact was made bet. Allied and Soviet forces in Second World War. Univ. at Halle. State was constituted after 1945 and placed in Soviet occupation zone; the administrative division [Ger. *Regierungsbezirk*] Erfurt (□ 1,438; 1939 pop. 650,840) of former Prussian Saxony prov. was inc. into Thuringia; several Brunswick exclaves were absorbed by Saxony-Anhalt. Became (1949) one of the states of the German Democratic Republic (East German state).

Saxton, borough (pop. 1,093), Bedford co., S Pa., 23 mi. SW of Huntingdon and on Raystown Branch of Juniata R.; railroad shops; bituminous coal; timber; agr. Inc. 1867.

Saxtons River, Vt.: see ROCKINGHAM.

Say (sī), town (pop. c.2,200), SW Niger territory, Fr. West Africa, on right bank of the Niger and 30 mi. SSE of Niamey; gum, millet; hides, livestock. Sleeping sickness and leprosy clinics.

Sayabec (sä'bĕk, Fr. säyäbĕk') or **Saindon** (sēdō'), village (pop. 2,115), SE Que., on L. Matapedia, 22 mi. SSW of Matane; lumbering, dairying.

Sayaboury (sůyä'bōōrē'), town (1941 pop. 3,882), ⊙ Sayaboury prov. (□ 7,100; 1947 pop. 79,000), NW Laos, near right bank of Mekong R. Trading center. In Thailand 1941–46; called Paklay until 1946.

Sayago (sīä'gō), N suburb of Montevideo, S Uruguay, c.5 mi. from the city (linked by rail and tram lines). Site of agr. col. and experiment station; cement plants. Founded 1867.

Sayalonga (sīälōng'gä), Málaga prov., S Spain, town (pop. 853), 24 mi. E of Málaga; raisins, grapes, oranges, apricots, almonds, olives.

Sayán (sīän'), town (pop. 1,229), Lima dept., W central Peru, on Huaura R. and 28 mi. E of Huacho; rail terminus; distributing center for surrounding cotton- and sugar-growing region.

Sayan Mountains (sůyän'), mountain system partly on Siberia-Mongolia border. **Eastern Sayan Mountains** extend SE from Yenisei R. in Russian SFSR, along right watershed of Mana R., to the area S of, and within 100 mi. of, SW end of L. Baikal; form boundary bet. Russian SFSR and Mongolia in E section. Small glaciers exist on highest peak, Munku Sardyk (11,453 ft.). Irkutsk-Jibhalanta highway passes through Eastern Sayans at Mondy. **Western Sayan Mountains** (rising to 9,180 ft.), entirely in USSR, extend NE from Altai Mts. to central section of Eastern Sayan Mts.; form border bet. Krasnoyarsk Territory and Tuva Autonomous Oblast. Yenisei R. and Kyzyl-Minusinsk highway pass through them. Sayan Mts. yield gold, coal, graphite, silver, and lead. Lumber is floated down N slopes to Trans-Siberian RR.

Sayantui or **Sayantuy** (sīŭntōō'ē), village (1948 pop. over 500), S Buryat-Mongol Autonomous SSR, Russian SFSR, on Selenga R. and 7 mi. S of Ulan-Ude, in agr. area (wheat, livestock).

Sayapullo (sīäpōō'yō), town (pop. 944), Cajamarca dept., NW Peru, in Cordillera Occidental, 28 mi. W of Cajabamba; silver- and copper-mining center.

Sayasan, Russian SFSR: see RITLYAB.

Sayat (sůyät'), town (1933 pop. over 3,000), E Chardzhou oblast, Turkmen SSR, near the Amu Darya, 28 mi. SE of Chardzhou; cotton; metalworks.

Sayausí (sī-ousē'), village Azuay prov., S Ecuador, in the Andes, 5 mi. WNW of Cuenca; platinum deposits.

Sayaxché (sīäkh-chā'), town (1950 pop. 318), Petén dept., N Guatemala, on Pasión R. and 35 mi. SW of Flores; livestock.

Saybrook. 1 Town, Conn.: see DEEP RIVER; village, see OLD SAYBROOK. **2** Village (pop. 758), McLean co., E central Ill., 24 mi. E of Bloomington; grain, dairy products, livestock, poultry.

Saybrook Point, Conn.: see OLD SAYBROOK.

Saybusch, Poland: see ZYWIEC.

Sayda (zī'dä), town (pop. 1,546), Saxony, E central Germany, in the Erzgebirge, 15 mi. S of Freiberg, near Czechoslovak border; woodworking, toy mfg.

Sayda-Guba, Russian SFSR: see SAIDA-GUBA.

Saydanaya, Syria: see SAIDNAYA.

Sayghan, Afghanistan: see SAIGHAN.

Sayhut, Aden: see SEIHUT.

Sayiadha, Greece: see SAGIADA.

Sayida, Lebanon: see SAIDA.

Sayla (sī'lŭ), town (pop. 5,346), NE Saurashtra, India, 16 mi. SW of Wadwan; local trade in cotton and millet. Was ⊙ former Eastern Kathiawar state of Sayla (□ 222; pop. 15,352) of Western India States agency; state merged 1948 with Saurashtra.

Saylesville, village (1940 pop. 2,490) in Lincoln town, Providence co., NE R.I., on Moshassuck R. and 5 mi. N of Providence; textiles, textile dyeing and finishing.

Saylorsburg, resort village, Monroe co., NE Pa., 9 mi. SW of Stroudsburg. Small lake near by.

Saylyugem Range, Mongolia: see SAILYUGEM RANGE.

Säynätsalo (sä'ünätsä"lō), village (commune pop. 2,968), Häme co., S central Finland, on islet at N end of L. Päijänne, 6 mi. S of Jyväskylä; lumber, plywood, and joinery mills.

Sayn Shanda, Mongolia: see SAIN SHANDA.

Sayo (sä'yō), town (pop. 5,250), Hyogo prefecture, S Honshu, Japan, 23 mi. NW of Himeji; rice-producing center.

Saypan, Marianas Islands: see SAIPAN.

Sayr, Lebanon: see SIR.

Sayram, Kazakh SSR: see SAIRAM.

Sayram Nuur, China: see SAIRAM NOR.

Sayre (sâr). **1** City (pop. 3,362), ⊙ Beckham co., W Okla., on North Fork of Red R. and 16 mi. WSW of Elk City, in dairying and agr. area (grain, broomcorn, cotton; dairy products; livestock). Natural-gas fields near by. Oil refineries, carbon-black plant, railroad shops. City is a broomcorn market. Seat of Sayre Jr. Col. Settled 1901; inc. as town 1903, as city 1910. **2** Borough (pop. 7,735), Bradford co., NE Pa., 17 mi. ESE of Elmira, N.Y., and on Susquehanna R.; railroad shops; lumber and metal products; dairying, agr. Laid out 1871, inc. 1891.

Sayreville (sâr'vĭl), borough (pop. 10,338), Middlesex co., E N.J., on Raritan R. and 5 mi. ESE of New Brunswick; bricks, tiles, chemicals. Inc. 1919. Includes industrial Parlin village (chemicals, fabrics, photographic products).

Sayr Usa, Mongolia: see SAIR USU.

Sayula (sīōō'lä). **1** City (pop. 9,340), Jalisco, central Mexico, near S shore of L. Sayula, on interior plateau, on railroad and 45 mi. NNE of Colima; alt. 5,278 ft. Processing and agr. center (grain, sugar cane, alfalfa, cotton, tobacco, livestock); flour milling, lumbering, sugar refining, vegetable-oil pressing, tanning. **2** Town (pop. 2,898), Veracruz, SE Mexico, on Isthmus of Tehuantepec, 29 mi. WSW of Minatitlán; fruit.

Sayula, Lake (□ 79; alt. 4,511 ft.), in Jalisco, central Mexico, on central plateau, SW of L. Chapala and 40 mi. SSW of Guadalajara; 16 mi. long NNE-SSW, 2–6 mi. wide. Town of Sayula near S shore.

Sayulilla (sīōōlē'yä), town (pop. 1,323), Nayarit, W Mexico, in Pacific lowland, on Acaponeta R. and 70 mi. NNW of Tepic; tobacco, corn, sugar cane, fruit, vegetables, stock.

Sayville, resort village (pop. 4,251), Suffolk co., SE N.Y., on S shore of Long Isl., on Great South Bay, 8 mi. E of Bay Shore; yachting center; oysters; flower growing. Mfg.: aircraft parts, barrels, fishing tackle, cement blocks.

Sayward, village, SW B.C., on NE Vancouver Isl., on Johnstone Strait, at mouth of small Salmon R., 50 mi. ESE of Alert Bay; steamship landing for lumbering and farming area. Just S is Hkusam, Indian village.

Sayyun, Aden: see SEIYUN.

Saza, Japan: see SASA.

Saza (sä'zä), village, Southern Highlands prov., SW Tanganyika, 34 mi. WNW of Chunya, near SE tip of L. Rukwa; gold-mining center in Lupa gold field.

Sazaire, Angola: see SANTO ANTÓNIO DO ZAIRE.

Sazan or **Sazani,** Albania: see SASENO.

Sazanovka, Kirghiz SSR: see ANANYEVO.

Sazava (sä'zävä), Czech *Sázava,* village (pop. 1,435), E central Bohemia, Czechoslovakia, on Sazava R., on railroad and 17 mi. WSW of Kutna Hora, in wheat and potato region; glassmaking. Has 14th-cent. monastery.

Sazava River, Czech *Sázava,* E Bohemia, Czechoslovakia, rises in Bohemian-Moravian Heights, 8 mi. SW of Devet Skal mtn.; flows WNW, past Pribyslav, Havlickuv Brod, and Sazava, and W to Vltava R. at Davle; 135 mi. long.

Sazhino (sä'zhĭnŭ), village (1939 pop. over 500), SW Sverdlovsk oblast, Russian SFSR, 25 mi. SE of Krasnoufimsk; wheat, livestock.

Sazlika River, Sazliika River, or **Sazliyka River** (säzlĭ'kä), central Bulgaria, rises in Sirnena Gora 8 mi. S of Kazanlik; flows 61 mi. generally SE, through Stara Zagora Basin, to Maritsa R. just E of Simeonovgrad. Sometimes called Syutlika R. in upper course. Formerly Rakitnitsa R.

Sazonovo (sůzō'nůvŭ), town (1926 pop. 392), SW Vologda oblast, Russian SFSR, on railroad and 33 mi. SW of Babayevo, in Chagoda glassworking dist. Glassworks at adjacent (N) Zavod Imeni Sazonova (formerly Pokrovski Steklyanny Zavod; 1926 pop. 928) and at Smerdomlya (10 mi. NW; 1926 pop. 979). Until 1947, Belye Kresty.

Sbeitla (zbātlä'), anc. *Sufetula,* town (pop. 2,415), Kasserine dist., W central Tunisia, on Sousse-Tozeur RR, and 19 mi. ENE of Kasserine; dry-farming (modern irrigation project); experimental orchards and olive groves. Esparto trade and handicraft. Extensive ruins (3 temples, triumphal arch, aqueduct) of a once-prosperous Roman colony.

Sbiba (zbēbä'), village, Kasserine dist., W central Tunisia, 30 mi. NE of Kasserine; center of irrigated agr. settlement (orchards, pastures, vegetable gardens). Horse and cattle raising.

Sbikha (zbēkä'), village, Kairouan dist., E central Tunisia, 19 mi. N of Kairouan; irrigated forage crops; sheep raising.

Scaër (skäär'), village (pop. 1,716), Finistère dept., W France, 19 mi. E of Quimper; fruit and vegetable preserving.

Scafati (skäfä'tē), town (pop. 9,049), Salerno prov., Campania, S Italy, on Sarno R. and 4 mi. E of Torre Annunziata; cotton milling, tomato canning, metalworking, castor-oil mfg.

Scafell or **Scaw Fell** (both: skô'fĕl'), mountain group of the Cumbrians, S Cumberland, England, in the Lake District bet. Wastwater and Esk R., 14 mi. S of Keswick. Includes the peaks of Scafell Pike (3,210 ft., highest mountain in England), Scafell (3,162 ft.), Great End (2,984 ft.), and Lingmell (2,649 ft.). The region is natl. property and much visited by tourists.

Scala, Cyprus: see LARNACA, city.

Scalabis, Portugal: see SANTARÉM.

Scalambri, Cape, Sicily: see SCARAMIA, CAPE.

Scalanuova, town, Turkey: see KUSADASI.

Scalanuova, Gulf of, Turkey: see KUSADA, GULF OF.

Scalasaig, Scotland: see COLONSAY.

Scalby (skôl, skô–), residential urban district (1931 pop. 2,771; 1951 census 6,225), North Riding, E Yorkshire, England, near North Sea 2 mi. NW of Scarborough. Church dates from 12th cent.

Scald Law, Scotland: see PENTLAND HILLS.

Scalea (skälā'ä), town (pop. 2,513), Cosenza prov., Calabria, S Italy, port on Tyrrhenian Sea, 22 mi. W of Castrovillari, in fruitgrowing region; bathing resort; olive oil, wine. Cape Scalea (39°51'N 15°46'E) is 2 mi. NW, on SE shore of Gulf of Policastro.

Scaleby, village and parish (pop. 307), N Cumberland, England, 5 mi. NE of Carlisle; cattle, sheep, oats. Near by are remains of 14th-cent. Scaleby Castle.

Scale Force, England: see CRUMMOCK WATER.

Scales Mound, village (pop. 385), Jo Daviess co., extreme NW Ill., near Wis. line, 21 mi. E of Dubuque (Iowa), in agr. area. Near by is Charles Mound (alt. 1,241 ft.), highest point in state.

Scalloway (skă'lōwā, –lůwā), village in Tingwall parish (pop. 1,552), Shetlands, Scotland, on SW coast of Mainland isl., 5 mi. WSW of Lerwick; fishing port. Harbor protected by Trondra isl. Has castle built 1600 by Earl Patrick. Scalloway is former ⊙ Shetlands.

Scalpay (skăl'pů). **1** Island (pop. 27), Inner Hebrides, Inverness, Scotland, just off E coast of Skye, 8 mi. WNW of Kyle; 4½ mi. long, 3½ mi. wide; rises to 1,298 ft. in S. Has noted oyster fisheries in Loch na Cairidh, which separates isl. from Skye. **2** Island (pop. 636), Outer Hebrides, Inverness, Scotland, at entrance to East Loch Tarbert, Harris; 3 mi. long, 1½ mi. wide; rises to 341 ft. At SE extremity is lighthouse (58°48'N 6°46'W).

Scalp Level, borough (pop. 1,756), Cambria co., SW central Pa., 6 mi. SSE of Johnstown. Inc. 1898.

Scamander (skůmăn'důr), village, E Tasmania, 60 mi. E of Launceston, on Tasman Sea; resort.

Scamander River, Turkey: see KUCUK MENDERES RIVER.

Scammon, city (pop. 561), Cherokee co., extreme SE Kansas, 11 mi. SW of Pittsburg, in diversified agr. area. Coal mines near by.

Scammon Bay, Eskimo village (pop. 94), W Alaska, on Bering Sea, 60 mi. SW of Akulurak; supply point.

Scandia: see SCANDINAVIA.

Scandia (skăn'dēů), city (pop. 611), Republic co., N Kansas, on Republican R. and 8 mi. WSW of Belleville, in grain region; cement products.

Scandiano (skändyä'nô), town (pop. 2,441), Reggio nell'Emilia prov., Emilia Romagna, N central Italy, 7 mi. SSE of Reggio nell'Emilia and on branch of Secchia R.; liquor, sausage, cement. M. M. Boiardo and L. Spallanzani b. here.

Scandinavia (skăn"dĭnā'vēů), anc. *Scandia,* region of N Europe, comprising territory of SWEDEN, NORWAY, and DENMARK (total □ 315,181; pop. c.14,000,000). FINLAND is often included. From anthropological and cultural viewpoint, Iceland and Faeroe Isls. are often considered as part of Scandinavia. From purely geographical viewpoint, region is confined to Scandinavian peninsula, bounded by the Skagerrak and the Baltic (S), North Sea and Norwegian Sea of Atlantic (W), Barents Sea of Arctic Ocean (N), and Gulf of Bothnia and Baltic (E), and comprising only Norway and Sweden (total □ 298,605; pop. c.9,850,000), while Denmark is, geographically, N extension of North German plain. Scandinavian peninsula is c.1,150 mi. long (NNE–SSW), 230–500 mi. wide. From central mtn. range along Swedish-Norwegian border, surface slopes steeply W to fjord-indented rugged coast of Norway, and more gently E to low, level coast of Sweden on the Baltic and Gulf of Bothnia. N part of peninsula lies within Arctic Circle and includes W part of LAPLAND. Galdhoppigen (8,097 ft.), in Jotunheim Mts., Norway, is highest elevation of peninsula; W of this range is Jostedal Glacier, largest ice field of Europe. Kebnekaise (6,965 ft.), in N Sweden, is highest peak of central mtn. range. Numerous lakes dot peninsula, especially its S part; largest are Vaner, Vatter, Malar, and Hjalmar, all in S Sweden. Short rapid rivers flow W into North Sea and Norwegian Sea; among large rivers emptying into Gulf of Bothnia are the Torne, Dal, Lule, Pite, Skellefte, Angerman, Indal, and Ljusna rivers. Chief isls. off Scandinavia are Gotland and Oland (Baltic), the Lofoten and Vesteralen groups (Norwegian Sea), as well as numerous other isls. off Norwegian coast. Chief cities of peninsula are Stockholm, Oslo, Goteborg, Bergen, Malmo, and Trondheim. The peninsula is rich in timber and minerals (notably iron and copper pyrites); coastal waters, especially off Norway, are major fishing grounds. The languages of Scandinavia (Danish, Norwegian, Swedish) are of common origin and retain considerable similarity, especially bet. Danish and Norwegian; a distinct literary Norwegian language is of very recent origin. Lapp and Finnish are spoken in N extremity of the peninsula. Since 18th cent. the Finno-Ugric Lapp language has, in W Lapland, absorbed a large number of Scandinavian loan words. The oldest Germanic literature flourished in Scandinavia and Iceland.

Scandinavia, village (pop. 286), Waupaca co., central Wis., 20 mi. ESE of Stevens Point, in timber and farm area; lumbering.

Scania, Sweden: see SKANE.

Scanlon, village (pop. 572), Carlton co., NE Minn., on St. Louis R., near Fond du Lac Indian Reservation, and 16 mi. W of Duluth, in grain and potato area. State forests in vicinity.

Scanno (skän'nô), village (pop. 3,571), Aquila prov., Abruzzi e Molise, S central Italy, 10 mi. SSW of Sulmona; resort (3,379 ft.) just S of Lago di Scanno (1 mi. long).

Scansano (skänsä'nô), town (pop. 1,985), Grosseto prov., Tuscany, central Italy, 12 mi. ESE of Grosseto, in area raising grapes, olives; livestock.

Scantic, village, Conn.: see EAST WINDSOR.

Scantic River (skăn'tĭk), Mass. and Conn., rises SSE of Springfield, Mass.; flows c.35 mi. generally SW, through Conn., to the Connecticut near South Windsor.

Scapa Flow (skă'pů), area of water (□ 50) in the Orkneys, Scotland, c.15 mi. long, up to 8 mi. wide, bounded by isls. of Pomona (N and E), Hoy (W), Flotta and South Ronaldsay (S), and Burray (SW). Opens S on Pentland Firth, W on Sound of Hoy, E on Sound of Holm. Scapa Flow is a major naval anchorage. In First World War it was one of chief bases of the British Grand Fleet; in spite of mines, the *Vanguard* was torpedoed here in 1917. Part of the Ger. fleet interned here was scuttled by their crews in 1919. In Oct., 1939, a Ger. submarine passed the boom defenses, considered impregnable, and sank the *Royal Oak.*

Scappoose, town (pop. 659), Columbia co., NW Oregon, 20 mi. NW of Portland; potatoes, pickles.

Scaramia, Cape (skärä'myä), point on SE coast of Sicily, 6 mi. W of Irminio R. mouth; 36°47'N 14°30'E. Also called Cape Scalambri.

Scarba (skär'bů), island (pop. 5) of the Inner Hebrides, Argyll, Scotland, just N of Jura, from which it is separated by 1-mi.-wide strait of Corryvreckan; 4 mi. long, 3 mi. wide; rises to 1,470 ft. Has deer forest.

Scarboro or **Scarborough,** (skär'bů"rō, –bůrů), town (pop. 4,600), Cumberland co., SW Maine, just S of Portland, at mouth of Nonesuch R., includes villages of Dunstan and Prouts Neck. Fishing and resort area; sea food canned. Settled in 1630s, inc. 1658. Rufus King b. here.

Scarborough (skär'brů), municipal borough (1931 pop. 41,788; 1951 census 43,983), North Riding, E Yorkshire, England, on North Sea 40 mi. N of Hull; seaside and spa resort with small port. Spreads inland from a peninsula bet. 2 bays. Peninsula was site of 4th-cent. Roman signal station; castle built here 1136 was later converted into a fort by Henry II. Town has a marine drive linking South Bay and North Bay. Has several parks, and a church dating partly from 1198. St. Martin's church has windows by Burne-Jones, Rossetti, and Morris. Scene of annual music festival. George Fox, founder of the Society of Friends, was imprisoned here. In First World War town was shelled by German submarines.

Scarborough, town (pop. 908), ⊙ Tobago isl., B.W.I., 65 mi. NE of Port of Spain; 11°11'N 60°44'W. In coconut-growing region, situated picturesquely at base of a hill. Vessels anchor offshore. Has govt. stock farm, botanical station, administrative bldgs. Govt. House is ½ mi. away. Sawmilling, extracting of lime oil. On top of the hill stand ruins of Fort King George (built 1770). Scarborough succeeded Georgetown (now Mount Saint George) as capital in 1796. It was formerly called Port Louis.

Scarborough (skär'bů"rō, –bůrů). **1** Town, Maine: see SCARBORO. **2** Village, Westchester co., SE N.Y., 2 mi. S of Ossining; seat of Scarborough School.

Scarborough, Lake, Texas: see COLEMAN.

Scarborough Beach, R.I.: see NARRAGANSETT.

Scarborough Shoal, China: see MACCLESFIELD BANK.

Scarbro, village (pop. 2,459, with near-by Glen Jean and Hilltop), Fayette co., S central W.Va., 12 mi. N of Beckley, in coal region.

Scarcies River, Fr. Guinea and Sierra Leone: see GREAT SCARCIES RIVER; LITTLE SCARCIES RIVER.

Scarcliffe, town and parish (pop. 3,039), NE Derby, England, 8 mi. E of Chesterfield; agr. market.

Scardona, Yugoslavia: see SKRADIN.

Scariff (skă'rĭf), Gaelic *Scairbh,* town (pop. 342), E Co. Clare, Ireland, on W shore of Lough Derg, 8 mi. NNW of Killaloe; agr. market (grain, potatoes; dairying). Has anc. round tower.

Scariff, islet (366 acres, 1 mi. long; rises to 830 ft.) of the Hog Isls., in the Atlantic, off SW Co. Kerry, Ireland, near mouth of Kenmare R., 5 mi. W of Lamb's Head.

Scarisbrick (skârz'–), agr. village and parish (pop. 2,597), W Lancashire, England, 3 mi. SE of Southport.

Scarlatizza, peak, Yugoslavia: see SKRLATICA.

Scarpanto, Greece: see KARPATHOS.

Scarperia (skärpĕrē'ä), village (pop. 1,716), Firenze prov., Tuscany, central Italy, S of Il Giogo pass, 16 mi. NNE of Florence; cutlery. Has early-14th-cent. palace.

Scarpe River (skärp'), Pas-de-Calais and Nord depts., N France, rises just above Aubigny, flows generally ENE, past Arras (head of canalization and navigation), Douai, and Saint-Amand, to the Escaut at Mortagne-du-Nord (near Belg. border); c.60 mi. long. Traverses large coal basin of N France; connected with canals of Flanders plain. Important battle line in First World War.

Scarsdale (skärz'–), residential village (pop. 13,156), Westchester co., SE N.Y., bet. Yonkers (SW) and White Plains, in New York city metropolitan area; mfg. (wood products, machinery). Settled c.1701, inc. 1915.

Scarville, town (pop. 105), Winnebago co., N Iowa, near Minn. line, 14 mi. N of Forest City; feed, dairy products. Sand and gravel pits near by.

Scatari Island (6 mi. long). NE N.S., off E Cape Breton Isl., 15 mi. SE of Glace Bay; 46°2'N 59°47'W.

Scattery Island (186 acres; 1 mi. long) in the Shannon, SW Co. Clare, Ireland, just SW of Kilrush. There are remains of 6 primitive churches; an anc. round tower; and 16th-cent. castle, built by Limerick citizens, to whom isl. was given by Queen Elizabeth.

Scaw Fell, England: see SCAFELL.

Sceaux (sō), town (pop. 8,320), Seine dept., N central France, a residential SSW suburb of Paris, 6 mi. from Notre Dame Cathedral. Its 19th-cent. castle was erected on the site of a château built by Colbert in 17th cent.; part of sumptuous park became a public garden in 1922.

Scebeli, Uebi, Ethiopia and Ital. Somaliland: see SHEBELI, WEBI.

Scedro Island (shchĕ'drô), Serbo-Croatian *Šćedro,* Ital. *Torcola* (tôr'kôlä), Dalmatian island in Adriatic Sea, S Croatia, Yugoslavia, c.30 mi. S of Split; 4 mi. long, 1 mi. wide. Sometimes spelled Shchedro.

Sceptre, village (pop. 205), SW Sask., near South Saskatchewan R., 40 mi. S of Kindersley; wheat, stock.

Scerni (shĕr'nē), village (pop. 2,163), Chieti prov., Abruzzi e Molise, S central Italy, 7 mi. W of Vasto. Agr. school.

Scesaplana, Alpine peak: see RHÄTIKON.

Scey-sur-Saône (sā-sür-sōn'), village (pop. 1,161), Haute-Saône dept., E France, on Saône R. and 9 mi. WNW of Vesoul; iron foundry, textile mill.

Schaaksvitte, Russian SFSR: see KASHIRSKOYE.

Schaal Lake (shäl), Ger. *Schaalsee* (shäl'zā"), lake (□ 8.5), Mecklenburg, N Germany; extends 9 mi. N from Zarrentin, 1–3 mi. wide; greatest depth 234 ft., average depth 59 ft. Indented shore line; contains several isls. Drained (S) into the Elbe by small Schaale R.

Schaan (shän), town (pop. 1,845), Liechtenstein, near the Rhine (Swiss border), on Arlberg Express (via Buchs and Feldkirch), 2.5 mi. NNW of Vaduz. Mfg. of leather goods, perfumes, artificial teeth; lumberyards. Anc. settlement, believed to be of Celtic origin, originally on a lake. Has Dux chapel; graveyard with Romanesque belfry; convent. Roman and Allemanic remains near by.

Schaarbeek, Belgium: see SCHAERBEEK.

Schaasberg, Netherlands: see SCHAESBERG.

Schacht-Audorf (shäkht'-ou'dôrf), village (pop. 2,979), in Schleswig-Holstein, NW Germany, on Kiel Canal, 2.5 mi. E of Rendsburg; furniture mfg.

Schaefferstown (shā'fůrztoun), village (1940 pop. 537), Lebanon co., SE Pa., 8 mi. ESE of Lebanon.

Schaerbeek or **Schaarbeek** (skhär'bāk), town (pop. 124,292), Brabant prov., central Belgium, NE industrial suburb of Brussels; rail junction with switch and freight yards; electric-power station.

Schaesberg (skhäz'bĕrkh), town (pop. 8,720), Limburg prov., SE Netherlands, 2 mi. E of Heerlen; coal-mining center. Sometimes spelled Schaasberg.

Schafberg (shäf'bĕrk), peak (5,850 ft.) in Salzburg, W central Austria, on E shore of Sankt Wolfgangsee, in the Salzkammergut. Cogwheel railroad from Sankt Wolfgang.

Schafer (shā'fůr), village and township (pop. 94), McKenzie co., W N.Dak., 5 mi. E of Watford City. Was ⊙ 1906–41; succeeded by Watford City.

Schaffhausen (shäf-hou'zůn), Fr. *Schaffhouse* (shäf-ōōz'), canton (□ 115; 1950 pop. 57,448), N Switzerland, N of the Rhine; ⊙ Schaffhausen. In S spurs of Black Forest, nearly surrounded by Germany. Pop. German speaking and largely Protestant. Forests, cultivated fields (cereals), and meadows; some orchards, gardens, and vineyards. Pop. (over half) and industry are concentrated in the capital and in Neuhausen am Rheinfall.

Schaffhausen, town (1950 pop. 25,901), ⊙ Schaffhausen canton, N Switzerland, on right bank of the Rhine, near Ger. border. Originally an abbey (founded c.1050), Schaffhausen became a free imperial city (c.1208); joined Swiss Confederation in 1501. Several hydroelectric plants on the Rhine, here noted for the RHEINFALL, 2 mi. SSW of town. Produces metal goods (notably cables and fittings), woolen textiles, playing cards, beer, watches. Many old houses and some medieval fortifications (notably the Munot, or Unnot, castle) remain. Important buildings include old (15th cent.) and new (17th cent.) town halls, 11th-cent. minster (Romanesque), and monastic buildings, including historical mus.

Area in square miles is indicated by the symbol □, capital city or county seat by the symbol ⊙.

Schafstädt (shäf'shtĕt), town (pop. 3,778), in former Prussian Saxony prov., central Germany, after 1945 in Saxony-Anhalt, 11 mi. SW of Halle; agr. market (sugar beets, wheat).

Schagen (skhä'khŭn), village (pop. 3,889), North Holland prov., NW Netherlands, 11 mi. N of Alkmaar; dairy farming.

Schaghticoke (skă'tĭkŏŏk", shă'–) village (pop. 687), Rensselaer co., E N.Y., on Hoosic R. and 13 mi. NNE of Troy, in dairying, and grain- and potato-growing area.

Schaken, Lithuania: see SAKIAI.

Schalchen (shäl'khŭn), town (pop. 2,802), W Upper Austria, 11 mi. SSE of Braunau; scythe mfg.

Schalkau (shäl'kou), town (pop. 2,704), Thuringia, central Germany, in Thuringian Forest, 8 mi. WNW of Sonneberg; toy mfg., woodworking; sandstone quarrying. Near by are ruins of medieval Schaumburg castle.

Schaller (shä'lŭr, shä'–), town (pop. 841), Sac co., W Iowa, 22 mi. SE of Cherokee; popcorn, feed.

Schallerbach, Austria: see BAD SCHALLERBACH.

Schallihorn (shä'lēhôrn"), peak (13,050 ft.) in Pennine Alps, S Switzerland, NNW of Zermatt.

Schanck, Cape, S Victoria, Australia, S extremity of peninsula separating Port Phillip Bay from Western Port; 38°30'S 144°53'E; lighthouse.

Schandau, Bad, Germany: see BAD SCHANDAU.

Schanfigg (shän'fĭk), valley of lower Plessur R., Grisons canton, E Switzerland, known for its bridges, viaducts, tunnels.

Schänis (shā'nĭs), residential town (pop. 2,111), St. Gall canton, NE central Switzerland, bet. lakes of Zurich and Wallenstadt.

Schans, Nieuwe, Netherlands: see NIEUWE SCHANS.

Schanzer Kopf (shän'tsŭr kôpf'), peak (2,113 ft.) of the Hunsrück, W Germany, 10 mi. W of Bingen.

Schardenberg (shärd'ŭnbĕrk), town (pop. 2,400), W Upper Austria, 5 mi. NNE of Schärding; vineyards.

Schärding (shĕr'dĭng), town (pop. 6,259), NW Upper Austria, on Inn R. (Ger. border), 8 mi. S of Passau, Germany; dairying (butter, cheese). Granite quarries near by.

Scharfenort, Poland: see OSTROROG.

Scharfenwiese, Poland: see OSTROLEKA.

Scharhörn (shär'hûrn"), uninhabited North Sea island (□ 1.8) of East Frisian group, NW Germany, 13 mi. NW of Cuxhaven.

Scharmbeck, Germany: see OSTERHOLZ-SCHARMBECK.

Scharmer (skhär'mŭr), village (pop. 593), Groningen prov., NE Netherlands, 6 mi. E of Groningen; potato-flour milling.

Scharmützel Lake, Ger. *Scharmützelsee* (shärmü'tsŭlzā"), lake (□ 5.3), Brandenburg, E Germany, 6 mi. S of Fürstenwalde; 7 mi. long, 1–1.5 mi. wide, greatest depth 91 ft., average depth 30 ft. Drained by Storkow Canal towards Dahme R.

Scharmützel Lake-Dahme Canal, Germany: see STORKOW CANAL.

Scharnitz Pass (shär'nĭts), anc. *Porta Claudia,* defile (alt. 3,140 ft.) on Austro-Ger. border just S of Mittenwald; cut by Isar R. bet. Wettersteingebirge (W) and Karwendelgebirge (E) of the Bavarian Alps. Followed by road and railroad, it connects Innsbruck and Munich. Was used by the Romans.

Scharrel (shä'rŭl), village (commune pop. 6,422), in Oldenburg, NW Germany, after 1945 in Lower Saxony, 7 mi. WNW of Friesoythe, in peat region. Commune is called Saterland (zä'tŭrlänt).

Scharster-Rhine Canal (skhär'stŭr-rīn'), Du. *Scharster-Rijn,* Friesland prov., N Netherlands; extends 16 mi. N-S, bet. the Ijsselmeer at Lemmer and Sneek. Crosses several lakes; connects with Grouw Canal at Sneek L.

Schässburg, Rumania: see SIGHISOARA.

Schattendorf (shät'ŭndôrf), village (pop. 2,527), Burgenland, E Austria, 4 mi. WNW of Sopron, Hungary; sugar beets.

Schatzlar, Czechoslovakia: see ZACLER.

Schauen (shou'ŭn), village (pop. 857), in former Prussian Saxony prov., central Germany, after 1945 in Saxony-Anhalt, at N foot of the upper Harz, 9 mi. NNW of Wernigerode, 7 mi. E of Vienenburg.

Schauenburg, Germany: see SCHAUMBURG-LIPPE.

Schauenstein (shou'ŭn-shtīn), town (pop. 1,824), Upper Franconia, NE Bavaria, Germany, in Franconian Forest, 8 mi. W of Hof; mfg. of precision instruments, thread; metalworking. Chartered 1386.

Schauinsland (shou'ĭnslänt), mountain (4,223 ft.) in the Black Forest, S Germany, 5 mi. S of Freiburg (cable railroad). Climatic health resort and winter-sports center.

Schaulen, Lithuania: see SIAULIAI.

Schaumburg-Lippe (shoum'bŏŏrk-lĭ'pŭ), former state (□ 131; 1939 pop. 53,195), NW Germany, after 1945 comprised in Lower Saxony; ⊙ was Bückeburg. Extending NE from the Porta Westfalica, it was surrounded by former Prussian provs. of Hanover and Westphalia. County of Schaumburg or Schauenburg (⊙ was Rinteln) occupied large part of Westphalia in 12th cent. and received Holstein in 1111. Direct line died out in 1459; succeeding branch line retained only Schaumburg and Pinneberg in Holstein. When it in turn became extinct (1640), Pinneberg passed to Danish crown and Schaumburg was divided among Brunswick-Lüneburg, Hesse-Kassel, and LIPPE. Divisions among various branches of Lippe family resulted in creation of county, later principality, of Schaumburg-Lippe. Last prince abdicated in 1918, and state joined Weimar Republic.

Schedewitz (shā'dŭvĭts), S suburb of Zwickau, Saxony, E central Germany, on the Zwickauer Mulde.

Scheemda (skhām'dä), town (pop. 1,282), Groningen prov., NE Netherlands, on the Winschoter Diep and 4 mi. NW of Winschoten; strawboard, building stone. Site of 1st battle (1568) in Netherlands' struggle against Spaniards.

Scheer (shâr), town (pop. 1,336), S Württemberg, Germany, after 1945 in Württemberg-Hohenzollern, on the Danube and 3 mi. ESE of Sigmaringen; paper milling.

Scheerhorn or **Grosses Scheerhorn** (grō'sŭs shâr'hôrn), peak (10,820 ft.) in Glarus Alps, E central Switzerland, 9 mi. ESE of Altdorf. Kleines Scheerhorn (10,610 ft.) is near by.

Scheessel (shā'sŭl), village (pop. 4,063), in former Prussian prov. of Hanover, NW Germany, after 1945 in Lower Saxony, 5 mi. NE of Rotenburg; mfg. of textile ornaments, leather goods, paints; metalworking, food processing.

Scheggia Pass (skĕd'jä) (alt. 1,886 ft.), bet. N and central Apennines, central Italy, 25 mi. NE of Perugia; crossed by road bet. Gubbio and Sassoferrato. Site of Scheggia village (pop. 602).

Scheibbs (shīps), town (pop. 3,371), W Lower Austria, 16 mi. SE of Amstetten; scythe mfg.; summer resort.

Scheibenberg (shī'bŭnbĕrk), town (pop. 2,768), Saxony, E central Germany, in the Erzgebirge, 5 mi. SW of Annaberg, near Czechoslovak border, in uranium-mining region; ribbon, lace mfg.

Scheidegg or **Grosse Scheidegg** (grō'sŭ shī'dĕk), mountain (6,445 ft.), with a fine view, in Bernese Alps, S central Switzerland, 12 mi. ESE of Interlaken. Kleine Scheidegg (6,773 ft.), with another notable view, is 8 mi. SSE of Interlaken.

Scheidt (shīt), town (pop. 5,897), S Saar, 3.5 mi. E of Saarbrücken; metal- and woodworking.

Scheinfeld (shīn'fĕlt), town (pop. 2,147), Middle Franconia, W Bavaria, Germany, 25 mi. ESE of Würzburg; metalworking, printing. Cattle. Sandstone quarries in area.

Schela (skä'lä), village (pop. 774), Gorj prov., SW Rumania, 10 mi. N of Targu-Jiu; anthracite mines.

Schelde River, Belgium and Netherlands: see SCHELDT RIVER.

Scheldt-Meuse Junction Canal (skĕlt-mûz), NE Belgium, runs from Albert Canal near Herentals E to the ZUID-WILLEMSVAART S of Hamont. Serves Neerpelt. Crossed by Canal d'Embranchement 4 mi. NE of Mol.

Scheldt River (skĕlt), Fr. *Escaut* (ĕskō'), Flemish and Du. *Schelde* (skhĕl'dŭ), rises in N France, crosses Belgium, enters Netherlands below Antwerp, and forms estuary on North Sea; 270 mi. long. From its source in Aisne dept. near Le Catelet (whence it is paralled by SAINT-QUENTIN CANAL to Cambrai), it flows generally NNE, past Valenciennes, through W central Belgium, past Tournai, Ghent, Dendermonde, and Antwerp. Its estuary, the WESTERN SCHELDT, separating Walcheren and South Beveland isls. from Flanders mainland, is in Du. territory. The EASTERN SCHELDT, formerly a N branch of estuary, is now cut off by dyke linking South Beveland isl. with mainland, and is reached from Western Scheldt only by SOUTH BEVELAND CANAL. Thanks to its regular volume and intensive regulation, the Scheldt is navigable along most of its course; it is the master stream of a dense network of canals in N France and Belgium. Chief tributaries are the Scarpe and Lys (left), the Dender and Rupel (right). From 1648 to 1863, Dutch levied dues on foreign shipping ascending the Scheldt.

Schelklingen (shĕl'klĭng-ŭn), town (pop. 2,240), S Württemberg, Germany, after 1945 in Württemberg-Hohenzollern, in Swabian Jura, 12 mi. W of Ulm; rail junction. Has ruined castle.

Schell City (shĕl), city (pop. 400), Vernon co., W Mo., near Osage R., 18 mi. NE of Nevada.

Schelle (skhĕ'lŭ), town (pop. 4,958), Antwerp prov., N Belgium, near Scheldt R., 7 mi. SSW of Antwerp; electric-power station.

Schellenberg, Germany: see MARKTSCHELLENBERG.

Schellenberg (shĕ'lŭnbĕrk), village (pop. 406), N Liechtenstein, 7 mi. N of Vaduz and 2.5 mi. W of Feldkirch (Austria); cattle raising. Nunnery. Founded in 12th cent. by dukes of Schellenberg.

Schellsburg (shĕlz'bûrg), borough (pop. 305), Bedford co., S Pa., 8 mi. WNW of Bedford.

Schemnitz, Czechoslovakia: see BANSKA STIAVNICA.

Schenectady (skŭnĕk'tŭdē), county (□ 209; pop. 142,497), E N.Y.; ⊙ SCHENECTADY. Bounded N by Schoharie Creek; intersected by Mohawk R. and the Barge Canal. Dairying, fruitgrowing, general farming. Formed 1809.

Schenectady, city (pop. 91,785), ⊙ Schenectady co., E N.Y., on Mohawk R. (bridged) and the Barge Canal, and 13 mi. NW of Albany; important electrical-equipment mfg. center; hq. (since 1894) of the General Electric Company. Knolls atomic research laboratory is near by. Large locomotive plants. Also mfg. of athletic equipment, sports goods, varnish, mica products, wire and cable products. Charles P. Steinmetz's home and laboratory, now state-owned, serves as science mus. Seat of Union Col. and Univ. Among points of historic interest is pre-Revolution St. George's Episcopal Church. City founded by Arent Van Curler in 1662; inc. 1798. Grew commercially after coming of railroads in 1830s; industrial growth came after establishment (1848) of locomotive works and of Edison's electrical-machinery plant (1886), forerunner of huge General Electric works.

Schenefeld (shā'nŭfĕlt), village (pop. 5,178), in Schleswig-Holstein, NW Germany, 8 mi. WNW of Hamburg city center; mfg. of chemicals. Has 11th–12th-cent. church.

Schenevus (skŭnē'vŭs), village (pop. 568), Otsego co., central N.Y., 12 mi. SSE of Cooperstown, in the Catskills; glovemaking. Summer resort; small Schenevus L. is near by.

Schengen (shĕng'ŭn), village (pop. 375), extreme SE Luxembourg, on Moselle R., at Saar–Fr. border, and 4 mi. ESE of Mondorf-les-Bains; grape and plum growing.

Schepdaal (skhĕp'däl), town (pop. 2,829), Brabant prov., central Belgium, 7 mi. W of Brussels; market center for strawberry area. Formerly spelled Schepdael.

Scheppenstedt, Germany: see SCHÖPPENSTEDT.

Schererville (shĕr'ŭrvĭl), town (pop. 1,457), Lake co., extreme NW Ind., 10 mi. SW of Gary, near Ill. line.

Scherfede (shâr'fā"dŭ), village (pop. 3,050), in former Prussian prov. of Westphalia, NW Germany, after 1945 in North Rhine-Westphalia, near the Diemel, 6 mi. NW of Warburg; rail junction.

Scherpenheuvel (skhĕr'pŭnhû"vŭl), Fr. *Montaigu* (mōtĕgü'), village (pop. 5,226), Brabant prov., N central Belgium, 3 mi. W of Diest; agr. market; tree nurseries. Has 1st baroque church in Belgium, built in 17th cent.

Scherwiller (shĕrvēlâr'), Ger. *Scherweiler* (shĕr'vīlŭr), town (pop. 1,954), Bas-Rhin dept., E France, at E foot of the Vosges, 3 mi. NW of Sélestat; wool spinning, winegrowing.

Schesslitz (shĕs'lĭts), town (pop. 1,731), Upper Franconia, N Bavaria, Germany, 9 mi. NE of Bamberg; grain, livestock. Has 15th-cent. Gothic church.

Scheur (skhûr), channel, South Holland prov., SW Netherlands; formed by junction of NEW MAAS RIVER and OLD MAAS RIVER 7 mi. WSW of Rotterdam; flows 6.5 mi. WNW, past Maassluis, to E end of the NEW WATERWAY 4 mi. SE of Hook of Holland. Forms part of Rotterdam–North Sea waterway. Navigable by ocean-going ships.

Scheveningen (skhā'vŭnĭng-ŭn), town, South Holland prov., W Netherlands, on North Sea, 2 mi. NW of The Hague; popular seaside resort; herring-fishing port; mfg. (furniture, ice, fishing equipment), fish canning. Lighthouse; marine radio station. Considerable destruction in Second World War.

Schiedam (skhē'däm), town (pop. 69,728), South Holland prov., W Netherlands, on New Maas R. and 3.5 mi. W of Rotterdam; rail junction; major gin- and liquor-distilling center; shipbuilding; mfg. of glass, bottles, chemicals, asbestos, machinery, bridging material, lumber products, crates, cardboard. Has 15th-cent. church, 17th-cent. town hall. Chartered 1273; became fishing and grain-trade center in Middle Ages, later superseded by Rotterdam.

Schiefbahn (shēf'bän), village (pop. 5,626), in former Prussian Rhine Prov., W Germany, after 1945 in North Rhine-Westphalia, 5 mi. NE of München Gladbach; grain, cattle.

Schiehallion (shĭhăl'yŭn), mountain (3,547 ft.), N Perthshire, Scotland, 10 mi. WNW of Aberfeldy, near Loch Rannoch. In 1774 Nevil Maskelyne here experimented to determine density of the earth.

Schienhorn (shēn'hôrn), peak (12,490 ft.) in Bernese Alps, S central Switzerland, 8 mi. SSE of Mürren.

Schieratz, Poland: see SIERADZ.

Schierke (shēr'kŭ), village (pop. 1,310), in former Prussian Saxony prov., central Germany, after 1945 in Saxony-Anhalt, in the upper Harz, at foot of the Brocken, 8 mi. SW of Wernigerode; popular climatic health resort and winter-sports center.

Schiermonnikoog (skhērmônĭkōkh'), island (□ 10; pop. 767), one of West Frisian Isls., Friesland prov., N Netherlands, bet. North Sea (N) and the Waddenzee (S); 8 mi. long, 2 mi. wide. Lighthouse (NW); navigation school. S part of isl. consists of reclaimed Banckspolder (□ 1.6), with fertile soil. Chief village, Schiermonnikoog (pop. 665), 13 mi. NE of Dokkum; resort; ferry to Oostmahorn.

Schiers (shĭrs), town (pop. 2,192), Grisons canton, E Switzerland, on Landquart R. and 11 mi. NE of Chur.

Schierstein (shēr'shtīn), suburb (pop. 6,241) of Wiesbaden, W Germany, on right bank of the Rhine and 3 mi. SW of city center; fruit.

Schifferstadt (shĭ'fŭr-shtät), village (pop. 11,741), Rhenish Palatinate, W Germany, 5 mi. NW of Speyer; rail junction; flour milling. Vineyards; corn, tobacco. Roman remains excavated near by.

Schifflange (shĭflăzh′), town (pop. 5,077), S Luxembourg, on Alzette R., just ENE of Esch-sur-Alzette; iron mining.
Schiffweiler (shĭf′vī″lůr), town (pop. 6,549), E Saar, 3 mi. NW of Neunkirchen; coal mining; tobacco-products mfg.
Schildau (shĭl′dou), town (pop. 2,473), in former Prussian Saxony prov., central Germany, after 1945 in Saxony-Anhalt, 8 mi. SSW of Torgau; agr. market (grain, sugar beets, potatoes, livestock). Field Marshal Gneisenau b. here.
Schildberg, Poland: see OSTRZESZOW.
Schilde (skhĭl′dů), residential town (pop. 3,857), Antwerp prov., N Belgium, 8 mi. E of Antwerp. Barony of Schilde founded (1723) by Charles VI.
Schildpad Islands, Indonesia: see TOGIAN ISLANDS.
Schiller Park, village (pop. 1,384), Cook co., NE Ill., NW suburb of Chicago.
Schillingsfürst (shĭ′lĭngsfürst″), village (pop. 2,449), Middle Franconia, W Bavaria, Germany, 14 mi. W of Ansbach; brewing; oats, wheat, cattle, sheep. Has baroque castle. Sandstone quarries in area.
Schiltach (shĭl′täkh), village (pop. 2,378), S Baden, Germany, in Black Forest, on the Kinzig and 4 mi. NNW of Schramberg; textile and machinery mfg., woodworking, lumber milling. Summer resort.
Schilthorn or **Grosses Schilthorn** (grō′sůs shĭlt′hôrn), peak (9,757 ft.) in Bernese Alps, S central Switzerland, 3 mi. W of Mürren. Kleines Schilthorn (9,400 ft.) is near by.
Schiltigheim (shĕltēkĕm′, Ger. shĭl′tĭkh-hīm), N industrial suburb (pop. 22,168) of Strasbourg, Bas-Rhin dept., E France, on the Ill and Marne-Rhine Canal; metalworks (textile and agr. machinery, mining equipment, iceboxes, tools), breweries, distilleries, woodworking plants. Fruit, vegetable, and *pâté de foie gras* preserving, candy and malt coffee mfg. Railroad freight yards.
Schinnen (skhĭ′nůn), village (pop. 1,462), Limburg prov., SE Netherlands, 6 mi. NW of Heerlen; building stone; fruit syrup.
Schin op Geul (skhĭn′ ôb khûl′), town (pop. 358), Limburg prov., SE Netherlands, 8 mi. E of Maastricht; rail junction.
Schinousa or **Shinusa,** Greece: see SCHOINOUSA.
Schio (skyô), town (pop. 11,959), Vicenza prov., Veneto, N Italy, 15 mi. NW of Vicenza. Rail terminus; woolen center; also produces mill machinery (textile, marble, lumber), cutlery, furniture, leather goods, dyes, marmalade, lime, and cement. Has church (begun 1436) and 18th-cent. cathedral. Kaolin quarries and lead mines near by.
Schiphol (skhĭp′hōl), village (pop. c.1,000), North Holland prov., W Netherlands, on the Ringvaart and 6 mi. SW of Amsterdam; air transportation center at Schiphol airport; hq. of Royal Dutch Airlines. Entirely destroyed toward end of Second World War; rebuilt and enlarged since.
Schippenbeil, Poland: see SEPOPOL.
Schirgiswalde (shĭr′gĭsväl″dů), town (pop. 4,704), Saxony, E Central Germany, in Upper Lusatia, at N foot of Lusatian Mts., on the upper Spree and 7 mi. S of Bautzen, near Czechoslovak border; textile milling; stone quarrying.
Schirmeck (shĕrmĕk′, Ger. shĭr′mĕk), village (pop. 1,446), Bas-Rhin dept., E France, in Bruche R. valley of the E Vosges, and 13 mi. WSW of Molsheim; resort; mfg. (cord, hosiery), sawmilling. Col du DONON (or Schirmeck Pass) is 4 mi. NW.
Schirnding (shĭrn′dĭng), village (pop. 1,980), Upper Franconia, NE Bavaria, Germany, in the Fichtelgebirge, 7 mi. SE of Selb, near Czechoslovak border; glassworks. Lignite mined in area.
Schirwindt, Russian SFSR: see KUTUZOVO.
Schisò, Cape (shēzô′), point on E coast of Sicily, near mouth of Alcantara R.; 37°49′N 20°17′E. Formed by anc. lava flow. Site of NAXOS.
Schist Lake, village, W Man., on Schist L. (9 mi. long), 8 mi. SE of Flin Flon; copper mining.
Schitu-Golesti or **Golesti** (skē′tōō-gôlĕsht′), Rum. *Schitu-Goleşti*, village (pop. 1,291), Arges prov., S central Rumania, on railroad and 5 mi. S of Campulung; coal mining, textiles.
Schivelbein, Poland: see SWIDWIN.
Schiza or **Skhiza** (both: skhē′zů), largest island (□ 9) of Oinousai Isls., in Ionian Sea off SW Peloponnesus, Greece, 5 mi. W of Cape Akritas; 6 mi. long, 2 mi. wide; uninhabited. Formerly Cabrera.
Schkeuditz (shkoi′dĭts), town (pop. 17,463), in former Prussian Saxony prov., central Germany, after 1945 in Saxony-Anhalt, on the White Elster and 10 mi. NW of Leipzig, 12 mi. SE of Halle; 51°23′N 12°14′E. Paper milling, metalworking; mfg. of machinery, tarred paper. Site of airport for Halle and Leipzig; meteorological observatory. Lignite mined near by.
Schkölen (shkû′lůn), town (pop. 2,412), in former Prussian Saxony prov., central Germany, after 1945 in Saxony-Anhalt, 8 mi. S of Naumburg; flour milling, brick mfg.; grain, sugar beets.
Schkopau (shkō′pou), town (pop. 6,572), in former Prussian Saxony prov., central Germany, after 1945 in Saxony-Anhalt, on the Saxonian Saale and 6 mi. S of Halle, in lignite-mining region; mfg. of chemicals, synthetic rubber. Power station.
Schlachtensee (shläkh′tůnzā″), residential section of Zehlendorf dist., SW Berlin, Germany, on small lake, 10 mi. SW of city center; popular excursion resort. After 1945 in U.S. sector.
Schladen (shlä′důn), village (pop. 4,736), Brunswick, NW Germany, after 1945 in Lower Saxony, on the Oker and 10 mi. NE of Goslar; metalworking, sugar refining. Until 1941 in former Prussian prov. of Hanover.
Schladming (shlät′mĭng), village (pop. 2,813), Styria, central Austria, on Enns R. and 40 mi. SE of Salzburg; rail junction; textiles, brewery, tannery; summer resort with mineral springs. The Dachstein is N.
Schlaggenwald, Czechoslovakia: see HORNI SLAVKOV.
Schlakenwerth, Czechoslovakia: see OSTROV, Bohemia.
Schlan, Czechoslovakia: see SLANY.
Schlanders, Italy: see SILANDRO.
Schlangenbad (shläng′ůnbät), village (pop. 1,245), in former Prussian prov. of Hesse-Nassau, W Germany, after 1945 in Hesse, in the Taunus, 6 mi. W of Wiesbaden; resort with warm springs.
Schlarigna, Switzerland: see CELERINA.
Schlawa, Poland: see SLAWA.
Schlawe, Poland: see SLAWNO.
Schlehdorf (shlā′dôrf), village (pop. 1,142), Upper Bavaria, Germany, on N slope of the Bavarian Alps, on N shore of the Kochelsee, 14 mi. SSE of Weilheim; brewing, lumber milling. Has former Augustinian abbey (1140–1803; founded c.740 as Benedictine monastery).
Schlei (shlī), Baltic estuarine inlet, NW Germany; 25 mi. long, 433 ft.–2.5 mi. wide (average width .6 mi.), 50 ft. deep. Abounds in fish (eel, pike, herring). Schleswig is at W end. Formerly also spelled Schley.
Schleicher (shlī′kůr, slī′kůr), county (□ 1,331; pop. 2,852), W Texas; ⊙ Eldorado. On Edwards Plateau; alt. c.2,100–2,500 ft. Sheep-ranching region; also cattle, goats, poultry; ships wool, mohair. Some agr. (grain sorghums, oats, wheat, cotton). Some oil, natural gas, clay, limestone. Hunting in E. Formed 1887.
Schleiden (shlī′důn), town (pop. 2,351), in former Prussian Rhine Prov., W Germany, after 1945 in North Rhine-Westphalia, 16 mi. SW of Euskirchen; sawmills, paper mills.
Schleisingerville, Wis.: see SLINGER.
Schleiz (shlīts), town (pop. 7,493), Thuringia, central Germany, 15 mi. WNW of Plauen; metal- and woodworking, bookbinding, textile milling, tanning, machinery and tobacco-products mfg. Has castle (rebuilt c.1500) and late-Gothic church. Originally Slav settlement.
Schlesien, region, Europe: see SILESIA.
Schlesiersee, Poland: see SLAWA.
Schlesisch-Ostrau, Czechoslovakia: see SLEZSKA OSTRAVA.
Schlestadt, France: see SÉLESTAT.
Schleswig (shlĕz′wĭg, shlĕs′–, Ger. shlās′vĭkh), Dan. *Slesvig* (slās′vĭkh), S part of Jutland peninsula, S Denmark and N Germany, N of Eider R. Region was Danish duchy from 11th cent. until annexed in 1864–66 by Prussia, and, with HOLSTEIN (S of the Eider), was constituted into Prussian prov. of SCHLESWIG-HOLSTEIN. Following First World War, N part of Schleswig passed to Denmark as result of plebiscite (1920) and became known as North Schleswig, Dan. *Nordslesvig* (nôr′slās′vĭkh); it includes Aabenraa, Haderslev, Sonderborg, and Tondern. Ger. portion forms N part of Schleswig-Holstein.
Schleswig, residential town (1939 pop. 26,015; 1946 pop. 36,935), Schleswig-Holstein, NW Germany, at W end of the Schlei, 27 mi. NW of Kiel, at SW tip of the Angeln; airport (SSW); small harbor. Some mfg.: cordage, leather goods, chemicals, furniture; food processing. Seat of higher courts; Lutheran bishopric. Town consists of 4 dists. (united 1712): old town, Lollfuss, Friedrichsberg (S), and Holm (E; fishermen's quarter). Romanesque-Gothic cathedral has noted carved altar and tomb of Frederic I of Denmark. Just off Friedrichsberg, on isl. in the Schlei, is 16th–17th-cent. Gottorp castle, residence of dukes of Schleswig and later (1544–1713) of dukes of Schleswig-Holstein-Gottorp; now houses state archives and (since 1948) state mus. Town 1st mentioned c.800. Was R.C. bishopric from 947 until Reformation. Was ⊙ Schleswig-Holstein until 1917, when seat was transferred to Kiel. A. J. Carstens b. here.
Schleswig (shlĕs′wĭg), town (pop. 751), Crawford co., W Iowa, 11 mi. NNW of Denison; agr. shipping point.
Schleswig-Holstein (shlĕz′wĭg, shlĕs′–, –hōl′stīn, Ger. shlās′vĭkh-hôl′shtīn), state (□ 6,045; 1939 pop. 1,589,284; 1946 pop. 2,590,210, including displaced persons 2,650,488; 1950 pop. 2,593,617), NW Germany; ⊙ Kiel. Situated at base of Jutland peninsula; bordered by Denmark (N), Lower Saxony (S), and Mecklenburg (SE); Hamburg forms (S) partial enclave. Fronted by Baltic Fehmarn isl. and North FRISIAN ISLANDS. Low region (highest elevation 538 ft.) with irregular shore line; calm Baltic coast (E) affords excellent natural harbors (Flensburg, Kiel, Lübeck); rough wave action of North Sea (W) necessitates extensive diking of low, sandy shore. Drained by Eider, Trave, and Elbe (S border) rivers; traversed (E-W) by Kiel Canal. Noted cattle raising (especially in North Friesland); wheat (E), rye (W), intensive vegetable growing in the Dithmarschen; noted tree nurseries in Pinneberg region (S). Heath and moor predominate in center (N–S) strip. Industries (shipbuilding; machinery, leather, textiles) are centered at Elmshorn, Flensburg, Itzehoe, Kiel, Lübeck, Neumünster, Pinneberg, and Rendsburg; state-wide food processing (fish, dairy products, vegetables). Univ. at Kiel. Danish duchy of SCHLESWIG (N of Eider R.) became hereditary fief of German county of HOLSTEIN (S of Eider R.) in 1386 (confirmed 1440). After 1460, both were in personal union with Danish king, an arrangement constantly challenged by Ger. nobles. Holstein (created duchy in 1474) was member of Holy Roman Empire and, after 1815, of German Confederation, while Schleswig remained outside of imperial, later German, jurisdiction. Attempts (after 1846) of Denmark to annex the 2 duchies led to war of 1864, in which Austria and Prussia defeated Denmark, forcing her to relinquish Schleswig, Holstein, and Lauenburg (see RATZEBURG). Disagreement bet. Austria and Prussia over administration of duchies resulted in Austro-Prussian War (1866). Victorious Prussia annexed Holstein, Lauenburg, and Schleswig, from which the prov. of Schleswig-Holstein was constituted (1867, 1876). Following First World War, N part of SCHLESWIG passed to Denmark as result of a plebiscite (1920). After dissolution (1946) of Prussia, Schleswig-Holstein was reconstituted as state in Br. occupation zone. Due to influx of displaced persons and of refugees from E Germany, pop. of region increased 60% over 1939 figure. Joined (1949) the German Federal Republic (West German state).
Schlettau (shlĕ′tou), town (pop. 3,335), Saxony, E central Germany, in the Erzgebirge, 3 mi. SW of Annaberg, in uranium-mining region; ribbon, lace; woodworking, electrical-equipment mfg.
Schlettstadt, France: see SÉLESTAT.
Schleusingen (shloi′zĭng-ůn), town (pop. 5,717), in former Prussian Saxony prov. exclave, central Germany, after 1945 in Thuringia, in Thuringian Forest, 8 mi. SSE of Suhl; metal- and woodworking, paper milling; mfg. of glass (scientific instruments), china, leather. Has 13th-cent. Bertholdsburg castle, seat (1274–1583) of counts of Henneberg; and 18th-cent. church.
Schley, Germany: see SCHLEI.
Schley (shlī), county (□ 162; pop. 4,036), W central Ga.; ⊙ Ellaville. Coastal plain agr. (cotton, corn, truck, peanuts, pecans, peaches) and sawmilling area. Formed 1857.
Schlichtingsheim, Poland: see SZLICHTYNGOWA.
Schlieben (shlē′bůn), town (pop. 2,402), in former Prussian Saxony prov., central Germany, after 1945 in Saxony-Anhalt, 15 mi. WNW of Finsterwalde; flour milling; grain, potatoes, livestock.
Schlierbach (shlēr′bäkh), town (pop. 2,240), SE central Upper Austria, 15 mi. SW of Steyr; wheat, cattle.
Schlieren (shlē′růn), town (pop. 4,761), Zurich canton, N Switzerland, 4 mi. WNW of Zurich; heavy metalworks, silk textiles, chemicals.
Schliersee (shlēr′zā″), village (pop. 7,687), Upper Bavaria, Germany, in the Bavarian Alps, on N shore of the lake Schliersee (□ c.1), 14 mi. SW of Rosenheim; mfg. (pharmaceuticals; tobacco). Summer resort and winter-sports center (alt. 2,549 ft.).
Schlitz (shlĭts), town (pop. 4,543), central Hesse, W Germany, in former Upper Hesse prov., 9 mi. NNW of Fulda; artificial-silk and linen mfg. Has several Renaissance castles.
Schlochau, Poland: see CZLUCHOW.
Schlock, Latvia: see SLOKA.
Schloppe, Poland: see CZLOPA.
Schlossbach, Russian SFSR: see NEVSKOYE.
Schlossberg, Russian SFSR: see DOBROVOLSK.
Schlotheim (shlōt′hīm), town (pop. 5,527), Thuringia, central Germany, 9 mi. ENE of Mühlhausen; mfg. (electrical equipment, cordage).
Schluchsee (shlŏŏkh′zā″), lake (□ 1.4), S Baden, Germany, in Black Forest, 17 mi. SE of Freiburg; 4 mi. long, ½ mi. wide, 213 ft. deep; alt. 2,953 ft. Dammed at S tip; water is led to large hydroelectric plant 4 mi. S. Climatic health resort (alt. 3,117 ft.) of Schluchsee (pop. 835) on N shore.
Schlucht, Col de la (kôl dů lä shlŏŏkht′), chief pass (alt. 3,737 ft.) of the high Vosges, E France, on Vosges-Haut-Rhin dept. border, on Gérardmer-Colmar road, and 7 mi. E of Gérardmer, just N of the Hohneck (road). Winter sports. Formed Franco-German border, 1871–1919.
Schlüchtern (shlükh′tůrn), town (pop. 5,604), in former Prussian prov. of Hesse-Nassau, W Germany, after 1945 in Hesse, on the Kinzig and 15 mi. SSW of Fulda; mfg. of metal cloth.
Schluckenau, Czechoslovakia: see SLUKNOV.
Schlüsselburg (shlü′sůlbŏŏrk), town (pop. 1,674), in former Prussian prov. of Westphalia, NW Germany, after 1945 in North Rhine-Westphalia, on left bank of the Weser and 15 mi. NE of Minden.
Schlüsselburg, Russian SFSR: see PETROKREPOST.
Schmadribach (shmä′drēbäkh″), small stream in Bernese Alps, S central Switzerland, branch of White Lütschine R., SW of the Jungfrau; noted for its fine waterfall.

Schmalenbeck, Germany: see GROSSHANSDORF-SCHMALENBECK.

Schmalkalden (shmäl'käl"dŭn), town (pop. 12,663), in former Prussian Saxony prov. exclave, central Germany, after 1945 in Thuringia, at foot of Thuringian Forest, on small Schmalkalde R. near its mouth on the Werra, and 30 mi. SW of Erfurt, in iron-mining region; metalworking center (tools, kitchen utensils); mfg. of glass, tobacco products. Resort with mineral springs and tuberculosis sanitariums. The town hall (1419) was scene of founding (1531) of Schmalkaldic League by Protestant princes against Charles V; at the Crown Inn (rebuilt), the Schmalkaldic Articles of faith were drawn up (1537) by Luther. Has house where Luther stayed; town church (1437–1509); remains of fortifications. First mentioned 874. Chartered in 13th cent. Passed to Hesse-Kassel in 1583, and with it to Prussia in 1866. Until 1944 it was in exclave of former Prussian prov. of Hesse-Nassau. Sometimes called Smalcald or Smalkald. Niederschmalkalden village, with steelworks, is 4 mi. W.

Schmallenberg (shmä'lŭnbĕrk), town (pop. 3,402), in former Prussian prov. of Westphalia, W Germany, after 1945 in North Rhine-Westphalia, on the Lenne and 19 mi. SE of Arnsberg; forestry. Has 13th-cent. church.

Schmalleningken, Lithuania: see SMALININKAI.

Schmelz (shmĕlts), town (pop. 5,464), N central Saar, on Prims R. and 10 mi. NNE of Saarlouis; agr. market (stock, grain); woodworking. Created 1937.

Schmiden (shmē'dŭn), village (pop. 3,567), N Württemberg, Germany, after 1945 in Württemberg-Baden, 3 mi. NE of Stuttgart; wine.

Schmidgaden (shmĭt'gä"dŭn), village (pop. 551), Upper Palatinate, E Bavaria, Germany, 10 mi. ESE of Amberg; lignite mining.

Schmidt, Cape, Russian SFSR: see SHMIDT, CAPE.

Schmidt Island, Russian SFSR: see SHMIDT ISLAND.

Schmiedeberg (shmē'dŭbĕrk), village (pop. 3,184), Saxony, E central Germany, in the Erzgebirge, on Red Weisseritz R. and 14 mi. SW of Pirna, near Czechoslovak border; woodworking; climatic health resort and winter-sports center.

Schmiedeberg, Poland: see KOWARY.

Schmiedeberg, Bad, Germany: see BAD SCHMIEDEBERG.

Schmiedefeld (shmē'dŭfĕlt). **1** or **Schmiedefeld am Rennsteig** (äm rĕn'shtĭk), town (pop. 3,414), in former Prussian Saxony prov. exclave, central Germany, after 1945 in Thuringia, in Thuringian Forest, 6 mi. E of Suhl; china and glass (scientific instruments) mfg. Climatic health and winter-sports resort. Magnetite deposits have been largely exhausted. **2** Village (pop. 1,441), Thuringia, central Germany, in Thuringian Forest, 10 mi. SW of Saalfeld; iron-mining center supplying Maxhütte steelworks at Unterwellenborn-Röblitz.

Schmiegel, Poland: see SMIGIEL.

Schmittenhöhe, Austria: see KITZBÜHEL ALPS.

Schmölln (shmûln), town (pop. 15,084), Thuringia, central Germany, 12 mi. E of Gera; mfg. of buttons, button-making machinery, machine tools, leather, shoes, zipper fasteners; woolen milling, woodworking. Has 15th-cent. church.

Schnabelwaid (shnä'bŭlvīt), village (pop. 766), Upper Franconia, N Bavaria, Germany, 4 mi. NE of Pegnitz; tiles, beer.

Schnackenburg (shnä'kŭnbo͝ork), town (pop. 775), in former Prussian prov. of Hanover, NW Germany, after 1945 in Lower Saxony, on left bank of the Elbe and 8 mi. WNW of Wittenberge (E Germany).

Schnaitheim (shnīt'hīm), N suburb of HEIDENHEIM, Germany.

Schnaittach (shnīt'täkh), village (pop. 3,641), Middle Franconia, N central Bavaria, Germany, 5 mi. NE of Lauf; textile mfg., woodworking. Hops, horseradish, hogs.

Schnaittenbach (shnī'tŭnbäkh), village (pop. 2,888), Upper Palatinate, N central Bavaria, Germany, 9 mi. NE of Amberg; mfg. (precision instruments, pottery, rugs). Kaolin quarried in area.

Schnauder River (shnou'dŭr), E central Germany, rises NE of Gera, meanders 30 mi. generally N, past Meuselwitz, Wintersdorf, and Groitzsch, to the White Elster 2 mi. N of Groitzsch.

Schneealpe (shnā'älpŭ), outlier of Eastern Alps, on Styria–Lower Austria border, just W of the Raxalpe; rises to 6,247 ft. Summer resort of Neuberg at S foot.

Schneeberg (shnā'bĕrk), mountain, SE Lower Austria, an E outlier of the Alps, 12 mi. WNW of Neunkirchen; rises to 6,808 ft. in the Klosterwappen. Ski center, here, reached by cogwheel railroad from Puchberg.

Schneeberg (shnā'bĕrk). **1** Village (pop. 1,248), Lower Franconia, W Bavaria, Germany, 4 mi. S of Miltenberg; rye, potatoes, hogs, cattle. **2** Town (pop. 13,602), Saxony, E central Germany, in the Erzgebirge, 11 mi. SE of Zwickau; mining center (uranium, bismuth, nickel, cobalt, wolframite); textile milling and knitting, metalworking; mfg. of lace, embroidery, paints, toys. Has 16th-cent. church with paintings by Lucas Cranach the Elder. Town founded 1477, when important silver deposits were found here.

Schneeberg, highest peak (3,448 ft.) of the Fichtelgebirge, Bavaria, Germany, 6 mi. WNW of Wunsiedel. Separated from neighboring (SW) Ochsenkopf mtn. by a wide moor.

Schneeberg, Yugoslavia: see SNEZNIK.

Schneekoppe (shnā'kô"pŭ), Czech *Sněžka* (snyĕsh'kä), Pol. *Sniezka* (snyĕsh'kä), highest peak (5,259 ft.) of the Riesengebirge, on Czechoslovak-Pol. border, 12 mi. S of Hirschberg (Jelenia Gora), 3 mi. SSW of Karpacz, 5 mi. ENE of Spindleruv Mlyn; 50°44'N 15°45'E. Winter-sports resort. Site of observatory and 17th-cent. chapel.

Schneidemühl (shnī'dŭmül) or **Pila** (pē'wä), Pol. *Piła*, town (1939 pop. 45,791; 1946 pop. 10,671) in Pomerania, after 1945 in Poznan prov., NW central Poland, 50 mi. N of Poznan. Rail junction on Berlin–East Prussia main line; hemp and linen milling, mfg. of agr. machinery, wire netting, cardboard; metalworking, sawmilling, beet-sugar refining. Chartered 1380. Creation of Polish Corridor (1919) resulted in rapid growth of town's commerce. Was (1922–38) ⊙ former Prussian Grenzmark Posen–Westpreussen prov. Until 1939, Ger. frontier station on Pol. border, opposite Ujscie. In Second World War, c.85% destroyed.

Schneider (snī'dŭr), town (pop. 356), Lake co., NW Ind., near Kankakee R., 29 mi. S of Gary.

Schneverdingen (shnā"fĕr'dĭng-ŭn), village (pop. 5,276), in former Prussian prov. of Hanover, NW Germany, after 1945 in Lower Saxony, 9 mi. N of Soltau; leatherworking (boots), sugar refining, flour- and sawmilling.

Schnierlach, France: see LAPOUTROIE.

Schocken, Poland: see SKOKI.

Schoden, Lithuania: see SKUODAS.

Schodnica, Ukrainian SSR: see SKHODNITSA.

Schoelcher (shûlkā'), town (pop. 1,006), W Martinique, 2 mi. W of Fort-de-France; cacao, coffee, and sugar growing.

Schoenbrunn Memorial State Park (shān'brŭn, –bro͞on), Tuscarawas co., E Ohio, near New Philadelphia; site of Schoenbrunn, 1st town (1772; restored) established in Ohio.

Schoenchen (shĕn'shĕn), city (pop. 170), Ellis co., W central Kansas, on Smoky Hill R. and 11 mi. S of Hays; grain, livestock.

Schofield (skō'–), village (pop. 1,948), Marathon co., central Wis., at confluence of Wisconsin and Eau Claire rivers, just S of Wausau; sawmilling. Settled c.1849, inc. 1904.

Schofield Barracks (skō'–), central Oahu, T.H., 19 mi. NW of Honolulu; large U.S. army military post (established 1909) on central plateau.

Schogen, Rumania: see SIEU.

Schoharie (skōhă'rē, skŭ–), county (□ 625; pop. 22,703), E central N.Y.; ⊙ Schoharie. Partly in the Catskills; traversed by The Helderbergs; drained by Schoharie Creek (dam impounds Schoharie Reservoir) and Catskill Creek. Dairying, farming (hay, fruit, truck, hops, potatoes), poultry raising. Resorts in the Catskills; includes several scenic caverns. Formed 1795.

Schoharie, village (pop. 1,059), ⊙ Schoharie co., E central N.Y., on Schoharie Creek and 28 mi. W of Albany; trade center in resort and farm area; mfg. (rubberized cloth products, cider). Has 18th-cent. bldgs., including Old Stone Fort (1772), now a mus. Inc. 1867.

Schoharie Creek, E central N.Y., rises in the Catskills in Greene co., flows c.85 mi. E and N, past Prattsville and Middleburg, to Mohawk R. 5 mi. W of Amsterdam. At Gilboa, Gilboa Dam impounds **Schoharie Reservoir** (1,145 acres; c.5 mi. long), which supplies water to New York city via Shandaken Tunnel to ASHOKAN RESERVOIR, and thence through CATSKILL AQUEDUCT.

Schoinousa or **Skhoinousa** (both: skhēno͞o'sŭ), Aegean island (□ 3.4; pop. 239) of the Cyclades, Greece, S of Naxos; 36°52'N 25°32'E. Also spelled Schinousa, Schinoussa, and Schinusa.

Schokland (skhŏk'länt), former island in the Ijsselmeer, N central Netherlands, 18 mi. WSW of Meppel; 3 mi. long, ½ mi. wide; now part of North East Polder.

Scholeion, Greece: see OLYMPUS.

Scholes (skōlz). **1** Town in NEW MILL urban dist., West Riding, Yorkshire, England. **2** Town in SPENBOROUGH urban dist., West Riding, Yorkshire, England.

Schomberg (shŏm'bûrg), village (pop. estimate 500), S Ont., 28 mi. NW of Toronto; dairying, mixed farming.

Schömberg (shûm'bĕrk), town (pop. 1,400), S Württemberg, Germany, after 1945 in Württemberg-Hohenzollern, in Swabian Jura, 7 mi. ENE of Rottweil; cattle.

Schömberg, Poland: see CHELMSKO SLASKIE.

Schomberg, Poland: see CHRUSZCZOW.

Schöna (shû'nä), village (pop. 1,168), Saxony, E central Germany, in Saxonian Switzerland, on the Elbe and 14 mi. ESE of Pirna; frontier station on Czechoslovak border, opposite Hrensko; grain, livestock.

Schonach or **Schonach im Schwarzwald** (shō'näkh ĭm shvärts'vält), village (pop. 2,974), S Baden, Germany, in Black Forest, 13 mi. NW of Villingen; watch industry; metal- and woodworking. Climatic health resort; winter-sports center; alt. 3,903 ft.

Schönaich (shû'nīkh), village (pop. 4,051), N Württemberg, Germany, after 1945 in Württemberg-Baden, 3 mi. SE of Böblingen; cattle.

Schönanger (shûnäng'ŭr), village (pop. 2,191), Lower Bavaria, Germany, in Bohemian Forest, 15 mi. SE of Zwiesel; glass grinding, woodworking.

Schönau (shû'nou). **1** Town (pop. 2,949), N Baden, Germany, after 1945 in Württemberg-Baden, in the Odenwald, 5 mi. ENE of Heidelberg; leatherworking, paper milling. **2** Town, Saxony, Germany: see SIEGMAR-SCHÖNAU.

Schönau, Poland: see SWIERZAWA.

Schönberg (shûn'bĕrk). **1** Village (pop. 2,579), Lower Bavaria, Germany, in Bohemian Forest, 13 mi. SE of Zwiesel; brewing. Chartered in early 13th cent. **2** Town (pop. 5,498), Mecklenburg, N Germany, 11 mi. E of Lübeck; agr. market (grain, potatoes, sugar beets, stock). **3** Village (pop. 5,188), in Schleswig-Holstein, NW Germany, 11 mi. NE of Kiel; seed-selection station. On the Baltic, 2 mi. NE, is Schönberger Strand (shûn'bĕr"gŭr shtränt'), popular seaside resort.

Schönberg, Poland: see SULIKOW.

Schönbrunn (shûn'bro͞on), former royal palace in Hietzing dist. of Vienna, Austria, built in 18th cent. by Maria Theresa. Treaty signed here 1809 bet. France and Austria. Damaged in Second World War.

Schönebeck (shû'nŭbĕk), city (pop. 44,578), in former Prussian Saxony prov., central Germany, after 1945 in Saxony-Anhalt, port on the Elbe and 9 mi. SE of Magdeburg; 52°1'N 11°44'E. Rock-salt and potash mining and shipping center; chemical and explosives mfg., metalworking. Includes spa Bad Salzelmen (bät" zälts'ĕl"mŭn), 2 mi. SSW.

Schöneberg (shû'nŭbĕrk), residential district (1939 pop. 277,880; 1946 pop. 173,409), SW Berlin, Germany, 4 mi. SW of city center. Mfg. (electrical equipment, radios, clothing). After 1945 in U.S. sector.

Schöneck (shû'nĕk), town (pop. 4,521), Saxony, E central Germany, in the Erzgebirge, 11 mi. SE of Plauen; cotton milling, musical-instruments mfg.

Schöneck, Poland: see SKARSZEWY.

Schönefeld (shû'nŭfĕlt), NE suburb of Leipzig, Saxony, E central Germany.

Schöneiche (shûn"ī'khŭ), village (pop. 8,799), Brandenburg, E Germany, 13 mi. E of Berlin; market gardening.

Schönenwerd (shû'nŭnvĕrt), town (pop. 3,313), Solothurn canton, N Switzerland, on Aar R. and 2 mi. WSW of Aarau; shoes, knit goods, beer. Romanesque church (12th cent.).

Schönewalde (shû'nŭväl"dŭ), town (pop. 1,368), in former Prussian Saxony prov., central Germany, after 1945 in Saxony-Anhalt, 14 mi. SE of Jüterbog; grain, potatoes, livestock.

Schönfeld, Czechoslovakia: see KRASNO.

Schönfliess in Neumark, Bad, Poland: see TRZCINSKO ZDROJ.

Schongau (shōn'gou), town (pop. 5,850), Upper Bavaria, Germany, on the Lech and 12 mi. W of Weilheim; lumber and paper milling, printing, brewing, tanning. Has 17th–18th-cent. church. Chartered c.1321.

Schönhausen (shûnhou'zŭn), village (pop. 3,281), in former Prussian Saxony prov., central Germany, after 1945 in Saxony-Anhalt, near the Elbe, 8 mi. SE of Stendal. Bismarck b. here. Church dates from 1212.

Schönheide (shûnhī'dŭ), village (pop. 6,942), Saxony, E central Germany, in the Erzgebirge, near the Zwickauer Mulde, 10 mi. SW of Aue, near Czechoslovak border, in uranium-mining region; brush-mfg. center; woodworking, textile knitting; mfg. of enamelware, machinery.

Schönholthausen (shûn'hôlt'hou"zŭn), village (pop. 9,956), in former Prussian prov. of Westphalia, W Germany, after 1945 in North Rhine-Westphalia, 14 mi. SSW of Arnsberg; forestry.

Schöningen (shû'nĭng-ŭn), town (pop. 14,057), in Brunswick, NW Germany, after 1945 in Lower Saxony, 6 mi. SSW of Helmstedt; has saline. Mfg. of agr. machinery, rubber products, pharmaceuticals, rope, shoes; weaving, food processing. Has Romanesque-Gothic church. First mentioned 747.

Schönkirchen (shûn'kĭr"khŭn), residential suburb (pop. 2,353), in Schleswig-Holstein, NW Germany, 4 mi. NE of Kiel city center. Has early-Gothic church.

Schönlanke, Poland: see TRZCIANKA.

Schönlinde, Czechoslovakia: see KRASNA LIPA.

Schönsee (shûn'zā"), town (pop. 1,844), Upper Palatinate, E Bavaria, Germany, in Bohemian Forest, 21 mi. SE of Weiden, near Czechoslovak border; rail terminus; rye, oats, cattle. Chartered c.1366. Peat bogs in area.

Schönsee, Poland: see KOWALEWO.

Schönstein, Yugoslavia: see SOSTANJ.

Schönwald (shûn'vält"), village (pop. 4,040), Upper Franconia, NE Bavaria, Germany, 4 mi. SE of Rehau; glass and porcelain mfg. Mineral spring.

Schoodic Island (sko͞o'dĭk), Hancock co., S Maine, small isl. just SE of Schoodic Peninsula, off entrance to Frenchman Bay.

Schoodic Lake, Piscataquis co., central Maine, 17 mi. NE of Dover-Foxcroft; 9 mi. long.

Schoodic Peninsula, Hancock co., S Maine, extending into the Atlantic at E side of Frenchman Bay; terminates at Schoodic Head, a bold promontory 440 ft. high, just off which lies small isl. whose seaward tip is Schoodic Point. Peninsula is partly in ACADIA NATIONAL PARK.

Schoolcraft, county (□ 1,199; pop. 9,148), S Upper Peninsula, Mich.; ⊙ Manistique. Bounded S by L. Michigan; drained by Indian R. and by Manistique R. and its affluents. Indian L. is in SW. Includes part of Hiawatha Natl. Forest. Dairying and agr. area (potatoes, grain, hay). Some mfg. at Manistique. Lumbering, commercial fishing. Resorts (hunting, fishing). Fish hatchery, wildlife refuge, and two state parks are in co. Organized 1871.

Schoolcraft, village (pop. 1,078), Kalamazoo co., SW Mich., 13 mi. S of Kalamazoo, in dairying and grain-growing area; mfg. of trailers.

Schooleys Mountain (skōō'lēz), village, Morris co., NW N.J., on Schooleys (or Schooley) Mtn., 17 mi. W of Morristown; mineral springs. Mtn. (alt. c.1,000 ft.) is flat-topped ridge of the Appalachians, extending NE–SW bet. valleys of Musconetcong R. and South Branch of the Raritan.

Schoolfield, village (pop. 4,872, with near-by Jaffa), Pittsylvania co., S Va., just SW of Danville.

Schoonebeek, Oud, Netherlands: see OUD SCHOONEBEEK.

Schoonhoven (skhōn'hōvün), town (pop. 4,869), South Holland prov., W Netherlands, on Lek R. and 7 mi. SE of Gouda; white lead, paint, varnish, sealing wax, tiles, gold- and silverware, fruit wines; dairying. Has 15th-cent. town hall, 17th-cent. St. Bartholomew's Church, 17th-cent. gateway (*Veerpoort*).

Schoorisse, Belgium: see SCHORISSE.

Schoorl (skhōrl), village (pop. 1,463), North Holland prov., NW Netherlands, 5 mi. NNW of Alkmaar, near North Sea, behind dunes; sand quarries; cattle raising, agr.

Schooten, Belgium: see SCHOTEN.

Schopfheim (shôpf'hīm), town (pop. 4,649), S Baden, Germany, in Black Forest, 8 mi. ENE of Lörrach; rail junction; mfg. of chemicals, textiles, machinery; paper milling.

Schöpfl, Austria: see WIENER WALD.

Schöppenstedt (shû'pün-shtĕt), town (pop. 5,826), in Brunswick, NW Germany, after 1945 in Lower Saxony, 10 mi. E of Wolfenbüttel; foundry; mfg. of chemicals (pharmaceuticals, cosmetics, paints, plastics, artificial fiber), rubber goods, toys; sugar refining. Formerly also Scheppenstedt (shĕ'pün-).

Schoppinitz, Poland: see SZOPIENICE.

Schörfling (shûrf'lĭng), town (pop. 2,716), SW central Upper Austria, on N shore of the Attersee and 9 mi. WNW of Gmunden; summer resort (alt. 1,675 ft.) in the Salzkammergut.

Schorisse (skhō'rĭsü), agr. village (pop. 1,874), East Flanders prov., W central Belgium, 5 mi. SE of Oudenaarde. Has 16th-cent. Gothic church. Formerly spelled Schoorisse.

Schorndorf (shôrn'dôrf), town (pop. 12,268), N Württemberg, Germany, after 1945 in Württemberg-Baden, on the Rems and 14 mi. E of Stuttgart; rail junction; mfg. of agr. machinery, iron and steel goods, textiles, hats; food processing, leather- and woodworking, lumber milling, tanning. Brickworks. Has 15th-cent. church, 18th-cent. town hall. Inventor Daimler b. here.

Schoten (skhō'tün), town (pop. 17,317), Antwerp prov., N Belgium, on Antwerp-Turnhout Canal and 5 mi. NE of Antwerp; mfg. (artificial silk, chemicals, metal and wood products), food processing. Has 13th-cent. gateway. Formerly spelled Schooten.

Schötmar (shût'mär), town (pop. 7,168), in former Lippe, NW Germany, after 1945 in North Rhine-Westphalia, on the Werre and 1 mi. S of Bad Salzuflen; woodworking.

Schottegat (skhō'tügät), lagoon (3 mi. long, 1½ mi. wide), S Curaçao, Du. West Indies; deep, sheltered inlet just N of Willemstad, and linked with the Caribbean through Sint Anna Bay; harbor and seaplane anchorage.

Schotten (shô'tün), town (pop. 3,598), central Hesse, W Germany, in former Upper Hesse prov., on the Nidda and 20 mi. ESE of Giessen; textile mfg., lumber milling. Has 14th-cent. church.

Schottwien (shôt'vēn), village (pop. 919), SE Lower Austria, 11 mi. SW of Neunkirchen; resort (alt. 1,935 ft.). Pilgrimage church near by.

Schouten Island (shōō'tün), in Tasman Sea, 1 mi. S of Freycinet Peninsula, E Tasmania; forms SE shore of Oyster Bay; 5 mi. long, 3 mi. wide. Livestock.

Schouten Islands (skhou'tün, skōō'-, skou'-), archipelago (□ 1,231; pop. 25,487) at entrance of Geelvink Bay, off NW New Guinea; 0°20'–1°20'S 135°12'–136°50'E. Consists of BIAK, SUPIORI, NUMFOR, and several small isls. Agr., fishing. First visited (1616) by Dutch navigator Schouten. Sometimes called Misore Isls.

Schouten Isles, small volcanic group (pop. c.2,000), Sepik dist., Territory of New Guinea, SW Pacific, c.25 mi. NE of New Guinea; 3°15'S 144°34'E; comprise several isls.; largest is Vokeo (3 mi. long); mountainous.

Schouwen (skhou'ün), island, Zeeland prov., SW Netherlands, NW of Bergen op Zoom; bounded by North Sea (N, W), the Eastern Scheldt (S), Duiveland isl. (E); forms, with Duiveland isl., isl. of Schouwen-Duiveland. Agr. (vegetables, grains, potatoes, sugar beets, flax); dairying. Chief town, Zierikzee. Isl. flooded in Second World War.

Schramberg (shräm'bĕrk), town (pop. 15,439), S Württemberg, Germany, after 1945 in Württemberg-Hohenzollern, 28 mi. NE of Freiburg; rail terminus; a center of Black Forest watchmaking industry; mfg. of furniture, springs, household goods, paper, majolica. Summer resort (alt. 1,391 ft.). Has 4 ruined castles. Chartered 1867.

Schram City (shrăm), village (pop. 793), Montgomery co., S central Ill., just NE of Hillsboro, in agr. and bituminous-coal-mining area.

Schraplau (shräp'lou), town (pop. 2,687), in former Prussian Saxony prov., central Germany, after 1945 in Saxony-Anhalt, 9 mi. SE of Eisleben, in lignite- and potash-mining region.

Schreckenstein, Czechoslovakia: see STREKOV.

Schreckhorn, Gross (grōs shrĕk'hôrn), peak (13,390 ft.) in Bernese Alps, S central Switzerland, 4 mi. SE of Grindelwald. Klein Schreckhorn (klīn) (11,474 ft.) is NW.

Schreiber (shrī'bür), village (pop. estimate 1,000), W Ont., on L. Superior, 90 mi. ENE of Port Arthur; gold mining.

Schreiberhau, Poland: see SZKLARSKA POREBA.

Schremingen-Ersingen, France: see SERÉMANGE-ERZANGE.

Schrems (shrĕms), town (pop. 2,998), NW Lower Austria, 4 mi. ENE of Gmünd; linen mfg.

Schriesheim (shrēs'hīm), village (pop. 5,735), N Baden, Germany, after 1945 in Württemberg-Baden, 5 mi. N of Heidelberg; tobacco. Has ruined castle.

Schrimm, Poland: see SREM.

Schrobenhausen (shrō"bünhou'zün), town (pop. 8,070), Upper Bavaria, Germany, on Paar R. and 16 mi. SSW of Ingolstadt; mfg. of chemicals, paper, textiles; brewing, woodworking, flour and lumber milling. Has church dating from 2d half of 15th cent. Chartered before 1388. Franz von Lombach b. here.

Schröcken (shrû'kün), village (pop. 185), Vorarlberg, W Austria, on river Bregenzer Ache, in the Bregenzerwald, and 23 mi. E of Feldkirch; tourist and winter sports center (alt. 4,133 ft.).

Schroda, Poland: see SRODA.

Schroffenstein (shrô'fünstīn"), mountain (7,224 ft.), S South-West Africa, 55 mi. SE of Keetmanshoop, highest peak of Grosse Karras Mts.; 27°10'S 18°44'E.

Schroon Lake (skrōōn), resort village (1940 pop. 575), Essex co., NE N.Y., in the Adirondacks, 37 mi. NNW of Glens Falls, at N end of Schroon L. (□ c.6½; 9 mi. long, ½–1½ mi. wide), a widening of **Schroon River,** which rises in E Essex co., flows c.60 mi. generally S to the Hudson just below Warrensburg.

Schröttersburg, Poland: see PLOCK.

Schruns (shrōōnz), town (pop. 2,872), Vorarlberg, W Austria, on Ill R., in Montafon valley, and 18 mi. SE of Feldkirch; textiles, lumberyards. Summer and winter resort (alt. 2,260 ft.).

Schübelbach (shü'bülbäkh), town (pop. 2,614), Schwyz canton, NE central Switzerland, 16 mi. NE of Schwyz; cotton textiles. Siebnen hydroelectric plant is W of town.

Schubin, Poland: see SZUBIN.

Schuermann Heights (shōōr'mün), town (pop. 306), St. Louis co., E Mo.

Schukmansburg (skōōk'mänsbōōrg), village, NE South-West Africa, in E part of CAPRIVI ZIPFEL, on Zambezi R. and 70 mi. WNW of Livingstone, 4 mi. SW of Sesheka; cattle.

Schulenburg (shōō'lünbûrg), town (pop. 2,005), Fayette co., S central Texas, 31 mi. NNE of Yoakum; trade, processing center in dairy, poultry, cotton area; evaporated milk plants, flour milling, cotton ginning. Inc. 1873.

Schulitz, Poland: see SOLEC.

Schull or **Skull,** Gaelic *Sgoil Mhuire,* town (pop. 353), SW Co. Cork, Ireland, on Roaringwater Bay, 11 mi. W of Skibbereen, at foot of Mt. Gabriel; fishing port; former copper-mining center.

Schulpforte (shōōl"pfôr'tü) or **Schulpforta** (-pfôr'tä), suburb of Bad Kösen, central Germany. Formerly site of noted school founded 1543 by the Elector Maurice of Saxony in bldgs. of former Cistercian monastery (established 1134). Among its graduates were Klopstock, Fichte, Ranke, and Nietzsche. Became Nazi party school after 1933. Formerly also called Pforta.

Schuls (shōōls), Romansh *Scuol* (shkōō'ôl), village (pop. 1,346), Grisons canton, E Switzerland, on Inn R. and 22 mi. E of Davos, in Lower Engadine; resort (alt. 4,080 ft.) noted for its mineral springs. Consists of Upper Schuls, with curative baths, and Lower Schuls, with an old church.

Schulter (shōōl'tür), village (1940 pop. 805), Okmulgee co., E central Okla., 7 mi. S of Okmulgee; coal mining.

Schultz Lake (□ 110), central Keewatin Dist., Northwest Territories; 64°42'N 97°30'W; 35 mi. long, 11 mi. wide. Drained E by Thelon R.

Schulzendorf (shōōl'tsündôrf), village (pop. 7,738), Brandenburg, E Germany, 13 mi. SE of Berlin; market gardening.

Schumacher (shōō'măkûr), town (pop. estimate 3,000), NE Ont., 2 mi. E of Timmins, in gold-mining region.

Schüpfen (shüp'fün), town (pop. 2,273), Bern canton, NW Switzerland, 7 mi. NNW of Bern; cement, tiles, flour.

Schüpfheim (shüpf'hīm), town (pop. 3,677), Lucerne canton, central Switzerland, on Kleine Emme R. and 14 mi. WSW of Lucerne; farming; mineral waters. Has 17th-cent. monastery.

Schussenried (shōō'sünrēt), town (pop. 4,370), S Württemberg, Germany, after 1945 in Württemberg-Hohenzollern, 8.5 mi. SW of Biberach; rail junction; dairying. Has former Premonstratensian abbey.

Schussen River (shōō'sün), S Germany, rises in small lake 3 mi. SSE of Schussenried, flows 35 mi. S, past Ravensburg, into L. of Constance 1.5 mi. NNW of Langenargen.

Schüss River (shüs) or **Suze River** (süz), NW Switzerland, rises in the Jura SE of La Chaux-de-Fonds, flows 25 mi. E to L. Biel at Biel.

Schütt (shüt), 2 isls. formed by the Danube just below Bratislava, at Czechoslovakia-Hungary line, one (the Great Schütt) belonging to Czechoslovakia, the other (Little Schütt) to Hungary. The main stream of the Danube flows bet. them. On N is the **Great Schütt,** Slovak *Ostrov* or *Velký Ostrov Žitný* (vĕl'kē ô'strôf zhĭt'nē), Hung. *Csallóköz* (chŏl'lōkûz), in SW Slovakia; 53 mi. long, 9–18 mi. wide. Fertile agr. region (wheat, corn, sugar beets, tobacco, melons, paprika, sunflowers), with large orchards, vineyards, and willow fields. The city of KOMARNO is on its SE tip; other centers are Guta and Dunajska Streda. On S is the **Little Schütt,** Hung. *Szigetköz* (sĭ'gĕtkûz), Slovak *Malý Ostrov Žitný* (mä'lē), in Györ-Moson co., NW Hungary; c.30 mi. long, 6 mi. average width. Swampy in parts; wheat, rye; dairy farming. Main town, Hedervar.

Schüttenhofen, Czechoslovakia: see SUSICE.

Schutterwald (shōō'türvält), village (pop. 3,295), S Baden, Germany, 3 mi. WSW of Offenburg; corn, tobacco.

Schüttorf (shüt'tôrf), town (pop. 6,767), in former Prussian prov. of Hanover, NW Germany, after 1945 in Lower Saxony, on the Vechte and 9 mi. NW of Rheine; cotton weaving.

Schuyler (skī'lür). **1** County (□ 434; pop. 9,613), W Ill.; ⊙ Rushville. Bounded SE by Illinois R.; drained by La Moine R. Agr. (livestock, poultry, corn, wheat, fruit; dairy and meat products). Bituminous-coal mining. Formed 1825. **2** County (□ 306; pop. 5,760), N Mo.; ⊙ Lancaster. Bounded W by Chariton R.; drained by North Fabius R.; grain (corn, wheat, oats), cattle, poultry; coal. Formed 1845. **3** County (□ 331; pop. 14,182), W central N.Y.; ⊙ Watkins Glen. Situated in Finger Lakes region; includes S end of Seneca L., and Lamoka and Cayuta lakes. Drained by Cayuta and Catherine creeks. Fruitgrowing and general-farming area (grain, poultry, livestock, hay; dairy products). Diversified mfg. at Watkins Glen, Montour Falls. Contains scenic Watkins Glen State Park, and several waterfalls and gorges. Formed 1854.

Schuyler. 1 City (pop. 2,883), ⊙ Colfax co., E Nebr., 60 mi. WNW of Omaha and on Platte R., in prairie region; rail and trade point for agr. region; beverages, flour; grain, livestock, dairy and poultry produce. Near-by canal, part of Loup R. public power project, conducts water from diversion dam near Genoa to powerhouse at Columbus. Founded 1869. **2** Village, Nelson co., central Va., on Rockfish R. and 20 mi. SSW of Charlottesville; soapstone quarrying, processing.

Schuyler, Fort, N.Y.: see THROGS NECK.

Schuylerville (skī'lürvĭl), village (pop. 1,314), Saratoga co., E N.Y., on the Hudson and 11 mi. E of Saratoga Springs; summer resort; mfg. (wallboard, paper products, gloves). Scene of Burgoyne's surrender to Gates in Saratoga campaign of the Revolution. Saratoga Monument (155 ft. high) is here. Revolutionary battles fought in vicinity are commemorated by natl. historical park 9 mi. SE of SARATOGA SPRINGS. Settled in 17th cent. as Saratoga; inc. 1874.

Schuylkill (skōōl'kĭl", skōō'kŭl), county (□ 783; pop. 200,577), E central Pa.; ⊙ Pottsville. Mountainous region at S end of anthracite fields; drained by Schuylkill R.; Blue Mtn. along S border. Anthracite; mfg. (clothing, leather products), meat packing, brewing. Formed 1811.

Schuylkill Haven, borough (pop. 6,597), Schuylkill co., E central Pa., 4 mi. SSE of Pottsville and on Schuylkill R.; shoes, clothing. Settled 1748, laid out 1829, inc. 1840.

Schuylkill River, SE Pa., rises in anthracite region in central Schuylkill co., flows 130 mi. SE, past industrial towns of Pottsville, Reading, Pottstown, and Norristown, to Delaware R. at Philadelphia. Joined by West Branch (c.20 mi. long) at Schuylkill Haven. Navigable for canal boats as far as Port Clinton, 98 mi. upstream; here it passes through Blue Mtn. and receives from N Little

Schuylkill R. (c.35 mi. long). A project to dredge anthracite culm from the river bed was begun in 1948.

Schwaan (shvän), town (pop. 6,600), Mecklenburg, N Germany, on the Warnow and 11 mi. S of Rostock; mfg. of chemicals, bricks; fish canning. Near by was site of anc. fortress of Werle, until 12th cent. one of chief Wendish strongholds in Mecklenburg.

Schwabach (shvä'bäkh), city (1950 pop. 19,448), Middle Franconia, W central Bavaria, Germany, on small Schwabach R. and 8 mi. SSE of Nuremberg; metal (aluminum, bronze, gold leaf; needles, screws, springs, wire), chemical (soap, soap powder, soda), and food-processing (preserves, gingerbread, bakery products, beer) industries. Other mfg.: heating equipment, felt, mattresses, sports apparatus; lumber and paper milling, printing. Has late-Gothic church with carvings by Veit Stoss and tabernacle by Adam Krafft; and city hall (1509). First mentioned 1117, Schwabach came to the Hohenzollern in 1364. Articles of Schwabach, drawn up here (1529), were used in drafting (1530) the Augsburg Confession of the Lutheran faith.

Schwabegg (shvä'bĕk), village (pop. 474), Carinthia, S Austria, on Drau R. and 13 mi. S of Wolfsberg; hydroelectric plant.

Schwaben, Germany: see SWABIA.

Schwäbische Alb, Germany: see SWABIAN JURA.

Schwäbische Rezat, Germany: see SWABIAN REZAT.

Schwäbischer Jura, Germany: see SWABIAN JURA.

Schwäbisch Gmünd (shvā'bĭsh gŭmünt'), city (pop. 30,748), N Württemberg, Germany, after 1945 in Württemberg-Baden, at N foot of Swabian Jura, on the Rems and 27 mi. E of Stuttgart; 48°48'N 9°48'E. Rail junction; long known as precious metalworking center (gold and silver wares); iron and light-metal foundries; produces construction machinery, machine tools, engines, pumps, gears, drills, die casts, pressure and casting molds. Also mfg. of optical goods, watches, costume jewelry, light bulbs, pharmaceuticals, cosmetics, soap, textiles. Glassworks. Has 13th- and 14th-cent. churches; many monasteries; and remains of medieval fortifications. Site of teachers col.; and technical school for precious metalworking. Chartered 1162. Created free imperial city in 1268.

Schwäbisch Hall (häl'), town (pop. 16,589), N Württemberg, Germany, after 1945 in Württemberg-Baden, on the Kocher and 23 mi. E of Heilbronn; rail junction; iron and steel construction; machinery and gypsum mfg., metal- and woodworking. Resort with saline baths. Baroque town hall burned down in 1945. Anc. settlement; developed around salt spring. Chartered in 12th cent. Was free imperial city.

Schwabmünchen (shväp'mün'khŭn), village (pop. 5,613), Swabia, SW Bavaria, Germany, in the Lechfeld, 14 mi. SSW of Augsburg; cotton mfg., dairying (cheese), brewing, printing, woodworking. Has late-15th-cent. chapel, and 17th-cent. church. Chartered c.1562.

Schwager (shwä'gĕr), N mining suburb (1930 pop. 5,842) of Coronel, Concepción prov., S central Chile, on the Pacific, and 14 mi. SSW of Concepción; coal-mining center; copper smelters.

Schwaigern (shvī'gŭrn), town (pop. 3,187), N Württemberg, Germany, after 1945 in Württemberg-Baden, 7 mi. W of Heilbronn; grain. Has late-Gothic church; castle.

Schwalbach (shväl'bäkh), town (pop. 6,642), SW Saar, 3 mi. ESE of Saarlouis; coal mining.

Schwalbach, Bad, Germany: see BAD SCHWALBACH.

Schwalenberg (shvä'lŭnbĕrk), town (pop. 1,587), in former Lippe, NW Germany, after 1945 in North Rhine-Westphalia, 10 mi. NW of Höxter; woodworking. Has 13th-cent. castle (renovated 1913), and 16th-cent. paneled town hall.

Schwand or **Schwand bei Nürnberg** (shvänt' bī nürn'bĕrk), village (pop. 1,037), Middle Franconia, W central Bavaria, Germany, 8 mi. SE of Schwabach; potatoes, hops, cattle, hogs.

Schwanden (shvän'dŭn), town (pop. 2,748), Glarus canton, E Switzerland, on the Linth and 3 mi. S of Glarus; hydroelectric plant; electrothermic apparatus, cotton textiles.

Schwandorf or **Schwandorf in Bayern** (shvän'dôrf ĭn bī'ŭrn), city (1950 pop. 13,332), Upper Palatinate, E Bavaria, Germany, at W foot of the Bohemian Forest, on the Nab and 14 mi. SE of Amberg; rail junction; lignite-mining center; metalworking, clay burning, pottery mfg. Chartered 1299.

Schwanebeck (shvä'nŭbĕk), town (pop. 5,220), in former Prussian Saxony prov., central Germany, after 1945 in Saxony-Anhalt, 6 mi. NE of Halberstadt; agr. market (sugar beets, grain, vegetables).

Schwanenkirchen (shvä'nŭn-kĭr"khŭn), village (pop. 1,049), Lower Bavaria, Germany, on SW slope of the Bohemian Forest, 9 mi. SE of Deggendorf; lignite mining.

Schwanenstadt (–shtät), town (pop. 3,205), S central Upper Austria, near Ager R., 9 mi. N of Gmunden; food products.

Schwangau (shväng'ou), resort (pop. 2,969), Swabia, SW Bavaria, Germany, 2 mi. ENE of Füssen; alt. 2,690 ft. Near by are 2 imposing castles: the anc. Hohenschwangau (renovated in 19th cent.), formerly called Schwanstein, which passed in 1567 from the Guelphs to the dukes of Bavaria; and the Neuschwanstein, built (1869–86) by Louis II of Bavaria.

Schwanheide (shvän"hī'dŭ), village (pop. 808), Mecklenburg, N Germany, 5 mi. NNW of Boizenburg, 4 mi. SE of Büchen (Schleswig-Holstein). After 1945 traffic check point bet. East and West Germany.

Schwanheim (shvän'hīm), W district (pop. 11,527) of Frankfurt, W Germany, on left bank of the canalized Main.

Schwartau, Bad, Germany: see BAD SCHWARTAU.

Schwarza (shvär'tsä), town (pop. 4,517), Thuringia, central Germany, at foot of Thuringian Forest, on the Thuringian Saale, at mouth of Schwarza R., and 3 mi. SSW of Rudolstadt, 20 mi. S of Weimar; mfg. (china, synthetic fiber). Scene (Oct., 1806) of victory of French under marshals Lannes and Augereau over Prussians commanded by Prince Louis Ferdinand.

Schwarzach (shvär'tsäkh), town (pop. 2,420), Salzburg, W central Austria, on the Salzach and 7 mi. SSW of Bischofshofen; brewery. N terminus of Tauern RR. Schernberg castle near by.

Schwarza River (shvär'tsä), SE Lower Austria, rises on N slope of the Schneeberg, flows SE and NE 40 mi., past Gloggnitz and Neunkirchen, joining Pitten R. just NE of Erlach to form Leitha R. Its beautiful valley bet. the Raxalpe and the Schneeberg is called Höllental.

Schwarza River, central Germany, rises in the Thuringian Forest NNE of Zella-Mehlis, flows 20 mi. W and SSW to the Werra, 4 mi. SE of Meiningen.

Schwarzburg-Rudolstadt (shvärts'bōōrk-rōō'dôlshtät), former principality, Thuringia, central Germany; ⊙ was Rudolstadt. Became principality in 1710. In 1920 it was inc. into THURINGIA.

Schwarzburg-Sondershausen (–zôn"dŭrs-hou'zŭn), former principality, Thuringia, central Germany; ⊙ was Sondershausen. Became principality in 1697. In 1920 it was inc. into THURINGIA. Until 1945 it formed Thuringian exclave in former Prussian Saxony prov.

Schwarze Elster, Germany: see ELSTER RIVER.

Schwarzenau, Poland: see CZERNIEJEWO.

Schwarzenbach (shvär'tsŭnbäkh). **1** or **Schwarzenbach an der sächsischen Saale** (än dĕr zĕk'sĭ-shŭn zä'lŭ), town (pop. 6,912), Upper Franconia, NE Bavaria, Germany, on the Saxonian Saale and 7 mi. S of Hof; mfg. of cotton, excelsior, porcelain; leather- and metalworking, brewing, distilling. Clay pits near by. **2** or **Schwarzenbach am Wald** (äm vält'), village (pop. 3,318), Upper Franconia, NE Bavaria, Germany, in Franconian Forest, 13 mi. WSW of Hof; mfg. of precision instruments, weaving.

Schwarzenbach, Yugoslavia: see CRNA.

Schwarzenbek (–bĕk), village (pop. 5,885), in Schleswig-Holstein, NW Germany, 20 mi. E of Hamburg; summer resort.

Schwarzenberg, mountain, Czechoslovakia: see JANSKE LAZNE.

Schwarzenberg (–bĕrk), town (pop. 12,117), Saxony, E central Germany, in the Erzgebirge, 18 mi. SE of Zwickau, near Czechoslovak border, in uranium-mining region; paper-milling center; lace mfg., metal- and woodworking. Power station. Has 17th-cent. church; old castle.

Schwarzenborn (–bôrn), town (pop. 1,318), in former Prussian prov. of Hesse-Nassau, W Germany, after 1945 in Hesse, 12 mi. WNW of Hersfeld; lumber milling.

Schwarzenburg, Switzerland: see WAHLERN.

Schwarzenfeld (–fĕlt), village (pop. 4,273), Upper Palatinate, E Bavaria, Germany, on the Nab and 13 mi. ESE of Amberg; brick-, tile-, glassworks; tanning, woodworking. Lignite mining in area.

Schwarzer Regen, Germany: see BLACK REGEN RIVER.

Schwarzheide (shvärts"hī'dŭ), town (pop. 7,449), Brandenburg, E Germany, in Lower Lusatia, 8 mi. WSW of Senftenberg; lignite mines; synthetic-oil plant. Until 1936 called Zschornegosda (chôr"-nŭgôs'dä).

Schwarzhofen (shvärts"hō'fŭn), village (pop. 1,549), Upper Palatinate, E Bavaria, Germany, in Bohemian Forest, on small Schwarzach R. and 11 mi. ENE of Schwandorf; brewing, tanning.

Schwarzort, Lithuania: see JUODKRANTE.

Schwarzwald, Germany: see BLACK FOREST.

Schwarzwasser, Poland: see STRUMIEN.

Schwarzwasser, river, Poland: see WDA RIVER.

Schwaz (shväts), town (pop. 9,373), Tyrol, W Austria, on Inn R. and 15 mi. ENE of Innsbruck, at foot of Tuxer Alps; mfg. (tobacco, majolica). Copper and silver mined near by since Middle Ages. Has medieval Fugger House; 15th-cent. church with copper roof.

Schwebach, Luxembourg: see SAEUL.

Schwebsingen (shwāp'sĭng-ŭn), Fr. *Schwebsange* (shvĕpsäzh'), village (pop. 229), SE Luxembourg, on Moselle R. and 3 mi. S of Remich, on Ger. border; grape and plum growing.

Schwechat (shvĕ'khät), outer SE district (□ 85; pop. 38,675) of Vienna, Austria, on right bank of the Danube. Formed (1938) through inc. of 28 towns, including Ebergassing, Fischamend, Gramatneusiedl, Himberg, Oberlaa, and Schwechat (pop. 7,782; 7 mi. SE of city center; airport; oil refining, brewing, flour milling).

Schwechat River, E Lower Austria, rises on Schöpfl mtn. in the Wiener Wald, flows 35 mi. E, past Baden, and N to the Danube near Schwechat.

Schwedt or **Schwedt an der Oder** (shvät' än dĕr ō'dŭr), town (pop. 5,961), Brandenburg, E Germany, on the West Oder (Berlin-Stettin Canal) and 30 mi. SSW of Stettin; center of tobacco- and vegetable-growing region; cigar mfg. Tobacco growing introduced by Huguenots who settled here in late-17th cent. Has 17th-cent. palace.

Schweidnitz (shvīt'nĭts) or **Swidnica** (shvēdnē'tsä), Pol. *Świdnica*, town (1939 pop. 39,052; 1946 pop. 21,448) in Lower Silesia, after 1945 in Wroclaw prov., SW Poland, at N foot of the Eulengebirge, on Bystrzyca R. and 33 mi. SW of Breslau (Wroclaw); textile milling (linen, cotton, woolen), sugar refining, mfg. of agr. machinery, electric motors, clocks, watches, refractory bricks, wire, chemicals, soap, leather, gloves, furniture, toys. Has 14th-cent. parish church and 17th-cent. church (one of 3 conceded 1648 to Silesian Protestants under Treaty of Westphalia). Founded early-13th cent.; was ⊙ independent principality under Pol. Piast princes until it passed (late-14th cent.) to Bohemia; ceded 1526 to Hapsburgs. Reformation introduced 1561. In Thirty Years War, sacked by imperial forces; later (1642) captured by Swedes under Torstensson. Passed 1742 to Prussia; fortified by Frederick the Great. In Seven Years War, besieged several times; captured 1807 by French; fortifications razed 1867.

Schweighausen (shvĕgōzĕn', Ger. shvīk'houzŭn), town (pop. 2,063), Bas-Rhin dept., E France, on the Moder and 3 mi. W of Haguenau; paper milling, brewing, oil drilling. Hops grown in area.

Schweina (shvī'nä), town (pop. 4,762), Thuringia, central Germany, in Thuringian Forest, 10 mi. S of Eisenach; textile and paper milling, woodworking, tool mfg. Fröbel died here.

Schweinfurt (shvīn'fōōrt), city (1939 pop. 49,321; 1946 pop. 37,331; 1950 pop. 45,901), Lower Franconia, NW Bavaria, Germany, on the Main (canalized) and 31 mi. NW of Bamberg; 50°3'N 10°14'E. Rail junction; mfg. of machine tools, chemicals (noted for its dyes); paper milling, brewing, printing. Hydroelectric plant. The center of Ger. ball- and roller-bearing industry until 1945, city was subjected to severe air attacks (April, 1943–Oct., 1944) in second World War, and was heavily damaged. First mentioned 791. Became free imperial city c.1280. Captured by U.S. troops in April, 1945. Rückert b. here.

Schweinitz, Czechoslovakia: see TRHOVE SVINY.

Schweinitz (shvī'nĭts), town (pop. 1,808), in former Prussian Saxony prov., central Germany, after 1945 in Saxony-Anhalt, on the Black Elster and 17 mi. ESE of Wittenberg; grain, potatoes, livestock.

Schweinsberg (shvīns'bĕrk), town (pop. 1,291), in former Prussian prov. of Hesse-Nassau, W Germany, after 1945 in Hesse, on the Ohm and 9 mi. ESE of Marburg; grain.

Schweiz, Ger. name for SWITZERLAND.

Schweizer Reneke (shvī'zŭr rĕ'nŭkŭ), village (pop. 2,427), SW Transvaal, U. of So. Afr., near Cape Prov. border, on Hartz R. and 90 mi. WSW of Klerksdorp; farming center (irrigation).

Schwelm (shvĕlm), town (pop. 26,020), in former Prussian prov. of Westphalia, W Germany, after 1945 in North Rhine-Westphalia, in the Ruhr, just E of Wuppertal; rail junction; mfg. of textiles (linen, ribbons, trimmings), pianos; metalworking.

Schwenksville or **Schwenkville,** (shwĕnks'vĭl, shwĕnk'–), resort borough (pop. 563), Montgomery co., SE Pa., on Perkiomen Creek and 11 mi. NW of Norristown; handbags; agr.

Schwenningen or **Schwenningen am Neckar** (shvĕ'-nĭng-ŭn äm nĕ'kär), town (pop. 20,694), S Württemberg, Germany, after 1945 in Württemberg-Hohenzollern, in Black Forest, on the Neckar (near its source) and 31 mi. E of Freiburg; extensive watchmaking industry; mfg. of electrical equipment, shoes; metalworking. Chartered 1908.

Schwerin (shvārēn'), city (pop. 88,164), ⊙ Mecklenburg, N Germany, on SW shore of Schwerin L., 60 mi. E of Hamburg, 110 mi. NW of Berlin; 53°37'N 11°25'E. Rail junction; commercial center of dairying and agr. region. Distilling; mfg. of pharmaceuticals, soap, cosmetics. Site of Mecklenburg state conservatory; and of theological seminary. Has 14th–15th-cent. cathedral; former ducal palace (1845–57) on isl. in lake; and mus. Originally Wendish settlement, 1st mentioned 1018; chartered 1161 by Henry the Lion. Seat (1167–1648) of bishopric. Was ⊙ county of Schwerin and with it passed (1358) to Mecklenburg. Reformation introduced 1524. In Thirty Years War, occupied (1624–31) by imperial forces under Wallenstein. Was ⊙ MECKLENBURG-SCHWERIN from 1621 to 1934, then became ⊙ unified Mecklenburg.

Schwerin, Poland: see SKWIERZYNA.

Schwerin Lake, Ger. *Schweriner See* (shvārē'nŭr zā"), lake (□ 24) in Mecklenburg, N Germany, just E of Schwerin; 14 mi. long, 1–4 mi. wide. Drained (via 12-mi.-long canal) into Elde R. (S).

Schwersenz, Poland: see SWARZEDZ.

Schwertberg (shvĕrt′bĕrk), town (pop. 3,121), NE Upper Austria, 13 mi. E of Linz, N of the Danube; earthenware.

Schwerte (shvĕr′tŭ), town (pop. 21,199), in former Prussian prov. of Westphalia, W Germany, after 1945 in North Rhine-Westphalia, on the Ruhr and 7 mi. NE of Hagen; iron foundries; nickel and copper refining. Has 12th-cent. church, 16th-cent. town hall. Chartered 1242.

Schwetz, Poland: see Swiecie.

Schwetzingen (shvĕ′tsĭng-ŭn), town (pop. 12,861), N Baden, Germany, after 1945 in Württemberg-Baden, 5 mi. WSW of Heidelberg; rail junction; asparagus- and tobacco-growing center. Railroad repair shops. Food processing (vegetable preserves, beer); metal (brewing machinery and apparatus) and tobacco (cigars, cigarettes) industries, silk mfg., woodworking. Medieval castle, rebuilt c.1700, was summer residence (1720–77) of electors palatine; in noted park modeled after Fr. baroque and English landscape designs.

Schwiebus, Poland: see Swiebodzin.

Schwieloch Lake, Ger. *Schwielochsee* (shvē′lôkh-zā″), lake (□ 4.5), Brandenburg, E Germany, 3 mi. SW of Friedland; 6 mi. long, 1–2 mi. wide, greatest depth 25 ft., average depth 12 ft. Traversed by Spree R.

Schwielow Lake (shvē′lō), lake (□ 3.3), Brandenburg, E Germany, 5 mi. SW of Potsdam; 4 mi. long, 1–1.5 mi. wide, greatest depth 29 ft., average depth 13 ft. Traversed by Havel R.

Schwientochlowitz, Poland: see Swietochlowice.

Schwörstadt (shvûr′shtät), village (pop. 1,116), S Baden, Germany, at S foot of Black Forest, on the Rhine (Swiss border) and 5 mi. ENE of Rheinfelden; site of hydroelectric plant Ryburg-Schwörstadt.

Schwyz (shvēts), canton (□ 351; 1950 pop. 71,246), central Switzerland, borders L. of Zurich (N), L. of Lucerne (SW); ⊙ Schwyz. Forests, meadows, and pastureland, with some cultivated fields and orchards. Alpine mts. rise in S. Well-developed hydroelectric system extends along the Wäggital and S shore of L. of Zurich. Mfg. (cotton and silk textiles). Numerous resorts on L. of Lucerne, on the Rigi, and elsewhere (e.g., Einsiedeln). Pop. German speaking and Catholic. In 1291 Schwyz concluded a pact with Uri and Unterwalden which became basis of Swiss liberty. With Lucerne, these cantons became known as the Four Forest Cantons. Switzerland derives its name from Schwyz.

Schwyz, town (1950 pop. 10,192), ⊙ Schwyz canton, Switzerland, 16 mi. E of Lucerne; tourist center. Cotton textiles, flour, knives; cement works, woodworking. Federal Archives, 17th-cent. town hall, baroque church, R.C. col. The Great Mythen (mē′tŭn) (6,240 ft.) and the Little Mythen (5,955 ft.) rise NE of town.

Schyl River, Rumania: see Jiu River.

Schynige Platte (shē′nĭgŭ plä′tŭ), place with notable view (6,823 ft.) in Bernese Alps, S central Switzerland, 3 mi. SE of Interlaken; reached by rack-and-pinion railway.

Sciacca (shäk′kä), town (pop. 17,265), Agrigento prov., W Sicily, port on Mediterranean Sea, 30 mi. NW of Agrigento; agr. center (cereals, wine, olive oil, macaroni, citrus fruit), mfg. (cement, soap). Health resort (sulphur baths 5 mi. E). Important royal town in Middle Ages; has town walls (built c.1330), ruins of castles, palace, medieval cathedral.

Sciascia, Ethiopia: see Shasha.

Sciasciamanna, Ethiopia: see Shashamana.

Scicli (shē′klē), town (pop. 17,355), Ragusa prov., SE Sicily, 9 mi. S of Ragusa. Asphalt mines near.

Science Hill, town (pop. 445), Pulaski co., S Ky., in Cumberland foothills, 6 mi. NNW of Somerset; makes concrete products.

Scilla (shĕl′lä), town (pop. 4,608), Reggio di Calabria prov., Calabria, S Italy, fishing port at NE end of Strait of Messina, 10 mi. NNE of Reggio di Calabria, in citrus-fruit and olive region; bathing resort. Severely damaged by earthquakes of 1783 and 1908. Situated on a small promontory, the rock of Scylla of anc. legend. Opposite it, near Punta del Faro, Sicily, is Garofalo whirlpool, the supposed Charybdis.

Scilly (sĭ′lē), fishing village, S Co. Cork, Ireland, on Kinsale Harbour, just E of Kinsale.

Scilly Island (sĭ′lē), uninhabited atoll, one of most westerly of Society Isls., Fr. Oceania, S Pacific; 3°52′N 159°22′W; owned by Fr. copra company. Also called Fenua Ura.

Scilly Islands or **Scilly Isles** (sĭ′lē), archipelago (□ 6.3; pop. 1,740), Cornwall, England, in the Atlantic, at entrance to English Channel, 28 mi. SW of Land's End; 49°55′N 6°20′W. There are some 140 islets and rocks, 5 of which are inhabited: Saint Mary's (largest; with chief town, Hugh Town), Tresco, Saint Martin's, Saint Agnes, Bryher. Generally identified with the *Cassiterides* (tin isls.) of the Phoenicians. Flower-growing center; fishing; tourist resort, with mild, even climate. Samson isl. has anc. stone monuments and is scene of Besant's *Armorel of Lyonesse;* Annet isl. is a bird-breeding ground. Called the "Flower Garden of England."

Scinawa (shŭtsĕnä′vä), Pol. *Ścinawa,* Ger. *Steinau* (shtīn′ou), town (1939 pop. 6,529; 1946 pop. 1,895) in Lower Silesia, after 1945 in Wroclaw prov., SW Poland, on the Oder and 19 mi. NE of Liegnitz (Legnica); cotton milling; power station. In Second World War, c.80% destroyed.

Scio, Greece: see Chios.

Scio (sī′ō). **1** Village (1940 pop. 532), Allegany co., W N.Y., 4 mi. NW of Wellsville; oil wells; makes hardware. **2** Village (pop. 1,152), Harrison co., E Ohio, 9 mi. NNW of Cadiz and on small Conotton Creek; pottery, chinaware, paperboard containers. **3** City (pop. 448), Linn co., NW Oregon, on small affluent of Willamette R. and 19 mi. SE of Salem in livestock, fruit, and poultry area; lumber milling, logging.

Scionzier (sēōzyā′), village (pop. 1,633), Haute-Savoie dept., SE France, in Faucigny valley near the Arve, 2 mi. W of Cluses; clock- and watch-making.

Sciota (sī′ō″tŭ), village (pop. 128), McDonough co., W Ill., 8 mi. NNW of Macomb, in agr. and bituminous-coal area.

Scioto (sīō′tŭ, –tō), county (□ 609; pop. 82,910), S Ohio; ⊙ Portsmouth. Bounded S by Ohio R., here forming Ky. line; intersected by Scioto and Little Scioto rivers. Includes Shawnee State Forest and Roosevelt Game Preserve. Agr. area (livestock, dairy products, grain, fruit); mfg. at Portsmouth. Formed 1803.

Scioto River, central and S Ohio, rises in region W of Kenton, flows SE into Marion co., then S, past Columbus and Chillicothe, to the Ohio at Portsmouth; c.237 mi. long. Tributaries include Olentangy R. and several creeks.

Scipio (sĭ′pēō), town (pop. 491), Millard co., W central Utah, 25 mi. ESE of Delta; alt. 5,300 ft.; sheep, cattle, hay, grain. Pavant Mts. near by.

Scituate (sĭ′chŏŏwăt″, –wĭt). **1** Town (pop. 5,993), including Scituate village (pop. 1,457), Plymouth co., E Mass., on Massachusetts Bay and 20 mi. SE of Boston; summer resort; fishing; truck, poultry, fruit. Irish moss, sand, gravel found here. Settled c.1630, inc. 1636. Includes resort villages of Egypt, Greenbush, Minot (mī′nŭt), Rivermoor, Sandhills, Shore Acres, North Scituate (1940 pop. 669), Scituate Center. **2** Town (pop. 3,905), Providence co., central R.I., on North Branch of Pawtuxet R. (here dammed to form Scituate Reservoir) and 11 mi. W of Providence. Includes villages of Hope and North Scituate (administrative center). In Revolution, cannon cast at ironworks here. Stephen and Esek Hopkins b. in Scituate. Set off from Providence in 1731, town inc. in 1739.

Scituate Reservoir, central R.I., 9 mi. W of Providence, for which it is chief water supply. Kent (or Scituate) Dam (180 ft. high, 3,200 ft. long; completed 1928) impounds North Branch of Pawtuxet R.; reservoir receives Ponaganset R. in W arm (c.5 mi. long) and short Moswansicut R. in N arm (c.7 mi. long).

Sclayn (sklē), town (pop. 1,716), Namur prov., S central Belgium, on Meuse R. and 8 mi. ENE of Namur; chalk quarrying; limekilns. Romanesque church.

Sclessin (sklĕsē′), town, Liége prov., E Belgium, on Meuse R. and 2 mi. SSW of Liége; blast furnaces; mfg. (steam and Diesel engines, machine tools).

Scobey (skō′bē), city (pop. 1,628), ⊙ Daniels co., NE Mont., port of entry on Poplar R., near Sask. line, and 50 mi. N of Poplar; coal mines; flour; livestock, grain. Inc. 1919.

Scodra, Albania: see Scutari.

Scoffera, Colle della (kôl′lĕ dĕl-lä skôf-fā′rä), pass (alt. 2,225 ft.) in Ligurian Apennines, N Italy, 10 mi. NE of Genoa. Crossed by road bet. Genoa and Piacenza. Site of village of Scoffera (pop. 49).

Scofield, town (pop. 236), Carbon co., central Utah, 20 mi. NW of Price, in mtn. region; alt. 7,702 ft. Scofield Dam is N, on Price R. Coal, ozocerite deposits near by.

Scofield Dam, Utah: see Price River.

Scone (skōōn), municipality (pop. 2,253), E New South Wales, Australia, 80 mi. NW of Newcastle; dairying center.

Scone (skōōn), parish (pop. 2,559), SE Perthshire, Scotland. Includes agr. village of Old Scone, on the Tay, 3 mi. NE of Perth. It is site of Scone Palace, present structure dating from early 19th cent. Abbey founded here 1115 by Alexander I for Augustinian canons was destroyed 1559 by people from Perth fired by Knox's preaching. From 1157 until 1488 Scone was residence of kings of Scotland; all Scottish kings until time of James I were crowned here, though the Stone of Scone (also called Stone of Destiny or Coronation Stone) was carried off to England by Edward I in 1297, and has long been in Westminster Abbey (on Christmas morning, 1950, it was stolen by Scottish nationalists and was recovered the following April). Last coronation in Scone was that of Charles II (1651). In anc. times Scone was ⊙ Pictavia. Just E of Old Scone is agr. village of New Scone.

'Sconset, Mass.: see Nantucket Island.

Scooba, town (pop. 734), Kemper co., E Miss., 35 mi. NNE of Meridian, near Ala. line. Has dist. jr. col.

Scoonie, N suburb of Leven, SE Fifeshire, Scotland.

Scopi (skō′pē), peak (10,506 ft.) in the Alps, SE central Switzerland, 9 mi. S of Disentis.

Scopus, Mount (skō′pŭs) (2,736 ft.), central Palestine, just NNE of Jerusalem. Site of bldgs. of Hebrew Univ. (founded 1925) and of Hadassah Medical Center. Held by Israelis after May, 1948; as all approaches were Arab-controlled, univ. was transferred to Terra Sancta Col. in Rehavia, W suburb of Jerusalem.

Scordia (skôrdē′ä), town (pop. 10,672), Catania prov., E Sicily, 19 mi. ENE of Caltagirone, in citrus-fruit region; olive oil, wine.

Scoresby Land (skōrz′bē), region, E Greenland, on Greenland Sea, bet. King Oscar Fjord (N) and N arm of Scoresby Sound (S); 71°50′N 25°W.

Scoresby Sound, deep inlet and fjord system of Greenland Sea, E Greenland; 69°55′–72°2′N 22°–28°57′W. Greatest length (to head of NW arm), 200 mi. Sound extends 70 mi. E from mouth, thence numerous fjords radiate WSW, W, and NW, to edge of inland icecap, where they receive extensive glaciers. Contains Milne Land, an isl. (70 mi. long, 25 mi. wide; rises to 6,234 ft.), and several small isls. Scoresbysund settlement at N side of mouth. Sound charted (1822) by William Scoresby.

Scoresbysund (skōrz′bēsōōn″), fishing and hunting settlement (pop. 90), E Greenland, on small bay at N side of mouth of Scoresby Sound; 70°29′N 21°57′W. Radio station, seaplane landing. Founded 1924. Near by are several small trading and hunting posts (dist. pop. 251); seal and polar-bear hunting.

Scorff River (skôrf), Morbihan dept., W France, rises on S slope of Armorican Massif 13 mi. NW of Pontivy, flows 30 mi. S, past Guémené and Pont-Scorff (head of navigation), to Bay of Biscay forming a common estuary with the Blavet above Lorient.

Scorno, Point, Sardinia: see Caprara, Point.

Scorrano (skôr-rä′nô), village (pop. 3,472), Lecce prov., Apulia, S Italy, 2 mi. S of Maglie.

Scorteni (skôrtsān′), Rum. *Scorţeni.* **1** Village (pop. 1,644), Bacau prov., E central Rum., 11 mi. W of Bacau. **2** Village (pop. 1,687), Prahova prov., S central Rumania, 6 mi. ESE of Campina; oil and natural-gas center.

Scorzè (skôrtsā′), village (pop. 337), Venezia prov., Veneto, N Italy, 14 mi. NW of Venice; nail factory.

Scotby, England: see Wetheral.

Scotch Plains, residential village (1940 pop. 4,229), Union co., NE N.J., 9 mi. W of Elizabeth; makes toys; truck farming. Settled 1684 by Scotch Presbyterians and Quakers.

Scotia (skō′shŭ). **1** Village (pop. 1,017), Humboldt co., NW Calif., 22 mi. S of Eureka and on Eel R.; a "company town," built around large redwood-lumber mill. **2** Village (pop. 474), Greeley co., central Nebr., 10 mi. SW of Greeley and on N.Loup R.; grain, livestock, dairy and poultry produce. **3** Residential village (pop. 7,812), Schenectady co., E N.Y., on Mohawk R. and the Barge Canal (bridged), opposite Schenectady. Settled before 1660, inc. 1904. **4** Town (pop. 226), Hampton co., SW S.C., 45 mi. N of Savannah, Ga.

Scotland, political division (□ 30,405, including its isls. and 609 sq. mi. of inland water; 1931 pop. 4,842,980; 1951 census pop. 5,095,969) and N part of isl. of Great Britain and of the United Kingdom of Great Britain and Northern Ireland; ⊙ Edinburgh. It is separated from England (S) by Tweed R., Cheviot Hills, Liddell Water, and Solway Firth; bounded by the Atlantic (N and W), the North Sea (E), and the North Channel (SW). Its greatest length is c.280 mi., bet. Cape Wrath (N) and the Mull of Galloway (SW extremity); width ranges from 26 mi. bet. head of Loch Broom (W) and head of Dornoch Firth (E) to c.150 mi. bet. Applecross (W) and Buchan Ness (E extremity). Its N extremity, Dunnet Head, on Pentland Firth, is northernmost point of Great Britain, though near-by John o'Groat's House is popularly considered so. Rugged and rocky coast line of Scottish mainland is irregular in shape, has a total length of c.2,300 mi., and is deeply indented by numerous sea lochs and firths (narrow and wide inlets respectively); largest are Solway Firth, Firth of Clyde, lochs Fyne and Long, Firth of Lorne, lochs Linnhe and Broom (W coast), Loch Eriboll and the Kyle of Tongue (N coast), Dornoch, Moray, Cromarty, and Inverness firths, Firth of Tay, and Firth of Forth (E coast). Of Scotland's numerous isls. the most important groups are Orkney Islands and Shetland Islands (N), and the Inner and Outer Hebrides, or Western Isles (NW). Mainland is largest isl. of the Shetlands. Pomona and Hoy are chief isls. of the Orkneys; Scapa Flow, bay on SE coast of Pomona, is one of chief British naval bases and scene (1918) of scuttling of German fleet. Among important isls. of the Inner Hebrides are Skye, Rum, Mull, Iona, Colonsay, Jura, and Islay; the Outer Hebrides include Lewis with Harris, North Uist, South Uist, and Barra. In the Firth of Clyde are isls. of Arran and Bute. Extending N from English border are the Southern Uplands, a region rising to 2,756 ft. on Broad Law in Peeblesshire, at source of the Tweed. Rolling moorland tracts abound, cut by numerous valleys and drained by Tweed, Esk,

Annan, Nith, Dee, Doon, Ayr, Clyde, and Teviot rivers. St. Marys Loch is principal lake of this region; its chief city is Dumfries. N of the line Girvan (Ayrshire)-Edinburgh, the terrain drops abruptly into the Lowlands region of Scotland. This has a NE-SW trend and extends N to line bet. firths of Clyde (W) and Tay(E); general elevation here is c.500 ft., with deeper valleys cut by several small rivers and by lower Tay R. Almost two-thirds of Scotland's pop. live in the Lowlands, in which are the cities of Glasgow (2d largest of the United Kingdom), Edinburgh, Dundee, Paisley, Greenock, Motherwell and Wishaw, Clydebank, Kirkcaldy, Coatbridge, Ayr, Kilmarnock, Hamilton, Dunfermline, Falkirk, Perth, Rutherglen, Stirling, and Dumbarton. This region contains industrial heart of Scotland. Entire N half of country is occupied by the Highlands, a mountainous region divided into NW and SW Highlands by depression of the Great Glen, which extends from Moray Firth (NE), through Inverness Firth, the beautiful and noted Loch Ness, lochs Oich and Lochy, to Loch Linnhe (SW). The lochs are connected by short canals and entire route constitutes the transversal Caledonian Canal. Grampian Mts. are chief range in SW Highlands; here is Ben Nevis (4,406 ft.), highest peak of Great Britain. Other noted peaks in the range are Ben Macdhui (4,296 ft.), Cairngorm (4,084 ft.), Ben Lawers (3,984 ft.), Ben More (3,843 ft.), Ben Wyvis (3,429 ft.), and Ben Lomond (3,192 ft.). On S slope of the Grampian Mts. are numerous lochs, noted for their rugged and beautiful scenery and for their fishing; these include lochs Rannoch, Tay, Earn, and Katrine, with its near-by valley of the Trossachs, immortalized by Scott. At S edge of Highlands is the celebrated Loch LOMOND. Principal rivers draining Highlands are the upper Tay, North and South Esk, Dee, Don, Spey, Findhorn, and Helmsdale rivers, all emptying into North Sea. Highland watershed is close to W coast, so that only short streams empty into the Atlantic. All Highland streams abound in salmon and trout; valley of the Dee is especially noted for its fishing. On the Dee are Braemar, scene of annual Highland games, and Balmoral Castle, royal summer residence. Chief cities of the Highlands are Aberdeen and Inverness. Important granite quarries near Aberdeen. Rugged, mountainous isls. of the Hebrides are usually considered as part of the Highlands. Scottish rail network is comparatively sparse; main lines run N-S along E and W coasts; a central line cuts through S part of the Highlands from Perth to Inverness. Road, water, and air transportation play a far greater part in Scotland that in other parts of Great Britain. Prestwick (Ayrshire) is Scotland's principal international airport. Wick and Thurso (N) are communications centers for Orkneys and Shetlands (sea and air traffic). Off N Scotland are major fishing grounds; principal fishing ports are Aberdeen, Wick, Peterhead, Fraserburgh, Rothesay, Montrose, Leith, and Orkneys and Shetlands. Scotland's important coal fields are concentrated in the Lowlands: in Lanarkshire, SE and E of Glasgow; in Ayrshire; and in Midlothian, SE of Edinburgh. Iron is mined in Ayrshire; some nonferrous metals are worked in uplands near English border. Important Scottish steel industry is centered in Coatbridge and Motherwell and Wishaw region, SE of Glasgow. Scotland's shipbuilding industry is one of considerable importance and high repute; it is largely concentrated on the Clyde estuary (Clydebank, Dumbarton, Greenock, and Gourock). There is also some shipbuilding at Leith and Dundee, on E coast. In the Glasgow-Kilmarnock region is a major concentration of mfg. industries, including large locomotive and machinery plants. Region is also center of Scotland's cotton-milling industry and is site of silk, rayon, linen, and carpet mills. Dundee is principal British jute-milling center; coarse floor coverings (from jute and hemp) are made at Kirkcaldy. Tweed milling is important in Clackmannanshire (Alloa, Tillicoultry) and in the Hebrides (especially on Harris) and Shetlands (also noted for hand-knitted hosiery). Whisky distilling is a major Scottish industry; tobacco processing is also important. Large oil refinery at Ardrossan. Principal British alumina-reduction plants are at Foyers, Kinlochleven, and Inverlochy, all in the Highlands, where hydroelectric power has been developed in recent times, especially through the Lochaber scheme, near Fort William. Only about one quarter of Scotland's surface is under cultivation; barley, oats, wheat, potatoes, turnips, and beans are principal crops. Sheep raising is important, especially in S uplands and in the Highlands. Central Clyde valley is noted for its fruit. Precarious livelihood earned by crofters of the Hebrides, who support themselves by sheep raising, peat digging, and hand looming of tweed, has in recent years encouraged a considerable shift of pop. to the mainland. Under 3% of Scotland's pop. are Gaelic-speaking. Country has an intense cultural life, largely independent of that of England; Edinburgh is Scottish cultural and intellectual center and also one of the world's publishing centers; since 1948 it has been scene of annual music and drama festival. There are universities at Edinburgh, Glasgow, Aberdeen, and St. Andrews. Local Government Board of Scotland (established 1894) is presided over by the Secretary of State for Scotland, a member of British cabinet. The Church of Scotland (established 1560, confirmed 1688) is Presbyterian; it was merged (1929) with the United Free Church. Scottish law is based upon Roman, rather than upon common law as in England. Scotland's climate is a cool maritime one, with cool summers and cold winters; in the Hebrides mild winters are prevalent. Rainfall is heavy in W and N Scotland. Inhabitants of Scotland at beginning of historic times were the Picts who, together with roving bands of Gaels or Celts from Ireland prevented Roman penetration of the country until A.D. 80, when Agricola invaded S Scotland. Successive walls built by Romans to contain N Scottish tribes were inadequate, and while Roman influence in the country was slight, Scotland had been Christianized by St. Ninian and his disciples before Romans left Britain in 5th cent. Post-Roman era in Scotland saw establishment of kingdoms of the Picts (N), the Scots (W), the Britons (SW, bet. Mersey and Clyde), and that of Northumbria (SE). In 6th cent., St. Columba, from his monastery on Iona, brought Christianity in the form practiced in Ireland to the Picts; he was followed by St. Mungo, St. Cuthbert, and St. Aidan, who converted other parts of Scotland. Synod of Whitby (644) decided disagreements that had arisen bet. S Britain, where Roman church usage predominated, and Scotland, orientated toward Ireland. Decision led to reorientation of Scotland toward continental Europe rather than toward Ireland and Scandinavia. Bet. 8th and 12th cent. Scotland was subjected to continuous Norse raids; by 870 Norsemen were established in the Hebrides, Caithness, and Sutherland. In 11th cent. Duncan was king of greater part of Scotland; he was murdered and succeeded by Macbeth, who was in turn killed and succeeded by Duncan's son, Malcolm III who, with his wife, St. Margaret (an English princess), began to anglicize or modernize Scottish Lowlands. His daughter, Maude, married Henry I of England, and a period of peace with England allowed the growth of Scottish feudalism, which differed from that of Europe or of Norman England by emphasizing blood ties of the clan and personal loyalty to a chieftain rather than land rights of lord and vassal. Latter form of feudalism, however, became general in the Lowlands in 11th and 12th cent. A united Scotland was achieved (1122) by David I upon death of his brother Alexander; David encouraged growth of walled burghs, organized responsible govt., and promoted foreign trade. William the Lion (1165–1214) was captured (1174) by Henry II of England; under treaty of Falaise, extorted from William, Scotland became English vassal. It was allowed to purchase (1187) its freedom by Richard I, who needed funds for his Crusade; ambiguous wording of the agreement allowed later English kings to revive their claim to Scotland. Alexander III expelled Norsemen from N Scotland after decisively defeating them (1263) at Largs. Orkneys and Shetlands remained in Norse hands until 1469, when they passed to Scotland by marriage. On death (1286) of Alexander III the only heiress was infant Margaret Maid of Norway; she was betrothed to son of Edward I of England, but d. (1290) before being married. In ensuing struggle for the throne Edward I, while claiming overlordship of Scotland, declared for John Baliol, who was crowned, 1293. Edward began (1295) war with Philip of France and demanded Scottish troops, but Scottish nobles and burghs allied themselves with Philip, beginning the long relationship with France which distinguishes Scottish history. Edward invaded (1296) Scotland, captured Baliol, and forced submission of Scots, who then rose under Wallace to fight for Baliol's return, but Wallace was defeated and executed (1305), and Scotland came under English rule. Baliol's heir was killed (1306) by Robert Bruce, another claimant to Scottish throne, who had himself crowned (1309) at Scone, traditional coronation place of Scottish kings. He then captured Edinburgh and defeated (1314) Edward II of England at Bannockburn; later Robert and his brother Edward invaded Ireland. In 1328 Edward III acknowledged Scotland's free status. In 1424 James I, after long imprisonment in England, ascended throne in Scotland; he did much to regulate Scottish law, improved foreign relations, curbed powerful nobility, and married his daughter to the future Louis XI of France. His murder (1437) led to a long period of civil conflict. In 1513 Scots suffered major defeat at Flodden Field; James IV (who had married a Tudor princess) and great part of Scottish nobility fell in battle. Under James V, who married Mary of Guise, French influence grew; in opposition, the people and nobility became favorably inclined toward the Reformation, which progressed rapidly under the rule of Mary of Guise as regent for her daughter, Mary Queen of Scots. In 1603 James VI of Scotland became king of England as James I. Under Charles I the Covenanters rose against religious forms imposed by the king. A brief constitutional union of England and Scotland took place during Commonwealth under Cromwell; final union bet. England and Scotland was voted (1707) by both Parliaments to insure Hanoverian succession after Queen Anne; provision was made for Scottish representation in Parliament of GREAT BRITAIN. Unsuccessful risings by Scottish Jacobites (1715 and 1745) were quickly put down. Economically Scotland benefited from the union. Enclosure of grazing land in the Highlands in late 18th and early 19th cent. led to large-scale emigration to Canada, the United States, and Australia. A Scottish nationalist movement, which demands great autonomy for the country, is still active. For further information, see the separate articles on cities, towns, physical features, and the following 33 counties into which Scotland is administratively divided: N of the Grampians are CAITHNESS, Buteshire (BUTE), SUTHERLAND, ORKNEY, ROSS AND CROMARTY, Inverness-shire (INVERNESS), Nairnshire (NAIRN), SHETLAND, Morayshire (MORAY), Banffshire (BANFF), Aberdeenshire (ABERDEEN); S of the Grampians are Argyllshire (ARGYLL), Perthshire (PERTH), ANGUS, and the more populous counties of Kincardineshire (KINCARDINE), Dumbartonshire (DUMBARTON), Sterlingshire (STERLING), Clackmannanshire (CLACKMANNAN), Kinross-shire (KINROSS), Fifeshire (FIFE), Renfrewshire (RENFREW), Ayreshire (AYRE), Lanarkshire (LANARK), WEST LOTHIAN, MIDLOTHIAN, EAST LOTHIAN, Peeblesshire (PEEBLES); the counties of the Southern Uplands are Wigtownshire (WIGTOWN), Kirkcudbrightshire (KIRKCUDBRIGHT), Berwickshire (BERWICK), Dumfriesshire (DUMFRIES), Selkirkshire (SELKIRK), Roxburghshire (ROXBURGH).

Scotland, village (pop. estimate 450), S Ont., 10 mi. SW of Brantford; dairying, mixed farming.

Scotland. 1 County (□ 441; pop. 7,332), NE Mo.; ⊙ Memphis. Drained by North Fabius R. and North and South Wyaconda rivers; grain, livestock, dairying. Formed 1841. **2** County (□ 317; pop. 26,336), S N.C., on S.C. line; ⊙ Laurinburg. Coastal plain and sand hills region; drained by Lumber R. Farming (cotton, tobacco, corn), textile mfg. (Laurinburg), sawmilling. Formed 1899.

Scotland. 1 Town (pop. 513), Windham co., E Conn., near Little R., 6 mi. E of Willimantic; agr. (dairy products, poultry); summer resort. Has 18th-cent. houses, including birthplace of Samuel Huntington. **2** Town (pop. 218), Telfair and Wheeler cos., S central Ga., 5 mi. E of McRae and on Little Ocmulgee R. **3** Village, La: see SCOTLANDVILLE. **4** Village (1940 pop. 708), Franklin co., S Pa., 4 mi. NE of Chambersburg; agr. (fruit, truck, grain). **5** City (pop. 1,188), Bon Homme co., SE S.Dak., 25 mi. NW of Yankton, near James R.; diversified farming; dairy products, grain. Artificial lakes near by. Founded 1879. **6** Hamlet, Surry co., SE Va., on the James (ferry) opposite Jamestown Isl. and 35 mi. E of Petersburg.

Scotland Neck, town (pop. 2,730), Halifax co., NE N.C., 25 mi. NE of Rocky Mount; hosiery, lumber, and peanut mills. Settled 1722.

Scotlandville, village (1940 pop. 1,963), East Baton Rouge parish, SE central La., on E bank (levee) of the Mississippi and 5 mi. N of Baton Rouge. Seat of Southern Univ. and Agr. and Mechanical Col. Also called Scotland.

Scotlandwell, agr. village in Portmoak parish (pop. 891), Kinross, Scotland, near Loch Leven, 4 mi. E of Kinross.

Scot's Dyke, England: see LONGTOWN.

Scotstown, town (pop. 1,273), S Que., on Salmon R., a tributary of St. Francis R., and 30 mi. ENE of Sherbrooke, in dairying, stock-raising region.

Scott, town (pop. 263), W Sask., 35 mi. SW of North Battleford; wheat.

Scott. 1 County (□ 898; pop. 10,057), W Ark.; ⊙ Waldron. In Ouachita Mts., and bounded W by Okla. line; drained by Poteau and Fourche La Fave rivers. Coal mining, lumbering, agr. (livestock, cotton, corn, lespedeza, dairy products). Includes part of Ouachita Natl. Forest and a U.S. wildlife preserve. Formed 1883. **2** County (□ 251; pop. 7,245), W central Ill.; ⊙ Winchester. Bounded W by Illinois R.; drained by small Sandy and Mauvaise Terre creeks. Agr. (corn, wheat, oats, livestock, poultry). Formed 1839. **3** County (□ 193; pop. 11,519), SE Ind.; ⊙ Scottsburg. Bounded N by Muscatatuck R., and drained by its small tributaries. Agr. (grain, tobacco, truck, livestock, poultry); timber; limestone. Industry at Scottsburg and Austin. Formed 1820. **4** County (□ 453; pop. 100,698), E Iowa; ⊙ Davenport. Bounded E and S by Mississippi R. (forms Ill. line here), and N mainly by Wapsipinicon R. Prairie agr. area (hogs, cattle, poultry, corn, wheat, oats), with industry at Davenport; coal deposits (SW), limestone quarries. Formed 1837. **5** County (□ 723; pop. 4,921), W Kansas; ⊙ Scott City. Sloping to rolling plains region. Grain, livestock. Formed 1886. **6** County (□ 284; pop. 15,141), N Ky.; ⊙ Georgetown. Bounded SW by Elkhorn Creek; drained by Eagle Creek and North Branch of Elkhorn Creek. In Bluegrass region; gently rolling upland agr. area (burley tobacco, corn, wheat); limestone quarries. Some mfg. at Georgetown. Formed 1792. **7**

County (□ 352; pop. 16,486), S Minn.; ⊙ Shakopee. Agr. area bounded N and W by Minnesota R. Dairy products, livestock, corn, oats, barley. Formed 1853. **8** County (□ 615; pop. 21,681), central Miss.; ⊙ Forest. Drained by Strong and Leaf rivers and small Tuscolameta Creek. Agr. (cotton, corn); lumbering. Formed 1833. **9** County (□ 418; pop. 32,842), SE Mo.; ⊙ Benton. On Mississippi R. (E); drainage canals. Grows and processes cotton; corn, wheat, oats, hay, livestock; lumber. Formed 1821. **10** County (□ 549; pop. 17,362), N Tenn.; ⊙ Huntsville. Bordered N by Ky.; a rugged region of the Cumberlands; drained by South Fork Cumberland R. and small New R. Lumbering, coal and clay mining, farming (corn, fruit, tobacco, hay, livestock, vegetables). Formed 1849. **11** County (□ 539; pop. 27,640), SW Va.; ⊙ Gate City. Mainly in the Alleghenies; bounded S by Tenn.; parts of Clinch and Powell mts. in W; Natural Tunnel through Powell Mtn. attracts tourists. Drained by Clinch R., North Fork of Holston R. Includes part of Jefferson Natl. Forest. Agr. (fruit, tobacco, wheat, corn); livestock raising, dairying, lumbering, bituminous-coal mining. Formed 1814.

Scott. 1 Town (pop. 194), Johnson co., E central Ga., 14 mi. E of Dublin. **2** Village (pop. 688), Lafayette parish, S La., 4 mi. W of Lafayette; cotton gins; mfg. of concrete products, patent medicines. Pecan orchards near by. **3** Village (pop. 347), on Van Wert–Paulding co. line, W Ohio, 8 mi. N of Van Wert, in agr. area.

Scott, Cape, SW B.C., NW extremity of Vancouver Isl.; 50°47'N 128°26'W; lighthouse.

Scott, Mount, Oregon: see CRATER LAKE NATIONAL PARK.

Scott Air Force Base, Ill.: see BELLEVILLE.

Scottburgh (-bŭrŭ), town (pop. 1,601), SE Natal, U. of So. Afr., on Indian Ocean, 35 mi. SSW of Durban; fishing port, resort; sugar milling.

Scott Channel (7 mi. wide), in the Pacific, SW B.C., separates Scott Isls. from NW tip of Vancouver.

Scott City, city (pop. 3,204), ⊙ Scott co., W Kansas, 34 mi. N of Garden City; trade and shipping center for agr. and stock-raising area. Oil wells in vicinity. Last battle (1878) with Indians in Kansas was fought in near-by canyon. State park (N) has remains of Indian pueblo. Inc. 1887.

Scottdale, borough (pop. 6,249), Westmoreland co., SW Pa., 31 mi. SE of Pittsburgh, bituminous coal; metal and wood products, coffins, coke; railroad shops; agr. Laid out 1872, inc. 1874.

Scott Island (¼ mi. long, ⅛ mi. wide), in the Pacific off Antarctica, 315 naut. mi. NE of Cape Adare, Victoria Land; 67°24'S 179°55'W. Discovered 1902 by William Colbeck, Br. explorer.

Scott Jonction (zhōksyō'), village (pop. estimate 500), S Que., on Chaudière R. and 22 mi. SSE of Quebec; mfg. of clothing, biscuits; lumbering; in agr. region (dairying, grain, potatoes).

Scott Mountains, Calif.: see KLAMATH MOUNTAINS.

Scotts Bluff, county (□ 726; pop. 33,939), W Nebr.; ⊙ Gering. Irrigated agr. area bounded W by Wyo.; drained by L. Minatare and N.Platte R. Wildcat Hills, highest at Wildcat Mtn. (5,038 ft.), in SE. Scotts Bluff Natl. Monument is near Scottsbluff, commercial center of co. Beet sugar, flour; livestock, grain, beans, potatoes, dairy and poultry produce. Formed 1888.

Scottsbluff, city (pop. 12,858), Scotts Bluff co., W Nebr., 80 mi. NE of Cheyenne, Wyo., and on left bank of N.Platte R.; trade center for irrigated agr. region in W Nebr. and E Wyo.; tourist trade; oil refinery; beet sugar, flour; grain, livestock, dairy and poultry produce, potatoes. Jr. col., hosp., and agr. experiment station here. Settled after 1885, platted 1899, inc. 1900. Across river is **Scotts Bluff National Monument** (3.4; established 1919), prominent elevation (4,649 ft.) that served as landmark on Oregon Trail; includes mus. of historical relics and fossils.

Scottsboro, city (pop. 4,731), ⊙ Jackson co., NE Ala., near Tennessee R., at edge of Cumberland Plateau, 30 mi. E of Huntsville; cotton products, clothing, lumber. Scene of famous Scottsboro Case, *cause célèbre* in which conviction (1931) of 9 Negro boys for rape was fought for years by liberals who felt the conviction was a miscarriage of justice infringing upon the civil rights of the accused. The long, bitter legal struggle gradually secured the release of the defendants, and by 1946 only 1 was in prison; he later escaped.

Scottsburg. 1 Town (pop. 2,953), ⊙ Scott co., SE Ind., 28 mi. N of New Albany, in agr. area (grain, truck, poultry); mfg. (canned goods, work clothes); limestone quarries; timber. **2** Town (pop. 222), Halifax co., S Va., 35 mi. ENE of Danville.

Scottsdale, town (pop. 1,194), N Tasmania, 27 mi. NE of Launceston; butter, dehydrated vegetables, sawmills; orchards.

Scottsdale, village (pop. 2,032), Maricopa co., S central Ariz., 8 mi. E of Phoenix.

Scotts Hill, town (pop. 299), on Decatur-Henderson co. line, W Tenn., 8 mi. SW of Decaturville.

Scotts Mills, city (pop. 217), Marion co., NW Oregon, 20 mi. ENE of Salem.

Scotts Mountain, NW N.J., ridge (1,000–1,200 ft.) of the Appalachians extending SW from Oxford (on its N slope) to point NE of Phillipsburg.

Scottsville. 1 City (pop. 108), Mitchell co., N Kansas, 10 mi. NE of Beloit; grain, livestock. **2** Town (pop. 2,060), ⊙ Allen co., S Ky., 22 mi. SW of Glasgow, in agr. (dairy products, livestock, poultry, fruit, burley tobacco), oil, and timber region; mfg. of nitroglycerine, tobacco products, lumber products, clothing; sawmills. **3** Village (pop. 1,025), Monroe co., W N.Y., on Genesee R. and 12 mi. SSW of Rochester. **4** Town (pop. 396), Albemarle and Fluvanna counties, central Va., on James R. and 16 mi. S of Charlottesville; mfg. of rayon cord.

Scottville, village (pop. 242), E Queensland, Australia, 110 mi. SSE of Townsville; coal mines.

Scottville. 1 Village (pop. 200), Macoupin co., SW central Ill., 32 mi. SW of Springfield, in agr. and bituminous-coal area. **2** City (pop. 1,142), Mason co., W Mich., 9 mi. E of Ludington and on Pere Marquette R., in dairying and agr. area (potatoes, beans, livestock); grist mill, creamery, cannery. Indian mounds near by. Settled 1876; inc. as village 1889, as city 1907.

Scrabster, port, N Caithness, Scotland, on Thurso Bay of the Atlantic, 2 mi. NW of Thurso; terminal of steamers to the Orkneys. Just N is promontory of Holborn Head, sheltering Thurso Bay; lighthouse (58°38'N 3°33'W).

Scranton (skrăn'tŭn). **1** Town (pop. 283), Logan co., W Ark., 23 mi. W of Russellville, near Arkansas R. **2** Town (pop. 891), Greene co., central Iowa, 33 mi. W of Boone; concrete products. Sand and gravel pits near by. **3** City (pop. 487), Osage co., E Kansas, 19 mi. SSW of Topeka; shipping and marketing point in livestock and grain region. Coal mines near by. **4** City (pop. 360), Bowman co., SW N.Dak., 13 mi. E of Bowman; lignite mines; grain and poultry farms; dairy products. **5** Industrial city (pop. 125,536), ⊙ Lackawanna co., NE Pa., c.135 mi. NW of New York city and on Lackawanna R.; 41°24'N 75°42'W. A leading anchracite center of U.S.; mfg. (textiles, especially laces; clothing, metal products, heating equipment, electrical appliances, machinery, furniture, plastics, tobacco products); railroad shops. Marywood Col., Univ. of Scranton, Internatl. Correspondence Schools here. Settled in late 18th cent.; named successively Unionville c.1798, Slocum Hollow 1816, Harrison 1845, Scrantonia c.1850, and Scranton 1851; inc. 1866. **6** Town (pop. 602), Florence co., E central S.C., 20 mi. S of Florence; sawmill.

Scraper, village (pop. 2,922, with adjacent Moecherville), Kane co., NE Ill.

Scratchley, Mount, New Guinea: see OWEN STANLEY RANGE.

Screven (skrĭ'vĭn), county (□ 651; pop. 18,000), E Ga.; ⊙ Sylvania. Bounded E by S.C. line (formed here by Savannah R.) and SW by Ogeechee R. Coastal plain agr. (cotton, corn, potatoes, peanuts, livestock) and forestry (lumber, naval stores) area drained by Brier Creek. Formed 1793.

Screven, town (pop. 752), Wayne co., SE Ga., 11 mi. SW of Jesup, near Little Satilla R.

Screven, Fort, Ga.: see TYBEE ISLAND.

Screw Auger Falls, Maine: see BEAR RIVER.

Scribner, city (pop. 913), Dodge co., E Nebr., 17 mi. NNW of Fremont and on Elkhorn R.; trading point in livestock region; flour, grain. Has autumn livestock show.

Scridain, Loch, Scotland: see MULL.

Scrivia River (skrē'vyä), N Italy, rises in Ligurian Apennines 14 mi. NNE of Genoa, flows 55 mi. W and N, past Tortona, to Po R. NW of Voghera.

Scrooby, agr. village and parish (pop. 215), N Nottingham, England, on Ryton R. and 8 mi. NE of Worksop; home of William Brewster and center of group known as Pilgrims after migration to Holland. Has 14th-cent. church.

Scrub Island, islet (2 mi. long) of Leeward Isls., B.W.I., just NE of Anguilla; 18°17'N 62°57'W.

Scrub Island, islet, Br. Virgin Isls., 4 mi. E of Tortola isl.; 18°29'N 64°30'W.

Scudai, Malaya: see SKUDAI.

Scugog, Lake (16 mi. long, 7 mi. wide), SE Ont., 36 mi. NE of Toronto, in Kawartha lake region. Contains Scugog Isl. (9 mi. long, 3 mi. wide). Drained N into Sturgeon L. by Scugog R. On shore are several resorts.

Sculcoates, England: see HULL.

Sculeni, Moldavian SSR: see SKULYANY.

Scullin (skŭ'lĭn), town (pop. 21), Murray co., S Okla., 19 mi. SSW of Ada.

Sculthorpe, agr. village and parish (pop. 531), N Norfolk, England, just NW of Fakenham; farm-implement works. Has 14th-cent. church, rebuilt by Sir Robert Knolles.

Scunthorpe, formerly **Scunthorpe and Frodingham** (frŏ'dĭng-ŭm), municipal borough (1931 pop. 33,761; 1951 census 54,245), Parts of Lindsey, NW Lincolnshire, England, near Trent R., 26 mi. N of Lincoln; steel-milling center (blast furnaces, rolling mills, iron smelters) in ironstone-quarrying region; mfg. of pharmaceuticals. In the borough are towns of Frodingham (SE), with steel mills, and site of church with 13th-cent. tower; Crosby (N), with ironstone quarries; and Appleby (E), with steel mills.

Scuol, Switzerland: see SCHULS.

Scupi, Yugoslavia: see SKOPLJE.

Scuppernong River (skŭ'pŭrnŏng). **1** In N.C.: see COLUMBIA. **2** In SE Wis., rises in Waukesha co., flows 20 mi. generally W to Rock R. at Fort Atkinson. Receives Bark R.

Scurdie Ness, Scotland: see MONTROSE.

Scurelle (skōōrĕl'lĕ), village (pop. 774), Trento prov., Trentino–Alto Adige, N Italy, 18 mi. E of Trent, in Valsugana; paper mill.

Scurry, county (□ 909; pop. 22,779), NW central Texas; ⊙ Snyder. Rolling plains (alt. 2–3,000 ft.); drained by Colorado R. Agr., dairying, cattle-ranching, oil-producing region; cotton, grain sorghums, wheat, oats, peanuts, peaches, some truck; sheep, poultry. Produces oil, natural gas, bentonite; deposits of coal, magnesium, limestone, caliche. Formed 1876.

Scusciuban, Ital. Somaliland: see SKUSHUBAN.

Scutari (skōō'tŭrē), Albanian *Shkodër* (shkô'dŭr) or *Shkodra* (shkô'drŭ), Serbo-Croatian *Skadar*, Turkish *Iskenderiye*, anc. *Scodra*, largest city (1945 pop. 33,852) of N Albania, 55 mi. NNW of Tirana, in plain at SE end of L. Scutari where the navigable Bojana issues from lake; industrial and commercial center; mfg. (textiles, cement, cigarettes, soap, tobacco and flour products), auto repair shops, airport. City consists of large bazaar [Albanian *treg*] at outlet of Bojana R., adjoined (E) by fortified hill crowned by 15th-cent. Venetian citadel, and the new 19th-cent. town with gardens, mosques, Jesuit col. and mus., R.C. cathedral (archbishopric since 1867). The anc. ⊙ of Illyria, Scutari became (168 B.C.) a Roman colony, passed (A.D. 395) to Byzantine Empire and to Serbs (7th cent.); held by Venetians 1396–1479, and by Turks until 1913, when it was briefly occupied by Montenegro. During First World War, Scutari was occupied (1916) by Austrians and (1918) by Allied forces (withdrawn 1920).

Scutari, city, Turkey: see USKUDAR.

Scutari, Lake, Serbo-Croatian *Skadarsko Jezero*, Albanian *Liqen i Shkodrës* (lēkyĕn' ē shkô'drŭs), largest (□ 146-205) in Balkan Peninsula, on Albanian-Yugoslav border, at south end of Dinaric Alps; over 25 mi. long, 4–7.5 mi. wide. Normally only 20 to 23 ft. deep, it gains 7 to 10 ft. in winter and floods near-by plains, its area varying correspondingly. Has several whirlpools (26 to 144 ft. deep) in SW section. Freezes seldom and then only along N shores. Navigable by small steamers bet. Vir, Plavnica (shipyards), and Scutari. Rich in fish, which are important to local economy. Fed partly by Moraca R. (NW) and drained by Bojana R. (SE). Once an inlet of the Adriatic, it was separated from the sea by an alluvial isthmus.

Scy (sē), W suburb (pop. 390) of Metz, Moselle dept., NE France, on left bank of the Moselle; winegrowing.

Scylla, Italy: see SCILLA.

Scyllaeum, Cape, Greece: see SKYLLAION, CAPE.

Scyros or **Scyrus,** Greece; see SKYROS.

Scythia (sĭ'thēŭ), anc. region of S Europe inhabited by the Scythians. Its extent varied with the power of the Scythians, but heart of the region was on N shore of the Black Sea, on lower courses of the Don and the Dnieper, and in the Crimea. A Scythian kingdom was established long before end of 9th cent. B.C. After 7th cent. B.C. the Scythians—the barbarians par excellence to the Greeks—traded grain and their service as mercenaries for Greek wine, Greek ornaments, and other luxury items. They successfully invaded the Assyrian Empire and late in the 7th cent. held Palestine. They also pushed down into the Balkan Peninsula. In 3d cent. B.C. the Scythians were replaced by the related Sarmatians, and part of their shadowy empire became SARMATIA.

Scythopolis, anc. city, NE Palestine; on site is modern BEISAN.

Sde Eliyahu (sŭdā' ĕlēyähōō'), settlement (pop. 300), NE Israel, in Jordan valley, 4 mi. SSE of Beisan; fruit, olives; fish breeding. Founded 1939. Also spelled Sede Eliyahu and Sde Eliahu.

Sde Nahum (nähōōm'), settlement (pop. 450), NE Israel, at SE end of Plain of Jezreel, on railroad and 2 mi. NW of Beisan; mixed farming, fruit-growing; fish ponds. Fish cannery. Founded 1937. Also spelled Sede Nahum.

Sde Warburg (vär'bōōrg), settlement (pop. 220), W Israel, in Plain of Sharon, 5 mi. NE of Herzliya; citriculture, horticulture. Founded 1938. Also spelled Sede Warburg.

Sde Ya'aqov or **Sde Yaakov** (both: yä-äkōv'), settlement (pop. 500), NW Israel, at NW end of Plain of Jezreel, at SE foot of Mt. Carmel, on Kishon R., on railroad and 12 mi. SE of Haifa; mixed farming. Children's home. Founded 1927. Also spelled Sede Ya'aqov or Sede Yaakov.

Sdom, Israel: see SODOM.

Sdot Yam (sŭdōt' yäm), settlement (pop. 240), NW Israel, on Mediterranean, at edge of Plain of Sharon, 22 mi. S of Haifa; fishing port; boatyards. Modern village founded 1940, then called Kesaria, on site of anc. city of CAESAREA. Also spelled Sedot Yam.

Se [river]. For Laos names beginning thus and not found here, see under following part of the name.

Seaboard, town (pop. 745), Northampton co., NE N.C., 12 mi. E of Roanoke Rapids.

Seabra (sä'brů), **1** City, Acre territory, Brazil: see TARAUACÁ. **2** City (pop. 823), central Bahia, Brazil, on the Chapada Diamantina, 32 mi. WNW of Andaraí; diamond mining. Formerly called Dr. Seabra.

Sea Bright (sē' brīt″), resort borough (pop. 999), Monmouth co., E N.J., bet. Shrewsbury R. inlet and the Atlantic, 4 mi. N of Long Branch, in estate area; boatbuilding. Natl. and internatl. tennis and polo matches held here.

Seabrook. 1 Village (1940 pop. 535), Prince Georges co., central Md., 12 mi. ENE of Washington. **2** Town (pop. 1,788), Rockingham co., SE N.H., 13 mi. S of Portsmouth, on Mass. line; shoe mfg. Settled 1638, inc. 1768. **3** Locality, N.J.: see BRIDGETON. **4** Village, S.C.: see PORT ROYAL ISLAND. **5** Village (1940 pop. 862), Harris co., S Texas, 24 mi. SE of Houston and on Galveston Bay, in summer-resort area.

Seabrook Island, Charleston co., S S.C., one of Sea Isls., at E side of North Edisto R. mouth, 13 mi. SW of Charleston; c.5 mi. long.

Seabrook Landing, village, Beaufort co., S S.C., 20 mi. ENE of Savannah, Ga.; ships oysters.

Sea Cliff, residential village (pop. 4,868), Nassau co., SE N.Y., on N shore of W Long Isl., on Hempstead Harbor, just S of Glen Cove; summer resort. Inc. 1883.

Seacombe, England: see WALLASEY.

Sea Cow Island, Seychelles: see BIRD ISLAND.

Seadrift, resort city (pop. 567), Calhoun co., S Texas, on Hynes Bay (an arm of San Antonio Bay), 33 mi. SE of Victoria; fishing.

Seafield, Scotland: see KINGHORN.

Seaford (sē″fôrd', sē'fůrd), urban district (1931 pop. 6,570; 1951 census 9,023), S Sussex, England, on the Channel, 8 mi. E of Eastbourne; resort, with beach. Has Norman to 15th-cent. church. In urban dist. (NW) is East Blatchington, resort town.

Seaford (sē'fůrd). **1** Town (pop. 3,087), Sussex co., SW Del., 13 mi. W of Georgetown and at head of navigation on Nanticoke R.; a nylon-industry center; canning, oyster packing, shipbuilding. Inc. 1865. **2** Village (1940 pop. 2,216), Nassau co., SE N.Y., on S shore of Long Isl., 5 mi. E of Freeport, in summer-resort area. State park near by.

Seaforth, town (pop. 1,668), S Ont., on Bayfield R. and 24 mi. NW of Stratford; tanning, woodworking, dairying; mfg. of shoes, furniture, agr. machinery, pottery, bricks, tiles.

Seaforth, England: see WATERLOO WITH SEAFORTH.

Seaforth, village (pop. 136), Redwood co., SW Minn., on Redwood R. and 11 mi. WSW of Redwood Falls, in grain area.

Seaforth, Loch (lŏkh), sea inlet on SE coast of Lewis with Harris isl., Outer Hebrides, Scotland, extending 16 mi. inland from The Minch; it is up to 2 mi. wide and contains small Seaforth Isl. Loch forms part of boundary bet. Harris (in Inverness) and Lewis (in Ross and Cromarty).

Sea Gate, N.Y.: see CONEY ISLAND.

Sea Girt (sē' gûrt″), resort borough (pop. 1,178), Monmouth co., E N.J., on the coast and 6 mi. S of Asbury Park. State natl. guard encampment near by.

Seagoville (sē'gōvĭl), town (pop. 1,927), Dallas co., N Texas, 17 mi. SE of Dallas, in agr. area (cotton, fruit, truck); sand, gravel pits.

Seagraves (sē'grāvz), city (pop. 2,101), Gaines co., NW Texas, on S Llano Estacado, 60 mi. SW of Lubbock, near N.Mex. line; market, shipping center for cattle-ranching and oil-producing region, with some agr. (cotton, corn). Carbon-black plant. Inc. 1928.

Seagrove, town (pop. 319), Randolph co., central N.C., 12 mi. S of Asheboro; lumber milling.

Seagull Lake, Cook co., NE Minn., near Ont. line, c.45 mi. ENE of Ely in vacation and resort area; 6 mi. long, 2 mi. wide. Has N outlet into Saganaga L. Lies within Superior Natl. Forest.

Seaham Harbour (sē'ům), urban district (1931 pop. 19,399; 1951 census 26,138), E Durham, England, on North Sea 6 mi. SSE of Sunderland; coal-mining center and coal-shipping seaport. At near-by Seaham Hall, Byron and Anne Isabella Milbanke were married in 1815.

Seahorse Point, E extremity of Southampton Isl., E Keewatin Dist., Northwest Territories, on Hudson Bay, at S end of Foxe Channel; 63°46'N 80°9'W.

Sea Island (c.5 mi. long, 2 mi. wide), one of the Sea Isls., in Glynn co., SE Ga., just off the coast. Near S end is Sea Island, a resort (pop. c.300) connected by causeway to adjacent St. Simons Isl. and Brunswick, 8 mi. W on mainland.

Sea Islands, a chain of low islands along the coast of S.C., Ga., and N Fla. bet. the mouths of Santee and St. Johns rivers. Chief isls. in S.C. are: Folly, James, Johns, Wadamalaw, Kiawah, Edisto, SAINT HELENA, Ladies, PORT ROYAL, Hunting, PARRIS, Hilton Head, and Daufuskie; in Ga.: Tybee, Wilmington, Skidaway, Ossabaw, St. Catherines, Sapelo, SAINT SIMONS, JEKYLL, and Cumberland (c.23 mi. long, 1–5 mi. wide; largest of the Sea Isls.); in Fla.: AMELIA ISLAND. Isls. are generally sandy along the Atlantic side and marshy along the mainland side, where the Intracoastal Waterway passes; some are forested. Causeways and bridges connect the more important isls. to the mainland. Fishing and farming are carried on; some isls. are popular resorts and some are uninhabited. Others serve as wildlife refuges and state parks. Spanish established missions and garrisons in the isls., but later lost control to the English. From early 19th cent. until Civil War, the isls., especially St. Helena and Port Royal (most important of S.C. group), became seat of plantations devoted to fine, long-staple Sea Isl. cotton. Rice was also important. After the War, the federal govt. parcelled out land to newly freed slaves. The Carolina isls. are still largely inhabited by Negroes, who, virtually isolated until the 1920s, developed a distinct set of customs and dialects (Gullah is the best known). With coming of the boll weevil c.1920, cotton culture gave way to diversified farming (corn, potatoes, peanuts, poultry); oystering and shrimping are also important.

Sea Isle City, resort city (pop. 993), Cape May co., SE N.J., on Ludlom Beach and 20 mi. SW of Atlantic City; printing.

Seal, town and parish (pop. 2,078), W Kent, England, 2 mi. NE of Sevenoaks; agr. market. Has 15th-cent. church.

Sealand, agr. village and parish (pop. 2,834), Flint, Wales, on the Dee and 4 mi. WNW of Chester.

Seal Beach, city (pop. 3,553), Orange co., S Calif., on the coast, just SE of Long Beach; bathing beaches; fishing. Chemical plant here. Oil fields near by. Inc. 1915.

Seale, agr. village and parish (pop. 1,355), W Surrey, England, 7 mi. W of Guildford. Church dates from 14th cent.

Seale (sēl), town (pop. 343), a ⊙ Russell co., E Ala., 15 mi. SW of Phenix City; turpentine.

Seal Harbor, Maine: see MOUNT DESERT.

Seal Island (2 mi. long), off SW N.S., 30 mi. SSE of Yarmouth; 43°25'N 66°1'W.

Seal Island, Maine: see MATINICUS ISLE.

Seal Islands, Peru: see LOBOS ISLANDS.

Sealkote, W Pakistan: see SIALKOT.

Seal Rocks Point, Australia: see SUGARLOAF POINT.

Sealy, city (pop. 1,942), Austin co., S Texas, c.50 mi. W of Houston, near the Brazos; trade, market center for cotton, corn area; mattress factory; cotton ginning, cottonseed-oil milling, broom mfg. Inc. after 1940.

Seaman, village (pop. 736), Adams co., S Ohio, 17 mi. S of Hillsboro, in agr. area.

Sea Mill, Scotland: see WEST KILBRIDE.

Searcy (sûr'sē), county (□ 664; pop. 10,424), N Ark.; ⊙ Marshall. Intersected by Buffalo R.; drained by Middle Fork of Little Red R.; situated in Ozark region. Agr. (grain, cotton, hay, truck, livestock). Timber. Formed 1838.

Searcy, city (pop. 6,024), ⊙ White co., central Ark., c.45 mi. NE of Little Rock, near Little Red R.; shipping point in strawberry-growing area; cotton ginning, woodworking, pecan shelling. Seat of Harding Col. Inc. 1854.

Searight, town (pop. 82), Crenshaw co., S Ala., on Conecuh R. and 12 mi. NNE of Andalusia.

Searles, locality, Calif.: see RANDSBURG.

Searles Lake, Calif.: see TRONA.

Searsboro, town (pop. 183), Poweshiek co., central Iowa, 20 mi. N of Oskaloosa, in agr. area.

Searsburg, town (pop. 84), Bennington co., SW Vt., on Deerfield R. (power plant) and 12 mi. E of Bennington, in Green Mts.

Sears Island (sērz), St. Lawrence co., N N.Y., in the St. Lawrence, at Ont. line, in group of small isls. just SW of Cardinal, Ont.; c.½ mi. long.

Searsmont, town (pop. 558), Waldo co., S Maine, 8 mi. SW of Belfast; in agr., recreational area; wood products.

Searsport, town (pop. 1,457), Waldo co., S Maine, on W shore of Penobscot Bay and c.25 mi. S of Bangor, near Belfast; terminus of Bangor and Aroostook RR. Chemical and fertilizer plants. Village of Searsport, now resort, flourished in sailing-ship days; maritime mus. opened in 1936. Set off from Belfast 1845.

Seascale, village and parish (pop. 493), SW Cumberland, England, on Irish Sea and 4 mi. NW of Ravenglass; dairy farming; seaside resort.

Seashore State Park, SE Va., recreational area (c.3,000 acres) on Cape HENRY, 17 mi. E of Norfolk; beaches, sand dunes, cypress and live-oak forests, many bays, small lakes; recreational facilities.

Seaside. 1 Village (pop. 10,226), Monterey co., W Calif., on S shore of Monterey Bay, 3 mi. E of Monterey; grows bulbs, flower seed. **2** A section of S Queens borough of New York city, SE N.Y., on Rockaway Peninsula; shore resort. **3** City (pop. 3,886), Clatsop co., NW Oregon, on the Pacific, 13 mi. S of Astoria; summer resort. Inc. 1899.

Seaside Heights, resort borough (pop. 862), Ocean co., E N.J., on peninsula (here bridged to mainland) bet. Barnegat Bay and the Atlantic, and 7 mi. E of Toms River; boatyards, recreational facilities.

Seaside Park, resort borough (pop. 987), Ocean co., E N.J., on peninsula bet. Barnegat Bay and the Atlantic, just S of Seaside Heights, 7 mi. ESE of Toms River; yachting center. Includes Berkeley village.

Seaton. 1 Village and parish (pop. 1,941), W Cumberland, England, 2 mi. NE of Workington; dairy farming. **2** Urban district (1931 pop. 2,349; 1951 census 2,903), E Devon, England, on Lyme Bay of the Channel, at mouth of Axe R., 6 mi. SW of Axminster; seaside resort. Has 14th-cent. church.

Seaton, village (pop. 285), Mercer co., NW Ill., 24 mi. WNW of Galesburg, in agr. area.

Seaton Burn, England: see WEETSLADE.

Seaton Carew, England: see WEST HARTLEPOOL.

Seaton Delaval (sē'tůn dĕ'lůvůl), former urban district (1931 pop. 7,377), SE Northumberland, England, 8 mi. NNE of Newcastle-upon-Tyne; coal mining. Seaton Delaval Hall (1720–29) was designed by Vanbrugh. Here are coal-mining town of New Hartley (NE) and (3 mi. E, on North Sea) market town of Hartley. Seaton Delaval inc. 1935 in Seaton Valley.

Seaton Valley, urban district (1951 census pop. 26,435), SE Northumberland, England, 7 mi. NNE of Newcastle-upon-Tyne; coal mining. Formed 1935 out of Seaton Delaval, Cramlington, Earsdon, Seghill, and Weetslade.

Seatonville, village (pop. 405), Bureau co., N Ill., 4 mi. NW of Spring Valley, in agr. and coal area.

Seat Pleasant, town (pop. 2,255), Prince Georges co., central Md., E of Washington. Inc. 1931.

Seattle (sēă'tůl), city (□ c.81; 1940 pop. 368,302; 1950 pop. 467,591), ⊙ King co., W central Wash., on E shore of Puget Sound; 47°37'N 122°19'W. Largest city in the state and a metropolis of the Pacific Northwest, beautifully situated on hilly isthmus bet. the Sound and L. Washington (E); a great port, with harbor facilities along Elliott Bay and Smith Cove of the Sound, and on freshwater L. Union (in city's heart) and L. Washington, both joined to Sound by L. Washington Ship Canal. Its location as closest U.S. port to the Orient and at S terminus of Inside Passage to Alaska has made it a commercial center controlling much of the Alaskan and Far Eastern trade; port of entry, with a foreign trade zone (free port) opened 1949; served by 6 railroads (Great Northern; Chicago, Milwaukee, St. Paul, and Pacific; Northern Pacific; Union Pacific; Canadian Pacific; Pacific Coast), an international airport (opened 1949), steamer and ferry lines to other Puget Sound cities (including Victoria, B.C.), and by network of highways. Foreign and coastwise shipments include lumber, canned and fresh fish, fruit, manufactured goods, and a variety of food products; port receives coconut oil, hemp, spices, tea, coffee, silk, jute, wool, cotton, minerals, woodpulp, canned salmon (from Alaska), petroleum. Large aircraft and shipbuilding plants, lumber and woodworking mills, railroad yards, and plants producing aluminum, iron, and steel products, flour, canned fruits and fish, packed meat, textiles, and clothing. City is an important fur market, and home port for large fishing fleet (generally leading world in halibut catch) working in coastal and Alaskan waters. At heart of some of the Northwest's finest scenery, Seattle has as background the lofty Cascades to the E (Mt. Baker is NE, Mt. Rainier, in a natl. park, is SE); to the W, across the Sound, tower the Olympic Mts., also site of a natl. park. The scenic isls., sport fishing (notably for salmon), yachting afforded by Puget Sound, and mild climate (Jan. mean 40°F., July mean 64°F.) attract vacationers. In Seattle are Univ. of Washington (opened 1861), Seattle Univ., Seattle Pacific Col., a Bible institute, the state mus., an art mus., Episcopal (1931) and R.C. (1907) cathedrals, a U.S. marine hosp., Sand Point naval air station, and U.S. Fort Lawton (established 1897). Other points of interest: large locks of L. Washington Ship Canal; Salmon Bay (fishing port); Pike Place Public Market; the Aquarium; the Frozen Fish Mus.; several parks; L. Washington Bridge (partly pontoon-supported); L. C. Smith Bldg. (42 stories; city's highest); Civic Auditorium group. Municipally-owned power system is served by hydroelectric dams on Skagit R. Settled 1852, Seattle remained a small lumber town until coming of the railroad (1884); rapid growth followed despite labor trouble, anti-Chinese riots, and the fire of 1889. The Alaska gold rush (1897) made it a boom town and, together with the opening of the Panama Canal (1914), opened a new era of expansion. The Alaska-Yukon-Pacific Exposition was held here, 1909. The Second World War started a new period of industrial growth which centered on the shipbuilding and aircraft industries.

Seattle, Mount (10,070 ft.), on Yukon-Alaska border, in St. Elias Mts., 150 mi. WSW of Whitehorse, 40 mi. NNE of Yakutat; 60°5'N 139°12'W.

Seavey's Island, SW Maine, in Piscataqua R. bet. Kittery, Maine, and Portsmouth, N.H.; □ c..3. U.S. navy yard installations.

Sea View, Mass.: see MARSHFIELD.

Seawell, airfield, E Barbados, B.W.I., 8 mi. ESE of Bridgetown.

Sebaâ Aïoun (sĕbä-ä' äyōōn'), agr. village, Meknès region, N central Fr. Morocco, on railroad and 10 mi. E of Meknès; fruit and vegetable preserving, essential-oil distilling.

Sébaco (sä'bäkō), town (1950 pop. 1,339), Matagalpa dept., W central Nicaragua, 13 mi. WSW of Matagalpa, on Inter-American Highway; corn, onions, rice, coffee.

Sebago (sĭbā'gō), resort town (pop. 577), Cumberland co., SW Maine, on Sebago L. and 28 mi. NW of Portland.
Sebago Lake, village, Maine: see STANDISH.
Sebago Lake, second largest lake in Maine, in central Cumberland co.; 12 mi. long, 1–8 mi. wide. Center of resort area; Sebago L. State Park on N shore. Water supply for Portland.
Sebangka, Indonesia: see LINGGA ARCHIPELAGO.
Sebaou, Oued (wĕd' sĕbou'), stream in Alger dept., N central Algeria, rises in Djurdjura range of Great Kabylia, flows c.60 mi. generally NW to the Mediterranean just W of Cape Bengut.
Sebasco, Maine: see PHIPPSBURG.
Sebascodegan Island, Maine: see HARPSWELL.
Sebaste, Turkey: see SIVAS, city.
Sebastian (sĭbăs'chŭn, sĭbă'stĭn), county (□ 529; pop. 64,202), W Ark.; ⊙ FORT SMITH and Greenwood. Bounded W by Okla. line, N by Arkansas R.; drained by Petit Jean R.; Ouachita Mts. in S. Coal-mining region; also stock raising, agr. (cotton, truck, fruit), dairying, poultry raising. Mfg. at Fort Smith. Oil refining, zinc smelting; natural gas. Formed 1851.
Sebastian (sĭbăs'chŭn), resort town (pop. 376), Indian River co., central Fla., 14 mi. NNW of Vero Beach, on Indian R. lagoon.
Sebastian, Cape (sĭbăs'chŭn), SW Oregon, promontory c.700 ft. high, 8 mi. S of Gold Beach.
Sebastianópolis (sĭbŭstyŭnô'pōōlēs), town (pop. 356), NW Rio Grande do Norte, NE Brazil, on Apodi R. and 25 mi. SW of Mossoró; gypsum quarries. Until 1944, called São Sebastião.
Sebastián Vizcaíno Bay (săbästyän' vēskäē'nō), large inlet of the Pacific on W coast of Lower California, NW Mexico; c.60 mi. in diameter, 40 mi. wide. Bounded W by Cedros Isl. Eugenia Point at SW entrance.
Sebasticook Lake (sĭbă'stĭkōōk), Penobscot co., S central Maine, resort lake near Newport, 22 mi. WNW of Bangor; 4 mi. long.
Sebasticook River, central Maine, rises in SE Somerset co., flows c.40 mi. generally S and SW to the Kennebec at Winslow.
Sebastopol, Australia: see BALLARAT.
Sebastopol, Russian SFSR: see SEVASTOPOL.
Sebastopol (sĭbă'stŭpŭl, -pōl"). **1** City (pop. 2,601), Sonoma co., W Calif., 5 mi. W of Santa Rosa; fruit (especially apples; also grapes), hops, vegetables. Inc. 1902. **2** Town (pop. 330), Scott co., central Miss., 39 mi. WNW of Meridian.
Sebastye, Palestine: see SAMARIA, city.
Sebbe, Fr. Togoland: see ZÉBÉ.
Sebec (sē'bĭk), resort town (pop. 442), Piscataquis co., central Maine, on Piscataquis R. and Sebec L. and 9 mi. NE of Dover-Foxcroft.
Sebec Lake, village, Maine: see WILLIMANTIC.
Sebec Lake, Piscataquis co., central Maine, 4 mi. N of Dover-Foxcroft; 11 mi. long, .5–3 mi. wide. Resort center. Source of **Sebec River,** which flows c.9 mi. E and SE to the Piscataquis.
Sebeka (sŭbē'kŭ), village (pop. 802), Wadena co., W central Minn., on tributary of Leaf R. and 14 mi. N of Wadena, in grain, livestock, poultry area; dairy products.
Sebenico, Yugoslavia: see SIBENIK.
Sebennytos or **Sebennytus** (sĕbĕ'nĭtŭs), city of anc. Egypt, on Sebennytic branch of the Nile, near site of present SAMANNUD, Gharbiya prov., central Lower Egypt. Famous historian and priest Manetho b. here (3d cent. B.C.).
Sebes (sĕ'bĕsh), Rum. *Sebeş*, Ger. *Mühlbach* (mül'-băkh), Hung. *Szászsebes* (säs'shĕ"bĕsh), town (1948 pop. 10,080), Sibiu prov., central Rumania, on railroad and 8 mi. S of Alba-Iulia, in winegrowing region; mfg. of hosiery, hats, footwear; trade in agr. produce; woodworking. One of the original 7 towns founded (12th–13th cent.) in Transylvania by Saxon colonists, it still has a noted 13th–14th-cent. Evangelical church. A second Ger. group of colonists settled here in 18th cent. from Baden.
Sebesi (sŭbā'sē), volcanic islet (3 mi. long, 3 mi. wide), Indonesia, in Sunda Strait, off S coast of Sumatra, near entrance to Lampung Bay, 36 mi. SSE of Telukbetung; 5°57'S 105°29'E. Hilly, wooded, rising to 2,649 ft. Sometimes called Tamarind Isl.
Sebes Körös, Hungary and Rumania: see KÖRÖS RIVER.
Sebewaing (sē'bŭwĭng), village (pop. 1,911), Huron co., E Mich., 23 mi. NE of Bay City, on Saginaw Bay, in farm area (grain, beans, sugar beets, poultry; dairy products); beet-sugar refining, commercial fishing. Settled 1835, inc. 1879.
Sebezh (sĭbyĕsh'), city (1926 pop. 5,753), SW Velikiye Luki oblast, Russian SFSR, 75 mi. W of Velikiye Luki, near Latvian border; flax processing, brewing. Chartered 1535 under Lithuania; briefly held (1667–78) by Muscovy; passed 1772 from Poland to Russia.
Sebgag, Oued, Algeria: see CHÉLIFF RIVER.
Sebha (sĕb'hä), town (pop. 1,702), ⊙ Fezzan, Libya, on road and 175 mi. SW of Hun, in a Saharan oasis (dates, cereals, vegetables); 27°4'N 14°25'E. Communication center; airport, motor repair shop; flour mill, ice factory. Has fort and mosque.
Sébikotane (sĕbēkōtän'), village, W Senegal, Fr. West Africa, on railroad and 18 mi. E of Dakar; brick making. Normal school.
Sebinkarahisar (shĕbĭn'kärähĭsär"), Turkish *Şebinkarahisar*, town (pop. 7,542), Giresun prov., N Turkey, 45 mi. S of Giresun, 80 mi. NE of Sivas; alt. c.4,200 ft.; alum mines; grain trade. Formerly also Karahisar or Karahissar; Shabin Karahisar.
Sebino, Lago di, Italy: see ISEO, LAGO D'.
Sebinus, Lacus, Italy: see ISEO, LAGO D'.
Sebis (shĕ'bēsh), Rum. *Şebiş*, Hung. *Borossebes* (bô'rôsh-shĕ"bĕsh), village (pop. 2,314), Timisoara prov., W Rumania, on White Körös R., on railroad and 40 mi. SE of Arad; wine industry. Health resort and lumbering center of Moneasa or Baile-Moneasa (bû'ĕlĕ-mōnyä'sä) is 8 mi. NE.
Sebnitz (zăp'nĭts), town (pop. 13,653), Saxony, E central Germany, in Saxonian Switzerland, 24 mi. E of Dresden; frontier station on Czechoslovak border, opposite Dolni Poustevna; paper and textile (cotton, wool) milling, metalworking, artificial-flower mfg.
Seboeis Lake (sŭbōō'ĭs), Penobscot co., N central Maine, 42 mi. N of Millinocket; 7 mi. long. Source of Seboeis R. Formerly sometimes spelled SEBOOIS LAKE, the name of another lake in Piscataquis co.
Seboeis River. **1** Stream in Penobscot co., central Maine, rises in 2 branches S of Millinocket, flows c.20 mi. SE to join the Piscataquis 2 mi. above Howland. **2** River in Penobscot co., central Maine, rises in Seboeis L., flows c.20 mi. S to East Branch of Penobscot R.
Seboekoe, Indonesia: see SEBUKU.
Sebol (säbōl'), village (pop. 750), Alta Verapaz dept., central Guatemala, 31 mi. NE of Cobán, at N foot of Sierra de Chamá; corn, stock; lumbering.
Seboois Lake (sŭbōō'ĭs), Piscataquis co., central Maine, 15 mi. SW of Millinocket, in recreational area; 7 mi. long, 1 mi. wide. Formerly sometimes spelled SEBOEIS LAKE, the name of another lake in Penobscot co.
Seboomook (sĭbōō'mŭk), township (pop. 18), Somerset co., W central Maine, at N end of Moosehead L., 32 mi. NE of Jackman; hunting, fishing area.
Seboomook Lake, Somerset co., W central Maine, just NW of Moosehead L., 23 mi. NE of Jackman; 11 mi. long, 1 mi. wide.
Seboruco (säbōrōō'kō), town (pop. 1,015), Táchira state, W Venezuela, in Andean spur, 29 mi. NNE of San Cristóbal; coffee, grain, cattle.
Sebou River (sĕbōō'), in N and NW Fr. Morocco, rises in the Middle Atlas as the Guigou, 25 mi. SSE of Azrou, flows generally N past E outskirts of Fez (head of barge navigation), then W, draining the low Rharb plain in a meandering course, to the Atlantic at Mehdia; c.280 mi. long. Port-Lyautey, 10 mi. above its mouth, is reached by ocean-going vessels. Chief tributaries are the Oued Beth (left) and the oueds Inaouene and Ouergha (right). Also spelled Sebu.
Seboyeta (sĕbôyĕ'tŭ), village (pop. c.250), Valencia co., W N.Mex., on branch of San Jose R., just E of San Mateo Mts., and 40 mi. WNW of Albuquerque; alt. c.7,000 ft. Penitente church is here; shrine of Our Lady of Lourdes near by. Laguna Pueblo Indian village is 12 mi. S.
Sebree (sē'brē), town (pop. 1,158), Webster co., W Ky., 16 mi. S of Henderson, in agr. (tobacco, corn, wheat) and timber area; gas wells, coal mines; flour and planing mills, hatchery. Settled c.1850; inc. 1872.
Sebring (sē'brĭng). **1** City (pop. 5,006), ⊙ Highlands co., S central Fla., c.50 mi. SE of Lakeland, on L. Jackson (c.3 mi. long); citrus-fruit packing, fertilizer mfg. Founded 1912 by George Sebring. Highlands Hammock State Park is near by. **2** Village (pop. 4,045), Mahoning co., E Ohio, 5 mi. E of Alliance; makes pottery, china, enamelware.
Sebringville (sē'brĭngvĭl"), village (pop. estimate 550), S Ont., 5 mi. NW of Stratford; lumber and grist milling, leather mfg., dairying.
Sebryakovo, Russian SFSR: see MIKHAILOVKA, Stalingrad oblast.
Sebta, N Africa: see CEUTA.
Sebu, Fr. Morocco: see SEBOU RIVER.
Sebuku or **Seboekoe** (both sŭbōō'kōō). **1** Island (pop. 4,984), Indonesia, in Macassar Strait, off SE coast of Borneo, E of Pulu Laut; 3°30'S 116°20'E; 20 mi. long, 6 mi. wide. Pepper, rubber. **2** Volcanic islet (4 mi. long), Indonesia, in Sunda Strait, off S tip of Sumatra, at entrance to Lampung Bay, 33 mi. SSE of Telukbetung. Wooded, hilly, rising to 1,438 ft. Lumbering.
Sebungwe, district, Southern Rhodesia: see GOKWE.
Sebzewar, Afghanistan: see SHINDAND.
Sec, Czechoslovakia: see VAPENNY PODOL.
Seca, La (lä sä'kä), town (pop. 2,201), Valladolid prov., N central Spain, 7 mi. NNE of Medina del Campo; brandy distilling, flour milling; cereals, vegetables, wine, sheep.
Secaucus (sēkô'kŭs), town (pop. 9,750), Hudson co., NE N.J., 4 mi. N of Jersey City, near Hackensack R.; mfg. (clothing, silk, metal products, fertilizers, cleansers); fat-rendering plants; agr. (truck, livestock). Inc. 1917.
Secchia River (sĕk'kyä), N central Italy, rises on Alpe di Succiso in Etruscan Apennines, flows 97 mi. NNE and N, past Concordia sulla Secchia and Quistello, to Po R. 6 mi. W of Ostiglia. With its tributary, the Dolo, forms S half of Modena-Reggio nell'Emilia prov. boundary.
Seccondee, Gold Coast: see SEKONDI.
Sechelt (sē'shĕlt), village (pop. estimate 350), SW B.C., at base of Sechelt Peninsula, 33 mi. WNW of Vancouver; resort; shingle milling. Near by is Sechelt Indian village.
Sechenovo (syĕ'chĭnŭvŭ), village (1926 pop. 2,315), SE Gorki oblast, Russian SFSR, 27 mi. SE of Sergach; hemp processing. Until 1945, Teply Stan.
Sechibaru (sächē'bärōō) or **Sechibara** (–bärä), town (pop. 9,130), Nagasaki prefecture, NW Kyushu, Japan, on NW Hizen Peninsula, 6 mi. N of Sasebo; coal-mining center. Sometimes called Sechihara.
Séchilienne (säshēlyĕn'), village (pop. 359), Isère dept., SE France, near W end of Romanche R. gorge, 10 mi. SSE of Grenoble, in Dauphiné Alps; calcium carbide mfg.
Sechtem (zĕkh'tŭm), village (pop. 7,697), in former Prussian Rhine Prov., W Germany, after 1945 in North Rhine-Westphalia, 10 mi. S of Bonn.
Sechura (sächōō'rä), city (pop. 3,826), Piura dept., NW Peru, on lower Piura R., near its mouth on Sechura Bay of the Pacific, 29 mi. SW of Piura, at SW edge of irrigated cotton area; also salt-mining and fishing center. A beach resort is 2 mi. W.
Sechura Bay, inlet of Pacific Ocean, in Piura dept., NW Peru; 15 mi. long, 40 mi. wide. Sechura is on NE coast, Bayovar on S shore.
Sechura Desert, Piura dept., NW Peru, bet. W outliers of Cordillera Occidental and the Pacific, SE of Piura R. and just SE of city of Sechura; 50 mi. long, 40 mi. wide. Continued in SE by MÓRROPE DESERT and OLMOS DESERT. Sulphur deposits near Cerro Illesca (W); salt mining.
Seckenburg, Russian SFSR: see ZAPOVEDNOYE.
Seckenheim (zĕ'kŭnhīm), ESE suburb of Mannheim, Germany.
Seclin (sŭklē'), town (pop. 6,914), Nord dept., N France, 6 mi. S of Lille; beet-sugar refining, vegetable-oil mfg., tanning, cotton-waste processing. Also spelled Séclin.
Seco (sē'kō), mining town (pop. 644), Letcher co., SE Ky., in the Cumberlands, on North Fork Kentucky R. and 5 mi. W of Jenkins; bituminous coal.
Seco, El, Mexico: see EL SECO.
Seco, Río (rē'ō sä'kō). **1** River in NE Salta prov., Argentina, rises at NE foot of Sierra del Itaú, 10 mi. NW of Aguaray, flows S to lose itself in marshland near the Bermejo. **2** River in central Tucumán prov., Argentina, rises at SE foot of Nevado del Aconquija, flows c.50 mi. ESE to the Río Salí 12 mi. SSE of Leales.
Seco, Río, river in Tabasco, SE Mexico, arm of lower Grijalva R.; formed 2 mi. S of Cárdenas, flows c.40 mi. NNE, past Comalcalco and Paraíso, to Gulf of Campeche.
Second Baku (băkōō'), Rus. *Vtoroye Baku* (ftŭroi'yĕ bŭkōō'), vast oil-bearing region of E European Russian SFSR, bet. the middle Volga and the Urals. Main production centers are Syzran, Zhigulevsk, Stavropol, Buguruslan, Ishimbai, Oktyabrski, and Krasnokamsk. Oil was 1st struck 1929 at Verkhne-Chusovskiye Gorodki and the 1st productive well was drilled (1932) at Ishimbai. Originally, most of the oil came from Carboniferous and Permian horizons; considerably greater oil reserves were revealed (1944) when the deeper Devonian strata were penetrated.
Second Connecticut Lake, N.H.: see CONNECTICUT LAKES.
Secondigliano-Capodichino (sĕkôndēlyä'nô käpôdēkē'nô), two contiguous towns (pop. 27,734), Napoli prov., Campania, S Italy, 2 mi. N of Naples; sausage factories.
Secondigny (sŭkōdēnyē'), village (pop. 787), Deux-Sèvres dept., W France, on Thouet R. and 8 mi. WSW of Parthenay; dairying. Has 12th-cent. church.
Second Roach Pond, Piscataquis co., central Maine, 20 mi. NE of Greenville, in recreational area; 3 mi. long, ½ mi. wide. Joined by stream to First Roach Pond.
Secor (sē'kôr), village (pop. 375), Woodford co., central Ill., 25 mi. E of Peoria, in agr. and bituminous-coal area.
Secos Islands (sĕ'kōōsh), group of uninhabited rocky islets in the Atlantic, forming part of Cape Verde Isls., c.5 mi. N of Brava. Largest are Ilhéu Grande (□ ¾), Luís Carneiro, and Ilhéu de Cima. Also called Rombo Isls.
Secovce (sĕ'chôftsĕ), Slovak *Sečovce*, Hung. *Gálszécs* (gäl'säch), town (pop. 3,354), SE Slovakia, Czechoslovakia, on railroad and 18 mi. E of Kosice; wheat, sugar beets.
Secretary, fishing town (pop. 344), Dorchester co., E Md., c.10 mi. above Cambridge, on Choptank R.; clothing factory, oyster-packing plant. My "Lady Sewall's Manor" (c.1665) is here.
Secretary Island, Fiordland Natl. Park, SW S. Isl., New Zealand, bet. Thompson and Doubtful sounds of Tasman Sea; c.10 mi. long, 8 mi. wide; mountainous.
Secret Caverns, N.Y.: see HOWES CAVE.
Section, town (pop. 476), Jackson co., NW Ala., 7 mi. SSE of Scottsboro.

Secueni (sākwăn′), village (pop. 1,235), Bacau prov., NE Rumania, 6 mi. SW of Roman.

Secunderabad (sĭkŭn′dŭrŭbăd″), town (pop., including military administration centers of Bolarum and Trimulgherry, 113,642), central Hyderabad state, India, N suburb of Hyderabad; a major Indian Army cantonment. Researches by Sir Ronald Ross led to his discovery here (1898) that malaria is conducted by mosquitoes.

Secureni, Ukrainian SSR: see SEKIRYANY.

Secure River (sākōō′rā), Beni dept., N Bolivia, rises in several branches on NE slopes of Cordillera de La Paz 40 mi. ESE of Huachi, flows 150 mi. E and NE, across the llanos, to Mamoré R. 12 mi. W of Loreto. Receives Isiboro R. (right). Navigable for 120 mi.

Security Bay, fishing village (1939 pop. 13), SE Alaska, on NW shore of Kuiu Isl., 15 mi. SW of Kake; 56°52′N 134°20′W.

Sedalia (sĭdāl′yŭ). **1** (also sĭdā′yŭ) Town (pop. 240), Graves co., SW Ky., on Mayfield Creek and 8 mi. S of Mayfield. **2** City (pop. 20,354), ⊙ Pettis co., central Mo., 75 mi. ESE of Kansas City; agr. center. Railroad shops; mfg. (disinfectants, dairy products, work clothes); limestone quarries. State fair held here. Laid out 1859. **3** Village (pop. 276), Madison co., central Ohio, 10 mi. S of London. Also called Midway.

Sedam, India: see SERAM.

Sedam Kastela, Yugoslavia: see KASTELANSKA RIVIJERA.

Sedan, village (pop. 128), SE S Australia, 45 mi. NE of Adelaide; rail terminus; wheat.

Sedan (sŭdăn′, Fr. sŭdā′), town (pop. 12,987), Ardennes dept., N France, on the Meuse (canalized) and 50 mi. NE of Rheims, at foot of the Ardennes, near Belg. border; important woolen cloth mfg. center. Also produces metal plate, mirrors, and rugs. Citadel incorporates fragments of 15th-cent. castle. Long ⊙ duchy of Bouillon, it passed to France in 1642. During 16th and 17th cent. Sedan was Protestant stronghold with renowned Calvinist acad. Scene (1870) of decisive Fr. defeat in Franco-Prussian War and of capture of Napoleon III. Occupied by Germans in First World War. In May, 1940, Germans broke through here once more, thus opening the "battle of France." Sedan was heavily damaged. Turenne b. here.

Sedan (sēdăn′, sĭ-). **1** City (pop. 1,640), ⊙ Chautauqua co., SE Kansas, 30 mi. WNW of Coffeyville, in stock-grazing area. Oil wells near by. Founded 1875, inc. 1876. **2** Village (pop. 134), Pope co., W Minn., 9 mi. SE of Glenwood; dairy products.

Sedano (sā-dhä′nō), town (pop. 465), Burgos prov., N Spain, 25 mi. N of Burgos, in agr. region (La Lora); flour milling; stock raising, lumbering.

Sedaví (sā-dhävē′), S suburb (pop. 2,452) of Valencia, Valencia prov., E Spain, in rice-growing and truck-farming area; mfg. of fans.

Sedbergh (sĕd′bŭr, -bŭrŭ), town and parish (pop. 2,234), West Riding, W Yorkshire, England, 8 mi. E of Kendal; woolen milling, mfg. of textile-machinery parts. Has grammar school (16th cent.).

Seddin (zĕ′dĭn), village (pop. 439), Brandenburg, E Germany, on Stepenitz R. and 8 mi. NE of Perleberg; site of largest early Bronze Age grave discovered in Germany.

Seddin Lake, Brandenburg, E Germany, 15 mi. SE of Berlin city center; 4 mi. long, c.1 mi. wide. Traversed by Dahme R., which connects Oder-Spree Canal (W terminus here) with the Spree.

Seddon, township (pop. 361), ⊙ Awatere co. (□ 1,019; pop. 1,443), NE S.Isl., New Zealand, 50 mi. SE of Nelson; agr. center; linen factory.

Seddonville, township (pop. 221), W S. Isl., New Zealand, 75 mi. NNE of Greymouth; rail terminus in coal-mining area. Mokihinui mine near by.

Seddouk (sĕdōōk′), village (pop. 662), Constantine dept., NE Algeria, near the Oued Soummam, 26 mi. SW of Bougie; olive-oil pressing.

Sede, for names in Israel beginning thus: see SDE.

Sedeh (sĕdĕ′), village, Tenth Prov., W central Iran, 8 mi. E of Isfahan; grain, melons, cotton, opium.

Sedeir, Saudi Arabia: see SUDAIR.

Sedella (sā-dhĕ′lyä), town (pop. 1,109), Málaga prov., S Spain, 24 mi. ENE of Málaga; grapes, raisins, olives, cereals, livestock.

Sedelnikovo or **Sedel'nikovo** (sĭdyĕl′nyĭkŭvŭ), village (1926 pop. 570), NE Omsk oblast, Russian SFSR, 33 mi. E of Tara, in flax-growing area.

Sedenak (sŭdĕnäk′), village (pop. 420), S Johore, Malaya, on railroad and 23 mi. NW of Johore Bharu; rubber and pineapple plantations.

Séderon (sādrō′), village (pop. 348), Drôme dept., SE France, 22 mi. SE of Nyons, in the Baronnies; lavender-essence processing.

Sedes, Greece: see THERME.

Sedgefield, town and parish (pop. 3,451), SE central Durham, England, 10 mi. NNE of Darlington; agr. market. Site of county mental hosp.

Sedgemoor, marshy tract, central Somerset, England, 4 mi. ESE of Bridgwater. Scene of battle (1685) in which James II defeated duke of Monmouth.

Sedgewick, village (pop. 417), E Alta., 35 mi. W of Wainwright; cereal-food mfg., mixed farming.

Sedgewickville, town (pop. 92), Bollinger co., SE Mo., on Whitewater R., near Mississippi R. and 16 mi. NW of Jackson.

Sedgley, urban district (1931 pop. 19,262; 1951 census 23,104), S Stafford, England, 3 mi. S of Wolverhampton; coal and iron mining, metalworking.

Sedgwick. **1** County (□ 544; pop. 5,095), extreme NE Colo.; ⊙ Julesburg. Irrigated agr. area bordering Nebr.; watered by S.Platte R. Sugar beets, beans, livestock. Formed 1889. **2** County (□ 999; pop. 222,290), S Kansas; ⊙ Wichita. Sloping to gently rolling plain, drained by Arkansas and Little Arkansas rivers. Wheat, livestock. Scattered oil and gas fields. Industries at Wichita. Formed 1870.

Sedgwick. **1** Town (pop. 196), Lawrence co., NE Ark., 13 mi. NW of Jonesboro. **2** Town (pop. 332), Sedgwick co., NE Colo., on South Platte R., near Nebr. line, and 13 mi. WSW of Julesburg; shipping point in sugar-beet area. **3** City (pop. 732), Harvey co., S central Kansas, on Little Arkansas R. and 16 mi. NNW of Wichita; grain-shipping point; alfalfa milling. **4** Town (pop. 614), Hancock co., S Maine, on Penobscot Bay and 20 mi. SE of Belfast; foods canned. Includes village of Sargentville.

Sedhes, Greece: see THERME.

Sedhiou (sĕdyōō′), town (pop. c.2,350), SW Senegal, Fr. West Africa, landing on right bank of Casamance R. and 50 mi. E of Ziguinchor; peanuts, timber, subsistence crops.

Sedico (sā′dēkō), village (pop. 571), Belluno prov., Veneto, N Italy, 6 mi. SW of Belluno, in Piave R. valley; macaroni, wood products, whetstones.

Sedilo (sā′dēlō), village (pop. 3,157), Cagliari prov., central Sardinia, near L. Tirso, 10 mi. SE of Macomer. Nuraghi near by.

Sedjenane (sĕjnän′), village, Bizerte dist., N Tunisia, on railroad and 23 mi. N of Béja; tobacco growing, hog raising. Iron and zinc mines near by.

Sedjoumi (sĕjōōmē′), agr. village, N Tunisia, 5 mi. SW of Tunis; winegrowing, truck gardening. Saltworks on near-by Sedjoumi salt flat (5 mi. long, 3 mi. wide).

Sedlcany (sĕ′dŭlchänĭ), Czech *Sedlčany*, Ger. *Seidlitz* or *Sedlitz* (zī′dlĭts, zĕ′–), town (pop. 2,888), S Bohemia, Czechoslovakia, 15 mi. SW of Benesov, in rye and potato region; rail terminus; mfg. of razor blades. Seidlitz powders derive their name from mineral springs in the area.

Sedlec (sĕd′lĕts). **1** Village (pop. 1,666), central Bohemia, Czechoslovakia, just NNE of Kutna Hora; rail junction; tobacco-processing industry. Known for its 12th-cent. church of Holy Virgin and 13th-cent. charnel house. Picturesque 19th-cent. castle of Kacina (kä′chĭnä), Czech *Kačina*, with park, is 3 mi. NE. **2** Town (pop. 773), S Bohemia, Czechoslovakia, in W foothills of Bohemian-Moravian Heights, 19 mi. E of Pribram, in lumbering dist.

Sedlets, Poland: see SIEDLCE.

Sedley, village (pop. 209), S Sask., 35 mi. SE of Regina; wheat.

Sedlitz, Czechoslovakia: see SEDLCANY.

Sedom, Israel: see SODOM.

Sedot, for names in Israel beginning thus: see SDOT.

Sedova, Imeni G. Ya. (ē′mĭnyē gĕ yä syĭdô′vŭ), town (1939 pop. over 500), S Stalino oblast, Ukrainian SSR, on Sea of Azov, 3 mi. SE of Budennovka; fish canning.

Sedrata (sĕdrätä′), village (pop. 3,025), Constantine dept., NE Algeria, on the High Plateaus, 24 mi. S of Guelma, in wheat-growing region; flour milling.

Sedro-Woolley (sē′drō-wŏŏ′lē), city (pop. 3,299), Skagit co., NW Wash., 20 mi. SE of Bellingham and on Skagit R., in rich agr. region; fruit, truck, dairy products, talc; railroad equipment. State mental hosp. near by. Sedro and Woolley, founded separately, were consolidated in 1898.

Seduva or **Sheduva** (shĕ′dōōvä), Lith. *Šeduva*, Pol. *Szadów*, Rus. *Shadov*, city (pop. 3,736), N central Lithuania, 23 mi. W of Panevezys; shoe mfg., sawmilling, flour milling. In Rus. Kovno govt. until 1920.

Sedziszow (sĕjē′shōōf), Pol. *Sędziszów*, town (pop. 2,519), Rzeszow prov., SE Poland, on railroad and 14 mi. W of Rzeszow; flour milling; metalworks.

Sée, river, France: see SÉE RIVER.

Seeberg Pass (zā′bĕrk) or **Jezerski Vrh** (yĕ′zĕrskē vŭrkh′), pass (alt. c.3,990 ft.) in the Karawanken, on Austro-Yugoslav frontier, 6 mi. SSW of Eisenkappel. Road over the pass leads from Völkermarkt (Austria) to Kranj.

Seeboden (zā′bōdŭn), town (pop. 3,602), Carinthia, S Austria, on N shore of the Millstättersee and 2 mi. NNE of Spittal; summer resort.

Seeburg, Poland: see JEZIORANY.

Seechelt Inlet (sē′shĕlt), SW arm of Jervis Inlet, SW B.C., bet. Seechelt Peninsula (W) and mainland (E), in lumbering and fishing area; 22 mi. long, 1–2 mi. wide. Sechelt village at S end. Narrows Arm and Salmon Arm branch off (W).

Seedorf (zā′dôrf), town (pop. 2,616), Bern canton, NW Switzerland, 9 mi. NW of Bern.

Seeduwa, Ceylon: see SIDUWA.

Seefeld (zā′fĕlt), town (pop. 1,867), Tyrol, W Austria, 10 mi. WNW of Innsbruck, on S slopes of Bavarian Alps; summer resort, winter sports center (alt. 3,870 ft.) on road to Scharnitz Pass. Has 14th-cent. Gothic church. Oil shale found near by.

Seefingan (sēfĭng′gŭn), mountain (2,364 ft.), N Co. Wicklow, Ireland, 12 mi. W of Bray, in the Wicklow Mts.

Seehausen (zā′hou″zŭn). **1** Town (pop. 4,951), in former Prussian Saxony prov., central Germany, after 1945 in Saxony-Anhalt, 8 mi. S of Wittenberge; agr. market (grain, sugar beets, potatoes, livestock). Has church, rebuilt in 15th cent.; 15th-cent. town gate. **2** Town (pop. 3,745), in former Prussian Saxony prov., central Germany, after 1945 in Saxony-Anhalt, 15 mi. W of Magdeburg; agr. market (sugar beets, grain, vegetables).

Seeheim (zā′hīm), village, S South-West Africa, on Fish R. and 30 mi. SW of Keetmanshoop; rail junction in Karakul sheep-raising region.

Seekirchen (zā′kĭrkhŭn), town (pop. 3,124), Salzburg, W central Austria, at SW tip of small Wallersee and 7 mi. NNE of Salzburg; summer resort. Has oldest church in Salzburg.

Seekonk (sē′kŏngk), residential town (pop. 6,104), Bristol co., SE Mass., 5 mi. E of Providence, at R.I. line. Settled 1636, set off from Rehoboth 1812.

Seekonk River, R.I.: see BLACKSTONE RIVER, Mass. and R.I.

Seeland, Denmark: see ZEALAND.

Seelbach (zāl′băkh), village (pop. 2,467), S Baden, Germany, in Black Forest, 4 mi. SE of Lahr; cigarette mfg., woodworking.

Seeley Lake, W Mont., in Missoula co., 45 mi. NE of Missoula, just E of Mission Range; 4 mi. long, ½ mi. wide; drained by short branch of Blackfoot R. Recreation center.

Seelisberg (zā′lĭsbĕrk″), village (pop. 681), Uri canton, central Switzerland, near L. of Uri, 4 mi. SW of Schwyz; resort (alt. 2,764 ft.). Has 17th-cent. chapel.

Seelman, Russian SFSR: see ROVNOYE, Saratov.

Seelow (zā′lō), town (pop. 2,765), Brandenburg, E Germany, 15 mi. NNW of Frankfurt; grain.

Seelowitz, Czechoslovakia: see ZIDLOCHOVICE.

Seelyville, town (pop. 898), Vigo co., W Ind., 8 mi. ENE of Terre Haute, in agr. and bituminous-coal area.

Seelze (zāl′tsŭ), village (pop. 5,484), in former Prussian prov. of Hanover, W Germany, after 1945 in Lower Saxony, bet. Leine R. and Weser-Elbe Canal, 6 mi. WNW of Hanover city center.

Seer, Lebanon: see SIR.

Sée River (sā), Manche dept., NW France, rises in Normandy Hills ESE of Sourdeval, flows c.25 mi. W, past Brécey, to the Bay of Saint-Michel (English Channel) below Avranches.

Sées (sā, sāĕs), town (pop. 2,728), Orne dept., NW France, on the Orne and 13 mi. NNE of Alençon; poultry shipping, distilling, horse breeding. Porphyry quarries near by. Episcopal see. Has fine 13th–14th-cent. Gothic cathedral.

Seesen (zā′zŭn), town (pop. 10,355), Brunswick, NW Germany, after 1945 in Lower Saxony, at NW foot of the upper Harz, 11 mi. W of Goslar; rail junction; food processing (flour and dairy products, canned goods, beer), metalworking. Has 17th-cent. church.

Seewalchen (zā′välkhŭn), town (pop. 3,080), SW central Upper Austria, on N shore of the Attersee and 5 mi. SSW of Vöcklabruck; resort.

Séez (sāĕz′), village (pop. 366), Savoie dept., SE France, in upper Tarentaise Valley (Savoy Alps) 20 mi. ESE of Albertville; customhouse near Ital. border at junction of Little Saint Bernard and Col de l'Iseran roads.

Seez River (zāts), E Switzerland, rises in SW St. Gall canton, flows NE through the Weisstannental, past Mels, thence NW through the Seeztal and Seez Canal to L. of Wallenstadt near Wallenstadt; length, 18 mi.

Sefadu (sĕfä′dōō), town (pop. 1,503), South-Eastern Prov., E Sierra Leone, 70 mi. NE of Bo; trade center; palm oil and kernels, cacao. Hq. Kono dist.

Sefagnuk, Alaska: see SFAGANUK.

Seferihisar (sĕfĕrē′hēsär″), town (pop. 4,975), Smyrna prov., W Turkey, near Aegean Sea 23 mi. SW of Smyrna; raisins, olives. Formerly sometimes Sivri-Hissar.

Sefid Koh, Afghanistan: see SAFED KOH.

Sefid Rud (sĕfēd′ rōōd′), river in Gilan, N Iran, formed in Elburz mtn. gorge at Manjil by union of the QIZIL UZUN and the Shah Rud, flows 60 mi. NE, through Gilan lowland, forming delta on Caspian Sea E of Resht. Dam for irrigation and power is projected in gorge below Manjil.

Sefkerin (sĕf′kĕrĭn), Hung. *Szekerény* (sĕk′ĕrānyŭ), village (pop. 5,566), Vojvodina, N Serbia, Yugoslavia, 12 mi. NW of Pancevo, in the Banat.

Sefrou (sĕfrōō), city (pop. 17,594), Fez region, N central Fr. Morocco, on N slope of the Middle Atlas, 19 mi. SSE of Fez; alt. 2,800 ft. Wool trade; carpet mfg. City is surrounded by cherry orchards and lavender trees. Large Jewish minority. Occupied by French 1912.

Sefton, Mount, peak (10,354 ft.) in Southern Alps, W Central S.Isl., New Zealand, near Mueller Glacier.

Sefwi Bekwai (sĕ′fwē bĕkwī′), town, Western Prov., W Gold Coast colony, 4 mi. SW of Awaso, in bauxite-mining area; cacao, cassava, corn.

Ségala Plateau (sāgälä′) (□ c.2,000), in Aveyron dept., S France, bounded by Aveyron R. (N and W), Tarn R. (S), and Lévézou range (E); average alt. 2,300 ft. A poor rye-growing region until 19th-cent., when wheat, rye, oats, vegetables, livestock were introduced as a result of use of locally produced fertilizer. Crossed by Viaur R. and Rodez-Albi RR. Sometimes spelled Ségalas.

Segama River (sŏgä′mŏ), N Borneo, rises in E central highlands, flows c.300 mi. ENE to Sulu Sea 60 mi. SE of Sandakan; navigable for c.75 mi. by small craft.

Segamat (sŏgämät′), town (pop. 7,289), NW Johore, Malaya, on railroad, and 95 mi. NNW of Johore Bharu; rubber-growing center; airfield.

Segangan (sägäng′gän), town (pop. 2,005), Kert territory, E Sp. Morocco, 10 mi. SW of Melilla; barley, livestock. Just S is Beni bu Ifrur iron mine, from which ore is exported via Melilla (mining railroad).

Segaon, India: see SEVAGRAM.

Segargea (sägär′jä), village (pop. 7,090), Dolj prov., S Rumania, on railroad and 15 mi. SSW of Craiova; noted for its red wines; extensive vineyards, medicinal-herb gardens.

Segbwema (sĕgbwĕ′mä), town (pop. 2,614), South-Eastern Prov., E Sierra Leone, on railroad and 8 mi. W of Daru; palm oil and kernels, cacao, coffee. Wesleyan Methodist mission.

Segeberg, Bad, Germany: see BAD SEGEBERG.

Segeltorp (sā′gŭltôrp″), residential village (pop. 2,442), Stockholm co., E Sweden, near L. Malar, 6 mi. WSW of Stockholm city center.

Segendorf, Germany: see NIEDERBIEBER-SEGENDORF.

Segesta (sŭjĕ′stŭ), ancient city of NW Sicily, represented by Greek and Roman ruins 2 mi. NW of Calatafimi. Has notable unfinished Doric temple (begun 430 B.C.), necropolis, and Greek theater (later altered by Romans). Its seaport was Castellammare del Golfo.

Segesvar, Rumania: see SIGHISOARA.

Segewold, Latvia: see SIGULDA.

Segezha (syĕ′gĭzhŭ), Finnish *Sekehen* (sĕ′kĕhĕn), city (1941 pop. 5,400), E central Karelo-Finnish SSR, on NW shore of lake Vygozero, at mouth of Segezha R. (outlet of lake Segozero), on Murmansk RR and 135 mi. N of Petrozavodsk; lumber- and paper-milling center; rosin, turpentine.

Seghill (sĕg′hĭl), former urban district (1931 pop. 2,582), SE Northumberland, England, 7 mi. NNE of Newcastle-upon-Tyne; coal mining. Inc. 1935 in Seaton Valley.

Segl, Switzerland: see SILS IM ENGADIN.

Segna, Yugoslavia: see SENJ, Croatia.

Segni (sā′nyē), town (pop. 7,864), Roma prov., Latium, central Italy, 13 mi. E of Velletri; mfg. (machinery, explosives, fertilizer); sugar refinery. Bishopric. Occupies site of anc. Signia; has cyclopean walls.

Segodunum, France: see RODEZ.

Segond Canal, New Hebrides: see ESPIRITU SANTO.

Segontium, Wales: see CAERNARVON.

Segonzac (sŏgōzäk′), village (pop. 759), Charente dept., W France, 7 mi. SE of Cognac; high-grade cognac distilling.

Segorbe (sägôr′vä), city (pop. 6,048), Castellón de la Plana prov., E Spain, in Valencia, finely situated bet. two castle-crowned hills, 27 mi. SW of Castellón de la Plana; cotton- and silk-textile mfg., olive-oil processing, tanning, flour- and sawmilling. Agr. trade (fruit, vegetables, hogs, cattle). Episcopal see since early medieval times. Has cathedral, a church with fine paintings, and seminary. On site of anc. *Segobriga*. Limestone and gypsum quarries near by.

Ségou or **Segu** (both: sāgōō′), town (pop. c.14,750), S Fr. Sudan, Fr. West Africa, landing on right bank of the Niger and 125 mi. ENE of Bamako. Trading center for agr. region (peanuts, cotton, shea-nut butter, kapok, sisal, subsistence crops, livestock). Cotton ginning; mfg. of rugs. Airfield; R.C. mission. Once capital of a Moslem kingdom (Amadou). Seat of Niger authority for hydroelectric and irrigation projects.

Segovia (sägō′vyä), town (pop. 1,973), Antioquia dept., NW central Colombia, in Cordillera Central, 45 mi. NNW of Puerto Berrío; alt. c.2,950 ft.; gold mining.

Segovia (sĭgō′vēŭ, Sp. sägō′vyä), province (□ 2,683; pop. 189,190), central Spain, in Old Castile; ⊙ Segovia. On the Meseta (central plateau), separated E from New Castile (Madrid and Guadalajara provs.) by the rugged Sierra de Guadarrama, which rises in the Peñalara to 7,972 ft. Burgos and Valladolid provs. are N, Ávila prov. is SW. Watered by tributaries of the Duero or Douro (e.g., Eresma, Riaza rivers). Climate is of the rigorous continental type (cold winters, hot summers); sufficient rains only in spring. Chiefly of historic and artistic interest, the prov. is sparsely populated. Apart from extensive forests, which yield fine timber and naval stores, natural resources are negligible. The tablelands, however, permit large-scale grain growing and pasturing. Also grows, in more fertile valleys, grapes, chick-peas, sugar beets, potatoes, flax, hemp, and fruit. Among little-exploited mineral resources are copper, iron, gold-quartzite, marble, lime, gypsum, feldspar, kaolin, mineral waters. Prov. is crossed by Madrid–La Coruña RR, which passes through Segovia, the only city of some importance. The E mtn. slopes have become a favorite tourist region (El Espinar, San Rafael, San Ildefonso). Except for the Sierra de Guadarrama region, Segovia was taken early in Sp. civil war (1936–39) by the Nationalist forces.

Segovia, city (pop. 24,253), ⊙ Segovia prov., central Spain, in Old Castile, on W slope of the Sierra de Guadarrama, 40 mi. NW of Madrid, and on Madrid–Zamora–La Coruña RR; 40°56′N 4°8′W; alt. c.3,250 ft. Chiefly important for its venerable history and outstanding architecture. Once a leading textile center, it now has only minor industries, among them liquor distilling, tanning, sawmilling, woolwashing; mfg. of textile goods, naval stores, glassware, sanitary fixtures, ceramics, biscuits, meat products, processed chicory. The region produces wheat, barley, rye, chick-peas, and livestock. Segovia stands upon a rocky hill, below which join the Eresma and another small river, tributaries of the Douro (Duero) system. Above the precipitous confluence rises the imposing, turreted alcazar (begun in 11th cent., built mostly in 15th cent., and restored in 19th cent.), where Isabella I was crowned. The Gothic cathedral (begun 1525), among the finest in Spain, commands the highest spot and has a magnificently decorated interior. The most impressive landmark is, however, the lofty Roman aqueduct (SE), the largest and best conserved of its kind in the country (815 yards long, 92 ft. high, with some 170 arches), still supplying the city with water. Segovia consists of a labyrinth of narrow, winding streets, lined by innumerable architectural treasures, such as the following churches: San Andrés, the Mudejar San Lorenzo, Corpus Cristi (formerly a synagogue), Romanesque-Byzantine San Martín and San Esteban. Outside the anc. walls (N) is Santa María de Parral or El Parral monastery. A mecca of Sp. art, the city's splendid past is captured in its archives and archaeological mus. It is a bishopric. Has artillery school. Of Iberian origin, Segovia was developed by the Romans, who left ample remains. Repeatedly taken from the Moors, who made it a flourishing capital and most likely introduced the great textile industry (which declined after 16th cent.), it was finally reconquered (1085) by Alfonso VI after he took Toledo. Suffered during Peninsular War (1808–14).

Segovia Highlands (sägō′vyä), NW Venezuela, bet. W extremity of coastal range and N spur of the Andes, arid tableland around Barquisimeto. It is sometimes considered to include area N to Falcón state and Paraguaná Peninsula. Consists of dry plains occasionally broken by small ranges. Alt. 1,500–3,000 ft. Goat grazing in hills; some coffee and cacao plantations.

Segovia River, Nicaragua: see COCO RIVER.

Segowlie, India: see SAGAULI.

Segozero (syĕg′ô″zyĭrŭ), Finnish *Seesjärvi* (sās′yăr″-vē), lake (□ c.300) in S central Karelo-Finnish SSR, 20 mi. NW of Medvezhyegorsk; 20 mi. wide, 20 mi. long, 300 ft. deep; drains through Segezha R. (NE) into lake Vygozero. Padany on W shore; talc factory of Liste-Guba on SE shore.

Segré (sŭgrā′), town (pop. 4,536), Maine-et-Loire dept., W France, on Oudon R. and 21 mi. NW of Angers; commercial center; leatherworking, cider milling, winegrowing. Iron mines and slate quarries near by.

Segre River (sĕ′grä), Fr. *Sègre* (sĕ′grŭ), in S France and NE Spain, rises above Saillagouse (Pyrénées-Orientales dept., S France) in the E Pyrenees, flows generally SW, through Cerdaña (entering Spain at Puigcerdá), past Seo de Urgel and Lérida, to the Ebro at Mequinenza; c.165 mi. long. Receives Cinca, Noguera Pallaresa, Noguera Ribagorzana, and Valira rivers (right). Feeds Urgel Canal and other irrigation canals of Lérida prov. Hydroelectric plants on the Segre and tributaries (at Adrall, Capdella, Tremp, Camarasa) power Catalonian industries.

Segu, Fr. West Africa: see SÉGOU.

Seguam Island (sē′gwäm) (13 mi. long, 8 mi. wide), Aleutian Isls., SW Alaska, at E end of the Andreanof Isls., 180 mi. WSW of Umnak; 52°20′N 172°25′W; rises to 3,457 ft. on Pyre Peak (center).

Séguéla (sĕgĕ′lä), town (pop. c.4,200), central Ivory Coast, Fr. West Africa, 260 mi. NW of Abidjan; coffee, palm kernels, rubber, cotton, rice, corn, potatoes, tobacco. Cotton ginning.

Segui (sä′gē), town (pop. estimate 1,000), W Entre Ríos prov., Argentina, on railroad and 28 mi. SE of Paraná, in grain and livestock area.

Seguin (sŭgēn′), city (pop. 9,733), ⊙ Guadalupe co., S central Texas, on Guadalupe R. and 33 mi. ENE of San Antonio; trade, shipping, processing center for agr. area (cotton, corn, pecan, poultry), also producing cattle and oil; flour, feed, and cottonseed-oil milling, cotton ginning, nut shelling, dairying, poultry packing, mfg. of clay products, dusters, clothing, food products. Seat of Texas Lutheran Col. Recreational areas on Guadalupe R. and L. McQueeney (W) attract visitors; hunting, fishing. Settled 1832, laid out 1838, inc. 1853.

Seguin Island (sēgwĭn′), SW Maine, island at mouth of the Kennebec, with lighthouse built 1795, rebuilt 1857.

Segundo (sŭgŭn′dō, sŭgōōn′dō), village (1940 pop. 827), Las Animas co., S Colo., on Purgatoire R. and 12 mi. WSW of Trinidad; alt. c.6,400 ft. Coal mines near by.

Segundo, Río (rē′ō sāgōōn′dō), river in central Córdoba prov., Argentina, rises in the Sierra de Córdoba SW of Córdoba, flows c.200 mi. E and NE, past Despeñaderos, Pilar, Río Segundo town, Villa del Rosario, and Concepción, to the marshy Mar Chiquita. Used for hydroelectric power in its upper reaches.

Segura (sĭgōō′rŭ), village (pop. 1,237), Castelo Branco dist., central Portugal, on Erges R. and 30 mi. E of Castelo Branco; customs station on Sp. border, opposite Piedras Albas.

Segura, Sierra de (syĕ′rä dhā sägōō′rä), group of mountain ranges, Jaén prov., S Spain, extending c.50 mi. NNE-SSW from the border of Albacete prov. to area E of Cazorla; rises to 7,812 ft. Includes the Sierra de Cazorla, where the Guadalquivir rises. Segura R. originates on NE slopes.

Segura de León (sägōō′rä dhā lāōn′), town (pop. 4,716), Badajoz prov., W Spain, in Sierra Morena, 19 mi. SE of Jerez de los Caballeros; agr. center (cereals, olives, acorns, livestock). Limekiln, potteries; mfg. of olive oil, meat products.

Segura River, SE Spain, rises on NE slopes of the Sierra de Segura in Jaén prov., flows 200 mi. generally E, across Albacete, Murcia, and Alicante provs., past city of Murcia, to the Mediterranean 20 mi. SSW of Alicante. Its waters feed irrigation canals fertilizing garden regions of Cieza, Murcia, and Orihuela. Several gorges and falls (hydroelectric plants). Chief tributary, Mundo R.

Segurilla (sägōōrē′lyä), town (pop. 1,317), Toledo prov., central Spain, 4 mi. NW of Talavera de la Reina; olives, grapes, cereals, livestock.

Segusio, Italy: see SUSA.

Sehkuha or **Sehkoha** (both: sĕkōhä′), ruined town in Seistan, E Iran, 18 mi. SSW of Zabul, which it preceded as capital of Iranian Seistan.

Sehma (zā′mä), village (pop. 3,797), Saxony, E central Germany, in the Erzgebirge, 3 mi. S of Annaberg, near Czechoslovak border, in uranium-mining region; cotton, rayon, and paper milling.

Sehore (sŭhôr′), town (pop. 16,831), W Bhopal state, India, 20 mi. W of Bhopal; trades in grain, cotton, sugar cane, cloth fabrics; sugar milling, cotton ginning, hand-loom weaving; distillery.

Sehwan (sā′vän), town (pop. 4,364), Dadu dist., W Sind, W Pakistan, near Indus R., 20 mi. SSE of Dadu; trade center (wheat, rice, cloth fabrics, fish); rice milling, mfg. (aerated water, toys), handicraft cloth and carpet weaving, pottery making. Has tomb of 13th-cent. Persian saint; annual religious fair here.

Seia (sā′ŭ), village (pop. 1,539), Guarda dist., N central Portugal, on NW slope of Serra da Estrêla and 21 mi. SSE of Viseu; cheesemaking center. Hydroelectric plant. Has restored Romanesque church.

Sei'ar, Aden: see HUSN AL 'ABR.

Seibert (sī′bûrt, sē′–), town (pop. 346), Kit Carson co., E Colo., 32 mi. W of Burlington; alt. 4,705 ft.

Seibo or **El Seibo** (ĕl sä′bō), province (□ 1,287; 1935 pop. 75,882; 1950 pop. 97,873), E Dominican Republic; ⊙ Seibo. Borders N on Samaná Bay; crossed W-E by the Cordillera Central. Fertile agr. region (Seibo lowland), yielding coffee, cacao, sugar cane, rice, corn, tropical fruit; also cattle raising, dairying. Main trading and processing centers are Seibo, Hato Mayor, Higüey, and port of Sabana de la Mar. Prov. was set up 1845; in 1944 La Altagracia prov. was formed from it.

Seibo or **El Seibo**, officially Santa Cruz del Seibo, city (1935 pop. 2,593; 1950 pop. 3,164), ⊙ Seibo prov., E Dominican Republic, in interior valley, on Soco R. and 60 mi. ENE of Ciudad Trujillo; 18°45′N 69°2′W. Agr. center (cacao, coffee, sugar cane, corn, cattle, beeswax, medicinal plants). Has notable church. Founded 1502.

Seibo or **El Seibo**, lowland, SE Dominican Republic, extensive fertile plain stretching E c.100 mi. along the Caribbean from Ozama R. near Ciudad Trujillo to Mona Passage; c.20 mi. wide. Mainly a sugar-growing region; other products include cacao, rice, corn, coffee, tobacco, tropical fruit, cattle.

Seica-Mare (shä′kä-mä′rä), Rum. *Şeica-Mare*, Hung. *Nagyselyk* (nŏ′dyŭ-shäk), Ger. *Markt-Schelken* (märkt′-shĕl′kŭn), village (pop. 1,799), Sibiu prov., central Rumania, on railroad and 13 mi. SW of Medias; bathing resort with mineral springs; also winegrowing center.

Seicheprey (sĕshprā′), village (pop. 94), Meurthe-et-Moselle dept., NE France, 12 mi. E of Saint-Mihiel.

Seiches-sur-le-Loir (sĕsh-sür-lŭ-lwär′), village (pop. 1,436), Maine-et-Loire dept., W France, on Loir R. and 12 mi. NE of Angers; winegrowing, woodworking, tanning.

Seidenberg, Poland: see ZAWIDOW.

Seidlitz, Czechoslovakia: see SEDLCANY.

Seiffen (zī′fŭn), village (pop. 4,534), Saxony, E central Germany, in the Erzgebirge, 20 mi. SSE of Freiberg, near Czechoslovak border; toy-mfg. center. Tin formerly mined here.

Seifhennersdorf (zīf″hĕ′nûrsdôrf″), town (pop. 9,181), Saxony, E central Germany, in Upper Lusatia, in Lusatian Mts., 10 mi. WNW of Zittau; frontier station on Czechoslovak border, opposite Rumburk; cotton and woolen milling, lumbering; mfg. of pianos, glass, furniture.

Seiglingville (sī′glĭngvĭl), town (1940 pop. 143), Allendale co., SW S.C., 40 mi. SW of Orangeburg.

Seigne, Col de la (kôl dù lä sĕ′nyù), Alpine pass (alt. 8,242 ft.) in S Mont Blanc massif, on Fr.-Ital. border, 7 mi. SSW of Mont Blanc.

Seignelay (sĕnyùlā′), village (pop. 981), Yonne dept., N central France, near the Serein, 8 mi. N of Auxerre; belt mfg.

Seigneury Drift (sē′nūrē), village, Salisbury prov., central Southern Rhodesia, in Mashonaland, on Umfuli R. and 17 mi. ESE of Hartley; gold mining.

Seihut, Saihut, or **Sayhut** (sä′hōōt), town, on Mahri coast, Eastern Aden Protectorate, 35 mi. WSW of Qishn, at mouth of the main Wadi Hadhramaut. Residence of a junior Mahri sultan. Caravan center for trade with E Wadi Hadhramaut.

Seiki, Korea: see SOGWI.

Seikpyu (sīk′pyōō), village, Pakokku dist., Upper Burma, on right bank of Irrawaddy R. (landing) opposite Chauk, at mouth of Yaw R.; head of road to Kanpetlet (S Chin Hills).

Seil (sēl), island (pop. 367) of the Inner Hebrides, Argyll, Scotland, in the Firth of Lorne, 8 mi. SW of Oban, separated from mainland by a narrow strait; 5 mi. long, 2 mi. wide; rises to 479 ft. Just off W coast is EASDALE.

Seiland (sā′län), island (□ 216; pop. 986) in Norwegian Sea, Finnmark co., N Norway, at mouth of Alta Fjord, 5 mi. SW of Hammerfest; 26 mi. long (NNE-SSW), 15 mi. wide. Glacier-covered central portion rises to 3,527 ft. (W). There are iron deposits. In summer, reindeer from mainland are swum across narrow strait to graze heights of isl. Rugged Stjernoy (styärn′ûü), Nor. *Stjernøy*, isl. (□ 89; pop. 229) is 2 mi. SW.

Seilhac (sĕyäk′), village (pop. 462), Corrèze dept., S central France, 7 mi. NNW of Tulle; road junction; vegetable preserving.

Seiling (sē′lĭng), city (pop. 700), Dewey co., W Okla., 33 mi. SE of Woodward, near North Canadian R., in agr. area (wheat, cotton); flour and feed milling, cotton ginning.

Seille River (sā). **1** In Jura and Saône-et-Loire depts., E central France, rises in the Jura near Baume, flows c.70 mi. SW, through the Bresse region past Louhans (head of navigation) and Cuisery, to the Saône 3 mi. below Tournus. **2** In Moselle dept., NE France, rises in lake dist. just SE of Dieuze, flows 80 mi. W, then N, to the Moselle at Metz. Not navigable.

Seilles (sā), town (pop. 4,197), Liége prov., E Belgium, 7 mi. WSW of Huy, near Meuse R.; ceramics, cement mfg.

Seimchan or **Seymchan** (syämchän′), village (1948 pop. over 500), N Khabarovsk Territory, Russian SFSR, on Kolyma R. and 235 mi. N of Magadan, in gold-mining region.

Seimen, Bulgaria: see SIMEONOVGRAD.

Seimenli, Bulgaria: see SIMEONOVGRAD.

Seim River or **Seym River** (syām), SW European USSR, rises W of Stary Oskol in Central Russian Upland, flows generally W, past Kursk and Lgov, S, past Rylsk, and W to Desna R. SE of Sosnitsa; 435 mi. long. Navigable in lower course.

Sein (sē), island (pop. 1,144), in the Atlantic off Pointe du Raz, Finistère dept., W France, 29 mi. SW of Brest; 1.5 mi. long, .5 mi. wide; fisheries.

Seinäjoki (sā′năyō″kē), Swedish *Östermyra* (ûs′tûrmü″rä), town (pop. 7,390), Vaasa co., W Finland, 45 mi. SE of Vaasa; rail junction in lumbering region. Large grain elevator.

Seine (sān, Fr. sĕn), department (□ 185; pop. 4,775,711), in Île-de-France, N central France; ⊙ Paris. Forming an enclave within Seine-et-Oise dept., it is wholly urbanized, consisting of Paris proper (21% of dept. area) and of a ring of industrial and residential suburbs (*banlieue*), which together constitute the metropolitan area (sometimes called Greater Paris). An outer ring of suburbs extends into Seine-et-Oise and Seine-et-Marne depts. Seine dept. occupies center of Paris Basin at the influx of Marne R. into the Seine. Agr. limited to truck gardening. Several canals facilitate intensive river navigation centered on port of Paris. Dept. is highly industrialized, with important metalworks (automobile, aircraft, bicycle, and machine bldg.), perfume, chemical, textile, and leather manufactures, and diversified consumer industries which supply almost 15% of France's pop., concentrated in metropolitan area. Seine dept., unlike other Fr. depts. which are each administered by one prefect, has 2 prefects, the prefect of Seine and the prefect of the police. Principal suburbs of Paris within limits of Seine dept. are Asnières, Aubervilliers, Boulogne-Billancourt, Clichy, Colombes, Courbevoie, Issy-les-Moulineaux, Ivry-sur-Seine, Levallois-Perret, Montreuil, Neuilly-sur-Seine, Pantin, Puteaux, Saint-Denis, Saint-Maur-des-Fossés, Saint-Ouen, Vincennes, and Vitry-sur-Seine. They are reached by Paris subway (*métropolitain*) and dense suburban rail net. Seine is smallest dept. of France, but ranks 1st in pop.

Seine, river, France: see SEINE RIVER.

Seine, Bay of the, on English Channel, off Normandy coast, NW France, extending from Barfleur Point (W) to Antifer Cape (E); 65 mi. wide, 25 mi. long; indented by estuary of Seine R. Also receives Vire, Orne, Touques, Dives, and Risle rivers. Chief ports: Le Havre, Honfleur, Trouville. Numerous bathing resorts (Deauville, Cabourg, Houlgate). On its SW and S shore, Allies landed (June 6, 1944) in Normandy invasion of Second World War.

Seine Bight, village (pop. 505), Stann Creek dist., Br. Honduras, on Caribbean coast, 25 mi. SSW of Stann Creek; coconuts, bananas; fisheries.

Seine-et-Marne (sĕn-ā-märn′), department (□ 2,290; pop. 407,137), N central France, formed of part of Île-de-France and Champagne; ⊙ Melun. Near center of Paris Basin, it lies across E approaches to Paris. Drained by the Marne, its tributaries (Petit-Morin, Grand-Morin, Ourcq), and by the Seine and its affluents (Loing, Yères). Bet. Seine and Marne lies fertile wheat-growing and cheese-mfg. Brie region. Forest of Fontainebleau (S center) largest of wooded tracts. Dept. supplies Paris with fruit (especially grapes), cattle, and dairy products. Chief industries: metalworking, (Montereau, Nangis), glass, paper and sugar milling, mfg. of millstones, pharmaceuticals, refractory products, woodworking. Principal towns are Melun, Fontainebleau, Meaux, Provins, and Montereau.

Seine-et-Oise (-ā-wäz′), department (□ 2,185; pop. 1,414,910), in Île-de-France, N central France; ⊙ Versailles. Situated in central part of Paris Basin, it completely surrounds Seine dept. (Paris and its immediate suburbs.) Drained by the Seine and its tributaries. All agr. output directed toward Paris: cereals from the Beauce (S), truck produce from belt area nearest capital. Cattle raising in Rambouillet-Étampes area. Largest wooded tracts are forests of Rambouillet, Saint-Germain, and Montmorency. Industry in belt of outer Parisian suburbs primarily for consumer market of Paris metropolitan area. Outstanding are natl. porcelain works at Sèvres, mfg. of musical instruments (Mantes-Gassicourt), and miscellaneous metalworks (Argenteuil, Rueil-Malmaison, Pontoise).

Seine-Inférieure (-ēfārēûr′) [Fr.,=lower Seine], department (□ 2,448; pop. 846,131), in E Normandy, N France; ⊙ Rouen. Bounded by the lower Seine and its estuary (S), and by English Channel (NW and N). Physically divided into Bray dist. (cattle raising, dairying), chalky Caux tableland (flax, sugar beets, cereals) which juts out into Channel at Cape La Hève, and meandering Seine R. valley (wooded areas, marshes near estuary). Chalk cliffs along coast bet. Le Tréport and Fécamp. Industry and commerce centered on ROUEN and LE HAVRE. A leading textile-milling dept.: Elbeuf (woolens), Lillebonne, Bolbec, Yvetot, and Rouen area (cotton). Glassworks in Bresle R. valley. Clocks made at Saint-Nicolas-d'Aliermont; Benedictine liqueur at Fécamp. Important petroleum refineries at Port-Jérôme, Le Petit-Couronne, Gonfreville-l'Orcher. Chief ports: Rouen, Le Havre, Dieppe, Fécamp—all heavily damaged in Second World War. Bathing resorts: Sainte-Adresse (suburb of Le Havre), Étretat, Saint-Valery-en-Caux, Le Tréport.

Seine River (sān), W Ont., issues from Lac des Milles Lacs, flows 150 mi. SW, through the lake region N of Minn. border to Rainy L.

Seine River (sān, Fr. sĕn), anc. *Sequana*, N central France, rises in Plateau of Langres (Côte-d'Or dept.) 1,545 ft. above sea level, flows generally NW, through Champagne, past Bar-sur-Seine and Troyes (where it is but 300 ft. above sea level), thence in an ever more meandering course through Île-de-France (past Melun, Corbeil, and Paris), Vexin, and Normandy (past Mantes-Gassicourt, Vernon, Elbeuf, Rouen, Caudebec), to the English Channel which it enters in an estuary 6 mi. wide bet. Le Havre and Honfleur. Length: 482 mi. With its tributaries (Aube, Marne, Oise, right; Yonne, Loing, Eure, left), the Seine drains entire Paris Basin. It is the most navigable river of France because of its mature profile, the permeability of Paris Basin soils, and the staggered flood-stages of its principal affluents. Navigable for river tugs below Bar-sur-Seine (beginning of lateral canal), and for ocean shipping at Rouen. Large cities of Paris, Rouen, and Le Havre, owe their growth to the Seine, and carry on the bulk of France's internal and foreign trade. Through a system of canals the Seine is connected with the Scheldt, Meuse, Rhine, Rhone, and Loire.

Seini (sān′), Hung. *Szinér- Váralja* (sē′nâr-vä′räl-yŏ), village (pop. 5,628), Baia-Mare prov., NW Rumania, on railroad and 20 mi. E of Satu-Mare; noted for white-wine production; mfg. of alcohol, yeast, paper and emery cloth; andesite and trachyte quarrying. In Hungary, 1940–45.

Seiny, Poland: see SEJNY.

Seira, Formosa: see SILEI.

Seis de Septiembre, Argentina: see MORÓN.

Seisen, town, Korea: see SONGCHON.

Seisen River, Korea: see CHONGCHON RIVER.

Seishin, Korea: see CHONGJIN.

Seishu. 1 City, N.Chungchong prov., Korea: see CHONGJU. **2** Township, N.Kyongsang prov., Korea: see SONGJU.

Seisin, Korea: see CHONGJIN.

Seiskari or **Seyskari** (syā′skŭ), fortified island in Gulf of Finland, in Leningrad oblast, Russian SFSR, 65 mi. W of Leningrad. Finnish beach resort until 1940.

Seistan (sästän′) or **Sistan** (sē–), region and inland lake depression (alt. 2,000 ft.) of E Iran and SW Afghanistan; 31°N 61°E. Its dominant feature is the Hamun-i-Helmand, or simply Hamun, a reed lagoon 70 mi. long in flood, when it discharges its overflow through SHELAGH RIVER (S) to the GAUD-I-ZIRREH. The regime of the Hamun is conditioned chiefly by the spring floods of the HELMAND RIVER, but also of the Khash Rud, Farah Rud, and Harut Rud of Afghanistan. At low-water stage, the Hamun is reduced to 2 vestigial lagoons—the Hamun-i-Sabari (NW) and the Hamun-i-Puzak (NE). Bet. floods, Seistan produces wheat, barley, cotton. The anc. *Drangiana*, the region was crossed in 325 B.C. by Craterus, one of Alexander the Great's generals, on his return from India. It was held (2d–3d cent. A.D.) by the Sacae or Sakas (Scythians) and called Sakastan (Sagastan), whence the modern name is derived. During Sassanian times, it was a center of Zoroastrian worship. Under Arab rule (8th cent.), Seistan's capital was Zaranj (20 mi. E of modern Zabul), home of Saffarid dynasty, which briefly ruled (867–908) E Persia under the Abbasid caliphate. The next capital, ZAHIDAN, was razed (1383) by Tamerlane, who also destroyed the Helmand river-control system and ended the prosperity of Seistan. In modern times, the area was disputed by Persia and Afghanistan, from 16th cent. until the border settlement, begun 1872 and completed 1903–05. Zabul is chief town of Iranian Seistan (□ 50,000; pop. 190,000), which became part of Eighth Prov. (see KERMAN) in 1938. The center of Afghan Seistan (part of Farah prov.) is Chakhansur.

Seisyu, Korea: see CHONGJU.

Seitenstetten (zī′tùnshtĕtùn), town (pop. 2,575), W Lower Austria, 10 mi. E of Steyr. Has Benedictine abbey with large library. Includes Seitenstetten Dorf and Seitenstetten Markt.

Seitler, Russian SFSR: see NIZHNEGORSKI.

Seival (sävăl′), town (pop. 511), S Rio Grande do Sul, Brazil, on railroad and 40 mi. SE of Bagé; copper mining.

Seix (sā), village (pop. 788), Ariège dept., S France, in central Pyrenees, on Salat R. and 9 mi. SSE of Saint-Girons; brick- and tileworks, cheese factory. Marble quarries near by.

Seixal (sāshäl′), town (pop. 3,247), Setúbal dist., S central Portugal, an industrial suburb of Lisbon on S shore of Lisbon Bay (ferry), 5 mi. SSE of city center; rail-spur terminus; cork processing; mfg. of chemical fertilizer, hardware, textiles; canning, codfish drying.

Seiyo, Korea: see CHONGYANG.

Seiyu, Korea: see CHONGUP.

Seiyun, Saiun, Seyyun, or **Sayyun** (all: sā′yōōn), town (1946 pop., with near-by villages, 9,707), ⊙ Kathiri sultanate (one of the Hadhramaut states), in the Wadi Hadhramaut, 100 mi. NNW of Mukalla; 15°57′N 16°37′E. Agr. center in date-growing area; native handicrafts (gold- and silver-work); lime burning. Situated at foot of S wadi walls, Seiyun consists of old town and modern garden city, separated by imposing white sultan's palace. Radio station; airfield. Sometimes spelled Saiwun.

Sejera, Israel: see ILANIYA.

Sejero Bay (sā′yûrû″), NW Zealand, Denmark, bet. Rosnaes peninsula (S) and Sjaellands Odde (N); 24 mi. wide. Sejero isl. (□ 4.8; pop. 817) at mouth. Nekselo isl. (□ .86; pop. 45) forms inner Nekselo Bay.

Sejny (sā′nĭ), Rus. *Seiny* (sā′nyĭ), town (pop. 1,678), Bialystok prov., NE Poland, 17 mi. E of Suwalki; mfg. (bricks, turpentine), dairying, tanning. Monastery.

Seke (sĕ′kā), village, Lake Prov., NW Tanganyika, on railroad and 22 mi. NNE of Shinyanga; cotton peanuts, corn; cattle, sheep, goats.

Sekenke, Tanganyika: see SINGIDA.

Sek Harbour, New Guinea: see ALEXISHAFEN.

Seki (sä′kē). **1** Town (pop. 21,610), Gifu prefecture, central Honshu, Japan, 10 mi. ENE of Gifu; cutlery, agr. implements. Known in feudal times for its master swordsmiths. Sometimes called Mino-seki. **2** Town (pop. 5,114), Mie prefecture, S Honshu, Japan, 11 mi. WSW of Suzuka, in agr. area (rice, tea); raw silk, cotton textiles.

Sekia el Hamra, Sp. West Africa: see SAGUIA EL HAMRA.

Sekigahara (säkēgä′härä), town (pop. 7,020), Gifu prefecture, central Honshu, Japan, 8 mi. W of Ogaki; rice, persimmons, raw silk. Here in a decisive battle (1601) against his rivals, Tokugawa Ieyasu won a victory setting foundation for the Tokugawa shogunate.

Sekihara (säkē′härä), town (pop. 4,626), Niigata prefecture, central Honshu, Japan, 4 mi. W of Nagaoka; rice, tobacco; makes writing brushes.

Sekimon, Formosa: see SHIHMEN.

Sekimoto (sākē'mōtō), town (pop. 6,686), Ibaraki prefecture, central Honshu, Japan, 14 mi. SE of Tochigi; lumbering, rice growing.

Sekirovo (sĕkē'rôvô), village (pop. 5,668), Plovdiv dist., central Bulgaria, 13 mi. NE of Plovdiv; wheat, rice, fruit, truck. Formerly Baltadzhii.

Sekiryany (sĭkĭryä'nē), Rum. *Secureni* (sĕkōōrĕn'), village (1941 pop. 4,386), E Chernovtsy oblast, Ukrainian SSR, in Bessarabia, near Dniester R. and Moldavian SSR border, 16 mi. W of Mogilev-Podolski.

Sekitei, Formosa: see SHIHTING.

Sekiyado (sākē'yädō), town (pop. 3,635), Chiba prefecture, central Honshu, Japan, 9 mi. SE of Koga; rice, wheat, raw silk.

Sekken (sĕk'kŭn), island (□ 7; pop. 277) in Romsdal Fjord, More og Romsdal co., W Norway, 5 mi. SE of Molde; 6 mi. long, 3 mi. wide. Site of naval battle (1162) in which Haakon II Herdebred was finally defeated.

Sekondi (sĕ'kŭndē), town, ⊙ Western Prov., (□ 12,990; pop. 865,811), Gold Coast colony, port on Gulf of Guinea, 110 mi. WSW of Accra; since 1946, forms a single municipality (pop. 44,130) with its new port, TAKORADI (5 mi. SW). Terminus of railroad to Kumasi (Ashanti); workshops. Sawmilling, fishing. Trade in cacao, palm oil and kernels. Has remains of Du. Fort Orange (now a lighthouse). Founded in 16th cent. by Dutch; held jointly by Dutch and British until in 1872 British gained full control. Flourished after construction (1898–1903) of railroad to Tarkwa and Obuasi gold dists., and became colony's chief port. Superseded by modern deep-water Takoradi harbor in 1928. Formerly spelled Seccondee.

Sekretarka (sĕkrĭtär'kŭ), village (1939 pop. over 500), NW Chkalov oblast, Russian SFSR, 25 mi. SSE of Bugulma; wheat, sunflowers, livestock.

Sel, Norway: see OTTA.

Sel, Le (lŭ sĕl'), village (pop. 299), Ille-et-Vilaine dept., W France, 15 mi. SSE of Rennes. Megalithic monuments.

Sela, Palestine: see PETRA.

Selah (sē'lŭ), town (pop. 2,489), Yakima co., S Wash., just N of Yakima and on Yakima R.; fruit, dairy products.

Selama (sŭlä'mä), village (pop. 1,269), NW Perak, Malaya, 25 mi. N of Taiping, on Krian R. (Kedah line) opposite Kuala Selama at mouth of small Selama R.; rice, rubber.

Selamat, Mount, Indonesia: see SLAMET, MOUNT.

Selangor (sŭlăng'gôr, sŭlăng'ōōr), most densely populated state (□ 3,166; pop. 710,788; including transients, 715,531) of Malaya, on Strait of Malacca; ⊙ Kuala Lumpur, ⊙ of Federation of Malaya. Bounded N by Perak along Bernam R., E by Pahang along central Malayan range, and SE by Negri Sembilan, it is fertile alluvial plain drained by Selangor, Klang, and Langat rivers. Agr.: rubber, rice (in upland valleys and NW marshes), coconuts (along coast), pineapples. Fisheries. Coal mining at Batu Arang; tin at Ampang, Sungei Besi, Rawang and Serendah. Served by W coast railroad and deep-water port of Port Swettenham. Pop. is 50% Chinese, 20% Indian, 15% Malay. One of the original Negri Sembilan states under rule of old Malacca, Selangor had first contacts with Dutch in 18th cent. Present dynasty ascended throne c.1780. Br. trade was allowed (1818) by treaty, and Br. protectorate declared 1874. Ruled by a sultan (residence at Klang), Selangor was one of the Federated Malay States and joined the Federation of Malaya after Second World War.

Selangor River, Selangor, W Malaya, rises in central Malayan range on Pahang line and at Semangko Gap, flows 100 mi. SW, past Kuala Kubu Bharu and Rasa, to Strait of Malacca at Kuala Selangor.

Selanovtsi (sĕlä'nôftsē), village (pop. 7,259), Vratsa dist., NW Bulgaria, 4 mi. SSE of Oryakhovo; grain, fruit, truck.

Selargius (sĕlär'jūs), town (pop. 4,568), Cagliari prov., S Sardinia, 3 mi. NE of Cagliari; wine distilleries.

Selaroe, Indonesia: see TANIMBAR ISLANDS.

Selaru, Indonesia: see TANIMBAR ISLANDS.

Selatan, Cape (sŭlä'tŭn), southernmost point of Borneo, on Java Sea, S of Banjermasin; 4°10'S 114°40'E.

Selatpandjang or **Selatpanjang,** Indonesia: see TEBINGTINGGI, island.

Selawik (sĕ'lŭwĭk), Eskimo village (pop. 269), NW Alaska, on Selawik L., 70 mi. ESE of Kotzebue, on Arctic Circle; trapping, hunting, fishing; fox and mink farming. Has Friends Mission, native school.

Selawik Lake (45 mi. long, 5–20 mi. wide), NW Alaska, SE arm of Hotham Inlet, 60 mi. ESE of Kotzebue, on Arctic Circle. Selawik village, E.

Selb (zĕlp), city (1950 pop. 18,822), Upper Franconia, NE Bavaria, Germany, 14 mi. SE of Hof, near Czechoslovak border; rail junction; porcelain-mfg. center (Rosenthal porcelain, technical ceramics); precision instruments; metalworking. Has Gothic church; and school for porcelain workers. Chartered 1426. First porcelain factory opened 1857.

Selb Horn, Austria and Germany: see STEINERNES MEER.

Selbitz (zĕl'bĭts), village (pop. 3,698), Upper Franconia, NE Bavaria, Germany, in Franconian Forest, on small Selbitz R. and 7 mi. W of Hof; mfg. of leather products, precision instruments; metalworking, weaving, brewing; lumber, flour milling.

Selbo, Norway: see SELBU LAKE.

Selborne (sĕl'bôrn), agr. village and parish (pop. 1,144), E Hampshire, England, 7 mi. N of Petersfield. Known for *Natural History and Antiquities of Selborne*, by vicar Gilbert White, who was b. here, lived in "The Wakes," and is buried in 13th-cent. church.

Selbu Lake (sĕl'bōō), Nor. *Selbusjø*, Sor-Trondelag co., central Norway, on Nea (Nid) R., 15 mi. SE of Trondheim; □ 23; 18 mi. long, 442 ft. deep. Selbu village is at SE tip; formerly spelled Selbo.

Selby, urban district (1931 pop. 10,064; 1951 census 10,217), West Riding, SE central Yorkshire, England, on Ouse R. and 12 mi. S of York; textile bleaching, beet-sugar refining, barge building; also produces agr. machinery, twine, brick, cement, feed cakes. The church was part of Benedictine abbey founded 1069 by William the Conqueror. Traditional birthplace of Henry I.

Selby. 1 Village (pop. c.400), Contra Costa co., W Calif., at W end of Carquinez Strait, opposite Vallejo; lead smelter. **2** City (pop. 706), ⊙ Walworth co., N S.Dak., 80 mi. N of Pierre; trade center for farming and cattle-raising area; livestock, dairy produce, poultry, grain.

Selbyville, town (pop. 1,086), Sussex co., SE Del., near Md. line, 50 mi. SSE of Dover; canning, strawberry shipping.

Selce (sĕl'tsĕ), village, NW Croatia, Yugoslavia, on Adriatic Sea, 19 mi. SE of Rijeka (Fiume), opposite Krk Isl.; bathing resort.

Selcuk, Turkey: see KUSADASI.

Selden. 1 City (pop. 438), Sheridan co., NW Kansas, 28 mi. ENE of Colby, in agr. and livestock region. **2** Village (pop. 1,743), Suffolk co., SE N.Y., on central Long Isl., 6 mi. S of Port Jefferson, in agr. area (truck, potatoes).

Seldovia (sĕldō'vyŭ), village (pop. 428), S Alaska, on Kachemak Bay, S Kenai Peninsula, 90 mi. SW of Seward; distribution center for Cook Inlet towns; fishing, fish processing; undeveloped coal deposits near by.

Sele, Cape (sä'lä), westernmost point of New Guinea, on Vogelkop peninsula, opposite S coast of Waigeu across narrow Sele Strait; 1°26'S 130°56'E.

Selecka Mountains or **Selechka Mountains** (both: sĕ'lĕchkä), Serbo-Croatian *Selečka Planina*, Macedonia, Yugoslavia, surrounded on 3 sides by the Crna Reka; c.15-mi. long NNE-SSW. Highest peak, Visoko (4,828 ft.), is 10 mi. SSE of Prilep.

Selefkeh, Turkey: see SILIFKE.

Sele La (sä'lä lä), pass (alt. 12,000 ft.) in W Assam Himalayas, SW Bhutan, 16 mi. SW of Paro, at junction of 2 routes from S.

Selemdzha River (sĕlyĭmjä'), Amur oblast, Russian SFSR, rises in N Bureya Range, flows 425 mi. SW, past Ekimchan (head of navigation) and Norsk, to Zeya R. near Novo-Kiyevka. Extensive gold-mining area along upper course, with centers at Ekimchan, Zlatoustovsk, Lukachek, and Stoiba.

Selemiya or **Salamiyah** (both: sĕ'lĕmĭyŭ), Fr. *Sélémié*, town, Hama prov., W Syria, 20 mi. ESE of Hama; cotton, cereals.

Selenduma (sĕlyĭndōō'mŭ), town (1948 pop. over 500), S Buryat-Mongol Autonomous SSR, Russian SFSR, on Selenga R. (landing) and 40 mi. NNW of Kyakhta; cattle raising.

Selenga (sĕlĕng-gä') or **Selenge** (sĕ'lĕng-gĕ), aimak (□ 19,000; pop. 25,000), N Mongolian People's Republic; ⊙ Altan Bulak. Bounded N by Buryat-Mongol Autonomous SSR of USSR, it is largely wooded steppe watered by Selenga and Orkhon rivers; includes forested Kentei Mts. (E). Has Buryat and Russian minorities. One of the country's leading agr. areas.

Selenga River or **Selenge River,** chief stream of Mongolian People's Republic, formed by union of Muren and Ider rivers SE of Muren town, flows generally ENE to USSR border near Sukhe Bator, and N through Buryat-Mongol Autonomous SSR, past Novo-Selenginsk and Ulan-Ude, to L. Baikal, forming delta N of Kabansk. It receives the Egin Gol and Dzhida rivers (left), and Orkhon, Chikoi, and Uda rivers (right). Navigable in ice-free season (May–Oct.) below Sukhe Bator. The Selenga has long been considered to be c.750 mi. long with the Ider (c.550 mi. without the Ider), but a recent study gives its length as 897 mi. (616 mi. without the Ider).

Selenginsk, Russian SFSR: see NOVO-SELENGINSK.

Selenicë (sĕlĕnē'tsŭ) or **Selenica** (–nē'tsä), Ital. *Selenizza*, village (1930 pop. 451), S Albania, on lower Vijosë R. and 9 mi. NE of Valona (linked by Decauville); bitumen and ozocerite mining. First worked by Turks in 19th cent.

Selennyak River (sĕlyĭnyäk'), NE Yakut Autonomous SSR, Russian SFSR, rises in N Cherski Range, flows c.275 mi. SE and E to Indigirka R. above Druzhina.

Sele River (sä'lĕ), anc. *Silarus*, in Campania, S Italy, rises in the Apennines W of Caposele, flows 40 mi. S and ESE to Gulf of Salerno 16 mi. SSE of Salerno. Receives Tanagro R. (left). Furnishes water to APULIA.

Sélestat (sālĕstä'), Ger. *Schlettstadt* (shlĕt'shtät), town (pop. 10,225), Bas-Rhin dept., E France, on the Ill and 27 mi. SW of Strasbourg, in Alsatian lowland near E foot of the Vosges; rail junction; mfg. (metal belt conveyors, morocco leather, bricks and tiles, straw matting). Vegetable shipping, sawmilling, wool spinning. Old town, crowded within its fortifications, contains 11th-cent. church of Sainte-Foy and 13th–14th-cent. Gothic cathedral. Became a free imperial city in 13th cent. Captured by Swedes in Thirty Years War, it then remained in France until 1871. Former Fr. name, Schlestadt. Castle of HAUT-KOENIGSBOURG is 5 mi. WSW.

Seletin (syĭlyĕ'tyĭn), village (1941 pop. 1,784), SW Chernovtsy oblast, Ukrainian SSR, in the Carpathians, on Suceava R. (Rum. border) and 45 mi. SW of Chernovtsy, in N Bukovina; rail terminus; climatic resort; mud baths.

Selety River (syĭlyĕ'tē), in Akmolinsk and Kokchetav oblasts, Kazakh SSR, rises in N Kazakh Hills near Akmolinsk, flows c.180 mi. NNE to **Selety-Tengiz,** a salt lake (□ 350; 11 ft. deep) in NE Kazakh SSR, 100 mi. S of Omsk.

Seleucia (sŭlū'shŭ), anc. city of Mesopotamia, whose site is in modern Iraq, 20 mi. SE of Baghdad and on the right bank of the Tigris opposite the ruins of anc. CTESIPHON. Founded c.312 B.C. by Seleucus I (Seleucus Nicator), a general of Alexander the Great. It was the Seleucid's eastern capital. Ctesiphon, across the river, grew as its rival, and when the Parthians conquered (140 B.C.) the area, they made Ctesiphon their capital. Sacked and burned (A.D. 164) by the Romans, Seleucia never recovered, and nothing significant remains today. Sometimes called Sur by the Arabs. The Arabs, who conquered the region in 7th cent., applied the name Al Maidan to Seleucia-Ctesiphon.

Seleucia. 1 or **Seleucia Pieria** (pīē'rēŭ), anc. city on the Mediterranean, once an important port, the sea outlet for Antioch; site was just N of Orontes mouth, S Turkey, near Suveydiye. Founded 300 B.C. by Seleucus Nicator, captured by Egyptians c.245 B.C., recovered by Antiochus III; later an independent city, it had all but disappeared by 5th cent. A.D. **2** or **Seleucia Trachea:** see SILIFKE, Turkey.

Selevac or **Selevats** (both: sĕ'lĕväts), village (pop. 5,986), N central Serbia, Yugoslavia, 10 mi. NNW of Palanka.

Selfoss (sĕl'fôs"), town (pop. 902), ⊙ Arne co., S Iceland, near the coast, 35 mi. ESE of Reykjavik; agr., dairying center.

Selfridge, village (pop. 343), Sioux co., S N.Dak., 54 mi. S of Bismarck; wheat, livestock.

Selfridge Field, Mich.: see MOUNT CLEMENS.

Sélibaby (sālēbäbē'), town (pop. c.22,000), S Mauritania, Fr. West Africa, 130 mi. NW of Kayes, 290 mi. ESE of Saint-Louis, Senegal. Exports gum, beef, mutton. Region produces also millet, corn, peanuts, rice, dates.

Selidovka (syĭlyĕ'dŭfkŭ), village (1926 pop. 6,065), W Stalino oblast, Ukrainian SSR, in the Donbas, 26 mi. WNW of Stalino; metalworks.

Seligdar (syĕlyĭgdär'), town (1933 pop. 2,080), SE Yakut Autonomous SSR, Russian SFSR, 6 mi. W of Aldan; gold mining; power plant.

Seligenstadt (zā'lēgŭn-shtät"), town (pop. 7,481), S Hesse, W Germany, in former Starkenburg prov., on left bank of the canalized Main and 13 mi. ESE of Frankfurt; lignite mining. Has Benedictine abbey (founded 9th cent.) with 13th-cent. bldgs.

Seliger, Lake (syĕlyĭgyĕr') (□ 103), in Valdai Hills, W European Russian SFSR, largely in W Kalinin oblast; formed by several small lakes of glacial origin connected by narrow channels; 45 mi. long. Ostashkov on S shore. Empties (S) via navigable Selizharovka R. to the Volga at Selizharovo.

Seligman (sŭlĭg'mŭn), village (1940 pop. 764), Yavapai co., NW central Ariz., c.70 mi. W of Flagstaff; alt. 5,242 ft. Trade and shipping center for mining, ranching area.

Selima (sĕlē'mŭ), locality, Northern Prov., Anglo-Egyptian Sudan, in Libyan Desert oasis, on caravan route and 145 mi. WSW of Wadi Halfa; salt mining.

Selino, Crete: see PALAIOCHORA.

Selinous (sĕlĭnōōs'), town (pop. 3,154), Elis nome, W Peloponnesus, Greece, 10 mi. ESE of Pyrgos; road center; livestock, Zante currants, wine. Formerly called Krestena or Krestaina.

Selinous River, N Peloponnesus, Greece, rises in Erymanthos mts., flows 24 mi. N to Gulf of Corinth 3 mi. E of Aigion; site of hydroelectric plants. Non-navigable. Formerly Vostitsa R.

Selinsgrove (sē'lĭnzgrōv), borough (pop. 3,514), Snyder co., central Pa., 6 mi. SW of Sunbury and on Susquehanna R.; paper boxes, hosiery, steel tools, medicines, flour. Susquehanna Univ. here. Settled 1755, laid out 1790, inc. 1827.

Selinunte, Sicily: see MARINELLA.

Selinus, Sicily: see MARINELLA.

Seli River, Sierra Leone: see ROKEL RIVER.

Selishche (syĭlyē'shchĭ), town (1940 pop. over 500), W Kalinin oblast, Russian SFSR, on L. Volgo, near issuance of Volga R., 7 mi. WNW of Selizharovo; lignite-mining center, supplying Leningrad.

Selitë (sĕlē'tĕ) or **Selita** (–tä), village, central Albania, 10 mi. NE of Tirana; alt. 5,600 ft. Underground hydroelectric plant (SW; begun 1950) serves Tirana.

Selivanovo. 1 Village, Tomsk oblast, Russian SFSR: see BAKCHAR. **2** Village, Vladimir oblast, Russian SFSR: see KRASNAYA GORBATKA.

Selivanovskaya (syĕlyĕvä'nŭfskīŭ), village (1939 pop. over 500), E Rostov oblast, Russian SFSR, 37 mi. N of Morozovsk; wheat, sunflowers.

Selizharovo (syĕlyēzhä'rŭvŭ), town (1939 pop. 2,057), W Kalinin oblast, Russian SFSR, on Volga R., at mouth of navigable Selizharovka R. (outlet of L. Seliger), and 60 mi. WSW of Torzhok; dairying, flax processing. Limestone works. Lignite mines at Selishche (W).

Selje (sĕl'yŭ), tiny island (□ c.2) in bay of North Sea, Sogn og Fjordane co., W Norway, 1 mi. off Stadland peninsula, 33 mi. N of Floro. Has cave sanctuary with relics of St. Sunniva (11th cent.); and tower of 12th-cent. Benedictine monastery. Canton (pop. 3,634) of Selje largely on mainland.

Seljord (sĕl'yōr), village and canton (pop. 3,147), Telemark co., S Norway, 40 mi. NW of Skien; cattle, lumber.

Selkirk. 1 Town (pop. 5,408), SE Man., on Red R. and 22 mi. NE of Winnipeg; transshipment center for L. Winnipeg fish; lumber and steel mills; dairying, truck gardening. Center of Red River Settlement region, established by earl of Selkirk; near by is Lower Fort Garry, built 1832 by the colonists. **2** Village (pop. estimate 400), S Ont., near L. Ontario, 27 mi. SE of Brantford; dairying, mixed farming. **3** Village, Yukon; see FORT SELKIRK.

Selkirk or **Selkirkshire** (–shĭr), county (□ 266.8; 1931 pop. 22,608; 1951 census pop. 21,724), S Scotland; ⊙ Selkirk. Bounded by Dumfries (S), Peebles (W and NW), Midlothian (N), and Roxburgh (E and SE). Drained by Tweed, Ettrick Water, and Yarrow Water rivers. Surface is generally hilly, becoming mountainous in W. Co. was formerly densely wooded and contained Ettrick Forest, a royal hunting ground. There are several lochs; largest, St. Mary's Loch. Good salmon fishing. Sheep raising is main agr. occupation; woolen milling (tweeds, tartan) is important, centered on Galashiels. Besides Selkirk, Galashiels is only other burgh. Co. has associations with Scott and James Hogg, the "Ettrick Shepherd."

Selkirk, burgh (1931 pop. 5,667; 1951 census 5,853), ⊙ Selkirkshire, Scotland, in E part of co., on Ettrick Water and 30 mi. SE of Edinburgh; woolen (tweed) milling and textile printing. In 1113 the future David I here founded abbey, later moved to Kelso. Statues commemorate Sir Walter Scott (deputy sheriff of Selkirk for some years) and Mungo Park (b. near by). Also a memorial to battle of Flodden. Term "souters of Selkirk" dates from times when shoemaking was major industry here; the souters distinguished themselves at battle of Flodden. W, 5 mi., are ruins of 15th-cent. Newark castle.

Selkirk Mountains, range (extending 200 mi. NW–SE) of Rocky Mts., mostly in SE B.C., W of main body of the Rocky Mts., bet. apex of Columbia R. loop (N), Columbia R. and Arrow Lakes (W), and upper Columbia and Kootenay rivers (E); they extend S into the U.S. just over the borders of Idaho and Mont. The highest peaks include Mt. Sir Sanford (11,590 ft.), Mt. Farnham (11,342 ft.), Jumbo Mtn. (11,217 ft.), Mt. Dawson (11,123 ft.), Adamant Mtn. (10,980 ft.), Grand Mtn. (10,842 ft.), Iconoclast Mtn. (10,630 ft.), Sorcerer Mtn. (10,387 ft.), and Mt. Rogers (10,525 ft.). Glacier Natl. Park is in N part of range. Canadian Pacific RR crosses range bet. Revelstoke and Banff, passing through Connaught Tunnel near Glacier.

Selkirkshire, Scotland: see SELKIRK, county.

Sella (sĕ'lyä), town (pop. 1,208), Alicante prov., E Spain, 13 mi. SE of Alcoy; pinewoods; olive oil, almonds, cereals, fruit.

Sellano (sĕl-lä'nō), village (pop. 287), Perugia prov., Umbria, central Italy, 15 mi. NE of Spoleto; files, rasps.

Sella River (sĕ'lyä), Oviedo prov., NW Spain, rises in the Cantabrian Mts., flows 40 mi. N to Bay of Biscay at Ribadesella.

Selle, Massif de la (mäsēf' dŭ lä sĕl'), range in SE Haiti, just S of Port-au-Prince; extends c.50 mi. E to Dominican Republic border; rises in Mont la Selle to 8,793 ft., the highest peak in Haiti.

Selle River (sĕl), Nord dept., N France, rises S of Le Cateau, flows c.25 mi. NNW, past Solesmes, to the Escaut just above Denain. Battlefield in Oct., 1918.

Sellero, Italy: see CEDEGOLO.

Sellers, town (pop. 530), Marion and Dillon counties, NE S.C., 18 mi. ENE of Florence; lumber.

Sellersburg, residential town (pop. 1,664), Clark co., SE Ind., near small Silver Creek, 8 mi. NNE of New Albany, in agr. area.

Sellersville, borough (pop. 2,373), Bucks co., SE Pa., 27 mi. NNW of Philadelphia; cigars, metal products; agr.; sandstone quarrying. Settled c.1730, inc. 1874.

Selles-sur-Cher (sĕl-sür-shâr'), town (pop. 2,498), Loir-et-Cher dept., N central France, on Cher R. and 9 mi. WSW of Romorantin; winegrowing; cotton milling. Has 12th–14th-cent. church, part of a former abbey.

Sellières (sĕlyâr'), village (pop. 952), Jura dept., E France, 11 mi. N of Lons-le-Saunier; makes heating equipment.

Sellin (zĕ'lĭn), village (pop. 2,744), in former Prussian Pomerania prov., N Germany, after 1945 in Mecklenburg, on E Rügen isl., on the Baltic, 11 mi. ESE of Bergen; seaside resort, fishing port.

Selling Tso, Tibet: see ZILLING TSO.

Sello (sĕ'lyō), SW suburb (pop. 1,392) of Vigo, Pontevedra prov., NW Spain; flour, sawmilling.

Sellore Island (sŭlōr'), in central Mergui Archipelago, Lower Burma, in Andaman Sea, 25 mi. SSW of Mergui town; consists of 3 isls. linked by mangrove swamps; 16 mi. long, 4 mi. wide.

Sells, village (1940 pop. 903), Pima co., S Ariz., 57 mi. SW of Tucson. Hq. and trade center for Gila Bend, Papago, and San Xavier Indian reservations. U.S. Indian school and mission school are here.

Selly Oak, SW industrial suburb (pop. 28,558) of Birmingham, NW Warwick, England. Site of a group of Quaker colleges.

Selm (zĕlm), village (pop. 12,452), in former Prussian prov. of Westphalia, NW Germany, after 1945 in North Rhine-Westphalia, 6 mi. NNW of Lünen; grain, cattle, hogs.

Selma (sĕl'mŭ). **1** City (pop. 22,840), ⊙ Dallas co., S central Ala., on Alabama R. and 40 mi. W of Montgomery; trade and rail center (with railroad repair shops) for livestock and cotton area; food processing (meat, dairy, and bakery products, canned fruits and vegetables), mfg. of cigars, clothing, wood and foundry products, bricks, cottonseed and peanut oil, fertilizer. Settled 1816, inc. 1920. Ravaged during Civil War. Recovery followed diversification of agr. in vicinity and introduction of livestock and dairying. Has fine ante-bellum homes and Selma Univ. (Negro). U.S. military aviation school was opened (1941) at near-by Craig Air Force Base. **2** Town (pop. 5,964), Fresno co., central Calif., 15 mi. SE of Fresno, in irrigated San Joaquin Valley; fruit (especially grapes), truck, cotton, flax, dairy products, poultry; packing plants, canneries, wineries. Inc. 1893. **3** Town (pop. 499), Delaware co., E Ind., 6 mi. E of Muncie, in agr. area. **4** Town (pop. 2,639), Johnston co., central N.C., 19 mi. NW of Goldsboro, near Neuse R.; trade and mfg. center (textiles, fertilizer, cottonseed oil); lumber milling. **5** Village (1940 pop. 759), Alleghany co., W Va., on Jackson R. and just SW of Clifton Forge, in the Alleghenies.

Selma, Jebel, Saudi Arabia: see SHAMMAR, JEBEL.

Sema'il, Wadi, Oman: see SAMA'IL, WADI.

Selmec-es-belabanya, Czechoslovakia: see BANSKA STIAVNICA.

Selmer, town (pop. 1,759), ⊙ McNairy co., SW Tenn., 33 mi. SSE of Jackson, in timber, cotton, corn area; makes shoes.

Selmes (sĕl'mĭsh), village (pop. 1,453), Beja dist., S Portugal, 10 mi. NE of Beja; grain, wine, olives, oranges.

Seloignes (sŭlwä'nyŭ), village (pop. 917), Hainaut prov., S Belgium, 4 mi. SW of Chimay; butter-making center.

Selommes (sŭlôm'), village (pop. 453), Loir-et-Cher dept., N central France, 6 mi. ESE of Vendôme; flour milling. Stone quarries.

Seloncourt (sŭlõkōōr'), town (pop. 3,739), Doubs dept., E France, 5 mi. SE of Montbéliard and part of its industrial dist. Produces automobile and bicycle parts and accessories, clocks and precision tools.

Selongey (sŭlõzhā'), village (pop. 1,091), Côte-d'Or dept., E central France, 20 mi. NNE of Dijon; tinplate and wood products.

Selsbakk (sĕls'bäk), village (pop. 2,994) in Strinda canton, Sor-Trondelag co., central Norway, on Nid R., on railroad and 4 mi. S of Trondheim; produces carpets, mattresses, dairy products. Formerly spelled Selsbak. Includes Byasen (byô'sŭn), Nor. *Byåsen*, village.

Selsey (sĕl'sē), town and parish (pop. 2,514), SW Sussex, England, on the Channel, 7 mi. S of Chichester; resort. Was site of Saxon cathedral and monastery founded by St. Wilfrid in 7th cent., and was seat of bishopric until 1075, when see was transferred to Chichester. Has 13th-cent. church. Just S is promontory of Selsey Bill. Sometimes spelled Selsea.

Selston, town and parish (pop. 8,905), W Nottingham, England, 11 mi. NW of Nottingham; coal-mining center. Has 15th-cent. church.

Selters, Germany: see NIEDERSELTERS.

Seltso or **Sel'tso** (syĭltsô'), town (1939 pop. over 500), NE Bryansk oblast, Russian SFSR, on Desna R. and 8 mi. WNW of Bezhitsa; lumber mill (prefabricated houses).

Selty (syĭltē'), village (1948 pop. over 2,000), W Udmurt Autonomous SSR, Russian SFSR, 50 mi. NW of Izhevsk; flax processing, grain, livestock.

Seltz (sĕlts), Ger. *Selz* (zĕlts), anc. *Saletio*, village (pop. 1,752), Bas-Rhin dept., E France, on the Sauer, near its mouth on the Rhine, and 13 mi. SE of Wissembourg, at NE edge of Forest of Haguenau; customhouse near Ger. border, opposite Plittersdorf (near Rastatt). Damaged in Second World War.

Selukwe (sĕlōō'kwä), town (pop. 1,474), Gwelo prov., central Southern Rhodesia, in Matabeleland, on railroad and 20 mi. SE of Gwelo; alt. 4,734 ft. Major chrome-mining center. Hq. of native commissioner; police post. Near by are WANDERER MINE (gold) and township of Chrome Railway Block (chrome).

Seluma, China: see NANGTSIEN.

Sélune River (sälün'), Manche dept., NW France, rises near Le Teilleul, flows c.35 mi. W, past Saint-Hilaire-du-Harcouët, to the Bay of Saint-Michel (English Channel) 4 mi. S of Avranches; 2 dams and hydroelectric plants above Ducey.

Selva (sĕl'vä), town (pop. estimate 1,000), ⊙ Rivadavia dept. (□ 1,625; 1947 pop. 5,474), SE Santiago del Estero prov., Argentina, on railroad and 105 mi. SE of Añatuya; agr. center (wheat, flax, alfalfa, livestock); sawmill.

Selva or **Seuva** (sĕ'ōōvä), town (pop. 1,660), Majorca, Balearic Isls., 18 mi. NE of Palma; grain, vegetables, carobs, olives, almonds, apricots, livestock; lumber.

Selva, Chile: see COPIAPÓ.

Selva del Campo, La (lä sĕl'vä dhĕl käm'pō), town (pop. 2,591), Tarragona prov., NE Spain, 4 mi. N of Reus; cotton spinning, olive-oil processing; hazelnut shipping. Mineral deposits (iron, lead, nickel) near by. Has 16th-cent. church.

Selvagens (sĕlvä'zhĕnsh), group of uninhabited volcanic islets in the Atlantic, c.180 mi. S of Madeira (to which they belong) and c.120 mi. N of the Canary Isls. Consist of Selvagem Grande isl. (515 ft. high) with surrounding reefs (30°8'N 15°52'W), and 10 mi. SW, the Pitones isls. (Piton Grande, Piton Pequeno) in 30°2'N 16°2'W. Also called Salvage Isls.

Selva Oscura (sĕl'vä ōskōō'rä), village (1930 pop. 906), Malleco prov., S central Chile, on railroad and 50 mi. SE of Angol; agr. center (wheat, oats, potatoes, fruit); lumbering.

Selve, island, Yugoslavia: see SILBA ISLAND.

Selway River, N central Idaho, rises in N half of Bitterroot Range, flows 100 mi. N and W, through Idaho co., to Middle Fork Clearwater R. 22 mi. ESE of Kamiah.

Selwyn (sĕl'wĭn), village, W central Queensland, Australia, 60 mi. S of Cloncurry; rail terminus; sheep. Cobalt mine.

Selwyn, New Zealand: see HORORATA.

Selz, France: see SELTZ.

Selzach (zĕl'tsäkh), town (pop. 2,109), Solothurn canton, NW Switzerland, 4 mi. W of Solothurn; watches.

Selzaete, Belgium: see ZELZATE.

Selzthal (zĕlts'täl), town (pop. 2,237), Styria, central Austria, 40 mi. WNW of Leoben; rail junction; dairy farming.

Sem (sĕm), village (pop. 994; canton pop. 12,094), Vestfold co., SE Norway, on railroad and 3 mi. NW of Tonsberg; market gardening; shipyards on Stein Canal, 2 mi. E.

Semangka Bay (sŭmäng'kŭ), inlet (40 mi. long, 35 mi. wide at entrance) of Sunda Strait, S Sumatra, Indonesia, W of Lampung Bay. Contains Tabuan isl. (8 mi. long, 3 mi. wide). Kotaagung is at head of bay. Also spelled Semangko.

Semangko Gap (sŭmäng'kō), commonly called **The Gap,** pass (2,793 ft.) in central Malayan range, Malaya, 37 mi. N of Kuala Lumpur, on Selangor-Pahang line, just S of Fraser's Hill; used by highway from Kuala Lumpur to Pahang.

Seman River (sĕ'män) or **Semani River** (sĕ'mänē), S central Albania, formed 8 mi. NW of Berat by union of Devoll and Osum rivers, flows generally W in meandering course through fertile Myzeqe plain to the Adriatic, forming a delta S of Kravasta Lagoon. Length, 50 mi.; length with Devoll R., c.150 mi.

Semans (sē'mŭnz), village (pop. 348), S central Sask., 65 mi. N of Regina; wheat, stock.

Semaoe, Indonesia: see SEMAU.

Semara, Sp. West Africa: see SMARA.

Semarang (sŭmŭräng', sŭmä'räng), city (pop. 217,796), N Java, Indonesia, port on Java Sea, at mouth of small Semarang R., 160 mi. W of Surabaya; 6°58'S 110°26'E; principal trade center for central Java, connected by rail with Jakarta and Surabaya. Unprotected harbor is unsafe during monsoon period. Industries: mfg. of textiles, machinery, electrical equipment, glass, shoes. Has shipyards and railroad workshops. Exports tobacco, sugar, copra, rubber, kapok, cassava, teak, coffee, cacao.

Semau or **Semaoe** (both: sŭmou'), coral island (pop. 4,208; 17 mi. long, 8 mi. wide), Indonesia, in Savu Sea, off W tip of Timor across narrow Semau Strait; 10°13'S 123°23'E. Copra; fishing.

Sembehun (sĕmbāhōōn'), town (pop. 1,290), South-Western Prov., SW Sierra Leone, on road and 17 mi. SSW of Moyamba; trade center; palm oil and kernels, piassava, rice.

Semberija or **Semberiya** (both: sĕm'bĕrēä), agr. region, NE Bosnia, Yugoslavia, along Sava and lower Drina rivers; borders on Serbia.

Sembilan Islands (sŏŏmbēlän'), island group in Strait of Malacca, 10 mi. off W Perak, Malaya; 4°N 100°30'E. Ceded 1826 (confirmed 1874) by Perak to Great Britain; part of Penang settlement until retroceded (1935) to Perak as part of the Dindings.

Sembiyam (sĕm'bĭyŭm), town (pop. 37,625), Chingleput dist., E Madras, India, suburb (5 mi. NW) of Madras; tanning center. Large workshops in adjacent railway settlement of Perambur. Formerly spelled Sembiem.

Semdinli (shĕmdĕnlē'), Turkish *Şemdinli*, village (pop. 554), Hakari prov., SE Turkey, 45 mi. ESE of Hakari; millet, wheat. Also called Navsar.

Séméac (sāmāäk'), E suburb (pop. 3,184) of Tarbes, Hautes-Pyrénées dept., SW France; metalworking, macaroni mfg.

Semeikino or **Semeykino** (sĭmyā'kĭnŭ), town (1939 pop. over 500), SE Voroshilovgrad oblast, Ukrainian SSR, in the Donbas, 11 mi. WNW of Krasnodon; coal mines.

Semen or **Semeni**, river, Albania: see SEMAN RIVER.

Semendria, Yugoslavia: see SMEDEREVO.

Semenov (sĭmyô'nŭf), city (1939 pop. 12,000), central Gorki oblast, Russian SFSR, 37 mi. NNE of Gorki; metal- and woodworking center. Teachers col. Handicraft work (wooden spoons) near by. Chartered 1779.

Semenovka (sĭmyô'nŭfkŭ). **1** Town (1948 pop. over 10,000), S Maritime Territory, Russian SFSR, on Daubikhe R. and 90 mi. NE of Voroshilov, in agr. area (grain, soybeans, rice, perilla). **2** Town (1926 pop. 16,394), NE Chernigov oblast, Ukrainian SSR, 30 mi. WNW of Novgorod-Severski; leather products; peat cutting. **3** Town (1926 pop. 2,913), S central Poltava oblast, Ukrainian SSR, 30 mi. SSE of Lubny; sugar-refining center; flour mill.

Semenovskoye (–skŭyŭ). **1** Village (1939 pop. over 2,000), SW central Archangel oblast, Russian SFSR, on Northern Dvina R., near mouth of Vaga R., and 130 mi. SE of Archangel; potatoes. **2** Village (1948 pop. over 2,000), S Kostroma oblast, Russian SFSR, 25 mi. N of Kineshma; flax.

Semenud, Egypt: see SAMANNUD.

Semenyih (sŏŏmĕnyē'), town (pop. 2,321), SE Selangor, Malaya, on highway and 17 mi. SE of Kuala Lumpur; rubber-growing center.

Semerah or **Semerah Kanan** (sŏŏmĕrä' kä"nän'), village (pop. 664), NW Johore, Malaya, on Strait of Malacca, 8 mi. WNW of Bandar Penggaram; coconuts.

Semerah Kiri (kē'rē), village (pop. 202), NW Johore, Malaya, on Strait of Malacca just NW of Semerah, 18 mi. SE of Bandar Maharani; coconuts.

Semerak, Malaya: see CHERANG RUKU.

Semeru Mountains or **Semeroe Mountains** (both: sŏŏmĕ'rōō), volcanic range (c.30 mi. long) in E Java, Indonesia, S of Pasuruan; rises to 12,060 ft. in Mt. Mahameru, highest peak of Java.

Semeykino, Ukrainian SSR: see SEMEIKINO.

Semgallia, Latvia: see ZEMGALE, province.

Semibratovo (syĕmēbrä'tŭvŭ), town (1948 pop. over 500), SE Yaroslavl oblast, Russian SFSR, 10 mi. NNE of Rostov; mfg. of construction materials. Until 1948, Isady.

Semichi Islands (sŏŏmē'chē), group of 3 small isls. of Aleutian Isls., SW Alaska, 20 mi. ESE of Attu; 52°43'N 174°1'E. Consists of SHEMYA ISLAND, Nizki Isl., and Alaid Isl.

Semien, range, Ethiopia: see SIMEN MOUNTAINS.

Semikarakorskaya (syĕmēkŭrŭkôr'skīŭ), village (1926 pop. 4,212), central Rostov oblast, Russian SFSR, on Don R., near mouth of the Sal, and 30 mi. ESE of Shakhty; flour mill, metalworks; wheat, sunflowers; vineyards.

Semiluki (syĕmēlōō'kē), town (1938 pop. estimate 7,300), W Voronezh oblast, Russian SFSR, on Don R. and 8 mi. WNW of Voronezh; cement and brickworks; chalk and refractory-clay quarries.

Semily (sĕ'mĭlĭ), Ger. *Semil* (zā'mēl), town (pop. 5,480), N Bohemia, Czechoslovakia, on Jizera R., on railroad and 17 mi. SE of Liberec; textile mfg. (notably linen); barley.

Seminara (sĕmēnä'rä), town (pop. 4,217), Reggio di Calabria prov., Calabria, S Italy, 2 mi. SE of Palmi, in olive- and grape-growing region; pottery mfg. Destroyed by earthquakes of 1783, 1908.

Seminary, town (pop. 345), Covington co., S central Miss., 20 mi. NNW of Hattiesburg.

Seminoe Dam (sĕ'mĭnō), S central Wyo., on N.Platte R. and 55 mi. SW of Casper; concrete dam 295 ft. high, 525 ft. long; finished 1939. Used for hydroelectric power and irrigation. Seminoe Reservoir (□ 32; 25 mi. long, average width 2 mi.; capacity 1,026,000 acre-ft.) is fed by Medicine Bow R. Dam and reservoir are units in Kendrick irrigation project.

Seminole (sĕ'mĭnōl). **1** County (□ 321; pop. 26,883), E central Fla.; ⊙ Sanford. N and E boundaries formed by St. Johns R., including lakes Monroe and Harney. Contains L. Jessup and many smaller lakes. Truck-growing area noted for its celery; also produces citrus fruit, corn, poultry, livestock. Some wood- and food-processing plants. Formed 1913. **2** County (□ 274; pop. 7,904), extreme SW Ga.; ⊙ Donalsonville. Bounded W by Ala. and Fla. lines (formed here by Chattahoochee R.) and E by Spring Creek. Coastal plain agr. (cotton, corn, truck, peanuts, livestock) and sawmilling area. Formed 1920. **3** County (□ 629; pop. 40,672), central Okla.; ⊙ Wewoka. Bounded S by Canadian R., N by North Canadian R.; drained by Little R.; includes L. Wewoka (recreation). Agr. area (cotton, corn, cattle, peanuts, poultry; dairy products). Mfg. at Seminole, Konawa, and Wewoka. Oil and natural-gas fields; oil refineries, gasoline plants. Formed 1907.

Seminole. 1 City (pop. 11,863), Seminole co., central Okla., c.50 mi. ESE of Oklahoma City, in oil-producing and agr. area; oil refineries; mfg. of oil-field equipment, carbon black, machine-shop products, dairy products, mattresses, lumber, concrete blocks. Seat of Seminole Jr. Col. Settled 1890; inc. as town 1908, as city 1926. **2** Town (pop. 3,479), ⊙ Gaines co., NW Texas, on S Llano Estacado, 75 mi. SW of Lubbock, near N.Mex. line; retail center for oil and cattle-ranching region. Founded 1908, inc. 1936.

Semion (sĭmēôn'), village (1939 pop. over 500), central Ryazan oblast, Russian SFSR, 25 mi. N of Ryazhsk; wheat, tobacco.

Semiozerny or **Semiozernyy** (syĕmēŭzyôr'nē, –zyĕr'–), village (1926 pop. 3,144), N Kustanai oblast, Kazakh SSR, near S.Siberian RR (Aman-karagai station), 60 mi. SSE of Kustanai; agr.; sawmilling.

Semipalatinsk (syĕmēpŭlä'tyĭnsk), oblast (□ 67,600; 1946 pop. estimate 400,000), E Kazakh SSR; ⊙ Semipalatinsk. Drained by Ayaguz R. (S) and Irtysh R. (N); bisected E–W by Chingiz-Tau and Tarbagatai Range. Agr. economy (wheat, millet, sunflowers, opium) in E, with partial irrigation in SE, and livestock raising (cattle, sheep) in W. Extensive gold mines in Akzhal area. Some lumbering in extreme N. Industry at Semipalatinsk and Ayaguz. Turksib RR crosses oblast N–S; highway from Ayaguz to China. Pop.: Kazakhs, Russians. Formed 1939.

Semipalatinsk, city (1939 pop. 109,779), ⊙ Semipalatinsk oblast, Kazakh SSR, on Irtysh R., on Turksib RR. and 560 mi. NNE of Alma-Ata; 50°25'N 80°15'E. Transportation hub; important meat-packing center; flour milling, wool washing, tanning (leather goods), textile milling, woodworking; railroad shops. Rail branch to Kulunda and Tatarsk. Teachers col. Pop.: Russians, Kazakhs, Tatars. Founded 1718 as Rus. frontier post.

Semirara Islands (sāmērä'rä) (□ c.50; 1948 pop. 4,779), Antique prov., Philippines, bet. Tablas Strait (N) and Cuyo East Pass (S), c.20 mi. off NW tip of Panay; 11°57'N 121°27'E. Comprises 3 isls.: Semirara Isl. (largest, □ 22; 9 mi. long, 3 mi. wide; 1939 pop. 1,033), Caluya Isl. (kälōō'yä) (□ 9; 4.5 mi. long, 2.5 mi. wide; 1939 pop. 916), and Sibay Isl. (sēbī') (□ 16; 8 mi. long, 3 mi. wide; 1939 pop. 931), surrounded by several islets. Isls. are generally low. Coal mining, coconut growing, fishing. Chief center is Caluya on Caluya Isl.

Semirechye or **Semirech'ye,** Kazakh SSR: see DZHETY-SU.

Semirom, Iran: see SAMIRUM.

Semisopochnoi Island (sĕmĕsŭpŏsh'noi) (12 mi. long, 10 mi. wide), Rat Isls., Aleutian Isls., SW Alaska, 35 mi. NE of Amchitka Isl.; 51°57'N 179°38'E; rises to 4,285 ft. Uninhabited; important as landmark for vessels sailing down the Aleutian chain.

Semiyarskoye (syĕmēyär'skŭyŭ), village (1939 pop. over 500), SE Pavlodar oblast, Kazakh SSR, on Irtysh R. and 110 mi. SE of Pavlodar; sheep breeding. Clay quarry near by. Founded 1720 as Rus. frontier post.

Semiz-Bugu (syĭmēs"-bŏŏgōō'), town (1939 pop. over 2,000), NE Karaganda oblast, Kazakh SSR, 70 mi. ENE of Karaganda; corundum.

Semizovac or **Semizovats** (both: sĕ'mēzō"väts), village, SE Bosnia, Yugoslavia, on Bosna R. and 7 mi. NW of Sarajevo; rail junction for CEVLJANOVICI area; manganese ore-dressing plant.

Sem Kolodezei or **Sem' Kolodezey** (syĕm kŭlô'-dyĭzyā) [Rus.,=seven springs], village (1939 pop. over 500), E Crimea, Russian SFSR, on railroad and 33 mi. W of Kerch; metalworks; wheat, cotton.

Semlevo (syĕm'lyĭvŭ), village (1939 pop. over 500), E central Smolensk oblast, Russian SFSR, 16 mi. SW of Vyazma; flax.

Semliki River (sĕmlē'kē), E central Africa, partly in Belgian Congo, partly along Uganda–Belgian Congo border. Issues from NW end of L. Edward 10 mi. SW of Kalindi and meanders for c.130 mi. NNE around W foot of the Ruwenzori to L. Albert; most of its course lies in Albert Natl. Park. Reached by Henry Stanley in 1888.

Semlin, Yugoslavia: see ZEMUN.

Semmama, Djebel (jĕ'bĕl sĕmämä'), mountain (4,311 ft.) in Kasserine dist., W Tunisia, 10 mi. NNE of Kasserine; NE flank of Kasserine Pass.

Semmaya (säm-mä'yä), town (pop. 6,527), Iwate prefecture, N Honshu, Japan, 11 mi. E of Ichinoseki; rice, tobacco, silk cocoons; sake brewing.

Semmering (zĕm'ŭrĭng), village (pop. 1,265), SE Lower Austria, in Semmering Pass, 12 mi. SW of Neunkirchen; health resort, tourist center (alt. 2,952 ft.).

Semmering, scenic resort region of Eastern Alps in Austria, on Styria–Lower Austria border, SW of Vienna. A mtn. saddle, **Semmering Pass** (3,215 ft.), here crosses the Alps 23 mi. SW of Wiener Neustadt; 275 ft. beneath it is a great railroad tunnel (1 mi. long; built 1848–54), 1st mtn. railroad in the world. From Gloggnitz in Lower Austria to Mürzzuschlag in Styria the railroad runs through 15 tunnels and is carried over 16 viaducts.

Semna (sĕm'nŭ), village, Northern Prov., Anglo-Egyptian Sudan, on right bank of the Nile and 40 mi. SW of Wadi Halfa. Has ruined fortress of Middle Empire period (2100–1700 B.C.) which marked S limit of Egypt.

Semnan, Iran: see SAMNAN.

Semois River or **Semoy River** (both: sŭmwä'), SE Belgium and N France, rises in the Ardennes just W of Arlon, flows 110 mi. WNW in meandering course through the Ardennes, past Tintigny, Chimy, and Bouillon, into France near Les Hautes-Rivières, and to the Meuse just above Monthermé. Its valley is favorite tourist area.

Semoy River, Belgium and France: see SEMOIS RIVER.

Sempach (zĕm'päkh), town (pop. 1,229), Lucerne canton, N central Switzerland, on L. of Sempach, 7 mi. NNW of Lucerne. Here Swiss decisively defeated Austrians in 1386.

Sempach, Lake of, Ger. *Sempachersee* (zĕm'päkh-ŭrzā"), Lucerne canton, N central Switzerland; □ 5, alt. 1,653 ft., max. depth 295 ft.; numerous fish. Outlet (NW): Suhr R. Sempach and Sursee are main towns on lake.

Sempang Mangayau Point, Borneo: see SAMPANMANGIO POINT.

Sempst, Belgium: see ZEMST.

Semtin (sĕm'tyēn), Czech *Semtín*, village, E Bohemia, Czechoslovakia, 3 mi. NE of Pardubice; large chemical plants; explosives and munitions mfg.

Semur-en-Auxois (sŭmür'ānōswä'), town (pop. 2,913), Côte-d'Or dept., E central France, 9 mi. S of Montbard, on rocky escarpment in bend of Armançon R.; market. Has 13th–14th-cent. Gothic church, massive towers of 13th-cent. fortress.

Semur-en-Brionnais (–ā-brēōnā'), agr. village (pop. 429), Saône-et-Loire dept., E central France, 15 mi. N of Roanne; 12th-cent. Romanesque church.

Semyatichi, Poland: see SIEMIATYCZE.

Sen, Yugoslavia: see SENJE.

Sen, Cape (sān), Jap. *Sen-zaki*, E Kyushu, Japan, in Philippine Sea, at N end of Hyuga Sea; 32°50'N 132°E.

Sen, Stung (stŏŏng' sĕn'), river of Cambodia, formed 20 mi. W of Melouprey by several streams rising in Dangrek Mts. on Thailand-Cambodia frontier, flows 200 mi. S, past Kompong Thom, into S extremity of the lake Tonle Sap.

Sena (sä'nä), village, Pando dept., NW Bolivia, on Madre de Dios R., at mouth of Sena R., and 80 mi. WSW of Riberalta; rubber.

Sena (sĕ'nä), village, Manica and Sofala prov., central Mozambique, on right bank of Zambezi R. and 170 mi. N of Beira. Bet. here and Mutarara (on left bank), the Trans-Zambezia RR (serving Nyasaland) crosses Zambezi R. on steel bridge (12,064 ft. long; opened 1935). Formerly also spelled Senna.

Sena (sä'nä), village (pop. 1,065), Huesca prov., NE Spain, on Alcanadre R. and 8 mi. SE of Sariñena; lumber; sugar beets, melons.

Senachwine Lake (sŭnă'chŭwīn), N Ill., bayou lake (c.8 mi. long) of Illinois R. along its right bank S of Hennepin.

Senado or **Central Senado** (sĕnträl' sänä'dō), sugar-mill village (pop. 1,993), Camagüey prov., E Cuba, on railroad and 23 mi. ENE of Camagüey.

Senador Pompeu (sĭnŭdôr' pōmpĕ'dōō), city (pop. 3,670), central Ceará, Brazil, on Fortaleza-Crato RR and 140 mi. SSW of Fortaleza; cattle-raising center.

Senafe (sĕnä'fä), town (pop. 2,000), Adi Caieh div., central Eritrea, near Ethiopian border, on road and 55 mi. SE of Asmara, near Mt. Soira; alt. c.7,700 ft.; trade center.

Senahú (sānäōō'), town (1950 pop. 5,338), Alta Verapaz dept., central Guatemala, in N highlands, 29 mi. E of Cobán; alt. 3,850 ft.; coffee, cacao, sugar cane; livestock.

Senai (sŭnī'), village (pop. 1,488), S Johore, Malaya, on railroad and 12 mi. NW of Johore Bharu; rubber plantations.

Senaki, Georgian SSR: see MIKHA-TSKHAKAYA.

Sena Madureira (sĕ'nŭ mŭdōōrā'rŭ), city (pop. 1,502), Acre territory, westernmost Brazil, head of navigation and hydroplane landing on Iaco R. (near its influx into the Purus), near Amazonas line, and 80 mi. NW of Rio Branco (connected by road); rubber, Brazil nuts, medicinal plants. Formerly spelled Senna Madureira.

Senami (sänä'mē), town (pop. 2,917), Niigata prefecture, N Honshu, Japan, on Sea of Japan, 2 mi. NW of Murakami; rice, tea; cotton textiles.

Senanga (sĕnäng'gä), township (pop. 216), Barotse prov., SW Northern Rhodesia, on left bank of Zambezi R. and 60 mi. S of Mongu; cattle, sheep, goats; corn, millet. Airfield.

Sénart, Forest of, France: see BRUNOY.

Senath (sē'nŭth), city (pop. 1,528), Dunklin co., extreme SE Mo., near St. Francis R., 10 mi. SW of Kennett; cotton. Founded 1882.

Senatobia (sĕnùtō'bēù), town (pop. 2,108), ⊙ Tate co., NW Miss., 35 mi. S of Memphis (Tenn.), in agr., stock-raising, and timber area; sawmills, cotton gins, creamery. Has a jr. col. Founded 1856; burned by Union troops in Civil War.

Sencha (syĕn'chŭ), village (1926 pop. 3,322), N Poltava oblast, Ukrainian SSR, on Sula R. and 22 mi. NNE of Lubny; flour mill.

Senchi (sĕn'chē), village, Eastern Prov., SE Gold Coast colony, on Volta R. (rapids) and 9 mi. NNW of Akuse; ferry station on Accra-Br. Togoland road. Dam and hydroelectric plant projected for Ajena, 6 mi. N.

Senchoa, India: see NOWGONG, town, Assam.

Sendai (sän'dī'). **1** City (1940 pop. 34,289; 1947 pop. 40,705), Kagoshima prefecture, SW Kyushu, Japan, 22 mi. NW of Kagoshima; commercial center for agr. area (rice, sweet potatoes, wheat, millet); raw silk, paper. **2** Principal city (□ 26; 1940 pop. 223,630; 1947 pop. 293,816) of N Honshu, Japan, ⊙ Miyagi prefecture, on W Ishinomaki Bay, 190 mi. NNE of Tokyo; mfg. center (silk textiles and yarn, lacquer ware, pottery), woodworking; sake and beer breweries. Seat of Tohoku Imperial Univ. (1907) and Industrial Art Research Inst. (1928). Once stronghold of powerful 17th-cent. feudal lord Date Masamune.

Sendamangalam (sĕndŭmŭng'gŭlŭm), town (pop. 13,674), Salem dist., S central Madras, India, 26 mi. SSE of Salem; rice, cotton, peanuts, castor beans. Magnetite workings E in Kollaimalai Hills.

Send and Ripley, residential parish (pop. 3,278), central Surrey, England, 5 mi. NNE of Guildford, near the Wey. Includes towns of Send, with 15th-cent. church, and Ripley, with church of Norman origin. Ruins of 12th-cent. Newark Priory near by.

Sendenhorst (zĕn'dùnhôrst), town (pop. 3,891), in former Prussian prov. of Westphalia, NW Germany, after 1945 in North Rhine-Westphalia, 11 mi. SE of Münster; pumpernickel; hog raising.

Sendhwa (sänd'vŭ), town (pop. 5,635), SW Madhya Bharat, India, 34 mi. WSW of Khargon, in N foothills of Satpura Range; local trade in millet, cotton, timber, rice; cotton ginning.

Sendurjana (sän'dŏŏrjŭnŭ), town (pop. 7,152), Amraoti dist., W Madhya Pradesh, India, 4 mi. NNE of Warud; cotton, millet, oilseeds. Sometimes spelled Shendurjana.

Senec (sĕ'nyĕts), town (pop. 5,659), SW Slovakia, Czechoslovakia, on railroad and 14 mi. ENE of Bratislava; agr. center (wheat, barley, rye).

Seneca (sĕ'nùkù). **1** County (□ 330; pop. 29,253), W central N.Y.; ⊙ Ovid and Waterloo. In Finger Lakes region, bounded E by Cayuga L. and Seneca R., partly W by Seneca L.; crossed by the Barge Canal in NE. Dairying and farming area (truck, fruit, wheat, potatoes, hay, beans); diversified mfg. Formed 1804. **2** County (□ 551; pop. 52,978), N Ohio; ⊙ Tiffin. Drained by Sandusky R. and tributaries. Agr. area (livestock, grain, poultry, dairy products); limestone quarries, clay pits; mineral springs (resort). Mfg. at Fostoria and Tiffin. Formed 1824.

Seneca. **1** (sĕ'nùkù) Village (pop. c.1,500), La Salle co., N Ill., on Illinois R. and 30 mi. WSW of Joliet, in agr. area. Was a shipbuilding center (barges) during Second World War, when it had a max. pop. of c.11,000. **2** (sùnē'kù, sĕ'nùkù) City (pop. 1,911), ⊙ Nemaha co., NE Kansas, on South Fork Nemaha R. and 55 mi. NNW of Topeka; shipping point for livestock and grain region; wood planing; grain storage. State park near by. Laid out 1857, inc. 1870. **3** (sĕ'nùkù) City (pop. 1,195), Newton co., SW Mo., in the Ozarks, 17 mi. S of Joplin; grain; tripoli mined and processed. Platted c.1869. **4** (sĕ'nùkù) Village (pop. 219), Thomas co., central Nebr., 13 mi. WNW of Thedford and on Middle Loup R. **5** (sĕ'nùkù) Town (pop. 3,649), Oconee co., NW S.C., 34 mi. WSW of Greenville; cotton and woolen textiles, fertilizer, lumber, feed, cottonseed oil; cotton, corn. Founded 1874. **6** (sĕ'nùkù) Town (pop. 204), Faulk co., N central S.Dak., 20 mi. W of Faulkton; diversified farming; grain.

Seneca Caverns (sĕ'nùkù). **1** In Ohio: see BELLEVUE. **2** In Pendleton co., E W.Va., in the Alleghenies, 9 mi. NNW of Franklin; 2 series of underground caves, with varied rock formations; tourist attraction.

Seneca Falls, village (pop. 6,634), Seneca co., W central N.Y., in Finger Lakes region, on Seneca R. (water power) and 9 mi. E of Geneva; mfg. (machinery, metal products, rulers, electrical and electronic equipment, hosiery, rugs, textiles); summer resort. Cayuga L. (with state park) is E. Elizabeth Cady Stanton lived here and helped organize 1st woman's-rights convention in U.S., held here in 1848. Settled 1787, inc. 1831.

Seneca Gardens, town (pop. 868), Jefferson co., N Ky.

Seneca Lake, W central N.Y., largest (□ c.67) and 2d longest of the Finger Lakes, lying bet. Keuka and Cayuga lakes and extending 35 mi. S from Geneva to Watkins Glen (site of scenic Watkins Glen State Park) at its head. Its outlet is Seneca R. Linked to Barge Canal system by Cayuga and Seneca Canal. Resorts. Naval training base (at SAMPSON) was here in Second World War.

Seneca Oil Spring, N.Y.: see CUBA.

Seneca River. **1** In W central N.Y., issues from N end of Seneca L., flows NE, supplying water power at Waterloo and Seneca Falls, to N end of Cayuga L., thence generally NE and E, traversing Cross L. and receiving outlets of the E Finger Lakes, and joining Oneida R. to form Oswego R. near Phoenix. Length, c.65 mi. Section connecting Cayuga and Seneca lakes is canalized (Cayuga and Seneca Canal) as part of N.Y. State Barge Canal system. **2** In NW S.C., formed as Keowee R. (kē'ùwē) near N.C. line by headstreams rising in the Blue Ridge; flows 50 mi. S, joining Tugaloo R. 13 mi. WSW of Anderson to form Savannah R.

Seneca Rocks, Pendleton co., E W.Va., castlelike rock formation (c.900 ft. high) in the Alleghenies, along highway and 26 mi. E of Elkins; trail to summit.

Senecaville, village (pop. 586), Guernsey co., E Ohio, 9 mi. SE of Cambridge. Dam near by impounds Senecaville Reservoir (capacity 88,500 acre-ft.; for flood control) in a tributary of Wills Creek.

Seneca Vista, town (pop. 363), Jefferson co., N Ky.

Sened (sĕnĕd'), village, Gafsa dist., S central Tunisia, on Sfax-Tozeur RR, and 28 mi. ENE of Gafsa; esparto, sheep, camels.

Seneffe (sùnĕf'), town (pop. 3,270), Hainaut prov., S central Belgium, 12 mi. NW of Charleroi; cable mfg. French under Prince of Condé here defeated (1674) Dutch under William of Orange; French under Marceau defeated Austrians (1794).

Senegal (sĕnùgôl', sĕ'nùgôl), Fr. *Sénégal,* French overseas territory (□ c.75,750; pop. c.1,895,000), Fr. West Africa, on the Atlantic; ⊙ SAINT-LOUIS. Principal city is DAKAR, ⊙ Fr. West Africa. Lying bet. 12°20' and 16°40'N, it borders N (along Senegal R.) on Mauritania, E on Fr. Sudan (mostly along Falémé R.), S on Portuguese Guinea, and SE on Fr. Guinea. The Br. colony of Gambia forms a long narrow enclave along Gambia R. Leading interior rivers are the Saloum and Casamance, which are partly navigable and form large tidal deltas; but the Senegal R. serves as chief water artery. The territory is generally a flat, monotonous region with verdant tropical vegetation only in river basins and in the Casamance. The climate is excessively hot and unhealthful. During the dry season, roughly Nov.-June, the harmattan wind sweeps S from the Sahara. The rainy season is even hotter. Yearly average temp. is 73°F. The Senegal is a one-crop (peanut) country; it exports peanuts and its processed products (vegetable oil, fats, glycerine, etc.). Other products: gums, cotton, rice, bananas, sisal, indigo, manioc, shea-nut butter, castor beans, subsistence crops (corn, millet, potatoes). Also hides and skins; hardwoods. Mineral products include titanium and zirconium ores from coastal area. Fishing is becoming of increasing importance. Dakar, an international air center and transoceanic port, ships quantities of peanuts, as do Kaolack and Ziguinchor. From Dakar radiate railroads to Rufisque, Thiès, and Saint-Louis, and also to the Niger (Fr. Sudan) via Kayes on the Senegal. Senegal coast was 1st explored properly by the Portuguese in 15th cent. Other European nations followed. The French established themselves at the time of Richelieu, under whom were founded trading companies. Saint-Louis (c.1658) and Gorée isl., seized from Dutch in 1677, became centers of flourishing slave trade to the Antilles. The French were dislodged several times, last by British during Napoleonic Wars, until their return in 1817. Actual occupation of the colony began under General Faidherbe (governor 1854–65), who fought the Negro and Moorish rulers of interior kingdoms. Senegal became (1895) part of Fr. West Africa, with Saint-Louis as capital, replaced 1902 by Dakar. Dakar and its environs formed (1924–46) a separate unit called "Dakar and Dependencies." The territory sends 2 deputies to the National Assembly of France, and is also represented in the Council of the Republic and the Assembly of the French Union.

Senegal River, in Fr. West Africa, formed by union of BAFING RIVER (left) and BAKOY RIVER (right) at Bafoulabé in Fr. Sudan, flows generally NW past Kayes and, after receiving the Falémé R., forms Mauritania-Senegal border, passing towns of Bakel, Kaédi, and Podor, and turns W to fall into the Atlantic below Saint-Louis, forming an irregular delta of several arms, swamps, and isls. Total length, including the Bafing (rising in Fouta Djallon), c.1,000 mi.; from Bafoulabé, c.650 mi. Navigable for ocean-going vessels of 10-ft. draught upstream to a little beyond Podor (c.200 mi.) all year round, and to Kayes (c.565 mi.) during high-water season (July-Oct.). Its Bafing course is impeded by rapids. The Dakar-Niger RR links its basin with that of the Niger.

Senegambia (sĕnùgăm'bēù), name formerly much used for the region of W Africa now included in the Fr. West Africa territories of Senegal and Fr. Sudan; watered by Senegal and Gambia rivers. It was once part of a territorial dependency which France set up in 1902 and called Senegambia and Niger Territories.

Seneghe (sā'nĕgĕ), village (pop. 2,435), Cagliari prov., W Sardinia, 12 mi. N of Oristano. Iron deposits near by.

Senekal (sĕ'nùkäl), town (pop. 4,422), SE central Orange Free State, U. of So. Afr., on Zand R. and 50 mi. SE of Kroonstad; alt. 4,748 ft.; agr. center (sheep, wool, wheat); grain elevator.

Sene River (sĕ'nā), in Ashanti, S central Gold Coast, rises near Ejura, flows c.100 mi. E to Volta R. at Kete Krachi.

Senetosa, Cape (sĕnĕtō'zä), SW Corsica, on the Mediterranean, 22 mi. NW of Bonifacio; 41°43'N 8°45'E.

Seney (sē'nē), village, Schoolcraft co., S Upper Peninsula, Mich., 31 mi. NE of Manistique. Was a notoriously wild lumber camp in 1880s and '90s. Large Seney Natl. Wildlife Refuge is here.

Senez (sùnĕz'), village (pop. 72), Basses-Alpes dept., SE France, on the Asse and 7 mi. NW of Castellane, in Provence Alps. Former episcopal see (5th cent. to 1790) with 11th-cent. Romanesque church. Also spelled Sénez.

Senftenberg, Czechoslovakia: see ZAMBERK.

Senftenberg (zĕnf'tùnbĕrk), town (pop. 17,783), Brandenburg, E Germany, in Lower Lusatia, on the Black Elster and 22 mi. SW of Cottbus; lignite-mining center; mfg. of glass, electrical equipment; metalworking. Power station (SW). Airfield. Has remains of anc. town walls. Originally Slav settlement, fortified by Germans c.1000; chartered c.1200. In Middle Ages, staging point at intersection of salt-trade route from Halle to Poland and of main road from Hamburg to Silesia and Bohemia.

Senga (sĕng'gä), village, Leopoldville prov., on Kwango R. (Angola border) and 180 mi. SW of Kikwit; terminus of navigation on the Kwango.

Senge or **Sengge** (sĕng'gĕ), Chinese *Hsin-chi-pu-k'o* (shĭn'jē'bōō'kŭ'), village, SW Tibet, in Kailas Range, on upper Indus (Senge) R. and 75 mi. ESE of Gartok; alt. 16,944 ft. Sometimes spelled Singi; also called Senge Khambab.

Senge Khambab River, Tibet: see INDUS RIVER.

Sengés (sĕnzhĕs'), city (pop. 896), E Paraná, Brazil, on railroad and 10 mi. W of Itararé (São Paulo); sawmilling, rice milling, distilling, tanning. Diamond washings.

Senggarang (sĕng-gäräng'), town (pop. 1,787), SW Johore, Malaya, 11 mi. SE of Bandar Penggaram; coconuts, bananas, tapioca.

Senghenydd (sĕng-hĕ'nĭdh), town (pop. 5,326) in Caerphilly urban dist., E Glamorgan, Wales, on Rhymney R.; coal mining.

Sengilei or **Sengiley** (syĕn-gĭlyā'), city (1938 pop. over 9,500), E Ulyanovsk oblast, Russian SFSR, port on right bank of the Volga and 30 mi. SE of Ulyanovsk; cement making, metalworking, food processing; marl and tripoli quarrying. Became city in 1943.

Sengkang, Indonesia: see SINGKANG.

Sengkawang, Indonesia: see SINGKAWANG.

Senglea (sĕng-glā'ä), town (pop. 2,756), SE Malta, one of the "Three Cities," together with COSPICUA (S) and VITTORIOSA (E), on small narrow peninsula bet. French Creek (W) and Dockyard Creek (E), inlets of Grand Harbour, across which (N) lies Valletta, linked by ferry. Has coaling station, ship repair yards. Was almost entirely destroyed by Second World War air raid (Jan. 16, 1941). Only Church of St. Paul at promontory's tip escaped severe damage. Town was founded by grand master De La Sengle in 1554. It is sometimes called L'Isla.

Sengsengebirge (zĕngs'ĕn-gùbĭr"gù), range in SE Upper Austria, extending 10 mi. E from Steyr R.; rises to 6,432 ft. in the Hohe Nock (hō'ù nôk').

Senguerr River (sĕng-gĕr'), in Patagonia, in Comodoro Rivadavia military zone, Argentina, rises in L. Fontana near Chile border, flows E until it receives Genoa R., then SSE, past Ensanche Colonia Sarmiento, and bends NNE to L. Musters 7 mi. W of Sarmiento; 210 mi. long. Receives Mayo R. Also spelled Senguer.

Senguio (sĕng'gyō), town (pop. 912), Michoacán, central Mexico, 45 mi. E of Morelia; cereals.

Sengule (sĕng-gōō'lä), village, Eastern Prov., NE Belgian Congo, near right bank of Ituri R., 60 mi. WSW of Irumu; gold mining.

Senhor do Bonfim (sĭnyôr' dōō bōfĕn'), city (pop. 7,213), N Bahia, Brazil, 200 mi. NNW of Salvador; rail junction on Alagoinhas-Juàzeiro line (spur to Campo Formoso and Mundo Novo). Ships coffee, rice, tobacco, sugar. Manganese mining, kaolin quarrying. Until 1944, called Bonfim, sometimes spelled Bomfim.

Senhur, Egypt: see SANHUR.

Sénia, La (lä sänyä'), S suburb (pop. 1,434) of Oran, NW Algeria, at NE edge of the Oran Sebkha; chemical works (sulphuric acid, superphosphates), distilleries. Site of Oran airport.

Senica (sĕ'nyĭtsä), Hung. *Szenice* (sĕ'nĭtsĕ), town (pop. 4,772), W Slovakia, Czechoslovakia, in S foothills of the White Carpathians, on railroad and 21 mi. ESE of Breclav; artificial-silk production. Health resort of Smrdaky (smŭr'däkĭ), Slovak *Smrdáky,* with sulphurous springs and peat baths, is 4 mi. NW.

Senigallia (sĕnēgäl'lyä), anc. *Sena Gallica,* town (pop. 11,394), Ancona prov., The Marches, central

Italy, port on the Adriatic, 16 mi. WNW of Ancona. Bathing resort; mfg. (linen, agr. tools, spectacles, macaroni, liquor). Bishopric. Has 15th-cent. castle and walls. Near by is church with a Madonna by Perugino. A Roman center; in 6th cent. one of 5 cities of the Pentapolis; later became a papal fief. Pope Pius IX b. here. Formerly Sinigaglia.

Senio River (sä'nyô), N central Italy, rises in Etruscan Apennines 6 mi. W of Marradi, flows 50 mi. NNE, past Riolo dei Bagni, Cotignola, and Alfonsine, to Reno R. 4 mi. NNE of Alfonsine.

Senise (sĕnē'zĕ), town (pop. 5,422), Potenza prov., Basilicata, S Italy, near Sinni R., 23 mi. SW of Pisticci; wine, olive oil, dairy products.

Senj (sĕ'nyů), **1** Ital. *Segna* (sĕn'yä), Ger. *Zengg* (tsĕngk), village (pop. 2,572), W Croatia, Yugoslavia, port on Adriatic Sea, opposite SE coast of Krk Isl., 30 mi. SE of Rijeka (Fiume). Bishopric. Has Romanesque cathedral, many old bldgs., parts of old walls, ruined fortress. Originally a Roman settlement; passed to Croatia in 7th cent. and is allegedly the oldest Croatian town. Long known as former hide-out of pirates. Sometimes called Sinj. **2** Village, Serbia, Yugoslavia: see SENJE.

Senja (sĕn'yä), island (□ 614; pop. 10,148) in Norwegian Sea, Troms co., N Norway, just offshore, 50 mi. N of Narvik; 45 mi. long, 25 mi. wide. Coast line is deeply indented; rugged surface rises to 3,022 ft. in Istind mtn. (N). Graphite mining (at Senjehopen, N), fishing. Formerly Senjen.

Senje or **Senye** (both: sĕ'nyĕ), village, central Serbia, Yugoslavia, on railroad and 6 mi. NE of Cuprija. Sometimes called Senj, Sen, or Sen'.

Senjski Rudnik, Senski Rudnik, or **Sen'ski Rudnik** (sĕ'nyůshē rōōd'nĭk), a group of brown or subbituminous coal mines, is on railroad, 5 mi. ENE of Senje. Ravanica (Ravanitsa) monastery is just NE of Senje.

Senjehopen (sĕn'yůhōpůn), village (pop. 209) in Berg canton (pop. 1,414), N Senja isl., Troms co., N Norway, 40 mi. WSW of Tromso; graphite mining and processing.

Senjen, Norway: see SENJA.

Senjirli, Sinjirli (sĭnjĭrlē'), or **Samal** (sämäl'), Turkish *Zincirlihöyük*, village, Gaziantep prov., S Turkey, 45 mi. NNE of Iskenderun (Alexandretta), just NE of Fevzipasa. Here ruins of anc. Hittite city have been excavated.

Senjski Rudnik, Yugoslavia: see SENJE.

Senju (sän'jōō), town (pop. 5,540), Niigata prefecture, central Honshu, Japan, on Shinano R. and 18 mi. SE of Kashiwazaki; rice, silk cocoons, cotton flannel. Has hydroelectric plant.

Senkaku-gunto (sän'käkō-gōōntō), small, uninhabited island group (□ 8) of Sakishima Isls., in the Ryukyus, in East China Sea, 90 mi. NNW of Ishigaki; comprises 5 coral isls. and scattered islets. Uotsuri-shima (2.5 mi. long, 1 mi. wide) is largest isl. Generally low. Rattan-palm and banyan trees. Visited by inhabitants of Ishigaki-shima.

Senkerah, Iraq: see LARSA.

Senkevichevka (sĭnkyĕ'vĭchĕfkŭ), Pol. *Sienkiewiczówka*, village (1939 pop. over 500), SE Volyn oblast, Ukrainian SSR, 11 mi. E of Gorokhov; wheat, rye, potatoes.

Senkobo (sĕngkō'bō), township (pop. 40), Southern Prov., Northern Rhodesia, on railroad and 18 mi. N of Livingstone; tobacco, wheat, corn; market gardening.

Senlac Hill, England: see BATTLE.

Senlis (sälēs'), town (pop. 6,049), Oise dept., N France, 27 mi. NNE of Paris; road center and agr. market; popular excursion resort surrounded by forests. Mfg. (rubber, furniture, fertilizer). Has inner city wall (largely embedded in present houses) dating from Gallo-Roman times, and vestiges of medieval ramparts. The church of Notre Dame (cathedral until Fr. Revolution), with its fine spire, is one of earliest large Gothic structures (12th cent.). Senlis also has Gallo-Roman arenas, archaeological mus., and several other old churches. A royal residence from time of Clovis I. Here, in 1493, a treaty was signed bet. Charles VIII and Emperor Maximilian I. Damaged in both world wars.

Senmanat or **Sentmanat** (both: sĕnmänät'), town (pop. 1,765), Barcelona prov., NE Spain, 5 mi. NNE of Sabadell; cotton and silk mfg., olive-oil processing, flour milling. Summer resort with mineral springs. Anc. castle near by.

Senna, Mozambique: see SENA.

Sennaar, Anglo-Egyptian Sudan: see SENNAR.

Sennabra, Bridge of, Palestine: see DEGANIYA.

Senna Madureira, Brazil: see SENA MADUREIRA.

Sennar (sĕn-när'), town, Blue Nile prov., E central Anglo-Egyptian Sudan, on left bank of the Blue Nile, on railroad, and 160 mi. SE of Khartoum; cotton, wheat, barley, corn, fruits, durra; livestock. Sennar dam (3,300 yards long, 119 ft. high) was built here 1922–25; called Makwar dam until 1930s. The storage reservoir (which, when full, extends 93 mi. upstream) is filled during flood period (July-Dec.). It feeds the Gezira irrigation scheme through main canal extending 35 mi. N parallel to the Blue Nile from W end of dam. Old Sennar, ruined town (⊙ Fung kingdom, 15th–19th cent.) destroyed 1885 by the Khalifa, lies 6 mi. NNW bet. the Blue Nile and main irrigation canal. Sennar Junction (or Old Sennar Junction), with rail lines from Kassala, Khartoum, and El Obeid, is on left bank of main irrigation canal opposite ruined site. Sometimes spelled Sennaar.

Senne I (zĕ'nů), village (pop. 8,419), in former Prussian prov. of Westphalia, NW Germany, after 1945 in North Rhine-Westphalia, 6 mi. NE of Gütersloh; grain. **Senne II** (pop. 4,032) is 3 mi. E.

Sennebec Pond (sĕ'nůbĕk), Knox co., S Maine, near Appleton, in agr., recreational area; 2 mi. long, ¾ mi. wide.

Sennecey-le-Grand (sĕnsā'lů-grā'), village (pop. 1,489), Saône-et-Loire dept., E central France, 10 mi. S of Chalon-sur-Saône; agr. market.

Senneterre (sĕntâr'), village (pop. estimate 1,500), W Que., at S end of L. Parent, 30 mi. NE of Val d'Or; gold mining; trout-fishing center.

Senneville (sĕ'nĭvĭl, Fr. sĕnvēl'), village (pop. 555), S Que., on W shore of Montreal Isl., on L. of the Two Mountains, 20 mi. WSW of Montreal; dairying; resort.

Sennheim, France: see CERNAY.

Senno (syĕ'nů), city (1939 pop. 3,493), SW central Vitebsk oblast, Belorussian SSR, 33 mi. SW of Vitebsk; flax processing.

Sennwald (zĕn'vält), town (pop. 2,759), St. Gall canton, NE Switzerland, near the Rhine, 14 mi. NNE of Wallenstadt, at Liechtenstein border; woolen textiles; farming.

Senny Bridge, Wales: see DEVYNOCK.

Seno (sänō'), airfield, Savannakhet prov., S Laos, 20 mi. NE of Savannakhet; 16°41'N 105°2'E.

Senohraby (sĕ'nôhräbĭ), village (pop. 776), SE central Bohemia, Czechoslovakia, near Sazava R., on railroad and 19 mi. SSE of Prague; fashionable recreation center (summer and winter sports).

Senoia (sĭnoi'ů), city (pop. 770), Coweta co., W Ga., 15 mi. ESE of Newnan; textile and paper products.

Senonches (sůnōsh'), village (pop. 1,275), Eure-et-Loir dept., NW central France, in wooded Perche hills, 22 mi. WNW of Chartres; limekilns; agr.-machinery mfg., sawmilling.

Senones (sůnôn'), town (pop. 3,682), Vosges dept., E France, in NW Vosges, 8 mi. N of Saint-Dié; cotton and silk milling, granite quarrying. Heavily damaged during First World War.

Senoo (sänō'), town (pop. 9,622), Okayama prefecture, SW Honshu, Japan, just SW of Okayama; agr. center (rice, wheat, grapes); floor mats, sake.

Senorbì (sĕnôrbē'), village (pop. 2,153), Cagliari prov., S central Sardinia, 21 mi. N of Cagliari, in corn-growing area.

Sens (sã), anc. *Agendicum* or *Agedincum*, town (pop. 15,936), Yonne dept., N central France, on right bank of Yonne R. and 37 mi. WSW of Troyes; road and market center. Mfg. (railroad and cycle accessories, agr. machinery, razors, brushes, essential oils, biscuits); bronze foundry, brickworks. Its 12th–16th-cent. cathedral of St. Étienne is one of France's oldest Gothic bldgs., with windows painted by Jean Cousin. An important center of Roman Lugdunensis prov.; later became a countship; annexed to Fr. crown in 1055. Scene of several medieval ecclesiastical councils. Massacre (1562) of town's Huguenots rekindled Wars of Religion during which Sens was stronghold of the League. Occupied by Russians (1814) and by Germans (1870–71). Town and cathedral suffered some damage (1940) in Second World War. Sometimes called Sens-sur-Yonne.

Sensburg, Poland: see MRAGOWO.

Sensée Canal (säsā'), Nord dept., N France, connects the Scarpe (at Douai) with the Escaut (above Bouchain), using marshy valley of small Sensée R.; 15 mi. long. Important coal, metal, building material shipments.

Sensen, Korea: see SONCHON.

Sense River (zĕn'sů), W Switzerland, formed by 2 headstreams joining 4 mi. N of the Kaiseregg; flows 29 mi. N and W to Saane R. at Laupen.

Senshin-ko, Korea: see SOMJIN RIVER.

Senski Rudnik, Yugoslavia: see SENJE.

Sensui-jima, Japan: see TOMO.

Sensuntepeque (sĕnsōōntāpā'kā), city (pop. 3,966), ⊙ Cabañas dept., N Salvador, 40 mi. ENE of San Salvador; alt. 2,297 ft.; 13°53'N 88°37'W. Commercial center in agr. area; grain, indigo, henequen, sugar cane, coffee. Formerly a major indigo-growing center.

Senta (sĕn'tä), Hung. *Zenta* (zĕn'tŏ), city (pop. 24,916), Vojvodina, N Serbia, Yugoslavia, port on Tisa R. (head of passenger navigation) and 23 mi. SE of Subotica, in the Backa. Rail junction (lines to Subotica, Novi Sad, Hungary, and Rumania); flour milling. Truck gardening, natural-gas wells in vicinity. Scene of victory (1697) of Prince Eugene of Savoy over Turks.

Sentani, Lake (sĕntä'nē), in Cyclops Mts., N New Guinea, 7 mi. SW of Hollandia; 20 mi. long, 4 mi. wide, c.160 ft. deep. In Second World War nearby Jap. air base taken by U.S. troops April, 1944.

Sentas (syĭntäs'), town (1948 pop. over 2,000), E Semipalatinsk oblast, Kazakh SSR, 55 mi. ENE of Zhangis-Tobe; gold mining.

Sentein (sãtē'), village (pop. 280), Ariège dept., S France, in central Pyrenees, on the Lez (small tributary of the Salat) and 12 mi. SW of Saint-Girons; lead mining. Hydroelectric station.

Senthal (sän'tŭl), town (pop. 4,845), Bareilly dist., N central Uttar Pradesh, India, 15 mi. NE of Bareilly; sugar refining; wheat, rice, gram, sugar.

Sentier, Le, Switzerland: see Le CHENIT.

Sentinel, city (pop. 1,131), Washita co., W Okla., 28 mi. SSW of Clinton, in agr. area (grain, cotton, alfalfa, livestock); cotton ginning; mfg. of farm machinery, wood products, trucks, trailers, feed. Settled 1901, inc. 1906.

Sentinel Butte (būt), village (pop. 229), Golden Valley co., W N.Dak., 8 mi. E of Beach. Lignite mines near by.

Sentinel Dome, Calif.: see KINGS CANYON NATIONAL PARK; YOSEMITE NATIONAL PARK.

Sentinelle, La (lä sätēnĕl'), SW suburb (pop. 2,745) of Valenciennes, Nord dept., N France.

Sentinel Mountains, group in Ellsworth Highland, Antarctica, bet. 77° and 78°S and 86°–92°30'W. Highest peak is Mt. Ulmer (12,500 ft.). Discovered 1935 by Lincoln Ellsworth.

Sentinel Peak, Oregon: see WALLOWA MOUNTAINS.

Sentinel Ridge, Wis.: see WYALUSING STATE PARK.

Sentis, Switzerland: see SÄNTIS.

Sentmanat, Spain: see SENMANAT.

Sento Sé (sĕn'tōō sĕ'), city (pop. 686), N Bahia, Brazil, on right bank of São Francisco R. (navigable) and 50 mi. WSW of Juàzeiro; rock-crystal extracting; iron deposits. Ships maniçoba rubber.

Sent Peter na Krasu (shĕnt pĕ'tĕr nä krä'sōō), Slovenian *Sent Peter na Krasu*, Ital. *San Pietro del Carso* (sän pyĕt'rô dĕl kär'sô), village (1936 pop. 666), SW Slovenia, Yugoslavia, 20 mi. E of Trieste; rail junction. Until 1947, in Italy.

Sentul, Malaya: see KUALA LUMPUR.

Sentyanovka, Ukrainian SSR: see FRUNZE, town, Voroshilovgrad oblast.

Senyavin Islands (sĕn'yůvĭn), island group, E Caroline Isls., W Pacific; consist of ANT, PAKIN, and PONAPE.

Senye, Yugoslavia: see SENJE.

Senzaki (sänzä'kē), town (pop. 9,325), Yamaguchi prefecture, SW Honshu, Japan, on Sea of Japan, S of Omi-shima, 11 mi. W of Hagi; fishing port; makes whalebone products.

Senzeille (säzā'), village (pop. 707), Namur prov., S Belgium, 16 mi. S of Charleroi; marble quarrying.

Seo de Urgel or **Urgel** (sĕ'ō dhā ōōrhĕl'), fortified city (pop. 3,914), Lérida prov., NE Spain, in Catalonia, in the central Pyrenees, 11 mi. SSW of Andorra, on Segre R. at mouth of Valira R. Stock raising, dairying, lumbering, tanning. Agr. trade (cereals, olive oil, wine, hemp). Hydroelectric plant 3 mi. SW. Has 11th-cent. Romanesque-Gothic cathedral. Seat, since 840, of a bishop, who, with President of France, is joint suzerain of Andorra. Played important role in Carlist Wars. Also called La Seo.

Seohara (sāōhä'rů), town (pop. 11,799), Bijnor dist., N Uttar Pradesh, India, 30 mi. ESE of Bijnor; sugar processing; trades in rice, wheat, gram, barley, sugar cane, oilseeds.

Seon (zā'ôn), town (pop. 2,530), Aargau canton, N Switzerland, 6 mi. SE of Aarau; textiles, flour, tobacco; canneries.

Seonath River (sā'ōnät), in E Madhya Pradesh, India, rises in S outlier of E Satpura Range, SW of Raj Nandgaon; flows c.220 mi. NE and E, through canal-irrigated rice lands, to Mahanadi R. 32 mi. SE of Bilaspur.

Seondha (syōn'dŭ), town (pop. 5,445), NW Vindhya Pradesh, India, on Sind R. and 39 mi. NNE of Datia; markets millet, gram, wheat.

Seoni (sā'ōnē). **1** Village, central Himachal Pradesh, India, on Sutlej R. and 9 mi. NNW of Simla; local market for corn, spices, potatoes. Hot sulphur springs (just W) have medicinal value. Was ⊙ former Punjab Hill state of Bhajji. **2** Town (pop. 20,570), Chhindwara dist., central Madhya Pradesh, India, 39 mi. E. of Chhindwara; sawmilling, essential-oil (*rosha* or Andropogon) distilling, shellac mfg.; silk growing; wheat, rice, oilseeds. Was ⊙ former Seoni dist. until dist. merged in early 1930s with Chhindwara dist. Bauxite deposits (SE).

Seoni-Malwa (–mäl'vŭ), town (pop. 6,427), Hoshangabad dist., NW Madhya Pradesh, India, in fertile Narbada valley, 26 mi. SW of Hoshangabad; wheat, millet, cotton, oilseeds; betel farming. Sometimes called Banapura; sometimes written Seoni Malwa.

Seoul (sōl, sā-ōōl', sā'ōōl; Kor. sŭ'ōōl') or **Kyongsong** (kyŭng'sŭng'), Jap. *Keijo* or *Keizyo* (both: kā'jō'), city (1949 pop. 1,446,019), traditional ⊙ Korea and ⊙ Kyonggi prov., central Korea, on Han R. and 200 mi. NW of Pusan; 37°34'N 127°E; cultural and industrial center. In scenic setting at foot of Mt. Pukhan (2,940 ft.), the anc. city was formerly enclosed by high wall. In 1st half of 20th cent. it was thoroughly modernized and built up. Seoul has an airport at Kimpo (NW) and is connected by railroad with Chemulpo, its port. Industrial establishments include cotton and textile mills, tanneries, railroad workshops, flour mills, and breweries. Here are Univ. of Seoul (formerly Keijo Imperial Univ.), Severance Union Medical Col., Union Women's Christian Col. (in suburb),

Christian Col. (1915), Confucian Institute, and R.C. cathedral. There are 3 imperial palaces, including the beautiful 14th-cent palace built by founder of Yi dynasty (the last imperial line). In center of city is a huge bronze bell cast in1468; the 3 remaining wall gates are of architectural interest. Seoul became ⊙ Korea in 1393, succeeding Kaesong, and was seat (1910–45) of Jap. governor-general. After Second World War, city became hq. of U.S. occupation zone comprising the area S of 38°N. In 1948, it became ⊙ Republic of Korea (South Korea). The seesaw battles in the Korean war (1950–51), during which Seoul was taken and retaken by opposing forces, left it a shattered ruin.

Sepandjang, Indonesia: see KANGEAN ISLANDS.

Sepanjang, Indonesia: see KANGEAN ISLANDS.

Separation Point, settlement (pop. 51), SE Labrador, at head of Sandwich Bay; 53°36′N 57°27′W; lumbering.

Separation Point, N S.Isl., New Zealand, separates Tasman Bay from Golden Bay of Tasman Sea; 40°47′S 173°1′E.

Sepetiba Bay (sĭpĭtē′bù), on the Atlantic coast of Rio de Janeiro state, Brazil, 30 mi. W of Rio; 30 mi. wide, 8 mi. deep; almost closed off from the open Atlantic by Marambaia Isl. and sand bar. Bounded (E) by Federal Dist.

Sephorie, Palestine: see TSIPORI.

Sepik River (sĕ′pĕk), NE New Guinea, rises near boundary bet. Netherlands New Guinea and Territory of New Guinea, drains N Victor Emmanuel and S Torricelli ranges, flows 700 mi. NE to Bismarck Sea. Navigable for 180 mi.; largest tributary, Potter R. Formerly Kaiserin-Augusta R. Sepik R. basin forms Sepik dist. (⊙ Wewak) of Territory of New Guinea.

Sepino (sĕpē′nô), village (pop. 2,537), Campobasso prov., Abruzzi e Molise, S central Italy, 11 mi. S of Campobasso. Near by are ruins of anc. Altilia, destroyed (9th cent.) by Saracens.

Sepolno or **Sepolno Krainskie** (sĕpôl′nô krī′nyùskyĕ), Pol. *Sępolno Kraińskie*, Ger. *Zempelburg* (tsĕm′pùlbŏŏrk), town (pop. 4,214), Bydgoszcz prov., NW Poland, on railroad and 30 mi. NW of Bydgoszcz; agr. center; lumbering, furniture mfg., brewing, flour milling.

Sepopol (sĕpô′pôl), Pol. *Sępopol*, Ger. *Schippenbeil* (shĭ′pùnbīl), village (1939 pop. 3,434; 1946 pop. 1,465) in East Prussia, after 1945 in Olsztyn prov., NE Poland, near USSR border, on Lyna R. and 40 mi. NNE of Allenstein (Olsztyn); grain and cattle market. Ruins of medieval Prussian fortifications near by. After 1945, briefly called Szepopol or Sepopel.

Sepotuba River (sĭpŏŏtŏŏ′bù), central Mato Grosso, Brazil, rises on S slopes of the Serra dos Parecis, flows 150 mi. S to the Paraguay above Cáceres. Not navigable.

Sepphoris, Palestine: see TSIPORI.

Sepsibodok, Rumania: see BODOC.

Sepsiszentgyörgy, Rumania: see SFANTU-GHEORGHE.

Septemvri (sĕp′tĕmvrē), village (pop. 2,700), Plovdiv dist., W central Bulgaria, 10 mi. W of Pazardzhik; rail junction; vineyards; rice, fruit, truck. Formerly called Saranbei, later (until 1950) Saranovo.

Septfonds (sĕfō′), village (pop. 1,045), Tarn-et-Garonne dept., SW France, 17 mi. NE of Montauban; produces straw and felt hats; food preserving; tanning.

Septfontaines, Luxembourg: see LUXEMBOURG, city.

Septiembre, 6 de, Argentina: see MORÓN.

Sept Îles (sĕtēl′) or **Seven Islands,** village (pop. estimate 600), E Que., on Seven Islands Bay of the St. Lawrence, and 100 mi. NNE of Matane, 300 mi. NE of Quebec; 50°12′N 66°23′W; fur-trapping and fishing trading post. Radio station, airfield. Established as fortified trading post 1650, later under North West Co. and Hudson's Bay Co.

Sept-Îles [Fr.,=seven islands], group of islands in English Channel, off coast of Côtes-du-Nord dept., W France, c.10 mi. N of Lannion; extend over area 5 mi. long, 2 mi. wide. Île aux Moines is largest. Bird sanctuary. Lighthouse.

Septimanca, Spain: see SIMANCAS.

Septimania (sĕptĭmā′nēù), historic region of S France. In Roman times, a narrow strip along the Mediterranean around Narbonne, named for the Seventh Legion. In Frankish days it included whole area from upper Garonne to the Rhone, and from the Pyrenees to the Cévennes.

Septimer Pass (zĕp′tēmùr), Ital. *Passo di Sett* (pä′sô dē sĕt′) (7,582 ft.), in the Alps, SE Switzerland, 25 mi. SE of Chur. Road, which crosses pass, leads from valley of Hinterrhein R. (NW) to Maloja (4 mi. E).

Septmoncel (sĕtmōsĕl′), village (pop. 358), Jura dept., E France, in the Jura, 3 mi. ESE of Saint-Claude; alt. 3,280 ft. Produces cheese of Roquefort type; gem cutting. Winter sports.

Sept Pagodes (sĕt pägôd′), Annamese *Phaoson* (fou′shôn′), town, Haiduong prov., N Vietnam, 35 mi. ENE of Hanoi; river navigation hub at confluence of the Song Cau, Canal des Rapides, and united Lucnam and Thuong rivers; rice-trading center.

Sepulcro Hilario (sāpōōl′krō ēlä′ryō), village (pop. 1,022), Salamanca prov., W Spain, 20 mi. ENE of Ciudad Rodrigo; vegetables, livestock.

Sepulga River (sùpŭl′gù), S Ala., rises in N Conecuh co., flows c.50 mi. SE and S to Conecuh R. 18 mi. SW of Andalusia.

Sepúlveda (sāpōōl′vā-dhä), town (pop. 1,322), Segovia prov., central Spain, 31 mi. NE of Segovia; cereals, vetch, carobs, livestock; flour milling. Historic town built on precipitous rock. Has remains of old wall; also churches of Our Lady of Peña, Salvador, and San Justo; castle. After several attempts, it was taken from Moors in 1002.

Sepulveda, Calif.: see SAN FERNANDO VALLEY.

Sequals (sĕkwäls′), village (pop. 862), Udine prov., Friuli-Venezia Giulia, NE Italy, 20 mi. WNW of Udine; agr. tools.

Sequana, France: see SEINE RIVER.

Sequatchie (sùkwŏ′chē), county (□ 273; pop. 5,685), SE central Tenn.; ⊙ Dunlap. Partly in the Cumberlands; Walden Ridge in SE; drained by Sequatchie R. Coal mining, lumbering, agr. (livestock, feed crops, fruit, tobacco). Formed 1857.

Sequatchie River, E Tenn., rises in Crab Orchard Mts. in S Cumberland co., flows c.80 mi. SSW past Pikeville and Dunlap, to Tennessee R. 3 mi. S of Jasper. Its valley separates Cumberland Plateau and Walden Ridge.

Sequeros (sākā′rōs), town (pop. 806), Salamanca prov., W Spain, 36 mi. SW of Salamanca; olive oil, wine; lumber. Summer resort.

Sequim (skwĭm), town (pop. 1,044), Clallam co., NW Wash., 15 mi. E of Port Angeles; trade center for agr. area.

Sequoia National Park (sùkwoi′ù) (□ 601.7; established 1890), E central Calif., c.55 mi. ESE of Fresno; adjoins Kings Canyon Natl. Park (N). Vast primitive area of massive peaks, canyons, and giant sequoia groves, extending up W slope of the Sierra Nevada, across Great Western Divide and spectacular KERN RIVER canyon, to high E crest of range; here, on park's E boundary, are Mt. WHITNEY (14,495 ft.), highest point in U.S., and mounts Williamson, Russell, Langley, Tyndall, and Barnard, all over 14,000 ft. W of Kern R. canyon is Mt. Kaweah (kùwē′ù), 13,816 ft., highest of the 4 Kaweah Peaks, all above 13,000 ft. Giant Forest (in NW) is best known of 35 sequoia groves; includes General Sherman Tree (272.4 ft. high, more than 30 ft. in diameter; c.3,500 yrs. old). Other points of interest are Marble Falls (dropping 2,000 ft. in 7 cascades), in Marble Fork of Kaweah R.; Muir Grove, Crescent Meadow, Moro Rock (massive granite dome; alt. 6,719 ft.). John Muir Trail traverses park.

Sequoyah (sùkwoi′ù), county (□ 703; pop. 19,773), E Okla.; ⊙ Sallisaw. Hilly region (Boston Mts.), bounded E by Ark. line, S by Arkansas R.; drained by Illinois R. Agr. (vegetables, cotton, livestock, corn, potatoes); farm-products processing, some mfg. Coal mines; natural-gas wells; salt deposits. Formed 1907.

Sera (sĕ′rä) [Tibetan,=rose fence], lamasery (pop. c.7,700), SE Tibet, 3 mi. N of Lhasa. One of the 3 great lamaseries of Tibet (the others are Drepung and Ganden). Founded in 14th cent. by Tsong Kapa; divided into 4 colleges.

Seradz, Poland: see SIERADZ.

Serae, Eritrea: see ADI UGRI.

Serafimovich (syĕrŭfē′mùvĭch), city (1926 pop. 6,010), W Stalingrad oblast, Russian SFSR, on Don R., opposite Medveditsa R. mouth, and 100 mi. NW of Stalingrad; flour milling; wheat, fruit. Pop. largely Cossack. Until 1933 (when it became a city) called Ust-Medveditskaya.

Serai, Turkey: see SARAY.

Seraikela, India: see SARAIKELA.

Seraing (sùrē′), town (pop. 43,100), Liége prov., E Belgium, on Meuse R. and 3 mi. WSW of Liége; major steel center; mfg. (locomotives, ship machinery, munitions); coal mining.

Serajevo, Yugoslavia: see SARAJEVO.

Sérakab, Syria: see SERAQAB.

Serakhs (syĭräkhs′), town (1948 pop. over 2,000), SE Ashkhabad oblast, Turkmen SSR, on Tedzhen R. (Iran border) and 180 mi. SE of Ashkhabad; wheat, pistachio woods. USSR frontier station opposite Sarakhs (Iran).

Seram or **Serum** (sā′rŭm), town (pop. 5,619), Gulbarga dist., SW central Hyderabad state, India, 32 mi. ESE of Gulbarga; limestone quarrying and dressing; cotton ginning, oilseed milling. Has 13th-cent. Sivaite temple. Sometimes Sedam.

Serampore (sä′rùmpôr, sä′rùmpŏŏr), town (pop. 55,339), Hooghly dist., S central West Bengal, India, on Hooghly R. and 12 mi. N of Calcutta city center; jute, rice, and cotton milling, mfg. of chemicals, rope, jewelry, hand looms, metal polish. Col. (noted library), Govt. Weaving Inst. Originally a Danish settlement, called Fredericksnagar; acquired 1845 by English. Formerly called Srirampur. Largest Jagannath car festival in India (except for Puri) held just S, at Mahesh; betel gardens 1 mi. NW, at Chatra.

Serang (sùräng′), town (pop. 11,163), NW Java, Indonesia, 50 mi. W of Jakarta; trade center for rice-growing region; machine shops.

Serang, island, Indonesia: see CERAM.

Serang Sea, Indonesia: see CERAM SEA.

Serapeum (sĕ″rùpē′ùm), village, Canal Governorate, NE Egypt, on Suez Canal, on Cairo-Suez RR, and 8 mi. SSE of Ismailia. Named by the French (c.1860) because of neighboring ruins of a temple believed to be erected to Serapis, the composite god of later Egyptian religion.

Seraqab or **Saraqab** (both: sĕrä′käb), Fr. *Sérakab*, village, Aleppo prov., NW Syria, 31 mi. SW of Aleppo; cotton, cereals.

Serasan, Indonesia: see SOUTH NATUNA ISLANDS.

Seravezza (sĕrävĕ′tsä), town (pop. 1,896), Lucca prov., Tuscany, Italy, in SW foothills of Apuane Alps, 8 mi. SE of Carrara. Extensive quarrying and processing of marble; mfg. (marble-working machinery, hydraulic pumps).

Serawak, Borneo: see SARAWAK.

Serayevo, Yugoslavia: see SARAJEVO.

Serbal, Gebel (gĕ′bĕl sĕrbăl′), **Jebel Serbal** (jĕ′bĕl), or **Jabal Sirbal** (jĕ′bĕl sĭrbăl′), mountain peak (6,791 ft.), Sinai Peninsula, NE Egypt, 21 mi. WNW of Gebel Katherina.

Serban-Voda (shĕr′bän-vô′dù), Rum. *Şerban-Vodă*, S suburb (1948 pop. 31,548) of Bucharest, in Bucharest municipality, S Rumania; site of Vacaresti prison, formerly a monastery with noted church.

Serbariu, Sardinia: see CARBONIA.

Serbia (sûr′bēù), Serbo-Croatian *Srbija* or *Srbiya* (sŭr′bĭyä), constituent republic (□ 34,194; pop. 6,523,224), E Yugoslavia; ⊙ Belgrade. Bounded by Croatia (NW), Bosnia and Montenegro (W), Albania (SW), Macedonia (S), Bulgaria and Rumania (E), and Hungary (N). Includes autonomous territory of VOJVODINA and autonomous oblast of Kosovo-METOHIJA; Serbia proper, Serbo-Croatian *Uža Srbija* or *Uzha Srbiya* (ōō′zhä), the remaining part (□ 21,514; pop. 4,134,416) of the republic, is generally mountainous. It lies within several mountain systems: Dinaric Alps (W), North Albanian Alps and Sar Mts. (SW), and Balkan Mts. (E). Serbia proper slopes generally northward toward the Danube and the Sava, which form its N border; drained chiefly by Drina (which forms W border), Kolubara, Morava, Mlava, and Timok rivers and their tributaries. Serbia proper is predominantly agr., with 80% of pop. engaged in cultivation. Chief crops are wheat and corn; barley, rye, oats also grown; truck gardening (beans, potatoes, cabbage, paprika) near cities. Among industrial crops, hemp and sugar beets are most important, followed by flax and tobacco. Serbia proper is one of leading European fruitgrowing areas, noted for plum brandy (slivovits), and an important winegrowing region. Raising of cattle (N, NW), horses (N), sheep (S, E), swine, poultry, silkworms, and bees is also well developed. Fishing chiefly along the Danube and the Sava. Serbia proper is rich in coal (E) and lignite (near ARANDJELOVAC and KOSTOLAC); also mining of copper (BOR), gold, antimony, marble, and millstone. Some of its many health resorts are very well known, e.g., VRNJACKA BANJA, VRANJSKA BANJA, and KOVILJACA. Home industry and handicraft are important. Industry, based primarily on local agr. and stock raising, includes flour and beet-sugar milling, fruit and vegetable canning, meat packing, brewing, dairying, tanning, and tobacco processing; also mfg. of paper, glass, textiles, footwear, and chemical products. Metallurgical industry (development begun 1949) at BELGRADE, VALJEVO, SMEDEREVO, PALANKA, and KRUSEVAC. Belgrade-Salonika RR, with branches to Istanbul and the Adriatic coast, internatl. highways, linking Europe with the Near East, and navigable rivers (Danube and Sava) stimulate trade. Besides Belgrade, chief cities are NIS, KRAGUJEVAC, and LESKOVAC. The Serbs, a South Slavic people, settled in the region (Roman *Moesia Superior*) in 7th cent. Their petty princes, at first under Byzantine suzerainty, were converted (9th cent.) to Orthodox Eastern church, and formed (12th cent.) an independent kingdom which flourished under Stephen Dushan (1331–55), who ruled over Bosnia, Macedonia, Epirus, and Albania, and proclaimed himself emperor of Serbs and Greeks. After his death the empire disintegrated, the Serbs were decisively defeated (1389) at Kosovo by the Turks, and Serbia became (1459) part of Ottoman Empire. N Serbia was temporarily held (1718–39) by Austria. Revolts in early-19th cent., under Karageorge in 1804–13 and Milosh Obrenovich in 1815–17, forced Turkey to recognize (1817) the prince of Serbia, who gained (after 1830) increasingly greater autonomy, until complete independence was secured in 1878. In 1882, Serbia was proclaimed a kingdom. The Greater Serbia movement, aimed chiefly at Austria-Hungary, resulted in friction. Austria's annexation (1908) of Bosnia and Herzegovina, long coveted by Serbia, increased the friction. In the Balkan Wars which followed, Serbia's territory was doubled (1913) by the incorporation of N Macedonia. The assassination of Archduke Francis Ferdinand of Austria at Sarajevo in 1914 precipitated the First World War. In 1918 Serbia joined with the Croats, Slovenes, and Montenegrins to form the Kingdom of the Serbs, Croats, and Slovenes, or YUGOSLAVIA. Serbia was organized until 1921 as 2 separate provs., North Serbia and South Serbia, and later (1929–41) as the banovinas of Dunav, Drin, Zeta, Morava, and

Vardar. In 1946, Serbia became a people's republic. Formerly called Servia.

Serbin, Texas: see GIDDINGS.

Sercaia (shěrkä'yä), Rum. *Şercaia*, Hung. *Sárkány* (shär'känyŭ), village (pop. 1,790), Sibiu prov., central Rumania, on Olt R., on railroad and 7 mi. E of Fagaras; agr. center noted for well-preserved folkways.

Serchio River (sěr'kyô), Tuscany, central Italy, rises in Etruscan Apennines 6 mi. SE of Alpe di Succiso, flows SE, through the Garfagnana, past Castelnuovo di Garfagnana, and S, turning SW near Lucca, to Ligurian Sea 8 mi. NW of Pisa; total length 64 mi. Used in mfg., and, along coast, for irrigation. Receives Lima R.

Sercq, Channel Isls.: see SARK.

Serdán or **Ciudad Serdán** (syōōdädh' sěrdän'), city (pop. 7,791), Puebla, central Mexico, near W foot of Pico de Orizaba, 50 mi. E of Puebla; alt. 8,541 ft. Rail junction; wheat- and corn-growing center; stock raising; textile milling, salt quarrying. Until 1934 named Chalchicomula, still name of municipio.

Serdang (sŭrdäng'). **1** Village (pop. 1,965), S Kedah, Malaya, 23 mi. SE of George Town; rubber plantations. **2** Village (pop. 815), S central Selangor, Malaya, on railroad and 9 mi. S of Kuala Lumpur; tin mining.

Serdash, Iraq: see SURDASH.

Serdeles (sěrdělěs'), village (pop. 120), Fezzan, Libya, on road and 60 mi. NNE of Ghat, in a Saharan oasis; date growing, alum extracting. Placed under Algerian administration c.1945.

Serdica, Bulgaria: see SOFIA, city.

Serditoye (syĭrdyē'tŭyŭ), town (1939 pop. over 500), E Stalino oblast, Ukrainian SSR, in the Donbas, on railroad and 10 mi. W of Chistyakovo; coal mines.

Serdj, Djebel (jě'běl sârj'), mountain (4,452 ft.) in Maktar dist., central Tunisia, 20 mi. ENE of Maktar; zinc mines.

Serdobol, Karelo-Finnish SSR: see SORTAVALA.

Serdobsk (syĭrdôpsk'), city (1926 pop. 18,616), S Penza oblast, Russian SFSR, on Serdoba R. (left branch of Khoper R.) and 60 mi. SSW of Penza; agr. center (wheat, sunflowers, sugar beets); brickworks; food processing, flour milling, sawmilling. Peat deposits near by. Chartered 1780.

Serdtse-Kamen, Cape, or **Cape Serdtse-Kamen'** (syěr'tsĭ-kä'mĭnyŭ), on N coast of Chukchi Peninsula, NE Siberian Russian SFSR; 66°54'N 171°32'W. Govt. arctic station; trading post, airfield. Silver-lead deposits near by.

Serebryanka (sěrĭbryän'kŭ), village (1926 pop. 2,689), W Sverdlovsk oblast, Russian SFSR, on Serebryanka R. (right tributary of Chusovaya R.) and 38 mi. WNW of Nizhni Tagil; lumbering.

Serebryanye Prudy or **Serebryanyye Prudy** (sĭrěb'ryŭnēŭ prōōdē'), village (1926 pop. 5,366), S Moscow oblast, Russian SFSR, 20 mi. NNW of Mikhailov; flour milling, distilling. Until c.1928, Sergiyevy Prudy.

Sered (sě'rět), Hung. *Szered* (sě'rěd), town (pop. 5,863), SW Slovakia, Czechoslovakia, on Vah R. and 30 mi. ENE of Bratislava; rail junction; agr. center (wheat, barley); noted for timber trade; sugar refining. Vineyards in vicinity.

Sereda (syěrĭdä'). **1** City, Ivanovo oblast, Russian SFSR: see FURMANOV. **2** Village (1926 pop. 421), E Yaroslavl oblast, Russian SFSR, 20 mi. SE of Danilov; flax, wheat.

Seredina-Buda (syěrĭdyē'nŭ-bōō'dŭ), town (1926 pop. 7,265), N Sumy oblast, Ukrainian SSR, 35 mi. N of Glukhov; hemp growing.

Seredka (sĭryôt'kŭ), village (1939 pop. over 500), W Pskov oblast, Russian SFSR, 23 mi. N of Pskov; flax processing.

Serefli Kochisar (shěrěflē' kôchĭsär'), Turkish *Şerefli Koçhisar*, village (pop. 3,396), Ankara prov., central Turkey, near E shore of L. Tuz, 75 mi. SSE of Ankara; grain, fruit, mohair goats. Formerly Kochisar.

Seregelyes (shě'rěgālyěsh), Hung. *Seregélyes*, town (pop. 4,753), Fejer co., W central Hungary, 9 mi. SE of Szekesfehervar; wheat, corn, beans, lentils; cattle, hogs.

Seregno (sěrā'nyô), town (pop. 14,770), Milano prov., Lombardy, N Italy, 13 mi. N of Milan. Rail junction; industrial center; cotton and silk mills, foundries; mfg. of furniture, soap, glass, alcohol.

Seregovo (syěrĭgô'vŭ), village (1926 pop. 724), W Komi Autonomous SSR, Russian SFSR, on Vym R. and 45 mi. N of Syktyvkar; saltworks; mineral springs.

Serein River (sŭrē'), Côte-d'Or and Yonne depts., E central France, rises 6 mi. NNW of Arnay-le-Duc, flows 115 mi. NW, past Précy-sous-Thil and Chablis, to the Yonne 9 mi. NNW of Auxerre.

Serémange-Erzange (sŭrāmäzh'-ěrzäzh'), Ger. *Schremingen-Ersingen* (shrā'mĭng-ŭn-ěr'zĭng-ŭn), commune (pop. 3,838), Moselle dept., NE France, 5 mi. SW of Thionville; blast furnaces, forges.

Seremban (sŭrěmbän'), town (pop. 35,274; with suburbs 37,539), ⊙ Negri Sembilan, Malaya, on W coast railroad and Linggi R., 35 mi. SE of Kuala Lumpur; linked by rail with Port Dickson on Strait of Malacca; center of rubber-growing area. Tin mining near by.

Serena, La, Chile: see LA SERENA.

Serena, La (lä sārā'nä), region of Estremadura, in Badajoz prov., SW Spain, along left bank of the Guadiana, N of Castuera. Though fertile, it suffers from occasional droughts. Chiefly stock raising (sheep, hogs).

Serendah (sŭrěndä'), town (pop. 1,544), N central Selangor, Malaya, on railroad and 17 mi. NNW of Kuala Lumpur; tin mining.

Serendib, Asia: see CEYLON.

Serengeti Plains (sěrěng-gě'tē), section of Tanganyika's central plateau SE of L. Victoria near Kenya border; average alt. 5,000 ft. Nomadic grazing. Sometimes spelled Serengetti.

Serenje (sěrěn'jā), township (pop. 112), Central Prov., Northern Rhodesia, 180 mi. NE of Broken Hill; tobacco, corn; cattle, sheep, goats. Was ⊙ former Serenje prov.

Serere (sōōrě'rā), town, Eastern Prov., E central Uganda, 16 mi. SSW of Soroti; cotton, peanuts, sesame; livestock. Has govt. agr. experimental station.

Seres, China: see SERICA.

Seres, Greece: see SERRAI.

Sereth, town, Rumania: see SIRET.

Sereth River, Ukrainian SSR and Rumania: see SIRET RIVER.

Seret River (sĭryět'), W Ukrainian SSR, rises SE of Olesko in Volyn-Podolian Upland, flows 153 mi. S, past Zalozhtsy, Mikulintsy, Budanov, and Chortkov, to Dniester R. 5 mi. E of Zaleshchiki.

Serga or **Ser'ga** (sĭrgä'), village (1926 pop. 783), E central Molotov oblast, Russian SFSR, on Sylva R. and 55 mi. ENE of Okhansk; grain, livestock.

Sergach (syĭrgäch'), city (1926 pop. 3,575), SE Gorki oblast, Russian SFSR, 80 mi. SE of Gorki; metalworking. Chartered 1779.

Sergeant Bluff (sär'jŭnt), town (pop. 569), Woodbury co., W Iowa, near Missouri R., 8 mi. S of Sioux City; livestock, grain.

Sergei Kirov Islands or **Sergey Kirov Islands** (sĭrgā" kē'rŭf), in Kara Sea of Arctic Ocean, 100 mi. off N Taimyr Peninsula, in Krasnoyarsk Territory, Russian SFSR; 77°N 90°E. Main isls.: Kirov, Isachenko, Voronin.

Sergeyevka (sĭrgā'ŭfkŭ), village (1939 pop. over 500), NW Stalino oblast, Ukrainian SSR, in the Donbas, 8 mi. WSW of Kramatorsk; metalworks.

Sergey Kirov Islands, Russian SFSR: see SERGEI KIROV ISLANDS.

Sergines (sěrzhēn'), agr. village (pop. 749), Yonne dept., N central France, 10 mi. N of Sens.

Sergiopol, Kazakh SSR: see AYAGUZ, city.

Sergipe (sěrzhě'pĭ), smallest state (□ 8,130; 1940 pop. 542,326; 1950 census 650,132) of Brazil, in NE; ⊙ Aracaju. Of triangular shape, it is bounded N by São Francisco R. (Alagoas border), E by the Atlantic, S and W by Bahia. Its low coastal plain merges gradually with interior plateau. Drained by lower course of the São Francisco, and by intermittent-flowing Vasa Barris, Cotinguiba, and Sergipe rivers. Chief crops: sugar, cotton, and rice (in irrigated river valleys); also manioc, tobacco, oranges. Livestock raised in the interior. Rock salt extracted near Cotinguiba. Chief industries are textile and sugar milling, one of the country's largest sugar plants being situated at Riachuelo. Principal cities are Aracaju (seaport), Propriá (N terminus of railroad from Salvador which crosses entire state), and Estância. State has tropical monsoon climate (average temp. 76°F.; rainy season, March–July) with periodic droughts in the interior. Sandy coast line is navigation hazard. First settled in 16th cent. Held by Dutch in mid-17th cent. Was dependency of Bahia until 1821, then became an independent captaincy, and in 1824 a prov. of Brazilian Empire with old ⊙ at São Cristóvão. Since 1889, a state of federal republic. Old name, Sergipe d'el Rey.

Sergipe River, Sergipe, NE Brazil, rises near Bahia border at 10°S 38°W, flows c.100 mi. SE to the Cotinguiba above Aracaju. Intermittent-flowing stream.

Sergiyev, Russian SFSR: see ZAGORSK.

Sergiyevo, Russian SFSR: see VOLODARSKI.

Sergiyevsk (syěr'gēŭfsk), village (1932 pop. estimate 6,100), N central Kuibyshev oblast, Russian SFSR, on right bank of Sok R., opposite Surgut, and 70 mi. NE of Kuibyshev; flour milling. Health resort of Sernovodsk is 5 mi. E.

Sergiyevskaya (–skīŭ), village (1939 pop. over 500), N central Stalingrad oblast, Russian SFSR, on Medveditsa R. and 27 mi. NE of Mikhailovka; wheat, sunflowers.

Sergiyevski or **Sergiyevskiy** (–skē), town (1939 pop. over 2,000), central Udmurt Autonomous SSR, Russian SFSR, on railroad and 39 mi. SSE of Glazov; glassworking center. Quartz sand deposits near by.

Sergiyevski Posad, Russian SFSR: see ZAGORSK.

Sergo, Ukrainian SSR: see KADIYEVKA.

Sergokala (syěrgŭkŭlä'), village (1939 pop. over 500), E Dagestan Autonomous SSR, Russian SFSR, on Caspian coastal plain, 37 mi. SSE of Makhachkala; wheat (irrigation), livestock.

Sergunia (sěrgōōnē'ä) or **Szirguni** (sērgōōnē'), settlement (pop. 150), NE Israel, Lower Galilee, 2 mi. SW of Tiberias; mixed agr. Founded 1939 as Hazorim or Hazor'im; name changed after 1948. Sometimes spelled Serguniah. Modern village on site of anc. Jewish village of Sergunin.

Sergy (sěrzhē'), village (pop. 150), Aisne dept., N France, 3 mi. ESE of Fère-en-Tardenois. Captured by Americans (July, 1918) after changing hands 9 times during fierce fighting.

Seria (sŭrē'ŭ), town (dist. pop. 5,525) in W section of Brunei, NW Borneo, on S.China Sea, 10 mi. E of Kuala Belait; has oil fields linked by pipe line with Lutong (23 mi. WSW, in Sarawak). Severely damaged during Second World War.

Serian (sŭrēän'), town, S Sarawak, in W Borneo, 32 mi. SSE of Kuching; sago, coconuts, livestock.

Seriate (sěrēä'tě), town (pop. 5,696), Bergamo prov., Lombardy, N Italy, on Serio R. and 2 mi. ESE of Bergamo; silk and cotton mills, brewery; metalworking.

Serica (sě'rĭkŭ), Roman name for China, derived from the Latin *sericum* (silk). Seres was the Roman name applied to the Chinese.

Sérifontaine (sārēfōtěn'), village (pop. 1,152), Oise dept., N France, on the Epte and 15 mi. WSW of Beauvais; metalworks.

Serifos, Greece: see SERIPHOS.

Sérignan (sārēnyā'), town (pop. 2,261), Hérault dept., S France, on Orb R. near its mouth on the Gulf of Lion, and 5 mi. SE of Béziers; winegrowing.

Serik (sěrĭk'), village (pop. 1,500), Antalya prov., SW Turkey, 22 mi. E of Antalya; wheat, sesame. Near by are ruins of anc. Aspendus. Formerly Kukes (Turkish *Kükes*) or Kokes (*Kökes*).

Serinam (sěrēnäm'), village, Tuléar prov., W Madagascar, on Tsiribihina R. (head of navigation), 10 mi. E of Belo-sur-Tsiribihina; rice, beans. R.C. and Protestant missions.

Seringapatam (sěrĭng'gŭpŭtŭm) or **Srirangapatan** (srērŭng'gŭpŭtŭn), town (pop. 7,678), Mandya dist., S Mysore, India, on W end of isl. in Cauvery R., 7 mi. NNE of Mysore city center. Named for its 12th-cent. temple to Sri Ranga, town (originally fortified in 15th cent.) became (1610) seat of Mysore rajas and (1761) of Mysore sultans; archaeological and historical sites include Hindu monuments (mostly 17th cent.) and palace and large mosque built by Tippoo Sahib. Near E suburb of Ganjam are Tippoo's elaborate summer palace (1784) and the mausoleum in which he and his father, Hyder Ali, rest. Treaty bet. Tippoo and the British signed here 1792. Ceded to the British after the siege of 1799, in the course of which Tippoo was killed.

Seringes-et-Nesles (sŭrēzh'-ā-něl'), commune (pop. 346), Aisne dept., N France, 2 mi. ENE of Fère-en-Tardenois. Here Americans took part in heavy fighting (July–Aug., 1918) during First World War. Site of Oise-Aisne American Cemetery.

Serinhaem, Brazil: see SIRINHAÉM.

Serio River (sā'rēō), Lombardy, N Italy, rises in Bergamasque Alps 15 mi. NNE of Clusone, flows 77 mi. S, past Crema, to Adda R. 7 mi. S of Crema. Used for hydroelectric power in upper course.

Seriphos or **Serifos** (both: sě'rĭfôs), Lat. *Seriphus* (sŭrī'fŭs), Aegean island (□ 29; 1940 pop. 2,749) in the Cyclades, Greece, SW of Syros isl., bet. Kythnos and Siphnos; 37°10'N 24°30'E; 5 mi. long, 5 mi. wide; rises to 1,585 ft. Produces grain, wine, olives, figs. Iron mining; copper and lead deposits. Main town, Seriphos (1928 pop. 1,621), is on E shore. Settled by Ionians from Athens. Under Turkish rule (1537–1832).

Serivara Point (sŭrēvä'rŭ) or **Sevivara Point** (sŭvēvä'rŭ), easternmost point of Timor, in Wetar Strait, opposite Jaco isl.; 8°24'S 127°18'E.

Sermadevi (särmŭdā'vē) or **Shermadevi** (shār–), since 1949 officially **Cheranmahadevi** (chārŭnmŭhä'dāvē), town (pop. 8,958), Tinnevelly dist., S Madras, India, 9 mi. WSW of Tinnevelly, in agr. area; sesame-oil extraction.

Sermaize-les-Bains (sěrměz'-lā-bē'), resort (pop. 2,120), Marne dept., N France, on Marne-Rhine Canal and 11 mi. W of Bar-le-Duc; chalybeate springs; sugar refining. Ravaged, 1914, in First World War.

Sermata (sŭrmä'tŭ), island (14 mi. long, 4 mi. wide; pop. 2,714), S Moluccas, Indonesia, in Banda Sea, bet. Babar Isls. (E) and Leti Isls. (W), 105 mi. E of Timor; 8°13'S 128°55'E; hilly, wooded. Coconut growing, fishing.

Sermide (sěr'mědě), town (pop. 2,471), Mantova prov., Lombardy, N Italy, on Po R. and 20 mi. NW of Ferrara; dairy products, macaroni, linen, beet sugar.

Sermilik, Greenland: see EGEDE AND ROTHE FJORD.

Sermin or **Saramin** (both: särmēn'), Fr. *Sarmine*, village, Aleppo prov., NW Syria, 33 mi. SW of Aleppo; cotton, cereals.

Sermione, Italy: see SIRMIONE.

Sernancelhe (sěrnäsā'lyĭ), town (pop. 785), Viseu dist., N central Portugal, 28 mi. NE of Viseu, in the Serra da Lapa; stock raising, wheat growing.

Sernovodsk (syěrnŭvôtsk'), village (1939 pop. over 2,000), N central Kuibyshev oblast, Russian SFSR, 5 mi. E of Sergiyevsk; health resort (sulphur springs, mud baths).

Sernur (syĭrnōōr'), village (1948 pop. over 500), NE Mari Autonomous SSR, Russian SFSR, 45 mi. ENE of Ioshkar-Ola; wheat, rye, oats.

Serny Zavod or **Sernyy Zavod** (syĕr′nē zŭvôt′), town (1938 pop. 1,812), NE Ashkhabad oblast, Turkmen SSR, in Kara-Kum desert, 155 mi. N of Ashkhabad; sulphur works.

Serock (sĕ′rôtsk), Rus. *Serotsk* (syĭrôtsk′), town (pop. 2,123), Warszawa prov., E central Poland, on the Narew, opposite Bug R. mouth, and 20 mi. N of Warsaw; soap mfg., sawmilling, flour and groat milling.

Serodino (sārōdē′nō), town (pop. estimate, 2,000), S central Santa Fe prov., Argentina, 30 mi. NNW of Rosario; agr. center (sunflowers, corn, wheat, flax, hogs, cattle). Liquor distilling, dairying, grain processing.

Seroei, Indonesia: see JAPEN ISLANDS.

Seroetoe, Indonesia: see KARIMATA ISLANDS.

Serom (sûrōm′), village (pop. 992), NW Johore, Malaya, 10 mi. NNE of Bandar Maharani; rubber plantations.

Serón (sārōn′), town (pop. 2,097), Almería prov., S Spain, on Almanzora R. and 35 mi. N of Almería; wool- and cotton-cloth mfg., olive-oil and meat processing. Pop. fluctuates according to degree of activity at iron, lead, and silver mines in near-by Sierra de los Filabres (aerial tramway, roads). Has ruins of Moorish castle.

Serón de Nájima (sārōn′ dhā′ nä′hēmä), town (pop. 815), Soria prov., N central Spain, 23 mi. SE of Soria; cereals, barley, anise, potatoes, truck produce, livestock; timber; flour milling.

Serós (sārōs′), town (pop. 2,314), Lérida prov., NE Spain, near Segre R. and the Aragon and Catalonia Canal, 15 mi. SW of Lérida; olive-oil processing; agr. trade (cereals, wine, vegetables). Hydroelectric plant near by, at end of an irrigation canal.

Serotsk, Poland: see SEROCK.

Serov (syĕ′rŭf), city (1939 pop. 64,719), N Sverdlovsk oblast, Russian SFSR, in E foothills of the central Urals, near FILKINO, and 190 mi. N of Sverdlovsk. Rail junction; leading metallurgical center, based on RUDNICHNY and VORONTSOVKA magnetite, MARSYATY manganese, SAMA hematite, Uglezhzheniye charcoal, and Karpinsk coking coal; produces quality steels and pig iron; woodworking, light mfg. Developed in 1890s as ironworks called Nadezhdinski Zavod (later Nadezhdinsk); became city in 1926. Renamed Kabakovsk (1935), again Nadezhdinsk (1938), and finally (1939) Serov, for Rus. aviator Anatoli Serov. Largely industrialized in 1930s and during Second World War.

Serovo, Uzbek SSR: see BAGDAD.

Serowe (sĕrō′wä), town (pop. 15,935), ⊙ Ngwato dist., E Bechuanaland Protectorate, 200 mi. SW of Bulawayo, 250 mi. NNE of Mafeking; agr. center. Hq. of Bamangwato tribe; hosp.

Serpa, Brazil: see ITACOATIARA.

Serpa (sĕr′pù), town (pop. 6,873), Beja dist., S Portugal, 15 m . SE of Beja; agr. trade center (grain, olives, livestock); pottery and cheese mfg. Has Moorish castle and fortifications.

Serpa Pinto (sĕr′pù pēn′tōō), town (pop. 387), Bié prov., S central Angola, 170 mi. SSE of Silva Pôrto; 14°39′S 17°48′E. Until 1930s, called Menongue. Became ⊙ Cuando-Cubango dist. (formed 1946).

Serpeddi, Monte (môn′tĕ sĕrpĕd′dē), or **Punta Serpeddi** (pōōn′tä), mountain (3,506 ft.), SE Sardinia, 14 mi. NE of Cagliari.

Serpentine Mountains (–tīn), ridge (2,240 ft.) in N central N.B., 40 mi. ENE of Grand Falls.

Serpent Mound, Adams co., S Ohio, prehistoric Indian mound c.1,330 ft. long, representing a serpent swallowing an egg. With adjacent mounds, it is now in a state park (trails, picnic grounds, and a mus.).

Serpent's Mouth, Sp. *Boca de la Sierpe* (bō′kä dā lä syĕr′pā), channel bet. NE Venezuela and Trinidad, linking Gulf of Paria with the Atlantic, at Orinoco R. delta.

Serpets, Poland: see SIERPC.

Serpukhov (syĕr′pōōkhŭf), city (1939 pop. 90,766), S Moscow oblast, Russian SFSR, on Oka R., at mouth of the Nara, and 60 mi. S of Moscow. Major cotton-milling center (spinning and weaving mills); woolen milling, flax processing, sawmilling, metalworking, mfg. of motorcycles, paper. Fortress (1556) at center of city, with well-preserved walls and gates. Chartered 1328; in 14th and 15th cent., one of principal fortified centers protecting S approaches of Moscow. During Second World War, resisted Ger. assault (1941) in Moscow campaign.

Serqueux, France: see FORGES-LES-EAUX.

Serra (sĕ′rù), city (pop. 1,439), central Espírito Santo, Brazil, 14 mi. N of Vitória; coffee, bananas, pineapples, oranges.

Serra (sĕ′rä), village (pop. 1,176), Valencia prov., E Spain, 9 mi. W of Sagunto; olive-oil and meat processing; cork, figs, almonds. Stone and gypsum quarries.

Serra Alta, Brazil: see SÃO BENTO DO SUL.

Serra Azul (sĕ′rù äzōōl′), city (pop. 1,142), NE São Paulo, Brazil, on railroad and 18 mi. ESE of Ribeirão Prêto; coffee, grain, cotton.

Serra Branca (sĕ′rù brăng′kù), city (pop. 644), central Paraíba, Brazil, 60 mi. WSW of Campina Grande; cotton, corn, livestock. Called Itamorotinga, 1944–48.

Serracapriola (sĕr″räkäprēō′lä), town (pop. 7,569), Foggia prov., Apulia, S Italy, 14 mi. NW of San Severo; olive oil, wine.

Serra de El-Rei (sĕ′rù dĕlrā′), village (pop. 1,438), Leiria dist., W central Portugal, 6 mi. ESE of Peniche. Has restored 14th-cent. royal castle.

Serradifalco (sĕr″rädēfäl′kô), town (pop. 7,398), Caltanissetta prov., central Sicily, 10 mi. WSW of Caltanissetta. Rich sulphur mines near by.

Serradilla (sĕrä-dhē′lyä), town (pop. 4,162), Cáceres prov., W Spain, near the Tagus, 15 mi. SSW of Plasencia; olive-oil processing, flour milling; produces cereals, cork, honey.

Serra-di-Scopamène (sĕrä′-dē-skôpämĕn′), village (pop. 1,058), S central Corsica, 11 mi. NNE of Sartène; alt. 2,800 ft.

Serra Dolcedorme, Italy: see POLLINO.

Serrai (sĕr′ā), nome (□ 1,566; pop. 231,660), Macedonia, Greece; ⊙ Serrai. Bounded N by Bulgaria, S by the Vertiskon and Aegean Sea, E by the Pangaion and the Menoikion; drained by lower Struma R. (partly canalized). Agr.: cotton, tobacco, barley, corn, potatoes. Fisheries in L. Kerkinitis. Main centers are: Serrai, Siderokastron, Nigrita.

Serrai, Lat. *Serrae* or *Serrhae* (both: sĕ′rē), city (1951 pop. 36,297), ⊙ Serrai nome, Macedonia, 40 mi. ENE of Salonika; trading center for tobacco; also cotton, barley, corn, wheat, sesame; cotton textile and cigarette mfg. Bishopric. Antimony and lignite mining near by. Known as Siris during Byzantine era, when it flourished with a pop. of more than 50,000, it became capital (14th cent.) of Serbian emperor Stephen Dushan. Known as Siroz under Turkish rule, from 15th cent. to Balkan Wars (1912–13). Later called Seres or Serres. Sometimes spelled Serre.

Serramanna (sĕr″rämän′nä), town (pop. 5,178), Cagliari prov., S Sardinia, near Flumini Mannu R., 17 mi. NNW of Cagliari.

Serramazzoni (sĕr″rämätsō′nē), village (pop. 539), Modena prov., Emilia-Romagna, N central Italy, 17 mi. SSW of Modena; resort (alt. 2,595 ft.). Called Monfestino in Serra Mazzoni until 1948.

Serrana Bank (sĕrä′nä), coral reef in the Caribbean c.200 mi. off Mosquito Coast of Nicaragua, belonging to Colombia, in SAN ANDRÉS Y PROVIDENCIA intendancy; 14°25′N 80°16′W. Claimed 1919 by U.S.

Serra Negra (sĕ′rù nĕ′grù), city (pop. 2,979), E São Paulo, Brazil, 29 mi. NE of Campinas; rail-spur terminus; hydro-mineral resort. Produces Panama hats, textiles, furniture, rum, perfumes.

Serra Negra do Norte (dōō nôr′tĭ), city (pop. 729), S Rio Grande do Norte, NE Brazil, on Piranhas R. (irrigation dam projected) and 25 mi. SW of Caicó, near Paraíba border; manioc, vegetables, livestock. Rock crystals found here. Airfield. Until 1944, called Serra Negra.

Serranilla Bank (sĕränē′yä), coral reef in the Caribbean c.225 mi. off Mosquito Coast of Nicaragua and Honduras, belonging to Colombia, in SAN ANDRÉS Y PROVIDENCIA intendancy; 15°51′N 79°46′W.

Serranillos (sĕränē′lyōs), town (pop. 1,174), Ávila prov., central Spain, on N slopes of the Sierra de Gredos, 23 mi. SW of Ávila; potatoes, cherries, livestock; flour milling.

Serrano Island (sĕrä′nō). **1** or **Little Wellington Island,** off coast of Aysén prov., S Chile, just N of Wellington Isl., bet. 48°7′–48°40′S; c.40 mi. long. **2** Islet just off N coast of Chile, protecting harbor of Iquique; 20°13′S 70°9′W.

Serraria (sĕrûrē′ù), city (pop. 1,143), E Paraíba, NE Brazil, 55 mi. WNW of João Pessoa; cotton, rice, sugar.

Serra San Bruno (sĕr′rä sän brōō′nô), town (pop. 6,736), Catanzaro prov., Calabria, S Italy, 14 mi. ESE of Vibo Valentia; summer resort (alt. 2,625 ft.). Lumbering, stoneworking, wrought-iron products. Damaged 1783 by earthquake.

Serra San Quirico (kwē′rēkô), village (pop. 790), Ancona prov., The Marches, central Italy, 10 mi. NE of Fabriano; silk mill; limekilns.

Serrastretta (sĕr″rästrĕt′tä), town (pop. 2,898), Catanzaro prov., Calabria, S Italy, 5 mi. ENE of Nicastro, in grape- and olive-growing region.

Serrat, Cape (sĕrät′), headland on the Mediterranean coast of N Tunisia, 35 mi. W of Bizerte; 37°15′N 9°13′E. Lighthouse.

Serra Talhada (sĕ′rù tŭlyä′dù), city (pop. 2,999), central Pernambuco, NE Brazil, 70 mi. W of Sertânia; cotton, corn, tobacco. Until 1939, called Villa Bella.

Serravalle, Italy: see VITTORIO VENETO.

Serravalle Libarna (sĕr″rävälʹlĕ lēbär′nä), village (pop. 2,433), Alessandria prov., Piedmont, N Italy, on Scrivia R., 5 mi. SE of Novi Ligure; mfg. (metal products, pottery, leather goods, paper, fertilizer); resort. SE are ruins (theater, aqueduct) of Libarna, Roman town of 2d cent. B.C. Called Serravalle Scrivia until early 1930s.

Serravalle Pistoiese (pēstōyä′zĕ), village (pop. 307), Pistoia prov., Tuscany, central Italy, 4 mi. WSW of Pistoia; ceramics.

Serravalle Scrivia, Italy: see SERRAVALLE LIBARNA.

Serravalle Sesia (sā′zyä), village (pop. 2,897), Vercelli prov., Piedmont, N Italy, near Sesia R., 15 mi. NE of Biella. Has large paper mill.

Serrazzano (sĕr-rätsä′nô), village (pop. 430), Pisa prov., Tuscany, central Italy, 13 mi. SSW of Volterra. Has *soffioni* used to produce boric acid and electricity.

Serre, Greece: see SERRAI.

Serre (sĕr′rĕ), village (pop. 2,719), Salerno prov., Campania, S Italy, 7 mi. ESE of Eboli.

Serrejón (sĕrāhōn′), town (pop. 1,312), Cáceres prov., W Spain, 22 mi. SE of Plasencia; cereals, olive oil, livestock.

Serrenti (sĕr-rĕn′tē), village (pop. 3,526), Cagliari prov., S Sardinia, 20 mi. NNW of Cagliari. Kaolin mine near by.

Serre River (sâr), Ardennes and Aisne depts., N France, rises 8 mi. ENE of Rozoy-sur-Serre, flows c.50 mi. W, past Marle and Crécy-sur-Serre, to the Oise at La Fère.

Serres (sâr), village (pop. 754), Hautes-Alpes dept., SE France, on rocky spur above Buëch R. and 20 mi. SW of Gap, in Dauphiné Alps; flour products. Has 12th-cent. church.

Serres, Greece: see SERRAI.

Serrezuela (sĕräswä′lä), town (pop. estimate 700), NW Córdoba prov., Argentina, 90 mi. NW of Córdoba; rail junction; corn, vegetables, livestock; lumbering, sawmilling. Sierra de Serrezuela, a range of the Sierra de Córdoba, is S.

Serrhae, Greece: see SERRAI.

Serrières (sĕrēâr′), village (pop. 1,227), Ardèche dept., S France, on right bank of Rhone R. and 7 mi. NE of Annonay; fruitgrowing.

Serrinha (sĭrē′nyù). **1** City (pop. 2,765), NE Bahia, Brazil, on railroad and 50 mi. NW of Alagoinhas; ships tobacco, cattle, hides. **2** Town, Paraíba, Brazil: see JURIPIRANGA.

Sêrro (sā′rōō), city (pop. 2,776), central Minas Gerais, Brazil, in the Serra do Espinhaço, 27 mi. SSE of Diamantina; diamond washings, talc quarries. Gold-mining town in colonial times.

Serro Azul, Brazil: see CÊRRO AZUL.

Sers, Le (lù sârs′), village, Le Kef dist., N central Tunisia, on railroad, and 18 mi. ESE of Le Kef; horse-breeding center; flour milling.

Sersale (sĕrsä′lĕ), town (pop. 4,838), Catanzaro prov., Calabria, S Italy, in La Sila foothills, 10 mi. NE of Catanzaro. Two hydroelectric stations near.

Sersou Plateau (sĕrsōō′), in N central Algeria, high tableland (alt c.2,500 ft.) at S edge of the Tell Atlas (Ouarsenis Massif), extending c.50 mi. ENE from Tiaret; fertile wheat-growing dist. settled by European colonists.

Sert, Turkey: see SIIRT.

Sertã (sĕrtã′), town (pop. 1,297), Castelo Branco dist., central Portugal, 33 mi. W of Castelo Branco, in fruitgrowing region; gunpowder mfg., sawmilling, resin extracting. Has 15th-cent. church.

Sertânia (sĕrtä′nyù), city (pop. 4,288), central Pernambuco, NE Brazil, near Paraíba border, 160 mi. W of Recife; W terminus (1949) of railroad from Recife; ships cotton, tobacco, cattle. Has chalk and saltpeter quarries. Until 1944, called Alagoa de Baixo.

Sertanópolis (sĕrtŭnô′pōōlēs), city (pop. 2,803), N Paraná, Brazil, near Tibagi R., on road, and 18 mi. NNE of Londrina, in pioneer agr. zone; corn milling, coffee and rice processing, cotton ginning. Brick kilns.

Sertãozinho (sĕrtã″ōzē′nyōō). **1** City, Alagoas, Brazil: see MAJOR ISIDORO. **2** City (pop. 5,074), NE São Paulo, Brazil, on railroad and 11 mi. WNW of Ribeirão Prêto; sugar milling, distilling; coffee, cotton, fruit, sugar.

Serui, Netherlands New Guinea: see JAPEN ISLANDS.

Serum, India: see SERAM.

Serutu, Indonesia: see KARIMATA ISLANDS.

Servance (sĕrvãs′), village (pop. 250), Haute-Saône dept., E France, in the S Vosges, 13 mi. NE of Lure; resort. Weaving, hardware mfg. Granite quarries near by.

Servance, Ballon de (bälō dù), summit (3,900 ft.) of the S Vosges, E France, on Vosges–Haute-Saône dept. border, 4 mi. S of Le Thillot, topped by a fort.

Servia (sĕr′vēù), town (pop. 3,236), Kozane nome, Macedonia, Greece, on highway and 14 mi. SE of Kozane; timber, charcoal, wine; livestock; dairy products.

Servia, Yugoslavia: see SERBIA.

Servian (sĕrvyã′), town (pop. 2,681), Hérault dept., S France, 7 mi. NE of Béziers; distilling, winegrowing. Produces tools for viticulture.

Servoz (sĕrvōz′), Alpine village (pop. 150), Haute-Savoie dept., SE France, in Arve R. gorge and 5 mi. W of Chamonix; resort. Just NE is gorge of the Diosaz.

Seryshevo (syĕrĭshĕ′vù), town (1948 pop. over 500), S Amur oblast, Russian SFSR, on Trans-Siberian RR and 65 mi. NNE of Blagoveshchensk, in agr. area (wheat, livestock).

Sesa (sĕ′sä), village, Katanga prov., SE Belgian Congo, near railroad, 16 mi. NW of Jadotville; copper mining. Also copper mining at Shangulowe (shäng-gōōlō′wä), 8 mi. WNW.

Sesana, Yugoslavia: see SEZANA.

Seschi, Greece: see SESKLI.

Sescli, Greece: see SESKLI.

Sese (sĕ′sä), village, Western Prov., SW Gold Coast colony, on Butre R. (small coastal stream) and 11 mi. WSW of Takoradi; palm-oil mill.

Sese Islands (sĕ'sä), S Uganda, archipelago in NW L. Victoria, S of Entebbe. Includes c.15 isls.; largest, Bugala Isl. (W).

Seseña (säsä'nyä), town (pop. 1,180), Toledo prov., central Spain, 22 mi. S of Madrid; beans, potatoes, grapes, sugar beets, cereals, sheep.

Sesheke (sĕshĕ'kä), township (pop. 124), Barotse prov., SW Northern Rhodesia, on Zambezi R., at border of Caprivi Strip of South-West Africa, opposite Schukmansburg, and 70 mi. WNW of Livingstone; cattle, sheep, goats; corn, millet. Mission. Airfield.

Sesia River (sä'zyä), anc. *Sessites*, N Italy, rises 3 mi. N of Alagna Valsesia on Monte Rosa, flows S and E, past Varallo, and S, past Borgosesia and Vercelli, to Po R. 6 mi. E of Casale Monferrato; length, 86 mi. Irrigates over 130,000 acres. Crossed by Cavour Canal. Chief affluent, Cervo R. (right).

Sesimbra or **Sezimbra** (sĭzēm'brů), town (pop. 6,539), Setúbal dist., S central Portugal, on the Atlantic at foot of the Serra da Arrábida, 13 mi. SW of Setúbal; sardine-canning center; processing of fish fertilizer, textile and cordage weaving. Its castle was recaptured from the Moors (1165) by Alfonso I.

Seskaro (sĕs'kärû"), Swedish *Seskarö*, village (pop. 1,091), Norrbotten co., N Sweden, on Seskaron, Swedish *Seskarön*, isl. (□ 8) in Gulf of Bothnia, 13 mi. SW of Haparanda; sawmilling.

Seskli (sĕ'sklē), Ital. *Seschi* (sĕs'kē), Aegean island (□ .7; pop. 7) in the Dodecanese, Greece, off S tip of Syme isl., 20 mi. W of Rhodes city; 36°30'N 27°52'E. Sometimes spelled Sescli.

Sesma (sĕ'zmä), town (pop. 1,881), Navarre prov., N Spain, 14 mi. SSW of Estella; wine, cereals, olive oil. Gypsum quarries near by.

Sesori (säsō'rē), city (pop. 993), San Miguel dept., E Salvador, on Sesori R. (left affluent of the Lempa) and 20 mi. NW of San Miguel; grain, livestock raising. Gold, silver, and limestone mines near by. Became city in 1922.

Sesqui-Centennial State Park, S.C.: see COLUMBIA.

Sesquilé (säskēlā'), village (pop. 432), Cundinamarca dept., central Colombia, 36 mi. NE of Bogotá; alt. 8,661 ft.; saltworks.

Sessa Aurunca (sĕs'sä ourōōng'kä), town (pop. 5,017), Caserta prov., Campania, S Italy, near Monte Massico, 32 mi. NW of Naples, in wine- and fruitgrowing region. Bishopric. On site of anc. *Suessa Aurunca;* has Roman ruins (theater, bridge).

Ses Salines (sĕs' sälē'nĕs), town (pop. 1,233), Majorca, Balearic Isls., on railroad and 26 mi. SE of Palma; grain growing, stock raising; flour milling, mfg. of magnesium carbonate.

Sesser, city (pop. 2,086), Franklin co., S Ill., 17 mi. SSW of Mount Vernon; livestock, dairy products, corn, wheat. Inc. 1906.

Sessites, Italy: see SESIA RIVER.

Sesslach (zĕs'läkh), town (pop. 875), Upper Franconia, N Bavaria, Germany, on the Rodach and 7 mi. SW of Coburg; brewing, flour and lumber milling. Partly surrounded by medieval wall; has late-Gothic church. Chartered 1335.

Sestanovac (shĕ'stänôvăts), Serbo-Croatian *Šestanovac*, village, S Croatia, Yugoslavia, on Cetina R. and 10 mi. E of Omis, in Dalmatia. Hydroelectric plant, at Gubavica Falls of Cetina R., is at near-by Zadvarje. Sometimes spelled Shestanovats.

Sestao (sĕstä'ō), outer NW suburb (pop. 18,625) of Bilbao, Vizcaya prov., in the Basque provs., N Spain, on left bank of Nervión R. near its mouth; with Baracaldo (SE), it is leading siderurgical center of Spain. Terminus of mining railroads, with 1 mi. of ore-shipping docks and large basin protected by mole. Blast furnaces, coke ovens, tin-plate factory; shipyards construct boats up to 10,000 tons; also makes tubes, boilers, locomotives, and other machinery; cementworks. Iron mines in vicinity.

Sesteadero, El, Panama: see EL SESTEADERO.

Sestino (sĕstē'nô), village (pop. 575), Arezzo prov., Tuscany, central Italy, on upper Foglia R. and 13 mi. NE of Sansepolcro.

Sestín River, Mexico: see ORO, RÍO DEL.

Sesto Calende (sĕ'stô kälĕn'dĕ), town (pop. 2,842), Varese prov., Lombardy, N Italy, near efflux of Ticino R. from Lago Maggiore, 12 mi. SW of Varese. Rail junction; airplane mfg. center; textiles, glass, pottery.

Sesto Fiorentino (sĕ'stô fyôrĕntē'nô), town (pop. 10,021), Firenze prov., Tuscany, central Italy, 5 mi. NW of Florence; large ceramics industry (porcelain); mfg. (soap, cement, straw hats, candy, metal products).

Sestos or **Sestus** (sĕ'stŭs), anc. town on Thracian shore of the Hellespont (Dardanelles) opposite Abydos, scene of legend of Hero and Leander and site of Xerxes' crossing by means of a bridge of boats. Its site is just NE of modern town of Eceabat, Turkey in Europe.

Sesto San Giovanni (sĕ'stô sän jôvän'nē), industrial NE suburb (pop. 31,394) of Milan, Lombardy, N Italy; foundries, rolling mills, glassworks; mfg. (elevators, chemicals, alcohol, plastics).

Sestriere (sĕstrēä'rē), village (pop. 108), Torino prov., Piedmont, NW Italy, in Cottian Alps, 8 mi. E of Montgenèvre Pass. Summer resort (alt. 6,668 ft.); also winter sports. Formerly Sestrières, its Fr. name.

Sestri Levante (sä'strē lĕvän'tĕ), town (pop. 5,063), Genova prov., Liguria, N Italy, port on Gulf of Genoa and 25 mi. ESE of Genoa; shipyard; fisheries; canneries. Winter resort, bathing place. Copper mine at Libiola, 3 mi. NE.

Sestri Ponente (pônĕn'tĕ), town (pop. 26,374), Genova prov., Liguria, N Italy, port on Gulf of Genoa and 4 mi. W of Genoa, within Greater Genoa; industrial center; iron- and steelworks, shipyards, railroad shops, tanneries, mfg. (soap, tobacco, munitions), cooperage. Wine and flower trade.

Sestroretsk (syĕstrŭrĕtsk'), former city (1935 pop. 24,400), NW Leningrad oblast, Russian SFSR; since 1946 within Leningrad city limits, on Gulf of Finland, 16 mi. NW of city center; bathing and health resort.

Sestu (sä'stōō), village (pop. 4,392), Cagliari prov., S Sardinia, 5 mi. N of Cagliari, in vineyard area.

Sesupe River, Lithuania and Russian SFSR: see SHESHUPE RIVER.

Sesvenna, Piz, Switzerland: see PIZ SESVENNA.

Seta (sä'tä), town (pop. 9,629), Shiga prefecture, S Honshu, Japan, on S shore of L. Biwa, at mouth of Seta R. (upper course of Yodo R.), and 10 mi. ESE of Kyoto; commercial center for agr. area (rice, sweet potatoes, market produce). Connected with Otsu (NW) by bridge.

Setabganj, E Pakistan: see DINAJPUR, town.

Setaka (sätä'kä), town (pop. 20,083), Fukuoka prefecture, W Kyushu, Japan, 11 mi. SE of Saga; agr. center (rice, wheat, millet, sweet potatoes); mulberry groves.

Setamai (sätämī'), town (pop. 6,244), Iwate prefecture, N Honshu, Japan, 19 mi. WSW of Kamaishi; gold, silver, copper mining.

Setana (sätä'nä), town (pop. 5,847), SW Hokkaido, Japan, on Sea of Japan, 50 mi. SW of Iwanai; fishing, agr. (soybeans, rice, potatoes).

Seta River, Japan: see YODO RIVER.

Setauket (sĕtô'kĭt, sĭ-), resort village, Suffolk co., SE N.Y., on N shore of Long Isl., on Setauket Harbor (W arm of Port Jefferson Harbor), 2 mi. W of Port Jefferson village. Caroline Church (1729) is one of oldest on Long Isl.

Sète (sĕt), city (pop. 29,914), Hérault dept., S France, on the Mediterranean, on a tongue of land bet. Étang de THAU and the Gulf of Lion, 17 mi. SW of Montpellier; 43°24'N 3°42'E. France's second Mediterranean commercial port, at terminus of Canal du MIDI and RHONE-SÈTE CANAL. Wine-shipping center. Has important chemical factories (salt, superphosphates, sulphur); produces vermouth, wine casks, and electrical equipment; petroleum refining, sardine canning, olive preserving. Site of marine zoological station of Montpellier univ. Lies at the foot of rocky Mont-Saint-Clair (alt. 591 ft.), which once was an offshore isl. City was founded in 17th cent. by Colbert and fortified in 18th cent. Heavily damaged during Second World War. Formerly spelled Cette.

Sete Cidades (sĕ'tĭ sēdä'dĭsh), village (pop. 602), Ponta Delgada dist., E Azores, in W part of São Miguel Isl., 11 mi. NW of Ponta Delgada; resort at edge of the Lagoa Grande, the largest of several crater lakes within the huge Caldeira das Sete Cidades (crater, 3 mi. in diameter; formed by prehistoric eruptions; assumed present shape in 1445). The contrasting blue and green waters of neighboring lakes constitute the chief object of tourist interest.

Seteia or **Sitia** (both: sētē'ŭ), town (pop. 3,207), Lasethi nome, E Crete, on small Gulf of Seteia on N coast, 26 mi. E of Hagios Nikolaos. Trades in carobs, olives, raisins; olive oil.

Sete Lagoas (sĕ'tĭ lŭgō'ŭs), city (pop. 10,537), central Minas Gerais, Brazil, on railroad and 35 mi. NW of Belo Horizonte. State's chief marble-quarrying and quartz-crystal-mining center; textile mills. Ships sugar, cotton, cereals. Has experimental wheat station.

Setenil (sätänēl'), town (pop. 3,535), Cádiz prov., SW Spain, in N spur of the Cordillera Penibética, 8 mi. N of Ronda; olives, acorns, cereals, livestock; olive-oil pressing, flour milling, liquor distilling, dairying.

Setentrional, Cordillera (kôrdĭyä'rä sätĕntrēōnäl'), range, N Dominican Republic, parallel to the Cordillera Central and along the Atlantic coast, extending c.120 mi. ESE from Monte Cristi to Escocesa Bay; rises to 4,003 ft.

Sete Pontes (sĕtĭ pōn'tĭs), NE suburb (pop. 24,017) of Niterói, Rio de Janeiro state, Brazil, just E of Neves.

Sete Quedas, Ilha das, Brazil: see GRANDE, ILHA.

Sete Quedas Falls, Brazil and Paraguay: see GUAIRA FALLS.

Setesdal (sä'tŭsdäl), steep, narrow, long valley largely in Aust-Agder co., S Norway, extending from the highlands of Haukelifjell (in Hordaland co.) S through Bykle Mts., whence it is drained by the Otra to the Byglandsfjord N of Kristiansand. Long an isolated area, the valley people have retained their ancient dress, speech, architecture, and customs. Agr., fishing, lumbering, cattle raising; handicrafts. Sometimes spelled Saetersdal.

Seth, village (pop. 1,033), Boone co., SW W.Va., 11 mi. ENE of Madison, in coal-mining and agr. region.

Seth Ward, village (pop. 1,035), Hale co., NW Texas.

Sétif (sātēf'), anc. *Sitifis*, city (pop. 39,883), Constantine dept., NE Algeria, in the High Plateaus (alt. 3,600 ft.) just S of Little Kabylia's Babor range, 70 mi. WSW of Constantine; grain and livestock market, and communications center on Algiers-Constantine railroad; flour milling, woodworking, carpet mfg. Zinc mines in mts. (N). Founded as a veterans' colony in 1st cent. A.D., it became a leading city of Mauretania in 3d cent. French established a fortified post here in 1838.

Setiles (sätē'lĕs), town (pop. 759), Guadalajara prov., central Spain, 16 mi. ESE of Molina; iron mining. Also produces grain and sheep.

Seti River, Nepal: see GOGRA RIVER.

Setit River, Ethiopia and Anglo-Egyptian Sudan: see TAKKAZE RIVER.

Set Mahet (sät' mŭhät'), extensive Buddhist ruins on Gonda-Bahraich dist. border, NE Uttar Pradesh, India, 10 mi. NW of Balrampur. Site of anc. *Sravasti* where the Buddha performed his miracle of levitation while preaching to 6 heretics. Kushan inscriptions, monastery ruins; many antiquities removed to Provincial Mus. at Lucknow. One of 8 great places of Buddhist pilgrimage in anc. times. Also spelled Saheth Maheth.

Seto (sä'tō). **1** City (1940 pop. 45,775; 1947 pop. 42,788), Aichi prefecture, central Honshu, Japan, 12 mi. E of Nagoya; terminus of electric railroad from Nagoya; important porcelain center since 13th cent. Site of natl. ceramic experiment station. **2** Town (pop. 6,758), Nagasaki prefecture, W Kyushu, Japan, on W coast of Sonogi Peninsula, 18 mi. NW of Nagasaki; rice, wheat, sweet potatoes. Fishing. **3** Town (pop. 4,121), Okayama prefecture, SW Honshu, Japan, 7 mi. NE of Okayama, in agr. area (rice, wheat, citrus fruit); raw silk, floor mats, sake. Sawmilling. **4** Town, Tokushima prefecture, Japan: see MUYA. **5** Town, Wakayama prefecture, Japan: see SHIRAHAMA.

Seto-chi-umi, Japan: see INLAND SEA.

Setoda (sätō'dä), largest town (pop. 10,972) on Ikuchi-jima, Hiroshima prefecture, Japan, on W coast of isl.; fishing port; agr. center (rice, wheat).

Seto-kanayama, Japan: see SHIRAHAMA, Wakayama prefecture.

Seton, Scotland: see COCKENZIE AND PORT SETON.

Seto-naikai, Japan: see INLAND SEA.

Seton Lake (sē'tŭn) (14 mi. long, 1 mi. wide), SW B.C., in Coast Mts., 3 mi. WSW of Lillooet, just E of Anderson L. Drains E into Fraser R.

Settat (sĕt-tät'), city (pop. 27,064), Casablanca region, W Fr. Morocco, on railroad and 40 mi. S of Casablanca, in wheat-growing area; agr. trade and flour-milling center; active commerce in skins, leather, wool, grain, truck produce; mfg. of soap and fruit preserves. Occupied by Fr. in 1908.

Setté-Cama (sĕtā-kämä'), village, W Gabon, Fr. Equatorial Africa, on the coast near the mouth of Setté Cama lagoon (also called N'Dogo lagoon), 140 mi. SSE of Port-Gentil; shipping point for hardwood-lumbering area; fisheries.

Sette Comuni, Italy: see ASIAGO.

Settimo Torinese (sĕt'tēmô tôrēnä'zē), town (pop. 7,598), Torino prov., Piedmont, NW Italy, near Po R., 6 mi. NNE of Turin; rail junction; bricks, cement, buttons, automatic pencils.

Setting Lake (□ 65), central Man., 70 mi. N of L. Winnipeg; 28 mi. long, 3 mi. wide. Drains N into Nelson R.

Settle, town and parish (pop. 2,455), West Riding, W Yorkshire, England, on Ribble R. and 13 mi. NW of Skipton; leather tanning, cotton and paper milling. Has mus. and many 17th-cent. houses. Just E is Castleberg hill.

Settlement Island, Tasmania: see MACQUARIE HARBOUR.

Settons, Les, France: see MONTSAUCHE.

Settsu (sät'tsōō), former province in S Honshu, Japan; now part of Osaka and Hyogo prefectures.

Settur (sät'tōōr), town (pop. 15,348), Ramnad dist., S Madras, India, 6 mi. SW of Rajapalaiyam, in agr. area.

Setúbal (sĭtōō'bŭl), district (□ 1,971, including interior waters 2,016; pop. 268,884), S central Portugal, forming part of Baixo Alentejo and Estremadura provinces; ⊙ Setúbal. Borders on the Atlantic; in N, it is separated from Lisbon dist. by Tagus estuary (Lisbon Bay). The mouth of the Sado (which drains dist.) forms an almost enclosed inlet of the sea, thus providing Setúbal city with a sheltered harbor. Intensive agr. (vineyards, citrus and olive groves, cereals), especially on peninsula bet. Tagus and Sado estuaries. Cork-oak forests, rice fields. Principal industry of Setúbal city and smaller fishing ports (Sines, Sesimbra) is sardine canning. Saltworks along lower Sado R. Diversified consumer industries in Lisbon's suburbs lining S shore of Lisbon Bay.

Setúbal, city (pop. 37,071), ⊙ Setúbal dist., in Estremadura prov., S central Portugal, seaport at mouth of Sado R. and 20 mi. SE of Lisbon; 3d-largest city of continental Portugal, with a harbor next only to that of Lisbon; major sardine-canning center; industries include mfg. of fertilizer, cement, pottery, biscuits, corks, soft drinks; boatbuilding, distilling. Important commerce in noted muscatel wine and in fine oranges grown in area. Saltworks in Sado R. marshes. Setúbal was a royal residence (1481–95) under John II. Its old historic buildings were destroyed in the disastrous earthquake of 1755. Along coast W of city rises the scenic Arrábida range. City is noted for its delightful climate. Formerly frequently called, in English, Saint Ubes or Saint Yves.

Setúbal Bay, inlet of the Atlantic off W coast of Portugal, bounded by Cape Espichel (NW) and by Cape Sines (S); 35 mi. wide, 20 mi. long. Receives Sado R. Setúbal city on Sado estuary is sheltered from the bay by a sand bar reaching almost across river mouth.

Seudre River (sû'drů), Charente-Maritime dept., W France, rises near Saint-Genis-de-Saintonge, flows 43 mi. NW, past Saujon, to the Bay of Biscay opposite S end of Île d'Oléron, forming 12-mi.-long marshy estuary rich in oyster- and mussel-beds.

Seugne River (sû'nyů), Charente-Maritime dept., W France, rises near Montlieu, flows 47 mi. NNW, past Jonzac and Pons, into the Charente 7 mi. above Saintes.

Seui (sĕōō'ē), village (pop. 2,973), Nuoro prov., E central Sardinia, 33 mi. S of Nuoro. Anthracite mines here and at Seulo (5 mi. NW).

Seul, Lac (läk sûl'), lake (□ 416), NW Ont.; 50°30'N 92°W; alt. 1,172 ft. Drained W by English R. Near SE shore is Sioux Lookout.

Seulles River (sûl), Calvados dept., NW France, rises in Normandy Hills near Villers-Bocage, flows c.25 mi. NNE to the Channel at Courseulles.

Seulo, Sardinia: see SEUI.

Seurre (sûr), town (pop. 2,090), Côte-d'Or dept., E central France, on Saône R. and 14 mi. E of Beaune; produces prosthetic devices, cheese, starch.

Seuva, Balearic Isls.: see SELVA.

Sevagram (sā'vŭgrŭm, shā'vŭ–) [Hindi,=village of service], until 1940 called **Segaon** (sā'goun), village, Wardha dist., central Madhya Pradesh, India, 4 mi. ESE of Wardha. Model community, founded by Mahatma Gandhi in 1936; his residence until his death in 1948 (in New Delhi) and the focus of his efforts in behalf of India's independence and of other landmarks of his lifework. Here Gandhi developed his 2 major institutions for revival of village economy, the All-India Spinners' Assn. (hq. and training center here) and the All-India Village Industries Assn. (hq. and training center at Wardha). Other institutions here continuing Gandhi's work include associations for furthering his scheme of education centering on a craft, spreading Hindustani as a natl. language of India, improving social conditions of casteless Hindus (formerly called untouchables; designated scheduled castes by constitution of 1950), and studying methods of nonviolence. Gandhi's own domicile, a small mud hut, is now a natl. shrine. Adjacent village of Gopuri (called Nalwadi until 1940) is a center for *charka* (spinning wheel) mfg. and has experimental farm (dairying, cattle breeding) and tannery.

Sevan (syĭvän'), town (1939 pop. 2,700), central Armenian SSR, on NW shore of L. Sevan, at Zanga R. outlet, 35 mi. NNE of Erivan; sawmills, metalworks; fisheries. Site of Ozernaya underground hydroelectric station, powered by 4-mi. tunnel draining water from L. Sevan into Zanga R. Until c.1935, called Yelenovka.

Sevan, Lake, largest (□ 546) lake in Transcaucasia, in central Armenian SSR; 45 mi. long, 25 mi. wide, 325 ft. deep; alt. 6,285 ft.; rocky shores. Fed by c.30 inlets, it has only one outlet, the ZANGA RIVER. Remains ice-free in winter; abounds in trout. Sevan Isl., 1 mi. offshore, in extreme NW, is site of old Armenian monastery, now a rest home. Sevan-Zanga hydroelectric project (started in 1930) began to drain larger, shallower SE section, restricting lake area to smaller, deeper NW part and reducing yearly evaporation loss. Formerly called Gokcha, Turkish *Gökçe*.

Sevaruyo (sävärōō'yō), village (pop. c.1,300), Oruro dept., W Bolivia, in the Altiplano, 100 mi. S of Oruro, on Oruro-Uyuni RR; alt. 12,300 ft.; barley, potatoes, quinoa; mineral springs, salt deposits.

Sevastopol (sĭvă'stūpōl', Rus. syĕvŭstô'pŭl), city (1939 pop. 111,946), S Crimea, Russian SFSR, port on Black Sea, 190 mi. SE of Odessa, 37 mi. SW of Simferopol; 44°37'N 33°32'E. Major Black Sea naval base and shipbuilding center; fish processing (refrigerating plant), light mfg., tanning, flour milling. Site of institute of physiotherapy, biological marine research station, regional mus., picture gall., mus., and panoramic replica of 19th-cent. defense of Sevastopol. Its Peter-Paul cathedral is copy of temple of Theseus at Athens. City proper is on S shore of Bay of Sevastopol or Severnaya Bukhta [Rus.,=northern bay], an inlet (4 mi. long, ½ mi. wide) of Black Sea; bounded E by Yuzhnaya Bukhta [Rus.,=southern bay], an arm of N bay. Across S bay lies E suburb of Korabelnaya Storona [Rus.,=ship's side], dominated by MALAKHOV hill. Across Bay of Sevastopol, in N suburb, is common grave of over 100,000 participants of siege of Sevastopol (1854–55). Included within city limits are major part of so-called Chersonese peninsula (projection of land bet. Bay of Sevastopol and Black Sea), a littoral strip extending 15 mi. N from city, and INKERMAN. On peninsula, 3 mi. W of Sevastopol, are excavations and mus. of ruins of anc. Gr. colony of Chersonesus Heracleotica (founded 5th cent. B.C. by Heraclea Pontica), which flourished later as Byzantine trade center, known to Slavs as Korsun. Sevastopol was founded (16th cent.) as Tatar village of Akhtiar; renamed after annexation (1783) by Russians; became their chief Black Sea naval base and important commercial port. During Crimean War, stormed and destroyed by allied Fr., Br., and Turkish troops following memorable 11-month siege (1854–55). Fortified again after 1870, it ceased to be (1890) a trading port and remained solely a major military base. During First World War, shelled (1914) by Germans; hq. of Wrangel army in Rus. civil war. Besieged 8 months during Second World War; fell (July, 1942) to Germans and recaptured (1944) by Soviet troops. In 1948, Sevastopol was constituted into an independent administrative-economic unit within the Russian SFSR. Formerly also spelled Sebastopol.

Sevelen (zā'vůlůn), town (pop. 2,137), St. Gall canton, E Switzerland, near the Rhine and Liechtenstein border, 2 mi. SW of Vaduz, Liechtenstein; woolen textiles, woodworking.

Seven Brothers Mountain (8,547 ft.), SW N.Mex., in Mimbres Mts., 30 mi. ENE of Silver City.

Seven Devils Mountains, in Adams and Idaho counties, W Idaho, in Weiser Natl. Forest; extend N–S and form E wall of Grand Canyon of the Snake R. (part of Oregon line). Chief peaks are Monument Peak (8,956 ft.) and HE DEVIL MOUNTAIN (9,387 ft.).

Seven Falls, Colo: see COLORADO SPRINGS.

Seven Harbors, village (pop. 1,385, with adjacent White Lake), Oakland co., SE Mich., 15 mi. WNW of Pontiac.

Seven Hills, village (pop. 1,350), Cuyahoga co., N Ohio, a S suburb of Cleveland.

Seven Hundred Acre Island (□ c.2), Waldo co., S Maine, in Penobscot Bay off Lincolnville.

Seven Hunters, Scotland: see FLANNAN ISLES.

Seven Islands, village, Que.: see SEPT ÎLES.

Seven Islands, group of 7 islets in the St. Lawrence, E Que., off Sept Îles village, opposite Gaspé Peninsula, at entrance at Seven Islands Bay. High, steep, and rocky; rise to 500 ft.

Seven Islands, France: see SEPT-ÎLES.

Seven Islands Bay, shallow inlet (10 mi. long, 12 mi. wide at mouth) of the Atlantic, NE Labrador, at entrance of Kangalaksiorvik Fiord (extends 10 mi. W inland); 59°25'N 63°40'W. Contains several isls. and islets; largest are Avigalik or Whale Isl. and Amiktok Isl. Bay is surrounded by high mts.

Seven Mile, village (pop. 569), Butler co., extreme SW Ohio, 6 mi. N of Hamilton and on small Seven Mile Creek; cement products.

Seven Mile Beach, S N.J., barrier isl. (c.7 mi. long) bet. Great Sound and the Atlantic, off Cape May Peninsula; site of Avalon and Stone Harbor resorts; 2 bridges to mainland.

Sevenoaks, residential urban district (1931 pop. 10,484; 1951 census 14,834), W Kent, England, near Darent R. 15 mi. W of Maidstone. Has 15th-cent. church and grammar school founded 1432. Near by is "Knole," seat of Lord Sackville, built mainly by Archbishop Bourchier in 15th cent.; has large park.

Seven Pagodas, India: see MAHABALIPURAM.

Seven Pines, village (pop. 3,902, with near-by Sandston), Henrico co., E central Va., E of Richmond. Civil War battle of FAIR OAKS is sometimes called battle of Seven Pines.

Seven Sisters, mountain (9,140 ft.), W B.C., in Coast Mts., 100 mi. ENE of Prince Rupert.

Seven Sisters Falls, waterfalls, SE Man., on Winnipeg R., at N end of Natalie L., 50 mi. ENE of Winnipeg; hydroelectric-power center.

Seven Springs, town (pop. 197), Wayne co., E central N.C., 13 mi. SE of Goldsboro and on Neuse R. State park near by. Officially Whitehall.

Seven Troughs Range, NW Nev., in Pershing co., SE of Black Rock Desert. Rises to 7,497 ft. in Seven Troughs Mtn., 27 mi. NW of Lovelock. Small-scale mining (chiefly gold and silver).

Seven Valleys, borough (pop. 437), York co., S Pa., 8 mi. S of York.

Seven Weeks Poort (pōōrt), mountain (7,628 ft.), SW Cape Prov., U. of So. Afr., in Little Swartberg range, 8 mi. NE of Ladismith; 33°24'S 21°23'E; highest peak in W Cape Prov.

Sévérac-le-Château (sāvārăk'-lŭ-shätō'), village (pop. 924), Aveyron dept., S France, near the Aveyron, 15 mi. N of Millau; agr. market. Bituminous schists mined near by.

Severance (sĕ'vůrůns). **1** Town (pop. 108), Weld co., N Colo., 10 mi. NW of Greeley, in irrigated grain area; alt. 4,900 ft.; sugar beets. **2** City (pop. 197), Doniphan co., NE Kansas, 20 mi. W of St. Joseph, Mo.; agr. (chiefly apples).

Sever do Vouga (sĕvĕr' dōō vō'gů), town, Aveiro dist., N central Portugal, near Vouga R., 17 mi. ENE of Aveiro; paper milling.

Severgin Peak, Russian SFSR: see KHARIMKOTAN ISLAND.

Severgin Strait (sĕ'vyĭrgĭn), Jap. *Shasukotan-kaikyo*, in N main Kurile Isls. group, Russian SFSR; separates Kharimkotan Isl. (N) and Shiashkotan Isl. (S); 17 mi. wide.

Severin, Rumania: see CARANSEBES.

Severn (sĕ'vůrn), town (pop. 340), Northampton co., NE N.C., 7 mi. NW of Murfreesboro.

Severna Park (sĭvûr'nů), resort village (pop., with adjacent Round Bay, 1,095), Anne Arundel co., central Md., on Severn R. c.7 mi. above Annapolis.

Severnaya [Rus.,=NORTH, NORTHERN], in Rus. names: see also SEVERNIYE, SEVERNOYE, SEVERNY, SEVERO-.

Severnaya Dvina River, Russian SFSR: see DVINA RIVER (Northern Dvina).

Severnaya Zemlya (sĕ'vyĭrnŭ zĭmlyä') [Rus.,= north land or northern land], archipelago (□ 14,300) in Arctic Ocean, N of Taimyr Peninsula, in Krasnoyarsk Territory, Russian SFSR; extends from 77°50'N to 81°15'N; separates Kara and Laptev seas. Main isls.: Komsomolets, Pioner, Oktyabrskaya Revolyutsiya, Bolshevik. Discovered 1913 by Vilkitski. Formerly called Zemlya Imperatora Nikolaya II [Rus.,=Emperor Nicholas II Land].

Severniye [Rus.,=NORTH, NORTHERN], in Rus. names: see also SEVERNAYA, SEVERNY, SEVERO-.

Severnoye [Rus.,=NORTH, NORTHERN], in Rus. names: see also SEVERNAYA, SEVERNY, SEVERO-.

Severnoye (sĕ'vyĭrnŭyů). **1** Village (1939 pop. over 500), NW Novosibirsk oblast, Russian SFSR, on Tartas R. and 70 mi. N of Barabinsk. **2** Town (1939 pop. over 500), E Stalino oblast, Ukrainian SSR, 4 mi. NNW of Snezhnoye; coal mines.

Severn River, Australia: see DUMARESQ RIVER.

Severn River (sĕ'vůrn). **1** In S central Ont., leaves N end of L. Couchiching (short channel connects S with L. Simcoe), flows 30 mi. WNW to Georgian Bay of L. Huron N of Waubaushene. Forms part of inland waterway system, linking Georgian Bay and L. Ontario, via L. Simcoe and Trent Canal. **2** In NW Ont., rises in Finger Lake area of Patricia dist., flows 420 mi. NE to Hudson Bay. At its mouth is Fort Severn, trading post.

Severn River, anc. *Sabrina*, Wales and England, rises on E slope of Plinlimmon Fawr, Wales, flows c.200 mi. NE, SE, S, and SW, past Llanidloes, Welshpool, Shrewsbury, Bridgnorth, Stourport, Worcester, Gloucester, and Avonmouth, where it enters Bristol Channel. Receives Teme, Wye, Usk, Taff, Upper Avon, and Lower Avon rivers. It is connected by canals with Thames, Mersey, Trent, and other rivers, and forms important inland transportation route. Navigable below Welshpool. Rail tunnel, c.4 mi. long, built by Sir John Hawkshaw in 1886, passes under river below Chepstow.

Severn River, central Md., estuary (c.15 mi. long) entering Chesapeake Bay in Anne Arundel co.; Annapolis (site of U.S. Naval Acad.) is on right bank, at head of deep-water channel. Greenbury Point (site of naval radio station and offshore light) is at N side of mouth.

Severny or **Severnyy** [Rus.,=NORTH, NORTHERN], in Rus. names: see also SEVERNAYA, SEVERNOYE, SEVERO-.

Severny, Russian SFSR: see KYSHTYM.

Severny Cape, Russian SFSR: see SHMIDT, CAPE.

Severnykh Promyslov Ozera No. 6, Poselok, Turkmen SSR: see SARTAS.

Severny Kommunar or **Severnyy Kommunar** (sĕ'vyĭrnē kŭmōōnär'), town (1942 pop. over 500), W Molotov oblast, Russian SFSR, 34 mi. NW of Vereshchagino; mfg. (paper, cardboard).

Severny Suchan or **Severnyy Suchan** (sōōchän'), town (1947 pop. over 500), S Maritime Territory, Russian SFSR; N suburb of Suchan; coal mining.

Severnyy Donets River, USSR: see DONETS RIVER.

Severo-[Rus. combining form,=NORTH, NORTHERN], in Rus. names: see also SEVERNAYA, SEVERNIYE, SEVERNOYE, SEVERNY.

Severokamsk, Russian SFSR: see KRASNOKAMSK.

Severo-Kazakhstan, oblast, Karakh SSR: see NORTH KAZAKHSTAN.

Severo-Kurilsk or **Severo-Kuril'sk** (sĕ'vyĭrŭ-kōōrēlsk'), city (1947 pop. over 2,000), on NE coast of Paramushir Isl., Kurile Isls., Russian SFSR, port on Second Kurile Strait opposite Baikovo (Shumshu Isl.); 50°41'N 156°08'E. Fish-canning center; naval installations, airfield. Sulphur deposits near by. Under Jap. rule (until 1945), called Kashiwabara (kä'shēwä'bärä).

Severouralsk or **Severoural'sk** (–ōōrälsk'), city (1939 pop. under 2,000; 1946 pop. estimate 30,000), N Sverdlovsk oblast, Russian SFSR, in E foothills of the N Urals, on right tributary of Sosva R. and 43 mi. NE of Serov, near railroad (Boksity station). Major bauxite-mining center, based on Krasnaya Shapochka mtn. deposits. Supplies Krasnoturinsk aluminum works. Largely developed during Second World War; became city in 1944. Formerly called Petropavlovski.

Severovostochny Cape, Russian SFSR: see CHELYUSKIN, CAPE.

Severo-Yeniseiski or **Severo-Yeniseyskiy** (–yĕnyĭsyā'skē), town (1933 pop. estimate 5,100), central Krasnoyarsk Territory, Russian SFSR, on Yenisei Ridge, 140 mi. NE of Yeniseiski; gold-mining.

Severskaya (–skīŭ), village (1926 pop. 7,956), W Krasnodar Territory, Russian SFSR, on railroad and 7 mi. SW of Krasnodar, in tobacco and wheat area; flour and sunflower-oil milling.

Severski, Russian SFSR: see POLEVSKOI.

Severy (sĕ'vûrē), city (pop. 477), Greenwood co., SE Kansas, 14 mi. SSE of Eureka, in grain, poultry, and livestock region. Oil wells near by.

Seveso (sä'vězô), town (pop. 6,753), Milano prov., Lombardy, N Italy, 13 mi. N of Milan; rail junction; furniture mfg. center; silk textiles, tanning, glass.

Sevier (sůvēr'). **1** County (□ 585; pop. 12,293), SW Ark.; ⊙ De Queen. Bounded W by Okla. line, S by Little R., E by Saline R.; drained by small Rolling Fork and Cossatot R. Rich truck-farm area (fruit, vegetables); cotton, livestock, dairy products; timber. Mfg. at De Queen. Formed 1828. **2** County (□ 603; pop. 23,375), E Tenn.; ⊙ Sevierville. Bounded S and SE by N.C.; Great Smoky Mts. along S border, with Clingmans Dome (6,643 ft.; highest point in state), Mt. Guyot (6,621 ft.; on N.C. line), and Mt. Le Conte (6,593 ft.). Drained by French Broad R. and small Little Pigeon R. Includes Douglas Dam and part of Douglas Reservoir. Lumbering, agr. (livestock, fruit, tobacco, corn, hay). Formed 1794. **3** County (□ 1,932; pop. 12,072), central Utah; ⊙ Richfield. Mtn. and plateau region crossed by Sevier R. Sections of Fishlake Natl. Forest throughout. Livestock, hay, sugar beets, fruit, truck. Formed 1865.

Sevier Lake, shrinking salt lake in Great Basin, Millard co., W Utah, 35 mi. SW of Delta; 18 mi. long, max. width 7 mi. (formerly 24 mi. long, 9 mi. wide). Receives Sevier R.

Sevier Plateau, in Sevier, Piute, and Garfield counties, S Utah; extends N–S along E bank of Sevier R. through parts of Fishlake and Powell natl. forests. Mt. Dutton (10,800 ft.) is S of East Fork Sevier R. (crossing plateau E–W). SIGNAL PEAK (11,223 ft.) and MONROE PEAK (11,226 ft.) are in N half of plateau.

Sevier River, formed by confluence of Panguitch and Assay creeks just N of Panguitch, SW Utah, flows 240 mi. N, past Tushar and Pavant mts., then 85 mi. SW, past Delta and through desert area, to Sevier L.; total length, 325 mi. Piute Reservoir (4 mi. long, half dry; near Junction), Sevier Bridge Reservoir (11 mi. long; NNW of Gunnison), and Sevier River Reservoir (3.5 mi. long; NE of Delta), formed by small dams, are used for irrigation. Livestock and agr. (especially alfalfa seed) in river valley. Tributaries: San Pitch and East Fork Sevier rivers.

Sevierville (sůvēr'vĭl), town (pop. 1,620), ⊙ Sevier co., E Tenn., 22 mi. ESE of Knoxville; trade center for timber and farm area; mfg. of hosiery, furniture, canned foods; lumber and flour milling. Great Smoky Mts. Natl. Park is S, Douglas Dam (French Broad R.) is N. Laid out 1795.

Sevilla (sävē'yä), town (pop. 10,450), Valle del Cauca dept., W Colombia, in Cauca valley, 33 mi. S of Cartago; agr. center (coffee, sugar cane, tobacco, cacao, bananas, yucca, cereals, stock). Silver, gold, platinum are mined near by.

Sevilla de Niefang, Sp. Guinea: see NIEFANG.

Sevilla la Nueva (sävē'lyä lä nwä'vä), town (pop. 460), Madrid prov , central Spain, 18 mi. W of Madrid; cereals, grapes, livestock.

Sevilla Nueva, Jamaica: see SAINT ANN'S BAY.

Sevilla River (sävē'yä), Camagüey prov., E Cuba, rises just E of Hatuey, flows c.50 mi. S to the Gulf of Guacanayabo opposite small Sevilla keys.

Seville, Jamaica: see SAINT ANN'S BAY.

Seville (sůvĭl'), Sp. *Sevilla* (sävē'lyä), province (□ 5,409; pop. 963,044), SW Spain, in ANDALUSIA; ⊙ Seville. Bounded by Badajoz prov. (N), Córdoba prov. (E), Málaga prov. (SE), Cádiz prov. (S), Huelva prov. (W). Though an interior prov., it is close to the Atlantic, easily reached by the navigable Guadalquivir, which crosses it, watering a wide, fertile plain. Low, broken mtn. ranges are formed in N by the Sierra Morena, in SE by spurs of the Cordillera Penibética. The climate is remarkable for its mildness, but excessive temperatures occur in summer. Marshlands, called here Las Marismas, adjoin the Guadalquivir estuary, and are a network of river arms and isls., well suited for stock raising; rice culture was introduced here in 1930s. The prov. is predominantly agr., exporting olives and olive oil, grapes, wine, wheat and other grain, beet sugar, oranges, chick-peas, cotton. Processing industries: vegetable-oil distilling, flour milling, canning, tanning, wine and liquor making. Mining is also important; main resources are in the Sierra Morena and include copper, iron, lead, silver, barite, manganese, aluminum silicate, graphite, salt, and coal. The wooded ranges yield various kinds of timber (oak, poplar, pine, etc.); also cork and acorns. The Guadalquivir and its many affluents (Genil, Carbones, Guadaira) are good fishing grounds. Game abounds. Industrial center and major port is Seville city. Other important cities are Écija, Utrera, Carmona, Morón, Osuna, Lebrija, Marchena. One of Spain's most historic regions, with great wealth of Roman and Moorish remains.

Seville, Sp. *Sevilla*, anc. *Hispalis*, leading city (pop. 270,126; commune pop. 312,123) of Andalusia, ⊙ Seville prov., SW Spain, major inland port (c.50 mi. from the Atlantic) on left bank of the tidal Guadalquivir, and 60 mi. NNE of Cádiz, 240 mi. SW of Madrid; 37°2'N 6°1'W. The 4th largest city of Spain and one of its most colorful, it is universally known for its great artistic and historic tradition, though equally important as commercial and industrial center of the entire region. Situated on a fertile plain, surrounded by beautiful gardens, Seville has a delightful, mild winter climate, with excessive temperatures only in summer. This most typical of Andalusian cities is celebrated for its grace and gay fiestas, which make it a popular tourist mecca. Upon the city converge railroad lines from Madrid, Córdoba, Granada, Cádiz, and Huelva. A transatlantic port since the discovery of America, it now exports chiefly wine, olives and olive oil, fruit, wool, cork, mercury, iron and lead pyrites. Dredging and the construction of canals, which circumvent the windings of the Guadalquivir, have enabled it to maintain its status as leading outlet for the interior. Its numerous mfg. establishments include tobacco factories, govt.-owned ammunition plants, metalworks and foundries, railroad shops, potteries, flour and rice mills, liquor distilleries, breweries, fish canneries. Mfg. also of fertilizers, pharmaceuticals, perfumes, soap, glass- and chinaware, carpets, yarns, silk cloth, cotton and woolen goods, furniture, matches, electrical equipment, bicycles, processed olives, and cork. Seville is an archbishopric (since time of the Visigoths), and seat of a univ. (founded 1502). With its many low, mostly one-storied houses, the city covers a relatively large area. Modernization has not destroyed its unique, primarily Moorish character. In the old quarters are tortuous, narrow streets, intersected by fine squares, along which lie the typical whitewashed houses with their balconies, patios, and wrought-iron work. Its admirable monuments include the alcazar, the Moorish palace built in pure Mudejar style during 12th cent. and equaling the Alhambra in its exquisite decorations, beautiful halls, chapels, fountains, and gardens. The adjoining cathedral is among the largest in Christendom; it was begun in 1402 on site of an old mosque; Arabic and plateresque features have been added to its immense Gothic structure. The chapels are adorned with works of the great Sp. painters, such as Murillo, Zurbarán, Valdés Leal, El Greco, Alonso Cano, who are, however, represented to even greater advantage in the art gallery or provincial mus. (former La Merced convent). In the S transept of the cathedral is the monument to Columbus with a sarcophagus believed to contain his remains. Part of the cathedral forms the city's landmark, the lofty Giralda, a minaret more than 300 ft. high (erected towards end of 12th cent.). Other chief relics of the Moorish era are the Torre del Oro, originally a part of the walls surrounding the alcazar, and the Casa de Pilatos. Some of Seville's many convents and baroque churches are decorated in the sumptuous Churrigueresque manner. Notable, too, are the palace of las Duenas belonging to duke of Alba, the palace of San Telmo (now a seminary), the baroque tobacco factory, the Renaissance Ayuntamiento, the Lonja (exchange) built in Greco-Roman style and housing the invaluable Archive of the Indies, archbishop's palace, and town hall. Parts of the city's wall remain. Modern bldgs. were added by the Hispanic-American Exhibition (1929). Seville's beauty is enhanced by its public squares and attractive boulevards. The fashionable promenade Paseo de las Delicias leads to the María Luisa park. The renowned bull ring is the 2d largest in Spain. From the Roman period are the Alameda de Hercules and remains of an aqueduct. The ruined town of Italica, founded by Scipio Africanus, is near by (NW). Among the oldest and quaintest sections of the city is Santa Cruz with the Judería (Jewish quarter). Triana, across the Guadalquivir (W) and linked by bridges, is chiefly a working-class suburb, and center for ceramics industry. The origin of the anc. Hispalis has been attributed to Iberians and Phoenicians. It was captured (43 B.C.) by Caesar, who renamed it Julia Romula. Already an important city, it became, during Roman domination, ⊙ Baetica (approximately coextensive with present-day Andalusia). It was successively taken by Vandals and Visigoths, who made it their chief city in S Spain. Seville was conquered by the Moors in 712, changing hands bet. different Arab dynasties, and becoming capital of flourishing Arab kingdoms. Its decline began with its capture (1248) by Ferdinand III of Castile, who allegedly expelled the majority of its citizens. The discovery of America and the virtual monopoly of trade with the Indies (with the establishment of the Casa de Contratación or Loja) brought enormous prosperity. However, it lost out in early 18th cent. to Cádiz, to which the Council of the Indies was transferred. Seville was frequently ravaged by bubonic plague, yellow fever, and floods. After the rising in 1808 against the French, it was occupied until 1812. Since beginning of 20th cent., Seville has undergone an economic and industrial revival. Early during Sp. civil war (1936–39) the city was taken by Nationalist forces and became a base for the conquest of Estremadura and central Spain, profiting considerably from the ensuing influx. Seville is the birthplace of 3 of Spain's greatest painters, Valdés Leal, Murillo, and Velázquez. The colorful city has frequently been depicted in literature and music; among the most notable examples are *Carmen, Don Juan*, and *The Barber of Seville*.

Seville. 1 City (pop. 427), Volusia co., NE Fla., 30 mi. WNW of Daytona Beach; citrus-fruit packing. **2** Town (pop. 187), Wilcox co., S central Ga., 11 mi. E of Cordele. **3** Village (pop. 963), Medina co., N Ohio, 9 mi. S of Medina, and on small Chippewa Creek, in agr. area; cement blocks.

Sevilleja de la Jara (sävēlyä'hä dhä lä hä'rä), village (pop. 1,009), Toledo prov., central Spain, 28 mi. SSW of Talavera de la Reina; grain, livestock; flour milling. Hydroelectric plant.

Sevivara Point, Timor: see SERIVARA POINT.

Sevliyevo (sĕvlē'ůvô), city (pop. 9,856), Gorna Oryakhovitsa dist., N Bulgaria, on Rositsa R. and 36 mi. SE of Pleven; market center in fruitgrowing dist.; mfg. of cotton textiles, tanning, flour milling. Important industrial center under Turkish rule; when by-passed by rail construction it reverted to handicrafts and horticulture as its main activities. Sometimes spelled Sevlievo or Sevlijevo.

Sevljus, Ukrainian SSR: see VINOGRADOV.

Sevnica (sĕv'nĭtsä), Ger. *Savenstein* (zä'vůnshtīn"), village, E Slovenia, Yugoslavia, on Sava R. and 16 mi. S of Celje; rail junction. Until 1918, in Styria.

Sevo, Pizzo di (pē'tsô dē sä'vô), peak (7,946 ft.) in Monti della Laga, S central Italy, 3 mi. ENE of Amatrice.

Sevran (sĕvrā'), town (pop. 9,860), Seine-et-Oise dept., N central France, an outer NE suburb of Paris, just E of Aulnay-sous-Bois, 10 mi. from Notre Dame Cathedral, on Ourcq Canal; natl. powder works. Mfg. (railroad brakes, paints, photo equipment).

Sèvre Nantaise River (sĕ'vrů nãtĕz'), in Deux-Sèvres, Vendée, and Loire-Inférieure depts., W France, rises 10 mi. W of Parthenay, flows 85 mi. NW past Mortagne-sur-Sèvre and Vertou to the Loire opposite Nantes. Receives Maine R. (left).

Sèvre Niortaise River (nyôrtĕz'), in Deux-Sèvres and Charente-Maritime depts., W France, rises 5 mi. NE of Melle, flows 95 mi. generally W, past La Mothe-Saint-Héray, Saint-Maixent-l'École, and Niort (head of navigation), across the Marais Poitevin, to the Pertuis Breton of the Bay of Biscay. Receives the Vendée (right).

Sèvres (sĕ'vrů), town (pop. 15,112), Seine-et-Oise dept., N central France, a WSW suburb of Paris, 6 mi. from Notre Dame Cathedral, on left bank of Seine R. opposite Boulogne-Billancourt; famous for its Sèvres chinaware. Small-arms ammunition, brewing, mica processing. The natl. porcelain factory, with ceramics school and mus. (damaged), is located at W end of Seine R. bridge, on S edge of Saint-Cloud park. Just N of it is the Pavillon Breteuil, hq. of International Bureau of Weights and Measures.

Sèvres, Deux-, France: see DEUX-SÈVRES.

Sevsk (syĕfsk), city (1926 pop. 8,574), SE Bryansk oblast, Russian SFSR, 75 mi. S of Bryansk, in hemp area; hemp-oil extraction; hemp, starch, and vegetable processing; metalworks. Dates from 12th cent.; passed (1503) to Moscow.

Sewall, Lake (sōō'ůl, sū'ůl), W central Mont., in Lewis and Clark co. and Broadwater co., 15 mi. E of Helena; 7 mi. long, 2 mi. wide; formed by widening of Missouri R.

Sewall Point, SE Va., point of land at E side of Elizabeth R. mouth on Hampton Roads, in Norfolk city; site of U.S. naval operating base.

Sewanee (sůwä'nē, swä'nē), village (pop. 1,407), Franklin co., S Tenn., 35 mi. WNW of Chattanooga, near edge of Cumberland Plateau. Univ. of the South (1857) and Sewanee Military Acad. are located here.

Seward, (sōō'ůrd, sū'–) town (pop. 2,063), S Alaska, on Kenai Peninsula at head of Resurrection Bay, 80 mi. S of Anchorage; 60°6'N 149°27'W. Ocean terminus of Alaska RR, its ice-free port is the most important transfer point for supplies to interior Alaska; supply center for fishing, logging, and gold-mining activities. Cannery, sawmill; airfield. Founded 1902 as supply base for Alaska RR survey crews. Supply port and site of U.S. Army base during Second World War.

Seward (sōō'ůrd, sū'–). **1** County (□ 639; pop. 9,972), SW Kansas; ⊙ Liberal. Plains region, bordered S by Okla.; drained by Cimarron R. Grain, livestock. Formed 1886. **2** County (□ 572; pop. 13,155), SE Nebr.; ⊙ Seward. Agr. area drained by Big Blue R. and its branches. Grain, livestock, dairy and poultry produce. Formed 1865.

Seward. 1 City (pop. 130), Stafford co., S central Kansas, 13 mi. S of Great Bend, in wheat region. **2** City (pop. 3,154), ⊙ Seward co., SE Nebr., 20 mi. WNW of Lincoln and on Big Blue R., in prairie region; bricks, cement, flour, feed; dairy and poultry produce. Concordia Teachers Col. here. City founded 1868, inc. 1874. **3** Town (pop. 75), Logan co., central Okla., 7 mi. SW of Guthrie. A U.S. demonstration farm is near by. **4** Borough (pop. 852), Westmoreland co., SW central Pa., 9 mi. NW of Johnstown and on Conemaugh R.

Seward Glacier, SE Alaska and SW Yukon, in St. Elias Mts. glacier system, S of Mt. Logan. S arm flows to Malaspina Glacier.

Seward Mountain (4,404 ft.), Franklin co., NE N.Y., in the Adirondacks, 14 mi. SW of Lake Placid village.

Seward Peninsula (210 mi. long, 90–140 mi. wide), W Alaska, bet. Norton Sound of Bering Sea (S), Bering Strait (W), and Chukchi Sea and Kotzebue Sound (N). W extremity is Cape PRINCE OF WALES (most westerly point of North American continent), opposite Cape Dezhnev, Siberia. Nome city in SW. Undulating surface consists mainly of perpetually frozen muskeg tundra; rises to 4,720 ft. (SW). Gold mining, trapping are main occupations; there are tin, lead, and other metal deposits.

Sewaren (sē'wŏrŭn), village (1940 pop. 1,284) in WOODBRIDGE township, Middlesex co., E N.J., on Arthur Kill just E of Woodbridge; chemicals, metal and petroleum products; detinning plant; large power plant.

Sewa River (sä'wä), E central Sierra Leone, formed 18 mi. WNW of Sefadu by junction of Bagbe and Bafi rivers, rising in hills on Fr. Guinea frontier; flows c.150 mi. generally SW, past Baoma and Sumbuya, joining Waanje R. 30 mi. ESE of Bonthe to form KITTAM RIVER. Sometimes called Bum R., a name also applied to the Kittam. Receives Tabe R. (right).

Sewell (sōō'ĕl), mining settlement (1930 pop. 7,556), O'Higgins prov., central Chile, in the Andes, on Santiago prov. border, 25 mi. ENE of Rancagua; rail terminus; copper-mining and -smelting center near the EL TENIENTE deposits.

Sewell, England: see HOUGHTON REGIS.

Sewickley (sŭwĭ'klē), residential borough (pop. 5,836), Allegheny co., W Pa., 12 mi. NW of Pittsburgh and on Ohio R.; agr. Inc. 1853.

Sewickley Heights, borough (pop. 679), Allegheny co., W Pa., 11 mi. NW of Pittsburgh.

Sexey-aux-Forges (sĕksā'-ō-fôrzh'), village (pop. 405), Meurthe-et-Moselle dept., NE France, on Moselle R. and 8 mi. SW of Nancy; iron mining.

Sexmoan (sĕksmwän'), town (1939 pop. 1,421; 1948 municipality pop. 9,804), Pampanga prov., central Luzon, Philippines, 8 mi. SW of San Fernando; sugar cane, rice. Sometimes called Santa Lucia.

Sexsmith, village (pop. 302), W Alta., near B.C. border, 13 mi. N of Grande Prairie; coal mining, lumbering, wheat, mixed farming.

Seybouse, Oued (wĕd' sābōōz'), stream of Constantine dept., NE Algeria, rises c.20 mi. E of Constantine, flows generally E past Guelma, then N, past Duvivier, to the Mediterranean just S of Bône; length, 145 mi. Has most constant volume of Algeria's rivers. Course followed by Constantine-Bône RR.

Seychelles (sāshĕlz', sāshĕl'), island group in Indian Ocean, c.700 mi. NE of Madagascar, c.1,000 mi. E of Zanzibar; 3°40'–6°5'S 53°55'–59°10'E. Located at the center of a vast submerged bank (□ c.12,000; average water depth 150–200 ft.), they consist of c.30 isls., including Mahé (□ 56), Praslin, Silhouette, and La Digue isls. Receive SE tradewinds in winter (May–Nov.) and NW monsoons in summer (74°–86°F.). Rainfall (heaviest Nov.–April) averages 90 in. a year. Fertile soils produce coconuts (to alt. of 300–500 ft.), cinnamon, patchouli, and vanilla. Pop., descended largely from European settlers and African slaves (augmented by liberated slaves) brought (18th cent.) from Mauritius, is of R.C. faith and speaks French or a Creole patois. Of volcanic origin, these rugged mountainous isls. (rising to 2,993 ft. in the Morne Seychellois on Mahé Isl.) are said to be peaks of the hypothetical Gondwana continent of the Mesozoic era. Uninhabited when discovered 1505 by Portuguese, they were a pirates' rest until occupation (middle 18th cent.) by French. Captured 1794 by British, became dependency of Br. colony of Mauritius in 1810, formally ceded by France in 1814. Separation of the Seychelles from Mauritius began 1872 and was completed 1903 when they were constituted as separate crown colony. The **Seychelles** crown colony (□ 156¼; 1947 pop. 34,632; ⊙ Victoria, on Mahé Isl.) includes the Seychelles proper and outlying coral isls. (Aldabra, Farquhar, Amirante, Alphonse, and Coëtivy groups) bet. the Seychelles and Madagascar, a total of 92 isls. bet. 4° and 10°S, 46° and 57°E. Govt. is by a governor assisted by executive and legislative councils. Exports are copra, essential oils (cinnamon, palmarosa, patchouli), vanilla, and (largely from outlying isls.) tortoise shell, calipee, and guano.

Seychellois, Morne (môrn' sāshĕlwä'), highest point (2,993 ft.) of Mahé Isl., Seychelles, in central range 2 mi. SW of Victoria.

Seyches (sĕsh), village (pop. 352), Lot-et-Garonne dept., SW France, 8 mi. ENE of Marmande; chemicals, cereals, plums.

Seyda (zī'dä), town (pop. 1,704), in former Prussian Saxony prov., central Germany, after 1945 in Saxony-Anhalt, 11 mi. E of Wittenberg; grain, potatoes, livestock.

Seydisehir (sādĭ'shĕhĭr'), Turkish *Seydişehir*, village (pop. 3,965), Konya prov., SW central Turkey, near L. Sugla, 45 mi. SW of Konya; barley, wheat, chick-peas, vetch.

Seydisfjordur or **Seydhisfjordhur** (sā'dhĭsfyûr"-dhŭr), Icelandic *Seyðisfjörður*, city (pop. 772), ⊙ and in but independent of Nordur-Mula co., E Iceland, at head of Seydis Fjord (10-mi.-long inlet of Atlantic); 65°16'N 14°W; fishing port. Terminus of cable to Denmark (completed 1906).

Seyd Naya, Syria: see SAIDNAYA.

Seyé (sĕyā'), town (pop. 2,496), Yucatan, SE Mexico, 18 mi. SE of Mérida; henequen, sugar, corn.

Seyhan (sāhän'), prov. (□ 6,663; 1950 pop. 509,600), S Turkey; ⊙ Adana. On Mediterranean Sea, bordered NW by Tahtali Mts., E by Amanos Mts., both part of Taurus Mts. Drained by Ceyhan and Seyhan rivers. Resources include copper, iron, arsenic. Agr. (wheat, oats, millet, rice, sesame, legumes, onions, linseed, cotton); citrus fruits. Formerly Adana.

Seyhan River, anc. *Sarus* (sâ'rŭs), S central Turkey, rises in the Anti-Taurus Mts. as the Yenice Irmak (or Zamanti) c.40 mi. SSW of Sivas, flows 320 mi. SSW, past Pinarbasi and Adana, to the Mediterranean 15 mi. E of Mersin. Receives the Goksu (left). Formerly sometimes spelled Sihun.

Seyitgazi (sĕyĭt'gäzĭ"), village (pop. 1,871), Eskisehir prov., W central Turkey, on Sakarya R. and 24 mi. SSE of Eskisehir; cereals, potatoes; mohair goats.

Seymchan, Russian SFSR: see SEIMCHAN.

Seymour (sē'môr,–mŭr), town (pop. 3,016), central Victoria, Australia, on Goulburn R. and 55 mi. N of Melbourne, in livestock area.

Seymour. 1 Town (pop. 7,832), including Seymour village (pop. 5,342), New Haven co., SW Conn., on Naugatuck R. and 10 mi. NW of New Haven; agr. Mfg. (metal products, wire and cable, hard rubber goods, textiles, tools, hardware) at Seymour village. Settled c.1680. inc. 1850. **2** City (pop. 9,629), Jackson co., S Ind., 17 mi. S of Columbus, in agr. area; mfg. of automobile parts, home appliances, furniture, wood products, woolen goods, canned foods, flour, fertilizer, cheese, leather products, metal products, drugs; printing, lumber milling. Aviation school here. A state forest is near by. Settled c.1850. **3** Town (pop. 1,223), Wayne co., S Iowa, near Mo. line, 13 mi. WSW of Centerville, in stock-raising and bituminous-coal-mining area; mfg. (concrete blocks, feed). Inc. 1874. **4** City (pop. 1,015), Webster co., S central Mo., in the Ozarks, 30 mi. E of Springfield; agr.; lumber. **5** City (pop. 3,779), ⊙ Baylor co., N Texas, on Brazos R. and c.45 mi. SW of Wichita Falls; trade, shipping center for cotton, cattle, wheat area; mfg. (tile, mattresses, cottonseed oil); oil wells. Kemp and Diversion lakes (fishing) to N and NE. Settled 1878 at crossing of Dodge City and California trails; inc. 1906. **6** City (pop. 1,760), Outagamie co., E Wis., 15 mi. W of Green Bay; dairy products, flour, canned goods. Settled 1871, inc. 1879.

Seymour, Mount (4,120 ft.), Franklin co., NE N.Y., in the Adirondacks, 13 mi. SW of Lake Placid village.

Seymour Canal, SE Alaska, N–S inlet on E side of Admiralty Isl., Alexander Archipelago, c.45 mi. long.

Seymour Island (8 naut. mi. long, 4 naut. mi. wide), Antarctica, off NE Palmer Peninsula, E of Ross Isl., in Weddell Sea; 64°18'S 56°50'W. Discovered 1843 by Sir James Clark Ross.

Seymour Island, islet (□ 1; 1950 pop. 17) of the Galápagos Isls., Ecuador, in the Pacific, off N coast of Chaves Isl.

Seymour Lake, NE Vt., resort lake 9 mi. E of Newport, in hunting, fishing area; c.3 mi. long.

Seymour Narrows, B.C.: see DISCOVERY PASSAGE.

Seym River, European USSR: see SEIM RIVER.

Seyne (sĕn), village (pop. 539), Basses-Alpes dept., SE France, 19 mi. NNE of Digne, at W foot of Montagne de la Blanche; alt. 3,970 ft. Resort. Also called Seyne-les-Alpes.

Seyne-sur-Mer, La (lä sĕn-sür-mâr'), SW suburb (pop. 18,490) of Toulon, on E shore of Cape Sicié peninsula; port and shipbuilding center on Toulon roadstead. Ostreiculture. Surrounded by fortifications. Damaged in Second World War. Just SE, in bay sheltered by Saint-Mandrier Peninsula, is bathing resort of Tamaris-sur-Mer, with Lyons univ. laboratory of marine zoology.

Seyskari, Russian SFSR: see SEISKARI.

Seyssel (sĕsĕl'), village (pop. 952), Ain dept., E France, on right bank of Rhone R., opposite Seyssel (pop. 889), Haute-Savoie dept., and 15 mi. WNW of Annecy; produces mining explosives and sparkling wines. Asphalt mining near by. Construction of a hydroelectric installation, to be linked with GÉNISSIAT dam, was begun here 1946.

Seyyun, Aden: see SEIYUN.

Sezana (sĕ'zhänä), Slovenian *Sežana*, Ital. *Sesana* (sezä'nä), village (pop. 2,001), SW Slovenia, Yugoslavia, 5 mi. NE of Trieste, on Free Territory line. Until 1947, in Italy.

Sézanne (säzän'), town (pop. 4,680), Marne dept., N France, 14 mi. N of Romilly-sur-Seine; agr. trade center; winegrowing, mfg. (refractories, hosiery). In area of Marshes of Saint-Gond (c.8 mi. NE), Fr. army repulsed Germans in 1st battle of the Marne (1914).

Sezibwa River, Uganda: see KYOGA, LAKE.

Sezimbra, Portugal: see SESIMBRA.

Sezimovo Usti (sĕ'zĭmôvo ōō'styē), Czech *Sezimovo Ústí*, village (pop. 3,264), S Bohemia, Czechoslovakia, on Luznice R. and 2 mi. SSE of Tabor, in barley- and oat-growing dist. Eduard Benes, who had summer residence here, buried here.

Sezze (sĕ'tsĕ), anc. *Setia*, town (pop. 7,879), Latina prov., Latium, S central Italy, 19 mi. SE of Frosinone, on hill overlooking Pontine Marshes, in agr. (corn, wheat, vegetables) and livestock-raising region. Bishopric. Has cathedral, medieval houses, anc. walls.

Sfaganuk, Eskimo village (1939 pop. 33), SW Alaska, in Kuskokwim R. delta, 90 mi. WSW of Bethel; trapping. Also spelled Sefagnuk.

Sfakia, Crete: see SPHAKIA.

Sfaktiria, Greece: see SPHAKTERIA.

Sfanta-Ana (sfûn'tä-ä'nä), Rum. *Sfânta-Ana*, Hung. *Újszentánna* (ōō'ēsĕntän"nŏ), village (pop. 5,838), Arad prov., W Rumania, 13 mi. NE of Arad; rail junction; brick making.

Sfantu-Gheorghe or **Sfantul-Gheorghe** (sfûn'tōō-gyôr'gĕ,–tōōl–), Rum. *Sfântu-Gheorghe* or *Sfântul-Gheorghe*. **1** Village (pop. 1,366), Galati prov., SE Rumania, on Black Sea, at the mouth of Sfantu-Gheorghe arm of the Danube delta, 17 mi. S of Sulina; fishing harbor. **2** Hung. *Sepsiszentgyörgy* (shĕ'pēsĕntyûr"dyŭ), town (1948 pop. 14,224), Stalin prov., central Rumania, in Transylvania, on Olt R. and 95 mi. NNW of Bucharest; rail junction and trading center (livestock, leather, woodwork); mfg. of textiles and clay products, distilling, tobacco processing. Has 15th-cent. Protestant church, mus. with prehistoric and ethnographical collections. Noted finds of Neolithic period have been made near by. About 90% pop. are Magyars. In Hungary, 1940–45.

Sfax (sfäks), city (pop. 54,637), ⊙ Sfax dist. (□ 3,408; pop. 285,559), E Tunisia, seaport on N shore of Gulf of Gabès (central Mediterranean), 150 mi. SSE of Tunis; 34°45'N 10°46'E. Second-largest city of Tunisia and its principal phosphate-shipping center, connected with the mines in Gafsa area (c.130 mi. WSW) by mining railroad. Other exports are olive oil of high quality, sponges, almonds, dates (from Saharan oases), and esparto grass (for European paper mills). Also a growing industrial center with new (1950) superphosphate plant (also producing sulphuric acid), olive-oil and soap factories; tanning, perfume mfg.; handicraft carpet industry; saltworks. Airfield. The coastal region around Sfax is noted for its fine olive groves. The Kerkennah isls. are c.20 mi. offshore. The native dist., built around the great mosque and surrounded by old walls, is a beehive of activity. S of it, in back of the harbor (laid out 1895; considerably improved) is the European city with rectangular street pattern. A Phoenician and a Roman colony, Sfax early enjoyed a prosperous trade. Occupied 12th cent. by Sicilians and 16th cent. by Spaniards. Later a stronghold of Barbary pirates. Bombarded (1881) by French prior to occupation. Taken by British (April, 1943) near end of Tunisian campaign in Second World War.

Sfira or **Safirah** (both: sfē'rŭ), Fr. *Sfiré*, village, Aleppo prov., NW Syria, 15 mi. SE of Aleppo; cotton, cereals, pistachios.

Sgonico (zgô'nēkō), Slovenian *Zgonik* (zgô'nĭk), village (pop. 234), N Free Territory of Trieste, in the Karst, 6 mi. NNW of Trieste, near Yugoslav line. Pop. is Slovenian. Placed 1947 under Anglo-American administration.

's Gravenbrakel, Belgium: see BRAINE-LE-COMTE.

's Gravendeel (skrä'vŭndāl), village (pop. 4,194), South Holland prov., SW Netherlands, on the Dortsche Kil and 3 mi. SW of Dordrecht; flax processing, fishing, agr.

's Gravenhage, Netherlands: see HAGUE, THE.

's Gravenmoer (–mōōr), village (pop. 1,413), North Brabant prov., SW Netherlands, on Donge R. and 10 mi. NW of Tilburg; leather tanning, shoe mfg.

's Gravenzande (–zändŭ), village (pop. 5,140), South Holland prov., W Netherlands, 13 mi. SW of The Hague, near North Sea, in Westland agr. area; vegetable-growing center; cattle raising.

's Greveldiun-Capelle (skrĕ'vŭldoin-käpĕ'lŭ), town, North Brabant prov., SW Netherlands, 10 mi. NNW of Tilburg; leather tanning, shoe mfg. Also called Kapelle.

Sgur Alasdair, Scotland: see CUILLIN HILLS.

Sha, China: see SHA RIVER.

Sha'am, Trucial Oman: see SHA'M.

Shaar Haamakim or **Sha'ar ha Amaqim** (both: shä'är hä-ämäkēm'), settlement (pop. 410), NW Israel, bet. Zebulun Valley and Plain of Jezreel, near SE slope of Mt. Carmel, near Kishon R., 9 mi. SE of Haifa; mixed farming. Founded 1935.

Shaar Hagolan or **Sha'ar ha Golan** (both: hägōlän'), settlement (pop. 450), NE Israel, Lower Galilee, near Syrian and Jordan borders, near S shore of Sea of Galilee, bet. the Jordan (W) and the Yarmuk (SE), 8 mi. SSE of Tiberias; mixed farming (fruit, bananas, viticulture); fish ponds. Traces of neolithic culture excavated here. Founded 1937; destroyed in Arab invasion, 1948; later rebuilt.

Shaarikhan, Uzbek SSR: see STALINO, village, Andizhan oblast.

Shaartuz (shŭärtōōs'), town (1948 pop. over 2,000), SW Stalinabad oblast, Tadzhik SSR, on Kafirnigan

R. and 50 mi. SW of Kurgan-Tyube, in long-staple-cotton area; cotton ginning; salt deposits.
Shaar Yashuv, Israel: see SHEAR YASHUV.
Shabalino, Russian SFSR: see LENINSKOYE, Kirov.
Shabani (shäbä'nē), asbestos-mining center (pop. 8,883), Gwelo prov., S central Southern Rhodesia, in Matabeleland, on road and 95 mi. E of Bulawayo. Consists of township (pop. 7,572) of Shabani Mine and Birthday Mine, which is adjoined SW by New Shabani (pop. 420; rail terminus and asbestos shipping point) and NE by Old Shabani (pop. 891).
Shabas el Shuhada or **Shabas al-Shuhada'** (both: shăbăs' ĕsh-shoo͞hădă'), village (pop. 10,316), Gharbiya prov., Lower Egypt, 6 mi. ESE of Disuq; cotton.
Shabats, Yugoslavia: see SABAC.
Shabbaz (shŭbäs'), village (1948 pop. over 2,000), S Kara-Kalpak Autonomous SSR, Uzbek SSR, on the Amu Darya and 75 mi. SE of Nukus; metalworks. Formerly Sheikh-Abbaz.
Shabbona (shă'bŭnŭ), village (pop. 667), De Kalb co., N Ill., 28 mi. W of Aurora, in rich agr. area; makes cheese.
Shabelkovka or **Shabel'kovka** (shŭbĭlkôf'kŭ), town (1939 pop. over 500), N Stalino oblast, Ukrainian SSR, in the Donbas, 4 mi. WNW of Kramatorsk.
Shabestar, Iran: see SHABISTAR.
Shabin Karahisar, Turkey: see SEBINKARAHISAR.
Shabistar or **Shabestar** (both: shäbĕstär'), village, Third Prov., in Azerbaijan, NW Iran, 30 mi. WNW of Tabriz; grain, tobacco.
Shablykino (shŭblĭ'kĭnŭ), village (1939 pop. over 500), SW Orel oblast, Russian SFSR, 20 mi. SSE of Karachev; hemp milling.
Shabo (shä'bŭ), Rum. *Şaba* (shä'bä), village (1941 pop. 3,736), E Izmail oblast, Ukrainian SSR, on Dniester Liman, 5 mi. SSE of Belgorod-Dnestrovski; climatic resort (grape cure); vineyards. Founded 1822 as Swiss agr. colony.
Shabrovski or **Shabrovskiy** (shŭbrôf'skē), town (1940 pop. over 500), S Sverdlovsk oblast, Russian SFSR, 7 mi. SW of Aramil; manganese mining.
Shabunda (shäbo͞on'dä), village, Kivu prov., E Belgian Congo, on Ulindi R. and 105 mi. WSW of Costermansville; gold and tin mining. Protestant mission.
Shabwa or **Shabwah** (shăb'wŭ), town, Eastern Aden Protectorate, 115 mi. WSW of Shibam, on caravan route to Upper Aulaqi country; rock-salt deposits.
Sha Ch'i, China: see SHA RIVER, Fukien prov.
Shackelford, county (□ 887; pop. 5,001), N central Texas; ⊙ Albany. Drained by Clear Fork of Brazos R.; includes part of L. Fort Phantom Hill. A leading Texas cattle-ranching co.; some sheep, turkeys; agr. in E and NE (wheat, cotton, grain sorghums). Oil, natural-gas wells. Formed 1856.
Shackleford Banks, E N.C., section (c.7 mi. long) of the Outer Banks, extending NW from Cape Lookout to Beaufort Inlet (entrance to Beaufort Harbor).
Shackleton, Mount (10,800 ft.), SE B.C., near Alta. border, in Rocky Mts., in Hamber Provincial Park, 50 mi. S of Jasper; 52°11'N 117°54'W.
Shadadi, Tall, Syria: see SHEDADI, TELL.
Shade Gap, borough (pop. 157), Huntingdon co., S central Pa., 14 mi. S of Mt. Union.
Shadehill Dam, S.Dak.: see GRAND RIVER.
Shadek, Poland: see SZADEK.
Shade Mountain, central Pa., NE–SW ridge (1,800–2,000 ft.), runs c.30 mi. NE from Juniata R. just E of Lewistown to Snyder co.; forms part of border bet. Juniata and Mifflin counties.
Shadgan (shädgän'), town (1940 pop. 5,744), Sixth Prov., in Khuzistan, SW Iran, 20 mi. N of Abadan and on Karun R.; grain, rice, dates.
Shadmot Dvora (shädmōt' dvōră'), settlement (pop. 200), Lower Galilee, N Israel, at E foot of Mt. Tabor, 9 mi. SW of Tiberias; mixed farming. Founded 1939. Also spelled Shadmot Devora or Shadmot Dvorah.
Shadov, Lithuania: see SEDUVA.
Shadow Mountain Dam, N Colo., on N fork of Colorado R. bet. Grand L. and Granby, and c.55 mi. NW of Denver. Earth and rockfill dam (78 ft. high, 3,100 ft. long, including dike) built (1943–46) as unit in Colorado–Big Thompson project; forms Shadow Mountain L. (continuous with Grand L., just NE). Water pumped from GRANBY Reservoir into Shadow Mountain and Grand lakes, then conducted through ALVA B. ADAMS TUNNEL to E slope of Continental Divide and used for irrigation and power.
Shadrinsk (shä'drĭnsk), city (1926 pop. 19,203), NW Kurgan oblast, Russian SFSR, on Iset R. (head of navigation), on Trans-Siberian RR and 75 mi. NW of Kurgan; agr. center; flour and linen milling, distilling, sawmilling, meat packing. Teachers col. In 18th and 19th cent., on main access route to Siberia.
Shadwell, village, Albemarle co., central Va., 4 mi. ESE of Charlottesville. Near by is Shadwell estate, birthplace of Thomas Jefferson.
Shady Dale, town (pop. 253), Jasper co., central Ga., 9 mi. NE of Monticello; sawmilling.
Shadypoint, village, Le Flore co., SE Okla., 21 mi. SW of Fort Smith (Ark.), and on Poteau R.; cotton ginning, grain milling. Grew from early Choctaw settlement near by.
Shady Side or **Shadyside,** village (1940 pop. 749), Anne Arundel co., central Md., on an inlet of Chesapeake Bay; 10 mi. S of Annapolis.
Shadyside, village (pop. 4,433), Belmont co., E Ohio, on the Ohio and 8 mi. SSW of Wheeling, W.Va.; makes caskets. Platted 1901, inc. 1913.
Shafarud (shäfäro͞od'), town (1940 pop. 4,995), First Prov., in Gilan, N Iran, 33 mi. NW of Resht; Caspian fishing port.
Shafer, village (pop. 127), Chisago co., E Minn., near St. Croix R., 35 mi. NNE of St. Paul; dairy products.
Shafer Lake, NW central Ind., resort lake (c.10 mi. long) impounded by power dam on Tippecanoe R. near Monticello. Receives Big Monon Creek.
Shafranovo (shŭfrä'nŭvŭ), town (1948 pop. over 2,000), W central Bashkir Autonomous SSR, Russian SFSR, 55 mi. WNW of Sterlitamak; health resort; dairying (kumiss); grain.
Shafrikan (shŭfrēkän'), village (1926 pop. 542), S Bukhara oblast, Uzbek SSR, 10 mi. W of Gizhduvan; cotton. Formerly called Khodzha-Arif and, c.1935–37, Bauman.
Shafter (shăf'tŭr). **1** City (pop. 2,207), Kern co., S central Calif., 17 mi. NW of Bakersfield, in potato-growing dist. Air Force base (Minter Field) here in Second World War. Inc. 1938. **2** Mining village, Presidio co., extreme W Texas, c.40 mi. SSW of Marfa, in Chinati Mts.; alt. c.3,900 ft.; silver mines are largely shut down.
Shafter, Fort, S Oahu, T.H., 3 mi. NW of Honolulu; U.S. military hq. of Hawaiian Dept.; 1st military post to be occupied (1907) after annexation of Hawaii.
Shafter Lake, Texas: see ANDREWS.
Shaftesbury, municipal borough (1931 pop. 2,367; 1951 census 3,297), N Dorset, England, on hill 18 mi. WSW of Salisbury: agr. market in dairying region; agr.-equipment works. Has remains of abbey founded 880 by Alfred the Great. There are traces of British, Roman, and Saxon occupation. Town is locally known as Shaston.
Shaftsbury, town (pop. 1,673), Bennington co., SW Vt., on N.Y. line, just N of Bennington; steel squares, wood products made at South Shaftsbury village. Chartered 1761, settled 1763.
Shagamu (shägä'mo͞o), town, Ijebu prov., Western Provinces, SW Nigeria, 20 mi. W of Ijebu-Ode; agr. trade center; cacao industry; cotton weaving, indigo dyeing; palm oil and kernels, rice.
Shagany Lagoon (shŭgä'nē), Rum. *Şagani* (shägän'), Black Sea coastal lagoon, SE Izmail oblast, Ukrainian SSR, E of Sasyk Lagoon; closed off by narrow sandspit; 6 mi. long, 5 mi. wide.
Shagawa Lake (shă'gŭwä), St. Louis co., NE Minn., at Ely, in Superior Natl. Forest; 4 mi. long, 2 mi. wide. Resorts. Burntside L. is just W.
Shageluk (shă'gŭlŭk), village (pop. 99), W Alaska, on Innoko R. and 30 mi. N of Holy Cross; fur-trading post; supply point. School.
Shag Harbour, village (pop. estimate 200), SW N.S., on the Atlantic, 30 mi. SE of Yarmouth; lobster, halibut, haddock fisheries. De Monts here established trading post.
Shaghra, Maltese Isls.: see XAGHARA.
Shag Island, subantarctic island, actually several tiny rocks in S Indian Ocean, just N of Heard Isl. and c.280 mi. SE of Kerguelen Isls., approximately at 53°S 72°30'E.
Shagonar (shŭgŭnär'), city (1945 pop. over 1,000), N Tuva Autonomous Oblast, Russian SFSR, on Yenisei R. and 75 mi. W of Kyzyl; trading center.
Shahabad (shä'häbäd), district (□ 4,408; pop. 2,328,581), W Bihar, India; ⊙ Arrah. Mainly on Ganges Plain (extension of Vindhya Range in S); bounded by the Ganges (N) and Son R. (E, S); drained by tributaries of the Ganges; irrigated by Son Canals system. Largely alluvial soil; rice, wheat, gram, oilseeds, barley, corn, sugar cane, tobacco; bamboo in forest area (S). Saltpeter extracting, oilseed, flour, sugar, and paper milling, mfg. of sugar-mill accessories, carpets, pottery, cement, chemicals, soap, plywood. Main centers: Dehri, Jagdispur, Sasaram (tomb of Sher Shah). Experimental agr. farm at Dumraon. Arrah figured in Sepoy Rebellion of 1857. Decisive English victory, 1764, over Indian forces at Buxar.
Shahabad. 1 Town (pop. 5,904), Atraf-i-Balda dist., S central Hyderabad state, India, 27 mi. SW of Hyderabad; rice, oilseeds. **2** Town (pop. 10,152), Gulbarga dist., W Hyderabad state, India, near Kagna R., 15 mi. SSE of Gulbarga; cement-mfg. center (limestone and clay quarries near by); limestone dressing, oilseed milling. Major rail junction of Wadi is 7 mi. SE. **3** Town (pop. 14,745), Karnal dist., E Punjab, India, 35 mi. NNW of Karnal; market center for wheat, corn, gram, cotton; glass factory; handicraft silver products, lacquered woodwork, and musical instruments. Sometimes called Shahabad Markanda. **4** Town (pop. 22,213), Hardoi dist., central Uttar Pradesh, India, 16 mi. S of Shahjahanpur; sugar milling; trades in wheat, gram, barley, millet, rice. Has 17th-cent. mosque. Founded 1677 by an Afghan. Important during Mogul rule. Fruit and vegetable gardens near by. **5** Town (pop. 5,934), Rampur dist., N central Uttar Pradesh, India, near the Ramganga, 16 mi. S of Rampur; corn, wheat, rice, gram, sugar cane.
Shahabad (shä"häbäd'), town (1940 pop. 15,667), Fifth Prov., in Kermanshah, W Iran, 35 mi. SW of Kermanshah; road junction on Qasr-i-Shirin–Kermanshah road; sugar beets, grain, tobacco, opium, dairy products, wool. Sugar refinery. Developed rapidly in 1930s. Formerly known as Harunabad.
Shah Abdul Azim, Iran: see RAI.
Shahada (shähä'dŭ), town (pop. 9,092), West Khandesh dist., N Bombay, India, 50 mi. NNW of Dhulia; peanuts, millet; cotton ginning, hand-loom weaving, oilseed pressing.
Shahapur (shä'häpo͞or). **1** Town (pop. 13,512), Belgaum dist., S Bombay, India, 1 mi. S of Belgaum; trade center; agr. market (rice, jaggery, chili); cotton and silk dyeing, mfg. (hosiery, handicraft cloth, gold and silver products). **2** Village (pop. 3,160), Thana dist., W Bombay, India, 30 mi. NE of Thana; rice milling, cotton and silk handicraft weaving, dyeing, carpet mfg.
Shaharak, Afghanistan: see SHAHRAK.
Shahat, Cyrenaica: see CYRENE.
Shahba (shäbă'), Fr. *Chahba*, town, Jebel ed Druz prov., S Syria, 10 mi. NNE of Es Suweida; cereals. Founded as *Philippopolis* by Philip the Arabian, Roman emperor (A.D. 244–49); extensive ruins.
Shahbazgarhi, W Pakistan: see MARDAN, town.
Shahbazpur River, E Pakistan: see DAKHIN SHAHBAZPUR ISLAND.
Shahdad (shädäd'), town, Eighth Prov., in Kerman, SE Iran, 40 mi. ENE of Kerman, at W edge of the Dasht-i-Lut; dates, oranges, grain, tobacco, henna; rugs, hand-woven textiles. Formerly known as Khabis.
Shahdadpur (shä'dädpo͝or), town (pop. 11,768), Nawabshah dist., central Sind, W Pakistan, 25 mi. SSE of Nawabshah; cotton, millet, tobacco; cotton ginning, handicraft mfg. of cloth fabrics, camel fittings.
Shahdara (shä'dŭrŭ), town (pop. 15,955), E Delhi, India; residential suburb of Delhi, 4 mi. ENE of city center; hand-loom weaving, pottery. Headworks of Agra Canal are near by.
Shahdara (shä'dŭrŭ), industrial suburb of Lahore, Sheikhupura dist., E Punjab, W Pakistan, on right bank of Ravi R. and 2 mi. N of Lahore. Rail junction; agr. market (wheat, rice, cotton, oilseeds); flour, rice, and oilseed milling, cotton ginning, hand-loom weaving, tanning, mfg. of matches, metal products, chemicals, woolen goods, electric appliances, agr. machinery, truck bodies; engineering and enamel works, sawmill, electric power station. Mausoleum of Mogul emperor Jahangir, with halls of inlaid marble, here.
Shahganj (shä'gŭnj). **1** Town (pop. 2,423), S Bhopal state, India, on Narbada R. and 38 mi. SE of Bhopal; trades in wheat, cotton, teak, oilseeds. **2** Town (pop. 6,550), Jaunpur dist., SE Uttar Pradesh, India, 22 mi. N of Jaunpur; road center; sugar processing; trades in barley, rice, corn, wheat, cotton, gram. Founded 18th cent.
Shahgarh, India: see SULTANPUR, town, Uttar PRADESH.
Shahi (shä'hē), town (pop. 6,669), Bareilly dist., N central Uttar Pradesh, India, on tributary of the Ramganga and 14 mi. NNW of Bareilly; sugar refining; wheat, rice, gram, sugar cane.
Shahi (shähē'), town (1941 pop. 7,407), Second Prov., in E Mazanderan, N Iran, on Talar R. (short Caspian coastal stream), on road and railroad from Teheran across Elburz mts., and 10 mi. SE of Babul; industrial center, with cotton spinning, rice cleaning, jute-sack mfg. Until mid-1930s, called Aliabad.
Shahidmena (shŭhĕd'mānŭ), village, Khyber agency, central North-West Frontier Prov., W Pakistan, at NE end of Safed Koh Range, 18 mi. NW of Peshawar. Marble quarried near by.
Shahi Island, Iran: see URMIA, LAKE.
Shahin Dezh (shähēn' dĕzh'), town (1940 pop. 9,660), Fourth Prov., in Azerbaijan, NW Iran, in Kurd country, 55 mi. SSE of Maragheh and on Zarineh R.; sheep raising; rugmaking. Sulphur and lead deposits near by. Formerly known as Sain Qaleh.
Shahjahanabad, India: see DELHI, city.
Shahjahanpur (shäjŭhän'po͝or), district (□ 1,770; pop; 983,385), Rohilkhand div., central Uttar Pradesh, India; ⊙ Shahjahanpur. On W Ganges Plain; bounded SW by the Ganges; drained by the Ramganga; irrigated by Sarda Canal system. Agr. (wheat, rice, gram, oilseeds, sugar cane, pearl millet, barley, jowar); bamboo, sissoo, toon, sal (N), and babul forests. Main centers: Shahjahanpur, Tilhar, Jalalabad, Miranpur Katra.
Shahjahanpur. 1 Town, Madhya Bharat, India: see SHAJAPUR, town. **2** City (pop. including cantonment, 110,163), ⊙ Shahjahanpur dist., central Uttar Pradesh, India, on tributary of the Ramganga and 125 mi. ENE of Agra; road junction; trade center (grains, sugar cane, oilseeds); sugar milling, mfg. of chemicals, carpet weaving; distillery. Has 17th-cent. mosque. Founded 1647. Sugar milling, rum distillery at Rosa village, 3 mi. S of city center.
Shahjui (shä'jo͞oē), town (pop. 10,000), Kandahar prov., SE Afghanistan, 120 mi. NE of Kandahar, and on Tarnak R. and highway to Kabul; alt.

6,975 ft.; oasis; irrigated agr. Sometimes spelled Shahjoi.

Shaho (shä'hŭ'). **1** or **Shahochen,** city, Liaotung co., Manchuria, China: see ANSHAN. **2** Town, ⊙ Shaho co. (pop. 139,472), SW Hopeh prov., China, 10 mi. S of Singtai and on Peking-Hankow RR; cotton, wheat, kaoliang, millet.

Sha Ho, river, China: see SHA RIVER, Honan prov.

Shah Pass (shä) (alt. 7,240 ft.), in the Zagros mts., W central Iran, NW of the Alwand, 20 mi. W of Hamadan, and on highway to Asadabad, for which the pass is also named. Snow-blocked in winter.

Shahpur (shä'po͝or). **1** Town (pop. 5,146), Gulbarga dist., SW Hyderabad state, India, 45 mi. S of Gulbarga; millet, cotton. **2** Town (pop. 4,112), Muzaffarnagar dist., N Uttar Pradesh, India, 12 mi. SW of Muzaffarnagar; wheat, gram, sugar, oilseeds.

Shahpur, town (1941 pop. estimate 14,000), Fourth Prov., in Azerbaijan, NW Iran, on road and 45 mi. NNW of Rizaiyeh; grain, fruit, tobacco; stock grazing; carpetmaking. Known as Dilman or Salmas until destructive earthquake (1930). Rebuilt town was renamed Shahpur.

Shahpur, dist. (□ 4,770; 1951 pop. 1,149,000), central Punjab, W Pakistan; ⊙ Sargodha. Bounded SE by Chenab R.; crossed NW by Salt Range, NE-SW by Jhelum R.; section W of the Jhelum lies in Sind-Sagar Doab; E section, in Chaj Doab, irrigated by branches of Lower Jhelum Canal. Agr. (wheat, cotton, millet, oilseeds); cattle breeding, cotton ginning, hand-loom weaving. Rock salt and coal mined in Salt Range. Trade centers: Sargodha, Bhera, Khushab.

Shahpur or **Shahpur Sadar** (sä'dŭr), town (1941pop. 3,958), Shahpur dist., central Punjab, W Pakistan, 16 mi. NW of Sargodha; local agr. market (wheat, cotton, oilseeds); cotton ginning. Sometimes called Shahpur Chhauni.

Shahpura (shä'po͝orŭ). **1** Town (pop. 9,939), S central Rajasthan, India, 105 mi. SW of Jaipur; markets millet, cotton, barley, gram; cotton ginning, handicraft cloth weaving and dyeing; lacquered woodwork. Was ⊙ former princely state of Shahpura (□ 405; pop. 61,173) in Rajputana States, India; state established 1629 by Sesodia Rajputs; in 1948, merged with union of Rajasthan. **2** Town (pop. 4,695), E Rajasthan, India, 33 mi. NNE of Jaipur; millet, gram, barley.

Shahpur Chhauni, W Pakistan: see SHAHPUR, town.

Shahpur City (shä'po͝or), town (pop. 5,515), Shahpur dist., central Punjab, W Pakistan, near Jhelum R., 5 mi. E of Khushab; wheat, cotton. Sometimes called Shahpur Shahr.

Shahpur Sadar, W Pakistan: see SHAHPUR, town.

Shahpur Shahr, W Pakistan: see SHAHPUR CITY.

Shahr [Persian,=city], for names in Iran beginning thus and not found here: see under following part of the name.

Shahraban, Iraq: see MUQDADIYAH.

Shahrak (shä'rŭk) or **Qala Shahrak** (kŭ'lŭ), town (pop. over 500), Herat prov., NW Afghanistan, 130 mi. E of Herat, in W outliers of the Hindu Kush. Pop.: Persian-speaking Taimanis. Also spelled Shaharak or Qala Shaharak.

Shahr-e-Babak, Iran: see SHAHR-I-BABAK.

Shahr-e-Kord, Iran: see SHAHR-I-KURD.

Shahreza, Iran: see SHAHRIZA.

Shahr-i-Babak or **Shahr-e-Babak** (both: shä'hŭrēbäbäk'), village, Tenth Prov., in Yezd, central Iran, 130 mi. SSE of Yezd; grain, opium, cotton; carpet weaving.

Shahrig (shä'rĭg), village, Sibi dist., NE central Baluchistan, W Pakistan, in N Central Brahui Range, 45 mi. NNW of Sibi; wheat; coal mined. S.

Shahr-i-Kurd or **Shahr-e-Kord** (both: kōrd'), town (1940 pop. 13,469), Tenth Prov., in Isfahan, W central Iran, 50 mi. WSW of Isfahan; wheat, opium. Formerly known as Deh Kurd.

Shahriza (shärĭzä') or **Shahreza** (–rēzä'), town (1940 pop. 23,980), Tenth Prov., in Isfahan, W central Iran, 50 mi. S of Isfahan and on Isfahan-Shiraz road; fruit gardens; opium, cotton; cotton-spinning factory. Formerly known as Qumisheh or Kumisheh, it was renamed for Shah Riza, grandson of the Imam Riza, whose blue-tiled tomb is here.

Shahr Rey. **1** Town, Seventh Prov., in Fars, Iran: see RISHAHR. **2** Town, Second Prov., in Teheran, Iran: see RAI.

Shahrud (shäro͞od'), town (1941 pop. 23,132), Second Prov., NE Iran, on railroad to Meshed, and 200 mi. ENE of Teheran and 45 mi. SE of Gurgan across Elburz mts.; alt. 4,319 ft. Trade center of former Shahrud prov.; cotton, wheat, fruit; lumbering; match mfg., rugmaking, leatherworking. Airfield. Reached by railroad in 1941. Shahrud prov., bounded E by Khurasan and W by Samnan and Gurgan, was inc. (1938) into Iran's Second Prov. (see TEHERAN).

Shah Rud (shä'ro͞od'), river in N Iran, rises 30 mi. NW of Teheran, flows 130 mi. WNW, joining the Qizil Uzun at Manjil to form the Sefid Rud.

Shahsawar or **Shahsavar** (both: shäsävär'), town (1940 pop. 5,046), First Prov., in W Mazanderan, N Iran, on Caspian Sea, 80 mi. ESE of Resht.

Shahsien (shä'shyĕn'), town (pop. 19,431), ⊙ Shahsien co. (pop. 97,937), central Fukien prov., China, 30 mi. WSW of Nanping and on Sha R. (tributary of Min R.); rice, sugar, peanuts, beans.

Shahyar (shähyär'), Chinese *Shaya* (shä'yä'), town and oasis (pop. 59,304), W central Sinkiang prov., China, 40 mi. S of Kucha, near Tarim R.; pear-growing center; grain, cattle.

Shahzand (shäzänd'), town, First Prov., in Arak, W central Iran, 20 mi. SW of Arak and on Trans-Iranian RR; sugar beets, fruit. Sugar refinery.

Shaibah, Iraq: see SHU'AIBA.

Shaibi, Sheibi, or **Sha'ibi** (all: shĕē'bē), tribal area of Western Aden Protectorate, on Yemen *status quo* line; ⊙ Awabil (former ⊙, Bakhal). Formerly considered part of Upper Yafa confederation, it began to be regarded as a separate sheikdom after 1940s. A protectorate treaty dates from 1903.

Shaidan or **Shaydan** (shīdän'), village (1939 pop. over 2,000), NE Leninabad oblast, Tadzhik SSR, on S slope of Kurama Range, 45 mi. NE of Leninabad; irrigated area (wheat, cotton). Until c.1940, called Asht.

Shaikh, for Arabic names beginning thus and not found here: see under SHEIKH.

Shaikhabad (shī'khäbäd"), town (pop. over 2,000), Kabul prov., E Afghanistan, 40 mi. SW of Kabul, and on highway to Ghazni, at crossing of Logar R.

Shaikhpura, India: see SHEIKHPURA.

Shaikh Sa'ad or **Shaykh Sa'd** (shīkh' sä'-äd), town, 'Amara prov., E Iraq, on Tigris R. and 70 mi. NW of 'Amara; dates, rice, corn, millet, sesame.

Shaikh Shu'aib or **Sheykh Sho'eyb** (both: shākh' shōāb'), island in Persian Gulf, off S Iran, 95 mi. WNW of Lingeh; 53°15'E 26°50'N; c.14 mi. long, 4 mi. wide. Sparsely populated.

Shaikhupura, W Pakistan; see SHEIKHUPURA, dist.

Shaistaganj, E Pakistan: see HABIGANJ.

Shaitanski Zavod, Russian SFSR: see PERVOURALSK.

Shajapur (shä'jäpo͝or), town (pop. 10,757), ⊙ Shajapur dist., central Madhya Bharat, India, 55 mi. NNE of Indore; market center for cotton, wheat, millet; cotton ginning. Founded c.1640 by emperor Shah Jahan; present name corrupted from Shahjahanpur.

Shakardarah or **Shakardarrah** (shŭkŭr'dŭrŭ) [Pashto,=sugar valley], town, Kabul prov., E Afghanistan, 15 mi. NW of Kabul, at foot of Paghman Mts.; agr. center in Samt-i-Shimali dist.

Shakargarh (shŭkŭr'gŭr), village, Sialkot dist., E Punjab, W Pakistan, 40 mi. ESE of Sialkot; local market for wheat, corn.

Shaker Heights, residential city (pop. 28,222), Cuyahoga co., N Ohio, a SE suburb of Cleveland. Founded 1905; inc. 1912 as village, 1931 as city.

Shakertown or **Pleasant Hill,** former Shaker settlement, Mercer co., central Ky., on Kentucky R. and 20 mi. SW of Lexington. Settled 1805; last member of Shaker colony here died 1925. Guest house, now a mus., contains relics.

Shakespeare Cliff, England: see DOVER.

Shakhbuz (shŭkhbo͞os'), village (1932 pop. estimate 920), N Nakhichevan Autonomous SSR, Azerbaijan SSR, 15 mi. NNE of Nakhichevan; wineries.

Shakh-Dag (shŭkh-däk'), range in the Lesser Caucasus, on Armenian-Azerbaijan SSR border, on N shore of L. Sevan; rises to c.10,900 ft. Dashkesan iron mines on N slopes.

Shakhimardan (shŭkhēmŭrdän'), village, S Fergana oblast, Uzbek SSR, 27 mi. S of Fergana and on Shakhimardan R. Center of small Uzbek enclave in Kirghiz SSR.

Shakhimardan River, in Kirghiz and Uzbek SSR, rises on N slope of Alai Range, flows c.50 mi. N, past Shakhimardan, Frunze, and Vuadil. In its lower reaches it fans out into irrigation canals which disappear into sands of Fergana Valley.

Shakhmatovo, Russian SFSR: see KRASNY TEKSTILSHCHIK.

Shakhovichi, Yugoslavia: see SAHOVICI.

Shakhovskaya (shŭkhŭfskī'ŭ), village (1939 pop. over 2,000), NW Moscow oblast, Russian SFSR, 16 mi. W of Volokolamsk; flax processing, agr.-machinery mfg.

Shakhrinau (shŭkhrēnou'), village (1932 pop. estimate 2,220), NW Stalinabad oblast, Tadzhik SSR, near railroad, 23 mi. W of Stalinabad; cotton, vineyards. Formerly Cheptura.

Shakhristan (–stän'), village (1948 pop. over 2,000), W Leninabad oblast, Tadzhik SSR, on N slope of Turkestan Range, 13 mi. SW of Ura-Tyube, on Leninabad-Stalinabad highway; wheat, truck.

Shakhrisyabz (–syäps'), city (1932 pop. estimate 14,200), NE Kashka-Darya oblast, Uzbek SSR, 4 mi. S of Kitab station; metalworking, silk milling, food processing. On site of anc. Kesh, home of Tamerlane. Formerly spelled Shakhrizyabs.

Shakhta (shäkh'tŭ) [Rus.,=mine], town (1944 pop. over 500), E central Molotov oblast, Russian SFSR, 3 mi. from (under jurisdiction of) Kizel; bituminous-coal mining.

Shakhta [Rus.,=mine]. Name of numerous mining towns in the Ukraine, usually followed by numbers. **1 Shakhta No. 1,** town (1939 pop. over 500), E Stalino oblast, Ukrainian SSR, in the Donbas, 4 mi. E of Snezhnoye; coal mines. **2 Shakhta No. 2,** town, E Stalino oblast, Ukrainian SSR, in Donbas coal region: see PERVOMAISKI. **3 Shakhta No. 3/3 bis,** town (1939 pop. over 500), SE Voroshilovgrad oblast, Ukrainian SSR, in the Donbas, near Krasnodon; coal mines. **4 Shakhta No. 5 bis,** town (1939 pop. over 500), S Voroshilovgrad oblast, Ukrainian SSR, in the Donbas, near Krasny Luch; coal mines. **5 Shakhta No. 7/7 bis,** town (1939 pop. over 500), S Voroshilovgrad oblast, Ukrainian SSR, in the Donbas, 2 mi. S of Bokovo-Antratsit; anthracite mining. **6 Shakhta No. 7/8,** town (1926 pop. 1,862), S Voroshilovgrad oblast, Ukrainian SSR, in the Donbas, near Krasny Luch; coal mines. Formerly called Karlomarksovski No. 7/8 Rudnik. **7 Shakhta No. 8,** town, E Stalino oblast, Ukrainian SSR, in Donbas coal region: see OREKHOVSKI. **8 Shakhta No. 8/9,** town (1926 pop. 1,138), S Voroshilovgrad oblast, Ukrainian SSR, in the Donbas, just N of Bokovo-Antratsit; anthracite mining. **9 Shakhta No. 12,** town (1939 pop. over 500), SE Voroshilovgrad oblast, Ukrainian SSR, in the Donbas, near Krasnodon; coal mines. **10 Shakhta No. 18,** town, E Stalino oblast, Ukrainian SSR, in Donbas coal region: see NOVY DONBASS. **11 Shakhta No. 19,** town (1939 pop. over 500), E Stalino oblast, Ukrainian SSR, in the Donbas, c.5 mi. NNW of Snezhnoye; coal mines. **12 Shakhta No. 22/53,** town (1939 pop. over 500), S Voroshilovgrad oblast, Ukrainian SSR, in the Donbas, 3 mi. SW of Bokovo-Antratsit; anthracite mining. **13 Shakhta No. 33/37,** town (1926 pop. 926), S Voroshilovgrad oblast, Ukrainian SSR, in the Donbas, 6 mi. NE of Bokovo-Antratsit; anthracite mines. Formerly Lobovski No. 33/37 Rudnik.

Shakhta Imeni Dimitrova (ē'mĭnyē dyĭmē'trŭvŭ), town (1939 pop. over 500), W Stalino oblast, Ukrainian SSR, in the Donbas, near Krasnoarmeiskoye.

Shakhtersk (shŭkh-tyôrsk'), city (1940 pop. 28,599), S Sakhalin, Russian SFSR, on W coast, 7 mi. N of Uglegorsk; coal-mining center. Under Japanese rule (1905–45), called Toro (tōrō').

Shakhty (shäkh'tē). **1** Town (1948 pop. over 500), S Buryat-Mongol Autonomous SSR, Russian SFSR, just NE of Gusinoye L., 60 mi. SW of Ulan-Ude; lignite mining. **2** City (1926 pop. 41,043; 1939 pop. 155,081), SW Rostov oblast, Russian SFSR, 40 mi. NE of Rostov; major anthracite-mining center in E Donets Basin; mfg. (machinery, apparel, furniture), agr. processing (dairy products, meat). City includes Shakhty proper (until early 1920s, Aleksandrovsk-Grushevski) at Shakhtnaya station and (since c.1940) Artemovski (5 mi. NE; mines; power plant). Town of Kamenolomni adjoins (S).

Shakhunya or **Shakhun'ya** (shŭko͞o'nyŭ), city (1939 pop. over 2,000), NE Gorki oblast, Russian SFSR, on railroad and 135 mi. NE of Gorki; metalworking. Became city in 1943.

Sha Ki, China: see SHA RIVER, Fukien prov.

Shaki (shä'kē), town, Oyo prov., Western Provinces, SW Nigeria, 65 mi. NW of Oyo; cotton weaving, shea-nut processing; cattle raising.

Shaklawa, Iraq: see SHAQLAWA.

Shako, Korea: see CHAHO.

Shakopee (shä'kŭpē), city (pop. 3,185), ⊙ Scott co., SE central Minn., on Minnesota R. and 18 mi. SW of Minneapolis; trading and mfg. center for farming area; ice cream, malt, beverages, bricks, ironware. Settled 1851, inc. 1870. State reformatory for women is here.

Shakotan, Russian SFSR: see MALOKURILSKOYE.

Shaktolik (shăktō͞o'lĭk), Eskimo village (pop. 123), W Alaska, at E end of Norton Sound, 130 mi. E of Nome; trading post. Has territorial school. Sometimes spelled Shaktoolik.

Shakyai, Lithuania: see SAKIAI.

Shal, W Pakistan: see QUETTA.

Shala (shä'lŭ), **Shalski,** or **Shal'skiy** (shäl'skē), town (1949 pop. over 500), SE Karelo-Finnish SSR, on L. Onega, at mouth of Vodla R. and 16 mi. W of Pudozh; granite quarries.

Shala, Lake (shä'lä) (□ c.175), S central Ethiopia, in Great Rift Valley, bet. lakes Hora Abyata and Awusa, 105 mi. S of Addis Ababa; 7°25'N 38°30'E; alt. 5,141 ft.; 16 mi. long (E-W), 12 mi. wide. Receives many short tributaries (S) and during flood periods, receives overflow of L. Hora Abyata (N). Has no outlet and water is saline.

Shalagh River, Iran and Afghanistan: see SHELAGH RIVER.

Shalakusha (shŭlŭko͞o'shŭ), town (1941 pop. over 500), SW Archangel oblast, Russian SFSR, on railroad and 40 mi. N of Nyandoma; sawmill.

Shalalth, village (pop. estimate 250), S B.C., on Seton L., 13 mi. W of Lillooet, in lumbering and mining (gold, silver) region.

Shaler (shā'lŭr), urban township (pop. 16,430), Allegheny co., SW Pa., on Allegheny R. opposite N Pittsburgh; residential. Post office is Glenshaw.

Shalford, residential town and parish (pop. 3,447), W central Surrey, England, on the Wey just S of Guildford; mfg. of electrical equipment.

Shali, Russian SFSR: see MEZHDURECHYE.

Shalimar, India: see HOWRAH, city.

Shalimar, town (pop. 694), Okaloosa co., NW Fla., on Choctawhatchee Bay 38 mi. E of Pensacola.

Shalinskoye (shŭlyēn'skŭyŭ), village (1939 pop. over 2,000), SE Krasnoyarsk Territory, Russian SFSR, 35 mi. SE of Krasnoyarsk; metalworks.

Shalkot, W Pakistan: see QUETTA.

Shallal, El, Esh Shallal, or **Al-Shallal** (all: ĕshshăl-lăl'), village (1937 pop. 954; 1947 commune pop. 6,485), Aswan prov., S Egypt, 3 mi. S of

Aswan, at 1st Nile cataract; rail terminus and transfer point for Nile steamers to Wadi Halfa in the Anglo-Egyptian Sudan; cereals, dates. Sometimes spelled Shellal.

Shallotte (shŭlōt′) or **Shallotte City,** fishing town (pop. 493), Brunswick co., SE N.C., 31 mi. SW of Wilmington and on short Shallotte R., entering the Atlantic near by through Shallotte Inlet.

Shallowater, village (pop. c.800), Lubbock co., NW Texas, on the Llano Estacado, 10 mi. NW of Lubbock; a shipping, trading point in agr. region.

Shallow Lake, village (pop. 304), S Ont., on small Shallow L., 8 mi. WNW of Owen Sound; dairying, mixed farming, fruitgrowing.

Shalshalamun (shăl″shălămōōn′), village (pop. 6,521), Sharqiya prov., Lower Egypt, 10 mi. SW of Zagazig; cotton.

Shalski, Karelo-Finnish SSR: see SHALA.

Shalu (shä′lōō′), Jap. *Sharoku* (shärō′kōō), town (1935 pop. 6,630), W central Formosa, near W coast, 10 mi. NW of Taichung, and on railroad; sugar milling; mfg. of pottery, wooden and bamboo articles; rice, sugar cane, pumpkins, livestock. Its port is Wusi.

Shalya (shä′lyŭ), town (1948 pop. over 2,000), SW Sverdlovsk oblast, Russian SFSR, in W foothills of the central Urals, on railroad and 50 mi. WSW of Kirovgrad; lumbering, charcoal burning. Gold placers near by.

Shalygino (shŭlĭ′gĭnŭ), village (1939 pop. over 2,000), E Sumy oblast, Ukrainian SSR, 10 mi. SE of Glukhov; sugar refining, peat cutting.

Shalym (shŭlĭm′), town (1948 pop. over 2,000), S Kemerovo oblast, Russian SFSR, in the Gornaya Shoriya, 2 mi. N of Tashtagol; iron mines.

Sha'm or **Sha'am** (shäm), village, Trucial Oman, in Ras al Khaima sheikdom, on Persian Gulf, 18 mi. NNE of Ras al Khaima town and just S of the cape Ras Sha'm.

Sham, El, or **Esh Sham,** Syria: see DAMASCUS; SYRIA.

Sham, Jabal, Oman: see AKHDAR, JABAL.

Shama (shä′mä), town, Western Prov., S Gold Coast colony, on Gulf of Guinea, at mouth of Pra R., and 6 mi. NE of Sekondi; fishing center. Has remains of 17th-cent. European castle. A major trading post until 19th cent.

Shamailiya, Trucial Oman: see FUJAIRA.

Shamary (shŭmä′rē), town (1946 pop. over 500), SW Sverdlovsk oblast, Russian SFSR, on Sylva R. and 19 mi. ENE of Shalya, on railroad; sawmilling.

Shamats, Yugoslavia: see SAMAC.

Shambat (shăm′băt), village (pop. 4,069), Khartoum prov., central Anglo-Egyptian Sudan, on right bank of the Nile and 3 mi. N of Khartoum, opposite Omdurman; site of large govt. experimental farm and agr. school.

Shambaugh (shăm′bô), town (pop. 251), Page co., SW Iowa, on West Nodaway R. and 5 mi. S of Clarinda, in bituminous-coal-mining area; farm equipment.

Shambe (shăm′bē), village, Upper Nile prov., S Anglo-Egyptian Sudan, on the Bahr el Jebel (White Nile) and 180 mi. SSW of Malakal, in Sudd swamps.

Shameen, China: see CANTON.

Shamganj (shăm′gŭnj), village, Mymensingh dist., E central East Bengal, E Pakistan, 12 mi. NE of Mymensingh; rail junction, with spurs to Jaria Jhanjail (12 mi. NNE) and Mohanganj (26 mi. E; fish trade center).

Shamgarh (shăm′gŭr), village, W Madhya Bharat, India, 36 mi. ENE of Mandasor; local market for cotton, millet, wheat; cotton ginning. Excavations at Dhamnar village, 9 mi. W; medieval Buddhist and Brahmanic rock-cut caves and shrines.

Shamir (shämēr′) settlement (pop. 300), Upper Galilee, NE Israel, near Syrian border, at W foot of Bashan hills, 16 mi. NE of Safad; mixed farming. Founded 1944; withstood Arab attacks, 1948.

Shamiran or **Shemiran** (shĕmērän′), foothills of the Elburz mts., N Iran, N and NE of Teheran; contain summer resorts of Tajrish, Darband, Gulhek.

Shamiya, Ash, Al Shamiya, or **Al-Shamiyah** (all: äsh-shämē′yŭ), village, Diwaniya prov., SE central Iraq, on the Euphrates and 20 mi. W of Diwaniya; rice, dates. Has a floating bridge. Also called Umm al-Ba'rur.

Shamkhor (shŭmkhôr′), city (1926 pop. 2,166), W Azerbaijan SSR, on railroad and 20 mi. NW of Kirovabad; wine-producing center; distilleries; cheese. Called Annenfeld or Annino, c.1928–37.

Shamkhor River, W Azerbaijan SSR, rises in Shakh-Dag section of the Lesser Cacasus, on Armenian border; flows 53 mi. NNE to Kura R. 10 mi. NE of Shamkhor. Used for irrigation.

Shamli (shämlē), town (pop. 12,416), Muzaffarnagar dist., N Uttar Pradesh, India, near Eastern Jumna Canal, 23 mi. W of Muzaffarnagar; wheat, gram, sugar cane, oilseeds.

Shamlug (shŭmlōōk′), town (1926 pop. 814), NE Armenian SSR, 5 mi. NE of Alaverdi; copper mining.

Shammar, Jebel, or **Jabal Shammar** (both: jĕ′bĕl shăm-mär′), highland province (pop. 200,000) of N Nejd, Saudi Arabia; ⊙ Hail. Extending from the N Nafud desert to the Wadi Rima (S), it is astride lat. 28°N and rises to 6,000 ft. Its 2 main mtn. ranges (oriented SW–NE)—the Jabal Aja and the Jabal Salma (Jebel Selma)—enclose the principal populated dist. around Hail. Pop. is largely Bedouin, but also includes agr. oasis dwellers. Prov. includes the outlying W oases of Taima and Khaibar. Ruled after late-18th cent. by the Rashid family, Jebel Shammar was briefly under Wahabi influence, but then asserted its independence against Riyadh, which it controlled in late-19th cent. The Rashid house resisted Ibn Saud during his drive to conquer all Arabia, but was finally overwhelmed by the ruler of Nejd in 1921.

Shamo, Mongolia: see GOBI.

Shamo, Lake, Ethiopia: see CHAMO, LAKE.

Shamokin (shŭmō′kĭn), borough (pop. 16,879), Northumberland co., E central Pa., 12 mi. ESE of Sunbury; anthracite; textiles, clothing, machinery, meat products, fertilizers. Laid out 1835.

Shamokin Dam, borough (pop. 730), Snyder co., E central Pa., on Susquehanna R. opposite Sunbury.

Shamrock. 1 Village (1940 pop. 2,530), Dixie co., N Fla., 1 mi. WNW of Cross City; sawmilling. **2** Town (pop. 263), Creek co., central Okla., 28 mi. WSW of Sapulpa, in agr. and oil-producing area. **3** City (pop. 3,322), Wheeler co., extreme N Texas, in E part of huge Panhandle natural-gas and oil field, c.50 mi. SE of Pampa, near North Fork of Red R.; shipping, commercial, mfg. center for petroleum, cotton, truck, livestock area; oil and gas wells, mfg. (gasoline, carbon black, cottonseed oil, dairy products); cotton gins, hatchery. Settled 1901, inc. 1911.

Shamsabad (shŭm′säbäd). **1** Town (pop. 5,077), Agra dist., W Uttar Pradesh, India, 13 mi. SSE of Agra; pearl millet, gram, wheat, barley, oilseeds. **2** Town (pop. 8,475), Farrukhabad dist., central Uttar Pradesh, India, 13 mi. NW of Farrukhabad; wheat, gram, jowar, corn, potatoes, tobacco. Old town founded c.1228 by Shams-ud-din Altamsh (Iltutmish); new town founded c.1585. Also spelled Shamshabad.

Shamsherpur, India: see NAHAN.

Shamva (shäm′vä), village (pop. 339), Salisbury prov., NE Southern Rhodesia, in Mashonaland, 50 mi. NE of Salisbury; alt. 3,385 ft. Rail terminus; gold-mining and agr. center; tobacco, cotton, peanuts, corn, citrus fruit; dairy products. Hq. of native commissioner; police post.

Shana, Russian SFSR: see KURILSK.

Shanafiyah, Iraq: see SHINAFIYA.

Shanagolden (shă″nŭgōl′dŭn), Gaelic *Seana-Ghualainn*, town (pop. 229), NW Co. Limerick, Ireland, near the Shannon, 21 mi. W of Limerick; agr. market (grain, potatoes; dairying). It was site of Shanid Castle, fortress of the Desmonds.

Shanawan (shănăwăn′), village (pop. 9,917), Minufiya prov., Lower Egypt, 4 mi. S of Shibin el Kom; cereals, cotton, flax.

Shancheng, China: see NANTSING.

Shanchow, China: see SHANHSIEN, Honan prov.

Shandaken (shăndā′kŭn), resort village, Ulster co., SE N.Y., in the Catskills, on Esopus Creek and 25 mi. NW of Kingston.

Shandaken Tunnel, N.Y.: see ASHOKAN RESERVOIR.

Shandur Pass (shŭndōōr′), mountain pass (alt. c.12,250 ft.) in the Hindu Kush, bet. Chitral and Gilgit, W Pakistan, 100 mi. WNW of Gilgit town.

Shandwe, Belgian Congo: see LUISHIA.

Shanesville (shānz′vĭl), village (pop. 460), Tuscarawas co., E Ohio, 11 mi. W of New Philadelphia; makes ceramics.

Shangaly (shŭn-gä′lē), village (1939 pop. over 500), SW Archangel oblast, Russian SFSR, on railroad, on right affluent of Vaga R. and 40 mi. E of Velsk; dairying.

Shangani (shäng-gä′nē), township (pop. 57), Bulawayo prov., central Southern Rhodesia, in Matabeleland, on upper Shangani R., on railroad and 55 mi. ENE of Bulawayo; alt. 4,504 ft. Tobacco, corn; cattle, sheep, goats. Shangani village, 65 mi. NNW, is hq. of native commissioner for Shangani dist.

Shangani River, W Southern Rhodesia, rises N of Fort Rixon, flows 220 mi. NW and W, through Shangani dist. to Gwaai R. 22 mi. NW of Dett.

Shangcheng or **Shang-ch'eng** (shäng′chŭng′), town ⊙ Shangcheng co. (pop. 209,353), S Honan prov., China, near Anhwei line, 80 mi. ESE of Sinyang; wheat, millet, beans. Coal mines near by.

Shangchih (shäng′jŭ′), town, ⊙ Shangchih co. (pop. 133,383), W Sungkiang prov., Manchuria, 75 mi. SE of Harbin and on railroad; road-rail junction; grain market. Called Wuchuho or Wuchimiho until 1927, and Chuho, 1927–49.

Shang-chin, China: see SHANGKIN.

Shang-chiu, China: see SHANGKIU.

Shangchow, China: see SHANGHSIEN.

Shang-ch'uan Island, China: see SAINT JOHN ISLAND.

Shangchwan Island, China: see SAINT JOHN ISLAND.

Shanghai (shăng′hī′, shäng′-) [Chinese,=above (at) the sea], city (1947 pop. 4,300,630) in, but independent of, Kiangsu prov., China, port on Whangpoo R. (a narrow tributary of Yangtze estuary) and 170 mi. ESE of Nanking; 31°14′N 121°30′E. Largest city on continent of Asia and one of the world's leading seaports, Shanghai is the natural seaward trade focus of central China, normally handling ½ of the country's overseas trade. Its preeminent commercial position, caused primarily by the vast, productive, and densely settled Yangtze R. hinterland, is further enhanced by the large coastwise trade funneled into the port. Situated at the gateway to one of China's richest regions and at the former hub of Western interests, Shanghai has also become the chief mfg. center of the country, based almost entirely on imported fuel and raw materials. Its leading industries are cotton milling (half of China's spindles), silk spinning, rice milling, tanning, match and paper mfg., shipbuilding, and machine mfg. It also produces cigarettes, egg products, meat and canned goods. Next to Peking the foremost educational city of China, Shanghai has many universities, including Chi Nan, Fuh Tan, Aurora, and St. John's, and technical and scientific institutions. It is also a great publishing center. Connected by rail with Nanking and, via Pukow, with N China, and with Hangchow, Nanchang, and S China. Main civil airport is at Lunghwa. The greater part of the city is situated on a tidal flat on left bank of Whangpoo R. at the mouth of Soochow Creek. Shanghai's commercial core is in the former International Settlement at the river confluence, where broad streets and handsome boulevards are lined by imposing bldgs., including banks, business houses, hotels, and department stores. The Bund (which runs along the waterfront), Nanking Road, and Bubbling Well Road are the best-known thoroughfares. Industrial Hongkew, the Settlement's NE section, is thickly studded with factories and warehouses along the waterfront, as is the right-bank suburb of Pootung across the Whangpoo. The former French Concession and the teeming outlying dists., including the N Chapei suburb, form the residential sections of Shanghai. Dredged at considerable cost to admit ocean-going vessels via the Yangtze estuary, the wharf-lined Whangpoo R. is the shipping route for the city's exports, which consist chiefly of raw silk, hog bristles, hides, tea, and vegetable oils. The name Shanghai dates from 11th cent.; but the town, made a walled city in 14th cent., continued as an unimportant fishing port to the middle of 19th cent. By the Treaty of Nanking (1842), Shanghai became one of the original treaty ports, and the ensuing Western influence launched the city on its phenomenal growth. The greater part of the metropolis was inc. into the British concession (1843), just N of the old walled city, and into the U.S. concession of Hongkew (1862), which were consolidated (1863) into the International Settlement; the French Concession (1849) continued as a separate unit W of the old city. Separate administrations for the foreign zones existed until the Second World War. Shanghai was the scene (1932) of a Sino-Japanese incident. During Sino-Japanese War, city was occupied (1937–45) by Japanese. It fell to the Chinese Communists in 1949. Shanghai became an independent municipality in 1927. It was ⊙ Shanghai co. (1946 pop. 118,265) until 1937, when co. seat was moved to village of Pehkiao, 12 mi. S, thereafter also known as Shanghai.

Shanghang (shäng′häng′), town (pop. 11,020), ⊙ Shanghang co. (pop. 196,438), SW Fukien prov., China, 50 mi. S of Changting and on Ting R.; rice, wheat, sweet potatoes. Manganese and iron mines near by.

Shangho (shäng′hŭ′), town, ⊙ Shangho co. (pop. 157,000), N Shantung prov., China, on railroad and 45 mi. NNE of Tsinan; cotton weaving; wheat, kaoliang, beans.

Shanghsien (shäng′shyĕn′), town (pop. 6,445), ⊙ Shanghsien co. (pop. 252,501), SE Shensi prov., China, 55 mi. SE of Sian and on road to Honan; commercial center; cotton weaving, papermaking; rice, wheat, kaoliang, indigo. Until 1913 called Shangchow.

Shang-hsin-ho, China: see SHANGSINHO.

Shangi (shäng′yē′), town, ⊙ Shangi co. (pop. 37,916), N Chahar prov., China, 55 mi. NW of Kalgan; cattle; grain. Until 1935 called Tatsingkow.

Shangjao (shäng′rou′), town (pop. 30,937), ⊙ Shangjao co. (pop. 309,326), NW Kiangsi prov., China, on Kwangsin R., on Chekiang-Kiangsi RR and 135 mi. E of Nanchang; commercial center; rice, peanut oil, ramie. Coal mines. Until 1912 called Kwangsin.

Shangkao (shäng′gou′), town (pop. 8,100), ⊙ Shangkao co. (pop. 104,266), NW Kiangsi prov., China, 65 mi. WSW of Nanchang and on Kin R.; rice, cotton, ramie, sesame oil. Coal mining.

Shangkin or **Shang-chin** (both: shäng′jĭn′), town, ⊙ Shangkin co. (pop. 52,826), SW Kwangsi prov., China, 30 mi. WSW of Tsungshan and on Li R.; millet, beans, peanuts, sugar cane.

Shangkiu or **Shang-chiu** (both: shäng′jyō′), town (1947 pop. estimate 70,000), ⊙ Shangkiu co. (1937 pop. 625,104), NE Honan prov., China, 80 mi. ESE of Kaifeng and on Lunghai RR; agr. center; silk weaving; exports hides, wheat, kaoliang, beans, mushrooms. An anc. city, it was an imperial residence of the Northern Sung dynasty (960–1127).

Shanglin (shäng′lĭn′), town, ⊙ Shanglin co. (pop. 219,054), SW central Kwangsi prov., China, 50 mi. NNE of Nanning; millet, beans. Gold mines near.

Shangnan (shäng′nän′), town, ⊙ Shangnan co. (pop. 68,036), SE Shensi prov., China, 115 mi. SE of Sian, on Honan line; rice, wheat, kaoliang.
"Shangri-La," Md.: see CATOCTIN MOUNTAIN.
Shangshui (shäng′shwā′), town, ⊙ Shangshui co. (pop. 266,153), E Honan prov., China, 33 mi. E of Yencheng; cotton weaving; rice, wheat.
Shangsinho or **Shang-hsin-ho** (both: shäng′shĭn′-hŭ′), town, S Kiangsu prov., China, 3 mi. SW of Nanking and on Yangtze R.
Shangsze or **Shang-ssu** (both: shäng′sû′), town, ⊙ Shangsze co. (pop. 92,719), SW Kwangsi prov., China, 45 mi. SSW of Nanning, near Kwangtung line; rice, wheat, millet.
Shangtsai or **Shang-ts'ai** (shäng′tsī′), town, ⊙ Shangtsai co. (pop. 506,405), central Honan prov., China, 28 mi. SE of Yencheng; wheat, beans, kaoliang.
Shangtsichang, Manchuria: see SUILENG.
Shangtu (shäng′dōō′). **1** Town, ⊙ Shangtu co. (pop. 66,395), NW Chahar prov., China, 85 mi. NW of Kalgan; cattle raising; wheat, beans, kaoliang. **2** or **Shangtuho** (shäng′dōō′hŭ′), village, NE Chahar prov., China, 10 mi. NW of Tolun and on upper Lwan R. (here called Shangtu R.). Was site of China's imperial summer residence during Mongol Yüan dynasty; built 1260 by Kublai Khan.
Shangtu River, China: see LWAN RIVER.
Shangugu (shäng-gōō′gōō), village (1949 pop. 447), W Ruanda-Urundi, in Ruanda, on S shore of L. Kivu opposite Costermansville, near Belgian Congo border, 85 mi. SW of Kigali; alt. 4,768 ft.; center of native trade; coffee plantations; cattle.
Shangulowe, Belgian Congo: see SESA.
Shangyiu or **Shang-yu** (both: shäng′yōō′), town (pop. 8,351), ⊙ Shangyiu co. (pop. 124,727), SW Kiangsi prov., China, 15 mi. WNW of Kanchow and on Tsang R.; rice. Tungsten, tin, gold mines.
Shangyü (shäng′yü′), town (pop. 10,357), ⊙ Shangyü co. (pop. 307,132), NE Chekiang prov., China, 35 mi. W of Ningpo; rice, wheat, peanuts, cotton.
Shang-yu, Kiangsi prov., China: see SHANGYIU.
Shangyütung, China: see KINTANG, Sikang prov.
Shanhaikwan or **Shan-hai-kuan** (shän′hī′gwän′), city (1922 pop. estimate 70,000), northeasternmost Hopeh prov., China, at Liaosi line, on Tientsin-Mukden RR, and 180 mi. E of Peking, on Gulf of Chihli; strategic gateway to Manchuria, at easternmost end of the Great Wall. Called LINYÜ from 1912 until 1949, when it became an independent municipality and Linyü co. seat was transferred to Haiyang. The Shanhaikwan corridor extends NE from here bet. Jehol and the sea, connecting Manchuria and N China.
Shan-hsi, China: see SHANSI; SHENSI.
Shanhsien (shän′shyĕn′). **1** Town, ⊙ Shanhsien co. (pop. 127,415), NW Honan prov., China, on Yellow R. (Shansi line), opposite Pinglu, on Lunghai RR and 75 mi. W of Loyang; commercial center; cotton and wool weaving; exports hides and sheepskins. Saltworks near by. Until 1913 called Shanchow. **2** Town, ⊙ Shanhsien co. (pop. 450,602), southeasternmost Pingyuan prov., China, 45 mi. SE of Hotseh; cotton weaving; wheat, kaoliang, millet. Until 1949 in Shantung prov.
Shan-hua, Formosa: see SHANHWA.
Shanhwa or **Shan-hua** (both: shän′hwä′), Jap. *Zenka* (zäng′kä), town (1935 pop. 1,415), W central Formosa, 11 mi. NE of Tainan, in oil field.
Shani, China: see TAOSHA.
Shani (shä′nē), town (pop. 7,951), Bornu prov., Northern Provinces, E Nigeria, port on Hawal R. (left affluent of Gongola R.) and 28 mi. SSW of Biu; peanuts, cassava, millet, durra; cattle, skins.
Shaniko (shă′nĭkō), town (pop. 61), Wasco co., N Oregon, 45 mi. SE of The Dalles; alt. 3,340 ft.; rail terminus.
Shanivarsante, India: see SANIVARSANTE.
Shankhouse, England: see CRAMLINGTON.
Shanklin, former urban district (1931 pop. 5,072) now in urban dist. of Sandown-Shanklin (1948 pop. estimate 13,170), on E coast of Isle of Wight, Hampshire, England, on Sandown Bay of the Channel, 7 mi. SE of Newport; seaside resort, with beaches and pier. Has fountain with verses by Longfellow, who visited town in 1868.
Shanks Village, N.Y.: see ORANGEBURG.
Shanksville, borough (pop. 342), Somerset co., SW Pa., 9 mi. E of Somerset and on Stony Creek.
Shanmulung (shän′mōō′lōōng′), town, westernmost Yunnan prov., China, 45 mi. SW of Tengchung. Officially known as Lungchwan or Lung-ch'uan (lōōng′chwän) in winter and spring, when LUNGCHWAN dist. seat, moved from CHANGFENGKAI (30 mi. SW), is situated here.
Shannock, mill village (pop. c.500) in Charlestown and Richmond towns, Washington co., SW R.I., on Pawcatuck R. and 11 mi. ENE of Westerly; silks, elastic webbing.
Shannon, borough (pop. 922), S N.Isl., New Zealand, 60 mi. NNE of Wellington; dairy plants, linen mills.
Shannon, village, central Tasmania, 65 mi. NNW of Hobart and on Shannon R. (S outlet of Great L.); hydroelectric plant; sheep.
Shannon or **Shannon Valley,** residential town (pop. 2,069), W Orange Free State, U. of So. Afr., 4 mi. ESE of Bloemfontein; alt. 4,507 ft.
Shannon. 1 County (□ 999; pop. 8,377), S Mo.; ⊙ Eminence. In the Ozarks; drained by Current R. Agr.; lumber mills; copper, manganese mines. Parts of Clark Natl. Forest here. Formed 1841. **2** County (□ 2,100; pop. 5,669), SW S.Dak., on Nebr. line, in Pine Ridge Indian Reservation; drained by White R. Livestock. Shannon, formerly a smaller unorganized co. (□ 960; 1940 pop. 5,366) was combined 1943 with adjacent (N) unorganized co. of Washington (□ 1,140; 1940 pop. 1,789). New co. of Shannon is attached to Fall River co. for judicial purposes.
Shannon. 1 Village (pop. 1,676), Floyd co., NW Ga., 8 mi. NNE of Rome. **2** Village (pop. 668), Carroll co., NW Ill., 11 mi. SSW of Freeport, in rich agr. area. **3** Town (pop. 520), Lee co., NE Miss., 10 mi. S of Tupelo, in agr. area.
Shannon Airport or **Rineanna** (rĭ″nē-ă′nŭ), international airport, S Co. Clare, Ireland, on the Shannon and 15 mi. W of Limerick; 52°41′N 8°59′W; European terminal of North Atlantic air routes.
Shannonbridge (–brĭj′), Gaelic *Rachra,* town (pop. 127), NW Co. Offaly, Ireland, on the Shannon (bridge), at mouth of Suck R., and 3 mi. NE of Banagher; agr. market (cattle; hops, barley, potatoes).
Shannon City, town (pop. 171), on Ringgold-Union co. line, S Iowa, on Grand R. and 12 mi. SSE of Creston, in livestock and grain area.
Shannon Dam, Wash.: see BAKER RIVER.
Shannon Harbour, Gaelic *Cluaine Uaine Bheag,* agr. village (district pop. 431), W Co. Offaly, Ireland, on the Shannon at mouth of Brosna R. and at junction with Grand Canal, 9 mi. N of Birr. Formerly important inland port.
Shannon Island (35 mi. long, 5–15 mi. wide), in Greenland Sea, NE Greenland; 75°10′N 18°15′W. Separated from mainland by Shannon Sound (7–10 mi. wide). Surface is low and level; E coast deeply indented by Frosne Bay. During Second World War isl. was site of German weather station until captured by U.S. forces.
Shannon River, principal river of Ireland, rises on slope of Cuilcagh mtn., Co. Cavan, flows generally S through a series of lakes (Allen, Boderg, Ree, Derg) to Limerick, where it turns W in a broad estuary (c.70 mi. long), past Foynes (head of navigation for large vessels) and Kilrush to its mouth (c. 13 mi. wide) on the Atlantic bet. Loop Head and Kerry Head; c.220 mi. long. Towns on upper course include Carrick-on-Shannon, Athlone, Banagher, Portumna, and Killaloe. Main tributaries are Suck, Brosna, Little Brosna, Deel, and Feale rivers. Grand and Royal canals link the Shannon with the Irish Sea at Dublin. At Ardnacrusha, near Limerick, is major hydroelectric power station. River navigable for small craft for most of its length. Fishing is important.
Shannontown, village (pop. 5,828), Sumter co., central S.C., just S of Sumter; residential, industrial (woodworking plants).
Shannon Valley, U. of So. Afr.: see SHANNON.
Shanpa, China: see SHENPA.
Shanshan (shän′shän′), town, ⊙ Shanshan co. (pop. 43,936), E Sinkiang prov., China, on highway, S of the Bogdo Ola, at E end of Turfan depression, 50 mi. ESE of Turfan; silk and cotton textiles; winegrowing; sericulture. Copper and coal mines, gypsum quarrying near by. Also called Pichan.
Shansi or **Shan-hsi** (both: shăn′sē′, Chinese shän′-shē′) [Chinese,=W of the mountains], province (□ 50,000; pop. 10,000,000) of N China, W of the Taihang Mts.; ⊙ Taiyüan. Bounded W by Shensi and S by Honan along the Yellow R., SE by Pingyuan and E by Hopeh along the Taihang Mts., N by Chahar along S section of the Great Wall, and NW by Suiyuan. Shansi is a loess-covered plateau, overlooking N China plain (E), varying in average alt. bet. 5,000 ft. (N) and 2,500 ft. (S). In addition to the Taihang Mts. on its SE edge, the plateau rises in the Wutai, Taiyo, and Luliang mts. The Fen R., which bisects the prov., flows from N to S through a series of Tertiary lake basins that are the chief centers of pop. and economic activity. Shansi's climate is continental, and only the Fen valley offers protection against cold N winds. Agr., concentrated in the former lake basins of Taiyüan and Linfen, yields N grain (wheat, barley, millet, kaoliang), as well as corn, tobacco, and cotton in sheltered locations. Persimmons, pears, and grapes (made into wine, liquor, vinegar) are also produced. On the open plateau, animal husbandry (fat-tailed sheep, goats) predominates. The entire prov. is underlaid with thick, horizontal layers of coal (anthracite in E, bituminous in W), and contains 50% of China's reserves. Coal is mined by primitive methods wherever it appears on the surface in eroded river valleys. Modern mines exist near Taiyüan, Pingting, and Wutai. Iron abounds in the Taihang Mts., and salt is obtained at the Lutsun salt pan (S). Industrial towns lie mainly along the Tatung-Puchow (Yüngtsi) RR in the Fen valley; they are, in addition to Taiyüan (steel milling), Fenyang, Linfen, Yütze, and Ningwu. Other centers are Pingting (E; with its modern satellite town of Yangchüan), Changchih, and Tsincheng (SE). Pop. belongs entirely to the N Mandarin-speaking group. The prov. is one of the earliest settlement areas of China; Siahsien in S Shansi is associated with the Hsia dynasty (2205–1766 B.C.). The traditional name of Shansi is Chin or Tsin, for a kingdom that existed in the area, 737–420 B.C. Situated in an exposed location near the Mongol areas, the region was protected (300 B.C.) by the older Great Wall. Coal and iron served to make it the earliest Chinese ironworking region, with smelters at Pingting and Tsechow (Tsincheng). It acquired its present name under the Ming dynasty, and came in 1661 under Manchu control. After the Chinese revolution, the prov. became identified with the stable administration of "model" governor Yen Hsi-shan. It was largely occupied by the Japanese during Sino-Japanese War, and passed 1948–49 to Communist control. The area of Shansi prov. of Manchu times was reduced after 1911, when the section (including Kweisui) beyond the N Great Wall went to Suiyuan, and again in 1949, when the area (including Tatung) beyond the S section of the Great Wall was added to Chahar.
Shan State (shăn, shän), constituent unit (□ 61,090; 1941 pop. 1,699,585) of Burma, in E Upper Burma; ⊙ Lashio. Bounded N by Burma's Kachin State, E by China's Yunnan prov. and, along the Mekong, by Laos, and S by Thailand (along the Tanen Taunggyi Range) and by Burma's Karenni State. The state's area coincides essentially with the Shan plateau, a crystalline massif (mean alt. 3,000 ft.) rising abruptly (E) from the Irrawaddy-Sittang valley. Much dissected, it is cut N–S by deep Salween R. gorge. Predominant rocks are gneisses, yielding the rubies and sapphires of MOGOK. The rich silver-lead deposits of Bawdwin occur in anc. volcanic rocks. Average yearly rainfall is 45–50 in. Agr.: hill rice, cotton, opium, vegetables and potatoes, fruit, tea, tung oil. Extensive teak forests. Main centers, Lashio, Taunggyi, and Kengtung, are reached by branches of the axial Rangoon-Mandalay RR and by connecting highways, such as the Burma Road and the Kengtung-Lampang (Thailand) route. The leading modern industry is the smelting of Bawdwin ores at Namtu. The nominal ethnic group, the Shans, constitute 45% of total pop. They are a Thai people resembling the true Thai (Siamese) and the Laos in language and customs. Other groups are the Burmese (20%), the Was and Palaungs of the Mon-Khmer group (10%), the Karens (10%; largely in S), and the Kachins and Chinese (each 4%; largely in N). The Shans, who had migrated after 7th cent. from China's Yunnan prov. via Thailand, entered Burma in 13th cent. and dominated N Burma (until 16th cent.) and Assam where they founded the Ahom kingdom in 1229. They came under Br. rule upon Br. annexation (1885) of Upper Burma. In late 19th cent. the Shans were distributed among 30 petty states ruled as feudatories of the Br. crown by their hereditary chiefs, known as sawbwas, myosas, and ngegunhmus, in decreasing order of their power and importance. In 1922, most of the states were joined into a federation, the Federated Shan States, under a commissioner who also administered the Wa States. Following the Second World War, a single Shan State (including the Wa States) was formed within the Union of Burma, by the terms of the 1947 Constitution. For administrative purposes, the constituent petty states are grouped in the **Southern Shan State** (□ 36,408; 1941 pop. 927,094; ⊙ Taunggyi), which includes the sawbwaships of KENGTUNG, LAIHKA, LAWKSAWK, MAWKMAI, MONGKUNG, MONGNAI, MONGPAI, MONGPAN, MONGPAWN, SAMHKA, and YAWNGHWE; the myosaships of HOPONG, HSAHTUNG, HSAMONGHKAM, KEHSI-MANSAM, LOILONG, MAW, MONGHSU, MONGNAWNG, PWELA, SAKOI, WANYIN; and the ngegunhmus of KYONG, PANGMI, PANGTARA, and YENGAN; and in the **Northern Shan State** (□ 24,682; 1941 pop. 772,491; ⊙ Lashio), which includes the sawbwaships of NORTH HSENWI and SOUTH HSENWI, HSIPAW, MANGLUN, MONGMIT, TAWNPENG, and the WA STATES.
Shantan (shän′dän′), town, ⊙ Shantan co. (pop. 35,959), central Kansu prov., China, on the Silk Road to Sinkiang, and 38 mi. ESE of Changyeh, at the Great Wall; coal-mining center; pottery mfg.; kaolin quarrying. Gold deposits near by.
Shantar Islands (shŭntär′) (□ 965), in SW Sea of Okhotsk, in Lower Amur oblast, Khabarovsk Territory, Russian SFSR; 55°N 137°E. Consists of 4 large, 8 small isls. Largest, Bolshoi (or Bol'shoy) Shantar Isl. (35 mi. long, 28 mi. wide) and Feklistov Isl. (W). Inhabitants chiefly Russians. Fishing, hunting. Discovered 1645 by Rus. explorer Poyarkov.
Shantiniketan, India: see SANTINIKETAN.
Shan-t'ou, China: see SWATOW.
Shantung (shăn′tŭng′, shän′tōōng′, shän′dōōng′) [Chinese,=E of the mountains], province (□ 55,000; pop. 36,000,000) of E China; ⊙ Tsinan. Bounded NW by Hopeh, W by Pingyuan along the Grand Canal, and S by Kiangsu along Lunghai RR, Shantung prov. extends as a rocky, indented peninsula into the Yellow Sea, forming the S shore of the Gulf of Chihli. The prov. consists of 2 barren

elevated regions of igneous rocks, the sacred Tai Shan (W; 5,069 ft.) and the peninsular heights rising to 3,707 ft. in the Lao Shan. These are connected by sedimentary lowlands of loess and the alluvial deposits of the Yellow R., which in its repeated course changes has entered the sea N and S of the Shantung peninsula. After 1946 the Yellow R. again traversed NW Shantung. The climate is of the N China continental type, though moderated by proximity to the sea. July and Aug. have the greatest rainfall. Coal, bauxite, kaolin, iron, gold are the chief mineral deposits. Shantung ranks 3d as China's coal producer, with mines at Poshan, Tzechwan, Fangtze (near Weifang), and Tsaochwang (near Yihsien). Bauxite and kaolin are mined in the Poshan-Tzechwan dist., iron at Kinlingchen and Kiawang, gold at Mowping and Chaoyüan. Agr. is predominantly of the N type: millet, kaoliang, wheat, and sweet potatoes are grown in the hilly areas; and wheat, peanuts, cotton, ramie, beans, and tobacco in the alluvial lowlands. The prov. is a noted fruitgrowing area (grapes and jujubes). Wild yellow silk, a traditional local product, is woven into Shantung pongee silk (production center is Chowtsun). There are fisheries along the coast. Straw plait, egg and flour products (noodles), bean cake, as well as pongee are the leading export products. Industry is concentrated in Tsinan and Tsingtao (the largest city and chief port), which are connected by railroad. Other ports are Lienyün (deepwater harbor of Sinhai), Weihai, Chefoo, and Lungkow. Inland cities lie mainly along N–S Tientsin-Pukow RR; in addition to Tsinan, these are Tehchow, Taian, Tzeyang, Tsining, and Süchow (junction for Lunghai RR). One of China's most densely settled provs., Shantung has a homogeneous pop. speaking N Mandarin dialect. One of the earliest areas of Chinese settlement, the peninsula is traditionally called Lu, for an early local kingdom that produced the Chinese sages Confucius (b. at Küfow) and Mencius (b. at Tsowhsien). Known since 12th cent. as Shantung (so named with reference to the Taihang Mts.), it was set up as a separate prov. under the Ming dynasty and at 1st included the Liaotung peninsula. As a result of its strategic location, the peninsula was partly leased to Great Britain (Weihaiwei) and Germany (Kiaochow). It was under Jap. occupation during 1914–22, and again (1937–45) during Sino-Japanese War. It passed in 1948 to Communist control.

Shanwei, China: see SWABUE.

Shanyang (shän'yäng'), town, ⊙ Shanyang co. (pop. 106,314), SE Shensi prov., China, 70 mi. SE of Sian, near Hupeh line; wheat, millet, beans.

Shanyin (shän'yĭn'), town, ⊙ Shanyin co. (pop. 59,226), SW Chahar, prov., China, on road and 45 mi. SSW of Tatung, near Shansi line; kaoliang, millet, beans, indigo, ramie. Until 1949 in N Shansi.

Shaochiufang, China: see ANFUCHEN.

Shaochow, China: see KÜKONG.

Shaohing or **Shao-hsing** (both: shou'shĭng'), town (pop. 92,533), ⊙ Shaohing co. (pop. 854,273), N Chekiang prov., China, on railroad and 30 mi. SE of Hangchow; commercial center; rice-wine processing, silk weaving; mfg. of paper fans, joss paper. Rice, wheat, corn, cotton.

Shaopo (shou'bŭ'), town, S Kiangsu prov., China, 8 mi. NNE of Yangchow and on Grand Canal.

Shaowu (shou'wōō'), town (pop. 12,328), ⊙ Shaowu co. (pop. 105,669), NW Fukien prov., China, near Kiangsi line, 65 mi. NW of Nanping, and on Futun (Shaowu) R. (headstream of Min R.); coal-mining center; rice, sugar cane, sweet potatoes, wheat. Exports tea, bamboo shoots, paper, ramie.

Shaoyang (shou'yäng'), town, ⊙ Shaoyang co. (pop. 1,013,104), S Hunan prov., China, 75 mi. WNW of Hengyang; timber, wheat, beans. Coal and iron mining. Until 1926 called Paoking.

Shap, former urban district (1931 pop. 1,228), central Westmorland, England, 10 mi. SSE of Penrith; agr. market for cattle- and sheep-raising area. Has remains of Shap Abbey, founded in 13th cent. Many remains of Stone Age (stone circle, graves) near by. Shap Summit, a pass (alt. 914 ft.) 3 mi. S, is highest point of W coast railroad line to Scotland. Just W, Shap granite works.

Shapaja (shäpä'hä), town (pop. 782), San Martín dept., N Peru, landing at confluence of Mayo and Huallaga rivers, 9 mi. SSE of Tarapoto, in agr. region (tobacco, sugar cane, cotton, coffee).

Shapinsay (shă'pĭnsā), island (□ 10.6, including Hellior Holm isl.; pop. 576) of the Orkneys, Scotland, bet. Pomona and Stronsay isls.; 5 mi. long, 5 mi. wide; generally level. On SW coast is harbor of Ell Wick, overlooked by anc. Balfour Castle. Just off SW coast is islet of Hellior Holm or Hellyor Holm, site of lighthouse (59°1'N 2°54'W).

Shapkino (shäp'kēnŭ), village (1926 pop. 8,552), SE Tambov oblast, Russian SFSR, 25 mi. NE of Borisoglebsk; wheat, sunflowers.

Shapleigh (shăp'lē), town (pop. 531), York co., SW Maine, 20 mi. WNW of Biddeford.

Shap Summit, England: see SHAP.

Shapur (shäpōōr'), anc. city of S Persia, 60 mi. WNW of Shiraz and 12 mi. NW of Kazerun. Founded by Shapur I (ruled A.D. 241–72) of Sassanian dynasty, the city declined after Arab conquest (7th cent.). Remains include colossal statue of Shapur I and several bas-reliefs.

Shaqlawa or **Shaqlawah** (shäklä'wù), town, Erbil prov., N Iraq, in Kurdistan, 25 mi. NE of Erbil; sesame, millet, corn. Sometimes spelled Shaklawa.

Shaqra or **Shaqrah** (shä'krù), town (pop. 12,000), central Nejd, Saudi Arabia, 100 mi. WNW of Riyadh; 25°15'N 45°15'E. Center of Washm dist.; dates, grain; stock raising.

Shara, Mountains, Yugoslavia: see SAR MOUNTAINS.

Sharafkhaneh, Iran: see SHARIFKHANEH.

Sharakpur (shŭrŭk'pōōr), town (pop. 6,764), Sheikhupura dist., E Punjab, W Pakistan, 18 mi. SSE of Sheikhupura; local agr. market (wheat, rice, cotton); rice husking. Also spelled Sharqpur.

Shara Muren, Manchuria: see LIAO RIVER.

Sharan (shŭrän'), village (1948 pop. over 2,000), W Bashkir Autonomous SSR, Russian SFSR, 80 mi. W of Ufa; lumbering; grain, livestock.

Sharanga (shŭrän'gŭ), village (1926 pop. 702), SW Kirov oblast, Russian SFSR, 35 mi. S of Shakhunya; flax processing.

Sharangad, Mongolia: see MANDAL GOBI.

Sharasume (shäräsōōmä'), Chinese *Chenghwa* or *Ch'eng-hua* (chŭng'hwä'), town, ⊙ Sharasume co. (pop. 24,672), northernmost Sinkiang prov., China, on S slopes of the Altai Mts., on tributary of the Black Irtysh and 280 mi. N of Urumchi; 47°52'N 74°54'E. Trade center near Mongolian border. Gold mining near by. It is administrative hq. of the dist. Altai [Chinese *Aerhtai* or *Ashan*], by which name the town is sometimes called, and which formed part (1944–50) of the East Turkestan Republic. Altai dist. was part of Mongolia until 1907.

Sharavati River (shŭrä'vŭtē), in NW Mysore and S Bombay, India, rises in Western Ghats SE of Hosanagara; flows NW past Hosanagara, and W to Arabian Sea at Honavar; c.70 mi. long. Hydroelectric plant at Jog, 1.5 mi. E of famous Gersoppa Falls. Sometimes called Swarna Nadi below Gersoppa village, 12 mi. WNW of falls. Sometimes spelled Shiravati.

Sharbatat, Ras (räs' shärbătăt'), cape on SE Oman coast, at NE side of Kuria Muria Bay of Arabian Sea; 17°55'N 56°23'E.

Sharbot Lake (shär'bŭt), village (pop. estimate 550), SE Ont., on Sharbot L. (5 mi. long), 40 mi. NNW of Kingston; dairying, farming; resort.

Sharchino (shär'chēnŭ), village (1939 pop. over 2,000), N Altai Territory, Russian SFSR, on Kulunda R. and 45 mi. SSE of Kamen, in agr. area.

Shardlow with Great Wilne, parish (pop. 1,012), SE Derby, England. Includes town of Shardlow, on Trent and Mersey Canal, 7 mi. ESE of Derby, with wire factory and 17th-cent. mansion, now a school; and, just NE, agr. village of Great Wilne.

Shargol, Kashmir: see KARGIL.

Shargorod (shär'gŭrŭt), town (1948 pop. over 10,000), SW Vinnitsa oblast, Ukrainian SSR, 23 mi. NNE of Mogilev-Podolski; flour mill.

Shari (shä'rē), town (pop. 14,200), E Hokkaido, Japan, on S shore of Abashiri Bay, 22 mi. ESE of Abashiri; agr. (rice, potatoes), fishing.

Shariakandi (shär″yäkän'dē), village, Bogra dist., N central East Bengal, E Pakistan, on tributary of the Karatoya and 13 mi. ENE of Bogra; trades in rice, jute, rape and mustard, sugar cane.

Shari Bay, Japan: see ABASHIRI BAY.

Sharifkhaneh or **Sharafkhaneh** (shäräf-khänĕ'), town, Third Prov., in Azerbaijan, NW Iran, port on L. Urmia, 45 mi. W of Tabriz; rail terminus, connected by steamer service with Gelma Khaneh, lake port of Rizaiyeh.

Shariin, Korea: see SARIWON.

Shari River (shä'rē, sharē'), NE Belgian Congo, rises 30 mi. W of Mahagi, flows c.100 mi. SSW and SW, past Kilo-Mines, to Ituri R. just below Irumu. Site of 3 important hydroelectric plants supplying power to Kilo-Mines gold fields.

Shari River (shä'rē), Fr. *Chari* (shärē'), main tributary of L. Chad, in N Ubangi-Shari and W Chad territories, Fr. Equatorial Africa, formed by Bamingui and Gribingui rivers 105 mi. W of N'Délé, flows c.500 mi. NW, past Fort-Archambault and Bousso, to join with Logone R. at Fort-Lamy and form the Fr. Cameroons border before entering S part of L. Chad in a wide delta. Receives Bahr Aoûk and Bahr Salamat (right), Bahr Sara and Logone (left). Its length with Bamingui is 660 mi.; with Bahr Sara (sometimes considered its main headstream) c.900 mi. At times of high water, 2 strong arms branch off the main stream, one to rejoin the Shari further on, another to be lost in swamps near L. Fittri. Shari R. system is also occasionally linked with Benoué (Benue) system through Logone and Mayo-Kebbi. Navigable for small steamers through part of the year. Was explored by Heinrich Barth (1852) and Gustav Nachtigal (1872–73).

Sha River (shä). **1** Chinese *Sha Ki* or *Sha Ch'i* (both: shä' chē'), SW headstream of Min R., in Fukien prov., China, rises in the Bohea Hills on Kiangsi border, flows 150 mi. E, past Ninghwa (river is sometimes called Ninghwa), Tsingliu, and Yungan, and NE, past Shahsien, to Min R. above Nanping. **2** Chinese *Sha Ho* (shä' hŭ'), chief right affluent of Ying R., in Honan prov., China, rises in Funiu Mts., flows 200 mi. generally E, past Lushan and Yencheng, joining Ying R. in 2 arms at Chowkiakow and Fowyang (Anhwei prov.). Sometimes called Tasha R.

Sharja or **Sharjah** (shär'jù), most important sheikdom (□ 1,000; pop. 3,000) of TRUCIAL OMAN, extending 20 mi. along Trucial Coast of Persian Gulf, interrupted by AJMAN enclave, and 30 mi. inland to DHAID oasis. Main town is Sharja, port on Persian Gulf coast, 8 mi. NE of Dibai. It has boatbuilding and wool-weaving industries, and wheat, rice, and date warehouses; and is a center of pearling and fishing fleets. It is residence of British political agent and has international airport. Sharja's suzerainty formerly extended over the sheikdoms of RAS AL KHAIMA and KALBA, recognized in 1919 and 1937, respectively, as trucial members; and over the sheikdom of FUJAIRA, which has no treaty relations with Britain.

Sharkan (shŭrkän'), village (1948 pop. over 2,000), E Udmurt Autonomous SSR, Russian SFSR, 19 mi. NNW of Votkinsk; wheat, livestock. Limestone deposits near by.

Shark Bay, inlet of Indian Ocean, W Western Australia, bet. Bernier, Dorre, Dirk Hartogs isls. (W) and mainland (E and S); 150 mi. long, 60 mi. wide. Outlets: Geographe and Naturaliste channels. Peron Peninsula divides S part into 2 arms: Denham Sound (W), leading into Freycinet Estuary; Hopeless Reach (E), leading into Hamelin Pool. Carnarvon and whaling station on E shore.

Sharkey, county (□ 436; pop. 12,903), W Miss.; ⊙ Rolling Fork. Drained by Sunflower R. and other streams of Yazoo system. Agr. (cotton, corn, oats); timber. Much of co. is in Delta Natl. Forest. Formed 1876.

Shark Island, Fla.: see FORT JEFFERSON NATIONAL MONUMENT.

Sharkovshchina (shŭrkôf'shchĭnŭ), Pol. *Szarkowszczyzna*, town (1939 pop. over 500), W central Polotsk oblast, Belorussian SSR, on Disna R. and 19 mi. NNW of Glubokoye; fruit gardening; rye, flax, potatoes.

Sharkoy, Turkey: see SARKOY.

Shark River, E N.J., rises in E Monmouth co., flows c.7 mi. SE to irregularly-shaped Shark R. Inlet, estuary (c.2 mi. long) opening into the Atlantic bet. Belmar and Avon by the Sea; has improved harbor for yachts, fishing boats. Short North Branch enters river just above estuary.

Sharlston, England: see NEW SHARLSTON.

Sharlyk (shŭrlĭk'), village (1926 pop. 4,577), N Chkalov oblast, Russian SFSR, 65 mi. SE of Abdulino; road center; metalworking; wheat, sunflowers, livestock. Formerly called Sharlyk-Mikhailovskoye.

Sharma Bay, Aden: see DIS.

Shar Mountains, Yugoslavia: see SAR MOUNTAINS.

Sharoku, Formosa: see SHALU.

Sharon (shâ'rŭn, shă'–). **1** Resort town (pop. 1,889), Litchfield co., NW Conn., in Taconic Mts., bet. N.Y. line and the Housatonic, 19 mi. WNW of Torrington. State park, state forest here. Noah Webster wrote his *Spelling Book* while teaching here. Inc. 1739. **2** City (pop. 224), Taliaferro co., NE Ga., 6 mi. E of Crawfordville. **3** City (pop. 278), Barber co., S Kansas, on small affluent of Salt Fork of Arkansas R. and 9 mi. ESE of Medicine Lodge; grain, cattle. **4** Residential town (pop. 4,847), including Sharon village (pop. 2,815), Norfolk co., E Mass., 9 mi. WNW of Brockton; makes wooden boxes. Settled c.1650, inc. 1775. **5** Town (pop. 62), Hillsboro co., S N.H., 23 mi. WNW of Nashua; agr. **6** Village (pop. 312), Steele co., E N.Dak., 7 mi. N of Finley; grain refining, dairy products. **7** Village (pop. 2,858), Trumbull co., NE Ohio, 12 mi. NE of Youngstown and adjacent to Sharon, Pa. **8** Town (pop. 133), Woodward co., NW Okla., 11 mi. SSE of Woodward, in livestock and grain area. **9** Industrial city (pop. 26,454), Mercer co., W Pa., 11 mi. NE of Youngstown, Ohio, and on Shenango R., at Ohio line; has large steel plant; also mfg. of electrical products, railroad cars, hardware, clothing. Settled c.1800, laid out 1815, inc. as borough 1841, as city 1918. **10** Town (pop. 365), York co., N S.C., 18 mi. W of Rock Hill. **11** Town (pop. 880), Weakley co., NW Tenn., 19 mi. SE of Union City, in farm area; ships fruit, vegetables. **12** Town (pop. 470), Windsor co., E Vt., on White R. and 29 mi. NE of Rutland; lumber. Joseph Smith, founder of Mormonism, b. here. **13** Village (pop. 1,013), Walworth co., SE Wis., on Ill. line, 16 mi. E of Beloit, in agr. area; concrete burial vaults, dairy products, feed.

Sharon, Plain of (shâ'rŭn, shă'–), part of coastal plain of W Israel, bet. Samarian Hills (E) and Mediterranean (W), extends c.50 mi. NNW-SSE bet. Tel Aviv and Hills of Ephraim near Haifa. Coast line is even, lined with sand dunes; soil is generally fertile; citriculture and mixed farming are chief agr. occupations. Plain is most densely populated region of Israel; centers of population are Tel Aviv, Petah Tiqva, Ramat Gan, Herzliya, Natanya, and Hadera. Region is repeatedly mentioned in the Bible.

Sharon Hill, borough (pop. 5,464), Delaware co., SE Pa., SW suburb of Philadelphia; metal products, bricks. Inc. 1890.

Sharon Springs. 1 City (pop. 994), ⊙ Wallace co., W Kansas, 31 mi. S of Goodland, near Smoky Hill R.; trading center for livestock and grain region. Has railroad roundhouse. Highest point (4,135 ft.) in Kansas is 15 mi. W, on Colo. line. **2** Resort village (pop. 361), Schoharie co., E central N.Y., 24 mi. WSW of Amsterdam; health resort, with sulphur springs.

Sharonville, village (pop. 1,318), Hamilton co., extreme SW Ohio, 12 mi. NNE of downtown Cincinnati; freight yards, railroad shops; mfg. of motor vehicles. Surveyed 1796.

Sharovka (shä'rŏŏfkŭ), town (1939 pop. over 500), NW Kharkov oblast, Ukrainian SSR, 10 mi. SSW of Bogodukhov; distilling.

Sharp, county (□ 596; pop. 8,999), N Ark.; ⊙ Evening Shade and Hardy. Bounded N by Mo. line; drained by Strawberry and Spring rivers. Agr. (cotton, corn, hay, poultry, livestock); timber. Resorts (fishing). Formed 1868.

Sharp, Cape, on Minas Channel, N N.S., 4 mi. SW of Parrsboro, at entrance to Minas Basin.

Sharpness, sub-port of city of Gloucester, W central Gloucester, England, in parish of Hinton (pop. 1,450), on Severn R., at end of GLOUCESTER AND BERKELEY SHIP CANAL, and 16 mi. SW of Gloucester; 51°44'N 2°28'W; has important dock installations. Just N the Severn is crossed by a 4,000-ft. railroad bridge, built in 19th cent. Agr. village of Hinton is just E.

Sharp Park, coast resort (1940 pop. 834, with adjoining Salada Beach), San Mateo co., W Calif., on the Pacific, just S of San Francisco, whose municipal golf course is here.

Sharp Peak, Nev.: see ANTELOPE RANGE.

Sharps, fishing and resort village, Richmond co., E Va., on the Rappahannock and 55 mi. SE of Fredericksburg; cans and ships fish, oysters.

Sharpsburg. 1 Town (pop. 133), Coweta co., W Ga., 9 mi. ESE of Newnan. **2** Town (pop. 147), Taylor co., SW Iowa, 23 mi. SW of Creston, in agr. region. **3** Town (pop. 405), Bath co., NE central Ky., 17 mi. E of Paris. **4** Town (pop. 866), Washington co., W Md., 13 mi. S of Hagerstown; farm trade center. Civil War battle of Antietam (or Sharpsburg) was fought here and near by, along Antietam Creek; town is hq. for ANTIETAM NATIONAL BATTLEFIELD SITE. **5** Town (pop. 415), Nash, Edgecombe, and Wilson counties, E central N.C., 5 mi. SSW of Rocky Mount. **6** Industrial borough (pop. 7,296), Allegheny co., SW Pa., on Allegheny R. opposite N Pittsburgh; hardware, chemicals, grease, beverages, cement; agr. Inc. 1842.

Sharps Island, islet, Talbot co., E Md., in Chesapeake Bay just off mouth of Choptank R., 16 mi. WNW of Cambridge; Sharps Isl. Lighthouse is 1 mi. NNW.

Sharpsville. 1 Town (pop. 508), Tipton co., central Ind., 8 mi. SSE of Kokomo, in agr. area. **2** Borough (pop. 5,414), Mercer co., W Pa., 13 mi. NE of Youngstown, Ohio, and on Shenango R.; metal products. Settled 1798, inc. 1874.

Sharp Top, Va.: see OTTER, PEAKS OF.

Sharptown, town (pop. 680), Wicomico co., E Md., 14 mi. NNW of Salisbury, near Del. line and on Nanticoke R., in truck-farm and pine-timber area; clothing, basket factories.

Sharqat or **Qal'a Sharqat** (käl'ä shärkät'), town, Mosul prov., N Iraq, on the Tigris, on railroad, and 60 mi. S of Mosul; barley, wheat, fruits. Near by is the site of the anc. Assyrian city of ASHUR. Also spelled Shergat and Kalah Shergat.

Sharqi, Jebel esh, Lebanon: see ANTI-LEBANON.

Sharqiya or **Sharqiyah** (shärkē'yŭ), province (□ 1,908; pop. 1,356,798), Lower Egypt; ⊙ ZAGAZIG. Bounded E by Suez Canal, N by L. Manzala and Daqahliya prov., W and S by Daqahliya and Qalyubiya provs. Main industry: cotton ginning. Agr.: cotton, cereals, dates. Main urban centers: BILBEIS, Zagazig. Served by railroads from Cairo through Bilbeis and Zagazig and by the Bahr Saft and the Ismailia Canal. TELL EL KEBIR is a village of historical importance and at San el Hagar are the ruins of anc. TANIS.

Sharqiya or **Sharqiyah,** interior district of Oman, on landward side of the Eastern Hajar and extending to the desert Rub' al Khali; main towns, Ibra and Mudhaibi. Ja'lan dist. adjoins SE.

Sharqpur, W Pakistan: see SHARAKPUR.

Sharuna or **Sharunah** (shärōō'nŭ), village (pop. 7,385), Minya prov., Upper Egypt, on E bank of the Nile and 3 mi. SSE of Maghagha; cotton, cereals, sugar cane. Has tombs dating from end of VI dynasty.

Sharya or **Shar'ya** (shŭryä'), city (1939 pop. over 10,000), E Kostroma oblast, Russian SFSR, near Vetluga R., 150 mi. W of Kirov; metalworking, sawmilling.

Sharypovo (shŭrĭpô'vŭ), village (1948 pop. over 500), SW Krasnoyarsk Territory, Russian SFSR, 30 mi. NW of Uzhur; metalworks.

Shasan, Formosa: see SHASHAN.

Shasha (shä'shä), Ital. *Sciascia,* village, Kaffa prov., SW Ethiopia, near Omo R., 37 mi. NE of Maji; market.

Shashamana (shä'shämänä), Ital. *Sciasciamana,* village, Arusi prov., S central Ethiopia, near L. Awusa, on road and 55 mi. SW of Asselle, in cattle-raising region.

Shashan (shä'shän'), Jap. *Shasan* (shä'sän), village (1935 pop. 4,738), W central Formosa, on W coast, 4 mi. WNW of Erhlin; fish, oysters.

Sha-shih, China: see SHASI.

Shashi River (shä'shē), S Africa, rises in NE Bechuanaland Protectorate at Southern Rhodesia border W of Plumtree, flows c.225 mi. in a wide arc S and SE, forming part of the border, to Limpopo R. 40 mi. W of Beitbridge.

Shasi or **Sha-shih** (both: shä'sē', Chinese shä'shû'), town (1931 pop. 113,526), S central Hupeh prov., china, port on left bank of Yangtze R. and 120 mi. WSW of Hankow, 5 mi. SW of Kiangling; industrial and commercial center; cotton and silk weaving, flour milling. Major cotton market and shipping point; airport. A treaty port of call after 1876 and an open port after 1895, it supplanted the anc. city of Kiangling.

Shasima, Tibet: see YATUNG.

Shasta (shă'stŭ), county (□ 3,846; pop. 36,413), N Calif.; ⊙ Redding. Largely mountainous; Klamath Mts. (W) here meet Cascade Range (E) at N end of the Central Valley. SHASTA DAM, a unit of Central Valley project, impounds Shasta L. here in valleys of Sacramento, Pit, and McCloud rivers. In SE is Lassen Peak (10,453 ft.; only active volcano in U.S.), in LASSEN VOLCANIC NATIONAL PARK. Much of co. is included in Shasta and Lassen natl. forests. Castle Crags and McArthur-Burney Falls state parks are here. Lumbering, (chiefly pine; also fir, cedar), stock raising (beef and dairy cattle, hogs, sheep, poultry), irrigated fruitgrowing, general farming (alfalfa, grain, vegetables, berries), winegrowing. Working of pyrite (a leading Calif. co. in production), gold, sand and gravel, zinc, copper deposits. Lumber milling and woodworking, and processing of farm products are principal industries. Hunting, fishing, camping attract vacationers. Formed 1850.

Shasta, Mount (14,162 ft.), in Cascade Range, SE Siskiyou co., N Calif., c.60 mi. N of Redding. Impressive, symmetrical extinct volcano, with steam vents on its slopes; has 5 glaciers on E and NE flanks. Discovered 1827 by P. S. Ogden, scaled 1854 by E. D. Pearce. Mount Shasta town is at SW base.

Shasta Dam, N Calif., on Sacramento R., near Redding; one of largest (3,500 ft. long, 602 ft. high) in the world; built 1939–45. Chief unit in CENTRAL VALLEY project, the dam (with auxiliary Keswick Dam, just downstream) regulates the flow of the Sacramento and its tributaries for navigation and flood-control purposes, creates hydroelectric power. Its reservoir, **Shasta Lake** (shore line of 365 mi.; c.16 mi. long; capacity 4,500,000 acre-ft.), formed by the backed-up waters of Sacramento, Pit, and McCloud rivers, supplies water for Central Valley irrigation and reclamation development.

Shasta River, N Calif., rises in central Siskiyou co., flows c.40 mi. N, past Montague (where it is joined by the Little Shasta), to Klamath R. c.10 mi. N of Yreka.

Shasukotan-kaikyo, Russian SFSR: see SEVERGIN STRAIT.

Shasukotan-to, Russian SFSR: see SHIASHKOTAN ISLAND.

Shat [Arabic,=river; sometimes lake], for names in Arabic-speaking countries beginning thus and not found here, see under following proper noun; see also under SHATT.

Shat, Am (ăm'shät'), village, Subeihi tribal area, Western Aden Protectorate, 70 mi. WNW of Aden; 12°54'N 44°1'E. Administrative center of Abdali sultanate for W Subeihi area.

Shat al Arab, Iraq and Iran: see SHATT AL ARAB.

Shatalovka (shŭtä'lŭfkŭ), village (1926 pop. 2,192), W Voronezh oblast, Russian SFSR, 21 mi. ESE of Stary Oskol; wheat.

Shat el Arab, Iraq and Iran: see SHATT AL ARAB.

Shatki (shät'kē), village (1939 pop. over 2,000), S Gorki oblast, Russian SFSR, on railroad and 18 mi. SE of Arzamas; wheat, hemp, potatoes.

Shato, Formosa: see SHETOW.

Shatoi, Russian SFSR: see SOVETSKOYE, Grozny.

Shator Mountains, Yugoslavia: see SATOR MOUNTAINS.

Shatow or **Sha-t'ou** (shä'tō'), town, SE Kiangsu prov., China, 35 mi. NW of Taitsang; commercial center.

Shatra or **Shatrah** (shä'trŭ), town, Muntafiq prov., SE Iraq, on the Shatt al Gharraf and 25 mi. N of Nasiriya; dates, sesame, barley, wheat. Sometimes spelled Shattrah.

Shatrat al-'Amara, Iraq: see QAL'A SALIH.

Shatrovo (shŭtrô'vŭ), village (1926 pop. 2,759), N Kurgan oblast, Russian SFSR, 50 mi. NE of Shadrinsk; dairy plant, metalworks.

Shatsk (shätsk). **1** City (1926 pop. 15,120), SE Ryazan oblast, Russian SFSR, 90 mi. SE of Ryazan; distilling center. Founded 1553 on border of Mordvinian territory; 1st called Shatskiye Vorota [Rus.,=Shatsk gates]. **2** Pol. *Szack* (shätsk), village (1939 pop. over 500), NW Volyn oblast, Ukrainian SSR, 38 mi. NW of Kovel; grain, potatoes; lumbering.

Shatt [Arabic,=river; sometimes lake], for names in Arabic-speaking countries beginning thus and not found here, see under following proper noun.

Shatt al Arab or **Shatt al 'Arab** (shät' äl ä'räb), river formed by the union of the Euphrates and the Tigris in extreme SE Iraq; formed at Al Qurna, 40 mi. NW of Basra, it flows c.120 mi. SE through a marshy area, past Ma'qil (port for Basra; head of navigation for ocean-going vessels) and Basra in Iraq, and forms Iraq-Iran line for the rest of its course to the head of the Persian Gulf. It passes Iranian towns of Khorramshahr and Abadan and washes SW shore of Abadan Isl. Receives Karun R. from Iran. Sometimes spelled Shat al Arab and Shat el Arab.

Shattrah, Iraq: see SHATRA.

Shattuck (shă'tŭk), town (pop. 1,692), Ellis co., NW Okla., 30 mi. WSW of Woodward, in agr. area (broomcorn, livestock; dairy products); cement and sheet-metal products, flour. Settled 1904, inc. 1906.

Shattuckville, Mass.: see COLRAIN.

Shattura or **Shatturah** (shät-tōō'rŭ), village (pop. 9,835), Girga prov., central Upper Egypt, 4 mi. N of Tahta; cotton, cereals, dates, sugar cane.

Shatura (shŭtōō'rŭ), city (1939 pop. over 10,000), E Moscow oblast, Russian SFSR, on S shore of small Svyatoye L., 75 mi. E of Moscow, in major peat-producing center. Local peat-fed power plant, one of main Moscow suppliers (in operation since 1919), is served by peat works at Baksheyevo, Kerva, Tugolesski Bor, and Shaturtorf. Called SHATURTORF until 1928; became city in 1936.

Shaturtorf (shŭtōōrtôrf'), town (1939 pop. over 500), E Moscow oblast, Russian SFSR, 4 mi. W (under jurisdiction) of Shatura; peat-producing center; developed in 1930s. The name Shaturtorf applied, until 1928, to SHATURA city.

Shaulder or **Shaul'der** (shŭōōldyĕr'), village (1948 pop. over 2,000), central South Kazakhstan oblast, Kazakh SSR, near Trans-Caspian RR (Timur station), 30 mi. S of Turkestan, in cotton area. Near by, on the Syr Darya, are ruins of old city of Otrar (c.12th to 16th cent.).

Shaulyai, Lithuania: see SIAULIAI.

Shaumyan (shŭōōmyän'), district of Greater Baku, Azerbaijan SSR. on S shore of Apsheron Peninsula, E of Baku. Main center, Akhmedly.

Shaumyani (–yä'nyē), town (1926 pop. 5,587), S Georgian SSR, on railroad and 22 mi. S of Tiflis; cotton-ginning center; clothing mfg. Formerly called Shulavery, then (until 1936) Shaumyan.

Shaumyanovsk (–nŭfsk), village (1939 pop. over 2,000), W Azerbaijan SSR, 20 mi. SE of Kirovabad; livestock. Until 1938, Nizhni Agdzhakend.

Shaunavon (shô'nŭvŭn), town (pop. 1,643), SW Sask., in the Cypress Hills, 55 mi. SW of Swift Current; alt. 3,012 ft.; coal mining; grain elevators, cold-storage plant, flour mills.

Shauwamiya, Oman: see SHUWAMIYA.

Shavano Peak (shŭvä'nō) (alt. 14,179 ft.), central Colo., in S tip of SAWATCH MOUNTAINS, 14 mi. WNW of Salida. Melting snow in fissures on peak creates figure known as Angel of Shavano.

Shavat (shŭvät'), village (1939 pop. over 500), W Khorezm oblast, Uzbek SSR, in Khiva oasis, 19 mi. WNW of Urgench; cotton.

Shavei Zion (shävā'), settlement (pop. 250), W Galilee, NW Israel, on Mediterranean, on railroad and 13 mi. NNE of Haifa, just S of Nahariya; mixed farming; seaside resort. Sanitarium. Founded 1938. Sometimes spelled Shave Zion.

Shaver Lake, Fresno co., E central Calif., in the Sierra Nevada, 35 mi. NE of Fresno; c.4 mi. long; summer and winter resort. Impounded in a tributary of San Joaquin R. by Shaver Lake Dam (184 ft. high, 2,220 ft. long; for power; completed 1927).

Shavers Fork, E W.Va., rises in N Pocahontas co. W of Cass, flows NNE bet. Cheat Mtn. (W) and Shavers Mtn. (E), briefly W near Elkins to cross Cheat Mtn., and NNE, joining Black Fork at Parsons to form Cheat R.; 83 mi. long.

Shavers Mountain, E W. Va., ridge of the Alleghenies; from Black Fork of Cheat R. in S Tucker co. extends c.50 mi. SSW, parallel to course of Shavers Fork (W), into W Pocahontas co. Rises to 4,842 ft. in Bald Knob, just N of Cass.

Shavgaon, India: see SHEVGAON.

Shavli, Lithuania: see SIAULIAI.

Shavnik, Yugoslavia: see SAVNIK.

Shaw, England: see CROMPTON.

Shaw, town (pop. 1,892), Bolivar co., W Miss., 22 mi. NE of Greenville, in rich cotton-growing area; cotton compress, lumber mill.

Shaw Air Force Base, S.C.: see SUMTER, city.

Shawan (shä'wän'), town and oasis (pop. 20,327), N Sinkiang prov., China, 30 mi. NW of Manas, near Manas R.; petroleum center; saltworks.

Shawangunk Kill (shŏng'gŭm, –gŭngk), stream in SE N.Y., rises in Orange co. E of Port Jervis, flows c.35 mi. generally E, along E base of the Shawangunk range, to Wallkill R. just W of Gardiner.

Shawangunk Mountain or **Shawangunk Mountains,** SE N.Y., range (mainly a single ridge) of the Appalachians, extending SW from Rondout Creek near Kingston to junction with Kittatinny Mtn. ridge in Orange co. near Port Jervis; c.45 mi. long; max. alt. 2,289 ft. Sam's Point (2,255 ft.), near Ellenville, is best-known peak. Resort area, with small lakes.

Shawano (shô'nō, shô'wŭnō), county (□ 1,176; pop. 35,249), E central Wis.; ⊙ Shawano. Drained by Wolf and Embarrass rivers. Largest of several lakes in co. is Shawano L. Generally forested area, with sawmills and dairy farms. Part of Menominee Indian Reservation is here. Formed 1853.

Shawano, city (pop. 5,894), ⊙ Shawano co., NE Wis., on Wolf R. and 35 mi. NW of Green Bay city, near Shawano L.; trade center for lumbering and agr. area; paper milling, woodworking, vegetable canning. Menominee Indian Reservation is near by. Settled c.1840, it was an early lumbering center. Inc. 1874.

Shawano Lake, Shawano co., NE Wis., just E of Shawano; c.5 mi. long, c.3 mi. wide. Drained by small stream entering Wolf R.

Shawbridge, village (pop. 628), S Que., on North R. and 35 mi. NW of Montreal; dairying.

Shawclough, England: see ROCHDALE.

Shawforth, England: see WHITWORTH.

Shawinigan Falls (shŭwĭ'nĭgŭn), city (pop. 20,325), S Que., on St. Maurice R. and 17 mi. NW of Trois Rivières; paper milling, mfg. of aluminum, abrasives, electrodes, chemicals, cellophane, shoes. Just NE are picturesque waterfalls, 150 ft. high, with large hydroelectric power station.

Shawmut. 1 Village (pop. 3,266), Chambers co., E Ala., on Chattahoochee R. and 27 mi. NNW of Columbus, Ga.; cotton fabrics. **2** Village, Maine: see FAIRFIELD.

Shawnee (shô"nē'), county (□ 545; pop. 105,418), NE Kansas; ⊙ Topeka. Dissected plain, drained by Kansas R. Stock raising; grain growing, general agr. Industries at Topeka. Formed 1855.

Shawnee. 1 Village, Park co., central Colo., in Front Range, 35 mi. SW of Denver; alt. 8,125 ft.; resort. Christ of the Rockies, 52-ft. figure, is near by. **2** City (pop. 845), Johnson co., E Kansas, 8 mi. SW of Kansas City, Kansas; residential suburb and trading point in dairying and general-farming region. Near by is Shawnee Methodist Mission (established 1839; partially restored), the temporary meeting place (1855) of the rump (proslavery) territorial legislature. **3** Village (pop. 1,145), Perry co., central Ohio, 7 mi. S of New Lexington, in coal-mining area; clay products. **4** City (pop. 22,948), ⊙ Pottawatomie co., central Okla., 35 mi. ESE of Oklahoma City, and on North Canadian R.; market and distribution center in rich agr. and oil-producing area. Mfg. of dairy products, clothing, mattresses, canvas articles, peanut products, packed meat and produce, flour, feed, electric motors, medicine, oil burners, lumber, sweeping compound; cotton ginning. Seat of Okla. Baptist Univ. and a Benedictine jr. col.; and has a U.S. tuberculosis sanatorium for Indians. Inc. 1894. **5** Village (pop. c.75), Converse co., E Wyo., 18 mi. E of Douglas; alt. c.5,000 ft. Coal and oil near by.

Shawnee, Lake, W.Va.: see PRINCETON.

Shawnee Hills, village (pop. 338), Delaware co., central Ohio, 14 mi. NNW of Columbus.

Shawnee State Forest, Scioto co., S Ohio, W of Portsmouth; largest forest area in Ohio (c.60,000 acres). Small lakes; fishing, camping. Roosevelt Game Preserve is adjacent.

Shawneetown (shô'nētown), city (pop. 1,917), ⊙ Gallatin co., SE Ill., on Ohio R. (ferry here) and 20 mi. E of Harrisburg; trade and shipping center in agr. and bituminous-coal-mining area; wheat, corn, livestock, dairy products, poultry; wood products. One of state's oldest towns, settled after 1800, laid out 1808, inc. 1814; important port and trading center in early-19th cent. Has 1st bank chartered in state. Lafayette was entertained here. After 1937 flood, part of town was moved W to higher ground. In 1940, the state purchased part of the old Shawneetown area.

Shawnigan Lake (shô'nĭgŭn), village (pop. estimate 400), SW B.C., on SE Vancouver Isl., on Shawnigan L. (5 mi. long), 20 mi. NW of Victoria; lumbering, mixed farming, fruitgrowing.

Shawomet, R.I.: see WARWICK.

Shawsheen Village, Mass.: see ANDOVER.

Shawville, village (pop. 892), SW Que., near Ottawa R., 40 mi. WNW of Ottawa; dairying, lumbering; brick, tile mfg.

Shawwamiyah, Oman: see SHUWAMIYA.

Shaya, China: see SHAHYAR.

Shayang (shä'yäng'), town, S central Hupeh prov.; China, 100 mi. W of Hankow and on Han R.; commercial center.

Shaydan, Tadzhik SSR: see SHAIDAN.

Shaykh, for Arabic names beginning thus: see under SHAIKH; SHEIKH.

Shaykh, Jabal al-, Lebanon: see HERMON, MOUNT.

Shaykh Sa'd, Iraq: see SHAIKH SA'AD.

Shchara River (shchä'rŭ), Pol. *Szczara* (shchä'rä), W Belorussian SSR, rises 10 mi. N of Baranovichi, flows S, W, and generally NNW, past Byten and Slonim, to Neman R. 5 mi. E of Mosty; 200 mi. long. Connected with Vygonovo L.; forms N part of Dnieper-Neman waterway.

Shchebreshin, Poland: see SZCZEBRZESZYN.

Shchedrin (shchĭdrēn'), town (1939 pop. over 2,000), SE Bobruisk oblast, Belorussian SSR, 22 mi. SE of Bobruisk; truck produce.

Shchedro Island, Yugoslavia: see SCEDRO ISLAND.

Shcheglovsk, Russian SFSR: see KEMEROVO, city.

Shchekino (shchĕkēnô'), city (1948 pop. over 10,000), central Tula oblast, Russian SFSR, 14 mi. S of Tula, in Moscow Basin; major lignite-mining center; refractory clays. Power plant.

Shchekotsiny, Poland: see SZCZEKOCINY.

Shchelkovo (shchôl'kŭvŭ), city (1926 pop. 12,330), E Moscow oblast, Russian SFSR, 19 mi. NE of Moscow; textile-milling center; cotton and woolen goods, chemicals, metal products.

Shcherbakov (shchĕrbŭkôf'), city (1926 pop. 55,494; 1939 pop. 139,011), N central Yaroslavl oblast, Russian SFSR, Volga R., at its efflux from Rybinsk Reservoir, and 50 mi. NW of Yaroslavl. Major river port and lumber center; shipyards, mfg. (agr., match-making, road-building, and printing machinery, aircraft motors, matches, linen); fish canneries, numerous flour mills and sawmills. Site of Rybinsk Reservoir dam and hydroelectric station (completed 1941 at NW suburb of Sheksninski), with adjoining river-port suburb of Perebory (until c.1940, Abbakumovo). Has mid-19th-cent. cathedral and regional mus. City 1st mentioned (1504) as Rybnaya Sloboda, later Rybinsk. Developed into major trading and transshipment center after founding of St. Petersburg (1703) and construction of Volga-Neva canal systems. Chartered 1777. Shipments include grain, salt, fish, petroleum (upstream) and lumber (downstream). Importance of port increased following filling (1941) of Rybinsk Reservoir. Renamed (1946; from Rybinsk) for Shcherbakov, a Bolshevik leader b. here. Was ⊙ short-lived Rybinsk govt. (1921–23).

Shcherbakty (shchĭrbäk'tē), village, E Pavlodar oblast, Kazakh SSR, on S. Siberian RR and 50 mi. E of Pavlodar; metalworks.

Shcherbinka (shchĭrbēn'kŭ), town (1939 pop. over 500), S central Moscow oblast, Russian SFSR, 18 mi. S of Moscow, 5 mi. N of Podolsk; woolen milling. At village of Ostafyevo (W) is one of Moscow's civil airports.

Shcherbinovka, Ukrainian SSR: see DZERZHINSK, Stalino oblast.

Shchetovo (shchô'tŭvŭ), town (1939 pop. over 500), S Voroshilovgrad oblast, Ukrainian SSR, in the Donbas, 4 mi. N of Bokovo-Antratsit; rail junction; coal-mining center.

Shchigry (shchĭgrē'), city (1926 pop. 7,043), N Kursk oblast, Russian SFSR, 30 mi. ENE of Kursk; phosphate works; metalworking, flour milling, fruit canning. Chartered 1779.

Shchirets (shchĕryĕts'), Pol. *Szczerzec*, town (1931 pop. 1,210), S Lvov oblast, Ukrainian SSR, 15 mi. SSW of Lvov; gypsum quarrying. A thriving Ruthenian settlement in 12th cent., destroyed by several 16th-cent. Tatar and Swedish attacks.

Shchors (shchôrs), city (1926 pop. 6,850), N Chernigov oblast, Ukrainian SSR, 35 mi. NE of Chernigov; metalworking, flax processing. Until c.1935, called Snovsk.

Shchorsk (shchôrsk), town (1939 pop. over 500), W central Dnepropetrovsk oblast, Ukrainian SSR, 19 mi. E of Pyatikhatki; flour mill. Until c.1940, Bozhedarovka.

Shchuchin, Poland: see SZCZUCZYN.

Shchuchin (shchōō'chĭn), Pol. *Szczuczyn* or *Szczuczyn Nowogródzki* (shchōō'chĭn nôvôgrōōdz'kē), town (1937 pop. 3,000), N central Grodno oblast, Belorussian SSR, 30 mi. SW of Lida; plywood mfg., pitch processing, flour milling, sawmilling.

Shchuchinsk (–chĭnsk), city (1939 pop. over 10,000), S Kokchetav oblast, Kazakh SSR, on railroad (Kurort Borovoye station) and 40 mi. SE of Kokchetav, in wooded area. Until 1939, called Shchuchye.

Shchuchye or **Shchuch'ye** (shchōō'chyĭ). **1** City, Kokchetav oblast, Kazakh SSR: see SHCHUCHINSK. **2** City (1926 pop. 2,300), W Kurgan oblast, Russian SFSR, on Trans-Siberian RR (Chumlyak station) and 50 mi. E of Chelyabinsk; agr. center; flour milling. Became city in 1945. **3** Village, W Yamal-Nenets Natl. Okrug, Tyumen oblast, Russian SFSR, on short Shchuchya R. and 80 mi. NE of Salekhard; trading post in tundra adjoining Baidarata Bay of Kara Sea. **4** Village (1926 pop. 3,232), N Voronezh oblast, Russian SFSR, 55 mi. E of Voronezh; metalworks.

Shchugor River (shchōō'gôr'), Komi Autonomous SSR, Russian SFSR, rises in the N Urals at c.63°20'N, flows c.175 mi. N and generally W to Pechora R. at Ust-Shchugor, 125 mi. NE of Ukhta.

Shchunat Beilinson, Israel: see BEILINSON.

Shchunat Ono, Israel: see KFAR ONO.

Shchurovo (shchōō'rŭvŭ), city (1948 pop. over 10,000), SE Moscow oblast, Russian SFSR, on Oka R., opposite mouth of the Moskva, and 3 mi. SE of Kolomna; cement works; limestone and quartz quarries.

Shdemot, Israel: see NIR AM.

Sheakleyville (shā'klēvĭl), borough (pop. 141), Mercer co., NW Pa., 14 mi. SSW of Meadville.

Shear Yashuv (shĕ-är' yäshōōv') or **Shaar Yashuv** (shä-är'), settlement (pop. 200), Upper Galilee, NE Israel, near Syrian border, at SW foot of Mt. Hermon, 20 mi. NNE of Safad; mixed farming. Founded 1940; withstood Arab attacks 1948.

Sheba (shē'bŭ), Arabic *Saba* (sŭ'bŭ), biblical name of region in SW Arabian Peninsula, corresponding to modern YEMEN. The Sabaean (or Sabean) civilization (950–115 B.C.) succeeded the Minaean period (see JAUF) and was in turn replaced by the Himyaritic kingdom (⊙ ZAFAR). All 3 civilizations are associated with dialects of South Arabic, an extinct language deciphered (19th cent.) from inscriptions found in Najran and Jauf oases. Sabaean culture and prosperity are also evidenced in the remains of the great irrigation works of MARIB, the Sabaean capital, and in the biblical story of the visit of the queen of Sheba (called Balkis in the Koran) to Solomon (1 Kings 10).

Shebalino (shĭbä'lyĭnŭ), village (1948 pop. over 2,000), W Gorno-Altai Autonomous Oblast, Altai Territory, Russian SFSR, 50 mi. SSW of Gorno-Altaisk; maral breeding.

Shebandowan Lake (25 mi. long, 3 mi. wide), NW Ont., 40 mi. WNW of Port Arthur, 10 mi. S of Lac des Milles Lacs; alt. 1,474 ft. Drains E into L. Superior.

Shebar Strait (shē'bär), SW Sierra Leone, connects S arm of Sherbro R. and Atlantic Ocean; separates Sherbro Isl. (W) from Turner's Peninsula (E); 1½ mi. wide.

Shebekino (shĕbĭkē'nŭ), city (1948 pop. over 2,000), S Kursk oblast, Russian SFSR, 18 mi. SE of Belgorod; sugar-refining center; machine works; distilling, tanning; chalk quarrying. Became city in 1938.

Shebeli, Webi, Webi Shibeli, or **Webbe Shibeli** (all: wĕ'bĕ shĕbĕ'lē), Ital. *Uebi Scebeli*, river over 1,200 mi. long in Ethiopia and Ital. Somaliland. Rises in Ethiopian highlands on Mt. Guramba (edge of Great Rift Valley) near source of the Ganale Dorya, flows NE then SE, past Imi, Callafo, and Mustahil, into Ital. Somaliland; continues S, past Belet Uen, Bulo Burti, and Villaggio, and turns SW near Mogadishu paralleling coastal sand dunes, to a swamp 25 mi. inland from the Indian Ocean and 20 mi. from Juba R. Has 2 flood seasons (April-June, Sept.-Nov.) and is generally dry Feb.-March; lower course 130–260 ft. wide. The upper course, explored 1928–29 by the duke of Abruzzi, is called Wabi (Ital. *Uabi*) or Webbe. Its lower valley, together with that of the Juba, is the chief agr. region (durra, corn, sesame) of Ital. Somaliland; major plantations at Genale and Villabruzzi.

Sheboygan (shĭboi'gŭn), county (□ 506; pop. 80,631), E Wis.; ⊙ Sheboygan. Bordered E by L. Michigan; drained by Sheboygan R. One of the leading dairying and cheese-producing areas in U.S.; has diversified mfg. (especially enamel, porcelain, and wood products) in Sheboygan, Kohler, Sheboygan Falls, and Plymouth. Includes Terry Andrae State Park, and a state forest. Formed 1836.

Sheboygan, city (pop. 42,365), ⊙ Sheboygan co., E Wis., on L. Michigan, at mouth of Sheboygan R., 50 mi. N of Milwaukee; port of entry, with lake harbor; industrial center of rich dairying and cheese-making co. Mfg. of furniture, enamelware, iron and steel products, wood products, clothing, knit goods, machinery, beer, cheese; oil refining; fisheries. Settled c.1835 on site of fur-trading post established 1795; inc. as village in 1846, as city in 1853. Grew as shipping, industrial, and dairying center. Liberal German refugees came in mid-19th cent.

Sheboygan Falls, city (pop. 3,599), Sheboygan co., E Wis., at falls of Sheboygan R., 5 mi. W of Sheboygan, in dairy and grain area; mfg. (furniture, magnets, plumbing fixtures, woodenware, woolen goods, canned peas, cheese, butter). Inc. as village in 1854, as city in 1913.

Sheboygan River, E Wis., rises in Fond du Lac co., flows generally N and then SE, past Sheboygan Falls, to L. Michigan at Sheboygan; c.40 mi. long. Navigable c.2½ mi. by small craft.

Shebshi (shĕp'shē), town, Adamawa prov., Northern Provinces, E Nigeria, in Shebshi Mts., 25 mi. SE of Jalingo; tin deposits; cassava, durra, yams; cattle raising.

Shebshi Mountains, Br. Cameroons, bet. Temba R. (SW) and Benue R. (NE); c.100 mi. long; rise to over 6,000 ft. Town of Toungo is on E slopes.

Shebunino (shĕbōō'nĭnō), town (1947 pop. over 500), S Sakhalin, Russian SFSR, on W coast, 17 mi. S of Nevelsk and on railroad. Under Japanese rule (1905–45), called Minami-nayoshi.

Shechem, Palestine: see NABLUS.

She-ch'i, China: see SHEKI.

Shedadi, Tell, or **Tall Shadadi** (both: tĕl shĕdä'dē), Fr. *Chadadé*, town, Jezire prov., NE Syria, on Khabur R. and 33 mi. S of El Haseke. Rich oil deposits in region.

Shediac (shĕ'dēăk), town (pop. 2,147), E N.B., on Northumberland Strait 15 mi. NE of Moncton; resort; oyster, lobster, smelt fisheries; seaplane base.

Sheduva, Lithuania: see SEDUVA.

Sheelin, Lough (lŏkh shē'lĭn), lake (5 mi. long, 3 mi. wide), S Co. Cavan, Ireland, 5 mi. E of Granard.

Sheen, England: see RICHMOND.

Sheenjik River (shēn'jĭk), NE Alaska, rises in Davidson Mts. near 68°30'N 143°20'W, flows c.200 mi. S to Porcupine R. at 66°44'N 144°32'W.

Sheep Haven, inlet of the Atlantic, N Co. Donegal, Ireland, extends 7 mi. inland from Horn Head.

Sheep Head or **Muntervary** (mŭn″tûrvâ′rē), Atlantic cape, SW Co. Cork, Ireland, bet. Bantry Bay and Dunmanus Bay, 25 mi. W of Skibbereen; 51°33′N 9°50′W.

Sheep Islands, Iran: see URMIA, LAKE.

Sheep Mountain, peak (12,800 ft.) in Rocky Mts., Park co., central Colo.

Sheep Range, SE Nev., in N Clark co., N of Las Vegas. Rises to 9,706 ft. in Sheep Peak, in S.

Sheepscot Bay, SW Maine, bet. Georgetown and Southport; c.5 mi. wide; receives Sheepscot R.

Sheepscot River, S Maine, rises in Sheepscot Pond, SW Waldo co., near Palermo; flows c.30 mi. SW to Sheepscot Bay.

Sheepshead Bay (shēps′hĕd″), SE N.Y., a section of S Brooklyn borough of New York city, on Sheepshead Bay, an indentation in SW shore of Long Isl.; commercial- and pleasure-fishing center. Coney Isl. is near by.

's Heer Arendskerke (sār ä′rụntskĕr″kụ), village (pop. 688), Zeeland prov., SW Netherlands, on South Beveland isl., 3 mi. W of Goes; chicory drying.

's Heerenberg (sā′rụnbĕrkh), town (pop. 4,041), Gelderland prov., E Netherlands, 16 mi. ESE of Arnhem, on Ger. frontier; mfg. of brushes, baking machinery. Town since 1379; property (1749–1912) of Hohenzollern-Sigmaringen family.

Sheerness, village (pop. estimate 100), SE Alta., 15 mi. SE of Hanna; coal mining.

Sheerness, urban district (1931 pop. 16,738; 1951 census 15,727), on Isle of Sheppey, N Kent, England, on Thames estuary at mouth of the Medway, 11 mi. ENE of Chatham; 51°26′N 0°45′E; port and govt. dockyard, protecting Chatham naval base. Garrison area is known as Blue Town; E district is a bathing resort. The dockyards were established and fortified by Charles II, with aid of Samuel Pepys. Town was taken by Dutch (1667) under de Ruyter.

Sheet Harbour, village (pop. estimate 1,200), SE N.S., on Sheet Harbour, at mouth of a stream, 60 mi. ENE of Halifax; site of major hydroelectric power station; pulp milling. Near by is extensive game sanctuary.

Shefayim, Israel: see SHFAYIM.

Shefer (shĕ′fĕr) or **Ramat Naftali** (rämät′näftälē′), agr. settlement (pop. 80), Upper Galilee, NE Israel, on Lebanese border, on E slope of Hills of Naftali, 8 mi. NNW of Safad. Founded 1945; entirely destroyed by Arabs, 1948; later rebuilt.

Shefeya, Israel: see SHFEYA.

Sheffield, county borough (1931 pop. 511,757; 1951 census 512,834) and city, West Riding, S Yorkshire, England, on Don R. and 35 mi. E of Manchester; 53°23′N 1°28′W; major steel center, with foundries, rolling mills, and machine shops. Mfg. (armorplate, rails, artillery, cutlery, tools, wire). A cutlery center since 14th cent.; the Cutlers' Company was established in 1624. Site of 1st Bessemer steelworks (1858). Sheffield Univ. (1905) has medical school and technical col. Notable bldgs.: Ruskin Mus., the observatory, Mappin Art Galleries, Cutlers' Hall (1832), Church of St. Peter's (14th–15th cent., seriously damaged by bombing in Second World War), Renaissance town hall (1897). Mary Queen of Scots was held prisoner (1569–84) in the old Norman castle taken 1644 by Parliamentarians and later dismantled. In Second World War the city and surrounding area were heavily damaged (especially in Dec., 1940) by air raids. In county borough are TINSLEY, ATTERCLIFFE, DARNALL, ECCLESALL, HANDSWORTH.

Sheffield, township (pop. 179), ⊙ Malvern co. (□ 250; pop. 3,605), E central S Isl., New Zealand, 35 mi. W of Christchurch; agr. center.

Sheffield, village (pop. 656), N Tasmania, 40 mi. W of Launceston; dairying center.

Sheffield. **1** City (pop. 10,767), Colbert co., NW Ala., on Tennessee R. (bridged) opposite Florence, in iron and coal area. Metalworking center, with boat connections; aluminum products (ingots, wire, sheets, tubing, roofing), ferroalloys, structural castings, stoves, ranges. Large Listerhill aluminum plant (built 1941) is E. Industries stimulated by construction of Wilson Dam (4 mi. ENE) and development of TVA. Sheffield founded 1883, inc. 1885. **2** Village (pop. 995), Bureau co., N Ill., 12 mi. NE of Kewanee, in agr. and bituminous-coal area; shale products, feed. **3** Town (pop. 1,163), Franklin co., N central Iowa, 18 mi. S of Mason City; brick, tile, hybrid seed corn, dairy and wood products. Clay and gravel pits near by. Inc. 1876. **4** Resort town (pop. 2,150), Berkshire co., SW Mass., in the Berkshires, on Housatonic R. and 7 mi. S of Great Barrington. Settled 1726, inc. 1733. Includes village of Ashley Falls. **5** Village (pop. 1,147), Lorain co., N Ohio, 4 mi. N of Elyria. Inc. 1933. **6** Village (pop. 2,087), Warren co., NW Pa., 11 mi. SE of Warren; bottles, wood products. Founded 1864. **7** Village (pop. c.100), Pecos co., extreme W Texas, on the Pecos and c.65 mi. E of Fort Stockton; trading point in sheep-ranching region. **8** Town (pop. 451), Caledonia co., NE Vt., 15 mi. NW of St. Johnsbury; lumber, dairy products.

Sheffield Lake (□ 9), W central N.F., 15 mi. E of Sandy L. (into which it drains); 5 mi. by 3 mi.

Sheffield Lake, village (pop. 2,381), Lorain co., N Ohio, near L. Erie, 4 mi. ENE of Lorain. Inc. 1920.

Shefford, county (□ 567; pop. 33,387), S Que., on upper Yamaska R.; ⊙ Waterloo.

Shefford, town and parish (pop. 715), E central Bedford, England, on Ivel R. and 9 mi. SE of Bedford; agr. market. Has 15th-cent. church.

Shegaon (shā′goun), town (pop. 15,294), Buldana dist., W Madhya Pradesh, India, 21 mi. WNW of Akola; millet, wheat; cotton ginning, oilseed milling. Sometimes spelled Sheogaon.

Shegarskoye, Russian SFSR: see MELNIKOVO.

Sheho (shē′hō), village (pop. 248), SE central Sask., near small Sheho L., 40 mi. NW of Yorkton; mixed farming.

Shehsien (shŭ′shyĕn′), town, ⊙ Shehsien co. (pop. 149,500), SW Hopeh prov., China, on road and 50 mi. SW of Singtai; millet, kaoliang. Until 1950 in Honan prov.

Shehung (shŭ′hŏŏng′), town (pop. 17,747), ⊙ Shehung co. (pop. 468,473), NW central Szechwan prov., China, 15 mi. SE of Santai and on right bank of Fow R.; sweet-potato and indigo center; cotton textiles; rice, wheat, kaoliang, tobacco.

Shehy Mountains (shā), small range, SW Co. Cork, Ireland; rises to 1,797 ft. 12 mi. NE of Bantry.

Sheibi, Aden: see SHAIBI.

Sheikh, for Arabic names beginning thus and not found here: see under SHAIKH.

Sheikh, Br. Somaliland: see UPPER SHEIKH.

Sheikh, Jebel esh, Lebanon: see HERMON, MOUNT.

Sheikh Fadl, El, Esh Sheikh Fadl, or **Al-Sheikh Fadl** (all: ĕsh-shākh′ fă′dụl), town (pop. 9,686), Minya prov., Upper Egypt, 45 mi. N of Minya; sugar mill.

Sheikh Othman or **Sheikh 'Othman** (shākh′ ōthmăn′), largest Arab village (1946 pop. 18,424) of mainland Aden Colony, in oasis, 7 mi. NNW of Crater, at Aden Protectorate line; Arab trading center and terminus for caravans from the protectorate and Yemen; dyeing and weaving, distilling, pottery making. Scottish medical mission. Large public gardens, with deep wells furnishing Aden with its water supply. Inc. 1882 into Aden Colony.

Sheikhpura (shākh′pŏŏrŭ), town (pop. 16,333), Monghyr dist., central Bihar, India, 45 mi. WSW of Monghur; road and trade (rice, wheat, corn, grain, barley) center; hookah-tube mfg. Also spelled Shaikhpura.

Sheikh Said, Shaikh Said, or **Shaykh Sa'id** (shākh′-săĕd′), village, Taiz prov., SW Yemen, on southwesternmost point of Arabian Peninsula, 100 mi. W of Aden, on the strait Bab el Mandeb, opposite Perim isl. Acquired in 1869 by French for construction of a telegraph station, it passed in 1870 to the Turks and after First World War to Yemen.

Sheikhupura or **Shekhupura** (shā″khōō′pŏŏrŭ), district (□ 2,303; 1951 pop. 922,000), E Punjab, W Pakistan; ⊙ Sheikhupura. In Rechna Doab; bounded E by Ravi R., NE by Indian Punjab; irrigated by Upper and Lower Chenab canal systems. Wheat, rice, millet, cotton, oilseeds, sugar cane widely cultivated; rice milling, cotton ginning, hand-loom weaving. Chief centers: Shahdara, Sheikhupura. Sometimes spelled Shaikhupura.

Sheikhupura, town (1941 pop. 22,272), ⊙ Sheikhupura dist., E Punjab, W Pakistan, 20 mi. WNW of Lahore; commercial center; agr. market (wheat, cotton, rice, oilseeds); cotton ginning, flour, rice, and oilseed milling, ice mfg., hand-loom weaving, shoe mfg.; metal- and enamel works. Also called Qila Sheikhupura.

Shějak or **Shějaku,** Albania: see SHIJAK.

Shekar (shĕ′kär), Chinese *Hsieh-ka-erh* (shyĕ′gär′), town [Tibetan *dzong*], S Tibet, in N Nepal Himalayas (alt. 14,620 ft.), on Katmandu-Lhasa trade route and 120 mi. WSW of Shigatse; barley. Lamasery.

Shekhman or **Shekhman'** (shĕkh′mŭnyŭ), village (1926 pop. 4,736), W Tambov oblast, Russian SFSR, 26 mi. S of Michurinsk; grain.

Sheki or **She-ch'i** (both: shŭ′chē′), town, SW Honan prov., China, 25 mi. E of Nanyang and on Tang R. (head of navigation); commercial center.

Shekki, China: see CHUNGSHAN, Kwangtung prov.

Shekluk (sĕk′lŏŏk′), Mandarin *Shihlu* (shŭ′lōō′), town, W Hainan, Kwangtung prov., China, 25 mi. E of Cheongkong; iron-mining center, linked by rail with ports of Paso (near Pakli) and Yülin. Developed by the Japanese during the Second World War.

Sheklung (sĕk′lŏŏng′), Mandarin *Shihlung* (shŭ′-lŏŏng′), town, S Kwangtung prov., China, at head of East R. delta, on Canton-Kowloon RR and 37 mi. E of Canton; sugar- and rice-producing center; ceramics industry (pottery, bricks, tiles); mfg. of bamboo articles, lace.

Shekpaiwan, Hong Kong: see ABERDEEN.

Shekran, W Pakistan: see KHUZDAR.

Shekshing, China: see LIMKONG.

Sheksna River (shĭksnä′), Vologda oblast, Russian SFSR, issues from lake Beloye Ozero E of Belozersk, flows S, past Nikolskoye, and W to Rybinsk Reservoir at Cherepovets; 100 mi. long. Navigable as part of Mariinsk canal system; connects with Northern Dvina R. basin via Northern Dvina Canal. Until filling (1941) of Rybinsk Reservoir, it joined the Volga at Shcherbakov.

Sheksninski, Russian SFSR: see SHCHERBAKOV.

Shelabolikha (shĕlŭbô′lyĭkhŭ), village (1926 pop. 3,416), N Altai Territory, Russian SFSR, on Ob R. and 45 mi. W of Barnaul; flour mill.

Shelagh River or **Shalagh River** (shäläg′), in Seistan, E Iran and SW Afghanistan, seasonal stream conducting overflow of Seistan lake depression to Gaud-i-Zirreh salt tract; c.50 mi. long.

Shelagski, Cape, or **Cape Shelagskiy** (shĭläg′skē), on Chaun Bay of E.Siberian Sea, NE Siberian Russian SFSR; 70°4′N 171°E. Govt. arctic station, trading post, airfield.

Shelbina (shĕlbī′nŭ), city (pop. 2,113), Shelby co., NE Mo., near Salt R., 36 mi. W of Hannibal; agr. (corn), horses, poultry. Founded 1857.

Shelburn, town (pop. 1,412), Sullivan co., SW Ind., 21 mi. S of Terre Haute, in agr. area (grain, livestock, poultry; dairy products); oil wells, bituminous-coal mines; timber. Inc. 1872.

Shelburne, county (□ 979; pop. 13,251), SW N.S., on the Atlantic; ⊙ Shelburne.

Shelburne. **1** Town (pop. 1,605), ⊙ Shelburne co., SW N.S., at head of Shelburne Harbour (10-mi.-long inlet of the Atlantic) at mouth of Roseway R., 40 mi. E of Yarmouth; shipbuilding, fish curing and packing, lumbering; mfg. of boxes and barrels. Granite is quarried near by. **2** Village (pop. 1,005), S Ont., 14 mi. NNW of Orangeville; tanning, dairying, lumber and flour milling, sandstone quarrying.

Shelburne. **1** Town (pop. 1,756), Franklin co., NW Mass., on Deerfield R. and 4 mi. W of Greenfield. Settled c.1756, set off from Deerfield 1768. Includes part of SHELBURNE FALLS village. **2** Town (pop. 184), Coos co., NE N.H., on the Androscoggin and 12 mi. SE of Berlin, near White Mts. **3** Town (pop. 1,365), Chittenden co., NW Vt., on L. Champlain and 7 mi. S of Burlington; dairying. Macdonough's fleet wintered here in War of 1812. Granted 1763, 1st settled 1768, organized 1787.

Shelburne Falls, village (pop. 2,364), in Buckland and Shelburne towns, Franklin co., NW Mass., on both banks of Deerfield R. and 7 mi. W of Greenfield, near crest of Mohawk Trail. Makes cutlery, tools.

Shelby. **1** County (□ 801; pop. 30,362), central Ala.; ⊙ Columbiana. Hilly agr. region lying bet. Coosa and Cahaba rivers. Cotton, corn, livestock; coal mining, quarrying. Formed 1818. **2** County (□ 772; pop. 24,434), central Ill.; ⊙ Shelbyville. Agr. (wheat, corn, hay, soybeans; dairy products; livestock, poultry) and bituminous-coal-producing area. Mfg. (farm machinery, hairpins). Drained by South Fork of Sangamon R., and by Kaskaskia and Little Wabash rivers. Formed 1827. **3** County (□ 409; pop. 28,026), central Ind.; ⊙ Shelbyville. Drained by Big Blue R., Flatrock and Sugar creeks. Rich farming (corn, hay, grain), stock-raising, and dairying region. Mfg. at Morristown and Shelbyville. Formed 1821. **4** County (□ 587; pop. 15,942), W Iowa; ⊙ Harlan. Prairie agr. area (cattle, hogs, poultry, corn, alfalfa) drained by West Nishnabotna R. and by Keg, Silver, and Mosquito creeks; bituminous-coal deposits. Formed 1851. **5** County (□ 384; pop. 17,912), N Ky.; ⊙ Shelbyville. Bounded NW by Floyds Fork; drained by several creeks. Gently rolling upland agr. area (burley tobacco, dairy products, livestock, corn), in Bluegrass region. Some mfg. at Shelbyville. Formed 1792. **6** County (□ 502; pop. 9,730), NE Mo.; ⊙ Shelbyville. Drained by North and Salt rivers. Agr. (corn, wheat, oats, hay, soy beans), livestock (notably poultry, dairying); coal; lumber. Formed 1835. **7** County (□ 409; pop. 28,488), W Ohio; ⊙ Sidney. Intersected by Great Miami R. and Loramie Creek; L. Loramie is in W. Agr. area (livestock, grain, dairy products); mfg. at Sidney and Jackson Center; gravel pits. Formed 1819. **8** County (□ 751; pop. 482,393), extreme SW Tenn.; ⊙ MEMPHIS. Bounded S by Miss. line, W by Mississippi R. and Ark.; drained by Loosahatchie and Wolf rivers. Cotton growing, dairying, livestock raising. Memphis is an important commercial and mfg. center of Tenn. and adjoining states. Formed 1819. **9** County (□ 819; pop. 23,479), E Texas; ⊙ Center. Bounded E by Sabine R. (here the La. line), W by Attoyac Bayou; includes part of Sabine Natl. Forest. Hilly, wooded area (pine, hardwood); lumbering is chief industry. Also natural-gas wells, some oil, agr. (truck, cotton, corn, peanuts, pecans), beef and dairy cattle, poultry. Hunting, fishing. Formed 1836.

Shelby. **1** Town (pop. 592), Shelby co., W Iowa, 26 mi. NE of Council Bluffs; grain, livestock. **2** Village (pop. 1,500), Oceana co., W Mich., 27 mi. NNW of Muskegon, in fruitgrowing and dairying area; produces canned foods, fruit packages, flour, lumber. Wildlife sanctuary. Inc. 1885. **3** Town (pop. 2,148), Bolivar co., NW Miss., 20 mi. SSW of Clarksdale, in rich cotton-growing area; cottonseed products; cotton compress, feed mill. **4** City (pop. 3,058), ⊙ Toole co., N Mont., near Marias R., 75 mi. NNW of Great Falls; oil and gas wells; highest gasoline; livestock, dairy and poultry products, grain. Discovery of near-by oil (1921) was important factor in growth of town. Inc. 1914. **5** Village (pop. 624), Polk co., E central Nebr., 6 mi. E of Osceola; dairying, feed, grain, livestock, poultry. **6** City (pop. 15,508), ⊙ Cleveland co., SW N.C., 40 mi. W of Charlotte, in the piedmont; textile-mfg. center. Inc. as city 1929. **7** City (pop. 7,971), Richland co., N central Ohio, 11 mi. NW of Mansfield, and on Black Fork of Mohican R., in rich agr. region (livestock, poultry, grain); mfg. (steel tubing, cutlery, bicycles).

Shelbyville. **1** City (pop. 4,462), ⊙ Shelby co., central Ill., on Kaskaskia R. and 30 mi. SSW of Decatur; bituminous-coal mines; mfg. (farm machinery, hairpins); agr. (soybeans, corn, wheat, hay, poultry, livestock; dairy products). Inc. 1839. **2** City (pop. 11,734), ⊙ Shelby co., central Ind., on Big Blue R. and 27 mi. SE of Indianapolis; trade center in rich corn, livestock, and dairy area. Mfg.: furniture, paper products, stoves, lawn mowers, clothing, dairy products, packed meat, canned foods. Platted 1822. **3** City (pop. 4,403), ⊙ Shelby co., N Ky., 30 mi. E of Louisville, in Bluegrass agr. (livestock, corn, dairy products, burley tobacco) area. Trade center; mfg. of clothing, dairy products, concrete products; flour and feed mills, oil refinery. Airport. Science Hill School (for girls; opened 1825). City founded 1792. **4** City (pop. 635), ⊙ Shelby co., NE Mo., near Salt R., 36 mi. WNW of Hannibal; agr. (grain), livestock; lumber. **5** Town (pop. 9,456), ⊙ Bedford co., central Tenn., on Duck R. and 50 mi. SSE of Nashville. Trade and shipping center in agr., dairying, timber region; mfg. of rubber goods, pencils, clothing, hosiery, paper boxes, electric heaters, harnesses, cotton mats, staves. Region known for breeding the Tenn. "walking horse." Laid out 1810; inc. 1819. **6** Village (pop. c.450), Shelby co., E Texas, 8 mi. SE of Center; canning, shipping point in truck-farming area; lumber milling; oil wells.

Sheldahl (shĕl'dôl), town (pop. 211), on Boone-Polk-Story co. line, central Iowa, 18 mi. N of Des Moines.

Sheldon. **1** Village (pop. 1,114), Iroquois co., E Ill., 28 mi. SSE of Kankakee, near Ind. line; ships grain. Founded 1860 at railroad; inc. 1901. **2** City (pop. 4,001), O'Brien co., NW Iowa, on Floyd R. and 55 mi. NNE of Sioux City; rail junction; concrete products, feed, beverages. Sand and gravel pits near by. Has a jr. col. Inc. 1876. **3** City (pop. 427), Vernon co., W Mo., 13 mi. S of Nevada. **4** Village (pop. 267), Ransom co., SE N.Dak., 13 mi. NE of Lisbon. **5** Town (pop. 1,352), Franklin co., NW Vt., on Missisquoi R. and 8 mi. NE of St. Albans. Includes Sheldon Springs village (paper milling). Granted 1763, settled 1789–90, organized 1791. **6** Village (pop. 271), Rusk co., N central Wis., 13 mi. SSE of Ladysmith; dairying.

Sheldon's Point, village (pop. 43), W Alaska, near Yukon R. delta.

Shelekhov Gulf (shĕ'lyĭkhŭf), NE section of Sea of Okhotsk, NE Siberian Russian SFSR; includes (N) Gizhiga and Penzhina bays, separated by Taigonos Peninsula. Named for 18th-cent. Rus. merchant. Formerly Penzhina Gulf.

Shelekhovo (shĕ'lyĭkhŭvŭ), fishing village on Paramushir Isl., N Kurile Isls., Russian SFSR, on W shore, 30 mi. SW of Severo-Kurilsk; ship repair yard. Under Jap. rule (until 1945), called Kakumabetsu.

Shelemishevo (shĕlyĭmĕ'shĭvŭ), village (pop. over 500), SW central Ryazan oblast, Russian SFSR, 10 mi. W of Ryazhsk; wheat, tobacco.

Shelf, former urban district (1931 pop. 2,600) now in Queensbury and Shelf urban dist. (1948 pop. estimate 9,005), West Riding, SW Yorkshire, England, 3 mi. NE of Halifax; woolen milling.

Sheliff River, Algeria: see CHÉLIFF RIVER.

Shelikof Bay (shĕ'lĭkŏf) (4 mi. long, 5 mi. wide), SE Alaska, on W side of Kruzof Isl., on Gulf of Alaska, 20 mi. W of Sitka.

Shelikof Strait (130 mi. long, 30 mi. wide), S Alaska, bet. Alaska Peninsula (W) and Kodiak and Afognak isls. (E); connects Gulf of Alaska and its Cook Inlet (NE) with N Pacific (SW). W shore is uncharted; constantly overcast, due to volcanic dust from Katmai Volcano field (W). Fish canneries on E shore.

Shelikot (shĕlĕkōt'), village, Tigre prov., NE Ethiopia, 8 mi. S of Makale, salt market.

Shelkovskaya (shĭlkôf'skīŭ), village (1948 pop. over 10,000), SE Grozny oblast, Russian SFSR, on railroad, on Terek R. and 35 mi. ENE of Grozny, in cotton area; canned goods, flour, metalware.

Shella (shäl'lŭ), village, Khasi and Jaintia Hills dist., W Assam, India, on tributary of the Surma and 31 mi. SSW of Shillong; rice, sesame, cotton. Limestone quarries near by.

Shellal, Egypt: see SHALLAL, EL.

Shellbrook, village (pop. 506), central Sask., 26 mi. W of Prince Albert; grain elevators, flour mills, dairying.

Shell Camp, village (pop. 1,573), Gregg co., E Texas.

Shell Creek, E central Nebr., rises in Boone co., flows 74 mi. SE and E, past Newman Grove, to Platte R. near Schuyler.

Shell Creek Range (12–13,000 ft.), E Nev., in White Pine co., E of Ely, W of Snake Range. Lies in Nevada Natl. Forest. Highway crosses range in S at Connors Pass (6,997 ft.; also spelled Conners Pass).

Shellen (shĕl'ŭn), town (pop. 1,218), Adamawa prov., Northern Provinces, E Nigeria, on Gongola R. and 30 mi. N of Numan; peanuts, cassava, durra; cattle raising.

Shelley, former urban district (1931 pop. 1,566), West Riding, S Yorkshire, England, 5 mi. SE of Huddersfield; coal mining. Inc. 1938 in Kirkburton.

Shelley, city (pop. 1,856), Bingham co., SE Idaho, on Snake R. and 8 mi. SSW of Idaho Falls; alt. 4,627 ft.; potato-shipping point in livestock and agr. area (potatoes, grain, poultry); beet sugar, flour. Settled 1884, inc. 1904.

Shellharbour, municipality (pop. 3,117), New South Wales, Australia, on E coast, 55 mi. SSW of Sydney, near S shore of Illawarra L.; coal-mining center. Sometimes written Shell Harbour.

Shell Haven, England: see STANFORD-LE-HOPE.

Shell Lake, village (pop. 954), ⊙ Washburn co., NW Wis., on small Shell L., 5 mi. S of Spooner, in dairying and farming area (corn, peas, potatoes); boatbuilding, cheese making.

Shellman, city (pop. 1,090), Randolph co., SW Ga., 11 mi. E of Cuthbert, in agr. area. Settled 1837.

Shell Point, village (pop. 4,674), Contra Costa co., W Calif., near Pittsburg.

Shell River, rises in Shell L. (4 mi. long, 1.5 mi. wide), Becker co., W Minn., flows 40 mi. SE and E, through several small lakes, to Crow Wing R. 11 mi. SE of Park Rapids. Straight R. is tributary.

Shell Rock, town (pop. 1,013), Butler co., N central Iowa, on Shell Rock R. and 19 mi. NW of Waterloo, in agr. area; feed. Limestone quarries, sand and and gravel pits near by.

Shell Rock River, rises in L. Albert Lea, S Minn., flows SSE into N Iowa, past Northwood and Clarksville, to Cedar R. NW of Waterloo; 102 mi. long.

Shellsburg, town (pop. 632), Benton co., E central Iowa, 13 mi. NW of Cedar Rapids; corn cannery. Limestone quarries near by.

Shelly, village (pop. 329), Norman co., NW Minn., in Red R. valley, c.40 mi. N of Fargo, N. Dak.; dairying.

Shelmerdine (shĕl'mûrdĭn"), town (pop. 32), Pitt co., E N.C., 13 mi. SSE of Greenville.

Shelocta (shĭlŏk'tŭ), borough (pop. 105), Indiana co., W central Pa., 8 mi. WNW of Indiana.

Shelon River or **Shelon' River** (shĭlôn'yŭ), W European Russian SFSR, rises in marshes SE of Porkhov, flows NW, past Porkhov, and NE, past Soltsy (head of navigation; 25 mi. above mouth), to L. Ilmen near Shimsk; 160 mi. long. Part of anc. Pskov-Novgorod water route.

Shelopugino (shĕlŭpōō'gĭnŭ), village (1948 pop. over 2,000), SE Chita oblast, Russian SFSR, 175 mi. E of Chita; wheat, livestock.

Shelter Island, summer-resort village (pop. 928), Suffolk co., SE N.Y., 9 mi. N of Bridgehampton, on irregularly shaped Shelter Isl. (c.7 mi. long, 6 mi. wide), which lies bet. E peninsulas of Long Isl. at W end of Gardiners Bay. Ferries from isl. to Greenport (N), to North Haven (S). Shelter Island Heights (resort) is NW of Shelter Island village; Dering Harbor is N. Settled in 17th cent.

Shelton. **1** City (pop. 12,694), coextensive with Shelton town, Fairfield co., SW Conn., on the Housatonic (dammed here) opposite Derby, and 9 mi. W of New Haven; textiles, silverware, clothing, tools, machinery, metal products. State tuberculosis sanatorium, state park are here. Settled 1697, town inc. 1789, city inc. 1915. **2** Village (pop. 1,032), Buffalo co., S Nebr., 20 mi. ENE of Kearney; grain, stock, sugar beets, potatoes. **3** Village, Fairfield co., N central S.C., on Broad R. and 20 mi. WNW of Winnsboro; mineral springs; beverage plant. **4** City (pop. 5,045), ⊙ Mason co., W Wash., 15 mi. NW of Olympia and on arm of Puget Sound; oysters, lumber, dairy products; cellulose plant. Inc. 1889.

Sheltozero (shĕlt'ô"zyĭrŭ), village (1948 pop. over 500), S Karelo-Finnish SSR, on L. Onega, 45 mi. SE of Petrozavodsk; grain. Formerly called Sheltozerski. Quarries on L. Onega at Shoksha (quartzite, sandstone), 13 mi. NW, and at Rop-Ruchei, Finnish *Ruoppoja*, 8 mi. SE. Dist. largely inhabited by Veps.

Shelyakino (shĭlyä'kĕnŭ), village (1939 pop. over 500), SW Voronezh oblast, Russian SFSR, 23 mi. WNW of Rossosh; wheat.

Shemakha (shĕmŭkhä'), city (1926 pop. 3,665), E Azerbaijan SSR, at SE foot of the Greater Caucasus, 65 mi. W of Baku; silk-milling center; wines (champagne); orchards. Frequent earthquakes, one of which destroyed it in 1902. Founded in 6th cent.; silk trade with Venice and Hungary (16th cent.). Until 17th cent., ⊙ Shirvan khanate; conquered 1805 by Russians.

Shemiran, Iran: see SHAMIRAN.

Shemonaikha (shĕmŭnŭē'khŭ), town (1948 pop. over 10,000), NW East Kazakhstan oblast, Kazakh SSR, on railroad and 55 mi. NW of Ust-Kamenogorsk; metalworks.

Shemordan (shĕmŭrdän'), town (1939 pop. over 500), NW Tatar Autonomous SSR, Russian SFSR on railroad and 21 mi. ENE of Arsk; food processing, grain trading.

Shemshak, Iran: see SHIMSHAK.

Shemursha (shĕmōōrshä'), village (1926 pop. 560), SE Chuvash Autonomous SSR, Russian SFSR, 45 mi. S of Kanash; sawmilling.

Shemya Island (shĕm'yŭ) (4 mi. long, 2 mi. wide), Semichi Isls., W Aleutian Isls., SW Alaska, 150 mi. WNW of Kiska Isl. and 50 mi. ESE of Attu Isl.; 52°43'N 174°9'W. Airport, important refueling point on N air route bet. U.S. and the Far East (1,450 mi. from Anchorage, 2,050 mi. from Tokyo); radio station, hosp. On NW side is Alcan Harbor, anchorage with breakwater.

Shemysheika or **Shemysheyka** (shĕmĭshā'kŭ), village (1932 pop. estimate 3,500), central Penza oblast, Russian SFSR, 27 mi. SE of Penza, in wheat and sunflower area; food processing.

Shenandoah (shĕnŭndō'ŭ), county (□ 507; pop. 21,169), NW Va.; ⊙ Woodstock. In Shenandoah Valley; bounded W and NW by W.Va. and ridges of the Alleghenies, E and SE by Massanutten Mtn.; drained by North Fork of Shenandoah R. and Cedar Creek. Diversified agr.: livestock (especially poultry, dairy and beef cattle), wheat, fruit, hay; limestone quarrying; lumbering. Mineral springs (health resorts), George Washington Natl. Forest, limestone caverns attract tourists. Strasburg, Woodstock are trade, processing centers. Formed 1772.

Shenandoah. **1** City (pop. 6,938), Page co., SW Iowa, on East Nishnabotna R. (hydroelectric plant) and c.40 mi. SE of Council Bluffs; rail junction, and a major shipping center for large nurseries, seed houses, and poultry hatcheries. Also has feed mills, bottling works, rendering plant, railroad shops; mfg. of dairy products, packed poultry, neon signs, paint, chemicals, leather articles, gloves, fur garments. Inc. 1871. **2** Borough (pop. 15,704), Schuylkill co., E central Pa., 9 mi. N of Pottsville; anthracite; clothing mfg., brewing, meat packing. Settled 1835, laid out 1862, inc. 1866. **3** Town (pop. 1,903, Page co., N Va., on South Fork of Shenandoah R. and 22 mi. NNE of Waynesboro, bet. Massanutten Mtn. (W) and Blue Ridge (E); rail station in agr. area; clothing mfg. Inc. 1884.

Shenandoah Caverns, Va.: see MOUNT JACKSON.

Shenandoah Heights, village (pop. 1,798), Schuylkill co., E central Pa., near Shenandoah.

Shenandoah Mountain, in Va. and W.Va., a ridge of the Alleghenies; from Bath co., Va., extends c.80 mi. NW, partly along state line, into Hardy co., W.Va.; rises to over 4,400 ft. W of Harrisonburg, Va.

Shenandoah National Park (□ 302.3), N Va., extends for c.75 mi. along crest of the Blue Ridge from Front Royal (N) to point near Waynesboro (S); width varies from 1–13 mi. Heavily wooded mtn. area noted for scenic views (Shenandoah Valley to W, the piedmont to E), abundance of wildlife and flowers, picturesque trails, and recreational facilities. Reaches max. elevations in N, where Stony Man peak rises to 4,010 ft. and Hawks Bill peak to 4,049 ft. Skyline Drive (97 mi. long; max. alt. 3,680 ft.) extends through length of park, joining Blue Ridge Parkway in S. Park is traversed by 94 mi. of Appalachian Trail. Area 1st explored (1669) by John Lederer; deeded to U.S. and established as natl. park in 1935.

Shenandoah River, in Va. and W.Va., formed near Front Royal, Va., by North Fork (c.100 mi. long) and South Fork (c.95 mi. long), both flowing generally NE through Shenandoah Valley, on either side of 45-mi.-long Massanutten Mtn., at whose N end they join; flows 55 mi. NE, through N portion of the valley, across Eastern Panhandle of W.Va., to Potomac R. at Harpers Ferry, W.Va. The beautiful **Shenandoah Valley** is part of Great Appalachian Valley (which continues N as Hagerstown Valley of Md. and Cumberland Valley of Pa.); c.150 mi. long, 10–20 mi. wide, bet. the Alleghenies (W) and Blue Ridge (E). Famed for its rich farmlands, orchards (especially apples), and pastures; chief centers are Winchester, Front Royal, Luray, Staunton, Waynesboro, Lexington. In Civil War, valley was avenue for Confederates' attempts to invade the North (Stonewall Jackson's 1862 campaign; Gettysburg campaign, 1863; Early's raid in 1864), and was a chief supply source for Lee's army. Federal troops under Sheridan finally drove out the Confederates and laid region waste; by 1865 the valley's resources were lost to the South.

Shenango River (shĭnăng'gō), mainly in W Pa., rises in NW Pa. and NE Ohio, flows S c.60 mi., past Greenville and Sharon, joining Mahoning R. at New Castle to form Beaver R. Flood-control dam in upper course forms Pymatuning Reservoir.

Shenchih or **Shen-ch'ih** (shŭn'chŭ'), town, ⊙ Shenchih co. (pop. 49,084), N Shansi prov., China, 10 mi. NW of Ningwu, near S section of Great Wall (Chahar line); wheat, beans, ramie.

Shen-ch'iu, China: see SHENKIU.

Shenchow. **1** Town, Hopeh prov., China: see SHENHSIEN. **2** Town, Hunan prov., China: see YÜANLING.

Shen-ch'uan, China: see SHUMCHÜN.

Shencottah (shĕngkō'tä), city (pop. 14,814), SE Travancore, India, E of Ariankavu pass (in Western Ghats; 18 mi. long; rail tunnel), 50 mi. E of Quilon; rubber, tea, and coffee processing (plantations near by), sawmilling. Papanasam and Pallivasal (MUNNAR) hydroelectric systems linked here. Rail junction of Tenkasi is 4 mi. ESE, in Madras. Also spelled Shenkottah.

Shendam (shĕn'dŭm), town, Plateau Prov., Northern Provinces, central Nigeria, 80 mi. SE of Jos; tin mining.

Shendi (shĕn'dē), town (pop. 14,600), Northern Prov., Anglo-Egyptian Sudan, on right bank of the Nile, on railroad and 100 mi. NNE of Ed Damer; industrial center; mfg. of cotton goods, dyeing, metalworking. An important town of Fung kingdom (17th–19th cent.). At El Metemma, opposite Shendi, the khedive of Egypt defeated the Mahdists in 1885.

Shendurjana, India: see SENDURJANA.

Shendurni (shăn'dŏŏrnē), town (pop. 10,005), East Khandesh dist., E Bombay, India, 24 mi. S of Jalgaon; agr. market (cotton, millet, wheat); cotton ginning.

Shenfield, residential town and parish (pop. 3,501), SW Essex, England, just NE of Brentwood. Has 13th-cent. church.

Shenge (shĕng'gā), town (pop. 1,400), South-Western Prov., SW Sierra Leone, minor port on Atlantic Ocean, opposite Plantain Isl., and 40 mi. WSW of Moyamba, on road; fishing. United Brethren in Christ mission.

Shëngjin (shŭng-gyĕn') or **Shëngjini** (–gyē'nē), Ital. *San Giovanni di Medua* (sän jôvän'nē dē mĕ'dŏŏä), village (1930 pop. 14), N Albania, minor Adriatic port on Drin Gulf, 18 mi. SSE of Scutari, serving Scutari and N Albania. Dates from 1313. Also spelled Shingjin or Shingjini.

Shengking, Manchuria: see MUKDEN.

Sheng-tse, China: see SHINGTSEH.

Shenhsien (shŭn'shyĕn'), town, ⊙ Shenhsien co. (pop. 369,790), SW Hopeh prov., China, 55 mi. E of Shihkiachwang; peaches, chestnuts, cotton, peanuts. Until 1913 called Shenchow.

Shenick's Island, islet of The Skerries, in the Irish Sea, just SE of Skerries town, NE Co. Dublin, Ireland.

Shenipsit Lake or **Snipsic Lake,** N Conn., lake (c.2 mi. long) just N of Rockville; drained by Hockanum R.

Shenkeng or **Shen-k'eng** (shŭn'kŭng'), Jap. *Shinko* (shĕng'kō), town (1935 pop. 1,344), N Formosa, 7 mi. SE of Taipei; coal mining.

Shenkiu or **Shen-ch'iu** (both: shŭn'chyō'). **1** Town, Anhwei prov., China: see LINCHÜAN. **2** Town, ⊙ Shenkiu co. (pop. 329,801), E Honan prov., China, on Anhwei line, 70 mi. ESE of Yencheng; cotton weaving; rice, wheat, millet.

Shenkottah, India: see SHENCOTTAH.

Shenkursk (shĭn-kōōrsk'), city (1926 pop. 2,536), SW central Archangel oblast, Russian SFSR, on Vaga R. and 75 mi. NNE of Velsk; metalworking, sawmilling; food processing. Dates from 14th cent.; chartered 1762; formerly a trading center on White Sea route.

Shenley, town and parish (pop. 2,349), S Hertford, England, 5 mi. SSE of St. Albans. Has 15th-cent. church.

Shenmu (shŭn'mōō'), town, ⊙ Shenmu co. (pop. 83,365), northernmost Shensi prov., China, 50 mi. NE of Yülin, at Great Wall (Suiyuan line); wheat, millet, beans.

Shenpa (shŭn'bä') or **Shanpa** (shän'–), town, ⊙ Shenpa dist. (pop. 18,183), W Suiyuan prov., China, 25 mi. NW of Linho, in Howtao oasis; agr. settlement; cattle raising; grain.

Shensi (shĕn'sē'), Chinese *Shan-hsi* (shän'shē'), province (□ 75,000; pop. 10,000,000) of NW central China; ⊙ Sian. Bounded E by Shansi (along Yellow R.), SE by Honan and Hupeh, S by Szechwan along Tapa Shan, W by Kansu, and NW by Ningsia and Suiyuan along the Great Wall, Shensi falls into 2 distinct natural regions separated by the E–W Wei R. valley, the economic center of the prov. To the N is the heart of China's loess lands, extending S from the Ordos Desert and ending abruptly at Wei R. This region, drained by Lo R. and dominated climatically by the near-by deserts, has dry, cold winters marked by dust storms. Wheat, millet, and kaoliang are the principal food crops, and cotton and tobacco are raised in the Wei valley. S of Wei R. rises the great barrier of the Tsinling Mts., which overlook upper Han R. valley. This natural region resembles the adjoining Red Basin of Szechwan (S) in physiography, climate, and agr. products. It is marked by cloudy winters and hot summers, and produces fruit, corn, cotton, tea, ramie, and tobacco. Shensi is one of China's chief oil producers (main fields at Yenchang and Yenchwan) and has ⅓ of the country's coal deposits. Coal mining is restricted, however, to Hancheng (on Yellow R.) and Tungchwan (on spur of Lunghai RR). Iron deposits are found in Tsinling Mts. The chief urban centers are: Nancheng and Ankang, in the Han valley; Tungkwan, Tali, Sian, and Paoki, in the Wei valley; and Yenan and Yülin, in the N loess lands. Pop., almost entirely Chinese, speaks N Mandarin (N of Tsinling Mts.) and SW Mandarin (in Han valley). There are small Mongolian elements along the Ordos Desert frontier (N). One of the original areas (Wei R. valley) of Chinese settlement, the region, with its center at Sian, played a major role in early Chinese history. Traditionally called Chin (Ch'in) or Tsin (Ts'in) for an early kingdom (897–221 B.C.) on its site, the prov. became known as Shensi under the 13th-cent. Mongol dynasty. The spelling Shensi (properly written Shansi) is used to differentiate this prov. from the prov. of Shansi. The name Shensi (Shansi), meaning W of Shan, refers to the Yellow R. town of Shan (modern Shanhsien), originally situated on Shensi's E border. The prov. passed in 1644 to Manchu control, when it acquired its present limits; it suffered greatly in the Moslem rebellion of the 1860s. In the late 1930s, N Shensi became the center of the Chinese Communist party (⊙ Yenan). Prov. remained in Free China during Second World War, and in 1949 came entirely under Chinese Communist control.

Shentala (shĕntŭlä'), village (1939 pop. over 500), N Kuibyshev oblast, Russian SFSR, on railroad and 37 mi. NNE of Sergiyevsk; woodworking; wheat, sunflowers.

Shentseh or **Shen-tse** (shŭn'dzŭ'), town, ⊙ Shentseh co. (pop. 114,773), SW Hopeh prov., China, 40 mi. ENE of Shihkiachwang and on Huto R.; cotton, wheat, millet.

Shenyang, Manchuria: see MUKDEN.

Sheo (shā'ō), village, W Rajasthan, India, 32 mi. NNW of Barmer, on Thar Desert; camel breeding.

Sheoganj (shā'ōgŭnj), town (pop. 4,166), S Rajasthan, India, 22 mi. NNE of Sirohi, 1 mi. E of Erinpura; market for millet, wheat, corn.

Sheogaon, India: see SHEGAON.

Sheopur (shā'ōpŏŏr), town (pop. 8,378), N Madhya Bharat, India, 95 mi. WSW of Lashkar; rail terminus; agr. market (millet, wheat, oilseeds, gram); lacquered woodwork. Sometimes called Sheopur Kalan.

Shepaug River (shĭpôg'), W Conn., rises W of Goshen, flows c.35 mi. generally S, forming Shepaug Reservoir near Warren, to the Housatonic 9 mi. NE of Danbury.

Shepetovka (shĕpyĭtôf'kŭ), city (1926 pop. 14,693), N Kamenets-Podolski oblast, Ukrainian SSR, 50 mi. N of Proskurov; rail junction; sugar refining, meat packing, sawmilling. Developed as rail town. In Second World War, held (1941–43) by Germans.

Shepherd, village (pop. 899), Isabella co., central Mich., 6 mi. SE of Mt. Pleasant, in stock raising, dairying, and agr. area.

Shepherd Islands, small volcanic group, New Hebrides, SW Pacific, 35 mi. N of Efate. Largest isl. is Tongoa (pop. 1,453; 8 mi. in circumference), 2d largest is Mai (pop. 299; 6 mi. long). Produce copra, mother-of-pearl.

Shepherdstown, town (pop. 1,173), Jefferson co., NE W.Va., in Eastern Panhandle near the Potomac, 9 mi. ESE of Martinsburg. Shepherd State Col., Rumsey State Park here. One of 2 oldest towns in state; settled 1762. Rumsey demonstrated his steamboat here in 1787. The *Potomac Guardian* (started here 1790) was 1st newspaper in what is now W.Va.

Shepherdsville, town (pop. 953), ⊙ Bullitt co., NW Ky., near Salt R., 16 mi. S of Louisville, in agr. area; flour, feed, and lumber milling.

Shepley, former urban district (1931 pop. 1,668), West Riding, S Yorkshire, England, 5 mi. SE of Huddersfield; woolen milling. Inc. 1938 in Kirkburton.

Shepody Bay (shĕ'pŭdē), NW arm (10 mi. long, up to 5 mi. wide) of Chignecto Bay of the Bay of Fundy, SE N.B., 20 mi. SSE of Moncton. Receives Petitcodiac and Memramcook rivers.

Sheppard Air Force Base, Texas: see WICHITA FALLS.

Sheppard Park, village (pop. 1,419, with adjacent Pinehurst), Dorchester co., S.C.

Shepparton, municipality (pop. 7,914), N Victoria, Australia, on Goulburn R. and 100 mi. NNE of Melbourne; rail junction in agr., livestock area; fruit and vegetable canneries, meat-packing plant; wheat, wool, dairy products, tobacco, wine. Hydroelectric plant.

Shepperton, England: see SUNBURY-ON-THAMES.

Sheppey, Isle of, island (9 mi. long, 4 mi. wide) in the Thames estuary, N Kent, England, separated from mainland by the Swale, a narrow inlet. Largely flat, with low cliffs in N. Fertile agr. land supports grain, vegetables, sheep. Main towns: Sheerness, Queensborough, Minster-in-Sheppey.

Shepshed, urban district (1931 pop. 5,758; 1951 census 6,235), N Leicester, England, 4 mi. W of Loughborough; hosiery-knitting center; shoe industry. Has 13th-cent. church. Formerly an important sheep market.

Shepton Mallet, urban district (1931 pop. 4,108; 1951 census 5,131), E Somerset, England, 5 mi. ESE of Wells; agr. market; cheese making, bacon and ham curing, brewing. Has 13th–15th-cent. church and 14th-cent. market cross.

Shequaga Falls, N.Y.: see MONTOUR FALLS.

Sherada (shĕrä'dä), Ital. *Sciaradda*, village, Kaffa prov., SW Ethiopia, near Gojab R., 15 mi. ENE of Bonga; coffeegrowing.

Sherbakul or **Sherbakul'** (shĕrbŭkōōl'), village (1934 pop. over 2,000), SW Omsk oblast, Russian SFSR, 45 mi. SW of Omsk, in agr. area.

Sherborn (shûr'bûrn), town (pop. 1,245), Middlesex co., E Mass., near Charles R., 5 mi. SE of Framingham. Settled 1652, inc. 1674.

Sherborne (shûr'bûrn), urban district (1931 pop. 6,542; 1951 census 5,987), N Dorset, England, on elevated site in Vale of Blackmore, on Yeo R. and 5 mi. E of Yeovil; agr. market; silk milling and dairying. Became seat of bishopric under St. Aldhelm in 705; in 1075 see was removed to Old Sarum. Abbey church (Norman to 15th cent.) was part of Benedictine abbey founded 998. Castle, built 1594 by Sir Walter Raleigh, adjoins remains of Saxon castle. Site of Sherborne School, public school founded 1550 by Edward VI, with library containing notable musical scores.

Sherborne Saint John, town and parish (pop. 2,348), NE Hampshire, England, 2 mi. NNW of Basingstoke; agr. market. Site of mental hosp. Has 15th-cent. church. Near by is 16th-cent. mansion, rebuilt by Inigo Jones.

Sherbro Island (shûr'brō), in the Atlantic just off Sierra Leone, 65 mi. SSE of Freetown; 30 mi. long, up to 15 mi. wide; separated from mainland (N and E) by Sherbro R. and Shebar Strait; covered with mangrove-swamp forest. Terminates W in Cape St. Ann, off which lie Turtle Isls. Port of Bonthe on E coast. Fisheries; rice, cassava. Historically part of the colony; isl. (except Bonthe town) is administered under South-Western Prov. of the protectorate.

Sherbrooke, county (□ 238; pop. 46,574), S Que., on St. Francis R.; ⊙ Sherbrooke.

Sherbrooke. 1 Village (pop. estimate 500), SE N.S., on St. Mary R. and 45 mi. SE of New Glasgow; lumbering; pulpwood-shipping point. Founded 1662 as French post. **2** City (pop. 35,965), ⊙ Sherbrooke co., S Que., on St. Francis R., at mouth of Magog R., and 80 mi. E of Montreal; commercial center of the Eastern Townships and hosiery-mfg. center, with rayon and knitting mills and also steel foundries, railroad workshops; lumbering, milk canning; mfg. of mining machinery, rubber products, clothing, underwear, gloves, furniture. Hydroelectric power station. Has 2 colleges and a technical school. Seat of R.C. bishop. Copper and asbestos are mined near by. Market for surrounding lumbering, dairying, cattle-raising region. Originally settled by United Empire Loyalists, region is now mainly French.

Sherbrooke Lake (8 mi. long, 2 mi. wide), W N.S., 18 mi. N of Bridgewater. Drains into Lahave R.

Sherbro River, arm of the Atlantic, in SW Sierra Leone, bet. Sherbro Isl. and mainland; extends c.50 mi. from Shebar Strait N and W, around Sherbro Isl., to 25-mi.-wide mouth bet. Cape St. Ann (S) and Shenge (N); average width 5 mi. Receives Kittam, Jong, and Bagru rivers. Contains York Isl., opposite Bonthe (chief port).

Sherburn, town and parish (pop. 3,182), E central Durham, England, 3 mi. E of Durham; coal.

Sherburn (shûr'bûrn), village (pop. 1,221), Martin co., S Minn., 14 mi. W of Fairmont near Iowa line, in grain, livestock, poultry area; dairy products. Small lakes near by. Also written Sherburne.

Sherburne (shûr'bûrn), county (□ 438; pop. 10,661), central Minn.; ⊙ Elk River. Agr. area bounded W and S by Mississippi R. and drained by Elk R. Dairy products, livestock, grain, poultry; marl deposits. Co. formed 1856.

Sherburne. 1 Town (pop. 100), Fleming co., NE Ky., on Licking R. and 29 mi. ESE of Cynthiana, in outer Bluegrass agr. region. **2** Village (pop. 1,604), Chenango co., central N.Y., on Chenango R. and 33 mi. SSW of Utica, in dairying area; mfg. (knit goods, animal foods, lumber, concrete products). Summer resort. State game farm near by. Settled 1793, inc. 1830. **3** Town (pop. 283), Rutland co., S central Vt., in Green Mts., 10 mi. ENE of Rutland; wood products. Killington Peak is here.

Sherburn-in-Elmet, town and parish (pop. 1,877), West Riding, S central Yorkshire, England, 6 mi. S of Tadcaster; agr. market. Former site of a palace of the archbishops of York.

Shercock (shûrkŏk'), Gaelic *Searcóg*, town (pop. 235), E Co. Cavan, Ireland, 8 mi. WNW of Carrickmacross; agr. market (flax, potatoes; cattle, pigs); flax-scutching center.

Shere (shēr), residential town and parish (pop. 3,070), central Surrey, England, 5 mi. E of Guildford. Church (Norman to 13th cent.) has old glass.

Sheremetyevka or **Sheremet'yevka** (shĕrĭmĕ'tyĭfkŭ), village (1932 pop. estimate 2,500), central Tatar Autonomous SSR, Russian SFSR, near Kama R., 35 mi. E of Chistopol; saddle making; leathercrafts; wheat, livestock.

Shereshevo (shĕrĭshĕ'vŭ), Pol. *Szereszów* (shĕrĕ'shŏŏf), town (1931 pop. 3,554), N central Brest oblast, Belorussian SSR, in Bialowieza Forest, 10 mi. W of Pruzhany; flour-milling center; flaxseed processing. Has old churches and synagogue.

Shergat, Iraq: see SHARQAT.

Sherghati (shărgä'tē), town (pop. 6,014), Gaya dist., W central Bihar, India, on tributary of the Ganges and 20 mi. SW of Gaya; road center; rice, gram, wheat, barley; mfg. of brass utensils.

Shergol, Kashmir: see KARGIL.

Sheridan (shĕr'ĭdŭn). **1** County (□ 893; pop. 4,607), NW Kansas; ⊙ Hoxie. Rolling plain area drained by South Fork of Solomon R. and Saline R. Grain, livestock. Formed 1880. **2** County (□ 1,700; pop. 6,674), extreme NE Mont.; ⊙ Plentywood. Well-watered agr. area bordering on Sask. and N.Dak.; drained by Medicine L. and Big Muddy Creek. Grain. Part of Fort Peck Indian Reservation in SW. Formed 1913. **3** County (□ 2,466; pop. 9,539), NW Nebr.; ⊙ Rushville. Agr. area bounded N by S.Dak.; drained by Niobrara R. and numerous small lakes. Grain, livestock, dairy and poultry produce. Formed 1885. **4** County (□ 995; pop. 5,253), central N.Dak.; ⊙ McClusky. Agr. area watered by Sheyenne R. Dairy products, livestock, poultry. Formed 1908. **5** County (□ 2,531; pop. 20,185), N Wyo.; ⊙ Sheridan. Irrigated agr. and coal-mining area, bordering on Mont.; watered by Little Bighorn, Tongue, and Powder rivers. Grain, livestock, sugar beets, beans. Part of Bighorn Natl. Forest and Bighorn Mts. in W. Formed 1888.

Sheridan. **1** Town (pop. 1,893), ⊙ Grant co., central Ark., 23 mi. WNW of Pine Bluff, in timber and farm area (corn, cotton, peanuts); cotton ginning, woodworking. **2** S suburb (pop. 1,715) of Denver, Arapahoe co., N central Colo.; alt. 5,394 ft. **3** Village (pop. 476), La Salle co., N Ill., on Fox R. (bridged here) and 24 mi. SW of Aurora, in agr. and bituminous-coal area. **4** Town (pop. 1,965), Hamilton co., central Ind., 25 mi. N of Indianapolis, in livestock, grain, and dairy area; cement products, canned goods, condensed milk, flour, chemicals, packed meat. **5** Village (pop. 535), Montcalm co., central Mich., 34 mi. NE of Grand Rapids, in farm area; mfg. of fire extinguishers. **6** Town (pop. 370), Worth co., NW Mo., on Little Platte R. and 18 mi. NE of Maryville. **7** Town (pop. 572), Madison co., SW Mont., on branch of Beaverhead R., in Jefferson R. system, and 40 mi. SSE of Butte; livestock, grain. Silver, lead, gold mined in near-by Tobacco Root Mts. **8** Village (pop. c.250), Chautauqua co., extreme W N.Y., 5 mi. E of Dunkirk; canned foods, paving material; ships seed. **9** City (pop. 1,922), Yamhill co., NW Oregon, on South Yamhill R. and 20 mi. NW of Salem; lumber milling, dairying, fruit processing. Settled 1847, inc. 1880. **10** Village (pop. 1,314, with adjacent Newmanstown), Lebanon co., SE central Pa., 11 mi. E of Lebanon. **11** City (pop. 11,500), ⊙ Sheridan co., N Wyo., at confluence of Goose Creek and Little Goose creek, near Mont. line, 130 mi. SE of Billings, Mont. Largest city in N Wyo.; railroad div. point, with railroad shops; tourist stop for visitors to Bighorn Mts., 20 mi. W. Food processing (beet sugar, flour, dairy products, cereals); mfg. of iron products, beverages, bricks, tiles. Coal mines and dude ranches in vicinity; livestock, truck products raised. Veterans' hosp. (on site of Fort MacKenzie), state industrial school for girls, Bighorn Natl. Forest near by. Points of interest to S: site of Fetterman Massacre (1866), where Indians wiped out force of soldiers; reproduction of Fort Phil Kearney, military post in 1860s. City settled 1878, laid out 1882, inc. 1884. Grew with arrival of railroad and development of near-by coal deposits.

Sheridan, Cape, NE extremity of Ellesmere Isl., NE Franklin Dist., Northwest Territories, on Lincoln Sea of the Arctic Ocean, at NW entrance of Robeson Channel; 82°27'N 61°27'W. The *Alert* of the Nares expedition wintered here 1875–76; Peary's expedition vessel, the *Roosevelt,* wintered here 1905–06 and again 1908–09. Notes left by Peary in a cairn, 1906, found by U.S. icebreakers in 1948.

Sheridan, Fort, Ill.: see HIGHLAND PARK.

Sheridan, Mount, Wyo.: see RED MOUNTAINS.

Sheriffmuir, Scotland: see DUNBLANE.

Sheringham, urban district (1931 pop. 4,142; 1951 census 4,803), N Norfolk, England, on North Sea, 4 mi. WNW of Cromer; seaside resort and small fishing port.

Sherkin (shûr'kĭn), island (1,247 acres; 3 mi. long, 1 mi. wide) just off Baltimore, SW Co. Cork, Ireland; site of ruins of Dunalong Castle and of Franciscan abbey founded 1460 by the O'Driscolls. At E end is lighthouse (51°28'N 9°24'W).

Sherkot (shär'kōt), town (pop. 17,027), Bijnor dist., N Uttar Pradesh, India, on tributary of the Ramganga and 27 mi. E of Bijnor; trades in rice, wheat, sugar cane. Sacked 1805 by Pindaris. Founded 16th cent.

Sherlovaya Gora (shĭrlô"vĭŭ gŭrä'), town (1948 pop. over 2,000), SE Chita oblast, Russian SFSR, on branch of Trans-Siberian RR and 13 mi. NNW of Borzya; tin-mining center. Developed in late 1930s.

Shermadevi, India: see SERMADEVI.

Sherman. **1** County (□ 1,055; pop. 7,373), NW Kansas; ⊙ Goodland. Gently rolling agr. area, bordering W on Colo.; watered by headstreams of Beaver and Sappa creeks. Grain, livestock. Formed 1886. **2** County (□ 570; pop. 6,421), central Nebr.; ⊙ Loup City. Farming region drained by Middle Loup R. Grain, livestock, dairy and poultry produce. Formed 1873. **3** County (□ 830; pop. 2,271), N Oregon; ⊙ Moro. Bounded and drained by Columbia R. (N), Deschutes R. (W), and John Day R. (E); borders on Wash. Wheat, barley, oats. Formed 1889. **4** County (□ 914; pop. 2,443), extreme N Texas; ⊙ Stratford. In high Panhandle plains, and bounded N by Okla. line; alt. c.3,100–3,800 ft. Drained by North Canadian R. (intermittent here) and tributaries. Large-scale grain farming; beef cattle; some dairying, poultry. Natural-gas wells; some oil. Formed 1876.

Sherman. **1** Town (pop. 549), Fairfield co., W Conn., bet. N.Y. line and L. Candlewood, 13 mi. N of Danbury; hunting, fishing. **2** Town (pop. 1,029), Aroostook co., E central Maine, 20 mi. NE of Millinocket, in Molunkus Stream valley; farming, lumbering, hunting, fishing. **3** Town (pop. 386), on Pontotoc-Union co. line, N Miss., 12 mi. NE of Pontotoc, in agr., dairying, and timber area. **4** Village (pop. 861), Chautauqua co., extreme W N.Y., 19 mi. WNW of Jamestown; metal products, tools; dairy products, poultry. **5** Town (pop. 120), Minnehaha co., E S.Dak., 20 mi. NE of Sioux Falls, near Minn. line, on branch of Big Sioux R. **6** City (pop. 20,150), ⊙ Grayson co., N Texas, c.60 mi. N of Dallas, in Red R. valley; trade, industrial, wholesale distribution center, in fertile agr. region; highway, rail junction, with railroad shops. Flour, feed milling, cotton ginning, cottonseed-oil milling; mfg. of cereal and other food products, textiles, clothing, foundry and machine-shop products. Seat of Austin Col. Perrin Air Force Base near. Settled 1849, inc. 1854.

Sherman, Mount, peak (14,037 ft.) in Park Range, central Colo., 7 mi. ESE of Leadville.

Sherman Air Force Base, Kansas: see LEAVENWORTH.

Sherman Oaks, suburban residential section of Los ANGELES city, Los Angeles co., S Calif., in San Fernando Valley, c.9 mi. S of San Fernando.

Sherm Rabigh, Saudi Arabia: see RABIGH.

Sherm Wejh, Saudi Arabia: see WEJH.

Sherpur (shär'po͝or), town (pop. 12,623), Ghazipur dist., E Uttar Pradesh, India, on an arm of the Ganges and 13 mi. E of Ghazipur; trades in rice, barley, gram, oilseeds.

Sherpur. **1** Anc. *Salimnagar,* town (pop. 5,145), Bogra dist., N central East Bengal, E Pakistan, on Karatoya R. (tributary of the Atrai) and 12 mi. S of Bogra; trades in rice, jute, rape and mustard, sugar cane. Mogul frontier post in 15th cent. Formerly called Sherpur Murcha. **2** Town (pop. 24,210), Mymensingh dist., NE East Bengal, E Pakistan, 30 mi. NW of Mymensingh; trade center (jute, rice, mustard, sugar cane). Anc. fort ruins near by.

Sher Qila (shär kĭ'lŭ), village, Punial state, Gilgit Agency, NW Kashmir, on Gilgit R. and 20 mi. NW of Gilgit. Fort; residence of a raja.

Sherrard (shĕ'rärd), village (pop. 484), Mercer co., NW Ill., 12 mi. SSE of Rock Island, in agr. and bituminous-coal area.

Sherridon, town (pop. estimate 1,500), W Man., on Kississing L., 40 mi. NE of Flin Flon; copper-mining center, largely replaced in early 1950s by Lynn Lake copper-nickel center, 120 mi. N.

Sherrill. **1** Town (pop. 263), Jefferson co., central Ark., 11 mi. NNE of Pine Bluff. **2** Town (pop. 162), Dubuque co., E Iowa, 8 mi. NW of Dubuque. **3** City (pop. 2,236), Oneida co., central N.Y., near Oneida Creek, 12 mi. SSW of Rome; makes silverware, machinery. Summer resort. Inc. 1916.

Sherrodsville, village (pop. 426), Carroll co., E Ohio, 21 mi. SSE of Canton and on small Conotton Creek.

Shershell, Algeria: see CHERCHEL.

Sherston, agr. village and parish (pop. 1,145), NW Wiltshire, England, on the Avon and 5 mi. W of Malmesbury. Has Norman church. Scene of Saxon-Danish battle (1016).

Shertallai (shĕrtŭ'lī), town (pop. 6,765), NW Travancore, India, 13 mi. N of Alleppey; coir rope and mats, copra; hand-loom weaving, rice and betel farming. Also spelled Shertally or Sherthala.

's Hertogenbosch (sĕr'tōkh-ŭnbôs"), Fr. *Bois-le-Duc* (bwä-lü-dük') [Du., and Fr.,=the duke's woods], city (pop. 53,208), ⊙ North Brabant prov., S central Netherlands, at confluence of Dommel and Aa rivers and the Zuid-Willemsvaart (here forming Dieze R.), 13 mi. NE of Tilburg; 51°38'N 5°19'E. Rail junction; mfg. (electric light bulbs, bicycles, food products, cigars); iron foundry; shipbuilding; cattle market. Has 15th-cent. cathedral, 16th-cent. town hall. Chartered 1184 by Duke Henry I of Brabant; remained fortified until 1876. Sustained considerable damage by bombardment (1944–45) during Second World War. Also known as Den Bosch.

Sherwood. **1** Town (pop. 717), Pulaski co., central Ark., near North Little Rock. **2** Village (pop. 362), Branch co., S Mich., 13 mi. NW of Coldwater, in farm area. **3** City (pop. 421), Renville co., N N.Dak., port of entry 15 mi. N of Mohall, near Can. line. **4** Village (pop. 570), Defiance co., NW Ohio, on Maumee R. and 10 mi. W of Defiance, in farming area. **5** Town (pop. 575), Washington co., NW Oregon, 13 mi. SW of Portland; fruit canning. **6** Village (pop. c.1,300), Franklin co., S Tenn., 34 mi. W of Chattanooga, in the Cumberlands; makes lime. **7** Village, Texas: see MERTZON.

Sherwood, Lake, Ventura co., S Calif., small lake (resort) on N slope of Santa Monica Mts., 23 mi. WNW of Santa Monica.

Sherwood Forest, anciently a forest of England, covering one-fifth of Nottingham and parts of Derby and Yorkshire. Of the forest there remain sections near Mansfield and Rotherham, including the park district of The Dukeries. It is most celebrated as the home of Robin Hood and his band.

Sherwood Forest, resort village, Anne Arundel co., central Md., on Severn R., 5 mi. NW of Annapolis.

Sherwood Park, village (pop. 2,523), Elizabeth City co., SE Va., near Hampton and Newport News.

Sherwood Star, township (pop. 1,055), Gwelo prov., central Southern Rhodesia, in Matabeleland, 7 mi. N of Que Que; gold-mining center.

Sheshma River (shĕ'shmŭ), E European Russian SFSR, rises c.15 mi. SW of Bugulma, in Kuibyshev oblast; flows 90 mi. generally NNW, past Novo-Sheshminsk, to Kama R. 18 mi. ENE of Chistopol. Receives Kuchni R. (right). Petroleum and asphalt deposits in upper valley, at SHUGUROVO.

Sheshupe River or **Sheshupa River** (shĕ-sho͞opä'), Lith. *Šešupė,* Ger. *Scheschupe,* in Poland, Lithuania, and Kaliningrad oblast (Russian SFSR); rises in extreme NE Poland, N of Suwalki; flows N past Kalvarija and Marijampole, W past Naumiestis, and NW past Krasnoznamensk (Kaliningrad oblast), to Neman R. E of Neman; 191 mi. long. Nonnavigable.

Shestaki (shĕstŭkē'), village, N Kirov oblast, Russian SFSR, on Vyatka R. and 14 mi. N of Slobodskoi; grain. Formerly Shestakovo.

Shestanovats, Yugoslavia: see SESTANOVAC.

Shetek, Lake (shŭtĕk'), Murray co., SW Minn., 7 mi. N of Slayton; 7 mi. long, 2 mi. wide. Summer resorts and state park are here. Lake has S outlet into Des Moines R.

Shetland or **Zetland,** insular county (□ 550.5; 1931 pop. 21,421; 1951 census 19,343) of Scotland, consisting of the **Shetland Islands,** an archipelago 95 mi. long and 45 mi. wide, made up of several hundred isls. and islets, of which 24 are inhabited. They lie in 60°25'N 1°25'W, about 55 mi. NE of the Orkneys. The largest isl., MAINLAND, embraces ¾ of the entire area; other isls. include Unst, Yell, Fetlar, Bressay, Whalsay, East and West Burra, and Fair Isle. Lerwick, the ⊙, on Mainland, is the only burgh. Isls. have irregular and rocky coast lines. There is little arable land and few trees; fishing, fish curing, home weaving and knitting of woolens are main industries. Other occupations are growing of oats, barley, and root crops; raising of cattle and sheep (a small breed, noted for quality of their wool, is named after isls.); and breeding of Shetland ponies, formerly extensively used as work horses in British coal mines, now mainly used as children's mounts and pets. There are deposits of peat, copper, iron. Vestiges of anc. habitation, mainly brochs (round stone towers), are numerous and many Norse customs and traces of speech survive. History of Shetland parallels that of ORKNEY. In Second World War, isls. were target of 1st German air raid on Great Britain (Nov., 1939) and were frequently bombed after that.

Shetow or **She-t'ou** (both: shŭ'tō'), Jap. *Shato* (shä'tō), town (1935 pop. 2,068), W central Formosa, 4 mi. SSE of Yüanlin; mfg. (wood and bamboo products, bamboo hats); rice, oranges, bananas.

Shetrunja, hill, India: see PALITANA, town.

Shettleston, SE industrial suburb (pop. 28,692) of Glasgow, Lanark, Scotland; machinery, machine tools, glass, cement.

Shetucket River (shĭtŭ'kĭt), E Conn., formed at Willimantic by junction of Willimantic and Natchaug rivers; flows c.25 mi. SE and S to the Thames at Norwich; receives Quinebaug R. 4 mi. NE of mouth.

Sheungshui (shyo͝ong'shwä'), town, Hong Kong colony, in the New Territories, on Canton-Kowloon RR and 13 mi. N of Kowloon; vegetables, rice; hog raising. Has govt. agr. experiment station.

Shevaroy Hills (shĕ'vŭroi), outlier of S Eastern Ghats, S central Madras, India, N of Salem; 17 mi. long, 12 mi. wide; rise to 5,341 ft. in Shevarayan peak. Extensive coffee plantations (factories); sandalwood, Casuarina, bamboo, rubber plants; fruit farming. Bauxite workings. Yercaud lies on S plateau.

Shevchenko (shĭfchĕn'kŭ), town (1926 pop. 1,589), W Stalino oblast, Ukrainian SSR, in the Donbas, 5 mi. SSW of Krasnoarmeiskoye; coal mines. Formerly called Lysaya Gora.

Shevchenkovo (–kŭvŭ). **1** Village (1939 pop. over 500), E central Kharkov oblast, Ukrainian SSR, on railroad (Bulatselovka station) and 19 mi. W of Kupyansk; flour. **2** Town, Kirovograd oblast, Ukrainian SSR: see DOLINSKAYA.

Shevchenko Vtoroye (–kŭ ftŭroi'ŭ), town (1939 pop. over 500), E central Zaporozhe oblast, Ukrainian SSR, on Konka R., just W of Pologi; wheat, sunflowers, mustard.

Shevgaon (shāv'goun), town (pop. 5,548), Ahmadnagar dist., E Bombay, India, 35 mi. NE of Ahmadnagar; road center; cotton, millet, gur; cotton ginning, handicraft cloth weaving. Sometimes spelled Shavgaon.

Shevington, agr. village and parish (pop. 1,936), S Lancashire, England, 3 mi. NW of Wigan.

Shevlin, village (pop. 242), Clearwater co., NW Minn., near Clearwater R., 18 mi. W of Bemidji; dairy products.

Sheyenne (shīĕn′, –ăn′), village (pop. 469), Eddy co., central N.Dak., 11 mi. N of New Rockford and on Sheyenne R.

Sheyenne River, N.Dak., rises in central N.Dak., flows E and S 325 mi., past Valley City and Lisbon, where it turns NE and flows to Red River of the North 10 mi. N of Fargo.

Sheykh Sho'eyb, Iran: see SHAIKH SHU'AIB.

Shfayim or **Shefayim** (both: shfä′yēm), settlement (pop. 600), W Israel, in Plain of Sharon, near Mediterranean, 4 mi. NNW of Herzliya; dairying, mixed farming; health resort.

Shfeya or **Shefeya** (both: shfĕyä′), settlement (pop. 500), NW Israel, at N end of Plain of Sharon, 2 mi. NE of Zikhron Ya'aqov; limekilns; mixed farming. Has children's settlement, agr. school, and training farm. Founded 1892; suffered Arab attacks, 1948. Also called Meir Shfeya or Meir Shefeya.

Shiashkotan Island (shēäsh′kŭtŭn), Jap. *Shasukotan-to* (□ 35), one of N main Kurile Isls. group, Russian SFSR; separated from Kharimkotan Isl. (N) by Severgin Strait, from Lovushki Isl. (S) by Fortuna Strait; 48°50′N 154°6′E; 15 mi. long. Consists of 2 volcanic peaks (c.3,000 ft.), linked by low, narrow isthmus. Small fishing pop.

Shiawassee (shīuwô′sē), county (□ 540; pop. 45,967), S central Mich.; ⊙ Corunna. Drained by Shiawassee, Maple, and Lookingglass rivers. Agr. (beans, grain, corn, potatoes, hay, livestock; dairy products). Mfg. at Owosso. Oil and gas fields, coal mines. Organized 1837.

Shiawassee River, S central and E central Mich., rises in NW Oakland co., flows NW, past Holly, Fenton, and Owosso, then NNE, past Chesaning, to its confluence with the Tittabawassee to form Saginaw R. just SW of Saginaw city; c.85 mi. long.

Shibam (shĭbăm′), town (1946 pop. 7,500), ⊙ Shibam prov., Quaiti state, Eastern Aden Protectorate, in the upper Wadi Hadhramaut, 100 mi. NNW of Mukalla, at Kathiri line; commercial center of the W Hadhramaut, linked by road with Mukalla; caravan center, linked with Yemen and Aden hinterland. Mat weaving, dyeing of cloth and skins. Airfield. Town is remarkable for the height of its houses, generally 6 stories high, grouped on a slight eminence in the wadi.

Shibam, town (pop., including adjoining Kaukaban, 7,000), Sana prov., N central Yemen, 25 mi. WNW of Sana; center of the Wadi Ahjar (Ahjir) agr. area, on seaward slope of watershed range. Kaukaban (W) also appears as Haukaban.

Shibarghan or **Shibirghan** (shĭbûrgän′), town (pop. 15,000), Mazar-i-Sharif prov., N Afghanistan, in Afghan Turkestan, on Sar-i-Pul R. and 80 mi. W of Mazar-i-Sharif, and on highway to Andkhui; center of irrigated oasis.

Shibar Pass (shē′bûr) (alt. 9,800 ft.), in the Hindu Kush, E central Afghanistan, 60 mi. NW of Kabul and on highway bet. Chorband valley (E) and Bamian (W).

Shibata (shĭbä′tä), city (1940 pop. 24,977; 1947 pop. 35,327), Niigata prefecture, central Honshu, Japan, 15 mi. E of Niigata; rice-collection center; silk, woodworking. Sometimes spelled Sibata.

Shibeli, Webi, Ethiopia and Ital. Somaliland: see SHEBELI, WEBI.

Shibenik, Yugoslavia: see SIBENIK.

Shibetoro, Russian SFSR: see SLAVNOYE.

Shibetsu (shĭbä′tsōō), town (pop. 19,612), N central Hokkaido, Japan, on Teshio R. and 29 mi. N of Asahigawa; fish processing, dairying.

Shibin el Kom or **Shibin al-Kum** (both: shĭbēn ĕl-kōōm′), town (pop. 41,836), ⊙ Minufiya prov., Lower Egypt, 37 mi. NNW of Cairo; rail and canal center in a rich agr. area; woolen weaving, cigarette mfg.; cotton, flax, cereals.

Shibin el Qanatir or **Shibin al-Qanatir** (both: ĕlkănă′tĭr), village (pop. 11,610; with suburbs, 12,664), Qalyubiya prov., Lower Egypt, on railroad and 18 mi. NNE of Cairo; cotton ginning, cigarette mfg.; cotton, flax, cereals, fruits.

Shibirghan, Afghanistan: see SHIBARGHAN.

Shiblanga (shĭblăn′gŭ) or **Shiblanjah** (–jŭ), village (pop. 7,038), Qalyubiya prov., Lower Egypt, on railroad and 5 mi. ENE of Benha; cotton, flax, cereals, fruits.

Shibotsu Island (shĭbô′tsōō), one of lesser Kurile Isls. chain, Russian SFSR, 16 mi. NE of Cape Noshappu, Hokkaido, Japan; 43°30′N 146°8′E; 5 mi. square. Fish and crab canning.

Shibr, Ash, or **Al-Shibr** (both: ăsh-shĭ′bûr), town, ⊙ Hadhrami sheikdom of Upper Yafa, Western Aden Protectorate, 6 mi. NNE of Mahjaba.

Shibukawa (shĭbōō kăwä), town (pop. 19,634), Gumma prefecture, central Honshu, Japan, 8 mi. NNW of Maebashi; spinning.

Shibushi (shĭbōō′shē), town (pop. 24,355), Kagoshima prefecture, S Kyushu, Japan, on NE Osumi Peninsula, port on Ariake Bay, 35 mi. SW of Miyazaki; commercial center for agr. area (rice, sweet potatoes, millet); medical powder made from antlers. Exports charcoal, lumber.

Shibushi Bay, Japan: see ARIAKE BAY.

Shichijo, Japan: see ICHIJO.

Shichinohe or **Shichinoe** (both: shĭchē′nōā), town (pop. 12,685), Aomori prefecture, N Honshu, Japan, 23 mi. ESE of Aomori; apple growing, horse breeding; sake brewing, soybean processing. Sericulture experiment station.

Shichito, Formosa: see CHITU.

Shichi-to, Ryukyu Isls.: see TOKARA-GUNTO.

Shickley, village (pop. 316), Fillmore co., SE Nebr., 10 mi. SW of Geneva.

Shickshinny (shĭk′shĭ′nē), borough (pop. 2,156), Luzerne co., NE central Pa., 16 mi. WSW of Wilkes-Barre and on Susquehanna R.; silk, clothing; anthracite; agr. Inc. 1861.

Shickshock Mountains, range in E Que., extension of Notre Dame Mts., extends c.100 mi. E-W near N coast of Gaspé Peninsula, rising to 4,160 ft. on Mt. Jacques Cartier, 70 mi. W of Gaspé. In center of range is Gaspesian Provincial Park.

Shid, Yugoslavia: see SID.

Shidler (shĭd′lûr), town (pop. 840), Osage co., N Okla., 20 mi. WNW of Pawhuska; oil and gas wells; gasoline plant.

Shidlovets, Poland: see SZYDLOWIEC.

Shido (shē′dō), town (pop. 8,710), Kagawa prefecture, N Shikoku, Japan, on Harima Sea, 7 mi. E of Takamatsu; commercial center for agr. area (rice, wheat); makes sake, soy sauce, cast-iron braziers, wooden clogs (*geta*). Site of 17th-cent. Buddhist temple. Sometimes spelled Sido.

Shidzuoka, Japan: see SHIZUOKA, city.

Shiel, Loch (lŏkh shēl′), lake on border bet. SW Inverness and NW Argyll, Scotland, 17 mi. long (SW-NE), c.1 mi. wide. Outlet: Shiel R. (3 mi. long), flowing to sea at Loch Moidart (SW). At head is village of Glenfinnan, where Prince Charles Edward, the Young Pretender, raised his standard in 1745.

Shields, North, England: see TYNEMOUTH.

Shields, South, England: see SOUTH SHIELDS.

Shifnal (shĭf′nŭl, –nôl), town and parish (pop. 3,266), E Shropshire, England, 16 mi. E of Shrewsbury; leather tanning; agr.-machinery works. Has 13th-cent. church and 14th-cent. inn.

Shiga (shē′gä), prefecture [Jap. *ken*] (□ 1,564; 1940 pop. 703,679; 1947 pop. 858,367), S Honshu, Japan, surrounding L. Biwa; ⊙ OTSU. Generally fertile terrain, drained by Seta R. (upper course of Yodo R.). Agr. (rice, tea, wheat, market produce). L. Biwa is important for fisheries and tourist trade. Principal centers: Otsu, HIKONE, NAGAHAMA; all produce textiles.

Shigali, India: see SIGLI.

Shigano-shima (shĭgä′nō-shĭmä), island (□ 5; pop. 11,442), Fukuoka prefecture, Japan, in Genkai Sea; forms E side of entrance to Hakata Bay, N Kyushu; 2 mi. long, 1.3 mi. wide. Fishing.

Shigaraki (shēgä′rä′kē), town (pop. 6,650), Shiga prefecture, S Honshu, Japan, 20 mi. SE of Kyoto; rail terminus; agr. center (rice, wheat, tea).

Shigatse (shēgä′tsĕ) or **Zhikatse** (zhē′kätsĕ), Chinese *Jih-k'o-tse* (rŭ′kô′dzĕ′), second-largest town [Tibetan *dzong*] of Tibet, SE Tibet, on the Nyang Chu, on main Leh-Lhasa trade route and 135 mi. WSW of Lhasa. Has large fort, built in 17th cent.; captured 1791 by Gurkhas. Famous lamasery of TASHI LUMPO is 1 mi. SSW. Printing establishment is 7 mi. SW, at Narthang or Natang.

Shiggaon (shĭg′goun), town (pop. 5,720), Dharwar dist., S Bombay, India, 35 mi. SSE of Dharwar; millet, rice, cotton.

Shighnan or **Shignan,** USSR: see SHUGNAN.

Shigli, India: see SIGLI.

Shigony (shĭgô′nē), village (1926 pop. 2,446), W Kuibyshev oblast, Russian SFSR, 19 mi. NE of Syzran; distilling; wheat, sunflowers, potatoes.

Shigri (shĭg′rē), locality, Kangra dist., NE Punjab, India, in Punjab Himalayas, 75 mi. E of Dharmsala. Deposits of antimony ore, here, are occasionally worked.

Shihcheng or **Shih-ch'eng** (both: shû′chŭng′), town (pop. 10,494), ⊙ Shihcheng co. (pop. 81,333), SE Kiangsi prov., China, 90 mi. SSW of Nancheng, in the Bohea Hills, near Fukien border; rice, tea; iron mining.

Shihchi, China: see SHIHCHŬ.

Shih-chia-chuang, China: see SHIHKIACHWANG.

Shih-chiao-ching, China: see SHIHKIAOTSING.

Shih-ch'ien, China: see SHIHTSIEN.

Shihchih (shû′jû′), Jap. *Shiodome* (shēō′dōmä), town (1935 pop. 5,860), N Formosa, on Keelung R. and 9 mi. E of Taipei, and on railroad; coal mining; iron foundry; tea processing.

Shih-ching-shan, China: see SHIHKINGSHAN.

Shihchŭ or **Shih-ch'ü** (shû′chü′), town, ⊙ Shihchü co. (pop. 11,690), N Sikang prov., China, on upper Yalung R. and 170 mi. NW of Kantse, near Tsinghai border; melons, beans, cabbage. Until 1912 called Shihshu; sometimes spelled Shihchi. Placed 1950 in Tibetan Autonomous Dist.

Shihchu (shû′jōō′), town (pop. 10,036), ⊙ Shihchu co. (pop. 226,714), E Szechwan prov., China, 45 mi. NE of Fowling, near Hupeh border; tung oil, indigo, rice, millet, wheat, beans, rapeseed.

Shihchüan or **Shih-ch'üan** (shû′chwän′), town (pop. 4,766), ⊙ Shihchüan co. (pop. 84,097), S Shensi prov., China, 50 mi. NW of Ankang and on Han R.; rice, wheat, beans. Gold washing near by.

Shihchwan, China: see PEHCHWAN.

Shiheir, Shuhair, or **Shuhayr** (all: shûhär′), town (1946 pop. 3,000), Quaiti state, on Gulf of Aden, on road and 20 mi. ENE of Mukalla; fishing. Also spelled Shuheir. Sometimes confused with SHIHR, 14 mi. ENE.

Shiherhwei (shû′ûr′hwā′) or **Shih-erh-hsü** (–shü′), town, N Kiangsu prov., China, 3 mi. ESE of Icheng and on Yangtze R.; commercial center; exports salt.

Shihfang (shû′fäng′), town (pop. 28,420), ⊙ Shihfang co. (pop. 202,766), NW Szechwan prov., China, 35 mi. N of Chengtu; paper milling, tea processing; sugar cane, rice, wheat, sweet potatoes, tobacco.

Shih-hsing, China: see CHIHING.

Shihhweiyao, China: see HWANGSHIHKANG.

Shihkiachwang or **Shih-chia-chuang** (both: shû′jyä′jwäng′), city (1935 pop. 217,327; 1947 pop. 125,651), W central Hopeh prov., China, 160 mi. SW of Peking; major rail center on Peking-Hankow and Tehchow-Taiyüan railroads; railroad repair shops; cotton milling, glass mfg. Became independent municipality in 1947. Called Shihmen, 1947–49.

Shihkiaotsing or **Shih-chiao-ching** (both: shû′jyou′-jĭng′), town, W central Szechwan prov., China, 30 mi. SE of Chengtu; commercial center.

Shihkingshan or **Shih-ching-shan** (both: shû′jĭng′-shän′), W industrial suburb of Peking, China, 12 mi. W of city, on Yungting R.; metallurgical center; iron- and steelworks, coking plant (based on near-by Mentowkow coal mines).

Shihkiu Lake (shû′jyō′), Chinese *Shihkiu Hu* or *Shih-chiu Hu* (hōō), on Kiangsu-Anhwei border, China, 40 mi. S of Nanking; 15–20 mi. long, 10–20 mi. wide (N-S). Connected with Yangtze R. by Chinhwai R. Near lake are towns of Kaoshun (SE) and Lishui (NE). W section is called Tanyang L.

Shihlin (shû′lĭn′), Jap. *Shirin* (shē′rēn), town (1935 pop. 4,638), N Formosa, 2 mi. N of Taipei and on railroad; coal mining; limestone quarry; mfg. of cutlery, rope, paper; tea processing.

Shihlow or **Shih-lou** (shû′lō′), town, ⊙ Shihlow co. (pop. 34,982), W Shansi prov., China, 55 mi. WSW of Fenyang; kaoliang, chestnuts, wheat.

Shihlu, China: see SHEKLUK.

Shihlung, China: see SHEKLUNG.

Shihma (shû′mä′), town, SE Fukien prov., China, port on estuary of Lung R., 10 mi. SE of Lungki; commercial center.

Shihmen (shû′mŭn′). **1** Town, Chekiang prov., China: see TSUNGTEH. **2** City, Hopeh prov., China: see SHIHKIACHWANG. **3** Town, ⊙ Shihmen co. (pop. 310,088), N Hunan prov., China, on Li R. and 40 mi. NNW of Changteh; rice, wheat, beans. Sulphur and coal mining near by.

Shihmen (shû′mŭn′), Jap. *Sekimon* (sä′kĕmōn), village (1935 pop. 1,338), N Formosa, on N coast, 14 mi. NW of Keelung; tea center; rice, sweet potatoes; stock raising; fishing.

Shihnan, China: see ENSHIH.

Shihpai or **Shih-p'ai** (shû′pī′), town, N Anhwei prov., China, 25 mi. WSW of Anking; commercial center; tanning, cotton weaving.

Shih-pan-to, Tibet: see SHOBANDO.

Shihping. 1 (shû′bĭng′) Town, Kweichow prov., China: see SHIPING. **2** or **Shih-p'ing** (shû′pĭng′), town, Pingyuan prov., China: see CHIHPING. **3** or **Shih-p'ing** (shû′pĭng′), town, ⊙ Shihping co. (pop. 92,679), S Yunnan prov., China, 90 mi. S of Kunming; rail terminus on NW shore of small lake; alt. 5,750 ft.; coal mining; timber, rice, wheat, millet, beans.

Shihpu or **Shih-p'u** (shû′pōō′). **1** Town, NE Chekiang prov., China, minor port on E. China Sea, at entrance to Sanmen Bay, 18 mi. S of Siangshan. **2** Town, Shensi prov., China: see HWANGLUNG.

Shihr or **Ash Shihr** (ăsh shĭ′hûr), town (1946 pop. 12,500), ⊙ Shihr prov., Quaiti state, Eastern Aden Protectorate, port on Gulf of Aden, 35 mi. ENE of Mukalla; main distributing center for E Hadhramaut; fishing center and principal port for the Kathiri country (linked by highway). Fish curing, dhow building, cloth weaving and dyeing. Airfield; radio station. A town of low houses, wide streets, and open spaces, Shihr was once the most important town of the Hadhramaut, but has been largely superseded by Mukalla. Shihr is sometimes confused with SHIHEIR, 14 mi. WSW.

Shihshow or **Shih-shouh** (sû′shō′), town (pop. 19,123), ⊙ Shihshow co. (pop. 189,130), S Hupeh prov., China, on Hunan line, 45 mi. SSE of Kiangling, and on right bank of Yangtze R.; cotton weaving; rice, wheat, tea, beans.

Shihshu, China: see SHIHCHŬ.

Shihtai (shû′dī′), town, ⊙ Shihtai co. (pop. 47,264), S Anhwei prov., China, 55 mi. ESE of Anking; rice, tea, tung oil, silk.

Shihting (shû′dĭng′), Jap. *Sekitei* (säkē′tä), village (1935 pop. 666), N Formosa, 10 mi. SE of Taipei; coal mining.

Shihtowhotze or **Shih-t'ou-ho-tzu** (both: shû′tō′-hŭ′dzŭ′), town, S Sungkiang prov., Manchuria, on Chinese Eastern RR and 50 mi. WNW of Mutankiang; lumbering center; plywood mill.

Shihtsien or **Shih-ch'ien** (both: shû′chyĕn′), town (pop. 13,983), ⊙ Shihtsien co. (pop. 134,253), NE Kweichow prov., China, 30 mi. SSW of Szenan; cotton textiles; timber, wheat, millet, Gypsum quarry, salt deposits near by.

Shihtsung (shŭ'dzŏŏng'), town, ⊙ Shihtsung co. (pop. 36,545), E Yunnan prov., China, 80 mi. E of Kunming, in mtn. region; rice, millet, beans, pears. Antimony and tungsten deposits near by.

Shihtu, Tibet: see SHOBANDO.

Shihwei (shŭ'wā'), town, ⊙ Shihwei dist. (pop. 2,942), N Inner Mongolian Autonomous Region, Manchuria, in the Barga, 150 mi. N of Hailar and on Argun R. (USSR line); gold-mining center. Until 1920 called Chilalin.

Shihwei, peak, Manchuria: see KHINGAN MOUNTAINS.

Shiida (shē'dä), town (pop. 5,597), Fukuoka prefecture, N Kyushu, Japan, on Suo Sea, 21 mi. SE of Yawata; rice; fishing. Sometimes called Tsuida.

Shijak (shēyäk') or **Shijaku** (shēyäk'ŏŏ), town (1945 pop. 2,777), W central Albania, on railroad and 6 mi. ENE of Durazzo; agr. market; livestock trade. Also spelled Shějak or Shějaku.

Shikabe (shĭkä'bā), village (pop. 4,215), SW Hokkaido, Japan, on the Pacific, 20 mi. SSW of Muroran; hot-springs resort.

Shikama (shĭkä'mä), city (1940 pop. 35,061; 1945 estimate 38,355), Hyogo prefecture, S Honshu, Japan, port on Harima Sea, just S of Himeji; mfg. center (textiles, pottery). Exports rice, fertilizer. Since early 1940s, includes former town of Mega. Sometimes spelled Sikama. Since c.1947, part of Himeji.

Shikano (shĭkä'nō), town (pop. 3,253), Tottori prefecture, SW Honshu, Japan, 10 mi. WSW of Tottori; commercial center in rice-growing area; makes tissue paper.

Shikari Pass (shĭkä'rē), defile in the Hindu Kush, NE Afghanistan, on Surkhab R. and 75 mi. NW of Kabul, on highway to Mazar-i-Sharif.

Shikarpur (shĭkär'pŏŏr). **1** Town (pop. 5,785), Shimoga dist., NW Mysore, India, 25 mi. NNW of Shimoga; local cloth market; rice, betel nuts, sugar cane. **2** Town (pop. 11,783), Bulandshahr dist., W Uttar Pradesh, India, 12 mi. SE of Bulandshahr; hand-loom cotton weaving, wood carving; wheat, oilseeds, barley, cotton, sugar cane. Large unfinished Moslem tomb (begun c.1718) near by.

Shikarpur, city (pop. 62,746), Sukkur dist., NE Sind, W Pakistan, in hot, low-lying tract, 22 mi. NW of Sukkur; trade center for grain (wheat, rice, millet), cloth fabrics, jewelry; rice, silk, and flour milling, cotton ginning, mfg. of hosiery, chemicals; engineering works. Handicrafts include woolen goods, carpets, palm mats and baskets, pottery, leather articles. Has col. Until building of railroad, city was important trade depot on caravan route through Bolan Pass to Afghanistan.

Shikhany (shĭkhä'nē), town (1939 pop. over 500), N Saratov oblast, Russian SFSR, 10 mi. WNW of Volsk; cement-rock quarries.

Shikhazany (shĭkhŭzä'nē), village (1939 pop. over 500), E central Chuvash Autonomous SSR, Russian SFSR, on Lesser Tsivil R. and 5 mi. NW of Kanash; wheat, rye, oats.

Shikhikaya (shĭkhē'kīŭ), town (1945 pop. over 500) in Molotov dist. of Greater Baku, Azerbaijan SSR, c.20 mi. SW of Baku; oil wells (developed in 1940s).

Shikhirdany, Russian SFSR: see CHKALOVSKOYE, Chuvash Autonomous SSR.

Shiki (shē'kē), town (pop. 14,882), Saitama prefecture, central Honshu, Japan, 5 mi. W of Urawa; rice growing.

Shikine-jima, Japan: see NII-JIMA.

Shikirlikitai, Ukrainian SSR: see SUVOROVO.

Shikiu, China: see PUNYÜ.

Shiko, Formosa: see SINKANG.

Shikohabad (shĭkō'häbäd), town (pop. 14,061), Mainpuri dist., W Uttar Pradesh, India, near Lower Ganges Canal distributary, 28 mi. WSW of Mainpuri; road center; glass mfg.; wheat, gram, pearl millet, corn, barley. Ruins of 18th-cent. Mahratta fort. Glass mfg. at village of Makhanpur (also spelled Makkhanpur), 7 mi. W.

Shikoku (shĭkō'kōō), island (□ c.6,860; including offshore isls.: □ 6,869; 1940 pop. 3,337,102; 1947 pop. 4,074,708), Japan, S of Honshu, E of Kyushu, bet. Inland Sea and Philippine Sea; 140 mi. long, 30-95 mi. wide; smallest of 4 major isls. of Japan. Several mtn. ranges extend E-W in interior; highest peak, Mt. Ishizuchi (6,497 ft.). Drained by many rivers; Yoshino R., largest. Mild climate; mean annual temp. 60°F. Rainfall, ranging from 105 in. (S) to 65 in. (N), is particularly heavy on E coast. Sparsely populated interior is heavily forested (pine, Japan cedar, cypress, bamboo); plum, pear, and orange orchards. Rice, wheat, tobacco, soybeans grown in fertile valleys and on coastal strips. Mining is confined to a small N area at Besshi copper field. Mfg. (paper, textiles, pottery; woodworking). Most of the towns are on the coast; many are fishing ports, with saltmaking centers in NE. Chief exports: salt, copper, tobacco, lumber, fruit. Isl. contains 4 prefectures: EHIME (N), KOCHI (S), TOKUSHIMA (E), KAGAWA (NE). Sometimes spelled Sikoku.

Shikotan Island (shēkŭtän'), northernmost and largest (□ 70) of lesser Kurile Isls. chain, Russian SFSR; separated from Kunashir Isl. (NW) by 30-mi.-wide strait; 43°47'N 146°45'E; 17 mi. long, 5.5 mi. wide. Unlike other isls. of lesser Kuriles chain, it is volcanic in origin and hilly (up to 1,355 ft.). Main village, Malokurilskoye, on NW shore. Majority of Ainu pop. of the Kuriles was settled here (1880s) by Japanese and subsequently died out.

Shikotsu Lake (shĭkō'tsōō), Jap. *Shikotsu-ko* (□ 29), SW Hokkaido, Japan, 12 mi. NW of Tomakomai, in mtn. area; 7 mi. long, 5 mi. wide.

Shikuka, Russian SFSR: see PORONAISK.

Shilbottle, town and parish (pop. 1,088), E Northumberland, England, 3 mi. S of Alnwick; coal.

Shildon, urban district (1931 pop. 12,691; 1951 census 14,513), central Durham, England, 2 mi. SE of Bishop Auckland; coal mining. In urban dist. (S) is coal-mining town of New Shildon (pop. 3,152).

Shile, Turkey: see SILE.

Shilka (shēl'kŭ), town (1939 pop. over 10,000), central Chita oblast, Russian SFSR, on Trans-Siberian RR, on Shilka R. and 110 mi. E of Chita; metalworks.

Shilka River, E Chita oblast, Russian SFSR, formed by union of Ingoda and Onon rivers 15 mi. below Shilka; flows 345 mi. ENE, past Shilka, Sretensk, and Ust-Karsk, joining Argun R. to form Amur R. on USSR-Manchuria frontier. Navigable for entire length. Tributaries, Nercha and Amazar rivers (left).

Shilla, Mount (shĭl'lŭ), peak (23,050 ft.) in Zaskar Range of SE Punjab Himalayas, NE Punjab, India, 110 mi. ENE of Dharmsala, at 32°23'N 78°13'E.

Shillanwali, W Pakistan: see SILLANWALI.

Shillelagh (shĭlā'lŭ), Gaelic *Siól Éiligh*, town (pop. 114), S Co. Wicklow, Ireland, 16 mi. WSW of Arklow; agr. market (dairying; cattle, sheep; potatoes). Anc. Forest of Shillelagh provided wood for the characteristic Irish oak or blackthorn cudgel, or *shillalah*.

Shilling, Cape, S point of Sierra Leone Peninsula, W Sierra Leone, 22 mi. S of Freetown; 8°11'N 13°10'W. Site of Kent village.

Shillington, agr. village and parish (pop. 1,622), E Bedford, England, 5 mi. NW of Hitchin.

Shillington, borough (pop. 5,059), Berks co., SE central Pa., 3 mi. SW of Reading; building blocks, textiles; lumber; limestone. Founded 1860, inc. 1908.

Shillong (shĭl'lông), Khasi *Yeddo* (yĕd'dō), town (pop. 38,192), ⊙ Assam and Khasi and Jaintia Hills dist., W Assam, India, on Shillong Plateau, 305 mi. NE of Calcutta; 25°35'N 91°54'E. Trades in rice, cotton, sesame, oranges, potatoes, betel nuts; pisciculture. Has Pasteur Inst., St. Edmund's Art Col., St. Mary's Col.; citrus fruit and silk-growing research stations. City is divided administratively into 2 sections, one (pop. 24,990) within Khasi and Jaintia Hills dist., the other (pop. 13,202) directly under Assam govt. Became ⊙ Khasi States in 1864 and ⊙ Assam in 1874, when Assam became a separate prov. Town rebuilt after total destruction by earthquake in 1897.

Shillong Plateau, undulating tableland, W Assam, India; bounded by Jaintia Hills and Khasi Hills which form N and S escarpments respectively; rises to isolated Shillong Peak (c.4,435 ft.), 3 mi. S of Shillong. Rice, sesame, cotton, potatoes, soybeans, oranges.

Shiloango River, Belgian Congo and Angola: see CHILOANGO RIVER.

Shiloh (shī'lō). **1** Town (pop. 41), Cleburne co., N central Ark., 7 mi. WNW of Heber Springs, in the Ozarks. **2** Village (pop. 453), St. Clair co., SW Ill., 14 mi. ESE of East St. Louis, in bituminous-coal and agr. area. **3** Borough (pop. 427), Cumberland co., SW N.J., 4 mi. NW of Bridgeton, in agr. region. **4** Village (pop. 655), Richland co., N central Ohio, 15 mi. NNW of Mansfield and on West Branch of Huron R.

Shiloh National Military Park (□ 5.8; established 1894), SW Tenn., on Tennessee R. near Pickwick Landing Dam, and 8 mi. SW of Savannah. Includes field of battle of Shiloh (April 6 and 7, 1862; also called battle of Pittsburg Landing), 2d major engagement of Civil War, in which Confederates, after successful attack on Union positions at Pittsburg Landing, were forced back by Federal reinforcements. Here also are Shiloh Natl. Cemetery (10.3 acres; established 1866) and well-preserved Indian mounds. Park hq. at Pittsburg Landing, on E boundary.

Shilovo (shē'lŭvŭ). **1** Agr. town (1948 pop. over 2,000), central Ryazan oblast, Russian SFSR, on Oka R. and 50 mi. SE of Ryazan; road center; truck produce. **2** Village (1939 pop. under 500), SE Tula oblast, Russian SFSR, 18 mi. ENE of Yefremov; wheat.

Shilute, Lithuania: see SILUTE.

Shimabara (shĭmä'bärä), city (1940 pop. 30,411; 1947 pop. 41,074), Nagasaki prefecture, W Kyushu, Japan, on E coast of Shimabara Peninsula, 28 mi. E of Nagasaki, port on Shimabara Bay; textile mill; agr. (rice, wheat, sweet potatoes). Exports cotton textiles, rice. Site of castle where Christians made their last stand (1641) against Tokugawa shogunate. Sometimes Simabara.

Shimabara Bay, NE arm of Amakusa Sea, W Kyushu, Japan, sheltered W by Shimabara Peninsula, S by Amakusa Isls.; opens N into the Ariakeno-umi; semi-circular; c.30 mi. long, 13 mi. wide. Shimabara is on W shore. Sometimes called Shimbara Gulf, a name which includes Ariakeno-umi.

Shimabara Peninsula, W Kyushu, Japan, SE projection of Hizen Peninsula, bet. Tachibana Bay (W) and Shimabara Bay (E), N of Amakusa Isls.; 20 mi. long, 11 mi. wide. Site of Unzen Natl. Park, containing hot springs. Shimabara on E, Obama on W coast.

Shimada (shĭmä'dä), town (pop. 30,635), Shizuoka prefecture, central Honshu, Japan, 15 mi. SW of Shizuoka; agr. (rice, fruit, bamboo shoots).

Shimada-shima (-shĭmä), island (□ 5; pop. 7,480), Tokushima prefecture, Japan, in Naruto Strait, bet. NE coast of Shikoku and SW coast of Awaji-shima; 3 mi. long, 1.5 mi. wide. Hilly, fertile. Produces rice, wheat, raw silk. Fishing.

Shimando River (shĭmän'dō), Jap. *Shimando-gawa*, SW Shikoku, Japan, rises in mts. 15 mi. NE of Nomura, flows 112 mi. S, W, and SSE, past Nakamura, to Tosa Bay at Shimoda. Carp fishing.

Shimane (shĭmä'nā), prefecture [Jap. *ken*] (□ 1,558; 1940 pop. 740,940; 1947 pop. 894,267), SW Honshu, Japan; ⊙ MATSUE, its chief port. Bounded N by Sea of Japan; includes isl. group OKI-GUNTO. Interior is generally mountainous and forested; many fertile valleys with rice fields. Extensive stock raising, sawmilling, and fishing. Other products: charcoal, raw silk. Mfg. (textiles, yarn, soy sauce, sake). Principal centers: MATSUE, IZUMO, HAMADA (major fishing center). Sometimes spelled Simane.

Shimanovski or **Shimanovskiy** (shēmä'nŭfskē), town (1926 pop. 2,703), S Amur oblast, Russian SFSR, on Trans-Siberian RR and 115 mi. NNW of Blagoveshchensk, in agr. area (wheat, livestock); metalworks.

Shimba, Russian SFSR: see DACHNOYE.

Shimbara Gulf, Japan: see SHIMABARA BAY.

Shime (shē'mä), town (pop. 17,973), Fukuoka prefecture, N Kyushu, Japan, 5 mi. E of Fukuoka, in coal-mining, rice-growing area. Sometimes spelled Sime.

Shimizu (shĭmē'zōō). **1** or **Shimisu** (-sōō), town (pop. 12,237), S central Hokkaido, Japan, 17 mi. WNW of Obihiro; agr. (rice, potatoes, sugar beets). **2** Town (pop. 14,754), Kochi prefecture, SW Shikoku, Japan, on Philippine Sea, 38 mi. SE of Uwajima; fishing port. Chief product, dried bonito. Sometimes spelled Simizu. **3** City (1940 pop. 68,617; 1947 pop. 80,515), Shizuoka prefecture, central Honshu, Japan, port on NW Suruga Bay, 7 mi. NE of Shizuoka, in rice-growing area; exports tea, oranges. Sometimes spelled Simizu.

Shimmachi, Japan: see SHIN-MACHI.

Shimmikuriya, Japan: see SHIN-MIKURIYA.

Shimminato, Japan: see TAKAOKA, Toyama prefecture.

Shimmi-to, Korea: see SINMI ISLAND.

Shimo-aso (shĭmō-äsō'), town (pop, 2,025), Gifu prefecture, central Honshu, Japan, 13 mi. N of Tajimi; rice, wheat.

Shimoda (shĭmō'dä). **1** Town (pop. 5,099), Kochi prefecture, SW Shikoku, Japan, on Tosa Bay, 31 mi. SE of Uwajima, at mouth of Shimando R.; fishing port; rice. **2** Town (pop. 8,973), Shizuoka prefecture, central Honshu, Japan, on SE Izu Peninsula, on Sagami Sea, 30 mi. SSE of Numazu; seaside resort. Hot springs. Under U.S.-Japanese treaty of 1854, port of Shimoda was to be opened to Amer. trade, but its poor harbor prevented this from being done. First Amer. consulate established here, 1856.

Shimodate (shĭmō'dä'tā), town (pop. 16,344), Ibaraki prefecture, central Honshu, Japan, 15 mi. ESE of Tochigi, in generally swampy area; rail junction; textiles.

Shimoga (shĭmō'gŭ), district (□ 4,058; pop. 551,149), NW Mysore, India; ⊙ Shimoga. On Deccan Plateau; bounded W by Bombay (Kanara dist.) and Madras (South Kanara dist.), with Western Ghats (rise to over 4,000 ft. on crest) along W border. Drained by Sharavati (famous Gersoppa Falls on Bombay border) and Tungabhadra rivers. Timber and sandalwood in thickly wooded W foothills (average annual rainfall here over 200 in.); rice (terrace farming), millet, sugar cane, chili. Rice milling, charcoal burning, tile mfg.; handicrafts (wickerwork, sandalwood and ivory carving, lacquerware). Manganese mines near Kumsi and Shimoga supply large steel plant at Bhadravati. Other chief towns: Sagar, Tirthahalli. Hydroelectric works at Jog.

Shimoga, town (pop. 27,712), ⊙ Shimoga dist., NW Mysore, India, on Tunga R. (headstream of the Tungabhadra) and 135 mi. NNW of Mysore; road center. Manganese works here (mines in near-by hills) supply steel plant at Bhadravati. Rice and sugar milling, match mfg., sandalwood-oil processing, sawmilling. Industrial col.

Shimoichi (shĭmō'ēchē), town (pop. 12,102), Nara prefecture, S Honshu, Japan, on N central Kii Peninsula, 25 mi. SE of Osaka; collection center for lumber, fruit (oranges, persimmons). Copper mine near by. Sometimes spelled Simoiti.

Shimoji (shĭmô'jē), town (1950 pop. 5,842), on W coast of Miyako-shima, in the S Ryukyus, 3 mi. S of Hirara; fishing port.

Shimo-jima (shĭmō'-jĭmä), largest island (□ 227; pop. 149,597, including offshore islets) of Amakusa Isls., in E.China Sea, Japan, in Kumamoto prefecture, off W coast of Kyushu; 25 mi. N–S, 13 mi. E–W; deeply indented SW coast. Mountainous; rises to 1,726 ft. Hot springs in NW. Extensive fishing industry. Agr. (rice, wheat, sweet potatoes); produces camellia oil, dolls, coal, charcoal. Chief town and port, Ushibuka. Sometimes spelled Simo-zima.

Shimoji-shima, Ryukyu Isls.: see IRABU-SHIMA.

Shimo-kamakari-jima (shē'mō-kämä'-kä'rē-jĭmä), or **Shimo-kamagari-jima** (-gä'rē–), island (□ 3; pop. c.4,500), Hiroshima prefecture, Japan, in Hiuchi Sea (central section of Inland Sea), just SE of Kure on SW Honshu; roughly circular, 2 mi. in diameter. Produces rice, sweet potatoes. Fishery.

Shimo-koshiki-shima (shē'mō-kōshē'kē-shĭmä), island (□ 26; pop. 13,670) of isl. group Koshiki-retto, Kagoshima prefecture, Japan, in E.China Sea, 22 mi. off SW coast of Kyushu; 13 mi. long, 4 mi. wide; has long, narrow peninsula; mountainous. Produces rice, wheat. Fishing.

Shimoni (shēmō'nē), town, Coast Prov., SE Kenya in coastal protectorate, port on Indian Ocean, 50 mi. SSW of Mombasa, near Tanganyika border; fisheries; sisal, cotton, copra, sugar cane.

Shimonita (shĭmō'nētä), town (pop. 7,425), Gumma prefecture, central Honshu, Japan, 7 mi. WSW of Tomioka; rice, raw silk.

Shimo-no-isshiki, Japan: see NAGOYA.

Shimonoseki (shĭ"mŭnŭsä'kē, shē'mōnō"sākē), city (1940 pop. 196,022; 1947 pop. 176,666), Yamaguchi prefecture, at extreme SW tip of Honshu, Japan, port on Shimonoseki Strait, opposite Moji (on Kyushu); 33°58'N 130°58'E. Rail and industrial center; engineering works, shipyards, metalworks, chemical plants; textile making, fish canning. Exports coal, tobacco, metalwork, textiles. Connected by ferry with Pusan (Korea), across Tsushima and Korea straits. Includes isl. of Hiko-shima or Hike-shima (3.5 mi. long, 3 mi. wide), connected with mainland by short bridges and with Moji by a tunnel under Shimonoseki Strait. Former nearby towns included in city are Chofu and Yasuoka (1937) and Ozuki (1939). Shimonoseki is site of Shinto shrines dedicated to Emperor Antoku (12th cent.) and to Gen. Maresuke Nogi. City bombarded (1864) by Br., Fr., U.S., and Du. ships in retaliation for firing (1863) on foreign ships. Treaty of Shimonoseki (ending Sino-Japanese War) was signed here, 1895. Bombed (1945) in Second World War. Formerly called Akamagaseki and Bakan. Sometimes spelled Simonoseki.

Shimonoseki Strait, Jap. *Shimonoseki-kaikyo,* channel of Japan connecting Sea of Japan (W) with Inland Sea (E), bet. Shimonoseki on SW Honshu and Moji on N tip of Kyushu; 10 mi. long, $\frac{1}{2}$–$\frac{1}{4}$ mi. wide. A tunnel was built (1942) bet. Hiko-shima (isl. belonging to Shimonoseki) and Moji.

Shimorski or **Shimorskiy** (shĭmôr'skē), town (1926 pop. 2,788), SW Gorki oblast, Russian SFSR, on Oka R. and 5 mi. W of Vyksa; metalworks.

Shimosa (shĭmō'sä), former province in central Honshu, Japan; now part of Chiba and Ibaraki prefectures.

Shimosato (shĭmō-sä'tō) or **Shimozato** (–zä'tō), town (pop. 4,311), Wakayama prefecture, S Honshu, Japan, on Kumano Sea, on SE Kii Peninsula, 11 mi. SSW of Shingu; charcoal making. Fishing.

Shimo-suwa (shĭmō'sōōwä), town (pop. 18,912), Nagano prefecture, central Honshu, Japan, on N shore of L. Suwa, 13 mi. SSE of Matsumoto; raw-silk center; hot-springs resort.

Shimotsu (shĭmō'tsōō), town (pop. 5,791), Wakayama prefecture, S Honshu, Japan, on Kii Channel, on W Kii Peninsula, 8 mi. S of Wakayama; fishing port; raw silk, agr. products (rice, wheat). Until 1938, called Hamanaka.

Shimotsui (shĭmō'tsōōē), town (pop. 9,918), Okayama prefecture, SW Honshu, Japan, on strait bet. Hiuchi and Harima seas, 16 mi. SW of Okayama; tourist center in agr. area. Part of town is in Inland Sea Natl. Park. Sometimes spelled Simotui.

Shimotsuke (shĭmō'tsōōkä), former province in central Honshu, Japan; now Tochigi prefecture.

Shimotsuma (shĭmō'tsōōmä), town (pop. 10,688), Ibaraki prefecture, central Honshu, Japan, 19 mi. SE of Tochigi; commercial center for agr., lumbering area; makes agr. implements.

Shimo-yoshida (shĭmō'-yō'shĭdä), town (pop. 18,039), Yamanashi prefecture, central Honshu, Japan, 18 mi. SE of Kofu; tourist resort (starting point for ascent of Fujiyama). Until 1928, called Yoshida.

Shimozato, Japan: see SHIMOSATO.

Shimpo, Formosa: see SINPU.

Shimsa Falls (shĭm'sŭ), cataract on Shimsa R., S Mysore, India, 38 mi. E of Mysore, 3.5 mi. NW of Shimsa-Cauvery confluence; descend 310 ft. Harnessed 1940 for hydroelectric power (plant at nearby village of Shimshapura) to augment pivotal hydroelectric works near SIVASAMUDRAM isl.

Shimsa River, S Mysore, India, rises ESE of Tumkur, flows W past Gubbi, and S past Maddur to Cauvery R. 40 mi. E of Mysore, 4 mi. E of Sivasamudram isl.; c.140 mi. long. Hydroelectric works at Shimsha Falls, 3.5 mi. NW of mouth.

Shimshak or **Shemshak** (both: shĕmshäk'), village, Second Prov., in Teheran, N Iran, in Elburz mts., 24 mi. N of Teheran; chief Iranian coal mine.

Shimshapura, India: see SHIMSA FALLS.

Shimsk (shēmsk), village (1939 pop. over 500), W Novgorod oblast, Russian SFSR, near L. Ilmen, on Shelon R. and 29 mi. SW of Novgorod; road center; flax, wheat.

Shimushir Island, Russian SFSR: see SIMUSHIR ISLAND.

Shimushiru-kaikyo, Russian SFSR: see DIANA STRAIT.

Shimushu-kaikyo, Russian SFSR: see KURILE STRAIT.

Shimushu-to, Russian SFSR: see SHUMSHU ISLAND.

Shin, Japan: see SHIN-MACHI.

Shin, Loch (lôkh), lake (17 mi. long, 1 mi. wide; 162 ft. deep), S Sutherland, Scotland. Outlet: Shin R., issuing at Lairg and flowing 6 mi. S to the Oykell.

Shinafiya (shĭnäfē'yŭ) or **Shanafiyah** (shä–), village, Diwaniya prov., SE central Iraq, on the Euphrates and 34 mi. SW of Diwaniya; rice, dates.

Shinano (shĭnä'nō), former province in central Honshu, Japan; now Nagano prefecture.

Shinano, town (pop. 8,051), Aichi prefecture, central Honshu, Japan, 2 mi. NNE of Seto; pottery.

Shinano River, Jap. *Shinano-gawa,* longest river of Honshu, Japan, in Niigata and Nagano prefectures; rises in mts. c.20 mi. N of Kofu; flows 229 mi. generally NNE, past Ueda, Senju (hydroelectric plant), Nagaoka, and Sanjo, to Sea of Japan at Niigata. Drains large fertile plain. Sometimes spelled Sinano.

Shinanshu, Korea: see SINANJU.

Shinas (shĭnäs'), town (pop. 2,000), Batina dist., N Oman, port on Gulf of Oman, 30 mi. NW of Sohar; fishing; date cultivation. Airfield.

Shinbwiyang (shĭn-bwē-yän'), village, Myitkyina dist., Kachin State, Upper Burma, in Hukawng Valley, on road and 34 mi. NW of Maingkwan.

Shinchiku, Formosa: see SINCHU.

Shindand (shĭn'dŭnd), Persian *Sabzawar* or *Sebzewar* (sŭb"zŭwär'), town (pop. over 10,000), Herat prov., W Afghanistan, on the Harut Rud and 70 mi. S of Herat, and on road to Farah; oasis center, serving sheep-raising nomads. Pop.: Durani Afghans. Old walled town and remains of anc. *Isfazar* on right bank; new garden town developed on left bank.

Shinei, Formosa: see SINYING.

Shiner, town (pop. 1,778), Lavaca co., S Texas, 11 mi. N of Yoakum; processing center in dairy, poultry, grain, cotton area; brewery. Settled 1887, inc. 1890.

Shinfield, residential town and parish (pop. 2,671), S Berkshire, England, 3 mi. SSE of Reading; dairy market.

Shingak-Kul or **Shingak-Kul'** (shĭn-gäk"-kōōl'), village (1926 pop. 792), W central Bashkir Autonomous SSR, Russian SFSR, on railroad and 37 mi. SW of Ufa; wheat, livestock.

Shingishu, Korea: see SINUIJU.

Shingjin or **Shingjini,** Albania: see SHENGJIN.

Shinglehouse, borough (pop. 1,201), Potter co., N Pa., 15 mi. NW of Coudersport; grist and planing mills; gas and oil wells; agr. Settled 1808, inc. 1902.

Shingmun (shĭng'mōōn'), town, Hong Kong colony, in the New Territories, on reservoir formed by small Shingmun R., 6 mi. NNW of Kowloon; tungsten mines.

Shingtseh or **Sheng-tse** (both: shĭng'dzŭ'), town, S Kiangsu prov., China, on railroad and 28 mi. S of Soochow, on Chekiang line; silk-weaving center.

Shingu (shĕng'gōō). **1** Town (pop. 4,496), Hyogo prefecture, S Honshu, Japan, 11 mi. NW of Himeji; rice, wheat. **2** City (1940 pop. 32,403; 1947 pop. 31,437), Wakayama prefecture, S Honshu, Japan, on E coast of Kii Peninsula, on Kumano Sea, at mouth of Kumano R., 60 mi. SE of Wakayama; lumber-collection center. Fishery. Copper, silver, gold mined near by. Sometimes spelled Singu.

Shinhama, Japan: see MATSUYAMA, Ehime prefecture.

Shinho, Korea: see SINPO.

Shinichi (shĭnē'chē), town (pop. 4,622), Hiroshima prefecture, SW Honshu, Japan, 7 mi. NW of Fukuyama; rice, raw silk.

Shining Tor, mountain (1,833 ft.), in The Peak, NW Derby, England, 5 mi. E of Macclesfield.

Shinji (shēn'jē), town (pop. 6,139), Shimane prefecture, SW Honshu, Japan, on SW shore of L. Shinji, 10 mi. WSW of Matsue; raw silk, charcoal, livestock.

Shinji, Lake, Jap. *Shinji-ko,* lagoon (□ 32), Shimane prefecture, SW Honshu, Japan, separated from Naka-no-umi (a lagoon) by an isthmus; 10 mi. long, 4 mi. wide. On one of its islets is a shrine. Sometimes spelled Sinzi.

Shinjo, Formosa: see SINCHENG.

Shinjo (shēn'-jō'). **1** Town (pop. 7,314), Nara prefecture, S Honshu, Japan, on NW Kii Peninsula, 16 mi. SE of Osaka; commercial center for agr. area (rice, wheat, watermelons). **2** Town, Toyama prefecture, Japan: see TOYAMA, city. **3** Town (pop. 25,234), Yamagata prefecture, N Honshu, Japan, 36 mi. N of Yamagata; rail junction; collection center for rice and lumber; spinning, sawmilling, pottery making. Sometimes spelled Sinzyo.

Shinka, Formosa: see SINHWA.

Shinkai (shĭng'kī), town, Kandahar prov., SE Afghanistan, 35 mi. ESE of Kalat-i-Ghilzai.

Shinkawa (shēng'-kä'wä). **1** Town (pop. 13,632), Aichi prefecture, central Honshu, Japan, 3 mi. E of Handa across Chita Bay; fishing center; copperware, cotton textiles, tiles. **2** Town (pop. 14,783), Aichi prefecture, central Honshu, Japan, just W of Nagoya; textiles, paper, woodworking.

Shinko, Formosa: see SHENKENG; SINKANG.

Shinko, Korea: see SINHUNG.

Shinkolobwe (shĭngkōlōb'wā), village, Katanga prov., SE Belgian Congo, 12 mi. WSW of Jadotville; pitchblende-mining center; also gold mining. Most of its uranium output is shipped to U.S.A.

Shin-machi (shēn'-mä'chē) or **Shimmachi** (shēm'–), town (pop. 11,478), Gumma prefecture, central Honshu, Japan, 7 mi. ESE of Takasaki; raw silk. Sometimes called Shin.

Shinmi-do, Korea: see SINMI ISLAND.

Shin-mikuriya (shēn'-mēkōō'rēyä), town (pop. 10,471), Nagasaki prefecture, W Kyushu, Japan, on NW Hizen Peninsula, 13 mi. NNW of Sasebo; raw silk, rice. Called Mikuriya until 1943. Sometimes spelled Shimmikuriya.

Shinnecock Bay (shĭ'nŭkŏk"), SE N.Y., inlet of the Atlantic indenting SE shore of Long Isl., W of Southampton; c.12 mi. long E–W; max. width c.2$\frac{1}{2}$ mi. Sheltered from ocean by barrier beach, which is pierced by Shinnecock Inlet 6 mi. WSW of Southampton. Connected with Great Peconic Bay (N) by Shinnecock Canal (c.1 mi. long; partly a land cut; crossed by highway bridges). Resort area; yachting; duck hunting.

Shinnecock Hills, Suffolk co., SE N.Y., low rolling region of SE Long Isl., bet. Great Peconic Bay (N) and Shinnecock Bay, c.4 mi. W of Southampton. Shinnecock Indian Reservation is here.

Shinnston, city (pop. 2,793), Harrison co., N W.Va., on the West Fork and 8 mi. N of Clarksburg, in bituminous-coal, gas, oil, and agr. (corn, livestock, fruit, tobacco) region; coke ovens. Settled 1818.

Shinogi, Japan: see KASUGAI.

Shinonoi (shĭnōnō'ē) or **Shinoi** (shĭnō'ē), town (pop. 10,943), Nagano prefecture, central Honshu, Japan, 6 mi. SW of Nagano; spinning.

Shinpo, Formosa: see SINPU.

Shinrone (shĭnrōn'), Gaelic *Suidhe an Róin,* town (pop. 398), SW Co. Offaly, Ireland, 8 mi. S of Birr; agr. market (barley, potatoes; cattle).

Shinsen, Korea: see SINCHON.

Shinshiro (shēn'shĭrō), town (pop. 9,900), Aichi prefecture, central Honshu, Japan, 11 mi. NE of Toyohashi; agr. center (rice, cherries). Sericulture and agr. schools.

Shinsho, Formosa: see SINCHWANG.

Shinshu. 1 Town, S. Hamgyong prov., Korea: see SINCHANG. **2** City, S.Kyongsang prov., Korea: see CHINJU.

Shinso, Korea: see SINCHANG.

Shintainin, Korea: see SINTAEIN.

Shinten, Formosa: see SINTIEN.

Shintoku (shēn'tōkōō), town (pop. 9,890), S central Hokkaido, Japan, 22 mi. NW of Obihiro; rice, sugar beets, potatoes, soybeans.

Shin-usa (shēn-ōō'sä), town (pop. 10,622), Kochi prefecture, S Shikoku, Japan, on Tosa Bay, 9 mi. SW of Kochi; fishing port; truck gardening. Formed in early 1940s by combining Usa and Nii.

Shinyanga (shēnyäng'gä), town (pop. c.3,000), NW Tanganyika, on railroad and 90 mi. SSE of Mwanza; center of diamond-mining dist. The noted Williamson mine is at Mwadui, 15 mi. NE (rail spur). Agr. trade: cotton, peanuts, corn, rice, livestock. Tsetse research station.

Shinyo, Korea: see SINPO.

Shio (shē'ō), town (pop. 8,962), Ishikawa prefecture, central Honshu, Japan, 15 mi. SW of Nanao; lumbering, rice growing. Mineral springs.

Shiobara (shēō'bärŭ), town (pop. 5,003), Tochigi prefecture, central Honshu, Japan, 29 mi. N of Utsunomiya; hot-springs resort.

Shiocton (shĭŏk'tŭn), village (pop. 673), Outagamie co., E Wis., on Wolf R. and 15 mi. NW of Appleton; vegetable canning.

Shiodome, Formosa: see SHIHCHIH.

Shiogama (shēō'gämŭ), city (1940 pop. 35,890; 1947 pop. 42,428), Miyagi prefecture, N Honshu, Japan, on W inlet of Ishinomaki Bay, 8 mi. ENE of Sendai; outer port for Sendai; major fishing center. Trade chiefly imports of salt and coal for Sendai. Sometimes spelled Siogama.

Shiojiri (shēō'jĭrē), town (pop. 13,765), Nagano prefecture, central Honshu, Japan, 9 mi. S of Matsumoto; produces lime, carbide.

Shiokawa (shēō'käwŭ), town (pop. 2,843), Fukushima prefecture, N central Honshu, Japan, 7 mi. NNW of Wakamatsu; rice.

Shio Point (shē'ō), Jap. *Shio-no-misaki,* southernmost point of Honshu, Japan, at SE end of Kii Peninsula, opposite O-shima; 33°26'N 135°45'E; lighthouse. Sometimes spelled Sio.

Shiota (shēō'tä), town (pop. 6,678), Saga prefecture, W Kyushu, Japan, on E Hizen Peninsula, 22 mi. ESE of Sasebo; rice, millet. Sometimes Siota.

Shiotsu, Japan: see KATAYAMAZU.

Shiozawa (shēō'zäwŭ), town (pop. 9,626), Niigata prefecture, central Honshu, Japan, 29 mi. S of Nagaoka, in rice-growing area; textiles.

Shipan Island, Yugoslavia: see SIPAN ISLAND.
Ship Bottom, resort borough (pop. 533), Ocean co., E N.J., on Long Beach isl. (here bridged to mainland) and 20 mi. S of Toms River village; fishing. Beach Arlington is adjacent.
Shiping or **Shihping** (both: shû'bĭng'), town (pop. 3,191), ⊙ Shiping co. (pop. 42,750), E Kweichow prov., China, 100 mi. ENE of Kweiyang and on main road to Hunan; cotton textiles, embroideries; rice, millet, beans, fruit. Salt deposits near by.
Ship Island, islet, E N.F., on W side of Bonavista Bay, 25 mi. WNW of Cape Bonavista; 48°45'N 53°39'W.
Ship Island, SE Miss., in the Gulf of Mexico, one of isl. chain lying bet. Mississippi Sound (N) and Chandeleur Sound (S), 11 mi. S of Biloxi; c.8 mi. long. A lighthouse (30°13'N 88°58'W), old Fort Massachusetts (built just before Civil War; later destroyed and rebuilt), and a former quarantine station are here. Surf bathing, boating. Was a port of entry for French and Spanish vessels from end of 17th cent. to 1720s. Isl. was held alternately by Union and Confederate forces in Civil War. To W is deepwater channel (Ship Island Pass) connecting the Gulf with harbors of Biloxi, Gulfport, and other ports.
Shipka (shĕp'kä), village (pop. 2,209), Stara Zagora dist., central Bulgaria, in Shipka Mts., 7 mi. NNW of Kazanlik; sheep raising. A 19th-cent. monastery commemorates defeat (1877–78) of Turks by Bulgarians. **Shipka Mountains,** part of central Balkan Mts., extend c.15 mi. bet. Kalofer Mts. (W) and Tryavna Mts. (E), just N of Shipka; rise to 4,500 ft. Yantra R. headstreams rise in N slope. Crossed by **Shipka Pass** (alt. 4,166 ft.), 2 mi. N of Shipka, on highway linking Kazanlik and Gabrovo.
Shipki Pass (shĭp'kē) (alt. c.15,400 ft.), in S Zaskar Range, at NW end of Kumaun Himalayas, near India-Tibet border (undefined), 95 mi. W of Gartok, on caravan route; overlooks Sutlej R. (N). Also called Shipki La.
Shiplake, town and parish (pop. 1,624), SE Oxfordshire, England, on the Thames and 5 mi. NE of Reading; agr. market. Its church contains noted French glass collection.
Shipley. 1 Town and parish (pop. 735), E Derby, England, 2 mi. NW of Ilkeston; coal mining. **2** Urban district (1931 pop. 30,242; 1951 census 32,585), West Riding, SW central Yorkshire, England, on Aire R. and 3 mi. NNW of Bradford; woolen milling, leather tanning; mfg. (machine tools, metal products, paint, pharmaceuticals). In urban dist., on Aire R. just W, is the model woolen-milling town of Saltaire, founded 1851 by Sir Titus Salt.
Shipley or **Shipley Heights,** village, Anne Arundel co., central Md., 7 mi. SSW of downtown Baltimore.
Shipman. 1 Town (pop. 376), Macoupin co., SW Ill., 17 mi. NNE of Alton, in agr. and bituminous-coal area. **2** Village, Va.: see LOVINGSTON.
Shippensburg, borough (pop. 5,722), Cumberland and Franklin counties, S Pa., 11 mi. NE of Chambersburg; clothing, furniture, paper products, flour. State teachers col. here. Settled 1733, inc. 1819.
Shippenville, borough (pop. 522), Clarion co., W central Pa., 5 mi. NW of Clarion.
Shippigan (shĭ'pĭgŭn), village (pop. estimate c.550), NE N.B., fishing port on Shippigan Sound, bet. the Gulf of St. Lawrence and Chaleur Bay, 45 mi. ENE of Bathurst, opposite Shippigan Isl.; cod, herring, mackerel, lobster.
Shippigan Island (13 mi. long, 8 mi. wide), in the Gulf of St. Lawrence at entrance of Chaleur Bay, just off NE N.B. across narrow Shippigan Sound; 47°47'N 64°36'W. Just N is Miscou Isl. There are clam, lobster, mackerel, herring, and cod fisheries, and oyster beds. Peat is worked.
Shippingport, borough (pop. 408), Beaver co., W Pa., on Ohio R. just above Midland.
Shiprock, village (pop. c.250), San Juan co., extreme NW N.Mex., on San Juan R., near Chuska Mts., and 38 mi. W of Aztec, in Navajo Indian Reservation; alt. 4,903 ft. Oil and natural-gas fields in vicinity. Ship Rock Peak (7,178 ft.), prominent rock mass that rises 1,400 ft. above surrounding countryside, is 10 mi. SW.
Shipshaw River (shĭp'shô), S Que., Canada, flows c.100 mi. S to the Saguenay near Kenogami; hydroelectric plant.
Shipshewana (shĭp"shŭwä'nŭ), town (pop. 277), Lagrange co., NE Ind., 20 mi. E of Elkhart, in farm area.
Shipston-on-Stour (stour, stō'ŭr), town and parish (pop. 1,373), S Warwick, England, on Stour R. and 10 mi. SSE of Stratford-on-Avon; agr. market; woolen milling. Has church with 15th-cent. tower.
Shipunovo (shĭpōō'nŭvŭ), village (1929 pop. over 2,000), central Altai Territory, Russian SFSR, on Turksib RR, on Alei R. and 27 mi. SW of Aleisk; dairy farming.
Shipwreck Point, cape on NE coast of P.E.I., on the Gulf of St. Lawrence, 12 mi. NW of Souris; 46°28'N 62°26'W.
Shira (shē'rŭ), village (1939 pop. over 500), N Khakass Autonomous Oblast, Krasnoyarsk Territory, Russian SFSR, 75 mi. NNW of Abakan and on Achinsk-Abakan RR; health resort on L. Shira (alkaline bitter-salt water); metalworks.
Shirabad (shērŭbät'), village (1926 pop. 3,159), SW Surkhan-Darya oblast, Uzbek SSR, 35 mi. NW of Termez; cotton.
Shirahama (shĭrä'hämŭ). **1** Town (pop. 6,039), Chiba prefecture, central Honshu, Japan, on S Chiba Peninsula, on the Pacific, 6 mi. SE of Tateyama; summer resort; fishing, agr. **2** Town (1945 pop. estimate 6,778), Hyogo prefecture, S Honshu, Japan, on Harima Sea, 4 mi. SSE of Himeji; rice; saltmaking. Since c.1947, part of Himeji. **3** Town (pop. 5,523), Wakayama prefecture, S Honshu, Japan, on S Kii Peninsula, on Philippine Sea, 4 mi. SSW of Tanabe; hot-springs resort. Lead mining, fishing, agr. (rice, wheat, sweet potatoes). Has marine experimental laboratory of Kyoto Imperial Univ. Until early 1940s, called Seto-kanayama and Seto.
Shiraishi (shĭrī'shē) or **Shiroishi** (shĭrō'ēshē), town (pop. 4,841), Saga prefecture, W Kyushu, Japan, 9 mi. WSW of Saga; agr. center (rice, wheat); raw silk. Agr. school. Sometimes spelled Siraisi; until 1936, Fukuji.
Shiraiwa (shĭrī'wä), town (pop. 6,772), Yamagata prefecture, N Honshu, Japan, 12 mi. NNW of Yamagata; rice growing, stock raising; mining (gold, silver, copper).
Shirakami, Cape (shĭrä'-kä'mē), Jap. *Shirakami-saki,* southernmost point of Hokkaido, Japan, at NW side of entrance to Tsugaru Strait; 41°24'N 140°12'E; lighthouse.
Shirakata (shĭrä'kätŭ), town (pop. 6,439) Chiba prefecture, central Honshu, Japan, on E Chiba Peninsula, 13 mi. N of Ohara; summer resort; agr., fishing.
Shirakawa (shĭrä'käwŭ), town (pop. 27,866), Fukushima prefecture, central Honshu, Japan, on Abukuma R. and 21 mi. SSW of Koriyama; horse trading, spinning, sake brewing. Sometimes spelled Sirakawa.
Shiraki Steppe (shĭrä'kē). **1** or **Leninakan Steppe** (lyĕ'nyĭnŭkän'), W Armenian SSR, on Turkish border; irrigated by the Western Arpa-Chai; wheat, sugar beets. Main center, Leninakan. **2** In SE Georgian SSR, bet. Alazan and Iora rivers; dry petroleum-bearing region, with main oil field at Mirzaani.
Shirako, Japan: see YAMATO, Saitama prefecture.
Shirala (shĭrä'lŭ), village, Satara South dist., S central Bombay, India, 30 mi. WNW of Sangli; millet; lamp mfg.
Shiralkoppa (shĭräl'kŏpŭ) or **Siralkoppa** (sĭ–), town (pop. 3,321), Shimoga dist., NW Mysore, India, 38 mi. NNW of Shimoga; local agr. market (rice, betel nuts, sugar cane); handicraft sandalwood carving. Also written Shiral-Koppa.
Shira Muren, Manchuria: see LIAO RIVER.
Shirane, Mount (shĭrä'nā), Jap. *Shirane-san,* peak (10,534 ft.), Yamanashi prefecture, central Honshu, Japan, 20 mi. W of Kofu. Highest point, Kitadake. Mtn. climbing.
Shiranuhino-umi, Japan: see YATSUSHIRO BAY.
Shiraoi (shĭrä'ōē), village (pop. 9,169), SW Hokkaido, Japan, on the Pacific, 14 mi. WSW of Tomakomai; fishing, agr.; iron mining. Inhabitants are Ainus.
Shirasato (shĭrä'sä'tō), town (pop. 9,242), Chiba prefecture, central Honshu, Japan, on E coast of Chiba Peninsula, 5 mi. SSE of Togane; seaside resort; fishing, agr.
Shirasgaon-Kasba, India: see SIRASGAON KASBA.
Shirasuka (shĭrä'sōōkä), town (pop. 5,504), Shizuoka prefecture, central Honshu, Japan, on Philippine Sea, 8 mi. SE of Toyohashi; rice, livestock.
Shiratorihon (shĭrä'tōrē-hō) or **Shirotorihon** (shĭrō'–), town (pop. 5,373), Kagawa prefecture, NE Shikoku, Japan, on Harima Sea, 16 mi. NW of Tokushima; mfg. center (gloves, medicine, sake, soy sauce).
Shiraura, Russian SFSR: see VZMORYE, Sakhalin oblast.
Shiravati River, India: see SHARAVATI RIVER.
Shiraz (shēräz', –räz'), city (1941 pop. 129,023), ⊙ Seventh Prov., S central Iran, 115 mi. ENE of Bushire, its port on Persian Gulf; alt. 5,200 ft.; 29°38'N 52°35'E. Chief city of Fars, and trade and road center of central Zagros ranges, linked by highways with Bushire, Isfahan, Yezd, and Kerman; airfield. Situated in agr. lowland (sugar beets, wine; roses; well-known gardens), it is noted for its rugs, hand-woven textiles, silverwork, and mosaics, and has flour mills, distilleries, and cement plant. Its many mosques include the 9th-cent. Masjid-i-Jama, the Masjid Nau (new mosque; one of the largest in Iran), and the unfinished Masjid-i-Khan. Other sights are a large bazaar and the blue-tiled dome of the Shah Chiragh mausoleum. Prominent in the history of Persian literature, Shiraz is the birthplace of 2 great Persian poets, Sadi (13th cent.) and Hafiz (14th cent.), whose much-visited tombs are in the N garden suburbs. The founder of Babism is also a native of Shiraz. Founded in 7th cent. after the Arab conquest, the city flourished under the Abbasid caliphate, was sacked (1393) by Tamerlane, was rebuilt and prospered in 15th cent. It lost much of its importance under the Safavids (1499–1736), but became ⊙ Zand dynasty (1750–94), whose founder, Karim Khan, adorned the city with many of its fine bldgs. Repeatedly damaged by earthquakes during 19th cent.
Shirbin (shĭr'bēn), town (pop. 13,293; with suburbs, 16,366), Gharbiya prov., Lower Egypt, on Damietta branch of the Nile, on railroad, and 23 mi. SW of Damietta; cotton, cereals, rice, fruits.
Shirebrook. 1 Town and parish (pop. 11,091), E Derby, England, 4 mi. N of Mansfield; coal-mining center. **2** Town, Nottingham, England: see WARSOP.
Shirehampton, industrial suburb of Bristol, SW Gloucester, England, on Avon R. and 4 mi. NW of the city. Landing place (1690) of William III after battle of the Boyne.
Shire Highlands (shē'rā), upland in S Nyasaland, E of Shire R.; extend from Blantyre to Zomba; rise to 3,500 ft. Chief region of European settlement.
Shiremanstown, borough (pop. 887), Cumberland co., S central Pa., 5 mi. WSW of Harrisburg.
Shire River (shē'rā), Port. *Chire* (shē'rĭ), in S Nyasaland and central Mozambique, issues from S end of L. Nyasa, flows c.250 mi. S in a low, swampy valley, past Fort Johnston, Chiromo, Port Herald (last town in Nyasaland), to the lower Zambezi (left bank) 30 mi. below Sena and 100 mi. above latter's mouth on Mozambique Channel of Indian Ocean. Receives Ruo R. (left). Navigable in lower course below Murchison Rapids (bet. Matope and Chikwawa, W of Blantyre). River's volume varies with changes in level of L. Nyasa, of which it is the only outlet. Also spelled Shiré.
Shiretoko, Cape (shĭrä'tōkō), Jap. *Shiretoko-saki,* E Hokkaido, Japan, at tip of narrow peninsula, in Sea of Okhotsk; forms NW side of entrance to Nemuro Strait; 44°20'N 145°20'E. Sometimes called Shiritoko.
Shirgah (shērgä'), railroad town, Second Prov., in E Mazanderan, N Iran, 10 mi. S of Shahi, on line to Teheran; creosoting plant.
Shirhatti (shĭr'hŭt-tē), town (pop. 6,415), Dharwar dist., S Bombay, India, 40 mi. ESE of Dharwar; market center for cotton, millet, peanuts; handicraft cloth weaving.
Shiribeshi-yama (shĭrĭbāsh'yämŭ) or **Ezo-Fuji** (ā'zō-fōō"jē), volcanic cone (6,211 ft.), SW Hokkaido, Japan, 35 mi. NNW of Muroran.
Shirin, Formosa: see SHIHLIN.
Shiringushi (shĭrēn-gōō'shē), town (1926 pop. 1,404), SW Mordvinian Autonomous SSR, Russian SFSR, 25 mi. NNE of Zemetchino; woolen milling.
Shirinki Island (shĭrēn'kē), Jap. *Shirinki-to,* uninhabited island (□ 3.3) of N main Kurile Isls. group, Russian SFSR; separated from Paramushir Isl. (E) by Third Kurile Strait; 50°12'N 154°59'E; 2.5 mi. long, 2 mi. wide. Consists of extinct volcano rising to 2,464 ft.
Shirinki-kaikyo, Russian SFSR: see KURILE STRAIT.
Shiritoko, Cape, Japan: see SHIRETOKO, CAPE.
Shiritori, Russian SFSR: see MAKAROV.
Shiriya, Cape (shĭrē'yä), Jap. *Shiriya-saki,* at NE tip of Honshu, Japan, in Aomori prefecture, at E entrance to Tsugaru Strait; 41°26'N 141°28'E; lighthouse.
Shirland and Higham (hī'ŭm), parish (pop. 4,406), E Derby, England. Includes coal-mining towns of Shirland, 2 mi. NNW of Alfreton, with 15th-cent. church; and Higham, 3 mi. NNW of Alfreton.
Shirley. 1 Suburb, Hampshire, England: see SOUTHAMPTON. **2** Town, Warwick, England: see SOLIHULL.
Shirley. 1 Town (pop. 259), Van Buren co., N central Ark., c.40 mi. N of Conway and on Middle Fork of Little Red R., in farm area. Caverns with Indian relics near by. **2** Town (pop. 1,087), on Hancock-Henry co. line, E central Ind., 32 mi. ENE of Indianapolis, in agr. area. **3** Town (pop. 212), Piscataquis co., central Maine, 22 mi. NW of Dover-Foxcroft; agr., lumbering. Includes Shirley Mills village. **4** Town (pop. 4,271), including Shirley Village (pop. 1,082), Middlesex co., N Mass., on Nashua R. and 8 mi. ESE of Fitchburg; suspenders, cordage, elastic webbing. Settled c.1720, inc. 1753. Shaker community established here 1793.
Shirley City, Ind.: see WOODBURN CITY.
Shirleysburg, borough (pop. 241), Huntingdon co., S central Pa., 6 mi. S of Mount Union; brick clay.
Shiroda, India: see VENGURLA.
Shiroishi (shērō'ĭshē). **1** Town (pop. 17,738), Miyagi prefecture, N Honshu, Japan, 23 mi. SW of Sendai, in agr. area (rice, wheat); flour, charcoal, raw silk. Sometimes spelled Siroisi. **2** Town, Saga prefecture, Japan: see SHIRAISHI.
Shirokaya Balka (shĭrô'kĭŭ bäl'kŭ), town (1939 pop. over 2,000), S Nikolayev oblast, Ukrainian SSR, 2 mi. S of Nikolayev.
Shirokaya Pad' or **Shirokaya Pad'** (pät'yŭ), village (1939 pop. over 500), N Sakhalin, Russian SFSR, on Tatar Strait, 40 mi. S of Aleksandrovsk; fish cannery.
Shiroki Briyeg, Yugoslavia: see SIROKI BRIJEG.
Shiroki Buyerak or **Shirokiy Buyerak** (shĭrô'kē bōōyĭräk'), village (1926 pop. 4,506), N Saratov oblast, Russian SFSR, on right bank of Volga R. and 16 mi. ENE of Volsk; agr. center; wheat, sunflowers.

Shiroki Karamysh or **Shirokiy Karamysh** (kŭrŭmĭsh′), village (1926 pop. 2,368), S Saratov oblast, Russian SFSR, 40 mi. WSW of Saratov; flour mill; wheat, sunflowers.

Shiroko, Japan: see SUZUKA.

Shirokolanovka (shĭrô″kŭlä′nŭfkŭ), village (1926 pop. 2,781), W Nikolayev oblast, Ukrainian SSR, 28 mi. NW of Nikolayev; flour mill. Originally a Ger. agr. colony (Landau); called (c.1935–45) Karla Libknekhta.

Shirokoye (shĭrô′kŭyŭ), town (1939 pop. over 10,000), SW Dnepropetrovsk oblast, Ukrainian SSR, on Ingulets R. and 15 mi. SSW of Krivoi Rog, in iron-mining basin; truck produce.

Shirol (shĭrōl′), town (pop. 6,953), Kolhapur dist., S Bombay, India, 27 mi. E of Kolhapur; market center for millet, peanuts, cotton, sugar cane; handicraft cloth weaving.

Shirone (shĭrō′nā), town (pop. 10,568), Niigata prefecture, central Honshu, Japan, 12 mi. SSW of Niigata; bulb nurseries. Sometimes spelled Sirone.

Shirotori (shĭrō′tōrē), town (pop. 5,556), Gifu prefecture, central Honshu, Japan, 10 mi. NW of Hachiman; livestock.

Shirotorihon, Japan: see SHIRATORIHON.

Shirpula, Iraq: see LAGASH.

Shirpur (shĭr′po͝or), town (pop. 12,829), West Khandesh dist., NE Bombay, India, 32 mi. NNE of Dhulia; market center for millet, wheat, timber; cotton ginning, oilseed milling.

Shirutoru, Russian SFSR: see MAKAROV.

Shirvan (shērvän′), town, Ninth Prov., in Khurasan, NE Iran, on Atrek R. and 40 mi. NW of Quchan, and on road to Bujnurd; alt. 3,447 ft. Grain, raisins, melons; woolen textiles.

Shirvan Steppe, Azerbaijan SSR: see KURA LOWLAND.

Shirvintos, Lithuania: see SIRVINTOS.

Shirwa, Lake, Nyasaland: see CHILWA, LAKE.

Shiryayevo (shĭryī′ŭvŭ), village (1926 pop. 2,673), central Odessa oblast, Ukrainian SSR, 65 mi. NNW of Odessa; wheat, corn.

Shisa (shē′sä), town (pop. 8,459), Nagasaki prefecture, W Kyushu, Japan, on N coast of Hizen Peninsula, 12 mi. N of Sasebo; rice; coal. Sometimes spelled Sisa.

Shisen, Korea: see SACHON.

Shishaki (shĕshä′kē), village (1926 pop. 4,735), central Poltava oblast, Ukrainian SSR, on Psel R. and 30 mi. NW of Poltava; clothing mill, metalworks.

Shishaldin Volcano (shĭshôl′dĭn) (c.9,500 ft.; its alt. is variously given from 9,372 ft. to nearly 10,000 ft.), on central Unimak Isl., SW Alaska, 44 mi. NE of Unimak village; 54°45′N 163°58′W. Mildly active for at least 150 years; several eruptions recorded in recent years.

Shisha Pangma, peak, Tibet: see GOSAINTHAN, peak.

Shishawen, Sp. Morocco: see XAUEN.

Shishgarh (shēsh′gŭr), town (pop. 3,246), Bareilly dist., N central Uttar Pradesh, India, 25 mi. NNW of Bareilly; rice, wheat, gram, pearl millet, oilseeds, corn.

Shishido (shē′shĭdō), town (pop. 11,088), Ibaraki prefecture, central Honshu, Japan, 10 mi. WSW of Mito; lumbering, agr.

Shishi-jima (shĭshē′jĭmä), island (□ c.9; pop. c.6,000) of Amakusa Isls., in Yatsushiro Bay of E.China Sea, Japan, in Kagoshima prefecture, off W coast of Kyushu, N of Naga-shima; 4 mi. long, 3 mi. wide; mountainous. Fishing.

Shishikui (shēshĭko͞o′ē), town (pop. 5,529), Tokushima prefecture, SE Shikoku, Japan, on Philippine Sea, 37 mi. SSW of Tokushima, in agr. area; fishing port; rice, lumber, charcoal, dried bonito. Sometimes spelled Sisikui.

Shishmaref (shĭsh′mŭrĕf), village (pop. 193), NW Alaska, on small Sarichet Isl., at entrance of Shishmaref Inlet, NW Seward Peninsula, on Chukchi Sea; 66°9′N 166°8′W; Eskimo settlement. Has territorial school and Lutheran mission. Airfield. Fox farming; fishing.

Shishmaref Inlet, bay (10 mi. long, 9 mi. wide), NW Alaska, on NW Seward Peninsula, on Chukchi Sea; 66°9′N 165°49′W; Eskimo settlers in region; fishing, trapping. Shishmaref village on Sarichet Isl. at entrance of bay.

Shisui (shĭso͞o′ē) or **Shushui** (sho͞osho͞o′ē), town (pop. 6,253), Chiba prefecture, central Honshu, Japan, 2 mi. E of Sakura, in forested area; rice growing.

Shitka (shēt′kŭ), village (1948 pop. over 2,000), W Irkutsk oblast, Russian SFSR, on Biryusa R. and 30 mi. N of Taishet; lumbering.

Shitlingthorpe, England: see NETHERTON.

Shituru, Belgian Congo: see JADOTVILLE.

Shiuchow, China: see KÜKONG.

Shiuhing, China: see KOYIU.

Shiveluch (shēvyĭlo͞och′), active volcano (10,825 ft.) in E range of Kamchatka Peninsula, Russian SFSR, 50 mi. NW of Ust-Kamchatsk.

Shively (shĭv′lē), town (pop. 2,401), Jefferson co., NW Ky., 5 mi. S of downtown Louisville, within Louisville metropolitan dist.; mfg. of whisky, concrete blocks; feed milling, mushroom growing. Settled c.1885; inc. 1938.

Shivpuri (shĭv′po͞orē), town (pop. 15,490), ⊙ Shivpuri dist., N central Madhya Bharat, India, 60 mi. SSW of Lashkar, in forested area; rail terminus; market center (millet, wheat, gram, oilseeds, forest produce). Forest training school. Big game and wild fowl abound in near-by jungles. Formerly also called Sipri.

Shivrajpur (shĭvräj′po͝or), village, Panch Mahals dist., N Bombay, India, 23 mi. S of Godhra; local market for wheat, corn, timber. Manganese and bauxite mining near by.

Shivwits Plateau (shĭv′wĭts), NW Ariz., N of Colorado R. and W of Uinkaret Plateau; tableland c.7,000 ft. high. W escarpment is Grand Wash Cliffs.

Shiwa Ngandu (shē′väng-gän′do͞o), agr. estate, Northern Prov., N Northern Rhodesia, in Muchinga Mts., 45 mi. NNE of Mpika; tobacco, wheat, corn, potatoes.

Shiyali (shĭyä′lē, shē′älē), since 1949 officially **Sirkali** (sĭr′kŭlē), town (pop. 12,804), Tanjore dist., SE Madras, India, in Cauvery R. delta, 50 mi. NE of Tanjore; rice milling, rush-mat weaving; confectionery. Sivaite shrine.

Shizukawa (shĭzo͞o′käwŭ), town (pop. 9,524), Miyagi prefecture, N Honshu, Japan, fishing port on inlet of the Pacific, 19 mi. NNE of Ishinomaki; rice, wheat, soybeans; spinning.

Shizuki (shēzo͞o′kē), town (pop. 6,805) on Awaji-shima, Hyogo prefecture, Japan, port on Osaka Bay, 7 mi. N of Sumoto; exports salt, rice.

Shizukuishi (shĭzo͞o′-ko͞o′ishē), town (pop. 4,455), Iwate prefecture, N Honshu, Japan, 9 mi. W of Morioka; agr., livestock.

Shizunai (shĭzo͞onī′), town (pop. 13,638), S Hokkaido, Japan, on the Pacific, 55 mi. SSE of Yubari; agr., fishing, stock raising.

Shizuoka (shĭzo͞o′ōkä), prefecture [Jap. *ken*] (□ 3,000; 1940 pop. 2,017,860; 1947 pop. 2,353,005), central Honshu, Japan; ⊙ Shizuoka. Bounded S by Suruga Bay; Shimizu is principal port. Mountainous terrain, drained by Tenryu R.; Fujiyama (highest peak of Japan) is in Fuji-Hakone Natl. Park. Many hot springs on Izu Peninsula. Prefecture is chief tea-producing area of Japan; extensive orange orchards; rice growing. Paper milling, mfg. (musical instruments, textiles, lacquer ware). Centers: Shizuoka, HAMAMATSU, NUMAZU, SHIMIZU, ATAMI.

Shizuoka, city (1940 pop. 212,198; 1947 pop. 205,737), ⊙ Shizuoka prefecture, central Honshu, Japan, on W shore of Suruga Bay, 90 mi. WSW of Tokyo; 34°58′N 138°23′E. Collection center for tea and oranges; mfg. (cotton textiles, lacquer ware, wooden and metal products). Site of castle of last shogun. Statue of Ieyasu (founder of Tokugawa shogunate) is in Hodai-in, a Buddhist temple. Bombed (1945) in Second World War. Includes (since 1936) former town of Hikuma. Sometimes spelled Sizuoka, Shidzuoka.

Shkhara (shŭkhŭrä′), peak (17,037 ft.) in main range of the central Greater Caucasus, on Russian SFSR–Georgian SSR border, just SE of the Dykh-Tau, 40 mi. SW of Nalchik.

Shkhunat Beilinson, Israel: see BEILINSON.

Shkhunat Ono, Israel: see KFAR ONO.

Shklov (shklôf), city (1926 pop. 8,293), N Mogilev oblast, Belorussian SSR, on Dnieper R. and 22 mi. N of Mogilev; paper-milling center; flax processing; metalworks. Pop. 40% Jewish until Second World War.

Shkodër or **Shkodra,** Albania: see SCUTARI.

Shkotovo (shkô′tŭvŭ), town (1926 pop. 2,522), SW Maritime Territory, Russian SFSR, on Ussuri Bay of Sea of Japan, 25 mi. NNE of Vladivostok, on branch of Trans-Siberian RR; fishing flotilla base; fish canning, sawmilling.

Shkumbi River (shko͞om′bē) or **Shkumbini River** (–bēnē), main river of central Albania, rises near L. Ochrida, flows over 90 mi. NW and W, past Librazhd, Elbasan, and Peqin to the Adriatic 20 mi. S of Durazzo. Lower valley is used by Durazzo-Elbasan RR. Forms linguistic border bet. Gheg (N) and Tosk dialects.

Shkurinskaya (shko͞o′rĭnskĭŭ), village (1926 pop. 9,752), N Krasnodar Territory, Russian SFSR, on Yeya R. and 12 mi. W of Kushchevskaya; flour mill, metalworks; wheat, sunflowers, castor beans.

Shlisselburg, Russian SFSR: see PETROKREPOST.

Shmakovo, Ukrainian SSR: see KARLA LIBKNEKHTA, IMENI, Dnepropetrovsk oblast.

Shmidt, Cape, or **Cape Schmidt** (shmĭt), on coast of Chukchi Sea, NE Siberian Russian SFSR; 68°55′N 179°25′W. Govt. arctic station; trading post, airfield. Formerly Severny Cape [Rus., =north].

Shmidt Island or **Schmidt Island** (□ 290), in Kara Sea of Arctic Ocean, 25 mi. off NW Komsomolets Isl. of Severnaya Zemlya; 81°10′N 91°E. Discovered 1930; named for Soviet scientist.

Shoa (shō′ä), province (□ c.30,400), central Ethiopia; ⊙ Addis Ababa. Mountainous region situated bet. the Blue Nile (NW) and Omo R. (SW), rising to c.13,120 ft. in the Abuya Myeda; includes much of Gurage dist. Drained by Awash R. Pop. largely Amhara and Galla. Agr. (cereals, coffee, vegetables, bananas, tobacco) and stock raising. Has extensive trade (coffee, hides, beeswax). Chief centers: Addis Ababa, Addis Alam, Ankober, Awash, Debra Birhan, Fiche. Long a kingdom, Shoa expanded in 19th cent., especially bet. 1875–98 under Menelik II, to include remainder of Ethiopia and become chief prov. of the empire.

Shoa Gimirra, Ethiopia: see WOTA.

Shoal Bay, B.C.: see THURLOW ISLANDS.

Shoal Creek. 1 In SW Ill., formed SW of Greenville by junction of East Fork (c.40 mi. long) and Middle Fork (c.45 mi. long), both rising in SW central Ill.; flows c.75 mi. S and SW to Kaskaskia R. 8 mi. SE of New Baden. West Fork (c.30 mi. long) enters Middle Fork S of Hillsboro. **2** In Tenn. and Ala., rises in Lawrence co., S Tenn.; meanders c.75 mi. generally S past Lawrenceburg, into NW Ala., to L. Wilson 5 mi. NE of Wilson Dam.

Shoalhaven River, SE New South Wales, Australia, rises in Great Dividing Range (bet. Australian Capital Territory and SE coast), flows NNE and E, past Nowra, to the Pacific 75 mi. SSW of Sydney; 206 mi. long.

Shoalhaven South, municipality (pop. 781), E New South Wales, Australia, on the Pacific, 70 mi. SSW of Sydney; dairying.

Shoal Lake, village (pop. 683), SW Man., on Shoal L. (6 mi. long), 50 mi. NW of Brandon; grain elevators; lumbering, dairying. Resort.

Shoal River, NW Fla., rises 12 mi. N of De Funiak Springs in Walton co., flows c.45 mi. WSW to Yellow R. 8 mi. SW of Crestview in Okaloosa co.

Shoals, town (pop. 1,039), ⊙ Martin co., SW Ind., on East Fork of White R. and 21 mi. E of Washington, in agr. area; lumber milling; mfg. of furniture, buttons. A state forest is near by. Settled 1818, inc. c.1845.

Shoals, Isles of, Maine and N.H.: see ISLES OF SHOALS.

Shoalwater Bay, inlet of Coral Sea, E Queensland, Australia, bet. Cape Townshend and Stanage Point, just E of Broad Sound; 26 mi. long, 20 mi. wide.

Shobak, El, Esh Shobak, or **Al-Shobak** (all: ĕsh-shō′băk), village (pop. c.3,000), S Jordan, in hills 26 mi. NNW of Ma'an; alt. 4,380 ft.; trade center; wheat, barley, fruit. Manganese deposits (N). Sometimes spelled Shobek.

Shobando (shō′bändō) or **Shopando** (–pändō), Chinese *Shih-pan-to* (shû′bän′dô′), after 1913 *Shihtu* (–do͞o′), town, E Tibet, in Kham prov., 80 mi. WSW of Chamdo, and on road to Lhasa; timber, agr. products; gold mining.

Shobar or **Shubar** (both: sho͞o′bär), village (pop. 6,519), Gharbiya prov., Lower Egypt, 5 mi. NNW of Tanta; cotton.

Shobara (shō′bärŭ) or **Shohara** (shō′härŭ), town (pop. 9,572), Hiroshima prefecture, SW Honshu, Japan, 32 mi. NNW of Onomichi; commercial center for agr. area (rice, wheat); raw silk, charcoal. Hot springs.

Shobu (shō′bo͞o), town (pop. 5,739), Saitama prefecture, central Honshu, Japan, 13 mi. ESE of Kumagaya; rice, wheat.

Shodo-shima (shō′dō-shĭmä), island (□ 60; pop. 50,965), Kagawa prefecture, Japan, in Harima Sea (E section of Inland Sea), just off NE coast of Shikoku, 9 mi. NE of Takamatsu; 11 mi. long, 6 mi. wide; has 3 large peninsulas. Mountainous, with scenic valleys. Building-stone quarries. Agr. (tobacco, sweet potatoes, rice). Spinning mills, soy-sauce factories. Tonosho (on W peninsula) is chief town and port. Sometimes spelled Syodo-sima.

Shoeburyness (sho͞o′bürĕnĕs′), former urban district (1931 pop. 6,720), SE Essex, England, on N shore of mouth of Thames estuary, 4 mi. E of Southend-on-Sea, opposite Sheerness. Site of extensive barracks, gunnery school, and artillery proving ground. Has Norman church. Inc. 1933 in Southend.

Shoemakersville, borough (pop. 1,066), Berks co., E central Pa., 11 mi. NNW of Reading; brickworks. Founded 1833.

Shohara, Japan: see SHOBARA.

Shohsien or **Shuo-hsien** (both: shwô′shyĕn′), town, ⊙ Shohsien co. (pop. 173,928), SW Chahar prov., China, 70 mi. SW of Tatung and on railroad; timber. Coal mining near by.

Shoin (shō′ēn), town (pop. 3,556), Ishikawa prefecture, central Honshu, Japan, on NE Noto Peninsula, on Sea of Japan, 22 mi. ENE of Wajima; rice, raw silk.

Shoina or **Shoyna** (shoi′nŭ), village (1939 pop. over 500), W Nenets Natl. Okrug, Archangel oblast, Russian SFSR, on W coast of Kanin Peninsula, 230 mi. W of Naryan-Mar; fish cannery.

Shojo. 1 Township, N.Hamgyong prov., Korea: see CHONGSONG. **2** Township, N.Pyongan prov., Korea: see CHANGSONG.

Shoka, Formosa: see CHANGHWA.

Shokalski Strait or **Shokal'skiy Strait** (shŭkäl′skē), joins Kara and Laptev seas of Arctic Ocean at c.100°E; separates Oktyabrskaya Revolyutsiya and Bolshevik isls. of Severnaya Zemlya, in Krasnoyarsk Territory, Russian SFSR; 100 mi. long, 15–30 mi. wide.

Shokan (shō′kŭn, shō′kăn″), resort village, Ulster co., SE N.Y., in the Catskills, on Ashokan Reservoir, 12 mi. WNW of Kingston.

Shokei, Formosa: see TSIAOKI.

Shoko, Korea: see SUNGHO.

Shoksha, Karelo-Finnish SSR: see SHELTOZERO.

Sholapur (shōlä′po͝or), district, E Bombay, India; ⊙ Sholapur. Bordered E by Hyderabad state, NW and S by Bhima R., SW by Satara South dist. Agr.

(millet, wheat, cotton, oilseeds, sugar cane); handloom weaving, oilseed pressing, dyeing. Sholapur and Barsi are cotton-milling and trade centers; Pandharpur is noted place of Hindu pilgrimage. Under Bijapur and Ahmadnagar kingdoms in 16th–17th cent.; annexed 1795 by Mahrattas. Original dist. (□ 4,572; 1941 pop. 1,014,670) enlarged by inc. (1949) of parts of former Deccan states of Akalkot, Sangli, Kurandvad Junior, Jath, Miraj Senior, Miraj Junior, and Jamkhandi, and by exchange (1950) of enclaves with Hyderabad. Pop. 87% Hindu, 8% Moslem.

Sholapur, city (pop. 203,691; including suburban area, 212,620), ⊙ Sholapur dist., E Bombay, India, 220 mi. SE of Bombay. Road and rail junction; major cotton-milling center; trades in cotton, grain, oilseeds, hides; mfg. of leather goods, glass, chemicals, metal furniture, carpets; handicraft cloth weaving and dyeing; engineering works, motion picture studio. Cols., technical institute. Large reservoir and irrigation works just N. Ruled by Bijapur kings in 16th cent.

Sholashahar (shō'lāshŭhŭr), village, Chittagong dist., SE East Bengal, E Pakistan, 1 mi. N of Chittagong; rail spur junction, with spurs to Nazirhat (18 mi. N) and Dohazari (21 mi. SE).

Sholavandan, India: see SOLAVANDAN.

Sholdaneshty (shŭldŭnyĕsh'tē), Rum. *Şoldăneşti* (shôldŭnĕsht'), village (1941 pop. 1,242), E Moldavian SSR, on railroad and 10 mi. NW of Rezina; tobacco center.

Sholes, village (pop. 32), Wayne co., NE Nebr., 15 mi. WNW of Wayne.

Sholinghur or **Shollingur** (both: shō'lĭngōōr), town (pop. 9,977), North Arcot dist., E central Madras, India, 23 mi. NE of Vellore; peanuts, sugar cane, sesame. Granite quarries near by.

Sholkhi, Russian SFSR: see KARTSA.

Shollar (shŭlär'), town (1939 pop. over 500), NE Azerbaijan SSR, near Caspian coast, 105 mi. NW of Baku, just NW of Khudat, in orchard dist.; fruit and vegetable canning.

Shollingur, India: see SHOLINGHUR.

Sholski Zavod, Russian SFSR: see ZUBOVO.

Sholta Island, Yugoslavia: see SOLTA ISLAND.

Shona (shō'nŭ), island (pop. 62) off W Inverness, Scotland, 8 mi. S of Arisaig, separated from mainland by narrow inlets of the Sea of the Hebrides; 3 mi. long, 1½ mi. wide.

Shonai (shō'nī). **1** Town, Aichi prefecture, Japan: see NAGOYA. **2** Town (pop. 11,880), Miyazaki prefecture, S Kyushu, Japan, 26 mi. WSW of Miyazaki; agr. center (rice, wheat). **3** Town (pop. 12,524), Osaka prefecture, S Honshu, Japan, just N of Amagasaki, in rice-growing area.

Shonga (shông-gä'), town (pop. 3,878), Ilorin prov., Northern Provinces, W Nigeria, near the Niger, 20 mi. ESE of Jebba; shea-nut processing, cotton weaving; dried fish, cassava, corn, yams. A Br. commercial station in 19th cent.

Shongar (shŭn-gär'), town (1945 pop. over 500) in Molotov dist. of Greater Baku, Azerbaijan SSR, c.20 mi. SW of Baku; oil wells (developed 1936).

Shoni or **Shuni** (both: shōō'nē), village (pop. 7,111), Minufiya prov., Lower Egypt, 5 mi. NNW of Tala; cereals, cotton, flax.

Shooter's Hill, conspicuous height (425 ft.) and residential district of Woolwich, London, England, S of the Thames, 9 mi. ESE of Charing Cross.

Shooters Hill, village, Manchester parish, S central Jamaica, 20 mi. WNW of May Pen; processing of spices.

Shooters Hill, town (pop. 13), Marion co., central Ind., NW suburb of Indianapolis.

Shooters Island, Richmond co., SE N.Y., small island at entrance to Newark Bay from Kill Van Kull, just off N shore of Staten Isl.; part of Richmond borough of New York city.

Shopando, Tibet: see SHOBANDO.

Shopian, Kashmir: see SHUPIYAN.

Shoping, China: see YUYÜ.

Shora, Iraq: see SHURA.

Shoranur (shō'rŭnōōr), town (pop. 8,587), Malabar dist., SW Madras, India, on Ponnani R. and 50 mi. SE of Calicut; rail junction; metalworks; rice milling; cassava, pepper, ginger. Rail spur serves extensive teak plantations 35 mi. N, near village of Nilambur. Agr. research station 6 mi. WNW, at village of Pattambi.

Shorapani (shŭrŭpä'nyē), town (1939 pop. over 500), W central Georgian SSR, on railroad and 20 mi. ESE of Kutaisi; junction of rail branch to Chiatura and Sachkhere; metalworks.

Shorapur (shō'räpōōr), town (pop. 11,836), Gulbarga dist., SW Hyderabad state, India, 55 mi. S of Gulbarga; millet, oilseeds, rice; cotton ginning. Formerly spelled Surapur.

Shoreacres, village (pop. estimate 500), S B.C., on Kootenay R. at mouth of Slocan R., and 12 mi. WSW of Nelson, in lumbering and mining (gold, silver, tungsten) region.

Shore Acres, Mass.: see SCITUATE.

Shoreacres, town (pop. 183), Harris co., S Texas.

Shoreditch, metropolitan borough (1931 pop. 97,042; 1951 census 44,885) of London, England, N of the Thames, 2.5 mi. NE of Charing Cross. Workers' residential and industrial region, furniture-mfg. center. Suffered heavy air-raid damage 1940–41. James Burbage built (c.1576) London's 1st theater in Shoreditch.

Shoreham (shô'rŭm). **1** Village (pop. 391), Berrien co., extreme SW Mich., 2 mi. SW of St. Joseph, on L. Michigan. **2** Village (pop. 90), Suffolk co., SE N.Y., near N shore of Long Isl., 8 mi. E of Port Jefferson, in summer-resort, and truck and poultry area. Just N is Shoreham Beach, resort village. **3** Town (pop. 829), Addison co., W Vt., on L. Champlain and 25 mi. NW of Rutland, in agr. area. Levi P. Morton b. here. Chartered 1761, settled after Revolution.

Shoreham Beach, N.Y.: see SHOREHAM.

Shoreham-by-Sea (shô'rŭm), urban district (1931 pop. 8,757; 1951 census 13,052), S Sussex, England, on the Channel at mouth of Adur R., 6 mi. W of Brighton; seaside resort, with metalworking industry. Has early-12th-cent. church. Its harbor was important in Middle Ages. In urban dist. (NE) is Kingston-by-Sea.

Shores Acres, town (pop. 9), Marion co., central Ind.

Shorewood, residential village (pop. 16,199), Milwaukee co., SE Wis., on L. Michigan, just N of Milwaukee; has numerous recreational facilities. Settled c.1834; inc. as East Milwaukee in 1900; renamed 1917.

Shorewood Hills, residential village (pop. 1,594), Dane co., S Wis., just W of Madison, near L. Mendota. Inc. 1927.

Shorey (shōrā'), village (pop. 414), Libertad dept., NW Peru, in Cordillera Occidental, 2 mi. WSW of Quiruvilca, in mining region (copper, gold, silver); foundry.

Shoriya, Gornaya, Russian SFSR: see GORNAYA SHORIYA.

Shorkot (shōr'kōt), town (pop. 5,786), Jhang dist., S central Punjab, W Pakistan, 33 mi. SSW of Jhang-Maghiana; local market for wheat, cotton, dates. Shorkot Road, rail junction, is 11 mi. E; cotton ginning.

Shorncliffe, England: see SANDGATE.

Shorsu (shŭrsōō'), town (1939 pop. over 500), SW Fergana oblast, Uzbek SSR, 17 mi. SSW of Kokand; oil fields; chemical works (based on local sulphur, potash and ozocerite deposits).

Shortandy (shŭrtŭndē'), town (1948 pop. over 2,000), N Akmolinsk oblast, Kazakh SSR, on railroad and 40 mi. NNW of Akmolinsk; mfg. (furniture, musical instruments, wagon parts).

Short Beach, Conn.: see BRANFORD.

Shor Tepe or **Shor Tepah** (shōr' tä'pŭ), village, Mazar-i-Sharif prov., N Afghanistan, on the Amu Darya (USSR line) and 30 mi. E of Kelif, 45 mi. NNW of Mazar-i-Sharif; salt and oil deposits.

Short Heath, former urban district (1931 pop. 5,047), S central Stafford, England, 5 mi. NE of Wolverhampton; coal mining, metalworking. Inc. 1934 in Willenhall.

Short Hills, village, N.J.: see MILLBURN.

Short Hills, mountains, Va.: see SOUTH MOUNTAIN, Pa. and Md.

Shortland Islands, volcanic group (□ c.200; pop. c.1,300), Solomon Isls., SW Pacific, 5 mi. SE of Bougainville. Comprise Shortland Isl. (largest isl., 10 mi. long, 8 mi. wide), Fauro (10 mi. long, 6 mi. wide), and many smaller isls.; coconuts. Faisi, islet off E coast of Shortland Isl., is site of chief town and port; in Second World War, site of Jap. base.

Shortsville, village (pop. 1,314), Ontario co., W central N.Y., 25 mi. SE of Rochester, in Finger Lakes region; mfg. (paper, machinery, canned foods). Inc. 1889.

Shoshone (shōshō'nē), county (□ 2,609; pop. 22,806), N Idaho; ⊙ Wallace. Mining and lumbering area bounded on E by Mont. and crossed by Coeur d'Alene and St. Joe rivers. Includes Coeur d'Alene mining district, in Coeur d'Alene Mts., and parts of Coeur d'Alene and St. Joe natl. forests. Lead, silver, zinc, copper. Formed 1858.

Shoshone, village (pop. 1,420), ⊙ Lincoln co., S Idaho, on Little Wood R. and 25 mi. N of Twin Falls, in valley of Snake R.; alt. 3,968 ft. Wool-shipping point in sheep-raising and irrigated farming area. Founded (1882) with coming of railroad. At first a cattle town. After construction (1907) of Magic Dam and development of Minidoka irrigation project, village became trade center for productive agr. region.

Shoshone Cavern National Monument (212.4 acres; established 1909), NW Wyo., on Shoshone R. and 5 mi. WSW of Cody. Subterranean chambers display dripstone and crystal formations.

Shoshone Dam, Wyo.: see SHOSHONE RIVER.

Shoshone Falls, cascade in Snake R., S Idaho, near city of Twin Falls. Once spectacular, the falls (more than 200 ft. high) have been reduced in volume by irrigation works upstream.

Shoshone Lake, Wyo.: see YELLOWSTONE NATIONAL PARK.

Shoshone Mountains, central Nev., W of Toiyabe Range and Reese R., in Toiyabe Natl. Forest; barium mines. North Shoshone Peak (10,322 ft.) and South Shoshone Peak (10,072 ft.) are chief elevations.

Shoshone River, NW Wyo., rises in several branches in Absaroka Range in Yellowstone Natl. Park, flows c.100 mi. NE, past Cody and Lovell, to Bighorn R. at Kane, near Mont. line. Chief crops in river valley are sugar beets, grain, beans. Shoshone power and irrigation project on river includes 161,654 acres. Consists of system of canals and dams; Buffalo Bill (formerly Shoshone) Dam is largest; concrete dam 325 ft. high, 200 ft. long; finished 1910; forms Shoshone Reservoir (c.10 mi. long, 4 mi. wide). Project serves Cody, Powell, and Lovell.

Shoshong, Bechuanaland Protectorate: see SHUSHONG.

Shoshoni (shōshō'nē), town (pop. 891), Fremont co., central Wyo., near Bighorn R., 42 mi. NE of Lander; alt. 4,820 ft.; sheep.

Shoshu, Korea: see SANGJU.

Shoshuenco Volcano (shōshwĕng'kō), Andean peak (7,740 ft.) in Valdivia prov., S central Chile, in Chilean lake dist., 70 mi. ESE of Valdivia.

Shostka (shŭstkä'), city (1932 pop. estimate 13,390), N Sumy oblast, Ukrainian SSR, 21 mi. NW of Glukhov, in hemp-growing region; photographic-film mfg., sawmilling. In Second World War, held (1941–43) by Germans.

Shotb or **Shutb** (both: shōō'tŭb), village (pop. 5,600), Asyut prov., central Upper Egypt, on railroad and 8 mi. NW of Abu Tig; cereals, dates, sugar cane. Has a necropolis of the Roman period. Sometimes spelled Chatb.

Shotei, Korea: see SONGJONG.

Shotland High Quarter, England: see BLANCHLAND.

Shotley, agr. village and parish (pop. 2,005), SE Suffolk, England, bet. Orwell R. and Stour R. estuaries, 3 mi. NW of Harwich. Site of naval school.

Shottermill, town and parish (pop. 2,440), SW Surrey, England, just W of Haslemere; agr. market. George Eliot lived here.

Shottery, England: see STRATFORD-ON-AVON.

Shotton, town and parish (pop. 19,529), E Durham, England, 9 mi. E of Durham; coal-mining center.

Shotton, town in Connah's Quay urban dist., Flint, Wales, on the Dee just SE of Connah's Quay; steel milling.

Shotts, town and parish (pop. 20,538), N Lanark, Scotland, 8 mi. ESE of Airdrie; steel milling, coal and iron mining.

Shou-, for Chinese names beginning thus and not found here: see under SHOW-.

Shou-kuang, China: see SHOWKWANG.

Shoultes, village (pop. 1,973), Snohomish co., NW Wash.

Shoval (shōväl'), agr. settlement (pop. 100), S Israel, in N part of the Negev, 12 mi. N of Beersheba. On Negev water pipe line. Founded 1946.

Show or **Shou** (both: shō), Jap. *Kotobuki* (kōtō'bōōkē), village, E central Formosa, on railroad and 9 mi. SW of Hwalien; sugar mill.

Showa (shō'wä). **1** Town (pop. 15,503), Akita prefecture, N Honshu, Japan, 11 mi. NNW of Akita, on lagoon Hachiro-gata; fishing, agr. (rice, wheat, fruit). Formed in early 1940s by combining former towns of Okubo (1940 pop. 5,393) and Iidakawa (1940 pop. 4,716). **2** Town (pop. 5,209), Chiba prefecture, central Honshu, Japan, on W Chiba Peninsula, on Tokyo Bay, just N of Kisarazu; rice, poultry, raw silk. **3** Town (pop. 26,705), Greater Tokyo, central Honshu, Japan, just W of Tachikawa, in forested area; mulberry fields.

Showchang. 1 or **Shou-ch'ang** (shō'chäng'), town (pop. 7,870), ⊙ Showchang co. (pop. 81,282), W Chekiang prov., China, 22 mi. SW of Kienteh; rice, wheat, vegetable oil, tea. **2** or **Shou-ch'ang** (shō'chäng'), town, Hupeh prov., China: see OCHENG. **3** or **Shou-chang** (shō'jäng'), town, ⊙ Showchang co. (pop. 233,705), NE Pingyuan prov., China, on main road and 75 mi. SW of Tsinan, near Yellow R.; cotton weaving, straw matting; wax, wheat, peanuts. Until 1949 in Shantung prov.

Showhsien or **Shou-hsien** (shō'shyĕn'), town, ⊙ Showhsien co. (pop. 419,475), N Anhwei prov., China, 55 mi. NNW of Hofei, in lake dist.; rice, wheat, cotton, tobacco, beans. Until 1912, Showchow.

Showkija, Maltese Isls.: see XEWKIJA.

Showkwang or **Shou-kuang** (both: shō'gwäng'), town, ⊙ Showkwang co. (pop. 563,080), E central Shantung prov., China, 20 mi. NE of Yitu; agr. center (wheat, millet, kaoliang, peanuts).

Show Low, village (pop. c.300), Navajo co., E Ariz., 45 mi. S of Holbrook, in Sitgreaves Natl. Forest; alt. 6,500 ft.; livestock, agr.

Showning or **Shou-ning** (both: shō'nĭng'), town (pop. 13,775), ⊙ Showning co. (pop. 107,326), NW Fukien prov., China, on Chekiang line, 45 mi. NW of Siapu; rice, sweet potatoes, sugar cane, wheat.

Showyang or **Shou-yang** (both: shō'yäng'), town, ⊙ Showyang co. (pop. 156,764), E Shansi prov., China, 30 mi. E of Taiyüan and on railroad; coal mining.

Shoyna, Russian SFSR: see SHOINA.

Shpikov (shpēkôf'), village (1926 pop. 3,422), central Vinnitsa oblast, Ukrainian SSR, 30 mi. S of Vinnitsa; sugar refining.

Shpikulovo (shpēkōō'lŭvŭ), village (1939 pop. over 500), SE Tambov oblast, Russian SFSR, 27 mi. NW of Borisoglebsk; wheat.

Shpola (shpô'lŭ), city (1926 pop. 15,107), S Kiev oblast, Ukrainian SSR, 40 mi. SW of Cherkassy; sugar-refining center; flour and sawmills; light mfg.

Shramkovka (shräm′kŭfkŭ), village (1939 pop. over 2,000), W Poltava oblast, Ukrainian SSR, 17 mi. SW of Piryatin; sugar beets, wheat.

Shravan Belgola, India: see SRAVANA BELGOLA.

Shreve (shrēv), village (pop. 1,287), Wayne co., N central Ohio, 9 mi. SSW of Wooster, in gas- and oil-producing area.

Shreveport (shrēv′pôrt), city (pop. 127,206), ⊙ Caddo parish, NW La., on Red R., near Ark. and Texas lines, and 205 mi. NW of Baton Rouge; 2d-largest city in state, and center of rich oil and natural-gas area. Oil refineries, pipelines, railroad shops. Mfg. of cotton and cottonseed products; lumber; wood, metal, and paper articles; machinery, glass, chemicals, clay, concrete products. Seat of Centenary Col., a parochial col., a jr. col.; also has state fairgrounds. Cross L. (resort) and U.S. Barksdale Air Force Base are near by. Founded c.1834, inc. 1839. Important in antebellum period; made the Confederate capital 1863, it remained the last place over which the Confederate flag flew. Oil discovery in 1906 caused its rapid growth.

Shrewsbury (shrōōz′brē, shrōz′–), municipal borough (1931 pop. 32,372; 1951 census 44,926), ⊙ Shropshire, England, in center of co., on the Severn and 140 mi. NW of London; 52°42′N 2°45′W; anc. Saxon and Norman stronghold, protected by the river on 3 sides. Has a medieval atmosphere, with a number of old churches and bridges and oak-timbered houses. Has ruins of 11th-cent. castle and abbey. The public school, founded 1551 by Edward VI, was attended by Sir Philip Sydney, Fulke Greville, and Charles Darwin. Chief industries: mfg. of leather, electrical equipment, and pharmaceuticals. The battle of Shrewsbury (1403) was fought at near-by BATTLEFIELD.

Shrewsbury (shrōōz′bĕ″rē, –bŭrē). **1** Village (1940 pop. 2,845), Jefferson parish, SE La., a NW suburb of New Orleans. **2** Residential town (pop. 10,594), Worcester co., central Mass., just ENE of Worcester; agr.; leather products. Settled 1722, inc. 1727. Township bounded W by L. Quinsigamond. **3** City (pop. 3,382), St. Louis co., E Mo., W of St. Louis. **4** Borough (pop. 1,613), Monmouth co., E N.J., near head of Shrewsbury estuary, just S of Red Bank. Has 18th-cent. church. Settled 1665, inc. 1926. **5** Agr. borough (pop. 787), York co., S Pa., 14 mi. SSE of York. **6** Town (pop. 464), Rutland co., central Vt., 9 mi. SE of Rutland; dairy products; winter sports center. Includes Cuttingsville village (molybdenum deposits here).

Shrewsbury River, NE N.J., short stream entering navigable estuary (c.8 mi. long) which extends ENE from Oceanport (head of navigation) to junction with Navesink R. estuary at entrance to passage to Sandy Hook Bay (N). Monmouth Beach, Sea Bright, and other resorts are on sandy peninsula sheltering estuary from the Atlantic.

Shrewton, agr. village and parish (pop. 631), central Wiltshire, England, 10 mi. NW of Salisbury.

Shrigley, village (district pop. 629), E Co. Down, Northern Ireland, just NW of Killyleagh; tanning.

Shrigonda (shrē′gōndŭ), village (pop. 7,668), Ahmadnagar dist., E Bombay, India, 32 mi. S of Ahmadnagar; agr. market (sugar cane, millet, wheat).

Shrine Pass, Colo.: see GORE RANGE.

Shrivardhan, India: see SRIVARDHAN.

Shrivenham (shrĭ′vŭnŭm), village and parish (pop. 592), NW Berkshire, England, 6 mi. NE of Swindon; technical military col.

Shropshire (shrôp′shĭr, –shŭr) or **Salop** (să′lŭp), county (□ 1,337.2; 1931 pop. 244,156; 1951 census pop. 289,844), W England; ⊙ Shrewsbury. Bounded by Welsh cos. of Radnor, Montgomery, Denbigh, and Flint (W), Cheshire (N), Stafford (E), Worcester (SE), and Hereford (S). Drained by Severn R. and Tern R. Mountainous in S (Clee Hills), level in N. Dairying, cattle and sheep raising. Coal and limestone deposits. Chief industries are metallurgy (Wellington area), carpet weaving (Bridgnorth), and varied light industries. Other important towns are Oswestry, Wenlock, and Market Drayton. Many Roman remains, and vestiges of castles guarding Welsh border.

Shtepovka (shtyĕ′pŭfkŭ), village (1939 pop. over 2,000), S central Sumy oblast, Ukrainian SSR, 20 mi. WSW of Sumy; sugar beets.

Shtergres (shtyĭrgryĕs′), town (1939 pop. over 2,000), SW Voroshilovgrad oblast, Ukrainian SSR, in the Donbas, on Mius R. and 3 mi. S of Krasny Luch. Large coal-fed power station here.

Shterovka (shtyĕ′rŭfkŭ), town (1939 pop. over 500), S Voroshilovgrad oblast, Ukrainian SSR, in the Donbas, 12 mi. N of Krasny Luch; coal mines. Shterovka rail junction is 6 mi. S.

Shterovski Zavod Imeni Petrovskogo (–skē zŭvôt′ ē″mĭnyē′ pētrôf′skŭvŭ), town (1926 pop. 1,545), S Voroshilovgrad oblast, Ukrainian SSR, in the Donbas, on Mius R. and 3 mi. S of Krasny Luch; machinery works.

Shtimlye, Yugoslavia: see STIMLJE.

Shtip, Yugoslavia: see STIP.

Shtraklovo or **Shtrakl'ovo** (shtrŭklyô′vô), village (pop. 4,392), Ruse dist., NE Bulgaria, 8 mi. SSE of Ruse; sugar beets, sunflowers, truck.

Shu, China: see SZECHWAN.

Shu'aiba (shōō-ī′bŭ) or **Shaibah** (shī′bŭ), village, Basra prov., SE Iraq, 10 mi. SW of Basra, an oasis on the edge of the desert; military air base.

Shuang-, for Chinese names beginning thus and not found here: see under SHWANG-.

Shuang-ch'i, Formosa: see SHWANGKI.

Shuang-chiang, China: see SHWANGKIANG.

Shubany (shōōbä′nē), town (1939 pop. over 500) in Molotov dist. of Greater Baku, Azerbaijan SSR, 4 mi. W of Baku; oil wells (developed 1910–11).

Shubar, Egypt: see SHOBAR.

Shubar-Kuduk (shōōbär″-kōōdōōk′), oil town (1939 pop. over 500), central Aktyubinsk oblast, Kazakh SSR, on railroad and 80 mi. SSW of Aktyubinsk, in Emba oil fields. Until c.1940, Chubar-Kuduk.

Shubenacadie (shōō″bĕnă′kŭdē), village (pop. estimate 800), central N.S., on Shubenacadie R. and 20 mi. SSW of Truro; dairying and lumbering center. Center of Micmac Indian settlements of central N.S.

Shubenacadie Lake (7 mi. long, 2 mi. wide), S central N.S., 16 mi. N of Halifax. Drained by Shubenacadie R.

Shubenacadie River, central N.S., issues from Shubenacadie L. 16 mi. N of Halifax, flows 45 mi. N to Cobequid Bay 12 mi. WSW of Truro.

Shubert, village (pop. 295), Richardson co., SE Nebr., 13 mi. N of Falls City, near Missouri R.; fruit, grain.

Shubra el Kheima or **Shubra al-Khaymah** (both: shōōbrä′ ĕl-khā′mŭ), village (pop. 14,712), Qalyubiya prov., Lower Egypt, 4 mi. N of Cairo city center; cotton ginning, tarboosh mfg.; cotton, flax, cereals, fruits.

Shubra Khit (shōōbrä′ khēt′), village (pop. 5,609), Beheira prov., Lower Egypt, on Rosetta branch of the Nile and 14 mi. E of Damanhur; cotton ginning, wool weaving; cotton, rice, cereals.

Shubuta (shōōbōō′tŭ), town (pop. 782), Clarke co., E Miss., 35 mi. S of Meridian and on Chickasawhay R.; asphalt.

Shucheng or **Shu-ch'eng** (shōō′chŭng′), town, ⊙ Shucheng co. (pop. 488,747), N Anhwei prov., China, 30 mi. SW of Hofei; rice, cotton, lacquer, hemp, tung oil.

Shuchi (shōō′chē), town (pop. 3,182), Kyoto prefecture, S Honshu, Japan, 22 mi. NW of Kyoto, in agr. area (rice, wheat); raw silk, charcoal.

Shufu, China: see KASHGAR.

Shugnan (shōōgnän′), village (1939 pop. over 500), SW Gorno-Badakhshan Autonomous oblast, Tadzhik SSR, in the Pamir, on Gunt R. and 3 mi. E of Khorog; wheat, cattle. Formerly Verkhni Khorog. The Shugnan (Shighnan or Shignan) area passed in 1895 from Afghanistan to Russia.

Shugozero (shōōg′ô″zyĭrŭ), village, E Leningrad oblast, Russian SFSR, 31 mi. NE of Tikhvin; coarse grain.

Shugurovo (shōōgōō′rŭvŭ), village (1932 pop. estimate 2,180), SE Tatar Autonomous SSR, Russian SFSR, near Sheshma R., 28 mi. W of Bugulma; petroleum extracting, asphalt mining. Deve oped, after Second World War, as center of upper Sheshma R. valley petroleum and asphalt region.

Shuha (shōōhä′), village (pop. 7,409), Daqahliya prov., Lower Egypt, 6 mi. E of Mansura; cotton, cereals.

Shuhada, El, Esh Shuhada', or **Al-Shuhada'** (all: ĕsh-shōōhădä′), village (pop. 5,077), Minufiya prov., Lower Egypt, on railroad and 7 mi. WNW of Shibin el Kom; cereals, cotton, flax.

Shuhair, Shuhayr, or **Shuheir,** Aden: see SHIHEIR.

Shuichang, China: see JUICHANG.

Shuicheng or **Shui-ch'eng** (shwā′chŭng′), town (pop. 3,177), ⊙ Shuicheng co. (pop. 150,883), W Kweichow prov., China, 35 mi. ESE of Weining and on Wu R. (upper course of Kien R.); timber, grain. Important iron and coal mines, lead and salt deposits, asbestos quarry near by.

Shui-chi, China: see SHUIKI.

Shuifeng, Korea: see SUPUNG.

Shuiki or **Shui-chi** (both: shwā′jē′), town (pop. 10,455), ⊙ Shuiki co. (pop. 60,027), N Fukien prov., China, 25 mi. N of Kienow; rice, sweet potatoes.

Shuikin, China: see JUIKIN.

Shuikow or **Shui-k'ou** (both: shwā′kō′), town, E central Fukien prov., China, 40 mi. NW of Foochow, and on Min R. at mouth of Kutien R.; head of regular Min R. navigation.

Shuikowshan or **Shui-k'ou-shan** (both: –shān), hill in S Hunan prov., China, 11 mi. NE of Changning, 30 mi. S of Hengyang; major lead-zinc mining center, producing silver as a by-product. Linked by short mining railroad with landing on Siang R.

Shuishio Island (shōōēshēō′), Jap. *Suisho-shima* (sōōēshō′-shĭmŭ), southernmost island of lesser Kurile Isls. chain, Russian SFSR; separated from Cape Noshappu, Hokkaido, Japan, by 5-mi.-wide Goyomai Strait; 43°26′N 145°55′E; 5 mi. long, 3.5 mi. wide.

Shuiskoye or **Shuyskoye** (shōō′ēskŭyŭ), village (1939 pop. over 500), S Vologda oblast, Russian SFSR, on Sukhona R. and 40 mi. ENE of Vologda; dairying.

Shuitau (shwā′tou′), town, Hong Kong colony, in the New Territories, 11 mi. NNW of Kowloon; vegetables, rice, peanuts, sugar cane.

Shujabad (shōōjäbäd′), town (pop. 8,206), Multan dist., S Punjab, W Pakistan, 23 mi. SSW of Multan; wheat, millet, rice; cotton ginning. Also spelled Shujaabad.

Shujalpur (shōōjäl′pōōr), town (pop. 7,878), central Madhya Bharat, India, 27 mi. E of Shajapur; local market for cotton, wheat, millet; cotton ginning. Near by is cenotaph of Ranoji Sindhia (d. 1745), founder of house of Gwalior.

Shukkoko, Formosa: see CHUKWANGKENG.

Shuksan, Mount (shōōk′sŭn), peak (9,038 ft.), N Wash., in Cascade Range, in Mt. Baker Natl. Forest, c.40 mi. ENE of Bellingham.

Shulan (shōō′län′), town, ⊙ Shulan co. (pop. 295,633), W central Kirin prov., Manchuria, 38 mi. NNE of Kirin, near railroad; gold deposits; coal and molybdenum mining; brick- and tilemaking plant. Called Chaoyangchwan until 1910.

Shulaps Peak (shōō′lăps) (9,450 ft.), S B.C., in Coast Mts., 120 mi. NNE of Vancouver.

Shulavery, Georgian SSR: see SHAUMYANI.

Shuleh, town, China: see YANGI SHAHR.

Shuleh River or **Sulo River** (both: sōō′lŭ′), Chinese *Su-lo Ho* (hŭ′), Mongolian *Bulungir* or *Bulunzir* (both: bōōlōōnjĭr′), river in NW Kansu prov., China, rises in the Nan Shan, flows over 350 mi. N and W, past Yümen and Ansi, to the salt lake Khara Nor N of Tunhwang.

Shulgino or **Shul'gino** (shōōl′gĭnŭ), village (1939 pop. over 500), SW Tambov oblast, Russian SFSR, 40 mi. SW of Tambov; sugar beets.

Shullsburg, city (pop. 1,306), Lafayette co., S Wis., on a branch of Galena R. and 23 mi. ENE of Dubuque (Iowa), in dairy-farming area; cheese; zinc mines. Inc. 1889.

Shulmak, Tadzhik SSR: see NOVABAD.

Shulu (shōō′lōō′), town, ⊙ Shulu co. (pop. 370,817), SW Hopeh prov., China, 45 mi. ESE of Shihkiachwang; cotton, rice, beans, wheat.

Shumadiya, region, Yugoslavia: see SUMADIJA.

Shumagin Islands (shōō′mŭgĭn), SW Alaska, group of c.20 isls. and islets in N Pacific off S coast of Alaska Peninsula; 54°54′–55°20′N 159°15′–160°45′W. Largest isls. are Unga, Popof, and Nagai. Covered by low scrub elder and willow; mild, damp climate. Cod fishing and canning. Discovered 1741 by Vitus Bering.

Shumailiya, Trucial Oman: see FUJAIRA.

Shumanai or **Shumanay** (both: shōō′mŭnī), village (1950 pop. over 500), Kara-Kalpak Autonomous SSR, Uzbek SSR, 20 mi. NW of Khodzheili, in cotton and wheat area, irrigated in 1940s. Until 1950 called Taza-Bazar.

Shumatovo, Russian SFSR: see SOVETSKOYE, Chuvash Autonomous SSR.

Shumbat (shōōm′bät) or **Shumbati** (shōōm′bätē), village (1930 pop. 336), E central Albania, 7 mi. NW of Peshkopi.

Shumchün (shōōm′chün′), Mandarin *Shen-ch'uan* (shŭn′chwän′), town, S Kwangtung prov., China, on Hongkong border, 15 mi. N of Kowloon and on railroad to Canton; customs and trading post.

Shume, Tanganyika: see MKUMBARA.

Shumen, Bulgaria: see KOLAROVGRAD.

Shumerlya (shōōmĭrlyä′), city (1939 pop. over 10,000), W Chuvash Autonomous SSR, Russian SFSR, on Sura R., on railroad and 55 mi. SW of Cheboksary, in woodland; lumber-milling center (mainly oak); woodworking, tannin extracting. Developed in 1930s; became city in 1937.

Shumikha (shōōmē′khŭ), city (1948 pop. over 10,000), W Kurgan oblast, Russian SFSR, on Trans-Siberian RR and 80 mi. W of Kurgan; agr. center (wheat, butter, flax, poultry); processing plants. Became city in 1944.

Shumilino (shōōmĭlyē′nŭ), town (1926 pop. 1,042), NW Vitebsk oblast, Belorussian SSR, 25 mi. NW of Vitebsk; food products, flax.

Shumkai (sŭm′kī′), Mandarin *Ts'en-ch'i* (tsŭn′-chē′), town, ⊙ Shumkai co. (pop. 211,159), SE Kwangsi prov., China, near Kwangtung line, 45 mi. SW of Wuchow; litchi nuts, rice, wheat, beans, millet.

Shumla, Bulgaria: see KOLAROVGRAD.

Shumna, Bulgaria: see KOLAROVGRAD.

Shumshu Island (shōōm′shōō), Jap. *Shimushu-to* (shēmōōshōō-tō′) (□ 89), one of the Kurile Isls. group, Russian SFSR; separated from Cape Lopatka (S end of Kamchatka Peninsula) by First Kurile Strait, from Paramushir Isl. by Second Kurile Strait; 50°45′N 156°22′E; 18 mi. long, 12 mi. wide. Rises to 620 ft. Main village, Baikovo, on SW shore.

Shumski or **Shumskiy** (shōōm′skē), town (1943 pop. over 500), SW Irkutsk oblast, Russian SFSR, 5 mi. SE of Nizhneudinsk and on Trans-Siberian RR.

Shumskoye (shōōm′skŭyŭ), Pol. *Szumsk* (shōōmsk), village (1931 pop. 2,345), NE Ternopol oblast, Ukrainian SSR, on right tributary of Goryn R. and 18 mi. E of Kremenets; flour milling, distilling, brick mfg. Has ruins of 16th-cent. castle. An old settlement, assaulted by Tatars in 12th cent.; became ⊙ independent principality in 13th cent.; passed to Poland (14th cent.). Ceded to Russia (1795); reverted to Poland (1919); ceded to USSR in 1945.

Shumway (shŭm′wā), village (pop. 248), Effingham co., SE central Ill., 7 mi. NW of Effingham, in agr. area.

Shumyachi (sho͝omyä′chē), village (1926 pop. 3,258), SW Smolensk oblast, Russian SFSR, 18 mi. WSW of Roslavl; flax processing.

Shuna (sho͞o′nu̇), island (pop. 12) of the Inner Hebrides, Argyll, Scotland, bet. Luing and the mainland, 15 mi. SSW of Oban; 2 mi. long, 1 mi. wide; rises to 296 ft.

Shuna, El, Esh Shuna, or **Al-Shunah** (all: ĕsh-sho͞o′nu̇), town (pop. c.1,000), N central Jordan, on main Amman-Jerusalem road and 18 mi. WSW of Amman, just N of Dead Sea; fire-clay quarries. Site of royal winter palace. Also spelled Shuneh.

Shunan (sho͝on′än′), Mandarin *Ch′un-an* (cho͝on′-än′), town (pop. 6,351), ⊙ Shunan co. (pop. 238,737), W Chekiang prov., China, near Anhwei line, 34 mi. W of Kienteh and on Sinan R. (tributary of Tsientang R.); tea-growing center; timber, ramie, rice.

Shunchang or **Shun-ch′ang** (sho͝on′chäng′), town (pop. 4,394), ⊙ Shunchang co. (pop. 61,025), NW Fukien prov., China, 28 mi. WNW of Nanping and on Min R.; rice, sugar cane, sweet potatoes, wheat.

Shuneh, Jordan: see SHUNA, EL.

Shunga or **Shun′ga** (sho͝on′yu̇gŭ), village, S central Karelo-Finnish SSR, on L. Onega, 25 mi. SE of Medvezhyegorsk; grain. Schungite, a Silurian type of anthracite, found here.

Shungnak (shu̇ng′năk), village (pop. 141), NW Alaska, on Kobuk R.; 66°54′N 156°55′W; placer gold mining. Has Friends mission, Federal school for natives; airfield.

Shungopovi or **Shungopavy** (both: shu̇ng-ō′pä″vē″, shu̇ng-ō′pu̇vē), Indian pueblo, NE Ariz., on high mesa (alt. c.6,560 ft.), 55 mi. N of Winslow, in Hopi Indian Reservation. Sometimes Chimopavy (shu̇mō′pä″vē″).

Shunhwa or **Hsün-hua** (both: shün′hwä′), town, ⊙ Shunhwa co. (pop. 32,602), E Tsinghai prov., China, 60 mi. SE of Sining and on Yellow R.; cattle raising; agr. products. Until 1928 in Kansu prov.

Shun-i, China: see SHUNYI.

Shuni, Egypt: see SHONI.

Shunkengshan (sho͝on′gŭng′shän′), town, N Anhwei prov., China, near Hwai R., 30 mi. SW of Pengpu, at foot of the peak Shunkeng Shan; coal-mining center.

Shunking, China: see NANCHUNG.

Shunning (sho͝on′nĭng′), town, ⊙ Shunning co. (pop. 130,703), W Yunnan prov., China, 80 mi. SSW of Tali; alt. 5,800 ft.; tea-growing center; cotton textiles; timber, rice, millet, beans. Lead and iron mines near by.

Shunsen, Korea: see CHUNCHON.

Shuntak (so͝on′dŭk′), Mandarin *Shunte* (sho͝on′dŭ′), town (pop. 22,975), ⊙ Shuntak co. (pop. 623,196), S Kwangtung prov., China, in Canton R. delta, 20 mi. S of Canton; silk-raising center; rice; fisheries.

Shunteh, China: see SINGTAI.

Shunyi or **Shun-i** (sho͝on′yē′), town, ⊙ Shunyi co. (pop. 171,541), N Hopeh prov., China, 20 mi. NE of Peking and on railroad; cotton, wheat, kaoliang, beans.

Shuo-hsien, China: see SHOHSIEN.

Shuotsu, Korea: see CHUURONJANG.

Shuotsuonjo, Korea: see CHUURONJANG.

Shupiyan or **Shopian** (sho͞opē′ŭn), town (pop. 4,359), Anantnag dist., SW central Kashmir, in foothills of Pir Panjal Range, 25 mi. S of Srinagar; rice, corn, oilseeds, wheat.

Shuqra or **Shuqrah** (sho͝o′kru̇), town (pop. 5,000), ⊙ Fadhli sultanate, Western Aden Protectorate, port on Gulf of Aden, 60 mi. NE of Aden; trading center on Aden-Lodar route; fishing industry; exports ambergris, coffee, millet, ghee. Saltworks (E). Town consists of sultan's palace (E) and fishing and commercial quarter (W). Airfield.

Shuqualak (sho͝o′gu̇lŏk), town (pop. 714), Noxubee co., E Miss., 9 mi. S of Macon; lumber milling. Annual bird-dog trials held here.

Shur, river, Iran: see SHUR RIVER.

Shura or **Shurah** (sho͝o′ru̇), town, Mosul prov., N Iraq, on railroad and 25 mi. SSE of Mosul; barley, wheat, fruit. Oil deposits near by. Sometimes spelled Shora.

Shurab (sho͝oräp′), town (1932 pop. estimate 3,000), E Leninabad oblast, Tadzhik SSR, on rail spur and 17 mi. SSE of Kanibadam; coal mining.

Shuragat (sho͝orŭgät′), village (1939 pop. over 500), N Dagestan, Russian SFSR, 14 mi. W of Khasavyurt; cotton, wheat. Until 1944 (in Chechen-Ingush Autonomous SSR), called Alleroi.

Shurala (sho͝orŭlä′), village (1926 pop. 2,378), SW central Sverdlovsk oblast, Russian SFSR, on Neiva R. and 4 mi. S of Nevyansk; rail junction; metalworks; truck gardening. Former site (until c.1930) of ironworks called Shuralinski Zavod.

Shurchi (sho͝orchē′), village (1939 pop. over 500), E central Surkhan-Darya oblast, Uzbek SSR, on railroad and 55 mi. NNE of Termez; cotton, cattle; metalworks.

Shuri (sho͞o′rē), city (1950 pop. 20,006), on Okinawa of Okinawa Isls., in Ryukyu Isls., 3 mi. ENE of Naha; mfg. and educational center; makes Panama hats. Teachers col. Site of feudal castle. Formerly anc. ⊙ Ryukyus; ⊙ (1879–1881) of Okinawa prefecture, preceding Naha.

Shurma (sho͝or′mu̇), village (1939 pop. over 2,000), SE Kirov oblast, Russian SFSR, on Vyatka R. (landing) and 33 mi., NNW of Malmyzh; sawmilling, woodworking.

Shuroabad (sho͞o″ru̇ŭbät′), village (1939 pop. over 2,000), SE Kulyab oblast, Tadzhik SSR, 17 mi. ESE of Kulyab; wheat, truck produce.

Shur River (sho͞or′), N Iran, rises in 2 branches joining S of Kazvin, flows 100 mi. SE to Namak salt lake.

Shuruppak (sho͝oro͝o′păk), anc. Sumerian city, S Mesopotamia, whose site (modern Fara) is in SE central Iraq, in Diwaniya prov., 60 mi. NW of Nasiriya, 35 mi. W of site of Lagash. Excavations.

Shuryshkary (sho͝orĭshkä′rē), village, SW Yamal-Nenets Natl. Okrug, Tyumen oblast, Russian SFSR, on arm of Ob R. and 50 mi. SSW of Salekhard; fish cannery.

Shusf (sho͞osf), town, Ninth Prov., in Khurasan, E Iran, 90 mi. SE of Birjand and on highway to Zahidan; orchards (peaches, grapes). Also spelled Shusp.

Shush, Iran: see SUSA.

Shusha (sho͞oshä′), city (1926 pop. 5,104), central Nagorno-Karabakh Autonomous Oblast, Azerbaijan SSR, on E slope of the Lesser Caucasus, 5 mi. S of Stepanakert; alt. over 5,000 ft. Silk spinning, rug mfg. Flourished as ⊙ Karabakh khanate, conquered 1805 by Russians. Pop. once exceeded 40,000, mainly Armenians, until 1920, when the Armenians were massacred by Moslem mountaineers and nearly entire city was destroyed. Has been replaced as economic center by new city of Stepanakert.

Shushal (sho͞oshäl′), village, Ladakh dist., E Kashmir, in Ladakh Range (alt. 14,230 ft.), near Tibet border, 70 mi. SE of Leh; trade route center. Sometimes called Chushul.

Shushan, Iran: see SUSA.

Shushanna Junction, Alaska: see McCARTHY.

Shushartie (sho͞oshär′tē), village, SW B.C., on extreme N Vancouver Isl., on Queen Charlotte Strait, 45 mi. WNW of Alert Bay; lumbering.

Shushenskoye (sho͞o′shĭnskŭyu̇), village (1926 pop. 3,104), S Krasnoyarsk Territory, Russian SFSR, on Yenisei R. and 28 mi. SSE of Minusinsk, in agr. area. Lenin exiled here, 1897–1900.

Shushong (sho͞o′shông), village (pop. 6,957), Ngwato dist., E Bechuanaland Protectorate, 40 mi. SSW of Serowe, in low Shushong Hills. Hq. Bamangwato Chief Khama until shortly after proclamation of British protectorate, when hq. was moved to Old Palapye. Sometimes Shoshong or Mangwato.

Shushtalep, Russian SFSR: see OSINNIKI.

Shushtar (sho͞oshtär′) or **Shushter** (–tĕr′), town (1940 pop. 23,654), Sixth Prov., in Khuzistan, SW Iran, 34 mi. SE of Dizful and 50 mi. NNE of Ahwaz, and on Karun R., where river divides into 2 arms; agr. trade center; grain, onions, garlic; cotton rugs, canvas, and glassware. Pop. is largely Arab and Iranian. Has imposing citadel on rock; and Valerian's Bridge across Karun R., just SW. Site of projected dam on Karun R. Dating from 3d cent. A.D., the town flourished as provincial center under the Safavids (16th–18th cent.) until eclipsed by Dizful. Sometimes spelled Shustar or Shuster.

Shushu, Formosa: see TSITSI.

Shushui, Japan: see SHISUI.

Shusp, Iran: see SHUSF.

Shustar or **Shuster,** Iran: see SHUSHTAR.

Shuswap Lake (sho͞os′wŏp) (□ 123), S B.C., 35 mi. W of Revelstoke; 87 mi. long, including Seymour and Anstey arms (NE) and Salmon Arm (S); 1–3 mi. wide. Receives Shuswap R. (SE); drained W by South Thompson R.

Shuswap River, S B.C., rises in Selkirk Mts. SW of Revelstoke, flows in a wide arc SSE and then N to Mabel L., thence W to Enderby, where it turns N, through Mara L., to Shuswap L. at Sicamous; 160 mi. long.

Shutb, Egypt: see SHOTB.

Shutesbury, town (pop. 213), Franklin co., W central Mass., 14 mi. NE of Northampton, near Quabbin Reservoir; lumber.

Shuttington, town and parish (pop. 588), N Warwick, England, 3 mi. ENE of Tamworth; coal mining. Has remains of priory founded 1159.

Shuttleworth, England: see WALMERSLEY CUM SHUTTLEWORTH.

Shuvelyany (sho͞ovĭlyä′nē), town (1939 pop. over 500) in Azizbekov dist. of Greater Baku, Azerbaijan SSR, on E Apsheron Peninsula, 20 mi. NE of Baku; seaside resort; vineyards.

Shuwaikh, Bandar Shuwaikh, or **Bandar Shuwaykh** (băndär′ sho͞owīkh′), SW suburb and port of Kuwait town, on Kuwait Bay of Persian Gulf; anchorage. Linked by pipe line with Ahmadi oil tank farm.

Shuwamiya (sho͞owămē′yu̇), **Shauwamiya,** or **Shawwamiyah** (both: shou–), cape on Kuria Muria Bay of Arabian Sea, on SE Oman coast; 17°55′N 55°45′E. Airfield.

Shwangki or **Shuang-ch′i** (both: shwäng′chē), Jap. *Sokei* (sō′kā), village (1935 pop. 2,519), N Formosa, 10 mi. SE of Keelung and on railroad; rice milling; sweet potatoes, livestock. Wutankeng gold mine is 3 mi. N.

Shuya (sho͞o′yŭ), city (1939 pop. 57,950), S central Ivanovo oblast, Russian SFSR, on Teza R. and 19 mi. SE of Ivanovo; rail junction; cotton-milling center; mfg. (sheepskins, textile machinery). Teachers col. City dates from late 14th cent.; chartered 1539.

Shuyang (sho͞o′yäng′), town (1935 pop. 54,839), ⊙ Shuyang co. (1946 pop. 659,751), N Kiangsu prov., China, 40 mi. NNW of Hwaiyin; agr. center (wheat, beans, corn, cotton).

Shuya River, Finnish *Suojujoki* (so͞o′ōyo͞oyô″kē), in S Karelo-Finnish SSR, rises in lake Suoyarvi, flows 145 mi. SE and E to L. Onega N of Petrozavodsk; low shores. Timber floating.

Shuyskoye, Russian SFSR: see SHUISKOYE.

Shuzan (sho͞ozä′), town (pop. 2,141), Kyoto prefecture, S Honshu, Japan, 13 mi. NW of Kyoto; rice, raw silk, lumber.

Shuzenji (sho͞ozān′jē), town (pop. 7,893), Shizuoka prefecture, central Honshu, Japan, on N central Izu Peninsula, 9 mi. SE of Numazu; hot-springs resort; mushrooms; makes camellia oil, corn starch; paper milling.

Shvartsevskiy or **Shvartsevskiy** (shvär′tsvĭfskē), town (1939 pop. over 500), E Tula oblast, Russian SFSR, near railroad (Obolenskoye station), 17 mi. ESE of Tula, in Moscow Basin; lignite mining, metalworking.

Shvenchenelyai, Lithuania: see SVENCIONELIAI.

Shvenchenis, Lithuania: see SVENCIONYS.

Shventoji, Lithuania: see SVENTOJI.

Shventoyi River, Lithuania: see SVENTOJI RIVER.

Shwangcheng or **Shuang-ch′eng** (both: shwäng′-chŭng′), town, ⊙ Shwangcheng co. (pop. 578,025), W Sungkiang prov., Manchuria, on railroad and 32 mi. SW of Harbin, near Lalin R. (Kirin line); lumbering center.

Shwangkiang or **Shuang-chiang** (both: shwäng′-jyäng′), town, ⊙ Shwangkiang co. (pop. 37,517), SW Yunnan prov., China, 120 mi. SSE of Paoshan, in mtn. region; cotton textiles; rice, millet, beans.

Shwangliao or **Shuang-liao** (both: shwäng′lyou′), town ⊙ Shwangliao co. (pop. 191,910), N Liaosi prov., Manchuria, 50 mi. NW of Szeping, and on W branch of Liao R. (shallow-draught navigation head) near confluence with E branch; rail junction, and outlet for Mongolian products; horse and cattle market; hides, skins, soybeans, licorice. Originally known as Chengkiatun, it was later called Liao-yüan, until 1949, when the co. absorbed Shwangshan, 25 mi. NE. Was ⊙ Liaopeh prov. (1946–49).

Shwangliu or **Shuang-liu** (both: shwäng′lyō′), town (pop. 8,320), ⊙ Shwangliu co. (pop. 153,933), W Szechwan prov., China, 10 mi. SW of Chengtu, on Chengtu plain; rice, wheat, rapeseed, potatoes, beans.

Shwangliuchen, Manchuria: see TAONAN.

Shwangmiaotze, Manchuria: see LANSI.

Shwangpo or **Shuang-po** (both: shwäng′bŭ′), town (pop. 3,160), ⊙ Shwangpo co. (pop. 44,658), central Yunnan prov., China, 13 mi. S of Tsuyung, in mtn. region; cotton textiles; rice, wheat, millet, beans. Until 1913, Nanan; called Mochu, 1913–29.

Shwangshan, Manchuria: see SHWANGLIAO.

Shwangtaitze, Manchuria: see PANSHAN.

Shwangyang or **Shuang-yang** (both: shwäng′yäng′), town, ⊙ Shwangyang co. (pop. 258,289), SW Kirin prov., Manchuria, 30 mi. SE of Changchun; coal, kaolin deposits; beans, rye, barley, millet, corn.

Shwebo (shwā′bō), district (□ 5,735; 1941 pop. 496,185), Sagaing div., Upper Burma; ⊙ Shwebo. Located W of Irrawaddy R., in dry zone (annual rainfall 34 in.), it is largely lowland drained by Mu R. and irrigated by Yeu and Shwebo canals. Agr.: rice, cotton, corn, sesame. Pottery mfg.; salt extraction. Served by railroads from Mandalay to Myitkyina and Yeu and by Irrawaddy steamers. Pop. is 95% Burmese.

Shwebo, town (pop. 11,286), ⊙ Shwebo dist., Upper Burma, on railroad and 50 mi. NNW of Mandalay, on Shwebo irrigation canal (opened 1906; fed by Mu R.); army cantonment, airfield. Ruins of old city wall and pagodas. The home of Alaungpaya, it was temporary ⊙ (1753–63) of Ava kingdom. In Second World War, captured (1945) by Br. troops.

Shwedaung (shwā′doung), town (pop. 8,408), Prome dist., Lower Burma, on left bank of Irrawaddy R. and 8 mi. S of Prome; silk industry; gold washing in Irrawaddy R.

Shwegon (shwāgo͞on′), village, Thaton dist., Lower Burma, in Tenasserim, on left bank of Salween R. (head of regular navigation) and 45 mi. N of Moulmein; head of road to Hlaingbwe. Also spelled Shwegun or Shwegoon.

Shwegu (shwā-go͞o′), village, Bhamo dist., Kachin State, Upper Burma, on left bank of Irrawaddy R. and 30 mi. WSW of Bhamo; pottery.

Shwegun, Burma: see SHWEGON.

Shwegyin (shwā′jĭn), town (pop. 5,876), Toungoo dist., Lower Burma, on left bank of Sittang R. and 50 mi. NE of Pegu. Placer mining (gold) on W edge of forested area.

Shweli River (shwā′lē), Chinese *Juili* (rwā′lē′), left tributary of the Irrawaddy, in China and Burma, rises as Lungchwan R. in westernmost Yunnan prov. (China) in Kaolikung Mts., flows 400 mi. S and SW, along N edge of the Shan plateau, to the Irrawaddy at Inywa.

Shwenyaung (shwā-nyoun′), village, Yawnghwe state, Southern Shan State, Upper Burma, 5 mi. W of Taunggyi; rail terminus of S Shan State branch (completed 1928) of Burmese rail system. Serves Taunggyi and Yawnghwe.

Shyok River (shyōk), in Ladakh dist., central Kashmir, rises (as Chip Chap R.) in Aghil-Karakoram Range, at 35°17'N 78°26'E; flows W, S, making a great bend at SE end of the main Karakoram, and NW past Khapalu to Indus R. 17 mi. ESE of Skardu; c.340 mi. long. Separates Kailas-Karakoram Range (N) from Ladakh Range (S). Disastrous floods caused periodically by damming of river by a glacier. Main tributary, Nubra R. (right).

Si, lake, China: see WEST LAKE.

Si, river, China: see WEST RIVER.

Sia, China: see TANGUT.

Siachen Glacier (syä'chĕn), one of longest mtn. glaciers of the world, in Karakoram mtn. system, N Kashmir, bet. main range (E) and Kailas-Karakoram Range (W); c.45 mi. long NNW-SSE, bet. 35°40'N 76°45'E and 35°10'N 77°15'E. At S end, gives rise to c.50-mi.-long Nubra R., right tributary of Shyok R.

Siadehan, Iran: see TAKISTAN.

Siahan Range (syä'hän), hill system (5,000 ft. average height) in W Baluchistan, W Pakistan; from Iran border extends c.170 mi. ENE, along Kharan-Makran state border, merging with N end of Central Makran Range; c.20 mi. wide. Rugged and abrupt; rises to c.6,770 ft. in NE peak. Watered mainly by tributaries of Rakhshan R. Koh-i-Sabz is S spur.

Siah Koh or **Siah Kuh** (sē'ä kō') [Pashto,=black mountain]. **1** SW outlier of the Hindu Kush, in W Afghanistan; one of the Firoz Koh ranges; rises to c.12,000 ft. 80 mi. ENE of Shindand. Iron deposits. **2** Mountain (4,262 ft.) on Iran-Afghanistan line, at N edge of Seistan depression; 31°29'N 60°51'E.

Siaho or **Hsia-ho** (both: shyä'hŭ'), town, ⊙ Siaho co. (pop. 46,967), SE Kansu prov., China, near Tsinghai border, 90 mi. SW of Lanchow; Lamaist center; monastery. Cattle and sheep raising; exports wool. Until 1928 called Labrang.

Siahsien or **Hsia-hsien** (both: shyä'shyĕn'), town, ⊙ Siahsien co. (pop. 127,178), SW Shansi prov., China, 12 mi. NE of Anyi, near railroad; wheat, corn, millet. Home of Hsia dynasty (2205–1766 B.C.) and its original residence until 2188 B.C.

Siakiang or **Hsia-chiang** (both: shyä'jyäng'), town (pop. 4,039), ⊙ Siakiang co. (pop. 33,507), W central Kiangsi prov., China, 30 mi. NNE of Kian and on Kan R.; rice, wheat, beans, cotton. Anthracite and iron mines.

Siakiutai, Manchuria: see KIUTAI.

Siakwan or **Hsia-kuan** (both: shyä'gwän'). **1** Suburb, Kiangsu prov., China: see NANKING. **2** Town, W Yunnan prov., China, on Burma Road and 10 mi. SE of Tali, on SW shore of the lake Erh Hai; commercial center.

Sialkot (syäl'kōt), dist. (□ 2,063; 1951 pop. 1,480,-000), Punjab, W Pakistan; ⊙ Sialkot. In Rechna Doab; bounded NW by Chenab R., SE by Ravi R. and Indian Punjab. Fairly level tract, irrigated W by Upper Chenab Canal. Agr. (wheat, corn, millet, sugar cane); metalwork; hand-loom weaving. Chief towns: Sialkot, Daska, Narowal, Pasrur. Original dist. (□ 1,576; 1941 pop. 1,190,497) enlarged by inc. (1947) of W portion of Gurdaspur dist. of former Br. Punjab prov. Formerly spelled Sealkote.

Sialkot, city (1951 pop., with N cantonment area, 152,000), ⊙ Sialkot dist., E Punjab, W Pakistan, 65 mi. NNE of Lahore. Rail junction; major trade and industrial center; agr. depot (wheat, rice, millet, sugar cane). Noted for mfg. of surgical instruments and sports goods (cricket, tennis, hockey, soccer, etc.); engineering and metalworks; cotton ginning, hand-loom weaving, rice and flour milling, tanning, food processing, mfg. of steel tools and boxes, hospital furniture, musical instruments, bicycle parts, tents, carpets, toothbrushes, slates, ink, leather goods. Has col. Shrine of Guru Nanak, founder of Sikhism, here. Site of fortress built (1181) by Mohammed of Ghor. Formerly spelled Sealkote.

Siam: see THAILAND.

Siam, Gulf of (sīăm'), arm of South China Sea separating Malay Peninsula (SW) from Indochina (NE) bet. Cape Pattani and Point Camau; 300–350 mi. wide, 450 mi. long. Borders W and N on Thailand, and NE on Cambodia and Cochin China (S Vietnam). At the head, it receives the Chao Phraya R. (Mae Nam or Menam) below Bangkok, its leading port. Other harbors are Pattani, Songkhla, Pak Phanang (port of Nakhon Sithammarat), and Chanthaburi (in Thailand), Ream, Kampot, and Kep (in Cambodia), and Rachgia (in S Vietnam).

Sian or **Hsi-an** (both: sē'än', Chinese shē'än'). **1** City (1938 pop. 32,475), ⊙, but independent of, Sian co. (1946 pop. 391,990), N Liaotung prov., Manchuria, China, 50 mi. ESE of Szeping and on railroad; anthracite mining; basalt quarry; brick and tile plant. Briefly called Peifeng, 1947–49. **2** City (1947 pop. 502,988), ⊙ Shensi prov., NW China, in Wei R. valley, 600 mi. SW of Peking, and on Lunghai RR; 34°16'N 108°54'E. Trading and cultural center; cotton and wool weaving, flour milling, tanning, printing, mfg. of glassware and chemicals. Exports wheat, rice, tea, tobacco, cereals, silk, porcelain. Seat of Northwestern univ., and col. of engineering. Situated 10 mi. S of Wei R. and 80 mi. from Yellow R., Sian has a major airport and is the hub of overland trade routes. One of China's oldest capitals, the city is built in a walled rectangle (2.5 mi. by 1.5 mi.), with small walled suburbs adjoining outside the 4 gates. Near by (S) is the Peilin mus. of stone tablets, including an 8th-cent. Nestorian inscription. Succeeding SIENYANG as ⊙ China under the Han dynasty (206 B.C.-A.D. 220), the city (just NW of modern site) was originally called Changan. It continued intermittently as residence of later dynasties, flourishing as the W capital [Chinese *Siking*] under the Tang dynasty (618–906). From this period date the important remains of foreign religious colonies (Mazdean, Manichaean, Nestorian). It was visited (13th cent.) by Marco Polo, who called it Quengianfu. The name Sian dates from the Ming dynasty. It was besieged (1868–70) during the Moslem rebellion, and was an imperial refuge (1900–02) following the Boxer Rebellion. Sian was the scene of the kidnapping (1936) of Chiang Kai-shek by Chang Hsueh-liang. It remained in Free China during the Second World War, and passed in 1949 to Communist control. Known as Sian also under the Manchu dynasty, it became in 1913 ⊙ CHANGAN co. and assumed the name of Changan. City was separated 1932 from the co., becoming an independent municipality called Siking (1932–43) and then Sian (since 1943). Formerly spelled Singan.

Siana, India: see SIYANA.

Siang, province, China: see HUNAN.

Siang. **1** River, Hunan prov., China: see SIANG RIVER. **2** River, Kwangsi prov., China: see YÜ RIVER.

Siangcheng or **Hsiang-ch'eng** (both: shyäng'chŭng'), town, ⊙ Siangcheng co. (pop. 342,188), E Honan prov., China, on Anhwei line, 50 mi. SE of Yencheng; cotton weaving, tobacco processing; wheat, kaoliang.

Siangchow, China: see SIANGHSIEN.

Siangho or **Hsiang-ho** (both: shyäng'hŭ'), town, ⊙ Siangho co. (pop. 143,727), N Hopeh prov., China, 35 mi. ESE of Peking, near Grand Canal; cotton, fruit, grain.

Sianghsien or **Hsiang-hsien** (both: shyäng'shyĕn'), town, ⊙ Sianghsien co. (pop. 132,273), E central Kwangsi prov., China, 30 mi. SE of Liuchow and on Liu R.; grain, vegetable oil, sugar cane. Until 1912 called Siangchow.

Sianghwaling, China: see LINWU.

Siang Kiang, China: see SIANG RIVER.

Siangkow, China: see WULUNG.

Siangling or **Hsiang-ling** (both: shyäng'lĭng'), town, ⊙ Siangling co. (pop. 78,018), S Shansi prov., China, 8 mi. SW of Linfen, across Fen R.; cotton weaving, paper mfg., flour milling; winegrowing; rice, kaoliang, millet, beans.

Siangning or **Hsiang-ning** (both: shyäng'nĭng'), town, ⊙ Siangning co. (pop. 67,386), S Shansi prov., China, 40 mi. W of Linfen; cotton weaving; kaoliang, millet.

Siang River (shyäng), Chinese *Siang Kiang* or *Hsiang Chiang* (both: shyäng' jyäng'). **1** Main stream of Hunan prov., China, rises S of Hingan in NE Kwangsi prov., flows NE past Chüanhsien and Lingling, and N past Hengyang and Changsha, to Tungting L. below Siangyin in a delta merging with that of Tzu R.; 715 mi. long. Receives Lei R. (right). Navigable for small vessels below Lingling, and for large vessels below Changsha. Upper course of Siang R. is connected by canal with upper Kwei R. **2** River, Kwangsi prov., China: see YÜ RIVER.

Siangshan or **Hsiang-shan** (both: shyäng'shän'), town (pop. 18,741), ⊙ Siangshan co. (pop. 208,200), NE Chekiang prov., China, on S shore of Siangshan Bay on E.China Sea, 35 mi. SE of Ningpo; cotton and ramie weaving; saltworks; rice, wheat.

Siangshan Bay, inlet of E.China Sea, in Chekiang prov., China, 20 mi. SE of Ningpo; penetrates 40 mi. inland; 3–5 mi. wide (10 mi. at mouth); well-sheltered anchorage. Also called Nimrod Bay.

Siangsiang or **Hsiang-hsiang** (both: shyäng'shyäng'), town, ⊙ Siangsiang co. (pop. 1,041,218), E Hunan prov., China, on branch of Siang R., on railroad and 45 mi. SW of Changsha; coal-mining center; rice, cotton. Tseng Kuo-fan (1811–72), leader against Taiping Rebellion, b. here.

Siangtan or **Hsiang-t'an** (both: shyäng'tän'), town (1943 pop. 82,589), ⊙ Siangtan co. (1946 pop. 917,500), NE Hunan prov., China, commercial port on Siang R., on railroad and 20 mi. SSW of Changsha; tea-processing center; rice, cotton, hemp, medicinal herbs. Coal mining in vicinity. Mao Tse-tung was b. 1893 in near-by village.

Siangtu or **Hsiang-tu** (shyäng'dōō'), town, ⊙ Siangtu co. (pop. 91,159), SW Kwangsi prov., China, 55 mi. SE of Poseh; agr. products. Gold mines, antimony and bauxite deposits near by.

Siangyang or **Hsiang-yang** (both: shyäng'yäng'), town (pop. 17,966), ⊙ Siangyang co. (pop. 448,706), NW Hupeh prov., China, on right bank of Han R., opposite FANCHENG, and 165 mi. NW of Hankow; an anc. city, dating from Han dynasty (1st cent. B.C.). It has been largely superseded by the new commercial center of Fancheng, across the river.

Siangyin or **Hsiang-yin** (both: shyäng'yĭn'), town, ⊙ Siangyin co. (pop. 565,650), N Hunan prov., China, commercial port on Siang R. delta, 32 mi. N of Changsha, near Tungting L.; rice-producing center; tea, wheat, fiber crops (cotton, hemp); sawmilling.

Siangyüan or **Hsiang-yüan** (both: shyäng'yüän'), town, ⊙ Siangyüan co. (pop. 142,182), SE Shansi prov., China, 30 mi. N of Changchih; cotton weaving, furniture mfg.; wheat, rice, millet, cattle. Coal mining near by.

Siangyün or **Hsiang-yün** (both: shyäng'yün'), town (pop. 22,219), ⊙ Siangyün co. (pop. 101,486), NW central Yunnan prov., China, on Burma Road and 30 mi. SE of Tali; tung-oil processing; rice, wheat, millet, beans. Coal mines near by. Until 1929 called Yunnan.

Sianow (shä'nōōf), Pol. *Sianów*, Ger. *Zanow* (tsä'-nō), town (1939 pop. 3,050; 1946 pop. 1,930) in Pomerania, after 1945 in Koszalin prov., NW Poland, near the Baltic, 5 mi. NE of Köslin (Koszalin); mfg. of chemicals, matches. After 1945, briefly called Canow, Pol. *Canów*.

Siantan, Indonesia: see ANAMBAS ISLANDS.

Siao, China: see SIU RIVER.

Siaochengtze, Manchuria: see NINGCHENG.

Siaoching River or **Siaotsing River** (both: shyou'-chĭng'), Chinese *Hsiao-ch'ing Ho* (shyou'chĭng' hŭ'), former arm of Yellow R. delta, in NW Shantung prov., China; 125 mi. long. Navigable in entire course, it links, by means of a canal, Tsinan to Gulf of Chihli, at Yangkiokow.

Siaoe, Indonesia: see SIAU.

Siaofeng or **Hsiao-feng** (both: shyou'fŭng'), town (pop. 10,777), ⊙ Siaofeng co. (pop. 88,798), NW Chekiang prov., China, on Anhwei line, 45 mi. NW of Hangchow, N of Tienmu Mts.; rice, wheat, bamboo shoots, tobacco, timber.

Siaofengman, Manchuria: see FENGMAN.

Siaohsien or **Hsiao-hsien** (both: shyou'shyĕn'), town, ⊙ Siaohsien co. (pop. 578,368), N Anhwei prov., China, 15 mi. WSW of Süchow; wheat, beans, kaoliang, cotton. Coal deposits near by. Until 1949 in Kiangsu.

Siaokan or **Hsiao-kan** (both: shyou'gän'), town (pop. 6,990), ⊙ Siaokan co. (pop. 562,218), NE central Hupeh prov., China, 35 mi. NW of Hankow, near Peking-Hankow RR; cotton and ramie weaving, sugar milling.

Siao River, China: see SIU RIVER.

Siaoshan or **Hsiao-shan** (both: shyou'shän'), town (pop. 8,756), ⊙ Siaoshan co. (pop. 458,432), N Chekiang prov., China, 10 mi. SE of Hangchow, across Tsientang R.; rail junction for Ningpo; silk textiles; rice, wheat, beans, berries. Lime and alum quarries.

Siaotsing River, China: see SIAOCHING RIVER.

Siaoyi or **Hsiao-i** (both: shyou'yē'). **1** Town, ⊙ Siaoyi co. (pop. 130,129), central Shansi prov., China, 10 mi. S of Fenyang; wheat, corn, cotton. **2** Town, Shensi prov., China: see TSOSHUI.

Siapu or **Hsia-p'u** (both: shyä'pōō'), town (pop. 12,661), ⊙ Siapu (pop. 180,939), NE Fukien prov., China, 70 mi. NE of Foochow, on E.China Sea; tea, tobacco, sweet potatoes, rice; saltworks, fisheries. Until 1913 called Funing.

Siargao Island (syärgä'ō, –gou') (□ 169; 1939 pop. 21,252), Surigao prov., Philippines, off NE tip of Mindanao; 22 mi. long. Coconuts. Numancia and General Luna are chief towns.

Siasconset, Mass.: see NANTUCKET ISLAND.

Siashih or **Hsia-shih** (both: shyä'shŭ'), town, N Chekiang prov., China, 35 mi. NE of Hangchow and on railroad to Shanghai.

Siasi Island (syä'sē) (□ 29.6; 1939 pop. 12,662; 1948 municipal dist. pop., including offshore isls., 29,836), chief island of Tapul Group, Sulu prov., Philippines, in the Sulu Archipelago, 25 mi. SW of Jolo.

Siatanshui Ki, Formosa: see TANSHUI RIVER.

Siatista (sēä'tĭstŭ), town (pop. 4,743), Kozane nome, Macedonia, Greece, 13 mi. W of Kozane; alt. 3,120 ft.; trade center; tobacco, wine, wheat, livestock; dairy products.

Siaton (syä'tōn, syätōn'), town (1939 pop. 2,616; 1948 municipality pop. 17,926), Negros Oriental prov., extreme SE Negros isl., Philippines, near Siaton Point, 25 mi. SW of Dumaguete; agr. center (corn, coconuts, sugar cane).

Siaton Point, southernmost point of Negros isl., Philippines, in Sulu Sea, near Siaton town; 9°2'N 123°E.

Siatsing or **Hsia-ching** (both: shyä'jĭng'), town, ⊙ Siatsing co. (pop. 197,915), S Hopeh prov., China, 55 mi. WNW of Tsinan, on Pingyuan line; cotton weaving; grain, peanuts.

Siatsun or **Hsia-t'sun** (both: shyä'tsōōn'), town, E Shantung prov., China, 22 mi. NE of Haiyang, near Yellow Sea; commercial center.

Siau or **Siaoe** (both: sēou'), island (□ 60; pop. 30,858), Sangi Isls., Indonesia, bet. Celebes Sea and Molucca Passage, 65 mi. NNE of Celebes; 2°49'N 125°23'E; 12 mi. long, 7 mi. wide; mountainous, forested. Lumbering, agr., fishing. Main town is Hulusiau.

Siauliai, Shaulyai, or **Shaulyay** (shou'lī), Lith. *Šiauliai*, Ger. *Schaulen*, Rus. *Shavli*, city (pop. 31,641), N Lithuania, 75 mi. NNW of Kaunas. Rail and industrial hub; principal Lithuanian shoe-mfg. and tanning center; mfg. of bicycles, agr. implements, metalware, linen and woolen textiles, knitwear, paper, furniture; meat packing, vegetable-oil and starch processing, dairying. Alabaster works (near-by gypsum quarries). Sugar milling near by. Dates from 15th cent.; in Rus. Kovno govt. until 1920.

Siayi or **Hsia-i** (both: shyä'yē'), town, ⊙ Siayi co. (pop. 288,854), NE Honan prov., China, on Anhwei line, 28 mi. ESE of Shangkiu; rice, wheat, millet.

Sib (sēb), town (pop. 2,000), Batina dist., N Oman, on Gulf of Oman, at mouth of the Wadi Sama'il, 25 mi. W of Muscat; fishing; date cultivation.

Sibai or **Sibay** (sēbī'), town (1948 pop. over 2,000), SE Bashkir Autonomous SSR, Russian SFSR, in the S Urals, 20 mi. ENE of Baimak; copper mining.

Siba'iya, El, Es Siba'iya, or **Al-Siba'iyah** (all: ĕs-sĭbă-ē'yŭ), village (pop. 7,230), Aswan prov., S Egypt, on W bank of the Nile and 19 mi. NW of Idfu; cereals, dates. Phosphate deposits near by.

Sibajak, Mount, Indonesia: see SIBAYAK, MOUNT.

Sibalom (sēbälōm'), town (1939 pop. 2,525; 1948 municipality pop. 28,558), Antique prov., SW Panay isl., Philippines, 39 mi. WNW of Iloilo; agr. center (rice, sugar cane).

Sibambe (sēbäm'bā), village, Chimborazo prov., S central Ecuador, in the Andes, rail junction on Guayaquil-Quito RR, and 4 mi. SW of Alausí, in cattle region. Near by is the famed Nariz del Diablo (Devil's Nose) gorge, through which passes the railroad. Sulphur mining in vicinity.

Sibanicú (sēbänēkōō'), town (pop. 2,513), Camagüey prov., E Cuba, on Central Highway and 27 mi. ESE of Camagüey; cattle, sugar cane.

Sibata, Japan: see SHIBATA.

Sibayak, Mount, or **Mount Sibajak** (both: sēbäyäk'), active volcanic peak (7,251 ft.) of Barisan Mts., N Sumatra, Indonesia, just N of Brastagi, 25 mi. SSW of Medan.

Sibay Island, Philippines: see SEMIRARA ISLANDS.

Sibbhult (sĭb'hŭlt"), village (pop. 890), Kristianstad co., S Sweden, 17 mi. N of Kristianstad; grain, potatoes.

Sibchar (sĭb'chŭr), village, Faridpur dist., S central East Bengal, E Pakistan, on Arial Khan R. and 12 mi. N of Madaripur; trades in rice, jute, oilseeds, sugar cane.

Sibenik (shē'bĕnĭk), Serbo-Croatian *Šibenik*, Ital. *Sebenico* (sĕbā'nēkô), town (pop. 16,015), W Croatia, Yugoslavia, major Adriatic seaport, above Krka R. mouth (joined with sea by Sibenik Channel), 30 mi. WNW of Split, in Dalmatia. Naval harbor; bathing resort, rail spur terminus; electrochemical mfg. (calcium carbide, cyanamide, fertilizer). Exports timber, bauxite, coal, nonmineral oils, marble, wine, maraschino, cement, cellulose, cyanamide. Marasca grown in vicinity. Brown-coal deposits (NE); hydroelectric plants on the Krka (N). R.C. bishopric since 1298; also Orthodox Eastern bishopric. Picturesquely situated on steep karst slope; built mainly in Gothic and Renaissance styles (14th–16th cent.). Has large cathedral (begun 1430) built entirely of stone, loggia (built 1522), several castles. Includes N suburb of Crnica. Known since 10th cent.; contested by Venice, Byzantine Empire, and Croatia until 1412, when it passed to Venice; included in Austria 1815–1919. Sometimes spelled Shibenik.

Siberia (sībē'rēŭ), Rus. *Sibir* or *Sibir'* (sĭbēr'), vast region of the USSR in Asia, comprising roughly the Asiatic part (□ 5,000,000; pop. c.20,000,000) of the Russian SFSR. Occupying the N 3d of Asia, Siberia extends from the Ural Mts. to the Pacific Ocean (specifically the Bering Sea, Sea of Okhotsk, and Sea of Japan), and from the Arctic Ocean (specifically the Kara Sea, Laptev Sea, East Siberian Sea) to Kazakhstan and the S land border bet. the USSR and China and Mongolia. Its W–E extent is 130° of long. bet. 60°E (in the Urals) and 170°W (in Cape Dezhnev, on Bering Strait). Generally situated N of 50°N, Siberia reaches its and Asia's northernmost point in Cape Chelyuskin (77°44'N). Among the Arctic isls. off the Siberian coast are the New Siberian Isls., Severnaya Zemlya, and Wrangel Isl. Off its Pacific coast are Sakhalin and the Kurile Isls. Physiographically, Siberia consists of 3 major divisions: the West Siberian plain, one of the world's largest and flattest lowlands, bounded W by the Urals, E by the Yenisei R. and drained by the Ob-Irtysh river system; the Central Siberian Plateau, E of the Yenisei and watered by the Lena R.; and the E Siberian highlands (Yablonovy, Stanovoi, Verkhoyansk, Cherski, Kolyma, and Anadyr ranges). Along Siberia's S margins are the Amur R., the Sayan Mts., and the Altai Mts., rising in the Belukha (15,157 ft.) to Siberia's highest non-volcanic summit. It is exceeded only by the Klyuchevskaya Sopka (15,912 ft.) in the volcanic Kamchatka Peninsula. With exception of the Amur, Siberia's mighty rivers (Ob, Yenisei, Lena), among the world's longest, flow into the Arctic seas (frozen 9 months every year), with consequent limitation to navigability. In S Siberia lies sickle-shaped L. Baikal, the world's deepest lake and Eurasia's 3d largest. Siberia's climate is of the extreme continental type. While Atlantic influence is negligible and the Pacific monsoon affects only the Far Eastern littoral, the entire region is directly exposed to Arctic air masses. Thus, the area of Verkhoyansk and Oimyakon (NE) is the world's cold pole, with a Jan. mean of −60° to −65°F. At the same time, however, summer temperatures are relatively high, with July averages of 60° to 65°F. in the cold pole area. Precipitation is generally low, except on the E Kamchatka slopes and in the coastal areas exposed to the Pacific summer monsoon. As a result of the long and rigorous winters and the thin snow cover, permafrost conditions exist throughout most of Siberia E of the Yenisei. The region may be divided, from N to S, into zones of vegetation that run across the entire USSR—the tundra of moss and lichen along the Arctic shore; the taiga (coniferous forest), whose spruce, larch, and fir occupy most of Siberia; and the steppe, best developed in the SW, where it has been largely put under cultivation. Among Siberia's chief fur-bearing animals are the squirrel, marten, ermine, and, in remote mtn. areas, the now rare sable. Ivory of the mammoth, an extinct member of the Siberian fauna, has been found along the Arctic shore. Siberia's mineral wealth is still in the early stages of development, in spite of the great strides toward industrialization made by the Soviet regime. Coal is mined in the Kuznetsk Basin at Chernogorsk, Cheremkhovo, Chita, Artem, and Suchan, while vast deposits in the Tunguska, Lena, and Bureya basins are still largely unexploited. Iron is mined in the Shornaya Goriya (just S of the Kuznetsk Basin), lead-zinc in the Altai Mts. and at Tetyukhe, and gold in the Kolyma, Aldan, and Bodaibo areas. Molybdenum, tungsten, tin, salt, graphite, barite, and mica are also exploited. Agr. is particularly well developed in the SW steppe, the Zeya-Bureya Lowland, and near Yakutsk. Wheat and other grains (rye, oats), sunflower, flax, sugar beets (in Altai foothills), and rice and soybeans (near L. Khanka) are the chief crops. Meat and dairy cattle (Baraba and Ishim steppes) are widely raised. In the forest areas, lumbering, fur trapping, fishing, and reindeer raising are the leading occupations. Industry has developed on the basis of mineral resources (particularly in the Kuznetsk Basin), and the processing of agr. products and timber. The leading cities (Novosibirsk, Omsk, Krasnoyarsk, Irkutsk, Khabarovsk, and Vladivostok) all lie on the Trans-Siberian RR, the only E–W route. Pop. is very unevenly distributed, with 90% (nearly all Russian and, to a lesser extent, Ukrainian) concentrated in the vicinity of the Trans-Siberian RR and its branches. The non-Russian pop. includes Turkic groups: the Altaic (Oirot) tribes, Khakass, Tuvinians, and Yakuts; Buryat-Mongols; Finno-Ugric groups: Khanty (Ostyaks), Mansi (Voguls), and the related Nentsy (Samoyedes); Tungusic groups: Evenki (Tungus), Eveny (Lamuts), and Nanai (Golds); and various Hyperborean (Paleoasiatic) tribes: the Luoravetlany (Chukchi), Nymylany (Koryaks), Itelmeny (Kamchadales), Eskimos, and Aleuts. These indigenous peoples were gradually pushed N into the taiga during the early historical period, while warlike Turkic and Mongolian tribes roamed the S steppes. The 1st Russian penetration of NW Siberia was that of Novgorod traders in 13th cent. However, the actual Russian conquest of the territory did not begin until the Cossack Yermak and his band crossed the Urals in 1581–82 and conquered the Tatar khanate of SIBIR. The Cossacks rapidly extended their gains, penetrating eastward by land and river, building a string of small posts, and within less than 60 years reached the Pacific by 1640. While Siberia soon began to be used as a penal colony and place of exile and fur tribute was exacted from the indigenous pop., no organized Russian colonization developed until the late 19th cent. Settlement on a large scale was speeded with the construction (1892–1905) of the Trans-Siberian RR, after which the eastward migration reached gigantic proportions (over 3 millions in 1905–14). After the Bolshevik revolution, counter-revolutionary groups and Allied and Japanese interventionists occupied large sections of Siberia and it was only in 1922 that the last Siberian territory passed to Soviet control. Under the Five Year Plans, the agr. settlement and the industrialization of Siberia made remarkable progress, leading to the gradual eastward shift of the industrial center of gravity of the USSR. Part of Soviet agr. colonization was carried out through the forced resettlement of expropriated kulaks, while forced labor continued to be used in industrial and mining projects. Prior to the Bolshevik revolution, Siberia was divided into the govts. or oblasts of the Amur, Irkutsk, Sakhalin, Tobolsk, Tomsk, Yakutsk, Yeniseisk, and the Maritime Oblast. After order had been reestablished following the civil war, Siberia consisted (middle 1920s) of the Siberian Territory (formed 1925), the Buryat-Mongol and the Yakut Autonomous SSRs, and the Far Eastern Territory. The Siberian Territory was later subdivided (1930–37) into the West Siberian Territory and the East Siberian Territory. In 1951 the administrative divisions by Siberia's major regions were as follows: Western Siberia—oblasts of Kurgan, Tyumen (including Khanti-Mansi and Yamal-Nenets natl. okrugs), Omsk, Novosibirsk, Tomsk, Kemerovo, and Altai Territory (including Gorno-Altai Autonomous Oblast); Eastern Siberia—Krasnoyarsk Territory (including Khakass Autonomous Oblast, Evenki and Taimyr natl. okrugs), Tuva Autonomous Oblast, Irkutsk oblast (including Ust-Orda Buryat-Mongol Natl. Okrug), Chita oblast (including Aga Buryat-Mongol Natl. Okrug), and Buryat-Mongol and Yakut Autonomous SSRs; Soviet Far East—Amur and Sakhalin oblasts, Maritime Territory and Khabarovsk Territory (including Kamchatka oblast with the Koryak and Chukchi natl. okrugs, Lower Amur oblast, and the Jewish Autonomous Oblast). For further information, see the articles on those administrative divisions and on the cities and physical features of Siberia.

Siberut or **Siberoet** (both: sēbŭrōōt'), largest island (pop. 9,314; 70 mi. long, 25 mi. wide) of MENTAWAI ISLANDS, Indonesia, off W coast of Sumatra, 90 mi. WSW of Padang; 1°25'S 98°55'E. Generally low, rising in W area to 1,260 ft. Agr. (sago, sugar, tobacco, coconuts), fishing. Chief settlement and port is Murasiberut or Moerasiberoet (both: mōō"rŭsēbŭrōōt'). Sometimes called Groot Fortuin.

Sibganj (sĭb'gŭnj), village, Rajshahi dist., W East Bengal, E Pakistan, on tributary of the Mahananda and 10 mi. NW of Nawabganj; rice, wheat, oilseeds.

Sibi (sĭb'ē), dist. (□ 11,457; 1951 pop. 209,000), NE Baluchistan, W Pakistan; ⊙ Sibi. Crossed N by N Central Brahui Range; drained mainly by upper course (Beji R.) of Nari R.; SW strip irrigated by North Western Canal of Sukkur Barrage system. Agr. (wheat, millet, rice); fruitgrowing (melons, grapes) in NW section. Handicrafts (woolen weaving; felts, saddlebags, mats, rope); cattle raising in plain around Sibi. Coal mined near Khost and Shahrig; gypsum deposits (central area). Part of Ghaznevid kingdom (10th–12th cent.); later under Moguls; ceded to British in 1879. Includes Marri-Bugti Territory, a large tribal tract (□ c.7,000). Pop. 95% Moslem, 4% Hindu.

Sibi, town (1941 pop. 8,854), ⊙ Sibi dist., NE central Baluchistan, W Pakistan, on N Kachhi plain, 65 mi. SE of Quetta; rail junction; E terminus of Bolan Pass road from Quetta; wheat, millet; handicrafts (woolen, felt); cattle raising.

Sibillini, Monti (môn'tē sēbēl-lē'nē), range of the Apennines, central Italy, c.20 mi. NNW of Gran Sasso d'Italia; extend c.20 mi. N–S. Highest peak, Monte Vettore (8,130 ft.). Source of Nera, Aso, and Tenna rivers.

Sibinal (sēbēnäl'), town (1950 pop. 357), San Marcos dept., SW Guatemala, in the Sierra Madre, near Mexican border, 19 mi. NW of San Marcos; alt. 8,465 ft.; coffee, sugar cane, grains.

Sibir or **Sibir'** (sĭbēr'), 16th-cent. capital of Tatar Siberian khanate, on right bank of Irtysh R., SE of modern Tobolsk. Captured (1581) by Yermak, Cossack conqueror of Siberia; abandoned by its pop. following founding of Tobolsk. The name Sibir, first applied to the Tatar khanate along Irtysh, Tobol, and Ishim rivers, was later extended to all SIBERIA. The old town was also known as Isker and Kashlyk.

Sibirski or **Sibirskiy,** Russian SFSR: see NOVO-NAZYVAYEVKA.

Sibiti (sēbētē'), village, S Middle Congo territory, Fr. Equatorial Africa, 130 mi. WNW of Brazzaville; oil-palm center with large experimental plantations, nurseries, and agr. school; some gold mining. Komono (kōmōnō') rubber plantations are c.20 mi. NNW.

Sibiu (sēbē'ōō), Ger. ***Hermannstadt*** (hĕr'mänshtät), Hung. ***Nagyszeben***, city (1948 pop. 60,602), ⊙ Sibiu prov., central Rumania, in Transylvania, 130 mi. NW of Bucharest; 45°48'N 29°9'E. Rail junction, industrial, historical, military, and commercial center. Produces industrial machinery, iron and steel structural forms, scales, hardware, electrical appliances, automobile bodies, paper, clay products, pencils, hosiery, textiles, knitwear, blankets, hats, driving belts, cordage, pharmaceuticals, varnishes, candles, inks, glue, confectionery, alcohol, vinegar, flour, dairy products; specializes in preparation of salami; brewing and tanning. Art printing and publishing are important. Tourist center. Orthodox bishopric. Educational establishments include theological seminary, military academy and law school. Founded in 12th cent. by Saxon colonists and laid out on 2 terraces, Sibiu still preserves much of its Ger. medieval character and has 25% Ger. pop. Notable are: 14th–15th-cent. Gothic Evangelical church with religious mus.; 15th-cent. fortifications; 15th-cent. town hall, 16th-cent. tower; 16th-cent. Parish House; 18th-cent. fountain and Jesuit church; large Byzantine-style Orthodox cathedral. There are several museums and a major art gallery. In 14th cent. city was already an important industrial and commercial center and became temporary ⊙ Transylvania when it passed (1699) to Austria.

Sible Hedingham (hĭ'nĭgŭm, –nĭng-gŭm), town and parish (pop. 2,149), N Essex, England, on Colne R. and 7 mi. N of Braintree; agr. market. Has 14th-cent. church. Near by is Norman keep of Castle Hedingham (c.1100).

Sibley, county (□ 581; pop. 15,816), S Minn.; ⊙ Gaylord. Agr. area bounded E by Minnesota R.; has small lakes. Livestock, dairy products, corn, oats, barley. Formed 1853.

Sibley. 1 Village (pop. 345), Ford co., E central Ill., 32 mi. ENE of Bloomington, in rich agr. area. **2** City (pop. 2,559), ⊙ Osceola co., NW Iowa, near Minn. line, c.70 mi. NNE of Sioux City, in livestock, dairy, and farm area; center for some of the chief Iowa cooperatives. Named 1872, inc. 1875. **3** Town (pop. 623), Webster parish, NW La., 27 mi. E of Shreveport, in agr. and natural-gas area.

Sibolga or **Siboga** (sēbŏl'gŭ, –bō'gŭ), town (pop. 10,765), NW Sumatra, Indonesia, port on Tapanuli Bay (inlet of Indian Ocean), 130 mi. S of Medan; 1°44'N 98°48'E; ships rubber, coffee, timber, resin, camphor, copra. Harbor is protected by isl. of Musala or Moesala (12 mi. long, 4 mi. wide).

Siboney (sēbōnā'), village, Oriente prov., E Cuba, on the Caribbean, 9 mi. ESE of Santiago de Cuba. One of the points where Amer. troops disembarked (July, 1898) in Spanish-American War.

Sibonga (sēbông'gä), town (1939 pop. 2,772; 1948 municipality pop. 19,230), central Cebu isl., Philippines, on Bohol Strait, on railroad and 28 mi. SW of Cebu city; agr. center (corn, coconuts).

Sibpur, India: see HOWRAH, city.

Sibsagar (sĭbsä'gŭr), district, E central Assam, India; ⊙ Jorhat. Mainly in Brahmaputra valley; bounded N by Subansiri R., E by Naga Hills; traversed by Brahmaputra R. Largely agr.; tea (major tea garden dist.), rice, rape and mustard, sugar cane, jute; calamus palms on Majuli Isl.; silk growing. Extensive tea processing, oilseed milling, sawmilling, railroad shops. Coal mining near Nazira (weaving, printing, and dyeing factory). Projected oil wells in hill region (E). Assamese jewelry-mfg. center at Jorhat (sugar-cane research station). Silk-growing and rice research stations at Titabar. Dist. formed important part of anc. Ahom (Shan) kingdom, with capitals at Nazira, Sibsagar, Jorhat. Suffered greatly in 1950 earthquake. Original dist. (□ 5,138; 1941 pop. 1,074,741; 59% Hindu, 33% tribal) reduced in 1950, when W area with tribal Mikir majority was separated to form Mikir Hills dist.

Sibsagar, town (pop. 7,559), Sibsagar dist., E central Assam, India, in Brahmaputra valley, on tributary of the Brahmaputra and 30 mi. ENE of Jorhat; tea, rice, rape and mustard, jute; tea processing. Extensive tea gardens near by. Has 17th- and 18th-cent. Ahom temple ruins. Was ⊙ Ahom (Shan) kingdom, 1699–1786; called Rangpur.

Sibu (sē'bōō), town (pop. 9,983), S Sarawak, in W Borneo, port at confluence of Rajang and small Igan R., 115 mi. NE of Kuching; 2°18'N 111°49'E; trade center for area producing rubber, rice, sago, livestock. Ships rubber, sago flour.

Sibuguey Bay (sēbōōgā'), inlet of Moro Gulf in SW coast of Mindanao, Philippines, along E shore of lower part of Sibuguey or Zamboanga Peninsula. Several isls. along W shore.

Sibulan (sēbōō'län), town (1939 pop. 1,599; 1948 municipality pop. 8,096), Negros Oriental prov., Philippines, SE Negros isl., near entrance to Tañon Strait, opposite S end of Cebu isl., 3 mi. NNW of Dumaguete; agr. center (corn, coconuts, sugar).

Sibun River (sēbōōn'), Br. Honduras, rises in NE Maya Mts., flows 90 mi. NE to Caribbean Sea 7 mi. SW of Belize. Timber floating.

Sibutu Island (sēbōōtōō', sēbōō'tōō) (□ 39; 1939 pop. 3,129), Sulu prov., Philippines, westernmost of Sulu Archipelago, 22 mi. SE of NE tip of Borneo, 20 mi. SW of Tawitawi across Sibutu Passage; 19 mi. long; 4°50'N 119°25'E. It is largest isl. of Sibutu Group, which includes near-by Tumindao Isl. and other islets, all comprised in Si Tangkay municipality (1948 pop. 9,228). Sibutu, inadvertently omitted from 1898 treaty with Spain, was ceded (with Cagayan Sulu Isl.) to U.S. in 1900.

Sibuyan Island (sēbōō'yän, sēbōōyän') (□ 173; 1939 pop. 19,764), Romblon prov., Philippines, in Sibuyan Sea, S of Luzon and N of Panay, bet. Tablas Isl. (W) and Masbate isl. (E); 12°25'N 122°34'E; 18 mi. long, 14 mi. wide. Mountainous, rising to 6,750 ft. in Mt. Guitinguitin in central part of isl. Rice, coconuts. Chief centers: Magdiwang (N), Cajidiocan (E), and San Fernando (S).

Sibuyan Sea, central Philippines, bet. Luzon (N), Mindoro (W), Panay (S), Masbate (E); Marinduque isl. is in N. Opens NW to S.China Sea via Verde Isl. Passage, S to Visayan Sea via Jintotolo Channel, SW to Sulu Sea via Tablas Strait.

Sicalpa (sēkäl'pä), town, Chimborazo prov., central Ecuador, in the Andes, on Pan American Highway, on Guayaquil-Quito RR, adjoined N by Cajabamba, 9 mi. WSW of Riobamba; cereals, potatoes, livestock. In 1949 earthquake zone.

Sicamous (sĭ'kŭmōōs), village (pop. estimate 200), S B.C., on Shuswap L. at mouth of Shuswap R., 35 mi. WSW of Revelstoke; dairying, lumbering, fruitgrowing. Just S is Mara L.

Sicasica (sēkäsē'kä) or **Villa Aroma** (vē'yä ärō'mä), town (pop. c.8,600), ⊙ Sicasica (or Aroma) prov., La Paz dept., W Bolivia, in the Altiplano, 65 mi. SSE of La Paz, on La Paz–Oruro road, in agr. area; alt. 13,041 ft.; livestock (sheep, llamas).

Sicasica, Serranía de (sěrănē'ä dā), the Eastern W outlier of Cordillera of the Andes, La Paz dept., W Bolivia; extends c.90 mi. NW from Colquiri to point S of La Paz; rises to 16,000 ft. at SE end. Luribay, Caracato, and Sapahaqui lie in Luribay Valley at its NE foot.

Sicawei, China: see ZIKAWEI.

Sicaya (sēkī'ä), town (pop. 2,700), Junín dept., central Peru, on Mantaro R. and 6 mi. NW of Huancayo; barley, wheat, sheep.

Sicca Veneria, Tunisia: see KEF, LE.

Siccawei, China: see ZIKAWEI.

Sicciole (sētchō'lā), Slovenian *Sičole* (sē'chôlā), village, S Free Territory of Trieste, on Pirano Bay, 4 mi. SE of Pirano; coal mining. Placed 1947 under Yugoslav administration.

Sichang or **Hsi-chang** (both: shē'jäng'), town, ⊙ Sichang co. (pop. 154,486), SE Sikang prov., China, 150 mi. S of Kangting and on highway; agr. and trading center; wax processing, lacquer-ware mfg., cotton weaving; wheat, rice, beans. Iron found near by. Until 1913, Ningyüan. Until 1938 in Szechwan.

Sichang, Ko (kô' sē'chäng'), island in Gulf of Siam, 45 mi. SSE of Bangkok; outer deepwater port of Bangkok, used by ocean-going vessels which cannot clear bar at mouth of Chao Phraya R.; cargo-transfer station. Also spelled Koh Sichang.

Sichelberg, Poland: see SIERPC.

Sichem, Belgium: see ZICHEM.

Sichhübel, peak, Czechoslovakia: see JIZERA.

Sichi or **Hsi-chi** (both: shē'jē'), town, ⊙ Sichi co. (pop. 69,918), SE Kansu prov., China, 45 mi. NW of Pingliang; wheat, beans, kaoliang. Until 1941 called Mukiaying.

Sichirlichitai, Ukrainian SSR: see SUVOROVO.

Sichomovi (sŏchōō'mō"vē"), Hopi Indian pueblo, NE Ariz., on a mesa in Hopi Indian Reservation, c.65 mi. NNE of Winslow; alt. c.6,200 ft. Sometimes Sichomivi or Sichomoir.

Sichon (sē'chōn'), village (1937 pop. 3,300), Nakhon Sithammarat prov., S Thailand, minor Gulf of Siam port on E coast of Malay Peninsula, 40 mi. ESE of Suratthani; granite quarries; iron deposits near by. Also spelled Sijol.

Sichow. 1 (shē'jō') Town, Shansi prov., China: see SIHSIEN. **2** or **Hsi-ch'ou** (shē'chō'), town, ⊙ Sichow co. (pop. 68,250), SE Yunnan prov., China, 32 mi. E of Wenshan, near Vietnam border; tung-oil processing; rice, millet, beans. Until 1929 called Sisakai.

Sichung or **Hsi-ch'ung** (both: shē'chōōng'), town (pop. 30,551), ⊙ Sichung co. (pop. 334,440), central Szechwan prov., China, 20 mi. NW of Nanchung; sweet-potato center; tung-oil processing; rice, kaoliang, beans, wheat, cotton. Saltworks near by.

Sichwan or **Hsi-ch'uan** (both: shē'chwän'), town, ⊙ Sichwan co. (pop. 172,038), W Honan prov., China, near Hupeh line, 65 mi. W of Nanyang, and on Tan R. (tributary of Han R.); wheat, kaoliang, beans. Asbestos quarrying.

Sicié, Cape (sēsyā'), headland of Var dept., SE France, forming S tip of peninsula 6 mi. SSW of Toulon; 43°4'N 5°51'E. Meteorological station. Peninsula (fortified) shelters Toulon harbor from W. Near its base is La Seyne-sur-Mer. Also spelled Cicié.

Sicilies, The Two, Italy: see TWO SICILIES, THE.

Sicily (sĭ'sŭlē, sĭ'sĭlē), Ital. *Sicilia* (sēchē'lyä), anc. *Trinacria*, largest and most populous island (□ 9,831; pop. 3,961,719) in Mediterranean Sea, forming with some small neighboring isls., chiefly Pantelleria, Ustica, and Lipari and Egadi isls., an autonomous region (□ 9,926; pop. 4,000,078) of Italy; ⊙ Palermo. Separated from SW Italy by Strait of Messina (2–10 mi. wide); lies 260 mi. SW of Rome, 95 mi. NE of Cape Bon, Africa. Isl. is 180 mi. long, 120 mi. wide; triangular-shaped. Situated bet. 36°38'N (Cape Correnti) and 38°18'N (Cape Rasocolmo), and bet. 12°25'E (Cape Boeo) and 15°39'E (Punta del Faro). Has 9 provs.: AGRIGENTO, CALTANISSETTA, CATANIA, ENNA, MESSINA, PALERMO, RAGUSA, SIRACUSA, and TRAPANI. Isl. is continuation of the Apennines; mountainous terrain (average alt. 1,450 ft.) includes (N to NE) Madonie, Nebrodi, and Peloritani mts., with SE spur ending near coast in Monti Iblei. Along E coast is large earthquake zone, culminating in Mt. ETNA, highest point (10,705 ft.) of isl., flanked on S by only large lowland, Plain of Catania. Virtually only remaining forests are in Madonie and Nebrodi mts. (chestnut, oak, beech) and on Mt. Etna (chestnut, pine, birch). Drained mostly by intermittent streams (torrential during winter rains, dry in summer), and by a few rivers, including Simeto, Salso, Platani, Belice, and Alcantara. Mild, subtropical climate, with few snowfalls and light rainfall. Subjected to occasional siroccos in summer. Malaria in lowlands. Pop. ⅓ along coast. Primary occupations are agr. (cereals, grapes, olives, citrus fruits) and stock raising (sheep, goats, mules). Leads Italy in production of citrus fruit. Has important tunny fisheries. Produces ⅔ of Italy's sulphur (bet. Caltanissetta and Agrigento), much of its asphalt (Ragusa prov.), ⅙ of its marine salt (Trapani, Syracuse), pumice (Lipari), and rock salt. Hydroelectric power plants at L. Piana dei Greci, and on Alcantara and Cassibile rivers. Industry concentrated at Palermo, Catania, Messina, Syracuse, and Trapani. Exports citrus fruit, wheat, wine, sulphur. Main railroad around coast, with secondary lines traversing interior. Earliest civilized settlers were Phoenicians, on W coast, with chief colony at Panormus (Palermo), Carthaginians at Lilybaeum (Marsala) and Drepanum (Trapani), and Greeks, who founded (8th–6th cent. B.C.) many colonies on E and SE coasts, including Syracuse, Catania, Zancle (Messina), Gela, and Selinus. Became Roman colony in 241 B.C. Passed to Byzantines (A.D. 535), Arabs (9th cent.), Normans (11th cent.), Aragonese (1302), Spain, and Bourbon house of Naples (1738). With kingdom of Naples, it formed the Kingdom of the Two Sicilies. Garibaldi freed isl. from Bourbons in 1860; inc. into Italy in 1861. Under the republican constitution (1947), received administrative autonomy. In Second World War its air and naval bases were heavily bombed, and on July 9–10, 1943, an Allied landing was effected from N Africa. After heavy fighting, Allied conquest completed with fall of Messina on Aug. 8, 1943.

Sicily Island, village, Catahoula parish, E La., near Tensas and Boeuf rivers, 25 mi. NW of Natchez, Miss.; lumber milling, cotton ginning. Called "island" because of its location on high ground in often-flooded area.

Sicinus, Greece: see SIKINOS.

Sicole, Free Territory of Trieste: see SICCIOLE.

Sico River (sē'kō), in Mosquitia region of E Honduras, rises in Sierra de Agalta SW of Gualaco, flows c.150 mi. generally NE, past Gualaco and San Esteban, to Caribbean Sea 14 mi. E of Iriona, here forming Criba Lagoon. Receives Paulaya R. (right). Also called Río Negro or Río Tinto.

Sicuani (sēkwä'nē), city (pop. 7,036), ⊙ Canchis prov. (□ 1,244; pop. 72,150), Cuzco dept., S Peru, on Vilcanota R., on railroad and highway to Cuzco, and 70 mi. SE of Cuzco; alt. 11,495 ft. Trading in agr. products (wool, grain, potatoes), flour milling, mfg. of woolen and leather goods. Picturesque market. Hydroelectric station near by.

Siculiana (sēkōōlyä'nä), town (pop. 7,374), Agrigento prov., S Sicily, 8 mi. WNW of Agrigento. Sulphur mines near by.

Sicyon (sĭ'sēŭn), anc. town in Argolis and Corinthia nome, NE Peloponnesus, Greece, 12 mi. WNW of Corinth, near Gulf of Corinth. There are ruins of theater and stadium. A center of art (school of painting) and philosophy, it flourished 6th–3d cent. B.C. and was home of Gr. sculptors Canachus and Lysippus. Member of Achaean League under Aratus (3d cent. B.C.). It declined after brief rise under Romans. Just E of ruins is modern town of Sikyon or Sikion (both: sēkēōn') (pop. 1,191), trading in Zante currants, wine, livestock. Formerly called Vasilikon; now sometimes Sykion. Modern town of Sikyonia is 2 mi. N, on the coast.

Sid or **Shid** (both: shēt), Serbo-Croatian *Šid*, village (pop. 6,471), Vojvodina, NW Serbia, Yugoslavia, 65 mi. WNW of Belgrade, in the Srem, near Croatia border; rail junction.

Sidamo-Borana (sē'dämō-bō'ränä), province (□ 39,500), S Ethiopia bordering on Kenya; ⊙ Yirga-Alam. Situated bet. Ganale Dorya (E) and Galana Sagan (W) rivers; includes L. Awusa (N) and parts of lakes Stefanie and Abaya (W). Consists of mtn. region (alt. 6,000–10,000 ft.), partly forested, in N and plateau (alt. 3,000–6,000 ft.) in S. Watered by Dawa River. Agr. (coffee, plantain, corn, cereals) and cattle raising in N; pastoralism (sheep, camels) in S. Cotton growing N of L. Abaya. Gold mining (Adola) and salt extracting (Mega). Inhabited by Sidamo, Galla, and Somali tribes. Trade centers: Mega, Hula, Soddu, Yirga-Alam, Yavello, Cheichei, Burji. Crossed (N–S) by road to Addis Ababa. Prov. formed c.1941.

Sidcup, residential former urban district (1931 pop. 12,355) now in Chislehurst and Sidcup urban dist. (1948 pop. estimate 72,750), NW Kent, England, 5 mi. ENE of Bromley; makes radios. Just S, on Cray R., is residential town of Foot's Cray.

Siddapur (sĭd-dä'pōōr), village (pop. 3,252), Kanara dist., S Bombay, India, 60 mi. SE of Karwar; trades in rice, betel nuts; sugar, cardamom, chili.

Siddapura, India: see MOLAKALMURU.

Siddeswaram (sĭd-dā'svŭrŭm), village, Kurnool dist., N Madras, India, on Kistna R. and 23 mi. NE of Kurnool. River dammed here, 1949; headworks planned as initial step of irrigation and hydroelectric project.

Siddhavattam (sĭd'dŭvŭtŭm), village, Cuddapah dist., central Madras, India, on Penner R. and 9 mi. E of Cuddapah; melon farming. Rail station 4 mi. SW, at Sidhout, is also called Siddhavattam.

Siddipet (sĭd'dĭpāt), town (pop. 12,865), Medak dist., central Hyderabad state, India, 55 mi. NNE of Hyderabad; rice; silk and cotton weaving.

Sideling Hill (sĭd'lĭng), NE–SW ridge (1,600–2,000 ft.), N Md. and S Pa., runs from Potomac R. in

W part of Washington co., Md., c.65 mi. NE to Juniata R. just above Mapleton, Pa.

Sidell (sī'dĕl', sĭdĕl'), village (pop. 554), Vermilion co., E Ill., near Little Vermilion R., 17 mi. SSW of Danville, in agr. and bituminous-coal area.

Siderno Marina (sēdĕr'nô märē'nä), town (pop. 6,164), Reggio di Calabria prov., Calabria, S Italy, port on Ionian Sea, 25 mi. E of Palmi, in citrus-fruit and olive region; bathing resort; olive oil refining.

Siderokastron or **Sidhirokastron** (both: sĭdhērô'-kästrôn) [Gr.,=iron castle], town (pop. 12,359), Serrai nome, Macedonia, Greece, on railroad and 13 mi. NW of Serrai, 9 mi. from Bulg. line; chief town of Sintica; trade center for tobacco, cotton, silk. Sulphur springs near by. Connected during Second World War with Bulg. railroad net. Under Turkish rule, called Demir-Hissar; also spelled Sidirokastron.

Sideros, Cape, or **Cape Sidheros** (both: sē'dhĕrôs), NE extremity of Crete, on Aegean Sea; 35°19'N 26°19'E.

Siders, Switzerland: see SIERRE.

Sidestrand, village and parish (pop. 94), N Norfolk, England, on North Sea, 3 mi. ESE of Cromer; chemical works.

Sidfa (sĭdfä'), village (pop. 5,916), Asyut prov., central Upper Egypt, on W bank of the Nile, on railroad, and 6 mi. SE of Abu Tig; cereals, dates, sugar cane.

Sidhauli (sĭdou'lē), village, Sitapur dist., central Uttar Pradesh, India, 22 mi. SSE of Sitapur; wheat, rice, gram, barley.

Sidheros, Cape, Crete: see SIDEROS, CAPE.

Sidhi (sĭd'ē), village ⊙ Sidhi dist., E central Vindhya Pradesh, India, 38 mi. ESE of Rewa; millet, wheat, gram. Sometimes spelled Sidi.

Sidhirokastron, Greece: see SIDEROKASTRON.

Sidhnai Canal (sĭdnī'), irrigation channel in Multan dist., S Punjab, W Pakistan; from left bank of Ravi R. (headworks 11 mi. WNW of Talamba) runs c.30 mi. SW, where 2 main branches continue to area SE of Multan.

Sidhout, India: see SIDDHAVATTAM.

Sidhpur (sĭd'po͝or), town (pop. 24,565), Mehsana dist., N Bombay, India, on Saraswati R. and 21 mi. N of Mehsana; market center (millet, pulse, wheat, oilseeds); cotton ginning and milling, cloth printing and dyeing, opium mfg. (extensive poppy cultivation near by). Hindu pilgrimage center.

Sidi, India: see SIDHI.

Sidi Abdallah, Tunisia: see BIZERTE.

Sidi-Ahmed (sē'dē-ämĕd'), village, Béja dist., N Tunisia, 17 mi. N of Béja; calamine mining.

Sidi Ahmed el Magrun, Cyrenaica: see SIDI MAGRUN.

Sidi-Aich (-äēsh'), village (pop. 1,072), Constantine dept., NE Algeria, in Oued Soummam valley, on railroad and 24 mi. SW of Bougie; figs, olives, wine.

Sidi-Aïssa (-ēsä'), town (pop. 3,088), Alger dept., N central Algeria, on the High Plateaus, on road to Bou-Saâda and 18 mi. SSE of Aumale; trade center for nomadic tribesmen; sheep and horse raising.

Sidi-Ali-ben-Nasser-Allah (-ä'lē-bĕn-näsär'-ällä'), village, Kairouan dist., central Tunisia, 26 mi. SW of Kairouan; sheep raising, esparto weaving.

Sidi Ali el Mekki, Ras (räs', ĕl mĕkē'), cape on the Mediterranean coast of N Tunisia, 23 mi. ESE of Bizerte, forming NW limit of Gulf of Tunis; 37°11'N 10°17'E. Sometimes called Cape of Porto-Farina.

Sidi-Amor-ben-Salem (sē'dē-āmôr-bĕn-sälĕm'), village, Le Kef dist., W Tunisia, on railroad, and 26 mi. SW of Le Kef; lead mine. Iron mined near by.

Sidi-Athman (-ätmän'), agr. village, Tunis dist., N Tunisia, on railroad and 18 mi. NW of Tunis.

Sidi-Ayed (-äyĕd), agr. village, Medjez-el-Bab dist., N central Tunisia, on railroad and 10 mi. SE of Teboursouk; distilling.

Sidi Barrani (sē'dē bärä'nē), town (pop. 3,308), Western Desert prov., NW Egypt, on Mediterranean coast, 235 mi. W of Alexandria, 45 mi. E of Salum. Caravan route leads S to the Siwa oasis. Has airfield. In Second World War, was important objective (1941–42) in the desert fighting.

Sidi-bel-Abbès (-bĕl-äb-bĕs'), city (pop. 52,881), Oran dept., NW Algeria, on the Mékerra and 35 mi. S of Oran, in the Tell; commercial center of a fertile agr. region (c.1,500 ft. high, along back slope of the Tessala Mts.) settled by European colonists since mid-19th cent. A leading grain market (wheat, oats, barley) with important trade in wines, olives, and livestock. Mfg. of cement, agr. equipment, furniture, hosiery, biscuits, cheese, olive oil; flour milling, lumbering. Has railroad shops and agr. school. An old walled town, it became a Fr. military post after occupation of Algeria, and later the hq. of the Foreign Legion. City now has modern layout and appearance.

Sidi Bennour (bĕno͞or'), village, Casablanca region, W Fr. Morocco, 40 mi. S of Mazagan; palm-fiber processing, stock raising.

Sidi-bou-Ali (-bo͞o-älē'), village, Sousse dist., E Tunisia, on railroad and 12 mi. NW of Sousse; cattle raising, beekeeping. Olive groves.

Sidi-bou-Rouis (-ro͞oēs'), village, Le Kef dist., N central Tunisia, on railroad and 20 mi. SSW of Teboursouk; pine forests.

Sidi-bou-Saïd (-säēd'), residential town (pop. 1,642), Tunis dist., N Tunisia, on rocky Cape Carthage overlooking Gulf of Tunis, 10 mi. ENE of Tunis; orange groves and vineyards. A picturesque native town known for its Moorish coffee houses.

Sidi-bou-Zid (-zēd'), village, Gafsa dist., central Tunisia, 40 mi. ESE of Kasserine, in irrigated agr. region; wool and cereal market of the interior. Horse raising, almond trees. Faïd Pass 8 mi. E.

Sidi Chalifa, Cyrenaica: see SIDI KHALIFA.

Sidi-Chami (-shämē'), village (pop. 1,059), Oran dept., NW Algeria, 7 mi. SE of Oran; vineyards.

Sidi-Daoud (-doud'), village, Grombalia dist., NE Tunisia, near tip of Cape Bon Peninsula, on Gulf of Tunis, 40 mi. ENE of Tunis; tuna fisheries.

Sidi el Aïdi (ĕl īdē'), village, Casablanca region, W Fr. Morocco, 33 mi. S of Casablanca; rail junction (spur to Khouribga and Oued Zem).

Sidi-el-Hani (hänē'), village, Sousse dist., E Tunisia, on railroad and 12 mi. E of Kairouan; agr. settlement. Near by is L. Sidi-el-Hani, a salt flat (20 mi. long, 10 mi. wide), flooded periodically.

Sidi-Ferruch, Cape (-fĕrŭsh'), headland of Alger dept., N central Algeria, on the Mediterranean, 12 mi. W of Algiers; 36°46'N 2°50'E. Here Fr. invasion army landed in 1830.

Sidi Harazem (häräzĕm'), spa, Fez region, N central Fr. Morocco, on the Sebou and 7 mi. E of Fez; thermal springs.

Sidi Ifni, town, NW Africa: see IFNI.

Sidi-Khaled (-kälĕd'), village and Saharan oasis, in Touggourt territory, N central Algeria, on the Oued Djedi, 5 mi. SW of Ouled-Djellal; date palms.

Sidi Khalifa (sē'dē khälē'fä), Ital. *Sidi Chalifa*, village (pop. 1,295), W Cyrenaica, Libya, near Mediterranean Sea, on coastal road and 13 mi. NE of Benghazi; olives, dates, grapes, livestock.

Sidi Magrun (sē'dē mägro͞on'), village, W Cyrenaica, Libya, near Gulf of Sidra, on coastal road and 45 mi. S of Benghazi. Formerly also Sidi Ahmed el Magrun.

Sidi-Meskine (-mĕskēn'), village, Souk-el-Arba dist., NW Tunisia, on Medjerda R., on railroad and 18 mi. N of Le Kef; cereals, livestock.

Sidi-Okba (-ôkbä'), village (pop. 7,410), Touggourt territory, NE Algeria, oasis in the Ziban region of the N Sahara, 12 mi. SE of Biskra; date palms. Its mosque, containing tomb of the Arab conqueror Sidi Okba, is a Moslem pilgrimage place.

Sidi Omar (sē'dē ō'mär), on Egypt-Cyrenaica line, 20 mi. SW of Salum; fighting here (1941–42) in Second World War.

Sidi Rafa, Cyrenaica: see BEDA LITTORIA.

Sidi Rahal (rähäl'), town (pop. 2,200), Marrakesh region, W central Fr. Morocco, at N foot of the High Atlas, 30 mi. E of Marrakesh; olive-oil pressing.

Sidi Rezegh (sē'dē rĕzĕg') or **Rezegh,** village, E Cyrenaica, Libya, 20 mi. SE of Tobruk. Scene of fighting (1941–42) bet. Axis and British in Second World War.

Sidirokastron, Greece: see SIDEROKASTRON.

Sidi-Saad (-sä-äd'), village, Kairouan dist., central Tunisia, on railroad and 28 mi. SW of Kairouan; lead and zinc mines near by.

Sidi Said Machou Dam, Fr. Morocco: see OUM ER RBIA.

Sidi Slimane (slēmän'), town (pop. 4,321), Rabat region, NW Fr. Morocco, on the Oued Beth, on railroad and 37 mi. E of Port-Lyautey; center of citrus- and cotton-growing area irrigated from El Kansera Dam (15 mi. S); cotton ginning, essential-oil processing. Air base.

Sidi-Tabet (-täbĕt'), village, Tunis dist., N Tunisia, near Medjerda R., 11 mi. NW of Tunis; cattle-, poultry- and horse-breeding center (experimental laboratories); intensive agr. (cereals, wine). Stone quarries near by.

Sidi-Toui (-twē'), frontier station near Lybian border, in Southern Territories, SE Tunisia, 55 mi. ESE of Foum-Tatahouine; 32°44'N 11°24'E.

Sidi Yahya du Rharb (yähyä' dü gärb'), village, Rabat region, NW Fr. Morocco, on railroad and 15 mi. E of Port-Lyautey, at N edge of Mamora Forest; tobacco, fruits and vegetables cultivated by European settlers. Experimental tobacco farm. Cork gathering. Also spelled Sidi Yahia du Gharb.

Sidlaghatta (sĭd'lŭgŭtŭ), town (pop. 7,263), Kolar dist., E Mysore, India, 25 mi. NW of Kolar; silk milling, hand-loom silk and woolen weaving.

Sidlaw Hills, range in E Perthshire and SW Angus, Scotland, extends 27 mi. SW–NE. Highest point is Auchterhouse Hill (1,399 ft.), 5 mi. SW of Glamis. DUNSINANE is a hill of this range.

Sidley, Mount (12,000 ft.), in the Executive Committee Range, Antarctica, in Marie Byrd Land; 77°25'S 129°W. Discovered 1934 by R. E. Byrd.

Sidmouth (sĭd'mŭth), urban district (1931 pop. 6,126; 1951 census 10,403), E Devon, England, on Lyme Bay of the Channel, at mouth of Sid R. and 9 mi. ENE of Exmouth; seaside resort. Has 15th-cent. church.

Sidmouth, Cape (sĭd'mŭth), N Queensland, Australia, in Coral Sea, on E Cape York Peninsula, N of Princess Charlotte Bay; 13°25'S 143°36'E. Rises to 205 ft.

Sidney. 1 Town (pop. estimate 1,000), SW B.C., on SE Vancouver Isl., on Haro Strait, 15 mi. N of Victoria; center of lumbering, dairying, and agr. (fruit, poultry, bees) region; fruit, salmon, and clam canning, brick and cement mfg. Resort. Site of Dominion Pathological Laboratory and of Dominion experimental farm. Near by are fox fur farms. Car ferries to mainland. **2** Village (pop. estimate 150), S Man., 35 mi. WSW of Portage la Prairie; stock, grain.

Sidney. 1 Town (pop. 120), Sharp co., N Ark., 15 mi. N of Batesville. **2** Village (pop. 653), Champaign co., E Ill., 10 mi. SE of Champaign; agr. (corn, soybeans, oats, alfalfa). **3** Town (pop. 168), Kosciusko co., N Ind., 32 mi. W of Fort Wayne, in agr. area. **4** Town (pop. 1,132), ⊙ Fremont co., extreme SW Iowa, 15 mi. W of Shenandoah, in livestock and grain area. Annual championship rodeo held here (Aug.). Inc. 1870. **5** Town (pop. 918), Kennebec co., S Maine, bet. Kennebec R. and Messalonskee L., just NW of Augusta. **6** City (pop. 3,987), ⊙ Richland co., NE Mont., on Yellowstone R., near N.Dak. line, and 50 mi. NNE of Glendive; trade center for irrigated wheat and sugar-beet area; flour, beet sugar, culverts; livestock, dairy produce, grain. Near by is Three Buttes, colorful scenic spot on edge of badlands region. Inc. 1911. **7** City (pop. 4,912), ⊙ Cheyenne co., W Nebr., 60 mi. SE of Scottsbluff and on Lodgepole Creek, bet. N.Platte and S.Platte rivers; trade and shipping center in Great Plains region; farm implements; grain, livestock, dairy and poultry produce, potatoes. Has military ordnance depot. Founded 1867 by Union Pacific RR, city grew around Fort Sidney (1867–94) and was a supply station during Black Hills gold rush (1876–77). **8** Village (pop. 4,815), Delaware co., S N.Y., in the Catskills, on Susquehanna R. and 30 mi. NE of Binghamton; mfg. (magnetos, spark plugs, textiles); timber; blue-stone quarrying. Inc. 1888. **9** City (pop. 11,491), ⊙ Shelby co., W Ohio, 35 mi. N of Dayton and on Great Miami R.; machine tools, refrigerators, washing machines, foundry products, motor vehicles, road machinery; also leather, packed meat. Gravel pits. Settled 1820.

Sido, Japan: see SHIDO.

Sidoarjo or **Sidoardjo** (both: sēdōär'yō), town (pop. 12,082), E Java, Indonesia, on Madura Strait, 15 mi. S of Surabaya; trade center for Brantas delta (rice and corn growing); textile mills.

Sidoktaya (zēdōk"tŭyä'), village, Minbu dist., Upper Burma, on Mon R. and 45 mi. WNW of Minbu, at foot of the Arakan Yoma.

Sidon, Lebanon: see SAIDA.

Sidon (sī'dŭn), town (pop. 361), Leflore co., W central Miss., 8 mi. S of Greenwood and on Yazoo R.

Sidra, Gulf of (sĭ'drŭ), Ital. *Gran Sirte* or *Golfo di Sidra*, anc. *Syrtis Major*, inlet (275 mi. wide) of Mediterranean Sea indenting the coast of Libya, bet. Benghazi (E; Cyrenaica) and Misurata (W; Tripolitania); fisheries (tunny, sponge). Its shore, mostly desert with salt marshes and scattered oases, is followed by a highway. Sirte is chief port.

Siduwa or **Seeduwa** (sĭd'o͞ovŭ), village (pop. 1,577), Western Prov., Ceylon, near Negombo Lagoon, 6.5 mi. SSE of Negombo; major govt. arrack distillery. Research institute.

Siebenbrunnen, Luxembourg: see LUXEMBOURG, city.

Siebenbürgen, Rumania: see TRANSYLVANIA.

Siebengebirge (zē'bŭngŭbĭr"gŭ) [Ger.,=Seven Mountains], small E range of the Westerwald, W Germany, extending 10 mi. along right bank of the Rhine S of Bonn, and rising to 1,509 ft. in the Grosser Ölberg. Of volcanic origin. The Drachenfels is best-known among the peaks. Range became natural preserve in 1923.

Siebenhirten (zē'bŭnhĭr"tŭn), town (pop. 2,634), after 1938 in Liesing dist. of Vienna, Austria, 6 mi. SW of city center; wine.

Siebenlehn (zē'bŭnlān), town (pop. 2,860), Saxony, E central Germany, on the Freiberger Mulde and 12 mi. SW of Meissen; shoe mfg.

Siebnen (zēb'nŭn), hamlet, Schwyz canton, NE central Switzerland, on the Wäggitaler Aa, 16 mi. NNE of Schwyz; hydroelectric plant; textiles, woodworking.

Siedlce (shĕ'dŭltsĕ), Rus. *Sedlets* (syĕd'lyĭts), city (pop. 25,562), Lublin prov., E Poland, 55 mi. E of Warsaw. Rail junction; trade center; mfg. of scales, locks, cement, glass, soap; tanning, flour milling, distilling; brickworks. Has town hall, church in Ital. style, palace (formerly of the Czartoryskis), arch of triumph (built for Stanislaus II; now bell tower). Became a town in 16th cent.; passed (18th cent.) to Austria and (1815) to Rus. Poland; was ⊙ Sedlets govt.; returned to Poland in 1921. Before Second World War, pop. was 40% Jewish. Heavily damaged (1939) by Germans.

Siegburg (zēk'bo͝ork), town (pop. 24,266), in former Prussian Rhine Prov., W Germany, after 1945 in North Rhine-Westphalia, on the Sieg and 6 mi. ENE of Bonn; 50°48'N 7°13'E. Rail junction; mfg.: machinery, tools, chemicals, artificial fiber, dyes, furniture, shoes, accordions. Has old Benedictine abbey (founded c.1065, suppressed 1803); bldgs. were restored in 17th–18th cent.; 12th-cent. church. Noted in Middle Ages for its pottery.

Siegen (zē′gŭn), city (1939 pop. 40,269; 1946 pop. 29,922; 1950 pop. 38,510), in former Prussian prov. of Westphalia, W Germany, after 1945 in North Rhine-Westphalia, on Sieg R. and 42 mi. SE of Remscheid, in iron-ore-mining region; rail junction; foundries. Second World War destruction (c.55%) included all noteworthy bldgs. Rubens b. here.

Siegenburg (zē′gŭnbo͝ork), village (pop. 2,310), Lower Bavaria, Germany, 11 mi. S of Kelheim; brewing, tanning, lumber and flour milling. Chartered early 14th cent.

Siegendorf (zēg′ŭndôrf), village (pop. 304), central Lower Austria, 10 mi. WSW of Sankt Pölten; sugar refinery.

Siegendorf im Burgenland (ĕm bo͞or′gŭnlänt), Hung. *Cinfalva* (tsĭn′fōlvŏ), town (pop. 2,248), Burgenland, E Austria, 4 mi. S of Eisenstadt; sugar refining.

Sieglar (zēk′lär), village (pop. 13,525), in former Prussian Rhine Prov., W Germany, after 1945 in North Rhine-Westphalia, 3 mi. W of Siegburg.

Siegmar-Schönau (zēk′mär-shûn′ou), town (pop. 21,591), Saxony, E central Germany, 5 mi. W of Chemnitz; hosiery-knitting center; mfg. of automobiles, machine tools, office machinery. Inc. former commune of Schönau.

Sieg River (zēk), W Germany, rises on the Ederkopf, flows 80 mi. W, past Siegen and Siegburg, to the Rhine just N of Bonn. Iron and some manganese mined in upper valley.

Siegsdorf (zēks′dôrf), village (pop. 3,296), Upper Bavaria, Germany, in Salzburg Alps, on small Weisse Traun R. and 3 mi. S of Traunstein; mfg. of precision instruments, lumber milling, woodworking. Summer resort (alt. 2,011 ft.), with mineral springs and mud baths.

Siemensstadt (zē′mŭns-shtät″, zē′mŭn-shtät″), industrial section of Spandau dist., W Berlin, Germany, on the Spree and 7 mi. WNW of city center; noted for electrical-equipment mfg. After 1945 in British sector.

Siemianowice or **Siemianowice Slaskie** (shĕmyänô-vē′tsĕ shlō′skyĕ), Pol. *Siemianowice Śląskie*, Ger. *Siemianowitz* (zĕmyä′nōvĭts), city (pop. 32,708), Katowice prov., S Poland, 3 mi. N of Katowice; coal mining; ironworks; mfg. of boilers, machines, screws; brewing. During Second World War, under Ger. rule, called Laurahütte, which had been, until First World War, name of a separate village, later inc. with Siemianowice.

Siemiatycze (shĕmyätĭ′chĕ), Rus. *Semyatichi* (syĭm-yŭtē′chĭ), town (pop. 4,106), Bialystok prov., E Poland, 50 mi. SSW of Bialystok; mfg. of cement, bricks, tiles, trunks, stockings, artificial wool; flour milling, tanning, sawmilling, woodworking. Before Second World War, pop. ⅔ Jewish.

Siempang (syĕm′päng′), town, Stungtreng prov., NE Cambodia, on the Se Khong and 45 mi. NE of Stungtreng, near Laos line.

Siemreap (syĕm′ryäp′), town, ⊙ Siemreap prov. (□ 6,700; 1948 pop. 235,081), NW Cambodia, 140 mi. NNW of Pnompenh, on Siemreap R. (affluent of lake Tonle Sap; navigable at high water), in rice-growing area; irrigation works. Airport. Noted ANGKOR ruins are 4 mi. N. Prov. was in Thailand prior to 1907 and (except for Siemreap town) again in 1941–46.

Siena (sēĕ′nŭ, Ital. syä′nä), province (□ 1,475; pop. 268,459); Tuscany, central Italy; ⊙ Siena. Has mtn. and hill terrain, watered by Elsa R. and by upper Ombrone R. and its tributaries. Agr. (grapes, olives, cereals, fruit, raw silk) and stock raising (cattle, sheep) widespread. Noted for its wine (Monti Chianti) and its marble (Chianciano, Sovicille, Casole d'Elsa) of a rich orange with purple and black veinings. Travertine quarries at Rapolano. Lignite mines (Pienza, Sinalunga, Montefollonico); mercury mines (Abbadia San Salvador, Piancastagnaio) on Monte Amiata. Mfg. at Siena, Colle Val d'Elsa, and Poggibonsi.

Siena, city (pop. 36,064), ⊙ Siena prov., Tuscany, central Italy, 31 mi. S of Florence, in center of rich agr. region noted for its wine and marble; 43°19′N 11°20′E. Produces agr. machinery, statues, glass, furniture, chemicals, fertilizer, cork articles, liquor, sausage. Seat of archbishopric and university (founded 13th cent.). Noted for art treasures, school of painting (13th–14th cent.), and Palio, the annual horse race of medieval origin held in the main square. Around this square are medieval palaces, slender Mangia tower, and imposing Gothic town hall with frescoes by Ambrogio Lorenzetti and Martini. Cathedral, with its elaborate façade of polychrome marble, is one of finest examples of Ital. Gothic. Adjoining is Piccolomini Library, with Pinturicchio's famous frescoes. There are many fine Gothic and Renaissance palaces. Home of St. Catherine of Siena, who was b. here, is a frequented shrine with frescoed chapels.

Sienfeng or **Hsien-feng** (both: shyĕn′fŭng′), town (pop. 13,449), ⊙ Sienfeng co. (pop. 153,292), southwesternmost Hupeh prov., China, 45 mi. SW of Enshih; rice, wheat, cotton, ramie.

Sienhsien or **Hsien-hsien** (both: shyĕn′shyĕn′), town, ⊙ Sienhsien co. (pop. 444,589), S central Hopeh prov., China, 55 mi. SE of Paoting and on Huto R.; cotton, melons, pears.

Sieniawa (shĕnyä′vä), town (pop. 936), Rzeszow prov., SE Poland, on San R. and 11 mi. N of Jaroslaw; flour milling, lumbering; brickworks. Castle.

Sienkiewiczowka, Ukraine: see SENKEVICHEVKA.

Sienkü or **Hsien-chü** (both: shyĕn′jü′), town (pop. 9,543), ⊙ Sienkü co. (pop. 211,748), E Chekiang prov., China, 25 mi. W of Linhai and on headstream of Ling R.; rice, wheat, medicinal herbs.

Sienne River (syĕn), Manche dept., NW France, rises in Normandy Hills near Saint-Sever-Calvados, flows c.35 mi. NW, past Villedieu and Gavray, to the Channel W of Coutances.

Sienning or **Hsien-ning** (both: shyĕn′nĭng′), town pop. 3,574), ⊙ Sienning co. (pop. 143,223), SE Hupeh prov., China, 40 mi. S of Hankow and on Canton-Hankow RR; tea-growing center; hemp.

Siennümiao or **Hsien-nü-miao** (both: shyĕn′nü′-myou′), town, N Kiangsu prov., China, 8 mi. ENE of Yangchow, across Grand Canal; commercial center.

Sientaochen or **Hsien-tao-chen** (both: shyĕn′dou′ jŭn′), town, SE central Hupeh prov., China, 50 mi. WSW of Hankow and on left bank of Han R.; commercial center; cotton and silk weaving; lotus seeds.

Sienyang or **Hsien-yang** (both: shyĕn′yäng′), town (pop. 16,008), ⊙ Sienyang co. (pop. 102,835), S central Shensi prov., China, on Wei R. (head of navigation) and 15 mi. WNW of Sian, and on Lunghai RR; cotton-weaving center. The oldest Chinese capital in the Sian area, Sienyang dates from 4th cent. B.C. and was residence (350–206 B.C.) of the Tsin dynasty. It was succeeded as capital by SIAN under the Han dynasty.

Sienyu or **Hsien-yu** (both: shyĕn′yō′), town (pop. 19,856), ⊙ Sienyu co. (pop. 298,306), SE Fukien prov., China, 65 mi. SW of Foochow; rice, wheat, sweet potatoes, rapeseed.

Sieradz (shĕ′räts), Rus. *Seradz* (syĕ′rŭts), town (pop. 9,813), Lodz prov., central Poland, on Warta R., on railroad and 33 mi. WSW of Lodz; flour milling, sawmilling, tanning, mfg. of yeast, cement; distilling. Monastery. During Second World War, under Ger. rule, called Schieratz.

Sierakow (shĕră′ko͞of), Pol. *Sieraków*, Ger. *Zirke* (tsĭr′kŭ), town (1946 pop. 2,782), Poznan prov., W Poland, on Warta R. and 40 mi. WNW of Poznan; glass mfg., sawmilling; stallion breeding.

Sierck or **Sierck-les-Bains** (sērk-lā-bē′), village (pop. 1,144), Moselle dept., NE France, on right bank of Moselle R., near Saar and Luxembourg borders, and 11 mi. NE of Thionville; iron founding, steel milling. Mineral springs. Damaged in Second World War.

Sierning (zērn′ĭng), town (pop. 7,084), E Upper Austria, 5 mi. W of Steyr; mfg. of knives.

Sierpc (shĕrpts), Rus. *Serpets* (syĕr′pĭts), town (pop. 9,282), Warszawa prov., N central Poland, 70 mi. NW of Warsaw. Rail and road junction; mfg. of agr. machinery, cement, tiles; tanning, flourmilling. Castle ruins near by. During Second World War, under administration of East Prussia, called Sichelberg.

Sierpe, Boca de la, Venezuela-Trinidad: see SERPENT'S MOUTH

Sierra (sēĕ′rŭ). **1** County (□ 958; pop. 2,410), NE Calif.; ⊙ Downieville. In the Sierra Nevada, here crossed by Yuba Pass; rises to 8,615 ft. at Sierra Buttes. Bounded E by Nev. line. Drained by Yuba R. and tributaries. Parts of Tahoe and Plumas natl. forests are in co. Gold L., other lakes (fishing) in N. Gold mining (rich quartz lodes have yielded since 1850s); some lead, silver, and copper mining, sand and gravel quarrying. Lumbering (pine, fir, cedar); cattle and sheep grazing; some farming and dairying in Sierra Valley (NE). Old mining camps, hunting, fishing, winter sports attract vacationers. Formed 1852. **2** County (□ 3,034; pop. 7,186), SW N.Mex.; ⊙ Truth or Consequences (Hot Springs). Livestock-grazing area; drained by Rio Grande, flowing through Elephant Butte and Caballo reservoirs. Placer mining for gold. Part of Black Range and Gila Natl. Forest in W. Formed 1884.

Sierra, La, Costa Rica: see LA SIERRA.

Sierra, La, Uruguay: see LA SIERRA.

Sierra Ancha (ăn′chŭ), mountain range, central Ariz., N of Roosevelt Reservoir; rises to 6,505 ft. in LOOKOUT MOUNTAIN.

Sierra Baya, Argentina: see SIERRAS BAYAS.

Sierra Blanca (sēĕ′rŭ blăng′kŭ, sēr′ŭ), village (1940 pop. 671), ⊙ Huspeth co., extreme W Texas, c.80 mi. SE of El Paso and c.15 mi. from Mex. border; alt. c.4,500 ft. Railroad junction; shipping, trading point in ranching, mining, tourist region. Sierra Blanca Mtn. is 7 mi. NW; Quitman Mts. are SW.

Sierra Blanca (sēĕ′rŭ blăng′kŭ). **1** In S Colo., range of Sangre de Cristo Mts., in parts of Alamosa, Huerfano, and Costilla counties. Highest points: Old Baldy (14,125 ft.), BLANCA PEAK (c. 14,363 ft.). **2** In S central N.Mex., range of Sacramento Mts. in Lincoln and Otero counties; iron-ore deposits, soft-coal mines. Chief peaks: Nogal Peak (9,983 ft.), Sierra Blanca (12,003 ft.; 33 mi. NNE of Alamogordo; highest point in Sacramento Mts.). Range extends through part of Mescalero Indian Reservation and Lincoln Natl. Forest. **3** Peak (c.6,950 ft.), Hudspeth co., extreme W Texas, 7 mi. NW of Sierra Blanca village.

Sierra-Bullones (syĕ′rä-bo͝olō′näs), town (1939 pop. 2,813; 1948 municipality pop. 19,385), central Bohol isl., Philippines, 32 mi. ENE of Tagbilaran; agr. center (rice, coconuts).

Sierra Buttes (sēĕ′rŭ bŭts′), Sierra co., NE Calif., jagged twin peaks of the Sierra Nevada, 17 mi. SW of Portola; the higher summit is 8,615 ft. Gold-bearing quartz mines here have yielded since 1850s.

Sierra Chica (syĕ′rä chē′kä), town (pop. estimate 1,000), central Buenos Aires prov., Argentina, 6 mi. NE of Olavarría; state prison.

Sierra Chivato, N.Mex.: see SAN MATEO MOUNTAINS, Valencia co.

Sierra City (sēĕ′rŭ), gold-mining village (pop. c.200), Sierra co., NE Calif., on North Yuba R., at foot of Sierra Buttes, and 18 mi. SSW of Portola. Winter-sports area near by. Yuba Pass is E.

Sierra Colorada (syĕ′rä kōlōrä′dä), village (pop. estimate 400), ⊙ Nueve (9) de Julio dept. (1947 census 4,652), central Río Negro natl. territory, Argentina, on railroad and 240 mi. W of Viedma; stock raising (sheep, goats, horses).

Sierra de Fuentes (syĕ′rä dhā fwĕn′tĕs), village (pop. 2,728), Cáceres prov., W Spain, 6 mi. ESE of Cáceres; cereals, olive oil, livestock.

Sierra del Caballo Muerto, Texas: see CARMEN, SIERRA DEL.

Sierra del Carmen, Texas: see CARMEN, SIERRA DEL.

Sierra de Yeguas (syĕ′rä dhā yā′gwäs), town (pop. 4,638), Málaga prov., S Spain, in the Sierra de YEGUAS, 17 mi. WNW of Antequera; olives and olive oil, cereals, livestock. Mfg. of plaster.

Sierra Diablo (sēĕ′rŭ dēä′blō), extreme W Texas, mtn. group extending E and N from point NE of Sierra Blanca; max. alt. c.6,600 ft. Forms part of S and E boundary of Diablo Bolson.

Sierra Estrella (sēĕ′rŭ ĕstrĕ′lŭ), mountain range, SW central Ariz., near Gila R., SW of Phoenix. Rises to 4,508 ft.

Sierra Leone (sēĕ′rŭ lēō′nē, lēōn′), British colony and protectorate (□ 27,968; pop. 1,858,275), W Africa; ⊙ FREETOWN. Bounded N by Fr. Guinea, SE by Liberia (along Mano R.); Atlantic coast line is 210 mi. long. The colony portion (□ 269; pop. 124,657) consists of Sierra Leone Peninsula (on which Freetown is situated), near-by Tasso and Banana Isls., and the township of BONTHE (on Sherbro Isl.) with adjacent York Isl. Some other small areas (a coastal strip ¼ to 1 mi. w de, Sherbro Isl. outside of Bonthe township, and several inland dists.), though historically a part of the colony, are administered under the protectorate (□ 27,699; pop. 1,733,618) which constitutes the bulk of Sierra Leone. The coastal region is low, with many tidal inlets and mangrove swamps; in W and S is a rain-forest plain, broken in places by low hills. In N and NE the country rises to a savanna plateau (average alt. 1,500 ft.), topped by Loma Mts. (Bintimane peak, 6,390 ft.) and Tingi Hills (6,080 ft.). Numerous short streams (Little and Great Scarcies, Rokel or Sierra Leone, Jong, Sewa, Moa) rise in the plateau and form deep inlets on the Atlantic; their lower courses are navigable for small craft. The monsoon tropical climate is not healthful; average temperatures 75°–85°F.; rainfall (up to 150 in. per year in Freetown; higher inland) concentrated in rainy season (May–Nov.); during virtually rainless Jan.–Feb. the Saharan harmattan blows from NE. Rice (both paddy and upland variety) is chief subsistence crop; cassava (manioc), sweet potatoes, and peanuts are also grown. Palm kernels, piassava fiber, kola nuts, ginger, and cacao are exported. Mineral resources are abundant; iron is mined in large quantities at Marampa (or Lunsar) and shipped from tidewater loading point at Pepel (NE of Freetown); diamonds are washed at Yengema (in NE), chromite is mined at Hangha (near Kenema). Platinum and ilmenite are recovered on Sierra Leone Peninsula. Only industries are sawmilling, oil pressing, ship and railroad repairing. Sierra Leone has an adequate rail net (311 mi. long) linking Freetown (Br. West Africa's best port) with the interior of the protectorate (termini at Pendembu and Makeni); there are c.500 mi. of roads. A new airport was built after 1948 near Lungi, 8 mi. N of Freetown, across the bay. Pop. is predominantly Christian in the colony and pagan in the protectorate, with some Moslems in N. Principal tribes are the Temne, Limba, Loko, Fula, and Mandingo in N, the Mende, Sherbro, Gallina, and Gola in S. There is a Kru community in Freetown. Sierra Leone coast was 1st visited by Portuguese in 1462; English slave traders followed. Through the efforts of British abolitionists, a settlement was established (1787) by liberated slaves on Sierra Leone Peninsula. Became a crown colony in 1808, and for several short periods during 19th cent. Freetown was hq. of West African Settlements which also included Gambia and Gold Coast. After gradual penetration of unhealthful hinterland, the protectorate was established in 1896. Sierra Leone is ruled by an appointed governor (for both colony and protectorate) with the aid of a nominated executive council and a partly elective legislative council. For administration, the protectorate (⊙ Bo) is divided into provinces, districts, and chiefdoms; the provinces are Northern (⊙ Makeni), South-Western (⊙ Bo), and South-Eastern (⊙ Kenema). The colony has separate administrations for Freetown municipality, the rural areas on Sierra Leone Peninsula, and the Sherbro Judicial Dist. (Bonthe and York Isl.).

Sierra Leone, Cape, NW point of Sierra Leone Peninsula, W Sierra Leone, at mouth of Sierra Leone R., 4 mi. W of Freetown; 8°30'N 13°18'W. Lighthouse.

Sierra Leone Peninsula (□ 256; pop. 117,045), on Atlantic Ocean, in W Sierra Leone, bet. Bunce and Sierra Leone rivers (N) and Yawri Bay (S); 25 mi. long, c.10 mi. wide; constitutes major part of SIERRA LEONE colony. Formed by range of wooded igneous mts., rising to 2–3,000 ft. in Picket Hill, Sugar Loaf Mtn., and Leicester Peak. Terminates NW in Cape Sierra Leone, W in False Cape, and S in Cape Shilling. One of W Africa's rare mountainous coastal areas. Mining of platinum and ilmenite. Some agr. (cassava, fruit, vegetables); fisheries. Main centers (served by railroad): FREETOWN, Kissy, Hastings, Waterloo, York.

Sierra Leone River, estuary on the Atlantic, in W Sierra Leone, N of Sierra Leone Peninsula; formed 17 mi. SW of Port Loko by junction of Port Loko Creek and ROKEL RIVER; c.25 mi. long, 4–10 mi. wide. Contains Tasso Isl. Its ports are Freetown (S bank, near mouth) and Pepel (N bank; hematite shipping point). Excellent deepwater natural harbor. Name Sierra Leone R. sometimes applied to Rokel R.

Sierra Madre (syĕ'rä mä'dhrā), chief mountain system of MEXICO, including the Sierra Madre Oriental, the Sierra Madre Occidental, and the Sierra Madre del Sur, which enclose the great central plateau, itself an integral part of this formation, broken by block ranges and depressions (*bolsons*). To a large measure the Sierra Madre *is* Mexico. It thrusts c.1,500 mi. SE from U.S. border towards the Isthmus of Tehuantepec. A subrange extends farther beyond the isthmus into Guatemala (Sierra Madre de Guatemala), followed by the main cordillera of Central America, which connects with the Andean ridges near Panama-Colombia boundary. In NE the Sierra Madre Oriental is separated by the Rio Grande from corresponding ranges of the S Rockies in Texas. However, a structural relationship bet. the Sierra Madre and the great W chains of South America and the U.S. has not been conclusively established. In general, the mts. were formed by Tertiary folding and faulting of Cretaceous deposits. There are volcanic rocks in the W, and the plateau just S of Mexico city is flanked by the formidable transverse E–W axis of volcanoes—sometimes called Cordillera de Anáhuac—rising in the Pico de ORIZABA or Ciltaltépetl (18,700 ft.) to highest elevation of the entire range. Other well-known peaks include the POPOCATEPETL, IXTACIHUATL, and the recently formed (1943) PARICUTÍN. The Sierra Madre of Guatemala has the volcano TACANÁ on international line and TAJUMULCO (13,816 ft.), highest peak in Central America. Altogether this mtn. region takes up about ¾ of Mexico, representing a giant triangle—based on U.S. border—wedged bet. the narrow tropical lowlands on the Pacific and Gulf of Mexico coasts. Lofty massifs tower over hot valleys and temperate highlands, blocking passage with rough ridges and impassable canyons (*barrancas*). The ranges hold an enormous store of minerals (silver, lead, copper, arsenic, manganese, gold, iron, tungsten, and other metals). They determine climate, crops, communication, and wealth. As in the Andean countries of South America, the sierras are responsible for the characteristic patterning of vegetation zones into hot, temperate, and cold zones—*tierra caliente, tierra templada*, and *tierra fría*. Drainage is provided by moderately large, unnavigable river systems, such as Santiago-Lerma (with L. Chiapas), Río de las BALSAS, and PÁNUCO RIVER. There are several interior drainage basins, foremost CASAS GRANDES and LAGUNA DISTRICT (NAZAS RIVER). The **Sierra Madre Oriental** (ōryĕntäl'), beginning in barren hills of Coahuila and Nuevo León S of the Rio Grande, runs parallel to the coastal strip (10–200 mi. wide) of the Gulf of Mexico, merging in S near Orizaba at about 19°N with the volcanic belt. It supports on its SE slopes a luxuriant vegetation. The **Sierra Madre Occidental** (ōksēdĕntäl'), paralleling the Gulf of California and the Pacific, is the wider and more forbidding mtn. mass. Its main, deeply incised escarpment is more abrupt and rugged, rendering ascent from the coast extremely difficult. The width increases from c.100 mi. in Sonora and Chihuahua (S of Arizona) to 300 mi. further SSE, where it also merges with the volcanic axis. Average height is c.7,000 ft. There are several subranges (e.g., sierras of Durango and Nayarit) and many snow-capped peaks, among them Cerro del PIMAL, the Nevado de COLIMA (14,240 ft.), and Volcán de Colima (12,631 ft.). In its S section of Jalisco lies L. Chapala, largest of Mexican lakes. The **Sierra Madre del Sur** (del sōōr') is a tumbled mass of uplifted mts. in Guerrero and Oaxaca, touching the Pacific coast, but forming nowhere a clearly defined range. It slopes down to the Isthmus of Tehuantepec, beyond which it is continued by the Chiapas highlands and the Sierra Madre of Guatemala.

Sierra Madre, range in the Philippines, extends over 200 mi. along E coast of Luzon; rises above 6,000 ft.

Sierra Madre (sēĕ'rū mă'drē, mä'drā), city (pop. 7,273), Los Angeles co., S Calif., just E of Pasadena, at foot of Mt. Wilson; orange groves. Inc. 1907.

Sierra Madre, range in Continental Divide, S Wyo., just W of North Platte R. Chief peaks: Vulcan Mtn. (10,700 ft.), Bridger Peak (11,007 ft.). Range is NW extension of Park Range. BRIDGER'S PASS is in NW tip.

Sierra Mojada (syĕ'rä mōhä'dhä), town (pop. 959), Coahuila, N Mexico, at foot of Sierra Mojada, on railroad and 120 mi. N of Torreón; alt. 4,120 ft. Mining center (silver, gold, copper, lead, zinc).

Sierra Morena (syĕ'rä mōrā'nä), town (pop. 1,734), Las Villas prov., central Cuba, near N coast, 30 mi. WNW of Sagua la Grande; sugar cane, fruit, cattle.

Sierra Morena or **Cordillera Mariánica** (kôr-dhēlyā'rä märyä'nēkä), mountain range in S Spain, flanks the great central Meseta (plateau) along the N boundary of Andalusia, forms divide bet. the valleys of the Guadiana (N) and the Guadalquivir (S). Highly eroded, partly wooded. The main pass, the historic Despeñaperros, is crossed by the Málaga-Madrid RR in E section. Range extends c.375 mi. E-W to Port. border, rising to 4,340 ft. Particularly rich in mines (copper, iron, galena, pyrite, manganese, tin, nickel, sulphur, antimony, tungsten, coal), such as those at La Carolina, Linares, Santa Elena (Jaén prov.), Espiel, Peñarroya-Pueblonuevo, Bélmez (Córdoba prov.), Cala, Ríotinto, Nerva, Tharsis (Huelva prov.). On its slopes olives, grapes, cereals, fruit, and cereals are grown, and livestock raised.

Sierra Nevada (sēĕ'rū nūvă'dū, nūvä'dū, Sp. syĕ'rä nävä'dhä), Andalusian mtn. range of S Spain, in Granada and Almería provs., chief chain of the Cordillera PENIBÉTICA; extends c.60 mi. W–E parallel to, and within 25–30 mi. of, the Mediterranean. Rises to highest point in continental Spain in the Mulhacén (11,411 ft.); other snow-capped peaks: Veleta (11,128 ft.), Alcazaba (11,043). Part of watershed separating waters flowing to the Mediterranean and to the Atlantic. Rich in minerals (iron, lead, copper, zinc, mercury). Vineyards, olive and fruit orchards, sugar-cane fields on S slopes. Railway and road from Granada to foot of the Veleta. Botanical station; observatory built by Granada univ.

Sierra Nevada, great mountain range, mainly in E Calif., forming the wall bet. Central Valley (W) and the Great Basin; extends more than 400 mi. SE from gap S of Lassen Peak, at S end of CASCADE RANGE, to Tehachapi Pass (tĭhă'chŭpē) SE of Bakersfield, whence transverse Tehachapi Mts. swing SW to meet the Coast Ranges. Mt. WHITNEY (14,495 ft.) is highest peak in U.S. outside Alaska. Structurally a single colossal block with a granitic core, range has been repeatedly uplifted and eroded, partly overlaid by volcanic flows (especially in N part), subjected to faulting (along E margin), and extensively glaciated at higher altitudes. Its steep, barren E front rises sharply, as the result of faulting and tilting, above the Great Basin; the longer, more gradual W slope runs out into grass-covered foothills bordering the Central Valley. Highest portion (often called the High Sierras) is S of L. Tahoe (partly in Nev.), which lies in fault basin bet. main chain and CARSON RANGE, here the E front range. Besides Mt. Whitney, range includes many summits over 14,000 ft.: Mt. Williamson (14,384 ft.), North Palisade (14,254 ft.), Mt. Russell (14,190 ft.), Split Mtn. (14,051 ft.), Mt. Langley (14,042 ft.), Mt. Tyndall (14,025 ft.), Mt. Muir (14,025 ft.), Mt. Barnard (14,003 ft.); and many others over 13,000 ft. Main (E) divide, called John Muir Crest, is paralleled W of Mt. Whitney region by short secondary divide (Great Western Divide). Range is famed for its wilderness recreational resources and some of finest mtn. scenery in North America, much of it in magnificent natl. parks. (YOSEMITE, KINGS CANYON, and SEQUOIA), which include stupendous gorges (canyons of Kings, Kern, Merced, Tuolumne rivers), towering peaks, granite monoliths (e.g., Half Dome), some of world's most beautiful waterfalls (notably Yosemite Falls), groves of giant redwoods, and glacial lakes and meadows famed for their beauty. Heavy snowfall feeds streams of W slope (Feather, Yuba, American, Stanislaus, Tuolumne, Merced, Kings, Kern rivers), which produce much power and supply irrigation water to Central Valley; from drier E slope, the Truckee, Carson, East Walker, and West Walker rivers flow E into Nev., and Owens R. flows S through Owens Valley along E base. Gold-bearing belt (including MOTHER LODE) of W has yielded richly since discovery of gold was made here in 1848. Highway passes across range (N-S) are Beckwourth (alt. c.5,250 ft., also railroad), Yuba (alt. 6,700 ft.), Donner (alt. 7,135 ft., also railroad), Truckee (alt. c.5,800 ft.), Carson (alt. 8,600 ft.), Ebbetts (alt. 8,800 ft.), Sonora (alt. c.9,625 ft.), Tioga (alt. 9,946 ft.), Kearsarge (alt. 11,823 ft.), Walker (alt. c.5,250 ft.).

Sierra Nevada de Mérida (dā mā'rēdä), mountain range, W Venezuela, spur of the Andes beginning at Colombian border and extending c.300 mi. from Cordillera Oriental of Colombia NE bet. the Orinoco llanos and Maracaibo lowlands to Barquisimeto at foot of Caribbean coastal range; 30–50 mi. wide. Includes a number of snow-capped peaks; rises, in peak La Columna (or Bolívar), to 16,411 ft. Other mountains are La CORONA (or Humboldt), La CONCHA, and Pico El León. Crops vary from bananas in lowlands, and coffee, the major crop, in middle altitudes, to wheat below 10,000 ft.; cattle are raised above on windswept grasslands called *páramos*. The transandine highway travels the range's entire length. City of Mérida is in Chama R. valley.

Sierra Oscura (sēĕ'rū ŏskōō'rū), S central N.Mex., range in SW tip of Chupadera Mesa, just NE of San Andres Mts., E of Rio Grande. Highest at Oscura Peak (8,732 ft.). First atomic bomb was exploded (July 16, 1945) in desert region just W.

Sierrapando (syĕräpän'dō), E suburb (pop. 1,984) of Torrelavega, Santander prov., N Spain; cheese processing, cordage mfg.

Sierra Prieta (sēĕ'rū prēā'tū), small range, just W of Prescott, central Ariz.; highest point is GRANITE MOUNTAIN (7,700 ft.).

Sierras Bayas (syĕ'räs bī'äs), town (pop. 2,437), central Buenos Aires prov., Argentina, 9 mi. ESE of Olavarría, in the Sierra Baya hills; cement-milling center; limestone, stone, sand quarries.

Sierra Valley (sēĕ'rū), NE Calif., mountain basin (c.20 mi. long, up to 10 mi. wide; alt. c.5,000 ft.), largest in the Sierra Nevada, c.25 mi. NW of Reno, Nev. Farming, stock raising, dairying, lumbering. Loyalton is chief settlement. Middle Fork Feather R. rises here. Beckwourth Pass across Sierra Nevada crest is E.

Sierra Vieja (vēā'hū) or **Vieja Mountains,** Jeff Davis and Presidio counties, extreme W Texas, generally parallel to the Rio Grande (W), c.35 mi. to W and NW of Marfa; c.30 mi. long; rise to 6,467 ft. Sometimes called Tierra Vieja Mts.

Sierre (syâr), Ger. *Siders* (zē'dūrs), town (pop. 6,306), Valais canton, S Switzerland, on the Rhone and 9 mi. ENE of Sion; on hilly (alt. 1,771 ft.) remains of a prehistoric landslip. Former monastery, 13th-cent. tower, 16th-cent. castle. Chippis lies across the Rhone; resorts NW of town.

Sierro (syĕ'rō), town (pop. 1,222), Almería prov., S Spain, near Almanzora R., 26 mi. WSW of Huércal-Overa; olive oil, cereals, potatoes.

Siersburg (zērs'bŏŏrk), town (pop. 2,508), W Saar, near Fr. border, 5 mi. NW of Saarlouis; stock, grain.

Siete Aguas (syā'tā ä'gwäs), town (pop. 1,192), Valencia prov., E Spain, 11 mi. ESE of Requena; olive oil, wine, saffron. Mineral springs.

Siete de Abril (dā äbrēl') or **7 de Abril,** town (pop. estimate 500), NE Tucumán prov., Argentina, 55 mi. NE of Tucumán; lumbering and agr. (alfalfa, corn, sugar cane, grapes, livestock).

Siete Iglesias de Trabancos (ēglā'syäs dā trävāng'kōs), town (pop. 1,699), Valladolid prov., N central Spain, 14 mi. WNW of Medina del Campo; cereals, wine, sheep.

Sieu (syĕ'ōō), Ger. *Schogen* (shō'gūn), Hung. *Nagysajó* (nŏ'dyŭ-shŏyō), village (pop. 1,549), Rodna prov., N central Rumania, 12 mi. SE of Bistrita. In Hungary, 1940–45.

Sieve River (syā'vĕ), Tuscany, central Italy, rises in several headstreams in Etruscan Apennines, joining 8 mi. SSW of La Futa pass; flows E, past Borgo San Lorenzo, and S, past Dicomano, to Arno R. at Pontassieve; 33 mi. long. Its upper valley is called the Mugello.

Sievershausen (zē"fūrs-hou'zūn), village (pop. 1,617), in former Prussian prov. of Hanover, W Germany, after 1945 in Lower Saxony, 5 mi. NW of Peine. Scene (1553) of battle bet. Maurice of Saxony and Albert, margrave of Brandenburg. Maurice was mortally wounded, but his forces were victorious.

Sife, Lake (sĭfĕ') (□ 13), central Turkey, 12 mi. ENE of Kirsehir; 6 mi. long, 4 mi. wide; alt. 3,540 ft.

Sifeng or **Hsi-feng** (both: shē'fŭng'), town (1938 pop. 33,886), ⊙ Sifeng co. (1946 pop. 265,779), N Liaotung prov., Manchuria, 37 mi. SE of Szeping, and on railroad, at Liaosi prov. line; coal and iron mining; soybeans, kaoliang, hemp, tobacco, furs; sericulture.

Sifengkow or **Hsi-feng-k'ou** (both: –kō'), town, N Hopeh prov., China, on Lwan R. and 100 mi. ENE of Peking, at gate in Great Wall (Jehol line).

Sifnos, Greece: see SIPHNOS.

Sig (sēg), name given to lower course of Oued Mékerra, in Oran dept., NW Algeria, below Saint-Denis-du-Sig; and to fertile coastal lowland (growing cereals, citrus, cotton, truck), irrigated by that stream.

Sigacik, Gulf of (sŭäjŭk'), Turkish *Sığacık*, inlet of Aegean Sea, W Turkey, 25 mi. SW of Izmir; 15 mi. wide, 11 mi. long.

Sigao (sēgou'), village, central Goa dist., Portuguese India, in Western Ghats, 28 mi. SE of Pangim; sugar milling, jaggery mfg. Teak in near-by forests.

Sigean (sēzhã'), town (pop. 2,007), Aude dept., S France, near Bages and Sigean L. (lagoon of Gulf of Lion), 11 mi. S of Narbonne; slaked-lime mfg.; saltworks, vineyards.

Sigel (sē'gŭl), town (pop. 296), Shelby co., central Ill., 19 mi. SSW of Mattoon; grain, soybeans, dairy products, livestock, poultry.

Siggenthal, Switzerland: see OBERSIGGENTHAL.

Siggiewi (sĭj-jā'wē) or **Sijuwi** (sĭgōō'wē), Maltese *Siġġiewi*, town (pop. 4,583), W central Malta, 5 mi. SW of Valletta, in agr. region (citrus fruit, wheat; goats, sheep). Has several old baroque churches, several fortified houses, Palace of the Inquisitor. Remarkable troglodyte village L'Ghar il Gbir is near by.

Sighet (sē'gĕt), Hung. *Máramarossziget* (mä'rŏmŏ-rôsh-sē"gĕt) or *Sziget* (sē'gĕt), town (1948 pop. 18,329), Baia-Mare prov., on Tisa R. (USSR border), NW Rumania, in Crisana-Maramures, in W foothills of the Carpathians, 270 mi. NNW of Bucharest; rail junction and trading center (salt, lumber, fruit, livestock, animal products). Mfg. (knitwear, scarves, cardboard and paper goods, clay products, furniture, brushes, buttons); tanning. Extensive kaolin deposits in vicinity. Originally a colony of Slavs, Sighet was chartered in 16th cent. Formerly had a large Jewish pop; c.30% pop. are Magyars. In Hungary, 1940–45.

Sighisoara (sēgēshwä'rä), Rum. *Sighișoara*, Ger. *Schässburg* (shäs'bŏŏrk), Hung. *Segesvár* (shĕ'gĕsh-vär), town (1948 pop. 18,284), Sibiu prov., central Rumania, in Transylvania, 110 mi. NW of Bucharest, 40 mi. NE of Sibiu; rail junction, summer resort and tourist center; mfg. of cotton, wool, and silk textiles, knitwear, furniture, bricks, tiles; metalworking, flour milling. Extensive trade (wine, cattle). The Upper Town, also called the Citadel, is surrounded by fortified walls. Within the walls are well-preserved medieval buildings; 15th-cent. Tower of the Clock, now a mus.; and several 15th-cent. churches. The town was in existence in 12th cent. and was settled in 13th cent. by Ger. colonists; it received the title of royal free city. During the Middle Ages, it became noted as a center of craft guilds. Hungarian revolutionaries of 1849 were defeated by the Russians near by.

Sigiriya (sĭg'ĭrĭyŭ), village (pop. 497), Central Prov., Ceylon, 45 mi. NNE of Kandy; airfield. On summit of near-by isolated rock (1,144 ft.) are noted Buddhist ruins (5th cent. A.D.) of palace, baths, and frescoes; in 5th cent., used as fortress and, for 18 years, as ⊙ Ceylon.

Siglap (sĭglăp'), village (pop. 4,755), Singapore isl., on SE coast, 5 mi. E of Singapore.

Sigli (sĭg'lē), town (pop. 4,676), Dharwar dist., S Bombay, India, 30 mi. SE of Dharwar; market center for cotton, peanuts, wheat; handicraft cloth weaving. Also spelled Shigli or Shigali.

Sigli (sē'glē), town (pop. 3,327), N Sumatra, Indonesia, port on Strait of Malacca, 45 mi. ESE of Kutaraja, on railroad; ships resin, pepper.

Siglingen (zēk'lĭng-ŭn), village (pop. 1,307), N Württemberg, Germany, after 1945 in Württemberg-Baden, on the Jagst and 11 mi. NNE of Heilbronn; cement mfg.

Siglo Veinte or **Siglo XX** (sē'glō vān'tā), tin-mining settlement (pop. c.8,700), Potosí dept., W central Bolivia, adjoining Catavi.

Siglufjordur or **Siglufjordhur** (sĭk'lüfyûr"dhür), Icelandic *Siglufjörður*, city (pop. 3,069), in but independent of Eyjafjardar co., N Iceland, on small inlet of Greenland Sea, 160 mi. NE of Reykjavik; 66°9'N 18°55'W. Chief center of Icelandic herring fisheries, with freezing, curing, and canning plants.

Sigma (sĕg'mä), town (1939 pop. 1,251; 1948 municipality pop. 10,898), Capiz prov., N Panay isl., Philippines, 13 mi. SW of Capiz; agr. center (tobacco, rice, hemp).

Sigmaringen (zēk'märĭng"ŭn), town (pop. 6,158), former ⊙ Hohenzollern, S Germany, after 1945 Württemberg-Hohenzollern, at S foot of Swabian Jura, on the Danube and 28 mi. NW of Ravensburg; rail junction; furniture mfg. On a rock rising abruptly from the Danube is large castle, rebuilt after fire of 1893. First mentioned 1077. Town passed to counts, later dukes, of Hohenzollern in 1534; residence of Hohenzollern-Sigmaringen line until 1849, when it came to Prussia. Kings Carol I and Ferdinand I of Rumania b. here.

Signa (sē'nyä), town (pop. 4,694), Firenze prov., Tuscany, central Italy, on the Arno and 8 mi. W of Florence; mfg. center; straw hats, terra cotta, machinery (agr., wine, hat), soap, paint, liquor. Heavily damaged by bombing (1943–44) in Second World War.

Signakhi (sēgnä'khē), city (1926 pop. 4,853), E Georgian SSR, in Kakhetia, 60 mi. ESE of Tiflis, in winegrowing area; orchards, cotton, wheat; handicraft industry. In 18th cent., a fortress against Lezghian attacks. Until 1936, Signakh.

Signal Hill, city (pop. 4,040), Los Angeles co., S Calif., surrounded by LONG BEACH; covered with oil wells (1st gusher in 1921). Inc. 1924.

Signal Mountain, town (pop. 1,786), Hamilton co., SE Tenn., 8 mi. N of Chattanooga, on slope of Signal Mtn. (1,400 ft.; S spur of Walden Ridge). Scene of Civil War fighting in Chattanooga campaign; battlefield area now included in Chickamauga and Chattanooga Natl. Military Park. Settled 1911; inc. 1919.

Signal Peak (11,223 ft.), in Sevier Plateau, SW central Utah, 6 mi. E of Monroe.

Signau (zĭg'nou), town (pop. 2,644), Bern canton, W central Switzerland, in the EMMENTAL, 13 mi. E of Bern.

Signo, Yugoslavia: see SINJ, S Croatia.

Signy Island (sēnyē') (4 naut. mi. long, 3 naut. mi. wide), South Orkney Isls., S of Coronation Isl., in the South Atlantic; 60°43'S 45°37'W. Discovered in 1825.

Signy-l'Abbaye (-läbā'), village (pop. 1,455), Ardennes dept., N France, 14 mi. WSW of Mézières; sawmilling, hosiery mfg.

Signy-le-Petit (-lŭ-pŭtē'), village (pop. 1,160), Ardennes dept., N France, 17 mi. ENE of Vervins; customhouse near Belg. border. Mfg. of heating equipment.

Sigoulès (sēgōōlĕs'), village (pop. 282), Dordogne dept., SW France, 7 mi. SSW of Bergerac; wine.

Sigourney (sĭ'gûrnē), city (pop. 2,343), ⊙ Keokuk co., SE Iowa, 23 mi. E of Oskaloosa, in livestock and grain area; mfg. (feed, concrete blocks). Limestone quarries near by. Inc. 1868.

Sigriswil (zĭ'grĭsvēl"), residential town (pop. 3,788), Bern canton, central Switzerland, near L. of Thun, 5 mi. ESE of Thun.

Sigsbee Deep: see MEXICO, GULF OF.

Sigsig (sēgsēg'), town (1950 pop. 1,632), Azuay prov., S Ecuador, in the Andes, on highway and 17 mi. WSW of Cuenca; agr. center (cereals, fruit, sugar cane, cotton, livestock); mfg. of *toquilla* hats. Gold mines in vicinity.

Sigtuna (sĭg'tü"nä), city (pop. 1,432), Stockholm co., E Sweden, on N arm of L. Malar, 20 mi. NNW of Stockholm; cultural center, with noted people's high school, theological research institute, and several boarding schools. Has remains of many 11th- and 12th-cent. churches and of 13th-cent. monastery. Stones with runic inscriptions near by. One of Sweden's oldest cities, it was founded in early 11th cent.; after destruction (1187) by Estonians its importance declined.

Siguatepeque (sēgwätāpā'kā), city (pop. 2,618), Comayagua dept., W central Honduras, on road and 15 mi. NW of Comayagua; commercial center; tobacco, coffee, sugar cane, livestock. Dates from 17th cent.

Sigüenza (sēgwĕn'thä), anc. *Segontia* or *Saguntia*, city (pop. 4,395), Guadalajara prov., central Spain, in New Castile, on Henares R., on railroad and 40 mi. NE of Guadalajara. Bishopric, and one of oldest cities of the prov. Trading center in rich agr. region (wheat, truck produce, livestock). Tanning, lumbering, flour milling, lime quarrying; mfg. of woolen goods, soap, chocolate, plaster. Fortress-like cathedral (damaged during civil war; reopened 1946) has Romanesque, Gothic, and Renaissance elements. Neolithic caverns are near by.

Siguiri (sēgē'rē), town (pop. c.11,000), NE Fr. Guinea, Fr. West Africa, on left bank of the Niger and 120 mi. SW of Bamako (Fr. Sudan), 335 mi. ENE of Conakry; 11°25'N 9°5'W. Trading and agr. center, exporting rubber, millet, corn, hides, gold. Stock raising (goats, sheep). Airfield; R.C. and Protestant missions. The near-by gold placers of the upper Guinea are visited during dry season by great numbers of natives. Bauxite and manganese deposits in vicinity.

Sigulda (sē'gōōldä), Ger. *Segewold*, city (pop. 1,618), N central Latvia, in Vidzeme, on the Gauja and 32 mi. ENE of Riga; excursion center for "Livonian Switzerland"; summer resort. Has 13th-cent. castle ruins. Across the Gauja are Turaida and Krimulda castle ruins, visited by tourists.

Sigurd (sĭ'gûrd), town (pop. 431), Sevier co., central Utah, 8 mi. NE of Richfield and on Sevier R.; alt. 5,308 ft.; agr., gypsum mines.

Sihasinaka (sēhäsēnä'kŭ), village, Fianarantsoa prov., E Madagascar, on railroad and 30 mi. NNW of Manakara; native market and coffee center.

Sihfeng or **Hsi-feng** (both: shē'fŭng'), town (pop. 2,709), ⊙ Sihfeng co. (pop. 62,067), central Kweichow prov., China, 35 mi. N of Kweiyang and on main road to Szechwan; alt. 3,524 ft.; papermaking; wheat, millet. Bauxite deposits near by.

Sihiyoun, Syria: see SAHYUN.

Sihl River (zēl), NE central Switzerland, rises in S Schwyz canton, flows 45 mi. NNW, through the Sihlsee, to Limmat R. at Zurich. Etzel hydroelectric plant is on river.

Sihlsee (zēl'zā), lake, Schwyz canton, NE central Switzerland, traversed by Sihl R.; □ 4, alt. 2,913 ft., max. depth 82 ft. Dam of Etzel hydroelectric works here. Bridge and viaduct connect W and S shores.

Siho or **Hsi-ho** (both: shē'hŭ'), town, ⊙ Siho co. (pop. 127,237), SE Kansu prov., China, 50 mi. SW of Tienshui; paper mfg., tobacco processing; winegrowing; rice, beans, millet, wheat, timber. Coal and iron mines.

Sihor (sĭhōr'), town (pop. 11,256), E Saurashtra, India, 13 mi. WSW of Bhaunagar; trades in cotton, millet, oilseeds, building stone; pottery and glassworks; oilseed pressing, cloth dyeing, handicrafts (copper-, brassware; snuff). Was ⊙ Rajput clan.

Sihora (sĭhō'rŭ), town (pop. 7,026), Jubbulpore dist., N Madhya Pradesh, India, 25 mi. NNE of Jubbulpore; agr. market (wheat, rice, gram, oilseeds). Bauxite workings near by. Rock edict of Asoka 22 mi. N, near village of Bahuriband.

Sihsien or **Hsi-hsien** (both: shē'shyĕn'). **1** Town, ⊙ Sihsien co. (pop. 343,500), S Anhwei prov., China, on railroad and 100 mi. S of Wuhu; rice, tea, corn, tung oil, lacquer. An anc. city dating from the Mongol Yüan dynasty (1280–1368), it was traditionally known for its tea (TUNKI) and India ink (SIUNING) production. Until 1912 called Hweichow. **2** Town, ⊙ Sihsien co. (pop. 476,966), SE Honan prov., China, 60 mi. ENE of Sinyang, near Anhwei line; rice, wheat, beans, kaoliang. Until 1935 called Paosintsi. The old Sihsien is 20 mi. SW, on Hwai R. **3** Town, ⊙ Sihsien co. (pop. 64,139), SW Shansi prov., China, 50 mi. NW of Linfen; medicinal herbs; cattle raising. Oil deposits. Until 1912 called Sichow.

Si Hu, China: see WEST LAKE.

Sihuas (sē'wäs), city (pop. 1,432), Ancash dept., W central Peru, in Cordillera Occidental, 23 mi. NW of Pomabamba; alt. 8,858 ft. Weaving of native textiles; agr. products (wheat, corn, alfalfa). Silver and copper mining near by.

Sihun River, Central Asia: see SYR DARYA.

Sihun River, Turkey: see SEYHAN RIVER.

Sihunta (sĭhōōn'tä), village, N Himachal Pradesh, India, 18 mi. S of Chamba; local market for corn, rice, tea.

Sihwa or **Hsi-hua** (both: shē'hwä'), town, ⊙ Sihwa co. (pop. 275,004), E Honan prov., China, 30 mi. NE of Yencheng and on Ying R.; wheat, rice, beans.

Siirt (sērt), prov. (□ 4,383; 1950 pop. 158,838), SE Turkey; ⊙ Siirt. Bordered E by Hakari Mts., S by Tigris R.; also drained by Buhtan and Perveri rivers. Mountainous and unproductive. Sometimes spelled Sairt or Sert.

Siirt, anc. *Tigranocerta*, town (1950 pop. 15,574), ⊙ Siirt prov., SE Turkey, on Buhtan R. 95 mi. E of Diyarbakir; wheat. Founded by the Armenian king Tigranes, who was later defeated here (69 B.C.) by the Roman Lucullus. Sometimes spelled Sairt and Sert.

Sija or **San Carlos Sija** (sän kär'lōs sē'hä), town (1950 pop. 954), Quezaltenango dept., SW Guatemala, at S foot of volcano Sija, on headstream of Samalá R. and 9 mi. N of Quezaltenango; alt. 10,500 ft.; corn, wheat, fodder grasses, livestock.

Siján (sēhän'), village (pop. estimate 300), S Catamarca prov., Argentina, 30 mi. NW of Catamarca; kaolin deposits; cattle.

Sijilmassa, Fr. Morocco: see TAFILALET.

Sijol, Thailand: see SICHON.

Sijuwi, Malta: see SIGGIEWI.

Sik (sēk), village (pop. 631), central Kedah, Malaya, on road from Gurun station and 22 mi. NE of Sungei Patani; rice.

Sikaiana, Solomon Isls.: see STEWART ISLANDS.

Sikama, Japan: see SHIKAMA.

Sikandarabad (sĭkŭn'dŭrābäd'), town (pop. 23,307), Bulandshahr dist., W Uttar Pradesh, India, 10 mi. WNW of Bulandshahr; road junction; hand-loom cotton-weaving center; wheat, oilseeds, barley, jowar, cotton. Also spelled Sikandrabad.

Sikandarpur (sĭkŭn'dŭrpōōr), town (pop. 7,506), Ballia dist., E Uttar Pradesh, India, near the Gogra, 21 mi. NNW of Ballia; perfume mfg.; rice, gram, barley, oilseeds, sugar cane. Afghan fort ruins. Founded 15th cent.

Sikandra (sĭkŭn'drŭ), village, Agra dist., W Uttar Pradesh, India, near the Jumna, 5 mi. WNW of Agra city center. Noted as the site of Akbar's mausoleum (red sandstone inlaid with white marble) which stands in 150 acres of garden, flanked by massive walls and gateways; built c.1612 by Akbar's son Jahangir. Also other protected Mogul monuments.

Sikandrabad, India: see SIKANDARABAD.

Sikandra Rao (rou), town (pop. 13,032), Aligarh dist., W Uttar Pradesh, India, on Upper Ganges Canal and 23 mi. SE of Aligarh; hand-loom cotton-weaving center; glass mfg.; wheat, barley, pearl millet, cotton, gram. Has 16th-cent. mosque. Founded (15th cent.) by Sikandar Lodi.

Sikang or **Hsi-k'ang** (sē'kăng', shē'kăng') [Chinese, =western Kang or KHAM], province (□ 90,000; pop. 2,000,000) of SW China; ⊙ Yaan. Bounded W by Tibet (along Yangtze R.), N by Tsinghai, E by Szechwan, and S by Yunnan, Sikang prov. occupies the SE dissected margins of the Tibetan plateau. High, abrupt ranges, extending generally NW–SE and rising to 24,900 ft. in the Minya Konka, are separated from each other by the sheer, canyon-like gorges of some of Asia's mightiest rivers, the Yangtze and the Yalung. The climate is distinguished by warm, rainy summers (mainly in SE), and cold, dry winters, governed by the SE Asia monsoons. Among Sikang's chief mineral resources are gold, copper, and salt. Agr. is possible in the few level areas and produces wheat, beans, sweet potatoes, tea, and fruit. The raising of sheep, goats, and cattle is important in the economy, and yields wool and skins for export. Other important products are musk, deer horns, and medicinal plants. Prov. is traversed by the chief trade route linking Lhasa and S China. On it are Sikang's chief towns:

Yaan, Kangting (whence another road leads NW past Kantse to Jyekundo), Lihwa, and Paan. Poor roads and the precipitous relief generally render transportation difficult. Pop. is Chinese (speaking SW Mandarin dialect) only in Kangting-Yaan area adjoining Szechwan border (E); but Chinese colonization has proceeded into the Tibetan area as far as Paan (on Yangtze R.). Lolo and Moso aborigines are found in SE and S. Sikang has had a confused administrative history. It was formed originally (1914) as the special administrative dist. of Chwanpien, out of Kham (E Tibet) and W Szechwan. Chwanpien was renamed Sikang in 1924 and became a full prov. in 1928. It was enlarged (SE) in 1938 through a further territorial addition from Szechwan. The Chinese have long claimed that Sikang's W border was at c.93°W (so as to include what is KHAM prov. of Tibet), although Tibet's E frontier is at the Yangtze (c.99°W). In 1950 the Tibetan-majority area of W Sikang prov. E of the Yangtze was established as TIBETAN AUTONOMOUS DISTRICT (⊙ Kangting, former prov. capital).

Sikang River, India: see DIBANG RIVER.

Sikanni Chief River (sĭkă'nē), NE B.C., rises in Stikine Mts. near 57°15'N 124°40'W, flows c.275 mi. in a wide arc ENE and NE to confluence with Muskwa R. at Fort Nelson, forming Fort Nelson R.

Sikar (sē'kŭr), town (pop. 32,334), ⊙ Sikar dist., E central Rajasthan, India, 65 mi. NW of Jaipur; rail junction; trade center (millet, gram, wool, cotton, salt, cattle); handicrafts (cloths, pottery, enamel work, lacquered goods). Col.

Sikaram, Mount (sĭkŭräm'), highest peak (15,620 ft.) in Safed Koh Range, on Afghanistan-Pakistan border, 55 mi. SE of Kabul, at N end of Durand Line, just N of Paiwar Pass; 34°3'N 69°55'E.

Sikasso (sēkä'sō), town (pop. c.14,250), S Fr. Sudan Fr. West Africa, near Upper Volta border, on road to Bobo-Dioulasso and 180 mi. SE of Bamako; cotton-growing center. Cattle and hog raising.

Sikes, village (pop. 342), Winn parish, N central La., 15 mi. NE of Winnfield.

Sikeston (sĭks'tŭn), city (pop. 11,640), on New Madrid-Scott co. line, SE Mo., in Mississippi flood plain, 25 mi. WSW of Cairo, Ill.; agr. center, processes and ships cotton; shoe factory. Inc. 1874.

Sikhim, India: see SIKKIM.

Sikhiu, Thailand: see CHANTHUK.

Sikhote-Alin Range or **Sikhote-Alin' Range** (sēkhŭtě'-ŭlyĕn'yŭ), Maritime and Khabarovsk territories, Russian SFSR, in parallel ranges along Sea of Japan, from Vladivostok N to lower Amur R.; rises to 5,200 ft. Extensive, dense forests abound in valuable woods processed in sawmilling centers along the Ussuri (Lesozavodsk, Iman, Bikin). Rich in mineral resources: gold, silver, coal, iron, nonferrous, and rare metals. Site of game reserves.

Si Kiang, China: see WEST RIVER.

Siking, China: see SIAN.

Sikinos (sē'kēnôs), Lat. *Sicinus* (sĭ'sĭnŭs), Aegean island (□ 16; 1940 pop. 688) in the Cyclades, Greece, SW of Naxos isl.; 36°40'N 25°5'E; 8 mi. long, 2 mi. wide; produces wine, figs, wheat. Main town, Sikinos (1928 pop. 267), is on W shore. Used as penal colony under Romans.

Sikion, Greece: see SICYON.

Sikionia, Greece: see SIKYONIA.

Sikkim (sĭk'kĭm) [Tibetan *Denjong*, =rice country], protectorate (□ 2,745; 1951 pop. 135,646) of India, in the E Himalayas, S central Asia; ⊙ Gangtok. Bounded W by Singalila Range (Nepal border), N by Tibet, NE by Dongkya Range (Tibet border), SE by Bhutan, S by Darjeeling dist. of India; drained by upper Tista R. Predominantly a mountainous area, with Nepal (W) and Assam (E) Himalayas, separated by the Tista and intersected by deep river valleys. Highest point (28,146 ft.) is the Kanchenjunga, 3d-highest peak in the world, with Zemu Glacier (largest in Sikkim) on E slope. State divided into 3 zones: tropical (up to 5,000 ft.), temperate (5–13,000 ft.), and alpine (13,000 ft. to perpetual snowline at 16,000 ft.). Botanically one of richest areas in India; includes c.4,000 species of flowering plants, orchids (660 recorded species), ferns (250 species), rare fungi, and huge thickets of rhododendron; also several thousand species of moths and butterflies. Temperate zone includes both deciduous and evergreen forests; Siberian flora in alpine zone. Crops: corn, rice, pulse, oranges, cardamom, wheat, barley, apples. Copper mines at Pachikhani. Hand-loom cotton weaving is chief handicraft industry. There are 44 Buddhist monasteries, the most noted being Sangachelling, Pemiongchi, Tashiding, Rumtek, and Tulung (art collection). Main India-Tibet trade route, in SE, runs through Jelep La Pass. Lepchas, the original inhabitants, were ruled after 17th cent. by rajas of Tibetan descent. Twice invaded by Gurkhas in 18th, once in 19th cent. In 1835, site of Darjeeling was ceded to English; in 1849, the Sikkim Terai and lower course of the Tista were annexed by the English, while China claimed N section, but recognized Br. sovereignty over whole area in 1890. State religion is Buddhism, but majority of inhabitants profess Hinduism. Pop. mainly Nepalese tribes (including the Limbu, Gurung, Kami, Newar), also Bhotiya (Tibetan) and Lepcha (Rong), all of whom speak Tibeto-Burman languages and dialects. State became independent following Br. withdrawal from India in 1947; negotiations begun 1949 resulted in India's assumption of responsibility for state's administration, with treaty signed in 1950. Also spelled Sikhim.

Siklos (shĭk'lōsh), Hung. *Siklós*, town (pop. 5,927), Baranya co., S Hungary, at S foot of Villany Mts., 16 mi. S of Pecs; brickworks, wine.

Siknas (sēk'nĕs"), Swedish *Siknäs*, village (pop. 416), Norrbotten co., N Sweden, on small inlet of Gulf of Bothnia, 20 mi. NE of Lulea; sawmilling, woodworking.

Sikoku, Japan: see SHIKOKU.

Siku or **Hsi-ku** (both: shē'gōō'), town, ⊙ Siku co. (pop. 52,084), SE Kansu prov., China, 100 mi. SW of Tienshui; rice, wheat, millet.

Sikwangshan, China: see SINHWA.

Sikyon, Greece: see SICYON.

Sikyonia or **Sikionia** (both: sēkēōnē'ŭ), town (pop. 5,210), Argolis and Corinthia nome, NE Peloponnesus, Greece, port on Gulf of Corinth, on railroad and 11 mi. WNW of Corinth; trades in Zante currants, citrus fruits, olive oil. Summer resort. Formerly called Kiaton. Site of anc. SICYON is 2 mi. inland.

Sil, Lake, Swedish *Silen* (sē'lŭn) (25 mi. long, 1–4 mi. wide), W Sweden, near Norwegian border, 15 mi. NW of Amal; drains S into L. Vaner.

Sila, La (lä sē'lä), massif (□ 1,275) of the Apennines, S Italy, in Cosenza and Catanzaro provs. Forms central part of toe of Ital. boot. Average height, 4,250–4,600 ft.; descends abruptly to Crati R. valley (W) and gradually toward Gulf of Taranto (E). Divided into Sila Greca (N), Sila Grande (center), and Sila Piccola (S). Chief peaks: BOTTE DONATO (6,329 ft.), MONTENERO (6,171 ft.). Sparsely settled; chief industries are stock raising and forestry. Recently its lakes have been converted into reservoirs (on the Ampollino and Arvo) for hydroelectric power (chief plants near SAN GIOVANNI IN FIORE and COTRONEI). Source of Crati and NETO rivers.

Silacayoápan (sēläkīwä'pän), town (pop. 2,375), Oaxaca, S Mexico, in Sierra Madre del Sur, 33 mi. NW of Tlaxiaco; alt. 5,518 ft.; cereals, sugar cane, fruit, stock.

Silandro (sēlän'drô), Ger. *Schlanders*, town (pop. 1,841), Bolzano prov., Trentino–Alto Adige, N Italy, in Val Venosta, 19 mi. W of Merano.

Silang (sēläng'), town (1939 pop. 3,870; 1948 municipality pop. 20,292), Cavite prov., S Luzon, Philippines, 26 mi. S of Manila; agr. center (rice, fruit, coconuts).

Silanus (sēlä'nōōs), village (pop. 2,674), Nuoro prov., central Sardinia, 23 mi. W of Nuoro. Nuraghe near by.

Silao (sēlä'ō), city (pop. 13,880), Guanajuato, central Mexico, on affluent of Lerma R. and 13 mi. WSW of Guanajuato; alt. 5,830 ft. Rail junction; agr. center (corn, wheat, alfalfa, beans, chili, sugar cane, livestock). Mineral springs near by. Founded 1537.

Silas, town (pop. 383), Choctaw co., SW Ala., 21 mi. N of Chatom.

Silay (sēlī'), town (1939 pop. 7,941; 1948 municipality pop. 35,570), Negros Occidental prov., NW Negros isl., Philippines, port on Guimaras Strait, 9 mi. N of Bacolod; sugar milling, sulphur mining.

Silba Island (sēl'bä), Ital. *Selve* (sĕl'vĕ), Dalmatian island in Adriatic Sea, W Croatia, Yugoslavia, 32 mi. NW of Zadar; 5 mi. long, 1 mi. wide. Chief village, Silba.

Silberberg, Poland: see SREBRNA GORA.

Silberhorn, Mount (sĭl'bûrhôrn), peak (10,757 ft.) in Tasman Natl. Park Southern Alps, W central S.Isl., New Zealand.

Silbitz (zĭl'bĭts), village (pop. 615), in former Prussian Saxony prov., central Germany, after 1945 in Saxony-Anhalt, on the White Elster and 7 mi. NNW of Gera; mfg. of steel products.

Silbury Hill, England: see AVEBURY.

Silceastre, England: see SILCHESTER.

Silchar (sĭl'chŭr) town (pop. 16,601), ⊙ Cachar dist., S Assam, India, in Surma Valley, on Barak (Surma) R. and 78 mi. SE of Shillong; rail spur terminus; road and trade center (rice, tea, cotton, sugar cane, rape and mustard, timber); tea processing, rice milling, paper and tea-box mfg.

Silchester (sĭl'chĭstŭr), agr. village and parish (pop. 443), N Hampshire, England, 6 mi. N of Basingstoke. Site of ruins of the Romano-British town of *Calleva Atrebatum*, of which extensive remains were found. Most of the relics are now in Reading Mus. Has 13th–15th-cent. parish church. Silchester was the Saxon *Silceastre*.

Sile (shĭ'lĕ), Turkish *Şile*, village (pop. 2,772), Istanbul prov., NW Turkey in Asia, on Black Sea, 36 mi. ENE of Istanbul; commercial and residential suburb. Sometimes spelled Shile.

Sileby, town and parish (pop. 3,598), N Leicester, England, 7 mi. N of Leicester; hosiery, leather, shoe industry. Has church dating from 13th cent.

Silei or **Hsilei** (both: shē'lā'), Jap. *Seira* (sā'rä), town (1935 pop. 10,394), W central Formosa, 20, mi. N of Kiayi and on Choshui R.; mfg. (noodles, flour, gold and silver paper, wood products, tile). Also spelled Silo or Hsilo.

Silene, Mount (5,000 ft.), NE Labrador, near head of Nachvak Fiord; 58°58'N 64°2'W.

Silenen (zē'lŭnŭn), town (pop. 2,202), Uri canton, central Switzerland, on Reuss R. and 6 mi. S of Altdorf. Amsteg hydroelectric plant is S of town.

Siler City (sī'lŭr), town (pop. 2,501), Chatham co., central N.C., 30 mi. SE of Greensboro; furniture factories, textile and grain mills. Settled 1855; inc. 1885.

Sile River (sē'lĕ), Veneto, N Italy, rises 5 mi. W of Castelfranco Veneto, flows c.50 mi. E, in many meanders, past Treviso, and SE, past Casale sul Sile, to Lagoon of Venice near Burano.

Silerton (sī'lŭrtŭn), town (pop. 121), Hardeman co., SW Tenn., 19 mi. S of Jackson, in pine-timber and farm area.

Sileru River, India: see MACHKUND RIVER.

Siles (sē'lĕs); agr. town (pop. 3,830), Jaén prov., S Spain, 34 mi. NE of Villacarrillo; olive-oil processing, flour milling. Lumbering. Salt mining. Has remains of anc. walls and towers.

Silesia (sĭlē'zhŭ, –shŭ, sī–), Czech *Slezsko* (slĕs'kô), Ger. *Schlesien* (shlā'zyŭn), Pol. *Śląsk* (shlōsk), region (□ c.20,000; 1946 pop. c.6,250,000), E central Europe, extending along both banks of the upper Oder R. and bordering S on the Sudetes and W Beskids. Almost all the region is politically divided bet. SW Poland and N central Czechoslovakia. The Polish part (□ c.17,500), by far the largest, borders S on Czechoslovakia and W on Lusatian Neisse and Oder rivers (German line). The greater part of Silesia was a prov. of Germany until 1919, when it was divided into provs. of Lower Silesia (Ger. *Niederschlesien;* □ 10,419; 1939 pop. 3,286,539; ⊙ Breslau) and Upper Silesia (Ger. *Oberschlesien;* 1939 area □ 3,880; 1939 pop. 1,582,225; ⊙ Oppeln). Treaty of Versailles provided for plebiscite to determine whether Upper Silesia was to remain German or to pass to Poland. The plebiscite, preceded by considerable violence on both sides, was held in 1921; only easternmost part of Upper Silesia voted for transfer to Poland. After Pol. armed rising (1922), League of Nations accepted partition of Upper Silesia; the larger part of the industrial region, including Katowice, passed to Poland and was formed into prov. of Silesia (□ 1,628; 1931 pop. 1,295,027; ⊙ Katowice). In 1945 all of Ger. Silesia (i.e.,Lower Silesia and the remaining part of Upper Silesia) was placed under Pol. administration, pending final settlement by a peace conference. This placed all of the pre-1919 area of Ger. Silesia under Polish control, except for a small part W of the Lusatian Neisse R., which was inc. into Saxony. The Pol. govt. at once (1945) redistricted the whole area and by 1950 it was divided among WROCLAW (⊙ BRESLAU), OPOLE, and KATOWICE provs. and part of ZIELONA GORA prov. Czech Silesia, at SE edge of Ger. Silesia, lies N of the Moravian Gate and is centered on Opava. It was an Austro-Hungarian crownland (□ 1,987; 1910 pop. 756,949) until 1919, when most of it became part of the new republic of Czechoslovakia. The TESCHEN city and dist. were partitioned, 1920, bet. Poland and Czechoslovakia by the Conference of Ambassadors. In 1920 Czech Silesia also received the dist. of Hultschin (Hlucin) from Germany. Munich Pact, 1938, partitioned Czech Silesia bet. Germany and Poland, but in 1945 Czech Silesia was restored to its pre-1938 boundaries (□ 2,132; 1948 pop. 840,841), and Ger. pop. was expelled. Until 1949, it was part of Moravia and Silesia prov., after 1949 part of the Czech Lands, one of the 2 constituent states of Czechoslovakia (the other is Slovakia). Silesia in general consists of mountainous, partly forested, region, cut by numerous N–S valleys along N slopes of the Sudetes and W Beskids, and of undulating lowland region along the Oder. Highest elevation is the Schneekoppe (5,259 ft.) in the Riesengebirge, central range of the Sudetes. Region is drained by the Oder, Kwisa (Queis), Bobrawa (Bober), Kaczawa (Katzbach), Lusatian Neisse (Nysa Luzycka), Glatzer Neisse (Nysa Klodzka), and Opava rivers, and by headstreams of Vistula and Warta (Warthe) rivers. Soil is generally fertile; region produces rye, potatoes, oats, wheat, barley, flax, and sugar beets. Stock raising. In E part of Pol. Silesia, at N foot of W Beskids, is one of principal European industrial regions; it has extensive deposits of coal, lignite, zinc, lead, and iron. Mines, iron and steel furnaces and mills, coke and chemical plants are centered on Katowice, Beuthen (Bytom), Gleiwitz (Glywice), Chorzow, Zabrze (Hindenburg), and Czestochowa. Central part of Pol. Silesia, with cities of Oppeln (Opole) and Brieg (Brzeg), is generally agr. and has many tanneries and sugar refineries; Ratibor (Raciborz) has machinery works. In W part of region the Oder valley has extensive agr., while N slope of the Sudetes is industrialized; its principal cities are Breslau (Wroclaw); Waldenburg (Walbrzych), with important coal mines and glassworks; Liegnitz (Legnica); Hirschberg (Jelenia Gora); Glatz (Klodzko); and Szklarska Poreba (Schreiberhau), with major glassworks. Other industries of the region are textile and paper milling, machinery mfg., and metalworking Among numerous health and winter-sports resorts of Pol. Silesia are Szklarska Poreba, Karpacz

(Krummhübel), Kudowa Zdroj (Bad Kudowa), and Duszniki Zdroj (Bad Reinerz). Czech Silesia adjoins Bohemia (W), Moravia (S), and Slovakia (E), and (since 1949) is coextensive with most of Ostrava and N part of Olomouc provs. Greater part of region lies on N slopes of the Jeseniky (4,920 ft.); Beskids rise to 4,346 ft. on Lysa Hora near Slovak border. Both ranges are popular resort areas. Ridges are forested and in pasture. Region is noted for mineral wealth; local metallurgical industry, centered around Ostrava and Karvina, is based on coal and iron mined here. Other industries are chemical mfg., petroleum refining, textile milling, brewing. Principal cities: Opava, Karvina, Slezska Ostrava. Silesia was settled (A.D. c.500) by Slavic tribes; by 11th cent. it was integral part of Poland. In early 12th cent. it became one of the 4 hereditary duchies into which King Boleslaus III of the Piast dynasty divided the kingdom. Duchy soon fell apart into many minor principalities; Ger. colonization was encouraged by the various Piast princes and Silesia was rapidly Germanized; in early 14th cent. the princes accepted suzerainty of king of Bohemia and thus became mediate princes of the Holy Roman Empire. During Hussite Wars (15th cent.) Silesia, with Moravia, was temporarily under Hungarian rule, but both reverted (1490) to Bohemia, with which they passed, 1526, to the Hapsburgs. Principality of Sagan (Zagan), Saxon since 1472, came to Bohemia in 1547. In Thirty Years War (1618–48) Silesia suffered heavily under Saxon, imperial, and Swedish occupation; at Peace of Westphalia it reverted to Austria. With extinction (1675) of Silesian Piast dynasty the individual principalities and fiefs disappeared and Silesia was inc. by Austria with Bohemian crown domain. In 1532 the margraviate of Jägerndorf (Krnov) had been purchased by a cadet branch of the Hohenzollern dynasty of Brandenburg, which later also claimed inheritance to other Silesian fiefs. Under treaty (1537) bet. Elector Joachim II of Brandenburg and Piast duke of Liegnitz, Brieg, and Wohlau, Brandenburg was to inherit Piast principalities if their dynasty became extinct, but King Ferdinand I of Bohemia (later Emperor Ferdinand I) declared treaty invalid. John George of Jägerndorf, brother of elector of Brandenburg, lost (1621) his fief for having supported Frederick the Winter King. In 1740 however, Frederick II of Prussia, as heir of house of Brandenburg, claimed part of Silesia on basis of the treaty of 1537. Prussians invaded Silesia even before Maria Theresa, who had just assumed succession to Austria, Bohemia, and Hungary, had rejected Frederick's claim. Silesian Wars of 1740–42 and 1744–45 were part of the general War of the Austrian Succession. In Treaty of Berlin (1742) Maria Theresa ceded all of Silesia except the present Czech part and Teschen to Prussia; cession ratified by Treaty of Dresden (1745). Industrial revolution had serious effect on Silesia; bad working conditions and unemployment among the weavers led to frequent outbreaks, landholding conditions were iniquitous, and many social problems arose from industrialization of Upper Silesia. Treaty of Versailles (1919) gave E part of Ger. Silesia to Poland, while Austro-Hungarian part passed to Czechoslovakia, and thus began the series of complex divisions of the territory which continued down through the post-Second World War period.

Silet (sēlĕt'), oasis, Saharan Oases territory, S Algeria, in the Ahaggar Mts., 60 mi. WSW of Tamanrasset; 22°43'N 4°30'E. Date palms.

Siletz (sĭlĕts'), city (pop. 570), Lincoln co., W Oregon, on Siletz R. (c.70 mi. long; flowing to Pacific Ocean near Taft) and 7 mi. N of Toledo.

Silex (sī'lĭks), town (pop. 188), Lincoln co., E Mo., on N. Fork of Cuivre R. and 11 mi. NNW of Troy.

Silgarhi Doti, Nepal: see DOTI.

Silghat (sĭl'gät), village, Nowgong dist., central Assam, India, on the Brahmaputra and 23 mi. NE of Nowgong; rail terminus; rice, jute, rape and mustard, tea.

Silhouette Island, westernmost (4,900 acres; pop. 502) of the Seychelles proper, in Indian Ocean, 15 mi. NW of Victoria; 4°30'S 55°15'E; 4 mi. long, 3 mi. wide; granite formation. Copra, essential oils; fisheries.

Siliana (sēlyänä'), town (pop. 1,807), Maktar dist., N central Tunisia, on Siliana R. and 18 mi. NE of Maktar; agr. trade center.

Siliana River, N central Tunisia, rises near Maktar, flows c.70 mi. N, past Siliana and El-Aroussa, to the Medjerda near Testour.

Silica Caves, Czechoslovakia: see SLOVAKIAN KARST.

Silifke (sĭlĭfkĕ'), anc. *Seleucia Trachea* or *Saleucia Tracheotis*, town (pop. 5,728), Icel prov., S Turkey, on Goksu R., 10 mi. from its mouth, and 50 mi. SW of Mersin; wheat, barley, sesame, vetch, beans. Formerly also Selefkeh. There are ruins of the anc. town, a center of Cilicia.

Siliguri (sĭlē'gŏŏrē), town (pop. 10,487), Darjeeling dist., N West Bengal, India, on the Mahananda and 25 mi. SSE of Darjeeling; focal point of trade from Tibet and Sikkim; sawmilling, rice milling; general-engineering factory; trades in tea, rice, corn, cardamom, oranges, jute, wheat.

Silikow, China: see TULAN.

Silin or **Hsi-lin** (both: shē'lĭn'), town, ⊙ Silin co. (pop. 59,105), W Kwangsi prov., China, 60 mi. NW of Poseh, near Yunnan line; rice, wheat, millet.

Silingol (sēlĭng-gōl'), Chinese *Hsi-lin-kuo-lo*, Mongolian league in SW Inner Mongolian Autonomous Region, Manchuria. Bounded N by Mongolian People's Republic, it was in N Chahar until 1949.

Silipica, Argentina: see SIMBOL.

Siliqua (sēlē'kwä), village (pop. 2,893), Cagliari prov., SW Sardinia, 17 mi. NW of Cagliari; rail junction.

Silistat, Turkey: see BOZKIR.

Silistea (sēlēsh'tyä), Rum. *Siliştea*, village (pop. 1,597), Bucharest prov., S Rumania, 45 mi. NW of Giurgiu, in grain and tobacco region.

Silistra (sĭlē'strä), anc. *Durostorum*, city (pop. 16,180), Ruse dist., NE Bulgaria, in S Dobruja, port on right bank of the Danube (Rum. border), opposite Calarasi, and 65 mi. ENE of Ruse, on railroad. Agr. and commercial center; exports grain, wool, wine, fish; weaving, tanning. Beekeeping, truck gardening near by. Has teachers col., theater. Founded by Romans in 29 B.C.; became important town of Moesia Inferior; later ruled successively by Bulgarians, Kievan Russians, Byzantines, Pecheneges, Wallachians, and Turks (15th–19th cent.). Subjected to several Rus. assaults in 19th cent.; finally captured (1877) and ceded to Bulgaria. In Rumania (1913–1940), it was ⊙ Durostor dept. (□ 1,245; 1930 pop. 211,433). Sometimes spelled Silistria.

Silivri (sĭlĭvrē'), village (pop. 4,129), Istanbul prov., Turkey in Europe, port on Sea of Marmara 37 mi. W of Istanbul; grain.

Silja, Lake, Swedish *Siljan* (sĭl'yän"), expansion (□ 137, including L. Orsa) of East Dal R., central Sweden, 25 mi. NW of Falun; 25 mi. long (NW–SE), 1–7 mi. wide; 394 ft. deep. Noted tourist center of Dalarna; shore resorts include Mora, Leksand, and Rattvik. Just N is L. Orsa, Swedish *Orsasjön* (ōōr'sä-shûn"), 7 mi. long, 1–4 mi. wide.

Silkeborg (sĭl'kûbôr), city (1950 pop. 23,372), Skanderborg amt, E Jutland, Denmark, on Guden R. and small lake Langso, 25 mi. W of Aarhus; health resort surrounded by woods and lakes; famous for scenery. Mfg. (paper, farm machinery, margarine, textiles), meat canning.

Silk Road or **Silk Route**, ancient caravan track linking China proper with the West. It passed through the neck of Kansu prov., left the protection of the Great Wall near Tunhwang through the Jade Gate, and passed S of the Taklamakan Desert to Kashgar. This route was followed by Marco Polo in c.1275. Later variants of this route passed N and S of the Tien Shan.

Silksworth, town and parish (pop. 1,769), NE Durham, England, 3 mi. WSW of Sunderland; coal mining. Just E is coal-mining town of New Silksworth.

Sill, Fort, Okla.: see LAWTON.

Sill, Mount, Calif.: see KINGS CANYON NATIONAL PARK.

Silla (sē'lyä), town (pop. 6,168), Valencia prov., E Spain, near Albufera lagoon, 8 mi. SSW of Valencia, in rice-growing area; mfg. of fertilizer, burlap, tiles, sirups; fruit, peanuts, cereals.

Silla de Caracas (sē'yä dä kärä'käs), mountain with 2 peaks (Pico Occidental, 8,163 ft.; and Pico Oriental or Aguilón, 8,661 ft.), N Venezuela, in coastal range, 6 mi. ENE of Caracas.

Sillajhuay (sĭyäkh-wī'), peak (19,695 ft.) in the Andes, on Chile-Bolivia line, NW of the Salar de Uyuni; 19°45'S.

Sillamae or **Sillamyae**, Est. *Sillamäe* (all: sē'lämää), town (1949 pop. over 500), on Gulf of Finland, 14 mi. W (under jurisdiction) of Narva, 1 mi. N of Vaivara rail junction; refines oil shale from Vivikond mine; bathing resort.

Sillanwali (sĭl-län'välē), town (pop. 3,926), Shahpur dist., central Punjab, W Pakistan, 19 mi. SSW of Sargodha, on branch of Lower Jhelum Canal; wheat, cotton, millet; cotton ginning. Sometimes spelled Shillanwali.

Sillaro River (sēl-lä'rô), N central Italy, rises in Etruscan Apennines 6 mi. N of Firenzuola, flows 40 mi. NE, past Castel San Pietro dell'Emilia, to Reno R. 3 mi. SE of Argenta. Canalized in lower course; used for irrigation.

Sillein, Czechoslovakia: see ZILINA.

Silleiro, Cape (sēlyā'rō), Pontevedra prov., NW Spain, at S entrance of Vigo Bay, 2 mi. W of Bayona; 42°7'N 8°54'W. Lighthouse.

Sillé-le-Guillaume (sēyā'-lü-gēyōm'), town (pop. 2,264), Sarthe dept., W France, 19 mi. NW of Le Mans; road center; hosiery mfg. Has dungeon of 15th-cent. castle.

Sillery (sĭ'lürē, Fr. sēyürē'), SW suburb (pop. estimate 500) of Quebec, S Que., on the St. Lawrence.

Sillery (sēyürē'), village (pop. 505), Marne dept., N France, on Aisne-Marne Canal and 6 mi. SE of Rheims; noted champagne wines.

Sillod (sĭl-lōd'), village (pop. 3,228), Aurangabad dist., NW Hyderabad state, India, 35 mi. NE of Aurangabad; millet, wheat, oilseeds; cotton ginning. Sometimes spelled Sillode.

Sillon de Bretagne (sēyō' dü brütä'nyü), range of hills in Loire-Inférieure dept., W France, extending 25 mi. WNW–ESE from Pontchâteau to Nantes, and rising to 300 ft. near Savenay.

Silloth (sĭ'lŭth), town in former Holme Cultram (hōm kŭl'trŭm) urban dist. (1931 pop. 4,743), NW Cumberland, England, on Solway Firth 18 mi. W of Carlisle; flour-milling center, seaside resort, and port for Carlisle. Founded 1855.

Sill River (zĭl), in Tyrol, W Austria, rises in Zillertal Alps near Brenner Pass, flows 25 mi. N, through the Wipptal, to Inn R. at Innsbruck.

Silly (sēyē'), Flemish *Opzullik* (ôp'sûlĭk), village (pop. 1,570), Hainaut prov., SW central Belgium, 7 mi. E of Ath, in chicory-growing area.

Silo, Formosa: see SILEI.

Siloam (sīlō'ŭm, sīlōm'), town (pop. 324), Greene co., NE central Ga., 6 mi. ESE of Greensboro.

Siloam Springs (sī'lōm"), city (pop. 3,270), Benton co., extreme NW Ark., 22 mi. WNW of Fayetteville, near Okla. line, in the Ozarks; trade, shipping center for fruit, livestock, poultry area. Health resort, with mineral springs. Seat of John Brown Univ. Laid out and inc. 1880.

Silos, Los (lōs sē'lōs), town (pop. 1,120), Tenerife, Canary Isls., 38 mi. WSW of Santa Cruz de Tenerife; bananas, tomatoes, potatoes, wheat, onions, livestock. Limekilns; cheese processing, embroidery making.

Silos, Los, N suburb (pop. 3,846) of Calañas, Huelva prov., SW Spain, 30 mi. N of Huelva; copper mine.

Silperk, Czechoslovakia: see STITY.

Sil River (sēl), chief tributary of the Miño, NW Spain, rises in Leon prov. 30 mi. NE of Ponferrada, flows 150 mi. WSW across Orense and Lugo prov. to Miño R. 10 mi. NE of Orense. Gold placer mining in Roman times.

Sils, Lake of (zĭls), Ger. *Silsersee* (zĭl'sûrzā), lake (3 mi. long, □ 2, alt. 5,894 ft.), Grisons canton, SE Switzerland. Sils im Engadin is on NE shore.

Silsbee (sĭlz'bē), city (pop. 3,179), Hardin co., E Texas, near Neches R., 20 mi. N of Beaumont; trade center in agr. area (fruit, truck, cotton), with oil wells, lumbering, cattle raising; railroad shops; sawmill. Founded c.1892, inc. as town 1906, as city 1938.

Silsden (sĭlz'dŭn), urban district (1931 pop. 4,889; 1951 census 5,820), West Riding, W Yorkshire, England, near Aire R., 11 mi. NW of Bradford; cotton and rayon milling.

Silsersee, Switzerland: see SILS, LAKE OF.

Sils im Engadin (zĭls' ĭm ĕng-gädēn'), Romansh *Segl* (sĕ'lyü), village (pop. 270), Grisons canton, SE Switzerland, bet. L. of Sils and L. of Silvaplana, on Inn R. and 6 mi. SW of St. Moritz; resort (alt. 5,945 ft.) in Upper Engadine. Consists of hamlets of Sils-Maria (märē'ä) and Sils-Baselgia (bäsĕl'jä).

Silt, town (pop. 361), Garfield co., W Colo., on Colorado R. and 18 mi. W of Glenwood Springs; alt. 5,338 ft. Shipping point for livestock and potatoes.

Siltepec (sēltāpĕk'), town (pop. 1,259), Chiapas, S Mexico, in Sierra Madre, 45 mi. SSW of Comitán; sugar cane.

Silung or **Hsi-lung** (both: shē'lŏŏng'), town, ⊙ Silung co. (pop. 78,683), W Kwangsi prov., China, 90 mi. NW of Poseh, near Hungshui R. (Kweichow line); rice, wheat, millet.

Siluria, village (1940 pop. 710), Shelby co., central Ala., 20 mi. S of Birmingham; cotton products, lime.

Silute or **Shilute** (shēlōōtā'), Lith. *Šilutė*, Ger. *Heydekrug* (hī'dŭkrōōk"), city (1941 pop. 5,236), W Lithuania, 30 mi. SSE of Memel; fisheries; cheese making; vegetables. In Memel Territory, 1920–39.

Silva Jardim (sēl'vŭ zhär'dēn'), city (pop. 697), central Rio de Janeiro state, Brazil, on railroad and 55 mi. ENE of Rio; distilling, manioc-flour milling; coffee. Until 1943, called Capivari (old spelling, Capivary).

Silvan (sĭlvän'), village (pop. 3,155), Diyarbakir prov., E Turkey, 45 mi. ENE of Diyarbakir; wheat, barley. Formerly Mayafarkin.

Silvani (sĭlvä'nē), town (pop. 2,425), E Bhopal state, India, 65 mi. E of Bhopal. Sometimes spelled Silwani.

Silvânia (sēlvä'nyü), city (pop. 1,675), S Goiás, central Brazil, near railroad, 30 mi. SE of Anápolis; textile milling; ships livestock, rice, cheese, tobacco. Rutile deposits. Until 1944, called Bonfim (formerly spelled Bomfim).

Silvaplana (sēl"väplä'nä), village (pop. 295), Grisons canton, SE Switzerland, 3 mi. SW of St. Moritz; resort (alt. 5,955 ft.) in Upper Engadine. Late-Gothic church. Road leads W to Julier Pass. Village is on **Lake of Silvaplana**, Ger. *Silverplanersee* (zĭl'vûrplä"nûrzā') (□ 1), which is joined at N to small L. of Campfèr by narrow neck.

Silva Pôrto (sĕl'vŭ pōr'tōō), town (pop. 4,671), ⊙ Bié prov., central Angola, on Benguela RR and 230 mi. E of Lobito; 12°24'S 16°57'E; alt. 5,645 ft., on Bié plateau. Agr. trade center in one of Angola's healthiest and richest regions. Ships rice, grain, beeswax, meat. Processing industry (rice hulling, meat processing); sawmilling. Airfield. Formerly called Bié or Bihé.

Silvares (sēlvä'rĭsh), town (pop. 2,136), Castelo Branco dist., central Portugal, on Zêzere R. and 14 mi. SW of Covilhã; there are extensive tungsten deposits.

Silvassá (sēlväsä'), town (pop. 1,721), Damão dist., Portuguese India, 13 mi. SE of Damão, in Nagar Aveli enclave; local market for rice, wheat, tobacco; palm-mat weaving.

Silveiras (sēlvā'rŏos), city (pop. 813), extreme SE São Paulo, Brazil, in the Serra da Bocaina, 8 mi. SE of Cruzeiro; coffee, livestock.

Silver Bank, shoal (c.35 mi. wide) with reefs, in the West Indies, 55 mi. NE of Puerto Plata (Dominican Republic), separated by 20-mi.-wide Silver Bank Passage from Mouchoir Bank (W).

Silver Bay, resort village, Warren co., E N.Y., on W shore of L. George, 12 mi. SSW of Ticonderoga.

Silver Beach, Mass.: see FALMOUTH.

Silver Bow, county (□ 716; pop. 48,422), SW Mont.; ⊙ Butte. Mtn. region crossed by Continental Divide; bounded SW by Big Hole R. Copper, zinc, lead, silver, manganese; livestock, dairy products; smelters at Butte. Formed 1881.

Silver Bow Park, village (pop. 5,128, with near-by Floral Park), Silver Bow co., SW Mont., a suburb of Butte.

Silver City, residential town (pop. 5,732), Cristobal dist., N Panama Canal Zone, on transisthmian highway just SSE of Cristobal.

Silver City. 1 Town (pop. 311), Mills co., SW Iowa, near Silver Creek, 15 mi. SE of Council Bluffs, in agr. area. 2 Town (pop. 381), Humphreys co., W Miss., on the Yazoo and 6 mi. S of Belzoni, in cotton region. 3 Hamlet, Lyon co., W Nev., 4 mi. S of Virginia City in Virginia Range; alt. c.5,000 ft. Formerly great silver producer (near Comstock Lode); mines mostly inactive. 4 Town (pop. 7,022), ⊙ Grant co., SW N.Mex., in foothills of Pinos Altos Mts., near Ariz. line, 130 mi. NW of El Paso, Texas; alt. 5,931 ft. Health resort, trade and shipping center for irrigated agr. and livestock area. Copper, zinc, and silver mines in vicinity. State teachers col., hq. of near-by Gila Natl. Forest here. Founded 1870, inc. 1878. Grew as silver- and gold-mining camp. Gila Cliff Dwellings Natl. Monument is 32 mi. N.

Silver Cliff, town (pop. 217), ⊙ Custer co., S central Colo., bet. Sangre de Cristo and Wet mts., 45 mi. WSW of Pueblo; alt. 8,000 ft. Boomed as silver camp in 1881.

Silver Creek. 1 Village (pop. 3,234, with adjoining Lindale), Floyd co., NW Ga., 5 mi. S of Rome. 2 Town (pop. 275), Lawrence co., S central Miss., c.50 mi. SSE of Jackson. 3 Village (pop. 444), Merrick co., E central Nebr., 17 mi. WSW of Columbus and on Platte R.; flour; stock, grain. 4 Village (pop. 3,068), Chautauqua co., extreme W N.Y., on L. Erie, 10 mi. NE of Dunkirk, in agr. area (grapes, cherries, tomatoes); summer resort; mfg. (milling machinery, railroad cars). Inc. 1848. 5 Town, Pa.: see NEW PHILADELPHIA.

Silver Creek. 1 In SW Ill., rises near Mount Olive, flows c.75 mi. generally S to Kaskaskia R. opposite New Athens. 2 In SW Iowa, rises near Westphalia in Shelby co., flows c.70 mi. S to West Nishnabotna R. 4 mi. S of Malvern.

Silverdale, town, NW Stafford, England, in the Potteries area; part of Newcastle-under-Lyme.

Silverdale, borough (pop. 384), Bucks co., SE Pa., 26 mi. NNW of Philadelphia; clothing mfg.

Silver Grove, village (1940 pop. 859), Campbell co., N Ky., on the Ohio, 7 mi. SE of downtown Cincinnati.

Silverheels, Mount (13,825 ft.), in Rocky Mts., Park co., central Colo.

Silverhill, farming town (pop. 354), Baldwin co., SW Ala., 22 mi. SE of Mobile.

Silver Hill, village (1940 pop. 546), Prince Georges co., central Md., SE of Washington.

Silver Islet, village, W Ont., on L. Superior, 20 mi. E of Fort William; silver mining.

Silver Lake. 1 Town (pop. 472), Kosciusko co., N Ind., 40 mi. W of Fort Wayne; ships vegetables. Resort lakes (fishing) near by. 2 City (pop. 331), Shawnee co., NE Kansas, 10 mi. WNW of Topeka, in fertile agr. valley of Kansas R. 3 Village (pop. 2,024), in Tewksbury and Wilmington towns, Middlesex co., NE Mass., 8 mi. SE of Lowell. 4 Village (pop. 603), McLeod co., S central Minn., c.45 mi. W of Minneapolis, in livestock and poultry area; dairy products, lumber. Small lakes near by. 5 Village, N.H.: see MADISON. 6 Resort village, Wyoming co., W N.Y., on Silver L. (c.3 mi. long), c.40 mi. SSW of Rochester. Here is a Methodist Church institute. 7 Village (pop. 1,040), Summit co., NE Ohio, 6 mi. NE of downtown Akron, near Cuyahoga R. 8 Town (1940 pop. 97), Lake co., S central Oregon, 65 mi. SSE of Bend; alt. 4,345 ft. Silver L., a dry lake bed, is E, near by. 9 Resort village (pop. 603), Kenosha co., extreme SE Wis., on Silver L., 17 mi. WSW of Kenosha.

Silver Lake. 1 In Amador co., E Calif., in the Sierra Nevada, 18 mi. S of L. Tahoe; c.2 mi. long; resort. 2 Lake (c.2 mi. long), Kent co., central Del., just N of Dover; drained by St. Jones R. Has waterfowl sanctuary. 3 Lake (c.2 mi. long), New Castle co., N central Del., just SE of Middletown; fishing. 4 In Clinton co., extreme NE N.Y., in the Adirondacks, 24 mi. SW of Plattsburg; c.2½ mi. long, ½–¾ mi. wide. 5 In Richmond co., N.Y.: see STATEN ISLAND.

Silvermine, Conn.: see NORWALK.

Silver Mine Bay, Chinese *Ngang Kong* (ŭngäng' kông'), inlet of S.China Sea, in E Lan Tao isl., Hong Kong colony; 1½ mi. long, 1 mi. wide. Lead deposits on NE shore.

Silverpeak, village, Esmeralda co., W Nev., in E foothills of Silver Peak Mts., 22 mi. W of Goldfield; Alt. 4,307 ft.; formerly important silver-mining center.

Silver Peak Mountains, W Nev., in Esmeralda co., near Calif. line. Chief peaks: Magruder Mtn. (9,057 ft.), 25 mi. SW of Goldfield, and Piper Peak (9,500 ft.), c.15 mi. WSW of Silverpeak town.

Silver Plume, town (pop. 136), Clear Creek co., N central Colo., on head stream of Clear Creek, in Front Range, and 40 mi. W of Denver; alt. 9,175 ft. Granite quarry near by. Grays Peak 6 mi. SW.

Silver Spring, residential suburb (pop. c.65,000), Montgomery co., central Md., just N of Washington; mfg. of scientific instruments; lumber milling. Seat of applied physics laboratory of Johns Hopkins Univ. Naval ordnance laboratory is at near-by White Oak.

Silver Springs. 1 Famous limestone spring and resort, Marion co., N central Fla., 6 mi. E of Ocala. Anc. spring with large basin c.80 ft. deep and with variable rate of flow of c.25,000,000 gallons per hour; has outlet c.7 mi. long to Oklawaha R. 2 Village (pop. 830), Wyoming co., W N.Y., 24 mi. SSE of Batavia; saltmaking; mfg. of rulers, maple syrup.

Silver Strand Beach, village (pop. 1,000, with adjacent Hollywood-by-the-Sea), Ventura co., S Calif.

Silver Strand Fall, Calif.: see YOSEMITE NATIONAL PARK.

Silverstreet, town (pop. 201), Newberry co., NW central S.C., 6 mi. SW of Newberry.

Silverthrone, Mount (13,130 ft.), S central Alaska, in Alaska Range, in Mt. McKinley Natl. Park, 130 mi. N of Anchorage, 10 mi. ENE of Mt. McKinley; 63°7'N 150°40'W.

Silverthrone, Mount (9,700 ft.), SW B.C., in Coast Mts., 210 mi. NW of Vancouver.

Silverton, village (pop. 103), W New South Wales, Australia, 15 mi. WNW of Broken Hill, near South Australia border; copper-mining center.

Silverton, village (pop. 272), SE B.C., in Selkirk Mts., on Slocan L., 30 mi. N of Nelson; silver, lead, zinc mining.

Silverton, town and parish (pop. 1,129), E central Devon, England, 7 mi. NNE of Exeter; paper milling.

Silverton, residential village (pop. 1,898), S central Transvaal, U. of So. Afr., 7 mi. ENE of Pretoria; tannery.

Silverton. 1 Town (pop. 1,375), ⊙ San Juan co., SW Colo., in San Juan Mts., on Animas R. and 39 mi. NNE of Durango; alt. 9,302 ft. Tourist and trade center. Lead, silver, copper, gold mines in vicinity. Founded 1874, inc. 1885. 2 Village (pop. 4,827), Hamilton co., extreme SW Ohio, a NE residential suburb of Cincinnati. Inc. 1904. 3 City (pop. 3,146), Marion co., NW Oregon, 12 mi. ENE of Salem; lumber and flour milling, canning, metalworking. Founded c.1853, inc. 1891. 4 Town (pop. 857), ⊙ Briscoe co., NW Texas, on Llano Estacado, 30 mi. NE of Plainview, near Cap Rock escarpment; alt. 3,261 ft. Trade center for farm, ranch area (grain, cotton, livestock, dairy products); ships grain; fuller's earth, clay products.

Silvertown, industrial city (pop. 3,387), Upson co., W central Ga., just N of Thomaston. Founded 1926 around large tire-fabric plant. Inc. 1929.

Silver Zone Pass, Nev.: see TOANO MOUNTAINS.

Silves (sĕl'vĭsh), city (pop. 4,326), Faro dist., S Portugal, 6 mi. NE of Portimão; cork-processing center; trade in figs, almonds, olive oil, wine, alcohol. Has ruined Moorish castle and a small Gothic cathedral. Settled by Phoenicians; ⊙ of Algarve under Moorish domination. Sacked 1060 by Ferdinand I of Castile; finally recaptured from Moors 1242. Almost leveled by 1755 earthquake.

Silvestre Ferraz (sēlvĕ'strĭ fĕrăz'), city (pop. 2,194), S Minas Gerais, Brazil, on N slope of the Serra da Mantiqueira, on railroad and 30 mi. NE of Itajubá; coffee, tobacco, dairy products.

Silvi (sēl'vē), village (pop. 961), Teramo prov., Abruzzi e Molise, S central Italy, near the Adriatic, 9 mi. NW of Pescara; licorice-extraction factory.

Silvia (sēl'vyä), town (pop. 2,203), Cauca dept., SW Colombia, in Cordillera Central, 20 mi. NE of Popayán; alt. 8,320 ft.; cacao, tobacco, sugar cane, fique, cereals, stock.

Silvianópolis (sēlvyŭnô'pŏolēs), city (pop. 1,660), S Minas Gerais, Brazil, on N spur of the Serra da Mantiqueira, 18 mi. NE of Pouso Alegre; coffee, tobacco, dairy products.

Silvies River, E central Oregon, rises near Strawberry Mts. in Malheur Natl. Forest, flows c.90 mi. S, past Burns, to Malheur L.

Silvis, residential city (pop. 3,055), Rock Island co., NW Ill., just E of East Moline; has railroad yards. Inc. 1920.

Silvretta Group (sēlvrĕt'tä), mountain group in Rhaetian Alps, extending along Swiss-Austrian border from E of Klosters to N of Schuls, Switzerland. Its highest peak, Piz Linard (11,200 ft.), is in Switzerland. Piz Buin is its high point in Austria.

Silvrettahorn, peak (10,656 ft.) in Silvretta Group of Rhaetian Alps, on Swiss-Austrian border, 10 mi. E of Klosters.

Silwa or **Silwah** (sĭl'wŭ), village (pop. 5,233), Aswan prov., S Egypt, on E bank of the Nile and 18 mi. SSE of Idfu; cereals, dates.

Silwani, India: see SILVANI.

Sim (sēm), city (1938 pop. estimate 9,600), W Chelyabinsk oblast, Russian SFSR, in the S Urals, on Sim R. and 15 mi. E of Asha, on rail spur; agr.-machinery mfg. center. Founded 1784; became city in 1942. Until c.1928, Simski Zavod.

Sim, river, Russian SFSR: see SIM RIVER.

Sim, Cape (sēm), headland of SW Fr. Morocco on the Atlantic, 10 mi. SSW of Mogador; 31°24'N 9°51'W. Lighthouse.

Sima or **Fort Morton** (sē'mä), village, Myitkyina dist., Kachin State, Upper Burma, on Chinese Yunnan prov. border, 30 mi. SE of Myitkyina.

Simabara, Japan: see SHIMABARA, city.

Simacota (sēmäkō'tä), town (pop. 1,422), Santander dept., N central Colombia, in W valley of Cordillera Oriental, 5 mi. SW of Socorro; alt. 3,937 ft. Rice, corn, cotton, sugar cane, coffee, cacao, cattle, hogs. Petroleum deposits near by.

Simaluguri, India: see NAZIRA.

Simalur, Indonesia: see SIMULUE.

Simancas (sēmäng'käs), anc. *Septimanca*, town (pop. 1,075), Valladolid prov., N central Spain, 7 mi. SW of Valladolid; cereals, wine, sugar beets, fruit. Anc. castle (rebuilt in 15th cent.) contains Spain's natl. archives (over 30,000,000 documents).

Simane, Japan: see SHIMANE.

Simanggang (sēmäng-gäng'), town (pop. 2,449), S Sarawak, in W Borneo, on Lupar R. and 80 mi. ESE of Kuching; trade center for lumbering, rubber-growing, and agr. area.

Simão Dias (sēmã'ō dē'ŭs), city (pop. 3,941), W Sergipe, NE Brazil, near Bahia border, 50 mi. WNW of Aracaju; livestock market; grows sugar, coffee, cereals. Until 1944, called Anápolis (formerly spelled Annapolis).

Simara Island (sēmä'rä) (□ 8; 1948 pop. 5,158), Romblon prov., Philippines, bet. Tablas Strait and Sibuyan Sea, 10 mi. N of Tablas Isl.; 12°48'N 122°3'E; 5½ mi. long, ½–2½ mi. wide; hilly. Rice, coconuts.

Simard, Lac, Que.: see EXPANSE, LAKE.

Simat de Valldigna (sēmät' dhä väldē'nyä), village (pop. 3,225), Valencia prov., E Spain, 11 mi. SE of Alcira, in fertile area producing oranges, strawberries, beans. Furniture mfg.

Simav (sĭmäv'), town (pop. 5,180), Kutahya prov., W Turkey, on Simav R. and 60 mi. WSW of Kutahya; chromium deposits; carpet mfg.; opium, potatoes, onions, wheat, barley, corn.

Simav Dag (dä), Turkish *Simav Dağ*, peak (5,909 ft.), W Turkey, in Demirci Mts., 3 mi. W of Simav.

Simav River, anc. *Macestus*, NW Turkey, rises 6 mi. E of Simav, flows 160 mi. W and N, past Simav, Sindirgi, Susurluk, and Karacabey, to Sea of Marmara 19 mi. W of Mudanya. Receives Koca R. (left), Kirmasti and Nilufer rivers (right). Also called Susurluk R.

Simaxis (sēmäk'sēs), village (pop. 1,203), Cagliari prov., W Sardinia, near Tirso R., 6 mi. ENE of Oristano.

Simba (sēm'bä), village, Eastern Prov., N central Belgian Congo, on Lopari R. and 150 mi. W of Stanleyville; terminus of navigation; native trade (copal, palm products). R.C. mission.

Simba, village, Central Prov., S central Kenya, on railroad and 80 mi. SE of Nairobi; sisal, rubber, corn. Derives its name, a Swahili word meaning "lion," from the many lions formerly found here.

Simbach (zĭm'bäkh). 1 Village (pop. 2,008), Lower Bavaria, Germany, 7 mi. S of Landau; rye, wheat, cattle, horses. 2 or **Simbach am Inn** (äm ĭn'), village (pop. 7,858), Lower Bavaria, Germany, on the Inn, opposite Braunau (Austria); machine shops; mfg. (leather products, chemicals).

Simberi, volcanic island (□ c.30), New Ireland dist., Bismarck Archipelago, Territory of New Guinea, SW Pacific, c.30 mi. NE of New Ireland; 6 mi. long.

Simbillawein, El, Es Simbillawein, or **Al-Simbillawayn** (all: ĕs-sĭmbĭlä'wān), town (pop. 23,831; with suburbs, 25,639), Daqahliya prov., Lower Egypt, on railroad and 12 mi. SSE of Mansura; cotton ginning. A canal and branch-railway center.

Simbirsk, Russian SFSR: see ULYANOVSK, city.

Simbol (sēmbōl') village (pop. estimate 400), ⊙ Silipica dept. (□ 445; 1947 pop. 7,604), W Santiago del Estero prov., Argentina, on railroad and 20 mi. S of Santiago del Estero; agr. and lumbering center; wheat, alfalfa, livestock.

Simbor (sĭmbôr'), small detached section of Diu dist., Portuguese India, 11 mi. ENE of Diu, on S Kathiawar peninsula, W India; fishing. Just offshore, in mouth of Gulf of Cambay, is Pani Kota isl. and fort, obtained c.1720 by Portuguese.

Simcoe (sĭm'kō), county (□ 1,663; pop. 87,057), S Ont., bet. Georgian Bay and L. Simcoe; ⊙ Barrie.

Simcoe, town (pop. 6,037), ⊙ Norfolk co., S Ont., on Lynn R. and 35 mi. SW of Hamilton; woolen and lumber milling, glove mfg.; dairy and meat market, fruit and vegetable canning.

Simcoe, Lake (□ 280), S Ont., 40 mi. N of Toronto; 28 mi. long, 26 mi. wide. Indented by Cook Bay (S) and Kempenfelt Bay (W), it is connected with L. Couchiching (N), through which it drains into Georgian Bay of L. Huron by Severn R. On shore are Orillia, Barrie, Beaverton, and numerous small resorts. Contains several isls.

Simcoe Island (4 mi. long, 1 mi. wide), SE Ont., one of the Thousand Isls., at head of L. Ontario, near entrance to the St. Lawrence, opposite Kingston and just W of Wolfe Isl.

Sime, Japan: see SHIME.

Simeiz (sēmyĕ'ēs), town (1926 pop. 592), S Crimea, Russian SFSR, port on Black Sea, 10 mi. SW of Yalta; resort; tobacco, vineyards. Has large park with former estate of 19th-cent. industrialist S.I. Maltsev, now a sanatorium. Simeiz observatory (founded 1908) is branch of Pulkovo observatory. Simeiz developed as fashionable resort in early 20th cent.

Simel (zē'mŭl), peak (7,710 ft.) in Glarus Alps, E Switzerland, 8 mi. WNW of Chur.

Simen Mountains (sĭmĕn'), Ital. *Semien*, highest range in Ethiopia, in Begemdir prov., NE of Gondar, in a large bend of Takkaze R. Rises to 15,157 ft. in the Ras Dashan.

Simeonof Island (sĭ'mēŭnôf) (4 mi. long, 3 mi. wide; pop. 13), SW Alaska, 55 mi. ESE of Unga; 54°54'N 159°15'W; rises to c.1,600 ft.; fishing.

Simeonovgrad (sĭmēô'nôvgrät), after 1950 called **Maritsa** (mŭrĭ'tsŭ), city (pop. 4,252), Khaskovo dist., S central Bulgaria, on the Maritsa and 9 mi. NNW of Kharmanlii; sericulture center; cotton textiles. Has textile school. Formerly Seimen or Seimenli. Zlati-dol (pop. 2,102), rail junction, is just S, across the Maritsa.

Simeto River (sēmā'tô), principal river of Sicily, rises in several branches on Mt. Sori in Nebrodi Mts., flows S, along W foot of Mt. Etna, and SE, through Plain of Catania, to Gulf of Catania 6 mi. S of Catania; 70 mi. long. Chief tributaries: Dittaino and Salso rivers. Used for irrigation. Fisheries in lower course. Necropolis of anc. town of Symaethus on S bank, 4 mi. above mouth.

Simeuloee, Indonesia: see SIMULUE.

Simeulu, Indonesia: see SIMULUE.

Simferopol or **Simferopol'** (sēmfyĭrô'pŭl), city (1939 pop. 142,678), ⊙ Crimea, Russian SFSR, on Salgir R., on railroad and 37 mi. NE of Sevastopol; 44°57'N 34°6'E. Administrative and industrial center in orchard, vineyard, and tobacco region; canning of fruits and vegetables, flour milling, tanning, mfg. of canning machinery, woodworking. Has agr., medical, and teachers colleges. Modern Rus. administrative and industrial section (N) and old Gr. and Tatar part (S) of Oriental appearance are on right bank of Salgir R., opposite new residential city. In anc. times, Gr. settlement of Neapolis and a Scythian capital; site was occupied (after 16th cent.) by Tatar town of Ak-Mechet. Renamed Simferopol after Rus. conquest in 1783.

Simhachalam, India: see VIZAGAPATAM, city.

Simi, Greece: see SYME.

Simikot (sĭm'ĭkōt), village, NW Nepal, near upper Karnali (Gogra) R., 55 mi. NNW of Jumla. Nepalese military post.

Similkameen River (sĭmĭl'kŭmēn"), N Wash. and S B.C., rises in N Wash. at N end of Cascade Range, flows N, crossing into B.C., past Copper Mountain, to Princeton, thence SE, crossing back into Wash. 35 mi. S of Penticton; then flows in winding course E along Wash. side of border, to Okanogan R. at Oroville; 140 mi. long. Valley has rich copper and gold deposits.

Simin Han or **Simin Khan,** Yugoslavia: see TUZLA.

Simisa Island (sēmē'sä) (□ 5.6), in Samales Group, Sulu prov., Philippines, at NE end of Sulu Archipelago, 9 mi. E of Jolo Isl.

Simití (sēmētē'), town (pop. 1,575), Bolívar dept., N Colombia, in Magdalena basin, 40 mi. N of Puerto Wilches; livestock. Airport.

Simitli (sēmĭtlē'), village (pop. 1,850), Gorna Dzhumaya dist., SW Bulgaria, on Struma R. and 8 mi. S of Gorna Dzhumaya; tobacco, vineyards; thermal springs and baths. Lignite mining on slope of Pirin Mts. (E).

Simizu, Japan: see SHIMIZU, Kochi and Shizuoka prefectures.

Simla (sĭm'lŭ), former district (□ 80; pop. 38,576) in E Punjab prov., India; consisted of several small detached areas around town of Simla (its ⊙). Since 1948, merged with Himachal Pradesh.

Simla, town (pop. 18,348), ⊙ Himachal Pradesh, India, in small exclave of Punjab within Himachal Pradesh, 100 mi. ESE of Jullundur, 170 mi. N of New Delhi; 31°6'N 77°10'E. Picturesquely situated on wooded ridge (c.7,100 ft.) of outer Kumaun Himalayas, Simla is one of most popular hill resorts in India; average temp. c.35°F. (Jan.), c.75°F. (June); annual rainfall, 61 in. Rail terminus (linked with Ambala); market center (grain, potatoes, spices, timber, wool, spirits). Mfg. of cigarettes, plywood; hand-loom weaving, dairy farming; distillery, brewery. Area is dotted with numerous bungalows, hotels, and govt. bldgs.; crowded bazaars in E section. After Anglo-Gurkha War (1814–16) retained by British as military sanatorium. From 1864 to 1947, was summer ⊙ India. It became temporary ⊙ Punjab until completion of that state's new ⊙ near Chandigarh (31 mi. SW). Simla dist. of Punjab (in 1941: □ 80; pop. 38,576) consists since 1950 reorganization only of Simla town and suburbs.

Simla, town (pop. 424), Elbert co., E central Colo., on Big Sandy Creek and 45 mi. NE of Colorado Springs; alt. 6,090 ft. Grain, livestock, poultry and dairy products, beans.

Simla Hill States, India: see PUNJAB HILL STATES.

Simleul-Silvaniei (shēmlĕ'ōōl-sēlvänyä'), Rum. *Şimleul-Silvaniei*, Hung. *Szilágysomlyó* (sĕ'lädyŭshômlyō), town (1948 pop. 7,931), Bihor prov., NW Rumania, in Transylvania, on railroad and 12 mi. WNW of Zalau amid extensive vineyards and orchards; trading center (grain, livestock, hides, cheese, fruit); wine industry; flour mills, alcohol and vinegar production. Has remains of 16th-cent. fortress, other ruins of fortresses in vicinity. Most of pop. are Magyars. In Hungary, 1940–45.

Simmental (zĭ'mŭntäl), valley of Simme R., Bern canton, SW central Switzerland, embracing dists. of Niedersimmental (N; pop. 13,902) and Obersimmental (S; pop. 7,333).

Simmering (zĭ'mŭrĭng), district (□ 8; pop. 39,849) of Vienna, Austria, 4 mi. SE of city center; mfg. of machinery.

Simme River (zĭ'mŭ), SW central Switzerland, rises SSE of Lenk, in Bernese Alps; flows 33 mi. N and E, past Zweisimmen (here joined by Kleine Simme R.), to Kander R. 5 mi. S of Thun. Spiez hydroelectric plant is on Simme and Kander rivers.

Simmern (zĭ'mŭrn), town (pop. 3,972), in former Prussian Rhine Prov., W Germany, after 1945 in Rhineland-Palatinate, 17 mi. W of Bingen; main town of the Hunsrück; rail junction. Has late-Gothic church. Was property of counts palatine (1358–1794).

Simmesport (sĭmz'pôrt), fishing village (pop. 1,510), Avoyelles parish, E central La., 45 mi. SE of Alexandria and on Atchafalaya R.; cotton gins, sawmill. Hunting near by.

Simms', village, S central Bahama Isls., on N Long Isl., 31 mi. NNW of Clarence Town; 23°27'N 75°15'W. Stock, sisal.

Simms. 1 Village (pop. c.450), Cascade co., W central Mont., on Sun R. and 30 mi. W of Great Falls, in irrigated region; grain, livestock. **2** Town, N.C.: see SIMS.

Simoca (sēmō'kä), town (pop. estimate 1,000), central Tucumán prov., Argentina, on railroad and 32 mi. SSW of Tucumán; agr. center (sugar cane, corn, oats, livestock).

Simoïs (sĭ'mōĭs), small river of Troas, NW Asia Minor (now in Turkey), flowing from Ida Mts. to the Scamander (modern Kucuk Menderes); scene of many events in the Trojan War.

Simoiti, Japan: see SHIMOICHI.

Simojovel (sēmōhōvĕl'), officially Simojovel de Allende, city (pop. 1,816), Chiapas, S Mexico, 37 mi. NE of Tuxtla; cereals, sugar cane, fruit.

Simonoseki, Japan: see SHIMONOSEKI, city.

Simonovany, Czechoslovakia: see PARTIZANSKE.

Simón Patiño (sēmōn' pätē'nyō), tin-mining settlement (pop. c. 1,900), Potosí dept., W central Bolivia, near Catavi.

Simon Peak (10,899 ft.), W Alta., on B.C. border, in Rocky Mts., in Jasper Natl. Park, 18 mi. SW of Jasper; 52°40'N 118°17'W.

Simonstown (sĭ'mŭnz–), Afrikaans *Simonstad* (–stät), town (pop. 7,315), SW Cape Prov., U. of So. Afr., on False Bay of the Atlantic, 20 mi. S of Cape Town, 12 mi. N of Cape of Good Hope; 34°11'S 18°26'W; major British naval base, with extensive dockyard facilities and hosp.; seaside resort. Has oldest English church (1814) in So. Afr. Established 1741 as Dutch naval and military base; scene (1795) of British landing. Later became commercial port, frequented by American whalers. Naval base established 1814; ceded by Cape Prov. to British Admiralty 1898. Played important part in Second World War operations in S Atlantic and Indian Ocean.

Simonsvik, Norway: see LAKSEVAG.

Simonszand (sēmōnsänt'), uninhabited island, Groningen prov., N Netherlands, bet. North Sea and the Waddenzee, 12 mi. NW of Warffum; 2 mi. long, 1.5 mi. wide.

Simontornya (shĭ'môntôrnyŏ), town (pop. 4,755), Tolna co., W central Hungary, on Sio-Kapos Canal and 17 mi. W of Dunaföldvar; tanneries, shoe factory, distillery, brickworks.

Simoom Sound (sĭmōōn'), village (pop. estimate 250), SW B.C., on Queen Charlotte Strait, opposite N Vancouver Isl., 25 mi. NE of Alert Bay; lumbering.

Simotui, Japan: see SHIMOTSUI.

Simo-zima, Japan: see SHIMO-JIMA.

Simpang (sĭmpäng'), village (pop. 623), NW Perak, Malaya, on rail spur, 3 mi. W of Taiping; rubber.

Simpang Ampat (ämpät'). **1** Village (pop. 459), NW Perak, Malaya, 10 mi. NW of Taiping, in Krian rice dist. **2** Village (pop. 1,950), W Perak, Malaya, 2 mi. S of SITIAWAN and 4 mi. E of Lumut; rubber. Airfield. Sometimes called Sitiawan. **3** Village, Prov. Wellesley, Penang, NW Malaya, on railroad and 10 mi. SE of Butterworth; coconuts, rubber.

Simpang Kachau (kächou'), village (pop. 595), SE Selangor, Malaya, 3 mi. NNE of Semenyih; rubber, rice.

Simpang Lima (lē'mä), village (pop. 307), NW Perak, Malaya, 23 mi. NW of Taiping and on railroad, in Krian rice dist.

Simpele (sĭm'pĕlā), village (commune pop. 3,383), Kymi co., SE Finland, in lake region, 35 mi. SE of Savonlinna; frontier station near USSR border, opposite Elisenvaara; rail junction; pulp and paper mills.

Simpelveld (sĭm'pŭlvĕlt), town (pop. 4,733), Limburg prov., SE Netherlands, 5 mi. S of Heerlen; frontier station near Ger. border; site of Sophia coal mine.

Simplício Mendes (sēmplē'syōō mĕn'dĭs), city (pop. 916), S central Piauí, Brazil, 100 mi. SE of Floriano; stock raising; carnauba wax, skins.

Simplon Pass (sĭm'plŏn, Fr. sĕplō') (6,589 ft.), over the Alps, S Switzerland, in Valais canton. Forms divide bet. Pennine (W) and Lepontine (E) Alps. Simplon Road (built 1800–06 by Napoleon) crosses the pass and connects Brig with Domodossola, Italy. Bet. pass and Ital. line, road leads through Gallery of Gondo, a 735-ft. tunnel, and along Ravine of Gondo, one of wildest in the Alps. Simplon Hospice (6,563 ft.), in the pass, is 4 mi. W of Monte Leone. Simplon Tunnel, longest (12.3 mi.) in the world, pierces Monte Leone and carries the railroad from Brig to Iselle, Italy, it is lowest (2,313 ft.) of the great Alpine tunnels; opened in 1906.

Simpson, village (pop. 283), S Sask., 16 mi. S of Watrous; wheat, stock.

Simpson. 1 County (□ 239; pop. 11,678), S Ky.; ⊙ Franklin. Bounded S by Tenn. line; drained by West Fork of Drake Creek. Rolling agr. area (dark tobacco, strawberries, grain, livestock). Timber; limestone quarries. Some mfg. at Franklin. Formed 1819. **2** County (□ 587; pop. 21,819), S central Miss.; ⊙ Mendenhall. Bounded W by Pearl R.; also drained by Strong R. and small Okatoma Creek. Agr. (cotton, corn); lumbering. Formed 1824.

Simpson. 1 Village (pop. 119), Johnson co., S Ill., 22 mi. SSW of Harrisburg, in fruitgrowing region of Ill. Ozarks. **2** City (pop. 234), Cloud and Mitchell cos., N central Kansas, on Solomon R. and 11 mi. ESE of Beloit; grain, livestock. **3** Town (pop. 278), Pitt co., E central N.C., on Tar R. and 6 mi. ESE of Greenville. **4** Village (1940 pop. 4,145), Lackawanna co., NE Pa., just N of Carbondale, in anthracite region.

Simpson Desert (□ 43,500), SE Northern Territory, Australia, extends c.200 mi. W from Queensland border and 150 mi. N from South Australia border; uninhabited; scrub, sand dunes. First crossed in 1939 by Dr. Cecil Madigan. Sometimes spelled Simpson's Desert; also called Arunta Desert.

Simpson Harbour, Bismarck Archipelago: see BLANCHE BAY.

Simpson Island (10 mi. long, 6 mi. wide), W Ont., in L. Superior, at entrance of Nipigon Bay, 70 mi. ENE of Port Arthur, just E of Isle St. Ignace. Just E are small Salter, Silson, and Copper isls.

Simpson Island, Chile: see CHONOS ARCHIPELAGO.

Simpson River, Aysén prov., S Chile, rises in the Andes on Argentina border SSW of Balmaceda, flows c.75 mi. NW, past Baquedano, to Aysén R. 10 mi. ESE of Puerto Aysén.

Simpson Strait, S Franklin Dist. and N Keewatin Dist., Northwest Territories, arm (40 mi. long, 2–10 mi. wide) of the Arctic Ocean, bet. King William Isl. (N) and Adelaide Peninsula of mainland (S); 68°25'N 97°30'W. Opens W on Queen Maud Gulf.

Simpsonville. 1 Town (pop. 247), Shelby co., N Ky., 25 mi. E of Louisville, in Bluegrass agr. region. Near by are Lincoln Inst. (an endowed vocational and agr. high school for Negroes) and Lincoln Inst. model farm. **2** Town (pop. 1,529), Greenville co., NW S.C., 12 mi. SE of Greenville; textiles.

Simrishamn (sĭm"rĭs-hä'mŭn), city (pop. 3,215), Kristianstad co., S Sweden, on the Baltic, 35 mi. SSW of Kristianstad; port, with machinery and brickworks, tanneries. Has 12th-cent. church and mus. Chartered in early-13th cent. Formerly also spelled Cimbrishamn.

Sim River (sēm), E European Russian SFSR, rises in the S Urals c.20 mi. WSW of Ust-Katav, flows NNW, past Sim and Minyar, and generally SW to Belaya R. 25 mi. SE of Ufa; c.150 mi. long. Receives Inzer R. (left).

Sims. 1 Village (pop. 408), Wayne co., SE Ill., 19 mi. E of Mount Vernon, in agr. area; oil wells. **2** Town (pop. 207), Wilson co., E central N.C., 8 mi. WNW of Wilson. Sometimes written Simms.

Simsbury, town (pop. 4,822), including Simsbury village (pop. 1,771), Hartford co., N central Conn., on Farmington R. and 10 mi. NW of Hartford; tobacco packing; mfg. (safety fuses, metal products). Includes Tariffville village (1940 pop. 668). Has state forest, part of McLean Game Refuge. Westminster school for boys, Ethel Walker school for girls here. Settled 1660, inc. 1670.

Simski Zavod, Russian SFSR: see SIM, city.

Simssee (zĭms'zā", zĭm'sā"), lake (□ 2.5), Upper Bavaria, Germany, 4 mi. E of Rosenheim; 3.5 mi. long, 1 mi. wide, 74 ft. deep; alt. 1,542 ft.

Simuleu, Rumania: see MERCUREA-CIUC.

Simulue or **Simeuloee** (both: sēmŭlōō'ŭ), island (□ 712; pop. 19,302), Indonesia, in Indian Ocean, off NW coast of Sumatra, 170 mi. WSW of Medan; 2°45'N 96°E; 65 mi. long, 20 mi. wide. Hilly, rising to 1,860 ft. Coconuts, timber; buffalo raising. Its port, Sinabang, is on SE coast. Also spelled Simalur and Simeulu.

Simunul Island (sēmōōnōōl') (□ 15.8; 1948 pop., with offshore Manuk Manka Isl., 5,413), in Tawi-tawi Group, Sulu prov., Philippines, in Sulu Archipelago, off S tip of Tawitawi Isl. Manuk Manka (mänōōk' mängkä') has □ 6.4.

Simushir Island or **Shimushir Island** (sēmōō'shĕr, shē–), Jap. *Shimushiru-to* (□ 126), one of central main Kurile Isls. chain, Russian SFSR; separated from Ketoi Isl. (N) by Diana Strait, from Chernye Bratya isls. (S) by Boussole Strait; 46°55'N 152°E; 36 mi. long, 9 mi. wide. Consists of 4 volcanic groups (rising to 5,007 ft.) linked by lower ridges. Settlements at NE tip and on SW coast.

Simvolon, Mount, Greece: see SYMVOLON, MOUNT.

Sin, Egypt: see PELUSIUM.

Sinaai (sĭ'nī), agr. village (pop. 5,150), East Flanders prov., N Belgium, 4 mi. W of St-Nicolas. Formerly spelled Sinay.

Sinai (sī'nī, sī'nēī, sī'nāī), Arabic *Sina* (sē'nă), triangular peninsula, constituting the easternmost part of Egypt, extending from a broad base (c.150 mi. wide) on the Mediterranean S c.230 mi. to the N tip of the Red Sea, whose two arms bound it W by Gulf of Suez (extended N by Suez Canal), E by Gulf of Aqaba. It is usually regarded as part of Asia rather than Africa. In the N coastal area are high sand dunes extending along the coast to Palestine. In central area is the sandy plateau of El TIH, which rises in the S to a barren massif of crystalline rocks, the highest being Gebel KATHERINA (8,651 ft.). Just NE of Katherina is Gebel MUSA [Arabic,=mount of Moses], sometimes identified with the biblical Mt. Sinai (perhaps also Horeb), as are also Gebel Serbal and Gebel Umm Shomer, both near by. At N foot of this group is the famed Greek Orthodox monastery of St. Catherine, founded c.250. Here was found (1844) the Codex Sinaiticus, one of oldest MSS of the New Testament. It was purchased from the USSR by the British Museum in 1933. Today Sinai, a barren area inhabited by nomads, constitutes a so-called frontier prov. (settled area □ 34; pop. 37,897) of Egypt. Manganese and iron are mined near ABU ZENIMA, some crude oil is produced at ABU DURBA; both towns are on the Gulf of Suez.

Sinai, town (pop. 181), Brookings co., E S.Dak., 13 mi. WSW of Brookings.

Sinai, Mount, peak (2,329 ft.), S Grenada, B.W.I., 4 mi. ENE of St. George's.

Sinaia (sēnä'yä), town (1948 pop. 6,531), Prahova prov., S central Rumania, in Walachia, at SE foot of the Bucegi Mts. of Transylvanian Alps, on railroad and 37 mi. NW of Ploesti; leading health resort (alt. 2,953 ft.), with noted winter-sports facilities and numerous tourist attractions. Also mfg. of hardware, munitions, mosaics, plaster, cement, sausages; sawmilling, stone quarrying. Former summer residence of Rumanian kings to whom most of the development since 1860 is due. Its Ger. Renaissance castle of Peles, built 1873–83 by Carol I, enlarged 1896–1914, contains one of the most valuable art collections in Rumania. Pelisor castle (1899–1903) was noted as summer home of Ferdinand I and Queen Marie. The famous Sinaia monastery dates from 17th cent. Sinaia also has a zoological institute and a military rehabilitation center.

Sinajana (sēnähä'nyä), town (pop. 3,068) and municipality (pop. 9,159), central Guam, S of Agana; coconut plantations.

Sinaloa (sēnälō'ä), state (□ 22,582; 1940 pop. 492,821; 1950 pop. 618,439), NW Mexico; ⊙ Culiacán. Extends long and narrow along the Pacific and the Gulf of California, backed by outliers of the Sierra Madre Occidental. Bordered (N-S) by Sonora, Chihuahua, Durango, Nayarit. Narrow coastal lowlands are cut by many streams, including the Río del Fuerte, and Sinaloa, Culiacán, and Piaxtla rivers. The long, alluvial coast line includes many islets, lagoons, and marshes. Temperate to subtropical climate; fertile plains have extremely hot, sometimes rainy, summers; winters are dry and mild. Area is rich in minerals, with silver, gold, and copper mines near Contra Estaca, Concordia, Cosalá, and Culiacán. The irrigated river valleys produce sugar cane, cotton, coffee, tobacco, rice, chick-peas, corn, tomatoes, peppers, bananas, citrus fruit. State's forested ranges, rich in dyewood and rubber, are little exploited. Fishing along coast. Leather industry, sugar refineries, food canneries, cotton gins, and foundries concentrated at Culiacán and Mazatlán; latter is only important port. Sinaloa was made a state in 1830.

Sinaloa, town (pop. 1,290), Sinaloa, NW Mexico, on Sinaloa R. and 90 mi. NW of Culiacán; agr. center (corn, chick-peas, tomatoes, sugar cane, fruit).

Sinaloa River, NW Mexico, rises as Petatlán R. in Sierra Madre Occidental near Sinaloa border, flows c.200 mi SW through fertile coastal lowlands, past Sinaloa and Guasave, to Gulf of California 17 mi. SW of Angostura.

Sinalunga (sēnälōōng'gä), town (pop. 1,148), Siena prov., Tuscany, central Italy, 22 mi. ESE of Siena; mfg. (soap, floor wax). Lignite mines near by.

Sinamaica (sēnämī'kä), town (pop. 629), Zulia state, NW Venezuela, in Maracaibo lowlands near Gulf of Venezuela, 35 mi. NNW of Maracaibo; livestock.

Sinan or **Hsin-an** (both: shĭn'än'). **1** Town, ⊙ Sinan co. (pop. 152,043), NW Honan prov., China, 18 mi. W of Loyang, on Lunghai RR; millet, wheat, beans. **2** Town, Kwangtung prov., China: see POON.

Sinancha (sēnŭnchä'), town (1946 pop. over 500), E Maritime Territory, Russian SFSR, on short Sinancha R. and 18 mi. N of Tetyukhe; tin mines.

Sinanché (sēnänchā'), town (pop. 1,221), Yucatan, SE Mexico, 30 mi. NE of Mérida; henequen.

Sinanju (sĕn'än'jōō'), Jap. *Shinanshu*, township (1944 pop. 16,493), S.Pyongan prov., N Korea, on Chongchon R. and 40 mi. NNW of Pyongyang, in coal-mining and agr. area. Formerly an important city; there are ruins of the old walls that once enclosed it.

Sinano, Greece: see MEGALOPOLIS.

Sinano River, Japan: see SHINANO RIVER.

Sinan River, Chinese *Sinan Kiang* or *Hsin-an Chiang* (both: shĭn'än' jyäng'), E China, rises in S Anhwei prov., flows c.90 mi. ESE, past Sihsien, into Chekiang prov., past Shunan, to Tsientang R. at Kienteh.

Sinaouen, Fezzan: see SINAUEN.

Sinarcas (sēnär'käs), town (pop. 1,480), Valencia prov., E Spain, 18 mi. NW of Requena; lumbering, stock raising; wine, cereals.

Sinarskaya, Russian SFSR: see KAMENSK-URALSKI.

Sinauen (sēnäwĕn'), Arabic *Sinawen*, Fr. *Sinaouen* or *Sinaouène*, village (pop. 703), N Fezzan, Libya, 90 mi. NE of Ghadames, in an oasis; date growing. Has Turkish fort.

Sinay, Belgium: see SINAAI.

Sinbaungwe (sĭnboun'jŭwĕ''), village, Thayetmyo dist., Upper Burma, on left bank of Irrawaddy R. and 27 mi. N of Thayetmyo.

Sinbyugyun (sĭnbyōōjōōn'), town (pop. 4,369), Minbu dist., Upper Burma, on right bank of Irrawaddy R. at mouth of Salin R., 35 mi. NNW of Minbu. Rice, sesame, tobacco, wheat; trade center for palm sugar, silk cloth, catechu.

Sincé (sēnsā'), town (pop. 8,287), Bolívar dept., N Colombia, in savannas, 35 mi. S of Carmen; agr. center (corn, sugar cane, tobacco, fruit, stock).

Sincelejo (sēnsālā'hō), town (pop. 11,014), Bolívar dept., N Colombia, 80 mi. S of Cartagena; commercial and agr. center (sugar cane, tobacco, corn, cattle); sugar refining; produces honey.

Sinchang or **Hsin-ch'ang** (both: shĭn'chäng'). **1** Town (pop. 17,875), ⊙ Sinchang co. (pop. 244,184), NE central Chekiang prov., China, 45 mi. SW of Ningpo; tobacco, medicinal herbs, rice, wheat. **2** Town, Kiangsi prov., China: see IFENG. **3** Town, Kweichow prov., China: see KINSHA.

Sinchang (sĕn'chäng'), Jap. *Shinshu* or *Shinso*, town (1944 pop. 21,770), S.Hamgyong prov., N Korea, on E.Korea Bay, 50 mi. ENE of Hungnam; fishing center.

Sinchen, China: see SINWEN.

Sincheng. **1** or **Hsin-cheng** (shĭn'jŭng'), town, ⊙ Sincheng co. (pop. 198,634), N Honan prov., China, 25 mi. S of Chengchow; rice, wheat, kaoliang, beans. Coal mines near by. **2** or **Hsin-ch'eng** (shĭn'chŭng'), town, ⊙ Sincheng co. (pop. 251,021), N central Hopeh prov., China, 40 mi. NE of Paoting; willow plaiting; wheat, kaoliang, peanuts. **3** or **Hsin-ch'eng** (shĭn'chŭng'), town, Kiangsi prov., China: see LICHWAN. **4** or **Hsin-ch'eng** (shĭn'chŭng'), town, ⊙ Sincheng co. (pop. 116,243), central Kwangsi prov., China, 38 mi. WSW of Liuchow, near Hungshui R.; rice, wheat, beans. **5** or **Hsin-ch'eng** (shĭn'chŭng'), town, Kweichow prov., China: see HINGJEN. **6** or **Hsin-ch'eng** (shĭn'chŭng'), town, Shantung prov., China: see HWANTAI.

Sincheng or **Hsin-ch'eng** (both: shĭn'chŭng'), Jap. *Shinjo* (shĕn'jō), village, E central Formosa, on E coast, 10 mi. N of Hwalien; sugar cane, rice.

Sinchin, Manchuria: see SINKIN.

Sincholagua, Cerro (sĕ'rō sēnchōlä'gwä), volcanic Andean peak (14,846 ft.), Pichincha prov., N central Ecuador, N of Cotopaxi volcano, 23 mi. SSE of Quito.

Sinchon (sĕn'chŭn'), Jap. *Shinsen*, town (1944 pop. 22,611), Hwanghae prov., central Korea, N of 38° N, 25 mi. NNW of Haeju; wheat-growing center.

Sinchow, China: see SINHSIEN, Shansi prov.

Sinchu or Hsinchu (both: shĭn'jōō'), Jap. *Shinchiku* (shĕn'chĭkōō), town (1940 pop. 57,957), NW Formosa, on W coast, 38 mi. SW of Taipei and on railroad; industrial center; produces synthetic oil, fertilizer (cyanamide, ammonium sulphate), glass, paper, wood products. Trades in rice, tea, fruit. Has Confucianist and Buddhist temples. One of oldest centers of Formosa, it was called Chuchien or Teukchan until 1875. The name Sinchu was also applied (1945–50) to TAOYÜAN, 25 mi. NE.

Sinchula (sĭn'chōōlŭ), village, SW Bhutan, 35 mi. NNE of Cooch Behar, on a main Bhutan-India route. Treaty made here, 1865, bet. Bhutan and British, ending Bhutan War.

Sinchula Pass, India and Bhutan: see BUXA DUAR.

Sinchwang or **Hsin-chuang** (both: shĭn'jwäng'), town, S Kiangsu prov., China, 10 mi. SW of Shanghai and on Shanghai-Hangchow RR; commercial center.

Sinchwang or **Hsin-chuang,** Jap. *Shinsho* (shĕn'shō), town (1935 pop. 6,371), N Formosa, 4 mi. N of Taipei across Tanshui R.; rice milling, woodworking; confectionery. Dates from 1732; originally called Haishankow.

Sinclair, town (pop. 775), Carbon co., S Wyo., 7 mi. E of Rawlins; alt. c.6,590 ft. Refinery processes oil from Lost Soldier field. Town named Parco until 1943.

Sinclairtown, Scotland: see KIRKCALDY.

Sinclairville, village (pop. 672), Chautauqua co., extreme W N.Y., 12 mi. N of Jamestown; canned foods, dairy products; lumbering.

Sincorá, Serra do (sĕ'rŭ dōō sĕngkōōrä'), range in central Bahia, Brazil, extending S and SE of the Chapada Diamantina bet. Andaraí and Jiquié; rises to 3,500 ft. Forms watershed bet. Paraguaçu R. (N) and the Rio de Contas (S).

Sind (sĭnd), prov. (□ 50,443; 1951 pop. 4,619,000), W Pakistan, comprising lower INDUS RIVER valley; ⊙ Hyderabad (until early 1950s ⊙ was Karachi). Bounded SW by Arabian Sea and Karachi administrative area, W by Baluchistan, Kirthar Range, and Hab R., NE by Bahawalpur, E by Khairpur and Indian state of Rajasthan, S by Rann of Cutch. Prov. consists of 3 well-defined areas: hilly country along W border, including KOHISTAN region (SW); central alluvial plain, drained by the Indus and irrigated by noted SUKKUR BARRAGE canal system; and arid E section (W edge of Thar Desert). Shifting course of the Indus has left numerous traces of anc. river beds, now utilized for irrigation purposes. Deltaic tract from Karachi administrative area to Rann of Cutch is low swamp land, occasionally submerged, and intersected by many tidal creeks. Annual rainfall is very scanty (3–10 in.); N Sind is known for its intense summer heat (especially at Jacobabad). Agr. (wheat, millet, rice, cotton, oilseeds) entirely dependent on irrigation; mango trees and date palms are common. Agr. processing and salt mfg. (solar evaporation) are chief industries; cementworks at Sukkur and Rohri. Handicrafts include cloth weaving and dyeing, embroidering, mfg. of carpets, pottery, leather goods, lacquer- and metalware. Cattle, camel, goat, sheep raising; buffaloes in delta area. Fishing off coast (sardines, sharks, pomfrets, seerfish, prawns) and in the Indus (shad); shallow lakes (carp fishing) in W section attract snipe, partridge, geese, and quail. HYDERABAD (rail junction), SUKKUR, Shikarpur are main commercial centers. Sind Univ. is at Karachi. Literacy in Sind is low (c.10%). Indus valley was site of highly-developed prehistoric civilization, to which noted ruins at MOHENJO-DARO attest. Area was part of anc. Aryan kingdom of *Sindhu* when Alexander the Great moved down the Indus in 325 B.C. on return to Persia. Soon after, Mauryans became dominant power (c.3d cent. B.C.). The Arab invaders of Sind in A.D. 712 were the 1st permanent Moslem settlers in India; their control lasted until conquest by Ghaznevids in early-11th cent. Although briefly inc. into Mogul empire by Akbar in 1592, Sind remained for centuries semi-independent under local Moslem dynasties. Amirs or Mirs of Sind, chieftains of Baluch descent, held power in late 18th and early 19th cent. and successfully resisted Br. penetrations until 1843, when Sir Charles Napier defeated them at Miani and Dabo near Hyderabad. Sind was then annexed to Br. India and made prov. within Bombay presidency; constituted (1937) an autonomous prov.; became a prov. of Pakistan in 1947. Prov. (in 1941: □ 48,136; pop. 4,535,008) was reduced in 1948 when Karachi administrative area (includes Karachi city) was detached. Comprises 8 dists.: Dadu, Hyderabad, Tatta, Larkana, Nawabshah, Sukkur, Thar Parkar, Upper Sind Frontier. Chief language is Sindhi. Sometimes spelled Sindh.

Sindal (sĭn'dăl''), town (pop. 1,366), Hjorring amt, N Jutland, Denmark, 8 mi. E of Hjorring; cement, toy mfg.

Sindañgan (sēndä'nyŭgän), town (1939 pop. 4,849; 1948 municipality pop. 30,484), Zamboanga prov., W Mindanao, Philippines, 40 mi. NW of Pagadian, on Sindañgan Bay (inlet of Sulu Sea).

Sindara (sēndärä'), village, S Gabon, Fr. Equatorial Africa, on N'Gounié R. and 60 mi. NNW of Mouila; gold mining and hardwood-lumbering center; also manganese mining. R.C. mission.

Sindel (sēndĕl'), village (pop. 955), Stalin dist., E Bulgaria, on Provadiya R. and 15 mi. WSW of Stalin; rail junction; winegrowing, horticulture. Sawmilling in near-by woodland. Formerly Sendel.

Sindelfingen (zĭn'dŭlfĭng''ŭn), town (pop. 10,027), N Württemberg, Germany, after 1945 in Württemberg-Baden, 9 mi. SW of Stuttgart; mfg. of vehicles, machinery, tools, precision instruments (watches), textiles, shoes; lumber milling. Concrete- and brickworks. Has 11th-cent. church.

Sindgi (sĭnd'gē), village, Bijapur dist., S Bombay, India, 36 mi. ENE of Bijapur; millet, peanuts, linseed, cotton.

Sindhia's Dominions, India: see GWALIOR, former princely state.

Sindhnur (sĭnd′nŏŏr), town (pop. 6,377), Raichur dist., SW Hyderabad state, India, 50 mi. SW of Raichur; road center; millet, oilseeds; gins cotton.

Sindhos, Greece: see SINDOS.

Sindhuli Garhi (sĭndōō′lē gŭr′hē) or **Sindhuli,** town, E central Nepal, in Mahabharat Lekh range, 45 mi. SE of Katmandu. Nepalese military post.

Sindi (sēn′dē), Ger. *Zintenhof,* city (pop. 1,854), SW Estonia, on Parnu R. (head of navigation) and 6 mi. E of Parnu; woolen and cotton textiles, tiles; peat works.

Sindi (sĭn′dē), town (pop. 5,856), Wardha dist., central Madhya Pradesh, India, 18 mi. ENE of Wardha; cotton ginning; millet, wheat, oilseeds.

Sindiki, Greece: see SINTICA.

Sindirgi (sŭndŭrgŭ′), Turkish *Sındırgı,* village (pop. 3,209), Balikesir prov., NW Turkey, near Simav R., 33 mi. SSE of Balikesir; wheat, rye, sesame, potatoes.

Sindkheda (sĭndkā′dŭ), town (pop. 7,095), West Khandesh dist., NE Bombay, India, 26 mi. N of Dhulia; trades in cotton, peanuts, wheat, millet; cotton ginning.

Sindos or **Sindhos** (both: sĭn′dhôs), village (pop. 2,979), Salonika nome, Macedonia, Greece, on railroad and 7 mi. NW of Salonika. Formerly called Tekele or Tekeli.

Sindri (sĭn′drē), village, Manbhum dist., SE Bihar, India, 10 mi. WNW of Purulia; large chemical-fertilizer factory, cement works.

Sindringen (zĭn′drĭng-ŭn), town (pop. 534), N Württemberg, Germany, after 1945 in Württemberg-Baden, on the Kocher and 15 mi. NE of Heilbronn; wine.

Sind River, mainly in NE Madhya Bharat, India, rises c.15 mi. WSW of Sironj, flows c.320 mi. generally NNE, past Seondha (NW Vindhya Pradesh), to Jumna R. 18 mi. W of Auraiya. Sometimes spelled Sindh.

Sind-Sagar Doab (sĭnd′-sŭ′gŭr dō′äb), extensive tract, W Punjab, W Pakistan, bet. Indus R. (W) and Jhelum R. (E). Consists of Potwar Plateau (N) and sandy THAL region (S), separated by Salt Range. Comprises dists. of Attock, Rawalpindi, Jhelum, Muzaffargarh, and parts of Mianwali, Shahpur, and Jhang.

Sinegorsk (sēnyĭgôrsk′), town (1940 pop. 5,776), S Sakhalin, Russian SFSR, on rail spur and 18 mi. NW of Yuzhno-Sakhalinsk; coal-mining center; carbonic springs. Under Jap. rule (1905–45), called Kawakami or Kawakami-tanzan (käwä′kä′mē-tän′zä′).

Sinegorski or **Sinegorskiy** (–skē), town (1939 pop. over 2,000), W central Rostov oblast, Russian SFSR, on right bank of Northern Donets R. and 12 mi. SSE of Belaya Kalitva; coal-mining center (mine at Krasnodonetskaya, 3 mi. E, across river).

Sinelitsovka (sēnyĕ′lyĭtsŭfkŭ), town (1939 pop. over 500), N central Kharkov oblast, Ukrainian SSR, on railroad (Kuryazh station) and 8 mi. W of Kharkov city center; sawmill.

Sinelnikovo or **Sinel'nikovo** (sēnyĕl′nyĭkŭvŭ), city (1933 pop. 16,300), S Dnepropetrovsk oblast, Ukrainian SSR, 20 mi. ESE of Dnepropetrovsk; rail junction; metalworks, flour mill; food processing; refractory clays. In middle 1930s, called Imeni Tovarishcha Khatayevicha.

Sinepuxent Bay (sĭ″nēpŭk′sŭnt), SE Md., narrow lagoon c.12 mi. long, protected from the Atlantic by Assateague Isl. (E); communicates directly with Chincoteague Bay (S), and with ocean through Ocean City Inlet, at N end of bay.

Sines (sē′nĭsh), town (pop. 3,937), Setúbal dist., S central Portugal, port on the Atlantic, near Cape Sines, 40 mi. S of Setúbal; rail-spur terminus; fish canning and drying, cork processing. Bathing beach. Vasco da Gama b. here 1469.

Sines, Cape, headland on the Atlantic on SW coast of Portugal, 40 mi. S of Setúbal and just W of Sines; 37°57′N 8°52′W; lighthouse.

Sinéu (sēnĕ′ōō), town (pop. 3,573), Majorca, Balearic Isls., on railroad and 20 mi. E of Palma; agr. center (wheat, almonds, grapes, grain, vegetables, figs, livestock, poultry). Liquor distilling, rug mfg.; lignite mining.

Sinevka (sē′nyĭfkŭ), village (1926 pop. 2,282), S Sumy oblast, Ukrainian SSR, 30 mi. ESE of Romny; wheat, hemp.

Sinfãis (sēnfā′ēsh), town (pop. 254), Viseu dist., N central Portugal, 16 mi. W of Lamego, in Douro R. valley; hat mfg.; olives, oranges, wine. Old spelling, Sinfães.

Sinfan or **Hsin-fan** (both: shĭn′fän′), town (pop. 14,870), ⊙ Sinfan co. (pop. 101,936), W Szechwan prov., China, 15 mi. NNW of Chengtu, on Chengtu plain; rice, wheat, rapeseed, potatoes.

Sinfeng or **Hsin-feng** (both: shĭn′fŭng′), town (pop. 15,616), ⊙ Sinfeng co. (pop. 228,862), SW Kiangsi prov., China, 32 mi. S of Kanchow; tobacco, rice. Tungsten mines.

Sinfra (sĕn′frä), village (pop. c.1,000), S central Ivory Coast, Fr. West Africa, 160 mi. WNW of Abidjan; cacao, coffee, palm kernels.

Sing-, for Chinese names beginning thus and not found here: see under HING-.

Singa (sĭng′gä), town (pop. 10,650), Blue Nile prov., E central Anglo-Egyptian Sudan, on left bank of the Blue Nile, on road and 90 mi. SSE of Wad Medani; cotton, wheat, barley, corn, fruits, durra; livestock. Hq. Fung dist.

Singa (sēng′gä), town (pop. 1,082), Huánuco dept., central Peru, on E slopes of Cordillera Blanca of the Andes, on Marañón R. and 11 mi. NNE of Llata; barley, corn, potatoes; sheep raising.

Singac, N.J.: see LITTLE FALLS.

Singaing (sĭng-gīn′), village, Kyaukse dist., Upper Burma, 17 mi. S of Mandalay and on railroad.

Singalila Range (sĭng-gä′lĭlŭ), S spur of E Nepal Himalayas, S central Asia, along Nepal-India (mainly Sikkim) border; c.50 mi. long N-S. Highest point (28,146 ft.) is in KANCHENJUNGA mtn. Jongsong La (jôngsông′ lä′), a N pass (alt. 20,334 ft.), lies 11 mi. N of highest Kanchenjunga peak; leads from Sikkim into NE Nepal.

Singan, China: see SIAN.

Singanallur (sĭng′gŭnŭlōōr), town (pop. 13,230), Coimbatore dist., SW Madras, India, on Noyil R. and 5 mi. E of Coimbatore; cotton and sugar mills; betel farming.

Singapore (sĭng′ŭpôr, sĭng′-gŭ–), island (□ 224, including adjacent islets; pop. 938,144) off S tip of Malay Peninsula, constituting chief component of Br. colony of Singapore; 27 mi. long, 14 mi. wide. Strategic Br. naval base is on N coast; Singapore city on S shore. Roughly diamond shaped, but broken by long tidal inlets, Singapore isl. is separated from Malay Peninsula by Johore Strait (N; crossed by rail and road causeway) and is bounded S by Singapore Strait. It has mangrove coast line (W and N) and low cliff (E) and rises to 581 ft. in the Bukit Timah. In central portion are 3 water reservoirs supplying Singapore city. Agr. (on predominantly red laterite and clay soils) consists of intensive market gardening, rubber, coconut, tobacco, and pineapple plantations. Hogs are raised and fishing is of importance. Outside of municipal area (□ 31) of Singapore city, rural isl. portion contains large villages of Bukit Timah, Changi, Geylang Serai, Nee Soon, and Paya Lebar. Pop. is 78% Chinese, 12% Malay, and 7% Indian. On N shore, E of Johore Strait causeway, is Br. air and naval base area (built in 1930s). Island's major civil airports are Kallang, Changi, and Tengah. The Br. crown colony of **Singapore** (□ 286; pop. 940,824; ⊙ Singapore city) consists of Singapore isl. and its adjacent isls. (including Pulau BRANI, Pulau BUKUM, BLAKANG MATI, and SAINT JOHN'S ISLAND), as well as the far-off CHRISTMAS ISLAND in Indian Ocean. Cocos (Keeling) ISLANDS, formerly part of the colony, were transferred to Australia in 1951. One of the original STRAITS SETTLEMENTS from 1826 to Jap. occupation (1942) in Second World War, Singapore was set up (1946) as a separate crown colony.

Singapore, city (□ 31; pop. 679,659), ⊙ Singapore crown colony, on Singapore Strait and at S side of Singapore isl.; 1°17′N 103°50′E. Leading trade focus, rubber market, and one of the great cities of SE Asia, Singapore is the principal port of call on Europe–Far East route, midway bet. India and China. Although politically detached (since 1946) from Malaya, it continues to handle three-fourths of the Federation's exports (rubber, tin, copra and coconut oil) and imports. Singapore's premier commercial position is further enhanced by its focal role in the entrepôt trade with Indonesia. A major international air center, Singapore is served by KALLANG and Tangah civil airports. Among its industries are the important tin-smelting works on off shore isl. of Pulau BRANI, pineapple canneries, rubber factories, and sawmills; it also produces coconut oil, soap, bricks, glass, asbestos, concrete and steel pipes, shoes, soft drinks, beer, and alcohol. Within the limits of the port area (□ 36) are the Inner Harbor (NE) for small ships, protected from the NE monsoon by mile-long granite mole separating it from the Outer Roadstead, and the deep-water channel of Keppel Harbor (SW), land locked bet. Singapore isl. (N) and Blakang Mati and Pulau Brani (S). On Singapore side of Keppel Harbor, in the dock area known as Tanjong Pagar, are the bulk of the city's harbor installations (wharves, quays, and docks, including the ½-mi. long Empire Dock), extending for 3 mi. along water front. Here is the Singapore railroad station, terminus of the Malayan rail system leading to Kuala Lumpur, Penang, and Bangkok (Thailand). Singapore city proper, NE of Keppel Harbor, is commanded by low (140–150 ft.) hills (Fort Canning, Pearls Hill) topped by reservoirs, and by Government Hill (129 ft.) with the governor's residence. The city spans the Singapore and Rochore rivers, tidal inlets filled with coastal native craft. Among the notable downtown buildings are the govt. and municipal offices, Victoria Theater, and Memorial Hall with Raffles Statue, Raffles Library and Mus., Anglican St. Andrews Cathedral (1862), and the imposing Sultan Mosque. In extensive W residential suburbs are the Botanical Gardens (where rubber was first cultivated, 1891), and Raffles Col. (1928) and King Edward VII Medical Col. (1905), combined 1949 into a univ. Situated 77 mi. N of the equator, Singapore has a uniformly hot, humid climate without notable seasonal changes, but conditioned by the NE (Oct.–March) and SW (May–Aug.) monsoons. The city has a cosmopolitan aspect with a pop. nearly 80% Chinese, 7% Indian, 7% Malay, and 1% European. A prosperous commercial center in 13th and 14th cents., Singapore was destroyed by Javanese c.1377, abandoned for Malacca, and disappeared from history for 400 years. Its revival and the founding of the modern city are associated with the name of T.S. Raffles, an official of the Br. East India Company, who sought a trading station on route to the Far East to rival the Dutch trading centers of Indonesia. Then a small Johore fishing village, Singapore and its isl. were ceded 1819 (confirmed 1824) to the British. A policy of free trade, encouragement to settlers, and the natural advantage as a port led to the phenomenal rise of Singapore during the 19th cent., spurred above all by large-scale Chinese immigration. Singapore became (1826) one of the Straits Settlements, soon overshadowing Penang and Malacca in importance, and succeeding (1836) George Town (Penang) as the capital. The development of Br. Malaya made Singapore one of the world's leading ports for the export of tin and rubber. Although considered with its naval base (on isl's. N shore) the key point in defense of SE Asia, Singapore was rapidly overwhelmed in the final phase of the Japanese Malaya campaign (Feb., 1942) in Second World War. Known as Shonan under Jap. occupation, which continued to end of Second World War. After the war, Singapore rapidly reassumed its dominant position in SE Asia, in spite of internal political unrest.

Singapore River, tidal inlet on S shore of Singapore isl., in Singapore city; anchorage for native coastal craft. At its mouth is the civic center of the city.

Singapore Strait, channel bet. Singapore isl. and Indonesian Riouw Archipelago, linking Strait of Malacca with South China Sea; 65 mi. long, 10 mi. wide; strewn with small isls. As the sea approach to Singapore, it is a great shipping route of SE Asia.

Singaradja, Indonesia: see SINGARAJA.

Singaraja or **Singaradja** (both: sĭng-ŭrä′jŭ), town (pop. 12,345), ⊙ Bali, Indonesia, near N coast of isl.; 8°8′S 115°6′E; trade center for agr. area (rice, coffee); its port is near-by Buleleng. Metalworking, weaving. Has many Hindu temples.

Singareni Collieries, India: see YELLANDLAPAD.

Singatoka River (sĭng″ätō′kä), central Viti Levu, Fiji, SW Pacific, rises in mtn. range near Vatukoula, flows 75 mi. SW to the sea; drains agr. area.

Singburi (sĭng′bŏŏrē′), town (1947 pop. 5,430), ⊙ Singburi prov. (□ 326; 1947 pop. 115,961), S Thailand, on Chao Phraya R. and 80 mi. N of Bangkok, in rice-growing region; river fisheries. Also spelled Singhaburi.

Singen (zĭng′ŭn), town (pop. 18,978), S Baden, Germany, at E foot of the Hohentwiel (a Württemberg exclave), on the Aach and 17 mi. WNW of Constance; rail junction; aluminum rolling mill; mfg. of cotton, machinery, vegetable extract; woodworking. Tourist center. Chartered 1899. Sometimes called Singen am Hohentwiel (äm hōūntvēl′).

Singers Glen, town (pop. 126), Rockingham co., NW Va., in Shenandoah Valley, 28 mi. NNE of Staunton.

Singhaburi, Thailand: see SINGBURI.

Singhana (sĭng-gä′nŭ), town (pop. 5,152), E Rajasthan, India, 7 mi. NNE of Khetri, at N end of Aravalli Range; millet, barley.

Singhbhum (sĭng′bōōm), district (□ 4,528; pop. 1,350,141), SE Bihar, India, in Chota Nagpur div.; ⊙ Chaibasa. Mainly in E foothills of Chota Nagpur Plateau; bounded NE by Subarnarekha R., S by Orissa. Original dist. (□ 3,905; 1941 pop. 1,144,717) enlarged 1948 by inc. of former Orissa states of Saraikela (asbestos and limestone quarries) and Kharsawan (major cyanite and copper mining), which had divided dist. into E and W areas. Agr. (rice, oilseeds, corn, jowar, sugar cane, tobacco), lac and silk growing; sal, kusum, bamboo, bhabur, in dispersed forest areas. Major hematite-mining centers (Noamundi, Manoharpur), copper and cyanite mining (Mosaboni; copper-smelting plant), chromite mining (Chaibasa); limestone and asbestos quarries. Principal iron- and steelworks of India are located at Jamshedpur, in this district.

Singhjani, E Pakistan: see JAMALPUR.

Singi, Tibet: see SENGE.

Singida (sĭng-gē′dä), town, Central Prov., central Tanganyika, 65 mi. N of Manyoni; 4°49′S 34°42′E. Peanuts, gum arabic, beeswax. Salt mining. Gold mined at Sekenke (50 mi. NW) and Kinyangiri (25 mi. N). Rail spur from Manyoni removed 1947.

Singidunum, Yugoslavia: see BELGRADE.

Singirg (sĭn′gĭrg) or **Sinjirj** (–jĭrj), village (pop. 6,178), Minufiya prov., Lower Egypt, on Baguriya Canal, on railroad, and 3 mi. NNE of Minuf; cereals, cotton, flax.

Singisyu, Korea: see SINUIJU.

Singitic Gulf (sĭnjĭ′tĭk) or **Gulf of Hagion Oros** (ä′yēôn ō′rôs), Ital. *Golfo di Monte Santo* (gōl′fō dē mōn′tā sän′tō), arm of Aegean Sea, bet. Sithonia and Akte (Athos) prongs of Chalcidice peninsula, Greek Macedonia; 30 mi. long, 15 mi. wide. Named for anc. Singus, on W shore.

Singkaling (sĭng″kŭlĭng′), village, ⊙ Naga Hills dist., Upper Burma, on left bank of Chindwin R. and 90 mi. NE of Homalin; 26°N 95°42′E. Was (until 1947) ⊙ Shan state of Singkaling Hkamti, Shan *Kanti* (□ 981; pop. 2,157).

Singkang or **Sengkang** (both: sĭngkäng′), town (pop. 5,847), Celebes, Indonesia, 80 mi. NNE of Macassar, on SW peninsula; 4°49′S 119°41′E; trade center for corn-growing region.

Singkarak, Lake (sĭngkäräk′) (□ 43; 14 mi. long, 4 mi. wide), W central Sumatra, Indonesia, in Padang Highlands, 7 mi. SE of Padangpanjang.

Singkawang (sĭngkäwän′), town (pop. 7,127), W Borneo, Indonesia, port on S.China Sea, 70 mi. NNW of Pontianak; 0°55′N 109°E; trade center, shipping rubber, copra, pepper. Sometimes spelled Sengkawan.

Singkep (sĭngkĕp′), island (□ c.320; 23 mi. long, 20 mi. wide), Lingga Archipelago, Indonesia, in S.China Sea, off E coast of Sumatra and S of Lingga isl., 120 mi. SSE of Singapore. Generally low, becoming hilly on E coast. There are important tin mines, employing Chinese labor. Agr. (sago, gambier, pepper), fishing, lumbering; rattan, copra. Chief town and port: Dabo (dä′bō) or Dabosingkep, on E coast.

Singles, France: see TAUVES.

Singleton, municipality (pop. 3,940), E New South Wales, Australia, on Hunter R. and 40 mi. NW of Newcastle; dairying and fruitgrowing center. Coal mines near by.

Singora, Thailand: see SONGKHLA.

Singri (sĭng′grē), village, Darrang dist., NW Assam, India, on Brahmaputra R. and 20 mi. W of Tezpur; rail spur terminus; tea, rice, rape and mustard; tea processing.

Singsas (sĭngs′ōs), Nor. *Singsås*, village and canton (pop. 1,810), Sor-Trondelag co., central Norway, on railroad and 35 mi. S of Trondheim; agr., lumbering. At Flottum (S) is pyrite mine. Sometimes spelled Singsaas.

Sing Sing, N.Y.: see OSSINING.

Singtai or **Hsing-t'ai** (both: shĭng′tī′), town, ⊙ Singtai co. (pop. 807,723), SW Hopeh prov., China, 60 mi. S of Shihkiachwang and on Peking-Hankow RR; wool weaving, fur dressing. Until 1912 called Shunteh.

Singtang or **Hsing-t'ang** (both: shĭng′täng′), town, ⊙ Singtang co. (pop. 161,499), W Hopeh prov., China, 30 mi. N of Shihkiachwang; wheat, beans, kaoliang. Sometimes Hangtang or Hangt'ang.

Singtze or **Hsing-tzu** (both: shĭng′dzŭ′), town (pop. 5,804), ⊙ Singtze co. (pop. 74,373), N Kiangsi prov., China, 20 mi. S of Kiukiang, on Poyang L. at outlet of Hukow Canal; porcelain mfg.; kaolin quarrying. Until 1912 called Nankang.

Singu (sĭng-gōō′, Burmese sŭgōō′). **1** Village, Mandalay dist., Upper Burma, landing on left bank of Irrawaddy R. and 40 mi. N of Mandalay. **2** Village, Myingyan dist., Upper Burma, on left bank of Irrawaddy R. and 4 mi. NE of Chauk. The Singu oil field, the 2d largest in Burma, includes the production centers of Chauk, Yenangyat, and Lanywa.

Singu, Japan: see SHINGU, Wakayama prefecture.

Singuilucan (sĕng-gēlōō′kän), town (pop. 1,514), Hidalgo, central Mexico, 19 mi. SE of Pachuca; grain, maguey, stock.

Singwen, China: see HINGWEN.

Sinhai or **Hsin-hai** (both: shĭn′hī′). **1** Town, Hopeh prov., China: see HWANGHWA. **2** City (1948 pop. 48,158), S Shantung prov., China, on Lunghai RR and 125 mi. SW of Tsingtao, on Kiangsu line, near Yellow Sea; commercial center, trading in wheat and cotton. Saltworks and fisheries on coast near by. Potash is found in area. Called Haichow until 1912, when as Tunghai it became ⊙ Tunghai co. (1948 pop. 301,314). It developed greatly with construction (1930s) of Lunghai RR. In 1949, the city was renamed Sinhai and was constituted as the independent municipality of Sinhailien, including its deepwater port of LIENYÜN. Until 1949 in Kiangsu prov.

Sinhailien, China: see LIENYÜN; SINHAI.

Sinho or **Hsin-ho** (both: shĭn′hŭ′). **1** Town, Chahar prov., China: see CHANGPEH. **2** Town, ⊙ Sinho co. (pop. 94,186), SW Hopeh prov., China, 55 mi. W of Tehchow; cotton, wheat, beans, kaoliang, corn. **3** Town and oasis, Sinkiang prov., China: see DUSHAMBA.

Sinhsien or **Hsin-hsien** (both: shĭn′shyĕn′). **1** Town, ⊙ Sinhsien co. (pop. 122,840), SE Honan prov., China, on Hupeh line, 55 mi. SE of Sinyang; wheat, beans, kaoliang. Called Kingfu until 1949. **2** Town, ⊙ Sinhsien co. (pop. 127,208), NE Pingyuan prov., China, 75 mi. ENE of Anyang; cotton weaving; timber, wheat, millet, kaoliang. Until 1949 in Shantung prov. **3** Town, ⊙ Sinhsien co. (pop. 232,703), N Shansi prov., China, 35 mi. N of Taiyüan; commercial center; grain, kaoliang, wheat. Rail junction for coal mines of Kiatzewan, 30 mi. NE, near Wutai. Until 1912 called Sinchow.

Sinhung (sĕn′hōōng′), Jap. *Shinko*, town (1944 pop. 7,583), S.Hamgyong prov., N Korea, 19 mi. N of Hamhung; lumbering and gold-mining center.

Sinhwa or **Hsin-hua** (both: shĭn′hwä′), town, ⊙ Sinhwa co. (pop. 738,880), central Hunan prov., China, 32 mi. N of Shaoyang; major antimony-mining center, with chief mine at Sikwangshan, 15 mi. ENE.

Sinhwa or **Hsin-hua** (shĭn′hwä′), Jap. *Shinka* (shēn′kä), town (1935 pop. 6,820), W central Formosa, 7 mi. ENE of Tainan; mfg. (tiles, incense, soy sauce). Petroleum wells near by.

Sini (sē′nē), S Bulgaria, highest peak (5,042 ft.) in NE Rhodope Mts., 13 mi. SE of Asenovgrad. Sometimes called Kokez.

Sini, China: see SUNYI.

Sini, India: see SARAIKELA.

Siniatsikon (sēnēä′tsĭkôn), mountain in Greek Macedonia, rises to 6,935 ft. 15 mi. NW of Kozane; lignite mining. Also called Askion.

Sinigaglia, Italy: see SENIGALLIA.

Siniloan (sēnēlō′än), town (1939 pop. 4,184; 1948 municipality pop. 5,450), Laguna prov., S Luzon, Philippines, 26 mi. NNE of San Pablo; agr. center (rice, coconuts, sugar cane).

Sining or **Hsi-ning** (both: shē′nĭng′). **1** Town, Chahar prov., China: see YANGYÜAN. **2** City (1947 pop. 59,266), ⊙ Tsinghai prov., China, on Sining R., 110 mi. WNW of Lanchow and E of the lake Koko Nor; 36°37′N 101°49′E. Major trading center on route to Tibet; wool weaving, tanning. Exports wool, salt, timber. Long the extraterritorial ⊙ Koko Nor territory, it remained in Kansu prov. until 1928, when it became ⊙ newly formed Tsinghai prov. Raised to municipality in 1945.

Sining River, in NE Tsinghai and Kansu provs., China, rises in the Nan Shan NE of lnke Koko Nor, flows 200 mi. ESE, past Sining, to the Yellow R. 25 mi. W of Lanchow. Sometimes called Hwang Shui.

Siniscola (sēnēskô′lä), village (pop. 4,625), Nuoro prov., NE Sardinia, 26 mi. NE of Nuoro, near coast.

Sini Shikhan or **Siniy Shikhan** (sē′nyē shĕkhän′), town (1948 pop. over 2,000), NE Chkalov oblast, Russian SFSR, in E foothills of the S Urals, 13 mi. SE of Kvarkeno, near railroad; gold mining.

Sinissippi Lake, Wis.: see HUSTISFORD.

Siniye Lipyagi (sē′nyĭ lyĕpyä′gē), village (1926 pop. 8,056), W Voronezh oblast, Russian SFSR, 35 mi. SW of Voronezh; wheat.

Sinj (sē′nyŭ). **1** Ital. *Signo* (sē′nyô), village (pop. 6,091), S Croatia, Yugoslavia, near Cetina R., 17 mi. NE of Split, in Dalmatia. Rail terminus; chief village of the Zagora; cigar mfg. Center of bauxite area which includes Visoka mine SW of Sinj; gypsum deposits. Flourished in medieval Croatian kingdom; gained importance in wars against Turks (15th-17th cent.); passed (1699) to Venetian Dalmatia. Formerly called Fsinj. **2** Village, W Croatia, Yugoslavia: see SENJ, Croatia.

Sinjajevina or **Sinyayevina** (both: sē′nyäyĕvēnä), mountain in Dinaric Alps, N central Montenegro, Yugoslavia, bet. Tara and Piva rivers. Highest point, the Korman (6,130 ft.), is 12 mi. ENE of Savnik.

Sinjawi, W Pakistan: see SANJAWI.

Sinjirj, Egypt: see SINGIRG.

Sinjirli, Turkey: see SENJIRLI.

Sinkaisze or **Hsin-k'ai-ssu** (both: shĭn′kī′sŭ′), town, SW Szechwan prov., China, 5 mi. WSW of Omei, on N slope of Omei Shan; summer resort.

Sinkan (sĭn′kän), village, Bhamo dist., Kachin State, Upper Burma, on Irrawaddy R. and 15 mi. SW of Bhamo, at E end of the river's 2d defile (15 mi. long).

Sinkan or **Hsin-kan** (both: shĭn′gän′), town (pop. 8,280), ⊙ Sinkan co. (pop. 81,536), central Kiangsi prov., China, 70 mi. SW of Nanchang and on Kan R.; rice, cotton, wheat.

Sinkang, Hsinkang (both: shĭn′gäng′), or **Hsin-chiang** (-jyäng′). **1** Jap. *Shiko* (shē′kō), town (1935 pop. 2,461), W central Formosa, on W coast, 20 mi. WNW of Kiayi. **2** Jap. *Shinko* (shĕn′kō), village (1935 pop. 3,000), SE Formosa, on E coast, 28 mi. NE of Taitung; fishing center; cold-storage plant.

Sinkao Shan, Formosa: see MORRISON, MOUNT.

Sinkat (sĭng-kăt′), town, Kassala prov., NE Anglo-Egyptian Sudan, on railroad and 60 mi. SSW of Port Sudan; cotton, corn, fruit; livestock. Pop. is largely Beja-Hadendoa.

Sinkiang or **Hsin-chiang** (both: sĭn′kyăng′, shĭn′jyäng′) [Chinese, =new territory], largest province (□ 700,000; pop. 4,000,000) of China, NW China; ⊙ Urumchi (Tihwa). Bounded S by Tibet and Kashmir along the Kunlun mts., W and NW by the USSR, NE by Mongolia (in part along the Altai Mts.), and E and SE by China's Kansu and Tsinghai provs., Sinkiang is roughly coextensive with Chinese TURKESTAN and is divided by the Tien Shan into 2 unequal sections, the Dzungaria tableland (N) and the Tarim basin (S), occupied by the Taklamakan Desert. It is a region of interior drainage, where the rivers descending from the high peripheral mts. flow into salt lakes or disappear into the desert. The Tarim R., skirting the Taklamakan Desert on the N, is the longest stream. Only the waters of the Black Irtysh (extreme N) reach the ocean. Sinkiang has a dry, continental climate with less than 10 inches of rainfall and extreme summer and winter temperatures. The Turkic Uigurs make up nearly 80% of the people. Other ethnic groups are Kazakhs and Chinese (each 8%), Kirghiz, and Mongols. Pop. is engaged in nomadic pastoralism in Dzungaria, in oasis farming on the rim of the Taklamakan Desert, and in dry farming in the mtn. valleys (notably along the upper Ili R.). Cotton and silk (spun and woven) are the leading commercial crops, followed by grain (wheat, rice, millet, corn), fruit, melons. Transportation is mainly along the motor highway from Kansu, which forks at Turfan into the road N of the Tien Shan (Chinese *T'ien-Shan Pei-lu*) and the road S of the Tien Shan (Chinese *T'ien-Shan Nan-lu*), the terms having been extended by the Chinese to the regions N (Dzungaria) and S (Tarim basin) of the Tien Shan, respectively. The leading centers are Urumchi, Yarkand, Kashgar, Khotan, Aksu, Turfan, and Hami. Sinkiang's trade is largely with the USSR via the border-crossing points of Chimunai (near Zaisan, Kazakh SSR), Chuguchak, Horgos (near Kuldja), and Irkestan (near Kashgar). In 1950, the USSR obtained the right to exploit the provincial mineral resources, mainly petroleum (Wusu, Kucha), tungsten (Arasan, Fuyün), gold, salt, and jade. Hemp narcotics are exported to Kashmir and India via Karakoram Pass. Traversed by the anc. Silk Road by which China traded with the West, S Sinkiang was controlled by China in the Han period (200 B.C.–A.D. 220), was long ruled by the Uigurs, conquered (13th cent.) by Jenghiz Khan and under his successors became part of the Jagatai domain, and later passed to the Kalmucks (Kalmyks). The area was 1st annexed (1724, 1760) by the Chinese Manchu Empire and consolidated under effective Chinese control after a Moslem (Dungan) revolt (1861–78) had been crushed. Sinkiang became a Chinese prov. in 1885, but her ties with China remained tenuous because of geographical remoteness and economic orientation toward the USSR. Following a Turki revolt for greater autonomy, an autonomous East Turkestan Republic was set up in 1944 in the dists. of Kuldja (Ili), Chuguchak, and Sharasume (Altai), but was dissolved in 1950 when the prov. passed to the Chinese Communists. Under the new regime, the Uigur pop. has assumed the leadership of the provincial govt.

Sinkiang or **Hsin-chiang,** town, ⊙ Sinkiang co. (pop. 98,820), SW Shansi prov., China, on Fen R. (head of navigation) and 35 mi. SSW of Linfen, near railroad; industrial and commercial center; cotton weaving, flour milling, iron smelting, match mfg. Wheat, beans, kaoliang, rice.

Sinkien or **Hsin-chien** (both: shĭn′jyĕn′), town (pop. 7,098), ⊙ Sinkien co. (pop. 199,774), N Kiangsi prov., China, on railroad and 6 mi. N of Nanchang; rice, cotton; mfg. (wine, paper).

Sinkin, Sinchin, or **Hsin-chin** (all: shĭn′jĭn′), town, ⊙ Sinkin co., SW Liaotung prov., Manchuria, on Liaotung peninsula, on railroad and 55 mi. NE of Dairen, on Korea Bay. In Kwantung territory (1905–45). Until 1949 it was called Pitzewo or Pitzuwo, Jap. *Hishika*.

Sinking Spring. 1 Village (pop. 187), Highland co., SW Ohio, 28 mi. SW of Chillicothe. Near by are Fort Hill and SERPENT MOUND, prehistoric earthworks. **2** Borough (pop. 1,982), Berks co., SE central Pa., 5 mi. W of Reading; foundry; textiles. Settled 1793, laid out 1831, inc. 1913.

Sin-le-Noble (sē-lŭ-nô′blŭ), E residential suburb (pop. 11,379) of Douai, Nord dept., N France, in coal-mining basin; mfg. of heating equipment; truck gardening.

Sinlitun or **Hsin-li-t'un** (both: shĭn′lē′tōōn′), town, central Liaosi prov., Manchuria, 70 mi. WNW of Mukden; 4-way rail junction at Willow Palisade.

Sinlo or **Hsin-lo** (both: shĭn′lŭ′), town, ⊙ Sinlo co. (pop. 126,283), W Hopeh prov., China, 30 mi. NE of Shihkiachwang and on Peking-Hankow RR; peanuts, millet, sesame.

Sinlumkaba (sĭn′lōōmkŭbä′), village, Bhamo dist., Kachin State, Upper Burma, 17 mi. E of Bhamo.

Sinmi Island (sĕn′mē′), Korean *Shinmi-do*, Jap. *Shimmi-to* (□ c.40; pop. c.15,000), N.Pyongan prov., Korea, in Korea Bay, just off NW coast; 10 mi. long, 5 mi. wide; has rugged terrain. Tourist resort (fishing).

Sinmin or **Hsin-min** (both: shĭn′mĭn′), town (1938 pop. 32,995), ⊙ Sinmin co. (pop. 506,247), central Liaosi prov., Manchuria, 36 mi. WNW of Mukden and on right bank of lower Liao R.; rail junction; soybean oil, bean cake; kaoliang, rice.

Sinminshih or **Hsin-min-shih** (both: shĭn′mĭn′shŭ′), town, SW Honan prov., China, 30 mi. WNW of Nanyang; Buddhist monastery. Formerly called Shihfosze.

Sinnai (sĕn′nī), town (pop. 5,243), Cagliari prov., S Sardinia, 6 mi. NE of Cagliari.

Sinnamary (sēnämärē′), town (commune pop. 1,373), N Fr. Guiana, on Sinnamary R. near its mouth on the Atlantic, 50 mi. WNW of Cayenne; coffee, cacao, fruit, hogs. Radio station.

Sinnamary River, central and N Fr. Guiana, rises at W foot of Chaîne Granitique, flows c.110 mi. N, through tropical forests, to the Atlantic just below Sinnamary. Navigable for small craft in lower course. Gold placers near mid-course.

Sinnar (sĭn′nŭr), town (pop., including suburban area, 12,380), Nasik dist., central Bombay, India, 17 mi. SE of Nasik; market center (gur, betel leaf, rice, plantains); cotton and silk handicraft weaving, oilseed pressing, biri mfg.

Sinneh, Iran: see SANANDAJ.

Sinnemahoning Creek (sĭ″nŭmŭhō′nĭng), N central Pa., rises in several branches in mts. of Cameron co., flows c.40 mi. SE, past Emporium, receiving Bennett Branch (from W) and First Fork (from N), to West Branch of Susquehanna R. 8 mi. WSW of Renovo.

Sinning or **Hsin-ning** (both: shĭn′nĭng′). **1** Town, ⊙ Sinning co. (pop. 210,051), SW Hunan prov., China, 50 mi. WNW of Lingling, near Kwangsi line; antimony mining. **2** Town, Kwangsi prov., China: see FUNAN. **3** Town, Szechwan prov., China: see KAIKIANG.

Sinni River (sēn′nē), anc. *Siris*, in Basilicata, S Italy, rises in the Apennines 6 mi. ENE of Lagonegro, flows 58 mi. S and ENE to Gulf of Taranto 9 mi. E of Rotondella.

Sin Nombre, Cerro (sĕ′rō sēn nōm′brā), peak (7,395 ft.), Aysén prov., S Chile, on NW bank of L. Buenos Aires, 55 mi. SSE of Puerto Aysén.

Sinnuris or **Sinuris** (sĭnōō′rĭs), town (pop. 23,537; with suburbs, 25,839), Faiyum prov., Upper Egypt, on railroad and 8 mi. NNE of Faiyum; cotton ginning and dyeing; cereals, sugar cane, fruits.

Sino, town, Liberia: see GREENVILLE.

Sinob, Turkey: see SINOP, town.

Sinoe (sī′nō), county, SE Liberia, on Atlantic coast; ⊙ Greenville. Bounded E by Grand Cess R., W by Sangwin R.; drained by Sinoe and Nana Kru rivers; extends c.40 inland. Agr. (citrus fruit), coconuts, palm oil and kernels, coffee, cacao, raffia, cassava, rice); cattle raising. Gold mining; graphite deposits. Main centers: Greenville, Nana Kru, Sangwin. Sometimes spelled Sino.

Sinoe, town, Liberia: see GREENVILLE.

Sinoe, Lake, Rumania: see RAZELM, LAKE.

Sinoe River, SE Liberia, rises in Niete Mts., flows c.70 mi. SW to the Atlantic at Greenville.

Sinoia (sēnō′yä), village (pop. 756), Salisbury prov., N Southern Rhodesia, in Mashonaland, on Hunyani R., on railroad and 65 mi. WNW of Salisbury; alt. 3,818 ft. Tobacco-growing center; corn, peanuts, cotton, citrus fruit. Gold deposits. Hq. Lomagundi dist. Sinoia limestone caves c.5 mi. W.

Sinop (sĭnôp′), prov. (□ 2,353; 1950 pop. 225,427), N Turkey, on Black Sea; ⊙ Sinop. Drained by Gok R.; flax, olives, tobacco.

Sinop, anc. *Sinope* (sĭnō′pē), town (1950 pop. 5,780), ⊙ Sinop prov., N Turkey, port on Black Sea, 75 mi. WNW of Samsun, 190 mi. NE of Ankara; 42°2′N 35°12′E. Though situated on a peninsula sheltering one of the finest harbors on N coast of Asia Minor, its lack of land communications makes it only of minor importance as a port. Some shipbuilding; exports tobacco, fruit, timber. The anc. Sinope was founded c.780 B.C. by Milesian colonists, was rebuilt after its destruction (7th cent. B.C.) by the Cimmerians, rose to great commercial and political importance, and established numerous colonies on the Euxine shores. One of its chief exports was cinnabar. The city fell (early 2d cent. B.C.) to the kings of Pontus, whose capital it became. The Romans under Lucullus captured it from Mithridates VI in the Third Mithridatic War (74–63 B.C.) and made it a free city. Sinope was occupied and devastated by Pharnaces II but was restored by Julius Caesar. Under the Roman Empire, the city again reached great prosperity, which continued under the Byzantine Empire. When the Byzantine Empire broke up (1204) as a result of the Fourth Crusade, Sinope joined the Greek empire of Trebizond, but within a few years it was conquered by the Seljuk Turks and its decline began. Diogenes and Mithridates the Great b. here. Formerly sometimes spelled Sinob.

Sinopoli (sēnô′pôlē), village (pop. 2,756), Reggio di Calabria prov., Calabria, S Italy, on N slope of the Aspromonte, 16 mi. NE of Reggio di Calabria; flour milling.

Sinor (sĭnōr′), town (pop. 6,804), Baroda dist., N Bombay, India, near Narbada R., 27 mi. SSE of Baroda; local trade in cotton, millet, rice; handicraft cloth weaving and printing.

Sinos River (sē′nōōs), NE Rio Grande do Sul, Brazil, rises in the Serra do Mar, flows c.70 mi. W and S, past Taquara (head of navigation) and São Leopoldo, to Jacuí R. just N of Pôrto Alegre.

Sinpin or **Hsin-pin** (both: shĭn′bĭn′), town, ⊙ Sinpin co. (pop. 118,359), central Liaotung prov., Manchuria, 55 mi. W of Tunghwa; gold-mining center; tobacco. Until 1929 called Hingking. Was ancestral home of China's Manchu dynasty.

Sinping or **Hsin-p'ing** (both: shĭn′pĭng′), town, ⊙ Sinping co. (pop. 47,686), central Yunnan prov., China, 80 mi. SW of Kunming; alt. 5,361 ft.; rice, wheat, millet, beans.

Sinpo (sĕn′pô′), Jap. *Shinyo*, town (1944 pop. 26,086), S.Hamgyong prov., N Korea, on E.Korea Bay, 35 mi. ENE of Hungnam; fishing port.

Sinpu or **Hsin-p'u** (both: shĭn′pōō′), town, SW Shantung prov., China, 3 mi. NE of Sinhai, and on Lunghai RR and Yen R.; commercial center; exports flour, bean oil, bean cake, salt. Sometimes called Sinpuchen. Until 1949 in Kiangsu prov.

Sinpu or **Hsin-pu** (both: shĭn′bōō′), Jap. *Shimpo* or *Shinpo* (shēm′pō), village (1935 pop. 3,574), NW Formosa, 7 mi. E of Sinchu; rice milling; bricks and tiles, wooden articles. Agr.: rice, oranges, tea.

Sinsheim (zĭns′hīm), town (pop. 5,430), N Baden, Germany, after 1945 in Württemberg-Baden, on the Elsenz and 13 mi. SE of Heidelberg; metal stamping and enameling.

Sinsiang or **Hsin-hsiang** (both: shĭn′shyäng′), city, ⊙ Pingyuan prov., E China, on Wei R. and 360 mi. SSW of Peking; rail center on Peking-Hankow RR; cotton weaving, flour milling, match mfg.; wheat, beans, kaoliang. Was ⊙ Sinsiang co. (pop. 252,410) until 1949, when city became an independent municipality and co. seat was transferred to a village 7 mi. S, thereafter also called Sinsiang. Until 1949, city was in Honan prov.

Sinsicap (sēnsēkäp′), town (pop. 1,047), Libertad dept., NW Peru, on W slopes of Cordillera Occidental, 13 mi. WNW of Otusco; wheat, corn, alfalfa.

Sinsinawa (sĭnsĭ′nŭwŭ), village (pop. c.200), Grant co., extreme SW Wis., 6 mi. E of Dubuque, Iowa; stock raising. Seat of St. Clara Acad. for girls (1848).

Sinsing, China: see YÜKI, Yunnan prov.

Sinsyu, Korea: see CHINJU.

Sintaein (sēn′tā′ēn′), Jap. *Shintainin*, town (1949 pop. 20,961), N.Cholla prov., S Korea, 17 mi. SW of Chonju; agr. center (rice, soybeans, cotton, hemp); rope making.

Sint-Agatha-Berchem, Belgium: see BERCHEM-SAINTE-AGATHE.

Sintai or **Hsin-t'ai** (both: shĭn′tī′), town, ⊙ Sintai co. (pop. 228,096), central Shantung prov., China, on rail spur and 70 mi. SE of Tsinan; peanuts, melon, cotton, silk, honey.

Sintaluta (sĭn″tŭlōō′tŭ), town (pop. 341), SE Sask., 50 mi. E of Regina; grain elevators.

Sint-Amands (sĭnt-ä′mänz), Fr. *Saint-Amand* (sĕtämä′), town (pop. 4,010), Antwerp prov., N Belgium, on Scheldt R. and 13 mi. W of Mechlin; agr. market (vegetables, potatoes).

Sint-Amandsberg (sĭnt-ä′mänzbĕrk), Fr. *Mont-Saint-Amand* (mō-sĕtämä′), town (pop. 21,445), East Flanders prov., NW Belgium, E suburb of Ghent.

Sint-Andries (sĭnt-än′drēs), Fr. *Saint-André* (sĕtädrā′), town (pop. 10,650), West Flanders prov., NW Belgium, WSW suburb of Bruges.

Sint Andries, village (pop. 57), Gelderland prov., central Netherlands, 7 mi. SSW of Tiel. Near by is Sint Andries Canal (3 mi. long), joining Maas and Waal rivers.

Sintang (sĭntäng′), town (pop. 4,474), W central Borneo, Indonesia, on the Kapuas and 180 mi. E of Pontianak; 0°5′N 111°30′E; trade center in forested area (rubber, timber, coconuts).

Sint Anna Bay (sĭnt ä′nä) or **Santa Anna Bay** (sän′tŭ ä′nŭ), harbor of Willemstad, SW Curaçao isl., Du. West Indies. A narrow, deep channel c.1 mi. long, 110–325 yards wide. The city is built on both sides; along it stretch several wharves. The bay widens into Schottegat, a deep lagoon.

Sint Anna-Parochie (–pärō-khē′), village (pop. 2,035), Friesland prov., N Netherlands, in commune of 't Bildt, 7.5 mi. NW of Leeuwarden; cattle raising, dairying, truck gardening.

Sint Christoffelberg (krĭ′stôfŭlbĕrkh″), highest elevation (1,220 ft.) on Curaçao isl., Du. West Indies, 20 mi. NW of Willemstad.

Sinteng or **Hsin-teng** (both: shĭn′dŭng′), town (pop. 6,697), ⊙ Sinteng co. (pop. 64,396), NW Chekiang prov., China, near Tsientang R., 35 mi. SW of Hangchow; mfg. of paper umbrellas; rice, wheat, watermelons, fruit, cotton.

Sint Eustatius, Du. West Indies: see SAINT EUSTATIUS.

Sint Filipsland, Netherlands: see SINT PHILIPSLAND.

Sint-Genesius-Rode (sĭnt-gŭnā′sēŭs-rō′dŭ), Fr. *Rhode-Saint-Genèse* (rōd-sĕ-zhŭnĕz′), town (pop. 8,366), Brabant prov., central Belgium, 7 mi. S of Brussels; paper mfg.

Sint-Gillis, Brabant prov., Belgium: see SAINT-GILLES.

Sint-Gillis-bij-Dendermonde, Belgium: see SAINT-GILLES-LEZ-TERMONDE.

Sint-Gillis-Waas, East Flanders prov., Belgium: see SAINT-GILLES-WAAS.

Sinti or **Hsin-ti** (both: shĭn′dē′), town, SE Hupeh prov., China, 70 mi. SW of Hankow and on left bank of Yangtze R.; commercial center.

Sintica (sĭntē′kä), Gr. *Sintike* or *Sindiki* (both: sĭndē′kē), region of Greek Macedonia, in Serrai nome, on Bulg. border, astride Struma R.; chief town, Siderokastron.

Sintien or **Hsin-t'ien** (both: shĭn′tyĕn′), town, ⊙ Sintien co. (pop. 148,706), S Hunan prov., China, 55 mi. WNW of Chenhsien; rice, wheat, cotton, timber.

Sintien or **Hsin-tien** (both: shĭn′dyĕn′), Jap. *Shinten* (shēn′tän), town, N Formosa, 5 mi. S of Taipei and on Sintien R. (right tributary of Tanshui R.); black-tea center; coal mining; lumbering; camphor.

Sintike, Greece: see SINTICA.

Sint Jacobi-Parochie, Netherlands: see 'T BILDT.

Sint-Jans-Molenbeek, Belgium: see MOLENBEEK-SAINT-JEAN.

Sint-Joost-ten-Node, Belgium: see SAINT-JOSSE-TEN-NOODE.

Sint-Katelijne-Waver (sĭnt-kätŭlī′nŭ-vä′vŭr), Fr. *Wavre-Sainte-Catherine* (väv′rŭ-sĕt-kätärēn′), town (pop. 10,418), Antwerp prov., N Belgium, 4 mi. NE of Mechlin; agr. market (vegetables, potatoes).

Sint-Kruis (–krois′), Fr. *Sainte-Croix* (sĕt-krwä′), town (pop. 8,225), West Flanders prov., NW Belgium, E suburb of Bruges.

Sint-Lambrechts-Woluwe, Belgium: see WOLUWE-SAINT-LAMBERT.

Sint-Lenaarts (sĭnt-lā′närts), Fr. *Saint-Léonard* (sĕ-lāōnär′), town (pop. 4,067), Antwerp prov., N Belgium, on Antwerp-Turnhout Canal and 14 mi. NE of Antwerp; brick-mfg. center.

Sint-Michiels (–mĭ′khēŭls), Fr. *Saint-Michel-lez-Bruges* (sĕ-mēshĕl-lā-brüzh′), town (pop. 5,564), West Flanders prov., NW Belgium, 2 mi. S of Bruges; blast furnaces; mfg. of railroad stock.

Sint Michielsgestel (–khē′stŭl), town (pop. 3,041), North Brabant prov., S central Netherlands, on Dommel R. and 4 mi. SSE of 's Hertogenbosch. Deaf-and-dumb institution.

Sint Nicolaas (sĭnt nē′kôläs), town, S Aruba, Du. West Indies, 11 mi. SE of Oranjestad. Adjoining E is the large Lago petroleum refinery.

Sint Nicolaas Punt, Indonesia: see SAINT NICHOLAS POINT.

Sint-Niklaas, Belgium: see SAINT-NICOLAS.

Sinton (sĭn′tŭn), town (pop. 4,254), ⊙ San Patricio co., S Texas, 19 mi. NNW of Corpus Christi; shipping, trade center in cotton, cattle, truck, oil area; cotton processing, oil refining. Settled c.1892, inc. 1916.

Sint Philipsland or **Sint Filipsland** (sĭnt fĭ′lĭpslänt), former island (□ 12) of Zeeland prov., SW Netherlands, bet. the Krammer (N), the Mastgat (W), and the Eendgracht (S); NNW of Bergen op Zoom; 4.5 mi. long, 2.5 mi. wide; now linked with mainland. Grows vegetables, sugar beets, potatoes, wheat, oats. Chief village, St. Philipsland (pop. 1,350), 11 mi. NNW of Bergen op Zoom. Isl. flooded in Second World War.

Sint-Pieters-Leeuw (–pē′tŭrs-lyōō′), Fr. *Leeuw-Saint-Pierre* (lû-sĕ-pyâr′), town (pop. 10,856), Brabant prov., central Belgium, on Charleroi Canal and 8 mi. SW of Brussels; distilling, mfg. of chemicals, electrical equipment. Has 17th-cent. castle and Gothic church.

Sint-Pieters-Woluwe, Belgium: see WOLUWE-SAINT-PIERRE.

Sintra, Portugal: see CINTRA.

Sintra, Serra de (sĕ′rŭ dĭ sēn′trŭ), short mtn. range of Lisboa dist., W central Portugal, extending from Cintra to the Atlantic at Cape Roca. Rises to 1,736 ft. just S of Cintra. Its lush vegetation and mild climate make it a favorite tourist region.

Sintsai or **Hsin-t'sai** (both: shĭn′tsī′), town, ⊙ Sintsai co. (pop. 330,454), S Honan prov., China, on Anhwei line, 65 mi. NE of Sinyang; cotton weaving; rice, wheat, beans.

Sintsing or **Hsin-ching** (both: shĭn′jĭng′), town (pop. 15,480), ⊙ Sintsing co. (pop. 163,160), W Szechwan prov., China, 22 mi. SW of Chengtu, on Chengtu plain; cotton spinning and weaving, winegrowing, sugar milling; rice, sugar cane, potatoes, wheat, tobacco, ramie.

Sintsiu, Manchuria: see KIENPING.

Sint-Truiden, Belgium: see SAINT-TROND.

Sintu or **Hsin-tu** (both: shĭn′dōō′). **1** Town, ⊙ Sintu co. (pop. 59,640), E Kwangsi prov., China, 45 mi. NNE of Wuchow, near Kwangtung line; rice, wheat, beans. The name of Sintu was formerly applied to a town 6 mi. S; present locality was then known as Kwantan. **2** Town (pop. 21,956), ⊙ Sintu co. (pop. 159,187), W Szechwan prov., China, 11 mi. NNE of Chengtu, on Chengtu plain; rice, wheat, rapeseed, beans.

Sinuapa (sēnwä′pä), town (pop. 901), Ocotepeque dept., W Honduras, near Lempa R., 3 mi. NW of Nueva Ocotepeque; wheat, corn, coffee, tobacco.

Sinuiju (sĕn′ōō′ē′jōō′), Jap. *Shingishu* or *Singisyu* (both: shēng-gē′shōō), city (1944 pop. 118,414), ⊙ N.Pyongan prov., N Korea, on Yalu R. opposite Antung in Manchuria; 40°6′N 124°24′E; commercial center for sawmilling area. Its port is YONGAMPO. Industries: paper milling, soybean processing, alcohol distilling. The city's rise dates from opening (1910) of international bridge (3,047 ft. long) across the Yalu. Became provincial ⊙ in 1923, succeeding Uiju. Heavily bombed (1950) in Korean war.

Sinuris, Egypt: see SINNURIS.

Sinú River (sēnōō′), Bolívar dept., N Colombia, rises at N foot of Cordillera Occidental in Antioquia dept., flows c.250 mi. N, past Montería and Lorica, to Gulf of Morrosquillo of Caribbean Sea, 13 mi. WSW of Tolú, forming a delta. Along its course are rich soils supporting a fourth of the dept.'s pop. Along upper Sinú are mainly precious woods; along middle course, livestock; and along lower course, rice. Navigable for small craft.

Sinus Gallicus, France: see LION, GULF OF.

Sinwen or **Hsin-wen** (both: shĭn′wŭn′), town, ⊙ Sinwen co. (pop. 163,664), N central Hopeh prov., China, 45 mi. WSW of Tientsin; cotton, wheat, kaoliang, millet. Called Wenan until 1949. A former co. seat, Sinchen, is 10 mi. NW.

Sinyang or **Hsin-yang** (both: shĭn'yäng'), town, ⊙ Sinyang co. (pop. 416,695), S Honan prov., China, 180 mi. S of Chengchow and on Peking-Hankow RR; head of navigation of headstream of Hwai R.; commercial center of S Honan. Cotton and silk weaving, mfg. of bamboo articles. Tung oil, lacquer, hides, rice, beans, millet. Projected junction for railroad E to Hofei (Anhwei prov.).

Sinyavino (sēnyä'vēnŭ), town (1939 pop. over 2,000), central Leningrad oblast, Russian SFSR, 6 mi. NNE of Mga; peat working.

Sinyayevina, mountain, Yugoslavia: see SINJAJEVINA.

Sinyeh or **Hsin-yeh** (both: shĭn'yĕ'), town, ⊙ Sinyeh co. (pop. 272,019), SW Honan prov., China, 30 mi. SW of Nanyang, near Hupeh line; wheat, beans, kaoliang.

Sinying or **Hsinying** (both: shĭn'yĭng'), Jap. *Shinei* (shē'nā), officially *Tainan* (dī'nän'), town (1935 pop. 10,522), W central Formosa, on railroad and 22 mi. NNE of Tainan; sugar milling, distilling; drugs, tropical vegetables.

Sinyü or **Hsin-yü** (both: shün'yü'), town (pop. 4,394), ⊙ Sinyü co. (pop. 139,454), N Kiangsi prov., China, on Yüan R., on Chekiang-Kiangsi RR and 35 mi. E of Ichun; coal mining.

Sinzheim (zĭnts'hīm), village (pop. 4,301), S Baden, Germany, at W foot of Black Forest, 3.5 mi. W of Baden-Baden; woodworking.

Sinzi, Lake, Japan: see SHINJI, LAKE.

Sinzig (zĭn'tsĭkh), town (pop. 4,396), in former Prussian Rhine Prov., W Germany, after 1945 in Rhineland-Palatinate, on the Ahr near its mouth on the Rhine, and 14 mi. SSE of Bonn; mosaic tiles; bottles. Has late-Romanesque church.

Sinzyo, Japan: see SHINJO, Yamagata prefecture.

Siocon (syō'kōn, syōkōn'), town (1939 pop. 1,930; 1948 municipality pop. 11,751), Zamboanga prov., W Mindanao, Philippines, 55 mi. N of Zamboanga city; coconuts, corn, rice.

Siofok (shĭ'ōfôk), Hung. *Siófok*, resort town (pop. 4,545), Veszprem co., W central Hungary, on L. Balaton, at efflux of Sio R., and 26 mi. SW of Szekesfehervar; rail junction; steamship connection to Balatonfüred. Vineyards, wheat, corn, cattle in vicinity.

Siogama, Japan: see SHIOGAMA.

Sion (syō), Ger. *Sitten* (zĭ'tŭn), town (1950 pop. 11,031), ⊙ Valais canton, SW Switzerland, on the Rhone, at mouth of Sionne R., 30 mi. SE of Vevey; alt. 1,621 ft. Metal- and woodworking, printing; flour, tobacco. An old town (anc. *Sedunum*), Sion has been an episcopal see since the 6th cent., with several churches: Gothic cathedral, Notre-Dame-de-Valère (12th–13th cent.), St. Théodule (16th cent.), 14th-cent. chapel. Here are castle remains of Tourbillion (13th cent.), Valère (or Valeria; on anc. foundations), and Majoria. Other notable bldgs.: governmental palace, bishop's palace, town hall, archaeological mus. Chandoline and Bramois hydroelectric plants near by; coal mining in the vicinity.

Sio Point, Japan: see SHIO POINT.

Sio River (shĭ'ō), Hung. *Sió*, W central Hungary, only outlet of L. Balaton; efflux at Siofok, here regulated by sluices; flows E, receiving Kapos R., thence S at Simontornya as Sio-Kapos Canal, parallel to Sarviz R. and joining it 6 mi. W of Szekszard. Length, 45 mi.

Siota, Japan: see SHIOTA.

Sioule River (syōōl), Puy-de-Dôme and Allier depts., central France, rises in a crater lake of the Monts Dore, 4 mi. SE of Rochefort-Montagne, flows 95 mi. NNE, past Pontgibaud and Ébreuil, to the Allier 5 mi. below St-Pourçain-sur-Sioule. Traverses a narrow gorge near Queuille, where it powers 3 hydroelectric plants. Receives the Bouble (left).

Sioux (sōō). **1** County (□ 766; pop. 26,381), NW Iowa, on S.Dak. line (formed here by Big Sioux R.); ⊙ Orange City. Prairie agr. area (hogs, cattle, poultry, corn, oats, hay) drained by Rock R. and Floyd and West Branch Floyd rivers. Formed 1851. **2** County (□ 2,063; pop. 3,124), extreme NW Nebr.; ⊙ Harrison. Agr. region bordering on S.Dak. and Wyo.; drained by branches of White and Niobrara rivers. Toadstool Park, area of curious stone formations, in NE. Livestock, grain, dairy and poultry produce. Formed 1877. **3** County (□ 1,124; pop. 3,696), S N.Dak.; ⊙ Fort Yates. Livestock, poultry, grain. Part of Standing Rock Indian Reservation is here; hq. at Fort Yates. Formed 1914.

Sioux Center, town (pop. 1,860), Sioux co., NW Iowa, 42 mi. NNE of Sioux City; agr. trade center with several cooperatives; dairy products, feed, dressed poultry. Inc. 1891. Many people of Dutch descent in the area.

Sioux City, city (pop. 83,991), ⊙ Woodbury co., W Iowa, c.155 mi. WNW of Des Moines, and on Missouri R. at influx of Big Sioux and Floyd rivers; 2 bridges span the Missouri here to South Sioux City, Nebr. The 2d-largest city in the state, it is a major market (livestock, grain) and meat-packing center for an extensive area, including near-by states. Served by many railroads, roads, and airport; has large stockyards. Manufactures dairy products, flour, feed, animal serums, popcorn, wind-propelled generators, batteries, tools, machinery, brick and tile. Morningside Col. (Methodist; coeducational; 1894) and Briar Cliff Col. (Catholic; for women) are here. Holds annual (March) stock show. Near by are Stone State Park and Floyd Monument commemorating death and burial in 1804 of Sgt. Charles Floyd of the Lewis and Clark expedition. Settled 1848, inc. 1857.

Sioux Falls, city (pop. 52,696), ⊙ Minnehaha co., SE S.Dak., largest city in state, c.75 mi. N of Sioux City, Iowa, and on Big Sioux R. (falls furnish water power); 43°30'N 96°45'W; alt. 1,400 ft. Business center for large farming region; meat products, soy beans, biscuits, candy, soap, paint, cement blocks and silos, acetylene gas, granite. Two cathedrals (Episcopal and R.C.), several hospitals, state penitentiary, and airport are here. Seat of Sioux Falls Col., Augustana Col., and state school for deaf. Founded 1857, abandoned 1862, resettled 1865 with establishment here of Fort Dakota; inc. as village 1877, chartered as city 1883.

Sioux Lookout (sōō), town (pop. 1,756), NW Ont., on Pelican L. (4 mi. long), near Lac Seul, 180 mi. NW of Fort William; alt. 1,198 ft.; gold-mining and lumbering center; creosote works. Distributing point for surrounding region.

Sioux Rapids, town (pop. 1,010), Buena Vista co., NW Iowa, on Little Sioux R. and 17 mi. S of Spencer; mfg. of metal products. Sand pits near by. Platted 1858, replatted 1869.

Sipan Island (shē'pän), Serbo-Croatian *Šipan*, Ital. *Giuppana* (jōōp-pä'nä), Dalmatian island in Adriatic Sea, S Croatia, Yugoslavia, 12 mi. NNW of Dubrovnik; c.5 mi. long. Chief village, Sipanjska Luka, Serbo-Croatian *Šipanjska Luka*, is on W coast. Sometimes spelled Shipan.

Siparia (sĭpâ'rēŭ), village (pop. 4,455), SW Trinidad, B.W.I., rail terminus 10 mi. S of San Fernando, in cacao-growing region. Formerly a Sp. mission; has a church, founded by Capuchins (1758), with shrine to Black Virgin. Petroleum wells near by.

Sip Canal, Yugoslavia: see IRON GATE.

Sipesipe (sēpäsē'pā), town (pop. c.8,200), Cochabamba dept., central Bolivia, on S slopes of Cordillera de Cochabamba, 14 mi. WSW of Cochabamba; alt. 8,323 ft.; barley, corn; livestock.

Siphnos or **Sifnos** (both: sĭf'nôs), Lat. *Siphnus* (sĭf'nŭs), Aegean island (□ 31; pop. 3,325) in the Cyclades, Greece, W of Paros; 37°N 24°40'E; 11 mi. long, 4 mi. wide; rises to 2,280 ft. Produces wheat, wine, olive oil, silk. Silver-lead deposits. Main town, Apollonia (pop. 2,061), is on E shore. In anc. times noted for its gold and silver mines.

Sipí (sēpē'), village (pop. 205), Chocó dept., W Colombia, landing on affluent of San Juan R. and 36 mi. S of Istmina; sugar cane, corn, bananas, cattle.

Siping or **Hsi-p'ing** (both: shē'pĭng'), town, ⊙ Siping co. (pop. 271,431), central Honan prov., China, 15 mi. S of Yencheng and on Peking-Hankow RR; wheat, beans, kaoliang.

Siple, Mount (15,000 ft.), Antarctica, at E entrance of Wrigley Gulf, Marie Byrd Land; 73°15'S 123°W. Discovered 1940 by U.S. expedition.

Sipó, Brazil: see CIPÓ.

Sipoera, Indonesia: see SIPORA.

Sipolilo (sēpōlē'lō), village, Salisbury prov., N Southern Rhodesia, in Mashonaland, 85 mi. NNW of Salisbury; gold mining; police post.

Siponzh, Tadzhik SSR: see BARTANG.

Sipora, Sipura, or **Sipoera** (all: sēpōō'rŭ), island (pop. 3,892), Mentawai Isls., Indonesia, in Indian Ocean, off W coast of Sumatra, 30 mi. SE of Siberut; 30 mi. long, 12 mi. wide; hilly. Agr. (sago, sugar, tobacco, coconuts), fishing.

Sipote or **Sipotele** (shēpō'tā), Rum. *Şipote*, village (pop. 898), Jassy prov., NE Rumania, 28 mi. NW of Jassy.

Sippar (sĭpär'), anc. city of N Babylonia, on the Euphrates, in present-day Iraq, 20 mi. SW of Baghdad. According to Sumerian tradition it existed before the flood. It was one of the capitals of Sargon and had a great temple to the sun-god Shamash. Excavations begun in 1882 have yielded over 125,000 tablets here and in the neighboring mounds of Abu Habba. Sippar is probably the biblical Sepharvaim.

Sipra River (sĭ'prŭ), S central Madhya Bharat, India, rises 12 mi. SE of Indore, flows c.125 mi. NNW, past Ujjain and Mehidpur, to Chambal R. 10 mi. SE of Sitamau. Sacred to Hindus.

Sipri, India: see SHIVPURI.

Sipsey, village (1940 pop. 926), Walker co., NE Ala., on Mulberry Fork and 25 mi. NW of Birmingham, in coal-mining and agr. area.

Sipsey Creek, NW Ala. and NE Miss., rises in NW Marion co., Ala., flows c.35 mi. SW to Buttahatchee R. 15 mi. ENE of Aberdeen, Miss.

Sipsey Fork, NW Ala., rises in Lawrence co., flows c.60 mi. SE to Mulberry Fork of Black Warrior R. 12 mi. E of Jasper.

Sipsey River, W Ala., rises in SE Marion co., flows c.100 mi. S and SW to Tombigbee R. 8 mi. S of Aliceville.

Sipura, Indonesia: see SIPORA.

Siputeh (sēpōōtĕ'), village (pop. 680), central Perak, Malaya, on slopes of Kledang Range, 10 mi. SW of Ipoh; tin mining.

Siqueira Campos (sēkā'rŭ kăm'pōōs). **1** City, Espírito Santo, Brazil: see GUAÇUÍ. **2** City (pop. 1,789), NE Paraná, Brazil, on railroad and 45 mi. S of Cambará; coffee, rice, and corn-meal processing; pottery mfg. Coal mines and clay quarries near by. Until c.1935, called Colonia Mineira.

Siqueros (sēkā'rōs), town (pop. 1,096), Sinaloa, NW Mexico, on Presidio R., in coastal lowland, and 14 mi. NE of Mazatlán; chick-peas, tobacco, coffee, cotton, corn, fruit.

Siquia River (sē'kyä), S Nicaragua, rises near Camoapa, flows c.100 mi. E, past Santo Domingo and La Libertad goldfields (hydroelectric plant for El Jabalí mine), joining Mico and Rama rivers at Rama to form Escondido R. Navigable for launches in lower course.

Siquijor (sēkēhôr'), island (□ 130; 1939 pop. 59,507), Negros Oriental prov., Philippines, in Mindanao Sea, 11 mi. off SE coast of Negros isl., S of Cebu isl.; 9°11'N 123°34'E; 14 mi. long, 11 mi. wide. Mountainous, rising to 2,060 ft. in central area. Agr. (rice, sweet potatoes), manganese mining, fishing. Chief centers are LAZI and Siquijor. The isl. constitutes a sub-prov. of Negros Oriental prov.; ⊙ Siquijor (1939 pop. 614; 1948 municipality pop. 14,681), on NW coast.

Siquinalá (sēkēnälä'), town (1950 pop. 756), Escuintla dept., S Guatemala, in Pacific piedmont, 11 mi. W of Escuintla; sugar cane (mill at Pantaleón), cacao, coffee, fodder grasses; livestock.

Siquirres (sēkē'rēs), town (1950 pop. 326), Limón prov., E Costa Rica, 34 mi. ENE of Limón rail center, near La Junta junction; abacá, bananas, cacao, fodder crops. Formerly a major banana center. Pop. is largely Jamaican Negro.

Siquisique (sēkēsē'kā), town (pop. 1,616), Lara state, NW Venezuela, on Tocuyo R., in fertile section of otherwise arid Segovia Highlands, and 45 mi. NW of Barquisimeto; coffee, cacao, cattle.

Sir (sēr) or **Sayr** (sär), Fr. *Seer*, village, N Lebanon, 11 mi. ESE of Tripoli; alt. 3,300 ft.; summer resort; fruit orchards.

Sira (sē'rŭ), town (pop. 6,797), Tumkur dist., E Mysore, India, 30 mi. NNW of Tumkur; local trade in coconuts, coir products (rope, mats), grain. In late-18th cent., a Deccan administrative hq. of Mogul empire.

Sir Abu Nu'air (sēr' ă'bōō nōōīr'), uninhabited island in Persian Gulf, off Trucial Coast; 25°15'N 54°14'E.

Siracha (sē'rä'chä'), village (1937 pop. 3,848), Chonburi prov., S Thailand, minor port on Gulf of Siam, 14 mi. S of Chonburi. Sometimes spelled Sriracha and Sriraja.

Siracusa (sērăkōō'zä), province (□ 849; pop. 277,572), SE Sicily; ⊙ Syracuse. Hilly terrain, rising to 3,231 ft. in Monti Iblei; drained by Tellaro and Anapo rivers. Agr. (wheat, olives, citrus fruit, grapes); sheep raising (NE). Tunny fishing. Saltworks (Syracuse, Augusta). Limestone deposits (NE). Industry concentrated at Syracuse and Augusta. Anc. ruins at Syracuse and Pantalica. Suffered widespread destruction in earthquake of 1693. In Second World War, 1st Allied invasion of isl. (July 10, 1943) made along E coast.

Siracusa, city, Sicily: see SYRACUSE.

Siraha, Nepal: see SIRHA.

Siraisi, Japan: see SHIRAISHI.

Sirajganj (sĭrăj'gŭnj), town (pop. 42,075), Pabna dist., central East Bengal, E Pakistan, on the Jamuna (main course of the Brahmaputra) and 46 mi. NE of Pabna; rail terminus; trade center (rice, jute, rape and mustard, wheat); jute pressing, rice milling, soap and brick mfg.

Sirakawa, Japan: see SHIRAKAWA.

Sir Alexander, Mount (10,740 ft.), E B.C., in Rocky Mts., 100 mi. E of Prince George.

Siralkoppa, India: see SHIRALKOPPA.

Siran (shĭrän'), Turkish *Şiran*, village (pop. 843), Gumusane prov., NE Turkey, 24 mi. SW of Gumusane; wheat, barley, vetch, potatoes. Formerly Karaca.

Sira River (sē'rä), Nor. *Sira*, *Sireelv*, or *Siredalselv*, Vest-Agder co., S Norway, rises in the Ruven Mts., flows c.85 mi. S, through Sirdal L. and Lund L., to North Sea 6 mi. SE of Sogndal.

Sirasgaon Kasba (sĭrŭs'goun käs'bä), town (pop. 7,351), Amraoti dist., W Madhya Pradesh, India, 12 mi. ENE of Ellichpur; cotton, millet, wheat. Also spelled Shirasgaon-Kasba. Formerly called Sirasgaon.

Sirathu (sĭrä'tōō), village, Allahabad dist., SE Uttar Pradesh, India, 35 mi. WNW of Allahabad; gram, rice, barley, wheat, linseed, sugar cane.

Sirauli or **Sarauli** (sŭrou'lē), town (pop. 6,003), Bareilly dist., N central Uttar Pradesh, India, on the Ramganga and 22 mi. WNW of Bareilly; sugar refining; wheat, rice, gram, sugar cane. Also called Sirauli-Pyas.

Sirault (sērō'), agr. village (pop. 2,842), Hainaut prov., SW Belgium, 8 mi. WNW of Mons.

Sirbal, Jabal, Egypt: see SERBAL, GEBEL.

Sirdal Lake (sēr'däl), Nor. *Sirdalsvatn*, formerly *Siredalsvand*, Vest-Agder co., S Norway, a widening of the river Sira; □ 7; 17 mi. long, c.1 mi. wide. On N shore is Tonstad.

Sir Douglas, Mount (11,174 ft.), SW Alta., near B.C. border, in Rocky Mts., 35 mi. SSE of Banff.

Siredalselv, Norway: see Sira River.

Siredalsvand, Norway: see Sirdal Lake.

Sir Edward Pellew Islands (pŭlyōō', pĕl'yōō), group (□ 800) in Gulf of Carpentaria, just off E coast of Northern Territory, Australia, near mouth of McArthur R.; form N shore of Port McArthur. Comprise Vanderlin Isl. (largest; 17 mi. long, 9 mi. wide), S.W.Isl., W.Isl., Centre Isl., N.Isl., many islets and rocks. Sandstone; hilly, barren.

Sireelv, Norway: see Sira River.

Siren (sī'rŭn), village (pop. 613), Burnett co., NW Wis., 16 mi. E of Grantsburg.

Siret (sē'rĕt, sĭrĕt'), Ger. *Sereth* (zā'rĕt), town (1948 pop. 8,058), Suceava prov., N Rumania, in Bukovina, near USSR border, on Siret R., and 8 mi. NE of Radauti; trading center (grain, livestock, lumber) with brewing, milling, tanning industries. Founded in 13th-14th cent. Has 14th-cent. monastery ruins and 14th-cent. church recently restored.

Siret River (sē'rĕt, sĭrĕt'), **Siretul** (sē'rĕtōōl), or **Sereth River** (zā'rĕt), Russian *Seret* (syĕ'rĕt), largely in E Rumania, rises in Ukrainian SSR on E slopes of the Carpathians 45 mi. SW of Chernovtsy, flows SE for c.50 mi., crossing the border into Rumania, and flows SSE to join the Danube 3 mi. above Galati; total length, 280 mi. Swampy in mid and lower course. Receives Suceava, Bistrita, and Moldava rivers (right), Barlad R. (left).

Sireuil (sērû'ē), village (pop. 97), Charente dept., W France, on Charente R. and 7 mi. WSW of Angoulême; tanning, stone quarrying.

Sir Francis Drake's Channel, small strait in Br. Virgin Isls., bet. NE Tortola and S Virgin Gorda.

Sirguja, India: see Surguja, district.

Sirha or **Siraha** (sĭr'ŭhŭ), town, SE Nepal, in the Terai, 7 mi. NE of Jaynagar (Bihar, India); trades in rice, wheat, barley, corn, millet, jute, oilseeds.

Sirhan, Wadi (wä'dē sĭrhän'), structural depression in N Saudi Arabia, at Jordan border, NW of Jauf; 200 mi. long, 20–30 mi. wide; 1,000 ft. below elevation of adjoining plateau. Main town, Kaf.

Sirhind (sĭr'hĭnd), town (pop. 5,823), E central Patiala and East Punjab States Union, India, 21 mi. N of Patiala; agr. market (sugar cane, millet, wheat); cotton ginning. Fruit farm 2 mi. N; rail junction just S. In 16th-17th cent., flourished under Moguls; several mosques and tombs remain. Name formerly applied to extensive surrounding plain.

Sirhind Canal, extensive irrigation system in Punjab and Patiala and East Punjab States Union, India. From headworks on Sutlej R. at Rupar (Ambala dist.) runs 39 mi. WSW and then divides into 3 branches: W branch flows c.140 mi. WSW to Rajasthan border W of Abohar (Ferozepore dist.); central branch flows c.130 mi. WSW, past Bhatinda, to Rajasthan border S of Abohar; E branch flows c.50 mi. SSE to Patiala, with 2 longer branches extending WSW into Hissar dist. System has numerous distributaries; irrigates wheat, gram, millet, rice, cotton, and sugar-cane fields. Opened 1883.

Sirhowy, town, England: see Tredegar.

Sirhowy River (sĭrou'ē), in Brecon (Wales) and Monmouth (England), rises N of Brynmawr, flows 18 mi. SE, past Tredegar, to Ebbw R. just W of Risca.

Siri (sē'rē), village (pop. 800), Arusi prov., S central Ethiopia, 25 mi. SE to Hadama.

Siri, India: see Delhi, state.

Siria (shē'ryä), Rum. *Şiria*, Hung. *Világos* (vē'lägōsh), village (pop. 5,878), Arad prov., W Rumania, on railroad and 15 mi. NE of Arad; noted for its wine production and remains of 14th-cent. fortress, former seat of Janos Hunyadi. Hung. revolutionary army under General Gorgei surrendered here (1849) to Russians.

Sirina, Greece: see Syrnai.

Sirinhaém (sĕrĕnyäān'), city (pop. 1,682), E Pernambuco, NE Brazil, near the Atlantic, 37 mi. SSW of Recife; sugar, coconuts. Has historic Franciscan convent. Formerly spelled Serinhaem.

Siriri (sĕrĕrē'), city (pop. 1,154), central Sergipe, NE Brazil, 32 mi. NW of Aracaju; cotton, livestock. Formerly spelled Siriry.

Sir James McBrien, Mount (9,049 ft.), SW Mackenzie Dist., Northwest Territories, in Mackenzie Mts.; 62°7'N 127°45'W.

Sirjan (sērjän'), town (1941 pop. 8,074), Eighth Prov., in Kerman, SE Iran, 100 mi. SW of Kerman; road junction on highways to Shiraz and Bandar Abbas; cotton ginning, metalworking; pistachios, fruit, opium, gum arabic. Was ⊙ Kerman under the Abbasids (8th-13th cent.). Formerly called Saidabad.

Sir John Abbott, Mount (11,250 ft.), E B.C., in Premier Group of Rocky Mts., 75 mi. W of Jasper.

Sir John Thompson, Mount (11,250 ft.), E B.C., in Premier Group of Rocky Mts., 70 mi. W of Jasper; 52°45'N 119°39'W. The large Thompson Icefield extends ESE of the peak.

Sir Joseph Banks Islands, in Spencer Gulf, 5 mi. off SE coast of Eyre Peninsula, South Australia; shelters Louth Bay. Comprise c.20 islands, islets, and rocks. Largest isls.: Spilsby Isl. (2 mi. long, 1.5 mi. wide), Reevesby Isl. (3 mi. long, .5 mi. wide). Wooded, hilly; geese, sheep. Wolframite on Langton Isl.

Sirk (sĭrk), Hung. *Szirk* (sĭrk), village (pop. 1,217), S central Slovakia, Czechoslovakia, in Slovak Ore Mts., 20 mi. WSW of Roznava; iron mining here and in vicinity, notably on Zeleznik mtn. (2,660 ft.), just E.

Sirkali, India: see Shiyali.

Sir Lowry Pass, U. of So. Afr.: see Hottentots Holland Mountains.

Sir Mackenzie Bowell, Mount (11,000 ft.), E B.C., in Premier Group of Rocky Mts., 70 mi. W of Jasper; 52°52'N 119°46'W.

Sirmia, region, Yugoslavia: see Srem.

Sirmione (sērmyô'nĕ), anc. *Sirmio*, village (pop. 601), Brescia prov., Lombardy, N Italy, port on peninsula of Sirmione (2.5 mi. long; in S part of Lago di Garda), 19 mi. ESE of Brescia. Health resort (hot mineral springs) and fishing center. Has picturesque castle (built 1259; restored), church (rebuilt 1320), and ruins of Roman baths. Formerly Sermione.

Sirmium, Yugoslavia: see Mitrovica, Vojvodina, Serbia.

Sirmur (sĭrmōōr'), former princely state (□ 1,091; pop. 156,026) of Punjab Hill States, India; ⊙ was Nahan. Since 1948, merged with Himachal Pradesh. Sometimes spelled Sirmoor.

Sirmur, district, S Himachal Pradesh, India; ⊙ Nahan; includes former Simur state.

Sir Muttra (sĭr' mōōt'trŭ), village, E Rajasthan, India, 35 mi. WSW of Dholpur; rail terminus; millet, wheat.

Sirnach (zĭr'näkh), town (pop. 2,434), Thurgau canton, N Switzerland, 8 mi. SSE of Frauenfeld; cotton textiles, metal products.

Sirnai, Greece: see Syrnai.

Sirnak (shĭrnäk'), Turkish *Şirnak*, village (pop. 3,730), Siirt prov., SE Turkey, 40 mi. SE of Siirt; grain.

Sirnena Gora, Bulgaria: see Sredna Gora.

Sirodá (sērōdä'), town (pop. 8,267), central Goa dist., Portuguese India, 17 mi. SE of Pangim; rice, cashew nuts, timber.

Sirohi (sĭrō'hē), former princely state (□ 1,988; pop. 233,879) in Rajputana States, India; ⊙ was Sirohi. In 1949, administered by Bombay for govt. of India; partitioned in 1950, with SE section (including Abu) merging with Banas Kantha dist. of Bombay and rest of area joining union of Rajasthan.

Sirohi, town (pop. 9,501), ⊙ Sirohi dist., S Rajasthan, India, 95 mi. S of Jodhpur; trades in millet, maize, wheat, barley; handicraft metal work (knives, sword blades). Was ⊙ former Rajputana state of Sirohi.

Siroisi, Japan: see Shiroishi, Miyagi prefecture.

Siroki Brijeg or **Shiroki Briyeg** (both: shē'rôkē brē'yĕk), Serbo-Croatian *Široki Brijeg*, village (pop. 2,288), W Herzegovina, Yugoslavia, on Mostar–Adriatic Sea road and 12 mi. W of Mostar, near Mostar L.; bauxite mine.

Sirolo (sērô'lô), village (pop. 981), Ancona prov., The Marches, central Italy, on Adriatic coast, 8 mi. SSE of Ancona; cement works. Stone quarries near by.

Siron, India: see Lalitpur.

Sironcha (sĭrōn'chŭ), village, Chanda dist., S Madhya Pradesh, India, on Pranhita R., 3 mi. NE of Godavari-Pranhita confluence and 90 mi. SSE of Chanda; rice, millet, oilseeds; betel farming. Sawmilling 40 mi. N, at village of Alapillai or Allapilli.

Sirone, Japan: see Shirone.

Sironj (sĭrōnj'), town (pop. 13,906), S Rajasthan, India, 45 mi. SSE of Guna, in enclave in Madhya Bharat; local trade center (wheat, millet, gram); hand-loom cotton weaving, wood carving.

Siros, Greece: see Syros.

Sirotino (sērô'tyĭnŭ), town (1939 pop. over 500), W Voroshilovgrad oblast, Ukrainian SSR, in the Donbas, 4 mi. E of Lisichansk, across the Northern Donets; coal mines.

Sirotinskaya (sērô'tyĭnskīŭ), village (1939 pop. over 500), central Stalingrad oblast, Russian SFSR, on right bank of Don R. and 14 mi. WSW of Ilovlinskaya; wheat farming. Iron and fireproof-clay deposits (N). Pop. largely Cossack.

Siroua, Djebel (jĕ'bĕl sērwä'), volcanic mtn., SW Fr. Morocco, forming a bridge bet. the High Atlas (N) and the Anti-Atlas (S), just E of the Sous valley; rises to 10,840 ft.; 30°42'N 7°39'W.

Sirpur (sĭr'pōōr), village (pop. 4,521), Adilabad dist., NE Hyderabad state, India, near Wardha R., 70 mi. ESE of Adilabad; rice, oilseeds. Paper mill 11 mi. SW, at Kothapet.

Sirri Island (sĭr'rē), in Persian Gulf, 50 mil SW of Lingeh; 25°55'N 54°32'E; 3–4 mi. across. Arab pop. Former dependency of Sharja sheikdom of Trucial Oman; belongs to Iran since First World War.

Sirsa (sĭr'sŭ). **1** Town (pop. 20,718), Hissar dist., S Punjab, India, 50 mi. NW of Hissar; trades in grain, oilseeds, salt, cotton, wool; hand-loom weaving; leather goods, fibre matting; electric supply works. Large summer cattle fair. **2** Town (pop. 3,744), Allahabad dist., SE Uttar Pradesh, India, on the Ganges and 20 mi. SE of Allahabad; trades in gram, rice, barley, wheat, oilseeds.

Sirsaganj (sĭr'sägŭnj), town (pop. 4,563), Mainpuri dist., W Uttar Pradesh, India, 23 mi. WSW of Mainpuri; trade center (wheat, gram, pearl millet, corn, barley, cotton, hides). At village of Rapri (important town under Afghans and Moguls), 9 mi. SW, are 14th-cent. inscriptions, mosque, and tomb ruins.

Sir Sandford, Mount (11,590 ft.), SE B.C., in Selkirk Mts., on edge of Hamber Provincial Park, 55 mi. NNW of Revelstoke; 51°39'N 117°52'W.

Sirs el Laiyana or **Sirs al-Layanah** (both: sĭrs' ĕl-lăyă'nŭ), town (pop. 20,009), Minufiya prov., Lower Egypt, on railroad and 3 mi. SE of Minuf; linen mfg.; cereals, cotton, flax.

Sirsi (sĭr'sē). **1** Town (pop. 10,451), Kanara dist., S Bombay, India, 50 mi. ESE of Karwar; road center; agr. market (betel nuts, rice, cardamum, pepper); betel processing, sandalwood and ivory carving. **2** Town (pop. 6,875), Moradabad dist., N central Uttar Pradesh, India, 6 mi. NE of Sambhal; hand-loom cotton weaving; wheat, rice, pearl millet, oilseeds, sugar cane.

Sirsilla (sĭrsĭl'lŭ), town (pop. 6,836), Karimnagar dist., E central Hyderabad state, India, 21 mi. W of Karimnagar; rice, oilseeds.

Sirte (sēr'tä), town (pop. 2,500), Tripolitania, Libya, minor port on Gulf of Sidra, on coastal highway and 120 mi. SE of Misurata, in livestock (sheep, camels) and agr. (barley, dates) region. Caravan junction. Has restored Turkish castle built 1842 and 19th cent. mosque.

Sirtis Major, Libya: see Sidra, Gulf of.

Siruela (sērwā'lä), town (pop. 5,118), Badajoz prov., W Spain, 13 mi. S of Herrera del Duque; olives, grapes, livestock; flour milling.

Siruguppa (sĭrōōgōō'pŭ), town (pop. 6,037), Bellary dist., NW Madras, India, near Tungabhadra R., 34 mi. N of Bellary; rice milling; bamboo coracles; coconut palms, plantain. Irrigation research station here.

Sirumalai Hills (sĭ'rōōmŭlī"), outlier of S Western Ghats, SW Madras, India, N of Madura; c.40 mi. long, up to 25 mi. wide; rise to over 4,000 ft. Chief products of W forested areas are coffee, plantain, turmeric. SW segments called Alagar Hills and Nattam Hills.

Sirur (sĭrōōr'), town (pop., including suburban area, 6,124), Poona dist., central Bombay, India, 39 mi. NE of Poona; trades in cotton, millet, cattle; handicraft cloth weaving.

Sirur Tajband, India: see Ahmadpur, Hyderabad state.

Sirvan (shĭrvän'), Turkish *Şirvan*, village (pop. 562), Siirt prov., SE Turkey, 8 mi. NNE of Siirt; cereals. Formerly Kufre.

Sirvintos or **Shirvintos** (shērvēn'tōs), Lith. *Širvintos*, Rus. *Shirvinty*, town (pop. 2,119), E central Lithuania, 28 mi. NNW of Vilna; flour milling, distilling. In Rus. Vilna govt. until 1920. Formerly called Sirvintai.

Sirw, El, Es Sirw, or **Al-Sirw** (all: ĕs-sĭr'wŭ), village (pop. 7,455), Daqahliya prov., Lower Egypt, on Damietta branch of the Nile and 16 mi. SW of Damietta; cotton, cereals.

Sirwan River, Iran and Iraq: see Diyala River.

Sir Wilfrid, Mount (2,569 ft.), SW Que., in the Laurentians, 10 mi. NNW of Mont Laurier; 46°42'N 75°35'W. Named for Sir Wilfrid Laurier.

Sir Wilfrid Laurier, Mount (11,750 ft.), E B.C., in Premier Group of Rocky Mts., 70 mi. W of Jasper; 52°48'N 119°45'W.

Sis, Turkey: see Kozan.

Sisa, Japan: see Shisa.

Sisa, Peru: see San José de Sisa.

Sisagarhi, Nepal: see Chisapani Ghari.

Sisak (sē'säk), Hung. *Sziszek* (sĭs'ĕk), anc. *Segestica* and *Siscia*, town (pop. 12,334), N Croatia, Yugoslavia, major port on Sava R. (head of navigation for freight vessels), at Kupa R. mouth, on railroad and 29 mi. SSE of Zagreb. Terminus of canal to Podsused (begun 1947). Trade center for grain, timber; mfg. (alcohol, tannin, leather, hats, glass, bricks, beer). Petroleum, natural gas, and mineral springs near by. Industrial center of Caprag just S. Anc. Roman colony; seat (910–21) of early Croat ruler. A major communications center since Roman period; strategic center in wars against Turks. Castle (built 1544) remains.

Sisakai, China: see Sichow, Yunnan prov.

Sisaket or **Srisaket** (both: sē'sùkät'), town (1947 pop. 6,520), ⊙ Sisaket prov. (□ 3,444; 1947 pop. 451, 576), SE Thailand, in Korat Plateau, on railroad and 40 mi. WSW of Ubon; rice, tobacco, lac. Silver mining near by.

Sisal (sēsäl'), town (pop. 165), Yucatan, SE Mexico, on bar off N coast, 29 mi. NW of Mérida; fishing village with fine beaches. Has colonial church, monastery.

Sisante (sēsän'tā), town (pop. 3,944), Cuenca prov., E central Spain, in upper La Mancha of New Castile, 35 mi. NW of Albacete; agr. center (saffron, grapes, olives, cereals). Olive-oil extracting, liquor distilling, woolen-goods mfg.

Sisargas Islands (sēsär'gäs), archipelago of 3 islets off Atlantic NW coast of Spain, 21 mi. W of La Coruña, and opposite Malpica. On the largest one (□ 2½) is a lighthouse.

Sisauli (sĭsou'lē), town (pop. 6,641), Muzaffarnagar dist., N Uttar Pradesh, India, 14 mi. WSW of

Muzaffarnagar; wheat, gram, sugar cane, oilseeds.
Sisavan, Armenian SSR: see SISIAN.
Sisha, China: see PARACEL ISLANDS.
Sishui or **Hsi-shui** (both: shē'shwä'). **1** Town (pop. 12,329), ⊙ Sishui co. (pop. 514,334), SE Hupeh prov., China, 60 mi. E of Hankow; cotton, beans, wheat, ramie, medicinal herbs. Until 1933 called Kishui. **2** Town (pop. 5,846), ⊙ Sishui co. (pop. 154,410), N Kweichow prov., China, on Szechwan border, 45 mi. SE of Luhsien; cotton textiles; wheat, millet, beans. Coal mines near by.
Sisi (sĭs'ē), village, Lakhimpur dist., E central Assam, India, on Brahmaputra R. and 19 mi. WSW of Dibrugarh; tea, rice, jute, sugar cane; sawmilling. Also spelled Sissi.
Sisian (sēsēän'), village (1948 pop. over 2,000), S Armenian SSR, on road and 40 mi. NE of Nakhichevan in Karabakh Highland; wheat. Originally called Karaklis or Karakilisa, and, c.1935–39, Sisavan.
Sisiang or **Hsi-hsiang** (both: shē'shyäng'), town (pop. 12,467), ⊙ Sisiang co. (pop. 144,628), SW Shensi prov., China, 35 mi. E of Nancheng; tea, gums and resins.
Sisikui, Japan: see SHISHIKUI.
Siskiwit Bay and **Siskiwit Lake,** Mich.: see ISLE ROYALE NATIONAL PARK.
Siskiyou (sĭ'skēyōō), county (□ 6,313; pop. 30,733), N Calif.; ⊙ Yreka. Bounded N by Oregon line. In W, Klamath Mts. (peaks up to c.9,000 ft.) are drained by Klamath R. and tributaries; in E center is part of Cascade Range, here rising to 14,162 ft. at Mt. SHASTA, whose glacier-fed springs are sources of Sacramento and McCloud rivers. To E of the Cascades lies a semiarid farming and lumbering region (partly irrigated) of volcanic soils and lava beds (including LAVA BEDS NATIONAL MONUMENT); here are Tule and Lower Klamath lakes. Much of co. included in Klamath, Shasta, Modoc natl. forests. Part of Klamath irrigation project in N. Lumbering, lumber milling; stock grazing, farming (potatoes, hay, barley, wheat); mining and quarrying (gold, pumice, sand, gravel, diatomite). Mtn. scenery, hunting, fishing attract vacationers. Formed 1852.
Siskiyou Mountains, N Calif. and SW Oregon, a range of KLAMATH MOUNTAINS extending NE from Calif. coast S of Crescent City, into Josephine and Jackson counties, Oregon; mark divide bet. Rogue R. (N) and Klamath R. (S). Chief peaks in Oregon are Mt. Ashland (7,530 ft.), Dutchman Peak (7,411 ft.), and Siskiyou Peak (7,147 ft.), all S of Medford. Preston Peak (7,310 ft.) is in Calif., c.30 mi. E of Crescent City. OREGON CAVES NATIONAL MONUMENT attracts tourists. Lumbering (pine, fir, spruce), hunting, fishing. Fruitgrowing (especially pears) and agr. in Rogue R. valley.
Sisophon (sēsōpôn'), town (1941 pop. 3,496), Battambang prov., W Cambodia, on railroad and 180 mi. NW of Pnompenh, near Thailand border; transportation hub on Bangkok-Saigon route; customs station. In Thailand before 1907 and again 1941–46.
Sisquoc River (sĭskwŏk'), SW Calif., rises in E Santa Barbara co., flows c.50 mi. W to Cuyama R. SE of Santa Maria; flow is intermittent.
Sissach (zĭ'säkh), town (pop. 3,040), Basel-Land half-canton, N Switzerland, on Ergolz R. and 12 mi. SE of Basel; metal products (notably electrical apparatus), foodstuffs; woodworking.
Sisseton (sĭ'sŭtŭn), city (pop. 2,871), ⊙ Roberts co., NE S.Dak., 70 mi. ENE of Aberdeen, 10 mi. W of L. Traverse; trade center for diversified farming region; agency hq. for Sisseton Indian Reservation. Resort. Cattle feed, dairy products livestock, poultry. Fort Sisseton, 20 mi. W, is historic military outpost established 1864. Inc. 1892.
Sissi, India: see SISI.
Sisson, Calif.: see MOUNT SHASTA.
Sissonne (sēsôn'), village (pop. 1,535), Aisne dept., N France, 12 mi. E of Laon; military camp near by.
Sistan, Iran: see SEISTAN.
Sister Bay, village (pop. 429), Door co., NE Wis., on inlet of Green Bay, on Door Peninsula, 27 mi. NE of Sturgeon Bay; dairying, cherry growing. Offshore are small Sister Isls.
Sisteron (sēstûrō'), anc. *Segustera,* town (pop. 2,859), Basses-Alpes dept., SE France, in a defile of Durance R. (just below influx of the Buëch), and 16 mi. NW of Digne; agr. trade; flour and paper milling, toy mfg. Terraced above river, it has 12th-cent. Romanesque former cathedral, picturesque *Provençal* old quarter, and a 13th-17th-cent. citadel. Damaged in Second World War.
Sisters, city (pop. 723), Deschutes co., central Oregon, 20 mi. NW of Bend, in Cascade Range; alt. 3,182 ft.; outfitting point for hunting and fishing region. Three Sisters are SW.
Sisters, The, group of 3 islets, S Ont. and NE Ohio, at W end of L. Erie, 10–25 mi. W of Pelee Isl.; East Sister Isl. and Middle Sister Isl. belong to Ont., West Sister Isl. to Ohio.
Sisters, The, two islets (each 1 mi. long) of the Seychelles, in Indian Ocean, 6 mi. ENE of Praslin Isl.; 4°18'S 55°52'E; granite formation.
Sistersville, city (pop. 2,313), Tyler co., NW W.Va., on the Ohio and 38 mi. SSW of Wheeling; mfg. of glass, boilers, machine-shop products, dairy products; gasoline and oil refineries. Settled 1802.
Siston, town and parish (pop. 1,616), SW Gloucester, England, 6 mi. ENE of Bristol; agr. market, with flour mills and shoe industry. Has 13th-14th-cent. church.
Sistova, Bulgaria: see SVISHTOV.
Siswa Bazar (sĭs'vŭ bäzär'), town (pop. 7,867), Gorakhpur dist., E Uttar Pradesh, India, 36 mi. NE of Gorakhpur; trades in rice, wheat, barley, oilseeds; sugar milling.
Sitabaldi, hill, India: see NAGPUR, city.
Sita-Buzaului (sē'tä-bōōzŭ'ōōlōōē), Rum. *Sita-Buzăului,* Hung. *Szitabodza* (sē'tŏbō"dzō), village (pop. 950), Stalin prov., central Rumania, on Buzau R., on railroad and 23 mi. E of Stalin (Brasov); lignite mining, lumbering.
Sitakund, India: see MONGHYR, city.
Sitakund (sē'täkōōnd), village, Chittagong dist., SE East Bengal, E Pakistan, near Sandwip Channel, 20 mi. NNW of Chittagong; rice, oilseeds, tobacco. Pilgrimage center (noted Hindu temples). Buddhist ruins near by.
Sitamarhi (sētä'mŭrē), town (pop. 12,437), Muzaffarpur dist., N Bihar, India, on Ganges tributary and 33 mi. NNE of Muzaffarpur; road junction; trades in rice, wheat, barley, oilseeds, saltpeter, hides; rice milling. Annual cattle fair.
Sitamau (sētä'mou), town (pop. 7,600), W Madhya Bharat, India, 18 mi. E of Mandasor; agr. market (millet, cotton, wheat); cotton ginning, hand-loom weaving. Was ⊙ former princely state of Sitamau (□ 191; pop. 33,461) of Central India agency; since 1948, state merged with Madhya Bharat.
Si Tangkay, Philippines: see SIBUTU ISLAND.
Sitao or **Hsi-t'ao** (both: shē'tou'), name applied to Ningsia section of Inner Mongolia, China, consisting of Alashan Desert and Etsin Gol regions. Inc. 1914 into Kansu and 1928 into Ningsia.
Sitapur (sē'täpōōr), district (□ 2,207; pop. 1,293,554), central Uttar Pradesh, India; ⊙ Sitapur. On Ganges Plain; bounded S by Gumti, E by Gogra rivers; drained by the Sarda; irrigated by Sarda Canal system. Agr. (wheat, rice, gram, barley, corn, oilseeds, sugar cane, pearl millet, jute); scattered sissoo and toon groves; a major Indian sugar-processing dist. Main towns: Sitapur, Khairabad, Laharpur, Biswan.
Sitapur. 1 Town (pop. 2,270), Banda dist., S Uttar Pradesh, India, 39 mi. SE of Banda; gram, jowar, wheat, oilseeds. **2** Town (pop., including notified area, 35,249), ⊙ Sitapur dist., central Uttar Pradesh, India, on tributary of the Gumti and 50 mi. NNW of Lucknow; rail and road junction; trade center (grains, oilseeds, sugar cane); sugar processing, plywood mfg. Has a leading Indian eye hospital. Former Br. military cantonment. Sugar processing 14 mi. NNE, at village of Hargaon.
Sitarampur (sētä'rämpōōr), village, Burdwan dist., W West Bengal, India, 6 mi. WNW of Asansol; rail junction; oilseed milling; electrical-engineering factory. Coal mining near by.
Sitawaka (sĭt'ŭvŭkŭ), E section (pop. 899) of Avissawella town, Western Prov., Ceylon. Anc. royal Singhalese city; palace and temples destroyed 16th cent. by Portuguese.
Sitges (sē'chĕs), town (pop. 5,879), Barcelona prov., NE Spain, on the Mediterranean, 5 mi. E of Villanueva y Geltrú; noted for its muscatel and malvasia wines. Mfg. of shoes, tiles, knit goods. Trades in olive oil, hazelnuts, fruit. Fashionable summer and winter resort. Airport. Rusiñol mus. contains fine metalware.
Sitgreaves Mountain (sĭt'grēvz), (9,600 ft.), N central Ariz., 22 mi. WNW of Flagstaff.
Sithammarat Range (sē'täm-mŭrät'), S Thailand, in Malay Peninsula, bet. Tapi R. valley and E coast; rises to 5,860 ft., 16 mi. WNW of Nakhon Sithammarat. Tin mining (Ronphibun). Also called Nakhon Range. Its S continuation, the Kalakhiri, forms Thailand-Malaya border.
Sithonia (sĭthônēä') or **Longos** (lông'gôs), middle prong of Chalcidice peninsula, Greek Macedonia, on Aegean Sea, bet. Toronaic (W) and Singitic (E) gulfs; 30 mi. long 11 mi. wide; rises to 2,650 ft. Terminates in Cape Drepanon (SE).
Sitia, Crete: see SETEIA.
Sitiawan (sētēäwän'), village, W Perak, Malaya, on inlet of Dindings R., 4 mi. E of Lumut. Once minor Perak port, declined after retrocession (1935) of the Dindings and Lumut to Perak. The name Sitiawan is sometimes applied to SIMPANG AMPAT (2 mi. S).
Sitifis, Algeria: see SÉTIF.
Sítio da Abadia (sē'tyōō dä äbŏdē'ŭ), city (pop. 598), E Goiás, central Brazil, on Minas Gerais border, 90 mi. NE of Formosa; hides, sugar, tobacco. Formerly spelled Sítio da Abbadia.
Sitio del Niño (sē'tyō dĕl nē'nyō), village (pop. estimate 600), La Libertad dept., W central Salvador, 6 mi. WSW of Quezaltepeque; rail junction.
Sitionuevo (sētyōnwä'vō), town (pop. 4,630), Magdalena dept., N Colombia, river port on lower Magdalena R. and 15 mi. S of Barranquilla; cotton-growing center.
Sitka (sĭt'kŭ), town (pop. 2,080), SE Alaska, on W shore of Baranof Isl., in Alexander Archipelago, 100 mi. SSW of Juneau; 57°3'N 135°20'W; trading and commercial center, and port of entry; fishing, canning, cold-storage operations, lumbering. Excellent harbor and airport. Site of Sheldon Jackson school for natives, Pioneers' Home for elderly Alaskans, and Russian Orthodox Cathedral of St. Michael, built 1844. Town founded 1799 as Novo-Arkhangelsk or New Archangel by Baranov, who moved his hq. here (1804) from Kodiak, changed its name to Sitka, and made it ⊙ Russian America. It was here that the transfer of Alaska from Russia to U.S. took place, Oct. 18, 1867, and Sitka remained ⊙ until 1900. Since 1940 it has been an important naval base. At Sitka is Sitka Natl. Monument. During Second World War other naval installations were built on Japonski Isl., just W; site now occupied by Mt. Egecumbe School of Alaska Native Service.
Sitkalidak Island (sĭtkŭlē'dăk) (23 mi. long, 3–6 mi. wide), S Alaska, in Gulf of Alaska, off SE Kodiak Isl., 50 mi. SW of Kodiak; 57°7'N 153°10'W; rises to 2,047 ft. Port Hobron bay (N) was formerly site of whaling station. Cattle ranching.
Sitka National Monument (sĭt'kŭ) (57 acres), SE Alaska, on W Baranof Isl., just S of Sitka; preserves collection of Indian totem poles, Indian stockade (scene 1804 of last Indian stand against Russians), and replica of Russian blockhouse. Established 1910.
Sitka Sound, SE Alaska, on W side of Baranof Isl., Alexander Archipelago; entrance to Sitka from Gulf of Alaska; washes SE shore of Kruzof Isl.
Sitkovtsy (sēt'kŭftsē), village (1939 pop. over 2,000), E Vinnitsa oblast, Ukrainian SSR, 10 mi. NW of Gaisin; sugar mill.
Sitnica or **Sitnitsa** (both: sĭt'nētsä), village (pop. 5,585), NW Bosnia, Yugoslavia, 8 mi. E of Kljuc.
Sitnica or **Sitnitsa,** mountain (4,654 ft.) in Dinaric Alps, S Herzegovina, Yugoslavia, 7 mi. ENE of Ljubinje.
Sitnica River or **Sitnitsa River,** S Serbia, Yugoslavia, rises in N Sar Mts., flows c.50 mi. N, through the Kosovo, to Ibar R. at Kosovska Mitrovica.
Sitniki (sēt'nyĭkē), town (1946 pop. over 500), W Gorki oblast, Russian SFSR, 7 mi. N of Bor; peat works. Until 1946, Kozlikha.
Sitoebondo, Indonesia: see SITUBONDO.
Sitpur (sēt'pōōr), village, Muzaffargarh dist., SW Punjab, W Pakistan, 60 mi. SSW of Muzaffargarh; dates, wheat; handicraft toys, palm-mat weaving.
Sitra or **Sitrah** (sēträ'), island of Bahrein archipelago, in Persian Gulf, just off NE shore of main Bahrein isl. (separated by ¼-mi.-wide channel); 4 mi. long, 1½ mi. wide. Site of tank farm and loading terminal of Bahrein, linked by pipe line with refinery and producing field on Bahrein proper.
Sitsang: see TIBET.
Sittang River (sĭ'tăng, Burmese sĭt'toun), one of chief rivers of Burma, rises on edge of Shan plateau NE of Yamethin, flows c.350 mi. S bet. Pegu Yoma (W) and Shan plateau and Karenni hills (E), past Toungoo, to Gulf of Martaban of Andaman Sea, forming a funnel-shaped estuary crossed by a bar 9 ft. high and subject to heavy sedimentation. Little navigation. Linked in lower course by canal with Pegu R.
Sittard (sĭ'tärt), town (pop. 17,165), Limburg prov., SE Netherlands, 13 mi. NE of Maastricht; rail junction; leather industry; stone quarrying.
Sittaung (sĭt'toun"), village, Upper Chindwin dist., Upper Burma, on left bank of Chindwin R. and 17 mi. E of Tamu (linked by road), near Manipur (India) border.
Sitten, Switzerland: see SION.
Sittingbourne and Milton (sĭ'tĭngbôrn), urban district (1931 pop. 20,177; 1951 census 21,904), N Kent, England, 10 mi. ENE of Maidstone; agr. market; mfg. of paper, paint, cement. Has 13th-cent. church with Norman tower. It is on the old pilgrimage route to Canterbury. In urban dist. (N) is town of Milton Regis, with brickworks; church has large 14th-cent. tower.
Sittona (sĭt'tōnä), village, Agordat div., W Eritrea, on Setit R. (Ethiopian border) and 55 mi. SSW of Barentu in doom palm- and acacia-growing region.
Situ, China: see HENGYANG.
Situbondo or **Sitoebondo** (both: sētōōbôn'dō), town (pop. 15,238), E Java, Indonesia, near Madura Strait, 95 mi. ESE of Surabaya; 7°42'S 114°1'E; trade center for agr. area (rice, sugar, peanuts, corn).
Siu, China: see SIU RIVER.
Siuna (sū'nä), town, Zelaya dept., E Nicaragua, 95 mi. ESE of Puerto Cabezas, in spur of Cordillera Isabelia; major gold-mining center for La Luz mine.
Siungchow or **Hsiung-chou** (both: shyōōng'jō'), island of SW Kwangtung prov., China, in Kwangchow Bay of S.China Sea, SE of Tunghai isl.; forms part of CHANKIANG municipality.
Siuning or **Hsiu-ning** (both: shyō'nĭng'), town, ⊙ Siuning co. (pop. 214,447), S Anhwei prov., China, 10 mi. WNW of Tunki; tung oil, tea, rapeseed; noted for mfg. of India ink. Antimony deposits near by.
Siu River (shyō'), Chinese *Hsiu Shui* (shyō' shwā'), NW Kiangsi prov., China, rises on Hunan-Hupeh

line, flows 170 mi. E, past Siushui, Wuning, and Yungsiu, to Poyang L. at Wucheng. Sometimes spelled Siao.

Siuro (sē'ōōrō), village in Pirkkala commune (pop. 3,642), Häme co., SW Finland, on Kokemäki R. and 14 mi. W of Tampere; lumber and pulp mills, machine shops.

Siushan or **Hsiu-shan** (both: shyō'shän'), town (pop. 6,365), ⊙ Siushan co. (pop. 346,413), southeasternmost Szechwan prov., China, 50 mi. NE of Szenan (Kweichow prov.); rice-growing center; tung oil, sweet potatoes, millet, indigo, wheat, rapeseed. Antimony and mercury deposits near by.

Siushui or **Hsiu-shui** (both: shyō'shwā'), town (pop. 10,100), ⊙ Siushui co. (pop. 258,881), NW Kiangsi prov., China, 80 mi. WNW of Nanchang and on Siu R.; tea, rice; cotton weaving. Gold mines. Until 1912 called Ining.

Siuslaw River (sīōō'slô), W Oregon, rises in Coast Range S of Eugene, flows 110 mi. WNW and W to the Pacific, near Florence.

Siut, Egypt: see ASYUT, city.

Siuwen or **Hsiu-wen** (both: shyō'wŭn'), town (pop. 4,247), ⊙ Siuwen co. (pop. 73,708), central Kweichow prov., China, 16 mi. NNW of Kweiyang; rice, wheat, millet, beans. Bauxite deposits and coal mines near by.

Siuwu or **Hsiu-wu** (both: shyō'wōō'), town, ⊙ Siuwu co. (pop. 42,102), SW Pingyuan prov., China, on Wei R., on railroad and 22 mi. WSW of Sinsiang; agr. center. Coal mining near by. Until 1949 in Honan prov.

Siuyen or **Hsiu-yen** (both: shyō'yĕn'), town, ⊙ Siuyen co. (pop. 268,236), S Liaotung prov., Manchuria, 60 mi. W of Antung; coal mining; gold and iron deposits; wild silk.

Siva (sē'vŭ), village (1926 pop. 891), W Molotov oblast, Russian SFSR, 25 mi. NNW of Vereshchagino; flax processing.

Sivac or **Sivats** (both: sē'väts), Hung. *Szivác* (sĭ'väts), village (pop. 10,705), Vojvodina, N Serbia, Yugoslavia, on Danube-Tisa Canal and 13 mi. ESE of Sombor, in the Backa. Consists of larger old Sivac, Serbo-Croatian *Stari Sivac*, Hung. *Ószivác* (S; Serbian pop.), and new Sivac, Serbo-Croatian *Novi Sivac*, Hung. *Újszivác* (N; Ger. pop.).

Sivaganga (sĭvŭgŭng'gŭ), town (pop. 12,106), Ramnad dist., S Madras, India, 25 mi. E of Madura; road center in cotton area; peanut-oil extraction.

Sivagiri (sĭv'ŭgĭrē), town (pop. 15,176), Tinnevelly dist., S Madras, India, 27 mi. NNE of Tenkasi; grain, cattle.

Sivakasi (sĭvŭkä'sē), city (pop. 16,626), Ramnad dist., S Madras, India, 14 mi. SW of Virudhunagar; match-mfg. center; agr. trade.

Sivaki (sēvä'kē), town (1948 pop. over 2,000), S Amur oblast, Russian SFSR, on Trans-Siberian RR, 150 mi. ESE of Skovorodino, in lumber area.

Sivas (sŭväs'), Turkish *Sivas*, province (□ 11,174; 1950 pop. 540,412), central Turkey; ⊙ Sivas. Ak Mts. on W; drained by Kizil Irmak, Kelkit, Calti, and Tohma rivers. Deposits of lead, copper, antimony, lignite. Wheat, barley, vetch, potatoes, apples, pears, apricots; poultry.

Sivas, Turkish *Sivas*, anc. *Sebaste*, *Sebastia*, and *Cabira*, city (1950 pop. 52,269), ⊙ Sivas prov., central Turkey, on the Kizil Irmak, on railroad, 220 mi. E of Ankara; 39°40'N 37°12'E; alt. 4,185 ft. Mfg. of tiles, cement, rugs; railroad repair shops; trade center for agr. area (wheat, barley, potatoes). Copper mining near by. Has Pasteur Institute. City was important under the Romans, Byzantines, and Seljuks. Its former large Armenian pop. is largely gone. Here in Sept., 1919, Mustafa Kemal (Ataturk) held a Nationalist Congress, leading to the revolution. Sivas has preserved many fine relics of medieval Moslem art.

Sivasamudram (sē"vŭsŭmōō'drŭm, sĭvŭsŭmōō'drŭm), island bet. 2 arms of Cauvery R., on Mysore-Madras border, India, 35 mi. E of Mysore; c.3 mi. long, ¾ mi. wide; one of the 2 series of rapids of CAUVERY FALLS is on each surrounding river arm. Generating plant (just NW, on mainland) utilizes falls of river's left channel; hub of state's extensive hydroelectric system. Initial works built 1902 to power mines of Kolar Gold Fields, 80 mi. NE; by late 1920s, Krishnaraja Sagara (reservoir above dam at KRISHNARAJASAGARA) was tapped and plant's increased power used to develop industries in Bangalore and Mysore cities; auxiliary works installed 1940 at near-by SHIMSA FALLS. In 1948, power connections were projected bet. these and new hydroelectric works at JOG, in NW part of state.

Sivash (sēväsh') or **Putrid Sea**, Rus. *Gniloye More* (gnyĭloi'ŭ môr'yŭ), salt lagoon (□ c.1,000) on NE side of Crimea, Russian SFSR; separated from Sea of Azov by Arabat Tongue; joined (N) with sea by narrow Genichesk Strait. Consists of deeply indented W portion (50 mi. long), bet. Crimea and Ukrainian mainland, and 70-mi.-long E portion, bet. Crimea and Arabat Tongue, which receives Salgir R. Of high salinity (up to 20%); has variable water level.

Sivashskoye (-skŭyŭ), village (1926 pop. 7,251), SE Kherson oblast, Ukrainian SSR, 20 mi. NW of Genichesk; cottonseed oil. Until c.1935, called Rozhdestvenskoye.

Sivats, Yugoslavia: see SIVAC.

Siverek (sĭvĕrĕk'), town (pop. 17,264), Urfa prov., S Turkey, 50 mi. NE of Urfa; wheat, barley, rice, chick-peas, lentils, cotton, tobacco.

Siveric (sē'vĕrĭch), Serbo-Croatian *Siverić*, village, W Croatia, Yugoslavia, on railroad and 2 mi. NE of Drnis, at S foot of the Promina, in Dalmatia; brown-coal mine; briquette plant. Sometimes spelled Siverich.

Siverski or **Siverskiy** (sē'vyĭrskē), town (1926 pop. 3,491), central Leningrad oblast, Russian SFSR, 15 mi. S of Gatchina; rail junction; molding-sand quarry; lumber milling.

Siversov Canal, Russian SFSR: see MSTA RIVER.

Sivrice (sĭvrĭjĕ'), village (pop. 290), Elazig prov., E central Turkey, on railroad near W end of L. Hazar, 15 mi. S of Elazig; grain. Also called Kurk and Hoh.

Sivrihamam, Turkey: see HAYMANA.

Sivrihisar (sēvrē'hĭsär). **1** Town (pop. 6,722), Eskisehir prov., W central Turkey, 60 mi. ESE of Eskisehir; grain, mohair goats. **2** Town, Smyrna prov., Turkey: see SEFERIHISAR.

Sivrihisar Mountains, W central Turkey, extend 70 mi. ESE from Eskisehir bet. Porsuk R. (N) and Sakarya R. (E and S); rise to 5,970 ft. in Arayit Dag. Chromium and magnesite in W.

Sivry (sēvrē'), village (pop. 1,593), Hainaut prov., S Belgium, 10 mi. NNW of Chimay; dairying.

Siwa or **Siwah** (sē'wŭ), anc. *Ammonium*, oasis (pop. 3,799), in Libyan Desert, Western Desert prov., Egypt, 290 mi. SW of Alexandria, 160 mi. S of Sidi Barrani, and 15 mi. E of Cyrenaica frontier. It lies in a basin (c.100 ft. below sea level) c.50 mi. long, 10 mi. wide. Has several small salt lakes. Olives and dates are grown in the small cultivated area (□ 1.5) around the village of Siwa (29°15'N 25°30'E; pop. 878). The oasis was seat of the oracle of Jupiter Ammon, and at Siwa are anc. temples and rock tombs of Ptolemaic and Roman period. Alexander the Great visited Siwa and may have consulted the oracle.

Siwalik Range (sĭvä'lĭk) [Sanskrit, =belonging to Siva], southernmost range of HIMALAYAS, S central Asia; from SW Kashmir it extends c.1050 mi. ESE through NW corner of India and S Nepal to Tista R., S of Darjeeling; average height, 2–3,500 ft.; sometimes considered to continue c.400 mi. E across S Bhutan to bend of Brahmaputra R. as S foothills of Assam Himalayas; parallels (c.90 mi. apart from) main range of Himalayas and separates mtn. system from Indo-Gangetic plain (S). In places separated (20–50 mi.) from outer Himalayas by longitudinal, alluvial valleys (*duns*), as in Dehra Dun dist. (N Ganges–Jumna Doab). Composed of conglomerates, clays, and sandstones of fresh-water origin (Himalayan river deposits), Siwaliks have many vertebrate fossil remains. Deforestation and monsoon torrents (*chos*) have caused severe erosion in W section. Known as Churia Range in Nepal.

Siwan (sĭvän'), town (pop. 18,386), Saran dist., NW Bihar, India, on Ganges Plain, 38 mi. NW of Chapra; rail junction (Savan station); trades in rice, wheat, barley, corn, oilseeds; sugar milling; pottery and brasswork. Large sugar-milling plant 10 mi. NNW, at Hathwa. Formerly also called Aliganj Siwan.

Siwhe Mountain (9,280 ft.), SW B.C., in Coast Mts., 80 mi. N of Chilliwack.

Siwo, China: see OSHAN.

Sixaola (sēksou'lä), village, Limón prov., E Costa Rica, on railroad, on Sixaola R. (Panama border), opposite Guabito (Panama), and 45 mi. SE of Limón; bananas.

Sixaola, Panama: see GUABITO.

Sixaola River, SE Costa Rica, rises in the Cordillera de Talamanca W of Durika peak, flows 85 mi. N and E, past Suretka, Sixaola, and Guabito (Panama), to the Caribbean 45 mi. SE of Limón. Forms Panama–Costa Rica border in navigable lower course. Called Tarire R. in upper reaches.

Six-Fours-la-Plage (sēs-fōōr-lä-plăzh'), commune (pop. 4,750), Var dept., SE France, occupying Cape Sicié peninsula, SSW of Toulon; salt- and tileworks.

Six Islands, uninhabited coral atoll (□ 664 acres) of Chagos Archipelago, in Indian Ocean, a dependency of Mauritius; 6°40'S 71°22'E. Encloses lagoon 5 mi. long, 1.5 mi. wide. Coconuts. Also called Egmont Isls.

Six Madun (sēs mädū') or **Badus** (bädōōs'), peak (9,616 ft.) in Lepontine Alps, S central Switzerland, 3 mi. E of Andermatt.

Six Mile, town (pop. 157), Pickens co., NW S.C., 24 mi. W of Greenville.

Sixmilebridge, Gaelic *Droichead Abhann Uí Chearnaigh*, town (pop. 304), SE Co. Clare, Ireland, 8 mi. NW of Limerick; woolen milling; agr. market (grain, potatoes; dairying).

Sixmilecross, agr. village (district pop. 689), central Co. Tyrone, Northern Ireland, at foot of Slievemore, 16 mi. WNW of Dungannon; oats, flax, potatoes; cattle.

Six Mile Run, Pa.: see COALDALE, Bedford co.

Sixt (sēkst), Alpine resort (pop. 125), Haute-Savoie dept., SE France, on the Giffre and 18 mi. E of Bonneville; alt. 2,497 ft. Has Gothic church of former abbey (founded 1145). Near headwaters of Giffre R., 4 mi. ENE, is spectacular Cirque du Fer-à-Cheval (Horseshoe cirque), with numerous waterfalls.

Sixtymile, village, W Yukon, near Alaska border, 40 mi. W of Dawson; gold mining.

Siyana (sĭyä'nŭ), town (pop. 10,882), Bulandshahr dist., W Uttar Pradesh, India, 20 mi. NE of Bulandshahr; trades in wheat, oilseeds, barley, cotton, corn. Also spelled Siana.

Siyang or **Hsi-yang** (both: shē'yäng'), town, ⊙ Siyang co. (pop. 129,423), E Shansi prov., China, 12 mi. SSE of Pingting; millet, beans, corn.

Siyanis, Turkey: see BAYKAN.

Siyeh, Mount, Mont.: see LEWIS RANGE.

Siying or **Hsi-ying** (both: shē'yĭng'), central district and town of CHANKIANG municipality, SW Kwangtung prov., China, port on Kwangchow Bay of S.China Sea; shipping and administrative offices. While under French rule (1898–1945), called Fort-Bayard.

Sizeboli, Bulgaria: see SOZOPOL.

Sizewell, England: see LEISTON CUM SIZEWELL.

Sizun (sēzŭ'), town (pop. 919), Finistère dept., W France, 19 mi. E of Brest; slate quarry near by. Has 16th-cent. calvary and ossuary.

Sizuoka, Japan: see SHIZUOKA, city.

Sjaelland, Denmark: see ZEALAND.

Sjaellands Odde, Denmark: see SEJERO BAY.

Sjalevad (shĕ'lŭväd), Swedish *Själevad*, village (pop. 830), Vasternorrland co., NE Sweden, 4 mi. W of Ornskoldsvik; timber yards.

Sjenica or **Syenitsa** (both: syĕ'nĭtsä), village (pop. 3,873), W Serbia, Yugoslavia, 27 mi. WNW of Novi Pazar, in the Sanjak; sheep raising; carpet making.

Sjobo (shû'bōō"), Swedish *Sjöbo*, village (pop. 1,451), Malmohus co., S Sweden, 15 mi. NNW of Ystad; rail junction; grain, potatoes, sugar beets, cattle.

Sjögren Fiord (shō'grĭn, shû'–), Antarctica, inlet of E extremity of Nordenskjöld Coast, Palmer Peninsula; 64°10'S 58°45'W. Discovered 1903 by Otto Nordenskjöld, Swedish explorer.

Sjoholt (shû'hôlt), Nor. *Sjøholt*, village (pop. 484) in Orskog (Nor. *Ørskog*) canton (pop. 1,974), More og Romsdal co., W Norway, port on N shore of Norddal Fjord (an arm of Stor Fjord), 22 mi. E of Alesund; furniture mfg. Formerly spelled Soholt, Nor. *Søhølt*.

Sjomarken (shû'mär"kŭn), Swedish *Sjömarken*, village (pop. 923), Alvsborg co., SW Sweden, 3 mi. W of Boras; woodworking.

Sjonsta (shûn'stä), Nor. *Sjønsta*, village in Fauske canton, Nordland co., N Norway, on Finneid Fjord (arm of Salt Fjord), 35 mi. E of Bodo; terminus of railroad from Sulitjelma metal mines and transfer point for metals shipped to Finneid and Bodo. Sometimes spelled Skjonsta or Sjonnstaa.

Sjotorp (shû'tôrp"), Swedish *Sjötorp*, village (pop. 449), Skaraborg co., S Sweden, on E shore of L. Vaner, 10 mi. NE of Mariestad; W terminus of central section of Gota Canal; shipbuilding, sawmilling, furniture mfg.

Sjuntorp (shŭn'tôrp"), village (pop. 1,067), Alvsborg co., SW Sweden, 6 mi. SSW of Trollhattan; woolen milling.

Sjuoyane, Spitsbergen: see NORTHEAST LAND.

Skaanevik, Norway: see SKANEVIK.

Skaatoy, Norway: see KRAGERO.

Skadar, Albania: see SCUTARI.

Skadovsk (skŭdôfsk'), town (1926 pop. 3,897), S Kherson oblast, port on Karkinit Gulf of Black Sea, 39 mi. SSE of Kherson; cotton ginning; saltworks, metalworks.

Skaelskor (skĕl'skûr), Dan. *Skælskør*, city (pop. 2,921) and port, Soro amt, W Zealand, Denmark, on the Great Belt and 55 mi. SW of Copenhagen; meat and fruit canning, fishing. Has 13th-cent. church.

Skaerbaek (skâr'bĕk), town (pop. 1,666), Tonder amt, S Jutland, Denmark, 16 mi. NNW of Tonder; livestock.

Skafta, Iceland: see LAKI.

Skafta (skäf'tô), Nor. *Skaftå*, village in Bruvik canton, Hordaland co., SW Norway, on SE shore of Osteroy, 12 mi. ENE of Bergen; limestone quarrying.

Skaftareldahraun, Iceland: see LAKI.

Skagafjardar or **Skagafjardhar** (skä'gäfyär"dhär), Icelandic *Skagafjarðar*, county [Icelandic *sýsla*] (pop. 2,722), N Iceland; ⊙ Saudarkrokur, a city in but independent of the co. Surrounds the Skaga Fjord. Includes fertile valley of Heradsvotn R. Sheep and horse raising; fishing.

Skaga Fjord (skä'gŭ, –gä), Icelandic *Skagafjörður* (skä'gäfyûr"dhŭr), inlet (25 mi. long, 7–17 mi. wide) of Greenland Sea, N Iceland; 65°55'N 19°40' W. Receives several rivers from Hofsjokull, glacier; contains Drangey islet.

Skagastolstind, Nor. *Skagastølstindane* (skä'gästŭl'-stĭn-nänŭ) [=the peaks], peaks in SW Jotunheim Mts., Sogn og Fjordane co., W Norway, near Luster Fjord, 29 mi. NE of Sogndal. Highest peak, 7,887 ft. Tourist area.

Skagastrond (skä'gästrûnt"), Icelandic *Skagaströnd*, town (pop. 547), Hunavatn co., NW Iceland, on Huna Bay, 60 mi. W of Akureyri; supply point and fishing port.

Skagen (skă'yŭn), city (pop. 6,446) and port, Hjorring amt, N Jutland, Denmark, near N tip of peninsula, on the Kattegat and 30 mi. NE of Hjorring; 57°44'N 10°37'E. Rail terminus; fisheries, shipyards. City dates from 14th cent.

Skagen, Cape, Denmark: see SKAW, THE.

Skager, Lake, Swedish *Skagern* (skä'gŭrn) (12 mi. long, 3–5 mi. wide), S central Sweden, 9 mi. W of Laxa. Drains W into L. Vaner.

Skagerrak (skă'gŭrăk), arm of North Sea bet. Norway and Jutland (Denmark), continued (SE) by the Kattegat toward the Danish sounds and the Baltic Sea; 150 mi. long, 80–90 mi. wide. Shallow along the Danish shore, it deepens toward the Norwegian coast and reaches a depth of more than 2,000 ft. The naval battle of the Skagerrak (1916) was fought c.60 mi. W of JUTLAND.

Skagersvik (skä"gŭrsvēk'), village (pop. 495), Skaraborg co., S Sweden, on E shore of L. Skager, 20 mi. NE of Mariestad; woodworking; furniture.

Skagit (skă'jĭt), county (□ 1,735; pop. 43,273), NW Wash.; ⊙ Mount Vernon. Bounded W by Rosario Strait; rises to Cascade Range in E. Includes Swinomish Indian Reservation and part of Mt. Baker Natl. Forest; drained by Skagit R. Dairy products, fish, truck, seeds, poultry, timber, wood products, cement. Formed 1883.

Skagit, resort village, Whatcom co., NW Wash., at site of Diablo Dam, on Skagit R. and 65 mi. E of Bellingham, in Cascade Range.

Skagit River, in British Columbia and NW Wash., rises in Cascade Range in British Columbia, flows 163 mi. SW, through Wash., to Skagit Bay of Puget Sound, 25 mi. NW of Everett. Near its source, 3 power dams (Ross DAM, DIABLO DAM, and Gorge Dam) have been constructed by city of Seattle.

Skagway, city (pop. 761), SE Alaska, at head of Chilkoot Inlet of Lynn Canal, c.75 mi. NNW of Juneau, in a mtn. valley at foot of White Pass; 59°27'N 135°19'W; trade and shipping center for the interior mining area; tourist trade; port of entry. Coastal terminus of White Pass and Yukon RR; seaport and airport. Founded in 1890s, it was gateway to the Klondike and Yukon gold fields; reached its peak 1897–98, when it had pop. of 10–20,000. Canol pipe line (closed down at present), built during Second World War, links town with Whitehorse and Fairbanks.

Skakavets (skäkä'vĕts), peak (8,969 ft.) in central Rila Mts., W Bulgaria, 10 mi. S of Samokov.

Skala (skä'lŭ), town (pop. 2,024), Laconia nome, SE Peloponnesus, Greece, on Eurotas R. and 20 mi. SE of Sparta; citrus fruits, olives; livestock raising (sheep, cattle).

Skala or Skala nad Zbruczem, Ukrainian SSR: see SKALA-PODOLSKAYA.

Skaland (skä'län), village in Berg canton, N Senja isl., Troms co., N Norway, on Bergs Fjord of Norwegian Sea, 45 mi. WSW of Tromso; graphite mining and processing.

Skala-Podolskaya or **Skala-Podol'skaya** (skŭlä'-pŭdôl'skīŭ), village (1931 pop. 5,094), SE Ternopol oblast, Ukrainian SSR, on Zbruch R. and 7 mi. NE of Borshchev; tanning, distilling, flour milling; tobacco, hogs; textile trade. Has ruins of 16th-cent. castle. An old Pol. settlement, frequently assaulted (14th–17th cent.) by Tatars, Walachians, and Swedes. Passed to Austria (1772); reverted to Poland (1919); ceded to USSR in 1945. Until 1940, called *Skała* or *Skała nad Zbruczem* (skä'-wä näd zbrōō'chĕm).

Skalat (skŭlät'), Pol. *Skałat* (skä'wät), city (1931 pop. 6,949), E Ternopol oblast, Ukrainian SSR, on artificial lake formed by tributary of Zbruch R., 18 mi. SE of Ternopol; flour milling, winemaking, brick mfg. Has ruins of old palace. Passed from Poland to Austria (1772); reverted to Poland (1919); ceded to USSR in 1945.

Skalbmierz (skälb'myĕsh), Rus. *Skalbmerzh* or *Skal'bmerzh* (both: skä'lyŭbmyĭrsh), town (pop. 1,878), Kielce prov., S central Poland, 30 mi. SSW of Kielce; flour milling.

Skalby (shĕl'bü"), Swedish *Skälby,* residential village (pop. 1,241), Stockholm co., E Sweden, near L. Malar, 9 mi. NW of Stockholm city center.

Skalderviken (shĕl'dŭrvē"kŭn), Swedish *Skälderviken,* village (pop. 575), Kristianstad co., SW Sweden, on Skalder Bay of the Kattegat, 2 mi. NNW of Angelholm; seaside resort.

Skalholt (skoul'hôlt"), Icelandic *Skálholt,* anc. locality, Arne co., SW Iceland, on the Olfusa and 40 mi. E of Reykjavik. Upon establishment (1056) of Catholic bishopric it became cultural and educational center; after introduction of Reformation, see was abolished (1550) and last bishop executed.

Skalica (skä'lĭtsä), Hung. *Szakolca* (sŏ'kôltsŏ), Ger. *Skalitz* (shkä'lĭts), town (pop. 5,259), W Slovakia, Czechoslovakia, on railroad and 16 mi. NE of Breclav, in wheat and barley region; distilling. Former printing center of Moravian Brethren. Extensive winegrowing area.

Skalkaho Pass, Mont.: see SAPPHIRE MOUNTAINS.

Skalna (skäl'nä), Czech *Skalná,* formerly *Vildštejn,* Ger. *Wildstein* (vĭld'shtīn), town (pop. 1,253), W Bohemia, Czechoslovakia, 6 mi. N of Cheb; leather industry; cattle breeding.

Skalny or **Skal'nyy** (skäl'nē), town (1943 pop. over 500), E Molotov oblast, Russian SFSR, 9 mi. ENE (under jurisdiction) of Chusovoi, near railroad; quartzite quarrying, bituminous-coal mining.

Skamania (skŭmā'nēŭ), county (□ 1,676; pop. 4,788), SW Wash., on Oregon line; ⊙ Stevenson. Mtn. area watered by Lewis and Columbia rivers; includes part of Columbia Natl. Forest. Lumber, cattle, dairy products, fruit, nuts. Formed 1854.

Skanderborg (skä'nŭrbôr), amt (□ 664; 1950 pop. 134,133), E Jutland, Denmark; ⊙ Skanderborg. HIMMELBJAERGET hills, wooded and famous for scenery, in center. Mos and Jul lakes, largest; drained by Guden R. Land not very fertile. Other cities: Horsens, Silkeborg.

Skanderborg, city (1950 pop. 5,091), ⊙ Skanderborg amt, E Jutland, Denmark, on Skanderborg L. and 13 mi. SW of Aarhus; 56°2'N 9°56'E. Mfg. (machinery, bicycles, cement), meat canning; rail junction.

Skane (skō'nŭ), Swedish *Skåne,* province [Swedish *landskap*] (□ 4,356; pop. 804,887), S Sweden, on the Baltic and the Oresund. Included in Malmohus co. and Kristianstad co. Scene of numerous battles bet. Swedes and Danes, it was ceded (1658) to Sweden by Denmark. Sometimes called Scania (skā'nēŭ).

Skaneateles (skĭnēăt'lŭs, skă–), resort village (pop. 2,331), Onondaga co., central N.Y., in Finger Lakes region, at outlet and N end of Skaneateles L., 16 mi. SW of Syracuse; mfg. (fiber, paper, and wood containers; canned foods, feed, boats). Agr. (hay, cabbage). Settled before 1800, inc. 1833.

Skaneateles Lake (□ c.14), central N.Y., one of the Finger Lakes, 17 mi. SW of Syracuse; 15 mi. long; furnishes water to Syracuse. Skaneateles is on its N end. Drained by **Skaneateles Outlet,** flowing c.13 mi. NNW to Seneca R. near Weedsport.

Skanee (skănē'), village (pop. c.250), Baraga co., NW upper Peninsula, Mich., 15 mi. NE of L'Anse, on Huron Bay; ships apples, potatoes, dairy products. Commercial fishing.

Skanes Fagerhult (skō'nŭs fä'gŭrhŭlt"), Swedish *Skånes Fagerhult,* village (pop. 655), Kristianstad co., S Sweden, 18 mi. NW of Hassleholm; grain, potatoes, livestock.

Skanevik (skô'nüvĕk, –vĭk), Nor. *Skånevik,* village (pop. 122; canton pop. 2,966), Hordaland co., SW Norway, port at mouth of Akra Fjord, 31 mi. SW of Odda; boatbuilding, shipping, fishing, fish and meat canning; tanning, mfg. of furniture. Sometimes spelled Skaanevik.

Skanninge (shĕ'nĭng-ŭ), Swedish *Skänninge,* city (pop. 1,880), Ostergotland co., S Sweden, 19 mi. W of Linkoping; rail junction; agr. center (grain, sugar beets, stock); light industries. Scene of annual fair. Has 13th-cent. church and town hall (1770). Known since 10th cent.; of commercial importance in 12th and 13th cent.

Skanor med Falsterbo (skänûr' mā fäl'stŭrbōō"), Swedish *Skanör med Falsterbo,* city (pop. 999), Malmohus co., S Sweden, on Falsterbo Peninsula, on the Baltic, on SE side of mouth of the Oresund. Formed by 2 parishes: Skanor (pop. 582), at mouth of Oresund, 14 mi. SSW of Malmo, a herring-fishing port, has 13th-cent. church and old castle ruins; Falsterbo (pop. 417), on Baltic, 17 mi. SSW of Malmo, a seaside resort, has Gothic church. In Middle Ages and during Hanseatic period both localities were herring-fishing and commercial centers; scene of important fairs.

Skansen (skän'sŭn), settlement (pop. 112), Godhavn dist., W Greenland, on SE Disko isl., on Disko Bay, 30 mi. ENE of Godhavn; 69°26'N 52°26'W; lignite deposits.

Skantzoura (skändzōō'rŭ), uninhabited Aegean island (□ 2) in the Northern Sporades, Magnesia nome, Greece, 40 mi. off Thessalian mainland; 39°5'N 24°6'E; 3 mi. long, ½ mi. wide.

Skara (skä'rä"), city (pop. 7,761), Skaraborg co., SW Sweden, 25 mi. SW of Mariestad; rail junction; agr. center (grain, sugar beets, stock); metalworking, shoe mfg. See of Lutheran bishop; site of veterinary col. (1775). Has 12th-cent. cathedral, mus. One of Sweden's oldest towns; bishopric established in 11th cent. Skaraborg Castle (16th cent.) burned (1612) by Danes. First Swedish high school founded here, 1641.

Skaraborg (skä'räbôr"yŭ), county [Swedish *län*] (□ 3,269; 1950 pop. 248,567), S Sweden; ⊙ Mariestad. Bet. lakes Vaner and Vatter; forms N part of Vastergotland prov. Hilly, rising to c.1,000 ft.; drained by Tida and several smaller rivers. Among its many small lakes are lakes Skager, Und, and Vik. Agr. (wheat, rye, sugar beets), stock raising, dairying. Industries include textile, paper, and lumber milling, stone quarrying, metalworking. Cities are Mariestad, Lidkoping, Falkoping, Skara, Hjo, and Tidaholm.

Skara Brae (skă'rŭ brā'), Stone Age village on W coast of POMONA, Orkneys, Scotland.

Skarblacka-Ljusfors (shâr'blä"kä-yüs'fôrs", –fôsh"), Swedish *Skärblacka-Ljusfors,* village (pop. 2,376), Ostergotland co., SE Sweden, on Gla L., Swedish *Glan* (9 mi. long, 2–5 mi. wide), at mouth of Motala R., 9 mi. W of Norrkoping; paper mills, sulphite works.

Skardu (skär'dōō), town (pop. 2,537), ⊙ Baltistan and Skardu tahsil (□ 8,522; pop. 106,271), Ladakh dist., W central Kashmir, in Deosai Mts., on the Indus and 95 mi. NNE of Srinagar; wheat, pulse, corn. Has 16th-cent. fort; residence of local raja. Fighting here in 1948, during India-Pakistan struggle for control.

Skare (skō'rŭ), Swedish *Skåre,* village (pop. 1,211), Varmland co., W Sweden, on Klar R., near its mouth on L. Vaner, 4 mi. NNW of Karlstad; sawmilling, woodworking.

Skarhamn (shâr"hä'mŭn), Swedish *Skärhamn,* fishing village (pop. 1,051), Goteborg och Bohus co., SW Sweden, on W coast of Tjorn isl., on the Skagerrak, 6 mi. N of Marstrand; fish canning.

Skarishev, Poland: see SKARYSZEW.

Skarszewy (skär-shĕ'vĭ), Ger. *Schöneck* (shûn'ĕk), town (1946 pop. 2,741), Gdansk prov., N Poland, 21 mi. SSW of Danzig; rail junction; lumbering, distilling, flour milling, mfg. of agr. machinery.

Skaryszew (skärĭ'shĕf), Rus. *Skarishev* (skŭrē'shĭf), town (pop. 2,228), Kielce prov., E central Poland, 7 mi. SSE of Radom; flour mills, distilleries, cement works.

Skarzysko-Kamienna (skär-zhĭ'skô-kämyĕ'nä), Pol. *Skarżysko-Kamienna,* town (pop. 15,451), Kielce prov., E central Poland, on Kamienna R. (bridged) and 20 mi. NNE of Kielce. Rail junction; ironworks; mfg. of munitions, cutting stones, tiles, dyes; flour milling, sawmilling.

Skatoy, Norway: see KRAGERO.

Skat River (skŭt), NW Bulgaria, rises NE of Vratsa in outlier of W Balkan Mts., flows 75 mi. generally N, past Byala Slatina, to the Danube 4 mi. W of Oryakhovo. Sometimes spelled Skit.

Skattkarr (skät'chĕr"), Swedish *Skattkärr,* village (pop. 960), Varmland co., W Sweden, on N shore of L. Vaner, 7 mi. ENE of Karlstad; sawmilling, woodworking.

Skaw, The (skô), or **Cape Skagen** (skä'gŭn), N tip of Jutland, Denmark, at junction of the Skagerrak (W) and the Kattegat (E). Lighthouse (57°43'N 10°36'E) is ½ mi. from point.

Skawa River (skä'vä), Krakow prov., S Poland, rises c.10 mi. E of Babia Gora, flows 57 mi. NNW, past Jordanow, Makow, Sucha, Wadowice, and Zator, to Vistula R. 2 mi. N of Zator. Nearly entire course followed by railroad. Noted for salmon and trout.

Skawina (skävē'nä), town (pop. 3,638), Krakow prov., S Poland, near the Vistula, 8 mi. SW of Cracow; rail junction; ceramic industry, petroleum refinery, brickworks; brewing, flour milling, sawmilling. During Second World War, under Ger. rule, called Konradshof.

Skedee (skē'dē), town (pop. 170), Pawnee co., N Okla., 6 mi. NE of Pawnee, in agr. area.

Skedsmo, Norway: see STROMMEN, Akershus co.

Skeena River (skē'nŭ), W B.C., rises in Stikine Mts. at about 57°10'N 128°30'W, flows S, past Hazelton, thence SW to Hecate Strait of the Pacific 12 mi. SE of Prince Rupert; 360 mi. long. Navigable c.100 mi. Receives Bulkley R.

Skegness (skĕg'nĕs'), urban district (1931 pop. 9,122; 1951 census 12,554), Parts of Lindsey, E Lincolnshire, England, on North Sea, 20 mi. NE of Boston; seaside and golfing resort; cast-stone industry.

Skeldon or **Skeldon Plantation,** village (pop. 2,654), Berbice co., NE Br. Guiana, on Courantyne R. mouth (Du. Guiana), near the Atlantic, and 38 mi. SE of New Amsterdam; sugar growing.

Skelleftea (shĕlĕf'tüō"), Swedish *Skellefteå,* city (1950 pop. 14,065), Vasterbotten co., N Sweden, on Skellefte R., near its mouth on Gulf of Bothnia, 65 mi. SSW of Lulea; port; ships metal ores, timber, tar; center of rich metal-mining region (copper, arsenic, antimony, zinc, lead, silver, gold). Founded 1845. Outport at Skelleftehamn, 8 mi. ESE.

Skellefte River, Swedish *Skellefte älv* (shĕlĕf'tŭ ĕlv'), Lapland, N Sweden, rises on Norwegian border SW of Mt. Sulitelma, flows 255 mi. SE, through lakes Hornavan, Uddjaur, and Storavan, over several falls (power stations), past Skelleftea, to Gulf of Bothnia at Ronnskar. Important logging route.

Skelligs, The, or **Skellig Rocks,** group of 3 islets in the Atlantic, off Bolus Head, SW Co. Kerry, Ireland. Largest isl., Great Skellig (44 acres), 8 mi. W of Bolus Head, rises to 714 ft.; site of lighthouse (51°46'N 10°33'W) visible for 18 mi. There are anc. monastic ruins, said to date from time of St. Finan, and evidence of Danish landing here in 9th cent. Climbing summit of isl. was part of anc. means of penance. Little Skellig, 7 mi. W of Bolus Head, rises to 440 ft. and is breeding ground of sea birds. Lemon Rock is 5 mi. WNW of Bolus Head.

Skelmanthorpe, former urban district (1931 pop. 3,712), West Riding, S Yorkshire, England, 6 mi. SE of Huddersfield; woolen milling. Inc. 1938 in Denby Dale.

Skelmersdale, urban district (1931 pop. 6,177; 1951 census 6,211), SW Lancashire, England, 7 mi. W of Wigan; coal mining; mfg. of shoes.

Skelmorlie (skĕl'mŭrlē), town in Largs parish, N Ayrshire, Scotland, on Firth of Clyde, 8 mi. SW of Greenock; bathing resort. Just S is Skelmorlie Castle, dating partly from 1502.

Skelton, village and parish (pop. 594), E Cumberland, England, 6 mi. NW of Penrith; cattle, sheep.

Area in square miles is indicated by the symbol □, capital city or county seat by the symbol ⊙.

Skelton and Brotton, urban district (1931 pop. 13,655; 1951 census 12,999), North Riding, NE Yorkshire, England. Includes iron-mining town of Skelton, 6 mi. SE of Redcar, with remains of 11th-cent. castle, and iron-mining and steel-milling town of Brotton, 7 mi. SE of Redcar, with church of 12th-cent. origin. Just S is iron-mining village of Lumpsey.

Skene, Scotland: see KIRKTON OF SKENE.

Skene (shā'nŭ), village (pop. 3,189), Alvsborg co., SW Sweden, on Viska R. and 19 mi. SW of Boras; textile mills, chemical works.

Skern (skĕrn), town (pop. 3,461), Ringkobing amt, W Jutland, Denmark, 14 mi. SE of Ringkobing; textiles, machinery.

Skerne River, Durham, England, rises 2 mi. NNW of Sedgefield, flows 19 mi. S, past Aycliffe and Darlington, to the Tees 2 mi. S of Darlington.

Skernevitsy, Poland: see SKIERNIEWICE.

Skerries (skĕ'rēz), Gaelic *Sgeirí*, town (pop. 2,305), NE Co. Dublin, Ireland, on the Irish Sea, 19 mi. NE of Dublin; fishing port, resort; also shirt mfg. Offshore are The Skerries.

Skerries, The, group of islets in the Irish Sea off NE coast of Co. Dublin, Ireland, near Skerries town. Group includes Red, St. Patrick's, Shenick's, Colt, and Rockabill isls.; last is site of lighthouse.

Skerries, The, group of islets off NW coast of Co. Antrim, Northern Ireland, just N of Portrush; 55°13'N 6°38'W.

Skerries, The, Welsh *Ynysoedd y Moelrhoniard*, group of rock islets in Irish Sea off NW coast of Anglesey, Wales, 2 mi. NW of Carmel Head; lighthouse (53°25'N 4°36'W).

Skerrow, Loch (lôkh skĕ'rō), small lake in W Kirkcudbright, Scotland, 12 mi. NW of Kirkcudbright; drains into Dee R.

Skerryvore (skĕrĭvôr'), islet (pop. 3), Hebrides, Argyll, Scotland, 11 mi. SW of SW end of Tiree; lighthouse (56°18'N 7°2'W).

Skervuile (skûr'vŭl), rock islet of the Inner Hebrides, Argyll, Scotland, in the Sound of Jura, bet. Jura and Kintyre peninsula; lighthouse (55°51'N 5°51'W).

Sketty, Wales: see SWANSEA.

Skhira, La, or **La Cekhira** (lä sŭkērä'), village, Sfax dist., E Tunisia, small port on Gulf of Gabès, 27 mi. N of Gabès; sponge and shell gathering. Esparto trade.

Skhirat (skērät'), village, Rabat region, NW Fr. Morocco, near the Atlantic, on Casablanca-Rabat road, 17 mi. SW of Rabat; livestock raising, palm-fiber processing.

Skhiza, Greece: see SCHIZA.

Skhodnitsa (sŭkhôd'nyĭtsŭ), Pol. *Schodnica* (sŭkhôdnyē'tsä), town (1931 pop. 2,730), central Drogobych oblast, Ukrainian SSR, in East Beskids, 5 mi. SW of Borislav; petroleum extraction; flour- and sawmilling.

Skhodnya (–nyŭ), town (1938 pop. 7,800), central Moscow oblast, Russian SFSR, 18 mi. NW of Moscow; glass, furniture. During Second World War, reached (1941) by advance Ger. units in Moscow campaign.

Skhoinousa, Greece: see SCHOINOUSA.

Skholion, Greece: see OLYMPUS.

Ski (shē), village (pop. 2,620; canton pop. 5,250), Akershus co., SE Norway, 14 mi. S of Oslo; rail junction; explosives works.

Skiathos (skē'ŭthôs), Lat. *Sciathus* (sī'ŭthŭs), Aegean island (□ 18.8; pop. 3,433) in the Northern Sporades, Magnesia nome, Greece, 2.5 mi. off Thessalian mainland (separated by Strait of Skiathos); 39°12'N 23°28'E; 8 mi. long, 4 mi. wide. Olives, figs, wheat, citrus fruit; fisheries. Marble quarries. Its only town and port, Skiathos, is on SE shore.

Skiatook (skītŏŏk', –tŏŏk'), town (pop. 1,734), Osage and Tulsa cos., NE Okla., 15 mi. N of Tulsa and on Bird Creek, in agr. area; cotton ginning, feed milling; poultry hatchery; oil wells. Settled 1886, inc. 1907.

Skibbereen (skĭ'bŭrēn, –ēn'), Gaelic *Sciobairín*, urban district (pop. 2,363), SW Co. Cork, Ireland, on Ilen R. and 42 mi. SW of Cork; agr. market (grain, potatoes, oats; dairying), with agr.-implement works and near-by slate quarries. There are ruins of Cistercian abbey, where victims of 1847 famine, especially severe in this district, are buried. Town has cathedral and bishop's palace of R.C. diocese of Ross.

Skibby (skĭ'bü), town (pop. 771), Frederiksborg amt, Zealand, Denmark, 18 mi. SW of Hillerod; cement- and brickworks.

Skibotn, Norway: see LYNGEN FJORD.

Skidaway Island, one of the Sea Isls., in Chatham co., SE Ga., just off the coast, 10 mi. SSE of Savannah, bet. 2 distributaries of Savannah R.; c.10 mi. long and wide; marshy.

Skiddaw, mountain (3,054 ft.) of the Cumbrians, in the Lake District, central Cumberland, England, 3 mi. N of Keswick. On E slope is Skiddaw Forest.

Skidegate (skĭ'dŭgĭt), village, W B.C., on SE Graham Isl., on Skidegate Inlet, 3 mi. E of Queen Charlotte; lumbering; stock, potatoes. Adjoining is a village of Haida Indians.

Skidegate Inlet (16 mi. long, 1–7 mi. wide), arm of Hecate Strait, W B.C., bet. Graham Isl. (N) and Moresby Isl. (S), in lumbering and cattle-raising area. Queen Charlotte village is on N shore; Skidegate Channel (18 mi. long) joins inlet with the Pacific.

Skidel or **Skidel'** (skēdyĕl'), town (1931 pop. 3,814), NW central Grodno oblast, Belorussian SSR, 19 mi. SE of Grodno; sugar-refining center; tanning, flour milling, brewing.

Skidmore. 1 Village (pop. 1,279, with adjacent East Kingsford), Dickinson co., SW Upper Peninsula, Mich. **2** City (pop. 485), Nodaway co., NW Mo., on Nodaway R. and 12 mi. SW of Maryville; grain, bluegrass seed, livestock. **3** Village (1940 pop. 643), Bee co., S Texas, 12 mi. SSE of Beeville; farm-trade and shipping point.

Skien (shā'ŭn, shē'ŭn), city (pop. 15,006), ⊙ Telemark co., S Norway, on Skien R. and 65 mi. SW of Oslo; 59°11'N 9°37'E. Industrial center and port, with sawmills, tanneries, breweries, and mfg. of wood pulp, cellulose, paper, food products, soap, shoes, and electrical appliances. Outlet for interior lumbering, cattle-raising, and mining region, to which it is joined by the BANDAK-NORSJA CANAL; the Skien R. leads to Frier Fjord and the Skagerrak. The town, which grew around a monastery founded 1110, was called Skida in the Middle Ages; inc. 1346. It suffered a severe fire in 1886. Henrik Ibsen was b. here. Seat of co. mus.

Skien River, Telemark co., S Norway, issues from Nor L., flows 10 mi. SE and S, past Skien (waterfall here) and Porsgrunn, to Frier Fjord and the Skagerrak. Above Skien it is also called the Far, and at Porsgrunn, the Porsgrunn.

Skierniewice (skyĕrnyĕvē'tsĕ), Rus. *Skernevitsy* (skyĕrnyĭvē'tsĭ), town (pop. 17,666), Lodz prov., central Poland, 22 mi. ENE of Lodz; rail junction; mfg. of electrical equipment, bricks, tiles, cereals; sawmilling, brewing, flour milling. Glass and ceramics made in region.

Skiervoy (shē'ŭrv-ûü), Nor. *Skjervøy*, fishing village (pop. 608; canton pop. 4,418), Troms co., N Norway, on Skiervoy, an isl. (□ 3.5; pop. 613) in Kvaenang Fjord of Norwegian Sea, 60 mi. ENE of Tromso. Nansen's ship *Fram* returned here (1896) after 3-year polar voyage.

Skiff Lake (□ 2.75; 3 mi. long, 2 mi. wide), SW N.B., near Maine border, 22 mi. S of Woodstock.

Skiftesvik, Norway: see ASKOY.

Skihist Mountain (9,660 ft.), S B.C., in Coast Mts., 70 mi. N of Chilliwack.

Skilak Lake (skē'lăk, skī–) (15 mi. long), S Alaska, central Kenai Peninsula, 30 mi. WNW of Seward; 60°24'N 150°22'W; game fishing, hunting. Drained WNW by Kenai R.

Skillaion, Cape, Greece: see SKYLLAION, CAPE.

Skillet Fork, S Ill., rises NE of Salem, flows c.100 mi. SE to Little Wabash R. 5 mi. above Carmi.

Skillingaryd (shĭ'lĭng-ärüd"), village (pop. 1,816), Jonkoping co., S Sweden, on Lage R. and 17 mi. N of Varnamo; woodworking, agr.-implement mfg. Hydroelectric power station near by.

Skillinge (shĭ'lĭng-ŭ), fishing village (pop. 780), Kristianstad co., S Sweden, on the Baltic, 12 mi. SSW of Simrishamn.

Skinnskatteberg (shĭn"skä'tŭbĕr"yŭ), village (pop. 896), Vastmanland co., central Sweden, in Bergslag region, 14 mi. SSW of Fagersta, in iron-mining region; sawmilling and woodworking. Large ironworks not now in operation.

Skipton, urban district (1931 pop. 12,461; 1951 census 13,210), West Riding, W Yorkshire, England, near Aire R. 16 mi. NW of Bradford; cotton, rayon, and paper milling, leather tanning; agr. market. Has castle dating from 11th cent. and grammar school founded in 16th cent.

Skiropoula, Greece: see SKYROPOULA.

Skiros, Greece: see SKYROS.

Skit River, Bulgaria: see SKAT RIVER.

Skivarp (shē'värp"), village (pop. 702), Malmohus co., S Sweden, 10 mi. W of Ystad; sugar refining; grain, sugar beets, potatoes, stock.

Skive (skē'vŭ), city (1950 pop. 14,497) with near-by port, Viborg amt, central Jutland, Denmark, on SE Salling peninsula, on Skive Fjord and 16 mi. WNW of Viborg. Iron foundries, machine shops; meat packing, margarine, tobacco; fisheries.

Skive Fjord, inlet of Lim Fjord, Denmark, E of Salling peninsula, joined to Lim Fjord by the Hvalpsund (välp'sōōn) (c.1 mi. wide).

Skjaak, Norway: see SKJAK.

Skjaeggedalsfoss, Norway: see SKJEGGEDALSFOSS.

Skjak (shôk), Nor. *Skjåk*, village and canton (pop. 2,990), Opland co., S central Norway, on Otta R. and 90 mi. SSE of Kristiansund; lumber and flour mills. Sometimes spelled Skjaak.

Skjalfandafljot (skoul'väntäfŭlyöt", skyoul'–), Icelandic *Skjálfandafljót*, river, N Iceland, rises in several headstreams at N edge of Vatnajokull, flows 120 mi. N to **Skjalfandi,** bay (10 mi. long, 17 mi. wide at mouth) of Greenland Sea.

Skjeggedalsfoss (shĕg'gŭdälsfôs"), waterfall (525 ft.) in Hordaland co., SW Norway, 9 mi. ENE of Odda; popular tourist attraction of the Hardanger region. Sometimes spelled Skjegedalsfoss or Skjaeggedalsfoss.

Skjerdalen, Norway: see TYRISTRAND.

Skjerstad Fjord, Norway: see SALT FJORD.

Skjold (shôl), village and canton (pop. 2,364), Rogaland co., SW Norway, at head of Skjold Fjord (13-mi.-long N arm of Bokn Fjord), 12 mi. NE of Haugesund; agr., lumbering.

Skjolden (shôl'dŭn), village in Luster (formerly Lyster) canton (pop. 2,957), Sogn og Fjordane co., W Norway, at head of Luster Fjord, 25 mi. NE of Sogndal; agr., notably tobacco- and fruitgrowing; tourist center. Many viking monuments and archaeological findings near by. At Dale (dä'lŭ) village, 7 mi. SW, are medieval stone church and Luster Sanatorium. At Fortun (fôr'tōōn) village, 2 mi. E, is original site of Fantoft stave church, now moved to Fjosanger near Nesttun.

Skjoldungen Island (shŭ'lōōngŭn), Dan. *Skjøldungen* (30 mi. long, 4–8 mi. wide), SE Greenland, in bay of Atlantic. Meteorological station at SE tip (63°13'N 41°8'W).

Skjonsta, Norway: see SJONSTA.

Skjorn, Norway: see RAKVAG.

Sklene Teplice, Czechoslovakia: see VYHNE.

Sklenov (sklĕ'nôf), village (pop. 1,170), NE Moravia, Czechoslovakia, 15 mi. S of Ostrava; noted for large 13th-cent. Hukvaldy castle (just S), with adjoining game park.

Skobelev, Uzbek SSR: see FERGANA, city.

Skocjan, Yugoslavia: see DIVACA.

Skoczow (skô'chōōf), Pol. *Skoczów*, Ger. *Skotschau* (skô'chou), town (pop. 4,480), Katowice prov., S Poland, on the Vistula and 8 mi. ENE of Cieszyn; rail junction; mfg. of cement goods, machinery, clothing; distilling, tanning.

Skodsborg (skōs'bôr), town (pop. 1,496) and port, Copenhagen amt, Zealand, Denmark, on the Oresund and 9 mi. N of Copenhagen.

Skofde, Sweden: see SKOVDE.

Skofja Loka (shkô'fyä lô'kä), Slovenian *Škofja Loka*, Ger. *Bischoflack* (bĭsh'ŏf-läk), village, W Slovenia, Yugoslavia, on Sora R., on railroad and 12 mi. NW of Ljubljana. Summer resort; lumbering; textile and lace making; barium mining. First mentioned as trade center in 1274. Held by bishops of Freising from 973 to 1803. Until 1918, in Carniola.

Skoger (skō'gŭr), village and canton (pop. 10,867), Vestfold co., SE Norway, 4 mi. S of Drammen; mfg. of paper, cellulose, glass, bricks, gold foil; lumber mills. Abandoned zinc mines. Tourist hotel at Konnerudkollen (kôn'nŭrōōkôl"lŭn), 4 mi. NW.

Skoghall-Vidon (skōōg'häl"-vĭd'ŭn"), Swedish *Skoghall-Vidön*, village (pop. 4,542), Varmland co., W Sweden, on NW coast of Hammar Isl., on L. Vaner, 4 mi. SSW of Karlstad; lumber, pulp, and paper mills, sulphite works.

Skogn (skông'ŭn), canton (pop. 4,208), Nord-Trondelag co., central Norway, on Trondheim Fjord, on railroad and 4 mi. SW of Levanger; agr., dairying, lumber milling. At Alstadhaug (äl'stähoug") is medieval parish church (antedating 1250) and viking burial mound.

Skogsbo (skōōks'bōō"), residential village (pop. 1,626), Kopparberg co., central Sweden, just NE of Falun. Site of sanitarium. Includes residential villages of Rutbo (rŭt'bōō") and Hogbo (hûg'bōō"), Swedish *Högbo*.

Skogslund, Sweden: see SURAHAMMAR.

Skogstorp (skōōks'tôrp"), residential village (pop. 972), Sodermanland co., E Sweden, 3 mi. SW of Eskilstuna. Includes Rosenfors (rōō"sŭnfôrs', –fôsh') village.

Skokholm, Wales: see SKOMER.

Skoki (skô'kē), Ger. *Schocken* (shô'kŭn), town (1946 pop. 1,567), Poznan prov., W Poland, 21 mi. NNE of Poznan; rail junction; mfg. of cement, furniture; brewing, flour milling, sawmilling.

Skokie (skō'kē), village (pop. 14,832), Cook co., NE Ill., N suburb of Chicago; mfg. (wood and concrete products, tools, drugs, novelties, archery equipment, lumber, brick); greenhouses. Inc. 1888. Until 1940, called Niles Center.

Skokloster (skōōklō'stŭr), castle, Uppsala co., E Sweden, on NE arm of L. Malar, 10 mi. S of Uppsala. Built (1650) by Field Marshal Wrangel on site of earlier Dominican and Cistercian monastery; contains noted collection of art and of arms of Thirty Years War.

Skokomish River (skōkō'mĭsh), W Wash., formed NW of Shelton by North Fork (c.25 mi. long) and South Fork (c.25 mi. long), both rising in Olympic Mts.; flows c.10 mi. E and NE to S end of Hood Canal. On North Fork are Cushman No. 1 Dam (280 ft. high, 1,200 ft. long) and Cushman No. 2 Dam (240 ft. high), hydroelectric dams owned by city of Tacoma which impound L. Cushman (c.8 mi. long).

Skoldinge (shŭl'dĭng-ŭ), Swedish *Sköldinge*, village (pop. 893), Sodermanland co., E Sweden, 7 mi. ENE of Katrineholm; iron mining and smelting. Includes Kantorp (kän'tōrp") village.

Skole (skô'lyĭ), city (1931 pop. 7,543), SE Drogobych oblast Ukrainian SSR, in E Beskids, on tributary of Stry R. and 22 mi. S of Drogobych; summer resort; sawmilling, candle mfg. Has old castle, several wooden Ruthenian churches. Passed from Austria to Poland in 1919; ceded to USSR in 1945.

Skomer, island in the Atlantic just off W coast of Pembroke, Wales, 12 mi. WNW of Milford Haven; 2 mi. long, 1 mi. wide. S, 2 mi., is small isl. of Skokholm (1 mi. long, ½ mi. wide), site of lighthouse (51°41'N 5°16'W).

Skonsberg (shûns'bĕr"yû), Swedish *Skönsberg*, village (pop. 4,734), Vasternorrland co., NE Sweden, on small inlet of Gulf of Bothnia, just ENE of Sundsvall, opposite Alno isl.; sawmilling, woodworking.

Skonsmon (shûns'mōōn"), Swedish *Skönsmon*, village (pop. 3,540), Vasternorrland co., NE Sweden, on inlet of Gulf of Bothnia, just ESE of Sundsvall, opposite Alno isl.; foundries, sawmills; wood- and metalworking. Includes suburb of Kubikenborg, with aluminum works.

Skonvik (shûn'vēk"), Swedish *Skönvik*, village (pop. 790), Vasternorrland co., NE Sweden, on small inlet of Gulf of Bothnia, opposite Alno isl., 6 mi. N of Sundsvall; sawmilling, metalworking. Includes Skyttberg (shüt'bĕr'yû) village.

Skopelos (skô'pĕlôs), town (pop. 4,132), SE Lesbos isl., Greece, 7 mi. SW of Mytilene; olive oil, barley, wine, peaches; fish (especially lobsters).

Skopelos, anc. *Peparethus* (pĕpûrē'thûs), Aegean island (□ 35.5; pop. 6,006) in the Northern Sporades, Magnesia nome, Greece, 13 mi. off Thessalian mainland and separated from Skiathos isl. (W) by Strait of Skopelos; 39°10'N 23°40'E; 13 mi. long, 5 mi. wide. Olives, wine, livestock. Main town and port, Skopelos (pop. 3,536), is on E shore.

Skopin (skŭpēn'), city (1926 pop. 10,135), W central Ryazan oblast, Russian SFSR, 55 mi. S of Ryazan; lignite-mining center in Moscow Basin; machine mfg.; flour mills. Principal mines at OKTYABRSKI (SW) and POBEDINSKI (S). Chartered 1663.

Skoplje (skôp'lyĕ), Macedonian *Skopje* (skô'pyĕ), Turkish *Üsküb*, anc. *Scupi* and *Justinana Prima*, city (pop. 91,557), ⊙ Macedonia and Skoplje oblast (formed 1949), Yugoslavia, on Vardar R., on Belgrade-Salonika RR and 210 mi. SSE of Belgrade, in fertile valley. Economic and cultural center of Macedonia; rail and road junction; trade center for tobacco- and vegetable-growing region; food processing (fish cannery, flour mill, brewery, winery), mfg. of soap, cigarettes, opium, cement, asbestos, carpets, leather goods; woodworking; handicrafts (pottery making). City consists of old and new sections (on right and left banks of Vardar R., respectively) connected by bridge of Emperor Dushan (probably built by Romans). Has a Macedonian univ., medical school, many museums, churches, and mosques, including mosques of Mustafa Pasha (15th cent.) and Sultan Murad (1430), a dervish monastery, the *Kuršumli Han* (a caravanserai), bazaar, gypsy quarter, and many anc. relics (fortress, aqueduct, theater). Was ⊙ Roman prov. of Dardania; fell (14th cent.) to Stephen Dushan, who was crowned emperor here in 1346. Under Turkish rule, Skoplje was the capital of an eyalet until 1878. Reverted to Serbia in 1913.

Skopska Crna Gora, Yugoslavia: see CRNA GORA, Macedonia and Serbia.

Skorcz (skōōrch), Pol. *Skórcz*, Ger. *Skurz* (skōōrts), town (1946 pop. 2,857), Gdansk prov., N Poland, 12 mi. S of Starogard; rail junction; mfg. of agr. machinery, flour milling, sawmilling.

Skorodnoye (skô'rŭdnŭyŭ), village (1926 pop. 4,016), E central Kursk oblast, Russian SFSR, 29 mi. SW of Stary Oskol; wheat, sunflowers, essential oils.

Skorovas, Norway: see GJERSVIKA.

Skorping (skûr'pĭng), Dan. *Skørping*, town (pop. 1,193), Aalborg amt, N Jutland, Denmark, 14 mi. S of Aalborg; fruitgrowing; lumber, furniture mfg.

Skosyrskaya (skŭsĭr'skĭŭ), village (1939 pop. over 500), central Rostov oblast, Russian SFSR, 25 mi. WNW of Morozovsk; flour milling, distilling; wheat, sunflowers.

Skotfoss (skōt'fôs), village (pop. 1,882) in Solum canton (pop. 9,032), Telemark co., S Norway, on Skien R. and 3 mi. W of Skien; paper mfg. The 30-ft.-high falls, which drive sawmill and hydroelectric plant, are by-passed by a canal with locks.

Skothammeren, Norway: see TORVIK.

Skotovataya (skŭtŭvä'tĭŭ), town (1926 pop. 2,542), central Stalino oblast, Ukrainian SSR, in the Donbas, 17 mi. N of Stalino; glassworks.

Skotschau, Poland: see SKOCZOW.

Skotterud (skôt'tŭrōōd), village (pop. 485) in Eidskog canton, Hedmark co., SE Norway, near Swedish border, 15 mi. SSE of Kongsvinger; rail junction; lumbering, woodworking.

Skotthamar, Norway: see TORVIK.

Skottsund (skôt"sŭnd'), residential village (pop. 637), Vasternorrland co., NE Sweden, on Ljunga R., just above its mouth on Gulf of Bothnia, 7 mi. SE of Sundsvall.

Skoun (skōōn), village, Kompong Cham prov., S Cambodia, 35 mi. N of Pnompenh; road junction.

Skouriotissa (skōōryô'tēsä), mining village (pop. 169), Nicosia dist., NW Cyprus, in Evrykhou Valley, 27 mi. W of Nicosia; alt. c.800 ft. Pyrite and ocher mining. Ore is crushed and shipped at Karavostasi.

Skovde (shûv'dû), Swedish *Skövde*, city (1950 pop. 17,723), Skaraborg co., S Sweden, 40 mi. N of Jonkoping; rail junction; garrison town. Mfg. of chemicals, bricks, cement, insulating materials; stone quarrying. Has Church of St. Elin (Helen), dating from 1250, and 18th-cent. town hall. Known since 12th cent., it early became place of pilgrimage, associated with St. Elin (buried here). Chartered 1526; suffered (1759) destructive fire. Formerly spelled Skofde, Swedish *Sköfde*.

Skovorodino (skŭvŭrŭdyĭnô'), city (1939 pop. over 10,000), SW Amur oblast, Russian SFSR, on Trans-Siberian RR and 450 mi. NE of Chita; junction of railroad to Dzhalinda; center of gold-mining area; lumber milling, food processing; metalworks, distillery. Until c.1940, Rukhlovo.

Skowhegan (skouhē'gĭn), town (pop. 7,422), including Skowhegan village (pop. 6,183), ⊙ Somerset co., central Maine, on the Kennebec above Waterville. Mfg. (textiles, shoes, boats and canoes, wood products); supply point for resort area. Holds annual agr. fair. Seat of state reformatory for women. Lakewood, resort 5 mi. N on Hayden L., has summer theater (opened 1901). Settled 1771, set off from Canaan as Milburn 1823, renamed 1836.

Skraava, Norway: see SKROVA.

Skradin (skrä'dĭn), Ital. *Scardona* (skärdô'nä), village, W Croatia, Yugoslavia, on Krka R. and 6 mi. N of Sibenik, in Dalmatia. Hydroelectric plant is at Skradinski Buk [Serbo-Croatian,=Skradin waterfall] of the Krka. Known since Roman times; medieval R.C. bishopric.

Skraekken Bay, Greenland: see KIALINEK BAY.

Skrapar or **Skrapari**, Albania: see ÇOROVODË.

Skrava, Norway: see SKROVA.

Skraven, Norway: see SKROVA.

Skrim, Norway: see HEDENSTAD.

Skrimkolla, Norway: see DOVREFJELL.

Skripou, Greece: see ORCHOMENUS.

Skrlatica (shkûr'lätĭtsä), Slovenian *Škrlatica*, Ital. *Scarlatizza* (skärlätēt'tsä), peak (8,983 ft.) in Julian Alps, NW Slovenia, Yugoslavia, 4 mi. N of the Triglav; 3d-highest peak in Yugoslavia.

Skromberga (skrōm'bĕr"yä), village (pop. 2,778), Malmohus co., S Sweden, 12 mi. ESE of Halsingborg; coal mining, brick making. Includes Valleberga (vä'lübĕr"yä) and Truedstorp (trü'ăts'tôrp") villages.

Skrova (skrō'vä), fishing village (pop. 497) in Vagan canton, Nordland co., N Norway, on Skrova islet (□ 1) of Lofoten Isls., in Vestfjord, 6 mi. SE of Svolvaer; summer resort. Sometimes spelled Skrava (Nor. *Skråva*), Skraava, or Skraven.

Skruv (skrüv), village (pop. 648), Kronoberg co., S Sweden, 20 mi. ESE of Vaxjo; glass, furniture.

Skudai (skōō"dī'), village (pop. 998), S Johore, Malaya, 7 mi. NW of Johore Bharu; pineapple canning. Sometimes spelled Scudai.

Skudeneshavn (skōō'dûnās-häv"ûn), town (pop. 1,310), Rogaland co., SW Norway, port at S end of Karmoy, 11 mi. S of Kopervik; exports fresh and canned fish, lobsters, fish oil. Lighthouses. Inc. 1857. Sometimes spelled Skutesnaeshamn.

Skull, Ireland: see SCHULL.

Skultuna (skŭl"tü'nä), village (pop. 1,395), Vastmanland co., central Sweden, 7 mi. NNW of Vasteras; copper smelter, brassworks, sawmills.

Skulyany (skōōlyä'nē), Rum. *Sculeni* (skōōlĕn'), village (1941 pop. 2,181), W Moldavian SSR, on Prut R. (Rum. border) and 11 mi. N of Jassy; corn, wheat, oilseeds. Pop. largely Jewish until Second World War.

Skuna River (skōō'nû), N central Miss., rises in Pontotoc co., flows c.75 mi. SW, past Bruce, to Yalobusha R. just above Grenada.

Skunk River, central and SE Iowa, rises in NE Hamilton co., flows 264 mi. SE, past Ames, to the Mississippi 7 mi. S of Burlington. Main tributary is North Skunk R., rising in Marshall co., flowing c.100 mi. SE to Skunk R. 11 mi. SE of Sigourney.

Skuo (skōō'û), Dan. *Skuø*, Faeroese *Skúvoy*, island (□ 4; pop. 162) of the SW Faeroe Isls., separated from SW Sando by Skuo Fjord; highest point 1,282 ft. Fishing, sheep raising.

Skuodas (skwō'däs), Ger. *Schoden*, Pol. *Szkudy*, city (pop. 4,410), NW Lithuania, 28 mi. NNE of Kretinga, on Latvian border; shoe-mfg. center.

Skuratovski or **Skuratovskiy** (skōōrä'tŭfskē), town (1948 pop. over 500), central Tula oblast, Russian SFSR, S of Kosaya Gora, in Moscow Basin; lignite mining. Until 1948, Yuzhny.

Skuru (skü'rü"), Finnish *Pohjankuru* (pō'yän-kōō"rōō, pōhk'yän-), village in Pojo commune (pop. 6,507), Uusimaa co., SW Finland, at head of Pojo Bay of Gulf of Finland, 4 mi. WNW of Karis; port, serving Fiskars iron and steel mills.

Skuru (skü'rü), residential village (pop. 1,655), Stockholm co., E Sweden, on Saltsjo, fjord of Baltic, 5 mi. E of Stockholm city center. Includes Ektorp (āk'tôrp") village.

Skurup (skü'rŭp"), town (pop. 2,112), Malmohus co., S Sweden, 13 mi. WNW of Ystad; agr. center (grain, sugar beets, potatoes, stock); brickworks, mechanical workshops. Site of agr. school.

Skurz, Poland: see SKORCZ.

Skushuban (skōōshōōbän'), Ital. *Scusciuban*, village, in the Mijirtein, N Ital. Somaliland, in Daror Valley, 70 mi. W of Hafun; water hole, livestock market.

Skutari, Turkey: see USKUDAR.

Skutec (skōō'tĕch), Czech *Skuteč*, Ger. *Skutsch* (skōōch), town (pop. 2,998), E Bohemia, Czechoslovakia, 17 mi. SE of Pardubice; rail junction; hand-worked footwear industry; lace making; granite quarrying.

Skutesnaeshamn, Norway: see SKUDENESHAVN.

Skuthamn, Sweden: see MUNKSUND.

Skutsch, Czechoslovakia: see SKUTEC.

Skutskar (sküt'shâr"), Swedish *Skutskär*, village (pop. 3,616), Uppsala co., E Sweden, on Gulf of Bothnia, at mouth of Dal R., 9 mi. ESE of Gavle; sawmilling center.

Skuvoy, Faeroe Isls.: see SKUO.

Skvira (skvē'rŭ), city (1926 pop. 13,912), W Kiev oblast, Ukrainian SSR, 20 mi. WSW of Belaya Tserkov; rail terminus; sugar refining, metalworking, food processing.

Skwentna (skwĕnt'nû), village (pop. 33), S Alaska, 70 mi. NW of Anchorage, on Yentna R. at mouth of the Skwentna; airfield.

Skwentna River, S Alaska, rises in Mt. Gerdine glacier system near 61°40'N 152°45'W, flows 55 mi. in an arc N and E to Yentna R. at 61°58'N 151°10'W.

Skwierzyna (skvyē-zhĭ'nä), Ger. *Schwerin* (shvārēn'), town (1939 pop. 8,952; 1946 pop. 2,822) in Brandenburg, after 1945 in Zielona Gora prov., W Poland, on Warta R. and 15 mi. SE of Landsberg (Gorzow Wielkopolski); agr. center (grain, tobacco, potatoes, livestock); agr.-machinery mfg., sawmilling. First mentioned 1251; chartered 1406.

Skye, Isle of (skī), island (□ 670, including surrounding small isls.; pop. 9,908), largest of the Inner Hebrides, Inverness, Scotland, separated from mainland by the Sound of Sleat, Loch Alsh, the Inner Sound, and Sound of Raasay, and from the Outer Hebrides by the Little Minch and the Sea of the Hebrides. It is 48 mi. long and up to 28 mi. wide, and has irregular coastline with deep inlets. Chief elevations are the Cuillin Hills (SE), rising to 3,309 ft. In N part of isl. highest elevation is The Starr (2,360 ft.). There is little arable land; climate is moist and mild. Chief industries are cattle and sheep raising, and growing of oats, potatoes, turnips. Fishing is important, some marble is quarried, and isl. attracts many tourists. Chief town is Portree, fishing port on E coast, 21 mi. NW of Kyle on mainland. On the coast NE of Portree is cave where Prince Charles Edward was sheltered in 1746. Near Dunvegan (dûnvĕg'ûn), fishing port on NW coast, 14 mi. W of Portree, at head of Loch Dunvegan (7 mi. long), is Boreraig Castle, seat of the Macleods and once site of bagpipers' school of the MacCrimmons, pipers to the Macleods. Carbost, on W coast, 10 mi. SW of Portree, is fishing port with whisky distillery. Ord, on SW coast, is fishing port. Uig (ōō'ĭg) is a resort on Loch Snizort, 14 mi. NNW of Portree. At Kilmuir, 4 mi. N of Uig, is grave of Flora Macdonald. N of Uig, 6 mi., is anc. Duntulm Castle (restored), stronghold of the Macdonalds, lords of the Isles.

Skykomish (skīkō'mĭsh), town (pop. 497), King co., W central Wash., in Cascade Range, 45 mi. E of Seattle and on Skykomish R.; railroad center; sawmills.

Skykomish River, NW Wash., formed near Index by North Fork (c.30 mi. long) and South Fork (c.35 mi. long), both rising in Cascade Range; flows c.30 mi. W to junction with Snoqualmie R., forming Snohomish R. SW of Monroe.

Skyland. **1** Summer resort, Buncombe co., W N.C., 7 mi. S of Asheville. **2** Summer resort, Page co., N Va., on crest of the Blue Ridge in Shenandoah Natl. Park, 8 mi. SE of Luray; alt. c.3,500 ft. Near by are Stony Man and Hawks Bill peaks.

Skylight, Mount (4.920 ft.), Essex co., NE N.Y., peak of the Adirondacks, just S of Mt. Marcy and 13 mi. S of Lake Placid village.

Skyline Caverns, Va.: see FRONT ROYAL.

Skyline Drive, Va.: see SHENANDOAH NATIONAL PARK.

Skyllaion, Cape, or **Cape Skillaion** (both: skĭl'āôn), Lat. *Scyllaeum* (sĭlē'ûm), easternmost point of Peloponnesus, Greece, and of Argolis Peninsula, on Aegean Sea bet. Gulf of Argolis (S) and Saronic Gulf (N); 37°35'N 23°30'E. Also spelled Skylaion, Skilaion, or Skyli.

Skyring Peninsula, Aysén prov., S Chile, a W arm of TAITAO PENINSULA.

Skyring Sound (60 mi. long, 5–20 mi. wide), off Patagonian coast of S Chile, 55 mi. S of Puerto Natales; bounded by mainland (N), Riesco Isl. (S), and Muñoz Gamero Peninsula (W). Almost completely landlocked, it is connected by narrow channels with Strait of Magellan (SW) and Otway Sound (SE).

Skyropoula or **Skiropoula** (both: skērôpōō'lû), uninhabited island (□ 1.3) in Aegean Sea, Euboea nome, Greece, 4 mi. off E coast of isl. of Skyros; 1.3 mi. long, 1 mi. wide. Also spelled Skyropoulo and Skyropulo.

Skyros or **Skiros** (both: skē'rôs), Lat. *Scyros* or *Scyrus* (sī'rûs), largest island (□ 81; 1940 pop. 3,395) of Northern Sporades, in Aegean Sea, Euboea nome, Greece, 22 mi. off E coast of Euboea; 18 mi. long, 2–9 mi. wide; rises to 2,608 ft. Mainly agr.: wheat, figs, olive oil. Marble, chromite, and iron deposits; fisheries. Its cheese is well-known. On NE shore lies town and port of Skyros (1928 pop. 2,878); sponge fishing, trading. Skyroupoula and Valaxa isls. lie off W shore. In anc. legend, Thetis here concealed her son Achilles (in woman's attire) among the daughters of Lycomedes; here Neoptolemus, son of Achilles by Deidamia, was reared; and here Theseus was killed by Lycomedes. Skyros was conquered in 469 B.C. by the Athenians under Cimon, who discovered Theseus' bones and conveyed them to the Theseum in Athens. Rupert Brooke, who died in the Gallipoli campaign of 1915, was buried on Skyros.

Skytop, resort village, Monroe co., NE Pa., in Pocono Mts., 16 mi. N of Stroudsburg; alt. 1,575 ft.

Skyttberg, Sweden: see SKONVIK.

Slab Fork, village (1940 pop. 1,069), Raleigh co., S W.VA., 10 mi. SW of Beckley, in coal-mining region.

Slade, village (pop. c.400), Powell co., E central Ky., in Cumberland Natl. Forest, 30 mi. ESE of Winchester. Tourist resort; gateway to NATURAL BRIDGE STATE PARK.

Sladkovo (slät'kůvŭ), village (1926 pop. 1,035), SE Tyumen oblast, Russian SFSR, 50 mi. SE of Ishim; dairy farming.

Slaettaratinde or **Slaettaratindur,** Faeroe Isls.: see OSTERO.

Slagelse (slä'yůlsů), city (pop. 19,184), Soro amt, Zealand, Denmark 50 mi. WSW of Copenhagen; rail junction; mfg. center (margarine, spirits, tobacco, chemicals, machinery), meat canning, woodworking.

Slaithwaite (slăth'wăt, slăth'–, slō'ĭt), former urban district (1931 pop. 5,183), West Riding, SW Yorkshire, England, on Colne R. and 4 mi. WSW of Huddersfield; woolen and cotton milling; mfg. of textile machinery, chemicals. Has medicinal mineral spring. Inc. 1937 in Colne Valley.

Slamannan (slůmă'nůn), town and parish (pop., 2,959), SE Stirling, Scotland, 5 mi. SSW of Falkirk; coal mining.

Slamet, Mount (slä'mĕt), volcanic peak (11,327 ft.), central Java, Indonesia, 55 mi. SE of Cheribon. Also called Mount Selamat and Tegal Peak.

Slana River, Czechoslovakia and Hungary: see SAJO RIVER.

Slane, Gaelic *Baile Shláinghe,* town (pop. 155), NE Co. Meath, Ireland, on the Boyne and 9 mi. W of Drogheda; agr. market (cattle, horses; potatoes). Has ruins of anc. abbey church and col., rebuilt 1512. Near by are a rath and remains of a hermitage.

Slaney River, Ireland, rises in Wicklow Mts., flows 60 mi. S through Co. Carlow and Co. Wexford, past Baltinglass, Tullow, and Enniscorthy, to Wexford Harbour. Navigable below Enniscorthy. Receives Bann R.

Slangerup (släng'ŭrŏŏp), town (pop. 1,256), Frederiksborg amt, N Zealand, Denmark, 8 mi. SW of Hillerod; sugar refinery. Important trade center until 1809, when city charter was revoked.

Slanic (slůnĕk'), Rum. *Slănic,* town (1948 pop. 6,495), Prahova prov., S central Rumania, in Walachia, 21 mi. N of Ploesti; rail terminus; major salt-mining center and summer resort, with mineral springs.

Slanic-Moldova, Rumania: see BAILE-SLANIC.

Slankamen (slän'kämĕn), village, Vojvodina, N Serbia, Yugoslavia, on the Danube, opposite Tisa R. mouth, and 18 mi. NNW of Belgrade; mineral waters. Consists of Stari Slankamen and Novi Slankamen. Here, in 1691, Margrave Louis of Baden defeated Turks.

Slano (slä'nô), village, S Croatia, Yugoslavia, on Adriatic Sea, 14 mi. NW of Dubrovnik.

Slantsy (slän'tsē), city (1935 pop. 6,700), SW Leningrad oblast, Russian SFSR, on Plyussa R. and 18 mi. S of Narva; oil-shale-mining center; sawmilling, metalworking. Became city in 1949.

Slany (slä'nē), Czech *Slaný,* Ger. *Schlan* (shlän), town (pop. 9,105), W central Bohemia, Czechoslovakia, on railroad and 18 mi. NW of Prague; mfg. of chemicals, batteries, glue; ironworks (locomotives, machinery); sugar refining; coal mining.

Slashchevskaya (slä'shchĭfskĭŭ), village (1939 pop. over 500), W Stalingrad oblast, Russian SFSR, on Khoper R. and 40 mi. WSW of Mikhailovka; wheat, fruit, sunflowers.

Slask, region, Europe: see SILESIA.

Slask Dabrowski, province, Poland: see KATOWICE prov.; OPOLE prov.

Slask Dolny, province, Poland: see WROCLAW.

Slata (slätä'), village, Le Kef dist., W Tunisia, 26 mi. SW of Le Kef; rail terminus. Iron mines at Djebel Slata (1 mi. E) and Djebel Hameïma (5 mi. W).

Slate Islands, group of 11 isls. in L. Superior, W Ont., 100 mi. E of Port Arthur. Largest is Patterson Isl. (5 mi. long, 3 mi. wide).

Slate Peak, Colo.: see PURPLE PEAK.

Slater. 1 Village (1940 pop. 503), Lee co., SW Fla., 7 mi. N of Fort Myers. **2** Town (pop. 583), Story co., central Iowa, 19 mi. N of Des Moines; dairy products, feed. **3** City (pop. 2,836), Saline co., central Mo., near Missouri R., 10 mi. NE of Marshall; agr. (grain), livestock; mfg. (flour, underwear); rock quarry. **4** Textile-mill village (1940 pop. 726), Greenville co., NW S.C., 13 mi. NNW of Greenville; rayon.

Slate River, W central Colo., rises in Elk Mts., flows c.40 mi. SE, past Crested Butte town, joining Taylor R. at Almont to form Gunnison R.

Slatersville, R.I.: see NORTH SMITHFIELD.

Slatersville Reservoir, R.I.: see BRANCH RIVER.

Slaterville, village (pop. 611), E central Alaska, near Fairbanks.

Slate Spring or **Slate Springs,** village (pop. 134), Calhoun co., N central Miss., 25 mi. E of Grenada.

Slatina (slä'tĕnä). **1** Village (pop. 2,719), Pleven dist., N Bulgaria, 8 mi. N of Lovech; wheat, corn, livestock. **2** Village (pop. 11,810), Sofia dist., W Bulgaria, SE suburb of Sofia; light mfg.; poultry, truck, dairying.

Slatina (slä'tēnä), town (1948 pop. 13,136), Arges prov., S Rumania, in Walachia, near Olt R., on railroad and 80 mi. W of Bucharest; trading center (grain, lumber); flour milling, tanning, woodworking, mfg. of bricks and tiles. Has 17th- and 18th-cent. churches. Dates probably from 14th cent.

Slatina or **Podravska Slatina** (pô'dräfskä slä'tēnä), village (pop. 6,000), N Croatia, Yugoslavia, in the Podravina, 17 mi. ESE of Virovitica, in Slavonia; local trade center; rail junction; lumbering.

Slatina Ilidze, Yugoslavia: see BANJA LUKA.

Slatina Radenci (rä'dĕntsē), Ger. *Bad Radein* (bät' rä'dīn), village, NE Slovenia, Yugoslavia, on Mura R., on railroad and 4 mi. SE of Gornja Radgona, near Austrian border, at E foot of the Slovenske Gorice. Health resort with mineral waters. Also called Radenci, formerly Radinci. Until 1918, in Styria.

Slatington, borough (pop. 4,343), Lehigh co., E Pa., 12 mi. NW of Allentown and on Lehigh R.; slate quarrying; potatoes. Settled 1737, inc. 1864.

Slatinice (slä'tyĭnyĭtsĕ), village (pop. 1,201), N central Moravia, Czechoslovakia, on railroad and 7 mi. WSW of Olomouc; health resort with sulphurous and ferruginous springs.

Slaton (slā'tůn), city (pop. 5,036), Lubbock co., NW Texas, near Cap Rock escarpment of Llano Estacado, 15 mi. SE of Lubbock, near Double Mtn. Fork of Brazos R.; railroad division point; grain elevator, cottonseed-oil mills, cotton gins and compresses; mattresses, dairy products.

Slaugham (slă'fům, slä'–), agr. village and parish (pop. 1,531), central Sussex, England, 5 mi. NW of Haywards Heath. Has 13th-cent. church. Just SSW is village of Warninglid, for some time residence of Tennyson.

Slaughter, town (pop. 290), East Feliciana parish, SE central La., 19 mi. N of Baton Rouge, in agr. area.

Slaughter Beach, resort town (pop. 85), Sussex co., E Del., 7 mi. E of Milford and on Delaware Bay; fishing, bathing.

Slaughters or **Slaughtersville,** town (pop. 326), Webster co., W Ky., 12 mi. N of Madisonville.

Slav (släf), peak (7,576 ft.) in W Rhodope Mts., SW Bulgaria, 27 mi. WSW of Pazardzhik. Also called Dzhaferitsa.

Slave Coast, the coastal region of W Africa along the Bight of Benin section of the Gulf of Guinea, bet. the Gold Coast (W) and the mouths of the Niger (E); 0°–6°E. Bordering it are Togoland, Dahomey, and Nigeria. Named for its former trade in slaves.

Slave Falls, waterfalls, SE Man., on Winnipeg R. and 75 mi. ENE of Winnipeg; hydroelectric-power center.

Slave River, NE Alta. and S Mackenzie Dist., Northwest Territories, issues from NW end of L. Athabaska, flows 258 mi. NNW, past Fort Fitzgerald, into Northwest Territories at Fort Smith, to Great Slave L. 9 mi. NNE of Fort Resolution. Receives Peace R. N of outflow from L. Athabaska. Bet. Fort Fitzgerald and Fort Smith are rapids, bypassed by portage road. At mouth, on Great Slave L., is river-lake transshipment point of Res-delta. Sometimes called Great Slave R.

Slavesti (slůvĕsht'), Rum. *Slăvești,* village (pop. 1,182), Teleorman prov., S Rumania, 18 mi. NE of Rosiorii-de-Vede; extensive orchards.

Slavgorod (släv'gůrůt). **1** Town (1926 pop. 4,420), S Mogilev oblast, Belorussian SSR, on Sozh R., at mouth of the Pronya, and 40 mi. SE of Mogilev; woodworking, dairying, flax processing. Until 1945, Propoisk. **2** City (1935 pop. estimate 18,000), W Altai Territory, Russian SFSR, on railroad and 215 mi. W of Barnaul, on Kulunda Steppe; agr. processing center; mfg. of agr. machinery; agr. and livestock products (grain, meat, wool, butter). Chartered 1917. **3** Town (1939 pop. over 500), E central Dnepropetrovsk oblast, Ukrainian SSR, 23 mi. NE of Zaporozhe; machine mfg.; metalworking, flour. Kaolin quarries.

Slavkov, Czechoslovakia: see AUSTERLITZ.

Slavkovichi (släf'kůvēchē), village (1926 pop. 299), central Pskov oblast, Russian SFSR, 30 mi. ESE of Pskov; flax processing.

Slavnoye (släv'nŭyů), fishing village (1940 pop. 1,200) on Iturup Isl., S Kuriles, Russian SFSR, on NW coast, 40 mi. NE of Kurilsk; whale factory. Under Jap. rule (until 1945), called Shibetoro (shĭbā'tōrō).

Slavonia (slůvō'nēů), Serbo-Croatian *Slavonija* (slävō'nēä), Ger. *Slavonien* (slävō'nyůn), Hung. *Szlavonország* (slŏ'vônôrság), region of Croatia, Yugoslavia, largely bet. the Drava (N) and the Sava (S). Fertile and generally flat; noted for forests and mineral springs. Largest city is OSIJEK. The hist. of Slavonia is closely linked with that of CROATIA. With Croatia, Slavonia was recovered by Hungary from the Turks by Treaty of Karlowitz (1699). As result of Revolution of 1848–49, Hungary lost Slavonia, which was made an Austrian crownland, but in 1868 Slavonia was restored to Hungarian crown and was united with Croatia. Has been part of Yugoslavia since 1918.

Slavonice (slä'vônyĭtsĕ, Ger. *Zlabings* (zlä'bĕnks), village (pop. 1,980), SW Moravia, Czechoslovakia, on railroad, 29 mi. SSW of Jihlava, on Austrian border; oat growing; lumbering.

Slavonska; Slavonski [Serbo-Croatian,=Slavonian]. For Yugoslav names beginning thus and not found here, see under following part of the name.

Slavosovce (slä'vôshôftsĕ), Slovak *Slavošovce,* Hung. *Nagyszabos* (nŏ'dyůsŏ'bôsh), village (pop. 1,038), S Slovakia, Czechoslovakia, on railroad and 12 mi. WNW of Roznava; paper mills.

Slavovitsa (slävôvē'tsä), village (pop. 2,604), Pleven dist., N Bulgaria, on Iskar R. and 18 mi. NNW of Pleven; wheat, corn, livestock.

Slavsk (släfsk), city (1939 pop. 3,460), N Kaliningrad oblast, Russian SFSR, 8 mi. WSW of Sovetsk, in marshy wooded dist.; lumber milling. Until 1945, in East Prussia and called Heinrichswalde (hīn'rĭkhsvăldů).

Slavsko (släf'sků), Pol. *Sławsko* (swäf'skô), village (1939 pop. over 500), SE Drogobych oblast, Ukrainian SSR, in the Beshchady, on right tributary of Stry R. and 15 mi. S of Skole; winter resort (skiing grounds); logging, sheep raising.

Slavskoye (släf'skŭyů), town (1939 pop. 2,007), W Kaliningrad oblast, Russian SFSR, on rail spur and 15 mi. S of Kaliningrad; agr. market. Remains of 13th-cent. castle. Until 1945, in East Prussia and called Kreuzburg (kroits'bŏŏrk).

Slavuta (slä'vŏŏtů), city (1926 pop. 10,478), N Kamenets-Podolski oblast, Ukrainian SSR, on Goryn R. and 12 mi. NW of Shepetovka, in dry forest region; health resort; sawmilling, paper mfg., food processing. Feldspar quarries.

Slavyanka (slůvyän'kŭ). **1** Village (1926 pop. 2,277), S South Kazakhstan oblast, Kazakh SSR, 15 mi. S of Ilich; cotton. **2** Town (1943 pop. over 500), SW Maritime Territory, Russian SFSR, port on Peter the Great Bay, 30 mi. SSW of Vladivostok; fish canneries.

Slavyanoserbsk (slůvyä"nŭsyĕrpsk'), village (1926 pop. 3,170), S central Voroshilovgrad oblast, Ukrainian SSR, in the Donbas, on the Northern Donets and 16 mi. NW of Voroshilovgrad; truck produce.

Slavyanovo (slävyä'nôvô), village (pop. 6,700), Pleven dist., N Bulgaria, 15 mi. S of Nikopol; flour milling; livestock, truck, oil-bearing plants. Formerly Turski Trastenik or Trastenik.

Slavyansk (slůvyänsk'), city (1926 pop. 28,771; 1939 pop. 75,542), N Stalino oblast, Ukrainian SSR, in the Donbas, 60 mi. NNW of Stalino. Industrial center; mfg. (concrete mixers, soda chemicals, porcelain insulators); salt and limestone works. Teachers col. City founded 1676 as fortress Tor. Health resort (mud baths) just NE.

Slavyanskaya (slůvyän'skĭů), village (1926 pop. 18,931), W Krasnodar Territory, Russian SFSR, on Protoka (right) arm of Kuban R. delta mouth and 45 mi. WNW of Krasnodar; agr.-processing center; flour mill, cotton gin, winery.

Slawa (swä'vä), Pol. *Sława,* Ger. *Schlesiersee* (shlā'zyůrzā"), town (1939 pop. 1,803; 1946 pop. 1,602) in Lower Silesia, after 1945 in Zielona Gora prov., W Poland, on small lake, 25 mi. ESE of Grünberg (Zielona Gora); agr. market (grain, vegetables, fruit, potatoes). Until 1937, called Schlawa; after 1945, briefly called Slawa Slaska, Pol. *Sława Śląska.*

Slawi (slä'wē), town (pop. 17,115), N central Java, Indonesia, 45 mi. ESE of Cheribon; trade center for agr. area (sugar, rice, peanuts); textile mills.

Slawiecice (swä"vyĕ-chē'tsĕ), Pol. *Sławięcice,* Ger. *Slawentzitz* (slä'vůntsĭts) and (c.1935–45) *Ehrenforst* (â'růnfôrst), village, Upper Silesia, after 1945 in Opole prov., S Poland, 5 mi. E of Kedzierzyn, chemical col. Former Hohenlohe estate.

Slawno (swäv'nô), Pol. *Sławno,* Ger. *Schlawe* (shlä'vů), town (1939 pop. 9,768; 1946 pop. 4,845) in Pomerania, after 1945 in Koszalin prov., NW Poland, 17 mi. WSW of Stolp (Slupsk); rail junction; mfg. (furniture, food products), fruit and vegetable processing. Chartered 1317. In Second World War, c.50% destroyed.

Slawsko, Ukrainian SSR: see SLAVSKO.

Slayden (slā'důn), town (pop. 90), Dickson co., N central Tenn., 40 mi. WNW of Nashville, in timber and farm area.

Slayton, village (pop. 1,887), ⊙ Murray co., SW Minn., on Des Moines R. and 28 mi. E of Pipestone; trade center in grain and livestock area; settled 1881.

Sleaford (slē'fůrd), urban district (1931 pop. 7,025; 1951 census 7,282), Parts of Kesteven, central Lincolnshire, England, on Slea R. and 17 mi. SSE of Lincoln; mfg. of agr. machinery and electrical equipment; malt processing. Has medieval church and fragments of castle built 1130.

Sleaford Bay, inlet of Indian Ocean, SE Eyre Peninsula, S South Australia, just W of Cape Catastrophe; 10 mi. E–W, 5 mi. N–S.

Slea Head (slā), cape on the Atlantic, W Co. Kerry, Ireland, 35 mi. WSW of Tralee, at foot of Mt. Eagle and at N entrance to Dingle Bay; 52°6′N 10°27′W. Offshore are Blasket Isls. Just NW is Dunmore Head, W extremity of Irish mainland.

Sleat, Sound of (slāt), strait (23 mi. long, 2–7 mi. wide) bet. Isle of Skye and mainland of Inverness, Scotland; connects with the Inner Sound (N) through Kyle Rhea and Loch Alsh, and with the Sea of the Hebrides (S). Point of Sleat, S tip of Skye, is at 57°2′N 6°2′W.

Sledge, town (pop. 383), Quitman co., NW Miss., 12 mi. N of Marks, in cotton-growing area.

Sleeper, town (pop. 131), Laclede co., S central Mo., in the Ozarks, near Gasconade R., 7 mi. NE of Lebanon.

Sleeper Islands, SE Keewatin Dist., Northwest Territories, group of c.30 small isls. and islets in Hudson Bay, off W Ungava Peninsula; 57°30′N 79°45′W. Group extends 60 mi. N–S.

Sleeping Bear Point, Mich.: see GLEN HAVEN.

Sleepy Eye, city (pop. 3,278), Brown co., S Minn., on Cottonwood R. and 14 mi. W of New Ulm; food-processing center in grain and livestock area; dairy products, canned vegetables, poultry. Platted 1872. State park is here.

Sleepy Hollow. 1 Ravine in Greene co., SE N.Y., near PALENVILLE, where legendary Rip Van Winkle took his 20-year nap. **2** Locality at NORTH TARRYTOWN, Westchester co., SE N.Y., setting of Washington Irving's "Legend of Sleepy Hollow." Old Dutch church here (restored) was built 1684–97; Irving is buried in its graveyard.

Sleetmute, village (pop. 120), W Alaska, on Kuskokwim R. at mouth of Holitna R., 90 mi. ESE of Holy Cross; fur farming, mercury mining. Sometimes spelled Sleitmut.

Sleidinge (slī′dĭng-ů), town (pop. 5,711), East Flanders prov., NW Belgium, 6 mi. NNW of Ghent; textiles, wood products, furniture; agr. market. Formerly spelled Sleydinge.

Sleitmut, Alaska: see SLEETMUTE.

Slemish (slā′mĭsh), hill (1,437 ft.) in central Co. Antrim, Northern Ireland, 7 mi. E of Ballymena. According to tradition St. Patrick was a herdsman here in his youth.

Sleptsovskaya, Russian SFSR: see ORDZHONIKIDZEVSKAYA.

Slesin (shlĕ′sēn), Pol. *Ślesin*, town (pop. 2,167), Poznan prov., W central Poland, on L. Slesin, 11 mi. N of Konin; brewing, flour milling. L. Slesin, here, is 5 mi. long.

Slesvig, Denmark and Germany: see SCHLESWIG.

Sletten (slĕ′tůn), fishing settlement (pop. 248), Julianehaab dist., SW Greenland, on Agdluitsok Fjord (25-mi. inlet of the Atlantic), 25 mi. ENE of Julianehaab; 60°33′N 45°21′W. Radio station.

Sleydinge, Belgium: see SLEIDINGE.

Slezska Ostrava (slĕ′skä ô′strävä), Czech *Slezská Ostrava*, Ger. *Schlesisch-Ostrau* (shlā′zĭsh-ô′strou), town (pop. 18,109), NE Silesia, Czechoslovakia, on right bank of Ostravice R., just E of and across from Ostrava; rail junction; coal-mining and metallurgical center; part of industrial complex of Greater OSTRAVA. Because of large Polish pop., it was formerly known as *Polnish-Ostrau*. First coal mining of Ostrava-Karvina field began here in 1770.

Slezsko, region, Europe: see SILESIA.

Sliac, Czechoslovakia: see ZVOLEN.

Slick, town (pop. 151), Creek co., central Okla., 20 mi. WNW of Okmulgee, in agr. and oil-producing area.

Slickville, village (pop. 1,266), Westmoreland co., SW Pa., 11 mi. N of Greensburg.

Slidell (slīdĕl′), town (pop. 3,464), St. Tammany parish, SE La., on short Bayou Bonfouca (navigable), near L. Pontchartrain (bridged near here to New Orleans, 27 mi. SW); shipbuilding; machine-shop products, lumber, creosoted products, packed sea food, fertilizer, brick, tile. Hunting, fishing near by. Settled after Civil War; inc. 1888.

Slide Mountain (4,204 ft.), Ulster co., SE N.Y., highest peak of the Catskills, c.18 mi. W of Kingston.

Sliedrecht (slē′drĕkht), town (pop. 15,088), South Holland prov., SW Netherlands, on Lower Merwede R. and 4 mi. E of Dordrecht; mfg. of machinery, dredges, steam engines, cement, oil cakes.

Sliema (slē′mä), town (pop. 24,294), E Malta, on peninsula bet. 2 Mediterranean inlets, terminating in Fort Tigné, which guards entrance to Marsamuscetto Harbour. Ferry to Valletta (SE) across the harbor. Modern residential town, favored by the British. Has a fine beach. Severely damaged by Second World War air raids.

Slieve Anierin (slēv), mountain (1,922 ft.), central Co. Leitrim, Ireland, 5 mi. NE of Drumshambo; coal mines.

Slieve Bloom, mountain range, Ireland, extending 15 mi. NE–SW along border of cos. Laoighis and Offaly; rises to 1,733 ft. at Arderin, 15 mi. W of Port Laoighise.

Slieve Car (kär′), peak (2,369 ft.) in Nephin Beg Range, W Co. Mayo, Ireland, 14 mi. NNW of Newport.

Slieve Commedagh (kŏ′můdä), peak (2,512 ft.) of the Mourne Mts., S Co. Down, Northern Ireland, 2 mi. WSW of Newcastle.

Slieve Donard (dŏ′nůrd), peak (2,796 ft.), highest point of Mourne Mts., S Co. Down, Northern Ireland, 2 mi. SW of Newcastle.

Slieve Gamph (gămf′) or **Ox Mountains,** range, W Co. Sligo and NE Co. Mayo, Ireland, extending 20 mi. NE–SW; rises to 1,778 ft. on Knockalongy, WSW of Sligo.

Slieve Gullion (gŭl′yůn), mountain (1,893 ft.), S Co. Armagh, Northern Ireland, 6 mi. SW of Newry.

Slieve Mish (mĭsh′), mountain range, W central Co. Kerry, Ireland, extending 12 mi. E–W, bet. Tralee Bay and Castlemaine Harbour (an extension of Dingle Bay); rises to 2,796 ft. on Baurtregaum, 7 mi. SW of Tralee.

Slieve Miskish (mĭskĭsh′, mĭs′–), mountain range, SW Co. Cork, Ireland, extending 10 mi. NE–SW along peninsula bet. Bantry Bay and Kenmare R.; rise to 2,044 ft. 4 mi. NE of Castletown Bere. Range is continued N by Caha Mts.

Slieve Mor (môr′), mountain (2,204 ft.) near N coast of Achill Isl., W Co. Mayo, Ireland; highest point of isl.

Sligo (slī′gō), Gaelic *Sligeach*, county (□ 693.6; pop. 62,375), in Connacht, NW Ireland; ⊙ Sligo. Bounded by cos. Roscommon (S), May (S and W), Leitrim (E), and the Atlantic (N). Drained by Moy, Unshin, and other rivers. Loughs Gill and Arrow are largest lakes of co. Surface is mountainous in center; Slieve Gamph or Ox Mts. rise to 1,778 ft. on Knockalongy; leveling toward coast, Sligo Bay, and Moy R. valley. Coast is low and sandy, indented by Killala, Drumore, Sligo, and Drumcliff bays. Coney and Inishmurray isls., off coast, have anc. remains. Sea fisheries are important; cattle raising and potato growing are main agr. occupations. Barites are mined at Glanaff. Industries include iron founding, dairying, bacon curing, mfg. of fertilizer. Besides Sligo, other towns are Ballymote, Tubbercurry, and Easky. Drumcliff has remains of anc. monastic establishment; megalithic stone monuments at Carrowmore. Stone mausoleum (c.2000 B.C.) was excavated (1923–26) at Creevykeel by archaeologists.

Sligo, Gaelic *Sligeach*, urban district (pop. 12,920), ⊙ Co. Sligo, Ireland, in NE part of co., at head of Sligo Bay, at mouth of Garrogue R., and near Lough Gill, 110 mi. NW of Dublin; 54°16′N 8°28′W; seaport and fishing center, with dock installations, terminus of shipping lines from England and Scotland. Industries include iron founding, bacon and ham curing, mfg. of fertilizer; there is important woolen trade. Features are 17th-cent. St. John's Church and ruins of Sligo Abbey, founded 1252 by Maurice Fitzgerald. Town is 1st mentioned (c.800) as target for Danish raid; Sligo became (1245) hq. of Maurice Fitzgerald, earl of Kildare, who built castle here. In 1641 town was sacked and abbey burned by Parliamentarians under Sir Frederick Hamilton; it was taken 1645 by Sir Charles Coote. At near-by Carrowmore is large group of megalithic stone monuments.

Sligo, borough (pop. 913), Clarion co., W central Pa., 9 mi. SW of Clarion; bituminous coal.

Sligo Bay, inlet (10 mi. wide, 7 mi. long) of the Atlantic, NE Co. Sligo, Ireland. At head of bay is Sligo; Drumcliff Bay extends E from Sligo Bay.

Slijk-Ewijk (slīk-ā′vīk), village (pop. 341), on right bank of Waal R., Gelderland prov., E central Netherlands, 5 mi. NW of Nijmegen; fruit, raspberries, strawberries; wooden-shoe mfg. Sometimes spelled Slyk-Ewyk. On left bank of the Waal, 2 mi. SW, is village (pop. 605) of Ewijk or Ewyk.

Slikkerveer (slĭ′kůrvār), town (pop. 5,060), South Holland prov., W Netherlands, on New Maas R. and 7 mi. ESE of Rotterdam; mfg. (electric motors, electric appliances).

Slim, village (pop. 647), S Perak, Malaya, on Slim R. and 12 mi. N of Tanjong Malim, in rubber growing dist. Its railroad station, **Slim River** (pop. 747), is on W coast line, 6 mi. W, on Slim R. (right affluent of Bernam R.); scene of decisive Jap. victory in 1942.

Slinger, village (pop. 919), Washington co., E Wis., 27 mi. NW of Milwaukee; mfg. (electrical equipment, musical instruments, beer). Near by is Cedar L. (resort). Formerly Schleisingerville.

Slioch (slē′ůkh), mountain (3,217 ft.) in W Ross and Cromarty, Scotland, 13 mi. ESE of Gairloch, overlooking Loch Maree.

Slippery Rock, residential borough (pop. 2,294), Butler co., W Pa., 16 mi. NW of Butler; farming center; bituminous coal; timber; potatoes, corn, hay. State teachers col. Inc. 1851.

Slissen (slēsĕn′), village (pop. 600), Oran dept., NW Algeria, in the Tell Atlas, on railroad and 26 mi. SSW of Sidi-bel-Abbès; sheep raising, lumbering.

Slite (slē′tů), town (pop. 2,139), Gotland co., SE Sweden, on NE coast of Gotland isl., 18 mi. ENE of Visby; port and resort; cement mfg.; limestone quarries. Grain, sugar beets, potatoes, flax.

Sliven (slē′vĕn), city (pop. 35,553), Yambol dist., E central Bulgaria, on SE slope of central Balkan Mts., 60 mi. W of Burgas; agr. and mfg. center; woolen textiles, carpets, hand embroidery. Textile school. Has ruins of fortresses, Turkish mosques. Health resort is 7 mi. SE, with mineral baths. Bituminous coal mines near by (NW). Under Turkish rule (15th–19th cent.). Known as Sliven after 1153; later also called Slivno.

Slivenec (slĭ′vĕnĕts), village (pop. 1,726), central Bohemia, Czechoslovakia, 6 mi. SW of Prague; marble quarrying.

Slivnitsa (slēv′nĭtsä), village (pop. 4,574), Sofia dist., W Bulgaria, 18 mi. NW of Sofia; grain, livestock. Defeat here (1885) of Serbs by Bulgarians commemorated by monument.

Slivno, Bulgaria: see SLIVEN.

Sloan. 1 Town (pop. 654), Woodbury co., W Iowa, 21 mi. SSE of Sioux City; feed milling. **2** Village (pop. 4,698), Erie co., W N.Y., just E of Buffalo; railroad shops. Inc. 1896.

Sloatsburg, village (pop. 2,018), Rockland co., SE N.Y., on Ramapo R., in the Ramapos, near N.J. line, 4 mi. NW of Suffern; lumber milling, textile mfg. Settled before 1775, inc. 1929.

Sloboda (slŭbůdä′). **1** Village (1939 pop. over 500), NW Smolensk oblast, Russian SFSR, 25 mi. ESE of Velizh; flax. **2** Town (1948 pop. over 500), central Voronezh oblast, Russian SFSR, near Khrenovoye.

Slobodka (slŭbôt′kŭ), town (1948 pop. over 2,000), NW Odessa oblast, Ukrainian SSR, 13 mi. W of Balta; rail junction. Village of Slobodzeya or Slobodzeya Russkaya (1926 pop. 5,945) is just W.

Slobodskoi or **Slobodskoy** (slŭbůtskoi′), city (1936 pop. 18,600), N central Kirov oblast, Russian SFSR, on Vyatka R. and 20 mi. ENE of Kirov; rail spur terminus; fur-processing, tanning center; food processing. Chartered 1546.

Slobodzeya (slŭbůdzyā′ů), village (1926 pop. 5,471), SE Moldavian SSR, on left bank of Dniester R. and 7 mi. SSE of Tiraspol; vineyards, orchards; distilling. Sometimes called Slobodzeya Moldavskaya. Another Slobodzeya or Slobodzeya Russkaya (1926 pop. 5,945) is just W of SLOBODKA, Odessa oblast, Ukrainian SSR.

Slobozia (slôbô′zyä), town (1948 pop. 7,714), Ialomita prov., SE Rumania, on Ialomita R. and 25 mi. N of Calarasi; rail junction and cattle market; flour milling, mfg. of candles. Stud farm. Has 17th-cent. church. Amara health resort is 4 mi. to N, on Saline Lake.

Slocan (slōkăn′), city (pop. 183), SE B.C., on Slocan R. at S end of Slocan L., and 21 mi. NNW of Nelson; silver, lead, zinc mining.

Slocan Lake (□ 24), S B.C., 22 mi. NNW of Nelson; 25 mi. long, 1–2 mi. wide. At S end is Slocan. Drained S by Slocan R.

Slocan River, S B.C., issues from S end of Slocan L. at Slocan, flows 35 mi. SSW to Kootenay R. at Shoreacres, 12 mi. WSW of Nelson.

Slocomb (slō′kům), town (pop. 1,219), Geneva co., SE Ala., 15 mi. SW of Dothan, near Fla. line; farming. Settled 1884, inc. 1900.

Slocum, village, R.I.: see NORTH KINGSTOWN.

Slocum, Fort, N.Y.: see NEW ROCHELLE.

Sloe, Het (hĕt slōō′), SW Netherlands, inlet of Western Scheldt, W of Flushing; extends c.8 mi. N; separated by dyke connecting Walcheren isl. (W) and South Beveland isl. (E) from Veersche Gat (N).

Sloinge (slû′ĭng-ů), Swedish *Slöinge*, village (pop. 657), Halland co., SW Sweden, near the Kattegat, 13 mi. NNW of Halmstad; grain, flax, sugar beets.

Sloka (slō′kä), Ger. *Schlock*, city (pop. 4,651), W central Latvia, in Vidzeme, 18 mi. W of Riga, bet. Gulf of Riga and lower Lielupe R.; industrial center; mfg. (sulphite pulp, paper), sawmilling, stone cutting.

Slomikhino, Kazakh SSR: see FURMANOVO.

Slomniki (swômnē′kē), Pol. *Słomniki*, town (pop. 4,303), Krakow prov., S Poland, on railroad and 16 mi. NNE of Cracow; sawmilling, flour milling.

Slonim (slô′nyĭm), Pol. *Słonim* (sōōō′nyēm), city (1931 pop. 16,284), SW Baranovichi oblast, Belorussian SSR, on Shchara R. and 29 mi. W of Baranovichi; mfg. of agr. machinery, matches, soap, candles, bricks, woolen textiles; tanning, distilling, flour milling, sawmilling (prefabricated houses). Phosphorite deposits near by (NE). Has 17th-cent. palace and several old churches. Founded 11th cent.; successively under Lithuania, duchy of Galich, and Poland; chartered 1552. Developed as trading center following opening (1777) of Dnieper-Neman Canal. Passed (1795) from Poland to Russia; reverted (1921) to Poland; ceded to USSR in 1945.

Slonta (slôn′tä), town (pop. 2,000), W Cyrenaica, Libya, on road and 18 mi. SW of Cyrene, on the plateau Gebel el Akhdar. Has troglodyte dwellings and noted grotto with anc. wall carvings. Scene of fighting (1942) in Second World War.

Slope, county (□ 1,226; pop. 2,315), SW N.Dak., on Mont. line; ⊙ Amidon. Rich agr. area with black loam soil and extensive lignite deposits. Drained by Little Missouri R. Livestock, wheat, hay. Black Butte, highest point in state (alt. 3,468 ft.), is here. Formed 1915.

Slot, The, Solomon Isls.: see NEW GEORGIA SOUND.

Slottsbron (slôts′brōōn″), village (pop. 937), Varmland co., W Sweden, on NW shore of L. Vaner, 14 mi. WSW of Karlstad; lumber and pulp mills.

Slough (slou), municipal borough (1931 pop. 33,530; 1951 census 66,439), SE Buckingham, England, 6 mi. E of Maidenhead, 18 mi. W of London; modern industrial center with varied light industries (aircraft parts, radios, asbestos, metal products, pharmaceuticals, chemicals, food products, leather goods). Town's industrial growth dates from 1930s, when the Slough Trading Estate was established here to attract light industries and provide employment for men thrown out of work in the large staple industries in other regions of Great Britain. Site of Br. Orphan Asylum. The Herschel family, noted astronomers, lived here. Borough includes industrial towns of Farnham (NW; pop. 6,127), Burnham (NW; pop. 2,889), and Langley (E; pop. 3,535).

Sloup, Czechoslovakia: see MORAVIAN KARST.

Slovakia (slōvä'kēů, –vă'–), Slov. *Slovensko* (slô'-věnskô), Ger. *Slowakei* (slōväkī'), Hung. *Szlovákia* (slōvä'kyä), E region (in 1948: □ 18,902; pop. 3,434,369) and one of the 2 constituent states (Czech *Země*) of CZECHOSLOVAKIA, bounded by Austria (SW), Hungary (S), Ruthenia (E; part of Soviet Ukraine), Poland (N), and adjoining Moravia and Silesia (W); ⊙ Bratislava. Largely mountainous, it is traversed E-W by W wing of the Carpathians and dominated in N by the Tatra Mts. or High Tatra (highest peak, 8,737 ft.); the Low Tatra (6,707 ft.) are in the center; the Beskids (5,658 ft.) along Polish border; the White Carpathians (3,175 ft.) and Little Carpathians (2,473 ft.) in W. N and central Slovakia are extensively forested; upland pastures and meadows support intensive sheep grazing (wool, meat, cheese). Broken crystalline massifs are separated by deep valleys. Mountain climate varies with exposure and altitude; lowest winter temp. is registered in Orava valley (severe N winds). Upper Vah and adjacent valleys noted for lumbering (spruce, pine, birch) and woodworking industries, with major centers at Ruzomberok and Liptovsky Svaty Mikulas; Hron R. vicinity is known for trout fishing and hunting. S Slovakia belongs to Alföld plain of Hungary. The Little Alföld and Great Schütt isl. (W) are drained by Lower Vah and the Danube, E lowlands by Ondava and Laborec rivers. Mild climate and fertile soils favor wide variety of crops (wheat, barley, sugar beets, corn, clover, tobacco, green vegetables, paprika, melons, sunflowers, pickling herbs); here are extensive vineyards and orchards (including almond trees), livestock breeding, poultry farming. Main industries are connected with agr. (food processing, wine making, agr.-machinery mfg.). Bratislava, first Czechoslovak port on internationalized Danube, specializes in cable production and petroleum refining. Mining concentrates in Slovak Ore Mts. (high-grade iron ore, copper, mercury at Gelnica), and W offshoots (gold, silver, lead); lignite deposits are worked at Handlova. SW corner of Slovakia has been thoroughly prospected for oil; there are producing wells at Gbely. Other mineral resources: magnesite, limestone, salt, semi-precious stones (milky opals), important antimony deposits near Roznava. Mineral springs are abundant. Principal cities are Bratislava, Kosice, Trnava, Nitra. Komarno is second port on the Danube. Levoca and Bardejov are famous as late-Gothic and Renaissance towns. The High Tatra area is known for winter-sports and health resorts. Former communication difficulties left imprint on Slovak population (Slavs), R.C. and mostly dependent on soil for subsistence, who have preserved their handicrafts and colorful regional folklore. Post-war economic plans have encouraged industrialization; major water-power works are in construction on Orava, Vah, and Hron rivers. Although the Slovaks and Czechs are ethnically and linguistically closely related, they have been politically and culturally separate for 1,000 years. The region was settled by Slavic tribes in 5th-6th cent.; part of Great Moravian Empire (9th cent.); occupied by Magyars in 10th cent., and absorbed by Hungarian kingdom thereafter, until 1918. Right bank of Vah R. belonged to Moravia till 12th cent. Tatar invaders overran most of land in 13th cent. German colonists in Spis area (12th cent.) acquired great privileges. Hussites sought asylum here in 14th-15th cent. Germanization was introduced under Maria Theresa. Indirect contact with Bohemia was intermittently maintained through several rulers (Wenceslaus II and III, Jagellons, and Hapsburgs) combining sovereignty over Bohemia and Hungary. National consciousness awoke 1790–1840. Because of concentration of land in hands of Magyar landowners, large immigration to U.S. took place (1900–10). The Slovak independence movement grew and when agreement bet. Czech and Slovak leaders was reached in 1918, the union of Slovak and Czech lands was proclaimed. Treaty of Trianon incorporated into prov. of Slovakia 1,000,000 Magyars, creating minority problem. Slovakian agitation for greater autonomy continued bet. the 2 world wars. After Munich pact (1938) Poland seized parts of Orava and Spis area (Javornica), and Hungary a large strip of lowlands S of Bratislava-Kosice line. Antagonism between Slovaks and Czechs culminated in secession from Prague organized by Joseph Tiso (who was supported by Hitler), first as autonomous area within the Republic (1938–39) then as independent state (March, 1939). Slovakia was proclaimed Ger. protectorate (Aug., 1939), declared war on U.S. (1941). Liberated in 1944–45 by USSR troops after Slovak uprising against Germans (Aug., 1944). Pending Ger. withdrawal from W Czechoslovakia, Benes coalition government resided at Kosice (April–May, 1945). Reincorporated into Czechoslovakia (1945), Slovakia recovered its 1938 status and territories lost to Hungary and Poland. Since 1949, it has been subdivided into 6 provinces (Czech *Kraj*), Bratislava, Zilina, Banska Bystrica, Kosice, Presov, Nitra. The Potsdam Conference (1945) made provision for an exchange of Magyar and Slovak minorities.

Slovakian Karst (slōvä'kēůn kärst", –vă'–), Slovak *Jihoslovenský Kras* (yĭ'hôslô"věnskē kräs"), hilly region in S Slovakia, Czechoslovakia; extends ENE-WSW, bet. Plesivec and Moldava nad Bodvou, and partly across Hung. border. Local limestone formations are studded with stalactite caves and caverns, many of which provided shelter for Stone Age man. Greatest tourist attractions are the scenic Domica labyrinth (c.5 mi. SE of Plesivec; the latest discovered), BARADLA CAVES, Ardova and Silica caves (respectively just SE and 5 mi. E of Plesivec).

Slovak Ore Mountains (slō'väk, –văk), Slovak *Slovenské Rudohorie* (slô'věnskā rōō'dôhôryě), Hung. *Gömör-Szepesi Érchegység* (gů'môr-sě'pěshě ārts'-hĕdyůsäg), range of Carpathian mtn. system in S Slovakia, Czechoslovakia; extend c.85 mi. bet. Zvolen (W) and Kosice (E); rise to 4,554 ft. in Stolica. Noted for mineral resources, which play an important part in Czechoslovak economy. Mining of high-grade iron ore, especially in S and E, antimony ore near Roznava, mercury and copper at Gelnica, magnesite at Kosice, Lucenec, and Jelsava. Semi-precious stones (agates, amethysts). Ipel R. rises on SW, Slana R. on N slopes. Famous ice cavern of Dobsina is on N slope.

Slovan, village (pop. 1,885, with adjacent Atlasburg), Washington co., SW Pa., 20 mi. WSW of Pittsburgh.

Slovechno (slŭvyĕch'nů), agr. town (1926 pop. 2,223), N Zhitomir oblast, Ukrainian SSR, on S edge of Pripet Marshes, 32 mi. NNW of Korosten; flax, buckwheat, potatoes.

Slovenia (slōvē'nēů), Slovenian *Slovenija* (slôvě'-nēä), constituent republic (□ 7,796; pop. 1,389,084), NW Yugoslavia; ⊙ Ljubljana. Bounded by Italy (W), Austria (N), Hungary (NE), Croatia (S), and Free Territory of Trieste (SW). Generally mountainous, it lies in Dinaric Alps and Eastern Alps (here called Slovenian Alps), separated by Sava R.; highest peak, the Triglav (c.9,395 ft.), is in Julian Alps. Chief rivers, Sava and Drava; largest lakes, Bohinj and Bled. Only 20% of the area, chiefly plains and river valleys, is cultivated, but c.65% of pop. engage in agr. Potatoes are leading crop (13% of cultivated area); various grains (wheat, corn, rye, barley, oats, buckwheat, millet), vegetables, industrial plants (hops, flax, rape, chicory), fruit (notably apples) also grown; vineyards. Forests occupy 40% of area and forestry is well developed. Many fine pastures (notably in Julian Alps) are used for stock raising (chiefly dairy cattle). Poultry raising, beekeeping, fishing. Coal mined at Trbovlje, Zagorje, Hrastnik, Velenje, and Kocevje, metal ore at Litija (lead) and Idrija (mercury). Chief hydroelectric plant is at Fala; health resorts at Bled, Lasko, Rimske Toplice, Dobrna, Rogaska Slatina, and Slatina Radenci. Mfg. (notably heavy metallurgy) and home industry are well developed. Slovenia has good roads and a thick rail network. Besides Ljubljana, the only cities are Maribor and Celje. After being settled (6th cent.) by Slovenians, region passed to an early Slav state, and later (748) to the Franks. At the division of Charlemagne's empire, the region was divided bet. dukes of Bavaria and Friuli. By 14th cent. it passed to the Hapsburgs, who controlled it until 1918, when Slovenia prov. of Yugoslavia was carved out of several Austrian provs. (mainly Carniola and Styria). Prov. was reorganized into 2 oblasts in 1921 and, 1929–41, into Drava banovina. After Second World War, during which Slovenia was divided bet. Germany (upper Carniola and lower Styria), Italy (lower Carniola), and Hungary (Prekmurje), it reverted to Yugoslavia; became a people's republic in 1946; gained some Italian territory in 1947.

Slovenjgradec (slô'věngrä"děts), Ger. *Windischgraz* (vĭn'dĭshgräts"), anc. *Colatio*, village, N Slovenia, Yugoslavia, on railroad and 22 mi. NNW of Celje, in brown-coal area. Summer resort; leather and lumber industries. Until 1918, in Styria.

Slovenska Bistrica, Yugoslavia: see BISTRICA, NE Slovenia.

Slovenska Lupca (slô'věnskä lyōōp'chä), Slovak *Slovenská L'upča*, Hung. *Zólyomlipcse* (zoi'ômlĭp-chě), village (pop. 2,095), central Slovakia, Czechoslovakia, in the Low Tatra, on Hron R., on railroad and 6 mi. ENE of Banska Bystrice. Has 13th-cent. castle, former hunting lodge of Hung. kings, now an orphanage. Area known for wild-boar hunting, trout fishing. Health resort of Brusno (brōō'snô) (alt. 1,286 ft.), with sulphurous thermal springs and peat baths, is c.5 mi. ENE.

Slovenske Gorice (–skě gô'rĭtsě), Ger. *Windisch Büheln* (vĭn'dĭsh bü'ůln), hilly region, NE Slovenia, Yugoslavia, bet. Drava and Mura rivers. Very fertile and well cultivated; wine- and fruit-growing. LJUTOMER, GORNJA RADGONA, SLATINA RADENCI at E, MARIBOR and PTUJ at S foot.

Slovenske Konjice, Yugoslavia: see KONJICE.

Slovenske Rudohorie, Czechoslovakia: see SLOVAK ORE MOUNTAINS.

Slovensko, Czechoslovakia: see SLOVAKIA.

Slovinky, Czechoslovakia: see KROMPACHY.

Slowakei, Czechoslovakia: see SLOVAKIA.

Sloy, Loch (lŏkh sloi'), small mtn. lake in Dumbarton, Scotland, near Argyll border, 3 mi. W of N tip of Loch Lomond; hydroelectric plant (opened 1950) on its short outlet into Loch Lomond.

Slubice (swōōbē'tsě), Pol. *Słubice*, Ger. *Damm-Vorstadt* (däm'-fôr'shtät), town (1946 pop. 1,689), Zielona Gora prov., W Poland, before 1945 an E suburb of FRANKFURT, Germany, on right bank of the Oder. Chartered after 1945.

Sluch River or **Sluch' River** (slōōch), Pol. *Słucz* (swōōch). **1** In S central Belorussian SSR, rises N of Slutsk in Lithuanian-Belorussian Upland, flows c.90 mi. S, past Slutsk and Starobin, to Pripet R. 10 mi. W of Turov. Lower course formed (1921–39) Poland-USSR border. **2** In NW Ukrainian SSR, rises W of Bazaliya in Volyn-Podolian Upland, flows E, past Staro Konstantinov, N, past Novograd-Volynski, NNW, and N, past Sarny, to Goryn R. 4 mi. NNE of Dubrovitsa; length, 273 mi.

Sluis (slois), Fr. *L'Écluse* (läklüz'), town (pop. 1,615), Zeeland prov., SW Netherlands, on Flanders mainland, at Belg. border, 10 mi. NE of Bruges (Belgium); mfg. of ether, lace, furniture, roofing tiles, building stone. Has 14th-cent. town hall. Sluis was founded in 13th cent. as an additional port of Bruges, and it accorded trading privileges to the Hanseatic League. In 1340 Edward III of England defeated, off Sluis, the fleet of Philip VI of France, which had tried to prevent an English landing. The naval battle of Sluis was 1st important engagement in the Hundred Years War. During the Dutch struggle for independence, Sluis fell to the Spanish in 1587 and was recovered by the Dutch in 1604. It subsequently lost its importance as a port and its harbor silted up. Also spelled Sluys.

Sluiskil (slois'kĭl), town, Zeeland prov., SW Netherlands, on Flanders mainland and 4 mi. S of Terneuzen, on Ghent-Terneuzen Canal; coke ovens; mfg. (coal-tar products, nitrogen fertilizer, hydrogen).

Sluiskin Falls (slōō'skĭn), W central Wash., waterfall 300 ft. high, in S Rainier Natl. Park.

Sluknov (shlōōk'nôf), Czech *Šluknov*, Ger. *Schluckenau* (shlōō'kůnou), town (pop. 3,617), N Bohemia, Czechoslovakia, on railroad and 30 mi. NE of Usti nad Labem; mfg. of cotton and rayon textiles, linen, artificial flowers, feather ornaments.

Slunj (slōō'nyů), village (pop. 2,129), NW Croatia, Yugoslavia, on Korana R. and 26 mi. S of Karlovac; local trade center. Formerly called Sluin or Slovinj Grad.

Slupca (swōōp'tsä), Pol. *Słupca*, Rus. *Sluptsy* (slōōp'tsyĭ), town (pop. 5,133), Poznan prov., W central Poland, on railroad and 40 mi. E of Poznan; flour milling, brick mfg. Until 1919, in Rus. Poland, near Ger. frontier.

Slupia River (swōō'pyä), Pol. *Słupia*, Ger. *Stolpe* (shtôl'pů), in Pomerania, after 1945 in NW Poland, rises in lake area SW of Kartuszy, flows W and WNW past Stolp (Slupsk) to the Baltic at Ustka; 90 mi. long.

Slupsk, Poland: see STOLP.

Sluptsy, Poland: see SLUPCA.

Slutsk (slōōtsk). **1** City (1926 pop. 15,687), W Bobruisk oblast, Belorussian SSR, on Sluch R. and 60 mi. S of Minsk, in grain region; flour and meat industries; mfg. (apparel, enamelware). Passed from Poland to Russia in 1793. During Second World War, held (1941–44) by Germans. **2** City, Leningrad oblast, Russian SFSR: see PAVLOVSK.

Sluys, Netherlands: see SLUIS.

Slyk-Ewyk, Netherlands: see SLIJK-EWIJK.

Slyne Head (slīn), westernmost of group of rocky islets in the Atlantic off W Co. Galway, Ireland, 10 mi. SW of Clifden Just E is islet of Illaunamid.

Slyudyanka (slyōōdyän'kŭ), city (1939 pop. over 10,000), S Irkutsk oblast, Russian SFSR, at SW end of L. Baikal, 50 mi. SSW of Irkutsk, on Trans-Siberian RR; mica-mining center; metalworks. Marble, quartz, radioactive ore deposits near by.

Smaalandsfarvand (smô'lănsfär"vän), sometimes called **Vordingborg Bay** (vôr'dhĭng-bôr), strait, Denmark, extending E from the Great Belt, bet. Zealand isl. (N) and Lolland, Falster, and Moen isls. (S). In NW are Agerso and Omo isls.; in S are Nejro, Fejo, Femo, Asko isls., many small uninhabited islets. Outlets to Baltic Sea: Bogestrom, bet. Zealand and Nyord isl.; Gronsund, bet. Moen and Falster isls.; Guldborg Sound, bet. Falster and Lolland isls. Inner straits: Masnedsund, bet. Zealand and small Masnedo isl., crossed by rail and highway bridge from Vordingborg which also crosses Storstrom strait, bet. Masnedo and Falster isls.; Ulvsund, bet. Zealand and Moen.

Smaalenene, Norway: see OSTFOLD.
Smackover (smăˈkōvûr), city (pop. 2,495), Union co., S Ark., 12 mi. NNW of El Dorado; oil wells, refineries. Vocational school for Negroes near by. Inc. 1922.
Sma' Glen, Scotland: see GLENALMOND.
Smala-des-Souassi (smälä'-dā-swäsē'), village, Sousse dist., E Tunisia, 33 mi. S of Sousse; seat of nomadic Souassi tribe. Horse breeding, olive-oil pressing, artisan mfg.
Smaland (smō'länd), Swedish *Småland*, province [Swedish *landskap*] (□ 12,239; pop. 612,472), S Sweden, on the Baltic. Included in Jonkoping co., Kronoberg co., and part of Kalmar co.
Smalands Anneberg (smō'länts ä'nûbĕr"yû), Swedish *Smålands Anneberg*, village (pop. 861), Jonkoping co., S Sweden, 13 mi. W of Varnamo; grain, potatoes, stock.
Smalands Rydaholm (rü"dähôlm'), Swedish *Smålands Rydaholm*, village (pop. 878), Jonkoping co., S Sweden, 17 mi. NW of Vaxjo; woodworking. Has Romanesque church.
Smalandsstenar (–tā"när), Swedish *Smålandsstenar*, village (pop. 1,490), Jonkoping co., S Sweden, 20 mi. W of Varnamo; metal- and woodworking. Anc. cairns near by.
Smalands Taberg (tä'bĕr"yû), Swedish *Smålands Taberg*, village (pop. 1,693), Jonkoping co., S Sweden, at foot of the Taberg, a mtn. (1,125 ft.) 7 mi. SSW of Jonkoping; iron mining, begun in 17th cent., abandoned in 19th cent., resumed 1939. Woolen milling, metalworking, furniture mfg. Tourist resort.
Smalcald, Germany: see SCHMALKALDEN.
Smale (smôl), town (pop. 48), Monroe co., E central Ark., 11 mi. E of Clarendon.
Smalininkai or **Smalininkay** (smälēnēn'kī), Ger. *Schmalleningken* (shmä'lûnĭng-kûn), city (1941 pop. 1,321), SW Lithuania, on Neman R. and 20 mi. E of Sovetsk; shipbuilding, sawmilling. In Memel Territory, 1920–39.
Smalkald, Germany: see SCHMALKALDEN.
Small, Cape, SW Maine, peninsula marking NE boundary of Casco Bay; summer colony. Small Point and Bald Head are seaward extensions.
Smallbridge, England: see ROCHDALE.
Small Heath, E industrial suburb (pop. 32,127) of Birmingham, NW Warwick, England.
Small Isles, insular parish (□ 59; pop. 281), Inner Hebrides, Inverness, Scotland, comprising Canna, Eigg, Hyskier, Muck, Rum, and Sanday isls.
Smara or **Semara** (sämä'rä), village and oasis (pop. 266), Saguia el Hamra, Sp. West Africa, 100 mi. ESE of Aiun; 26°34'N 11°30'W. Junction of caravan tracks. Occupied by Spaniards 1934.
Smarje or **Smarje pri Jelsah** (shmär'yĕ prē yĕl'shä), Slovenian *Šmarje pri Jelšah*, Ger. *Sankt Marein* (zängkt mä'rīn), village, E Slovenia, Yugoslavia, on railroad and 12 mi. E of Celje, in brown-coal area; hydroelectric plant. Until 1918, in Styria.
Smarts Mountain (3,240 ft.), Grafton co., W N.H., near the Connecticut, 6 mi. ENE of Lyme.
Smeaton (smē'tûn), village (pop. 250), central Sask., 45 mi. ENE of Prince Albert; dairying, wheat.
Smederevo (smĕ'dĕrĕvô), Ger. *Semendria* (zĕmĕn'drēä), town (pop. 15,455), N Serbia, Yugoslavia, port on the Danube at mouth of W arm of Morava R., and 24 mi. ESE of Belgrade. Rail terminus (repair shops); steel plant; petroleum refinery; mfg. of rolling stock, agr. machinery; flour milling, fishing; trade center for winegrowing region (noted for grapes, white wine). Site of Serbian fortress (begun in 1429; seat of Serbian ruler George Brankovich) which fell to Turks in 1459.
Smederevska Palanka, Yugoslavia: see PALANKA, central Serbia.
Smedjebacken (smā'dyûbä"kûn), town (pop. 2,847), Kopparberg co., central Sweden, 7 mi. E of Ludvika; N terminus of Stromsholm Canal; ironworks. Tourist resort.
Smedovo (smĕ'dôvô), village (pop. 5,939), Kolarovgrad dist., E Bulgaria, 15 mi. SSE of Kolarovgrad; vineyards, grain, livestock.
Smedstad, Norway: see SMESTAD.
Smedstorp (smāts'tôrp"), village (pop. 402), Kristianstad co., S Sweden, 9 mi. W of Simrishamn; grain, potatoes, sugar beets, livestock.
Smeerenburg, Spitsbergen: see AMSTERDAMOYA.
Smela (smyĕ'lŭ), city (1926 pop. 23,324), SE Kiev oblast, Ukrainian SSR, 17 mi. SSW of Cherkassy; rail junction; sugar-refining center; flour milling, machine mfg., woodworking. Developed in 19th cent. In Second World War, held (1941–43) by Germans.
Smeloye (smyĕ'lŭyû), village (1926 pop. 7,014), W central Sumy oblast, Ukrainian SSR, 13 mi. NNE of Romny; flour milling.
Smeltertown, industrial suburb (1940 pop. 2,289), El Paso co., extreme W Texas, just NW of El Paso, on the Rio Grande; metallurgical plants.
Smelterville, town (pop. 76), Shoshone co., N Idaho, 5 mi. W of Kellogg, in mining (lead, zinc) dist.
Smerdomlya, Russian SFSR: see SAZONOVO.
Smerdzonka (smĕr'jôn-kä), Slovak *Smerdžonka*, village, N Slovakia, Czechoslovakia, on NE slope of the High Tatra, NNE of Poprad; health resort (alt. 1,590 ft.) with alkaline sulphur springs.
Smestad (smā'stä), suburb (pop. 5,817) of Oslo, SE Norway, 3 mi. WNW of city center. Until 1948, in Akershus co. Sometimes spelled Smedstad.
Smethport (smĕth'–), borough (pop. 1,797), ⊙ McKean co., N Pa., 18 mi. S of Olean, N.Y.; chemicals, novelties, petroleum products, butter, lumber; bituminous coal, clay. Laid out 1807, inc. 1853.
Smethwick (smĕ'dhĭk), county borough (1931 pop. 84,406; 1951 census 76,397), S Stafford, England, 3 mi. W of Birmingham; steel-milling center, with railroad workshops; mfg. (light metals, chemicals, paint, soap, glass and glassware, electrical equipment, metal products. Near by are the Soho ironworks, established by James Watt, where 1st steam engine was built. Has early 18th-cent. chapel. In county borough is town of Bearwood (pop. 7,913) with machinery, electrical-equipment industries.
Smichov (smĭ'khôf), SSW suburb (pop. 62,444) of Prague, Czechoslovakia, on left bank of Vltava R.; mfg. and industrial area with metallurgical and construction works, breweries, and railroad yards. New residential area with fine villas has sprung up at Barrandov (bä'rändôf) (SE), around Czechoslovak motion-picture hq. on rock above Vltava R.
Smicksburg, borough (pop. 92), Indiana co., W central Pa., 11 mi. WSW of Punxsutawney.
Smidovich (smē'dûvĭch). **1** Town (1926 pop. 2,495), NE Jewish Autonomous Oblast, Khabarovsk Territory, Russian SFSR, on Trans-Siberian RR and 40 mi. E of Birobidzhan; sawmills, metalworks. Formerly named In. **2** Settlement, Novaya Zemlya, Russian SFSR: see ADMIRALTY PENINSULA.
Smigiel (shmē'gyĕl), Pol. *Śmigiel*, Ger. *Schmiegel* (shmē'gûl), town (1946 pop. 3,566), Poznan prov., W Poland, 7 mi. SSW of Koscian; flour milling, sawmilling; cattle trade.
Smiginitsa or **Smiginova,** Greece: see MENOIKION.
Smilde (smĭl'dû), town (pop. 4,981), Drenthe prov., N Netherlands, on the Smildervaart and 6 mi. WSW of Assen; potato flour, sandstone; center of peat-digging and sugar-beet area.
Smildervaart (smĭl'dûrvärt) or **Drentsche Hoofdvaart** (drĕnt'sû hōft'färt), canal, in Drenthe prov., N Netherlands, extends 28 mi. NE-SW, bet. the Meppelerdiep at Meppel and Assen. Serves Smilde.
Smiley, city (pop. 503), Gonzales co., S central Texas, c.55 mi. ESE of San Antonio; poultry-hatching and shipping center.
Smiley Mountain, Idaho: see PIONEER MOUNTAINS.
Smiltene (smĕl'tĕnä), Ger. *Smilten*, city (pop. 3,754), NE Latvia, in Vidzeme, near main Riga-Pskov highway, 20 mi. ESE of Valmiera (linked by railroad); flax milling, pottery mfg.
Smilyan (smĕlyän'), village (pop. 1,261), Plovdiv dist., S Bulgaria, in SE Rhodope Mts., on Arda R. and 7 mi. SSE of Smolyan; tobacco, rye, potatoes, livestock. Scattered lead, copper, silver, and zinc deposits near by. Formerly Ismilan. Lead and silver mined at Rudozem (pop. 518), 6 mi. E.
Smindja, Tunisia: see DEPIENNE.
Smirnovo (smērnô'vû), village (1926 pop. 1,684), S Gorki oblast, Russian SFSR, 23 mi. E of Arzamas; wheat.
Smirnovski or **Smirnovskiy** (smērnôf'skē), town (1948 pop. over 500), N North Kazakhstan oblast, Kazakh SSR, on railroad and 25 mi. S of Petropavlovsk, in wheat and cattle area. Formerly Chulakdoshchan.
Smith or **Mirror Landing,** village (pop. estimate 350), central Alta., on Athabaska R. at mouth of Lesser Slave R., and 45 mi. NW of Athabaska; mixed farming, wheat, stock.
Smith. 1 County (□ 893; pop. 8,846), N Kansas; ⊙ Smith Center. Corn-belt region, bordering N on Nebr.; drained by North Fork Solomon R. Corn, livestock. Geographic center of U.S. (39°50'N 98°35'W) is 2 mi. NW of Lebanon. Formed 1872. **2** County (□ 642; pop. 16,740), S central Miss.; ⊙ Raleigh. Drained by Leaf and Strong rivers; includes part of Bienville Natl. Forest. Agr. (corn, cotton); lumbering; bentonite mining. Formed 1833. **3** County (□ 325; pop. 14,098), N central Tenn.; ⊙ Carthage. In central basin; drained by Cumberland R. and its tributaries. Livestock raising, dairying, lumbering; agr. (tobacco, corn). Formed 1799. **4** County (□ 939; pop. 74,701), E Texas; ⊙ TYLER, commercial, transportation, industrial center. Bounded N by Sabine R., W by Neches R. Diversified agr.; rose growing; livestock raising, dairying; oil fields, mining (iron ore, salt, silica, lignite, clays). Chief crops: sweet potatoes, tomatoes, other truck and fruit, cotton, corn, forage crops, pecans; a leading Texas mule-raising co.; also cattle, hogs, poultry. Some lumbering. Formed 1846.
Smith, Camp, N.Y.: see PEEKSKILL.
Smith and Sayles Reservoir, R.I.: see CHEPACHET RIVER.
Smith Bay, N Alaska, inlet (20 mi. wide) of Beaufort Sea, 60 mi. SE of Point Barrow; 70°54'N 153°50'W.
Smithboro, village (pop. 253), Bond co., S central Ill., 14 mi. WSW of Vandalia, in agr. area.
Smith Center, city (pop. 2,026), ⊙ Smith co., N Kansas, 85 mi. NW of Salina, in livestock and corn region; grain storage; produce packing. Founded 1871, inc. 1886.
Smithers, village (pop. 759), W central B.C., on Bulkley R. and 130 mi. ENE of Prince Rupert; railroad division point; silver- and lead-mining center; lumbering, fur trapping.
Smithers (smĭ'dhûrz), city (pop. 2,208), Fayette co., S central W.Va., on Kanawha R. and 22 mi. SE of Charleston, in coal-mining and agr. region. Inc. 1938.
Smithfield, market in the City of London, England, N of the Thames, 1.5 mi. NE of Charing Cross; site of Central Meat Market, where London's meat supplies are distributed. From 12th cent. it was scene of tournament jousts, fairs (including St. Bartholomew Fair), markets, and executions. William Wallace (1305) and Wat Tyler (1381) were executed here. Adjoining market is St. Bartholomew's Hosp., founded 1123 and refounded 1547 by Henry VIII; it has famous medical school.
Smithfield, town (pop. 2,322), SW Orange Free State, U. of So. Afr., 35 mi. NNW of Aliwal North; alt. 4,400 ft.; stock, grain, fruit.
Smithfield. 1 Village (pop. 355), Fulton co., W central Ill., 14 mi. WSW of Canton, in agr. and bituminous-coal area. **2** Town (pop. 121), Henry co., N Ky., 26 mi. WNW of Frankfort. **3** Resort town (pop. 354), Somerset co., S Maine, 11 mi. NE of Waterville, in Belgrade Lakes resort area. **4** Village (pop. 102), Gosper co., S Nebr., 22 mi. WNW of Holdrege. **5** Town (pop. 5,574), ⊙ Johnston co., central N.C., 25 mi. SE of Raleigh and on Neuse R.; tobacco market and processing center; cotton and lumber milling, meat packing. Settled before 1746; inc. 1861. **6** Village (pop. 1,255), Jefferson co., E Ohio, 10 mi. SW of Steubenville, in coal-mining area. **7** Agr. borough (pop. 1,066), Fayette co., SW Pa., 8 mi. SW of Uniontown; railroad shops. **8** Village (pop. 1,134, with adjacent Crooked Creek), Huntingdon co., S central Pa. **9** Town (pop. 6,690), Providence co., N R.I., on the Woonasquatucket R. (bridged here) and 10 mi. NW of Providence, in agr. area (milk, poultry, apples); mfg. (yarns, blankets), textile bleaching, dyeing, and finishing. Includes Georgiaville (pop. 1,247; administrative center), Greenville, Stillwater, and ESMOND villages. Settled (mainly by Friends) in early 18th cent., inc. 1731. **10** City (pop. 2,383), Cache co., N Utah, 6 mi. N of Logan, near Idaho line and Bear R., in Cache Valley; alt. 4,595 ft.; processing center for dairying and irrigated agr. area; canned vegetables, dried fruit, bricks and tiles. Settled 1859. Newton Dam is 10 mi. NW, on Clarkston Creek. **11** Town (pop. 1,180), Isle of Wight co., SE Va., on Pagan R. (head of navigation), near the James, and 20 mi. NW of Portsmouth. Noted for its hams; also ships peanuts. Near by are one of oldest Protestant churches in America (at BENNS CHURCH) and Bacon's Castle (1655), which was fortified (1676) in Bacon's Rebellion. Rail station at Windsor, 14 mi. SW. Settled c.1633; inc. 1752. **12** Town (pop. 390), Wetzel co., N W.Va., 23 mi. W of Fairmont, in oil, gas, and agr. area.
Smith Hill, town (1940 pop. 280), Bibb co., central Ala., 21 mi. SW of Bessemer.
Smith Island, Northwest Territories: see CAPE SMITH.
Smith Island, Jap. *Sumisu-shima* (sōōmēsōō'shĭmä), rocky islet of isl. group Izu-shichito, Greater Tokyo, Japan, in Philippine Sea, 110 mi. SSE of Hachijo-jima.
Smith Island (15 naut. mi. long, 6.5 naut. mi. wide), South Shetland Isls., 42 mi. W of Deception Isl., off Palmer Peninsula, Antarctica; 62°55'S 62°30'W. Rises to c.6,500 ft.
Smith Island. 1 In SE Md. and E Va., low-lying marshy archipelago (c. 8 mi. long, 4 mi. wide), consisting of islets divided by narrow creeks, in Chesapeake Bay 8 mi. W of Crisfield (ferry); S tip is in Va. Most remote of Md. isls. Has isolated crabbing, oystering villages of Ewell (ū'ûl), Tylerton (tī'lûrtûn), and Rhodes Point. Angling, duck shooting attract sportsmen. **2** In Brunswick co., S N.C., 3 mi. SE of Southport, at the mouth of Cape Fear R.; c.5 mi. long, 3 mi. wide. Southern tip is Cape FEAR. **3** In E Va., low sandy island (c.7 mi. long) just SE of Cape Charles, at entrance to Chesapeake Bay from the Atlantic; Cape Charles lighthouse is here.
Smithland. 1 Town (pop. 373), Woodbury co., W Iowa, on Little Sioux R. and 30 mi. SE of Sioux City. **2** Town (pop. 498), ⊙ Livingston co., W Ky., on left bank (levee) of the Ohio, at Cumberland R. mouth, and 12 mi. ENE of Paducah, in agr. (burley tobacco, corn), fluorspar-mine, stone-quarry area. Kentucky Reservoir is SE.
Smithonia, town (pop. 80), Oglethorpe co., NE Ga., 13 mi. ENE of Athens.
Smith Point, E Va., low promontory in Chesapeake Bay, at S side of mouth of Potomac R.; lighthouse.
Smith River, trading post, N B.C., near Yukon border, on Smith R. (tributary of Liard R.), on branch of Alaska Highway; 59°53'N 126°26'W; radio station, airfield.
Smith River, village (pop. c.300), Del Norte co., NW Calif., near mouth of Smith R. on the Pacific, 12 mi. N of Crescent City; trade center for lumbering, dairying area. Smith River Indian Reservation near by.

Smith River. 1 In NW Calif., formed by its South and Middle Forks 8 mi. NE of Crescent City, flows 20 mi. NNW to the Pacific just below Smith River village. **2** In W central Mont., rises in Meagher co., flows SW, past White Sulphur Springs, thence NNW to Missouri R. SW of Great Falls; c.100 mi. long. **3** In central N.H., rises near Grafton, flows c.20 mi. SE and E, past Danbury, to the Pemigewasset below Bristol. **4** In W Oregon, rises in Coast Ranges W of Cottage Grove, flows 70 mi. W to Umpqua R. near its mouth. Fishing; lumbering, dairying in valley. **5** In Va. and N.C., rises in Patrick co., Va., flows NE, then SE, past Bassett and Fieldale, into N.C., to Dan R. near Leaksville. Site of Philpott Dam (for flood control and power) is just above Bassett.

Smith's, parish (1939 pop. 1,311), central Bermuda, on Bermuda Isl.

Smithsburg, town (pop. 641), Washington co., W Md., at W base of South Mtn., 8 mi. E of Hagerstown, in fruitgrowing area; cannery.

Smiths Falls, town (pop. 7,159), SE Ont., on Rideau R. and 40 mi. SSW of Ottawa; railroad center; mfg. of electrical appliances, agr. implements, castings, clothing, woodwork; resort.

Smiths Ferry, Pa.: see GLASGOW.

Smiths Grove, town (pop. 683), Warren co., S Ky., 14 mi. ENE of Bowling Green, in agr. area.

Smith's Island (¾ mi. long, ¼ mi. wide), NE Bermuda, at entrance of St. George's Harbour, just N of St. David's Isl.

Smith Sound, Arctic sea passage (55 mi. long, 30–45 mi. wide) bet. E Ellesmere Isl. (Canada) and NW Greenland; 78°30′N 74°W. Opens N on Kane Basin, S on Baffin Bay. Limited navigation is possible after break-up of winter ice in late summer. Sound was discovered 1616 by William Baffin, who here reached northernmost latitude of any explorer prior to mid-19th cent.

Smithton, town (pop. 1,668), NW Tasmania, 110 mi. WNW of Launceston and on Duck Bay; butter, dehydrated vegetables.

Smithton. 1 Village (pop. 515), St. Clair co., SW Ill., 17 mi. SSE of East St. Louis, in bituminous-coal and agr. area. **2** Town (pop. 339), Pettis co., central Mo., 8 mi. E of Sedalia; ships dairy products. **3** Borough (pop. 690), Westmoreland co., SE Pa., on Youghiogheny R. and 24 mi. SSE of Pittsburgh.

Smith Town, village (1940 pop. 964), McCreary co., S Ky., in the Cumberlands, 26 mi. SSE of Somerset, in Cumberland Natl. Forest.

Smithtown. 1 Village, Suffolk co., SE N.Y., on Nissequogue R. and just W of Smithtown Branch, in agr. area (potatoes, cauliflower). **2** Village (pop. 182), Yadkin co., NW N.C., 20 mi. NW of Winston-Salem, near Yadkin R.

Smithtown Bay, SE N.Y., open bight on N shore of Long Isl., bet. Eatons Neck (W) and Crane Neck (E), 3 mi. N of Smithtown; c.8½ mi. wide. Receives Nissequogue R. in SW. Stony Brook Harbor (c.2½ mi. long) is shallow SE arm.

Smithtown Branch, residential village (pop. 1,424), Suffolk co., SE N.Y., on central Long Isl., 13 mi. ESE of Huntington; mfg. (clothing, machinery); poultry, hogs, vegetables.

Smithville, village (pop. estimate 750), S Ont., on Twenty Mile Creek and 19 mi. SE of Hamilton; dairying, lumber and grist milling; fruit.

Smithville. 1 Town (pop. 676), Lee and Sumter cos., SW central Ga., 12 mi. S of Americus, in agr. area; sawmilling. **2** Village (pop. 419), Monroe co., E Miss., 23 mi. ESE of Tupelo, near Ala. line. **3** Town (pop. 947), Clay co., W Mo., on Little Platte R. and 20 mi. N of Kansas City; wheat, corn, oats, fruit; stock, poultry. **4** Village (pop. 755), Wayne co., N central Ohio, 6 mi. NE of Wooster; lumber, agr. machinery, meat products. **5** Town (pop. 256), McCurtain co., extreme SE Okla., c.40 mi. N of Idabel, near Ark. line. **6** Town (pop. 1,558), ⊙ De Kalb co., central Tenn., 19 mi. N of McMinnville, in the Cumberlands; makes hosiery; fruit tree nurseries. Center Hill Dam is near by. **7** City (pop. 3,379), Bastrop co., S central Texas, on Colorado R. and c.40 mi. ESE of Austin; trade, shipping center in cattle, cotton, fruit area; railroad shops; lumber, cottonseed-oil mills. Settled 1827, inc. 1895.

Smiyinitsa or **Smiyinova,** Greece: see MENOIKION.

Smoaks, town (pop. 130), Colleton co., S central S.C., 28 mi. S of Orangeburg.

Smock, village (pop. c.2,000), Fayette co., SW Pa., 7 mi. NNW of Uniontown, in bituminous-coal area.

Smogen (smû′gûn), Swedish *Smögen,* village (pop. 1,411), Goteborg och Bohus co., SW Sweden, on islet of same name in the Skagerrak, 9 mi. NW of Lysekil; fishing center, with fish canneries and shipyards. Seaside resort.

Smoke Bend, village (pop. 1,619, with adjacent Port Barrow), SE La., on the Mississippi just W of Donaldsonville.

Smoke Creek Desert, NW Nev., N of Pyramid L., near Calif. line; SW extension (c.40 mi. long) of Black Rock Desert.

Smoke Hole, E W.Va., wooded gorge (c.16 mi. long) of South Branch of the Potomac, just E of the Allegheny Front and SW of Petersburg, in Monongahela Natl. Forest; traversed by highway. Smoke Hole village is here. Hunting, fishing; has spectacular rock formations and caves, including Smoke Hole Caverns, whose use by pioneers gave region its name.

Smokemont (smōk′mŏnt), resort village, Swain co., W N.C., 12 mi. NNE of Bryson City, in Great Smoky Mts. Natl. Park.

Smoky Bay, inlet of Great Australian Bight, S South Australia, at NW base of Eyre Peninsula; sheltered by Nuyts Archipelago; 11 mi. long, 5 mi. wide.

Smoky Cape, E New South Wales, Australia, forms S end of Trial Bay of Pacific Ocean; 30°56′S 153°6′E; consists of 3 hills.

Smoky Hill River, in Colo. and Kansas, formed by confluence of 2 headstreams near Cheyenne Wells in E Colo., flows E into Wallace co. in W Kansas, continues E past Wallace and Russell Springs, and turns SE at Ellsworth, N at Lindsborg, and ENE at Salina; passing Solomon and Abilene in lower course, it joins Republican R. at Junction City to form Kansas R. Length, 560 mi. Receives Saline R. E of Salina and Solomon R. at Solomon. Flood-control dam near KANOPOLIS was one of 1st units of Missouri R. Basin project. The North Fork (80 mi. long; in Colo. and Kansas) is sometimes referred to as part of main stream. Cutting through Great Plains in W Kansas, river has exposed colored chalk formations; fossil beds in vicinity.

Smoky Lake, village (pop. 457), central Alta., near Smoky L. (10 mi. long) and near North Saskatchewan R., 60 mi. NE of Edmonton; wheat, cattle, poultry.

Smoky Mountains, N.C. and Tenn.: see GREAT SMOKY MOUNTAINS.

Smoky River, Alta., rises in Rocky Mts. in N part of Jasper Natl. Park, flows in a winding course generally NNE to Peace R. 5 mi. SSW of Peace River; 245 mi. long. Receives Little Smoky and Wapiti rivers.

Smola (smû′lä), Nor. *Smøla,* island (□ 83; pop. 2,696) in North Sea, More og Romsdal co., W Norway, 15 mi. NNE of Kristiansund; 14 mi. long, 10 mi. wide. Dyrnesvagen (dür′năsvô″gûn) (Nor. *Dyrnesvågen*), in NW, is chief village (pop. 103). Fishing, fish canning. Formerly called Smolen.

Smolensk (smōlĕnsk′, Rus. smŭlyĕnsk′), oblast (□ 18,900; 1946 pop. estimate 1,800,000) in W European Russian SFSR; ⊙ Smolensk. In Smolensk-Moscow Upland, serving as watershed for Western Dvina, Volga, and Dnieper river basins; drained by upper Dnieper R. (timber drives). Moderate continental climate. Mixed forest region; clayey and sandy podsolic soils; peat and building materials are chief mineral resources. Economy based on extensive flax growing, furnishing fiber and linseed oil; fodder grasses sown as alternate crop. Coarse grain grown; wheat recently introduced. Dairy farming, hog raising important. Rural industries: flax processing, dairying, tanning, sawmilling, woodworking. Industrial centers: Smolensk, Vyazma, Yartsevo. Formed 1937 out of Western Oblast.

Smolensk, city (1926 pop. 78,520; 1939 pop. 156,677), ⊙ Smolensk oblast, Russian SFSR, on Dnieper R. and 220 mi. WSW of Moscow; 54°47′N 32°3′E. Rail junction; linen-milling center; produces machinery (textile machines, road graders), electrical goods, clothing; flour milling, distilling, brewing, sawmilling, woodworking. Remains of old walled kremlin in center of city. Has medical and teachers colleges, cathedral (former place of pilgrimage), several parks, regional mus., and art gall. Monuments to Rus. composer Glinka and to a Napoleonic battle of 1812. Founded 882 on left bank of Dnieper R.; later expanded to right bank. Because of excellent location on river routes, city developed early into important commercial center. Long a prize of Polish-Russian struggles, it was finally acquired (1667) by Russia. Was ⊙ Smolensk govt. until 1929; then, until 1937, ⊙ Western Oblast. In Second World War, occupied (1941) by Germans and recaptured (1943) by Russians, after heavy fighting had largely razed the city.

Smolensk-Moscow Upland, Rus. *Smolensko-Moskovskaya Vozvyshennost,* in W European USSR, extends from Berezina R. 350 mi. E, past Smolensk, to area N of Moscow, where it is called KLIN-DMITROV RIDGE. Formed of moraine ridges; rises to 950 ft.; forms divide bet. upper Dnieper and Volga rivers (N) and Oka R. (S). Sometimes regarded as part of Central Russian Upland.

Smolenskoye (smŭlyĕn′skŭyŭ), village (1926 pop. 8,379), central Altai Territory, Russian SFSR, 15 mi. SSW of Bisk, in agr. area.

Smolevichi (smŭlyĕ′vĕchē), town (1926 pop. 3,120), central Minsk oblast, Belorussian SSR, 25 mi. ENE of Minsk; peat works.

Smolikas (smô′lĭkûs), highest massif in Pindus system, S Epirus, Greece, bet. upper Aoos and Sarandaporos rivers; rises to 8,650 ft. 30 mi. NNE of Ioannina.

Smolnik (smôl′nyĕk), Slovak *Smolník,* Hung. *Szómolnok* (sō′mōlnôk), village (pop. 1,745), S Slovakia, Czechoslovakia, in Slovak Ore Mts., 10 mi. NE of Roznava; iron and copper mining; pyrite processing. Popular health resort of Stos (shtôs), Slovak *Štos* (alt. 2,197 ft.), is 4 mi. ESE.

Smolyan (smôlyän′), city (pop. 3,395), Plovdiv dist., S Bulgaria, in SE Rhodope Mts., on left branch of Arda R. and 38 mi. S of Plovdiv; agr. center (tobacco, rye, potatoes), livestock; weaving, dairying, sawmilling, lumbering. Has woodworking school. Linked by road across Rhodope Mts. with Xanthe (Greece). Until 1934, Pashmakli.

Smolyaninovo (smŭlyŭnyē′nŭvŭ), town (1948 pop. over 2,000), S Maritime Territory, Russian SFSR, 25 mi. NE of Vladivostok, on branch of Trans-Siberian RR; junction of branch line to Dunai (S).

Smooth Rock Falls, town (pop. 953), E Ont., on Mattagami R. (28-ft. falls) and 30 mi. NW of Cochrane, in mining region; mixed farming.

Smoothstone Lake (□ 110), central Sask., 110 mi. NNW of Prince Albert; 16 mi. long, 11 mi. wide. Drains N into Snake L. and Churchill R.

Smorgon or **Smorgon'** (smŭrgô′nyŭ), Pol. *Smorgonie* (smôrgô′nyĕ), city (1931 pop. 4,090), central Molodechno oblast, Belorussian SSR, near Viliya R., 45 mi. SE of Vilna; agr.-processing center (linen, wool, hides, hops); sawmilling, brick mfg. Has ruins of 16th-cent. church. Passed (1793) from Poland to Russia; reverted (1921) to Poland; ceded to USSR in 1945.

Smotrich (smŭtrēch′), agr. town (1926 pop. 3,868), SW Kamenets-Podolski oblast, Ukrainian SSR, on Smotrich R. (left affluent of the Dniester) and 18 mi. N of Kamenets-Podolski; sugar beets.

Smrciny, Czechoslovakia and Germany: see FICHTELGEBIRGE.

Smrdaky, Czechoslovakia: see SENICA.

Smrk (smŭrk), Ger. *Tafelfichte* (tä′fŭlfĭkh″tŭ), highest peak (3,681 ft.) of the Isergebirge, on Czechoslovak-Pol. border, 12 mi. NE of Liberec. Nove Mesto pod Smrkem is at NW foot; Jizera R. rises on S slope.

Smrzovka (smŭr′zhôfkä), Czech *Smržovka,* Ger. *Morchenstern* (môr′khŭnshtĕrn″), village (pop. 4,040), N Bohemia, Czechoslovakia, in the Sudetes, 7 mi. ESE of Liberec; rail junction; glassmaking, cotton spinning.

Smugglers Notch, Vt.: see MANSFIELD, MOUNT.

Smuttynose Island, Maine: see ISLES OF SHOALS.

Smychka (smĭch′kŭ), town (1926 pop. 2,814), NW Moscow oblast, Russian SFSR, 2 mi. NW of Volokolamsk; cotton milling. Until 1929, Ivanovskoye.

Smyge (smü′gû), fishing village (pop. 494), Malmohus co., S Sweden, on the Baltic, 8 mi. ESE of Trelleborg. Just ESE is Cape Smyge, Swedish *Smygehuk,* 55°20′N 13°21′E, S extremity of Sweden.

Smyre (smīr) or **Smyre Mills,** village (pop. 2,929, with adjacent Ranlo), Gaston co., S N.C., 3 mi. E of Gastonia.

Smyrna (smûr′nû) or **Izmir** (ĭzmĭr′), Turkish *İzmir,* prov. (□ 4,952; 1950 pop. 767,374), W Turkey, on Aegean Sea; ⊙ Izmir. Bordered N by Kozac and Boz Mts., S by Aydin Mts. Rich in both forest and mineral resources, including antimony, copper, silver in N near Bergama, emery, iron, copper, and manganese in S near Torbali, arsenic, emery, iron, copper, and mercury in E at Tire and Odemis, mercury in W near Karaburun, zinc, chromium, and emery near Smyrna. Valonia, gallnuts, chestnuts, and olives; raisins, figs, apples, pears, plums, and citrus fruit; tobacco, hemp, cotton, licorice, and dye plants; sesame, wheat, barley, and beans; alum, salt, fish, poultry, Merino sheep.

Smyrna or **Izmir,** Turkish *İzmir,* city (1950 pop. 230,508), ⊙ Smyrna prov., W Turkey, at head of Gulf of Smyrna of the Aegean Sea, 210 mi. SSW of Istanbul; 38°25′N 27°10′E. Located on a magnificent harbor and backed by mts., Smyrna is the chief exporting port of Turkey and a rail and mfg. center long known for its export of figs. Produces soap, dyes, hides, tobacco products (though Samsun has largely superseded it as a tobacco port), cotton textiles, leather goods, tannin extract, olive oil, valonia. Has teachers col. City was an early Ionian colony, was destroyed by the Lydians in 627 B.C., restored 3 centuries later by Antigonus, enlarged and beautified by Lysimachus. Conquered by the Romans, it became an early seat of Christianity, one of the "seven churches of Asia." Tomb of St. Polycarps is on hillside overlooking city. It fell to the Seljuks in 11th cent., was recaptured for Byzantine Empire during the First Crusade, and formed part of the empire of Nicaea from 1204 to 1261, when Byzantine Empire was restored. In 1261 also the Genoese obtained trading privileges at Smyrna, which they retained until it fell once more to the Seljuks in 1300. The Byzantines regained it 1344 and the Genoese privileges were restored. In 1402 Tamerlane took Smyrna, which had been defended by the Knights Hospitalers, and sacked the city. The Mongols were succeeded in 1424 by the Ottoman Turks, who kept it until 1919. A Greek Orthodox archiepiscopal see, Smyrna remained a center of Greek culture and the chief Mediterranean port of Asia Minor, and it retained its large Greek population. After the collapse of the Ottoman Empire in the First World War, the city was occupied (1919) by Greek forces. The Treaty of Sèvres (1920) assigned Smyrna and its hinterland to Greek administration and provided for a plebiscite to be held in 1925 to determine the permanent status of the area, but Greek forces, with the consent of the Allies, undertook (July, 1920) their campaign against the Turkish nationalists under Kemal Ataturk, who had refused to recognize the treaty. The Greeks were crushed and Smyrna fell to the Turks in Sept., 1922; a few days later it was nearly destroyed by fire. Thousands of Greek civilian refugees fled. The Treaty of Lausanne (1923) restored Smyrna to Turkey. A separate convention bet. Greece and Turkey provided for the exchange of their minorities, which was carried out under League of Nations supervision. The population of Smyrna thus became predominantly Turkish. With the loss of most of its Greek inhabitants, Smyrna declined considerably as a trade center. It suffered further from severe earthquakes in 1928 and 1939. Among the cities that claim to have given birth to Homer, Smyrna is the most likely.

Smyrna. **1** Town (pop. 2,346), Kent and New Castle counties, central Del., 12 mi. NNW of Dover, near Smyrna R., in agr. region (poultry, fruit, grain); food canning and packing. State welfare home near by; L. Como (fishing) is S. Inc. 1859. **2** Town (pop. 2,005), Cobb co., NW central Ga., 11 mi. NW of Atlanta; furniture mfg. **3** Agr. town (pop. 349), Aroostook co., E Maine, on East Branch of Mattawamkeag R. and 14 mi. W of Houlton. **4** Village (pop. 269), Chenango co., central N.Y., 32 mi. SW of Utica, in dairying and lumbering area. **5** Town (pop. 105), York co., N S.C., 30 mi. ENE of Spartanburg. **6** Town (pop. 1,544), Rutherford co., central Tenn., 18 mi. SE of Nashville; makes cedar chests. Air Force base here. Near by are home and grave of Sam Davis, Confederate hero.

Smyrna, Gulf of, or **Gulf of Izmir,** Turkish *İzmir,* inlet of Aegean Sea in W Turkey; 35 mi. long, 14 mi. wide. Smyrna is at its head, isl. of Lesbos opposite its mouth.

Smyrna River, central Del., rises W of Smyrna near Md. line, flows E, past Smyrna, and NE to Delaware Bay just N of Bombay Hook Isl.; c.15 mi. long. Navigable for c.10 mi. in lower course.

Smyth (smĭth), county (□ 435; pop. 30,187), SW Va.; ⊙ Marion. In Great Appalachian Valley; Walker Mtn. in NW, part of Iron Mts., including Mt. Rogers (highest peak in Va.) in SE. Includes Hungry Mother State Park and part of Jefferson Natl. Forest; traversed by Appalachian Trail. Drained by headstreams of Holston R. Agr. (cabbage, fruit), stock raising, dairying, mfg. (at Marion). Salt and gypsum mining, limestone quarrying. Formed 1832.

Smyth, town, N.C.: see BALFOUR, Henderson co.

Smyth Channel, Sp. *Canal Smyth,* arm of the Pacific, off Magallanes prov., S Chile, connecting Strait of Magellan and Nelson Strait at c.74°W; 100 mi. long. Separates Adelaide and Rennell isls. (W) from the Muñoz Gamero Peninsula. Sometimes spelled Smith.

Snaasa, Norway: see SNASA.

Snaasavand, Norway: see SNASA LAKE.

Snaefell (snā'fĕl), mountain (2,034 ft.), highest point of Isle of Man, England, 8 mi. N of Douglas.

Snaefellsjokull (snĭ'fĕls"yû"kütûl), Icelandic *Snæfellsjökull,* glacier, W Iceland, on Snaefellsnes peninsula, near the coast; rises to 4,744 ft. at 64°48'N 23°47'W, on extinct volcano.

Snaefellsnes (snĭ'fĕls"nĕs"), county [Icelandic *sýsla*] (pop. 3,171), W Iceland; ⊙ Stykkisholmur. Coextensive with Snaefellsnes peninsula, which extends 50 mi. into Denmark Strait, bet. Breidi Fjord (N) and Faxa Bay (S), 50 mi. NW of Reykjavik. Mts. here rise to 4,744 ft. on Snaefellsjokull glacier. Fishing ports are Stykkisholmur, Sandur, Olafsvik. Ondverdarnes cape is W extremity.

Snag, village, W Yukon, near Alaska border, on White R. and 120 mi. S of Dawson; 62°24'N 140°28'W; trading post, airfield, radio and weather station. Record low temperature of —81°F. was recorded here, Feb., 1947.

Snagov (snä'gôv), village (pop. 1,175), Bucharest prov., S Rumania, on Snagov L., 20 mi. N of Bucharest; popular recreation center with large park. Also site of 14th-cent. Snagov monastery, formerly an important cultural center. Called sometimes Dobrosesti. Caldarasani monastery with noted frescoes is 3 mi. SE.

Snailbeach, England: see MINSTERLEY.

Snaipol (snīpôl'), town, Preyveng prov., S Cambodia, 20 mi. ENE of Pnompenh; rice, corn, tobacco; fisheries.

Snaith and Cowick, parish (pop. 1,641), West Riding, S Yorkshire, England. Includes woodworking village of Snaith, on Aire R. and 6 mi. W of Goole, with 13th–15th-cent. church; and, just SE, agr. villages of West Cowick and East Cowick.

Snake Island, uninhabited island (□ 18) in Bass Strait just off S coast of Victoria, Australia; forms E side of entrance to Corner Inlet; 8.5 mi. long, 3 mi. wide; low, sandy, with sparse vegetation. Deer, wild pigs, wallabies, kangaroos.

Snake Lake (34 mi. long, 10 mi. wide), N central Sask., expansion of the Churchill R. 150 mi. N of Prince Albert.

Snake Mountain (5,594 ft.), in the Appalachians, on Tenn.-N.C. line, 8 mi. N of Boone, N.C.

Snake Range, E Nev., in White Pine co., E of Shell Creek Range, near Utah line; extends N-S through 2 sections of Nevada Natl. Forest. Rises to 12,049 ft. in Mt. Moriah and 13,058 ft. in WHEELER PEAK. Lehman Caves Natl. Monument in S. Highway crosses range at Sacramento Pass (c.7,160 ft.).

Snake River. **1** In NW U.S., the chief tributary (1,038 mi. long) of the Columbia; rises in NW Wyo. in Yellowstone Natl. Park S of Yellowstone L., flows S through Jackson L. and Jackson Hole Natl. Monument, then W into Bonneville co., Idaho, and across S part of state in wide arc, passing through Snake River Plain; it makes a bend into Oregon and turns N (forming part of Idaho-Oregon line and Idaho-Wash. line) to Lewiston, Idaho, where it turns W into Wash. and flows to Columbia R. 4 mi. ESE of Pasco. Tributaries: in Wyo., Lewis R.; in Idaho, Henrys Fork, Boise R., Payette R., Salmon R., Clearwater R.; in Oregon, Malheur R., Owyhee R.; in Wash., Palouse R. Drains □ 109,000. High-water navigation (for shallow drafts) to Lewiston. Greatest of its numerous gorges is Grand Canyon of the Snake R. (sometimes called Hell's Canyon), one of deepest in world; with a total length of 125 mi., it averages 5,500 ft. in depth for c.40 mi. and reaches maximum depth of 7,900 ft.; it extends N-S bet. Wallowa Mts., Oregon, and Seven Devils Mts., Idaho. SHOSHONE FALLS are best-known of several cascades on main stream. Rexburg, Idaho Falls, Pocatello, Burley, and Twin Falls are in its Idaho valley, which is served by large irrigation and hydroelectric projects. Most notable of private irrigation projects is at TWIN FALLS. Minidoka project (served by JACKSON LAKE Dam in Wyo., and by MINIDOKA DAM and AMERICAN FALLS DAM in Idaho) was developed by Bureau of Reclamation. River discovered (1805) by Lewis and Clark expedition. Formerly called Lewis R. or Lewis Fork of Columbia R. **2** In E Minn., rises in marshy area of Aitkin co., flows S, past Mora, then E, past Pine City, to St. Croix R. (on Wis. line) in Pine co.; 80 mi. long. **3** In NW Minn., rises in marshy area of Marshall co., flows W, past Warren, then N, past Alvarado, to Red R. on N.Dak. line; 70 mi. long.

Snake River Plain, S Idaho, crescent-shaped lava tableland (alt. c.3–5,000 ft.) traversed by Snake R., from Wash. to Wyo. line; separates Northern Rocky Mts. (N) from the Great Basin and Middle Rocky Mts. on S. Irrigation has made it cultivable. U.S. Atomic Energy Commission established a reactor testing station (□ 700) near Arco in 1949.

Snares Islands, uninhabited volcanic group (600 acres) in S Pacific, one of outlying isl. groups of New Zealand, 56 mi. SW of Stewart Isl.; 6 islets.

Snartemo (snär'tümô), village (pop. 217) in Haegebostad canton (pop. 1,087), Vest-Agder co., S Norway, on the Lygna, on railroad and 30 mi. WNW of Kristiansand, bet. Kvineshei Tunnel (9,913 yards long; W) and Haegebostad Tunnel (9,267 yards long; E). Stone Age finds made near by.

Snasa (snô'sä), Nor. *Snåsa,* village and canton (pop. 3,158), Nord-Trondelag co., central Norway, on N shore of Snasa L., on railroad and 16 mi. S of Grong; cattle raising, lumbering, hunting, fishing. Brick factories and sawmills near by. Sometimes spelled Snaasa.

Snasa Lake, Nor. *Snåsavatn,* lake (□ 46), Nord-Trondelag co., central Norway; extends 26 mi. SW from Snasa village (16 mi. S of Grong) to within 7 mi. of Steinkjer on Trondheim Fjord, into which it empties via several lesser lakes; 443 ft. deep. Nordland railway follows its E shore. Formerly spelled Snaasavand.

Sneads, town (pop. 1,074), Jackson co., NW Fla., near Ga. line, 19 mi. ESE of Marianna.

Sneads Ferry, resort village (pop. c.100), Onslow co., E N.C., 38 mi. N of Wilmington and on New R. near its mouth; sport fishing.

Sneedville, town (pop. c.300), ⊙ Hancock co., NE Tenn., 55 mi. NE of Knoxville, in mtn. farm area.

Sneek (snāk), town (pop. 18,834), Friesland prov., N Netherlands, on Scharster-Rhine and Grouw canals, and 13 mi. SSW of Leeuwarden; dairy market; machinery, shoes, bicycles, tinplate, flour, oleomargarine. Has 16th-cent. church, 17th-cent. Renaissance gateway, 18th-cent. town hall.

Sneek Lake, Du. *Sneekermeer* (snā'kürmār), Friesland prov., N Netherlands, 3 mi. E of Sneek; 2 mi. long, 2 mi. wide. Water-sports center; annual regatta.

Sneem, Gaelic *Snaidhm,* town (pop. 340), SW Co. Kerry, Ireland, on Kenmare R. and 14 mi. W of Kenmare; fishing port. Near by is resort of Parknasilla.

Sneeuwberg (snā'ōōbĕrkh), mountain range (extends 30 mi. E–W), SE central Cape Prov., U. of So. Afr., at E edge of the Great Karroo; rises to 8,209 ft. on Compass Berg, 35 mi. N of Graaff Reinet, highest peak of Cape Prov.

Sneeuw Gebergte, Netherlands New Guinea: see SNOW MOUNTAINS.

Sneffels, Mount (14,143 ft.), SW Colo., in San Juan Mts., 5 mi. N of Telluride.

Snekkersten (snĕ'kurstùn), town (pop. 1,673), Frederiksborg amt, Zealand, Denmark, on the Oresund and 12 mi. NE of Hillerod; fishing, shipbuilding.

Snelling, town (pop. 34), Barnwell co., W S.C., 26 mi. SSE of Aiken, just E of Atomic Energy Commission's Savannah R. Plant.

Snelling, Fort, Minn.: see MINNEAPOLIS.

Snellville, town (pop. 309), Gwinnett co., N central Ga., 22 mi. ENE of Atlanta.

Snezhnoye (snyĕzh'nŭyû), city (1939 pop. over 10,000), E Stalino oblast, Ukrainian SSR, in the Donbas, 45 mi. E of Stalino; anthracite mining.

Snezka, mountain, Czechoslovakia: see SCHNEEKOPPE.

Sneznik (snĕzh'nĭk), Slovenian *Snežnik,* Ital. *Monte Nevoso* (môn'tĕ nĕvō'zô), Ger. *Schneeberg* (shnā'bĕrk), mountain (5,892 ft.) in Dinaric Alps, S Slovenia, Yugoslavia, 17 mi. N of Rijeka. Climbed from Ilirska Bistrica (at W foot). In Italy until 1947; title of Prince of Monte Nevoso was conferred on d'Annunzio in 1924.

Sniardwy, Lake (shnyärd'vĭ), Pol. *Śniardwy,* Ger. *Spirding* (shpĭr'dĭng) largest (□ 47) of Masurian Lakes, in East Prussia, after 1945 in NE Poland, 5 mi. N of Pisz, 50 mi. E of Allenstein (Olsztyn); 12 mi. long; 3–9 mi. wide; drains S into L. Ros.

Sniatyn, Ukrainian SSR: see SNYATYN

Snibston, England: see COALVILLE.

Sniezka, mountain, Poland: see SCHNEEKOPPE.

Snieznik, peak, Czechoslovakia and Poland: see KRALICKY SNEZNIK.

Snigirevka (snyĭgēryôf'kŭ), village (1926 pop. 4,231), E Nikolayev oblast, Ukrainian SSR, on Ingulets R. (landing) and 37 mi. ENE of Nikolayev; rail junction; metalworks, flour mill.

Snijeznica or **Sniyezhnitsa** (both: snē'yĕzhnĭtsä), Serbo-Croatian *Snježnica,* mountain (4,048 ft.) in Dinaric Alps, Yugoslavia, on Dalmatia-Herzegovina border, 12 mi. ESE of Dubrovnik.

Snina (snyĭ'nä), Hung. *Szinna* (sĭn'nŏ), town (pop. 4,349), E Slovakia, Czechoslovakia, on railroad and 31 mi. E of Presov; lumbering, woodworking.

Snipatuit Pond (snĭpūtū'ĭt), Plymouth co., SE Mass., 9 mi. NNE of New Bedford; 1¼ mi. long. Joined by stream to Great Quittacas Pond (NW); drains S into small Mattapoisett R.

Snipsic Lake, Conn.: see SHENIPSIT LAKE.

Snizort, Loch (lŏkh snē'zôrt), N inlet of Isle of Skye, Scotland; 10 mi. long, 8 mi. wide at mouth, narrowing toward its head.

Snodland, town and parish (pop. 4,168), central Kent, England, on Medway R. and 5 mi. NW of Maidstone; paper milling. Has 13th-cent church.

Snohetta, Norway: see DOVREFJELL.

Snohomish (snōhō'mĭsh), county (□ 2,100; pop. 111,580), NW Wash.; ⊙ Everett. Includes parts of Mt. Baker and Snoqualmie natl. forests and Tulalip Indian Reservation; Cascade Range is in E. Drained by Skykomish and Snoqualmie rivers. Timber; gold, silver, copper, nickel; fruit, dairy products, poultry. Formed 1861.

Snohomish, city (pop. 3,094), Snohomish co., NW Wash., 7 mi. SE of Everett and on Snohomish R.; dairy products, truck, lumber, berries. Settled in 1850s, inc. 1890.

Snohomish River, NW Wash., formed near Monroe by junction of Snoqualmie and Skykomish rivers; flows c.25 mi. NW to Everett Harbor at Everett.

Snoqualmie (snōkwäl'mē), town (pop. 806), King co., W central Wash., 25 mi. E of Seattle and on Snoqualmie R.; lumber, dairy products, poultry.

Snoqualmie Falls, Wash.: see SNOQUALMIE RIVER.

Snoqualmie Pass (alt. 3,004 ft.), W central Wash., highway pass through Cascade Range, c.45 mi. SE of Seattle. Winter-sports areas.

Snoqualmie River, W central Wash., formed near Snoqualmie by junction of North Fork (c.30 mi. long), Middle Fork (c.35 mi. long), and South Fork (c.40 mi. long), rising in Cascade Range E of Seattle; flows c.45 mi. W and NW to junction with Skykomish R., forming Snohomish R. near Monroe. Snoqualmie Falls (c.270 ft.) near Snoqualmie is power-plant site.

Snota, Norway: see TROLLHEIMEN.

Snoul (snōōl), town, Kratie prov., SE Cambodia, 35 mi. SE of Kratie, near Vietnam line, on main road to Saigon; lumbering.

Snovsk, Ukrainian SSR: see SHCHORS.

Snowbank Lake, Lake co., NE Minn., near Ont. line, 20 mi. ENE of Ely, in Superior Natl. Forest; 4.5 mi. long, 3 mi. wide.

Snow Basin, Utah: see OGDEN.

Snowbird Mountains, W N.C., E extension of Unicoi Mts., along Cherokee and Graham co. line, bet. Haw Knob and Nantahala R.; rise to 4,743 ft. in Teyahalee Peak, 4 mi. N of Andrews.

Snowcrest Mountains, range of Rocky Mts. in SW Mont., rise W of Ruby R., near Idaho line; extend c.45 mi. N. Largely within Beaverhead Natl. Forest. Highest peaks: Sunset Peak (10,573 ft.), Hogback Mtn. (10,605 ft.).

Snow Dome, mountain (11,340 ft.), on Alta.–B.C. border, in Rocky Mts., on S edge of Jasper Natl. Park, 60 mi. SE of Jasper; 52°11'N 117°19'W.

Snowdon, Welsh *Eryri* (ĕrŭ'rē), highest mountain (3,560 ft.) in Wales, in Caernarvonshire 10 mi. SE of Caernarvon; consists of 5 peaks, separated by passes. Rack-and-pinion railroad ascends summit from Llanberis. District is noted for beautiful scenery and for the splendid view from the summit. A large part of the area is owned by the National Trust.

Snowdrift, trading post, S Mackenzie Dist., Northwest Territories, on E side of Great Slave L., at mouth of Snowdrift R.; 62°24′N 110°45′W; radio station.

Snowflake, farming town (pop. 929), Navajo co., E Ariz., on small affluent of Little Colorado R. and 28 mi. S of Holbrook; alt. 5,600 ft.

Snow Hill. 1 Town (pop. 2,091), ⊙ Worcester co., SE Md., 18 mi. SE of Salisbury, at head of navigation on Pocomoke R.; ships truck; vegetable canneries; makes baskets, crates, clothing, textiles, fertilizer. All Hallows Church (1756) here has a Bible dated 1701, given by Queen Anne. Near by are Pocomoke State Forest and ruins of Nassawango Furnace (1832). Founded 1686. **2** Town (pop. 946), ⊙ Greene co., E central N.C., 14 mi. NNW of Kinston, in tobacco area. Founded 1799; inc. 1855.

Snow Hill Island (20 naut. mi. long, 6 naut. mi. wide), Antarctica, in Weddell Sea, off Palmer Peninsula, just S of Ross Isl.; 64°25′S 57°15′W. Discovered 1842 by Sir James Clark Ross.

Snow Island (11 naut. mi. long, 8 naut. mi. wide), South Shetland Isls., 5 mi. SW of Livingston Isl., off Palmer Peninsula, Antarctica; 62°45′S 61°30′W.

Snow Lake, village, W Man., 70 mi. E of Flin Flon; gold-mining center.

Snow Lake, town (pop. 96), Desha co., SE Ark., c.40 mi. SW of Helena, near the Mississippi.

Snowmass Peak (14,077 ft.), W central Colo., in Elk Mts., 13 mi. WSW of Aspen.

Snow Mountains, Du. *Sneeuw Gebergte,* collective name for mountain ranges extending c.400 mi. E-W in central New Guinea; main sections are NASSAU RANGE (W) and ORANGE RANGE (E).

Snows, The, islands, Mich.: see LES CHENEAUX ISLANDS.

Snow Shoe, borough (pop. 670), Centre co., central Pa., 12 mi. NW of Bellefonte; clay, bituminous coal.

Snowtown, village (pop. 525), S South Australia, 45 mi. SSE of Port Pirie; rail junction; agr. center.

Snow Valley, Vt.: see MANCHESTER.

Snowville, town (pop. 199), Box Elder co., NW Utah, near Idaho line, 25 mi. W of Portage; alt. 4,544 ft.; dairy, agr.

Snowy Mountain (3,903 ft.), Hamilton co., NE central N.Y., in the Adirondacks, just W of Indian L. and 6 mi. SW of Indian Lake village.

Snowy Range, Australia: see MUNIONG RANGE.

Snowy Range. 1 In Mont.: see BEARTOOTH RANGE. **2** In Wyo.: see MEDICINE BOW MOUNTAINS.

Snowy River, SE Australia, in SE New South Wales and E Victoria, rises in Australian Alps near Mt. Kosciusko, flows SE past Adaminaby (water power), turns W, then generally S through Gippsland to Bass Strait 50 mi. E of Bairnsdale; 265 mi. long.

Snug Corner, town (pop. 359), S Bahama Isls., on central Acklins Isl., c.250 mi. SE of Nassau; 22°33′N 73°52′W. Cascarilla bark.

Snyatyn (snyä′tĭn), Pol. *Śniatyn* (shnyä′tĭn), city (1931 pop. 10,915), E Stanislav oblast, Ukrainian SSR, on Prut R. and 24 mi. ESE of Kolomyya; agr. center, processing hides, cereals, vegetable oil, fruit. An anc. Roman settlement, later dominated by Walachians and Ruthenians; ceded to Poland in 1340. Frequently assaulted by Walachians (15th–16th cent.); passed to Austrians (1772); reverted to Poland (1919); Rumanian frontier station (until 1939–40); ceded to USSR in 1945.

Snyder, county (□ 329; pop. 22,912), central Pa.; ⊙ Middleburg. Agr. region, bounded E by Susquehanna R.; drained by Penn Creek. Jacks Mtn. runs NE-SW across NW part. Fruitgrowing; mfg. (leather goods, textiles, clothing, bricks). Formed 1855.

Snyder. 1 Village (pop. 369), Dodge co., E Nebr., 25 mi. NW of Fremont and on branch of Elkhorn R.; grain. **2** Town (pop. 1,646), Kiowa co., SW Okla., 22 mi. E of Altus and SW of Wichita Mts., in agr. (grain, livestock; dairy products) and granite-quarrying area; cotton ginning, cottonseed milling, monument mfg. Inc. 1903. **3** Town (pop. 12,010), ⊙ Scurry co., NW central Texas, 35 mi. NW of Sweetwater; market, shipping, processing center for agr., oil, dairying, livestock region; mfg. (cottonseed oil, machine-shop products, tile, mattresses); cotton gins. Settled 1876, inc. 1907.

Snydertown, borough (pop. 314), Northumberland co., E central Pa., 6 mi. E of Sunbury.

Soacha (swä′chä), town (pop. 2,006), Cundinamarca dept., central Colombia, on railroad and highway, in Cordillera Oriental, and 10 mi. W of Bogotá; alt. 9,242 ft.; coal mining; iron.

Soairieng or **Svayrieng** (swī′rēĕng′), town, ⊙ Soairieng prov. (□ 1,500; 1948 pop. 206,942), S Cambodia, on West Vaico R. and 70 mi. SE of Pnompenh, on main highway to Saigon, near Vietnam line; important rice-growing center. Pop. is largely Annamese and Chinese.

Soalala (swälä′lŭ), town, Majunga prov., NW Madagascar, small port on Mozambique Channel, 70 mi. WSW of Majunga; also cattle market. Formerly an active center of Arab slave trade.

Soalara (swälä′rŭ), town, Tuléar prov., SW Madagascar, at mouth of Onilahy R., on St. Augustin Bay of Mozambique Channel, 20 mi. SSE of Tuléar; coal port (rail line to Sakoa coal basin).

Soalheira (swŭlyā′rŭ), village (pop. 1,378), Castelo Branco dist., central Portugal, on railroad and 14 mi. N of Castelo Branco; grain, corn, olives, wine; oak forests.

Soaner, India: see KHAPA.

Soanierana or **Soanierana-Ivongo** (swänyĕrä′nŭ-ēvōōng′gōō), town, Tamatave prov., E Madagascar, on coast opposite Sainte-Marie Isl., 80 mi. N of Tamatave; clove plantations, vanilla processing.

Soan River (sōän′) or **Sohan River** (sōhän′), stream in N Punjab, W Pakistan, rises S of Murree in SW offshoots of Punjab Himalayas, flows c.155 mi. SW and WSW, across Potwar Plateau, to Indus R. 9 mi. NE of Kalabagh. Paleolithic artifacts found in its valley are among earliest archaeological remains on Indian subcontinent.

Soap Lake, town (pop. 2,091), Grant co., central Wash., 7 mi. NNE of Ephrata; health resort on medicinal Soap L., near S end of the Grand Coulee; wheat, apples, poultry.

Soar River, Leicester, England, rises 6 mi. SE of Hinckley, flows 40 mi. NE and NW, past Leicester and Loughborough, to Trent R. 2 mi. S of Long Eaton. Navigable below Leicester. Receives Wreak R. just E of Rothley.

Soatá (swätä′), town (pop. 2,272), Boyacá dept., central Colombia, in Cordillera Oriental, on Pan-American Highway and 45 mi. NNE of Sogamoso; alt. 6,709 ft. Potatoes, wheat, sugar cane, coffee, dates; textile milling. Founded 1547.

Soave (sōä′vĕ), town (pop. 2,860), Verona prov., Veneto, N Italy, 14 mi. E of Verona; soap factory. Noted for its white wine. Encircled by medieval walls and towers.

Soavinandriana (swävēnändrē′nŭ), town, Tananarive prov., central Madagascar, S of L. Itasy and 55 mi. WSW of Tananarive; alt. 5,340 ft.; agr. center (coffee, corn, rice), communications point; mfg. of edible oils, rice processing. R.C. and Protestant missions.

Soay (sō′ŭ). **1** Island (pop. 64), Inner Hebrides, Inverness, Scotland, just off SW coast of Skye; 3 mi. long, 2 mi. wide; rises to 455 ft. **2** Island (1½ mi. long, 1 mi. wide) just NW of St. Kilda, Outer Hebrides, Inverness, Scotland.

Soba (sō′bŭ), village (pop. 4,071), Khartoum prov., Anglo-Egyptian Sudan, on right bank of the Blue Nile and 11 mi. SE of Khartoum. Has ruins of anc. Soba, ⊙ Christian kingdom of S Sudan (6th–15th cent.).

Soba (sōbä′), town (pop. 2,031), Zaria prov., Northern Provinces, N central Nigeria, on railroad and 25 mi. ESE of Zaria; agr. trade center (cotton, peanuts, ginger).

Sobat River (sō′bät, –băt), Upper Nile prov., SE Anglo-Egyptian Sudan, formed by junction of Pibor and Baro rivers on Ethiopian border SE of Nasir, flows 205 mi. NW, past Nasir and Abwong, to White Nile SW of Malakal. Navigable (June-Dec.) to Gambela (Ethiopia) on Baro R. Contributes heavily to main Nile during flood period.

Sobernheim (zō′bûrnhīm), town (pop. 4,736), in former Prussian Rhine Prov., W Germany, after 1945 in Rhineland-Palatinate, on the Nahe and 10 mi. WSW of Bad Kreuznach; grain. Has late-Gothic church.

Sobeslav (sô′byĕsläf), Czech *Soběslav,* Ger. *Sobieslau* (zō′byĕslou), town (pop. 4,299), S Bohemia, Czechoslovakia, on Luznice R., on railroad and 11 mi. SSW of Tabor; mfg. (silk textiles, sewing machines), wood processing. Large apiaries produce honey for export. Has 15th-cent. Gothic church, folk art mus. Peat beds near by.

Sobibor (sôbē′bŏŏr), Pol. *Sobibór,* village, Lublin prov., E Poland, on Bug R. (USSR border) and 6 mi. SSE of Wlodawa. Ger. extermination camp here in Second World War.

Sobiecin (sôbyĕ′chēn), Pol. *Sobięcin,* Ger. *Hermsdorf* (hĕrms′dôrf), town (1939 pop. 11,233; 1946 pop. 12,156) in Lower Silesia, after 1945 in Wroclaw prov., SW Poland, in N foothills of the Sudetes, 3 mi. WSW of Waldenburg (Walbrzych); coal mining; major power station. Chartered after 1945 and briefly called Weglewo, Pol. *Węglewo.*

Sobieski, village (pop. 189), Morrison co., central Minn., on small affluent of Mississippi R. and 7 mi. SW of Little Falls; grain, potatoes, livestock.

Sobieslau, Czechoslovakia: see SOBESLAV.

Sobinka (sô′bĭnkŭ), city (1939 pop. 19,000), W Vladimir oblast, Russian SFSR, on Klyazma R. (head of navigation) and 18 mi. WSW of Vladimir; cotton-milling center. Called Komavangard in early 1920s. Became city in 1939.

Soboba Hot Springs, Calif.: see SAN JACINTO.

Sobolevo (sô′bŭlyĭvŭ), village (1947 pop. over 500), Kamchatka oblast, Khabarovsk Territory, Russian SFSR, on W coast of Kamchatka Peninsula, 100 mi. N of Ust-Bolsheretsk; fish canneries.

Soborsin, Rumania: see SAVARSIN.

Sobotin, Czechoslovakia: see LOUCNA NAD DESNOU.

Sobotka (sô′bôtkä), town (pop. 1,873), N Bohemia, Czechoslovakia, on railroad and 21 mi. SSE of Liberec; sugar beets, barley. Has 16th-cent. church, old town hall. In vicinity are 13th- and 17th-cent. castles.

Sobotka (sôbōōt′kä), Pol. *Sobótka,* Ger. *Zobten* (tsôp′tŭn), town (1939 pop. 3,524; 1946 pop. 5,899) in Lower Silesia, after 1945 in Wroclaw prov., SW Poland, 12 mi. ENE of Schweidnitz (Swidnica), at N foot of Sobotka mtn. (2,356 ft.); magnetite and nickel mining, granite quarrying. Prehistoric remains. Chartered 1399.

Sobradillo (sōvrä-dhē′lyō), town (pop. 1,211), Salamanca prov., W Spain, near Port. border, 27 mi. NW of Ciudad Rodrigo; olive-oil processing; livestock, rye, almonds, figs.

Sobradinho (sōōbrŏŏdē′nyōō), city (pop. 707), central Rio Grande do Sul, Brazil, in Jacuí valley, 45 mi. N of Cachoeira do Sul; wheat, tobacco. Until 1938, called Jacuí (old spelling, Jacuhy).

Sobral (sōōbräl′), city (1950 pop. 23,003), NW Ceará, Brazil, on Camocim-Crateús RR, 125 mi. W of Fortaleza; commercial and cotton-milling center; ships cotton yarn and cloth, carnauba wax, vegetable fibers, sugar, alcohol, and cattle. Bishopric.

Sobral da Adiça (dädē′sŭ), village (pop. 2,272), Beja dist., S Portugal, near Sp border, 33 mi. E of Beja; grain, olive oil, sheep. Copper mine near.

Sobral de Monte Agraço (dĭ mōn′tĭ ägrä′sōō), town (pop. 682), Lisboa dist., central Portugal, 20 mi. N of Lisbon; winegrowing center; cherries and other fruit shipped to Lisbon markets.

Sobrance (sô′bräntsĕ), Hung. *Szobránc* (sô′bränts), town (pop. 1,398), E Slovakia, Czechoslovakia, 16 mi. SE of Presov; health resort with saline and sulphur springs.

Sobraon (sōbroun′), village, Amritsar dist., W Punjab, India, on Sutlej R. and c.20 mi. NNE of Ferozepore. Near by is site of Br. victory (Feb., 1846) in 1st Anglo-Sikh War.

Sobrarbe (sōvrär′vä), historic district of Aragon, now in Huesca prov., NE Spain, in the central Pyrenees S of Fr. border, bet. Cinca (E) and Gállego (W) rivers; chief town, Boltaña. Resisted Moors (8th–9th cent.). Annexed (11th cent.) by kings of Aragon. The *fueros* [=privileges] of Sobrarbe were long considered the Magna Carta of Aragonese nobles.

Sobremonte, Argentina: see SAN FRANCISCO DEL CHAÑAR.

Sobrio, Monte di (môn′tĕ dē sô′brēō), mountain range (7,939 ft.) in Lepontine Alps, S Switzerland, 4 to 9 mi. NNW of Biasca.

Sobue (sōbōō′ā), town (pop. 15,583), Aichi prefecture, central Honshu, Japan, 13 mi. NW of Nagoya; rice-growing center; textiles.

Sobun River, Formosa: see TSENGWEN RIVER.

Soca (sō′kä), town (pop. 1,200), Canelones dept., S Uruguay, on highway, and 30 mi. ENE of Montevideo, in agr. region (grain, flax, stock). Formerly called Mosquitos; sometimes Doctor Francisco Soca.

Soca River, Yugoslavia and Italy: see ISONZO RIVER.

Soccorro, Brazil: see SOCORRO, São Paulo.

Soccoths (sŭ′kŭths), village (pop. 399), Cayo dist., central Br. Honduras, on Belize R. (western branch) and 1 mi. NE of Benque Viejo; corn, chicle, lumber. Also spelled Succotz.

Sochaczew (sô-khä′chĕf), Rus. *Sokhachev* (sŭ-khä′-chĭf), town (pop. 10,116), Warszawa prov., central Poland, on Bzura R. and 33 mi. W of Warsaw. Rail junction; mfg. (cement, artificial silk, flour). Castle ruins. Before Second World War, pop. was 50% Jewish.

Sochaux (sôshō′), outer NE suburb (pop. 2,831) of Montbéliard, Doubs dept., E France; important automobile factory.

Soche, China: see YARKAND.

Sochi (sô′chē), city (1939 pop. c.50,000), S Krasnodar Territory, Russian SFSR, port and subtropical resort on Black Sea, at foot of the Greater Caucasus, at mouth of short Sochi R., 105 mi. SSE of Krasnodar, on coastal railroad. One of main health and seaside resorts of USSR, with many hotels, sanatoriums, and rest homes; visited yearly by c.100,000 tourists. Tobacco- and food-processing industry; meat canning, dairying; tobacco, tea, citrus fruit. Consists of lower, older business section on left bank of Sochi R., and newer resort and residential parts amid extensive parks on hill slopes. Originally developed as resort in 1910–12; expanded considerably under Soviets. Became city in 1926; placed (1948) under direct jurisdiction of Russian SFSR govt.

Sochiapa (sōchyä′pä), town (pop. 339), Veracruz, E Mexico, in Sierra Madre Oriental, 4 mi. NE of Huatusco; fruit

Sochos or **Sokhos** (both: sôkhôs′), town (pop. 4,465), Salonika nome, Macedonia, Greece, 25 mi. ENE of Salonika; wheat, cotton, tobacco, silk.

Soci (sô′chē), village (pop. 1,384), Arezzo prov., Tuscany, central Italy, 3 mi. N of Bibbiena; macaroni mfg.

Social Circle, city (pop. 1,685), Walton co., N central Ga., 10 mi. S of Monroe; cotton and lumber milling. Inc. 1831.

Society Hill, town (pop. 645), Darlington co., NE S.C., 25 mi. N of Florence; chairs.

Society Islands, Fr. *Îles de la Société,* group (□ c.650; pop. 42,129), in FRENCH ESTABLISHMENTS IN OCEANIA, S Pacific, 4,200 mi. SW of San Francisco; 16°30′–17°47′S 148°–157°20′W. There are 2 clusters of volcanic and coral isls. in 450-mi. chain: Windward Isls. (Fr. *Îles du Vent* or *Archipel de Tahiti*), which include TAHITI (largest isl. of Fr.

Oceania, seat of Papeete, ⊙ colony), MOOREA, MAIAO, MEHETIA, TETIAROA; and Leeward Isls. (Fr. *Îles sous le Vent*), which include RAIATEA, largest isl. of group, HUAHINE, BORA-BORA, MAUPITI, TAHAA, MOPIHAA, MOTU ITI, SCILLY ISLAND, BELLINGSHAUSEN ISLAND. MAKATEA is only phosphate isl. of group. Highest peak (Mt. Orohena, 7,618 ft.) is on Tahiti. Breadfruit, pandanus, coconut trees; wild pigs, rats, small lizards. Isls. produce copra, sugar, rum, mother-of-pearl, vanilla, phosphates. Discovered 1767 by the British; visited 1769 by Capt. Cook and members of Royal Society, in honor of which the isls. were named; English missionaries arrived 1797, followed by the French. Fr. protectorate established 1843, group became colony 1880. Polynesian natives.

Sockburn, town (pop. 700), ⊙ Paparua co. (□ 136; pop. 6,652), E S.Isl., New Zealand, 5 mi. S of Christchurch; abattoirs, steel mills.

Sockenbacka, Finland: see PITAJANMAKI.

Socna, Tripolitania: see SOKNA.

Soco, El, Chile: see EL SOCO.

Sococha (sōkō'chä), town (pop. 3,500), Potosí dept., S Bolivia, near Argentina border, 9 mi. NE of Villazón; fruit, orchards, corn.

Socoltenango (sōkōltänäng'gō), town (pop. 1,410), Chiapas, S Mexico, in Sierra Madre, 8 mi. W of Comitán; cereals, sugar cane, fruit, livestock.

Socompa, Cerro (sĕ'rō sōkōm'pä), Andean peak (19,787 ft.) on Argentina-Chile border, 125 mi. WSW of San Antonio de los Cobres (Salta prov.) Argentina; 24°24'S. At SW foot is **Socompa Pass** (12,657 ft.), for railroad and road, bet. Chile and Argentina; 24°27'S 68°18'W. The Transandine RR of the North, over the pass, was opened 1948 bet. Salta (Argentina) and Antofagasta (Chile).

Soconusco (sōkōnōō'skō), town (pop. 1,273), Veracruz, SE Mexico, on Isthmus of Tehuantepec, 2 mi. ENE of Acayucan; fruit, livestock.

Socorro (sōōkô'rōō). **1** City, Piauí, Brazil: see FRONTEIRAS. **2** City (pop. 3,771), E São Paulo, Brazil, in the Serra da Mantiqueira, 40 mi. NE of Campinas; rail terminus; health resort; coffee, rice, sugar cane. Formerly Soccorro. **3** City, Sergipe, Brazil: see COTINGUIBA.

Socorro (sōkō'rō), town (pop. 7,891), Santander dept., N central Colombia, in valley of Cordillera Oriental, on road to Bogotá, and 45 mi. SSW of Bucaramanga; alt. 4,035 ft. Trading, processing, and agr. center (tobacco, sugar cane, coffee, cotton, corn, rice, vegetables, fruit, cattle); mfg. of cotton goods, footwear, tobacco products, leather goods, construction materials, food preserves. Lime and coal deposits near by. Old colonial town, founded in late 17th cent. Has fine bldgs. and cultural activities; sericulture school. Scene of one of 1st rebellions against Sp. rule in the Americas (1771).

Socorro (sukō'rō), county (□ 7,772; pop. 9,670), central N.Mex.; ⊙ Socorro. Grain and livestock-grazing area watered by Rio Grande, which flows through Elephant Butte Reservoir in S. Magdalena Mts. are W of Socorro, San Mateo Mts. in SW, part of Gallina Mts. in NW, sections of Cibola Natl. Forest in W and NE. Formed 1852.

Socorro. 1 City (pop. 4,334), ⊙ Socorro co., W central N.Mex., on Rio Grande, E of Magdalena Mts., and 70 mi. S of Albuquerque, in dairying, grain, livestock region; alt. 4,582 ft. Gold, silver, copper, lead, galena, and zinc mined in near-by mts. City is on site of Piro Pueblo, visited (1598) by Juan de Oñate. Church of San Miguel (part of which dates back to same year) and N.Mex. School of Mines here. Migratory waterfowl refuge and part of Cibola Natl. Forest near by. **2** Village, El Paso co., extreme W Texas, on the Rio Grande and 13 mi. S of El Paso, in irrigated farm area. One of oldest communities in Texas, founded in early 1680s around Sp. mission of Concepción del Socorro (extant; rebuilt from ruins).

Socorro, El, Venezuela: see EL SOCORRO.

Socorro Island, Chile: see GUAMBLIN ISLAND.

Socorro Island, Mexico: see REVILLAGIGEDO ISLANDS.

Socosani (sōkōsä'nē), village (pop. 78), Arequipa dept., S Peru, at W foot of the Chachani, 25 mi. NW of Arequipa; bottling of mineral waters.

Socotra, Sokotra, or **Soqotra** (sōkō'trŭ), island (□ 1,400; pop. 8,000) in Indian Ocean, 150 mi. off Cape Guardafui of Africa, forming insular section of MAHRI sultanate of Qishn and Socotra, Eastern Aden Protectorate; ⊙ Hadibu (Tamrida). Mountainous in interior (rises to nearly 5,000 ft.), the isl. is 85 mi. long, 25 mi. wide. Pop. engages in fishing and stock raising. Ghee, aloes, dragon's blood, pearls, and dried fish are the chief exports. British air base on cape Ras Karma, near QADHUB. Occupied 1834 by East India Company; placed 1886 under British protection, isl. is residence of senior Mahri sultan. British garrison was posted here in Second World War. Pop. speaks South Arabic dialect, similar to that of the Mahri coast and differing from the standard North Arabic language.

Socovos (sōkō'vōs), town (pop. 1,719), Albacete prov., SE central Spain, 20 mi. SW of Hellín; perfume mfg., olive-oil processing, flour milling; wine, esparto, cereals.

Socrum (sŏ'krŭm), village (1940 pop. 512), Polk co., central Fla., on Hillsboro R. and 9 mi. NNW of Lakeland.

Soctrang (shouk'träng), town (1936 pop. 7,754), ⊙ Soctrang prov. (□ 900; 1943 pop. 244,200), S Vietnam, in Cochin China, near Bassac R. mouth, 95 mi. SW of Saigon; airport. Road and canal center in intensive rice-growing area.

Socuéllamos (sōkwĕ'lyämōs), town (pop. 11,580), Ciudad Real prov., S central Spain, in New Castile, on railroad to Albacete and 23 mi. E of Alcázar de San Juan; viticultural center; also winegrowing and stock raising. Alcohol distilling, flour milling, cheese processing.

Soda, Gebel es- (jĕ'bĕl ĕs-sō'dä) [Arabic,=black mountain], Saharan range in W central Libya, along Tripolitania-Fezzan border, 250 mi. S of Misurata; c.125 mi. long E–W. Basalt formation. Rises to c.2,700 ft. The Giofra oases (Sokna, Hun) are at N foot.

Soda Lake, Calif.: see MOJAVE RIVER.

Sodankylä (sō'dän-kü"lä), village (commune pop. 8,015), Lapi co., N Finland, on Arctic Highway (Rovaniemi-Pechenga) and 65 mi. NNE of Rovaniemi; Lapp trade center. Site of Lapland People's Col.; has 17th-cent. church. Suffered heavy damage in Second World War.

Soda Springs. 1 Hamlet, Nevada co., E Calif., in the Sierra Nevada, near Donner Pass, 10 mi. W of Truckee; alt. c.6,700 ft. Summer, winter resort. **2** Village (pop. 1,329), ⊙ Caribou co., SE Idaho, 50 mi. ESE of Pocatello, near Bear R., in mining (phosphates), agr., grazing area; alt. 5,779 ft.; dairy products. Phosphorus plant (just N) begun 1951. Carbonic-acid-charged springs. Settled 1863, laid out 1870 by Brigham Young.

Sodaville, town (pop. 157), Linn co., NW Oregon, 15 mi. SE of Albany.

Soddu (sō'dōō), town, Sidamo-Borana prov., S Ethiopia, N of L. Abaya, 55 mi. WNW of Yirga-Alam, in cotton-growing region; alt. c.6,800 ft.; road junction. Commercial center; cotton ginning. Airfield. Near by are iron deposits.

Soddy, village (pop. 2,157), Hamilton co., SE Tenn., near Chickamauga Reservoir (Tennessee R.), 18 mi. N of Chattanooga.

Soden, Bad, Germany: see BAD SODEN.

Soderfors (sû"dûrfôrs', -fôsh'), Swedish *Söderfors*, village (pop. 1,505), Uppsala co., E Sweden, on Hedesunda Fjord (hā"dŭsŭn'dä), Swedish *Hedesundafjärden*, 15-mi.-long expansion of lower Dal R., 20 mi. S of Gavle; large iron- and steelworks.

Soderhamn (-hä'mŭn), Swedish *Söderhamn*, city (1950 pop. 11,514), Gavleborg co., E Sweden, on small bay of Gulf of Bothnia, 40 mi. N of Gavle; seaport, exporting timber, fish, iron ore, and wood pulp; rail junction. Lumber milling, metal- and woodworking. Had 17th-cent. church. Inc. 1620. Burned 1721 by Russians.

Soderi or **Sodiri** (sō'dĭrē), village, Kordofan prov., central Anglo-Egyptian Sudan, on road and 110 mi. NW of El Obeid; gum arabic, sesame, corn, durra; livestock.

Soderkoping (sû'dûrchû"pĭng), Swedish *Söderköping*, city (pop. 2,873), Ostergotland co., SE Sweden, on Gota Canal and 9 mi. SE of Norrkoping; health resort, with medicinal springs. Has two 14th-cent. churches, one of Sweden's earliest printing presses, and mus. One of country's oldest towns; noted trade center bet. 10th and 16th cent.

Sodermanland (-mänlănd"), Swedish *Södermanland*, county [Swedish *län*] (□ 2,634; 1950 pop. 214,254), E Sweden; ⊙ Nykoping. On the Baltic, bounded by L. Malar (N) and by L. Hjalmar (W), it forms W part of Sodermanland province [Swedish *landskap*] (□ 3,462; pop. 571,021), which also includes S part of Stockholm co. Lowland region with fertile soil, co. is dotted with numerous small lakes. Agr. (grain, fruit), stock raising, dairying. Industries are iron mining, woodworking, paper milling; Eskilstuna is center of important steel industry. Cities are Nykoping, Eskilstuna, Katrineholm, Strangnas, Torshalla, Mariefred, and Trosa. Prov. noted for purity of Swedish spoken here.

Sodertalje (sû"dûrtĕl'yû), Swedish *Södertälje*, city (1950 pop. 25,266), Stockholm co., E Sweden, bet. S shore of L. Malar (N) and head of Himmer Fjord, Swedish *Himmerfjärden*, 25-mi.-long inlet of the Baltic, 16 mi. SW of Stockholm; rail junction; popular seaside resort. Mfg. of chemicals, automobiles, machinery, matches, textiles, tobacco products. One of Sweden's oldest cities, in former times called Talje (tĕl'yû), Swedish *Tälje*. Sodertalje Canal (1 mi. long), connecting L. Malar with the Baltic, was built 1819, enlarged 1917–24.

Sodhra (sōd'rŭ), town (pop. 6,164), Gujranwala dist., E Punjab, W Pakistan, 4 mi. ENE of Wazirabad; wheat, rice; plywood factory. Sometimes spelled Sohdra.

Sodom (sŏ'dŭm), **Sdom,** or **Sedom** (both: sŭdōm'), village, SE Israel, on SW shore of Dead Sea, 40 mi. ESE of Beersheba; 1,292 ft. below sea level; important potash works (refinery is 4 mi. SE). The site of the Sodom of the Bible, destroyed for its wickedness, is unknown.

Sodra Vi (sû"drä vē'), Swedish *Södra Vi*, village (pop. 918), Kalmar co., SE Sweden, on Kro L., Swedish *Krön* (krŭn) (8 mi. long), 5 mi. NNW of Vimmerby; health resort; sawmilling, woodworking.

Sodus (sō'dŭs), resort village (pop. 1,588), Wayne co., W N.Y., near L. Ontario, 28 mi. ENE of Rochester; mfg. (gears, baskets, cement products, chemicals, canned foods). Agr. (fruit, truck). The lotuses of near-by Sodus Bay are famous. Inc. 1918.

Sodus Bay, W N.Y., inlet of L. Ontario, indenting N shore of Wayne co., 32 mi. E of Rochester; c.5 mi. long. Summer resorts; has noted lotus beds.

Sodus Point, resort village (pop. c.600), Wayne co., W N.Y., on L. Ontario, at entrance of Sodus Bay, 33 mi. ENE of Rochester; port of entry. Fired by British in War of 1812.

Soebang, Indonesia: see SUBANG.

Soebi Besar, Indonesia: see SOUTH NATUNA ISLANDS.

Soeda (sōä'dä), town (pop. 22,671), Fukuoka prefecture, N Kyushu, Japan, 26 mi. E of Fukuoka; commercial center for rice-growing, coal-mining area; raw silk.

Soegi, Indonesia: see SUGI.

Soekaboemi, Indonesia: see SUKABUMI.

Soekaradja, Indonesia: see SUKARAJA.

Soela Islands, Indonesia: see SULA ISLANDS.

Soela Sound (sō'ĕlä), Est. *Soela Vain*, arm of Baltic Sea, bet. Estonian isls. of Hiiumaa (N) and Saare (S); 3 mi. wide.

Soemba, Indonesia: see SUMBA.

Soembawa, Indonesia: see SUMBAWA.

Soembing, Mount, Indonesia: see SUMBING, MOUNT.

Soemedang, Indonesia: see SUMEDANG.

Soemenep, Indonesia: see SUMENEP.

Soenda Islands, Indonesia: see SUNDA ISLANDS.

Soenda Strait, Indonesia: see SUNDA STRAIT.

Soengaigerong, Indonesia: see SUNGAIGERONG.

Soengeigerong, Indonesia: see SUNGAIGERONG.

Soepiori, Netherlands New Guinea: see SUPIORI.

Soerabaja, Indonesia: see SURABAYA.

Soerakarta, Indonesia: see SOLO.

Soesdyke (sōōs'dīk), village (pop. 1,178), Demerara co., N Br. Guiana, on right bank of lower Demerara R. and 20 mi. SSW of Georgetown; rice, sugar cane, stock.

Soest (zōst), town (pop. 25,454), in former Prussian prov. of Westphalia, W Germany, after 1945 in North Rhine-Westphalia, 28 mi. E of Dortmund; rail junction; mfg. of machinery, wire, light bulbs, furniture; food processing (sugar, fruit preserves). Trades in agr. produce and cattle of region. Has Romanesque and Gothic churches, all damaged in Second World War (total destruction 30–40%). First mentioned in 7th cent. In Middle Ages it was Westphalia's leading town and a flourishing member of the Hanseatic League.

Soest (sōōst), town (pop. 17,140), Utrecht prov., central Netherlands, 10 mi. NE of Utrecht; mfg. (photographic film, linoleum, oleomargarine), dairy products. Painter Pieter van der Faes (Sir Peter Lely) b. here.

Soestdijk (sōōst'dīk), village (pop. 4,871), Utrecht prov., central Netherlands, 10 mi. NE of Utrecht. Royal summer palace here. Sometimes Soestdyk.

Soesterberg (sōō'stûrbĕrkh), town (pop. 1,860), Utrecht prov., central Netherlands, 9 mi. ENE of Utrecht; oleomargarine.

Sofades, Greece: see SOPHADES.

Sofala (sōfä'lä), village, Ngwato dist., E Bechuanaland Protectorate, near U. of So. Afr. border, 210 mi. SSW of Bulawayo, 70 mi. SE of Serowe; road junction. Hosp.

Sofala, village, Mozambique: see NOVA SOFALA.

Sofara (sōfä'rä), village, S Fr. Sudan, Fr. West Africa, on Bani R., in mid-Niger depression, and 35 mi. S of Mopti; rice, millet, livestock, hides. Has 2 beautiful mosques. Picturesque market for salt, dried fish, leatherware, blankets.

Sofia (sō'fēŭ, sōfē'ŭ, Bulg. sô'fēä), anc. *Serdica* or *Sardica*, Bulg. *Sofiya*, city (pop. 366,925), ⊙ Bulgaria and ⊙ (but independent of) Sofia dist. (formed 1949), W Bulgaria, in Sofia Basin, N of Vitosha Mts., on small left tributary of near-by Iskar R ; 42°48'N 23°18'E; alt. 1,820 ft. Largest city of Bulgaria; major transportation (5 rail lines, 2 airports) and mfg. center with heavy (metallurgy, armaments, machinery), light (textile, rubber, leather), and food-processing (cereals, sugar, meat, fruit, vegetables, hops, cocoa) industries. Mfg. also of electrical equipment (radios, telephones), chemicals, furniture, cigarettes, carpets, cosmetics. Important commercial center, with banking and financial cooperatives; central market for Sofia Basin agr. output (rye, oats, corn, livestock, fruit, vegetables). A leading cultural center of Bulgaria; site of univ. (established 1880), Polytechnical Inst., academies of science, art, and music, schools of military sciences, physical education, commerce, and handicrafts, and theological seminary. Has opera house, theaters, natl. library, astronomical observatory, archaeological, ethnographical, zoological, and other museums. Noted for architecture are chapel of St. George (originally a Roman bath), cathedral of St. Alexander Nevski (19th cent.), church of St. Sophia (6th cent.), Banya Bashi mosque (picturesque minaret), Black Mosque (transformed into church), town hall, and medieval synagogue. Royal palace has a picture gall. and collections of anc. relics. Several Bulg. kings and natl. heroes are commemorated by monuments and mausoleums. Statue of Rus. tsar Alexander II marks liberation of Bulgaria from Turkish rule.

Sofia's W suburb Krasno-selo (pop. 18,787) has mineral baths. Outlying residential and health resorts include Knyazhevo (SW) and Gorna-banya (W). Once a Thracian settlement; occupied (A.D. 29) by Romans and became military camp of Ulpia Serdica under Emperor Trajan (early 2d cent. A.D.). Destroyed (447) by Huns; restored and fortified by Byzantines. Successively under First Bulg. Kingdom (809–1018) and Byzantium (1194–1386); sacked by Turkish governor of Plovdiv. Developed as residence of Turkish governor-general for Balkan Peninsula and became important strategic center. Subject to Rus. assaults in 19th cent.; finally captured (1877) and ceded to Bulgaria; ⊙ Bulgaria since 1878. Modernized (extensive parks, residential dists.) and industrialized, it suffered severely from air raids during Second World War. Called Sredets by Slavs; renamed Triaditsa by Byzantines; known as Sofia since 1329. Was ⊙ former Sofia oblast (1934–47). Sometimes spelled Sophia.

Sofia Basin, synclinal valley (□ 458; average alt. 1,800 ft.) in W Bulgaria, bet. W Balkan Mts. (N) and Sredna Gora and Vitosha Mts. (S); drained by Iskar R. Fertile soil. Lignite mining N of Kurilo, mineral springs W of Sofia. Extensive agr. (rye, oats, corn, truck, fruit, livestock). Main center, Sofia.

Sofi-Kurgan, Kirghiz SSR: see SUFI-KURGAN.

Sofisk or **Sofiysk** (sŭfēsk′), town (1942 pop. over 500), SW Khabarovsk Territory, Russian SFSR, in N Bureya Range, 180 mi. WNW of Komsomolsk; gold-mining center.

Sofiya, Bulgaria: see SOFIA.

Sofiyevka (sŭfē′ufkŭ). **1** Village (1926 pop. 10,350), SW Dnepropetrovsk oblast, Ukrainian SSR, on road and 25 mi. NE of Krivoi Rog; flour milling. **2** Town, Zaporozhe oblast, Ukrainian SSR; see CHERVONOARMEISKOYE, Zaporozhe oblast.

Sofiyevski or **Sofiyevskiy** (–skē), town (1939 pop. over 500), S Voroshilovgrad oblast, Ukrainian SSR, 12 mi. NNE of Krasny Luch; coal mining.

Sofroniyevo (sôfrô′nē-ĕvô), village (pop. 3,849), Vratsa dist., NW Bulgaria, on Ogosta R. and 12 mi. SW of Oryakhovo; vineyards, grain, livestock. Formerly Sarbenitsa.

Softeland, Norway: see SYFTELAND.

Sofu-gan, Japan: see LOT'S WIFE.

Sofye-Kondratyevka or **Sof'ye-Kondrat'yevka** (sô′-fyĭ kŭndrä′tyĭfkŭ), town (1939 pop. over 500), E central Stalino oblast, Ukrainian SSR, in the Donbas, 3 mi. W of Yenakiyevo.

Sog (sôkh), river, SW Iceland, issues from the Thingvallavatn, flows 15 mi. S to join the Hvita 10 mi. NE of Eyrarbakki, forming the Olfusa. Ljosafoss, large waterfall, is site of largest Icelandic power station.

Soga, Japan: see CHIBA, city.

Soga (sō′gä), town, Eastern Prov., Tanganyika, on railroad and 25 mi. W of Dar es Salaam; sisal, cotton, copra.

Sogamoso (sōgämō′sō), town (pop. 5,216), Boyacá dept., central Colombia, on headstream of Chicamocha R., in Cordillera Oriental, and 33 mi. ENE of Tunja; alt. 8,432 ft. Rail terminus, connected by road and rail with Bogotá and with a highway to interior of llanos. Trading and agr. center (wheat, corn, potatoes, cotton, livestock); flour and textile milling; mfg. of footwear. Anc. sacred city of Chibcha Indians. Coal mines near by.

Sogamoso River, Santander dept., N central Colombia, rises in Cordillera Oriental foothills, flows c.100 mi. from the influx of Suárez R. (SE of Zapatoca) WNW to Magdalena R. 12 mi. N of Barrancabermeja. Navigable; carries most of import and export trade of the dept.

Soganli River, Turkey: see YENICE RIVER.

Sogdiana, Uzbek SSR: see TRANSOXIANA.

Sogn, region, Norway: see SOGN OG FJORDANE.

Sogndal (sông′ụndäl). **1** Village in Sokndal canton (pop. 3,127), Rogaland co., SW Norway, port on North Sea, 14 mi. W of Flekkefjord, in the Dalane. Iron-mining village (pop. 671) of Hauge (hou′gụ) is 3 mi. N. **2** or **Sogndal i Sogne** (ē sông′nụ), village (pop. 677; canton pop. 3,661), Sogn og Fjordane co., W Norway, on Sogndal Fjord (11-mi. NE arm of Sogne Fjord), 65 mi. ESE of Floro; fruitgrowing. At Kaupanger (koup′ängụr) village, 6 mi. SE, is 12th-cent. stave church and parsonage. At Amla (äm′lä) (formerly Amle) village, 7 mi. SE, is 17th-cent. manor house with Heiberg art collection.

Sognefjell (sông′nụfyĕl), SW section of JOTUNHEIM MOUNTAINS, in Sogn og Fjordane co., W Norway, NE of Luster Fjord; rises to 6,808 ft. 20 mi. NNE of Ardalstangen. Mtn. road from Skjolden and Fortun leads through pass (alt. c.5,250 ft.) to the Gudbrandsdal. Sometimes called Dolefjell, Nor. *Dølefjell.*

Sogne Fjord (sông′nụ), inlet (112 mi. long, 3 mi. wide) of North Sea, W Norway. Up to 4,081 ft. deep at mouth, it is Norway's longest and deepest fjord. Mouth, 45 mi. N of Bergen, is protected by Solund Isls. Fjord cuts into mts. over 5,000 ft. high; magnificent scenery attracts numerous tourists. Extends several arms: Fjaerlands Fjord extends 15 mi. N; Luster Fjord or Lyster Fjord extends 30 mi. NE to Skjolden, where it receives glacier stream from the Jostedalsbre; Ardal Fjord (Nor. *Årdalsfjord*) extends 12 mi. E, cutting into Jotunheim Mts.; and Aurlands Fjord extends 20 mi. S, with 2 arms cutting into the Hemsedalsfjell. Fjord is partly icebound in winter. Inhabitants are noted for their dialect; region is rich in viking tradition.

Sogn og Fjordane (sông′ụn ô fyō′ränụ), county [Nor. *fylke*] (□ 7,142; pop. 96,849), SW Norway; ⊙ FLORO. Includes the mountainous Sogn region around the inner SOGNE FJORD with its many branches; and the Fjordane region (formerly spelled Fjordene, originally Firdafylke), which covers Sunnfjord (formerly Sondfjord)—a mountainous coastal area with many lesser fjords—and the area around NORD FJORD. Coast is deeply indented. Contains many isls., notably the Solund and Bremanger. There are many mts. (part of the Jotunheim is E), glaciers (notably Jostedalsbre and Alfotbre), lakes, and waterfalls which attract tourists. Agr. (fruit and tobacco); fowl, cattle, and horse breeding; active fishing. Road net around Nord Fjord connects with the Gudbrandsdal. Until 1918, the co. (then called *amt*) was named Nordre Bergenhus or Nordre Bergenhuus.

Sogod (sō′gōd). **1** Town (1939 pop. 2,135; 1948 municipality pop. 15,687), N Cebu isl., Philippines, on Camotes Sea, 33 mi. NNE of Cebu city; agr. center (corn, tobacco). **2** Town (1939 pop. 2,291; 1948 municipality pop. 31,848), S Leyte, Philippines, at head of Sogod Bay, 60 mi. S of Tacloban; agr. center (rice, corn, hemp).

Sogod Bay, inlet of Mindanao Sea, S Leyte, Philippines, sheltered SE by Panaon Isl.; 25 mi. long.

Sogut (sụ̂üt′), Turkish *Söğüt*, village (pop. 2,630), Bilecik prov., NW Turkey, 15 mi. SE of Bilecik; grain, sugar beets, cotton. Birthplace of Osman, founder of Ottoman dynasty; near by is tomb ascribed to Osman's father Ertogrul. Sometimes spelled Sugut, Turkish *Sügüt.*

Sogut, Lake, Turkish *Söğüt* or *Söğütlü* (□ 17), SW Turkey, 40 mi. W of Antalya; 9 mi. long, 3 mi. wide; alt. 4,426 ft. Also called Manay.

Sogwi (sŭ′gwē′), Jap. *Seiki*, township (1946 pop. 17,495), S Cheju Isl., Korea, 18 mi. SSE of Cheju, on E.China Sea; agr. (grains, soybeans, cotton), fish canning.

Sohag (sō′hăg), **Suhag** (sōō′–), or **Suhaj** (–hăj), city (pop. 43,234), ⊙ Girga prov., central Upper Egypt, on W bank of the Nile, on railroad, and 190 mi. NNW of Aswan; cotton ginning, pottery making, dairying; cotton, cereals, dates, sugar cane. Has ruins of 2 fine 5th–6th cent. Coptic churches.

Sohagpur (sō′hägpŏŏr), town (pop. 8,629), Hoshangabad dist., NW Madhya Pradesh, India, 32 mi. E of Hoshangabad; trades in timber (teak, sal), lac, cutch; wheat, millet, oilseeds. Forests (S).

Soham (sō′ụm), town and parish (pop. 4,747), N Cambridge, England, 5 mi. SE of Ely; agr. market. Has 12th-cent. church with 15th-cent. tower.

Sohano (sōhä′nō), town, N Solomon Isls., on islet off S tip of Buka isl.; 5°25′S 154°40′E. Administrative center of Bougainville dist. of Territory of New Guinea, comprising Buka and Bougainville isls. Replaced Kieta (on Bougainville isl.) after Second World War.

Sohan River, W Pakistan: see SOAN RIVER.

Sohar or **Suhar** (both: sōhär′), chief town (pop. 7,500) of Batina dist., N Oman, 125 mi. NW of Muscat; port of supply for Western Hajar hill country, and date-exporting center; also ships ghee, dried limes, cowhides, goatskins. Mfg. (silk turbans, lungis). Airfield.

Sohara (sōhä′rä), town (pop. 8,724), Gifu prefecture, central Honshu, Japan, 7 mi. E of Gifu; sweet potatoes, market produce, flowers, raw silk.

Sohawal (sōhä′vŭl), village, central Vindhya Pradesh, India, 5 mi. W of Satna; ochre and limestone works; markets millet, gram, wheat. Was ⊙ former princely state of Sohawal (□ 251; pop. 50,435) of Central India agency; since 1948, state merged with Vindhya Pradesh.

Sohdra, W Pakistan: see SODHRA.

Sohland or **Sohland an der Spree** (zō′länt än dĕr shprā′), village (pop. 6,581), Saxony, E central Germany, in Upper Lusatia, near the Spree, 10 mi. S of Bautzen, near Czechoslovak border; lignite mining; textiles (cotton, linen, jute), button mfg.

Sohna (sō′nụ), town (pop. 5,710), Gurgaon dist., SE Punjab, India, 15 mi. SSE of Gurgaon; millet, gram, oilseeds; mfg. of glass bangles. Medicinal hot sulphur spring.

Soho (sōhō′, sụ–). **1** NW industrial suburb (pop. 25,407) of Birmingham, NW Warwick, England. **2** District of Westminster, London, England, N of the Thames, 1 mi. NW of Charing Cross, bounded by Oxford Street (N), Regent Street (W), Leicester Square (S), and Tottenham Court Road (E); known for its French and Italian restaurants. District is traversed by Shaftesbury Avenue, site of numerous theaters. After revocation of Edict of Nantes (1685) Soho became resort of French Protestant exiles and was fashionable residential dist. until early 19th cent.; later many artists and writers settled here. Among famous residents were Dryden, Hazlitt, William Blake, De Quincey, Ernest Dowson, Edmund Burke, Mrs. Siddons, Charles Kemble, and the duke of Monmouth.

Soholt, Norway: see SJOHOLT.

Sohrau, Poland: see ZORY.

Sohwal, India: see FYZABAD, city.

Soignies (swänyē′), Flemish *Zinnik* (zĭ′nĭk), town (pop. 10,387), Hainaut prov., S central Belgium, 10 mi. NE of Mons; granite, chalk, and blue-limestone quarrying center; leather tanning; mfg. (electric lamps, blown glass). Center of horse-breeding area. Has 11th-cent. Romanesque church.

Sointula (swŏntū′lụ), village (pop. estimate 500), SW B.C., on Malcolm Isl., just off NE Vancouver Isl., 170 mi. NW of Nanaimo; 50°38′N 127°1′W; fishing port; lumbering.

Soira, Mount (soi′rä), or **Mount Suaira** (swī′rä), highest mtn. group (9,885 ft.) in Eritrea, near Senafe, 60 mi. S of Massawa.

Soissons (swäsō′), anc. *Noviodunum*, later *Augusta Suessionum* and *Suessiona*, town (pop. 17,136), Aisne dept., N France, on left bank of Aisne R. (canalized) and 60 mi. NE of Paris; transportation and commercial (grain, beans) center. Foundries and metalworks (boilers, agr. implements), tanneries; mfg. of rubber articles, champagne bottles, sugar. Important town of Roman Belgica prov. Early episcopal see. Scene of decisive victory (486) of Clovis I over Syagrius. Became ⊙ several Merovingian kings. Often besieged in Middle Ages. Fell to Allies in 1814 and 1815, to Prussians in 1870. Captured twice (1914, 1918) by Germans, and near front lines throughout First World War, it suffered considerable damage. Heaviest fighting in area took place at the Chemin des Dames (NE). The 13th-cent. cathedral and the former abbey of Saint-Jean-des-Vignes (where Thomas à Becket lived for several years) were damaged in both world wars. In suburb of Saint-Vaast (right bank of Aisne R.) are ruins of abbey of St. Médard, a burial place of Merovingian kings.

Soisy-sous-Montmorency (swäzē′-sōō-mōmôrăsē′), town (pop. 5,618), Seine-et-Oise dept., N central France, an outer NNW suburb of Paris, just W of Montmorency, 10 mi. from Notre Dame Cathedral; foundry; mfg. of electric furnaces, metal mirrors.

Soja (sō′jä). **1** Town (pop. 5,049), Gumma prefecture, central Honshu, Japan, just NW of Maebashi; rice, raw silk. **2** Town (pop. 10,348), Okayama prefecture, SW Honshu, Japan, 10 mi. W of Okayama; rail junction; agr. center (rice, wheat, persimmons); mfg. (floor mats, raw silk, sake).

Sojat (sō′jŭt), town (pop. 11,790), central Rajasthan, India, 45 mi. SE of Jodhpur; trades in grain, wool, cotton, metal, oilseeds; cotton ginning; handicraft leather work (saddlery), cutlery, swords.

Sojitra (sō′jĭtrŭ), town (pop. 11,604), Kaira dist., N Bombay, India, 7 mi. NW of Petlad; trades in tobacco, millet, pulse, rice; handicraft cloth weaving, copper and brass utensils.

Sok, river, Russian SFSR: see SOK RIVER.

Soka (sō′kä), town (pop. 13,630), Saitama prefecture, central Honshu, Japan, 6 mi. ENE of Kawaguchi; rice growing.

Sokal or **Sokal'** (sŭkäl′), city (1931 pop. 12,135), N Lvov oblast, Ukrainian SSR, on Bug R. (Pol. border) and 45 mi. NNE of Lvov; mfg. center (machinery, cement, pottery, soap); agr. processing (cereals, fruit, vegetables), sawmilling. Has old monastery. Passed (1772) from Poland to Austria; reverted (1919) to Poland; ceded to USSR in 1945. The area (□ 185) W of Sokal, including Belz and Krystynopol, passed in 1951 from Lublin prov., Poland, to Lvov oblast, Ukrainian SSR.

Soke (sụ̂kĕ′), Turk. *Söke*, town (1950 pop. 13,791), Aydin prov., W Turkey, rail terminus 25 mi. WSW of Aydin, near Menderes R.; large grain crop; also tobacco, figs, olives; emery deposits, with iron near by. Sometimes spelled Sokia.

Sokei, Formosa: see SHWANGKI.

Sokelven, Norway: see SYKKYLVEN.

Soke of Peterborough, England: see PETERBOROUGH.

Sokh (sôkh), village (1939 pop. over 500) SW Fergana oblast, Uzbek SSR, on Sokh R. and 40 mi. S of Kokand; pasture area.

Sokhachev, Poland: see SOCHACZEW.

Sokhondo (sŭkhŭndô′), highest peak (8,136 ft.) of Borshchovochny Range, SW Chita oblast, Russian SFSR, 195 mi. SW of Chita, near Mongolian border; extensive tin deposits.

Sokhos, Greece: see SOCHOS.

Sokh River (sôkh), Kirghiz and Uzbek SSR, rises in W Alai Range, flows c.75 mi. N, past Sokh, into Fergana Valley, where it fans out into an irrigation canal network (near Kokand) and disappears into the sands.

Sokia, Turkey: see SOKE.

Sok-Karmala (sôk′-kŭrmŭlä′), village (1926 pop. 1,708), NW Chkalov oblast, Russian SFSR, 30 mi. SSW of Bugulma; wheat, sunflowers, livestock. Sometimes called Sok-Karmalinskoye or Sok-Karmalinsk.

Sokkelven, Norway: see SYKKYLVEN.

Sokna or **Socna** (sŏk′nä), oasis (1950 pop. 1,500), SE Tripolitania, Libya, near Fezzan border, 10 mi. WSW of Hun, on N slope of the Gebel es-Soda; alt. c.820 ft. Agr. (dates, figs, barley) and camel breeding.

Sokna River (sôk′nä), Sor-Trondelag co., central Norway, rises N of Kvikne (Hedmark co.) and flows N, joining the Gaula at Storen; 80 mi. long.

Sokndal, canton, Norway: see SOGNDAL, Rogaland.

Soko Banja or **Soko Banya** (sô'kô bä'nyä), village (pop. 3,844), E Serbia, Yugoslavia, 22 mi. N of Nis; health resort.

Sokodé (sōkō'dā), town (pop. 3,913), Fr. Togoland, on road, 190 mi. N of Lomé; projected terminus of railroad extension from Blitta. Commercial and agr. center; cotton, peanuts, shea nuts and butter; livestock. Kapok ginning; pottery mfg. Hosp., R.C. mission.

Sokol (sô'kŭl). **1** Town (1947 pop. over 500), S Sakhalin oblast, Russian SFSR, on E coast railroad and 7 mi. SSW of Dolinsk, in agr. area (oats, potatoes, vegetables). Under Jap. rule (1905–45), called Otani. **2** City (1939 pop. 26,000), S central Vologda oblast, Russian SFSR, on railroad, on Sukhona R. and 20 mi. NNE of Vologda; paper-milling, celluloid-mfg. center; sawmills, condensed-milk plant. Includes NW suburb of Pechatkino (celluloid works).

Sokolac, Yugoslavia: see GLASINAC.

Sokolka (sôkōō'ōōkä), Pol. *Sokółka*, town (pop. 4,879), Bialystok prov., NE Poland, on railroad and 24 mi. NE of Bialystok; cement mfg., sawmilling, tanning, flour milling, dairying. During Second World War, under administration of East Prussia.

Sokolniki or **Sokol'niki** (sŭkôl'nyĭkē), village (1939 pop. over 500), S Lvov oblast, Ukrainian SSR, 5 mi. S of Lvov; summer resort with sulphur springs.

Sokolo (sōkō'lō), village, S Fr. Sudan, Fr. West Africa, in mid-Niger basin (irrigation) and 85 mi. N of Ségou; peanuts, cotton, wheat, livestock.

Sokolov (sô'kôlôf), town (pop. 8,112), W Bohemia, Czechoslovakia, on Ohre R. and 11 mi. WSW of Carlsbad; rail junction; lignite mining; leather and chemical works. Until 1948, called Falknov or Falknov nad Ohri, Czech *Falknov nad Ohří*, Ger. *Falkenau*.

Sokolov (sŭkŭlôf'), village (1926 pop. 742), W central Zhitomir oblast, Ukrainian SSR, 8 mi. WNW of Chervonoarmeisk; potatoes, flax, buckwheat.

Sokolovka (–kŭ). **1** Village (1939 pop. over 500), N North Kazakhstan oblast, Kazakh SSR, on Ishim R. and 15 mi. N of Petropavlovsk; agr.; metalworks. **2** Town (1943 pop. over 500), SE Maritime Territory, Russian SFSR, on Sea of Japan and 100 mi. ENE of Vladivostok; fish canning.

Sokolovo (–lô'vŭ), village (pop. 2,215), E Tambov oblast, Russian SFSR, 16 mi. ENE of Tambov; wheat, sunflowers.

Sokolovo-Kondryuchenskoye (–kŭndryōō'chĭnskŭyŭ), village (1939 pop. over 500), SW Rostov oblast, Russian SFSR, 7 mi. SW of Krasny Sulin; truck produce.

Sokolow (sôkô'wōōf), Pol. *Sokołów*. **1** or **Sokolow Malopolski** (mäwôpôl'skē), Pol. *Sokołów Małopolski*, town (pop. 2,415), Rzeszow prov., SE Poland, 14 mi. NNE of Rzeszow; flour milling, tanning, lumbering; brickworks. **2** or **Sokolow Podlaski** (pôdlä'skē), Pol. *Sokołów Podlaski*, Rus. *Sokolov* (sŭkŭlôf'), town (pop. 7,515), Warszawa prov., E Poland, on railroad and 55 mi. ENE of Warsaw; stone quarrying; mfg. of bricks, caps; tanning, flour milling. Sugar mill near by. Before Second World War, pop. 50% Jewish.

Sokolskoye or **Sokol'skoye** (sŭkôl'skŭyŭ), town (1948 pop. over 2,000), E Ivanovo oblast, Russian SFSR, on Volga R. and 12 mi. SSE of Yuryevets; shipbuilding.

Sokoly (sôkô'wĭ), Pol. *Sokoły*, town (pop. 1,070), Bialystok prov., NE Poland, 21 mi. WSW of Bialystok.

Sokone (sōkō'nā), village, W Senegal, Fr. West Africa, landing on Saloum R. delta, 32 mi. NNE of Bathurst (Br. Gambia); peanut growing.

Sokota (sō'kōtä). **1** Village (pop. 800), Begemdir prov., NW Ethiopia, in Simen Mts., 55 mi. SW of Aduwa, in agr. and livestock region. **2** Town, Wallo prov., Ethiopia: see SAKOTA.

Sokoto (sōkōtō', sōkō'tō), province (□ 39,965; pop. 1,869,160), Northern Provinces, NW Nigeria; ⊙ Sokoto. Bounded N and W by Fr. West Africa; includes savanna (S) and thorn scrub (N); drained by Niger and Kebbi rivers. Gold, diamonds, limestone mined. Agr. (cotton, millet, tobacco); cattle raising. Main centers: Sokoto, Birnin Kebbi, Gusau, Kaura Namoda. Pop. largely Hausa and Fulah. Sokoto or Fulah empire (formed early 19th cent. from several smaller Moslem sultanates) extended throughout N Nigeria to Bornu. Came under full British control early in 20th cent.

Sokoto, town (pop. 20,084), ⊙ Sokoto prov., Northern Provinces, NW Nigeria, on Kebbi R., at mouth of Sokoto R., and 200 mi. NW of Kano; alt. 1,160 ft.; 13°3'N 5°14'E. Agr. trade center (cotton, rice, millet; cattle, skins); rice milling. Has hosp., domestic science school, airfield. Seat of spiritual leader of Nigerian Moslems. Founded 1809 at site of hunters' camp. Was capital (with Wurno) of 19th-cent. Sokoto or Fulah empire.

Sokoto River, NW Nigeria, rises near Funtua, flows 200 mi. NW, past Gusau, to Kebbi R. just W of Sokoto. Also called Gandi R. The name Sokoto R. is sometimes applied to the lower course of Kebbi R., below Sokoto R. mouth.

Sokotra, Aden: see SOCOTRA.

Sok River (sôk), SE European Russian SFSR, rises c.20 mi. S of Bugulma, flows generally W past Kamyshla and Isakly, and SW past Sergiyevsk and Krasny Yar (Kuibyshev oblast), to the Volga just N of Kuibyshev city; 210 mi. long. Navigable for 20 mi. Receives Kondurcha R. (right).

Sol (sōl) or **Sul** (sōōl), village (pop. 9,635), Giza prov., Upper Egypt, 2 mi. NE of El Wasta; cotton, sugar cane, corn.

Sol, Isla del, Bolivia: see TITICACA ISLAND.

Sol, Piz, Switzerland: see PIZ SOL.

Sola (sō'lä), village and canton (pop. 4,071), Rogaland co., SW Norway, 7 mi. SW of Stavanger; large airport (S) serves Stavanger. Formerly Sole.

Sola de Vega (sō'lä dā vā'gä), officially San Miguel Sola de Vega, town (pop. 1,704), Oaxaca, S Mexico, in Sierra Madre del Sur, on affluent of Atoyac R. and 40 mi. SSW of Oaxaca; cereals, sugar cane, coffee, vegetables, fruit.

Solai, Kenya: see LAKE SOLAI.

Solan, India: see SOLON.

Solana, La (lä sōlä'nä), town (pop. 13,407), Ciudad Real prov., S central Spain, in New Castile, 37 mi. E of Ciudad Real; processing center on La Mancha plain; grapes, olives, cumin, cereals, saffron, sheep, goats. Wine making, alcohol distilling, olive-oil extracting, flour milling, sawmilling, plaster mfg. Limekilns.

Solana Beach, village (pop. c.450), San Diego co., S Calif., on the coast, 20 mi. N of San Diego; flowers, truck, citrus fruit.

Solana de los Barros (dhā lōs bä'rōs), town (pop. 1,653), Badajoz prov., W Spain, 26 mi. ESE of Badajoz; olives, cereals, livestock. Mfg. of tiles.

Solander, Cape (sōlăn'dŭr), E New South Wales, Australia, on Pacific Ocean; forms S side of entrance to Botany Bay; 34°1'S 151°14'E.

Solander Island, uninhabited volcanic island (□ .5) in S Pacific, one of outlying isls. of New Zealand, 70 mi. WSW of Invercargill. Discovered 1770 by Capt. Cook.

Solano (sōlä'nō), town (1939 pop. 9,203; 1948 municipality pop. 19,840), Nueva Vizcaya prov., central Luzon, Philippines, on Magat R., just NE of Bayombong, and 40 mi. E of Baguio; trade center for agr. area (rice, corn).

Solano, county (□ 827; pop. 104,833), central and W Calif.; ⊙ Fairfield. Bounded SW by San Pablo Bay, S by Carquinez Strait (bridged) and Suisun Bay, SE by Sacramento R. Low ranges in NW; rest of co. generally level. Rich low-lying delta lands near the Sacramento are protected by dikes. Stock raising (principally sheep), farming (especially asparagus; also other truck, grain, sugar beets, alfalfa, fruit, nuts), dairying. Most industries process farm products. Shipbuilding (Mare Isl. navy yard at Vallejo). U.S. arsenal at Benicia, U.S. Travis Air Force Base near Fairfield. Natural-gas wells, sand and gravel pits. Waterfowl hunting. Formed 1850.

Solano del Pino (dhĕl pē'nō), town (pop. 1,661), Ciudad Real prov., S central Spain, in the Sierra Morena, near Jaén prov. border, 36 mi. SSW of Ciudad Real; cork, goats, cattle; flour milling, olive-oil pressing. Mines lead, copper, iron, and pitchblende.

Solano Mission, Calif.: see SONOMA, city.

Solano Point, Colombia: see SAN FRANCISCO SOLANO POINT.

Solares (sōlä'rĕs), village (pop. 958), Santander prov., N Spain, 7 mi. SSE of Santander; iron mines and mineral springs.

Solari (sōlä'rē), town (pop. estimate 600), S central Corrientes prov., Argentina, on railroad and 15 mi. SSW of Mercedes; stock raising, farming; stone quarries. Since c.1945 also called Villa Mariano y Loza.

Solarino (sôlärē'nô), village (pop. 4,971), Siracusa prov., SE Sicily, near Anapo R., 9 mi. WNW of Syracuse; lime- and cementworks.

Sola River (sō'wä), Pol. *Soła*, S Poland, rises on Czechoslovak border c.20 mi. SSW of Zywiec, flows 43 mi. N, past Zywiec and Oswiecim, to Vistula R. just NE of Oswiecim. Upper course followed by railroad.

Solar Point (sōlär'), on the Pacific, in Lima dept., W central Peru, 8 mi. S of Lima; 12°13'S 77°3'W.

Solarussa (sôlärōō'sä), village (pop. 1,906), Cagliari prov., W Sardinia, near Tirso R., 5 mi. NNE of Oristano; wine.

Solavandan (sō"lŭvŭndän') or **Sholavandan** (shō"lŭ–), town (pop. 10,804), Madura dist., S Madras, India, on Vaigai R. and 13 mi. NW of Madura. Main irrigation canal of PERIYAR LAKE project begins at Peranai Dam, 8 mi. WNW. Also spelled Cholavandan.

Solbad Hall in Tirol (zōl'bat häl' ĭn tērōl'), city (pop. 10,535), Tyrol, W Austria, on Inn R. (head of navigation), 5 mi. E of Innsbruck; resort with mineral springs; saltworks, tanneries, breweries. Many medieval bldgs.; 15th-cent. Gothic church rebuilt in rococo style in 18th cent. Large salt mines near by have been worked from antiquity. Before 1938, called Hall.

Solbiate Arno (sôlbyä'tē är'nô), village (pop. 1,029), Varese prov., Lombardy, N Italy, 7 mi. S of Varese; mfg. (elevators, hardware, cutlery); iron foundry.

Solca (sôl'kä), Ger. *Solka* (zôl'kä), town (1948 pop. 2,212), Suceava prov., N Rumania, 20 mi. WNW of Suceava; summer and health resort (alt. 1,640 ft.), in foothills of E Carpathians. Brewing; lumbering. Has church with old frescoes.

Solco River, Argentina: see GASTONA RIVER.

Soldados, Cerro (sĕ'rō sōldä'dōs), Andean peak (13,576 ft.), Azuay prov., S Ecuador, 13 mi. W of Cuenca.

Soldanesti, Moldavian SSR: see SHOLDANESHTY.

Soldato-Aleksandrovskoye (sŭldä'tŭ-ŭlyĭksän'drŭfskŭyŭ), village (1926 pop. 9,156), S Stavropol Territory, Russian SFSR, on right bank of Kuma R. and 16 mi. NE of Georgiyevsk, in winegrowing area; flour mill, metalworks; wheat, cotton. Until early 1940s, Soldatsko-Aleksandrovskoye.

Soldatskaya (sŭldät'skīŭ), village (1926 pop. 4,291), N Kabardian Autonomous SSR, Russian SFSR, on railroad, on Malka R. and 10 mi. WNW of Prokhladny, in wheat and corn area; metalworks.

Soldatskoye (–skŭyŭ), village (1948 pop. over 2,000), W Tashkent oblast, Uzbek SSR, on Angren R. and 35 mi. SSW of Tashkent; metalworking, fiber-plant processing, cotton ginning. Until c.1930, called Yangi-Bazar.

Soldau, Poland: see DZIALDOWO.

Soldeu (sōldĕ'ōō), village (pop. c.200), Andorra, 9 mi. NE of Andorra la Vella; lumbering. Iron ore mines near by. One of the highest villages (5,987 ft.) in Iberian Peninsula.

Soldier. 1 Town (pop. 323), Monona co., W Iowa, on Soldier R. and 16 mi. ESE of Onawa. **2** City (pop. 193), Jackson co., NE Kansas, on small affluent of Kansas R. and 35 mi. NNW of Topeka; livestock, grain.

Soldier River, W Iowa, rises in Ida co., flows c.80 mi. SW to Missouri R. near Modale.

Soldiers Grove, village (pop. 781), Crawford co., SW Wis., on Kickapoo R. and 37 mi. SE of La Crosse, in agr. area (tobacco, corn); cheese and other dairy products, flour, feed.

Soldier Summit, town (pop. 93), Wasatch co., central Utah, in mtn. region, 40 mi. SE of Provo, on dividing line bet. Great Basin and Colorado R. drainage system; alt. 7,440 ft.; shipping point.

Soldin, Poland: see MYSLIBORZ.

Sole (sō'lā), village, Sidamo-Borana prov., S Ethiopia, E of L. Awusa, on road and 33 mi. NNE of Yirga-Alam, in agr. (coffee, corn, plantain) and cattle-raising region.

Sole, Norway: see SOLA.

Sole, Val di (väl dē sô'lĕ), valley of upper Noce R., N Italy; extends 35 mi. ENE from Tonale Pass. Forestry, agr. (cereals, potatoes, fruit), stock raising. Chief center, Malè.

Soleb (sō'lĕb), village, Northern Prov., Anglo-Egyptian Sudan, on left bank of the Nile and 55 mi. N of Kerma, bet. 2d and 3d cataracts; site of Amon temple ruins (14th cent. B.C.).

Sole Bay, England: see SOUTHWOLD.

Solec or **Solec Kujawski** (sô'lĕts kōōyäf'skē), Ger. *Schulitz* (shōō'lĭts), town (pop. 3,774), Bydgoszcz prov., N central Poland, on the Vistula and 10 mi. ESE of Bydgoszcz; mfg. of tires, bricks; sawmilling, canning, flour milling.

Soledad (sōlādädh'), town (pop. estimate 800), central Santa Fe prov., Argentina, 70 mi. NNW of Santa Fe; rail terminus and agr. center (flax, corn, alfalfa, cattle, horses).

Soledad, town (pop. 11,500), Atlántico dept., N Colombia, on Magdalena R., in Caribbean lowlands, 4 mi. S of Barranquilla; agr. center (cotton, corn, sugar cane, yucca, fruit, stock). Airfield. Old colonial town, with cathedral.

Soledad, officially Soledad Atzompa, town (pop. 656), Veracruz, E Mexico, in Sierra Madre Oriental, 7 mi. SW of Orizaba; coffee, fruit. Sometimes Atzompa.

Soledad (sŏ'lĭdăd), city (pop. 2,441), Monterey co., W Calif., in Salinas valley, 23 mi. SE of Salinas; truck farming, stock raising, dairying. Ruined Soledad (or Nuestra Señora de la Soledad) Mission, founded 1791, is near by.

Soledad (sōlādädh'), town (pop. 2,563), Anzoátegui state, E Venezuela, landing on Orinoco R. opposite Ciudad Bolívar (linked by ferry); communication center in cattle country.

Soledad de Doblado (dā dōblä'dō), town (pop. 3,817), Veracruz, E Mexico, in Gulf lowland, on railroad and 20 mi. SW of Veracruz; agr. center (coffee, tobacco, fruit, vanilla).

Soledad Díez Gutiérrez (dyās' gōōtyĕ'rĕs), town (pop. 2,227), San Luis Potosí, N central Mexico, on interior plateau, 4 mi. NE of San Luis Potosí; rail terminus; corn, wheat, beans, cotton. Sometimes Díez Gutiérrez.

Soledade (sōōlĭdä'dĭ). **1** City (pop. 509), central Paraíba, NE Brazil, 38 mi. WNW of Campina Grande; cotton, hides and skins. Called Ibiapinópolis, 1944–48. **2** City (pop. 2,589), N central Rio Grande do Sul, Brazil, in the Serra Geral, 85 mi. NE of Santa Maria; stock raising, lumbering; rice, corn, maté, peanuts. Manganese deposits near by.

Soledade de Minas (dĭ mē'nŭs), city (pop. 2,127), S Minas Gerais, Brazil, on N slope of the Serra da Mantiqueira, 35 mi. NE of Itajubá; rail center. Called Soledade until 1944; and Ibatuba, 1944–48.

Soleduck River, NW Wash., rises in Olympic Natl. Park N of Mt. Olympus, flows c.70 mi. NW then

SW to junction with Bogachiel R., forming Quillayute R. E of Lapush.

Solenhofen, Germany: see SOLNHOFEN.

Soleniama, Belgian Congo: see KILO-MINES.

Solenoye (sŭlyô'nŭyŭ), village (1926 pop. 2,206), S Dnepropetrovsk oblast, Ukrainian SSR, 18 mi. SSW of Dnepropetrovsk; metalworks.

Solent, The (sō'lŭnt), W part of channel bet. Isle of Wight and mainland of Hampshire, England, from The NEEDLES to Southampton Water and the Spithead; 15 mi. long and ¾ to 5 mi. wide, it is the main navigational channel from W part of the English Channel to ports of Southampton and Portsmouth.

Solentiname Islands (sōlĕntēnä'mä), S Nicaragua, archipelago in SE L. Nicaragua, W of San Juan R. outlet at San Carlos. Includes 4 larger isls.: Mancarón (4 mi. long, 3 mi. wide), Mancaroncita, Fernando, Venada.

Solero (sôlä'rô), village (pop. 2,259), Alessandria prov., Piedmont, N Italy, in Tanaro R. valley, 5 mi. W of Alessandria.

Solesmes (sōlĕm'). **1** Town (pop. 4,884), Nord dept., N France, on the Selle and 12 mi. E of Cambrai; rail center; mfg. (linen, hosiery, iron-steel tubes); flour milling, sugar distilling. **2** Village (pop. 244), Sarthe dept., W France, on Sarthe R. and 15 mi. NW of La Flèche; marble quarries. Its Benedictine abbey (where the Gregorian chant was revived in 19th cent.) was founded in 1010 and enlarged in 19th cent. The 15th–16th-cent. church contains fine sculptures.

Soleto (sôlä'tô), town (pop. 3,993), Lecce prov., Apulia, S Italy, 12 mi. S of Lecce.

Soleure, Switzerland: see SOLOTHURN.

Solfatara (sôlfätä'rä), half-extinct volcanic crater in Phlegraean Fields, Campania, S Italy, just NE of Pozzuoli; fumaroles, hot mineral waters.

Solferino (sôlfĕrē'nô), village (pop. 936), Mantova prov., Lombardy, N Italy, 18 mi. NW of Mantua; peat digging. Here French and Sardinians defeated Austrians in 1859, freeing Lombardy from Austrian rule.

Solhan (sôlhän'), village (pop. 528), Bingol prov., E central Turkey, 31 mi. ENE of Bingol; grain.

Solhem (sōōl'hăm"), residential village (pop. 3,038), Stockholm co., E Sweden, 8 mi. NW of Stockholm. Has old church with 15th-cent. murals.

Soli (sō'lī), ruined city, Nicosia dist., NW Cyprus, on Morphou Bay and 30 mi. W of Nicosia. According to legend founded (c.1180 B.C.) by Acamas after the Trojan War. Besieged c.500 B.C. by the Persians. Known in antiquity for its copper mines. Ruins include a theater, Vouni palace, and other Hellenistic remains recently excavated.

Soli, anc. town on Cilician coast, SE Asia Minor (now in Turkey), 3 mi. SW of Mersin; flourished at time of Alexander, destroyed by Tigranes, restored by Pompey, who renamed it Pompeiopolis. Ruins.

Solice Zdroj, Poland: see SZCZAWNO ZDROJ.

Soliera (sôlyä'rä), town (pop. 1,621), Modena prov., Emilia-Romagna, N central Italy, 6 mi. N of Modena; wine.

Soligalich (sŭlyĕgä'lyĭch), city (1945 pop. 6,243), NW Kostroma oblast, Russian SFSR, on Kostroma R. and 50 mi. NNE of Bui, in flax, wheat region. Limestone quarries near by. Dates from 1380.

Solignac (sôlēnyäk'), village (pop. 606), Haute-Vienne dept., W central France, on Briance R. and 5 mi. S of Limoges; mfg. of clothing. Has 12th-cent. Romanesque church. Its abbey, founded 631 by St. Eloy, was school for goldsmiths and enamel artisans in Middle Ages.

Solignac-sur-Loire (sür-lwär'), village (pop. 395), Haute-Loire dept., S central France, near Loire R., 5 mi. S of Le Puy; lacemaking.

Soligny-la-Trappe (sôlēnyē'-lä-träp'), village (pop. 221), Orne dept., NW France, 7 mi. N of Mortagne; charcoal, pharmaceuticals. Noted monastery of La Trappe (founded c.1140), the parent house of Trappist order, is 2 mi. NE.

Solihull (sōlĭhŭl'), urban district (1951 census pop. 67,977), NW Warwick, England, 7 mi. SE of Birmingham; automobile, machinery, and metallurgical industries. Has 15th-cent. Old Berry Hall. In parish (SW) is town of Shirley, with electrical industry.

Solikamsk (sŭlyĭkämsk'), city (1926 pop. 3,685); 1945 pop. c.47,000), Molotov oblast, Russian SFSR, port on left bank of Kama R. and 15 mi. N of Berezniki. Rail spur terminus; major mining and processing center, based on extensive potash (carnallite, silvinite), magnesium, and common-salt deposits; chemical and woodworking industries; mfg. (paper, cellulose, agr. machinery), meat packing. Rare earths (cesium, rubidium). Has teachers col., old churches and houses. Known in 15th cent. as salt-mining settlement of Sol Kamskaya [Rus.,=Kama salt]. Chartered 1504; developed in 17th cent. as center on N trade route to Siberia; declined in 18th cent. following southward shift of Siberian colonization. Gained industrial significance after development of potash deposits (1925) and construction of major processing works (1934). Projected power plant and dam on the Kama (near Solikamsk waterfront section at suburban Borovsk) will render Vishera R. navigable.

Sol-Iletsk or **Sol'-Iletsk** (sôl"-ēlyĕtsk'), city (1926 pop. 11,096), S Chkalov oblast, Russian SFSR, near Ilek R., on Trans-Caspian RR (Iletsk station) and 40 mi. S of Chkalov. Rail junction; major salt-mining and -processing center; gypsum and alabaster quarrying; brick mfg., flour milling. Health resort (mud baths). Founded (1754) as stronghold of Iletskaya Zashchita [Rus.,=Iletsk defense]. Developed in 1890s, following exploitation of abundant salt deposits (known since 16th cent.). Became city and renamed Sol-Iletsk in 1945. Formerly sometimes called Iletsk.

Soliman (sôlēmän'), town (pop. 6,980), Grombalia dist., NE Tunisia, on Cape Bon Peninsula, near Gulf of Tunis, 18 mi. ESE of Tunis; road center; olive-oil processing. Saltworks near by. Founded 17th cent. by Moors from Spain. Damaged during Second World War.

Solimanca, Nudo (nōō'dō sōlēmäng'kä), Andean massif in Arequipa dept., S Peru, in Cordillera Occidental, 30 mi. NNW of Chuquibamba. Its highest peak rises to 20,728 ft.

Solimões, river, Brazil: see AMAZON RIVER.

Solin (sô'lĭn), Ital. *Salona* (sälō'nä), anc. *Salonae*, village, S Croatia, Yugoslavia, in Dalmatia, on Adriatic Sea, on railroad and 3 mi. NE of Split, at W foot of the Mosar; cement mfg. Anc. Christian city and ⊙ Roman prov., fell to Goths (535, 547); destroyed by Avars (614). Regained some importance in 10th cent., but later again declined. Foundations of 3 basilicas, baths, and an amphitheater remain, as well as numerous sarcophagi and traces of walls.

Solingen (zō'lĭng-ŭn), city (□ 31; 1950 pop. 147,782), in former Prussian Rhine Prov., W Germany, after 1945 in North Rhine-Westphalia, on the Wupper, adjoining Wuppertal (NE) and Remscheid (E); 51°10'N 7°4'E. Rail junction; center of Ger. cutlery mfg. (knives, scissors, razors, razor blades, tonsorial instruments, made of fine Solingen steel). Foundries; agr. machinery, bicycles, machine tools, automobile and bicycle parts. Other products: surgical and precision instruments, electrical and household goods, umbrella frames, textiles, artificial fiber, glass. Leather- and woodworking, sugar refining, brewing, distilling. Bridge across the Wupper (350 ft. above river) connects city with Remscheid (E). Solingen, noted for its fine blades in Middle Ages, was chartered 1374 and belonged to duchy of Berg until 1600; passed to Prussia in 1815. In 1929 it inc. neighboring towns of Gräfrath, Höhscheid, Ohligs, and Wald.

Solís (sōlēs'). **1** or **Solís de Mataojo** (dā mätäō'hō), town (pop. 1,800), Lavalleja dept., SE Uruguay, on Montevideo-Minas highway and 18 mi. SW of Minas; wheat, corn, cattle, sheep. Also called Solís Grande. Its rail station is N on Montevideo-Minas RR, 10 mi. W of Minas. **2** Beach resort, Maldonado dept., S Uruguay, on railroad and 45 mi. E of Montevideo, 23 mi. WNW of Maldonado, in pleasant hilly surroundings. Adjoining E are the Las Flores and Playa Verde resorts.

Solitude Island, Russian SFSR: see UYEDINENIYE ISLAND.

Solivar (sô'lĭvär), Hung. *Tótsóvár* (tō'tsōvär), village (pop. 1,959), E Slovakia, Czechoslovakia, on railroad and 2 mi. SE of Presov; saltworks.

Solivella (sōlēvĕ'lyä), village (pop. 1,303), Tarragona prov., NE Spain, 5 mi. N of Montblanch; trades in wine, sheep, cereals.

Solka, Rumania: see SOLCA.

Solkhat, Russian SFSR: see STARY KRYM, Crimea.

Sollana (sōlyä'nä), village (pop. 2,697), Valencia prov., E Spain, near Albufera lagoon, 7 mi. NNE of Alcira, in rice-growing dist.; rice mills; cereals, peanuts, vegetables. Mineral springs.

Sollebrunn (sōō'lŭbrŭn"), village (pop. 539), Alvsborg co., SW Sweden, 14 mi. SW of Trollhattan; furniture mfg., woodworking. Has 17th-cent. church.

Solleftea (sôlĕf'tŭō"), Swedish *Sollefteå*, city (pop. 7,763), Vasternorrland co., NE Sweden, on Angerman R. and 50 mi. N of Sundsvall; tourist and winter-sports center; mfg. of oxygen, leather goods, bricks; metalworking. Has 18th-cent. church, several prehistoric grave mounds. Known since 13th cent.; inc. 1917 as city.

Sollenau (zô'lŭnou), town (pop. 2,531), E Lower Austria, on Piesting R. and 6 mi. N of Wiener Neustadt; rail junction; mfg. of machines.

Sollentuna (sōō'lŭntü"nä), residential town (pop. 15,571), Stockholm co., E Sweden, 9 mi. NNW of Stockholm city center.

Sóller (sō'lyĕr), city (pop. 7,146), Majorca, Balearic Isls., on railroad and 14 mi. N of Palma; agr. and trading center; ships oranges and wine through its port Puerto de Sóller (also a submarine base), 2 mi. N. Wine making, olive-oil pressing, sawmilling, liquor distilling; mfg. of butter, sausages, ceramics, cement.

Sollerod, Denmark: see HOLTE.

Solliès-Pont (sôlyĕs'-pō'), town (pop. 2,058), Var dept., SE France, 7 mi. NE of Toulon; fruit (especially cherries) and vegetable shipping and preserving; winegrowing.

Söllingen (zû'lĭng-ŭn), village (pop. 3,980), N Baden, Germany, after 1945 in Württemberg-Baden, on the Pfinz and 6 mi. E of Karlsruhe; paper.

Sollstedt (zôl'shtĕt), village (pop. 1,690), in former Prussian Saxony prov., central Germany, after 1945 in Thuringia, on Wipper R., and 13 mi. WSW of Nordhausen; potash mining.

Sollum, Egypt: see SALUM.

Solna (sōl'nä", sôl'-), city (1950 pop. 37,311), Stockholm co., E Sweden, 4 mi. NW of Stockholm city center; rail junction; mfg. of machinery, electrical equipment, chocolate; paper milling. Seat of Swedish motion-picture industry. Has large institute for the blind, hosp.; football stadium.

Solnechnogorsk (sŭlnyĕchnŭgôrsk'), city (1945 pop. 14,600), N Moscow oblast, Russian SFSR, on Senezh L., 39 mi. NW of Moscow; metalworking, garment mfg.; glassworks, sawmill. Called Solnechnogorski after 1928, until it became city in 1938. During Second World War, briefly held (1941) by Germans in Moscow campaign.

Solnhofen (zōln'hō"fŭn), village (pop. 1,514), Middle Franconia, W central Bavaria, Germany, on the Altmühl and 10 mi. S of Weissenburg; cement mfg. Known for large lithographic stone quarries in area. Here in 1861 and 1872 were found skeletons of the prehistoric bird archaeopteryx. Formerly spelled Solenhofen.

Solntsedar, Russian SFSR: see GELENDZHIK.

Solntsevo (sôln'tsyĭvŭ), village (1926 pop. 441), central Kursk oblast, Russian SFSR, on Seim R. and 31 mi. SE of Kursk; flour milling.

Solo (sō'lō), formerly also **Surakarta** or **Soerakarta** (both: sōōrŭkär'tŭ), city (pop. 165,484), central Java, Indonesia, on Solo R. and 120 mi. WSW of Surabaya; 7°33'S 110°50'E; trade center for agr. area (rice, rubber, corn, indigo, cassava, sugar). Industries: tanning, textile milling, mfg. of machinery, batik making. Here is the vast walled palace of sultan of Surakarta. Town is divided into European, Chinese, and Arab quarters; European section resembles an old Du. town. Here is Fort Vastenburg (1779).

Solo, river, Indonesia: see SOLO RIVER.

Solo, Cerro (sĕ'rō sō'lō), Andean peak (20,300 ft.) on Argentina-Chile border, 26 mi. WSW of the Cerro Incahuasi; 27°7'S.

Solobkovtsy (sŭlŭpkôf'tsē), agr. town (1926 pop. 3,340), S central Kamenets-Podolski oblast, Ukrainian SSR, 22 mi. S of Proskurov; wheat.

Solodcha (sŭlŭchä'), village (1939 pop. over 500), central Stalingrad oblast, Russian SFSR, on Ilovlya R. and 25 mi. NNE of Ilovlinskaya; flour mill; wheat, cattle.

Solofra (sôlô'frä), town (pop. 4,651), Avellino prov., Campania, S Italy, 7 mi. SSE of Avellino; tanning center; hosiery factories.

Sologne (sôlô'nyŭ), region (□ 200) of N central France, comprised in Loir-et-Cher, Cher, and Loiret depts., and situated in great bend of the Loire S of Orléans; formerly a barren and marshy area, the Sologne is now drained and planted with pines, grows vegetables and cereals, and provides good hunting grounds. No important pop. centers.

Sologne Bourbonnaise (bōōrbônĕz'), poorly drained dist. of Allier dept., central France, bet. Loire and Allier rivers, E of Moulins. Formerly a barren sheep-raising area; agr. and poultry raising have been initiated by Trappist monks at a model farm near Dompierre-sur-Besbre.

Solok (sôlôk'), town (pop. 6,214), W Sumatra, Indonesia, in Padang Highlands, on railroad and 23 mi. ENE of Padang; rice and tea-growing center.

Solokija River (sôwôkē'yä), Pol. *Sołokija*, Rus. *Solokiya* (sŭlŭkē'yŭ), E Poland, rises 2 mi. NW of Tomaszow Lubelski, flows SE, past Tomaszow Lubelski, and E to Bug R. 7 mi. S of Sokal; 52 mi. long. In lower course forms Poland–Ukrainian SSR border.

Sololá (sōlōlä'), department (□ 410; 1950 pop. 82,850), SW central Guatemala; ⊙ Sololá. In central highlands; bounded by Nahualate R. (W) and Madre Vieja R. (E); includes L. ATITLÁN (tourist resort area) and volcanoes of Atitlán, Tolimán, and San Pedro. Mainly agr. (corn, beans, wheat); cattle and hog raising. Coffee grown on S shore of L. Atitlán. Cotton and woolen milling; lake fisheries. Main centers: Sololá and Panajachel (on Inter-American Highway), Atitlán and San Lucas (on S shore of L. Atitlán).

Sololá, city (1950 pop. 3,308), ⊙ Sololá dept., SW central Guatemala, near N shore of L. Atitlán, on Inter-American Highway and 45 mi. WNW of Guatemala; 14°46'N 91°10'W; alt. 6,900 ft. Trade center for local agr. produce (vegetables, grain, coffee). Has 16th-cent. church (rebuilt after 1902 earthquake). Flour milling near by.

Soloma or **San Pedro Soloma** (sän pā'drō sōlō'mä), town (1950 pop. 900), Huehuetenango dept., W Guatemala, on E slope of Cuchumatanes Mts., 26 mi. N of Huehuetenango; alt. 7,438 ft.; corn, wheat, livestock.

Solombala, Russian SFSR: see ARCHANGEL, city.

Solomennoye (sŭlô'myĭnŭyŭ), town (1948 pop. over 2,000), S Karelo-Finnish SSR, on L. Onega, 3 mi. NNE (under jurisdiction) of Petrozavodsk, across an inlet of lake; sawmilling.

Solomon (sŏ'lŭmŭn), village (pop. 63), W Alaska, on S Seward Peninsula, on N shore of Norton Sound, 30 mi. E of Nome; gold mining; supply point and port for gold-mining region.

Solomon. **1** Village (1940 pop. 753), Graham co., SE Ariz., 5 mi. E of Safford, on Gila R., at mouth of San Simon Creek; cotton, alfalfa, grain. Settled 1876. Formerly Solomonsville. **2** City (pop. 834), Dickinson co., central Kansas, on Smoky Hill R. at mouth of Solomon R., and 14 mi. ENE of Salina; shipping point for agr. region; poultry packing.

Solomon Islands (sŏ'lŭmŭn), volcanic group (□ 16,000; 1947 pop. estimate 160,000), SW Pacific, 1,500 mi. N of Sydney; 4°31'–11°38'S 154°11'–160°14'E. 900-mi. chain of isls. and isl. groups, including BUKA, BOUGAINVILLE (largest), CHOISEUL, NEW GEORGIA, SANTA ISABEL, GUADALCANAL, MALAITA, SAN CRISTOBAL, SANTA CRUZ ISLANDS, SHORTLAND ISLANDS, and many small volcanic and coral isls. Mountainous, with highest peak (Mt. Balbi, 10,170 ft.) on Bougainville; fertile. SE trade winds (April-Nov.). Temp. range, 95°–72°F.; annual mean rainfall, 120 in. Malarial area. Coconut palms, kauri pine; crocodiles, small lizards, cockatoos, parrots. Some gold. Melanesian and Polynesian natives. Produces copra, ivory nuts (fruit of sago palm, *metroxylon salomonense*). Discovered 1567 by Mendaña; Br. protectorate proclaimed 1893 over some of the Solomons (Guadalcanal, SAVO ISLAND, Malaita, San Cristobal, New Georgia); Santa Cruz Isls. and RENNELL ISLAND were added 1898 to protectorate. N Solomons (Santa Isabel, Choiseul, ONTONG JAVA) were transferred (1900) by treaty from Germany to Great Britain. Governed by High Commissioner of Western Pacific at Suva, Fiji, with ⊙ group at Honiara on Guadalcanal; Tulagi was formerly ⊙. The protectorate comprises □ 11,500, pop. (1947 estimate) 94,965. Buka and Bougainville are governed separately by Australia as part of former mandated Territory of New Guinea, placed 1947 under U.N. trusteeship. In Second World War, the Solomons, occupied early 1942 by the Japanese, were the scene (Aug. 7, 1942) of 1st Allied push northward. Heaviest fighting was on Guadalcanal.

Solomon River, formed 17 mi. W of Beloit in N Kansas by confluence of the North Fork and South Fork, flows c.140 mi. SE, past Beloit, to Smoky Hill R. at Solomon. North Fork and South Fork rise in Thomas co. near Colby, NW Kansas: former flows c.210 mi. generally E, past Logan and Gaylord; latter, c.150 mi. generally E, past Hill City and Stockton.

Solomons (sŏ'lŭmŭnz), town (pop. 270), Calvert co., S Md., on small Solomons Isl. (causeway to mainland) in Patuxent R. and 17 mi. SSE of Prince Frederick. Fishing resort and yachting center; has deep-draft harbor. Commercial fishing, oyster packing, boat building. Chesapeake Biological Laboratory (marine biology) is here.

Solomonsville, Ariz.: see SOLOMON.

Solon (sō'lŭn), town (pop. 2,142), W Himachal Pradesh, India, 14 mi. SSW of Simla; local trade in grain, cloth, potatoes, timber; match mfg. Site of East Punjab Univ. (founded 1947). Brewery 1 mi. N. Formerly in Punjab Hill state of Baghat. Sometimes spelled Solan.

Solon (sō'lŭn). **1** Town (pop. 527), Johnson co., E Iowa, 10 mi. N of Iowa City, in agr. area. **2** Town (pop. 746), Somerset co., central Maine, on the Kennebec and 14 mi. NNE of Skowhegan; dairying, wood products, sporting goods. **3** Village (pop. 2,570), Cuyahoga co., N Ohio, 15 mi. SE of downtown Cleveland; agr. machinery, electrical apparatus. Inc. 1927.

Soloneshnoye (sŭlô'nyĭshnŭyŭ), village (1926 pop. 2,272), S Altai Territory, Russian SFSR, 70 mi. SW of Bisk; dairy farming.

Solonópole (sōōlōōnô'pōōlĭ), city (pop. 349), central Ceará, Brazil, 32 mi. SE of Senador Pompeu; cattle. Until 1944, Cachoeira.

Solon Springs (sō'lŭn), village (pop. 480), Douglas co., NW Wis., 26 mi. SSE of Superior, in timber area. Near by is the co. bird sanctuary.

Solopaca (sōlôpä'kä), town (pop. 4,968), Benevento prov., Campania, S Italy, near Calore R., 14 mi. NE of Caserta; wine making.

Solor (sōlôr'), smallest island (□ 86; pop. 14,761) of Solor Isls., Lesser Sundas, Indonesia, in Savu Sea, just off E coast of Flores, adjacent to Adonara (N); 22 mi. long, 5 mi. wide. Has rugged terrain. Agr., fishing.

Solor Islands (sōlôr'), group (pop. 69,428), Lesser Sundas, Indonesia, in Flores Sea, just E of Flores; 8°20'S 123°20'E; comprise isls. of LOMBLEM (largest), ADONARA, SOLOR; largely mountainous. Fishing, copra production.

Solo River (sō'lō), longest river of Java, Indonesia, rises in mts. in S central part of isl., 40 mi. SE of Solo, flows N past Solo, thence E past Ngawi, turning NE past Chepu and Bojonegro to NE coast opposite Madura, 27 mi. NW of Surabaya; 335 mi. long. Lower course is canalized for 15 mi. above its mouth. Also called Bengawan R. At TRINIL was found Java man (1891) and, near by, Homo Soloensis (1931).

Solosancho (sōlōsän'chō), town (pop. 764), Avila prov., central Spain, on Adaja R. and 10 mi. WSW of Ávila; grain growing, stock raising.

Solotcha (sŭlŭchä'), village (1939 pop. over 500), NW Ryazan oblast, Russian SFSR, in Oka R. valley, 12 mi. NNE of Ryazan; garment mfg.

Solothurn (zō'lōtōōrn), Fr. *Soleure* (sôlûr'), canton (□ 306; 1950 pop. 170,325), NW Switzerland; ⊙ Solothurn. Pop. German speaking, Catholic. Fertile valley of Aar R. (cereals, cattle), with spurs of the Jura in N (marble quarries). Mfg. (metal products, watches, clothes).

Solothurn, Fr. *Soleure*, anc. *Salodurum*, town (1950 pop. 16,745), ⊙ Solothurn, NW Switzerland, on Aar R. and 25 mi. S of Basel; gas and electrical apparatus, radios, watches, other metal products, flour, pastry; printing. Solothurn joined Swiss Confederation in 1481. Points of interest: Cathedral of St. Ursus (18th-cent. Ital. baroque; see of bishop of Basel and Lugano), 17th-cent. arsenal (with historical collections), municipal mus. (mainly art), central library (valuable incunabula and MSS), 15th-cent. town hall, 13th-cent. clock tower, old fortifications, gates, fountains.

Solotvin (sŭlŭtvēn'), Pol. *Solotwina* (sôwôtvē'nä), town (1931 pop. 2,310), central Stanislav oblast, Ukrainian SSR, in East Beskids, on Bystritsa Solotvinskaya R. and 8 mi NE of Nadvornaya; petroleum extraction; sawmilling.

Solotvino (sô'lŭtvēnŭ), Czech *Solotvina* (sô'lôtvĭnä), Hung. *Szlatina* (slŏ'tĭnŏ), village (1941 pop. 8,941), SE Transcarpathian Oblast, Ukrainian SSR, on Tissa R. (Rum. border), opposite Sighet, on railroad and 30 mi. SE of Khust; salt-mining center.

Solotwina, Ukrainian SSR: see SOLOTVIN.

Solovetski Islands or **Solovetskiye Islands** (sŭlŭvyĕt'-skē), island group (□ c.150) in White Sea, part of Archangel oblast, Russian SFSR, at entrance to Onega Bay, 30 mi. E of Kem. Solovetski Isl. (□ 110; 15 mi. long, 10 mi. wide), largest of 3 main isls., is site of 15th-cent. monastery, once the economic and political center of Rus. White Sea littoral. It was used as a military fortress against Sweden in 16th and 17th cent. and later became a dreaded place of exile for political prisoners under both the tsarist and Communist regimes.

Solovyevsk or **Solov'yevsk** (sŭlŭvyôfsk'). **1** Town (1939 pop. over 2,000), SW Amur oblast, Russian SFSR, on Never-Yakutsk highway and 25 mi. NE of Skovorodino; gold mines. **2** Village (1948 pop. over 500), S Chita oblast, Russian SFSR, 50 mi. SW of Borzya and on branch (to Choibalsan, Mongolia) of Trans-Siberian RR; frontier station on Mongolian border.

Solre-le-Château (sôr-lŭ-shätō'), village (pop. 1,603), Nord dept., N France, near Belg. border, 8 mi. ENE of Avesnes; woolens, livestock.

Solsona (sōlsō'nä), city (pop. 3,103), Lérida prov., NE Spain, on S slopes of E Pyrenees, 25 mi. NW of Manresa. Flour- and sawmilling; agr. trade (cereals, livestock, vegetables). Chapel in parochial church is place of pilgrimage. Was once seat of univ. transferred (1717) by Philip V to Cervera. Has archaeological mus.

Solt (shôlt), town (pop. 7,875), Pest-Pilis-Solt-Kiskun co., central Hungary, 33 mi. WSW of Kecskemet; rail junction; distilleries.

Solta Island (shôl'tä; Ital. sōl'tä), Serbo-Croatian *Šolta*, Dalmatian island in Adriatic Sea, S Croatia, Yugoslavia, 12 mi. SW of Split; 12 mi. long. Chief village, Grohote, Ital. *Grocote*, on N shore; beekeeping. Sometimes spelled Sholta.

Soltaniyeh, Iran: see SULTANIYEH.

Soltau (zôl'tou), town (pop. 13,453), in former Prussian prov. of Hanover, NW Germany, after 1945 in Lower Saxony, 20 mi. SW of Lüneburg; rail junction; foundry; mfg. of knitwear, felt, sack fabrics, apparel, leather goods; food processing (flour products, canned goods, beer), woodworking.

Soltepec (sōltāpĕk'), town (pop. 1,407), Puebla, central Mexico, 33 mi. ENE of Puebla; cereals, maguey, livestock.

Solton (sŭltôn'), village (1926 pop. 2,052), E Altai Territory, Russian SFSR, 55 mi. ENE of Bisk, in agr. area.

Soltsy or **Sol'tsy** (sôl'tsē), city (1940 pop. 9,000), W Novgorod oblast, Russian SFSR, on Shelon R. (head of navigation) and 45 mi. SW of Novgorod; lumber center; sawmilling, woodworking, dairying, flax processing. Health resort (salt springs). Chartered 1781.

Soltvadkert (shôlt'vŏtkĕrt), town (pop. 8,936), Pest-Pilis-Solt-Kiskun co., S central Hungary, 26 mi. SW of Kecskemet; flour mills. Resort of Sziksosfürdö near by.

Soluch, Soluk, or **Suluk** (all: sōlōōk', sōō–), town (pop. 600), W Cyrenaica, Libya, 32 mi. SSE of Benghazi, in cereal-growing, stock-raising (sheep, goats) region; rail terminus; carpet weaving.

Solum, Egypt: see SALUM.

Solum, Norway: see SKOTFOSS.

Solun (sô'lōōn'), town, ⊙ Solun co. (pop. 8,519), N Inner Mongolian Autonomous Region, Manchuria, on railroad and 55 mi. NW of Ulan Hoto. Until 1917 called Solunshan; named for Tungusic Solon tribe in vicinity.

Solund Islands (sō'lōōn), Nor. *Solundøyane*, island group in North Sea, Sogn og Fjordane co., W Norway, at mouth of Sogne Fjord. Includes Indre [Nor.,=inner] Solundoy (Nor. *Solundøy*), an isl. (□ 45; pop. 724) 27 mi. S of Floro, separated from mainland by a sound dotted with lesser isls.; Ytre [Nor.,=outer] Solundoy, an isl. (□ 12; pop. 389) 5 mi. SW of Indre Solundoy; and Steinsundoy or Steinsoy (Nor. *Steinsundøy* or *Steinsøy*, formerly *Stenøy*), Norway's westernmost isl. (□ 7; pop. 54), with Utvaer beacon light, 61°2'8"N 4°27'27"E. Group forms Solund canton (pop. 1,910). Formerly spelled Sulen.

Solunska Glava, peak, Yugoslavia: see JAKUPICA.

Solusuchiapa (sōlōōschyä'pä), town (pop. 260), Chiapas, S Mexico, 40 mi. S of Villahermosa; fruit.

Solutré (sôlütrā'), village (pop. 241), Saône-et-Loire dept., E central France, in the Monts du Mâconnais, 5 mi. W of Mâcon; noted wines. A near-by rock shelter and burial place of prehistoric man (discovered 1867) gives name to Solutrean period.

Solva, Wales: see WHITCHURCH.

Solvang (sôl'văng), village (1940 pop. 659), Santa Barbara co., SW Calif., on Santa Ynez R. and 4 mi. WSW of SANTA YNEZ (old mission here). Established 1912 by Danes, it has preserved many Danish customs.

Solvay (sŏl'vā), village (pop. 7,868), Onondaga co., central N.Y., just E of Syracuse; mfg. (soda ash, salt, chinaware, electrical and metal products, coke). Inc. 1894.

Solvayhall, Germany: see BERNBURG.

Solvesborg (sŭl"vŭsbôr'yŭ), Swedish *Sölvesborg*, city (pop. 4,362), Blekinge co., S Sweden, at N end of Hano Bay of the Baltic, at base of Listerland peninsula, 17 mi. E of Kristianstad; seaport, with shipyards; mfg. of starch, flour products, glass, paint, machinery; stone quarrying, tanning. Has 13th–14th-cent. church and remains of old castle. Founded in 13th cent., chartered 1836.

Solvychegodsk or **Sol'vychegodsk** (sŭlvĭchĭgôtsk'), city (1939 pop. 4,200), S Archangel oblast, Russian SFSR, on Vychegda R. and 10 mi. NE of Kotlas; metalworks. Salt springs near by. Chartered 1492; was noted 16th-cent. salt-trading center. Stalin exiled here (1908–11).

Solway (sŏl'wā), village (pop. 124), Beltrami co., NW Minn., 12 mi. WNW of Bemidji; grain, potatoes.

Solway Firth (sŏl'wā), arm of the Irish Sea bet. S coast of Kircudbrightshire and Dumfriesshire, Scotland, and NW coast of Cumberland, England, extends 40 mi. inland; 20 mi. wide at mouth, 2 mi. wide at NE end. Receives the rivers Esk, Eden, Derwent, Dee, Annan, Nith, and Urr. Chief ports are Kircudbright, Silloth, Maryport, and Whitehaven. It is crossed by a railroad bridge near Annan. Has many sandbanks and dangerous tides. Salmon-fishing ground.

Solway Moss, drained moor area, N Cumberland, England, just W of Esk R. at Longtown, near Scottish border, c.7 mi. in circumference. Scene (1542) of battle bet. Scots and English in a Border War.

Solwezi (sōlwĕ'zē), township (pop. 38), Western Prov., NW Northern Rhodesia, 100 mi. NNE of Kasempa, near Belgian Congo border; corn, wheat, beeswax; hardwood. Transferred 1946 from Kaonde-Lunda prov.

Solymar (shô'ĭmär), Hung. *Solymár*, town (pop. 4,096), Pest-Pilis-Solt-Kiskun co., N central Hungary, in Buda Mts., 9 mi. NW of Budapest; brickworks. Lignite mine near by.

Soma (sō'mä), town (pop. 3,856), Ibaraki prefecture, central Honshu, Japan, 4 mi. WNW of Ryugasaki; rice growing.

Soma (sômä'), town (pop. 6,325), Manisa prov., W Turkey, on railroad and 40 mi. NNE of Manisa; lignite; wheat, barley, sugar beets, cotton, tobacco.

Somabula (sōmäbōō'lä), village, Gwelo prov., central Southern Rhodesia, in Matabeleland, 20 mi. SSW of Gwelo; alt. 4,638 ft. Rail junction; agr. (tobacco, cotton, citrus fruit, dairy products). Diamond deposits.

Somain (sômē'), town (pop. 9,679), Nord dept., N France, 9 mi. E of Douai; coal-mining center. Rail junction. Damaged in Second World War.

Somalia, E Africa: see ITALIAN SOMALILAND.

Somaliland (sōmä'lēlănd), region (□ c.350,000) of E Africa, occupying the continent's "horn" bet. Gulf of Aden (N) and the Indian Ocean (E), bordering inland on Ethiopia. The name is derived from the Somali, the dominant native people, who are Moslems and speak a Hamitic language. It is a generally arid area, where nomadic stock raising is the chief occupation. Politically, it is divided into FRENCH SOMALILAND (NW; at entrance to Red Sea), BRITISH SOMALILAND (on Gulf of Aden), ITALIAN SOMALILAND (a coastal strip on Indian Ocean S of the "horn"), and the OGADEN region of SE Ethiopia.

Somanathpur, temple, India: see TALAKAD.

Somanya (sōmä'nyä), town, Eastern Prov., SE Gold Coast colony, in Akwapim Hills, 8 mi. W of Akuse; cacao, palm oil and kernels, cotton, cassava.

Somapah (sōmäpä') **1** Village (pop. 1,066), E Singapore isl., 4 mi. SW of Changi and 8 mi. ENE of Singapore. **2** Village (pop. 9,171), E central Singapore isl., just N of Paya Lebar and 5 mi. NNE of Singapore.

Somapura, E Pakistan: see PAHARPUR.

Sombernon (sōbĕrnō'), agr. village (pop. 478), Côte-d'Or dept., E central France, on W slope of the Côte d'Or, 16 mi. W of Dijon. Here, in Sept., 1944, Allied troops which had landed in S France made contact with U.S. Third Army, driving E from Normandy.

Sombor (sôm'bôr), Hung. *Zombor* (zôm'bôr), city (pop. 34,321), Vojvodina, NW Serbia, Yugoslavia, on Danube-Tisa Canal and 34 mi. SW of Subotica, in the Backa. Rail junction (lines to Subotica, Belgrade, Zagreb); flour milling, mfg. of dairy products; grain trade. Winegrowing, hemp raising, carpet making in vicinity.

Sombreffe (sõbrĕf'), town (pop. 2,529), Namur prov., central Belgium, 13 mi. WNW of Namur; sugar refinery.

Sombrerete (sōmbrārā'tā), city (pop. 5,628), Zacatecas, N central Mexico, on interior plateau, 90 mi. NW of Zacatecas; alt. 7,805 ft.; rail terminus; mining center (silver, gold, lead, copper).

Sombrero (sŏmbrâ'rō), islet (pop. 5), dependency of St. Kitts-Nevis presidency, Leeward Isls., B.W.I., separated from Br. Virgin Isls. by Anegada Passage, and 100 mi. NW of Basseterre, St. Kitts. The bare rock rises to 40 ft. at 18°36'N 63°29'W; lighthouse. Phosphate of lime used to be quarried here. Belonged formerly to the Br. Virgin Isls.

Sombrero, El, Venezuela: see EL SOMBRERO.

Sombrero Channel, connects Bay of Bengal (W) and Andaman Sea (E) along c.7°35'N; runs bet. Little Nicobar (S) and Katchall (N) isls.

Sombrero River (sōmbrĕ'rō), S Nigeria, a main outlet of Niger R., flows past Degema and Abonema in E part of delta to Gulf of Guinea 20 mi. W of Bonny. Sometimes spelled Sombreiro.

Somcuta-Mare (shômkōō'tsä-mä'rā), Rum. *Şomcuta-Mare*, Hung. *Nagysomkút* (nŏ'dyùshôm"kōōt), village (pop. 3,213), Baia-Mare dept., NW Rumania, 34 mi. SE of Satu-Mare; rail terminus; noted for its cheese production. In Hungary, 1940–45.

Someitsun, China: see TEHJUNG.

Somercotes, England: see ALFRETON.

Somerdale (sŭ'mürdāl), borough (pop. 1,417), Camden co., SW N.J., 9 mi. SE of Camden. Inc. 1929.

Somerfield, former borough, Somerset co., SW Pa., 24 mi. SW of Somerset; site inundated by reservoir dammed (1944) in Youghiogheny R.

Somerghem, Belgium: see ZOMERGEM.

Somers (sŭ'mürz). **1** Town (pop. 2,631), Tolland co., N Conn., at Mass. line, on Scantic R. and 19 mi. NE of Hartford; dairying. Somersville village (1940 pop. 874) makes woolens. Organized 1734 as Mass. town, transferred to Conn. 1749. **2** Town (pop. 217), Calhoun co., central Iowa, 15 mi. SW of Fort Dodge; dairy products. **3** Village (1940 pop. 528), Flathead co., NW Mont., at N end of Flathead L., 10 mi. SSE of Kalispell; sawmill.

Somersby, agr. village and parish (pop. 43), Parts of Lindsey, E central Lincolnshire, England, 6 mi. ENE of Horncastle. Tennyson b. in the rectory here.

Somerset (sŭ'mürsĕt), settlement, N Queensland, Australia, on Cape York Peninsula, near Cape York, 470 mi. NNW of Cairns; pearl shell.

Somerset, village (pop. estimate 300), S Man., in Pembina Mts., 45 mi. SW of Portage la Prairie; grain elevators, flour mills; dairying.

Somerset or **Somersetshire** (-shĭr), county (□ 1,613; 1931 pop. 475,142; 1951 census 551,188), SW England; ⊙ Taunton. Bounded by Devon (W), Bristol Channel (N), Gloucester (NE), Wiltshire (E), and Dorset (S). Drained by Exe, Tone, Brue, Yeo, and Parrett rivers. Cut by several hill ranges (Mendip Hills, Quantock Hills, and Blackdown Hills), with moorland tract of Exmoor in W. Dairying is major industry (Cheddar and Yeovil cheeses are famous) and there are fruitgrowing and sheep raising; fishing in Bristol Channel. Coal-mining industry is centered on Radstock (NE); other industries include leather mfg., woolen milling, brickmaking, pottery mfg. Other important towns are resorts of Bath, Weston-super-Mare, Burnham-on-Sea, and Minehead; also Frome, Norton Radstock, Yeovil, and Wells. There are many tourist attractions, including Cheddar Gorge. Numerous vestiges of Roman hill forts; chief Roman centers were Bath and Ilchester. Co. has associations with King Alfred, and Glastonbury is important in Br. religious history.

Somerset, town (pop. 741), N Tasmania, 75 mi. WNW of Launceston and on Bass Strait; meat-packing plant, plywood.

Somerset. **1** County (□ 3,948; pop. 39,785), central and W Maine, on Que. line; ⊙ Skowhegan. Resorts in Belgrade Lakes region along Kennebec co. line. Mfg. (textiles, shoes, boats and canoes, paper, pulp, and wood products) at Skowhegan, Madison, Fairfield, Norridgewock on the Kennebec, and Pittsfield on the Sebasticook; farming, dairying. Moosehead L. and Jackman-Moose R. regions are known for hunting, canoeing, and excellent fishing. In NW are lumber camps. The Kennebec is dammed at Bingham and furnishes power to several towns along its course. Formed 1809. **2** County (□ 332; pop. 20,745), SE Md.; ⊙ Princess Anne. Peninsula on the Eastern Shore, bounded SE by Pocomoke R., S by Pocomoke Sound (forms Va. line here), W by Tangier Sound of Chesapeake Bay. Shores indented by Wicomico, Manokin, Big Annemessex river estuaries. In bay are Smith and South Marsh isls. Sandy, partly marshy tidewater area; agr. dists. produce fruit (especially strawberries), white potatoes, truck, poultry, dairy products. Timber; large seafood industry (especially at Crisfield and Deal Isl.); some vegetable and seafood canneries, lumber mills, fishing equipment and clothing factories. Popular sport-fishing, wild-fowl hunting grounds; muskrat trapping. Formed 1666. **3** County (□ 307; pop. 99,052), N central N.J., bounded NE by Passaic R.; ⊙ Somerville. Dairying, agr. (truck, poultry, grain); mfg. (textiles, asbestos goods, clothing, metal products). Estate region in N includes Bedminster and Far Hills. Appalachian ridges in NW; part of Watchung Mts. in NE. Drained by Millstone R. and North and South branches of Raritan R. Formed 1688. **4** County (□ 1,084; pop. 81,813), SW Pa.; ⊙ Somerset. Mountainous coal-mining and agr. area; bounded S by Md., Allegheny Mts. in E, Laurel Hill along W border; drained by Casselman R. and by Youghiogheny R. on SW border. Mt. Davis (3,213 ft.) in S part is highest point in Pa. Bituminous coal; agr. (oats, buckwheat, maple products, livestock, poultry); mfg. (clothing, lumber, food products, liquors, fertilizer, crushed stone). Formed 1795.

Somerset. **1** City (pop. 7,097), ⊙ Pulaski co., S Ky., in Cumberland foothills, 70 mi. S of Lexington, in agr. (livestock, poultry, corn, burley tobacco, hay), coal, oil, timber, and stone-quarry area. Rail, trade, and industrial center; mfg. of stoves, fertilizer, dairy products, furniture, clothing; flour, feed, and lumber milling; oil and gas refineries, bottling works; railroad shops; airport. Natl. cemetery, Zollicoffer Memorial Park are near by. **2** Residential town (pop. 430), Montgomery co., central Md., just NNW of Washington. **3** Residential town (pop. 8,566), Bristol co., SE Mass., on Taunton R. and 5 mi. N of Fall River; resort. Settled 1677, set off from Swansea 1790. Includes village of Pottersville. **4** Village (pop. 1,383), Perry co., central Ohio, 18 mi. WSW of Zanesville, in agr. area; petroleum refining; coal mining. Laid out 1810. **5** Borough (pop. 5,936), ⊙ Somerset co., SW Pa., 65 mi. SE of Pittsburgh; maple sugar, lumber; bituminous coal, limestone; agr. Settled 1771, laid out 1787, inc. 1804. **6** Village (pop. c.700), Bexar co., S central Texas, 16 mi. SW of San Antonio, in oil field; oil refining. **7** Town (pop. 8), Windham co., S Vt., in the Green Mts. 15 mi. ENE of Bennington. **8** Town, Va.: see MADISON. **9** Village (pop. 531), St. Croix co., W Wis., on Apple R. and 11 mi. NNE of Hudson, in dairying and stock-raising area.

Somerset Dam, Windham co., S Vt., in a headstream of Deerfield R., c.25 mi. NW of Brattleboro; 104 ft. high, 2,101 ft. long; for power; completed 1913. Impounds Somerset Reservoir (c.1,600 acres).

Somerset East, Afrikaans *Somerset-Oos* (ōōs'), town (pop. 7,447), SE Cape Prov., U. of So. Afr., on Little Fish R. and 70 mi. NW of Grahamstown; rail terminus; agr. center (stock, wool, meat, dairying, citrus fruit). Founded 1825 on site of govt. tobacco farm established 1815.

Somerset Island (2 mi. long, ½–1 mi. wide), W Bermuda, on Great Sound, 5 mi. W of Hamilton, separated from Bermuda Isl. (S) by narrow channel. Road connection with neighboring isls.

Somerset Island (□ 9,594), central Franklin Dist., Northwest Territories, in the Arctic Ocean, separated from Boothia Peninsula (S) by Bellot Strait, from Prince of Wales Isl. (W) by Peel Sound, from Cornwallis Isl. (N) and Devon Isl. (NE) by Barrow Strait, and from Baffin Isl. (E) by Prince Regent Inlet; 71°57'–74°10'N 90°10'–95°45'W. Isl. is 160 mi. long, 22–105 mi. wide. Creswell Bay in SE; E coast has steep cliffs, backed by hills rising to c.2,500 ft. At SE extremity is Fort Ross trading post. Isl. was discovered 1819 by Sir William Parry.

Somerset Reservoir, Vt.: see SOMERSET DAM.

Somersetshire, England: see SOMERSET.

Somerset West, Afrikaans *Somerset-Wes* (vĕs'), town (pop. 5,043), SW Cape Prov., U. of So. Afr., near False Bay of the Atlantic, 25 mi. ESE of Cape Town, at foot of Hottentots Holland Mts.; center of winegrowing and agr. area (fruit, vegetables); mfg. of chemicals, explosives, paints. Near by is seaside resort of Strand.

Somersham (sŭ'mür-shùm), agr. village and parish (pop. 1,417), E Huntingdon, England, 5 mi. NE of St. Ives. Has 13th-cent. church.

Somers Islands: see BERMUDA.

Somers Point (sŭ'mürz), city (pop. 2,480), Atlantic co., SE N.J., 2 mi. NW of Ocean City, on Great Egg Harbor Bay. Settled c.1695, inc. 1886.

Somersville, Conn.: see SOMERS.

Somersworth (sŭ'mürzwûrth), industrial city (pop. 6,927), Strafford co., SE N.H., on Salmon Falls R. opposite Berwick, Maine; shoes, textiles, yarn, electrical machinery; cotton mills 1st established here 1822. Part of Dover (S) until 1729, known as Great Falls until 1893.

Somerton, town and parish (pop. 1,937), central Somerset, England, 9 mi. NNW of Yeovil; agr. market in dairying region; shirt mfg., milk canning, cheese making. Has 15th-cent. church. Important town in Saxon times.

Somerton (sŭ'mürtùn), city (pop. 1,825), Yuma co., extreme SW Ariz., on Colorado R. and 10 mi. SSW of Yuma; shipping point for vegetables in irrigated agr. and livestock area.

Somervell (sŭ'mürvĭl), county (□ 197; pop. 2,542), N central Texas; ⊙ Glen Rose. Wooded, hilly region (alt. c.600–1,250 ft.), drained by Brazos R. and Paluxy Creek. Scenic resort area (bathing, hunting, fishing; mineral springs). Some agr. (grains, peanuts, fruit, pecans), cattle, poultry, dairying. Formed 1875.

Somerville (sŭ'mürvĭl). **1** Town (pop. 353), Gibson co., SW Ind., 23 mi. NNE of Evansville, in agr. and bituminous-coal area. **2** Plantation (pop. 227), Lincoln co., S Maine, on Sheepscot R. and 16 mi. NE of Gardiner; lumber mills. **3** Residential city (pop. 102,351), Middlesex co., E Mass., on Mystic R. just N of Boston; meat packing; mfg. (paper, food, and metal products, woolens, oil, furniture); automobile assembling. Settled 1630, inc. as town 1842, as city 1871. **4** Borough (pop. 11,571), ⊙ Somerset co., N central N.J., on Raritan R. and 10 mi. SW of Plainfield; mfg. (metal products, linoleum, clothing, lace, soft drinks); residential; farm trade center (poultry, dairy products). Has army supply depot. Wallace House (residence of the Washingtons, 1778–79) and old Dutch parsonage (1751; now a D.A.R. mus.) are here. Settled 1683; inc. as town 1864, as borough 1909. **5** Village (pop. 383), Butler co., extreme SW Ohio, 12 mi. NNW of Hamilton. **6** Town (pop. 1,760), ⊙ Fayette co., SW Tenn., on Loosahatchie R. and 37 mi. ENE of Memphis, in timber, cotton, corn, livestock area; makes furniture. Founded 1825. **7** City (pop. 1,425), Burleson co., S central Texas, near Yegua Creek, c.70 mi. ESE of Austin; trade center in cotton, corn area; railroad shops; creosoting plant.

Somes River (sô'mĕsh), Rum. *Someş*, Hung. *Szamos* (sŏ'môsh), in N Rumania and NE Hungary, formed at Dej by the union of the Great Somes, Rum. *Someşul-Mare* (sô'mĕshōōl-mä'rā), rising in Moldavian Carpathians, and the Little Somes, Rum. *Someşul-Mic* (-mēk'), rising in Apuseni Mts.; flows c.145 mi. NW, past Satu-Mare and forming Ecsed Marsh, to Tisa R. 2 mi. SE of Vasarosnameny. Receives Kraszna R. Total length, including either headstream, c.250 mi.

Somes Sound, Maine: see MOUNT DESERT ISLAND.

Somjin River (sŭm'jĕn'), Korean *Somjin-gang*, Jap. *Senshin-ko*, S Korea, rises in mts. c.20 mi. SE of Chonju, flows generally S, turning SE past Hadong to inlet of Korea Strait; 157 mi. long; navigable 25 mi. by small craft. Lower course forms boundary bet. S.Cholla and S.Kyongsang provinces.

Somlo, Mount (shôm'lō), Hung. *Somló* (1,427 ft.), W central Hungary, in Bakony Mts., near Torna R.; excellent vineyards on slopes.

Somlovasarhely (shôm'lōvä-shärhĕl), Hung. *Somlóvásárhely*, town (pop. 1,544), Veszprem co., W Hungary, on Torna R. and 25 mi. W of Veszprem; wine, potatoes, corn, hogs.

Somma, Monte (môn'tĕ sôm'mä), semicircular ridge, S Italy, on N and E sides of VESUVIUS; separated from central cone by a deep valley, the Atrio del Cavallo; rises to 3,714 ft. in Punta del Nasone.

Somma Lombardo (sôm'mä lômbär'dô), town (pop. 4,885), Varese prov., Lombardy, N Italy, near Ticino R., 4 mi. NW of Gallarate; cotton, silk, and rayon mills, alcohol distillery, rubber-tube factory.

Sommariva del Bosco (sôm-märē'vä dĕl bô'skô), village (pop. 3,890), Cuneo prov., NW Italy, 21 mi. SSE of Turin. Also written Sommariva Bosco.

Sommatino (sôm-mätē'nô), town (pop. 10,579), Caltanissetta prov., S Sicily, 12 mi. SSW of Caltanissetta, in major sulphur-mining region.

Somma Vesuviana (sôm'mä vĕzōōvyä'nä), town (pop. 7,075), Napoli prov., Campania, S Italy, on N slope of Vesuvius, N of Monte Somma, 9 mi. ENE of Naples.

Somme (sôm), department (□ 2,424; pop. 441,368), in Picardy, N France; ⊙ Amiens. Bounded by English Channel (W). Bisected E-W by canalized Somme R. flowing through marshy valley. Level, fertile, agr. area: high wheat and oat yields; sugar beets, market vegetables (especially artichokes); good pastures; apple orchards (for cider distilling). Small-scale metalworking (founding, locksmithing, mfg. of precision tools and instruments). Well-known textile industry (velvet, plush, cotton and linen cloth, carpets) centered at Amiens; flax and jute milling in Somme valley. Chief towns: Amiens, Abbeville, Albert, Péronne (all damaged in Second World War). Entire dept. ravaged in First World War during battles of the Somme (1916) and of Amiens (1918). Fr. army made short stand on the Somme in 1940 during "battle of France."

Sommedieu (sômdyû'), village (pop. 862), Meuse dept., NE France, 6 mi. SSE of Verdun; furniture making.

Sommen (sōō'mùn), village (pop. 935), Jonkoping co., S Sweden, at NW end of L. Somme, Swedish *Sommen* (□ 51; 25 mi. long, 1–7 mi. wide), 6 mi. N of Tranas; furniture works.

Sommepy (sômpē'), village (pop. 589), Marne dept., N France, 12 mi. SSW of Vouziers. Atop Blanc Mont Ridge (3 mi. N) is American memorial commemorating fighting in the Champagne region during First World War.

Sommerance (sômrãs'), village (pop. 103), Ardennes dept., N France, 17 mi. ESE of Vouziers.

Sömmerda (zû'mürdä"), town (pop. 13,932), in former Prussian Saxony prov., central Germany, after 1945 in Thuringia, on the Unstrut and 13 mi.

NNE of Erfurt; rail junction; mfg. of machinery, light metals, chemicals, bricks; metalworking.

Sommerein (zôm'ûrīn), village (pop. 707), E Lower Austria, on W slope of Leitha Mts. and 20 mi. SE of Vienna. Large limestone quarry near by.

Sommerfeld, Poland: see LUBSKO.

Sommerhausen (zô″mûrhou'zûn), village (pop. 1,450), Lower Franconia, W Bavaria, Germany, on the Main (canalized) and 6 mi. WSW of Kitzingen; basket weaving, brewing; plums. Surrounded by medieval walls. Town archives contain a catechism dated 1528. Sandstone quarries near by.

Somme River (sŏm), Aisne and Somme depts., N France, rises above Saint-Quentin, flows SW to Saint-Simon (paralleled by Saint-Quentin Canal), thence NW, past Ham and Péronne, continuing generally W, past Corbie, Amiens, and Abbeville (followed by a lateral navigation canal), through a marshy valley to the English Channel (in a sandy, poorly accessible estuary 15 mi. long) off Saint-Valéry-sur-Somme. Length, 150 mi. Receives the Ancre (right) and the Avre (left). Connected by canals with Escaut and Oise rivers. Has given its name to a major battle (July-Nov., 1916) of First World War. Here, Fr. army made brief stand, 1940, in "battle of France."

Sommevoire (sômvwär'), village (pop. 688), Haute-Marne dept., NE France, 14 mi. NNE of Bar-sur-Aube; metalworks.

Sommières (sômyâr'), town (pop. 2,474), Gard dept., S France, on the Vidourle and 14 mi. WSW of Nîmes; fruit and vegetable processing, soap mfg.

Somnath (sōm'nät), town (pop. 11,377), S Saurashtra, India, on Arabian Sea, 45 mi. S of Junagarh, 3 mi. ESE of Veraval; handicrafts (cotton cloth, metalware); fishing. An anc. site, celebrated for its wealthy temple which was plundered c.1025 by Mahmud of Ghazni. Near by is spot where, in Hindu mythology, Krishna was killed. Also called Patan Somnath, Patan, or Prabhas Patan.

Somnathpur, temple, India: see TALAKAD.

Somno River (sō'nōō), N Goiás, N central Brazil, rises in the Serra Geral de Goiás (near Bahia border), flows c.170 mi. NW to the Tocantins at Pedro Afonso. Not navigable.

Somogy (shô'môdyû), Ger. *Sümeg*, county (□ 2,569; pop. 358,307), SW Hungary; ⊙ KAPOSVAR. Hilly region bounded by L. Balaton (N) and Drava R. (S), drained by Rinya, Fekete, and Kapos rivers. Agr. (wheat, corn, potatoes, beans, wine), livestock (hogs, cattle, horses), poultry, garden products (honey, apples, pears, nuts). Home industries, especially embroidery; industrial centers at Kaposvar and Barcs.

Somogy, town (pop. 2,329), Baranya co., S Hungary, 5 mi. NE of Pecs; wine, nuts, plums.

Somogyvar (shô'môdyûvär), Hung. *Somogyvár*, town (pop. 2,247), Somogy co., SW Hungary, 16 mi. NNW of Kaposvar; wheat, wine, corn.

Somogyvisonta, Hungary: see CSOKONYAVISONTA.

Somonauk (sō'mûnôk), village (pop. 721), De Kalb co., N Ill., 20 mi. WSW of Aurora; livestock, grain.

Somorja, Czechoslovakia: see SAMORIN.

Somorrostro (sōmôrō'strō), small district (□ c.90) of Vizcaya prov., N Spain, near Bilbao, bet. Bay of Biscay (N) and Nervión R. (SE); contains richest iron mines in Spain (Monte Triano, Matamoros).

Somosierra (sōmōsyĕ'rä), town (pop. 187), Madrid prov., central Spain, in the Sierra de Guadarrama, on highway to Burgos just S of Somosierra Pass, and 50 mi. N of Madrid; rye, potatoes, oak wood, livestock.

Somosierra, NE spur of the Sierra de Guadarrama, central Spain, extends c.12 mi. along Madrid-Guadalajara-Segovia prov. border, 50 mi. N of Madrid. Rises to 7,421 ft. (Lobo peak). Crossed by Madrid-Burgos highway via the **Somosierra Pass** (alt. 4,585 ft.). The source of Jarama R. is on its W slopes.

Somoskö (shô'môsh-kû), Hung. *Somoskő*, town (pop. 887), Nograd-Hont co., N Hungary, 5 mi. NNE of Salgotarjan; near Czechoslovak line; lignite mines and basalt quarry near by.

Somoskőújfalu (shô'môsh-kûōōīfŏlōō), Hung. *Somoskőújfalu*, town (pop. 2,863), Nograd-Hont co., N Hungary, on Zagyva R. and 4 mi. N of Salgotarjan, on Czechoslovak frontier; basalt quarry near by.

Somosomo Strait, bet. Taveuni and E peninsula of Vanua Levu, Fiji, SW Pacific; c.5 mi. wide.

Somotillo (sōmōtē'yō), town (1950 pop. 1,052), Chinandega dept., W Nicaragua, near Honduras border, 32 mi. NNE of Chinandega and on Somotillo R. (short right affluent of Río Negro); road center; cotton weaving; agr. (sugar cane, rice, corn, beans).

Somoto (sōmō'tō), city (1950 pop. 2,322), ⊙ Madríz dept., NW Nicaragua, 95 mi. NNW of Managua, on Inter-American Highway; commercial center; dairying (butter making), hammock mfg.

Somovit (sô'môvēt), village (pop. 1,790), Pleven dist., N Bulgaria, port on right bank of the Danube (Rumanian border), near mouth of Vit R., and 7 mi. W of Nikopol; grain exports, customhouse. Sometimes spelled Samovit.

Sompa (sōm'pä), town (1949 pop. over 500), NE Estonia, 3 mi. W of Johvi; oil-shale mining.

Sompeta (sōm'pĕtŭ), town (pop. 8,083), Vizagapatam dist., NW Madras, India, 95 mi. NE of Vizianagaram; coconut oil; coir mats, rope.

Somport (sōpôr') or **Port d'Urdos** (pôr' dürdôs'), pass (alt. 5,354 ft.), in the Pyrenees, on Franco-Spanish border, 15 mi. N of Jaca. Crossed by trans-Pyrenean road. RR tunnel goes underneath it.

Sompuis (sõpwē'), village (pop. 335), Marne dept., N France, 10 mi. WSW of Vitry-le-François; sheep.

Somra Tract (sōm'rä), hilly region (□ 847; pop. 7,981) of S Naga Hills dist., Upper Burma, on Manipur (India) border; jungle-covered mts. (mean alt. 5,000 ft.). Pop.: Nagas and Chin (Kuki) tribes. Main village is Heirnkut.

Somvarpet or **Somwarpet** (sōmvär'pāt), town (pop. 2,061), N Coorg, India, 15 mi. NNE of Mercara; sandalwood, rice (terrace farming). Also spelled Somwarpett.

Son (sōn), town (pop. 549), Akershus co., SE Norway, on E shore of Oslo Fjord, 7 mi. N of Moss; seaside resort.

Son (sōn), town (pop. 2,277), La Coruña prov., NW Spain, fishing port on inlet of the Atlantic, 25 mi. WSW of Santiago; fish processing (shellfish, sardines), boatbuilding. Summer resort.

Soná (sōnä'), town (pop. 1,411), Veraguas prov., W central Panama, on Inter-American Highway, on San Pablo R. and 22 mi. WSW of Santiago; coffee, sugar cane; stock raising, lumbering. Gold mines, magnesium deposits.

Sonada (sōnä'dŭ), village, Darjeeling dist., N West Bengal, India, 5 mi. S of Darjeeling, in SE Nepal Himalayan foothills; brewery; tea, rice, corn, cardamom, oranges. Cinchona plantation 6 mi. ENE.

Sonaguera (sōnägā'rä), town (pop. 521), Colón dept., N Honduras, in Aguán R. valley, near railroad, 29 mi. SW of Trujillo; commercial center in banana area; rice, sugar cane.

Sonai (sō'nī), town (pop. 6,526), Ahmadnagar dist., E Bombay, India, 21 mi. N of Ahmadnagar; market center for grain, cotton, millet.

Sonamukhi (sōnä'mōōkē), town (pop. 14,667), Bankura dist., W West Bengal, India, 22 mi. ENE of Bankura; cotton weaving, shellac mfg.; rice, wheat, barley, mustard.

Sonargaon (sō'närgŭnj), village, Dacca dist., E central East Bengal, E Pakistan, 12 mi. ESE of Dacca; rice, jute. Was ⊙ Bengal under Khiljis (1296), Tughlaks (1330), and Afghan governors of Bengal (1351–1608); E terminus of 16th-cent. Grand Trunk Road built by Sher Shah. Ruins near.

Sonari (sōnä'rē), village, Sibsagar dist., E central Assam, India, on tributary of the Brahmaputra and 54 mi. ENE of Jorhat; tea, rice, rape and mustard. Extensive tea gardens near by.

Sonar River (sō'när), central India, rises in central Vindhya Range, in 2 headstreams joining in Saugor dist.; flows c.120 mi. NE, past Rehli, Garhakota, and Hatta, to Ken R. 27 mi. SSW of Panna.

Son Bonet (sōn' bōnĕt'), airfield, Majorca, Balearic Isls., 4 mi. NE of Palma.

Son Canals (sōn), irrigation system in W Bihar, India; from dam across Son R. at Dehri 3 main canals, including Arrah Canal (60 mi. long), extend from left bank NW to the Ganges, irrigating area bet. the rivers; Patna Canal (79 mi. long; steamer service) extends NE, along right bank of the Son, to the Ganges just W of Patna. Total acreage irrigated, c.490,000. Project begun 1869.

Sonchon (sŭn'chŭn'), Jap. *Sensen*, town (1944 pop. 22,725), N.Pyongan prov., N Korea, 34 mi. SE of Sinuiju, in agr. area (rice, soybeans). Gold and silver mines are near by.

Soncino (sônchē'nô), town (pop. 4,329), Cremona prov., Lombardy, N Italy, on Oglio R. and 8 mi. N of Soresina, in agr. region (cereals, sericulture, cattle raising); silk and flour mills, food and wood industries. Has castle (built 1473) and church (founded 1492).

Soncy, Texas: see AMARILLO.

Sonda (sōn'dä), town (pop. 529), NE Estonia, 18 mi. E of Rakvere, in oil-shale mining area; rail junction (spur to Aseri).

Sondeled (sûn'nŭlād), Nor. *Søndeled*, village and canton (pop. 2,983), Aust-Agder co., S Norway, on an inlet of the Skagerrak, 24 mi. NE of Arendal; mfg. of wood pulp, lumber.

Sonderborg, district, Denmark: see AABENRAA-SONDERBORG, amt.

Sonderborg (-nûrbôr), Dan. *Sønderborg*, Ger. *Sonderburg*, city (1950 pop. 16,204) and port, ⊙ Sonderborg dist. of Aabenraa-Sonderborg amt, S Jutland, Denmark, 39 mi. SW of Odense; 54°55'N 9°48'E. At S outlet of Als Sound, mostly on Als isl., with newer section on mainland; connected by 750-ft. pontoon bridge (built 1856). Textile mills, machine shops; margarine, tobacco. Founded around 13th-cent. castle (now a mus.). After 1864 in Germany until 1920 plebiscite.

Sonderjylland, Denmark: see JUTLAND.

Sonder Omme (sû'nûr ô'mû), Dan. *Sønder Omme*, town (pop. 1,120), Vejle amt, central Jutland, Denmark, 27 mi. WNW of Vejle; peat, brick.

Sondershausen (zôn″dûrs-hou'zûn), town (pop. 13,118), Thuringia, central Germany, near W foot of the Kyffhäuser, on the Wipper and 30 mi. NNW of Erfurt; potash mining; mfg. of electrical equipment, machinery, musical instruments, tobacco products; printing. Oil deposits near by. Site of music col. Has 16th-cent. palace; 17th-cent. church; house where Brahms lived. Until 1918, ⊙ principality of Schwarzburg-Sondershausen.

Sondfjord, Norway: see SOGN OG FJORDANE.

Sondhordland, Norway: see HORDALAND.

Sondmor, Norway: see MORE.

Sondre Bergenhus or **Sondre Bergenhuus,** Norway: see HORDALAND.

Sondre Strom Fjord (sûn'rû strûm' fyōr'), Dan. *Søndre Strømfjord*, inlet (120 mi. long, 1–5 mi. wide) of Davis Strait, SW Greenland, on Arctic Circle, extends NE from mouth at 66°N 53°30'E, 60 mi. S of Holsteinsborg, to edge of inland icecap, where several small arms receive glacier streams. Near its head, at 67°1'N 50°43'W, is Bluie West 8, U.S. base built during Second World War. Fjord was starting point of several expeditions.

Sondre Trondhjem, Norway: see SOR-TRONDELAG.

Sondre Upernavik (ōōpĕr'nävĭk) or **Sondre Upernivik** (-nĭvĭk), Dan. *Søndre Upernavik* or *Søndre Upernivik*, hunting settlement (pop. 120), Upernavik dist., W Greenland, on S Kekertarsuak (kĕkĕkhtäkh'swäk), isl. (20 mi. long, 2–10 mi. wide) in Baffin Bay, 45 mi. SSE of Upernavik; 72°9'N 55°33'W.

Sondrio (sôn'drēō), province (□ 1,239; pop. 142,919), Lombardy, N Italy; ⊙ Sondrio. Bounded N by Switzerland. The VALTELLINA runs through center and NE area, with Liro and lower Mera river valleys, which meet near CHIAVENNA, in NW.

Sondrio, town (pop. 7,639), ⊙ Sondrio prov., Lombardy, N Italy, on Adda R., near mouth of short Mallero R., and 35 mi. NNE of Bergamo; 46°10'N 9°52'E. Chief center of the picturesque Valtellina; resort (alt. 1,007 ft.); agr. trade center; wine, tanning, textile (silk, cotton), food (macaroni, sausage), sawmilling, furniture, and mica industries. Has technical school, old castle (now a barracks). Near by, on Armisa R. (6 mi. long; right branch of Adda R.), is a major hydroelectric plant.

Sone (sō'nā). **1** Town, Fukuoka prefecture, Japan: see KOKURA. **2** Town (pop. 5,150), Hyogo prefecture, S Honshu, Japan, on Harima Sea, 5 mi. SE of Himeji; rice, wheat, salt. **3** Town (pop. 5,619), Niigata prefecture, central Honshu, Japan, 12 mi. SW of Niigata; rice.

Sône, La (lä sōn'), village (pop. 596), Isère dept., SE France, on the Isère and 22 mi. SW of Grenoble; plastics, braids and laces; silk spinning.

Soneja (sōnā'hä), town (pop. 1,656), Castellón de la Plana prov., E Spain, 14 mi. NW of Sagunto; hardware and plaster mfg., flour milling; olive oil.

Sonepat (sōnā'pŭt), town (pop. 17,781), Rohtak dist., SE Punjab, India, 28 mi. ENE of Rohtak; trades in millet, wheat, gur, mangoes, cotton; cotton ginning, sugar milling, hand-loom weaving.

Sonepore, India: see SONPUR, Bihar.

Sonepur or **Sonpur** (both: sōn'pōōr), former princely state (□ 948; pop. 248,873) in Orissa States, India; ⊙ was Sonepur. In 1949, part inc. into Sambalpur dist., part into newly-created Bolangir dist., Orissa.

Sonepur. 1 or **Sonpur,** town (pop. 9,065), Bolangir dist., W central Orissa, India, on Mahanadi R. and 28 mi. ENE of Bolangir; trades in rice, timber, oilseeds; handicrafts (metal products, cloth fabrics). Was ⊙ former princely state of Sonepur. **2** Town, Saran dist., Bihar, India: see SONPUR.

Sone River, India: see SON RIVER.

Song (sōō'ŭng), village (1937 pop. 6,173), Phrae prov., N Thailand, on Yom R. and 23 mi. N of Phrae; rice, cotton. Locally known as Klang.

Song [Annamese,=river]: for names in Vietnam beginning thus and not found here, see under following part of the name.

Songarh (sōng'gŭr), town (pop. 2,591), Surat dist., N central Bombay, India, 45 mi. E of Surat; market center for pulse, cotton, rice; handicraft cloth weaving. Also spelled Songadh.

Songcau (shông'kou'), town, ⊙ Phuyen prov. (□ 1,400; 1943 pop. 282,800), S central Vietnam, in Annam, fishing port on South China Sea, on railroad and 235 mi. SSE of Hue; agr., cattle raising; coconuts. Formerly called Phuyen.

Songchin, Korea: see SONGJIN.

Songchon (sŭng'chŭn'), Jap. *Seisen*, township (1944 pop. 9,148), S.Pyongan prov., N Korea, 30 mi. NE of Pyongyang; rail junction; silk cocoons.

Songchon River, Korea: see TONGSONGCHON RIVER.

Songdo, Korea: see KAESONG.

Songe, Norway: see NES, village, Aust-Agder co.

Songea (sông-gä'ä), town, Southern Prov., S Tanganyika, on road and 280 mi. WSW of Lindi; 10°42'S 35°40'E. Agr. trade center; tobacco, coffee, wheat, sesame, rice; livestock. Talc and limestone deposits.

Songeons (sõzhō'), village (pop. 696), Oise dept., N France, on Thérain R. and 13 mi. NW of Beauvais; cheese mfg.

Songhor, Iran: see SUNQUR.

Songjin (sŭng'jĕn'), Jap. *Joshin* or *Zyosin* (both: jō'shĕn), city (1944 pop. 67,778), N.Hamgyong prov., N Korea, port at mouth of small Susong R., on Sea of Japan, 80 mi. SSW of Chongjin; industrial center (pig iron, steel, magnesium). Paper milling. Port was opened 1899 to foreign trade; exports fish, livestock, graphite, soybeans. Sometimes spelled Songchin.

Songjong (sông'jŭng'), Jap. *Shotei*, town (1949 pop. 21,768), S.Cholla prov., S Korea, 7 mi. W of Kwangju; commercial center in agr. area (rice, barley, cotton); grass linen, silk cocoons.

Songju (sŭng'jōō'), Jap. *Seishu*, township (1946 pop. 16,004), N.Kyongsang prov., S Korea, 18 mi. WNW of Taegu; rice, soybeans, silk cocoons.

Songkhla (sông'klä'), town (1947 pop. 17,842), ⊙ Songkhla prov. (□ 2,758; 1947 pop. 351,847), S Thailand, Gulf of Siam port on E coast of Malay Peninsula, on rail spur (from Hat Yai) and 450 mi. S of Bangkok, at outlet of the Thale Sap; 7°10'N 100°35'E. Major trade center and coastwise port of call (shipping rubber and copra); rice, coconuts; fisheries. Tin mining near by. Pop. is Thai, Malay, and Chinese. Developed in early 19th cent. as Chinese colony. Also called Singora.

Song Khone (shông' kôn'), town, Savannakhet prov., central Laos, 40 mi. SE of Savannakhet.

Songo or **Songo Town** (sông'gō), town (1931 pop. 600), Sierra Leone colony, on the protectorate border, on railroad and 22 mi. ESE of Freetown; kola nuts, ginger, rice.

Songololo (sông-gōlō'lō), village, Leopoldville prov., W Belgian Congo, on railroad and 60 mi. ENE of Boma, near Angola border; customs station and trading center; growing of native staples.

Songo River (sŏng'gō), SW Maine, short navigable stream with several locks; links Long and Sebago lakes, Cumberland co.

Songo Town, Sierra Leone: see SONGO.

Songsan (sŭng'sän'), Jap. *Jozan*, township (1946 pop. 14,098), on E coast of Cheju Isl., Korea, 24 mi. ESE of Cheju; fishing, agr. (rice, sweet potatoes, cotton).

Songwe (sông'gwä), village, Kivu prov., E Belgian Congo, 80 mi. NNE of Kasongo; gold mining.

Songwe, village, Southern Highlands prov., S Tanganyika, small port on NW shore of L. Nyasa, at mouth of small Songwe R. (Nyasaland border), 38 mi. SSE of Tukuyu; 9°44'S 33°55'E. Tea, coffee, rice.

Sonhat, India: see BAIKUNTHPUR.

Sonico (sô'nēkô), village (pop. 811), Brescia prov., Lombardy, N Italy, in Val Camonica, on Oglio R. and 2 mi. SE of Edolo. Has one of major Ital. hydroelectric plants.

Sonkach (sông'kŭch), town (pop. 4,222), S central Madhya Bharat, India, on Kali Sindh R. and 38 mi. SE of Ujjain; cotton, millet; cotton ginning. Sometimes spelled Sonkatch.

Sonkh (sōngk), town (pop. 4,084), Muttra dist., W Uttar Pradesh, India, 14 mi. SW of Muttra; gram, jowar, wheat, cotton, oilseeds. Also spelled Saunk.

Sonkovo (sôn'kŭvŭ), town (1938 pop 3,900), E Kalinin oblast, Russian SFSR, 17 mi. E of Bezhetsk; rail junction; food and flax processing.

Son-Kul or **Son-Kul'** (sŭn-kōōl'), lake (□ 100) in NW Tyan-Shan oblast, Kirghiz SSR, 40 mi. NW of Naryn: 17 mi. long; alt. 1,000 ft. Fresh water; frozen in winter. Outlet: Son-Kul (SE), a tributary of Naryn R.

Sonla (shŭn'lä'), town, ⊙ Sonla prov. (□ 4,200; 1943 pop. 118,700), N Vietnam, in Tonkin, 125 mi. W of Hanoi.

Sonmiani (sōnmyä'nē), village, Las Bela state, SE Baluchistan, W Pakistan, on creek, 4 mi. inland from Arabian Sea, and 45 mi. NW of Karachi; small port; fishing (catfish), salt panning. Sometimes called Miani. **Sonmiani Bay,** an inlet of Arabian Sea, extends from Cape Monze c.80 mi. W, along S coast of Las Bela.

Sonnblick (zôn'blĭk), peak (10,187 ft.) of the Hohe Tauern, S Austria, on Carinthia-Salzburg line. Has highest permanently inhabited meteorological station in Europe.

Sonneberg (zô'nŭbĕrk), town (pop. 21,534), Thuringia, central Germany, at foot of Thuringian Forest, 36 mi. SE of Meiningen, 3 mi. NE of Neustadt, in slate-quarrying region; toymaking and woodcarving center; mfg. of china, glass, electrical equipment. Resort. Has warehouses, serving surrounding toymaking villages; toy mus. and industrial school; remains of castle 1st mentioned 1216.

Sonnenberg, Austria: see LEITHA MOUNTAINS.

Sonnenberg (zô'nŭnbĕrk), residential suburb (pop. 5,464) of Wiesbaden, W Germany, 2 mi. NW of city center.

Sonnewalde (zô'nŭväl"dŭ), town (pop. 1,498), Brandenburg, E Germany, in Lower Lusatia, 5 mi. NNW of Finsterwalde, in lignite-mining region; grain, potatoes, stock.

Sonning Eye, residential village in parish of Eye and Dunsden (pop. 1,752), SE Oxfordshire, England, on the Thames opposite Sonning, and 4 mi. S of Henley-on-Thames. Just N is agr. village of Dunsden Green.

Sonnino (sôn-nē'nô), town (pop. 4,691), Latina prov., Latium, S central Italy, 9 mi. N of Terracina, in agr. region (olives, grapes, cereals).

Sonntagberg (zôn'täkbĕrk), town (pop. 4,041), W Lower Austria, 10 mi. SSW of Amstetten; grain, cattle.

Sonobe (sōnō'bā), town (pop. 9,381), Kyoto prefecture, S Honshu, Japan, 18 mi. WNW of Kyoto; agr. center (rice, wheat); raw silk.

Sonogi (sōnō'gē) or **Sonoki** (sōnō'kē), town (pop. 7,483), Nagasaki prefecture, W Kyushu, Japan, 15 mi. SE of Sasebo, on Omura Bay; agr. center (rice, wheat, sweet potatoes).

Sonogi Peninsula, W Kyushu, Japan, SW projection of Hizen Peninsula, bet. E.China Sea (W) and Omura Bay (E); 25 mi. long, 12 mi. wide. Nagasaki is at SE corner of base, where peninsula joins Nomo Peninsula. Sometimes spelled Sonoki.

Sonoita (sōnoi'tŭ), village, Santa Cruz co., S Ariz., port of entry 27 mi. NNE of Nogales. Sometimes spelled Sonoyta.

Sonoma (sŭnō'mŭ), county (□ 1,579; pop. 103,405), W Calif., on Pacific coast; ⊙ Santa Rosa. In the Coast Ranges; Mt. St. Helena is on E border. Bounded S by San Pablo Bay; drained by Russian R. and short coastal streams. Large poultry industry centered at Petaluma. Also dairying, winegrowing (notably in Sonoma Valley and Asti dists.), cattle raising, fruit and nut growing (apples, prunes, pears, cherries, berries, walnuts), farming (hops, vegetables, hay, grain). A leading Calif. co. in quicksilver mining; also stone quarries, oil and natural-gas wells. Many vacation resorts along lower Russian R.; mineral and hot springs (including The Geysers) attract health seekers. Redwood groves; some lumbering. Processing industries, some mfg. at Santa Rosa, Sonoma, Petaluma, Healdsburg. Formed 1850.

Sonoma. 1 City (pop. 2,015), Sonoma co., W Calif., 17 mi. NW of Vallejo; trade center of winegrowing Sonoma Valley; dairying, fruit canning. Founded 1835 by Gen. M. G. Vallejo on site of Serra's Mission San Francisco de Solano (1823; now restored). Bear Flag of the California republic was raised here in 1846. Mission and the home of Gen. Vallejo are state historic monuments. Hot springs (resorts) near by. **2** Town (pop. 210), Ellis co., N Texas.

Sonoma Range, N Nev., S of Winnemucca. Sonoma Peak (9,421 ft.) is at N end, Mt. Tobin (9,779 ft.) at S. Pleasant Valley Fault, a 25-mi., 15-ft. vertical displacement caused by an earthquake (1915), runs along W side of range.

Sonora (sŭnô'rŭ, Sp. sōnō'rä), state (□ 70,484; 1940 pop. 364,176; 1950 pop. 503,095), NW Mexico, on Gulf of California, S of Arizona; ⊙ Hermosillo. Bounded by Chihuahua (E), Sinaloa (S), and Lower California (NW). Mountainous region except for a coastal strip along the coast, it contains many broken ranges, plateaus, and desert areas amid the outliers of the Sierra Madre Occidental. It is intersected by several rivers which occasionally reach the gulf (e.g., Magdalena, Sonora, Mayo, and Yaqui rivers) and which, used for irrigation, have opened large areas to cultivation. Arid country with temperate (N) to semitropical climate, it has highest temperatures along the coast; late summer months sometimes bring rain, but desert areas and drought increase toward N. Its wealth lies in its mines: there are silver, gold, lead, and copper deposits in abundance. Cananea (NW) is one of the world's eading copper centers; other important mines are at La Colorada (silver, lead, copper, zinc), Pitiquito (copper, zinc), Arizpe (gold, silver, copper), Soyopa (coal), Agua Prieta (gypsum). Along irrigated river valleys are grown wheat, corn, cotton, rice, sugar cane, chick-peas, citrus fruit, alfalfa, winter vegetables (tomatoes, beans, etc.) on large scale. Cattle raising and corn and wheat growing on plateaus. Food-processing plants, tanneries, foundries, textile plants, cement mills are concentrated at Hermosillo, Ciudad Obregón, Navojoa, and Guaymas, the last being the only important port on the gulf coast. Nogales (N) is chief point of entry from U.S. The area was 1st explored by the Spanish in middle of 16th cent.; it formed, together with Chihuahua, Durango, and Sinaloa, the prov. of Nueva Viscaya. In 1830 Sonora was set up as a separate state. It took a leading part in the revolutionary wars in early 20th cent. Some of its native tribes, notably the Yaqui and Seri, are still wild and primitive.

Sonora. 1 Village (pop. 1,821), Pinal co., SE central Ariz., 16 mi. SSW of Miami in copper-mining region. **2** City (pop. 2,448), ⊙ Tuolumne co., central Calif., c.50 mi. E of Stockton, in the Mother Lode gold-mining country; site of Big Bonanza mine. Hq. for Stanislaus Natl. Forest. Limestone quarrying, fruitgrowing, lumbering in area. Old gold town of COLUMBIA is 4 mi. N. Sonora Pass across the Sierra Nevada is c.50 mi. NE. Founded 1848, inc. 1851. **3** Town (pop. 292), Hardin co., central Ky., 11 mi. S of Elizabethtown. **4** Town (pop. 2,633), ⊙ Sutton co., W Texas, on intermittent Dry Fork of Devils R. and 70 mi. S of San Angelo; retail point for ranching (sheep, goats, cattle) region; ships livestock, wool, mohair. Has annual wool and mohair show, quarter horse races. Ranch experiment station c.30 mi. SE; hunting near by. Settled 1888, inc. 1917.

Sonora Pass, E Calif., highway pass (alt. c.9,625 ft.) across the Sierra Nevada, N of Yosemite Natl. Park and c.50 mi. NE of Sonora.

Sonora Peak (11,429 ft.), E Calif., in the Sierra Nevada, on Mono-Alpine co. line, 35 mi. NW of Mono L.

Sonora River, Sonora, NW Mexico, rises on plateau near Cananea close to U.S. border, flows c.250 mi. S and SW, past Arizpe, Banámichi, Ures, and Hermosillo, to Gulf of California opposite Tiburón Isl. Receives San Miguel R. Used for irrigation, especially in Hermosillo dist. and in fertile delta; there cereals, vegetables, and subtropical fruit are grown. Reaches ocean only in years of heavy rain.

Sonoyta, Ariz.: see SONOITA.

Sonpur, former princely state, India: see SONEPUR.

Sonpur (sōn'pōōr). **1** Town, Saran dist., NW Bihar, India, on Gandak R. just above its mouth and 6 mi. N of Patna; rail junction (workshops); elephant-trade center; rice, wheat, barley, corn. Large annual Hindu bathing festival and fair. Also spelled Sonepur, Sonepore. **2** Town, Bolangir dist., Orissa, India: see SONEPUR.

Sonqor, Iran: see SUNQUR.

Son River (sōn), right tributary of the Ganges, NE central India, rises on plateau at E junction of Vindhya and Satpura ranges in NE Madhya Pradesh; flows NW, through E Vindhya Pradesh, to Kaimur Hills, then bends ENE, across SE Uttar Pradesh into Bihar, where it turns NE to the Ganges 8 mi. SE of Chapra; 475 mi. long. Receives (right) Rihand and N.Koel rivers. At Dehri (Bihar) are headworks of Son Canals. River liable to floods during rainy season; lower course 2–3 mi. wide. Sometimes spelled Sone.

Son San Juan (sōn' sän hwän'), village (pop. 1,586) and airport, Majorca, Balearic Isls., 4 mi. E of Palma.

Sonseca or **Sonseca con Casalgordo** (sōnsā'kä kōn käsälgôr'dhō), town (pop. 5,263), Toledo prov., central Spain, in New Castile, 13 mi. S of Toledo; agr. center (cereals, turnips, grapes, olives, potatoes, sheep, cattle). Alcohol distilling, cheese processing; mfg. of pottery, chocolate, marzipan and nougat confections, woolen goods. Hydroelectric plant.

Son Servera (sōn sĕrvä'rä), town (pop. 2,525), Majorca, Balearic Isls., on railroad and 38 mi. E of Palma; fruit, olives, carobs, almonds, pepper, hogs; olive-oil pressing.

Sonski or **Sonskiy** (sôn'skē), town (1926 pop. 1,408), E Khakass Autonomous Oblast, Krasnoyarsk Territory, Russian SFSR, on Achinsk-Abakan RR and 60 mi. NW of Abakan; sawmilling. Called Son until 1940.

Sonsón (sōnsōn'), town (pop. 8,984), Antioquia dept., NW central Colombia, in valley of Cordillera Central, on highway, and 40 mi. SSE of Medellín; alt. 8,350 ft. Mining (silver, gold, iron), agr. center (coffee, sugar cane, cereals, potatoes, fruit, stock); trading in dairy products and hides. Iron foundry; mfg. of coffee-processing and mining machinery. Founded 1785. Waterfalls and marble grottoes near by.

Sonsonate (sōnsōnä'tā), dept. (□ 866; 1950 pop. 119, 431), W Salvador, on the Pacific; ⊙ Sonsonate. Bounded N by coastal range, including volcano Izalco; slopes S to the coast; drained by Río Grande. Agr. (coffee, sugar cane, cacao, grain, tropical fruit), livestock raising. Balsam of Peru extraction and salt production on coastal plain. Hardwood lumbering. Main centers, Sonsonate and its port, Acajutla, are linked by rail and road with San Salvador. Formed 1855.

Sonsonate, city (1950 pop. 17,661), ⊙ Sonsonate, SW Salvador, on Río Grande and 36 mi. W of San Salvador, on railroad; alt. 145 ft.; 13°43'N 89°44'W. Commercial center connected with its port, Acajutla, by rail and road; processes livestock products, tropical fruit, coffee, sugar cane; exports skins and hides. Notable buildings: municipal palace, church of El Pilar, cathedral with 17 cupolas. Founded 1524; ⊙ Salvador, 1833–34.

Sonsorol (sôn'sŭrôl), coral island (pop. 122), Palau dist., W Caroline Isls., W Pacific, 42 mi. NNE of Pulo Anna; 5°20'N 132°15'E; sponges.

Sonta (sôn'tä), Hung. *Szond* (sônd), village (pop. 7,018), Yugoslavia, NW Serbia, Yugoslavia, 9 mi. SSW of Sombor, near the Danube (Croatia frontier), in the Backa; rail junction.

Sontay (shŭn'tī'), town (1936 pop. 7,000), ⊙ Sontay prov. (□ 400; 1943 pop. 210,600), N Vietnam, in Tonkin, on Red R. and 20 mi. WNW of Hanoi; coffee plantations, sericulture. Home industry: silk and cotton weaving, pottery. Has citadel (1830), captured 1883 by French. Military training center of Tong is just SW.

Sontheim or **Sontheim an der Brenz** (zônt'hīm än dĕr brĕnts'), village (pop. 2,281), N Württemberg, Germany, after 1945 in Württemberg-Baden, 11 mi. SE of Heidenheim; rail junction; mfg. of shoes, thread; metalworking.

Sonthofen (zônt'hō"fŭn), town (pop. 9,291), Swabia, SW Bavaria, Germany, in Allgäu Alps, on the Iller and 15 mi. SSW of Kempten; iron foundry; mfg. of precision instruments, textiles; dairying, printing, woodworking. Summer and winter resort (alt. 2,434 ft.). Chartered 1429. Site of military training school under Nazi regime.

Sontra (zôn'trä), town (pop. 6,376), in former Prussian prov. of Hesse-Nassau, W Germany, after 1945 in Hesse, 9 mi. SW of Eschwege; chemicals; woodworking. Has 17th-cent. town hall.

Soo, The, region, Mich. and Ont.: see SAULT SAINTE MARIE, city, Mich.

Soo Canals, Mich. and Ont.: see SAULT SAINTE MARIE CANALS.

Soochow, Suchow, or **Su-chou** (all: sōō'chou', Chinese sōō'jō'), city (1948 pop. 381,288), S Kiangsu prov., China, on Grand Canal, E of Tai L., and 50 mi. W of Shanghai, 40 mi. from mouth of Yangtze R.; rail junction. One of Kiangsu's largest cities, Soochow is important as a cotton- and silk-milling center, noted particularly for its silk goods. It has an active rice trade, and jade-carving and embroidery handicrafts. Seat of univ. and of Col. of Social Education. Soochow is situated in a scenic lake and hill dist. with numerous canals ("Venice of China"). The rectangular walled town (5 mi. by 2.5–3 mi.) is adjoined NW by industrial and commercial suburbs and contains palaces, temples, and the 12th-cent. Great Pagoda (250 ft. high). One of the oldest and best-known Chinese cities, Soochow dates from c.1000 B.C., when it was located on Tai L. (the lake has since receded). It was ⊙ Wu kingdom in 5th cent. B.C. Received its present name in 7th cent. A.D. It was visited by Marco Polo in 13th cent. City suffered in the Taiping Rebellion. Became a treaty port in 1896. During Sino-Japanese War, it was held (1937–45) by the Japanese. Passed 1949 to Communist control. It was called Wuhsien (1912–49) while ⊙ Wuhsien co. (1948 pop. 1,088,085). In 1949, Soochow became an independent municipality, regaining its old name; and the co. seat was moved to Hushukwan, 10 mi. NW on railroad, thereafter known as Wuhsien.

Soochow Creek, river of S Kiangsu prov., China, rises in canals of Soochow area, flows 60 mi. E to Whangpoo R. at Shanghai. Also Woosung R.

Sooden, Bad, Germany: see BAD SOODEN-ALLENDORF.

Soof, Jordan: see SUF.

Soo Junction, Luce co., NE Upper Peninsula, Mich., 12 mi. SSE of Newberry; departure point for excursions to Tahquamenon Falls in TAHQUAMENON RIVER.

Sooke (sōōk), village (pop. estimate 500), SW B.C., on SE tip of Vancouver Isl., on Sooke Harbour of Juan de Fuca Strait, 18 mi. W of Victoria; farming, fishing, lumbering.

Soomjam, Kashmir: see SUMJAM.

Sopachuy (sōpächōō'ē), town (pop. c.5,080), Chuquisaca dept., S central Bolivia, on Azero R. and 17 mi. SW of Padilla; wheat, corn, potatoes, vegetables, fruit.

Soper (sō'pûr), town (pop. 337), Choctaw co., SE Okla., 11 mi. W of Hugo, in rich farming area; cotton ginning.

Soperton (sō'pûrtûn). **1** City (pop. 1,667), ⊙ Treutlen co., E central Ga., 22 mi. ESE of Dublin, in agr. and timber area; mfg. (naval stores, clothing). **2** Village, Wis.: see WABENO.

Sopetrán (sōpäträn'), town (pop. 2,866), Antioquia dept., NW central Colombia, in Cauca valley, 23 mi. NW of Medellín; agr. center (corn, coffee, bananas, sugar, rice, cacao, cattle, hogs).

Sophades or **Sofadhes** (both: sôfä'dhĭs), town (pop. 4,046), Karditsa nome, S Thessaly, Greece, on narrow-gauge railroad and 9 mi. E of Karditsa; corn, vegetables; livestock. Also spelled Sofades.

Sophia, Bulgaria: see SOFIA, city.

Sophia (sūfē'ù), town (pop. 1,430), Raleigh co., S W.Va., 6 mi. SSW of Beckley, in semibituminous-coal region. Inc. 1912.

Sophia Island, Ellice Isls.: see NIULAKITA.

Soplaviento (sōplävyĕn'tō), town (pop. 2,782), Bolívar dept., N Colombia, on Canal del Dique and 28 mi. E of Cartagena; corn, sugar, livestock.

Sopockinie, Belorussian SSR: see SOPOTSKIN.

Sopor, Kashmir: see SOPUR.

Sopot (sô'pôt), after 1950 called **Vazovgrad** (vä'zôvgrät), city (pop. 3,248), Plovdiv dist., central Bulgaria, at S foot of Troyan Mts., in Karlovo Basin, 3 mi. W of Karlovo; armaments mfg.; rose-oil extracting, weaving; horticulture (tulips). Has mus. of Bulg. poet Ivan Vazov. Once a Turkish commercial town; declined under Bulg. rule.

Sopot (sô'pôt), Ger. *Zoppot* (tsô'pôt), residential city (1946 pop. 26,917), Gdansk prov., N Poland, on Gulf of Danzig, 7 mi. NNW of Danzig; seaside resort. Formerly fashionable gambling casino here.

Sopot (sô'pôt), village, N central Serbia, Yugoslavia, 21 mi. S of Belgrade.

Sopotskin (sŭpùtskēn'), Pol. *Sopockinie* (sôpôtskē'nyĕ), town (1931 pop. 3,000), NW Grodno oblast, Belorussian SSR, 13 mi. NW of Grodno, near Pol. border; rye, flax, livestock.

Sopris (sō'prùs, sō'–), village (1940 pop. 540), Las Animas co., S Colo., on Purgatoire R., E of Sangre de Cristo Mts., and 5 mi. SW of Trinidad; alt. c.6,100 ft.; coal-mining point.

Sopris Peak, Colo.: see ELK MOUNTAINS.

Sopron (shôp'rôn), county (□ 699; pop. 141,798), W Hungary; ⊙ SOPRON. Predominantly level region; some heavily forested mts. in W; includes S part of L. Neusiedler. Agr. area (wine, wheat, corn, sugar beets, some flax, beans, clover, fruit), dairy farming, hogs. Sopron is main industrial center. Lignite mined near Brennbergbanya. Large Ger. pop. along Austrian border.

Sopron, Ger. *Ödenburg,* city (pop. 42,255), ⊙ but independent of Sopron co., W Hungary, on Ikva R. and 37 mi. SSE of Vienna; near Austrian line; rail center; mfg. (starch, chemicals, bells, rugs, wool, silk); breweries, brick-, soap-, and candle-works. Its 1st sugar refinery established 1794. One of Hungary's oldest cultural centers. Celtic and Roman relics in Natl. Mus. Has 13th-cent. churches, 15th-cent. palace, univ., school of mines and forestry. Sopron, given to Austria after First World War, was returned to Hungary in 1921 after a plebiscite. Large Ger. pop. engaged in truck farming, wine making.

Sopronbanfalva (shôp'rômbänfôlvô), Hung. *Sopronbánfalva,* W suburb (pop. 3,391) of Sopron, Sopron co., W Hungary.

Sopur (sō'pōōr), town (pop. 11,770), Baramula dist., W central Kashmir, in Vale of Kashmir, on Wular L., at efflux of Jhelum R., 9 mi. NW of Srinagar; rice, corn, wheat, oilseeds. Named after noted 9th-cent. Kashmiri engineer, Suyya. Scene of fighting in 1947, during India-Pakistan struggle for control. Also spelled Sopor.

Soqotra, Aden: see SOCOTRA.

Soquel (sōkĕl'), village (1940 pop. 1,037), Santa Cruz co., W Calif., in Soquel Creek canyon, 5 mi. E of Santa Cruz, near Monterey Bay; bulb gardens, orchards, vineyards.

Sor (sôr), E suburb of Saint-Louis, NW Senegal, Fr. West Africa, on Sor isl. in Senegal R. estuary, linked by bridge with Saint-Louis. Railroad station. Experimental gardens; bacteriological station. Formerly Sohr.

Sora (sô'rä), town (pop. 7,443), Frosinone prov., Latium, S central Italy, on Liri R. and 15 mi. ENE of Frosinone; woolen and paper mills, soap factories, macaroni mfg. Has cathedral. On a rocky height above the town are remains of polygonal walls and medieval castle.

Sorá (sōrä'), village (pop. 132), Panama prov., central Panama, 10 mi. NW of Chame; stock raising.

Sorab (sō'rŭb), town (pop. 2,425), Shimoga dist., NW Mysore, India, 45 mi. NW of Shimoga; rice, betel nuts, cinnamon; handicraft sandalwood carving.

Soracte (sōrăk'tē), mountain (2,267 ft.) in the Apennines, central Italy, 25 mi. N of Rome. Celebrated by Vergil and Horace; in anc. times crowned with a temple of Apollo. Now has convent near its summit.

Sorada or **Surada** (both: sōōrä'dŭ), town (pop. 6,339), Ganjam dist., SE Orissa, India, on Rushikulya R. and 38 mi. NNW of Berhampur; exports sal timber, bamboo, hides.

Soragna (sôrä'nyä), town (pop. 1,378), Parma prov., Emilia-Romagna, N central Italy, 13 mi. NW of Parma.

Soraker (sûr'ō"kûr), Swedish *Söråker,* village (pop. 2,172), Vasternorrland co., NE Sweden, on Klinger Fjord (klĭng'ùr), Swedish *Klingerfjärden,* 10-mi.-long inlet of Gulf of Bothnia, 10 mi. NE of Sundsvall; pulp mills.

Sorano (sôrä'nô), village (pop. 1,463), Grosseto prov., Tuscany, central Italy, 20 mi. W of Orvieto; agr. products (cereals, wine, olive oil), livestock.

Soraon (sō'roun), village, Allahabad dist., SE Uttar Pradesh, India, 12 mi. N of Allahabad city center; rice, gram, barley, wheat, sugar cane.

Sora River (sô'rä), Ger. *Zeier* (tsī'ùr), NW Slovenia, Yugoslavia, formed by junction of Selska Sora, Slovenian *Selška Sora,* and Poljanska Sora rivers at Skofja Loka; flows 6 mi. ESE to Sava R. at Medvode.

Soras (sō'räs), town (pop. 1,238), Ayacucho dept., S Peru, in Cordillera Occidental, 70 mi. SE of Ayacucho; livestock center (cattle, sheep, llamas); agr. products (corn, wheat, potatoes, beans, quinoa).

Sorata (sōrä'tä), town (pop. c.6,500), ⊙ Larecaja prov., La Paz dept., W Bolivia, at foot of the ILLAMPU, 65 mi. NNW of La Paz, on road; alt. 8,717 ft. Trading center for subtropical agr. area (sugar cane, coffee, bananas); tourist resort. Scene of massacre by Indians in revolt of 1781. Formerly an active gold-collecting center.

Sorata, Mount, Bolivia: see ILLAMPU.

Sorath (sō'rŭt), district, S Saurashtra, India; ⊙ JUNAGARH.

Sorau (zō'rou) or **Zary** (zhä'rĭ), Pol. *Żary,* town (1939 pop. 25,902; 1946 pop. 6,109) in Brandenburg, after 1945 in Zielona Gora prov., W Poland, 35 mi. NNE of Görlitz, in Lower Lusatia. Center of lignite-mining region; rail junction; textile milling (woolen, cotton, linen, hemp, jute), mfg. of ceramics, glass, refractory bricks. Has 15th-cent. church. Salt market in Middle Ages; passed in 1785 to Saxony, in 1815 to Prussia. Heavily damaged in Second World War (c.80% destroyed).

Sor-Audnedal (sûr'-oud'nùdäl), Nor. *Sør-Audnedal,* or **Valle** (väl'lù), village and canton (pop. 2,361), Vest-Agder co., S Norway, on Audna R., on railroad and 25 mi. W of Kristiansand; wood products. Formerly called Sor-Undal.

Soraya (sörī'ä), town (pop. 530), Apurímac dept., S central Peru, in the Andes, 50 mi. SW of Abancay; grain, alfalfa, livestock. Gold and silver mining.

Sorbas (sôr'väs), town (pop. 1,402), Almería prov., S Spain, 26 mi. NE of Almería; pottery mfg.; cereals, olive oil, fruit, esparto.

Sorberge (sûr'bĕr"yù), Swedish *Sörberge,* residential village (pop. 2,340), Vasternorrland co., NE Sweden, on Indal R. near its mouth on Gulf of Bothnia, 9 mi. NNE of Sundsvall.

Sorbhog (sōr'bōg), village, Kamrup dist., W Assam, India, near Mora Manas R., 58 mi. WNW of Gauhati; rice, mustard, jute.

Sorbie, agr. village and parish (pop. 1,096), SE Wigtown, Scotland, 5 mi. S of Wigtown.

Sorbiodunum, England: see OLD SARUM.

Sorbolo (sôr'bôlô), town (pop. 1,805), Parma prov., Emilia-Romagna, N central Italy, on Enza R. and 6 mi. NE of Parma; packing boxes, canned tomatoes, hardware.

Sorcerer Mountain (10,387 ft.), SE B.C., in Selkirk Mts., 30 mi. NNE of Revelstoke.

Sorcy-Saint-Martin (sôrsē'-sē-märtē'), village (pop. 677), Meuse dept., NE France, on the Meuse and Canal de l'Est, 4 mi. SSE of Commercy; rail junction; limekilns. Stone quarries.

Sorde-l'Abbaye (sôrd'-läbā'), village (pop. 410), Landes dept., SW France, on the Gave d'Oloron and 12 mi. S of Dax; woodworking. Has noted 12th–13th-cent. Romanesque abbey church with Gallic-Roman mosaic.

Sordevolo (sôrdā'vôlô), village (pop. 912), Vercelli prov., Piedmont, N Italy, 4 mi. W of Biella; machinery.

Sore (sôr), village (pop. 707), Landes dept., SW France, 30 mi. N of Mont-de-Marsan; woodworking, lumber shipping.

Sorède (sôrĕd'), village (pop. 1,005), Pyrénées-Orientales dept., S France, at foot of the Monts Albères, 11 mi. ENE of Céret; whip mfg.; fruit- and winegrowing.

Sorel (sôrĕl'), city (pop. 12,251), ⊙ Richelieu co., S Que., on the St. Lawrence, at mouth of Richelieu R., and 45 mi. NNE of Montreal; grain-shipping center; shipbuilding, iron and steel founding, titanium refining, tanning, clothing mfg.; fruit, butter market. Site of former Fort Richelieu (1665). Sorel is hq. of St. Lawrence dredging fleet.

Sorell (sôrĕl'), town (pop. 522), SE Tasmania, 14 mi. ENE of Hobart and on N shore of Pitt Water; confectionery; oats, legumes.

Sorell, Cape, W Tasmania, in Indian Ocean, near entrance to Macquarie Harbour; 42°12'S 145°8'E.

Sorell, Lake, central Tasmania, 2d largest in Tasmania, 50 mi. N of Hobart; □ 19; 6 mi. long, 5 mi. wide; contains small isl. Interlaken at S shore. Just S is L. Crescent.

Sorel-Moussel (sôrĕl'-mōōsĕl'), commune (pop. 709), Eure-et-Loir dept., NW central France, on the Eure and 7 mi. N of Dreux; paper mill.

Sorento (sôrĕn'tō, sù–), village (pop. 692), Bond co., SW central Ill., 24 mi. ENE of Edwardsville, in agr. area (corn, wheat, poultry, oats; dairy products).

Soresina (sôrēsē'nä), town (pop. 8,895), Cremona prov., Lombardy, N Italy, 13 mi. NW of Cremona, in cattle-raising and sericulture region. Rail junction; agr. center, with largest dairy in Lombardy; flour mills, mfg. (fertilizer, machinery). Raw silk market.

Sorèze (sôrĕz'), village (pop. 864), Tarn dept., S France, on W slope of Montagne Noire, 11 mi. NNE of Castelnaudary; sawmilling, brickworks. Its former Benedictine abbey contained a well-known ecclesiastical school, headed (19th cent.) by Father Lacordaire.

Sor Fjord (sûr), Nor. *Sørfjord.* **1** Long, narrow arm of Hardanger Fjord (inlet of the North Sea), Hordaland co., SW Norway, begins near Kinsarvik and extends c.22 mi. S of Odda. W shore is mountainous, rising to Folgefonn glacier; E shore slopes have rich farms and orchards. Ullensvang, Espe, and Tyssedal are located here. **2** Inlet of the North Sea in Hordaland co., SW Norway, extends SE from point c.10 mi. N of Bergen, then curves NE and N, joining Oster Fjord and separating Osteroy from mainland; c.40 mi. long, 1 mi. wide. On it are Bruvik and Haus.

Sorfolda, Norway: see FOLDA.

Sorges (sôrzh), village (pop. 183), Dordogne dept., SW France, 11 mi. NE of Périgueux; truffles.

Sorgono (sôr'gônô), village (pop. 2,054), Nuoro prov., central Sardinia, 24 mi. SSW of Nuoro; rail terminus. San Mauro (14th-cent. church) is SW.

Sorgue River (sôrg), Vaucluse dept., SE France, rises just E of Fontaine-de-Vaucluse in a "fountain" (celebrated by Petrarch), flows c.15 mi. NW in a braided course across Rhone plain, past L'Isle-sur-la-Sorgue, to the Ouvèze at Bédarrides.

Sorgues or **Sorgues-sur-l'Ouvèze** (sôrg-sür-lōōvĕz'), town (pop. 5,911), Vaucluse dept., SE France, on the Ouvèze near its mouth into the Rhone, and 6 mi. NNE of Avignon, in winegrowing area (*Côtes-du-Rhône*); fertilizer, soda, and grindstone mfg., silk working. Has natl. gunpowder plant.

Sorgun (sôrgōōn'), village (pop. 2,528), Yozgat prov., central Turkey, 20 mi. E of Yozgat; barley, mohair goats. Formerly Yesilova.

Sor-Helgeland, Norway: see HELGELAND.

Sori (sô'rē), village (pop. 2,162), Genova prov., Liguria, N Italy, port on Gulf of Genoa and 9 mi. ESE of Genoa; foundries. In Second World War, partly destroyed by air bombing.

Sori, Mount, highest peak (6,060 ft.) in Nebrodi Mts., N Sicily, 17 mi. E of Mistretta.

Soria (sō'ryä), province (□ 3,977; pop. 159,824), N central Spain, in Old Castile; ⊙ Soria. Borders on Logroño prov. (N), Saragossa prov. (E), Guadalajara prov. (S), Segovia prov. (SW), and Burgos prov. (NW). Occupying N section of the Meseta (great central plateau), it is a largely forested, bleak region with an average alt. of c.3,000 ft. Duero (Douro) R., the prov.'s chief stream, rises in the Urbión massif (N). Climate is of the continental type (hot summers, cold winters). Rain is scarce. While stock raising (predominantly sheep) is the mainstay, some agr. crops (cereals, grapes, vegetables, hemp, fruit, sugar beets) are grown in the irrigated interior basins. The yield in timber and naval stores is considerable. Also flour milling, dairying, wine making, tanning; mfg. of woolen goods, soap, chocolate. Among little-exploited mineral resources are salt, ocher, iron, copper, lead, coal, peat, asphalt, petroleum, jasper, marble, clay, lime. The prov. is crossed by the Madrid-Saragossa-Barcelona RR. Soria, principal trading and communications center, is its only important city.

Soria, city (pop. 12,470), ⊙ Soria prov., N central Spain, in Old Castile, on right bank of the Duero (Douro) and 115 mi. NE of Madrid; 41°45′N 2°29′E; alt. 3,460 ft. Railroads to Saragossa, Madrid, and Burgos. Minor provincial city on the monotonous central plateau, the Meseta; center for a grazing region where some wheat, grapes, and fruit are also grown. Sawmilling, flour milling, canning, tanning, dairying, meat packing, wine making; mfg. of sweets, woolen goods, cement products, tiles, soap. Rich in history and art, it has several fine Romanesque (12th–14th cent.) churches and the sumptuous palace of the counts of Gómara. There are remains of a 13th-cent. wall and near-by citadel. Ruins of San Juan del Duero convent are just N. Has archaeological mus. (inaugurated 1919). Founded to replace NUMANTIA (3 mi. N), Soria achieved prominence during Christian reconquests.

Soriano (sōryä′nō), department (□ 3,561; pop. 93,490), SW Uruguay; ⊙ Mercedes. Bordered by the Río Negro (N), the Arroyo Grande (E), the Cuchilla San Salvador (S), and the Uruguay (W). Drained by the San Salvador and the Arroyo Grande. The Cuchilla del Bizcocho crosses dept. SE–NW. Includes Vizcaíno and Lobos isls. Mainly agr. region (wheat, corn, oats, linseed) and sheep- and cattle-raising area. Trades in wool; exports grain; flour milling. Main centers: Mercedes, Soriano, Santa Catalina. Served by railroad and highway from Montevideo, and by steamship lines on the Uruguay, San Salvador, and Río Negro. Dept. was formed 1816.

Soriano or **Santo Domingo de Soriano** (sän′tō dōmēng′gō dā), town (pop. 2,050), Soriano dept., SW Uruguay, at confluence of the Río Negro and Uruguay R., on highway, and 18 mi. SW of Mercedes; trade center for animal fat and wool; cattle and sheep raising. Said to be the oldest Uruguayan settlement, founded 1624 by an Indian tribe on Vizcaíno Isl., and transferred to its present site in 1708.

Soriano Calabro (sōrēä′nô kä′läbrô), town (pop. 4,095); Catanzaro prov., Calabria, S Italy, 9 mi. SE of Vibo Valentia, in cereal-growing, stock-raising region.

Soriano nel Cimino (nĕl chēmē′nô), town (pop. 4,654), Viterbo prov., Latium, central Italy, 7 mi. E of Viterbo; resort (alt. 1,673 ft.); wine, olive oil. Has palace designed by Vignola. Near by is 13th-cent. castle.

Sorihuela del Guadalimar (sōrēwā′lä dhĕl gwädhälēmär′), town (pop. 3,086), Jaén prov., S Spain, near the Guadalimar, 9 mi. NNE of Villacarrillo; olive-oil processing, fruit and vegetable canning, soap mfg. Esparto, cereals, truck produce. Mineral springs; sandstone quarries.

Sor Islands (sûr), Nor. *Sørøyane* (sûr′û″yänů) [=south islands], group in the North Sea, More og Romsdal co., W Norway, paralleling the coast c.25 mi. SW of Alesund. Include isls. of HAREID, GURSKOY, SANDOY.

Soritor (sōrētōr′), town (pop. 452), San Martín dept., N central Peru, in E outliers of the Andes, 8 mi. WSW of Moyobamba; coca, rice, sugar cane; mfg. of straw hats.

Sormovo, Russian SFSR: see GORKI, city, Gorki oblast.

Sorn, agr. village and parish (pop. 3,369), central Ayrshire, Scotland, on Ayr R. and 5 mi. NNW of Cumnock. Parish includes CATRINE.

Sornac (sôrnäk′), village (pop. 423), Corrèze dept., S central France, on Plateau of Millevaches, 10 mi. NW of Ussel; flour milling. Has 12th-cent. church.

Soro (sô′rů), Dan. *Sorø*, amt (□ 571; pop. 125,884), SW Zealand, Denmark; ⊙ Soro. Chief cities: Slagelse, Korsor. Gyldenloves Height (413 ft.), here, is highest point in Zealand. Some wooded areas in center. Agr., dairy farming.

Soro, Dan. *Sorø*, city (pop. 5,503), ⊙ Soro amt, Zealand, Denmark, 45 mi. WSW of Copenhagen; 55°26′N 11°34′E. Meat canning; furniture, machinery. Has 12th-cent. church, acad. founded 1584.

Soro, Fr. Equatorial Africa: see BAHR EL GHAZAL.

Soro (sō′rō), town (pop. 586), Sucre state, NE Venezuela, on S shore of Paria Peninsula, on Gulf of Paria, 10 mi. WSW of Güiria; goats, coconuts.

Soroca, Moldavian SSR: see SOROKI.

Sorocaba (sōōrōōkä′bů), city (1950 pop. 69,631), SE São Paulo, Brazil, on Sorocaba R. (affluent of the Tietê) and 55 mi. W of São Paulo; commercial and textile-milling center; historically, São Paulo's leading mule and cattle market. Situated in an important cotton- and citrus-growing dist., and at E end of a fertile agr. pioneer region—called Sorocabana after the railroad which serves it—extending 300 mi. W to Paraná R. in S São Paulo, the city channels agr. output of the interior to São Paulo and to Santos (coffee), with which it is linked by rail. In addition to textiles (knitwear, flannels, cotton prints), city produces lime and cement, footwear, hats, soap, wine, cottonseed oil. Large apatite deposits, worked at near-by Ipanema, are concentrated into superphosphates. Hydroelectric plant. Bet. early 17th cent. and arrival of railroads in late 19th cent., Sorocaba was a flourishing frontier town noted throughout Brazil for its livestock fairs.

Sorochinsk (sŭrŭchēnsk′), city (1926 pop. 11,179), W central Chkalov oblast, Russian SFSR, on Samara R., on railroad and 90 mi. WNW of Chkalov; flour-milling, meat-packing center. Became city in 1945. Until c.1935, Sorochinskoye.

Soroka, Karelo-Finnish SSR: see BELOMORSK.

Soroki (sŭrô′kē), Rum. *Soroca* (sôrô′kä), city (1930 pop. 15,001; 1941 pop. 8,042), N Moldavian SSR, in Bessarabia, on Dniester R. (Ukrainian border), S of Yampol, and 85 mi. NNW of Kishinev, in orchard area; flour and oilseed milling, brewing, soap and brick mfg. Ruins of 15th-cent. Genoese-Moldavian citadel. Developed on site of anc. Olgionia (5th cent. B.C.); trading center in 15th cent. Pop. largely Jewish until Second World War. While in Rumania (1918–40, 1941–44), it was ⊙ Soroca dept. (□ 1,672; 1941 pop. 314,440).

Sorokino (sŭrô′kēnŭ). **1** Village (1939 pop. over 2,000), NE Altai Territory, Russian SFSR, on Chumysh R., on S.Siberian RR and 55 mi. NE of Barnaul, in agr. area. **2** Village, Tyumen oblast, Russian SFSR: see BOLSHOYE SOROKINO. **3** Village, Voroshilovgrad oblast, Ukrainian SSR: see KRASNODON.

Soroksar (shô′rôk-shär), Hung. *Soroksár*, town (pop. 18,894), Pest-Pilis-Solt-Kiskun co., N central Hungary, on arm of the Danube and 7 mi. S of Budapest; rail junction; mfg. (velvet, ribbons, paint, soap, candles).

Sorol (sô′rôl), atoll (pop. 10), Yap dist., W Caroline Isls., W Pacific, 180 mi. SE of Yap; 6.5 mi. long, 1.5 mi. wide; 17 wooded isls. of which Sorol isl. (c.2 mi. long) is largest.

Soron (sō′rōn), town (pop. 12,886), Etah dist., W Uttar Pradesh, India, on tributary of the Ganges and 8 mi. NE of Kasganj; handicraft cotton spinning, sugar refining; pilgrimage center. Anc. Hindu fort ruins; c.12th-cent. Vishnuite temple, destroyed by Aurangzeb and rebuilt in 19th cent.

Sorong (sôrông′), town (dist. pop. 6,499), Netherlands New Guinea, on W coast of Vogelkop peninsula, on Sele Strait (here 12 mi. wide) 200 mi. W of Manokwari; 0°54′S 131°15′E; oil-shipping port, linked by 30-mi.-long pipe line with inland oil fields; also exports copra, resin. Important Jap. base in Second World War.

Soroti (sōrō′tē), town (1948 pop. c.4,000), E central Uganda, near L. Kyoga, 60 mi. NW of Mbale; agr. trade center; cotton, peanuts, sesame; livestock. Has hosp. Hq. Tesu dist. Soroti station (rail terminus) is 7 mi. NNE.

Sorovits, Greece: see AMYNTAION.

Soroy (sōr′ûü), Nor. *Sorøy*, island (□ 315; pop. 2,450) in Norwegian Sea, Finnmark co., N Norway, 11 mi. W of Hammerfest; 40 mi. long (NE–SW), 3–18 mi. wide; rises to 2,136 ft. Fishing.

Soroyane, Norway: see SOR ISLANDS.

Sorraia River (sôrä′yů), central Portugal, formed by junction of 2 headstreams (Sor and Raia) 15 mi. E of Coruche, crosses low-lying S part of Santarém dist., entering lower Tagus R. (left bank) below Benavente, in several marshy, meandering branches. Length, c.35 mi.

Sor-Rana, Norway: see FINNEIDFJORD.

Sorrel Hill, mountain (1,875 ft.), N Co. Wicklow, Ireland, 4 mi. ESE of Blessington.

Sorrento (sůrĕn′tō), village (pop. 1,045), S Victoria, Australia, 38 mi. S of Melbourne, on S shore of Port Phillip Bay; seaside resort.

Sorrento (sůrĕn′tō, It. sôr-rĕn′tô), anc. *Surrentum*, town (pop. 7,031), Napoli prov., Campania, S Italy, on S shore of Bay of Naples, 17 mi. SSE of Naples. Beautifully situated amid orange and lemon groves on the mountainous peninsula of Sorrento (c.15 mi. long), which separates Bay of Naples from Gulf of Salerno; rises to 4,734 ft. in Monte Sant'Angelo (W); terminates in Punta della Campanella, opposite Capri. A popular resort town; also noted for its wine and olive oil. Archbishopric. Tasso b. here.

Sorrento, fishing, resort town (pop. 201), Hancock co., S Maine, on Frenchman Bay, just NE of Mt. Desert Isl.

Sorsakoski (sōr′säkōs″kē), village in Leppävirta commune (pop. 14,278), Kuopio co., S central Finland, in Saimaa lake region, 30 mi. S of Kuopio; metalworking; machine shop.

Sorsele (sôr′sälů), village (pop. 789), Vasterbotten co., N Sweden, on Vindel R. and 70 mi. NW of Lycksele; sawmilling, woodworking.

Sorso (sôr′sô), town (pop. 7,405), Sassari prov., NW Sardinia, 4 mi. N of Sassari; rail terminus; domestic rope and cord production.

Sorsogon (sôrsōgōn′), province (□ 793; 1948 pop. 291,138), extreme SE Luzon, Philippines, bounded W by Ticao Pass, NE by Albay Gulf, SE by San Bernardino Strait; ⊙ Sorsogon. The W coast is deeply indented by Sorsogon Bay. Mountainous, rising to 5,115 ft. in Mt. Bulusan. Abacá is chief product; coconuts and rice are also grown.

Sorsogon, town (1939 pop. 8,153; 1948 municipality pop. 26,004), ⊙ Sorsogon prov., extreme SE Luzon, Philippines, port on NE shore of Sorsogon Bay, 22 mi. ESE of Legaspi; trade center for agr. area (hemp, coconuts, rice); fishing. Exports hemp, copra.

Sorsogon Bay, landlocked inlet of extreme SE Luzon, Philippines, opens NW into Burias Pass and SW into Ticao Pass; 13 mi. long, 5 mi. wide, with narrow entrance 1½–3 mi. wide.

Sort (sôrt), town (pop. 721), Lérida prov., NE Spain, on S slopes of central Pyrenees, on the Noguera Pallaresa and 17 mi. WNW of Seo de Urgel; agr. trade (livestock, cereals).

Sortavala (sôr′tävälä), Rus. *Serdobol* or *Serdobol′* (syĕrdŭbôl′), city (1941 pop. 13,000) SW Karelo-Finnish SSR, port on N shore of L. Ladoga, on railroad and 120 mi. W of Petrozavodsk; cultural and economic center of N Ladoga section of Karelia and summer resort; sawmilling (plywood); mfg. (woolens, furniture, felt, leather), brewing, dairying. Has teachers col., Karelian folk mus. (1883). Founded 1632; prospered in 19th cent. Former see of Greek Orthodox archbishop of Finland. Passed (1940) to USSR. In Second World War, held (1941–44) by Finns and Germans.

Sortino (sôrtē′nô), town (pop. 10,058), Siracusa prov., SE Sicily, near Anapo R., 15 mi. NW of Syracuse, in cereal- and olive-growing region. Necropolis of Pantalica, 2 mi. S on cliffs above the Anapo, is largest in Sicily; has c.4,000 Siculian tombs dating from 15th to 9th cent. B.C.

Sortland (sôrt′län), fishing village (pop. 828; canton pop. 5,359), Nordland co., N Norway, on W Langoy of the Vesteralen group, on Sortland Sound, 40 mi. NE of Svolvaer; fish canning, fish-oil and peat processing, tanning; stock raising. Iron and graphite deposits. Sortland Sound, Nor. *Sortlandsund*, is a strait (50 mi. long, 1–4 mi. wide) bet. Langoy and Hinnoy.

Sor-Trondelag (sûr′ trûn′nůläg), Nor. *Sør-Trøndelag*, county [Nor. *fylke*] (□ 7,268; pop. 193,912), central Norway; ⊙ Trondheim. Includes area bet. outer Trondheim Fjord and Swedish border, taking in Trollheimen mts. and the N Dovrefjell; drained by Gaula and Orkla rivers; has several large lakes, notably Selbu (N), Aursund (SE), and part of Femund (SE). Chief occupations: agr. (barley, potatoes), lumbering, fishing (cod). Copper mining in Roros, Lokken, and Alen areas; production of copper, sulphur, chromite at Trondheim, Roros, Orkanger. Tourist traffic in mts. (SW) and around Trondheim Fjord. Railroads from Dombas and from Glomma valley join at Storen and continue N to Trondheim; a short electric railroad connects Lokken mining center with the sea at Orkanger. Until 1918, co. (then called *amt*) was named Sondre Trondhjem, Nor. *Søndre Trondhjem.*

Sorumsand (sû′rōōmsän), Nor. *Sørumsand*, village (pop. 642) in Sorum (Nor. *Sørum*) canton (pop. 3,601), Akershus co., SE Norway, on Glomma R., on railroad and 18 mi. ENE of Oslo; mfg. of machinery, turbines.

Sor-Undal, Norway: see SOR-AUDNEDAL.

Sorvagen (sûr′vôgůn), Nor. *Sørvågen*, sometimes *Sørvaagen*, village (pop. 334) in Moskenes canton (pop. 2,027), Nordland co., N Norway, on E shore of Moskenesoy, Lofoten Isls., 50 mi. SW of Svolvaer; fishing port and summer resort, as is Reine village (pop. 332), 4 mi. NNE.

Sor-Vagsoy, Norway: see VAGSOY.

Sor-Varanger (sûr′ vär′äng-ůr), Nor. *Sør-Varanger*, canton (pop. 7,993), Finnmark co., N Norway, on USSR border, S of Kirkenes. Bjornevatn (byûr′-nůvätůn) (Nor. *Bjørnevatn*) village, 5 mi. S of Kirkenes, is center of important iron-mining region. Deposits discovered 1902, mining began 1910. Destroyed in Second World War, mines were subsequently rebuilt.

Sorve Peninsula or **Syrve Peninsula,** Est. *Sõrve* (sûr′vā), Ger. *Sworbe*, SW extremity of Saare isl., Estonia, in Baltic Sea; extends c.20 mi. SSW toward Latvia (separated by Irbe Strait), closing off Gulf of Riga; densely populated; orchards, vegetables.

Sosa (zō′zä), village (pop. 2,722), Saxony, E central Germany, in the Erzgebirge, on small tributary of the Zwickauer Mulde and 7 mi. SSW of Aue, near Czechoslovak border, in uranium-mining region; woodworking. Construction of major power and irrigation dam begun here 1949.

Sosa (sô′sä′), Jap. *Sosha*, town (1949 pop. 26,376), Kyonggi prov., central Korea, S of 38°N, 5 mi. SW of Seoul; rice, wheat, soy beans, silk cocoons.

Sosan (sŭ′sän′). **1** Jap. *Zuisan*, town (1949 pop. 21,202), S Chungchong prov., S Korea, 60 mi. SW of Seoul; rice, soy beans, cotton, tobacco. **2** Township, S Pyongan prov., Korea: see CHUNGSAN.

Sosdala (sŭs'dä"lä), Swedish *Sösdala*, village (pop. 925), Kristianstad co., S Sweden, 9 mi. SSW of Hassleholm; peat digging; grain, potatoes, livestock. Near by is extensive Iron Age burial ground.

Sos del Rey Católico (sōs' dhĕl rā' kätō'lēkō), town (pop. 2,226), Saragossa prov., N Spain, on S slopes of the Pyrenees, 36 mi. NNE of Tudela; agr. trade center (cereals, potatoes, livestock); lumber. King Ferdinand the Catholic b. here in Camporeal palace.

Sosedka (sŭsyĕt'kŭ), village (1939 pop. over 500), W Penza oblast, Russian SFSR, 17 mi. S of Zemetchino, in sugar-beet area.

Sosei, Japan: see O-o.

Soses (sō'sĕs), village (pop. 1,139), Lérida prov., NE Spain, on Segre R. and 10 mi. SW of Lérida; olive-oil processing; agr. trade (livestock, sugar beets, cereals, wine).

Sosha, Korea: see Sosa.

Soskovo (sôs'kŭvŭ), village (1939 pop. over 500), SW Orel oblast, Russian SFSR, 30 mi. SW of Orel; hemp.

Sosna River (sŭsnä'), Orel oblast, Russian SFSR, rises in Central Russian Upland NE of Maloarkhangelsk, flows c.125 mi. generally ENE, past Kolpny, Livny, and Yelets, to Don R. N of Vodopyanovo.

Sosneado, El, Argentina: see El Sosneado.

Sosninskaya, Novgorod oblast, Russian SFSR: see Kominterna, Imeni.

Sosnitsa (sŭsnyē'tsŭ), town (1926 pop. 6,948), E Chernigov oblast, Ukrainian SSR, near Desna R., 25 mi. NNW of Bakhmach; dairying.

Sosnovets (sŭsnô'vĭts), town (1948 pop. over 500), N central Karelo-Finnish SSR, on railroad and 10 mi. S of Belomorsk; sawmilling, woodworking.

Sosnovka (sŭsnôf'kŭ). **1** Town (1939 pop. over 500), N Chuvash Autonomous SSR, Russian SFSR, on left bank of the Volga, opposite (under jurisdiction of) Cheboksary; sawmilling. Quartz sand deposits near by. **2** Town (1926 pop. 950), SE Kirov oblast, Russian SFSR, on railroad, on Vyatka R. and 7 mi. E of Vyatskiye Polyany; sawmilling, woodworking, shipbuilding. **3** Village (1926 pop. 7,562), N Tambov oblast, Russian SFSR, 22 mi. SW of Morshansk; rail terminus; distillery.

Sosnovo (sŭsnô'vŭ), village (1940 pop. over 500), NW Leningrad oblast, Russian SFSR, on Karelian Isthmus, 40 mi. N of Leningrad; rail junction. Called Rautu while in Finland (until 1940) and, until 1948, in USSR.

Sosnovoborsk (sŭsnô"vŭbôrsk'), town (1926 pop. 2,534), E Penza oblast, Russian SFSR, 19 mi. NW of Kuznetsk; woolen milling. Until c 1940, Litvino.

Sosnovo-Ozerskoye (-vŭ-ŭzyôr'skŭyŭ), village (1948 pop. over 500), E Buryat-Mongol Autonomous SSR, Russian SFSR, on small Yeravnoye L., 175 mi. ENE of Ulan-Ude; highway center; lake fisheries. Coal deposits.

Sosnovoye (sŭsnô'vŭyŭ), village (1939 pop. over 500), E Rovno oblast, Ukrainian SSR, on Sluch R. and 35 mi. ENE of Rovno; rye, potatoes, livestock; lumbering. Until 1946, Lyudvipol, Pol. *Ludwipol*.

Sosnovskoye (sŭsnôf'skŭyŭ), town (1926 pop. 3,296), W Gorki oblast, Russian SFSR, 11 mi. S of Pavlovo; metalworking center.

Sosnovy Solonets or **Sosnovyy Solonets** (sŭsnô'vē sŭlŭnyĕts'), village (1939 pop. over 2,000), W Kuibyshev oblast, Russian SFSR, in Zhiguli Mts., in Samara Bend of the Volga, 25 mi. WNW of Kuibyshev; wheat, fruit.

Sosnowiec (sôsnô'vyĕts), Rus. *Sosnovets* (sŭsnô'-vyĭts), city (1950 pop. 95,147), Katowice prov., S Poland, on the Czarna Przemsza and 6 mi. ENE of Katowice. Rail junction; metallurgical center (blast furnace, foundry, rolling mill); mfg. of machinery, construction materials, chemicals, bricks, beer; flour milling, woodworking. Major power station. Passed (1795) to Prussia and (1815) to Rus. Poland; returned 1919 to Poland. Developed in late-19th cent. (1880 pop. 10,000; 1937 pop. 120,110) because of near-by mines; it now reaches Bedzin on N. During Second World War, under Ger. rule, called Sosnowitz; relatively little damaged.

Soso, village (pop. 171), Jones co., SE Miss., 9 mi. WNW of Laurel.

Sospel (sôspĕl'), village (pop. 1,471), Alpes-Maritimes dept., SE France, 15 mi. NE of Nice, near Ital. border, on Nice-Turin RR and road; plaster mfg., olive oil processing. Gorge of Bévère R. (small tributary of Roya R.) just NW.

Sostanj (shô'shtänyŭ), Slovenian *Šoštanj*, Ger. *Schönstein* (shûn'shtīn), village, N Slovenia, Yugoslavia, on railroad and 15 mi. NW of Celje; summer resort; mfg. (leather, footwear, glue). Hydroelectric plant. Until 1918, in Styria.

Sosúa (sōsōō'ä), village (1935 pop. 1,877), Puerto Plata prov., N Dominican Republic, on the Atlantic, 11 mi. E of Puerto Plata, in agr. region (coffee, cacao, rice, bananas, cattle). Fishing and swimming resort.

Sosva or **Sos'va** (sŭsvä'), town (1926 pop. 2,334), central Sverdlovsk oblast, Russian SFSR, on left bank of Sosva R. (landing) and 50 mi. SE (under jurisdiction) of Serov, on railroad; woodworking center. Until 1938, Sosvinski Zavod.

Sosva River or **Sos'va River. 1** In Sverdlovsk oblast, Russian SFSR, rises in the central Urals at 60°10'N, c.20 mi. W of Pokrovsk-Uralski; flows N, E, SSE, past Maslovo, Marsyaty, and Filkino, and NW, past Sosva and Gari, joining Lozva R. 8 mi. N of Gari to form Tavda R.; 345 mi. long. Navigable below Filkino. Receives Vagran, Turya, Kakva, and Lyalya (right) rivers. **2** or **Northern Sosva River**, Rus. *Severnaya Sosva*, in Khanty-Mansi Natl. Okrug, Tyumen oblast, Russian SFSR, rises on E slope of the N Urals at 62°10'N, flows E, past Nyaksimvol (head of navigation), N, ESE, and ENE, past Berezovo, to an arm of the Ob; c.400 mi. long. Receives Lesser Sosva R. (right).

Sotaquí (sōtäkē'), village (1930 pop. 951), Coquimbo prov., N central Chile, on Limarí R., on railroad and 5 mi. SE of Ovalle; fruitgrowing, stock-raising center.

Sotará Volcano (sōtärä') (15,026 ft.), Cauca dept., SW Colombia, in Cordillera Central, 13 mi. S of Popayán.

Sotavento (sōtävĕn'tō), lowlands in Veracruz, SE Mexico, on Gulf of Campeche, around port of Alvarado and along upper Papaloápam R. Noted cattle-raising country; sugar cane, coffee, fruit, timber.

Soteapan (sōtäă'pän), town (pop. 1,468), Veracruz, SE Mexico, 29 mi. W of Coatzacoalcos; tobacco, fruit.

Sotik (sō'tĭk), village (pop. c.1,500), W Kenya, on road and 30 mi. SSE of Kericho; tea, coffee, flax, corn. Also called Sotik Post.

Sotillo de la Adrada (sōtē'lyō dhä lä ädhrä'dhä), town (pop. 2,913), Ávila prov., central Spain, in SE Sierra de Gredos, 25 mi. NE of Talavera de la Reina; agr. center in region irrigated by Tiétar R. Grapes, cereals, chestnuts, figs, vegetables, livestock; pine cones, timber. Liquor distilling, flour milling.

Sotillo de la Ribera (rēvā'rä), town (pop. 1,199), Burgos prov., N Spain, 10 mi. NW of Aranda de Duero; grapes, cereals, vegetables, livestock; apiculture.

Sotkamo (sōt'kämō), village (commune pop. 14,644), Oulu co., central Finland, in lake region, 20 mi. ESE of Kajaani; rail terminus; quartz quarrying, lumbering. Summer and winter-sports resort.

Sotla River (sôt'lä) or **Sutla River** (sōōt'lä), N Yugoslavia, rises 5 mi. E of Rogatec, flows c.50 mi. S, past Rogatec, along Slovenia-Croatia border, to Sava R. 5 mi. SE of Brezice.

Sotnikovskoye (sôt'nyĭkŭfskŭyŭ), village (1926 pop. 8,613), central Stavropol Territory, Russian SFSR, 24 mi. WNW of Budennovsk; flour milling; wheat, cotton, livestock. Village of Burlatskoye (1926 pop. 3,318) is 8 mi. NW; metalworks.

Soto, Argentina: see Villa de Soto.

Soto la Marina (sō'tō lä märē'nä), town (pop. 202), Tamaulipas, NE Mexico, on Gulf plain, on Soto la Marina R. and 60 mi. E of Ciudad Victoria; henequen, sugar cane, corn, stock.

Soto la Marina River, in Tamaulipas, NE Mexico, rises in Sierra Madre Oriental at Nuevo León border SW of Linares, flows c.160 mi. E, past Padilla and Soto la Marina, to Gulf of Mexico 30 mi. E of Soto la Marina. Irrigates fertile Gulf plains. Mouth barred by sand banks. Sometimes Santander R.

Soton, Formosa: see Tsaotun.

Sotonera, Spain: see Alcalá de Gurrea.

Sotra, Norway: see Store Sotra.

Sotrondio (sōtrōn'dyō), village (pop. 1,074), Oviedo prov., NW Spain, on Nalón R. and 14 mi. SE of Oviedo; coal mines near by.

Sotsgorodok (sŭts"gŭrŭdôk'), town (1940 pop. over 500), SE Kursk oblast, Russian SFSR, SE suburb of Valuiki.

Sottegem, Belgium: see Zottegem.

Sotteville-lès-Rouen (sôtvēl'-lā-rōōä'), S suburb (pop. 18,271) of Rouen, Seine-Inférieure dept , N France, on the Seine; cotton mills, ship-repair yards; vinegar, varnish mfg., cider distilling Damaged in Second World War.

Sottomarina (sôt"tômärē'nä), town (pop. 9,308), Venezia prov., Veneto, N Italy, at S end of Lagoon of Venice, opposite Chioggia, with which it is connected by a bridge; bathing resort. Agr. experimental station.

Sottrum (zôt'rōōm), village (pop. 2,060), in former Prussian prov. of Hanover, NW Germany, after 1945 in Lower Saxony, 7 mi. W of Rotenburg; metal- and woodworking.

Sotuba (sōtōō'bä), rapids of the Niger and an irrigation area in S Fr. Sudan, Fr. West Africa, just E of Bamako.

Sotuta (sōtōō'tä), town (pop. 2,923), Yucatan, SE Mexico, 45 mi. SE of Mérida; rail terminus; henequen, sugar cane, fruit. Grotto and Maya ruins near by.

Souanké (swäng-kā'), village, N Middle Congo territory, Fr. Equatorial Africa, 135 mi. WNW of Ouesso, near Fr. Cameroons border; center of native trade (groundnuts, hides). Sometimes spelled Zouanké.

Soubré (sōō'brā), village (pop. c.300), SW Ivory Coast, Fr. West Africa, on Sassandra R. and 70 mi. NNW of Sassandra; bananas, coffee.

Souchez (sōōshā'), village (pop. 1,161), Pas-de-Calais dept., N France, 7 mi. NNW of Arras, in ravine bet. Vimy Ridge (SE) and Notre-Dame-de-Lorette hill (NW). Destroyed in battle of Arras (1917) of First World War.

Soucook River (sōō'kōōk), S central N.H., rises in ponds SW of L. Winnipesaukee, flows c.30 mi. SW to the Merrimack below Concord.

Souda, Crete: see Suda.

Soudan, Africa: see Sudan; French Sudan.

Soudan (sōōdăn'), village (1940 pop. 972), St. Louis co., NE Minn., on Vermilion iron range, 25 mi. NE of Virginia. Its mine has been rich source of iron ore since 1884. Vermilion L. is just N.

Souderton (sou'dûrtŭn), industrial borough (pop. 4,521), Montgomery co., SE Pa., 24 mi. NNW of Philadelphia; clothing, textiles, shoes, dairy products, piston rings, cigar boxes. Settled 1860, inc. 1887.

Soudha, Crete: see Suda.

Soueida, Syria: see Suweida, Es.

Soues (sōō), S suburb (pop. 1,312) of Tarbes, Hautes-Pyrénées dept., SW France; mfg. of turbines, electric locomotives.

Souf (sōōf), group of Saharan oases in Touggourt territory, E Algeria, amidst the sand dunes of the Great Eastern Erg, S of the Chott Melrhir, and c.50 mi. NE of Touggourt. The oases (El-Oued, Guémar, Kouinine) are noted for their Deglet Nur dates shipped to Biskra (120 mi. NNW) and to Tozeur, Tunisia (80 mi. NE).

Soufflenheim (sōōflĕnĕm'), Ger. *Sufflenheim* (zōō'-flŭnhīm), town (pop. 3,364), Bas-Rhin dept., E France, at E edge of Forest of Haguenau, 8 mi. E of Haguenau; pottery-mfg. center.

Soufli or **Souflion**, Greece: see Souphlion.

Soufrière (sōōfrēâr'), village (pop. 893), SW Dominica, B.W.I., on Soufrière Bay, 5 mi. SSE of Roseau; cacao, limes.

Soufrière or **La Grande Soufrière** (lä grăd), highest peak (4,869 ft.) of Guadeloupe and of the Lesser Antilles, Fr. West Indies, on S Basse-Terre isl., 4 mi. NE of Basse-Terre city; 16°2'N 61°40'W. Dormant, but with numerous small craters, some emitting sulphurous fumes.

Soufrière, volcanic hill (2,999 ft.), S Montserrat, Leeward Isls., B.W.I., just E of Plymouth; 16°42'N 62°11'W.

Soufrière, town (pop. 3,088), SW St. Lucia, B.W.I., at head of beautiful Soufrière Bay, 11 mi. SSW of Castries, in agr. region (coconuts, limes); fishing. Soufrière volcano with *solfataras* is just above the town. Outside the town are the Ventine mineral springs (2½ mi. SE), the properties of which are said to be identical with those of Aix-les-Bains. Soufrière Bay is flanked (SE) by famed The Pitons twin peaks, pyramidical cones rising from the sea.

Soufrière, volcano (4,048 ft.), N St. Vincent, B.W.I., 13 mi. NNE of Kingstown. It erupted violently in 1812 and, especially, on May 7, 1902 (a day in advance of Mont Pelée on Martinique), when it caused great destruction. Dormant since 1903. The Baleine Falls are at its N foot.

Sougné-Remouchamps, Belgium: see Remouchamps.

Souhegan River (sōōhē'gŭn), N Mass. and S N.H., rises just W of Ashby, Mass.; flows c.35 mi. NE and E, past Wilton and Milford, N.H., to Merrimack R. near Merrimack.

Souillac (sōōyäk'), town (pop. 2,552), Lot dept., SW France, on the Dordogne and 18 mi. S of Brive-la-Gaillarde; food-processing center; truffle and vegetable canning, flour milling, tanning, tobacco growing. Has noteworthy 12th-cent. abbey church.

Souillac, town (pop. 1,905), S Mauritius, port on Indian Ocean, 25 mi. S of Port Louis; railhead for rich sugar-growing region; ships sugar, alcohol. Founded c.1780.

Souilly (sōōyē'), village (pop. 390), Meuse dept., NE France, 10 mi. SSW of Verdun; hq. of Pétain and Nivelle in battle of Verdun (1916–17); of Pershing during Meuse-Argonne offensive (1918).

Souirah, Fr. Morocco: see Mogador.

Souk-Ahras (sōōk'-äräs'), anc. *Tagaste* or *Thagaste*, town (pop. 17,025), Constantine dept., NE Algeria, in the Tell Atlas (Medjerda Mts.), near headwaters of Medjerda R., 75 mi. E of Constantine; rail center on Algiers-Tunis line, shipping phosphates (from Tebessa area) and iron ore (from Ouenza) to Bône (45 mi. NNW; rail spur) for export. Cattle market; winemaking, olive-oil and cork processing. Zinc mines near by. Saint Augustine b. here.

Souk-el-Arba (sōōk'ĕl-ärbä'), town (pop. 6,469), ⊙ Souk-el-Arba dist. (□ 733; pop. 114,104), NW Tunisia, on railroad and 22 mi. N of Le Kef; agr. center (cereals, livestock) of fertile Medjerda valley. Cork shipping. Airfield. Extensive and partially underground ruins of near-by *Bulla Regia* (which antedates Roman period) include Roman mansions, thermae, a temple, and an amphitheater.

Souk el Arba du Rharb (dü gärb'), town (pop. 5,800), Rabat region, N Fr. Morocco, in N Rharb lowland, on Tangier-Fez RR and 45 mi. NE of Port-Lyautey; agr. trade center; livestock market. Oil wells in Aïn el Hamra area just N. Also spelled Souk el Arba du Gharb.

Souk el Gharb, Lebanon: see Suq el Gharb.

Souk-el-Khemis (-kĕmēs'), town (pop. 2,448), Souk-el-Arba dist., NW Tunisia, on Medjerda R., on railroad, and 14 mi. SW of Béja; road center and agr. market; vineyards. Lead mines at Sidi bou Anouane (4 mi. N) and Djebel Hallouf (6 mi. N; rail spur).

Soukhné, Syria: see SUKHNE, Es.

Soukra, La (lä sōōkrä'), village, Tunis dist., N Tunisia, 6 mi. NE of Tunis; distilling. Vineyards and truck farms.

Soulac-sur-Mer (sōōläk'-sür-mâr'), village (pop. 1,156), Gironde dept., SW France, near N tip of Médoc, 55 mi. NNW of Bordeaux; fishing. Bathing resort with pine groves and sandy beach (3 mi. long) on Bay of Biscay. Ferry to Royan. Damaged during Second World War.

Soulaines-Dhuys (sōōlān'-dwē'), village (pop. 393), Aube dept., NE central France, 10 mi. N of Bar-sur-Aube; bricks.

Soulanges (sōōlãzh'), county (□ 136; pop. 9,328), S Que., on the St. Lawrence and on Ont. border; ⊙ Coteau Landing.

Soulanges, village, S Que., on the St. Lawrence, at NE end of L. St. Francis, 3 mi. W of Valleyfield; W end of Soulanges Canal; hydroelectric center, supplying Montreal.

Soulanges, village (pop. 284), Marne dept., N France, on the Marne and its lateral canal, 5 mi. NNW of Vitry-le-François; cementworks.

Soulanges Canal, S Que., extends 14 mi. bet. L. St. Francis (W) and L. St. Louis (E), on N side of the St. Lawrence, by-passing rapids. Completed 1899, with 5 locks, it superseded original Beauharnois Canal, on S side of the St. Lawrence. Earlier canal on same route was opened 1783, enlarged 1848. Canal is now used for power purposes only.

Soule (sōōl), small historical region of SW France, now in Basses-Pyrénées dept., in the Basque country, near Sp. border.

Souli, Greece: see SULI.

Soulme (sōōlm), village (pop. 153), Namur prov., S Belgium, 9 mi. SW of Dinant; marble quarrying.

Soulom (sōōlõ'), village (pop. 517), Hautes-Pyrénées dept., SW France, on Gave de Pau R. and 3.5 mi. SSE of Argelès-Gazost; electrometallurgical (silicomanganese) and electrochemical (fertilizer) plants. Lead mines near by.

Soultz (sōōts), Ger. *Sulz* (zōōlts), town (pop. 4,015), Haut-Rhin dept., E France, at SE foot of the Vosges, 2 mi. SSE of Guebwiller; mfg. of textile machinery, silk spinning. Damaged in First World War during struggle (1915) for near-by Hartmannswillerkopf.

Soultzbach-les-Bains (sōōzbäk'-lā-bē'), Ger. *Sulzbach* (zōōlts'bäkh), village (pop. 568), Haut-Rhin dept., E France, on E slopes of the Vosges, 8 mi. WSW of Colmar; mineral springs.

Soultzeren (sōōtsĕrĕn'), Ger. *Sulzern* (zōōlt'sûrn), village (pop. 744), Haut-Rhin dept., E France, in the high Vosges, 12 mi. W of Colmar; cotton weaving, Munster cheese mfg.

Soultzmatt (sōōtsmät'), Ger. *Sulzmatt* (zōōlts'mät), village (pop. 1,689), Haut-Rhin dept., E France, on E slopes of the Vosges, 4 mi. N of Guebwiller, in winegrowing area; cotton and silk spinning. Mineral springs.

Soultz-sous-Forêts (sōōtsōō-fôrē'), Ger. *Sulz unterm Wald* (zōōlts' ŏontŭrm vält'), village (pop. 1,397), Bas-Rhin dept., E France, 9 mi. NNE of Haguenau; hosiery mfg. Oil refining (wells at near-by Merkwiller-Péchelbronn).

Soumagne (sōōmä'nyù), town (pop. 4,606), Liége prov., E Belgium, 7 mi. E of Liége; coal mining.

Soummam, Oued (wĕd' sōōmäm'), stream in NE Algeria, rises in the Tell Atlas (Biban range) E of Aumale, flows generally NE, in a deep, widening valley bet. Great Kabylia (W) and Little Kabylia (E), to the Gulf of Bougie (Mediterranean Sea) just S of Bougie. Length, 126 mi. Its upper course, along S slopes of the Djurdjura range as far as influx of the Oued Bou Sellam, is called Oued Sahel. Valley, followed by Algiers-Bougie RR, grows olives, figs, citrus fruit.

Soumont, France: see POTIGNY.

Sound, The, Scandinavia: see ORESUND.

Soundatti, India: see SAUNDATTI.

Sound Island (□ 6; pop. 391), SE N.F., at head of Placentia Bay, 35 mi. NNW of Argentia; 3 mi. long, 3 mi. wide; 47°49'N 54°10'W. Fishing.

Sounds, county (□ 505; pop. 946), NE S.Isl., New Zealand; St. Omer is largest of settlements on shores of Pelorus and Queen Charlotte sounds. Tourist resorts; sheep.

Soundwell, England: see MANGOTSFIELD.

Sounion, Cape (sōōn'yôn), Lat. *Sunium* (sōō'nēŭm, sū-), S extremity of Attica Peninsula, E central Greece, on Aegean Sea, bet. Gulf of Petalion (E) and Saronic Gulf (W); 37°39'N 24°2'E. Site of ruins of anc. temple of Poseidon, with 12 remaining columns. Silver, lead, and zinc mining near Laurion (N). Formerly called Cape Kalones or Cape Colonna.

Souphlion or **Souflion** (both: sōōflē'ōn), city (pop. 8,127), Hevros nome, W Thrace, Greece, on railroad and 32 mi. NE of Alexandroupolis on Maritsa R. (Turkish line); trading center in silk, wheat, barley, beans, cotton; cattle, sheep; dairy products. Also called Souphli, Soufli, or Sufli.

Souppes-sur-Loing (sōōp-sür-lwē'), village (pop. 1,619), Seine-et-Marne dept., N central France, on Loing R. (canalized) and 16 mi. S of Fontainebleau; market; sugar and paper milling. Stone quarries in area.

Souq Wadi Barada, Syria: see SUQ WADI BARADA.

Sour, Lebanon: see TYRE.

Sourdeval (sōōrdväl'), industrial village (pop. 1,453), Manche dept., NW France, in Normandy Hills, 8 mi. S of Vire; mfg. (steel table tops, cutlery, wooden kitchen utensils). Heavily damaged in Second World War.

Sourdnahunk Lake, Maine: see NESOWADNEHUNK LAKE.

Sourdough, village (1939 pop. 28), S Alaska, on Gulkana R. and 100 mi. NNE of Valdez, on Richardson Highway; supply point for prospectors, trappers, and sportsmen (hunting and fishing).

Soure (sō'rĭ). **1** City, Ceará, Brazil: see CAUCAIA. **2** City (pop. 4,452), NE Pará, Brazil, on E shore of Marajó isl., on Pará R. (Amazon delta) and 50 mi. N of Belém (steamer connection); health resort (sanatorium) amidst cattle pastures.

Soure, town (pop. 1,430), Coimbra dist., N central Portugal, on railroad and 15 mi. SW of Coimbra; textile milling, resin extracting.

Souris. 1 (sōōr'ĭs) Town (pop. 1,517), SW Man., on Souris R. and 21 mi. SW of Brandon; railroad shops, foundries, grain elevators; dairying. Resort. **2** (sōōr'ē) Town (pop. 1,114), NE P.E.I., small port on the Gulf of St. Lawrence, 40 mi. ENE of Charlottetown; 46°21'N 62°15'W; fishing center. Settled by Acadians 1748.

Souris (sōōr'ĭs), city (pop. 206), Bottineau co., N N.Dak., 12 mi. WNW of Bottineau, near branch of Souris R.

Souris River, N.Dak. and Canada, rises in SE Saskatchewan, flows SE into N.Dak., passing Minot, then turns N into Manitoba and enters Assiniboine R. Not extensively navigable, little used for irrigation; c.435 mi. long.

Sour Lake, city (pop. 1,630), Hardin co., E Texas, 20 mi. WNW of Beaumont, in oil field; oil pipeline station and storage point. Settled 1836, inc. 1939.

Sournia (sōōrnēä'), village (pop. 339), Pyrénées-Orientales dept., S France, 8 mi. N of Prades; grazing, winegrowing.

Sous (sōōs), fertile alluvial region of SW Fr. Morocco, coextensive with valley of Sous R.; bounded by the High Atlas (N), Djebel Siroua (E), and Anti-Atlas (S). Agadir is its gateway on the Atlantic. Sheltered from Saharan climatic influences, region grows early fruits and vegetables for export, cotton, and sugar. Olive and argan trees line valley slopes. Chief center is Taroudant. Sous R., which rises at Djebel Toubkal and enters the Atlantic 5 mi. S of Agadir, is 112 mi. long. Also spelled Souss.

Sousa, Tunisia: see SOUSSE.

Sousel (sōzĕl'), town (pop. 3,798), Portalegre dist., central Portugal, on railroad and 27 mi. SSW of Portalegre; agr. trade center (olives, grain, cork sheep).

Souss, Fr. Morocco: see SOUS.

Sousse (sōōs), anc. *Hadrumetum*, city (pop. 36,566), ⊙ Sousse dist. (pop. 264,157), E Tunisia, port on the Gulf of Hammamet (central Mediterranean), 70 mi. SSE of Tunis; 35°50'N 10°38'E. Commercial center of highly fertile coastal region (*Sahel*), noted for its olives and cereals Exports phosphates from mines in Gafsa area (160 mi. SW; rail link), oil, esparto (for European paper mills), skins, almonds, sponges. Local trade in wool and cereals. Olive-oil milling is principal industry. Founded c.9th cent. B.C. by Phoenicians, it became subject to Carthage, which it antedates. An important colony and port under Romans. Destroyed (A.D. 434) by Vandals and rebuilt by Justinian. Anc. remains include early Christian catacombs. Damaged by bombing during Tunisian campaign, it was captured by British in April, 1943. Mahdia dist. was carved out of Sousse dist (old □ 2,447) in 1941. Formerly spelled Susa or Sousa.

Soustons (sōōstõ'), town (pop. 2,193), Landes dept., SW France, 14 mi. WNW of Dax; cork-mfg. center; lumber trade.

Souterraine, La (lä sōōtĕrĕn'), town (pop. 2,992), Creuse dept., central France, on Paris-Toulouse RR and 19 mi. W of Guéret; cattle shipping center. Has a Romanesque and early-Gothic 12th-cent. church, and two 14th-cent. fortified gates.

South, for names beginning thus and not found here: see under SOUTHERN.

South, Southern, in Rus. names: see also YUZHN.

South Acton, Mass.: see ACTON.

South Africa, Union of, Afrikaans *Unie van Suid Afrika*, dominion (including Walvis Bay: □ 472,494; pop. 11,418,349, of which 9,045,659 are nonwhites, mostly Bantu) of the British Commonwealth of Nations; administrative ⊙ PRETORIA, though legislature convenes at CAPE TOWN. Largest city, JOHANNESBURG, is industrial and financial center. Most westernized of African countries, it occupies S subcontinental section of Africa, bet. Atlantic Ocean (W) and Indian Ocean (E). Cape AGULHAS, continent's southernmost point, is at 34°52'S 19°59'E. Greatest width c.1,050 mi., bet. 16°29'E and 32°56'E. Northernmost point is 22°7'S. Borders NE on SWAZILAND, Mozambique, and Southern Rhodesia (along Limpopo R.). The upper Limpopo and Molopo rivers separate it in N from Bechuanaland Protectorate. NW boundary with SOUTH-WEST AFRICA is formed by the lower Orange R. Walvis Bay (□ 374; pop. 2,424), an enclave in South-West Africa, belongs to Cape of Good Hope Prov. BASUTOLAND, an enclave (E) within South Africa, forms with Swaziland and Bechuanaland Protectorate the High Commission Territories—actually native reserves—administered by the crown, but in close contact with South Africa. PRINCE EDWARD ISLAND and MARION ISLAND, c.1,200 mi. SE of Cape Town, were formally annexed in 1947. The Union consists of 4 provs.: CAPE OF GOOD HOPE (S, W), including TRANSKEIAN TERRITORIES, ⊙ Cape Town; NATAL (E), including ZULULAND, ⊙ PIETERMARITZBURG; ORANGE FREE STATE (E central), ⊙ BLOEMFONTEIN; and TRANSVAAL (NE), ⊙ Pretoria. Geologically, South Africa is an old land block of Devonian and Triassic origin. Vast interior plateaus, largely flat or gently undulating, and with local ridges, vary in altitude (2–6,000 ft.), generally rising towards N. Among the more arid tablelands of the W, in Cape Prov., are the LITTLE KAROO, GREAT KAROO, and Northern Karoo. The elevated grasslands—well suited for stock raising—mainly in Orange Free State and Transvaal and also of Karoo formation, are called the VELD or Veldt, of which are distinguished a Low Veld (500–2,000 ft.), Middle Veld (2–4,000 ft.), and a High Veld or Northern Karoo (4–6,000 ft.). Within the High Veld lies the famous WITWATERSRAND, one of the world's richest gold-bearing reefs, with a cluster of cities of which Johannesburg (alt. 5,740 ft.) is the center. Escarpments bound the plateaus and fall to the coastal strip along the even and rocky shore lines. These escarpments, winding in a wide curve of c.1,400 mi., rise to over 11,000 ft. in the DRAKENSBERG range (E); other ranges are SNEEUWBERG and SWARTBERG of Cape Prov. Rivers are few. Even the only major stream, Orange R.—rising in the Drakensberg and flowing W to the Atlantic—with its chief affluent VAAL RIVER, is not navigable; it is used for irrigation, as is the Limpopo or Crocodile R. Almost all rivers are seasonal. There are, apart from Cape Town, hardly any natural harbors; the other leading ports (DURBAN, PORT ELIZABETH, EAST LONDON) are artificial. The climate—generally mild—is cooler than at corresponding latitudes of the N hemisphere, partly because of the cold Benguella Current of the South Atlantic. Despite the long N-S axis of the country, temperatures are—due to equalizing effect of the high plateau—remarkably uniform, so that Cape Town on the S coast has an annual mean of 62.5°F. and Pretoria, c.850 mi. NE, at 4,593 ft., an annual mean of 64.5°F. Rainfall, c.25 in. at Cape Town and about 30 in. at Johannesburg. The S part of the Cape has winter rains (April-Oct.), whereas summer rains predominate elsewhere. The W and NW is arid, permitting only some sheep grazing and giving way to desert in N. The Natal lowland, semitropical and humid, is a productive sugar-cane growing area. Durban has an annual mean of c.70°F. and a rainfall of 45 in. Here occurs occasionally the oppressive *Bergwind* of a foehn type, sweeping down from the uplands. Tropical conditions prevail in NE Low Veld of Transvaal, where is KRUGER NATIONAL PARK, a reserve (lions, buffaloes, elephants, zebras, giraffes, hippopotamuses, crocodiles, leopards, hyenas, cheetahs, warthogs, antelopes, monkeys, etc.). In KALAHARI NATIONAL PARK (NW) and NATAL NATIONAL PARK (E) are the springbok, steenbok, wildebeest, hartebeest, eland, kudu, and ostrich. The intense sunlight and dry, clear atmosphere make the country especially healthful for sufferers from pulmonary diseases, but the entrance of tuberculosis patients is forbidden. The clear atmosphere has also made South Africa popular for astronomic investigations (U.S.-owned Boyden Southern Station of Harvard is at MAZELSPOORT near Bloemfontein; Lamont-Hussey observatory of Univ. of Michigan is on NAVAL HILL near Bloemfontein; and the Yale-Columbia Southern Station is within Milner Park in Johannesburg). There are limited timber resources. On Drakensberg slopes of Natal grow wattle (yield much of world's supply in wattle bark) and eucalyptus (used for pit props) trees, both introduced from Australia. Apart from minerals, wool, hides, skins, and mohair are among leading exports. Though poor in agr. resources, but well adapted to stock raising (merino and karakul sheep, cattle, goats, pigs, donkeys, horses, mules, poultry), the country nevertheless is self-sufficient in almost all agr. products; only wheat has to be imported on a large scale. The staples corn, barley, rye, wheat, potatoes, kaffir corn are widely grown. Also tobacco, peanuts, cotton, sunflower seeds, citrus. The High Veld of Transvaal and Orange Free State leads in agr. production. The fertile coastal area of Cape Prov. is known for its grapes, fruit (apples, pears, peaches, cherries, etc.), and wine and brandy distilleries. Here, and in other sections, are raised citrus fruit (mostly oranges), which are shipped mainly to England. Sugar-growing Natal, rich in semitropical fruit, also yields cotton, tea, and tobacco. Important fisheries on the coast. Canned rock lobsters are shipped to the U.S. Durban has become the base of a whaling fleet. The hub of the nation's entire economy, however, is its enormous mineral wealth. Gold alone makes up 50–70% of the export volume. The fabulous gold resources of the Witwatersrand yield about ⅓ of the world's production. This region mines 97% of the Union's gold output. A new gold field (opened 1946) at Odendaalsrust (Orange Free State) promises to be as rich. Almost equally famed are the diamond fields of Kimberley in N Cape Prov. There are substantial though low-grade coal deposits in Witbank area E of Johannesburg and at Vryheid (Natal). The Transvaal abounds in all kinds of minerals, chiefly iron in Rustenburg dist. (with Thabazimbi mines, practically a mtn. of iron ore) and mines around Pretoria. Other minerals of the country include chromium, nickel, asbestos (Prieska), cryolite, platinum, tungsten (Little Namaqualand), lead, osmiridium, talc, mica, vermiculite (used in building trade), ocher, etc. Copper, longest mined in South Africa, is extracted at Messina (N Transvaal) and O'Okiep in Little Namaqualand (NW Cape Prov.) and shipped through Port Nolloth. The major manganese-mining center is Postmasburg in N central Cape Prov. Limestone quarries are at Port Shepstone (Natal). On the mineral resources is based an extensive heavy industry, which is, however, handicapped by a relatively small population, the low living standard of the majority of the people, and remoteness from the world's principal markets. Chief industrial region is the Witwatersrand, with the cities of Johannesburg, Krugersdorp, Germiston, Benoni, Boksburg, Springs. Here are metallurgical, chemical, and textile plants with ancillary consumer industries. Pretoria has Union's leading iron- and steelworks. Other steel mills are at Vereeniging and Vanderbijl Park. Chemical plants are at Somerset West in Cape Prov. Cape Town itself has engineering works and other industries. Durban—like Cape Town a favored seaside resort—the busiest port, serves the Rand. Automobile assembly and tire mfg. is centered in the Cape Prov. at Uitenhage and at Port Elizabeth, the 3d largest port, which is also a wool-trading and shoe-mfg. center. Automobiles are also assembled at East London. Simonstown, near Cape Town, is a naval base. The country is served by 13,340 mi. of govt.-owned railroads, communicating with the Rhodesias, Angola, and Belgian Congo. A Cape-to-Cairo RR has so far not materialized. At Johannesburg converge natl. and international airlines. There are now 8 universities or university colleges: the Univ. of South Africa at Pretoria, the universities of Pretoria, Cape Town, Stellenbosch (near Cape Town), Witwatersrand (at Johannesburg), Natal (at Pietermaritzburg and Durban), and Orange Free State (at Bloemfontein), and Rhodes Univ. (at Grahamstown). While schooling is compulsory for the white pop., the educational level of the native and colored people, who only in Cape Prov. enjoy a limited franchise, is low. The complex structure of the nation—racially, culturally, politically—is South Africa's gravest problem. The nonwhite peoples, comprising ⁴/₅ of the population, and largely disenfranchized, are rigidly contained by a "democracy of the elite"—a white minority, which is in turn divided into 2 factions, English-speaking (c.40% of the whites) and Afrikaans (a variant of Dutch)-speaking, of Dutch and Huguenot descent. Many are bilingual. The region is believed to have been originally peopled by the Bushman, a, strictly-speaking, non-Negro pygmy race, who left some astonishingly competent cave drawings. Few of them remain, though they form a strong component of the "Cape Colored" (with substantial white admixture). The Hottentots, believed by some to be related to the Bushman or to be a blend of Bushman and Hamite blood, survive as tribes only in South-West Africa. South Africa was continuously subject to influx of the Negroid Bantus, who practically superseded the aboriginals in the entire area. The Bantu—rather a linguistic than racial term—possess strong Hamite strains, but incidence of Semitic or Arab blood is rare. Among principal Bantu tribes in the Union are the Kafir (S), Zulu (NE), Basuto (E), and Matabeli (N), who put up a fierce resistance against European expansion. South Africa entered Western history when the Port. navigator Bartholomew Diaz rounded the Cape of Good Hope in 1488. The Cape, about midway on the shipping route to India (reached by Vasco da Gama in 1497), was an ideal supply station, of ever-increasing importance until completion of the Suez Canal. The British took possession of the Cape in 1620, but no permanent settlement was made until Jan van Riebeeck (or Riebeek) founded (1652) Cape Town on behalf of the Dutch East India Company. After revocation of Edict of Nantes (1685) Huguenots fled here. The British occupied the Cape region 1795–1803. Captured the colony again in 1806. English immigrants entered in large numbers after 1820. In 1836 began the great trek, i.e., the exodus of many Dutch or Boers into the interior Veld. These pioneers, notably Andries Pretorius, are the celebrated *voortrekkers* who have attained legendary stature in South African history and literature. The Boers eventually founded the republic of Transvaal, Orange Free State, and Natal. Wars against Kafirs and Zulus raged during the century. The Cape Colony received parliamentary govt. in 1852, the same year that the British recognized the independence of Transvaal, which became in 1853 the South African Republic, presided over by Martinus Pretorius. The republic was briefly annexed (1877–80) by the British. Meanwhile Natal had become a prov. of the Cape in 1844 and a separate crown colony in 1856. The Orange River Sovereignty set up (1848) by the British was opposed by the Boers. In the Orange Free State republic (established 1854), the Boer element was, however, dominant. A new phase opened with the gold discoveries in Witwatersrand, proclaimed a gold field 1886. The crisis was precipitated by the political discontent of newly-arrived Br. immigrants (called *Uitlanders* [foreign settlers] by the Boers) to this region, and the ambitious vision of Cecil Rhodes—onetime premier of the Cape Colony and the force behind the Kimberley mines—who conceived a great Br. dominion in Africa. The abortive Jameson Raid (1895–96) into Transvaal was followed in 1899 by the South African War, in which the 2 peasant republics of Transvaal and Orange Free State, rallying behind Kruger, fought for their independence against Great Britain. After initial successes, the Boers were defeated. Peace was concluded by Treaty of Vereeniging (1902). The position of the Boer population was recognized by continuing the Roman-Dutch common law of Holland, and by making Afrikaans an official language along with English. Transvaal and Orange Free State became crown colonies. Both acquired self-government in 1907. In 1910 they were joined through South Africa Act with Natal and Cape of Good Hope as provs. of the Union of South Africa. Rapprochement bet. the British and Boer elements was fostered under the able administration of Lord Milner; and former Boer generals like Louis Botha (1st prime minister of the Union) and Jan Smuts (leader of the Unionist party) became prominent statesmen. The 1920s saw, however, the resurgence of less conciliatory elements, led by the Nationalists. However, the Union actively participated on the Allied side in the 2 world wars. Union troops conquered South-West Africa from the Germans in 1915. They distinguished themselves during Second World War in Ethiopia, North Africa, and Italy, and took part in the Madagascar campaign. In the post-war years race relations deteriorated: riots broke out in Durban, and India ended (1946) diplomatic relations because of the treatment of the Indian minority (c.280,000), for whose rights Gandhi had struggled as a young lawyer early in the century. The Nationalists came to power in 1948. The country refused to sign an agreement making South-West Africa a U.N. trust territory and moved toward annexing the area. For further information see separate articles on towns, cities, physical features, regions, and the 4 provs. The term **South Africa,** in a wider, geographical sense, comprises all of the African continent S of the Zambezi R., i.e., the region including Southern Rhodesia, S section of Mozambique, Bechuanaland Protectorate, South-West Africa, the U. of So. Afr., Swaziland, and Basutoland.

South African Republic, former state, coextensive with Transvaal, U. of So. Afr.; founded 1853, with M. W. Pretorius as 1st president; annexed 1877 by Great Britain, restored 1880. Under Treaty of Vereeniging (1902) it became British colony and reverted to name of Transvaal.

Southall, formerly **Southall Norwood,** residential and industrial municipal borough (1931 pop. 38,940; 1951 census 55,900), Middlesex, England, 11 mi. W of London; mfg. of trucks and other vehicles, pharmaceuticals, food products. Has 17th-cent. manor house.

South Alligator River, N Northern Territory, Australia, rises in hills 55 mi. NE of Katherine, flows 100 mi. N to Van Diemen Gulf; mangroves, alligators. Parallel with it on either side are East Alligator R. (85 mi. long) and West Alligator R. (50 mi. long).

South Alloa, Scotland: see Alloa.

Southam, town and parish (pop. 1,761), E Warwick, England, 6 mi. ESE of Leamington; limestone quarrying; lime- and cementworks. Has 14th-cent. church.

South Amboy (ăm′boi), city (pop. 8,422), Middlesex co., E N.J., opposite Perth Amboy, with a harbor at mouth of Raritan R. (bridged here); mfg. (clay products, cigars, clothing, aquariums); clay (dug here since early 19th cent.); truck; transships coal. Terminal (1832) of the Camden and Amboy, state's 1st railroad; became an important coal port. Settled 1651; inc. as borough 1888, as city 1908. Damaged (1950) by explosion of munitions.

South America, continent (□ c.6,850,000; pop. c.110,000,000), the southern of the 2 continents of the Western Hemisphere, connected with Central America (which is considered part of North America) by the c.40-mi.-wide Isthmus of Panama. It is washed N by Caribbean Sea, NE and E by the Atlantic, W by the Pacific, and S by the Antarctic waters. It extends from Point Gallinas (12°28′N) in N Colombia c.4,750 mi. southward, narrowing to the islet of Cape Horn (55°59′S) in Tierra del Fuego, pointing toward Antarctica; Froward Cape (53°54′S) on Brunswick Peninsula, on the Strait of Magellan, is southernmost point of the mainland. Across the Atlantic is Africa, 1,850 mi. away (Natal-Dakar). The continent is c.3,100 mi. E–W just below the equator bet. Cabo Branco and Pedras Point (7°9′S 34°47′W) in Brazil and Pariñas Point (4°40′S 81°20′W) in Peru. Three-fourths of its area is in the tropics, but its climate also includes temperate and subantarctic zones. Most of its land mass lies E of the longitude of New York, and almost all of it lies E of the longitude of Florida. Politically, the continent is divided into the 10 Latin American republics of Argentina, Bolivia, Brazil, Chile, Colombia, Ecuador, Paraguay, Peru, Uruguay, and Venezuela, and the 3 colonies of Guiana. Of the 10 republics all are Spanish-speaking but Brazil, which is Portuguese-speaking. Only Paraguay and Bolivia do not have a coast line. Although it has a coast line of c.15,000 mi., the continent does not have many good bays. Few isls. fringe its shore. The only large isls. are in Tierra del Fuego and along the submerged, fjord-like coast of S Chile. The Falkland Islands are off the SE coast, Margarita off the coast of Venezuela, and the Galápagos Islands off Ecuador. South America's topography is extremely varied. In the Andes, 2d only to the Himalayas in alt., South America possesses the globe's longest mtn. chain, extending N over 4,000 mi. from the Strait of Magellan along the Pacific coast to the Caribbean. The Aconcagua (22,835 ft.) is the highest elevation in the Western Hemisphere. Numerous other peaks, some of them mighty volcanoes, exceed 20,000 ft. Few of the passes lie below 12,000 ft. Towering above a narrow coastal strip, the giant cordilleras are generally only 200 mi. wide, except in Bolivia and S Peru, where they enclose the Altiplano. Here is L. Titicaca, highest large lake (□ c.3,200; alt. 12,507 ft.) in the world. Though obstacles to communication are enormous and account for the pattern of isolated colonization, some of the continent's main centers of population are high in the Andes, where altitude offsets latitude, and vegetation is characterized by the altitudinal zoning into *tierra caliente* (warm), *tierra templada* (temperate), and *tierra fría* (cool); the tundra-like *páramos* are below the perpetual snow fields. In the E the central plateau of Brazil, above which rise several subdued ranges, occupies most of Brazil S of the Amazon lowlands. This plateau contains much of Brazil's fabulous mineral wealth, and here, too, especially in S, are the productive coffee and cotton lands. The Guiana Highlands are remote and undeveloped, but noted for their gold fields, iron mines, and gigantic waterfalls. Bet. the Andes in the W and the highlands in the E are the continent's vast lowlands, in the drainage basins of the large river systems. The largest is that of the Amazon River, comprising an area of almost the size of the U.S., with the globe's greatest expanse of virgin forests. The Amazon, though not the earth's longest stream, exceeds all others in water volume. It rises less than 100 mi. from the Pacific and flows to the Atlantic; it can be navigated by ocean-going vessels up to Iquitos (Peru), c.2,300 mi. from its mouth. Some of its affluents exceed 1,000 mi. in length. The Amazon system is linked through the Casiquiare with the Orinoco River, life stream of Venezuela. Here the tropical rain-drenched selvas give way to predominantly savanna land of the llanos; similar grazing lands are in the Oriente, Montaña, and Yungas regions and in the Chaco plain. In terms of communication and economic impact, the Río de la Plata system (with the Uruguay, Paraná, and Paraguay rivers) is the most important, with the great ports of Buenos Aires and Montevideo on its estuary. The Argentine Pampa is one of the world's great granaries and cattle-raising regions. Among other large rivers are the Magdalena River in Colombia, the São Francisco River in E Brazil, the Río Salado, Río Colorado, Río Negro, and Chubut River in Argentina. Extremes of temperature in South America are moderate. Temperatures above 90°F. are rare even in the Amazon basin, and in Tierra del Fuego, at 55°S, the coldest month (July) averages only 32°F. The NE and SE trade winds have a tempering effect in the tropical E section, while the cold Peru or Humboldt Current is responsible for the desert strip which stretches along the Pacific from N Chile through Peru into S Ecuador. Patagonia is semi-arid. Rainfall is highest in the Amazon basin, on the NW coast, and in S Chile. It is sufficient for agr. in the "Wet Pampa," for most of the Central Valley of Chile, and for parts of the Andean uplands and of the Brazilian highlands. The great forests are rich in hardwoods, medicinal plants, and rubber. Among indigenous plants are corn, potatoes, yams, cacao, tomatoes, pineapples, peanuts, beans, cassava, coca, tobacco, perennial cotton; cinchona,

Brazil nuts, maté, quebracho are also indigenous. The animal life is distinguished by its many kinds of insects, birds, and reptiles. Mammals are comparatively few. Neither horses, nor sheep, nor cattle were known to the pre-Columbian inhabitants. In the Andes are ruminants related to the camel (i.e., vicuña, alpaca, llama, and guanaco), the guemal mtn. goat, and the giant condor. The large majority of the people are engaged in agr. and stock raising. Coffee dominates the economy of Brazil and Colombia, and cocoa that of Ecuador. Wheat, flax, and corn are important in Argentina. Argentina, Uruguay, and Brazil are the chief livestock producers. N Argentina and Paraguay furnish quebracho extract and maté. Brazil is the principal supplier of carnauba wax, Peru of cinchona, Bolivia and Peru of coca, Ecuador of the light balsa wood. Both Brazil and Peru grow large amounts of cotton. The mineral wealth, largely foreign owned and only partly exploited, is considerable. Venezuela ranks as the world's 3d producer of petroleum (drilled chiefly in and around L. Maracaibo). Important oil wells are also in Argentina, S Chile, Peru, Ecuador, Bolivia, and Colombia. Brazil is reputed to have the world's largest deposits of iron and of manganese. It has also been for many years a source of diamonds and other precious stones. Iron from Venezuela, Brazil, and Chile is shipped to the U.S. At least as profitable are the copper mines of Chile and Peru. Peru is said to lead the world in bismuth and vanadium. Venezuela ships asphalt, and Colombia has large emerald and platinum resources. Bolivia is 1st in antimony and 3d in tin mining. Du. and Br. Guiana have valuable bauxite mines. Gold is found in many parts, and silver (particularly from Potosí, Bolivia) yielded great riches to the colonial Spanish. Industries, though increasing, are still of limited domestic importance. Vast tracts of the continent, such as the Amazon basin, the Guiana Highlands, and the S Pampa remain virtually empty and constitute one of the world's great frontiers. Most of the wealth is still owned by foreign capital and a small white upper class, descendants of the Sp. and Port. settlers. Only in Argentina and Uruguay has there developed a large, stable middle class. These are the only countries peopled by an overwhelmingly white population. All of the Andean countries, including Paraguay, are predominantly mestizo, with pure Indians forming an important segment but virtually out of touch with the national life of the republics. The Negro element is strong on the Caribbean coast, in the Guianas, and NE Brazil. The American cowboy has his counterpart in the *llanero* of Venezuela and the gaucho of the Pampa. In recent years millions of immigrants have gone to South America—Italians, Spaniards, Portuguese, Germans, Eastern Europeans, Levantines, and Japanese. South America saw the flowering of 2 great pre-Columbian civilizations of the Americas, the Incas of Peru, whose empire extended from present-day Ecuador to N Chile, and the Chibchas of Colombia, whose art has some astonishing affinities to that of the Far East. Apart from the Chibchas and Incas (who were rather a ruling class than a nation), principal tribes include the Arawak and Carib (N and NE), Tupí (E), Guaraní (center), Aymará and Quichua (Peru, Bolivia), Araucanian (S Chile). South America's coast was probably 1st sighted by Columbus, who reached the Orinoco estuary on his 3d voyage (1498). Contemporaneous with Columbus were the voyages by the Spaniards Alonso de Ojeda, Vicente Yáñez Pinzón, and Diego de Lepe, and the Portuguese Pedro Alvares Cabral, who on his way to India accidentally landed (1500) on the Brazilian coast. Famous explorers to follow were Amerigo Vespucci, Ferdinand Magellan on his voyage around the world (1520), and Sebastian Cabot. In 1513, Balboa crossed the Isthmus of Panama and discovered the Pacific. In the wake of the explorers came the conquistadors, spurred by greed and proselytizing fervor. With little regard for the natives, the European masters established the encomienda and repartimiento system which forced the Indians to virtual slave labor in the mines and fields. There evolved eventually the viceroyalties of Brazil, of New Granada (present-day Venezuela, Colombia, Panama, and Ecuador), of Peru (including present-day Chile), and of La Plata (Argentina, Uruguay, Paraguay, and most of Bolivia). These were generally subdivided into audiencias and captaincies. Rigid application of mercantilist policy hindered the economic development during the colonial regime. Though isolated revolts broke out earlier, the struggle for independence was kindled—as elsewhere in Spanish America—by the Peninsular War (1808–14), when Napoleon had taken Spain. Brazil, however, became the center of the Port. empire upon the arrival (1808) of John VI, and became a separate empire under Pedro I in 1822. Independence of the other South American republics (though not quite in their present form) was effected by the brilliant campaigns of Simón Bolívar and José de San Martín, sealed (1824) by the victory of Ayacucho. The French, Dutch, and British kept control of the Guianas. The Monroe Doctrine (1823) recognized the newly formed sister republics. Torn by social inequities and by civil and foreign wars, the political situation remained turbulent, characterized by unstable govts., short-lived democratic institutions, and frequent *coups d'état* and dictatorships. Boundary disputes and outbreaks of local warfare have been frequent. For further information see separate articles on countries, physical features, regions, and cities.

South Amherst (ă'mŭrst), village (pop. 1,020), Lorain co., N Ohio, 7 mi. W of Elyria; large sandstone quarries are just N.

Southampton (sou"thămp'tŭn, –ăm'tŭn, south"-hămp'tŭn), parish (1939 pop. 1,316), W Bermuda, on Bermuda Isl.

Southampton, town (pop. 1,600), S Ont., on L. Huron, at mouth of Saugeen R., 22 mi. WSW of Owen Sound; lumbering, furniture mfg.

Southampton, administrative county, England: see HAMPSHIRE

Southampton, county borough (1931 pop. 176,007; 1951 census 178,326), county in itself, and major seaport, S Hampshire, England, on peninsula bet. Test R. and Itchen R. (here forming Southampton Water) 70 mi. SW of London; 50°54'N 1°23'W. The dock area lines both rivers, and the port is principal European terminal of most transatlantic shipping lines, also handling important European, African, and Asiatic traffic. The graving and floating docks accommodate the world's largest ships. There is also an airport, and a flying boat base at Hythe, in Dibden. Town retains remnants of anc. Saxon walls (later rebuilt) with Norman towers and gates, including Bar Gate, surmounted by the Guildhall. Among notable bldgs. are 12th-cent. King John's Palace, Norman church of St. Michael, 14th-cent. Holy Rood Church, Watts Memorial Hall, Univ. Col., and modern Civic Center. Mfg.: marine engines, boilers, cables, paint, asbestos, chemicals, shoes, biscuits, oleomargarine. Southampton was site of Roman station of *Clausentum.* It is reputed scene of Canute's command to the waves. After Norman conquest it became important military port; Crusade of Richard I sailed from here in 1189, Henry V embarked here for France in 1415. The Pilgrim Fathers originally sailed from Southampton in 1620 (commemorated by memorial). In First and Second World Wars, it was a major military transport station. In Second World War the town suffered heavy air-raid damage, especially 1940–41, when the center of the city was completely destroyed. Southampton is birthplace of John Alden, Isaac Watts, Charles Dibdin, Sir John Millais, George Saintsbury, and Lord Jellicoe. Suburbs include Shirley (NW; pop. 17,342), Bitterne (NE; pop. 23,582), Freemantle (W; pop. 7,354) with large graving dock, and Bassett (N). The administrative county of Southampton (1931 pop. 1,014,316; 1948 estimate 1,106,310; □ 1,502.6) is the mainland part of Hampshire.

Southampton (south"hămp'tŭn, sou"thămp'tŭn), county (□ 607; pop. 26,522), SE Va.; ⊙ Courtland. In tidewater region; bounded S by N.C., W by Meherrin R., E by Blackwater R.; drained by Nottoway R. Diversified agr. (especially cotton, peanuts; also truck, fruit, grain), livestock (especially hogs). Lumber, paper milling at Franklin, its largest city. Set off 1748 from one of original Va. shires (formed 1634) and renamed Southampton.

Southampton. 1 Agr. town (pop. 1,387), Hampshire co., W central Mass., 8 mi. SSW of Northampton. Settled 1732, inc. 1775. **2** Residential village (pop. 4,042), Suffolk co., SE N.Y., on SE Long Isl., 14 mi. ESE of Riverhead, in potato- and truck-farming area; summer resort, known for its many fine estates. Mfg. (photographic reproduction equipment, knitted gloves). Parrish Memorial Art Mus. is here. Shinnecock Indian Reservation is W. Settled 1640, inc. 1894.

Southampton, Cape, SW extremity of Coats Isl., E Keewatin Dist., Northwest Territories, on Hudson Bay; 62°9'N 83°42'W.

Southampton Island (□ 16,936), E Keewatin Dist., Northwest Territories, at entrance of Hudson Bay; 64°N 83°W. Separated from mainland (W) by Roes Welcome Sound and from Melville Peninsula (N) by Repulse Bay and Frozen Strait. Isl. is 210 mi. long, 20–200 mi. wide. Plateau in NE part of isl. rises to c.2,000 ft. At head of South Bay is Coral Harbour trading post, with near-by air base. Off N coast is White Isl. (40 mi. long, 6–10 mi. wide).

Southamptonshire, England: see HAMPSHIRE.

Southampton Water, inlet of The Solent, S Hampshire, England, formed at Southampton by confluence of Test R. and Itchen R.; 6 mi. long, 2 mi. wide. Major shipping lane, forming approach to Southampton.

South Andaman Island: see ANDAMAN ISLANDS.

South Anna River, central Va., rises in the piedmont E of Charlottesville, flows c.85 mi. SE and E, joining North Anna R. c.20 mi. N of Richmond to form Pamunkey R.

South Arcot (är'kŏt), Tamil *Then Arkadu* (tān' ŭr'-kŭdōō), district (□ 4,205; pop. 2,608,753), SE, Madras, India; ⊙ Cuddalore. Bordered E by Coromandel Coast of Bay of Bengal, SE by Coleroon R., SW by Kalrayan Hills (magnetite deposits). Fr. settlement of Pondicherry (several isolated tracts) is a coastal enclave. Mainly lowland; drained by Ponnaiyar, Gadilam, and Vellar rivers. Agr. (rice, peanuts, sugar cane, sesame, cotton); extensive cashew-nut and Casuarina plantations along coast (mangrove tracts, lignite deposits, saltworks). Rice and sugar milling, peanut- and sesame-oil extraction, hand-loom cotton and silk weaving. Widespread quarrying of granite and other building stone. Chief towns: Chidambaram, Cuddalore, Nellikuppam, Panruti, Tindivanam, Villupuram. Historic rock fortress at Gingee. Under Chola kingdom and successive Indian powers until it became in 18th cent. a chief center of struggle bet. French, English, Mysore sultans and nawabs of Arcot in French-English contest for supremacy in India; ceded to English 1801 by nawab of Arcot.

Southard (sŭ'dhŭrd), village, Blaine co., W central Okla., 15 mi. NNW of Watonga; makes gypsum products.

South Ardmore, Pa.: see HAVERFORD.

South Aulatsivik Island (22 mi. long, 12 mi. wide), NE Labrador, at entrance of Webb's Bay on the Atlantic; Isl. contains several lakes. At N end is Mt. Thoresby (3,007 ft.), 56°54'N 61°28'W.

South Australia, state (□ 380,070; pop. 646,073) of Commonwealth of Australia; bounded by Northern Territory (N), Indian Ocean (S), Western Australia (W), Queensland (NE), New South Wales (E), Victoria (SE); bet. meridians of 129° and 141°E long., S of parallel of 26°S lat.; includes KANGAROO ISLAND and numerous isls. off S coast; ⊙ Adelaide. S coast is indented by Gulf St. Vincent, Spencer Gulf, and part of Great Australian Bight. Principal coastal features are Yorke and Eyre peninsulas. Greater part of state is wasteland, with large arid area in N and W; fertile region in S and SE. Generally low mtn. chains: Musgrave Ranges (containing Mt. Woodroffe, highest peak of state); Flinders and Mt. Lofty ranges with fertile valleys. Temp. range, 52°–74°F. Rainfall: less than 10 in. (N), 10–40 in. (S). Large lakes and rivers in N are usually dry. Murray R. (only navigable river) enters state in SE. Typically Australian flora and fauna: she-oak (*Casuarina*), tea tree (*Melaleuca*), eucalyptus (*Eucalyptus obliqua*); dingo (wild dog), marsupials (kangaroos, wombats). Granite, marble, limestone, gypsum, salt, talc, soapstone. Opal field in Stuarts Range. Mineral pigments: barite, ochre, malachite, azurite. Chief products: wheat, wine, wool, dairy products. Silver-lead smelting and superphosphate works, sawmills. Principal ports are Port Adelaide, Port Pirie, Port Lincoln, exporting pig lead, silver, wheat, wool, fruits, wine, meat. S coast surveyed 1802 by British; Murray R. explored 1830. Became 1836 Br. crown colony, and in 1901 state of Commonwealth of Australia. Northern Territory was included in 1863; transferred (1911) to Commonwealth govt.

South Bakersfield, village (pop. 12,120), Kern co., S central Calif., near Bakersfield.

South Baldy, peak (10,787 ft.) in Magdalena Mts., W central N.Mex., 17 mi. WSW of Socorro.

South Bank, England: see ESTON.

South Barre, Mass.: see BARRE.

South Bass Island, largest of Bass Isls., N Ohio, in L. Erie, 15 mi. NNW of Sandusky; c.3½ mi. long, 1½ mi. wide, it is site of PUT-IN-BAY village and natl. monument commemorating Perry's victory in battle of L. Erie. Isl. has extensive vineyards, wineries.

South Bay, town (pop. 1,050), Palm Beach co., SE Fla.

South Beach, SE N.Y., a shore-resort section of Richmond borough of New York city, along E shore of Staten Isl., SW of Fort Wadsworth; boardwalk, amusement park. Near by are Graham, New Dorp, Midland, Woodland, and Oakland beaches.

South Belmar, borough (pop. 1,294), Monmouth co., E N.J., on the coast 4 mi. S of Asbury Park.

South Beloit (bĭloit'), industrial city (pop. 3,221), Winnebago co., N Ill., on Rock R. (bridged here), across Wis. line from Beloit; mfg. (air-conditioning equipment, foundry and machine-shop products). Inc. 1917.

South Bend. 1 Town (pop. 2), Lincoln co., SE Ark., near Arkansas R., 34 mi. ESE of Pine Bluff. **2** City (pop. 115,911), ⊙ St. Joseph co., N Ind., on the great bend of St. Joseph R. and c.75 mi. ESE of Chicago, near Mich. line; mfg. and distribution center in farming and dairying area. Mfg.: automobiles and accessories, aircraft and parts, industrial and farm machinery, foundry products, ranges, sewing machines, paint, paper, clothing, textiles, watches, toys, asphalt insulation, beer, sporting goods. Has historical mus. The Univ. of Notre Dame (nō"tŭr dām') (at Notre Dame, just N) and St. Mary's Col. (at Notre Dame and at Holy Cross) are near by. City was settled in 1820, laid out in 1831 on site of Miami Indian village and a later French mission and trading post; an American Fur Company post was here in 1820. A monument to La Salle and a marker commemorating his 1st portage in the area are here. **3** Village (pop. 100), Cass co., SE Nebr., 25 mi. SW of Omaha and on Platte R., near Ashland. **4** City (pop. 1,857), ⊙ Pacific co., SW Wash., port of entry 22 mi. S of Aberdeen and on Willapa R., near Willapa Bay; oysters, fish, lumber, cranberries, poultry. Settled c.1860.

South Berwick (bûr'wĭk), town (pop. 2,646), including South Berwick village (pop. 1,701), York co., SW Maine, on Salmon Falls R. and just N of Kittery, opposite Dover, N.H.; mfg. (textiles, shoes). Seat of Berwick Acad. (founded 1791). Sarah Orne Jewett birthplace is preserved. Settled 1623, set off from Berwick 1814.

South Bethlehem (bĕth'lēŭm), borough (pop. 489), Armstrong co., W Pa., on Redbank Creek opposite New Bethlehem.

South Beveland, Du. *Zuid Beveland* (zoid bā'vŭlänt), island (□ 135), Zeeland prov., SW Netherlands, W of Bergen op Zoom; bounded by Het Sloe (W), the Western Scheldt (S), the Eastern Scheldt (NE), the Zandkreek (N); 18 mi. long, 11 mi. wide. Cattle, pig, and sheep raising; agr. (potatoes, flowers, vegetables, gherkins, raspberries, strawberries). Chief town, Goes. Railroad connection along dykes with mainland (E) and Walcheren isl. (W).

South Beveland Canal, SW Netherlands, extends 6.5 mi. S–N, bet. the Western Scheldt at Hansweert and the Eastern Scheldt near Wemeldinge. Part of Antwerp-Germany inland shipping route.

South Bimini, Bahama Isls.: see BIMINI ISLANDS.

South Bisbee, Ariz.: see LOWELL.

South Bishop, Wales: see BISHOP AND CLERKS.

South Bloomfield, village (pop. 250), Pickaway co., S central Ohio, 17 mi. S of Columbus, near Scioto R.

South Boca Grande, Fla.: see GASPARILLA ISLAND.

South Borden Island, Northwest Territories: see BORDEN ISLANDS.

Southboro or **Southborough,** town (pop. 2,760), Worcester co., E central Mass., 15 mi. E of Worcester; pork products, dairying. Settled 1660, inc. 1727. Includes village of Cordaville.

Southborough, residential urban district (1931 pop. 7,350; 1951 census 8,823), SW Kent, England, 2 mi. N of Tunbridge Wells; brick- and tileworks.

Southborough, Mass.: see SOUTHBORO.

South Boston. 1 Community, Mass.: see BOSTON. **2** Town (pop. 6,057), Halifax co., S Va., on Dan R. and 28 mi. ENE of Danville, in agr. area (tobacco, grain). Rail junction; important tobacco market; mfg. of textiles, flour, lumber, foundry products, beverages, dairy products. A state park is 12 mi. E. Chartered 1796; inc. 1884.

South Boulder, village (pop. 3,807), Boulder co., N central Colo., near Boulder.

South Boulevards, former village, Richland co., N central Ohio; annexed 1948 by MANSFIELD.

South Bound Brook, industrial borough (pop. 2,905), Somerset co., N central N.J., on Raritan R. opposite Bound Brook; mfg. (asphalt, asbestos products). Baron von Steuben had hq. here, 1778–79. Inc. 1907.

South Braintree, Mass.: see BRAINTREE.

Southbridge, agr. town (pop. 375), E S.Isl., New Zealand, 30 mi. SW of Christchurch, near L. Ellesmere; rail terminus.

Southbridge, town (pop. 17,519), including Southbridge village (pop. 16,748), Worcester co., S Mass., on Quinebaug R. and 18 mi. SW of Worcester; optical goods, textiles, metal products. Settled 1730, inc. 1816.

South Brisbane (brĭz'bŭn), city (pop. 31,063), SE Queensland, Australia, on S shore of Brisbane R., opposite Brisbane; govt. dry docks, flour mills. Horse racing.

South Bristol, resort town (pop. 631), Lincoln co., S Maine, partly on Rutherford Isl. and 11 mi. SE of Wiscasset. Includes villages of Walpole, with church built 1772, and Christmas Cove, port for coastal steamers.

South Britain, Conn.: see SOUTHBURY.

South Broadway, village (pop. 3,229), Yakima co., S Wash.

South Brooklyn, SE N.Y., a section of Brooklyn borough of New York city, along shore of Upper New York Bay. Its port area includes Erie and Atlantic shipping basins, N.Y. State Barge Canal terminal, and Red Hook section (partly residential). Adjacent are Gowanus (gŭwä'nŭs) dist. around Gowanus Bay (shipping), and huge Bush Terminal.

South Brother Island (7 acres), New York city, SE N.Y., in East R. bet. Rikers and North Brother isls.; part of Manhattan borough.

South Brother Mountain (3,951 ft.), Piscataquis co., N central Maine, 25 mi. NW of Millinocket, in Katahdin State Game Preserve.

South Brownsville, Pa.: see BROWNSVILLE.

South Bruny, Tasmania: see BRUNY.

South Burlington, town (pop. 3,279), including South Burlington village (pop. 1,527), Chittenden co., NW Vt., adjacent to Burlington.

Southbury, residential town (pop. 3,828), New Haven co., SW Conn., on the Housatonic, at mouth of Pomrepaug R., and 10 mi. SW of Waterbury, in agr., summer resort area. Steel traps made at South Britain village. State park near Southford village. Settled 1673, set off from Woodbury 1782.

South Caicos (kī'kōs, kī'kŭs), island (□ 9.4; pop. 826), Turks and Caicos Isls., dependency of Jamaica, at SE end of the Caicos Isls., on Turks Island Passage; 21°30'N 71°30'W. Salt panning. Has an airfield at S end.

South Cairo (kâ'rō), resort village, Greene co., SE N.Y., on Catskill Creek and 6 mi. NW of Catskill, in Catskill Mts.

South Canaan, Conn.: see CANAAN, town.

South Canadian River, SW U.S.: see CANADIAN RIVER.

South Canara, India: see SOUTH KANARA.

South Canon (kăn'yŭn), town (pop. 1,588), Fremont co., S central Colo., on Arkansas R. opposite Canon City, and 35 mi. WNW of Pueblo; alt. 5,300 ft. Inc. 1891.

South Cape, Nor. *Sør Kapp* (sûr' käp'), S tip of West Spitsbergen, in the Arctic Ocean; 76°34'N.

South Carolina, state (land only □ 30,594, with inland waters □ 31,055; 1950 pop. 2,117,027; 1940 pop. 1,899,804), SE U.S., on the Atlantic, bordered by N.C. (N and NE) and Ga. (S and W); 39th in area, 27th in pop., one of the original 13 states; ⊙ Columbia. CHARLESTON is largest city and chief mfg. and shipping center. The "Palmetto State" is almost triangular, c.250 mi. long (NW–SE) and 100–200 mi. wide. It descends gradually from the BLUE RIDGE (front range of Appalachians) in NW to the Atlantic. The hilly piedmont (c.⅓ of the area) is 1,200–500 ft. high, the low coastal plain (c.⅔ of the area) up to 500 ft. high. The Blue Ridge, a rugged area largely included in Sumter Natl. Forest, occupies only a small area in S.C. and rises to 3,560 ft. in SASSAFRAS MOUNTAIN, the highest point in the state. The piedmont is an old mtn. mass of granites, gneisses, and schists, worn down to rolling hills. It has red clay and sandy loam soils and is c.50% forested (pine, poplar, oak, gum, hickory). The fall line (the piedmont boundary) crosses state from Chesterfield co. to Aiken co., marking the shore line of earlier geologic times; below it runs a narrow sand-hill belt. The coastal plain is a gently rolling area, c.60% forested (pine, oak, gum, cypress), with a flat and generally swampy tidewater area traversed by the INTRACOASTAL WATERWAY and bordered below the mouth of the Santee R. by the SEA ISLANDS. S.C. is drained by the Pee Dee, Santee, Edisto, and Savannah river systems. Hydroelectric power has been extensively developed, especially in the Santee R. system, and furnishes c.85% of the state's electricity. Most of the lakes, including Wateree Pond, Catawba, Murray, Marion, Moultrie, and Greenwood lakes, are formed by power dams. The state has a humid subtropical climate characterized by long, hot summers (average temp. 80°F.) and short, mild winters (average temp. 48°F.), with only a few inches of snow in the upper piedmont and mts. Rainfall is evenly distributed and averages 48 in. annually, with the Blue Ridge receiving up to 65 in. The long growing season ranges from 200 days in the upper piedmont to 280 days along the coast. Farming (c.75% of pop. is rural) and mfg. are the primary bases of the state's economy. Erosion (especially in the piedmont) and soil depletion are major problems. S.C. uses more fertilizer than any other state except N.C., and 16% of its area is severely eroded. Corn, a major food staple, occupies the largest acreage, but cotton and tobacco are the chief cash crops. Other important crops include peaches, truck, wheat, oats, barley, hay, and peanuts. Livestock (beef and dairy cattle, hogs, poultry) is a major source of farm income. The principal industry is cotton milling, largely concentrated in the piedmont—at Spartanburg, Greenville, Anderson, Rock Hill, Greenwood, and Gaffney—and at Columbia, on the fall line. Forests (c.⅔ pine) cover c.55% of the state, and the forestry industry (lumber, paper and pulp, furniture, boxes) ranks 2d. Important wood-processing centers include the ports of Charleston, Georgetown, and Beaufort, and the coastal plain towns of FLORENCE, SUMTER, and ORANGEBURG. Other industries include food processing (meat packing, truck and fish canning, dairy and poultry products), fertilizer mixing, metal fabricating, and mining (clay, granite, sand and gravel, limestone). The better clays are found in the sand-hill belt and the principal granite quarrying area across the state just N of the fall line. U.S. Atomic Energy Commission's huge Savannah R. Plant is in W, in Aiken and Barnwell counties. Some fishing (oysters, shrimp, menhaden) is also carried on. Tourist attractions include resorts of the Blue Ridge, the sand hills (AIKEN, CAMDEN), the Sea Isls., old coastal cities (notably Charleston, BEAUFORT, PORT ROYAL, GEORGETOWN), and fine old gardens (especially BROOKGREEN). The Spanish founded an unsuccessful colony along the coast in 1526. Later De Soto explored (1540) the Savannah R. region. In 1562 the Frenchman Jean Ribaut established a Huguenot settlement in the Sea Isls. which was short-lived because of the Spanish expansion northward from Florida. The English supplanted the Spaniards and in 1680 founded Charleston. By 1729 S.C. was a crown colony, and on the eve of the Revolution the pop. (enlarged by an influx of German, Swiss, Scotch-Irish, and Welsh settlers) numbered c.140,000. At the time Negroes, who were imported for the tidewater rice and indigo plantations, outnumbered the whites 4 to 3. The long rivalry bet. the small independent farmers of the up country and the planters caused the capital to be moved in 1786 from Charleston to a more centrally located site, Columbia. Mounting tariffs after the war resulted in the adoption of Calhoun's nullification act in 1832, but secession was averted by compromise. S.C. was the 1st state to secede (Dec. 20, 1860) from the Union and the firing on Fort SUMTER 4 months later opened the Civil War. The state suffered little destruction until early in 1865 when Sherman laid waste large areas. The Reconstruction period (lasting until 1876) further impoverished the state. Farm tenancy became widespread, replacing the old plantation system. The continued reliance upon cotton, which had supplanted rice and indigo, after the invention of the cotton gin in 1793, resulted in much eroded land and more poverty. Some help to the state's economy came with expansion of textile mfg. (aided by Northern capital) in the piedmont following the Civil War. The coming of the cotton boll weevil after the First World War encouraged crop diversification and livestock raising, resulting in a more balanced farm economy. The two world wars saw a large emigration of Negroes (43% of the pop. in 1940) to the North. In the period following the Second World War the state continued to encourage the expansion of industry and better use of its land. See also articles on cities, towns, geographic features, and the 46 counties: ABBEVILLE, AIKEN, ALLENDALE, ANDERSON, BAMBERG, BARNWELL, BEAUFORT, BERKELEY, CALHOUN, CHARLESTON, CHEROKEE, CHESTER, CHESTERFIELD, CLARENDON, COLLETON, DARLINGTON, DILLON, DORCHESTER, EDGEFIELD, FAIRFIELD, FLORENCE, GEORGETOWN, GREENVILLE, GREENWOOD, HAMPTON, HORRY, JASPER, KERSHAW, LANCASTER, LAURENS, LEE, LEXINGTON, MCCORMICK, MARION, MARLBORO, NEWBERRY, OCONEE, ORANGEBURG, PICKENS, RICHLAND, SALUDA, SPARTANBURG, SUMTER, UNION, WILLIAMSBURG, YORK.

South Carrollton, town (pop. 289), Muhlenberg co., W Ky., on Green R. and 20 mi. E of Madisonville, in bituminous-coal-mining and agr. area.

South Casco, Maine: see CASCO.

South Charleston. 1 Village (pop. 1,452), Clark co., W central Ohio, 11 mi. ESE of Springfield; rural trade center; makes veterinary medicines; flour, lumber milling. Founded 1815. **2** Town (pop. 16,686), Kanawha co., W W.Va., on the Kanawha just W of CHARLESTON, in coal-mining area; mfg. of chemicals. U.S. naval ordnance plant, Indian burial mound here. Settled c.1900.

South Chatham, Mass.: see CHATHAM.

South Chicago Harbor, Ill.: see CALUMET HARBOR.

South Chicago Heights, residential village (pop. 2,129), Cook co., NE Ill., S suburb of Chicago, in industrial area near Ind. line. Inc. 1907.

South China, Maine: see CHINA.

South China Sea, Chinese *Nan Hai*, arm of Pacific Ocean, bet. SE Asian mainland and Malay Archipelago; 1,800 mi. long, 600 mi. wide. It is bounded by S China, the Indochinese states of Vietnam and Cambodia, Thailand, Malaya, Borneo, and the Philippine Isls. It is linked with East China Sea by the Formosa Strait, with the Philippine Sea of the Pacific by Luzon Strait, with Sulu Sea by Mindoro and Balabac Straits, with Java Sea by Karimata Strait, and with Andaman Sea by Strait of Malacca. The South China Sea penetrates deeply into SE Asia in the Gulf of Siam and the Gulf of Tonkin. It receives the West R. of China, the Red and Mekong rivers of Vietnam, and the Chao Phraya of Thailand. The leading ports are Singapore, Bangkok, Saigon, Haiphong, Canton, Hong Kong, Swatow, as well as Kaosiung on Formosa, and Manila in the Philippines. The sea includes the Indonesian Natuna, Anambas, Tambelan, Riouw, and Lingga isl. groups, and, N of 4°N, the Chinese isl. groups of Nansha Isls., Macclesfield (Chungsha) Bank, Paracel (Sisha) Isls., and Pratas (Tungsha) Isl., as well as Hainan isl. The sea is a region of violent storms (typhoons). Its S half, part of the geologic Sunda platform, is quite shallow (600 ft.), while depths of over 15,000 ft. are found in N.

South Cholla (chŭl'lä'), Korean *Cholla-namdo*, Jap. *Zenra-nando*, province [Jap. and Korean *do*] (□ 5,362; 1949 pop. 3,042,442), S Korea, bounded W by Yellow Sea, S by Cheju Strait, and E by Somjin R.; ⊙ KWANGJU. Chief ports are MOKPO and YOSU. The prov. includes 370 inhabited isls. (the largest being CHIN ISLAND and WAN ISLAND) and 1,377 uninhabited islets. Partly mountainous and largely fertile terrain, drained by Somjin R. The prov. is a major producer of raw silk. Agr. products are rice, cotton, potatoes, ramie, tobacco. Stock raising, fishing, and lumbering, gold and coal mining. Home industries (paper making, weaving, metalworking) are important.

South Chungchong (chōōng'chŭng'), Korean *Chungchong-namdo*, Jap. *Chusei-nando*, province [Jap. and Korean *do*] (□ 3,130; 1949 pop. 2,028,188), S Korea, bounded W by Yellow Sea; ⊙ TAEJON. Generally low terrain, drained by Kum R. Primarily agr. (grains, soy beans, ginseng), the prov. also has gold, silver, and tungsten mines. Other industries: lumbering, fishing, stock raising.

South Church, England: see SAINT ANDREW AUCKLAND.
South City, village (pop. 4,611, with adjacent Bond), Leon co., N Fla.
South Cle Elum (klē ĕ'lŭm), town (pop. 442), Kittitas co., central Wash., S of CLE ELUM across Yakima R.
South Coatesville, borough (pop. 1,996), Chester co., SE Pa., just SE of Coatesville. Inc. 1921.
South Coffeyville, town (pop. 527), Nowata co., NE Okla., 20 mi. N of Nowata, near Kansas line.
South Connellsville, borough (pop. 2,610), Fayette co., SW Pa., on Youghiogheny R. just above Connellsville and 37 mi. SE of Pittsburgh.
South Corning, village (pop. 880), Steuben co., S N.Y., just S of Corning.
South Cousin Island, one of the Seychelles, in Indian Ocean, 5 mi. SSW of Praslin Isl.; 4°21'S 55°38'E; granite formation.
South Coventry, Conn.: see COVENTRY.
South Creake, agr. village and parish (pop. 626), N Norfolk, England, 6 mi. NW of Fakenham; cereal mfg. Has 14th–15th-cent. church. Just N is agr. village and parish (pop. 466) of North Creake, with remains of 13th-cent. Creake Abbey.
South Creek, town (pop. 108), Beaufort co., E N.C., 26 mi. SE of Washington and on Pamlico R.
South Crosland, former urban district (1931 pop. 2,985), West Riding, SW Yorkshire, England, 3 mi. SW of Huddersfield; woolen milling. Site of Huddersfield reservoir. Here is woolen-milling town of Netherton. Inc. 1938 in Huddersfield.
South Dakota (dŭkō'tŭ), state (land only □ 76,536; with inland waters □ 77,047; 1950 pop. 652,740; 1940 pop. 642,961), N central U.S., bounded N by N.Dak., W by Mont. and Wyo., S by Nebr., E by Iowa and Minn.; 15th in area, 40th in pop., admitted 1889 as 40th state; ⊙ Pierre. S.Dak. is rectangular in shape (200 mi. N–S; 380 mi. E–W) and bisected by Missouri R. State is largely in Great Plains, except for granite Black Hills in SW, where Harney Peak rises to 7,242 ft.; alt. is lowest at Big Stone L. (962 ft.; in NE, on Minn. line). Most of S.Dak. is treeless, short-grass country. E part is rolling plain (becoming hilly in Coteau des Prairies) with abundance of rich, glacial soil and small lakes. Area W of the Missouri is dissected plateau, including Badlands region bet. Cheyenne and White rivers. NW, semiarid and not widely cultivated, includes area of gumbo soil (Pierre clay) difficult to farm when dry and impossible to work when wet. W and central S.Dak. are drained by Missouri R. and right tributaries (Grand, Moreau, Cheyenne, Bad, and White rivers), E and E central by left tributaries (James, Vermillion, and Big Sioux rivers); central S.Dak. is in artesian basin. Climate is continental, characterized by hot summers (up to 115°F.) and cold winters (down to −43°F.), with heavy snowfall and blizzards; diurnal temperature range is great. Rainfall varies from 20–25 in. in E to 15–20 in. in W. Growing season in E is c.145 days, sometimes less than 105 days in SW (Black Hills); average for state is 135 days. S.Dak. is primarily agr., ranking 1st in production of rye and 3d in production of spring wheat and barley. Cattle feed, grain, and hogs are raised in SE; small grain, livestock, and potatoes in E; spring wheat in NE. Grazing and diversified farming predominate in central S.Dak.; small grain, corn, and livestock are raised in N. In W, where soil is lightly glaciated and derived from shale and sandstone, grazing is prevalent, although sugar beets are grown in irrigated area served by BELLE FOURCHE RESERVOIR, and garden truck and fruit are grown near Spearfish. Dairying (especially for butter) is important in NE. Most of state is in farms, 34% in harvested cropland, 47% in pasture. Principal industry is processing of farm products (meat, dairy, poultry, and bakery products; flour, ice cream, beverages). Manufactures are farm implements and wood products. Mineral resources (chiefly in Black Hills) are gold (mined in Homestake Mine, at Lead), precious gems, silver, feldspar, tantalum, and lithium; manganese and limestone (in Paha Sapa formation, rimming Black Hills); bentonite (near Belle Fourche). SIOUX FALLS is largest city in state and distribution and food-processing point. Other cities are Aberdeen, Rapid City, Huron, Mitchell, Watertown, Lead, Yankton, Brookings, and Madison. Institutions of education are Univ. of S.Dak. (Vermillion), S.Dak. School of Mines and Technology (Rapid City), Augustana and Sioux Falls colleges (Sioux Falls), Dak. Wesleyan Univ. (Mitchell), Huron Col. (Huron), S.Dak. State Col. of Agr. and Mechanic Arts (Brookings), Yankton Col. (Yankton). There are 4 state teachers colleges (at Spearfish, Madison, Aberdeen, and Springfield). Much of S.Dak. has been set aside in Indian reservations. Pine Ridge and Rosebud Indian reservations occupy most of S S.Dak., bet. Missouri R. and Black Hills; and Cheyenne R. and Standing Rock Indian reservations extend through 5 counties in N. Others are Sisseton Indian Reservation, in NE; Lower Brule and Crow Creek Indian reservations SE of Pierre and on opposite banks of Missouri R.; and Yankton Indian Reservation, in SE, on left bank of Missouri R. (here forming Nebr. line). Black Hills and Harney Natl. forests (chiefly Ponderosa pine) are in SW, extending through Black Hills; small sections of Custer Natl. Forest in NW. Badlands Natl. Monument, in the Badlands, includes colorful and deeply eroded area which has large deposits of land and marine fossils. Wind Cave Natl. Park and Jewel Cave and Fossil Cycad natl. monuments have been set aside in Black Hills to preserve features of geological and scenic interest; Mt. Rushmore Natl. Memorial consists of gigantic carvings of great presidents. Earliest exploration occurred in middle of 18th cent., when sons of Pierre de la Vérendrye visited site of Ft. Pierre; Lewis and Clark later used Missouri R. in traveling to and from Pacific Northwest and twice (1804, 1806) passed through area now included in the Dakotas. Earliest settlement was fur-trading post (founded 1817; later known as Ft. Pierre) on Missouri R.; 1st agr. settlement (1856) was Sioux Falls. Dak. Territory was organized in 1861 (⊙ Yankton); states of N.Dak. and S.Dak. formed from it in 1889; Pierre selected as ⊙ S.Dak. 1889. In 1860s settlement was hampered by droughts, Indian raids, and insect plagues. Gold rush began in 1870s, after rumors of gold in Black Hills had been confirmed by military expedition under Gen. Custer, and Deadwood and Lead experienced phenomenal growth as gold-mining centers. Activity continued in spite of war (caused by white occupation of Indian territory) in which Custer and his men were massacred at the Little Bighorn. Gold boom stimulated cattle ranching in W S.Dak., and completion of railroads to the Missouri caused increased settlement in E. Unusually severe winter of 1886–87 destroyed much livestock and led to use of smaller herds and better provision for winter shelter and winter feeding. After period (1889–97) of recurrent droughts, cooperative movement of Farmers' Alliance received additional support. Populist party won decisive victory in 1896, and initiative and referendum were adopted in 1899. Expansion of agr. occurred after extension of railroad to Rapid City, but drought of 1910–11 caused abandonment of many farms. By 1935, agr. production and pop. had dropped far below 1929 level because of droughts, dust storms, and natl. depression of late 1920s and early 1930s. Partial recovery was effected as result of relief measures and irrigation, power, and soil-conservation projects; further recovery occurred during Second World War. Additional measures for water conservation, power, and land reclamation are included in proposed plan for development of basin of MISSOURI RIVER. Crop diversification and extensive raising of poultry and livestock have been encouraged in broad agr. program sponsored by the state agr. col., the Grange, the Farmers Union, and the Farm Bureau. See also articles on the cities, towns, geographic features, and the 68 counties: ARMSTRONG, AURORA, BEADLE, BENNETT, BON HOMME, BROOKINGS, BROWN, BRULE, BUFFALO, BUTTE, CAMPBELL, CHARLES MIX, CLARK, CLAY, CODINGTON, CORSON, CUSTER, DAVISON, DAY, DEUEL, DEWEY, DOUGLAS, EDMUNDS, FALL RIVER, FAULK, GRANT, GREGORY, HAAKON, HAMLIN, HAND, HANSON, HARDING, HUGHES, HUTCHINSON, HYDE, JACKSON, JERAULD, JONES, KINGSBURY, LAKE, LAWRENCE, LINCOLN, LYMAN, MCCOOK, MCPHERSON, MARSHALL, MEADE, MELLETTE, MINER, MINNEHAHA, MOODY, PENNINGTON, PERKINS, POTTER, ROBERTS, SANBORN, SHANNON, SPINK, STANLEY, SULLY, TODD, TRIPP, TURNER, UNION, WALWORTH, WASHABAUGH, YANKTON, ZIEBACH.
South Darenth, England: see DARENTH.
South Darley, England: see DARLEY.
South Dartmouth, Mass.: see DARTMOUTH.
South Dayton, village (pop. 727), Cattaraugus co., W N.Y., 16 mi. SE of Dunkirk; makes evaporated milk.
South Daytona (dātō'nŭ), town (pop. 692), Volusia co., NE Fla., suburb of Daytona Beach.
South Deerfield, Mass.: see DEERFIELD.
South Dennis, Mass.: see DENNIS.
South Dos Palos, Calif.: see DOS PALOS.
South Downs, England: see DOWNS.
South Durham, village (pop. estimate 350), S Que., 11 mi. W of Richmond; dairying; cattle, pigs.
South Duxbury, Mass.: see DUXBURY.
Southeast Cape, southernmost point of Tasmania, in Tasman Sea, S of D'Entrecasteaux Channel; 43°39'S 146°50'E.
South East Island, one of the Seychelles, in Indian Ocean, off E coast of Mahé Isl., 7 mi. SE of Victoria; 4°41'S 55°32'E; ½ mi. long, ¼ mi. wide.
South East Point, cape at E extremity of Jamaica, on Jamaica Channel, just S of Morant Point, and 40 mi. E of Kingston; 17°54'N 76°12'W.
Southeast Vineland, village (pop. 6,376), Cumberland co., S N.J., near Vineland.
South Edisto River, S.C.: see EDISTO RIVER.
South Eel River, Calif.: see EEL RIVER.
South Egremont, Mass.: see EGREMONT.
South Elgin (ĕl'jĭn), village (pop. 1,220), Kane co., NE Ill., on Fox R. (bridged here), just S of Elgin.
South Eliot, Maine: see ELIOT.
Southend, fishing village and parish (pop. 640), S Argyll, Scotland, at S extremity of Kintyre peninsula, 8 mi. S of Campbeltown; seaside resort. Offshore is SANDA.
Southend-on-Sea, residential county borough (1931 pop. 120,115; 1951 census 151,830), SE Essex, England, on N bank of the Thames estuary, near its mouth, and 35 mi. E of London; 51°33'N 0°43'E; popular seaside resort with long pier, and scene of annual yachting events. Mfg. (paint, pharmaceuticals, electrical appliances, metal products). In county borough are residential towns of Leigh-on-Sea (W; pop. 11,532) and Westcliff (W).
South English, town (pop. 248), Keokuk co., SE Iowa, near South Fork English R., 34 mi. NNE of Ottumwa; livestock, grain.
Southern, for names beginning thus and not found here: see under SOUTH.
Southern, in Rus. names: see also YUZHN.
Southern Alps, mountain range, W central S.Isl., New Zealand, extending c.200 mi. NE-SW. Contains Mt. Cook (12,349 ft.), highest peak of New Zealand. Arthur Pass and Tasman natl. parks contain many glaciers.
Southern Anyui Range, Russian SFSR: see ANYUI.
Southern Bug River, Ukrainian SSR: see BUG RIVER.
Southern Cross, town (pop. 760), SW central Western Australia, 210 mi. ENE of Perth; rail junction; center of Yilgarn Goldfield (□ 15,593).
Southern Desert, Arabic *Al-Sahra' al-Janubiyah*, part of the Libyan Desert in SW Egypt, its small settled area constituting a so-called frontier prov. (□ 47; pop. 32,291) of Egypt; ⊙ Kharga, in Kharga oasis. Bordered E by the Nile valley, N by the Western Desert, W by the Libyan frontier (25°E), S by Anglo-Egyptian Sudan. In it are the oases of KHARGA and DAKHLA, which, irrigated by springs, grow palm trees, fruit, rice, cereals. Kharga is reached by rail from Nag Hammadi. Both oases have important archaeological remains, especially temples of the Roman period.
Southern Highlands, province (□ 45,472; pop. 848,861), S Tanganyika; ⊙ Mbeya. Bounded SW by Northern Rhodesia, S by Nyasaland and L. Nyasa; drained by Great Ruaha R. Agr. (coffee, tea, rice, peanuts, corn, wheat, pyrethrum) and livestock region. Gold mining in Lupa goldfield near Chunya and Saza. Salt, mica, coal, iron, copper, potash deposits. Chief centers: Iringa, Mbeya, Chunya.
Southern Hills, village (1940 pop. 2,022), Montgomery co., W Ohio, a S suburb of Dayton.
Southern Indian Lake (□ 1,200), N Man., on Churchill R.; 105 mi. long, 16 mi. wide; 57°N 99°W.
Southern Karroo or **Little Karroo** (kŭrōō'), plateau region, SW Cape Prov., U. of So. Afr., bet. Langeberg and Outeniqua ranges (S) and Wittebergen and Swartberg ranges (N); c.15 mi. wide; average alt. 1,500 ft. Crossed E-W by several small ranges.
Southern Mahratta States, India: see DECCAN STATES.
Southern Morava River (mô'rävä), Serbo-Croatian *Južna Morava* (yōōzh'nä), S Serbia, Yugoslavia, formed at NE foot of Crna Gora, 16 mi. WSW of Vranje, by junction of Binacka Morava and Morava rivers; flows c.125 mi. N, past Vranje, Vladicin Han, Grdelica, Aleksinac, and Stalac, joining Western Morava R. near Stalac to form Morava R. Receives Vlasina, Toplica, and Nisava rivers. Entire course followed by Belgrade-Salonika RR. Hemp growing in its valley.
Southern Penner River, India: see PONNAIYAR RIVER.
Southern Pines, town (pop. 4,272), Moore co., central N.C., 28 mi. WNW of Fayetteville, in agr. (peaches, truck) and timber area; winter resort noted for its mild climate and recreation facilities. Settled 1885, inc. 1887.
Southern Protectorate of Morocco, Spanish protectorate (□ c.12,700; pop. 9,836) on NW coast of Africa, politically part of Sp. West Africa; ⊙ Villa Bens, on Cape Juby. A territory of vague political status, it lies just SW of Fr. Morocco, S of the Dra wadi (Oued Dra) and N of 27°40'N, its boundary with Saguia el Hamra (a part of the administrative division called Spanish Sahara). See the articles on RÍO DE ORO and SPANISH WEST AFRICA.
Southern Province, Pashto *Samt-i-Junubi* (sŭmt'-ĭ-jōōnōō'bē), province (□ 5,000; pop. 500,000), E Afghanistan; ⊙ Gardez. Bounded E by Pathan tribal areas of Pakistan's North-West Frontier Prov., it is a mountainous region at N end of the Sulaiman Range. Pop. consists largely of Ghilzai and other tribal Afghans, engaged in nomadic and seminomadic stock raising. Lumbering is an important industry, yielding pine timber exports. Main centers are Gardez, Matun, and Urgun.
Southern Province, administrative division (□ 2,146; pop., including estate pop., 961,790), S Ceylon; ⊙ Galle. Bounded S by Indian Ocean; mainly lowland, with S spurs of Sabaragamuwa Hill Country in NW; drained by Gin Ganga and Walawe Ganga rivers. Largely agr.; rice, vegetables, coconuts, tea, rubber, citronella grass (main area is Matara dist.), cinnamon, fruit; cotton growing in Hambantota dist. Fishing along coast. Major govt. salterns of Ceylon at Hambantota. Moonstone-mining center at Mitiyagoda; graphite mines (Ampegama, Dodanduwa); iron-ore, sapphire, and beryl deposits (Matara); thorium deposits (Bentota). Land development projects on Walawe Ganga and Kirindi Oya rivers. Main centers:

Galle, Matara. Archaeological landmarks at Tissamaharama and Wiraketiya. Created 1833.

Southern Rhodesia (rōdē'zhŭ), self-governing Br. colony (□ 150,333; 1949 pop. estimate 2,021,900), SE Africa; ⊙ Salisbury. Bounded NW by Northern Rhodesia (along Zambezi R.), N and E by Mozambique, S by Transvaal (U. of So. Afr.; along Limpopo R.), SW by Bechuanaland Protectorate. Part of great S African plateau (average alt. 2–5,000 ft.); only the N fringe and SE corner are in the low veld (below 2,000 ft.). A broad ridge of high veld (4–6,000 ft.) crosses colony SW-NE, from Bulawayo to Salisbury, where it branches N to the Umvukwe Range and SE to Umtali. Along Mozambique border are colony's highest ranges, the Inyanga Mts. rising to 8,517 ft. Flanking the high veld is the middle veld (2–4,000 ft.) which occupies ⅔ of territory. From the high veld (where all European settlements are concentrated) streams flow NW to the Zambezi (chief tributaries here: Gwaii, Shangani, Sanyati) and SE to the Limpopo and Sabi. Mazoe R. (an affluent of the lower Zambezi) drains NE. Climate varies with altitude, latitude, and distance from ocean. The 3 marked seasons are Sept.-Nov. (hot), Nov.-March (rainy), May-Aug. (cool). Mean annual temp. at 5,000 ft. is 65°F. Rainfall ranges from 40 in. along E mtn. frontier, to 32 in. at Salisbury and 24 in. at Bulawayo (SW). Most of colony is savanna; tropical forests (teak mahogany) are found in low veld and NW of Bulawayo. Chief occupations are farming and mining. Principal crops are corn (grown on ⅔ of cultivated land), tobacco (especially near Salisbury), peanuts, wheat, potatoes, and citrus fruit (NE). Livestock is reared throughout territory (except in tse-tse fly region along the Zambezi); dairying near urban centers. Gold deposits are widely distributed but predominate in high veld; principal mines are at Eiffel Flats, Que Que, Selukwe, Penhalonga (near Umtali), Gatooma, Filabusi, and in Gwelo, Hartley, Gwanda, and Victoria dists. Asbestos is mined at Shabani and Mashaba, Chromite in the Great Norite Dike (which crosses colony N-S) and at Selukwe, coal in the Wankie basin. A fairly good railroad system carries all of colony's exports (gold, asbestos, chrome, coal, tobacco, meat, corn). Main lines follow the watershed of the high veld; the Salisbury-Bulawayo line continues across Bechuanaland Protectorate to Mafeking (U. of So. Afr.); the Salisbury-Beira (Mozambique) line is nearest outlet to the Indian Ocean. A spur leading NW from Bulawayo, past Wankie, enters Northern Rhodesia at Victoria Falls. A good roadnet roughly parallels railroads; Beitbridge (head of Transvaal RR on Limpopo R.) is linked by road with Salisbury. Airfields at Salisbury, Gatooma, Gwelo, Bulawayo. Principal tourist attractions are VICTORIA FALLS and ZIMBABWE ruins (near Fort Victoria). Little is known of region's history before early 19th cent., when it was inhabited by the Mashona tribe. The war-like Matabele, expulsed from Transvaal (1837), occupied area and absorbed the Mashona. After these tribes were named Southern Rhodesia's 2 chief divisions (MASHONALAND in NE, MATABELELAND in SW), no longer of administrative importance. Territory came under Br. South Africa Company after 1888. In 1923, on partition of Rhodesia, Southern Rhodesia became a colony with responsible govt. It is ruled by an appointed governor with the aid of an executive council and an elected legislative assembly, with franchise limited to white British subjects. For native administration the colony is divided into 5 provinces (SALISBURY, GWELO, VICTORIA, BULAWAYO, UMTALI) and 36 dists. headed by native commissioners. Over ⅕ of colony's area has been set aside for native reserves. Pop. breakdown (1946) was 82,388 Europeans, 4,558 Coloured (mixed), 2,911 Asiatics, and 1,674,000 Natives. Immigration of European settlers increased after Second World War.

Southern Shan State, Burma: see SHAN STATE.

Southern Territories, Fr. *Territoires du Sud*, division (□ 765,158; 1948 pop. 816,993) of Algeria, comprising entire area (mostly in the Sahara) S of N Algeria's 3 depts. of Oran, Alger, and Constantine. Consists of 4 military territories (AÏN-SEFRA, GHARDAÏA, TOUGGOURT, and SAHARAN OASES) centrally administered from Algiers, with 4 military commandants (residing at Colomb-Béchar, Laghouat, Touggourt, and Ouargla respectively) responsible directly to governor-general of Algeria. Established 1902, Southern Territories are to be incorporated into N Algeria's 3 depts. The Ghat-Serdèles area of the Fezzan was temporarily joined to Southern Territories in 1945.

Southern Territories, Fr. *Territoires du Sud*, military territory (□ c.17,800; 1946 pop. 210,695), S Tunisia, comprising that protectorate's Saharan region S of the shott depressions and of the Gulf of Gabès; ⊙ Médenine. Triangle-shaped with apex in S, territory is bounded by Tripolitania (E) and Algeria (W), and reaches the Fezzan at Ghadames (extreme S), whose area was placed (1948) under Tunisian administration.

Southern View, village (pop. 898), Sangamon co., central Ill., just S of Springfield, in agr. and bituminous-coal area.

South Esk River. 1 In Angus, Scotland, rises in the Grampians, flows 48 mi. SE and E, past Brechin, to North Sea at Montrose. 2 In Midlothian, Scotland: see ESK RIVER.

South Esk River, longest of Tasmania, rises in mts. N of Ben Lomond, flows 120 mi. SE, SW, and NW, past Fingal, Evandale, and Longford, to Launceston, here joining North Esk R. to form Tamar R. Receives Lake R. and its tributary Macquarie R. (73 mi. long) on left.

South Essex, Mass.: see ESSEX.

South Euclid (ū'klĭd), city (pop. 15,432), Cuyahoga co., N Ohio, a NE residential suburb of Cleveland. Seat of Notre Dame Col. Inc. as village in 1917; became city after 1940.

Southey (sou'thē), village (pop. 334), S Sask., 35 mi. N of Regina; wheat.

South Fabius River, Mo.: see FABIUS RIVER.

South Fairbanks, S suburb (pop. 63) of Fairbanks, Alaska.

South Fallsburg or **South Fallsburgh,** resort village (pop. 1,147), Sullivan co., SE N.Y., 5 mi. NE of Monticello.

South Fayetteville (fā'ŭtvĭl), village (pop. 3,428), Cumberland co., S central N.C., near Fayetteville.

South Featherstone, England: see FEATHERSTONE.

Southfield, Mass.: see NEW MARLBORO.

Southfields, village, Orange co., SE N.Y., on Ramapo R. and 9 mi. NNW of Suffern; mfg. of hosp. equipment. Bear Mtn. recreational area is just E.

Southfleet, agr. village and parish (pop. 1,216), NW Kent, England, 3 mi. SW of Gravesend; fruitgrowing. Has 15th-cent. church.

South Flomaton (flō'mŭtŭn), town (pop. 395), Escambia co., extreme NW Fla.

South Floral Park, residential village (pop. 572), Nassau co., SE N.Y., on W Long Isl., just S of Floral Park. Until 1931, called Jamaica Square.

Southford, Conn.: see SOUTHBURY.

South Foreland, promontory, E Kent, England, on the Strait of Dover; 3 mi. ENE of Dover, at S end of The Downs roadstead; 51°8'N 1°22'E. Site of 2 lighthouses, one of which was 1st to use electricity (1858). Adjacent sea lane was under Ger. long-range artillery fire (1940–44) in Second World War.

South Fork, village (pop. estimate 100), SW Sask., in the Cypress Hills, 15 mi. W of Shaunavon; alt. 3,011 ft.; coal mining.

South Fork, borough (pop. 2,616), Cambria co., SW central Pa., 7 mi. ENE of Johnstown and on Conemaugh R. Break in dam near here, 1889, caused Johnstown flood.

South Fork, for river names beginning thus and not found here, see the article on the main stream.

South Fork Cumberland River, N Tenn. and S Ky., formed in Scott co., Tenn., by confluence of several headstreams; flows 77 mi. N into McCreary co., Ky., to Cumberland R. at Burnside. Sometimes known as Big South Fork.

South Fork Owyhee River (ōwī'ē, ōwī'hē), in Nev., Idaho, and Oregon, rises in NW corner of Elko co., N Nev., flows c.140 mi. generally NW, through SW corner of Idaho, into Malheur co., SE Oregon, where it joins N.Fork and Middle Fork (small affluents rising in Idaho) to form Owyhee R. Longest tributary is East Fork Owyhee R.

South Fork Range, Calif.: see KLAMATH MOUNTAINS.

South Fork Republican River, Colo., Kansas, and Nebr., rises in Kit Carson co., E Colo., flows 151 mi. ENE, past St. Francis, NW Kansas, to Republican R. at Benkelman, S Nebr. Dam (building begun 1948) in E Colo. near Kansas line.

South Fork White River, S S.Dak., rises in Shannon co., flows c.156 mi. E then NNE to White R. near town of White River.

South Fort Mitchell, residential town (pop. 3,142), Kenton co., N Ky., SW of Covington, within Cincinnati metropolitan dist. Inc. 1927.

South Fort Smith, village (1940 pop. 4,285), Sebastian co., W Ark., suburb 5 mi. S of Fort Smith.

South Fox Island, Mich.: see FOX ISLANDS.

South Fulton (fŏŏl'tŭn), city (pop. 2,119), Obion co., NW Tenn., on Ky. line adjacent to FULTON, Ky.; dairying.

South Gamboa (găm̆bō'ŭ), Sp. *Gamboa Sur* (gämbō'ä sŏŏr'), village (pop. 200), Balboa dist., central Panama Canal Zone, on Chagres R., on transisthmian railroad, and 15 mi. NW of Panama city, in jungle country. Prison. Oranges, livestock.

South Gardiner, Maine: see GARDINER.

South Gastonia (găstō'nēŭ), village (pop. 6,465), Gaston co., S N.C., 3 mi. S of Gastonia. Post office name, Pinkney.

Southgate, residential municipal borough (1931 pop. 55,577; 1951 census 73,376), Middlesex, England, N suburb of London.

South Gate, city (pop. 51,116), Los Angeles co., S Calif., suburb 7 mi. S of downtown Los Angeles, in industrial dist.; mfg. (furniture, building materials, tires, machinery, paper products, paint, chemicals, tile). Inc. 1923.

Southgate, town (pop. 1,903), Campbell co., N Ky., near the Ohio, just S of Newport, within Cincinnati metropolitan dist.; food processing.

South Georgia, mountainous, barren island (□ 1,450; c.100 mi. long, 20 mi. wide) in the South Atlantic, c.800 mi. E of Falkland Isls. and c.1,200 mi. E of Cape Horn; 54°30'S 37°W. Bleak antarctic climate (mean annual temp. c.35°F.); snow-covered most of the year. Whaling is its important industry, and there are several whaling stations, but Grytviken (grüt'vēkŭn), its only village, holds most of pop., which reaches c.700 during summer whaling season, c.250 at other periods. Whale and seal oil and tallow are exported. Capt. James Cook claimed it in 1775 for Great Britain, in whose Falkland Island Dependencies it lies. Sir Ernest Shackleton, the explorer, is buried here.

South Gifford, town (pop. 128), Macon co., N central Mo., on Chariton R. and 22 mi. NNW of Macon.

South Glastonbury, Conn.: see GLASTONBURY.

South Glens Falls, village (pop. 3,645), Saratoga co., E N.Y., on the Hudson (bridged), opposite Glens Falls; mfg. (clothing, textiles, paper). Inc. 1895.

South Gobi (gō'bē), Mongol *Umuni Gobi* or *Ömönö Gobi* (both: ŭ'mŭnē), aimak (□ 61,150; pop. 30,000), S Mongolian People's Republic; ⊙ Dalan Dzadagad. Bounded S by China's Ningsia and Suiyuan provs., it lies in the Gobi desert and is the most sparsely settled part of Mongolia. Oil-shale deposits.

South Gorin (gôr'ĭn), town (pop. 303), Scotland co., NE Mo., near North Fabius R., 10 mi. SE of Memphis, just S of Gorin.

South Grafton, municipality (pop. 3,742), NE New South Wales, Australia, 160 mi. S of Brisbane and on S shore of Clarence R., opposite Grafton; dairying center; bananas, timber.

South Grand River, W Mo., rises 30 mi. S of Kansas City, flows c.125 mi. SE to a W arm of L. of the Ozarks in Benton co.

South Greenfield, town (pop. 186), Dade co., SW Mo., on branch of Sac R. just S of Greenfield.

South Greensburg, borough (pop. 2,980), Westmoreland co., SW central Pa., just S of Greensburg; metal products. Inc. 1891.

South Greenwood, village (pop. 3,712), Greenwood co., W S.C., 2 mi. S of Greenwood.

South Groveton, town (1940 pop. 619), Trinity co., E Texas, c.30 mi. SW of Lufkin, near Groveton, in lumber, agr. area.

South Hadley, town (pop. 10,145), Hampshire co., S Mass., on Connecticut R. and 12 mi. N of Springfield, near Holyoke Range; bricks, dairy products, paper. Seat of Mount Holyoke Col. Settled c.1660, set off from Hadley 1753. Includes industrial village (pop. 2,446) of South Hadley Falls (water power).

South Hamgyong (häm'gyông'), Jap. *Kankyonando*, Korean *Hamgyong-namdo*, largest province [Jap. and Korean *do*] (□ 12,192; 1944 pop. 2,014,388) of Korea, bounded E by E.Korea Bay, N by Yalu R. (on border of Antung prov., Manchuria); ⊙ HAMHUNG. Chief port is WONSAN. Interior is extremely mountainous, rising to c.8,000 ft., and drained by Changjin and Puchon rivers. Agr. is largely confined to narrow coastal area: soy beans, millet, hemp, tobacco. Principal industry is mining (gold, coal, iron, tungsten, and graphite). Fishing and stock raising are also important. Principal center is industrial HUNGNAM.

South Hampton. 1 Town (pop. 314), Rockingham co., SE N.H., 18 mi. SW of Portsmouth, on Mass. line. 2 or **Southampton,** suburb (pop. 5,924, with near-by North Hampton) of Hampton, Elizabeth City co., SE Va.

South Hangay, Mongolia: see SOUTH KHANGAI.

South Harriman, village (pop. 2,761), Roane co., E Tenn.

South Harwich, Mass.: see HARWICH.

South Haven. 1 City (pop. 358), Sumner co., S Kansas, on small affluent of Chikaskia R. and 14 mi. S of Wellington; wheat. 2 Resort city (pop. 5,629), Van Buren co., SW Mich., 21 mi. NNE of Benton Harbor, on L. Michigan at mouth of Black R.; has sand beach. Port of entry; supply center for resort and fruitgrowing area; mfg. (pianos, organs, auto parts, wood and building products, baskets, canned goods); fisheries. Mich. State Col. maintains a horticultural experiment station here. Settled before 1840; inc. as village 1869, as city 1902. 3 Resort village (pop. 305), Wright co., S central Minn., near Clearwater L., c.50 mi. WNW of Minneapolis; corn, oats, barley, livestock, poultry.

South Hayling, town and parish (pop. 3,254), SE Hampshire, England, at S end of Hayling Isl., on the Channel, 5 mi. E of Portsmouth; agr. market and seaside resort. Has 13th-cent. church.

South Head, promontory, W N.F., on S side of entrance of the Bay of Islands, 25 mi. NW of Corner Brook; 49°9'N 58°23'W; lighthouse.

South Heights, borough (pop. 691), Beaver co., W Pa., on Ohio R. opposite Ambridge.

South Helgeland, Norway: see HELGELAND.

South Hero, town (pop. 567), Grand Isle co., NW Vt., on S end of Grand Isle, in L. Champlain, and 16 mi. SW of St. Albans; orchards; bridge to Vt. mainland here.

South Hill, town (pop. 2,153), Mecklenburg co., S Va., 55 mi. SW of Petersburg; an important tobacco and cotton market; textile milling. Inc. 1901.

South Hills, town (pop. 412), Kenton co., extreme N Ky.

South Hingham, Mass.: see HINGHAM.

South Holland, Du. *Zuidholland* (zoit'hō'länt), province (□ 1,085; pop. 2,284,080), W Netherlands; ⊙ The Hague. Bounded by North Sea (W), North Holland prov. (N), Utrecht prov. (E), North Brabant prov. (SE), the Krammer (SW). Low-lying, with fertile soil; protected by dunes along North Sea coast. Drained by Old Rhine, Hollandsche Ijssel, Lek, Upper Merwede, Lower Merwede, and New Merwede rivers. Prov. includes isls. of Ijsselmonde, Voorne, Putten, Beijerland, Goeree, and Overflakkee. Agr. centers in N (flower bulbs), in Westland, bet. The Hague and Hook of Holland (grapes, peaches, potatoes), and on Ijsselmonde isl. (vegetables); shipbuilding, machine mfg., various other mfg. industries, mainly concentrated in Rotterdam and Dordrecht areas. Main towns: The Hague, Rotterdam, Dordrecht, Gorinchem, Gouda, Leiden. Formed 1840 by division of Holland into North Holland and South Holland.

South Holland, village (pop. 3,247), Cook co., NE Ill., S suburb of Chicago; trade and shipping center for truck-growing region. Settled by Dutch in 1840; inc. 1894.

South Holston Dam, Tenn.: see HOLSTON RIVER.

South Houston (hū'stŭn), town (pop. 4,126), Harris co., S Texas, SE suburb of Houston, absorbed 1948 by Houston.

South Hsenwi (shăn'wē), S state (sawbwaship) (□ 2,351; pop. 82,672), Northern Shan State, Upper Burma, E of Salween R.; ⊙ Mongyai. Broken, hilly country and rolling downs (E) bisected by mtn. range (8,777 ft.). Drained by the Nam Pang. Tobacco, opium, garden crops; cattle breeding. Served by Lashio-Loilem road. Pop.: Shans, Kachins, Chinese.

South Hsingan (shĭng'än'), former province (□ 29,680; 1940 pop. 1,026,635) of Manchukuo; ⊙ was Wangyehmiao (present Ulan Hoto). Until 1932 in Liaoning, it was formed 1934 out of Hsingan prov.; it was inc. 1946 into Liaopeh prov. and 1949 into the Inner Mongolian Autonomous Region. Contained Mongolian Khingan (N) and Jerim (S) leagues.

South Huntington, village (pop. 1,274), Suffolk co., SE N.Y.

South Hutchinson, city (pop. 1,045), Reno co., S central Kansas, on right bank of Arkansas R., opposite Hutchinson.

South Hylton (hĭl'-), town in Ford parish (pop. 3,056), NE Durham, England, on Wear R. and 2 mi. W of Sunderland; paper milling, iron casting.

Southill, agr. village and parish (pop. 1,105), E central Bedford, England, 3 mi. SW of Biggleswade. Has 14th-cent. church.

Southington (sŭ'dhĭngtŭn), town (pop. 13,061), including Southington village (pop. 5,955), Hartford co., central Conn., on Quinnipiac R. and 8 mi. NE of Waterbury; mfg. (hardware, metal products, tools; airplane, automobile, and radio parts; furniture, lumber, paper boxes); agr. (fruit, dairy products, poultry). Includes mfg. villages of Milldale (1940 pop. 521) and Plantsville (pop. 1,536). Settled 1696, inc. 1779.

South International Falls, village (pop. 1,840), S suburb of International Falls, Koochiching co., N Minn.; grain, potatoes.

South Invercargill (ĭn"vûrkär'gĭl), borough (pop. 1,161), S S.Isl., New Zealand; residential suburb of Invercargill.

South Island (□ 58,093; pop. 556,006), NEW ZEALAND, the larger of its 2 main isls.; separated from N.Isl. by Cook Strait, and from Stewart Isl. by Foveaux Strait; 480 mi. from Cape Farewell (N) to Bluff (S), 210 mi. wide. W central mtn. range (S.Alps) contains Mt. Cook (12,349 ft.), highest peak of New Zealand. Largest river of isl. is Clutha R. Otira tunnel connects railroad bet. E and W coasts. Many sounds and mts. in Fiordland Natl. Park (SW); glaciers and lakes in Arthur Pass and Tasman natl. parks in S.Alps. Fertile plains in coastal areas. Coal and gold mines in W; grain belt in E. Chief ports are Lyttelton, near Christchurch on E coast, and Bluff, near Invercargill in S. Chief centers: Christchurch, Dunedin. Isl. is divided into provincial dists. of MARLBOROUGH, NELSON, WESTLAND, CANTERBURY, OTAGO. Formerly called Middle Isl.

South Island, S.C.: see WINYAH BAY.

South Jacksonville. 1 Community, Fla.: see JACKSONVILLE. **2** Village (pop. 1,165), Morgan co., W central Ill., adjacent to Jacksonville.

South Jamesport, village (pop. c.300), Suffolk co., SE N.Y., on NE peninsula of Long Isl., on Great Peconic Bay, 4 mi. E of Riverhead, in summer-resort area.

South Jordan, town (pop. 1,048), Salt Lake co., N central Utah, 12 mi. NNW of Lehi. Inc. 1935.

South Jutland, Denmark: see JUTLAND.

South Kanara (kä'nŭrŭ), district (□ 4,045; pop. 1,523,516), W Madras, India; ⊙ Mangalore. Lies bet. Western Ghats (E) and Malabar Coast of Arabian Sea (W). Agr.: rice (over 80% of cultivated area), coconuts, areca nuts, mangoes, cashew nuts, sugar cane. Timber (teak, blackwood) in the Ghats (pepper plantations). Kaolin-clay pits (largely along upper course of Netravati R.) supply numerous tileworks (mainly at Mangalore). Chief towns: Mangalore, Udipi, Kasaragod. Formed part of Kanara dist. of Madras presidency until 1864, when dist. was divided to form Kanara dist. of Bombay presidency and South Kanara dist. of Madras presidency. Dist. administration includes Amin Divi Isls. (N group of the Laccadives). Formerly spelled South Canara.

South Kazakhstan (kä"zäkstän'), Rus. *Yuzhno-Kazakhstan*, oblast (□ 61,500; 1946 pop. estimate 700,000), S Kazakh SSR; ⊙ Chimkent. Drained by the Syr Darya and Arys R.; includes range Kara-Tau (NE) and desert Kyzyl-Kum (SE). Chief cotton region of Kazakh SSR: cotton ginning at Turkestan, Chimkent, Saryagach, Ilich. Extensive lead-zinc mines at Achisai and Kantagi in the Kara-Tau (lead works at Chimkent); lignite mines (Lenger). Sheep raising in deserts (SW and N). Trans-Caspian RR and Turksib RR join at Arys. Pop.: Kazakhs, Uzbeks, Russians. Formed 1932.

South Kensington, London, England: see KENSINGTON.

South Kent, Conn.: see KENT.

South Khangai or **South Hangay** (both: khäng'gī), Mongolian *Ubur Khangai* or *Öbör Hangay* (ŭ'bûr), aimak (□ 27,000; pop. 65,000), central Mongolian People's Republic; ⊙ Arbai Khere. Situated on SE slopes of Khangai Mts., the aimak is traversed by the Ongin Gol and extends from the forested mtn. slopes (N) to the Gobi desert (S). Has high livestock density.

South Killingholme Haven, England: see IMMINGHAM.

South Killingly, Conn.: see KILLINGLY.

South Kingstown (kĭng'stŭn, kĭngz'toun"), town (pop. 10,148), ⊙ Washington co., S R.I., 26 mi. SSW of Providence and on Block Isl. Sound; textile milling, agr. (potatoes, corn). Includes villages of KINGSTON (seat of R.I. State Col.), WAKEFIELD, Green Hill, Matunuck (mŭtōō'nŭk) (resort), West Kingston, PEACE DALE, Perryville, and part of USQUEPAUG. Settled 1641, inc. 1674 as Kingstown, divided (1723) into North Kingstown and South Kingstown. Narragansett Indians made final stand (1675) at Great Swamp near Kingston.

South Koel River (kō'ăl), S Bihar and N Orissa, India, rises on Chota Nagpur Plateau W of Ranchi, flows c.200 mi. W, generally S, and W, joining Sankh R. 14 mi. ENE of Raj Gangpur to form Brahmani R.

South Kyongsang (kyŭng'säng'), Korean *Kyongsang-namdo*, Jap. *Keisho-nando*, province [Jap. and Korean *do*] (□ 4,751; 1949 pop. 3,134,829), S Korea, bounded S by Korea Strait and SW by Somjin R.; ⊙ PUSAN, major port. Partly mountainous, with wide plains drained by Naktong R. Agr. (rice, barley, soy beans, fruit) and fishing are important. There are salt fields along the coast, and scattered gold mines in central area. Paper making, weaving, and metal-working in many towns. Principal centers are Pusan (industrial), MASAN, CHINJU; a naval base is at CHINHAE.

South Lancaster, Mass.: see LANCASTER.

South Lancing, town in parish of Lancing (pop. 4,498), S Sussex, England, on the Channel, 3 mi. ENE of Worthing; seaside resort, with large railroad shops. Just N is town of North Lancing, site of Lancing Col., a public school founded 1849.

Southland, land district, New Zealand: see OTAGO.

Southland, county, New Zealand: see INVERCARGILL.

Southland. 1 Village (pop. 2,425, with adjacent Woodland), Jackson co., S Mich. **2** Town (pop. 210), Garza co., NW Texas, 20 mi. SE of Lubbock; shipping point in cattle and agr. area.

South Langhorne, Pa.: see PENNDEL.

South La Porte, village (pop. 2,285), La Porte co., NW Ind.

South Lebanon (lĕ'bŭnŭn), village (pop. 1,291), Warren co., SW Ohio, 24 mi. NE of Cincinnati and on Little Miami R.; chemicals.

South Lee, Mass.: see LEE.

South Lineville, town (pop. 92), Mercer co., N Mo., near Weldon R., 13 mi. NNE of Princeton.

South Lockport, village (pop. 3,291, with adjacent Fairmont), Will co., NE Ill., near Lockport.

South Loup River, Nebr.: see LOUP RIVER.

South Lowestoft, England: see LOWESTOFT.

South Lyon, city (pop. 1,312), Oakland co., SE Mich., 13 mi. NNE of Ann Arbor, in farm area (potatoes, grain, hay); mfg. of steel tubing. Inc. as village 1873, as city 1930.

South Manchester, Conn.: see MANCHESTER.

South Manchuria Railroad, name of S Manchurian trunk line bet. Changchun and Dairen, originally part of the CHINESE EASTERN RAILROAD, but acquired by Japan after Russo-Japanese War (1904–5). Following Second World War, the entire Manchurian rail system, renamed Chinese Changchun RR, passed to joint Soviet-Chinese control.

South Manistique Lake, Mich.: see MANISTIQUE LAKE.

South Manitou Island, Mich.: see MANITOU ISLANDS.

South Mansfield, village (pop. 276), De Soto parish, NW La., just S of Mansfield, in agr., oil, and timber area.

South Marsh Island, low, marshy isl. (c.5 mi. long, 3 mi. wide), Somerset co., SE Md., in Chesapeake Bay, 12 mi. NW of Crisfield, across Tangier Sound; oystering.

South Medford, village (pop. 1,226), Jackson co., SW Oregon, a suburb of Medford.

South Melbourne (mĕl'bûrn), municipality (pop. 43,452), S Victoria, Australia, on S bank of Yarra R., opposite Melbourne, in metropolitan area; industrial center; automobile plants, steel and lead products, chemicals.

South Miami (mīă'mē), city (pop. 4,809), Dade co., S Fla., suburb of Miami; packs truck produce, citrus fruit. Inc. 1926.

South Mills, town (1940 pop. 479), Camden co., NE N.C., 11 mi. NNW of Elizabeth City, on Dismal Swamp Canal; sawmilling.

South Milwaukee (mĭlwô'kē), industrial city (pop. 12,855), Milwaukee co., SE Wis., on L. Michigan, 10 mi. S of Milwaukee; iron castings, excavating machinery, electrical equipment, glue, tile; wood, leather, and metal products. Settled 1835, platted 1891, inc. 1897.

South Mimms. 1 Suburb, Hertford, England: see BARNET. **2** Village, Middlesex, England: see POTTERS BAR.

Southminster, village, W Sask., on Alta. border, 5 mi. SSE of Lloydminster; alt. 2,086 ft.; oil and natural-gas production.

South Modesto (mōdĕ'stō), village (pop. 4,672, with adjacent River Road), Stanislaus co., central Calif., near Modesto.

South Molton (mōl'-), municipal borough (1931 pop. 2,832; 1951 census 3,125), N Devon, England, 11 mi. ESE of Barnstaple; agr. market; tanneries, mfg. of agr. implements, biscuits. Has 15th-cent. church.

South Monroe, village (pop. 2,275), Monroe co., SE Mich., near Monroe.

Southmont, borough (pop. 2,278), Cambria co., SW central Pa., adjoining SW Johnstown.

South Mountain, in S Pa. and NW Md., northernmost section of the BLUE RIDGE; begins in region SE of Carlisle, Pa., extends c.65 mi. SW, across Md., and into N Va., where S tip (here called Short Hills) overlaps Va. section of Blue Ridge. Near Harpers Ferry, W.Va., the Potomac flows in gap through range. Lowest (c.1,000 ft.) in S; rises to 2,145 ft. at Quirauk Mtn. (kwĭ'rôk), just S of Md. line. In Md., South Mtn. splits into 2 prongs embracing Middletown Valley; E prong is Catoctin Mtn. (kŭtŏk'tĭn). Yields quartz, manganese-iron ore, sandstone, dolomite, clay. Civil War battle of South Mtn., fought near Burkittsville, Md., Sept. 14, 1862, was a victory for McClellan over Lee's rear guard of Confederates.

South Mount Vernon, village (pop. 1,322), Knox co., central Ohio.

South Nahanni River, SW Mackenzie Dist., Northwest Territories, rises in mts. on Yukon line, flows c.250 mi. SE to Liard R.; Virginia Falls (316 ft.) are on it.

South Naknek (năk'nĕk), village (1939 pop. 134), S Alaska, on Alaska Peninsula, on Naknek R., near its mouth on Bristol Bay, opposite Naknek; fishing, fish processing; supply point for trappers.

South Natick, Mass.: see NATICK.

South Natuna Islands (nŭtōō'nŭ), Du. *Zuid Natoena Islands* (zoit), group (pop. 2,805), Natuna Isls., Indonesia, in S.China Sea, near Cape Datu of W Borneo; 2°31'N 109°2'E. Comprise 2 low-lying isls. surrounded by many islets. The main isls. are Subi Besar or Soebi Besar (both: sōō'bē bŭsär'; 12 mi. long, 5 mi. wide) and Serasan (10 mi. long, 4 mi. wide). Chief products: timber, coconuts, mother-of-pearl, trepang.

South Negril Point (nĭgrĭl', nē–), westernmost cape of Jamaica, 33 mi. WSW of Montego Bay; 18°16'N 78°23'W. The minor port Negril is just N. North Negril Point is 6 mi. N.

South Nelson, village (pop. estimate c.500), NE N.B., on Miramichi R., opposite Newcastle; lumber-shipping port.

South New Castle, borough (pop. 993), Lawrence co., W Pa., on Beaver R. adjacent to New Castle.

South Norfolk (nôr'fŭk), city (pop. 10,434), in but independent of Norfolk co., SE Va., along branches of Elizabeth R., adjoining NORFOLK (N); lumber milling. Limestone deposits near by. Inc. 1921.

South Normanton (nôr'mŭntŭn), town and parish (pop. 6,988), E Derby, England, 2 mi. ENE of Alfreton; coal mining. Has Norman church, rebuilt in 14th cent.

South Norwalk, Conn.: see NORWALK.

South Norwood, England: see CROYDON.

South Nyack (nī'ăk"), residential suburban village (pop. 3,102), Rockland co., SE N.Y., on W bank of the Hudson, just S of Nyack. A state park is near by. Inc. 1878.

South Ogden (ŏg'dŭn), town (pop. 3,763), Weber co., N Utah, just S of Ogden; alt. 4,300 ft. Settled 1848 by Mormons. Inc. 1936.

Southold (south'hōld, sou'thōld), summer-resort village (pop. 1,027), Suffolk co., SE N.Y., on N peninsula of E Long Isl., 16 mi. NE of Riverhead, in agr. area (potatoes, truck); boat yards.

South Orange, residential village (pop. 15,230), Essex co., NE N.J., 5 mi. W of Newark; some mfg.

(toilet preparations, concrete products, plastics, radio parts, metal products); stone quarries. Seton Hall Col. (1856) here. Inc. 1869.

South Orkney Islands (ôrk'nē), Sp. *Islas Orcades del Sur* (ēs'läs ôrkä'dās dĕl sōōr'), group (□ c.400) in the South Atlantic, NE of Palmer Peninsula (Antarctica), c.850 mi. ESE of Cape Horn and c.450 mi. SW of South Georgia; 60°15'–60°55'S 44°20'–46°45'W. Consist of 2 large isls. (Coronation and Laurie), 2 smaller isls. (Powell, Signy), and a number of surrounding rocks (such as the Inaccessible Isls.). Barren and antarctic in character, they were discovered 1821 jointly by George Powell (British) and Nathaniel Palmer (American). Claimed by Great Britain as part of its Falkland Island Dependencies, but Argentina, too, claims them and maintains a meteorological and wireless station on Laurie Isl. Also called Powell Isls.

South Orleans, Mass.: see ORLEANS.

South Oromocto Lake (ôrŏmŏk'tō) (□ 3.6; 4 mi. long), SW N.B., 28 mi. WNW of St. John.

South Ossetian Autonomous Oblast (ŏsē'shŭn), Rus. *Yugo-Osetinskaya Avtonomnaya Oblast*, administrative division (□ 1,500; 1946 pop. estimate 116,000) of N Georgian SSR, on S slopes of the central Greater Caucasus; ⊙ Stalinir. Adjoins North Ossetian Autonomous SSR. Pop. (70% Ossetian, 25% Georgian), engaged primarily in livestock raising (goats, sheep) and lumbering (N), orchard and grain agr. (S). Metal- and woodworking, dairying at Stalinir. Tourist area (mineral springs at Dzhava). Formed 1922 as separate political administrative unit for Ossetian minority.

Southowram, former urban district (1931 pop. 2,570), West Riding, S Yorkshire, England, SE suburb of Halifax; woolen milling. Inc. 1937 in Brighouse.

South Pagi, Indonesia: see PAGI ISLANDS.

South Paris, Maine: see PARIS.

South Park. 1 Village (pop. 1,837), Sonoma co., W Calif. **2** Village (pop. 2,063), Kane co., NE Ill. **3** Village (pop. 2,391), St. Clair co., E Mich., near Port Huron.

South Parkersburg, village (pop. 10,808), Wood co., W W.Va., on Little Kanawha R. opposite Parkersburg.

South Pasadena (păsudē'nù), residential city (pop. 16,935), Los Angeles co., S Calif., bet. Pasadena and Los Angeles. Citrus-fruit orchards; lion, alligator, ostrich farms. Light mfg. Inc. 1888.

South Pass, La.: see MISSISSIPPI RIVER.

South Pass (c.7,550 ft.), W central Wyo., in Wind River Range of Rocky Mts., 35 mi. SSW of Lander. Broad, level valley, now crossed by road; formed important unit in Oregon Trail; used by pioneers moving W across Continental Divide.

South Pass City, village (pop. c.50), Fremont co., W central Wyo., in foothills of Wind River Range, 26 mi. S of Lander; alt. 7,805 ft. Gold dredging. Now a ghost town; in 1870 center of gold-mining dist., with pop. of c.4,000.

South Pekin (pē'kĭn), village (pop. 1,043), Tazewell co., central Ill., 4 mi. S of Pekin. Inc. 1917.

South Petherton, town and parish (pop. 1,983), SE Somerset, England, 5 mi. ENE of Ilminster; agr. market. Its church is Norman to 15th cent.

South Philipsburg, borough (pop. 512), Centre co., central Pa., just S of Philipsburg.

South Pittsburg, town (pop. 2,573), Marion co., S Tenn., on the Tennessee and 22 mi. W of Chattanooga, in timber, coal-mining, agr. area; mfg. of hosiery, cooking utensils, wood products, cement.

South Plainfield, residential borough (pop. 8,008), Middlesex co., NE N.J., adjacent to Plainfield. Inc. 1926.

South Plains, Texas: see LLANO ESTACADO.

South Platte River (plăt), in Colo. and Nebr., formed by confluence of several branches E of Leadville, central Colo., in Rocky Mts., flows E then NNE, through narrow canyon, passes Denver, where it receives Cherry Creek, turns E near Greeley, crossing NE Colorado, and joins North Platte R., at city of North Platte, central Nebr., to form Platte R.; 450 mi. long. CHEESMAN DAM and ELEVEN MILE RESERVOIR are in upper course. Part of river basin is privately irrigated. Most of Colo. section is served by Colorado–Big Thompson project. Similar project for Blue and South Platte rivers has been planned. On CHERRY CREEK is a dam. These and other developments are part of comprehensive Missouri R. Basin plan for flood control, irrigation, and power.

South Pleasureville or **Pleasureville,** town (pop. 355), Henry and Shelby counties, N Ky., 26 mi. ENE of Louisville, in Bluegrass agr. region. Renamed South Pleasureville after 1930; still often called Pleasureville.

South Point, village (pop. 804), Lawrence co., S Ohio, on Ohio R., opposite Catlettsburg (Ky.), and 9 mi. SE of Ironton; makes chemicals.

South Pole, S end of earth's axis, at lat. 90°S, long. 0°, in ANTARCTICA. The S magnetic pole is on George V Coast at 70°S 148°E. The South Pole was 1st reached (Dec. 14, 1911) by Roald Amundsen, followed by Scott (a month later) and by Byrd (1929).

South Pomfret, Vt.: see POMFRET.

South Porcupine, town (pop. estimate 6,000), NE Ont., on Porcupine L., 7 mi. E of Timmins; gold and barite mining center.

Southport, town (pop. 8,430), SE Queensland, Australia, 40 mi. SSE of Brisbane, at southernmost end of Moreton Bay; seaside resort.

Southport, county borough (1931 pop. 78,925; 1951 census 84,057), W Lancashire, England, on Irish Sea and 17 mi. N of Liverpool; seaside resort; also mfg. of leather goods, hosiery and knitted textiles, machine tools; metallurgy. Has mile-long pier, observatory, and several technical and art schools.

Southport. 1 Village, Conn.: see FAIRFIELD, town. **2** Town (pop. 730), Marion co., central Ind., 9 mi. S of Indianapolis. **3** Village (1940 pop. 1,266), SE La., on Jefferson-Orleans parish line, a W suburb of New Orleans. **4** Fishing and resort town (pop. 435), Lincoln co., SW Maine, on isl. just S of Boothbay and 10 mi. SE of Bath; includes Squirrel Isl. resort community. **5** Resort city (pop. 1,748), ⊙ Brunswick co., S N.C., 22 mi. SSW of Wilmington, on Atlantic coast, at Cape Fear R. mouth; shrimp fisheries. Fort Johnston (built 1764, destroyed 1776, rebuilt after 1794) is preserved. Founded 1792.

South Portland, residential city (pop. 21,866), Cumberland co., SW Maine, on Casco Bay and across Fore R. from Portland. Shipyards, foundries, marine-hardware plants. Site of U.S. Fort Preble. Set off from Cape Elizabeth 1895, chartered as city 1898.

South Portsmouth (pôrts'mŭth), village (1940 pop. 846), Greenup co., NE Ky., on left bank (levee) of the Ohio (toll bridge here) opposite Portsmouth, Ohio, in agr. area. On site of Lower Town, 1st white village in Ky.; established by Fr. traders with help of Shawnee Indians in early-18th cent. and abandoned during French and Indian Wars.

South Pottstown, village (pop. 1,504), Chester co., SE Pa., near Pottstown.

South Prairie, town (pop. 207), Pierce co., W central Wash., 18 mi. SE of Tacoma, in agr. region.

South Pyongan (pyŏng'än'), Korean *Pyongannamdo*, Jap. *Heian-nando*, province [Jap. and Korean *do*] (□ 5,764; 1944 pop. 1,826,651), N Korea, bounded N by Chongchon R. and W by Korea Bay (arm of Yellow Sea); ⊙ PYONGYANG. Chief port is CHINNAMPO. The terrain is generally low, except for mountainous interior. Taedong R. drains large agr. area: millet, soy beans, fruit, and rice. There are extensive coal fields and several gold mines. Silk cocoons are produced in scattered areas. Stock raising and lumbering in interior.

South Queensferry, Scotland: see QUEENSFERRY.

South Raccoon River, Iowa: see RACCOON RIVER.

South Range, village (pop. 712), Houghton co., NW Upper Peninsula, Mich., 5 mi. SW of Houghton, on Keweenaw Peninsula; iron ore-shipping point; mfg. of cheese.

South Rangeley, Maine: see RANGELEY.

South Reddish, England: see REDDISH.

South Renovo (rĭnō'vū), borough (pop. 862), Clinton co., N central Pa., on West Branch of Susquehanna R. opposite Renovo.

South River, village (pop. 838), S Ont., on South R. and 33 mi. S of North Bay; lumbering.

South River, industrial borough (pop. 11,308), Middlesex co., E N.J., on South R. and 4 mi. SE of New Brunswick, in clay-, sand-producing region; mfg. (embroideries, bricks, clay products, handkerchiefs, cigars, soft drinks, meat products). Has municipal power plant. Settled 1720, inc. 1897.

South River. 1 In N central Ga., rises near Atlanta, flows c.50 mi. SE to LLOYD SHOALS RESERVOIR 8 mi. NE of Jackson. **2** In S central Iowa, rises in NW Clarke co., flows 53 mi. NE to Des Moines R. 16 mi. SE of Des Moines. **3** In E central N.J., rises in S Middlesex co., flows c.10 mi. NE and N, past Old Bridge and South River, to Raritan R. above Sayreville. **4** In SE N.C., rises near Angier, flows c.75 mi. generally SSE to Black R. 30 mi. NW of Wilmington. **5** In NW Va., rises in S Augusta co., flows c.50 mi. NE, joining North R. near Port Republic to form South Fork of Shenandoah River.

South River Peak (13,145 ft.), SW Colo., in San Juan Mts., 19 mi. S of Creede.

South Rockwood, village (1940 pop. 566), Monroe co., SE Mich., 12 mi. NNE of Monroe and on Huron R., near L. Erie. State park near by.

South Ronaldsay (rō'nùldsā), island (□ 23.5, including Burray, Hunda, Swona isls., and Pentland Skerries; pop. 1,303) of the Orkneys, Scotland, 6 mi. NNE of Duncansbay Head, Caithness, across Pentland Firth, and 4 mi. E of SE end of Hoy isl.; 8 mi. long, 5 mi. wide; rises to 389 ft. Widewall Bay provides good anchorage; on it is chief village of Widewall. Isl. is noted for its fertility.

South Roxton, village (pop. estimate 500), S Que., 10 mi. NE of Granby; woodworking, cigar mfg.

South Royalton, Vt.: see ROYALTON.

South Russell, village (pop. 349), Geauga co., NE Ohio, 19 mi. ESE of downtown Cleveland.

South Ryegate, Vt.: see RYEGATE.

South Saint Paul, city (pop. 15,909), Dakota co., E Minn., on Mississippi R. just S of St. Paul; livestock and industrial center with railroad repair shops; meat products, beverages, ice cream, leather goods. Has stockyards and foundries.

South Salem (sā'lùm), village (pop. 206), Ross co., S Ohio, 17 mi. W of Chillicothe.

South Salt Lake, residential town (pop. 7,704), Salt Lake co., N Utah; suburb of Salt Lake City. Inc. 1938.

South Sandia Peak, N.Mex.: see SANDIA MOUNTAINS.

South Sandisfield, Mass.: see SANDISFIELD.

South Sandwich Islands, group of small, volcanic, antarctic islets in the South Atlantic N of the Weddell Sea, c.450 mi. SE of South Georgia; 56°18'–59°25'S 26°15'W. Discovered 1775 by Capt. James Cook. Included in Br. Falkland Islands Dependencies.

South Sandwich Trench, submarine depression of South Atlantic Ocean, on convex side of South Sandwich Isls.; 55°S 26°W. Until 1929, the depth of 26,443 ft. (55°7'S 26°46'W) was the deepest sounding in the Antarctic Ocean. During 1930s, however, soundings reaching to 27,110 ft. were obtained off the South Sandwich group, and BYRD DEEP (28,152 ft.) off the Ross Sea was found to be the greatest depth in the Antarctic.

South San Francisco (săn frŭnsĭ'skō), industrial city (pop. 19,351), San Mateo co., W Calif., S suburb of San Francisco, from which it is separated by San Bruno Mts.; steel mills, metal smelters and refineries, foundries, lumberyards, meat-packing plants. San Francisco municipal airport is S. Inc. 1908.

South Santee River, S.C.: see SANTEE RIVER.

South Saskatchewan River, Canada: see SASKATCHEWAN RIVER.

Southsea, England: see PORTSMOUTH.

South Sea or **South Seas:** see PACIFIC OCEAN.

South Shaftsbury, Vt.: see SHAFTSBURY.

South Shetland Islands, antarctic archipelago (c.280 naut. mi. ENE–WSW) in the South Atlantic S of South America and just off N tip of Palmer Peninsula (Antarctica); 61°–63°S 54°–63°W. Consist of several isls. (e.g., Deception, Greenwich, King George, Elephant, Livingston, Smith) and a number of rocks. The isls., barren and snow-covered, had whaling activity, 1906–31, and have figured in Antarctic exploration. Discovered 1819 by Capt. William Smith and claimed for Great Britain, which includes them in its Falkland Island Dependencies. Argentina and Chile have challenged Britain's claim to the South Shetlands.

South Shields, county borough (1931 pop. 113,455; 1951 census 106,605), NE Durham, England, on Tyne R. estuary, on North Sea, and 8 mi. E of Newcastle-upon-Tyne; seaport; ships coal; produces metal products, chemicals, paint, glass, food products, and engages in fishing. On Lawe hill are remains of a Roman station. There are a marine school and 2 long piers. The principle of the life boat was evolved here in 1785 and 1st boat launched in 1790. North Shields is across the river in TYNEMOUTH. In county borough (S) is coal-mining town of Harton (pop. 8,480).

South Shore, town (pop. 269), Codington co., E S.Dak., 16 mi. NE of Watertown; livestock, dairy produce, poultry, grain.

South Siberian Railroad, major rail line in SW Siberia, USSR, parallel to Trans-Siberian RR. Begun in late 1930s in Akmolinsk-Magnitogorsk section, the railroad is planned to extend ultimately from the Kuibyshev area on the Volga, past Sterlitamak, Magnitogorsk, Akmolinsk, Pavlodar, Barnaul, Stalinsk, and Abakan, to a junction with Trans-Siberian RR at Taishet. All but the extreme W and E sections were near completion in 1951.

Southside, village (pop. 1,734, with adjacent Green Hills), Maury co., central Tenn.

Southside Place, city (pop. 1,263), Harris co., S Texas, SW suburb of Houston, absorbed 1948 by Houston.

South Sioux City (sōō), city (pop. 5,557), Dakota co., NE Nebr., on right bank of the Missouri opposite Sioux City, Iowa, in rich agr. region; dairy and truck produce, grain. Founded 1887.

South Sioux Falls (sōō), town (pop. 1,586), Minnehaha co., SE S.Dak., on Big Sioux R.; suburb of Sioux Falls.

South Solon (sō'lùn), village (pop. 414), Madison co., central Ohio, 13 mi. SW of London, in stock-raising and farming area.

South Stack, Wales: see HOLYHEAD.

South Standard, Ill.: see STANDARD CITY.

South Stradbroke Island, in Pacific Ocean off SE coast of Queensland, Australia, near Southport, just S of N.Stradbroke Isl.; forms SE shore of Moreton Bay; 14 mi. long, 1 mi. wide; sandy.

South Streator (strē'tùr), village (pop. 1,508), Livingston co., E central Ill., just S of Streator, in agr. and mineral area.

South Suburban, town (pop. 63,479), 24-Parganas dist., SE West Bengal, India, 4.5 mi. SSW of Calcutta city center; extensive rice milling; chemical and brick mfg. Formed 1901 by separation of Tollygunge (E) and Garden Reach (W). Main areas are Behala and Barisa. Also called South Suburbs.

South Sudbury, Mass.: see SUDBURY.

South Sulphur Island, Volcano Isls.: see MINAMI-IWO-JIMA.

South Superior, suburb (pop. 780) of Superior, Sweetwater co., SW Wyo.; alt. c.6,900 ft. Coal mines.
South Swansea, Mass.: see SWANSEA.
South Taft, Calif.: see TAFT.
South Tamworth, N.H.: see TAMWORTH.
South Taranaki Bight (tă″rŭnä′kē), Tasman Sea, W N.Isl., New Zealand, separated from N.Taranaki Bight by Cape Egmont. Hawera is near SE shore.
South Tawton, town and parish (pop. 1,182), central Devon, England, on Taw R. and 4 mi. E of Okehampton; agr. market. Has 15th-cent. church.
South Tent, peak (12,300 ft.) in Wasatch Plateau, central Utah, 17 mi. NE of Manti.
South Teton Wyo.: see GRAND TETON NATIONAL PARK.
South Texarkana (tĕk″särkă′nŭ), town (pop. 317), NE Texas.
South Thomaston, town (pop. 654), Knox co., S Maine, on Weskeag R. inlet and just S of Rockland; resorts, fishing. Includes Spruce Head village.
South Thompson River, B.C.: see THOMPSON RIVER.
South Tidworth, town and parish (pop. 4,358), NW Hampshire, England, 13 mi. NNE of Salisbury; agr. market, adjoining military training area of Tidworth, Wiltshire. Near by is an observatory (51°14′N 1°39′W).
South Toms River, borough (pop. 492), Ocean co., E N.J., on Toms R. opposite Toms River village.
South Torrington (tŏ′rĭngtŭn), industrial suburb (1940 pop. 930) of Torrington, Goshen co., SE Wyo., on N.Platte R.; beet-sugar refinery.
South Truro, Mass.: see TRURO.
South Tucson (tōō′sŏn, tōōsŏn′), city (pop. 2,364) and S suburb of Tucson, Pima co., SE Ariz. Inc. 1939.
South Turlock (tûr′lŏk), village (pop. 1,492), Stanislaus co., central Calif., near Turlock.
South Twin Lake (□ 14), central N.F., 20 mi. W of Botwood; 10 mi. long, 2 mi. wide; drains into Exploits R.
South Twin Mountain, N.H.: see FRANCONIA MOUNTAINS.
South Tyne River, England: see TYNE RIVER.
South Ubian Island (ōōbyän′) (□ 2.5; 1939 pop. 2,809; 1948 municipality pop., including near-by isls., 10,286), in Tawitawi Group, Sulu prov., Philippines, in Sulu Archipelago, E of Tawitawi Isl.
South Uist (yōō′ĭst, ōō′ĭst), island (pop. 2,810) and parish (□ 141; pop. 4,236, including surrounding small isls.), of the Outer Hebrides, Inverness, Scotland, bet. Benbecula (N) and Barra (S), W of Skye, from which it is separated by the Sea of the Hebrides. It is 21 mi. long, up to 8 mi. wide. E part is mountainous, chief elevations being Beinn Mhor (2,034 ft.) and Mt. Hecla (1,988 ft.). In a hut bet. the mts. Prince Charles Edward hid for some time in 1746. E coast is sharply indented; main inlets are Loch Eynort (E center) and Loch Boisdale (SE). Chief town is Lochboisdale, fishing port, with radio station, at head of Loch Boisdale. At Milton, 5 mi. NW of Lochboisdale, Flora Macdonald was b. Fishing and crofting are chief occupations. The term The Uists is sometimes used to include South and NORTH UIST and BENBECULA.
South Ukrainian Canal, canal project in S Ukraine, extending from Zaporozhe on the Dnieper, past Molochnaya R. (reservoir) and Askaniya-Nova to Sivash lagoon; continued by NORTH CRIMEAN CANAL. Begun 1951.
South Uniontown, village (pop. 3,425), Fayette co., SW Pa., near Uniontown.
South Vernon, Mass.: see NORTHFIELD.
South Victoria Land, Antarctica: see VICTORIA LAND.
South Vienna or **Vienna** (vēĕ′nŭ), village (pop. 424), Clark co., W central Ohio, 11 mi. E of Springfield, in agr. area.
South Vizagapatam, district, India: see VIZAGAPATAM, dist.
South Wadesboro, town (pop. 390), Anson co., S N.C., suburb of Wadesboro.
South Wareham, Mass.: see WAREHAM.
Southwark (sŭ′dhûrk, south′wûrk), residential metropolitan borough (1931 pop. 171,695; 1951 census 97,171) of London, England, on S bank of the Thames (here crossed by Blackfriars, Southwark, and London bridges), 1.5 mi. ESE of Charing Cross. Includes quarter of BANKSIDE (on the Thames). Southwark was wholly or partly annexed to London in 1327, and is still known as "the Borough." St. Saviour's Church or Southwark Cathedral was part of 11th-cent. Augustinian priory of St. Mary Overy; considerably restored in 19th cent.; contains tomb of the poet Gower and chapel in memory of John Harvard, b. in Southwark. Pilgrim Fathers' Memorial Church (1864) is on site of London's oldest Congregational church (founded 1616). In 16th and 17th cent. Southwark was amusement center, site of Globe Theater and other places associated with Shakespeare; it also had a number of famous inns, including the White Hart and Talbot or Tabard Inn. The 17th-cent. George Inn is now operated by National Trust. In borough is Guy's Hosp. (1721), with noted medical school. The large Barclay brewery is here. Clink and Marshalsea prisons were in Southwark. Heavy damage (especially to churches) resulted from air raids in 1940–41.
South Waukegan (wôkē′gŭn), village (pop. 2,830), Lake co., NE Ill., just S of Waukegan.
South Waverly, borough (pop. 1,298), Bradford co., NE Pa., near Chemung R., just below Waverly, N.Y. Inc. 1878.
South Wayne, village (pop. 328), Lafayette co., S Wis., near Pecatonica R., 12 mi. W of Monroe. in dairy-farming area; cheese, feed.
South Waziristan, W Pakistan: see WAZIRISTAN.
South Weald (wēld), residential town and parish (pop. 6,370), SW Essex, England, just W of Brentwood; site of county mental hosp.
South Weber, town (pop. 244), Davis co., N Utah, 6 mi. S of Ogden.
South Webster, village (pop. 663), Scioto co., S Ohio, 14 mi. ENE of Portsmouth, in agr. area; makes refractories.
Southwell (south′wŭl, sŭdh′ŭl), cathedral town and parish (pop. 2,991), central Nottingham, England, 6 mi. W of Newark. Its minster, begun c.1110, was raised to rank of cathedral in 1884. Remains of 14th-cent. palace of the archbishops of York are now incorporated into the palace of the bishop of Southwell. In 7th cent. Paulinus founded a church here. Byron stayed with his mother at Burgage Manor House. Southwell does some silk milling.
South Wellfleet, Mass.: see WELLFLEET.
South Wellington, village (pop. estimate 200), SW B.C., on SE Vancouver Isl., 5 mi. SSE of Nanaimo; coal mining.
Southwest, Cape, SW extremity of Axel Heiberg Isl., N Franklin Dist., on Norwegian Bay; 78°11′N 92°10′W.
South-West Africa, formerly German Southwest Africa, mandated territory (□ 317,725, excluding Walvis Bay enclave; pop. 384,627), SW Africa, bounded by U. of So. Afr. across Orange R. (S and SE), the Atlantic (W), Angola (N), Bechuanaland Protectorate (E); ⊙ Windhoek. Territory includes narrow strip of the CAPRIVI ZIPFEL, which extends E to Zambezi R.; WALVIS BAY enclave (□ 374; pop. 2,424) forms part of Cape Prov., U. of So. Afr., but is administered by South-West Africa. Territory is a plateau rising rapidly from arid coastal plain of the Namib Desert to c.2,500 ft. (S) and to c.5,000 ft. (N), where the Kaokoveld Mts. rise abruptly. Highest peak of territory is Brandberg mtn. (8,550 ft.). There are no important perennial streams; numerous dry river beds carry water only after heavy rains. In N and E part of country are numerous pans, shallow depressions without outlet; largest of the salt-water depressions is Etosha Pan (N; □ 1,404). Cattle and sheep raising and grain growing are chief agr. occupations; introduction of Karakul sheep from Bessarabia after First World War has been major asset to territory's economy. Minerals worked include copper, tin, gold, vanadium, lithium, cadmium, fluorspar, tantalite, corundum; near Lüderitz and at mouth of Orange R. are important diamond deposits; garnets are found near Swakopmund. Walvis Bay is territory's chief seaport; towns include Lüderitz, Keetmanshoop, Swakopmund, Gobabis, Otjiwarongo, Grootfontein, Rehoboth, Outjo. Native inhabitants include a variety of Bantu tribes, among them Namaquas, Hereros, Hottentots, Ovambos, Damaras. Entire S and central part of territory consists of the "Police Zone" (□ 210,505), reserved for European development, but comprising several reserves for native peoples; in urban areas natives are confined to segregated locations. In N third of territory European settlement is restricted; this region includes Ovamboland and several other large native reserves. In S is Great NAMAQUALAND. Bartholomew Diaz was 1st European to visit territory, landing at Lüderitz (Angra Pequena) in 1486. In late-18th cent. several explorers from the Cape crossed Orange R. and visited Herero tribes; Walvis Bay was annexed 1792 by Dutch. In early 19th cent. German missions were established in S part of territory. British annexed Walvis Bay 1878. German settlement established at Lüderitz, 1883; German Colonial Co. chartered 1885 with trading rights over greater part of present territory. In 1892 area became German colony as German Southwest Africa. Caprivi Zipfel was ceded by Great Britain 1893. The Hottentot tribes were conquered by the Hereros, who were defeated (1904–08) by German troops. Upon outbreak of First World War, Union forces occupied Lüderitz and Swakopmund; early in 1915 major campaign against Germans was led by General Louis Botha; Germans surrendered (July 9, 1915) at Korab and Union troops occupied entire territory. Under Treaty of Versailles (1919) South-West Africa was declared a League of Nations mandate of U. of So. Afr. Eastern Caprivi Zipfel was annexed 1939 by the U. of So. Afr., where a strong movement favored annexation of entire territory. After the Second World War, the U. of So. Afr., refusing to sign an agreement making South-West Africa a trust territory of the United Nations, ignored the U.N. and moved toward annexation of South-West Africa.
Southwest Cape, Tasmania, in Indian Ocean, S of Port Davey; 43°34′S 146°2′E.
South West City, town (pop. 595), McDonald co., extreme SW Mo., in the Ozarks, near Elk R., 28 mi. SW of Neosho; agr.
Southwest Dillon, mill village (pop. 1,048), Dillon co., E S.C., adjoining Dillon; cotton-yarn mills.
Southwestern Louisiana Canal, Lafourche parish, extreme SE La., shallow-draught canal joining Timbalier Bay (W) to Caminada Bay and thence to Barataria Bay (E); c.11½ mi. long. Crosses navigable Bayou Lafourche at Leeville (oil field). W of bayou, canal is called West Louisiana Canal: to E, it is known as East Louisiana Canal.
South West Fargo, city (pop. 1,032), Cass co., E N. Dak., 5 mi. W of Fargo; meat-packing center, with stockyards. Inc. 1937.
Southwest Gander River, E central N.F., headstream of Gander R., rises 50 mi. SSE of Grand Falls, flows 50 mi. NE to Gander L.
Southwest Greensburg, borough (pop. 3,144), Westmoreland co., SW central Pa., adjoining Greensburg. Inc. 1890.
Southwest Harbor, town (pop. 1,534), Hancock co., S Maine; resort on S Mt. Desert Isl.; boat yards. Set off from Tremont 1905.
Southwest Lanett, village (pop. 1,631), Chambers co., E Ala., near Lanett.
Southwest Miramichi River, New Brunswick: see MIRAMICHI.
South Westport, Mass.: see WESTPORT.
Southwest Vineland, village (pop. 2,834), Cumberland co., S N.J., near Vineland.
Southwest Wausau (wô′sô), village (pop. 2,677), Marathon co., central Wis., near Wausau.
South Weymouth, Mass.: see WEYMOUTH.
South Whitley (hwĭt′lē), town (pop. 1,299), Whitley co., NE Ind., on Eel R. and 25 mi. W of Fort Wayne, in grain and livestock area; makes railroad equipment; ships grain.
Southwick (south′wĭk). **1** Suburb, Durham, England: see SUNDERLAND. **2** Urban district (1931 pop. 6,138; 1951 census 10,718), S Sussex, England, on the Channel, 5 mi. W of Brighton; seaside resort. Church dates from 13th cent. Traces of Roman and Saxon occupation have been found.
Southwick, town (pop. 2,855), Hampden co., SW Mass., 11 mi. WSW of Springfield; tobacco, potatoes. Inc. 1770.
South Wigston, England: see WIGSTON.
South Williamson, village (pop. 1,144), Pike co., E Ky., on Tug Fork (of the Big Sandy) opposite Williamson, W.Va.
South Williamsport, borough (pop. 6,364), Lycoming co., N central Pa., on West Branch of Susquehanna R. opposite Williamsport; furniture, hardware, textiles. Inc. 1886.
South Willington, Conn.: see WILLINGTON.
South Wilmington, village (pop. 662), Grundy co., NE Ill., 26 mi. SSW of Joliet, in agr. and bituminous-coal area.
South Wilton, Conn.: see WILTON.
South Windham (wĭn′dŭm). **1** Village, Conn.: see WINDHAM, town. **2** Village (pop. 1,569) in Windham and Gorham towns, Cumberland co., SW Maine, 10 mi. NW of Portland.
South Windsor (wĭn′zŭr), town (pop. 4,066), Hartford co., N Conn., on the Connecticut and 6 mi. NE of Hartford, in agr. region; tobacco growing, packing. Oliver Walcott, Jonathan Edwards b. here. Set off from Windsor 1845.
South Wisconsin Rapids, village (pop. 1,836), Wood co., central Wis., near Wisconsin Rapids.
Southwold (south′wōld), municipal borough (1931 pop. 2,753; 1951 census 2,473), NE Suffolk, England, on North Sea, at mouth of Blyth R., 11 mi. S of Lowestoft; seaside resort; woolen milling. Has 15th-cent. church. Offshore was fought (1672) naval battle of Southwold Bay or Sole Bay, bet. Dutch under De Ruyter and English and French under duke of York.
South Yarmouth, Mass.: see YARMOUTH.
South Zanesville (zānz′vĭl), village (pop. 1,477); Muskingum co., central Ohio, just S of Zanesville, on small Jonathan Creek near its mouth on Muskingum R.; pottery, lumber, crates.
Souto (sō′tōō), agr. village (pop. 1,993), Guarda dist., N central Portugal, near Sp. border, 22 mi. NE of Guarda.
Souvigny (sōōvēnyē′), village (pop. 1,270), Allier dept., central France, 7 mi. WSW of Moulins; glassworks; quartz mining. Has noted 12th–15th cent. abbatial church.
Souvret (sōōvrā′), town (pop. 4,226), Hainaut prov., S central Belgium, 5 mi. WNW of Charleroi; coal mining.
Souyen (sou′yŭn′), Mandarin *Hsiu-jen* (shyō′rŭn′), town, ⊙ Souyen co. (pop. 67,204), NE central Kwangsi prov., China, 45 mi. E of Liuchow; rice, wheat, beans, millet.
Souza (sō′zŭ), city (pop. 2,889), W Paraíba, NE Brazil, on railroad and 25 mi. NE of Cajàzeiras; center of irrigated agr. area (2 dams and reservoirs are SW on Piranhas R.) producing cotton, sugar, rice, fruit, and vegetables; cotton ginning and shipping. Airfield.
Sovana (sôvä′nä), village (pop. 195), Grosseto prov., Tuscany, central Italy, 28 mi. ESE of Grosseto. Has Etruscan necropolis, medieval castle, and cathedral (12th–13th cent.). Pope Gregory VII b. here.

Sovata (sôvä'tä), Hung. *Szováta* (sô'vätŏ), village (pop. 4,060), Mures prov., central Rumania, in Transylvania, on railroad and 23 mi. ENE of Targu-Mures; popular health and summer resort (alt. 1,706 ft.) in W foothills of the Carpathians in a region of salt lakes; thermal and mud baths; fishing. In Hungary, 1940–45.

Sövenyhaza (sû'vänyůhä"zŏ), Hung. *Sövényháza*, town (pop. 5,655), Csongrad co., S Hungary, 16 mi. N of Szeged; market center (grain, cattle).

Sovere (sô'vĕrĕ), village (pop. 1,664), Bergamo prov., Lombardy, N Italy, near N shore of Lago d'Iseo, 3 mi. W of Lovere; steelworks.

Sovetsk (sŭvyĕtsk'). **1** Formerly **Tilsit** (tĭl'zĭt, –sĭt), city (1939 pop. 58,468), N Kaliningrad oblast, Russian SFSR, port on Neman R. (Lith. line) and 30 mi. NE of Kaliningrad; lumber-milling center; mfg. (wood pulp, soap, leather, tobacco products, dairy goods). Its cheese is well-known. Has 18th-cent. baroque town hall. By treaties of Tilsit signed here (July 7–9, 1807) bet. Prussia, Russia, and France, Prussia was stripped of nearly half her territories. The city developed around a castle (1408) of the Teutonic Knights; chartered 1552 as Tilse. Tilsit passed (1945) to USSR along with N part of East Prussia and was renamed. **2** City (1926 pop. 4,827), S Kirov oblast, Russian SFSR, on Vyatka R. and 70 mi. SSW of Kirov, in grain and wheat area; food processing, sawmilling. Until 1919 called Kukarka.

Sovetskaya (sŭvyĕt'skīŭ). **1** Village (1926 pop. 13,182), SE Krasnodar Territory, Russian SFSR, on Urup R. and 15 mi. SSE of Armavir; metalworks, flour mill; wheat, sunflowers, castor beans. Formerly called Urupskaya. **2** Village (1926 pop. 6,185), SE Stavropol Territory, Russian SFSR, 30 mi. ESE of Georgiyevsk; flour mill, metalworks; wheat, cotton.

Sovetskaya Gavan or **Sovetskaya Gavan'** (gä'vŭnyŭ) [Rus., =Soviet harbor], city (1948 pop. over 50,000), SE Khabarovsk Territory, Russian SFSR, port and naval base on Tatar Strait of Sea of Japan, 180 mi. ESE of Komsomolsk (linked by railroad); sawmills, fisheries. Became city 1941; boomed with construction of railroad in Second World War.

Sovetski or **Sovetskiy** (sŭvyĕt'skē). **1** Town (1939 pop. over 500), E Crimea, Russian SFSR, on railroad and 30 mi. NW of Feodosiya; flour mill, metalworks; wheat. Until 1944, Ichki or Ichki-Grammatikovo. **2** Village (1926 pop. 898), NE Kursk oblast, Russian SFSR, 37 mi. N of Stary Oskol; sugar refinery. Kshen village is just N. **3** Town (1939 pop. over 500), NW Leningrad oblast, Russian SFSR, on Karelian Isthmus, 12 mi. S of Vyborg, on Vyborg Bay; cellulose mill. Once site of Rus. imperial glassworks (founded 1794). Called Johannes, Rus. *Iokhannes*, while in Finland (until 1940) and, until 1948, in USSR.

Sovetskoye (–skŭyŭ). **1** Village (1939 pop. under 500), W Chuvash Autonomous SSR, Russian SFSR, 26 mi. NNE of Shumerlya; wheat, rye, oats. Until 1939, Shumatovo. **2** Village (1926 pop. 968), SE Grozny oblast, Russian SFSR, in the central Greater Caucasus, on upper Argun R. and 30 mi. S of Grozny, near Georgian SSR border; health resort; grain, livestock; lumbering. Until 1944, Shatoi. **3** Village (1939 pop. over 500), SE Kabardian Autonomous SSR, Russian SFSR, on Cherek R. and 12 mi. S of Nalchik; lumbering, woodworking. Until 1944, Kashkatau. **4** Village (1926 pop. 4,257), central Saratov oblast, Russian SFSR, 25 mi. E of Engels; flour mill, metalworks; wheat, sunflowers, tobacco. Until 1941 (in German Volga Autonomous SSR), Mariyental or Mariental.

Sovicille (sôvēchēl'lĕ), village (pop. 287), Siena prov., Tuscany, central Italy, 6 mi. WSW of Siena; marble quarries.

Sovico (sôvē'kô), village (pop. 3,023), Milano prov., Lombardy, N Italy, adjacent to Macherio, 4 mi. N of Monza; cotton-milling center; organ factory.

Soviet Central Asia: see CENTRAL ASIA.

Soviet Far East, term applied to the easternmost part of Siberia, i.e., AMUR oblast, KHABAROVSK territory, MARITIME TERRITORY, and SAKHALIN oblast—all part of Russian SFSR.

Soviet Harbor, Russian SFSR: see SOVETSKAYA GAVAN.

Soviet Union: see UNION OF SOVIET SOCIALIST REPUBLICS.

Sovinec, Czechoslovakia: see RYMAROV.

Sowerby (sour'–, sôr'–). **1** Town and parish (pop. 2,076), North Riding, N central Yorkshire, England, on a tributary of Swale R. just S of Thirsk; agr. market. **2** or **Sowerby Bridge**, urban district (1931 pop. 14,680; 1951 census 18,770), West Riding, SW Yorkshire, England, on Calder R. and 3 mi. SSW of Halifax; NE terminal of Rochdale Canal; woolen and cotton milling, leather tanning and mfg. Also produces carpets, textile machinery, machine tools. Has church rebuilt in 1763.

Sowia, Gora, mountain, Poland: see HOHE EULE.

Sowie, Gory, Poland: see EULENGEBIRGE.

Soy (soi), village, Rift Valley prov., W Kenya, on rail spur and 15 mi. NNW of Eldoret; coffee, wheat, corn, wattle growing, dairying.

Soya, Cape, Jap. *Soya-misaki*, northernmost point of Hokkaido, Japan, in La Pérouse Strait; 45°31'N 141°57'E; lighthouse.

Soya Bay (sō'yä), Jap. *Soya-wan*, inlet of La Pérouse Strait, N Hokkaido, Japan, bet. capes Noshappu and Soya; 15 mi. long, 5 mi. wide. Wakkanai is on W side. Formerly sometimes called Romanzov.

Soya-kaikyo: see LA PÉROUSE STRAIT.

Soyalô (soiälō'), town (pop. 1,025), Chiapas, S Mexico, in spur of Sierra Madre, 17 mi. NE of Tuxtla; alt. 3,740 ft.

Soyapango (soiäpäng'gō), residential town (pop. 3,200), San Salvador dept., S central Salvador, on Inter-American Highway and 2.5 mi. E of San Salvador; rail junction; grain, sugar cane; poultry farming.

Soya Strait: see LA PÉROUSE STRAIT.

Soyatla (soiät'lä), town (pop. 1,175), Hidalgo, central Mexico, 13 mi. NE of Metztitlán; corn, beans, fruit, cotton, stock.

Soyatlán, Mexico: see ZOYATLÁN.

Soyea (sô'yů), small island (1 mi. long), SW Sutherland, Scotland, at mouth of Loch Inver.

Soyland, England: see RIPPONDEN.

Soyons (swäyŏ'), village (pop. 365), Ardèche dept., S France, on right bank of Rhone R. and 4 mi. SSW of Valence; foundry. Pyrite mine near by.

Soyopa (soiō'pä), town (pop. 590), Sonora, NW Mexico, on Yaqui R. and 85 mi. ESE of Hermosillo; stock raising, coal mining.

Sozan, Formosa: see TSAOSHAN.

Sozan, Korea: see CHOSAN.

Sozh River (sôsh), W European USSR, rises just S of Smolensk in Smolensk-Moscow Upland, flows 402 mi. generally SSW, past Khislavichi, Krichev (head of navigation), Slavgorod, Chechersk, and Gomel, to Dnieper R. at Loyev. Navigable for 200 mi. above mouth.

Sozopol (sôzô'pôl), anc. *Apollonia*, city (pop. 3,178), Burgas dist., E Bulgaria, port on Black Sea, 13 mi. ESE of Burgas; fishing center, summer resort. Has school of pisciculture, interesting ruins of anc. walls, fortress, and monastery. Founded 610 B.C. by Hellenes and sacked 72 B.C. by Romans. Known as important commercial center of Sozopolis in Middle Ages; called Suzeboli or Sizeboli under Turkish rule (15th–19th cent.).

Spa (spä), town (pop. 8,929), Liége prov., E Belgium, 7 mi. S of Verviers; popular tourist and health resort (known since 16th cent.), with mineral springs. Ger. hq. here in 1918; site of conference of Allied Supreme Council in 1920.

Spa (spä), Gaelic *Baile Garrán*, seaside resort, W Co. Kerry, Ireland, on Tralee Bay, 4 mi. W of Tralee. Noted oyster fisheries.

Spaccaforno, Sicily: see ISPICA.

Spada, Cape, Crete: see SPATHA, CAPE.

Spadafora (spädäfô'rä), village (pop. 3,010), Messina prov., NE Sicily, on Gulf of Milazzo and 10 mi. WNW of Messina, in citrus-fruit region; factory produces oil from gourd seeds. Before 1937, Spadafora San Martino.

Spaichingen (shpī'khĭng-ŭn), town (pop. 4,114), S Württemberg, Germany, after 1945 in Württemberg-Hohenzollern, in Swabian Jura, 7 mi. NNW of Tuttlingen; rail junction; cigar and furniture mfg., woodworking. Summer resort and winter-sports center (alt. 2,195 ft.).

Spain, Sp. *España* (äspä'nyä), anc. *Hispania* (hĭspä'nēŭ, –nyŭ), state (including Canary and Balearic isls.: □ 194,232; 1940 pop. 25,877,971; 1950 pop. 27,909,009), SW Europe; ⊙ MADRID. Continental Spain, including bulk of Iberian Peninsula, of which Portugal occupies an Atlantic section, is bet. 36°–42°53'N and 3°19'E–9°18'W. From its base along the PYRENEES (NE), which it shares with France, it extends c.500 mi. southward to GIBRALTAR (British since 1713) and Cape Marroquí, where the narrow Strait of Gibraltar separates it by c.8 mi. from North Africa (Sp. Morocco). On N Spain has the Bay of Biscay, on NW and SW the Atlantic, on S and E the Mediterranean. The BALEARIC ISLANDS (□ 1,936; pop. 407,497) in W Mediterranean and the CANARY ISLANDS (□ 2,808 or 2,912; pop. 680,294) in Atlantic off NW Africa constitute provs. of metropolitan Spain, while the Moroccan cities CEUTA and MELILLA are administered by Cádiz and Málaga respectively. Tiny sovereign ANDORRA in the Pyrenees is wedged bet. France and Spain. The coast line of some 1,500 mi. is in general little indented—the major embayments being the gulfs of Valencia and Alicante in E and Gulf of Cádiz in SW—but projects into a number of sharp promontories, such as capes Finisterre, Toriñana, Ortegal (NW); Creus (NE); Tortosa, Naos, and Palos (E); Gata (SE); Marroquí, Gibraltar, and Trafalgar (S). There are fine, sheltered bays (*rías*) in Galicia. The shore is steep and rocky on the Bay of Biscay, level and sandy on SW Atlantic coast. Beaches, lagoons, and marshes stretch along the Mediterranean, though the Catalan coast is partly rocky. The country's varied climate and vegetation is largely accounted for by the complexity of its relief. In spite of its long sea frontage, the predominantly mountainous land is not as marine as might be expected. Spain is almost isolated by the formidable Pyrenees from the rest of Europe, with which it has, in many respects, less tangible affinities than with oriental Africa. The Pyrenees rise to 11,168 ft. in Spain, in the Pico de Aneto of the Maladetta massif. Geologically related to this alpine crest are the wooded CANTABRIAN MOUNTAINS which continue it westward and merge in NW with GALICIAN MOUNTAINS. The MESETA, a massive plateau (average alt. c.2,000 ft.), surrounded by mts., covers the entire interior of Spain. Made up largely of mountainous steppes (among them La MANCHA), with some forests and pastures on slopes, it includes the historic regions of Leon, Estremadura, and, especially, Old Castile (N) and New Castile (S), which are separated by the Sierra de GUADARRAMA, Sierra de GREDOS, and Sierra de GATA. Smaller escarpments bound it in E, the SIERRA MORENA in S. The extreme S of Spain near Mediterranean coast of Andalusia is folded by another imposing range, 2d in Western Europe only to the Alps, the SIERRA NEVADA of the Cordillera Penibética system, where rises the highest elevation (MULHACÉN; 11,411 ft.) on the Spanish mainland. (The volcanic Pico de Teide, c.12,200 ft., in Canary Isls., is higher, however.) Bet. plateaus and mtn. blocks are the valleys of Spain's major rivers: the Ebro in Aragon (La RIOJA), the Duero (Douro) in Old Castile, and the Tagus and Guadiana in New Castile. The great alluvial plain of the GUADALQUIVIR in Andalusia is among Spain's most fertile and populated regions. Several other narrow lowlands stretch along the coast, notably those near VALENCIA, MURCIA, and ALICANTE, with their productive huertas. The valley of the Ebro, the only one of the larger rivers to drain into the Mediterranean, is mostly arid but has been turned fertile through irrigation around SARAGOSSA, an oasis city and rail center. All of the larger rivers, apart from the Ebro, flow westward to the Atlantic. The Miño R. (NW) forms part of the border with Portugal. Júcar and Segura rivers water Mediterranean E coast. Only the Guadalquivir is of good navigability, rendering SEVILLE a major inland port. The climate of Spain is on the whole marked by extremes of temp. and scarcity of rainfall. In the mountainous NW and along Bay of Biscay is the highest rainfall in the country. The lowlands of S and SE Spain are Mediterranean, i.e., wet winters, hot dry summers. The region of MÁLAGA, climatically one of the most favored in Europe, is subtropical. ELCHE has the only palm groves (dates) in Europe. The vast plateau is truly continental, having cold winters and hot summers. Altogether an area of low rainfall; about ⅓ of it is semi-desert. Madrid, the approximate geographical center, has a Jan. mean temp. of 39°F., Aug. 73.5°F.; temperatures are known to drop there 40° in a day. At Seville in S, temperatures may climb to 115°F. Deciduous forests and rich grasslands (cattle grazing) are ample only in maritime N. While the cork oak is typical for the central plateaus, olive trees abound in the S, especially in Andalusia. The drier sections support esparto grass. Wheat, mainly grown in Old Castile and Andalusia, is still the largest crop, though of low yield and supplemented by imports. Also barley, corn, rye, potatoes, onions, and high-quality rice (from irrigated S and SE). Grapes, largely grown for local consumption, are, with olives, Spain's leading industrial crops. There are vineyards in practically all parts, notably in Andalusia (JEREZ, Málaga, MONTILLA), on E coast (ALICANTE, TARRAGONA), in N (La Rioja), and on slopes of the valleys. Fresh grapes are shipped from ALMERÍA. The Balearic Isls., Andalusia, and the irrigated huertas along Mediterranean yield also citrus fruit, sugar cane, almonds, cotton, hemp, figs, vegetables, tobacco. Sericulture in Valencia and Murcia region. The Canaries export bananas. Olives and olive oil, grapes and wine, cork, almonds, and subtropical fruit make up more than half of Spain's exports. Cattle grazing is only prominent in N. On arid plateau originated well-known Merino sheep, which have helped Sp. textile industry in past ages, but have contributed to soil exhaustion. Horses, mules, goats, and bulls for the ring are also raised widely. Hogs thrive on acorns from wooded slopes. Extensive fisheries and canneries (sardines, tuna, anchovies, shellfish, etc.) are based in Galicia (La CORUÑA, VIGO, PONTEVEDRA) and on Atlantic S coast (HUELVA, ISLA-CRISTINA). Though canned fish is exported, cod from Norway is imported to supplement the diet. Spain is still predominantly an agr. country, but it has been famed since the dawn of history for its great mineral resources, which attracted Phoenicians, Cretans, Carthaginians, Romans, and others. To this day most of the mines are foreign owned. A drawback to the industrial development is the shortage of coal. There are minor deposits in Asturias and Leon. Iron, chiefly mined in Cantabrian Mts., represents the largest export item, the bulk of which is shipped to England from BILBAO, SANTANDER, and GIJÓN (also metallurgical centers). The Cantabrian Mts. in N and the Sierra Morena in S are the principal mining regions (copper, iron, galena, pyrite, manganese, tin, nickel, zinc, sulphur, antimony, tungsten, silver, gypsum, clay, coal, graphite, peat, limestone, marble, jasper). Among leading mines are copper at RÍOTINTO (Huelva prov.), mercury at ALMADÉN (Ciudad Real prov.), lead at LINARES, La CAROLINA, and SANTA-ELENA (Jaén prov.), phosphate at LOGROSÁN (Cáceres prov.). There are substantial tungsten deposits in the Sierra de Gata near Portuguese border. Since coal is scarce and oil is almost entirely lacking, industry has come to rely largely on hydroelectric developments. There are 2 major mfg. areas, the metalworks of Bilbao, Santander, Irún, and, especially, Oviedo in Basque Provs., and the foremost industrial center of Spain, Barcelona, which is the country's 2d city and largest port (cotton trade), outstanding for its textile mills. It is surrounded by a number of smaller industrial towns. Madrid, though little favored by nature, has evolved as the cultural, political, and financial hub of the nation, with important industries (machinery, vehicles, chemicals, and consumer goods). From it radiate railroads and highways. Valencia, Málaga, Alicante, Almería, La Línea, Algeciras, Seville, Jerez, and Huelva are, together with Barcelona, Valencia, and Bilbao, the principal ports. Cádiz has been since colonial days hq. for transatlantic shipping. There are naval bases at Cartagena on the Mediterranean and El Ferrol on the Atlantic. The flourishing cities of densely populated Andalusia still reflect their great Moorish past, exemplified in Mozarabic bldgs., such as the famous Alhambra of Granada, the Giralda of Seville, and the mosque (cathedral since 1238) of Córdoba. Apart from Madrid, Valladolid is the only large city of the Meseta. The traditional Castilian cities of Salamanca (old univ.), Burgos (Gothic cathedral), Ávila, Leon, Segovia (Roman aqueduct), Zamora, Alcalá de Henares (birthplace of Cervantes), and above all Toledo (famed through Greco's paintings, residence of R.C. primate) testify to Spain's history and venerable art, but have not kept up with modern times. Santiago de Compostela in Galicia has the country's most celebrated shrine of pilgrimage. Spain's art treasures, attracting tourists and scholars from all nations, are innumerable. The Prado mus. of Madrid houses one of the world's finest collections of paintings. Imposing castles, for which Castile and Catalonia are named, strew the countryside; notable are Escorial, Aranjuez, and San Ildefonso (La Granja) near Madrid. Beaches of San Sebastián near Biarritz (France), Málaga, and others rank with finest of the continent. Mild, subtropical Balearic Isls. and exotic Canary Isls. have become fashionable winter resorts. Spain's inland communications are generally poor. Railroads, unlike those of the rest of Europe outside Russia, use wide-gauge tracks; purposedly built to harass invading forces from N, they hinder trade with France. The country still has a high percentage of illiteracy, but possesses some of the West's great universities: Barcelona, Granada, Madrid, Oviedo, Salamanca, Santiago, Seville, Valencia, Valladolid, and Saragossa. Though the Castilian dialect has become the standard Sp. language, Catalan (akin to Provençal), Galician (akin to Portuguese), and Basque (totally unrelated to any other tongue) are still widely spoken and written in their respective dists. Separatist tendencies remain particularly strong among the Catalans and Basques. Overwhelming majority of the people adhere to R.C. church. Civilization in Spain dates back to the Stone Age. The Basques may be descended from Cro-Magnon man, whose art has been preserved in the Altamira caves. They antedated the Iberians, who mixed with Celtic invaders at an early period. Because of its mineral wealth and its position guarding Strait of Gibraltar (the "Pillars of Hercules"), Spain has been known to Mediterranean peoples from early times. Phoenicians established colonies in Andalusia, notably at Cádiz and Tartessus. They were followed by Greeks, Ligurians, and Carthaginians, who in 3d cent. B.C. conquered most of the peninsula and established Cartagena as capital. Victory over Hannibal in Second Punic War (218–201 B.C.) resulted in Roman infiltration. Most of Spain became latinized, divided into provs. of Tarraconensis (N, E, and SE), Lusitania (comprising present Portugal and W central Spain), and Baetica (roughly present Andalusia). In A.D. 409 Spain was overrun by 1st wave of Germanic invaders, the Suevi and Vandals, in turn replaced by Visigoths, who set up their capital at Toledo. A Moslem army under Tarik crossed Strait of Gibraltar and defeated (711) last Visigothic king, Roderick. The Moors, mostly of Berber stock, conquered entire peninsula save Asturias and Basque country. Córdoba became (756) ⊙ of separate Caliphate. In NE Charlemagne carved out (778) the Spanish March, from which evolved Catalonia. Asturias, focus of Christian reconquests, eventually controlled Navarre, Aragon, and Castile under Sancho III (1000–1035). Under Moorish rule the arts, industries, and agr. reached a level hardly ever attained again in Sp. history. In battle of Navas de Tolosa (1212) Moorish rule was reduced to Granada, which held out until conquest (1492) by Ferdinand and Isabella, who by their marriage merged Castile and Aragon, thus becoming rulers of all Spain. Portugal had won its independence in 12th cent. Moorish and Jewish elements were persecuted and finally expelled (1609), though leaving a great legacy to Sp. culture. Discovery (1492) of America inaugurated enormous expansion of Sp. empire. It included in 16th cent. almost all of the Americas, and the Philippines. The Treaty of Tordesillas (1494) bet. Spain and Portugal virtually divided the world into 2 spheres of influence. The Italian Wars (1494–1554) added kingdom of Naples and duchy of Milan as dependencies. Under Charles V (elected emperor 1519) Spain was at the peak of its power, holding also sway over Austria and the Netherlands. During reign of his son Philip II power of crown and church was strengthened. Introduction of the Inquisition hastened Dutch struggle for independence. Naval victory at Lepanto (1571) was followed by decisive defeat of the Armada (1588) in attempted conquest of England. From then on Sp. power began to decline step by step, and France replaced it after Thirty Years War (1648) as leading European country. The War of Spanish Succession (1700–14) transferred Sp. Netherlands, Milan, Naples, and Sardinia to Austria, and Sicily to Savoy. In Peninsular War (1803–14) Spain reached its greatest humiliation, occupation by Fr. troops, and installation of Joseph Bonaparte as puppet king. Latin American colonies rose. However, in 1814 the Spanish, with assistance of the British under Wellington, had expelled the French. Two years before, a liberal constitution was drawn up at Cádiz by 1st national Cortes. By 1825 all Latin America, except several territories in the West Indies, had gained independence. Through Sp. American War (1898) Puerto Rico, Cuba, and the Philippines were lost. During turbulent reign of Isabella II (1833–64) and after her abdication Spain was torn by civil war (Carlist Wars), military coups, and dictatorships. Short-lived Sp. republic (1873–74) led to another Carlist civil war. Towards end of 19th cent. the Socialist and Syndico-Anarchist parties began to gain a wide following. Strikes and uprisings became frequent. Spain remained neutral in the First World War. Military dictatorship under Primo de Rivera 1923–30. In 1931 Alfonso XIII abdicated and a republic was established. Disturbances continued. The Popular Front (Republicans, Socialists, Communists, and Syndicalists) won a victory in 1936 elections. This precipitated a military rebellion in Sp. Morocco and the great civil war of 1936–39. Insurgents under leadership of Gen. Francisco Franco faced the Loyalist forces, which were supported by parties of the Popular Front and the nationalists in Catalonia and Basque Provs., who had been granted autonomy under the Republic. Spain eventually lent itself to a dress rehearsal for the Second World War. German and Italian contingents actively aided the rebels, while the Loyalists received help only from an international brigade and some meager aid from the USSR. Catalonia and Madrid held out until 1939. With the fall of Madrid Franco established a dictatorship over Spain, the Falange became the sole party, and a corporative state was established which maintained the disproportion bet. the wealth of the land-owning aristocracy and an impoverished people. Catalan and Basque autonomy was abolished. Despite its sympathies for the Axis, Spain remained neutral during Second World War. In 1947 Spain was declared a monarchy. The eventual succession to Franco by a king or regent was to be determined by the regency council. Spain was refused admission to the U.N. The country still suffers from the destruction of the civil war. Remaining Sp. colonies in Africa include Spanish Morocco, Spanish West Africa (Ifni enclave, Southern Protectorate of Morocco, Saguia el Hamra, and Rió de Oro), and Spanish Guinea (including continental section and Fernando Po isl.). The international zone of Tangier was occupied 1940–45 by Spain. For further information see articles on cities, towns, physical features, the 13 historic regions, and the following 50 administrative provs.: in Andalusia—Almería, Cádiz, Córdoba, Granada, Huelva, Jaén, Málaga, Seville; in Aragon—Huesca, Saragossa, Teruel; in Asturias—Oviedo; in Basque Provinces—Álava, Guipúzcoa, Vizcaya; in Catalonia—Barcelona, Gerona, Lérida, Tarragona; in Estremadura—Badajoz, Cáceres; in Galicia—La Coruña, Lugo, Orense, Pontevedra; in Leon—Leon, Palencia, Salamanca, Valladolid, Zamora; in Murcia—Albacete, Murcia; Navarre; in New Castile—Ciudad Real, Cuenca, Guadalajara, Madrid, Toledo; in Old Castile—Ávila, Burgos, Logroño, Santander, Segovia, Soria; in Valencia—Alicante, Castellón de la Plana, Valencia; besides prov. of Balearic Islands, and Las Palmas and Santa Cruz de Tenerife provs. in Canary Islands.

Spakenburg (spä'kŭnbûrkh), village (pop. 4,403), Utrecht prov., central Netherlands, on the IJsselmeer, 7 mi. N of Amersfoort; mfg. (buttons, shoes); fishing, fish processing.

Spalato, Yugoslavia: see Split.

Spalding, village (pop. 240), S South Australia, 40 mi. SE of Port Pirie; rail terminus; wheat, wool, wine, livestock, dairy products.

Spalding, village (pop. 251), S central Sask., 28 mi. ENE of Humboldt; wheat, stock.

Spalding, urban district (1931 pop. 12,595; 1951 census 11,031), Parts of Holland, S Lincolnshire, England, on Welland R. and 15 mi. SSW of Boston; fruit and vegetable market and canning center; beet-sugar refining. Has parish church dating from 1284, and 15th-cent. Ascough Fee (or Ascoughfee) Hall, site of founding (1710) of oldest literary and scientific association in England, the Gentlemen's Society of Spalding.

Spalding, county (□ 201; pop. 31,045), W central Ga.; ⊙ Griffin. Bounded W by Flint R. Piedmont agr. (cotton, corn, peppers, fruit, livestock) and timber area; mfg. at Griffin. Formed 1851.

Spalding, village (pop. 713), Greeley co., E central Nebr., 13 mi. NE of Greeley and on Cedar R.; flour; livestock, grain. Recreation grounds near by.

Spaldings, town (pop. 2,160), Clarendon parish, central Jamaica, partly in Manchester parish, 22 mi. NW of May Pen; agr. center (sugar cane, ginger, tropical fruit, stock); exports honey.

Spalt (shpält), town (pop. 3,006), Middle Franconia, W central Bavaria, Germany, on the Franconian Rezat and 11 mi. SSW of Schwabach; center of Franconian hop-growing region; toy mfg., brewing. Has late-Romanesque church. Chartered c.1296. Spalatin b. here.

Spandau (shpän'dou), residential and industrial district (1939 pop. 170,384; 1946 pop. 159,599), W Berlin, on the Havel at mouth of the Spree, and 9 mi. W of city center; port at W end of Berlin-Spandau Canal. Steel milling, metalworking. Has former citadel, later a political prison. Originally Wendish fortress; became German c.1230. Inc. 1920 into Berlin. After 1945 in British sector. Includes Gatow (airport) and Siemensstadt sections.

Spangenberg (shpäng'ŭnbĕrk), town (pop. 3,169), in former Prussian prov. of Hesse-Nassau, W Germany, after 1945 in Hesse, 5 mi. ESE of Melsungen; mfg. (textiles, chemicals, precision instruments). Has late-Gothic church.

Spangle, town (pop. 242), Spokane co., E Wash., 15 mi. S of Spokane, in wheat-growing region.

Spangler, borough (pop. 3,013), Cambria co., SW central Pa., 23 mi. NNE of Johnstown and on West Branch of Susquehanna R.; bituminous coal. Inc. 1893.

Spaniard's Bay, town (pop. 1,239), SE N.F., on SW side of Conception Bay, N Avalon Peninsula, 6 mi. SW of Harbour Grace; fishing settlement; also furniture mfg., lumbering.

Spanish America, collective term referring in its present usage to the Spanish-speaking countries of Latin America, thus including Mexico, Central America (except British Honduras), South America (except Brazil and Guiana), Cuba, the Dominican Republic, and generally also Puerto Rico. Hispanic America is also used. As a historic concept Spanish America sometimes applies to all the areas settled by the Spanish in colonial times, such as S, SW, and W sections of the U.S.

Spanish Fork or **Spanish Fork City**, city (pop. 5,230), Utah co., N central Utah, 8 mi. S of Provo, at foot of Wasatch Range, near Utah L.; alt. 4,552 ft. Processing center for livestock and agr. area (sugar beets, grain, fruit) irrigated by water from Strawberry R.; beet sugar, flour, dairy products, canned goods, lumber. Settled 1850, inc. 1855. Spanish Fork Peak (10,185 ft.) is 7 mi. E in Wasatch Range.

Spanish Fork, stream rising in Wasatch Range, central Utah, and flowing 48 mi. WNW to Utah L. Receives water from Strawberry Reservoir (on Strawberry River). Used for irrigation and hydroelectric power.

Spanish Guinea (gĭ'nē), Sp. colony (□ c.10,800; 1942 pop. 170,582), W Africa, on Gulf of Guinea. It comprises the isl. of Fernando Po (on which is the ⊙, Santa Isabel), Annobón isl., and a square section of the African coast called Continental Sp. Guinea or Río Muni (rē'ō mōō'nē). The offshore isls. of Corisco and Elobey are considered part of the mainland division. Continental Spanish Guinea (□ c.10,000; 1942 pop. 135,223) is bounded N by Fr. Cameroons (along 2°21'N) and E and S by Gabon (Fr. Equatorial Africa), along 11°20'E and 1°1'N respectively. Its low Atlantic coast line extends from Campo R. (N) to mouth of the Río Muni (S). A narrow coastal plain is backed by a dissected tableland (average alt. 2,000 ft.). Humid tropical climate is characterized by 2 rainy (April–May, Sept.–Dec.) seasons; rainfall averages 80 in. per year. Principal export products are valuable cabinetwoods, shipped from colony's 3 ports (Río Benito, Bata, Kogo). Coffee, cocoa, palm oil, and palm kernels are also shipped, primarily to Spain. Bata (seat of sub-governor for continental Sp. Guinea) has air link with Santa Isabel. Though Fernando Po's history dates back to its discovery in 15th cent., the Sp. Guinea mainland was 1st occupied by Spain 1843. Present boundaries established 1885 by Treaty of Berlin.

Spanish Main, mainland of Spanish America, especially coastal region of N South America bet. Panama and mouth of Orinoco R., off which English freebooters attacked Sp. treasure vessels. The term is now indiscriminately used to describe entire Caribbean area associated with pre-19th-cent. pirate romance.

Spanish March, anc. region in Spain along S foot of the Pyrenees, set up by Charlemagne.

Spanish Morocco, N Africa: see MOROCCO.

Spanish Peaks, S Colo., in Sangre de Cristo Mts., bet. Huerfano and Las Animas counties, NW of Trinidad. West Spanish Peak (13,623 ft.) is 4 mi. WSW of East Spanish Peak (12,683 ft.); both are of volcanic origin.

Spanish Point, promontory on the Atlantic, W Co. Clare, Ireland, 20 mi. W of Ennis; 52°51′N 9°27′W.

Spanish River, SE central Ont., issues from Spanish L., 100 mi. NW of Sudbury, flows S through Biskotasi and Agnew lakes to Espanola, thence W to L. Huron opposite Manitoulin Isl.; 153 mi. long.

Spanish Sahara, Africa: see SPANISH WEST AFRICA.

Spanish Town, city (pop. 12,007), ⊙ St. Catherine parish, S Jamaica, inland on Cobre R., and 11 mi. W of Kingston; 17°59′N 76°57′W. Second largest town of Jamaica, and leading communications center, linked by railroad with Kingston, Montego Bay (NW), and Port Antonio (NE). Serves rich agr. region (annatto, breadfruit, coffee, cacao, bananas, sugar cane, citrus fruit, stock). Dyewood extracting, sugar milling, rum distilling, canning, cassava processing. The old city has fine colonial bldgs. grouped around central square, such as St. Catherine Cathedral (built 1655), ruins of old King's House (destroyed by fire 1925), Rodney Memorial, House of Assembly. Spanish Town was probably laid out by Diego Columbus c.1523, being originally called St. Jago de la Vega (sometimes Santiago de la Vega). It was ⊙ Jamaica from 1535 to 1872.

Spanish Town, village, S Anegada, Br. Virgin Isls., 13 mi. E of Road Town, Tortola; 18°25′N 64°25′W. Charcoal burning; livestock, vegetables.

Spanish Wells, settlement and district (□ ½; pop. 665), central Bahama Isls., comprises 3 small islets —Royal Isl., Egg Isl., and St. George's Cay (on which is Spanish Wells village)—just off N tip of Eleuthera Isl., 50 mi. NE of Nassau. Products: fruit, vegetables, fish. Spanish Wells was burned by an Amer. vessel during War of 1812.

Spanish West Africa, political term for the Spanish possessions (□ c.117,000; pop. c.95,000) in NW Africa. It consists of 2 areas—one a large coastal region of the Sahara SW of Fr. Morocco, the other a tiny enclave (called IFNI, seat of the ⊙, Sidi Ifni) c.60 mi. further up the coast in Fr. Morocco. It does not include Sp. Morocco (which is a protectorate). The nomenclature of the Sp. part of the Saharan coastal region has long been confused (the name Río de Oro has often been applied to the whole region), but from its N frontier with Fr. Morocco—the Dra wadi (Oued Dra)—it is now administratively divided, N–S, into: (1) a politically amorphous region S of the Dra and N of 27°40′N called, vaguely, the SOUTHERN PROTECTORATE OF MOROCCO or the "Zone South of the Dra"; (2) SAGUIA EL HAMRA, whose S boundary is 26°N; and (3) RÍO DE ORO, whose S boundary is 21°20′N. Saguia el Hamra and Río de Oro are, in addition, the components of a subdivision of Sp. West Africa called Spanish Sahara (□ 103,600; pop. 37,000; ⊙ Aiun).

Spannarhyttan, Sweden: see KARRGRUVAN.

Sparagio, Monte (môn′tē spärä′jō), highest mountain (3,742 ft.) in Trapani prov., W Sicily, 14 mi. ENE of Trapani.

Sparbu (spär′bōō), village (pop. 226; canton pop. 3,592), Nord-Trondelag co., central Norway, on an inlet of Trondheim Fjord, on railroad and 7 mi. S of Steinkjer. Agr., lumbering, sawmilling, wool spinning in the area. At Maere (măr′ů) village, 2 mi. N, is agr. school.

Sparkbrook, SE industrial suburb (pop. 31,741) of Birmingham, NW Warwick, England.

Sparkill (spär′kĭl″), village (1940 pop. 584), Rockland co., SE N.Y., near W bank of the Hudson, 4 mi. S of Nyack; lumber; sand, gravel. A state park is near by.

Sparkman, sawmilling town (pop. 964), Dallas co., S central Ark., 19 mi. SE of Arkadelphia.

Sparks. 1 Town (pop. 887), Cook co., S Ga., 19 mi. E of Moultrie, in agr. area; food canning. **2** City (pop. 8,203), Washoe co., W Nev., just E of Reno, near Truckee R.; alt. c.4,400 ft.; railroad division point, with repair shops, in irrigated agr. area (hay, potatoes, onions) supplied by Truckee storage project. Gold, silver mines near by. **3** Town (pop. 233), Lincoln co., central Okla., 6 mi. SSE of Chandler, in agr. area.

Sparland, village (pop. 509), Marshall co., N central Ill., on Illinois R. (bridged here), opposite Lacon, and 23 mi. NNE of Peoria, in agr. and bituminous-coal area.

Sparlingville, village (pop. 1,393), St. Clair co., E Mich., near Port Huron.

Sparreholm (spä″rŭhôlm′), village (pop. 630), Sodermanland co., E Sweden, on L. Bav, Swedish *Båven* (bō′vŭn) (12 mi. long, 1–6 mi. wide), 20 mi. NNW of Nykoping; sawmilling, woodworking. Has 18th-cent. castle.

Sparrow Bush, resort village (1940 pop. 617), Orange co., SE N.Y., on the Delaware and 2 mi. NW of Port Jervis.

Sparrows Point, industrial dist. in Baltimore co., central Md., on navigable Patapsco R. and 9 mi. SE of downtown Baltimore. Here is one of world's largest steel mills (founded 1887), with large shipyards (founded 1890). Deep-water ore docks and rail terminal receive foreign and domestic ore and Appalachian coal.

Sparta (spär′tŭ), Gr. *Sparti* or *Sparte* (both: spär′tē), city (pop. 9,700), ⊙ LACONIA nome, S Peloponnesus, Greece, on right bank of Eurotas R. and 90 mi. SSE of Patras; commercial and industrial center of Laconia; citrus fruits, olive oil. Just S are the scanty ruins of anc. Sparta (at 1st also known as Lacedaemon), founded c.900 B.C. by Dorians. Sparta became the strongest city in Greece, and legend has it that after a Messenian revolt in the 7th cent. B.C. the reforms of Lycurgus turned it into an armed camp. At any rate, by 5th cent. B.C. the ruling class, the Spartiates, gave themselves wholly to war, and Sparta made little contribution to Greek literature, art, or philosophy. Perhaps the most notable Spartan achievement was the courageous defense of THERMOPYLAE (480 B.C.) by Leonidas in the Persian Wars (500–449 B.C.). The Spartans, however, reached Marathon too late to take part in that victory (490 B.C.) because their religious belief prevented them from setting out before the full of the moon. They fought in the battle of Salamis (480 B.C.), and a Spartan, Pausanias, commanded in the victory of Plataea (479 B.C.). The power of Sparta continued to grow and the military city, with its allies of the Peloponnesian League, defeated Athens in the Peloponnesian War (431–404 B.C.). Thebes, by the victory of Epaminondas at Leuctra (371 B.C.), took the ascendancy in Greece. Sparta then fell easy prey to Philip II of Macedon and declined.

Sparta, Turkey: see ISPARTA, town.

Sparta. 1 City (pop. 1,954), ⊙ Hancock co., E central Ga., c.50 mi. NE of Macon; trade, processing, and shipping center for farm and timber area; mfg. (clothing, furniture, lumber). Inc. 1805. **2** City (pop. 3,576), Randolph co., SW Ill., c.40 mi. SSE of East St. Louis; mfg. of clothing, plows; railroad shops; agr. (corn, wheat; dairy products; livestock, poultry); bituminous-coal mines; timber. Inc. 1873. **3** Town (pop. 298), Gallatin and Owen counties, N Ky., on Eagle Creek and 33 mi. N of Frankfort; lumber; nurseries. **4** Village (pop. 2,327), Kent co., SW Mich., 14 mi. NNW of Grand Rapids, in dairy- and fruit-farming area; mfg. (auto parts, furniture, paper and milk products). Platted 1869, inc. 1883. **5** Town (pop. 244), Christian co., SW Mo., in the Ozarks, 18 mi. SE of Springfield. **6** Village (pop. 1,873, with near-by Lake Mohawk village), Sussex co., NW N.J., at N end of L. Mohawk, 6 mi. E of Newton, in recreational area. Has reproductions of historic colonial houses. **7** Resort town (pop. 820), ⊙ Alleghany co., NW N.C., 23 mi. NW of Elkin, in the Blue Ridge; pipe mfg., sawmilling. **8** Village (pop. 223), Morrow co., central Ohio, 12 mi. W of Mount Vernon. **9** Town (pop. 4,290), ⊙ White co., central Tenn., 60 mi. NNW of Chattanooga, on Cumberland Plateau, in coal, limestone, timber region; makes wood products, shirts. Great Falls and Center Hill dams in Caney Fork of the Cumberland are near by. Founded 1809. **10** City (pop. 5,893), ⊙ Monroe co., W central Wis., on La Crosse R. and 23 mi. ENE of La Crosse, in agr. area (tobacco; dairy products; poultry); creameries, tobacco warehouses; mfg. of doors, brushes, pumps. Seat of state school for children. U.S. Camp McCoy is near by. Settled c.1850, inc. 1883.

Spartanburg, county (□ 830; pop. 150,349), NW S.C.; ⊙ Spartanburg. Bounded N by N.C. line, SW by Enoree R.; drained by Tyger R. Mfg. (especially textiles) in Spartanburg and its surrounding mill villages; agr. (especially peaches; also cotton, corn). Formed 1785.

Spartanburg, city (pop. 36,795), ⊙ Spartanburg co., NW S.C., 90 mi. NW of Columbia, in piedmont area, near N.C. line. Important commercial, transportation (rail, highway, air), and market center for large industrial area of mill villages. Noted textile-milling center with numerous cotton mills; railroad shops; mfg. (foundry and machine-shop products, lumber, cottonseed, and grain products, fertilizer, tobacco and food products); printing; shipping center for peaches. Seat of Wofford Col. and Converse Col. Near by are state school for deaf and blind and Textile Inst. (industrial jr. col.). In Civil War Spartanburg was busy supply point; in Second World War, near-by Camp Croft was a large U.S. army training camp. City site selected as co. seat 1785, courthouse begun 1787, city inc. 1831.

Spartansburg, borough (pop. 482), Crawford co., NW Pa., 7 mi. SSW of Corry.

Sparte, Greece: see SPARTA.

Spartel, Cape (spärtĕl′), Fr. and Sp. *Espartel* (ĕspärtĕl′), northwesternmost headland of Africa, at W entrance to Strait of Gibraltar opposite (27 mi. S of) Cape Trafalgar (Spain) and 7 mi. W of Tangier, in International Zone; 35°48′N 5°56′W. Lighthouse. Jebel Kebir, just above the cape, rises to 1,073 ft.

Sparti, Greece: see SPARTA.

Spartivento, Cape (spärtēvĕn′tô), SE extremity of "toe" of Italy, in Calabria, 16 mi. W of Melito di Porto Salvo; 37°55′N; 16°4′E; lighthouse.

Spartivento, Cape, point on S coast of Sardinia; 38°52′N 8°50′E.

Spas-Demensk (spŭs-dyĭmyĕnsk′), city (1948 pop. over 10,000), W Kaluga oblast, Russian SFSR, 25 mi. NW of Kirov; metalworking, garment mfg., paper milling. Became city in 1917. During Second World War, held (1941–43) by Germans.

Spas-Klepiki (spŭs-klyĕ′pēkē), city (1926 pop. 2,411), NW Ryazan oblast, Russian SFSR, 38 mi. NNE of Ryazan; cotton-milling center (surgical cotton, clothing goods); food products. Peat works near by. Became city in 1920.

Spassk. 1 City, Penza oblast, Russian SFSR: see BEDNODEMYANOVSK. **2** City, Tatar Autonomous SSR, Russian SFSR: see KUIBYSHEV, city.

Spasskaya Guba (spä′skŭ gōōbä′), village (1926 pop. 341), S Karelo-Finnish SSR, 33 mi. NNW of Petrozavodsk; dairying.

Spassk-Dalni or **Spassk-Dal'niy** (spŭsk′-däl′nyē), city (1939 pop. estimate 23,000), SW Maritime Territory, Russian SFSR, 70 mi. NNE of Voroshilov, on Trans-Siberian RR (Yevgenyevka station); cement-milling center; power plant; food processing. Until c.1930, called Spassk.

Spasski Zaton, Russian SFSR: see KUIBYSHEVSKI ZATON.

Spasski Zavod, Kazakh SSR: see USPENSKI.

Spasskoye (spä′skŭyŭ), village (1926 pop. 3,974), E Gorki oblast, Russian SFSR, 23 mi. NNE of Sergach; wheat, flax.

Spassk-Ryazanski or **Spassk-Ryazanskiy** (späsk″-ryŭzän′skŭyŭ), city (1926 pop. 6,324), central Ryazan oblast, Russian SFSR, on low left bank of Oka R. and 30 mi. SE of Ryazan; garment mfg. Chartered 1778. Across Oka R., on high right bank, lie well-preserved ruins of Staraya Ryazan [Rus.,= old Ryazan], former ⊙ Ryazan principality, founded 1095. After its destruction (1237) by Tatars, seat of principality was moved 30 mi. NW to the place now known as RYAZAN.

Spata (spä′tŭ), town (pop. 4,787), Attica nome, E central Greece, 10 mi. E of Athens; wheat, vegetables; olive oil, wine; stock raising (cattle, sheep). Site of anc. cave tombs, discovered 1877.

Spatha, Cape (spä′thŭ), headland of W Crete, on Aegean Sea, bet. gulfs of Kisamos (W) and Canea (E); 35°42′N 23°44′E. Northernmost point of Crete. Also called Spada.

Spaulding, village (pop. 211), Sangamon co., central Ill., 7 mi. ENE of Springfield, in agr. and bituminous-coal area.

Spaulding, Lake, Calif.: see YUBA RIVER.

Spavinaw (spă′vĭnô), town (pop. 213), Mayes co., NE Okla., 16 mi. ENE of Pryor. Spavinaw L. is just NE. Inc. 1930.

Spavinaw Lake, NE Okla., just NE of Spavinaw, in the Ozark foothills, c.55 mi. ENE of Tulsa, for which it is principal source of water supply; formed by dam across small Spavinaw Creek; c.6 mi. long. Resort; fishing.

Spean Bridge (spē′ŭn), agr. village and resort, SW Inverness, Scotland, on Spean R. and 9 mi. NE of Fort William. First engagement of 1745 Jacobite uprising was fought near by.

Spean River, Inverness, Scotland, issues from SW end of Loch Laggan, flows 21 mi. W, past Spean Bridge, to Loch Lochy just E of Gairlochy.

Spear, Cape, E extremity of N.F., on Avalon Peninsula, 5 mi. SE of St. John's; 47°32′N 52°38′W; lighthouse.

Spearfish (spēr′–), city (pop. 2,755), Lawrence co., W S.Dak., 10 mi. NW of Lead and on Spearfish Creek, in Black Hills; alt. 3,647 ft. Tourist center, trading point for farming region; timber; truck farms; grain, sugar beets. Black Hills Teachers Col. and U.S. fish hatchery are here.

Spearman, town (pop. 1,852), ⊙ Hansford co., extreme N Texas, in high grassy plains of the Panhandle, 80 mi. NNE of Amarillo; trade, storage, shipping point for wheat and cattle area. Inc. 1921.

Spearville, city (pop. 610), Ford co., SW Kansas, 16 mi. ENE of Dodge City; grain, livestock.

Spearwood, town (pop. 1,046), SW Western Australia, 12 mi. SW of Perth; butter factory.

Spectacle Island, E Mass., in Boston Bay SE of downtown Boston and near Long Isl. (SE); c.½ mi. long. Site of city garbage-disposal plant.

Speculator, resort village (pop. 370), Hamilton co., E central N.Y., in the Adirondacks, at N end of L. Pleasant, c.50 mi. NE of Utica, in winter- and summer-resort area; skiing; lumbering.

Spednik Lake, Maine and N.B.: see CHIPUTNETICOOK LAKES.

Speed. 1 City (pop. 70), Phillips co., N Kansas, on North Fork of Solomon R. and 8 mi. SW of Phillipsburg; corn, livestock. **2** Town (pop. 103), Edgecombe co., E central N.C., 7 mi. NE of Tarboro.

Speedway, town (pop. 5,498), Marion co., central Ind., just W of Indianapolis; site of Indianapolis motor speedway (annual international races). Mfg. (storage batteries, electrical goods). Laid out 1912, inc. 1926.

Speers, borough (pop. 1,089), Washington co., SW Pa., on Monongahela R. just above Charleroi.

Speer's Point, town (pop. 2,021), E New South Wales, Australia, on N shore of L. Macquarie and 9 mi. WSW of Newcastle; coal-mining center; jetty. Also spelled Speers Point.

Speicher (shpī'khŭr), town (pop. 2,137), Appenzell Ausser Rhoden half-canton, NE Switzerland, 3 mi. ESE of St. Gall; embroideries, cotton textiles.

Speiden Island, Ellice Isls.: see NIUTAO.

Speier, Germany: see SPEYER.

Speightstown (spāts'–), town (pop. 2,128), NW Barbados, B.W.I., 11 mi. N of Bridgetown; market for flying-fish catch. Surrounded by sugar plantations. Formerly an important shipping place. Its old Denmark Fort is now an almshouse.

Speke, village and parish (pop. 384), SW Lancashire, England, near Mersey R. 7 mi. SE of Liverpool; mfg. of chocolate, pharmaceuticals, electrical switch-gear. Site of Liverpool airport.

Speke Gulf (spēk), SE inlet of L. Victoria, in Tanganyika, bet. Mwanza (S) and Ukerewe Isl. (N); 65 mi. long, 10–25 mi. wide.

Spekholzerheide (spĕk'hōlzŭrhī"dŭ), town (pop. 6,746), Limburg prov., SE Netherlands, 3 mi. SE of Heerlen; coal mining.

Speldhurst, town and parish (pop. 1,937), SW Kent, England, 2 mi. NW of Tunbridge Wells; agr.

Speldorf (shpăl'dôrf), industrial suburb of MÜLHEIM, W Germany, near left bank of the Ruhr, 2 mi. W of city center.

Spello (spĕl'lō), anc. *Hispellum*, town (pop. 2,731), Perugia prov., Umbria, central Italy, 3 mi. NW of Foligno; wine, olive oil. Has Roman ruins, 12th-cent. church of Santa Maria Maggiore with frescoes by Pinturicchio.

Spelter, village (pop. 1,054), Harrison co., N W.Va., on the West Fork and 5 mi. N of Clarksburg, in coal-mining region.

Spenard, village (pop. 2,168), S Alaska, just S of Anchorage.

Spenborough, urban district (1931 pop. 30,963; 1951 census 36,977), West Riding, S Yorkshire, England. Includes towns of: Cleckheaton (pop. 8,426), 5 mi. SSW of Bradford, with woolen, leather, machinery, and chemical industries; Scholes (pop. 2,455), just W of Cleckheaton, with silk-milling and printing industry; Gomersal (pop. 4,159), 5 mi. SE of Bradford, with woolen and rayon milling, leather tanning, and machinery industry; Liversedge (pop. 14,304), just S of Cleckheaton, with woolen and cotton milling and important leather-mfg. industry; and Hightown (pop. 3,356), just W of Liversedge, with woolen and cotton milling. Parish of Gomersal includes town of Birkenshaw, 4 mi. SE of Bradford, with woolen milling and mfg. of textile machinery. Parish of Cleckheaton includes (N) town of Hunsworth.

Spencer. 1 County (□ 396; pop. 16,174), SW Ind.; ⊙ Rockport. Bounded S by Ohio R., here forming Ky. line; drained by small Anderson R. and Little Pigeon Creek. Agr. area (grain, livestock, poultry). Mfg. of brick, tile, concrete blocks, buttons; flour and lumber milling; food products. Clay pits. Formed 1818. **2** County (□ 193; pop. 6,157), NW central Ky.; ⊙ Taylorsville. Rolling upland agr. area (livestock, burley tobacco, corn), in Bluegrass region; drained by Salt R. and several creeks. Formed 1824.

Spencer. 1 Town (pop. 70), Clark co., E Idaho, 13 mi. N of Dubois. **2** Town (pop. 2,394), ⊙ Owen co., SW central Ind., on West Fork of White R. and c.45 mi. SW of Indianapolis, in agr. area (corn, fruit, livestock); food products, drugs, typewriter ribbons, lumber. Bituminous-coal mining, limestone quarrying. Settled c.1815. William Vaughn Moody was b. here. **3** City (pop. 7,446), ⊙ Clay co., NW Iowa, on Little Sioux R. at mouth of Ocheyedan R., and c.75 mi. ENE of Sioux City; rail junction; mfg. and trade center; meat packing, poultry dressing, feed milling; dairy, concrete, metal, and wood products. Fourth of July fire in 1931 destroyed most of business section. The annual county fair, held here, is famous. Founded 1859, inc. 1890. **4** Town (pop. 7,027), including Spencer village (pop. 5,259), Worcester co., central Mass., 10 mi. W of Worcester; shoe mfg.; dairying, poultry. Settled 1721, inc. 1775. **5** Village (pop. 540), Boyd co., N Nebr., 8 mi. ESE of Butte and on Ponca Creek, near S.Dak. line; beverages, grain. Dam near by. **6** Village (pop. 694), Tioga co., S N.Y., 18 mi. NE of Elmira, in agr. area (dairy products, poultry, grain); feed milling. Small Spencer L. (resort) is 3 mi. N. **7** City (pop. 3,242), Rowan co., W central N.C., just NE of Salisbury; railroad div. point with shops and roundhouse. **8** Village (pop. 740), Medina co., N Ohio, 13 mi. WSW of Medina, in agr. area. **9** City (pop. 552), McCook co., SE S.Dak., 10 mi. W of Salem; trading point for farming region; building stone and crushed rock, harnesses. **10** Town (pop. 721), ⊙ Van Buren co., central Tenn., 12 mi. S of Sparta, in the Cumberlands; livestock raising. Great Falls Dam is near by. **11** City (pop. 2,587), ⊙ Roane co., W W.Va., 35 mi. SSE of Parkersburg, in livestock, grain, natural-gas and oil area; mfg. of wood products, beverages, plastics. State hosp. for insane here. Inc. 1858. **12** Village (pop. 757), Marathon co., central Wis., 36 mi. WSW of Wausau; makes cheese, butter.

Spencer, Cape, SE Alaska, on Gulf of Alaska, on N shore of ocean entrance to Cross Sound, 80 mi. W of Juneau; 58°13'N 136°40'W. Radio beacon.

Spencer, Cape, S South Australia, southernmost point of SW projection of Yorke Peninsula at E entrance to Spencer Gulf; 35°18'S 136°53'E.

Spencer Gulf, large inlet of Indian Ocean, South Australia, bet. Eyre Peninsula (W) and Yorke Peninsula (E); 200 mi. long, 80 mi. wide. Thistle Isl., Neptune and Gambier isls. at entrance. Port Augusta at head. Port Pirie on NE shore; Wallaroo on E shore; Port Lincoln on SW shore. Sometimes called Spencer's Gulf.

Spencer Lake, Somerset co., W Maine, 14 mi. SSW of Jackman, in recreational area; 5 mi. long.

Spencer Mountain (3,035 ft.), Piscataquis co., central Maine, E of Moosehead L., 23 mi. NNE of Greenville, in recreational area.

Spencerport, village (pop. 1,595), Monroe co., W N.Y., on the Barge Canal and 10 mi. W of Rochester; chemicals, flour; sand and gravel pits. Site of John T. Trowbridge's boyhood home. Inc. 1867.

Spencerville, village (pop. estimate 400), SE Ont., on South Nation R. and 9 mi. N of Prescott; dairying, mixed farming.

Spencerville, village (pop. 1,826), Allen co., W Ohio, 13 mi. W of Lima; trade center in agr. area (dairy products, livestock, grain, soybeans). Mfg.: furniture, metal products, cement, tile. Oil wells. Laid out 1844–45, inc. 1866.

Spences Bridge, village (pop. estimate 400), S B.C., on Thompson R. and 50 mi. WSW of Kamloops; fruit, vegetables; lumbering.

Spenge (shpĕng'ŭ), village (pop. 5,318), in former Prussian prov. of Westphalia, NW Germany, after 1945 in North Rhine-Westphalia, 8 mi. WNW of Herford; grain.

Spennymoor, urban district (1931 pop. 16,369; 1951 census 19,784), central Durham, England, 6 mi. S of Durham; coal mining, ironworking.

Spenser Mountains (8,000 ft.), N central S.Isl., New Zealand, N of Southern Alps, W of Kaikoura Ranges; extend 20 mi. N–S.

Speonk (spē'ŏngk), village, Suffolk co., SE N.Y., near S shore of Long Isl., 16 mi. E of Patchogue. Shore resorts, duck farms near by.

Spercheios River or **Sperkhios River** (both: spĕr-khēōs'), Lat. *Spercheus* (spûrkē'ŭs), in Phthiotis nome, E central Greece, rises in Tymphrestos massif of S Pindus system, flows 53 mi. E to Malian Gulf 7 mi. ESE of Lamia. Hydroelectric plant W of Lamia. Formerly called Alamanas and Hellada.

Sperillen (spä'rĭl-lŭn), lake expansion (□ 10) of Begna R., Buskerud co., SE Norway, 15 mi. NNW of Honefoss; 18 mi. long, 1–2 mi. wide, up to 354 ft. deep.

Sperkhios River, Greece: see SPERCHEIOS RIVER.

Sperlonga (spĕrlông'gä), village (pop. 2,508), Latina prov., Latium, S central Italy, port on Gulf of Gaeta, 10 mi. ESE of Terracina.

Sperrin Mountains (spĕ'rĭn), range extending 15 mi. E–W along border of Cos. Tyrone and Londonderry, Northern Ireland; rise to 2,240 ft. in Sawel, 17 mi. SE of Londonderry.

Sperry, town (pop. 665), Tulsa co., NE Okla., 10 mi. N of Tulsa, in agr. area.

Sperryville, village (pop. c.350), Rappahannock co., N Va., on Thornton R. and 19 mi. NW of Culpeper; ships apples. A gateway to Shenandoah Natl. Park (W).

Spessart, The (shpĕs'ärt), low mountain range in W Germany, extends 40 mi. NNE bet. the Odenwald and the Hohe Rhön; rises to 1,918 ft. in the Geyersberg. Forested slopes; wine- and fruitgrowing at W foot (Main valley). Woodworking; numerous sandstone quarries.

Spetsai (spĕ'tsā), anc. *Pityussa* (pĭtēŭ'sŭ), Ital. *Spezzia* (spĕt'sēä), island (□ 7; pop. 3,628) in Gulf of Argolis of Aegean Sea, in Argolis and Corinthia nome, Greece, 1 mi. off E Peloponnesus; 5 mi. long, 3 mi. wide. Its seafaring pop. distinguished itself in Gr. war of independence. Almost all of its people live in town and port of Spetsai on N shore. Fishing (notably for sponges), trading. It prospered during Napoleonic wars. Sometimes spelled Spetzia. Off SE coast is small isl. of Spetsopoula (pop. 5), 1½ mi. long, ½ mi. wide.

Speyer (shpī'ŭr), sometimes, in English, *Spires* (spīrz), Fr. *Spire* (spēr), city (1950 pop. 31,706), Rhenish Palatinate, W Germany, port on left bank of the Rhine (rail bridge), at mouth of Speyer R., and 12 mi. S of Ludwigshafen; 49°19'N 8°26'E. Rail junction; cultural center of historic importance. Shipbuilding; textiles (cotton, felt); tobacco (cigarettes, cigars, pipe tobacco). Other products: machinery, telephones, celluloid, shoes, paper. Food processing (beer, sparkling wine). Potteries and brickworks. Noted Romanesque cathedral, several times restored, contains tombs of 8 Ger. emperors. City has remains of medieval wall and gates. Site of Palatine Historical Mus. with large collection of pre-Roman and Roman antiquities, including a sealed bottle of wine over 16 cent. old. An anc. Celtic and later Roman (*Noviomagus, Civitas Nemetum, Augusta Nemetum*) settlement, Speyer was destroyed by Huns c.450. Rebuilt and created bishopric in 7th cent. Became free imperial city in 1111. Scene of numerous diets; at Diet of 1529 (commemorated by 19th–20th-cent. Memorial Church), Luther's followers protested against Edict of Worms, and were henceforth called Protestants. Seat (1527–1689) of Imperial Chamber of Justice. After unification with Bavaria (1816), it became ⊙ (replaced since 1945 by Neustadt) of Rhenish Palatinate. Captured by U.S. troops in March, 1945. Henry Villard b. here. Formerly also spelled Speier.

Speyerdorf, Germany: see LACHEN-SPEYERDORF.

Speyer River (shpī'ŭr), Rhenish Palatinate, Germany, rises in Hardt Mts., flows 35 mi. generally E, past Neustadt, to the Rhine at Speyer.

Speymouth (spā'mouth'), parish (pop. 611), NE Moray, Scotland, on Spey Bay of Moray Firth. Includes KINGSTON and GARMOUTH.

Spey River (spā), in Inverness, Moray and Banffshire, Scotland, rises in small lake E of Loch Lochy, flows 107 mi. NE, through Inverness, forming border bet. Moray and Banffshire in its lower course and passing Kingussie, Aviemore, Boat-of-Garten, Grantown-on-Spey, Aberlour, and Foachabers, to Moray Firth just N of Garmouth. It is most rapid river in Scotland, and 2d longest after the Tay. Its salmon fisheries are important. River valley is called Strathspey.

Speyside (spā'sīd"), village (pop. 944), NE Tobago, B.W.I., 16 mi. NE of Scarborough; cacao, coconuts.

Spezia or **La Spezia** (lä spā'tsyä), city (pop. 80,399), ⊙ La Spezia prov., Liguria, N Italy, Mediterranean port at head of Gulf of Spezia, 50 mi. SE of Genoa; 44°6'N 9°49'E. Chief naval station of Italy, with large shipyards (damaged in Second World War), drydocks (damaged), and arsenal (built 1861–69; badly damaged) containing naval mus. (1924); rail junction. Commercial and industrial center: mfg. (electrical machinery, munitions, porcelain, silk textiles, jute bags, leather goods, flour, macaroni, wine); ironworks, railroad shops, sawmills, thermo-electric plant, sulphur refineries, storage tanks (mineral oils). Exports oil, pig lead, silver, flour, wine, marble. Imports coal, iron, timber, grain, raw jute, mineral oils. Frequented as winter resort. Bishopric. Has church of Santa Maria (1371–1550), 14th-cent. castle, 16th-cent. cathedral (badly damaged), mus. of natural history. An important fortified seaport from medieval times; modern expansion began in 1857 when Cavour transferred naval hq. here from Genoa because of better harbor facilities. Became capital of prov. 1923. In Second World War, heavily bombed (especially 1943–44); c.42,000 residences damaged or destroyed.

Spezia, Gulf of, anc. *Portus Lunae*, N Italy, inlet (□ 30) of Gulf of Genoa, bet. promontory of Portovenere and Palmaria islet (W) and mainland (E); 8 mi. long, 2–5 mi. wide. Forms one of largest and safest harbors in Mediterranean Sea. Long protected by a series of fortifications. Chief ports: SPEZIA, Lerici.

Spezia, La, province (□ 345; pop. 221,634), Liguria, N Italy; ⊙ Spezia. Comprises E RIVIERA di Levante and lower Magra R. valley, enclosed by Ligurian Apennines. Forests cover 55% of area. Agr. (cereals, grapes, olives, citrus fruit) chiefly in Magra R. valley; cattle raising, fishing. Commerce and industry at Spezia and Sarzana. Marble quarries (Palmaria, Portovenere, Levanto). Resorts along Riviera di Levante. Anc. ruins at Luna. Formed 1923, largely from Genova prov.

Spezzano Albanese (spĕtsä'nô älbänä'zĕ), town (pop. 4,685), Cosenza prov., Calabria, S Italy, 11 mi. SSE of Castrovillari; mfg. (agr. machinery, licorice).

Spezzia, Greece: see SPETSAI.

Sphacteria, Greece: see SPHAKTERIA.

Sphagia, Greece: see SPHAKTERIA.

Sphakia or **Sfakia** (both: sfäkēä'), officially *Chora Sphakion* or *Khora Sfakion* (both: khô'rŭ sfäkē'-ôn), village (pop. 600), Canea nome, W Crete, port on S coast, 26 mi. SSE of Canea. Allied troops were evacuated from here following battle of Crete (1941) in Second World War. The rugged Sphakia dist. remained untouched in Middle Ages by Venetian and Turkish control.

Sphakteria or **Sfaktiria** (both: sfäktĭrē'ŭ), Lat. *Sphacteria* (sfăktē'rēŭ), uninhabited island (□ 1.5) in Ionian Sea off W coast of Messenia Peninsula, SW Peloponnesus, Greece, at mouth of Pylos Bay; 3 mi. long, ¾ mi. wide. Site of Athenian victory (425 B.C.) over Sparta. Formerly Sphagia.

Sphinx, Egypt: see GIZA, town.

Sphinx, Switzerland: see JUNGFRAU.

Spice Islands, Indonesia: see MOLUCCAS.

Spiceland, town (pop. 739), Henry co., E central Ind., 8 mi. SSW of New Castle, in agr. area.

Spicer, resort village (pop. 566), Kandiyohi co., S central Minn., on Green L. and 10 mi. NE of Willmar; grain.

Spicheren (spēkrĕn'), Ger. *Spichern* (shpĭkh'ŭrn), village (pop. 1,064), Moselle dept., NE France, near Saar border, 3 mi. E of Forbach; here the French lost the first engagement of the Franco-Prussian War.

Spickard or **Spickardsville** (spĭ'kŭrd–), city (pop. 517), Grundy co., N Mo., on Weldon R. and 12 mi. N of Trenton.

Spielberg, Czechoslovakia: see BRNO.

Spiesen (shpē'zůn), town (pop. 5,736), E Saar, 3 mi. SSW of Neunkirchen; coal mining.

Spiez (shpēts), town (pop. 5,679), Bern canton, central Switzerland, on L. of Thun and 5 mi. SSE of Thun; year-round resort; metal- and woodworking, printing, cement. Medieval castle with 11th-cent. basilica. Hydroelectric plant near by.

Spijkenisse (spī'kůnĭssů), village (pop. 2,291), South Holland prov., SW Netherlands, on Putten isl. and 8 mi. SW of Rotterdam; mfg. (cement, steel window frames). Sometimes spelled Spykenisse.

Spike Island (¾ mi. long and wide), in Cork Harbour, SE Co. Cork, Ireland, just SE of Cóbh; site of Fort Westmorland, used as prison 1847–85. Isl. was garrisoned by the British until 1938, when it was handed over to Ireland.

Spikeroog (shpē'kůrōk), North Sea island (□ 5.5; pop. 768) of East Frisian group, Germany, 8 mi. NE of Esens; 6 mi. long (E–W), 1.5 mi. wide (N–S). Nordseebad Spikeroog is W.

Spila, Albania: see SPILË.

Spilamberto (spēlämběr'tô), town (pop. 2,245), Modena prov., Emilia-Romagna, N central Italy, on Panaro R. and 9 mi. SSE of Modena; rail junction; sausage, wine, music instruments, explosives.

Spilberk, Czechoslovakia: see BRNO.

Spilë (spē'lů) or **Spila** (spē'lä), Ital. *Porto Spilio,* village, S Albania, port (2 mi. S) of Himarë, on Strait of Otranto.

Spilimbergo (spēlēmběr'gô), town (pop. 3,089), Udine prov., Friuli-Venezia Giulia, NE Italy, near Tagliamento R., 16 mi. WNW of Udine; alcohol, liquor, soap, sausage. Has cathedral (begun 1284), school of mosaics.

Spillertown, village (pop. 196), Williamson co., S Ill., 7 mi. ESE of Herrin, in bituminous-coal-mining and agr. area.

Spillimacheen, B.C.: see GALENA.

Spillville, town (pop. 363), Winneshiek co., NE Iowa, on Turkey R. and 10 mi. SW of Decorah. Here in this Czech community Anton Dvorak spent the summer of 1893 and composed part of his symphony, *From the New World.* His house later became a mus. of famous clocks.

Spilsby, town and parish (pop. 1,372), Parts of Lindsey, E Lincolnshire, England, 15 mi. NNE of Boston; agr. market, producing synthetic fertilizer, brick and tile. Has 14th-cent. church and grammar school founded 1550. Sir John Franklin b. here.

Spilsby Island, Australia: see SIR JOSEPH BANKS ISLANDS.

Spinazzola (spēnätsô'lä), town (pop. 11,862), Bari prov., Apulia, S Italy, 8 mi. S of Minervino Murge; cereal-growing area; flour milling, metalware mfg.

Spinbaldak or **Spinboldak** (spēn'bůldůk), town (pop. over 2,000), Kandahar prov., SE Afghanistan, 60 mi. SE of Kandahar, on Pakistan line, opposite Chaman. Next to Khyber Pass route, it is chief Afghanistan-Pakistan border crossing point. Formerly called Qala-i-Jadid or Qala-Jadid.

Spincourt (spēkōōr'), agr. village (pop. 421), Meuse dept., NE France, 17 mi. NE of Verdun.

Spindale, town (pop. 3,891), Rutherford co., S N.C., 22 mi. ENE of Shelby; cotton, hosiery, and lumber mills.

Spindleruv Mlyn (shpĭn'dlĕrōōf mlēn"), Czech *Špindlerův Mlýn,* Ger. *Spindelmühl* (shpĭn'důlmül), village (pop. 1,318), NE Bohemia, Czechoslovakia, at W foot of the Schneekoppe, on Elbe R. near its source and 24 mi. ESE of Liberec, near border of Pol.-administered Germany; leading summer and winter-sports resort. International skiing competitions held here.

Spindletop, Texas: see BEAUMONT.

Spinea (spēnā'ä), village (pop. 946), Venezia prov., Veneto, N Italy, 8 mi. NW of Venice; brushes, brooms.

Spineni (spēnān'), village (pop. 688), Arges prov., S Rumania, 20 mi. NE of Slatina; orchards.

Spinetta Marengo (spēnĕt'tä märĕng'gô), two adjacent villages (pop. 4,669), Alessandria prov., Piedmont, N Italy, 3 mi. SE of Alessandria; cork, furniture.

Spin Ghar, Afghanistan and Pakistan: see SAFED KOH.

Spink, county (□ 1,506; pop. 12,204), NE central S.Dak.; ⊙ Redfield. Agr. area drained by James R. Dairy produce, livestock, poultry, grain. Formed 1873.

Spinoso (spēnô'zô), village (pop. 2,122), Potenza prov., Basilicata, S Italy, 6 mi. ENE of Moliterno.

Spion Kop or **Spioen Kop** (both: spī'ůn kŏp, Afrikaans spēōōn' kôp'), hill (4,812 ft.), W Natal, U. of So. Afr., near Tugela R., 17 mi. SW of Ladysmith. In South African War, scene of battle (1900) during British efforts to relieve Ladysmith.

Spiral Tunnels, SE B.C., 2 tunnels on Canadian Pacific RR transcontinental line, in Rocky Mts., in Yoho Natl. Park, bet. Hector and Field; tunnels are 3,255 ft. and 2,922 ft. long; in each, the rail line almost completes a circle.

Spirding Lake, Poland: see SNIARDWY, LAKE.

Spire, Germany: see SPEYER.

Spires, Germany: see SPEYER.

Spirit Lake. 1 City (pop. 823), Kootenai co., N Idaho, near Wash. line, 35 mi. NE of Spokane and on Spirit L.; lumbering; resort activities. **2** Town (pop. 2,467), ⊙ Dickinson co., NW Iowa, 19 mi. N of Spencer, bet. Spirit and East Okoboji lakes; mfg., farm-trade, and resort center; dried eggs, beverages, chemicals, boats, boxes, cabinets, concrete blocks, farm equipment, hardware. Sand and gravel pit near by. Several state parks in vicinity. Settled 1856, inc. 1879.

Spirit Lake. 1 In N Idaho, fresh-water lake in Kootenai co., c.30 mi. NE of Spokane, Wash.; 5 mi. long, 1 mi. wide. Resort city of Spirit Lake is on NE shore. **2** In NW Iowa, largest glacial lake (4 mi. long, 3 mi. wide) in state, on Minn. line, just N of Spirit Lake town; fed by several small lakes in Minn. Resort area with state park (N). Region was scene of Indian massacre (1857), commemorated by monument at near-by Arnolds Park. **3** In SW Wash., lake in recreational area of Columbia Natl. Forest, just N of Mt. St. Helens; c.3 mi. long. Noted for great depth (more than 1,300 ft.), fine fishing.

Spirit River, village (pop. 362), W Alta., near B.C. border, 40 mi. N of Grande Prairie; lumbering, furniture mfg., mixed farming, wheat. In oil-bearing region.

Spiritwood, village (pop. 278), central Sask., near Witchekan L. (10 mi. long, 3 mi. wide), 75 mi. W of Prince Albert; grain; lumbering.

Spiro (spī'rō), town (pop. 1,365), Le Flore co., SE Okla., near Arkansas R., 15 mi. SW of Fort Smith (Ark.), in agr. area (potatoes, cotton, corn); cotton ginning, fruit and vegetable canning. Founded c.1895 near site of old Fort Coffee (1834). Indian mounds are near by.

Spirovo (spē'růvů), town (1948 pop. over 2,000), central Kalinin oblast, Russian SFSR, 18 mi. SE of Vyshni Volochek; glassworks; flax processing.

Spis (spĭsh), Slovak *Spiš,* Ger. *Zips* (tsĭps), Hung. *Szepes* (sĕ'pĕsh), Pol. *Spisz* (spēsh), historic area formerly in dispute bet. Hungary, Austria, and Poland. Since 1920 plebiscite, it is partly in N and central Slovakia (Czechoslovakia) and partly in Poland. Represents original "free cities" founded in 1750 in Magyar-occupied Slovakia by Ger. colonists. It was a former co. in N Hungary (19th–20th cent.). After Munich Pact (1938), Poland seized JAVORINA area, which was returned to Slovakia by Germany after 1939 partition of Poland.

Spisska Bela (spĭsh'skä bĕ'lä), Slovak *Spišská Belá,* Hung. *Szepesbéla* (sĕ'pĕshbā"lŏ), town (pop. 3,072), N Slovakia, Czechoslovakia, in the High Tatra, on Poprad R., on railroad and 12 mi. NE of Poprad. Has 13th-cent. church, old belfry, mineral springs. Former free town founded by Saxon colonists in 12th cent.

Spisska Nova Ves (nô'vävĕs"), Slovak *Spišska Nová Ves,* Ger. *Neudorf* (noi'dôrf), Hung. *Igló* (ĭg'lō), town (pop. 13,139), E central Slovakia, Czechoslovakia, in the Low Tatra, on Hornad R. and 35 mi. NW of Kosice; rail junction; health resort; noted for iron-mining and woodworking industries. Has picturesque late-Gothic remains. Former free town founded in 12th cent. by Saxon colonists.

Spisska Stara Ves (stä'rä vĕs"), Slovak *Spišská Stará Ves,* Hung. *Szepesófalu* (sĕ'pĕsh-sōfŏlŏŏ), town (pop. 1,282), N Slovakia, Czechoslovakia, in NE foothills of the High Tatra, 23 mi. N of Poprad, near Pol. border; oats, potatoes.

Spisske Podhradie (spĭsh'skā pôt'hrädyĕ), Slovak *Spišské Podhradie,* Ger. *Kirchdrauf* (kĭrkh'drouf), Hung. *Szepesváralja* (sĕ'pĕshvä"rŏlyŏ), town (pop. 2,535), E central Slovakia, Czechoslovakia, 29 mi. NW of Kosice; rail terminus; woodworking industry. Noted for picturesque remains of Spis castle (spĭsh), Slovak *Spiš,* Ger. *Zips* (tsĭps), Hung. *Szepes* (sĕ'pĕsh), built in 11th–13th cent., destroyed in 1780. Also has 13th–15th-cent. church, 16th-cent. town hall, bishop's residence. Near-by health resort of Baldovce (bäl'dôftsĕ), 2 mi. WSW, has large children's sanatorium, alkaline and acidulous springs.

Spisz, Czechoslovakia and Poland: see SPIS.

Spital (shpĭ'täl). **1** or **Spital am Pyhrn** (äm pürn'), town (pop. 2,803), SE Upper Austria, 26 mi. S of Steyr; scythes. Has baroque church. **2** or **Spital am Semmering** (äm zĕm'ůrĭng), town (pop. 2,514), Styria, E central Austria, at S foot of the Semmering, 4 mi. E of Mürzzuschlag; resort (alt. 2,522 ft.).

Spitalfields (spĭ'tůl–), district of Stepney, London, England, N of the Thames, 3 mi. ENE of Charing Cross, named for priory and hosp. of St. Mary (St. Mary Spital), founded here 1197. In 17th cent. Huguenot weavers introduced silk industry, of which district is still a center. Spitalfields was formerly also noted for its shoemakers and bird fanciers. Samuel Gompers b. here.

Spithead (spĭt'hĕd), E part of channel bet. Hampshire mainland and Isle of Wight, England, joining Southampton Water and The Solent to the English Channel; navigation approach to Portsmouth and Southampton. Scene of defeat (1545) of French by the English. In 1797 Spithead was scene of a mutiny in which crews won their demands.

Spiti (spĭt'ē), E subdivision of Kangra dist., NE Punjab, India; crossed by Punjab Himalayas (average height, 18,000 ft.; highest peak, 23,050 ft.); bordered N by Kashmir, W by Lahul and Kulu subdivisions, S by Himachal Pradesh, E by Tibet (frontier undefined). Largely rugged mtn. ridges, snow fields, rock-strewn valleys; forests, animal wild life. Several Buddhist monasteries.

Spitler Woods State Park, Ill.: see DECATUR.

Spitsbergen (spĭts'bûrgůn), archipelago in the Arctic Ocean belonging to Norway, c.400 mi. N of Norway, bet. Greenland (W) and Franz Josef Land (E). Spitsbergen is usually considered to include all the isls. in the area, but the Norwegians consider the Spitsbergen archipelago (□ 23,658) to include the isls. of WEST SPITSBERGEN, NORTHEAST LAND, EDGE ISLAND, BARENTS ISLAND, PRINCE CHARLES FORELAND, and offshore islets (all bet. 76°34'–80°50'N and 10°30'–27°10'E), while a few isls. on E edge of the group—KVITOYA, KONG KARLS LAND, and HOPEN—and BEAR ISLAND farther to S are included, along with Spitsbergen, in the Norwegian possession of Svalbard (sväl'bär) (□ 23,979; pop. in winter of 1946–47 was 1,034 Norwegians and 505 Russians), whose boundaries are 74°–81°N and 10°–35°E. Longyear City, on West Spitsbergen, is seat of governor of Svalbard. A dissected plateau, cut by deep fjords, some of which receive glaciers, Spitsbergen rises to 5,633 ft. in Mt. Newton on West Spitsbergen. The North Atlantic Drift washes the W coasts and makes navigation possible for more than half the year. Some 130 species of arctic vegetation flourish near the coast and on patches of interior tundra. Waterfowl, especially the eider duck, abound; but land game (reindeer, blue and white fox, polar bear, and arctic hare) has been rendered nearly extinct by hunting expeditions and is now protected. Sealing, whaling, and fishing are important occupations, but the chief resource of the isls. is coal, mostly on West Spitsbergen. There also are asbestos, copper, gypsum, iron, marble, mica, zinc, and phosphate deposits. Discovered by the vikings in the 12th cent. and named Svalbard by them, the isls. were again forgotten until their rediscovery by Willem Barents in 1596. For a decade after Henry Hudson reported (1607) good whaling at Spitsbergen, English and Dutch whalers quarreled over the territory; in 1618 they compromised, the Dutch limiting their operations to N Spitsbergen (based at Smeerenburg or Amsterdamoya), leaving the rest to the English, the French, and the Hanseatic League. The Danes at the same time claimed Spitsbergen as part of Greenland. After the decline of whaling, Spitsbergen became (18th cent.) a hunting ground for Russian, and later also Scandinavian, fur traders. In late 19th cent., the isls. were mapped by many notable explorers and scientists, and important coal deposits were discovered. Spitsbergen also served as a base for expeditions by Nordenskjöld, S. A. Andrée, Roald Amundsen, R. E. Byrd, Sir George H. Wilkins, and others. For half a century after the discovery of coal, Spitsbergen was the subject of negotiations by Norway, Russia, and Sweden. By a treaty signed at Paris in 1920 and subsequently ratified by the other claimants, Spitsbergen was awarded to Norway. The treaty prohibited military installations on the isls. and insured recognition of claims of other countries to parts of the coal fields. Norwegian sovereignty was proclaimed Aug., 1925. In Second World War, Spitsbergen was raided in 1941 by an Allied party which evacuated the civilian pop. to England and set fire to the mines. A German garrison was expelled in 1942 by a small Norwegian force. In 1943 German raid completed the devastation of the mines and mining installations; they were rebuilt after 1945. The Ger. spelling Spitzbergen was formerly often used.

Spitsevka (spē'tsyĭfků), village (1926 pop. 3,754), W Stavropol Territory, Russian SFSR, 25 mi. ENE of Stavropol, in wheat and sunflower area. Until c.1940, Spitsevskoye.

Spittal or **Spittal an der Drau** (shpĭt'äl, än dĕr drou'), town (pop. 9,672), Carinthia, S Austria, on Drau R. and 21 mi. NW of Villach; highway junction; S terminus of Tauern RR; leather goods, lumber and paper mills, breweries; resort.

Spittal, England: see BERWICK-UPON-TWEED.

Spittel, France: see HÔPITAL, L'.

Spitzbergen: see SPITSBERGEN.

Spitzhorn (shpĭts'hôrn), peak (9,219 ft.) in Bernese Alps, SW Switzerland, 10 mi. N of Sion.

Spivey (spī'vē), city (pop. 109), Kingman co., S Kansas, on Chikaskia R. and 12 mi. S of Kingman; wheat.

Spjelkavik (spyĕl'kävēk), village (pop. 744) in Borgund canton (pop. 11,431), More og Romsdal co., W Norway, port on a North Sea inlet, 8 mi. E of Alesund; mfg. (shoes, furniture). Agr., and fisheries near by. Medieval trading center at Borgund village (4 mi. W), ruins of which are preserved though heavily damaged by fire (1904). Peat bogs, forests, mtn. caves near by. Formerly spelled Spilkevik.

Splane Place, village (pop. 1,665, with adjacent Highland Park), Ouachita parish, N La.

Split (splĭt, splēt), Ital. *Spalato* (spä'lätô), chief Dalmatian city (pop. 49,885), ⊙ Dalmatia oblast (formed 1949), S Croatia, Yugoslavia, major seaport on Adriatic Sea, 155 mi. S of Zagreb, on small promontory, at E foot of the Marjan (584 ft.); approached by Split Channel (SW) of Adriatic

Sea. Rail terminus; tourist center; seaside resort. Has shipyards, fish canneries; cement works (at SOLIN, KASTEL SUCURAC) based on local argillaceous marl; mfg. (carpets, roofing materials, alcohol, flour products). Marasca is grown in vicinity. Brown-coal area (NW) includes SIVERIC mine. Formerly seat of R.C. archbishop (established 920); bishopric since 1820. Split is noted for palace of Diocletian (begun A.D. 295), which, despite considerable devastation, is still one of finest examples of Roman architecture. Has cathedral dating from Roman period, old town hall in Venetian Gothic style, archaeological mus., oceanographic institute, and numerous antiquities (notably at SOLIN). Split has 2 harbors: the larger is in S, but the northern one is better-equipped and exports chiefly cement. Docks, destroyed by Germans, were repaired after Second World War. A refuge for Christians who fled near-by Salonae (see SOLIN), city was built (c.620) within walls of palace of Diocletian. Later passed to Byzantine Empire, Croatian and Hung. kingdoms, Venice (1420), Austria (1797), France (1808), Austria (1814), and Yugoslavia (1919).

Split, Cape, on S side of Minas Channel, NW N.S., at entrance to Minas Basin, 18 mi. N of Kentville; 45°20′N 64°29′W.

Split Lake (34 mi. long, 10 mi. wide), N Man., on Nelson R.; 56°10′N 96°W.

Split Mountain, Calif.: see KINGS CANYON NATIONAL PARK.

Split Peak (9,601 ft.), SE B.C., near Alta. border, in Rocky Mts., on SE edge of Kootenay Natl. Park, 25 mi. SW of Banff; 50°53′N 115°56′W.

Spluga, Passo dello, Italy and Switzerland: see SPLÜGEN PASS.

Splügen Pass (shplü′gůn), Ital. *Passo dello Spluga* (alt. 6,945 ft.), on Italo-Swiss border, 23 mi. N of L. Como, bet. Lepontine and Rhaetian Alps, 13 mi. NNW of Chiavenna, (Italy). Crossed by Splügen Road (built 1819–21) bet. CHIAVENNA and Splügen (village 11 mi. SSW of Thusis, Switzerland).

Spodnji Dravograd, Yugoslavia: see DRAVOGRAD.

Spofford, town (pop. 246), Kinney co., SW Texas, 31 mi. ESE of Del Rio; rail junction; shipping point in ranching area (sheep, goats, cattle).

Spofford Lake, Cheshire co., SW N.H., resort lake near Chesterfield, 8 mi. W of Keene; 2 mi. long.

Spokane (spōkăn′), county (□ 1,763; pop. 221,561), E Wash.; ⊙ SPOKANE. Drained by Spokane R. Lumber, wheat, hay, truck, dairy products, livestock. Formed 1858.

Spokane, city (pop. 161,721), ⊙ Spokane co., E Wash., 230 mi. E of Seattle, at falls of Spokane R.; 47°40′N 117°25′W. Commercial and railroad center for the "Inland Empire," a rich lumbering, mining, and wheat-, stock-, and fruit-producing area; its industries include processing of wheat, meat, dairy products, petroleum, lumber; magnesium and aluminum reduction plants, aluminum rolling mill, machine and railroad shops. Port of entry. Points of interest: art center, mus., Episcopal and R.C. cathedrals, Gonzaga Univ., Whitworth Col., several fine parks. Spokane Air Force Base (post office address is Fairchild, formerly Bong) is 11 mi. W. Fort George Wright is just NW. Settled c.1872 in an area populated as early as 1810; inc. 1881 as Spokane Falls. Coming of the railroad (1883) aided early expansion. A great fire (1889) destroyed most of the town, but regrowth was rapid and the next year the new town was reincorporated as a city; has since become 2d largest city in Wash.

Spokane, Mount (5,878 ft.), E Wash., peak c.25 mi. NE of Spokane, in state park. Road to summit.

Spokane River, in Idaho and Wash., flows generally W from N tip of Coeur d'Alene L., NW Idaho, past Spokane, Wash., to Columbia R. 20 mi. NNW of Davenport; 100 mi. long. Farming, lumbering, mining are chief activities in river basin. Long Lake Dam (completed 1915; 247 ft. high), 25 mi. WNW of Spokane, furnishes power.

Spokoinaya or **Spokoynaya** (spŭkoi′nīŭ), village (1926 pop. 6,914), SE Krasnodar Territory, Russian SFSR, in N foothills of the Greater Caucasus, 55 mi. SSE of Armavir; dairying, flour milling, livestock raising.

Spokoiny or **Spokoynyy** (–nē), town (1942 pop. over 500), SE Yakut Autonomous SSR, Russian SFSR, 120 mi. SE of Aldan; gold mines.

Spokojna Gora, Poland: see MIRSK.

Spoleto (spôlā′tô), anc. *Spoletium*, town (pop. 10,579), Perugia prov., Umbria, central Italy, 13 mi. NNE of Terni; cotton and woolen mills, tannery; soap, macaroni. Archbishopric. Has Roman ruins (bridge, triumphal arch, theater), castle (1355–67; now a penitentiary), and several medieval churches with early mosaics and paintings. In 11th-cent. cathedral are frescoes by Filippo Lippi. An Umbrian and later Etruscan town; flourished under Romans. Became seat (A.D. c.570) of extensive autonomous Lombard duchy. Destroyed by Frederick Barbarossa in 1155; rebuilt and passed to Papal States in 13th cent.

Spondon (spŏn′dŭn, spōōn′–), town and parish (pop. 4,881), SE Derby, England, on Derwent R. and 3 mi. E of Derby; rayon center; chemical industry. Has 14th-cent. church.

Spongdal (spông′däl), village in Byneset (formerly Bynaeset) canton (pop. 1,877), Sor-Trondelag co., central Norway, on an inlet of Trondheim Fjord, 10 mi. SW of Trondheim; dairying, grain milling. Has medieval church.

Spooner. 1 Village (pop. 420), Lake of the Woods co., N Minn., on Rainy R. (at Ont. line) and just E of Baudette; dairying. **2** Village (pop. 1,264), Orange co., SE Texas. **3** City (pop. 2,597), Washburn co., NW Wis., on Yellow R. and 60 mi. S of Superior, in woods and lake region; rail junction; trade and shipping center for farming and dairying area. A state fish hatchery and a Univ. of Wisconsin branch agr. experiment station are near by. Settled c.1883, inc. 1909.

Spoon River, NW central Ill., rises in SW Bureau co., meanders S, SW, and SE, to Illinois R. opposite Havana; c.160 mi. long.

Sporades (spô′rŭdēz, spŏ′–), Gr. *Sporades* or *Sporadhes* (both: spôrä′dhĕs) [=the scattered], name applied in its broadest sense to all Greek islands of the Aegean outside of the Cyclades. In opposition to the Cyclades, which clustered in a circle around Delos, the name was applied in antiquity to the scattered isls. of the SE Aegean Sea off the W coast of Asia Minor, including generally the Dodecanese, Icaria, and Samos. Sometimes Chios and Lesbos are added to the list. While the name Sporades is no longer applied to this S grouping, it persists in the Northern Sporades [Gr. *Voriai Sporades*] (39°N; off the coasts of Thessaly and Euboea), which include the isls of Skyros and Skyropoula in Euboea nome, and Skopelos, Alonissos, Skiathos, Pelagonesi, and Peristera in the Thessalian Magnesia nome.

Sporny or **Spornyy** (spôr′nē), town (1948 pop. over 2,000), N Khabarovsk Territory, Russian SFSR, on small Orotukan R. (right branch of Kolyma R.) and 190 mi. N of Magadan (linked by road); 62°20′N 151°7′E. Road center in Kolyma goldmining region.

Spotland, England: see ROCHDALE.

Spotswood, borough (pop. 2,325), Middlesex co., E N.J., 8 mi. SE of New Brunswick; site of Revolutionary ironworks. Inc. 1908.

Spotsylvania (spŏtsůlvā′nyů), county (□ 413; pop. 11,920), NE Va.; ⊙ Spotsylvania. Historic FREDERICKSBURG (trade, mfg. center) is in but independent of co. Bounded N by Rapidan and Rappahannock rivers (here joining), SW and S by North Anna R.; drained by short Ny and Po rivers. Major Civil War battles are commemorated by Fredericksburg and Spotsylvania Co. Battlefields Memorial (hq. at Fredericksburg). Agr. (corn, wheat, tobacco, truck), dairy products, poultry, livestock. Formed 1720.

Spotsylvania, village, ⊙ Spotsylvania co., NE Va., 10 mi. SW of Fredericksburg. In Civil War, village (then called Spotsylvania Courthouse) gave its name to bloody but indecisive 13-day battle bet. Union forces under Grant and Confederates under Lee; severest action took place on May 12, 1864, when Union assault on salient (the Bloody Angle) in Confederate line was repulsed. Part of battle area now included in Fredericksburg and Spotsylvania Co. Battlefields Memorial (hq. at FREDERICKSBURG).

Spotted Islands, island (4 mi. long, 4 mi. wide) and settlement, just off SE Labrador; 53°28′N 55°47′W; fishing port and seaplane anchorage.

Sprague (sprāg). **1** Town (pop. 2,320), New London co., E Conn., on Shetucket R. and 6 mi. N of Norwich; mfg. (textiles, paperboard, hosp. supplies), agr. Includes mfg. villages of Baltic (pop. 1,345), Hanover (hă′nōvůr), and Versailles (vůrsālz′, vûr–). Inc. 1861. **2** Town (pop. 29), Bates co., W Mo., near Marais des Cygnes R., 5 mi. W of Rich Hill. **3** Village (pop. 110), Lancaster co., SE Nebr., 12 mi. S of Lincoln and on branch of Platte R. **4** City (pop. 598), Lincoln co., E Wash., 35 mi. SW of Spokane, in Columbia basin agr. region; wheat, hay, oats. Colville L. (SW), 6 mi. long, is recreational center. **5** Village (pop. 2,626), Raleigh co., S W.Va., just N of Beckley, in coal-mining area.

Sprague River, S Oregon, formed in Cascade Range, flows c.75 mi. W to join Williamson R. and enter Upper Klamath L.

Spragueville, town (pop. 115), Jackson co., E Iowa, 12 mi. E of Maquoketa; creamery.

Sprang (spräng), town (pop. 1,826), North Brabant prov., S Netherlands, 8 mi. N of Tilburg; leather tanning, shoe mfg.

Spranger, Mount (9,920 ft.), E B.C., in Cariboo Mts., 75 mi. E of Quesnel; 52°54′N 120°44′W.

Spratly Island (sprăt′lē), Chinese *Nanwei* (nän′wā′), Chinese dependency in S.China Sea, part of Kwangtung prov.; 111°55′E 8°38′N; 500 yds. long, 300 yds. wide. Sea-birds' eggs, turtles. Occupied by France, 1933–39; and by Japan during 1939–45, when it was developed as submarine base. Also called Storm Island.

Spray (sprā), textile village (pop. 5,542), Rockingham co., N N.C., adjacent to Leaksville, 12 mi. NNW of Reidsville, near Va. line; cotton and woolen mills.

Spreca River or **Sprecha River** (both: sprĕ′chä), Serbo-Croatian *Spreča*, NE Bosnia, Yugoslavia, rises W of Zvornik, flows c.60 mi. WNW, past Gracanica, to Bosna R. opposite Doboj. Lower course followed by Tuzla-Doboj RR.

Spreckels, village, Monterey co., W Calif., just S of Salinas; a "company town" for large beet-sugar refinery.

Spreckelsville, town (1940 pop. 2,634), N Maui, T. H., near Kahului; sugar plantations.

Spree Forest (shprā), Ger. *Spreewald* (shprā′vält), marshy wooded region, E Germany, in Lower Lusatia, astride the Spree bet. Cottbus (SE) and Lübben (NW); noted for its vegetables, pickled cucumbers, and horse-raddish. Crisscrossed by innumerable small waterways on which flat-bottomed boats are chief means of transportation. Almost entirely Wendish pop. has retained its local costumes and colorful traditions. Favorite excursion resort for near-by Berliners.

Spree-Oder Canal, Germany: see ODER-SPREE CANAL.

Spree River (shprā), E Germany, rises in Lusatian Mts. just N of Neugersdorf, meanders generally N, past Bautzen and Cottbus, through Spree Forest and Schwieloch L., past Fürstenwalde (river bed here used by ODER-SPREE CANAL), then continues WNW through Müggel L., traversing Berlin and joining the Havel (with which it is also connected by TELTOW CANAL) at NW Spandau dist. Length, c.250 mi. Navigable (for small vessels) to Cottbus. Receives Dahme (left) and Malxe (right) rivers.

Spreewald, Germany: see SPREE FOREST.

Spremberg (shprĕm′bĕrk). **1** Town (pop. 17,498), Brandenburg, E Germany, in Lower Lusatia, on the Spree and 14 mi. S of Cottbus; lignite-mining center; woolen and paper milling, wood- and metal-working; mfg. of glass, chemicals, plastics, machinery. Old part of town is on isl. in the Spree. Has late-Gothic church; and palace, the former seat of dukes of Saxe-Merseburg. Captured (April, 1945) by Soviet forces. Just S is important Trattendorf power station. **2** Town, Saxony, Germany: see NEUSALZA-SPREMBERG.

Sprendlingen (shprĕnt′lĭng-ůn), town (pop. 9,158), S Hesse, W Germany, in former Starkenburg prov., 2.5 mi. S of Neu-Isenburg; leatherworking, paper milling. Just N is large Rhine-Main airport.

Spresiano (sprĕzyä′nô), town (pop. 2,442), Treviso prov., Veneto, N Italy, near Piave R., 8 mi. N of Treviso; sawmill, box factory. Hydroelectric plant

Sprimont (sprĕmō′), town (pop. 4,059), Liége prov., E central Belgium, 10 mi. SSE of Liége; granite quarrying.

Spring Arbor, village (pop. c.500), Jackson co., S Mich., 11 mi. WSW of Jackson; has a jr. col.

Spring Bay, village (pop. 203), Woodford co., central Ill., on L. Peoria (widening of Illinois R.), 10 mi. NNE of Peoria, in agr. and bituminous-coal area.

Springbok (sprĭng′bôk), town (pop. 1,608), ⊙ Namaqualand dist., W Cape Prov., U. of So. Afr., 300 mi. N of Cape Town, in copper-mining region; 39°41′S 17°53′E; first shaft (unsuccessful in search for copper) sunk here 1685 by Governor Van der Stel's expedition.

Springboro. 1 Village (pop. 516), Warren co., SW Ohio, 14 mi. S of Dayton. **2** Borough (pop. 611), Crawford co., NW Pa., 27 mi. SW of Erie.

Springbrook, town (pop. 109), Jackson co., E Iowa, 26 mi. SSE of Dubuque, in agr. area.

Spring Brook or **Springbrook,** village (pop. 51), Williams co., W N.Dak., 11 mi. NE of Williston.

Springburn, village (pop. 132), E S.Isl., New Zealand, 60 mi. WSW of Christchurch; rail terminus; sheep raising.

Spring City. 1 Borough (pop. 3,258), Chester co., SE Pa., 6 mi. SE of Pottstown and on Schuylkill R.; metal products, clothing, paper boxes, flags. Inc. 1867 as Springville; renamed 1872. **2** Town (pop. 1,725), Rhea co., E Tenn., at head of arm of Watts Bar Reservoir, 50 mi. NE of Chattanooga, in Tennessee valley; mfg. of hosiery, underwear; lumbering. **3** City (pop. 703), Sanpete co., central Utah, 17 mi. NNE of Manti, in irrigated agr. area; alt. 5,685 ft.

Spring Creek. 1 In SW Ga., rises W of Edison, flows c.75 mi. S, past Colquitt, to Flint R. near its junction with the Chattahoochee R. at the Fla. line. **2** In E Ill., rises N of Paxton, flows c.40 mi. generally NNE to Iroquois R. 6 mi. NW of Watseka. **3** In W central N.Dak., rises in Dunn co., flows E c.90 mi., past Goldenvalley and Zap, to Knife R. near Beulah.

Springdale. 1 City (pop. 5,835), Washington co., NW Ark., 9 mi. N of Fayetteville, in the Ozarks; ships fruit (apples, peaches, grapes, strawberries), poultry; makes grape and other fruit juices, vinegar, wine. Settled c.1850, inc. 1878. **2** Village, Conn.: see STAMFORD. **3** Residential borough (pop. 4,939), Allegheny co., W central Pa., 13 mi. NE of Pittsburgh and on Allegheny R. Inc. 1906. **4** Village (pop. 4,313, with adjacent Lancaster Mills), Lancaster co., N S.C., just W of Lancaster; textile milling. **5** Village, Washington co., SW Utah, 30 mi. E of St. George; S gateway to Zion Natl. Park. Bryce Canyon Natl. Park is 45 mi. NE. **6** Town (pop. 268), Stevens co., NE Wash., 32 mi. NNW of Spokane and on Colville R.; dairying; hay, potatoes, lumber.

Springe (shprĭng'ů), town (pop. 7,464), in former Prussian prov. of Hanover, W Germany, after 1945 in Lower Saxony, 14 mi. SW of Hanover; rug mfg.

Springer. 1 Village (pop. 1,558), Colfax co., NE N.Mex., on smaller of 2 Cimarron rivers, near Sangre de Cristo Mts., and 38 mi. SSW of Raton; alt. c.5,840 ft. Trade center and shipping point (lumber, sugar beets, stock feed) in sheep and cattle region. Coal mines in vicinity. State industrial school for boys here. Inc. 1910. **2** Village (pop. c.300), Carter co., S Okla., 10 mi. N of Ardmore, in agr. and stock-raising area.

Springerton, village (pop. 279), White co., SE Ill., 30 mi. ESE of Mount Vernon, in agr. area.

Springerville, town (pop. 689), Apache co., E Ariz., on Little Colorado R. and 27 mi. S of St. Johns; alt. c.7,000 ft. Hunting center; livestock, poultry, grain.

Springfield, village (pop. 451), S Ont., 14 mi. ENE of St. Thomas; dairying, farming, fruitgrowing.

Springfield, Lancashire, England: see COPPULL.

Springfield, township (pop. 271), ⊙ Tawera co. (□ 941; pop. 622), E central S.Isl., New Zealand, 40 mi. WNW of Christchurch; agr.; health resort.

Springfield. 1 Town (pop. 2,041), ⊙ Baca co., SE Colo., 65 mi. SE of La Junta; alt. 4,400 ft.; grain, livestock, dairy products, beans. Inc. 1889. **2** Town (pop. 1,084), Bay co., NW Fla., suburb of Panama City. **3** City (pop. 627), ⊙ Effingham co., E Ga., 24 mi. NNW of Savannah. **4** City (pop. 81,628), ⊙ Ill. and Sangamon co., central Ill., on Sangamon R. and c.175 mi. SW of Chicago; 39°47'N 89°38'W; alt. c.600 ft. Trade, industrial, and distribution center in agr. (Corn Belt) and bituminous-coal-mining area; mfg. of farm machinery, food products, feed, beverages, clothing, footwear, soybean and tobacco products, clocks, radio parts, radiators, clay products, automotive and garage equipment, electric meters and parts, construction machinery, foundry and machine-shop products, wood products; railroad shops. Limestone, clay, oil, sand, gravel deposits near by. Abraham Lincoln, who was instrumental in making Springfield the state capital in 1837, lived and practiced law here during 1837–61. Here he is buried, with his wife and 3 of their children, in a tomb and monument designed by L. G. Mead. The Centennial Bldg. contains the state mus. and offices and libraries of the state historical society, with valuable Lincoln collections. Lincoln's home is preserved as a shrine. Other places of interest include the capitol (1867–87); the court house (1837), which served as the capitol for many years; the governor's mansion (1853–57); Ill. State Library; and state fairgrounds. Seat of Concordia Theological Seminary, Lincoln Col. of Law, a jr. col., and several preparatory schools. Near by are New Salem State Park, Camp Butler Natl. Cemetery, and artificial L. Springfield, the city's water supply and resort (swimming, fishing). Vachel Lindsay was b. here. Settled 1818; inc. as town in 1832, as city in 1840. **5** Town (pop. 2,032), ⊙ Washington co., central Ky., 25 mi. W of Danville. Trade center for Bluegrass agr. region (livestock, dairy products, poultry, burley tobacco, corn, wheat); mfg. of clothing, cheese; flour and feed mills, tobacco warehouses. Courthouse contains marriage certificate of Thomas Lincoln and Nancy Hanks. Near by are Lincoln Homestead State Park, with reproduction of home of Lincoln's paternal grandmother and a memorial to Nancy Hanks; St. Rose's Priory (Dominican school founded 1806; attended 1816–18 by Jefferson Davis); St. Catharine convent (1820); and Indian mounds. Town founded 1793. **6** Town (pop. 414), Penobscot co., E central Maine, 35 mi. SE of Millinocket, in hunting, fishing area. **7** Industrial city (pop. 162,399), ⊙ Hampden co., SW Mass., on the Connecticut (bridged) and 5 mi. N of Conn. line, 80 mi. WSW of Boston. Produces electrical and other machinery, machine tools, firearms, motorcycles, plastics, food products, printing and publishing, clothing, toys. Port of entry. U.S. armory, here, was founded by Washington. Seat of American International Col., art museums, Springfield Col. Westover Air Force Base is 7 mi. N. The annual Eastern States Fair is held at Storrowton, site of reconstructed colonial village. Metal products are made at Indian Orchard village. Springfield settled 1636 by Puritans, inc. as town 1641, as city 1852. Was a scene in Shay's Rebellion (1786–87), station on Underground Railroad. **8** City (pop. 2,574), Brown co., SW Minn., on Cottonwood R. and 26 mi. W of New Ulm; trading point in agr. area; dairy products, flour, feed, bricks and tiles. Platted 1877, inc. as village 1881, as city 1923. **9** City (pop. 66,731), ⊙ Greene co., SW Mo., in Ozarks resort area, near James R., 145 mi. SE of Kansas City; alt. 1,264 ft. Agr., industrial center; railroad shops, stockyards, lime plant, ironworks, steel mill; steel products, clothing, chemicals, food, lumber products. Large poultry market. Seat of Drury Col., Southwest Mo. State Col., Central Bible Inst. and Seminary. Near by are U.S. hosp. for criminal insane, state park, and fish hatchery. Inc. 1855. **10** Village (pop. 377), Sarpy co., E Nebr., 15 mi. SW of Omaha, near Platte R.; grain, livestock, fruit, poultry. **11** Town (pop. 324), Sullivan co., W N.H., 13 mi. NE of Newport. **12** Village (1940 pop. 3,087), Union co., NE N.J., 7 mi. W of Newark; mfg. (chemicals, clothing, radio equipment, rubber goods); nurseries; truck farming. Settled c.1717. Church and several other buildings burned by British, 1780; Bret Harte's poem "Caldwell of Springfield" commemorates Chaplain James Caldwell's aid to defenders. Present church was built 1791. **13** A residential section of E Queens borough of New York city, SE N.Y. **14** City (pop. 78,508), ⊙ Clark co., W central Ohio, 22 mi. ENE of Dayton and on Mad R.; industrial center making agr. and construction machinery, motor vehicles, foundry and machine-shop products, electrical goods, engines and turbines, printed matter, leather goods, paper products, measuring instruments. Wittenberg Col. is here. George Rogers Clark Memorial Park is near by. Settled 1799, laid out 1801, inc. 1850. **15** City (pop. 10,807), Lane co., W Oregon, on Willamette R. and just E of Eugene; lumber milling. Inc. 1893. **16** Town (pop. 782), Orangeburg co., W central S.C., 24 mi. W of Orangeburg; grist mill. **17** City (pop. 801), Bon Homme co., SE S.Dak., 10 mi. SSW of Tyndall and on Missouri R.; window sashes, dairy products, grain. State teachers col. **18** City (pop. 6,506), ⊙ Robertson co., N Tenn., 24 mi. N of Nashville, in tobacco, timber area; an important tobacco market; mfg. of woolen blankets, wood products; flour milling; stone quarries. Founded c.1798. **16** Town (pop. 9,190), including industrial Springfield village (pop. 4,940), Windsor co., SE Vt., on Connecticut and Black rivers and 33 mi. SE of Rutland. Mfg. (machinery, machine tools, textiles, metal products, printing, building materials); agr. (poultry, dairy products); winter sports. Settled before Revolution; its machinery and tool factories were flourishing by 1900.

Springfield Gardens, SE N.Y., a section of SE Queens borough of New York city; mainly residential. Fur dyeing; mfg. of clothing, machinery.

Springfield Place, village (pop. 13,161, with adjacent Lakeview), Calhoun co., S Mich.

Springfontein (sprĭng'fôntān"), town (pop. 2,093), SW Orange Free State, U. of So. Afr., 80 mi. SSW of Bloemfontein; alt. 4,985 ft.; rail junction; grain, stock. Airfield.

Spring Forest, Ill.: see WILLOW SPRINGS.

Spring Garden. 1 Town (pop. 46), Miller co., central Mo., near Osage R., 6 mi. E of Olean. **2** Village (pop. 2,176, with adjacent Standard), Westmoreland co., SW Pa., just N of Mt. Pleasant.

Spring Glen, resort village, Ulster co., SE N.Y., near W base of the Shawangunk range, 4 mi. SSW of Ellenville.

Spring Green, village (pop. 1,064), Sauk co., S Wis., near Wisconsin R., 35 mi. WNW of Madison, in timber, dairying, and livestock area; cheese, lumber, flour, feed.

Spring Grove. 1 Village (pop. 269), McHenry co., NE Ill., near Fox L., 20 mi. WNW of Waukegan, in agr. and lake-resort area. **2** Town (pop. 333), Wayne co., E Ind., just N of Richmond, in agr. area. **3** Village (pop. 1,093), Houston co., extreme SE Minn., near Iowa line, 25 mi. SW of La Crosse, Wis., in grain, potato, livestock area; dairy products, beverages. **4** Borough (pop. 1,238), York co., S Pa., 9 mi. SW of York; paper. Laid out 1747, inc. 1882.

Springhead, former urban district (1931 pop. 4,834), West Riding, SW Yorkshire, England, 2 mi. E of Oldham; cotton milling. Inc. 1937 in Saddleworth.

Springhill, town (pop. 7,170), N N.S., 15 mi. SE of Amherst; coal-mining center. Coal is shipped via Parrsboro.

Springhill, village (1930 pop. 128), Magallanes prov., S Chile, in N part of main isl. of Tierra del Fuego, 75 mi. NE of Punta Arenas; oil wells; sheep raising.

Spring Hill. 1 Unincorporated residential W suburb (1940 census dist. pop. 2,357) of Mobile, Ala. Spring Hill Col. is here. **2** Town (pop. 86), Warren co., S central Iowa, 12 mi. S of Des Moines, in agr. area. **3** City (pop. 619), Johnson co., E Kansas, 25 mi. SSW of Kansas City, Kansas; dairying, agr. **4** Village (pop. 91), Stearns co., central Minn., 33 mi. W of St. Cloud, in grain and livestock area. **5** Village (pop. 1,030), Cambria co., central Pa., 15 mi. NE of Johnstown. **6** Town (pop. 541), Maury co., central Tenn., 28 mi. SSW of Nashville, in timber, livestock, farm area.

Springhill, town (pop. 3,383), Webster parish, NW La., near Ark. line, 38 mi. NE of Shreveport, in agr. area (cotton, corn, potatoes); lumber, pulp, and paper milling; cotton ginning. Inc. 1922.

Spring Hills, town (pop. 27), Marion co., central Ind., NW suburb of Indianapolis.

Spring Hope, town (pop. 1,275), Nash co., E central N.C., 17 mi. W of Rocky Mount, in farm area; mfg. of cottonseed oil, lumber milling. Settled 1886; inc. 1889.

Spring Lake. 1 Village (pop. 1,824), Ottawa co., SW Mich., 29 mi. WNW of Grand Rapids, at mouth of Grand R. on Spring L. (c.3 mi. long; drains SW through short outlet to L. Michigan). Resort and shipping point for orchard and farm area; mfg. (auto parts, trailers, metal products); commercial fishing. Indian mounds near by. Inc. 1869. **2** Resort borough (pop. 2,008), Monmouth co., E N.J., near the Atlantic, 5 mi. S of Asbury Park; fruit, truck. Small lakes near by. Inc. 1892.

Spring Lake Heights, borough (pop. 1,798), Monmouth co., E N.J., just W of Spring Lake. Inc. 1927.

Spring Lake Park, town (pop. 156), Hancock co., central Ind., on Sugar Creek and 15 mi. E of Indianapolis.

Springlands or **Springlands Plantation,** village (pop. 181), Berbice co., NE Br. Guiana, on the coast, at mouth of Courantyne R. (Du. Guiana border), 36 mi. SE of New Amsterdam, in sugar-growing region. A port through which passes trade bet. Br. Guiana and Du. Guiana. Exports cattle, rice, edible oils, canned fish, salt.

Spring Mill, village (pop. 1,553, with adjacent Cedar Heights), Montgomery co., SE Pa., just SE of Conshohocken.

Spring Mills. 1 Village (pop. c.600), Centre co., central Pa., 16 mi. ENE of State College; textile milling. **2** Textile-mill village (pop. 1,210), Lancaster co., N S.C., adjacent to Lancaster.

Spring Mill State Park, Ind.: see MITCHELL.

Spring Mountains, SE Nev., in W Clark co., near Calif. line, in Nevada Natl. Forest; gold, silver, platinum, vanadium deposits. Rises to 11,910 ft. in Charleston Peak, 32 mi. W of Las Vegas.

Spring Peak, Nev.: see SANTA ROSA RANGE.

Spring Place, town (pop. 214), Murray co., NW Ga., 8 mi. E of Dalton.

Springport. 1 Town (pop. 217), Henry co., E Ind., 10 mi. S of Muncie, in agr. area. **2** Village (pop. 598), Jackson co., S Mich., 17 mi. NW of Jackson, in agr. area; mfg. of paint, varnish.

Spring River. 1 In S Mo. and N Ark., rises in Howell and Oregon counties, flows c.100 mi. S and SE to Black R. above Black Rock, Ark. At Mammoth Spring, Ark., receives flow of large springs. **2** In SW Mo., SE Kansas, and NE Okla., rises in Lawrence co., Mo.; flows W into Kansas, then S to L. of the Cherokees E of Miami, Okla.; 120 mi. long.

Springs, New Zealand: see SPRINGSTON.

Springs, city (pop. 111,141), S Transvaal, U. of So. Afr., on E Witwatersrand, 25 mi. E of Johannesburg; alt. 5,338 ft.; rail junction; gold-mining center. Site of technical col.

Springs of Moses, Egypt: see SUEZ.

Springston, township (pop. 248), ⊙ Springs co. (□ 91; pop. 1,878), E S.Isl., New Zealand, 16 mi. SW of Christchurch; dairy.

Springsure, village (pop. 719), E central Queensland, Australia, 165 mi. WSW of Rockhampton; rail terminus; sheep.

Springtown, town (pop. 102), Benton co., extreme NW Ark., 20 mi. NW of Fayetteville, in the Ozarks.

Spring Vale, residential suburb (pop. 2,768) of Melbourne, S Victoria, Australia, 15 mi. SE of Melbourne.

Springvale. 1 Town (pop. 127), Randolph co., SW Ga., 6 mi. NW of Cuthbert. **2** Village, Maine: see SANFORD.

Spring Valley. 1 Village (1940 pop. 1,051), San Diego co., S Calif., just E of San Diego, in citrus-fruit area. **2** City (pop. 4,916), Bureau co., N Ill., on Illinois R. (bridged here), just W of Peru, in agr. and mineral area (bituminous coal, sand, gravel); makes clothing, cigars. Inc. 1886. **3** Village (pop. 2,467), Fillmore co., SE Minn., on branch of Root R., near Iowa line, and 23 mi. S of Rochester; trade center for agr. area; dairy products, beverages. Settled 1855, inc. 1856. **4** Resort and residential village (pop. 4,500), Rockland co., SE N.Y., near N.J. line, 7 mi. W of Nyack, in diversified-farming area; mfg. (fur coats, uniforms, rubber stamps, leather and paper products, cutlery, smoking pipes); stone quarrying. Inc. 1902. **5** Village (pop. 645), Greene co., S central Ohio, 6 mi. SW of Xenia, in fruit and truck-farming area; mineral water bottled here. **6** Village (pop. 975), Pierce co., W Wis., on Eau Galle R. and 36 mi. W of Eau Claire, in dairying, poultry-raising, and lumbering area; flour milling.

Springview, village (pop. 298), ⊙ Keya Paha co., N Nebr., 20 mi. N of Ainsworth, near S.Dak. line; trade center; flour, feed; grain, livestock, dairy and poultry produce.

Springville. 1 Town (pop. 553), St. Clair co., N central Ala., 25 mi. NE of Birmingham; soap, lumber. **2** Town (pop. 680), Linn co., E Iowa, 12 mi. ENE of Cedar Rapids; dairy products. **3** Village (pop. 3,322), Erie co., W N.Y., 28 mi. SSE of Buffalo; mfg. (dental anesthetics, cutlery, castings, canned foods, amusement equipment, machinery, glass, aircraft parts); stone quarrying; lumbering. Dairy, poultry farms. Settled 1807, inc. 1834. **4** City (pop. 6,475), Utah co., N central Utah, 5 mi. SSE of Provo, near Utah L.; alt. 4,563 ft. Fruit-shipping point in agr. area (sugar beets, fruit) irrigated by water from Strawberry R.; flour, canned goods, lumber. Settled 1850 by Mormons. Has art gallery (1937). Fish hatcheries near by.

Springwater, village (pop. c.500), Livingston co., W central N.Y., 22 mi. N of Hornell; farm trade center; mfg. (electrical equipment, canned foods).

Springwood, town (pop. 1,921), E New South Wales, Australia, 40 mi. WNW of Sydney; cattle center; orchards.

Sproat Lake (□ 19), SW B.C., on S central Vancouver Isl., 5 mi. W of Port Alberni; 14 mi. long, 1 mi. wide; fishing.

Sprottau, Poland: see SZPROTAWA.

Spruce Creek, village, Blair co., central Pa., on Little Juniata R. and 7 mi. SE of Tyrone. Indian cave, with artifacts, attracts tourists.

Spruce Island (6 mi. long, 2–3 mi. wide), S Alaska, in Gulf of Alaska, 6 mi. N of Kodiak Isl.; 57°55′N 152°26′W; rises to 1,595 ft.; fishing, canning, fur farming. Inhabitants primarily Russian and Aleut; settled by Russians c.1800. Uzinki village in W.

Spruce Knob, peak (4,860 ft.) of the Alleghenies, in W Pendleton co., E W.Va.; highest point in state. BIG SPRUCE KNOB (4,695 ft.) is SW, in Pocahontas co.

Spruce Mountain. 1 Peak in Nev.: see PEQUOP MOUNTAINS. **2** Peak in W.Va.: see BIG SPRUCE KNOB.

Spruce Pine, resort town (pop. 2,280), Mitchell co., W N.C., 35 mi. NE of Asheville, in the Blue Ridge; mining and processing of mica, flint, kaolin, feldspar; mfg. of ceramics, hosiery; lumber milling. Settled c.1908.

Spui River (spoi), SW Netherlands, navigable branch of Old Maas R.; leaves main stream 6 mi. SSW of Rotterdam; flows 11 mi. SW to the Haringvliet 14 mi. SW of Rotterdam. Divides Putten isl. (NW) from Beijerland isl. (SE).

Spulico, Cape (spōō′lēkô), on W shore of Gulf of Taranto, S Italy, 2 mi. ENE of Amendolara; 39°57′N 16°38′E.

Spullersee (shpŏŏl′ûrzā), small lake in Vorarlberg, W Austria, 23 mi. E of Feldkirch; alt. 5,910 ft.; feeds hydroelectric plant c.2,600 ft. below.

Spungabera, Mozambique: see ESPUNGABERA.

Spur, city (pop. 2,183), Dickens co., NW Texas, on plains just below Cap Rock escarpment, c.55 mi. E of Lubbock; market, shipping, processing point for cattle-ranching and agr. area (cotton, grain, dairy products). Has state agr. experiment station. Hq. for large Spur Ranch, which once included this site. Settled 1909, inc. 1911.

Spurgeon, town (pop. 327), Pike co., SW Ind., 26 mi. NE of Evansville, in agr., oil, and bituminous-coal area.

Spurn Head, England: see HOLDERNESS.

Spurr, Mount (11,069 ft.), S Alaska, in Alaska Range, W of upper Cook Inlet, 80 mi. W of Anchorage; 61°18′N 152°15′W.

Spuyten Duyvil Creek, N.Y.: see HARLEM RIVER.

Spuz or **Spuzh** (spōōsh), Serbo-Croatian *Spuž*, village, S Montenegro, Yugoslavia, on Zeta R., on Titograd–Danilov Grad road and 6 mi. NNW of Titograd. Under Turkish rule until 1878.

Spuzh, Yugoslavia: see SPUZ.

Spy (spē), town (pop. 3,198), Namur prov., S central Belgium, near Sambre R., 7 mi. W of Namur; agr. market. In grotto here prehistoric bones have been found from which neolithic "Spy man" has been reconstructed.

Spykenisse, Netherlands: see SPIJKENISSE.

Spynie (spī′nē), village and parish, N Moray, Scotland, near Elgin. There are remains of Spynie Palace, castle of the bishops of Moray from early 15th cent. until 1686.

Squamish (skwô′mĭsh), village (pop. estimate 500), SW B.C., at head of Howe Sound, at mouth of Squamish R., 30 mi. N of Vancouver; rail terminus; pulp and lumber milling; hydroelectric power. In mining (copper, gold, silver, limonite) region.

Squam Lake (skwäm), central N.H., irregularly shaped lake (c.7 mi. long) 14 mi. NNW of Laconia, in resort area; drains SW through Little Squam L. into Pemigewasset R. Also known as Asquam L.

Squamscott River, N.H.: see EXETER RIVER.

Squannacook River (skwŏ′nùkŏŏk), N Mass., rises in region N of Fitchburg, flows c.25 mi. E and SE to Nashua R. NW of Ayer.

Squantum, Mass.: see QUINCY.

Squapan Lake (skwô′păn), Aroostook co., NE Maine; narrow V-shaped lake 13 mi. SW of Presque Isle; c.16 mi. long.

Square Island (4 mi. long, 3 mi. wide), in St. Michael's Bay, SE Labrador; 52°45′N 55°53′W. On S coast is fishing settlement of Square Island Harbour.

Square Lake, Maine: see FISH RIVER LAKES.

Squaw Harbor, village (pop. 44), SW Alaska, on E coast of Unga Isl.

Squaw Island, N.Y.: see CANANDAIGUA LAKE.

Squaw Lake, resort village (pop. 132), Itasca co., N Minn., c.40 mi. NW of Grand Rapids, in Greater Leech Lake Indian Reservation. Small lakes near by.

Squaw Mountain, peak (11,733 ft.) in Front Range, Clear Creek co., N central Colo.

Squaw Valley, Placer co., E Calif., valley in the Sierra Nevada, just NW of L. Tahoe; ski resort, with ski lifts and trails on Squaw Peak (8,960 ft.).

Squillace (skwēl-lä′chĕ), anc. *Scylacium*, town (pop. 2,401), Catanzaro prov., Calabria, S Italy, near Gulf of Squillace, 10 mi. SSW of Cantanzaro, in olive- and grape-growing region. Bishopric. Has monastery and ruined castle.

Squillace, Gulf of, inlet of Ionian Sea, Calabria, S Italy, bet. Cape Rizzuto (NE) and Cape Stilo (SW); 45 mi. long, 20 mi. wide.

Squinzano (skwēntsä′nô), town (pop. 10,438), Lecce prov., Apulia, S Italy, 9 mi. NW of Lecce; wine-making center; alcohol distilling, soap mfg.

Squire, village (pop. 1,240), McDowell co., S W.Va., 12 mi. S of Welch, near Va. line; coal.

Squirrel Island, Maine: see SOUTHPORT.

Sraburi, Thailand: see SARABURI.

Sragen (sùrä′gùn), town (pop. 15,382), E central Java, Indonesia, 17 mi. NE of Solo; trade center for agr. area (rice, rubber, sugar, corn); textile mills.

Sravana Belgola (srŭ′vŭnŭ bĕlgō′lŭ) or **Shravan Belgola** (shrŭvŭn′), town (pop. 2,709), Hassan dist., W central Mysore, India, 27 mi. ESE of Hassan; handicrafts (brass and copper vessels, glass bangles). Jain religious center and archaeological site, noted for huge, 57-ft.-high monolithic statue of a Jain saint (built A.D. c.980), standing on 470-ft.-high hill. Many elaborately carved temples (10th-17th cent.). Also written Sravanabelgola or Shravanbelgola.

Sravasti, India: see SET MAHET.

Srbica or **Srbitsa** (both: sûr′bĭtsä), village (pop. 2,718), S Serbia, Yugoslavia, 10 mi. SSW of Mitrovica, in the Kosovo.

Srbija, Yugoslavia: see SERBIA.

Srbitsa, Yugoslavia: see SRBICA.

Srbiya, Yugoslavia: see SERBIA.

Srbobran (sûr′bôbrän), Hung. *Szenttamás* (sĕnt′-tŏmäsh), village (pop. 13,177), Vojvodina, N Serbia, Yugoslavia, on Danube-Tisa Canal, on railroad and 21 mi. N of Novi Sad, on international highway, in the Backa.

Srebnoye (sryĕb′nŭyŭ), village (1939 pop. over 500), SE Chernigov oblast, Ukrainian SSR, 22 mi. ENE of Priluki; metalworks.

Srebrenica or **Srebrenitsa** (both: srĕ′brĕnĭtsä), town (pop. 5,751), E Bosnia, Yugoslavia, 45 mi. ENE of Sarajevo. Lead (formerly mined by Romans, Saxons, and Austrians), silver (mined in Middle Ages), and mercury deposits near by. Health resort of Crni Guber is 1 mi. E.

Srebrna Gora (srĕ′brŭnä gōō′rä), Pol. *Srebrna Góra*, Ger. *Silberberg* (zĭl′bûrbĕrk), town (1939 pop. 1,154; 1946 pop. 1,604) in Lower Silesia, after 1945 in Wroclaw prov., SW Poland, in the Eulengebirge, 10 mi. N of Glatz (Klodzko); mining (coal, galena, tetrahedrite); mfg. of electrical equipment, clocks; woolen milling, metalworking. Fortress, built (1765–77) by Frederick the Great, razed 1867; novelist Reuter spent part (1834–37) of his prison term here.

Sredets (srĕ′dĕts). **1** Village (pop. 3,928), Burgas dist., SE Bulgaria, on Mandra R. and 18 mi. SW of Burgas; vineyards. Until 1934, Karabunar. **2** City, Sofia dist., Bulgaria: see SOFIA, city.

Sredna Gora (srĕd′nä gôrä′) [Bulg.,=central mountains], mountain range in central Bulgaria; extend c.140 mi. bet. Iskar R. (W) and Tundzha R. (E); separated from Balkan Mts. (N) by Sofia, Zlatitsa, Karlovo, and Kazanlik basins; bounded S by W Rhodope Mts., and Thracian Plain. It may be considered in 3 sections: Ikhtiman Sredna Gora (W; bet. Iskar and Topolnitsa rivers); central Sredna Gora (highest; rise to 5,061 ft. at the Bogdan); Sirnena Gora (E; bet. Strema and Tundzha rivers). Copper deposits and mineral springs in central Sredna Gora. Forest utilization and livestock raising. Main center, Panagyurishte.

Sredne-Kamchatsk (sryĕ″dnyĭ-kŭmchätsk′), village (1948 pop. over 500), Kamchatka oblast, Khabarovsk Territory, Russian SFSR, on central Kamchatka Peninsula, on Kamchatka R. and 185 mi. N of Petropavlovsk, in agr. area.

Sredne-Kolymsk (–kŭlĭmsk′), city (1946 pop. estimate 2,000), NE Yakut Autonomous SSR, N of Arctic Circle, on Kolyma R. and 550 mi. N of Magadan, in reindeer-raising area; river port (ship repair); trading post. Founded 1646; 19th-cent. exile center.

Sredne-Krayushkino (–krĭyōōsh′kēnŭ), village (1939 pop. over 2,000), N Altai Territory, Russian SFSR, 27 mi. NNE of Barnaul, in agr. area.

Sredne-Serebrovsk, Russian SFSR: see VTOROI OROCHEN.

Sredne-Uralsk or **Sredne-Ural'sk** (–ōōrälsk′), town (1939 pop. 8,800), S Sverdlovsk oblast, Russian SFSR, on Iset L., 3 mi. NW (under jurisdiction) of Verkhnyaya Pyshma, on rail spur; has large coal-fed power plant. Developed in 1930s. The Sredneuralsk copper-refining plant is at REVDA.

Sredneye Selo, Russian SFSR: see KINGISEPP.

Srednikan, Russian SFSR: see UST-SREDNIKAN.

Sredni Strait or **Sredniy Strait** (sryĕd′nyē), Rus. *Proliv Srednego*, Jap. *Suride-kaikyo*, in central main Kurile Isls. group, Russian SFSR, bet. Rasshua Isl. (N) and Ushishir Isls. (S); 11 mi. wide. Reefs make it one of most hazardous straits in Kuriles.

Sredni Urgal or **Sredniy Urgal** (sryĕd″nyē ōōrgäl′) [Rus.,=middle Urgal], town (1942 pop. over 500), SW Khabarovsk Territory, Russian SFSR, on Urgal R. (left branch of Bureya R.) and 180 mi. WNW of Komsomolsk, in Bureya coal basin, on branch of Trans-Siberian RR.

Srednyaya Akhtuba (–nyī̆ŭ ŭkhtōō′bŭ), village (1926 pop. 7,645), E Stalingrad oblast, Russian SFSR, on left bank of Akhtuba R. and 15 mi. E of Stalingrad; truck produce, fruit.

Srednyaya Nyukzha (nyōōk′zhŭ), town (1939 pop. over 2,000), NW Amur oblast, Russian SFSR, near Nyukzha R. (branch of Olekma R.), 90 mi. NNW of Skovorodino; gold mines. In late 1930s, called Blyukherovsk.

Srednyaya Tunguska River, Russian SFSR: see STONY TUNGUSKA RIVER.

Srekhtum (srĕk′tŏŏm′), town, Kratie prov., SE Cambodia, at foot of SW extension of Annamese Cordillera, 60 mi. ESE of Kratie, near Vietnam line.

Srem (shrĕm), Pol. *Śrem*, Ger. *Schrimm* (shrĭm), town (1946 pop. 8,308), Poznan prov., W Poland, on Warta R. and 22 mi. S of Poznan; mfg. of bricks, machinery, furniture, chemicals; flour milling, sawmilling, weaving.

Srem (srĕm), Hung. *Szerém* (sĕr′ām), Ger. *Syrmien* (zür′mēŭn), Lat. *Sirmia* or *Syrmia*, region, Vojvodina, N Serbia, Yugoslavia; bounded by the Danube (N), the Sava (S), and Croatia (W). Intensive agr. (corn, wheat, wine). Includes FRUSKA GORA (N). Chief town, MITROVICA; largest village, RUMA. Easternmost co. of Croatia-Slavonia until 1918, extending into present Croatia; included Vukovar and Vinkovci. Present Srem became part of Danube banovina (1929–41); was returned (1941–44) to Croatia; since 1946, a section of Vojvodina autonomous territory.

Sremska Mitrovica, Yugoslavia: see MITROVICA, Vojvodina, Serbia.

Sremski Karlovci, Yugoslavia: see KARLOVCI.

Sretensk (sryĕ′tyĭnsk), city (1939 pop. 12,800), central Chita oblast, Russian SFSR, on Shilka R., on spur of Trans-Siberian RR and 180 mi. E of Chita; rail-river transfer point; tanning center; mfg. of sheepskins. Shipbuilding at Kokui (W). A convict station in 18th cent.; active trading center as temporary terminus (1910s) of Trans-Siberian RR.

Sreumbell (srŭm′bĕl′), village, Kampot prov., SW Cambodia, 45 mi. NW of Kampot, on the small Kompong Som R. near its mouth in Kompong Som Bay of Gulf of Siam.

Sri Dungargarh (srē dŏŏng′gŭrgŭr), town (pop. 11,671), N Rajasthan, India, 40 mi. E of Bikaner; local trade in wool, leather goods, handicraft jewelry.

Sri Ganganagar (srē gŭng′gänŭgŭr), town (pop. 16,136), ⊙ Sri Ganganagar dist., N Rajasthan, India, 135 mi. NNE of Bikaner; market center for millet, wheat, sugar cane, gram, cotton; sugar milling, hand-loom weaving. Has col. Camel and sheep breeding near by. Sometimes Ganganagar.

Sriharikota (srēhŭrĭkō′tŭ), narrow island along E coast of Madras, India; separates Pulicat L. from Bay of Bengal; c.45 mi. long N–S. Sea entrance to lake at S tip; Buckingham Canal along W edge; lighthouse at Armagon. Casuarina plantations.

Srihatta, E Pakistan: see SYLHET, district.

Srikanta (srē′kŭntŭ), peak (21,449 ft.) in W Kumaun Himalayas, in Tehri dist., N Uttar Pradesh, India, 9 mi. WSW of Gangotri.

Sri Karanpur (srē′ kŭrŭn′pŏŏr), town (pop. 7,410), N Rajasthan, India, 125 mi. N of Bikaner; local market for millet, wheat, gram.

Srikolayatji, India: see KOLAYAT.

Sri Madhopur (srē′ mä′dōpŏŏr), town (pop. 7,693), E Rajasthan, India, 40 mi. NNW of Jaipur; agr. (millet, gram); hand-loom weaving. Rail junction 7 mi. SSW, at Ringus (or Reengus).

Srimangal (srĭmŭng′gŭl), town (pop. 2,523), E East Bengal, E Pakistan, 40 mi. SSW of Sylhet; rice, tea, oilseeds; umbrella mfg.; tea processing near by.

Srimangala (srĭmŭng′gŭlŭ), village (pop. 454), S Coorg, India, 33 mi. SSE of Mercara; rice (terrace farming), oranges.

Sri Menanti (srē′mŭnän′tē), village, central Negri Sembilan, Malaya, in central Malayan range, 15 mi. ESE of Seremban; residence of Malay ruler (the Yang di-Pertuan Besar) of Negri Sembilan.

Sri Mohangarh (srē mō′hŭngŭr), village, W Rajasthan, India, 28 mi. NE of Jaisalmer; camel and sheep grazing. Natural salt deposits (S); worked on small scale.

Srimushnam or **Srimushnum** (both: srē′mŏŏshnŭm), town (pop. 5,679), South Arcot dist., SE Madras, India, 34 mi. SW of Cuddalore; rice, plantain, cassava; sugar milling. Vishnuite temple is site of annual pilgrimage and market.

Srinagar (srēnŭ′ŭr, srē′nŭgŭr), town (pop. 1,957), Garhwal dist., N Uttar Pradesh, India, on the Alaknanda and 26 mi. NNE of Lansdowne; trades in wheat, barley, rice, rape and mustard. New town built in 1894, after flood washed away old site. Rudraprayag, 13 mi. ENE, is at one of 5 sacred confluences of Alaknanda R.; pilgrimage center; Hindu temple.

Srinagar, anc. *Pravarapura*, city (□ 11; pop. 207,787; including cantonment area of Badami Bagh, 209,595), ⊙ Kashmir (winter ⊙ at Jammu) and Kashmir prov., in Anantnag dist., W central Kashmir, in Vale of Kashmir, on both banks of Jhelum R. (crossed by 7 wooden bridges) and 400 mi. NNW of New Delhi; 34°5′N 74°50′E; alt. 5,227 ft. Famed as one of most beautiful resorts in the East; intersected with canals and waterways, with principal mode of transportation by boat. Center of houseboat tours to floating gardens of DAL LAKE (just NE), MANASBAL LAKE (13 mi. NW), and other resorts in the Vale. Shawl-weaving industry for which city was famous has now almost disappeared; replaced by silk and woolen (carpets) mills; also mfg. of papier-mâché and leather goods, gold, silver-, and copperware; wood carving. Has Srinagar Mus. (archaeological exhibits). Founded 6th cent. A.D. In NE area are Jami Masjid (completed 1402; burned and rebuilt several times) and sacred hill (5,617 ft.) of Hari Parbat, surmounted by rampart and fort built late-16th cent. by Akbar. On right bank of river is wooden mosque of Shah Hamadan; opposite it is Stone Mosque, built 1623 by a Mogul empress. To SE is summit (6,210 ft.) of Takht-i-Sulaiman; has Sankaracharya temple, built c.7th cent. A.D. Parihasapura (excavated 1914), 4 mi. WNW, has extensive 8th-cent. Buddhist ruins, including monastery, stupa, and chaitya; chosen (8th cent.) as site of new ⊙ city by King Lalitaditya and noted for enormous blocks of limestone used in construction. Nara Nag, 20 mi. NNE, is pilgrimage center with extensive Hindu temples (damaged 11th–12th cent. A.D.).

Sringeri (srĭng'gĕrē), town (pop. 2,493), Kadur dist., W Mysore, India, on Tunga R. (headstream of the Tungabhadra) and 36 mi. WNW of Chikmagalur; rice milling, tile mfg. Hindu religious center; monastery, Sanskrit library. Original monastery founded 9th cent. by Shankaracharya (Hindu philosopher). Tea and coffee estates in near-by hills.

Sriniketan, India: see SANTINIKETAN.

Srinivaspur (srēnĭväs'po͝or), town (pop. 4,412), Kolar dist., E Mysore, India, 15 mi. NNE of Kolar; cotton ginning, oilseed milling, goldsmithing; handicraft glass bangles.

Sri Padastanaya, Ceylon: see ADAM'S PEAK.

Sriperumbudur (srēpĕro͝ombo͞o'do͞or), town (pop. 4,302), Chingleput dist., E Madras, India, 25 mi. WSW of Madras; road center. Shrine to Ramanuja (11th-cent. Vishnuite saint) here; pilgrimage center.

Sriracha or **Sriraja,** Thailand: see SIRACHA.

Srirampur, India: see SERAMPORE.

Sri Ranbirsinghpura, Kashmir: see NAWANSHAHR.

Srirangam (srē'rŭng-gŭm), city (pop. 26,676), Trichinopoly dist., S Madras, India, on Srirangam Isl., just N of Trichinopoly across Cauvery R.; fruit and vegetable gardens. Hindu pilgrimage center; has large 17th-cent. Dravidian (Vishnuite) temple complex (structural remains and inscriptions from 10th cent.). Earlier Dravidian (Sivaite) temple 1 mi. SE, at village of Tiruvanaikkaval (or Thiruvanaikoil; formerly Jambukeswaram).

Srirangam Island, in Trichinopoly dist., S Madras, India, bet. COLEROON RIVER (N) and CAUVERY RIVER (S), 180 mi. SW of Madras; 17 mi. long, 1–1¼ mi. wide; crossed by rail and road bridges. Alluvial lowland (coconut groves). Pilgrimage center of Srirangam in W. Grand Anicut at E end; irrigation works. Was strategic English-French-Indian military base during 18th-cent. struggle for Trichinopoly.

Srirangapatan, India: see SERINGAPATAM.

Srisailam, India: see ATMAKUR, Kurnool dist., Madras.

Srisaket, Thailand: see SISAKET.

Srivaikuntam (srēvī'ko͞ontŭm), town (pop. 9,524), Tinnevelly dist., S Madras, India, on Tambraparni R. and 17 mi. ESE of Tinnevelly; cotton, palmyra products, betel. Extensive prehistoric burial place at Adichanallur village, 2 mi. W, across river.

Srivardhan (shrē'vŭrdŭn), town (pop. 7,738), Kolaba dist., W Bombay, India, port on Arabian Sea, 65 mi. SSE of Bombay; fish-supplying center (mackerel, pomfrets); rice, coconuts; betel farming, handicraft cloth weaving. Also Shrivardhan.

Srivilliputtur (srē″vĭl-lĭpo͞ot-to͞or'), city (pop. 34,652), Ramnad dist., S Madras, India, 45 mi. SW of Madura; trade center for plantain, coffee, cardamom (from Varushanad Hills; NW), and millet.

Srnetica or **Srnetitsa** (both: sûr'nĕtĭtsä), mountain in Dinaric Alps, W Bosnia, Yugoslavia; highest point (4,125 ft.) is 13 mi. NE of Drvar; skirted by Prijedor-Knin RR. Bosanski Petrovac at NW foot.

Sroda (shrô'dä), Pol. *Środa*, Ger. *Schroda* (shrō'dä), town (1946 pop. 9,872), Poznan prov., W central Poland, on railroad and 20 mi. SE of Poznan; machine mfg., beet-sugar and flour milling, weaving. Medieval bldgs.

Sroda Slaska (shlō'skä), Pol. *Środa Śląska*, Ger. *Neumarkt* (noi'märkt), town (1939 pop. 6,428; 1946 pop. 4,301) in Lower Silesia, after 1945 in Wroclaw prov., SW Poland, 20 mi. W of Breslau (Wroclaw); agr. market (grain, potatoes, livestock); leather mfg. Known as market center before 1217.

Srostki (srôst'kē), village (1926 pop. 2,735), E Altai Territory, Russian SFSR, on Katun R. and 20 mi. ESE of Bisk; dairy farming.

Srpska Crnja or **Srpska Tsrnya,** Yugoslavia: see CRNJA.

Srpske Moravice (sûrp'skĕ mô'rävĕtsĕ), village, NW Croatia, Yugoslavia, on railroad and 29 mi. E of Rijeka (Fiume); local trade center; summer resort.

Srpski Itebej, Yugoslavia: see ITEBEJ.

Srungavarappukota (sro͞ong-gŭvŭrŭ'po͞okōtŭ), town (pop. 7,380), Vizagapatam dist., NE Madras, India, 17 mi. W of Vizianagaram; rice and oilseed milling; lacquerwork. Mango groves. Timber, coffee, tanning bark, lac in Eastern Ghats (W). Also spelled Srungavarapukota.

Ssu-, for Chinese names beginning thus and not found here: see under SZE-.

Staab, Czechoslovakia: see STOD.

Staaken (shtä'kŭn), section of Spandau dist., W Berlin, Germany, 12 mi. W of city center; metal refining. After 1945 in British sector.

Stabekk (stä'bĕk), village (pop. 4,474) in Baerum canton, Akershus co., SE Norway, at head of Oslo Fjord, on railroad and 4 mi. W of Oslo city center.

Stabiae, Italy: see CASTELLAMMARE DI STABIA.

Stabroek (stä'bro͝ok), residential town (pop. 4,768), Antwerp prov., N Belgium, 9 mi. NNW of Antwerp.

Stabroek, Br. Guiana: see GEORGETOWN.

Stachy (stä'khĭ), village (pop. 1,246), S Bohemia, Czechoslovakia, 6 mi. NW of Vimperk; skiing resort in Bohemian Forest.

Stackeln, Latvia: see STRENCI.

Stacksteads, town in Bacup urban dist., E Lancashire, England; coal mining, cotton milling, shoe mfg. Granite quarrying near by.

Stacy, village (pop. 150), Chisago co., E Minn., on small affluent of St. Croix R. and 32 mi. N of St. Paul; grain, livestock.

Stacyville. **1** Town (pop. 544), Mitchell co., N Iowa, near Minn. line, on Little Cedar R. and 10 mi. N of Osage; creamery. Sand and gravel pits near by. **2** Plantation (pop. 679), Penobscot co., central Maine, 18 mi. NE of Millinocket.

Stad, Norway: see STADLAND.

Stadacona (stŭdä'kōnŭ), former Indian village, S Que., on the St. Lawrence; now dist. of Quebec city.

Stade (shtä'dŭ), town (pop. 25,974), in former Prussian prov. of Hanover, NW Germany, after 1945 in Lower Saxony, port on small Schwinge R. near its mouth on Elbe estuary, and 22 mi. WNW of Hamburg city center; contains large saline. Shipbuilding, oil refining; mfg. of chemicals, rubber and leather goods, apparel, wood products; food processing. Has 2 Gothic churches, 17th-cent. town hall. Of anc. origin; was long the predominant trade center on Elbe estuary. Chartered in 12th cent. Was powerful member of Hanseatic League. Belonged successively to Bremen, Sweden, and Denmark until it came (1719) to Hanover.

Staden (stä'dŭn), town (pop. 5,407), West Flanders prov., NW Belgium, 5 mi. WNW of Roulers; agr. market (grain, stock).

Stadland (stä'län), peninsula in Sogn og Fjordane co., W Norway, 40 mi. N of Floro; protrudes 16 mi. NW into North Sea. Its tip is called Stad or Stadt. Sometimes spelled Stadtland, Statland, Stattland.

Stadl Paura (shtäd'ŭl pou'rä), town (pop. 6,221), central Upper Austria, on Traun R. and 8 mi. SW of Wels; textiles.

Stadsbygd or **Statsbygd** (both: stäts'bügd), village and canton (pop. 2,045), Sor-Trondelag co., central Norway, on N shore of Trondheim Fjord, 12 mi. WNW of Trondheim; agr., lumbering. Brickworks, lumber mills near by.

Stadskanaal (stäts″känäl'), town (pop. 6,234), Groningen prov., NE Netherlands, 10 mi. SSW of Winschoten; peat-digging center; potato-flour mill; strawboard, machinery, lumber.

Stadt, Norway: see STADLAND.

Stadtamhof (shtät'ämhōf'), N suburb of Regensburg, Upper Palatinate, E Bavaria, Germany, on opposite side of the Danube, at its confluence with the Regen. Inc. 1924 into Regensburg.

Stadtbredimus (stät-brā'dĭmüs), village (pop. 329), SE Luxembourg, on Moselle R., just N of Remich, on Ger. border; grape and plum growing.

Städterdorf, Rumania: see RASINARI.

Stadthagen (shtät'hä″gŭn), town (pop. 12,443), in former Schaumburg-Lippe, W Germany, after 1945 in Lower Saxony, 12 mi. ENE of Minden; sugar refining. Has 14th–15th-cent. church, 16th-cent. castle and town hall.

Stadtilm (shtät″ĭlm'), town (pop. 4,497), Thuringia, central Germany, on Ilm R. and 7 mi. SE of Arnstadt; mfg. of china, shoes, leather, chemicals; woodworking. Has 17th-cent. town hall.

Stadtland, Norway: see STADLAND.

Stadtlengsfeld (shtät'lĕngs'fĕlt″), town (pop. 2,580), Thuringia, central Germany, at N foot of Rhön Mts., 15 mi. SW of Eisenach; china mfg. Sometimes called Lengsfeld.

Stadtlohn (shtät″lōn'), town (pop. 5,410), in former Prussian prov. of Westphalia, NW Germany, after 1945 in North Rhine-Westphalia, on Berkel R. and 11 mi. NW of Coesfeld; grain, cattle.

Stadtoldendorf (shtät'ôl'dŭndôrf″), town (pop. 7,192), in former Prussian prov. of Hanover, NW Germany, after 1945 in Lower Saxony, 8 mi. ENE of Holzminden; mfg. of textiles, paints, wood and tobacco products; sawmilling. Gypsum mills. Until 1941 in Brunswick. Romanesque basilica of former Cistercian monastery Amelungsborn near by.

Stadtprozelten (shtät'prōtsĕl'tŭn), town (pop. 988), Lower Franconia, NW Bavaria, Germany, on the Main (canalized) and 17 mi. SE of Aschaffenburg; wood trade; brewing, lumber milling. Chartered 1333. Has 16th-cent. town hall. Just W are ruins of 12th-cent. castle. Sandstone quarries near by.

Stadtremda, Germany: see REMDA.

Stadtroda (shtät″rō'dä), town (pop. 6,261), Thuringia, central Germany, 8 mi. SE of Jena; knitting and flour mills; food canning, brewing, tanning; mfg. of musical instruments, tobacco products. Has 17th-cent. palace, Gothic church, remains of 13th-cent. Cistercian convent. Until 1922, Roda.

Stadtschlaining (shtät'shlī'nĭng), Hung. *Városszalónak* (vä'rôsôlōnŏk), village (pop. 835), Burgenland, E Austria, 17 mi. WNW of Szombathely, Hungary. Antimony mined near by.

Stadtschwarzach (shtät″shvärts'äkh), village (pop. 852), Lower Franconia, W Bavaria, Germany, near the Main, 13 mi. E of Würzburg; wheat, barley, hogs. Has Gothic church.

Stadtsteinach (shtät″shtīn'äkh), village (pop. 2,524), Upper Franconia, NE Bavaria, Germany, on small Steinach R. and 4 mi. NE of Kulmbach; textile mfg., paper milling, brewing. Summer resort. Clay pits in area.

Stadtsulza, Germany: see BAD SULZA.

Stadt Tepl, Czechoslovakia: see TEPLA.

Stäfa (shtā'fä), town (pop. 4,809), Zurich canton, N Switzerland, on L. of Zurich, 14 mi. SE of Zurich; silk textiles, metalworking, printing.

Staffa (stă'fŭ), uninhabited islet of the Inner Hebrides, Argyll, Scotland, 7 mi. W of Mull. It is noted for its numerous basaltic caves, best known of which is the beautiful Fingal's Cave, whose entrance is an archway 227 ft. long, supported by tall basaltic columns; the crown of the arch is 66 ft. above the sea, which is 25 ft. deep at low tide.

Staffanstorp (stä'fänstôrp″), village (pop. 838), Malmohus co., S Sweden, 8 mi. ENE of Malmo; rail junction; sugar refining.

Staffelden (stäfĕldĕn', Ger. shtäf'fĕldŭn), village (pop. 391), Haut-Rhin dept., E France, 8 mi. NW of Mulhouse; potash mining.

Staffelsee (shtä'fŭlzā″), lake (□ 3), Upper Bavaria, Germany, at N foot of the Bavarian Alps, 34 mi. SSW of Munich; 2 mi. long, 2 mi. wide, 115 ft. deep; alt. 2,126 ft. Resort of Murnau at SE tip.

Staffelstein (shtä'fŭl-shtīn″), town (pop. 3,455), Upper Franconia, N Bavaria, Germany, near the Main, 15 mi. NNE of Bamberg; mfg. of textiles, precision instruments, pottery; wood- and metalworking, brewing, tanning, flour and lumber milling. Has late-Gothic church; 17th-cent. town hall. Chartered 1130.

Stäffis, Switzerland: see ESTAVAYER-LE-LAC.

Stafford or **Staffordshire** (stă'fŭrd, -shĭr), county (□ 1,153.3; 1931 pop. 1,431,359; 1951 census 1,621,013), W Midlands, England; ⊙ Stafford. Bounded by Cheshire (NW), Derby (E), Warwick (SE), Worcester (S), and Shropshire (W). Drained by Trent R. and Sow R. Consists of moorland in N and center (Cannock Chase); otherwise mainly undulating plain. Has major coal fields in Stoke-on-Trent, Tipton, and Cannock Chase areas, and important pottery industry, concentrated in Stoke-on-Trent area. Other mfg.: important iron and steel industry (Wolverhampton area, BLACK COUNTRY), silk milling (Leek), and brewing (Burton-on-Trent). Other towns are West Bromwich and Walsall. In S of co. is a small enclave of Worcestershire. Abbr. is Staffs.

Stafford, municipal borough (1931 pop. 29,485; 1951 census 40,275), ⊙ Stafford or Staffordshire, England, in W central part of co., on Sow R. above junction with Trent R., 25 mi. NNW of Birmingham; mfg. of shoes; also metal products, chemicals. Castle built by the Saxon princess Æthelflæd has been replaced by a great unfinished castle. Site of St. Chad's (Norman) Church and St. Mary's Church, restored by Scott. Izaak Walton b. in Stafford; his cottage at Shallowford near by is a museum. City has fine library. Sheridan, the dramatist, represented the city in Parliament, 1780–1806.

Stafford. **1** County (□ 794; pop. 8,816), S central Kansas; ⊙ Saint John. Gently rolling area, watered by Rattlesnake Creek. Wheat, corn, livestock. Scattered oil fields. Formed 1879. **2** County (□ 271; pop. 11,902), NE Va.; ⊙ Stafford. Bounded E by the Potomac, SW and S by the Rappahannock; drained by Aquia Creek. Agr. (grain, tobacco, legumes, truck), dairying, livestock, poultry; river fisheries. Gold formerly mined here. Formed 1664.

Stafford. **1** Town (pop. 6,471), including Stafford Springs borough (pop. 3,396), Tolland co., NE Conn., on Mass. line and Willimantic R., and 22 mi. NE of Hartford. Agr., mfg. (textiles, turbines, buttons, buckles) at Stafford Springs and West Stafford. Staffordville village (1940 pop. 533), near L. Stafford (1.5 mi. long) is resort. Settled and inc. 1719, Stafford Springs borough inc. 1873. **2** City (pop. 2,005), Stafford co., S central Kansas, 37 mi. W of Hutchinson, in wheat area; grain storage. Inc. 1885. Growth stimulated by discovery (1938) of oil near by. **3** Village (pop. 141), Monroe co., E Ohio, 19 mi. SSW of Barnesville. **4** Village (pop. c.100), ⊙ Stafford co. (since 1715), NE Va., near the Potomac, 9 mi. NNE of Fredericksburg, in agr. area.

Staffordshire, England: see STAFFORD, county.

Stafford Springs, Conn.: see STAFFORD.

Staffordsville, village (1940 pop. 659), Johnson co., E Ky., 31 mi. NW of Pikeville, in coal, oil, and agr. region.

Staffordville, Conn.: see STAFFORD.

Staffs, England: see STAFFORD, county.

Stagira (stůjī'rů) or **Stagirus** (stůjī'rŭs), anc. city of Gr. Macedonia, on Chalcidice peninsula, 9 mi. ENE of modern Arnaia, near Strymonic Gulf. Colonized (7th cent. B.C.) by Greeks from Andros, it is noted as birthplace of Aristotle. Modern Gr. village of Stageira or Stayira (pop. 586) near by.

Stagno (stä'nyô) [Ital., =basin], in Italian names: for names beginning thus and not found here, see main part of name; e.g., for Stagno di Cagliari, see CAGLIARI, STAGNO DI.

Stagno or **Stagno Grande,** Yugoslavia: see STON.

Stagnone Islands (stänyô'nĕ) (□ 2; pop. 37), in Mediterranean Sea just off W Sicily, 3–5 mi. N of Marsala. Chief islets: Grande (saltworks), Santa Maria, and San Pantaleo. San Pantaleo is site of *Motya* or *Motye*, Phoenician fortress with ruins of walls and necropolises of 8th to 7th cent. B.C. Tunny fisheries.

Stahnsdorf (shtäns'dôrf), residential village (pop. 6,375), Brandenburg, E Germany, on Teltow Canal and 11 mi. SW of Berlin city center.

Staines, residential urban district (1931 pop. 21,213; 1951 census 39,983), Middlesex, England, on the Thames at mouth of Colne R., and 18 mi. WSW of London; automobile works. Has granite bridge (1831) built by Rennie. Scene of trial (1603) of Sir Walter Raleigh. Near by is the London stone, 1st set up in 1285 to mark limits of authority of City of London. There are traces of Roman occupation. In urban dist. are residential towns of Ashford (E), with large London reservoir, Stanwell (NNE), and Laleham (SE), birthplace of Matthew Arnold.

Stainforth, town and parish (pop. 7,989), West Riding, S Yorkshire, England, on Don R. and 7 mi. NE of Doncaster; coal-mining center.

Stainland, former urban district (1931 pop. 4,246), West Riding, SW Yorkshire, England, 3 mi. S of Halifax; woolen and paper milling. Inc. 1937 in Elland.

Stains (stẽ), town (pop. 18,308), Seine dept., N central France, an outer N suburb of Paris, 7 mi. from Notre Dame Cathedral, just NE of Saint-Denis; metalworks, paper mill; mfg. of linoleum products.

Stainz (shtīnts), village (pop. 1,344), Styria, S Austria, 14 mi. SW of Graz; mfg. of matches; vineyards.

Stair, agr. village and parish (pop. 1,034), central Ayrshire, Scotland, on Ayr R. and 7 mi. E of Ayr.

Staithes, England: see HINDERWELL.

Stajerlakanina, Rumania: see STEIERDORFANINA.

Staked Plain, Texas and N.Mex.: see LLANO ESTACADO.

Stakhanovets, Russian SFSR: see MONINO.

Stakhanovo, Russian SFSR: see ZHUKOVSKI.

Stakhr, Iran: see PERSEPOLIS.

Stalac or **Stalach** (both: stä'läch), Serbo-Croatian *Stalać*, village, central Serbia, Yugoslavia, on the Southern Morava, just SE of its confluence with the Western Morava, and 13 mi. S of Paracin; rail junction.

Stalbridge, town and parish (pop. 1,249), N Dorset, England, 6 mi. E of Sherborne; agr. market in dairying region. Has 14th-cent. market cross and 15th-cent. church.

Stalden (shtäl'dŭn), village (pop. 874), Valais canton, S Switzerland, at confluence of Mattervisp and Saaservisp rivers (headstreams of Visp R.), 4 mi. S of Visp; alt. 2,608 ft.; chemicals. Ackersand hydroelectric plant N.

Staley (stā'lē), town (pop. 236), Randolph co., central N.C., 23 mi. SSE of Greensboro; mfg. of hosiery, furniture.

Stalheim, Norway: see NAEROY FJORD.

Stalin, Albania: see KUÇOVË.

Stalin (stä'lĭn, stä'–), formerly **Varna** (vär'nů), city (pop. 77,792), ⊙ Stalin dist. (formed 1949), E Bulgaria, on sandy isthmus bet. Stalin Gulf of the Black Sea and E shore of Stalin L., 230 mi. ENE of Sofia; 43°13'N 27°54'E. Major seaport and rail terminus; noted summer resort (mineral baths); commercial (fishing trade) and mfg. center with metal, textile, leather, tobacco, and food-processing (flour, meat, fruit, vegetables) industries; soap mfg. Grain elevators, railroad shops, and shipyards on Stalin L. Livestock, tobacco, canned fish (sardines), and grain exports. Winegrowing and truck gardening near by. Has univ., polytechnical inst., naval acad., archaeological mus., theater, old churches and mosques, monuments and ruins of 6th-cent. fortifications. Founded (6th cent. B.C.) as Greek town of Odessos or Odessus; became a commercial center under Thracian rule. Dominated by Romans (1st cent. A.D.), by Byzantines and Bulgarians (13th-14th cent.). Sacked by Turks in 1391; site of defeat (1444) of Wladislaw III, king of Poland and Hungary, by Turkish sultan Murad II. Subjected to several Rus. assaults in 19th cent.; finally captured (1877) and ceded to Bulgaria. Called Varna until 1949. Was ⊙ former Varna oblast (1934–47).

Stalin, formerly **Brasov** (bräshôv'), Rum. *Braşov*, Ger. *Kronstadt* (krōn'shtät), Hung. *Brassó* (brŏsh'-shō), city (1948 pop. 82,984), ⊙ Stalin (Brasov) prov., central Rumania, in Transylvania, in NE foothills of the Transylvanian Alps, 75 mi. NNW of Bucharest; 45°38'N 25°34'E. Major commercial and mfg. center known for its metallurgical industry and its textiles (mainly woolens); rail hub. Also produces armaments, aircraft, tractors, rolling stock, industrial machinery, ballbearings, oil-drilling equipment, tin plate, copper plate, paper, cellulose, leather goods, pianos and organs, furniture, chemicals, paints and varnishes, cement, clay products. Petroleum refining, printing, brewing, distilling, food processing, woodworking. It is also a climatic resort (alt. 1,941 ft.) and winter-sports center with noted skiing facilities near by (2 mi. S). Educational institutions include a music conservatory and a summer university. City preserves characteristic medieval appearance with 14th-15th-cent. Black Church (so called because damaged by great fire in 1689), one of the largest in Rumania; 14th-15th-cent. St. Nicholas de Schei church; 15th-16th-cent. citadel with 4 bastions, now a military prison; 15th-cent. council house restored in 18th cent.; 16th-cent. marketplace. Also noteworthy are 15th-cent. town hall restored in 18th cent., baroque R.C. church, regional mus. Founded 1211 by Teutonic Knights and refounded by Saxon colonists (1225), the city soon became the main center of a Saxon district and largest city in Transylvania. Extensive commercial privileges were granted to its merchants by Walachian voivodes. It played an important part in 16th-cent. reform movement, with 1st printing presses of Transylvania. Efforts of Austria to re-establish catholicism (17th cent.) brought about the predominance of Rumanians over the Saxon pop. Was occupied (1916) by Rumania, to whom it was formally transferred in 1918. Still has large Magyar and Ger. pop. Renamed Stalin or Orasul Stalin [city of Stalin] in 1950.

Stalin (Rus. stä'lyĭn), district of Greater Baku, Azerbaijan SSR, on Caspian Sea, SW of Baku.

Stalin, city, Ukrainian SSR: see STALINO, city.

Stalin, Mount (9,500 ft.), N B.C., in Rocky Mts.; 58°15'N 124°45'W.

Stalina, Imeni, Uzbek SSR: see STALINO, village, Andizhan oblast.

Stalinabad (stä"lyĭnŭbät'), former oblast (□ 9,700; 1946 pop. c.500,000), SW Tadzhik SSR; ⊙ Stalinabad. Bounded S by Afghanistan (Panj R.), W by Uzbek SSR, N by Gissar Range; drained by Vakhsh and Kafirnigan rivers. Chiefly agr.; wheat on mtn. slopes, cotton in irrigated valleys (Vakhsh, Kafirnigan); extensive cattle, goat, and sheep (karakul) raising; pistachio-nut woods on low hill ranges (S); sericulture near Stalinabad. Cotton ginning, cotton and silk milling, meat packing. Chief cities: Stalinabad, Kurgan-Tyube. Pop.: Tadzhiks, Uzbeks. Formed 1939, dissolved 1951.

Stalinabad, city (1926 pop. 5,607; 1939 pop. 82,540; 1948 pop. c.110,000), ⊙ Tadzhik SSR, on Dyushambinka R. (branch of the Kafirnigan), on railroad from Kagan and 200 mi. S of Tashkent (linked by road), 1,900 mi. SE of Moscow; 38°35'N 68°47'E. Cotton- and silk-milling center; meat packing, tanning (fine leather), wine and rum distilling, tobacco processing, machine mfg. (hydroelectric turbines, agr. implements, hardware), printing. An important transportation center; hub of a narrow-gauge rail net; linked by highway and air with Leninabad and Khorog in the Pamir. Near by (N) are hydroelectric plants on Varzob R. Seat of Tadzhik state univ., teachers, medical, and agr. colleges. Developed (after 1929) as a new city of broad, tree-lined thoroughfares, on site of old Tadzhik village of Dyushambe.

Stalin Dam (stă'lĭn, stä'–), in W Bulgaria, on Iskar R. and 20 mi. SE of Sofia. Construction project (begun 1951) includes 3 hydroelectric stations below the dam—Pasarel (at dam site), Kokalyane (12 mi. SE of Sofia), and Sofia (just NE of the city). A multi-purpose project, the reservoir irrigates the semiarid Sofia plain. Formerly called Pasarel Dam.

Stalindorf, Ukrainian SSR: see STALINSKOYE, Dnepropetrovsk oblast.

Stalingrad (stă'lĭngrăd, stä–, Rus. stŭlyĭngrät'), oblast (□ 47,500; 1946 pop. estimate 1,800,000) in S European Russian SFSR; ⊙ Stalingrad. In lower Volga region; includes hilly right-bank section (Volga and Yergeni hills) and Caspian Lowland on left bank of the Volga. Drained by Volga and Don rivers (which approach within 40 mi. of each other; projected canal) and by Khoper, Medveditsa, and Ilovlya rivers (left affluents of the Don). Dry steppe climate; brown soils. Mineral resources: iron deposits along Khoper R., natural gas (Frolovo), salt (L. Elton). Major agr. region; grain farming (mainly wheat), sunflowers, mustard seed; beef cattle, sheep (on right bank of Volga R.); melons and other garden crops in Volga R. valley; sheep raising and semi-nomadic horse breeding in semi-desert left-bank section. With exception of Stalingrad, industry is on agr. basis. Main centers: Kamyshin, Frolovo, Mikhailovka, Uryupinsk. Exports wheat, livestock, wool, tractors, quality steels. Formed 1934 out of Lower Volga Territory; it was a territory [Rus. *krai* or *kray*] containing Kalmyk Autonomous Oblast until 1936, when it became an oblast. In 1941, absorbed S section of dissolved German Volga Autonomous SSR. During Second World War, SW section was held (1942–43) by Germans.

Stalingrad, city (1926 pop. 151,490; 1939 pop. 445,476), ⊙ Stalingrad oblast, Russian SFSR, port on Volga R., at mouth of small Tsaritsa R., and 230 mi. NW of Astrakhan, 580 mi. SE of Moscow; 48°45'N 44°30'E. One of leading commercial and industrial centers in Volga region, at nearest approach to Don R. and Donets Basin. A rail hub, linked to Moscow, the Ukraine, and the Caucasus; serves as transfer point for Volga and Caspian traffic; handles petroleum, fish, lumber, coal. Industries developed mainly under Soviet regime; mfg. of tractors, quality steels, machine tools, railway-car parts, oil-drilling machinery, ballbearings, canned goods, shoes, clothing; oil refining (crude petroleum from Baku), lumber milling, shipbuilding. Has medical, teachers, and agr. colleges, agr.-machinery trade school. City (served by circular belt railroad) extends in narrow belt 30 mi. along right bank of the Volga; formed by amalgamation of separate industrial riverside settlements, from the tractor plant (built 1930; at extreme N outskirts), the Barricade machinery works, and the Red October steel plant (founded 1897; rolling and wire mills), past central part of city (on small Tsaritsa R.), to Yelshanka (lumber mills), Beketovka (steam electric plant), and Krasnoarmeisk (shipyards, railroad shops; at S outskirts). Founded (1589) as a Rus. strategic center safeguarding Volga communications and named Tsaritsyn; held by Stenka Razin (1670) and Pugachev (1774). During 19th cent., it rapidly became an important commercial center, thanks to its favorable location on the Volga-Don route. Repeatedly besieged during civil war by counter-revolutionary troops; briefly abandoned (1919–20) by Soviets. A govt. capital (1919–28); renamed (1925) Stalingrad; during Five-Year Plans underwent considerable industrialization and urban reconstruction. During Second World War, scene (1942–43) of one of the war's decisive battles. Ger. troops, in an attempt to cross the Volga, occupied N half of city, but were stopped in their drive. Following a 3-month battle, Ger. attackers were encircled and finally captured in Feb., 1943. Almost depopulated at end of siege, Stalingrad undertook a vast rebuilding project; regained its pre-war pop. by 1950.

Stalingrad Dam, on lower Volga R., Russian SFSR, 10 mi. NE of center of Stalingrad, at fork of Volga and Akhtuba rivers. Construction project (begun 1951) includes hydroelectric plant (1,700,000 kw capacity), concrete spillway, and navigation locks on left bank, and a main earth-dam section. A multi-purpose project, the dam improves navigation of the lower Volga, furnishes power to Moscow, the Central Black-Earth region, and lower Volga region. The Stalingrad reservoir gives rise to the 400-mi.-long Stalingrad trunk canal extending E to the Ural R. and irrigating the N Caspian lowland. The hydroelectric station also provides power for irrigation pumps, lifting Volga R. water into the Sarpa Lakes depression on right bank for the irrigation of the NW Caspian lowland.

Stalin Gulf or **Gulf of Varna,** W inlet of Black Sea, E Bulgaria; 3 mi. wide, 4 mi. long; 65 ft. deep. Connected with Stalin L. (W lagoon; □ 7) by navigable canal (16 ft. deep). Port of Stalin (Varna) is on W shore, summer resort Galata (pop. 911) (S), and palace and park of Yevksinograd (N) at entrance.

Stalinir (stŭlyĭnyēr'), Georgian *Staliniri* (stŭlyĭnyē'rē), city (1939 pop. 15,000), ⊙ South Ossetian Autonomous Oblast, Georgian SSR, on rail spur from Gori and 55 mi. NW of Tiflis; 42°14'N 43°58'E. Orchards; metal- and woodworking, dairying, fruit canning. Teachers col. Until 1936, called Tskhinval or Tskhinvali.

Stalinissi, Georgian SSR: see KHASHURI.

Stalinka (stä'lyĭn-kŭ), town (1939 pop. over 500), N Poltava oblast, Ukrainian SSR, 7 mi. NE of Lokhvitsa; sugar refining.

Stalino (stä'lyĭnŭ), oblast (□ 10,230; 1946 pop. estimate 3,000,000), E Ukrainian SSR; ⊙ Stalino. N and central area in DONETS BASIN, S area (Azov Upland) borders on Sea of Azov. Agr. chiefly wheat, with sunflowers (N) and cotton (S); dairy farming and truck produce in urban and industrial areas. Major coal, metallurgical, and machinery mfg. region, with centers at Stalino, Makeyevka, Gorlovka, Kramatorsk, and Konstantinovka. Salt mining (Artemovsk), mercury (Nikitovka); deposits of limestone, quartzite, refractory clays. Dense rail network. Chief port, Zhdanov. Fisheries on Sea of Azov. Formed 1938 out of Donets oblast.

Stalino. 1 Village (1939 pop. under 500), S Evenki Natl. Okrug, Krasnoyarsk Territory, Russian SFSR, 260 mi. S of Tura and on Stony Tunguska R. Formerly called Bachinski. **2** Town (1948 pop. over 2,000), central Mary oblast, Turkmen SSR, on railroad (near Semenik station) and 10 mi. SE of Mary; metalworks; cotton. **3** City (1926 pop. 174,230; 1939 pop. 462,395), ⊙ Stalino oblast, Ukrainian SSR, in the Donbas, 380 mi. SE of Kiev; 47°59'N 37°48'E. Major coal and metallurgical center; iron and steel mills, machinery works, nitrate plant, clothing and food industries. Has Donets industrial school, medical and teachers college. Includes (W) suburbs of Rutchenkovo, Petrovski Rudnik, and Lidiyevski Rudnik, absorbed since 1926. Founded (1870s) by Scot industrialist Hughes and named Yuzovka; changed to Stalin after Bolshevik revolution, later (c.1935) to Stalino. **4** Village (1926 pop. 10,206), W Andizhan oblast, Uzbek SSR, on Great Fergana Canal (hydroelectric station) and 9 mi. NW of Leninsk (linked by railroad); cotton ginning. Formerly Shaarikhan and, later (1937–c.1940), Imeni Stalina.

Stalinogorsk (stŭ″lyĭnŭgôrsk′), city (1939 pop. 76,207), S Moscow oblast, Russian SFSR, 120 mi. S of Moscow; major lignite-mining and industrial center in Moscow Basin; machine mfg., chemical plants (sulphuric acid, plastics, nitrate fertilizers), ceramics. Has coal-fed power plant; near-by lignite centers at Donskoi, Zadonye, and Novougolny. Founded 1930; consists of residential section (S) and industrial city (7 mi. N). Called Bobriki until 1934. During Second World War, briefly held (1941) by Germans in Moscow campaign.

Stalin Peak (stä′lĭn, stä′lĭn), highest peak (9,596 ft.) of Bulgaria and of Rhodope Mts., in E Rila Mts., W Bulgaria, 9 mi. S of Samokov. Meteorological observatory. Called Musala or Mus-Allah until 1949.

Stalin Peak, highest peak (alt. 8,737 ft.) of the Carpathians and of Czechoslovakia, in the High Tatra, in N Slovakia, near Pol. border, 10 mi. NW of Poprad. Until 1949, called Gerlach or Gerlachovka (Ger. *Gerlsdorfer Spitze* or *Franz Josef Spitze,* Hung. *Gerlachfalvi-Csúcs* or *Ferenc Jozsef Csúcs,* Pol. *Gierlach*) and sometimes Masaryk. Tatranska Polianka and Vysne Hagy are at its S foot.

Stalin Peak (Rus. stä′lyĭn), highest point (24,590 ft.) in USSR, at junction of AKADEMIYA NAUK RANGE and PETER THE FIRST RANGE of Pamir-Alai mtn. system, on border of Gorno-Badakhshan Autonomous Oblast and Garm oblast, Tadzhik SSR; 38°56′N 72°3′E. Originally called Garmo Peak, it was determined (1932–33) the highest peak of USSR and renamed. LENIN PEAK had previously been considered the highest.

Stalinsk (stä′lyĭnsk). **1** City (1926 pop. 3,894; 1939 pop. 169,538; 1945 pop. estimate 223,000), W Kemerovo oblast, Russian SFSR, on Tom R. (head of navigation), on branch of Trans-Siberian RR (Novokuznetsk station) and 115 mi. S of Kemerovo. Industrial center of Kuznetsk Basin; site of one of leading metallurgical plants of USSR; chemical and coking installations; mfg. (locomotives, rolling stock, machines, building materials), ferroalloy and aluminum production. Coal mining at Kuibyshevo (W). Has metallurgical and teachers colleges. Consists of old city of Kuznetsk (founded 1618 as Rus. fortress, on right bank of Tom R.) and new industrial left-bank section (developed after 1929; called Novo Kuznetsk until 1932). Kuznetsk and Novo Kuznetsk were combined in 1932 to form city of Stalinsk. City developed rapidly in 1930s as one of the links of the Ural-Kuzbas coal and iron-ore exchange. Since c.1940, however, iron ore has been increasingly supplied by Gornaya Shoriya mines. **2** Village (1939 pop. over 500); S Jewish Autonomous Oblast, Khabarovsk Territory, Russian SFSR, on Amur R. and 95 mi. SSW of Birobidzhan. Formerly Nagibovo.

Stalinski or **Stalinskiy** (–skē). **1** Town (1948 pop. over 2,000), N Akmolinsk oblast, Kazakh SSR, 50 mi. SE of Stepnyak. **2** Town (1939 pop. over 500), central Moscow oblast, Russian SFSR, 11 mi. NE of Moscow, on branch of Moscow Canal; a site of Moscow waterworks. **3** Town (1926 pop. 4,650), central Moscow oblast, Russian SFSR, on Klyazma R. and 3 mi. NE of Mytishchi; cotton- and silk-milling center; metalworking; peat digging. Until 1928, Bolshevo.

Stalinskoye (stä′lyĭnskŭyŭ). **1** Village (1939 pop. over 2,000), W Frunze oblast, Kirghiz SSR, in Chu valley, on railroad (Belovodskaya station) and 25 mi. W of Frunze; sugar beets (refinery at adjoining Pervomaiski); metalworking, fruit canning. Until 1937, Belovodskoye. **2** Village (1939 pop. over 500), SW Dnepropetrovsk oblast, Ukrainian SSR, 20 mi. E of Krivoi Rog; metalworks. Formerly a Jewish settlement called Izluchistaya; later (c.1928–44), Stalindorf.

Stallarholmen (stä′lärhôl″mŭn), village (pop. 680), Sodermanland co., E Sweden, on an isl. in L. Malar, 5 mi. E of Strangnas; iron- and brickworks.

Stalldalen (stĕl′dä″lŭn), Swedish *Stålldalen,* village (pop. 1,249), Orebro co., S central Sweden, in Bergslag region, on Hork R. and 15 mi. SW of Ludvika; rail junction; paper and lumber mills, foundries, sulphite works.

Stallogargo (stäl′lōgärgô), village in Kvalsund canton, on S Kvaloy (isl.), Finnmark co., N Norway, on narrow sound opposite Kvalsund (ferry) on mainland, 12 mi. SW of Hammerfest; site of anc. Lapp sacrificial and worship ground.

Stallupönen, Russian SFSR: see NESTEROV.

Stallworthy, Cape, N extremity of Axel Heiberg Isl., N Franklin Dist., Northwest Territories, on the Arctic Ocean; 81°20′N 93°W.

Stalowa Wola (stälô′vä vô′lä), town (pop. 5,086), Rzeszow prov., SE Poland, on railroad and 36 mi. N of Rzeszow, near San R.; iron and steel industry, established in 1930s.

Stalpeni (stûlpän′), Rum. *Stâlpeni,* village (pop. 930), Arges prov., S central Rumania, on railroad and 15 mi. SSW of Campulung.

Stalybridge (stā′–), municipal borough (1931 pop. 24,831; 1951 census pop. 22,544), NE Cheshire, England, on Tame R. and 8 mi. E of Manchester; cotton mills, foundries, machine shops; mfg. of leather goods, paper, cables. Has library and art gall. Holy Trinity Church contains a bible of 1541. BUCKTON VALE is in the borough.

Stambaugh (stăm′bô), city (pop. 1,969), Iron co., SW Upper Peninsula, Mich., opposite Iron River city, in Menominee iron range; iron mining. Settled c.1878; inc. as village 1895, as city 1923.

Stambul, Turkey: see ISTANBUL.

Stamford, municipal borough (1931 pop. 9,947; 1951 census 10,899), Parts of Kesteven, SW Lincolnshire, England, on Welland R. and 11 mi. WNW of Peterborough; agr. market with brickworks and agr.-machinery works. It is supposed to be site of a defeat of the Picts and Scots by the Saxons in 449 and was one of the Five Burghs (Danelagh) of the Danes. Many of its historic bldgs. have been destroyed (some of them when town was sacked by the Lancastrians in 1461), but extant are: 6 old churches (including St. Mary's, All Saints, St. Martin's, St. John's, and St. George's); part of 12th-cent. Benedictine priory of St. Leonard; a gate of Brasenose Col. (founded by a group from Oxford in 1333, when Stamford vied with Oxford as a seat of learning); several almshouses (called "callises," since they were founded by Calais merchants), including Browne's Hosp. E of town, in Northampton, is Burghley House (16th cent.), containing collections of art treasures and built by Lord Burghley, who was buried in St. Martin's.

Stamford. 1 City (pop. 74,293), coextensive with Stamford town, Fairfield co., SW Conn., at mouth of Rippowam R., on Long Isl. Sound and 8 mi. SW of Norwalk; N.Y. commuters' residential area, mfg. center (locks, hardware, machinery, chemicals, drugs, plastics, clothing, airplane and automobile parts, optical goods, paint, oil burners, rubber, metal, and glass products); boat yards on Stamford Harbor. Seat of St. Basil's Col. Includes residential Shippan Point, and Glenbrook and Springdale villages (mfg. and residential). Cummings Park here has childrens' mus. Settled 1641, city inc. 1893, town and city govts. consolidated 1947. **2** Village (pop. 265), Harlan co., S Nebr., 12 mi. W of Alma and on Beaver Creek; livestock, grain. **3** Summer-resort village (pop. 1,162), Delaware co., S N.Y., in the Catskills, on West Branch of Delaware R. and 24 mi. ESE of Oneonta. Mt. Utsayantha (3,213 ft.) is just SE. Inc. 1870. **4** City (pop. 5,819), Jones co., W central Texas, 34 mi. N of Abilene; trade, processing center in cotton, cattle area (cotton gins and compress; mfg. of wood products, mattresses, flour, feed, dairy products); oil, natural-gas wells. Has annual Cowboy Reunion. Founded 1900, inc. 1901. **5** Town (pop. 514), Bennington co., SW Vt., in Green Mts., on Mass. line, just N of North Adams.

Stamford Bridge, agr. village, East Riding, E central Yorkshire, England, on Derwent R. and 7 mi. ENE of York. King Harold here defeated (1066) Harold Hardrada (Harold III) and Tostig.

Stamford Hill, England: see TOTTENHAM.

Stamford Hill, N residential suburb of Durban, E Natal, U. of So. Afr., on Indian Ocean; site of Durban airport.

Stammersdorf (shtäm′ûrsdôrf), town (pop. 3,977), E Lower Austria, 5 mi. N of Vienna; vineyards.

Stamnes, Norway: see SANDNESSJOEN.

Stampalia, Greece: see ASTYPALAIA.

Stamphanes, Greece: see STROPHADES.

Stamping Ground, town (pop. 396), Scott co., N Ky., 12 mi. ENE of Frankfort; makes whisky.

Stamps, city (pop. 2,552), Lafayette co., SW Ark., 31 mi. E of Texarkana, in oil, cotton, and timber area; cotton ginning, lumber milling.

Stamsund (stäm′sŏŏn), fishing village (pop. 676) in Hol canton (pop. 3,070), Nordland co., N Norway, on E Vestvagoy of the Lofoten Isls., 20 mi. WSW of Svolvaer; fish-oil, guano, and fodder processing; summer resort. Ure (ōō′rŭ) fishing village (pop. 100) is 5 mi. SW.

Stana-de-Vale (stû′nä-dā-vä′lā), Rum. *Stâna-de-Vale,* village, Bihor prov., W Rumania, in W of the Apuseni Mts. c.35 mi. SE of Oradea; summer and winter resort (alt. 3,614 ft.), and base for mountain excursions into the Bihor.

Stanardsville (stă′nŭrdzvĭl), town (pop. 182), ⊙ Greene co., N central Va., 18 mi. N of Charlottesville. Rail station at Barboursville, 12 mi. SE.

Stanberry, city (pop. 1,651), Gentry co., NW Mo., near Grand R., 35 mi. NE of St. Joseph; agr., livestock, poultry; ships hogs.

Stancomb-Wills Ice Tongue (stăn′kŭm-wĭlz′) (50 naut. mi. long, 45 naut. mi. wide), Antarctica, along Caird Coast; 74°10′S 25°W. Discovered 1915 by Ernest Shackleton, Br. explorer.

Standard, village (pop. 244), S Alta., 27 mi. SSW of Drumheller; coal mining.

Standard. 1 Village (pop. 290), Putnam co., N central Ill., 7 mi. SSW of La Salle, in agr. and bituminous-coal area. **2** Village (pop. 2,176, with adjacent Spring Garden), Westmoreland co., SW Pa., just N of Mt. Pleasant.

Standard City, village (pop. 192), Macoupin co., SW central Ill., 7 mi. NE of Carlinville, in agr. and bituminous-coal area. Post office is South Standard.

Standard Hill, England: see NORTHALLERTON.

Standerton, town (pop. 9,277), SE Transvaal, U. of So. Afr., on Vaal R. (bridges) and 90 mi. SE of Johannesburg; alt. 5,022 ft.; agr. center (stock, potatoes, oats, mealies, teff); grain elevator. Coal deposits in region.

Standish. 1 Agr. town (pop. 1,786), Cumberland co., SW Maine, 12 mi. NW of Portland and on Sebago L. Includes resort village of Sebago Lake. Mfg. (clothing, wood products). **2** City (pop. 1,186), ⊙ Arenac co., E Mich., 26 mi. NNW of Bay City, and on South Branch of Pine R. Trade and shipping center for farm area; flour mill, grain elevator, condensed-milk plant. Hunting, fishing. Inc. as city 1903.

Standish with Langtree, urban district (1931 pop. 7,261; 1951 census 8,991), S central Lancashire, England. Includes town of Standish, 3 mi. NNW of Wigan; bacon and ham curing. Coal mining near by. Has church rebuilt in 16th cent.

Standley Lake, small lake (1½ mi. wide), just NW of Denver, N central Colo. Standley L. Dam (113 ft. high, 7,000 ft. long; completed 1911) is at E end of lake. Used for irrigation.

Standon, town and parish (pop. 2,469), E Hertford, England, 8 mi. NE of Hertford; agr. market. Has 15th-cent. church.

Stanfield. 1 Mining village, Harlan co., SE Ky., S of Harlan. **2** City (pop. 845), Umatilla co., N Oregon, 21 mi. WNW of Pendleton and on Umatilla R.; sheep.

Stanford. 1 Village (pop. 457), McLean co., central Ill., 11 mi. WSW of Bloomington, in rich agr. area. **2** City (pop. 1,861), ⊙ Lincoln co., central Ky., near Herrington L., 11 mi. SE of Danville. Residential community in outer Bluegrass agr. region; some mfg. of dairy products, cabinets, office fixtures, caskets; flour and feed mills. Near by is site of fort built 1775 by Col. Benjamin Logan on old Wilderness Road. Stanford founded 1786 by Va. legislature. **3** Town (pop. 542), ⊙ Judith Basin co., central Mont., 55 mi. SE of Great Falls; shipping point for grain and livestock; coal mines; flour, wool, dairy and poultry products, timber.

Stanford-le-Hope (-lŭ-), town and parish (pop. 4,311), S Essex, England, near the Thames, 5 mi. NE of Tilbury. In parish, 4 mi. E, on the Thames, are Coryton, Shell Haven, and Thames Haven, important petroleum-refining and storage centers.

Stanga (stông′ä″), Swedish *Stånga,* village (pop. 252), Gotland co., SE Sweden, in S central part of Gotland isl., 25 mi. SSE of Visby; grain, sugar beets, potatoes, flax. Has 13th-cent. church.

Stange (stäng′ŭ), village (pop. 972; canton pop. 8,665), Hedmark co., SE Norway, on E shore of L. Mjosa, on railroad and 6 mi. S of Hamar; lumbering, woodworking, agr.

Stanger (stăng′ûr), town (pop. 3,510), E Natal, U. of So. Afr., on Indian Ocean, 40 mi. NNE of Durban; sugar-milling center; wattles, tea, mealies, vegetables grown in region. Chaka, a venerated Zulu chief, buried here.

Stanghella (stäng-gĕl′lä), village (pop. 1,485), Padova prov., Veneto, N Italy, 5 mi. N of Rovigo; beet-sugar refinery.

Stang River, Swedish *Stångån* (stông′ōn″), SE Sweden, rises NW of Vimmerby, flows SE to Vimmerby, thence in winding course generally N, through several small lakes, past Linkoping, to L. Rox 2 mi. N of Linkoping; 120 mi. long.

Stanground, England: see OLD FLETTON.

Stangvik (stäng′vēk, –vĭk), village and canton (pop. 2,303), More og Romsdal co., W Norway, on E shore of Halse Fjord, 27 mi. SE of Kristiansund. Agr., cattle raising, lumbering in near-by mts. Sawmills, furniture and barrel factories; boatbuilding. Village of Todalen (tō′dälŭn) is at head of fjord.

Stanhope (stă′nŭp), former urban district (1931 pop. 1,746), W Durham, England, on Wear R. and 6 mi. W of Wolsingham; stone-quarrying center; agr. market. Has 13th-cent. church and Roman altar in rectory.

Stanhope. 1 (stăn′hōp″) Town (pop. 420), Hamilton co., central Iowa, 12 mi. S of Webster City, in agr. area. **2** (stăn′hōp″, stă′nŭp) Borough (pop. 1,351), Sussex co., NW N.J., on old Morris Canal, near L. Hopatcong, and 13 mi. NW of Morristown; mfg. (mineral wool, beverages), agr. (poultry, dairy products). Settled 1714, inc. 1904. Produced iron in Revolution.

Staniard Creek (stă′nyŭrd), town (pop. 618), W Bahama Isls., on NE shore of Andros Isl., 40 mi. WSW of Nassau; 24°51′N 77°54′W. Fishing, lumbering.

Stanichno-Luganskoye (stŭnyēch′nŭ-lōōgän′skŭyŭ), town (1926 pop. 3,139), E Voroshilovgrad oblast, Ukrainian SSR, in the Donbas, near Kondrashevskaya junction, on the Northern Donets and 12 mi. NE of Voroshilovgrad; truck produce, wheat. Called Kosiorovo in mid-1930s.

Stanimaka, Bulgaria: see ASENOVGRAD.

Stanisesti (stŭnĕshĕsht'), Rum. *Stănişeşti*, village (pop. 1,017), Barlad prov., E Rumania, 40 mi. N of Tecuci.

Stanisic or **Stanishich** (both: stä'nĭshĭch), Serbo-Croatian *Stanišić*, Hung. *Őrszállás* (ûr'säl-läs), village (pop. 7,465), Vojvodina, NW Serbia, Yugoslavia, near Hung. border, 12 mi. NNE of Sombor, in the Backa.

Stanislaus (stă'nĭslô, -lôs), county (□ 1,506; pop. 127,231), central Calif.; ⊙ Modesto. Level land in San Joaquin Valley, bordered by Coast Ranges (W); watered by San Joaquin, Tuolumne, and Stanislaus rivers. Irrigation water supplied by Modesto, Turlock, Don Pedro reservoirs. Dairy and beef cattle, dairy products, poultry, fruit (peaches, melons, grapes, apricots), nuts, alfalfa, beans, grain, truck. Processing industries (fruit canning and drying, wine making, dairying). Working of sand and gravel, gold, clay, silver deposits; natural-gas wells. Formed 1854.

Stanislaus Peak (11,202 ft.), Alpine co., E Calif., in the Sierra Nevada, c.40 mi. SSE of L. Tahoe.

Stanislaus River, central Calif., formed by its North and Middle forks c.17 mi. E of San Andreas, flows c.75 mi. SW to San Joaquin R. 13 mi. W of Modesto. About 7 mi. W of Sonora is Melones Dam (mĭlō'nēz), completed 1926, for irrigation and power, to be replaced by New Melones Dam (and Tulloch Dam) of CENTRAL VALLEY project.

Stanislav (stŭnyĭslăf'), oblast (□ 5,350; 1946 pop. estimate 1,300,000), W Ukrainian SSR; ⊙ Stanislav. On N slopes of E Beskids; extends N into Dniester R. valley; bounded SE by Cheremosh R. Drained by right tributaries of the Dniester (Bystritsa, Lomnitsa, and Svitsa rivers), and by Prut R. Has dark prairie soils; loess (N); humid continental climate (short summers). Mining region: petroleum, natural gas, ozokerite, and salt in E Beskids; potassium (Kalush, Dolina), lignite, and gypsum. Grain, potatoes (N), sugar beets, tobacco, hogs, fruit and truck gardens (Pokutye upland), sheep (in mts.). Industries based on mining (petroleum refining, saltworks), agr. (sugar refining, flour milling, tanning, distilling, brewing, vegetable-oil extracting), and timber (sawmilling, paper and plywood mfg.). Metalworking and light industries in main urban centers (Stanislav, Kolomyya, Kalush). Health resorts (Yaremcha, Vorokhta) in E Beskids. Formed 1939 out of Pol. Stanislawow prov., following Soviet occupation of E Poland; held by Germany (1941–44); ceded to USSR in 1945.

Stanislav, Pol. *Stanisławów* (stänyēswä'vo͝of), Ger. *Stanislau* (stä'nĭslou), city (1931 pop. 61,256), ⊙ Stanislav oblast, Ukrainian SSR, in Bystritsa Solotvinskaya R. valley, 70 mi. SSE of Lvov; 48°56'N 24°44'E. Rail junction (repair shops); industrial center; iron casting, mfg. of machinery, railroad cars, chemicals, textiles, leather goods, furniture, ceramics; petroleum refining (gasoline, artificial asphalt, lubricating oil); agr. processing (cereals, fruit, vegetables, hops). Teachers and medical colleges, technical schools, mus., theaters. Has old castle, town hall, and numerous churches. An old Pol. town, frequently assaulted (17th cent.) by Tatars and Turks; chartered and fortified in 1683. Passed to Austria (1772); occupied by Russians during First World War; reverted to Poland (1919); ceded to USSR in 1945. Its Jewish pop. was largely exterminated during Second World War.

Stanislavchik (stŭnyĭslăf'chĭk), village (1926 pop. 6,034), W Vinnitsa oblast, Ukrainian SSR, 5 mi. S of Zhmerinka; sugar beets, wheat, fruit.

Stanislavovo, Belorussian SSR: see ROSSONY.

Stanislawow, Ukrainian SSR: see STANISLAV, city.

Stanjel na Krasu (shtä'nyĕl nä krä'so͞o), Slovenian *Štanjel na Krasu*, Ital. *San Daniele del Carso* (sän dänyā'lĕ dĕl kär'sō), village (1936 pop. 304), W Slovenia, Yugoslavia, on railroad and 13 mi. N of Trieste. Until 1947, in Italy.

Stankov (stä'nyŭkôf), Czech *Staňkov*, village (pop. 2,783), SW Bohemia, Czechoslovakia, on Radbuza R., on railroad and 6 mi. SW of Horsovsky Tyn; mirror mfg.

Stanley, Chinese *Chikchu* (chĕk'chü'), village, S Hong Kong isl., on Stanley Bay, 5 mi. SSE of Victoria; fisheries. Site of war-internee camp during Jap. occupation (1941–45).

Stanley. 1 Town and parish (pop. 4,881), SE Derby, England, 3 mi. W of Ilkeston; coal mining. Has 13th-cent. church with some remains of Norman chapel. **2** Urban district (1931 pop. 24,460; 1951 census 48,123), N Durham, England, 8 mi. SSW of Newcastle-upon-Tyne; coal-mining center. Absorbed (1937) Tanfield and Annfield Plain. **3** Residential urban district (1931 pop. 14,565; 1951 census 16,672), West Riding, S central Yorkshire, England, on Calder R. (here crossed by Aire and Calder Canal) and 2 mi. NNE of Wakefield; site of several mental hospitals.

Stanley, town (1948 pop. c.1,200), ⊙ FALKLAND ISLANDS, on Port William inlet, NE coast of East Falkland Isl., 1,100 mi. S of Montevideo, its main overseas connection; 51°45'S 57°58'W. Main port and trading center; exports wool, skins, tallow, seal oil; imports foodstuffs, coal, oil, timber. Wireless station and power plant. During Second World War a Br. garrison was stationed here. Also called Port Stanley.

Stanley, town and port (pop. 797), NW Tasmania, at E tip Circular Head peninsula in Bass Strait, 105 mi. WNW of Launceston; rail terminus; agr. center; sawmills. Exports wheat, oats. Formerly called Circular Head.

Stanley, county (□ 1,495; pop. 2,055), central S. Dak.; ⊙ Fort Pierre. Farming and cattle-raising area bounded N by Cheyenne R., E by Missouri R., and drained by Bad R. Livestock, wheat, barley, oats, alfalfa. Formed 1873.

Stanley. 1 Town (pop. 33), Custer co., central Idaho, 40 mi. WSW of Challis. **2** Town (pop. 158), Buchanan co., E Iowa, 5 mi. ESE of Oelwein. **3** Town (pop. 1,644), Gaston co., S N.C., 17 mi. NW of Charlotte; cotton mills. Settled 1840; inc. 1879. **4** City (pop. 1,486), ⊙ Mountrail co., NW central N.Dak., 51 mi. W of Minot, in fertile farm area; coal mines; dairy products, wheat, flax, corn. Inc. 1910. **5** Town (pop. 399), Page co., N Va., in Shenandoah Valley, 7 mi. S of Luray. **6** City (pop. 2,014), Chippewa co., W central Wis., 29 mi. ENE of Eau Claire, in dairying and farming area; produces clover honey, cheese, canned vegetables, wood and leather products. Settled c.1881, inc. 1898.

Stanley, Mount, Belgian Congo and Uganda: see RUWENZORI.

Stanley Baldwin, Mount (10,900 ft.), E B.C., in Premier Group of Rocky Mts., 65 mi. W of Jasper.

Stanley Bridge, village (pop. estimate 100), N P.E.I., on New London Bay, 16 mi. ENE of Summerside; cod, hake, oyster fisheries.

Stanley Falls, 7 cataracts in Lualaba R., NE central Belgian Congo, extending for c.60 mi. along curve of the river bet. Stanleyville and Ponthierville; total fall, c.200 ft. The 7th cataract, the largest, is 800 yards wide. Beyond the falls, the Lualaba becomes the Congo R. A rail line bet. Stanleyville and Ponthierville circumvents the falls.

Stanley Peak (10,351 ft.), on Alta.–B.C. border, in Rocky Mts., on W edge of Banff Natl. Park, 20 mi. W of Banff; 51°10'N 116°2'W.

Stanley Pool, lakelike expansion (□ 320) of Congo R. along Belgian Congo–Fr. Equatorial Africa border, c.350 mi. from river's mouth, above Livingstone Falls; c.20 mi. long, 13 mi. wide; max. depth 52 ft., alt. 852 ft. Discovered by Henry M. Stanley in 1877. Leopoldville is on its SW shore, Brazzaville on W shore. Large (□ 70), swampy, Bamu or M'Bamou Isl. (ŭmbä'mo͞o), belonging to Fr. Equatorial Africa, is in its center; it has extensive pastures for stock.

Stanley Reservoir (□ 60), in Salem dist., W Madras, India, on Cauvery R. NW of Salem; impounded by Mettur Dam; 33 mi. long; part of Mettur hydroelectric system.

Stanleyville, province, Belgian Congo: see EASTERN PROVINCE.

Stanleyville, town (1948 pop. 25,278), ⊙ Eastern Prov. and of Stanleyville dist. (□ 86,462; 1948 pop. c.650,000), NE central Belgian Congo, on both banks of Congo R. just below Stanley Falls, and 775 mi. NE of Leopoldville; 0°26'N 25°14'E. Air communications hub (5 airlines), important transshipment point (terminus of railroad circumventing the falls to Ponthierville, head of steam navigation on Congo R.), commercial and distributing center. Pharmaceuticals mfg., printing, rice and cotton processing. Has 2 hospitals for Europeans, school for European children, agr., medical, business and teachers school for natives, a Pasteur institute. Also known as a tourist center because of picturesque native fisheries in the river rapids, scenic falls to N, and near-by settlements of Arabicized natives. H. M. Stanley 1st reached area in 1877. Kisangani post (also known as Falls Station) was established by him (1882) on isl. just SE and was repeatedly attacked and burned down by Arab slave traders from their near-by camp Singitini. Stanleyville proper dates from 1898 and is still called Kisangani by Swahili-speaking natives. R.C. mission of Saint Gabriel des Falls (3 mi. WNW), founded 1897, is now seat of vicar apostolic of Stanley Falls and has teachers and trade schools for natives.

Stanlow, England: see ELLESMERE PORT.

Stanly (stăn'lē), county (□ 399; pop. 37,130), S central N.C.; ⊙ Albemarle. Piedmont region; bounded E by Yadkin R., here becoming Pee Dee R. (Badin and Tillery lakes; power dams). Farming (cotton, lespedeza, corn, wheat), dairying, poultry raising; timber (pine, oak). Textile mfg., lumbering. Formed 1841.

Stanmore, residential town constituted by parishes of Great Stanmore (pop. 2,688) and Little Stanmore (pop. 6,918), Middlesex, England, 3 mi. NW of Hendon; mfg. of electrical equipment. There are 2 ponds, named Julius Caesar's Ponds, believed to have served a near-by Roman station.

Stannard (stă'nûrd), town (pop. 116), Caledonia co., NE Vt., 13 mi. NW of St. Johnsbury.

Stannard Rock, Mich., reef and lighthouse in L. Superior, off Upper Peninsula 27 mi. SE of Keweenaw Point.

Stann Creek (stăn), district (□ 840, including 13 sq. mi. of cays; pop. 6,373) of central Br. Honduras; ⊙ Stann Creek. Coastal plain with mountainous interior (Cockscomb Mts., rising to 3,681 ft. in Victoria Peak). Citrus fruit, bananas, coconuts, sugar cane; lumbering. Plantation railroad serves the banana industry in Stann Creek valley; coastal craft service with Belize.

Stann Creek, town (pop. 3,414), ⊙ Stann Creek dist., central Br. Honduras, at mouth of the Stann Creek (20 mi. long), 40 mi. S of Belize. Trading center for bananas, timber, coconuts; fisheries. Port facilities, lighthouse; regular coastal craft service with Belize. Terminus of 25-mi. railroad serving banana plantations. Founded (19th cent.) by Caribs fleeing from Sp. Honduras.

Stanninghall, England: see HORSTEAD.

Stanningley, town in Leeds county borough, West Riding, S central Yorkshire, England, 5 mi. W of Leeds; woolen milling, knitting; also makes textile machinery, chemicals, lubricating oil.

Stannington, town and parish (pop. 1,920), SE Northumberland, England, 10 mi. N of Newcastle-upon-Tyne; agr. market.

Stanovoi Range or **Stanovoy Range** (stŭnŭvoi'), mountain divide in SE Siberian Russian SFSR, extending from Olekma R. c.450 mi. E to Maya R. (left affluent of Uda R.). Here continued by Dzhugdzhur Range, along Yakut Autonomous SSR–Amur oblast border. Forms watershed bet. Lena and Amur river basins. Rises to 8,143 ft. in Skalisty [Rus.,=rocky] Mtn., 400 mi. N of Blagoveshchensk. Consists basically of crystalline schists and gneiss and grey granite intrusives.

Stans (shtäns), village (pop. 755), Tyrol, W Austria, near Inn R., 18 mi. W of Innsbruck. Large Cistercian monastery (founded 1271).

Stans (shtäns), town (pop. 3,449), ⊙ Nidwalden half-canton, central Switzerland, 7 mi. SSE of Lucerne. Has town hall (1715), baroque church (1641–47), charnel house (1482), historical mus., monument to Arnold von Winkelried. Cable railway up the Stanserhorn (6,237 ft.), 2 mi. SSW.

Stansbury, village and port (pop. 314), S South Australia, on E Yorke Peninsula, 45 mi. W of Adelaide across Gulf St. Vincent; exports agr. products.

Stansbury Mountains, in Wasatch Natl. Forest, Tooele co., NW Utah; extend N from Onaqui Mts. Rise to 11,031 ft. in DESERET PEAK.

Stanserhorn, Switzerland: see STANS.

Stansstad (shtäns'shtät), village (pop. 1,174), Nidwalden half-canton, central Switzerland, on L. of Lucerne and 2 mi. NW of Stans, bet. the Bürgenstock and a spur of the Pilatus. It forms, together with near-by Fürigen (alt. 2,133 ft.), a summer resort. A watchtower dates from 1308.

Stanstead, county (□ 432; pop. 27,972), S Que., on Vt. border; ⊙ Coaticook.

Stanstead or **Stanstead Plain**, village (pop. 876), S Que., 30 mi. SSW of Sherbrooke, near Rock Island, at Vt. border; dairying, granite quarrying.

Stanstead Abbots, residential town and parish (pop. 1,362), E Hertford, England, on Lea R. and 2 mi. SE of Ware. Has 14th-cent. church.

Stansted, town in Stansted Mountfitchet parish (pop. 2,488), NW Essex, England, on Stort R. and 3 mi. NE of Bishop's Stortford; agr. market. Has church of Norman origin.

Stansty (stăn'stē), parish (pop. 2,410), E Denbigh, Wales, just NW of Wrexham; coal mining.

Stanthorpe, town (pop. 2,380), SE Queensland, Australia, on New South Wales border, 105 mi. SW of Brisbane; alt. 2,650 ft. Health resort; chief fruitgrowing center of state. Tin mines and limestone quarries near by.

Stanton, trading post, N Mackenzie Dist., Northwest Territories, at head of Liverpool Bay, inlet (30 mi. long, 5–10 mi. wide) of the Beaufort Sea, at mouth of Anderson R.; 69°45'N 128°52'W; radio station.

Stanton. 1 County (□ 676; pop. 2,263), SW Kansas; ⊙ Johnson. Sloping to rolling plain, bordering W on Colo. Grain (chiefly wheat). Formed 1887. **2** County (□ 431; pop. 6,387), NE Nebr.; ⊙ Stanton. Farming region drained by Elkhorn R. Grain, livestock, dairy and poultry produce. Formed 1867.

Stanton. 1 Village (pop. 1,762), Orange co., S Calif., 20 mi. NW of Santa Ana. **2** Village (pop. c.400), New Castle co., N Del., 5 mi. SW of Wilmington. Delaware Park race track here. **3** Town (pop. 570), Montgomery co., SW Iowa, on Tarkio R. and 7 mi. ESE of Red Oak; grain. **4** Town (pop. 635), ⊙ Powell co., E central Ky., near Red R., 37 mi. ESE of Lexington, in agr. area; oil wells, timber, coal mines, clay pits, stone quarries. Cumberland Natl. Forest is near by. Good hunting. **5** City (pop. 1,123), ⊙ Montcalm co., central Mich., 38 mi. NE of Grand Rapids, in farm area (livestock, grain, potatoes, beans; dairy products). **6** City (pop. 1,403), ⊙ Stanton co., NE Nebr., 12 mi. SE of Norfolk and on Elkhorn R.; dairying; livestock. Settled 1869, inc. 1871. **7** City (pop. 571), ⊙ Mercer co., central N.Dak., 45 mi. NNW of Bismarck and on Missouri R. at mouth of Knife R. **8** Town (pop. 503), Haywood co., W Tenn., 11 mi. SW of Brownsville, in timber and farm area. **9** City (pop. 1,603), ⊙ Martin co., W Texas, 20 mi. SW of Big Spring; trade, shipping point for cattle-ranching and agr. region (grain, cotton); makes glycerine. Oil fields to E. Inc. 1925.

Stanton and Newhall, England: see SWADLINCOTE DISTRICT.
Stanton-by-Dale, town and parish (pop. 606), SE Derby, England, 3 mi. S of Ilkeston; metalworks. Has Norman church, rebuilt in 14th cent.
Stantonsburg, town (pop. 627), Wilson co., E central N.C., 10 mi. SSE of Wilson; lumber milling.
Stantsiya Gorchakovo, Uzbek SSR: see GORCHAKOVO STANTSIYA.
Stantsiya Kermine, Uzbek SSR: see KERMINE.
Stanway, agr. village and parish (pop. 1,750), NE Essex, England, 4 mi. W of Colchester.
Stanwell, England: see STAINES.
Stanwick (stă'nĭk), town and parish (pop. 928), E Northampton, England, 6 mi. ENE of Wellingborough; shoe mfg. Has 13th-cent. church.
Stanwood. 1 Town (pop. 547), Cedar co., E Iowa, 27 mi. ESE of Cedar Rapids, in agr. area. **2** Village (pop. 189), Mecosta co., central Mich., 9 mi. S of Big Rapids, in farm area. **3** Town (pop. 710), Snohomish co., NW Wash., 20 mi. NW of Everett, near mouth of Stillaguamish R.; peas, oysters, dairy products; food processing.
Stanz (shtänts), village (pop. 2,103), Styria, E central Austria, 27 mi. N of Graz; paper mill, lumberyards.
Stanzertal (shtän'tsûrtäl), valley in Tyrol, W Austria, extending from the Arlberg c.15 mi. E along Rosanna R. to the Inn at Landeck. Main town, Sankt Anton am Arlberg.
Staouéli (stäwālē'), village (pop. 2,498), Alger dept., N central Algeria, 10 mi. WSW of Algiers; vineyards, citrus groves, truck gardens. Near-by is a former Trappist monastery.
Stapelburg (shtä'pŭlbŏŏrk), village (pop. 1,738), in former Prussian Saxony prov., central Germany, after 1945 in Saxony-Anhalt, at N foot of the upper Harz, 8 mi. NW of Wernigerode, 4 mi. E of Eckertal; flour milling. Has remains of 14th-cent. castle.
Stapleford, town in Beeston and Stapleford urban dist., SW Nottingham, England, 6 mi. WSW of Nottingham; coal mines, lace mills, textile-printing plants, pencil works. Has 14th-cent. church and a Saxon cross.
Staplehurst, town and parish (pop. 1,713), central Kent, England, 8 mi. S of Maidstone; agr. market, with brick- and tileworks. Has 14th–15th-cent. church.
Staplehurst, village (pop. 224), Seward co., SE Nebr., 27 mi. WNW of Lincoln and on Big Blue R.
Staples, city (pop. 2,782), Todd co., central Minn., near Crow Wing R., 30 mi. W of Brainerd; trade center for grain, livestock, truck-farming area; dairy products. Settled 1881, platted 1885, inc. 1906.
Staples, The, England: see FARNE ISLANDS.
Stapleton (stā'pŭltŭn). **1** Town (pop. 355), Jefferson co., E Ga., 32 mi. WSW of Augusta; clothes mfg. **2** Village (pop. 363), ⊙ Logan co., central Nebr., 25 mi. NNE of North Platte and on S.Loup R.; livestock, grain. **3** A port and industrial section of Richmond borough of New York city, SE N.Y., on NE Staten Isl., S of St. George. First U.S. foreign trade zone (free port), established 1936, and a U.S. marine hosp. are here. Mfg.: clothing, sirens, furniture, machinery, artificial flowers, dental equipment, paper and mineral products, knit goods.
Star or **Star'** (stär), town (1940 pop. 4,450), NE Bryansk oblast, Russian SFSR, 7 mi. W of Dyatkovo; glassworks.
Star, town (pop. 677), Montgomery co., central N.C., 21 mi. S of Asheboro; hosiery, lumber.
Stara [Serbo-Croatian and Czech,=old]. For names beginning thus and not found here, see under following part of the name.
Stara Boleslav (stä'rä bô'lĕsläf), Czech *Stará Boleslav*, Ger. *Altbunzlau* (ältbŏŏnts'lou), town (pop. 4,744), N central Bohemia, Czechoslovakia, on right bank of Elbe R. opposite Brandys nad Labem, on railroad and 14 mi. NE of Prague; pilgrimage center with noted church, on site of assassination (929) of St. Wenceslaus. Health resort of Houstka (hōsh'tyŏŏkä), Czech *Houšťka*, with ferruginous springs and peat baths, is just SSE.
Starachowice (stärä-khôvē'tsĕ), village, Kielce prov., E central Poland, on Kamienna R., just NW of Wierzbnik; iron mines; foundry, truck factory.
Stara Dala, Czechoslovakia: see HURBANOVO.
Stara Gradiska (stä'rä grä'dĭshkä), Serbo-Croatian *Stara Gradiška*, Hung. *Ógradiska* (ō'grädĭshkŏ), village, N Croatia, Yugoslavia, on the Sava and 10 mi. SW of Nova Gradiska, opposite Bosanska Gradiska, in Slavonia; trade center for plum-growing region.
Stara Lubovna (stä'rä lyŏŏ'bôvnyä), Slovak *Stará L'ubovňa*, Ger. *Lublau* (lŏŏb'lou), Hung. *Ólubló* (ō'lŏŏblō), town (pop. 1,989), N Slovakia, Czechoslovakia, in E foothills of the High Tatra on Poprad R. and 24 mi. NE of Poprad. Has picturesque castle ruins (partly restored), 18th-cent. church. Health resort of Lubovna (alt. 1,824 ft.), with mineral springs and peat baths, is 3 mi. SE.
Stara Moravica or **Stara Moravitsa** (stä'rä mô'rävĭtsä), Hung. *Bácskossuthfalva* (bäch'kôshŏŏtfŏ"lvŏ), village (pop. 6,695), Vojvodina, NW Serbia, Yugoslavia, 19 mi. SW of Subotica, in the Backa.
Staranzano (stäräntsä'nô), village (pop. 1,231), Gorizia prov., Friuli-Venezia Giulia, NE Italy, 1 mi. W of Monfalcone.
Stara Paka, Czechoslovakia: see NOVA PAKA.
Stara Pazova (stä'rä pä'zôvä), Hung. *Ópázova* (ō'päzôvŏ), village (pop. 9,069), Vojvodina, N Serbia, Yugoslavia, 19 mi. NW of Belgrade, in the Srem; rail junction.
Stara Planina, Bulgaria: see BALKAN MOUNTAINS.
Stara Reka, river, Yugoslavia: see STRUMICA RIVER.
Stara Sol, Ukrainian SSR: see STARAYA SOL.
Stara Wyzwa, Ukrainian SSR: see STARAYA VYZHVA.
Staraya [Rus.,=old], in Rus. names: see also STARO- [Rus. combining form], STAROYE, STARY, STARYE.
Staraya Barda (stä'rīŭ bär'dŭ), village (1926 pop. 2,804), E Altai Territory, Russian SFSR, 45 mi. ESE of Bisk; dairy farming.
Staraya Degtyanka, Russian SFSR: see DEGTYANKA.
Staraya Kriusha (krēŏŏ'shŭ), village (1926 pop. 7,224), SE Voronezh oblast, Russian SFSR, 17 mi. SSE of Kalach; wheat.
Staraya Kulatka (kŏŏlät'kŭ), village (1939 pop. over 2,000), S Ulyanovsk oblast, Russian SFSR, 45 mi. SW of Syzran; wheat, sunflowers.
Staraya Kupavna (kŏŏpäv'nŭ), town (1939 pop. over 10,000), E central Moscow oblast, Russian SFSR, 22 mi. E of Moscow; woolen textiles, chemicals; peat. Formerly called Kupavna.
Staraya Lyalya (lyä'lyŭ), village (1926 pop. 708), W Sverdlovsk oblast, Russian SFSR, on Lyalya R. and 20 mi. NNE of Is, on rail spur; lumbering. Gold placers near by. Former site of lumber works called Staro-lyalinski Zavod.
Staraya Maina or **Staraya Mayna** (mī'nŭ), village (1926 pop. 3,692), NE Ulyanovsk oblast, Russian SFSR, near Volga R., 30 mi. NE of Ulyanovsk; flour milling; grain, sunflowers, legumes.
Staraya Matveyevka (mŭtvyā'ufkŭ), village (1939 pop. over 500), E Tatar Autonomous SSR, Russian SFSR, on Ik R. and 14 mi. SSE of Menzelinsk; grain, legumes, livestock.
Staraya Pokrovka (pŭkrôf'kŭ), village (1939 pop. over 500), NE Frunze oblast, Kirghiz SSR, in Chu valley, near Tokmak; orchards, truck produce.
Staraya Poltavka (pŭltäf'kŭ), village (1939 pop. over 2,000), NE Stalingrad oblast, Russian SFSR, on Yeruslan R. and 35 mi. SE of Rovnoye; wheat, cattle.
Staraya Russa (rōō'sŭ), city (1935 pop. 32,000), W central Novgorod oblast, Russian SFSR, on Polist R. and 36 mi. S of Novgorod, across L. Ilmen; road, rail center; sawmilling, veneering; agr.-machinery shops, flour mill. Health resort (salt springs, mud baths). Has 12th-cent. monastery and Dostoyevskiy mus. One of oldest Rus. settlements, 1st mentioned in 1167. During Second World War, held (1941–44) by Germans.
Staraya Sinyava (sēnyä'vŭ), town (1926 pop. 2,749), E Kamenets-Podolski oblast, Ukrainian SSR, 30 mi. NE of Proskurov; sugar refining.
Staraya Sol or **Staraya Sol'** (sôl'), Pol. *Stara Sól* (stä"rä sōōl'), town (1931 pop. 1,152), W Drogobych oblast, Ukrainian SSR, on N slope of E Beskids, 11 mi. WSW of Sambor; lumbering; rye, oats, sheep.
Staraya Ushitsa (ōōshē'tsŭ), agr. town (1926 pop. 3,009), S Kamenets-Podolski oblast, Ukrainian SSR, on Dniester R., and 26 mi. ESE of Kamenets-Podolski; wheat, corn.
Staraya Vichuga (vē'chōōgŭ), town (1939 pop. over 500), N Ivanovo oblast, Russian SFSR, 3 mi. NNW of Vichuga.
Staraya Vyzhevka (vĭ'zhĭfkŭ), Pol. *Stara Wyżwa*, village (1939 pop. over 500), central Volyn oblast, Ukrainian SSR, in Pripet Marshes, 18 mi. NW of Kovel; rye, potatoes. Also called Staraya Vyzhva.
Stara Zagora (stä'rä zägô'rä), city (pop. 37,057), ⊙ Stara Zagora dist. (formed 1949), central Bulgaria, on S slope of Sirnena Gora, 120 mi. E of Sofia; commercial and mfg. center; textiles, chemicals (vitriol), tobacco and food (wheat, meat, fruit, sunflowers) processing; rail junction. Winegrowing and truck gardening near by. Has teachers col., technical schools, opera house, theater, mus., monuments, and excavations of anc. town of Beroea. Founded as Roman town of Augusta Trajana; developed under Byzantine rule. Became a market for Stara Zagora Basin under Turkish rule (15th–19th cent.), when it was called Eski-Zagra or Yeski-Zagra. Destroyed during Russo-Turkish war; ceded to Bulgaria (1877) and rebuilt in modern fashion. Was ⊙ former Stara Zagora oblast (1934–47).
Stara Zagora Basin (□ 610; average alt. 500 ft.), central Bulgaria, E part of Thracian Plain, bet. Sirnena Gora (N), Tundzha R. (E), and Plovdiv (W) and Khaskovo (SW) basins. Drained by Tundzha and Maritsa rivers. Extensive agr. (wheat, oats, barley, corn, truck, fruit), cattle, horse and donkey raising. Main centers: Stara Zagora, Chirpan, Nova Zagora.
Starbuck, village (pop. estimate 250), S Man., 22 mi. WSW of Winnipeg; grain, stock.
Starbuck. 1 Resort village (pop. 1,143), Pope co., W Minn., at W end of L. Minnewaska, 8 mi. WSW of Glenwood; dairy and cement products. **2** City (pop. 194), Columbia co., SE Wash., on Tucannon R. and 33 mi. NNE of Walla Walla, in wheat-growing region.
Starbuck Island, uninhabited coral island (□ 1), Line Isls., S Pacific, 160 mi. SW of Malden Isl.; 5°37'S 155°53'W. Discovered 1823 and claimed 1866 by British. Formerly worked for guano. Formerly Volunteer Isl.
Star City, town (pop. 470), central Sask., 65 mi. ESE of Prince Albert; grain; lumbering.
Star City. 1 Town (pop. 1,296), ⊙ Lincoln co., SE Ark., 22 mi. SSE of Pine Bluff; agr. (cotton, corn, fruit, truck); cotton ginning, woodworking. **2** Town (pop. 1,205), Monongalia co., N W.Va., on Monongahela R. just NW of Morgantown, in coal-mining, gas- and oil-producing area; makes glass. Inc. 1907.
Stare Mesto (stä'rĕ myĕ'stô, Czech *Staré Město*. **1** Ger. *Altstadt* (ält'shtät), town (pop. 6,174), SE Moravia, Czechoslovakia, 14 mi. SW of Gottwaldov and on right bank of Morava R., opposite Uherske Hradiste; part of its urban commune. Excavations of Stone Age remains, made here, have greatly contributed to knowledge of Central European prehistory. Early Slavonic graves found here in 1948. **2** Ger. *Mährisch-Altstadt* (mâ'rĭsh-ält'shtät), village (pop. 1,280), N Moravia, Czechoslovakia, in the Jeseniky, 14 mi. NNW of Sumperk; rail terminus; graphite mining.
Stare Splavy, Czechoslovakia: see DOKSY.
Staretina Mountains (stä'rĕtēnä), in Dinaric Alps, W Bosnia, Yugoslavia, NNW of Livno; c.10 mi. long; rise to c.6,000 ft.
Stargard or **Stargard in Mecklenburg,** Germany: see BURG STARGARD.
Stargard or **Stargard in Pommern** (shtär'gärt ĭn pô'mŭrn), town (1939 pop. 39,760; 1946 pop. 9,733) in Pomerania, after 1945 in Szczecin prov., NW Poland, on Ina R. and 20 mi. ESE of Stettin; rail junction (workshops); flour mills, cosmetics and soap mfg. First mentioned in early-12th cent. as Slav fortress; chartered in mid-13th cent.; joined Hanseatic League. Heavily damaged (1635) in Thirty Years War. Under Treaty of Westphalia, passed (1648) to Brandenburg with Farther Pomerania, of which it had been capital. In Second World War, c.75% destroyed.
Stari [Serbo-Croatian,=old]. For Yugoslav names beginning thus and not found here, see under following part of the name.
Starigrad (stä'rēgrät). **1** Ital. *Cittavecchia* (chēttävĕk'kyä), village, S Croatia, Yugoslavia, on N coast of Hvar Isl., 8 mi. E of Hvar. Also written Stari Grad. **2** or **Starigrad Paklenica** (pä'klĕnĭtsä), village, W Croatia, Yugoslavia, small port on Velebit Channel of Adriatic Sea, at SW foot of Velebit Mts., 15 mi. S of Gospic, in Dalmatia. Built on Roman site; archaeologically important. Church of Franciscan cloister has 900-year-old statue of the Madonna, which is carried in yearly processions commemorating salvation of Starigrad from a cholera epidemic. Vaganjski Vrh peak rises 6 mi. NE of village; Manita Pec, Serbo-Croatian *Manita Peć*, a large stalactite cave, is 2 mi. NE. Also written Stari Grad.
Stari Majdan, Stari Maidan, or **Stari Maydan** (all: stä'rē mī'dän), village, NW Bosnia, Yugoslavia, 5 mi. NNW of Sanski Most; iron mining.
Star Island. 1 In Minn.: see CASS LAKE. **2** In N.H.: see ISLES OF SHOALS.
Stari Trg or **Stari Trg pri Rakeku** (stä'rē tŭrk' prē rä'kĕkōō), village, S Slovenia, Yugoslavia, 23 mi. S of Ljubljana.
Staritsa (stä'rētsŭ), city (1926 pop. 3,911), S Kalinin oblast, Russian SFSR, on Volga R. and 30 mi. NE of Rzhev; leather working, vegetable drying, flax processing; marble quarries. Has ruins of castle of Ivan the Terrible and 16th-cent. monastery, now a mus. Dates from 13th cent.; chartered 1376. Passed 1486 to Moscow. During Second World War, held (1941–42) by Germans.
Staritsy, Belorussian SSR: see KIROVSK, Bobruisk oblast.
Starjunction or **Star Junction,** village (pop. 1,027), Fayette co., SW Pa., on the Monongahela and 12 mi. NNW of Uniontown.
Stark. 1 County (□ 291; pop. 8,721), N central Ill.; ⊙ Toulon. Agr. (corn, oats, wheat, livestock, poultry). Bituminous coal. Mfg. (horse collars, dairy products, cement blocks, monuments). Drained by Spoon River and small Indian Creek. Formed 1839. **2** County (□ 1,319; pop. 16,137), W N.Dak.; ⊙ Dickinson. Agr. area drained by Heart R. Rich in lignite and clay (bricks and pottery are made). Stock raising; dairy products, poultry, wheat. Formed 1879. **3** County (□ 580; pop. 283,194), E central Ohio; ⊙ CANTON. Intersected by Tuscarawas R. and small Nimishillen, Sandy, and Sugar creeks. Includes Fort Laurens State Park. Agr. (livestock, grain, fruit; dairy products); mfg. at Canton, Massillon, Alliance. Coal mining; limestone quarries, sand and gravel pits. Formed 1808.
Stark. 1 City (pop. 157), Neosho co., SE Kansas, 15 mi. E of Chanute; stock raising, general agr. **2** Town (pop. 373), Coos co., N N.H., on Upper Ammonoosuc R. and 10 mi. NW of Berlin; partly in White Mtn. Natl. Forest. Percy village, near Christine L. (2 mi. long), is summer resort.
Stark City, town (pop. 154), Newton co., SW Mo., in the Ozarks, 10 mi. E of Neosho.

Starke (stärk), county (□ 311; pop. 15,282), NW Ind.; ⊙ Knox. Bounded NW by Kankakee R.; drained by Yellow R. and other tributaries of the Kankakee. Rich agr. area, producing large mint and onion crops, livestock, poultry, truck; some mfg. at Knox. Formed 1835.
Starke, town (pop. 2,944), ⊙ Bradford co., N Fla., 23 mi. NE of Gainesville, in truck-produce, timber, and naval-stores area; noted for its strawberries; sawmilling, plastics mfg. Camp Blanding, a U.S. army station, was built near by in 1941.
Starkenbach, Czechoslovakia: see JILEMNICE.
Starkenburg (shtär'kunbŏŏrk), former province (□ 1,099; 1939 pop. 657,721) of Hesse (see HESSE-DARMSTADT), W Germany. Bounded W by the Rhine, N by former Prussian prov. of Hesse-Nassau, E by Bavaria, S by N Baden. Includes the Odenwald (E); drained by Rhine and canalized Main rivers. Fruit and vineyards on the Bergstrasse. Industry concentrated at Darmstadt and Offenbach (leather). Region was deeded to Hesse in 1479. Prov. abolished 1945.
Starkenburg, Palestine: see MONTFORT.
Starks, town (pop. 421), Somerset co., W central Maine, 8 mi. NE of Norridgewock; canneries.
Starksboro, town (pop. 576), Addison co., W central Vt., 19 mi. SE of Burlington; dairying.
Starkville. 1 Village (1940 pop. 795), Las Animas co., S Colo., just S of Trinidad, near N.Mex. line, in dairying, grain, and sugar-beet region; alt. c.6,400 ft. **2** City (pop. 7,107), ⊙ Oktibbeha co., E Miss., 23 mi. W of Columbus, in stock-raising, dairying, and farming area (cotton, corn, hay); condensed milk, textiles, lumber. Mississippi State Col. is at near-by State College (SE). Founded c.1834, inc. 1884.
Starkweather, village (pop. 229), Ramsey co., NE N.Dak., 23 mi. N of Devils Lake.
Starlake or **Star Lake,** resort village, St. Lawrence co., N N.Y., in the Adirondacks, on Star L. (c.1 mi. long), 31 mi. ENE of Carthage.
Star Lake. 1 In Otter Tail co., W Minn., 18 mi. NE of Fergus Falls; 6 mi. long, 3 mi. wide. Drains into Dead L., just SE. Fishing and bathing resorts. **2** In N.H.: see PRESIDENTIAL RANGE.
Starnberg (shtärn'bĕrk"), town (pop. 8,540), Upper Bavaria, Germany, at NW tip of the Starnberger See, 15 mi. SW of Munich; mfg. of textiles and chemicals, metalworking, printing. Has mid-16th-cent. castle, mid-18th-cent. church.
Starnberger See (shtärn'bĕr"gŭr zā") or **Würmsee** (vürm'zā"), lake (□ 22), Upper Bavaria, Germany, 14 mi. SW of Munich; 12 mi. long, 1–3 mi. wide, 403 ft. deep; alt. 1,916 ft. Fishing (char, pike, salmon). Drained by Würm R. Town of Starnberg at NW tip.
Staro- [Rus. combining form,=old], in Rus. names: see also STARAYA, STAROYE, STARY, STARYE.
Staro-Aleiskoye or **Staro-Aleyskoye** (stä"rŭ-ŭlā'-skŭyŭ), village (1939 pop. over 2,000), S Altai Territory, Russian SFSR, 15 mi. SW of Zmeinogorsk and on Alei R.; dairying; wheat, sugar beets.
Staro-Baltachevo (stä"rŭ-bŭltŭchĕ'vŭ), village (1939 pop. over 2,000), N Bashkir Autonomous SSR, Russian SFSR, 90 mi. N of Ufa; dairying center; livestock, grain.
Starobelsk or **Starobel'sk** (stŭrŭbyĕlsk'), city (1926 pop. 13,973), N central Voroshilovgrad oblast, Ukrainian SSR, on Aidar R. and 50 mi. NNW of Voroshilovgrad; agr. center in wheat and sunflower region; metalworks, flour mills, tanneries. Teachers col. here.
Staro-Beshevo (stä"rŭ-byĕ'shĭvŭ), village (1939 pop. over 2,000), S central Stalino oblast, Ukrainian SSR, in the Donbas, on Kalmius R. and 19 mi. SE of Stalino; metalworks.
Starobin (stŭrŭbēn'), town (1926 pop. 2,633), SW Bobruisk oblast, Belorussian SSR, on Sluch R. and 21 mi. SSW of Slutsk; food products.
Starodub (–dōōp'), city (1926 pop. 12,486), SW Bryansk oblast, Russian SFSR, on rail spur and 75 mi. SW of Bryansk; vegetable drying; brewing. Dates from 11th cent.; chartered 1218.
Starodubskoye (–skŭyŭ), village (1940 pop. 4,844), S Sakhalin, Russian SFSR, minor port on Sea of Okhotsk, 6 mi. N of Dolinsk; former N terminus of E coast railroad; declined following extension of line to Poronaisk. Under Jap. rule (1905–45), called Sakaehama (säkī'hämŭ).
Star of the Congo, Fr. *Étoile du Congo* (ātwäl'dü kōgō'), village, Katanga prov., SE Belgian Congo, 10 mi. ENE of Elisabethville; rail terminus and former major copper-mining center, now preserved as historic site.
Starogard (stärô'gärt), Ger. *Preussisch Stargard* (proi'sĭsh shtär'gärt), town (1946 pop. 15,081), Gdansk prov., N Poland, on Wierzyca R. and 27 mi. S of Gdansk; rail junction; lumber industry; mfg. of chemicals, liqueur, beer, furniture, roofing materials, machinery, leather, tobacco.
Starokazachye or **Starokazach'ye** (stä"rŭkŭzä'chyĭ), Rum. *Cazaci* or *Cazacii-Vechi* (käzäch', –zä'chē-vĕ'kē), village (1941 pop. 3,729), NE Izmail oblast, Ukrainian SSR, on road and 20 mi. NW of Belgorod-Dnestrovski; agr. center.
Staro-Konstantinov (stä"rŭ-kŭnstŭntyē'nŭf), city (1926 pop. 16,807), E central Kamenets-Podolski oblast, Ukrainian SSR, on Sluch R. and 25 mi. NNE of Proskurov; rail junction; sugar refinery, dairy plant, clothing and metal industries.
Staro-Maryevka or **Staro-Mar'yevka** (–mär'yĭfkŭ), village (1926 pop. 5,969), W Stavropol territory, Russian SFSR, on railroad and 12 mi. ENE of Stavropol; flour mill, metalworks; wheat, sunflowers. Until c.1940, Staro-Maryevskoye.
Staro-Mikhailovka or **Staro-Mikhaylovka** (–mēkhī'-lŭfkŭ), town (1939 pop. over 500), central Stalino oblast, Ukrainian SSR, in the Donbas, 9 mi. W of Stalino; coal mining.
Staro-Minskaya (–mēn'skīŭ), village (1926 pop. 22,604), N Krasnodar Territory, Russian SFSR, 40 mi. ESE of Yeisk; rail junction; agr. center in wheat and cotton area; meat packing, flour milling; metalworking, ceramics.
Staro-Mlinovka (–mlyē'nŭfkŭ), village (1926 pop. 3,790), W Stalino oblast, Ukrainian SSR, 50 mi. SW of Stalino; wheat. Until 1946, Stary Kermenchik.
Staro-Nikolayevka, Kirghiz SSR: see PANFILOVSKAYA.
Staro-Nizhestebliyevskaya (–nyĕzhĭstyĕb'lyĕŭf-skīŭ), village (1926 pop. 12,274), W Krasnodar Territory, Russian SFSR, 35 mi. NW of Krasnodar; flour mill, metalworks, dairying; rice, cotton, vineyards.
Staro Oryakhovo, Bulgaria: see DOLNICHIFLIK.
Staro-Pyshminsk (–pĭsh'mĕnsk), town (1926 pop. 1,595), S Sverdlovsk oblast, Russian SFSR, on Pyshma R. and 3 mi. NE (under jurisdiction) of Berezovski; gold mining, lumbering. Until 1943, Pyshminski Zavod.
Starosel (stärôsĕl'), village (pop. 3,915), Plovdiv dist., W central Bulgaria, at S foot of central Sredna Gora, 24 mi. NNW of Plovdiv; rye, potatoes, livestock. Formerly Staro-novo-selo.
Staroseltsi (stärôsĕl'tsē), village (pop. 3,809), Pleven dist., N Bulgaria, on Iskar R. and 20 mi. WNW of Pleven; wheat, corn, livestock.
Staro-Shaigovo, Russian SFSR: see STAROYE SHAIGOVO.
Staro-Shcherbinovskaya (–shchĭrbē'nŭfskīŭ), village (1926 pop. 16,997), N Krasnodar Territory, Russian SFSR, near Yeya R. mouth, 20 mi. ESE of Yeisk, in wheat and cotton area; flour milling, dairying, metalworking.
Starosielce (stärôsyĕl'tsĕ), Rus. *Staroseltsy* or *Staro-sel'tsy* (both: stŭrŭsĕ'lyŭtsĭ), town (pop. 2,511), Bialystok prov., NE Poland, 3 mi. W of Bialystok; rail junction; mfg. of cement, bricks, stockings.
Staro-Soldatskoye (stä"rŭ-sŭldät'skŭyŭ), village (1939 pop. over 500), central Omsk oblast, Russian SFSR, on Osha R. and 27 mi. NE of Tyukalinsk; dairy farming.
Staro-Timoshkino (–tyĭmôsh'kĭnŭ), town (1939 pop. over 2,000), central Ulyanovsk oblast, Russian SFSR, 16 mi. ENE of Barysh; woolen milling.
Staroturukhansk, Russian SFSR: see TURUKHANSK.
Staroutkinsk (stŭrŭōōt'kĭnsk), town (1939 pop. 5,900), SW central Sverdlovsk oblast, Russian SFSR, in the central Urals, on Chusovaya R. and 22 mi. E of Shalya, near railroad (Utkinski Zavod station); pig-iron production; sawmilling. Until 1933, Utkinski Zavod.
Staroverovka (–vyĕ'rŭfkŭ), village (1926 pop. 3,468), W Kharkov oblast, Ukrainian SSR, 15 mi. NE of Krasnograd; flour.
Staroye [Rus.,=old], in Rus. names: see also STARAYA, STARO- [Rus. combining form], STARY, STARYE.
Staroye Shaigovo or **Staroye Shaygovo** (stä'rŭyŭ shī'gŭvŭ), village (1932 pop. estimate 2,340), central Mordvinian Autonomous SSR, Russian SFSR, 25 mi. NW of Ruzayevka; hemp, legumes. Also called Staro-Shaigovo.
Staroye Shaimurzino or **Staroye Shaymurzino** (shī-mōōr'zĭnŭ), village (1926 pop. 2,912), SW Tatar Autonomous SSR, Russian SFSR, 20 mi. SW of Buinsk; grain, livestock. Phosphorite deposits near by.
Staroye Sindrovo (sēndrô'vŭ), village (1926 pop. 3,132), central Mordvinian Autonomous SSR, Russian SFSR, 12 mi. E of Krasnoslobodsk; grain, hemp. Formerly spelled Staroye Sindorovo.
Staro-Yuryevo or **Staro-Yur'yevo** (stä"rŭ-yōōr'yĭ-vŭ), village (1926 pop. 6,888), NW Tambov oblast, Russian SFSR, on right headstream of Voronezh R. and 28 mi. NNE of Michurinsk; grain.
Starozhilovo (stŭrŭ-zhē'lŭvŭ), village (1926 pop. 2,494), W central Ryazan oblast, Russian SFSR, 28 mi. SSE of Ryazan; coarse grain, wheat, fruit.
Star Peak, Nev.: see HUMBOLDT RANGE.
Star Prairie, village (pop. 288), St. Croix co., W Wis., 19 mi. NE of Hudson; dairying.
Starr, county (□ 1,207; pop. 13,948), extreme S Texas; ⊙ Rio Grande City. Bounded SW and S by Rio Grande (Mex. border), whose irrigated valley produces truck, citrus, other fruit; also cotton, corn, grain, peanuts. Uplands have large ranches (cattle, sheep, goats, horses, mules). Oil, natural-gas wells; clay. Formed 1848.
Starr, town (pop. 282), Anderson co., NW S.C., 10 mi. S of Anderson; brooms.
Starr King, Mount. 1 Peak (9,166 ft.) of the Sierra Nevada, E Calif., in Yosemite Natl. Park, SE of Yosemite Valley. There is a Mt. KING in Kings Canyon Natl. Park. **2** Peak (3,913 ft.) of White Mts., S Coos co., N.H., near Jefferson, 13 mi. NW of Mt. Washington.
Starrucca (stŭrōō'kŭ), borough (pop. 326), Wayne co., NE Pa., 36 mi. NNE of Scranton. Formerly spelled Starucca.
Startex or **Tucapau** (tŭ'kŭpô), textile-mill village (pop. 1,638), Spartanburg co., NW S.C., 9 mi. W of Spartanburg.
Start Point, promontory on the Channel, S Devon, England, at S extremity of Start Bay (7 mi. wide, 3 mi. long), 10 mi. SSW of Dartmouth; lighthouse (50°14'N 3°38'W). Site of radio transmitter.
Start Point, Scotland: see SANDAY.
Starucca, Pa.: see STARRUCCA.
Star Valley, Wyo. and Idaho: see SALT RIVER.
Starvation Cove, locality, N Adelaide Peninsula, N Keewatin Dist., Northwest Territories, on Simpson Strait; 68°10'N 97°1'W. Here c.40 skeletons and other relics of Franklin expedition (1847–48) have been found.
Starvation Peak (9,300 ft.), SE B.C., near Alta. and Mont. borders, in Rocky Mts., 50 mi. SE of Fernie; 49°2'N 114°16'W.
Starved Rock, cliff (140 ft. high), N Ill., along left bank of Illinois R. bet. La Salle and Ottawa; now included in Starved Rock State Park (established 1912; oldest in Ill.). Visited by Jolliet and Marquette (1673), by La Salle and Henri de Tonti (1679); here, in 1680, Tonti began building Fort St. Louis, completed by him and La Salle in 1682. Cliff is legendary scene of starvation of a band of Illinois supposed to have been driven here by Ottawa Indians in 18th cent.
Stary or **Staryy** [Rus.,=old], in Rus. names: see also STARAYA, STARO- [Rus. combining form], STAROYE, STARYE.
Stary Bykhov, Belorussian SSR: see BYKHOV, Mogilev oblast.
Stary Chardzhui, Turkmen SSR: see KAGANOVICHESK.
Stary Dashev, Ukrainian SSR: see DASHEV.
Starye or **Staryye** [Rus.,=old], in Rus. names: see also STARAYA, STARO- [Rus. combining form], STAROYE, STARY.
Starye Atagi, Russian SFSR: see PREDGORNOYE, Grozny oblast.
Starye Dorogi or **Staryye Dorogi** (stä"rēŭ dŭrô'gē), city (1948 pop. over 2,000), central Bobruisk oblast, Belorussian SSR, 40 mi. W of Bobruisk; food processing, light mfg.
Starye Zyattsy or **Staryye Zyattsy** (zyä'tsē), village (1926 pop. 660), central Udmurt Autonomous SSR, Russian SFSR, 39 mi. NNW of Izhevsk; flax processing, grain, livestock.
Stary Kermenchik, Ukrainian SSR: see STARO-MLINOVKA.
Stary Krym or **Staryy Krym** (stä'rē krĭm) [Rus.,= old Crimea]. **1** City (1926 pop. 4,740), E Crimea, Russian SFSR, on road and 14 mi. W of Feodosiya; climatic health resort in orchard and tobacco region. Has ruins of anc. fortifications. A major 13th–14th-cent. caravan center (named Solkhat) on route to India; original ⊙ Crimean Tatar khanate; declined following removal of capital to Bakhchisarai in 15th cent. Formerly called Eski Krym. **2** Town (1926 pop. 2,172), S Stalino oblast, Ukrainian SSR, 5 mi. N of Zhdanov; graphite quarries.
Stary Lesken or **Staryy Lesken** (stä"rē lyĭskyĕn'), village (1939 pop. over 2,000), E Kabardian Autonomous SSR, Russian SFSR, on Lesken R. (a left affluent of the Terek) and 19 mi. SE of Nalchik; bast-fiber plants (common and ambary hemp), orchards.
Stary Merchik or **Staryy Merchik** (myĕr'chĭk), town (1926 pop. 3,793), NW Kharkov oblast, Ukrainian SSR, on railroad and 17 mi. SE of Bogodukhov, in Kharkov metropolitan area; sawmilling, furniture mfg.
Stary Oskol or **Staryy Oskol** (stä"rē ŭskôl'), city (1926 pop. 20,192), E Kursk oblast, Russian SFSR, on Oskol R. and 75 mi. ESE of Kursk; agr. industries (flour, sunflower oil, alcohol); metalworks, hemp mill. Teachers col. Founded 1593 as Oskol. During Second World War, held (1942–43) by Germans.
Stary Sacz (stä'rĭ sŏch'), Pol. *Stary Sącz*, Ger. *Alt Sandec* (ält" zän'dĕts), town (pop. 4,586), Krakow prov., S Poland, in the Carpathians, on railroad and 4 mi. SSW of Nowy Sacz, near confluence of Dunajec and Poprad rivers; fur processing and trading; flour milling, sawmilling, tanning. Dates from at least 13th cent.
Stary Salavan or **Staryy Salavan** (stä"rē sŭlŭvän'), town (1948 pop. over 2,000), NE Ulyanovsk oblast, Russian SFSR, on Greater Cheremshan R. and 25 mi. ENE of Melekess; peat digging, lumbering.
Stary Saltov or **Staryy Saltov** (säl'tŭf), village (1926 pop. 4,014), N Kharkov oblast, Ukrainian SSR, on the Northern Donets and 23 mi. ENE of Kharkov; truck produce.
Stary Sambor or **Staryy Sambor** (säm'bŭr), city (1931 pop. 4,867), W Drogobych oblast, Ukrainian SSR, on the Dniester and 11 mi. SW of Sambor; tanning, flour milling.
Stary Smokovec (stä'rē smô'kôvĕts), Slovak *Starý Smokovec*, Ger. *Altschmecks* (ält'shmĕks), Hung. *Tátrafüred* (tä'trŏfü"rĕd), village, N Slovakia, Czechoslovakia, in the High Tatra, on rack-and-

pinion railroad and 7 mi. NNW of Poprad; popular summer resort with mineral springs; winter-sports (alt. 3,345 ft.); part of Vysoke Tatry commune.

Stashev, Poland: see STASZOW.

Stassfurt (shtäs'fŏŏrt), town (pop. 29,762), in former Prussian Saxony prov., central Germany, after 1945 in Saxony-Anhalt, on the Bode and 18 mi. S of Magdeburg; potash and rock-salt mining center (since 1843); chemical and machinery mfg. After 1945 it inc. Leopoldshall (lā'ōpôlts-häl") town (1939 pop. 7,483), just SE, in former Anhalt exclave.

Staszow (stä'shōōf), Pol. *Staszów*, Rus. *Stashev* (stä'shĭf), town (pop. 4,586), Kielce prov., SE central Poland, 27 mi. WSW of Sandomierz; tanning, flour milling, distilling.

State Center, town (pop. 1,040), Marshall co., central Iowa, 14 mi. W of Marshalltown; dairy products. Laid out 1865, inc. 1867.

State College. 1 Village, Miss.: see STARKVILLE. **2** Hamlet, Dona Ana co., S N.Mex., near Rio Grande, just SE of Las Cruces; shipping point for fruit and cotton. N.Mex. Col. of Agr. and Mechanic Arts here. Railroad station is at Mesilla Park (pop. c.500), just SW. **3** Residential borough (pop. 17,227), Centre co., central Pa., 35 mi. NE of Altoona. Pennsylvania State Col. here. Settled 1859, inc. 1896.

State Line. 1 Village (pop. 52), Kootenai co., N Idaho. **2** Town (pop. 152), Warren co., W Ind., on Ill. line, 7 mi. NE of Danville (Ill.), in agr. area. **3** Village, Mass.: see WEST STOCKBRIDGE. **4** Town (pop. 492), on Greene-Wayne co. line, SE Miss., c.45 mi. ESE of Laurel, at Ala. line.

Staten Island (stă'tŭn), Sp. *Isla de los Estados,* rocky island (□ 209) in the South Atlantic, 18 mi. E of SE tip of main isl. of Tierra del Fuego, Argentina, across Le Maire Strait; c.45 mi. long. Rises to 3,000 ft. Has cold, humid climate and is sparsely populated. Some goat and sheep raising, seal and nutria hunting. Has seismographic station. A small port, San Juan de Salvamento, is on E coast. Its E tip is Cape San Juan (54°42'S 63°43'W). Just N of Staten Isl. are the small NEW YEAR'S ISLANDS.

Staten Island, SE N.Y., island in New York Bay close to N.J. shore, 5 mi. SW of the Battery of Manhattan; with small adjacent isls., comprises Richmond borough (□ 57; pop. 191,555) of NEW YORK city and Richmond co. of N.Y. state. Co. courthouse and borough hall are at St. George. Max. length c.14 mi., max. width c.7 mi. It is separated from N.J. mainland on N by Kill Van Kull (văn kŭl'), spanned by Bayonne Bridge; on W is Arthur Kill, bridged to N.J. by Goethals Bridge and Outerbridge Crossing. On E, the Lower Bay and the Narrows separate isl. from Brooklyn borough on W tip of Long Isl.; plans are being made for bridge across the Narrows. Ferries ply bet. St. George (on NE shore) and Manhattan and Brooklyn. Passenger railroad connects isl.'s communities. Has 5 airports, including U.S. Miller Field. Chief centers are St. George (transportation hub), Port Richmond, and Stapleton; other communities include Tompkinsville, Tottenville, New Dorp, West New Brighton. Generally level, except for 6-mi. range of hills (highest alt. c.400 ft.) extending SW from St. George, and smaller E–W ridge in N; has beaches (bathing and amusement resorts) on E shore, and a marshy, thinly inhabited region (drained by Richmond and Main creeks and Fresh Kills) in W. Its communities are mainly residential, and isl. is semirural in parts (S). Its recreational areas include La Tourette, Silver Lake, Wolfes Pond, and Marine parks. Industries (shipbuilding and repairing, oil refining, lumber milling, printing; mfg. of soap and fertilizer, of mica, asphalt, paper, and lead products, and of dental equipment, dyes, clothing, plaster and other building materials) are mainly in N. Port region in NE (St. George, Tompkinsville, Stapleton, Clifton) is part of Port of New York, and includes Foreign Trade Zone No. 1, established in 1936 as 1st free port in U.S. Isl. receives water (via pipe line under the Narrows) from the Catskill Aqueduct; Silver L. is chief reservoir. On the Narrows opposite Fort Hamilton, Brooklyn, is U.S. Fort Wadsworth (1st established 1663). Isl. has U.S. quarantine station, a U.S. marine hosp., Halloran (hă'lŭrŭn) General Hosp. (U.S. army), Sailors' Snug Harbor (home for retired seamen), Wagner Memorial Lutheran Col., Notre Dame Col. of Staten Isl., and Staten Isl. Inst. of Arts and Sciences. Among its points of interest are the Billopp (or Conference) House (built before 1688), where Lord Howe negotiated with Continental patriots in 1776; Church of St. Andrew (1708); a Moravian church and cemetery; a Huguenot church; and the house where Garibaldi lived in the mid-1850s. Isl. was visited (1609) by Henry Hudson; called Staaten Eylandt by the Dutch. Permanent community was established by 1661, after 1st settlement was wiped out by Indians. Consolidated (as Richmond borough) with New York city in 1898.

Statenville (stā'tŭnvĭl), village (pop. c.1,000), ⊙ Echols co., S Ga., 17 mi. ESE of Valdosta and on Alapaha R., near Fla. line; mfg. (lumber, naval stores).

Statesboro, city (pop. 6,097), ⊙ Bulloch co., E Ga., c.50 mi. WNW of Savannah; market center for tobacco, livestock, and agr. area; mfg. (lumber, Venetian blinds, naval stores); meat packing, peanut processing, feed milling. Ga. Teachers Col. is at Collegeboro (2 mi. S). Statesboro laid out 1803.

States of the Church, Italy: see PAPAL STATES.

Statesville, city (pop. 16,901), ⊙ Iredell co., W central N.C., 38 mi. N of Charlotte, in the piedmont; trade and mfg. center (cotton textiles, hosiery, furniture, veneer, machinery, bricks, flour, dairy products). Seat of Mitchell Col. (jr.; coeducational). Agr. experiment station near by. Founded 1789.

Statham (stă'tŭm), town (pop. 626), Barrow co., NE central Ga., 13 mi. W of Athens; mfg. (work clothes).

Stathelle (stät'hĕl-lŭ), town (pop. 720) in Bamble canton, Telemark co., S Norway, on the Langesund Fjord at mouth of Frier Fjord, opposite Brevik (ferry), 11 mi. SSE of Skien; lumber trade; ice mfg.

Stathern (stăt'hŭrn), agr. village and parish (pop. 525), NE Leicester, England, 7 mi. N of Melton Mowbray; cheese making. Has 13th–14th-cent. church.

Statia, Du. West Indies: see SAINT EUSTATIUS.

Station Island, islet in S part of Lough Derg, S Co. Donegal, Ireland, 5 mi. NNW of Pettigo; important place of pilgrimage (since c.1150), scene of St. Patrick's vision of Purgatory. Just N is Saint's Isl.

Statland, Norway: see STADLAND.

Statsbygd, Norway: see STADSBYGD.

Statte (stät), town, Liége prov., E central Belgium, on Meuse R., just NW of Huy; rail junction; coal mines.

Stattland, Norway: see STADLAND.

Statue of Liberty National Monument (10.38 acres), New York city, SE N.Y., on Bedloe's Isl. in Upper New York Bay, c.2 mi. SW of the Battery of Manhattan. Here is colossal copper statue (*Liberty Enlightening the World*) sculptured by Frederic Bartholdi and presented (1884) by the people of France in commemoration of alliance of France and America in American Revolution. Dedicated 1886, it was made a natl. monument in 1924. Statue is 152 ft. high above its 150-ft. pedestal; elevator and stairs carry visitors to observation platform within its head.

Staubbach (shtoub'bäkh), stream in Bernese Alps, S central Switzerland, branch of White Lütschine R.; noted for its waterfall, which drops 980 ft. over a precipice near Lauterbrunnen.

Stauding, Czechoslovakia: see STUDENKA.

Staufen (shtou'fŭn), town (pop. 2,100), S Baden, Germany, at W foot of Black Forest, 9 mi. SW of Freiburg; textile mfg., metal- and leatherworking, lumber milling. Winegrowing. Summer resort. Has 16th-cent. town hall. On near-by hill are ruins of anc. Staufen castle, connected with legend of Dr. Faust.

Staunton. 1 (stôn'tŭn, stŏn'tŭn) City (pop. 4,047), Macoupin co., SW Ill., 22 mi. ENE of Alton; trade center for agr. and bituminous-coal-mining area. Settled 1817, laid out 1835, inc. 1859. **2** (stôn'tŭn) Town (pop. 487), Clay co., W Ind., 12 mi. E of Terre Haute, in agr. and bituminous-coal area. **3** (stăn'tŭn) City (pop. 19,927), in but independent of Augusta co., W Va., in S Shenandoah Valley, 32 mi. WNW of Charlottesville; co. courthouse is here. Trade, shipping, industrial center for rich agr. area (fruit, wheat, livestock, poultry); mfg. of clothing, textiles, furniture, dairy products, foundry and wood products; flour milling, rock quarrying. Seat of Staunton Military Acad., Mary Baldwin Col., state school for deaf and blind, Western State Hosp. Here is Woodrow Wilson's birthplace, made a natl. shrine in 1941. Shenandoah Natl. Park is c.15 mi. E. Settled c.1738; inc. as town 1801, as city 1871. Was ⊙ Northwest Territory, 1738–70. First city to adopt (1908) city-manager govt.

Staunton River, Va.: see ROANOKE RIVER.

Stavanger, county, Norway: see ROGALAND.

Stavanger (stäväng'ŭr), city (pop. 50,320), ⊙ Rogaland co., SW Norway, on S shore of Bokn Fjord of the North Sea, 100 mi. S of Bergen, 200 mi. WSW of Oslo; 58°58'N 5°44'E. Major seaport; has extensive trade with Great Britain and the Continent; terminus of railroad from Oslo and Kristiansand; airport at SOLA. Fishing and fish-canning center; also shipyards, steel and textile mills, metal- and woodworking plants, meat-packing plants; dairying; mfg. of chemicals, soap, tools, bicycles. Has 11th-cent. cathedral of St. Swithin, 13th-cent. chapel, ethnological and archaeological mus., and art gall. Seat of fish-canning industry research laboratory. One of Norway's oldest cities, it was founded in 8th cent.; in 11th cent. it became seat of bishopric which was moved to Kristiansand in 1682. Lutheran bishopric created 1924. In Second World War captured by Germans on April 9, 1940.

Stave Falls, village, SW B.C., on Stave R. at S end of Stave L., and 7 mi. NNW of Mission; site of dam and hydroelectric plant; lumbering.

Stave Lake (□ 24), SW B.C., 35 mi. E of Vancouver; 18 mi. long, 1–5 mi. wide; alt. 270 ft. Drained S by short Stave R. into Fraser R.

Staveley, urban district (1931 pop. 16,653; 1951 census 17,941), NE Derby, England, 4 mi. NE of Chesterfield; coal-mining center; metalworking. Has church dating partly from Saxon times, and 16th-cent. rectory.

Stavelot (stävùlō'), town (pop. 4,735), Liége prov., E Belgium, on Amblève R. and 5 mi. WSW of Malmédy, in N Ardennes; leather tanning. Has 13th-cent. shrine of St. Remaclus. Founded 651 as Benedictine abbey, whose abbots became princes of Holy Roman Empire.

Stavely, town (pop. 299), S Alta., 55 mi. SSE of Calgary; mixed farming, wheat.

Stavenhagen (shtä"fŭnhä'gŭn), town (pop. 6,521), Mecklenburg, N Germany, 7 mi. ESE of Malchin; agr. market (grain, sugar beets, potatoes, stock); sugar refining. Fritz Reuter b. here.

Stavern (stä'vŭrn), city (pop. 1,121), Vestfold co., SE Norway, on the Skagerrak, at mouth of Larvik Fjord, 4 mi. S of Larvik; woodworking, welding-equipment mfg. Site of Fredriksvern, 18th-cent. sea fortress, now military school. Novelist Jonas Lie buried here. Until 1929, called Fredriksvern.

Stavertsi (stä'vĕrtsē), village (pop. 5,262); Vratsa dist., NW Bulgaria, 20 mi. ESE of Oryakhovo; wheat, corn, livestock.

Stavishche (stŭvē'shchĭ), town (1926 pop. 5,029), W Kiev oblast, Ukrainian SSR, on road and 28 mi. S of Belaya Tserkov; sugar beets.

Stavishin, Poland: see STAWISZYN.

Staviski, Poland: see STAWISKI.

Stavoren (stä'vōrŭn), town (pop. 1,166) and port, Friesland prov., N Netherlands, on the Ijsselmeer and 16 mi. SW of Sneek; shipbuilding. Ferry to Enkhuizen. In early Middle Ages it was trade center, chief port, and ⊙ Friesland, reaching its zenith in 13th cent.

Stavropol or **Stavropol'** (stäv'rŭpŭl), territory [Rus. *krai* or *kray*] (□ 2,950; 1946 pop. estimate 1,500,000) in S European Russian SFSR, in the N Caucasus; ⊙ Stavropol. Touches main Caucasus range only in SW; extends N, through Stavropol Plateau, to Manych Depression. Includes CHERKESS AUTONOMOUS OBLAST. Dry climate (12–16 in. annual rainfall) causes poorly-developed river network and treeless steppe vegetation. Drained by Kuma R. (SE) and Kuban and Yegorlyk rivers (W), the once drought-ridden territory is watered (since mid 1940s) by Kuban-Yegorlyk irrigation scheme (including Nevinnomyssk Canal). Agr. (winter wheat, corn, sunflowers, cotton, castor beans, coriander); sheep raising. Vineyards, fruit, garden crops along Kuma R. Main agr.-processing centers: Stavropol, Georgiyevsk, Nevinnomyssk, Budennovsk, Mineralnye Vody. Territory contains major Pyatigorsk resort dist. with satellite spas of Zheleznovodsk, Kislovodsk, and Yessentuki; mineral-water bottling. Pop. largely Russian and Ukrainian, with some semi-nomadic Turkmen and Nogai Tatar herdsmen near Manych Depression (N). Main transportation route is double-tracked Rostov-Baku RR, with spurs to Stavropol, Budennovsk, Cherkessk, and Kislovodsk. Formed 1924 as North Caucasus Territory; renamed Ordzhonikidze (1937) and Stavropol (1943). Occupied (1942–43) by Germans, during Second World War.

Stavropol or **Stavropol'. 1** City (1926 pop. 6,485), W Kuibyshev oblast, Russian SFSR, on left bank of the Volga (landing) and 35 mi. WNW of Kuibyshev, on N side of Samara Bend; petroleum-extracting center; agr. processing (grain, sunflower seed). Site of projected dam and hydroelectric plant on the Volga. Became city in 1946. Oil production begun during Second World War. **2** City (1939 pop. 85,100), ⊙ Stavropol Territory, Russian SFSR, on Stavropol Plateau, on short rail spur and 180 mi. SE of Rostov, 750 mi. SSE of Moscow; 45°2'N 41°59'E. Major agr. center in wheat and sunflower dist.; food processing (flour, butter, meat), tanning, machine mfg., construction industry. Rail workshops, grain elevators. Agr., teachers, and medical colleges, regional mus. Founded 1777 as Rus. stronghold on St. Petersburg-Tiflis route; served as important base in 1830s for Rus. conquest of Caucasus. Administrative center of N Caucasus in late-19th cent. Was ⊙ Stavropol govt. until 1924. Called Voroshilovsk (c.1935–43). During Second World War, held (1942–43) by Germans.

Stavropol Plateau or **Stavropol Upland,** hilly region in the N Caucasus, Russian SFSR, bet. middle courses of Kuban (W) and Kuma (E) rivers and Manych Depression (N); rises to 2,713 ft. in Mt. Strizhament, 10 mi. NNE of Nevinnomyssk. A watershed bet. Sea of Azov and Caspian Sea, the plateau slopes gradually into surrounding plains and joins the Greater Caucasus (S).

Stavrovo (stä'vrŭvŭ), village (1926 pop. 1,662), W central Vladimir oblast, Russian SFSR, 15 mi. W of Vladimir; wheat, rubber-bearing plants.

Stawell (stô'ŭl), municipality (pop. 4,840), SW central Victoria, Australia, 130 mi. WNW of Melbourne; commercial center for livestock and agr. area; woolen and flour mills. There are gold mines near by.

Stawiski (stävē'skē), Rus. *Staviski,* town (pop. 1,687), Bialystok prov., NE Poland, 14 mi. N of Lomza; mfg. of caps, liqueur; sawmilling.

Stawiszyn (stävē'shĭn), Rus. *Stavishin* (stŭvē'shyĭn), town (1946 pop. 1,776), Poznan prov., W central Poland, 10 mi. N of Kalisz; flour, sandal mfg.

Stayner (stā'nŭr), town (pop. 1,085), S Ont., near Georgian Bay, 45 mi. ESE of Owen Sound; stockyard, cider mills.

Stayton, town (pop. 1,507), Marion co., NW Oregon, on North Santiam R. and 15 mi. SE of Salem; wool, flour, and lumber milling, canning. Platted 1872, inc. 1891.

Stazzema (stätsä'mä), village (pop. 459), Lucca prov., Tuscany, central Italy, in Apuane Alps, 12 mi. SE of Carrara; marble quarrying; explosives.

Steamboat or **Steamboat Springs,** village, Washoe co., NW Nev., 8 mi. NW of Virginia City; hot springs (small resorts) here are geologically interesting for their demonstration of mineral-deposition processes.

Steamboat Rock, town (pop. 395), Hardin co., central Iowa, on Iowa R. and 4 mi. NNE of Eldora.

Steamboat Springs, town (pop. 1,913), ⊙ Routt co., NW Colo., on Yampa R., just W of Park Range, and 110 mi. NW of Denver; alt. 6,762 ft. Resort and skiing center; hq. of near-by Routt Natl. Forest; livestock, grain, dairy and poultry products, silver foxes. Has hot mineral springs. Coal mines in vicinity. Founded 1875, inc. 1907.

Steamburg, village (pop. c.200), Cattaraugus co., W N.Y., 17 mi. E of Jamestown, near Allegany Indian Reservation; dairy products.

Steamer Point, W point of Aden peninsula, on strait linking Aden Bay and Gulf of Aden. Steamer Point section of Aden town is part of urban division of TAWAHI (E); it has overseas piers, govt. and business offices, and European residential section. Military reservation (S).

Stearns (stûrnz), county (□ 1,356; pop. 70,681), central Minn.; ⊙ St. Cloud. Agr. area bounded E by Mississippi R., watered by Sauk R. Has numerous small lakes. Dairy products, livestock, corn, oats, barley. Granite. Formed 1855.

Stearns, village (1940 pop. 1,548), McCreary co., S Ky., in the Cumberlands, 29 mi. SSE of Somerset, near Tenn. line; shipping point for coal and timber area.

Stebark, Poland: see TANNENBERG.

Stebbins, village (pop. 118), W Alaska, on SE shore of Norton Sound, 7 mi. WNW of St. Michael; supply point for trappers and prospectors.

Steben, Bad, Germany: see BAD STEBEN.

Stebnik (styĕb'nyĭk), town (1948 pop. over 500), central Drogobych oblast, Ukrainian SSR, 4 mi. SE of Drogobych; potassium and sodium-salt extracting center; mineral springs. Linked by gas pipe line with Drogobych.

Stechovice (shtyĕ'khôvĭtsĕ), Czech *Štěchovice*, village (pop. 1,086), S central Bohemia, Czechoslovakia, on Vltava R. and 16 mi. S of Prague; site of major waterworks (dam, locks, hydroelectric plant) operating conjointly with smaller waterworks at Vrane (vrä'nä), Czech *Vrané*, 6 mi. N. Has remains of 13th-cent. Cistercian monastery, later rebuilt as a castle. Both Vrane and Stechovice are popular summer resorts.

Steckborn (shtĕk'bôrn), town (pop. 2,329), Thurgau canton, N Switzerland, on the Untersee (L. Constance), 9 mi. NNE of Frauenfeld; artificial silk, sewing machines. Has 14th-cent. castle, town hall with finds from prehistoric lake dwellings.

Stecken, Czechoslovakia: see STOKY.

Stecknitz Canal, Germany: see ELBE-TRAVE CANAL.

Stederdorf (shtā'dŭrdôrf), village (pop. 3,241), in former Prussian prov. of Hanover, NW Germany, after 1945 in Lower Saxony, 2 mi. N of Peine; dairying.

Stedingen, Germany: see BERNE.

Stedman (stĕd'mŭn), town (pop. 424), Cumberland co., S central N.C., 10 mi. ESE of Fayetteville.

Stedum (stā'dŭm), village (pop. 1,034), Groningen prov., NE Netherlands, 9 mi. NE of Groningen; cattle raising, dairying, flax growing. Has church with 14th-cent. frescoes.

Steeg (shtāg), town, S Upper Austria, in the Salzkammergut, on N shore of L. of Hallstatt, 5 mi. S of Bad Ischl; hydroelectric station; aluminum plant.

Steeg, De, Netherlands: see DE STEEG.

Steele (shtā'lŭ), industrial district (since 1929) of ESSEN, W Germany, on the Ruhr and 3 mi. E of city center; coal mining.

Steele (stēl). **1** County (□ 425; pop. 21,155), SE Minn.; ⊙ Owatonna. Agr. area drained by Straight R. Dairy products, livestock, corn, oats, barley, poultry. Formed 1855. **2** County (□ 710; pop. 5,145), E N.Dak.; ⊙ Finley. Farming area watered by Goose R. Wheat processing: livestock, dairy products, potatoes. Formed 1883.

Steele. 1 City (pop. 2,360), Pemiscot co., extreme SE Mo., near Mississippi R., 12 mi. SW of Caruthersville; railroad shops, cotton gins. Inc. 1901. **2** City (pop. 762), ⊙ Kidder co., central N.Dak., 41 mi. E of Bismarck; grain elevators; shipping center for livestock; poultry, wheat, barley, rye.

Steele, Mount (16,439 ft.), SW Yukon, near Alaska border, in St. Elias Mts., 180 mi. W of Whitehorse; 61°5'N 140°23'W.

Steele City, village (pop. 214), Jefferson co., SE Nebr., 11 mi. SE of Fairbury and on Little Blue R.

Steele Island (15 naut. mi. long, 8 naut. mi. wide), Antarctica, in Weddell Sea off Richard Black Coast; 71°S 60°40'W. Discovered 1940 by U.S. expedition.

Steeles Tavern or **Midway Village,** hamlet, Augusta co., W Va., 17 mi. SSW of Staunton. Near by is "Walnut Hill," where Cyrus McCormick perfected his grain reaper.

Steeleville, village (pop. 1,353), Randolph co., SW Ill., c.50 mi. SSE of East St. Louis; agr. (corn, wheat, poultry) and dairying; bituminous-coal mines; mfg. (shoes, flour). Inc. 1851.

Steel Mill, village (pop. 4,296, with adjacent Roseland), Richland co., N central Ohio.

Steelton, borough (pop. 12,574), Dauphin co., S central Pa., 4 mi. SE of Harrisburg and on Susquehanna R.; steel; limestone. First practical production of Bessemer steel in U.S. here, 1867. Settled 1865.

Steelville, city (pop. 1,157), ⊙ Crawford co., E central Mo., in the Ozarks, near Meramec R., 75 mi. SW of St. Louis. Agr. and tourist trade; sulphur, iron mines. Founded 1835.

Steen, village (pop. 228), Rock co., extreme SW Minn., 10 mi. SSW of Luverne, near Iowa line.

Steenbergen (stān'bĕrkhŭn), town (pop. c.6,000), North Brabant prov., SW Netherlands, 6 mi. N of Bergen op Zoom; beet-sugar-refining center; flax growing.

Steene (stā'nŭ), town (pop. 5,384), West Flanders prov., NW Belgium, near North Sea, S suburb of Ostend. Has partly-Romanesque church, with tower dating from 1675. In 9th cent. it was important North Sea port; Flemish crusaders embarked here.

Steenkerque (stānkĕrk'), Flemish *Steenkerke* (stān'kĕrkŭ), agr. village (pop. 449), Hainaut prov., S central Belgium, 5 mi. N of Soignies. Has 15th-cent. Gothic church. English forces under William III defeated here (1692) by French under Marshal Luxembourg.

Steens Mountain (9,354 ft.), SE Oregon, is in Harney co., S of Burns.

Steenvoorde (stānvōrd'), town (pop. 1,842), Nord dept., N France, near Belg. border, 18 mi. SSE of Dunkirk, in hop-growing dist.; dairying. Customhouse.

Steenwijk (stān'vĭk), town (pop. 8,136), Overijssel prov., N central Netherlands, 19 mi. N of Zwolle; paint, tanning fluid, printer's ink, clothing, leather, wood products, silverware, oleomargarine, meat products. Has 13th- and 15th-cent. churches. Fortified town in Middle Ages; besieged (1572) by Spaniards. Sometimes spelled Steenwyk.

Steep, agr. village and parish (pop. 808), E Hampshire, England, just N of Petersfield. Bedales School here is well-known pioneer coeducational school. Church dates from late-Norman period.

Steep Holme Island (hōm) (47 acres), Somerset, England, in Bristol Channel, 6 mi. W of Weston-super-Mare; ½ mi. long, ¼ mi. wide. Uninhabited.

Steeples, The, mountain (9,100 ft.), SE B.C., in Rocky Mts., 16 mi. E of Cranbrook, overlooking the Kootenay valley; 49°34'N 115°25'W.

Steep Point, headland of Western Australia, in Indian Ocean, just S of Dirk Hartogs Isl.; westernmost point of Australia; 26°9'S 113°9'E.

Steep Rock Lake (4 mi. long, 3 mi. wide), NW Ont., on Seine R. and 120 mi. WNW of Fort William; iron-mining area. Lake has been drained for mining, and Seine R. diverted to new course.

Steese Highway (stēs), central Alaska, extends 162 mi. ENE from Fairbanks to Yukon R. at Circle; serves gold-mining region.

Steeton with Eastburn, parish (pop. 2,319), West Riding, W Yorkshire, England. Includes town of Steeton, near Aire R., 3 mi. NNW of Keighley; mfg. of pharmaceuticals, yarn bobbins.

Stefan-cel-Mare (shtā'fän-chĕl-mä'rā), Rum. *Stefan-cel-Mare*, village (pop. 511), Bacau prov., NE Rumania, 10 mi. NE of Piatra-Neamt.

Stefanesti (shtĕfŭnĕsht'), Rum. *Ştefăneşti*. **1** Village (1941 pop. 2,229), Arges prov., S central Rumania, 26 mi. SSW of Campulung. **2** Town (1948 pop. 7,770), Botosani prov., NE Rumania, in Moldavia, 25 mi. ENE of Botosani, near USSR border; trading center; flour milling, limestone quarrying.

Stefanie, Lake (stĕ'fŭnē), S Ethiopia, in Great Rift Valley bet. lakes Chamo (NE) and Rudolf (SW), 60 mi. SW of Gardula; 4°40'N 36°50'E; alt. 1,700 ft.; c.15 mi. long, 10 mi. wide. Because of desiccation, it has been greatly reduced (formerly □ c.200; 30–40 mi. long, 15–20 mi. wide) and is now largely occupied by malarial swamps. Its strongly saline waters provide salt for the natives. Receives the Galana Sagan (N). Native name is Basso Naebor. Discovered 1888 with L. Rudolf by Count Teleki. S tip extends into Kenya.

Steffisburg (shtĕ'fĭsbo͝ork), town (pop. 8,009), Bern canton, central Switzerland, 2 mi. N of Thun; fats, flour, tobacco, pottery, woolen textiles; metalworking.

Stege (stĕ'yŭ), city (pop. 2,623) and port, Praesto amt, Denmark, on Moen isl. and 50 mi. S of Copenhagen, on Stege Bay; sugar refinery, iron foundry, brewery, mfg. (cement, margarine); shipbuilding, fisheries.

Stege Bay, Denmark, bet. SE Zealand and Moen isls. Nyord isl. lies bet. it and Fakse Bay.

Steger (stē'gŭr), village (pop. 4,358), on Cook-Will co. line, NE Ill., near Ind. line, 28 mi. S of Chicago; mfg. of radio cabinets. Inc. 1896.

Stegersbach (shtā'gŭrsbäkh), town (pop. 2,660), Burgenland, E Austria, 21 mi. WSW of Szombathely, Hungary; sugar beets.

Stegi (stä'gē), village, E Swaziland, on main E-W road and 50 mi. ESE of Mbabane; customs station near Mozambique border.

Steglitz (shtā'glĭts, shtāk'lĭts), workers' residential district (1939 pop. 213,920; 1946 pop. 139,696), SW Berlin, Germany, on Teltow Canal and 7 mi. SW of city center; mfg. of electrical equipment, optical and precision instruments. After 1945 in U.S. sector.

Stehag (stā'häg''), village (pop. 559), Malmohus co., S Sweden, 5 mi. NE of Eslov; sawmilling; grain, livestock. Has medieval church.

Steierdorfanina (stĕyĕrdôrfä'nēnä) or **Anina** (ä'nēnä), Hung. *Stájerlakanina* (shtä'yĕrlŏkŏ''nēnŏ), village (pop. 8,811), Severin prov., SW Rumania, in Banat, on W slopes of the Transylvanian Alps, 9 mi. ENE of Oravita; rail terminus and coal and iron mining center. Has blast furnaces and rolling mills; mfg. of hardware, woodworking. Also known as health and winter-sports resort (alt. 2,558 ft.). Colonized by Germans in 18th cent.

Steiermark, Austria: see STYRIA.

Steilacoom (stĭ'lŭko͞om), town (pop. 1,233), Pierce co., W central Wash., on an arm of Puget Sound and 7 mi. SW of Tacoma. Founded 1850; inc. 1854; oldest inc. settlement in the state; has historic landmarks. State hosp. is here.

Steimke (shtĭm'kŭ), village (pop. 389), in former Prussian prov. of Hanover, NW Germany, after 1945 in Lower Saxony, 23 mi. NE of Celle, in oil region.

Stein or **Stein bei Nürnberg** (shtīn' bī nürn'bĕrk), SW suburb (pop. 6,326) of Nuremberg, Middle Franconia, N central Bavaria, Germany, on the Rednitz; mfg. of chemicals, pencils, slide rules, metal products; woodworking.

Stein (stīn), town (pop. 5,512), Limburg prov., SE Netherlands, on Juliana Canal and 5 mi. WSW of Sittard; coal-loading point for Limburg coal mines.

Stein, Yugoslavia: see KAMNIK, village.

Steinach (shtī'näkh), town (pop. 8,395), Thuringia, central Germany, in Thuringian Forest, 5 mi. N of Sonneberg, in slate-quarrying region; woodworking center; mfg. of glass, china, toys, slate products. Climatic health and winter-sports resort.

Steinamanger, Hungary: see SZOMBATHELY.

Stein am Rhein (shtīn' äm rīn'), town (pop. 2,107), Schaffhausen canton, N Switzerland, on right (N) bank of the Rhine (bridge), at its efflux from the Untersee (L. Constance), and 11 mi. E of Schaffhausen, on Ger. border; shoes, flour, pastry; woodworking. Has town hall (16th cent.), monastery bldgs. (11th cent.) with town church. Castle (12th cent.) N of town, priory (11th cent.) across the Rhine, pilgrims' chapel (15th cent.) on isl. in the Rhine.

Stein an der Donau, Austria: see KREMS.

Steinau (shtī'nou), town (pop. 3,762), in former Prussian prov. of Hesse-Nassau, W Germany, after 1945 in Hesse, on the Kinzig and 4 mi. SW of Schlüchtern; soap mfg. Has late-Gothic castle and town hall.

Steinau, Poland: see SCINAWA.

Steinauer (stī'nour), village (pop. 141), Pawnee co., SE Nebr., 7 mi. NNW of Pawnee City.

Steinbach (shtīn'bäkh), village (pop. 2,157), S Baden, Germany, at W slope of Black Forest, 2.5 mi. NNE of Bühl; wine trade.

Steinbach-Hallenberg (–hä'lŭnbĕrk), town (pop. 7,010), in former Prussian Saxony prov. exclave, central Germany, after 1945 in Thuringia, in Thuringian Forest, on small Schwarza R. and 5 mi. E of Schmalkalden; metalworking (kitchen utensils, tools, nails, locks, knives), wood carving, cigar mfg. Has 17th-cent. church; ruins of anc. castle. Until 1944 it was in exclave of former Prussian prov. of Hesse-Nassau.

Stein bei Nürnberg, Germany: see STEIN.

Steinbrück, Yugoslavia: see ZIDANI MOST.

Steinburg (shtīn'bo͝ork), district in Schleswig-Holstein, NW Germany: see ITZEHOE.

Stein Canal, Norway: see TONSBERG FJORD.

Steindorf, (shtīn'dôrf), town (pop. 2,666), Carinthia, S Austria, on NE shore of the Ossiachersee and 15 mi. WNW of Klagenfurt; summer resort.

Steiner Alpen, Yugoslavia: see SAVINJA ALPS.

Steinerkirchen an der Traun (shtīn'ŭrkĭr''khŭn än dĕr troun'), town (pop. 2,027), central Upper Austria, 6 mi. SW of Wels; wheat, cattle.

Steinernes Meer (shtī'nŭrnŭs mār'), small bare range of the Salzburg Alps, extending c.10 mi. along Austro-German border S of Berchtesgaden; rises (SE) to 8,710 ft. in the Selb Horn. Königssee is at N foot.

Steinfeld (shtīn'fĕlt), town (pop. 2,440), Carinthia, S Austria, on Drau R. and 13 mi. WSW of Spittal; paper mills; resort.

Steinfeld, village (commune pop. 5,730), in Oldenburg, NW Germany, after 1945 in Lower Saxony, 5 mi. S of Lohne; mfg. of cigars.

Steinförde, Germany: see WIETZE.
Steinfort (shtīn'fôrt), village (pop. 1,082), SW Luxembourg, 10 mi. WNW of Luxembourg city; mfg. of agr. machinery; potatoes, wheat, oats.
Steingaden (shtīn'gä"dŭn), village (pop. 3,061), Upper Bavaria, Germany, 16 mi. SW of Weilheim; textile mfg. Former Premonstratensian abbey has mid-12th-cent. church.
Steinhagen (shtīn'hä"gŭn), village (pop. 5,677), in former Prussian prov. of Westphalia, NW Germany, after 1945 in North Rhine-Westphalia, at S foot of Teutoburg Forest, 5 mi. W of Bielefeld; distilling (gin).
Steinheim (shtīn'hīm). **1** or **Steinheim am Main** (äm mīn'), town (pop. 8,046), S Hesse, W Germany, in former Starkenburg prov., on left bank of the canalized Main and 6 mi. E of Offenbach; leatherworking, paper milling. **2** Town (pop. 5,436), in former Prussian prov. of Westphalia, NW Germany, after 1945 in North Rhine-Westphalia, 10 mi. SE of Detmold; grain.
Steinhude (shtīn'hōō"dŭ), village (pop. 3,989), in former Schaumburg-Lippe, W Germany, after 1945 in Lower Saxony, on S shore of the Steinhuder Meer, 16 mi. WNW of Hanover; mfg. of chocolate.
Steinhuder Meer (-dŭr mār'), lake (□ 10) in W Germany, 15 mi. WNW of Hanover; 5 mi. long, 3 mi. wide, 10 feet deep; drains into the Weser. Fishing. On artificial isl. Wilhelmstein (near W shore) is former model fortress.
Steinkjer (stān'chăr), town (pop. 2,808), ⊙ Nord-Trondelag co., central Norway, port on Trondheim Fjord, at mouth of Steinkjer R., on railroad and 60 mi. NE of Trondheim; 64°1'N 11°31'E. Lumber milling, dyeing, tanning, wool spinning. Long ago known as Steinker; inc. 1857. In Second World War, its center was heavily damaged in 1940 campaign. Formerly also called Stenkjaer.
Steinpleis (shtīn'plīs), village (pop. 4,775), Saxony, E central Germany, 2 mi. SE of Werdau; cotton milling.
Steinschönau, Czechoslovakia: see KAMENICKY SENOV.
Steinsel (shtīn'zŭl), village (pop. 614), S central Luxembourg, 5 mi. N of Luxembourg city; roses, apple orchards; farinaceous food products. Just NE is agr. village of Müllendorf (pop. 336).
Steinshamn, Norway: see HAROY.
Steinsoy, Norway: see SOLUND ISLANDS.
Steinsundoy, Norway: see SOLUND ISLANDS.
Steinthal, France: see BAN-DE-LA-ROCHE.
Steinviksholm (stān'vēks-hôlm"), tiny island in Trondheim Fjord, Nord-Trondelag co., central Norway, 18 mi. NE of Trondheim, just off the mainland. Has ruins of the stronghold of the archbishops, built 1525, destroyed 1775. Formerly spelled Stenviksholm.
Steinwärder, Germany: see SANKT PAULI.
Steinwiesen (shtīn'vē"zŭn), village (pop. 2,504), Upper Franconia, N Bavaria, Germany, on the Rodach and 7 mi. NE of Kronach; porcelain mfg., tanning. Clay pits in area.
Stekene (stā'kŭnŭ), town (pop. 8,722), East Flanders prov., N Belgium, 5 mi. NW of St-Nicolas; textiles, bricks; agr. market.
Stella, England: see BLAYDON.
Stella. 1 Town (pop. 177), Newton co., SW Mo., in the Ozarks, 12 mi. SE of Neosho. **2** Village (pop. 324), Richardson co., SE Nebr., 15 mi. NW of Falls City, near Missouri R.; grain, livestock, dairy and poultry produce. **3** Residential village (1940 pop. 1,409), Broome co., S N.Y., suburb of Binghamton.
Stella, Pizzo di (pē'tsō dē stĕl'lä), glacier-topped peak (10,377 ft.) in Rhaetian Alps, N Italy, near Swiss border, 4 mi. N of Chiavenna.
Stellaland, former independent republic, now in NE Cape Prov., U. of So. Afr., near Transvaal and Bechuanaland Protectorate borders; ⊙ Vryburg. Founded 1883, it was proclaimed crown colony 1885 together with Bechuanaland.
Stellarton (stĕ'lŭrtŭn), town (pop. 5,351), N N.S., 3 mi. S of New Glasgow; coal mining, mfg. of steel products; large railroad shops.
Stellaville, town (pop. 69), Jefferson co., E Ga., 27 mi. SW of Augusta, in agr. area.
Stellenbosch (stĕ'lŭnbŏs", -bōōsh), town (pop. 15,292), SW Cape Prov., U. of So. Afr., 25 mi. E of Cape Town; educational center. Site of Univ. of Stellenbosch (1918), formerly Victoria Col; theological seminary; So. Afr. Conservatoire of Music; agr. col. at Elsenburg, 6 mi. NNW. Publishing. Center of tobacco, fruitgrowing, winegrowing region. Has several 17th- and 18th-cent. houses, including Dutch church (1717) and old Dutch arsenal. Founded 1679 by Simon van der Stel, it is 2d-oldest settlement in So. Afr.
Steller, Mount (10,000 ft.), S Alaska, in Chugach Mts., N of Bering Glacier, 90 mi. E of Cordova; 60°31'N 143°5'W.
Stellingen, Germany: see ALTONA.
Stelton, village (pop. c.100), Middlesex co., NE N.J., 2 mi. NE of New Brunswick; clothing, metal products. Settled by Baptists before 1700.
Stelvio Pass (stĕl'vyō), Ger. *Stilfser Joch* (alt. 9,048 ft.), N Italy, just S of Swiss border, at NW base of Ortles mtn. group, 6 mi. NNE of Bormio. Crossed by highest road in Alps; connects Valtellina with Val Venosta. At a junction 5 mi. N of Stelvio Pass branch road leads NW to the Lower Engadine, Switzerland.
Stem, town (pop. 217), Granville co., N N.C., 17 mi. NE of Durham.
Stembert (stābâr'), town (pop. 5,770), Liége prov., E Belgium, just E of Verviers; woolen mills.
Stenay (stŭnā'), town (pop. 2,000), Meuse dept., NE France, on Meuse R. and Canal de l'Est, and 18 mi. SE of Sedan; steel and paper mills. Former frontier fortress. Captured by Americans Nov. 11, 1918.
Sten Canal, Norway: see TONSBERG FJORD.
Stend (stĕn), village (pop. 753) in Fana canton, Hordaland co., SW Norway, 7 mi. S of Bergen; hemp spinning, mfg. of fishing equipment. Has agr. school.
Stendal (shtĕn'däl), city (pop. 40,325), in former Prussian Saxony prov., central Germany, after 1945 in Saxony-Anhalt, near the Elbe, 35 mi. NNE of Magdeburg; 52°37'N 11°51'E. Rail center; metalworking, sugar refining, food canning; mfg. of machinery, chemicals; railroad shops. Has basilica (founded 1188), 15th-cent. church of St. Mary, 13th–15th-cent. town gates, and 15th-cent. town hall. Winckelmann b. here. Stendhal took his pseudonym from city. Founded 1151 by Albert the Bear; chartered 1160. Seat (1258–1309) of elder line of Ascanian margraves of Brandenburg. Joined Hanseatic League c.1350. Reformation introduced 1539.
Stenen (stĕ'nŭn), agr. village (pop. 252), E Sask., near Assiniboine R., 50 mi. N of Yorkton.
Stenhousemuir (stĕn"housmūr'), town in Larbert parish, E Stirling, Scotland; coal mining, steel milling.
Stenkjaer, Norway: see STEINKJER.
Stenness (-nĕs'), locality on Pomona isl., Orkneys, Scotland, 9 mi. W of Kirkwall. The megalithic Standing Stones of Stenness consist of 2 circles, one originally of 12 stones (4 remain); the larger (Ring of Brogar), originally probably of 60 stones (36 remain).
Stenoy, Norway: see SOLUND ISLANDS.
Stenschewo, Poland: see STESZEW.
Stensele (stān'sā"lŭ), village (pop. 551), Vasterbotten co., N Sweden, on Ume R. and 50 mi. WNW of Lycksele; lumbering, stock raising, dairying; Lapp trading center.
Stensholm (stāns"hôlm'), village (pop. 771), Jonkoping co., S Sweden, near L. Vatter, just SE of Huskvarna; grain, livestock. Includes Ebbe (ĕ'bŭ) village.
Stenstorp (stāns'tôrp"), village (pop. 859), Skaraborg co., S Sweden, 9 mi. SW of Skovde; rail junction; grain, livestock.
Stenungsund (stā"nŭng"sŭnd'), village (pop. 271), Goteborg och Bohus co., SW Sweden, on narrow channel of the Skagerrak, opposite Tjorn isl., 15 mi. NNW of Kungalv; seaside resort.
Stenviksholm, Norway: see STEINVIKSHOLM.
Stepan (styĭpän'yŭ), Pol. *Stepań* (stĕ'pänyŭ), village (1937 pop. estimate 2,550), W Rovno oblast, Ukrainian SSR, on Goryn R. and 20 mi. SW of Sarny; flour milling, lumbering; livestock. Copper deposits in Mydzk, 8 mi. SW. Has ruins of fortified castle. Scene of defeat (1648) of Cossacks by Pol. general Stephen Czarniecki.
Stepanakert (styĕ"pŭnŭkyĕrt'), city (1944 pop. over 10,000), ⊙ Nagorno-Karabakh Autonomous Oblast, Azerbaijan SSR, on E slope of Karabakh Range, 60 mi. SSW of Yevlakh (linked by narrow-gauge railroad); silk mills, wineries; food processing. Teachers col. Originally the small village of Khankendy (renamed for Stepan Shaumyan, Baku revolutionary); developed greatly in 1930s and replaced the older Shusha.
Stepana Razina, Imeni (ē"mĭnyē styĭpä"nŭ rä'zĕnŭ). **1** Town (1939 pop. over 500) in Lenin dist. of Greater Baku, Azerbaijan SSR, on central Apsheron Peninsula, 7 mi. NE of Baku, on electric railroad. **2** Town (1926 pop. 899), S Gorki oblast, Russian SFSR, 12 mi. SW of Lukoyanov; glassworks.
Stepanavan (styĭpä"nŭvän') city (1945 pop. estimate 7,000), N Armenian SSR, on Lori Steppe, 16 mi. SW of Alaverdi; sawmilling, metalworking, rug mfg. Livestock, wheat, potatoes. Health resort (tuberculosis sanatorium). Formerly Dzhelaloglu.
Stepantsevo (styĭpän'tsyĭvŭ), town (1948 pop. over 500), E Vladimir oblast, Russian SFSR, 20 mi. WSW of Vyazniki; linen milling.
Stepenitz River (shtā'pŭnĭts), E Germany, rises just SE of Meyenburg, flows c.50 mi. generally SSW, past Perleberg, to the Elbe at Wittenberge.
Stephanskirchen (shtä'fänskĭr"khŭ), village (pop. 5,080), Upper Bavaria, Germany, near the Simssee, 2.5 mi. E of Rosenheim; grain, cattle.
Stephen, village, SE B.C., on Alta. border, in Rocky Mts., in Yoho Natl. Park, at W end of Kicking Horse Pass, 35 mi. NW of Banff; alt. 5,337 ft.; lumbering.
Stephen, village (pop. 877), Marshall co., NW Minn., on small tributary of Red R. and 19 mi. NNW of Warren; dairy products.
Stephen, Mount (10,494 ft.), SE B.C., near Alta. border, in Rocky Mts., in Yoho Natl. Park, 40 mi. WNW of Banff; 51°24'N 116°26'W.
Stephens. 1 County (□ 180; pop. 16,647), NE Ga.; ⊙ Toccoa. Bounded E by S.C. line, formed here by Tugaloo R. Piedmont agr. (cotton, corn, hay, sweet potatoes, livestock) and mfg. (textiles, furniture, metal products) area drained by headstreams of Broad R. W part in Chattahoochee Natl. Forest. Formed 1905. **2** County (□ 893; pop. 34,071), S Okla.; ⊙ Duncan. Drained by Wildhorse Creek; includes Comanche and Duncan lakes. Agr. (cotton, grain, corn, broomcorn, oats, watermelons); cattle ranching, dairying. Oil and natural-gas fields; oil refining, some mfg. Formed 1907. **3** County (□ 927; pop. 10,597), N central Texas; ⊙ Breckenridge. Drained by Clear Fork of Brazos R. and tributary creeks. Diversified agr., livestock raising: cattle, goats, sheep, hogs, horses, poultry (especially turkeys), corn, grain, grain sorghums, peanuts, fruit, truck. Oil, natural-gas wells. Part of Possum Kingdom L. (recreation) is in NE. Formed 1858; renamed from Buchanan, 1861.
Stephens, town (pop. 1,283), Ouachita co., S Ark., 18 mi. SW of Camden, in cotton-growing area. Oil refinery; oil wells near.
Stephens, Port, inlet of Pacific Ocean, E New South Wales, Australia, 25 mi. NE of Newcastle; 11 mi. E-W, 2 mi. N-S; generally shallow. Seafood canneries on shore.
Stephens City, town (pop. 676), Frederick co., N Va., in Shenandoah Valley, 8 mi. SSW of Winchester, in apple-growing region; lime.
Stephenson (stē'vŭnsŭn), county (□ 568; pop. 41,595), N Ill., bordered by Wis. (N); ⊙ Freeport. Dairying and agr. area (livestock, corn, wheat, oats, barley, nursery products, poultry). Drained by Pecatonica R. and small Yellow and Richland creeks. Formed 1837.
Stephenson. 1 Village (pop. 791), Menominee co., SW Upper Peninsula, Mich., 21 mi. N of Menominee and on Little Cedar R., in dairying and agr. area. **2** Town, Miss.: see CROSBY.
Stephens Passage, SE Alaska, channel (105 mi. long) bet. Admiralty Isl. and mainland, S of Juneau; part of Inside Passage to Alaska.
Stephenville, village (pop. 863), SW N.F., on N shore of St. George Bay, 40 mi. SW of Corner Brook; 48°32'N 58°36'W; fishing port. Site of Harmon Field, U.S. air base built 1941; transport and ferrying field during Second World War. Dairying, cattle and poultry raising in region; near Stephenville are magnetite ore deposits.
Stephenville (stē'vŭnvĭl), city (pop. 7,155), ⊙ Erath co., N central Texas, on Bosque R. and c.60 mi. SW of Fort Worth; processing center in agr. area (cotton, peanuts, grain, pecans, dairy products); nut shelling, dairying (cheese), feed milling; poultry hatcheries; nursery stock. Seat of Tarleton State Col., a junior branch of Texas A. and M. A state park is just N. Founded 1856, inc. 1888.
Stephenville Crossing, village (pop. 956), SW N.F., at head of St. George Bay, near mouth of St. George R., on railroad and 40 mi. SW of Corner Brook; fishing port and agr. market in dairying, cattle, and poultry region.
Stepney (stĕp'nē), residential and industrial metropolitan borough (1931 pop. 225,238; 1951 census 98,581) of London, England, on N bank of the Thames (here crossed by several tunnels), 3 mi. ENE of Charing Cross. Borough includes districts of Whitechapel (Jewish quarter), Limehouse (Chinese quarter), and Wapping (dock area). Noted landmarks and bldgs. are the Tower of London, London Hosp. (1740), the People's Palace (1887), Queen Mary's Col. of the Univ. of London, and Toynbee Hall, 1st university settlement in London, founded 1885. At Mile End, Richard II negotiated with Wat Tyler. Mainly industrial, Stepney suffered heavy bomb damage during the Second World War.
Stepney Depot, Conn.: see MONROE.
Stepnoi or **Stepnoy** (styĭpnoi'), city (1939 pop. 17,125), W Astrakhan oblast, Russian SFSR, in Yergeni Hills, 180 mi. W of Astrakhan; road junction; livestock-trading center; agr. processing (sheepskins, wool, meat, grain), mfg. (bricks, tanning extract). Founded 1928 as ⊙ Kalmyk Autonomous Oblast (Autonomous SSR after 1935; dissolved in 1943); became city in 1930; briefly occupied by Germans in 1942. Until 1944, called Elista.
Stepnoi Zai River, Russian SFSR: see ZAI RIVER.
Stepnoye (styĭpnoi'ŭ). **1** Village (1939 pop. over 500), S Rostov oblast, Russian SFSR, in Manych Depression, 40 mi. ESE of Salsk; wheat, sunflowers, livestock. Salt deposits. Until 1944 (in Kalmyk Autonomous SSR), called Esto-Khaginka. **2** Village (1926 pop. 7,500), SE Stavropol Territory, Russian SFSR, 38 mi. N of Mozdok, in wheat and cotton area; flour mill. Sometimes called Stepnovskoye.
Stepnyak (styĭpnyäk'), city (1939 pop. 25,000), Akmolinsk oblast, Kazakh SSR, in enclave within Kokchetav oblast, 65 mi. SE of Kokchetav; gold-mining center; food processing, sawmilling. Developed in 1930s.
Stepojevac or **Stepoyevats** (both: stĕ'pôyĕväts), village, N central Serbia, Yugoslavia, 21 mi. SSW of Belgrade, near Kolubara R.

Stepovak Bay (stĕ'pŭvăk) (17 mi. long, 17 mi. wide at mouth), SW Alaska, in S coast of Alaska Peninsula, N of Shumagin Isls.; 55°45'N 159°49'W; deep, sheltered anchorage.

Steppes, The, former general government of Russia, comprising govts. of Akmolinsk and Semipalatinsk; ⊙ was Omsk. So called for the Kirghiz Steppe, a name formerly applied to area of present central Kazakh SSR.

Stepps, residential town in Cadder parish, N Lanark, Scotland, 5 mi. NE of Glasgow.

Steppville, town (pop. 385), Cullman co., N central Ala., 11 mi. SE of Cullman, near Mulberry Fork.

Sterch-Kertychki (styĕrch'-kyĕrtĭchkē'), village (1939 pop. over 500), W Dagestan Autonomous SSR, Russian SFSR, 13 mi. E of Vedeno; petroleum deposits. Until 1944, in Chechen-Ingush Autonomous SSR.

Sterco (stûr'kō), village (pop. estimate 200), W Alta., in Rocky Mts., near E side of Jasper Natl. Park, 40 mi. SW of Edson; coal mining.

Stériles, Îles, Madagascar: see BARREN ISLANDS.

Sterkfontein (stĕrk'fôntān"), locality, S Transvaal, U. of S. Afr., 6 mi. NNW of Krugersdorp. Here are lime caves, scene of discovery (1936) of remains of prehistoric "Sterkfontein man" (*Plesianthropus transvaalensis*).

Sterkrade (shtĕrk'rä"dŭ), industrial suburb (1925 pop. 50,757) of OBERHAUSEN, W Germany, N of Rhine-Herne Canal, 3 mi. N of city center; ironworks; mfg. of synthetic oil. Coal mining. First Ger. steam engine built here in 1819. Inc. (1929) into Oberhausen.

Sterkstroom (stĕrks'trōōm"), town (pop. 3,415), E Cape Prov., U. of So. Afr., in Stormberg range, 30 mi. NW of Queenstown; rail junction; agr. center (stock, grain, wool).

Sterlegov, Cape (styĕr'lyĭgŭf), on Kara Sea coast of Taimyr Peninsula, in Taimyr Natl. Okrug, Krasnoyarsk Territory, Russian SFSR; 75°20'N 88°50'E. Govt. observation post.

Sterlibashevo (styĭrlyēbŭshĕ'vŭ), village (1948 pop. over 2,000), W Bashkir Autonomous SSR, Russian SFSR, on S.Siberian RR and 33 mi. SW of Sterlitamak; rye, oats, livestock.

Sterling, county (□ 914; pop. 1,282), W Texas; ⊙ Sterling City. In rolling prairies, drained by North Concho R.; alt. c.2,000–2,600 ft. Ranching region (sheep, goats, beef cattle); some poultry; wool, mohair marketed; some agr. (grain sorghums, Sudan grass). Organized 1891.

Sterling. **1** City (pop. 7,534), ⊙ Logan co., NE Colo., on South Platte R. and 80 mi. ENE of Greeley; trade and shipping center for sugar-beet, grain, and livestock region; beet sugar, dairy products, electrical appliances, beverages. Fish hatchery here. Buffalo ranch and co. mus. (in form of frontier fort) near by. Platted 1881, inc. 1884. **2** Town (pop. 1,298), Windham co., E Conn., on Moosup R., at R.I. line, and 17 mi. NE of Norwich, in hilly region; agr., granite quarrying. Mfg. (paper products, monuments) at Sterling and Oneco (ōnē'kō) villages. Set off from Voluntown 1794. **3** Industrial city (pop. 12,817), Whiteside co., NW Ill., on Rock R. (bridged here), opposite Rock Falls, and 45 mi. SW of Rockford, in farm and dairy area; mfg. (steel, petroleum products, hardware, electrical appliances, garden furniture, gas engines, toys, wire specialties, burial vaults, dairy products). Inc. 1841. **4** City (pop. 2,243), Rice co., S central Kansas, 18 mi. NW of Hutchinson, near Arkansas R., in wheat region; flour milling, salt refining. Salt mines and oil wells near by. Seat of Sterling Col. (Presbyterian; coeducational; 1887). Founded 1872, inc. 1876. **5** Town (pop. 2,166), Worcester co., central Mass., 12 mi. N of Worcester; cider. Settled 1720, inc. 1781. **6** Village (pop. 444), Arenac co., E Mich., 31 mi. NNW of Bay City, in farm area. State forest near by. **7** Village (pop. 547), Johnson co., SE Nebr., 30 mi. SSE of Lincoln and on N.Fork of Nemaha R.; grain, stock, poultry. **8** Town (pop. 447), Comanche co., SW Okla., 16 mi. NE of Lawton, in agr. area; cotton ginning. **9** Town (pop. 188), Sanpete co., central Utah, 5 mi. SSW of Manti and on San Pitch R.

Sterling City, village (1940 pop. 835), ⊙ Sterling co., W Texas, 40 mi. NW of San Angelo and on North Concho R.; trading, shipping point in ranching region (cattle, sheep, goats).

Sterlington, village (1940 pop. 733), Ouachita parish, NE central La., 13 mi. N of Monroe, near Ouachita R., in natural-gas area; makes carbon black, chemicals, fertilizer.

Sterlitamak (–tŭmäk'), city (1946 pop. estimate 55,000), W central Bashkir Autonomous SSR, Russian SFSR, port (head of navigation) on left bank of Belaya R. and 80 mi. S of Ufa, on S.Siberian RR. Rail junction; mfg. center (building machinery, oil-drilling tools, chemicals, shoes); agr. processing (grain, hides, meat), sawmilling. Phosphorite deposits near by. Has teachers col., technical schools, and regional mus. Founded 1781; salt-trading center in 19th cent. Largely expanded in 1930s, following development of Ishimbai (S) petroleum dist.

Sternberg (shtĕrn'bĕrk), town (pop. 4,479), Mecklenburg, N Germany, 18 mi. ENE of Schwerin; agr. market (grain, sugar beets, potatoes, stock); sawmilling. Has 14th-cent. church. Founded in 13th cent.; meeting place (1484–1918; after 1621, alternately with Malchin) of annual parliament of Mecklenburg-Schwerin and Mecklenburg-Strelitz. At 1545 parliament, Reformation was introduced into Mecklenburg.

Sternberk (shtĕrn'bĕrk), Czech *Šternberk*, Ger. *Sternberg* (shtĕrn'bĕrk), town (pop. 7,224), N central Moravia, Czechoslovakia, on railroad and 10 mi. N of Olomouc; textile mfg., iron mining, tobacco processing. Has large insane asylum. Town founded in 13th cent.

Sterpenich (stĕr'pŭnĭkh), village, Luxembourg prov., SE Belgium, 5 mi. ESE of Arlon; frontier station on Luxembourg border.

Sterzh, Lake (styĕrzh), northernmost of upper Volga lakes, Kalinin oblast, Russian SFSR, in Valdai Hills, near source of the Volga; 8 mi. long.

Sterzing, Italy: see VIPITENO.

Steszew (stĕ'shĕf), Pol. *Stęszew*, Ger. *Stenschewo* (shtän"shä'vō), town (1946 pop. 2,824), Poznan prov., W Poland, 13 mi. SW of Poznan; mfg. of bicycles, cotton wool; linen weaving, flour milling.

Steti (shtyĕ'tyē), Czech *Štětí*, Ger. *Wegstadl* (vĕk'-shtädŭl), town (pop. 1,716), N Bohemia, Czechoslovakia, on Elbe R. and 25 mi. NNW of Prague; vineyards.

Stetson, town (pop. 434), Penobscot co., S central Maine, 20 mi. WNW of Bangor, in agr. and lake area.

Stetsonville, village (pop. 334), Taylor co., N central Wis., 5 mi. S of Medford.

Stettin (shtĕtēn') or **Szczecin** (shchĕ'tsēn), city (1939 pop. 374,017; 1946 pop. 72,948; 1950 pop. c.200,000) in Pomerania, after 1945 ⊙ Szczecin prov., NW Poland, on Oder R. estuary 80 mi. NE of Berlin; 53°26'N 14°34'E. Rail junction; a major Baltic port, shipping coal, timber, industrial and agr. products; important trade with Scandinavia; handles much Czechoslovak transit traffic. Terminus of Berlin-Stettin Canal system. Industrial center; foundries, shipyards, coke ovens; woolen, paper, and wood-pulp mills, sugar refineries, food canneries; mfg. of chemicals, yeast, chocolate, candy, clothing; sawmilling, brewing, metalworking; power station. Medical acad., technical col. A Wendish fortress in 11th cent.; Christianity introduced in 1124; church built 1187. Town chartered 1243. From late 13th to 17th cent., residence of dukes of Pomerania; from 13th cent. an important member of Hanseatic League. Reformation introduced 1535 by Bugenhagen. In Thirty Years War, captured by Gustavus Adolphus; retained, with Hither Pomerania, by Sweden under Treaty of Westphalia (1648). Captured 1677 by Elector Frederick William of Brandenburg; returned to Sweden (1679) under Treaty of St. Germain; ceded (1720) to Prussia; occupied (1806–13) by French. In Second World War, c.45% destroyed. Until 1945, was ⊙ Prussian Pomerania prov. For some time after 1945 Soviet forces in E Germany had special port facilities in Stettin. Catherine the Great of Russia b. here. Suburbs include POLICE (N; inc. 1939) and GLINKI (NE).

Stettin Lagoon, Ger. *Stettiner Haff* (shtĕtē'nŭr häf'), Pol. *Zalew Szczecinski* (zä'lĕf shchĕchēn'skē) or *Zatoka Szczecinska* (zätô'kä –skä), expansion (□ 349) of Oder R. estuary mouth, in Pomerania, after 1945 divided bet. NW Poland and E Germany, 20 mi. N of Stettin; 35 mi. long E-W, 2-15 mi. wide. Separated from Baltic Sea by Usedom (Uznam) and Wolin isls. and draining into it via Peene, Swine, and Dievenow rivers. Receives Uecker R. On lagoon are Usedom town and Nowe Warpno. Also called Pommersches Haff (pô'-mŭr-shŭs).

Stettler, town (pop. 1,499), S central Alta., 50 mi. E of Red Deer; grain elevators, flour and grist mills, dairying; mfg. of cereal foods, chemicals. In coal-mining region.

Steuben (stōōbĕn', stū–). **1** County (□ 310; pop. 17,087), extreme NE Ind.; ⊙ Angola. Bounded N by Mich., E by Ohio; drained by Pigeon Creek. Resort lakes; timber; farming, stock raising, dairying. Formed 1835. **2** County (□ 1,408; pop. 91,439), S N.Y.; ⊙ Bath. Bounded S by Pa. line; extends N into Finger Lakes region; includes part of Keuka L. Drained by Canisteo, Cohocton, Tioga, and Chemung rivers. Dairying, and potato- and grape-growing area, with diversified mfg. at Corning, Hornell, Bath, Canisteo, Hammondsport. Timber; sand and gravel pits. Also grows grain, truck, hay. Formed 1796.

Steuben. **1** (stōōbĕn') Fishing town (pop. 784), Washington co., E Maine, on inlet of the Atlantic and 29 mi. SW of Machias; lumbering, resorts. **2** (stōō'bĭn) Village (pop. 264), Crawford co., SW Wis., on Kickapoo R. and 17 mi. NE of Prairie du Chien.

Steubenville (stōō'bŭnvĭl, stū'), city (pop. 35,872), ⊙ Jefferson co., E Ohio, on Ohio R. and 30 mi. W of Pittsburgh, Pa.; steel center, in coal- and clay-producing area; also makes tin plate, paper products, pottery, tools, electrical goods. Seat of Col. of Steubenville. Edwin M. Stanton b. here. Laid out c.1797; inc. as city in 1851. Canalization of the Ohio (completed 1929) spurred industrial growth.

Stevenage (stē'vŭnĭj), residential urban district (1931 pop. 5,476; 1951 census 6,627), N central Hertford, England, 5 mi. S of Letchworth; straw-plaiting, soap mfg. Has 13th-cent. church with Norman parts and 1558 grammar school. After Second World War it became proving ground of government town-planning scheme. Most of it is included in the new model residential community (1951 pop. 7,312) of Stevenage.

Stevens, village (pop. 84), N central Alaska, on Yukon R. and 90 mi. NNW of Fairbanks; gold mining, fur trapping, mink breeding. Airfield.

Stevens. **1** County (□ 729; pop. 4,516), SW Kansas; ⊙ Hugoton. Gently rolling plain, bordered S by Okla.; crossed in NW by Cimarron R. Large natural-gas field in W. Formed 1886. **2** County (□ 570; pop. 11,106), W Minn.; ⊙ Morris. Agr. area drained by Pomme de Terre R. Grain, livestock. Formed 1862. **3** County (□ 2,521; pop. 18,580), NE Wash., on British Columbia line; ⊙ Colville. Includes parts of Colville Natl. Forest and Spokane Indian Reservation. Watered by Columbia (W boundary), Kettle, and Colville rivers. Mining (copper, gold, silver, zinc, magnesite); agr. (grain, fruit, dairy products); magnesite and cement processing; stone quarries. Formed 1863.

Stevens Dam, Wash.: see WHITE RIVER.

Stevenson. **1** Town (pop. 927), Jackson co., NE Ala., on inlet of Tennessee R. and 33 mi. SW of Chattanooga, Tenn.; textiles. **2** Village, Conn.: see MONROE. **3** City (pop. 584), ⊙ Skamania co., SW Wash., 35 mi. ENE of Vancouver and on Columbia R., near Cascade foothills; lumbering, fruit raising, dairying.

Stevens Pass (alt. 4,061 ft.), central Wash., highway pass through Cascade Range, c.60 mi. SE of Everett. Univ. of Wash. ski center here.

Stevens Point, city (pop. 16,564), ⊙ Portage co., central Wis., on both banks of Wisconsin R. and 31 mi. S of Wausau; mfg. (paper, fishing equipment, furniture, toys, gas engines, dairy products). Has a state teachers col. Founded 1839, inc. 1858.

Stevens Pottery, village (pop. c.200), Baldwin co., central Ga., 9 mi. SSW of Milledgeville; mfg. (pottery, tile, fire brick, hollow pipe).

Stevenston, town and parish (pop. 11,572), N Ayrshire, Scotland, near Firth of Clyde, 2 mi. E of Saltcoats; coal mines, ironworks. Just SE, on Firth of Clyde, is dist. of Ardeer, with explosives works.

Stevensville. **1** Village, Md.: see KENT ISLAND. **2** Village (pop. 480), Berrien co., extreme SW Mich., 6 mi. SSW of St. Joseph, near L. Michigan. **3** Town (pop. 772), Ravalli co., W Mont., 25 mi. S of Missoula and on Bitterroot R., near Bitterroot Range and Idaho line; trade center in grain and sugar-beet region; canned goods; dairy products, fruit, potatoes. St. Mary's Mission is here; consists of small church and mus. containing mementos of religious settlement established here (1841) by Father De Smet.

Stevensweert (stā'vŭnsvārt), village (pop. 1,254), Limburg prov., SE Netherlands, on Maas R. and 7 mi. SW of Roermond, on Belg. border; wooden-shoe mfg. Also spelled Stevensweerd.

Steventon, England: see OVERTON.

Steveston (stē'vĭstŭn), town (pop. estimate 1,100), SW B.C., on the Strait of Georgia, at mouth of S arm of Fraser R. delta, 10 mi. SSW of Vancouver; fishing port. Ferry to Vancouver Isl.

Steward, village (pop. 270), Lee co., N Ill., on Kyte R. (bridged here) and 23 mi. E of Dixon, in rich agr. area.

Stewardson, village (pop. 666), Shelby co., central Ill., 20 mi. SW of Mattoon; grain, soybeans.

Stewart, village (pop. 446), W B.C., on Alaska border, at head of Portland Canal, at mouth of Bear R., 120 mi. N of Prince Rupert; port; mining (gold, silver, copper, lead, zinc) center.

Stewart or **Central Stewart,** sugar-mill village (pop. 1,157), Camagüey prov., E Cuba, 7 mi. S of Ciego de Ávila.

Stewart. **1** County (□ 463; pop. 9,194), SW Ga.; ⊙ Lumpkin. Bounded W by Ala. line, formed here by Chattahoochee R. Coastal plain agr. (cotton, corn, peanuts, fruit, livestock) and sawmilling area. Formed 1830. **2** County (□ 484; pop. 9,175), NW Tenn.; ⊙ Dover. Bounded N by Ky., W by Tennessee R. (Kentucky Reservoir); drained by Cumberland R. Livestock, dairying, agr. (corn, hay, tobacco). Includes Fort Donelson Natl. Military Park and Fort Henry. Formed 1803.

Stewart. **1** Village (pop. 695), McLeod co., S Minn., 17 mi. WSW of Glencoe, in agr. area; dairy products, feed. **2** Village (pop. 311), Montgomery co., central Miss., 17 mi. E of Winona, near Big Black R. **3** Village, Ormsby co., W Nev., 4 mi. S of Carson City, in valley of Carson R.; hq. for Duckwater, Fallon, Moapa, Pyramid Lake, Summit Lake, Walker River, and Yomba Indian reservations in Nev., and for Fort McDermitt Indian Reservation in Nev. and Oregon.

Stewart, Camp, Ga.: see HINESVILLE.

Stewart, Mount (10,871 ft.), SW Alta., in Rocky Mts., near NE edge of Banff Natl. Park, 70 mi. SE of Jasper; 52°13'N 116°57'W.

Stewart Air Force Base, N.Y.: see NEWBURGH.

Stewartby, England: see WOOTTON.

Stewart Island (22 mi. long), Tierra del Fuego, Chile, on the Pacific bet. Londonderry Isl. and Brecknock Peninsula; 54°50'S 71°20'W.

Stewart Island, volcanic island (□ c.660; pop. 343) of NEW ZEALAND, 20 mi. S of S.Isl., across Foveaux Strait; 39 mi. long, 20 mi. wide. Mountainous; Mt. Anglem (3,200 ft.) is highest peak. Tin, feldspar. Summer resort. Produces frozen fish, granite. Chief town is Oban (formerly Half-moon Bay), in NE. Port Pegasus in SE. Discovered 1808 by British, bought 1864 from Maori natives by Great Britain. Maori name is Rakiura. Stewart Isl. co. (□ 670; pop. 343), includes Ruapuke Isl., Mutton Bird Isls.

Stewart Islands, coral group (pop. c.200), Solomon Isls., SW Pacific, 110 mi. E of Malaita; 8°21'S 162°40'E; copra; Polynesian natives. Sikaiana (c.½ mi. long) is most important isl.

Stewart Manor, residential village (pop. 1,879), Nassau co., SE N.Y., on W Long Isl., bet. Garden City and Floral Park. Laid out 1926, inc. 1927.

Stewart Mountain Dam, S central Ariz., on Salt R. and 30 mi. ENE of Phoenix. Unit in Salt R. irrigation project; concrete arch dam (207 ft. high, 1,260 ft. long), completed 1930. Used for irrigation and power. Forms reservoir (10 mi. long) with capacity of 69,800 acre-ft.

Stewarton, burgh (1931 pop. 2,749; 1951 census 2,800), N central Ayrshire, Scotland, 5 mi. N of Kilmarnock; hosiery, lace, and woolen milling.

Stewart Peak (14,032 ft.), in Rocky Mts., Saguache co., S central Colo.

Stewart River, village, W Yukon, on Yukon R. at mouth of Stewart R., and 50 mi. S of Dawson; trading post, transshipment point for Mayo Landing mining region.

Stewart River, central Yukon, rises in Mackenzie Mts. near 63°40'N 130°45'W, flows generally W, past Mayo Landing, to Yukon R. at Stewart River; 320 mi. long. Navigable for greater part of its length. Discovered 1850 by Robert Campbell.

Stewartstown, town (pop. 1,137), E Co. Tyrone, Northern Ireland, 6 mi. NE of Dungannon; coal mining, linen milling.

Stewartstown. 1 Rural town (pop. 970), Coos co., NW N.H., on the Connecticut, near Canadian line. Inc. 1795 and 1799. West Stewartstown village is its commercial center. **2** Borough (pop. 1,133), York co., S Pa., 17 mi. SSE of York.

Stewartsville, city (pop. 414), De Kalb co., NW Mo., 18 mi. E of St. Joseph; agr., livestock.

Stewart Town, town, Trelawny parish, N Jamaica, 15 mi. ESE of Falmouth; fruit, sugar cane, stock. Settled by Germans, 1836–42.

Stewartville, village (pop. 1,193), Olmsted co., SE Minn., on branch of Root R. and 11 mi. S of Rochester, in grain and livestock area; dairy products, flour, feed. Settled 1858.

Stewiacke (stū'ĭăk), town (pop. 936), central N.S., on Stewiacke R. and 16 mi. SSW of Truro; agr. market in dairying region; furniture mfg.

Steyning (stĕ'nĭng), town and parish (pop. 1,885), central Sussex, England, near Adur R., 6 mi. NNE of Worthing; agr. market. Has Norman church and 1614 grammar school. King Alfred's father Æthelwulf buried here (858). In Norman times the town was one of largest in England, with port accessible to seagoing vessels.

Steynsrust (stāns'rŭst), town (pop. 1,934), central Orange Free State, U. of So. Afr., 30 mi. SE of Kroonstad; alt. 5,071 ft.; grain, stock.

Steynton, agr. village and parish (pop. 1,434), S Pembroke, Wales, just NE of Milford Haven.

Steyr (shtīr), city (1951 pop. 36,727), E Upper Austria, on the Enns, at confluence of Steyr R., and 17 mi. SSE of Linz; center of iron and steel industry. Seat of Daimler-Puch and Steyr auto factories; mfg. (cars, trucks, Diesel tractors, motorcycles, bicycles, ball bearings, machinery, scythes). Has 10th-cent. castle, 15th-cent. Gothic church.

Steyregg (shtī'rĕk), village (pop. 2,136), NE Upper Austria, 3 mi. E of Linz, N of the Danube; truck farming (poultry, fruit).

Steyrermühl (shtī'rŭrmūl), village, S central Upper Austria, on Traun R. and 5 mi. N of Gmunden; paper mill.

Steyr River (shtīr), Upper Austria, rises in the Totes Gebirge, flows 35 mi. N to Enns R. at Steyr.

Steytlerville (stāt'lŭrvĭl), town (pop. 1,794), SE Cape Prov., U. of So. Afr., on Groot R. and 85 mi. NW of Port Elizabeth; stock, fruit, grain, feed.

Stezzano (stĕtsä'nō), village (pop. 3,391), Bergamo prov., Lombardy, N Italy, 3 mi. S of Bergamo; piano factory.

Stia (stē'ä), village (pop. 1,706), Arezzo prov., Tuscany, central Italy, on the Arno and 9 mi. NW of Bibbiena; macaroni, woolen textiles, paper, inks. In parish church is a Madonna by A. della Robbia.

Stibnite, village (pop. 717), Valley co., central Idaho, in mtn. region c.45 mi. NE of Boise; alt. 5,270 ft.; potatoes, grain, dairy products. Deposits of stibnite near by.

Stickney. 1 Village (pop. 3,317), Cook co., NE Ill., W suburb of Chicago. Inc. 1913. **2** Town (pop. 388), Aurora co., S S.Dak., 8 mi. S of Plankinton; dairy products, livestock, poultry, grain.

Stidham (stĭ'dŭm), town (pop. 46), McIntosh co., E Okla., 8 mi. NW of Eufaula.

Stieringen-Wendel, France: see STIRING-WENDEL.

Stifford, residential town and parish (pop. 2,188), S Essex, England, 2 mi. N of Grays Thurrock.

Stigen (stē'gŭn), village (pop. 535), Alvsborg co., SW Sweden, 16 mi. NNE of Uddevalla; grain, livestock.

Stigler (stĭ'glŭr), city (pop. 2,125), ⊙ Haskell co., E Okla., 35 mi. SSE of Muskogee, in area yielding agr. produce, livestock, timber. Feed, lumber, canned foods; rendering plant, cotton gins, nurseries, poultry hatcheries. Coal mines.

Stigliano (stēlyä'nō), town (pop. 8,015), Matera prov., Basilicata, S Italy, 18 mi. W of Pisticci, in cereal-growing and stock-raising region.

Stikine Mountains (stĭkēn'), range (extending 250 mi. NW-SE), N B.C., bet. 56°N 126°W and 59°N 130°W. Highest elevation is Mt. Witt (8,200 ft.), 57°31'N 128°45'W. Stikine R. rises in SE part of range.

Stikine River, NW B.C. and SE Alaska, rises at about 57°30'N 128°10'W in Stikine Mts. in several headstreams which join at 58°4'N 130°45'W, flows in a wide arc W and SW, crossing into Alaska 24 mi. NE of Wrangell, to the Pacific N of Wrangell; 335 mi. long, navigable for 130 mi. upstream. Chief route to Cassiar mining region; noted salmon stream.

Stikine Strait, SE Alaska, in Alexander Archipelago, bet. Zarembo Isl. (N) and Etolin Isl. (S), SW of Wrangell; extends N from Clarence Strait; part of Inside Passage.

Stiklestad (stĭk'lŭstä), village in Verdal canton, Nord-Trondelag co., central Norway, 9 mi. NE of Levanger. A statue commemorates St. Olaf, who died here in battle (1030). Has 12th-cent. church. Catholic chapel (1930) is a pilgrimage center.

Stilesville, town (pop. 330), Hendricks co., central Ind., on Mill Creek and 27 mi. WSW of Indianapolis, in agr. area.

Stilfser Joch, N Italy: see STELVIO PASS.

Stilis, Greece: see STYLIS.

Stillaguamish River (stĭlŭgwä'mĭsh), NW Wash., formed near Arlington by North Fork (c.35 mi. long; rises E of Mt. Vernon) and South Fork (c.30 mi. long; rises E of Everett); flows c.20 mi. E to Skagit Bay of Puget Sound, near Stanwood. In South Fork near Granite Falls town is 350-ft. waterfall.

Stille Adler River, Czechoslovakia: see TICHA ORLICE RIVER.

Stillington, town and parish (pop. 247), SE Durham, England, 7 mi. NE of Darlington; lubricating-oil distilling.

Stillman Valley, village (pop. 362), Ogle co., N Ill., 11 mi. SSW of Rockford, in rich agr. area.

Stillmore, town (pop. 420), Emanuel co., E central Ga., 12 mi. SE of Swainsboro.

Still River, village, Mass.: see HARVARD.

Still River. 1 In SW Conn., rises W of Danbury, flows c.30 mi. generally NE, past Danbury and Brookfield, to the Housatonic S of New Milford. **2** In NW Conn., rises near Torrington, flows c.15 mi. generally N, past Winsted (water power), to West Branch Farmington R. at Riverton.

Stillwater, county (□ 1,797; pop. 5,416), S Mont.; ⊙ Columbus. Irrigated agr. region drained by Yellowstone R. Sugar beets, beans, livestock. Part of Custer Natl. Forest in SW. Formed 1913.

Stillwater. 1 Village, Maine: see OLD TOWN. **2** City (pop. 7,674), ⊙ Washington co., E Minn., on St. Croix R. and 16 mi. ENE of St. Paul; trade and industrial center; dairy products, flour, beverages; mfg. (farm equipment, clothing and shoes, twine, lumber and cement products). Settled before 1840, inc. 1854. Convention assembled here (1848) to draw up petition for organization of Minn. as territory. City grew as lumbering point. **3** Village (pop. 1,276), Saratoga co., E N.Y., on W bank of the Hudson opposite influx of Hoosic R., and 12 mi. SE of Saratoga Springs, in dairying area; textile milling. The Revolutionary battles (Sept. 19, 1777, and Oct. 7, 1777) fought near here are commemorated by natl. historical park 9 mi. SE of SARATOGA SPRINGS. **4** City (pop. 20,238), ⊙ Payne co., N central Okla., c.50 mi. NNE of Oklahoma City; trade and industrial center for agr. area (grain, cotton, livestock, poultry; dairy products). Cotton ginning, flour and lumber milling, meat packing; mfg. of mattresses, machine-shop products. Gas wells. Greenhouses. Seat of Okla. Agr. and Mechanical Col. L. Carl Blackwell (recreation) is 7 mi. W. Settled 1889, inc. 1899. **5** Borough (pop. 189), Columbia co., E central Pa., 12 mi. NNE of Bloomsburg. **6** Village, R.I.: see SMITHFIELD.

Stillwater Creek. 1 In E Ohio, rises in Belmont co., flows c.60 mi. N, past Freeport and Uhrichsville, to join the Tuscarawas at Midvale. Flood-control dam impounds Piedmont Reservoir (capacity 65,000 acre-ft.) just SE of Freeport. **2** In N central Okla., rises in Noble co., flows c.40 mi. SE, past Stillwater, to Cimarron R. near Ripley. Dam impounds L. Carl Blackwell (c.6½ mi. long; recreation area) c.7 mi. W of Stillwater.

Stillwater River. 1 In S Mont., rises near Wyo. line at NE corner of Yellowstone Natl. Park, flows c.70 mi. generally NE, bet. Absaroka and Beartooth ranges, to Yellowstone R. at Columbus. **2** In W Ohio, rises in Darke co. near Ind. line, flows SE, past Ansonia, to confluence with Greenville Creek at Covington, thence S to the Great Miami at Dayton; c.65 mi. long. Flood-control dam at Englewood.

Stilo (stē'lō), town (pop. 3,016), Reggio di Calabria prov., Calabria, S Italy, 7 mi. WNW of Cape Stilo, 17 mi. NNE of Siderno Marina, in agr. (olives, grapes, cereals) and stock-raising region.

Stilo, Cape, Calabria, S Italy, at SW end of Gulf of Squillace, 7 mi. ESE of Stilo; 38°26'N 16°35'E. Site of anc. CAULONIA.

Stilton, agr. village and parish (pop. 494), N Huntingdon, England, 6 mi. SSW of Peterborough; former distribution center for Stilton cheese, now chiefly made in Leicestershire. Has 13th-cent. church.

Stilwell, town (pop. 1,813), ⊙ Adair co., E Okla., near Ark. line, c.40 mi. E of Muskogee; resort in hill area (alt. c.1,100 ft.) producing timber, truck, strawberries. Stone and marble quarries. Mfg. (wood products, canned foods, machine-shop products).

Stilwell Road, Burma and India: see LEDO ROAD.

Stimfalia, Lake, Greece: see STYMPHALIA, LAKE.

Stimigliano (stēmēlyä'nō), village (pop. 859), Rieti prov., Latium, central Italy, near the Tiber, 17 mi. WSW of Rieti; alcohol distillery, ceramics.

Stimlje or **Shtimlye** (both: shtēm'lyĕ), Serbo-Croatian *Štimlje*, village (pop. 6,699), S Serbia, Yugoslavia, on Sitnica R. and 17 mi. SSW of Pristina, in the Kosovo.

Stimson, Mount, Mont.: see LEWIS RANGE.

Stinchar River (stĭn'kär), Ayrshire, Scotland, rises 5 mi. SSW of Straiton, flows 30 mi. SW, past Barr and Colmonell, to Firth of Clyde at Ballantrae.

Stinesville, town (pop. 355), Monroe co., S central Ind., 11 mi. NW of Bloomington, in agr. area.

Stinnett, oil town (pop. 1,170), ⊙ Hutchinson co., extreme N Texas, in high plains of the Panhandle, c.50 mi. NNE of Amarillo, near Canadian R.; oil and natural-gas wells, refineries; carbon-black plants. Ships cattle, grain.

Stinson Beach, resort village (pop. c.175), Marin co., W Calif., on the Pacific, 5 mi. W of Mill Valley; fishing. Mt. Tamalpais is near by.

Stip or **Shtip** (both: shtēp), Serbo-Croatian *Štip*, Turkish *Istib* or *Ishtib*, town (pop. 11,519), ⊙ Stip oblast (formed 1949), Macedonia, Yugoslavia, on Bregalnica R., on railroad and 40 mi. SE of Skoplje; poppy-oil and opium mfg.; mineral waters. Has castle ruins, 14th-cent. monastery.

Stira, Greece: see STYRA.

Stiring-Wendel (stērĕng'-vädĕl'), Ger. *Stieringen-Wendel* (shtē'rĭng-ŭn-vĕn"dŭl), town (pop. 7,627), Moselle dept., NE France, on Saar border just NE of Forbach, and 3 mi. SW of Saarbrücken; coal-mining center; ironworks, brewery.

Stirling. 1 Village (pop. 446), S Alta., on Stirling L. (5 mi. long), 19 mi. SE of Lethbridge; railroad junction; mixed farming, ranching. **2** Village (pop. 990), SE Ont., 12 mi. NW of Belleville; dairying, flour milling, woodworking.

Stirling or **Stirlingshire** (-shĭr), county (□ 251.5; 1931 pop. 166,477; 1951 census 187,432), S central Scotland; ⊙ Stirling. Bounded by Lanark (S), Dumbarton (S and W), Perthshire (N), Clackmannan and the Firth of Forth (E), and West Lothian (SE). Drained by the Forth, Endrick Water, and Carron rivers. Surface is mountainous in W; Ben Lomond (3,192 ft.) is highest point. SW is hilly (Campsie Fells and Kilsyth Hills), sloping toward the Forth valley. There are fertile farmland tracts (carse), pastures, peat bogs, and moorland. At W extremity of co. is Loch Lomond. Coal is mined in E and SE; ironworks at Carron. Other industries are woolen and cotton milling, ironstone, limestone, and sandstone quarrying, mfg. of chemicals, whisky distilling, shipbuilding, and oil refining (Grangemouth). Besides Stirling, other towns are Falkirk, Grangemouth, Carron, Denny, Kilsyth, and Bridge of Allan (spa resort). There are many historical associations, including battles of Stirling Bridge (1297), Falkirk (1297 and 1746), Bannockburn (1314), and Kilsyth (1647); Robert Bruce figures in Stirling's history. The Walls of Antoninus crossed in S.

Stirling, burgh (1931 pop. 22,593; 1951 census 26,960), ⊙ Sterlingshire, Scotland, in NE part of co., on the Forth (15th-cent. bridge) and 22 mi. NE of Glasgow, 30 mi. WNW of Edinburgh; agr. market with mfg. of chemicals, agr. machinery, feed cakes, bacon and ham, and carpets. On hill above the town is anc. Stirling Castle, within whose walls is the palace begun in 1540 and long rivaling Edinburgh as royal residence. James II and James V were b. here, and Mary Queen of Scots and James VI were crowned here. In 1304 castle was taken by Edward I after 3-month siege, retaken by the Scots after 1314 battle at near-by BANNOCKBURN. In 1297 William Wallace defeated the English at battle of Stirling Bridge. Other notable features are: 13th-cent. parish church; Cowane Hosp. (1639); Mar's Work (1570), unfinished fragment of Scottish architecture; and Argyll's Lodging (c.1630), a military hosp. since 1799. Just E of Stirling, on the Forth, is CAMBUSKENNETH.

Stirling, village (pop. 1,076), Morris co., N central N.J., 7 mi. NW of Plainfield, near Passaic R.; mfg. (pencils, metal products, clothing, clay products).

Stirling City, village (pop. c.450), Butte co., N central Calif., in foothills of the Sierra Nevada, 20 mi. NW of Chico; match factory.

Stirling Island, Solomon Isls.: see TREASURY ISLANDS.

Stirling Range, SW Western Australia, 40 mi. N of Albany; extends 40 mi. parallel with SW coast, rises to 3,640 ft. (Bluff Knoll); forested slopes.

Stirlingshire, Scotland: see STIRLING, county.

Stites (stīts), village (pop. 227), Idaho co., central Idaho, 15 mi. NE of Grangeville and on Clearwater R.; center of agr. area.

Stithians (stĭ'dhēūnz), agr. village and parish (pop. 1,463), SW Cornwall, England, 5 mi. WNW of Falmouth. Has 15th-cent. church.

Stitnik (shtyĕt'nyĭk), Slovak *Štítnik*, Hung. *Csetnek* (chĕt'nĕk), village (pop. 1,341), S Slovakia, Czechoslovakia, in Slovak Ore Mts., on railroad and 8 mi. W of Roznava; iron and copper mining.

Stity (shtē'tĭ), Czech *Štíty*, formerly *Šilperk*, Ger. *Schildberg* (shĭlt'bĕrk), village (pop. 855), NW Moravia, Czechoslovakia, 7 mi. NW of Zabreh; rail terminus; oats.

Stizharov (stē'zhärôf), village (pop. 3,208), Pleven dist., N Bulgaria, 11 mi. SW of Svishtov; wheat, corn, livestock.

Stjarnsund (shârn"sŭnd'), Swedish *Stjärnsund*, village (pop. 500), Kopparberg co., central Sweden, on L. Gryck, Swedish *Grycken* (grü'kûn) (4 mi. long, 2 mi. wide), 12 mi. NE of Hedemora; watch mfg., sawmilling. Large ironworks, founded in 18th cent., now closed down.

Stjernoy, Norway: see SEILAND.

Stjordal (styûr'däl), Nor. *Stjørdal*, village (pop. 2,015; canton pop. 4,337), Nord-Trondelag co., central Norway, at head of Strinda Fjord (a bay of Trondheim Fjord), at mouth of Stjordal R., on railroad and 17 mi. E of Trondheim; produces wood products, lime, peat, straw, potato flour. At Vernes (W) are airport and medieval parish church.

Stjordal River, Nor. *Stjørdalselv*, Nord-Trondelag co., central Norway, rises in a lake on Swedish border 13 mi. ESE of Meraker, flows 31 mi. W to Strinda Fjord (a bay of Trondheim Fjord) at Stjordal.

Stjorna, Norway: see RAKVAG.

Stobi, Yugoslavia: see GRADSKO.

Stobo (stō'bō), agr. village and parish (pop. 292), central Peebles, Scotland, on the Tweed and 5 mi. WSW of Peebles. Has medieval church and early-19th-cent. castle.

Stochek, Poland: see STOCZEK.

Stochod River, Ukrainian SSR: see STOKHOD RIVER.

Stocka (stô'kä"), village (pop. 794), Gavleborg co., E Sweden, on Gulf of Bothnia, 14 mi. NE of Hudiksvall; sawmills.

Stockach (shtôk'äkh), town (pop. 3,560), S Baden, Germany, 10 mi. NE of Singen; cotton mfg., metalworking. Has ruined castle. Archduke Charles here decisively defeated Jourdan in 1799.

Stockaryd (stô'kärüd"), village (pop. 822), Jonkoping co., S Sweden, 20 mi. S of Nassjo; sawmilling, woodworking.

Stockbridge, town and parish (pop. 826), W Hampshire, England, on Test R. and 6 mi. S of Andover; agr. market. Site of race course; race-horse training.

Stockbridge. 1 Town (pop. 717), Henry co., N central Ga., 17 mi. SSE of Atlanta; granite quarrying. **2** Resort town (pop. 2,311), Berkshire co., SW Mass., in the Berkshires, on Housatonic R. and 12 mi. S of Pittsfield. Has fine old houses, art colony, and Berkshire Playhouse, leading summer theater. Jonathan Edwards taught here, 1750–57. Includes villages of Glendale and Interlaken (ĭn'türlä"kûn) (just S of Stockbridge Bowl lake), and part of Tanglewood estate (near center of adjoining LENOX). Monument Mtn. Reservation is near by. Stockbridge founded 1736 as model village for Mahican Indians; inc. 1739. **3** Village (pop. 1,098), Ingham co., S central Mich., 18 mi. NE of Jackson, in farm area (dairy products; grain, onions). **4** Town (pop. 427), Windsor co., central Vt., on White R. and 16 mi. NE of Rutland; lumber. Partly in Green Mtn. Natl. Forest. **5** Village (pop. 409), Calumet co., E Wis., near L. Winnebago, 20 mi. NNE of Fond du Lac, in dairying and grain-growing area. Settled in 1820s by Stockbridge Indians.

Stockdale. 1 Borough (pop. 870), Washington co., SW Pa., 4 mi. SE of Charleroi and on Monongahela R. **2** Town (pop. 1,105), Wilson co., S Texas, 34 mi. ESE of San Antonio; shipping (rail, highway) point, in truck-farming area; peanut processing.

Stockdale, Mount (10,100 ft.), SE B.C., in Selkirk Mts., 65 mi. SW of Banff; 50°33'N 116°35'W.

Stockelsdorf (shtô'kûlsdôrf), village (pop. 10,752), in Schleswig-Holstein, NW Germany, 3 mi. N of Lübeck city center; metal- and woodworking, food processing. Until 1937 in Oldenburg.

Stockem (stōkĕm'), village, Luxembourg prov., SE Belgium, 2 mi. W of Arlon; railroad switching yards. Commune center of Heinsch (pop. 2,052) is 1 mi. NW.

Stockerau (shtôk'ûrou), city (pop. 10,790), E Lower Austria, on branch of the Danube and 12 mi. NW of Vienna; rail junction; mfg. (machine tools, glass, chemicals, wood products).

Stockertown, borough (pop. 757), Northampton co., E Pa., 5 mi. NNW of Easton; cement.

Stockes, Monte (mōn'tā stôks'), peak (7,000 ft.) in Patagonian Andes, on Argentina-Chile border, 8 mi. SW of S arm of L. Argentino; 50°49'S.

Stockett, village (pop. c.350), Cascade co., W central Mont., near Missouri R., 12 mi. SSE of Great Falls.

Stockham (stŏ'kûm), village (pop. 82), Hamilton co., SE central Nebr., 10 mi. S of Aurora and on W.Fork of Big Blue R.

Stockheim (shtôk'hīm), village (pop. 1,519), Upper Franconia, N Bavaria, Germany, 5 mi. NNW of Kronach; rail junction; coal-mining center.

Stockholm, village (pop. 225), SE Sask., 40 mi. SSE of Yorkton; wheat, stock.

Stockholm (stŏk'hōlm, -hōm, Swed. stôk'hôlm"), county [Swed. *län*] (□ 2,986; 1950 pop. 357,932), E Sweden; ⊙ Stockholm (not included in the co.). On the Baltic, it includes E part of Sodermanland prov. and SE part of Uppland prov. Fertile lowland, dotted with many lakes; coast line is deeply indented by fjords. Offshore are innumerable skerries. Iron mining (NE). Metalworking, paper milling; mfg. of machinery and electrical equipment are among leading industries. Center of pop. is in S part of co., which includes all suburbs of Stockholm city. Sodertalje, Solna, and Nynashamn are largest cities.

Stockholm, city (□ 55; 1945 pop. 671,284; 1950 census 745,936), ⊙ Sweden, on the E coast, beautifully situated bet. L. Malar (Malaren) and its outlet *Saltsjö* (sält'shû") on the near-by Baltic Sea; 59°20'N 18°4'E. A large seaport and rail center, and with an airport at BROMMA, it is the cultural, commercial, and industrial center of Sweden. Built partly on several peninsulas and partly on some small isls., it has wide waterways and canals which have led it often to be called "the Venice of the North." With the exception of Staden isl., its oldest part, which has preserved much of its medieval character, Stockholm is a modern city and a notable example of town planning, with extensive cooperative housing developments, wide avenues, and many parks. There are no slums. Seat of Lutheran archbishop; site of univ., Swedish Academy (1786), academies of letters and history, music, science, art, folklore, and agr., and of Nobel Institute. Annual Nobel Prize awards are made in Stockholm's concert hall. City is hq. of most large Swedish corporations; its industries include shipbuilding, mfg. of electrical and telephone equipment, machinery, textiles, chemicals, automobiles, and rubber products. Stockholm's new city hall (1911–23), facing L. Malar, built by Ragnor Ostberg, is its most celebrated landmark. On Staden isl. are the market square, where Stockholm Massacre (1520) began; 13th-cent. Storkyrka (great church), 17th-cent. Riddarhuset (hall of nobles), and Royal Palace (1760). On adjacent islet of Riddarholm is 13th-cent. Riddarholm Church, built by Franciscan monks, where Swedish kings and notables are buried. Other noted bldgs. are the Riksdag (parliament; completed 1905), Royal Opera, and Royal Dramatic Theater. Stockholm's many museums include National Mus. and, at Skansen, in E part of city, open-air folk mus. Among modern bldgs. are hq. of *Kooperativa Förbundet* (cooperatives' union), hq. of Swedish Match Co., several new hospitals, and the Stadium, built for Olympic Games of 1912. Kungsgatan, Drottningsgatan, and Birger Jarlsgatan are chief shopping streets. Among city's many statues are several noted modern ones by Carl Milles. Stockholm's annual temperature ranges from 29°F. (Jan.) to 62°F. (July); average annual rainfall is 20.7 inches. Founded 1255, city rapidly became a center of medieval trade, dominated by Hanseatic League. On occasion of his coronation (1520) as king of Sweden, Christian II of Denmark and Norway instigated massacre of anti-Danish nobility in Stockholm's market square; this led to Swedish rising under Gustavus Vasa, who, as Gustavus I of Sweden (1523), ended privileges of Hanseatic League. In 17th cent. city was beautified by Queen Christina, who made it a leading European intellectual center. As a neutral capital, Stockholm was scene of much diplomatic activity in First and Second World wars. It is ⊙ Stockholm co., which does not include the city. Among its chief suburbs are Danderyd, Djursholm, Stocksund (N), Sollentuna (NNW), Solna (NW), Drottningholm, with celebrated palace (W), Hasselby, Sundbyberg (WNW), Stuvsta (SW), Saltsjobaden (ESE), Vaxholm (ENE), and Lidingo (NE); all independent municipal entities in Stockholm co.

Stockholm. 1 Town (pop. 641), Aroostook co., NE Maine, on Little Madawaska R. and 14 mi. NNW of Caribou. Settled 1870 by Swedish immigrants, inc. 1911. **2** Town (pop. 114), Grant co., NE S.Dak., 12 mi. SW of Milbank. **3** Fishing village (pop. 124), Pepin co., W Wis., on L. Pepin, 14 mi. ESE of Red Wing, Minn.

Stockhorn (shtôk'hôrn), peak (7,196 ft.) in Bernese Alps, central Switzerland, 6 mi. SW of Thun.

Stockingford, England: see NUNEATON.

Stockmannshof, Latvia: see PLAVINAS.

Stockport, county borough (1931 pop. 125,490; 1951 census 141,660), NE Cheshire, England, on slopes of narrow valley of Mersey R., at confluence of Tame R. and Goyt R., 6 mi. SE of Manchester; 53°24'N 2°9'W; textile center (cotton and wool), metalworking, mfg. of textile machinery, electrical switchgear, light metals, pharmaceuticals, paint, paper, food products. Has 1,800-ft.-long railroad viaduct (built early 19th cent.) over the valley; 14th-cent. church; mus. and art gall.; statue of Richard Cobden, who was a member of Parliament for Stockport. Stockport was site of Roman and Norman stations. Borough includes (NE) cotton-mfg. suburb of Heaton Norris, in Lancashire.

Stockport. 1 Town (pop. 346), Van Buren co., SE Iowa, 12 mi. SSE of Fairfield; livestock, grain. **2** Village (pop. 404), Morgan co., E central Ohio, on the Muskingum and 20 mi. WNW of Marietta.

Stocksbridge, urban district (1931 pop. 9,255; 1951 census 10,277), West Riding, S Yorkshire, England, 8 mi. NW of Sheffield; steel milling.

Stocksund (stôk"sŭnd'), residential town (pop. 4,218), Stockholm co., E Sweden, on small fjord of the Baltic, 4 mi. N of Stockholm city center; machinery works.

Stockton, N suburb of Newcastle, E New South Wales, Australia, opposite Newcastle, on small peninsula forming N side of entrance to Port Hunter; shipyards.

Stockton, town and parish (pop. 935), E Warwick, England, 7 mi. E of Leamington; limestone quarrying; lime and cement works.

Stockton. 1 Village (pop. c.1,200), Baldwin co., SW Ala., 10 mi. NW of Bay Minette and on Tensaw R.; wood products. **2** City (pop. 70,853), ⊙ San Joaquin co., central Calif., on deepwater channel to San Joaquin R. and c.65 mi. SE of San Francisco; inland seaport (c.90 mi. from the Golden Gate), shipbuilding and mfg. center; railroad center (6 lines); has airport. Harbor development began 1928; became a U.S. port of entry in 1935. Ships agr. produce and livestock of San Joaquin Valley; produces farm implements and machinery, canned foods, paper products, flour and feed, lumber products, fertilizer, cans, leather goods. Has mus., art gall., state hosp. for insane, civic auditorium. Seat of Col. of the Pacific and Stockton Col. (jr.). Founded 1847 as Tuleburg; inc. 1852 as Stockton. Was an outfitting center in gold rush days. **3** Village (pop. 1,445), Jo Daviess co., NW Ill., 19 mi. WNW of Freeport; trade center in agr. area; dairy products. Inc. 1890. **4** Town (pop. 165), Muscatine co., SE Iowa, 15 mi. WNW of Davenport; foundry products. **5** City (pop. 1,867), ⊙ Rooks co., N Kansas, on South Fork Solomon R. and 36 mi. N of Hays; shipping point for grain and livestock area. Oil wells near by. Kansas-Nebr. Fair takes place here annually in Aug. State park near by. Settled 1872, inc. 1880. **6** Village, Worcester co., SE Md., 25 mi. SSE of Salisbury; rail-shipping point for Chincoteague Bay oysters; vegetable cannery. **7** Village (pop. 235), Winona co., SE Minn., 6 mi. W of Winona; dairying. **8** City (pop. 811), ⊙ Cedar co., W Mo., in Ozark region, near Sac R., 42 mi. NW of Springfield; grain, livestock. **9** Borough (pop. 488), Hunterdon co., W N.J., on Delaware R. and 17 mi. NW of Trenton. **10** Town (pop. 414), Tooele co., NW central Utah, 5 mi. SSW of Tooele; alt. 5,068 ft.; gold, silver, lead.

Stockton Heath, town and parish (pop. 4,844), N Cheshire, England, on Bridgewater Canal and Manchester Ship Canal, 2 mi. S of Warrington; metalworking, mfg. of electrical goods.

Stockton-on-Tees, municipal borough (1931 pop. 67,722; 1951 census 74,024), SE Durham, England, on the Tees and 3 mi. WSW of Middlesbrough; shipbuilding and steel center, with blast furnaces, boiler works, chemical and pharmaceutical plants. Developed after opening (1825) of Stockton and Darlington RR, the 1st in the United Kingdom. There are no remains of 13th-cent. castle, taken (1644) by Parliamentarians, and subsequently destroyed. In municipal borough are industrial suburbs of Hartburn (W; pop. 7,073), Norton (N; pop. 10,745), and Portrack (E; pop. 7,642).

Stockton Plateau, Texas: see EDWARDS PLATEAU.

Stockton Springs, town (pop. 949), Waldo co., S Maine, on Penobscot R. and 8 mi. NE of Belfast; includes Sandypoint village.

Stockvik (stôk"vēk'), village (pop. 1,431), Vasternorrland co., NE Sweden, on small inlet of Gulf of Bothnia, at mouth of Ljunga R., 4 mi. SE of Sundsvall; chemical works.

Stockville, village (pop. 181), ⊙ Frontier co., S Nebr., 25 mi. NNE of McCook and on Medicine Creek. Sites of prehistoric Indian villages near by.

Stoczek or **Stoczek Lukowski** (stô'chĕk wōōkôf'skē), Pol. *Stoczek Łukowski*, Rus. *Stochek* (stô'chĭk), town (pop. 1,922), Lublin prov., E Poland, 18 mi. W of Lukow; flour and groat milling, dairying, brewing.

Stod (stôt), Ger. *Staab* (shtäp), town (pop. 2,502), W Bohemia, Czechoslovakia, on Radbuza R., on railroad and 12 mi. SW of Pilsen; glassworks; zinc mining.

Stoddard, county (□ 837; pop. 33,463), SE Mo.; ⊙ Bloomfield. On St. Francis R. (W); drained by Castor R.; drainage canals. Agr. (grain), livestock; grows and processes cotton; lumber. Formed 1835.

Stoddard. 1 Town (pop. 200), Cheshire co., SW N.H., on Highland L. and 14 mi. NNE of Keene. **2** Village (pop. 459), Vernon co., SW Wis., on small Coon Creek, near the Mississippi, and 10 mi. S of La Crosse; fishing.

Stode (stû'dû), Swedish *Stöde* village (pop. 757), Vasternorrland co., NE Sweden, on Ljunga R. and 25 mi. W of Sundsvall; sawmills.

Stodolishche (stŭdô'lyĭshchĭ), village (1926 pop. 535), S Smolensk oblast, Russian SFSR, 18 mi. NW of Roslavl; sawmill.

Stoelmans (stōōl'mäns), village (pop. 47), Marowijne dist., E Du. Guiana, on isl. at confluence of Maroni (or Marowijne) and Tapanahoni rivers (Fr. Guiana border), 40 mi. SE of Dam, in gold-mining region.

Stog (stôg), peak (5,330 ft.) in central Carpathians, on USSR-Rumania line, 22 mi. ENE of Sighet. Formed (1918–39) meeting point of Polish, Czech, and Rum. borders.

Stogovo (stô'gôvô), mountain (7,534 ft.), in the Pindus system, W Macedonia, Yugoslavia, along right bank of the Black Drin, 8 mi. SSE of Debar.

Stoiba or **Stoyba** (stoibä'), town (1942 pop. over 500), NE Amur oblast, Russian SFSR, on Selemdzha R. and 250 mi. NNE of Blagoveshchensk; gold mines. Developed during Second World War.

Stoiceni (stoichĕn'), village, Arges prov., S central Rumania, 22 mi. NW of Pitesti.

Stoke. 1 Town, Surrey, England: see GUILDFORD. **2** Suburb, Warwick, England: see COVENTRY.

Stoke Climsland, agr. village and parish (pop. 1,464), E Cornwall, England, 7 mi. S of Launceston. Has 15th-cent. church.

Stoke D'Abernon (stōk dă'bŭnŭn), residential town and parish (pop. 1,036), N central Surrey, England, on Mole R. and 5 mi. W of Epsom. Church (dating partly from Saxon times) contains earliest English brasses (1277).

Stoke Ferry, agr. village and parish (pop. 610), SW Norfolk, England, 6 mi. ESE of Downham Market.

Stoke Gifford, agr. village and parish (pop. 1,255), SW Gloucester, England, 5 mi. NE of Bristol. Church dates from 14th cent.

Stokenchurch, agr. village and parish (pop. 1,916), SW Buckingham, England, 7 mi. WNW of High Wycombe. Has church dating from Norman times. The 1st English Sunday School was established here 1769.

Stoke Newington, metropolitan borough (1931 pop. 51,208; 1951 census 49,137) of London, England, N of the Thames, 4 mi. NNE of Charing Cross. Has 16th-cent. parish church of St. Mary. Edgar Allen Poe attended school here (1817–19), and Daniel Defoe lived here for some time.

Stokenham (stōkŭnhăm', stō'kŭnŭm), agr. village and parish (pop. 1,217), S Devon, England, 7 mi. SSW of Dartmouth. Church dates from 13th cent.

Stoke-on-Trent or **Stoke-upon-Trent,** county borough (1931 pop. 276,639; 1951 census 275,095), NW Stafford, England, on Trent R. and 35 mi. S of Manchester; 53°N 2°11'W; center of the pottery industry; site of China-clay and coal mines; has colliery equipment works, foundries; also tile, copper, tin, and pharmaceutical industries. The borough was formed in 1910 when Stoke-on-Trent was joined with the important pottery- and china-mfg. towns of Hanley, Burslem, Tunstall, Etruria, Fenton, Longton, and Longport. Has several museums, including Minton Memorial mus. and library. Closely connected with the well-known pottery manufacturers Josiah Wedgwood (Etruria), Josiah Spode, William Copeland, and Herbert Minton. The town and surrounding area of the upper Trent valley is also known as the POTTERIES or the "Five Towns." The pottery industry was introduced into the area in 16th cent. Josiah Wedgwood b. in Burslem, Arnold Bennet in Hanley.

Stoke Poges (pō'jĭz), residential town and parish (pop. 2,110), SE Buckingham, England, 2 mi. N of Slough. The churchyard of St. Giles (12th–14th cent.), generally considered to be scene of Gray's *Elegy*, contains Gray's grave.

Stoke Prior, town and parish (pop. 3,378), central Worcester, England, 4 mi. NE of Droitwich; brine springs, saltworks. Church has 12th-cent. tower.

Stokes (stōks), county (□ 459; pop. 21,520), N N.C., on Va. line; ⊙ Danbury. Piedmont agr. (tobacco, corn) and timber area; drained by Dan R. Formed 1798.

Stokes town (pop. 217), Pitt co., E central N.C., 10 mi. NE of Greenville.

Stoke Saint Gregory, agr. village and parish (pop. 1,266), S central Somerset, England, 8 mi. E of Taunton. Has 13th-cent. church.

Stokesay, agr. village and parish (pop. 1,112), S Shropshire, England, 7 mi. NW of Ludlow. Site of Stokesay Castle, oldest example of fortified, moated manor house in England, with 13th-cent. stone tower and banquet hall and 17th-cent. gatehouse.

Stokes Island, Chile: see CHONOS ARCHIPELAGO.

Stokesley, town and parish (pop. 1,688), North Riding, N Yorkshire, England, on Leven R. and 7 mi. SSE of Middlesbrough; agr. market. Has church of 14th-cent. origin.

Stokes State Forest, NW N.J., recreational area (c.12,500 acres) on Kittatinny Mtn., c.10 mi. N of Newton.

Stoke-sub-Hamdon or **Stoke-under-Ham,** town and parish (pop. 1,649), S Somerset, England, 6 mi. WNW of Yeovil; agr. market; mfg. of gloves and other leather goods. Stone quarries near by. Has Norman church. Traces of Roman occupation.

Stokhod River (stô'khŭt), Pol. *Stochód* (stô'khōōt), in Volyn oblast, Ukrainian SSR, rises NNW of Torchin in Volyn-Podolian Upland, flows 123 mi. generally N, past Lyubeshov (head of navigation), to Pripet R. 8 mi. NE of Lyubeshov.

Stokke (stôk'kù), village (pop. 466; canton pop. 5,268), Vestfold co., SE Norway, on railroad and 6 mi. SW of Tonsberg; lumbering, market gardening; tanning, flour- and sawmilling, carriage mfg.

Stokken, canton, Norway: see EYDEHAMN.

Stokkmarknes, Norway: see MELBU.

Stokkoy (stôk'ûü), Nor. *Stokkøy*, island (□ 7; pop. 538) in North Sea, Sor-Trondelag co., central Norway, 40 mi. NNW of Trondheim; agr. Harbor for herring fishing is at Stokkoy village in Stoksund canton (pop. 1,473), at E tip.

Stokkseyri (stôks'ā″rē), fishing village (pop. 413), Arne co., SW Iceland, 30 mi. SE of Reykjavik.

Stokmarknes, Norway: see MELBU.

Stoksund, Norway: see STOKKOY.

Stoky (shtô'kĭ), Czech *Štoky*, Ger. *Stecken* (shtĕ'kŭn), town (pop. 990), SE Bohemia, Czechoslovakia, on railroad and 7 mi. S of Havlickuv Brod.

Stol, peak, Austria and Yugoslavia: see HOCHSTUHL.

Stolac or **Stolats** (both: stô'läts), town (pop. 2,287), central Herzegovina, Yugoslavia, on the Bregava and 19 mi. S of Mostar; road junction; winegrowing center.

Stolbce, Belorussian SSR: see STOLBTSY.

Stolberg (shtôl'bĕrk). **1** Town (pop. 27,921), in former Prussian Rhine Prov., W Germany, after 1945 in North Rhine-Westphalia, 6 mi. E of Aachen; 50°46'N 6°14'E. Rail junction; a center of Ger. brass industry; extensive metalworking (brass, copper, lead, and zinc products; chains, cables). Other mfg.: cloth, felt, chemicals, soap, perfumes, glass; brewing. Brass industry was brought to town in 16th cent., when Aachen Protestants settled here. Chartered 1856. Captured (Nov., 1944) by U.S. troops after 6 weeks of heavy fighting. **2** or **Stolberg am Harz** (äm härts'), town (pop. 3,123), in former Prussian Saxony prov., central Germany, after 1945 in Saxony-Anhalt, in the lower Harz, 10 mi. NE of Nordhausen; coal mining; wood carving. Climatic health resort. Has 15th-cent. church and town hall. Münzer b. here.

Stolbishchi (stŭlbē'shchĭ), village (1939 pop. over 500), W Tatar Autonomous SSR, Russian SFSR, 10 mi. SSE of Kazan; truck.

Stolboukha (stŭlbŭōō'khŭ), town (1945 pop. over 500), E East Kazakhstan oblast, Kazakh SSR, in Altai Mts., 20 mi. NNE of Zyryanovsk.

Stolbovo (stôl'bŭvŭ), village, E central Leningrad oblast, Russian SFSR, 16 mi. ESE of Volkhov and on Syas R. By Treaty of Stolbovo (1617) Russia ceded Karelian littoral to Sweden.

Stolbovoi Island or **Stolbovoy Island** (stŭlbŭvoi'), one of Lyakhov Isls., in Laptev Sea, 120 mi. off Yakut Autonomous SSR, Russian SFSR; 74°N 136°E.

Stolbtsy (stŭlptsē'), Pol. *Stolbce* (stôlp'tsĕ), city (1931 pop. 6,278), E Baranovichi oblast, Belorussian SSR, on Neman R. (head of navigation) and 39 mi. NE of Baranovichi; flaxseed and pitch processing, flour milling, brick mfg.; fruit gardening. Has 17th-cent. church and monastery. Founded 16th cent.; developed as agr.-trading center. Passed (1793) from Poland to Russia; reverted (1921) to Poland; major customs rail station on Pol.-Soviet border until 1939; ceded to USSR in 1945.

Stolica (stô'lĭtsä), highest mountain (4,554 ft.) of Slovak Ore Mts., S central Slovakia, Czechoslovakia, 17 mi. NW of Roznava. Sajo (Slana) R. rises on NE slope.

Stolin (stô'lyĭn), city (1931 pop. 6,328), S Pinsk oblast, W Belorussian SSR, in Pripet Marshes, on Goryn R. and 35 mi. SE of Pinsk; grain-trading center; tanning, distilling, flour milling, sawmilling, mfg. of furniture, fireproof bricks. Passed (1793) from Poland to Russia; reverted (1919) to Poland; ceded to USSR in 1945.

Stollberg (shtôl'bĕrk), town (pop. 11,208), Saxony, E central Germany, at N foot of the Erzgebirge, 11 mi. SW of Chemnitz; hosiery-knitting center; metalworking; mfg. of radios, needles. Old Hoheneck castle overlooks town.

Stolovi (stô'lôvē), mountain, central Serbia, Yugoslavia; highest point (4,510 ft.) is 9 mi. SSW of Rankovicevo town.

Stolowe, Gory, Poland: see HEUSCHEUER MOUNTAINS.

Stolp (shtôlp) or **Slupsk** (swōōpsk), Pol. *Słupsk*, town (1939 pop. 50,377; 1946 pop. 33,948) in Pomerania, after 1945 in Koszalin prov., NW Poland, on Slupia R. and 65 mi. W of Danzig; 54°28'N 17°2'E. Rail junction; sawmilling, mfg. of chemicals, agr. implements, chocolate, candy, machinery; food canning, brewing, distilling, woodworking. First mentioned 1276; chartered 1310. Has 16th-cent. castle. Passed 1653 to Brandenburg. In Second World War, c.50% destroyed.

Stolpen (shtôl'pŭn), town (pop. 2,189), Saxony, E central Germany, in Saxonian Switzerland, 15 mi. E of Dresden, near Czechoslovak border; mfg. of buttons, artificial flowers; cotton milling, metalworking. Has remains of anc. castle.

Stolpe River, Poland: see SLUPIA RIVER.

Stolpmünde, Poland: see USTKA.

Stolzembourg (stôlzäbōōr'), Ger. *Stolzemburg* (shtôlts'ŭmbōōrk), agr. village (pop. 186), NE Luxembourg, on Our R. and 3 mi. NNW of Vianden, at Ger. border; chalk quarrying.

Stolzenhagen, Poland: see GLINKI.

Ston (stôn), Ital. *Stagno* or *Stagno Grande* (stä'nyô grän'dĕ), village, S Croatia, Yugoslavia, in Dalmatia, at base of Peljesac peninsula, 30 mi. NW of Dubrovnik, on Ston Canal (Serbo-Croatian *Stonski Kanal*, Ital. *Canale di Stagno* or *Canale di Stagno Grande*), an inlet of Adriatic Sea. Saltworking center; trade in tobacco, wine, olives, vegetable oil. Former R.C. (10th–13th cent.) and Orthodox Eastern (11th–14th cent.) bishopric. Mali Ston, Ital. *Stagno Piccolo*, village, is just NW, on Mali Ston Canal (Serbo-Croatian *Malostonski Kanal*, Ital. *Canale di Stagno Piccolo*), an inlet of Neretva Channel.

Stone. 1 Agr. village and parish (pop. 1,633), central Buckingham, England, 3 mi. WSW of Aylesbury. Has 14th-cent. church. Site of co. mental hosp. **2** Residential town and parish (pop. 6,661), NW Kent, England, on the Thames 4 mi. W of Gravesend. Has early-13th-cent. church. **3** Urban district (1931 pop. 5,952; 1951 census 8,299), N central Stafford, England, on Trent R. and 7 mi. S of Stoke-on-Trent; shoe mfg. Has remains of 7th-cent. priory.

Stone. 1 County (□ 610; pop. 7,662), N Ark.; ⊙ Mountain View. Bounded NE by White R.; situated in Ozark region. Agr. (livestock, cotton, grain, hay; dairy products). Some mfg. at Mountain View. Pine, hardwood timber. Part of Ozark Natl. Forest is in N. Formed 1873. **2** County (□ 488; pop. 6,264), SE Miss.; ⊙ Wiggins. Drained by Biloxi R. and Red and Black creeks. Agr. (cotton, corn; tung and pecan groves), dairying; lumbering. Formed 1916. **3** County (□ 509; pop. 9,748), SW Mo.; ⊙ Galena. In the Ozarks; drained by White and James rivers. Agr. region, especially for livestock; tomatoes, strawberries, corn; lead, zinc. Part of Mark Twain Natl. Forest here. Formed 1851.

Stone, mining village (1940 pop. 990), Pike co., E Ky., in the Cumberlands, 6 mi. S of Williamson, W.Va.; bituminous coal.

Stoneboro, borough (pop. 1,294), Mercer co., NW Pa., 9 mi. W of Polk. Inc. 1866.

Stone City. 1 Village (pop. c.100), Pueblo co., S central Colo., on branch of Arkansas R. and 18 mi. NW of Pueblo; alt. 5,200 ft.; limestone quarries. Petrified dinosaur skeleton is here. **2** Village (pop. c.175), Jones co., E Iowa, on Wapsipinicon R. and 19 mi. ENE of Cedar Rapids. Limestone quarries near by.

Stoneclough (stōn'klŭf), town in Farnworth municipal borough, S Lancashire, England; cotton milling, paper mfg.

Stone Creek, village (pop. 225), Tuscarawas co., E Ohio, 9 mi. SW of New Philadelphia; clay products, cheese.

Stonecutters Island, Chinese *Ngonshun Chau* (ŭngôn'sōōn' jou'), small island of Hong Kong colony, off W coast of Kowloon peninsula, 2 mi. N of Victoria; 1 mi. long, ¼ mi. wide. Radio station on E shore.

Stonefield, town in Blantyre parish, N Lanark, Scotland, just NW of Hamilton; steel milling.

Stonefort (stōn'fûrt), village (pop. 490), on Saline-Williamson co. line, S Ill., 13 mi. SW of Harrisburg, in agr. area. Until 1934, called Bolton. Ruins of prehistoric stone fort near by.

Stonega (stŭnē'gŭ), mining village (pop. 1,439, with near-by Possum Trot Hollow), Wise co., SW Va., 6 mi. E of Lynch, Ky.

Stoneham (stō'nŭm). **1** Town (pop. 216), Oxford co., W Maine, c.25 mi. SW of Rumford, in White Mtn. Natl. Forest. **2** Residential town (pop. 13,229), Middlesex co., E Mass., 9 mi. N of Boston; mfg. (leather goods, chemicals, furniture, drugs). Settled 1645, inc. 1725.

Stone Harbor, resort borough (pop. 670), Cape May co., S N.J., on Seven Mile Beach isl. (bridged to mainland), bet. Great Sound and the Atlantic, and 28 mi. SW of Atlantic City; yachting center; seafood, truck, dairy products.

Stonehaven (stōnhā'vŭn), burgh (1931 pop. 4,185; 1951 census 4,438), ⊙ Kincardine, Scotland, in E part of co., on North Sea, 14 mi. SSW of Aberdeen; agr. market, resort, and herring- and haddock-fishing port; tanneries, linen mills, mfg. of fish nets and fertilizer. Just S is DUNNOTTAR, with noted castle.

Stonehenge (stōn'hĕnj″), remains of prehistoric structure on Salisbury Plain, SE Wiltshire, England, 8 mi. N of Salisbury. Preeminent among megalithic monuments in the British Isles, it was presented to the nation in 1918. The structure, enclosed within a circular ditch 300 ft. in diameter, consists of stones arranged in 4 series, the 2 outermost forming circles, the third a horseshoe, and the innermost an oval. Of the outer circle (c.100 ft. in diameter), originally formed of 30 upright stones 13½ ft. high, 16 stones are in place, connected by dovetailed stone lintels; of the some 40 menhirs in the 2d circle (76½ ft. in diameter), 9 are upright and 11 lie overturned; the horseshoe-shaped group is made up of 5 huge sarsen trilithons, 2 of which still stand; within the ovoid lies the so-called Altar Stone, over 16 ft. long, now in 2 parts. The purpose of the structure has not been definitely established, but a recent theory holds that it dates from the Bronze Age and its purpose was perhaps sepulchral.

Stonehouse. **1** Town, Devon, England: see PLYMOUTH. **2** Town and parish (pop. 2,255), central Gloucester, England, on Frome R. and 8 mi. SSE of Gloucester; leatherworks and tanneries; woolen milling, fruit packing.

Stonehouse, town and parish (pop. 3,703), N Lanark, Scotland, 6 mi. S of Motherwell; coal mining.

Stoneleigh (stōn'lē), agr. village and parish (pop. 899), central Warwick, England, on Avon R. and 4 mi. S of Coventry; has large deer park, and abbey dating from 11th cent.

Stoneman, Camp, Calif.: see PITTSBURG.

Stone Mountain, city (pop. 1,899), De Kalb co., NW central Ga., 12 mi. ENE of Atlanta; quarrying. Near by is Stone Mtn. (alt. 1,686 ft.), a huge granite dome with Confederate Memorial Monument carved into one side.

Stone Mountains, range (3–4,000 ft.) of the Appalachians along Tenn.-N.C. line, paralleling Iron Mts. (W); from Watuga R. extend c.30 mi. NE to White Top Mtn., Va. Sometimes considered a range of Unaka Mts. Included in Cherokee and Pisgah natl. forests.

Stone Park, village (pop. 1,414), Cook co., NE Ill., W suburb of Chicago. Inc. 1939.

Stones River, central Tenn., formed 9 mi. N of Murfreesboro by confluence of East and West forks; meanders 39 mi. NNW to Cumberland R. 8 mi. E of Nashville. Stones River Natl. Military Park is near the West Fork, 3 mi. NW of Murfreesboro; includes site of Battle of Stones River (Dec. 31, 1862, to Jan. 2, 1863), a major Civil War battle that initiated Federal campaign to trisect Confederacy; Union troops, led by Gen. William Rosecrans, forced retreat of Confederates under Gen. Braxton Bragg and captured Murfreesboro. Stones River Natl. Cemetery (20.1 acres; established 1865) is in park.

Stoneville. **1** Village, Mass.: see AUBURN. **2** Town (pop. 786), Rockingham co., N N.C., 16 mi. NW of Reidsville; tobacco warehouses, cotton mills, furniture factory.

Stonewall, town (pop. 1,071), SE Man., 20 mi. NNW of Winnipeg; dairying; grain. Dolomitic limestone is quarried.

Stonewall, county (□ 927; pop. 3,679), NW central Texas; ⊙ Aspermont. Rolling plains, with hilly areas and mesquite woodlands; drained by Salt and Double Mtn. forks of Brazos R., joining in NE to form the Brazos. Cattle-ranching and farm area, with most of agr. in E (cotton, corn, grain, grain sorghums, dairy products, poultry); some sheep, hogs, goats. Oil wells; some minerals (gypsum, clays, stone, salt, copper). Formed 1876.

Stonewall. **1** Village (pop. 1,015), Clarke co., E Miss., near Chickasawhay R., 17 mi. SSW of Meridian; textiles, clothing. **2** Town (pop. 272), Pamlico co., E N.C., just SE of Bayboro. **3** Town (pop. 634), Pontotoc co., S central Okla., 12 mi. SE of Ada, in agr. area; cotton ginning.

Stonewood, town (pop. 2,066), Harrison co., N W.Va., 2 mi. SE of Clarksburg. Inc. after 1940.

Stoney Creek, village (pop. 1,007), S Ont., 4 mi. ESE of Hamilton; fruit canning, wine making, basket weaving. Scene of battle (1813) bet. Amer. and Br. forces.

Stoneykirk, agr. village and parish (pop. 2,092), W Wigtown, Scotland near Luce Bay, 5 mi. SSE of Stranraer.

Stonington (stō'nĭngtŭn). **1** Town (pop. 11,801), including Stonington borough (pop. 1,739), New London co., SE Conn., on Long Isl. Sound and R.I. line, 10 mi. E of New London; mfg. (textiles, machinery, printing presses, tools), agr., fishing, resorts. Important early fishing and shipping port. Includes villages of MYSTIC, Pawcatuck (pop. 5,269) on Pawcatuck R. opposite Westerly, R.I., and part of Old Mystic (mainly in Groton town). Settled 1649, town inc. 1662, borough inc. 1801. **2** Village (pop. 1,120), Christian co., central Ill., 18 mi. SW of Decatur, in agr. and bituminous-coal-mining area. Inc. 1885. **3** Town (pop. 1,660), Hancock co., S Maine, port on S shore of Deer Isl., in Penobscot Bay; fishing, granite quarrying. Inc. 1897.

Stonington Island (stō'-) (2,500 ft. long, 1,000 ft. wide), Antarctica, off the Fallières Coast of Palmer Peninsula, in Marguerite Bay; 68°12'S 67°3'W. It has been the base for a number of expeditions, notably the U.S. expeditions of 1939–41 and 1947–48.

Stono River, SE S.C., tidal channel SW of Charleston, a part of Intracoastal Waterway; entered from the Atlantic through Stono Inlet, bet. Folly and Kiawah isls.; runs E and N of Johns Isl. Channels join it to Charleston Harbor (E), North Edisto R. (W).

Stony Brook, resort and residential village (1940 pop. 768), Suffolk co., SE N.Y., on N shore of Long Isl., on Stony Brook Harbor (SE arm of Smithtown Bay), 15 mi. E of Huntington; wood products. Restored 1941 to resemble 18th-cent. village.

Stony Creek. **1** Village, Conn.: see BRANFORD. **2** Resort village, Warren co., E N.Y., in the Adirondacks, on a tributary of the Hudson and 16 mi. NW of Glens Falls. Lakes near by. **3** Town (pop. 482), Sussex co., SE Va., 18 mi. S of Petersburg; lumber milling, peanut cleaning.

Stony Creek. **1** In N central Calif., rises in the Coast Ranges NE of Clear L., flows c.80 mi. NE, N, and E, to the Sacramento near Hamilton City; flow is intermittent in lower course. Orland irrigation project is served by reservoirs impounded by Stony Gorge Dam (139 ft. high, 868 ft. long; completed 1928) and East Park Dam (137 ft. high, 249 ft. long; completed 1910). Plans of CENTRAL VALLEY project call for construction of Black Butte Reservoir for additional irrigation. **2** In SW Pa., rises in small branches in the Alleghenies in S Somerset co., flows c.45 mi. N to Conemaugh R. at Johnstown.

Stony Hill, town, St. Andrew parish, E Jamaica, in W foothills of Blue Mts., 8 mi. N of Kingston; dairying. Industrial school and radio station.

Stonyhurst, England: see CLITHEROE.

Stony Island, Jefferson co., N N.Y., in E part of L. Ontario, 8 mi. W of Sackets Harbor village; c.4 mi. long, ½–1 mi. wide.

Stony Lake (10 mi. long, 1–3 mi. wide), Kawartha Lakes, S Ont., 18 mi. NNE of Peterborough; drains S into the St. Lawrence. Clear L. (5 mi. long) is SW arm.

Stony Man, peak (4,010 ft.) of the Blue Ridge, N Va., in Shenandoah Natl. Park, c.14 mi. ENE of Shenandoah.

Stony Middleton, village and parish (pop. 513), N Derby, England, 11 mi. SW of Sheffield; lead mining, shoe mfg.

Stony Mountain, village (pop. estimate 200), SE Man., 14 mi. NNW of Winnipeg; grain; dairying. Site of Manitoba Penitentiary.

Stony Plain, town (pop. 720), central Alta., 20 mi. W of Edmonton, in Cree Indian reservation; grain elevators.

Stony Point. **1** Village (pop. 1,438), Rockland co., SE N.Y., on W bank of the Hudson and 5 mi. SW of Peekskill. Has state orthopedic hosp. for children. Near by is Stony Point Mus. (1936) in battlefield reservation (part of Palisades Interstate Park), commemorating storming of Stony Point by Anthony Wayne's Continental forces in July, 1779. **2** Village (pop. 1,020), Alexander co., W central N.C., 10 mi. NW of Statesville; cotton and woolen mills.

Stony River, village, W Alaska, on Kuskokwim R. at mouth of Stony R. and 65 mi. SE of Flat; outfitting point for trappers and prospectors.

Stony River, stream, W Alaska, rises on W slope of Alaska Range near 61°17'N 153°48'W, flows 170 mi. generally WNW to Kuskokwim R. at Stony River village.

Stony Stratford, England: see WOLVERTON.

Stony Tunguska River (to͞on-go͞o'skŭ), Rus. *Podkamennaya Tunguska* (pŭtkä'myĭnŭ), or **Middle Tunguska River,** Rus. *Srednyaya Tunguska* (sryĕd'nyŭ), in Krasnoyarsk Territory, Russian SFSR, rises on Central Siberian Plateau, 80 mi. NNW of Ust-Kut; flows 975 mi. generally NW, past Baikit, to Yenisei R. at Podkamennaya Tunguska. Navigable below rapids in lower course. Receives Chunya R. (right).

Stoob (shtōp), village (pop. 1,351), Burgenland, E Austria, 12 mi. SSW of Sopron, Hungary; pottery.

Stoppenberg (shtô'pŭnbĕrk), industrial district (since 1929) of ESSEN, W Germany, 2 mi. NE of city center; coal mining.

Stopsley, residential town and parish (pop. 1,474), SE Bedford, England, 2 mi. NNE of Luton.

Stor, lake, Sweden: see STOR LAKE; STORAVAN.

Stora (stôrä'), village (pop. 1,569), Constantine dept., NE Algeria, port on the Gulf of Philippeville of Mediterranean Sea, 3 mi. NW of Philippeville; fish salting, winegrowing. Anc. Roman port.

Stora, village, Sweden: see GULDSMEDSHYTTAN.

Stora, Gulf of, Algeria: see PHILIPPEVILLE, GULF OF.

Stora Barum, Sweden: see VALBERG.

Stora Le Lake (sto͞o'rä lā') (□ 53, including Fox L.), W Sweden, partly in E Norway, 17 mi. E of Halden. Stora Le L. is 30 mi. long (N–S), 1–2 mi. wide. Adjoining Fox L. (N), 8 mi. long, 1–4 mi. wide, is connected SE with Lelang L., through which it drains into L. Vaner.

Stora Lule Lake (sto͞o'rä lü'lù), Swedish *Stora Lulevatten,* expansion (□ 64) of Lule R., Lapland, N Sweden, 25 mi. W of Gallivare; 30 mi. long.

Stora Sjofallet (sto͞o'rä shû'fä"lŭt), Swedish *Stora Sjöfallet* [=great lake falls], waterfalls (131 ft. high; 197 ft. wide) bet. 2 small expansions of upper Lule R., Lapland, N Sweden, 55 mi. WSW of Kiruna. Site of dam. Surrounding region is natl. park.

Storavan (sto͞or'ä"vän), lake, an expansion (□ 66) of Skellefte R., Lapland, N Sweden, 90 mi. WNW of Pitea; 20 mi. long, 1–8 mi. wide. Connects NW with L. Uddjaur.

Storchnest, Poland: see OSIECZNA.

Stord or **Stordoy** (stōr'dü), Nor. *Stordøy,* formerly *Storøy,* island (□ 93; pop. 6,259), Hordaland co., SW Norway, 30 mi. S of Bergen, near mouths of Hardanger and Bjorna fjords; 17 mi. long (N–S), 8 mi. wide. Fishing, lumber milling, agr., mining. S part is in canton of Stord (pop. 5,030), with villages of LITLABO, LEIRVIK, SAGVAG; N part is in canton of FITJAR.

Storden, village (pop. 398), Cottonwood co., SW Minn., 15 mi. NW of Windom; dairy products.

Store (shtô'rĕ), Slovenian *Store,* village, E Slovenia, Yugoslavia, on railroad and 3 mi. E of Celje, in brown-coal area; iron and steel mills. Until 1918, in Styria.

Store Baelt, Denmark: see GREAT BELT.

Store Borgefjell, Norway: see BORGEFJELL.

Storebro (sto͞o'rùbro͞o"), village (pop. 629), Kalmar co., SE Sweden, 5 mi. S of Vimmerby; metal-working.

Store Dimon (stô'rù dē'mōn), Faeroese *Stóra Dimun,* island (□ 1; pop. 12) of the S Faeroe Isls., separated from N Sudero by Sudero Fjord and from S Sando by Dimon Fjord; highest point 1,266 ft.

Store Glacier, Greenland: see QARAJAQ ICE FJORD.

Store Heddinge (stô'rù hĕ'dĭng-ù), city (pop. 2,140), Praesto amt, Zealand, Denmark, 26 mi. S of Copenhagen; limestone quarries, egg-packing plant, furniture mfg.

Store Koldewey, Greenland: see GREAT KOLDEWEY.

Stor-Elvdal, Norway: see KOPPANG.

Storen (stû'rûn) Nor. *Støren,* village (pop. 171; canton pop. 2,357), Sor-Trondelag co., central Norway, on Gaula R. at mouth of Sokna R., and 28 mi. S of Trondheim; junction of railroads from Roros and Lillehammer to Trondheim. Sawmills, tanneries. Animal husbandry and lumbering near by.

Store Nup, Norway: see HAUKELIFJELL.

Store Sotra (stō'rù sō'trä) or **Sotra,** island (□ 68; pop. 5,745) in North Sea, Hordaland co., SW Norway, 8 mi. W of Bergen; 19 mi. long, 5 mi. wide; active fishing. Across a narrow strait (NE) is Lille Sotra isl. (□ 7; pop. 786). Formerly called Sartor or Sartoroy (Nor. *Sartorøy*).

Storey, county (□ 262; pop. 671), W Nev.; ⊙ Virginia City. Bounded N by Truckee R. Site of famous Comstock Lode, at Mt. Davidson. Silver, gold, copper; dairy farms. Formed 1861.

Stor Fjord (stōr), inlet (70 mi. long) of the North Sea, More og Romsdal co., W Norway, extends inland E and S from mouth (protected by several isls.) just S of Alesund. Chief arms are Hjorund Fjord, Nor. *Hjørundfjord* (extends 20 mi. S), and Norddal Fjord (extends 10 mi. E). GEIRANGER FJORD extends E from fjord's SE extremity. Noted for its imposing scenery, Stor Fjord is lined by sheer cliffs. Rockslides are frequent.

Storfors (sto͞or"fôrs', –fôsh'). **1** Village (pop. 486), Norrbotten co., N Sweden, on Pite R., near its mouth on Gulf of Bothnia, just W of Pitea; sawmilling. **2** Village (pop. 2,654), Varmland co., W Sweden, in Bergslag region, at S end of Oster L., Swedish *Östersjön* (ûs'tùr-shûn") (5 mi. long), 13 mi. SSE of Filipstad; iron-, steelworks, tube mill.

Storkow (shtôr'kō), town (pop. 4,738), Brandenburg, E Germany, on small Storkow L. and on Storkow Canal, and 10 mi. SW of Fürstenwalde; shoe and cigar mfg.

Storkow Canal, E Germany, extends 22 mi. E–W bet. Scharmützel L. and Dahme R.; 3 locks; navigable for ships up to 125 tons. Sometimes called Scharmützel Lake–Dahme Canal.

Storkyro, Finland: see ISOKYRÖ.

Stor Lake, Swedish *Storsjön* (sto͞or'shûn") [=great lake]. **1** Lake (□ 176), N central Sweden; 45 mi. long (N-S), 1–10 mi. wide; 285 ft. deep. Ostersund city on W shore. Drained NE by Indal R. Contains Froso isl. **2** Lake (10 mi. long, 1–5 mi. wide), E Sweden. Sandviken city on N shore. Receives Jadra R. (N); drained E by Gavle R.

Storli, Norway: see ALEN.

Storlien (sto͞or'lē"ŭn), village, Jamtland co., NW Sweden, 80 mi. W of Ostersund; frontier station on Norwegian border, E of Hell, on Stockholm-Trondheim main line. Winter-sports center.

Stormarn (shtôr'märn), district of Schleswig-Holstein, NW Germany: see BAD OLDESLOE.

Storm Bay, inlet of Tasman Sea, SE Tasmania, bet. North Bruny isl. (W) and Tasman Peninsula (E); connects (NW) with Derwent R. and D'Entrecasteaux Channel; opens (NE) into Frederick Henry Bay; 16 mi. long, 15 mi. wide, with small isl.

Stormberg (sto͞orm'bĕrkh), mountain range, E Cape Prov., U. of So. Afr., extends 80 mi. bet. Molteno (W) and Indwe (E), W continuation of Drakensberg range; rises to 7,114 on Morgenzon mtn., 10 mi. ENE of Molteno. SE limit of Northern Karroo.

Storm Island, China: see SPRATLY ISLAND.

Storm King, Orange co., SE N.Y., peak (1,355 ft.) near W bank of the Hudson, S of Newburgh and near West Point. Central feature of Storm King section (c.1,000 acres) of Palisades Interstate Park. Storm King Highway around mtn. is noted for fine views.

Storm Lake, city (pop. 6,954), ⊙ Buena Vista co., NW Iowa, on Storm L. (c.4 mi. long), c.65 mi. E of Sioux City; summer resort; meat and poultry packing, vegetable canning. Buena Vista Col. and a state park are here. Inc. 1873.

Storm Mountain (10,372 ft.), on Alta.–B.C. border, in Rocky Mts., on SW edge of Banff Natl. Park, 20 mi. W of Banff; 51°12'N 116°W.

Stormont (stôr'mŭnt), county (□ 412; pop. 40,905), SE Ont., on the St. Lawrence and on N.Y. border; ⊙ Cornwall.

Stormont (stŏr'mŭnt), E suburb of Belfast, N Co. Down, Northern Ireland, 4 mi. E of Belfast; site of Parliament House of Northern Ireland, begun 1928, completed 1932.

Stornara (stôrnä'rä), village (pop. 2,440), Foggia prov., Apulia, S Italy, 7 mi. WNW of Cerignola.

Stornarella (stôrnärĕl'lä), village (pop. 2,377), Foggia prov., Apulia, S Italy, 9 mi. W of Cerignola.

Stornoway (stôr'nùwā), village, S Que., 18 mi. NW of Megantic; dairying, lumbering, pig raising.

Stornoway (stôr'nùwā), burgh (1931 pop. 3,770; 1951 census 4,954), chief town of LEWIS WITH HARRIS isl., Outer Hebrides, Ross and Cromarty, Scotland, on E coast of isl., 38 mi. from the mainland and 60 mi. NW of Ullapool, the nearest mainland port; 58°13'N 6°23'W; port and center of Hebrides herring fisheries, with spinning and woolen mills (Harris tweeds). Modern castle replaces ruins of anc. castle, pulled down 1882. Near by is an airfield.

Storojinet, Ukrainian SSR: see STOROZHINETS.

Storoy, Norway: see STORD.

Storozhevsk (stŭrŭzhĕfsk'), village (1926 pop. 2,045), S Komi Autonomous SSR, Russian SFSR, on Vychegda R., 50 mi. ENE of Syktyvkar; flax.

Storozhinets (stŭrŭzhēnyĕts'), Rum. *Storojineţ* (stôrôzhēnĕts'), Ger. *Storozynetz,* city (1941 pop. 6,610), central Chernovtsy oblast, Ukrainian SSR, in N Bukovina, on Seret R., on railroad and 13 mi. SW of Chernovtsy; agr. center; flour milling, mfg. (leather, soap, alcohol). Probably dates from 14th cent. Passed (1775), with Bukovina, to Austria. While in Rumania (1918–40; 1941–44), it was ⊙ Storojinet dept. (□ 1,024; 1941 pop. 158,199).

Storrington, town and parish (pop. 1,754), central Sussex, England, 8 mi. NNW of Worthing. Church dates from 15th cent.

Stor River, Dan. *Storaa* (stō'rô), W Jutland, Denmark, rises ESE of Herning, flows c.60 mi. NW and W to Nissum Fjord of North Sea 12 mi. W of Holstebro. Sometimes called Holstebro R.

Stör River (shtûr), Schleswig-Holstein, NW Germany, rises 3 mi. WNW of Rickling, flows 50 mi. generally W, past Kellinghusen (head of navigation) and Itzehoe, to Elbe estuary just below Wewelsfleth.

Storrs (stôrz), village in Mansfield town, Tolland co., NE Conn., in agr. area. Seat of Univ. of Conn.

Storsjo (stōr'shû), Nor. *Storsjø,* expansion (□ 20) of Rena R., Hedmark co., E Norway, 35 mi. ENE of Lillehammer; 22 mi. long, 1 mi. wide, 987 ft. deep.

Storsjon, Sweden: see STOR LAKE.

Storsteinnes, Norway: see TROMSDALEN.

Storstrom, Denmark: see SMAALANDSFARVAND.

Stort River, Hertford and Essex, England, rises 8 mi. NNW of Bishop's Stortford, flows 22 mi. S and SW, forming boundary bet. Hertford and Essex, past Bishop's Stortford, to Lea R. just E of Hoddesdon.

Storuman (stōōr'ümän"), village (pop. 862), Vasterbotten co., N Sweden, at SE end of L. Storuma, Swedish *Storuman,* 30-mi.-long expansion of Ume R., 55 mi. WNW of Lycksele; rail junction; lumbering, stock raising, dairying; Lapp market.

Storvik (stōōr'vēk"), town (pop. 1,736), Gavleborg co., E Sweden, on Stor L., 8 mi. WSW of Sandviken; rail junction; metal- and woodworking, pulp milling.

Storvreta (stōōr"vrā'tä), village (pop. 561), Uppsala co., E Sweden, on Fyris R. and 7 mi. NNE of Uppsala; woodworking.

Story, county (□ 568; pop. 44,294), central Iowa; ⊙ Nevada. Prairie agr. area (hogs, cattle, poultry, corn, oats, soybeans) drained by Skunk R. Limestone quarries, sand and gravel pits, bituminous-coal deposits. Formed 1846.

Story, village (pop. c.350), Sheridan co., N Wyo., on branch of Clear Creek, just E of Bighorn Mts., and 16 mi. SSE of Sheridan; alt. 4,960 ft. Summer resort. Just S is reproduction of Fort Phil Kearny, near site of Fetterman Massacre, in which force of U.S. soldiers was wiped out (1866) by Indians.

Story, Fort, Va.: see HENRY, CAPE.

Story City, town (pop. 1,545), Story co., central Iowa, near Skunk R. 11 mi. N of Ames; mfg.: dairy products, butter tubs, cement products. Has pioneer schoolhouse. Inc. 1881.

Stos, Czechoslovakia: see SMOLNIK.

Stössen (shtû'sùn), town (pop. 2,004), in former Prussian Saxony prov., central Germany, after 1945 in Saxony-Anhalt, 7 mi. SSW of Weissenfels, in lignite-mining region.

Stosswihr (stôsvēr'), Ger. *Stossweier* (shtôs'vīûr), village (pop. 746), Haut-Rhin dept., E France, in Munster valley of the high Vosges, 12 mi. WSW of Colmar; cotton weaving, cheese mfg.

Stotesbury. 1 Town (pop. 71), Vernon co., W Mo., on Little Osage R. and 15 mi. NW of Nevada. **2** Village (pop. 1,612, with near-by McAlpin), Raleigh co., S W.Va., 10 mi. SW of Beckley.

Stotfold, town and parish (pop. 3,526), E Bedford, England, on Ivel R. and 5 mi. N of Hitchin; agr. market, with flour mills. Site of large mental hosp., serving 3 counties.

Stotsenburg, Fort (stŏt'sùnbûrg), chief U.S. military establishment in Philippines, in Pampanga prov., central Luzon, near Sapangbato, 50 mi. NW of Manila. Clark Field (U.S. air base) is near by. In U.S.-Philippines pact signed 1947, it was agreed that the U.S. would retain its control here.

Stötteritz (shtû'tùrĭts), SE suburb of Leipzig, Saxony, E central Germany.

Stotternheim (shtô'tùrnhīm), village (pop. 3,660), Thuringia, central Germany, 6 mi. N of Erfurt; spa; salt mines.

Stotts City, city (pop. 285), Lawrence co., SW Mo., in the Ozarks, near Spring R., 21 mi. E of Carthage.

Stottville, village (pop. 1,020), Columbia co., SE N.Y., 4 mi. NE of Hudson; textile milling.

Stouffville (stō'vĭl), village (pop. 1,253), S Ont., 24 mi. NNE of Toronto; dairying, mixed farming.

Stoughton (stou'tùn), village (pop. 334), SE Sask., 40 mi. E of Weyburn; rail junction; grain elevators.

Stoughton, England: see GUILDFORD.

Stoughton (stō'tùn). **1** Town (pop. 11,146), Norfolk co., E Mass., 5 mi. NW of Brockton; shoes, knit goods, elastic webbing, rubber specialties, confectionery, raincoats, shoemakers' supplies. Settled c.1713, inc. 1743. **2** City (pop. 4,833), Dane co., S Wis., on both banks of Yahara R. and 14 mi. SSE of Madison, in dairying and farming area; mfg. (automobile bodies, trailers, clothing, electric heaters and stoves, shoes, condensed milk, foundry products, canned foods); ships tobacco. Settled c.1847, inc. 1882.

Stoura, Greece: see STYRA.

Stourbridge (stour'brĭj, stōōr'–, stōr'–), municipal borough (1931 pop. 19,904; 1951 census 37,247), N Worcester, England, on Stour R. and 12 mi. W of Birmingham; steel-milling, glass-mfg. center (since 16th cent.); mfg. of refractory bricks, leather, machinery and machine tools, electrical equipment, boilers; fire-clay quarrying. In municipal borough are industrial suburbs of Wollaston (NW) and Upper Swinford (S).

Stourport-on-Severn (stour'pôrt-ŏn-sĕ'vùrn, stōōr'–), urban district (1931 pop. 5,949; 1951 census 10,140), N Worcester, England, on Severn R., at mouth of Stour R., 11 mi. N of Worcester; steel, electrical-equipment, carpet, and pharmaceutical industries. Site of important power station. Has 18th-cent. iron bridge over the Severn, 19th-cent. church designed by Sir Gilbert Scott. In urban dist. (N) is residential town of Upper Mitton.

Stour River (stour, stōōr, stōr). **1** In Dorset and Hampshire, England, rises 4 mi. NNW of Gillingham (Dorset), flows 55 mi. SE, past Gillingham, Sturminster Newton, Blandford, and Wimborne Minster, to the Channel at Christchurch, where it joins the Avon. **2** In Kent, England: see GREAT STOUR RIVER. **3** In Suffolk and Essex, England, formed by several headstreams 3 mi. SE of Haverhill, flows 47 mi. E, along Essex-Suffolk border, past Sudbury and Manningtree, to North Sea at Harwich, where it is joined by the Orwell. **4** In Worcester, England, rises near Halesowen, flows 20 mi. W and SW, past Stourbridge and Kidderminster, to Severn R. at Stourport-on-Severn.

Stout. 1 Town (pop. 135), Grundy co., central Iowa, 19 mi. W of Waterloo, in agr. area. **2** Village (pop. 151), Adams co., S Ohio, on the Ohio and 20 mi. WSW of Portsmouth. Also called Rome.

Stoutland, town (pop. 192), Camden co., central Mo., in the Ozarks, 13 mi. NE of Lebanon.

Stoutsville, town (pop. 146), Monroe co., NE central Mo., near Salt R., 9 mi. NE of Paris.

Stovall (stō'vôl, –vŏl), town (pop. 410), Granville co., N N.C., 10 mi. N of Oxford.

Stovepipe Wells, Calif.: see DEATH VALLEY NATIONAL MONUMENT.

Stover, city (pop. 693), Morgan co., central Mo., 9 mi. W of Versailles; agr.; timber.

Stovring (stûv'rĭng), Dan. *Støvring,* town (pop. 1,080), Aalborg amt, N Jutland, Denmark, 10 mi. S of Aalborg; machine shops, dairy products.

Stow (stō), town and parish (pop. 1,279), SE Midlothian, Scotland, on Gala Water and 6 mi. NNW of Galashiels; woolen milling.

Stow. 1 Town (pop. 147), Oxford co., W Maine, 37 mi. WNW of Auburn, partly in White Mtn. Natl. Forest. **2** Town (pop. 1,700), Middlesex co., E central Mass., 18 mi. NE of Worcester; dairying, apples; wooden boxes. Settled 1681, inc. 1683. **3** Resort village, Chautauqua co., extreme W N.Y., on Chautauqua L., 10 mi. NW of Jamestown. **4** Village (1940 pop. 1,507), Summit co., NE Ohio, 6 mi. NE of Akron; metal products, dairy products.

Stow Creek, SW N.J., rises NW of Bridgeton, flows c.20 mi. SW and S, forming part of Cumberland-Salem co. line, to Delaware Bay above mouth of Cohansey Creek.

Stowe, England: see BUCKINGHAM.

Stowe (stō). **1** Urban township (pop. 12,210), Allegheny co., SW Pa., on Ohio R. just NW of McKees Rocks; residential, mfg. of railroad equipment. Includes Pittock village. **2** Village (pop. 2,524), Montgomery co., SE Pa., on Schuylkill R. just W of Pottstown; mfg. (steam fittings, boilers, textiles). **3** Resort town (pop. 1,720), including Stowe village (pop. 556), Lamoille co., N central Vt., 15 mi. NW of Montpelier; winter sports center (ski lifts and trails on Mt. Mansfield, just NW); wood products, dairying. Chartered 1763, settled 1794.

Stowmarket, urban district (1931 pop. 4,297; 1951 census 7,325), central Suffolk, England, on Gipping R. and 12 mi. NW of Ipswich; agr. market; tanneries, chemical and pharmaceutical works. Has 13th-15th-cent. church and 16th-cent. vicarage.

Stow-on-the-Wold (wōld), former urban district (1931 pop. 1,266), E Gloucester, England, 15 mi. E of Cheltenham; agr. market. Formerly an important wool market. Scene (1646) of last important action in Civil War. Has medieval church and mus. with notable paintings.

Stowupland, agr. village and parish (pop. 1,619), central Suffolk, England, 2 mi. NE of Stowmarket.

Stoy, village (pop. 161), Crawford co., SE Ill., 26 mi. NW of Vincennes (Ind.), in oil, natural-gas, and agr. area.

Stoyba, Russian SFSR: see STOIBA.

Stoystown, borough (pop. 517), Somerset co., SW Pa., 9 mi. NE of Somerset and on Stony Creek.

Stozac or **Stozhats** (stô'zhäts), Serbo-Croatian *Stožac,* mountain (7,019 ft.) in Dinaric Alps, central Montenegro, Yugoslavia, bet. upper Zeta and Moraca rivers, 16 mi. E of Niksic.

Stra (strä), town (pop. 528), Venezia prov., Veneto, N Italy, on Brenta R. and 6 mi. E of Padua; shoes, soap. Near by is splendid Villa Nazionale or Pisani (built 1756) encircled by large park.

Strabane (strùbăn'), urban district (1937 pop. 5,600; 1951 census 6,620), NW Co. Tyrone, Northern Ireland, on Mourne R. at confluence with Finn R., here forming Foyle R., 13 mi. SSW of Londonderry; frontier station on Irish border; agr. market (flax, oats, potatoes; cattle); hosiery mfg.; salmon fishing.

Strabane (strùbăn', –bān'), village (pop. 2,861), Washington co., SW Pa., 7 mi. NE of Washington.

Strachan (strôn), agr. village and parish (pop. 546), NW Kincardine, Scotland, 3 mi. SW of Banchory.

Strachur (strùkh-ûr'), fishing village and parish (pop. 507), central Argyll, Scotland, on Loch Fyne, 5 mi. S of Inveraray; resort.

Stradbally (strădbă'lē), Gaelic *Sráidbhaile,* town (pop. 721), E Co. Laoighis, Ireland, 7 mi. W of Athy; agr. market (wheat, barley, potatoes, beets).

Stradbroke (străd'brōōk), town and parish (pop. 903), N Suffolk, England, 7 mi. NNW of Framlingham; agr. market.

Stradbroke Island, Australia: see NORTH STRADBROKE ISLAND.

Stradella (strädĕl'lä), town (pop. 6,529), Pavia prov., Lombardy, N Italy, near Po R., 10 mi. SE of Pavia, in grape-growing region. A major wine market of Lombardy; mfg. (cement, flour, macaroni, leather goods, musical instruments, hardware, plastics, paint).

Straelen (shträ'lùn), town (pop. 7,893), in former Prussian Rhine Prov., W Germany, after 1945 in North Rhine-Westphalia, in the Ruhr, 15 mi. NW of Krefeld, near Dutch border; textile mfg. Has 14th-cent. church.

Strafford, county (□ 377; pop. 51,567), SE N.H., on Maine line; ⊙ Dover. Mfg. (wood products, textiles, shoes, machinery, leather goods, brick), agr. (truck, poultry). Univ. of N.H. at Durham. Drained by Salmon Falls and Cocheco (water power) rivers. Formed 1769.

Strafford. 1 Town (pop. 770), Strafford co., SE N.H., on Bow L. (2 mi. long) and 15 mi. WNW of Dover. **2** Town (pop. 680), Orange co., E Vt., 23 mi. SSE of Barre; copper mines here opened 1793.

Strahan (strôn), town and port (pop. 446), W Tasmania, on NW inlet of Macquarie Harbour and 105 mi. WSW of Launceston; sawmills.

Strahlhorn (shträl'hôrn), peak (13,758 ft.) in Pennine Alps, S Switzerland, 7 mi. E of Zermatt.

Straid, village, SE Co. Antrim, Northern Ireland, 3 mi. E of Ballyclare; bauxite mining.

Straight River. 1 In SE Minn., formed by 2 forks in Steele co., flows 40 mi. N, past Owatonna, to Cannon R. at Faribault. **2** In W central Minn., rises in Straight L. (3 mi. long, .5 mi. wide) in Becker co., flows 20 mi. E and S to Shell R. 5 mi. SSE of Park Rapids. Fish Hook R. is tributary. Fishing resort is on lake.

Straiton, agr. village and parish (pop. 1,080), S Ayrshire, Scotland, on Girvan Water and 6 mi. ESE of Maybole.

Straits Settlements, former Br. crown colony (□ 1,357; 1931 pop. 1,114,015), constituting one of the former subdivisions of Br. Malaya; ⊙ was Singapore. Comprised, at its greatest extent (1907–42) the settlements of SINGAPORE (including CHRISTMAS ISLAND and COCOS ISLANDS), PENANG (including PROVINCE WELLESLEY and the DINDINGS), MALACCA, and LABUAN. A joint administration for the original settlements of Penang, Malacca, and

Singapore on the Strait of Malacca (for which they were named) was first established 1826 by the Br. East India Company. Following dissolution (1858) of the company, the Straits Settlements were briefly under the Indian Government and became a separate crown colony in 1867, joined 1912 by the settlement of Labuan. Its existence was ended by Jap. occupation during Second World War and, in 1946, Singapore was constituted as a separate crown colony, Penang and Malacca were attached to the Union (later Federation) of Malaya, and Labuan to Br. North Borneo.

Strakhilovo (sträkhē'lôvô), village (pop. 3,232), Pleven dist., N Bulgaria, 18 mi. SE of Svishtov; wheat, corn, livestock. Formerly Khibilii.

Strakonice (strä'kônyĭtsĕ), Ger. *Strakonitz* (shträ'kōnĭts), town (pop. 9,608), S Bohemia, Czechoslovakia, on Otava R. and 32 mi. NW of Budweis; rail junction; mfg. of fezzes, felt caps, hosiery, gloves, industrial machinery, motorcycles, arms, carpets; popular summer resort. Gold extraction in vicinity. Has castle of Knights of St. John, and, within castle walls, 13th-cent. church containing precious paintings; another castle has anc. torture tower. Czech poet F. L. Celakovsky b. here. Town founded in 7th-8th cent.

Straldzha (sträljä'), village (pop. 5,348), Yambol dist., E Bulgaria, 13 mi. NE of Yambol; grain, flax, sunflowers.

Stralsund (shträl'zo͝ont, shträlzo͝ont'), city (pop. 50,389), in former Prussian Pomerania prov., N Germany, after 1945 in Mecklenburg, on Bodden strait of the Baltic, 85 mi. NW of Stettin, opposite Rügen isl. (rail and road dam); 54°19'N 13°6'E. Rail center; seaport. Shipbuilding, metalworking, sugar refining, fish processing; mfg. of machinery, food products, jewelry, playing cards. Power station. Heavily bombed in Second World War (destruction about 45%). Founded 1209. Was a leading member of the Hanseatic League; peace treaty (1370) bet. Denmark and the league signed here. In Thirty Years War, Stralsund successfully withstood, with Danish and later Swedish aid, siege (1628) by Wallenstein. Passed to Sweden under Treaty of Westphalia (1648). Taken by French in 1807; went to Denmark in 1814, to Prussia in 1815. Remained fortified until 1872. Captured by Soviet troops in May, 1945.

Stramberk (shträm'bĕrk), Czech *Štramberk*, village (pop. 3,281), S central Silesia, Czechoslovakia, on railroad and 17 mi. SSW of Ostrava; limestone quarrying; cementworks. Has old wooden buildings, 13th-cent. ruins, 18th-cent. baroque church with wooden belfry, paleontological mus.

Strambino (strämbē'nô), village (pop. 2,040), Torino prov., Piedmont, NW Italy, near Dora Baltea R., 6 mi. S of Ivrea; woolen mills.

Strand, canton, Norway: see JORPELAND.

Strand, Sweden: see GUSTAVSBERG.

Strand, town (pop. 8,677), SW Cape Prov., U. of So. Afr., on False Bay 30 mi. SE of Cape Town; popular seaside resort.

Strand, The, street in W central London, England, running parallel with N bank of the Thames from Trafalgar Square (W) to Aldwych (E), continued E by Fleet Street; main artery bet. West End and the City. Here are hotels, theaters, and office bldgs. S, bet. the Strand and the Thames, are the Adelphi and Savoy.

Stranda (strän'tä), county [Icelandic *sýsla*] (pop. 1,945), NW Iceland; ⊙ Holmavik, a fishing village. Covers NE part of Vestfjarda Peninsula, on W shore of Huna Bay. Mountainous. Fishing, agr.

Stranda (strän'nä), village and canton (pop. 2,391), More og Romsdal co., W Norway, port on Stor Fjord, 30 mi. ESE of Alesund; cement, wood products; tourist center. Rebuilt after devastating landslide in 1731. LIABYGDA village is in canton.

Strandburg, town (pop. 144), Grant co., NE S.Dak., 13 mi. SSW of Milbank.

Strandquist, village (pop. 208), Marshall co., NW Minn., 29 mi. NNW of Thief River Falls; dairy products.

Strandvik (strän'vēk, -vĭk), village and canton (pop. 2,345), Hordaland co., SW Norway, on NE shore of Bjorna Fjord, 20 mi. SE of Bergen; fishing and canning center.

Strandzha Mountains, Bulgaria and Turkey: see ISTRANCA MOUNTAINS.

Strang. 1 Village (pop. 100), Fillmore co., SE Nebr., 8 mi. S of Geneva. **2** Town (pop. 201), Mayes co., NE Okla., 12 mi. NE of Pryor, near Neosho R.

Strangeville, town (pop. 626), Orangeburg co., S central S.C.

Strangford (străng'fŭrd), fishing village (district pop. 1,270), E Co., Down, Northern Ireland, on W shore of Strangford Lough, near its mouth on the Irish Sea, 7 mi. ENE of Downpatrick. Near by are remains of several anc. strongholds which formerly guarded entrance to lough.

Strangford Lough (lŏkh'), inlet (17 mi. long, 4 mi. wide) of the Irish Sea, E Co. Down, Northern Ireland. Its narrow entrance (S) is 5 mi. long; lough is separated from the sea (E) by Ards peninsula. There are numerous isls. Chief towns on lough are Portaferry and Killyleagh.

Strangnas (strĕng'nĕs"), Swedish *Strängnäs*, city (pop. 6,010), Sodermanland co., E Sweden, on S shore of L. Malar, 35 mi. W of Stockholm; metal- and woodworking. Seat of Lutheran bishop. Has cathedral (1290); former episcopal palace (1490), where Gustav Vasa was elected king; and present episcopal palace (1650). Dating back to pagan times, city was scene (1080) of St. Eskil's martyrdom. Bishopric created 1129. Suffered (1871) destructive fire.

Stranorlar (strănôr'lŭr), town (pop. 476), S Co. Donegal, Ireland, on Finn R. and 12 mi. W of Lifford, opposite Ballybofey; agr. market (flax, grain).

Stranraer (strŭnrär', străn-), burgh (1931 pop. 6,527; 1951 census 8,622), W Wigtown, Scotland, at head of Loch Ryan, inlet of Irish Sea; 54°55'N 5°0'W; seaport and agr. market; terminal of mail route to Larne, Northern Ireland. Fishing is chief industry. The 16th-cent. castle (now town jail) was occupied 1682 by Bonnie Dundee. Stranraer has been mail port for Ireland since 1849, when it superseded Portpatrick.

Strasbourg (străs'bûrg), town (pop. 459), S central Sask., 45 mi. NNW of Regina, at foot of Last Mtn.; grain elevators, lumbering.

Strasbourg (străs'bûrg, sträz'-, Fr. sträzbo͞or'), Ger. *Strassburg* (shträs'bo͝ork), anc. *Argentoratum*, city (pop. 167,149), ⊙ Bas-Rhin dept., E France, on the Ill, 2 mi. W of the Rhine (Ger. border), and 250 mi. E of Paris, 70 mi. N of Basel; 48°35'N 7°46'E. Economic and cultural center of Alsace, river port, and hub of communications, with rail and road bridges (damaged 1944) across Rhine R. to KEHL (Germany). Chief industries are metalworking (automobiles, rolling stock, household appliances), brewing, tanning, printing, flour and paper milling, woodworking, and food processing (kirsch and quetsch distilling, vegetable and meat preserving, sauerkraut and candy mfg.). Strasbourg is noted for its *pâté de foie gras*. Trade in Alsatian wines, vegetables (especially asparagus), hops (grown in Haguenau area), and tobacco. Commercial activity considerably enhanced by expansion (since 1945) of autonomous port of Strasbourg, (head of Rhine navigation) located just E of city, on isl. bet. the Rhine (E) and a W arm, at junction of Rhone-Rhine Canal (N terminus) and Marne-Rhine Canal (E terminus). Ger. port of KEHL now also under Strasbourg port administration. Port clears iron ore (from Lorraine), coal (from the Ruhr), Alsatian potash, cereals, metal and food products. All parts of the city suffered damage as a result of Second World War bombings. Old section, built on an isl bet. 2 arms of the Ill, contains the cathedral (begun in 1015, completed in 1439), a masterpiece of Rhenish architecture, with a single spire (466 ft. high), and a famous 16th-cent. astronomic clock. The Rohan château (former episcopal palace, now municipal art mus.) was damaged in 1944. Strasbourg has large univ. (founded 16th cent.) and holds a yearly fair (Sept.). Chief suburbs are Schiltgheim, Bischheim, Hoenheim (N), and Illkirch-Graffenstaden (S). An important Roman city of Upper Germany prov., it became episcopal see in 4th cent. Destroyed (455) by Huns, it rose again as *Strateburgum*. Here, in 842, Charles the Bald and Louis the German solemnized their alliance against their brother, Lothair I, by Oath of Strasbourg. After long rule by its bishops, Strasbourg became a free imperial city in 13th cent., and a center of medieval Ger. literary activity. Here Gutenberg may have invented the printing press. City accepted Reformation and, in 1608, joined Protestant Union. Seized (1681) by Louis XIV, it was confirmed in Fr. possession by Treaty of Ryswick (1697) and subsequently was fortified by Vauban. It embraced French Revolution and increasingly adopted Fr. customs and speech. Severely bombarded by Prussians in 1870, it passed to Germany by Treaty of Frankfurt (1871). Recovered by France in 1919; reincorporated into Germany (1940); liberated by Allies (Nov., 1944). Generals Kléber and Kellermann, painter Gustave Doré, and Oberlin b. here. In 1792 Rouget de Lisle composed the *Marseillaise* here for the army of the Rhine. Goethe studied at univ., his name being associated with many places in Strasbourg area.

Strasburg (shträs'bo͝ork), town (pop. 6,994), Brandenburg, E Germany, 14 mi. NNW of Prenzlau; rail junction; sugar refining; agr. market (sugar beets, grain, tobacco, stock). Has 13th-cent. church.

Strasburg, Poland: see BRODNICA.

Strasburg. 1 (străs'bûrg) Village (pop. c.250), Arapahoe co., N central Colo., 35 mi. E of Denver; alt. 5,576 ft. Grain, dairy and poultry products, beans. **2** (sträs'bûrg) Village (pop. 436), Shelby co., central Ill., 15 mi. SW of Mattoon, in agr. and bituminous-coal area. **3** (străs'bûrg) Town (pop. 180), Cass co., W Mo., 12 mi. NE of Harrisonville. **4** (străs'bûrg) City (pop. 733), Emmons co., S N.Dak., 10 mi. S of Linton. **5** (străs'bûrg, strôz'-) Village (pop. 1,366), Tuscarawas co., E Ohio, 8 mi. NNW of New Philadelphia, and on small Sugar Creek, in coal-mining area; firebrick, lumber. Settled 1810. **6** (străs'bûrg) Residential borough (pop. 1,109), Lancaster co., SE Pa., 7 mi. SE of Lancaster; tobacco packing; fishing tackle; agr. Settled c.1733, inc. 1816. **7** (străs'bûrg) Town (pop. 2,022), Shenandoah co., NW Va., on North Fork of Shenandoah R. and 17 mi. SSW of Winchester. Shipping, processing center in agr., limestone, timber area; mfg. of viscose rayon; apple juice, packed poultry; ships fluxing stone, lumber. Crystal Caverns (just N) attract tourists. Hupp's Fort (c.1755) and Harmony Hall or Fort Bowman (c.1755) are near by. At Fishers Hill (c.2 mi. S) Union troops won a Civil War engagement, Sept. 22, 1864. Founded c.1761.

Straschnitz, Czechoslovakia: see STRAZNICE.

Strasheny (strŭshĕ'nē), Rum. *Straşeni* (sträshĕn'), village (1941 pop. 5,157), central Moldavian SSR, on Byk R., on railroad and 13 mi. NW of Kishinev, in winegrowing dist.

Strassburg (shträs'bo͝ork), town (pop. 3,157), Carinthia, S Austria, on Gurk R. and 19 mi. N of Klagenfurt; mineral springs.

Strassburg, France: see STRASBOURG.

Strassen (shträ'sŭn), town (pop. 1,283), S Luxembourg, 3 mi. W of Luxembourg city; mfg. of railroad equipment; chalk quarrying.

Strasshof or **Strasshof an der Nordbahn** (shträs'hōf, än dĕr nôrt'bän), town (pop. 2,662), E Lower Austria, 14 mi. NE of Vienna; vineyards, corn.

Strasswalchen (shträs'välkhŭn), town (pop. 4,167), Salzburg, W central Austria, 16 mi. NE of Salzburg; brewery, tannery.

Strata Florida, agr. village in Caron Uwch Clawdd (kä'rŭn ūkh' kloudh') parish (pop. 376), E central Cardigan, Wales, on Teifi R. and 14 mi. SE of Aberystwyth; site of remains of Strata Florida Abbey, Cistercian monastery probably founded in 11th or 12th cent. Near by are lead mines.

Stratfield Mortimer, agr. village and parish (pop. 1,395), S Berkshire, England, 6 mi. SSW of Reading.

Stratford, city (pop. 17,038), ⊙ Perth co., S Ont., on Avon R., tributary of Thames R., and 80 mi. WSW of Toronto; locomotive repair shops, woolen and knitting mills; mfg. of furniture, leather and rubber products, felt shoes, clothing, agr. machinery, cigars, food products.

Stratford, borough (pop. 3,854), ⊙ Stratford co. (□ 419; pop. 4,751), W N.Isl., New Zealand, 22 mi. SSE of New Plymouth; rail junction; dairies, sheep and cattle ranches.

Stratford. 1 Town (pop. 33,428), Fairfield co., SW Conn., on Long Isl. Sound, at mouth of Housatonic R., just E of Bridgeport; mfg. (chemicals, asbestos, metal and asphalt products, hardware, tools, boats, machinery); resort; seafood, truck. Has early 18th-cent. houses. Settled 1639. **2** Town (pop. 673), on Hamilton-Webster co. line, central Iowa, near Des Moines R., 14 mi. N of Boone; livestock, grain. **3** Town (pop. 973), Coos co., NW N.H., on the Connecticut and 12 mi. N of Lancaster; wood products. Includes North Stratford village. Settled 1772. **4** Borough (pop. 1,356), Camden co., SW N.J., 10 mi. SE of Camden, in fruitgrowing region. Founded 1890, inc. 1925. **5** Town (pop. 1,065), Garvin co., S central Okla., 16 mi. W of Ada, in strawberry-producing area; cotton ginning, feed milling; oil wells. **6** Town (pop. 164), Brown co., NE S.Dak., 13 mi. SE of Aberdeen, near James R. **7** Town (pop. 1,385), ⊙ Sherman co., extreme N Texas, in high plains of the Panhandle, 32 mi. NE of Dalhart; ships grain, cattle. **8** Village (pop. 982), Marathon co., central Wis., 25 mi. SW of Wausau; dairy products, canned peas, cement blocks.

Stratford, historic estate of Lee family, in Westmoreland co., E Va., on the Potomac and 35 mi. ESE of Fredericksburg. A natl. shrine (dedicated 1935), it preserves Stratford Hall, built 1729–30 by Thomas Lee. Birthplace of Richard Henry Lee, Francis Lightfoot Lee, and Robert E. Lee; "Light Horse Harry" Lee lived here.

Stratford le Bow, London, England: see Bow.

Stratford-on-Avon or **Stratford-upon-Avon** (ā'vŭn, ă'-), municipal borough (1931 pop. 11,605; 1951 census 14,980), S Warwick, England, on right bank of the Avon (crossed by arched 16th-cent. bridge) and 21 mi. SSE of Birmingham; agr. market with some light metal and chemical industries, it is famed for its connection with Shakespeare. Has many bldgs. associated with the poet. A room in a gabled building on Henly Street is shown as the poet's birthplace. The site of the home he purchased in 1597 is marked, the building having been torn down by a local vicar in 1759; to this "New Place" Shakespeare retired in 1610, and here he died 6 years later. His grave is beside that of his wife, Anne Hathaway (whose cottage, in Shottery, 1 mi. W of Stratford, is preserved as natl. property), in the fine old Church of the Holy Trinity. This church, built partly in 14th cent., is said to be on the site of a 7th-cent. monastery, probably Stratford's earliest building; it has also a bust and memorial to the poet, and a stained-glass window (given by Americans) depicting Shakespeare's "seven ages of man." The town's principal memorial was a theater, built in late 19th cent. and thereafter the scene of annual Shakespeare festivals. In 1926 fire destroyed the theater, but the attached gall., library, and mus. were saved, and in 1932 a new theater was dedicated. Most of the various structures and places connected with the life of

Shakespeare were acquired by the nation in 19th cent. The grammar school of Edward VI, which Shakespeare may have attended, is also now natl. property.

Strathalbyn (străth-ôl'bĭn), town (pop. 1,201), SE South Australia, 30 mi. SE of Adelaide; center of poultry-raising area; hogs.

Stratham (stră'tŭm), town (pop. 759), Rockingham co., SE N.H., on Squamscott R. and 9 mi. WSW of Portsmouth; agr.

Strathaven (strā'vŭn, stră'thăvŭn), town in Avondale parish (pop. 5,529), W central Lanark, Scotland, on Avon Water and 7 mi. S of Hamilton; agr. market and textile-milling center, with breweries. Has remains of 15th-cent. Avondale Castle. Near by is DRUMCLOG.

Strathblane (străthblān'), town and parish (pop. 1,161), S Stirling, Scotland, 3 mi. N of Milngavie; resort; also has textile-printing works.

Strathbogie (străth-bō'gē, strŭth-), district in NW Aberdeen, Scotland, extending c.15 mi. E-W bet. upper courses of Deveron and Ythan rivers; chief town, Huntly.

Strathclair (străthklâr'), village (pop. estimate 250), SW Man., 45 mi. NW of Brandon; grain, stock.

Strathclyde and Cumbria (străth"klīd', kŭm'brēŭ), early medieval British kingdom in territory now in S Scotland and N England. One of the 4 great British units after the Anglo-Saxon invasion. Remained independent into 9th cent. and was fought over by Scots and English later. Principal towns were Dumbarton and Carlisle.

Strathcona, town, Alta.: see EDMONTON.

Strathcona (străth-kō'nŭ), village (pop. 143), Roseau co., NW Minn., 30 mi. N of Thief River Falls; grain, potatoes.

Strathcona Provincial Park (străth-kō'nŭ) (□ 828), SW B.C., on central Vancouver Isl., 20 mi. W of Courtenay; 40 mi. long, 11-36 mi. wide. Heavily forested, mountainous area, with many streams. Game sanctuary; stream and lake fishing; gold mining along rivers. Contains Golden Hinde mtn. (7,219 ft.) and other peaks over 5,000 ft. Includes S part of Buttle L.

Strathdon (străth'dŭn), agr. village and parish (pop. 809), W Aberdeen, Scotland, on Don R. and 11 mi. N of Ballater. Near by are ruins of 16th-cent. Colquhonnie Castle. Strathdon is scene of annual Lonach Gathering.

Strathearn, Scotland: see EARN RIVER.

Strathfield, municipality (pop. 15,751), E New South Wales, Australia, 10 mi. W of Sydney; rail junction; coal-mining center. Since 1947, includes HOMEBUSH.

Strathmiglo (strŭth-mĭ'glō), agr. village and parish (pop. 1,561), NW Fifeshire, Scotland, on Eden R. and 10 mi. WSW of Cupar. Village of Gateside, 3 mi. WSW, makes yarn bobbins.

Strathmoor Gardens (străth'-), town (pop. 329), Jefferson co., NW Ky., suburb of Louisville.

Strathmoor Manor, town (pop. 422), Jefferson co., N Ky., suburb of Louisville.

Strathmoor Village, town (pop. 466), Jefferson co., NW Ky., suburb of Louisville.

Strathmore (străth'-), town (pop. 603), S Alta., 30 mi. E of Calgary; railroad town, center of Canadian Pacific RR irrigation system, and site of C.P.R. supply farm.

Strathmore (străth-môr'), the "great valley" of Scotland, a plain extending c.100 mi. NE-SW across Scotland bet. Ardmore, Dumbarton (SW), and the North Sea bet. Stonehaven and Inverbervie, Kincardine (NE); flanked by the Grampians (N) and Lennox, Ochil, and Sidlaw hills (S). It is noted for scenic beauty and fertile soil.

Strathmore (străth'môr", străth"môr'), village (pop. c.500), Tulare co., S central Calif., at E side of San Joaquin Valley, bet. Lindsay and Porterville; packs citrus fruit, olives.

Strathpeffer (strŭth-pĕ'fŭr), resort town in Fodderty parish, SE Ross and Cromarty, Scotland, at foot of Ben Wyvis, 4 mi. W of Dingwall. Has noted medicinal springs. Just N is village of Achterneed, with 17th-cent. castle of countess of Cromartie.

Strathroy (străthroi'), town (pop. 3,016), S Ont., on Sydenham R. and 20 mi. W of London; fruit canning, woolen milling, woodworking, dairying, container mfg.

Strathspey, Scotland: see SPEY RIVER.

Strathy (stră'thē), agr. village, NE Sutherland, Scotland, on Strathy Bay, 17 mi. W of Thurso, at foot of Strathy Point promontory (58°37'N 4°1'W).

Stratonike or **Stratoniki** (both: strätônē'kē), village (pop. 1,401), Chalcidice nome, Macedonia, Greece, 20 mi. NE of Polygyros; iron pyrite mining. Formerly called Isvoron.

Strattanville, borough (pop. 562), Clarion co., W central Pa., 3 mi. E of Clarion.

Stratton, England: see BUDE-STRATTON.

Stratton. **1** Town (pop. 720), Kit Carson co., E Colo., 18 mi. W of Burlington; alt. 4,404 ft.; livestock, grain, poultry. **2** Village, Maine: see EUSTIS. **3** Village (1940 pop. 127), Newton co., E central Miss., 27 mi. WNW of Meridian. **4** Village (pop. 628), Hitchcock co., S Nebr., 32 mi. W of McCook and on Republican R., near Kansas line; farm implements; dairy and poultry produce, grain. **5** Village (pop. 467), Jefferson co., E Ohio, on Ohio R. and 11 mi. N of Steubenville; clay products. **6** Town (pop. 54), Windham co., SE Vt., in Green Mtn. Natl. Forest, 23 mi. NW of Brattleboro. Stratton Mtn. (3,859 ft.) is here.

Stratton and Bude, England: see BUDE-STRATTON.

Stratton-on-the-Fosse, agr. village and parish (pop. 341), NE Somerset, England, 3 mi. W of Radstock. Site of Downside Abbey, a Benedictine monastery and col. Has 14th-15th-cent. church.

Stratton Saint Margaret, residential town and parish (pop. 4,365), NE Wiltshire, England, 2 mi. NE of Swindon. Has 15th-cent. church.

Stratus (strā'tŭs), chief city of anc. Acarnania, W central Greece, on Achelous R. and 6 mi. NW of modern Agrinion. Site is marked by ruins and modern Gr. village of Stratos (pop. 642), formerly called Sorovigli.

Straubing (shtrou'bĭng), city (1950 pop. 36,314), Lower Bavaria, Germany, on the Danube and 24 mi. SE of Regensburg; 48°53'N 12°34'E. Airport; rail junction. Mfg. of machinery, precision instruments, textiles; printing, brewing. Truck farming (vegetables). Trades in grain, cattle, and horses. Has Romanesque church, Gothic church and city hall, 14th-cent. tower. Developed on site of Roman camp; chartered c.1307. Was ⊙ duchy of Bavaria-Straubing (1353-1425).

Straughn, town (pop. 345), Henry co., E Ind., 10 mi. SSE of New Castle, in agr. area.

Straumen (strou'mŭn), village (pop. 333) in Inderoy (Nor. *Inderøy*) canton (pop. 3,181), Nord-Trondelag co., central Norway, on Trondheim Fjord, 9 mi. N of Levanger; lumbering, cattle raising; limekiln. Formerly Strommen. At Kjerknesvagen (chărk'-năsvôgŭn) (Nor. *Kjerknesvågen*, formerly *Kirknesvåg*) village, 4 mi. NW, are sawmills, box factory.

Straumgjerde (stroum'yărdŭ), village in Sykkylven canton, More og Romsdal co., W Norway, on W shore of Sykkylven Fjord (a branch of Stor Fjord), 17 mi. SE of Alesund; furniture mfg.

Straumnes (strû'ümnĕs"), cape, NW extremity of Iceland, on Denmark Strait, at NW end of Vestfjarda Peninsula; 66°26'N 23°8'W. Lighthouse.

Strausberg (shtrous'bĕrk), town (pop. 9,716), Brandenburg, E Germany, on small Strausberg L., 20 mi. E of Berlin; market gardening. Racecourse. Has 13th-cent. church.

Strausstown (strous'toun), borough (pop. 368), Berks co., E central Pa., 17 mi. NW of Reading.

Strawberry, Calif.: see STRAWBERRY LAKE.

Strawberry Hill, residential district in Twickenham, S Middlesex, England, on the Thames, in S part of borough. It is named for 1747 mansion of Horace Walpole, who had private printing press here.

Strawberry Island, islet (1939 pop. 27), SE Alaska, in Glacier Bay, 12 mi. NW of Gustavus; 58°31'N 136°W; fishing.

Strawberry Lake, E Calif., resort lake (c.1 mi. long) in the Sierra Nevada, c.75 mi. ENE of Stockton. Pinecrest (summer and winter resort) is on lake; Strawberry (winter sports) is 2 mi. W.

Strawberry Mountain (9,052 ft.), E central Oregon, 10 mi. S of Prairie City, in Strawberry Mts., part of Blue Mts.

Strawberry Plains, village (pop. c.400), Jefferson co., E Tenn., on Holston R. and 14 mi. ENE of Knoxville; trade center for agr., zinc-mining region; limestone quarry.

Strawberry Point, town (pop. 1,247), Clayton co., NE Iowa, 45 mi. WNW of Dubuque; large creamery; poultry packing, feed milling. Inc. 1887. Near by is Backbone State Park, largest in the state, with a trout hatchery on Maquoketa R.

Strawberry River. **1** In N Ark., rises near Salem in Fulton co., flows c.125 mi. SE to Black R. 10 mi. N of Tuckerman. Flood-control dam on lower course. **2** In NE Utah, rises in Wasatch Range near Heber, flows c.70 mi. E to Duchesne R. near Duchesne. Strawberry Dam (77 ft. high, 488 ft. long; completed 1913) is near source of river, 30 mi. E of Provo. Water from Strawberry Reservoir is diverted to Spanish Fork and used in irrigation of 50,000 acres in Utah co.

Straw Island, islet of the Aran Isls., off SW Co. Galway, Ireland, in Galway Bay, 2 mi. E of Kilronan; lighthouse (53°7'N 9°39'W).

Strawn. **1** Village (pop. 173), Livingston co., E central Ill., 19 mi. SE of Pontiac, in agr. and bituminous-coal area. **2** City (pop. 922), Palo Pinto co., N central Texas, 22 mi. SW of Mineral Wells, in coal, oil, natural-gas, agr., ranching region.

Strazhitsa (strä'zhĭtsä), village (pop. 4,625), Gorna Oryakhovitsa dist., N Bulgaria, on headstream of Bregovitsa R. and 16 mi. NE of Gorna Oryakhovitsa; flour milling; stock, truck. Formerly Kadakoi.

Straznice (sträzh'nyĭtsĕ), Czech *Strážnice*, Ger. *Straschnitz* (shträsh'nĭts), town (pop. 4,989), S Moravia, Czechoslovakia, on railroad and 28 mi. SSW of Gottwaldov; soap mfg., wine and pottery making, farming. Its regional fairs, costumes, dance and song festivals are popular tourist attractions. Town was originally erected as a border fort to oppose Magyar incursions into Moravia.

Strba (shtŭr'bä), Slovak *Štrba*, Hung. *Csorba* (chôr'bŏ), village (pop. 2,047), N Slovakia, Czechoslovakia, on S slope of the High Tatra, 35 mi. E of Ruzomberok; mtn. rail junction (alt. 3,000 ft.); tourist center. Lucivna sanatorium (alt. 2,611 ft.) for the tubercular is 3 mi. E.

Strba Lake, Slovak *Štrbské Pleso*, Hung. *Csorbató* (chôr'bŏtō), lake (50 acres; 67 ft. deep) in N Slovakia, Czechoslovakia, on S slope of the High Tatra, on watershed bet. Vah and Poprad rivers, 12 mi. NW of Poprad; alt. 4,430 ft. Leading resort area with summer and winter-sports facilities. Part of commune of Vysoke Tatry.

Streaky Bay, village and port (pop. 546), S South Australia on NW Eyre Peninsula, 165 mi. NW of Port Lincoln and on S shore of Streaky Bay of Great Australian Bight; exports livestock.

Streaky Bay, inlet of Great Australian Bight, S South Australia, NW Eyre Peninsula; just below Smoky Bay; 17 mi. long, 16 mi. wide.

Streatham (strĕ'tŭm), residential district in Wandsworth, London, England, S of the Thames, 5 mi. S of Charing Cross. It is mentioned in *Domesday Book*, and it was site of Thrale Place, often visited by Samuel Johnson. Considerable damage was caused by air bombs (1940-41 and 1944); St. Leonard's Church (partly 14th cent.) was seriously damaged.

Streator (strē'tŭr), city (pop. 16,469), La Salle-Livingston co. line, N Ill., on Vermilion R. (bridged here) and c.50 mi. NE of Peoria; trade, industrial, and railroad center in agr. and mineral area (bituminous coal, shale, sand); mfg. of brick, tile, pipes, glass, dairy and farm machinery, truck bodies, iron castings; railroad shops. Corn, wheat, oats, livestock, dairy products, poultry. Laid out 1868, inc. 1882.

Strecno (strĕch'nô), Slovak *Strečno*, Hung. *Sztrecsény* (strĕ'chānyŭ), village (pop. 1,092), N Slovakia, Czechoslovakia, in the Lesser Fatra, on Vah R., on railroad and 6 mi. ESE of Zilina; asphalt quarrying. Its castle, now in ruins, was formerly of great strategic importance.

Street, urban district (1931 pop. 4,453; 1951 census 5,300), central Somerset, England, 2 mi. SW of Glastonbury; tanning, mfg. of shoes and other leather products; stone quarrying; agr. market in dairying region. Remains of prehistoric animals have been excavated here.

Streeter, village (pop. 602), Stutsman co., S central N.Dak., 35 mi. SW of Jamestown.

Streetman, town (pop. 419), on Freestone-Navarro co. line, E central Texas, 17 mi. SE of Corsicana, in cotton, truck area.

Street Mountain (4,216 ft.), Essex co., NE N.Y., in the Adirondacks, 8 mi. NW of Mt. Marcy and 6 mi. SSW of Lake Placid village.

Streetsville, village (pop. 709) S Ont., 16 mi. WSW of Toronto; flour milling, woodworking; mfg. of pumps, pickles.

Strefa, Greece: see PYLAIA.

Strehaia (strĕkhä'yä), town (1948 pop. 7,776), Gorj prov., SW Rumania, on railroad and 27 mi. E of Turnu-Severin; trade in grain, livestock, fruit; flour milling, mfg. of tiles. Has old monastery, restored in 17th cent.

Strehla (shtrā'lä), town (pop. 5,260), Saxony, E central Germany, on the Elbe and 4 mi. NW of Riesa; chemical mfg., woodworking. Has late-Gothic church, 15th-cent. castle.

Strehlen, Poland: see STRZELIN.

Strekov (stŭrzhĕ'kôf, Czech *Střekov*, Ger. *Schreckenstein* (shrĕ'kŭnshtīn), town (pop. 9,073), NW Bohemia, Czechoslovakia, on Elbe R., on railroad and 10 mi. E of Teplice, in urban area of Usti nad Labem; mfg. of edible fats. Site of major dam and hydroelectrical plant.

Strelcha (strĕl'chä), village (pop. 5,346), Plovdiv dist., W central Bulgaria, in central Sredna Gora, 6 mi. E of Panagyurishte; health resort; livestock, rye, fruit.

Streletskoye (stryĭlyĕt'skŭyŭ), village (1926 pop. 6,623), N central Kursk oblast, Russian SFSR, E suburb of Kursk; truck.

Strelitsa (-lyē'tsŭ), town (1947 pop. over 500), W Voronezh oblast, Russian SFSR, near Latnaya, W of Voronezh.

Strelitz (shtrā'lĭts), suburb of Neustrelitz, N Germany, 3 mi. SE of city center. Until destruction (1712) by fire of their palace, it was ⊙ and residence of grand dukes of Mecklenburg-Strelitz. New ⊙ founded (1733) at Neustrelitz.

Strelka (stryĕl'kŭ). **1** Village (1948 pop. over 500), SE Evenki Natl. Okrug, Krasnoyarsk Territory, Russian SFSR, on Chunya R. and 180 mi. SSE of Tura; trading point. **2** Village (1948 pop. over 500), S Krasnoyarsk Territory, Russian SFSR, on Yenisei R., at mouth of Angara R., and 140 mi. N of Krasnoyarsk. **3** Village, Molotov oblast, Russian SFSR: see KRASNOKAMSK.

Strelki (stryĭlkē'), Pol. *Strzyki*, village (1939 pop. over 500), W Drogobych oblast, Ukrainian SSR, on the Dniester and 24 mi. W of Drogobych; logging; rye, oats, sheep.

Strelno, Poland: see STRZELNO.

Strema (strĕ'mä), village (pop. 3,647), Plovdiv dist., S central Bulgaria, 11 mi. NE of Plovdiv; wheat, rye, rice, fruit, truck. Formerly Ine-bekchi.

Strema River, central Bulgaria, rises in central Balkan Mts. just NE of Koznitsa Pass, flows ESE, past Klisura, and generally S, through Karlovo and Plovdiv basins, to Maritsa R. 10 mi. E of Plovdiv;

71 mi. long. Separates central Sredna Gora and Sirnena Gora (E part of Sredna Gora).

Strenci or **Strenchi** (strĕn'chē), Lettish *Strenči*, Ger. *Stackeln*, city (pop. 1,763), NE Latvia, in Vidzeme, on Gauja R. and 11 mi. NE of Valmiera; flax and wool processing; flour mill.

Strengelbach (shtrĕng'ulbäkh), town (pop. 2,111), Aargau canton, N Switzerland, on Wigger R. and 5 mi. S of Olten; knit goods, woolen and cotton textiles; woodworking.

Strensall (strĕn'sôl), agr. village (pop. 824), North Riding, E central Yorkshire, England, on Fosse R. and 6 mi. NNE of York; leather tanning. Site of military camp.

Strepha, Greece: see PYLAIA.

Strépy (strāpē'), town, Hainaut prov., S Belgium, on Haine R. and 8 mi. E of Mons; coal mining. Town of Bracquegnies (bräkůnyē') is just N. Pop. of both towns, 9,123.

Stresa (strā'zä), village (pop. 2,074), Novara prov., Piedmont, N Italy, port on W shore of Lago Maggiore, 3 mi. S of Pallanza; boatbuilding, furniture mfg.; resort. Excursions to Monte Mottarone (W). In church of Rosminian Col. lies tomb of Antonio Rosmini-Serbati, who founded R.C. Inst. of Charity (Congregation of Rosminians) in 1828. Conference of Stresa held (1935) on Isola Bella in nearby BORROMEAN ISLANDS. Until 1947, also called Stresa Borromeo.

Streshin (stryĕ'shĭn), town (1926 pop. 2,679), W Gomel oblast, Belorussian SSR, on Dnieper R. and 13 mi. S of Zhlobin; food products.

Stretford, residential municipal borough (1931 pop. 56,791; 1951 census 61,532), SE Lancashire, England, on Bridgewater Canal and 4 mi. SW of Manchester; mfg. of chemicals and concrete; barge building.

Stretto, Yugoslavia: see MURTER ISLAND.

Streymoy, Faeroe Isls.: see STROMO.

Strezova, Greece: see DAPHNE.

Strib (strĭb), town (pop. 1,359) and port, Odense amt, Denmark, on N Fyn isl. and 26 mi. NW of Odense, on the Little Belt; leather tanning, machinery mfg.

Striberg (strē'bĕr"yů), village (pop. 495), Orebro co., S central Sweden, 5 mi. NW of Nora; iron-mining center.

Stribro (stûrzhē'brô), Czech *Stříbro*, Ger. *Mies* (mēs), town (pop. 3,950), W Bohemia, Czechoslovakia, on Mze R., on railroad and 17 mi. W of Pilsen; mfg. of furniture, glass products, carpets. Lead and zinc mining; formerly silver mining.

Strichen (strĭkh'ŭn), town and parish (pop. 2,024), N Aberdeen, Scotland, on Ugie R. and 8 mi. SSW of Fraserburgh; agr. market. Mormond Hill (769 ft.) here has figures of a white horse and stag cut into its side.

Strickland Ketel, parish (pop. 947), S Westmorland, England. Includes village of Burneside (bûr'nĭsīd, bûrn'sīd), 2 mi. NNW of Kendal; sheep grazing. Has 14th-cent. mansion.

Striegau, Poland: see STRZEGOM.

Strigno (strē'nyô), village (pop. 1,062), Trento prov., Trentino-Alto Adige, N Italy, 19 mi. E of Trent, in Valsugana.

Strigonium, Hungary: see ESZTERGOM.

Strijen (strī'ůn), village (pop. 2,460), South Holland prov., SW Netherlands, on Beijerland isl. and 7 mi. SW of Dordrecht; flax growing. Sometimes spelled Stryen.

Strimon River, Greece: see STRUMA RIVER.

Strinda (strĭn'nä), canton (pop. 25,171), Sor-Trondelag co., central Norway, just SE of Trondheim, along Strinda Fjord (inlet of Trondheim Fjord); gardening; mfg. of roofing materials. Industries at Lade (NW) and Ranheim (NE). Formerly spelled Strinden.

Stringtown, town (pop. 499), Atoka co., SE Okla., 7 mi. NNE of Atoka, in farm area.

Stripa, Sweden: see GULDSMEDSHYTTAN.

Strivali, Greece: see STROPHADES.

Strizhi (strē'zhē), town (1943 pop. over 500), central Kirov oblast, Russian SFSR, on railroad and 17 mi. WSW of Kirov; peat works.

Strizivojna-Vrpolje (strē'zhĭvoinä-vûr'pôlyĕ), Serbo-Croatian *Striživojna-Vrpolje*, village, N Croatia, Yugoslavia, 6 mi. S of Dakovo, in Slavonia; rail junction.

Strnisce (stûr'nĭshchĕ), Slovenian *Strnišče*, village, NE Slovenia, Yugoslavia, 4 mi. W of Ptuj, in brown-coal area; aluminum industry. Until 1918, in Styria.

Ströbeck (shtrû'bĕk), village (pop. 1,797), in former Prussian Saxony prov., central Germany, after 1945 in Saxony-Anhalt, 5 mi. WNW of Halberstadt. Inhabitants have for centuries been noted for their chess-playing skill.

Strobel Lake (□ 46; alt. 2,346 ft.), W central Santa Cruz natl. territory, Argentina, in Patagonia, 25 mi. N of L. Cardiel; c.12 mi. long, 5 mi. wide.

Ströbitz (shtrû'bĭts), village (pop. 5,306), Brandenburg, E Germany, in Lower Lusatia, just W of Cottbus.

Strobl (shtrōbl), town (pop. 2,287), Salzburg, W central Austria, on Sankt Wolfgangsee, in the Salzkammergut, 6 mi. W of Bad Ischl; health resort (alt. 1,781 ft.).

Strofadhes, Greece: see STROPHADES.

Strogonov Bay, Japan: see ISHIKARI BAY.

Strokestown, Gaelic *Béal Átha na mBuillí*, town (pop. 617), NE Co. Roscommon, Ireland, 11 mi. NNE of Roscommon; agr. market (cattle, sheep; flax, potatoes).

Strom (strûm), Swedish *Ström*, village (pop. 641), Gavleborg co., E Sweden, on Gulf of Bothnia, 12 mi. NE of Hudiksvall; sulphite works.

Stroma (strō'mů), island (pop. 193) in Pentland Firth, NE Caithness, Scotland, 4 mi. NW of Duncansbay Head; 2 mi. long, 1 mi. wide; rises to 167 ft. At N extremity is Langaton Point, site of lighthouse (58°42'N 3°7'W).

Stromberg (shtrôm'bĕrk), town (pop. 1,584), in former Prussian Rhine Prov., W Germany, after 1945 in Rhineland-Palatinate, 5 mi. WSW of Bingen; wine. Has ruined 12th-cent. castle.

Stromboli (strôm'bôlē), anc. *Strongyle*, island (□ 4.7; pop. 1,193), northernmost of Lipari Isls., in Tyrrhenian Sea off NE Sicily, 39 mi. N of Milazzo; 38°47'N 15°13'E. Is 3 mi. long, 2.5 mi. wide, with active volcano rising to 3,038 ft. Exports malmsey wine, capers. Noted since antiquity for volcanic activity, Stromboli is one of few European volcanoes constantly active. Serious eruptions rare; last occurred in 1921.

Strome, village (pop. 233), S central Alta., 35 mi. SE of Camrose; mixed farming, wheat.

Strome Ferry, village, SW Ross and Cromarty, Scotland, on S shore of Loch Carron, 8 mi. NE of Kyle; terminal of car ferry to N shore of loch.

Stromfors, Sweden: see BOLIDEN.

Stromm, Canton, Norway: see SVELVIK.

Strommen (strûm'mŭn). **1** Nor. *Strømmen*, village (pop. 5,519) in Skedsmo canton (pop. 8,632), Akershus co., SE Norway, 9 mi. E of Oslo; mfg. of railroad cars, ships' propellers, furniture; automobile assembly. **2** Village, Nord-Trondelag co., Norway: see STRAUMEN.

Stromnas, Sweden: see LUNDE.

Stromness (strŏm"nĕs'), burgh (1931 pop. 1,592; 1951 census 1,503), on SW coast of Pomona isl., Orkneys, Scotland, on inlet of Hoy Sound, 12 mi. W of Kirkwall; 58°57'N 3°16'W; port and fishing center, summer hq. of Scottish herring fleet. Main industries: shipbuilding, mfg. of herring barrels.

Stromo (strû'mû), Dan. *Strømø*, Faeroese *Streymoy*, largest island (□ 144; pop. 7,865) of the Faeroe Isls.; bounded E by Sundene strait and Nolso Fjord, S by Skopen Fjord, W by Hesto Fjord, Vaago Fjord, and Vestmansund; c.30 mi. long, 9 mi. wide. Terrain is rocky and mountainous; highest point c.2,590 ft. On SE coast is town of THORSHAVN, ⊙ Faeroes. Fishing, whaling, sheep raising.

Stromsburg, city (pop. 1,231), Polk co., E central Nebr., 50 mi. NW of Lincoln and on Big Blue R., near Platte R.; farm trade center in prairie region; grain, livestock, poultry. Settled 1872, inc. 1883.

Stromsdal, Finland: see JUANKOSKI.

Stromsholm (strûms"hôlm'), Swedish *Strömsholm*, residential village (pop. 812), Vastmanland co., central Sweden, at W end of L. Malar, at mouth of Kolback R., 10 mi. E of Koping; S terminus of Stromsholm Canal. Site of cavalry depot and riding school. Has 17th-cent. castle.

Stromsholm Canal, Sweden: see KOLBACK RIVER.

Stromsnasbruk (strûms"nĕsbrük'), Swedish *Strömsnäsbruk*, village (pop. 1,366), Kronoberg co., S Sweden, on Laga R. and 25 mi. E of Laholm; paper milling; sulphite works.

Stromso, Norway: see DRAMMEN.

Stromstad (strûm'städ"), Swedish *Strömstad*, city (pop. 3,069), Goteborg och Bohus co., SW Sweden, on the Skaggerak, 90 mi. NNW of Goteborg, near Norwegian border; port; food canning, stone quarrying, sawmilling. Seaside resort, with mud baths. Chartered 1666; fortified by Charles XII. Suffered heavily in Danish-Swedish wars.

Stromsund (strûm"sŭnd'), Swedish *Strömsund*, village (pop. 1,134), Jamtland co., N central Sweden, on expansion of Vangel R., Swedish *Vängelälven* (vĕng'ŭlĕl"vŭn), tributary of Angerman R., and 50 mi. NE of Ostersund; stone and talc quarrying and processing; tourist resort.

Strone, resort village, N central Inverness, Scotland, on W bank of Loss Ness, at mouth of Enrick R., 14 mi. SW of Inverness. Just E are remains of Urquhart Castle, dating from time of Edward I.

Strong. 1 Town (pop. 839), Union co., S Ark., 19 mi. ESE of El Dorado, near La. line; cotton, lumber. **2** City, Kansas: see STRONG CITY. **3** Agr. town (pop. 1,036), Franklin co., W Maine, 10 mi. N of Farmington and on Sandy R.; wood products. Maine's Republican party organized here in 1854. Settled 1784, inc. 1801.

Strong City. 1 City (pop. 680), Chase co., E central Kansas, on Cottonwood R. and 19 mi. W of Emporia; livestock, grain. Formerly Strong. **2** Town (pop. 107), Roger Mills co., W Okla., 5 mi. NE of Cheyenne, and on Washita R., in agr. area.

Stronghurst, village (pop. 741), Henderson co., W Ill., 12 mi. ESE of Burlington, Iowa; corn, livestock, dairy products.

Strongoli (strông'gôlē), town (pop. 4,568), Catanzaro prov., Calabria, S Italy, near Gulf of Taranto, 14 mi. NNW of Crotone. Sulphur mines near by. Occupies site of anc. *Petelia*.

Strong River, central Miss., rises in S Scott co., flows c.75 mi. SW to Pearl R. just SE of Georgetown.

Strongs, village (pop. c.250), Chippewa co., E Upper Peninsula, Mich., 31 mi. SW of Sault Ste. Marie, in Marquette Natl. Forest; hardwood timber, pulpwood.

Strongsville, village (pop. 3,504), Cuyahoga co., N Ohio, 15 mi. SSW of downtown Cleveland; dairy, meat, and grain products. Inc. 1927.

Strongyle, Sicily: see STROMBOLI.

Stronsay (strŏn'sā), island (□ 13.6, including surrounding small isls.; pop. 953) of the Orkneys, Scotland, 12 mi. NE of Kirkwall on Pomona isl.; 7 mi. long, 5 mi. wide. Chief village, Rothiesholm (SW). Just off N coast of Stronsay is islet of Holm of Huip, 1 mi. long.

Strontian (strŏntē'ůn), village, N Argyll, Scotland, near head of Loch Sunart, 20 mi. WSW of Fort William; lead mining. Village gives its name to the element strontium, 1st discovered here.

Strood, England: see ROCHESTER.

Stroombeek-Bever (strōm'bāk-bā'vůr), residential town (pop. 5,336), Brabant prov., central Belgium, N suburb of Brussels; market gardening, dairying, brewing.

Strophades or **Strofadhes** (strŏ'fůdēz, Gr. strôfä'-dhēs), Ital. *Strivali* (strēvä'lē), islets (□ 0.3; pop. 11) in Ionian Sea, Greece, in Zante nome, 28 mi. SSE of Zante isl., 37°16'N 20°59'E. Site of monastery. Sometimes called Stamphanes.

Stropkov (strôp'kôf), Hung. *Sztropkó* (strôp'kō), town (pop. 2,506), NE Slovakia, Czechoslovakia, on Ondava R. and 24 mi. NE of Presov, in agr. area; potatoes.

Stroppiana (strôp-pyä'nä), village (pop. 1,801), Vercelli prov., Piedmont, N Italy, 7 mi. S of Vercelli.

Stroud (stroud), village (pop. 686), E New South Wales, Australia, 37 mi. NNE of Newcastle; dairy products, hardwood.

Stroud, urban district (1931 pop. 8,364; 1951 census 15,977), central Gloucester, England, on Frome R. and 7 mi. S of Gloucester; mfg. of woolens, carpets, plastics. Town is noted for red dyes. Has art col. and mus. In urban dist. (N) is town of Uplands (pop. 1,386).

Stroud. 1 Town (pop. 79), Chambers co., E Ala., 12 mi. NNE of Lafayette. **2** City (pop. 2,450), Lincoln co., central Okla., c.45 mi. SW of Tulsa, in agr. and oil-producing area; mfg. of petroleum products, cottonseed and dairy products, frozen foods, concrete; cotton ginning. Inc. 1898.

Stroudsburg, resort borough (pop. 6,361), ⊙ Monroe co., E Pa., 21 mi. NE of Easton, in Pocono Mts. region; textiles, metal products; agr. Settled 1738, inc. 1815.

Stroudwater River, SW Maine, rises in N York co., flows 12 mi. generally NE to Fore R. above Portland.

Strovitsi, Greece: see LEPREUM.

Strovolos (strô'vôlôs), S suburb (pop. 3,252) of Nicosia, central Cyprus, in agr. region (wine, olives; sheep, cattle). Commercial airfield of Nicosia is 2 mi. W.

Struble (strōō'bůl), town (pop. 91), Plymouth co., NW Iowa, 7 mi. N of Le Mars.

Struer (strōō'ůr), city (pop. 6,754) and port, Ringkobing amt, W Jutland, Denmark, on Lim Fjord and 30 mi. NNE of Ringkobing; meat and fish packing, mfg. (machinery, bicycles), brewing, shipbuilding.

Struga (strōō'gä), village (pop. 5,243), Macedonia, Yugoslavia, near Albania border, on L. Ochrida, at efflux of the Black Drin, 70 mi. SSW of Skoplje; narrow-gauge rail spur terminus; fish-trading center. Pop. predominantly Moslem. Has mus. of L. Ochrida, old Turkish-style houses with large, luxuriant gardens. It was once very prosperous under Turkish rule.

Strugi Krasnye or **Strugi Krasnyye** (strōō'gē krä'-snēū), town (1948 pop. over 2,000), NE Pskov oblast, Russian SFSR, 40 mi. SW of Luga; metalworking, dairying.

Strum, village (pop. 542), Trempealeau co., W Wis., on Buffalo R. and 18 mi. SSE of Eau Claire, in dairy, poultry, and grain area; butter, cheese.

Struma River (strōō'mů), Gr. *Strymon* or *Strimon* (strī'mŭn, Gr. strēmôn'), Turkish *Kara-Su*, W Bulgaria and Greece, rises in Vitosha Mts. at S foot of the Cherni-vrakh; flows 215 mi. SSE, through fertile agr. dist. (Mediterranean crops), past Pernik, Radomir, and Gorna Dzhumaya, to Strymonic Gulf of Aegean Sea 30 mi. WSW of Kavalla (Greece). Receives Dzherman, Rila, Angistes (left), and Strumica (Bulg. *Strumeshnitsa*; right) rivers. Valley is direct route from Sofia to Aegean Sea. In connection with canalization (1930s) of lower course, L. ACHINOS was drained and L. KERKINITIS filled as a natural flood reservoir.

Strumble Head, Wales: see FISHGUARD.

Strumen River or **Strumen' River**, Belorussian SFSR: see PRIPET RIVER.

Strumica or **Strumitsa** (both: strōō'mĭtsä), Turkish *Üstrumça* or *Ustrumdja*, anc. *Astracum*, town (pop. 10,649), Macedonia, Yugoslavia, in Strumica R. valley, 70 mi. SE of Skoplje; trade center for agr. region (figs, tobacco, poppies, rice, cotton); cattle; silkworms. Once called Tiberiopolis, after Roman emperor Tiberius, who built a castle here. In Bulgaria, 1913–19.

Strumica River or **Strumitsa River,** Bulg. *Strumeshnitsa,* Yugoslavia and Bulgaria, rises in Yugoslavia on SW slope of the Plackovica, 11 mi. S of Kocane; flows SE, past Radovis, bet. Ograzden and Belasica mts., and E, into Bulgaria, to Struma R. 6 mi. NE of Petrich; c.65 mi. long. Its fertile valley produces cotton, rice, and poppies. Also called Radovis R. or Radovish R., Serbo-Croatian *Radoviška Reka,* in upper course and Stara Reka in middle course.

Strumien (stro͞o′myĕnyů), Pol. *Strumień,* Ger. *Schwarzwasser* (shvärts′vä″sůr), town (pop. 1,557), Katowice prov., S Poland, on the Vistula and 26 mi. SSW of Katowice; tile mfg.

Strunino (stro͞onyĭnô′), city (1938 pop. 15,200), NW Vladimir oblast, Russian SFSR, 6 mi. WSW of Aleksandrov; cottonmilling; food processing.

Strusov (stro͞o′sůf), Pol. *Strusów* (stro͞o′so͞of), village (1931 pop. 2,560), central Ternopol oblast, Ukrainian SSR, on Seret R. and 5 mi. NW of Terebovlya, in deciduous woodland; flour milling, distilling, brickmaking, lumbering; horse raising. Has old palace.

Strusshamn, Norway: see ASKOY.

Struthers (strŭ′dhůrz), city (pop. 11,941), Mahoning co., E Ohio, on Mahoning R., just SE of Youngstown; steel mills. Inc. as city in 1922.

Strvyazh River (stůrvyäsh′), Pol. *Strwiąż* (stůrvyōzh′), in SE Poland and W Ukrainian SSR, rises SE of Nizhniye Dolne in East Beskids, flows NNW past Nizhniye Dolne, and ENE past Khyrov, to Dniester R. SSW of Rudki; length, 60 mi.

Stry or **Stryy,** river, Ukrainian SSR: see STRY RIVER.

Stry or **Stryy** (strē), Pol. *Stryj* (strē), city (1931 pop. 30,682), E Drogobych oblast, Ukrainian SSR, on Stry R. and 16 mi. ESE of Drogobych; rail junction, airport; mfg. center in petroleum and natural-gas dist.; iron casting, mfg. of machinery, drilling tools, furniture, matches, textiles, dyes, candles, soap; sawmilling, petroleum refining, agr. processing (hides, cereals), fish canning. Technical schools. Scene of defeat (1664) of Turks by Russians. Passed from Poland to Austria (1772); scene of Russo-German battles during First World War; reverted to Poland (1919); ceded to USSR in 1945.

Strydpoort Mountains (strāt′po͝ort), N central Transvaal, U. of So. Afr., extend c.80 mi. ENE-WSW near N end of Drakensberg range, ESE of Pietersburg; rise to 6,974 ft. on Iron Crown.

Stryen, Netherlands: see STRIJEN.

Stryj, Ukrainian SSR: see STRY; STRY RIVER.

Stryker, village (pop. 1,026), Williams co., extreme NW Ohio, on Tiffin R. and 7 mi. ENE of Bryan; corn, wheat, hay; mfg. of ceramics.

Strykow (strĭ′ko͞of), Pol. *Stryków,* Rus. *Strykov* (strē′kůf), town (pop. 2,603), Lodz prov., central Poland, 12 mi. NNE of Lodz; tanning, brick mfg., flour milling.

Strymon, river, Bulgaria and Greece: see STRUMA RIVER.

Strymonic Gulf (strĭmŏ′nĭk), inlet of N Aegean Sea in Greek Macedonia, on E side of Chalcidice peninsula; 14 mi. wide, 17 mi. long. Receives Struma (Strymon) R. on N shore and outlet of L. Volve (W). In a wider sense, it is applied to the entire section of the Aegean Sea bet. isl. of Thasos and Acte (Athos) arm of Chalcidice peninsula. In anc. times, Stagira and Amphipolis were on its shores. Also called Gulf of Orphane (Orfani) for small village on N shore; also Rendina and Contessa.

Strymon River, Bulgaria and Greece: see STRUMA RIVER.

Stryn Lake (strün), Nor. *Strynsvatn,* lake (□ 9) in a fissure of the glacier Jostedalsbre, Sogn og Fjordane co., W Norway, on Stryn R., emptying into Nord Fjord, 65 mi. ENE of Floro; 9 mi. long, 1-2 mi. wide, 650 ft. deep. Tourist and skiing center.

Strypa River (strĭ′pŭ), Ternopol oblast, Ukrainian SSR, rises N of Zborov in Volyn-Podolian Upland, flows 93 mi. S, past Zborov and Buchach, to Dniester R. 5 mi. SE of Zolotoi Potok.

Stry River or **Stryy River** (strē), Pol. *Stryj,* in Drogobych oblast, Ukrainian SSR, rises in the Beshchady section of the Carpathians, 8 mi. SW of Slavsko, flows NW past Turka, E and NE past Stry and Zhidachov, to Dniester R. 2 mi. NE of Zhidachov; 137 mi. long.

Strzegom (stchĕ′gôm), Ger. *Striegau* (shtrē′gou), town (1939 pop. 15,918; 1946 pop. 7,137) in Lower Silesia, after 1945 in Wroclaw prov., SW Poland, 10 mi. NW of Schweidnitz (Swidnica); cotton milling, granite and kaolin quarrying, agr.-machinery mfg., metalworking, malt processing. Has late-Gothic church. Poet Günther b. here.

Strzelce (stchĕl′tsĕ), Ger. *Gross Strehlitz* (grōs″ shtrā′lĭts), town (1939 pop. 11,523; 1946 pop. 8,429) in Upper Silesia, after 1945 in Opole prov., S Poland, 20 mi. SE of Oppeln (Opole); mfg. of machinery, chemicals; lime processing.

Strzelce Krajenskie (kräyĕ′nyůskyĕ), Pol. *Strzelce Krajeńskie,* Ger. *Friedeberg in Neumark* (frē′dŭbĕrk ĭn noi′märk), town (1939 pop. 5,918; 1946 pop. 1,552) in Pomerania, after 1945 in Zielona Gora prov., W Poland, 16 mi. NE of Landsberg (Gorzow Wielkopolski), in lake region; sawmilling, brick mfg. Has 13th-cent. town walls. Founded c.1220. In Second World War, c.60% destroyed.

Strzelin (stchĕ′lēn), Ger. *Strehlen* (shtrā′lůn), town (1939 pop. 12,337; 1946 pop. 7,334) in Lower Silesia, after 1945 in Wroclaw prov., SW Poland, on Olawa R. and 25 mi. S of Breslau (Wroclaw); sugar refining, food canning, granite and kaolin quarrying. Heavily damaged in Second World War.

Strzeliska Nowe, Ukrainian SSR: see NOVYE STRELISHCHE.

Strzelno (stchĕl′nô), Ger. *Strelno* (shtrĕl′nō), town (pop. 5,264), Bydgoszcz prov., central Poland, 12 mi. SSW of Inowroclaw; mfg. of cement, machines; flour-and sawmilling, distilling; trades in cattle, grain.

Strzylki, Ukrainian SSR: see STRELKI.

Strzyzow (stchĭ′zho͞of), Pol. *Strzyżów,* town (pop. 2,834), Rzeszow prov., SE Poland, on Wislok R. and 14 mi. SW of Rzeszow; brewing, distilling, sawmilling, mfg. of cement products.

Stuart, Australia: see ALICE SPRINGS.

Stuart. 1 City (pop. 2,912), ⊙ Martin co., SE Fla., 18 mi. S of Fort Pierce, and on St. Lucie R. (bridged here), near E terminus of St. Lucie Canal; resort; shark-fishing and -processing center. **2** City (pop. 1,500), on Adair-Guthrie co. line, SW Iowa, 37 mi. W of Des Moines; grain, stock, and dairy farming; creamery. Has annual stock show (Aug.). Founded 1869, inc. 1877. **3** Village (pop. 785), Holt co., N Nebr., 27 mi. WNW of O'Neill and on Elkhorn R.; dairying; grain, livestock, poultry. **4** Town (pop. 303), Hughes co., central Okla., 19 mi. W of McAlester; cotton ginning. **5** Town (pop. 849), ⊙ Patrick co., S Va., on Mayo R. and 22 mi. W of Martinsville, in foothills of the Blue Ridge; trade center in agr. and timber area; makes knit goods, canned foods; lumber milling.

Stuart Channel, SW B.C., W arm of Strait of Georgia, separating Vancouver Isl. (W) from Gulf Isls. (E); 30 mi. long, 1–3 mi. wide. Chemanius and Ladysmith are on W shore. Saanich Inlet extends S from S end of channel.

Stuart Lake (□ 138), central B.C., 70 mi. NW of Prince George; 48 mi. long, 1–6 mi. wide. Drained E by Stuart R. and Nechako R. into Fraser R. At E extremity of lake is Fort St. James.

Stuarts Range, central South Australia, in arid region, 130 mi. W of L. Eyre; c.100 mi. long (NW-SE); rises to 2,000 ft. Site of town of Coober Pedy and opal fields.

Stubachtal (shto͞o′bäkhtäl), valley in Salzburg, W central Austria, on N slope of the Hohe Tauern, NNW of the Grossglockner; 7 mi. long. Small emerald deposits; hydroelectric station.

Stubai Alps or **Stubay Alps** (both: shto͞o′bī), in Tyrol, W Austria, a NE group of the Ötztal Alps; bordered by Inn R. (N), Ötztal (W), and Wipptal (E). Highest peak, Zuckerhütl (11,519 ft.). The Stubai Valley, Ger. *Stubaital,* descends (NE) from mts. 20 mi. to the Wipptal just S of Innsbruck; Fulpmes, largest town.

Stubbekobing (sto͞o′bůkûbĭng), Dan. *Stubbekøbing,* city (pop. 2,112) and port, Maribo amt, Denmark, on Falster isl. and 11 mi. NE of Nykobing, on Gronsund strait; brewing, machinery mfg. Formerly spelled Stubbekjobing.

Stubbenkammer (shto͞o′bůnkä″můr), cape, N Germany, on NE Rügen isl., on the Baltic, 4 mi. N of Sassnitz; sheer chalk bluff rising 400 ft.

Stubbins, town in Ramsbottom urban dist., SE Lancashire, England, 5 mi. N of Bolton; cotton milling.

Stuben (shto͞o′bůn), village, Vorarlberg, W Austria, on W slope of the Arlberg, 16 mi. E of Bludenz; ski center (alt. 4,370 ft.).

Stubnianske Teplice, Czechoslovakia: see TURCIANSKE TEPLICE.

Studenica or **Studenitsa** (both: sto͞o′dĕnĭtsä), monastery, S central Serbia, Yugoslavia, 17 mi. SW of Rankovicevo town; church built in 1183.

Studenka (sto͞o′dän-kä), Czech *Studénka,* Ger. *Stauding* (shtou′dĭng), village (pop. 2,729), NE Moravia, Czechoslovakia, 12 mi. SW of Ostrava; mfg. of railway cars.

Studenki, Belorussian SSR: see BORISOV.

Studland, agr. village and parish (pop. 455), SE Dorset, England, on E coast of Isle of Purbeck, 2 mi. N of Swanage; seaside resort. Has Norman church built on Saxon foundations.

Studley, town and parish (pop. 3,072), W Warwick, England, 3 mi. SE of Redditch; aluminum and electrical industries. Has 13th-cent. church; horticultural col. in 19th-cent. castle.

Stuhleck, peak, Austria: see FISCHBACH ALPS.

Stühlingen (shtü′lĭng-ůn), village (pop. 1,320), S Baden, Germany, in Black Forest, on the Wutach and 9 mi. WNW of Schaffhausen (connected by tramway), on Swiss border; cotton mfg. Summer resort.

Stuhlweissenburg, county, Hungary: see FEJER.

Stuhlweissenburg, city, Hungary: see SZEKESFEHERVAR.

Stuhm, Poland: see SZTUM.

Stump Lake, in Nelson co., E central N.Dak.; 10 mi. long. U.S. game reserve here.

Stung [Cambodian,=river]. For Cambodian names beginning thus and not found here, see under following part of the name.

Stungtreng (sto͝ong′trĕng′), town (1936 pop. c.3,000), ⊙ Stungtreng prov. (□ 7,300; 1948 pop. 40,034), NE Cambodia, on left bank of Mekong R. at confluence with the Se Khong, and 145 mi. NNE of Pnompenh; timber-trading center; big-game hunting. Precious stones (sapphires), alabaster, quartz, gold. Pop. is largely Lao.

Stupino (sto͞o′pēnů), city (pop. over 10,000), S Moscow oblast, Russian SFSR, near Oka R., 60 mi. SSE of Moscow; metallurgical plant, mfg. of electric locomotives, lumber; food processing. Developed in 1930s; called (c.1935–38) Elektrovoz.

Stupki, Ukrainian SSR: see MALO-ILINOVKA.

Stuppach (shto͝op′äkh), village (pop. 660), N Württemberg, Germany, after 1945 in Württemberg-Baden, 3 mi. SSW of Mergentheim; grain. Parish church houses noted *Madonna of Stuppach* by Grünewald.

Stura, Greece: see STYRA.

Stura di Demonte River (sto͞o′rä dē dĕmôn′tĕ), NW Italy, rises on SE slope of Maddalena Pass, flows 65 mi. NE, past Demonte, Cuneo, and Fossano, to Tanaro R. near Cherasco.

Sturbridge (stûr′–), agr. town (pop. 2,805), Worcester co., S Mass., on Quinebaug R. and 18 mi. SW of Worcester. Settled c.1730, inc. 1738. Includes village of Fiskdale.

Sturge Island (stûrj), Antarctica, largest (27 naut. mi. long, 8 naut. mi. wide) of Balleny Isls., in the Pacific off Victoria Land; 67°24′S 164°15′E. Discovered 1839 by John Balleny, Br. explorer.

Sturgeon (stûr′jůn). **1** Town (pop. 544), Boone co., central Mo., 8 mi. W of Centralia; agr.; chemical mfg. **2** Village (pop. 1,375, with adjacent Noblestown), Allegheny co., W Pa., 12 mi. WSW of downtown Pittsburgh.

Sturgeon Bay, city (pop. 7,054), ⊙ Door co., NE Wis., on Door Peninsula, port at head of Sturgeon Bay (small inlet of Green Bay), at W end of ship canal cutting across the peninsula and connecting Green Bay with L. Michigan; cherry-growing and resort center. Shipyards, dairy plants, fruit canneries; fisheries; limestone quarries. A state fish hatchery, an agr. experiment station, and Potawatomi State Park are near by. Inc. 1883.

Sturgeon Falls, town (pop. 4,567), E central Ont., on Sturgeon R., near its mouth on L. Nipissing, and 22 mi. W of North Bay; pulp- and lumber-milling center; garnet grinding, woodworking.

Sturgeon Falls, waterfalls (46 ft. high), NE Ont., on Mattagami R. and 25 mi. NNW of Timmins; hydroelectric power.

Sturgeon Lake. 1 Lake (□ 110), NW Ont., 50 mi. E of Sioux Lookout; 38 mi. long, 5 mi. wide. **2** Lake (□ 18), S Ont., in Kawartha lake region, 4 mi. N of Lindsay; 12 mi. long, 2 mi. wide. Drained E by Trent Canal.

Sturgeon Lake, resort village (pop. 189), Pine co., E Minn., on branch of Kettle R., near small lake, and c.45 mi. SW of Duluth in grain, potato, livestock area.

Sturgeon Point, village (pop. 16), S Ont., on Sturgeon L., 8 mi. N of Lindsay; resort.

Sturgeon River, SE central Ont., rises NE of Sudbury, flows 110 mi. SE, past Sturgeon Falls, to L. Nipissing 4 mi. SW of Sturgeon Falls.

Sturgeon River. 1 In NW Upper Peninsula, Mich., rises in SE Baraga co., flows WNW into Houghton co., then N to Portage L. c.7 mi. SE of Houghton; c.75 mi. long. **2** In N Mich., rises NE of Gaylord in Otsego co., flows N c.30 mi., past Wolverine, and through a state park to Burt L., near Indian River village; fishing.

Sturgis (stûr′jĭs), village (pop. 364), E Sask., on Assiniboine R. and 50 mi. N of Yorkton; mixed farming.

Sturgis. 1 City (pop. 2,222), Union co., W Ky., near Tradewater R., 30 mi. SW of Henderson; mining center in bituminous-coal and agr. (livestock, grain) area; makes clothing, concrete products; flour and feed mills; airport. **2** City (pop. 7,786), St. Joseph co., SW Mich., 35 mi. SSE of Kalamazoo, near Ind. line; mfg. (storage tanks, plumbing supplies, shears, furniture, Venetian blinds, curtain rods, paper products, bandages, chemicals, paint). Settled 1827; inc. as village 1855, as city 1895. **3** Town (pop. 402), Oktibbeha co., E Miss., 16 mi. WSW of Starkville. **4** City (pop. 3,471), ⊙ Meade co., W S.Dak., 25 mi. NNW of Rapid City and on branch of Belle Fourche R., at E edge of Black Hills. Business center for mining and farming region; timber; flour, dairy products, livestock, grain. Laid out near Fort Meade, an army post, after its establishment in 1878.

Sturminster Newton, town and parish (pop. 1,708), N Dorset, England, on Stour R. and 7 mi. SW of Shaftesbury; agr. market in dairying region. William Barnes b. here.

Sturovo (shto͞o′rôvô), Slovak *Štúrovo,* town (pop. 4,082) S Slovakia, Czechoslovakia, on left bank of Danube R. opposite Esztergom, Hungary, and 27 mi. E of Komarno; rail junction; river port noted for lumber and fruit export. Until 1949, known as Parkan, Slovak *Parkán,* Hung. *Párkány.*

Sturry, town and parish (pop. 2,291), NE Kent, England, on Great Stour R. and 3 mi. NE of Canterbury; coal mining. Has Norman church with 15th-cent. tower.

Sturt Bay, inlet of Investigator Strait, S Yorke Peninsula, South Australia; 17 mi. E-W, 5 mi. N-S.

Sturtevant, village (pop. 1,176), Racine co., SE Wis.,

5 mi. W of Racine, in truck-farming region; railroad shipping point.

Sturt Point, SE Victoria Isl., S Franklin Dist., Northwest Territories, on Queen Maud Gulf; 68°51'N 103°6'W.

Stutsman, county (□ 2,274; pop. 24,158), central N.Dak.; ⊙ Jamestown. Agr. area drained by James R. Dairying, farming; livestock, poultry, wheat, flax. Formed 1873.

Stutterheim (stŭ'tŭrhĭm"), town (pop. 6,503), SE Cape Prov., U. of So. Afr., at foot of Amatola Range, 40 mi. NW of East London; agr. (sheep, wool) and lumbering center; health resort.

Stuttgart (stŭt'gärt, Ger. shtŏŏt'gärt), city (□ 86; 1939 pop. 496,490; 1946 pop. 413,528; 1950 pop. 481,845), N Württemberg, Germany, after 1945 ⊙ Württemberg-Baden, on the Neckar and 95 mi. SSE of Frankfurt, 120 mi. WNW of Munich; 48°47'N 9°11'E. Rail hub strategically located on natural route connecting N Germany and Rhine valley with the Danube; airport (at Echterdingen, 6 mi. S); a seat of Ger. publishing (connected with flourishing paper industry); diversified industrial center (mfg. concentrated mainly at suburbs of Bad Cannstatt, Feuerbach, Untertürkheim, and Zuffenhausen). Major products: vehicles, all types of machinery; iron, steel, and other metal goods; construction supplies. Also precision and optical instruments (photographic equipment, radios, sound- and silent-film projectors). Mfg. of chemicals increased in post-war years, while textile mfg. declined considerably. Leather- (trunks, shoes) and woodworking (furniture, Venetian blinds, cabinets for radios, office equipment). Tourist center with frequent industrial fairs; suburbs Bad Cannstatt, Berg, and Degerloch are visited as resorts. Protestant bishopric. Site of technological institute (bldg. heavily damaged) with numerous research divisions, agr. col. (at suburb of Hohenheim), acad. of fine arts, conservatory. Chartered in 13th cent., Stuttgart became residence of counts of Württemberg in 1320; was capital of state, 1482–1945. Rapid development in 16th cent. was followed by decline during Thirty Years War and the invasions of Louis XIV. Because of its rapid expansion in 19th and 20th cent. (present area was reached after incorporation of numerous suburbs in 1942), Stuttgart, except for its core, is situated along slopes of surrounding hills. Thus, the industrial suburbs, with exception of Bad Cannstatt, escaped major damage in Second World War, while the city center, where most notable bldgs. are located, suffered almost complete destruction. Destroyed were: 2 of the 3 medieval churches; the Akademie, until 1794 the seat of the Karlsschule, where Schiller studied medicine. Heavily damaged were 14th–16th-cent. old castle, 18th-cent. new castle; 19th-cent. State Library, State Industrial Mus., Mus. of Art, and State Archive (housing Mus. of Natural History); 20th-cent. city hall, and noted main railroad station. Captured by Fr. troops in April, 1945; later in U.S. zone of occupation.

Stuttgart (stŭt'gärt, -gŭrt), city (pop. 7,276), a ⊙ Arkansas co., E central Ark., 33 mi. NE of Pine Bluff; trade center for rich rice-growing area, which also produces cotton, soybeans, feed crops, livestock; lumber, rice, and feed mills. State univ. has a rice experiment station near by. Duck, quail hunting. Inc. 1889.

Stützerbach (shtü'tsŭrbäkh), village (pop. 3,211), in former Prussian Saxony prov. exclave, central Germany, after 1945 in Thuringia, in Thuringian Forest, on Ilm R. and 5 mi. SW of Ilmenau; glass.

Stuvsta (stüv'stä"), residential village (pop. 4,836), Stockholm co., E Sweden, 6 mi. SW of Stockholm city center.

Stuyvesant (stī'vŭsŭnt), village (1940 pop. 660), Columbia co., SE N.Y., on E bank of the Hudson and 9 mi. N of Hudson.

Stuyvesant Heights, SE N.Y., a residential section of N Brooklyn borough of New York city. St. Johns Univ. is here.

Styal, town and parish (pop. 1,336), NE Cheshire, England, 5 mi. SW of Stockport; cotton milling. The textile industry was introduced here in 1784.

Stykkisholmur (stĭ'kĭs-hōl'mŭr), Icelandic *Stykkishólmur*, town (pop. 790), ⊙ Snaefellsnes co., W Iceland, trade center of Snaefellsnes peninsula, on SE shore of Breidi Fjord, at mouth of Hvamm Fjord; 65°4'N 22°44'W; fishing port.

Stylis or **Stilis** (both: stē'lĭs), town (pop. 3,606), Phthiotis nome, E central Greece, port of Lamia on N shore of Malian Gulf, on railroad and 10 mi. E of Lamia; ships tobacco, cotton, wheat; wine.

Stymphalia, Lake, or **Lake Stimfalia** (stĭmfă'lēŭ, stĭmfŭlē'ŭ) (□ 7), in Argolis and Corinthia nome, NE Peloponnesus, Greece, 24 mi. WSW of Corinth; 5.5 mi. long, 1.5 mi. wide; alt. 2,100 ft. In Gr. mythology associated with man-eating Stymphalian birds killed by Hercules. Formerly L. Zaraka.

Styra or **Stira** (both: stē'rŭ), uninhabited island (□ 1.3) in upper Gulf of Petalion, Euboea nome, Greece, 1.5 mi. off Euboea; 38°10'N 24°10'E; 2 mi. long, 1 mi. wide. Also called Stoura or Stura.

Styria (stĭ'rēŭ), Ger. *Steiermark* (shtī'ŭrmärk), autonomous prov. [*Bundesland*] (□ 6,326; 1951 pop. 1,106,581), SE and central Austria, bordering on Upper and Lower Austria (N), Burgenland (E), Yugoslavia (S), Carinthia (SW), and Salzburg (W); ⊙ Graz. Covered (except in SE) by Eastern Alps, it includes (NW) part of the Salzkammergut (Totes Gebirge, Dachstein), E portion of the Niedere Tauern, the Koralpe and Packalpe (on Carinthian border), and the Fischbach Alps and the Semmering (NE). Drained by Mur (largest), Enns, Mürz, and Raab rivers. Numerous resort towns in mts.; extensive mining (iron, lignite, magnesite), notably in the Erzberg; well-developed metal industry (Graz, Kapfenberg, Judenburg, Knittelfeld, Leoben). Cattle in upper valleys of Mur and Mürz rivers; agr. (corn, wine), fruit (apples, pears) and poultry in SE. Once part of Roman provs. of Noricum and Pannonia; became feudal state, then (12th cent.) duchy; passing to dukes of Austria. After 1276 became part of the Hapsburg dominions. Lost its S portion to Yugoslavia after 1918. Placed (1945) in Br. occupation zone.

Styr River or **Styr' River** (stĭr), W Ukrainian SSR, rises S of Brody in Volyn-Podolian Upland; flows 280 mi. generally N, past Berestechko, Lutsk, Rozhishche, and Kolki (head of navigation) to Pripet R. 20 mi. E of Pinsk. Receives Ikva R.

Styrso (stürs'ü"), Swedish *Styrsö*, fishing village (pop. 916), Goteborg och Bohus co., SW Sweden, on isl. (□ 1.5) of same name in the Kattegat, 9 mi. SW of Goteborg; seaside resort.

Styrum (shtü'rŏŏm), industrial suburb of MÜLHEIM, W Germany, on right bank of the Ruhr and 2.5 mi. NW of city center.

Styx, village, E Queensland, Australia, 65 mi. NW of Rockhampton; state coal mines.

Su, China: see KIANGSU.

Suaçuí River (swŭswē'), E Minas Gerais, Brazil, rises in the Serra da Penha E of Diamantina, flows 120 mi. E to the Rio Doce below Governador Valadares. Semiprecious stones found here. Also called Suaçuí Grande R. Formerly spelled Suassuí and Suassuhy.

Suadi, India: see SUNDARGARH, village.

Suaira, Mount, Eritrea: see SOIRA, MOUNT.

Suaita (swī'tä), town (pop. 1,573), Santander dept., N central Colombia, in W Cordillera Oriental, 29 mi. SSW of Socorro; alt. 5,282 ft. Cotton, sugar cane, coffee, potatoes, corn, stock; mfg. of hats, clothing; cotton spinning.

Suakin (swä'kĭn), town (pop. 5,750) Kassala prov., NE Anglo-Egyptian Sudan, port on Red Sea, 40 mi. S of Port Sudan; railhead. Ships cotton, livestock, hides in native craft. Quarantine station. Embarkation point for Mecca-bound pilgrims. The inner town, built on an isl., is connected by a causeway with outer town (rail station) on the mainland. Was chief African Red Sea port before founding (1906) of Port Sudan. Because of rapid growing up of coral reef, entrance is no longer safe for vessels drawing over 20 ft.

Sual (swäl), town (1939 pop. 1,102; 1948 municipality pop. 7,458), Pangasinan prov., central Luzon, Philippines, port on SW shore of Lingayen Gulf, 17 mi. WNW of Dagupan; fishing; copra production.

Suán (swän), town (pop. 2,411), Atlántico dept., N Colombia, minor inland port on Magdalena R., in Caribbean lowlands, and 45 mi. S of Barranquilla; cotton, corn, stock.

Suances (swän'thĕs), town (pop. 1,648), Santander prov., N Spain, fishing and ore-shipping port at mouth of Besaya R. on Bay of Biscay, 12 mi. WSW of Santander; fish processing, boatbuilding. Lumbering and cattle raising in area.

Süancheng or **Hsüan-ch'eng** (both: shüăn'chŭng'), town, ⊙ Süancheng co. (pop. 291,413), S Anhwei prov., China, 35 mi. SE of Wuhu, and on railroad, in rice region; tea, rapeseed; mfg. of paper. Until 1912 called Ningkwo.

Süanen or **Hsüan-en** (both: shüăn'ŭn'), town (pop. 8,610), ⊙ Süanen co. (pop. 133,576), southwesternmost Hupeh prov., China, 20 mi. S of Enshih; millet, wheat, beans.

Süanhan or **Hsüan-han** (both: shüăn'hän'), town (pop. 8,386), ⊙ Süanhan co. (pop. 475,139), NE Szechwan prov., China, 20 mi. NE of Tahsien; olive-growing center; rice, wheat, sweet potatoes, tea, tung oil. Until 1914 called Tungsiang.

Süanhwa or **Hsüan-hua** (both: shüăn'hwä'), town, ⊙ Süanhwa co. (pop. 222,928), central Chahar prov., China, on Yang R. and 14 mi. SSE of Kalgan, and on railroad; fur dressing, tanning. Center for Süanlung (or Lungyen) iron-mining dist., extending from the mtn. Yentung Shan (just ENE) toward Lungkwan (40 mi. ENE). Coal is mined at Chimingshan, 20 mi. SE. Until 1928 in Chihli (Hopeh).

Suani Ben Adem (swä'nē bĕn ä'dĕm), town (pop. 3,187), W Tripolitania, Libya, on railroad and 13 mi. SSW of Tripoli, in an oasis (cereals, vegetables, dates); road junction.

Süanlung, China: see SÜANHWA.

Süanping or **Hsüan-p'ing** (both: shüăn'pĭng'), town (pop. 5,171), ⊙ Süanping co. (pop. 74,480), SW Chekiang prov., China, 22 mi. NW of Lishui; tung-oil and vegetable-tallow processing, cotton weaving; tea, indigo, rice, wheat.

Suantar-Khayata, Russian SFSR: see SUNTAR-KHAYATA.

Süante, China: see AMPHITRITE GROUP.

Süanwei or **Hsüan-wei** (both: shüăn'wā'), town (pop. 7,476), ⊙ Süanwei co. (pop. 293,073), NE Yunnan prov., China, 115 mi. NE of Kunming; rice, wheat, millet, beans. Coal mines near by.

Suao (sōō'ou'), Jap. *Suo* (sōō'ō), town (1935 pop. 6,381), N Formosa, on E coast, 13 mi. SE of Ilan; railroad terminus; port and industrial center; cement mfg., fish processing (swordfish, tuna). Has one of best natural harbors of Formosa. Manganese and silica mined near by are processed in Lotung ferroalloys plant. Suao is linked (since 1931) by coastal highway with Hwalien.

Suapi (swä'pē), village (pop. c.2,100), La Paz dept., W Bolivia, on Beni R., opposite Santa Ana, and c.50 mi. NNE of Coroico; rice plantations.

Suaqui (swä'kē), town (pop. 1,144), Sonora, NW Mexico, near confluence of Yaqui and Moctezuma rivers, 80 mi. E of Hermosillo; cereals, fruit, stock.

Suaqui Grande (grän'dā), town (pop. 664), Sonora, NW Mexico, on affluent of Yaqui R. and 80 mi. SE of Hermosillo; livestock, cereals.

Suar (swŭr), town (pop. 6,217), Rampur dist., N central Uttar Pradesh, India, 15 mi. N of Rampur; corn, wheat, rice, gram, sugar cane.

Suárez or **Joaquín Suárez** (hwäkēn' swä'rĕs). **1** town (pop. 1,100), Canelones dept., S Uruguay, on railroad and 14 mi. NE of Montevideo; agr., wine-growing. Reform school near by. **2** Town (pop. 1,400), Colonia dept., SW Uruguay, on railroad (Tarariras station) and 19 mi. NE of Colonia, in agr. region (grain, fruit, stock); flour milling, dairying. Formerly called Tarariras.

Suárez Arana (swä'rĕs ärä'nä), military post (Fortín Suárez Arana), Santa Cruz dept., E Bolivia, 70 mi. SE of San José.

Suárez River, central and N central Colombia; its headstreams rise in Cordillera Oriental N of Zipaquirá (Cundinamarca dept.) and flow N into Laguna de Fúquene, from which the Suárez flows N c.150 mi., into Santander dept., to Sogamoso R. (affluent of the Magdalena) 5 mi. SE of Zapatoca. Fertile subandean valley.

Suassuí River, Brazil: see SUAÇUÍ RIVER.

Suaza (swä'sä) town (pop. 1,767), Huila dept., S central Colombia, in Cordillera Oriental, on affluent of Magdalena R. and 20 mi. SSW of Garzón; alt. 3,280 ft.; rice, cacao, stock.

Subaihi, Aden: see SUBEIHI.

Subang or **Soebang** (both: sōōbäng'), town (pop. 10,539), W Java, Indonesia, 25 mi. NNE of Bandung; trade center in rice region; lumber mills.

Subansiri River (sōōbŭn'sĭrē), in E Tibet prov., China, and N Assam, India, rises in Tibet prov., in E Assam Himalayas; flows SE and SW, past extensive tea gardens, to Brahmaputra R. 22 mi. NNW of Golaghat; 226 mi. long.

Subarctic Current: see ALEUTIAN CURRENT.

Subarn, Thailand: see SUPHANBURI.

Subarnarekha River (sōōbŭrnŭrā'kŭ), in S Bihar, SW West Bengal, and NE Orissa, India, rises on Chota Nagpur Plateau, c.10 mi. SW of Ranchi; flows E, past Ranchi, and SE, past Jamshedpur, through copper-mining area of Singhbhum dist., to Bay of Bengal 28 mi. E of Balasore; c.290 mi. long.

Subata (sōō'bätä), Ger. *Subbat*, city (pop. 1,489), SE Latvia, in Zemgale, 26 mi. WNW of Daugavpils, near Lith. border; flour milling.

Subathu, India: see SABATHU.

Subayhi, Aden: see SUBEIHI.

Subbat, Latvia: see SUBATA.

Subcarpathian Ruthenia, Ukrainian SSR: see TRANSCARPATHIAN OBLAST.

Subeihi, Subaihi, or **Subayhi** (all: sōōbā'hē), westernmost tribal area (pop. 16,000) of Western Aden Protectorate, bet. Gulf of Aden and Yemen, W of Aden; placed 1948 under administration of Abdali sultanate. Sparsely populated sandy desert, with little cultivation (wheat) and a predominantly pastoral, nomadic pop. (camel breeding). Area is divided into the sheikdoms of BARHIMI, ATIFI, RIJAI, MAKHDUMI, MANSURI, DUBEINI, and the minor Khalifi and Atawi. Centers of administration are at Am Shat and Tor al Baha. Although protectorate treaties were signed (1872–1912) bet. Britain and the sheiks, the Subeihi resisted Abdali influence in 1880s, and the tribe joined the Turks from Yemen in their advance on Aden in First World War. Order and security were later established, and the Subeihi area was administered by Abdali (W) and the Western Aden Protectorate agency (E) until the entire area passed in 1948 into the Abdali dominions. The Subeihi area was one of the original NINE CANTONS.

Subiaco (sōōbēä'kō), municipality (pop. 18,789), SW Western Australia, W suburb of Perth; porcelain, furniture, copperware, woodwork, steel products.

Subiaco (sōōbyä'kô), town (pop. 7,155), Roma prov., Latium, central Italy, on Aniene R. and 32 mi. E of Rome; mfg. (paper, coal briquettes, macaroni). Marble quarries near by. Has monastery of San Benedetto, founded by St. Benedict of Nursia, which achieved great power and wealth in Middle Ages; here 1st printing presses in Italy were established, 1464. There is also a convent, Santa Scolastica, named after its founder, St. Benedict's sister, which is 1st monastic community established for women.

Subiaco (sŭbēă'kō, sōōbē–), town (pop. 191), Logan co., W Ark., 27 mi. W of Russellville, in farm area. Seat of Subiaco Col. and Abbey (Benedictine).
Subi Besar, Indonesia: see SOUTH NATUNA ISLANDS.
Subic (sōō'bĭk), town (1939 pop. 1,257; 1948 municipality pop. 25,223), Zambales prov., central Luzon, Philippines, on N shore of Subic Bay, 55 mi. WNW of Manila; rice, sugar cane.
Subic Bay, inlet of S.China Sea, central Luzon, Philippines, near Bataan Peninsula; 9 mi. N–S, 5–8 mi. E–W. On its shores are Olongapo and Subic; near entrance is small Grande Isl. In Second World War, U.S. forces landed here in Jan., 1945.
Subk el Ahad or **Subk al-Ahad** (both: sōōb'kĕl-ăhăd'), village (pop. 8,954), Minufiya prov., Egypt, 3 mi. ENE of Ashmun; cereals, cotton, flax.
Subk el Dahhak, Subk ed Dahhak, or **Subk al-Dahhak** (all: sōōb'kĕdă'hăk), village (pop. 7,473), Minufiya prov., Lower Egypt, on railroad and 8 mi. ESE of Minuf; cereals, cotton, flax.
Sublette (sŭblĕt'), county (□ 4,876; pop. 2,481), W Wyo.; ⊙ Pinedale. Agr. region; watered by Green R. Livestock, hay. Part of Bridger Natl. Forest and Wind River Range in N. Formed 1921.
Sublette. 1 Village (pop. 290), Lee co., N Ill., 18 mi. SE of Dixon, in rich agr. area. **2** City (pop. 838), ⊙ Haskell co., SW Kansas, 29 mi. N of Liberal, in agr. region.
Sublimity, town (pop. 367), Marion co., NW Oregon, 13 mi. SE of Salem.
Suboskon, Greece: see ARDEA.
Subotica or **Subotitsa** (both: sōō'bôtĭtsä), Hung. *Szabadka* (sŏ'bŏkŏ), Ger. *Theresiopel* or *Maria-Theresiopel* (mä'rēä tŭrāzēō'pŭl), largest city (pop. 112,551) in Vojvodina, N Serbia, Yugoslavia, 100 mi. NNW of Belgrade, near Hung. border, on internatl. highway, in the Backa. Rail junction (lines to Belgrade, Zagreb, Budapest, Bucharest, and Szeged; repair shops); flour milling, meat packing, poultry fattening and exporting; electrical, chemical, and furniture industries. Peaches, apricots, grapes grown in vicinity. Law school (founded 1920). Settled in prehistoric times. Health resort of PALIC near by.
Subtiava, Nicaragua: see LEÓN, city.
Succasunna (sŭkŭsŭ'nŭ), village (pop. 2,383, with near-by KENVIL), Morris co., N N.J., 5 mi. W of Dover.
Success, town (pop. 311), Clay co., extreme NE Ark., 19 mi. NE of Pocahontas, near Mo. line.
Success Reservoir, Calif.: see TULE RIVER.
Success Village, village (pop. 6,730), NW Trinidad, B.W.I., just SE of Port of Spain; lime- and coconut-oil factories.
Succonesset, Mass.: see MASHPEE.
Succotz, Br. Honduras: see SOCCOTHS.
Suceava, province, Rumania: see CAMPULUNG.
Suceava (sōōchä'vä), Ger. *Suczawa* (zōōk-tsä'vä), town (1948 pop. 10,123), Suceava prov., N Rumania, in Bukovina, on Suceava R., on railroad and 70 mi. NW of Jassy; historic shrine of Rumania, and modern trading center; milling, tanning, meat processing. Original (1388–1564) ⊙ of Moldavia, it still preserves 14th-cent. Mirauti church, former cathedral of the first primate of Moldavia, 16th-cent. St. George Church (St. Jean Novi), a famous pilgrimage center because of its miraculous relics, and several other noted 16th- and 17th-cent. churches. There are also remains of a 14th-cent. fortress built by Stephen the Great and once residence of Suleiman II. Mus. has large pre historic and medieval collections. Jews form 25% of pop. Town is also sometimes called Cetatea-Sucevii. Among numerous mementoes of the past located near by, the most notable is the 17th-cent. Dragomirna monastery, 9 mi. N.
Suceava River, Ger. *Suczawa*, Rus. *Sutchava* (sōōchä'-vä), Ukrainian SSR and N Rumania, in Bukovina, rises on E slopes of the Moldavian Carpathians 30 mi. WSW of Radauti, flows E and SE c.110 mi., past Suceava, to Siret R. 19 mi. WNW of Harlau.
Sucevita, Rumania: see MARGINEA.
Sucha (sōō'khä), town (pop. 5,866), Krakow prov., S Poland, on Skawa R. and 27 mi. SSW of Cracow; rail junction; sawmilling. Castle.
Suchan (sōō'khänyŭ), Pol. *Suchań*, Ger. *Zachan* (tsä'khän), town (1939 pop. 1,302; 1946 pop. 529) in Pomerania, after 1945 in Szczecin prov., NW Poland, 12 mi. ESE of Stargard; grain, sugar beets, potatoes, livestock.
Suchan (sōōchän'), city (1939 pop. c.40,000), S Maritime Territory, Russian SFSR, 60 mi. ENE of Vladivostok, on branch of Trans-Siberian RR; major coal-mining center; power plant. Coal basin, exploited since 1901, developed largely in 1930s.
Suches (sōō'chĕs), village, La Paz dept., W Bolivia, on L. Suches (6 mi. long, 1 mi. wide), at outlet of Suches R., 55 mi. W of Apolo, on Peru border; alt. 15,062 ft.; gold mining. Sometimes spelled Súchez.
Suches River, La Paz dept., W Bolivia, rises in L. Suches at Suches, flows c.75 mi. SSE to L. Titicaca near Escoma. Forms part of Bolivia-Peru border in upper course.
Suchiapa (sōōchyä'pä), town (pop. 2,540), Chiapas, S Mexico, in Chiapas Valley, 9 mi. S of Tuxtla; agr. center (cereals, tobacco, coffee, sugar cane, fruit, livestock).
Suchiate (sōōchyä'tä), officially Mariscal Suchiate, town (pop. 1,412), Chiapas, S Mexico, in Pacific lowland, opposite Ayutla (Guatemala), 70 mi. SSE of Tapachula; rail terminus. Customhouse, airfield.
Suchiate River, on Mexico-Guatemala border, rises in Sierra Madre just S of Ixchiguán (Guatemala), flows c.100 mi. SW, past Ayutla and Suchiate, to the Pacific 3 mi. NW of Ocós.
Su-chia-t'un, Manchuria: see SUKIATUN.
Su-ch'ien, China: see SUTSIEN.
Súchil (sōō'chēl), town (pop. 3,044), Durango, N Mexico, on interior plateau, on railroad and 55 mi. SE of Durango; alt. 6,483 ft. Agr. center (grain, tobacco, sugar cane, cotton, vegetables, fruit).
Suchitán (sōōchētän'), extinct volcano (6,699 ft.), Jutiapa dept., SE Guatemala, 11 mi. NE of Jutiapa. Last erupted 1469.
Suchitepéquez (sōōchētāpā'kĕs), department (□ 960; 1950 pop. 123,373), SW Guatemala, on Pacific Ocean; ⊙ Mazatenango. In Pacific piedmont and coastal plain; drained by Nahualate and Madre Vieja rivers. Mainly agr.: coffee, sugar cane, cacao, rice, tobacco on mtn. slopes; corn, beans, bananas in coastal plain. Sugar milling (Palo Gordo), lumbering, textile milling, cotton ginning, oil extraction. Principal centers (along railroad; N): Mazatenango, Cuyotenango, San Antonio.
Suchitlán (sōōchētlän'), town (pop. 885), Colima, W Mexico, 10 mi. N of Colima; corn, beans, sugar cane, fruit, stock.
Suchitoto (sōōchētō'tō), city (pop. 10,619), Cuscatlán dept., W central Salvador, at NE foot of volcano Guazapa, 20 mi. NE of San Salvador; market center; processes livestock products; grain, livestock. Dept. ⊙, 1853–63. Village of La Bermuda (6 mi. S) was former site of San Salvador, 1528–39.
Suchow. 1 Town, Anhwei prov., China: see SUHSIEN. **2** Town, Kansu prov., China: see KIUCHÜAN.
Süchow or **Hsü-chou** (both: shü'jō'). **1** City (1935 pop. 160,013; 1947 pop. 339,517), SW Shantung prov., China, 175 mi. NNW of Nanking; rail center at junction of Tientsin-Pukow and Lunghai railroads. Tobacco mfg., ironworking, flour milling; winegrowing; wheat, beans, kaoliang, cotton. Meteorological station. As ⊙ Tungshan co. (1946 pop. 1,099,296), it was called Tungshan (1912–45), until it became an independent municipality in 1945. City was in Kiangsu prov. until 1949, when Tungshan co. seat was moved to a village 10 mi. NE, thereafter called Tungshan. **2** Town, Szechwan prov., China: see IPIN.
Süchteln (zükh'tŭln), town (pop. 11,798), in former Prussian Rhine Prov., W Germany, after 1945 in North Rhine-Westphalia, on the Niers and 7 mi. NNW of München Gladbach; textile mfg.
Sucilá (sōōsēlä'), town (pop. 883), Yucatan, SE Mexico, 11 mi. W of Tizimín; henequen.
Suckling, Cape, S Alaska, on Gulf of Alaska, 75 mi. SE of Cordova; 59°59'N 143°54'W. E extremity of Chugach Natl. Forest.
Suck River, Ireland, rises in a small lake 7 mi. W of Castlerea, Co. Roscommon, flows 60 mi. SSE along Roscommon-Galway border, past Castlerea, Ballymoe, and Ballinasloe, to the Shannon at Shannonbridge.
Sucre (sōō'krä), city (1949 pop. estimate 32,500), nominal ⊙ Bolivia and Chuquisaca dept., S central Bolivia, 260 mi. SE of La Paz, in E outliers of Eastern Cordillera of the Andes; 19°2'S 65°17'W; alt. 9,301 ft. Terminus of gasoline rail-car line from Potosí; road and commercial center for agr. products (corn, vegetables, wheat) and general merchandise; oil distilling, alcohol distilling, brewing, mfg. of shoes, candy, cigarettes. Seat of supreme court of Bolivia, old legislative and govt. palaces, cathedral (1553), Univ. of San Francisco Xavier (1624; considered oldest in South America), public library. Residence of archbishop of La Plata diocese. Surrounded by country seats of old Spanish families. Originally an Indian center named Charcas; Spanish city founded (1538) on orders of Francisco Pizarro as capital of Sp. *audiencia* of Charcas (or Upper Peru) and was called Chuquisaca (later La Plata). Early revolutionary center (1809). Became provisional ⊙ Bolivia in 1826, legal and de facto ⊙ in 1839, when it was renamed for General Sucre. Since c.1900 La Paz has been actual seat of Bolivian govt.
Sucre. 1 Town (pop. 2,485), Bolívar dept., N Colombia, 30 mi. S of Magangué; cattle raising. **2** Village, Caquetá commissary, S Colombia, on Orteguaza R., on E slopes of Cordillera Oriental, and 12 mi. NNW of Florencia; alt. 3,363 ft.
Sucre, town (1950 pop. 1,427), Manabí prov., W Ecuador, 15 mi. S of Portoviejo, in lowlands (cacao, coffee, rice, tagua nuts, balsa wood); rice- and sawmilling.
Sucre, city (pop. 1,615), Cajamarca dept., NW Peru, on E slopes of Cordillera Occidental, on road from Cajamarca, and 5 mi. S of Celendín; coca, corn. Until 1940 (when it became a city), called Huauco.
Sucre, state (□ 4,560; 1941 pop. 291,452; 1950 census 333,296), NE Venezuela, on the Caribbean; ⊙ Cumaná. Bordering E on Gulf of Paria and SE on San Juan R., it is traversed W–E by spurs of coastal range and includes Araya Peninsula on Gulf of Cariaco (W) and Paria Peninsula (E). Climate varies greatly, being generally tropical and humid, with some parts having rain all year round. Among mineral resources are the asphalt lake of Guanoco, saltworks on Araya Peninsula, gypsum near Macuro (or Cristóbal Colón), sulphur at Casanay; also iron, copper, coal, and petroleum deposits. Predominantly an agr. region, it produces mainly cacao, sugar cane, coffee, tobacco, corn, cotton, rice, yucca, bananas; and coconuts along coast. Fishing is one of the state's main activities; rural industries include sugar milling and liquor distilling. Processing plants are centered at Cumaná. Carúpano, Güiria, Irapa, Río Caribe, and Puerto Sucre are its ports.
Sucúa (sōōkōō'ä), village, Santiago-Zamora prov., SE central Ecuador, on E slopes of the Andes, 11 mi. SSW of Macas. Missionary settlement. Airfield.
Suçuapara or **Sussuapara** (sōōswŭpŭrä'), city (pop. 1,470), S Goiás, central Brazil, 30 mi. SE of Goiânia; coffee, tobacco, sugar, dairy products. Chromite deposits in area. Until 1944, called Bela Vista (formerly spelled Bella Vista).
Sucumbíos, town, Ecuador: see SANTA ROSA DE SUCUMBÍOS.
Sucumbíos River, Ecuador and Colombia: see SAN MIGUEL RIVER.
Sucuriú River (sōōkōōryōō'), SE Mato Grosso, Brazil, rises in the Serra das Araras near Goiás border, flows 200 mi. SE to the Paraná at Jupiá (crossing of São Paulo–Corumbá RR). Not navigable.
Sucy-en-Brie (süsē'-ā-brē'), town (pop. 6,458), Seine-et-Oise dept., N central France, an outer SE suburb of Paris, 9 mi. from Notre Dame Cathedral, near left bank of the Marne; rail junction; glassworks; mfg. (morocco leather, photo equipment, false pearls).
Suczawa, town, Rumania: see SUCEAVA, town.
Suczawa River, Ukrainian SSR and Rumania: see SUCEAVA RIVER.
Suda (sōō'dŭ), Gr. *Souda* or *Soudha* (both: sōō'dhŭ), town (pop. 1,854), Canea nome, W Crete, on N coast, 3 mi. SE of Canea; port and naval base on Suda Bay, best natural harbor of Crete, used as fleet anchorage for centuries.
Suda (sōō'dŭ), uninhabited island (□ 5) of the Kuria Muria group, off SE Oman; 17°30'N 55°54'E; rises to 1,290 ft.
Suda or **Sudah,** town (pop. 1,200), Hajja prov., N central Yemen, in maritime range, 21 mi. NE of Hajja.
Sudai or **Suday** (sōōdī'), village, NW Kostroma oblast, Russian SFSR, 25 mi. NNE of Galich; flax, wheat.
Sudair or **Sudayr** (sōōdăr'), oasis district of N central Nejd, Saudi Arabia; main towns, Majma'a and Zilfi. Sometimes spelled Sedeir.
Sudak (sōōdăk'), town (1938 pop. estimate 3,000), E Crimea, Russian SFSR, Black Sea port, 22 mi. SW of Feodosiya; beach resort; winegrowing center; orchards, tobacco, essential-oil plants (lavender, roses). Has ruins of 14th-cent. Genoese fortress. A Gr. city in 3d cent.; passed (7th cent.) to Byzantines; in 11th cent. a major transit point for Europe-Asia trade. After decline due to repeated Tatar assaults, it passed (1365) to Genoese and flourished anew as wine center; sacked 1475 by Turks.
Sudan (sōōdăn'), Fr. *Soudan*, a vast, vaguely-defined region of N central Africa, S of the Sahara and N of the rainy tropics and extending, in its largest sense, 3,500–4,000 mi. from the Atlantic (at W Africa's bulge) to the upper Nile valley and even beyond to the Ethiopian highlands and the Red Sea coast. It is not a political unit, and covers parts of Fr. West Africa (including the political division called FRENCH SUDAN), N Fr. Equatorial Africa (including the L. Chad depression), and N and central ANGLO-EGYPTIAN SUDAN (anc. NUBIA). The ethnographic sense of the term Sudan is also its origin [Sudan in Arabic means black, and the area is called "country of the blacks"], referring to the Negro tribes here who have been Moslem since medieval times. But the term perhaps means most today as descriptive of the vegetation: a transitional belt bet. the dry desert and the moist tropics, characterized by semi-arid scrub and desert plants in the N and progressing to tall grass and savannas in the S. Physiographically, the Sudan consists of 3 major drainage basins (Niger R., L. Chad, middle Nile R.), all of which have marshy internal drainage deltas at their centers. The drainage divides are isolated ranges which rise above an otherwise monotonous lowland. The economy is characteristically pastoral.
Sudan, city (pop. 1,348), Lamb co., NW Texas, on the Ilano Estacado, 50 mi. NW of Lubbock, in agr. area (grain, cotton). Inc. 1925.
Suda River (sōō'dŭ), Vologda oblast, Russian SFSR, rises in lake region S of L. Onega, flows c.150 mi. SE, past Borisovo-Sudskoye and Kadui, to Rybinsk Reservoir W of Cherepovets.
Sudauen, Poland: see SUWALKI.
Suday, Russian SFSR: see SUDAI.
Sudayr, Saudi Arabia: see SUDAIR.
Südbaden, Germany: see BADEN.
Sudbishche (sōōd'bĭshchĭ), village (1939 pop. over

500), N Orel oblast, Russian, SFSR, 20 mi. SW of Yefremov; coarse grain.

Sudbury, district (□ 18,058; pop. 80,815), SE central Ont., on L. Huron; ⊙ Sudbury.

Sudbury, city (pop. 32,203), ⊙ Sudbury dist., SE central Ont., 200 mi. NW of Toronto; one of world's most important nickel mining, smelting, and refining centers. Silver, lead, zinc, gold, copper, and platinum are also mined in region. There are machine shops, lumber mills, woodworking plants, brickworks.

Sudbury. 1 Suburb, Middlesex, England: see WEMBLEY. **2** Municipal borough (1931 pop. 7,007; 1951 census 6,614), S Suffolk, England, on Stour R. and 13 mi. NW of Colchester; agr. market; silk and rayon milling, mfg. of coconut-fiber matting. Has three 15th-cent. churches and a 15th-cent. town hall. Woolen industry, introduced by Flemish weavers in 14th cent., has ceased. Thomas Gainsborough b. here.

Sudbury. 1 Rural town (pop. 2,596), Middlesex co., E Mass., 18 mi. W of Boston; truck, dairying, fruit, poultry; greenhouses. Sudbury R. borders it (E). The restored Howe or Red Horse tavern here (built 1686), called Wayside Inn, was setting of Longfellow's *Tales of a Wayside Inn*. Settled 1638, inc. 1639. Includes South Sudbury village. **2** Town (pop. 263), Rutland co., W Vt., 17 mi. NW of Rutland, in resort region.

Sudbury Reservoir, E central Mass., unit in Boston water-supply system, just SE of Marlboro; c.3 mi. long.

Sudbury River, E Mass., rises in ponds in E Worcester co., flows c.30 mi. E and N, past Framingham, joining Assabet R. to form Concord R. in Concord town. Supplies reservoirs of Boston water system.

Sud Chichas, Bolivia: see TUPIZA.

Sud Cinti, Bolivia: see VILLA ABECIA.

Sudd (sŏŏd), swampy lowland region, S central Anglo-Egyptian Sudan, drained by the BAHR EL GHAZAL (W) and BAHR EL JEBEL (center), headstreams of the White Nile; 250 mi. long, 200 mi. wide. Here the course of the rivers is impeded by floating vegetation (sudd) consisting of papyrus and aquatic grass. Through dispersal and evaporation the Bahr el Jebel loses half its water. A canal by-passing the Sudd is projected bet. Jonglei and the area of Malakal. Region inhabited by Nilotic Nuer tribes.

Suddie (sŭ'dē), village (pop. 432), ⊙ Essequibo dist., Essequibo co., N Br. Guiana, landing on Atlantic coast, 32 mi. NW of Georgetown, in tropical forest region; coconut plantations; also rice, sugar cane, stock.

Süderbrarup (zü"dŭrbrä'rōōp), village (pop. 4,563), in Schleswig-Holstein, NW Germany, 12 mi. NE of Schleswig; rail junction; market center of the Angeln (wheat, cattle, hogs); flour milling, metalworking. Numerous prehistoric artifacts found near by.

Süderelbe, Germany: see ELBE RIVER.

Süderlügum (zü"dŭrlü'gōōm), village (pop. 1,315), in Schleswig-Holstein, NW Germany, 4 mi. S of Tonder (Denmark), in North Friesland; customs station.

Sudero (sōō'dhŭr-ŭ), Dan. *Suderø* or *Syderø*, Faeroese *Suðuroy*, island (□ 64; pop. 5,991) of the S Faeroe Isls., bounded N by Sudero Fjord; c.20 mi. long, 5 mi. wide. Coast is irregular with many inlets; terrain is rocky, highest point 2,000 ft. Less than 3 sq. mi. are cultivated; fishing, sheep raising.

Suderode, Bad, Germany: see BAD SUDERODE.

Sudero Fjord, strait of the Faeroe Isls., bet. Sudero isl. (S) and Store Dimon isl. (N); in center is Lille Dimon (Faeroese *Lítla Dímun*), a rocky, uninhabited isl. (□ ⅓; highest point 1,358 ft.).

Sudetenland (sōōdā'tŭnlănd", Ger. zōōdā'tŭnlänt"), border districts (□ 8,976) in Bohemia and Moravia, Czechoslovakia, which had large Ger. pop. (1930 pop. 3,000,000 Germans, 800,000 Czechs); involved in dramatic dispute bet. Czechoslovakia and Germany during July-September, 1938. The area was yielded to Germany after Munich Pact (Sept. 29–30, 1938) and inc. into Germany. This cession deprived Czechoslovakia of natural defense lines and important power resources (54.7% of its coal, 93.2% of its lignite), disrupted the natl. economy, and cut most of international communications. Returned to Czechoslovakia in 1945. After Second World War, Ger. nationals were deported in accordance with Potsdam Agreement (1945).

Sudetes (sōōdē'tēz) or **Sudetic Mountains** (sōōdĕ'tĭk), Ger. *Sudeten* (zōōdā'tŭn), Czech *Sudety* (sōō'dĕtĭ), Pol. *Sudety* (sōōdĕ'tĭ), mountain system along Ger.-Czechoslovak and Pol.-Czechoslovak border; extend c.170 mi. bet. valleys of the Elbe at Decin (ESE) and the Oder at Moravian Gate (WNW). The principal W ranges are Lusatian Mts. with Jested peak (3,314 ft.) and the Isergebirge with Smrk peak (3,681 ft.). The Riesengebirge, highest and central range of the Sudetes, rise to 5,259 ft. in the Schneekoppe. Beyond the Riesengebirge and running chiefly ESE are 2 generally parallel groups of ranges. The northernmost group comprises the Eulengebirge (rise to 3,327 ft.) lying entirely in Poland, Reichenstein Mts. (up to 2,959 ft.) running ESE into Czechoslovakia, and the Jeseniky (rise to 4,888 ft. in Praded peak) and Oder Mts. (to 2,234 ft.), both entirely in Czechoslovakia. The parallel S group of ranges includes Heuscheuer Mts. (up to 3,018 ft.; directly WSW of the Eulengebirge), the Adlergebirge (rise to 3,655 ft. in Velka Destna mtn.), largely in Czechoslovakia and paralleled in Poland (N) by Habelschwerdt Mts. (up to 3,025 ft.), and Kralicky Sneznik (rise to 4,672 ft.), which run NE, again along Czechoslovak-Pol. border, to E foothills of Reichenstein Mts. Range is rich in mineral resources; coal mined at Waldenburg (Walbrzych), Glatz (Klodzko), and in Nachod region. Iron, galena, and tetrahedryte are also worked. Important glass-mfg. industry flourishes on both slopes of the Sudetes, especially at Waldenburg and Szklarska Poreba (Schreiberhau). Of the numerous health and winter-sports resorts in the region, best known are Karpacz (Krummhübel), Szklarska Poreba, Spindleruv Mlyn, Kudowa Zdroj (Bad Kudowa), and Duszniki Zdroj (Bad Reinerz).

Sudharam, E Pakistan: see NOAKHALI, town.

Sudhureyri, Iceland: see SUDUREYRI.

Sudhur-Mula, Iceland: see SUDUR-MULA.

Sudislavl or **Sudislavl'** (sōōdyĕslä'vŭl), village (1948 pop. over 2,000), SW Kostroma oblast, Russian SFSR, 28 mi. E of Kostroma; flour mill; woodworking.

Sudlersville (sŭd'lŭrzvĭl), town (pop. 347), Queen Annes co., E Md., 18 mi. W of Dover, Del.

Sud Lípez, Bolivia: see SAN PABLO, Potosí dept.

Süd-Nord Canal (züt'-nôrt'), NW Germany, runs 30 mi. bet. NORDHORN (S) and Rütenbrock (N), where it joins Haren-Rütenbrock Canal. Connected by Coevorden-Piccardie Canal with Overijssel Canal (Netherlands).

Sudogda (sōōdŭgdä'), city (1926 pop. 4,491), central Vladimir oblast, Russian SFSR, on Sudogda R. (right affluent of the Klyazma) and 21 mi. SE of Vladimir; linen mills, glassworks. Founded 1552.

Sudostroi, Russian SFSR: see MOLOTOVSK, Archangel oblast.

Sudovaya Vishnya (sōōdô'vĭŭ vē'shnyŭ), Pol. *Sądowa Wisznia* (sôdô'vä vēsh'nyä), city (1931 pop. 4,765), N Drogobych oblast, Ukrainian SSR, on Vishnya R. and 31 mi. NNW of Drogobych; agr.-processing center (cereals, chicory); ceramics; lumbering; horse raising.

Sudr (sōō'dŭr), oil-mining settlement, Sinai, Egypt, on NE coast of Gulf of Suez, 25 mi. SSE of Suez.

Südtondern (züt"tôn'dŭrn), district of Schleswig-Holstein, NW Germany: see NIEBÜLL.

Sudureyri or **Sudureyri i Sugandafirdi** (sü'dhürā"-rē ē sōō'gäntäfĭr"dhē), Icelandic *Suðureyri í Súgandafirði*, fishing village (pop. 339), Isafjardar co., NW Iceland, on Vestfjarda Peninsula, 11 mi. WNW of Isafjordur, on Suganda Fjord, Icelandic *Súgandafjörður*, small inlet of Denmark Strait. Also spelled Sudhureyri i Sugandafirdhi.

Sudur-Mula or **Sudhur-Mula** (sü'dhür-mōō"lä), Icelandic *Suður-Múla*, county [Icelandic *sýsla*] (pop. 4,151), SE Iceland; ⊙ Eskifjordur. On SE coast, bordering edge of Vatnajokull glacier region. Many fjords. Generally mountainous. Sheep raising, fishing. Chief towns are Neskaupstadur (city in, but independent of, co.), Budir, and Eskifjordur.

Suduroy, Faeroe Isls.: see SUDERO.

Sud Yungas, Bolivia: see CHULUMANI.

Sudzal (sōōtsäl'), town (pop. 498), Yucatan, SE Mexico, 4 mi. SSE of Izamal; in henequen region. Maya ruins near by.

Sudzha (sōō'jŭ), city (1939 pop. over 10,000), W Kursk oblast, Russian SFSR, 50 mi. SW of Kursk; metalworking, cotton milling. Chartered 1672.

Sudzhenka, RSFSR: see ANZHERO-SUDZHENSK.

Sudzukh or **Sudzhukhe** (sōōdzōōkh', –jōōkhyĕ'), village (1939 pop. under 500), SE Maritime Territory, Russian SFSR, at mouth of short Sudzukh R., 90 mi. E of Vladivostok; fish canning.

Sueca (swā'kä), city (pop. 16,864), Valencia prov., E Spain, on the Júcar and 20 mi. S of Valencia; center of rich rice-growing dist.; rice mills. Mfg. of tiles, artificial flowers, candy. Also oranges, cereals, onions.

Süehfeng Mountains (shüĕ'fŭng'), Chinese *Hsüehfeng Shan* (shüĕ'fŭng' shän'), W central Hunan prov., China, forming divide bet. Yüan and Tzu rivers; rises to over 3,000 ft. Süehfeng peak is 20 mi. SE of Kienyang.

Suehn (swē, swĕn), town, Montserrado co., W Liberia, 21 mi. N of Monrovia; palm oil and kernels, citrus fruit, coffee. Mission station.

Sue Peaks, Texas: see CARMEN, SIERRA DEL.

Suero, Spain: see ALCIRA.

Suesca (swā'skä), village (pop. 303), Cundinamarca dept., central Colombia, in Cordillera Oriental, on railroad and 40 mi. NNE of Bogotá; alt. 8,645 ft.; coal mining.

Suessiona, France: see SOISSONS.

Suess Land (züs), peninsula (50 mi. long, 5–30 mi. wide), E Greenland, bet. Franz Josef Fjord (N) and W arm of King Oscar Fjord (S); 73°N 26°20'W. Rises to 7,283 ft. near its base, where narrow isthmus connects it with mainland.

Sueyoshi (sōōā'-yō'shē), town (pop. 27,779), Kagoshima prefecture, S Kyushu, Japan, 28 mi. ENE of Kagoshima; commercial center for agr. area (rice, wheat, sweet potatoes); lumber, charcoal, medical powder made from antlers.

Suez (sōōĕz', sōō'ĕz), city (pop. 108,250), NE Egypt, constituting the Suez Governorate, a port at head of Gulf of Suez, at S end of Suez Canal, and 80 mi. E of Cairo; 29°58'N 32°33'E. Has large oil refinery; rail lines to Cairo and Port Said. Its 2 harbors are Port Ibrahim and Port Taufiq (Port Tewfik), both parts of S Suez. Large fertilizer plant near by. In anc. times Suez was an important port and canals gave it access to the interior, but it was insignificant for centuries before its development in 19th cent. with building of SUEZ CANAL. In a near-by oasis, the Springs of Moses, is a spring which Moses is supposed to have made miraculously sweet.

Suez, Gulf of, NW arm of the Red Sea in E Egypt, c.180 mi. long and 20 mi. wide, bet. the Sinai Peninsula and Arabian Desert of Egypt; Suez Canal joins it with the Mediterranean.

Suez, Isthmus of, NE Egypt, connecting Asia and Africa, bet. Gulf of Suez (S) and the Mediterranean (N). Narrowest part is 72 mi. wide.

Suez Canal, waterway of NE Egypt joining the Mediterranean with the Gulf of Suez and thus with the Red Sea and the Orient. At N terminus is PORT SAID, at S is Port Taufiq (Port Tewfik), a part of the city of SUEZ. Built 1859–69 by Ferdinand de Lesseps, it proceeds S from Port Said in almost a straight line to small L. Timsah; from there a cutting leads to the Bitter Lakes (now one body of water), and a final cutting attains the Gulf of Suez; there are no locks. Canal is 107 mi. long (including 7 mi. of dredged approach channels); the depth, originally 26 ft., is now 42.5 ft., and the width, originally 72 ft., is now 197 ft. Average time of transit is 13¼ hours. Some 6,000 ships use it annually. The canal is owned by a company whose controlling interest has been held (since 1875) by Great Britain; the concession terminates 1968, when the canal reverts to the Egyptian govt. The desirability of a canal here was long appreciated in antiquity, and in 20th or 19th cent. B.C. a canal was built to L. Timsah, then the N end of the Red Sea. When the Red Sea receded, Xerxes I had the canal extended. It was restored several times (notably by Ptolemy II and Trajan) until 8th cent. A.D., when it closed and fell into disrepair.

Suf (sōōf), village (pop. c.3,500), N Jordan, 4 mi. NW of Jerash; grains, vineyards. Sometimes spelled Soof.

Sufetula, Tunisia: see SBEITLA.

Suffern, suburban residential village (pop. 4,010), Rockland co., SE N.Y., on Ramapo R., in the Ramapos, at N.J. line, c.27 mi. NW of downtown Manhattan; trade center, in diversified-farming area; mfg. (clothing, cosmetics, condiments, machinery, metal products, baskets); crushed stone. Has summer stock theater. Inc. 1896.

Suffield, town (pop. 4,895), Hartford co., N Conn., on the Connecticut, at Mass. line, and 16 mi. N of Hartford; grows and packs tobacco. Cigar making began in 1810. Suffield Acad. for boys here. Settled c.1670.

Sufflenheim, France: see SOUFFLENHEIM.

Suffolk (sŭ'fŭk), county (□ 1,481.7; 1931 pop. 401,114; 1951 census 442,439), SE England; ⊙ Ipswich. Bounded by Cambridge (W), Norfolk (N), North Sea (E), and Essex (S). Drained by Deben, Stour, Alde, Lark, Orwell, and Waveney rivers. Generally level country, rising toward W to low chalk hills, continuing the Chilterns. Wheat, barley, and vegetable growing; dairying; hog, sheep, and horse ("Suffolk punches") raising. Lowestoft is important North Sea fishing center; oyster fishing is carried on at Orford and in Orwell R. estuary. There are some metalworking and agr.-implement industries; printing industry is important in Beccles and Bungay. For administrative purposes, co. is divided into East Suffolk (□ 870.9; 1931 pop. 294,977; 1951 census 321,849) and West Suffolk (□ 610.8; 1931 pop. 106,137; 1951 census 120,590). Important towns include Ipswich, Lowestoft, Felixstowe (resort), Sudbury, Newmarket, Framlingham, Bury St. Edmunds, Eye, Stowmarket, Beccles, Saxmundham, and Bungay. Has many traces of Roman occupation, including fort at Burgh Castle. Co. was crossed by Icknield Way.

Suffolk. 1 County (□ 55; pop. 896,615), E Mass., on Massachusetts Bay and Boston Bay; ⊙ Boston. Comprises cities of Boston, Chelsea, Revere, Winthrop, and several small isls. in Boston Harbor and the bay. Formed 1643. **2** County (□ 922; pop. 276,129), SE N.Y.; ⊙ Riverhead. On central and E Long Isl., bounded W by Nassau co., S by the Atlantic, E by Block Island Sound, N by Long Island Sound. Traversed E-W by 2 parallel highways: along N shore to Orient Point, and along S shore to Montauk Point, the most easterly point of Long Isl. and N.Y. Served by lines of Long Isl. RR. Off S shore, barrier isls. shelter Great South, Moriches, and Shinnecock bays from the Atlantic; bet. E peninsulas ("flukes") of Long Isl. are Great Peconic, Little Peconic, and Gardiners bays, with many inlets; on N shore are Huntington and Smithtown bays and Port Jefferson Harbor. Ferries from Port Jefferson to Bridgeport, Conn., and from Orient Point to New London, Conn. Residential and summer-resort region, with areas of large estates (notably Southampton), picturesque villages (many among oldest in state). Principal centers:

Patchogue, Babylon, Amityville, Riverhead, Southampton. Huge duck-raising industry along S shore; large oyster beds, fisheries; offshore and surf sport fishing (especially at Montauk Point); yachting. Potato and truck farming, and dairying supply New York city metropolitan area (W). Some mfg. Includes Shinnecock Indian Reservation, many state parks (Montauk Point, Hither Hills, Orient Beach, Wildwood, Sunken Meadow, Belmont Lake, Heckscher). Formed 1683 as one of original N.Y. counties.

Suffolk, city (pop. 12,339), in but independent of Nansemond co., SE Va., on Nansemond R. (head of navigation) and 20 mi. SW of Norfolk; co. courthouse is here. Important peanut market and processing center; rail and highway junction; mfg. of agr. machinery, paper boxes, bldg. materials, fertilizer; lumber milling, meat packing, cotton ginning. Settled 1720; inc. as town 1808, as city 1910. Burned by British in 1779, occupied (1862) by Union troops in Civil War and besieged by Longstreet in April, 1863.

Sufian (sōōfēän'), village, Third Prov., in Azerbaijan, NW Iran, 20 mi. NW of Tabriz and on railroad to Julfa; junction for Sharifkhaneh; grain, fruit.

Sufi-Kishlak (sōōfē"-kēshläk'), village (1926 pop. 1,602), E Andizhan oblast, Uzbek SSR, near railroad, 15 mi. ESE of Andizhan; metalworks; quarrying.

Sufi-Kurgan (-kōōrgän'), village, SE Osh oblast, Kirghiz SSR, in Alai Range, on Osh-Khorog highway and 50 mi. SE of Osh; cattle, wheat. Formerly spelled Sofi-Kurgan or Sofi-Korgon.

Sufli, Greece: see SOUPHLION.

Suftgen, France: see ZOUFFTGEN.

Sufu, China: see KASHGAR.

Sug-Aksy (sōōk"-ŭksē'), village, W Tuva Autonomous Oblast, Russian SFSR, 130 mi. W of Kyzyl and on Khemchik R., in agr. area. Iron and asbestos mining near by.

Sugarbush Hill, NE Wis., in SE Forest co., SE of Crandon. Highest point (1,951 ft.) in state.

Sugar City. 1 Town (pop. 527), Crowley co., SE central Colo., near Arkansas R., 5 mi. E of Ordway; alt. 4,325 ft. Trade center in cattle and sugar-beet area; beet sugar. **2** or **Sugar,** village (pop. 684), Madison co., E Idaho, 4 mi. NNE of Rexburg; alt. 4,892 ft.; beet sugar.

Sugar Creek, city (pop. 1,858), Jackson co., W Mo., on Missouri R. just E of Kansas City. Agr. center; oil wells; oil refinery, cement plant. Inc. 1920.

Sugarcreek, village (pop. 889), Tuscarawas co., E Ohio, 10 mi. W of New Philadelphia and on small Sugar Creek; makes brick, tile, cheese; coal mining.

Sugar Creek. 1 In central and W Ind., rises in Clinton co., flows 85 mi. SW, past Crawfordsville, to the Wabash 6 mi. N of Montezuma. **2** In central Ind., rises in Henry co., flows c.65 mi. SSW to East Fork of White R. 5 mi. NNW of Edinburg.

Sugar Grove. 1 Village (pop. 434), Fairfield co., central Ohio, 6 mi. SSE of Lancaster, and on Hocking R., in agr. area. **2** or **Sugargrove,** borough (pop. 520), Warren co., NW Pa., 16 mi. ENE of Corry, near N.Y. line.

Sugar Hill. 1 Town (pop. 783), Gwinnett co., N central Ga., just W of Buford. **2** Village, N.H.: see LISBON.

Sugar Island, E Upper Peninsula, Mich., in St. Marys R. just below Sault Ste. Marie, bet. lakes Nicolet (W) and George (E); 16 mi. long, 2–9 mi. wide. Mich.-Ont. boundary passes to N and E. Resort; some farming, maple-sugar making.

Sugar Land, village (pop. 2,285), Fort Bend co., S Texas, near Brazos R., 21 mi. WSW of Houston; sugar refining; also oil, fig, vegetable processing, chemical mfg.; oil wells. State prison farms are near.

Sugar Loaf, mountain (1,955 ft.), NW Monmouth, England, 3 mi. NNW of Abergavenny; highest point of Monmouth.

Sugarloaf, mountain (1,887 ft.), SW Co. Cork, Ireland, near Bantry Bay, 8 mi. WNW of Bantry.

Sugarloaf Key, Fla.: see FLORIDA KEYS.

Sugar Loaf Mountain, Port. *Pão de Açúcar* (pä'ō dĭ äsōō'kŭr), granitic peak (1,296 ft.) in Rio de Janeiro city, Brazil, guarding entrance to Guanabara Bay. Summit reached by aerial railroad in 2 stages (stopover at Urca hill). Magnificent view of city and beaches; one of Rio's principal landmarks.

Sugar Loaf Mountain (2,494 ft.), Sierra Leone colony, on Sierra Leone Peninsula, 5 mi. S of Freetown.

Sugarloaf Mountain (4,237 ft.), Franklin co., W Maine, 26 mi. NW of Farmington.

Sugar Loaf Mountain (c.1,280 ft.), Frederick co., N Md., just E of Lilypons, in a park.

Sugarloaf Point, E New South Wales, Australia, in Pacific Ocean NE of Port Stephens; 32°26'S 152°34'E; lighthouse. Seal Rocks (cluster of small rocks) lie just off point. Sometimes called Seal Rocks Point.

Sugarloaf Reservoir, Australia: see EILDON WEIR.

Sugar Notch, borough (pop. 2,002), Luzerne co., NE central Pa., 5 mi. SW of Wilkes-Barre. Inc. 1867.

Sugar River. 1 In Sullivan co., SW N.H., rises in Sunapee L., flows c.25 mi. W, past Newport and Claremont (water power), to the Connecticut. **2** In S Wis. and N Ill., rises in Dane co., Wis., flows generally SE to Pecatonica R. in Winnebago co., Ill., 10 mi. SW of Beloit (Wis.); c.70 mi. long.

Sugar Valley, town (pop. 214), Gordon co., NW Ga., 5 mi. NW of Calhoun, in agr. area.

Suga-shima (sōōgä'shĭmä), island (□ 2; pop. 1,120), Mie prefecture, Japan, in Ise Bay (inlet of Philippine Sea), just E of Toba; 2.5 mi. long, 1 mi. wide; hilly, fertile. Pearling by women divers. Lighthouse at E end.

Sugat Pass, Kashmir and China: see SUGET PASS.

Sugaya (sōōgä'yä), town (pop. 5,620), Ibaraki prefecture, central Honshu, Japan, 5 mi. N of Mito; rice, wheat.

Sugden (sŭg'dŭn), town (pop. 105), Jefferson co., S Okla., 5 mi. S of Waurika, and on Beaver Creek.

Suget Pass (sōō'gĕt) or **Sugat Pass** (-gät) (alt. 17,600 ft.), in W Kunlun mts., on Kashmir-China border (undefined), 150 mi. N of Leh, and on main Kashmir-China trade route.

Sugh, India: see JAGADHRI.

Sugh el Giumaa, Tripolitania: see SUK EL GIUMA.

Sugi or **Soegi** (both: sōō'gē), island (□ c.40; 10 mi. long, 5 mi. wide), Riouw Archipelago, Indonesia, 30 mi. SSW of Singapore, just W of Chombal; lumbering, fishing.

Sugito (sōōgē'tō), town (pop. 5,670), Saitama prefecture, central Honshu, Japan, 11 mi. NE of Omiya; rice, wheat, raw silk.

Sugla, Lake (sōōlä'), Turkish *Suğla* (□ 48), SW central Turkey, 40 mi. SW of Konya; 8 mi. wide, 7 mi. long; alt. 3,410 ft. Receives outlet of L. Beysehir (NW).

Sugluk (sŭg'lŭk), village, N Que., on Sugluk Inlet (15 mi. long) of Hudson Strait; 64°14'N 75°31'W; Hudson's Bay Co. trading post.

Sügüt, Turkey: see SOGUT.

Suhag, Egypt: see SOHAG.

Suha Gora or **Sukha Gora** (sōō'khä gô'rä), mountain, NW Macedonia, Yugoslavia, extending c.10 mi. N-S bet. Vardar (W) and Treska (E) rivers; highest point (5,733 ft.) is 12 mi. NNE of Gostivar.

Suhaj, Egypt: see SOHAG.

Suhar, Oman: see SOHAR.

Suhe Bator, Mongolia: see SUKHE BATOR.

Suhl (zōōl), town (pop. 24,598), in former Prussian Saxony prov. exclave, central Germany, after 1945 in Thuringia, in Thuringian Forest, 25 mi. S of Gotha; automobile, bicycle, precision instruments, chemical, toy, china works. Formerly noted small-arms-mfg. center. Has 16th–17th-cent. castle and 18th-cent. church. Founded before 1200, and chartered 1527, town had important salt trade. During Thirty Years War, it became arms- and armor-mfg. center (industry based on local iron mines, now exhausted).

Suhr (zōōr), town (pop. 3,067), Aargau canton, N Switzerland, on Suhr R. and 2 mi. SE of Aarau; metalworking, clothes.

Suhr River, N Switzerland, rises in L. of Sempach near Sursee, flows 21 mi. N to the Aar near Aarau.

Suhsien (sōō'shyĕn'), town, ⊙ Suhsien co. (pop. 1,089,825), N Anhwei prov., China, 55 mi. NNW of Pengpu and on Tientsin-Pukow RR; coal-mining center; wheat, beans, rice, kaoliang, corn. Until 1912 called Suchow.

Suhum (sōōhōōm'), town, Eastern Prov., S central Gold Coast colony, 15 mi. WSW of Koforidua; cacao market; palm oil and kernels, cassava.

Suhut (shōōhōōt'), Turkish *Şuhut,* village (pop. 4,529), Afyonkarahisar prov., W central Turkey, 16 mi. S of Afyonkarahisar; grain, mohair goats.

Sui, China: see SUI RIVER.

Suian (swā'än'), town (pop. 5,112), ⊙ Suian co. (pop. 128,706), W Chekiang prov., China, near Anhwei line, 35 mi. NNW of Chühsien; rice, wheat, peanuts, sugar cane, vegetable oil.

Suibara (sōōē'bärŭ), town (pop. 12,681), Niigata prefecture, central Honshu, Japan, 11 mi. SE of Niigata; rice, silk cocoons.

Suichang or **Sui-ch'ang** (swā'chäng'), town (pop. 4,301), ⊙ Suichang co. (pop. 114,273), SW Chekiang prov., China, 40 mi. WNW of Lishui and on headstream of Wu R.; plums, apricots, chestnuts, tea, rice.

Sui-ch'i, China: see SUIKAI.

Sui-chiang, town, China: see SUIKIANG.

Sui Chiang, river, China: see SUI RIVER.

Suichow, China: see SUIHSIEN.

Sui-ch'uan, China: see SUICHWAN.

Suichung (swā'jōōng'), town, ⊙ Suichung co. (pop. 253,713), SW Liaosi prov., Manchuria, on railroad and 38 mi. NE of Shanhaikwan, near Gulf of Liaotung; gold deposits; salt; brick and tiles; cotton, kaoliang.

Suichwan or **Sui-ch'uan** (both: swā'chwän'), town (pop. 12,601), ⊙ Suichwan co. (pop. 140,510), SW Kiangsi prov., China, 55 mi. SW of Kian, in rice-growing region; tungsten and bismuth mining. Until 1914 called Lungchüan.

Suifenho (swā'fŭn'hŭ'), Rus. *Pogranichnaya* (pŭgrănyēch'nŭyŭ), town, SE Sungkiang prov., Manchuria, near branch of Suifun R., 95 mi. NNW of Vladivostok; frontier station on Chinese Eastern RR, on USSR border, opposite Grodekovo.

Suifen Ho, river, Manchuria: see SUIFUN RIVER.

Suifu, China: see IPIN.

Suifun River or **Suyfun River,** Chinese *Suifen Ho* (swā'fōōn' hŭ'), in E Manchuria and Maritime Territory of Russian SFSR, rises in 2 branches in Manchurian highlands, flows over 150 mi. E and S, past Tungning, Voroshilov, and Razdolnoye (head of navigation), to Amur Bay of Sea of Japan 15 mi. NW of Vladivostok. Shallow-draught navigation in lower reaches.

Suigen, Korea: see SUWON.

Suiho, Korea: see SUPUNG.

Suihsien (swā'shyĕn'). **1** Town, ⊙ Suihsien co. (pop. 336,077), N Honan prov., China, on road and 50 mi. SE of Kaifeng; cotton weaving; sericulture; wheat, beans, kaoliang, peanuts, sesame. Until 1913 called Suichow. **2** Town (pop. 31,179), ⊙ Suihsien co. (pop. 589,575), NE central Hupeh prov., China, 35 mi. NNW of Anlu; cotton weaving, vegetable-oil processing. Until 1912, Suichow.

Suihwa or **Sui-hua** (swā'hwä'), town, ⊙ Suihwa co. (pop. 316,712), SE Heilungkiang prov., Manchuria, on Sungkiang line, 60 mi. NNE of Harbin; rail junction in agr. dist.; flour and oilseed milling; soybeans, wheat, rye, millet. Formerly called Pehtwanlintze.

Suikai (swā'kī'), Mandarin *Sui-ch'i* (swā'chē'), town (pop. 934), ⊙ Suikai co. (pop. 244,832), SW Kwangtung prov., China, on N Luichow Peninsula, 17 mi. NW of Chankiang; hemp, fruit, sugar cane.

Suikiang or **Sui-chiang** (both: swā'jyäng'), town (pop. 4,759), ⊙ Suikiang co. (pop. 29,485), northeasternmost Yunnan prov., China, 40 mi. WSW of Ipin and on right bank of Yangtze R. (Szechwan border); tung-oil processing; ramie, rice, millet, timber. Coal deposits near by. Until 1914 called Tsingkiang.

Sui Kiang, river, China: see SUI RIVER.

Sui Kong, China: see SUI RIVER.

Suilai, China: see MANAS.

Suileng (swā'lŭng'), town, ⊙ Suileng co. (pop. 98,962), SE Heilungkiang prov., Manchuria, 100 mi. NNE of Harbin; soybeans, millet, barley, rye, kaoliang, tobacco. Until 1915, Shangtsichang.

Suilu (swā'lōō'), town, ⊙ Suilu co. (pop. 45,832), SW Kwangsi prov., China, on railroad, 40 mi. SW of Nanning; rice, wheat, ramie, bamboo, rattan.

Suining (swā'nĭng'). **1** Town, ⊙ Suining co. (pop. 164,118), SW Hunan prov., China, near Kwangsi line, 65 mi. SSE of Chihkiang; rice. Iron and copper mining near by. Gold deposits. **2** Town, ⊙ Suining co. (pop. 645,890), N Kiangsu prov., China, 50 mi. SE of Süchow; wheat, kaoliang, corn, cotton. **3** Town (pop. 57,891), ⊙ Suining co. (pop. 570,191), central Szechwan prov., China, 55 mi. NW of Hochwan and on Fow R. (sometimes called Suining R.); sweet-potato center; rice, sugar cane, wheat, cotton, beans. Oil deposits and saltworks near by.

Suining River, China: see FOW RIVER.

Suipacha (swēpä'chä), town (pop. 2,973), ⊙ Suipacha dist. (□ 365; pop. 6,410), N Buenos Aires prov., Argentina, 11 mi. WSW of Mercedes; grain, flax, livestock; dairying, flour milling.

Suipacha, town (pop. c.2,100), Potosí dept., SW Bolivia, on San Juan R., opposite Nazareno, and 12 mi. SE of Tupiza; orchards, corn.

Suipin (swā'bĭn'), town, ⊙ Suipin co. (pop. 50,000), N Sungkiang prov., Manchuria, 10 mi. WNW of Fuchin, across Sungari R.; beans, wheat, kaoliang, tobacco. The name Suipin was applied 1929–35 to a village 10 mi. ENE, on Sungari R.; and 1946–49 to a village 30 mi. NNE, on Amur R.

Suiping or **Sui-p'ing** (swā'pĭng'), town, ⊙ Suiping co. (pop. 263,277), S central Honan prov., China, 30 mi. S of Yencheng and on Peking-Hankow RR; beans, wheat, kaoliang.

Suippe River (swēp), Marne dept., N France, rises near Suippes in the Champagne badlands, flows c.45 mi. NW to the Aisne just below Neufchâtel-sur-Aisne.

Suippes (swēp), town (pop. 2,697), Marne dept., N France, on Suippe R. and 14 mi. NE of Châlons-sur-Marne; wool combing and spinning.

Suira, Fr. Morocco: see MOGADOR.

Sui River (swā), Cantonese *Sui Kong* (sōō'ē gông'), Mandarin *Sui Kiang* or *Sui Chiang* (swā' jyäng'), S China, rises in E Kwangsi prov., flows 100 mi. SE, past Waitsap, into Kwangtung prov., past Szewui, and empties into West and North rivers in area of Samshui. Sometimes called Bamboo R. for bamboo woods along its banks.

Suir River (shōōr), Ireland, rises in the Devilsbit Mts., N Co. Tipperary, flows S, past Thurles and Cahir, then E along Waterford border, past Clonmel and Currick-on-Suir, along Waterford-Kilkenny border, past Waterford, to join Barrow R. at head of Waterford Harbour; 85 mi. long. Navigable below Clonmel.

Suisho-shima, Russian SFSR: see SHUISHIO ISLAND.

Suisse, Fr. name for SWITZERLAND.

Suisun Bay (sŭsōōn'), extreme E arm of SAN FRANCISCO BAY, W Calif., connected with San Pablo Bay (W) by Carquinez Strait. Receives from E the united Sacramento and San Joaquin rivers. Port Chicago and Martinez are on S shore; at Martinez, drawbridge crosses bay to point near Benicia.

Suisun City or **Suisun,** town (pop. 946), Solano co., W central Calif., just S of Fairfield and on Suisun Slough (navigable connection with Suisun Bay), in fertile agr. region; canneries, packing houses, boat yards. Travis (formerly Fairfield-Suisun) Air Force Base is near by.

Suita (sōō'ē'tä), city (1940 pop. 65,812; 1947 pop. 72,197), Osaka prefecture, S Honshu, Japan, 7 mi. N of Osaka; beer and sake breweries.

Suiteh or **Sui-te** (swā'dŭ'), town, ⊙ Suiteh co. (pop. 157,398), NE Shensi prov., China, 75 mi. NE of Yenan; commercial center; trades in furs, wool, hides. Millet, wheat, kaoliang. Saltworks near by.

Suiting (swā'dĭng'). **1** Town, ⊙ Suiting co. (pop. 44,611), W Sinkiang prov., China, 30 mi. WNW of Kuldja, near USSR border and near Ili R.; trades in tea, carpets, livestock; wine and cheese processing, tanning. Opened to foreign trade in 1850. Sometimes called Ili. **2** Town, Szechwan prov., China: see TAHSIEN.

Suitland (sōōt'lŭnd), village (1940 pop. 1,169), Prince Georges co., central Md., ESE suburb of Washington. U.S. Bureau of the Census and Navy Hydrographic Office are here. Suitland Parkway (9 mi. long; made a unit of Natl. Capital Parks in 1949) extends bet. Washington and Andrews Air Force Base, Md.

Suitung (swā'dōōng'), town, NE Jehol prov., Manchuria, on road and 30 mi. SSW of Kailu; trading center. Called Pasientung until c.1910. The name Suitung previously applied to Kulunkai, 50 mi. SE.

Suiyang (swā'yäng'), town (pop. 8,767), ⊙ Suiyang co. (pop. 140,995), N Kweichow prov., China, 25 mi. NE of Tsunyi; cotton weaving, papermaking; grain, timber.

Suiyuan or **Suiyüan** (swā'yüän'), province (□ 135,000; pop. 2,000,000) of N China, partly in Inner Mongolia; ⊙ Kweisui. Bounded N by Mongolian People's Republic, W by Ningsia, S by Shensi and Shansi along the Great Wall, and E by Chahar, Suiyuan lies entirely on the Mongolian plateau astride the great Yellow R. bend. It consists of the Yeghe Jo league of the Ordos Desert inside the bend (SW), an agr. belt extending E–W through the prov.'s center; and the Olanchab league in the pasture lands N of the Tatsing Mts. Its desert and steppe climate permits agr. only in irrigated areas. These are mainly the Howtao and Saratsi areas, adjoining the Yellow R. Wheat, oats, kaoliang, beans, ramie, licorice are the principal products. Sheep, cattle, camels, and horses are raised in the nomadic dists. Coal is mined at S foot of the Tatsing Mts., and natron is extracted in the lake Yenhai Tze. Wool weaving (rugs), flour milling, fur and hide processing are local industries. Chinese pop. (speaking N Mandarin) and settled economy is concentrated in central agr. belt served (since early 1920s) by railroad from Peking. Here are the chief trade centers: Paotow, Kweisui, Tsining, and Fengchen. Mongol pop. lives in Olanchab area (N; main town is Polingmiao) and in Ordos Desert (SW). The prov., named for Chinese section of Kweisui city, was originally formed in 1914 out of Ordos and Olanchab sections of Inner Mongolia and out of N Shansi (including Kweisui). A section of Chahar passed to Suiyuan in 1928, when it became a full prov. During Sino-Japanese War (1937–45), Suiyuan was joined with Chahar to form MENGKIANG, a Jap. puppet state of Inner Mongolia. Prov. passed to Communists in 1948.

Suiyuan, town, Suiyuan prov., China: see KWEISUI.

Suiyüan, Manchuria: see FUYÜAN, Sungkiang prov.

Suiza, La, Costa Rica: see LA SUIZA.

Sujangarh (sōō'jängŭr), town (pop. 24,972), N central Rajasthan, India, 75 mi. ESE of Bikaner; trades in wool, hides, salt, leather goods; hand-loom weaving, pottery making; ivory products.

Sujanpur (sōōjän'pōōr), village, Gurdaspur dist., NW Punjab, India, on Upper Bari Doab Canal and 4 mi. NW of Pathankot; wheat, sugar cane, gram; sugar milling, mfg. of spirits, carbonic-acid gas; hand-loom woolen weaving.

Sukabumi or **Soekaboemi** (both: sōōkŭbōō'mē), town (pop. 34,191), W Java, Indonesia, 50 mi. S of Jakarta, at foot of Mt. Pangrango; 6°55'S 106°54'E; alt. 1,970 ft.; trade center for agr. area (rubber, rice, corn, cassava, copra); health resort. Has textile mills, machine shops.

Sukagawa (sōōkä'gäwŭ), town (pop. 24,625), Fukushima prefecture, central Honshu, Japan, 7 mi. S of Koriyama, in agr. area (rice, tobacco); horse breeding, spinning, sake brewing. Has large tree-peony garden.

Sukaraja, Sukaradja, or **Soekaradja** (all: sōōkŭrä'jŭ), town (pop. 16,632), S central Java, Indonesia, 80 mi. WNW of Jogjakarta; trade center for agr. area (sugar, rice, tobacco, corn, peanuts, cassava).

Suk el Giuma (sōōk' ĕl jōō'mä), Ital. *Sugh el Giumaa*, town (pop. c.1,300; 1950 dist. pop. 35,000), W Tripolitania, Libya, 4 mi. E of Tripoli, in an oasis on Mediterranean coast; commercial center (dates, cereals, tobacco, henna; livestock); olive oil, flour, bricks, barracans, leather goods, sickles.

Suk esh Sheyukh, Iraq: see SUQ ASH SHUYUKH.

Suket (sōōkāt'), former princely state (□ 392; pop. 71,092) of Punjab States, India; ⊙ was Sundarnagar (formerly called Suket). Since 1948, merged with Himachal Pradesh.

Sukhachevka (sōōkhŭchôf'kŭ), W suburb (1926 pop. 2,834) of Dnepropetrovsk, Dnepropetrovsk oblast, Ukrainian SSR, on right bank of Dnieper R. and 8 mi. W of city center.

Sukha Gora, Yugoslavia: see SUHA GORA.

Sukhaya Tes, Russian SFSR: see BAGRAD.

Sukhe Bator, Suhe Bator (both: sŭ'khä bä'tōr), or **Sühe Baatar** (bä'tär); aimak (□ 28,300; pop. 50,000), E Mongolian People's Republic; ⊙ Barun Urt. Bounded SE by China's Inner Mongolian Autonomous Region, it lies largely on a steppe plateau.

Sukhe Bator, Suhe Bator, or **Sühe Baatar**, city (pop. over 2,000), Selenga aimak, N Mongolian People's Republic, on Selenga R. at mouth of the Orkhon, on railroad and 165 mi. NNW of Ulan Bator, 15 mi. WSW of Altan Bulak; trade center and freight transshipment point on major USSR-Mongolia route. Developed c.1940 as upstream head of Selenga R. navigation, partly superseding Altan Bulak. Reached 1949 by railroad to Ulan Bator. Named for Mongolian revolutionary leader who died in 1923.

Sukhindol (sōōkhēn'dôl), village (pop. 4,737), Gorna-Oryakhovitsa dist., N Bulgaria, 11 mi. NNE of Sevliyevo; wine-making center; grain, livestock.

Sukhinichi (sōōkhē'nyĭchē, city (1938 pop. over 10,000), central Kaluga oblast, Russian SFSR, 45 mi. SW of Kaluga; rail junction; flour; woolen milling; brickworks. Chartered 1762.

Sukhne, Es, El Sukhne, or **Al-Sukhnah** (all: ĕs sōōkh'nŭ), Fr. *Soukhné*, town, Homs prov., central Syria, 40 mi. NE of Palmyra.

Sukhobezvodnoye (sōō"khŭbyĭzvôd'nŭyŭ), town (1944 pop. over 500), N central Gorki oblast, Russian SFSR, on railroad and 22 mi. NE of Semenov; sawmilling.

Sukhobuzimskoye (–bōōzēm'skŭyŭ), village (1939 pop. over 2,000), S Krasnoyarsk Territory, Russian SFSR, 37 mi. NNE of Krasnoyarsk; dairy farming.

Sukhodolski or **Sukhodol'skiy** (–dôl'skē), town (1948 pop. over 500), E Tula oblast, Russian SFSR, 3 mi. NNE of Kaganovich, in Moscow Basin; lignite mining.

Sukhoi Log or **Sukhoy Log** (sōōkhoi' lôk"), city (1938 pop. estimate 11,000), S Sverdlovsk oblast, Russian SFSR, on Pyshma R. and 50 mi. ENE of Sverdlovsk, on railroad; mfg. (cement, fireproof bricks). Became city in 1943. Kuri, village (1926 pop. 2,537), is 4 mi. E, on rail spur; refractory-clay quarrying, paper milling.

Sukhoi Nos or **Sukhoy Nos** (nôs"), cape on W coast of N isl. of Novaya Zemlya, Russian SFSR; 73°45'N 53°40'E.

Sukhona River (sōōkhô'nŭ), Vologda oblast, Russian SFSR, issues from SE Kubeno L., flows 358 mi. ENE, past Sokol, Totma, and Nyuksenitsa, joining Yug R. at Veliki Ustyug to form Lesser [Rus. *Malaya*] NORTHERN DVINA RIVER. Navigable for entire course. Receives Vologda R. (right). The name Sukhona is sometimes applied to the Lesser Northern Dvina bet. Veliki Ustyug and Kotlas.

Sukhothai (sōō'kō'tī'), town (1947 pop. 9,979), ⊙ Sukhothai prov. (□ 2,712; 1947 pop. 193,698), N Thailand, on Yom R. and 230 mi. NNW of Bangkok; rice, tobacco, beans, cotton. An early Thai settlement under Khmer rule, it became independent (13th cent.) and was 1st capital (1257–1350) of a unified Thai state until transfer of seat of government to Ayutthaya. Also spelled Sukotai, Sukhodhai, and Sukhoday. Local name, Thani.

Sukhov Vtoroi or **Sukhov Vtoroy** (sōō'khŭf ftŭroi') [Rus.,=Sukhov No. 2], village (1939 pop. over 500), N central Stalingrad oblast, Russian SFSR, near railroad (Rakovka station), 11 mi. SE of Mikhailovka; metalworks; wheat, sunflowers.

Sukhumi (sōōkhōō'mē), city (1939 pop. 44,350), ⊙ Abkhaz Autonomous SSR, Georgian SSR, port on Black Sea, on coastal railroad and 100 mi. NNW of Batum; 43°N 41°2'E. One of chief subtropical resorts of USSR; tobacco, fruit, and fish processing, metalworking, distilling; agr. (citrus fruit, tobacco, tea). S terminus of Sukhumi Military Road. Has botanic garden, Abkhaz scientific research institute, agr. experimental station, teachers col. Site of Roman sulphur baths and Byzantine fortifications. Power obtained from Sukhumi hydroelectric station (*Sukhumges*), 7 mi. N, on Gumista R. On site of Gr. colony of Dioscurias, later the Roman Sebastopolis, was (after 15th cent.) Turkish fortress of Sukhum-Kale, which passed (1810) to Russia. Called Sukhum until 1936, when the Georgian form of the name (Sukhumi) was officially adopted.

Sukhumi Military Road, road (c.120 mi. long) across the Greater Caucasus, linking Sukhumi (Georgian SSR) and Ust-Dzhegutinskaya (Russian SFSR). Uses Kuban, Teberda, and Kodor river valleys; crosses Caucasian crest at Klukhori Pass (alt. 9,239 ft.) as a trail. Main way stations: Klukhori, Teberda.

Suki or **Es Suki** (ĕs sōō'kē), town (pop. 6,600), Blue Nile prov., E central Anglo-Egyptian Sudan, on right bank of Blue Nile, on railroad and 10 mi. N of Singa; rail-steamer transfer point for Roseires; cotton, wheat, barley, corn, fruits, durra; livestock.

Sukiatun or **Su-chia-t'un** (both: sōō'jyä'tōōn'), town, W central Liaotung prov., Manchuria, 8 mi. SSW of Mukden; rail junction on South Manchuria RR for lines to Dairen, Antung, and Fushun.

Sukkari, El, Es Sukkari, or **Al-Sukkari** (all: ĕs-sōōk'kärē), town, Red Sea Frontier Prov., E Egypt, 85 mi. SSE of Kosseir; gold mining.

Sukkertoppen (sōō'kŭrtô"pŭn), Eskimo *Manitsoq*, town (pop. 821), ⊙ Sukkertoppen dist. (pop. 1,831), SW Greenland, at S tip of Sukkertoppen Isl. (6 mi. long, 4 mi. wide), on Davis Strait, 90 mi. NNW of Godthaab; 65°25'N 52°56'W. Fishing and hunting base. Meteorological and radio station, hosp., children's sanitarium. Founded 1761 on site of present Kangamiut settlement.

Sukkur (sōōk'kōōr), district (□5,550; pop. 692,556), NE Sind, W Pakistan; ⊙ Sukkur. Bordered SE by Rajasthan; crossed E by Thar Desert; irrigated (center) by canals from Indus R., including noted Sukkur Barrage system. Has 2 enclaves in Khairpur state (S). Agr. (millet, wheat, rice, gram, rapeseed); mangoes and dates cultivated; handicrafts (pottery, metal and leather goods, cloth fabrics). Sukkur and Shikarpur are trade centers. Fishing (chiefly shad) in the Indus. Area under Ghaznevid rule in 11th cent.

Sukkur, city (pop. 66,466), ⊙ Sukkur dist., NE Sind, W Pakistan, on Indus R. (bridged), on railroad (workshops) and 220 mi. NNE of Karachi; important commercial center; cotton ginning, silk milling, dyeing, rice and flour milling, boat building, mfg. of cement, tiles, leather goods, confectioneries, cigarettes, sewing thread, hosiery, playing cards; fodder presses, chemical and metalworks Markets millet, wheat, rice, oilseeds, cloth fabrics, fish. Technical school. Bukkur, an old isl. fortress, lies in the Indus (E), bet. Sukkur and Rohri.

Sukkur Barrage, irrigation dam across Indus R., in Sukkur dist., N Sind, W Pakistan, just below city of Sukkur; c.5,000 ft. long. Built 1923–32; controls one of largest irrigation systems in the world. Gates at both ends regulate supply of water to 7 canals: right-bank canals are Dadu, Rice, and North Western which extend S and W through Sukkur, Larkana, and Dadu dists., and SW Sibi (in Baluchistan); left-bank canals are Eastern Nara, Rohri, and 2 smaller channels, which extend S through Khairpur state and Nawabshah, Hyderabad, and Thar Parkar dists. Total length of all canals and distributaries is c.6,000 mi. (including subsidiary watercourses, c.50,000 mi.); total area irrigated is over 5,000,000 acres. Chief crops: wheat, cotton, millet, rice, oilseeds. Also known as Lloyd Barrage.

Suklatirtha (sōōk'lŭtēr"tŭ), village, Broach dist., N Bombay, India, on Narbada R. and 10 mi. ENE of Broach. Noted place of Hindu pilgrimage, with sacred bathing ghats. Also spelled Suklatirth.

Sukotai, Thailand: see SUKHOTHAI.

Sükow or **Hsü-kou** (both: shü'gō'), town, ⊙ Sükow co. (pop. 43,320), central Shansi prov., China, on railroad and 20 mi. S of Taiyüan; wheat, sweet potatoes, cabbage, melons.

Sukreml or **Sukreml'** (sōōkrĕ'mŭl), town (1926 pop. 2,306), SW Kaluga oblast, Russian SFSR, 3 mi. S of Lyudinovo; metalworking.

Suksun (sōōksōōn'), town (1939 pop. 5,300), SE Molotov oblast, Russian SFSR, on Sylva R. and 24 mi. SE of Kungur; machine mfg., metalworking. Formerly called Suksunski Zavod.

Sukumo (sōōkōō'mō), town (pop. 13,976), Kochi prefecture, SW Shikoku, Japan, on inlet of Hoyo Strait, 22 mi. SSE of Uwajima; agr. and fishing center; ornamental coral, tuna, rice, raw silk.

Sukuta (säkōō'tä), residential town (pop. 1,626), Western Div., Gambia, in Kombo North, 9 mi. WSW of Bathurst (linked by road); truck gardens.

Sul, Egypt: see SOL.

Sula (sōō'lä), island (□ 22.5; pop. 4,152) in North Sea, More og Romsdal co., W Norway, at mouth of Stor Fjord, 3 mi. S of Alesund; 10 mi. long, 4 mi. wide; rises to 2,600 ft. Fisheries.

Sula Besi, Indonesia: see SANANA.

Sulaco (sōōlä'kō), town (pop. 543), Yoro dept., N Honduras, on Sulaco R. and 22 mi. SSW of Yoro; sugar milling, ceramics; dairying; hogs; grain, sugar cane.

Sulaco, Sierra de (syĕ'rä dā), mountain range of N Honduras, N of Sulaco; rises to over 7,000 ft. Forms watershed bet. upper Aguán R. (N) and Sulaco R. (S).

Sulaco River, N central Honduras, formed by several branches joining SE of Sulaco; flows c.50 mi. W, past Sulaco, to Comayagua R. 13 mi. ENE of Santa Cruz de Yojoa. Forms Yoro-Comayagua dept. border.

Sulaimaniya or **Sulaymaniyah** (sōōlī"mänē'yŭ), province (□ 3,619; pop. 222,732), NE Iraq, in Kurdistan, bordering E on Iran; ⊙ Sulaimaniya. Mountainous. Grows tobacco, fruit; livestock raising. Sometimes spelled Suleimanieh.

Sulaimaniya or **Sulaymaniyah**, town (pop. 41,114), ⊙ Sulaimaniya prov., NE Iraq, in mts. of Kurdistan, near Iran line, 60 mi. E of Kirkuk, 160 mi. NNE of Baghdad; trade center; tobacco, livestock. Sometimes spelled Suleimanieh.

Sulaimanke (sōōlī'mŭngkä), village, Montgomery dist., E Punjab, W Pakistan, on left bank of Sutlej R.; headworks of canal-irrigation system; left-bank canals extend SW through N Bahawalpur, while right-bank Pakpattan Canal extends WSW through Montgomery and Multan dists. Also spelled Sulemanke.

Sulaiman Range (sōōlī'män), mountain mass in W Pakistan; from NE end of Central Brahui Range in Sibi dist. extends c.280 mi. N, along Baluchistan-Punjab border, into S North-West Frontier Prov.; c.40 mi. wide; at N end throws out E spurs. Rises in N to twin peaks (11,290 ft. and 11,085 ft.) known as TAKHT-I-SULAIMAN. Gumal R. cuts through pine-covered N end; olive trees in center; hill resort of Fort Munro toward S. Sometimes spelled Suliman.

Sula Islands or **Soela Islands** (sōō'lü), group (□ 1,873; pop. 20,137), N Moluccas, Indonesia, in Molucca Sea, bet. Celebes (W) and Obi Isls. (E); 1°45'S 125°10'E. Comprise TALIABU (largest isl.), MANGOLE, SANANA, and several islets. Group is generally mountainous, with fertile coastal strips. Agr. (coconuts, corn, sago, tobacco), fishing.

Sulaiyil or **Sulayyil** (sōōlā'yĭl), town, S Nejd, Saudi Arabia, 300 mi. SSW of Riyadh, in the Wadi Dawasir; trade center; framing (grain, dates), stock raising.

Sulak (sōōläk'), village (1926 pop. 2,986), E central Saratov oblast, Russian SFSR, on Greater Irgiz R. and 23 mi. SW of Pugachev; wheat, sunflowers, cattle.

Sulak River, N Dagestan Autonomous SSR, Russian SFSR, formed near Gimry by union of the Andi KOISU (right) and Avar-Koisu (left); flows N, through deep gorge bet. Caucasus outliers, and E, in lower course, through irrigation area (cotton, orchards, grain), to Caspian Sea, forming delta mouth at base of Agrakhan Peninsula; c.90 mi. long. Spring floods.

Sula River (sōōlä'), N Ukrainian SSR, rises SW of Sumy in Central Russian Upland, flows WSW past Romny, and generally S past Lubny, to Dnieper R. just W of Gradizhsk; 250 mi. long.

Sula Valley (sōō'lä), fertile alluvial lowland in NW Honduras, extends from Caribbean coast E of Puerto Cortés c.50 mi. S to vicinity of L. Yojoa; 10–25 mi. wide; drained by meandering courses of Chamelecón and Ulúa rivers. A major banana zone, producing also rice, sugar cane, fruit, vegetables, cotton; livestock raising. Hardwood lumbering. Main centers (served by dense rail network): San Pedro Sula, Choloma, Villaneuva.

Sulawesi, Indonesia: see CELEBES.

Sulaymaniyah, Iraq: see SULAIMANIYA.

Sulayyil, Saudi Arabia: see SULAIYIL.

Suldal Lake (sōōl'däl), Nor. *Suldalsvatn,* (□ 11), in Suldal canton (pop. 1,517), Rogaland co., SW Norway, 50 mi. NE of Stavanger, in scenic tourist area. Extends from Nesflaten 16 mi. SW to village of Suldalsosen; empties into Sand Fjord via Suldal R. Formerly spelled Suledal.

Suldeh (sōōldĕ'), town, Second Prov., in E Mazanderan, N Iran, on Caspian Sea, 40 mi. W of Babul.

Sul do Save (sōōl' dōō sä'vĭ), province (□ 59,317; 1950 pop. 1,247,399), S Mozambique; ⊙ Inhambane. Bounded N by lower Sabi R. (Port. *Save*), W by Southern Rhodesia and Transvaal, E and SE by Mozambique Channel of Indian Ocean. A wide, low coastal plain drained by Sabi, Limpopo, and Komati rivers. Commercial agr. (especially sugar plantations) along lower river courses and in vicinity of chief centers (Inhambane, Vila do João Belo). Chief exports are sugar, corn, cotton, copra, hardwoods. Prov. is subdivided into 2 dists. (Inhambane, Gaza). Lourenço Marques region, formerly in prov., became (1946) an autonomous dist.

Sulechow (sōōlĕ'khōōf), Pol. *Sulechów,* Ger. *Züllichau* (tsü'lĭ-khou), town (1939 pop. 9,897; 1946 pop. 3,284) in Brandenburg, after 1945 in Zielona Gora prov., W Poland, near the Oder, 12 mi. NNE of Grünberg (Zielona Gora); rail and road junction; agr. market (grain, vegetables, potatoes, livestock); brush mfg. Founded 1260; 1st mentioned as town in 1319; passed 1482 to Brandenburg. Scene (1759) of Austrian victory over Prussians. In Second World War, c.70% destroyed.

Sulecin (sōōlĕ'tsēn), Pol. *Sulęcin,* Ger. *Zielenzig* (tsēlĕn'tsĭkh), town (1939 pop. 6,568; 1946 pop. 2,566) in Brandenburg, after 1945 in Zielona Gora prov., W Poland, 20 mi. SSW of Landsberg (Gorzow Wielkopolski), in lake region; lignite mining, sawmilling; grain market. Remains of medieval town walls. Founded c.1240; chartered 1244. In Second World War, c.40% destroyed.

Suledal Lake, Norway: see SULDAL LAKE.

Suleimanieh, Iraq: see SULAIMANIYA.

Sulejow (sōōlĕ'yōōf), Pol. *Sulejów,* Rus. *Suleyev* (sōōlā'yĭf) or *Suleyov* (–ūf), town (pop. 4,329), Lodz prov., S central Poland, on Pilica R. and 9 mi. ESE of Piotrkow; rail spur terminus; soap mfg., sawmilling; lime kiln. Castle ruins.

Sulemanke, W Pakistan: see SULAIMANKE.

Sulen Islands, Norway: see SOLUND ISLANDS.

Suleyev, Poland: see SULEJOW.

Suleymanli, Turkey: see ZEYTUN.

Sülfeld (zül'fĕlt), village (pop. 979), in former Prussian prov. of Hanover, NW Germany, after 1945 in Lower Saxony, on Weser-Elbe Canal (lock; level difference: 30 ft.) and 12 mi. NE of Brunswick; distilling.

Sulgrave, agr. village and parish (pop. 319), S Northampton, England, 6 mi. N of Brackley. Site of the Tudor house of Sulgrave Manor, home of the ancestors of George Washington from 1539 until 1610. In 1914 it was presented to the George Washington-Sulgrave Institution; it has been restored, refurnished, and made into a mus.

Suli or **Souli** (both: sōō'lē), small mtn. district in S Epirus, Greece, 15 mi. ENE of Parga, N of Acheron R. Its inhabitants, the Suliotes, fought successfully (1790–1802) against Ali Pasha, Turkish governor of Ioannina, who massacred many of them (1803) after concluding a false truce. The remainder fled to the Ionian Isls. Permitted to return, the Suliotes were again decimated in a new rebellion (1820). Marco Bozzaris was a Suliote.

Sulikow (sōōlē'kōōf), Pol. *Sulików,* Ger. *Schönberg* (shûn'bĕrk), town (1939 pop. 1,935; 1946 pop. 1,598) in Lower Silesia, after 1945 in Wroclaw prov., SW Poland, in Upper Lusatia, 7 mi. SE of Görlitz, in lignite-mining region; tanning. After 1945, briefly called Szymbork.

Sulima (sōōlē'mä), town (pop. 664), South-Western Prov., S Sierra Leone, minor port on the Atlantic, at mouth of Moa R., and 28 mi. SSE of Pujehun; piassava center; fishing.

Suliman Range, W Pakistan: see SULAIMAN RANGE.

Sulima River, Sierra Leone: see MOA RIVER.

Sulimov, Russian SFSR: see CHERKESSK.

Sulin, Russian SFSR: see KRASNY SULIN.

Sulina (sōōlē'nä), town (1948 pop. 3,373), Galati prov., SE Rumania, in Dobruja, port on Black Sea at mouth of Sulina arm (c.50 mi. long) of the Danube delta, 41 mi. E of Tulcea; post of the International Danube Commission. Also naval station and bathing resort. Has fisheries and ship-repair installations.

Sulingen (zōō'lĭng-ün), town (pop. 6,206), in former Prussian prov. of Hanover, NW Germany, after 1945 in Lower Saxony, 17 mi. WNW of Nienburg, in peat region; rail junction.

Sulita (sōō'lētsä), Rum. *Sulița,* village (pop. 2,361), Botosani prov., NE Rumania, 14 mi. SE of Botosani; agr. center with flour mills. Also called Targu-Sulita.

Sulita, Ukrainian SSR: see NOVOSELITSA.

Sulitjelma (sōō'lĭtyĕlmä), village (pop. 2,155) in Fauske canton, Nordland co., N central Norway, at foot of Sulitjelma range, 45 mi. E of Bodo; mining and smelting center (copper, pyrites, lead, zinc). Mines opened 1887. Formerly spelled Sulitelma. Just SSW is Sandnes (sän'näs) village, terminus of railroad to Sjonsta port. Furulund (fōō'rōōlōōn) village, 2 mi. WNW, is residential and administrative center for the mines.

Sulitjelma, Swed. *Sulitelma* or *Sulitälma,* Lappish *Sullui Čielbma,* mountain range in Lapland, extending c.30 mi. NW-SE along border bet. N central Norway and NW Sweden; rises to 6,279 ft. 55 mi. E of Bodo; 67°7'N 16°25'E. Permanently snow-clad. Among the glaciers is Blamannsisen, Nor. *Blåmannsisen* (blô'mäns-ē'sün), Swed. *Åll-mallojekna* (ôl'mälōyĕk"nä), which extends N from Sulitjelma village; 10 mi. long.

Sullana (sōōyä'nä), city (pop. 22,344), ⊙ Sullana prov. (□ 1,815; pop. 55,697), Piura dept., NW Peru, on coastal plain, on Chira R., on Paita-Piura RR and 20 mi. N of Piura, on Pan American Highway; important trade and shipping center in irrigated cotton area; cottonseed-oil mills, cotton gins; charcoal burning, tanning. Cinchona bark gathered in the area.

Sulligent (sŭ'lŭjŭnt), town (pop. 1,209), Lamar co., NW Ala., near Miss. line, 80 mi. WNW of Birmingham; processes cottonseed, lumber. Settled 1887, inc. 1888.

Sullivan. 1 County (□ 457; pop. 23,667), SW Ind.; ⊙ Sullivan. Bounded W by Wabash R., here forming Ill. line; drained by small Busseron and Maria creeks. Agr. (grain, fruit, livestock, poultry; dairy products); bituminous-coal mines, limestone quarries, oil and natural-gas wells; timber. Mfg. at Sullivan and Farmersburg. Formed 1816. **2** County (□ 654; pop. 11,299), N Mo.; ⊙ Milan. Agr. (corn, oats), livestock. Formed 1845. **3** County (□ 537; pop. 26,441), SW N.H., on Vt. line; ⊙ Newport. Agr., (fruit, poultry, truck), mfg. (textiles, shoes, machinery and tools, paper); resorts in Sunapee L. area. Drained by Connecticut and Sugar rivers (water power) and Cold R. Formed 1827. **4** County (□ 986; pop. 40,731), SE N.Y.; ⊙ Monticello. Bounded W and SW by Delaware R. (here forming Pa. line); includes parts of the Catskills and the Shawangunk range. Drained by Neversink R., Shawangunk and Beaver kills, and small Willowemoc Creek. Vacation region, with many mtn. and lake resorts Poultry raising is important; also dairying, fruitgrowing. Some timber. Mfg. at Monticello. Formed 1809. **5** County (□ 478; pop. 6,745), NE Pa.; ⊙ Laporte. Scenic resort region of mtn. lakes; drained by Loyalsock and Muncy creeks. Anthracite; textiles, ice cream. Formed 1847. **6** County (□ 428; pop. 95,063), NE Tenn.; ⊙ Blountville. Bounded N by Va.; in Great Appalachian Valley, here traversed by mtn. ridges. Drained by South Fork of Holston R., site of TVA's South Holston Dam. Includes part of Cherokee Natl. Forest. Agr. (tobacco, corn, truck, fruit, hay), dairying, livestock raising; lumbering; limestone, iron-ore deposits. Industry at KINGSPORT and BRISTOL (partly in Va.). Formed 1779.

Sullivan. 1 City (pop. 3,470), ⊙ Moultrie co., central Ill., 25 mi. SE of Decatur, in agr. area (corn, soybeans, broomcorn, livestock, poultry); mfg. (shoes, concrete products, cheese and other dairy products). Inc. 1869. **2** City (pop. 5,423), ⊙ Sullivan co., SW Ind., near small Busseron Creek, 25 mi. S of Terre Haute, in dairy, poultry, and grain area; mfg. (machine-shop products, cheese, fertilizer); bituminous-coal mines, oil and gas wells; timber. Platted 1842. William H. Hays was b. here. **3** Town (pop. 762), Hancock co., S Maine, on Frenchman Bay, just NE of Mt. Desert Isl.; fishing, resorts, granite quarrying. **4** City (pop. 3,019), Crawford and Franklin counties, E central Mo., in Ozark region, near Meramec R., 55 mi. SW of St. Louis. Tourist and farm trade; mfg. (shoes, lumber products). Caverns, state park near by. Laid out c.1860. **5** Town (pop. 272), Cheshire co., SW N.H., 7 mi. NNE of Keene. **6** Village (pop. 349), Jefferson co., SE Wis., 11 mi. E of Jefferson, in dairying region.

Sullivan Island, in S Mergui Archipelago, Lower Burma, in Andaman Sea, 50 mi. NNW of Victoria Point; 20 mi. long, 2–4 mi. wide; hilly and forested; tin, tungsten, copper deposits.

Sullivan Lake (□ 62), SE central Alta., 40 mi. NE of Drumheller; 20 mi. long, 7 mi. wide. Drains S into Red Deer R.

Sullivan Lake, in Morrison co., central Minn., 22 mi. NE of Little Falls; 2.5 mi. long, 1.5 mi. wide. Platte L. is just N. Drained by Platte R. Has resorts.

Sullivans Island, Charleston co., SE S.C., at N side of entrance to Charleston Harbor; 3½ mi. long. Site of Fort MOULTRIE and Sullivans Isl., a resort village formerly called Moultrieville (mōōl'trēvĭl).

Sullurupeta, India: see SULURPET.

Sully (sülē'), village (pop. 174), Oise dept., N France, on Thérain R. and 16 mi. NW of Beauvais; optical glass mfg.

Sully (sŭ'lē), county (□ 1,061; pop. 2,713), central S.Dak.; ⊙ Onida. Agr. region bounded W by Missouri R. Cattle raising in W, dairy produce, poultry, grain in E. Formed 1877.

Sully, town (pop. 452), Jasper co., central Iowa, c.40 mi. E of Des Moines; dairy products.

Sully-sur-Loire (sülē'-sür-lwär'), town (pop. 2,051), Loiret dept., N central France, on left bank of the Loire and 24 mi. ESE of Orléans; livestock market. Biscuit and candy mfg., bicycle assembling, sawmilling. Its large 14th-cent. feudal castle was rebuilt (17th cent.) by Sully. Town and castle severely damaged in Second World War.

Sulmierzyce (sōōlmyĕ-zhĭ'tsĕ), Ger. *Sulmierschütz* (zōōlmĕr'shüts), town (1946 pop. 2,060), Poznan prov., W Poland, 7 mi. SSE of Krotoszyn; flour milling; cattle, horse, and produce trading.

Sulmona (sōōlmô'nä), town (pop. 16,854), Aquila prov., Abruzzi e Molise, S central Italy, 34 mi. SE of Aquila, in small, fertile plain surrounded by the Apennines. Rail junction; mfg. (agr. machinery, wrought iron, furniture, woolen textiles, macaroni, liquor). Bishopric. Has several fine churches and palaces. Ovid b. here. Badly damaged by air bombing (1943–44) in Second World War.

Sulo, town, China: see YANGI SHAHR.

Sulo River, China: see SHULEH RIVER.

Sulphur. 1 Town (pop. 5,996), Calcasieu parish, SW La., 10 mi. W of Lake Charles city, in agr. area. Sulphur dome here (now abandoned). Oil discovered near by in 1924. **2** City (pop. 4,389), ⊙ Murray co., S Okla., 24 mi. SW of Ada; resort, with mineral springs (ships mineral water). PLATT NATIONAL PARK is adjacent. Mfg. (cheese, cottonseed oil, feed, asphalt and metal products). Asphalt and glass-sand mining, gravel quarrying. Has a state school for the deaf and a state veterans' hosp. Near by (SW) are the Arbuckle Mts. (recreation area). Settled 1898.

Sulphur Island, Volcano Isls.: see IWO JIMA.

Sulphur River, NE Texas and SW Ark., formed in Delta co., Texas, by junction of North and South forks, flows c.110 mi. generally E to Red R. in Miller co., Ark., c.25 mi. SE of Texarkana. Site of Texarkana Reservoir (planned capacity c.2,000,000 acre-ft.; for conservation, flood control) is 8 mi. SW of Texarkana.

Sulphur Rock, town (pop. 179), Independence co., NE central Ark., 8 mi. E of Batesville.

Sulphur Springs. 1 Resort town (pop. 543), Benton co., extreme NW Ark., 33 mi. NNW of Fayetteville, in the Ozarks, at Mo. line; medicinal springs; boating, bathing. **2** Village (1940 pop. 4,968), Hillsborough co., W Fla., N suburb of Tampa; resort with mineral waters and a greyhound track. **3** Town (pop. 351), Henry co., E central Ind., 7 mi. NNW of New Castle, in agr. area. **4** City (pop. 8,991), ⊙ Hopkins co., NE Texas, 30 mi. E of Greenville; trade, shipping point in dairying, agr. region; dairy products, cottonseed oil, packed meat, brick, furniture; also ships fruit and truck produce.

Sultan, town (pop. 814), Snohomish co., NW Wash., 20 mi. ESE of Everett and on Skykomish R., timber, fruit, potatoes, peas.

Sultanabad (sōōltä'näbäd) or **Osmannagar** (ŏs'-män-nŭgŭr"), village (pop. 3,348), Karimnagar dist., E Hyderabad state, India, 14 mi. NE of Karimnagar; rice, oilseeds.

Sultanabad. 1 City, First Prov., in Arak, Iran: see ARAK. 2 Town, Ninth Prov., in Khurasan, Iran: see KASHMAR.

Sultanganj, India: see BHAGALPUR, city.

Sultangulovo (so͝oltän′go͞olŭvŭ), village, E Kuibyshev oblast, Russian SFSR, 10 mi. NNE of Pokhvistnevo; natural-gas extracting (pipe line to Pokhvistnevo).

Sultan Hamud (so͝oltän′ hämo͞od′), town, Central Prov., S central Kenya, on railroad and 65 mi. SE of Nairobi; alt. 5,025 ft. Sisal plantations. Cement plant. Game reserve (gazelles, ostriches, zebras, giraffes).

Sultaniye, Turkey: see KARAPINAR.

Sultaniyeh or Soltaniyeh (both: sōltänēyĕ′), town, First Prov., in Khamseh, N Iran, 25 mi. SE of Zenjan, and on road and railroad to Teheran. Dating from early-14th cent., it became residence of the Shiite Ilkhan Uljaitu (Sultan Mohammed Khudabanda), succeeding Tabriz. The Ilkhan's tomb towers above the town.

Sultan Mountain, peak (13,336 ft.) in San Juan Mts., SW Colo., near Silverton.

Sultan Mountains (sŭl′tŭn), W central Turkey, SE of Afyonkarahisar, extend 100 mi. SE bet. lakes Eber and Aksehir (N) and lakes Egridir and Beysehir (S); rise to 8,468 ft. in Sultan Dag. Towns of Yalvac and Sarkikaraagac on SW slope.

Sultanpur (so͝oltän′po͝or), district (□1,699; pop. 1,100,368), E central Uttar Pradesh, India; ⊙ Sultanpur. On Ganges Plain; drained by the Gumti. Rice, wheat, gram, barley, oilseeds, jowar, sugar cane, corn. Only town, Sultanpur.

Sultanpur. 1 Town (pop. 10,168), N Patiala and East Punjab States Union, India, 15 mi. SW of Kapurthala; agr. market (wheat, corn, gram, sugar); handicraft cloth weaving and printing. Here emperor Aurangzeb spent his early youth. 2 Village, Kangra dist., Punjab, India: see KULU, village. 3 Village, Saharanpur district, Uttar Pradesh, India: see CHILKANA. 4 Town (pop. 13,126), ⊙ Sultanpur dist., E central Uttar Pradesh, India, on the Gumti and 37 mi. S of Fyzabad; trades in grains, oilseeds, sugar cane. Annual fair. Extensive mango groves near by. Ruins of 16th-cent. fort built by Sher Shah 14 mi. ESE, at village of Dhopap (also called Shahgarh).

Sultan's Island, Maldive Isls.: see MALE ISLAND.

Sultanwind (so͝oltän′vĭnd), town (pop. 7,578), Amritsar dist., W Punjab, India, SE suburb of Amritsar; hand-loom weaving.

Sultepec (so͞oltäpĕk′), officially Sultepec de Pedro Ascencio Alquisiras, town (pop. 1,778), Mexico state, central Mexico, on central plateau, 36 mi. SW of Toluca; alt. 7,664 ft. Silver, gold, lead, copper, and zinc mining; fruitgrowing.

Sulu Archipelago (so͞o′lo͞o), group of islands coextensive with Sulu province (□ 1,086; 1948 pop. 240,826), Philippines, extending 200 mi. SW from Basilan Isl. (SW of Mindanao) to within 25 mi. of NE coast of Borneo, bet. Sulu Sea (N) and Celebes Sea (S); ⊙ Jolo, on Jolo Isl. Comprises nearly 400 isls. and islets and hundreds of rocks and reefs. Chief groups are Jolo, with JOLO ISLAND (largest and most important), PANGUTARAN GROUP, SAMALES GROUP, TAWITAWI GROUP, TAPUL GROUP, and Sibutu group with SIBUTU ISLAND. Of volcanic origin (and rising to 2,664 ft. on Jolo), but with numerous coral islets and reefs, they are thickly forested and have fertile soil. Rice, coconuts, cassava, and fruit are grown; but pearl-shell and pearl fishing are most important industries, centered on Jolo. Moros (Mohammedan Malays) form large part of pop. The inhabitants were converted to Mohammedanism in 14th cent.; withstood Sp. rule for centuries until mid-19th cent., when the Spaniards fortified Jolo. In 1899 the sultanate was formally recognized in a treaty with U.S.; this ended in 1940, when the reigning sultan ceded the Sulus to the Philippines.

Sulu Island, Philippines: see JOLO ISLAND.

Sulu Island (so͞olo͞o′) or **Granbusa Island** (grämbo͞o′sä), just E of Cape Gelidonya, SW Turkey, at entrance to Gulf of Antalya (Adalia).

Suluk, Cyrenaica: see SOLUCH.

Sulur (so͞o′lo͞or), town (pop. 6,850), Coimbatore dist., SW Madras, India, on Noyil R. and 12 mi. ENE of Coimbatore; cotton; betel farming.

Sulurpet (so͞o′lo͞orpĕt), town (pop. 6,798), Nellore dist., E Madras, India, on Coromandel Coast of Bay of Bengal, 45 mi. NNW of Madras, near Pulicat L.; palmyra sugar; cashew and Casuarina plantations. Gypsum deposits near by. Also spelled Sullurupeta, Sullurpeta, or Suluru.

Sulu Sea (so͞o′lo͞o), large sea in the W Pacific, bet. SW Philippines and Borneo, bordered by Cuyo Isls. (N), Panay (NE), Negros and Mindanao (E), Sulu Archipelago (SE), North Borneo (SW), Palawan (W); over 400 mi. long, E-W. In it are several groups of islets, including Cagayan Sulu Isl. and Cagayan Isls.

Sulyukta (so͞olyo͞oktä′), city (1939 pop. 10,078), W Osh oblast, Kirghiz SSR, in N foothills of Turkestan Range, on rail spur from Proletarsk and 21 mi. SSW of Leninabad; coal-mining center; power plant.

Sulz, France: see SOULTZ.

Sulz or **Sulz am Neckar** (zo͝olts′ äm nĕ′kär), town (pop. 2,958), S Württemberg, Germany, after 1945 in Württemberg-Hohenzollern, in Black Forest, on the Neckar and 13 mi. N of Rottweil; textile mfg. Has small saline bath.

Sulza, Bad, Germany: see BAD SULZA.

Sulz am Neckar, Germany: see SULZ.

Sulzbach, France: see SOULTZBACH-LES-BAINS.

Sulzbach or **Sulzbach an der Murr** (zo͝olts′bäkh än dĕr mo͝or′), village (pop. 3,377), N Württemberg, Germany, after 1945 in Württemberg-Baden, on the Murr (an affluent of the Neckar) and 11 mi. N of Schwäbisch Gmünd; cattle.

Sulzbach, city (pop. 22,130), S central Saar, on Sulz R. and 6 mi. NE of Saarbrücken; coal mining; woolen milling; mfg. of machinery, coke and by-products, margarine, furniture, clothing, food products, brushes; woodworking. Chartered 1346.

Sulzbach-Rosenberg (–rō′zünbĕrk), town (pop. 17,082), Upper Palatinate, N central Bavaria, Germany, 6 mi. NW of Amberg; iron-mining center; foundries; mfg. of chemicals and paper. Late-16th-cent. castle is prison (since 1919). Formed 1934 through union of Sulzbach and Rosenberg.

Sulzberger Bay (sŭlz′bûrgûr), large inlet (90 naut. mi. long, 100 naut. mi. wide) in NW coast of Marie Byrd Land, Antarctica, bet. Edward VII Peninsula and Ruppert Coast, in 77°S 151°W. Discovered 1929 by R. E. Byrd.

Sulzburg (zo͝olts′bo͝ork) village (pop. 1,137), S Baden, Germany, on W slope of Black Forest, 12 mi. SSW of Freiburg; lumber milling, winegrowing.

Sulzbürg (–bürk), village (pop. 1,516), Upper Palatinate, central Bavaria, Germany, 7 mi. SSW of Neumarkt; rye, oats, wheat, cattle. Has two 18th-cent. churches. Chartered 1540. Limestone quarries near by.

Sülze, Bad, Germany: see BAD SÜLZE.

Sulzer, Mount (sŭl′zûr) (10,920 ft.), S Alaska, in St. Elias Mts., 160 mi. ENE of Cordova; 61°27′N 141°37′W.

Sulzer Belchen, France: see GUEBWILLER, BALLON DE.

Sulzern, France: see SOULTZEREN.

Sulzfeld (zo͝olts′fĕlt), village (pop. 3,227), N Baden, Germany, after 1945 in Württemberg-Baden, on the Kraichbach (near its source) and 12 mi. ESE of Bruchsal; wine.

Sulzmatt, France: see SOULTZMATT.

Sulz River (zo͝olts), S Saar, rises 3 mi. SW of Neunkirchen, flows 11 mi. SW, past Sulzbach and Dudweiler, to Saar R. at Saarbrücken.

Sulzthal (zo͝olts′täl), village (pop. 1,033), Lower Franconia, NW Bavaria, Germany, 5 mi. SSW of Bad Kissingen; furniture mfg., brewing, flour and lumber milling.

Sulz unterm Wald, France: see SOULTZ-SOUS-FORÊTS.

Suma, Japan: see KOBE.

Suma (so͞o′mä), town (pop. 682), Yucatan, SE Mexico, 32 mi. ENE of Mérida; henequen.

Sumac, village (pop. 2,117), Yakima co., S Wash.

Sumadija or **Shumadiya** (both: sho͞o′mädēä), Serbo-Croatian *Šumadija* [Serbo-Croatian, =forest country], hilly region in central Serbia, Yugoslavia, S of Belgrade; bounded N by Danube and Sava rivers, E by Morava R., S and SW by Western Morava R., NW by Kolubara R. Heavily forested in early-19th cent.; now it has much arable land, grassland, and pastures; corn, wine, fruit (notably plums); cattle, swine. Lignite mining near ARANDJELOVAC; marble quarrying on VENCAC mtn. Highest point, the RUDNIK. The Sumadija is densely settled and has large villages. Economic and cultural center, KRAGUJEVAC.

Sumaika, Iraq: see DUJAIL.

Sumampa (so͞omäm′pä), town (pop. estimate 1,500), S Santiago del Estero prov., Argentina, 90 mi. SE of Loreto; lumbering (quebracho, carob), charcoal burning, sawmilling. Manganese mines near by.

Sumampa, Sierra de (syĕ′rä dā), low pampean range in S Santiago del Estero prov., Argentina, extends c.30 mi. S from area S of Quebrachos to Córdoba prov. border; rises to c.3,000 ft. Rich in minerals, of which manganese (near Sumampa) is exploited.

Sumapaz, Páramo de (pä′rämō dā so͞omäpäs′), Andean range in Cundinamarca dept., central Colombia, situated where the Cordillera Oriental splits into the high plateaus of Bogotá (Sabana de Bogotá) and Boyacá; extends c.45 mi. from Tolima–Cundinamarca–Meta border NNE to Bogotá; rises to 13,715 ft.

Sumartin, Yugoslavia: see BRAC ISLAND.

Sumas (so͞o′măs), city (pop. 658), Whatcom co., NW Wash., port of entry near British Columbia line, 20 mi. NE of Bellingham; sugar beets, berries, dairy products, livestock.

Sumatra (so͞omä′trŭ), 2d largest island (□ 163,557; 1950 pop. c.12,000,000) of Indonesia, one of Greater Sundas, in Indian Ocean, S and W of Malay Peninsula across Strait of Malacca and just NW of Java across Sunda Strait; 5°39′N–5°57′S 95°10′–106°5′E; 1,110 mi. long, 280 mi. wide, fringed with numerous isls. Volcanic Barisan Mts. traverse length of isl. along W coast and rise to 12,487 ft. in Mt. Kerinchi; E coast area is generally swampy. The volcanic isl. KRAKATOA is off S tip of Sumatra. Rising in Barisan Mts. are Asahan, Rokan, Indragiri, Hari, and Musi rivers, all flowing E. There are numerous mtn. lakes, largest being L. Toba in N central area. Climate is generally hot and humid (except in highland areas), with year-round rainfall which is especially heavy on W coast and in Deli region. Much of interior is impenetrable forest; wild animals include elephants, rhinoceroses, panthers, tapirs, tigers, snakes. Bird life includes weaver birds. Among the Malayan inhabitants are the Batak (in L. Toba area), the Achinese in N, and Menangkabau on W coast. On the coast are the Chinese and Arabs. Religion is predominantly Moslem; only the Batak are Christians. Economically, Sumatra is less advanced than Java, although there are extensive oil and coal fields, the latter being the most important in Indonesia. Other mineral resources are gold and silver. Lumbering (camphor, ebony, ironwood, rattan), agr. (tobacco —grown in Deli region—tea, coffee, sugar, pepper). Important forest products: rubber, copra, palm oil, resin. Chief centers are PALEMBANG, MEDAN, PADANG, KUTARAJA, JAMBI, SIBOLGA, BENKULEN, TELUKBETUNG. The Hindu-Sumatran kingdom of Sri Vijaya (with ⊙ at Palembang) flourished in 8th cent., extending its control over Malay Peninsula and large part of Indonesia; in 14th cent. it fell to the Javanese. First European visitors were the Portuguese. The Dutch came in 1596 and gradually gained control of all the native states, Achin being the last to accept Du. sovereignty. The British briefly controlled parts of isl. in late 18th and early 19th cent. In 1945 most of Sumatra (except 2 small sections in E and W) was included in original Republic of Indonesia; in 1946 the Du.-sponsored states of South Sumatra and East Sumatra were formed. In 1950, all Sumatra was absorbed into Indonesia and divided into 3 provs.

Sumava, Czechoslovakia: see BOHEMIAN FOREST.

Sumay (so͞omī′), port town and municipality (pop. 6,131), W Guam; U.S. naval base is at Apra Harbor. Has marine corps reservation; rice farms, coconut plantations.

Sumaykah, Iraq: see DUJAIL.

Sumba or **Soemba** (both: so͞om′bŭ), island (□ 4,306; pop. 182,326), Lesser Sundas, Indonesia, in Indian Ocean, 30 mi. S of Flores across Sumba Strait, 180 mi. W of Timor across Savu Sea; 9°16′–10°20′S 118°56′–120°53′E; 140 mi. long, 50 mi. wide. Mountainous, rises in W area to 2,913 ft.; has narrow coastal plains. Stock raising (horses, cattle), cotton spinning, weaving, and dyeing. Formerly important source of sandalwood and long known as Sandalwood Isl.

Sumbar River (so͞ombär′), in SW Turkmen SSR (USSR) and Iran, rises in Turkmen-Khurasan mts. just across Iranian border, flows 150 mi. W, past Kara-Kala, to Atrek R. on USSR-Iran line. Subtropical agr. (dates, figs) in valley.

Sumba Strait, channel (30–55 mi. wide) connecting Savu Sea (in Indonesia) with Indian Ocean, bounded N by Komodo isl. and W half of Flores, S by Sumba Isl. Formerly called Sandalwood Strait.

Sumbat (both: so͞ombät′), village (pop. 7,280), Gharbiya prov., Lower Egypt, 7 mi. NNW of Zifta; cotton.

Sumbawa or **Soembawa** (both: so͞ombä′wŭ), island (□ 5,965; pop. 314,843), Lesser Sundas, Indonesia, bet. Flores Sea (N) and Indian Ocean (S), 10 mi. E of Lombok across Alas Strait, 45 mi. W of Flores; 8°5′–9°8′S 116°47′–119°10′E; 165 mi. long, 10–60 mi. wide. Extremely irregular coast line is deeply indented by Sale Bay (55 mi. long, 15 mi. wide). Mountainous terrain has several volcanic peaks, highest being Mt. Tambora (9,255 ft.) in N. Climate is generally dry, with little rainfall. Cattle raising, agr. (rice, corn, tobacco). Chief towns are Raba (NE) and Sumbawa (N); chief port is Bima, on inlet of Flores Sea.

Sumbawanga (so͞ombäwäng′gä), town, Western Prov., SW Tanganyika, on Ufipa Plateau, 220 mi. SSW of Tabora; 7°57′S 31°35′E. Tobacco, sisal, wheat, corn. Coal deposits N.

Sumbing, Mount, or **Mount Soembing** (both: so͞ombĭng′), volcanic peak (11,059 ft.), central Java, Indonesia, 35 mi. NW of Jogjakarta.

Sumburgh Head, Scotland: see MAINLAND, Shetlands.

Sumbuya (so͞ombo͞o′yä), town (pop. 1,190), South-Western Prov., SW Sierra Leone, on Sewa R. and 25 mi. SW of Bo; palm oil and kernels, piassava.

Sumedang or **Soemedang** (both: so͞omĕdäng′), town (pop. 12,448), W central Java, Indonesia, in Preanger region, 20 mi. E of Bandung; alt. 1,507 ft.; trade center for agr. area (rice, rubber, tea).

Sümeg, county, Hungary: see SOMOGY.

Sümeg (shü′mĕg), town (pop. 5,585), Zala co., W Hungary, 30 mi. WSW of Veszprem; market center for wine, cattle area. Alexander Kisfaludy b. here. Mus. has collection of MSS and anc. relics (5th cent. B.C. to 2d cent. A.D.).

Sumène (sümĕn′), village (pop. 1,384), Gard dept., S France, in the Cévennes, 6 mi. E of Le Vigan; silk-hosiery mills.

Sumenep or **Soemenep** (both: so͞omŭnĕp′), town (pop. 17,824), SE Madura, Indonesia, near Madura Strait, 80 mi. ENE of Surabaya; 7°S 113°52′E; trade center for salt-panning and agr. area (rice, corn, cassava). Handicraft industry: working of gold, silver, leather.

Sumer (sōō'mûr), region of Mesopotamia, occupying the S part of later Babylonia. Here lived from earlier known times a non-Semitic speaking people who had established a flourishing civilization by 3500 B.C., though its beginnings went back at least to the 5th millennium. The sites of the great Sumerian cities—Kish, Erech, Ur, Nippur, Lagash, Larsa—are in S central Iraq. The Sumerians invented the cuneiform system of writing. The Semitic peoples of Mesopotamia, living perhaps further N, were in contact with the Sumerians from earliest times, and increasing Semitic strength culminated in the conquests of Sargon of Agade (c.2600 B.C.), who brought all Mesopotamia under Semitic rule, with his capital at AGADE (see also AKKAD) in the N. Sumerian rule had a final revival under the 3d dynasty at Ur (c.2300 B.C.). This dynasty fell to Elam. With the rise of Hammurabi and the founding of Babylonia, the country passed to the Semitic Babylonian dynasty and the Sumerians, as a nation, disappeared.

Sumerpur (sōōmār'pŏŏr), town (pop. 6,260), Hamirpur dist., S Uttar Pradesh, India, 9 mi. S of Hamirpur; gram, jowar, wheat, sesame. Also called Bharwa Sumerpur.

Sumgait (sōōmgēēt'), district of Greater Baku, Azerbaijan SSR, at NW base of Apsheron Peninsula, on Caspian Sea. Main centers: Sumgait, Nasosny, Dzharat.

Sumgait, town (1945 pop. over 2,000) in Sumgait dist. of Greater Baku, Azerbaijan SSR, on Caspian Sea, at mouth of short Sumgait R., 20 mi. NW of Baku, on railroad; major industrial center; pipe rolling (based on Dashkeson iron ore), mfg. of chemicals (caustic soda, hydrochloric acid), alunite processing (from Zaglik mine). Power station. Developed in 1940s.

Sumidouro (sōōmēdō'rōō), city (pop. 574), N Rio de Janeiro state, Brazil, on railroad and 17 mi. NNW of Nova Friburgo; coffee, tobacco, sugar cane, rice.

Sumino (sōōmē'nō), town (pop. 12,962), Ehime prefecture, N Shikoku, Japan, 3 mi. SE of Niihama; copper-mining center.

Suminodo (sōōmē'nōdō), town (pop. 9,658), Osaka prefecture, S Honshu, Japan, 6 mi. E of Osaka; rice, truck.

Sumisu-shima, Japan: see SMITH ISLAND.

Sumiswald (zōō'mĭsvält), town (pop. 5,638), Bern canton, NW central Switzerland, 15 mi. ENE of Bern; knit goods, watches, cement, linen textiles.

Sumiton (sŭ'mŭtŭn), village (pop. 1,334), Walker co., N central Ala., 10 mi. NW of Birmingham; coal mines.

Sumjam or **Soomjam** (sōōmjäm'), village, Doda dist., W central Kashmir, in the Himalayas, 40 mi. NNE of Kishtwar. Sometimes spelled Sumsam. Noted sapphire mines (alt. 15,000 ft.) 6 mi. SSW. Much-used pass of Umasi La (alt. 17,370 ft.) is 9 mi. ENE.

Summan (sōōm-măn'), barren plateau in Hasa, Saudi Arabia, E of Dahana desert; alt. 1,300 (W)–800 (E) ft.; 50–150 mi. wide. Ends in E scarp overlooking Persian Gulf coastal lowland.

Summer Cove, Ireland: see KINSALE.

Summerdale, town (pop. 489), Baldwin co., SW Ala., 25 mi. SE of Mobile; naval stores.

Summerfield. 1 Village (pop. 378), St. Clair co., SW Ill., 20 mi. E of East St. Louis, in agr. area. **2** City (pop. 305), Marshall co., NE Kansas, at Nebr. line, 19 mi. NE of Marysville, in grain area. **3** Village (pop. 368), Noble co., E Ohio, 27 mi. NNE of Marietta.

Summerhill, borough (pop. 849), Cambria co., SW central Pa., 9 mi. ENE of Johnstown and on Conemaugh R.

Summer Isles, group of islets at mouth of Loch BROOM, Ross and Cromarty, Scotland. Largest is Tanera, 2 mi. long, 1 mi. wide.

Summer Lake, S Oregon, partly dry body of water in Lake co., 9 mi. long, 4.5 mi. wide. Basin (□ c.60) is 15 mi. long, 5 mi. wide. Fed by short Ana R.

Summerland, town (pop. estimate 3,000), S B.C., on SW shore of Okanagan L., 9 mi. NW of Penticton; peach-growing center. Site of Dominion govt. experimental farm.

Summerland, village (pop. c.400), Santa Barbara co., SW Calif., on Santa Barbara Channel, just E of Santa Barbara; offshore oil field; oil refining.

Summerland Island, islet, Jefferson co., N N.Y., largest of the Summerland group of the Thousand Isls., in the St. Lawrence, at Ont. line, 4½ mi. NE of Alexandria Bay.

Summerland Key, Fla.: see FLORIDA KEYS.

Summers, county (□ 359; pop. 19,183), SE W.Va.; ⊙ Hinton. Mtn. region, on Allegheny Plateau; Keeney Knob (in E) rises to 3,945 ft. Drained by New R. and its branches (Greenbrier and Bluestone rivers); Bluestone Reservoir is in co. Livestock, dairy products, fruit, tobacco; some natural gas, timber. Railroad shops at Hinton. Formed 1871.

Summerseat, town in Ramsbottom urban dist., SE Lancashire, England, 3 mi. NNW of Bury; cotton milling.

Summerside, town (pop. 5,034), ⊙ Prince co., W central P.E.I., on Bedeque Bay, on railroad and 35 mi. WNW of Charlottetown; 46°23'N 63°49'W; port (ships dairy products, seed potatoes), resort, and fox fur-farming center. Site of Dominion Fox Experimental Station. Airport.

Summersville. 1 Town (pop. 306), on Shannon-Texas co. line, S central Mo., in the Ozarks, 33 mi. NNE of West Plains. **2** Town (pop. 1,628), ⊙ Nicholas co., central W.Va., 17 mi. WNW of Richwood, in agr. and coal-mining area; lumber milling. Carnifex Ferry State Park is 7 mi. SW.

Summerton, town (pop. 1,419), Clarendon co., central S.C., 22 mi. S of Sumter, in agr. area; lumber; tourist trade.

Summertown, England: see OXFORD.

Summertown, town (pop. 137), Emanuel co., E central Ga., 10 mi. NNE of Swainsboro.

Summerville. 1 Town (pop. 3,973), ⊙ Chattooga co., NW Ga., 18 mi. NW of Rome, near Chattooga R.; mfg. (clothing, yarn, cotton sacks). State fish hatchery near by. Inc. 1839. **2** Town (pop. 73), Union co., NE Oregon, 12 mi. NNE of La Grande. **3** Borough (pop. 933), Jefferson co., W central Pa., 6 mi. WSW of Brookville; ceramics, bricks. Settled c.1812, inc. 1887. **4** Town (pop. 3,312), Dorchester co., SE S.C., 21 mi. NW of Charleston; winter resort; lumber, bricks, bakery products. Near-by country was great plantation center in 18th and 19th cent.; has estates and homes of period. Settled c.1795, inc. 1847.

Summit, town (pop. 48), Balboa dist., S central Panama Canal Zone, on transisthmian railroad and 11 mi. NW of Panama city, in dairying and stock-raising region. Has agr. experiment station. Summit naval radio reservation is just S on E shore of the canal above Gaillard Cut.

Summit. 1 County (□ 615; pop. 1,135), N central Colo.; ⊙ Breckenridge. Mining and livestock-grazing region; drained by Blue R. Zinc, gold, silver. Includes part of Gore Range and Arapaho Natl. Forest. Formed 1861. **2** County (□ 413; pop. 410,032), NE Ohio; ⊙ AKRON. Drained by Cuyahoga and Tuscarawas rivers. Includes Portage Lakes (recreation). Agr. area (dairy products, corn, poultry, clover, livestock). Mfg. at Akron, Barberton, and Cuyahoga Falls. Limestone, sandstone quarries; sand, gravel, clay, salt deposits. Formed 1840. **3** County (□ 1,860; pop. 6,745), NE Utah; ⊙ Coalville. Mining and cattle-grazing area bordering on Wyo. and drained in W by Weber R. Wasatch Natl. Forest and Uinta Mts. here. Gold, silver, lead, coal mines. Truck crops in irrigated region around Coalville. Formed 1854.

Summit. 1 Town (pop. 268), Marion co., N Ark., 23 mi. E of Harrison, in the Ozarks. **2** Town, Ga.: see TWIN CITY. **3** Village (pop. 8,957), Cook co., NE Ill., on Des Plaines R., just W of Chicago; large corn-refining industry here and at adjacent Argo (just SW). Limestone quarrying near by. Inc. 1890. **4** Town (pop. 1,558), Pike co., SW Miss., 3 mi. N of McComb, in agr., dairying, and timber area; cotton and lumber milling; chenille articles. Has jr. col. Founded 1857. **5** Hamlet, Glacier and Pondera counties, NW Mont., on Continental Divide in Marias Pass, and 50 mi. SW of Cut Bank; alt. 5,216 ft. Statue of John F. Stevens, discoverer of pass, is here. **6** Residential city (pop. 17,929), Union co., NE N.J., 10 mi. W of Newark, in Watchung Mts.; mfg. (textiles, clothing, chemicals, lighting equipment, metal products); farming. Inc. 1899. **7** Village, R.I.: see COVENTRY. **8** Town (pop. 105), Lexington co., W central S.C., 22 mi. WSW of Columbia. **9** Town (pop. 431), Roberts co., NE S.Dak., 25 mi. S of Sisseton and on Coteau des Prairies; dairy products.

Summit Hill, resort borough (pop. 4,924), Carbon co., E Pa., 6 mi. WSW of Mauch Chunk. Burning Mine smoldering here since 1859.

Summit Mountain, Nev.: see MONITOR RANGE.

Summit Peak (13,272 ft.), SW Colo., in San Juan Mts., 18 mi. ENE of Pagosa Springs.

Summitville. 1 Town (pop. 1,061), Madison co., E central Ind., 15 mi. S of Marion, in agr. area; canned foods. **2** Resort village, Sullivan co., SE N.Y., in the Shawangunk range, 12 mi. ESE of Monticello. **3** Village (pop. 150), Columbiana co., E Ohio, 26 mi. ESE of Canton.

Sumner. 1 County (□ 1,183; pop. 23,646), S Kansas; ⊙ Wellington. Level to gently rolling plain, bordering S on Okla.; drained in SW by Chikaskia R., in NE by Ninnescah and Arkansas rivers. Wheat, corn, livestock. Oil and gas fields. Formed 1871. **2** County (□ 552; pop. 33,533), N Tenn.; ⊙ Gallatin. Bounded N by Ky., S by Cumberland R.; drained by headstreams of Red R. and by Drake Creek. Livestock, dairy products, tobacco, strawberries, corn. Formed 1786.

Sumner. 1 Town (pop. 226), Worth co., S central Ga., 6 mi. E of Sylvester. **2** City (pop. 1,170), Lawrence co., SE Ill., 10 mi. W of Lawrenceville, in oil, natural-gas, and agr. area. Inc. 1887. **3** Town (pop. 1,911), Bremer co., NE Iowa, on Little Wapsipinicon R. and 26 mi. NNE of Waterloo; poultry, dairy-products packing; mfg. of feed, chemicals, coops. Inc. 1892. **4** Town (pop. 526), Oxford co., W Maine, 14 mi. SSE of Rumford, in farming, recreational area; wood products. Village of East Sumner is partly in Hartford town. **5** Town (pop. 550), a ⊙ Tallahatchie co., NW central Miss., 19 mi. SE of Clarksdale; cottonseed products. **6** Town (pop. 309), Chariton co., N central Mo., near mouth of Locust Creek in Grand R., 13 mi. SW of Brookfield; grain, livestock. **7** Village (pop. 267), Dawson co., S central Nebr., 17 mi. NE of Lexington and on Wood R. **8** Town (pop. 46), Noble co., N Okla., 9 mi. ENE of Perry. **9** City (pop. 2,816), Pierce co., W central Wash., 10 mi. ESE of Tacoma, in Puyallup valley. Berries, bulbs, fruit, truck; wood products; food processing. Settled 1855, inc. 1891.

Sumner Strait, SE Alaska, in Alexander Archipelago, bet. Prince of Wales Isl. (S), Kupreanof Isl. (N), and Kuiu Isl. (W), extending from Iphigenia Bay on the Pacific to head of Clarence Strait.

Sumoto (sōōmō'tō), city (1940 pop. 29,461; 1947 pop. 36,505), on E coast of Awaji-shima, Hyogo prefecture, Japan, on Osaka Bay, 10 mi. SW of Kobe. Principal center of isl.; agr. (rice, wheat); cotton-textile mills.

Sumpango (sōōmpäng'gō), town (1950 pop. 4,512), Sacatepéquez dept., S central Guatemala, on Inter-American Highway and 5 mi. N of Antigua; alt. 5,974 ft. Market center; soap and candle mfg.; grain, black beans.

Sumperk (shōōm'pĕrk), Czech *Šumperk*, Ger. *Mährisch-Schönberg* (mâ'rĭsh-shûn'bĕrk), town (pop. 12,341), N Moravia, Czechoslovakia, in SW foothills of the Jesenicky, 28 mi. NNW of Olomouc; rail junction; textile-mfg. center (silk, linen, cotton); synthetic building materials, paper. Winter-sports facilities in vicinity.

Sumprabum (sōōmpräbōōm', Burmese sōōpŭyä"-bōōn'), village, Myitkyina dist., Kachin State, Upper Burma, on road to Putao and 80 mi. N of Myitkyina. In Second World War, a base for Kachin guerrillas.

Sumpter, city (pop. 146), Baker co., NE Oregon, 18 mi. W of Baker.

Sumpul River (sōōmpōōl'), SW Honduras and N Salvador, rises near Nueva Ocotepeque (Honduras), flows 36 mi. SE, along international border and into Salvador, to Lempa R. 17 mi. E of Chalatenango (Salvador).

Sumrall (sŭ'mŭrôl, sŭm'rôl), town (pop. 853), Lamar co., SE Miss., 16 mi. WNW of Hattiesburg, in agr. and pine-timber area; lumber milling.

Sumsam, Kashmir: see SUMJAM.

Sumski Posad or **Sumskiy Posad** (sōōm"skē pŭsät'), Finnish *Suma*, village (1926 pop. 1,136), E Karelo-Finnish SSR, port on Onega Bay of White Sea, on railroad and 27 mi. SE of Belomorsk; fisheries; sawmilling.

Sumter. 1 County (□ 914; pop. 23,610), W Ala.; ⊙ Livingston. In Black Belt, on Miss. line, bounded E by Tombigbee R. Cotton, livestock, corn, bees; lumber milling. Formed 1832. **2** County (□ 561; pop. 11,330), central Fla., bounded partly W and S by Withlacoochee R.; ⊙ Bushnell. Truck-farming area, with swamps in W and many scattered lakes, including L. Panasoffkee; also produces citrus fruit, corn, cattle, and poultry; some forestry (lumber, naval stores). Formed 1853. **3** County (□ 491; pop. 24,208), SW central Ga.; ⊙ Americus. Bounded E by Flint R., drained by Muckalee Creek. Coastal plain agr. (cotton, corn, watermelons, peaches, pecans, peanuts, livestock) and timber area; mfg. at AMERICUS. Formed 1831. **4** County (□ 689; pop. 57,634), central S.C.; ⊙ Sumter. Bounded W by Wateree R., NE by Lynches R.; drained by Black R.; N part of L. Marion is in S. Includes Poinsett State Park and Forest. Agr. and lumbering area, with mfg. center (Sumter); lumber, tobacco, corn, cotton, livestock, poultry, squabs. Formed 1785.

Sumter, commercial and mfg. city (pop. 20,185), ⊙ Sumter co., central S.C., 45 mi. ESE of Columbia; trade, processing, shipping center in lumbering, agr. area; rail junction. Produces lumber, furniture, and other wood products, foundry and machine-shop products, printing, clothing, textiles. Ships livestock and farm produce. Seat of Morris Col. (Negro). Shaw Air Force Base is NW. Settled in late 18th cent., laid out 1800, inc. as town 1845, as city 1887.

Sumter, Fort, S.C.: see FORT SUMTER NATIONAL MONUMENT.

Sumuncurá, Sierra (syĕ'rä sōōmōōngkōō'rä), pre-Andean mountain range in SE Río Negro natl. territory, Argentina, 35 mi. SW of Valcheta; extends c.25 mi. NE-SW in arid Patagonian plateau; 41°10'S 66°40'W. Rises to c.3,300 ft.

Sumy (sōō'mē), oblast (□ 9,400; 1946 pop. estimate 1,700,000), N Ukrainian SSR; ⊙ Sumy. In W outliers of Central Russian Upland; wooded steppe drained by upper Vorskla, Psel, Sula, and Seim rivers. Mainly agr., with hemp and wheat (N), sugar beets and wheat (S); lesser crops are potatoes and buckwheat (N), tobacco and mint (S). Chief mfg. cities: Sumy, Konotop, Romny, Akhtyrka; sugar refining, flour milling, hemp retting. Formed 1939.

Sumy, city (1939 pop. 63,883), ⊙ Sumy oblast, Ukrainian SSR, on Psel R. and 190 mi. ENE of Kiev; 50°55'N 34°48'E. Sugar-refining center; agr. machinery, chemicals (fertilizers), woolens, food products. Teachers col., city mus. Founded 1658. In Second World War, held (1941–43) by Germans.

Sün, China: see SÜN RIVER.

Sun, Island of the, Bolivia: see TITICACA ISLAND.

Suna (sōō'nä), village, Nyanza prov., W Kenya, near Tanganyika border, on road and 38 mi. SSW of Kisii; cotton, peanuts, sesame, corn.

Suna (sōō'nŭ), village (1939 pop. over 500), central Kirov oblast, Russian SFSR, 50 mi. SSE of Kirov and on Kirov–Vyatskiye Polyany road; grain, wheat.

Sunagawa (sōōnä'gäwŭ), town (pop. 41,323), W central Hokkaido, Japan, on Ishikari R. and 42 mi. NE of Sapporo; coal mining; stock raising, agr.

Sunam (sōōnäm'), town (pop. 14,187), central Patiala and East Punjab States Union, India, 38 mi. WSW of Patiala; agr. market (wheat, millet, gram); cotton ginning. An anc. place, attacked 1398 by Timur.

Sunamganj (sōōnäm'gŭnj), town (pop. 7,484), Sylhet dist., E East Bengal, E Pakistan, on Surma R. and 32 mi. WNW of Sylhet; trades in rice, oilseeds, cotton; fish curing.

Sunan, China: see KIANGSU.

Sunapee (sŭ'nŭpē), town (pop. 1,108), Sullivan co., SW N.H., 30 mi. NW of Concord. Granted 1768. It is on W shore of **Lake Sunapee** (9 mi. long, 3 mi. wide; alt. 1,100 ft.), boating, fishing resort. **Mt.** Sunapee (2,683 ft.) is just S; winter sports.

Suna River (sōō'nŭ), Finnish *Suunujoki*, in S Karelo-Finnish SSR, rises in forests SE of Reboly, flows 175 mi. SE, through lake Sunozero (25 mi. above mouth), to L. Onega at Sunski, S of Kondopoga. Of its many rapids, Por (55 ft. high) and Girvas (49 ft. high) falls (above lake Sunozero) and Kivach Falls (35 ft. high; below the lake) are noteworthy.

Sunart, Loch (lŏkh sōō'nŭrt), sea inlet (c.1 mi. wide) in NW Argyll, Scotland, extending 20 mi. inland from the Sound of Mull bet. Ardnamurchan and Morven peninsulas. Near its head is village of Strontian.

Sunbul Dag (sŭmbŭl' dä), Turkish *Sünbül Dağ*, peak (12,270 ft.), SE Turkey, in Hakari Mts., 5 mi. SE of Hakari.

Sunburst, town (pop. 845), Toole co., N Mont., 26 mi. N of Shelby near Alta. line; oil products. Kevin-Sunburst oil field near by.

Sunbury, town (pop. 953), S Victoria, Australia, 20 20 mi. NW of Melbourne, in livestock area.

Sunbury, county (□ 1,079; pop. 8,296), S central N.B., E of Fredericton; ⊙ Burton.

Sunbury. 1 Village (pop. 936), Delaware co., central Ohio, 12 mi. ESE of Delaware, in agr. area. **2** City (pop. 15,570), ⊙ Northumberland co., E central Pa., 40 mi. N of Harrisburg and on Susquehanna R.; textiles, clothing, metal products. Once an important Indian village; now an anthracite shipping center. Fort Augusta built here 1756. One of 1st electric lighting plants built here 1883 by Edison. Laid out 1772, inc. as borough 1797, as city 1921.

Sunbury-on-Thames (tĕmz), urban district (1931 pop. 13,337; 1951 census 23,396), Middlesex, England, on the Thames and 15 mi. WSW of London; mfg. of machine tools, light metals, plastics, lubricating oil. Site of important river locks. In urban dist. is residential town of Shepperton (1931 pop. 3,465), with motion-picture studios and former residence of Thomas Love Peacock.

Sunchales (sōōnchä'lĕs), town (pop. estimate 3,000), W central Santa Fe prov., Argentina, on railroad and 70 mi. NW of Santa Fe; mfg. and agr. center (wheat, flax, oats, livestock); mfg. of grain products, leather, dairy products, brushes.

Suncho Corral (sōōn'chō kōräl'), town (pop. estimate 1,200), ⊙ Matará dept. (□ c.3,400; 1947 pop. 13,210), central Santiago del Estero prov., Argentina, on left bank of the Río Salado, on railroad and 50 mi. ESE of Santiago del Estero; cotton-growing and stock-raising center; sawmill, cotton gin.

Sunchon (sōōn'chŭn'). **1** Jap. *Junten*, town (1949 pop. 43,933), S.Cholla prov., S Korea, 90 mi. WSW of Pusan; rail junction, in agr. area (rice, persimmons, soybeans). **2** Jap. *Junsen*, town (1944 pop. 20,682), S.Pyongan prov., N Korea, 29 mi. NNE of Pyongyang; gold-mining center.

Sunchong (sŭn'chŭrng'), Mandarin *Hsin-ch'ang* (shĭn'chäng'), town, S Kwangtung prov., China, port on Tam R. and 10 mi. NW of Toishan; commercial center.

Sünchow, China: see KWEIPING.

Sun City, city (pop. 231), Barber co , S Kansas, on Medicine Lodge R. and 19 mi. SSW of Pratt, in cattle and wheat area; gypsum mining.

Suncook, village, N.H.: see PEMBROKE.

Suncook River, S central N.H., rises in ponds E of Gilmanton, flows c.35 mi. S and SW, past Pittsfield, to Merrimack R. at Suncook village (water power).

Suncrest, town (1940 pop. 238), Monongalia co., N W.Va., just N of Morgantown.

Sund, Norway: see FLAKSTAD.

Sund (sŭnd), village (pop. 561), Vasternorrland co., E Sweden, on small inlet of Gulf of Bothnia, opposite Alno isl., 4 mi. NE of Sundsvall; sawmills.

Sunda Islands or **Soenda Islands** (both: sŭn'dŭ, sōōn'dŭ), Indonesia, comprise W part of Malay Archipelago, bet. S.China Sea and Indian Ocean, in Java, Flores, and Savu seas. Largest isls. (sometimes called Greater Sundas) are BORNEO (largest isl. of Indonesia), SUMATRA, JAVA, CELEBES. The Lesser Sundas, forming a prov. of Indonesia, are isls. E of Java: BALI, LOMBOK, SUMBAWA, SUMBA, FLORES, SOLOR ISLANDS, ALOR ISLANDS, TIMOR.

Sundals Fjord, Norway: see SUNNDALS FJORD.

Sundance, town (pop. 893), ⊙ Crook co., NE Wyo., just NW of Black Hills, 60 mi. NW of Rapid City, S.Dak.; alt. 4,750 ft. Trade point in livestock, grain region; coal mines, oil refinery. Devils Tower Natl. Monument and part of Black Hills Natl. Forest near by. Sundance Mtn. (5,800 ft.) just S.

Sundarbans (sōōn'dŭrbŭns), extensive, heavily-timbered swamp area in S Ganges Delta, India (S area of 24-Parganas dist.) and E Pakistan (S area of Khulna and Bakarganj dists.); consists of tidal creeks or rivers and half-reclaimed isls.; c.160 mi. wide E–W, 30–50 mi. N–S. Main timber trees: sundari, mangroves. Rice grown mostly in E, areca and coconut palms in W areas. Abundant wild life includes Bengal tigers, buffalo, hogs, crocodiles, cobras, and pythons. Main trade center, Khulna. Village of Iswaripur was ⊙ independent 16th-cent. Moslem kingdom. Ravaged by Arakanese and Port. pirates in 18th cent. Formerly ran 60 to 80 mi. inland, but gradual reclamation is increasing area under cultivation. Model land-reclamation project at Gosaba.

Sundargarh (sōōn'dŭrgŭr), district (□ 3,757; pop. 490,708), NW Orissa, India; ⊙ Sundargarh. Bordered N by Bihar, W by Madhya Pradesh; drained by Brahmani R. Fairly level area (N, W); SE area hilly and thickly forested (sal, lac; silk growing). Agr. (rice, oilseeds, sugar cane); valuable deposits (worked) of manganese, iron ore, limestone, dolomite. Hand-loom weaving. Created 1949 by merger of former princely states of Gangpur and Bonai.

Sundargarh, village, ⊙ Sundargarh dist., NW Orissa, India, 45 mi. N of Sambalpur and on left tributary of Mahanadi R.; market center for rice, sugar cane, oilseeds, timber, lac; handicraft metal working. Formerly called Suadi. Was ⊙ former princely state of Gangpur.

Sundarnagar (sōōn'dŭrnŭgŭr), town (pop. 1,725), central Himachal Pradesh, India, 32 mi. NW of Simla; wheat, rice, corn. Formerly called Suket or Baned. Was ⊙ former Punjab state of Suket.

Sunda Strait or **Soenda Strait** (both: sŭn'dŭ, sōōn'dŭ), strait connecting Java Sea (N) with Indian Ocean (S), Indonesia, bet. Java (E) and Sumatra (NW); 16–70 mi. wide. Contains numerous volcanic islets, including Krakatoa. In Second World War, U.S. suffered (March, 1942) severe losses in part of battle of Java Sea that was fought here.

Sunday Cove Island (□ 10; pop. 308), E N.F., in Notre Dame Bay, 45 mi. W of Twillingate; 7 mi. long, 3 mi. wide; 49°33'N 55°50'W. On S coast is fishing village of Port Anson.

Sunday Island, volcanic island (□ 11; pop. 23), largest and only inhabited isl. of KERMADEC ISLANDS, S Pacific; roughly triangular, 20 mi. in circumference; rises to 1,723 ft. Forested, mountainous. Sometimes called Raoul Isl.

Sundays River, SE Cape Prov., U. of So. Afr., rises NNE of Graaff Reinet, flows 250 mi. in winding course generally SE, past Graaff Reinet and Jansenville, to Algoa Bay of the Indian Ocean 20 mi. NE of Port Elizabeth. Along upper course are extensive irrigation works.

Sundbyberg (sŭnd"bŭbĕr'yŭ), city (1950 pop. 24,488), Stockholm co., E Sweden, on L. Malar, 6 mi. WNW of Stockholm city center; mfg. of cables, machinery, rubber products, chemicals, chocolate; paper milling. Founded 1877, inc. 1927 as city.

Sunde (sōōn'nŭ), village (pop. 549) in Kvinnherad (formerly Kvindherred) canton (pop. 5,701), Hordaland co., SW Norway, S of mouth of Hardanger Fjord, 33 mi. WSW of Odda; shipbuilding; fisheries and canneries; steatite quarries. At Rosendal (pop. 168), 16 mi. NE, is 17th-cent. baronial estate.

Sundene (sōōn'nĭnĭ), Faeroese *Sundini*, strait (c.25 mi. long) separating Ostero (NE) and Stromo (SE), the 2 largest isls. of the Faeroe Isls.; width varies from ½ to c.2 mi.

Sunderland, village (pop. estimate 800), S Ont., on Beaverton R. and 18 mi. WSW of Lindsay; dairying, mixed farming.

Sunderland, county borough (1931 pop. 185,824; 1951 census 181,515), NE Durham, England, on North Sea at mouth of the Wear 10 mi. ESE of Newcastle; 54°55'N 1°22'W; seaport, rail, and industrial center, shipping chiefly coal and importing timber (pit props); shipbuilding, coal mining, mfg. of steel, machinery, leather, paper, pottery, chemicals, light metal products; fishing center. On the S bank is Sunderland proper and Bishopwearmouth. The suburb (pop. 7,403) of Monkwearmouth (mŭngkwâr'mŭth), on N bank of the Wear, is site of Benedictine monastery founded 674 by Benedict Biscop; some remains of its abbey are incorporated in St. Peter's church. Bridge over Wear R., built 1796 by Rowland Burdon, was widened (1858) by Stephenson. There are technical col., art gall., libraries. In county borough are N suburbs of Roker (pop. 10,095), Southwick (pop. 15,789), and Pallion (pop. 13,731).

Sunderland. 1 Town (pop. 905), Franklin co., W Mass., on Connecticut R. and 10 mi. N of Northampton; tobacco, onions. **2** Town (pop. 493), Bennington co., SW Vt., on Batten Kill and 18 mi. N of Bennington, in Green Mts.; wood products.

Sunderland Bridge, town and parish (pop. 1,110), central Durham, England, on Wear R. and 3 mi. S of Durham; coal mining.

Sundern (zōōn'dŭrn), village (pop. 5,181), in former Prussian prov. of Westphalia, W Germany, after 1945 in North Rhine-Westphalia, 5 mi. SW of Arnsberg; forestry.

Sundeved or **Sundved** (sōōn'vĕdh), peninsula, S Jutland, Denmark, bounded by Aabenraa Fjord (N), Als Sound (E), and Flensburg Fjord (S). Region one of most fertile in Jutland.

Sundheim (zōōnt'hīm), village (pop. 1,392), S Baden, Germany, adjacent to Kehl. Formed out of suburbs of KEHL following transfer (1945) of town proper to Fr. administration.

Sundial Mountain (10,438 ft.), SW Alta., near B.C. border, in Rocky Mts., in Jasper Natl. Park, 50 mi. SSE of Jasper; 52°13'N 117°37'W.

Sundiken Mountains (sŭndĭkĕn'), Turkish *Sündiken*, W central Turkey, extend 95 mi. E from Bozuyuk, bet. Sakarya R. (N and E) and Porsuk R. (S); rise to 5,860 ft. in Sundiken Dag. Towns of Sogut and Mihaliccik on S slope. Gold and meerschaum in W; chromium, asbestos, and fuller's earth in E.

Sundon, agr. village and parish (pop. 460), S Bedford, England, 5 mi. NW of Luton; cement works. Has 14th-cent. church.

Sundown. 1 Resort village, Ulster co., SE N.Y., in the Catskills, 25 mi. WSW of Kingston. **2** City (pop. 1,492), Hockley co., NW Texas, on the Llano Estacado, 30 mi. ESE of Lubbock, in oil field. Inc. after 1940.

Sundridge, village (pop. 506), SE central Ont., on Bernard L., 40 mi. S of North Bay; lumbering.

Sundsvall (sŭnts'väl", sŭnts"väl'), city (1950 pop. 25,775), Vasternorrland co., E Sweden, on inlet of Gulf of Bothnia, near mouth of Ljunga R., 200 mi. N of Stockholm; 62°23'N 17°20'E. Seaport (icebound in winter) and chief timber-shipping center of Sweden; also exports pulp, cellulose, and other wood products. Numerous lumber and pulp mills. Founded 1621 by Gustavus Adolphus. Chief suburbs (administratively independent) are Skonsberg (ENE), Skonsmon, and Kubikenborg, with large aluminum mills (ESE).

Sundved, Denmark: see SUNDEVED.

Sunel (sōōnāl'), town (pop. 5,572), NW Madhya Bharat, India, 65 mi. ENE of Mandasor; millet, cotton, wheat; cotton ginning. Sacked by Tantia Topi in 1857.

Sunfield, village (pop. 400), Eaton co., S central Mich., 22 mi. W of Lansing, in farm area.

Sunflower, county (□ 693; pop. 56,031), W Miss.; ⊙ Indianola. Rich lowland cotton-growing region, drained by Sunflower R. Also produces corn, oats, hay, alfalfa; some lumbering. Formed 1844.

Sunflower. 1 Village (pop. 3,834), Johnson co., E Kansas, 24 mi. WSW of Kansas City (Kansas), near Kansas R., in general agr. region. **2 Town** (pop. 639), Sunflower co., W Miss., 20 mi. W of Greenwood, in cotton-growing area; lumber.

Sunflower River or **Big Sunflower River,** NW and W central Miss., rises in Coahoma co., flows 240 mi. S to Yazoo R. in SW Yazoo co.

Sunfung (sŭn'fōōng'), Mandarin *Hsin-feng* (shĭn'-fŭng), town (pop. 1,703), ⊙ Sunfung co. (pop. 86,681), central Kwangtung prov., China, 28 mi. SW of Linping; hemp, rice, beans. Until 1914 called Chongning.

Sungaigerong or **Soengaigerong** (both: sōōngī"-gŭrông'), suburb of Palembang, SE Sumatra, Indonesia, on Musi R. and 5 mi. E of Palembang; oil-refining center. Severely damaged before Jap. withdrawal at end of Second World War; subsequently rebuilt. Also spelled Sungeigerong or Soengeigerong.

Sungai Kolok, Thailand: see SUNGEI GOLOK.

Sungaria, China: see DZUNGARIA.

Sungari River (sōōng"gŭrē'), Chinese *Sunghwa Kiang* or *Sung-hua Chiang* (both: sōōng'hwä' jyäng'), largest river entirely in Manchuria and draining half its territory; 1,150 mi. long. It rises in 2 headstreams (the Erhtao and the Towtao) on Changpai mtn., flows NW, past Fengman (hydroelectric station), Kirin (head of navigation), and Fuyü (Petuna), to confluence with Nonni R., where the Sungari turns sharply ENE, past Harbin, Ilan, and Kiamusze, converging with Amur R. at Tungkiang. Receives, in addition to the Nonni, the Hulan (left) and the Lalin and Mutan (right). A mtn. river cut by rapids in upper course, the Sungari becomes a slow-flowing, meandering stream on the Manchurian plain (below Kirin city). Manchuria's chief waterway, it is frozen Oct.–April.

Sung-ch'i, China: see SUNGKI.

Sung-chiang, province, Manchuria: see SUNGKIANG.

Sung-chiang, town, China: see SUNGKIANG.

Sungei (sōōng"ā') [Malay,=river]. For Malaya names beginning thus and not found here, see under following part of the name.

Sungei Bakap (bäkäp'), village (pop. 2,495), Prov. Wellesley, Penang, NW Malaya, on railroad and 14 mi. SE of Butterworth; rubber plantations.

Sungei Besi (bŏo̅sē′), town (pop. 1,584), central Selangor, Malaya, on railroad and 7 mi. S of Kuala Lumpur; tin mining.
Sungei Chuah (chōō′ä′), town (pop. 2,505), SE Selangor, Malaya, on railroad, just S of Kajang; rubber.
Sungei Golok (sōōngĭ′ gôlôk′), Thai *Sungai Kolok* (sōōngĭ′ kôlôk′), rail station, Narathiwat prov., S Thailand, on east-coast line and 20 mi. SW of Kota Bharu, on the Sungei Golok (Malayan border stream); Thai customs.
Sungei Kusial, Malaya: see KUSIAL BHARU.
Sungei Lembing (sōōng″-ā′ lĕmbĭng′), town (pop. 3,846), NE Pahang, Malaya, 20 mi. WNW of Kuantan; major tin-mining center.
Sungei Limau or **Sungei Limau Dalam** (lēmou′ dä-läm′), village (pop. 636), W Kedah, Malaya, on Strait of Malacca, 15 mi. S of Alor Star; coconuts, rice.
Sungei Mati (mä′tē), village (pop. 660), NW Johore, Malaya, on Muar R., and 8 mi. N of Bandar Maharani; coconuts, rubber.
Sungei Patani (pŏotä′nē), second largest town (pop. 13,175) of Kedah, NW Malaya, on railroad and 20 mi. NE of George Town; center of rubber and tapioca plantations.
Sungei Pinang Kechil (pĕnäng′ kŏochĕl′), village (pop. 2,487) on E coast of Pangkor Isl., W Perak, Malaya, in the Dindings; fisheries.
Sungei Rengit (rĕng″ĭt′), village (pop. 879, S Johore, Malaya, on Singapore Strait, 33 mi. ESE of Johore Bahru; coconuts; fisheries.
Sungei Siput (sēpŏot′), town (pop. 5,967), N central Perak, Malaya, on railroad and 23 mi. E of Taiping; tin mining; rubber.
Sungho (sōōng′hô′), Jap. *Shoko,* town (1944 pop. 17,907) S.Pyongan prov., N Korea, 12 mi. E of Pyongyang, in coal-mining area.
Sunghsien (sōōng′shyĕn′), town, ⊙ Sunghsien co. (pop. 173,516), NW Honan prov., China, 45 mi. SSW of Loyang, in Sung Mts.; timber, medicinal herbs, fruit.
Sung-hua Chiang, Manchuria: see SUNGARI RIVER.
Sunghwa Kiang, Manchuria: see SUNGARI RIVER.
Sungkai (sōōng′gī′), town, S Szechwan prov., China, 50 mi. SW of Chungking city and on left bank of Yangtze R.; commercial center.
Sungkai (sōōng″kī′), village (pop. 891), S Perak, Malaya, on railroad and 45 mi. SSE of Ipoh; rubber.
Sungki or **Sung-ch'i** (both: sōōng′chē′), town (pop. 4,691), ⊙ Sungki co. (pop. 54,500), N Fukien prov., China, near Chekiang line, 50 mi. NNE of Kienow and on tributary of Min R.; iron mining; sweet potatoes, rice, wheat.
Sungkiang or **Sung-chiang** (both: sōōng′jyäng′), province (□ 75,000; pop. 6,000,000) of NE Manchuria; ⊙ Harbin. Bounded NE and E by USSR along Amur and Ussuri rivers and L. Khanka, S by Kirin prov., and NW by Heilungkiang prov., Sungkiang occupies the middle and lower Sungari valley (for which it is named) and the N portion of the E Manchurian highlands. It is drained by the Lalin and Mutan rivers (affluents of the Sungari) and the Naoli and Muling rivers (affluents of the Ussuri). The chief agr. areas are Harbin-Hulan and Ningan (Ninguta), producing wheat, soybeans, sugar beets, corn, and kaoliang. Coal is mined at Hingshan-Haoli (or Haolikang), Mishan, and Lishuchen (near Muling). Ilan and Lopeh are the chief gold-mining centers. Flour milling and soybean processing are the chief industries. Timber is cut in the E Manchurian highlands and milled along the Chinese Eastern RR at Mutankiang, Hailin, and Shihtowhotze. The leading cities are served by branches of the Chinese Eastern trunk line: they are Harbin, Mutankiang, and Kiamusze. Tungkiang and Hulin are river ports on the Soviet border. Pop. is overwhelmingly N Mandarin Chinese in the densely settled Sungari and Mutan river valleys; there are some Gold tribes in the sparsely populated NE. Sungkiang was 1st formed (1946) from Manchukuo's Pinkiang prov., and was enlarged (1949) through the incorporation of the Harbin area and Hokiang prov.
Sungkiang or **Sung-chiang,** town (1938 pop. 66,663), ⊙ Sungkiang co. (1946 pop. 380,739), S Kiangsu prov., China, 20 mi. SW of Shanghai and on Shanghai-Hangchow RR; silk weaving and dyeing, oil pressing, rice milling, iron smelting, match mfg.; rice, rapeseed, wheat, beans, cotton. Noted for its perch fisheries, and a square pagoda. Has meteorological station; and tomb of F. T. Ward, 19th-cent. U.S. adventurer.
Sungming (sōōng′mĭng′), town (pop. 2,793), ⊙ Sungming co. (pop. 82,643), NE central Yunnan prov., China, 30 mi. NE of Kunming; alt. 6,234 ft.; stone carving; rice, wheat, millet, beans, peanuts. Copper mines, gypsum quarries near by.
Sung Mountains, Chinese *Sung Shan* (sōōng′ shän′), E outlier of the Kunlun system, in NW Honan prov., China, on right bank of Lo R.; mts. rise to over 7,800 ft. 33 mi. ESE of Loyang. Noted for its monasteries.
Sungpan or **Sung-p'an** (sōōng′pän′), town (pop. 2,073), ⊙ Sungpan co. (pop. 26,989), NW Szechwan prov., China, on main trade route to Kansu, on upper Min R. and 150 mi. N of Chengtu, in mtn. region; tea-growing center; medicinal plants, millet. Gold mining at Changla or Changlaying, 13 mi. N.
Sung Shan, China: see SUNG MOUNTAINS.
Sungshan (sōōng′shän′), Jap. *Matsuyama* (mätsōō′-yämä), town, N Formosa, on Keelung R., on railroad and 3 mi. E of Taipei; site of main Taipei airport.
Sungtao or **Sung-t'ao** (sōōng′tou′), town (pop. 5,379), ⊙ Sungtao co. (pop. 182,031), NE Kweichow prov., China, near Szechwan-Hunan line, 50 mi. ENE of Szenan; cotton textiles; grain. Lead deposits near by.
Sungtze or **Sung-tzu** (both: sōōng′dzŭ′), town (pop. 12,542), ⊙ Sungtze co. (pop. 362,557), S Hupeh prov., China, 25 mi. WSW of Kiangling; rice, wheat, cotton. Iron deposits near by. Until 1947, the name Sungtze was applied to a town on the Yangtze, 13 mi. NNW.
Sungurlare (sōōn-gōōrlä′rĕ), village (pop. 2,546), Burgas dist., E Bulgaria, on S slope of E Balkan Mts., 13 mi. NW of Karnobat; wine making; sheep raising.
Sungurlu (sōōngōōrlōō′), town (pop. 5,562), Corum prov., N central Turkey, 40 mi. SW of Corum; timber, grain, mohair goats.
Sungyang (sōōng′yäng′), town (pop. 9,507), ⊙ Sungyang co. (pop. 112,676), SW Chekiang prov., China, 25 mi. W of Lishui and on headstream of Wu R. (head of junk navigation); tobacco, indigo, tea, timber.
Sunhing (sŭn′hĭng′), Mandarin *Hsin-hsing* (shĭn′-shĭng′), town (pop. 21,072), ⊙ Sunhing co. (pop. 231,697), W central Kwangtung prov., China, 28 mi. SW of Koyiu; rice, beans, sugar cane. Tungsten mines near by. Sometimes spelled Sanhing and Sanhsing.
Sünhsien or **Hsün-hsien** (both: shün′shyĕn′), town, ⊙ Sünhsien co. (pop. 310,000), W central Pingyuan prov., China, on railroad and 45 mi. NE of Sinsiang; agr. center. Until 1949 in Honan prov. Sometimes written Chünhsien.
Suni (sōō′nē), village (pop. 1,886), Nuoro prov., W Sardinia, 32 mi. S of Sassari.
Suning (sōō′nĭng′), town, ⊙ Suning co. (pop. 160,624), central Hopeh prov., China, 35 mi. SE of Paoting; cotton, rice, wheat, millet.
Sunium, Cape, Greece: see SOUNION, CAPE.
Sunja (sōō′nyä), village, N Croatia, Yugoslavia, 15 mi. SE of Sisak; rail junction.
Sunken Meadow State Park, N.Y.: see KINGS PARK.
Sunkesula, India: see KURNOOL, city.
Sün Kiang, China: see SÜN RIVER.
Sunkiatai, Manchuria: see KAIYÜAN, Liaosi prov.
Sünko or **Hsün-k'o** (both: shün′kŭ′), town, ⊙ Sünko co. (pop. 7,500), NE Heilungkiang prov., Manchuria, on Amur R. (USSR border), across from Poyarkovo, and 70 mi. SE of Aigun; corn, millet, kaoliang. Called Chike or Chiko until 1949.
Sun Kosi River (sōōn′ kō′sē), E Nepal, rises on SE slope of Gosainthan peak, E of Gosainkund; flows c.160 mi. SSW and ESE, joining Arun and Tamur rivers 13 mi. WSW of Dhankuta to form Kosi R. Also spelled San Kosi. Chief tributary, Dudh Kosi R.
Sunland, outlying part of LOS ANGELES city, Los Angeles co., S Calif., in foothills of San Gabriel Mts., 7 mi. ESE of San Fernando; olives, citrus fruit.
Sunlight Peak (14,060 ft.), SW Colo., in San Juan Mts., c.10 mi. SSE of Silverton.
Sunman, town (pop. 358), Ripley co., SE Ind., 23 mi. ESE of Greensburg, in agr. area.
Sun-Moon Lake, Formosa: see JIHYÜEH LAKE.
Sunnana (sŭn′änō″), Swedish *Sunnanå,* village (pop. 2,017), Vasterbotten co., N Sweden, on Skellefte R., near its mouth on Gulf of Bothnia, opposite Skelleftea, of which it is S suburb.
Sunndal River, Norway: see DRIVA RIVER.
Sunndals Fjord (sōōn′däls), inlet of the North Sea in More og Romsdal co., W Norway; extends inland (SE) from near Kristiansund c.30 mi. to mouth of the Driva. Entrance protected by many isls. Along it lie villages of Tingvoll, Opdol, Oksendal. Formerly spelled Sundals.
Sunndalsora (sōōn′dälsû″rä), Nor. *Sunndalsøra,* village (pop. 124), More og Romsdal co., W Norway, at head of Sunndal Fjord, 40 mi. SE of Kristiansund. Site of projected aluminum plant.
Sunne (sŭ′nû), town (pop. 1,902), Varmland co., W Sweden, on L. Fryk, 20 mi. NE of Arvika; tourist center for the Fryksdal; metalworking, sawmilling, brick mfg.
Sunnfjord, Norway: see SOGN OG FJORDANE.
Sunnhordland, Norway: see HORDALAND.
Sunniland, village (pop. c.100), Collier co., S Fla., c.40 mi. SE of Fort Myers, in Big Cypress Swamp; contains 1st successful oil wells drilled in Fla.
Sunning, China: see TOISHAN.
Sunningdale, town and parish (pop. 1,733), E Berkshire, England, just E of Sunninghill; agr. market. Golf courses near by.
Sunninghill, town and parish (pop. 5,788), E Berkshire, England, 6 mi. SSW of Windsor; agr. market. In parish, just W, is village of ASCOT.
Sunnmor, Norway: see MORE.
Sunny Brae (brā), town (pop. 1,368), SE N.B., N suburb of Moncton.
Sunnylven, Norway: see HELLESYLT.
Sunnyside. 1 Village (pop. 169), Spalding co., W central Ga., 6 mi. NNW of Griffin. **2** Section of NW Queens borough, New York city, SE N.Y.; large railroad yards; also residential. **3** Town (pop. 1,881), Carbon co., E Utah, 25 mi. E of Price; coal, coke. **4** City (pop. 4,194), Yakima co., S Wash., 30 mi. SE of Yakima, in irrigated farm area producing truck, fruit, sugar beets, dairy products; food-processing plants. Inc. 1902.
Sunnyslope, village (pop. 4,420), Maricopa co., SW central Ariz., 7 mi. N of Phoenix.
Sunnyvale. 1 City (pop. 9,829), Santa Clara co., W Calif., bet. Palo Alto and San Jose; alt. 4,195 ft. Ironworks; fruit canning. Near by is U.S. Moffett Field, with huge dirigible hangar. Inc. 1912. **2** Town (pop. 28), Newton co., SW Mo.
Sunol (sŭnōl′), village (pop. c.625), Alameda co., W Calif., in valley of Coast Ranges, 9 mi. SW of Livermore; cattle. Niles Canyon (recreational region) just W.
Sunomata (sōōnō′mätŭ), town (pop. 3,536), Gifu prefecture, central Honshu, Japan, 4 mi. E of Ogaki; rice, persimmons.
Sun Prairie, village (pop. 2,263), Dane co., S Wis., near small Koshkonong Creek, 11 mi. NE of Madison, in farm area; porcelain mfg.; canned foods, dairy products. Georgia O'Keeffe b. here. Settled c.1837, inc. 1868.
Sunqur or **Sonqor** (both: sông-kōr′), village, Fifth Prov., in Kermanshah, W Iran, 45 mi. NE of Kermanshah, in mountainous region producing grain and tobacco. Sometimes Songhor.
Sunray, town (pop. 1,530), Moore co., extreme N Texas, in high plains of the Panhandle, 40 mi. E of Dalhart; wheat; natural-gas wells, carbon-black plants. Inc. after 1940.
Sunrise. 1 Village (pop. 1,616), Falls co., E central Texas. **2** Village, Platte co., SE Wyo., near N.Platte R., 23 mi. NE of Wheatland; alt. 4,900 ft. Large open-pit iron mines (Sunrise Mines) here; ore shipped to smelters at Pueblo, Colo.
Sunrise Heights, village (pop. 1,094), Calhoun co., S Mich.
Sün River, Chinese *Sün Kiang* or *Hsün Chiang* (both: shün′ jyäng′), section of WEST RIVER in E Kwangsi prov., China, formed at Kweiping by union of Hungshui and Yü rivers, flows 60 mi. E, past Pingnam and Tengyün, joining Kwei R. at Wuchow to form West R. proper; navigable in entire length.
Sun River, NW Mont., rises in several branches near Continental Divide, flows c.130 mi. SE and E to Missouri R. at Great Falls. Sun River irrigation project is system of dams and reservoirs on branches of main stream. Main reservoir, Greenfield L.; largest dam, Gibson Dam (199 ft. high, 960 ft. long). Pishkun and Willow Creek Bird Reservations are on Pishkun and Willow Creek Reservoirs.
Sunsas, Serranía de (sĕrănē′ä dā sōōn′säs), range in Santa Cruz dept., E Bolivia, just N of Tucavaca R.; extends 90 mi. bet. San Juan (W) and Santo Corazón (E); rises to 2,300 ft.
Sunset. 1 Village (pop. 1,080), St. Landry parish, S central La., 10 mi. S of Opelousas; agr.; cotton gins. Oil and natural-gas fields near by. **2** Village (pop. c.500), Montague co., N Texas, c.50 mi. NNW of Fort Worth, in farm area. **3** Town (pop. 993), Davis co., N Utah, 5 mi. SW of Ogden, near Great Salt L.
Sunset Beach, resort village (pop. c.200), Orange co., S Calif., on the Pacific, 7 mi. SE of Long Beach.
Sunset Crater National Monument (□ 4.7; established 1930), N central Ariz., just E of San Francisco Peaks, 14 mi. NE of Flagstaff. Truncated volcanic cinder cone rising 1,000 ft. above base, with large crater (400 ft. deep, ¼ mi. in diameter) and brilliantly colored (red, yellow, and orange) summit. Extensive lava flows, ice cave, and other volcanic phenomena. WUPATKI NATIONAL MONUMENT is 15 mi. N.
Sunset Park, SE N.Y., a residential section of W Brooklyn borough of New York city.
Sunset Peak, Mont.: see SNOWCREST MOUNTAINS.
Sunshine, town (pop. 8,659), S Victoria, Australia, 6 mi. WNW of Melbourne; industrial center; mfg. (agr. machinery).
Sunshine Beach, town (pop. 469), Pinellas co., W Fla., 13 mi. W of St. Petersburg.
Sunshine Peak (14,018 ft.), SW Colo., in San Juan Mts., 15 mi. NE of Silverton.
Sunski or **Sunskiy** (sōōn′skē), town (1948 pop. over 2,000), S Karelo-Finnish SSR, on Suna R., near L. Onega, on Murmansk RR and 5 mi. S of Kondopoga; hydroelectric plant; sawmill.
Suntar (sōōntär′), village (1948 pop. over 2,000), SW Yakut Autonomous SSR, Russian SFSR, on Vilyui R. (head of navigation) and 160 mi. SW of Vilyuisk, in agr. area; river port.
Suntar-Khayata (–khĭŭtä′), highest mountain range in NE Siberia, Russian SFSR, S of Oimyakon, along Indigirka R. headwaters; rises to c.10,000 ft. Glaciers. Known since c.1930, but first explored c.1945. Formerly spelled Suantar-Khayata.
Sunth or **Sant** (sōōnt, sŭnt), former princely state (□ 390; pop. 94,257) in Gujarat States, Bombay, India; ⊙ was Santrampur. Inc. 1949 into Panch Mahals dist.

Süntien or **Hsün-tien** (both: shün'dyĕn'), town (pop. 4,489), ⊙ Süntien co. (pop. 104,641), E Yunnan prov., China, 45 mi. NE of Kunming; alt. 6,201 ft.; cotton textiles; rice, millet, beans, peanuts, sugar cane. Coal mines near by.

Suntikoppa or **Sunticoppa** (sōōntĭkōp'pŭ), village (pop. 437), N Coorg, India, 6 mi. ENE of Mercara; sandalwood; coffee estates.

Suntrana (sŭntră'nŭ), village (pop. 129), S central Alaska, 50 mi. SE of Nenana, 4 mi. E of Healy on spur of Alaska RR; coal mining; coal shipped to Fairbanks.

Suntso, China: see PUNYŪ.

Sunuapa (sōōnwä'pä), town (pop. 317), Chiapas, S Mexico, in Gulf lowland, 38 mi. SW of Villahermosa; cacao, rice.

Sun Valley, village (pop. 428), Blaine co., S central Idaho, bet. Sawtooth Range and Pioneer Mts., 12 mi. N of Hailey; alt. c.6,000 ft. Built (1936) by Union Pacific RR. Year-round resort known chiefly for winter sports. Railroad station is at Ketchum (pop. 757), on Big Wood R. 2 mi. SW. Mt. Hyndman is 11 mi. ENE.

Sunwapta Peak (sŭnwäp'tŭ) (10,875 ft.), SW Alta., near B.C. border, in Rocky Mts., in Jasper Natl. Park, 50 mi. SE of Jasper; 52°21'N 117°17'W.

Sunwu (sōōn'wōō'), town, ⊙ Sunwu co. (pop. 26,378), N Heilungkiang prov., Manchuria, 50 mi. S of Aigun and on railroad; gold mining; soybeans, wheat, rice, millet, corn.

Sünwu or **Hsün-wu** (both: shün'wōō'), town (pop. 7,310), ⊙ Sünwu co. (pop. 84,955), S Kiangsi prov., China, 80 mi. SE of Kanchow; rice, wheat, beans, cotton.

Sunwui (sŭn'wē'), Mandarin *Hsin-hui* (shĭn'hwā'), town (pop. 49,525), ⊙ Sunwui co. (pop. 624,397), S Kwangtung prov., China, near W branch of Canton R. delta, on railroad and 45 mi. SSW of Canton; center for production of palm-leaf fans. Exports silk, timber, oranges, meat, eggs. Fisheries. Tungsten mining near by. Opened to foreign trade in 1902. The name Sunwui was applied until 1931 to a town (now called Old Sunwui) 5 mi. SW. Present Sunwui was called Kongmoon, Mandarin *Kiangmen* or *Chiang-men,* until made co. ⊙ in 1931.

Sünyang or **Hsün-yang** (both: shün'yäng'), town, ⊙ Sünyang co. (pop. 145,040), S Shensi prov., China, 20 mi. NE of Ankang and on Han R.; wheat, millet, beans, fruit. Lead, copper, and mercury deposits near by.

Sunyani (sōōnyä'nē), town (pop. 4,670), Ashanti, W Gold Coast, 65 mi. NW of Kumasi; kola nuts, cacao, hardwood, rubber; brick- and tilemaking.

Sunyi (sōōn'yē'), Mandarin *Sini* or *Hsin-i* (both: shĭn'yē'), town (pop. 10,289), ⊙ Sunyi co. (pop. 412,733), SW Kwangtung prov., China, on Foshan R. and 28 mi. N of Mowming; rice, beans.

Sünyi or **Hsün-i** (both: shün'yē'), town (pop. 1,344), ⊙ Sünyi co. (pop. 95,559), W Shensi prov., China, 70 mi. NNW of Sian, near Kansu line; wheat, beans. Until 1914 called Sanshui.

Sunzha Range (sōōn'zhŭ), N outlier of the central Greater Caucasus, Russian SFSR, S of Terek Range; forms left watershed of Sunzha R., W of Grozny; rises to c.2,000 ft. Oil-bearing area.

Sunzha River, N Caucasus, Russian SFSR, rises in a front range of the central Greater Caucasus, SE of Dzaudzhikau; flows N, past Kosta-Khetagurovo, and E, past Ordzhonikidzevskaya and Grozny, to Terek R. N of Gudermes; c.150 mi. long. Receives Argun R. (right). Used for irrigation.

Suo, Formosa: see SUAO.

Suojärvi, Karelo-Finnish SSR: see SUOYARVI.

Suolahti (sōō'ōlä"tē, –läkh"tē), town (pop. 5,045), Vaasa co., S central Finland, at S end of L. Keitele, 20 mi. N of Jyväskylä; lumber, plywood, and veneer mills.

Suomenlinna (sōō'ōmĕnlĭn"nä), Swedish *Sveaborg* (svā"äbôr'yŭ), island fortress, S Finland, in Gulf of Finland, 2 mi. SE of Helsinki city center. Begun 1748–49; until 1918 called Viapori (vē'äpō"rē). Enlarged to cover 7 islets, it was taken (1808) by Russians; in Crimean War shelled (1855) by Anglo-French fleet. Captured (1918) by Finnish and German forces from the Finnish Bolsheviks.

Suomi: see FINLAND.

Suomussalmi (sōō'ōmŏŏs-säl"mē), village (commune pop. 11,356), Oulu co., N central Finland, 110 mi. E of Oulu, near USSR line.

Suong (swŭng), village, Kompong Cham prov., S Cambodia, on main road and 14 mi. SE of Kompong Cham; distillery (rice alcohol); rice, oil palm, timber, rosin. Monastery.

Suo Sea (sōō'ō), Jap. *Suo-nada,* W section of Inland Sea, Japan, bet. SW coast of Honshu and NE coast of Kyushu; connected with Hibiki Sea (W) by Shimonoseki Strait; merges with Iyo Sea (E) and Hoyo Strait (SE); c.60 mi. long, 30 mi. wide. Kunisaki Peninsula forms SE shore.

Suoyarvi (sōō'ŭyŭrvē), Finnish *Suojärvi* (sōō'ōyăr"-vē), city (1948 pop. over 500), SW Karelo-Finnish SSR, on N shore of lake Suoyarvi (10 mi. long, 3 mi. wide), 70 mi. WNW of Petrozavodsk; mfg. (paper, cardboard). Until 1940, in Finland. Suoyarvi rail junction is at S end of lake.

Supe (sōō'pā), town (pop. 2,180), Lima dept., W central Peru, on coastal plain, on Pan American Highway, on short Supe R. and 4 mi. SE of Barranca (connected by railroad), 2 mi. ENE of Puerto de Supe; cotton growing and ginning. Supe Viejo (pop. 1,211) is a SW suburb.

Supeh, China: see KIANGSU.

Supei, province, China: see KIANGSU.

Supei (sōō'bā'), village, ⊙ Supei dist. (pop. 1,050), NW Kansu prov., China, 35 mi. NNW of Yümen, at S edge of the Gobi. Until 1938, Wulungchüan.

Superbagnères (süpĕrbänyâr'), resort in central Pyrenees, Haute-Garonne dept., S France, just S of Luchon; alt. 5,895 ft. Winter sports. Has luxurious hotel.

Superior. 1 Village (1940 pop. 4,291), Pinal co., S central Ariz., near Pinal Mts., 19 mi. WSW of Globe in mining and livestock area; copper-smelting. Copper, silver, and gold mines in vicinity. **2** Town (pop. 134), Boulder co., N central Colo., just E of Front Range, 15 mi. NNW of Denver; alt. 5,512 ft.; coal mining. **3** Town (pop. 240), Dickinson co., NW Iowa, 22 mi. NNE of Spencer; livestock, grain. **4** Town (pop. 626), ⊙ Mineral co., W Mont., on the Clark Fork and 38 mi. WNW of Missoula; gold mines; grain, timber. **5** City (pop. 3,227), Nuckolls co., S Nebr., 40 mi. SSE of Hastings and on Republican R. at Kansas line; trade center; cement products, serum, flour; grain, dairy produce. Founded 1876. **6** Village (pop. 1,697, with adjacent Maitland), McDowell co., S W.Va., just SE of Welch. **7** City (pop. 35,325), ⊙ Douglas co., extreme NW Wis., opposite Duluth (Minn.), at W tip of L. Superior, on Superior Bay and St. Louis Bay (estuary of St. Louis R.), and on Nemadji R.; 46°42'N 92°6'W; alt. 629 ft. An industrial and railroad center, it is the principal port of entry of Wis., sharing an extensive harbor with DULUTH. City of Superior is equipped with large grain elevators, and iron-ore and dry docks; there also are shipyards, railroad and machine shops, woodworking factories, canneries, breweries, and flour mills. Oil refinery (begun 1951) near. Has a state col. and R.C. cathedral; Billings Park covers a large area bordering St. Louis Bay. Superior is known as a major consumer cooperative center. First explorers here were French: Radisson came in 1661 and Duluth in 1679. Fur-trading posts were established in late-18th cent. Platted 1852, inc. 1858. City's rise dates from 1883 with discovery of iron ore in Gogebic Range. **8** Village (pop. 339), Douglas co., NW Wis., near Superior city. **9** Town (pop. 1,580), Sweetwater co., SW Wyo., 18 mi. NE of Rock Springs, on rail spur; alt. c.7,100 ft.; coal mines.

Superior, Laguna (lägōō'nä sōōpĕryōr'), inlet of Gulf of Tehuantepec in Oaxaca, S Mexico, S of Juchitán; 18 mi. long, 5–12 mi. wide. Connected by narrow channel with Laguna Inferior.

Superior, Lake, in U.S. and Canada, westernmost and largest of the GREAT LAKES and largest fresh-water lake in the world; 350 mi. long, 160 mi. wide, it covers □ 31,820, of which 11,200 are in Canada; surface alt. is c.602 ft., max. depth 1,290 ft. It is bounded NW by Minn., S by Wis. and Mich., N and E by Ont.; its SE end is connected with L. Huron by St. Marys R. (Sault Sainte Marie Canals and locks here). It receives Nipigon and Kaministikwia rivers from Ont., Pigeon R. (part of international line) and St. Louis R. (Minn.) from W. Among its isls. are Isle Royale (a U.S. natl. park), Michipicoten, Caribou, Grand, and the Apostle group. In a glacially-scoured basin, lake has high and rocky shores; Pictured Rocks, near Munising, Mich., red sandstone formations carved into fantastic shapes by waves and wind, are famous. Lake region is one of richest mineral areas of continent; great iron deposits (the iron ranges) of Minn. and Mich. yield ore shipped from Duluth and Two Harbors, Minn.; Ashland and Superior, Wis.; Marquette, Mich. Copper (particularly on Keweenaw Peninsula, Mich.), silver, and nickel are also found. Fort William and Port Arthur, Ont., are grain-shipping ports. Navigation season is 6–7 months. Lake fisheries are of value. First white man to see lake was possibly Étienne Brulé; Radisson and the sieur des Groseilliers (1659–60) and the sieur Duluth (1678–79) visited Superior, and Father Allouez established a mission (1665) near Ashland, Wis.

Superior Bay, long narrow inlet of L. Superior, in extreme NW Wis. and NE Minn., sheltered by 2 sandspits and forming part of the harbor for the twin ports of Duluth and Superior; c.9 mi. long, c.1 mi. wide. A narrow neck of land forming W shore of the bay nearly divides it from St. Louis Bay (estuary of St. Louis R.). Sometimes called Allouez Bay (ă'lŭwā).

Superstition Mountains. 1 In S central Ariz., E of Mesa, S of Salt R.; rise to 5,057 ft. in Superstition Mtn. (site of legendary Lost Dutchman Mine), c.25 mi. E of Mesa. **2** In S Calif., low (c.700 ft.) desert range along W side of Imperial Valley; mining.

Supetar, Yugoslavia: see BRAC ISLAND.

Suphanburi (sōōpän'bōōrē'), town (1947 pop. 7,980), ⊙ Suphanburi prov. (□ 2,015; 1947 pop. 340,872), S Thailand, on Tha Chin R. (also called Suphanburi R.; head of navigation) and 55 mi. NNW of Bangkok, in rice-growing area; corn, tobacco; fisheries. An anc. walled town, it was originally ruled by the Mon, then by the Khmer (10th–13th cent.) before it became part of the Thai state. Also called Suphan or Subarn.

Suphanburi River, Thailand: see THA CHIN RIVER.

Suphan Dag (sōōp-hän' dä), Turkish *Suphan Dağ,* peak (14,547 ft.; also given as 14,630 ft.), E Turkey, on N shore of L. Van, 22 mi. SE of Malazgirt.

Supía (sōōpē'ä), town (pop. 2,035), Caldas dept., W central Colombia, on highway to Medellín, on E slopes of Cordillera Occidental, near Cauca R., 27 mi. NNW of Manizales; alt. 4,029 ft. Coffee-growing and gold mining. Silver, lead, and salt deposits near by.

Supino (sōōpē'nō), village (pop. 3,351), Frosinone prov., Latium, S central Italy, 7 mi. WSW of Frosinone.

Supiori or **Soepiori** (both: sōōpēō'rē), island, SCHOUTEN ISLANDS, Netherlands New Guinea, just W of Biak, at entrance to Geelvink Bay, 90 mi. E of Manokwari; 0°50'S 135°35'E. Agr., fishing. Also called Supuri.

Suppe (sōō'pā), town (pop. 600), Wallaga prov., W central Ethiopia, 35 mi. S of Gimbi; coffee market; flour milling, soap making.

Süpplingen (züp'lĭng-ŭn), village (pop. 2,731), in Brunswick, NW Germany, after 1945 in Lower Saxony, 4 mi. W of Helmstedt; mfg. of sack fabric.

Supply, Okla.: see FORT SUPPLY.

Suprasl (sōō'prä-shŭl), Pol. *Supraśl,* Rus. *Suprasl* or *Suprasl'* (both: sōō'prŭsŭlyŭ), town (pop. 2,445), Bialystok prov., NE Poland, on Suprasl R. and 9 mi. NE of Bialystok; mfg. of textiles, bricks; flour milling, sawmilling.

Suprasl River, Pol. *Supraśl,* NE Poland, rises E of Zabludow, flows WNW past Suprasl, and W past Wasilkow, to Narew R. 10 mi. WNW of Bialystok; 50 mi. long. In lower course, sometimes also called Biala, Pol. *Biała* (byä'wä).

Süpu or **Hsü-p'u** (both: shü'pōō'), town, ⊙ Süpu co. (pop. 343,214), W Hunan prov., China, on branch of Yüan R. and 65 mi. ENE of Chihkiang; tung oil, tea oil, cotton, timber. Coal mining near by.

Supung (sōō'pŏŏng'), Chinese *Shuifeng* (shwā'-fŭng'), Jap. *Suiho* (sōō'ēhō'), dam on Yalu R., on Korea-Manchuria line, 35 mi. NE of Antung. Its hydroelectric station (built in early 1940s) serves Antung, Dairen, and Mukden industrial areas.

Supuri, Netherlands New Guinea: see SUPIORI.

Supurul-de-Jos (shōō'pōōrōōl-dā-zhōs'), Rum. *Şupurul-de-Jos,* Hung. *Alsószopor* (ŏl'shōsô"pôr), village (pop. 1,842), Baia-Mare prov., NW Rumania, 24 mi. NW of Zalau. In Hungary, 1940–45.

Suq ash Shuyukh or **Suq al Shuyukh** (both: sōōk ăsh-shōōyōōkh'), village, Muntafiq prov., SE Iraq, in a swampy area on Euphrates R. and 18 mi. SE of Nasiriya; dates. Sometimes spelled Suk esh Sheyukh.

Suq el Gharb or **Suq al-Gharb** (both: sōōk' ĕl gărb'), Fr. *Souk el Gharb,* village (pop. 1,019), central Lebanon, 6 mi. SSE of Beirut; summer resort; sericulture, cereals, oranges.

Suq Wadi Barada (sōōk' wă'dē bärădä'), Fr. *Souq Wadi Barada,* village, Damascus prov., SW Syria, on Barada R., on railroad and 14 mi. NW of Damascus, in the Anti-Lebanon mts.; orchards. Near site of anc. ABILA. Roman tombs and Latin inscriptions on rocks.

Sur, Iraq: see SELEUCIA.

Sur, Lebanon: see TYRE.

Sur (sōōr), town (pop. 12,000), E Oman, port on Gulf of Oman, 90 mi. SE of Muscat, at foot of Eastern Hajar hill country, 20 mi. W of Ras al Hadd (E extremity of Arabian Peninsula); port for Ja'lan and Sharqiya dists.; exports dates.

Sur, Point (sŭr, sōōr), rugged promontory on W coast of Calif., 30 mi. S of Monterey; lighthouse (built 1889; 270 ft. above sea).

Surabaya, Surabaja, or **Soerabaja** (all: sōōrŭbä'yŭ), city (pop. 341,675), E Java, Indonesia, 420 mi. ESE of Jakarta, on Kali Mas R. just above its mouth at W end of Madura Strait; 7°15'S 112°45'E. Commercial and industrial center. Just N of Surabaya proper is its port, Tanjungperak or Tandjungperak (both: tänjōŏng"pŭrăk'), adjacent to Udjung or Oedjoeng (both: ōōjōōng'), site of chief naval base of Indonesia. Industries include shipbuilding, textile milling, metalworking, mfg. of machinery, chemicals, glass, oil, leather, and rubber goods. There are railroad workshops. Chief exports: sugar, tobacco, coffee, teak, rubber, petroleum products, tapioca, fibers, spices, vegetable oils. Oil refinery in S suburb of Wonokromo. In N part of city is a Du. fort (1835). There is a large mosque (1868). In Second World War, city was bombed (1942) and occupied by the Japanese; heavily bombed (1944) by Allied aircraft. Damaged in the post-war struggle for Indonesian independence.

Surada, India: see SORADA.

Surahammar (sü'rähä"mär), village (pop. 4,154), Vastmanland co., central Sweden, on Kolback R. and 13 mi. NW of Vasteras; steel and tinplate mills, foundries, boiler works. Remains of Viking fortress found near by. Includes Skogslund (skōōks'lŭnd") village.

Surajgarh (sōō'rŭjgŭr), town (pop. 6,829), NE Rajasthan, India, 24 mi. NE of Jhunjhunu; local market for millet, cattle, hides.

Surajpur, India: see PINJAUR.

Surakarta, Indonesia: see SOLO.

Surakhany (sōōrŭkhä'nē), town (1939 pop. over 2,000) in Ordzhonikidze dist. of Greater Baku, Azerbaijan SSR, on central Apsheron Peninsula, 10 mi. ENE of Baku, on electric railroad; oil fields (developed 1903); metalworks. Fire worshippers' temple near by.

Suramangalam, India: see SALEM, city.

Surami (sōōrä'mē), town (1939 pop. 6,346), central Georgian SSR, on rail spur and 3 mi. NW of Khashuri; health resort (mineral springs). Until 1936, Suram.

Surami Range, W central Georgian SSR, connects the Greater Caucasus and the Lesser Caucasus; forms border bet. E and W Transcaucasia. At 3,113 ft. is Surami Pass, with 2½-mi. railroad tunnel, W of Khashuri.

Surandai (sōō'rŭndī), town (pop. 13,021), Tinnevelly dist., S Madras, India, 8 mi. E of Tenkasi; grain, legumes.

Surany (shōō'rănī), Slovak *Šurany*, town (pop. 5,326), S Slovakia, Czechoslovakia, on Nitra R., on railroad and 16 mi. SSE of Nitra; rail junction; agr. center (wheat, potatoes).

Surapur, India: see SHORAPUR.

Sura River (sōōrä'), E central European Russian SFSR, rises NE of Kuznetsk (Penza oblast), flows W, past Chaadayevka, NE, past Penza, Bolshiye Berezniki (head of navigation), and Surskoye, and N, past Alatyr and Shumerlya, to Volga R. at Vasilsursk; 537 mi. long. Navigable for 400 mi. Frozen Dec.-April. Receives Inza (right), Alatyr and Pyana (left) rivers.

Surashtr, Thailand: see SURATTHANI.

Surashtra, India: see SAURASHTRA.

Surastradhani, Thailand: see SURATTHANI.

Surat (sōō'rŭt), village (pop. 406), S Queensland, Australia, on Balonne R. and 240 mi. WNW of Brisbane; cattle, wheat.

Surat (sōō'rŭt), district, N central Bombay, India; ⊙ Surat. Bounded W by Gulf of Cambay; E section crossed N-S by Western Ghats; drained by Tapti R. (N) and several mtn. streams. Agr. (rice, cotton, millet); some mangoes and plantains grown; teak, sandalwood, bamboo in E forests. Hand-loom weaving, fishing (pomfrets, Bombay duck). Surat and Navsari are large textile centers; Bulsar and Bilimora have local trade. Raided by Mahrattas in late-17th cent. Original dist. (□ 1,695; 1941 pop. 881,058) was enlarged by inc. (1949) of former Gujarat states of Dharampur, Bansda, and Sachin, and Navsari div. of former Baroda state.

Surat, city (pop. 171,443), ⊙ Surat dist., N Bombay, India, port on Gulf of Cambay, near Tapti R. mouth, 150 mi. N of Bombay. Road junction; trade center; markets and exports cotton, millet, wheat, rice; cotton and silk milling, handicraft cloth weaving, rice husking, fish curing (pomfrets, jewfish, Bombay duck), sandalwood carving, mfg. of gold and silver thread, hats, paper, aerated water, soap, tiles; a depot for cottage industries. Technical institute, col. Developed as port under Moguls; became rich trade center in 17th and 18th cent., with several European settlements (1st English trading post in India established here, 1612); in late-17th cent. hq. of English East India Co.; sacked by Sivaji in 1664. Old Fr. trading post (*loge*) transferred to India in 1947.

Suratgarh (sōō'rŭtgŭr), town (pop. 5,186), N Rajasthan, India, 100 mi. NNE of Bikaner; rail junction.

Suratthani (sōōrät'tä'nē'), town (1947 pop. 10,423), ⊙ Suratthani prov. (□ 5,225; 1947 pop. 208,390), S Thailand, Gulf of Siam port on E coast of Malay Peninsula, on railroad and 280 mi. SSW of Bangkok, on Tapi R. delta; rice, coconuts, fruit; fish processing, timber trade (sawmilling); tin mining (S). Lignite deposits (W). Local name, Ban Don or Bandon. Also called Surat and Surashtr and spelled Surastradhani. Until early 1930s, when govt. seat was moved here, the name Suratthani was applied to Tha Kham, 5 mi. WSW on railroad.

Suraz (sōō'räsh), Pol. *Suraż*, Rus. *Surazh* (sōō'rŭsh), town (pop. 1,071), Bialystok prov., NE Poland, on Narew R. and 15 mi. SW of Bialystok; brickworks.

Surazh (sōōräsh'). **1** Town (1926 pop. 2,107), NE Vitebsk oblast, Belorussian SSR, on Western Dvina R. and 27 mi. NE of Vitebsk; food products, lumber, flax. Until 1939, Surazh-Vitebski. **2** City (1926 pop. 5,778), W Bryansk oblast, Russian SFSR, on Iput R. and 15 mi. NW of Unecha; paper milling (cardboard), woodworking. Peat works near by. Chartered 1777.

Surbiton, residential municipal borough (1931 pop. 29,401; 1951 census 60,675), N Surrey, England, on the Thames and 11 mi. SW of London; mfg. of machine tools, radios; printing.

Surbo (sōōr'bô), town (pop. 4,657), Lecce prov., Apulia, S Italy, 3 mi. N of Lecce; wine, olive oil.

Sur Chichas, Bolivia: see TUPIZA.

Sur Cinti, Bolivia: see VILLA ABECIA.

Surco or **Santiago de Surco** (säntyä'gō dā sōōr'kō), S residential suburb (pop. 7,101), of Lima, Lima dept., W central Peru, just E of Barranco. Inc. 1940 into Lima proper.

Surdash (sōōrdäsh'), town, Sulaimaniya prov., NE Iraq, in the mts. of Kurdistan, near Iran border, 30 mi. NW of Sulaimaniya; tobacco, fruit, livestock. Also spelled Serdash.

Surduc Pass (sōōr'dōōk), Ger. *Szurduk* (sōōr'dōōk), narrow gorge (alt. 1,771 ft.) in S central Rumania, cut by Jiu R. across the Transylvanian Alps; highway corridor bet. Transylvania and Oltenia. Battleground (1916) in First World War. Also called Vulcan Pass.

Surdulica or **Surdulitsa** (both: sōōr'dōōlĭtsä), village, SE Serbia, Yugoslavia, 17 mi. NE of Vranje.

Sûre, river: see SÛRE RIVER.

Surendranagar (sōōrĕn'drŭnŭgŭr), town (pop. 21,622), ⊙ Zalawad dist., NE Saurashtra, India, on Kathiawar peninsula, 60 mi. ENE of Rajkot; trade center for cotton, grain, ghee, cloth fabrics, hides; cotton ginning, hand-loom weaving, soap mfg. Glassworks at neary-by village of Joravarnagar. Rail junction 4 mi. NW. Town, until c.1950 called Wadhwan (vŭd'vän), was ⊙ former princely state of Wadhwan.

Sûre River (sür), Ger. *Sauer* (zou'ŭr), SE Belgium and Luxembourg, rises 14 mi. NW of Martelange (Belgium), flows 100 mi. generally E and SE, past Martelange, Ettelbruck, Diekirch, Bettendorf, and Echternach, to Moselle R. at Wasserbilling. Chief tributaries: Wiltz, Wark, Alzette, and Our rivers. Navigable below Diekirch. Forms Luxembourg-German border below confluence of Our R.

Suresnes (sürĕn'), town (pop. 31,775), Seine dept., N central France, a W suburb of Paris, 6 mi. from Notre Dame Cathedral, on left bank of Seine R., opposite Bois de Boulogne, just SSW of Puteaux; automobile, aircraft, and bicycle construction. Just W is fortified Mont Valérien. At conference of Suresnes (1593), Henry IV agreed to become a Catholic.

Suretka (sōōrät'kä), village, Limón prov., SE Costa Rica, on Sixaola R. and 30 mi. SSE of Limón. Was railhead, center of Talamanca banana zone.

Surfaide, resort town (pop. 1,852), Dade co., S Fla., just N of Miami Beach.

Surf City, resort borough (pop. 291), Ocean co., E N.J., on Long Beach isl. and 25 mi. NE of Atlantic City. Settled 1690 by whalers.

Surgana (sōōrgä'nŭ), village, Nasik dist., central Bombay, India, in Western Ghats, 42 mi. NNW of Nasik; local market for timber (teak, blackwood), rice, and millet. Was ⊙ former princely state of Surgana (□ 131; pop. 18,292) in Gujarat States, Bombay; state inc. 1949 into Nasik dist.

Surgentes, Los, Argentina: see LOS SURGENTES.

Surgères (sürzhâr'), town (pop. 3,186), Charente-Maritime dept., W France, 15 mi. NE of Rochefort; center of Charente dairying industry (natl. milk research institute, dairy cooperatives; mfg. of dairying equipment); produces casein derivatives (galalith, plastics), brandy, biscuits. Has 12th-cent. Romanesque church.

Surgidero de Batabanó (sōōrhēdā'rō dā bätäbänō'), town (pop. 5,695), Havana prov., W Cuba, port for Batabanó (2½ mi. N), 30 mi. S of Havana; rail terminus and fishing center (lobster, tuna, sponge); charcoal burning, lumbering. Point of embarkation for Isle of Pines.

Surguja (sōōr'gōōjŭ), former princely state (□ 6,067; pop. 551,752) of Chhattisgarh States, India; ⊙ was Ambikapur. Since 1948, inc. into Surguja dist. of Madhya Pradesh.

Surguja, district (□ 8,613; pop. 699,892), NE Madhya Pradesh, India, on W Chota Nagpur Plateau; ⊙ Ambikapur. Bordered W and NW by Vindhya Pradesh, N by Uttar Pradesh, NE by Bihar; mainly in rugged E highlands of Satpura Range, rising to c.4,000 ft. in numerous ridges; drained by tributaries of Son R. Largely covered with dense sal jungles mixed with bamboo, khair, and myrobalan; lac cultivation. Agr. (rice, oilseeds) mainly in SW valleys. Extensive coal deposits; mines near Chirmiri (rail spur terminus). Deposits of iron ore, limestone, bauxite, lead, and mica. Dist. created 1948 by merger of former Chhattisgarh States of Changbhakar, Korea, and Surguja. Pop. 64% tribal, 35% Hindu, 1% Moslem. Sometimes spelled Sirguja.

Surgut (sōōrgōōt'). **1** Village (1939 pop. over 500), N Kuibyshev oblast, Russian SFSR, on left bank of Sok R., opposite Sergiyevsk, and 70 mi. NE of Kuibyshev; rail spur terminus; wheat, sunflowers. **2** Village (1948 pop. over 2,000), central Khanty-Mansi Natl. Okrug, Tyumen oblast, Russian SFSR, on Ob R. and 150 mi. E of Khanty-Mansisk; fish canning; airport. Founded 1594 on early Siberian colonization route.

Suri (sōō'rē), town (pop. 15,867), ⊙ Birbhum dist., W West Bengal, India, 110 mi. NNW of Calcutta; road and trade center (rice, gram, wheat, sugar cane); rice milling, cotton and silk weaving. Annual cattle and agr. fair. Barrage for Mor River irrigation project 5 mi. NW, at Khatanga.

Suria (sōō'ryä), town (pop. 3,788), Barcelona prov., NE Spain, on the Cardoner and 10 mi. NW of Manresa; cotton spinning and weaving; agr. trade. Extensive potassium-salt mines near by.

Suriapet or **Suryapet** (both: sōōr'yŭpăt), town (pop. 7,381), Nalgonda dist., SE Hyderabad state, India, 25 mi. ENE of Nalgonda; road center; rice milling, peanut-oil extraction. Experimental farm.

Suribachi, Mount, Volcano Isls.: see IWO JIMA.

Suride-kaikyo, Russian SFSR: see SREDNI STRAIT.

Surigao (sōōrēgä'ō, -gou'), province (□ 3,079; 1948 pop. 264,952), along extreme NE coast of Mindanao, Philippines, across Surigao Strait from Leyte; ⊙ Surigao. Offshore isls. of Dinagat, Siargao, Bucas Grande, and Nonoc are in prov. Though it is a fertile coconut-growing area, it has developed in recent years as a mining region, with some of the leading gold deposits and the largest iron deposits of the Philippines.

Surigao, town (1939 pop. 8,635; 1948 municipality pop. 46,109), ⊙ Surigao prov., Philippines, at NE tip of Mindanao, c.400 mi. SE of Manila; port and trade center for a rich hinterland mining area (gold, iron); also coconuts; fishing.

Surigao Strait, in the Philippines, leading from Leyte Gulf to Mindanao Sea, bet. Leyte and Mindanao; c.50 mi. long, 10–20 mi. wide. A scene of action, in the Second World War, of part of the battle of Leyte Gulf (Oct., 1944), also called 2d battle of the Philippine Sea, in which U.S. naval forces defeated the Jap. fleet.

Surimena (sōōrēmā'nä), village, Meta intendancy, E central Colombia, in llano lowlands, 25 mi. SE of Villavicencio; cattle.

Surin (sōō'rĭn'), town (1947 pop. 8,768), ⊙ Surin prov. (□ 3,556; 1947 pop. 435,382), E Thailand, in Korat Plateau, on railroad and 100 mi. WSW of Ubon; lac, rice. Also spelled Surindr or Surindra.

Surinam, colony: see GUIANA, DUTCH.

Surinam, district, Du. Guiana: see PARAMARIBO.

Surinam River (sōō'rĭnăm, sōōrĭnäm'), Du. *Suriname* (sürĕnä'mŭ), Du. Guiana, rises as the Gran Rio in outliers of the Guiana Highlands at about 3°20'N 56°10'W, flows c.300 mi. N, through tropical forest region and alluvial lowlands, past Paramaribo and Nieuw Amsterdam (where it receives the Commewijne), to the Atlantic c.10 mi. N of Paramaribo. It has a wide mouth and is navigable for ocean-going vessels to Paramaribo; smaller craft can proceed c.90 mi. inland. Upper course is impeded by many rapids. There are important bauxite deposits at Paranam, 16 mi. SSE of Paramaribo; extensive gold fields along its midcourse. Saramacca Canal links it with Saramacca R.

Suring (sōōr'ĭng), village (pop. 546), Oconto co., NE Wis., on Oconto R. and 38 mi. NW of Green Bay, in lumbering and dairying area.

Surisawa, Japan: see SURUSAWA.

Surite (sōōrē'tä), town (pop. 1,778), Cuzco dept., S central Peru, in the Andes, 23 mi. WNW of Cuzco; potatoes, grain. Has archaeological remains. Sometimes Zurite.

Surkhab River, Afghanistan: see KUNDUZ RIVER.

Surkhab River (sōōrkhäp'), central Tadzhik SSR, formed by junction of the MUK-SU and KYZYL-SU, 28 mi. ENE of Khait; flows c.80 mi. WSW, past Tadzhikabad and Garm, joining Obi-Khingou R. near Komsomolabad to form VAKHSH RIVER. Also spelled Surkhob.

Surkhan-Darya or **Surkhan-Dar'ya** (sōōrkhän"-dŭryä'), oblast (□ 7,700; 1946 pop. estimate 300,000), SE Uzbek SSR; ⊙ Termez. Bounded W by the Baisun-Tau, S by river Amu Darya; drained by the Surkhan Darya. Cotton growing in irrigated river valleys, dry farming (wheat) on mtn. slopes, sheep (karakul) and goat raising in dry flatlands. Cotton ginning. Oil fields at Khaudag and Uch-Kzyl. Kagan-Stalinabad RR runs N-S. Pop.: Uzbeks, Tadzhiks. Formed 1941; an earlier oblast of the same name existed 1924–26.

Surkhan Darya or **Surkhan Dar'ya,** river in Surkhan-Darya oblast, Uzbek SSR, rises in 2 main branches in Gissar Range, flows c.150 mi. SSW, through fertile cotton area, past Dzhar-Kurgan, to the Amu Darya near Termez. Joined to Kafirnigan R. by Gissar Canal (at Gissar).

Sur Lípez, Bolivia: see SAN PABLO, Potosí dept.

Surma River (sōōr'mŭ), in Assam (India) and East Bengal (E Pakistan), rises (as Barak R.) in N Manipur Hills, NW of Ukhrul; flows W and SSW, then sharply N along W Manipur border, and W through Surma Valley, past Silchar (here forming numerous arms, including KUSIYARA, BIBIYANA, and BARAK rivers) and Sylhet, and SSW (its arms rejoining along W part of Surma Valley; here called Kalni R.), becoming MEGHNA RIVER below southernmost arm. Total course, to Meghna R., c.320 mi. Called Barak in Manipur and Cachar dist., Assam.

Surma Valley, alluvial tract in Sylhet dist. (E Pakistan) and E Assam (India); bounded N by Assam Range, E by Manipur Hills, S by Tripura and Lushai hills, W by Kalni (lower Surma) R.; served by Surma R. system; rice, tea, oilseeds.

Surmene (sürmĕnĕ'), Turkish *Sürmene*, village (pop. 2,979), Trebizond prov., NE Turkey, port on Black Sea 17 mi. ESE of Trebizond; marble near by. Formerly Humurgan.

Suro, Portuguese Timor: see AINARO.

Surovikino (sōōrô'vēkēnŭ), town (1939 pop. over 2,000), SW Stalingrad oblast, Russian SFSR, on Chir R., on railroad and 22 mi. NW of Nizhne-Chirskaya; metalworks, condensed-milk factory; wheat.

Surprise, village (pop. 120), Butler co., E Nebr., 40 mi. NW of Lincoln and on Big Blue R.

Surprise Valley, Modoc co., NE Calif., along Nev. line, E of Warner Mts.; c.50 mi. long N–S. Cedarville is near its center, Fort Bidwell in N. Contains large, intermittently dry Alkali Lakes (Middle,

Upper, and Lower lakes). Farming, stock raising, lumbering.

Surrency (sŭ'rŭnsē), town (pop. 295), Appling co., SE central Ga., 8 mi. ESE of Baxley; lumber.

Surrentum, Italy: see SORRENTO.

Surrey, county (□ 721.6; 1931 pop. 1,180,810; 1951 census 1,601,555), S England; ⊙ Guildford. Bounded by Hampshire (W), Berkshire (NW), Buckingham, Middlesex, and London (N), Kent (E), and Sussex (S). Drained by Thames, Wey, and Mole rivers. Crossed E-W by North Downs. Truck gardening for London market. Urban areas are mainly residential; E part of co. is a London residential area. In W, sheep grazing and dairying predominate. Fuller's earth is found near Nutfield and Reigate. There are various light industries. Other urban centers are Croydon, Kingston-on-Thames, Richmond, Wimbledon, Dorking, Godalming, Epsom, Woking. Many towns are of historical and architectural interest.

Surrey, county (□ 820.1; pop. 359,634), E Jamaica, B.W.I., comprising E third of the isl., with Kingston, Port Royal, St. Andrew, St. Thomas, and Portland parishes. Set up in 1758, it is now a region without administrative functions.

Surrey, village and township (pop. 398), Ward co., central N.Dak., 7 mi. E of Minot; 2 branches of Great Northern RR join here.

Surry (sŭ'rē). **1** County (□ 537; pop. 45,593), NW N.C.; ⊙ Dobson. In piedmont region; bounded N by Va., S by Yadkin R. Farming (tobacco, corn), dairying, sawmilling, granite quarrying; mfg. at Elkin and Mt. Airy. Formed 1770. **2** County (□ 280; pop. 6,220), SE Va.; ⊙ Surry. In tidewater region; bounded N and NE by James, S by Blackwater rivers. Agr. (peanuts; also some corn, cotton); dairying; lumbering. Historic bldgs. at Bacons Castle and Claremont. Formed 1652.

Surry. 1 Fishing, resort town (pop. 448), Hancock co., S Maine, on Blue Hill Bay just SW of Ellsworth. **2** Town (pop. 291), Cheshire co., SW N.H., on the Ashuelot and 7 mi. N of Keene. **3** Town (pop. 248), ⊙ Surry co., SE Va., near the James, 33 mi. ESE of Petersburg. Home (c.1650) of Thomas Rolfe and BACONS CASTLE near by. Rail station at Wakefield, 15 mi. SW.

Sursaari (sōōr'sŭärē), Finnish *Suursaari* (sōōr'särē), Swedish *Hogland*, rocky island (1944 pop. 583) in Gulf of Finland, in Leningrad oblast, Russian SFSR, 110 mi. W of Leningrad, 25 mi. S of Kotka; 6 mi. long, 1–2 mi. wide. Its chief village and harbor is Surkyulya, Finnish *Suurkylä*, near N end. Resort while in Finland (until 1940).

Sursee (zōōr'zā), town (pop. 3,784), Lucerne canton, N central Switzerland, on Suhr R. and 11 mi. NW of Lucerne; stoves, clothes; printing. Has 16th-cent. town hall.

Surskoye (sōōr'skŭyŭ), town (1939 pop. over 2,000), NW Ulyanovsk oblast, Russian SFSR, on Sura R. and 26 mi. S of Alatyr; wood- and metalworking, flour milling. Until c.1930, Promzino.

Surte (sür'tù), residential village (pop. 1,871), Alvsborg co., SW Sweden, on Gota R. and 8 mi. N of Goteborg; mfg. of glassware, chemicals. Scene (1648, 1950) of destructive landslides.

Surtshellir, Iceland: see EIRIKSJOKULL.

Surubim (sōōrōō'bēn), city (pop. 2,672), E Pernambuco, NE Brazil, near Paraíba border, 20 mi. WNW of Limoeiro; cotton, coffee, cattle.

Suruc (sōōrōōch'), Turkish *Suruç* or *Sürüç*, village (pop. 3,632), Urfa prov., S Turkey, 24 mi. WSW of Urfa, near Syrian line; wheat, barley.

Suruga (sōōrōō'gä), former province in central Honshu, Japan; now Shizuoka prefecture.

Suruga Bay, Jap. *Suruga-wan*, inlet of Philippine Sea, in Shizuoka prefecture, central Honshu, Japan; sheltered E by Izu Peninsula; 35 mi. N-S, 15–35 mi. E-W. Shizuoka and Shimizu on W, Numazu on NE shore.

Suruli River (sōō'rōōlē), Madura dist., S Madras, India, rises on Madras-Travancore border in Western Ghats, flows 40 mi. NE, through fertile agr. Kambam Valley, to Vaigai R. 8 mi. SSW of Periyakulam; conducts waters of PERIYAR LAKE irrigation project.

Suru River (sōō'rōō), in Ladakh dist., central Kashmir, rises on glacier in W Punjab Himalayas SE of Nunkun peak, at 33°55'N 76°15'E; flows N, W, and N past Kargil to Indus R. 14 mi. NNE of Kargil; c.100 mi. long. Separates Zaskar Range (S) from Deosai Mts. (N). In upper course, also called Ringdom Sankpo or Sankpo.

Surusawa (sōōrōō'säwŭ) or **Surisawa** (sōōrē'–) town (pop. 4,658), Iwate prefecture, N Honshu, Japan, 11 mi. ENE of Ichinoseki; agr., lumbering, raw-silk culture; lacquer ware.

Suryapet, India: see SURIAPET.

Sury-le-Comtal (sürē'-lü-kōtäl'), town (pop. 2,089), Loire dept., SE central France, in Forez Plain, 7 mi. SE of Montbrison; mfg. of bicycle parts and hosiery.

Sur Yungas, Bolivia: see CHULUMANI.

Susa (sū'zū, –sū), biblical *Shushan* (shōō'shăn), Persian *Shush* (shōōsh), anc. city of Persia, capital of Elam (later Susiana), 15 mi. SW of modern Dizful, bet. the rivers Karkheh and Ab-i-Diz. It flourished after 1200 B.C. and was destroyed in 645 B.C. by Assur-bani-pal of Assyria. Revived (c.500 B.C.) by Darius, it became winter residence of the Achaemenian rulers of Persia and was scene of story of Esther. Conquered (331 B.C.) by Alexander the Great, but prospered again as capital of the Sassanian dynasty until the coming of the Arabs. Continued as a center of sugar-cane cultivation, but declined in the Middle Ages. Excavations, begun 1850 by W. K. Loftus and later carried on by M. A. Dieulafoy, disclosed ruins of palace and citadel, many cuneiform inscriptions in the Elamite language, the code of Hammurabi, and colored friezes (now in Paris Louvre). Near by is the so-called Daniel's Tomb, a Moslem structure.

Susa (sōō'zä), anc. *Segusio*, town (pop. 3,803), Torino prov., Piedmont, NW Italy, on Dora Riparia R. and 32 mi. WNW of Turin, in grape-growing, stock-raising region; textiles, chemicals, cement, asbestos; printing; hydroelectric plant. Bishopric. Has triumphal arch (8 B.C.) dedicated to Augustus, 11th-cent. cathedral of San Giusto, 13th-cent. houses. Sacked by Frederick Barbarossa in 1175. Long important as junction of Mont Cenis and Montgenèvre roads. In Val di Susa, formed by upper Dora Riparia R.; noted for Alpine scenery, resorts, hydroelectric plants.

Susa (sōō'sä), town (pop. 6,221), Yamaguchi prefecture, SW Honshu, Japan, on Sea of Japan, 18 mi. NE of Hagi, in agr. and forested area; citrus fruit; sake, soy sauce. Sawmilling, fishing.

Susa, Tunisia: see SOUSSE.

Susa, Val di, Italy: see DORA RIPARIA RIVER.

Susaa, Denmark: see SUS RIVER.

Susac Island (sōō'shäts), Serbo-Croatian *Sušac*, Ital. *Cazza* (kät'tsä), island in Adriatic Sea, S Croatia, Yugoslavia, 80 mi. W of Dubrovnik; 3 mi. long. In Zara prov., Italy (1920–47). Sometimes spelled Sushats.

Susak, Yugoslavia: see RIJEKA.

Susaki (sōōsä'kē), town (pop. 15,950), Kochi prefecture, S Shikoku, Japan, on Tosa Bay, 19 mi. SW of Kochi; fishing port; rice-growing center; dried bonito, raw silk, lumber.

Susam-Adasi, Greece: see SAMOS.

Susami (sōōsä'mē), town (pop. 6,066), Wakayama prefecture, S Honshu, Japan, on Philippine Sea, on S Kii Peninsula, 4 mi. SSE of Tanabe; fishing and agr. center (rice, wheat).

Susamyr (sōōsŭmĭr'), high mountain valley in NW Tyan-Shan oblast, Kirghiz SSR, 120 mi. NW of Naryn; fertile pastures (sheep, horses). Main village, Susamyr. Drained by Susamyr R., a tributary of the Naryn. The range Susamyr-Tau (a section of the Tien Shan) lies S.

Susangird or **Susangerd** (both: sōōsäng-gĕrd'), town (1940 pop. 9,565), Sixth Prov., in Khuzistan, SW Iran, on Karkheh R. and 30 mi. NW of Ahwaz, in Arab tribal area of Dasht-i-Mishan; grain, rice. Formerly called Khafajiyeh.

Susanino (sōōsä'nyĭnŭ), village (1948 pop. over 2,000), W Kostroma oblast, Russian SFSR, 22 mi. S of Bui; clothing mfg. Until 1939, Molvitino.

Susan Island, B.C.: see RODERICK ISLAND.

Susank (sōō'săngk), city (pop. 100), Barton co., central Kansas, 30 mi. WSW of Ellsworth.

Susan River, NE Calif., rises in SW Lassen co., flows c.40 mi. E, past Susanville, to Honey L.

Susanville, city (pop. 5,338), ⊙ LASSEN co., NE Calif., at E base of the Sierra Nevada, on Susan R., at head of fertile Honey L. valley; alt. 4,195 ft. Lumber and flour mills, creamery; cattle and hay market. Annual co. stock show and rodeo held here. Seat of Lassen Jr. Col. Lassen Volcanic Natl. Park is c.40 mi. W. Settled 1853; inc. as town in 1900; became city in 1940.

Suscallón, Nicaragua: see SUSUCAYÁN.

Susegana (sōōzä'nyä), village (pop. 569), Treviso prov., Veneto, N Italy, 13 mi. N of Treviso; lumber and silk mills, wine making. Has church with altarpiece by Pordenone. Near by is castle of Collato (13–14th cent.), ruined in First World War.

Susehri (sōō-shĕrē'), Turkish *Suşehri*, village (pop. 4,223), Sivas prov., central Turkey, near Kelkit R., 65 mi. NE of Sivas; wheat, barley. Formerly Endires.

Süsel (zü'zŭl), village (pop. 6,727), in Schleswig-Holstein, NW Germany, on small Süsel L., 5 mi. SE of Eutin; sawmilling. Until 1937 in Oldenburg.

Sushitsa (sōōshē'tsä), village (pop. 4,480), Gorna Oryakhovitsa dist., N Bulgaria, at head of branch of Cherni Lom R., 12 mi. NE of Gorna Oryakhovitsa; flour milling; livestock, sugar beets, oil-bearing plants, truck.

Süshui or **Hsü-shui** (both: shü'shwā'), town, ⊙ Süshui co. (pop. 229,800), NW central Hopeh prov., China, 13 mi. NE of Paoting and on Peking-Hankow RR; cabbage, bean sprouts, poultry. Until 1914 called Ansu.

Susiana, Iran: see ELAM.

Susice (sōō'shĭtsĕ), Czech *Sušice*, Ger. *Schüttenhofen* (shü'tŭnhō"fŭn), town (pop. 6,793), SW Bohemia, Czechoslovakia, on Otava R., on railroad and 15 mi. SE of Klatovy; mfg. (watches, shoes, lamp wicks), tanning. Has fish hatchery. Ruins of Rabi (Czech *Rabí*) castle, of Zizka memory, lie 5 mi. NE, on Otava R.

Susitna (sōōsĭt'nŭ), village (1939 pop. 12), S Alaska, on Susitna R. and 30 mi. NW of Anchorage; supply point.

Susitna River, S Alaska, rises in Susitna Glacier on Mt. Hayes in Alaska Range near 63°30'N 147°15'W, flows in winding course generally SW to Curry, thence S, past Talkeetna, Chulitna, and Susitna, to head of Cook Inlet 25 mi. W of Anchorage; 300 mi. long. Receives Talkeetna and Yentna rivers. Navigable 85 mi. to Talkeetna.

Susleny (sōōslyĕ'nē), Rum. *Susleni* (sōōslĕn'), village (1941 pop. 4,541), E Moldavian SSR, 8 mi. ENE of Orgeyev, in tobacco dist.

Suslonger (sōōslŭn-gyĕr'), town (1939 pop. over 500), S Mari Autonomous SSR, Russian SFSR, on railroad and 25 mi. SSE of Ioshkar-Ola; sawmilling.

Susner (sōōsnär'), town (pop. 3,851), central Madhya Bharat, India, 37 mi. NNW of Shajapur; cotton, millet; cotton ginning.

Susquehanna (sŭskwĭhă'nŭ), county (□ 836; pop. 31,970), NE Pa.; ⊙ Montrose. Hilly lake region drained by Susquehanna R. Lackawanna R. rises in E part. Lumber products; anthracite; dairying. Formed 1810.

Susquehanna Depot, borough (pop. 2,646), Susquehanna co., NE Pa., 37 mi. N of Scranton and on Susquehanna R.; railroad shops; agr.

Susquehanna Flats, NE Md., marshlands at mouth of Susquehanna R. on Chesapeake Bay; noted for waterfowl hunting.

Susquehanna River, in NE U.S., rises in Otsego L., N.Y.; winds 444 mi. generally S, past Binghamton, N.Y., and Wilkes-Barre, Harrisburg, and other industrial towns in Pa., to head of Chesapeake Bay at Havre de Grace, Md. Scenic in parts; navigation not extensive; supplies water power; drains □ 27,570. Above junction with West Branch, it is sometimes called North Branch. West Branch rises in Cambria co., SW central Pa.; winds c.230 mi. E, past Williamsport, to main stream at Northumberland, Pa. Other affluents: Chenango R. at Binghamton; Chemung R. at Athens, Pa.; Lackawanna R. near Pittston, Pa.; Juniata R. at Duncannon, Pa. Its course cuts through several ridges of the Appalachians and traverses WYOMING VALLEY. Anthracite is dredged from its bed bet. Wilkes-Barre and Md. line. Some units of Federal flood-control project (approved 1936) on river and its tributaries have been completed. Hydroelectric dams at Safe Harbor, Pa., and Conowingo, Md.

Susques (sōō'skĕs), village (pop. estimate 100), ⊙ Susques dept. (□ 2,785; 1947 pop. 1,442), SW Jujuy prov., Argentina, on a small river and 120 mi. NW of Jujuy. Copper mines near by.

Sus River, Dan. *Susaa* (sōō'sô), longest (52 mi.) in Zealand, Denmark. Rises WSW of Fakse; flows NW, W, and S, forming NW boundary of Praesto amt, past Naestved, through Dybso Fjord, to Smaalandsfarvand strait c.8 mi. from its source.

Süssen (zü'sŭn), village (pop. 5,385), N Württemberg, Germany, after 1945 in Württemberg-Baden, on the Fils and 5 mi. ESE of Göppingen; rail junction; grain, cattle. Has ruined castle.

Sussex, town (pop. 3,027), S N.B., on Kennebecasis R. and 40 mi. NE of St. John; dairying center; mfg. of refrigerators, furniture, agr. implements, soft drinks; trout fishing. Gypsum and salt are worked in region.

Sussex, county (□ 1,457; 1931 pop. 769,859; 1951 census 936,744), S England; ⊙ Lewes. Bounded by Hampshire (W), Surrey (N), Kent (NE), and English Channel (S). Drained by Arun, Adur, Ouse, and Rother rivers. Crossed by South Downs and The Weald region. Grain and hay cultivation in coastal plain, sheep raising and fruitgrowing in N, hop growing in E. Tourist industry is important; on Channel coast are seaside resorts and residential towns of Brighton, Hastings, Bexhill-on-Sea, Eastbourne, Hove, Worthing, Littlehampton, and Bognor Regis. Industries include mfg. of leather, paper, brick and tile. Chief port is Newhaven. For administrative purposes the co. is divided into East Sussex (□ 829; 1931 pop. 546,864; 1951 census 618,083), ⊙ Lewes; and West Sussex (□ 628; 1931 pop. 222,995; 1951 census 318,661), ⊙ Chichester. Co. has numerous historical associations; there are traces of prehistoric, Roman, and Saxon occupation. Pevensey and Battle are historic centers of Norman invasion.

Sussex. 1 County (□ 946; pop. 61,336), S Del.; ⊙ Georgetown. Bounded S and W by Md. line, N by Mispillion R., E by Delaware Bay and the Atlantic; drained by Broadkill, Indian, Pocomoke, and Nanticoke rivers. Mainly agr. area; poultry, fruit, dairy products, truck; some mfg., canning; fishing, shipbuilding, and resorts on coast. Formed 1683. **2** County (□ 528; pop. 34,423), extreme NW N.J., bounded W by the Delaware, N by N.Y. line; ⊙ Newton. Mtn. and lake recreational area, including Kittatinny Mtn. ridge, site of scenic and historic Stokes State Forest and High Point (alt. 1,801 ft.; in state park), highest point in state. Agr. (poultry, fruit, dairy products, livestock); zinc and limestone deposits; mfg. (textiles, metal products, paper, clothing, pocketbooks). Drained by Musconetcong, Wallkill, and Pequest rivers, and Paulins Kill. Formed 1753. **3** County (□ 496; pop. 12,785), SE Va.; ⊙ Sussex. In tidewater region; bounded NE by Blackwater R.; drained by Nottoway R. Agr. (especially peanuts; also cotton, corn), livestock (hogs, cattle). Lumbering, lumber milling, processing of farm products at Waverly. Formed 1754.

Sussex. 1 Borough (pop. 1,541), Sussex co., NW N.J., 6 mi. N of Franklin; trade center for dairying, poultry-raising area; nurseries; mfg. of life rafts. Settled 1734, inc. 1902. 2 Village, ⊙ Sussex co., SE Va., 21 mi. SSE of Petersburg. Co. courthouse dates from 1828. 3 Village (pop. 679), Waukesha co., SE Wis., on branch of Fox R. and 16 mi. NW of Milwaukee, in dairying and truck-farming area.

Sussuapara, Brazil: see SUÇUAPARA.

Sustenhorn (zōōs'tŭnhôrn), peak (11,507 ft.) in Alps of the Four Forest Cantons, S central Switzerland, 13 mi. E of Meiringen.

Susten Pass (zōōs'tŭn) (7,422 ft.), in the Alps, S central Switzerland, on border of Bern and Uri cantons, 2 mi. N of the Sustenhorn.

Sustiacán (sōōstyäkän'), town (pop. 866), Zacatecas, N central Mexico, 8 mi. WSW of García; alt. 6,857 ft.; grain, vegetables, maguey, livestock.

Susucayán (sōōsōōkïän'), village, Nueva Segovia dept., NW Nicaragua, 6 mi. WSW of El Jícaro; sugar cane, livestock. Sometimes spelled Suscallón.

Susuman (sŏŏsŏŏmän'), town (1942 pop. over 2,000), N Khabarovsk Territory, Russian SFSR, on Berelyakh R. (headstream of Kolyma R.) and 225 mi. NW of Magadan (linked by highway); 62°47'N 148°9'E. Gold-mining center in Kolyma region; developed in late 1930s. Berelyakh is just NE.

Susunai Range or **Susunay Range** (sŏŏsŏŏnī'), Jap. *Susuya-take* (sōōsōō'yä-täkĕ), section of E mtn. range in SE Sakhalin, Russian SFSR; rises to 3,428 ft. at Mt. Chekhov, 6 mi. NE of Yuzhno-Sakhalinsk. **Susunai Valley,** W of range, is main agr. area of S Sakhalin; contains cities of Dolinsk and Yuzhno-Sakhalinsk.

Susung (sōō'sōōng'), town, ⊙ Susung co. (pop. 345,229), N Anhwei prov., China, on Hupeh line, 60 mi. WSW of Anking, in lake dist.; rice, cotton, tobacco.

Susupuato (sōōsōōpwä'tō), officially Susupuato de Guerrero, town (pop. 242), Michoacán, central Mexico, 17 mi. S of Zitácuaro; silver deposits; stock.

Susurluk (sōōsŭrlŭk'), town (pop. 6,147), Balikesir prov., NW Turkey, on railroad and Simav R., 23 mi. NE of Balikesir; wheat. Sometimes spelled Susigirlik, Turkish *Susıgırlık.*

Susurluk River, Turkey: see SIMAV RIVER.

Susuya-take, Russian SFSR: see SUSUNAI RANGE.

Susz (sōōsh), Ger. *Rosenberg* (rō'zŭnbĕrk), town (1939 pop. 4,480; 1946 pop. 1,618), in East Prussia, after 1945 in Olsztyn prov., NE Poland, 17 mi. E of Marienwerder (Kwidzyn); sawmilling, limestone quarrying. Founded by Teutonic Knights; chartered 1315. Until 1919, in West Prussia prov. In Second World War, c.50% destroyed.

Sutanuti, India: see CALCUTTA.

Sutchava River, Ukrainian SSR and Rumania: see SUCEAVA RIVER.

Sutculer (sütchülĕr'), Turkish *Sütçüler,* village (pop. 2,416), Isparta prov., W central Turkey, on Aksu R. and 29 mi. SE of Isparta; cereals. Formerly Pavlucebel.

Sutera (sōōtä'rä), village (pop. 4,059), Caltanissetta prov., central Sicily, near Platani R., 19 mi. W of Caltanissetta.

Sutersville, borough (pop. 854), Westmoreland co., SW Pa., 21 mi. SE of Pittsburgh and on Youghiogheny R.

Sutherland (sŭ'dhûrlŭnd), town (pop. 4,375), E New South Wales, Australia, 14 mi. SW of Sydney; coal-mining center.

Sutherland, town (pop. 1,046), S central Sask., near South Saskatchewan R., E suburb of Saskatoon; railroad division point; Dominion forestry farm.

Sutherland or **Sutherlandshire** (-shĭr), highland county (□ 2,027; 1931 pop. 16,101; 1951 census 13,664), N Scotland, bet. the Atlantic (W and N) and the North Sea (E); ⊙ Dornoch. Bounded by Ross and Cromarty (S) and Caithness (NE). Drained by Helmsdale, Halladale, Oykell, Brora and Shin rivers. Surface is generally mountainous and wild, with extensive deer forests, frequented by sportsmen; highest peak is Ben More (3,273 ft.). There are numerous lochs (largest, Assynt and Shin). SE coastline, on Dornoch Firth, is regular; elsewhere coast is rugged and indented by numerous sea lochs. Sheep grazing and sea fisheries are important. Because of poor soil, heavy rainfall, and low temperature, little land is under cultivation. Besides Dornoch, other towns are Helmsdale, Brora, and Embo. Bet. 1810 and 1820 the 1st duke of Sutherland attempted to move c.15,000 poor inland crofters to the coast and to America by means of the "Sutherland clearances." Co. was the "Southern Land" (in relation to the Orkneys and Shetlands) of the Norsemen.

Sutherland. 1 Town (pop. 835), O'Brien co., NW Iowa, 16 mi. NNE of Cherokee; dairy products. 2 Village (pop. 856), Lincoln co., SW central Nebr., 19 mi. W of North Platte city and on S.Platte R.; grain. Reservoir and power plant, part of Platte valley power and irrigation project, are here; reservoir fed by water diverted through concrete conduit from Kingsley Dam.

Sutherland Falls, in Fiordland Natl. Park, SW S.Isl., New Zealand, 14 mi. SE of Milford Sound; drop from L. Quill into Arthur R.; 1,904 ft. high.

Sutherlandshire, Scotland: see SUTHERLAND.

Sutherland Springs, village (pop. c.300), Wilson co., S Texas, 29 mi. ESE of San Antonio; rail point in cotton, cattle area. Near by is Sutherland Springs Park, former resort, with mineral springs.

Sutherlin, city (pop. 2,230), Douglas co., SW Oregon, 13 mi. N of Roseburg; quicksilver mining, lumber milling.

Sutivan, Yugoslavia: see BRAC ISLAND.

Sutlac (sütlăch'), Turkish *Sütlâç,* village (pop. 725), Denizli prov., SW Turkey, 18 mi. SE of Civril; rail junction.

Sutla River, Yugoslavia: see SOTLA RIVER.

Sutlej River (sŭt'lĕj), anc. *Zaradros,* longest of the 5 rivers of the Punjab, extending through SW Tibet, N India, and W Pakistan. Rises in Rakas L., Tibet (lake receives water from Manasarowar L., just E), on S slope of Kailas Range at c.15,000 ft. alt.; considered by some to rise in source (c.60 mi. SE) of feeder stream of Manasarowar L. Flows NW as the Langchen Khambab to near Shipki Pass, where it cuts through Zaskar Range in a deep gorge and enters India; meanders WSW through the Himalayas, debouching onto Punjab plain at Rupar; continues W and then SW in broad channel, past Ferozepore, into Pakistan, past Bahawalpur, to confluence with Chenab R. just E of Alipur; combined stream (the Panjnad) flows c.50 mi. SW to the Indus. From Rakas L. to Chenab confluence, c.850 mi. long. The Sutlej descends to c.10,000 ft. near Shipki Pass, 3,000 ft. at Rampur (Himachal Pradesh), 1,000 ft. at Bilaspur, and 300 ft. at mouth. Fed by several glaciers in upper course; receives main tributary, Beas R., WSW of Sultanpur. Used extensively for irrigation: headworks at Rupar (Sirhind Canal), Ferozepore (Gang and Dipalpur canals), Sulaimanke (Pakpattan and other canals); large dam at Bhakra to impound reservoir for irrigation and power development. River partly navigable for light craft. In 19th cent., Sutlej R. was rough boundary bet. Sikh and Br. spheres of influence until Anglo-Sikh wars in 1840s and Br. annexation of Punjab (1849).

Sutor Rocks, headlands at entrance to CROMARTY FIRTH, Ross and Cromarty, Scotland. North Sutor is 400 ft. high, South Sutor 463 ft.

Sutri (sōō'trē), anc. *Sutrium,* town (pop. 2,556), Viterbo prov., Latium, central Italy, 14 mi. SSE of Viterbo; hosiery mfg. Has remains of anc. walls and Roman amphitheater. Etruscan tombs near.

Sutrio (sōō'trēō), village (pop. 1,165), Udine prov., Friuli-Venezia Giulia, NE Italy, 8 mi. N of Tolmezzo; cutlery.

Sutsien or **Su-ch'ien** (both: sōō'chyĕn'), town (pop. 28,603), ⊙ Sutsien co. (pop. 604,034), N Kiangsu prov., China, 50 mi. NW of Hwaiyin and on Grand Canal; wheat, corn, beans, kaoliang, cotton.

Sutter (sŭ'tûr), county (□ 607; pop. 26,239), N central Calif.; ⊙ Yuba City. Low-lying region in Sacramento Valley; bounded W by Sacramento R., E by Feather R. Sutter Buttes (natural-gas wells here) are in N. A leading Calif. peach-growing co.; also produces rice, beans, prunes and other fruit, nuts, sugar beets, grain, hay, vegetables, dairy products, sheep, poultry. Processing of farm products. Clay, sand, and gravel quarrying. Waterfowl hunting in marshes; fishing. Formed 1850.

Sutter, village (1940 pop. 958), Sutter co., N central Calif., in Sacramento Valley, 8 mi. W of Yuba City; agr.; waterfowl hunting. Sutter Buttes are near by.

Sutter Buttes (bŭts), N central Calif., isolated group (c.10 mi. in diameter) of 4 jagged volcanic peaks, in Sacramento Valley, just N of Sutter; highest (South Butte) is c.2,130 ft. Natural-gas wells. Also called Marysville Buttes.

Sutter Creek, city (pop. 1,151), Amador co., central Calif., on short Sutter Creek and c.40 mi. ESE of Sacramento, in Mother Lode country; gold mines; dairying, lumbering. Settled in 1850s, inc. 1874.

Sutter's Mill, Calif.: see COLOMA.

Süttö (shüt'tû), Hung. *Süttő,* town (pop. 1,434), Komarom-Esztergom co., N Hungary, on the Danube and 14 mi. W of Esztergom; basalt mined in near-by Gerecse Mts.

Sutton, village (1939 pop. 14), S Alaska, on Matanuska R. and 12 mi. NE of Palmer, on Glenn Highway; coal mining.

Sutton. 1 Village, Ont.: see SUTTON WEST. 2 Village (pop. 1,118), S Que., on Missisquoi R. and 20 mi. SSE of Granby; lumbering, dairying.

Sutton. 1 Agr. village and parish (pop. 1,553), in Isle of Ely, N Cambridge, England, 6 mi. W of Ely. Has 14th-cent. church with noted tower. 2 Town, Lincolnshire, England: see MABLETHORPE AND SUTTON.

Sutton, NE suburb of Dublin, Co. Dublin, Ireland.

Sutton, county (□ 1,493; pop. 3,746), W Texas; ⊙ Sonora. In broken uplands of Edwards Plateau; alt. c.2,000 ft. Drained by Devils R., North Llano R. Sheep- and goat-ranching region; ships wool, mohair; also beef cattle, horses, hogs, poultry. Formed 1887.

Sutton. 1 Agr. town (pop. 3,102), Worcester co., S central Mass., 9 mi. S of Worcester; woolens. Settled c.1715. Includes villages of Manchaug (măn'chôg) (1940 pop. 867) and Wilkinsonville (1940 pop. 564), on Blackstone R. and partly in Grafton town. 2 City (pop. 1,353), Clay co., S Nebr., 23 mi. E of Hastings and on branch of Big Blue R., in prairie region; grain, livestock, dairy and poultry produce. Settled 1869. 3 Town (pop. 554), Merrimack co., S central N.H., 23 mi. NW of Concord, in agr., resort area. Near-by Kezar L. (1 mi. long) has resorts, state park. 4 Town (pop. 528), Caledonia co., NE Vt., 15 mi. N of St. Johnsbury; includes part of Willoughby State Forest. 5 Trading town (pop. 1,070), ⊙ Braxton co., central W.Va., on Elk R. and 50 mi. NE of Charleston, in gas, oil, and agr. area (livestock, fruit, tobacco); lumber, flour, and feed milling; marble and granite working. Inc. 1826.

Sutton and Cheam (chēm), residential municipal borough (1931 pop. 46,500; 1951 census 80,664), NE Surrey, England. Includes towns of Sutton, 11 mi. S of London, with electrical, soap, and perfumery industries; and Cheam, just NW of Sutton, with machine-tool mfg.; site of grammar school founded 1665.

Sutton-at-Hone, residential town and parish (pop. 6,475), NW Kent, England, on Darent R. and 3 mi. SSE of Dartford; farm-equipment works. Has 15th-cent. church.

Sutton Bridge, village and small port in Parts of Holland, SE Lincolnshire, England, on Nene R., near The Wash, and 7 mi. N of Wisbech. A swing bridge built 1850 by Robert Stephenson was later replaced by a fixed bridge.

Sutton Coldfield, residential municipal borough (1931 pop. 29,928; 1951 census 47,590), N Warwick, England, 7 mi. NNE of Birmingham; also foundry, machinery, and pharmaceutical industries. Television transmitter. Sutton Park (over 2,000 acres) is public recreation ground. Mansion of New Hall dates from 13th cent.

Sutton cum Duckmanton, parish (pop. 3,270), NE Derby, England. Includes coal-mining towns of Duckmanton, 3 mi. E of Chesterfield, and, just SE, Sutton.

Sutton Heath, England: see SAINT HELENS.

Sutton-in-Ashfield, urban district (1931 pop. 25,153; 1951 census 40,521), W Nottingham, England, 13 mi. NNW of Nottingham; hosiery center, with cotton mills; mfg. also of lace, brick, lime, synthetic fertilizer. Has church dating partly from 12th–14th cent. A Stone Age burial ground has been found here. In urban dist. (SW) is coal-mining town of Sutton Woodhouse.

Sutton Island, Maine: see CRANBERRY ISLES.

Sutton Oak, England: see SAINT HELENS.

Sutton-on-the-Forest, village and parish (pop. c.500), North Riding, Yorkshire, 8 mi. N of York; Laurence Sterne lived here, 1738–59.

Sutton Place, SE N.Y., a residential dist. of Manhattan borough of New York city, along East R. in vicinity of 57th St. Beekman Place dist. adjoins on S.

Suttons Bay, village (pop. 485), Leelanau co., NW Mich., 15 mi. NNW of Traverse City, on West Arm of Grand Traverse Bay, in fruitgrowing and resort area; sawmills.

Sutton West, village (pop. 1,051), S Ont., near L. Simcoe, 30 mi. W of Lindsay; dairying, mixed farming. Sometimes Sutton.

Sutton Woodhouse, England: see SUTTON-IN-ASHFIELD.

Süttör (shüt'tûr), town (pop. 1,947), Sopron co., W Hungary, 14 mi. ESE of Sopron, in agr. area; fertilizer mfg.

Suttsu (sōōt'tsōō), town (pop. 5,197), SW Hokkaido, Japan, on inlet of Sea of Japan, 20 mi. SW of Iwanai; sulphur mining; fishing, agr.

Suure-Jaani or **Suure-Yani** (sōō'rä-yä'nē), Ger. *Gross Sankt Johannis,* city (pop. 1,031), central Estonia, 13 mi. NNW of Viljandi; felt mfg.

Suursaari, Russian SFSR: see SURSAARI.

Suva (sōō'vä), port town (pop. 11,398; Greater Suva, pop. 23,513), SE coast of Viti Levu, Fiji, SW Pacific; ⊙ Br. colony of Fiji. Harbor (3.5 mi. wide) extends inland 2.5 mi.; barrier reef forms breakwater. Port of call for Br. and U.S. steamship lines; airplane service. Factories produce coconut oil, soap. Chief exports: sugar, copra, gold, tropical fruits. Central Medical School (1928) trains native doctors.

Suvadiva Atoll (sōōvä'dĭvŭ), S group (pop. 9,339) of Maldive Isls., in Indian Ocean, bet. 0°11'N and 0°55'N; coconuts, breadfruit; fishing. Sometimes called Huvadu.

Suvali (sōōvä'lē), village, Surat dist., N Bombay, India, on Gulf of Cambay, near Tapti R. mouth, 12 mi. W of Surat; roadstead for coastal steamers. Formerly port of Surat and known to traders as Swally or Swally Hole.

Suvalki, Poland: see SUWALKI.

Suva Mountains (sōō'vä), SE Serbia, Yugoslavia, bet. Southern Morava and Nisava rivers; highest ponit (5,619 ft.) is 7 mi. SW of Bela Palanka.

Suva Reka (sōō'vä rĕ'kä), village (pop. 4,094), SW Serbia, Yugoslavia, 11 mi. NNE of Prizren, in the Metohija.

Suvarov: see SUWARROW.

Suvasra, India: see SUWASRA.

Suvereto (sōōvĕrā'tô), village (pop. 1,560), Livorno prov., Tuscany, central Italy, 4 mi. ENE of Campiglia Marittima; mfg. (bricks, tiles).

Suvero, Cape (sōō'vĕrô), Calabria, S Italy, at NE end of Gulf of Sant'Eufemia, 9 mi. WSW of Nicastro; 38°57'N 16°9'E.

Suveydiye (süvä'dĭyĕ), Turkish *Süveydiye*, town (pop. c.8,000), Hatay prov., S Turkey, minor port on the Mediterranean just N of mouth of the Orontes, 36 mi. SSW of Iskenderun and 13 mi. SW of Antioch, for which it was once an important port. The anc. SELEUCIA or Seleucia Pieria is near by.

Suvorov: see SUWARROW.

Suvorovo, Bulgaria: see NOVGRADETS.

Suvorovo (sōōvô'rûvŭ), village (1941 pop. 4,389), S Izmail oblast, Ukrainian SSR, 18 mi. NNE of Izmail, at N end of Katlabug Lagoon; agr. center. Until c.1930, called Shikirlikitai, Rum. *Şichirlichitai;* later, until 1940, Regele Carol II, and, 1941–44, Regele Mihai I.

Suvorovskaya (sōōvô'rûfskīŭ), village (1926 pop. 10,342), SW Stavropol Territory, Russian SFSR, in N foothills of the Greater Caucasus, on Kuma R. and 25 mi. WNW of Pyatigorsk; road center; flour mill; wheat, sunflowers, cotton, vineyards.

Suwa (sōō'wä), former province in central Honshu, Japan; now part of Nagano prefecture.

Suwa, city (1940 pop. 24,076; 1947 pop. 36,491), Nagano prefecture, central Honshu, Japan, on E shore of L. Suwa, 15 mi. SE of Matsumoto; spinning; agr. (wheat, beans, rice). Hot springs. Formed in early 1940s by combining former town of Kami-suwa (1940 pop. 24,076) and 2 villages.

Suwa, Lake, Jap. *Suwa-ko,* Nagano prefecture, central Honshu, Japan, bet. Okaya (W) and Suwa (E); 3.5 mi. long, 2.5 mi. wide, alt. 2,505 ft. Summer and winter sports.

Suwaiq (sōōwīk'), town, Batina dist., N Oman, port on Gulf of Oman, 75 mi. WNW of Muscat; fishing, date cultivating, stock raising.

Suwaira or **Suwayrah** (sōōwī'rŭ), town, Kut prov., E Iraq, on Tigris R. and 35 mi. SE of Baghdad; dates, sesame, millet. Also called Juwaimisa, Jumaisa, Djuwaymisah, or Djumaysah.

Suwalki (sōōvä'ōōkē), Pol. *Suwałki,* Rus. *Suvalki* (sōōväl'kē), town (pop. 13,670), Bialystok prov., NE Poland, on the Czarna Hancza and 70 mi. N of Bialystok. Rail junction; trade center; mfg. of chairs, stamps, electrical and knit goods, hosiery, gloves; flour milling, brewing, tanning. Founded (15th cent.) as a Lithuanian settlement; passed (1795) to Prussia; in Rus. Poland, 1815–1921, and ⊙ Suvalki govt.; returned to Poland in 1921. A short-lived agreement granting Vilna to Lithuania was signed here (1920) by Poles. During Second World War, inc. 1939 into USSR; passed (1941) to East Prussia and called Sudauen (zōō'dou"ŭn).

Suwanee (sùwô'nē, swô'nē, –wä'–), town (pop. 357), Gwinnett co., N central Ga., 26 mi. NE of Atlanta; shoe mfg.

Suwannee, county (□ 677; pop. 16,986), N Fla.; ⊙ Live Oak. Flatwoods area with small lakes, bounded by Suwannee (W,S) and Santa Fe (S) rivers. Farming (corn, peanuts, cotton, tobacco, vegetables), stock raising (hogs, cattle), and some lumbering. Formed 1858.

Suwannee River, in Ga. and Fla., rises in Okefenokee Swamp, SE Ga., meanders 250 mi. generally S, across N Fla., to the Gulf of Mexico 22 mi. S of Cross City. Receives Withlacoochee, Alapaha, and Santa Fe rivers. Its channel, tidal for 25 mi., is dredged 135 mi. to mouth of the Withlacoochee. Name used in Stephen Foster's famous song, *Old Folks at Home* or *The Swanee River.*

Suwanose-shima, Ryukyu Isls.: see TOKARA-GUNTO.

Suwaqa or **Suwaqah** (sōōwä'kù), village, central Jordan, on Hejaz RR and 25 mi. NE of Kerak; sheep, goat, camel raising. Ruins (W).

Suwar or **Tell es Suwar,** (tĕl' ĕs-sōō-wär'), town, Euphrates prov., NE Syria, on Khabur R. and 30 mi. ENE of Deir ez Zor.

Suwarof, Alaska: see NAKNEK.

Suwarrow (sōōvôr'ôf) or **Anchorage Island,** atoll (600 acres; pop. 5), Manihiki group, S Pacific, 515 mi. NW of Rarotonga; 13°17'S 163°7'W; c.25 islets. Discovered 1814 by Russians, claimed by Great Britain 1889, placed 1901 under N.Z. COOK ISLANDS administration. Sometimes spelled Suvorov, Suvarov, or Suwarroff.

Suwasra (sōōväs'rŭ), village, W central Madhya Bharat, India, 37 mi. E of Mandasor; millet, cotton, wheat, gram; cotton ginning, hand-loom weaving. Arts and crafts school. Also Suvasra.

Suwayda, Al-, Syria: see SUWEIDA, ES.

Suwaylih, Jordan: see SUWEILIH.

Suwayrah, Iraq: see SUWAIRA.

Suweida, Es, El Suweida, or **Al-Suwayda** (all: ĕs-sōōwä'dä), Fr. *Soueida,* town (pop. c.7,500), ⊙ Jebel ed Druz prov., S Syria, 25 mi. from Jordan border, on railroad, and 55 mi. SSE of Damascus. Built on site of Roman town, but few ruins remain.

Suweilih or **Suwaylih** (both: sōōwä'lē), town (pop. c.5,000), N central Jordan, on main Amman-Jerusalem road and 8 mi. NW of Amman; road junction; vineyards, kaolin quarries.

Süwen or **Hsü-wen** (both: shü'wŭn'), town (pop. 15,467), ⊙ Süwen co. (pop. 111,559), SW Kwangtung prov., China, on S Luichow Peninsula, near Hainan Strait, 35 mi. S of Hoihong; sugar cane, hemp, rice, peanuts. Fisheries and saltworks near by on coast. The port of Hoion is 10 mi. SSE.

Suwo (sōō'ō), former province in SW Honshu, Japan; now part of Yamaguchi prefecture.

Suwon (sōō'wŭn'), Jap. *Suigen,* walled town (1949 pop. 52,772), Kyonggi prov., central Korea, S of 38°N, 18 mi. S of Seoul; rail junction; agr. center (rice, wheat, soybeans). Has agr. experiment station, agr. col., and match factory.

Suyetikha (sōōyĭtyē'khŭ), town (1948 pop. over 2,000), W Irkutsk oblast, Russian SFSR, on Trans-Siberian RR and 5 mi. W of Taishet; sawmilling.

Suyetka (sōō'yĭtkŭ), village (1939 pop. over 2,000), W Altai Territory, Russian SFSR, on Kulunda Steppe, 60 mi. ENE of Slavgorod; dairy farming. Formerly Verkhne-Suyetka.

Suyfun River, Manchuria and USSR: see SUIFUN RIVER.

Suyi, China: see CHUYI.

Suyo (sōō'yō), town (pop. 744), Piura dept., NW Peru, on W slopes of Cordillera Occidental, near Peru-Ecuador border, 20 mi. WNW of Ayabaca; cattle raising.

Süyung or **Hsü-yung** (both: shü'yōōng'), town (pop. 20,782), ⊙ Süyung co. (pop. 316,835), SW Szechwan prov., China, 40 mi. S of Luhsien and on small Süyung R. (right affluent of Yangtze R.); paper milling; rice, sweet potatoes, wheat, beans. Coal mining, kaolin quarrying, copper deposits near by. Until 1913 called Yungning.

Suzak (sōōzäk'). **1** Village (1926 pop. 4,050), N South Kazakhstan oblast, Kazakh SSR, in N foothills of the Kara-Tau, 55 mi. N of Turkestan; cotton. Fell to Russians (1863). **2** Village (1939 pop. under 500), SW Dzhalal-Abad oblast, Kirghiz SSR, 5 mi. WSW of Dzhalal-Abad; phosphate works.

Suzaka (sōōzä'kä), town (pop. 24,883), Nagano prefecture, central Honshu, Japan, 7 mi. E of Nagano; spinning mills.

Suzana, Rumania: see VALENI.

Suzano (sōōzä'nōō), town (pop. 2,555), SE São Paulo, Brazil, on railroad and 20 mi. E of São Paulo, in truck-farming dist.

Suzdal or **Suzdal'** (sōōz'dŭl), city (1926 pop. 6,904), N Vladimir oblast, Russian SFSR, on left affluent of Nerl R. and 19 mi. N of Vladimir; flax processing, clothing mfg. Has old kremlin with 13th-cent. cathedral, monastery (1207), regional mus. Two 14th-cent. walled monasteries in N part of city. D. Pozharski is buried here. One of oldest cities of central European USSR; founded 1028. Became important city in Rostov-Suzdal principality after 1125, and religious center of NE Russia; destruction of city (1238) by Tatars marked beginning of decline; inc. (1451) into Muscovite state.

Suzemka (sōōzyĕm'kŭ), village (1926 pop. 2,022), SE Bryansk oblast, Russian SFSR, 65 mi. SSW of Bryansk; rail junction; sawmilling.

Suze River, Switzerland: see SCHÜSS RIVER.

Suze-sur-Sarthe, La (lä süz'-sür-särt'), village (pop. 1,493), Sarthe dept., W France, on Sarthe R. and 11 mi. SW of Le Mans; plastics. Has a 9-arch bridge built under Henry IV.

Suzuka (sōōzōō'kä), city (pop. 67,643), Mie prefecture, S Honshu, Japan, on W shore of Ise Bay, 27 mi. SW of Nagoya; commercial center for rice-growing area; raw silk. Summer resort. Formed in early 1940s by combining former towns of Shiroko (1940 pop. 7,572) and Kambe (1940 pop. 4,836), and many villages.

Suzun (sōōzōōn'), town (1926 pop. 3,098), SE Novosibirsk oblast, Russian SFSR, near Ob R., 50 mi. SW of Cherepanovo; dairy farming.

Suzu Point, Japan: see NAGATE POINT.

Suzzara (sōōtsä'rä), town (pop. 4,391), Mantova prov., Lombardy, N Italy, 12 mi. SSW of Mantua; rail junction; agr. market (dairy products, cereals, silk); mfg. (agr. machinery, macaroni).

Svab, Mount (shväb), Hung. *Svábhegy,* hill (1,522 ft.) in Buda Mts., N central Hungary. Zugliget residential area at foot.

Svabovce, Czechoslovakia: see POPRAD, town.

Svaelgfoss, Norway: see SVELGFOSS.

Svalava, Ukrainian SSR: see SVALYAVA.

Svalbard, in Norwegian Arctic: see SPITSBERGEN.

Svalenik (svä'lĕnĭk), village (pop. 3,422), Ruse dist., NE Bulgaria, 17 mi. SSE of Ruse; wheat, rye, sunflowers.

Svaljava, Ukrainian SSR: see SVALYAVA.

Svalov (svä'lûv"), Swedish *Svalöv,* village (pop. 1,512), Malmohus co., S Sweden, 11 mi. E of Landskrona; grain, potatoes. Has agr. school and large experimental seed nurseries.

Svalyava (svŭlyä'vŭ), Czech *Svalava* or *Svaljava* (svä'lävä,–lyä–), Hung. *Szolyva* (soi'vŏ), town (1941 pop. 8,400), W central Transcarpathian Oblast, Ukrainian SSR, on Latoritsa R., on railroad and 15 mi. NE of Mukachevo; wood cracking; limestone mining. Chalybeate springs in vicinity.

Svaneholm, Sweden: see VISKAFORS.

Svaneke (svä'nùkù), city (pop. 1,183) and port, Bornholm amt, Denmark, on E Bornholm isl.; fishing, shipbuilding.

Svanetia (svänē'shù), Rus. *Svanetiya* (svŭnyĕ'tyēŭ), isolated region in NW Georgian SSR, on S slopes of the Greater Caucasus, along upper Ingur R.; inhabited by the Svans. Chief towns: Mestia, Lentekhi. Passed 1858 to Russia.

Svanetian Range (svänē'shùn), spur of the central Greater Caucasus, in Svanetia, NW Georgian SSR; extends 50 mi. W from main range near the Dykh-Tau; forms left (S) watershed of upper Ingur R.; rises to c.13,120 ft.

Svangsta (svĕng'stä"), Swedish *Svängsta,* village (pop. 711), Blekinge co., S Sweden, on Morrum R. and 7 mi. NNW of Karlshamn; woolen milling; mfg. of typewriters, taxi meters, clocks.

Svano (svän'ü"), Swedish *Svanö,* village (pop. 561), Vasternorrland co., NE Sweden, on islet in Angerman R. estuary, 19 mi. NE of Harnosand; woodworking; sulphite works.

Svanoy (svän'üü), Nor. *Svanøy,* island (□ 4; pop. 62) in the North Sea, Sogn og Fjordane co., W Norway, 7 mi. S of Floro; 4 mi. long, 2 mi. wide. Has pyrite mines, no longer worked.

Svanvik (svän'vēk), village in Sor-Varanger canton, Finnmark co., NE Norway, on Pasvik R. (USSR line) opposite Salmiyarvi and 19 mi. S of Kirkenes.

Svarov (svä'rôf), Czech *Svárov,* town (pop. 2,956), N Bohemia, Czechoslovakia, in the Sudetes, 10 mi. ESE of Liberec; rail junction; mfg. of cotton textiles, cut glass, glass jewelry. Summer resort. Until 1949, called Tanvald (tän'vält), Ger. *Tannwald.*

Svartisen (svärt'ēsùn), glacier (□ c.200), Nordland co., N central Norway, on Arctic Circle, 12 mi. N of Mo; c.20 mi. long, 20 mi. wide; descends from alt. of 5,246 ft. on Snetind, 20 mi. NNW of Mo.

Svartvik (svärt'vēk"), village (pop. 1,047), Vasternorrland co., E Sweden, on Ljunga R., just above its mouth on Gulf of Bothnia, 4 mi. S of Sundsvall; lumber and pulp milling, woodworking.

Svata Hora, Czechoslovakia: see PRIBRAM.

Svatonovice, Czechoslovakia: see ZACLER.

Svatovo (svä'tùvŭ), city (1926 pop. 16,160), NW Voroshilovgrad oblast, Ukrainian SSR, 80 mi. NW of Voroshilovgrad; agr. center in wheat, sugar-beet area; flour mills, sunflower-oil press.

Svaty Jur (svä'tē yōōr"), Slovak *Svätý Jur,* Hung. *Szentgyörgy* (sĕnt-dyûr'dyù), village (pop. 4,399), W Slovakia, Czechoslovakia, on railroad and 8 mi. NNE of Bratislava; noted wine industry. Large vineyards in vicinity.

Svaty Kopecek, Czechoslovakia: see OLOMOUC.

Svaty Kriz nad Hronom (kùrzhēsh' nät' hrônôm), Slovak *Svätý Kříž nad Hronom,* Hung. *Garamszentkereszi* (gŏ'rŏmsĕntkĕ'rĕsē), village (pop. 1,407), W central Slovakia, Czechoslovakia, on Hron R., on railroad and 17 mi. SW of Banska Bystrica; summer resort. Summer residence of bishop of Banska Bystrica.

Svayrieng, Cambodia: see SOAIRIENG.

Sveaborg, Finland: see SUOMENLINNA.

Sveagruva (svä'ägrōō"vä), coal-mining settlement (pop. 218) and port, S central West Spitsbergen, Spitsbergen group, on NE shore of Van Mijen Fjord, 30 mi. SE of Longyear City, at foot of mts. rising to c.4,000 ft.; 77°54'N 16°45'E. Settlement burned down (1944) by German submarines; later rebuilt. Port ice-free July–Sept.

Svealand, Sweden: see SWEDEN.

Svearike, Sweden: see SWEDEN.

Svecha (svyĭchä'), town (1926 pop. 437), W Kirov oblast, Russian SFSR, on railroad and 30 mi. W of Kotelnich; flax processing.

Svedala (svā'dä"lä), town (pop. 2,060), Malmohus co., S Sweden, 12 mi. SE of Malmo; rail junction; iron foundry, sugar refinery; brick making, stone quarrying.

Sveg (svāg), town (pop. 1,515), Jamtland co., central Sweden, on Ljusna R. and 80 mi. S of Ostersund; rail junction; commercial center of Harjedal prov. Has folk mus.

Svelgen (svĕl'gùn), village (pop. 518) in Bremanger canton (pop. 3,148), Sogn og Fjordane co., W Norway, on an inlet of the North Sea, 15 mi. NE of Floro; industrial center, with hydroelectric plant, iron smelter.

Svelgfoss (svĕlg'fôs), falls (157 ft.) on Tinne R., Telemark co., S Norway, 3 mi. N of Notodden; hydroelectric plant for Notodden chemical works. Sometimes spelled Svaelgfoss.

Svelvik (svĕl'vēk,–vĭk), town (pop. 1,130), Vestfold co., SE Norway, on Drammen Fjord, 10 mi. SE of Drammen; lumber, paper, and woolen milling; shipbuilding, cement mfg.; mineral-water plant. Stromm (strûm), Nor. *Strømm,* canton (pop. 1,740) surrounds city; engages in lumbering.

Svencioneliai, Shvenchenelyai, or **Shvenchenelyay** (shvĕntsyōnā'lī), Lith. *Švenčionėliai,* Pol. *Nowo-Święciany,* Rus. *Novo-Sventsyany,* city (1931 pop. 3,715), E Lithuania, 45 mi. NE of Vilna; rail junction; summer resort; tanning, flour milling. In Rus. Vilna govt. until it passed (1921) to Poland; to Lithuania in 1939.

Svencionys or **Shvenchenis** (shvĕnchōnēs'), Lith. *Švenčionys,* Pol. *Święciany,* Rus. *Sventsyany,* city (1931 pop. 5,893), E Lithuania, 45 mi. NE of Vilna, on Belorussian border; processing of wool and hides, brickworking, flour milling. In Rus. Vilna govt. until it passed (1921) to Poland, 1939 to Belorussian SSR, and 1940 to Lithuania.

Svendborg (svĕn'bôr), amt (□ 644; pop. 149,671), Denmark, largely on S Fyn isl. and including Taasinge, Langeland, and Aero isls.; ⊙ Svendborg. Industry at Svendborg and Nyborg. Fruitgrowing, wine making, dairy and grain farming.

Svendborg, city (1950 pop. 23,069), ⊙ Svendborg amt, S Fyn isl., Denmark, port on Svendborg

Sound and 85 mi. SW of Copenhagen; 55°4'N 10°37'E. Shipping center. Shipbuilding, brewing, leather tanning, mfg. (tobacco, machinery, textiles, hardware).

Svendborg Sound, Denmark, strait bet. Fyn isl. (N) and Taasinge and Turo isls. (S); min. width, ½ mi.

Svenljunga (svĕn'yŭng"ä), town (pop. 2,296), Alvsborg co., SW Sweden, on Atra R. and 16 mi. SSE of Boras; woolen milling, tanning.

Sventoji or **Shventoji** (shvĕntō'yē), Lith. *Šventoji*, village (1925 pop. 310), W Lithuania, fishing port on Baltic Sea, 22 mi. N of Memel; has artificial harbor built in 1920s.

Sventoji River or **Shventoyi River,** Lith. *Šventoji*, E central Lithuania, rises in several small lakes S of Zarasai, flows 152 mi. SW, past Anyksciai and Ukmerge, to Viliya R. just E of Jonava.

Sventsyany, Lithuania: see SVENCIONYS.

Sverdlova, Imeni, Russian SFSR: see KAMESHKOVO.

Sverdlovo (svyĭrdlô'vŭ), village (1948 pop. over 2,000), S Saratov oblast, Russian SFSR, 19 mi. SSE of Balanda; wheat, sunflowers. Until 1941, a Ger. settlement called Nei-Valter or Neu-Walter.

Sverdlovsk (svĕrd'lŏfsk, Rus. svyĭrdlôfsk'), oblast (□ 70,550; 1939 pop. 2,512,175; 1946 pop. estimate 3,000,000) in W Siberian Russian SFSR; ⊙ Sverdlovsk. In the central and N Urals, extending E into W Siberian Plain; drained by Lozva, Sosva, Tavda, Tura, Tagil, Nitsa, Pyshma, Iset, and Chusovaya rivers. Humid continental climate (short summers; severe winters in N and NE). Noted industrial and leading mining region of USSR. Mineral resources, chiefly concentrated in the Urals (W), include magnetite (in Blagodat, Vysokaya, and Lebyashye mts.), copper (Krasnouralsk, Verkhnyaya Pyshma, Degtyarka, Kirovgrad), bauxite (Severouralsk, Kamensk-Uralski, Cheremukhovo, Kalya), iron (Alapayevsk), gold (Berezovski, Visim, Is), platinum (Kytlym), manganese (Marsyaty, Polunochnoye), bituminous coal (Karpinsk, Artemovski, Volchanka), asbestos (Asbest), precious stones (Izumrud), nickel (Rezh), chromium, titanium, nonmetals, and building stones. Heavily forested, with patches of agr. in SE part (rye, oats, potatoes) and in Tavda and Tura river valleys (wheat); livestock in woodland; truck gardening and dairy farming in densely populated SW. Industrial importance based on steel and pig-iron production (Sverdlovsk, Nizhni Tagil, Serov, Alapayevsk, Kushva, Polevskoi, Nizhnyaya Salda, Verkhnyaya Salda, Nizhniye Sergi, Nizhnyaya Tura) and nonferrous metallurgy (copper at Kirovgrad, Krasnouralsk, Verkhnyaya Pyshma, Revda; aluminum at Krasnoturinsk, Kamensk-Uralski; nickel at Rezh). Diversified machine mfg. and metalworking in numerous industrial centers (chiefly in SW part); among noted factories are Uralmash works of Sverdlovsk (mining and metallurgical equipment) and railroad-car mfg. plant of Nizhni Tagil. Also mfg. of paper, cellulose, chemicals, building materials, consumers goods; woodworking, lumbering. Main urban centers: Sverdlovsk, Nizhni Tagil, Serov. Well-developed rail net includes main branch of Trans-Siberian RR; river navigation, lumber floating. Formed 1934 out of Ural oblast. W section separated (1938) to form Molotov oblast. A center of Soviet war industry during Second World War.

Sverdlovsk. 1 City (1926 pop. 136,421; 1939 pop. 425,544; 1946 pop. estimate 600,000), ⊙ Sverdlovsk oblast, Russian SFSR, in E foothills of the central Urals, on dammed Iset R. and 850 mi. E of Moscow; 56°50'N 60°39'E. W terminus of Trans-Siberian RR; transportation center (7 rail lines; airport). Leading industrial city of the Urals and one of major machine-building centers of USSR. Uralmash works (city's industrial giant; constructed 1933) produce heavy metallurgical and mining equipment. Ferrous metallurgy (largely quality steels); mfg. of aircraft, ball bearings, lathes, turbines, railroad cars, radio, television, and electrical apparatus, industrial rubber goods, chemicals, building materials; wood-pulp processing, diamond cutting; consumer-goods industries (clothing, shoes, furniture, foodstuffs). Noted cultural center, with Urals state univ., medical, law, mining, forestry, art, and teachers colleges, polytechnic school, conservatory, and branch of USSR Acad. of Science. Has two 18th-cent. cathedrals, several monuments, museums, picture gall., opera house. City center is surrounded by Verkhne-Iset pond (W), Nizhne-Iset pond (S), Shartash L. (E; at recently developed university town), and Shuvakish L. (N; just NE of Uralmash works). On S shore of Nizhne-Iset pond are noted steel works of former town Nizhne-Isetski (1926 pop. 3,884; within Sverdlovsk city limits since 1928). Founded 1722 as fortress; named Yekaterinburg (or Ekaterinburg) for Rus. empress Catherine I. Building (1725) of Verkhne-Isetski ironworks (now producing steel and iron for electrical goods) marked city's industrial beginnings. Developed as gold-mining town in 1740s; major trading and resettlement center on route to Siberia in 1760s. Metallurgical center in 19th cent., gaining importance after building (1895) of Trans-Siberian RR. Nicholas II (last Rus. tsar) and his family executed here, 1918. Was ⊙ Yekaterinburg govt. (1919–23); renamed Sverdlovsk (1924) for Bolshevik revolutionary Yakov Sverdlov; became (1923) ⊙ Ural oblast, and (1934) ⊙ Sverdlovsk oblast. Assumed leading position in the Urals after modernization of metallurgical plants and development of machine building (largely in 1930s). During Second World War, evacuation of Soviet war industry to the Urals (partly to Sverdlovsk) resulted in further expansion; in 1943 city was placed under direct jurisdiction of Russian SFSR. **2** City (1939 pop. over 10,000), SE Voroshilovgrad oblast, Ukrainian SSR, in the Donbas, 37 mi. SSE of Voroshilovgrad; anthracite-mining center. Founded in 1930s; until 1938, called Imeni Sverdlova. **3** Village (1939 pop. under 500), S Bukhara oblast, Uzbek SSR, on Zeravshan R. and 12 mi. W of Bukhara; cotton. Formerly Dzhandar and, c.1935–37, Imeni Faizully Khodzhayeva.

Sverdlovski or **Sverdlovskiy** (–dlôf'skē), town (1926 pop. 1,867), E central Moscow oblast, Russian SFSR, on Klyazma R. and 4 mi. E of Shchelkovo; textiles. Until 1928, Sverdlovo.

Sverdlovski Priisk, Russian SFSR: see Is.

Sverdrup Channel, N Franklin Dist., Northwest Territories, arm (70 mi. long, 40 mi. wide) extending S from Arctic Ocean, bet. Axel Heiberg Isl. (E) and Meighen Isl. (W); 80°N 97°W.

Sverdrup Islands, archipelago, N Franklin Dist., Northwest Territories, in the Arctic Ocean; includes AXEL HEIBERG ISLAND, ELLEF RINGNES ISLAND, AMUND RINGNES ISLAND, MEIGHEN ISLAND, and many smaller isls.

Sverige: see SWEDEN.

Sverresborg, Norway: see BERGEN.

Svessa (svyĕ'sŭ), town (1926 pop. 1,256), N Sumy oblast, Ukrainian SSR, 19 mi. N of Glukhov; light mfg. Formerly spelled Svesa.

Sveti Andrija, Island of (svĕ'tē än'drēä), Ital. *Sant' Andrea* (säntändrĕ'ä), Dalmatian island in Adriatic Sea, S Croatia, Yugoslavia, c.50 mi. SW of Split; 2 mi. long, 1 mi. wide.

Sveti Ivan Zelina, Yugoslavia: see ZELINA.

Svetilovichi (svyĭtyĕ'lŭvĕchē), village (1939 pop. over 500), E Gomel oblast, Belorussian SSR, 28 mi. NE of Gomel.

Sveti Naum (svĕ'tē nä'ōōm), village, Macedonia, Yugoslavia, on Albanian border, on L. Ochrida, 14 mi. S of Ochrida. Site of monastery with church built (900–905) by St. Naum.

Sveti Nikola (nĭ'kô'lä) or **Sveti Nikole** (–lĕ), village (pop. 3,868), Macedonia, Yugoslavia, 26 mi. SE of Skoplje, in the Ovce Polje; local trade center.

Sveti Nikola Mountains, NW Bulgaria and E Yugoslavia, part of W Balkan Mts., on Bulg.-Yugoslav border, bet. Babin-nos Mts. (N) and Chiporov Mts. (SE), SE of Knjazevac (Yugoslavia); rise to 6,575 ft. Crossed by **Sveti Nikola Pass** (alt. 4,513 ft.), on road bet. Belogradchik (Bulgaria) and Nis (Yugoslavia).

Sveti Stevan (stĕ'vän), village, S Montenegro, Yugoslavia, on Adriatic coast, 3 mi. SE of Budva; summer resort. Formerly called Sveti Stefan.

Sveti Vrach, Bulgaria: see SANDANSKI.

Svetla nad Sazavou (svyĕt'lä nät' sä"zävō), Czech *Světlá nad Sázavou*, village (pop. 2,079), E Bohemia, Czechoslovakia, on Sazava R. and 9 mi. SE of Havlickuv Brod; rail junction; glassmaking, production of garnet abrasives, stone cutting.

Svetlaya (svyĕt'lĭŭ), town (1942 pop. over 500), NE Maritime Territory, Russian SFSR, port on Sea of Japan, 185 mi. NNE of Tetyukhe; fish canning.

Svetlogorsk (svyĕtlŭgôrsk'), city (1939 pop. 2,542), Kaliningrad oblast, Russian SFSR, 21 mi. NW of Kaliningrad; leading Baltic seaside resort amid pinewoods and orchards. With adjoining (W) OTRADNOYE, often called the "Northern Sochi." Until 1945, in East Prussia, called Rauschen (rou'shŭn). Developed greatly after Second World War.

Svetloye (svyĕt'lŭyŭ), village (1939 pop. 430), W Kaliningrad oblast, Russian SFSR, on railroad and 11 mi. SW of Kaliningrad; rail junction. Until 1945, in East Prussia and called Kobbelbude (kô'bŭlbōō"dŭ).

Svetly or **Svetlyy** (–lē), town (1948 pop. over 500), NE Irkutsk oblast, Russian SFSR, 75 mi. NE of Bodaibo; gold mines.

Svetogorsk (svyĕtŭgôrsk'), city (1940 pop. over 2,000), NW Leningrad oblast, Russian SFSR, on Vuoksi R. (rapids) and 27 mi. NNE of Vyborg, on Finnish border; pulp- and cellulose-milling center. Hydroelectric station supplies Leningrad with electricity. Called Enso (ĕn'sô) while in Finland (until 1940) and, until 1948, in USSR.

Svetozarevo (svĕ'tôzä"rĕvô), town (pop. 10,007), central Serbia, Yugoslavia, on railroad and 70 mi. SSE of Belgrade, near Morava R.; meat packing, brewing. Winegrowing in vicinity. Until 1947, called Jagodina or Yagodina.

Sviaga River, Russian SFSR: see SVIYAGA RIVER.

Sviazhsk, Russian SFSR: see SVIYAZHSK.

Svidnik (svĭd'nyĕk), Slovak *Svidník*, town (pop. 1,015), NE Slovakia, Czechoslovakia, in foothills of the Beskids, on Ondava R. and 26 mi. NNE of Presov; potato growing, lumbering. Formed c.1946 by union of Nizny Svidnik (Slovak *Nižný Svidník*, Hung. *Alsóvízköz*) and Vysny Svidnik (Slovak *Vyšný Svidník*; Hung. *Felsővízköz*).

Svid River or **Svid' River** (svē'tyŭ), SW Archangel oblast, Russian SFSR, rises in L. Vozhe, flows 39 mi. N to L. Lacha.

Svihov (shvĭ'hôf), Czech *Švihov*, village (pop. 1,348), SW Bohemia, Czechoslovakia, on Uhlava R., on railroad and 6 mi. N of Klatovy; summer resort with picturesque castle above river.

Svilaja (svē'läyä), mountain in Dinaric Alps, S Croatia, Yugoslavia, in Dalmatia; extends c.10 mi. SE-NW, near right bank of upper Cetina R., Highest peak (4,950 ft.) is 10 mi. NW of Sinj.

Svilajnac, Svilainats, or **Svilaynats** (all: svē'līnäts), village (pop. 5,398), ⊙ Resava co., E central Serbia, Yugoslavia, on Resava R. and 50 mi. SE of Belgrade, in sericulture region.

Svilengrad (svē'lĕn-grät), city (pop. 9,918), Khaskovo dist., SE Bulgaria, on left bank of the Maritsa (Gr. border) and 35 mi. ESE of Khaskovo; customs rail station; major sericulture center; silk textiles. A commercial town under Turkish rule; rebuilt in modern fashion following its destruction during First World War. Formerly called Mustafa-Pasha. Anc. relics have been excavated at Mezek (pop. 994), 6 mi. SW.

Svino (svē'nû), Dan. *Svinø*, Faeroese *Svínoy*, island (□ 11; pop. 198) of the NE Faeroe Isls., separated from Fuglo by Fuglo Fjord (N). Mountainous and rocky terrain; highest point 1,924 ft. Fishing, sheep raising.

Svir or **Svir'** (svēr), Pol. *Świr* (shvēr), village (1939 pop. over 500), NW Molodechno oblast, Belorussian SSR, on L. Svir (□ 11), 45 mi. ENE of Vilna; fisheries, lumbering.

Sviritsa (svē'rētsŭ), town (1939 pop. over 500), NE Leningrad oblast, Russian SFSR, port on L. Ladoga, at mouth of Svir R., 30 mi. SW of Lodeinoye Pole; metalworks.

Svir River or **Svir' River** (svēr), Leningrad oblast, Russian SFSR, issues from L. Onega at Voznesenye, flows 140 mi. W, past Podporozhye and Svirstroi (hydroelectric stations) and Lodeinoye Pole, to L. Ladoga at Sviritsa. Navigable for entire course as part of Mariinsk canal system. Receives Pasha and Oyat rivers (left).

Svirskoye (svēr'skŭyŭ), town (1939 pop. over 500), SE Irkutsk oblast, Russian SFSR, 12 mi. SE of Cheremkhovo, in Cheremkhovo coal basin.

Svirstroi or **Svir'stroy** (svērstroi'), town (1939 pop. over 10,000), NE Leningrad oblast, Russian SFSR, on Svir R. and 7 mi. NE of Lodeinoye Pole; large hydroelectric station; metalworks, flour mills, sawmills. During Second World War, a Rus. front-line position (1941–44).

Svishchevka (svē'shchĭfkŭ), village (1939 pop. over 2,000), SW Penza oblast, Russian SFSR, 16 mi. SE of Belinski; grain, hemp.

Svishtov (svēshtôf'), city (pop. 12,949), Pleven dist., N Bulgaria, port on right bank of the Danube (Rum. border), opposite Zimnicea, and 38 mi. ENE of Pleven; rail terminus; agr. and grain-trading center; weaving, hemp milling, tanning, flour milling, winegrowing. Has commercial acad., technical schools, mus. Ruins of Roman colony of Novae near by (W). Svishtov L. (W; □ 6) has fisheries. Became important commercial center, called Sistova, under Turkish rule (15th–19th cent.). Treaty signed here (1791) bet. Austria and Turkey. Burned and destroyed several times during Russo-Turkish wars; finally sacked (1878) by Russians after crossing of the Danube (commemorated by a monument).

Svisloch or **Svisloch'** (svē'slŭch), Pol. *Świslocz* (shvē'swôch), town (1931 pop. 3,731), SW Grodno oblast, Belorussian SSR, 18 mi. SW of Volkovysk, near Pol. border; mfg. of concrete blocks, bricks; tanning, distilling, flour milling, sawmilling. Has ruins of 17th-cent. church.

Svisloch River or **Svisloch' River,** central Belorussian SSR, rises NW of Zaslavl in Lithuanian-Belorussian Upland, flows c.100 mi. SE, past Minsk, to Berezina R. 20 mi. NNW of Bobruisk.

Svit or **Tatrasvit** (tä'träsvĭt), town (pop. 1,315), N Slovakia, Czechoslovakia, on S slope of the High Tatra, on railroad (Batizovce station), just S of Batizovce, and 6 mi. WNW of Poprad; rayon industry; mfg. of stockings, knitwear. Founded 1935; developed greatly after Second World War.

Svitava River (svĭ'tävä), W Moravia, Czechoslovakia, rises in N Bohemian-Moravian Heights just NW of Svitavy, flows c.60 mi. SSE, past Blansko, to Svratka R. 3 mi. S of Brno.

Svitavy (svĭ'tävĭ), Ger. *Zwittau* (tsvĭ'tou), town (pop. 8,983), W Moravia, Czechoslovakia, on Svitava R. and 36 mi. WNW of Olomouc; rail junction; mfg. (silk, cotton, and linen textiles, footwear), tobacco and jute processing. Has old houses, noted library.

Svitsa River (svē'tsŭ), Pol. *Świca*, in W Ukrainian SSR, rises in the Gorgany (section of the Carpathians) SE of Slavsko, flows 62 mi. generally N, past Vygoda, to Dniester R. at Zhuravno.

Sviyaga River (svēä'gŭ), E central European Russian SFSR, rises WNW of Kuzovatovo, flows NNE, past Bolshiye Klyuchishchi and Ulyanovsk (here forming 2-mi.-wide watershed with the Volga), and generally N (parallel with and in opposite direction to the Volga), past Isheyevka and Sviyazhsk, to Volga R. 15 mi. W of Kazan, opposite Vasilyevo;

245 mi. long. Navigation for 3 mi. in lower course; lumber floating for 30 mi. Sometimes Sviaga.

Sviyazhsk (svēäsh-sk'), village (1926 pop. 2,598), W Tatar Autonomous SSR, Russian SFSR, on Sviyaga R., near its confluence with the Volga, and 17 mi. W of Kazan; truck, grain. Has 16th-cent. monastery and cathedral (frescoes). Founded in 1550s by Ivan the Terrible as fortified trading outpost on road to Kazan; flourished as military and commercial center until end of 18th cent. Sviyazhsk rail junction is 6 mi. W. Sometimes spelled Sviazhsk.

Svoboda (svŭbô'dŭ). **1** Village (1926 pop. 2,941), N Kursk oblast, Russian SFSR, 15 mi. NNE of Kursk; metalworks. **2** City, Voronezh oblast, Russian SFSR: see LISKI.

Svobodny or **Svobodnyy** (svŭbôd'nē). **1** City (1938 pop. estimate 37,000), S Amur oblast, Russian SFSR, on Trans-Siberian RR, on Zeya R. and 80 mi. N of Blagoveshchensk; industrial center in agr. area (wheat, livestock); shipbuilding, metalworking, flour milling. Called Alekseyevsk until 1924, when it became a city. **2** Town (1943 pop. over 500), N Saratov oblast, Russian SFSR, on railroad (Karabulak station) and 5 mi. NNW of Bazarny Karabulak; wheat, sunflowers.

Svoge (svô'gĕ), village (pop. 2,651), Sofia dist., W Bulgaria, at S foot of W Balkan Mts., at mouth of Iskrets R. (short left tributary of Iskar R.), 18 mi. N of Sofia; health resort; chocolate mfg. Anthracite mined N.

Svolvaer (svōl'vär), chief town (pop. 3,300) of the Lofoten Isls., Nordland co., N Norway, on SE shore of Austvagoy, 70 mi. N of Bodo, at foot of 1,959-ft. mtn.; 68°14'N 14°35'E. Fishing port, center of Lofoten cod fisheries. Processing of guano, cod-liver oil, mineral oils; shipbuilding and -repair yards; mfg. of nails, barrels, cement castings. Summer resort. Inc. 1918.

Svorkmo (svôrk'mô), village (pop. 151) in Orkland canton (pop. 1,854), Sor-Trondelag co., central Norway, on Orkla R., on railroad and 10 mi. S of Orkanger; agr., lumbering; mfg. of cement.

Svratka River (svûrät'kä), W Moravia, Czechoslovakia, rises in Bohemian-Moravian Heights on N slope of Devet Skal, 10 mi. SE of Hlinsko; flows E, SE, past Tisnov and Brno, and S to Dyje R. just W of Dolni Vestonice; 106 mi. long. Receives Jihlava (right) and Svitava (left) rivers. Dammed c.7 mi. above Brno.

Svrljig or **Svrlyig** (both: svûr'lyĭk), village, (pop. 2,898) E Serbia, Yugoslavia, on railroad and 13 mi. ENE of Nis. **Svrljig Mountains** extend c.10 mi. along right bank of the Nisava; highest point (4,375 ft.) is 9 mi. ESE of Svrljig.

Svyatoi Krest, Russian SFSR: see BUDENNOVSK.

Svyatoi Nos or **Svyatoy Nos** (svyŭtoi'nôs"), cape on Murman Coast of Kola Peninsula, Russian SFSR, at NW end of headland (10 mi. long, 3 mi. wide) projecting into Barents Sea; forms W side of entrance to White Sea; 66°10'N 39°40'E.

Svyatoshino (svyŭtô'shĕnŭ), W suburb (1939 pop. over 10,000) of Kiev, Kiev oblast, Ukrainian SSR, 6 mi. from city center; summer resort; mfg. of bacterial fertilizer.

Svyatoslavka (svyŭtŭsläf'kŭ), village (1939 pop. over 500), SW Saratov oblast, Russian SFSR, 18 mi. SE of Balashov; wheat, sunflowers, cattle.

Swabi (swä'bē), village, Mardan dist., N central North-West Frontier Prov., W Pakistan, 25 mi. ESE of Mardan; wheat, sugar cane. Alluvial gold deposits in near-by Indus R. (S) worked locally on small scale.

Swabia (swā'bēŭ), Ger. *Schwaben* (shvä'bŭn), a historic region of SW Germany, the E part of which forms a contemporary administrative division or province of SW Bavaria. The modern province [Ger. *Regierungsbezirk*] (□ 3,818; 1946 pop. 1,196,274; 1950 pop. 1,255,595), with ⊙ at Augsburg, is bounded S by Austria, E by Upper Bavaria, N by Middle Franconia, W by Württemberg-Baden and Württemberg-Hohenzollern. It has grain and livestock in N; intensive cattle raising and dairying in the Allgäu Alps (S), concentrated at Kempten. Industrial (textile, metalworking) centers at Augsburg and Memmingen. Area of present administrative div. came to Bavaria during Napoleonic Wars. After Second World War, while the contemporary prov. of Swabia was placed, along with most of Bavaria, in U.S. zone, the dist. of LINDAU was placed under French occupation. The historic region of Swabia is generally understood to comprise SW Bavaria, S Württemberg, Hohenzollern, and S Baden. Its main physical features are the BLACK FOREST, the valley of the upper Danube, which rises here, the Swabian Jura, a range which extends parallel to, and N of, the Danube, and the valley of the upper Neckar. The Rhine and the L. of Constance (also called Swabian Sea) form W and S borders. All Swabia is predominantly agr. or forested country, famous for the loveliness of its landscape. Settled by the Germanic Suevi and Alamanni or Alemanni during the great migrations, the region was also known as Alamannia. The Alamanni were conquered by the Franks in late 5th cent. Swabia became one of the stem duchies of Germany in 9th cent., when it far exceeded its present boundaries, including also Alsace and Switzerland E of Reuss R. The duchy belonged to the house of Hohenstaufen from 1079 to 1268, when Swabia was broken up and lost its political identity. Territories in Alsace, S Baden, and Switzerland had already passed under control of house of Hapsburg. The Swiss part became independent in 1291 and Alsace passed to France in 1648, but Breisgau and the other Hapsburg domains in S Baden remained Austrian until 1803-6, except in 1469–77, when they were seized by Charles the Bold of Burgundy. The rest of Swabia was held in large part by the counts (later dukes) of Württemberg and by numerous other princes, bishops, abbots, counts, and knights. Most of the numerous and prosperous towns of Swabia had obtained status of free imperial cities (i.e., virtually independent republics) by 1300. Among them were AUGSBURG, ULM, Schwäbisch Gmünd, Reutlingen, Rauensburg, and Rottweil. They formed a series of powerful leagues. The Swabian League of 1376–89 defeated Emperor Charles IV and count of Württemberg. Most important Swabian League was that of 1488–1534, which had 26 cities by end of 1488. The chief Swabian cities accepted Reformation in 16th cent., but countryside has remained divided bet. Catholics and Protestants to the present day. The elimination of the small ecclesiastic and feudal holdings in favor of Baden, Württemberg, and Bavaria was largely the work of Napoleon I and was effected at diet of Regensburg of 1801–3. Swabia in its largest sense has remained a linguistic unit, the Alamannic or Swabian dialects of its various regions being closely related.

Swabian Jura (jŏŏ'rŭ, yŏŏ'rŭ), Ger. *Schwäbische Alb* (shvā'bĭ-shŭ ălp') or *Schwäbischer Jura* (shvā'-bĭ-shŭr yŏŏ'rä), mountain range in SW Germany, extends c.100 mi. SW–NE bet. Black Forest and Wörnitz R.; rises to 3,330 ft. in the Lemberg. Geologically a continuation of the Jura, range becomes plateaulike in NE, where it continues in the Franconian Jura. Sparsely populated, with raw climate and poor soil in uplands; grain (spelt, oats) and vegetables (potatoes, lentils, peas) grown up to 2,900 ft. elev.; cattle raising; fruit in valleys. Many large towns along N foot (Aalen, Göppingen, Reutlingen, Rottweil, Schwäbisch Gmünd).

Swabian Rezat (rä'tsät), Ger. *Schwäbische Rezat*, river in Bavaria, Germany, rises 2 mi. E of Weissenburg, flows 12 mi. N to Georgensgmünd, where it joins the FRANCONIAN REZAT to form REDNITZ RIVER.

Swabue (swä'bū', Cantonese sän'mā'), Mandarin *Shanwei* (shän'wā'), town, SE Kwangtung prov., China, port on Honghai Bay of S.China Sea, 14 mi. S of Hoifung; commercial center; fisheries, saltworks.

Swadlincote District (swäd'lĭnkōt), urban district (1931 pop. 20,308; 1951 census 20,909), S Derby, England, 4 mi. SE of Burton-upon-Trent; coal mining, pottery making, metalworking. In urban dist. are towns of Church Gresley (SW; pop. 8,926) and Stanton and Newhall (NW; pop. 6,412).

Swaffham (swŏ'fŭm), urban district (1931 pop. 2,783; 1951 census 2,863), W central Norfolk, England, 11 mi. W of East Dereham; agr. market, with farm-implement works. Has medieval church, rebuilt in 15th cent.

Swain (swān), county (□ 544; pop. 9,921), W N.C.; ⊙ Bryson City. Bounded N by Tenn., W by Little Tennessee R. (dammed to form Fontana and Cheoah reservoirs here). Heavily forested mtn. area; largely included in Great Smoky Mts. Natl. Park; contains Cherokee Indian reservation in E, adjacent to park. Farming (corn, potatoes), cattle and poultry raising, lumbering; resort region. Formed 1871.

Swaine Island, islet, E N.F., on N side of Bonavista Bay, 45 mi. ENE of Gander; 49°8'N 53°32'W; lighthouse.

Swainsboro, city (pop. 4,300), ⊙ Emanuel co., E central Ga., c.65 mi. SSW of Augusta; trade and shipping point for agr. and livestock area; mfg. (naval stores, lumber, clothing). Founded 1814, inc. 1853.

Swains Island, islet and district (pop. 164), American Samoa, S Pacific, c.200 mi. N of Tutuila; 11°3'S 171°15'W; ring of sand and coral 20 ft. high; luxuriant vegetation. Annexed 1925 to American Samoa.

Swakopmund (svä'kôpmûnt"), town (pop. 2,877), W South-West Africa, on the Atlantic, at mouth of Swakop R., 170 mi. W of Windhoek, 20 mi. N of Walvis Bay; 22°40'S 14°32'E; rail terminus; seaside resort. Chief seaport of South-West Africa under Germans; now silted up and closed to shipping. Salt pans and garnet deposits in region. At outbreak of First World War town was occupied by Union forces.

Swakop River (svä'kôp), intermittent stream, W South-West Africa, rises on inland plateau NNE of Windhoek, flows 250 mi. generally W to the Atlantic at Swakopmund.

Swale, England: see SHEPPEY, ISLE OF.

Swaledale, town (pop. 205), Cerro Gordo co., N Iowa, 13 mi. SSW of Mason City. Limestone quarry, sand and gravel pits near by.

Swale Island (5 mi. long, 1 mi. wide), E N.F., in Bonavista Bay, 28 mi. W of Bonavista.

Swale River, N Yorkshire, England, rises in the Pennines 4 mi. SE of Kirkby Stephen, at Westmorland line, flows 60 mi. E and SE, past Richmond, to Ure R. 1 mi. E of Aldborough.

Swallow Falls State Forest, Garrett co., NW Md., in the Alleghenies bet. Youghiogheny R. and W.Va. line, just NW of Oakland; recreational area containing Swallow Falls and Muddy Creek Falls (highest in Md., dropping c.70 ft.).

Swallowfield, agr. village and parish (pop. 1,540), S Berkshire, England, on Loddon R. at mouth of Blackwater R., 5 mi. S of Reading. Has 13th-cent. church.

Swallow Islands, small volcanic group, Solomon Isls., SW Pacific, c.25 mi. NE of Santa Cruz Isls.; largest of some 5 isls. is 4 mi. long; copra.

Swally, India: see SUVALI.

Swalmen (sväl'mŭn), town (pop. 3,334), Limburg prov., SE Netherlands, 3 mi. NNE of Roermond; roofing tiles, glass, mirrors, packing boxes. Sometimes spelled Zwalmen.

Swalwell, England: see WHICKHAM.

Swamihalli (svä'mĭhŭlē), village, NW Madras, India, 25 mi. SSE of Hospet; rail spur terminus; ships ore from important manganese mines (N). Also spelled Samehalli.

Swami Narayan Chhapia (svä'mē nä'räyŭn chŭp'yŭ), village, Gonda dist., NE Uttar Pradesh, India, 17 mi. NE of Nawabganj. Noted 19th-cent. Hindu religious reformer b. here; worshiped as incarnation of Krishna under the name of Swami Narayan. Large temple. Has 2 annual fairs. Sugar processing 7 mi. ESE, at village of Babhnan.

Swampscott (swŏmp'skŭt), residential town (pop. 11,580), Essex co., NE Mass., coast resort on N Nahant Bay, 11 mi. NE of Boston. Settled 1629, set off from Lynn 1852. Includes village of Beach Bluff.

Swamy Rock, Ceylon: see TRINCOMALEE.

Swan, town (pop. 194), Marion co., S central Iowa, near Des Moines R., 18 mi. ESE of Des Moines, in bituminous-coal-mining and agr. area.

Swanage (swŏ'nĭj), urban district (1931 pop. 6,247; 1951 census 6,853), SE Dorset, England, on SE coast of Isle of Purbeck and 8 mi. S of Poole; seaside resort and market; leather-goods mfg. Just S is promontory of Durlstone Head.

Swanee River, U.S.: see SUWANNEE RIVER.

Swan Hill, municipality (pop. 4,305), N Victoria, Australia, on New South Wales border, 190 mi. NNW of Melbourne and on Murray R., in agr., sheep-raising area; flour mill, vegetable cannery; dairy products, fruit.

Swan Island, Tasmania: see BANKS STRAIT.

Swan Island, SW Maine, island (4 mi. long), in the Kennebec, 10 mi. above Bath; formerly known as Perkins township.

Swan Islands, Sp. *Islas del Cisne* (ē'släs dĕl sē'snä), group of two isls. (pop. 20) in Bay Islands dept., N Honduras, in Caribbean Sea, c.110 mi. NNE of Patuca Point; 17°25'N 83°56'W. Of limestone formation; 2 mi. and 1 mi. long, ½ mi. wide. Guano deposits (formerly exploited by U.S.), hardwood; turtle fishing. Radio station, lighthouse. Discovered in early 16th cent. Formerly also called Santanilla Isls.

Swan Lake, village (pop. estimate 350), S Man., in Pembina Mts., 45 mi. SW of Portage la Prairie; grain, stock. Adjoining is Chippewa Indian Reserve.

Swan Lake (20 mi. long, 9 mi. wide), W Man., 30 mi. NE of Swan River. Drains N into L. Winnipegosis.

Swan Lake. 1 In Waldo co., S Maine, at Swanville, 7 mi. N of Belfast; 3 mi. long, 1 mi. wide. **2** In Itasca co., NE central Minn., 16 mi. ENE of Grand Rapids; 4 mi. long. Fishing resorts. Drains through Swan R. into Mississippi R. Village of Pengilly at N end of lake. **3** In Sullivan co., SE N.Y., 4 mi. SW of Liberty; 4 mi. long; resort village on shore.

Swanland, SW Western Australia, most populous and fertile region of state; extends SSE from Perth to Albany; borders W and S on Indian Ocean. Only area in Western Australia with year-round rivers. Wheat, timber (karri eucalyptus).

Swannanoa (swŏnŭnō'ŭ), resort and textile-mill village (pop. 1,913, with adjacent Grovemont), Buncombe co., W N.C., 9 mi. E of Asheville, in the Blue Ridge. Seat of Warren Wilson Col. Near by is Swannanoa railroad tunnel (1,800 ft. long; completed 1879).

Swan Peak, Mont.: see FLATHEAD RANGE.

Swanquarter or **Swan Quarter,** resort and fishing town (pop. 212), ⊙ Hyde co., E N.C., 18 mi. SE of Belhaven, on inlet of Pamlico Sound.

Swan Reach, village (pop. 223), SE South Australia, 65 mi. ENE of Adelaide and on Murray R.; livestock.

Swan River, SW Western Australia, rises as Avon R. in hills near Corrigin, flows 240 mi. NW and SW, past York, Northam, and Perth, to Indian Ocean at Fremantle. Widens into Perth Water (1 mi. wide) at E Perth and into Swan Estuary (2 mi. wide; sometimes called Melville Water). Receives Helena R. (40 mi. long; site of MUNDARING Weir) and Canning R. Swan River Settlement (1829) was 1st colonial settlement in Western Australia and included sites of Perth and Fremantle.

Swan River, town (pop. 1,175), W Man., on Swan R. and 80 mi. NW of Dauphin; lumbering and distributing center; grain, stock.

Swan River. 1 In NE Minn., rises near Hibbing, flows 60 mi. SW, through Swan L., and S, past Trout L. to Mississippi R. in NE corner of Aitkin co. **2** In NW Mont., rises in Mission Range, near McDonald Peak; flows c.80 mi. NNW, bet. Mission and Flathead ranges, through Swan L. (10 mi. long, 1 mi. max. width), to NE end of Flathead L. near Somers.

Swansboro, resort and fishing town (pop. 559), Onslow co., E N.C., 22 mi. W of Morehead City, on Atlantic coast.

Swanscombe (swŏnz'kŭm), urban district (1931 pop. 8,543; 1951 census 8,295), NW Kent, England, 3 mi. W of Gravesend; metalworking, chalk quarrying. In urban dist., just WNW, on the Thames, is town of Greenhithe (pop. 2,547), with mfg. of concrete, cement, paper, and foundry products. One of the world's oldest skulls excavated here, 1935.

Swansea (swŏn'zē, -sē), town (pop. 3,174), New South Wales, Australia, 60 mi. NNE of Sydney, on E coast; summer resort.

Swansea, residential village (pop. 6,988), S Ont., W suburb of Toronto.

Swansea, town (pop. 450), E Tasmania, 65 mi. NE of Hobart, on NW shore of Oyster Bay; summer resort. Small deposits of bauxite.

Swansea. 1 (swŏn'sē) Village (pop. 1,816), St. Clair co., SW Ill., just N of Belleville and within St. Louis metropolitan area. Inc. 1895. **2** (swŏn'zē, -sē) Town (pop. 6,121), Bristol co., SE Mass., on Mt. Hope Bay, 4 mi. NNW of Fall River; textile dyeing and finishing, mfg. (castings, curtains); resort. Formerly shipbuilding. Settled 1632, set off from Rehoboth 1668. Includes villages of Ocean Grove, Touisset, North Swansea, South Swansea. **3** (swŏn'sē) Town (pop. 762), Lexington co., central S.C., 20 mi. S of Columbia; wood products, beverages.

Swansea (swŏn'zē, -sē), Welsh *Abertawe* (ăbûrtou'ĕ), county borough (1931 pop. 164,797; 1951 census 160,832), SW Glamorgan, Wales, on Swansea Bay of Bristol Channel, at mouth of Tawe R., 35 mi. WNW of Cardiff; 51°37'N 3°56'W; seaport and metallurgical center. Exports coal, tinplate, and metallurgical products; imports timber, iron and tin ore. Important sheet-metal and tinplate mills, and foundries smelting tin, copper, iron, zinc, nickel, gold, silver; chemical works. Has extensive docks and shipyards, ruins of Norman castle, 15th-cent. church of St. Mary, and modern Guildhall. Site of Royal Institute of South Wales. In 1st half of 19th cent. Swansea ware, noted blue pottery, was made here. In co. borough are towns of Llandarcy (lăndär'sē) (E), with important petroleum refineries, Morriston (N; pop. 10,957), with tin-plate and zinc works, Llandore (lăndôr') (pop. 10,804), with steelworks, Sketty (W; pop. 6,358), Oystermouth (SW; pop. 9,646), including seaside resort of The Mumbles, Llansamlet (lănsăm'lĕt) (pop. 7,154), with coal mines, tinplate, copper, and zinc works, Clase (N; pop. 5,559), and Kilvey (NE; pop. 5,320), with tin-plate, zinc works. Swansea sustained heavy air raids in 1941.

Swans Island, town (pop. 468), Hancock co., S Maine, on Swans (6 mi. long, 1-4 mi. wide), Marshall, and other small isls. in Blue Hill Bay, just SW of Mt. Desert Isl.

Swanton (swŏn'tŭn, swän'-). **1** Village (pop. 203), Saline co., SE Nebr., 8 mi. SW of Wilber and on branch of Big Blue R. **2** Village (pop. 1,740), Fulton co., NW Ohio, 19 mi. W of Toledo; machinery, furniture, heaters, construction materials. **3** Town (pop. 3,740), including Swanton village (pop. 2,275), Franklin co., NW Vt., on Missisquoi R. and L. Champlain, and 7 mi. N of St. Albans; building materials, machinery, clothing; lime, marble; agr. (dairy products, poultry). Port of entry for planes. Jesuit mission established here c.1700; English settlement began 1765. Smugglers' hq. in early 19th cent. Town attacked by British in War of 1812.

Swan Valley, town (pop. 203), Bonneville co., SE Idaho, on Snake R. and 36 mi. E of Idaho Falls.

Swanville. 1 Resort town (pop. 437), Waldo co., S Maine, on Swan L., just N of Belfast; granite quarries. **2** Village (pop. 373), Morrison co., central Minn., on small affluent of Mississippi R. and 14 mi. WSW of Little Falls, in grain, livestock, poultry area; dairy products.

Swanwick, England: see ALFRETON.

Swanzey (swän'zē), town (pop. 2,806), Cheshire co., SW N.H., on Ashuelot R. just S of Keene; inc. 1753. West Swanzey village produces wood products, woolens.

Swarbacks Minn, inlet of St. Magnus Bay, Mainland isl., Shetland, Scotland, extending 5 mi. E, forming 2-mi.-wide channel bet. Muckle Roe (N) and Vementry (S) isls. E continuation of inlet is Olna Firth, 3 mi. long, former whaling station and cruiser base in First World War.

Swarland, village and parish (pop. 198), E central Northumberland, England, 7 mi. S of Alnwick; woolen milling.

Swartberg or **Zwartberg** (both: svärt'bĕrkh), mountain range, S Cape Prov., U. of So. Afr., extends 150 mi. E from E end of Wittebergen range near Laingsburg to Willowmore. Consists of the Little Swartberg (Klein Swartberg) (W), rising to 7,628 ft. on Seven Weeks Poort, 8 mi. NE of Ladismith; the Swartberg (center), separated from Little Swartberg range by Gamka R. valley, and rising to 6,645 ft. on Cango Berg, 14 mi. NE of Calitzdorp; and the Great Swartberg (E), rising to 7,060 ft. on Tygerberg, 20 mi. NNE of Oudtshoorn. Entire range forms part of S boundary of the Great Karroo.

Swarthmore (swôrth'môr, swŏth'-), borough (pop. 4,825), Delaware co., SE Pa., SW suburb of Philadelphia; paper products. Has Swarthmore Col. (chartered 1864, opened 1869).

Swartswood (swôrts'wŏŏd), village, Sussex co., NW N.J., 4 mi. WNW of Newton, on Swartswood L. (c.2 mi. long; drains SW into Paulins Kill). State park here. Scene of massacre by Indians (1756).

Swartz, village (1940 pop. 733), Ouachita parish, NE central La., 9 mi. NE of Monroe, in natural-gas field; makes carbon black.

Swartz Creek, village (1940 pop. 901), Genesee co., SE central Mich., 8 mi. SW of Flint, and on the small Swartz Creek, in farm area; makes farm implements.

Swarzedz (svä'zhĕts), Pol. *Swarzędz*, Ger. *Schwersenz* (shvâr'zĕnts"), town (1946 pop. 5,764), Poznan prov., W Poland, 7 mi. E of Poznan; lumber industry; brickworks.

Swastika, village (pop. estimate 1,000), E Ont., 5 mi. SW of Kirkland Lake; rail junction; gold mining; farming.

Swat (svät), princely state (□ 4,000; 1951 pop. 569,000), North-West Frontier Prov., W Pakistan, in Malakand agency; ⊙ Saidu. Bounded partly by Indus R. (E), Dir state (W), tribal areas (N); comprises valley of Swat R. and SE ranges of the Hindu Kush. Very mountainous region (several peaks over 15,000 ft. in N section) with deep, narrow valleys; largely inaccessible from outside. Agr. (wheat, rice, barley, sugar cane, corn); fruitgrowing, handicraft woolen weaving; trades in timber, ghee, fruit, honey, wool. Inhabitants are Pathan tribes. Present ruler, the Wali of Swat, is descendant of noted Akhund of Swat (1794-1877).

Swatara Creek (swŭtä'rŭ), E central Pa., rises in Schuylkill co. c.8 mi. W of Pottsville, flows 60 mi. SW, past Hummelstown, to Susquehanna R. at Middletown.

Swatara Station or **Swatara,** village (pop. 6,076, with adjacent Hershey), Dauphin co., S central Pa., 12 mi. E of Harrisburg.

Swat Canals, small irrigation system of Swat R. in N central North-West Frontier Prov., W Pakistan. Upper Swat Canal leaves left river bank in SW Swat state, runs S, through hills at Malakand via 2-mi.-long tunnel, past Dargai, then SE across Mardan dist.; c.75 mi. long. Lower Swat Canal leaves left bank 5 mi. WNW of Tangi, runs c.35 mi. ESE, past Takht-i-Bahi, to S of Mardan town.

Swatow (swä'tou', swä'tō'), Mandarin *Shan-t'ou* (shän'tō'), city (pop. 214,990), E Kwangtung prov., China, port in Han R. delta, on Swatow Bay of S.China Sea, 220 mi. E of Canton; 23°22'N 116°41'E. Head of railroad to Chaoan. Industrial and commercial center; produces pharmaceutical products, cigarettes, matches, linen (drawn work), embroidered goods; exports sugar, indigo, tobacco, rice, wheat, fruit. Originally a small fishing village, it was opened to foreign trade in 1858 and developed into a major commercial center and emigration port, supplanting Chaoan (N). It became a municipality in 1930. In Sino-Japanese War, it was held 1939-45 by Japanese.

Swat River (svät), in N central North-West Frontier Prov., W Pakistan, rises on SE spur of the Hindu Kush, flows S and SW, through Swat state, and SE, past Utmanzai, to Kabul R. just S of Charsadda; c.200 mi. long. Supplies irrigation canals in lower course. Receives Panjkora R. (right) in SW Swat state.

Swaythling, NE residential suburb of Southampton, S Hampshire, England, on Itchen R.; aircraft works.

Swayzee (swā'zē), town (pop. 690), Grant co., E central Ind., 9 mi. WSW of Marion, in agr. area; canned foods.

Swaziland (swä'zēlănd), British protectorate (□ 6,705; 1946 pop. 186,880), S Africa, on NE edge of U. of So. Afr., bounded by Natal (S), Transvaal (W and N), and Mozambique (E); ⊙ Mbabane. Sloping plateau, divided into mountainous high veld (3,500-5,000 ft. high) in W, middle veld (1,500-3,000 ft. high) in center, and low or bush veld (500-1,500 ft. high) in E. Mean annual temp. ranges (Mbabane) from 52.5°F to 72.3°F.; average annual rainfall 34.87 in. (Bremersdorp) to 53.99 in. (Mbabane). Stock raising (cattle, sheep, goats), dairying; wool, hides, skins; tobacco, fruit, grain. Chief export, cattle. Cotton growing is in experimental stage. Asbestos, tin, and gold are mined in N part of territory. Chief villages: Bremersdorp, Havelock, Piggs Peak, Hlatikulu, Stegi, Gollel. Swazi inhabitants settled in territory early in 19th cent. after being expelled from N Zululand. Swazi independence was guaranteed by Great Britain (1881) and South African Republic (1884), but a joint British-South African-Swazi govt. was set up in 1890. South African Republic established protectorate over territory, 1890. After South African War, territory came under administration of governor of Transvaal; British high commissioner for South Africa assumed control for British govt., 1907. Swaziland's judicial system is closely linked to that of Transvaal; Roman-Dutch law is in force. Swaziland, Basutoland, and Bechuanaland Protectorate constitute the High Commission Territories.

Swea City (swā), town (pop. 869), Kossuth co., N Iowa, 26 mi. E of Estherville; feed milling.

Swede Island, Caroline Isls.: see LAMOTREK.

Sweden, Swedish *Sverige* (svĕr'yŭ), kingdom (□ 158,486; with water area □ 173,423; 1950 pop. 7,046,920), N Europe; ⊙ STOCKHOLM. Occupies E, lake-covered, part of Scandinavian peninsula; bounded by the Oresund, Kattegat, and Skagerrak (SW), Norway, with which it has 1,030-mi.-long land frontier (W), Finland (NE), and the Baltic, including Gulf of Bothnia (S and E). Extends bet. 55°20'-69°4'N and 10°28'-24°10'E. Its greatest length (N-S) is 977 mi., greatest width is 310 mi. Mtn. range along Norwegian border rises to 6,965 ft. on Kebnekaise in Lapland; hilly central plateau slopes E to narrow coastal plain along Gulf of Bothnia. S part of Sweden is generally low and level, rising to low plateau S of L. Vatter. In this region are Sweden's largest lakes: Vaner (□ 2,141), Vatter (□ 733), Malar (□ 440), and Hjalmar (□ 190); lakes Vaner and Vatter, together with several smaller lakes, the Gota and other rivers, and short canal sections, form the Gota Canal, major E-W waterway across S third of Sweden. In N half of country, at foot of border mtn. range, are several other large lakes, including Stor, Hornavan, and Torne lakes. This region is drained by the great Torne, Dal, Lule, Pite, Skellefte, Angerman, Indal, and Ljusna rivers; they provide hydroelectric power on a vast scale and are major logging routes. Falls on Gota R. at Trollhattan (SE Sweden) supply power to almost whole of S Sweden. Largest Swedish isls., both in the Baltic, are Gotland and Oland. Almost 55% of country's surface is forested; lumbering, woodworking, paper and pulp milling are major industries. Cultivated land forms 9 percent of total area; intensive modern farming by small landowners results in a high yield of wheat, oats, rye, barley, flax, and potatoes. Sugar beets are grown and sugar refined in S Sweden. Livestock is raised; dairying is important. High-grade iron is leading mineral worked; largest mines are at Kiruna, Gallivare, and Malmberget, in Lapland; ore is shipped via Lulea or Narvik, Norway. Other mines (iron, copper, zinc, manganese) are in Bergslag region of central Sweden; some have been worked since late Middle Ages. The very important Swedish steel industry is concentrated in this region (Avesta is one of its main centers); here are steel smelters, mills, and foundries, and machinery, locomotives, turbines, generators, and other electrical-equipment are made. At Karlskoga are noted Bofors armament works; Eskilstuna is center of stainless-steel cutlery mfg. Swedish industry is among the most efficient and up-to-date in the world. Some coal is mined in SE part of country, centered on Hoganas. Jonkoping and Tidaholm are match-mfg. centers. Shipbuilding, shipping, and fishing are major industries; textile mills and shoe factories are also important in S Sweden. Motala is center of radio and electrical-appliance works. Noted throughout the world is Swedish glassware, especially that made at Orrefors. Swedish furniture and decorative and folk art also enjoy international reputation. Tourist trade is important. Sweden is exemplary for the fact that social progress has kept pace with industrial development; social legislation, as well as provision of such essential facilities as housing, public and welfare services, and education, are on an exceptionally high level, and a cultured and plentiful life is accessible to all. Wholly or largely govt.-owned are railroads, telephones, iron mines, and electric-power plants. Social legislation provides for old-age, disability, and maternity benefits, workmen's compensation insurance, family allowances, and compulsory health insurance (effective 1951). Mfg. and retailing cooperatives have developed rapidly in recent times, with great benefit to consumers. Goteborg licensing system, in force throughout Sweden, is one of the most advanced in the field of liquor legislation. Sweden is officially called Kingdom of the Swedes, Goths, and Wends. Executive power is vested in the king-in-council; legislative power rests in bicameral parliament (*Riksdag*), whose bills must receive royal assent before becoming law. Suffrage is universal. In practice Sweden is a parliamentary democracy; the king rarely fully uses his constitutional powers. Though there is a nobility, it has no political privileges. Established church is Lutheran; there are 13 dioceses; Uppsala is metropolitan see and is site of older of the 2 state universities, the other being at Lund. There are private universities at Stockholm and Goteborg. Sweden's leading cities are Stockholm, Goteborg, Malmo, Norrkoping, Halsingborg, Orebro,

Uppsala, Boras, Vasteras, Eskilstuna, Linkoping. Train ferries connect Sweden with Denmark (Malmo-Copenhagen and Halsingborg-Helsingor), with Germany (Trelleborg-Sassnitz), and with Poland (Trelleborg-Odra); Goteborg is chief transatlantic port. Except for c.30,000 Finns and c.7,000 Lapps, settled in LAPLAND, pop. is of Swedish stock, descended from Scandinavian tribes who have probably been settled here since Neolithic times. In early times country was divided into Gotaland, Swedish *Götaland* (yû'tälând"), or Gotarike, Swedish *Götarike* (yû'tärē"kû), in extreme S of country, settled by the Gotar, Swedish *Götar*, according to unproved tradition ancestors of the Goths; these were at war with their N neighbors, the Svear of Svealand (sfā'äländ") or Svearike (sfā'ärē"kû), mentioned as *Suiones* by Tacitus. By 6th cent. A.D. the Svear had conquered and merged with the Gotar. The N two thirds of the country was known as Norrland (nôr'länd"). Known in Russia as Varangians, Swedes had, by 10th cent., extended their influence to the Black Sea. Sweden was Christianized (c.829) by St. Ansgar, but paganism survived until reign (12th cent.) of Eric IX, who also conquered Finland. By 13th cent. royal power had been weakened by rise of independent feudal class and by demands for autonomy by the cities, which were strongly influenced by German merchants of the Hanseatic League. Bet. 1319 and 1343 Sweden and Norway were united under Magnus VII; in 1350 a uniform law was 1st codified. Queen Margaret, after becoming regent of Sweden, effected (1397) personal union of Sweden, Norway, and Denmark through the Kalmar Union, and had Eric of Pomerania proclaimed king of the 3 countries. Governed from Copenhagen, Swedes quickly became restive; after rebellion (1435) 1st Swedish diet met and, after another rising (1448), began to elect its own regents. Christian II of Denmark asserted his claim to Sweden by force of arms and instigated massacre (1520) of Swedish nobles at Stockholm. Swedes rose under Gustavus Vasa, who became (1523) king Gustavus I. While most of S Sweden remained in Danish hands, Gustavus built up country's military power, freed trade from grip of Hanseatic League, made Lutheranism state religion, and vested hereditary kingship in his dynasty. His successors turned attention toward E Europe and conquered (1561) N part of Livonia. John III of Sweden married sister of Sigismund II of Poland; their son, Sigismund III of Poland, a Catholic, acceded (1592) to Swedish throne. After brief civil war he was overthrown (1599) and crown passed to his uncle, Charles IX. Under Gustavus II (Adolphus) Sweden reached zenith of her power; she acquired (1617) Ingermanland and Karelia from Russia and (1629) most of Livonia from Poland. With her entry (1630) into Thirty Years War, Sweden became chief Protestant power of continental Europe. After death (1632) of Gustavus II, his chancellor, Oxenstierna, became dominant figure in Sweden during reign of Queen Christina. Under Treaty of Westphalia (1648) Sweden acquired Pomerania and archbishopric of Bremen. In a concurrent war (1643–45) with Denmark she regained part of S Sweden; Charles X, who succeeded (1654) Christina on her abdication, regained (1658) remainder of S Sweden from Denmark. Under Treaty of Oliva (1660) Poland renounced all claims to Swedish throne and ceded Livonia. Under Charles XI Sweden became absolute monarchy; in Northern War (1700–1721), under Charles XII, Sweden triumphed (1700) over Russia at Narva, but suffered crushing defeats after battle of Poltava (1709). Under treaties of Stockholm (1720) and Nystad (1721) Sweden ceded archbishopric of Bremen to Hanover, part of Pomerania to Prussia, and Livonia, Ingermanland, and Karelia to Russia, and was reduced to a secondary power. Throughout ensuing part of 18th cent. Sweden was torn by political intrigue and civil discord, dominated by pro- and anti-Russian factions of nobles. Late 18th cent. saw resurgence of absolutism under Gustavus III and Gustavus IV, who involved (1803) Sweden in war against Napoleon and lost (1809) Finland to Russia, and remainder of Pomerania to Prussia. Liberal revolution (1809) overthrew Gustavus IV, resulted in new constitution, and placed Charles XIII on throne. Charles' adopted heir, French Marshal Bernadotte (later Charles XIV), led Swedish policy from 1810 onward; in 1813 he joined the allies against Napoleon. This was Sweden's last war. In 1814 Congress of Vienna joined Sweden in personal union with Norway (dissolved 1905). During 19th cent. progressive political liberalization paralleled rapid industrial progress. Basis of present constitution was laid in 1864; in 1866 the *Riksdag* was made bicameral. Industrialization spurred rise of Social Democratic party, which dominated Swedish politics from 1920 onward. Bet. 1870 and 1914, c.1,500,000 Swedes emigrated to the United States (mostly to the Middle West). Sweden remained neutral in both wars. During depression of the 1930s electrification of almost whole Swedish railroad network provided stimulus to economy and made transportation system independent of imported fuel. Sweden joined (1946) the U.N. and, later, the European Recovery Program. Administratively Sweden is divided into 24 counties [Swedish *läner*] and the city of Stockholm; independent of these, and of little administrative importance, are 25 historical provs. [Swedish *landskapen*]. The counties are as follows: ALVSBORG, BLEKINGE, GAVLEBORG, GOTEBORG OCH BOHUS, GOTLAND, HALLAND, JAMTLAND, JONKOPING, KALMAR, KOPPARBERG, KRISTIANSTAD, KRONOBERG, MALMOHUS, NORRBOTTEN, OREBRO, OSTERGOTLAND, SKARABORG, SODERMANLAND, STOCKHOLM, UPPSALA, VARMLAND, VASTERBOTTEN, VASTERNORRLAND, VASTMANLAND.

Sweden, town (pop. 212), Oxford co., W Maine, 30 mi. W of Auburn.

Swedesboro, borough (pop. 2,459), Gloucester co., SW N.J., on Raccoon Creek and 17 mi. SW of Camden; baskets, canned goods, crates; truck, poultry. Settled by Swedes 1641, inc. 1902. Partly burned by British, 1778. Trinity Church built 1784.

Swedesburg, village (pop. 1,710, with adjacent Kings Manor), Montgomery co., SE Pa., near Norristown.

Swedru (swĕ'drōō), town, Western Prov., S Gold Coast colony, 15 mi. NNW of Winneba; road center; cacao market; palm oil and kernels, cassava.

Sweeny, town (pop. 1,393), Brazoria co., S Texas, 17 mi. E of Bay City; oil refining. Inc. after 1940.

Sweers Island, Australia: see WELLESLEY ISLANDS.

Sweet Briar, village, Amherst co., central Va., 11 mi. NNE of Lynchburg. Sweet Briar Col. for women (1901) here.

Sweet Grass, county (□ 1,846; pop. 3,621), S Mont.; ⊙ Big Timber. Agr. area drained by Yellowstone R. Livestock, grain. Part of Absaroka Natl. Forest and Absaroka Range in S. Formed 1895.

Sweetgrass, village (pop. c.350), Toole co., N Mont., on Alta. line 35 mi. N of Shelby; port of entry; trading point in agr. region.

Sweet Home. 1 Village (1940 pop. 694), Pulaski co., central Ark., just S of Little Rock, near Arkansas R. **2** Town (pop. 3,603), Linn co., W Oregon, on South Santiam R. and 25 mi. SE of Albany; lumber milling. Gold mines in vicinity. Willamette Natl. Forest near by. Settled in 1840s, inc. 1893.

Sweet Island, Maine: see ISLE OF SPRINGS.

Sweetsburg, village (pop. 492), S Que., on Yamaska R. and 2 mi. E of Cowansville; dairying, pig raising.

Sweet Springs, city (pop. 1,439), Saline co., central Mo., on Blackwater R. and 16 mi. SW of Marshall; agr.; cooperative creamery, shoe factory. Settled 1826.

Sweetsprings or **Sweet Springs,** village, Monroe co., S W.Va., 18 mi. SW of Covington, Va., near state line. Formerly a noted spa, whose heyday was in 1830s; large hotel here is now a home for the aged.

Sweetwater, county (□ 10,492; pop. 22,017), SW Wyo.; ⊙ Green River. Mining and sheep-raising area, bordering on Utah and Colo.; watered by Green R. Coal, oil. Formed 1867.

Sweetwater. 1 or **Sweet Water,** town (pop. 230), Dade co., S Fla., near Miami. **2** Town (pop. 4,199), Monroe co., SE Tenn., on small Sweetwater Creek and 40 mi. SW of Knoxville, in timber, farm, barite-mining area; mfg. of woolen goods, concrete blocks, staves, hosiery, dresses, cheese; lumbering. Craighead Caverns and Tenn. Military Inst. are near by. Settled c.1850; inc. 1875. **3** City (pop. 13,619), ⊙ Nolan co., W Texas, c.40 mi. W of Abilene; trade, processing, shipping, distribution center for ranching and agr. area; ships livestock, wool, mohair, grain, feed; oil refining, cotton ginning, cottonseed-oil milling, dairy-products processing, meat packing, mfg. of gypsum products, agr. machinery; railroad shops. Has annual stock show. Near by are L. Sweetwater (SE) and L. Trammel (SW), recreational areas. Founded c.1876, moved 1881 to site on railroad; grew as cattle-shipping point.

Sweetwater, Lake, W Texas, impounded by dam in small Bitter Creek (a S tributary of Clear Fork of Brazos R.), 6 mi. ESE of Sweetwater; c.1.5 mi. long; capacity 10,000 acre-ft.; resort.

Sweetwater Lake. 1 In Calif.: see SWEETWATER RIVER. **2** In Ramsey co., E central N.Dak., NNE of Devils L.; 3 mi. long.

Sweetwater Mountains, in Calif. and Nev., a N–S range just E of the Sierra Nevada, in Lyon co., W Nev., and Mono co., E Calif. Rises to 11,646 ft. at Wheeler Peak, 28 mi. NNW of Mono L.

Sweetwater River. 1 In S Calif., rises in mts. E of San Diego, flows c.55 mi. SW to San Diego Bay just S of National City. Dams impound water-supply reservoirs: Sweetwater L., 3 mi. long; L. Loveland, formed by Lake Loveland Dam (783 ft. long, 224 ft. high; completed 1945). **2** In S central Wyo., rises in S tip of Wind River Range, flows generally E, crossing Continental Divide near South Pass, through cattle-raising area, to Pathfinder Reservoir on N.Platte R.; 151 mi. long.

Swellendam (svĕ'lŭndäm'), town (pop. 4,003), SW Cape Prov., U. of So. Afr., near Breede R., 65 mi. ESE of Worcester; agr. center (wool, viticulture, grain, oranges); ostrich feathers were formerly important product. Founded c.1745, one of the oldest towns in Cape Prov. The Drostdy (1746), former residence of local governor, is now mus. The first of several South African republics was set up here in 1795 under the leadership of Hermanus Steyn.

Swepsonville (swĕp'sŭnvĭl), village (1940 pop. 640), Alamance co., N central N.C., on Haw R. and 6 mi. SE of Burlington; rayon milling.

Sweveghem, Belgium: see ZWEVEGEM.

Swevezeele, Belgium: see ZWEVEZELE.

Swica River, Ukrainian SSR: see SVITSA RIVER.

Swidnica, Poland: see SCHWEIDNITZ.

Swidwin (shvēd'vēn), Pol. *Świdwin*, Ger. *Schivelbein* (shē'fŭlbīn), town (1939 pop. 9,714; 1946 pop. 6,098) in Pomerania, after 1945 in Koszalin prov., NW Poland, on Rega R. and 30 mi. SW of Köslin (Koszalin), 18 mi. SSW of Bialogard; rail junction; agr. market (grain, sugar beets, potatoes, livestock); mfg. of mustard, vegetable oil. Has 15th-cent. castle of Teutonic Knights. Pathologist Virchow b. here.

Swiebodzice (shvyĕbôjē'tsĕ), Pol. *Świebodzice*, Ger. *Freiburg* or *Freiburg in Schlesien* (frī'bŏork ĭn shlā'zyŭn), town (1939 pop. 9,309; 1946 pop. 6,078) in Lower Silesia, after 1945 in Wroclaw prov., SW Poland, 7 mi. N of Waldenburg (Walbrzych); linen milling, furniture and clock mfg. After 1945, briefly called Frybork.

Swiebodzin (shvyĕbô'jĭn), Pol. *Świebodzin*, Ger. *Schwiebus* (shvē'bōōs), town (1939 pop. 10,432; 1946 pop. 6,144) in Brandenburg, after 1945 in Zielona Gora prov., W Poland, 20 mi. N of Grünberg (Zielona Gora); rail junction; mfg. of furniture, electrical equipment, clocks, soap, synthetic fertilizer, chocolate; metalworking, distilling. Has early-Gothic church, 16th-cent. town hall. First mentioned c.1300; chartered before 1319. Captured 1474 by Hungarians. Belonged to Brandenburg, 1686–95, then passed to Bohemia, and in 1742 to Prussia.

Swieciany, Lithuania: see SVENCIONYS.

Swiecie (shvyĕ'chĕ), Pol. *Świecie*, Ger. *Schwetz* (shvĕts), town (pop. 8,358), Bydgoszcz prov., N central Poland, on Wda R., near its mouth on the Vistula, and 27 mi. NNE of Bydgoszcz. Rail spur terminus; mfg. of cement, musical instruments, soap, potato flakes; sawmilling, beet-sugar milling.

Swieradow Zdroj (shvyĕrä'dŏof zdrōō'ē), Pol. *Świeradów Zdrój*, Ger. *Flinsberg* or *Bad Flinsberg* (bät" flĭns'bĕrk), town (1939 pop. 2,803; 1946 pop. 2,994) in Lower Silesia, after 1945 in Wroclaw prov., SW Poland, near Czechoslovak border, at N foot of the Isergebirge, on Kwisa R. and 18 mi. W of Hirschberg (Jelenia Gora); health and winter-sports resort. Chartered after 1945 and briefly called Wieniec Zdroj.

Swierzawa (shvyĕ'zhä'vä), Pol. *Świerzawa*, Ger. *Schönau* (shûn'ou), town (1939 pop. 1,911; 1946 pop. 1,253) in Lower Silesia, after 1945 in Wroclaw prov., SW Poland, on the Katzbach and 18 mi. SW of Liegnitz (Legnica); agr. market (grain, potatoes, livestock). Has 13th-cent. church. After 1945, briefly called Szunow, Pol. *Szunów*.

Swietochlowice (shvyĕtōkh-wôvē'tsĕ), Pol. *Świętochłowice*, Ger. *Schwientochlowitz* (shvēn"tôkh'lōvĭts), town (pop. 25,704), Katowice prov., S Poland, just SW of Chorzow; coal mining; ironworks. Inc. after 1946.

Swietokrzyskie, Gory (gōō'rĭ shvyĕtôk-zhĭ'skyĕ), Pol. *Góry Świętokrzyskie* [holy cross mountains], mountain group, SE central Poland, bet. Vistula (E) and Pilica (W) rivers. Highest point (2,005 ft.), the Lysica, Pol. *Łysica*, is 12 mi. E of Kielce.

Swift, county (□ 747; pop. 15,837), SW Minn.; ⊙ Benson. Agr. area drained by Pomme de Terre and Chippewa rivers. Grain, livestock. Formed 1870.

Swift Current, city (pop. 6,379), SW Sask., on Swiftcurrent Creek and 100 mi. W of Moose Jaw; distributing center for SW Sask., with grain elevators, lumber yards, coal yards, oil refinery, tanneries, dairies. Site of Dominion experimental station (700 acres).

Swift Diamond River, Coos co., N N.H., rises N of Dixville Notch, flows c.20 mi. ESE to Magalloway R. N of Umbagog L. Dead Diamond R. (c.18 mi. long), its N branch, joins it 2 mi. above mouth, N of Wentworth Location village.

Swifton, town (pop. 539), Jackson co., NE Ark., 25 mi. W of Jonesboro, in agr. area.

Swift River. 1 In Mass.: see QUABBIN RESERVOIR. **2** In W Maine, rises in Franklin co. S of Mooselookmeguntic L., flows c.20 mi. S to the Androscoggin at Rumford. **3** In E N.H., rises in White Mtn. Natl. Forest N of Waterville Valley, flows c.24 mi. E to Saco R. near Conway.

Swifts Beach, Mass.: see WAREHAM.

Swilly, Lough (lŏkh), long narrow inlet of the Atlantic, N Co. Donegal, Ireland, extends 25 mi. inland bet. Fanad Head (W) and Dunaff Head (E); receives Swilly R. Buncrana is on E shore, Letterkenny at head. In SE part of lough is Inch Isl. Inlet was British naval base in First World War; British-held fort evacuated under 1938 agreement.

Swilly River, Co. Donegal, Ireland, rises at foot of Derryveagh Mts., flows 10 mi. E to head of Lough Swilly at Letterkenny.

Swina River, Poland: see SWINE RIVER.

Swinburne, Cape, S tip of Prince of Wales Isl., S Franklin Dist., Northwest Territories, on McClintock Channel and Franklin Strait; 71°12'N 99°9'W.

Swinburne Island, SE N.Y., small artificial island in Lower New York Bay, just off E shore of Staten Isl.; former quarantine station. Part of Richmond borough of New York city.

Swindle Island (□ 120), SW B.C., in Hecate Strait; 52°34'N 128°47'W; 16 mi. long, 2–10 mi. wide. Klemtu fishing village on NE coast. Just S is Price Isl. (□ 47), 14 mi. long, 6 mi. wide.

Swindon, municipal borough (1931 pop. 62,401; 1951 census 68,932), NE Wiltshire, England, 28 mi. ENE of Bath; agr. market, with important railroad shops.

Swineford, Ireland: see SWINFORD.

Swinemünde (svēnůmün'dů) or **Swinoujscie** (shvē-nô-ōō'ēshchě), Pol. *Świnoujście,* town (1939 pop. 30,239; 1946 pop. 5,771) in Pomerania, after 1945 in Szczecin prov., NW Poland, Baltic port on E shore of Usedom isl., on Swine mouth of the Oder and 35 mi. NNW of Stettin; 53°54'N 14°14'E. Fishing center; popular seaside resort; mineral springs. Chartered 1765. In Second World War, Ger. naval base; c.70% destroyed. Odra Port, terminus of train ferry to Trelleborg (Sweden), is across the Swine, on W shore of Wolin isl.

Swine River (svē'nů) or **Swina River** (shvē'nä), Pol. *Świna,* central arm of Oder R. estuary mouth, in Pomerania, after 1945 in NW Poland, bet. Usedom isl. (W) and Wolin isl. (E); connects Stettin Lagoon (S) with the Baltic; 13 mi. long. Just below its mouth on the Baltic are Swinemunde (Swinoujscie; W) and Odra Port (E). For ocean-going ships, most navigable of the Oder's 3 mouths; winding S part is by-passed by 3-mi.-long navigation channel.

Swineshead, town and parish (pop. 1,990), Parts of Holland, SE central Lincolnshire, England, 6 mi. WSW of Boston; agr. market. Has church dating from 14th cent.

Swinford or **Swineford** (both: swĭn'fůrd), Gaelic *Béal Átha na Muice,* town (pop. 1,186), NE Co. Mayo, Ireland, 16 mi. ENE of Castlebar; agr. market (cattle, potatoes).

Swinica (shvēnē'tsä), Pol. *Świnica,* peak (7,549 ft.) in the High Tatra, on Pol.-Czechoslovak border, 5 mi. SSE of Zakopane, Poland; 2d-highest peak in Poland.

Swink. 1 Town (pop. 336), Otero co., SE Colo., on Arkansas R. and 5 mi. WNW of La Junta, in irrigated sugar-beet region; alt. 4,000 ft.; beet sugar. **2** Town (pop. 96), Choctaw co., SE Okla., 19 mi. E of Hugo, in farm area.

Swinoujscie, Poland: see SWINEMÜNDE.

Swinton, urban district (1931 pop. 13,821; 1951 census 11,922), West Riding, S Yorkshire, England, 9 mi. NE of Sheffield; coal mining; mfg. of bottles, pottery, metal products.

Swinton and Pendlebury, municipal borough (1931 pop. 32,761; 1951 census 41,294), SE Lancashire, England. Swinton, 5 mi. NW of Manchester, has cotton milling, metallurgy, mfg. of dry batteries, tobacco products. Pendlebury, 4 mi. NW of Manchester, has cotton milling and coal mining.

Swir, Belorussian SSR: see SVIR.

Swisher (swĭ'shůr), county (□ 888; pop. 8,249), NW Texas; ⊙ Tulia. On the Llano Estacado; alt. 3,100–3,600 ft. Cap Rock escarpment in E is broken by Tule Canyon. Wheat growing, cattle ranching, dairying; grain sorghums, oats, barley, alfalfa, fruit, truck, livestock (hogs, sheep, poultry). Formed 1876.

Swisher, town (pop. 205), Johnson co., E Iowa, 15 mi. NNW of Iowa City.

Swislocz, Belorussian SSR: see SVISLOCH.

Swisshelm Mountain (7,185 ft.), Cochise co., SE Ariz., 23 mi. N of Douglas.

Swissvale, industrial borough (pop. 16,488), Allegheny co., SW Pa., on Monongahela R. adjacent to E Pittsburgh; railroad equipment, glass products. Settled c.1760, inc. 1898.

Swissville, village (pop. 1,009), Lee co., N Ill.

Switchback, village (pop. 1,646, with adjoining Maybeury), McDowell co., S W.Va., 12 mi. ESE of Welch, in coal region. Also called Lick Branch.

Switz City, town (pop. 328), Greene co., SW Ind., 35 mi. NE of Vincennes, in agr. and bituminous-coal area.

Switzerland (swĭ'tsůrlůnd), Fr. *Suisse* (süēs'), Ger. *Schweiz* (shvīts), Ital. *Svizzera* (zvēt'tsärä), also **Swiss Confederation,** republic (□ 15,944; 1950 pop. 4,700,297), central Europe; ⊙ BERN. A mountainous country, of great scenic beauty and variety, Switzerland lies on intercontinental crossroads. The Alps, which transverse it NNE-SSW, fall sharply at its S boundary with Italy, with which it also shares L. LUGANO and Lago MAGGIORE. The lower JURA Mts. (W) and L. GENEVA (SW), formed by the Rhone, border on France. From Germany, in the N, it is separated by the Rhine and L. Constance. On E, partly along the upper Rhine, are Liechtenstein and Austria. Switzerland consists of 3 well-defined regions, paralleling one another NNE-SSW: the Jura, the *Mittelland* or Swiss Plateau, and the Alps. More than half the country is covered by central ranges of the Alps (BERNESE ALPS, RHAETIAN ALPS, GLARUS ALPS), a majestic line of glacier-clad massifs with snow-capped summits and numerous valleys. Though the highest peak of the Alps (MONT BLANC) is in France, there are in Switzerland countless lofty peaks (e.g., MATTERHORN, FINSTERAARHORN, JUNGFRAU), culminating in DUFOURSPITZE (15,203 ft.) of the Monte Rosa. Lower, semi-detached mtn. systems, like the famed RIGI and PILATUS, adjoin in N. The Swiss Alps are easily crossed at fine, but occasionally snow-bound passes, some used since ancient days, now adapted to international rail and motor traffic (GREAT SAINT BERNARD PASS, SPLÜGEN PASS, BERNINA PASS, MALOJA PASS, SAN BERNARDINO PASS, BRÜNIG PASS, SUSTEN PASS). Through the long tunnels of the SIMPLON PASS (12.3 mi. long), LÖTSCHBERG PASS (c.9 mi. long), and SAINT GOTTHARD PASS (c.7.5 mi. long) pass transcontinental express trains. In the Alps rise the Rhine, Rhone, and Inn (Danube affluent), which drain respectively into North Sea, Mediterranean, and Black Sea. The deeply incised valleys of upper Rhone and upper Rhine, converging upon FURKA PASS, form a striking link bet. E and W. As remarkable is the ENGADINE valley, in the Grisons, with its string of glittering mtn. lakes (at c.5,500 ft.) and a host of renowned summer and winter resorts; SAINT MORITZ, SILS, SILVAPLANA, DAVOS, PONTRESINA. Among the many other picturesque and healthful centers are ZERMATT, MONTANA, INTERLAKEN, GSTAAD, MÜRREN, FLIMS, KLOSTERS, LENZERHEIDE, AROSA. Spas and mineral springs abound in the region. The beautiful Alpine landscape attracts travelers from all nations and the tourist industry is an important source of revenue, compensating for Switzerland's unfavorable trade balance. On the mtn. slopes are also excellent pastures, where goats, sheep, and, especially, cattle are grazed. Dairying is of 1st importance, and Swiss cheese (Emmenthal, Gruyère) and condensed milk are internationally known. Principal winegrowing section is the Italian-speaking Ticino (centered on LUGANO, LOCARNO, and BELLINZONA), which lies at S piedmont and enjoys an almost subtropical vegetation. Excellent wines are also produced in Vaud canton of the Jura. The Jura is a much lower, calcareous range, geologically of the same origin as the Alps. It stretches from Rhone gorge near Geneva to Basel, extending into France (W) and Germany (NE). Predominantly an agr. and forested region, it also supports Switzerland's best-known export industry, watchmaking, whose centers are Le LOCLE and La CHAUX-DE-FONDS. The bulk of the Swiss population lives in the narrow, so-called plateau (about 1,200–1,800 ft. high) bet. the Jura and Alps, a country of rolling foothills, rich in forests and water-power resources, and dotted with pleasant villages and towns. The climate, varying greatly with altitude, is generally salubrious, with marked seasonal changes. Zurich has an annual mean temp. of c.49°F., with 44 inches of rainfall. Characteristic winds are the hot, dry foehn (which descends from the Alpine slopes) and the cold *bise* of W Switzerland. On the plateau are the major Swiss lakes, e.g., L. Constance. L. of Zurich, L. of Lucerne, L. of Neuchâtel, L. Geneva, along which some of the leading cities are located. Though Switzerland is not self-supporting, agr. is an important occupation, in which c.22% of the people are engaged. Principal crops are wheat, rye, potatoes, sugar beets, vegetables, tobacco, apples, pears. Switzerland is poor in mineral deposits. Only asphalt (Val de TRAVERS), salt (BEX, SCHWEIZERHALL, RHEINFELDEN), iron, and manganese (canton of St. Gall) are mined. The country owes its prosperity largely to the export of high-quality manufactures. Among these products, besides watches, are chemicals and dyes (Basel, Geneva, SCHAFFHAUSEN), metal goods (ZURICH, WINTERTHUR, BURGDORF, AARAU, BIENNE), textiles and embroidery (St. Gall, Zurich), foodstuffs, especially chocolate, beer, liquor (ZUG), newsprint and books (Zurich, Bern, FRAUENFELD, LAUSANNE). In banking and insurance, politically stable Switzerland holds a front rank. It is also renowned for its educational institutions. There are universities at Zurich, Basel, Bern, Geneva, LAUSANNE, NEUCHÂTEL, FRIBOURG; the Federal Inst. of Technology is at Zurich, and the School of Economics at St. Gall. The government-owned railroads are largely electrified. Major airports are near Geneva (COINTRIN) and Zurich (KLOTEN). Basel is an important inland port on the Rhine. Switzerland also owns a merchant marine (set up 1942), operated from Mediterranean and Atlantic ports. German, French, Italian, and Romansh (since 1938) are the official languages; 57% of the pop. are Protestant, 41% R.C. In anc. times inhabited by the Celtic Helvetii (hence Latin name, *Helvetia,* for Switzerland), region was conquered (58 B.C.) by Julius Caesar. Invaded (5th cent.) by Alemanni and Burgundii, passed to Franks in 6th cent. Under Holy Roman Empire after 1033. First nucleus of political unity was formed (1291) when the cantons of Uri, Schwyz, and Unterwalden concluded defensive league against Hapsburg. This led to victory of Morgarten (1315). After being joined by Lucerne, Zurich, Zug, Glarus, and Bern, the league defeated the Austrians at Sempach (1386) and Näfels (1388). Switzerland then rose to 1st rank as a military power. By 1513 Fribourg, Solothurn, Basel, Schaffhausen, and Appenzell were admitted, raising number of cantons to 13, maintained until 1798. Since Swiss defeat at Marignano (1515) and alliance (1516) with France, a policy of neutrality has been followed. Through activities of Calvin at Geneva and Zwingli at Zurich, Switzerland became a center of Reformation in 16th cent. French Revolution led to invasions and formation of *Helvetic Republic* (1798–1803). Restored (1815) at Paris when neutrality was guaranteed for all time, Switzerland emerged with its present boundaries and 22 cantons. The short *Sonderbund* civil war (1847) ended in defeat of Catholic cantons and adoption (1848) of new constitution, superseded in 1874. The country maintained neutrality throughout First and Second World Wars. Joined (1920) League of Nations, of which Geneva became hq. (still seat of several international agencies). The charter of the United Nations makes Swiss membership impossible without some modification of the strict Swiss interpretation of neutrality. For further information see separate articles on towns, cities, physical features, and the cantons. Three of the 22 cantons are divided into so-called half-cantons, making a total of 25 federated states: AARGAU, APPENZELL (AUSSER-RHODEN and INNER-RHODEN), BASEL (BASEL-LAND and BASEL-STADT), BERN, FRIBOURG, GENEVA, GRISONS, GLARUS, LUCERNE, NEUCHÂTEL, SAINT GALL, SCHAFFHAUSEN, SCHWYZ, SOLOTHURN, THURGAU, TICINO, UNTERWALDEN (OBWALDEN and NIDWALDEN), URI, VALAIS, VAUD, ZUG, ZURICH.

Switzerland, county (□ 221; pop. 7,599), SE Ind.; ⊙ Vevay. Bounded E and S by Ohio R., here forming Ky. line. Mfg. (dairy products, flour); agr. (grain, tobacco, stock, truck). Formed 1810.

Switzers, New Zealand: see WAIKAIA.

Swona (swō'nů), island (pop. 6) of the Orkneys, Scotland, in Pentland Firth bet. Hoy and South Ronaldsay, 6 mi. N of Duncansbay Head; 1½ mi. long. Lighthouse (58°44'N 3°3'W).

Sworbe Peninsula, Estonia: see SORVE PENINSULA.

Swords, Gaelic *Sórd Choluim Chille,* town (pop. 703), central Co. Dublin, Ireland, 9 mi. NNE of Dublin; agr. market in cattle-raising, potato-growing region. Abbey, founded here 550 by St. Columba, was held by William of Wykeham in 14th cent. Has anc. round tower and remains of 13th-cent. archbishop's palace and of abbey church.

Swoyersville (swoi'ůrzvĭl), borough (pop. 7,795), Luzerne co., NE central Pa., 3 mi. N of Wilkes-Barre and on Susquehanna R.; anthracite; textiles, metal products. Inc. 1888.

Syam (syä'), village (pop. 187), Jura dept., E France, near the Ain, 19 mi. ENE of Lons-le-Saunier; forges. Gruyère cheese making.

Syamnagar, India: see GARULIA.

Syamozero (syäm'ô"zyĭrů), Finnish *Säämäjärvi* (să'măyărvē), lake in S Karelo-Finnish SSR, 35 mi. WNW of Petrozavodsk; 15 mi. long, 8 mi. wide, max. depth 325 ft.; steep shores. Empties S into Shuya R. Formerly spelled Samozero.

Syamzha, Russian SFSR: see DYAKOVSKAYA.

Syangja (syäng'jů), village, central Nepal, on tributary of the Kali Gandaki and 3 mi. SSW of Nuwakot; rice, corn, wheat, millet, vegetables.

Syariin, Korea: see SARIWON.

Syas River or **Syas' River** (syäs), NW European Russian SFSR, rises in moraine region SE of Nebolchi, flows 160 mi. NNW to L. Ladoga just below Syasstroi. Receives Tikhvinka R. (right) which forms part of Tikhvin canal system below its confluence. Connected with Volkhov R. (W) by Syas Canal (6 mi. long) along S L. Ladoga shore.

Syasstroi or **Syas'stroy** (syůstroi'), town (1939 pop. over 7,500), N Leningrad oblast, Russian SFSR, on Syas R., near L. Ladoga, and 17 mi. NE of Volkhov; paper-milling center; peat works.

Syava (syä'vů), town (1948 pop. over 2,000), N Gorki oblast, Russian SFSR, 23 mi. NE of Vetluga; sawmilling.

Sybaris (sĭ'bůrĭs), anc. Greek city of S Italy, on Gulf of Tarentum (Taranto), bet. Sybaris (Coscile) and Crathis (Crati) rivers. Founded 720 B.C. by Achaeans and Troezenians; became a byword for wealth and voluptuousness of its citizens. The Achaeans drove out the Troezenians, who with the aid of the neighboring colony of Crotona destroyed Sybaris in 510 B.C. Near its site is Terranova di Sibari.

Sycaminum, Palestine: see HAIFA.

Sycamore (sĭ'kůmôr). **1** Village, Talladega co., E central Ala., 14 mi. SSW of Talladega, in part of Talladega Natl. Forest; cotton milling. **2** Town (pop. 624), Turner co., S central Ga., 2 mi. SSE of Ashburn. **3** City (pop. 5,912), ⊙ De Kalb co., N Ill., 20 mi. W of Elgin; trade, industrial, and shipping center in rich agr. area; mfg. (electrical and heating equipment, farm machinery, brass products); corn, oats, wheat, truck, livestock, dairy products, poultry. Founded c.1840, inc. 1859. **4** Village (pop. 935), Wyandot co., N central Ohio, 11 mi. S of Tiffin and on small Sycamore Creek; grain, livestock, dairy products, poultry, fruit. **5** Town (pop. 383), Allendale co., SW S.C., 38 mi. SSW of Orangeburg.

Sychevka (sĭchĕf′kŭ), city (1948 pop. over 10,000), NE Smolensk oblast, Russian SFSR, 40 mi. N of Vyazma; dairying, flax processing; metal- and brickworks, tobacco factory, tannery. Chartered 1776.

Sycow (sĭ′tsōōf), Pol. *Syców*, Ger. *Gross Wartenberg* (grōs″ vär′tûnbĕrk), town (1939 pop. 3,089; 1946 pop. 2,108) in Lower Silesia, after 1945 in Wroclaw prov., SW Poland, 35 mi. ENE of Breslau (Wroclaw); agr. market (grain, potatoes, livestock); sawmilling. Until 1939, Ger. frontier station on Pol. border.

Sydenham (sĭ′dûnûm, sĭd′nûm), village (pop. estimate 550), SE Ont., on small Sydenham L., 14 mi. NNW of Kingston; dairying, farming.

Sydenham, residential district of Lewisham, London, England, S of the Thames, 6 mi. SE of Charing Cross. Crystal Palace, built in Hyde Park of iron and glass by Sir Joseph Paxton for Great Exhibition of 1851, was re-erected here 1854. It was destroyed by fire in 1936; the remaining iron towers were taken down in Second World War.

Sydenham, E suburb of Belfast, N Co. Down, Northern Ireland, 2 mi. E of Belfast; site of Belfast airport.

Sydenham Island, Gilbert Isls.: see NONOUTI.

Sydenham River, S Ont., rises W of London, flows 100 mi. WSW, past Dresden and Wallaceburg, to L. St. Clair 14 mi. WNW of Chatham.

Sydero, Faeroe Isls.: see SUDERO.

Sydney, municipality (pop. 95,952; metropolitan Sydney 1,484,434), ⊙ New South Wales, Australia, on S shore of Port Jackson or Sydney Harbour (see JACKSON, PORT), c.4 mi. W of entrance to harbor; 33°52′S 151°12′E. Principal port, commercial and cultural center of the Commonwealth. Textile and knitting mills, brass foundries, automobile plants, sugar refinery; chemicals, sheet metal, flour. Port equipped for bulk loading of grain, coal, timber. Has floating drydocks. Chief exports: wool, wheat, coal, timber. Seat of Univ. of Sydney (1852), St. Paul's Col. (1854), St. John's Col. (1857), Wesley Col. (1910), Women's Col. (1889), St. Mary's Cathedral (R.C.), St. Andrew's Cathedral (Anglican), State Conservatorium of Music (1915), Natl. Art. Gall. (1904), Australian Mus. (1830). Mean annual temp., 63°F.; rainfall, 42 in. Founded 1788 as 1st penal settlement (see BOTANY BAY) of Australia. In Second World War, Sydney was site of Allied naval and army base. Large immediate suburbs are MANLY, MOSMAN, HUNTER'S HILL, RYDE, ERMINGTON AND RYDALMERE, VAUCLUSE, BALMAIN, DRUMMOYNE, CONCORD, KU-RING-GAI, HOLROYD. Bathing beaches are E.

Sydney, city (pop. 28,305), ⊙ Cape Breton co., E N.S., on coast of Cape Breton Isl., at head of South Arm of Sydney Harbour, 210 mi. NE of Halifax; 46°9′N 60°11′W; coal-mining and steel-milling center (iron ore is shipped in from Newfoundland); shipbuilding, metalworking, woodworking; mfg. of chemicals, bricks, food products. Founded 1783 by United Empire Loyalists, it was ⊙ Cape Breton prov. until 1820.

Sydney Harbour, Australia: see JACKSON, PORT.

Sydney Harbour, inlet (10 mi. long, 3 mi. wide at entrance) of the Atlantic, NE Nova Scotia, in E coast of Cape Breton Isl. At North Sydney, inlet divides into West Arm (4 mi. long) and South Arm (5 mi. long). On inlet are Sydney, North Sydney, and Sydney Mines. Sydney Harbour freezes over in Jan. for 3–4 months.

Sydney Island, triangular atoll (□ 1.6; pop. 294), Phoenix Isls., S Pacific, 110 mi. SE of Canton Isl.; base of triangle c.2 mi. Discovered 1823 by Americans, included 1937 in Br. colony of Gilbert and Ellice Isls. Sometimes called Manra.

Sydney Mines, town (pop. 8,198), E N.S., on E coast of Cape Breton Isl., on W shore of Sydney Harbour, 8 mi. NNW of Sydney; coal-mining center, with steelworks, foundries, machine shops. Coal is shipped from near-by North Sydney.

Sydproven (süd′prüvûn), Dan. *Sydprøven*, fishing settlement (pop. 266), Julianehaab dist., SW Greenland, on small isl. in the Atlantic, at mouth of Agdluitsok Fjord (25 mi. long), 20 mi. SE of Julianehaab; 60°28′N 45°33′W. Radio station. On mainland, 4 mi. NE, is site of former Moravian mission of Lichtenau.

Syene, Egypt: see ASWAN, town.

Syenitsa, Yugoslavia: see SJENICA.

Syfteland (süf′tülän), village (pop. 373) in Os canton, Hordaland co., SW Norway, 1 mi. NW of Os village; has furniture factory. Formerly spelled Softeland, Nor. *Søfteland*.

Syke (zü′kû), town (pop. 5,983), in former Prussian prov. of Hanover, NW Germany, after 1945 in Lower Saxony, 12 mi. S of Bremen; rail junction.

Sykeston (sīks′-), city (pop. 272), Wells co., central N.Dak., 17 mi. SE of Fessenden.

Sykesville. 1 Town (pop. 941), Carroll co., N Md., near S branch of Patapsco R., 20 mi. WNW of Baltimore, in agr. area; mfg. (clothing, woolens, boxes, wormseed oil); cannery. Near by are Springfield State Hosp. for the insane (established 1894) and Henrytown Sanatorium (tuberculosis; for Negroes). **2** Borough (pop. 1,652), Jefferson co., W central Pa., 5 mi. SW of Du Bois; clothing, bricks; bituminous coal; timber.

Sykion, Greece: see SICYON.

Sykkylven (sük′chülvûn), village (pop. 467; canton pop. 3,261), More og Romsdal co., W Norway, on E shore of Sykkylven Fjord, 16 mi. ESE of Alesund; industrial center producing furniture, cement, bricks, wood products. Formerly spelled Sokelven or Sokkelven, Nor. *Søkelven* or *Søkkelven.*

Syktyvkar (sĭktĭfkär′), city (1926 pop. 5,068; 1939 pop. 25,285), ⊙ Komi Autonomous SSR, Russian SFSR, on Vychegda R., at mouth of Sysola R., and 140 mi. ENE of Kotlas, 625 mi. NE of Moscow; 61°40′N 50°50′E. Lumbering center; sawmilling, paper and pulp milling, wood cracking, shipbuilding, tanning, shoe mfg.; metalworks. Teachers col. Founded 1780 as center of Rus. colonization; place of exile under Catherine the Great. Called Ust-Sysolsk until 1930.

Sylacauga (sĭlûkŏ′gû), city (pop. 9,606), Talladega co., E central Ala., 40 mi. SE of Birmingham; processing center for cotton and corn area; cotton milling (fabrics, work clothes), woodworking, marble quarrying and finishing, dairying; cottonseed oil, bricks, fertilizer. Part of Talladega Natl. Forest is just E. Inc. 1886.

Sylhet (sĭl′hĕt), dist. (□ 4,621; 1951 pop. 3,072,-000), East Bengal, E Pakistan; ⊙ Sylhet. In Surma Valley (extensions of Tripura Hills S); bounded N and E by Assam, S by Tripura state; drained by Surma R. and its tributaries. Mainly alluvial soil; rice, tea, oilseeds, jute, cotton, tobacco, sugar cane, potatoes, oranges. Extensive tea gardening; mfg. of cotton cloth, cement, perfume, iron implements, umbrellas, electrical supplies; sawmilling, handicraft mat weaving; fish curing; general engineering factories (Sylhet, Fenchuganj). Surma Valley Technical Inst. at Sylhet, rice research station at Habiganj. Main towns: Habiganj, Maulavi Bazar, Sunamganj, Sylhet. Former petty Hindu kingdom (Sylhet was ⊙); conquered 1384 by Moslems; passed to Mogul empire under Akbar in late-16th cent. Part of Dacca div., Br. Bengal, until placed (1874) under Assam. Major part of Sylhet, except E section (Patharkandi, Ratabari, Karimganj, Badarpur), transferred 1947 from Assam to East Bengal, following formation of E Pakistan. Formerly called Srihatta.

Sylhet, town (1941 pop. 28,128), ⊙ Sylhet dist., E East Bengal, E Pakistan, on the Surma R. and 123 mi. NE of Dacca; rail spur terminus; road junction; airport; trade (rice, tea, oilseeds, jute, cotton) and tea-processing center; mfg. of cotton cloth, electrical supplies; sawmilling; general engineering and construction factory. Surma Valley Technical Inst. Large mosque. Former ⊙ petty Hindu kingdom conquered 1384 by Moslems.

Syli, Lake (sē′lē) (□ 6), Akrotiri Peninsula, S Cyprus, 4 mi. SW of Limassol; 3 mi. long, 2½ mi. wide. Yields salt.

Sylmar, Calif.: see SAN FERNANDO VALLEY.

Sylt (zĭlt, zült), northernmost German North Sea island (□ 36; 1939 pop. 11,920; 1946 pop. 26,346) of North Frisian group, 7 mi. off Schleswig-Holstein coast (connected by Hindenburgdamm), near Danish border; 22 mi. long, average width 1 mi. (except for 8-mi.-wide peninsular extension in center). Dunes and heath predominate; W tip is cultivated. Harbor at Hörnum (S); Westerland is popular seaside resort; main village is Keitum. Fortified in 1930s; was 1st Ger. territory bombed in Second World War.

Sylte (sül′tû), village (pop. 178) in Norddal canton (pop. 2,477), More og Romsdal co., W Norway, on N shore of Norddal Fjord, 38 mi. ESE of Alesund; tourist center.

Sylva (sĭl′vŭ). **1** Town (1940 pop. over 500), S central Molotov oblast, Russian SFSR, on Sylva R. and 15 mi. ENE of Molotov city center, on railroad; glassworking center. **2** Village (1926 pop. 4,428), SW Sverdlovsk oblast, Russian SFSR, on Sylva R. and 5 mi. N of Shalya; lumbering; grain.

Sylva, town (pop. 1,382), ⊙ Jackson co., W N.C., 40 mi. SW of Asheville, near Tuckasegee R.; paper-board and lumber mills, tanning and tanning-extract plants. Inc. 1899.

Sylvan Beach, resort village, Oneida co., central N.Y., on E shore of Oneida L., 13 mi. W of Rome.

Sylvan Grove, city (pop. 506), Lincoln co., central Kansas, on Saline R. and 13 mi. W of Lincoln; livestock, grain.

Sylvania (sĭlvā′nēû). **1** City (pop. 2,939), ⊙ Screven co., E Ga., 21 mi. NNE of Statesboro, in farm and timber area; mfg. (veneer, lumber, naval stores, cottonseed oil, peanut products); cotton ginning. Founded 1847, inc. 1854. **2** Suburban village (pop. 2,433), Lucas co., NW Ohio, at Mich. line, 10 mi. WNW of downtown Toledo; building supplies, fertilizer. **3** Borough (pop. 211), Bradford co., N Pa., 20 mi. S of Elmira, N.Y.

Sylvan Lake, town (pop. 971), S central Alta., on Sylvan L. (9 mi. long, 2 mi. wide), 13 mi. W of Red Deer; mixed farming, dairying. Inc. 1946.

Sylvan Lake, city (pop. 1,165), Oakland co., SE Mich., just SW of Pontiac, on small Sylvan L. Inc. 1921 as village, as city 1946.

Sylvan Lake, lake, Ind.: see ROME CITY.

Sylvan Pass, Wyo.: see ABSAROKA RANGE.

Sylvarena, village (pop. 112), Smith co., S central Miss., 9 mi. E of Raleigh.

Sylva River (sĭl′vŭ), in Sverdlovsk and Molotov oblasts, Russian SFSR, rises in the central Urals 7 mi. E of Shalya, flows NW, past Sylva (village), SSW, past Shamary, and generally NNW, past Suksun, Kungur, Serga, and Sylva (town), to Chusovaya R. 10 mi. ENE of Molotov; 390 mi. long. Receives Iren R. (left).

Sylvester. 1 City (pop. 2,623), ⊙ Worth co., S central Ga., 20 mi. E of Albany, in farm and timber area; mfg. (lumber, naval stores, vegetable oil); peanut shelling. Inc. 1898. **2** Town (1940 pop. 405), Fisher co., NW central Texas, 20 mi. NNE of Sweetwater; shipping, trading point in agr. and cattle-ranching area.

Sylvia, city (pop. 496), Reno co., S central Kansas, on North Fork Ninnescah R. and 27 mi. WSW of Hutchinson, in wheat region; planing mill.

Sylvia, Mount, Chinese *Tzekao Shan* or *Tz'u-kao Shan* (both: tsŭ′gou′ shän′), Jap. *Tsugitaka-yama* (tsŏŏgē′täkä-yä′mä), second-highest peak (12,897 ft.) of Formosa, in N central range, 33 mi. SE of Sinchu. First climbed 1935 by Japanese.

Syme or **Simi** (sĭ′mē, Gr. sē′mē), Aegean island (□ 22; pop. 4,083) in the Dodecanese, Greece, NW of Rhodes, off Turkish Resadiye Peninsula; 36°35′N 27°50′E; 7 mi. long, 6 mi. wide, rises to 1,971 ft. Produces barley, olive oil, almonds, figs, tobacco, honey; sponge fisheries. Main town, Syme (pop. 3,756), is on N shore. Also spelled Symi.

Syme, Gulf of, or **Gulf of Symi,** Turkish *Hisarönü*, inlet (18 mi. long) of SW coast of Turkey, N of Rhodes; Syme isl. at its mouth.

Symerton (sĭ′mûrtûn), village (pop. 119), Will co., NE Ill., 14 mi. S of Joliet, in agr. and bituminous-coal area.

Symvolon or **Simvolon** (both: sĭm′vôlôn), mountain ridge (2,274 ft.) in Macedonia, Greece, 17 mi. WSW of Kavella, near Aegean Sea.

Syndicate, town (1939 pop. 6,365) in Aroroy municipality, Masbate isl., Philippines, 16 mi. WNW of Masbate town, in gold-mining area; agr. center (rice, coconuts).

Syntul (sĭntōōl′), town (1933 pop. estimate 2,500), N Ryazan oblast, Russian SFSR, 6 mi. NW of Kasimov; iron foundry. Iron, peat, clay deposits near by.

Synzhereya (sĭnzhĭryā′ŭ), Rum. *Sângerei* (sûnjĕrā′), village (1941 pop. 4,541), central Moldavian SSR, 14 mi. SE of Beltsy; corn, wheat, sugar beets.

Syodo-sima, Japan: see SHODO-SHIMA.

Syosset (sīō′sĭt), village (pop. 1,133), Nassau co., SE N.Y., on W Long Isl., 9 mi. NE of Mineola.

Syr, river, Luxembourg: see SYRE RIVER.

Syra, Greece: see SYROS.

Syracuse (sĭ′rûkūz), Ital. *Siracusa* (sērākōō′zä), anc. *Syracusae*, city (pop. 43,639), ⊙ Siracusa prov., SE Sicily, port on Ionian Sea, 33 mi. SE of Catania; 37°3′N 15°18′E; fisheries (oysters, sea mussels), cement and soap factories, saltworks; vegetable-oil refining, winemaking. Old town is on small isl. of Ortygia, connected by a bridge with the near-by mainland where the modern dists. are laid out. Its bay, Porto Grande, is one of the best natural harbors of Italy. Archbishopric. On Ortygia are the cathedral, built on remains of a Greek temple; the notable archaeological mus; anc. fountain of Arethusa; ruins of Temple of Apollo; and a castle erected by Emperor Frederick II. Among the remains on the mainland are the celebrated Greek theater (5th cent. B.C.), still used for classical performances; a Roman amphitheater, the castle of Euryelus (a Greek fortress); and extensive catacombs. Founded by Greek colonists in 743 B.C., grew rapidly and soon established colonies of its own. Taken (485 B.C.) by Gelon, who defeated (480) the Carthaginians at Himera, and made it leader of the Greek cities of Sicily. Under his successor, Hiero I, city became a great cultural center; Pindar and Aeschylus lived at the court. Syracuse later ruled all E Sicily, successfully resisted an Athenian siege (415–413), and reached peak of its power under the long rule (begun 406) of Dionysius the Elder. During Second Punic War, occupied by Romans under Marcellus after a siege (214–212), which brought death to Archimedes who directed the city's defense. Taken by Saracens (A.D. 878) and Normans (1085). Heavily bombed (1943) in Second World War.

Syracuse. 1 (sĭ′rûkūz, –kūs) Town (pop. 1,453), Kosciusko co., N Ind., on Wawasee L., 32 mi. SE of South Bend, in agr. area; resort; makes cedar chests. **2** (sĭ′rûkūz, –kūs) City (pop. 2,075), ⊙ Hamilton co., SW Kansas, on Arkansas R. and 45 mi. W of Garden City; shipping point for farm produce in livestock, poultry, and grain area. Inc. 1887. **3** (sĭ′rûkūz, –kūs) Town (pop. 221), Morgan co., central Mo., near Lamine R., 19 mi. E of Sedalia. **4** (sŭ′rûkūz) Village (pop. 1,097), Otoe co., SE Nebr., 30 mi. ESE of Lincoln and on Little Nemaha R.; flour, livestock, poultry produce, grain. **5** (sĭ′rûkūs, sē′–) City (pop. 220,583), ⊙ Onondaga co., central N.Y., at S end of Onondaga L., on the Barge Canal and 75 mi. ESE of Rochester; railroad center; port of entry. Mfg.: typewriters, farm machinery; metal, paper, food, wood, and soap products; steel, chemicals, wax candles, air-conditioning equipment, chinaware, clothing, furniture, automobiles, optical goods. Settled

1805; inc. as village in 1825, as city absorbing adjoining Salina village in 1847. Saltmaking, city's chief early industry, declined after Civil War; but industrial development came as result of location on Erie Canal (opened here in 1819) and on railroads. Seat of Univ. of Syracuse, with the state col. of forestry; Le Moyne Col.; a state school for mental defectives, and a state psychopathic hosp. Has Mus. of Fine Arts, with ceramic exhibits, and the Mills Rose Garden. Near by are the Onondaga Indian Reservation and state parks. Annual state fair held here since 1841. **6** (sĭ'rŭkŭs) Village (pop. 700), Meigs co., SE Ohio, 3 mi. SE of Pomeroy, and on Ohio R., in coal-mining and livestock area. **7** (sĭ'rŭkŭz, -kŭs) Town (pop. 837), Davis co., N Utah, 10 mi. SW of Ogden and on Great Salt L.; alt. 4,241 ft.; agr.

Syrallum, Turkey: see CORLU.

Syr-Darinski or **Syr-Dar'inskiy** (sĭr-dŭrēn'skē), town (1948 pop. over 2,000), W Tashkent oblast, Uzbek SSR, 45 mi. SW of Tashkent; cotton ginning. Until 1947, Syr-Novorossiysk.

Syr-Darya or **Syr-Dar'ya** (-dŭryä'), former oblast of Rus. Turkestan, including most of valley of the Syr Darya SE of Aral Sea; ⊙ was Tashkent. Became a govt. in 1917; passed (1921) to Turkestan Autonomous SSR, and in 1924 largely to Kazakh SSR. Abolished 1928.

Syr-Darya or **Syr-Dar'ya** (-dŭryä'), village (1939 pop. over 500), W Tashkent oblast, Uzbek SSR, on Trans-Caspian RR and 45 mi. WSW of Tashkent; food processing.

Syr Darya or **Syr Dar'ya** (sĭr där'yä, Rus. sĭr dŭryä'), anc. *Jaxartes or Yaxartes* (jăksär'tēz), Persian *Sihun*, one of main rivers of Central Asia; 1,327 mi. long. Formed by junction of NARYN RIVER and the KARA DARYA in Fergana Valley, Uzbek SSR; flows generally W past Leninabad in Tadzhik SSR, and N, re-entering Uzbek SSR at Begovat (site of Farkhad hydroelectric plant), through irrigated cotton area, into Kazakh SSR below Chinaz, past Chardara, forming E and N limits of the desert Kyzyl-Kum bet. Kzyl-Orda and Kazalinsk, to Aral Sea. Nonnavigable because of its shallowness. Trans-Caspian RR parallels lower course. Receives Angren, Chirchik, and Arys (right) rivers. Important for irrigation.

Syre River or **Syr River** (both: zēr), SE Luxembourg, rises 6 mi. ESE of Luxembourg city, flows 20 mi. NE, past Roodt-sur-Syr, Wecker, and Manternach, to Moselle R. at Mertert.

Syria (sĭ'rēŭ), Arabic *Esh Sham, El Sham*, or *Al-Sham* (all: ĕshäm'), also *Es Suriya, El Suriya*, or *Al-Suriyah* (all: ĕsōōrē'yŭ), republic (□ 66,063; 1946 pop. 3,006,028), SW Asia, on the Mediterranean, bordering N on Turkey, E on Iraq, S on Jordan, SW on Lebanon; ⊙ DAMASCUS. Most of Syria is covered by the Syrian Desert (central and SE), but the most heavily populated regions (all in the W) have varied terrain. In NW are mts. and valleys, in W are the ANTI-LEBANON mts. (on Lebanon line), rising to 9,232 ft. in Mt. Hermon, and in SW is the JEBEL ED DRUZ (5,900 ft.). W of the Jebel ed Druz stretches the fertile HAURAN plain toward the Sea of Galilee. N of the Hauran is the fertile oasis of Damascus, and further N the Orontes irrigates the regions near the cities of Homs and Hama. In the N and E the Euphrates cuts a fertile path across the desert. The climate varies from the generally mild Mediterranean type on the coast to the prevailing desert conditions of the SE, where there are fairly cold winters and very hot summers. Although rainfall is adequate in the mtn. areas in the W, the annual precipitation in most parts is extremely small. Syria is primarily a pastoral and agr. country. Large numbers of sheep, goats, cattle, and camels are raised, while the main crops are wheat, barley, millet, corn, figs, olives, apricots, and vegetables. Cotton is becoming an important cash crop, and in the NW (notably near Latakia) tobacco is grown extensively. Manufactures are on a small scale—chiefly cotton and silk textiles, leather goods, cement, and olive oil—and are mostly confined to the cities of Aleppo and Damascus. Other than bitumen and salt, there are few mineral resources, although oil drilling has been undertaken recently on an exploratory basis. Railroads link the major cities (Aleppo, Hama, Homs, and Damascus), but because Syria has no deep-water harbor on the Mediterranean, the bulk of Syrian exports are shipped from the Lebanese ports of Beirut and Tripoli. The pop. is largely of Arab origin, and Arabic is the chief language. About ¾ of the people are Moslems (predominantly Sunnites), while the rest are Syrian Christians (Catholics and Orthodox) and Jews. The Druses, of a separatist Moslem sect, dwell in the S, and the Syrian Desert is inhabited by several nomadic Bedouin tribes. Literacy is on a low level. Historically, the name Syria has comprised those lands of the Levant, or eastern littoral of the Mediterranean, which correspond to modern Syria and Lebanon, most of Israel and Jordan, and parts of N Arabia. Three geographic factors have played a major part in determining the history of Syria—its location on trade and military routes bet. the Mediterranean and Mesopotamia; its varied topography, which has made political unity difficult; and the encroaching desert, from which many of its peoples and cultural movements have come. From the dawn of history Syria was an object of conquest; it has through most of its long history been held by foreign powers. From the 19th to 13th cent. B. C. the area probably was part of the empire of the Hittites, although it fell under Egyptian rule for many years during that time. The 1st great indigenous culture was the Phoenician civilization (mostly in present Lebanon), which flourished after 1250 B.C. in a group of trading cities along the coast; later, in Palestine, appeared the Hebrew kingdoms. Syria was invaded and ruled by Assyrians, Babylonians, Egyptians, Persians, Alexander the Great (332–331 B.C.), and the Seleucidae. The Seleucidae founded colonies and strove successfully to introduce Hellenistic civilization, but when invasions began again with the Armenians under Tigranes and then the Parthians —both in the 1st cent. B.C.—the Hellenistic sheen was soon dulled. The Romans under Pompey conquered the region by 63 B.C. The old pagan gods of Syria were exported to Rome. More significant for the future, Christianity was born in Palestine and soon exerted some influence over all Syria; St. Paul was converted on the road to Damascus. In central Syria PALMYRA was allowed to grow to considerable power as an autonomous state after the 1st cent. A.D. but was cut down when it threatened the power of Rome. After the division of the Roman Empire into the Western Empire and the Eastern, Syria was under Byzantine rule, but control grew somewhat lax long before the Arabs appeared (633–36). Syria was largely converted to Islam. Damascus became the usual capital of the OMAYYAD caliph (661–750) and had a period of great splendor. Now the bonds bet. Moslem Syria and the predominantly Christian south (the later Lebanon) began to sever. The Christian hosts of the Crusades came into Syria at end of 11th cent. Already the Seljuk Turks had conquered most of the land, and the Christians warred against them, as well as against the conquering Saladin, who was dominant by end of 12th cent. His rule was followed by that of the Mamelukes, and Syria was visited again with furious invasions—this time by the Mongols—before the Ottoman Empire established its control by 1516. The fierce Druses grew very strong in their mtn. fastnesses and threatened the Christian Maronites. The adventure of Napoleon I in Egypt took the French into Syria in 1799, but the occupation was ephemeral. In the early 19th cent. Ibrahim Pasha of Egypt seized Syria from the Turks (1832–33) and held power there, reinforced by new campaigns in 1838–39, but the Egyptians were forced to withdraw under pressure from the European powers. The intermittent massacres of the Christians took place principally in present Lebanon, but all Syria was thrown into an uproar. Arab nationalism also began to take shape. In the First World War, the British encouraged nationalist ambitions in the warfare against the Turks. In the peace settlement France was given a mandate (1920) over the Levant States (roughly present Syria and Lebanon). The region was divided into dists., but after serious disturbances in 1925, resulting in a rebellion by the Druses and a French siege and bombardment of Damascus, the dists. of Aleppo and Damascus (roughly present Syria) were combined in 1925 to form a single state of Syria, and Lebanon was made a separate state in 1926. Latakia and the Jebel ed Druz were made separate territories. Nationalist agitation for independence continued and grew more bitter. Anti-French feeling ran particularly high after the troubles that resulted in the cession of the sanjak of Alexandretta (see ALEXANDRETTA, SANJAK OF) to Turkey, completed in 1939. In that year the French suspended the constitution, and in the Second World War they garrisoned Syria with a large number of troops, most of whom, after the fall of French in June, 1940, declared loyalty to the Vichy govt., while others left to join Free French forces. Relations with Great Britain deteriorated, and when it was discovered that Syrian airfields had been used by German planes en route to Iraq, British and Free French forces invaded and occupied Syria in June, 1941. In accordance with previous promises, the French proclaimed the creation of an independent Syrian republic in Sept., 1941, and an independent Lebanese republic in Nov., 1941. In Jan., 1942, the territories of Latakia and Jebel ed Druz were incorporated into the new Syrian state, and on Jan. 1, 1944, complete independence was achieved. However, not until April, 1946, were all foreign troops finally withdrawn from the country. Syria became a member of the U.N. A member of the Arab League, the republic joined the other Arab states in the unsuccessful war (1948) against Israel; an armistice was signed in July, 1949. Plans for a federation of the Arab states in a Greater Syria are supported by many Syrians, but mutual suspicions among the Arab rulers have so far thwarted any steps in this direction. For further information, see the articles on the cities, towns, anc. regions, and the 9 provs.: ALEPPO, DAMASCUS, EUPHRATES, HAMA, HAURAN, HOMS, JEBEL ED DRUZ, JEZIRE, LATAKIA.

Syriam (sĭ'rēăm), town (pop. 15,070), Hanthawaddy dist., Lower Burma, on E bank of Rangoon R., at mouth of Pegu R., opposite (SE of) Rangoon. Petroleum-refining center for Yenangyaung oil field. Has ruins of 18th-cent. R.C. church. Noted Kyaikkauk Pagoda, a landmark, is 3 mi. SSE. Founded 6th cent. B.C., it became the chief port of Burma and the earliest European settlement, with Portuguese post established c.1600, Dutch and Br. stations later in 17th cent., and a Fr. settlement in 18th cent. The town was sacked by the Mons in 1743 and by the Burmese under Alaungpaya in 1756. Following rise of Rangoon, it remained nearly deserted until industrialization in 1870s.

Syrian Desert, Arabic *Badiet esh Sham*, arid wasteland, SW Asia, bet. the cultivated lands along the E Mediterranean coast and the fertile Euphrates river valley. Extends N from the Arabian Desert and comprises central and SE Syria, W Iraq, E Jordan, and N Saudi Arabia. The famous Arabian horses are raised along the edges. In N it is crossed by oil pipe lines from Kirkuk (Iraq) to Haifa and Tripoli and from Abqaiq (Saudi Arabia) to Saida (Sidon). Other lines are in construction. There is a motor route from Damascus to Baghdad. Several nomadic tribes live in the desert, whose S central section is commonly known as Hamad or Hammad.

Syrian Gates, Turkey: see BELEN.

Syringa (sĭrĭng'gŭ), village, Bulawayo prov., SW Southern Rhodesia, in Matabeleland, on railroad and 15 mi. E of Plumtree; alt. 4,825 ft. Corn, cattle, sheep, goats.

Syrmia, region, Yugoslavia: see SREM.

Syrnai or **Sirnai** (both: sĕr'nä), Ital. *Sirina*, Aegean island (□ 3.1; pop. 6) in the Dodecanese, Greece, SE of Astypalaia; 36°21'N 26°41'E.

Syros or **Siros** (sĭ'rŏs, Gr. sē'rŏs), Lat. *Syrus* (sī'rŭs), Aegean island (□ 33; pop. 25,918) of the Cyclades, Greece, SW of Tenos; 37°25'N 24°55'E; 10 mi. long, 6 mi. wide; rises to 1,415 ft. The commercial center of the Cyclades; its capital and chief port is HERMOUPOLIS (also known as Syros). Rocky and mountainous, it produces some grain, vegetables, figs, olives, and wine. Under Turkish rule (1537–1832). Also called Syra.

Syr River, Luxembourg: see SYRE RIVER.

Syrski or **Syrskiy** (sĭr'skē), town (1939 pop. 6,900), NW Voronezh oblast, Russian SFSR, 5 mi. SW of Lipetsk; iron mining. Village of Syrskaya (1926 pop. 2,571) is on Voronezh R. and 3 mi. SSW of Lipetsk.

Syrtis Minor, Tunisia: see GABÈS, GULF OF.

Syrus, Greece: see SYROS.

Syrve Peninsula, Estonia: see SORVE PENINSULA.

Sysert or **Sysert'** (sĭsyĕrt'yŭ), city (1939 pop. 12,000), S Sverdlovsk oblast, Russian SFSR, on left tributary of Iset R. and 25 mi. SSE of Sverdlovsk; mfg. of polygraphic equipment, metal- and woodworking. Founded 1732; former site (until 1932) of metallurgical works called Sysertski Zavod. Became city in 1946.

Sysladobsis Lake (sĭs"lŭdŏb'sĭs), E Maine, 43 mi. NW of Machias; 9 mi. long. Joined to Pocumpus L. on E, Upper Sysladobsis L. on N.

Sysmä (sŭs'mă), village (commune pop. 9,884), Mikkeli co., S Finland, on E shore of L. Päijänne, 35 mi. N of Lahti; trade center of lumbering and agr. (grain, potatoes, cattle; dairying) region.

Sysola River (sĭsŏ'lŭ), N European Russian SFSR, rises in the Northern Uvals NW of Rudnichny (Kirov oblast), flows NW, past Kazhim, and N, past Nyuvchim, to Vychegda R. at Syktyvkar; c.200 mi. long. Iron and phosphorite found along banks. Navigable below Kazhim; timber floating.

Sysonby, England: see MELTON MOWBRAY.

Syston (sī'stŭn), town and parish (pop. 4,322), central Leicester, England, 5 mi. NE of Leicester; leather and shoe mfg., textile printing, paper milling. Has 16th-cent church.

Syuginski Zavod, Russian SFSR: see MOZHGA.

Syumsi (syōōmsē'), village (1948 pop. over 2,000) W Udmurt Autonomous SSR, Russian SFSR, near Kilmez R., 65 mi. WNW of Izhevsk; wood cracking, flax processing, lumbering.

Syunsen, Korea: see CHUNCHON.

Syuotu, Korea: see CHUURONJANG.

Syutlika River, Bulgaria: see SAZLIKA RIVER.

Syvulya (sĭvōō'lyŭ), Pol. *Sywula*, highest peak (6,023 ft.) in Gorgany Mts. of the Carpathians, SW Ukrainian SSR, 23 mi. W of Delyatin. Bystritsa Solotvinskaya R. rises at N foot.

Syzran or **Syzran'** (sĭzrän'yŭ, sĭz'rŭnyŭ), city (1939 pop. 77,679; 1946 pop. estimate 150,000), Kuibyshev oblast, Russian SFSR, 70 mi. W of Kuibyshev, extending c.20 mi. along right bank of the Volga. Major industrial and transportation (transshipment port; 3 rail lines) center; petroleum extracting and refining; mining and quarrying (oil shale, asphalt, phosphorite, potassium nitrate, slate, refractory clay, quartz sand, limestone); mfg. of locomotives, prefabricated houses, building materials, clothing, shoes; agr. processing and preserving (hides, meat, grain, hops, fruit, vegetables), sawmilling, wood-, metal-, and glassworking. Teachers col. Has old cathedral, monastery, and churches. City center is on a bend of the Volga, at mouth of Syzran R., near recently constructed oil wells. During Second World War, Syzran expanded c.10 mi. S, absorbing Kashpirovka (1939 pop. over 2,000; oil-shale mines). Eastward expansion (c.10 mi.) resulted in merger with grain-transshipping port of Batraki (1939 pop. over 10,000; asphalt and phosphorite mines). Included within E city limits is rail bridge (c.1 mi. long) across the Volga. Founded 1684 as Rus. military settlement; developed as grain-trading center in 19th cent. Major industrialization and expansion began after development of oil industry in 1936.

Syzran River or **Syzran' River,** SE central European Russian SFSR, rises 4 mi. E of Imeni V. I. Lenina (Ulyanovsk oblast), flows 70 mi. SSE and E, past Novo-Spasskoye, to Volga R. at Syzran city center.

Szabadbattyan (sŏ'bŏdbŏt-tyän), Hung. *Szabadbattyán,* town (pop. 1,543), Fejer co., W central Hungary, on Sarviz R. and 5 mi. S of Szekesfehervar; rail center.

Szabadka, Yugoslavia: see SUBOTICA.

Szabadszallas (sŏ'bŏtsäl-läsh), Hung. *Szabadszállás,* town (pop. 8,752), Pest-Pilis-Solt-Kiskun co., 22 mi. W of Kecskemet; flour mills; grain, tobacco, cattle, hogs.

Szabolcs (sŏ'bôlch), county (□ 1,718; pop. 422,420), NE Hungary; ⊙ Nyiregyhaza. Slightly hilly region including part of the Alföld; drained by the Tisza. Largest tobacco-producing co. of Hungary; rye, potatoes, wheat also grown; livestock (cattle, hogs, sheep); garden products (honey, apples, pears). Main industrial center is Nyiregyhaza (tobacco warehouses, flour mills, brickworks); other industry at Kisvarda (petroleum refinery), Nyirbator (distilleries), Ujfeherto, Büdszentmihaly.

Szack, Ukrainian SSR: see SHATSK, Volyn oblast.

Szacul, Rumania: see SACUL.

Szacvolkany, Rumania: see VULCAN.

Szadek (shä'dĕk), Rus. *Shadek* (shä'dyĭk), town (pop. 2,191), Lodz prov., central Poland, 21 mi. W of Lodz; flour milling, tanning.

Szajol (sŏ'yôl), town (pop. 2,955), Jasz-Nagykun-Szolnok co., E central Hungary, 6 mi. E of Szolnok; agr. Rail junction at near-by Pusztatenyö.

Szakcs (sŏkch), town (pop. 3,062), Tolna co., W central Hungary, 19 mi. NE of Kaposvar; wheat, barley, honey.

Szakolca, Czechoslovakia: see SKALICA.

Szalard, Rumania: see SALARD.

Szamocin (shämô'chēn), Ger. *Samotschin* (zämô'chĭn), town (1946 pop. 2,463), Poznan prov., W Poland, 9 mi. ENE of Chodziez; flour milling.

Szamos River, Rumania and Hungary: see SOMES RIVER.

Szamosszeg (sŏ'môsh-sĕg), town (pop. 3,140), Szatmar-Bereg co., NE Hungary, on Szamos R. and 30 mi. ENE of Nyiregyhaza; brickworks; grain, cattle.

Szamosujvar, Rumania: see GHERLA.

Szamotuly (shämôtōō'wĭ), Pol. *Szamotuły,* Ger. *Samter* (zäm'tůr), town (1946 pop. 8,780), Poznan prov., W Poland, 20 mi. NW of Poznan; rail junction; brick- and gypsum works; mfg. of machines, furniture, liqueur; flour and beet-sugar milling, distilling, tanning.

Szaraz River (sä'räs), Hung. *Száraz,* S Hungary and NE Rumania, intermittent arm of Mures R., branches off near Arad (Rumania), flows c.55 mi. W, past Battonya and Földeak, and rejoins the Mures E of Szeged.

Szarazvam, Austria: see MÜLLENDORF.

Szarkowszczyzna, Belorussian SSR: see SHARKOVSHCHINA.

Szarvas (sŏr'vŏsh), town (pop. 25,023), Bekes co., SE Hungary, 10 mi. S of Mezötur, near Körös R.; agr. center; flour mills, lumberyards, tanneries. Pop., mostly Slavs, engaged in agr., stock raising.

Szarvkö, Austria: see HORNSTEIN.

Szaszkabanya, Rumania: see SASCA-MONTANA.

Szaszkezd, Rumania: see SASCHIZ.

Szaszlekence, Rumania: see LECHINTA.

Szaszregen, Rumania: see REGHIN.

Szaszsebes, Rumania: see SEBES.

Szaszvaros, Rumania: see ORASTIE.

Szatmar-Bereg (sŏt'mär-bĕ'rĕg), Hung. *Szatmár-Bereg,* county (□ 829; pop. 161,836), NE Hungary; ⊙ Mateszalka. Flat region drained by the Tisza, Szamos, and Kraszna rivers. Agr. (grain, tobacco, potatoes); cattle, hogs; fruitgrowing (plums, apples, pears). Peat is cut in Ecsed marshes (S).

Szatmarnemeti, Rumania: see SATU-MARE, city.

Szava River, Yugoslavia: see SAVA RIVER.

Szczakowa (shchäkô'vä), town (pop. 4,285), Krakow prov., S Poland on Biala Przemsza R. and 12 mi. E of Katowice; rail junction; gasworks, cement plant, glassworks. Until First World War, Austro-Hungarian frontier station on border of Rus. Poland.

Szczara River, Belorussian SSR: see SHCHARA RIVER.

Szczawno Zdroj (shchäv'nô zdrōō'ē), Pol. *Szczawno Zdrój,* Ger. *Bad Salzbrunn* (bät" zälts'brōōn), town (1939 pop. 9,799; 1946 pop. 10,339) in Lower Silesia, after 1945 in Wroclaw prov., SW Poland, in N foothills of the Sudetes, 4 mi. N of Waldenburg (Walbrzych); health resort. Mineral springs, known since 16th cent. Chartered after 1945 and briefly called Solice Zdroj, Pol. *Solice Zdrój.* Gerhart Hauptmann b. here.

Szczebrzeszyn (shchĕb-zhĕ'shĭn), Rus. *Shchebreshin* (shchĕbrĕ'shĭn), town (pop. 5,122), Lublin prov., SE Poland, on Wieprz R., and 12 mi. W of Zamosc; mfg. (machinery, piping, wooden articles, cereals, flour, beer).

Szczecin (shchĕ'tsēn), province [Pol. *województwo*] (□ 4,869; pop. 307,568), NW Poland; ⊙ STETTIN (Szczecin). Borders W on Germany, N on the Baltic. Low level surface, dotted with lakes; drained by the Oder estuary and by Ina (Ihna) and Rega rivers. Coast line deeply indented by Stettin Lagoon. Prov. includes Wolin (Wollin) isl. and E tip of Usedom (Uznam) isl. Fishing is important. Principal crops are rye, potatoes, oats, barley, wheat; livestock. Industries (metallurgy, shipbuilding; textile, paper, and pulp milling; food processing, sugar refining, chemicals mfg.) are concentrated in Stettin; other important towns are Swinemünde (Swinoujscie; fishing center and seaside resort); and Gryfice (Greifenberg). New port of Odra is terminus of train ferry to Sweden. Until 1945, part of Ger. Pomerania prov.; subsequently briefly called Pomorze Zachodnie. After 1945, Ger. pop. was expelled and replaced by Poles. In 1950, E part of prov. was detached to form Koszalin prov.

Szczecin, city, Poland: see STETTIN.

Szczecinek (shchĕtsē'nĕk), Ger. *Neustettin* (noi"-shtĕtēn'), town (1939 pop. 19,942; 1946 pop. 12,413) in Pomerania, after 1945 in Koszalin prov., NW Poland, just SW of Wielim L., 55 mi. S of Stolp (Slupsk); food processing, dairying, brewing, sawmilling. Chartered 1310. Until 1938, in former Prussian prov. of Grenzmark Posen–Westpreussen. In Second World War, c.50% destroyed.

Szczecinski, Zalew, Poland and Germany: see STETTIN LAGOON.

Szczekociny (shchĕkôtsē'nĭ), Rus. *Shchekotsiny* (shchĕkůtsē'nyĭ), town (pop. 3,794), Kielce prov., S central Poland, on Pilica R. and 40 mi. WSW of Kielce; tanning, flour milling, sawmilling.

Szczerzec, Ukrainian SSR: see SHCHIRETS.

Szczuczyn or **Szczuczyn Bialostocki** (shchōō'chĭn byälôstôts'kē), Rus. *Shchuchin* (shchōō'chĭn), town (pop. 2,479), Bialystok prov., NE Poland, 45 mi. NW of Bialystok; mfg. of tiles, caps; tanning, flour milling, brewing, dairying.

Szczuczyn, Belorussian SSR: see SHCHUCHIN.

Szczytno (shchĭt'nô), Ger. *Ortelsburg* (ôr'tůlsbōōrk), town (1939 pop. 14,234; 1946 pop. 3,645) in East Prussia, after 1945 in Olsztyn prov., NE Poland, in Masurian Lakes region, 25 mi. ESE of Allenstein (Olsztyn); sawmilling, limestone quarrying, dairying, brewing. Teutonic Knights built castle here, 1266; settlement founded in mid-16th cent.; chartered 1723. In First World War, partly burned (Aug., 1914) by Russians during battle of Tannenberg. In Second World War, c.45% destroyed.

Szecheng, China: see LINGYÜN.

Szechow. 1 Town, Anhwei prov., China: see SZEHSIEN. **2** Town, Kweichow prov., China: see TSENKUNG.

Szechwan or **Szu-ch'uan** (sĕ'chwän, sŭ'chwän') [Chinese,=four rivers], province (□ 120,000; pop. 45,000,000) of SW China; ⊙ Chengtu. Entirely surrounded by mts., Szechwan is bounded N by Tsinghai, Kansu, and Shensi along outliers of the Kunlun system (Min Shan, Tapa Shan), W by Sikang along the Tahsüeh Mts. (Szechwan Alps), S by Yunnan and Kweichow, and E by Hunan and Hupeh. The prov. is traversed SW–NE by Yangtze R., which flows along the S edge of the Red Basin, the bed of a Tertiary lake. This basin, which constitutes the greater part of the prov., is an area of brick-red sandstone formations deeply dissected by Min, To, and Kialing rivers (left tributaries of the Yangtze). The only level area is the Chengtu plain, the most fertile section of the Red Basin, irrigated by canalized arms of Min R. Surrounding barrier mts. protect the interior of the prov. from temp. extremes. Average yearly rainfall is 40 inches. Because of the mild climate, Szechwan has exceptionally diversified agr., carried on largely on the terraced hillsides where 2–3 crops a year are raised. The leading summer crops are rice, corn, sugar cane, tobacco, beans, and potatoes; wheat and rapeseed, beans and peas are grown during the winter. Among the leading export products are skins and wool from peripheral mts., and, from the Red Basin, tung oil, silk, ramie, tea, tobacco, and medicinal plants (rhubarb, *tihwang*). The prov. is underlaid by coal-bearing strata and limestone, occasionally exposed by erosion. Coal is of poor average quality. The most important mineral resource is salt, obtained from brine wells. At Tzekung (Tzeliutsing), the traditional center of the salt industry, petroleum and natural-gas extraction has developed. Gold is mined in NW mts. and iron near Kikiang. Pop., concentrated in the Red Basin, where the density is 1,000 per sq. mi., is entirely Chinese. Aborigines (Hsi-fan) are found only in NW mts. Szechwan is served primarily by the Yangtze and its left tributaries (junk navigation), with the river acting as chief eastward trade outlet. The leading commercial centers are Chungking city, Chengtu, Wanhsien (tung oil), and Loshan (silk, Chinese wax). A railroad was under construction (1950) bet. Chungking and Chengtu. Other rail lines are projected to link the prov. with Tienshui (Kansu), Kangting (Sikang), and Kunming (Yunnan). The name Szechwan, in existence since the Mongol Yüan dynasty (1280–1368), refers to Min, To, and Kialing rivers (affluents of the Yangtze), and to a 4th river which, according to varying accounts, is the Yangtze proper, the Yalung (in Sikang), or the Fow (affluent of the Kialing). Depopulated in 17th-cent. rebellion and ensuing reprisals, Szechwan was later settled from other parts of China. In modern years its territory was considerably reduced in W to form the new prov. of Sikang. The traditional name of Szechwan prov. is Shu.

Szechwan Alps, China: see TAHSÜEH MOUNTAINS.

Szecseny (sā'chānyů), Hung. *Szécsény,* town (pop. 3,912), Nograd-Hont co., N Hungary, 10 mi. E of Balassagyarmat; brickworks, flour mills. Dates back to 15th cent.; has 17th-cent. castle.

Szefang or **Ssu-fang** (both: sŭ'fäng'), N industrial suburb of Tsingtao, E Shantung prov., China, on Tsingtao-Tsinan RR; cotton mills.

Szeged (sĕ'gĕd), city (1941 pop. 136,752), in, but independent of, Csongrad co., S Hungary, at junction of Tisza (here bridged) and Maros rivers, 50 mi. SSE of Kecskemet; rail and shipping center, metropolis of the Alföld. Sawmills, flour mills, mfg. (textiles, tobacco, soap, fertilizer, matches, brooms, brushes, salami), brickworks, breweries, paprika mills. Agr. (grain, paprika), dairy farming, fishing in area. Agr. experiment station (flax, hemp). City, partly destroyed by 1879 flood of Tisza R., was rebuilt in modern style; was Hungary's 2d largest city until the loss (1950) of its extensive rural suburban area reduced pop. to less than 100,000. Library holds 150,000 vols. and ethnographic collection. Has univ., Franciscan monastery, numerous churches. Landmark is 13th-cent. Romanesque tower. Horthy govt. formed here, 1919. Formerly called Szegedin.

Szeghalom (sĕg'hŏlŏm), town (pop. 10,712), Bekes co., SE Hungary, on Berettyo R. and 26 mi. E of Mezötur; flour mills; grain, tobacco, hogs, sheep.

Szegvar (sĕg'vär), Hung. *Szegvár,* town (pop. 7,961), Csongrad co., S Hungary, on Kurca arm of Tisza R. and 5 mi. S of Szentes; agr., fishing.

Szehai or **Ssu-hai** (both: sŭ'hī'), town, ⊙ Szehai co., E Chahar prov., China, 50 mi. N of Peking, at Great Wall; cattle raising; ramie, beans, corn. Until 1950 called Szehaipao.

Szehsien or **Ssu-hsien** (both: sŭ'shyĕn'). **1** Town, ⊙ Szehsien co. (pop. 619,613), N Anhwei prov., China, 50 mi. NE of Pengpu, near Kiangsu line; rice, wheat, beans, kaoliang, corn. Until 1912 called Szechow. **2** Town, Kweichow prov., China: see TSENKUNG.

Szekelyhid, Rumania: see SACUENI.

Szekelyudvarhely, Rumania: see ODORHEI.

Szekereny, Yugoslavia: see SEFKERIN.

Szekesfehervar (sā'kĕsh-fĕhärvär), Hung. *Székesfehérvár,* Ger. *Stuhlweissenburg* (shtōōl'wī"sůnbōōrk), anc. *Alba Regia,* city (pop. 47,968), ⊙ but independent of Fejer co., W central Hungary, 35 mi. SW of Budapest, 16 mi. NE of L. Balaton; rail, trade, market center for wine, truck, tobacco area. Mfg. (textiles, shoes, soap, candles); distilleries, tanneries, brickworks; mineral springs. One of Hungary's oldest cities, dating back to Roman period; mus. contains Roman artifacts. R.C. bishopric; has 18th-cent. cathedral on site of one built in 11th cent., Carmelite seminary, Franciscan and Dominican monasteries. Hungarian kings crowned here, 1027–1527; was ⊙ Hungary until 14th cent., when Budapest became residence of rulers. Has large Ger. pop. Formerly also called Fehervar.

Szekszard (sĕk'särd), Hung. *Szekszárd,* city (pop. 14,683), ⊙ Tolna co., S Hungary, 80 mi. SSW of Budapest; market center; winery, alcohol distillery, brickworks. Noted for its red Schiller wine. Paprika, wheat, potatoes, peaches, poultry raised in area. Mus. has Stone and Bronze Age remains.

Szeleveny (sĕ'lĕvānyů), Hung. *Szelevény,* town (pop. 2,446), Jasz-Nagykun-Szolnok co., central Hungary, on Körös R. and 7 mi. NNE of Csongrad.

Szelimluk Cave, Hungary: see BANHIDA.

Szelistye, Rumania: see SALISTE.

Szelo or **Ssu-lo** (both: sŭ'lŭ'), town, ⊙ Szelo co. (pop. 52,255), SW Kwangsi prov., China, on road and 60 mi. SW of Nanning; grain, sugar cane, peanut oil.

Szemao, Ssu-mao, or **Szu-mao** (all: sŭ'mou'), town (pop. 1,672), ⊙ Szemao co. (pop. 11,302), S Yunnan prov., China, near Laos border, 20 mi. S of Ningerh; alt. 4,698 ft.; rice, millet, beans. Opened to foreign trade in 1897, it was a major trade center (tea, salt) for Shan country until construction (1910) of Kunming-Hanoi RR.

Szeming, China: see AMOY.

Szenan or **Ssu-nan** (both: sŭ'nän'), town (pop. 8,386), ⊙ Szenan co. (pop. 205,468), NE Kweichow prov., China, on Wu R. (Kien R.; head of navigation) and 140 mi. NE of Kweiyang; cotton-textile and match mfg., tung-oil processing; rice, wheat, timber. Arsenic, sulphur deposits near by.

Szendrö (sĕn'drŭ), Hung. *Szendrő,* town (pop. 3,314), Borsod-Gömör co., NE Hungary, on the Bodva and 21 mi. N of Miskolc. Ruins of 14th-cent. fortress here.

Szengen (sŭng′ĕn) or **Ssu-en** (both: sŭ′ŭn′), town, ⊙ Szengen co. (pop. 89,536), N Kwangsi prov., China, 70 mi. NW of Liuchow, near railroad; cotton textiles; rice, beans. Until 1913 the name Szengen was applied to a fu city, 15 mi. N of Wuming, now a village called Chanhsü.

Szenice, Czechoslovakia: see SENICA.

Szentagota, Rumania: see AGNITA.

Szentendre (sĕn′tĕndrĕ), city (pop. 9,641), Pest-Pilis-Solt-Kiskun co., N central Hungary, on the Danube and 11 mi. N of Budapest; river port; beach, summer resort. Mfg. (tools, cement, paper); lumberyards; vineyards; plums, apples, pears.

Szentendre Island, N central Hungary, in the Danube, just N of Budapest; 19 mi. long, 2 mi. wide. Sandy and dry in N, some fruit (grapes, apples) in SE.

Szentes (sĕn′tĕsh), city (pop. 34,394), ⊙ Csongrad co., S Hungary, on Kurca arm of Tisza R. and 16 mi. N of Hodmezövasarhely; rail, market center; textile mills, distilleries, brickworks, pottery, sawmills, flour mills. Agr. (wheat, corn), dairy farming, fishing in vicinity.

Szentetornya (sĕn′tĕtôrnyŏ), town (pop. 4,318), Bekes co., SE Hungary, 23 mi. WSW of Bekescsaba; flour mills; grain, tobacco, cattle.

Szentgal (sĕnd′gäl), Hung. *Szentgál,* town (pop. 4,579), Veszprem co., NW central Hungary, in Bakony Mts., 8 mi. W of Veszprem; wheat, potatoes, corn, hogs, sheep.

Szentgotthard (sĕnd′gôt-härd), Hung. *Szentgotthárd,* town (pop. 3,548), Vas co., W Hungary, on Raba R. and 25 mi. SW of Szombathely, on Austrian frontier; mfg. (silk, agr. implements, tobacco); sawmills, brickworks. Montecucculi defeated Turks here, 1664. English form of name, Saint Gotthard.

Szentistvan (sĕn′tĭsht-vän), Hung. *Szentistván,* town (pop. 4,071), Borsod-Gömör co., NE Hungary, 23 mi. SSW of Miskolc; grain, tobacco, hemp, cattle, hogs.

Szentlörinc (sĕntlû′rĭnts), Hung. *Szentlőrinc,* town (pop. 2,906), Baranya co., S Hungary, at SW foot of Mecsek Mts., 12 mi. W of Pecs; rail center.

Szentmiklos, Ukrainian SSR: see CHINYADEVO.

Szenttamas, Yugoslavia: see SRBOBRAN.

Szepes, region, Czechoslovakia and Poland: see SPIS.

Szepes, castle, Czechoslovakia: see SPISSKE PODHRADIE.

Szepesofalu, Czechoslovakia: see SPISSKA STARA VES.

Szepesvaralja, Czechoslovakia: see SPISSKE PODHRADIE.

Szepetnek (sĕ′pĕdnĕk), town (pop. 2,054), Zala co., W Hungary, 5 mi. WSW of Nagykanizsa; potatoes, corn, hogs.

Szeping, Szuping, or **Ssu-p'ing** (all: sŭ′pĭng′), until 1947 called **Szepingkai** (–gī′) or **Ssu-p'ing-chieh** (–jyĕ′), city (1947 pop. 75,705), NE Liaosi prov., Manchuria, 105 mi. NNE of Mukden; rail junction on South Manchuria RR, and one of the chief agr. distributing centers of central Manchuria; soybean processing, flour milling; cement plant. City developed after 1900 in connection with railroad construction, flourished under Manchukuo regime, and became independent municipality in 1947.

Szepopol, Poland: see SEPOPOL.

Szepsi, Czechoslovakia: see MOLDAVA NAD BODVOU.

Szepvis, Rumania: see FRUMOASA.

Szerdahely, Rumania: see MERCUREA.

Szered, Czechoslovakia: see SERED.

Szerem, region, Yugoslavia: see SREM.

Szerencs (sĕ′rĕnch), town (pop. 7,613), Zemplen co., NE Hungary, in the Hegyalja, 19 mi. E of Miskolc; rail center; sugar refineries, chocolate mfg., flour mills; tobacco, grapes, beans, grain. Has 17th-cent. castle.

Szerep (sĕ′rĕp), town (pop. 2,445), Bihar co., E Hungary, 12 mi. SE of Karcag; wheat, corn, cattle.

Szereszow, Belorussian SSR: see SHERESHEVO.

Szeshui or **Ssu-shui** (both: sŭ′shwā′). **1** Town, ⊙ Szeshui co. (pop. 71,199), NW Honan prov., China, on Lunghai RR, on Yellow R. (head of seasonal navigation) and 25 mi. WNW of Kaifeng; chalk processing, grain. **2** Town, ⊙ Szeshui co. (pop. 190,835), SW Shantung prov., China, 25 mi. ENE of Tzeyang; cotton weaving; wheat, peanuts.

Szewui (sä′wē), Mandarin *Ssu-hui* (sŭ′hwā′), town, ⊙ Szewui co. (pop. 154,999), W central Kwangtung prov., China, on the Sui and 15 mi. NW of Samshui; tobacco, oranges.

Szeyang or **Ssu-yang** (both: sŭ′yäng′), town (pop. 8,198), ⊙ Szeyang co. (pop. 176,981), N Kiangsu prov., China, 22 mi. WNW of Hwaiyin and on Grand Canal; wheat, beans, kaoliang, corn. Until 1914 called Taoyüan.

Sziget, Hungary: see SZIGETVAR.

Sziget, Rumania: see SIGHET.

Szigetköz, Hungary: see SCHÜTT.

Szigetszentmiklos (sĭ′gĕtsĕntmĭ″klōsh), Hung. *Szigetszentmiklós,* town (pop. 5,997), Pest-Pilis-Solt-Kiskun co., N central Hungary, on Csepel Isl. in the Danube and 10 mi. S of Budapest; river port; grain, potatoes, cattle, hogs.

Szigetvar (sĭ′gĕtvär), Hung. *Szigetvár,* town (pop. 6,270), Somogy co., SW Hungary, 21 mi. W of Pecs; rail junction; brick mfg. Scene in 1566 of heroic stand by Hungarians, led by Nicholas Zrinyi, under Turkish siege led by Suleiman the Magnificent, who died during the battle. Formerly Sziget.

Sziksosfürdö, Hungary: see SOLTVADKERT.

Szikszo (sĭk′sō), Hung. *Szikszó,* town (pop. 5,570), ⊙ Abauj co., NE Hungary, 9 mi. NNE of Miskolc; flour mills; wheat, grapes, apples, pears. Has 15th-cent. church.

Szilagycseh, Rumania: see CEHUL-SILVANIEI.

Szilagysomlyo, Rumania: see SIMLEUL-SILVANIEI.

Szilberek, Yugoslavia: see BRESTOVAC, Vojvodina.

Szilvasfürdö, Hungary: see MAD.

Sziner-Varalja, Rumania: see SEINI.

Szinna, Czechoslovakia: see SNINA.

Szirguni, Israel: see SERGUNIA.

Sziszek, Yugoslavia: see SISAK.

Szitabodza, Rumania: see SITA-BUZAULUI.

Szivac, Yugoslavia: see SIVAC.

Szklarska Poreba (shklär′skä pôrĕ′bä), Pol. *Szklarska Poręba,* Ger. *Schreiberhau* (shrī′bŭrhou), commune (1939 pop. 7,601; 1946 pop. 7,406) in Lower Silesia, after 1945 in Wroclaw prov., SW Poland, near Czechoslovak border, in the Riesengebirge, 9 mi. WSW of Hirschberg (Jelenia Gora); popular health and winter-sports resort. First mentioned 1366. Includes Szklarska Poreba-Huta (–hōō′tä), Ger. *Josephinenhütte* (yōzĕfē′nŭnhü″tŭ), 3 mi. WSW; glass-mfg. center.

Szlatina, Ukrainian SSR: see SOLOTVINO.

Szlichtyngowa (shlēkh-tĭng-ô′vä), Ger. *Schlichtingsheim* (shlĭkh′tĭngs-hīm), town (1939 pop. 1,038; 1946 pop. 531) in Lower Silesia, after 1945 in Zielona Gora prov., W Poland, 8 mi. ENE of Glogau (Glogow); agr. market (grain, vegetables, potatoes, livestock). Founded c.1650.

Szlovakia, Czechoslovakia: see SLOVAKIA.

Szob (sôb), town (pop. 2,163), Nograd-Hont co., N Hungary, on the Danube and 6 mi. E of Esztergom, on Czechoslovak frontier; limestone quarry.

Szobranc, Czechoslovakia: see SOBRANCE.

Szöd (sûd), Hung. *Sződ,* town (pop. 5,021), Pest-Pilis-Solt-Kiskun co., N central Hungary, 15 mi. NNE of Budapest; wheat, corn, livestock.

Szolnok (sôl′nôk), city (pop. 42,011), ⊙ Jasz-Nagykun-Szolnok co., E central Hungary, at junction of Zagyva and Tisza (here bridged) rivers, 70 mi. SW of Debrecen; rail center, river port, tobacco market. Has sawmills, flour mills, sugar refineries, distillery, soap-, candle-, and brickworks, shoe and paper mills. Large Franciscan convent.

Szolyva, Ukrainian SSR: see SVALYAVA.

Szombathely (sôm′bŏt-hĕĭ), Ger. *Steinamanger,* city (pop. 42,872), ⊙ but independent of Vas co., W Hungary, on Gyöngyös R. and 68 mi. SSE of Vienna; rail, industrial center. Mfg. (agr. implements, cotton, thread, alcohol, chemicals); sawmills, flour mills, brickworks. Truck farming (fruit, honey, spices) in vicinity. Town was a Roman settlement, *Savaria* or *Sabaria,* founded A.D. 48; became seat of R.C. bishop in 17th cent. Bishop's palace (1781).

Szond, Yugoslavia: see SONTA.

Szöny (sû′nyŭ), Hung. *Szőny,* anc. *Brigetio,* town (pop. 4,066), Komarom-Esztergom co., N Hungary, on the Danube and 24 mi. ENE of Györ; petroleum refining, starch mfg.

Szopienice (shôpyĕnē′tsĕ), Ger. *Schoppinitz* (shô′pĭnĭts), town (pop. 20,854), Katowice prov., S Poland, just E of Katowice; rail junction; coal mining; smelting. Inc. after 1946.

Szöreg (sû′rĕg), Hung. *Szőreg,* town (pop. 4,660), Csanad co., S Hungary, 3 mi. ESE of Szeged; grain, cattle, hogs.

Szovata, Rumania: see SOVATA.

Szprotawa (shprôtä′vä), Ger. *Sprottau* (shprô′tou), town (1939 pop. 12,578; 1946 pop. 2,672) in Lower Silesia, after 1945 in Zielona Gora prov., W Poland, on Bobrawa R. and 25 mi. S of Grünberg (Zielona Gora); rail junction; textile milling and knitting, sawmilling, chemicals mfg. In Second World War, c.80% destroyed. Dramatist Laube b. here.

Sztropko, Czechoslovakia: see STROPKOV.

Sztum (shtōōm), Ger. *Stuhm* (shtōōm), town (1939 pop. 7,372; 1946 pop. 3,111) in East Prussia, after 1945 in Gdansk prov., N Poland, 9 mi. S of Marienburg (Malbork); grain and cattle market. Has remains of 14th-cent. hunting lodge of Teutonic Knights. Until 1919, in West Prussia prov.

Szu-, for Chinese names beginning thus and not found here: see under SZE-.

Szubin (shōō′bēn), Ger. *Schubin* (shōō′bĭn), town (pop. 3,742), Bydgoszcz prov., W central Poland, 14 mi. SW of Bydgoszcz; rail junction; mfg. of cement, liquor; sawmilling.

Szumsk, Ukrainian SSR: see SHUMSKOYE.

Szunow, Poland: see SWIERZAWA.

Szydlowiec (shĭdwô′vyĕts), Pol. *Szydłowiec,* Rus. *Shidlovets* (shĭdlô′vyĭts), town (pop. 4,010), Kielce prov., E central Poland, 18 mi. SSW of Radom; ironworks; mfg. of scales, bricks; flour milling, tanning; stone quarrying. Pop. 75% Jewish before Second World War.

Szymbork, Poland: see SULIKOW.

Szymrych, Poland: see CHELMSKO SLASKIE.

T

Taal (tä-äl′), town (1939 pop. 3,923; 1948 municipality pop. 26,044), Batangas prov., S Luzon, Philippines, just SE of Lemery, near Balayan Bay and L. Taal; rice, sugar cane, corn, coconuts.

Taal, Lake (□ 94), Batangas prov., S Luzon, Philippines, 35 mi. S of Manila; 15 mi. long, 9 mi. wide. Contains VOLCANO ISLAND and several other islets. Formerly called Bombon (bōmbōn′).

Taal, Mount, Philippines: see VOLCANO ISLAND.

Taalintehdas, Finland: see DALSBRUK.

Taan (dä′än′), Jap. *Taian* (tī′än), village, W central Formosa, on Formosa Strait, 3 mi. NW of Takia; fishing port and seaside resort.

Taanach (tā′ŭnăk) or **Tanach** (tā′năk), Biblical locality, N Palestine, at W edge of Plain of Jezreel, 5 mi. SE of Megiddo, 24 mi. SE of Haifa. Barak and Deborah here defeated (13th cent. B.C.) Sisera. Sometimes spelled Ta'anak.

Taancan Point (tä-äng′kän), southernmost point of Leyte, Philippines, in Mindanao Sea, at tip of peninsula separating Sogod Bay from Canigao Channel; 10°N 125°E.

Taarnby (tôrn′bü), town (pop. 8,148), Copenhagen amt, Denmark, on Amager isl. and 4 mi. S of Copenhagen.

Taasinge (tô′sĭng-ŭ), island (□ 27; pop. 4,432), Denmark, separated from S Fyn isl. by Svendborg Sound; fruitgrowing. Valdemar's Castle (17th cent.) on NE shore, just S of Troense, is its port.

Taastrup (tô′strōōp), town (pop. 4,351), Copenhagen amt, Zealand, Denmark, 11 mi. W of Copenhagen; orchards; cannery, chemical works.

Tab (tŏb), town (pop. 4,251), Somogy co., SW Hungary, 27 mi. NE of Kaposvar; flour mill.

Tab, river, Iran: see ZUHREH RIVER.

Taba (tä′bă), town (pop. 406), Sinai prov., NE Egypt, on Gulf of Aqaba 6 mi. SW of Aqaba, at Israel line.

Tabacal, Argentina: see EL TABACAL.

Tabaco (täbä′kō), town (1939 pop. 7,660, 1948 municipality pop. 33,209), Albay prov., SE Luzon, Philippines, 15 mi. N of Legaspi; minor port on Tabaco Bay, shipping abacá. Tabaco municipality includes SAN MIGUEL ISLAND.

Tabaco Bay, inlet of Lagonoy Gulf, Albay prov., SE Luzon, Philippines, sheltered E by San Miguel and Cagraray isls.; 12 mi. long, 3–6 mi. wide.

Tabacundo (täbäkōōn′dō), town (1950 pop. 2,553), Pichincha prov., central Ecuador, in the Andes, on Quito-Ibarra RR and 29 mi. NE of Quito; center for mfg. of Panama hats.

Tabaí, Paraguay: see TAVAÍ.

Tabaiana, Brazil: see ITABAIANA.

Tabalosos (täbälō′sōs), town (pop. 2,266), San Martín dept., N central Peru, in E outliers of the Andes, 7 mi. W of Lamas; sugar cane, tobacco, coffee, rice, cotton.

Taban Bogdo, Mongolia: see TABUN BOGDO.

Tabapuã (tŭbŭpwã′), city (pop. 1,814), N São Paulo, Brazil, 23 mi. ESE of São José do Rio Prêto; sawmilling, butter processing; coffee, sugar.

Tabapy, Paraguay: see ROQUE GONZÁLEZ DE SANTA CRUZ.

Tabaquite (täbäkē′tä, täbŭkē′tŭ) village (pop. 660), central Trinidad, B.W.I., on railroad and 20 mi. SE of Port of Spain; oil wells.

Tábara (tä′värä), town (pop. 1,265), Zamora prov., NW Spain, 25 mi. NNW of Zamora; flour milling; lumbering; livestock, cereals, grapes.

Tabarangué, Paraguay: see JESÚS.

Tabarca, Tunisia: see TABARKA.

Tabarcia (täbär′syä), village (dist. pop. 2,725), San José prov., W central Costa Rica, on W slopes of the Escazú, 6 mi. S of Villa Colón. Sugar cane, coffee, grain; mat and hat weaving. Pop. is largely Indian.

Tabar Islands (täbär′), small group (□ c.90; pop. c.1,900), New Ireland dist., Bismarck Archipelago, Territory of New Guinea, SW Pacific; 2°50′S 152°E; comprise single volcanic isl. and scattered coral islets. Tabar, main isl., is c.10 mi. long, rises to 1,500 ft.; timber.

Tabaristan, Iran: see MAZANDERAN.

Tabariya, Israel: see TIBERIAS.

Tabarka (täbärkä′), anc. *Thabraca,* town (pop. 1,006), ⊙ Tabarka dist. (□ 489; pop. 47,920), NW Tunisia, fishing port on the Mediterranean, near Algerian border, 55 mi. E of Bône (Algeria); terminus of railroad from Bizerte. Cork-processing center; sardine and anchovy fisheries. Tobacco growing. Iron, lead, and zinc mines in Medjerda Mts. near by. An important marble-shipping port in Roman and early Christian times. Has a 17th-cent. Genoan castle (on a small offshore isl.) and 2 Turkish forts. Sometimes spelled Tabarca.

Tabarz (tä'bärts), village (pop. 4,642), Thuringia, central Germany, in Thuringian Forest, 10 mi. WSW of Gotha; climatic health resort.

Tabas (täbäs') or **Golshan** (gōlshän'), town (1939 pop. 17,743), Ninth Prov., in Khurasan, NE Iran, 80 mi. WSW of Firdaus and on Meshed-Yezd road, at edge of desert; dates, grain, tobacco, oranges, asafetida; handmade woolen textiles.

Tabasará, Serranía de, or **Serranía de Tabazará** (both: sĕränē'ä dā täbäsärä'), section of continental divide in W Panama; c.50 mi. long. Rises to 9,272 ft. in the Cerros Santiago, 24 mi. NNE of Remedios. Pop. is largely Guaymie Indian.

Tabasará River or **Tabazará River,** W central Panama, rises in the Serranía de Tabasará, flows c.50 mi. S to Chiriquí Gulf of the Pacific 20 mi. W of Soná.

Tabasco (tŭbă'skō, Sp. täbä'skō), state (□ 9,783; 1940 pop. 285,630; 1950 pop. 351,106), SE Mexico, on the Gulf of Campeche; ⊙ Villahermosa. Bordered by Veracruz (W), Chiapas (S), Guatemala (SE), and Campeche (E). Except for Sierra Madre outliers in S, Tabasco consists mostly of jungle plain broken by numerous swamps, lagoons, and rivers. The streams are all tributary to the large Grijalva and Usumacinta rivers and serve as main lines of communication. Rainfall is heavy: c.120 inches annually. The fertile soil yields cacao, sugar cane, bananas, coffee, vanilla, rice, rubber, pepper, corn, chicle, fine tropical wood. Some oil deposits in NW, on Gulf of Tehuantepec. Villahermosa and Alvaro Obregón are trading and processing centers, the latter being also a port. Tabasco was crossed by Cortés on his march to Honduras (1524–25), and was conquered by Francisco de Montejo (1530). State since 1824.

Tabasco, town (pop. 1,458), Zacatecas, N central Mexico, on Juchipila R. and 27 mi. E of Tlaltenango; grain, tropical fruit, livestock. Formerly Villa del Refugio.

Tabat (täbät'), village, Blue Nile prov., E central Anglo-Egyptian Sudan, in the Gezira, 17 mi. WSW of Hasiheisa; cotton, wheat, barley.

Tabatinga (tŭbŭtĕng'gŭ). **1** Village, Amazonas, Brazil: see SAPURARA. **2** City (pop. 1,650), central São Paulo, Brazil, 33 mi. W of Araraquara; rail junction; distilling, sugar milling; cotton, rice, and grain processing.

Tabatinga, Serra da (sĕ'rŭ dä), range of NE Brazilian highlands on Maranhão-Goiás and Piauí-Bahia borders forming divide bet. the Parnaíba, Tocantins, and São Francisco drainage basins. Rises to 2,500 ft. Parnaíba R. rises here. Range is continued by Serra das Mangabeiras (NW), Serra da Gurgueia (E), and Serra do Duro (S).

Tabay or **Colonia Tabay** (kōlō'nyä täbī'), town (pop. estimate 500), W central Corrientes prov., Argentina, 60 mi. N of Mercedes; farming center (corn, alfalfa, cotton, manioc, livestock).

Tabayin (tŭbŭyĭn'), village, Shwebo dist., Upper Burma, on road and 8 mi. SW of Yeu.

Tabbowa (tŭb-bō'vŭ), village (pop. 1,163), North Western Prov., Ceylon, 10 mi. ENE of Puttalam, on small irrigation tank; land reclamation project.

Tabe (tä'bā), village (pop. 410), South-Western Prov., S central Sierra Leone, on Tabe R. (affluent of Sewa R.) and 15 mi. WNW of Bo, on railroad; palm oil and kernels, piassava, rice.

Tabelbala (täbĕlbälä'), Saharan military post, in Aïn-Sefra territory, W Algeria, surrounded by *areg* (sand dunes), 160 mi. SSW of Colomb-Béchar; 29°25'N 3°17'W.

Taber (tā'bŭr), town (pop. 1,760), S Alta., near Oldman R., 30 mi. ENE of Lethbridge; coal mining, oil and nautral-gas production, flour milling, vegetable canning, ranching; sugar beets.

Taberg, mountain, Sweden: see SMALANDS TABERG.

Tabernas (tävĕr'näs), town (pop. 2,883), Almería prov., S Spain, 15 mi. NNE of Almería; knitwear mfg., flour milling; ships grapes. Wine, olive oil, cereals, esparto; livestock market. Iron mines, and magnesium, copper, lead deposits near by.

Tabernes Blanques (bläng'kĕs), N suburb (pop. 2,115) of Valencia, E Spain; mfg. (chemical fertilizers, beer, candles). Olive and peanut oil, cereals in area.

Tabernes de Valldigna (dhä väldē'nyä), city (pop. 10,885), Valencia prov., E Spain, 11 mi. SE of Alcira, in rice- and orange-growing dist.; rice processing, sawmilling; agr. trade (strawberries, peanuts, beans, cereals). Dominated by hill topped by remains of anc. castle.

Tabgha, Palestine: see TABIGHA.

Tabia (täbyä'), village (pop. 832), Oran dept., NW Algeria, on the Mékerra and 13 mi. SSW of Sidi-bel-Abbès; rail junction; winegrowing.

Tabigha (tä'bĭgŭ) or **Tabgha** (täb'gŭ), Greek *Heptapegon* [=seven springs], locality, NW Palestine, Lower Galilee, on N shore of Sea of Galilee, 6 mi. N of Tiberias; site of Church of the Multiplication of the Loaves; reputed scene of the Feeding of Five Thousand. Sometimes spelled Tabga. In near-by cave were found traces of human habitation in Paleolithic times and parts of Mousterian skull (Galilee Man).

Tabio, Colombia: see CAJICÁ.

Tabiona (tăbēō'nŭ), town (pop. 160), Duchesne co., NE Utah, 22 mi. NW of Duchesne and on Duchesne R.; alt. 6,750 ft.; trade center for ranchers.

Tabiteuea (tä'bĭtä'ōōä'ä), atoll (□ 19; pop. 3,784), Kingsmill Group, W central Pacific, largest, most populous of Gilbert Isls., in Br. colony of Gilbert and Ellice Isls.; 1°23'S 174°51'E; 50-mi. reef; copra. Formerly Drummond Isl.

Tablada or **La Tablada** (lä tävlä'dä), town (pop. estimate 3,000) in Greater Buenos Aires, Argentina, 9 mi. WSW of Buenos Aires; agr. center (alfalfa, corn, flax); mfg. of chemicals, vegetable oils; lead mill.

Tablada, SW suburb (pop. 6,117) of Seville, SW Spain, on right bank of Alfonso XIII navigation channel of the Guadalquivir. Has military airport. Mfg. of airplanes.

Tablas, Las, Panama: see LAS TABLAS.

Tablas Island (tä'bläs), largest island (□ 265; 1939 pop. 52,241) of Romblon prov., Philippines, just N of Panay, 32 mi. E of Mindoro isl. across Tablas Strait, and separated from Romblon Isl. (E) by Romblon Pass; 12°23'N 122°2'E; 40 mi. long, 11 mi. wide. Mountainous, rising to 2,164 ft. Rice and coconut growing. Centers are BADAJOZ, LOOC, ODIOÑGAN.

Tablas Strait, Philippines, bet. Mindoro (W) and Tablas Isl. (E), leading S from Sibuyan Sea to Sulu Sea; c.30 mi. wide. Semirara Isls. at S end.

Tablat (täblät'), village (pop. 610), Alger dept., N central Algeria, in the Mitidja Atlas, 30 mi. SE of Algiers; winegrowing; wheat.

Tablazo (täblä'sō), village (pop. 1,317), Piura dept., NW Peru, on coastal plain, near Piura R., 15 mi. SSW of Piura, in irrigated cotton area.

Tablazo Bay, Zulia state, NW Venezuela, part of passage bet. Gulf of Venezuela (N) and L. Maracaibo (S), flanked NW by San Carlos Isl., 10 mi. N of Maracaibo; c.20 mi. W-E, 15 mi. N-S.

Table, Île de la (ēl' dü lä tä'blü), island of Faitsilong Archipelago, N Vietnam, in Gulf of Tonkin, opposite Campha; 20°55'N 107°30'E; 15 mi. long, 5 mi. wide; rises to 1,184 ft.

Table Bay (3 mi. long, 6 mi. wide), SW Cape Prov., U. of So. Afr., inlet of the Atlantic, extending N from Cape Town and overlooked by Table Mtn. Open anchorage, protected by breakwater. Discovered c.1500 by Portuguese voyagers to India; landing attempt was made here (1510) by Francisco de Almeida, viceroy of Portuguese Indies, who was killed by Hottentots. The shore was settled 1652 by Dutch, who founded Cape Town.

Table Cape, E extremity of Mahia Peninsula in Hawke Bay, E N.Isl., New Zealand; 39°6'S 178°3'E.

Table Cape, N Tasmania, in Bass Strait, N of Wynyard; 40°56'S 145°44'E; lighthouse.

Table Grove, village (pop. 481), Fulton co., W central Ill., 24 mi. SW of Canton, in agr. and bituminous-coal area; mfg. of tractor parts.

Tableland, village (pop. 2,412), S central Trinidad, B.W.I., 13 mi. E of San Fernando; cacao.

Table Mountain (3,549 ft.), SW Cape Prov., U. of So. Afr., just S of Cape Town, overlooking the city and Table Bay. Summit is flat, often shrouded in a white mist called the "tablecloth." Cable railway (built 1929) to summit.

Table Mountain, central Calif., mass of basaltic lava with a flat top (2,200 ft. high, c.30 mi. long, 1,200–1,500 ft. wide), W of Jamestown (Tuolumne co.). Rich source of gold in 1850s.

Table Rock, village (pop. 513), Pawnee co., SE Nebr., 7 mi. NNE of Pawnee City and on N.Fork of Nemaha R.; grain, livestock, dairy and poultry produce.

Table Rock (3,157 ft.), an outlier of the Blue Ridge, NW S.C., c.20 mi. NW of Greenville, in scenic Table Rock State Park (c.2,900 acres). Pinnacle Mtn. (c.3,400 ft.) and a peculiar formation called The Stool (2,500 ft.) are near by.

Tabletop, Que.: see JACQUES CARTIER, MOUNT.

Tabligbo (tablĕg'bō), village, S. Fr. Togoland, near Dahomey border, on road and 25 mi. N of Anécho; palm oil and kernels. Agr. experiment station.

Tabo (tŭbō'), village, Kangra dist., NE Punjab, India, 120 mi. E of Dharmsala, in Spiti subdivision. Site of noted Buddhist monastery, with sculptures and wall paintings. Ruins of many stupas near by.

Taboada (täbwä'dä), village (pop. estimate 500), ⊙ San Martín dept. (□ c.750; 1947 pop. 10,911), central Santiago del Estero prov., Argentina, on railroad and 35 mi. SE of Santiago del Estero; stock raising, lumbering.

Taboga Island (täbō'gä), in Bay of Panama of the Pacific, Panama prov., Panama, 11 mi. S of Panama city; 2 mi. long, 1 mi. wide. Pineapple plantations. Tourist resort. Village of Taboga (pop. 897) is on NE shore. Small Taboguilla Isl. is 1.5 mi. NE of Taboga Isl.

Tabogon (täbōgōn'), town (1939 pop. 1,060; 1948 municipality pop. 17,227), N Cebu isl., Philippines, on Camotes Sea, 45 mi. NNE of Cebu city; agr. center (corn, coconuts, tobacco).

Tabón Island (täbōn') (□ 3.7; pop. 563), Llanquihue prov., S central Chile, in Gulf of Ancud, NE of Chiloé Isl., 9 mi. S of Calbuco, 32 mi. SSW of Puerto Montt; 41°55'S 73°8'W. Potatoes, livestock; fishing.

Tabor (tä'bôr), Czech *Tábor*, town (pop. 17,956), S Bohemia, Czechoslovakia, on Luznice R. and 31 mi. NNE of Budweis, in barley- and rye-growing region; rail junction; trade center; wool and tobacco processing, tanning, mother-of-pearl industry. Kaolin quarrying in vicinity. Has several trade schools. Bathing and fishing just N, in Jordan pool. Founded in 1420 by Zizka and subsequently a stronghold of Hussites (Taborite sect); still retains part of its medieval fortifications. Has 13th-cent. tower, 16th-cent. Gothic town hall (now a Huss mus.), 16th-cent. Gothic church, Gothic and Renaissance houses. Historic ruins of Kozi Hradek castle are 3 mi. ESE, Pribenice castle is 5 mi. WSW, pilgrimage center of Klokoty just WNW.

Tabor (tā'bŭr). **1** Town (pop. 869), on Fremont-Mills co. line, SW Iowa, 27 mi. SSE of Council Bluffs; feed. **2** or **Tabor City,** city (pop. 2,033), Columbus co., SE N.C., 16 mi. SSW of Whiteville, near S.C. line; agr. trade and shipping center; sawmilling, crate mfg. **3** Town (pop. 373), Bon Homme co., SE S.Dak., 11 mi. ESE of Tyndall; livestock, grain. Founded by the Hutterische Community, an early communistic Christian group.

Tabor, Mount (tā'bŭr), mountain (1,929 ft.), Lower Galilee, N Palestine, 5 mi. E of Nazareth. In Biblical history Barak here assembled his forces prior to engaging Sisera at Taanach. Stronghold of Israelites against Canaan, and later against Romans, peak is reputed scene of Jesus' Transfiguration. Several chapels, remains of anc. fortifications.

Tabora (täbō'rä, tŭbô'rŭ), largest inland town (12,768), of Tanganyika, ⊙ Western Prov. (□ 78,405; pop. 943,067), 460 mi. WNW of Dares Salaam; 5°1'S 32°48'E. Alt. 3,900 ft. Junction of main E–W rail line with branch to Mwanza on L. Victoria (railroad shops); commercial and agr. center; cotton, millet, peanuts, corn, rice; beeswax; cattle. Has native technical school. Founded by Arabs c.1820 as a slave- and ivory-trading station. Became a hub of caravan routes bet. coast and lakes Tanganyika, Nyasa, and Victoria.

Tabor City, N.C.: see TABOR.

Tabory (tä'bŭrē), village (1948 pop. over 500), E Sverdlovsk oblast, Russian SFSR, on Tavda R. (landing) and 45 mi. NE of Turinsk; lumbering; grain, livestock.

Taboshar (tŭbŭshär'), town (1939 pop. over 500), N Leninabad oblast, Tadzhik SSR, on S slope of Kurama Range, 22 mi. N of Leninabad. Lead-zinc mine here has great variety of ores (uranium, vanadium, arsenic).

Tabou (tŭbōō'), town (pop. 1,400), SW Ivory Coast, Fr. West Africa, minor port on Gulf of Guinea (Atlantic) near Liberia border (Cavally R. mouth), 240 mi. WSW of Abidjan. Ships coffee, cacao, palm kernels, palm oil, rubber, and hardwood. Customhouse.

Tab River, Iran: see ZUHREH RIVER.

Tabriz (täbrēz', tä–) or **Tebriz** (tĕbrēz'), anc. *Tauris* (tô'rĭs), city (1940 pop. 213,542), ⊙ Third Prov., NW Iran, on Talkheh R. and 330 mi. NW of Teheran, 40 mi. from L. Urmia, at N foot of the Sahand; alt. 4,423 ft.; 38°5'N 46°17'E. Second-largest city of Iran and main commercial center of Azerbaijan; connected by railroad with Julfa (on USSR border), Teheran, and Sharifkhaneh (L. Urmia port); rail station in SW outskirts. Industrial center; rug weaving, cotton and wool spinning, leatherworking, flour milling; mfg. of soap, matches, alcohol. Has trade in dry fruit and carpets. Contains ruined 15th-cent. Blue Mosque, citadel, and univ. (late 1940s). Situated in earthquake zone: badly destroyed in 858, 1041, 1721, 1780. Mentioned as Armenian residence in 3d cent. A.D. Sacked 1392 by Tamerlane. Iranians captured it from Turks under early Safavids (1500), Abbas the Great (1618), and Nadir Shah (1730). In traditional Russian zone of influence after 1800, it was occupied by Russian troops in 1827–28, and in First and Second World Wars. In 1946, it was temporary hq. of autonomous Azerbaijan.

Tábua (tä'bwŭ), town (pop. 608), Coimbra dist., N central Portugal, 23 mi. ENE of Coimbra; resin extracting, textile milling.

Tabuaço (tŭbwä'sōō), town (pop. 1,277), Viseu dist., N central Portugal, 13 mi. E of Lamego; port wine, olives, figs, almonds, oranges.

Tabuk, Saudi Arabia: see TEBUK.

Tabulam (tă'bŭlŭm), village (pop. 322), NE New South Wales, Australia, on Clarence R. and 100 mi. SSW of Brisbane; mining center (gold, copper).

Tabun Bogdo, Tabyn Bogdo, or **Taban Bogdo** (tä'bŭn bŏg'dō), mountain knot in the Altai Mts., at junction of USSR, China, and Mongolia frontiers; 49°10'N 87°55'E; rises just inside Mongolian People's Republic to 15,266 ft. in the Khuitun or Hüyten, the highest point of the Altai. From here the Sailyugem Range extends toward the NE and the Mongolian Altai toward SE.

Tabuny (tŭbōōnē'), village (1939 pop. over 500), W Altai Territory, Russian SFSR, on railroad and 15 mi. S of Slavgorod, in agr. area.

Tabuse (täbōō'sä), town (pop. 8,959), Yamaguchi prefecture, SW Honshu, Japan, 16 mi. ESE of Tokuyama; agr. and livestock center; rice, raw silk; textiles.

Taby (tē'bü"), Swedish *Täby*, residential village (pop. 1,310), Stockholm co., E Sweden, 11 mi. N of Stockholm; has 15th-cent. church. Several stones with runic inscriptions found here.

Tabyn Bogdo, Mongolia: see TABUN BOGDO.

Tacabamba (täkäbäm'bä), city (pop. 857), Cajamarca dept., NW Peru, in Cordillera Occidental, 13 mi. NNE of Chota; wheat, corn, potatoes.

Tacajó (täkähō'), town (pop. 1,288), Oriente prov., E Cuba, 23 mi. E of Holguín; sugar cane, fruit. The sugar central Tacajó is 5 mi. NW.

Tacámbaro (täkäm'bärō), officially Tacámbaro de Codallos, city (pop. 4,173), Michoacán, W central Mexico, on central plateau, on railroad and 45 mi. SSW of Morelia; agr. center (cereals, sugar cane, tobacco, fruit); flour milling, tanning, alcohol distilling.

Tacaná (täkänä'), town (1950 pop. 857), San Marcos dept., SW Guatemala, in the Sierra Madre, 27 mi. NW of San Marcos; alt. 8,996 ft.; corn, wheat, livestock.

Tacaná, volcano (13,333 ft.), on Mexico-Guatemala border, in Sierra Madre, 19 mi. NE of Tapachula; 2d highest mtn. in Central America. Major eruptions 1855 and 1878. Emits sulphuric gases.

Tacanas River, Argentina: see ZÁRATE RIVER.

Tacara, Mount (täkä'rä), central Eritrea, peak (8,461 ft.) on central plateau, 15 mi. SW of Asmara. Source of Barka and Gash rivers.

Tacarcuna, Cordillera de (kôrdĭyä'rä dā täkärkōō'nä), section of continental divide on Panama-Colombia border, E of El Real; extends 40 mi. NW–SE along Caribbean coast; rises to 7,480 ft. Part of the Serranía del Darién.

Tacarigua (täkŭrĭ'gwŭ), village (pop. 2,378), N central Trinidad, B.W.I., on railroad and 10 mi. E of Port of Spain; rice growing (irrigation). Has industrial school.

Tacarigua (täkärē'gwä). **1** Town (pop. 1,137), Miranda state, N Venezuela, in Caribbean lowlands, 50 mi. ESE of Caracas; cacao, sugar cane, corn. **2** Town (pop. 1,277), in interior uplands of Margarita Isl. (E), Nueva Esparta state, NE Venezuela, 3 mi. NW of La Asunción; sugar cane, corn, fruit.

Tacarigua Lagoon (□ c.75), Miranda state, N Venezuela, 70 mi. ESE of Caracas; separated from the Caribbean by narrow bar; 17 mi. long NW–SE, c.4 mi. wide.

Tacazze, river, Ethiopia: see TAKKAZE RIVER.

Tachai, China: see KENGMA.

Tachanallur or **Tachchanallur** (tächä'nŭl-lōōr), town (pop. 8,772), Tinnevelly dist., S Madras, India, on Tambraparni R. and 2 mi. NE of Tinnevelly, in rice-growing area; produces jaggery, senna, betel; sugar refinery.

Tachang or **Ta-ch'ang** (dä'chäng'), village, Kiangsu prov., China, 8 mi. NNW of Shanghai; site of one of Shanghai's military airports.

Tachau, Czechoslovakia: see TACHOV.

Tacheng. 1 or **Ta-ch'eng** (dä'chŭng'), town, ⊙ Tacheng co. (pop. 170,236), E central Hopeh prov. China, 45 mi. SW of Tientsin, near Huto R.; wheat, rice, millet. **2** or **T'a-ch'eng** (tä'chŭng'), town, Sinkiang prov., China: see CHUGUCHAK.

Tachi, Formosa: see TAKI.

Tachia, Formosa: see TAKIA.

Ta-chiang, China: see TAKIANG.

Tachibana (täch ē'bänŭ), town (pop. 5,608), Tokushima prefecture, E Shikoku, Japan, on Kii Channel, 14 mi. SSE of Tokushima; fishing center; canneries, shipyards. Exports rice, sugar, soy sauce.

Tachibana Bay, N arm of Amakusa Sea, in S Hizen Peninsula, W Kyushu, Japan; formed by Nomo Peninsula (W) and Shimabara Peninsula (E); 11 mi. E-W, 7 mi. N-S. Chijiwa and Obama are on E shore. Sometimes called Chijiwa Bay and Tiziwa Bay.

Tachikawa (tächē'käwŭ), city (1940 pop. 33,849; 1947 pop. 45,302), Greater Tokyo, central Honshu, Japan, 20 mi. W of Tokyo; agr. (rice and mulberry fields). Has aviation schools, agr. and sericulture experiment stations.

Tachin, Thailand: see SAMUTSAKHON.

Ta-ching Shan, China: see TATSING MOUNTAINS.

Táchira (tä'chērä), inland state (□ 4,285; 1941 pop. 245,722; 1950 census 307,583), W Venezuela; ⊙ San Cristóbal. Bordering on Colombia (Táchira R.), it is a mountainous region traversed SW-NE by Sierra Nevada de Mérida. Its NW corner is in Maracaibo lowlands. Climate, depending on alt., is humid, tropical in N, semitropical in settled uplands. Venezuela's main coffee-producing region, it also grows corn, wheat, bananas, cacao, sugar cane, tobacco, potatoes, yucca, beans, peas, and raises cattle; in El Cobre area (NE) apples, peaches, and apricots are grown. Tropical forests yield timber. Mineral resources include gold, copper, sulphur, coal, and petroleum deposits.

Táchira River, on Venezuela-Colombia line, rises in Cordillera Oriental E of Pamplona, flows c.50 mi. N along international border, past San Antonio (Bolívar Bridge) and Ureña, to Pamplonita R. 4 mi. N of Cúcuta.

Tachov (tä'khôf), Ger. *Tachau* (tä'khou), town (pop. 4,230), W Bohemia, Czechoslovakia, on Mze R., on railroad, and 33 mi. W of Pilsen; lumber and mother-of-pearl industries. Site of victory (1427) of Procopius the Great over Crusaders.

Tachu (dä'jōō'), town (pop. 17,368), ⊙ Tachu co. (pop. 477,266), E central Szechwan prov., China, 100 mi. NNE of Chungking city; road center; paper milling; rice, wheat, sweet potatoes, indigo.

Tac Island (täk) (□ 2.8; pop. 442), bet Chiloé Isl. and mainland of S Chile; 42°23'S 73°8'W.

Tacloban (täklō'bän), town (1939 pop. 19,048; 1948 municipality pop. 45,421), ⊙ LEYTE prov., Philippines, on NE Leyte isl., port on NW shore of San Pedro Bay, at entrance to San Juanico Strait, 355 mi. SE of Manila; 11°14'N 125°E. Trade center for agr. area, exporting hemp, copra. In Second World War, town became (1944) temporary ⊙ Philippines after the U.S. landing on Leyte.

Tacna (täk'nä), department (□ 4,182; pop. 37,512), S Peru, on the Pacific, bordering on Chile (S) and Bolivia (W); ⊙ Tacna. Largely mountainous, sloping from high Cordillera Occidental to the ocean. Watered by Sama and Locumba rivers. Has dry, semitropical climate near the coast, cooler in the highlands. Its arid soil, made fertile by irrigation, produces sugar cane, cotton, grapes, fruit, alfalfa; wheat, barley, cattle, sheep in higher altitudes. Among its little-exploited mineral deposits are copper, silver, borax, gypsum, and sulphur. Main industries: cotton ginning, sugar milling, wine and liquor distilling, centered at Tacna city. The dept.'s SE section, comprising most of Tacna prov., was held by Chile after the War of the Pacific (1879–82) until the treaty of Lima (1929) settled the border dispute, giving Tacna city to Peru and Arica to Chile.

Tacna. 1 Town, Madre de Dios dept., Peru: see IÑAPARI. **2** City (pop. 11,378), ⊙ Tacna dept. and Tacna prov. (□ 3,946; pop. 21,705), S Peru, in W foothills of Cordillera Occidental, on Pan American Highway and 33 mi. N of Arica, Chile (linked by railroad), 630 mi. SE of Lima; 18°S 70°17'W; alt. 1,837 ft. Situated in a fertile oasis, it is a processing and agr. center (tobacco, wine, cotton, sugar cane, wheat, alfalfa, fruit); tanning, fruit canning, wine making, liquor distilling. Airport. Has cathedral. Its market serves Indians from Bolivian highlands. On a near-by hill, Campo de la Alianza, was fought a bloody battle (1880) of the War of the Pacific, in which the Chileans defeated the Peruvian-Bolivian forces. The peace treaty of Ancón (1883) ceded Tacna prov. together with Arica prov. to Chile; however, the former was returned to Peru in 1929 settlement, and Tacna city again became ⊙ Tacna dept.

Tacoma (tŭkō'mŭ), city (pop. 143,673), ⊙ Pierce co., W central Wash., on Commencement Bay of Puget Sound and 25 mi. S of Seattle, in sight of Mt. Rainier (c.40 mi. SE); 47°15'N 122°27'W. It is an important port (with extensive docks and wharves), port of entry, rail and air terminus, and industrial city, having lumber mills, electrochemical plants, flour mills, food-processing plants, smelters, and foundries. Ships lumber, grain, flour, copper, phosphate, explosives; receives tea, sugar, rubber, minerals, oil, nitrates. Fur market. McChord Air Force Base and Fort Lewis are near by. Points of interest: state historical society and Chinese museums, old Fort Nisqually, Col. of Puget Sound, an Indian sanatorium, Tacoma Narrows Bridge (1950) across Puget Sound. Settled 1852; named and laid out by Gen. McCarver (1868); arrival of transcontinental railroad (1887) aided in its growth.

Tacoma, Mount, Wash.: see MOUNT RAINIER NATIONAL PARK.

Tacoma Lake, Kennebec co., S Maine, just S of L. Cobbosseecontee, in resort area; c.2 mi. long.

Taconic, village, Conn.: see SALISBURY.

Taconic Mountains (tŭkŏ'nĭk), in New England and N.Y., range of the Appalachian system, lying E of the Hudson in N.Y. and W of Green Mts. in Vt.; it extends c.150 mi. S from point SW of Brandon, Vt., along N.Y. border with Mass. and Conn., to N Putnam co., N.Y., where it meets the highlands of the Hudson. S part is traversed by Appalachian Trail. Highest point is Mt. Equinox (3,816 ft.) near Manchester, Vt.; range includes Bear Mtn. (2,355 ft.), highest point in Conn. That part of range in Mass. is called BERKSHIRE HILLS. Taconic State Park along state line S of Hillsdale, N.Y., is a recreational area.

Taconite (tă'kŭnĭt), village (pop. 322), Itasca co., N central Minn., at W end of Mesabi range, 9 mi. NE of Grand Rapids. Iron mines.

Tacony (tăkō'nē), a NE section of Philadelphia, Pa.; Tacony-Palmyra Bridge (main span 2,324 ft.; opened 1929) here spans the Delaware to N.J.

Tacopaya (täkōpī'ä). **1** Town, Chuquisaca dept., Bolivia: see ZUDAÑEZ. **2** Town (pop. c.7,200), Cochabamba dept., central Bolivia, on S slopes of Cordillera de Cochabamba and 10 mi. W of Arque; on Oruro-Cochabamba RR; alt. 10,328 ft.; corn, vegetables.

Tacora (täkō'rä), village (pop. 42), Tarapacá prov., N Chile, at S foot of Cerro de Tacora, an Andean peak (19,520 ft.) on Peru border, 65 mi. NE of Arica. Sulphur mined near by.

Taco Ralo (tä'kō rä'lō), town (pop. estimate 500), S Tucumán prov., Argentina, on railroad and 70 mi. S of Tucumán; lumbering and stock-raising center. Mfg. of linoleum and gunpowder. Thermal waters near by.

Tacoronte (täkōrōn'tä), city (pop. 3,298), Tenerife, Canary Isls., 9 mi. W of Santa Cruz de Tenerife (linked by tramway); agr. center (corn, potatoes, wheat, grapes, tomatoes, bananas). Potteries; mfg. of barrels. Wine industry.

Taco-Taco (täkō-tä'kō), town (pop. 1,190), Pinar del Río prov., W Cuba, on railroad and 40 mi. NE of Pinar del Río; tobacco, sugar cane, fruit.

Tacotalpa (täkōtäl'pä), town (pop. 628), Tabasco, SE Mexico, on Tacotalpa (affluent of Grijalva) R. and 28 mi. S of Villahermosa; rice, beans, coffee.

Tacovo, Ukrainian SSR: see TYACHEVO.

Tactic (täktēk'), town (1950 pop. 1,255), Alta Verapaz dept., central Guatemala, in N highlands, 9 mi. S of Cobán; alt. 4,855 ft.; market center; weaving, soap and candle making; coffee, sugar cane, corn, beans.

Tacuaras (täkwä'räs), town (dist. pop. 1,198), Ñeembucú dept., S Paraguay, 24 mi. E of Pilar; cattle.

Tacuarembó (täkwärĕmbō'), department (□ 8,114; pop. 105,939), N central Uruguay; ⊙ Tacuarembó. Bordered S by the Río Negro. A major hydroelectric plant is at Rincón del Bonete on the Río Negro. Cattle and sheep raising; wheat, corn, vegetables. Main centers: Tacuarembó, Paso de los Toros. Dept. was formed 1837.

Tacuarembó, city (pop. 18,000), ⊙ Tacuarembó dept., N central Uruguay, on railroad and 220 mi. N of Montevideo, 115 mi. ESE of Salto; 31°38'S 56°3'W. Trade in wool and hides, agr. products (corn, wheat); livestock industry. Airport. Founded 1831 as San Fructuoso.

Tacuarembó River, N central Uruguay, rises in the Cuchilla Negra on Uruguay-Brazil border near Rivera, flows 140 mi. S, past Tranqueras and El Borracho, to the Río Negro 34 mi. S of El Borracho. Navigable for smaller boats upstream to El Borracho. Also called Tacuarembó Grande.

Tacuarendí (täkwärĕndē'), village (pop. estimate 1,000), NE Santa Fe prov., Argentina, on railroad and 55 mi. NNE of Reconquista; sugar refining.

Tacuari River (täkwärē'), Cerro Largo dept., NE Uruguay, rises in the Cuchilla Grande Principal NNE of Fraile Muerto, flows 100 mi. SE and E to L. Mirim 13 mi. NNW of Río Branco, forming part of Cerro Largo–Treinta y Tres dept. border.

Tacuatí (täkwätē'), town (dist. pop. 1,561), San Pedro dept., central Paraguay, on Ypané R. and 45 mi. E of Concepción; livestock, maté.

Tacuatimanu River, Peru: see PIEDRAS, RÍO DE LAS.

Tacuba (täkōō'bä), NW section of Mexico city, central Mexico; residential and mfg. suburb (machinery, rubber). San Gabriel church is notable; during Holy Week Indians enact a passion play. Many archaeological remains near by. Founded by Tepaneca Indians; was later admitted into Aztec confederacy. Was occupied by Spanish and was partly destroyed (1521).

Tacubaya (täkōōbī'ä), W section of Mexico city, central Mexico; fashionable residential suburb; textile, glass, clothing, dairy, and food industries. Site of Natl. Astronomical Observatory (19°24'17" N 99°11'38"W); alt. c.7,600 ft.

Tacurupucú, Paraguay: see HERNANDARIAS.

Tacutú River (tŏkōōtōō'), Rio Branco territory, northernmost Brazil, rises in the Serra Uassari near 1°45'N 59°40'W, flows N along Brazil–Br. Guiana border, then SW after receiving the Maú (or Ireng R.), to a junction with the Uraricoera 20 mi. above Boa Vista to form the Rio BRANCO. Length, 200 mi. Also spelled Takutu.

Tadanoumi (tä"dänō-ōō'mē), town (pop. 10,035), Hiroshima prefecture, SW Honshu, Japan, on Inland Sea, 24 mi. ENE of Kure; agr. (rice, wheat) and livestock (cattle, hogs) center. Fishery; raw-silk production.

Tadaoka (tädä'ōkä), town (pop. 9,089), Osaka prefecture, S Honshu, Japan, on Osaka Bay, bet. Izumi-otsu (N) and Kishiwada (S); mfg. (cotton textiles, yarn); stock raising, fishing.

Tadau or **Tada-u** (tŭdä'"ōō'), village, Sagaing dist., Upper Burma, 14 mi. SW of Mandalay and just S of Ava; road-rail junction.

Tadcaster, agr. village and parish (pop. 1,370), West Riding, central Yorkshire, England, on Wharfe R. and 9 mi. WSW of York. It was the Roman station *Calcaria*. Has 14th-15th-cent. church.

Tademaït Plateau (tädĕmäēt'), gravelly tableland of the Sahara, in central Algeria, in lat. 28°N bet. long. 1° and 5°E. Rises to 2,743 ft. Bounded by strings of oases: Gourara (NW), Touat (W), Tidikelt (S).

Tadepallegudem or **Tadepalligudem** (tŭdĕpŭ'lĭgōō-dĕm), town (pop. 9,396), West Godavari dist., NE Madras, India, in Godavari R. delta, 28 mi. ENE of Ellore; cotton-textile mfg., rice milling; oilseeds, tobacco, sugar cane.

Tadiandamol (tŭdēŭn'dŭmōl), peak, (5,724 ft.) in Western Ghats, S Coorg, India, 17 mi. SW of Mercara; highest point in Coorg.

Tadjerouine (täjĕrwēn'), village, Le Kef dist., W Tunisia, 22 mi. SSW of Le Kef; iron- and lead-mining center.

Tadjik-, in Rus. names: see TADZHIK-.

Tadjoura or **Tajura** (täjōō'rä), town (pop. 1,150), Fr. Somaliland, port on N shore of Gulf of Tadjoura (inlet of Gulf of Aden), 22 mi. NW of Djibouti; fisheries; livestock raising. Residence of Sultan. First mentioned in 12th cent., it was formerly the head of important caravan routes to interior. Declined since rise of Djibouti.

Tadjoura, Gulf of, inlet of Gulf of Aden, S of Bab el Mandeb strait, penetrating into Fr. Somaliland; 35 mi. wide at mouth, 50 mi. long. Contains Moucha Isls. Djibouti on S shore, Tadjoura and Obock on N shore.

Tadmor, Syria: see PALMYRA.

Tadó (tädō'), town (pop. 1,263), Chocó dept., W Colombia, on San Juan R. and 35 mi. S of Quibdó; platinum- and gold-placer mines.

Tadotsu (tädō'tsōō), town (pop. 12,904), Kagawa prefecture, N Shikoku, Japan, port on Hiuchi Sea, 3 mi. SW of Marugame; saltmaking center; seaside resort; artisan fan industry. Exports tobacco, rice, wheat, copper, machinery, hats, lumber. Industrial school.

Tadoussac (tä'dōōsăk, Fr. tädōōsäk'), village (pop. 766), ⊙ Saguenay co., SE Que., on Saguenay R., just above its mouth on the St. Lawrence, and 24 mi. NNW of Rivière du Loup; dairying, lumbering; resort. Mica is mined near by. Settlers arrived here 1600 and left in 1601; in 1640 a Jesuit mission was founded. Tadoussac became an important fur-trading post.

Tadpatri (täd'pŭtrē), city (pop. 15,184), Anantapur dist., NW Madras, India, on Penner R. and 31 mi. NE of Anantapur; trade center (silk and cotton cloth); cotton ginning, peanut milling, fruit canning. Has 15th-cent. Dravidian temples. Barite and steatite mines near by.

Tadzhikabad (tŭjĭkŭbät'), village (1939 pop. over 500), N Garm oblast, Tadzhik SSR, on Surkhab R. and 30 mi. ENE of Garm; gold placers; wheat. Until 1949, Kalai-Lyabiob.

Tadzhikistan or **Tadzhik Soviet Socialist Republic** (tŭjĭ'kĭstăn",–stän", täjĭ'–, Rus. tŭjĭkĭstän'; täjĭk', –jēk', Rus. tŭjĭk'), constituent republic (□ 55,000; 1947 pop. estimate 1,455,000) of the USSR, in Central Asia; ⊙ Stalinabad. Bounded by Kirghiz and Uzbek SSRs (N and W), Afghanistan (S), and China (E). Includes GORNO-BADAKHSHAN Autonomous Oblast (in the Pamir) and falls administratively into 4 oblasts: STALINABAD, LENINABAD, GARM, KULYAB. Essentially a high-mtn. country, with some of the highest points (Stalin and Lenin peaks) of the USSR and, in SE, the Pamir, an arid, high plateau (12-15,000 ft.). Only extensive lowlands are the Tadzhik section of Fergana Valley (N) and hot, dry Gissar and Vakhsh valleys (SW) on right tributaries of the Amu Darya. Pop. consists of Tadzhiks (Tadjiks, Tajiks; 78%; an Iranian people of Sunni Moslem religion), Uzbeks (18%), Kirghiz, Russians. Cotton is the leading agr. product, with ¼ of the area (in Vakhsh and Gissar valleys) sown in Egyptian long-staple cotton. Other irrigated crops are rice, lucerne, fruit; also vineyards and mulberry trees (sericulture). Two crops are frequently obtained, early wheat and barley being followed in July by a late sowing of corn, millet, sesame, legumes, or vegetables. Gissar and Vakhsh valleys specialize in dry, subtropical crops, such as almonds, figs, pistaccio, pomegranates, sugar cane, and essential oils. Gissar (Hissar) sheep, horses, and (in the Pamir) yaks are the principal livestock herds. Industry based in part on exploitation of mineral resources: lead-zinc-silver ores (Kara-Mazar), uranium (Taboshar), arsenic, antimony, bismuth, molybdenum, tungsten, feldspar, petroleum (Kim, Nefteabad), coal (Ziddy, Shurab), salt, and gold. Agr. processing (cotton, silk, fruit, flour) is important. Chief urban centers (linked in part by a narrow-gauge rail net) are Stalinabad, Leninabad, Kurgan-Tyube, Ura-Tyube, and Kanibadam. Cotton, silk, dried fruit, and lead-zinc ores are exported. The Tadzhiks descend from tribal inhabitants of anc. Sogdiana (in Zeravshan R. valley), who migrated into their present mtn. country under the pressure of conquerors and were ruled by the Uzbeks (Bukhara khanate) until 19th cent. Originally constituted (1924) as an autonomous SSR within Uzbek SSR, Tadzhikistan became (1929) a separate constituent republic within the USSR.

Taedong River (tă'dông'), Korean *Taedong-gang*, Jap. *Daido-ko*, S.Pyongan prov., N Korea, rises in mts. 50 mi. NW of Hungnam, flows 245 mi. generally SW, past Pyongyang and Kyomipo, to Korea Bay at Chinnampo; navigable 40 mi. by small steamer. Drains large agr. area. Sometimes spelled Taidong.

Taegu (tīgōō', Korean tă'gōō'), Jap. *Taikyu* (tī'kū'), city (1949 pop. 313,705), ⊙ N.Kyongsang prov., S Korea, 55 mi. NNW of Pusan; rail center; commercial center for agr. area (grains, fruit, tobacco). Silk-spinning and cotton-ginning mills. Large fairs are frequently held here. An important objective of North Korean forces in Korean war (1950–51), it formed a U.N. bastion in the perimeter defense of the Pusan beachhead in the 1st U.N. retreat. Sometimes called Taiku.

Taejon (tī'jŏn', Korean tă'jŭn'), Jap. *Taiden* (tī'dĕn), city (1949 pop. 126,704), ⊙ S.Chungchong prov., S Korea, 85 mi. SSE of Seoul; rail center in fruitgrowing area; commercial and mfg. center (silk reeling, leather tanning, brick making, brewing); railroad shops. Near by are hot springs. Severely damaged in the Korean war (1950–51).

Taejong (tă'jŭng'), Jap. *Taisei*, township (1946 pop. 16,938), SW Cheju Isl., Korea, 22 mi. SW of Cheju; agr. (grains, soybeans, cotton), fishing. Near-by anchorage (on E.China Sea) is called Mosulpo (Jap. *Boshippo*).

Taenarum, Cape, Greece: see MATAPAN, CAPE.

Tafahi (täfä'hē), volcanic island, N Tonga, S Pacific; 15°50'S 173°43'W; rises to 2,000 ft. Formerly Boscawen Isl.

Tafahna el 'Azab or **Tafahna al-'Azab** (both: tăfä'năl-äzăb'), village (pop. 6,966), Gharbiya prov., Lower Egypt, on Damietta branch of the Nile and 8 mi. S of Zifta; cotton.

Tafalla (täfä'lyä), city (pop. 6,036), Navarre prov., N Spain, road junction 20 mi. S of Pamplona, in fertile agr. area (wine, olive oil, fruit, cereals); flour- and sawmilling, tanning; mfg. of bicycles, brandy, alcohol, plaster. Has medieval castle and 2 Gothic churches.

Tafangshen, Manchuria: see TEHHWEI.

Tafelberg (tä'fûlbĕrkh), mountain (3,540 ft.), central Du. Guiana, at E end of Wilhelmina Mts.; 3°48'N 56°15'W; a triangular plateau of c.65 sq. mi. overlooking the surrounding jungle region.

Tafelfichte, peak, Czechoslovakia and Poland: see SMRK.

Tafelney, Cape (täfĕlnā'), headland of SW Fr. Morocco, on the Atlantic, 30 mi. S of Mogador. Here terminates a W spur of the High Atlas; 31°6'N 9°50'W. Also spelled Tafelneh.

Taff River, Brecknock and Glamorgan, Wales, rises on Brecon Beacons, flows 40 mi. SE, past Merthyr Tydfil, Pontypridd, and Llandaff, to Bristol Channel at Cardiff. Receives Rhondda R. and Cynon R.

Taff's Well, town (pop. 3,473) in Caerphilly urban district, E Glamorgan, Wales, on Taff R.; coal mining. Once noted for its tepid medicinal springs. Near by is 13th-cent. Castell Coch (restored).

Tafí, department, Argentina: see TAFÍ VIEJO.

Tafí del Valle (täfē' dĕl vä'yä) or **Tafí,** town (pop. estimate 500), W Tucumán prov., Argentina, at E foot of Nevado del Aconquija, 32 mi. W of Tucumán; agr. center (corn, alfalfa, wheat, livestock); flour milling, dairying.

Tafih (tă'fē), village, ⊙ Dubeini sheikdom, Subeihi tribal area, Western Aden Protectorate.

Tafila (tăfē'lū), **El Tafila, Et Tafila,** or **Al-Tafilah** (all: ĕt-tăfē'lū), town (pop. c.6,500), S central Jordan, 24 mi. SSW of Kerak; alt. 3,300 ft.; grain (wheat, barley). Manganese deposits (S). Sometimes spelled Tafile or Tafileh.

Tafilalet, Tafilalt, or **Tafilelt** (all: täfēlĕlt'), largest Saharan oasis (□ c.200; pop. c.50,000) of S Fr. Morocco, on the Oued Ziz (which here forms an alluvial fan), S of the High Atlas, in 31°20'N 4°15'W. Erfoud, at N edge, is its chief center. Oasis grows date-palms, fruit trees (especially figs), cereals, and vegetables. Tanning, mfg. of woolen and esparto products. Its old capital, Sijilmassa (now in ruins), was a Berber stronghold in 8th and 9th cent. A.D. Throughout the Middle Ages, Tafilalet was a prosperous oasis supporting considerably larger pop. than today. The ruling dynasty of Morocco's sultans, which came to power in 1649, originated here. Occupied by French since 1917, area was not completely pacified until early 1930s.

Tafion, Greece: see MEGANESI.

Tafira Alta (täfē'rä äl'tä), village (pop. 1,645), Grand Canary, Canary Isls., 5 mi. SW of Las Palmas; inland resort in agr. region (bananas, cereals, fruit, livestock). Tafira Baja (pop. 1,334) adjoins.

Tafí Viejo (täfē' vyā'hō), town (1947 census pop. 15,094), ⊙ Tafí dept. (□ c.1,300; 1947 census pop. 36,146), central Tucumán prov., Argentina, 7 mi. NNW of Tucumán; rail, processing, and commercial center for agr. area (sugar cane, corn, oranges, livestock). Resort. Has railroad shops and sugar refineries.

Tafna, Oued (wĕd' täfnä'), stream of Oran dept., NW Algeria, rises in Tlemcen Mts., flows c.100 mi. generally N to the Mediterranean W of Beni-Saf. Beni-Bahdel Dam (177 ft. high; 15 mi. SW of Tlemcen) stores water for irrigation in Marnia lowland and contributes to Oran water supply.

Tafnidilt (täfnēdĕlt'), Saharan military outpost, Agadir frontier region, southwesternmost Fr. Morocco, on right bank of the Oued Dra (border of Spanish Southern Protectorate of Morocco), 110 mi. SW of Tiznit; 28°33'N 11°1'W.

Tafo (tä'fō), town, Eastern Prov., central Gold Coast colony, on railroad and 10 mi. NNW of Koforidua; cacao center. Site of W African Cocoa Research Inst.

Tafos, Greece: see MEGANESI.

Taf River (täv), Pembroke and Carmarthen, Wales, rises on Mynydd Prescelly, flows 25 mi. S and SE, past St. Clears and Laugharne, to Carmarthen Bay of Bristol Channel 2 mi. SE of Laugharne.

Taft (täft), village (1932 pop. estimate 8,000), Tenth Prov., in Yezd, central Iran, 14 mi. SW of Yezd, in hilly region; agr. (grain, pomegranates, peaches).

Taft (tăft). **1** City (pop. 3,707), Kern co., S central Calif., in San Joaquin Valley, 30 mi. SW of Bakersfield; supply and refining center in productive oil region. Jr. col. here. Taft Heights (pop. 2,176), South Taft (pop. 2,918) are residential suburbs. Inc. 1910. **2** Town (pop. 541), Muskogee co., E Okla., 10 mi. W of Muskogee, in agr. area; an all-Negro community. Near by are a state home for handicapped and orphaned children, a state training school for girls, and a state hosp. for the insane, all for Negroes. Site of Taft Reservoir, a unit in Arkansas R. flood-control plan, is near. **3** City (pop. 450), Lincoln co., W Oregon, on Pacific Ocean, near mouth of Siletz R., and 22 mi. N of Toledo; summer resort. **4** City (pop. 2,978), San Patricio co., S Texas, 19 mi. N of Corpus Christi; trade, shipping, processing point in agr. area (cotton, grain sorghums, cattle); cotton, vegetable processing plants; oil, natural-gas field near by. Inc. 1929.

Taft Point, Calif.: see YOSEMITE NATIONAL PARK.

Taftville, Conn.: see NORWICH.

Taga (tä'gä), fortified town [Bhutanese *dzong*], S Bhutan, on right tributary of the Sankosh and 37 mi. S of Punakha, on a main India-Bhutan route; rice. Several lamaseries are near by. Formerly spelled Taka.

Taga (tä'gä). **1** Town (pop. 37,186), Ibaraki prefecture, central Honshu, Japan, on the Pacific, 4 mi. S of Hitachi; mining center (coal, copper, silver, gold); smelting. Formed in late 1930s by combining former town of Kawarago and several villages. **2** Town (pop. 7,127), Shiga prefecture, S Honshu, Japan, 4 mi. SSE of Hikone, in rice-growing, poultry-raising area; earthenware, walking canes, dried mushrooms.

Tagai or **Tagay** (tŭgī'), village (1926 pop. 3,079), N Ulyanovsk oblast, Russian SFSR, 31 mi. W of Ulyanovsk; wheat, livestock.

Taganana (tägänä'nä), village (pop. 637), Tenerife, Canary Isls., 9 mi. NNE of Santa Cruz de Tenerife; fruit, livestock.

Taganrog (tă'gŭnrŏg", Rus. tŭgŭnrôk'), city (1926 pop. 86,444; 1939 pop. 188,808), SW Rostov oblast, Russian SFSR, port on N shore of Taganrog Gulf (NE section of Sea of Azov), 35 mi. W of Rostov; metallurgical and machine-building center; steel milling (sheet metal, pipes, wheel rims), mfg. of aircraft, food-processing, chemical, and agr. machines, hydraulic presses, instruments, tools, boilers, leather goods; fish and agr. processing. Railroad shops, shipyards; extensive port installations. Exports coal, grain. Teachers col., institute for agr. mechanization. Has historical mus. (former imperial palace where Alexander I died, 1825) and memorial mus. of Chekhov (b. here). Founded originally as a fortress (1698) by Peter the Great on site of Ital. 13th–15th-cent. colony; twice destroyed and abandoned to Turks. Finally acquired by Russians in 1769; chartered 1775; fortress razed 1788. Developed a large trade in 19th cent., serving as a port for Donets Basin. Industrialized in 19th cent. (metallurgy, agr. processing). During Second World War, held by Germans in late 1941 and again in 1942–43.

Tagant (tägänt'), region and subdivision of S Mauritania, Fr. West Africa, separated from Adrar ridge (N) by sand ravine. Consists of a low sandstone plateau dissected by wadis which support oases, among them Tidjikja.

Tagapula Island (tägäpōōlä') (□ 11; 1939 pop. 3,826), Samar prov., Philippines, bet. Masbate and Samar isls.; 12°3'N 124°11'E; 6 mi. long, 3 mi. wide. Coconut growing, fishing.

Tagaste, Algeria: see SOUK-AHRAS.

Tagaung (tŭgoun'), village, Katha dist., Upper Burma, on left bank of Irrawaddy R. and 110 mi. N of Mandalay. Said to be most anc. ⊙ Burma, founded 6th cent. B.C. by Manipur prince (extensive ruins and Sanskrit inscriptions; pagodas). Occupied (1283) by Mongol army.

Tagawa (tä"gä'wä) or **Takawa** (tä"kä'wä), city (1940 pop. 70,225; 1947 pop. 75,899), Fukuoka prefecture, N Kyushu, Japan, 23 mi. E of Fukuoka; rail junction; chief mining center for Chikuho coal field. Includes (since early 1940s) former adjacent town of Ida or Ita (1940 pop. 30,640).

Tagaytay (tägītī'), city (1939 pop. 951; 1948 dist. pop. 5,233) in but independent of Cavite prov., S Luzon, Philippines, 35 mi. S of Manila, just N of L. Taal; agr. center (rice, fruit, coconuts). In NE part of dist. is Tagaytay Ridge, a small range rising to 2,467 ft.

Tagbilaran (tägbēlä'rän), town (1939 pop. 5,187; 1948 municipality pop. 16,051), ⊙ Bohol prov., Philippines, on SW Bohol isl., port on Bohol Strait, sheltered by Panglao Isl., 390 mi. SSE of Manila; 9°38'N 123°51'E. Trade center for agr. area (rice, coconuts). Exports copra, buri-palm hats.

Taggia (täd'jä), town (pop. 3,585), Imperia prov., Liguria, NW Italy, on Taggia R. and 4 mi. NE of San Remo; soap mfg.; market for flowers, bricks, wood, olives. Has medieval houses, 16th-cent. palace.

Taggia River, NW Italy, rises in Ligurian Alps on Mt. Saccarello, flows 21 mi. S, past Taggia, to Gulf of Genoa 4 mi. E of San Remo. Used for hydroelectric power. Called the Argentina in middle course. Its valley is flower-growing and perfume-making region.

Taghmon, Gaelic *Teach Munna*, town (pop. 361), S Co. Wexford, Ireland, 8 mi. WSW of Wexford; agr. market (dairying, cattle raising; wheat, barley, potatoes, beets).

Taghum (tă'gŭm), village, SE B.C., in Selkirk Mts., on Kootenay R. and 5 mi. W of Nelson; gold and silver mining.

Tagil River (tŭgēl'), Sverdlovsk oblast, Russian SFSR, rises in the central Urals c.15 mi. S of Kirovgrad, flows N, past Verkhni Tagil and Nizhni Tagil, and ENE, past Makhnevo, to Tura R. 35 mi. NW of Lenskoye; 260 mi. long. Navigable below Nizhni Tagil. Receives Salda R. (right).

Tagish Lake (tă'gĭsh) (□ 115), S Yukon and NW B.C., W of Atlin L., 40 mi. SE of Whitehorse; c.70 mi. long, 1–3 mi. wide. Several arms extend from main body of lake. Drained N by Lewes R.

Tagiura (tājōō'rä), town (pop. 600; 1950 dist. pop. 17,000), W Tripolitania, Libya, 8 mi. E of Tripoli in an oasis (dates, citrus fruit, cereals, tobacco; livestock) on Mediterranean coast; rail spur terminus; weaving (carpets, barracans). Moslem religious center with 16th-cent. mosque.

Tagliacozzo (tälyäkô'tsô), town (pop. 3,693), Aquila prov., Abruzzi e Molise, S central Italy, 10 mi. WNW of Avezzano. Resort (alt. 2,543 ft.); felt mills, hosiery factory. Has ducal palace (14th–15th cent.). Near by Charles I of Naples defeated the last Hohenstaufen, Conradin, in 1268.

Tagliamento River (tälyämĕn'tô), NE Italy, rises in Carnic Alps 13 mi. WNW of Ampezzo, flows 106 mi. E and S, past Latisana, to the Adriatic 14 mi. W of Grado. In lower course forms Venezia-Udine prov. boundary. Receives Fella and Degano rivers (left).

Taglio di Po (tä'lyō dē pô'), town (pop. 4,787), Rovigo prov., Veneto, N Italy, on Po R. and 8 mi. ESE of Adria; agr. machinery.

Tagliuno (tälyōō'nô), village (pop. 1,948), Bergamo prov., Lombardy, N Italy, 3 mi. NNE of Palazzolo sull'Oglio; bell foundries.

Tago (tägō'), town (1939 pop. 1,942; 1948 municipality pop. 23,036), Surigao prov., Philippines, on NE coast of Mindanao, just SE of Tandag, in mining and coconut-growing area.

Tagomago (tāgōmä'gō), islet, Balearic Isls., in the W Mediterranean, just E of Iviza isl.; 39°2'N 1°39'E.

Tagounite (tägōōnēt'), village and Saharan oasis, Marrakesh region, S Fr. Morocco, near undefined Algerian border, on the Oued Dra and 30 mi. SE of Zagora; 29°28'N 5°36'W. Date palms.

Tagua, La, Colombia: see LA TAGUA.

Taguatinga (tŏogwŏotĕng'gŏo), city (pop. 1,562), E Goiás, central Brazil, near Bahia border; 12°17'S 46°3'W. Stock raising.

Taguatinga, Serra, Brazil: see GERAL DE GOIÁS, SERRA.

Taguchi (tägōō'chē), town (pop. 5,020), Aichi prefecture, central Honshu, Japan, 28 mi. ESE of Seto. Mineral springs.

Tagudin (tägōōdēn'), town (1939 pop. 3,980; 1948 municipality pop. 15,637), Ilocos Sur prov., N Luzon, Philippines, 39 mi. S of Vigan, near W coast; rice-growing center.

Tagula (tägōō'lä), volcanic island, largest of Louisiade Archipelago, Territory of Papua, SW Pacific, 175 mi. SE of New Guinea; 50 mi. long, 15 mi. wide. Gold rush here in 1889. Formerly Sud-est.

Tagum, Philippines: see HIJO.

Tagus (tā'gŭs), village (pop. 101), Mountrail co., NW central N.Dak., 22 mi. E of Stanley.

Tagus River (tā'gŭs), Sp. *Tajo* (tä'hō), Port. *Tejo* (tā'zhōō), in Spain and Portugal; generally considered the longest river of the Iberian Peninsula, though some estimates of its length (565–625 mi.) are slightly smaller than some estimates of the Ebro's. In its basin (tributary to the Atlantic) are both Madrid and Lisbon. Rises c.15 mi. WSW of Albarracín in Teruel prov., E Spain, only c.100 mi. from the Mediterranean; flows generally SW through steep, mountainous region of S Guadalajara prov. (Serranía de Cuenca), and W through a fertile section of the central plateau (Meseta), past Aranjuez, Toledo, and Talavera de la Reina, crossing New Castile bet. the Sierra de Gredos (N) and Montes de Toledo (S), then passing through Estremadura, where again it cuts through deep gorges, frequently obstructed by falls; below Alcántara (Cáceres prov.), it follows the international line for c.30 mi., and in Portugal turns SW, passing Abrantes, Santarém; below Vila Franca de Xira begins Tagus estuary which consists of Lisbon Bay or Mar da Palha (12 mi. long, up to 7 mi. wide) and of a narrow, c.8-mi.-long channel on whose N shore lies the Atlantic seaport of Lisbon. Smaller vessels can navigate upstream to Abrantes. As its name (Tajo=cut) implies, the Tagus plunges through precipitous mtn. country. Thus, apart from its middle section, it is of little importance to agr., but has an enormous hydroelectric power potential. Among its chief tributaries are: right—Jarama, Tajuña, Alberche, Tiétar, Alagón; left—Guadiela, Almonte. Its Port. course is c.125 mi. long.

Tahaa (tähä'ä) or **Iripau** (ērēpä'ōō), volcanic island (□ 32; pop. 3,203), Leeward group, SOCIETY ISLANDS, Fr. Oceania, S Pacific, just N of Raiatea; circular, c.6 mi. in diameter. Mountainous; Mt. Ohiri (1,936 ft.) is highest peak.

Tahala (tähälä'), village, Fez region, N central Fr. Morocco, near railroad, 30 mi. E of Fez; Fr. agr. settlement.

Tahan, Gunong (gōōnōōng' tähän'), highest peak (7,186 ft.) of Malay Peninsula, on Pahang-Kelantan border and 33 mi. NNE of Kuala Lipis; 4°38'N 102°14'E.

Tahapanes (tăhă'pŭnēz), **Tahpanhes** (tä'pŭnhēz), or **Tehaphnehes** (tēhăf'nĭhēz), anc. city of NE Egypt, on L. Manzala, 9 mi. W of El Qantara. An anc. garrison city, called by the Greeks Daphnae (dăf'nē). Flourished in 6th cent. B.C. Excavations (1886) yielded artifacts. On site is present-day village of Kom Dafana or Tell Dafana (Tell Defenneh).

Tahara, Japan: see TAWARA.

Tahat (tähät'), highest peak (9,850 ft.) of Ahaggar Mts., in the Sahara of S Algeria; 23°21'N 5°26'E.

Tahcheng, China: see CHUGUCHAK.

Tahdziú (tätsū'), town (pop. 1,200), Yucatan, SE Mexico, 5 mi. N of Peto; henequen, sugar, fruit.

Taheiho or **Taheihotun,** Manchuria: see AIGUN.

Tahent, Djebel, Tunisia: see HILL 609.

Taher (tähâr'), village (pop. 895), Constantine dept., NE Algeria, near the Mediterranean, 8 mi. SE of Djidjelli; vineyards, olive groves.

Tahing or **Ta-hsing** (both: dä'shĭng'), town, ⊙ Tahing co. (pop. 145,883), N Hopeh prov., China, 10 mi. S of Peking and on Peking-Tientsin RR; wheat, millet, kaoliang. Until 1928, Hwangtsun.

Tahiti (tähē'tē, tĭ'tē), island (□ 402; pop. 24,820), Windward group, SOCIETY ISLANDS, S Pacific; 17°37'S 149°26'W; ⊙ Papeete, the capital of Fr. Establishments in Oceania. Largest (c.30 mi. long), most important isl. of Fr. Oceania. Isthmus of Taravao joins E and W Tahiti. Mountainous, with 4 prominent peaks; highest is Mt. Orohena (7,618 ft.); annual mean temp. 85°F. Produces fruits, copra, vanilla, sugar cane, phosphates; pearl fisheries. Polynesian inhabitants. Discovered 1767 by the British, visited 1788 by *Bounty*. Spaniards unsuccessfully attempted 1774 to colonize isl.; Br. and Fr. missionaries arrived 1797–1800. Queen Pomare was forced to agree 1843 to establishment of Fr. protectorate; Pomare V abdicated 1880, ceding isl. to France. During Second World War, Tahitians voted in 1940 plebiscite to support Free France. Gauguin did many paintings here. Formerly called Otaheite and King George III Isl.

Tahkilek (tä'kēlĕk"), village, Kengtung state, Southern Shan State, Upper Burma, 55 mi. SSE of Kengtung, on road to Lampang (Thailand) and 10 mi. from Thai border. Sometimes Monghopung.

Tahlequah (tă'lŭkwô), city (pop. 4,750), ⊙ Cherokee co., E Okla., 25 mi. ENE of Muskogee; trade and commercial center for agr., fruitgrowing, and stock-raising region; canned foods, dairy products, flour, feed, lumber, machine-shop products. Seat of Northeastern State Col., a U.S. school for Indian orphans, and an Indian hosp. Has a historical mus., with Indian relics. State fish hatchery near by. Settled by Cherokees in 1839, and made ⊙ Cherokee Nation.

Tahmek (tämĕk'), town (pop. 1,544), Yucatan, SE Mexico, 25 mi. ESE of Mérida; henequen.

Tahoe, Lake (tä'hō) (□ c.195), in E Calif. and W Nev. Beautifully situated bet. Sierra Nevada (W) and Carson Range; 21.6 mi. long, 12 mi. wide; surface alt. 6,225 ft.; great depth (over 1,600 ft.) prevents freezing. Discovered 1844 by J. C. Frémont. Supplies water through TRUCKEE RIVER (W outlet) for Newlands irrigation project in Nev. Tahoe City, on W shore, is one of several resorts on lake.

Tahoe City, resort village (pop. c.200), Placer co., E Calif., in the Sierra Nevada, on W shore of L. Tahoe. Also on lake are resorts of Tahoe Pines and Tahoe Vista, in Placer co., and Tahoe Valley, in El Dorado co.

Tahoelandang, Indonesia: see TAHULANDANG.

Tahoena, Indonesia: see SANGI ISLANDS.

Tahoka (tŭhō'kŭ), city (pop. 2,848), ⊙ Lynn co., NW Texas, on the Llano Estacado, 30 mi. S of Lubbock; trade, shipping, processing point for agr., dairying, and livestock region (cotton, black-eyed peas, poultry); cotton gins, compress, creameries. Silica mines. Small Tahoka L. is c.9 mi. N. Settled 1903, inc. 1915.

Taholah (tŭhō'lŭ), village (pop. c.350), Grays Harbor co., W Wash., on Pacific coast, at mouth of Quinault R., and 32 mi. NW of Hoquiam; hq. of Quinault Indian Reservation.

Tahopa, China: see HINGHAI.

Tahoua (tou'ä), town (pop. c.12,600), SW Niger territory, Fr. West Africa, on desert road and 225 mi. ENE of Niamey; trading and stock-raising center (goat, cattle, donkey). Airstrip, garrison.

Tahpanhes, Egypt: see TAHAPANES.

Tahquamenon River (tŭkwä'mŭnŭn, -mŭnŏn"), NE Upper Peninsula, Mich., rises in small lakes in W Luce co., flows SE and E, then N and E through wild forested area to W shore of Whitefish Bay of L. Superior; c.80 mi. long. Associated with Longfellow's *Hiawatha*, the scenic Tahquamenon Falls (2 cataracts, 6 mi. apart) attract tourists.

Tahsien (dä'shyĕn'), town (pop. 26,431), ⊙ Tahsien co. (pop. 670,375), NE Szechwan prov., China, 125 mi. NNE of Chungking city and on left tributary of Chü R. (head of navigation); paper milling; exports hog bristles; rice, sweet potatoes, millet, wheat, beans. Coal mines near by. Until 1913 called Suiting.

Ta-hsing, China: see TAHING.

Tahsüeh Mountains, Chinese *Tahsüeh Shan* (dä'shüĕ' shän'), outlier of the Tibetan plateau, in E Sikang prov., China, extending N-S bet. Yalung and Tatu rivers; range rises to 24,900 ft. in the Minya Konka. The name is sometimes extended to all ranges in E Sikang (until 1914 in W Szechwan), sometimes known as Szechwan Alps.

Tahta (tä'tä), town (pop. 36,125), Girga prov., central Upper Egypt, on the Nile, on railroad and 34 mi. SSE of Asyut; wool weaving, dairying (butter, cheese); cotton, cereals, dates, sugar.

Tahtali Mountains (tätälŭ'), Turkish *Tahtalı*, S central Turkey, part of the Anti-Taurus range, E of Kayseri; rise to 10,020 ft. in Bey Dag. Tahtali Dag is 8,845 ft. Iron and lignite deposits.

Tahtsa Lake (20 mi. long, 1–2 mi. wide), W central B.C., in Coast Mts., in Tweedsmuir Park, 180 mi. W of Prince George; alt. 2,783 ft. Drained E into Ootsa L. by short Tahtsa R.

Tahu (dä'hōō'), Jap. *Taiko* (tī'kō), village (1935 pop. 6,881), NW Formosa, 9 mi. SSE of Miaoli; camphor center; rice, sugar cane, sweet potatoes.

Tahua (tä'wä), village (pop. c.1,200), Potosí dept., SW Bolivia, at SW foot of Tahua peak (17,457 ft.), 60 mi. N of Colcha "K", with which it is connected by road across the Salar de Uyuni; saltworks.

Tahuamanu, Bolivia: see PORVENIR.

Tahuamanu, province, Peru: see IÑAPARI.

Tahuamanu River (täwämä'nōō), rises in Madre de Dios dept., E Peru, flows c.250 mi. E, into Bolivia, past Porvenir, joining Manuripi R. at Puerto Rico to form ORTON RIVER. Navigable in middle and lower course, c.100 mi. Rubber is exploited in tropical forests along its banks in Bolivia.

Tahuata (tähōōä'tä), volcanic island (pop. 305), Marquesas Isls., Fr. Oceania, S Pacific, 3 mi. SW of Hiva Oa across Bordelaise Channel; rises to c.3,280 ft. Many valleys; most fertile is Vaitahu. Formerly called Santa Cristina Isl., Resolution Isl.

Tahuenahuec Island, Chile: see CHONOS ARCHIPELAGO.

Tahuesco (täwĕ'skō), village (pop. 244), Suchitepéquez dept., SW Guatemala, on Pacific Ocean, 25 mi. SE of Champerico; fisheries, saltworks.

Tahulandang or **Tahoelandang** (both: tŭhōō"ländäng'), island (□ 24; pop. 9,950), Sangi Isls., Indonesia, bet. Celebes Sea and Molucca Passage, 45 mi. NNE of Celebes; 7 mi. long, 4 mi. wide; mountainous, forested. Lumbering, agr., fishing.

Tahuna, Indonesia: see SANGI ISLANDS.

Tahushan (dä'hōō'shän'), town, S central Liaosi prov., Manchuria, 60 mi. NE of Chinchow and on railroad to Mukden; junction for Heishan.

Tahwai or **Tahway** (tähwī'), village (pop. 7,720), Minufiya prov., Lower Egypt, on Rosetta branch of the Nile and 7 mi. NW of Ashmun; cereals, cotton, flax.

Ta-i, China: see TAYI.

Taï (tī), village (pop. c.900), SW Ivory Coast, Fr. West Africa, on Liberia border, 115 mi. NW of Sassandra, coffee, rice.

Taiabad or **Tayebat** (both: täyĕbät'), village, Ninth Prov., in Khurasan, NE Iran, 125 mi. SE of Meshed, and on highway to Herat, near Afghanistan border.

Taiama (täyä'mä), town (pop. 1,500), South-Western Prov., central Sierra Leone, on Jong R. and 12 mi. N of Mano, at head of road; palm oil and kernels, piassava, rice.

Taian or **T'ai-an** (both: tī'än'). **1** Town, W central Heilungkiang prov., Manchuria, China, on railroad and 75 mi. NE of Tsitsihar; soybeans, kaoliang, rye, hemp, indigo. **2** Town, ⊙ Taian co. (pop. 209,609), SE Liaosi prov., Manchuria, China, 50 mi. SW of Mukden, on Liao plain; kaoliang. Until 1914 called Pakiotai. **3** Town (1934 pop. 79,803), ⊙ Taian co. (1946 pop. 906,075), W Shantung prov., China, at foot of the Tai Shan, 30 mi. SSE of Tsinan, and on Tientsin-Pukow RR; peanut-growing center; silk weaving; wheat, beans, kaoliang.

Taian, Formosa: see TAAN.

Taiarapu (tīärä'pōō), peninsula, E Tahiti, Society Isls., S Pacific; joined to W Tahiti by isthmus. Also called Tahiti iti.

Taibique (tīvē'kä), village (pop. 1,247), Hierro, Canary Isls., 9 mi. SSW of Valverde; fig- and wine-growing. Iron deposits.

Taichao or **T'ai-chao,** Tibet: see GIAMDA.

T'ai-chiang, China: see TAIKIANG.

Taichow. 1 or **T'ai-chou** (tī'jō'), town, Chekiang prov., China: see LINHAI. **2** or **T'ai-chou** (tī'jō'), city (1948 pop. 131,058), N Kiangsu prov., China, 28 mi. ENE of Yangchow; rice center; wheat, beans, rapeseed, cotton; rice milling, oil pressing.

Called Taihsien (1912–49) while ⊙ Taihsien co. (1948 pop. 880,211). **3** or Tai-chou (dī'jō'), town, Shansi prov., China: see TAIHSIEN.

Taichu, Formosa: see TAICHUNG.

Taichung or **T'ai-chung** (tī'jŏŏng'), Jap. *Taichu* (tī'chōō), city (1940 pop. 82,259; 1950 pop. 207,009), W central Formosa, on railroad and 70 mi. SW of Taipei; agr. and commercial center; rice, bananas, sugar cane, jute, hemp, camphor; sugar milling, distilling. Has airfield and aircraft assembly plant. City has one of finest parks of Formosa (NE), industrial dist. (SE), and govt. and business section (NW). It was briefly considered (1890) as ⊙ Formosa. The name Taichung is also applied to YÜANLIN, 14 mi. SW.

Taiden, Korea: see TAEJON.

Taidong River, Korea: see TAEDONG RIVER.

Taiei, Russian SFSR: see UGOLNY, Sakhalin oblast.

Taien, Formosa: see TAYÜAN.

Taierhchwang or **T'ai-erh-chuang** (both: tīr'jwäng'), town, SW Shantung prov., China, 35 mi. NE of Süchow, near Kiangsu line, transportation hub on spur of Tientsin-Pukow RR, on highway and on Grand Canal.

Taieri, county, New Zealand: see MOSGIEL.

Taieri River (tī'rē), SE S.Isl., New Zealand, rises in Rock and Pillar Range 20 mi. E of Roxburgh, flows 125 mi. N and SE to the S Pacific 20 mi. SW of Dunedin; drains agr. area. Summer resort at mouth.

Taif or **Al-Ta'if** (ăl tä'ĭf), city (pop. 25,000), S central Hejaz, Saudi Arabia, on high plateau, 40 mi. ESE of Mecca; alt. 5,350 ft.; 21°16'N 40°24'E. Summer resort and summer capital of Hejaz; center of fruitgrowing dist. (grapes, apricots, pomegranates) noted for its wine and attar of roses (for Mecca pilgrim trade). Weaving handicrafts. Yemen–Saudi Arabia treaty was signed here, 1934.

Taiga or **Tayga** (tīgä'), city (1938 pop. estimate 33,800), NW Kemerovo oblast, Russian SFSR, on Trans-Siberian RR and 50 mi. NNW of Kemerovo; rail junction (branch railroad to Tomsk) mfg. (beverages, bricks); truck produce; beekeeping station.

Taigonos Peninsula or **Taygonos Peninsula** (tīgŭnôs'), on N Sea of Okhotsk, NE Siberian Russian SFSR; separates Gizhiga and Penzhina bays; c.150 mi. long, c.90 mi. wide.

Taihang Mountains, Chinese *Taihang Shan* (dī'häng' shän'), on SE edge of Shensi plateau, China, forming boundary bet. Shensi (W), Hopeh and Pingyuan (E); rise to over 4,500 ft. Have rich iron-ore deposits.

Taihape (tīhä'pē), borough (pop. 2,186), S central N.Isl., New Zealand, 65 mi. WSW of Napier; dairy plants, sawmills.

Taihei, Russian SFSR: see UDARNY.

Taiheizan, Formosa: see TAIPINGSHAN.

Taihing or **T'ai-hsing** (both: tī'shĭng'), town (pop. 30,488), ⊙ Taihing co. (pop. 404,144), N Kiangsu prov., China, 35 mi. E of Chinkiang, across Yangtze R.; rice, wheat, beans, kaoliang, rapeseed.

Taiho or **T'ai-ho** (both: tī'hŭ'). **1** Town, ⊙ Taiho co. (pop. 475,389), N Anhwei prov., China, 20 mi. NW of Fowyang and on Ying R.; wheat, beans, cotton, kaoliang, sweet potatoes. **2** Town (pop. 21,028), ⊙ Taiho co. (pop. 131,512), SW Kiangsi prov., China, 25 mi. SSW of Kian, and on Kan R., in rice-growing region. Tungsten and bismuth mining; limestone deposits.

Taihochen or **T'ai-ho-chen** (both: tī'hŭ'jŭn'), town, central Szechwan prov., China, 25 mi. SE of Santai and on right bank of Fow R.; cotton and salt-trading center.

Taihoku, Formosa: see TAIPEI.

Taihsien. 1 or **T'ai-hsien** (tī'shyĕn'), city, Kiangsu prov., China: see TAICHOW. **2** (dī'shyĕn') Town, ⊙ Taihsien co. (pop. 112,176), northernmost Shansi prov., China, on upper Huto R., on rail spur and 90 mi. NNE of Taiyüan, near S section of Great Wall (Chahar line); commercial center; wheat, millet, kaoliang. Until 1912, Taichow.

T'ai-hsing, China: see TAIHING.

Taihu or **T'ai-hu** (both: tī'hōō'), town, ⊙ Taihu co. (pop. 328,777), N Anhwei prov., China, 45 mi. W of Anking, near Hupeh line; rice, tea, cotton, lacquer, tung oil; vegetable-tallow processing (soap, candles), papermaking.

T'ai Hu, lake, China: see TAI LAKE.

Taiji (tī'jē) or **Daiji** (dī'jē), town (pop. 4,346), Wakayama prefecture, S Honshu, Japan, on Kumano Sea, on SE Kii Peninsula, 10 mi. SSW of Shingu; fishing, rice growing, stock raising.

Taikang or **T'ai-k'ang** (both: tī'käng'). **1** Town, ⊙ Taikang co. (pop. 10,046), SW Heilungkiang prov., Manchuria, 50 mi. SE of Tsitsihar; soybeans, wheat, kaoliang, corn, millet, rye. **2** Town, ⊙ Taikang co. (pop. 369,757), NE Honan prov., China, on road and 60 mi. SSE of Kaifeng; cotton weaving; grain, salt.

Taikei, Formosa: see TAKI.

Taikgyi, Burma: see TAIKKYI.

Taikiang or **T'ai-chiang** (both: tī'jyäng'), town (pop. 2,564), ⊙ Taikiang co. (pop. 43,710), E Kweichow prov., China, 32 mi. S of Chenyüan; cotton textiles, embroideries; wheat, beans, millet, kaoliang. Until 1942, Taikung.

Taikkyi (tĭk"chē'), village, Insein dist., Lower Burma, on Rangoon-Prome RR and 40 mi. NNW of Rangoon. Also spelled Taikgyi.

Taiko, Formosa: see TAHU; TAKIA.

Taikoktow (tīkŏktou', dī'gôk'tou'), island at mouth of Canton R., S Kwangtung prov., China, W of the Boca Tigris, 35 mi. SE of Canton. Sometimes spelled Tycocktow or Taikoktau.

Taiku or **T'ai-ku** (both: tī'gōō'), town, ⊙ Taiku co. (pop. 111,719), central Shansi prov., China, 40 mi. S of Taiyüan; rail junction and commercial center; copper articles, lacquer goods, felt; beans, wheat, cotton, indigo, watermelons.

Taiku, Korea: see TAEGU.

Taikung, China: see TAIKIANG.

Taikyu, Korea: see TAEGU.

Tailai or **T'ai-lai** (both: tī'lī'), town, ⊙ Tailai co. (pop. 140,246), SW Heilungkiang prov., Manchuria, 70 mi. SSW of Tsitsihar and on railroad; kaoliang, wheat, corn, beans, tobacco.

Tai Lake, Chinese *T'ai Hu* (tī' hōō') [great lake], one of China's largest lakes, on Kiangsu-Chekiang border, bet. Shanghai and Nanking; 40 mi. long (E–W), 35 mi. wide. Contains numerous isls. and is connected with Grand Canal. Sericulture and fisheries along shores. In lake vicinity are the urban centers of Wusih (N), Soochow (E), Wukiang (E), Ihing (W), Wuhing (S), and Changhing (SW).

Tailak-Paion, Uzbek SSR: see KOMSOMOLSK, Samarkand oblast.

Tailem Bend (tā'lŭm), town (pop. 1,307), SE South Australia, 55 mi. ESE of Adelaide and on Murray R.; rail junction; dairying and agr. center; wheat.

Tailfingen (tīl'fĭng-ŭn), town (pop. 10,349), S Württemberg, Germany, after 1945 in Württemberg-Hohenzollern, in Swabian Jura, 3 mi. N of Ebingen; mfg. of knitwear, machinery, furniture; woodworking. Site of chemical research institute.

Taillefer (tīfâr'), small range of Dauphiné Alps, in Isère dept., SE France, bet. lower Romanche (N) and Bonne (S) rivers, SW of Le Bourg-d'Oisans. Rises to 9,396 ft.

Taima or **Tayma** (tämă'), outlying town and oasis of Jebel Shammar prov., Nejd, Saudi Arabia, 200 mi. W of Hail; farming (dates, millet, fruit), stock raising. Formerly considered part of Hejaz and called Teima.

Taimatí (tīmätē'), village (pop. 368), Darién prov., E Panama, on Garachiné Bay of the Pacific, at mouth of small Taimatí R., and 18 mi. SSW of La Palma; fishing, lumbering; corn, rice, beans.

Taimi Canal (tī'mē), major irrigation channel in Lambayeque dept., NW Peru, branches off from Lambayeque R. 6 mi. ENE of Pucalá, flows 40 mi. through major rice and sugar-cane region to area of Ferreñafe. Feeds numerous irrigation channels. Also Taymi.

Taimo Shan (dī'mō' shän'), highest mountain (3,141 ft.) of Hong Kong colony, in the New Territories, 7 mi. NW of Kowloon.

Tai Mountains, Chinese *Tai Shan* or *T'ai Shan* (tī' shän'), W central Shantung prov., China, SE of Tsinan; rise to 5,069 ft. in the Tai Shan, 6 mi. N of Taian, one of China's sacred mts., which has several Buddhist and Taoist temples visited by pilgrims.

Taimyr, Lake, or **Lake Taymyr** (tīmĭr') (□ 2,700), on N Taimyr Peninsula, Krasnoyarsk Territory, Russian SFSR; 125 mi. long (E–W); traversed by Taimyra R. Coal deposits near by.

Taimyra River or **Taymyra River** (–mī'rŭ), on Taimyr Peninsula, Krasnoyarsk Territory, Russian SFSR, rises at center of peninsula, flows NE through L. Taimyr, and N to Taimyr Gulf of Kara Sea; 330 mi. long. Called Verkhnyaya Taimyra [Rus.,=upper Taimyra] above L. Taimyr.

Taimyr Island or **Taymyr Island**, in Kara Sea of Arctic Ocean, near Taimyra R. mouth, 2 mi. off N Taimyr Peninsula, Krasnoyarsk Territory, Russian SFSR.

Taimyr National Okrug or **Taymyr National Okrug**, administrative division (□ 316,700; pop. 25,000) of N Krasnoyarsk Territory, Siberian Russian SFSR; ⊙ Dudinka. Bounded S by Putorana Mts., N by Kara and Laptev seas. Tundra and forest area. Inhabitants are mainly nomad Nentsy (Samoyeds) and Dolgans. Reindeer raising, hunting, fishing. Mining at Norilsk. Formed 1930; formerly called Dolgan-Nenets Natl. Okrug for its 2 main ethnic groups.

Taimyr Peninsula or **Taymyr Peninsula**, northernmost projection of Siberian Russian SFSR, on Kara and Laptev seas, bet. Yenisei and Khatanga river mouths; 700 mi. long (NE–SW); covered by tundra. N extremity is Cape Chelyuskin. Contains Byrranga Mts. and L. Taimyr.

Tain (tān), burgh (1931 pop. 1,383; 1951 census 1,602), NE Ross and Cromarty, Scotland, on Dornoch Firth, 5 mi. S of Dornoch; port and agr. market. Has 15th-cent. hall, formerly church of St. Duthus. Tain was created a royal burgh by James VI in 1587. Near by are ruins of 13th-cent. chapel. Tain was site of Scottish estate of Andrew Carnegie.

Tainan or **T'ai-nan** (both: tī'nän'), Jap. *Tainan* (tī'nän), city (1940 pop. 142,133; 1950 pop. 229,452), W central Formosa, on W coast, 25 mi. N of Kaohiung, and on railroad; 23°N 120°12'E. Major economic and cultural center, with ANPING as its port; processing of agr. products (rice, castor beans, sugar cane, sweet potatoes, fruit); ironworks; mfg. of gunny bags. Has shrines of Confucius and Koxinga. Founded by the Dutch, who built Fort Providentia here (1650), the city became ⊙ Formosa under Koxinga's rule (1662–83). Called Taiwan or Taiwanfu, it remained political center of isl. until transfer of govt. to Taipei in 1885, when the city was renamed Tainan. The name Tainan is also applied officially to SINYING, 22 mi. NNE of here.

Tainaron, Cape, Greece: see MATAPAN, CAPE.

Taincha or **Tayncha** (tīnchä'), town (1948 pop. over 2,000), N Kokchetav oblast, Kazakh SSR, on railroad and 40 mi. NNE of Kokchetav; coal mining.

Taïneste (tīnĕst'), village (pop. 221), Fez region, N Fr. Morocco, on S slope of Rif Mts., 24 mi. N of Taza; alt. 4,750 ft.

Taining or **T'ai-ning** (both: tī'nĭng'). **1** Town (pop. 4,668), ⊙ Taining co. (pop. 45,254), NW Fukien prov., China, 65 mi. WNW of Nanping; rice, beans, peanuts, wheat, rapeseed. Talc quarrying. **2** Town, Sikang prov., China: see KIENNING.

Tainionkoski (tī'nēōn-kōs"kē), village in Joutseno commune (pop. 9,527), Kymi co., SE Finland, near USSR border, on Vuoksi R. (rapids) near its mouth on L. Saimaa, 2 mi. NW of Imatra; pulp, cellulose, paper, and bobbin mills, alcohol plant. Hydroelectric station.

Tain-l'Hermitage (tē-lĕrmētäzh'), town (pop. 3,220), Drôme dept., SE France, on left bank of Rhone R., opposite Tournon, and 10 mi. NNW of Valence; known for Hermitage wines grown on near-by hills. Mfg. (chocolate, fruit preserves, refractories).

Taiohae (tī"ōhä'ĕ), village (pop. 442), former ⊙ Marquesas Isls., on Taiohae Bay, S coast of Nuku Hiva, Marquesas Isls., Fr. Oceania, S Pacific. Bay is c.3 mi. long, 2 mi. wide; protected by ridges 3,000 ft. high.

Taipai Shan, China: see TSINLING MOUNTAINS.

Taipa Islands (dī'pä'), two islands (□ 2; pop. 6,148) of Macao colony, in S.China Sea, 4 mi. SSE of Macao peninsula; fisheries. Small port of Taipa is on SW shore of larger isl. (E).

Taipang Wan, Hong Kong: see MIRS BAY.

Taipeh, Formosa: see TAIPEI.

Taipei, Taipeh, or **T'ai-pei** (all: tī'bā'), Jap. *Taihoku* (tī'hōkōō), city (1940 pop. 326,407; 1950 pop. 450,777), ⊙ Formosa, on right bank of Tanshui R. and 15 mi. WSW of Keelung (its port), 10 mi. SE of Tanshui (its former port); 25°2'N 121°31'E. N terminus of W coast railroad, administrative and cultural center; rice and tea processing; steel foundry; glass mfg. Coal mining (S, SE). Taipei consists of the sections of Wanhwa (SW), Chengnai (SE), and Tataocheng (N), all amalgamated in 1920. Wanhwa, also known as Mankia (Jap. *Manka*), is the oldest section of the city and its former commercial and harbor quarter. Because of river silting, these activities were transferred (late-19th cent.) to Tataocheng (Jap. *Taitotei*), the more modern commercial and industrial quarter, with zoological garden. The SE section, Chengnai (Jap. *Jonai*), is the most modern part of Taipei, founded 1885 on site of anc. castle walls and developed under Jap. rule as the city's administrative and residential quarter. It has radio station, library, botanical garden, and, in its outskirts, Taipei univ. NE of Taipei are the major industrial plants, extending toward Sungshan, site of Taipei's airport. Founded 1708 by immigrants from Chüanchow in Fukien prov., China, who settled in the Wanhwa quarter, Taipei received another pop. influx (19th cent.) from Changchow, also in Fukien prov., which settled in Tataocheng. In 1885, the ⊙ Formosa was moved here from Tainan and the modern development of the city began under Jap. rule (1895–1945); Taipei underwent considerable modernization and expansion. The 3 city quarters were united in 1920, and the city limits were expanded in 1938 to include Sungshan. During the Second World War, Taipei suffered damage from bombing. In 1949 it became the refuge of the Nationalist Chinese regime expelled from the mainland. The name Taipei is also applied to PANKIAO, 4 mi. SW.

Taiping or **T'ai-p'ing** (both: tī'pĭng'). **1** Town, ⊙ Taiping co. (pop. 70,115), S Anhwei prov., China, 70 mi. SSW of Wuhu, in Hwang Mts.; tung oil, tea, silk. Until 1912, the name Taiping was applied to TANGTU, 15 mi. NNE of Wuhu. **2** Town, Chekiang prov., China: see WENLING. **3** Town, Kiangsu prov., China: see YANGCHUNG. **4** Town, Kwangsi prov., China: see TSUNGSHAN. **5** Town, S Kwangtung prov., China, fishing port on E shore of Canton R. estuary, 15 mi. SW of Tungkun, near the Boca Tigris; commercial center. Formerly also called Humen. **6** Town, Shansi prov., China: see FENCHENG. **7** Town, Szechwan prov., China: see WANYÜAN.

Taiping (tīpĭng'), town (pop. 41,361), ⊙ Perak, W Malaya, on railroad and 45 mi. SE of George Town; tin mining; rubber, rice. Has mus. Situated picturesquely at foot of Maxwell's Hill (E; alt. c.4,000 ft.), a noted hill station and holiday resort. Further E is Caulfield's Hill (alt. 4,558 ft.) with Br. residence. Once the leading tin-mining center of Malaya, Taiping has been supplanted by Kinta Valley.

Taiping Island, China: see ITU ABA ISLAND.
Taipingshan or **T'ai-p'ing-shan** (both: tī'pĭng'shän'), Jap. *Taiheizan* (tīhā'zän), village, N Formosa, on railroad and 21 mi. SW of Lotung; lumbering center of Formosan cypress forests.
Taipinsan, Ryukyu Isls.: see MIYAKO-JIMA.
Taipu (tīpōō'), city (pop. 855), E Rio Grande do Norte, NE Brazil, on railroad and 31 mi. WNW of Natal; cotton, corn, manioc.
Taipu (dī'bōō'), Mandarin *Tapu* (dä'bōō), town, ⊙ Taipu co. (pop. 262,104), E Kwangtung prov., China, on Han R. and 75 mi. N of Swatow, near Fukien border; grain. Kaolin quarrying.
Taira (tī'rä). **1** City (1940 pop. 30,126; 1947 pop. 31,595), Fukushima prefecture, central Honshu, Japan, 55 mi. SSE of Fukushima, in fruitgrowing, poultry-raising area; spinning, sake brewing, woodworking. **2** Town (pop. 6,148) on Uku-shima, of isl. group Goto-retto, Nagasaki prefecture, Japan, on E.China Sea; chief town of isl.; fishing.
Taira, Ryuku Isls.: see HIRARA.
Tairadate Strait, Japan: see TSUGARU STRAIT.
Tairetá (tīrĭtä'), town (pop. 3,251), W Rio de Janeiro state, Brazil, 28 mi. NW of Rio; coffee, sugar cane, fruit, cattle.
Tairin, Formosa: see TALIN.
Taisei, Korea: see TAEJONG.
Tai Seng (tī'sĕng'), NE suburb (pop. 4,427), of Singapore, Singapore isl., on city line, 4 mi. NE of city center. Pop. is Chinese.
Taisha (tī'shä), town (pop. 10,905), Shimane prefecture, SW Honshu, Japan, on Sea of Japan, 22 mi. WSW of Matsue; rail terminus; soy sauce, sake; raw silk. Poultry; fishing. Site of Izumo Taisha (great shrine of Izumo), which legend holds to be the oldest shrine in Japan. Present structure housing the shrine built 1874. Pine-covered grounds cover 20 acres. Mus. has historical relics. There are 68 smaller shrines near the main shrine. Bathing beaches near by. Sometimes spelled Taisya.
T'ai-shan, town, China: see TOISHAN.
Tai Shan or **Day Shan** (both: dī'shän'), island of Chusan Archipelago, in E.China Sea, Chekiang prov., China; 30°20'N 122°10'E; 8.5 mi. long, 6.5 mi. wide.
Tai Shan or **T'ai Shan,** mountains, China: see TAI MOUNTAINS.
Taishet or **Tayshet** (tīshĕt'), city (1939 pop. estimate 17,000), W Irkutsk oblast, Russian SFSR, on Trans-Siberian RR and 200 mi. E of Krasnoyarsk. Lumbering center; sawmilling, mfg. of railroad ties, brickmaking. Completion (after 1950) of Abakan-Taishet section of S.Siberian RR will make Taishet a major rail center. Construction of Baikal-Amur trunk railroad started here (1938); interrupted during Second World War.
Taishun or **T'ai-shun** (tī'shōōn'), town (pop. 11,014), ⊙ Taishun co. (pop. 174,305), S Chekiang prov., China, on Fukien line, 65 mi. SW of Wenchow; sweet potatoes, tea, berries, chestnuts, rice. Manganese mines near by.
Taiskirchen im Innkreis (tīs'kĭrkhůn ĭm ĭn'krīs), town (pop. 2,779), W Upper Austria, 5 mi. NE of Ried; potatoes, fruit.
Taisya, Japan: see TAISHA.
Taitao Peninsula (tītou'), Aysén prov., S Chile, on the Pacific S of Chonos Archipelago. Mountainous and irregular, with many sounds, adjoining islets, and smaller peninsulas, it is c.75 mi. long (N–S), c.70 mi. wide, connected with mainland by narrow Ofqui Isthmus (6 mi. wide), which borders beautiful L. San Rafael. NW part is Skyring Peninsula, SW Tres Montes Peninsula. Small settlement Istmo de Ofqui on L. San Rafael has radio station. Its NW cape, Point Taitao, is at 45°53'S 75°5'W.
Taito, Formosa: see TAITUNG.
Taitotei, Formosa: see TAIPEI.
Taitsang or **T'ai-ts'ang** (tī'tsäng'), town (pop. 24,068), ⊙ Taitsang co. (pop. 305,422), S Kiangsu prov., China, 27 mi. NW of Shanghai, in rice region; wheat, cotton; spinning, weaving.
Taitung or **T'ai-tung** (both: tī'dōōng'), Jap. *Taito* (tī'tō), town (1935 pop. 8,886), SE Formosa, port on E coast, 55 mi. E of Kaohiung; S terminus of E coast railroad; agr. center; sugar milling, cotton ginning; coffee, cacao. Has experimental station for tropical agr. Formerly called Pinan. Hot springs of Chihpen are 7 mi. SW.
Taitzesze, China: see NINGTING.
Taivaskero, Finland: see PALLAS MOUNTAINS.
Taivassalo (tī'väs-sä'lō), Swedish *Tövsala* (tûv'sälä"), village (commune pop. 3,032), Turku-Pori co., SW Finland, on small inlet of Gulf of Bothnia, 25 mi. WNW of Turku; granite quarries.
Taiwan, island: see FORMOSA.
Taiwan or **Taiwanfu,** city, Formosa: see TAINAN.
Taiwara, Afghanistan: see GHOR.
Taiwi, Oman: see TIWI.
Taiya Inlet (tī'ů), SE Alaska, NNE arm (12 mi. long) of Chilkoot Inlet, an arm of Lynn Canal, NNW of Juneau; 59°25'N 135°18'W; extends from Haines to Skagway.
Taiyetos, Greece: see TAYGETUS.
Taiyo Mountains (dī'yō') or **Hwo Mountains** (hwō), Chinese *Taiyo Shan* or *Hwo* (*Ho*) *Shan* (shän), on S central Shansi line, China, on E divide of Fen R.; rise to 8,500 ft. 15 mi. E of Hwohsien.
Taiyüan or **T'ai-yüan** (both: tī'yüän'), city (1934 pop. 251,566), ⊙ Shansi prov., N China, on Fen R., on railroad and 250 mi. SW of Peking; alt. 2,600 ft.; 37°52'N 112°35'E. Agr. and industrial center, in densely populated farming dist. (wheat, kaoliang, beans, tobacco, ramie, wine). Metallurgical plant (iron and steel production); cotton milling; mfg. of tractors, agr. implements, paper, cement, ceramic products; flour milling. Industry is supplied with coal from near-by mines of Lantsun (13 mi. NW) and Paikiachwang (10 mi. W). Seat of Shansi univ. Dating from 3d cent. B.C., Taiyüan was an early defense center against Mongol invasions. It was visited (13th cent.), while on anc. Peking-Sian route, by Marco Polo. Became ⊙ Shansi under the Ming dynasty. During Sino-Japanese War, it was held (1937–45) by the Japanese. Passed 1949 to Communist control. During 1912–47, city was called YANGKÜ, as ⊙ Yangkü co., while the name Taiyüan was applied to CHINYÜAN, 10 mi. SW. In 1947, Taiyüan became an independent municipality under its old name, and Yangkü co. seat was transferred to a village 10 mi. N.
Taiyün Mountains, Chinese *Taiyün Shan* (dī'yün' shän'), one of the coastal ranges of Fukien prov., China, 75 mi. inland, extending parallel to coast, bet. Kiulung and Min rivers; range rises to over 5,000 ft. 85 mi. WSW of Foochow.
Taiz, Ta'iz, or **Ta'izz** (tă-ĭz'), town (pop. 3,500), ⊙ Taiz prov. (pop. 425,000), SW Yemen, 85 mi. NW of Aden, and on motor road to Hodeida, in maritime range; alt. 4,500 ft. Center of the S coffee dist.; tanning, cotton weaving, jewelry mfg. Situated at N base of the Jabal Sabir (9,863 ft.), Taiz has 3 large mosques, rebuilt by Turks in 15th-16th cent. It was (c.1300) a ⊙ Yemen, had a univ. (c.1500), and was formerly a prosperous city trading through Mocha. Declined in 19th cent. and its trade has shifted to Aden.
Taiza (tī'zä), town (pop. 3,871), Kyoto prefecture, S Honshu, Japan, on Sea of Japan, 25 mi. NNW of Maizuru; fishing and agr. center; raw silk.
Tajewala (tůjä'välů), village, Ambala dist., E Punjab, India, on Jumna R. and 45 mi. E of Ambala; headworks of Jumna Canal system. Also called Bhogriwala.
Tajgarh (täj'gůr), town (pop. 823), Bahawalpur state, W Pakistan, 6 mi. NNW of Rahimyar Khan.
Tajik-, in Rus. names: see TADZHIK-.
Tajima (tä'jĭmä), former province in S Honshu, Japan; now part of Hyogo prefecture.
Tajima, town (pop. 9,697), Fukushima prefecture, central Honshu, Japan, 22 mi. SSW of Wakamatsu; rice, silk cocoons, hemp, charcoal.
Ta-jima (tä'jĭmä), island (□ 4; pop. 5,179), Hiroshima prefecture, Japan, in Inland Sea just off SW coast of Honshu, near Tomo; 3 mi. long, 1.5 mi. wide; mountainous. Produces rice, wheat, raw silk.
Tajimi (tä"jē'mē), city (1940 pop. 26,820; 1947 pop. 36,092), Gifu prefecture, central Honshu, Japan, 17 mi. NE of Nagoya; rail junction; ceramic center; persimmons, raw silk.
Tajiri (tä"jē'rē), town (pop. 6,606), Miyagi prefecture, N Honshu, Japan, 7 mi. NW of Wakuya; rice, silk cocoons.
Tajiro (tä"jē'rō), town (pop. 6,083), Saga prefecture, W Kyushu, Japan, 5 mi. N of Kurume; rice, wheat, raw silk; sake.
Taj Mahal, India: see AGRA, city.
Tajo River, Spain and Portugal: see TAGUS RIVER.
Tajrish (täjrēsh'), village, Second Prov., in Teheran, N Iran, 9 mi. N of Teheran, at foot of Elburz mts.; summer resort for Teheran; truck produce; gardens.
Tajumbina, Cerro (sĕ'rō tähōōmbē'nä), Andean peak (13,533 ft.), SW Colombia, on Nariño-Huila dept. border, 37 mi. ENE of Pasto.
Tajumulco (tähōōmōōl'kō), town (1950 pop. 188), San Marcos dept., SW Guatemala, at N foot of volcano Tajumulco, 11 mi. NNW of San Marcos; alt. 6,560 ft.; coffee, sugar cane, grain.
Tajumulco, extinct volcano (13,816 ft.); highest mtn. in Central America, in San Marcos dept., SW Guatemala. Climbed from San Marcos, 9 mi. SE. Sulphur deposits.
Tajuña River (tähōō'nyä), New Castile, central Spain, rises near Soria prov. border SE of Medinaceli, flows c.150 mi. SW, past Brihuega, through Guadalajara and Madrid provs., to the Jarama (affluent of the Tagus) 6 mi. N of Aranjuez. Used for irrigation.
Tajura, Fr. Somaliland: see TADJOURA.
Tak (täk), town (1947 pop. 8,246), ⊙ Tak prov. (□ 5,255; 1947 pop. 102,193), W Thailand, on Ping R. and 240 mi. NNW of Bangkok, on road from Phitsanulok; teak center; airport. Local name, Rahaeng or Raheng.
Taka, Bhutan: see TAGA.
Taka (tä'kä), uninhabited atoll, Ratak Chain, Kwajalein dist., Marshall Isls., W central Pacific, 190 mi. NE of Kwajalein; c.30 mi. in circumference.
Takab (täkäb'), town, Fifth Prov., in Garus, NW Iran, in the Kurd country, 75 mi. N of Sanandaj; grain, tobacco; sheep raising.
Takachiho (täkä'chĭhō). **1** Town (pop. 11,102), Miyazaki prefecture, E central Kyushu, Japan, on Gokase R. and 23 mi. WNW of Nobeoka; mtn. resort; rice, lumber, charcoal, livestock. **2** Village, Yamaguchi prefecture, Japan: see ONODA.
Takachiho-dake, Japan: see KIRISHIMA-YAMA.
Takada (tä"kä'dä). **1** Town (pop. 7,068), Fukushima prefecture, N central Honshu, Japan, 6 mi. WSW of Wakamatsu; rice, silk cocoons. **2** or **Takata** (tä"kä'tä), town (pop. 6,377), Gifu prefecture, central Honshu, Japan, 5 mi. SW of Ogaki; rice, market produce. **3** Town (pop. 6,269), Iwate prefecture, N Honshu, Japan, on the Pacific, 23 mi. SW of Kamaishi; agr. (rice, tobacco); spinning. **4** Town (pop. 31,334), Nara prefecture, S Honshu, Japan, 17 mi. SE of Osaka; textile center in agr. area (rice, watermelons). **5** City (1940 pop. 30,152; 1947 pop. 38,226), Niigata prefecture, central Honshu, Japan, 75 mi. SW of Niigata, in livestock-raising area; mfg. (dolls, skis). Ski resort. **6** Town, Oita prefecture, Japan: see TAKATA.
Takagawa, Japan: see ATAMI, Fukushima.
Takahagi (täkä'-hä'gē), town (pop. 17,855), Ibaraki prefecture, central Honshu, Japan, 8 mi. NE of Hitachi; mining center (anthracite coal). Until 1937, called Matsubara.
Takahama (täkä'hämů). **1** Town (pop. 18,691), Aichi prefecture, central Honshu, Japan, 3 mi. NE of Handa, across Chita Bay; fish hatcheries; makes ironware. **2** Town (pop. 5,959), Fukui prefecture, S Honshu, Japan, on S Wakasa Bay, 11 mi. W of Obama; pottery making. Fish hatcheries. Sometimes called Wakasa-takahama. **3** Town (pop. 4,462), Ibaraki prefecture, central Honshu, Japan, on lagoon Kasumi-ga-ura, 2 mi. SE of Ishioka; rice, wheat. **4** Town (pop. 3,779), Ishikawa prefecture, central Honshu, Japan, on Toyama Bay, 11 mi. WSW of Nanao, fishing port; raw silk. **5** Town (pop. 2,367), Niigata prefecture, central Honshu, Japan, on Sea of Japan, 7 mi. NNE of Kashiwazaki; fishing; summer resort.
Takaharu (täkä'-hä'rōō), town (pop. 15,406), Miyazaki prefecture, S central Kyushu, Japan, 24 mi. W of Miyazaki; agr. center (rice, wheat); raw silk, lumber. Starting point for ascent of Kirishima-yama.
Takahashi (täkä'-hä'shē), town (pop. 13,012), Okayama prefecture, SW Honshu, Japan, 20 mi. NW of Okayama, in agr. area (rice, wheat, peppermint); raw silk, wheat, straw; paper mills, stockyards.
Takahata (täkä'hätů), town (pop. 10,542), Yamagata prefecture, N Honshu, Japan, 8 mi. NE of Yonezawa; rice and mulberry fields; sandstone quarries.
Takaike (tä"kī'kä), town (pop. 2,727), Wakayama prefecture, S Honshu, Japan, on SE Kii Peninsula, 17 mi. SW of Shingu; rice, raw silk, lumber, livestock, fish.
Takaishi (tä"kī'shē), town (pop. 18,800), Osaka prefecture, S Honshu, Japan, on Osaka Bay, 10 mi. SW of Osaka; beach resort; rice, wheat, poultry. Fishing.
Takajo (täkäjō'), town (pop. 16,323), Miyazaki prefecture, E central Kyushu, Japan, 19 mi. WSW of Miyazaki; agr. center (rice, wheat); lumber, livestock.
Takaka (tä'kůků), town (pop. 512), ⊙ Takaka co. (□ 456; pop. 2,182), NW S.Isl., New Zealand, 40 mi. NW of Nelson, near SE shore of Golden Bay. Near-by Takaka Valley contains deposits of gold, silver, copper, tin, asbestos.
Takaki, Japan: see YAMOTO.
Takakkaw Falls or **Takkakaw Falls** (tă'kůkō), in Yoho Natl. Park, B.C., in the Rockies; drop an estimated 1,200–1,600 ft. in 3 leaps to Yoho R.
Takama (tůkä'mů), village, Berbice co., E central Br. Guiana, on left bank of Berbice R., just N of Paradise, and 55 mi. SSW of New Amsterdam. Terminus of Rupununi cattle trail.
Takamaka (täkämä'kä), village on W coast of Mahé Isl., Seychelles, port on the Anse Takamaka (inlet of Indian Ocean), 10 mi. S of Victoria; copra, essential oils; fisheries.
Takamatsu (täkä'-mä'tsōō). **1** Town (pop. 8,951), Ishikawa prefecture, central Honshu, Japan, on Sea of Japan, 15 mi. NNE of Kanazawa; rice, raw silk; mfg. (silk textiles, tiles); fishing. **2** City (1940 pop. 111,207; 1947 pop. 101,403), ⊙ Kagawa prefecture, N Shikoku, Japan, port on Harima Sea, 85 mi. WSW of Osaka; 34°20'N 134°3'E. Mfg. (cotton textiles, fans, lacquer ware, tissue paper, umbrellas, patent medicine) and cultural center. Exports tobacco, rice, wheat, raw silk, paper. Ritsurin Park (134 acres) is known for its landscape gardens. Site of 14th-cent. castle. Yashima (formerly an isl. just SE of Takamatsu) is part of city, connected to it by a narrow strip of land; site of Buddhist temple containing relics of feudal battles. Takamatsu bombed (1945) in Second World War.
Takamiya (täkä'mēyä), town (pop. 4,119), Shiga prefecture, S Honshu, Japan, just S of Hikone; hemp cloth.
Takamori (täkä'mōrē). **1** Town (pop. 4,684), Kumamoto prefecture, central Kyushu, Japan, 24 mi. E of Kumamoto; rail terminus; rice; bamboo articles. Mulberry groves. **2** Town (pop. 8,994), Yamaguchi prefecture, SW Honshu, Japan, 14 mi. E of Tokuyama; agr. center (rice, wheat, dried mushrooms), livestock; charcoal.

Takanabe (täkä'näbā), town (pop. 20,278), Miyazaki prefecture, E Kyushu, Japan, 14 mi. NNE of Miyazaki; agr. center (rice, wheat, barley); livestock.

Takanosu (täkä'nōsōō) or **Takasu** (tä"kä'sōō), town (pop. 7,465), Akita prefecture, N Honshu, Japan, 18 mi. E of Noshiro; rice-growing center.

Takanysh (tŭkŭnĭsh'), village (1939 pop. over 500), N Tatar Autonomous SSR, Russian SFSR, 20 mi. NW of Mamadysh; grain, legumes, livestock.

Takao, Formosa: see KAOHIUNG.

Takaoka (täkä'ôkä). **1** Town (pop. 9,817), Kochi prefecture, S Shikoku, Japan, on Niyodo R. and 8 mi. WSW of Kochi; paper-milling center; melon-growing. **2** Town (pop. 12,839), Miyazaki prefecture, E Kyushu, Japan, 7 mi. WNW of Miyazaki; commercial center for agr. area (rice, tea); raw silk, lumber, bamboo. **3** Town (pop. 11,580), Shizuoka prefecture, central Honshu, Japan; agr. center (rice, wheat). Hot springs. **4** City (1940 pop. 59,434; 1947 pop. 133,858), Toyama prefecture, central Honshu, Japan, 12 mi. WNW of Toyama; rice-trading and mfg. center (cotton textiles, lacquer and bronze ware). Has 17th-cent. castle of Maeda clan. Includes (since early 1940s) former towns of Shimminato (1940 pop. 24,330) and Fushiki (1940 pop. 14,132).

Takaono (täkä'ônō), town (pop. 11,964), Kagoshima prefecture, W Kyushu, Japan, 36 mi. NNW of Kagoshima; tobacco-producing center; sawmills.

Takapoto, Tuamotu Isls.: see TAKAROA.

Takapuna (tă"kŭpōō'nŭ), borough (pop. 10,272), N N.Isl., New Zealand, 6 mi. N of Auckland, on NE shore of Waitemata Harbour; residential suburb of Auckland.

Takarabe (täkä'räbā), town (pop. 17,663), Kagoshima prefecture, S Kyushu, Japan, 27 mi. ENE of Kagoshima; rail terminus; commercial center for agr. area (rice, wheat); livestock; lumber, raw silk.

Takarazuka, Japan: see KOHAMA.

Takaroa (täkärō'ä), atoll (pop. 257), N Tuamotu Isls., Fr. Oceania, S Pacific; 14°27'S 144°58'W; just N of Takapoto, with which it was discovered 1765 by Byron, who named them King George Isls.

Takasago (täkä'-sä'gō), town (pop. 15,456), Hyogo prefecture, S Honshu, Japan, port on Harima Sea (E section of Inland Sea), 9 mi. SE of Himeji; mfg. (textiles, paper, soy sauce). Exports textiles.

Takasaki (täkä'-sä'kē). **1** City (1940 pop. 71,002; 1947 pop. 88,483), Gumma prefecture, central Honshu, Japan, just SW of Maebashi, 58 mi. NW of Tokyo; rail junction; silk-textile and flour mills, packing houses. **2** Town (pop. 17,045), Miyazaki prefecture, S central Kyushu, Japan, 21 mi. W of Miyazaki; agr. center (rice, wheat); lumber; livestock.

Takashima (täkä'shĭmä), town (pop. 7,786), Shiga prefecture, S Honshu, Japan, on W shore of L. Biwa, 13 mi. W of Hikone; rice-growing center. Includes (since early 1940s) former town of Omizo (1940 pop. 2,486).

Taka-shima (täkä'shĭmä). **1** Island (256 acres; pop. 6,634), Nagasaki prefecture, Japan, in E. China Sea, 8 mi. SW of Nagasaki; 32°40'N 129°45'E; ½ mi. long, ½ mi. wide; hilly. Coal mine. Agr. (sweet potatoes). **2** Island (□ 8; pop. 5,066), Nagasaki prefecture, Japan, in Genkai Sea, just off NW coast of Kyushu, 12 mi. NW of Imari; 33°26'N 129°46'E; 5 mi. long, 3 mi. wide; irregularly shaped. Sweet potatoes, millet; fishing.

Takashimizu (täkä'-shē'mĭzōō), town (pop. 4,356), Miyagi prefecture, N Honshu, Japan, 10 mi. SW of Wakayanagi; rice, silk cocoons.

Takasu (tä"kä'sōō). **1** Town, Akita prefecture, Japan: see TAKANOSU. **2** Town (pop. 4,523), Gifu prefecture, central Honshu, Japan, 17 mi. W of Nagoya; rice; lumber.

Takata (tä"kä'tä). **1** Town, Gifu prefecture, Japan: see TAKADA. **2** or **Takada** (tä"kä'dä), town (pop. 14,918), Oita prefecture, NE Kyushu, Japan, on W Kunisaki Peninsula, 24 mi. NNW of Oita, on Suo Sea; rail terminus; agr. center (rice, wheat, barley).

Takato (täkä'tō), town (pop. 4,635), Nagano prefecture, central Honshu, Japan, 6 mi. E of Ina, in rice-growing area.

Takatomi (täkä'tōmē), town (pop. 3,629), Gifu prefecture, central Honshu, Japan, 5 mi. N of Gifu; rice, wheat, pears.

Takatori (täkä'tōrē), town (pop. 4,487), Nara prefecture, S Honshu, Japan, 17 mi. S of Nara; lumber, charcoal, rice, wheat.

Takatsu, Japan: see KAWASAKI, Kanagawa prefecture.

Takatsuki (täkä'tsōōkē), city (1940 pop. 31,011; 1947 pop. 37,714), Osaka prefecture, S Honshu, Japan, 15 mi. NNE of Osaka; commercial center for dairying, poultry-raising area; silk textiles, drugs, woodworking. Sometimes spelled Takatuki.

Takatu Mountain (tŭ'kŭtōō), N spur (c.11,340 ft.) of Central Brahui Range, in Quetta-Pishin dist., NE Baluchistan, W Pakistan, overlooking city of Quetta (S).

Takaungu (täkoung'gōō), village, Coast Prov., SE Kenya, small port on Indian Ocean, 5 mi. SSE of Kilifi; cotton, copra, sisal.

Takaw (tŭkô'), village, Kengtung state, Southern Shan State, Upper Burma, 60 mi. W of Kengtung, and on road to Taunggyi, at Salween R. (ferry).

Takawa, Japan: see TAGAWA.

Takaya (tä"kä'yä), town (pop. 4,732), Okayama prefecture, SW Honshu, Japan, 7 mi. NNE of Fukuyama, in agr. area (rice, wheat, peppermint, pears); raw silk; textiles.

Takayama (täkä'yämŭ), city (1940 pop. 34,145; 1947 pop. 41,877), Gifu prefecture, central Honshu, Japan, 38 mi. S of Toyama; woodworking, sake brewing. Includes (since 1936) former town of Onada.

Tak Bai (täk' bī'), village (1937 pop. 8,792), Narathiwat prov., S Thailand, minor South China Sea port on E coast of Malay Peninsula, 20 mi. SE of Narathiwat, at mouth of the Sungei Golok (Malaya border).

Takebu (tä"kā'bōō) or **Takefu** (tä"kā'fōō), town (pop. 27,220), Fukui prefecture, central Honshu, Japan, 11 mi. SSW of Fukui; mfg. (rayon textiles, cutlery, paper).

Takeda (tä"kā'dä). **1** Town (pop. 5,104), Hyogo prefecture, S Honshu, Japan, 17 mi. S of Toyooka; rice, wheat, cattle; raw silk, charcoal. **2** Town (pop. 15,647), Oita prefecture, E central Kyushu, Japan, 31 mi. NW of Nobeoka; agr. center; makes bamboo articles.

Takedazu, Japan: see TAKETAZU.

Takefu, Japan: see TAKEBU.

Takegahana (täkāgä'hänŭ), town (pop. 11,431), Gifu prefecture, central Honshu, Japan, 7 mi. SW of Gifu; textile-collection center; rice, persimmons.

Takehara (täkā'härŭ), town (pop. 12,903), Hiroshima prefecture, SW Honshu, Japan, on Hiuchi Sea, 20 mi. ENE of Kure; fishing and agr. center (rice, wheat, grapes); salt, sake, soy sauce.

Takeli (tŭkyĕ'lyē), town (1939 pop. over 500), N Leninabad oblast, Tadzhik SSR, on SW slope of Kurama Range, 18 mi. NNW of Leninabad; arsenic mine.

Takengon, Indonesia: see TAKINGUN.

Takeo (tä'kyō'), town, ⊙ Takeo prov. (□ 1,500; 1948 pop. 364,211), SW Cambodia, 40 mi. S of Pnompenh; agr. (rice, pepper, sugar palm, lac, hardwoods); sericulture. Cattle exports. R.C. mission. Pop. chiefly Chinese and Annamese.

Takeo (tä"kā'ō), town (pop. 14,812), Saga prefecture, W Kyushu, Japan, on central Hizen Peninsula, 17 mi. E of Sasebo; health resort (ferruginous hot springs); rice, wheat, raw silk.

Takestan, Iran: see TAKISTAN.

Taketazu (täkā'-tä'zōō) or **Takedazu** (–dä'zōō), town (pop. 3,741), Oita prefecture, NE Kyushu, Japan, on N Kunisaki Peninsula, 30 mi. N of Oita, on Suo Sea; mfg. (sake, silk textiles), lumbering; fishing.

Taketoyo (täkā'tōyō), town (pop. 10,849), Aichi prefecture, central Honshu, Japan, on E Chita Peninsula, port on Chita Bay, 3 mi. SSW of Handa; mfg. (cotton textiles, soy sauce, sake, dynamite). Exports raw silk, sake.

Takeyama, Formosa: see CHUSHAN.

Takfan (tŭkfän'), village, S Leninabad oblast, Tadzhik SSR, on Leninabad-Stalinabad highway and 40 mi. N of Stalinabad. Site of extensive coal and ore deposits extending 30 mi. W along Zeravshan Range to Ravat, Zauran, and Kshtut.

Takhia-Tash (tä'khēä-täsh'), town, S Kara-Kalpak Autonomous SSR, Uzbek SSR, on left bank of the Amu Darya and 10 mi. S of Nukus, on railroad from Urgench; site of hydroelectric station, dam, and headworks of the TURKMEN CANAL. Founded in 1950.

Takhing (dŭk'hĭng'), Mandarin *Te-ch'ng* (dŭ'-chĭng'), town (pop. 6,439), ⊙ Takhing co. (pop. 167,075), W Kwangtung prov., China, on West R. and 40 mi. SE of Wuchow; produces matting. Ink-stone quarries. Tin mining near by. Opened to foreign trade in 1897. Sometimes spelled Tehking.

Ta Khli (tä' klē'), village (1937 pop. 5,597), Nakhon Sawan prov., central Thailand, on Bangkok–Chiangmai RR and 110 mi. N of Bangkok; iron mining; foundry. Highway to Chainat on Chao Phraya R.

Takhmau (täk'mou'), village, Kandal prov., S Cambodia, on Bassac R. and 6 mi. SSE of Pnompenh; insane asylum.

Takhta (tŭkhtä'). **1** Village (1948 pop. over 500), SE Lower Amur oblast, Khabarovsk Territory, Russian SFSR, on Amur R. and 35 mi. W of Nikolayevsk; fisheries. **2** Village (1926 pop. 4,407), NW Stavropol Territory, Russian SFSR, 60 mi. N of Stavropol; flour mill, metalworks; wheat, sunflowers, castor beans. Sometimes called Takhtinskoye. Village of Dmitriyevskoye (1926 pop. 10,891) is 13 mi. SW, on Yegorlyk R.; metalworks. **3** Town, NE Tashauz oblast, Turkmen SSR, on Khiva oasis, 10 mi. S of Tashauz; cotton.

Takhta-Bazar (–bŭzär'), town (1933 pop. over 2,500), S Mary oblast, Turkmen SSR, on Murgab R., near Kushka-Mary RR, and 125 mi. SSE of Mary; cotton.

Takhta-Kupyr (–kōōpĭr'), village (1948 pop. over 2,000), E Kara-Kalpak Autonomous SSR, Uzbek SSR, 50 mi. NE of Nukus; cotton.

Takhtamukai or **Takhtamukay** (–mōōkī'), village (1926 pop. 2,003), W Adyge Autonomous Oblast, Krasnodar Territory, Russian SFSR, 6 mi. S of Krasnodar; metalworks; wheat, sunflowers, tobacco. Until 1938, Khakurate.

Takht-e-Jamshid or **Takht-i-Jamshid,** Iran: see PERSEPOLIS.

Takht-i-Bahi (tŭkht'-ē-bä'hē), village, Mardan dist., N central North-West Frontier Prov., W Pakistan, 8 mi. NW of Mardan, on Lower Swat Canal; sugar milling, distilling. Just N are ruins of anc. Buddhist monastery. Sometimes spelled Takht-i-Bhai.

Takht-i-Rustam, Afghanistan: see HAIBAK.

Takht-i-Sulaiman (–sōōlī'män), twin peaks and highest points (11,290 ft. and 11,085 ft.) in Sulaiman Range, S North-West Frontier Prov., W Pakistan, 55 mi. WSW of Dera Ismail Khan. Shrine here visited annually by pilgrims. Higher peak sometimes called Kaisargarh. Another Takht-i-Sulaiman, a foothill of Punjab Himalayas, is SE of Srinagar, Kashmir.

Taki, Tachi, or **Ta-ch'i** (all: dä'chē'), Jap. *Taikei* (tī'kā), town (1935 pop. 5,346), NW Formosa, on Tanshui R. and 6 mi. S of Taoyüan; coal mining; tea processing, sugar and rice milling; wooden articles.

Taki (tä'kē), town (pop. 11,051), 24-Parganas dist., SE West Bengal, India, on upper Jamuna (Ichamati) R., on rail spur and 37 mi. E of Calcutta; trades in rice, jute, pulse. Rail spur terminus 1 mi. SW, at Hasanabad.

Takia or **Tachia** (both: dä'jyä'), Jap. *Taiko* (tī'kō), town (1935 pop. 4,927), W central Formosa, 14 mi. NNW of Taichung and on railroad; home industries (hat- and capmaking, mat weaving); food canning, oilseed milling.

Takiang or **Ta-chiang** (both: dä'jyäng'), town, S Kiangsu prov., China, 10 mi. ESE of Chinkiang and on Yangtze R.; commercial center.

Tak-i-Bostan, Iran: see TAQ-I-BUSTAN.

Takigawa, Japan: see TAKIKAWA.

Takihara (täkē'härŭ), town (pop. 4,449), Mie prefecture, S Honshu, Japan, 18 mi. SW of Ujiyamada; rice, raw silk, lumber.

Takikawa (täkē'käwŭ), or **Takigawa** (–gäwŭ), town (pop. 26,276), W central Hokkaido, Japan, on Ishikari R. and 27 mi. WSW of Asahigawa; agr. (rice, potatoes, hemp, wheat), sheep raising.

Takine (tä"kē'nā), town (pop. 6,717), Fukushima prefecture, central Honshu, Japan, 17 mi. ESE of Koriyama; rice, silk cocoons, charcoal.

Takingun or **Takingeun** (both: täkĭng-gŭn'), town (pop. 1,411), N Sumatra, Indonesia, 120 mi. ESE of Kutaraja, on L. Tawar, in mountainous area; 4°38'N 96°50'E; alt. 3,953 ft. Trade center for tobacco-growing and buffalo-raising region. Also spelled Takengon.

Takino (tä"kē'nō), town (pop. 5,640), Hyogo prefecture, S Honshu, Japan, 17 mi. NE of Himeji; rice, wheat; charcoal; cattle raising, lumbering.

Takinoue (täkēnō'ā), town (pop. 12,053), E Hokkaido, Japan, 60 mi. WNW of Abashiri; agr. (rice, potatoes), lumbering.

Takistan or **Takestan** (both: täkĕstän'), town, First Prov., in Kazvin, N Iran, 20 mi. SW of Kazvin and on railroad to Tabriz; road center on highway to Kazvin, Zenjan, and Hamadan; extensive vineyards; exports raisins. Formerly called Siadehan.

Takiyah, Al-, Syria: see TEKIYE, ET.

Takkakaw Falls, Canada: see Takakkaw Falls.

Takkalakote, India: see TEKKALAKOTA.

Takkaze River (tä'käzä), Ital. *Tacazze*, in NW Ethiopia, rises SE of Mt. Abuna Josef in mts. forming W edge of Great Rift Valley, 60 mi. N of Dessye, flows in a deep valley generally NW, around Simen Mts., enters Anglo-Egyptian Sudan near Umm Hajar (Eritrea), and continues c.70 mi. to Atbara R. 35 mi. NE of Gedaref; total length, c.470 mi. Receives Tsellari, Gheva, and Weri rivers. Its lower course (dry c.9 mos. of yr.) below Sittona, is called Setit R. Forms section of Eritrea-Ethiopia border. Sometimes spelled Takazze.

Takko (täk'kō) or **Tako** (tä'kō), town (pop. 6,117), Aomori prefecture, N Honshu, Japan, 22 mi. WSW of Hachinohe; charcoal, lumber; millet, livestock.

Taklakot (tä'kläkōt) or **Taklakhar** (–kär), Chinese *T'a-la-k'o* (tä'lä'kŭ'), village, SW Tibet, near Karnali (Gogra) R., on Tanakpur-Gartok trade route (via Lipula pass) and 110 mi. SSE of Gartok; has fort. Formerly called Purang.

Takla Lake (□ 98), central B.C., 60 mi. ENE of Smithers; 57 mi. long, 2 mi. wide. Near SE end the Northwest Arm extends 18 mi. NW. Drains SE into Stuart L.

Taklamakan Desert (täklämäkän'), vast sandy desert in Sinkiang prov., China, bet. Kunlun mts. (S) and the Tien Shan (N). It occupies most of the Tarim basin (the river skirts it in N) in the SW third of Sinkiang prov. Entirely uninhabited, the desert is rimmed by numerous oases linked by caravan tracks along the N foot of the Kunlun mts. and the S foot of the Tien Shan. The chief oases are Yarkand and Khotan (SW).

Tako (tä'kō). **1** Town, Aomori prefecture, Japan: see TAKKO. **2** Town (pop. 8,535), Chiba prefecture, central Honshu, Japan, 5 mi. NW of Yokaichiba; rice, wheat, poultry.

Takoma Park (tŭkō'mŭ), residential town (pop. 13,341), Montgomery and Prince Georges counties, central Md., suburb just NNE of Washington. Seat of Seventh Day Adventist institutions (sanitarium, missionary col., jr. col.). Chartered 1890.

Takoradi (täkôrä'dē), town, Western Prov., S Gold Coast colony, major port on Gulf of Guinea, 115 mi. WSW of Accra. Since 1946, forms a single municipality (pop. 44,130) with SEKONDI (5 mi. NE). Modern, deep-water harbor (protected by 2 granite-rubble breakwaters), has manganese-loading facilities, cacao sheds, and oil-storage tanks; railroad from Kumasi comes alongside. Chief exports are cacao, manganese, bauxite, gold, diamonds, and timber. Cacao-butter factory. Has technical school, hosp., and airport. Port opened to shipping in 1928.

Takotna (tŭkŏt'nŭ), village (pop. 43), SW central Alaska, near upper Kuskokwim R., 15 mi. W of McGrath; placer gold mining. Airfield.

Takow, Formosa: see KAOHIUNG.

Takow, Manchuria: see LINGYÜAN.

Takshak or **Tuckshuck** (tŭk"shŭk'), village (pop. 39), W Alaska, on lower Yukon R.; 61°58'N 162°10'W.

Takshasila, W Pakistan: see TAXILA.

Taksony (tŏk'shônyû), town (pop. 6,098), Pest-Pilis-Solt-Kiskun co., N central Hungary, on arm of the Danube and 12 mi. S of Budapest; petroleum refineries, distilleries.

Taktaharkany (tŏk'tŏhŏrkänyû), Hung. *Taktaharkány,* town (pop. 3,154), Zemplen co., NE Hungary, 16 mi. E of Miskolc; grain, apples, pears, grapes; cattle.

Taku (tä'kōō, tä'–), village, NW B.C., near Alaska border, on Graham Inlet of Tagish L., 7 mi. NW of Atlin, 100 mi. NNE of Juneau; gold mining.

Taku (dä'gōō'), town, E Hopeh prov., China, port on Gulf of Chihli, 30 mi. ESE of Tientsin (linked by road), and on S bank of Pai R. mouth; outer port for Tientsin, and transshipment point. Main installations are at Tangku, across the river. **Taku Bar,** a silt bank off mouth of Pai R., is crossed by a dredged channel leading to the ports of Taku and Tangku.

Taku, Formosa: see KAOHIUNG.

Taku (tä'kōō), atoll (205 acres; pop. c.180), Solomon Isls., SW Pacific, 120 mi. NE of Bougainville; c.20 islets on reef; governed as part of Australian Territory of New Guinea under U.N. trusteeship. Sometimes called Mortlock Isl.

Ta-kuan, China: see TAKWAN.

Takua Pa (täkōō'ŭ pä'), village (1937 pop. 1,989), Phangnga prov., S Thailand, on W coast of Malay Peninsula, 30 mi. NNW of Phangnga; tin-mining center.

Taku Bar, China: see TAKU.

Taku Glacier (tä'kōō) (30 mi. wide, 30 mi. long), SE Alaska, in Coast Range, 30 mi. NNE of Juneau; 58°28'N 134°5'W; drains into Taku Inlet (S) and Lynn Canal (SW).

Taku Inlet, SE Alaska, opens on Stephens Passage, 10 mi. SE of Juneau; extends 25 mi. N. Receives Taku R. and Taku Glacier.

Takum (täkōōm'), town (pop. 3,991), Benue prov., Northern Provinces, E central Nigeria; 45 mi. SSE of Wukari; road junction; sesame processing; cassava, durra, yams.

Takuma (tä"kōō'mä), town (pop. 11,196), Kagawa prefecture, N Shikoku, Japan, port on Hiuchi Sea, 9 mi. SW of Marugame, saltmaking center; mfg. (insect powder, cayenne pepper). Exports tobacco, salt.

Takuran, Formosa: see CHOLAN.

Taku River (tä'kōō, tä'–), N B.C. and SE Alaska, rises W of Dease L., flows generally W to Coast Mts. SE of Atlin L., thence SW, crossing into Alaska 5 mi. SW of Tulsequah, to Taku Inlet 25 mi. NE of Juneau; 180 mi. long to head of longest tributary.

Takushan, Manchuria: see KUSHAN.

Takutea (täkōōtä'ä), uninhabited coral island (302 acres), COOK ISLANDS, S Pacific, c.118 mi. NE of Rarotonga; 19°49'S 158°18'W. Also Fenua Iti.

Takutu River, Brazil-Br. Guiana: see TACUTÚ RIVER.

Takwan or **Ta-kuan** (both: dä'gwän'), town, ⊙ Takwan co. (pop. 88,342), northeasternmost Yunnan prov., China, 28 mi. NNE of Chaotung; alt. 3,674 ft.; rice, millet, timber.

Tal (täl), village, W Madhya Bharat, India, 16 mi. ENE of Jaora; corn, cotton, millet.

Tala (tŭ'lŭ), village, Kataghan prov., NE Afghanistan, on N slopes of the Hindu Kush, 30 mi. SW of Doshi, and on Surkhab R., in coal-mining area. Ishpushta mine is 9 mi. SW.

Tala, department, Argentina: see ROSARIO TALA.

Tala (tä'lä), village (pop. estimate 500), S Salta prov., Argentina, on Tala R., on railroad and 95 mi. S of Salta, in agr. area (alfalfa, corn, livestock). Its adjoining railroad station is called Ruiz de los Llanos.

Tala, China: see KUNGSHAN.

Tala (tälä'), town (pop. 18,570), Minufiya prov., Lower Egypt, on railroad and 8 mi. SSW of Tanta; cereals, cotton, flax.

Tala (tä'lä), Ital. *Talo,* peak (13,451 ft.) in Choke Mts., NW Ethiopia.

Tala, town (pop. 5,460), Jalisco, W Mexico, 23 mi. W of Guadalajara; alt. 4,413 ft.; sugar-cane center.

Tala, town, Canelones dept., S Uruguay, on highway, and 45 mi. NE of Montevideo; grain, flax, stock.

Talaat n'Yakoub, Fr. Morocco: see AMIZMIZ.

Talabriga, Portugal: see AVEIRO.

Talacogon (täläkō'gōn), town (1939 pop. 1,614; 1948 municipality pop. 3,186), Agusan prov., Philippines, on N Mindanao, on Agusan R. and 30 mi. S of Butuan; coconuts.

Talagang (tŭl'ŭgŭng), town (pop. 8,828), Attock dist., NW Punjab, W Pakistan, 55 mi. S of Campbellpur; local trade in wheat, millet; hand-loom weaving; embroidered shoes. Sometimes spelled Talaganj.

Talagante (tälägän'tā), town (pop. 5,105), ⊙ Talagante dept. (□ 248; pop. 32,049), Santiago prov., central Chile, 20 mi. SW of Santiago; rail junction; resort in fruitgrowing area.

Talai (dä'lī'), town, ⊙ Talai co. (pop. 141,708), SW Heilungkiang prov., Manchuria, on Nonni R. and 80 mi. ENE of Taonan, and on railroad; kaoliang, corn, millet, beans. Until 1913, Choerhcheng.

Talaimannar (tŭlī'mŭn-när"), town (pop. 2,201), Northern Prov., Ceylon, on NW end of Mannar Isl., 15 mi. NW of Mannar; near E end of Adam's Bridge; rail terminus; coconut and palmyra palms. Steamer service to Dhanushkodi (India) is main passenger route bet. India and Ceylon. Lighthouse.

Talaja (tŭlä'jŭ), town (pop. 4,601), SE Saurashtra, India, 30 mi. SSW of Bhaunagar; millet, cotton, wheat.

Talakad or **Talkad** (tŭlkäd'), town (pop. 4,736), Mysore dist., S Mysore, India, near left bank of Cauvery R., 25 mi. ESE of Mysore, in sugar-cane and silk-growing area. Just S, on river bank, is partly sand-covered site of anc. city; some of its many Dravidian temple ruins are believed to date from 6th cent. A.D.; others (mostly 13th cent.) are notable examples of Chalukyan art. Massive star-shaped Chalukyan temple of Somanthpur or Somnathpur (A.D. 1270), noted for its richly-carved scenes of Hindu mythology, is 10 mi. NW.

Talakag (tälä'käg), town (1939 pop. 2,185; 1948 municipality pop. 9,661), Bukidnon prov., Philippines, N Mindanao, 15 mi. S of Cagayan; coconuts.

T'a-la-k'o, Tibet: see TAKLAKOT.

Talala (tŭlä'lŭ), town (pop. 210), Rogers co., NE Okla., 15 mi. NNW of Claremore.

Talalayevka (tŭlŭlī'ŭfkŭ), agr. town (1926 pop. 4,358), SW Sumy oblast, Ukrainian SSR, 17 mi. WNW of Romny; grain, sugar beets, tobacco.

Talamalai, hill, India: see KOLLAIMALAI HILLS.

Talamanca (tälämäng'kä), district (pop. 3,681) of E Costa Rica, on Atlantic slopes, adjoining Panama; drained by Sixaola R. and its affluents. Pop. largely Indian. Lower and middle courses of the Sixaola were formerly an important banana region. Main centers are Suretka and Sixaola.

Talamanca, Cordillera de (kôrdīyä'rä dā), section of continental divide in SE Costa Rica, extends 100 mi. NW-SE from area of Copey to Panama border; rises to 12,533 ft. in the Chirripó Grande. Other heights are Pico Blanco and Durika.

Talamanca de Jarama (härä'mä), town (pop. 632), Madrid prov., central Spain, on Jarama R. and 25 mi. NNE of Madrid, in fertile agr. region (cereals, grapes, olives, vegetables, fruit, sheep); flour.

Talamba (tŭlŭm'bŭ), town (pop. 5,606), Multan dist., S Punjab, W Pakistan, 50 mi. NE of Multan; local trade in wheat, oilseeds, millet, wool; cotton ginning, handicraft cloth printing. Sometimes spelled Tulamba and Tolamba.

Talamona (tälämō'nä), village (pop. 2,931), Sondrio prov., Lombardy, N Italy, in the Valtellina, 2 mi. E of Morbegno; sawmilling.

Talang, China: see MOKIANG.

Talanga (täläng'gä), town (pop. 2,312), Francisco Morazán dept., central Honduras, 21 mi. NNE of Tegucigalpa; road junction; market center; grain, sugar cane, plantains. Airfield.

Talanti, Gulf of, Greece: see EUBOEA, GULF OF.

Talara (tälä'rä), town (pop. 12,985), Piura dept., NW Peru, port on the Pacific, on Pan American Highway and 37 mi. NNW of Paita, in sandy desert. Center of Peruvian petroleum industry and central shipping point for oil and oil products; connected by pipe lines with surrounding fields of LA BREA, NEGRITOS, LAGUNITOS, and with petroleum center of LOBITOS (N). Petroleum refinery and distillery (gasoline, turpentine, tar), asphalt works, power plant, machine shops; mfg. (cans, barrels). Large-scale production was organized after 1914. Airport.

Talarrubias (tälärōō'vyäs), town (pop. 4,871), Badajoz prov., W Spain, 34 mi. E of Don Benito; agr. center (olives, grain, acorns, grapes, livestock); wax; potteries.

Talas or **Talass** (tŭläs'), oblast (□ 6,400; 1946 pop. estimate 125,000), NW Kirghiz SSR; ⊙ Talas. Bet. the Talas Ala-Tau and Kirghiz Range; drained by Talas R. Agr. (wheat, tobacco) in valley; livestock (cattle, sheep) on mtn. slopes. Arsenic mine at Uchimchak. Pop.: Kirghiz, Ukrainians, Russians. Formed 1939.

Talas or **Talass,** city (1939 pop. over 2,000), ⊙ Talas oblast, Kirghiz SSR, on Talas R. and 120 mi. WSW of Frunze, on highway to Dzhambul; 42°32'N 72°12'E. In wheat area; agr. processing. Until 1937, Dmitriyevskoye.

Talas Ala-Tau or **Talass Ala-Tau** (both: täläs' älä'-tou'), branch of the Tien Shan mountain system, in NW Kirghiz SSR, forming S watershed of upper Talas R. valley; rises to 13,200 ft.

Talasea (täläsä'ä), port, E Willaumez Peninsula, New Britain, Bismarck Archipelago, SW Pacific; exports copra, copper.

Talas River or **Talass River** (tŭläs'), Kirghiz and Kazakh SSR, rises in the Talas Ala-Tau, flows c.200 mi. W, through Talas valley, past Budenny, Talas, and Kirovskoye, and N, into Kazakh SSR, past Dzhambul, to the desert Muyun-Kum. Used for irrigation.

Talata Ko, Indonesia: see TOGIAN ISLANDS.

Talata Mafara (tä'lätä mäfärä'), town (pop. 9,234), Sokoto prov., Northern Provinces, NW Nigeria, on Sokoto R. and 35 mi. W of Kura Namoda; agr. trade center (cotton, millet, rice, cattle, skins).

Talatze, Manchuria: see HOLUNG.

Talaudière, La (lä tälōdyâr'), town (pop. 2,541), Loire dept., SE central France, in Monts du Lyonnais, 4 mi. NNE of Saint-Étienne; coal mining; ironworks; mfg. of cosmetics.

Talaud Islands or **Talaur Islands** (täloud', -our'), group (□ 495; pop. 23,825), Indonesia, in the Pacific, 180 mi. NE of Celebes, S of Mindanao; 4°N 126°50'E. Include KARAKELONG (largest), SALEBABU, KABURUANG, and many islets. Forested (iron-wood, ebony, rattan). Chief products: timber, sago, copra, nutmeg. Fishing. Also spelled Talaut.

Talaván (tälävän'), town (pop. 2,340), Cáceres prov., W Spain, 18 mi. NNE of Cáceres; cereals, livestock.

Talavera, Bolivia: see PUNA.

Talavera (tälävä'rä), town (pop. 1,544), Apurímac dept., S central Peru, in the Andes, 2 mi. W of Andahuaylas; grain, potatoes, livestock.

Talavera, town (1939 pop. 2,738; 1948 municipality pop. 24,353), Nueva Ecija prov., central Luzon, Philippines, 8 mi. NNW of Cabanatuan; agr. center (rice, corn).

Talavera de la Reina (dhā lä rā'nä), city (pop. 16,509), Toledo prov., central Spain, in New Castile, on right bank of the Tagus (spanned by 15th-cent. arched bridge) near influx of Alberche R., on railroad to Cáceres and 65 mi. SW of Madrid. Trading and industrial center in fertile *vega* (cereals, chick-peas, beans, carobs, potatoes, olives, grapes, livestock). An important silk center in the Middle Ages, it is now chiefly known for its ceramics. Also meat packing, vegetable canning, textile milling (rugs, tapestry, woolen goods, hats, etc.); mfg. of cork articles, soap, candles, shoe polish, paper bags and cardboard boxes, sweets. Livestock market. The historic town has several religious edifices, such as Santa María la Mayor church and old secularized convents. Here are anc. Roman and Moorish remains. It was taken (1085) by Alfonso VI of Castile. In the outskirts was fought (1809) a battle bet. Wellington and Joseph Bonaparte. The historian Juan de Mariana was b. here.

Talavera Island, Itapúa dept., SE Paraguay, formed by arms of upper Paraná R. (Argentina border), 30 mi. WSW of Encarnación; 13 mi. long, c.6 mi. wide. Forested.

Talavera la Real (lä rääl'), town (pop. 3,780), Badajoz prov., W Spain, on left bank of the Guadiana and 10 mi. E of Badajoz; trades in agr. produce of the region (cereals, vegetables, olives, tomatoes). Sawmilling; mfg. of tiles, soft drinks, meat products.

Talavera la Vieja (vyā'hä), town (pop. 1,464), Cáceres prov., W Spain, on the Tagus and 35 mi. NE of Trujillo; cereals, olive oil, livestock. Has some Roman remains.

Talawakele or **Talawakelle** (tŭlŭvŭkĕl'ă), village (pop., including near-by villages, 2,638), Central Prov., Ceylon, on Hatton Plateau, on right tributary of the Mahaweli Ganga and 8 mi. WSW of Nuwara Eliya; tea-transport center. Tea Research Inst. (founded 1925).

Talayan (tälä'yän), town (1939 pop. 10,013), Cotabato prov., Philippines, on S central Mindanao, 25 mi. SSE of Cotabato; rice, coconuts.

Talayuela (tälīwā'lä), town (pop. 1,030), Cáceres prov., W Spain, 26 mi. ESE of Plasencia; cereals, pepper, tobacco; stock raising.

Talayuelas (–läs), town (pop. 1,137), Cuenca prov., E central Spain, 36 mi. SSW of Teruel; cereals, grapes, saffron, livestock. Resin extracting, flour milling.

Talbahat (täl'bŭhŭt), town (pop. 3,671), Jhansi dist., S Uttar Pradesh, India, 30 mi. S of Jhansi; wheat, rice, jowar, oilseeds. Ruins of Rajput fort, built 1618. Sometimes spelled Talbehat.

Talbot (tôl'bŭt, tŏl'–). **1** County (□ 390; pop. 7,687), W Ga.; ⊙ Talbotton. Bounded NE by Flint R. Intersected by fall line. Agr. (cotton, corn, grain, peaches, livestock) and sawmilling area. Formed 1827. **2** County (□ 279; pop. 19,428), E Md.; ⊙ Easton. A peninsula on the Eastern Shore, bounded W by Chesapeake Bay. Tidewater agr. area (truck, grain, dairy products, poultry, cattle); canneries handle much produce. Has large seafood industry (fish, oysters, crabs). Resort area (yachting, hunting, fishing). Includes old colonial mansions and gardens, Wye Oak State Park (near Wye

Mills), and several Chesapeake Bay isls. (notably Tilghman Isl.). Formed 1661.

Talbot Island, Duval co., NE Fla., barrier island (7½ mi. long, 2 mi. wide) along Atlantic shore, separated from the mainland by salt marshes; at N end is Nassau Sound, separating it from Amelia Isl.; at S end is mouth of St. Johns R.

Talbotton (tôl'bŭtŭn, tŏl'-), town (pop. 1,175), ⊙ Talbot co., W Ga., 28 mi. ENE of Columbus; trade center for farm and timber area; lumber and textile milling. Founded 1828.

Talca (täl'kä), province (□ 3,722; 1940 pop. 157,141; 1949 estimate 164,311), central Chile; ⊙ Talca. Situated in the fertile central valley bet. the Andes and the Pacific, N of Maule R. Most important winegrowing area of Chile, it also produces wheat, barley, and vegetables on large scale, and raises cattle, goats, and mules. Dairying, flour milling, lumbering. Prov. was set up 1833.

Talca, city (1940 pop. 50,464; 1949 estimate 42,994), ⊙ Talca prov. and Talca dept.(□ 2,694; 1940 pop. 109,919), central Chile, 150 mi. SSW of Santiago; 35°27'S 71°39'W. Most important center in the central valley bet. Santiago and Concepción, it is rail junction and trade and mfg. center for an agr. area noted for its wines and producing also wheat and livestock. Paper mills, flour mills, distilleries, foundries, tobacco and shoe factories, clothing mills. Its match factory is largest in Chile. Airport. Town founded 1692. On Feb. 12, 1818, Bernardo O'Higgins here formally proclaimed Chile's independence. Destroyed by 1928 earthquake, city has been rebuilt on modern lines.

Talcahuano (tälkäwä'nō), city (1940 pop. 35,774, 1949 estimate 38,605), ⊙ Talcahuano dept. (□ 48; 1940 pop. 41,536), Concepción prov., S central Chile, on SW shore of Concepción Bay (sometimes also called Talcahuano Bay), 8 mi. NNW of Concepción; 36°43'S 73°7'W. One of Chile's major ports, it is an important trading, fishing, and mfg. center, and the country's foremost naval base (especially for submarines), with extensive dry docks. It is at terminus of rail spur from Concepción, for which it became the port after earthquake of 1730. Ships lumber, hides, wool, flour, vegetables, wine, coal; imports machinery. Has large fishing industry and engages in fish canning, flour milling, and petroleum refining. Just W is resort beach of San Vicente on San Vicente Bay, site of large modern Huachipato steel mill. In Talcahuano harbor is anchored the Peruvian ironclad *Huáscar*, whose capture (1879) in the War of the Pacific established Chile's naval supremacy. Formerly sometimes spelled Talcaguano.

Talcamávida (tälkämä'vēdä), village (1930 pop. 560), Concepción prov., S central Chile, on railroad, on Bío-Bío R. and 28 mi. SSE of Concepción, in agr. area (grain, vegetables, livestock).

Talcán Island (tälkän') (□ 19; pop. 238), off W coast of Chiloé prov., S Chile, 25 mi. E of Chiloé, Isl.; 42°45'S; 9 mi. long, 2–4 mi. wide.

Talcher (täl'chär), town (pop. 6,002), Dhenkanal dist., E central Orissa, India, on Brahmani R. and 31 mi. NW of Dhenkanal; rail terminus; exports coal, building stone, rice, lac; handicrafts (cloth, metalware). Coal mines near by. Was ⊙ former princely state of Talcher (□ 388; pop. 86,432) in Orissa States; state inc. 1949 into newly-created Dhenkanal dist.

Talco, oil city (pop. 917), Titus co., NE Texas, near North Fork of Sulphur R., 33 mi. SE of Paris; trade center for oil field (discovered 1935); asphalt, oil refineries. Inc. 1936.

Talcottville, Conn.: see VERNON.

Taldom (tŭldôm'), city (1938 pop. 9,900), N Moscow oblast, Russian SFSR, 65 mi. N of Moscow; shoe mfg.; metalworking, food processing. Called Leninsk 1921-29.

Taldyk Pass, Kirghiz SSR: see ALAI RANGE.

Taldy-Kurgan (tŭldĭ"-kōōrgän'), oblast (□ 46,200; 1946 pop. estimate 300,000), SE Kazakh SSR; ⊙ Taldy-Kurgan. Drained by Lepsa R. and by the Kara-Tal and Ak-Su, which rise in the Dzungarian Ala-Tau in E section of oblast; bounded NW by L. Balkhash, S by Ili R., E by China-USSR border. Includes desert areas (Sary-Ishik-Otrau) along L. Balkhash. Irrigated agr. (wheat, sugar beets, rice, opium) on slopes of the Dzungarian Ala-Tau; cotton around Panfilov; sheep and cattle raising. Extensive lead-zinc mines and works at Tekeli. Food processing at Taldy-Kurgan. Fisheries in L. Balkhash (Burlyu-Tobe). Turksib RR crosses N–S. Pop. mainly Kazakhs; some Russians, Ukrainians. Formed 1944.

Taldy-Kurgan, city (1939 pop. over 2,000), ⊙ Taldy-Kurgan oblast, Kazakh SSR, in N foothills of Dzungarian Ala-Tau, 135 mi. NNE of Alma-Ata; 45°N 78°20'E. Center of irrigated agr. area (rice, sugar beets); sugar refinery, metalworks. Taldy-Kurgan station, on Turksib RR and 20 mi. W of city, is junction for rail spur to Tekeli.

Taldy-Su (–sōō'), village, NE Issyk-Kul oblast, Kirghiz SSR, 7 mi. NE of Tyup; wheat, opium.

Talegaon Dabhade (tŭlā'goun däbä'dä), town (pop. including suburban area, 6,629), Poona dist., central Bombay, India, 19 mi. NW of Poona; glass and pottery mfg. Technical school. Ordnance factory and depot 5 mi. E, at Dehu.

Taleh (tä'lā), village, SE Br. Somaliland, in plateau, 90 mi. NE of Las Anod; stock raising.

Talence (tälãs'), S suburb (pop. 20,412) of Bordeaux, Gironde dept., SW France; glass- and metalworks; mfg. of chemicals, furniture, hosiery, chocolates, macaronis.

Talent, town (pop. 739), Jackson co., SW Oregon, 7 mi. SE of Medford.

Tale Sap, Thailand: see THALE SAP.

Talesh Mountains, Iran: see TALYSH MOUNTAINS.

Talgar (tŭlgär'), village, S Alma-Ata oblast, Kazakh SSR, 10 mi. E of Alma-Ata; irrigated agr. (wheat, tobacco, truck produce); distillery. Located at foot of Talgar peak (16,027 ft.), highest of the Trans-Ili Ala-Tau.

Talgarth (tăl'gärth), town and parish (pop. 1,882), E Brecknock, Wales, 8 mi. ENE of Brecknock; agr. market, with shoe mfg. Has 14th-cent. church and 13th-cent. fortified tower. Near by is 12th–13th-cent. Bronllys Castle.

Talgram (tăl'gräm), town (pop. 3,367), Farrukhabad dist., central Uttar Pradesh, India, 24 mi. S of Farrukhabad; wheat, gram, corn, jowar, oilseeds.

Talguppa (tŭlgōō'pŭ), village, Shimoga dist., NW Mysore, India, 8 mi. WNW of Sagar, 6 mi. E of hydroelectric works at Jog; rail spur terminus.

Talh Pass or **Tulh Pass** (both: täl), in the Kaur al Audhilla, Western Aden Protectorate, on main route from Aden to Upper Aulaqi country, and 60 mi. NE of Shuqra; 14°7'N 46°12'E.

Tali (dä'lē'). **1** Town (pop. 14,608), ⊙ Tali co. (pop. 120,237), E Shensi prov., China, on lower Lo R. and 65 mi. NE of Sian; commercial center; tanning, cotton weaving; fur farming. Saltworks near by. Until 1913 called Tungchow. **2** Town (pop. 8,575), ⊙ Tali co. (pop. 68,137), NW Yunnan prov., China, on spur of Burma Road and 160 mi. WNW of Kunming, in scenic location on W shore of lake Erh Hai; alt. 5,118 ft.; marble-quarrying center. Rice, wheat, beans, pears. Last stronghold of Moslem rebellion (1855–72).

Taliabu or **Taliaboe** (both: tälyäbōō'), largest island (68 mi. long, 25 mi. wide; pop. 3,606) of Sula Isls., N Moluccas, Indonesia, in Molucca Sea, 80 mi. E of Celebes, adjacent to Mangole (E); 1°45'S 124°50'E. Rugged terrain rises to 4,330 ft.; has fertile coastal strips. Agr. (coconuts, corn, sago), fishing.

Taliaferro (tŏ'lŭvŭr, tŭ'-), county (□ 195; pop. 4,515), NE Ga.; ⊙ Crawfordville. Drained by Little and Ogeechee rivers. Piedmont agr. (cotton, corn, grain, fruit, livestock) and sawmilling area. Formed 1825.

Talien, Manchuria: see DAIREN.

Táliga (tä'lēgä), town (pop. 1,495), Badajoz prov., W Spain, 24 mi. S of Badajoz; cereals, olives, livestock; mfg. of olive oil and tiles.

Talihina (tălŭhē'nŭ), town (pop. 965), Le Flore co., SE Okla., in the Ouachita Mts., c.40 mi. ESE of McAlester, in resort area; mfg. (lumber, furniture, shoes, harnesses). A state tuberculosis sanatorium and an Indian hosp. are near by. Founded 1888, inc. 1905.

Talikan or **Talikhan**, Afghanistan: see TALIQAN.

Talikota (tä'lĭkōtŭ), town (pop. 8,199), Bijapur dist., S Bombay, India, 50 mi. SE of Bijapur; cotton, millet; handicraft carpet making. Armies of allied Deccan Sultans defeated Vijayanagar forces on battlefield of Talikota (on right bank of Kistna R., 23 mi. S) in 1565. Also spelled Talikoti.

Talim Island (tälēm'), (□ 11; 1939 pop. 7,160), Rizal prov., S Luzon, Philippines, in Laguna de Bay, 20 mi. SE of Manila; 9 mi. long, 1 mi. wide, with small E peninsula (1 mi. wide); rises to 1,421 ft. Rice growing. Chief center is Talim (1939 pop. 711) at S tip of isl.

Talin (dä'lĭn'), Jap. *Tairin* (tī'rēn), town (1935 pop. 1,777), W central Formosa, 7 mi. N of Kiayi and on railroad; sugar, alcohol processing; rice, sweet potatoes, livestock.

Talin, Verkhni Talin, or **Verkhniy Talin** (vyĕrkh"nyē tŭlyēn') [Rus.,=upper Talin], village (1932 pop. estimate 1,450), NW Armenian SSR, at W foot of Mt. Aragats, 28 mi. S of Leninakan; road junction; wheat, livestock.

Talina (tälē'nä), town (pop. c.4,100), Potosí dept., S Bolivia, near Río Grande de San Juan, 22 mi. SSW of Tupiza; orchards, corn.

Talina River, Bolivia: see SAN JUAN RIVER.

Taliouine (tälēwēn'), village, Marrakesh region, SW Fr. Morocco, bet. the Anti-Atlas (S) and the Djebel Siroua (NE), 60 mi. E of Taroudant.

Taliparamba, India: see CANNANORE, city.

Taliqan, Talikan, or **Talikhan** (tälēkän'), town (pop. 10,000), Kataghan prov., NE Afghanistan, in Afghan Turkestan, 25 mi. E of Khanabad, and on highway to Faizabad; cottonseed mill. Salt deposits near by. Sometimes spelled Taloqan and Taluqan.

Talisay (tälē'sī). **1** Town (1939 pop. 2,094; 1948 municipality pop. 12,140), Batangas prov., S Luzon, Philippines, on N shore of L. Taal, 20 mi. W of San Pablo; fishing, agr. (rice, sugar cane, coconuts). **2** Town (1939 pop. 1,506; 1948 municipality pop. 22,442), central Cebu isl., Philippines, on Bohol Strait, 5 mi. SW of Cebu city; agr. center (corn, coconuts); sugar milling. **3** Town (1939 pop. 10,668; 1948 municipality pop. 43,610), Negros Occidental prov., W Negros isl., Philippines, on Guimaras Strait, 4 mi. NNE of Bacolod; trade center for agr. area (rice, sugar cane). Sugar mill, distillery.

Talisayan (tälēsä'yän), town (1939 pop. 5,755; 1948 municipality pop. 22,215), Misamis Oriental prov., N Mindanao, Philippines, at W side of entrance to Gingoog Bay, 39 mi. NNE of Cagayan; agr. center (corn, coconuts).

Talish Mountains, Iran: see TALYSH MOUNTAINS.

Talitsa (tä'lyĭtsŭ). **1** Village (1939 pop. over 500), E Kirov oblast, Russian SFSR, 40 mi. SSE of Zuyevka; flax, wheat. **2** Village (1939 pop. over 500), E Orel oblast, Russian SFSR, 10 mi. NE of Yelets; coarse grain. **3** City (1939 pop. 10,200), SE Sverdlovsk oblast, Russian SFSR, on Pyshma R. and 65 mi. N of Shadrinsk; wood-cracking center; mfg. (liquor, yeast). Became city in 1942. Until c.1928, Talitski Zavod.

Talitski Chamlyk or **Talitskiy Chamlyk** (tä'lyĭtskē chŭmlĭk'), village (1926 pop. 4,374), N Voronezh oblast, Russian SFSR, 38 mi. SE of Gryazi; meat-packing plant. Also spelled Talitski Chemlyk.

Talje, Sweden: see SODERTALJE.

Talkad, India: see TALAKAD.

Talkeetna (tăl"kēt'nŭ), village (pop. 108), S Alaska, on Susitna R. at mouth of Chalitna R., and 80 mi. N of Anchorage, on Alaska RR; gold mining; outfitting point for Cache Creek dist. gold fields. Airfield.

Talkeetna Mountains, range in S Alaska, N of Matanuska R., extending c.150 mi. NE–SW along Susitna R. NE of Anchorage; rises to c.8,000 ft.

Talkha (tälkhä'), town (pop. 13,216), Gharbiya prov., Lower Egypt, on Damietta branch of the Nile opposite Mansura, on railroad, and 36 mi. SW of Damietta; cotton, cereals, rice, fruits.

Talkhatan-Baba, Turkmen SSR: see KUIBYSHEVO, Mary oblast.

Talkheh River (tälkhĕ'), Turkic *Aji Chai* (äjē' chī'), in Azerbaijan, NW Iran, rises on Savalan mtn., flows over 100 mi. W, past Tabriz, to L. Urmia.

Talking Rock, town (pop. 94), Pickens co., N Ga., 12 mi. S of Ellijay.

Tall: for Arabic names beginning thus, see TEL; TELL.

Talla or **Tallah** (tăl'lŭ), village (pop. 11,950), Minya prov., Upper Egypt, 2 mi. SW of Minya; cotton ginning, woolen and sugar milling; cotton, cereals, sugar cane.

Tallaboa (täyäbō'ä), village, S Puerto Rico, on the coast, on railroad and 5 mi. W of Ponce; sugar milling. Along near-by bay are oil tanks.

Talladega (tălŭdē'gŭ), county (□ 750; pop. 63,639), E central Ala.; ⊙ Talladega. Bounded W by Coosa R.; drained by its affluents. Parts of Talladega Mts. and of Talladega Natl. Forest in E. Cotton, corn; iron mines. Textile milling at Talladega. Formed 1832.

Talladega, city (pop. 13,134), ⊙ Talladega co., E central Ala., c.40 mi. E of Birmingham; trade and processing center for cotton, corn, and hay region; work clothes, cotton yarn and fabrics, pipe fittings, textile repair parts, wood products. Andrew Jackson defeated Creek Indians (1813) on site of city. Settled in 1830s. Talladega Col. (Negro) and state schools for deaf, dumb, and blind are here. Talladega Mts. are E in sec. of Talladega Natl. Forest.

Talladega Mountains, E central Ala., low-lying range in Clay and Talladega counties, E of Birmingham. Rise to 2,407 ft. in CHEAHA MOUNTAIN, highest point in state. Occupies part of Talladega Natl. Forest.

Talladega Springs, town (pop. 222), Talladega co., central Ala., on Coosa R. and 30 mi. SW of Talladega.

Tallahala Creek (tălŭhă'lŭ), SE Miss., rises in N Jasper co., flows c.95 mi. generally S, past Laurel, to Leaf R. just W of New Augusta.

Tallahassee (tălŭhă'sē), city (pop. 27,237), ⊙ Fla. and Leon co., NW Fla., near Ga. line, c.160 mi. W of Jacksonville, in a hilly farming region with many lakes and springs in vicinity; 30°26'N 84°17'W. Trade and wood-processing center; boxes, furniture, lumber, naval stores; also dairy, meat, metal, and concrete products. Seat of Florida State Univ. and Florida Agr. and Mechanical Col. for Negroes. De Soto discovered an Indian settlement here in 1539; Spanish missionaries came to the area in 17th cent., and colonization by Spaniards followed. Tallahassee was established in 1824 as ⊙ Florida Territory. In 1861 the ordinance of secession was passed here; city was attacked by Union troops in Civil War; near by is a monument marking site of battle of Natural Bridge (1865), a Union defeat. Points of interest: the Capitol, with the state library; Walker Memorial Library; and mus. of the state geological survey. Prince Achille Murat and his wife are buried here.

Tallahatchie (tălŭhă'chē), county (□ 644; pop. 30,486), NW central Miss.; ⊙ Sumner and Charleston. Drained by Tallahatchie R. Agr. (cotton, corn, soybeans, livestock); timber. Formed 1833.

Tallahatchie River, N Miss., rises in Tippah co., flows 230 mi. SW and S, joining Yalobusha R. just N of Greenwood to form the Yazoo. Upper section (c.190 mi.) above influx of Yocona and Coldwater rivers is sometimes called Little Tallahatchie R.

Just SE of Sardis is Sardis Dam (117 ft. high above stream bed, 15,300 ft. long; completed 1940; for flood control), which impounds Sardis Reservoir (□ 91; capacity 1,570,000 acre-ft.).

Tall al-Kabir, Egypt: see TELL EL KEBIR.

Tallandoon (tă'lŭndōōn'), village (pop. 131), NE Victoria, Australia, on Mitta Mitta R. and 155 mi. NE of Melbourne; tin.

Tallangatta (tă"lŭn-gă'tŭ), village (pop. 853), NE Victoria, Australia, on Mitta Mitta R., at SE end of Hume Reservoir, and 165 mi. NE of Melbourne; irrigation center in livestock and agr. area.

Tallapoosa (tălŭpōō'sŭ), county (□ 711; pop. 35,074), E Ala.; ⊙ Dadeville. Piedmont region drained by Tallapoosa R. and Martin L. Cotton, potatoes, timber; textiles. Formed 1832.

Tallapoosa, city (pop. 2,826), Haralson co., NW Ga., 17 mi. NW of Carrollton, near Ala. line; mills (yarn, lumber), cooperage. Settled c.1856, inc. 1860.

Tallapoosa City, town (pop. 168), Tallapoosa co., E Ala.

Tallapoosa River, meandering stream in NW Ga. and E Ala.; rises in Paulding co. SW of Dallas, flows W, then SW into Cleburne co., Ala., turns S near Heflin, passes through Martin L. in Tallapoosa co., veers W below Tallassee, joining Coosa R. 10 mi. N of Montgomery to form Alabama R.; 268 mi. long. Receives Little Tallapoosa R. in upper course, 6 mi. W of Wedowee, Ala. Martin Dam (forming MARTIN LAKE) and YATES DAM are in lower course of main stream, above Tallassee; THURLOW DAM is at Tallassee.

Tallard (tälär'), village (pop. 545), Hautes-Alpes dept., SE France, on the Durance and 7 mi. S of Gap; winegrowing. Has ruined 14th-16th-cent. castle.

Tallarevu, India: see COCANADA.

Tallasen (täl'ō"sŭn), Swedish *Tallåsen*, village (pop. 1,226), Gavleborg co., central Sweden, near Ljusna R., 3 mi. NNW of Ljusdal; woodworking.

Tallassee (tă'lŭsē"), town (pop. 4,225), Elmore and Tallapoosa cos., E central Ala., on Tallapoosa R. (dammed for power here by Thurlow Dam) and 25 mi. ENE of Montgomery; work clothes, cotton yarn and fabrics. Site of Tukabatchee (Creek Indian town) is just S.

Tallaweka (tălŭwē'kŭ), town (pop. 609), Elmore co., E central Ala.

Tallinn or **Tallin** (tä'lĭn) [Est.,=Danes' city], Ger. *Reval* (rä'väl), Rus. (until 1917) *Revel* or *Revel'* (rā'vĕl), city (1934 pop. 137,792; 1947 pop. estimate 168,000), ⊙ Estonia, major Baltic port on S coast of Gulf of Finland, 200 mi. W of Leningrad; 59°26'N 24°46'E. Major industrial and commercial center; shipbuilding, mfg. of cotton textiles, agr. and oil-shale-mining equipment, electric motors, plastics, glass, pulp and paper, plywood, furniture; agr. processing (flour, meat, tobacco products). Port (frozen 45 days a year) exports textiles, paper, timber. Has polytechnical and teachers colleges, conservatory, schools of drama and applied arts. City consists of upper town on cathedral hill, an adjoining walled, medieval lower town, and modern industrial and residential sections. Within the walled town are (on the hill) 13th-cent. Danish Toompea castle (reconstructed 1935 as govt. bldg.) with 100-ft. Hermann tower, episcopal church (1233), and 16th-cent. watch tower *Kiek in de Kök;* in the lower town are late-Gothic (13th-cent.) church of St. Olai with 456-ft. steeple, Hanseatic "Black Heads" house, and 14th-cent. city hall with wood carvings, Gobelin tapestry, and wall paintings. Modern business bldgs. cluster around Liberty Sq. On E outskirts is Kadriorg Palace, a govt. residence built 1718 by Peter the Great; beyond (3 mi. ENE) is Pirita beach with ruins of Gothic cloister (built 1407–36; destroyed 1577). City founded 1219 by Danes on site of Estonian settlement; joined Hanseatic League in 1285; passed in 1346 to Livonian Knights, in 1561 to Sweden; occupied (1710) by Russia, to whom it was ceded (1721) by Sweden. Commercial development speeded after completion (1870) of railroad from St. Petersburg, which it served as a winter port. In Second World War it was occupied (1941–44) by the Germans and suffered much damage.

Tallmadge (tăl'mĭj), city (pop. 5,821), Summit co., NE Ohio, just E of Akron; metal and stone products, foodstuffs. Settled 1808, inc. 1936.

Tallman Mountain State Park (c.700 acres), Rockland co., SE N.Y., on bluff above W bank of the Hudson, SE of Piermont; recreational area (swimming, sports, picnicking); part of Palisades Interstate Park.

Talloires (tälwär'), village (pop. 239), Haute-Savoie dept., SE France, on E shore of L. of Annecy, 6 mi. SE of Annecy; summer resort.

Tallow (tă'lō), Gaelic *Tulach an Iarainn*, town (pop. 722), W Co. Waterford, Ireland, on Bride R. and 5 mi. SW of Lismore; agr. market (dairying, cattle raising; potatoes).

Tallula (tŭlōō'lŭ), village (pop. 527), Menard co., central Ill., 17 mi. WNW of Springfield, in agr. and bituminous-coal area.

Tallulah (tŭlōō'lŭ), village (pop. 7,758), ⊙ Madison parish, NE La., 19 mi. WNW of Vicksburg (Miss.), in rich lowland cotton-producing area; cotton ginning; cottonseed and soybean products, beverages, lumber; commercial fisheries; edible frogs. Has U.S. agr. experiment station. Oxbow lakes (fishing, camping), formed by the Mississippi, are near by.

Tallulah Falls, resort town (pop. 239), Rabun and Habersham cos., extreme NE Ga., at falls of Tallulah R. and 9 mi. S of Clayton; sawmilling. Power dams form several large reservoirs near by.

Tallulah Park, town (1940 pop. 6), Habersham co., NE Ga., on Tallulah R. 11 mi. S of Clayton.

Tallulah River (c.40 mi. long), extreme NE Ga., rises on Wine Spring Bald just across N.C. line, flows S and E through a deep gorge to join Chattooga R. at S.C. line 3 mi. SE of Tallulah Falls, forming Tugaloo R. Contains 6 power dams forming reservoirs, including lakes BURTON and RABUN.

Tallya (tä'lyŏ), Hung. *Tállya*, town (pop. 3,564), Zemplen co., NE Hungary, 21 mi. ENE of Miskolc; vineyards, agr., hogs.

Talmaciu (tŭlmä'chōō), Rum. *Tălmaciu*, Hung. *Bántolmács* (bän'tôlmäch), village (pop. 2,511), Sibiu prov., central Rumania, on Olt R., on railroad and 11 mi. SSE of Sibiu; lumbering center; textile mfg. Ruins of historical fortress near by.

Talmage (tăl'mĭj). **1** or **Talmadge,** town (pop. 66), Washington co., E Maine, 30 mi. NW of Calais. **2** Village (pop. 398), Otoe co., SE Nebr., 13 mi. SW of Nebraska City and on Little Nemaha R.; flour.

Talmenka or **Tal'menka** (tŭlmyĕn'kŭ), town (1939 pop. estimate 14,200), N Altai Territory, Russian SFSR, on Turksib RR (Ust-Talmenskaya station), on Chumysh R. and 32 mi. N of Barnaul; sawmilling, machine mfg.

Talmo, town (pop. 152), Jackson co., NE central Ga., 10 mi. SE of Gainesville.

Talmont (tälmō'), village (pop. 1,014), Vendée dept., W France, 8 mi. ESE of Les Sables-d'Olonne; limekilns. Has ruins of 15th-16th-cent. castle with older keep.

Talnoye or **Tal'noye** (täl'nŭyŭ), city (1926 pop. 10,652), S Kiev oblast, Ukrainian SSR, 25 mi. ENE of Uman; sugar-refining center.

Talo, peak, Ethiopia: see TALA.

Taloda (tŭlō'dŭ), town (pop. 10,973), West Khandesh dist., N Bombay, India, near Tapti R., 60 mi. NW of Dhulia; market center for grain and timber (teak, blackwood) from forests at foot of Satpura Range (N); palmarosa-oil extracting, wooden-cart mfg.

Talodi (tŭlō'dē), village, Kordofan prov., central Anglo-Egyptian Sudan, in Nuba Mts., on road and 170 mi. S of El Obeid; gum arabic, sesame, corn, durra; livestock.

Talofofo (tälōfō'fō), town (pop. 618) and municipality (pop. 914), S Guam; coconut plantations.

Taloga (tŭlō'gŭ), town (pop. 430), ⊙ Dewey co., W Okla., on Canadian R. and 37 mi. SE of Woodward, in stock-raising and agr. area (cotton, broomcorn); fuller's-earth mining.

Taloqan, Afghanistan: see TALIQAN.

Talovaya (tä'lŭvīŭ), village (1926 pop. 2,743), E central Voronezh oblast, Russian SFSR, 50 mi. E of Liski; rail junction; metalworks. Agr. acclimatization station. Formerly called Talovoye.

Talovoye (–vŭyŭ), town (1939 pop. over 500), SE Voroshilovgrad oblast, Ukrainian SSR, in the Donbas, 5 mi. WNW of Krasnodon; coal mines.

Talpa, town (pop. 234), Coleman co., central Texas, 17 mi. W of Coleman, in agr. area.

Talpa de Allende (täl'pä dā äyĕn'dā), town (pop. 2,722), Jalisco, central Mexico, in coastal ranges, 50 mi. WSW of Ameca; banana-growing center; sugar cane, cotton, rice, tobacco.

Talpaki (tŭlpä'kē), village (1939 pop. 415), central Kaliningrad oblast, Russian SFSR, on Pregel R. and 5 mi. ENE of Znamensk; road junction. Until 1945, in East Prussia and called Taplacken (täp'läkŭn).

Talpiyot or **Talpioth** (both: tälpēyōt'), residential SSE suburb of Jerusalem, E Israel.

Talquin, Lake, Fla.: see OCHLOCKONEE RIVER.

Talsi (täl'sē), Ger. *Talsen*, city (pop. 4,116), NW Latvia, in Kurzeme, 40 mi. ESE of Ventspils; lumber milling, tanning, starch mfg.; ceramics.

Taltal (tältäl'), town (pop. 5,659), ⊙ Taltal dept. (□ 9,115; pop. 12,765), Antofagasta prov., N Chile, port on the Pacific adjoining Taltal Point (25°25'S 71°37'W), and 125 mi. S of Antofagasta; rail terminus and nitrate-shipping center.

Taltson River (tôl'sŭn), trading post, S Mackenzie Dist., Northwest Territories, on S shore of Great Slave L., at mouth of small Taltson R., 35 mi. ENE of Fort Resolution; 61°23'N 112°45'W; radio station.

Taltsy or **Tal'tsy** (täl'tsē), town (1948 pop. over 2,000), SE Irkutsk oblast, Russian SFSR, on Angara R., on Trans-Siberian RR and 25 mi. SE of Irkutsk; porcelain mfg., sawmilling.

Taluban, Thailand: see SAIBURI.

Taluqan, Afghanistan: see TALIQAN.

Taly (tä'lē), village (1926 pop. 5,697), S Voronezh oblast, Russian SFSR, 21 mi. WSW of Boguchar; wheat, sunflowers.

Talya (täl'yă), village (pop. 9,139), Minufiya prov., Lower Egypt, 1 mi. E of Rosetta branch of the Nile, 3 mi. SE of Ashmun; cereals, cotton, and flax are grown.

Taly Klyuch, Russian SFSR: see KRASNOGVARDEISKI, Sverdlovsk oblast.

Talyllyn (tălŭth-lĭn'), agr. village and parish (pop. 1,135), SW Merioneth, Wales, at foot of Cader Idris, 7 mi. SE of Barmouth; tourist resort. Just E is Talyllyn Lake, 1 mi. long.

Talysh Mountains (tälĭsh'), Persian *Talish* or *Talesh* (both: tälĕsh'), NW extremity of the Elburz system, in NW Iran, extending from the lower Sefid Rud NW to USSR border; rise to over 8,000 ft. At E foot stretches humid subtropical coastal lowland on Caspian Sea, known as Lenkoran Lowland in Soviet Azerbaijan.

Talyzino (tŭlĭ'zĭnŭ), village (1926 pop. 2,078), SE Gorki oblast, Russian SFSR, 34 mi. SSE of Sergach; hemp, wheat.

Tam, China: see TAM RIVER.

Tama (tä'mä), village (pop. estimate 500), ⊙ Vélez Sarsfield dept. (□ 1,015; 1947 pop. 2,369), E central La Rioja prov., Argentina, at W foot of Sierra de los Llanos, 14 mi. SW of Chamical; stock-raising center (goats, cattle); embroidery.

Tama (tā'mŭ), county (□ 720; pop. 21,688), central Iowa; ⊙ Toledo. Prairie agr. area (hogs, cattle, poultry, corn, oats, soybeans) drained by Iowa R. and Wolf Creek. State parks. Formed 1843.

Tama, city (pop. 2,930), Tama co., central Iowa, on Iowa R. and 18 mi. ESE of Marshalltown; rail junction; mfg. (paperboard, wood preservatives, dairy products, cement blocks). Platted 1862, inc. 1869. Sac and Fox Indians own near-by area.

Tamaha (tŭmä'hä), town (pop. 117), Haskell co., E Okla., on Arkansas R. and 33 mi. SE of Muskogee.

Tamajón (tämähōn'), town (pop. 433), Guadalajara prov., central Spain, 26 mi. N of Guadalajara, in forested region; grain, livestock; glass mfg.

Tamaki River (tŭmä'kē), inlet of Tamaki Strait, N N.Isl., New Zealand, 3.5 mi. E of Auckland; 1.5 mi. wide across mouth (E–W), 10 mi. long. Otahuhu is on SW shore.

Tamaki Strait, of Hauraki Gulf, N N.Isl., New Zealand, S of Waiheke Isl. and E of Auckland; merges with Firth of Thames (SE); 3.5 mi. wide at narrowest point.

Tamala (tŭmä'lŭ), village (1932 pop. estimate 2,150), SW Penza oblast, Russian SFSR, on railroad and 23 mi. ESE of Kirsanov, in grain area; flour milling.

Tamalameque (tämälämä'kā), town (pop. 1,043), Magdalena dept., N Colombia, on Magdalena R. and 15 mi. SE of El Banco.

Tamale (tŭmä'lē), town (pop. 17,372), ⊙ Northern Territories, N central Gold Coast, 260 mi. NNW of Accra; 9°24'N 0°53'W. Road and agr. trade center in cotton area; cotton ginning and milling, shea-nut processing, cattle raising. Has teachers col., agr. experiment station, airfield. Hq. Dagomba dist. Canoe traffic on White Volta R. below Yapei (27 mi. SW).

Tamalín (tämälēn'), town (pop. 1,599), Veracruz, E Mexico, in Sierra Madre Oriental foothills, 39 mi. NW of Tuxpan; cereals, sugar cane, coffee, tobacco, fruit.

Tamalpais, Mount (tă'mŭlpī"ŭs), peak, Marin co., W Calif., rising steeply from the Pacific W of Mill Valley, across the Golden Gate from San Francisco; highest of its 3 crests is 2,604 ft. Auto road to summit. MUIR WOODS NATIONAL MONUMENT, a fine redwood grove at S base, adjoins Mount Tamalpais State Park (961 acres), which has many hiking trails, 3 lakes, ravines, campgrounds, varied plant life, and a natural amphitheater where plays are presented.

Tamames (tämä'mĕs), town (pop. 1,708), Salamanca prov., W Spain, 23 mi. ENE of Ciudad Rodrigo; tanning; cereals, livestock.

Tamampaya River (tämämpī'ä), La Paz dept., W Bolivia, rises in Cordillera de La Paz N of Chulumani, flows c.25 mi. E, joining La Paz R. ENE of Chulumani to form Bopi R.

Tamamura (tämä'mōōrä), town (pop. 7,548), Gumma prefecture, central Honshu, Japan, 6 mi. E of Takasaki; rice, raw silk.

Taman or **Taman'** (tŭmä'nyŭ), village (1926 pop. 7,190), W Krasnodar Territory, Russian SFSR, on Taman Gulf of Kerch Strait, opposite (15 mi. SE of) Kerch, on N shore of Taman Peninsula; terminus of branch line from Krymskaya; cotton, wheat, vineyards; fisheries. Mud baths near by. A Turkish fortress, captured (1777) by Russians. Sometimes called Tamanskaya. Near by (NE) are ruins of anc. Gr. colony of Phanagoria.

Tamana (tämä'nä), atoll (□ 2; pop. 883), Kingsmill group, S Gilbert Isls., W central Pacific; 2°30'S 175°58'E. Formerly Rotcher Isl.

Tamana (tä"mä'nä), town (pop. 13,640), Kumamoto prefecture, W Kyushu, Japan, 12 mi. NW of Kumamoto; agr. center (rice, millet). Airfield.

Tamaná, Cerro (sĕ'rō tämänä'), Andean peak (13,780 ft.), W central Colombia, on Caldas-Chocó dept. border, highest in Cordillera Occidental, 45 mi. W of Manizales.

Tamanar (tämänär'), village, Marrakesh region, SW Fr. Morocco, near the Atlantic, 37 mi. S of Mogador; almond trees.

Tamano (tä"mä'nō), city (1940 pop. 35,467; 1947 pop. 41,098), Okayama prefecture, SW Honshu, Japan, port on Inland Sea, 13 mi. S of Okayama

Rail terminus; commercial center for agr. area (rice, wheat, persimmons). Shipbuilding, salt- and sake making. Exports drugs, salt. Formed 1940 by combining former adjacent towns of Tamano, Hibi, and Uno. Connected by ferry with Takamatsu on Shikoku.

Tamanoura (tämänō'rä), town (pop. 7,659) on Fukae-shima of isl. group Goto-retto, Nagasaki prefecture, Japan, on small SW peninsula, 9 mi. W of Tomie; agr. center (sweet potatoes, grain); charcoal.

Taman Peninsula (tŭmä'nyŭ), on Kerch Strait, in Krasnodar Territory, Russian SFSR; 20 mi. long, 8 mi. wide. Forms S prong of lagoon-studded peninsula (to which name Taman is sometimes extended) bet. Sea of Azov (N) and Black Sea, separated from Crimea by Kerch Strait. Of recent formation (c.5th cent. A.D.); has small mud volcanoes, gas and petroleum deposits. On N shore is Taman, a small port on Taman Gulf (E inlet of Kerch Strait).

Tamanrasset (tämänräsĕt') or **Fort Laperrine** (läpŭrēn'), oasis (pop. 1,846) and military post in Saharan Oases territory, S Algeria, in Ahaggar Mts., on trans-Saharan auto track, 350 mi. SSE of In-Salah; 22°50'N 5°30'E. Date palms. Tuareg pop.

Tamanskaya, Russian SFSR: see TAMAN, village.

Tamanthi (tŭmän"dhē'), village, Upper Chindwin dist., Upper Burma, on Chindwin R. and 40 mi. NE of Homalin; head of path to Somra Tract.

Tamaqua (tŭmō'kwŭ), borough (pop. 11,508), Schuylkill co., E Pa., on Little Schuylkill R. and 15 mi. NE of Pottsville; anthracite; explosives, clothing, metal products. Settled 1799, laid out 1829, inc. 1832.

Támara (tä'märä), town (pop. 901), Casanare intendency, central Colombia, in E foothills of Cordillera Oriental, 55 mi. E of Sogamoso; alt. 3,793 ft.; coffee, corn, livestock. Salt deposits near by.

Tamarack, village (pop. 132), Aitkin co., E Minn., c.50 mi. W of Duluth in lake resort region. State forest just N.

Tamarai (tämärī'), town (pop. 3,335), Oita prefecture, E central Kyushu, Japan, 31 mi. NW of Nobeoka; rice, lumber.

Tamara Island (tämä'rä), largest of the LOS ISLANDS of Fr. Guinea, Fr. West Africa, 6 mi. W of Conakry. On its N tip is village of Fotoba.

Tamarida, Socotra: see HADIBU.

Tamarin (tämärē'), village (pop. 626), SW Mauritius, 13 mi. SSW of Port Louis, on Tamarin R.; railhead; sugar milling.

Tamarind Island, Indonesia: see SEBESI.

Tamarindo (tämärēn'dō) town (pop. 1,584), Piura dept., NW Peru, on coastal plain, near Chira R., on Pan American Highway and 17 mi. NE of Paita, in irrigated area; cotton, fruit.

Tamaris, Les, France: see ALÈS.

Tamaris-sur-Mer, France: see SEYNE-SUR-MER, LA.

Tamarite de Litera (tämärē'tā dhā lētā'rä), town (pop. 3,252), Huesca prov., NE Spain, 20 mi. NNW of Lérida, in irrigated agr. area (wine, cereals, fruit); olive-oil processing, mfg. of chocolate. Gypsum quarries near by.

Tamaro, Monte (môn'tē tämä'rô), peak (6,452 ft.) in the Alps, S Switzerland, 8 mi. NW of Lugano, 2 mi. E of Ital. border.

Tamaroa (tă"mŭrō'ŭ), village (pop. 849), Perry co., SW Ill., 27 mi. SSW of Centralia, in bituminous-coal-mining and agr. area; oil wells.

Tamar River (tā'mŭr), SW England, rises in N Cornwall near Morwenstow, flows 60 mi. SE, along border of Cornwall and Devon, to Plymouth Sound. Navigable almost to Launceston. Estuarial section is called Hamoaze.

Tamar River (tā'mŭr), N Tasmania, formed by junction of North Esk and South Esk rivers at Launceston; flows 40 mi. NW to Bass Strait (its mouth is known as Port Dalrymple); 2 mi. wide. Navigable by steamer for entire course.

Tamaru (tä"mä'rōō), town (pop. 3,594), Mie prefecture, S Honshu, Japan, 4 mi. W of Uji-yamada; rice, wheat, raw silk.

Tamarugal, Pampa del (päm'pä dĕl tämärōōgäl'), desert plateau (alt. c.3,200 ft.) in Tarapacá and Antofagasta provs., N Chile, a NW part of the arid Atacama Desert. Extends c.180 mi. N–S (c.20 mi. wide) bet. the Andes (E) and coastal range (W). Rainless and mostly devoid of vegetation, it is rich in nitrates, iodine, and borax.

Tamasaki, Japan: see EZAKI.

Tamashima (tämä'shĭmä), town (pop. 28,608), Okayama prefecture, SW Honshu, Japan, on Hiuchi Sea, 16 mi. WSW of Okayama; commercial center for agr. area (rice, wheat, persimmons); textile and spinning mills; mfg. (salt, sake, floor mats); raw silk.

Tamasi (tŏ'mä-shē), Hung. *Tamási*, town (pop. 7,222), Tolna co., W central Hungary, 28 mi. NW of Szekszard; market center; wheat, potatoes, hogs.

Tamasopo (tämäsō'pō), town (pop. 1,009), San Luis Potosí, N central Mexico, 38 mi. E of Río Verde; grain, cotton, fruit, stock.

Tamatam, Caroline Isls.: see PULAP.

Tamatave (tämätäv'), province (□ 33,860; 1948 pop. 757,500), E Madagascar; ⊙ Tamatave. Drained by Mangoro R. and L. Alaotra. Fertile coastal plain rising to dissected highlands in W. Coffee, vanilla, cloves, rice. Some graphite and gold mining. Mfg. of tapioca and cassava starch; sawmilling, distilling, rice and meat processing at Tamatave, main port of Madagascar and head of rail line to Tananarive. Canal des Pangalanes is an important transport route for local produce. Chief centers are Tamatave, Antalaha, Brickaville, Maroantsetra. Sainte-Marie Isl. is part of prov.

Tamatave, town (1948 pop. 28,194), ⊙ Tamatave prov., E Madagascar, on Indian Ocean coast and Canal des Pangalanes, 135 mi. NE of Tananarive; 18°8'S 49°22'E. Leading seaport and 2d largest town of Madagascar, commercial center, and terminus of railroad from Tanarive. Ships rice, corn, cassava products, sugar, rum, chilled pork, canned beef, coffee, spices, essential oils, fibers, hardwoods. Rice and meat processing, distilling (at near-by Salamazet), sugar milling (at Melville), sawmilling; mfg. of soap, horse carts, carbonated drinks; printing; machine shops. Large cinnamon, coffee, and cacao plantations in vicinity; also graphite mining. Airport. Has large military camp, 2 hospitals, R.C. and Protestant missions. The town was entirely reconstructed on modern lines after its destruction by hurricane in 1925. Its deep-water harbor was built 1929–35.

Tamatsukuri (tämä'tsōōkōōrē), town (pop. 4,038), Ibaraki prefecture, central Honshu, Japan, on NE shore of lake Katsumi-ga-ura, 12 mi. E of Tsuchiura; rice, wheat, silk cocoons.

Tamaulipas (tämoulē'päs), state (□ 30,734; 1940 pop. 458,832; 1950 pop. 716,029), NE Mexico, on the Gulf of Mexico, bordered N by the Rio Grande; ⊙ Ciudad Victoria. The central and W sections are situated in the Sierra Madre Oriental; S and N regions consist of cultivable plains, particularly in the long panhandle beginning at Nuevo Laredo and following the Rio Grande to Matamoros. Coast is low, sandy, fringed with lagoons, and (except for Matamoros and Tampico) virtually uninhabited. State's extreme SW portion, where there is some mining, borders on the vast semiarid basins of central Mexico. Except in the elevated interior, the climate is hot and humid. Tamaulipas is drained by San Fernando, Soto la Marina, and Tamesí (or Guayalejo) rivers. Minerals include gold, silver, lead, and copper, mined at San Nicolás, San Carlos, Güémez, and Ciudad Victoria; salt at Altamira. Most important resource is petroleum, found in the Tampico dist., which, next to Veracruz, has the largest deposits in Mexico. Produces cotton, cereals, sugar cane, beans, vegetables in fertile Rio Grande basin; sugar cane, corn, henequen, pineapples, bananas, citrus fruit on plateaus and in SE. Stock raising predominantly in N. Tarpon fishing on Gulf coast. Processing industries concentrated at Nuevo Laredo, Matamoros, Ciudad Victoria, and Tampico. Conquered in early 16th cent. by the Spanish, the region, called Pánuco, was abandoned until colonized (1747) by José de Escandón, who renamed it Nuevo Santander. Renamed Tamaulipas shortly after independence from Spain (1821). Occupied by U.S. forces (1846) during Mexican War; and invaded by the French (Tampico, 1862).

Tamayo (tämī'ō), town (1950 pop. 3,230), Bahoruco prov., SW Dominican Republic, on Yaque del Sur R. (Barahona prov. line), 14 mi. NW of Barahona.

Tamazato, Formosa: see YÜLI.

Tamazula (tämäsōō'lä). **1** Town (pop. 523), Durango, N Mexico, at W foot of Sierra Madre Occidental, near Sinaloa border, on affluent of Culiacán R. and 30 mi. ENE of Culiacán; silver, gold, copper mining. **2** Town (pop. 1,307), Sinaloa, NW Mexico, on lower Sinaloa R. near its mouth on Gulf of California, and 80 mi. NW of Culiacán; chickpeas, corn, sugar cane, tomatoes, fruit.

Tamazula de Gordiano (dā gôrdyä'nō), town (pop. 5,228), Jalisco, central Mexico, on interior plateau, 16 mi. ESE of Guzmán; agr. center (corn, chickpeas, alfalfa, fruit, sugar cane, tobacco, livestock).

Tamazulápan (tämäsōōlä'pän), officially Tamazulápan del Progreso, town (pop. 2,817), Oaxaca, S Mexico, on Inter-American Highway and 29 mi. NW of Nochixtlán; alt. 6,530 ft. Cereals, sugar cane, fruit, livestock.

Tamazunchale (tŏ"mŭsŭnchä'lē, Sp. tämäsōōnchä'lā), city (pop. 4,570), San Luis Potosí, E Mexico, in fertile Gulf plain on Moctezuma R., on Inter-American Highway and 70 mi. SW of Pánuco. Resort; agr. center (tobacco, sugar cane, coffee, cereals, fruit, livestock). Anc. Aztec town.

Tamba (täm'bä), former province in S Honshu, Japan; now part of Kyoto and Hyogo prefectures.

Tambach (täm'bäch), town, Rift Valley prov., W Kenya, on road and 20 mi. ENE of Eldoret; coffee, wheat, corn, wattle growing, dairying.

Tambach-Dietharz (täm'bäkh-dēt'härts), town (pop. 5,649), Thuringia, central Germany, in Thuringian Forest, 12 mi. SSW of Gotha; mfg. of china, glass, electrical equipment, cardboard; wood- and metalworking; stone quarrying. Town created 1919 by union of Tambach and Dietharz villages. Hydroelectric power station (S)

Tambacounda (tämbäkōōn'dä), town (pop. c.3,700), S Senegal, Fr. West Africa, on railroad to Niger and 260 mi. ESE of Dakar; trading and agr. center (cotton, sisal, millet, fruit, livestock). Exports peanuts, hardwood, bamboo, essential oils, gums. Airfield; missions.

Tambaichi (tämbī'chē), town (pop. 21,742), Nara prefecture, S Honshu, Japan, 6 mi. S of Nara, in agr. area (rice, wheat); rail junction; raw silk, medicine. Site of tomb of founder of Tenri-kyo (important Shinto sect). Sometimes spelled Tanbaichi.

Tambalagam Bay, Ceylon: see KODDIYAR BAY.

Tambara (tämbä'rä), town (pop. 4,764), Ehime prefecture, N Shikoku, Japan, 6 mi. W of Saijo; rice, wheat, raw silk.

Tambaram (tŭm'bŭrŭm), village, Chingleput dist., E Madras, India; outer suburb of Madras, 15 mi. SW of city center; rail settlement (workshops). Site of Madras Christian Col. (moved here 1937 from Madras city). Tuberculosis sanatorium.

Tambaú (tämbäōō'), city (pop. 3,123), NE São Paulo, Brazil, on railroad and 50 mi. SE of Ribeirão Prêto; pottery mfg.; coffee, sugar cane.

També (tämbĕ'), city (pop. 2,169), E Pernambuco, NE Brazil, on Paraíba border, opposite Pedras de Fogo and 50 mi. NNW of Recife; sugar milling, marble quarrying. Formerly called Itambé.

Tambei or **Tambey** (tŭmbyā'), village, N Yamal-Nenets Natl. Okrug, Tyumen oblast, Russian SFSR, on NE Yamal Peninsula, on Ob Bay, at mouth of Tambei R., 540 mi. NNE of Salekhard; trading post.

Tambelan Islands (tämbŭlän'), group of islets (pop. 2,692), Indonesia, in S.China Sea, bet. Borneo and Riouw Archipelago; 1°N 107°34'E; coconuts, copra, trepang.

Tamberías (tämbărē'äs), village (pop. estimate 500), ⊙ Calingasta dept. (□ c.2,500; 1947 census pop. 6,563), SW San Juan prov., Argentina, on the Río de los Patos (affluent of San Juan R.) and 45 mi. W of San Juan; apples, wine, grain, livestock (sheep, goats); flour milling, wine making.

Tambillo (tämbē'yō), village, Pichincha prov., N central Ecuador, in the Andes, on Pan American Highway and 15 mi. SSW of Quito. Cotton-textile milling; cereals, potatoes, fruit.

Tambillos (–yōs), village (1930 pop. 317), Coquimbo prov., N central Chile, on railroad and 20 mi. S of La Serena; copper mining.

Tambinh (täm'bĭng'), town, Vinhlong prov., S Vietnam, in Mekong delta, 14 mi. S of Vinhlong; rice.

Tambo or **El Tambo** (ĕl täm'bō), town (pop. 1,481), Nariño dept., SW Colombia, in the Andes at N foot of Galeras Volcano, 17 mi. NNW of Pasto; alt. 7,220 ft. Wheat, corn, potatoes, sugar cane, coffee, fruit, livestock.

Tambo or **El Tambo**, village, Cañar prov., S central Ecuador, in the Andes, on Pan American Highway, on railroad and 16 mi. NNW of Azogues; corn, barley, potatoes, sheep.

Tambo. 1 Village (pop. 168), Arequipa dept., S Peru, near mouth of Tambo R. (irrigation), on railroad and 50 mi. SSW of Arequipa; alfalfa, cotton, sugar cane, grain. **2** Town (pop. 1,462), Ayacucho dept., S central Peru, in Cordillera Central, 25 mi. NE of Ayacucho; road junction; coca, coffee, cacao, grain.

Tambo, El, Colombia: see EL TAMBO, Cauca dept.

Tambobamba (tämbōbäm'bä), town (pop. 1,033), Apurímac dept., S central Peru, in the Andes, 35 mi. SW of Cuzco; gold, silver mining; grain, stock.

Tambo de Mora (täm'bō dā mō'rä), town (pop. 928), Ica dept., SW Peru, port on the Pacific, 4 mi. SW of Chincha Alta (connected by road); cotton processing and shipping.

Tambo Grande (täm'bō grän'dā), town (pop. 4,078), Piura dept., NW Peru, on Piura R. and 26 mi. NE of Piura; alfalfa; cattle raising. Iron deposits near by.

Tambo Machay, Peru: see CUZCO, city.

Tambopota, province, Peru: see PUERTO MALDONADO.

Tambopata River (tämbōpä'tä), SE Peru, rises on Bolivian border in Cordillera Oriental of the Andes just W of Sandia, flows 170 mi. NW and NE, past Astillero, to Madre de Dios R. at Puerto Maldonado.

Tambor (tämbōr'), village, Puntarenas prov., W Costa Rica, small port on Gulf of Nicoya of the Pacific, on Nicoya Peninsula, 20 mi. SE of Puntarenas; livestock, lumbering.

Tambora, Mount (tämbô'rŭ), active volcano (9,255 ft. high), N Sumbawa, Indonesia. Destructive eruption in 1815.

Tamborada River, Bolivia: see ANGOSTURA.

Tamboraque (tämbōrä'kä), village (pop. 209), Lima dept., W central Peru, on Rímac R., on Lima–La Oroya RR, on highway, and 7 mi. ENE of Matucana; copper and silver mining.

Tamboras (tämbō'räs), village (pop. 171), Libertad dept., NW Peru, in Cordillera Occidental, near Santiago de Chuco; tungsten mining.

Tambo Real (täm'bō räál'), village (pop. 2,946), Ancash Dept., W central Peru, on coastal plain, in irrigated Santa R. valley, on railroad and 7 mi. SSW of Chimbote; major sugar- and cotton-producing center; sugar milling, cotton ginning.

Tambores (tämbō'rĕs), town (pop. 1,100), Tacuarembó dept., N central Uruguay, 18 mi. SW of Tacuarembó; grain, vegetables, cattle.

Tamboril (tämbōōrēl'), city (pop. 834), W Ceará, Brazil, on upper Acaraú R. and 30 mi. NE of Crateús; cattle raising.

Tambo River (tăm'bō). **1** In S Peru, rises in Cordillera Occidental E of Puno, flows c.140 mi. S and SW, through Andean foothills of Moquegua and Arequipa depts., to the Pacific 18 mi. SE of Mollendo. Used for irrigation in lower course. **2** In Cuzco-Junín provs., Peru: see APURÍMAC RIVER.

Tamboryacu River or **Tambor-yacu River** (tämbōr' yä'kōō), Loreto dept., NE Peru, rises at about 0°50'S 75°W, flows c.200 mi. SE, through virgin forest region, to Napo R. (Amazon basin) 85 mi. NNW of Iquitos.

Tambov (tŭmbôf'), oblast (□ 13,250; 1946 pop. estimate 1,650,000) in central European Russian SFSR; ⊙ Tambov. In level Oka-Don river lowland; drained by Tsna and Vorona rivers; black-earth steppe. Important agr. region; coarse grains (rye, oats, millet), wheat, potatoes (along Tsna R.), tobacco (near Morshansk), legumes (E), sugar beets. Cattle and hog raising (N), horse breeding (S). Industries (flour milling, distilling, meat packing) based on agr. production. Textile mills (Morshansk, Rasskazovo), metalworking and machine mfg. (Tambov, Michurinsk). Formed 1937 out of Voronezh oblast.

Tambov, city (1939 pop. 121,285), ⊙ Tambov oblast, Russian SFSR, on Tsna R. (head of navigation) and 260 mi. SE of Moscow; 52°44'N 41°27'E. Rail junction; industrial center; mfg. (synthetic rubber, railway-car lighting equipment, aircraft, electric motors); flour milling, distilling, tobacco processing, brickworking. Teachers col., medical and music schools. Has regional and art mus., 17th-cent. cathedral. Founded 1636 as fortress on SE frontier of Moscow domain; developed (18th cent.) into grain and wool-trading center. Was ⊙ Tambov govt. (1779–1928). Industrial SE suburban portion became (1940) separate adjoining city of KOTOVSK.

Tambovka (tŭmbôf'kŭ), village (1926 pop. 3,113), SE Amur oblast, Russian SFSR, 25 mi. SE of Blagoveshchensk, in agr. area (grain, soybeans).

Tamboya (támboi'ä), village (pop. 1,195), Piura dept., NW Peru, on W slopes of Cordillera Occidental, 35 mi. S of Ayabaca; potatoes, corn.

Tambraparni River (tŭm"brŭpŭr'nē), Tinnevelly dist., S Madras, India, rises on Agastya Malai peak in Western Ghats, flows 80 mi. E, through fertile agr. valley, past PAPANASAM (hydroelectric station), Ambasamudram, Tinnevelly, Palamcottah, and Srivaikuntam, to Gulf of Mannar, forming delta mouth N of Kayalpatnam. Extensively used for irrigation since 15th cent. Receives Chittar R.

Tambun (tämbōōn'), town (pop. 1,091), central Perak, Malaya, on W slopes of central Malayan range, 4 mi. E of Ipoh; tin mining.

Tamchakett (tămshākĕt'), village, SE Mauritania, Fr. West Africa, in the Sahara, 400 mi. ENE of Saint-Louis, Senegal; stock, gum arabic.

Tamchi (täm'chē), village, Gobi Altai aimak, SW Mongolian People's Republic, 200 mi. SW of Uliassutai.

Tamdao (täm'dou'), Fr. *Cascade d'Argent* [=silver cascade], village, Vinhyen prov., N Vietnam, in Tamdao Range, 10 mi. N of Vinhyen and 30 mi. NNW of Hanoi; noted hill station (3,050 ft.); views over Red R. delta.

Tamdy-Bulak (tŭmdĭ"-bōōläk'), village, E Bukhara oblast, Uzbek SSR, in the Kyzyl-Kum, 135 mi. N of Bukhara; karakul sheep; corundum deposits. Until 1943, in Kara-Kalpak Autonomous SSR.

Tame (tä'mā), town (pop. 1,154), Arauca commissary, E Colombia, at E foot of Saliente de Tame (9,450 ft.), on E spur of Cordillera Oriental, 80 mi. SW of Arauca; cattle raising. Airfield.

Tâmega River (tä'mĭgŭ), Sp. *Támega* (tä'mägä), in NW Spain and N Portugal, rises in Orense prov. E of L. Antela, flows c.100 mi. SW, past Chaves and Amarante, to the Douro (right bank) 18 mi. SE of Oporto. Not navigable.

Tamel Aike (tämĕl' ī'kä), village, N central Santa Cruz natl. territory, Argentina, on the Río Chico and 55 mi. NW of Cañadón León, in sheep-raising area. Airport.

Tamelelt (tämlĕlt'), village, Marrakesh region, W Fr. Morocco, 32 mi. ENE of Marrakesh, in fertile agr. area (olives, truck, fruits); olive-oil pressing. Also called Tamelelt el Djedid.

Tamengo Canal (tämĕng'gōō), on Brazil-Bolivia border, natural channel (6 mi. long) in marshy Paraguay flood plain, linking Corumbá (Mato Grosso) on Paraguay R. with Puerto Suárez (Santa Cruz dept.) on L. Cáceres.

Tamer, At, Aden: see THUMEIR, ATH.

Tamera (tämrä'), village, Bizerte dist., N Tunisia, on railroad and 22 mi. ENE of Tabarka; cork extracting, hog raising. Zinc and iron deposits near by.

Tame River (tām), Stafford and Warwick, England, rises just W of Walsall, flows 25 mi. E and N, past Birmingham and Tamworth, to Trent R. 7 mi. N of Tamworth. Receives Anker R. at Tamworth.

Tamerlan, Russian SFSR: see VARNA.

Tamerlanovka (tŭmyĭrlä'nŭfkŭ), village, S South Kazakhstan oblast, Kazakh SSR, on Arys R. and 25 mi. NW of Chimkent; cotton, cattle.

Tamerton Foliot (tā'mŭrtŭn fōl'yŭt), agr. village and parish (pop. 1,232), SW Devon, England, 4 mi. NNW of Plymouth. Has 15th-cent. church.

Tamerza (tämĕrzä'), village and oasis, Tozeur dist., SW Tunisia, frontier station near Algerian border, 33 mi. NNW of Tozeur; date palms; 34°23'N 7°58'E.

Tamesí River (tämäsē'), in Tamaulipas, NE Mexico, rises in Sierra Madre Oriental W of Ciudad Victoria, flows c.250 mi. SE and E, past Xicoténcatl and along Tamaulipas-Veracruz border, to Gulf lagoons (linked with Pánuco R.) NW of Tampico. Called Guayalejo R. in upper course.

Támesis (tä'māsēs), town (pop. 3,950), Antioquia dept., NW central Colombia, on E slopes of Cordillera Occidental, 40 mi. SSW of Medellín; alt. 5,374 ft. Coffeegrowing, gold-mining, lumbering center, in agr. region (corn, sugar, potatoes, rice, cacao, cattle, hogs). Founded 1850. Silver, iron, copper, coal, lime, salt deposits near by.

Tamesis, England: see THAMES RIVER.

Tamgué Massif (tăgā', tämgā'), N Fr. Guinea, Fr. West Africa, N outlier of the FOUTA DJALLON mts. just S of Senegal border; rises to 4,970 ft.

Tamia or **Tamiyah** (tä'mĭyŭ), village (pop. 8,893), Faiyum prov., Upper Egypt, 14 mi. NNE of Faiyum; cotton ginning; cereals, sugar, fruits.

Tamiahua (tämyä'wä), town (pop. 2,319), Veracruz, E Mexico, at S end of Tamiahua Lagoon, 23 mi. N of Tuxpan; agr. center (corn, sugar cane, fruit).

Tamiahua Lagoon, on Gulf coast of Veracruz, E Mexico; extends 65 mi. SSE from SE of Tampico to Tamiahua, where narrow channel opens on ocean; c.12 mi. wide. Contains number of large isls. Navigable for small craft.

Tamiami Trail (tă'mĭă"mē), S Fla., a road (U.S. 94; built 1917–28) across the Everglades, from Miami on the Atlantic to Naples, c.105 mi. W, on the Gulf; bordered by drainage canal. Joined at Naples by road to Tampa; hence name is contraction of Tampa-Miami. Noted for picturesque scenery along the way.

Tamiathis, Egypt: see DAMIETTA.

Tamilnad (tŭ'mĭlnäd), linguistic region in extreme SE India, where Tamil—a Dravidian tongue—is the dominant language. Comprises area of Madras state extending inland from E coast to an indefinite line running SW from a point N of Madras city along Eastern Ghats and then S along Travancore-Cochin and Madras border. From Asoka's time (c.250 B.C.) to coming of Moslems in 14th cent. A.D. area was ruled by Pandya, Pallava, and, primarily, Chola dynasties. Its inhabitants, the Tamils, are an enterprising race, many of them since early Middle Ages emigrating to Ceylon, Burma, Malaya, Singapore, and elsewhere throughout SE Asia, where they are active in industry and commerce.

Tamina River (tämē'nä), E Switzerland, short, turbulent stream which joins the Rhine at Bad Ragaz; Pfäfers Bad on it.

Tamines (tämēn'), town (pop. 6,887), Namur prov., S central Belgium, 8 mi. ENE of Charleroi; rail junction; mfg. (stoves, glassware, mirrors).

Taming (dä'mĭng'), town, ⊙ Taming co. (pop. 566,975), SW Hopeh prov., China, near Pingyuan line, 45 mi. ENE of Anyang; road center; kaoliang, millet, peanuts, cotton, wheat, beans.

Tamio, Formosa: see MINHIUNG.

Tamise, Belgium: see TEMSE.

Tamis River, Rumania and Yugoslavia: see TIMIS RIVER.

Tamiyah, Egypt: see TAMIA.

Tam Kong, China: see TAM RIVER.

Tamky (täm'kē'), town, Quangnam prov., central Vietnam, on railroad and 90 mi. SE of Hue; tea plantations; cinnamon trade from Tramy (linked by road).

Tamlang Nuevo (tämläng' nwā'vō, täm'läng), town (1939 pop. 5,799) in Escalante municipality, Negros Occidental prov., NE Negros isl., Philippines, 35 mi. ENE of Bacolod; agr. trade center (rice, sugar cane).

Tamlap, Cambodia: see PRABATCHEANCHUM.

Tamluk (tŭmlōōk'), Sanskrit *Tamralipta* [*Tamra*,= copper], town (pop. 12,079), Midnapore dist., SW West Bengal, India, on Rupnarayan R. and 34 mi. SW of Calcutta; chemical mfg.; general engineering works; rice, betel nuts, pulse, jute, sugar cane. Arts and Science Inst. Figured in anc. Hindu writings. Stronghold of Buddhism in 5th cent. B.C.; former Buddhist temple, now dedicated to Kali, surmounted by sacred disk of Vishnu. Was ⊙ anc. Hindu kingdom of Tamralipta or Suhma (early kings were Rajputs of Peacock dynasty); anc. port exporting copper. Visited 5th cent. A.D. by Chinese pilgrim Fa Hian, 7th cent. by Hiuen Tsiang.

Tammela (täm'mĕlä), village (commune pop. 7,950), Häme co., SW Finland, in lake region, 4 mi. E of Forssa; feldspar quarrying.

Tammerfors, Finland: see TAMPERE.

Tammerkoski, Finland: see TAMPERE.

Tammer Rapids, Finland: see TAMPERE.

Tamminkatti, India: see TUMINKATTI.

Tammisaari, Finland: see EKENAS.

Tamms, village (pop. 665), Alexander co., extreme S Ill., 16 mi. NNW of Cairo, in agr. area.

Tamok (tŭmōk'), village, Mergui dist., Lower Burma, in Tenasserim, on road and 15 mi. NE of Mergui.

Tamora (tŭmŏ'rŭ), village (pop. 91), Seward co., SE Nebr., 28 mi. WNW of Lincoln.

Tampa (tăm'pŭ). **1** City (pop. 124,681), ⊙ Hillsborough co., W Fla., port of entry with fine harbor on Hillsboro Bay (an arm of Tampa Bay), at mouth of Hillsboro R., c.200 mi. NW of Miami; chief cigar-mfg. center and phosphate-shipping port in U.S.; also a major citrus-fruit canner and shipper. Its other important industries manufacture boxes, cans, canned vegetables, metal window casements, millwork, portland cement, concrete products, feed, fertilizer, beverages (including beer), preserves, paper wrappers, clothing, dairy and meat products; has shipyards and railroad shops. Winter resort. Points of interest: the Univ. of Tampa in Plant Park, the municipal mus., De Soto Oak, the municipal auditorium and the state fair grounds; Ybor City (ē'bûr), hq. of cigar industry and center of the Spanish and Cuban community; Davis Isls. (artificial), the site of a residential development; and the bridges across Old Tampa Bay (W) to St. Petersburg and Clearwater. MacDill Air Force Base is near by. Town grew around Fort Brooke, built 1823 by Americans. It was captured by Federal forces in Civil War. Construction of railroads and beginning of cigar industry in late 1880s initiated city's modern development. Tampa was port of embarkation and training base for Theodore Roosevelt's Rough Riders during the Spanish-American War. **2** City (pop. 216), Marion co., central Kansas, 30 mi. ENE of McPherson, in grain-, stock-, and oil-producing area.

Tampa Bay, W Fla., large irregular arm of the Gulf of Mexico, with Tampa and St. Petersburg on its shores. Bay proper is c.25 mi. long, 7–12 mi. wide, and is partly sheltered on W by Pinellas peninsula (site of St. Petersburg); many small isls. are scattered across its mouth. A mid-bay peninsula separates N part into a NE arm called Hillsboro Bay (c.10 mi. long, 5–6 mi. wide), which has Tampa at N end, where it receives Hillsboro R. The NW arm, called Old Tampa Bay, is c.15 mi. long, 4–12 mi. wide, and is crossed by bridges connecting mid-bay peninsula with W shore. Bay has dredged shipping channels.

Tampacán (tämpäkän'), town (pop. 585), San Luis Potosí, E Mexico, in fertile Gulf plain, 45 mi. SSE of Valles; tobacco, coffee, sugar cane, livestock.

Tampamolón or **Tampamolón Corona** (tämpämōlōn' kōrō'nä), town (pop. 812), San Luis Potosí, E Mexico, 33 mi. SSE of Valles; sugar cane, tobacco, coffee, fruit, stock.

Tampere (täm'pĕrä), Swedish *Tammerfors* (tä"-mŭrfôrs',-fôsh'), city (pop. 95,753), Häme co., SW Finland, on Tammer Rapids, Finnish *Tammerkoski* (täm'mĕrkōs"kē), Swedish *Tammerfors*, which descend 59 ft. over distance of ½ mi. bet. lakes Näsi (N) and Pyhä (S), 100 mi. NNW of Helsinki; 61°30'N 23°45'E. Rail junction, lake port; airport. Industrial center with major textile, pulp, and paper mills, shoe factories, foundries; mfg. of locomotives, turbines, trucks, lumbering machinery, printing presses, tools, precision instruments. Hydroelectric plant, radio station. Seat (1923) of Lutheran bishopric; site of technical col. and women's physical-education col. Has cathedral (1907) and county mus. Founded 1779; created (1821) free city by Alexander I. Scene (April, 1918) of decisive victory of White forces under Mannerheim over Red troops in Finnish war of independence. Among industrial W suburbs are Lielahti, Epilä.

Tampico (tămpē'kō, Sp. tämpē'kō), city (pop. 82,475), Tamaulipas, NE Mexico, in Gulf plain, on Pánuco R. (7 mi. inland from its mouth on the Gulf), on Veracruz border, 215 mi. NE of Mexico city; major port and petroleum-producing center; trading and mfg. city; winter resort. Contains petroleum refineries, foundries, chemical plants, sugar refineries, flour mills, cordage factories. Has good harbor facilities, and rail connections W to San Luis Potosí and N to Monterrey and U.S.; exports petroleum, minerals, cattle, hides, cotton, bananas, fiber products, chicle, rubber, sarsaparilla, vanilla, beeswax, honey, coffee. Noted fishing grounds. Site of old pre-Sp. settlement and of Franciscan mission in early colonial days, it was 1st founded c.1554 and refounded 1823 by order of Santa Anna. Occupied by Amer. forces (1846) during Mexican War and by Fr. invaders 1862. With discovery of oil (c.1900) by English and Amer. geologists, rapid expansion and development of petroleum industries began. Before Mexico expropriated foreign-owned property (1938), about third of landowners were American and large element of pop. was foreign. Villa Cuauhtémoc (or Pueblo Viejo) is 3 mi. SE across Pánuco R. in Veracruz. Suburban seaside resorts La Barra and Miramar are 6 mi. NE, at mouth of Pánuco R. on the Gulf. Climate hot and humid; sometimes relieved in winter by cool winds.

Tampico (tămpē'kō, tăm'pĭkō), village (pop. 760), Whiteside co., NW Ill., 11 mi. SSW of Sterling, in agr. area; ships grain; cheese factory.

Tampico Alto or **Tampico el Alto** (tämpē'kō ĕl äl'tō), town (pop. 1,120), Veracruz, E Mexico, in Gulf lowland, 8 mi. SSE of Tampico; cereals, sugar cane, cattle.

Tampico Lagoon (□ 200), on Gulf coast of northernmost Veracruz, E Mexico, just S of Pánuco R. mouth. Also called Puerto Viejo Lagoon for Puerto Viejo (Villa Cuauhtémoc), on NE shore.

Tampin (tämpĭn'), town (pop. 2,204), S Negri Sembilan, Malaya, 18 mi. N of Malacca city, in rubber-growing dist. Just S, across Malacca border, is rail junction of Tampin, on W coast line.

Tampon, Le (lü tăpõ'), town (pop. 13,674; commune pop. 16,728), S Réunion isl., on cross-isl. road and 4 mi. NNE of Saint-Pierre; perfume distilling; geranium gardens.

Tamrida or **Tamridah,** Socotra: see HADIBU.

Tam River (täm), Mandarin *Tan Kiang* or *T'an Chiang* (both: tän' jyäng'), Cantonese *Tam Kong* (gông), S Kwangtung prov., China, formed by several branches near Chikhom, flows 80 mi. E and S, past Chikhom, Sunchong, and Kungyifow, to S.China Sea, merging its delta with West R. branch of Canton R. delta.

Tams, village (1940 pop. 1,045), Raleigh co., S W. Va., 10 mi. SW of Beckley; coal-mining area.

Tamsag Bulag, Mongolia: see TAMTSAK.

Tamshiyacu (täm-shēä'kōō), town (pop. 930), Loreto dept., NE Peru, landing on upper Amazon R. and 22 mi. SE of Iquitos; sugar cane, fruit, tropical forest products (rubber, timber).

Tamsui, Formosa: see TANSHUI.

Tamsweg (täms'vĕk), town (pop. 4,027), Salzburg, W central Austria, on Mur R. and 27 mi. NNE of Spittal; tin foundry, tannery; resort (alt. 3,350 ft.). Gothic church of Sankt Leonhard.

Tamtsak, Tamtsak Bulak, or **Tamsag Bulag** (täm'săkh bōō'läkh), village, Choibalsan aimak, easternmost Mongolian People's Republic, 115 mi. ESE of Choibalsan.

Tamu (tä"mōō'), village, Upper Chindwin dist., Upper Burma, in Kabaw Valley, 70 mi. N of Kalewa, on Manipur (India) line; frontier post on major Burma-India route.

Tamuin River, Mexico: see SANTA MARÍA RIVER.

Tamurejo (tämōōrā'hō), town (pop. 843), Badajoz prov., W Spain, 12 mi. SSE of Herrera del Duque; olives, cereals, livestock; textile milling.

Tamur River, Nepal: see KOSI RIVER.

Tamworth (tăm'wûrth), municipality (pop. 12,071), E central New South Wales, Australia, on Peel R. and 135 mi. NNW of Sydney; rail junction; dairying center; flour mill.

Tamworth, village (pop. estimate 500), SE Ont., on Salmon R. and 30 mi. NW of Kingston; dairying, mixed farming.

Tamworth, municipal borough (1931 pop. 7,509; 1951 census 12,889), SE Stafford, England, at confluence of Tame R. and Anker R., on Warwick border, 13 mi. NE of Birmingham; mfg. of glazed bricks, paper, metal products; brewing. St. Editha church was built (1345) on site of church originally built in 8th cent. Thomas Guy built the almshouse (1678). Town hall dates from 1701. Town was burned by Danes in 9th cent., rebuilt by Æthelflæd in 10th cent., and became residence of kings of Mercia. Sir Robert Peel was member of Parliament for the borough. Near by is Tamworth Castle.

Tamworth, town (pop. 1,025), Carroll co., E N.H., at S foot of White Mts., 14 mi. NW of Ossipee; resort center; winter sports. Includes villages of South Tamworth (woodcraft industry) and CHOCORUA.

Tamyang (täm'yäng'), Jap. *Tanyo,* town (1949 pop. 13,325), S.Cholla prov., S Korea, 12 mi. NNE of Kwangju, in agr. area (rice, soybeans, cotton); makes hemp and silk textiles.

Tan. 1 or **T'an,** river, Kwangtung prov., China: see TAM RIVER. **2** River, in Shensi, Honan, and Hupeh provs., China: see TAN RIVER.

Tana (tä'nä) or **Tsana** (tsä'nä), largest lake (□ c.1,400) in Ethiopia, in Begemdir and Gojjam provs., 20 mi. S of Gondar; 12°N 37°20'E; alt. c.6,000 ft.; max. depth 45 ft.; 50 mi. long, 40 mi. wide. Receives Little Abbai R. (SW), the longest (c.85 mi.) of c.60 affluents. Its outlet (SE), site of a projected dam, is the Blue Nile, 1,000 mi. long. Contains several isls., including Dek Isl. (5 mi. long, 4 mi. wide). Visited in 16th–17th cent. by Portuguese Jesuits who called it Dembea.

Tana, Quebrada de, Chile: see CAMIÑA, QUEBRADA DE.

Tanabe (tä"nä'bā). **1** Town (pop. 5,018), Kyoto prefecture, S Honshu, Japan, 15 mi. S of Kyoto; rice-producing center. **2** City (1940 pop. 28,131; 1947 pop. 36,472), Wakayama prefecture, S Honshu, Japan, on inlet of Philippine Sea, on SW Kii Peninsula, 36 mi. SSE of Wakayama; summer resort; rice, livestock; raw silk. Sometimes called Kii-tanabe.

Tanabesar, Indonesia: see ARU ISLANDS.

Tanabi (tŏnŏobē'), city (pop. 3,060), NW São Paulo, Brazil, near railroad, 21 mi. NW of São José do Rio Prêto; cotton ginning, pottery mfg., sugar milling; rice, butter, grain.

Tanabu (tä"nä'bōō), town (pop. 20,189), Aomori prefecture, N Honshu, Japan, on NE Mutsu Bay, 40 mi. NE of Aomori; agr. (rice, soybeans), lumbering, fishing.

Tanach, Palestine: see TAANACH.

Tanacross (tă'nä–), village (pop. 151), E Alaska, on upper Tanana R. and 130 mi. WSW of Dawson, on Alaska Highway; 63°24'N 143°20'W; supply center for prospectors, trappers. School; airfield, radio station. Sometimes called Tanana Crossing.

Tana Fjord (tä'nä), inlet (c.40 mi. long, 4–9 mi. wide) of Barents Sea of Arctic Ocean, Finnmark co., N Norway, 45 mi. NW of Vardo. Receives Tana R. at its head.

Tanaga Island (tă'nŭgŭ) (25 mi. long, 3–20 mi. wide), Andreanof Isls., Aleutian Isls., SW Alaska, 5 mi. W of Kanaga Isl.; 51°48'N 177°57'W; rises to 6,975 ft. on Tanaga Volcano (NW), reportedly dormant. Second World War airstrip on SW shore.

Tanagawa, Japan: see TANAKAWA.

Tanagra (tŭnăg'rŭ, tŭnäg'rŭ), village (pop. 626), Boeotia nome, E central Greece, near Asopus R., 12 mi. E of Thebes. Formerly called Bratsi. Anc. Tanagra was chief town of E Boeotia, with close ties to Attica, and an early rival of Thebes. Here the Spartans defeated the Athenians in 457 B.C. It declined in 4th cent. B.C. but flourished again in Roman times. Lively Hellenistic terra-cotta figures have been unearthed here. Birthplace of poet Corinna (5th cent. B.C.).

Tanagro River (tänä'grô), S Italy, rises in the Apennines 4 mi. SW of Moliterno, flows 55 mi. NNW, past Casalbuono, Polla, and Auletta, to Sele R. 1 mi. S of Contursi. Used for hydroelectric power (Pertosa).

Tanagura (tänä'gōōrä) or **Tanakura** (–kōōrä), town (pop. 7,416), Fukushima prefecture, central Honshu, Japan, 28 mi. W of Taira; rice, silk cocoons, wheat; horse breeding.

Tanah or **Tannah** (tän-nä'), village (pop. 5,890), Daqahliya prov., Lower Egypt, 10 mi. E of Mansura; cotton, cereals.

Tanahbala (tä"näbä'lŭ), island (25 mi. long, 14 mi. wide), Batu Isls., Indonesia, off W coast of Sumatra, just S of Tanahmasa; low, forested. Copra, resin, fish.

Tanahdjampea, Indonesia: see TANA JAMPEA.

Tanahmasa (tänämä'sŭ) or **Hamasa** (hämä'sŭ), island (pop. 1,548), Batu Isls., Indonesia, off W coast of Sumatra, just N of Tanahbala; 30 mi. long, 6 mi. wide. Low, forested; copra, resin, fish.

Tanah Merah (tänä'mŭrä'), village (pop. 407), N Kelantan, Malaya, on Kelantan R. and E coast railroad, 23 mi. SSW of Kota Bharu; rice, rubber.

Tanahmerah Bay (tänämŭrä'), inlet of the Pacific, N New Guinea, 25 mi. WNW of Hollandia; 6 mi. long, 5 mi. wide. In Second World War U.S. troops landed here April, 1944.

Tanah Rata (tänä' rä'tä), township (□ 8; pop. 2,596) of Cameron Highlands, NW Pahang, Malaya, on road and 22 mi. NNE of Tapah (Perak); hill station (alt. 4,750 ft.).

Tanaïs, Russian SFSR: see AZOV; DON RIVER.

Tana Jampea or **Tanahdjampea** (both: tänä' jämpĕ'ŭ), coral island (12 mi. long, 10 mi. wide; pop. 2,285), Indonesia, in Flores Sea, 80 mi. N of Flores; 7°5'S 120°41'E; rises to 1,647 ft.; fishing. Also called Djampea.

Tanaka, Formosa: see TIENCHUNG.

Tanakawa (tänä'käwŭ) or **Tanagawa** (–gäwŭ), town (pop. 6,668), Osaka prefecture, S Honshu, Japan, on Osaka Bay, 7 mi. NNW of Wakayama, in agr. and poultry-raising area; woodworking.

Tanakpur (tŭn'ŭkpŏŏr), village, Naini Tal dist., N Uttar Pradesh, India, on Sarda R. (Nepal border) and 47 mi. SE of Naini Tal; rail spur terminus; trades in goods from Tibet (including borax, wool, grain) and turmeric and chili from Nepal. Founded 1880.

Tanakura, Japan: see TANAGURA.

Tanalian Point (tŭnăl'yŭn), village (1939 pop. 18), S Alaska, on E shore of L. Clark, 170 mi. WSW of Anchorage; fishing resort; airstrip.

Tanalyk River (tŭnŭlĭk'), Baskkir Autonomous SSR, Russian SFSR, rises in the S Urals at Baimak, flows S, past Buribai, and generally E to Ural R. 10 mi. N of Iriklinski; 100 mi. long.

Tanami (tă'nŭmē), settlement, W Northern Territory, Australia, 360 mi. NW of Alice Springs; gold mines.

Tánamo or **Central Tánamo** (sĕntrăl' tä'nämō), sugar-mill village (pop. 1,716), Oriente prov., E Cuba, on Tánamo Bay, 20 mi. E of Mayarí.

Tánamo Bay, sheltered Atlantic inlet (6 mi. long, 4 mi. wide), Oriente prov., E Cuba, 20 mi. E of Mayarí; linked with ocean by narrow channel.

Tanan (tänän'), village (pop. 10,484), Qalyubiya prov., Lower Egypt, 5 mi. NNE of Qalyub; cotton, flax, cereals, fruits.

Tanan (tŭn'än'), town (1936 pop. 3,018), ⊙ Tanan prov. (□ 1,400; 1943 pop. 159,000), S Vietnam, in Cochin China, on West Vaico R. and Saigon-Mytho RR, 45 mi. SW of Saigon; rice, sugar cane, coconuts (oil extraction).

Tanana (tă'nŭnô), village (pop. 221), central Alaska, on Yukon R., at mouth of Tanana R. and 135 mi. WNW of Fairbanks; 65°10'N 152°12'W; supply center for placer gold-mining region; fox and mink breeding. On Yukon R. steamer line; airfield. Site of R.C. mission. Formerly site of Fort Gibbon, U.S. army post. Tanana Native Village (pop. 75), 3 mi. E, is site of St. James Episcopal Mission.

Tanana Crossing, Alaska: see TANACROSS.

Tananarive (tänänärēv'), province (□ 1,090; 1948 pop. 822,200), central Madagascar; ⊙ Tananarive. Consists primarily of IMERINA region and Ankaratra Highlands. Extensive rice fields; stock raising; tobacco, coffee. Temperate-zone fruit and vegetables are grown; silkworms are raised. Mimosa and eucalyptus plantations; winegrowing. Industries include graphite mining, sawmilling; mfg. of starch, tapioca, edible oils, canned beef. Tananarive is center of diversified mfg.; Antsirabe is a noted spa. Tamatave-Antsirabe RR serving the area is known as the "rice railroad."

Tananarive, also, in English, **Antananarivo** (ăn"-tŭnă"nŭrē'vō), city (1948 pop. 171,000; including suburbs, 238,000), ⊙ Madagascar and Tananarive prov., E central Madagascar, 135 mi. WSW of Tamatave; 18°52'S 47°35'E. Seat of the high commissioner, chief commercial, distributing, and mfg. center of the isl., a rail junction and hub of a road network, and outlet of a rice region. Produces shoes and other leather goods, garments, umbrellas, sackcloth, brushes, glue, soap, building materials, edible oils, chocolate, canned meat, oxygen, ice. Has foundries, railroad shops, flour mills, sawmills. Printing, woodworking, tobacco processing, working of semi-precious stones. Extensive truck gardening in vicinity. A picturesque highland city, built on a ridge (alt. 4,815 ft.) which rises c.700 ft. above the fertile rice fields of Betsimitatra plain (to W), it culminates in a rock supporting the former royal estate "Rova." To W, along the railroad, are factory districts (Isotry, Soanierana), to NW and NE the newest urban extension (Ankadifotsy). Business centers on the zoma, the great native market. The humid, warm climate is relieved somewhat by a dry, cooler season, May-Sept. Inside the "Rova" enclosure are the palace of the last queen, now a mus., and sepulchers and mementoes of other Imerina kings. Further notable features of Tananarive are the sacred lake Anosy, created by Radama I; baroque palace of the former prime minister Rainilaiarivony (now school of applied arts); Fort Voyron; R.C. and Anglican cathedrals. There is an observatory, several research institutes (including Pasteur Inst.), schools of law and medicine, R.C. seminary, numerous trade schools, 2 military camps. Airports at Ivato (8 mi. NW) and ARIVONIMANO. Nanisana agr. station near by experiments with horticulture, sericulture, viticulture, fruit trees. There are c.17,000 French and c.2,000 Chinese and Indians in the city. From the original village, founded in 17th cent. by a Hova chieftain, the town developed into royal stronghold under Andrianampoinimerina and Radama I. Many churches were built after conversion (1870) of Ranavalona II to Protestantism. France conquered Tananarive 1895; Gallieni administered it 1896–1905 and planned extensive urban modernization.

Tanana River (tă'nŭnô), Alaska, rises in W Yukon near Alaska border, near 62°40'N 140°30'W, flows WNW along N side of Alaska Range, past Tanacross and Big Delta, to Fairbanks (on Chena Slough, N branch of river), thence WSW to Nenana, N to Minto, finally WNW to Yukon R. at Tanana; c.600 mi. long. Receives Nabesna, Delta, Nenana, and Kantishana rivers. Prior to advent of air transportation river was important route to gold fields of the interior. Some agr. is carried on in valley. Mouth discovered c.1860 by Russian traders.

Tanao (tänä'ō), town (pop. 6,973), Aichi prefecture, central Honshu, Japan, 3 mi. SE of Handa, across Chita Bay; cotton textiles; fishing.

Tanap (tän'äp'), village, central Vietnam, on railroad and 45 mi. SSE of Vinh; rail junction on highway through Mugia Pass to Thakhek (Laos).

Tana River, Nor. *Tanaelv* (tä'näĕlv"), Finnish *Tenojoki* (tĕ'nōyō"kē), border stream bet. Finnmark co., N Norway, and Lapland co., N Finland, rises on border near 68°45'N, flows 200 mi. generally NE to head of Tana Fjord of Barents Sea. Noted for its salmon; has traces of alluvial gold.

Tana River (tä'nä), Kenya, rises on E slopes of Aberdare Range W of Nyeri, flows c.500 mi. E and S, around S and E flanks of Mt. Kenya, past Garissa, Bura, and Garsen, through arid Nyika plain, to Indian Ocean at Kipini. Navigable in lower reaches.

Tanaro River (tä'närô), anc. *Tanarus,* NW Italy, rises in Ligurian Alps on W slopes of Mt. Saccarello, flows 171 mi. NE, past Ceva, Alba, Asti, and Alessandria, to the Po 1 mi. E of Bassignana. Widely used for agr. and industry; forms major valley traveled by railroad bet. Turin and Savona. Chief affluents: Stura di Demonte, Bormida, and Belbo rivers.

Tanauan (tänä'wän). **1** Town (1939 pop. 3,396 1948 municipality pop. 30,203), Batangas prov., S Luzon, Philippines, on railroad and 12 mi. W of San Pablo; agr. center (rice, sugar cane, corn; coconuts). **2** Town (1939 pop. 5,241; 1948 municipality pop. 24,573), W Leyte, Philippines, on San Pedro Bay, 9 mi. S of Tacloban; agr. center (rice, hemp).

Tanawan, Philippines: see BUSTOS.

Tanbaichi, Japan: see TAMBAICHI.

Tancacha (tängkä'chä), town (pop. estimate 2,000), central Córdoba prov., Argentina, 6 mi. SE of Río Tercero; wheat, flax, alfalfa, peanuts, hogs, cattle.

Tancanhuitz, Mexico: see GENERAL PEDRO ANTONIO SANTOS.

Tancarville (tākärvēl'), village (pop. 210), Seine-Inférieure dept., N France, on right bank of the Seine just above its estuary and 16 mi. E of Le Havre. Has noted old castle (13th–15th cent.) adjoined by 18th-cent. château.

Tancarville Canal, Seine-Inférieure dept., N France, running alongside Seine R. estuary bet. Tancarville and Le Havre, via Harfleur; 15 mi. long; c.15 ft. deep.

Tanchai (dän'jī'), town (pop. 3,008), ⊙ Tanchai co. (pop. 44,708), SE Kweichow prov., China, 70 mi. ESE of Kweiyang; cotton textiles, embroideries; millet, beans. Iron and mercury mines, lead deposits near by. Until 1941 called Pachai.

Tanchau (tŭn'chou'), town, Chaudoc prov., S Vietnam, on right bank of Mekong R. (river port) and 10 mi. NE of Chaudoc, on Cambodia line, in rice-growing area; rice- and corn-trading center; rice- and silkgrowing experiment station.

Tancheng or **T'an-ch'eng** (tän'chŭng'), town, ⊙ Tancheng co. (pop. 433,959), S Shantung prov., China, 30 mi. S of Lini, near Kiangsu line; silk weaving; grain, peanuts, melons.

Tan Chiang, China: see TAN RIVER.

T'an Chiang, China: see TAM RIVER.

Tanchon (tän'chŭn'), Jap. *Tansen*, town (1944 pop. 32,761), S.Hamgyong prov., N Korea, on Sea of Japan, 80 mi. ENE of Hungnam; rail junction; magnesite, iron sulphide, bauxite mines.

Tanchow. 1 Town, Kwangsi prov., China: see SANKIANG. **2** Town, Hainan, Kwangtung prov., China: see TANHSIEN.

Tanchuk (dän'jŏŏk'), Mandarin *Tan-chu* (dän'jōō'), village, SE Kwangsi prov., China, 45 mi. W of Wuchow and on left bank of Sün R. In Second World War site of U.S. air base, held 1944–45 by Japanese.

Tancítaro (tänsē'tärō), officially Tancítaro de Medellín, town (pop. 1,858), Michoacán, W central Mexico, at S foot of Tancítaro volcano, 23 mi. SW of Uruapan; alt. 6,588 ft. Sugar cane, coffee, fruit.

Tancítaro, volcano (12,664 ft.), Michoacán, W Mexico, at S end of Sierra de los Terascos, 22 mi. WSW of Uruapan. Often snow-capped; surrounded by crest of c.250 smaller volcanoes. PARICUTÍN volcano is just N.

Tancoco (tängkō'kō), town (pop. 1,328), Veracruz, E Mexico, in Sierra Madre Oriental foothills, 33 mi. NW of Tuxpan; cereals, sugar, coffee, fruit.

Tancook Island or **Great Tancook Island** (3 mi. long, 1 mi. wide), largest isl. in Mahone Bay, S N.S., 7 mi. SE of Chester.

Tanda (tän'dŭ). **1** Town (pop. 26,128), Fyzabad dist., E Uttar Pradesh, India, on the Gogra and 36 mi. ESE of Fyzabad; rail spur terminus; hand-loom cotton weaving center; trades in rice, wheat, gram, oilseeds, barley. **2** Town (pop. 8,404), Rampur dist., N central Uttar Pradesh, India, 12 mi. NNW of Rampur; corn, wheat, rice, gram, sugar cane. Also called Tanda Badridan.

Tandaai (tändī'), village, Umtali prov., E Southern Rhodesia, in Mashonaland, in Chimanimani Mts., on road and 13 mi. NNW of Melsetter, near Mozambique border; tobacco, wheat, corn.

Tandag (tän'däg), town (1939 pop. 6,064; 1948 municipality pop. 14,099), Surigao prov., Philippines, on NE coast of Mindanao, 60 mi. SE of Surigao, in mining and coconut-growing area.

Tandarei (tsûndûrā'), Rum. *Țăndărei*, village (pop. 2,353), Ialomita prov., SE Rumania, on Ialomita R. and 34 mi. NE of Calarasi; rail junction.

Tanda-Urmar (tän'dŭ-ŏŏr'mŭr), town (pop. 12,734), Hoshiarpur dist., N Punjab, India, 18 mi. NW of Hoshiarpur; market center for wheat, gram, sugar, corn; piece goods; hand-loom weaving, pottery mfg. Sometimes called Urmar Tanda.

Tanderagee or **Tandragee** (both: tăndrŭgē'), urban district (1937 pop. 1,120; 1951 census 1,394), NE Co. Armagh, Northern Ireland, near Bann R., 10 mi. E of Armagh; agr. market (flax, potatoes, oats; cattle). Elizabethan castle is seat of duke of Manchester, on site of fortress of the O'Hanlons.

Tandil (tändēl'), city (pop. 39,084), ⊙ Tandil dist. (□ 1,867; pop. 59,967), S central Buenos Aires prov., Argentina, at N end of Sierra del Tandil, 100 mi. NW of Mar del Plata. Railhead; health and pleasure resort. Agr. center in rich dairying region (Tandil cheese); stone-quarrying industry (granite, diorite, quartzite). Founded 1823.

Tandil, Sierra del (syĕ'rä dĕl), hill range in S Buenos Aires prov., Argentina, extends c.30 mi. S from Tandil; rises to c.1,600 ft. Quarrying of granite, diorite, quartzite.

Tandjoeng, Tandjong, or **Tandjung,** in Indonesian names: see TANJUNG.

Tandlianwala (tŭndyän'välŭ), town (pop. 7,875), Lyallpur dist., E central Punjab, W Pakistan, 27 mi. S of Lyallpur; wheat, cotton, oilseeds, millet; cotton ginning, oilseed milling, ice mfg.

Tando Adam (tŭn'dō ä'dŭm), town (pop. 17,233), Nawabshah dist., central Sind, W Pakistan, in irrigated area, 36 mi. SSE of Nawabshah; rail junction; market center (grain, silk, cotton, ghee, sugar, oilseeds); cotton ginning. Sometimes called Adam-jo-Tando.

Tando Allahyar (ŭlä'hyär), town (pop. 8,406), Hyderabad dist., S Sind, W Pakistan, 21 mi. E of Hyderabad; market center (grain, cotton, oilseeds, sugar); cotton ginning, handicraft silk weaving, ivory carving; metalwork. Also spelled Tando Alahyar; and sometimes called Alahyar-jo-Tando.

Tando Bago (bä'gō), village, Hyderabad dist., S Sind, W Pakistan, 55 mi. SE of Hyderabad; agr. market (rice, cotton, sugar cane, wheat).

Tando Jam (jäm'), village, Hyderabad dist., S central Sind, W Pakistan, 11 mi. E of Hyderabad; textiles. Also called Jam jo Tando.

Tando Muhammad Khan (mŏŏhŭm'mŭd khän'), town (pop. 8,718), Hyderabad dist., S Sind, W Pakistan, on Fuleli Canal and 20 mi. SSE of Hyderabad; trades in grain, metal products, tobacco, dyes; handicraft mfg. (cotton and silk fabrics, woolen blankets, leather goods, pottery, copper- and ironware); distillery. Also spelled Tando Mohammad (Mahomed) Khan.

Tandou, Lake (tăn'dōō) (□ 60), W New South Wales, Australia, 50 mi. SSE of Broken Hill; 12 mi. long, 7 mi. wide; usually dry.

Tandragee, Northern Ireland: see TANDERAGEE.

Tandubas Island (tändōō'bäs) (□ 4.3; 1939 pop. 3,687), in Tawitawi Group, Sulu prov., Philippines, in Sulu Archipelago, just NE of Tawitawi Isl.

Tandubatu Island (tändōō'bätōō') or **Tandubato Island** (–bätō') (□ 16.6; 1939 pop. 177), in Tawitawi Group, Sulu prov., Philippines, in Sulu Archipelago, just off NE tip of Tawitawi Isl.

Tandur (tän'dŏŏr). **1** Village, Adilabad dist., Hyderabad state, India: see BELAMPALLI. **2** Town (pop. 9,280), Gulbarga dist., SW central Hyderabad state, India, on Kagna R. and 50 mi. E of Gulbarga; limestone quarrying and dressing, rice and oilseed milling; ceramics; matches.

Taneatua (tănē"ütōō'ŭ), township (pop. 437), N N.Isl., New Zealand, 70 mi. NW of Gisborne; rail terminus; dairying, fruit; wild ducks, pheasants.

Tanega-shima (tänä'gä-shĭmä), island (□ 176; pop. 55,646), Kagoshima prefecture, Japan, bet. E. China Sea and Philippine Sea, 20 mi. S of Kyushu, across Osumi Strait; 35 mi. long, 7 mi. wide; mountainous. Agr. (sugar cane, rice, sweet potatoes); livestock; fishing. Chief town, Nishinoomote (W). Portuguese landed here, 1543.

Tanen Taunggyi Range (tŭnĭn' toun-jē'), Thai *Thanon Thong Chai* (tŭnôn' tông' chī') and, in NE section, *Daen Lao* (dăn' lou'), mountain range on Burma-Thailand line; extends from Mekong R. along S edge of Shan Plateau, forming watershed bet. Salween (W) and Ping (E) rivers; rises to 7,000 ft. Continued S by the Tenasserim Range.

Tanera, Scotland: see SUMMER ISLES.

Tanew River (tä'nĕf), Rus. *Tanev* (tä'nyĭf), SE Poland, rises 16 mi. NE of Lubaczow, flows c.65 mi. generally WNW to San R. 4 mi. N of Rudnik.

Taney (tā'nē), county (□ 656; pop. 9,863), S Mo.; ⊙ Forsyth. In the Ozarks; drained by White R., which here forms L. Taneycomo. Resort and agr. area, especially for livestock; cedar, oak timber. Part of Mark Twain Natl. Forest here. Formed 1837.

Taneycomo, Lake, Mo.: see WHITE RIVER.

Taneytown (tô'nētoun), city (pop. 1,420), Carroll co., N Md., 22 mi. NE of Frederick, in agr. area; mfg. (clothing, rubber rainwear); cannery. Near by are co. fairgrounds, amusement park, and birthplace of Francis Scott Key. Roger Brooke Taney b. here. Settled c.1740; inc. as city 1931.

Taneyville (tā'nēvĭl), town (pop. 132), Taney co., S Mo., in the Ozarks, near White R., 13 mi. NE of Branson.

Tanezrouft (tänĕzrōōft'), section of the Sahara in S Algeria (S of 25°N) and extending into N Sudan (Fr. West Africa); noted for its extreme aridity. Long feared by caravans because of the absence of water and of topographic landmarks, it is now crossed by Colomb-Béchar–Gao auto track. Poste Cortier is a refueling station here.

Tanfield, former urban district (1931 pop. 9,236), N Durham, England, 7 mi. SW of Newcastle-upon-Tyne; coal mining. Inc. 1937 in Stanley.

Tanforan, Calif.: see SAN BRUNO.

Tang, China: see TANG RIVER.

Tanga (täng'gŭ, täng'gä), province (□ 13,803; pop. 556,325), NE Tanganyika; ⊙ Tanga. Bounded E by Indian Ocean, N by Kenya. Drained by Pangani R. which skirts Pare and Usambara mts. Important sisal-growing region. Coffee and tea plantations in uplands. Copra, cotton; hardwood. Mica, garnet, limestone deposits. Chief towns, Tanga, Pangani, Korogwe.

Tanga, town (pop. 20,619), ⊙ Tanga prov., NE Tanganyika, port on Indian Ocean, opposite Pemba Isl., 120 mi. N of Dar es Salaam; 5°4'S 39°7'E. Tanganyika's 2d port, exporting sisal, copra, cotton, rubber, hides and skins. Ocean terminus of railroad to Korogwe (at foot of Usambara Mts.), Moshi (at foot of Kilimanjaro), and Arusha, tapping rich sisal, coffee, and tea area. Airport. Formerly a starting point for caravans to the interior, it later became port of entry for German settlers. Captured by British in 1916. It is now overshadowed by Dar es Salaam.

Tangail (tŭng-gīl'), town (pop. 21,684), Mymensingh dist., central East Bengal, E Pakistan, on branch of the Jamuna and 45 mi. SW of Mymensingh; hand-loom cotton-weaving center; trades in rice, jute, oilseeds. Has col. Metalware mfg. just W, at Kagmari.

Tanga Islands (täng'ä), small group (□ 54; pop. c.1,700), New Ireland dist., Bismarck Archipelago, Territory of New Guinea, SW Pacific, 35 mi. NE of New Ireland; comprise c.10 volcanic and coral isls. Malendok (largest, c.8 mi. long), Boang, Lif, and Tefa are only inhabited isls.; coconuts.

Tangalla (tŭng-gŭl'lŭ), town (pop., including nearby village of Beliatta, 6,891), Southern Prov., Ceylon, on S coast, 40 mi. E of Galle; trades in vegetables, rice, citronella grass, coconuts. Fort. Beliatta is vegetable trade center.

Tangamandapio (täng-gämändä'pyō), town (pop. 2,573), Michoacán, central Mexico, 10 mi. WSW of Zamora; cereals, sugar cane, fruit, livestock.

Tangancícuaro (täng-gängkē'kwärō), officially Tangancícuaro de Arista, town (pop. 4,792), Michoacán, central Mexico, on central plateau, 10 mi. SE of Zamora; agr. center (cereals, sugar cane, tobacco, fruit, livestock).

Tanganda, Southern Rhodesia: see CHIPINGA.

Tanganyika (tăng"gŭnyē'kŭ, tăng"găn–), British-administered United Nations trust territory (□ 362,688, including 19,982 sq. mi. of lakes; pop. 7,412,327), E Africa; ⊙ Dar es Salaam. Fronting on the Indian Ocean (Zanzibar is 20 mi. offshore), it is bounded N by Kenya and Uganda (with which it shares most of L. Victoria), NW by Ruanda-Urundi, W by L. Tanganyika (through which passes frontier with Belgian Congo), S by Northern Rhodesia (part of border along L. Nyasa) and Mozambique (mostly along Ruvuma R.). Mafia Isl. belongs to Tanganyika. From a low coastal strip 10–40 mi. wide, country rises gradually to the central plateau (average alt. 4,000 ft.) which constitutes greater part of hinterland, only to fall off sharply to level of L. Tanganyika (2,534 ft.) in W. Territory's most prominent physical features are the massive volcanic cones of Kilimanjaro (19,565 ft.; highest summit in Africa) and Mt. Meru (14,979 ft.) rising boldly above the tableland along Kenya border. The Southern Highlands, overlooking N tip of L. Nyasa, rise to 9,713 ft. in Mt. Rungwe. E Africa's Great Rift Valley is occupied in N Tanganyika by lakes Natron and Eyasi; here too is the huge Ngorongoro Crater; the valley's S extension is occupied by L. Nyasa. L. Tanganyika lies in W spur (Albertine Rift) of Great Rift Valley. The climate, generally of the tropical savanna type, varies greatly with alt. Along the coast average temp. is 79°F.; for every 1,000 ft. of elevation it decreases c.3°F. Only the highlands above 4,000 ft. are suitable for European settlement. Distribution of rainfall is closely matched by pop. distribution, ⅔ of territory (notably the central plateau) being virtually uninhabited because of inadequate precipitation (less than 40 in.) and lacking ground water. The densely settled shores of L. Victoria, the N half of the coastal strip, and S Tanganyika receive 40–60 in., while on upper slopes of Kilimanjaro, Usambara Mts., and highlands rimming L. Nyasa rainfall exceeds 60 in. Tanganyika's principal streams (Pangani, Rufiji, Lukuledi, Ruvuma) drain territory's E portion to the Indian Ocean; the lower Kagera crosses NW corner before entering L. Victoria; the Malagarasi (W) flows to L. Tanganyika. Sisal, rice, cotton, coconuts, beans, and millet are chief crops in coastal area; E Africa's largest sisal plantations are in Tanga prov., and in coastal area adjoining Dar es Salaam; coffee is the chief crop on densely populated S slopes of Kilimanjaro and Mt. Meru and also along shores of L. Victoria. Wheat, pyrethrum, tea, and tobacco are also grown in upland areas. Semi-arid plateau yields beeswax, gum arabic, landolphia rubber, oilseeds. Cattle is raised chiefly in highlands free from tsetse fly. Almost ¾ of Br. East Africa's groundnut (peanut) scheme was planned to be undertaken in Tanganyika; areas initially cleared were in Kongwa-Hogoro dist. (Central Prov., E of Dodoma), at Urambo (Western Prov., W of Tabora), and in Nachingwa-Noli dist. (Southern Prov., 80 mi. SW of Lindi). In 1949, rail links and airfields were under construction and a new peanut-shipping port was projected near MIKINDANI, in extreme SE. Hardwoods in NE highland forests are cut for export. Tanganyika has become Br. East Africa's leading mining region. Most important by value are diamonds from a newly-developed mine at Mwadui, near Shinyanga (Lake Prov.); gold is mined along S and E shores of L. Victoria near Musoma and at Geita (SW of Mwanza), in the Lupa gold field N of Mbeya (Southern Highlands prov.) and near Kinyangiri (Central Prov.). Tin is worked at Murongo (in NW, along Kagera R.), lead at Mpanda (Western Prov.; new rail spur). Tungsten, mica (especially near Morogoro), and salt are also mined, and there are important coal, iron, limestone, copper, and corundum deposits. Tanganyika's industries are limited to agr. processing (rice and flour milling, sisal working, cotton ginning, coffee curing, dairying), sawmilling, and meat packing. Soap, cigarettes, leather articles, and furniture are also made. DAR ES SALAAM and TANGA are territory's principal export centers, its largest towns, and termini of 2 rail lines to the interior; the Central RR links Dar es Salaam with Kigoma on L. Tanganyika, crossing territory's entire width; a spur leads from Tabora (largest inland town) to Mwanza on L. Victoria. A rail line from Tanga to Moshi and Arusha taps the coffee and sisal plantations of the NE, and by a spur links up with Mombasa-Nairobi RR in Kenya. There are 3,000 mi. of main roads, especially the Great North Road from Northern Rhodesia to Nairobi. The 3 great lakes along Tanganyika's borders are all navigable. Chief exports are sisal, diamonds, gold, coffee, raw cotton, hides and skins, ivory, and rubber. Less than 1% of area is set aside for European plantations. In 1948, non-native pop. included 16,299 Europeans, 46,491 Indians, and 11,952 Arabs. The majority of natives are Bantu, but large areas in N are occupied by the Masai and other Hamitic tribes (especially in Masai Steppe), and in S by tribes of Zulu origin. Swahili is the *lingua franca*. The coast was explored c.1500 and loosely held until 17th cent. by Portuguese. Taken over by Arab sultans of Muscat and later of Zanzibar, coastal towns became termini for ivory and slave caravans to the hinterland. In mid-19th cent. the interior was explored by Burton (1856), Livingstone, and Stanley; the last 2 met at Ujiji on L. Tanganyika in 1871. Later, German influence became dominant, and beginning in 1884 Karl Peters concluded treaties with local rulers on behalf of German East Africa Co. Territory was declared a protectorate (called German East Africa) by Germany in 1885; recognized by Britain in 1886. Coastal strip was acquired 1890 from Sultan of Zanzibar. German occupation was followed by 15 years of Arab and native uprisings, climaxing in the Maji-Maji revolt of 1905. Territory captured (1916) by British during First World War. Br. mandate over the territory renamed Tanganyika (less NW region which became Belgian mandate of Ruanda-Urundi, and Kionga strip in SE, annexed by Mozambique) was approved by League of Nations in 1922. Under UN trusteeship since 1946, Tanganyika is the UN's largest and most populous trust territory. It has been ruled since 1920 by an appointed Br. governor with the aid of an executive and a legislative council; the latter now includes several native members. For administration, territory consists of 8 provs.: Central (⊙ Dodoma), Eastern (⊙ Dar es Salaam), Lake (⊙ Mwanza), Northern (⊙ Arusha), Southern (⊙ Lindi), Southern Highlands (⊙ Mbeya), Tanga (⊙ Tanga), Western (⊙ Tabora). The technical services (railroads, mail, customs, statistical services, etc.) of Tanganyika are coordinated with those of neighboring Kenya and Uganda under an administrative body called the East Africa High Commission (established 1948) composed of the governors of the 3 territories; administrative hq. are at Nairobi, Kenya.

Tanganyika, district, Belgian Congo; see ALBERTVILLE.

Tanganyika, former province, Northern Rhodesia; see ABERCORN.

Tanganyika, Lake, Fr. *Tanganika*, lake (□ 12,700) in Great Rift Valley of E central Africa, SW of L. Victoria; extends over 400 mi. NNW-SSE, forming boundary bet. Belgian Congo and Tanganyika; borders in N on Ruanda-Urundi, in S on Northern Rhodesia. Longest, 2d largest (L. Victoria is larger), and deepest (4,700 ft.) of Africa's great lakes, 2d in depth only to L. Baikal among the world's fresh-water bodies; 15–50 mi. wide; alt. 2,534 ft. Receives Ruzizi R. (N; outlet of L. Kivu), Malagarasi R. (E). Its only outlet (frequently silted up, thus periodically raising lake's level) is the Lukuga, which issues from W shore at Albertville and flows into the Congo basin. The lake's steep shores rise to over 9,000 ft. near N end. Entire lake is navigable; principal ports are Kigoma (Tanganyika) and Albertville (Belgian Congo), both termini on Congo–Indian Ocean rail-water link, and Usumbura (Ruanda-Urundi), at N tip. Lake was discovered in 1858 by John Speke and Sir Richard Burton. Region explored in 1870s by Henry Stanley and David Livingstone who met at Ujiji (near Kigoma) in 1871. Scene of miniature naval warfare bet. German and British sloops, 1915–16, during First World War. The lake's level may once have stood at 4,000 ft., so that it formed an extensive inland sea; 75% of its 400 animal species are endemic.

Tangar, China: see HWANGYÜAN.

Tangará (tãng-gürä'), city (pop. 715), W central Santa Catarina, Brazil, on Peixe R., on railroad and 15 mi. NE of Joaçaba; coal deposits. Until 1944, Rio Bonito.

Tangarakau (täng"gürükou'), village (pop. 63), W N.Isl., New Zealand, 75 mi. NE of New Plymouth; coal mine.

Tangasseri, India: see ANJENGO.

T'ang-ch'i, China: see TANGKI.

T'ang-chia-cha, China: see TANGKIACHA.

T'ang-chia-kuan, China: see TANGKIAKWAN.

Tang-e-Malavi, Iran: see MALAWI.

Tangen, Norway: see DRAMMEN.

Tangen (tông'ün), Swedish *Tången*, fishing village (pop. 604), Goteborg och Bohus co., SW Sweden, on isl. (104 acres) of same name in the Skagerrak, 8 mi. NW of Lysekil.

Tangerhütte (täng"ürhü'tü), town (pop. 6,679), in former Prussian Saxony prov., central Germany, after 1945 in Saxony-Anhalt, 12 mi. S of Stendal; mfg. (steel products, enamelware).

Tangermünde (–mün'dü), town (pop. 16,480), in former Prussian Saxony prov., central Germany, after 1945 in Saxony-Anhalt, on the Elbe and 6 mi. SE of Stendal, 30 mi. NNE of Magdeburg; sugar-refining and -shipping center; chocolate mfg., food canning. Has 15th-cent. church and town hall; and remains of 12th-cent. castle destroyed (1640) in Thirty Years War by Swedes. First mentioned 1009; became stronghold of Albert the Bear in 11th cent. In late-14th cent., castle was rebuilt by Emperor Charles IV, who frequently resided here. From 1412 until end of 15th cent. it was residence of margraves of Brandenburg. Reformation introduced 1538. Tangermünde repeatedly changed hands in Thirty Years War; greatly damaged.

Tanggot, China: see TANGUT.

Tangho or **T'ang-ho** (täng'hŭ'), town, ⊙ Tangho co. (pop. 494,082), SW Honan prov., China, on Tang R., on road and 22 mi. SE of Nanyang; wheat, rice, beans, millet. Until 1914 called Tanghsien; later, 1914–23, Piyüan.

Tang Ho, river, China: see TANG RIVER.

Tanghsien or **T'ang-hsien** (both: täng'shyĕn'). **1** Town, Honan prov., China: see TANGHO. **2** Town, ⊙ Tanghsien co. (pop. 191,515), W Hopeh prov., China, 30 mi. WSW of Paoting, near Peking-Hankow RR; cotton, wheat, beans, kaoliang.

T'ang-i, China: see TANGYI.

Tangi (tŭng'gē), town (pop. 12,906), Peshawar dist., central North-West Frontier Prov., W Pakistan, 20 mi. N of Peshawar, near Lower Swat Canal; market center for agr. produce of lower Swat valley (wheat, sugar cane, corn); fruitgrowing (grapes, melons, quince).

Tangier (tănjēr'), village (pop. estimate 300), S N.S., at head of Tangier Harbour of the Atlantic, 50 mi. ENE of Halifax; lumbering, fishing port; in gold-mining region.

Tangier, Fr. and Ger. *Tanger*, Sp. *Tánger*, Arabic *Tanja* or *Tanjah*, anc. *Tingis*, important seaport along northernmost coast of Morocco, on Strait of Gibraltar (near Cape Spartel, its W entrance), 36 mi. SW of Gibraltar; 35°47'N 5°48'W. With surrounding territory it forms International Zone of Tangier (□ 147; 1947 pop. c.151,000, largely in city) at NW tip of Africa, surrounded on landward side by Sp. Morocco. Its strategic location and international status have made it a busy port of call and a commercial entrepôt, with a flourishing tourist trade. Its industries (mfg. of soap, canned fish, flour paste, essential oils) are minor; commercial activity is concentrated chiefly in harbor dist. (chief exports are goatskins, canary seed, coriander, cork, almonds, and Morocco leather, mostly from Sp. Morocco) and in native markets (*soks*). Occupying low hills along S shore of Tangier Bay (sheltered from all but E winds by a curved mole), city has a walled Moorish dist. (W), typically Moroccan in appearance. Its white houses and painted minarets are reached by a labyrinth of narrow dead-end alleys. The *casbah*, overlooking the Strait of Gibraltar, dominates Tangier from the N. By contrast, the foreign pop. and diplomatic missions reside in a luxurious, thoroughly European garden suburb (S). Tangier has an equable subtropical climate with moderate winter rainfall (32 in.). It communicates with the hinterland by Tangier-Fez RR (which links with Fr. Morocco's rail lines at Petitjean) and by highways to Rabat (Fr. Morocco) and Tetuán (Sp. Morocco). There are powerful radio transmitters in the zone and an airport 8 mi. SW of city center. Probably founded by Phoenicians, anc. *Tingis*, a free city under Romans, gave its name to W Mauretania (*Mauretania Tingitana*). Held in turn by Vandals, Byzantines, and Arabs, city was captured 1471 by Portuguese. Under Sp. rule for 60 years after 1580, it later reverted to Portugal, but passed (1662) to England when Charles II married Catherine of Braganza. Abandoned to Moors in 1684. In mid-19th cent., as the principal gateway to Morocco, it became the diplomatic capital of the Sherifian Empire. The visit (1905) of German Emperor William II to Tangier led to the conference of Algeciras (1906). In 1923, England, France, and Spain signed a convention (effective 1925; later adhered to by other European nations; revised 1928) establishing the International Zone and providing for area's neutrality and for a govt. by international commission. Occupied by Spain (1940–45) during Second World War, the zone's international administration was restored in Oct., 1945, on an interim basis. The division of Morocco into Fr. and Sp. protectorates has deprived Tangier of its former dominating position in Moroccan affairs. Under the statute, the sultan of Morocco is represented in Tangier by the Mendoub, who is in charge of the native administration. In 1947, native Moslem pop. was 125,000. French, Spanish, and Arabic are the official languages of the zone.

Tangier, fishing town (pop. 915), Accomack co., E Va., on Tangier Isl. (c.5 mi. long, 1½ mi. wide) in Chesapeake Bay, 14 mi. SSW of Crisfield, Md. (boat connections across Tangier Sound). Isl. discovered 1608 by Capt. John Smith and settled in late-17th cent.; its people, long virtually isolated, developed a distinctive culture.

Tangier Sound, protected passage of Chesapeake Bay, off the Eastern Shore of Md. and Va.; c.30 mi. long, 3–7 mi. wide, it extends from Watts Isl. (S) to Fishing Bay (N), and is connected (NW) with the bay by Hooper Strait. On W, marsh isls. (among them Tangier, Smith, South Marsh, Bloodsworth) border it. In SE, it is separated from Pocomoke Sound (partly in Va.) by marsh isls. and shoals. Crisfield and Deal Island, Md., are centers of sound's large seafood industry.

Tang-i-Gharu (täng'-ē-gäroo'), gorge on Kabul R., E Afghanistan, 25 mi. E of Kabul.

Tang-i-Malawi, Iran: see MALAWI.

Tangipahoa (tăn'jĭpühō'ü, –pühō"), parish (□ 803; pop. 53,218), SE La.; ⊙ Amite. Bounded E partly by Tchefuncta R., S by L. Maurepas and L. Pontchartrain, N by Miss. line, W partly by Natalbany R.; drained by Tangipahoa R. Agr. (especially strawberries and truck; also corn, cotton). Cotton ginning, grain milling. Lumber, naval stores. Resorts; hunting, fishing. Formed 1869.

Tangipahoa, village (pop. 352), Tangipahoa parish, SE La., on Tangipahoa R. and 50 mi. NE of Baton Rouge, near Miss. line; truck farming, dairying.

Tangipahoa River, in Miss. and La., rises NW of McComb in SW Miss., flows c.110 mi. generally S, past Osyka (Miss.), into SE La., past Tangipahoa and Amite, to L. Pontchartrain; partly navigable.

Tangkak (täng"käk'), town (pop. 3,939), NW Johore, Malaya, 15 mi. N of Bandar Maharani, near Malacca line; rubber.

Tangki or **T'ang-ch'i** (both: täng'chē'), town (pop. 1,689), ⊙ Tangki co. (pop. 109,236), SW Chekiang prov., China, near Tsientang R., 32 mi. ENE of Chühsien, and on railroad; papermaking, brick and tile mfg.; tea, bamboo shoots, rice, wheat. Lead and silver mines near by.

Tangkiacha or **T'ang-chia-cha** (both: täng'jyä'jä'), NW industrial suburb of Nantung, N Kiangsu prov., China; cotton spinning and weaving, iron smelting, oil pressing, flour milling.

Tangkiakwan or **T'ang-chia-kuan** (both: täng'-jyä'gwän'), town (pop. 7,870), S Kwangtung prov., China, port on Canton R. estuary, 12 mi. N of Macao. Known as Chungshan during 1930–34, and as Chungshankong for some time thereafter.

T'ang-ko-la-yu-mu Hu, Tibet: see TANGRA TSO.

Tangku or **T'ang-ku** (täng'goo'), town, E Hopeh prov., China, port on Gulf of Chihli, on N bank of mouth of Pai R., opposite Taku, on Tientsin-Mukden RR and 30 mi. ESE of Tientsin; outer port for Tientsin, and transshipment point.

Tang La, China-Tibet: see TANG PASS.

Tang La (täng' lä'), pass (alt. 15,219 ft.) in W Assam Himalayas, SE Tibet, on main India-Lhasa trade route, 8 mi. NNE of Phari.

Tanglewood, Mass.: see LENOX.

Tanglha Range or **Thanglha Range** (täng'lä), Chinese *T'ang-la* (täng'lä'), mountain range, W China, on Chang Tang plateau, along Tsinghai-Tibet border; extends c.300 mi. E-W. Forms watershed of upper Yangtze, Mekong, and Salween rivers. Crossed (center) by important TANG PASS.

Tangmarg, Kashmir: see GULMARG.

Tango (täng'gō), former province in S Honshu, Japan; now part of Kyoto prefecture.

Tang Pass (täng), Tibetan *Tang La* or *Thang Lha* (täng' lä'), pass (alt. 16,760 ft.) in Tanglha Range, W China, on Tibet-Tsinghai border, on main Lhasa-Sining trade route and 95 mi. NNE of Nagchu. Also called Tsangne La.

Tangploch (täng'plôch'), town, Kompong Chhnang prov., central Cambodia, at foot of outlying hills of Cardamom Mts., 45 mi. NW of Pnompenh.

Tangra Tso or **Tangra Tsho** (täng'grä tsō'), Chinese *T'ang-ko-la-yu-mu Hu* (täng'gŭ'lä'yoo'moo' hoo'), salt lake (□ 500), central Tibet, on Chang Tang plateau, at 31°N 86°25'E; alt. 14,760 ft. Sometimes called Dangra Yum.

Tang River, Chinese *Tang Ho* or *T'ang Ho* (täng' hŭ'), W central China, rises in Funiu Mts. of W Honan prov., flows over 100 mi. SSW, past Tangho, into NW Hupeh prov., where it joins Pai R. before entering Han R. near Fancheng.

Tangrot (tŭng'grōt) or **Dhangrot** (dŭng'grōt), village, Jhelum dist., N Punjab, W Pakistan, on Jhelum R. and 19 mi. N of Jhelum; noted for mahseer fishing.

Tangshan. **1** (däng'shän') Town (pop. 64,808), ⊙ Tangshan co. (pop. 325,822), N Anhwei prov., China, 50 mi. WNW of Süchow and on Lunghai RR; agr. center (beans, wheat, kaoliang). Until 1949 in Kiangsu. **2** or **T'ang-shan** (täng'shän'), city, ⊙ Tangshan co. (1935 pop. 149,124; 1947 pop. 136,762), NE Hopeh prov., China, 60 mi. NE of Tientsin and on railroad to Mukden; coal-mining center, in Kailan dist.; iron and steel plant; pottery, cement, bricks, tiles. Has Col. of Engineering. Became independent municipality in 1947. **3** or **T'ang-shan** (täng'shän'), town, Hopeh prov., China: see LUNGYAO.

Tangtu or **Tang-t'u** (däng'tōō'), town, ⊙ Tangtu co. (pop. 347,627), SE Anhwei prov., China, near Kiangsu line, on Yangtze R. and 15 mi. NNE of Wuhu, and on railroad; rice, wheat, rapeseed. Until 1912 called Taiping. Iron mining at Tayao Shan, 10 mi. ENE.

Tangub (täng-ōōb', –gōōb'). **1** Town (1939 pop. 2,955; 1948 municipality pop. 20,353), Misamis Occidental prov., W Mindanao, Philippines, on Panguil Bay, 24 mi. NE of Pagadian; agr. center (corn, coconuts). **2** Town (1939 pop. 5,333) in metropolitan Bacolod, Negros Occidental prov., W Negros isl., Philippines, just SSW of Bacolod; agr. center (rice, sugar cane).

Tangui or **Tanguy** (tŭn-gōō'ē), village (1948 pop. over 2,000), SW central Irkutsk oblast, Russian SFSR, on Iya R. and 55 mi. NNE of Tulun; wheat, livestock.

Tanguiéta (täng-gyĕ'tä), village (pop. c.700), NW Dahomey, Fr. West Africa, 25 mi. NNW of Natitingou; horse breeding; peanuts, shea nuts.

Tangut or **Tanggot** (täng'gōōt'), Chinese *Sia Hsia* or *Hsi-hsia* (shē'shyä'), former N Tibetan kingdom in NW China, in area of modern Ningsia and Kansu provs. Its capital was Halachar, near modern Tingyüanying. Founded c.1000, it was conquered 1227 by Jenghiz Khan. The name Ningsia is derived from the Chinese name of Tangut.

Tangwangho, Manchuria: see TANGYÜAN.

Tangyan (tän'-jän), village, South Hsenwi state, Northern Shan State, on road and 50 mi. SE of Lashio, overlooking Salween R.

Tangyang (däng'yäng'), town (pop. 18,237), ⊙ Tangyang co. (pop. 275,179), W central Hupeh prov., China, 27 mi. ENE of Ichang; winegrowing; silk weaving, vegetable-oil processing.

Tangyi or **T'ang-i** (both: täng'yē'), town, ⊙ Tangyi co. (pop. 229,388), NE Pingyuan prov., China, on main road and 70 mi. WSW of Tsinan; cotton center; straw matting; wheat, millet, peanuts. Until 1949 in Shantung prov.

Tangyin or **T'ang-yin** (täng'yĭn'), town, ⊙ Tangyin co. (pop. 224,945), NW Pingyuan prov., China, 10 mi. S of Anyang and on Peking-Hankow RR; wheat, beans, kaoliang. Until 1949 in Honan prov.

Tangyüan or **T'ang-yüan** (täng'yüăn'), town, ⊙ Tangyüan co. (pop. 115,000), N Sungkiang prov., Manchuria, on railroad and 25 mi. WSW of Kiamusze, across Sungari R. Formerly called Tangwangho.

Tanhsien (dän'shyĕn'), town, ⊙ Tanhsien co. (pop. 133,649), NW Hainan, Kwangtung prov., China, 75 mi. WSW of Kiungshan; fisheries, saltworks. Tin mining near by. Until 1912 called Tanchow.

Tanhuato de Guerrero (tänwä'tō dā gĕrā'rō), town (pop. 4,788), Michoacán, central Mexico, on central plateau, 19 mi. WSW of La Piedad; agr. center (cereals, vegetables, stock).

Tanimbar Islands or **Tenimbar Islands** (both: tŭnĭmbär'), group (□ 2,172; pop. 31,847), S Moluccas, Indonesia, in Banda Sea, c.270 mi. ENE of Timor; 7°S 131°30'E. Largest of c.30 isls. is Yamdena or Jamdena (both: yämdĕ'nŭ) (pop. 15,685; 70 mi. long, 28 mi. wide), with chief town, Saumlaki, on S coast. Just SW of Yamdena is Selaru or Selaroe (both: sŭlärōō') (pop. 5,591; 30 mi. long, 10 mi. wide); and just N is Larat (lärät') (pop. 3,703; 20 mi. long, 5 mi. wide). Isls. are low and heavily wooded. Chief products: tortoise shell, copra, sago, trepang, fish. Textiles are main import. Group was discovered 1629 by the Dutch. Also called Timorlaut or Timorlaoet (both: tēmôrläōōt').

Taning (dä'nĭng'). **1** Town, ⊙ Taning co. (pop. 19,968), SW Shansi prov., China, 50 mi. NW of Linfen, near Yellow R. (Shensi border); exports cotton, sheepskins, wool; produces wheat, sesame, medicinal herbs. **2** Town, Szechwan prov., China: see WUKI.

Taninges (tänĕzh'), village (pop. 866), Haute-Savoie dept., SE France, near the Giffre, 9 mi. ENE of Bonneville, in Savoy Pre-Alps; road junction; metalworking, cheese mfg., diamond cutting.

Taninul, Mexico: see VALLES.

Tanis (tā'nĭs), anc. city of Lower Egypt, in the delta region. On the site is modern village of San el Hagar. Tanis was ⊙ XXI (Tanite) dynasty; possibly it was Avaris, the Hyksos capital. It was a great and flourishing city, but when threatened with inundation by near-by L. Manzala the city was abandoned (after 6th cent. A.D.) for Tennis. Site, excavated since 1940, has yielded statues and inscriptions. Tanis is the biblical Zoan (zō'ăn).

Tanis, Lake, Egypt: see MANZALA, LAKE.

Taniyama (tänē'yämŭ), town (pop. 40,799), Kagoshima prefecture, S Kyushu, Japan, on E Satsuma Peninsula, on Kagoshima Bay, 5 mi. SSW of Kagoshima; tin-mining center; pottery making.

Tanjay (tänghī'), largest town (1939 pop. 11,849; 1948 municipality pop. 33,064) of Negros Oriental prov., SE Negros isl., Philippines, 55 mi. SSE of Binalbagan; trade center for agr. area (corn, coconuts, tobacco, sugar cane).

Tanjong (tänjōōng') [Malay,=cape]. For Malaya names beginning thus and not found here, see under following part of the name.

Tanjong Dawai (däwī'), village (pop. 1,600), W Kedah, Malaya, on Strait of Malacca at mouth of small Merbok R., 8 mi. WNW of Sungei Patani; coconuts, rice; fisheries.

Tanjong Lumpur (lōōm'pōōr), village (pop. 919), NE Pahang, Malaya, just S of Kuantan, across Kuantan R. mouth; fisheries.

Tanjong Malim (mälĭm'), town (pop. 3,527), southernmost Perak, Malaya, on Bernam R. (Selangor line) opposite Ulu Bernam and railroad, 40 mi. NNW of Kuala Lumpur; rubber plantations. Malay teachers col.

Tanjong Piandang (pēän"däng'), village (pop. 2,749), NW Perak, Malaya, on Strait of Malacca, 28 mi. NW of Taiping; coconuts, rice, fisheries.

Tanjong Rambutan (rämbōōtän'), town (pop. 5,453), central Perak, Malaya, on railroad and Kinta R., 7 mi. NE of Ipoh, at foot of central Malayan range; a tin-mining center of Kinta Valley; has mental hospital.

Tanjong Tokong (tōkōōng'), village (pop. 3,389) on Penang isl., NW Malaya, on N coast, 4 mi. NW of George Town; fisheries.

Tanjong Tualang (tōōä"läng'), village (pop. 1,352), S central Perak, Malaya, near Kinta R., 18 mi. S of Ipoh; tin mining.

Tanjore (tănjôr'), Tamil *Tanjavur* (tŭnjä'vōōr), district (□ 3,738; pop. 2,563,375), SE Madras, India; ⊙ Tanjore. Bordered E by S Coromandel Coast of Bay of Bengal, S by Palk Strait, N by Coleroon R. Fr. settlement of Karikal is a coastal enclave. Cauvery R. delta (NE; c.30% alluvial) is drained by network of numerous river arms (including the Vennar) and canals, supplied and controlled by dams on CAUVERY RIVER (GRAND ANICUT control works at head of delta) and by METTUR irrigation system. Non-deltaic tract (SW); mainly red ferruginous soil (laterite and limestone workings) with small quartz-producing plateau in NW; c.300,000 acres are irrigated by GRAND ANICUT CANAL and Vadavar Canal and their distributaries. Salt flats of Vedaranniyam Swamp (lignite deposits) extend E–W along Palk Strait. Mainly agr.: rice (over 80% of sown area), plantain, millet, peanuts, sugar cane, tobacco; coconut palms, bamboo; betel and mulberry farms. Mettur hydroelectric system furnishes power to main industrial center of Negapatam (steel-rolling mills). Kumbakonam, Tanjore (architectural landmarks), Mayavaram, and Mannargudi are noted handicraft centers (gold and silver jewelry, inlaid copperware, pith-carved temple models). Saltworks, Casuarina plantations, fisheries along coasts. Seat of Chola and successive Hindu kingdoms until ceded (1799; except for city of Tanjore) to English by the Mahrattas.

Tanjore, Tamil *Tanjavur*, city (pop. 68,702), ⊙ Tanjore dist., SE Madras, India, on Vennar R. and 170 mi. SSW of Madras. Rail junction; road and rice-milling center; silk and cotton weaving; mfg. of musical instruments; noted for gold and silver jewelry, crystalware, inlaid copperwork; soap and perfume factories. Borstal School (handicrafts), industrial and medical schools. Has large Dravidian (Sivaite) temple complex (main temple built 11th cent.; others, 11th–17th cent.) and 16th-cent. palace (Sanskrit library). Was a chief city of Chola and successive Hindu kingdoms. City retained by Mahratta raja (by treaty of 1799, which ceded surrounding area to English) until it passed to Br. govt. in 1855.

Tanjung [Indonesian,=cape], for names beginning thus and not found here, see under following part of the name.

Tanjungbalai, Tandjungbalai, or **Tandjoengbalai** (all: tänjōōng"bälī'), town (pop. 2,883), NE Sumatra, Indonesia, port on Asahan R. near its mouth on Strait of Malacca, 90 mi. ESE of Medan; ships rubber, copra, palm oil, tea, gambir, fruit; bauxite reduction works. Also spelled Tandjongbalei.

Tanjungpandan, Tandjungpandan, or **Tandjoengpandan** (–pändän'), chief town (pop. 15,708) of Billiton, Indonesia, on W coast of isl., port on Karimata Strait (bet. S.China and Java seas), 200 mi. E of Palembang, Sumatra; 2°44'S 107°38'E. Ships tin, copra, resin, pepper, spices, trepang. Airport. Also spelled Tandjongpandan.

Tanjungperak, Indonesia: see SURABAYA.

Tanjungpinang, Tandjungpinang, or **Tandjoengpinang** (–pēnäng'), chief town (pop. 5,789) of Riouw Archipelago, Indonesia, on SW coast of Bintan isl., port on small strait of S.China Sea, 50 mi. SE of Singapore; 0°55'N 104°26'E. Ships bauxite, copra, gambier, pepper; airport. Has Du. fort built 1824. Also spelled Tandjongpinang.

Tanjungpriok, Tandjungpriok, or **Tandjoengpriok** (–prēôk'), principal port of Indonesia and port for Jakarta, NW Java, on Jakarta Bay (inlet of Java Sea), 5 mi. NE of Jakarta. Protected by breakwater and equipped with drydocks. Exports tea, cinchona bark, cassava, rubber, coffee, fibers, copra, vegetable oils, rice. Chief imports: coal, petroleum products. There is an automobile-assembly plant. Construction of port began 1877. In battle of Java Sea (Feb., 1942) during Second World War, port was used as temporary base by U.S. Navy. Also spelled Tanjongpriok.

Tanjungpura or **Tandjoengpoera** (both: –pōō'rŭ), town (dist. pop. 33,114), NE Sumatra, Indonesia, port on Sarangan R. (50 mi. long), near its mouth on Strait of Malacca, 30 mi. NW of Medan; ships rubber, resin, fruit, nutmeg. Also spelled Tandjongpoera.

Tanjungselor, Tandjungselor, or **Tandjoengselor** (–sălôr'), town (pop. 1,991), E Borneo, Indonesia, port on Kajan R. near its mouth and 230 mi. N of Samarinda; 2°50'N 117°22'E; trade center; ships timber, resin, rattan. Also spelled Tandjongselor.

Tanjunguban, Tandjunguban, or **Tandjoengoeban** (all: –ūbän'), town, NW Bintan isl., Indonesia; 1°4'N 104°14'E. Radio station.

Tank (tängk), town (pop. 9,089), Dera Ismail Khan dist., S North-West Frontier Prov., W Pakistan, 40 mi. NW of Dera Ismail Khan; market center for wheat, millet, ghee, tobacco; handicraft cloth weaving. Timber from near-by hills (W).

Tankara (tŭngkä'rŭ), town (pop. 3,848), N Saurashtra, India, 24 mi. N of Rajkot; cotton, millet; hand-loom weaving.

Tankersley, town and parish (pop. 2,349), West Riding, S Yorkshire, England, 8 mi. N of Sheffield; coal-mining center.

Tankhoi or **Tankhoy** (tŭn-khoi'), town (1939 pop. over 2,000), S Buryat-Mongol Autonomous SSR, Russian SFSR, on Trans-Siberian RR, on S shore of L. Baikal, and 110 mi. WSW of Ulan-Ude; metalworks. Lignite deposits near by.

Tankiang, town, China: see LEISHAN.

Tan Kiang. **1** River, Kwangtung prov., China: see TAM RIVER. **2** River, in Shensi, Honan, and Hupeh provs., China: see TAN RIVER.

Tanlajás (tänlähäs'), town (pop. 620), San Luis Potosí, E Mexico, 24 mi. SSE of Valles; cotton, sugar cane, coffee, fruit, livestock.

Tanleng (dän'lŭng'), town (pop. 12,780), ⊙ Tanleng co. (pop. 88,513), W Szechwan prov., China, 55 mi. SSW of Chengtu, near Sikang border; tea, rice, sweet potatoes, wheat.

Tann (tän). **1** Village (pop. 1,874), Lower Bavaria, Germany, 7 mi. NW of Simbach or Simbach am Inn; brewing. **2** Town (pop. 1,987), in former Prussian prov. of Hesse-Nassau, W Germany, after 1945 in Hesse, on N slope of the Hohe Rhön, 16 mi. ENE of Fulda; lumber milling. Was Bavarian until 1866.

Tanna (tä'nä), town (pop. 2,617), Thuringia, central Germany, 6 mi. SSE of Schleiz; fruit, grain, livestock.

Tanna (tä'nä), volcanic island (□ c.215; pop. 5,869), NEW HEBRIDES, SW Pacific, 300 mi. SE of Espiritu Santo; 19°29'S 169°20'E. Br. administrative hq. at Whitesands on NE coast, Fr. hq. at Lenakel on SW coast; 25 mi. long, 12 mi. wide. Most fertile isl. of group; coconuts, sugar cane, cotton, some sandalwood. Copra, livestock. Constantly active volcano 3 mi. from Port Resolution in SE.

Tannadice (tă'nŭdĭs"), agr. village and parish (pop. 975), central Angus, Scotland, on South Esk R. and 5 mi. NNE of Forfar. Near by are ruins of anc. Finhaven Castle.

Tannah, Egypt: see TANAH.

Tannay (tänā'), village (pop. 876), Nièvre dept., central France, near Yonne R. and Nivernais Canal, 7 mi. SSE of Clamecy; winegrowing.

Tannenberg (tă'nŭnbûrg, Ger. tä'nŭnbĕrk), Pol. *Stębark* (stĕ'bärk), village in East Prussia, after 1945 in Olsztyn prov., NE Poland, 25 mi. SW of Allenstein (Olsztyn), 7 mi. NE of Dabrowno. Scene (Aug., 1914) of major defeat of Russians under Samsonov and Rennenkampf by Germans under Hindenburg and Mackensen. Hindenburg buried here, 1934; body removed to Bernterode, Thuringia, during Second World War; reburied 1946 at Marburg, Hesse. Defeat (1410) of Teutonic Knights by Poles and Lithuanians under Wladislaw Jagiello at Grünfelde, Pol. *Grunwald*, 3 mi. WSW, is often also called battle of Tannenberg.

Tannersville, resort village (pop. 639), Greene co., SE N.Y., in the Catskills, 14 mi. W of Catskill.

Tannforsen, Swedish *Tännforsen* (tĕn'fôr"sŭn,–fô"-shŭn), waterfalls (121 ft. high, 230 ft. wide) on upper Indal R., NW Sweden, 60 mi. WNW of Ostersund, 5 mi. NW of Duved. Noted for spectacular scenery.

Tannroda (tän'rō"dä), town (pop. 1,875), Thuringia, central Germany, on Ilm R. and 9 mi. SSW of Weimar; paper milling; sandstone quarrying. Has ruins of medieval castle.

Tannu-Ola Range or **Tannu-Ula Range** (tŭnōō"-ōōlä'), S Tuva Autonomous oblast, Russian SFSR; extends 350 mi. E from Altai Mts.; 8,400–8,800 ft. high. N slopes are wooded; S slopes form border bet. USSR and Mongolia. Traversed by highways from Kyzyl to Kobdo and Uliassutai.

Tannu-Tuva People's Republic, Russian SFSR: see TUVA AUTONOMOUS OBLAST.

Tannwald, Czechoslovakia: see SVAROV.

Tano (tä'nō), town (pop. 4,785), Kochi prefecture, S Shikoku, Japan, on Tosa Bay, 29 mi. ESE of Kochi; rice, raw silk.

Tanokuchi, Japan: see KOTOURA.

Tanong, Philippines: see MALABON.

Tañon Strait (tänyōn'), Philippines, bet. Cebu (E) and Negros (W), extending c.100 mi. S from Visayan Sea to Mindanao Sea; 3–17 mi. wide.

Tano River (tä'nō), SW Gold Coast, rises in Ashanti, 40 mi. NW of Mampong, flows c.250 mi. S, past Tanoso (head of navigation) to Aby Lagoon 5 mi.

NNW of Half Assini. Forms part of Ivory Coast–Gold Coast border in lower course.

Tanoso (tänō'sō), village, Western Prov., SW Gold Coast colony, on Tano R (head of navigation) and 45 mi. NW of Axim; rice, cassava, corn.

Tanout (tänōōt'), town (pop. c.900), S central Niger territory, Fr. West Africa, 75 mi. N of Zinder; stock-raising center (cattle, sheep, goats); also trading in hides. Region also produces millet, beans, tomatoes, onions, melons. Airfield.

Tanpa (dän'bä'), town, ⊙ Tanpa co. (pop. 12,750), E Sikang prov., China, on Tatu R. and 60 mi. N of Kangting, at Szechwan border; iron-mining center; cattle raising.

Tanque (täng'kā), village (pop. 483), Tenerife, Canary Isls., 33 mi. WSW of Santa Cruz de Tenerife; potatoes, wheat, corn, bananas, tomatoes, lentils, fruit, wine; cheese processing.

Tanquián (tängkyän'), officially Tanquián Escobedo, town (pop. 1,639), San Luis Potosí, E Mexico, in fertile Gulf plain, on Moctezuma R. and 45 mi. SW of Pánuco; coffee, tobacco, sugar cane, fruit, livestock.

Tan River, Chinese *Tan Kiang* or *Tan Chiang* (both: dän' jyäng'), W central China, rises in southeasternmost Shensi prov., flows through SW Honan prov., past Kingtzekwan (head of navigation) and Sichwan, into NW Hupeh prov., to Han R. above Kwanghwa (Laohokow); 125 mi. long. An anc. trade route bet. Sian and Yangtze R. valley.

Tansen, Korea: see TANCHON.

Tanshi, Formosa: see TANTZE.

Tanshui (dän'shwā'), Jap. *Tamsui* or *Tansui* (tän'sōōē), town (1935 pop. 9,018), N Formosa, fishing port on Formosa Strait, at mouth of Tanshui R., 10 mi. NW of Taipei; fish-processing industry. Remains of Spanish castle of Santo Domingo (1626); seaside resort. Formerly one of leading ports of Formosa, Tanshui declined following silting at river mouth and was replaced by Keelung as chief harbor of N Formosa.

Tanshui River. 1 In N Formosa, rises on slopes of Mt. Sylvia, flows 89 mi. N, past Taki, Sinchwang, and Taipei, to Formosa Strait at Tanshui town. Receives Sintien and Keelung rivers (right) at Taipei. Navigable below Taipei. **2** or **Lower Tanshui River,** Chinese *Siatanshui Ki* or *Hsia-tan-shui Ch'i* (both: shyä'dän'shwā' chē'), Jap. *Shimo-tamsui-kei* (shē'mō-tän'sōōē-kā'), second longest stream of Formosa; 97 mi. long; rises at E foot of Mt. Morrison, flows SSW to Formosa Strait at Tungkang. Lower course (navigable for 30 mi.) is spanned by 5,000-ft. bridge carrying Pingtung-Kaohiung RR. Extensive reclamation works in lower reaches. Receives the parallel Nansinsien R. (right); called Szeshe R. above the confluence.

Tansing, Nepal: see PALPA.

Tansui, Formosa: see TANSHUI.

Tanta (tän'tä), city (pop. 139,816), ⊙ Gharbiya prov., Lower Egypt, 52 mi. NNW of Cairo and 70 mi. ESE of Alexandria, bet. Rosetta and Damietta branches of the Nile; 30°47'N 31°E. Important rail and cotton center; cotton ginning, cottonseed-oil extraction, wool spinning, tarboosh mfg. There are 3 annual festivals in honor of the 13th-cent. Moslem saint Ahmad al-Badawi, buried in the tomb-mosque here.

Tantabin (tän'dubĭn). **1** Village, Insein dist., Lower Burma, on Myitmaka R. (ferry) and 20 mi. NW of Rangoon. **2** Village, Toungoo dist., Lower Burma, on Sittang R. and 10 mi. SSE of Toungoo. **3** Village, Shwebo dist., Upper Burma, on railroad and 75 mi. NNW of Mandalay; rice area.

Tantalus, Mount (tăn'–), or **Puu Ohia** (pōō'ōō ōhē'ü), hill (2,013 ft.), just N of Honolulu, T.H.; steep, scenic drive to summit.

Tantan (tän'tän), village (pop. 2,530), Southern Protectorate of Morocco, Sp. West Africa, near left bank of the Uad Dráa; 28°27'N 11°8'W; date palms.

Tantangara, Mount (tăntăng'gürü) (5,850 ft.), SE New South Wales, Australia, in Muniong Range of Great Dividing Range, near Kiandra.

Tantanoola, village (pop. 315), SE South Australia, 220 mi. SSE of Adelaide, WNW of Mt. Gambier; dairy products, acacia bark.

Tantara, Belgian Congo: see MINDIGI.

Tantima (täntē'mä), town (pop. 684), Veracruz, E Mexico, in Sierra Madre Oriental foothills, 38 mi. NW of Tuxpan; cereals, fruit.

Tantonville (tãtõvēl'), village (pop. 685), Meurthe-et-Moselle dept., NE France, 15 mi. S of Nancy; brewery.

Tantoyuca (täntoiōō'kä), city (pop. 3,916), Veracruz, E Mexico, in E foothills of Sierra Madre Oriental, 60 mi. NW of Tuxpan; agr. center (cereals, coffee, sugar cane, tobacco, fruit).

Tantu, China: see CHINKIANG.

Tantura, Israel: see NASHOLIM.

Tantze or **T'an-tzu** (both: tän'dzŭ'), Jap. *Tanshi* (tän'shē), town (1935 pop. 3,025), W central Formosa, 4 mi. N of Taichung and on railroad; sugar milling; rice, vegetables, tobacco, fruit.

Tanuku (tŭ'nōōkōō), town (pop. 13,562), West Godavari dist., NE Madras, India, in Godavari R. delta, on rail branch and 40 mi. E of Ellore; rice and oilseed milling, hand-loom cotton weaving; tobacco, sugar cane.

Tanuma (tä"nōō'mä), town (pop. 17,181), Tochigi prefecture, central Honshu, Japan, 22 mi. SW of Utsunomiya, in agr. area (wheat, rice, tobacco); dyes, woodworking.

Tanunak (tă'nünăk), Eskimo village (pop. 112), W Alaska, on W Nelson Isl., on Bering Sea; 60°34'N 165°20'W; trading post. Airfield.

Tanunda (tŭnŭn'dŭ), town (pop. 1,391), SE South Australia, 35 mi. NNE of Adelaide; wineries; wheat, fruits.

Tanur (tänōōr'), town (pop. 9,370), Malabar dist., SW Madras, India, on Arabian Sea, 20 mi. SSE of Calicut; fishing center (sardines, mackerel, catfish); fish canning. Pop. almost entirely Moslem.

Tanus, France: see PAMPELONNE.

Tanushimaru (tänōō'-shē'märōō), town (pop. 6,222), Fukuoka prefecture, N central Kyushu, Japan, 11 mi. E of Kurume; rice, wheat, raw silk; vegetable wax.

Tanvald, Czechoslovakia: see SVAROV.

Tanyang (dän'yäng'), town (pop. 30,753), ⊙ Tanyang co. (pop. 470,276), S Kiangsu prov., China, on Grand Canal, on Shanghai-Nanking RR and 15 mi. SSE of Chinkiang; agr. center (rice, wheat, beans, hemp). Kaolin quarries near by.

Tanyang (tän'yäng'), Jap. *Tanyo*, township (1946 pop. 9,417), N.Chungchong prov., S Korea, 22 mi. E of Chungju; anthracite.

Tanyang Lake, China: see SHIHKIU LAKE.

Tanyo. 1 Township, N.Chungchong, Korea: see TANYANG. **2** Town, S.Cholla prov., Korea: see TAMYANG.

Tanyong Mas or **Tanyong Mat,** Thailand: see RA NGAE.

Tanyong Sata, Thailand: see YONG SATA.

Tanyong Star, Thailand: see YONG SATA.

Tanza (tän'sä), town (1939 pop. 2,144; 1948 municipality pop. 18,183), Cavite prov., S Luzon, Philippines, 17 mi. SW of Manila; agr. center (rice, fruit, coconuts, sugar cane).

Tao, China: see TAO RIVER.

Taoan or **T'ao-an** (tou'än'), town, ⊙ Taoan co. (pop. 144,200), SW Heilungkiang prov., Manchuria, 130 mi. SSE of Tsitsihar; rail junction and stock-raising center; kaoliang, soybeans, rye. Soda extraction near by. Called Tsingan until 1914; later, Paicheng or Paichengtze.

Taochen (dou'jŭn'), town (pop. 4,586), ⊙ Taochen co. (pop. 96,726), NE Kweichow prov., China, on Szechwan border, 70 mi. NW of Szenan; rice, tea. Until 1932 called Tukichang.

Taocheng or **Tao-ch'eng** (dou'chŭng'), town, ⊙ Taocheng co. (pop. 4,234), S Sikang prov., China, near Yunnan line, 65 mi. S of Lihwa; rice.

Taochow. 1 Town, Hunan prov., China: see TAOHSIEN. **2** Town, Kansu prov., China: see LINTAN.

Taochung or **T'ao-ch'ung** (tou'chōōng'), mining settlement, S Anhwei prov., China, just W of Fanchang, near Yangtze R.; iron-mining center, connected by short rail line with Yangtze R. shipping point of Tikang.

Taofu (dou'fōō'), town, ⊙ Taofu co. (pop. 4,146), N Sikang prov., China, 80 mi. NW of Kangting and on highway. Gold and iron mining near by. Until 1913 called Taowu, Tibetan *Dawu*.

Taoho, town, China: see LINSIA.

Tao Ho, river, China: see TAO RIVER.

Taohsien (dou'shyĕn'), town, ⊙ Taohsien co. (pop. 313,795), S Hunan prov., China, on Tao R. (branch of Siang R.) and 45 mi. S of Lingling; rice, tea, wheat, cotton. Tin mining near by. Until 1913 called Taochow.

Taohwaping or **T'ao-hua-p'ing** (both: tou'hwä'pĭng'), town, central Hunan prov., China, on Tzu R. and 20 mi. SW of Shaoyang.

Taokow or **Tao-k'ou** (both: dou'kō'), town, central Pingyuan prov., China, on railroad and 40 mi. NE of Sinsiang, and just NW of Hwahsien; head of navigation on Wei R.; commercial center.

Taolin or **T'ao-lin** (tou'lĭn'), town (pop. 4,259), ⊙ Taolin co. (pop. 66,663), E Suiyuan prov., China, 30 mi. NW of Tsining; cattle raising; oats, wheat. Until 1914 in N Shansi; 1914–28, in Chahar.

Taolo or **T'ao-lo** (tou'lô'), town, ⊙ Taolo co. (pop. 4,053), SE Ningsia prov., China, 35 mi. NE of Yinchwan, across Yellow R., near Suiyuan line; cattle raising; rice, wheat, millet.

Taonan or **T'ao-nan** (tou'nän'), town (pop. 48,000), ⊙ Taonan co. (pop. 230,481), SW Heilungkiang prov., Manchuria, 150 mi. SSE of Tsitsihar and on railroad; major trade center in grain and soybean dist.; has trade (sheep, cattle, wool, furs) with Inner Mongolia; cotton and hemp production. Called Shwangliuchen until 1905.

Taongi (tä-ōng'ē) or **Pokaakku** (pō'kä-äk'kōō), northernmost atoll of Ratak Chain, Kwajalein dist., Marshall Isls., W central Pacific, 400 mi. NNE of Kwajalein; 14°35'N 169°E; 11 isls.; uninhabited.

Taopi (tāō'pē), village (pop. 118), Mower co., SE Minn., near Iowa line, 19 mi. ESE of Austin; grain, livestock.

Tao River. 1 Chinese *Tao Ho* (dou'hŭ'), river in SE Kansu prov., China, rises on Tsinghai border, flows c.280 mi. E and N, past Choni, Minhsien, Lintao, and Taosha, to Yellow R. SW of Lanchow. **2** Chinese *Tao Ho* or *T'ao Ho* (tou'hŭ'), Mongol *Tor* (tōr), river in W Manchuria, China, rises in the Great Khingan Mts. at c.46°30'N, flows c.250 mi. ESE, past Ulan Hoto and Taonan, through Chinese agr. dist., to Nonni R. 110 mi. S of Tsitsihar.

Taormina (täôrmē'nä), anc. *Tauromenium*, town (pop. 4,293), Messina prov., E Sicily, on Ionian coast 27 mi. SW of Messina; resort; also sulphur mining, marmalade mfg. Has cathedral, ruined castle, and medieval palaces, including Palazzo Corvaia (built 1372; badly damaged in Second World War). Founded c.395 B.C. on earlier Siculian site; noted for large Greek theater (357 ft. in diameter) rebuilt by Romans in 2d cent. A.D. and partly restored in 1748. Siculian necropolis of 8th cent. B.C. near by.

Taos (tous), county (□ 2,256; pop. 17,146), N N.Mex.; ⊙ Taos. Grain, livestock-grazing area; watered by Rio Grande; borders on Colo. Sangre de Cristo Mts. extend N–S, rising to 13,151 ft. in WHEELER PEAK (highest point in state). Part of Carson Natl. Forest in E; Pueblo Indian areas at Taos and in S. Formed 1852.

Taos, village (pop. 1,815), ⊙ Taos co., N N.Mex., on branch of the Rio Grande, in Sangre de Cristo Mts. and in Taos Pueblo (□ 74), 55 mi. NNE of Santa Fe; alt. 7,098 ft. Resort, trade center for near-by ranches. Settled early in 17th cent. by Spaniards, it served for many years as center of Sp.-Indian trade. In 1680 Taos Indians joined other pueblos in general uprising against Spaniards, who were temporarily driven off. Second revolt occurred in 1847, when Indians, incited by Spaniards, killed Charles Bent, U.S. governor. After 1898 village developed as colony for painters and writers attracted by color and beauty of region. Heptagon Gallery, Harwood foundation (housing library, studios, and exhibition room), Kit Carson House (occupied by scout 1858–66), grave of Kit Carson, and hq. for near-by Carson Natl. Forest are here. Inc. 1934; also known as Don Fernando de Taos. Near by is Indian village of Taos, or San Geronimo de Taos (pop. 921). Consists of 2 large, adobe, communal houses surrounded by smaller dwellings and platforms used for grain storage. Inhabitants are Tigua-speaking Pueblo Indians who farm and raise livestock. Religious services take place in village mission; native rituals are practiced in kivas. Ceremonial dances are Corn Dance and Sundown Dance.

Taosha or **T'ao-sha** (tou'shä'), town, ⊙ Taosha co. (pop. 23,838), SE Kansu prov., China, 30 mi. S of Lanchow and on Tao R.; tobacco, grain. Until 1914 called Shani.

Taoudéni (toudĕ'nē), saltworks in the Sahara, N Fr. Sudan, Fr. West Africa, on caravan trails, below Tropic of Cancer, at 22°40'N 3°57'W. Sometimes Taoudenni or Taodéni.

Taounate (tounät'), village (pop. 1,475), Fez region, N Fr. Morocco, on S slope of Rif Mts., 38 mi. NNE of Fez; olive groves.

Taourirt (tourērt'), town (pop. 8,924), Oujda region, NE Fr. Morocco, on railroad and 60 mi. WSW of Oujda; trade center (cattle, sheep, wool, grains, esparto). Lead, zinc deposits near by. Smectic clay quarry at Camp Berteaux, 12 mi. NW.

Taouz (touz), village and oasis, Meknès region, SE Fr. Morocco, on the Oued Ziz, 40 mi. SSE of Erfoud; lead and zinc deposits; 30°54'N 4°W.

Taowu, China: see TAOFU.

Taoyüan. 1 or **T'ao-yüan** (tou'yüän'), town, ⊙ Taoyüan co. (pop. 539,585), NW Hunan prov., China, on Yüan R. and 16 mi. SW of Changteh; rice, tea, wheat, cotton. Gold mining. **2** (dou'yüän') Town, Kiangsu prov., China: see SZEYANG.

Taoyüan or **T'ao-yüan** (both: tou'yüän'), Jap. *Toen* (tō'ĕn), town (1935 pop. 8,492), N Formosa, 13 mi. WSW of Taipei, 25 mi. NE of Sinchu; rice- and tea-growing center; sugar cane, ramie, livestock. Officially called Sinchu, 1945–50.

Tapa (tä'pä), Ger. *Taps*, city (pop. 3,751), N Estonia, on Tallinn-Leningrad RR and 45 mi. ESE of Tallinn; rail junction (repair yards) of line to Riga; meat packing, sawmilling.

Tapacarí (täpäkärē'), town (pop. c.9,100), ⊙ Tapacarí prov., Cochabamba dept., W central Bolivia, on S slopes of Cordillera de Cochabamba and 28 mi. WSW of Cochabamba; alt. 9,514 ft.; barley, corn; livestock.

Tapachula (täpächōō'lä), city (pop. 15,187), Chiapas, S Mexico, on Inter-American Highway route, W of Guatemala border, and 140 mi. WNW of Guatemala city, on railroad; coffee-growing center in Pacific lowland; also sugar cane, tobacco, bananas, fruit, cattle; sugar refining, sawmilling, distilling. Radio station, airfield, custom house.

Tapah (täpä'), town (pop. 4,990), S central Perak, Malaya, 30 mi. SSE of Ipoh; road center in rubber-growing dist.; kaolin quarrying. Tapah Road village (pop. 777), 5 mi. W, is rail junction for Telok Anson.

Tapajós River or **Tapajoz River** (both: tüpüzhôs'), important right tributary of the Amazon, in W Pará, Brazil, formed at Amazonas–Pará–Mato Grosso border by junction of Juruena and São Manuel rivers, flows NNE past Itaituba (head of navigation) and the experimental rubber plantations of Fordlândia and Belterra, to the Amazon at Santarém. Numerous rapids in upper course. Length, c.500 mi.; including the Arinos (longest headstream), c.1,250 mi.

Tapalapa (täpälä'pä), town (pop. 550), Chiapas, S Mexico, in spur of Sierra Madre, 29 mi. N of Tuxtla; corn, fruit.

Tapalpa (täpäl'pä), town (pop. 2,856), Jalisco, W Mexico, 40 mi. SSE of Ameca; grain, alfalfa, fruit, vegetables.

Tapalqué (täpälkā'), town (pop. 3,802), ⊙ Tapalqué dist. (□ 1,602; pop. 11,503), central Buenos Aires prov., Argentina, on the Arroyo Tapalqué and 30 mi. NNW of Azul; agr. center; sheep, cattle.

Tapalqué, Arroyo (äroi'ō), river in central Buenos Aires prov., Argentina, rises S of Olavarría, flows c.75 mi. NNE, past Olavarría and Tapalqué, losing itself SE of General Alvear. Used for hydroelectric power.

Tapanahoni River (täpänähō'nē), SE Du. Guiana, rises in Tumuc-Humac Mts. near Brazil border, flows c.200 mi. NE, through tropical forests, to the Maroni or Marowijne R. (at mouth of the Lawa or Aoua) at Stoelmans on Fr. Guiana border. Gold fields near its lower reaches.

Tapanlieh (dä'bän'lyĕ'), Jap. *Daihanratsu* (dīhän'-rätsōō) or *Daibanretsu* (dībän'rātsōō), village, southernmost Formosa, 3 mi. SSE of Hengchun, on Nan Wan inlet W of Cape Olwanpi; fishing port and whaling station.

Tapanshang (dä'bän'shäng'), town, S Inner Mongolian Autonomous Region, Manchuria, 25 mi. NNW of Chihfeng; banner hq. in Jooda league. Was ⊙ West Hsingan prov. in Manchukuo; until 1949 in Jehol.

Tapanui (täpŭnōō'ē), borough (pop. 287), S central S.Isl., New Zealand, 55 mi. NE of Invercargill; linen mill; agr.

Tapaotze, Manchuria: see PAICHŬAN.

Tapa Shan (dä'bä' shän'), outlying spur of the Kunlun system, on Szechwan-Shensi prov. border, China, 90 mi. NE of Wanhsien; rises over 8,000 ft. Also known as Kiulung Mts. and Kiutiao Mts.

Tapasi, India: see RANIGANJ.

Tapaste (täpä'stā), town (pop. 1,556), Havana prov., W Cuba, at foot of Tapaste hills, 15 mi. ESE of Havana; sugar cane, livestock. Outside the town are the spectacular El Cura Caverns.

Tapaz (tä'päs, täpäs'), town (1939 pop. 1,382; 1948 municipality pop. 16,376), Capiz prov., central Panay isl., Philippines, 27 mi. SW of Capiz; agr. center (rice, sugar cane).

Tape (tä'pā), Hung. *Tápé,* town (pop. 4,654), Csongrad co., S Hungary, on Tisza R. and 3 mi. E of Szeged; dairy farming; paprika, wheat; fishing.

Tapenagá, Argentina: see LA SÁBANA.

Taperoá (tŭpĭrooä'). **1** City (pop. 1,843), E Bahia, Brazil, near the Atlantic, 35 mi. S of Nazaré; ships manioc, cacao, vegetable dyes. **2** City (pop. 1,475), central Paraíba, NE Brazil, on Borborema Plateau, 33 mi. ESE of Patos; cotton, livestock. Called Batalhão, 1944–48.

Tapes (tä'pĭs), city (pop. 2,317), E Rio Grande do Sul, Brazil, landing on W shore of Lagoa dos Patos, 45 mi. S of Pôrto Alegre; rice, fruit.

Tapes, Serra dos (sĕ'rŭ dōōs), hilly area (alt. to c.600 ft.), S Rio Grande do Sul, Brazil, bounded N by Camaquã R.

Taphion or **Taphos,** Greece: see MEGANESI.

Tapia de Casariego (tä'pyä dhā käsäryā'gō), town (pop. 1,107), Oviedo prov., NW Spain, port on Bay of Biscay, 6 mi. ENE of Ribadeo; lobster fishing; cereals, vegetables, livestock; lumber. Iron mines.

Tapiales (täpyä'lĕs), residential town (pop. estimate 3,000) in Greater Buenos Aires, Argentina, 9 mi. WSW of Buenos Aires.

Tapiantana Islands (täpyäntä'nä) (□ 3; 1939 pop. 11,134), small group, Zamboanga prov., Philippines, off S coast of Basilan Isl. (at SW tip of Mindanao).

Tapiau, Russian SFSR: see GVARDEISK.

Tapiche River (täpē'chā), Loreto dept., E Peru, rises near Brazil border at about 7°35'S, flows c.250 mi. N to Ucayali R. at 5°S 73°52'W. Its right affluent, the Río Blanco, joining it 30 mi. above its mouth, sometimes designates its lower course.

Tapieh Mountains, Chinese *Tapieh Shan* (dä'byĕ' shän'), hill range on Honan-Hupeh-Anhwei line, China, extending E into central Anhwei; mts. rise to 4,000 ft. S of Hwoshan. Crossed by Peking-Hankow RR in NW. Also called Hwaiyang Mts.

Tapijulapa (täpēhōōlä'pä), town (pop. 1,080), Tabasco, SE Mexico, on navigable affluent of Grijalva R. and 38 mi. SSE of Villahermosa; corn, rice, coffee, tobacco, fruit.

Tapilon Point (täpē'lōn, täpēlōn'), northernmost point of Cebu isl., Philippines, in Visayan Sea; 11°17'N 124°1'E.

Tapilula (täpēlōō'lä), town (pop. 1,492), Chiapas, S Mexico, in spur of Sierra Madre, 33 mi. NNE of Tuxtla; corn, sugar cane, tobacco, fruit.

Taping River (dä'bĭng'), left tributary of the Irrawaddy, in China and Burma, rises as Taying R. in westernmost Yunnan prov. (China) N of Tengchung, flows 150 mi. SW to Irrawaddy R. at Bhamo.

Tapiogyörgye (tä'pĭōdyûrdyĕ), Hung. *Tápiógyörgye,* town (pop. 5,927), Pest-Pilis-Solt-Kiskun co., N central Hungary, on Tapio R. and 15 mi. NNW of Szolnok; flour mills; wheat, barley, paprika, cattle.

Tapioszele (tä'pĭōsĕlĕ), Hung. *Tápiószele,* town (pop. 10,165), Pest-Pilis-Solt-Kiskun co., N central Hungary, on Tapio R. and 18 mi. NW of Szolnok; flour mills; grain, tobacco, cattle, hogs.

Tapioszentmarton (tä'pĭōsĕntmär'tôn), Hung. *Tápiószentmárton,* town (pop. 6,066), Pest-Pilis-Solt-Kiskun co., N central Hungary, near Tapio R., 23 mi. NW of Szolnok; stud farm.

Tapiratiba (tŭpĕrŭtē'bŭ), city (pop. 1,363), E São Paulo, Brazil, 13 mi. NE of São José do Rio Pardo; coffee, rice, sugar, beans, corn.

Tapi River (tä'pē'), chief river of S peninsular Thailand, in Malay Peninsula, rises in two headstreams in Sithammarat Range W of Nakhon Sithammarat, flows 100 mi. N, past Suratthani, to Gulf of Siam. Navigable in lower course. Sometimes called Luang R.

Tapi Town, Liberia: see TAPPI.

Taplacken, Russian SFSR: see TALPAKI.

Taplow, residential town and parish (pop. 1,031), SE Buckingham, England, on the Thames opposite Maidenhead; 2 mi. N and on the Thames is Cliveden, seat of Lord Astor.

Tapoco (tŭpō'kō), mountain resort, Graham co., W N.C., near Tenn. line, on Little Tennessee R. at Cheoah R. mouth, and 11 mi. NW of Robbinsville; aluminum plant. Cheoah Dam (hydroelectric plant) is just E.

Tapolca (tŏ'pôltsŏ). **1** or **Görömbölytapolca** (gû'rûmbûĭ-), warm-springs resort, Borsod-Gömör co., NE Hungary, suburb of Miskolc; mineral waters. **2** Town (pop. 7,534), Zala co., W Hungary, 26 mi. SW of Veszprem, in Bakony Mts.; rail center for agr., vineyard area; wineries, brickworks. Known for its Badacsony wine.

Tapoly River, Czechoslovakia: see TOPLA RIVER.

Tappahannock (tăpŭhă'nŭk), town (pop. 1,011), ⊙ Essex co., E Va., on the Rappahannock (bridged) and 40 mi. NE of Richmond; lumber mill, cannery. Founded 1680 as a port; inc. 1914.

Tappan (tăpăn', tă'păn), residential village (1940 pop. 1,249), Rockland co., SE N.Y., at N.J. line, 6 mi. SSW of Nyack, in diversified-farming area. De Wint Mansion was Washington's hq. in 1780 and 1783. John André, British spy in the Revolution, was tried and hanged here.

Tappan Reservoir, Ohio: see DENNISON.

Tappan Zee (tă'pŭn zā',–zē'), SE N.Y., widening of HUDSON RIVER bet. Irvington (S) and Croton Point (N); c.10 mi. long; 2–3 mi. wide bet. Nyack and Tarrytown.

Tappen, village (pop. 379), Kidder co., central N.Dak., 14 mi. E of Steele.

Tappi (tă'pē) or **Tappita** (tă"pētä'), town, Central Prov., N central Liberia, 90 mi. NE of Buchanan; palm oil and kernels, kola nuts, cassava, rice. Sometimes called Tapi Town.

Taprobane, Asia: see CEYLON.

Taps, Estonia: see TAPA.

Tapso (täp'sō), village (pop. estimate 500), on Catamarca and Santiago del Estero prov. border, Argentina, 40 mi. E of Catamarca, on Tucumán-Córdoba RR; timber cutting, cattle raising. Formerly I-riondo.

Tapti River (täp'tē), W central India, rises in central Satpura Range near Multai in Madhya Pradesh, flows generally W, past Burhanpur, into Bombay, past Bhusawal and Surat, into Gulf of Cambay 13 mi. SW of Surat; c.450 mi. long. Receives (left) Purna, Girna, and Panjhra rivers. Lower course only partly navigable.

Tapu, China: see TAIPU.

Tapuaenuku, New Zealand: see KAIKOURA RANGES.

Tápuc (tä'pōōk), town (pop. 1,681), Pasco dept., central Peru, on Yanahuanca R. and 23 mi. NNW of Cerro de Pasco; grain, potatoes, livestock.

Tapul Group (täpōōl') (□ c.90; 1948 pop. 46,437), Sulu prov., Philippines, in central Sulu Archipelago, bet. Jolo and Tawitawi; 5°40'N 120°50'E. Chief isl. is SIASI ISLAND; other isls. include Tapul Isl. (□ 10.5; 1939 pop. 12,187), Lugus, Lapac, Cabingaan, Taluc.

Tapuruquá (tŭpōōrōōkwä') or **Tapuruquara** (–rŭ), town (pop. 131), NW Amazonas, Brazil, head of navigation on left bank of the Rio Negro, and 130 mi. E of Uaupés; Brazil nuts, rubber. Until 1944, Santa Isabel.

Taq-i-Bustan or **Tak-i-Bostan** (both: täk'ĕbōstän'), village, Fifth Prov., in Kermanshah, W Iran, 5 mi. NE of Kermanshah; road junction and excursion spot. Arched recesses in rocks here contain bas-reliefs of Sassanian times.

Taquara (tŭkwä'rŭ), city (pop. 5,670), NE Rio Grande do Sul, Brazil, head of navigation on Sinos R., on railroad and 40 mi. NE of Pôrto Alegre; cotton, alfalfa, tobacco, maté.

Taquari (tŭkwŭrē'). **1** City (pop. 3,056), E central Rio Grande do Sul, Brazil, on Taquari R. and 40 mi. WNW of Pôrto Alegre; agr. center (rye, oats, manioc, rice, fruit); livestock. Has fruit experiment station. Amethyst and agates found in area. Founded 1760 by settlers from the Azores. Formerly spelled Taquary. **2** City, São Paulo, Brazil: see TAQUARITUBA.

Taquari River. 1 In S central Mato Grosso, Brazil, rises near Alto Araguaia (Goiás border), flows c.350 mi. WSW, past Coxim (head of navigation), to the Paraguay 20 mi. E of Corumbá, after crossing Paraguay flood plain. Diamond washings in headstreams. Formerly spelled Taquary. **2** In NE Rio Grande do Sul, Brazil, rises on W slope of the Serra do Mar as the Rio das Antas, flows c.200 mi. W and S, past Lajeado (head of navigation), Estrêla, and Taquari, to the Jacuí at Bom Jesus do Triunfo. Amethysts and agates found in Lajeado area. Winegrowing in upper valley. Formerly spelled Taquary.

Taquaritinga (tŭkwŭrētēng'gŭ), city (pop. 8,152), N central São Paulo, Brazil, on railroad and 45 mi. WSW of Ribeirão Prêto; agr.-processing center (corn-meal mfg., sugar and rice milling, coffee roasting, distilling). Also makes flour products, candies. Lumber and cattle shipping.

Taquarituba (–tōō'bŭ), city (pop. 909), S São Paulo, Brazil, 35 mi. SSW of Avaré; cotton, grain, cattle. Until 1944, Taquari (old spelling, Taquary).

Taquary, Brazil: see TAQUARI.

Taques, Los, Venezuela: see LOS TAQUES.

Tara (tä'rŭ), village (pop. 495), S Ont., 12 mi. SW of Owen Sound; dairying, mixed farming.

Tara (tă'rŭ), Gaelic *Teamhair Breagh,* agr. village (district pop. 794), central Co. Meath, Ireland, near the Boyne, 6 mi. SSE of An Uaimh. Here is the Hill of Tara (507 ft. high), from anc. times until 6th cent. seat of the Irish kings. There are 6 raths, largest of which is 850 ft. in diameter. On summit of one rath is statue of St. Patrick (who preached here), reputed to mark site of the Lia Fail or stone of destiny. There are many other anc. stone monuments. It was scene of triennial convention, or *feis,* and was site of bldgs. owned by the separate provinces. The hill is connected with several anc. Irish legends.

Tara (tä'rä), town (pop. 102), Southern Prov., Northern Rhodesia, on railroad and 20 mi. ENE of Kalomo; tobacco, wheat, corn.

Tara (tä'rŭ), city (1939 pop. over 10,000), NE Omsk oblast, Russian SFSR, on Irtysh R., below mouth of Tara R., 135 mi. NNE of Omsk, in flax-growing area; shipbuilding, sawmilling; marketing of grain and dairy products. Founded 1594 at mouth of Tara R.; moved 1669 to present site.

Tarabganj (tŭr'ŭbgŭnj), village, Gonda dist., NE Uttar Pradesh, India, on tributary of the Gogra and 12 mi. S of Gonda; rice, wheat, corn, gram.

Tarabuco (täräbōō'kō), town (pop. c.10,320), ⊙ Yamparáez prov., Chuquisaca dept., S central Bolivia, 22 mi. ESE of Sucre (connected by railroad); corn, vegetables, fruit.

Tarabulus el Gharb, Libya: see TRIPOLI.

Tarabulus el Sham or **Tarabulus esh Sham,** Lebanon: see TRIPOLI.

Taracköz, Ukrainian SSR: see TERESVA.

Taraclia, Moldavian SSR: see TARAKLIYA.

Taraco (tärä'kō), town (pop. c.6,600), La Paz dept., W Bolivia, on Gulf of Taraco of L. Titicaca and 40 mi. W of La Paz; alt. 12,637 ft.; potatoes, barley, sheep.

Taraco, Gulf of, S inlet of SE part (L. Uinamarca) of L. Titicaca, W Bolivia, near Peru border; 10 mi. long, 7 mi. wide. Taraco on NE shore, Guaqui on SE shore.

Taradell (tärädäl'), town (pop. 1,446), Barcelona prov., NE Spain, 4 mi. SSE of Vich; cotton- and woolen-fabric mfg., flour milling.

Taragi (tä"rä'gē) or **Taraki** (–kē), town (pop. 8,566), Kumamoto prefecture, S central Kyushu, Japan, 39 mi. SSE of Kumamoto; agr. center; sawmill.

Tarahti, India: see KALINJAR.

Tarahyra River, Colombia-Brazil: see TARAÍRA RIVER.

Tarai, region, India and Nepal: see TERAI.

Taraika-wan, Russian SFSR: see TERPENIYE GULF.

Taraíra River (täräē'rä), on Colombia-Brazil line, rises at 0°10'S, flows c.100 mi. SSE along international border to the Apaporis at 1°7'S. Formerly spelled Tarahyra.

Tarairí (tärīrē'), village, Tarija dept., SE Bolivia, on E slopes of Serranía de Aguaragüe and 14 mi. N of Villa Montes, on road; oil fields.

Tarakan (täräkän'), island (c.10 mi. long) of Indonesian Borneo, off E coast of isl., in Celebes Sea, 500 mi. NNE of Banjermasin; 3°25'N 117°35'E. Low lying, with swampy coastal areas; oil fields. On SW coast is important town of Tarakan (pop. 11,589), a port shipping oil to refineries at Balikpapan and Banjermasin. In Second World War, town was Jap. oil-supply center.

Taraki, Japan: see TARAGI.

Tarakliya (tŭräk'lyēŭ), Rum. *Taraclia* (täräk'lyä), town (1941 pop. 9,461), S Moldavian SSR, on railroad and 22 mi. E of Kagul; corn, barley; sheep.

Taralga (tŭräl'gŭ), village (pop. 483), E New South Wales, Australia, 90 mi. SW of Sydney; rail terminus; dairy products, sheep; marble quarries. Wombeyan limestone caves are 10 mi. NE.

Tarama-jima (tärä'mä-jĭmä), volcanic island (□11; 1950 pop. 3,561) of Sakishima Isls., in Ryukyu Isls., bet. East China Sea (W) and Philippine Sea (E), 22 mi. E of Ishigaki-shima; 3.5 mi. long, 2.5 mi. wide; generally low, fertile (sweet potatoes, sugar cane).

Taramangalam or **Tharamangalam** (tŭrŭmŭng'-gŭlŭm), town (pop. 6,666), Salem dist., S central Madras, India, 14 mi. WNW of Salem; castor beans, peanuts, millet; cotton weaving. Has 17th-cent. Sivaite temple with 13th-cent. architectural remains and inscriptions.

Tara Mountains (tä'rä), in Dinaric Alps, W Serbia, Yugoslavia; highest point (5,117 ft.) is 18 mi. W of Titovo Uzice.

Taramskoye, Ukrainian SSR: see TAROMSKOYE.

Tarana (tŭrä'nŭ), town (pop. 6,345), W central Madhya Bharat, India, 19 mi. NE of Ujjain; local market for millet, cotton; wheat; cotton ginning.

Taranagar (tä'rŭnŭgŭr), town (pop. 8,319), N Rajasthan, India, 115 mi. ENE of Bikaner; exports raw hides and locally-made chaguls; hand-loom woolen weaving. Has 10th-cent. Jain temple. Formerly called Reni.

Taranaki (tă"rŭnă'kē), provincial district (□ 3,750; pop. 76,833), W N.Isl., New Zealand. Coastal plain, bounded E by Wanganui R. Chief borough is New Plymouth, near Egmont Natl. Park. Produces butter, cheese, coal. Area roughly corresponds to Taranaki land dist.

Taranaki, county, New Zealand: see NEW PLYMOUTH.

Tarancón (täräng-kōn'), city (pop. 6,673), Cuenca prov., central Spain, in New Castile, communications center 45 mi. SE of Madrid (linked by rail) Processes and exports agr. produce of the region (grapes, olives, cereals, wool). Olive-oil pressing, flour milling, liquor and alcohol distilling. Lumbering; lime and gypsum quarrying. Silk factories. Mfg. also of chocolate, meat products, plaster, ceramics. Has palace of dukes of Riánsares. Site of Fr. defeat (1809) in Peninsular War.

Tarandacuao (tärändäkwä'ō), town (pop. 2,472), Guanajuato, central Mexico, on Lerma R. and 15 mi. E of Acámbaro; alt. 6,187 ft.; cereals, sugar cane, vegetables, stock.

Taranda Mohammad Panah, W Pakistan: see TARIND MUHAMMAD PANAH.

Tarangnan (tärängnän'), town (1939 pop. 2,363; 1948 municipality pop. 12,271), W Samar isl., Philippines, 14 mi. NW of Catbalogan; agr. center (rice, hemp).

Tarango, Indonesia: see PUTERAN.

Taransay (tă'rŭnsā), island (pop. 33), Outer Hebrides, Inverness, Scotland, just W of Harris, from which it is separated by the narrow Sound of Taransay; 4 mi. long, 3 mi. wide; rises to 875 ft.

Taranta Peligna (tärän'tä pĕlē'nyä), village (pop. 1,227), Chieti prov., Abruzzi e Molise, S central Italy, 19 mi. SSW of Lanciano; woolen mill.

Taranto, province, Italy: see IONIO.

Taranto (tŭrăn'tō, tă'rŭntō, Ital. tä'räntô), anc. *Taras* and *Tarentum*, city (pop. 103,306), ⊙ Ionio prov., Apulia, S Italy, on N inlet (Mare Grande) of Gulf of Taranto, on mainland and on an isl. (bridged to mainland) lying bet. Mare Grande (W) and Mare Piccolo (E; 4 mi. wide) inlets, 50 mi. SSE of Bari; 40°29'N 17°14'E. Chief naval base (after Spezia) of Italy; excellent harbor; shipyards; arsenal. Industrial, commercial, and fishing center; mfg. (ceramics, furniture, glass, shoes, hosiery, fertilizer); wine, olive oil, beer, canned foods. Exports wine, olive oil, fruit, tomatoes, fish. Inlet (Mare Piccolo) E of city is extensively used for raising oysters and mussels; saltworks S of inlet. Archbishopric. Has 11th-cent. cathedral (restored 18th cent.), Byzantine castle (restored 1480), and mus. of antiquities. A powerful town of Magna Graecia; resisted Romans until 272 B.C. Destroyed by Arabs (A.D. 972) and rebuilt by Byzantines. Later became part of kingdom of Naples and strongly fortified. In Second World War, its harbor sheltered much of Ital. fleet; heavily bombed.

Taranto, Gulf of, large arm (85 mi. long and wide) of Ionian Sea, S Italy, bet. Cape Santa Maria di Leuca (NE) and Cape Colonne (SW); forms instep of Ital. boot. Chief center of Ital. oyster and mussel industry, especially around Taranto. Principal ports: TARANTO, Gallipoli, Crotone.

Tarany (tŏ'rŏnyŭ), town (pop. 2,192), Somogy co., SW Hungary, 26 mi. SW of Kaposvar; corn, wheat.

Taraon (tŭroun'), former petty state (□ 26; pop. 3,841) of Central India agency, W of Karwi; one of CHAUBE JAGIRS. In 1948, merged with Vindhya Pradesh.

Tarapacá (täräpäkä'), province (□ 21,346; 1940 pop. 104,097, 1949 estimate 109,664), extreme N Chile, bet. the Andes and the Pacific, bordering Peru and Bolivia; ⊙ IQUIQUE. The high mts. in E (notably Isluga Volcano), give way W to the extremely dry Atacama Desert area, with warm days and cool nights. The Atacama is rich in nitrates (e.g., at Negreiros, Huara), long the mainstay of the economy, but subject to fluctuating demands of the world market; also iodine, copper (Guatacondo), sulphur, borax and salt (Salar Grande); some gold, silver, antimony, tungsten in the Andes. Guano deposits on the coast. Some agr. in the few oases of the Lluta and Azapa valleys: cotton, corn, fruit, sheep. Llamas, alpacas, vicuñas are bred in the Andes. Mfg. is centered at the ports of Iquique and ARICA. The area belonged to Peru until cession (1883) to Chile after the War of the Pacific. The treaty of Lima (1929) settled the border dispute and gave Tacna to Peru and Arica to Chile. Area frequently damaged by earthquakes.

Tarapacá, village (pop. 120), Tarapacá prov., N Chile, oasis in the Pampa del Tamarugal, 45 mi. ENE of Iquique; nitrate refining; fruitgrowing (citrus, olives).

Tarapaya (täräpī'ä), village (pop. c.2,400), Potosí dept., S central Bolivia, 9 mi. NNW of Potosí, and on road from Oruro; alt. 11,785 ft.; hot springs.

Tarapoto (täräpō'tō), city (pop. 9,249), ⊙ San Martín prov. (□ 1,154; enumerated pop. 31,815, plus estimated 8,000 Indians), San Martín dept., N central Peru, in E outliers of the Andes, on edge of the Amazon basin, 55 mi. SE of Moyobamba, and linked by road with Yurimaguas (Loreto dept., 45 mi. NNE); 6°31'S 76°19'W. In fertile farming region (cotton, tobacco, sugar cane, cacao, coffee); mfg. of straw hats, distilling of alcohol and liquor. Airfield. Called San Martín (1940–47).

Tarapur (tärä'pŏŏr), town (pop. 5,296), Kaira dist., N Bombay, India, 10 mi. N of Cambay; market center for cotton, millet, cloth fabrics.

Tarare (tärär'), town (pop. 9,130), Rhône dept., E central France, in the Monts du Beaujolais, 15 mi. SW of Villefranche; textile center (silk, rayon, and cotton mills), known for its plush, muslin, tulle, and velvet goods. Produces fine veils and curtains.

Tarariras, Uruguay: see SUÁREZ, Colonia dept.

Tara River (tä'rŭ), in Novosibirsk and Omsk oblasts, Russian SFSR, rises in Vasyuganye marshes, flows 280 mi. W, past Kyshtovka and Muromtsevo, to Irtysh R. at Ust-Tara. Navigable below Kyshtovka.

Tara River (tä'rä), SW Yugoslavia, rises at SW foot of the Komovi, flows N, past Kolasin and Mojkovac, and NNW, joining Piva R. 10 mi. S of Foca to form Drina R.; 87 mi. long. Navigable for 34 mi

Tararua Range (tă"rŭrōō'ŭ), S N.Isl., New Zealand, on Wellington peninsula; extends 35 mi. S from Shannon to Featherston; rises to 5,016 ft.; forested slopes.

Tarascon (täräskõ'). **1** or **Tarascon-sur-Ariège** (–sür-ärēĕzh'), town (pop. 2,294), Ariège dept., S France, in central Pyrenees, on Ariège R. and 8 mi S of Foix; industrial center; blast furnaces, chemical and plaster factories, sawmills. Cattle and lumber trade. **2** Town (pop. 4,919), Bouches-du-Rhône dept., SE France, on left bank of the Rhone opposite Beaucaire, and 9 mi. N of Arles; communications center and agr. market; fruit and vegetable shipping, hat and furniture mfg., winegrowing. Has medieval castle (once residence of "Good King" René) and Romanesque and Gothic church of St. Martha (heavily damaged in Second World War). Suspension bridge across the Rhone and its approaches were also damaged. Made famous by Alphonse Daudet in his *Tartarin de Tarascon.*

Tarashcha (tŭrăsh'chŭ), town (1926 pop. 10,710), central Kiev oblast, Ukrainian SSR, 24 mi. SE of Belaya Tserkov; food, metalworking, and leather industries.

Tarasovka, Russian SFSR: see VERKHNE-TARASOVKA.

Tarasp (täräsp'), village (pop. 310), Grisons canton, E Switzerland, on Inn R. and 20 mi. E of Davos, in Lower Engadine. Includes resorts of Bad Tarasp (NE; alt. 3,945), noted for curative mineral springs used for drinking and bathing, and Vulpera (ENE; alt. 4,135 ft.), with medieval castle.

Tarata (tärä'tä), town (pop. c.12,500), ⊙ Tarata prov., Cochabamba dept., central Bolivia, on S slopes of Cordillera de Cochabamba and 20 mi. SE of Cochabamba, on railroad; alt. 8,858 ft. Local trade center for agr. products (barley, corn, potatoes), sheep; mfg. (soap, textiles, hats, leather). Once of some importance; has govt. palace, fine churches, and mansions.

Tarata, town (pop. 2,917), ⊙ Tarata prov. (□ 976; pop. 15,807), Tacna dept., S Peru, on tributary of Sama R., in Cordillera Occidental, and 40 mi. NNE of Tacna; alt. 10,013 ft. Stock-raising center (cattle, mules, sheep).

Tarauacá (tärou-ŭkä'), city (pop. 1,481), Acre territory, westernmost Brazil, hydroplane landing on Tarauacá R. (right affluent of the Juruá), near Amazonas line, and 220 mi. NW of Rio Branco; rubber, Brazil nuts. Until 1944, Seabra.

Taravao, Isthmus of (tärävä'ō), Tahiti, Society Isls., S Pacific; joins Taiarapu peninsula to W Tahiti: Port Taravao at N end, 35 mi. NE of Papeete.

Tarawa (tŭrä'wŭ, tä'rä'wä'), atoll (□ 7.7; pop. 3,582), N Gilbert Isls., W central Pacific; 1°25'N 173°E; ⊙ Br. colony of GILBERT AND ELLICE ISLANDS. Consists of 9 large, many small islets on 22-mi. reef. Port of entry, commercial center; exports copra, pearl shell. Site of govt. hosp., leper station, colony jail; airfield on SW islet of Betio (bā'shēō). During Second World War ⊙ colony moved here from Ocean Isl. Tarawa was occupied (Dec., 1941) by Japanese; taken (Nov., 1943), after a fierce battle, by U.S. marines who landed on Betio beach.

Tarawera Mountain (tărŭwĕr'ŭ), volcanic peak (c.1,000 ft.), N central N.Isl., New Zealand, in Hot Springs Dist. L. Tarawera (5 mi. long) is near by. Eruption (1886) destroyed L. Rotomahana, containing unusual sinter terraces.

Tarazona (tärä-thō'nä), city (pop. 10,375), Saragossa prov., NE Spain, in Aragon, 40 mi. ENE of Soria; industrial and agr. trade center. Produces matches, woolen yarns and linen, liqueurs, jams, flour products; olive-oil and meat processing, tanning, flour and sawmilling. Hemp, potatoes, sugar beets, and fruit in area. Episcopal see. Has 12th-cent. cathedral with cloisters (16th cent.), Romanesque church, and episcopal palace. Cistercian abbey of Veruela (12th cent.) with Gothic cloister and fortified walls is c.7 mi. S.

Tarazona de la Mancha (dhā lä män'chä), town (pop. 5,892), Albacete prov., SE central Spain, 19 mi. N of Albacete; wine- and saffron-production and -shipping center. Chocolate mfg., alcohol and brandy distilling, olive-oil processing. Trades in cereals, lumber, sheep.

Tarbagatai, China: see CHUGUCHAK.

Tarbagatai or **Tarbagatay** (tär"bŭgŭtī'). **1** Village (1939 pop. over 2,000), SE Buryat-Mongol Autonomous SSR, Russian SFSR, near Selenga R., 25 mi. S of Ulan-Ude; dairy products. **2** Town (1946 pop. over 500), SW Chita oblast, Russian SFSR, on Trans-Siberian RR, on Khilok R. and 14 mi. SE of Petrovsk, lignite mining; motor-repair shops.

Tarbagatai Range or **Tarbagatay Range,** northern outlier of Tien Shan system, on China-USSR border, W of Ayaguz; rises to 8,400 ft. 40 mi. N of Chuguchak (Tarbagatai).

Tarbat Ness (tär'bŭt nĕs'), promontory on North Sea, at mouth of Dornoch Firth, NE Ross and Cromarty, Scotland, 10 mi. E of Dornoch; site of lighthouse (57°52'N 3°46'W).

Tárbena (tär'vänä), town (pop. 1,394), Alicante prov., E Spain, 20 mi. E of Alcoy; wine, olive oil, cereals, fruit.

Tarbert (tär'bŭrt), Gaelic *Tairbeart*, town (pop. 317), NE Co. Kerry, Ireland, on the Shannon estuary, 10 mi. NE of Listowel; small port. Just N, in the Shannon, is Tarbert Isl. (64 acres).

Tarbert. 1 Fishing village, S Argyll, Scotland, and isthmus (1-mi.-wide) bet. East Loch Tarbert (1-mi.-long inlet of Kilbrannan Sound) and West Loch Tarbert (10-mi.-long inlet of the Sound of Gigha), near base of Kintyre peninsula. The village, at head of East Loch Tarbert, 14 mi. W of Rothesay, is herring-fishing center; has ruins of 14th-cent. castle. **2** Village, chief town of HARRIS, Outer Hebrides, Inverness, Scotland, on the isthmus; fishing port; tweed weaving. Summer station for Norwegian whalers.

Tarbert, Loch (lŏkh), inlet (6 mi. long, 2 mi. wide at mouth) in W coast of JURA, Inner Hebrides, Scotland.

Tarbes (tärb), city (pop. 42,778), ⊙ Hautes-Pyrénées dept., SW France, on left bank of Adour R. and 70 mi. WSW of Toulouse; transportation center for central Pyrenees tourist industry; has arsenal, metalworks (agr. machinery, railroad rolling stock), tanneries, chemical factories, printing establishments. Extensive trade in horses and in agr. produce (corn, tobacco, vegetables, wine) grown in irrigated Adour lowland (N). Has 11th–13th-cent. largely Romanesque cathedral. Founded in Gallo-Roman period, it became an episcopal see in 6th cent. Old ⊙ Gascon countship of Bigorre. Théophile Gautier and Marshal Foch b. here.

Tarbet (tär'bŭt), resort village in Arrochar parish, NW Dumbarton, Scotland, on Loch Lomond, just E of Arrochar.

Tarbolton (tärbōl'tŭn), town and parish (pop. 5,131), central Ayrshire, Scotland, 7 mi. NE of Ayr; coal mining. In 1780 Burns here founded Bachelors' Club. Near by is "Castle o'Montgomery" where Burns's "Highland Mary" was in service; monument marks reputed spot of his parting from her.

Tarboro (tär'bŭrŭ, –bŭrō), town (pop. 8,120), ⊙ Edgecombe co., E central N.C., on Tar R. and 15 mi. E of Rocky Mount; agr. market (tobacco, cotton, peanuts); cotton, hosiery, and lumber mills. Laid out 1760; inc. 1775.

Tarcal (tŏr'tsŏl), town (pop. 4,004), Zemplen co., NE Hungary, at W foot of Mt. Tokaj, 21 mi. NW of Nyiregyhaza; vineyards, with wineries; brickworks. State school for viticulture.

Tarca River, Czechoslovakia: see TORYSA RIVER.

Tarcento (tärchĕn'tô), town (pop. 1,692), Udine prov., Friuli–Venezia Giulia, NE Italy, 10 mi. N of Udine; resort; alcohol distilleries, silk mill.

Tarchendo, China: see KANGTING.

Tárcoles River or **Río Grande de Tárcoles** (rē'ō grän'dā dā tär'kōlĕs), W central Costa Rica, rises in several branches on central plateau in area of San José, Heredia, and Alajuela, flows 45 mi. SW to Gulf of Nicoya 20 mi. SE of Puntarenas.

Tarcoola (tärkōō'lŭ), village (pop. 225), S central South Australia, 260 mi. NW of Port Pirie, on Trans-Australian RR; gold; some wool.

Tarcsa, Austria: see BAD TATZMANNSDORF.

Tarcu or **Tarcul** (tsär'kōō, –l), Rum. *Tarcu* or *Tarcul*, mountain group in W part of the Transylvanian Alps, SW Rumania, in Banat, c.20 mi. SW of Caransebes, NW of the Godeanu and WSW of the Retezat; rises to 7,402 ft. Extensive forests; magnetite deposits. Noted skiing facilities, especially in NW at Muntele Mic (alt. 5,290 ft.).

Tardajos (tär-dhä'hōs), town (pop. 1,036), Burgos prov., N Spain, 5 mi. W of Burgos; cereals, potatoes, livestock; cheese processing.

Tardelcuende (tär-dhĕlkwĕn'dā), town (pop. 697), Soria prov., N central Spain, on railroad and 15 mi. SW of Soria; cereals, truck produce, livestock; timber, resins. Mfg. of ceramics.

Tardes River (tärd), Creuse dept., central France, rises in Combrailles hills near Crocq, flows 40 mi. NNE, past Chambon-sur-Voueize, to the Cher 11 mi. above Montluçon.

Tardets-Sorholus (tärdā'-sôrôlüs'), village (pop. 870), Basses-Pyrénées dept., SW France, on Saison R. and 14 mi. WSW of Oloron-Sainte-Marie; woolen and linen milling. Basque pop.

Tardienta (tär-dhyĕn'tä), town (pop. 1,661), Huesca prov., NE Spain, 13 mi. SW of Huesca, in irrigated agr. area (sugar beets, cereals, alfalfa); flour milling, plaster mfg.

Tardoire River (tärdwär'), in Haute-Vienne and Charente depts., W France, rises near Chalus, flows 62 mi. NW, past Montbron and La Rochefoucauld to the Charente near Mansle. Waters lost by seepage reappear near Magnac-sur-Touvre to form the spring of Touvre R.

Tardosked (tär'dôshkĕt), Slovak *Tardošked*, village (pop. 6,689), S Slovakia, Czechoslovakia, 15 mi. S of Nitra; wheat, sugar beets.

Tarecuato (tärākwä'tō), town (pop. 2,146), Michoacán, central Mexico, on railroad and 15 mi. WSW of Zamora; corn, sugar cane, fruit, livestock.

Taree (tärē'), municipality (pop. 5,423), E New South Wales, Australia, on Manning R. and 80 mi. NE of Newcastle; dairying center.

Tarentaise (tärätĕz'), Alpine valley of upper Isère R., in Savoie dept., SE France, in Savoy Alps bet. Beaufortin (N) and Massif de la Vanoise (S). Extends c.30 mi. W from Little Saint Bernard Pass to Albertville. Its 10 hydroelectric plants power electrochemical works at Notre-Dame-de-Briançon, Saint-Marcel, La Bâthie. Chief town: Moutiers.

Tarentum, Italy: see TARANTO, city.

Tarentum (tûrĕn'tûm), industrial borough (pop. 9,540), Allegheny co., W central Pa., 17 mi. NE of Pittsburgh and on Allegheny R.; metal, wood, and paper products, glass, beverages; bituminous coal. On site of Indian village; laid out 1829, inc. 1842.

Taretan (tärä'tän), officially Taretan de Terán, town (pop. 1,836) Michoacán, central Mexico, 11 mi. SE of Uruapan; alt. 7,054 ft.; sugar cane, coffee.

Tarf (tärf), semi-arid depression in S High Plateaus of Constantine dept., NE Algeria, N of Khenchela. It is filled by several playa lakes (size changing in accordance with amount of rainfall), of which the Garaet et Tarf is largest. Livestock raising. Some cereals grown on N slope of the Aurès massif (S).

Tarfaia or **Tarfaya**, Sp. West Africa: see VILLA BENS.

Tarff Water (tärf), river, Kircudbright, Scotland, rises 7 mi. N of Kirkcudbright, flows 9 mi. S, past Tarff, to the Dee 2 mi. N of Kirkcudbright.

Tarf Water, river, Angus, Scotland, rises in Grampian Mts. 8 mi. S of Dinnet, flows 8 mi. SE to North Esk R. 9 mi. NW of Edzell.

Targhee Pass (tär"gē') (alt. 7,078 ft.), in Continental Divide, SW Mont., just S of Hebgen L. and W of Yellowstone Natl. Park. Used (1877) by Chief Joseph and Nez Percé Indians in retreat from U.S. troops.

Targon (tärgō'), village (pop. 281), Gironde dept., SW France, in Entre-deux-Mers, 12 mi. S of Libourne; winegrowing.

Targovishte (tŭrgô'vĭshtĕ), city (pop. 10,505), Kolarovgrad dist., E Bulgaria, on Vrana R. and 17 mi. W of Kolarovgrad; mfg. and handicraft center (cotton textiles, furniture); cartmaking, pottery. Developed as cultural center of Bulg. Moslems under Turkish rule. Captured 1878 by Russians and ceded to Bulgaria. Until 1909, Eski (Yeski) Dzhumaya.

Targoviste (tûrgô'vēshtĕ), Rum. *Târgoviște*, town (1948 pop. 26,038), Prahova prov., S central Rumania, in Walachia, on Ialomita R., on railroad and 48 mi. NW of Bucharest; commercial center; oil refining, distilling, flour milling, brick making. Seat of cavalry school Orthodox bishopric. Has several 16th- and 17th-cent. churches, of which the most remarkable is 16th-cent. cathedral with 9 towers. There are remains of 14th-cent. palace. The noted 15th-cent. monastery is now a cadets' school. It was ⊙ Walachia 1383–1698. The Turks were defeated here 1597. Pop. and importance decreased sharply with transfer of ⊙ to Bucharest.

Targu-Carbunesti or **Targul-Carbunesti** (tûr'gōō, –l, –kûrbōōnĕsht'), Rum. *Târgu-Cărbunesti* or *Târgul-Cărbunesti*, village (pop. 866), Gorj prov., SW Rumania, on railroad and 13 mi. SE of Targu-Jiu; lignite mining, lumbering, pottery making. Also called Carbunesti.

Targu-Cucului, Rumania: see PLAINESTI.

Targu-Frumos or **Targul-Frumos** (–frōō'môs), Rum. *Târgu-Frumos* or *Târgul-Frumos*, town (1948 pop. 4,665), Jassy prov., NE Rumania, in Moldavia, on railroad and 27 mi. W of Jassy; flour milling, wine trade. Has 16th-cent. church.

Targuist (tärgēst'), town (pop. 2,407), Rif territory; central Sp. Morocco, in Rif Mts., 30 mi. SW of Villa Sanjurjo; woodworking; pine and cedar forests.

Targu-Jiu or **Targul-Jiu** (–zhē'ōō), Rum. *Târgu-Jiu* or *Târgul-Jiu*, town (1948 pop. 17,698), ⊙ Gorj prov., SW Rumania, in Walachia, on Jiu R., on railroad and 140 mi. NW of Bucharest; trading center (notably for lumber, livestock, cheese); mfg. of cloth, furniture, woodwork, bricks; tanning. Has a school of ceramics, archaeological mus. Probably dates from 15th cent.

Targu-Lapus or **Targul-Lapus** (–lŭ'pōōs), Rum. *Târgu-Lăpuș*, or *Târgul-Lăpuș*, Hung. *Magyarlápos* (mŏ'dyŏrlä'pôsh), village (pop. 2,411), Baia-Mare prov., N Rumania, 22 mi. N of Dej. In Hungary, 1940–45.

Targu-Logresti or **Targul-Logresti** (–lôgrĕsht'), Rum. *Târgu-Logrești* or *Târgul-Logrești*, village (pop. 1,080), Gorj prov., SW Rumania, 14 mi. SE of Targu-Jiu.

Targu-Mures or **Targul-Mures** (–mōō'rĕsh), Rum. *Târgu-Mureș* or *Târgul-Mureș*, Ger. *Neumarkt* (noi'märkt), Hung. *Marosvásárhely* (mŏ'rôsh-vä"shärhā), city (1948 pop. 47,043), ⊙ Mures prov., central Rumania, in Transylvania, on Mures R. and 155 mi. NW of Bucharest; 46°33'N 24°34'E. Rail junction and cultural center of the Szekler land. Mfg. of sugar, beer, liquor, furniture, clay products, confectionery, meat preserves, soap, mirrors, dolls; oil refining. Brisk trade in lumber, grain, petroleum, wine, fruit, tobacco. Most of the city was rebuilt in 20th cent. after a great fire in 1876. Among remaining old structures are 15th-cent. Gothic Reformed Church within 17th-cent. fortifications (still partly preserved), 18th-cent. R.C. church. Targu-Mures is also known for its huge "Cultural Palace" which contains art gallery, ethnographical mus., city library, and music conservatory; Telekiana library, founded in 13th cent., has valuable manuscripts. Was first called Osorhei (14th cent.); became a royal free city (17th cent.). Rakoczy was crowned prince of Transylvania here (1704). Has predominantly Magyar (Szekler) pop. In Hungary, 1940–45.

Targu-Neamt or **Targul-Neamt** (–nyämts'), Rum. *Târgu-Neamț* or *Târgul-Neamț*, town (1948 pop. 8,948), Bacau prov., NE Rumania, in Moldavia, 24 mi. N of Piatra-Neamt; woodworking and trading center; mfg. of cloth, knitwear, cheese. Noted 14th-cent. Neamt monastery is 8 mi. NW.

Targu-Ocna or **Targul-Ocna** (–ôk'nä), Rum. *Târgu-Ocna* or *Târgul-Ocna*, town (pop. 9,796), Bacau prov., E central Rumania, in Moldavia, on railroad and 23 mi. SW of Bacau; large salt mines; stone quarrying; oil production; flour milling. Has 18th-cent. church.

Targu-Sacuesc or **Targul-Sacuesc** (–sŭkwĕsk'), Rum. *Târgu-Săcuesc* or *Târgul-Săcuesc*, Hung. *Kézdivásárhely* (käz'dēvä"shärhā), town (1948 pop. 5,424), Stalin prov., central Rumania, in Transylvania, on railroad and 19 mi. NE of Sfantu-Gheorghe; mfg. of alcohol and textiles; flour milling, brewing, lumbering. Over 90% pop. are Magyars. Also spelled *Târgu-Săcuiesc* and *Târgu-Secuesc*. In Hungary, 1940–45.

Targu-Sulita, Rumania: see SULITA.

Targyn (tŭrgĭn'), town (1948 pop. over 2,000), W East Kazakhstan oblast, Kazakh SSR, 30 mi. S of Ust-Kamenogorsk, in gold- and tin-mining area.

Tarhuna (tägōō'nä), town, Tripolitania, Libya, on the plateau Gebel Nefusa, on main road and 40 mi. SE of Tripoli; alt. 1,305 ft. Caravan center; barley, esparto grass, livestock.

Táriba (tä'rēbä), town (pop. 4,734), Táchira state, W Venezuela, in Andean spur, 3 mi. N of San Cristóbal; alt. 2,650 ft. Coffeegrowing center; sugar, tobacco, grain. Coal and sulphur deposits near by.

Tarifa (tärē'fä), city (pop. 6,362), Cádiz prov., S Spain, minor port on Strait of Gibraltar and southernmost town of continental Europe, adjoined S by Point Marroquí, 16 mi. SW of Gibraltar. Agr. (cereals, oranges, cattle, hogs) and fishing center (chiefly tuna). Tanning, fish canning, liquor distilling; lime quarrying. Of picturesque Moorish character; has near-by Roman ruins. Founded by Greeks, it became 1st Roman colony in Spain and was taken by the Moorish conqueror Tarik in 711.

Tariffville, Conn.: see SIMSBURY.

Tarija (tärē'hä), department (□ 9,570; 1949 pop. estimate 135,800), SE Bolivia; ⊙ Tarija. Bordered by San Juan (W) and Pilaya (N) rivers, Argentina (S), Paraguay (E). Situated on easternmost outliers of Eastern Cordillera of the Andes, descending toward the Chaco; drained by upper Pilcomayo, Bermejo, and Tarija rivers. Mainly an agr. area, with tropical products in lowlands (sugar cane, tobacco, cotton), vineyards in higher valleys (W) near Tarija, and barley and potatoes in hill slopes. Cattle raised near Villa Montes. Contains S portion of main Bolivian oil fields in Serranía de Aguaragüe (Sanandita, Bermejo oil fields). Highways lead to Villazón, Potosí, Santa Cruz, and Argentina. Main centers: Tarija, Villa Montes, Yacuiba.

Tarija, city (1949 pop. estimate 19,800), ⊙ Tarija dept. and Cercado prov., S Bolivia, on Tarija R. and 180 mi. SSE of Sucre, 400 mi. SE of La Paz, and on highway to Villazón; 21°34'S 64°47'W; alt. 6,421 ft. Important commercial center for local agr. products and Argentine imports; brewery. Airport. Site of city hall, cathedral, military hosp. Founded 1574 by Spaniards as trade center; named San Bernardo de Tarija. During its early years, suffered continuous attacks by Indians. One of purest nuclei of Sp. colonization. Troop concentration center during Chaco war.

Tarija River, Tarija dept., S Bolivia, rises in Serranía de Tarija 20 mi. NW of Tarija, flows 150 mi. SW and S to the Bermejo near Fortín Campero. Receives Itau R. (left), together forming part of Argentina-Bolivia border. Also called Guadalquivir R. (gwädälkēvēr') in upper course.

Tarikaikea River, New Guinea: see MAMBERAMO RIVER.

Tarikere (tŭ'rĭkĕrĕ), town (pop. 8,858), Kadur dist., W Mysore, India, 27 mi. N of Chikmagalur; rail junction; trades in rice, grain, betel nuts. Rail spur to Narasimharajapura serves iron mines and coffee, cardamom, and pepper estates in Baba Budan Range (SW).

Tarim (tärēm'), town (1946 pop. 8,264), Kathiri state, Eastern Aden Protectorate, 14 mi. ENE of Seiyun, at N side of the Wadi Hadhramaut; agr. center in date-growing area; native handicrafts (gold- and silverwork); lime burning. Was autonomous sultanate until merger with Seiyun in 1945. Sometimes spelled Terim.

Tarímbaro (tärēm'bärō), town (pop. 1,733), Michoacán, central Mexico, 6 mi. N of Morelia; alt. 6,178 ft.; cereals, fruit, livestock.

Tarime (tärē'mā), village, Lake Prov., N Tanganyika, near Kenya border, 40 mi. ENE of Musoma; coffee, cotton, peanuts, corn. Gold deposits along Mara R. (S).

Tarimoro (tärēmō'rō), town (pop. 4,105), Guanajuato, central Mexico, on central plateau, 30 mi. SW of Querétaro; alt. 5,813 ft.; agr. center (grain, alfalfa, sugar cane, fruit, vegetables, stock).

Tarim River (tärēm', därēm'), chief river of Sinkiang prov., China, formed 50 mi. SE of Aksu by union of Aksu and Yarkand rivers (intermittently joined by the Khotan R.), flows c.1,300 mi. E, along N rim of Taklamakan Desert, to the Lob Nor basin, where the shifting channels of the lower course gave rise to the LOB NOR "problem." The Tarim basin, a vast closed depression bet. the Kunlun mts. (S), the Pamir (W), and the Tien Shan (N), is occupied largely by the Taklamakan Desert.

Tarind Muhammad Panah (tŭrĭnd' mōōhŭm'mŭd pŭnä'), town (pop. 872), Bahawalpur state, W Pakistan, 50 mi. SW of Bahawalpur; local market for wheat, dates, rice. Other spellings: Tarinda Muhammad Panah, Taranda (Tarrandah) Mohammad Panah.

Tarire River, Costa Rica: see SIXAOLA RIVER.

Taritalu River, New Guinea: see IDENBURG RIVER.

Tarjan (tŏr'yän), Hung. *Tarján*, town (pop. 2,162), Komarom-Esztergom co., N Hungary, 28 mi. WNW of Budapest; vineyards, grain, horses.

Tarkany (tär'känyŭ), Hung. *Tárkány*, town (pop. 2,822), Komarom-Esztergom co., N Hungary, 17 mi. ESE of Györ; butter, cheese, dairy farming; grain, tobacco.

Tarkastad (tär'kŭstät"), town (pop. 2,869), SE Cape Prov., U. of So. Afr., at foot of Winterberg mts., 40 mi. W of Queenstown; rail terminus; sheep-raising center; grain, feed crops, fruit.

Tarkhan, Cape, or **Cape Tarkhankut** (tŭrkhän', –khŭnkōōt'), extreme W point of Crimea, Russian SFSR, on Black Sea; 45°20'N 32°30'E.

Tarkio (tär'kēō), city (pop. 2,221), Atchison co., NW Mo., on Tarkio R. and 55 mi. NW of St. Joseph. Grain; ships, cattle, hogs. Tarkio Col. here. Laid out 1880.

Tarkio River, in SW Iowa and NW Mo., rises in Montgomery co., Iowa, flows c.130 mi. generally S to the Missouri 33 mi. NW of St. Joseph.

Tarko-Sale (tŭrkô"-sŭlyĕ'), village, E Yamal-Nenets Natl. Okrug, Tyumen oblast, Russian SFSR, 350 mi. ESE of Salekhard; trading post. Formerly called Tarsale.

Tarkwa (tär'kwä), town (pop. 7,649), Western Prov., SW Gold Coast colony, 30 mi. NNW of Takoradi; rail junction (spur to Prestea); major gold-mining center. Rubber plantation. Hq. dept. of mines. Important manganese mines of Nsuta are 4 mi. S.

Tarlac (tär'läk), province (□ 1,175; 1948 pop. 327,018), central Luzon, Philippines; ⊙ Tarlac. Drained by tributaries of the Agno. Largely a plain; mountainous in W section. Chief crops: coconuts, rice, sugar.

Tarlac, town (1939 pop. 16,350; 1948 municipality pop. 64,597), ⊙ Tarlac prov., central Luzon, Philippines, 65 mi. NNW of Manila, and on Tarlac R. (tributary of Agno R.); rail junction; trade center for agr. area (coconuts, rice, sugar cane).

Tarleton, town and parish (pop. 2,407), W Lancashire, England, 7 mi. SW of Preston; cotton milling; agr. market.

Tarlton, village (pop. 371), Pickaway co., S central Ohio, 9 mi. ESE of Circleville.

Tarm, town (pop. 1,502), Ringkobing amt, W Jutland, Denmark, 17 mi. SE of Ringkobing; furniture.

Tarma (tär'mä), city (pop. 7,876), ⊙ Tarma prov. (pop. 77,801, including c.10,000 Indians), Junín dept., central Peru, in Cordillera Central of the Andes, on Tarma R. (a headstream of the Chanchamayo) and 15 mi. ENE of La Oroya (connected by highway); alt. 10,105 ft. Transit center on roads to Chanchamayo R. valley and E Peru; corn, fruit, vegetables.

Tarn (tärn), department (□ 2,232; pop. 298,117), in Languedoc, S France; ⊙ Albi. Region bet. Aquitaine Basin (W) and Massif Central (E and SE). Drained by the Tarn and its tributaries (Agout, Dadou, Aveyron). Agr. (wheat, vegetables, potatoes) in lowlands; dairying and livestock raising in the Monts de Lacaune and Montagne Noire (S and SE); winegrowing along streams. Dept. is heavily industrialized, with coal-mining dist. (Albi-Carmaux) and textile-mfg. region (Thoré and upper Agout R. valleys). Chief towns: Albi (metallurgy, glass and rayon plants), Castres (textile, furniture factories), Mazamet (wool, hides), Carmaux (coal mines), and Graulhet (leather working).

Tarnab (tŭrnäb′), village, Peshawar dist., central North-West Frontier Prov., W Pakistan, 7 mi. E of Peshawar; model agr. and fruit farm (research station).

Tarnak (tûrnäk′), village (pop. 3,117), Vratsa dist., NW Bulgaria, 5 mi. E of Byala Slatina; livestock, grain, legumes.

Tarnak River (tŭrnäk′), SE Afghanistan, rises 45 mi. SW of Ghazni, flows 210 mi. SW, along Kabul-Kandahar highway, past Shahjui, Kalat-i-Ghilzai, Jaldak, and Kandahar oasis, to Arghastan R. 17 mi. SW of Kandahar.

Tarna River (tŏr′nŏ), N Hungary, rises in Matra Mts., flows 50 mi. S, past Kal, to the Zagyva E of Jaszbereny.

Tarnava (tûrnä′vä), village (pop. 3,976), Vratsa dist., NW Bulgaria, 5 mi. NW of Byala Slatina; grain, livestock.

Tarnaveni (tûrnuvān′), Rum. *Târnăveni*, town (1948 pop. 7,585), Mures prov., central Rumania, in Transylvania, on railroad and 20 mi. NE of Blaj; noted for synthetic-nitrogen installations and other chemical works based on abundant local supplies of methane. Produces sulphuric acid and by-products, soda, ammonia, chlorine, carbides and fertilizers. Has glass and vulcanizing works, brick-kilns and foundries, and a large power plant. Was ⊙ Tarnava-Mica dept. until 1926. Former name, Diciosanmartin (Rum. *Diciosânmartin*, Hung. *Dicsőszenmárton*), official until 1930, still much used.

Tarn-et-Garonne (tärn-ā-gärôn′), department (□ 1,441; pop. 167,664), SW France; ⊙ Montauban. Lies in Aquitaine Basin. Drained by Garonne, Tarn, and Aveyron rivers. Rich agr. area (wheat, corn, wine, vegetables, fruits, cattle and poultry). Known for its plums and grapes. Food processing, hatmaking, and textile milling are chief industries. Principal towns are Montauban (commercial center), Moissac (fruit market), and Castelsarrasin. Dept., formed 1808 from parts of neighboring depts., includes portions of old Languedoc, Guienne, and Gascogne provinces.

Tarnobrzeg (tärnôb′zhĕk), town (pop. 4,140), Rzeszow prov., SE Poland, port on the Vistula, on railroad and 40 mi. NNW of Rzeszow; brewing, mfg. of baskets. Castle.

Tarnogski Gorodok or **Tarnogskiy Gorodok** (tŭrnôk″skē gŭrŭdôk′), village, N Vologda oblast, Russian SFSR, 45 mi. NE of Totma; flax.

Tarnopol, Ukrainian SSR: see TERNOPOL.

Tarnov (tär′nŭv), village (pop. 74), Platte co., E central Nebr., 14 mi. NNW of Columbus and on branch of Platte R.

Tarnova (tûr′nôvä), Rum. *Târnova*, Hung. *Tornova* (tôr′nôvŏ), village (pop. 2,719), Arad prov., W Rumania, 25 mi. NE of Arad; agr. center.

Tarnova, Moldavian SSR: see TYRNOVO.

Tarnow (tär′nōōf), Pol. *Tarnów*, city (pop. 33,108), Krakow prov., S Poland, near Biala R. mouth, 45 mi. E of Cracow. Rail junction; mfg. of machinery, sawmilling, flour milling; lace and embroidery work, weaving; brickworks. R.C. bishopric. Has cathedral (built c.1400), 14th-cent. town hall, castle ruins, mus. Founded 12th cent.; under Austrian rule, 1772–1919.

Tarnowskie Gory (tärnôf′skyĕ gōō′rĭ), Pol. *Tarnowskie Góry*, town (pop. 18,427), Katowice prov., S Poland, 15 mi. NNW of Katowice. Rail junction; coal and iron-ore mining; ironworks; lumbering, mfg. of bricks, cement ware; brewing. Passed from Germany to Poland in 1921. Formerly called Tarnowice, Ger. *Tarnowitz*.

Tarn River (tärn), in Lozère, Aveyron, Tarn, and Tarn-et-Garonne depts., S central and S France, rises in the Cévennes on S slopes of Mont Lozère, flows 235 mi. generally W, through the CAUSSES (where it forms the scenic Tarn gorge bet. Sainte-Énimie and Peyreleau), past Millau, Albi, Gaillac, and Montauban, to the Garonne 3 mi. below Moissac. Receives the Aveyron (right) and the Jonte, Dourbie, and Agout rivers (left).

Tarnsjo (târn′shû″), Swedish *Tärnsjö*, village (pop. 1,242), Vastmanland co., S central Sweden, 25 mi. E of Avesta; tanneries, flour mills, woodworks.

Tarn Taran (tŭrn′ tä′rŭn), town (pop. 16,607), Amritsar dist., W Punjab, India, 12 mi. SSE of Amritsar; agr. market center (wheat, oilseeds, cotton, gram); hand-loom weaving, cotton ginning, oilseed pressing, mfg. of rubber goods, iron vessels. Leper asylum 1 mi. W. Has sacred Sikh tank.

Taro (tä′rō), village, Naga Hills dist., Upper Burma, on Chindwin R. and 100 mi. NW of Myitkyina.

Taroetoeng, Indonesia: see TARUTUNG.

Taromskoye (tŭrôm′skŭyŭ), W suburb (1926 pop. 4,298), of Dnepropetrovsk, Dnepropetrovsk oblast, Ukrainian SSR, on right bank of Dnieper R. and 12 mi. from city center; granite quarries. Also spelled Taramskoye.

Taroom, village (pop. 468), E central Queensland, Australia, on Dawson R. and 135 mi. NW of Brisbane; rail terminus; cattle, wheat.

Taro River (tä′rô), N central Italy, rises in Ligurian Apennines 10 mi. NE of Chiavari, flows 78 mi. NNE, past Borgo Val di Taro and Fornovo di Taro, to Po R. 8 mi. W of Casalmaggiore. Receives Ceno and Stirone rivers (left).

Tarouca (tŭrō′kŭ), town (pop. 596), Viseu dist., N central Portugal, 6 mi. S of Lamego; cottage industry. Its church was founded in 12th cent.

Taroudant (tärōōdänt′), town (pop. 12,877), Agadir frontier region, SW Fr. Morocco, in fertile Sous valley bet. the High Atlas (N) and the Anti-Atlas (S), 45 mi. E of Agadir; 30°29′N 8°53′W; commercial center with active trade in fruits and early vegetables; olive-oil pressing, plaster mfg. Noted handicraft manufactures are leather bags and copperware. Bastioned walls (17th-18th cent.) enclose town and fine olive groves. Of anc. origin, Taroudant was occupied by the Almoravide and Merinide Berber dynasties, and was a residence of the Saadian sultans. In 16th cent. it traded with the Sudan. Taken by French 1917.

Tarpa (tŏr′pŏ), town (pop. 4,202), Szatmar-Bereg co., NE Hungary, near the Tisza, 38 mi. ENE of Nyiregyhaza; processes hemp, flax; grain, tobacco, cattle, sheep.

Tarpaulin Cove, SE Mass., small bight (c.½ mi. across) in S shore of Naushon Isl., c.6 mi. SW of Woods Hole; lighthouse. Was a pirates' haven; reputedly last port of call for Capt. Kidd.

Tarpon Springs, city (pop. 4,323), Pinellas co., W Fla., port on Anclote R. (bridged here) near its mouth on the Gulf, 23 mi. NW of Tampa; a major sponge-fishing center and market; mfg. of phosphoric compounds. Sponge industry founded by Greek divers in 1905. City has colorful Greek religious festivals which draw many visitors.

Tarporley (tär′pŭlē, tär′plē), former urban district (1931 pop. 2,452), W central Cheshire, England, 10 mi. ESE of Chester; agr. market for dairying region. Near by is a steeplechase course. Has medieval church and 16th-cent. mansion.

Tarpum Bay (tär′pŭm), town (pop. 611), central Bahama Isls., on W shore of S central Eleuthera Isl., 13 mi. S of Governor's Harbour, 70 mi. E of Nassau; 25°N 76°13′W. Pineapple growing.

Tarquinia (tärkwē′nyä), town (pop. 6,368), Viterbo prov., Latium, central Italy, on a height overlooking Tyrrhenian Sea, near Marta R., 11 mi. N of Civitavecchia; paper mills, foundry, cement-works. Saltworks 4 mi. SW. Bishopric. Has cathedral and two 13th-cent. Romanesque-Gothic churches. In Vitelleschi palace (enlarged 1436–39) is mus. of notable Etruscan antiquities collected from near-by necropolis of anc. Tarquinii, once a chief city of the Etruscan League, later (1307) destroyed by inhabitants of Corneto. Called Corneto and Corneto Tarquinia until 1922.

Tarraco, Spain: see TARRAGONA, city.

Tarraconensis (tă″rŭkōnĕn′sĭs), anc. Roman prov., comprising most of N, central, E, and SE Spain; ⊙ was Tarraco, the present-day TARRAGONA.

Tarrafal (tŭrŭfäl′), town, Cape Verde Isls., near N tip of São Tiago Isl., 30 mi. NW of Praia; 15°17′N 23°46′W. Anchorage; fishing.

Tarragona (tărŭgō′nŭ, Sp. tärägō′nä), town (1939 pop. 1,642), Davao prov., SE Mindanao, Philippines, on coast 65 mi. E of Davao; abacá, coconuts.

Tarragona, province (□ 2,426; pop. 339,299), NE Spain, in Catalonia, on the Mediterranean; ⊙ Tarragona. Occupied by coastal range of Catalonia and fertile coastal plain. Drained in SW by the Ebro, which forms delta projecting into sea. Saltworks in delta area. Lead, marble, and gypsum deposits. Predominantly agr., with large exports of wine and olive oil; grows almonds, fruit, hazelnuts, cereals, rice (Ebro delta). Mfg.: chemicals, liqueurs, soap, cotton fabrics, knit goods. Chief towns: Tarragona, Reus, Tortosa, Valls, San Carlos de la Rápita, Amposta, Gandesa, Vendrell.

Tarragona, anc. *Tarraco*, city (pop. 33,708), ⊙ Tarragona prov., NE Spain, in Catalonia, at mouth of small Francolí R. on the Mediterranean, 50 mi. SW of Barcelona, and on fertile coastal plain (Campo de Tarragona); 41°7′N 1°15′E. Communications and commercial center with large wine exports. Mfg. of liqueurs, tobacco, pharmaceuticals, electrical equipment, linen, laces; sulphur and olive-oil refining, aluminum processing. Fishing. Noted liqueur made by Fr. Carthusian monks who settled here after they were expelled (1903) from Grande Chartreuse monastery. Old town, with remains of Roman ramparts, is crowded on slope of steep hill crowned by fine Romanesque-transitional cathedral (12th-13th cent.) with adjoining cloister, and by archiepiscopal palace. Town hall contains provincial archaeological mus. Of Iberian origin, the town fell (3d cent. B.C.) to Romans and became ⊙ Hispania Tarraconensis prov. Passed (8th cent.) to Moors and (11th cent.) to Christians. Sacked by the French in 1811. Its prosperity declined with capture of much of its trade by Barcelona and Valencia. Its archbishop shares title of primate of Spain with archbishop of Toledo. Near by is impressive Roman aqueduct (c.22 mi. long; restored in 19th cent. and still in use).

Tarraleah (tă″rŭlē′ŭ), village (pop. 201), central Tasmania, 60 mi. NW of Hobart and on Derwent R.; hydroelectric plant; sheep.

Tarrandah Mohammad Panah, W Pakistan: see TARIND MUHAMMAD PANAH.

Tarrant (tă′rŭnt), county (□ 877; pop. 361,253), N Texas; ⊙ FORT WORTH, commercial, industrial center of wide region. Drained by West and Clear forks of Trinity R., here joining; includes Worth and Eagle Mtn. lakes (recreation, water supply). Dairying, agr. (grains, cotton, peanuts, fruit, truck), livestock (beef cattle, hogs, poultry, sheep, goats). Oil refining, meat packing, grain milling and shipping, diversified mfg. at Fort Worth. Formed 1849.

Tarrant or **Tarrant City**, city (pop. 7,571), Jefferson co., N central Ala.; N suburb of Birmingham; cast-iron pipe and pipe fittings, calcium carbide.

Tarra River (tä′rä), affluent (50 mi. long) of Catatumbo R., Zulia state, NW Venezuela; oil fields along its course, centered at La Paloma.

Tarrasa (tärä′sä), city (pop. 43,930), Barcelona prov., NE Spain, in Catalonia, 15 mi. NW of Barcelona; leading textile center; mfg. of knit goods, textile machinery, dyes, chemical fertilizers, soap, toys, cement, chocolate; tanning, sawmilling, olive-oil processing. Has textile trade school. Reservoir and hydroelectric plant near by. Has Romanesque church and Gothic town hall. Near by is ruined castle of Egara on site of a Roman colony.

Tarrazú, San Marcos de, Costa Rica: see SAN MARCOS.

Tárrega (tä′rāgä), city (pop. 5,891), Lérida prov., NE Spain, 7 mi. WSW of Cervera; industrial and commercial center on fertile Urgel plain; mfg. of flour products, soap, knit goods; olive-oil processing, flour milling. Livestock, cereals, wine, vegetables.

Tar River, NE N.C., rises in Person co. E of Roxboro, flows 217 mi. generally SE, past Louisburg, Rocky Mount, Tarboro, Greenville (head of navigation), and Washington to Pamlico Sound 10 mi. S of Belhaven. Below Washington, its estuary (38 mi. long, 1–5 mi. wide) is called Pamlico R.

Tarryall Creek, central Colo., rises in Front Range, NW Park co.; flows 50 mi. SE, past Tarryall Mts., to S.Platte R. NNW of Florissant.

Tarryall Mountains, in Front Range, central Colo., just W of South Platte R. and N of Tarryall Creek. Chief peaks: Tarryall Peak (11,300 ft.), North Tarryall Peak (11,400 ft.), Buffalo Peak (11,627 ft.), and Bison Peak (12,400 ft.). Buffalo Peak was formerly known as Freeman or Freemans Peak.

Tarrytown. **1** Village (pop. 250), Montgomery co., E central Ga., 11 mi. NW of Vidalia. **2** Residential village (pop. 8,851), Westchester co., SE N.Y., on E bank of the Hudson, opposite Nyack (ferry), and 6 mi. NW of White Plains; automobile assembly plants; mfg. of clothing, wood products. Summer resort. Seat of Marymount Col. for women. Near by are Washington Irving's home (at IRVINGTON) and Castle Philipse (in North Tarrytown). Settled by Dutch in 17th cent.; inc. 1870.

Tarsale, Russian SFSR: see TARKO-SALE.

Tarshiha, Israel: see MEONA.

Tarshin or **Tarshien**, Malta: see TARXIEN.

Tarsia (tär′syä), village (pop. 1,860), Cosenza prov., Calabria, S Italy, 14 mi. SSE of Castrovillari.

Tarsus (tär′sŭs), city (1950 pop. 33,822), Icel prov., S Turkey, in SE Asia Minor, on Tarsus R. (anc. Cydnus), on railroad, and 16 mi. ENE of Mersin, 22 mi. W of Adana, 10 mi. from the Mediterranean; agr. center (sesame, wheat, barley, beans); cotton milling. Copper, zinc, chromium, and coal near by. Ruins remain of the celebrated anc. city which became ⊙ of Cilicia and was the birthplace of St. Paul. Near the Cilician Gates, it flourished particularly under the Romans and was famed for its notable citizens.

Tarsus River, anc. *Cydnus* (sĭd′nŭs), S Turkey, flows c.95 mi. S from Taurus Mts., past Tarsus, to the Mediterranean.

Tarta, Turkmen SSR: see KIANLY.

Tartagal (tärtägäl′). **1** Town (1947 pop. 10,155), N Salta prov., Argentina, on railroad and 65 mi. NNE of Orán; petroleum and lumber center; sawmilling, plywood and furniture mfg. **2** Town (pop. estimate 500), N Santa Fe prov., Argentina, on railroad and 37 mi. NNW of Reconquista; lumbering center; sawmills and quebracho-extracting plants.

Tartar, in Rus. names: see TATAR.

Tartaro River (tärtä′rô), N Italy, formed near Isola della Scala by union of several streams, flows 50 mi. ESE and E, bet. Po and Adige rivers, through the Polesine, to the Adriatic, which it enters 15 mi. E of Adria as the Po di Levante. Canalized in several places. Receives Tione R. (right).

Tartary (tär′tŭrē), name applied after 13th cent. to the vast areas of Eurasia overrun by the Tatars

(Tartars) under Mongol leadership. At its greatest extent, Tartary was the area bet. the Russian principalities and the Pacific, bet. 35°N and 55°N. After the break-up of the empire of Jenghiz Khan, the name European Tartary or Little Tartary was applied to the area held by the Golden Horde, while Asiatic Tartary or Great Tartary applied to Siberia and Central Asia. The name Little Tartary was ultimately restricted to the Crimean khanate. An unusual, though etymologically correct form, is Tatary. Many Tatars live in the TATAR AUTONOMOUS SOVIET SOCIALIST REPUBLIC.

Tartas (tärtäs'), village (pop. 1,601), Landes dept., SW France, on Midouze R. and 15 mi. NE of Dax; market (lumber, livestock, cereals), mfg. of resinous products.

Tartas River (tŭrtäs'), NW Novosibirsk oblast, Russian SFSR, rises in Vasyuganye marshes, flows W, past Severnoye, and SW, past Vengerovo, to Om R. 40 mi. NE of Tatarsk; c.200 mi. long.

Tartous, Syria: see TARTUS.

Tartu (tär'tōō), Ger. and Swedish *Dorpat* (dôr'pät), Rus. (until 1917) *Yuryev* or *Yur'yev* (yōōr'yĕf), city (1934 pop. 58,876; 1947 pop. estimate 71,000), E Estonia, port on Ema R. and 100 mi. SE of Tallinn, on Tallinn-Riga RR; 58°23'N 26°23'E. Estonia's 2d-largest city and noted univ. town; rail junction; mfg. of agr. machinery, telephone equipment, aluminum ware, textiles, tobacco products; tile making, sawmilling, agr. processing (tanning, meat packing, brewing, starch mfg.). Univ. (founded 1632 by Gustavus Adolphus) has botanical garden and 18th-cent. observatory; art and teachers colleges. Built around old fortified hill topped by restored 13th-cent. cathedral (site of univ. library), modern Tartu has mainly 18th- and early 19th-cent. bldgs.; arched granite bridge over Ema R. was built (1783) under Catherine II. Natl. Mus. of Estonia is on NE outskirts. City's founding (1030) as Yuryev is ascribed to Kievan duke Yaroslav. Following its capture (1224) by Livonian Knights, it was named Dorpat and developed as one of Livonia's leading cities. Joined Hanseatic League in 14th cent.; passed in 1561 to Poland, in 1629 to Sweden; occupied (1710) by Russia and inc. into govt. of Livonia. First known as Derpt (Russified form of Dorpat), later (after 1893) under its original Rus. name of Yuryev; assumed Estonian name of Tartu after passing (1918) to Estonia. In Second World War, occupied (1941–44) by Germans.

Tartus (tärtōōs'), Fr. *Tartous*, town, Latakia prov., W Syria, on the Mediterranean, 40 mi. S of Latakia, opposite RUAD isl.; fishing, agr. (grapes, oranges, olives, cotton, cereals). Founded in anc. times by colonists from Ruad and called Antaradus, it flourished in Roman and Byzantine times, and in the Middle Ages, when it was renamed Tortosa, it was important base of the Crusaders. Partly destroyed (1188) by Saladin, finally captured (1291) by the Arabs. There is a cathedral built 12th–13th cent. by Crusaders and ruins of an old castle.

Tarua, Thailand: see THA RUA.

Tarucachi (tärōōkä'chē), town (pop. 806), Tacna dept., S Peru, 4 mi. SSE of Tarata.

Tarui (tärōō'ē). **1** Town (pop. 6,558), Gifu prefecture, central Honshu, Japan, 5 mi. WNW of Ogaki; rice, raw silk. **2** Town (pop. 4,533), Osaka prefecture, S Honshu, Japan, on Osaka Bay, 11 mi. NNE of Wakayama, in agr. area (rice, wheat, tobacco); poultry. Cotton textiles, sake, soy sauce.

Taruma, Japan: see KOBE.

Tarumizu (tärōō'mēzōō), town (pop. 27,511), Kagoshima prefecture, S Kyushu, Japan, on W Osumi Peninsula, on E shore of Kagoshima Bay, 11 mi. SE of Kagoshima; agr. center (rice, wheat); raw silk, lumber. Site of feudal castle.

Tarumovka (tŭrōōmôf'kŭ), village (1939 pop. over 500), E Grozny oblast, Russian SFSR, near railroad, on N delta arm of Terek R. (irrigation) and 18 mi. NNW of Kizlyar; wheat, corn, rice.

Tarusa (tŭrōō'sŭ), city (1938 pop. 3,800), NE Kaluga oblast, Russian SFSR, on Oka R. and 38 mi. ENE of Kaluga; garment mfg. Dates from 1260. During Second World War, an advanced position briefly held (1941) by Germans.

Tarutao, Pulo (pōō'lō tärōōtou'), Thai island in Strait of Malacca, 10 mi. off Satun; 15 mi. long, 5 mi. wide.

Tarutino (tŭrōō'tyĭnŭ), village (1930 pop. 5,795; 1941 pop. 528), NW Izmail oblast, Ukrainian SSR 60 mi. W of Belgorod-Dnestrovski; road junction; agr. center; mfg. of textiles, leather. Founded, after 1812, as Ger. agr. colony; Ger. pop. repatriated in 1940.

Tarut Island (tărōōt'), in Persian Gulf, Saudi Arabia, bet. Ras Tanura peninsula and Qatif, 8 mi. N of Dammam; 3 mi. long, 3 mi. wide; pearling; agr. (dates, vegetables, fruit).

Tarutung or **Taroetoeng** (both: tärōōtōōng'), town (pop. 3,436), N central Sumatra, Indonesia, 25 mi. NE of Sibolga, on high plateau; alt. 3,530 ft.; trade center in area producing coffee and resin.

Tarvast, Estonia: see MUSTLA.

Tarves (tär'vĭs), agr. village and parish (pop. 2,026), E Aberdeen, Scotland, 5 mi. NE of Old Meldrum.

Tarvin, village and parish (pop. 1,122), W Cheshire, England, 5 mi. E of Chester; dairy farming. Has church dating from 14th and 15th cent.

Tarvisio (tärvē'zyô), Ger. *Tarvis*, Slovenian *Trbiž*, town (pop. 1,985), Udine prov., Friuli-Venezia Giulia, NE Italy, near Austrian and Yugoslav borders, 34 mi. NNE of Udine. Commercial center; customs station on Camporosso Pass road; steelworks. Resort (alt. 2,464 ft.) picturesquely situated in Carnic Alps.

Tarvisio Pass, Italy: see CAMPOROSSO PASS.

Tarvisium, Italy: see TREVISO, city.

Tarvita (tärvē'tä), town (pop. c.2,400), Chuquisaca dept., S central Bolivia, on road and 12 mi. NNW of Azurduy; corn, wheat, barley. Known as Villa Orías in early 1940s.

Tarvo River, Bolivia: see PARAGUÁ RIVER.

Tarxien (tärshēn'), town (pop. 4,607), SE Malta, 2 mi. S of Valletta; forage, potatoes; goats, sheep. Famous for its enormous troglodyte temples with prehistoric paintings on ceilings. Has parish church (1610) and 18th-cent. St. Bartholomew church. Sometimes Tarshin or Tarshien.

Tarzana (tärză'nŭ), suburban section of LOS ANGELES city, Los Angeles co., S Calif., in San Fernando Valley, 9 mi. SW of San Fernando; residential; alfalfa, truck farms; nurseries.

Tarzo (tär'tsô), village (pop. 599), Treviso prov., Veneto, N Italy, 3 mi. W of Vittorio Veneto, in silk- and fruitgrowing region.

Tas-Buget (täs"-bōōgyĕt'), town (1948 pop. over 500), central Kzyl-Orda oblast, Kazakh SSR, on the Syr Darya, near Kzyl-Orda, on rail spur of Trans-Caspian RR. Site of Kzyl-Orda irrigation dam and reservoir.

Taschereau (täshŭrō'), village (pop. estimate 1,000), W Que., bet. small L. Taschereau (N) and Robertson L. (S), 30 mi. NNE of Rouyn; railroad junction; lumbering, dairying.

Täschhorn, Switzerland: see MISCHABELHÖRNER.

Tascosa (tăskō'sŭ), ghost town, Oldham co., extreme N Texas, in the Panhandle, on S Canadian R. and 30 mi. NW of Amarillo. Founded as sheep camp in 1870s, became a booming cow town of 1880s. In 1939, a boys' ranch for underprivileged youths established here.

Taseko, Mount (tŭsē'kō) (10,057 ft.), SW B.C., in Coast Mts., 140 mi. N of Vancouver.

Tasermiut (täsĕr'myōōt), inlet (45 mi. long, 1–3 mi. wide) of Atlantic, S Greenland; 60°15'N 44°45'W. Extends NE from mouth at Nanortalik to edge of inland icecap. In 10th cent., site of Norse settlements of *Vik in Ketilsfjord* or *Aroskikja* (site of Augustinian monastery), and of *Vatsdal* or *Vazdal*.

Taserssuag Lake, Greenland: see NUGSSUAK.

Taseyeva River (tŭsyä'ŭvŭ), S Krasnoyarsk Territory, Russian SFSR, formed 80 mi. E of Kazachinskoye by confluence of Chuna and Biryusa rivers; flows 72 mi. ESE to Angara R. 50 mi. above its mouth on the Yenisei. Length, including Chuna R., 675 mi.

Taseyevo (–ŭvŭ), village (1948 pop. over 500), SE Krasnoyarsk Territory, Russian SFSR, 80 mi. NW of Kansk, in agr. area.

Tasgaon (täs'goun), town (pop. 11,587), Satara South dist., S central Bombay, India, 12 mi. NNE of Sangli; market center for millet, wheat, peanuts.

Tasha River, China: see SHA RIVER, Honan prov.

Tashauz (tŭshŭōōs'), oblast (□ 29,000; 1946 pop. estimate 300,000), N Turkmen SSR; ⊙ Tashauz. Drained by arms of the Amu Darya (N); includes W Khiva oasis (N) and the desert Kara-Kum (S). Cotton, cattle, horses in irrigated oasis; goats, camels, karakul sheep in near-by desert. Chardzhou-Kungrad RR passes through extreme NE. Pop.: Turkmen, Uzbeks. Formed 1939.

Tashauz, city (1939 pop. over 10,000), ⊙ Tashauz oblast, Turkmen SSR, in Khiva oasis, 230 mi. NNE of Ashkhabad; 41°50'N 59°58'E. Cotton-ginning center; cottonseed oil, silk, rugs. Teachers col. Its port, on the Amu Darya, is Pristan-Lavak (linked by railroad).

Tashi Chho (tä'shē chô') or **Trashi Cho** (trä'shē) fortified town [Bhutanese *dzong*], W Bhutan, on upper Raidak R. and 16 mi. SW of Punakha. Major lamasery (pop. c.300) of Bhutan here. Former summer ⊙ Bhutan. Founded 1581.

Tashiding, India: see NAMCHI.

Tashigong (tä'shēgông), Chinese *T'a-shih-kang* (tä'-shŭgäng'), village, SW Tibet, on the upper Indus, on main Leh-Gartok trade route and 70 mi. NW of Gartok; alt. 13,030 ft. Lamasery.

T'a-shih-kang, Tibet: see TASHIGONG.

Tashihkiao or **Ta-shih-ch'iao** (both: dä'shŭ'chyou'), town, SW Liaotung prov., Manchuria, near Gulf of Liaotung, 95 mi. SW of Mukden; rail junction on South Manchuria RR, serving Yingkow; magnesite-mining center; soapstone mining; cotton, silk, fruit, vegetables.

T'a-shih-pu Hu, Tibet: see TRASHI BHUP TSO.

Tashi Lumpo or **Trashi Lhümpo** (tä'shē lōōm'pō) [Tibetan, =mount of blessing], lamasery (pop. c.4,000), SE Tibet, 1 mi. SSW of Shigatse. One of best-known and largest lamaseries in Tibet. Founded in 15th cent., its grand lama, known as Panchen Lama, Panchen Rimpoche, or Tashi Lama, is regarded as the reincarnation of the Buddha Amitabha and 2d in rank to the Dalai Lama. The 9th Panchen Lama fled (1924) to China, where he died in 1937. The living Buddha of KUMBUM lamasery became his successor. Mausoleums of Panchen Lamas.

Tashino (tä'shēnŭ), town (1939 pop. 7,650), S Gorki oblast, Russian SFSR, near Alatyr R., 36 mi. S of Arzamas; iron-mining center; iron smelter, sawmills.

Tashkala, Russian SFSR: see CHERNORECHYE.

Tashkent (tăshkĕnt', täsh–, Rus. tŭshkyĕnt'), oblast (□ 5,900; 1946 pop. estimate 1,200,000), NE Uzbek SSR; ⊙ Tashkent. Bounded NE by Chatkal Range, E by Kurama Range (sheep and goat raising on slopes); drained by the Syr Darya and its affluents, Chirchik and Angren rivers. Extensive irrigation in lowlands (including part of the Golodnaya Step); cotton, fiber plants, rice, orchards; some dry farming (wheat). Industrial area centered at Tashkent and Begovat (site of Farkhad hydroelectric plant; metallurgical works); cotton ginning, fiber-plant and food processing. Coal mining at ANGREN; copper at Almalyk. Trans-Caspian RR passes N-S. Pop.: Uzbeks, Russians, Kazakhs. Formed 1938; an earlier Tashkent oblast existed 1924–26.

Tashkent, city (1926 pop. 323,613; 1939 pop. 585,005), ⊙ Uzbek SSR and Tashkent oblast, in Tashkent oasis (watered by Chirchik R.), on Trans-Caspian RR and 1,800 mi. SE of Moscow; 41°20'N 69°18'E. Largest and one of oldest cities of Central Asia, at junction of historic trade routes. Important industrial center; large-scale cotton-textile and -ginning plants; mfg. of textile-making and cotton-picking tools, excavators, mining equipment, electric cables, abrasives; food processing (flour, wine, canned goods, meat, tobacco), light mfg. (shoes and other leather goods, radios, porcelain, abrasives), paper milling; railroad workshops. A major educational center, with Central Asian state univ. and industrial col., medical, agr., law, and teachers colleges, textile and railroad trade schools. Has Uzbek Acad. of Sciences, state library, historical mus., conservatory, and Uzbek academic theater. City consists of new Rus. section (E; built after 1860s) near railroad station and old Oriental city (largely reconstructed by Soviets) which contains ruins of 9th-cent. mausoleum, 15th- and 16th-cent. madrasas. Near by, in Tashkent oasis (fruit, truck, cotton, silk) are industrial suburbs of Keles (NW), Ordzhonikidze (NE), and Kuilyuk (SE). Irrigation canals of Chirchik R. power several hydroelectric plants, including Boz-Su (4.5 mi. NNE) and Kadyrya (8 mi. NE). Other power sources include coal and gas from Angren and Chirchik and Farkhad hydroelectric plants. City dates from 7th cent.; originally called Chachkent [Tadzhik, =stone city]. Ruled by Arabs to 11th cent.; later dominated by Turkish khans of Khorezm; came (1361) under Mongol rule, followed by Uzbek, Kazakh, and (1808) Kokand khans. It fell (1865) to Russians and became ⊙ general-govt. of Turkestan. Its trade boomed after it was reached (1898) by Trans-Caspian RR. After Bolshevik revolution, it was (1918–24) ⊙ former Turkestan Autonomous SSR and replaced (1930) Samarkand as ⊙ Uzbek SSR.

Tashkepri (tŭshkyĭprē'), town (1939 pop. over 500), S Mary oblast, Turkmen SSR, on railroad, on Murgab R. and 115 mi. SSE of Mary; irrigation dam and reservoir.

Tashkumyr (tŭshkōōmĭr'), city (1939 pop. 3,198), W Dzhalal-Abad oblast, Kirghiz SSR, on Naryn R. and 50 mi. NW of Dzhalal-Abad; coal-mining center; terminus (since 1935) of railroad from Uch-Kurgan. Developed during Second World War.

Tashkurghan or **Tashqurghan** (täsh'kōōrgän"), town (pop. 20,000), Mazar-i-Sharif prov., N Afghanistan, in Afghan Turkestan, 33 mi. E of Mazar-i-Sharif, at junction of roads from Kabul and Badakhshan; center of oasis irrigated by Khulm R.; fruit, vegetables, wine, coriander, opium. Rice and flour milling. Pop. is largely Tadzhik. Has noted park. Commonly identified with anc. *Aornos*, on line of march (330–329 B.C.) of Alexander the Great. The city, later known as Khulm, was destroyed in mid-18th cent. and pop. was resettled in Tashkurghan, just S of Khulm's ruins. Passed 1850 to Afghans.

Tash Kurghan or **Tash Qurghan** (täsh' kōōrgän'), Chinese *Puli* or *P'u-li* (both: pōō'lē'), town, ⊙ Tash Kurghan co. (pop. 13,926), westernmost Sinkiang prov., China, near USSR border, 125 mi. SSW of Kashgar, in Muztagh Ata Range, on E edge of the Pamir; 37°47'N 75°14'E. Cattle, sheep raising; grain. Located on road leading to Gilgit and Kashmir via Kilik Pass, it is inhabited by Sarikolis (Tadzhiks). Also spelled Tash Kurgan.

Tashla (tŭshlä'), village (1939 pop. over 500), SW Chkalov oblast, Russian SFSR, on right tributary of Ural R. and 50 mi. SSW of Sorochinsk; wheat, cattle, sheep.

Tashlak (tŭshläk'), village (1939 pop. over 500), E Fergana oblast, Uzbek SSR, just E of Margelan; cotton ginning.

Tashqurghan, Afghanistan: see TASHKURGHAN.

Tash Qurghan, China: see TASH KURGHAN.

Tashtagol (tŭshtŭgôl'), town (1948 pop. 17,000), S Kemerovo oblast, Russian SFSR, on Kondoma R.

and 75 mi. SSE of Stalinsk (linked by rail); iron-mining center in Gornaya Shoriya. Developed in 1940s.

Tashtyp (tŭshtĭp'), village (1926 pop. 2,667), S Khakass Autonomous Oblast, Krasnoyarsk Territory, Russian SFSR, 85 mi. SW of Abakan; metalworks.

Tasikmalaya or **Tasikmalaja** (both: täsĭkmälī'ä), town (pop. 25,605), W central Java, Indonesia, in Preanger region, 50 mi. ESE of Bandung; alt. 1,151 ft.; trade center for agr. area (rubber, rice, corn, peanuts). There is large mosque. In 1948 a short-lived Moslem state was established in the region; it was crushed by Du. forces.

Tasiko, New Hebrides: see EPI.

Tasili, Algeria: see TASSILI.

Tasiussak or **Tasiussaq** (both: tä'syōōshäk), sealing and whaling settlement (pop. 84), Upernavik dist., W Greenland, on small isl. in Baffin Bay, 40 mi. N of Upernavik; 73°22'N 56°5'W. Sometimes spelled Tasiusak.

Taskan River (tŭskän'), left affluent of upper Kolyma R., in N Khabarovsk Territory, Russian SFSR; flows 115 mi. SE from Cherski Range to Kolyma R. at Ust-Taskan (power plant; 50 mi. WSW of Seimchan; road center in Kolyma gold-mining region).

Tas-Khayakhtakh Mountains, Russian SFSR: see CHERSKI RANGE.

Taskopru (täshkûprü'), Turkish *Taşköprü*, village (pop. 4,247), Kastamonu prov., N Turkey, on Gok R. and 25 mi. ENE of Kastamonu; wheat, spelt, barley, onions; copper, chromium deposits near by.

Tasley (tăs'lē), hamlet, Accomack co., E Va., on Eastern Shore; rail station for Onancock (just W) and Accomac (2 mi. NE); ships potatoes.

Tasman, Mount (tăz'mŭn), peak (11,475 ft.) in Tasman Natl. Park, W central S.Isl., New Zealand, near Mt. Cook.

Tasman Bay, inlet of Tasman Sea, N S.Isl., New Zealand; separated from Golden Bay by Separation Point; 45 mi. E-W, 30 mi. N-S; D'Urville Isl. is at E entrance, Nelson on SE shore, Motueka on W shore. Sometimes called Blind Bay.

Tasman Glacier, largest glacier of New Zealand, in Tasman Natl. Park Southern Alps, W central S.Isl.; rises in Mt. Hochstetter, flows SE to Tasman R.; 18 mi. long, 1.25 mi. wide.

Tasmania (tăzmā'nēŭ), island (□ c.24,450), Australia, 150 mi. S of Victoria across Bass Strait, bet. Indian Ocean and Tasman Sea; 40°38'–43°39'S 144°39'–148°18'E; 180 mi. N-S, 190 mi. E-W. Geologically, isl. is continuation of Australian continent. High central plateau with alpine lakes, forested mts. in W, agr. regions in N and SE, much unexplored territory in SW. Highest range is Ben Lomond, containing Legge Tor (5,160 ft.; highest peak of isl.). Largest river, South Esk R.; Derwent and Tamar rivers are more important. Great L. (largest of Tasmania; in central area), is source of hydroelectric power. Mean annual temp., 55°F.; rainfall, 20 in. Natl. park comprises mountainous S central area. Native flora includes King William pine (*Athrotaxis*), Huon pine (*Dacrydium franklini*), beech, eucalyptus. Indigenous fauna includes monotremes (platypus and spiny anteater); marsupials (kangaroo, wallaby, wornbat); Tasmanian tiger (*Thylacinus*) and devil (*Sarcophilus*), which are animals peculiar to Tasmania; poisonous snakes. Meat, dairy products, grain produced primarily for domestic consumption. Exports metals (copper, zinc, tin, lead, gold, silver), coal, wool, canned fruit, potatoes. Largest city is Hobart, seat of Univ. of Tasmania. Chief port towns: Launceston, Burnie, Devonport, Franklin. Discovered 1642 by Tasman, who named it Van Diemen's Land; visited 1777 by Cook. Great Britain took possession of isl. 1803, and established penal colony. Last shipment of convicts was in 1853, when present name was given to isl. **Tasmania** (□ 26,215; pop. 257,078), a state of the Commonwealth of Australia, ⊙ Hobart, includes isl. of Tasmania and isls. off its coasts: BRUNY, MACQUARIE ISLAND, MARIA ISLAND, SCHOUTEN ISLAND, FURNEAUX ISLANDS, HUNTER ISLANDS, ROBBIN ISLAND, KING ISLAND, MAATSUYKER ISLANDS. It was made a penal colony (1803), and was dependent on New South Wales until 1825, when Tasmania became separate Br. colony. Became (1901) an Australian state.

Tasman Island, Solomon Isls.: see NUKUMANU.

Tasman Mountains (tăz'mŭn), N S.Isl., New Zealand, on Golden Bay peninsula, NNE of Karamea Bight; extends 30 mi. E–W; rises to 5,300 ft.; forested slopes.

Tasman National Park (□ 153), W central S.Isl., New Zealand, in Southern Alps; contains many mts. and glaciers, including Mt. COOK and TASMAN GLACIER, highest peak and largest glacier of New Zealand.

Tasman Peninsula, SE Tasmania, connected (N) with Forestier Peninsula by narrow isthmus; forms E shores of Storm Bay and Frederick Henry Bay; Norfolk Bay in N; 17 mi. long, 12 mi. wide; irregular coast line. Zinc-lead mines, coal. Site of Port Arthur, formerly chief penal colony of Australia. Southernmost points are Cape Pillar (E), Cape Raoul (W; at entrance to Storm Bay).

Tasman River, W central S.Isl., New Zealand, rises in Tasman, Murchison, Mueller, and Hooker glaciers in Southern Alps, flows 25 mi. S to L. Pukaki.

Tasman Sea, arm of South Pacific Ocean, bet. SE Australia and Tasmania on W and New Zealand on E; merges with Coral Sea (N) and Indian Ocean (SW).

Tasna or **Tazna** (both: täs'nä), village (pop. c.2,900), Potosí dept., SW Bolivia, on W slopes of Cordillera de Chichas and 33 mi. ESE of Uyuni, on road; tin-mining center.

Tasnad (tŭzhnäd'), Rum. *Taşnad*, Ger. *Trestenberg* (trĕ'stŭnbĕrkh), Hung. *Tasnád* (tŏzh'nät), village (pop. 5,521), Baia-Mare prov., NW Rumania, in Transylvania, on railroad and 30 mi. NW of Zalau; health resort and wine-production center. In Hungary, 1940–45.

Taso, China: see ITUN.

Tasova (tä-shôvä'), Turkish *Taşova*, village (pop. 796), Tokat prov., N central Turkey, 25 mi. ENE of Amasya; tobacco.

Tasquillo (täskē'yō), town (pop. 1,300), Hidalgo, central Mexico, on Tula R. and 45 mi. NW of Pachuca; alt. 5,643 ft. Cereals, maguey, beans, fruit, livestock. Thermal springs near by.

Tassiding, India: see NAMCHI.

Tassili (täsēlē'), name given to 2 arid plateau regions of the Sahara Desert of S Algeria. The Tassili des Adjjer (or Ajjer), a NE extension of the Ahaggar Mts., lies WNW of Ghat (Fezzan), in lat. 25°–26°N. The Tassili n' Ahaggar, in southernmost Algeria, lies bet. the Ahaggar Mts. (NE) and the Adrar des Iforas (SW). Also spelled Tasili.

Tassin (täsĕn'), village (pop. 1,625), Oran dept., NW Algeria, 18 mi. SW of Sidi-bel-Abbès; vineyards.

Tassin-la-Demi-Lune (täsĕ'-lä-dŭmē-lün'), W suburb (pop. 6,799) of Lyons, Rhône dept., E central France; mfg. of watches, jewelry, chemicals, toys, building materials. Breweries.

Tasso Island or **Tassoh Island** (tă'sō) (pop. 1,295), Sierra Leone colony, in Sierra Leone R. estuary, off Pepel, 12 mi. ENE of Freetown; 2.5 mi. long, 2 mi. wide. Town of Tasso or Tassoh (1931 pop. 784) is on NW shore; fishing. Site of early Br. trading post (established 1663). Ceded 1824 to the Crown.

Tastak (tŭstäk'), village (1939 pop. over 2,000) on W outskirts of Alma-Ata, Kazakh SSR; orchard.

Tasüeh Mountains, Chinese *Ta-hsüeh Shan* (dä'-shüä' shän'), outlier of the Tibetan highlands, NW Yunnan prov., China, extending c.300 mi. N–S bet. Yangtze (E) and Mekong (W) rivers.

Tata (tŏ'tŏ), Ger. *Dotis* or *Totis*, town (pop. 12,328), Komarom-Esztergom co., N Hungary, 31 mi. E of Györ; textiles (silk, artificial silk, wool, rugs, blankets), porcelain, faïence, champagne; tanneries, brickworks, flour mills. Town existed in 9th cent. Eszterhazy castle has a fine library. Tovaros, Hung. *Tóváros* (tô'värôsh), which became part of Tata in 1938, is on small lake fed by warm springs.

Tata (tätä'), Saharan oasis and military outpost, Agadir frontier region, SW Fr. Morocco, in the Djebel Bani, 65 mi. SE of Taroudant; 29°45'N 7°59'W.

Tatabanya (tŏ'tŏbänyŏ), Hung. *Tatabánya*, city (pop. 7,312), Komarom-Esztergom co., N Hungary, 30 mi. W of Budapest; lignite-mining center; briquettes; brickworks. School of mining. Ger. pop. in vicinity.

Tatahouine, Tunisia: see FOUM-TATAHOUINE.

Tatamagouche (tătŭmŭgōōsh'), village (pop. estimate 1,000), N N.S., at head of Tatamagouche Bay of Northumberland Strait, 32 mi. WNW of New Glasgow; dairying center.

Tatamy (tă'tŭmē), borough (pop. 681), Northampton co., E Pa., 4 mi. NNW of Easton.

Tatanagar (tŭtä'nŭgŭr), town (pop. 16,684), Singhbhum dist., SE Bihar, India, on tributary of the Subarnarekha and 3 mi. S of Jamshedpur; rail junction serving Jamshedpur. Also called Jugsalai.

Tataocheng, Formosa: see TAIPEI.

Tataouine, Tunisia: see FOUM-TATAHOUINE.

Tatarani (tŭtŭrän'), Rum. *Tătărani*, S suburb of Ploesti, S central Rumania, in oil region.

Tatarasti, Ukrainian SSR: see TATARBUNARY.

Tatar Autonomous Soviet Socialist Republic (tä'tŭr, Rus. tŭtär'), administrative division (□ 26,100; 1939 pop. 2,919,423) in E central European Russian SFSR; ⊙ Kazan. In middle Volga and lower Kama river valleys; also drained by Vyatka and Sviyaga rivers. Humid continental climate (short summers); black earth (S), podzolic soils (N). Mineral resources: petroleum and asphalt (Shugurovo), gypsum (Volga R. valley), alabaster (Kamskoye Ustye), floridin (S of Chistopol), phosphorite and sulphur (SW), cupriferous sandstone, limestone, lignite, peat (scattered). Extensive agr., with wheat (E, W), legumes (N), rye, oats, barley (scattered), fruit (along right bank of the Volga), truck (around Kazan), sunflowers (S), flax (NE); livestock raising, beekeeping; hay meadows in Kama R. flood plain. Deciduous forests in central area. Industries based on agr. (tanning, flour milling, distilling, food processing) and timber (sawmilling, shipbuilding, furniture mfg., veneering); fur processing (Kazan), felt-boot mfg. (Kukmor, Bugulma). Metalworking, machine and light mfg. (chemicals, textiles, leather and rubber products) in main urban centers (Kazan, Zelenodolsk, Chistopol, Bugulma, Yelabuga, Agryz). Served by Moscow-Sverdlovsk RR, with lateral line crossing at Sviyazhsk. Navigation on Volga, Kama, and Vyatka rivers. Exports chemicals (glycerin, acids, gunpowder, cosmetics) and agr. products. Pop. 49% Tatars, 43% Russians; Chuvash, Udmurt, and Mordvinians. The Tatars are Turkic steppe people of Mohammedan (Sunnite) religion and culture; settled in Volga region before Bronze Age period; dominated by Volga Bulgars after 10th cent.; submerged (1236) by Mongols; in Golden Horde and Kazan khanate until 16th cent.; conquered (1552) by Ivan the Terrible. Republic formed largely out of Kazan govt. in 1920.

Tatar Bazarjik, Bulgaria: see PAZARDZHIK.

Tatarbunary (tŭtär"bōōnä'rē), Rum. *Tatar-Bunar* (tätär'-bōōnär') and (after c.1930) *Tătărăşti* (tŭtŭ-rŭsht'), village (1941 pop. 6,250), SE central Izmail oblast, Ukrainian SSR, 40 mi. SW of Belgorod-Dnestrovski, at N end of Sasyk Lagoon; grain, cattle trade; mfg. of furniture, textiles.

Tatarka (tŭtär'kŭ), village, central Krasnoyarsk Territory, Russian SFSR, 50 mi. E of Yeniseisk; bauxite mining.

Tatar Pass, Ukrainian SSR: see YABLONITSA PASS.

Tatar Pazarjik, Bulgaria: see PAZARDZHIK.

Tatarsk (tŭtärsk'), city (1939 pop. over 10,000), W Novosibirsk oblast, Russian SFSR, on Baraba Steppe, on Trans-Siberian RR and 100 mi. E of Omsk; agr. center (flour, meat and dairy products); junction of railroad to Kulunda and Semipalatinsk. Chartered 1925.

Tatar Strait (tŭtär'), arm of Pacific Ocean joining Sea of Japan (S) and Sea of Okhotsk (N); separates Sakhalin isl. (E) and Asiatic mainland (W); 5–80 mi. wide, c.350 mi. long; generally shallow. Receives Amur R. (N). Main ports: Sovetskaya Gavan, Nikolayevsk, Aleksandrovsk, Uglegorsk. Also called Gulf of Tatary.

Tatary: see TARTARY.

Tatary, Gulf of, Russian SFSR: see TATAR STRAIT.

Tata Sabaya, Bolivia: see SABAYA, SERRANÍA DE.

Tatatila (tätätē'lä), town (pop. 387), Veracruz, E Mexico, 17 mi. NW of Jalapa; corn, coffee.

Tataurovo (tŭtŭōō'rŭvŭ), village, S central Kirov oblast, Russian SFSR, 22 mi. NW of Molotovsk; grain, wheat.

Tate, county (□ 411; pop. 18,011), NW Miss.; ⊙ Senatobia. Bounded W and NW by Coldwater R. and Arkabutla Reservoir. Farming (cotton, corn, hay), dairying; lumbering. Formed 1873.

Tate, village (pop. c.1,500), Pickins co., N Ga., 13 mi. NNE of Canton; marble-quarrying center.

Tate, Mount (tä'tä), Jap. *Tate-yama*, a collective name for 4 peaks (highest, 9,950 ft.), in Toyama prefecture, central Honshu, Japan, 25 mi. ESE of Toyama. Solfataras and rest huts on slopes; alpine flora.

Tatebayashi (tätäbä'yäshē), town (pop. 23,277), Gumma prefecture, central Honshu, Japan, 16 mi. SE of Kiryu, in agr. area; cotton textiles.

Tateishi (tätä'shē), town (pop. 4,439), Oita prefecture, NE Kyushu, Japan, on W Kunisaki Peninsula, 18 mi. NNW of Oita; straw mats, charcoal.

Tateoka (tätä'ōkä), town (pop. 10,991), Yamagata prefecture, N Honshu, Japan, 16 mi. NNE of Yamagata; textiles, sake, woodwork. Agr. school.

Tate Springs, resort village, Grainger co., E Tenn., 40 mi. NE of Knoxville; mineral springs.

Tatetsu (tä"tä'tsōō), town (pop. 14,513), Osaka prefecture, S Honshu, Japan, just E of Fuse; commercial center for rice-growing area; home industries (textiles, woodworking).

Tateyama (tätä'yämŭ), city (1940 pop. 28,591; 1947 pop. 36,599), Chiba prefecture, central Honshu, Japan, on SW Chiba Peninsula, 23 mi. SE of Yokosuka across Uraga Strait; summer resort; agr., poultry raising. Includes (since late 1930s) former towns of Tateyamahojo, Nako, and Funakata.

Tati (tä'tē) or **Francistown,** formerly **Tati Concession,** district (□ 2,069; pop. 17,530), E Bechuanaland Protectorate, on Southern Rhodesia border, 100 mi. SW of Bulawayo; ⊙ Francistown. Gold- and silver-mining region. Formerly part of Matabeleland, it was ceded 1887 by native chief to British interests who have rights to all minerals. Gold was discovered here 1864; the Monarch Mine is oldest (1872) now operating.

Tatien or **Ta-t'ien** (dä'tyĕn'), town (pop. 4,346), ⊙ Tatien co. (pop. 99,061), S central Fukien prov., China, 70 mi. SSW of Nanping; rice, sweet potatoes, beans. Coal and iron mines near by.

Tating (dä'dĭng'), town (pop. 27,116), ⊙ Tating co. (pop. 241,261), W Kweichow prov., China, 25 mi. SE of Pichieh; lacquer-producing center; cotton-textile mfg., pottery making, tobacco processing; timber, medicinal herbs.

Tatio Geysers (tä'tyō), in the Andes, at NW foot of Cerro de Tocorpuri, Antofagasta prov., N Chile, near Bolivia border; 22°20'S. Emit steam and boiling water.

Tatishchevo (tŭtyē'shchĭvŭ), village (1948 pop. over 2,000), central Saratov oblast, Russian SFSR, on railroad and 20 mi. WNW of Saratov; flour mill; wheat, sunflowers.

Tatitlek (tŭtĭt'lĭk), native village (pop. 89), S Alaska, on Prince William Sound, 40 mi. NW of Cordova; fishing; trading point.

Tatlow, Mount (tăt'lō) (10,050 ft.), SW B.C., in Coast Mts., 150 mi. NNW of Vancouver; 51°23'N 123°52'W.

Tatnam, Cape (tăt'nŭm), NE Man., on Hudson Bay, 50 mi. ENE of York Factory; 57°15'N 91°5'W.

Tatoi or **Tatoion,** Greece: see DEKELEIA.

Tatoosh Island, Wash.: see FLATTERY, CAPE.

Tatrafüred, Czechoslovakia: see STARY SMOKOVEC.

Tatra Mountains or **High Tatra** (tä'trŭ), Slovak *Vysoké Tatry* (vĭ'sôkā tä'trĭ), Ger. *Hohe Tatra* (hō'ŭ tä'trä), Hung. *Magas Tátra* (mŏ'gŏsh tä'trŏ), Pol. *Tatry Wysokie* (tä'trĭ vĭsô'kyĕ), highest mountain group of the Carpathians and highest range of Czechoslovakia, on Czechoslovak-Pol. border, bet. Orava (W), Vah (S), and Poprad (E) rivers; c.40 mi. long E–W, c.15 mi. wide. Rise to 8,737 ft. in STALIN PEAK (Gerlachovka), to 8,639 ft. in Lomnice Peak. Central semicircle of 16 jagged summits of over 8,000 ft. is a leading winter-sports and mountaineering region, famed for scenic beauty and resorts (e.g., Strba L. area, Stary Smokovec, and Tatranska Lomnica); inc. since 1949 into single commune of VYSOKE TATRY. Rack-and-pinion railroad and noted mtn. highway, "Freedom Road," connect most important settlements. Mostly of crystalline rocks, with snow line at c.8,500 ft. and tree line (mainly conifers) at c.4,750 ft.; strongly glaciated (extensive moraines; over 100 high-lying lakes; hanging valleys). Wild game, including chamois, in park reserve SE of Javorina. Poprad and Biely Vah rivers rise on SE, Bialy Dunajec and Czarny Dunajec rivers on N slopes. The Low TATRA lie S of the High Tatra.

Tatranska Kotlina (tä'tränskä kôt'lĭnä), Slovak *Tatranská Kotlina,* Hung. *Tátrabarlangliget* (tä'-trŏbŏr"lŏng-glĭ"gĕt), village, N Slovakia, Czechoslovakia, on E slope of the High Tatra, 11 mi. N of Poprad; health and summer resort (alt. 2,768 ft.) with sanatorium; part of commune of Vysoke Tatry. Stalactite caverns, near by (S), are tourist attractions.

Tatranska Lomnica (lôm'nyĭtsä), Slovak *Tatranská Lomnica,* Ger. *Tatra Lomnitz* (tä'trä lôm'nĭts), Hung. *Tátralomnic* (tä'trŏlômnĭts), village, N Slovakia, Czechoslovakia, at SE foot of Lomnice Peak in the High Tatra, on rack-and-pinion railroad and 8 mi. N of Poprad; part of commune of Vysoke Tatry; leading summer resort (alt. 2,952 ft.) and winter-sports center.

Tatranska Polianka (pô'lyän-kä), Slovak *Tatranská Polianka,* Ger. *Weszterheim* (vĕ'stŭrhĭm"), Hung. *Tátraszéplak* (tä'trŏsāp'lŏk), village, N Slovakia, Czechoslovakia, in the High Tatra, at SE foot of Stalin Peak, on rack-and-pinion railroad and 6 mi. NW of Poprad; health resort (alt. 3,260 ft.) with several sanatoria; part of commune of Vysoke Tatry.

Tatranske Matliary, Czechoslovakia: see MATLIARY.

Tatrasvit, Czechoslovakia: see SVIT.

Tatry, mountains, Czechoslovakia and Poland: see TATRA MOUNTAINS.

Tatry Nizne, mountains, Poland and Czechoslovakia: see LOW TATRA.

Tatry Wysokie, mountains, Poland and Czechoslovakia: see TATRA MOUNTAINS.

Tatsienlu, China: see KANGTING.

Tatsingkow, China: see SHANGI.

Tatsing Mountains, Chinese *Tatsing Shan* or *Taching Shan* (both: dä'jĭng' shän'), section of the Yin Mts. system, in central Suiyuan prov., China, bet. Kweisui and Paotow, N of railroad; mts. rise to c.6,000 ft. Coal mining on S slopes.

Tatsinskaya (tŭtsēn'skĭŭ), village (1926 pop. 2,543), central Rostov oblast, Russian SFSR, on railroad and 29 mi. WSW of Morozovsk; flour mill, metal-works; wheat, sunflowers, livestock.

Tatsu (dä'dzōō'), town (pop. 38,576), ⊙ Tatsu co. (pop. 359,750), S central Szechwan prov., China, 55 mi. WNW of Chungking city; rice, wheat, sugar cane, sweet potatoes, beans.

Tatsue (tä"tsōō'ā), town (pop. 4,520), Tokushima prefecture, E Shikoku, Japan, 7 mi. SSE of Tokushima; rice-growing center.

Tatsuike, Japan: see KONAN.

Tatsuno (tä"tsōō'nō). **1** Town (pop. 8,006), Hyogo prefecture, S Honshu, Japan, 9 mi. WNW of Himeji; soy sauce. **2** Town (pop. 11,627), Nagano prefecture, central Honshu, Japan, on Tenryu R. and 6 mi. SW of Okaya, in rice-growing area. Mulberry fields. Sometimes called Inatomi.

Tatsuruhama, Japan: see TAZURUHAMA.

Tatta (tŭt'tŭ), district (□ 7,545; 1951 pop. 303,000), SW Sind, W Pakistan; ⊙ Tatta. Bordered W by Baluchistan, Karachi administrative area, and Arabian Sea, SE by Rann of Cutch, N by Baran R.; drained by Indus R. delta and small seasonal streams (W); canal irrigation. Mostly a low-lying area, with offshoots of Kirthar Range (NW). Rice, millet, barley, sugar cane, mangoes, grapes are grown. Rice husking, hand-loom weaving, fishing (sardines, Bombay duck, prawns; shad in the Indus). Brine-salt deposits worked. From a point in dist. (generally considered near Tatta) Alexander the Great in 325 B.C. started march across Baluchistan to Persia. Was part of former Karachi dist. (□ 8,357; 1941 pop. 713,900; ⊙ Karachi), which was divided in 1948 into Karachi administrative area (□ 812; including Karachi city) and Tatta dist. of Sind.

Tatta (tŭt'tŭ), town (pop. 8,262), ⊙ Tatta dist., SW Sind, W Pakistan, 55 mi. ESE of Karachi, near Indus R.; market center (rice, sugar cane, barley, wheat, millet); handicraft cloth weaving, pottery mfg. Partridge, grouse, snipe hunting. A very prosperous Moslem city in 15th–17th cent.; many medieval remains, including mosque built by Moguls. Sacked by Portuguese in 1555; factory established by Br. in 1758, but withdrawn some years later.

Tattaiyangarpettai, India: see THATHIENGARPET.

Tattamangalam (tŭtŭmŭng'gŭlŭm), city (pop. 8,373), in E exclave of Cochin, in SW Madras, India, 35 mi. ENE of Trichur; trades in cotton, rice, oilseeds; handloom weaving.

Tattayyangarpettai, India: see THATHIENGARPET.

Tattershall (tă'tŭrshŭl), agr. village and parish (pop. 398), Parts of Lindsey, central Lincolnshire, England, on Bain R. and 17 mi. SE of Lincoln. Has castle built c.1240 (now a mus.) and 13th-cent. church.

Tattnall (tăt'nŭl), county (□ 493; pop. 15,939), E central Ga.; ⊙ Reidsville. Bounded SW by Altamaha R.; drained by Ohoopee R. Coastal plain agr. (cotton, tobacco, pecans, peanuts, livestock) and sawmilling area. Formed 1801.

Tatu Ho, China: see TATU RIVER.

Tatuí (tŭtwē'), city (pop. 10,347), S central São Paulo, Brazil, on railroad and 25 mi. WNW of Sorocaba; cotton-growing center, producing textiles, dairy products, hats, oil, soap. Formerly spelled Tatuhy.

Tatul, Sierra de (syĕ'rä dā tätōōl'), subandean mountain range in Atacama prov., N Chile, extends 40 mi. SE to Argentina line SE of Vallenar; rises to c.18,000 ft.

Tatum (tā'tŭm). **1** Village (pop. 688), Lea co., SE N.Mex., near Texas line, 22 mi. N of Lovington, in grain and livestock region. Oil deposits in vicinity. **2** Town (pop. 119), Marlboro co., NE S.C., 5 mi. ENE of Bennettsville; cannery. **3** Town (pop. 599), on Panola-Rusk co. line, E Texas, 17 mi. SSW of Marshall, in oil, agr. area.

Tatung or **Ta-t'ung** (dä'tōōng'). **1** Town, S Anhwei prov., China, 50 mi. SW of Wuhu and on Yangtze R.; was treaty port of call after 1876. **2** City (1947 pop. estimate 80,000), ⊙, but independent of, Tatung co. (1946 pop. 299,236), SW Chahar prov., China, 100 mi. SW of Kalgan; railroad and coal-mining center (mines are near Kowchüan, 10 mi. SW). Trading hub for the Tatung agr. basin (kaoliang, millet, wheat, beans; sheep raising); wool weaving, flour milling. Formerly the chief city of N Shansi, it passed in 1950 to Chahar. **3** Town, Sungkiang prov., Manchuria, China: see TUNGHO. **4** Town, ⊙ Tatung co. (pop. 87,964), NE Tsinghai prov., China, 28 mi. NNW of Sining; agr. products. Coal mines near by. Formerly called Maopaisheng; until 1928 in Kansu prov.

Tatungkow, Manchuria: see ANTUNG.

Tatung Mountains, section of the Nan Shan, NE Tsinghai prov., China, N of lake Koko Nor. Here rises the **Tatung River,** which flows 300 mi. SE, past Weiyüan, to Sining R. at Minho.

Tatun Shan or **Ta-t'un Shan** (both: dä'tōōn' shän'), Jap. *Daiton-zan* (dī'tōn-zän), mountain (3,567 ft.) in N Formosa, 9 mi. N of Taipei. Health resorts of Peitow and Tsaoshan are on S slope.

Tatura (tŭtōō'rŭ), town (pop. 1,595), N Victoria, Australia, 95 mi. N of Melbourne, in livestock and agr. area; flour mill, dairy plant. Horticultural research station.

Tatu River, Chinese *Tatu Ho* (dä'dōō' hŭ'), in E Sikang and W Szechwan provs., China, rises in outlier of the Kunlun system at 32°N 102°E, flows over 400 mi. S, past Tanpa and Luting, to Min R. at Loshan.

Tatvan (tätvän'), village (pop. 1,933), Bitlis prov., SE Turkey, on L. Van 14 mi. NE of Bitlis; grain.

Tatzekow, Manchuria: see LINGYÜAN.

Tatzmannsdorf, Austria: see BAD TATZMANNSDORF.

Tau (tä'ōō), isl. (pop. 1,698) and county (pop. 770), MANUA dist., American Samoa, S Pacific, c.70 mi. E of Tutuila; rises to 3,056 ft.; cone-shaped, with steep, forested slopes.

Tauá (tou-ä'), city (pop. 1,853), W Ceará, Brazil, on upper Jaguaribe R. and 60 mi. SSE of Crateús; cattle, cotton. Nitrate deposits. Formerly spelled Tauhá.

Taubaté (toubŏtĕ'). city (1950 pop. 35,779), SE São Paulo, Brazil, on São Paulo–Rio de Janeiro RR and 75 mi. NE of São Paulo; largest city and chief commercial center of the upper Paraíba valley; has important textile (cotton fabrics, jute products) and agr.-processing industry (dairy produce, orange wine, brandy, rice, tobacco). Oil-shale extracting (experimentally) in Taubaté-Tremembé area. Dolomite quarried near by for blast-furnace refractory lining. Founded 1645. Has 17th-cent. convent of Santa Clara, old cathedral, and historical mus. Center of Paraíba valley coffeegrowing region in early 19th cent.

Tauberbischofsheim (tou"bŭrbĭ'shôfs-hīm"), village (pop. 5,414), N Baden, Germany, after 1945 in Württemberg-Baden, on the Tauber and 11 mi. SSE of Wertheim; food processing, woodworking. Has church with late-Gothic sacrament house; late-Gothic chapel. Here (1866) Prussians decisively defeated Württemberg army.

Tauber River (tou'bŭr), S Germany, rises 6 mi. NNE of Crailsheim, flows 78 mi. generally NNW, past Rothenburg, to the Main at Wertheim.

Tauca (tou'kä), city (pop. 2,489), Ancash dept., W central Peru, in Cordillera Occidental, 5 mi. SSW of Cabana; barley, corn. Gold placers near by.

Taucha (tou'khä), town (pop. 16,940), Saxony, E central Germany, on the Parthe and 6 mi. NE of Leipzig; metalworking; mfg. of machinery, chemicals. Until 15th cent., a trade center and scene of important fairs.

Tauchen (tou'khŭn), village (pop. 223), Burgenland, E Austria, 23 mi. SSE of Neunkirchen; lignite and antimony mined near by.

Tauchik (tŏŏōchēk'), town (1948 pop. over 2,000), S Guryev oblast, Kazakh SSR, on road and 55 mi. ESE of Fort Shevchenko, on Mangyshlak Peninsula. Coal, manganese, and oil deposits near by.

Tauchira, Cyrenaica: see TOCRA.

Tauden, Thailand: see THA UTHEN.

Tauern, Hohe, Austria: see HOHE TAUERN.

Tauern, Niedere, Austria: see NIEDERE TAUERN.

Taufiq, Port, Egypt: see PORT TAUFIQ.

Taufiqi, Raiyah, or **Rayah Tawfiqi** (rä'yŭ toufē'kē), navigable canal of the Nile delta, Lower Egypt; extends c.35 mi. from Delta Barrage parallel to the Damietta branch of the Nile.

Taufkirchen an der Pram (touf'kĭrkhŭn än dĕr präm'), town (pop. 3,018), NW Upper Austria, 6 mi. SE of Schärding; vineyards.

Taughannock Falls State Park (tŭgă'nŭk), W central N.Y., on W shore of Cayuga L., c.8 mi. NNW of Ithaca. In deep gorge of small creek entering lake here is spectacular Taughannock Falls (215 ft. high). Sports facilities; swimming.

Tauhá, Brazil: see TAUÁ.

Taulé (tōlā'), village (pop. 755), Finistère dept., W France, 4 mi. WNW of Morlaix; fruits, early vegetables.

Tauler or **Minas del Tauler** (mē'näs dhĕl toulĕr'), iron mines, Huelva prov., SW Spain, in Sierra Morena, 3 mi. NW of Santa Olalla del Cala, 40 mi. NNW of Seville (linked by narrow-gauge railroad).

Taulihawa (tou'lĭhŭvŭ), town, S Nepal, in the Terai, 24 mi. WNW of Nautanwa (India); trades in rice, millet, wheat, barley, corn, vegetables. Sometimes spelled Taulia.

Taumarunui (tou"mărōōnōō'ē), borough (pop. 2,706), ⊙ Taumarunui co. (□ 878; pop. 3,057), W central N.Isl., New Zealand, 65 mi. ENE of New Plymouth at junction of short Ongarue R. with the Wanganui; center of lumber industry.

Taumaturgo (toumŭtōōr'gōō), town, Acre territory, westernmost Brazil, on upper Juruá R., near Peru border, and 95 mi. S of Cruzeiro do Sul.

Taum Sauk Mountain (tôm' sôk"), SE Mo., W of Ironton; highest peak (1,772 ft.) of St. Francois Mts., and highest point in state.

Taungbyo (toun'byō) or **Taungbro** (toun-brō'), village, Akyab dist., Lower Burma, on E Pakistan border, at head of Naaf R., 85 mi. NW of Akyab.

Taungdwingyi (toun-dwĭn-jē'), town (pop. 8,339), Magwe dist., Upper Burma, on Pyinmana-Kyaukpadaung RR, at foot of Pegu Yoma, 40 mi. ESE of Magwe, in fertile rice-growing plain; artesian wells; old walled town.

Taunggyi (toun-jē'), town (pop. 8,652), ⊙ Southern Shan State, Upper Burma, on Thazi-Kengtung road and 100 mi. SE of Mandalay; 20°46'N 97°2'E, alt. 4,712 ft.

Taungs (tŏngz), town (pop. 1,922) in Bechuanaland dist., NE Cape Prov., U. of So. Afr., near Orange Free State border, on Hartz R. and 80 mi. N of Kimberley; center of Taungs Native Reserve (□ 1,442; total pop. 32,540; native pop. 26,401); stock, grain. Prehistoric remains of Taungs man (*Australopithecus africanus*) were found here in 1924. Just ENE of town is fort, established (1884) during Bechuanaland expedition.

Taungtha (toun-dhä'), village, Myingyan dist., Upper Burma, on railroad and 12 mi. SSE of Myingyan; palm-sugar mfg.

Taungu, Burma: see TOUNGOO.

Taungup (toung-gōōp'), village, Sandoway dist., Lower Burma, on Arakan coast, 27 mi. N of Sandoway; W head of Taungup Pass route over the Arakan Yoma.

Taungup Pass, chief crossing (alt. 3,000 ft.) of Arakan Yoma, SW Burma, 34 mi. WSW of Prome; 18°40'N 94°45'E. Used by motor road bet. Irrawaddy R. opposite Prome (ferry) and Taungup on Arakan coast.

Taunsa (toun'sŭ), town (pop. 8,701), Dera Ghazi Khan dist., SW Punjab, W Pakistan, 45 mi. N of Dera Ghazi Khan; wheat, millet, oilseeds; handloom weaving.

Taunton (tôn'tŭn, tän'–), municipal borough (1931 pop. 25,178; 1951 census 33,613), ⊙ Somerset, England, in W center of co., on Tone R. and 40 mi. SW of Bristol, in Taunton Deane Valley; agr. market; tanneries, woolen mills, mfg. of leather goods and plastics. King Ine of Wessex built castle here, probably early in 8th cent. In 12th cent.

William Giffard, bishop of Winchester, founded a priory and built castle, parts of which now contain mus. Perkin Warbeck occupied castle in 1497; in Civil War Admiral Blake held it for Parliamentarians (1644–45); after Monmouth's Rebellion (1685) Lord Jeffreys held "Bloody Assizes" here. Taunton School was founded (1522) by Richard Foxe, bishop of Winchester. There are a 15th-cent. and a 16th-cent. church, and historic White Hart Inn.

Taunton. **1** City (pop. 40,109), a ⊙ Bristol co., SE Mass., on Taunton R. and 15 mi. N of Fall River; silverware, textiles, stoves, textile machinery, machine parts, oilcloth, plastics, ceramics. Once a great New England port. State insane asylum. Settled 1638, inc. as town 1639, as city 1864. **2** Village (pop. 217), Lyon co., SW Minn., 17 mi. NW of Marshall, in grain area.

Taunton River, SE Mass., rises in S Norfolk co., flows 44 mi. generally SW and S, past Taunton (head of navigation), to head of Mt. Hope Bay at Fall River city, where its mouth is part of harbor.

Taunus (tou'no͞os), mountain range in W Germany, extends 50 mi. ENE from the Rhine; rises to 2,887 ft. in the Grosser Feldberg. Two main ranges: Rheingau Mts. (W) and the Hochtaunus or Hoher Taunus [Ger.,=high Taunus]. Resort region noted for mild climate and numerous mineral springs (Wiesbaden, Bad Nauheim, Bad Homburg); excellent wine on S slopes (Rheingau region). Geologically it is considered part of Rhenish Slate Mts.

Taupo (tou'pō), township (pop. 723), ⊙ Taupo co. (□ 3,272; pop. 4,248), central N.Isl., New Zealand, on NE shore of L. Taupo and 110 mi. ENE of New Plymouth, in Hot Springs Dist.; health resort.

Taupo, Lake, largest lake (□ 238) of New Zealand, in central N.Isl., 90 mi. E of New Plymouth; 25 mi. long, 17 mi. wide, 534 ft. deep. Source of Waikato R. Town of Taupo is on NE shore. Surrounded by many volcanic mts. and hot springs. Known for rainbow trout.

Tauq (touk), village, Kirkuk prov., NE Iraq, 22 mi. SSE of Kirkuk, in a grain and sheep-raising area.

Taura (tou'rä), village (pop. 3,790), Saxony, E central Germany, 7 mi. NW of Chemnitz; hosiery mfg.

Taurage (tourägä'), Lith. *Tauragė*, Ger. *Tauroggen* (tourô'gŭn), city (pop. 10,561), W Lithuania, 20 mi. NE of Sovetsk; meat-packing center; mfg. of woolen and cotton textiles, furniture, leather goods; flour milling. Dates from 13th cent.; in Rus. Kovno govt. until 1920. The Convention of Tauroggen was concluded here 1812 by the Prussian general Yorck von Wartenburg with Russia.

Tauranga (tou'răng-gŭ), borough (pop. 4,712), ⊙ Tauranga co. (□ 609; pop. 11,662), N N.Isl., New Zealand, 95 mi. SE of Auckland and on Tauranga harbor in Bay of Plenty. Harbor is 20 mi. long, sheltered by narrow Matakana Isl. (19 mi. long). Exports dairy products, meat, lumber.

Taurasi (tourä'zē), village (pop. 1,964), Avellino prov., Campania, S Italy, 11 mi. NE of Avellino; wine, fireworks.

Taurasia, Italy: see TURIN.

Taurianova (tourēänô'vä), commune (pop. 18,710), Reggio di Calabria prov., Calabria, S Italy, 9 mi. E of Palmi, in agr. region (cereals, citrus fruit, olives). Formed 1928; includes adjacent towns of Radicena and Iatrinoli, which form commune seat, and Terranova Sappo Minulio (pop. 1,177), 2 mi. S. Towns damaged by earthquakes of 1783, 1908.

Taurica, Chersonesus: see CRIMEA, Russian SFSR.

Tauric Chersonese: see CRIMEA, Russian SFSR.

Taurida: see CRIMEA, Russian SFSR.

Taurignac-Castet (tōrēnyäk'-kästā'), village (pop 214), Ariège dept., S France, on Salat R. and 5 mi. NW of Saint-Girons; paper milling.

Taurinya (tōrēnyä'), village (pop. 248), Pyrénées-Orientales dept., S France, on N slope of the Massif du Canigou, 3 mi. S of Prades; iron mining.

Taurion River (tōrēō'), Creuse and Haute-Vienne depts., central France, rises in Plateau of Gentioux 8 mi. SSW of Felletin, flows 80 mi. W, past Pontarion and Bourganeuf, to the Vienne 9 mi. above Limoges. Hydroelectric plants at Châtelus-le-Marcheix and near its mouth into the Vienne.

Tauris, Iran: see TABRIZ.

Taurisano (tourēzä'nô), town (pop. 5,692), Lecce prov., Apulia, S Italy, 15 mi. SE of Gallipoli.

Tauroggen, Lithuania: see TAURAGE.

Tauromenium, Sicily: see TAORMINA.

Tauron, Greece: see NEA SPHAGEIA.

Taurus Mountains (tô'rŭs), Turkish *Toros Dağları*, great mtn. chain of S Turkey extending from L. Egridir in a great curve SE, E, and NE parallel to Mediterranean coast of Asia Minor, to approximately the middle Seyhan R., including the ALA DAG, its highest part, rising to 12,251 ft. Across the Seyhan and extending NE is an extension of the Taurus proper called the Anti-Taurus. Along the E shore of the Gulf of Iskenderun are the Amanos Mts., sometimes considered an offshoot of the Taurus. N of the Ala Dag and S of Kayseri, in an outlier of the Taurus, in the central Anatolian ranges, is Erciyas Dag (Mt. Argaeus), which reaches 12,848 ft. In the SE, N of Tarsus, bet. the Ala Dag (E) and the BOLKAR MOUNTAINS (W), are the CILICIAN GATES, a pass famous in anc. times. Mineral deposits include chromium, copper, silver, lignite, zinc, iron, arsenic.

Taus, Czechoslovakia: see DOMAZLICE.

Tausik or **Tausik el Bandeg** (tousĭk' ĕl bändĕg'), city (pop. c.50,000), French Morocco, 700 mi. SE of Fez, on the Saharan trade route to Egypt. Long a hub of caravan routes, it was ⊙ anc. Carthaginian prov. of Zamara. With the construction of a large airfield here after the Second World War, Tausik doubled its pop.

Tauste (tou'stā), town (pop. 5,814), Saragossa prov., NE Spain, near the Tauste Canal, 27 mi. NW of Saragossa; olive-oil processing, flour milling; agr. trade (cereals, sugar beets, alfalfa). Alabaster, gypsum, and limestone quarries near by.

Tauste Canal, in Navarre and Saragossa provs., NE Spain, starts from the Ebro below Tudela, runs 28 mi. along right bank of river, which it reenters 16 mi. NW of Saragossa; used for irrigation.

Tautra (tout'rä), island (□ c.1) in Trondheim Fjord, Nord-Trondelag co., central Norway, 11 mi. NW of Trondheim; 2 mi. long. Has ruins of 13th-cent. Cistercian abbey.

Tauves (tōv), village (pop. 464), Puy-de-Dôme dept., central France, in Auvergne Mts., 15 mi. E of Ussel; cheese making.

Tauz (tŭo͞os'), city (1926 pop. 2,154), W Azerbaijan SSR, on railroad and 45 mi. WNW of Kirovabad; cement-milling center; vineyards, wheat, cotton, livestock.

Tauzkala, Azerbaijan SSR: see BERD.

Tavaí (tävăē'), village (dist. pop. 2,000), Caazapá dept., S Paraguay, 60 mi. SE of Villarrica; maté, fruit, livestock; lumbering. Sometimes Tabaí.

Tavani (tă'vŭnē), trading post, SE Keewatin Dist., Northwest Territories, on Mistake Bay of Hudson Bay; 62°4'N 93°7'W; radio station; R.C. mission.

Tavannes (tävän'), Ger. *Dachsfelden* (dăkhs'fĕldŭn), town (pop. 3,444), Bern canton, NW Switzerland, on Birs R. and 6 mi. NNW of Biel; watches, lamps, flour; woodworking.

Tavaputs Plateau (tă'vŭpo͞ots), E Utah, name sometimes applied to EAST TAVAPUTS PLATEAU, WEST TAVAPUTS PLATEAU.

Tavares (tŭvä'rĭs, tŭvâ'rēz), town (pop. 1,763), ⊙ Lake co., central Fla., 28 mi. NW of Orlando, bet. lakes Eustis and Dora, in citrus-fruit and resort area.

Tavas (tăväs'), town (pop. 7,110), Denizli prov., SW Turkey, 13 mi. S of Denizli; valonia, wheat, barley, chick-peas. Also called Yarangum.

Tavastehus, Finland: see HÄMEENLINNA.

Tavastkyro, Finland: see HÄMEENKYRÖ.

Tavatui or **Tavatuy** (tŭvŭto͞o'ē), village, SW central Sverdlovsk oblast, Russian SFSR, on Tavatui L. (□ 15; 11 mi. long), on railroad and 4 mi. NW of Ayat; peat digging, woodworking.

Tavaux (tăvō'), village (pop. 958), Jura dept., E France, 6 mi. SW of Dôle; large chemical factory. Near by is Cités Solvay (pop. 1,770), a workers' residential community.

Tavda (tŭvdä'), city (1926 pop. 4,166; 1939 pop. 25,266), E Sverdlovsk oblast, Russian SFSR, port on Tavda R. and 60 mi. NNW of Tyumen; rail spur terminus (locomotive and car repair shops); major sawmilling, woodworking center; shipyards; mfg. (plywood, furniture, skis). Fisheries; dairying. Became city in 1937.

Tavda River, W Siberian Russian SFSR, formed 8 mi. N of Gari by confluence of Lozva and Sosva rivers; flows c.450 mi. generally SE, past Tabory and Tavda, to Tobol R. 45 mi. SW of Tobolsk. Navigable for entire length; lumber floating; fisheries. Receives Pelym R. (left).

Taveiro (tŭvā'ro͞o), village (pop. 1,148), Coimbra dist., N central Portugal, on Mondego R. and 4 mi. W of Coimbra, in fertile agr. region (rice, grain, horse beans, corn).

Taverna (tävĕr'nä), town (pop. 2,618), Catanzaro prov., Calabria, S Italy, 8 mi. N of Catanzaro, in livestock region.

Tavernelle in Val di Pesa (tävĕrnĕl'lĕ ēn väl dē pā'zä), village (pop. 1,393), Firenze prov., Tuscany, central Italy, 16 mi. SSW of Florence; agr. tools.

Tavernes (tăvârn'), village (pop. 446), Var dept., SE France, 23 mi. WNW of Draguignan; olives.

Tavernier, Fla.: see KEY LARGO.

Taverny (tävĕrnē'), town (pop. 5,468), Seine-et-Oise dept., N central France, 6 mi. ESE of Pontoise, at W edge of Forest of Montmorency; precision metalworks; mfg. of household appliances.

Taveta (tävĕ'tä), village, Coast prov., SE Kenya, on Tanganyika line, on railroad and 60 mi. W of Voi; coffee, sisal, tea, corn; dairy farming. Kyanite workings at near by Murka Hill.

Taveuni (tävāo͞o'nē), volcanic island (□ 168; pop. 3,044), Fiji, SW Pacific, across Somosomo Strait from Vanua Levu; 26 mi. long. Mtn. range rises to Uluingalau (4,072 ft.). Copra, cattle, coffee. Chief town, Waiyevo.

Taviano (tăvyä'nô), town (pop. 6,433), Lecce prov., Apulia, S Italy, 8 mi. SE of Gallipoli; olive oil, wine, dairy products.

Taviche or **San Jerónimo Taviche** (sän hārō'nēmō tăvē'chā), town (pop. 1,131), Oaxaca, S Mexico, in Sierra Madre del Sur, 25 mi. SSE of Oaxaca; alt. 5,502 ft. Silver and gold deposits. Silver was mined here in pre-Columbian days.

Tavignano River (tăvēnyänō', It. -nyä'nô), Corsica, rises in central range 7 mi. E of Evisa, flows 40 mi. ESE, past Corte, to Tyrrhenian Sea 2 mi. below Aleria. Around its marshy mouth is Corsica's only important lowland.

Tavil-Dara or **Tavil'-Dara** (tŭvēl"-dŭrä'), village (1948 pop. over 500), SW Garm oblast, Tadzhik SSR, on Obi-Khingou R. and 25 mi. S of Garm; wheat; gold placers. Until 1937, also spelled Tovil-Dara.

Tavira (tŭvē'rŭ), city (pop. 5,972), Faro dist., S Portugal, port on an inlet of the Atlantic (S coast), on railroad and 17 mi. ENE of Faro; fishing and canning center (sardines, tuna); trade in wines, olive oil. Moorish architecture is in evidence. Reconquered from the Moors in 1242.

Tavistock (tă'vĭstŏk"), village (pop. 1,066), S Ont., 8 mi. ESE of Stratford; textile and flour milling, agr.-implement mfg., dairying.

Tavistock, urban district (1931 pop. 4,471; 1951 census 5,889), SW Devon, England, on Tavy R. and 12 mi. N of Plymouth; agr. market; mfg. of chemicals and pharmaceuticals. Formerly tin- and copper-mining center. Abbey founded 961, destroyed by Danes in 10th cent.; church rebuilt 1285, rest of abbey in 15th cent. Another church, built 1381, has unusual tower. Sir Francis Drake b. near here (monument). Near by is Kelly Col., founded 1877 by Admiral Kelly.

Tavistock, borough (pop. 15), Camden co., SW N.J., 6 mi. SE of Camden. Started as golf course.

Tavolara Island (tävôlä'rä) (□ 2; pop. 27), off NE Sardinia, in Sassari prov., in Tyrrhenian Sea; 3 mi. long, 1 mi. wide; rises to 1,820 ft.

Tavolzhan (tŭvŭlzhän'), town (1948 pop. over 2,000), E Pavlodar oblast, Kazakh SSR, 35 mi. NE of Pavlodar and on spur of S.Siberian RR; salt-extraction plant.

Tavoy (tŭvoi'), Burmese *Tavai* (dŭwĕ'), district (□ 5,404; 1941 pop. 211,729), Tenasserim div., Lower Burma, bet. Andaman Sea and Thailand frontier; ⊙ Tavoy. In the Tenasserim Range, it is cut up by 3 parallel ranges of mts. Drained by Tenasserim and Tavoy Rivers. Rice in plains, forests in mts. Tin and tungsten mines; iron ore near Tavoy. Salt extraction on coast. Pop. is 85% Burmese, 7% Karen.

Tavoy, town (pop. 29,018), ⊙ Tavoy dist., Lower Burma, in Tenasserim, Andaman Sea port at head of Tavoy R. estuary, 165 mi. S of Moulmein; 14°4'N 98°12'E. Iron-ore mines near by; mfg. of silk cloth; trade in salt fish, wood oil, forest products. Airport. Anc. ⊙ independent kingdom, subjected in turn to Burma and Thailand.

Tavoy Island, in N Mergui Archipelago, Lower Burma, in Andaman Sea, off Tenasserim coast, 60 mi. S of Tavoy town; 21 mi. long, 5 mi. wide; mountainous; rises to 2,254 ft.

Tavoy Point, cape of Tenasserim coast, Lower Burma, on Andaman Sea, 38 mi. S of Tavoy town, W of Tavoy R. estuary; 13°32'N 98°10'E; lighthouse.

Tavoy River, in Tenasserim, Lower Burma, rises in extreme N of Tavoy dist., meanders c.90 mi. SSE bet. 2 mtn. ranges. Lower valley is densely inhabited, cultivated. Forms 30-mi.-long estuary on Andaman Sea below Tavoy town; tidal up to 60 mi. upstream.

Tavrichanka (tŭvrēchän'kŭ), town (1948 pop. over 2,000), SW Maritime Territory, Russian SFSR, on Amur Bay, near mouth of Suifun R., and 15 mi. NNW of Vladivostok, on spur of Trans-Siberian RR; lignite mines.

Tavricheskoye (tŭvrē'chĭskŭyŭ). **1** Village (1939 pop. over 2,000), NW East Kazakhstan oblast, Kazakh SSR, on Irtysh R. and 30 mi. NW of Ust-Kamenogorsk; cattle. **2** Village (1939 pop. over 500), S Omsk oblast, Russian SFSR, 30 mi. S of Omsk; metalworks.

Tavron, Greece: see NEA SPHAGEIA.

Tavsanli (täv-shänlŭ'), Turkish *Tavşanlı*, town (pop. 6,404), Kutahya prov., W Turkey, on railroad and 27 mi. WNW of Kutahya; chromium, lignite; wheat, barley.

Tavua (tävo͞o'ä), town (pop. 444), N Viti Levu, Fiji, SW Pacific, 60 mi. NW of Suva, overlooks Tavua Bay; sugar.

Tavy River (tā'vē), Devon, England, rises in Dartmoor 7 mi. S of Okehampton, flows 20 mi. SW, past Tavistock, to Tamar R. 4 mi. NNW of Plymouth.

Tawahi (tŭwä'hē), urban division (1946 pop., with adjoining STEAMER POINT, 12,729) of Aden town, on NW shore of Aden peninsula, 4 mi. WNW of Crater; European residential section; hq. of coaling and cargo work. It developed in latter part of 19th cent. with rise in Aden's trade and superseded the old port of Crater. A military reservation is just SW.

Tawar, Lake (täwär') (□ 21; 10 mi. long, 3 mi. wide, 246 ft. deep), N Sumatra, Indonesia, in mountainous area; Takingun on W shore.

Tawara (tä"wä'rä), town (pop. 18,210), Aichi prefecture, central Honshu, Japan, on N Atsumi Peninsula, on Atsumi Bay and 10 mi. SW of Toyohashi; commercial center for agr. area (rice, wheat); cement, raw silk. Building-stone quarrying. Sometimes called Tahara.

Tawaramoto (täwärä'mōtō), town (pop. 4,838), Nara prefecture, S Honshu, Japan, 9 mi. SSW of Nara; collection center for agr. area; makes medicine.

Tawas City (tô'wŭs), city (pop. 1,441), ⊙ Iosco co., NE Mich., c.50 mi. NNE of Bay City, on Tawas Bay (an inlet of Saginaw Bay), sheltered on E by Tawas Point peninsula. Resort, in region of lakes, streams, and farms. Commercial fishing, lumber milling; railroad shops, gypsum mines. The Lumbermen's Memorial and part of Huron Natl. Forest are near by. Settled c.1853; inc. as village 1885, as city 1895.

Tawas Lake, Iosco co., NE Mich., just N of Tawas City, near L. Huron; c.3 mi. long, 1½ mi. wide. Resort; fishing, duck hunting.

Tawau (täwou'), town (pop. 5,000, including environs), East Coast residency, Br. North Borneo, port on Cowie Harbour, 110 mi. S of Sandakan; trade center for area producing rubber, copra, hemp. Fishing, coal mining.

Tawenkow or **Ta-wen-k'ou** (both: dä'wŭn'kō'), town, W Shantung prov., China, on Tawen R. (tributary of Grand Canal) and 15 mi. S of Taian, and on Tientsin-Pukow RR; coal-mining center.

Tawera, New Zealand: see SPRINGFIELD.

Tawe River (tou'ē), Brecknock and Glamorgan, Wales, rises 9 mi. SSW of Llandovery, flows 36 mi. SW, past Pontardawe and Clydach, to Bristol Channel at Swansea.

Tawfiqi, Rayah, Egypt: see TAUFIQI, RAIYAH.

Tawitawi Group (tä'wētä'wē), island group (1948 pop. 40,030), Sulu prov., Philippines, in Sulu Archipelago, bet. Sulu Sea and Celebes Sea, c.40 mi. off NE coast of Borneo, 60 mi. SW of Jolo Isl.; 5°15'N 120°E. Largest isl. is Tawitawi (□ 229; 1939 pop. 2,922), a long (34 mi.), sparsely inhabited isl., rising to 1,800 ft. Most of the inhabitants of the group are in the small offshore isls. such as Simunul, Bilatan, South Ubian, Bongao, Sanga Sanga, Kinapusan, and Tandubas isls. Coconuts, rice, fruit are grown. Shell fishing. Manganese deposits. A U.S. naval base is here, by 1947 pact with the Philippines. Sometimes spelled Tawi-Tawi and Tawi Tawi.

Tawmaw (tô'mô), village, Myitkyina dist., Kachin State, Upper Burma, 65 mi. WNW of Myitkyina, in jade-mining area.

Tawngpeng (tông'pĕng), central state (sawbwaship) (□ 938; pop. 58,398), Northern Shan State, Upper Burma; ⊙ Namhsan. Broken, hilly country bisected by mtn. range (7,000 ft.). Drained by Myitnge R. Tea, rice; teak and pine forests. Lead and silver mines at Bawdwin; smelter at Namtu. Served by Mandalay-Lashio RR and network of roads. Pop.: Palaungs, Shans, Kachins.

Taw River (tô), Devon, England, rises in Dartmoor 3 mi. E of Okehampton, flows 50 mi. NE and NW, past South Tawton and Barnstaple, to Barnstaple Bay near Appledore.

Taxco (tä'skō), officially Taxco de Alarcón, city (pop. 4,963), Guerrero, SW Mexico, on S slope of central plateau, 70 mi. SSW of Mexico city; alt. 5,692 ft. Resort; mining (silver, gold, lead, copper, zinc), trading, and mfg. center; tanneries, foundries, textile mills. Famed for silverware; known also for jewelry and other native handicrafts. Picturesque colonial town with quaint bldgs. and steep cobbled streets; new building is restricted and colonial monuments are protected by Mex. govt. Silver discovered here under Hernando Cortés, who established a mining community 1529. Owes development to José de la Borda, Fr. miner, who after 1717 built roads and lavish colonial San Sebastián church. City's charm and delightful climate attract tourists, writers, artists.

Taxenbach (täk'sūnbäkh), town (pop. 2,549), Salzburg, W central Austria, near the Salzach, 14 mi. SW of Bischofshofen; rye, oats, horses.

Taxila (tăk'sĭlŭ), Sanskrit *Takshasila*, archaeological site, Rawalpindi dist., N Punjab, W Pakistan, 16 mi. NW of Rawalpindi. Remains excavated here of 3 successive cities, generally considered to have existed bet. c.7th cent. B.C. and 7th cent. A.D. Earliest city was famous seat of learning in anc. India; 2d city was built soon after invasion of Alexander the Great in 326 B.C. Third city rose up in Mauryan period and became ⊙ NW section of Asokan empire; occupied (c.1st–2d cent. A.D.) by Kushans; visited by Hsüan-tsang in 7th cent. Among ruins are Buddhist stupas and monasteries, streets and dwellings, and sculpture of Gandhara school of art. Coins, implements, and reliefs in local mus.

Taximaroa, Mexico: see HIDALGO, Michoacán.

Taxisco (täksē'skō), town (1950 pop. 1,686), Santa Rosa dept., S Guatemala, in coastal plain, 6 mi. W of Chiquimulilla; livestock-raising center; dairying; coffee plantations.

Tay, Firth of, Scotland: see TAY RIVER.

Tay, Loch (lŏkh tā'), lake (15 mi. long, 1 mi. wide; 508 ft. deep), W central Perthshire, Scotland, 6 mi. WSW of Aberfeldy. Inlet: Dochart R. (headstream of the Tay) at Killin (SW); outlet; Tay R. at Kenmore (NE). Ben Lawers rises on NW bank.

Tayabamba (tīäbäm'bä), city (pop. 1,243), ⊙ Patás or Pataz prov. (□ 1,958; pop. 47,033), Libertad dept., N central Peru, on W slopes of Cordillera Central of the Andes, 130 mi. ESE of Trujillo; alt. 8,317 ft. Wheat, corn, coca; goat raising.

Tayabas, province, Philippines: see QUEZON, province.

Tayabas (täyä'bäs), town (1939 pop. 5,921; 1948 municipality pop. 16,989), Quezon prov., central Luzon, Philippines, 18 mi. ESE of San Pablo; agr. center (coconuts, rice).

Tayabas Bay, inlet of S Luzon, Philippines, connected with S.China Sea (W) by Verde Isl. Passage, and with Sibuyan Sea (SE) by Mompog Pass; c.40 mi. long, c.20 mi. wide. Contains Pagbilao Grande Isl. Near N shore is town of Lucena.

Taya Bay (dä'yä'), inlet of S.China Sea, in S Kwangtung prov., China, NE of Hong Kong; 20 mi. wide, 15 mi. long. Fisheries. Formerly called Bias Bay.

Tayacaja, Peru: see PAMPAS, Huancavelica dept.

Tayao (dä'you'), town (pop. 3,699), ⊙ Tayao co. (pop. 93,309), N central Yunnan prov., China, 50 mi. NNW of Tsuyung; alt. 6,693 ft.; rice, wheat, millet, beans, timber.

Tayao Shan, China: see TANGTU.

Tayebat, Iran: see TAIABAD.

Tayeh (dä'yĕ') [Chinese,=great smelter], town (pop. 27,740), ⊙ Tayeh co. (pop. 323,715), SE Hupeh prov., China, 50 mi. SE of Hankow; major iron-mining center. Mines at Tiehshan (10 mi. NNW) are connected by rail with Shihhweiyao, just SE of Yangtze port of Hwangshihkang. Formerly smelted at Tayeh, ore is now largely shipped to Hanyang steelworks.

Tayenhai Tze, China: see YENHAI TZE.

Tayezhny or **Tayezhnyy** (both: tī'ĕzh-nyē), town (1949 pop. over 500), S Krasnoyarsk territory, Russian SFSR, near Kansk.

Tayga, Russian SFSR: see TAIGA.

Taygetus or **Taiyetos** (tāĭ'jutŭs, Gr. tī'yĕtôs), mountains in S Peloponnesus, Greece, extend 65 mi. from NW Laconia S to Cape Matapan, forming in part Messenia-Laconia border; rise to 7,895 ft. at Mt. Hagios Elias, SW of Sparta. Also called Pentadaktylon.

Taygonos Peninsula, Russian SFSR: see TAIGONOS PENINSULA.

Tayi or **Ta-i** (both: dä'yē'), town (pop. 13,477), ⊙ Tayi co. (pop. 249,222), W Szechwan prov., China, 34 mi. W of Chengtu, near Sikang line; tea, rice, sugar cane, wheat, rapeseed. Coal mines near by.

Taying River, China and Burma: see TAPING RIVER.

Taylor, village (1939 pop. 29), NW Alaska, on Seward Peninsula, 80 mi. N of Nome; 65°41'N 164°47'W; placer gold mining. Airfield.

Taylor. 1 County (□ 1,032; pop. 10,416), N Fla., on Gulf of Mexico (S) and bounded W by Aucilla R.; ⊙ Perry. Flatwoods area, with large swamps and many small lakes. Forestry (lumber, naval stores), cattle raising, farming (corn, peanuts), and fishing. Limestone deposits. Formed 1856. **2** County (□ 400; pop. 9,113), W central Ga.; ⊙ Butler. Bounded N and E by Flint R. Intersected by the fall line. Agr. (cotton, corn, peanuts, pecans, peaches, livestock) and sawmilling area. Formed 1852. **3** County (□ 528; pop. 12,420), SW Iowa, on Mo. line (S); ⊙ Bedford. Prairie agr. area (corn, hogs, cattle, poultry, hay) drained by One Hundred and Two, Little Platte, and East Nodaway rivers. Coal deposits mined in W. Formed 1847. **4** County (□ 284; pop. 14,403), central Ky.; ⊙ Campbellsville. Drained by Green R. and several creeks. Rolling agr. area (burley tobacco, corn, oats, hay, wheat, livestock); timber; limestone quarries. Some mfg. (especially wood products) at Campbellsville. Formed 1848. **5** County (□ 913; pop. 63,370), W central Texas; ⊙ ABILENE. Drained to N by tributaries of Brazos R., to S by Colorado R. tributaries; alt. c.1,700–2,400 ft. Diversified agr. (cotton, grain sorghums, wheat, peanuts, fruit, truck); livestock (cattle, sheep, goats, hogs, horses, mules, poultry); dairying. Oil, natural-gas wells. Recreation on L. Abilene (state park). Mfg., processing at Abilene. Formed 1858. **6** County (□ 175; pop. 18,422), N W.Va.; ⊙ Grafton. On Allegheny Plateau; drained by Tygart R. Includes part of Tygart R. Reservoir and its surrounding state park. Agr. (livestock, fruit, tobacco); coal mines, natural-gas field, timber; industry at Grafton. Formed 1844. **7** County (□ 979; pop. 18,456), N central Wis.; ⊙ Medford. Drained by Black, Yellow, Jump, and Rib rivers. Contains a section of Chequamegon Natl. Forest and several small resort lakes. Dairying, farming (potatoes, canning crops), stock raising; sawmilling. Formed 1875.

Taylor. 1 Town (pop. 547), Columbia co., SW Ark., 18 mi. SW of Magnolia, near La. line. **2** Village (pop. 125), Lafayette co., N Miss., 8 mi. SSW of Oxford, in agr. and timber area. **3** Village (pop. 311), ⊙ Loup co., central Nebr., 25 mi. NW of Ord and on N.Loup R.; dairy and poultry produce, livestock, grain. Near-by scenic spot is Cheesebrough Canyon. **4** Village (pop. 258), Stark co., W N.Dak., 17 mi. E of Dickinson. Near by are deposits of clay used for mfg. of paints, cleaners, linoleum, cosmetics. **5** Industrial borough (pop. 7,176), Lackawanna co., NE Pa., on Lackawanna R. just below Scranton. Settled c.1800. **6** Village, S.C.: see TAYLORS. **7** City (pop. 9,071), Williamson co., central Texas, 29 mi. NE of Austin; trade, shipping, processing center for rich agr. area (cotton, grain, truck); ships agr. produce; has mattress factory, meat and poultry-packing plants, oil refineries, flour, cottonseed-oil mills; dairying, pecan shelling. Platted 1876, inc. 1877. **8** Village (pop. 350), Jackson co., W central Wis., 38 mi. SSE of Eau Claire, in dairying region.

Taylor, Mount (11,389 ft.), NW N.Mex., volcanic cone and highest point in San Mateo Mts., c.55 mi. WNW of Albuquerque.

Taylor River, W central Colo., rises near Castle Peak in Elk Mts., flows c.50 mi. SE and SW, through Taylor Park Reservoir, joining Slate R. at Almont to form Gunnison R. Taylor Park Dam (206 ft. high, 675 ft. long) is 16 mi. NE of Almont; completed 1937 as unit in Uncompahgre reclamation project; forms Taylor Park Reservoir (capacity 106,200 acre-ft.).

Taylors or **Taylor,** village (pop. 1,518), Greenville co., NW S.C., on Enoree R. and 8 mi. NE of Greenville; residential, mfg. (textiles, clothing, pharmaceuticals). Grew on site of Chick Springs, former summer resort.

Taylors Falls, village (pop. 520), Chisago co., E Minn., on St. Croix R. and 38 mi. NE of St. Paul; dairy products. INTERSTATE PARK is here.

Taylors Island, low, marshy island (c.8 mi. long, 4 mi. wide), Dorchester co., E Md., in Chesapeake Bay 14 mi. WSW of Cambridge; separated from mainland (E) by narrow creeks (bridged). Center of Eastern Shore's muskrat-trapping industry; summer resort (fishing, duck hunting). Only village is Taylors Island (vegetable, seafood canneries). Isl. settled c.1659.

Taylor Springs, village (pop. 627), Montgomery co., S central Ill., just S of Hillsboro, in agr. and bituminous-coal-mining area.

Taylorsville. 1 Town (pop. 260), Bartow and Polk cos., NW Ga., 12 mi. WSW of Cartersville; iron mining. **2** Town (pop. 888), ⊙ Spencer co., NW central Ky., on Salt R. and 28 mi. SE of Louisville, in Bluegrass agr. area (livestock, burley tobacco, corn); mfg. of dairy and animal-fat products; feed and flour milling, hide curing. **3** Town (pop. 1,116), Smith co., S central Miss., 20 mi. WNW of Laurel and on Leaf R.; truck, cotton, lumber. **4** Town (pop. 1,310), ⊙ Alexander co., W central N.C., 18 mi. NW of Statesville; cotton, hosiery, lumber, and paper-box mills. Inc. 1887. **5** Village, Ohio: see PHILO.

Taylorville, city (pop. 9,188), ⊙ Christian co., central Ill., near South Fork of Sangamon R., 26 mi. SW of Decatur; trade center in bituminous-coal-mining and agr. area (livestock, grain, poultry; dairy products); mfg. (tools, feed, paper, cigars, stationery). Founded c.1840, inc. 1882.

Tayma, Saudi Arabia: see TAIMA.

Taymi Canal, Peru: see TAIMI CANAL.

Taymyr, in Rus. names: see TAIMYR.

Tayncha, Kazakh SSR: see TAINCHA.

Tayninh (tī'nĭng'), town (1936 pop. 2,748), ⊙ Tayninh prov. (□ 1,700; 1943 pop. 146,100), S Vietnam, in Cochin China; on Tayninh R. (small tributary of the East Vaico) and 55 mi. NW of Saigon. Rubber and timber center; rice, sugar, and coconut-oil mills. Religious center of Caodaism, a religious sect (founded 1926) embodying elements of Buddhism, Taoism, Catholicism, and Confucianism.

Tayoltita (tīōltē'tä), mining settlement (pop. 1,948), Durango, N Mexico, on W slope of Sierra Madre Occidental, 80 mi. W of Durango; silver, gold, lead, copper mining.

Tayport (tāpôrt'), burgh (1931 pop. 3,164; 1951 census 3,222), NE Fifeshire, Scotland, on the Firth of Tay, 4 mi. E of Dundee; 56°27'N 2°53'W; seaside resort and ferry port for Broughty Ferry, Angus. Formerly Ferryport-on-Craig.

Tay River (tā), largest river (118 mi. long) in Scotland, mainly in Perthshire. Its headstream, the Fillan, rises on Ben Lui at Argyll border, flows through Loch Dochart, where it becomes the DOCHART RIVER, into Loch Tay; Tay proper issues at E end of the loch and flows 54 mi. E and SE, past Aberfeldy, Dunkeld, and Perth, to confluence with Earn R. 3 mi. W of Newburgh. It here forms the tidal Firth of Tay, extending 25 mi. ENE and E, past Dundee and Broughty Ferry, to the North Sea at Buddon Ness. At DUNDEE the firth is crossed by Tay Bridge. Drainage area of the Tay includes most of Perthshire, and parts of Angus, Argyll, and Fifeshire. River has important salmon fisheries; chief tributaries are Garry, Tummel, and Earn rivers.

Tayshet, Russian SFSR: see TAISHET.

Taytay (tī'tī, tītī'). **1** Town (1939 pop. 460; 1948 municipality pop. 4,050), N Palawan, Philippines, on Taytay Bay (large inlet on NE coast). Founded in early 18th cent. as a fort by Spain. **2** Town (1939 pop. 10,484; 1948 municipality pop. 14,144), Rizal prov., S Luzon, Philippines, 10 mi. ESE of Manila; rail terminus; trade center (rice, sugar cane, fruit).

Tayü (dä'yü'), town (pop. 14,970), ⊙ Tayü co. (pop. 90,109), SW Kiangsi prov., China, on tributary of Kan R., N of Tayü Mts., and 45 mi. WSW of Kanhsien; major tungsten-mining center. Mfg. of bamboo paper. Until 1912 called Nanan.

Tayüan (dä'yüän'), Jap. *Taien* (tī'ān), village (1935 pop. 1,089), NW Formosa, on W coast, 10 mi. NW of Taoyüan; rice, sweet potatoes, vegetables, livestock.

Tayug (täyōōg'), town (1939 pop. 3,707; 1948 municipality pop. 19,782), Pangasinan prov., central

Luzon, Philippines, 28 mi. SSE of Baguio; agr. center (rice, corn).

Tayü Mountains, Chinese *Tayü Ling* (dä'yü' lĭng'), S China, section of the Nan Ling on Kwangtung-Kiangsi border; extend 40 mi. E–W along border in area S of Tayü (Kiangsi prov.); rise to over 2,000 ft. Crossed by Meiling Pass, one of the main routes bet. Kwangtung and Kiangsi. Also called Meiling Mts.

Tayung (dä'yŏŏng'), town, ⊙ Tayung co. (pop. 151,468), NW Hunan prov., China, on branch of Li R. and 75 mi. W of Changteh. Copper, silver, and coal found near by. Until 1914, Yungting.

Taz, river, Russian SFSR: see TAZ RIVER.

Taza (täzä'), city (pop. 28,457), Fez region, NE Fr. Morocco, 55 mi. ENE of Fez, strategically located on a pass (crossed by road and railroad) bet. Rif Mts. (N) and Middle Atlas (S), historically the chief land route of access to central and W Morocco; alt. 1,800 ft.; 34°13'N 4°1'W. Commercial center (wool, grain, cork, palm fibers); mfg. of building materials, footwear, carpets. Lead mine at the Djebel Chiker (9 mi. S). Summer resort area in spurs of the Middle Atlas (just S). Founded 11th cent. as a Berber fortress, Taza consists today of the walled Moslem city and of an adjacent (N) modern European garrison town. Occupied by French in 1914.

Taza-Bazar (tä'zä-bäzär'). **1** Village, Turkmen SSR: see ANDREYEVA, IMENI. **2** Village, Uzbek SSR: see SHUMANAI.

Tazacorte (tä-thäkôr'tä), village (pop. 2,808), Palma, Canary Isls., 7 mi. WSW of Santa Cruz de la Palma; bananas, tomatoes, sugar cane, cereals, livestock. Sugar mill.

Taza Khurmatli or **Tazah Khurmatli** (tä'zü khŏŏrmät'lē), village, Kirkuk prov., NE Iraq, on railroad and 12 mi. SSW of Kirkuk; barley, wheat.

Tazarjan (tăzärjän'), village, Tenth Prov., in Yezd, central Iran, 25 mi. SW of Yezd, in hilly region; noted summer resort.

Tazawa, Lake (tä"zä'wä), Jap. *Tazawa-ko* (□10), Akita prefecture, N Honshu, Japan, 27 mi. E of Akita; roughly circular, 4 mi. in diameter; deepest (1,400 ft.) in Japan.

Taz Bay (täs), E inlet of Ob Bay, NE Yamal-Nenets Natl. Okrug, Tyumen oblast, Russian SFSR, N of Arctic Circle; 250 mi. long, 25–40 mi. wide; tundra shores. Receives Taz R.

Taze (tä"zā'), village, Shwebo dist., Upper Burma, near Mu R., 32 mi. NNW of Shwebo.

Tazenakhte (täznäkt'), village, Marrakesh region, SW Fr. Morocco, on E slope of the Anti-Atlas, 20 mi. SW of Ouarzazate; date palms. Bou Azzer cobalt mines 15 mi. E.

Tazerbo (täzĕr'bō), oasis (1950 pop. 100), in Libyan Desert, S Cyrenaica, Libya, 165 mi. NW of El Giof.

Tazewell (tăz'wŭl, –wĕl). **1** County (□ 653; pop. 76,165), central Ill.; ⊙ Pekin. Bounded NW by Illinois R.; drained by Mackinaw R. Agr. (corn, oats, soybeans, wheat, livestock, poultry, hay). Bituminous-coal mining; sand and gravel deposits; timber. Diversified mfg.: farm machinery, clothing, food products, washing machines; clay, metal, wood, and leather products. Includes Fort Creve Coeur State Park. Formed 1827. **2** County (□ 522; pop. 47,512), SW Va.; ⊙ Tazewell. In the Alleghenies; bounded N by W.Va.; includes part of Jefferson Natl. Forest. Drained by Clinch R. and a headstream of the Holston. Bituminous-coal mining and livestock raising are important; also produces dairy products, fruit, clover, corn. Limestone quarrying; some mfg.; brickmaking, lumber milling. Formed 1799.

Tazewell. 1 Village (pop. c.800), ⊙ Claiborne co., NE Tenn., 38 mi. NNE of Knoxville, in mtn. timber and agr. area; woodworking, printing, canning; tobacco warehouses. **2** Town (pop. 1,347), ⊙ Tazewell co., SW Va., in the Alleghenies, 20 mi. SW of Bluefield; commercial center for bituminous-coal and agr. (livestock, corn, wheat, potatoes) area; lumber milling. Settled 1769; inc. 1866.

Tazlina Glacier (tăzlē'nü), S Alaska, rises in Chugach Mts. at 61°30'N 146°35'W; flows 20 mi. N to Tazlina L.

Tazlina Lake (18 mi. long, 1–4 mi. wide), S Alaska, 50 mi. NNE of Valdez; 61°50'N 146°29'W; fed by Tazlina and Nelchina glaciers; drained NE by Tazlina R.

Tazmalt (täzmält'), village (pop. 1,338), Constantine dept., NE Algeria, on the Oued Sahel at SE foot of Djurdjura range, on railroad and 45 mi. SW of Bougie; olive-oil pressing.

Tazovskoye, Russian SFSR: see KHALMER-SEDE.

Taz Peninsula (täs), NE Yamal-Nenets Natl. Okrug, Tyumen oblast, Russian SFSR, bet. Ob (W) and Taz (E) bays; tundra.

Taz River, E Yamal-Nenets Natl. Okrug, Tyumen oblast, Russian SFSR, rises in swampy Ob-Yenisei divide, flows 485 mi. N, past Krasnoselkup, to Taz Bay at Khalmer-Sede.

Tazuruhama (täzŏŏrŏŏ'hämü) or **Tatsuruhama** (tätsŏŏ–), town (pop. 3,586), Ishikawa prefecture, central Honshu, Japan, on W inlet of Toyama Bay, 5 mi. WNW of Nanao; health resort (saline hot springs). Until 1934, called Wakura.

't Bildt, 't Bilt (both: ŭt bĭlt'), **Het Bildt,** or **Het Bilt,** polder area in Friesland prov., N Netherlands, NW of Leeuwarden; reclaimed in 1508. Is also commune including parish villages of SINT ANNA-PAROCHIE, Sint Jacobi-Parochie (pop. 1,199), and Vrouwen-Parochie (pop. 620). Cattle raising, dairying, truck gardening.

Tbilisi, Georgian SSR: see TIFLIS.

Tbilisskaya (ŭtbĭlyē'skīŭ), village (1926 pop. 9,054), E Krasnodar Territory, Russian SFSR, on right bank of Kuban R. and 19 mi. WSW of Kropotkin; flour mill, metalworks; wheat, sunflowers, sugar beets. Until 1936, Tiflisskaya.

't Bilt, Netherlands: see 'T BILDT.

Tchad, territory, Fr. Equatorial Africa: see CHAD.

Tchad, Lake, Africa: see CHAD, LAKE.

Tchanak Kalessi, Turkey: see CANAKKALE, town.

Tchaourou (chou'rōō), village, S central Dahomey, Fr. West Africa, on railroad and 30 mi. S of Parakou; cotton, peanuts, shea nuts; cattle, sheep.

Tchatalja, Turkey: see CATALCA.

Tchefuncta River (chŭfŭngk'tü, –tē), SE La., rises near Miss. line E of Kentwood, flows c.40 mi. S, through Tangipahoa and St. Tammany parishes, to L. Pontchartrain at N end. Also called Chefuncte R. State park on L. Pontchartrain, SE of river's mouth.

Tchékam, Kwangtung prov., China: see CHIKHOM, commercial dist.

Tchepone (chā'pōn'), town, Savannakhet prov., central Laos, on Savannakhet-Dongha road and 90 mi. W of Hue; gold mines.

Tchibanga (chēbäng-gä'), town, ⊙ Nyanga region (formed 1949; pop. 34,700), SW Gabon, Fr. Equatorial Africa, on Nyanga R. and 210 mi. SSE of Port-Gentil; center of native trade; rice growing.

Tchien (chē, chĕ), town, Eastern Prov., SE Liberia, c.100 mi. NE of Greenville; trade center; palm oil and kernels, kola nuts, cassava. Gold dredging.

Tchirpan, Bulgaria: see CHIRPAN.

Tchoban Bey, Syria: see CHOBAN BEY.

Tchorlu, Turkey: see CORLU.

Tchula (chōō'lü), town (pop. 927), Holmes co., central Miss., 24 mi. S of Greenwood, near the Yazoo; lumber milling; fisheries.

Tczew (chĕf), Ger. *Dirschau* (dĭr'shou), city (1946 pop. 20,934), Gdansk prov., N Poland, on the Vistula (bridged) and 20 mi. SSE of Danzig. Rail junction; trade center, specializing in lumber and grain; mfg. of bricks, cement goods, roofing materials, agr. machinery, furniture, enamelware, cartons; flour milling, sawmilling, canning, brewing. Founded 1209; included (1466) in Poland; passed 1772 to Prussia; returned 1919 to Poland. Developed extensively following building (1857) of a bridge over the Vistula; became a rail center. Considered a seaport since 1928.

Tea, town (pop. 151), Lincoln co., SE S.Dak., 10 mi. SW of Sioux Falls; farm trading center.

Teabo (tää'bō), town (pop. 2,560), Yucatan, SE Mexico, 19 mi. E of Ticul; henequen, sugar cane, fruit, timber.

Teaca (tyä'kä), Hung. *Teke* (tĕ'kĕ), pop. 2,935), Mures prov., central Rumania, on railroad and 24 mi. NNW of Targu-Mures; noted for its white wines; extensive vineyards in vicinity. Has old Evangelical church. In Hungary, 1940–45.

Teacheys (tē'chēz), town (pop. 226), Duplin co., E N.C., 38 mi. N of Wilmington.

Teague (tēg), city (pop. 2,925), Freestone co., E central Texas, c.50 mi. E of Waco; trade, shipping center for cotton, truck, timber area; railroad shops; cotton gins, mfg. of mattresses, dairy products; fish hatchery. Founded 1906.

Teallach, Scotland: see AN TEALLACH.

Teamhair Breagh, Ireland: see TARA.

Team Valley Trading Estate, England: see GATESHEAD.

Te-an, China: see TEIAN.

Te Anau, Lake (tē" ănou'), second largest lake (□ 132) of New Zealand, in SW S.Isl., 75 mi. NNW of Invercargill; 33 mi. long, 6 mi. wide, 906 ft. deep; contains numerous islets; salmon, trout.

Teaneck (tē'nĕk"), residential suburban township (pop. 33,772), Bergen co., NE N.J., near Hackensack R., just E of Hackensack; some mfg. (chemicals, metal products, machinery, boxes); dairy products. Has jr. col. Inc. 1895. Developed rapidly since building of George Washington Bridge to New York.

Teano (tĕä'nô), anc. *Teanum Sidicinum,* town (pop. 4,422), Caserta prov., Campania, S Italy, at SE foot of extinct volcano Rocca Monfina, 13 mi. NW of Capua; agr. center (wine, fruit, vegetables). Bishopric. Roman ruins (theater, baths) near by. Damaged in Second World War.

Teapa (tää'pä), city (pop. 2,199), Tabasco, SE Mexico, on navigable affluent of Grijalva R., near Chiapas border, and 30 mi. S of Villahermosa; rice, beans, coffee, cacao, fruit, stock, timber.

Teapi Island, Chile: see EASTER ISLAND.

Teapot Dome, area near Casper, Wyo., set aside 1915 by President Wilson as naval oil reserve. Certain aspects of the way in which Albert B. Fall, U.S. Secretary of the Interior in Harding's administration, leased (1922) the govt. oil fields to Harry F. Sinclair led to an investigation (1923), great notoriety, and criminal prosecutions resulting in conviction (1929) of Fall.

Tearaght Island, Ireland: see BLASKET ISLANDS.

Te Araroa (tē" ürä'rōü), township (pop. 417), ⊙ Matakaoa co. (□ 295; pop. 1,850), NE N.Isl., New Zealand, near East Cape, 75 mi. NNE of Gisborne; agr. center; sheep.

Tear of the Clouds, Lake, Essex co., NE N.Y., small tarn on slope of Mt. Marcy; source of main headstream (Opalescent R.) of the Hudson.

Te Aroha (tē" ürō'ü), borough (pop. 2,426), ⊙ Piako co. (□ 444; pop. 5,165), N N.Isl., New Zealand, 70 mi. SE of Auckland and on Thames R.; one of chief health resorts of New Zealand; mineral springs.

Teate, Italy: see CHIETI, town.

Teaticket, Mass.: see FALMOUTH.

Te-Au-o-Tu, Cook Isls.: see MANUAE.

Te Awamutu (tē" äwämōō'tōō), borough (pop. 3,017), ⊙ Waipa co. (□ 435; pop. 14,658), N N.Isl., New Zealand, 85 mi. SSE of Auckland; brickworks, dairy plants.

Teba (tā'vä), town (pop. 6,392), Málaga prov., S Spain, in Andalusia, on affluent of the Guadalhorce, at S foot of the Sierra de Yeguas, and 20 mi. W of Antequera; processing and agr. center; olives and olive oil, truck produce, cereals and flour, grapes, livestock. Marble quarrying. Mfg. of shoes, liquor, esparto goods, plaster. Empress Eugenie had title of countess of Teba.

Tébar (tā'vär), town (pop. 1,491), Cuenca prov., E central Spain, 40 mi. S of Cuenca; olives, cereals, saffron, grapes, livestock.

Tebarya, Israel: see TIBERIAS.

Tebay (tē'bā), village and parish (pop. 977), central Westmorland, England, on Lune R. and 10 mi. NE of Kendal; livestock.

Teberda (tyĕbyĭrdä'), town (1939 pop. over 500), NW Georgian SSR, in the W Greater Caucasus, on Teberda R., on Sukhumi Military Road and 23 mi. SSW of Klukhori; mtn. health resort (alt. 4,200 ft.). Until 1944, in Karachai Autonomous Oblast.

Teberda River, NW Georgian SSR, rises on N slopes of W Greater Caucasus W of Klukhori Pass, flows 40 mi. N, past Teberda, to Kuban R. at Klukhori. Sukhumi Military Road runs through its valley.

Tebessa or **Tébessa** (tĕbĕ'sü), anc. *Theveste,* town (pop. 18,293), Constantine dept., NE Algeria, in the Tebessa Mts. (E range of the Saharan Atlas), near Tunisia border, 110 mi. SE of Constantine; 35°25'N 8°7'E. Center of important phosphate-mining dist., and strategic gateway to Tunisia's shott region. Mines at the Djebel Kouif (13 mi. NE; largest in Algeria) and Djebel Dir (6 mi. N) linked by railroad with Bône (100 mi. N), the chief shipping port. Tebessa also has rail line to Constantine and to Le Kef (Tunisia). Town produces fertilizer and is noted for native silk embroidery and carpets. Exports wool, esparto, and dates from the interior. Tebessa's importance is enhanced by iron mines at the Djebel Ouenza (37 mi. N) and Djebel bou Kadra (25 mi. N), and by important phosphate deposits at the Djebel Onk (50 mi. SSW). Extensive anc. remains include the Roman arch of Caracalla (3d cent. A.D.) and an adjoining temple; an early Christian basilica (c.4th cent. A.D.) and restored Byzantine walls (with 13 square towers and 4 gates). Occupied by French in 1851. In Second World War, Tebessa served as American base during battle for Tunisia.

Tebessa Mountains, easternmost range of the Saharan Atlas, on Algeria-Tunisia border, S and E of Tebessa; rise to 5,600 ft. Important phosphate mines at the Djebel Kouif and Djebel Dir.

Tebicuary River (täbēkwärē'), S Paraguay, rises near Tavaí, meanders c.250 mi. W, past Florida, to Paraguay R. 20 mi. NNE of Pilar. During rainy season, navigable for c.90 mi.

Tebingtinggi (tŭbĭng"tĭng'gē), town (pop. 14,026), NE Sumatra, Indonesia, 40 mi. ESE of Medan, in Deli region; rail junction; trade center for agr. area (rubber, tobacco, tea, fibers, palm oil, rice).

Tebingtinggi, island (45 mi. long, 15 mi. wide), Indonesia, in Strait of Malacca, just off E coast of Sumatra, c.60 mi. WSW of Singapore, adjacent to Padang isl. (NW) and Rangsang isl. (NE); 0°55'N 102°45'E; isl. is low, wooded, swampy. Produces sago and timber. On N coast is port of Selatpanjang or Selatpandjang. Also called Rantau.

Tebneen, Lebanon: see TIBNIN.

Teboulba (tĕbōōlbä'), village, Mahdia dist., E Tunisia, near the Mediterranean, 22 mi. SE of Sousse; olive and citrus groves. On the coast 5 mi. ESE are the ruins of anc. *Thapsus,* where Caesar decisively defeated the Pompeians under Cato the Younger in 46 B.C.

Tébourba (täbōōrbä'), town (pop. 2,603), Tunis dist., N Tunisia, on the Medjerda and 19 mi. W of Tunis; agr. market; olive-oil mfg., stallion breeding, wine making. Near-by 18th-cent. bridge, dam destroyed in Second World War. Moorish pop.

Teboursouk (tĕbōōrsōōk'), town (pop. 5,276), ⊙ Teboursouk dist. (□ 476; 1946 pop. 59,157), N central Tunisia, 55 mi. WSW of Tunis; market center in olive-growing and livestock-raising region. Has a Byzantine citadel. Ruins of DOUGGA 4 mi. SSW. Also spelled Téboursouk.

Teboursouk Mountains, low range of N Tunisia, extending c.60 mi. parallel to Medjerda R. bet. Nebeur (SW) and Tébourba (NE).

Tebrau Strait, Malaya: see JOHORE STRAIT.

Tebriz, Iran: see TABRIZ.

Tebuk or **Tabuk** (both: tĕbōōk'), village and oasis, N Hejaz, Saudi Arabia, in Madian hinterland, 350 mi. NW of Medina, on former Hejaz railway; 28°23'N 36°53'E.

Tecali (tākä'lē), officially Tecali de Herrera, town (pop. 1,409), Puebla, central Mexico, on central plateau, 18 mi. SE of Puebla; alt. 7,349 ft.; cereals, vegetables. Marble and onyx deposits near by.

Tecalitlán (tākälētlän'), town (pop. 4,828), Jalisco, central Mexico, 33 mi. NE of Colima; alt. 3,400 ft.; sugar-growing center.

Tecámac (tākä'mäk), officially Santa Cruz Tecámac, town (pop. 831), Mexico state, central Mexico, 23 mi. NE of Mexico city; maguey, cereals.

Tecamachalco (tākämächäl'kō), city (pop. 4,014), Puebla, central Mexico, on central plateau, on railroad and 33 mi. ESE of Puebla; alt. 6,604 ft. Agr. center (corn, wheat, maguey). Has colonial churches.

Tecapa (tākä'pä), volcano (5,367 ft.) in Usulután dept., E central Salvador, 11 mi. NNW of Usulután. One of its craters is occupied by L. Tecapa (sulphurous waters).

Tecate (tākä'tä), town (pop. 1,088), Northern Territory, Lower California, NW Mexico, on U.S. border, 33 mi. SW of San Diego (Calif.), 65 mi. W of Mexicali; agr. center in irrigated area (cotton, fruit, vegetables). On U.S. side is village of Tecate, a port of entry.

Tecer Mountains (tĕjĕr'), central Turkey, extend 130 mi. NE from Bunyan, bet. the Kizil Irmak (NW) and Yenice Irmak and Calti rivers (SE); rise to 9,160 ft. in Bey Dag.

Techado, Cerro (sĕ'rō tächä'dō), Andean peak (6,170 ft.) in Llanquihue prov., S central Chile, on NE bank of L. Todos los Santos, 55 mi. NE of Puerto Montt.

Techaluta (tächälōō'tä), town (pop. 1,687), Jalisco, W Mexico, on L. Sayula, on railroad and 45 mi. SE of Ameca; alt. 4,511 ft.; alfalfa, fruit, vegetables, stock.

Te-ch'ang, China: see TEHCHANG.

Teche, Bayou (bī'ō tĕsh'), La., formed by tributary bayous in St. Landry parish, winds c.125 mi. SE, through fertile sugar-growing area, past Arnaudville (head of navigation), Breaux Bridge, St. Martinville, New Iberia, Jeanerette, and Franklin, to Atchafalaya R. c.11 mi. above Morgan City. The "Teche country," with many winding bayous and picturesque towns, is setting for Longfellow's *Evangeline;* many of its inhabitants are descendants of Acadians.

Techendorf, Austria: see WEISSENSEE.

Te-chiang, China: see TEHKIANG.

Te-ch'in, China: see TEHTSIN.

Te-ch'ing. **1** Town, Chekiang prov., China: see TEHTSING. **2** Town, Kwangtung prov., China: see TAKHING.

Te-ch'ing, Tibet: see DECHEN.

Techirghiol (tĕkĕrgyôl'), town (1948 pop. 2,136), Constanta prov., SE Rumania, 8 mi. S of Constanta; summer and health resort on salt lake, with radioactive mud baths; rail terminus; flour milling, brick mfg.

Techo, airport, Colombia: see BOGOTÁ.

Te-chou, China: see TEHCHOW.

Tech River (tĕsh), Pyrénées-Orientales dept., S France, rises in E Pyrenees on Sp. border above Prats-de-Mollo, flows 50 mi. NE, through the VALLESPIR, past Amélie-les-Bains, Céret, and Le Boulou, to Gulf of Lion 10 mi. SE of Perpignan.

Teck (tĕk), peak (2,543 ft.) in the Swabian Jura, Germany, 4 mi. S of Kirchheim (N foot); there is excellent view of Black Forest and Swabian Jura. Has ruins of ancestral castle of dukes of Teck.

Tecka (tā'kä), village (pop. estimate 500), ⊙ Languiñeo dept.,W Chubut natl. territory, Argentina, on Tecka R. (100 mi. long, flows NNE to Chubut R.) and 45 mi. SE of Esquel; alfalfa, oats, wheat, goats, cattle, sheep. Gold, lignite deposits near by.

Teck Hock (tĕk"hôk'), village (pop. 2,033), E Singapore isl., 7 mi. NE of Singapore; rubber. Pop. is Chinese.

Tecklenburg (tĕk'lŭnbŏŏrk), town (pop. 2,144), in former Prussian prov. of Westphalia, NW Germany, after 1945 in North Rhine-Westphalia, in Teutoburg Forest, 10 mi. WSW of Osnabrück. Has ruined castle.

Teckomatorp (tĕkōō'mätôrp"), village (pop. 895), Malmohus co., S Sweden, 10 mi. E of Landskrona; rail junction; sugar refining; sugar beets, grain, potatoes.

Tecoanapa (tākwänä'pä), town (pop. 1,238), Guerrero, SW Mexico, in Pacific lowland, 30 mi. E of Acapulco; sugar cane, fruit, livestock.

Tecoh (tākō'), town (pop. 2,709), Yucatan, SE Mexico, 18 mi. SSE of Mérida; henequen, sugar, corn.

Tecolotlán (tākōlōtlän'), town (pop. 4,266), Jalisco, W Mexico, 23 mi. SSE of Ameca; alt. 4,200 ft.; agr. center (grain, sugar cane, cotton, fruit, stock).

Tecoluca (tākōlōō'kä), city (pop. 2,720), San Vicente dept., S central Salvador, at SE foot of volcano San Vicente, on railroad and 6 mi. S of San Vicente; grain, coffee, livestock raising.

Tecolutla (-lōōt'lä), town (pop. 533), Veracruz, E Mexico, minor port at mouth of Tecolutla R., in Gulf lowland, 21 mi. E of Papantla.

Tecom, Mexico: see TEKOM.

Tecomán (tākōmän'), town (pop. 3,295), Colima, W Mexico, on Armería R., on Pacific coastal plain, and 25 mi. SSW of Colima, on railroad; agr. center (rice, corn, sugar cane, tobacco, coffee, cocoa, fruit).

Tecomatlán (tākōmätlän'). **1** Town (pop. 1,546), Hidalgo, central Mexico, 22 mi. W of Pachuca; corn, beans, fruit, livestock. **2** Town (pop. 1,228), Puebla, central Mexico, on affluent of Atoyac R. and 37 mi. SSE of Matamoros; cereals, sugar cane, fruit, livestock.

Tecomitl or **San Antonio Tecomitl** (sän äntō'nyō tākōmē'tŭl), town (pop. 1,904), Federal Dist., central Mexico, 17 mi. SE of Mexico city; cereals, fruit, vegetables, stock.

Tecozautla (tākōsout'lä), town (pop. 2,025), Hidalgo, central Mexico, 12 mi. N of Huichapan; corn, beans, potatoes, fruit, livestock.

Tecpán or **Tecpán Guatemala** (tĕkpän' gwätämä'lä), city (1950 pop. 3,113), Chimaltenango dept., S central Guatemala, 15 mi. WNW of Chimaltenango, near branch of Inter-American Highway; alt. 7,579 ft. Market center; cotton weaving. Flour milling and sawmilling near by. Here 1st ⊙ Guatemala was established (1524) on site of Indian capitol of Iximché. Formerly Tecpam.

Tecpan (tĕk'pän), officially Tecpan de Galeana, city (pop. 3,232), Guerrero, SW Mexico, in Pacific lowland, 55 mi. WNW of Acapulco; agr. center (rice, sugar cane, fruit, livestock); pearl fisheries on coast. Anc. unexcavated pyramids near by.

Tecpatán (tĕkpätän'), town (pop. 1,218), Chiapas, S Mexico, 29 mi. NNW of Tuxtla; corn, sugar cane, tobacco, fruit.

Tecsö, Ukrainian SSR: see TYACHEVO.

Tecuaco or **San Juan Tecuaco** (sän' hwän' tākwä'kō), town (1950 pop. 692), Santa Rosa dept., S Guatemala, in Pacific piedmont, 8 mi. E of Chiquimulilla; fodder grasses; livestock.

Tecuala (tākwä'lä), town (pop. 6,456), Nayarit, W Mexico, on Pacific coastal plain, on Acaponeta R. and 70 mi. NW of Tepic; agr. center (corn, cotton, tobacco, sugar cane, bananas, tomatoes, livestock); tobacco processing.

Tecuamburro (tākwämbōō'rō), extinct volcano (6,384 ft.), Santa Rosa dept., S Guatemala, 12 mi. SW of Cuilapa.

Tecuanipan (tākwänē'pän), officially San Jerónimo Tecuanipan, town (pop. 1,556), Puebla, central Mexico, 13 mi. WSW of Puebla; cereals, fruit, maguey.

Tecuci (tĕkōōch'), town (1948 pop. 20,292), Putna prov., E Rumania, in Moldavia, on Barlad R. and 125 mi. NE of Bucharest, 40 mi. NW of Galati; rail junction and marketing center. Mfg. of candles, leather goods, bricks; flour milling; distilling. Has large military airfield. Dates from 15th cent.

Teculután (tākōōlōōtän'), town (1950 pop. 864), Zacapa dept., E Guatemala, on Motagua R. and 11 mi. W of Zacapa; livestock.

Tecumseh (tĭkŭm'sē), residential town (pop. 2,412), S Ont., on L. St. Clair, 6 mi. E of Windsor.

Tecumseh. **1** Village (pop. 4,020), Lenawee co., SE Mich., 9 mi. NE of Adrian and on Raisin R. Ships celery, sand, gravel; mfg. (refrigeration equipment, auto parts, trailers, paper products, bricks, tile-making machinery). Has Indian village sites and earthworks. Settled 1824, inc. 1837. **2** City (pop. 1,930), ⊙ Johnson co., SE Nebr., 40 mi. SE of Lincoln and on N.Fork of Nemaha R.; grain, livestock, poultry produce, fruit. Founded 1859. **3** City (pop. 2,275), Pottawatomie co., central Okla., 5 mi. S of Shawnee, in grain, livestock, and truck area; meat packing, lumber and feed milling. A state school for girls is here.

Tecumseh, Mount, peak (4,004 ft.) of White Mts., SE Grafton co., N.H., near Waterville Valley.

Tedders (tĕdârs'), agr. village, Rabat region, W central Fr. Morocco, 45 mi. SE of Rabat.

Teddington, residential former urban district (1931 pop. 23,369), Middlesex, England, SW suburb of London, just S of Twickenham, on the Thames. Here is large Bushey Park, site of Natl. Physical Laboratory, founded 1902; the large U.S. air weather station established in Bushey Park during Second World War was maintained after the war. Port of London begins officially at Teddington dock. Here are largest Thames R. locks. Stephen Hales was curate at 16th-cent. church of St. Mary's for over 50 years. Teddington was inc. (1937) in Twickenham.

Tedjeghi, Fezzan: see TEGERHI.

Teduzara (tādōōsä'rä), village, Pando dept., N Bolivia, on Orton R. and 32 mi. SE of Santa Rosa; rubber.

Tedzhen (tyĭjĕn'), city (1939 pop. over 2,000), SE Ashkhabad oblast, Turkmen SSR, on Trans-Caspian RR and 120 mi. ESE of Ashkhabad. Center of Tedzhen oasis (wheat, cotton, cattle); woolen milling, carpet mfg., metalworking. Near-by (S) Tedzhen reservoir is 2.5 mi. wide, 15 mi. long. On its shore is town of Tedzhenstroi or Tedzhenstroy (1946 pop. 1,600).

Tedzhen River, Turkmen SSR: see HARI RUD.

Tee Harbor, settlement (pop. 32), SE Alaska, on E shore of Lynn Canal, 16 mi. NW of Juneau, on Glacier Highway; supply point; fishing.

Tees River (tēz), England, rises on Cross Fell in E Cumberland, flows 70 mi. E, forming Durham-York border, past Barnard Castle, Stockton-on-Tees, Thornaby-on-Tees, and Middlesbrough, to North Sea 2 mi. N of Redcar. Receives Skerne R. 2 mi. S of Darlington. Navigable below Stockton-on-Tees.

Teeswater (tēz'wô"tŭr), village (pop. 819), S Ont., 12 mi. SW of Walkerton; dairying; lumber, flour mills.

Teewinot, Wyo.: see GRAND TETON NATIONAL PARK.

Tefé (tĭfĕ'), city (pop. 1,651), central Amazonas, Brazil, steamer and hydroplane landing on Tefé R. (here forming a lake) just above its influx into the Amazon, and 310 mi. W of Manaus; ships Brazil nuts, tobacco, copaiba oil, rubber, manioc flour, and dried fish. Mission settlement founded in 17th cent. as Nogueira. Formerly sometimes called Ega. Old spelling, Teffé.

Tefenni (tĕfĕnē'), village (pop. 2,136), Burdur prov., SW Turkey, 39 mi. SW of Burdur; wheat, barley, onions, opium.

Tefé River (tĭfĕ'), W central Amazonas, Brazil, flows c.550 mi. NNE to the Amazon (right bank) below Tefé. Forms lake above its mouth. Navigable in lower course.

Teffé, Brazil: see TEFÉ.

Tefía (tāfē'ä), village (pop. 314), Fuerteventura, Canary Isls., 10 mi. W of Puerto de Cabras; airfield.

Teg (tāg), village (pop. 2,755), Vasterbotten co., N Sweden, on Ume R., near its mouth on Gulf of Bothnia, opposite Umea; woodworking, brick mfg.

Tegal (tĕgäl'), town (pop. 43,015), central Java, Indonesia, port on Java Sea, 160 mi. ESE of Jakarta; 6°52'S 109°8'E; industrial center (cotton and sugar mills, iron foundries, machine shops); exports sugar. Fisheries' school.

Tegal Peak, Indonesia: see SLAMET, MOUNT.

Teganion or **Tiganion** (both: tēgä'nēôn), town (pop. 2,490), on SE shore of Samos isl., Greece, 4 mi. SW of Limen Vatheos; wine, olive oil, raisins, citrus fruit. On site of anc. Samos, which was destroyed by Persians under Darius; remains of harbor works, aqueduct, and a near-by temple of Hera.

Tegea (tĕjē'ŭ), anc. city of Arcadia nome, central Peloponnesus, Greece, 4 mi. SE of Tripolis. Ruins here include temple of Athena Alea, public market, and theater. Founded 9th–8th cent. B.C., traditionally by King Aleus, it was once the ruling city in Peloponnesus, but fell to Sparta in 6th cent. B.C.; it was under Sparta until battle of Leuctra (371 B.C.). Tegeans fought in Persian Wars at Thermopylae and Plataea and against Spartans at Mantinea (362 B.C.). Forced (222 B.C.) into Achaean League. Modern village of Tegea or Teyea (pop. 682), formerly called Piali, is just N; it raises sheep, goats.

Tegel (tā'gŭl), residential section of Reinickendorf dist., NW Berlin, on the Havel and 8 mi. NW of city center; 52°28'N 13°13'E. After 1945 in French sector; airstrip built (1948–49) during Soviet blockade of West Berlin.

Tegelen (tā'khŭlŭn), town (pop. 7,528; commune pop. 13,800), Limburg prov., SE Netherlands, 3 mi. SW of Venlo; iron foundry, machine shops; stone quarrying; mfg. (tiles, cigars, tobacco products). Annual Passion Play. Several monasteries near by.

Tegerhi or **Tedjeghi** (both: tĕjĕ'gē), Saharan oasis (pop. 140), S Fezzan, Libya, 40 mi. S of Gatrun; dates, dom nuts. Has ruins of old fort.

Tegernsee (tā'gŭrnzā"), village (pop. 6,072), Upper Bavaria, Germany, in the Bavarian Alps, on E shore of the lake Tegernsee (□ 3.5), 14 mi. ESE of Bad Tölz; rail terminus; woodworking, printing, brewing. Summer resort and winter-sports center (alt. 2,379 ft.). Has former Benedictine abbey (719–1803), now a castle. Small petroleum wells near by.

Teggiano (tĕd-jä'nô), town (pop. 2,485), Salerno prov., Campania, S Italy, near Tanagro R., 3 mi. WSW of Sala Consilina, in agr. region (grapes, olives, vegetables, cereals). Bishopric. Has cathedral and convents. Formerly Diano.

Teghra (tā'grŭ), town (pop. 16,159), Monghyr dist., N central Bihar, India, near the Ganges, 35 mi. W of Monghyr; rice, corn, wheat, gram, barley.

Teglas (tāg'läsh), Hung. *Téglás*, town (pop. 3,180), Hajdu co., E Hungary, 12 mi. N of Debrecen; wheat, tobacco, cattle, hogs.

Teglio (tā'lyō), village (pop. 1,211), Sondrio prov., Lombardy, N Italy, in the Valtellina, 9 mi. E of Sondrio; wine.

Tegrinna, Tripolitania: see TIGRINNA.

Tegua, New Hebrides: see TORRES ISLANDS.

Tegucigalpa, department, Honduras: see FRANCISCO MORAZÁN.

Tegucigalpa (tāgōōsēgäl'pä), city (pop., including COMAYAGÜELA, 55,755), ⊙ Honduras and Francisco Morazán dept., in high mtn. valley, on right bank of Choluteca R., at mouth of short Río Chiquito, and 120 mi. WNW of San Salvador; 14°6'N 87°13'W; alt. 3,070 ft. Industrial and commercial center, served by Interoceanic Highway and Toncontín airport (just S of city); food processing (flour, jams), distilling, brewing, soft-drink bottling, mfg. of footwear, textiles, clothing. Lumber mills, match and furniture factories, marble and brickworks. Untouched by earthquakes, city stands as originally laid out on right bank of Choluteca R. opposite Comayagüela, linked by old colonial Mallol bridge and new (1930s) Carías bridge. Centers on Plaza Morazán, site of cathedral (completed 1782), natl. mus., and municipal palace; has presidential and ministerial palaces, natl. theater, univ., hospitals. Residential dist. extends N, up slopes of Leona hill and Picacho mtn. (site of park and city reservoir). Founded 1578 as gold- and silver-mining settlement; became city in 1821; succeeded (1880) Comayagua as ⊙ Honduras. Administered jointly with Comayagüela (since 1938) as the Central District (pop. 86,462), which also includes the silver and gold-mining center of San Juancito.

Tegueste (tāgĕ'stā), village (pop. 612), Tenerife, Canary Isls., 6 mi. NW of Santa Cruz de Tenerife; cereals, potatoes, wine.

Teguise (tāgē'sā), inland town (pop. 891) of Lanzarote isl., Canary Isls., 7 mi. N of Arrecife; cereals, sweet potatoes, onions, chick-peas, corn, melons, livestock. Limekilns, flour mills.

Teguldet or **Tegul'det** (tyĕgŏŏldyĕt'), village (1948 pop. over 500), E Tomsk oblast, Russian SFSR, on Chulym R. and 135 mi. ENE of Tomsk.

Tehachapi (tĭhă'chŭpē), town (pop. 1,685), Kern co., S central Calif., c.40 mi. SE of Bakersfield, in valley (alt. 3,950 ft.) of Tehachapi Mts. Has state prison for women. Cement making; clay mining; agr., including fruitgrowing. Just E is Tehachapi Pass. Settled near by in 1854, moved here to railroad in 1876. Inc. 1909.

Tehachapi Mountains, S central Calif., transverse range (c.4–8,000 ft.) linking S end of the Sierra Nevada (E) with the Coast Ranges (W), and at S end of San Joaquin Valley; crossed by Tejon and Tehachapi passes.

Tehachapi Pass, S central Calif., rail and highway pass (alt. c.3,790 ft.) across Tehachapi Mts., c.45 mi. ESE of Bakersfield; marks S end of the Sierra Nevada.

Tehama, Arabia: see TIHAMA.

Tehama (tĭhă'mŭ), county (□ 2,974; pop. 19,276), N Calif.; ⊙ Red Bluff. Lies across N part of Central Valley (here drained by Sacramento R., navigable to Red Bluff); extensions of Klamath Mts. and the Coast Ranges are in W; in E is the Sierra Nevada. Part of Lassen Volcanic Natl. Park is in NE. Includes Paskenta Indian Reservation and parts of Lassen (E) and Mendocino and Trinity (W) natl. forests. Drained by creeks tributary to the Sacramento. A leading sheep- and wool-producing co. of Calif.; also poultry, Angora goats (for mohair), beef cattle, dairy products, hogs, fruit (peaches, prunes), olives, nuts, grain, and alfalfa. Lumbering (pine, fir, cedar); some chromite mining, sand and gravel quarrying. Has processing industries (notably olives and olive oil at Corning), fruit drying and canning, sawmilling. Formed 1856.

Tehama, town (pop. 314), Tehama co., N Calif., 12 mi. SSE of Red Bluff and on Sacramento R.; sugar beets, livestock, dairy products, poultry.

Tehamiam or **Tehamiyam** (tĕhă'mĭyăm), village, Kassala prov., NE Anglo-Egyptian Sudan, on railroad and 100 mi. SSW of Port Sudan.

Tehchang or **Te-ch'ang** (dŭ'chäng'), town, ⊙ Tehchang co. (pop. 68,230), SE Sikang prov., China, 35 mi. S of Sichang and on highway; agr. products. Zinc mining near by.

Tehchow or **Te-chou** (both: dŭ'jō'), city, ⊙, but independent of, Tehsien co. (pop. 180,000), NW Shantung prov., China, on Grand Canal and 65 mi. NW of Tsinan, near Hopeh line; rail junction on Tientsin-Pukow RR; cotton textiles, straw plait; exports hides, wool, beans; arsenal. Called Tehsien (dŭ'shyĕn'), 1913–49, until made independent.

Teh el Barud, Egypt: see ITYAI EL BARUD.

Teheran (tĕ"hŭrăn', -rän', tē"ŭrăn') or **Tehran** (tĕrän'), city (1940 pop. 540,087; 1950 pop. 989,871), ⊙ Iran and Second Prov., in former Teheran prov., N Iran, 70 mi. from Caspian Sea, at S foot of Elburz mts. and SW of Mt. Demavend; alt. 3,850 ft.; 35°40'N 51°25'E. Seat of govt., industrial and cultural center of Iran, and transportation hub of the country. It is linked by railroad with the Persian Gulf ports of Khurramshahr and Bandar Shahpur, Tabriz and Julfa on USSR border, the Caspian port of Bandar Shah, and Meshed in NE Iran. Also linked by road with all major provincial centers on the Iranian plateau and by Elburz passes with the Mazanderan lowland on the Caspian. Airports are at Doshan Tepe (military; 4 mi. ENE) and Mehrabad (civil; 4 mi. W). Situated on fertile agr. plain (wheat, sugar beets, fruit, cotton), Teheran harbors 25% of Iran's industries: metalworking (copper refining, armaments), chemical mfg. (ammunition), cotton spinning, leatherworking, food canning, lumber milling; and mfg. of matches, soap, glass. City has univ. (1935), mosques (notably the Masjid Shah, and the Masjid Sipah-Silar with theological col.), mus. of art and archaeology, and mus. of ethnology. Center of the city is the large square Maidan Sipah (the former Tup Maidan), once surrounded by army barracks, but since city's reconstruction the civic and govt. center with natl. bank and ministries. S of the central square is the Gulistan (Rose Garden), with royal throne hall, and with mus. containing the Peacock Throne, brought 1739 by Nadir Shah from Delhi. The bazaars and old section of Teheran are S beyond the Gulistan. N and NW of the central square is the city's modern section, with royal marble palace and foreign legations. Another square, the Maidan Baharistan, is a popular meeting place, adjoined by the parliament bldgs. Built in 12th cent. just N of anc. RAI, Teheran remained unimportant until 17th cent., when it served as the occasional residence of the later Safavids. With the rise of the Kajar (Qajar) dynasty under Agha Mohammed Khan, it became ⊙ Iran in 1788. The city was renovated by Fath Ali Shah, but particularly under Nasr-ed-Din Shah (1848–96). After 1925, under Riza Shah, Teheran was modernized and expanded beyond its 19th-cent. walls, whose ornamented gates were demolished in 1934. While its S section retains a typical Oriental aspect of crooked, narrow streets, the N part is one of broad, tree-lined avenues and European-style bldgs. Suburban summer resorts (Gulhek, Tajrish, Darband) cluster at the foot of the Elburz mts. (N). In Second World War, Soviet and British troops were stationed in the Teheran area after 1941, and the Teheran Conference was held here in 1943. Teheran prov. was joined (1938) with provs. of Gurgan, Mazanderan, Shahrud, Samnan, Kashan, Qum, and Mahallat to form Iran's Second Province (□ 60,000; 1940 pop. 2,304,677), to which the name Teheran is commonly applied.

Tehhing or **Te-hsing** (both: dŭ'shĭng'), town (pop. 5,477), ⊙ Tehhing co. (pop. 57,457), NE Kiangsi prov., China, 55 mi. ESE of Poyang and on upper Loan R.; rice, tea; exports indigo. Copper, gold, anthracite deposits.

Tehhwei or **Te-hui** (both: dŭ'hwā'), town, ⊙ Tehhwei co. (pop. 333,637), NW Kirin prov., Manchuria, 60 mi. NE of Changchun, near railroad and Sungari R. Called Tafangshen until 1910.

Tehipite Dome, Calif.: see KINGS CANYON NATIONAL PARK.

Tehjung or **Te-jung** (dŭ'rŏŏng'), town, ⊙ Tehjung co. (pop. 5,232), S Sikang prov., China, 95 mi. SSE of Paan, near Yangtze R. (Yunnan line); rice, wheat, potatoes. Until 1913, Someitsun.

Tehkiang or **Te-chiang** (both: dŭ'jyäng'), town (pop. 147,050), NE Kweichow prov., China, 15 mi. NW of Szenan; cotton textiles, embroidered goods, tung oil, lacquer; rice, wheat, beans. Until 1914 called Anhwa.

Tehking, China: see TAKHING.

Tehko or **Te-ko** (dŭ'gŭ'), Tibetan *Dege Gonchen* (dĕ'gĕ' gŏn'chĕn'), town, ⊙ Tehko co. (pop. 11,838), N Sikang prov., China, on highway and 80 mi. WNW of Kantse, near Yangtze R.; agr. Copper found near by. Until 1914 called Tehwa.

Tehping or **Te-p'ing** (dŭ'pĭng'), town, ⊙ Tehping co. (pop. 245,161), NW Shantung prov., China, 50 mi. N of Tsinan; rice, wheat, beans, kaoliang.

Tehran, Iran: see TEHERAN.

Tehri or **Tehri-Garhwal** (tā'rē-gŭr'väl), district (□ 4,516; pop. 397,369), Kumaun div., N Uttar Pradesh, India, in W Kumaun Himalayas; ⊙ Tehri. Bounded N by Patiala and East Punjab States Union, NE by Tibet (border undefined), where Kumaun Himalayas rise to 21,700 ft. in Gangotri Peak. Bhagirathi, Jumna, and Alaknanda rivers rise here. Agr. (rice, wheat, barley, oilseeds, potatoes, tea); valuable timber tracts (including chir, deodar, sal). Main villages: Tehri, Devaprayag. Has noted Hindu shrines of Gangotri and Jamnotri. Important offshoot of Kangra school of painting flourished here in late-18th cent. Formerly a princely state (Tehri) of Punjab Hill States; merged 1947–48 with United Provs.; inc. 1949 into Uttar Pradesh.

Tehri. 1 Village, ⊙ Tehri dist., N Uttar Pradesh, India, in W Kumaun Himalaya foothills, on the Bhagirathi and 27 mi. ENE of Dehra; trades in rice, wheat, barley, oilseeds, potatoes. Also called Tehri-Garhwal. **2** Town, Vindhya Pradesh, India: see TIKAMGARH.

Tehsien, China: see TEHCHOW.

Te-hsing, China: see TEHHING.

Tehtsin or **Te-ch'in** (both: dŭ'chĭn'), village, ⊙ Tehtsin dist. (pop. 3,511), northwesternmost Yunnan prov., China, 140 mi. NW of Likiang, near Sikang border and near Mekong R.; alt. 11,417 ft.; commercial center for Tibetan trade. Tea, tobacco; silk and cotton cloth. Lamasery. Until 1935 called Atentze or Atuntze.

Tehtsing or **Te-ch'ing** (both: dŭ'chĭng'), town (pop. 5,094), ⊙ Tehtsing co. (pop. 149,319), N Chekiang prov., China, 20 mi. N of Hangchow; silk, rice, wheat, beans.

Tehtu or **Te-tu** (both: dŭ'dŏŏ'), town, ⊙ Tehtu co. (pop. 40,851), N central Heilungkiang prov., Manchuria, 25 mi. NW of Pehan; kaoliang, corn, millet.

Te-hua, China: see TEHWA.

Tehuacán (tāwäkän'), city (pop. 16,278), Puebla, central Mexico, on plateau, 65 mi. SE of Puebla; alt. 5,410 ft. Rail junction; health resort; processing and agr. center (corn, sugar cane, rice, alfalfa, fruit, livestock); flour milling, tanning, wine and liquor distilling; mfg. of straw hats, yarns and fabrics, chemicals. Airfield, radio station. Called "Carlsbad of Mexico" because of famed mineral springs. Has old colonial churches.

Tehuacana (tŭwä'kŭnē), town (pop. 389), Limestone co., E central Texas, 38 mi. ENE of Waco; has a jr. col. Was seat of Trinity Univ., 1869–1902.

Tehuantepec (tŭwŏn'tŭpĕk, Sp. tāwäntāpĕk'), city (pop. 6,731), Oaxaca, S Mexico, port on Tehuantepec R. (12 mi. inland from its mouth on Pacific coast) and 110 mi. SE of Oaxaca; colorful market, trading, processing, and agr. center (rice, sugar cane, fruit, coffee, vegetables); sugar refining, tanning. Exports indigo, cochineal, cotton, leather. Hot mineral springs. Silver, lead, copper deposits near by. Climate hot and tropical. Pop. largely Zapotec.

Tehuantepec, Gulf of, large inlet of the Pacific, on coast of Oaxaca and Chiapas, S Mexico; extends 300 mi. WNW–ESE from Puerto Angel to Barra Suchiate (near Guatemala border). Salina Cruz is main port. Receives Tehuantepec R. Several large lagoons indent shore: Laguna Superior, Laguna Inferior, Mar Muerto.

Tehuantepec, Isthmus of, in Oaxaca and Veracruz, S Mexico, narrowest part (c.125 mi. N–S) of republic, bet. Gulf of Campeche (part of Gulf of Mexico) and Gulf of Tehuantepec (inlet of the Pacific). Mostly tropical lowland; broad foothill ridges of Sierra Madre (S). Railroad (completed 1907) crosses isthmus, connecting its main ports Salina Cruz (S) and Coatzacoalcos (N). Interoceanic canal long under consideration.

Tehuantepec River, Oaxaca, S Mexico, rises in Sierra Madre SE of Miahuatlán, flows c.150 mi. SE in large curve, past Tehuantepec, to Gulf of Tehuantepec 3 mi. E of Salina Cruz.

Tehuelches, Argentina: see JOSÉ DE SAN MARTÍN.

Te-hui, Manchuria: see TEHHWEI.

Tehuipango (tāwēpäng'gō), town (pop. 4,467), Veracruz, E Mexico, in Sierra Madre Oriental, 23 mi. S of Orizaba; alt. 7,815 ft.; agr. center (corn, coffee, sugar cane, fruit).

Tehuitzingo (tāwētsēng'gō), town (pop. 2,643), Puebla, central Mexico, 20 mi. SE of Matamoros; alt. 3,562 ft.; agr. center (sugar cane, fruit, corn, livestock).

Tehwa or **Te-hua** (both: dŭ'hwä'). **1** Town (pop. 9,721), ⊙ Tehwa co. (pop. 104,355), SE Fukien prov., China, 45 mi. NW of Tsinkiang; rice, sweet potatoes, wheat; mfg. of porcelain. Coal and iron mining. **2** Town, Sikang prov., China: see TEHKO.

Tehyang or **Te-yang** (both: dŭ'yäng'), town (pop. 22,833), ⊙ Tehyang co. (pop. 199,195), NW Szechwan prov., China, 35 mi. NNE of Chengtu; sugar milling; rice, sweet potatoes, wheat, millet.

Teian or **Te-an** (both: dā'än'). **1** Town, Hupeh prov., China: see ANLU. **2** Town (pop. 4,175), ⊙ Teian co. (pop. 41,352), N Kiangsi prov., China, near W shore of Poyang L., on Kiukiang-Nanchang RR and 40 mi. N of Nanchang; commercial center; rice, cotton, ramie; exports indigo.

Teide, Pico de (pē'kō dhā tā'dā), volcano (c.12,200 ft.), Tenerife, Canary Isls., highest peak on Sp. soil, dominating the entire isl., from which it rises pyramidally to its majestic, snow-capped cone. The main crater has a diameter of c.200 ft. and is c.100 ft. deep, but is dormant. Smaller, active volcanoes appear occasionally near the summit. The lower slopes are covered by luxuriant vegetation (bananas, sugar cane, coffee, flowers, etc.). The Izaña observatory is on its NE slopes. Sometimes spelled Pico de Teyde.

Teidemann, Mount, B.C.: see TIEDEMANN, MOUNT.

Teifi River (tī'vē), Wales, rises 2 mi. E of Strata Florida, Cardigan, flows 50 mi. SW and W, past Lampeter, Newcastle Emlyn, and Cardigan, to Cardigan Bay of Irish Channel 3 mi. NNW of Cardigan. Forms S Cardigan border with Carmarthen and Pembroke.

Teignmouth (tĭn'mŭth), urban district (1931 pop. 10,017; 1951 census 10,589), S Devon, England, on the Channel, at mouth of Teign R. (old bridge), 12 mi. S of Exeter; port, seaside resort. Exports clay, granite. Partially destroyed by French in 14th cent. and in 1690. Has church built 1044.

Teign River (tĭn, tēn), Devon, England, rises in Dartmoor 5 mi. W of Exeter, flows 30 mi. SE, past Newton Abbot, to the Channel at Teignmouth.

Teijo (tā'yō), Swedish *Tykö* (tük'ŭ"), village in Perniö commune (pop. 10,026), Turku-Pori co., SW Finland, on inlet of Gulf of Bothnia, 10 mi. SW of Salo; metalworking.

Teikovo or **Teykovo** (tyā'kŭvŭ), city (1938 pop. 27,000), central Ivanovo oblast, Russian SFSR, 19 mi. SW of Ivanovo; cotton-milling center; peat works; clothing mfg., food processing. Chartered 1918.

Teil, Le (lŭ tā'), town (pop. 5,737), Ardèche dept., S France, on right bank of Rhone R. and 3 mi. W of Montélimar; industrial center with limekilns, foundries, calcium-carbide and carton factories. Important limestone quarries in area. Also called Le Teil-d'Ardèche.

Teil-d'Ardèche, Le, France: see TEIL, LE.

Teilleul, Le (lŭ tāyŭl'), village (pop. 696), Manche dept., NW France, 11 mi. WSW of Domfront; footwear mfg., quarrying.

Teima, Saudi Arabia: see TAIMA.

Teinach, Bad, Germany: see BAD TEINACH.
Teisen, Korea: see CHECHON.
Teishu, Korea: see CHONGJU.
Teith River (tēth), Perthshire, Scotland, rises 16 mi. ENE of Inveraray, flows 33 mi. SE, through lochs Katrine, Achray, and Vennachar, and the Trossachs, past Callander and Doune, to the Forth 3 mi. NW of Stirling.
Teius (tĕyōōsh'), Rum. *Teiuç*, Hung. *Tövis* (tû'vĕsh), village (pop. 5,167), Hunedoara prov., central Rumania, 11 mi. NNE of Alba-Iulia; rail junction. Has 15th-cent. late-Gothic church founded by Janos Hunyadi and 17th-cent. church with noted 18th-cent. frescoes.
Teiwi, Oman: see TIWI.
Teixeira (tāshā'rŏŏ), city (pop. 1,264), central Paraíba, NE Brazil, in mtn. range bordering on Pernambuco, 12 mi. S of Patos; cotton, manioc, corn, cedarwood.
Teixeira de Sousa (dĭ sō'zŏŏ), town (pop. 870), Bié prov., E Angola, frontier station on Benguela RR, opposite Dilolo-Gare (Belgian Congo), and 180 mi. ENE of Vila Luso; 10°42'S 22°7'E.
Teixeira Pinto (pĕn'tōō), village, W Port. Guinea, 32 mi. NW of Bissau; palm oil, copra, almonds. Until 1948, called Canchungo.
Teixeira Soares (swä'rĭs), city (pop. 1,216), S Paraná, Brazil, on railroad and 26 mi. SSW of Ponta Grossa; sawmilling, lard and maté processing. Clay quarries near by.
Teixoso (tāshō'zōō), village (pop. 1,851), Castelo Branco dist., central Portugal, 2 mi. NNE of Covilhã; textile milling.
Teja Island (tä'hä), Valdivia prov., S central Chile, at confluence of Cruces and Calle-Calle rivers just W of Valdivia; 3 mi. long, 2 mi. wide.
Tejar or **El Tejar** (ĕl tähär'), town (pop. 7,289), ⊙ El Guarco canton, Cartago prov., central Costa Rica, in Guarco Valley, on Inter-American Highway and 2 mi. SW of Cartago. Industrial and agr. center. Ceramic industry (tiles, bricks, pottery); rope-making, charcoal burning. Agr.: coffee, corn, potatoes, beans; stock raising. Sometimes called Concepción.
Tejar, El, Guatemala: see EL TEJAR.
Tejares (tähä'rĕs), town (pop. 1,040), Salamanca prov., W Spain, on Tormes R. and 2 mi. WSW of Salamanca; tile mfg., meat processing.
Tejas Verdes (tä'häs vĕr'dĕs), resort, Santiago prov., central Chile, on the Pacific at mouth of Maipo R., 55 mi. WSW of Santiago, just SE of Llolleo.
Tejeda (tähā'dhä), village (pop. 774), Grand Canary, Canary Isls., at foot of the Cruz de Tejeda, 14 mi. SW of Las Palmas; almonds, fruit, cereals, sheep, goats. Mfg. of sweets.
Tejeda, Villa, Mexico: see VILLA TEJEDA.
Tejeda de Tiétar (dhä tyā'tär), town (pop. 1,155), Cáceres prov., W Spain, 11 mi. E of Plasencia; olive-oil processing.
Tejen or **Tejend,** river, Turkmen SSR: see HARI RUD.
Tejerías, Las, Venezuela: see LAS TEJERÍAS.
Tejon Pass (tĭhōn'), SW Calif., passage (alt. c.4,230 ft.) through Tehachapi Mts., near NW corner of Los Angeles co. Old Fort Tejon (1854) is near by.
Tejo River, Spain and Portugal: see TAGUS RIVER.
Tejuco, Brazil: see DIAMANTINA.
Te-jung, China: see TEHJUNG.
Tejupilco (tähōōpēl'kō), officially Tejupilco de Hidalgo, town (pop. 2,075), Mexico state, central Mexico, 40 mi. SW of Toluca; coffee, sugar cane, fruit, stock.
Tejutla (tähōōt'lä), town (1950 pop. 801), San Marcos dept., SW Guatemala, on headstream of Cuilco R. and 11 mi. N of San Marcos; alt. 8,300 ft.; corn, wheat, beans.
Tejutla, city (pop. 1,015), Chalatenango dept., NW Salvador, 31 mi. N of San Salvador, on road to Honduras border; agr., livestock raising.
Tekal (täkäl'), officially Tekal de Venegas, town (pop. 990), Yucatan, SE Mexico, 6 mi. NE of Izamal; henequen.
Tekamah (tŭkā'mŭ), city (pop. 1,914), ⊙ Burt co., E Nebr., 35 mi. N of Omaha, near Missouri R.; farm trade center; dairy produce, grain. Settled 1854, inc. 1855.
Tekantó (täkäntō'), town (pop. 2,069), Yucatan, SE Mexico, 33 mi. E of Mérida; henequen, sugar, corn.
Tekapo, Lake (tĕkä'pō) (□ 32), central S.Isl., New Zealand, 45 mi. NW of Timaru; 12 mi. long, 4 mi. wide; receives Godley R. Outlet: **Tekapo River,** which flows 40 mi. S, receiving Pukaki and Ohau rivers; joins Ahuriri R. to form WAITAKI RIVER.
Te Karaka (tē'' kärä'kŭ), town (pop. 371), ⊙ Waikohu co. (□ 947; pop. 3,202), E N.Isl., New Zealand, 17 mi. NW of Gisborne; sheep; dairying.
Tekari or **Tikari** (both: tĭkä'rē), town (pop. 6,712), Gaya dist., W central Bihar, India, 15 mi. NW of Gaya; rice, gram, wheat, barley, oilseeds.
Tekax (täkäks'), officially Tekax de Alvaro Obregón, city (pop. 6,061), Yucatan, SE Mexico, at foot of hilly range, on railroad and 55 mi. SSE of Mérida; agr. center (henequen, sugar cane, tobacco, corn, tropical fruit, timber). Has beautiful colonial church. Grottoes and Maya ruins near by.
Teke, Rumania: see TEACA.
Tekele or **Tekeli,** Greece: see SINDOS.
Tekeli (tyĭkyĕ'lyē), town (1945 pop. over 500), central Taldy-Kurgan oblast, Kazakh SSR, in the Dzungarian Ala-Tau, on spur of Turksib RR and 30 mi. SE of Taldy-Kurgan; zinc-lead-mining center; lead smelter. Developed in Second World War.
Tekeli Dag (tĕkĕlē' dä), Turkish *Tekeli Dağ*, peak (8,599 ft.), N central Turkey, 23 mi. NW of Zara.
Tekem, Fr. Equatorial Africa: see TICKEM.
Tekes (tĕkĕs'), Chinese *Tekesze* or *Te-k'o-ssu* (both: dŭkŭ'sŭ), town, ⊙ Tekes co. (pop. 46,049), W Sinkiang prov., China, 60 mi. S of Kuldja, and on Tekes R. (left headstream of Ili R.); livestock; agr. products.
Tekfur-Dagh, Turkey: see TEKIRDAG.
Tekija or **Tekiya** (both: tĕ'kēä), village, E Serbia, Yugoslavia, on the Danube opposite Orsova (Rumania), and 11 mi. NW of Kladovo; fishing.
Tekirdag (tĕkĭr'dä), Turkish *Tekirdağ*, province (□ 2,353; 1950 pop. 222,916), Turkey in Europe, on Sea of Marmara; ⊙ Tekirdag. Wheat, spelt, oats, corn, canary-grass, flax, linseed, onions, garlic. Some lignite produced. Sometimes spelled Tekir-Dagh; formerly Rodosto.
Tekirdag, Turkish *Tekirdağ*, anc. *Bisanthe*, later *Rhoedestus*, town (1950 pop. 15,680), ⊙ Tekirdag prov., Turkey in Europe, on Sea of Marmara 75 mi. W of Istanbul, in an agr. area; port and commercial center and important market for grain, flax, linseed. Founded by Gr. colonists from Samos; later important Byzantine stronghold. Sacked by Bulgarians in 1913. Sometimes spelled Tekir-Dagh, Tekfur-Dagh. Formerly called Rodosto.
Tekir Mountains (tĕkĭr'), Turkish *Tekir Dağları*, Turkey in Europe, extend 25 mi. SW from Tekirdag along NW shore of Sea of Marmara; rise to 3,100 ft. in Ganos Dag.
Tekit (täkēt'), town (pop. 2,548), Yucatan, SE Mexico, 33 mi. SE of Mérida; henequen, sugar cane, corn, fruit, timber.
Tekiya, Yugoslavia: see TEKIJA.
Tekiye, Et, El Tekiye, or **Al-Takiyah** (all: ĕt-tä'-kĭyŭ), Fr. *Tékiyé*, village, Damascus prov., SW Syria, on Barada R., on railroad and 15 mi. WNW of Damascus; alt. 3,610 ft.; summer resort; hydro-electric station.
Tekkalakota or **Tekkalakote** (tĕkŭlŭkō'tŭ), town (pop. 6,630), Bellary dist., NW Madras, India, 27 mi. N of Bellary; rice milling; bamboo coracles; coconut palms, plantain. Sometimes spelled Takkalakote.
Tekkali (tĕ'kŭlē), town (pop. 9,460), Vizagapatam dist., NE Madras, India, on rail spur and 65 mi. NE of Vizianagaram; road center; trades in products (bamboo, tanning bark, lac) of forested hills (W). Saltworks 4 mi. SE, on Bay of Bengal, at rail junction of Naupada.
Teknaf (täk'näf), southernmost village of Chittagong dist., SE East Bengal, E Pakistan, on Naaf R. (inlet of Bay of Bengal; Burma line) and 105 mi. SSE of Chittagong; road terminus; trades in rice, oilseeds, tobacco, jute.
Te-ko, China: see TEHKO.
Teko, Sierra Leone: see MAKENI.
Tekoa (tĭkō'ŭ), city (pop. 1,189), Whitman co., SE Wash., near Idaho line, 25 mi. NE of Colfax; lumber, wheat.
Tekom (täkōm'), town (pop. 807), Yucatan, SE Mexico, 5 mi. SSE of Valladolid; henequen, fruit, timber. Sometimes Tecom.
Tekong Besar, Pulau (pōōlou' tŏŏkōōng' bŏŏsär'), island (pop. 3,252) off NE Singapore isl., at E entrance of Johore Strait; 1°25'N 104°3'E; 4 mi. long, 2 mi. wide. Fisheries.
Tekonsha (tēkŏn'shŭ), village (pop. 647), Calhoun co., S Mich., 18 mi. SE of Battle Creek and on St. Joseph R., in farm area; flour milling, chicken canning.
Te-k'o-ssu, China: see TEKES.
Tekrit, Iraq: see TIKRIT.
Tekstilshchiki or **Tekstil'shchiki** (tyĭkstyĕl'shchĭkē), town (1939 pop. over 10,000), E central Moscow oblast, Russian SFSR, on Klyazma R. and 4 mi. NNE of Mytishchi; cotton-milling center.
Te Kuiti (tē kōōē'tē), borough (pop. 2,720), ⊙ Waitomo co. (□ 1,137; pop. 6,715), W central N.Isl., New Zealand, 80 mi. NE of New Plymouth; agr., timber center. Waitomo Caves near by.
Tel [Arabic, =hill], for Arabic names beginning thus and not found here, see under following part of the name.
Tela (tä'lä), city (pop. 10,454), Atlántida dept., N Honduras, Caribbean banana port on Tela Bay, 33 mi. E of Puerto Cortés; 15°46'N 87°27'W. Commercial center; exports bananas (from Sula Valley; linked by rail), coconuts, fruit. Soap mfg. Has hosp., radio station, airport. New section of Tela (hq. of banana plantations) lies on left bank of small Tela R., opposite old Tela.
Tel Adashim or **Tel 'Adashim** (tĕl ädäshēm'), settlement (pop. 400), N Israel, at N edge of Plain of Jezreel, 3 mi. S of Nazareth; mixed farming. Founded 1923.
Télagh, Le (lŭ täläg'), village (pop. 2,762), Oran dept., NW Algeria, in the Tell Atlas, 28 mi. S of Sidi-bel-Abbès; sheep raising.
Telares, Los, Argentina: see LOS TELARES.
Telavi (tyĭlä'vē), city (1939 pop. 13,100), E Georgian SSR, on railroad and 35 mi. NE of Tiflis; center of Kakhetian wine dist.; silk spinning, wine making. Has teachers col., ruins of medieval fortress. Monasteries near by. First mentioned in 13th cent.; was ⊙ Kakhetia in 17th cent. Until 1936, Telav.
Tel Aviv (tĕl' ävēv'), city (1946 pop. estimate 183,200; 1950 pop. estimate, including Jaffa, 310,000), W Israel, in Plain of Sharon, on Mediterranean, just S of mouth of the Yarkon, 35 mi. WNW of Jerusalem; 32°5'N 34°46'E. Largest city and commercial and industrial center of Israel; industries include textile milling and knitting, metal- and woodworking, handicrafts; mfg. of food and tobacco products, chemicals, pharmaceuticals, cosmetics, soap, glass and leather goods, artificial teeth, machine tools, electrical equipment, fire extinguishers, jewelry. Seaport; airfield (N); railroad terminus. Power station. Site of Herzlia Hebrew Col. and of teachers' seminary. Home of *Habima* theater; has municipal art mus., several art galleries, large hosp., zoological gardens, parks. Founded 1906, became township 1921; inc. 1934. Chief suburbs include Hakirya, Givatayim, and Nahalat Yits-haq (E). After evacuation (1948) of Jaffa (S) by part of Arab pop., Jaffa was inc. (1950) into Tel Aviv.
Telbes or **Tel'bes** (tyĭlbyĕs'), town (1939 pop. over 2,000), S Kemerovo oblast, Russian SFSR, in the Gornaya Shoriya, on rail spur and 40 mi. SSE of Stalinsk; iron mines.
Telc (tĕlch), Czech *Telč*, Ger. *Teltsch* (tĕlch), town (pop. 4,052), SW Moravia, Czechoslovakia, in Bohemian-Moravian Heights, on railroad and 16 mi. SSW of Jihlava; known since 15th cent. for its production of painted ceramics; mfg. (enamelware, machinery), woodworking. Former medieval fortress; has parts of old walls and moats, 13th-cent. watchtower, arcaded market place, 15th-cent. church, 16th-cent. town hall, picturesque castle. Granite quarrying at Mrakotin (mrä'kôtyĕn), Czech *Mrákotín*, 3 mi. E, at SE foot of the Javorice. Numerous fish ponds near by.
Telchac (tĕlchäk'), town (pop. 1,470), Yucatan, SE Mexico, 28 mi. NW of Mérida; in henequen-growing region.
Telchac Puerto (pwĕr'tō), town (pop. 321), Yucatan, SE Mexico, on bar offshore, 25 mi. E of Progreso; henequen.
Telchye or **Tel'ch'ye** (tyĕl'chyĭ), village (1926 pop. 2,292), NW Orel oblast, Russian SFSR, 11 mi. WNW of Mtsensk; grain. Formerly also Telchi.
Telde (tĕl'dā), city (pop. 8,584), Grand Canary, Canary Isls., near isl.'s E shore, 6 mi. S of Las Palmas; trading and agr. center (corn, wheat, barley, tomatoes, potatoes, sweet potatoes, bananas, oranges). Fishing, stock raising. Limekilns; mfg. of cement articles. Has fine parish church with noted Flemish altarpiece.
Teldeniya (tĕldā'nĭyŭ), village (pop. 1,996), Central Prov., Ceylon, in Dumbara Valley, 8 mi. E of Kandy; trades in rice, tea, rubber, cacao, vegetables. Last king of Kandy captured (1815) 4 mi. ESE, near Bombure.
Telechany, Belorussian SSR: see TELEKHANY.
Telega (tĕlā'gä), village (pop. 6,612), Prahova prov., S central Rumania, in Walachia, on railroad and 3 mi. NE of Campina; oil and natural-gas production center, and summer resort. Has knitting and weaving industries, large machine shops.
Telegino (tyĭlyĕ'gĭnŭ), village (1926 pop. 2,105), central Penza oblast, Russian SFSR, on Khoper R. and 28 mi. SW of Penza; wheat, legumes.
Telegraph Creek, village, NW B.C., on Stikine R. and 120 mi. ESE of Juneau; gold mining.
Telek, Afghanistan: see TULAK.
Telekhany (tyĕlyĭkhä'nē), Pol. *Telechany* (tĕlĕkhä'-nē), village (1931 pop. 2,000), NW central Pinsk oblast, Belorussian SSR, on Oginski Canal and 30 mi. NNW of Pinsk; flour milling, sawmilling, furniture mfg.
Tele-Kul, Kazakh SSR: see SARY-SU.
Tel el Amarna, Tell el Amarna, or **Tall al-'Amarna** (all: tĕl ĕl ämär'nŭ), the modern name of a mass of ruins and rock tombs on the E bank of the Nile 8 mi. SE of Mallawi and 58 mi. N of Asyut, in Upper Egypt. Here was the city of Akhetaton, capital of Ikhnaton (Amenhotep IV), built c.1360 B.C. Tablets discovered 1887–88 have told us much about the period.
Tel el Kebir, Egypt: see TELL EL KEBIR.
Telemark (tĕl'ŭmark, Nor. tä'lŭmärk), county [Nor. *fylke*] (□ 5,875; pop. 131,679), S Norway, extends from the Hardangervidda E to the Skagerrak; ⊙ SKIEN. Picturesque lake and mtn. region popular with tourists. Gausta (6,178 ft.) is highest peak. Many of the lakes are connected by rivers, and some such water courses have been improved to carry traffic; one of these is the BANDAK-NORSJA CANAL, which links Skien with the interior. There are numerous waterfalls supplying power, the largest being at RJUKAN. Co. engages in lumbering; in mfg. of cellulose, wood pulp, and paper; in mining (copper, iron, molybdenum), stock raising, agr.; and in chemical mfg. Industries are at Skien, Porsgrunn, Notodden, Kragero, Brevik, Rjukan. Before 1918, co. (then called *amt*) was named Bratsberg.

Telén (tälĕn'), town (pop. estimate 1,000), N central La Pampa natl. territory, Argentina, 75 mi. WNW of Santa Rosa; rail terminus; stock-raising center; sawmilling.

Teleneshty (tyĕlyĭnyĕsh'tē), Rum. *Telenești* (tĕlĕnĕsht'), town (1941 pop. 2,468), central Moldavian SSR, 23 mi. NW of Orgeyev; grain, livestock; cheese factory. Pop. largely Jewish until Second World War.

Teleorman, Rumania: see ROSIORII-DE-VEDE.

Telescope Peak (11,045 ft.), Inyo co., E Calif., in Panamint Range; rises steeply above Death Valley 17 mi. W of its lowest point (280 ft. below sea level).

Telese (tĕlā'zĕ), village (pop. 1,466), Benevento prov., Campania, S Italy, near Calore R., 15 mi. NNE of Caserta; macaroni mfg. Has warm mineral baths. Near by are ruins (walls, amphitheater) of anc. *Telesia.*

Teles Pires River, Brazil: see SÃO MANUEL RIVER.

Teletskoye Lake (tyĭlyĕt'skŭyŭ) (□ 89), NE Gorno-Altai Autonomous Oblast, Altai Territory, Russian SFSR, in Altai Mts.; 49 mi. long, 3 mi. wide, 1,066 ft. deep; abounds in fish. Inlets: Bashkaus and Chulyshman rivers. Outlet: Biya R. Formerly known as Altyn-Kol.

Telfair, county (□ 440; pop. 13,221), S central Ga.; ⊙ McRae. Bounded S by Ocmulgee R., NE by Little Ocmulgee R. Coastal plain agr. (cotton, corn, melons, pecans, fruit, livestock) and forestry (lumber, naval stores) area. Formed 1807.

Telfers Island, narrow, 3½-mi.-long islet in Panama Canal Zone, at Atlantic end of Panama Canal, bet. old Fr. canal mouth (E) and Limon Bay (W). At N tip (opposite Cristobal) is large coaling and oil-bunkering plant. On Limon Bay side at Mindi Point, 3 mi. S of Cristobal, is Mindi Dock (unloading of explosives).

Telford, borough (pop. 2,042), Montgomery and Bucks counties, SE Pa., 25 mi. NNW of Philadelphia. Settled 1860; Bucks co. part inc. 1886, Montgomery co. part inc. 1897. West Telford inc. with Telford 1935.

Telfs (tĕlfs), town (pop. 4,863), Tyrol, W Austria, on Inn R. and 15 mi. WNW of Innsbruck; cotton mills; waterproof cloth.

Telgart (tyĕl'gärt), Slovak *Telgárt,* Hung. *Garamfő,* village (pop. 1,677), central Slovakia, Czechoslovakia, on Hron R., on railroad and 48 mi. ENE of Banska Bystrica; winter-sports center at E end of the Low Tatra; woodworking, needlework.

Telgte (tĕlk'tŭ), town (pop. 4,456), in former Prussian prov. of Westphalia, NW Germany, after 1945 in North Rhine-Westphalia, on the Ems and 7 mi. ENE of Münster; dairying.

Tel Hai, Israel: see KFAR GILADI.

Telhara (tālhä'rŭ), town (pop. 6,051), Akola dist., W Madhya Pradesh, India, 25 mi. NNW of Akola; millet, wheat, oilseeds; cotton ginning.

Teli (tyĭlyē'), village, W Tuva Autonomous Oblast, Russian SFSR, on Kremchik R. and 170 mi. WSW of Kyzyl, in agr. area.

Telica (tālē'kä), town (1950 pop. 1,114), León dept., W Nicaragua, at S foot of volcano Telica, 7 mi. N of León; sesame, corn, beans.

Telica, active volcano (3,346 ft.) in Cordillera de los Marabios, W Nicaragua, 11 mi. N of León. Has several craters.

Télimélé (tĕlēmĕ'lē), town (pop. c.2,000), N Fr. Guinea, Fr. West Africa, in Fouta Djallon mts., 105 mi. NNE of Conakry; cattle raising.

Telingana, region, India: see ANDHRA.

Telingana (tä"lĭng-gä'nŭ), E division (□ 41,502; pop. 8,711,766) of Hyderabad state, India. Comprises Hyderabad city and dists. of Adilabad, Atraf-i-Balda, Baghat, Karimnagar, Mahbubnagar, Medak, Nalgonda, Nizamabad, and Warangal.

Telish (tĕlēsh'), village (pop. 4,104), Pleven dist., N Bulgaria, 11 mi. NNE of Lukovit; grain, legumes, livestock. Formerly Aziziye.

Teliuc, Rumania: see HUNEDOARA, town.

Telkalakh, Tell Kalakh, or **Tall Kalakh** (all: tĕl' kălăkh'), town, Latakia prov., W Syria, near Lebanese border, on railroad and 65 mi. SSE of Latakia; cereals, sericulture. NW, 11 mi., is Krak des Chevaliers, a fortress important in the Crusades.

Telkibanya (tĕl'kĭbänyŏ), Hung. *Telkibánya,* town (pop. 1,333), Abauj co., NE Hungary, in Tokaj-Eperjes Mts., 38 mi. NE of Miskolc. Some gold, silver, copper mined near by.

Tel Kotchek (tĕl' kō'chĕk), town, Mosul prov., N Iraq, on Syria border, 65 mi. NW of Mosul, with which it is linked (since 1940) by railroad, thus connecting Baghdad with Turkey and European rail net.

Telkwa (tĕl'kwŭ), village (pop. estimate 200), W central B.C., on Bulkley R., at mouth of Telkwa R., 8 mi. SE of Smithers; coal mining.

Tell [Arabic,=hill], for Arabic names beginning thus and not found here, see under following part of the name.

Tell, name given to the Mediterranean coastal region of French North Africa with a Mediterranean subtropical climate. The inland limit of the Tell (bordering on subhumid steppe country merging in S with the Sahara) is usually given as the 12-inch isohyet; varying in width from 50 to 120 mi., the Tell is widest in Constantine dept. (E Algeria), where it includes the High Plateaus as well as the coastal Atlas ranges (Tell Atlas). Coastal and intermontane valleys within the Tell produce all Mediterranean crops; wine and olives are grown on slopes. Almost the entire sedentary pop. of Algeria lives within the Tell.

Tella (tĕ'lyä), village (pop. 106), Huesca prov., NE Spain, in the central Pyrenees, 43 mi. NE of Huesca. Hydroelectric plant on Cinca R. near by.

Tell Abiad, Syria: see ET TELL EL ABYAD.

Tell ad-Duweir, Palestine: see LACHISH.

Tellaro River (tĕl-lä'rô), SE Sicily, rises W of Palazzolo Acreide in Monti Iblei, flows 25 mi. SE to Ionian Sea 5 mi. S of Avola. Ruins of anc. Helorus (walls, towers) dating from 5th cent. B.C. are N of its mouth.

Tell Atlas, N Africa: see ATLAS MOUNTAINS.

Tell Basta, Egypt: see BUBASTIS.

Tell City, city (pop. 5,735), Perry co., S Ind., on Ohio R. and 45 mi. W of Evansville; trade center in agr. and bituminous-coal area. Oil refinery, distillery, packing plants; mfg. of furniture, wood products, electronic equipment, woolen textiles. Settled 1857 by Swiss.

Tell Dafana, Egypt: see TAHAPANES.

Tell Defenneh, Egypt: see TAHAPANES.

Tell ed Duweir, Palestine: see LACHISH.

Tell el Abyad, El, Syria: see ET TELL EL ABYAD.

Tell el Amarna, Egypt: see TEL EL AMARNA.

Tell el Kadi, Israel: see DAN.

Tell el Kebir, Tel el Kebir, or **Tall al-Kabir** (all: tĕl' ĕl kĕbĭr'), village (1937 pop. 2,161; 1947 commune pop. 15,928), Sharqiya prov., Lower Egypt, on Ismailia Canal, on railroad, and 16 mi. E of Zagazig, at E edge of the delta. The Egyptians led by Arabi were defeated here by the British in 1882.

Tell el Kheleifeh, Palestine: see EZION-GEBER.

Tell el Maskhuta, Egypt: see ABU SUWEIR.

Tell el Obeid, Iraq: see OBEID, TELL EL.

Tell el Qadi, Israel: see DAN.

Teller or **Teller Mission,** village (pop. 267), W Alaska, W Seward Peninsula, on Port Clarence, bay of Bering Sea, 60 mi. NNW of Nome; supply center for gold-placer area; tin, graphite, and copper in vicinity. Has territorial school for natives and Lutheran mission. Airfield. NW terminus of proposed Alaska RR extension from Fairbanks via Nome. Amundsen and Ellsworth landed here (1926) after North Pole flight of dirigible *Norge.*

Teller, county (□ 554; pop. 2,754), central Colo.; ⊙ Cripple Creek. Mining, ranching, and livestock-grazing area; gold, silver. Includes part of Front Range and Pike Natl. Forest. Cripple Creek dist., famous gold-producing region, is in S. Formed 1899.

Tell es Sultan, Palestine: see JERICHO.

Tell es Suwar, Syria: see SUWAR.

Tellicherry (tĕ'lĭchĕrē), city (pop. 36,320), Malabar dist., SW Madras, India, port (roadstead with natural and cement wall) on Arabian Sea, 35 mi. NNW of Calicut. Exports copra and products of wooded hills of the Wynaad (coffee, pepper, sandalwood, tea, ginger, cardamom); coffee curing, sardine-oil extraction; coir products (rope, mats). Has col. (affiliated with Madras Univ.). Was 1st major English settlement on Malabar Coast; established 1683 to command pepper and cardamom trade; fort (built 1708) unsuccessfully besieged, 1780–82, by forces of Hyder Ali. Fr. settlement of Mahé is 4 mi. SE.

Tellico Plains, town (pop. 833), Monroe co., SE Tenn., on Tellico R. (tributary of Little Tennessee R.) and 45 mi. SW of Knoxville, in scenic Cherokee Natl. Forest. Large fish and game preserve here.

Tellier (tĕlyār'), village (pop. estimate 200), SE Comodoro Rivadavia military zone, Argentina, on railroad and 10 mi. NW of Puerto Deseado; agr. (alfalfa, oats, sheep, goats).

Telli Nor (tĕlē' nōr'), salt lake in NW Sinkiang prov., China, 130 mi. SE of Chuguchak. Receives Manas R. (S). Town of Bulun Tokhoi near S shore.

Tel Litwinsky or **Tel Litvinsky** (both: tĕl' lētvēn'skē), residential settlement (pop. 400), W Israel, in Plain of Sharon, 5 mi. ESE of Tel Aviv; brewing, distilling. Founded 1935. Also spelled Tel Litvinski.

Tello (tĕ'yō), town (pop. 1,863), Huila dept., S central Colombia, in upper Magdalena valley, 16 mi. NE of Neiva; rice, cacao, livestock.

Tello, Indonesia: see TELO.

Telloh, Iraq: see LAGASH.

Tell Qassila (tĕl' käsē'lŭ), locality, W Palestine, in Plain of Sharon, on N bank of the Yarkon, near its mouth on Mediterranean, just N of Tel Aviv. Site of excavations (1949), yielding remains of several layers of anc. habitations dating from Philistine and later times; believed to be site of port to which, in Biblical history, materials for Temple in Jerusalem were shipped.

Tell Sandahannah, Palestine: see MARESHAH.

Tellsplatte (tĕls'plätŭ), hamlet, Uri canton, central Switzerland, on L. of Uri and 5 mi. NNW of Altdorf. Tell's Chapel (probably originally medieval; rebuilt 1881) commemorates a place associated with legend of William Tell.

Telluride (tĕl'yŏŏrĭd), city (pop. 1,101), ⊙ San Miguel co., SW Colo., in San Juan Mts., 90 mi. SSE of Grand Junction; alt. 8,500 ft. Trade and tourist center in livestock, dairying, mining region. Gold, silver, lead mines. Pop. exceeded 5,000 at peak of gold production (c.1890). Inc. 1887. Bridal Veil Falls near by. Mt. Wilson 12 mi. SW., Mt. Sneffels 5 mi. N.

Telma or **Tel'ma** (tyĭlmä'), town (1940 pop. 5,500), S Irkutsk oblast, Russian SFSR, on Angara R., on Trans-Siberian RR and 5 mi. SE of Usolye. Woolen cloth and glass made here since 18th cent.

Telmana, Imeni, or **Imeni Tel'mana** (ē'mĭnyē tyĕl'mŭnŭ). **1** Town (1949 pop. over 500), NE Jewish Autonomous Oblast, Khabarovsk Territory, Russian SFSR, near Smidovich. **2** Village, NE Tashauz oblast, Turkmen SSR, 20 mi. NNW of Tashauz; cotton. Until c.1940, Taza-Kala.

Telmanovo or **Tel'manovo** (-mŭnŭvŭ), village (1939 pop. over 500), SE Stalino oblast, Ukrainian SSR, 31 mi. NE of Zhdanov; metalworks. Until mid-1930s called Ostgeim or Ostheim.

Tel Mond (tĕl' mōnd'), settlement (pop. 600), W Israel, in Plain of Sharon, 7 mi. SE of Natanya; citriculture, mixed farming. Founded 1929.

Telnovski or **Tel'novskiy** (tyĕlnôf'skē), town (1947 pop. over 500) on W coast of S Sakhalin, Russian SFSR, 3 mi. S of Lesogorsk. Under Japanese rule (1905–45) called Kita-kozawa.

Telo or **Tello** (both: tĕ'lō), island (5 mi. long, 2 mi. wide), Batu Isls., Indonesia, off W coast of Sumatra, just off NW coast of Tanahmasa. Here is Pulautelo or Poelautelo (both: pōōlou"tĕ'lō), chief port of Batu Isls., shipping copra and resin.

Teloekbetoeng, Indonesia: see TELUKBETUNG.

Telok Anson (tĕ'lŏk än'sŭn), town (pop. 23,055), S Perak, Malaya, 40 mi. S of Ipoh; leading seaport of Perak, on Perak R. 30 river mi. from Strait of Malacca, on rail spur from Tapah Road; ships tin from Kinta Valley, rubber, copra. Also spelled Teluk Anson.

Telok Kumbar (tĕ'lŏkŏŏmbär'), village (pop. 1,062) on Penang isl., NW Malaya, on S coast, 12 mi. SSW of George Town; fisheries.

Teloloapan (tālōlwä'pän), city (pop. 5,140), Guerrero, SW Mexico, on S slopes of central plateau, 25 mi. W of Iguala; alt. 5,282 ft. Agr. center (cereals, tobacco, coffee, fruit, resin, vanilla); mfg. (vegetable oils, soap).

Telo Martius, France: see TOULON.

Telonia, Greece: see ANTISSA.

Telos or **Tilos** (both: tē'lŏs, Gr. tē'lôs), Ital. *Piscopi,* Aegean island (□ 24.3; pop. 1,085) in the Dodecanese, Greece, NW of Rhodes; 36°25'N 27°20'E; 9 mi. long, 1–5 mi. wide. Mostly mountainous, rises to 2,010 ft.; steep shores. Produces barley, almonds, wine, olive oil; fishing. Main town, Telos or Megalochorio (pop. 436), is on N shore.

Telpaneca (tĕlpänä'kä), town (1950 pop. 669), Madríz dept., NW Nicaragua, 19 mi. ENE of Somoto; coffee center.

Telpos-Iz or **Tel'pos-Iz** (tyĕl'pôs-ēz"), peak (5,558 ft.) in Urals, Russian SFSR; 64°N. Considered highest point of Urals until discovery (1930s) of NARODA peak.

Telsen (tĕl'sĕn), village (pop. estimate 200), ⊙ Telsen dept., N Chubut natl. territory, Argentina, 105 mi. NW of Rawson; sheep-raising center; alfalfa- and winegrowing.

Telsiai, Telshai, or **Tel'shay** (tyĕl'shī), Lith. *Telšiai,* Ger. *Telschen,* Rus. *Telshi* or *Tel'shi,* city (pop. 5,874), NW Lithuania, on railroad and 40 mi. W of Siauliai; mfg. (linen goods, knitwear, furniture, matches, bricks, cement). Folk art mus. Dates from 16th cent.; in Rus. Kovno govt. until 1920.

Teltow (tĕl'tō), residential town (pop. 10,950), Brandenburg, E Germany, on Teltow Canal and 10 mi. SW of Berlin city center; radio mfg. Formerly noted for turnips grown here.

Teltow Canal, E Germany, extends c.25 mi. E–W bet. Spree R. in Köpenick dist. (E) of Berlin and Havel R. in E Potsdam; 1 lock; navigable for vessels up to 600 tons.

Teltsch, Czechoslovakia: see TELC.

Tel Tsur or **Tel Tzur** (both: tĕl' tsōōr'), settlement (pop. 130), NW Israel, at N end of Plain of Sharon, 2 mi. S of Zikhron Ya'aqov; citriculture. Founded 1932. Sometimes spelled Tel Zur.

Teluk Anson, Malaya: see TELOK ANSON.

Telukbajur or **Telukbayur,** Indonesia: see PADANG.

Telukbetung or **Teloekbetoeng** (both: tŭlōōk"bŭtōōng'), town (pop. 25,170), S Sumatra, Indonesia, port on Lampung Bay (inlet of Sunda Strait), 120 mi. WNW of Jakarta, on Palembang-Panjang RR; 5°27'S 105°16'E. Exports pepper, rubber, coffee, fibers, cinchona bark. Town was virtually destroyed in 1883 by eruption of Krakatoa. Also spelled Telokbetong.

Tely (tälē'), village, Eastern Prov., N Belgian Congo, on Bomokandi R., on Congo-Nile highway, and 170 mi. ENE of Buta; cotton ginning; coffee plantations, palm groves.

Tel Yits-haq or **Tel Yitzhak** (both: tĕl' yēts-häk'), settlement (pop. 230), W Israel, in Plain of Sharon, 5 mi. SSE of Natanya; mixed farming, citriculture. Founded 1938.

Tel Yosef (tĕl' yōsĕf'), settlement (pop. 1,000), NE Israel, in SE part of Plain of Jezreel, at N foot of Mt. Gilboa, on railroad and 7 mi. ESE of Afula; dairying and farming center (viticulture; citrus fruit, grain, olives, vegetables, stock, poultry); fish ponds; workshops. Founded 1929 on reclaimed swamp land.

Tel Zur, Israel: see TEL TSUR.

Tema (tĕmä') or **Tima** (tĭmä'), town (pop. 19,702), Girga prov., central Upper Egypt, on railroad and 10 mi. NNW of Tahta; cotton ginning, pottery making, dairying; cotton, cereals, dates, sugar cane.

Temacine (tĕmäsēn'), village and Saharan oasis, Touggourt territory, E Algeria, one of the Oued Rhir oases, 7 mi. SSW of Touggourt; date palms.

Temagami, Ont.: see TIMAGAMI.

Temamatla (tāmämät'lä), town (pop. 1,048), Mexico state, central Mexico, on railroad and 25 mi. SE of Mexico city; sugar cane, cereals, livestock.

Temangan (tůmäng"än'), village (pop. 546), N Kelantan, Malaya, on Kelantan R., and 30 mi. S of Kota Bharu, on E coast railroad; rice. Iron mining at Bukit Besi, 4 mi. S.

Temanggung or **Temanggoeng** (both: tůmäng"-gŏŏng'), town (pop. 12,676), central Java, Indonesia, 30 mi. SW of Semarang, at foot of Mt. Sumbing; alt. 1,900 ft.; trade center for agr. area (rubber, coffee, rice, corn, cassava). Also spelled Temanggang.

Temapache, Mexico: see ALAMO.

Temara (tĕmärä'), village, Rabat region, NW Fr. Morocco, near the Atlantic, on Casablanca-Rabat road, 8 mi. SW of Rabat; horse breeding, truck farming. Popular bathing beach just NW.

Temascalapa (tämäskälä'pä), town (pop. 1,348), Mexico state, central Mexico, 32 mi. NE of Mexico city; cereals, maguey, stock.

Temascalcingo (-sēng'gō), town (pop. 1,565), Mexico state, central Mexico, 15 mi. NE of El Oro; cereals, fruit, livestock.

Temascaltepec (-tāpĕk'), officially Temascaltepec de González, town (pop. 1,174), Mexico state, central Mexico, 30 mi. SW of Toluca; alt. 5,722 ft.; silver and gold mining.

Temassinin, Algeria: see FORT FLATTERS.

Temax (tāmäks'), town (pop. 3,312), Yucatan, SE Mexico, on railroad and 45 mi. ENE of Mérida; henequen center.

Temaxcalac (tāmäskäläk'), officially San Baltasar Temaxcalac, town (pop. 2,042), Puebla, central Mexico, on railroad and 19 mi. NW of Puebla; corn, wheat, maguey, stock.

Tembe, Vale of, Greece: see TEMPE, VALE OF.

Tembladera (tĕmblädä'rä), city (pop. 1,456), Cajamarca dept., NW Peru, on W slopes of Cordillera Occidental, on Jequetepeque R., on Pacasmayo–Chilete RR; and 24 mi. WNW of Contumasá. Sugar cane, wheat, corn.

Temblador (tĕmblädōr'), oil field in Monagas state, NE Venezuela, 60 mi. SSE of Maturín; pipe line to the Caño Mánamo (arm of Orinoco R. delta).

Tembleque (tĕmblā'kā), town (pop. 3,604), Toledo prov., central Spain, road junction 24 mi. S of Aranjuez; agr. center in upper La Mancha (wheat, barley, grapes, sheep). Olive-oil pressing, cheese processing. Potassium-nitrate deposits.

Temblor Range (tĕmblôr') (c.2,000–4,300 ft.), S central Calif., meets S end of Diablo Range in NW Kern co., and extends c.50 mi. SE, bordering San Joaquin Valley, to meet San Emigdio Mts. near S end of the valley. Oil fields at E base.

Tembuland (tĕm'bŏŏlănd), district (□ 3,448; total pop. 304,471; native pop. 296,750) of the TRANSKEIAN TERRITORIES, E Cape Prov., U. of So. Afr., bounded by Transkei dist. (S), Griqualand East (N), Pondoland (NE), and the Indian Ocean (E); center near 31°40'S 28°30'E; ⊙ Umtata. Generally hilly region; stock raising, dairying, wool production are chief activities. Largely a native reserve, dist. was annexed (1885) by Great Britain; it later came under administration of United Transkeian Territories General Council.

Temburong, Borneo: see BANGAR.

Temecula (tĭmĕ'kyŏŏlů), village (pop. c.250), Riverside co., S Calif., 25 mi. NE of Oceanside, in Temecula Valley (farming, dairying, cattle grazing).

Temerin (tĕ'mĕrēn), village (pop. 10,515), Vojvodina, N Serbia, Yugoslavia, on railroad and 11 mi. NNE of Novi Sad, in the Backa; health resort. Natural-gas wells near by.

Teme River (tēm), England and Wales, rises on Radnor-Montgomery border 5 mi. S of Newtown, flows 60 mi. SE, past Knighton, Ludlow, and Tenbury, to the Severn 2 mi. S of Worcester.

Temerloh (tůmĕrlō'), town (pop. 1,866), S central Pahang, Malaya, on Pahang R. and 55 mi. ENE of Kuala Lumpur; rubber-growing center.

Temeschburg, Rumania: see TIMISOARA.

Temesrekas, Rumania: see RECAS.

Temes River, Rumania and Yugoslavia: see TIMIS RIVER.

Temesvar, Rumania: see TIMISOARA.

Temesvar, Banat of: see BANAT.

Temiang, Indonesia: see LINGGA ARCHIPELAGO.

Temir (tyĭmĕr'), city (1926 pop. 4,126), central Aktyubinsk oblast, Kazakh SSR, near railroad, 80 mi. S of Aktyubinsk, in millet area; phosphorite deposits. Former trading center (livestock, wool).

Temirgoyevskaya (tyĭmĕr'gŭyĕf"skĭŭ), village (1926 pop. 12,626), E Krasnodar Territory, Russian SFSR, on Laba R. and 27 mi. SW of Kropotkin; flour mill, metalworks; wheat, sunflowers, ambary hemp.

Temir-Khan-Shura, Russian SFSR: see BUINAKSK.

Temir-Tau (tyĭmĕr"-tou'). **1** City (1950 pop. estimate c.50,000), NE Karaganda oblast, Kazakh SSR, on Nura R. and 15 mi. NNW of Karaganda (linked by railroad); metallurgical center; site of reservoir and hydroelectric power plant, serving Karaganda coal basin; iron and steelworks, mfg. of chemicals, sawmilling. Until 1945, Samarkand. Developed around steel plant (scrap conversion) built during Second World War. **2** Town (1939 pop. over 10,000), S Kemerovo oblast, Russian SFSR, in the Gornaya Shoriya, on railroad (Akhpun station) and 45 mi. SSE of Stalinsk; iron mines, dolomite deposits. Until c.1940, spelled Timer-Tau.

Temiscamingue or **Témiscamingue** (tůmĭ'skůmĭng, tāmē"skämēg'), county (□ 8,977; pop. 40,471), SW Que., on Ont. border; ⊙ Ville Marie.

Témiscamingue, town, Que.: see TIMISKAMING, town.

Temiscouata or **Témiscouata** (tĕmĭskwä'tů, Fr. tāmĕskwätä'), county (□ 1,151; pop. 23,182), SE Que., on Maine and N.B. borders; ⊙ Notre Dame du Lac.

Temiscouata, Lake, or **Lake Témiscouata** (28 mi. long, 3 mi. wide), SE Que., 30 mi. E of Rivière du Loup. Drained by Madawaska R.

Temixco (tāmē'skō), town (pop. 1,437), Morelos, central Mexico, 5 mi. S of Cuernavaca; sugar cane, rice, wheat, coffee, fruit, livestock.

Temkino tyôm'kēnŭ), village (1926 pop. 465), E Smolensk oblast, Russian SFSR, 28 mi. ESE of Vyazma; flour milling.

Temnikov (tyĕmnyĭkôf'), city (1926 pop. 4,522), NW Mordvinian Autonomous SSR, Russian SFSR, on Moksha R. and 85 mi. WNW of Saransk, in potato and grain area; paper-milling center; hog raising. Teachers col. Peat works near by. Founded 1536.

Temoac (tāmwäk'), town (pop. 1,563), Morelos, central Mexico, 12 mi. ESE of Cuautla; sugar cane, corn, fruit, stock.

Temoh (tĕmō'), village (pop. 1,523), S central Perak, Malaya, on railroad and 25 mi. S of Ipoh; tin mining.

Temora (tůmô'rů), municipality (pop. 4,179), S central New South Wales, Australia, 90 mi. NW of Canberra; rail junction; gold-mining center.

Temósachic (tāmō'sächēk), town (pop. 1,504), Chihuahua, N Mexico, in Sierra Madre Occidental, on headstream of Yaqui R. and 110 mi. W of Chihuahua, on railroad; alt. 6,158 ft. Corn, wheat, beans, cattle.

Temozón (tāmōsōn'), town (pop. 1,060), Yucatan, SE Mexico, 12 mi. N of Valladolid; henequen, corn, sugar cane.

Tempate (tĕmpä'tā), village (dist. pop. 3,960), Guanacaste prov., NW Costa Rica, 13 mi. NW of Santa Cruz; rice, corn, beans, livestock.

Tempe (tĕm'pē'), city (pop. 7,684), Maricopa co., S central Ariz., on Salt R. and 8 mi. E of Phoenix; trade center for agr. area; flour, condensed milk, canned fruit juice. Seat of Ariz. State Col., hq. for U.S. experimental farm project. Papago State Park near by. Founded 1871–72 as Hayden's Ferry, renamed Tempe c.1879, inc. 1894.

Tempe, Vale of (tĕm'pē), Gr. *Tembe* or *Tembi* (both: tĕm'bē), 5 mi.-long defile in NE Thessaly, Greece, bet. lower Olympus and Ossa mts., traversed by Peneus R. The Vale of Tempe was sacred to Apollo (ruins of temple); laurel for the wreaths of victors of the Pythian Games was gathered here. Its beauty was celebrated by anc. poets, as by Virgil in the *Georgics*. Strategically important as a by-pass of the Olympus and as an access route from Macedonia; here the Greeks attempted (480 B.C.) to stop Xerxes' army, and Alexander the Great moved (336 B.C.) against the Greek cities. Fortified by Rome and by Byzantium. In Second World War, the German army was briefly held here in its advance into Greece.

Tempeh (tĕmpĕ'), town (pop. 10,965), SE Java, Indonesia, near Indian Ocean, 70 mi. SSE of Surabaya; trade center for agr. area (coffee, tea, rubber, cinchona bark).

Tempelburg, Poland: see CZAPLINEK.

Tempelhof (tĕm'půlhōf), workers' residential district (1939 pop. 125,360; 1946 pop. 110,882), S central Berlin, Germany, 4 mi. S of city center; 52°28'N 13°25'E. Contains chief Berlin airport, enlarged (1948–49) during Soviet blockade of West Berlin, when it was main American terminus of the "air lift." Mfg. of electrical appliances, machinery, phonographs, records; metalworking. After 1945 in U.S. sector.

Temperance, village (pop. 1,062), Monroe co., SE Mich., 13 mi. SW of Monroe.

Temperley, town (pop. 24,932) in Greater Buenos Aires, Argentina, adjoining Lomas de Zamora, 11 mi. SSW of Buenos Aires; rail junction and residential dist.; also mfg. of silk goods, custom jewelry, toys, chemical products, food preserves.

Tempino (tĕmpē'nō), village, S central Sumatra, Indonesia, 15 mi. SSW of Jambi; oil-production center, linked by pipe line with Plaju.

Tempio Pausania (tĕm'pyō pouzä'nyä), town (pop. 7,046), Sassari prov., N Sardinia, 31 mi. ENE of Sassari; chief center of Sardinian cork industry; sawmills; livestock market (cattle, goats, swine). Bishopric.

Tempisque River (tĕmpē'skā), main stream of Guanacaste prov., NW Costa Rica, rises in the volcano Orosi, flows 80 mi. S and SE, past Palmira, Filadelfia, and Bolsón (head of navigation), to Gulf of Nicoya of the Pacific, 30 mi. NW of Puntarenas. Navigable 25 mi.; mainly for lumber. At high tide navigable to Bolsón.

Temple. 1 Town (pop. 676), Carroll co., W Ga., 11 mi. NNE of Carrollton. **2** Town (pop. 284), Franklin co., W central Maine, just NW of Farmington. **3** Town (pop. 330), Hillsboro co., S N.H., 21 mi. WNW of Nashua; agr. **4** Town (pop. 1,442), Cotton co., S Okla., 30 mi. NNE of Wichita Falls (Texas), near Red R., in agr. area (cotton, wheat); cotton ginning, flour milling. Settled 1902. **5** Borough (pop. 1,460), Berks co., SE central Pa., 5 mi. N of Reading; limestone quarries. Founded 1857. **6** City (pop. 25,467), Bell co., central Texas, 33 mi. SSW of Waco; market, trade, mfg. center in rich agr. area (cotton, corn, grain, pecans); textile, flour, cottonseed-oil milling, cotton ginning, stone cutting, mfg. of mattresses, tools, rock wool, machine-shop and foundry products, furniture, clothing, brooms; railroad shops. Has a jr. col., agr. experiment station, veterans' hosp. Cooperative soil-conservation project near by. Founded 1881 by Santa Fe RR; inc. 1882.

Temple, Mount (11,636 ft.), SW Alta., near B.C. border, in Rocky Mts., in Banff Natl. Park, 30 mi. WNW of Banff; 51°21'N 116°12'W.

Temple Bay, inlet of Coral Sea, NE Cape York Peninsula, N Queensland, Australia, bet. Cape Grenville (N) and Fair Cape (S); 26 mi. long, 11 mi. wide. Piper Isls. at entrance.

Templebrough, England: see ROTHERHAM.

Temple City, unincorporated town (1940 pop. 5,196), Los Angeles co., S Calif., suburb 11 mi. ENE of downtown Los Angeles; residential; citrus fruit, walnuts, poultry.

Templemore (tĕm"půlmôr'), Gaelic *Teampall Mór*, urban district (pop. 2,055), NE Co. Tipperary, Ireland, on Suir R. and 27 mi. NNE of Tipperary, at foot of Devilsbit Mts., agr. market (dairying; potatoes, beets). There are remains of anc. castle and church of the Knights Templars.

Temple Normanton (nôr'můntůn), town and parish (pop. 773), NE Derby, England, 3 mi. SE of Chesterfield; coal mining.

Temple Terrace, city (pop. 433), Hillsborough co., W Fla., on Hillsboro R. and 6 mi. NE of Tampa.

Templeton, Que.: see SAINTE ROSE DE LIMA.

Templeton. 1 Town (pop. 385), Carroll co., W central Iowa, 11 mi. SSW of Carroll, in agr. area. **2** Town (pop. 4,757), Worcester co., N central Mass., 13 mi. W of Fitchburg; furniture. Settled 1751, inc. 1762. Includes villages of Baldwinsville (pop. 1,407), seat of institution for crippled children, and East Templeton (1940 pop. 784). **3** Village (pop. c.750), Armstrong co., W Pa., on the Allegheny and 8 mi. N of Kittanning; clay mines.

Templeuve (täplûv'), agr. village (pop. 3,547), Hainaut prov., SW Belgium, 5 mi. WNW of Tournai, near Fr. border.

Templeuve, town (pop. 2,156), Nord dept., N France, 9 mi. SSE of Lille in irrigated agr. area; mfg. (lace, clothing, chicory); trades in seeds (wheat, oats, sugar beets).

Templeville, town (pop. 82), Caroline and Queen Annes counties, E Md., near Del. line, 13 mi. W of Dover, Del., in agr. area.

Templin (tĕmplēn'), town (pop. 9,970), Brandenburg, E Germany, on small Templin L., surrounded by several other small lakes draining into the Havel, 40 mi. N of Berlin; climatic health resort; forestry; brick mfg. Has 15th-cent. fortifications. Noted boys' school (Joachimthalsches Gymnasium, founded 1607 at Joachimsthal) moved here (1912) from Berlin.

Tempo, town (pop. 719), NE Co. Fermanagh, Northern Ireland, 8 mi. ENE of Enniskillen; cattle; potatoes.

Tempoal (tĕmpwäl'), town (pop. 2,211), Veracruz, E Mexico, on affluent of Moctezuma R. and 16 mi. NW of Tantoyuca; cereals, coffee, sugar cane, fruit, stock.

Tempy (tyĕm'pē), town (1941 pop. over 500), N Moscow oblast, Russian SFSR, on Moscow Canal and 10 mi. WSW of Taldom.

Temryuk (tyĭmryŏŏk'), city (1926 pop. 15,861), W Krasnodar Territory, Russian SFSR, port on Temryuk Gulf of Sea of Azov, at mouth of Kuban R., 80 mi. WNW of Krasnodar; fishing center; fish canning and processing, wine making. A fortress under Turkish rule (until 18th cent.). Became city in 1860.

Temryuk Gulf, S inlet of Sea of Azov, in Krasnodar Territory, Russian SFSR, just E of Kerch Strait; 35 mi. wide, 15 mi. long. Receives main Kuban R. delta mouth branch at Temryuk. Has low, marshy, lagoon shores.

Temse (tĕms'hů), Fr. *Tamise* (tämēz'), town (pop. 13,920), East Flanders prov., N Belgium, on Scheldt R. and 11 mi. SW of Antwerp; jute spinning and weaving. Formerly spelled Temsche.

Temù (tĕmŏŏ'), village (pop. 485), Brescia prov., Lombardy, N Italy, in upper Val Camonica, on Oglio R. and 2 mi. WSW of Ponte di Legno. Has one of major Ital. hydroelectric plants.

Temuco (tāmōō'kō), city (1940 pop. 42,035, 1949 estimate 37,375), ⊙ Cautín prov. and Temuco dept. (□ 2,275; 1940 pop. 152,737), S central Chile, on Cautín R. and 300 mi. SSW of Santiago; 38°44'S 72°37'W. Rail junction, commercial and agr. center (wheat, barley, oats, apples, livestock). Has tanneries, sawmills, flour mills, tannin-extracting plants. Military air base. A cathedral town and colorful market place for Araucanian Indians, this N gateway to Chilean lake dist. is a favorite tourist resort. Overlooking the town is the wooded hill El Cerro Ñielol, where in 1881 a treaty was signed with the Araucanians, putting an end to Indian wars. In the same year the city, often referred to as "capital of the frontier," was founded, owing much of its rise to European, chiefly German, immigrants.

Temuka (tŭmōō'kŭ), borough (pop. 2,081), E S.Isl., New Zealand, 85 mi. SW of Christchurch; sheep-raising, agr. area.

Tena (tä'nä), town (1950 pop. 331), ⊙ Napo-Pastaza prov., E central Ecuador, on E slopes of the Andes, on affluent of Napo R. and 70 mi. SE of Quito (connected by road); 1°S 77°50'W. A missionary settlement. Stock, fruit, timber.

Tenabo (tänä'bō), town (pop. 1,990), Campeche, SE Mexico, on NW Yucatan Peninsula, on railroad and 10 mi. SW of Hecelchakán; sugar cane, tobacco, henequen, fruit, livestock.

Tenabo, Mount, Nev.: see CORTEZ MOUNTAINS.

Tenafly (tĕ'nŭflī), residential borough (pop. 9,651), Bergen co., NE N.J., near Hudson R., just N of Englewood; mfg. (cleansers, building blocks, stone products, liqueurs); printing, publishing. Settled 1640, inc. 1894.

Tenaha (tĕ'nĭhô), town (pop. 715), Shelby co., E Texas, c.45 mi. SSE of Marshall; lumber milling, vegetable canning and shipping; oil, gas wells.

Tenakee or **Tenakee Springs** (tĕnŭkē'), village (pop. 137), SE Alaska, on E shore of Chichagof Isl., 45 mi. SW of Juneau, NW of Angoon; fishing and canning; fur trade.

Tenali (tänä'lē), city (pop. 40,639), Guntur dist., NE Madras, India, in Kistna R. delta, 14 mi. ESE of Guntur; rail junction (spur to Repalle); rice and oilseed milling, cotton ginning; tobacco, palmyra. Headworks of Kistna delta canals system 6 mi. N, at Duggirala.

Tenamaxtlán (tänämäslän'), town (pop. 3,243), Jalisco, W Mexico, 21 mi. SSW of Ameca; agr. center (oranges, cotton, sugar cane, rice, tobacco).

Tenampa (tänäm'pä), town (pop. 821), Veracruz, E Mexico, in Sierra Madre Oriental, 19 mi. S of Jalapa; corn, fruit.

Tenampúa, Honduras: see VILLA DE SAN ANTONIO.

Tenampulco (tänämpōōl'kō), town (pop. 1,159), Puebla, E Mexico, in Gulf lowland, 20 mi. SSW of Papantla; sugar cane, coffee, tobacco, fruit.

Tenan, Korea: see CHONAN.

Tenancingo (tänänsēng'gō). **1** or **Tenancingo de Degollado** (dā dāgōyä'dō), city (pop. 6,644), Mexico state, central Mexico, on central plateau, 26 mi. SSE of Toluca; alt. 6,043 ft. Agr. center (grain, sugar cane, fruit, vegetables, livestock); textile milling. **2** Officially San Miguel Tenancingo, town (pop. 2,800), Tlaxcala, central Mexico, 7 mi. N of Puebla; cereals, alfalfa, beans, livestock.

Tenancingo, town (pop. 1,492), Cuscatlán dept., central Salvador, 8 mi. NW of Cojutepeque; produces palm hats; grain, livestock raising.

Tenango (tänäng'gō). **1** or **Tenango del Valle** or **Tenango de Arista** (dĕl vä'yä, dā ärē'stä), town (pop. 5,462), Mexico state, central Mexico, in Toluca Valley, on railroad and 35 mi. SW of Mexico city; alt. 8,484 ft. Agr. center (cereals, vegetables, livestock); dairying. **2** Town (pop. 1,964), Puebla, central Mexico, adjoining Zacatlán; coffee, tobacco, sugar cane, fruit.

Tenango de Arista, Mexico: see TENANGO, Mexico state.

Tenango de Doria (dā dōr'yä), town (pop. 1,055), Hidalgo, central Mexico, 37 mi. NE of Pachuca; alt. 5,495 ft.; corn, wheat, sugar cane, fruit, stock.

Tenango del Aire (dĕl ī'rā) or **Tenango de Tepopula** (dā täpōpōō'lä), town (pop. 822), Mexico state, central Mexico, on railroad and 27 mi. SE of Mexico city; cereals, vegetables, stock.

Tenango del Valle, Mexico: see TENANGO, Mexico state.

Tenango de Tepopula, Mexico: see TENANGO DEL AIRE.

Tenango Tepexi (täpä'hē), town (pop. 424), Guerrero, SW Mexico, in Sierra Madre del Sur, 14 mi. W of Tlapa; cereals, livestock.

Tenants Harbor, Maine: see SAINT GEORGE.

Tenararo, Tuamotu Isls.: see ACTAEON ISLANDS.

Tenares or **Villa Tenares** (vē'yä tänä'rĕs), town (1950 pop. 1,286), Espaillat prov., N Dominican Republic, 12 mi. E of Moca; cacao, coffee, bananas, fruit.

Tenarunga, Tuamotu Isls.: see ACTAEON ISLANDS.

Tenasserim (tŭnă'sŭrĭm), Burmese *Taninthayi* (tŭnĭn'-thäyē), SE administrative division (□ 31,588; 1941 pop. 1,635,562) of Lower Burma; ⊙ Moulmein. Extends in narrow strip of coast, 400 mi. long, bet. Andaman Sea and Thailand frontier, from Karenni hills S to Victoria Point at isthmus of Kra. Includes dists. of Salween, Thaton, Amherst, Tavoy, Mergui. Large alluvial rice plain (N) astride Salween R. mouth is bounded by Karenni Hills, Dawna and Tenasserim ranges. Drained by Salween, Gyaing, Ataran (N), Tavoy, and Tenasserim rivers. Tenasserim coast, studded with reefs, is sheltered by Mergui Archipelago. Rainfall averages 200 in. yearly. Rice, garden vegetables, rubber, teak are chief agr. and forest products. The leading tin and tungsten-mining area of Burma, with mines in Tavoy and Mergui dists. Served by Pegu-Martaban and Moulmein-Ye railroads. Moulmein, Tavoy, and Mergui are chief towns. Pop. is 40% Burmese (Tavoyans, Merguese; speaking distinct dialect); 30% Karen (in N), 17% Mon, and 7% Indian. Long disputed by Burma and Thailand, it passed to Br. East India Company as result of 1st Anglo-Burmese War (1824–26); was separate Indian prov. until formation of Br. (Lower) Burma in 1862.

Tenasserim, village, Mergui dist., Lower Burma, in Tenasserim, at confluence of Tenasserim and Little Tenasserim rivers, 35 mi. SE of Mergui. Once of importance.

Tenasserim Range or **Tenasserim Yoma** (yō'mä), Thai *Tanao Si,* mountain range in Tenasserim, on Burma-Thailand border, forming a S extension of Karenni Hills; 400 mi. long. Consists of parallel N-S ridges cut by deep valleys; rises to 6,801 ft. 60 mi. SE of Tavoy. Forested; tin, tungsten ores.

Tenasserim River or **Great Tenasserim River,** in Tenasserim, Lower Burma; c.280 mi. long; formed by 2 headstreams 20 mi. ENE of Tavoy, flows S in the Tenasserim Range parallel to Thailand frontier, turns W receiving Little Tenasserim R., then flows NW to Andaman Sea at Mergui.

Tenasserim Yoma, Burma-Thailand: see TENASSERIM RANGE.

Tenaún (tänä-ōōn'), village (1930 pop. 136), Chiloé prov., S Chile, on E coast of Chiloé Isl., opposite Chauques Isls., 40 mi. SE of Ancud; potatoes, wheat, livestock; lumbering, fishing.

Tenay (tŭnā'), village (pop. 1,951), Ain dept., E France, in gorge of the Albarine and 14 mi. NW of Belley, in the S Jura; silk-waste milling; cement.

Tenayuca, Mexico: see TLALNEPANTLA, Mexico state.

Tenbury, town and parish (pop. 1,755), W Worcester, England, on Teme R. and 18 mi. WNW of Worcester; agr. market and resort with mineral springs.

Tenby (tĕn'bē), municipal borough (1931 pop. 4,108; 1951 census 4,597), SE Pembroke, Wales, on Carmarthen Bay of Bristol Channel, 9 mi. E of Pembroke; seaside resort and fishing port, with woolen mills. Just E is Carmarthen Hill with ruins of 12th-cent. castle. Town has remains of walls (c.1460). St. Mary's church dates from 13th cent. Tenby was Danish fishing station; c.1100 it became settlement of Flemish weavers. Later developed as resort.

Tence (tās), village (pop. 1,256), Haute-Loire dept., S central France, in Monts du Vivarais, on Lignon R. and 8 mi. ESE of Yssingeaux; silk spinning, dairying. Small summer resort.

Tenda, France: see TENDE.

Tendaparacua (tĕndäpärä'kwä), town (pop. 1,963), Michoacán, central Mexico, 27 mi. NW of Morelia; cereals, fruit, stock.

Tenda Pass (tĕn'dä), Fr. *Col de Tende,* Ital. *Col di Tenda* or *Colle di Tenda,* (alt. 6,135 ft.), in Maritime Alps, on Fr.-Ital. border S of Limone Piemonte, Italy. Important route bet. Turin and Nice; crossed by 2 parallel tunnels for road (2 mi. long) and rail (5 mi. long). In Italy until 1947, when border was moved 8 mi. N.

Tende (tād), Ital. *Tenda* (tĕn'dä), village (pop. 1,427), Alpes-Maritimes dept., SE France, in upper Roya R. valley of Maritime Alps, 31 mi. NE of Nice; and 5 mi. S of Tenda Pass (Ital. border); resort. Zinc and lead mines near by. Part of Italy until 1947.

Tende, Col de, Alps: see TENDA PASS.

Ten Degree Channel, seaway connecting Bay of Bengal (W) and Andaman Sea (E) along 10°N, bet. Little Andaman Isl. (N) and Nicobar Isls. (S; Car Nicobar Isl.); c.90 mi. wide.

Tendelti (tĕndĕl'tē), town, Blue Nile prov., E central Anglo-Egyptian Sudan, on railroad and 55 mi. WSW of Kosti; gum-arabic center; cotton, peanuts, sesame, corn, durra; livestock.

Tendilla (tĕndē'lyä), town (pop. 1,032), Guadalajara prov., central Spain, 12 mi. ESE of Guadalajara; olives, grapes, pears, plums, tomatoes, sheep, goats. Lumbering.

Tendo (tān-dō'), town (pop. 10,264), Yamagata prefecture, N Honshu, Japan, 7 mi. NNE of Yamagata; rice, silk cocoons.

Tendrara (tĕndrärä'), village, Oujda region, E Fr. Morocco, on Oujda-Bou Arfa RR and 110 mi. S of Oujda; wool trade.

Tendre, Mont (mō tä'drŭ), peak (5,520 ft.), highest in the Swiss Jura, 11 mi. NW of Morges.

Tenduruk Dag (tĕndürük' dä), Turkish *Tendürük Dağ,* peak (10,870 ft.), E Turkey, 16 mi. SE of Diyadin.

Tenedos (tĕ'nĕdŏs), Turkish *Bozcaada* (bôzjä'ädä") [Bozca Island], island (□ 15; pop. 1,765), Canakkale prov., NW Turkey, in Aegean Sea 3 mi. off coast of Asia Minor, S of Imbros and the entrance to the Dardanelles; 6 mi. long. Town of Bozcaada on E coast. Tenedos was naval station of the Greeks in the Trojan War, and of Xerxes in Persian Wars. Occupied 1915–16 by British in Gallipoli campaign. Ceded to Greece but returned to Turkey in 1923 by Treaty of Lausanne.

Tenejapa (tänähä'pä), town (pop. 618), Chiapas, S Mexico, in Sierra de Hueytepec, 9 mi. NE of San Cristóbal de las Casas; alt. 6,447 ft.; wheat, fruit.

Tenerife or **Teneriffe** (both: tĕnŭrĭf'; Sp. tänärē'fā), anc. *Pintuaria,* largest island (□ 794.5; pop. 261,817) of the Canary Isls., Santa Cruz de Tenerife prov., Spain; ⊙ Santa Cruz de Tenerife. Situated in W central part of the archipelago, bet. Grand Canary (E) and Gomera (W), c.220 mi. W of Cape Juby on coast of Sp. Morocco. Extends 55 mi. NE-SW from 28°33'N 16°6'W to 27°59'N 16°40'W; up to 33 mi. wide. Of volcanic origin, covered by masses of basalt and comparatively recent lava layers, the mountainous isl. rises from a rugged coast line to the majestic Pico de Teide (c.12,200 ft.), highest peak on Sp. soil, and among the globe's most impressive sights. The semitropical, dry climate, with little seasonal change and noted for its mildness, attracts many tourists. On the slope of the Teide and in the immensely fertile valleys, such as famed Orotava Valley, thrive all kinds of crops; bananas, sugar cane, citrus fruit, almonds, tomatoes, potatoes, cochineal, onions, grapes, tobacco, cereals. More elevated zones are rich in timber. Goats and sheep are widely raised. Industries are principally devoted to processing of agr. produce and fish, though native embroidery and linen are also exported. Chief trading center is Santa Cruz de Tenerife. Among other principal towns are the bishopric and university city La Laguna, and Güimar, La Orotava, Icod, Granadilla de Abona, Puerto de la Cruz. Active trade with Europe and America. Originally inhabited by the Guanches (probably of Berber stock); the Sp. element has become dominant since 15th-cent. conquest.

Tenerife (tänärē'fā), town (pop. 1,810), Magdalena dept., N Colombia, minor river port on the Magdalena and 25 mi. S of Calamar; corn, tagua, livestock.

Ténès (tănĕs'), anc. *Cartennae,* town (pop. 6,131), Alger dept., N central Algeria, port on the Mediterranean, 24 mi. N of Orléansville (linked by branch railroad); ships agr. output of middle Chéliff valley and of Dahra region; fish canning. Copper and iron mines near by. Founded by Phoenicians; Romans established a veterans' colony here. Occupied by French 1843. Harbor improved in 1927. Cape Ténès (36°37'N 1°21'E; lighthouse) is 3 mi. NNE.

Tenextepango (tänĕstäpäng'gō), village (pop. 1,418), Morelos, central Mexico, on railroad and 6 mi. S of Cuautla; alt. 3,773 ft.; sugar cane, rice, fruit, coffee, vegetables.

Tengah (tĕng"ä'), one of the civil airports of Singapore isl., 12 mi. NW of Singapore city; 1°23'N 103°43'E.

Tenga Islands (tĕng'ä, –ŭ), small group of Indonesia, in Flores Sea, c.40 mi. N of Sumbawa; 6°45'S 118°19'E. Comprise many islets, largest being Satengar or Satangar (pop. 470; 3 mi. long). Coconut growing, fishing. Sometimes called Great Paternoster Isls.; also spelled Tengah.

T'eng-ch'iao, China: see TENGKIU.

Tengchow. **1** Town, Honan prov., China: see TENGHSIEN. **2** Town, Shantung prov., China: see PENGLAI.

Teng-ch'uan, China: see TENGCHWAN.

Tengchung or **T'eng-ch'ung** (tŭng'chŏŏng'), town, ⊙ Tengchung co. (pop. 205,337), W Yunnan prov., China, 40 mi. W of Paoshan; center of trade with Burma, on road to Myitkyina; alt. 5,354 ft.; silk exports. Rice, wheat, millet, beans. Iron mines, lead deposits. Until 1913 called Tengyüeh. Opened to foreign trade in 1897. Occupied 1942–44 by Japanese, who invaded the region from Burma.

Tengchwan or **Teng-ch'uan** (both: dŭng'chwän'), town, ⊙ Tengchwan co. (pop. 38,370), NW Yunnan prov., China, 20 mi. NNW of Tali, on NW shore of the lake Erh Hai; rice, wheat, millet, beans. Coal mines near by.

Tengelic (tĕng'gĕlĭts), town (pop. 3,199), Tolna co., W central Hungary, 13 mi. N of Szekszard; wheat.

Tengeriin Nuur, Tibet: see NAM TSO.

Tengfeng (dŭng'fŭng'), town, ⊙ Tengfeng co. (pop. 155,881), N Honan prov., China, 32 mi. SE of Loyang, in Sung Mts.; rice, wheat, beans, millet.

Tenghai (tĕng'hī'), Mandarin *Ch'eng-hai* (chŭng'-hī'), town (pop. 33,182), ⊙ Tenghai co. (pop. 379,595), E Kwangtung prov., China, in Han R. delta, 9 mi. NE of Swatow, in rice-growing dist.; exports tobacco, sugar, camphor, sea food.

Tenghsien. **1** (dŭng'shyĕn') Town, ⊙ Tenghsien co. (pop. 598,442), SW Honan prov., China, 35 mi. SW of Nanyang; road junction; tobacco processing; wheat, millet, beans. Until 1913, Tengchow. **2** or **T'eng-hsien** (tŭng'shyĕn'), town, Kwangsi prov., China: see TENGYÜN. **3** or **T'eng-hsien** (tŭng'shyĕn'), town, ⊙ Tenghsien co. (pop. 740,714), SW Shantung prov., China, 40 mi. SSE of Tzeyang and on Tientsin-Pukow RR; silk weaving; peanuts, fruit, wheat, kaoliang.

Tengi-Kharam, Uzbek SSR: see DEKHKANABAD.

Tengiz (tyĭngĕs′), salt lake (□ 450) in SW Akmolinsk oblast, Kazakh SSR, 90 mi. SW of Akmolinsk; 20 ft. is greatest depth; low steppe shores. Receives Nura R.

Tengkiu (tăng′kyō′), Mandarin *T'eng-ch'iao* (tŭng′chyou′), town (pop. 1,500), S Hainan, Kwangtung prov., China, port on S.China Sea, 35 mi. E of Aihsien; commercial center and fishing port; exports timber, hides, rattan cane, rice, coconuts, mushrooms, livestock.

Tengko (dŭng′kŭ′), town, ⊙ Tengko co. (pop. 4,322), N Sikang prov., China, on upper Yangtze R., on highway and 140 mi. NW of Kantse; cattle raising. Lead-zinc mining.

Tengkow or **Teng-k'ou** (both: dŭng′kō′), town, ⊙ Tengkow co. (pop. 21,529), E Ningsia prov., China, on railroad and 105 mi. NNE of Yinchwan; landing on Yellow R. (Suiyuan line); exports salt, fur, wool, grain. Sometimes spelled Tingkow.

Tengkye, Tibet: see Tingkye.

Tenglo Island (tĕng′glō) (1,070 acres; pop. 416), Llanquihue prov., S central Chile, in Reloncaví Sound just off Puerto Montt; resort; dairying.

Tengri Khan, USSR: see Khan Tengri.

Tengri Nor, Tibet: see Nam Tso.

Tengushevo or **Ten'gushevo** (tyĕnyŭgōō′shĭvŭ), village (1926 pop. 5,278), NW Mordvinian Autonomous SSR, Russian SFSR, on Moksha R. and 22 mi. WNW of Temnikov; agr. center (hog, potatoes, hemp). Peat bogs near by.

Tengyeling, Tibet: see Lhasa.

Tengyüeh, China: see Tengchung.

Tengyün (dĕng′yün′), Mandarin *T'eng-hsien* (tŭng′shyĕn′), town, ⊙ Tengyün co. (pop. 402,135), SE Kwangsi prov., China, on Sün R. at mouth of Jung R., and 27 mi. WSW of Wuchow; sericulture; rice, wheat, sweet potatoes, peanuts.

Tenhult (tān′hŭlt″), village (pop. 1,029), Jonkoping co., S Sweden, 5 mi. SSE of Huskvarna; grain, stock.

Teni, India: see Allinagaram.

Teniente, El, Chile: see El Teniente.

Teniente Bullaín (tānyĕn′tā bōōyäēn′), town (pop. c.1,900), Oruro dept., W Bolivia, in the Altiplano, 7 mi. E of Oruro; alt. 12,746 ft.; barley, potatoes. Until early 1940s, Dalence.

Teniente General Pablo Ricchieri, Argentina: see Bella Vista, Buenos Aires prov.

Téniet-el-Haâd (tānyĕt′-ĕl-hä-äd′), town (pop. 2,587), Alger dept., N central Algeria, on a pass in the Ouarsenis Massif, 30 mi. SSW of Affreville; alt. 3,770 ft. Health resort (cool summers) amidst noted cedar forest. Also spelled Teniet-el-Had.

Tenimbar Islands, Indonesia: see Tanimbar Islands.

Teningen (tā′nĭng-ŭn), village (pop. 2,530), S Baden, Germany, on canalized Elz R. and 2 mi. W of Emmendingen; tobacco mfg., metalworking.

Tenino (tŭnī′nō), town (pop. 969), Thurston co., W Wash., 13 mi. S of Olympia; lumber, agr., quarries.

Tenira (tĕnērä′), village (pop. 1,107), Oran dept., NW Algeria, in the Tell Atlas, 13 mi. SE of Sidi-bel-Abbès; winegrowing.

Tenkar, China: see Hwangyüan.

Tenkasi (tăngkä′sē), town (pop. 22,862), Tinnevelly dist., S Madras, India, on Chittar R. and 85 mi. SW of Madura, in rich agr. area; rail junction; trade and cotton-weaving center; sesame-oil extraction. Health resort of Kuttalam is 3 mi. SW. Coffee grown in foothills (SW).

Tenke (tĕng′kā), village, Katanga prov., SE Belgian Congo, 50 mi. NW of Jadotville; railroad junction and trading center in copper-mining region.

Tenke, Rumania: see Tinca.

Tenki or **Ten'ki** (tyĭnyŭkē′), village (1939 pop. over 2,000), W Tatar Autonomous SSR, Russian SFSR, near Volga R., 25 mi. SSW of Kazan; fruit, grain, legumes, livestock. Old Rus. settlement.

Tenkiller Ferry Reservoir, Okla.: see Illinois River.

Tenkodogo (tĕngkōdō′gō), town (pop. c.6,000), S Upper Volta, Fr. West Africa, on road to Lomé, Fr. Togoland, and 85 mi. ESE of Ouagadougou; growing and processing of shea nuts; also produces peanuts, potatoes, corn, millet, rice, beans, onions; sheep, goats, cattle. Airfield; R.C. and Protestant missions. Customhouse.

Ten Mile Lake (□ 18), N N.F., 12 mi. E of Ferolle Point; 15 mi. long, 2 mi. wide; 51°5′N 56°40′W; drains into Gulf of St. Lawrence. Round L. just NE.

Tenmile Lake, Cass co., central Minn., near Leech L., 7 mi. S of Walker, in state forest; 5 mi. long, 2.5 mi. wide. Has boating, bathing, fishing resorts.

Ten Mile Peaks (12,800 ft.), central Colo., in Rocky Mts., 5 mi. NW of Breckenridge.

Tennant, town (pop. 95), Shelby co., W Iowa, 8 mi. SW of Harlan, in agr. area.

Tennant Creek, settlement (dist. pop. 695), central Northern Territory, Australia, 280 mi. N of Alice Springs; gold mines.

Tenna River (tĕn′nä), The Marches, central Italy, rises in Monti Sibillini 6 mi. E of Visso, flows 48 mi. NE, past Amandola, to the Adriatic 6 mi. NE of Fermo.

Tennenbronn (tĕ′nŭnbrôn), village (pop. 2,323), S Baden, Germany, in Black Forest, 3 mi. SSW of Schramberg; metalworking. Summer resort (alt. 2,165 ft.).

Tennengebirge (tĕ′nŭn-gŭbĭrgŭ), range in Eastern Alps, Salzburg, W Austria, extending c.15 mi. E from the river Salzach; rises to 7,965 ft. in the Raucheck.

Tennessee (tĕ′nŭsē′, tĕ″nŭsē′, tĕ′nŭsē″), state (land □ 41,961, with inland waters □ 42,246; 1950 pop. 3,291,718; 1940 pop. 2,915,841), S central U.S., bordered by Ky. and Va. (N), N.C. (E), Ga., Ala., and Miss. (S), Ark. and Mo. (W); 34th in area, 16th in pop.; admitted 1796 as 16th state; ⊙ Nashville. Tenn. extends c.430 mi. E–W, c.110 mi. N–S. The "Volunteer State" slopes from the Appalachians in the E, where Clingmans Dome rises to 6,642 ft. (highest point in the state), to the Mississippi (182 ft.) in the W; has mean alt. of c.900 ft. Because of its width and topographic diversity, the state's 3 sections are called East, Middle, and West Tenn. In E Tenn. the Unaka Mts. (a range of the Appalachians), largely included in Cherokee Natl. Forest and Great Smoky Mountains National Park, form a narrow, rugged belt (3,000–6,000 ft. high) descending from the N.C. line to the Great Appalachian Valley (here called the Valley of East Tennessee; c.45 mi. wide), which is a succession of parallel valleys and ridges; the Cumberland Plateau (c.50 mi. wide; average alt. 1,800 ft.), a rolling tableland, rises W of Tennessee valley in a steep escarpment, and descends gradually to the Highland Rim in Middle Tenn. Here the rim, a dissected plateau c.400–1,000 ft. high, encloses the Nashville or Central Basin and slopes downward to the W loop of the Tennessee R. West Tenn. is a broad rolling plain (c.300–800 ft. elev.) cut by ravines and sloping from the highly dissected lands along the Tennessee R. to the bluffs overlooking the flood plain of the Mississippi. Tenn. is drained by three great river systems. The Tennessee R. flows in a great bend SW through the Great Appalachian Valley, then turns W near Chattanooga, flows SW, then NW through N Ala., and N across Tenn. again. Large multi-purpose TVA dams have converted the Tennessee R. system into a series of vast reservoirs including Norris, Cherokee, South Holston, Watauga, Douglas, Fort Loudoun, Calderwood, Ocoee, Watts Bar, Chickamauga, Hales Bar, Pickwick Landing, and Kentucky reservoirs. The Cumberland R. and its tributaries drain most of Middle Tenn., including the Nashville Basin, and contain Dale Hollow and Great Falls dams. West Tenn. is drained by the Wolf, Hatchie, Forked Deer, and Obion rivers, which flow into the Mississippi. In the Mississippi bottoms are many swamps and Reelfoot Lake. Forests originally covered most of the state; today almost 50% of the area is timbered, especially in the Unakas, Cumberland Plateau, W Highland Rim, and lowlands of West Tenn. Oak and hickory forests predominate and the state is an important hardwood producer; pine, cedar, cypress, and gum are also plentiful. The climate is characterized by hot summers and short, generally mild winters, with only a few inches of snow, except in the mts. Its long growing season ranges (E–W) from 180 to 261 days. The average annual rainfall is c.50 in., with a late winter or early spring max. and mid-fall min. About ¾ of the state is in farms, and ⅔ of the pop. is rural. The best farm lands are in West Tenn., especially in the Mississippi bottoms; other fertile areas are the Nashville Basin, a bluegrass region, and the Great Appalachian Valley. Erosion is widespread, with c.40% of the state severely affected by sheet and gully erosion. Corn and hay occupy the largest acreages, but cotton and tobacco are the chief cash crops. Also important are wheat, truck (sweet and Irish potatoes, strawberries, beans, tomatoes), and fruit (peaches, apples). Cotton is concentrated chiefly in West Tenn.; tobacco, wheat, and Irish potatoes in Middle and East Tenn. The state generally ranks 3d as a U.S. strawberry producer. Livestock raising (dairy and beef cattle, hogs, mules, horses, chickens, sheep) is of great importance, especially in the Nashville Basin and Great Appalachian Valley. In recent years, with the increased development of its farm, forest, water power, and mineral resources, greatly aided by TVA, Tenn. has become one of the most industrialized states in the South. The chief manufactures are textiles (synthetic-fiber, cotton, and woolen goods), chemicals (plastics, fertilizer, cottonseed products, sulphuric acid), food products (dairy and grain products, meat packing, canned goods), wood products (lumber, furniture, paper), leather, metal products, and cement. East Tenn. is the chief mfg. area of the state; it is the core of the TVA, and is the chief region for coal and other minerals. Here are Knoxville, Chattanooga, Oak Ridge, Kingsport, Johnson City, and Bristol. In Middle Tenn. are Nashville, Clarksville, and Columbia; Memphis, the state's largest city, Dyersburg, and Jackson are in West Tenn. Tenn. ranks 1st as a U.S. producer of pyrites (East Tenn.), 2d in phosphate (Middle Tenn.), zinc (Mascot, Jefferson City dists.), and barite (Sweetwater dist.). Other important minerals are bituminous coal (Cumberland Plateau), copper (Ducktown area), clay (West Tenn.), iron (W Highland Rim), marble (Knoxville area), and limestone. Some oil and natural gas are produced in N part of state. E Tenn. is a national center for the reduction of aluminum ore from Ark. and the Guianas. The leading institutions of higher learning include the Univ. of Tenn. (at Knoxville), Vanderbilt Univ., George Peabody Col. for Teachers, and Fiske Univ. (all at Nashville), and the Univ. of the South (at Sewanee). East Tenn. was visited by De Soto in 1540; West Tenn. by La Salle, who built (c.1682) Fort Prudhomme, probably on the site of Memphis. The area was claimed by the French as part of Louisiana, but the Indians remained in actual possession until well into 18th cent. The French claim was completely lost (1763) by the British victory in the French and Indian Wars. Virginians, later joined by North Carolinians, made 1st permanent settlement (1769) in the Watauga valley. Jonesboro, the oldest town in the state, was founded (1779) in this area. After the Revolution, the independent state of Franklin (1784–88) was established in East Tenn. from the western lands of N.C. ceded to the Federal Government. In 1796, Tenn., with substantially its present boundaries, was admitted into the Union, with Knoxville as its 1st capital. By 1800 there were over 100,000 settlers, many of them recent arrivals via the Wilderness Road and Cumberland Gap, and a number of other routes. The state's early history was dominated by Andrew Jackson, who became President in 1829; his home, the Hermitage, is preserved. Other notable figures were Samuel Houston and David Crockett, who later migrated to Texas, and James Polk. In the Civil War most Tennesseans fought with the Confederacy, but some joined the Union forces. The many major battles (Shiloh, Stones River, Chattanooga, Nashville, Memphis) fought here made Tenn. the biggest and bloodiest battleground of the war, after Virginia. In recent times, the TVA program, established in 1933, has resulted in a tremendous increase in industrialization and brought higher living standards and increased tourism to much of the state. See also articles on the cities, towns, geographic features, and the 95 counties: Anderson, Bedford, Benton, Bledsoe, Blount, Bradley, Campbell, Cannon, Carroll, Carter, Cheatham, Chester, Claiborne, Clay, Cocke, Coffee, Crockett, Cumberland, Davidson, Decatur, De Kalb, Dickson, Dyer, Fayette, Fentress, Franklin, Gibson, Giles, Grainger, Greene, Grundy, Hamblen, Hamilton, Hancock, Hardeman, Hardin, Hawkins, Haywood, Henderson, Henry, Hickman, Houston, Humphreys, Jackson, Jefferson, Johnson, Knox, Lake, Lauderdale, Lawrence, Lewis, Lincoln, Loudon, McMinn, McNairy, Macon, Madison, Marion, Marshall, Maury, Meigs, Monroe, Montgomery, Moore, Morgan, Obion, Overton, Perry, Pickett, Polk, Putnam, Rhea, Roane, Robertson, Rutherford, Scott, Sequatchie, Sevier, Shelby, Smith, Stewart, Sullivan, Sumner, Tipton, Trousdale, Unicoi, Union, Van Buren, Warren, Washington, Wayne, Weakley, White, Williamson, Wilson.

Tennessee, village (pop. 249), McDonough co., W Ill., 9 mi. WSW of Macomb, in agr. and bituminous-coal area.

Tennessee Cave, Tenn.: see Chattanooga.

Tennessee Pass (10,424 ft.), central Colo., in Park Range, 8 mi. N of Leadville. Crossed by railroad and highway.

Tennessee River, a major stream of SE U.S., follows U-shaped course through E Tenn., N Ala., W Tenn., and SW Ky., and enters Ohio R. at Paducah. Formed just E of Knoxville, Tenn., bet. Cumberland and Great Smoky mts., by confluence of Holston and French Broad rivers; flows generally SW past Knoxville and Chattanooga (here forming sharp meander known as Moccasin Bend), NW and SW around Lookout Mtn., turns SW past Richard City, into Ala., past Guntersville, then WNW past Decatur, Florence, Sheffield, and Waterloo, and N, forming small part of Miss. line, re-entering Tenn. near Pickwick Landing Dam and forming Kentucky Reservoir, into Ky., to Ohio R. at Paducah (22.4 river mi. below Kentucky Dam); 652 mi. long; 900 mi. long, from headwaters of the Holston. Drainage basin (□ 40,600) includes much of Tenn. and Ala. and parts of N.C., Va., Ga., Miss., and Ky. Receives Little, Hiwassee, Little Tennessee, Clinch, and Sequatchie rivers in E Tenn., Paint Rock, Flint, and Elk rivers in N Ala., Duck and Big Sandy rivers in W Tenn., and Clarks R. in SW Ky. Traverses well-forested mtn. region in upper course, flat to rolling area in lower and middle course; drains part of Great Appalachian Valley in E Tenn.; 1940 pop. estimate in basin, 2,500,000; 1950 estimate, 3,000,000. Small farms, orchards, and pasture lands predominate in upper part of valley; cotton, corn, hay, sweet potatoes, peanuts, vegetables are raised in lower reaches; dairying occurs in NE Miss. and parts of Ala. Deposits of coal, iron, copper (in Polk co., Tenn.), zinc (in NE Tenn.), marble (E Tenn.), phosphate rock, ceramic clays, limestone, gypsum, barites, sand, gravel. Principal cities: Chattanooga and Knoxville, Tenn.; Florence, Ala. Business activity and industrial employment in river basin have expanded greatly since establishment of Tennessee Valley Authority. River was explored in 17th cent. by Fr. and English trappers and traders; served as means of transportation for settlers going W in 18th cent. First navigated by steamboat throughout entire length in 1828. Became important trade route in 19th cent. for agr. produce; used for military and naval operations during Civil War. Chief obstacles to navigation have been differences in volume of river flow, causing great variation in channel depths, and steep slopes in river bed that give rise to swift currents and rapids. Most celebrated of numerous rapids was Muscle Shoals (now submerged by Wilson and Wheeler reservoirs), which once extended 37 mi. upstream from Florence and had total fall of 134 ft. Shoals were canalized (unsuccessfully) in 1836 by state of Ala. and in 1890 by U.S. Army Engineers; later developments included Wilson Dam (opened to navigation 1927) and 2 govt. nitrate plants (both started during First World War; 1 no longer in use). Early power and navigation project was HALES BAR DAM (completed 1913; privately built; now owned and operated by TVA) in main stream W of Chattanooga. Other privately constructed dams now owned by TVA were built in tributary streams; they are Ocoee No. 1 and Ocoee No. 2 (completed, respectively, 1912 and 1913) in OCOEE RIVER E of Chattanooga, and BLUE RIDGE DAM (1931) in Ocoee (Toccoa) R., N Ga.; GREAT FALLS DAM (completed 1916; in Caney Fork of Cumberland R., NE of McMinnville, Tenn.) was also privately built and purchased by TVA. Culminating event in history of Tennessee Valley was creation (1933, by act of Congress) of Tennessee Valley Authority. Statute established TVA as corporate agency and empowered it to operate Muscle Shoals installations for purposes of natl. defense and fertilizer research; further provided for improvement of Tennessee R. and tributaries in interests of navigation, flood control, and power. Agency has since evolved program that is outstanding example of regional planning and development. Chief feature is system of multiple-purpose dams (power, flood control, and navigation) and reservoirs (total □ c.1,000) in main stream and tributaries. At beginning of flood season capacity of more than 11,000,000 acre-ft. is available in reservoirs for flood control. Power is distributed from TVA plants (1949 installed capacity, 2,400,000 kw.; 80% hydroelectric) by municipal and cooperative distributors to individual consumers, private industries, and utilities; integrated power system generated (1949) 15,750,000,000 kwh. (c.14,000,000,000 produced by TVA, remainder by private interests and U.S. Army Engineers), serving nearly 1,000,000 consumers and bringing electricity to more than 50% of farms in valley (as compared with 3.5% in 1933). Navigation works consist of 11 locks (including 2 at Wilson Dam) and 9-ft. channel (extending 630 mi. upstream from mouth) maintained by U.S. Army Engineers; traffic includes petroleum, automobiles, grain, aluminum, fertilizer, coal, and iron and steel products. TVA chemical works (outgrowth of U.S. nitrate plant) at town of MUSCLE SHOALS produce phosphate fertilizers and other plant nutrients and, in cooperation with land-grant colleges and agr. extension services, supply privately operated test-demonstration farms in Tennessee Valley and in 25 states outside watershed; results of research carried on in laboratories are made available to govt. agencies and private industry. Other services for which TVA provides assistance or guidance are reforestation, soil conservation, malaria control, development of mineral resources, fish and wildlife development, food processing, and education in use of electricity for domestic and agr. purposes; expansion of recreational resources is made possible by TVA reservoirs, now provided with privately and publicly owned facilities for bathing, boating, fishing, and camping. Major TVA dams: in Tenn., NORRIS DAM (completed 1936) on Clinch R., CHEROKEE DAM (1942) on Holston R., DOUGLAS DAM (1943) on French Broad R., WATAUGA DAM (1949) on Watauga R., Ocoee No. 3 (1943) on OCOEE RIVER, and FORT LOUDOUN DAM (1943), WATTS BAR DAM (1942), CHICKAMAUGA DAM (1940), and PICKWICK LANDING DAM (1938), all on Tennessee R.; in N.C., FONTANA DAM (1945) on Little Tennessee R., and CHATUGE DAM (1942), HIWASSEE DAM (1940), and APALACHIA DAM (1943), all on Hiwassee R.; in Ga., NOTTELY DAM (1942) on Nottely R.; in Ala., GUNTERSVILLE DAM (1939), WHEELER DAM (1936), and WILSON DAM (main structure finished 1925), all on Tennessee R.; in Ky., KENTUCKY DAM (1944) on Tennessee R. SOUTH HOLSTON DAM on South Fork of Holston R. under construction in 1950. A further plan is to connect Tennessee R. near Pickwick Landing Dam with Tombigbee R. and to provide waterway transportation to Gulf of Mexico.

Tennessee Valley, SE U.S.: see TENNESSEE RIVER.

Tenney, village (pop. 62), Wilkin co., W Minn., 17 mi. SSE of Breckenridge, in grain area.

Tennille (tĕ'nĭl), city (pop. 1,713), Washington co., E central Ga., 3 mi. S of Sandersville; textile, veneer, and lumber mills. Inc. 1875.

Tennis, ruins of medieval city, Lower Egypt, SW of Port Said, on an isl. in L. Manzala; founded when TANIS was abandoned. Also spelled Tinnis. Supposedly, *tinnisi* cloth made here was used to cover the balls in an earlier form of the game and supplied the name of tennis.

Tennstedt, Bad, Germany: see BAD TENNSTEDT.

Tennyson. 1 Town (pop. 409), Warrick co., SW Ind., 26 mi. ENE of Evansville, in agr. and bituminous-coal area. **2** Village (pop. 211), Grant co., SW Wis., 10 mi. WSW of Platteville.

Teno (tā'nō), town (pop. 1,884), Curicó prov., central Chile, 9 mi. NNE of Curicó; agr. center (grain, peas, beans, wine, fruit, livestock); dairying, flour milling.

Tenochitlán (tānōchētlän'), village (pop. 1,070), Veracruz, E Mexico, in Sierra Madre Oriental, 18 mi. NNW of Jalapa; coffee, fruit.

Tenochtitlán (–tētlän'), Aztec capital on which Cortés founded MEXICO city, Mexico.

Tenojoki, Finland and Norway: see TANA RIVER.

Tenom (tĕnôm'), town (pop. 800, including environs), Interior and Labuan residency, Br. North Borneo, near W coast, 20 mi. SE of Beaufort; on railroad; agr. center. Formerly ⊙ residency.

Teno Point (tā'nō), westernmost cape of Tenerife, Canary Isls., 40 mi. WSW of Santa Cruz de Tenerife; 28°20'N 16°55'W. Lighthouse.

Tenorio (tänōr'yō), extinct volcano (6,299 ft.) in the Cordillera de Guanacaste, NW Costa Rica, 17 mi. NNE of Cañas; 10°40'N 85°3'W.

Teno River (tā'nō), Curicó prov., central Chile, rises in the Andes at NE foot of Planchón volcano near Argentina border, flows c.65 mi. W to join Lontué R. 5 mi. WNW of Curicó, forming Mataquito R.

Tenos or **Tinos** (tē'nŏs, Gr. tē'nôs), Aegean island (□ 74; pop. 11,380) of the Cyclades, Greece, bet. Andros (NW) and Myknonos (SE); 38°35'N 25°10'E; 17 mi. long, 7 mi. wide; rises to 2,340 ft. Wine, figs, wheat, olive oil, and silk are produced. Green marble is quarried here. On S coast is the chief town, Tenos (pop. 2,861), formerly called St. Nicholas. Tenos shared the anc. history of Andros. In Middle Ages, it passed (1207) to an Ital. family and was held by the Venetians from 1390 until 1715, when it passed to the Turks. Monastery here is visited by pilgrims.

Tenosique (tānōsē'kā), officially Tenosique de Pino Suárez, city (pop. 3,545), Tabasco, SE Mexico, on Usumacinta R. and 115 mi. ESE of Villahermosa; rubber, fruit, tobacco, rice, timber. The railroad from Mérida, Yucatan, was extended (1950) W to connect with Mexico city.

Tenouchfi, Djebel, Algeria: see TLEMCEN MOUNTAINS.

Ten Pound Island, E Mass., lighthouse islet in harbor of Gloucester; has federal fish and wildlife station.

Tenryu River (tān'rū), Jap. *Tenryu-gawa*, central Honshu, Japan, in Shizuoka and Nagano prefectures; rises in L. Suwa near Okaya; flows 135 mi. generally S, past Ina, Akaho, and Iida, to Philippine Sea just SE of Hamamatsu. Known for scenic rapids. Hydroelectric plants.

Tensas (tĕn'sô), parish (□ 623; pop. 13,209), E La.; ⊙ St. Joseph. Bounded E and SE by Mississippi R., W almost completely by Tensas R.; part of lowland region called Tensas Basin. Agr. (cotton, corn, oats, hay, livestock, soybeans). Cotton gins; lumber, oil. Includes lakes St. Joseph and Bruin (fish hatchery); fishing. Formed 1843.

Tensas River, E La., rises in East Carroll parish as Tensas Bayou, meanders S to Madison parish, whence it continues SSW as Tensas R., joining the Ouachita R. at Jonesville; c.175 mi. long. Drains Tensas Basin, a portion (c.100 mi. long N-S) of the Mississippi R. lowland.

Tensaw River, SW Ala., E bayou of Mobile R., flowing 35 mi. S from Mobile R. near Mt. Vernon, through Baldwin co., to Mobile Bay E of Mobile.

Tensed (tĕn'sĕd), town (pop. 189), Benewah co., N Idaho, 30 mi. N of Moscow.

Tensift River (tĕnsēft'), W Fr. Morocco, rises in the High Atlas SE of Marrakesh, flows c.160 mi. W, through the Haouz lowland, to the Atlantic 20 mi. SSW of Safi near 32°N.

Ten Sleep, town (pop. 289), Washakie co., N central Wyo., on branch of Bighorn R., just W of Bighorn Mts., and 25 mi. E of Worland; alt. 4,206 ft. Supply point in sheep and cattle region. Powder River Pass is E.

Tenstrike, resort village (pop. 206), Beltrami co., N Minn., 16 mi. NE of Bemidji, in lake and forest region; grain.

Tenterden, municipal borough (1931 pop. 3,472; 1951 census 4,225), S Kent, England, 10 mi. SW of Ashford; agr. market, with tanneries. Has 13th–15th-cent. church; reputed birthplace of Caxton.

Tenterfield, municipality (pop. 3,046), NE New South Wales, Australia, near Queensland border, 125 mi. SW of Brisbane; sheep center; orchards. Silver-lead mines near by.

Ten Thousand Islands, group of numerous small islands in Gulf of Mexico, just off S Fla. coast, in Collier and Monroe counties, E of Cape Romano; they are covered with mangrove forests and surrounded by major clam bed.

Tentudia (tĕntōō'dhyä), mountain (3,622 ft.) in the Sierra Morena, Badajoz prov., W Spain, near Huelva prov. border, 30 mi. SE of Jerez de los Caballeros. On its summit is the sanctuary of the Virgin of Tentudia, which has been declared a natl. monument.

Tentyaksai, Uzbek SSR: see KOKAN-KISHLAK.

Teocalli Mountain (tēōkă'lē), peak (13,220 ft.) in Rocky Mts., Gunnison co., W central Colo.

Teocaltiche (tāōkältē'chā), city (pop. 7,909), Jalisco, central Mexico, on interior plateau, near Zacatecas border, 40 mi. SW of Aguascalientes; alt. 6,100 ft. Agr. center (grain, alfalfa, beans, chickpeas, fruit, livestock).

Teocelo (tāōsā'lō), city (pop. 3,508), Veracruz, E Mexico, in Sierra Madre Oriental, 10 mi. S of Jalapa; alt. 3,996 ft.; agr. center (corn, coffee, oranges).

Teocuitatlán or **Teocuitatlán de Corona** (tāōkwētätlän' dā kōrō'nä), town (pop. 4,617), Jalisco, central Mexico, 40 mi. S of Guadalajara; agr. center (grain, alfalfa, beans, fruit, tobacco, stock).

Teodo, Yugoslavia: see TIVAT.

Teodolina (tā"ōdōlē'nä), town (pop. estimate 2,500), S Santa Fe prov., Argentina, 40 mi. SE of Venado Puerto; agr. (corn, wheat, flax, oats, livestock); flour milling, dairying.

Teodoro River, Brazil: see ROOSEVELT RIVER.

Teófilo Otoni (tĭō'fēlōō ōōtō'nē), city (1950 pop. 20,204), NE Minas Gerais, Brazil, on Todos os Santos R. (flows to Mucuri R.), on railroad from Caravelas (Bahia), on Rio de Janeiro–Bahia highway and 220 mi. NE of Belo Horizonte. Noted for its semiprecious stones (especially aquamarines) cut by local artisans. Mica quarries in area. Lumbering. Formerly spelled Theophilo Ottoni.

Teofipol or **Teofipol'** (tyăūfē'pŭl), town (1926 pop. 3,676), W Kamenets-Podolski oblast, Ukrainian SSR, 36 mi. SW of Shepetovka; dairy plant.

Teojomulco or **Santo Domingo Teojomulco** (sän'tō dōmēng'gō tāōhōmōōl'kō), town (pop. 1,564), Oaxaca, S Mexico, in Sierra Madre del Sur, 45 mi. SW of Oaxaca; silver, gold, lead, copper mining.

Teolo (tĕō'lō), village (pop. 373), Padova prov., Veneto, N Italy, in Euganean Hills, 11 mi. WSW of Padua; trachyte quarries.

Teolocholco (tāōlōchōl'kō), officially San Luis Teolocholco, town (pop. 2,639), Tlaxcala, central Mexico, 15 mi. N of Puebla; corn, wheat, barley, alfalfa.

Teoloyucan (tāōloiōō'kän), town (pop. 1,167), Mexico state, central Mexico, on railroad and 23 mi. N of Mexico city; grain, livestock; alt. c.7,500 ft. Natl. magnetic observatory.

Teopantlán (tāōpäntlän'), town (pop. 2,045), Puebla, central Mexico, 23 mi. SSW of Puebla; cereals, sugar, fruit, stock.

Teopisca (tāōpē'skä), town (pop. 1,588), Chiapas, S Mexico, in Sierra de Hueytepec, 18 mi. SE of San Cristóbal de las Casas; corn, fruit, timber.

Teor (tĕôr'), village (pop. 1,165), Udine prov., Friuli-Venezia Giulia, NE Italy, 17 mi. SW of Udine; alcohol distilleries.

Teora (tĕô'rä), village (pop. 1,313), Avellino prov., Campania, S Italy, 22 mi. ESE of Avellino.

Teorama (tāōrä'mä), town (pop. 1,765), Norte de Santander dept., N Colombia, in Cordillera Oriental, 14 mi. NNE of Ocaña; alt. 3,799 ft.; coffee, cacao, tobacco, corn, stock.

Teos (tē'ŏs), anc. Ionian town in W Asia Minor, port on Aegean Sea SW of Smyrna, 2 mi. W of Seferihisar, Turkey. Anacreon b. here. Ruins.

Teotecacinte (tāōtäkäsēn'tā), peak (over 7,000 ft.) on Honduras-Nicaragua border, at E end of Sierra de Dipilto, 25 mi. E of Danlí (Honduras); 14°7'N 86°10'W. Marks E end of frontier section demarcated (1900–01) from Gulf of Fonseca of the Pacific. Bet. Teotecacinte and Caribbean Sea, undemarcated *de facto* boundary follows ranges of mts. (including Colón Mts.) along left watershed of Poteca and Coco rivers. Honduras claims boundary along POTECA RIVER and Coco River, while Nicaragua disputes entire MOSQUITO COAST region N to Aguán R. Sometimes spelled Totecacinte.

Teotepec, Cerro (sĕ'rō tāōtāpĕk'), highest mountain (12,149 ft.) in Guerrero, SW Mexico, in Sierra Madre del Sur, 40 mi. WSW of Chilpancingo.

Teotepeque (–pā'kā), town (pop. 1,884), La Libertad dept., SW Salvador, on Pacific slope of coastal range, 16 mi. WSW of Nueva San Salvador; balsam of Peru extraction; coffee, livestock.

Teotihuacán or **San Juan Teotihuacán** (sän hwän' tāōtēwäkän'), town (pop. 1,353), Mexico state, central Mexico, on central plateau, on railroad and 25 mi. NE of Mexico city. Noted for its remains of an anc. Toltec sacred city, which includes temples, courts, pyramids. The famous Pyramid of the Sun, greatest structure of its kind (though others are higher), has a base 761 by 721 ft. and rises to 216 ft. The site is one of the principal sources of information on the Toltecs (who occupied the region before the Aztecs) and one of the most important archaeological sites in Mexico. One of the oldest Sp. colonial churches, completed 1560, is at San Agustín near by (SW).

Teotitlán del Camino (tāōtētlän' dĕl kämē'nō), town (pop. 2,192), Oaxaca, S Mexico, 15 mi. W of Huautla; agr. center (cereals, beans, sugar cane, coffee, cotton, fruit, stock).

Teotitlán del Valle (vä'yä), town (pop. 2,290), Oaxaca, S Mexico, 17 mi. ESE of Oaxaca; weaving center, known for bright serapes with idol design. Was capital of the Zapotec during 11th and 12th cents. Temple and pyramid in honor of Quetzalcoatl are on hill near by.

Teotlalco (tāōtläl'kō), town (pop. 402), Puebla, central Mexico, 22 mi. SW of Matamoros; cereals, fruit, stock.

Teotlaltzingo (tāōtlältsēng'gō), officially San Felipe Teotlaltzingo, town (pop. 1,694), Puebla, central Mexico, 23 mi. NW of Puebla; corn, wheat, maguey.

Tepa, Indonesia: see BABAR ISLANDS.

Tepache (tāpä'chä), town (pop. 808), Sonora, NW Mexico, 90 mi. ENE of Hermosillo; cereals, livestock.

Tepakán (tāpäkän'), town (pop. 1,210), Yucatan, SE Mexico, 37 mi. E of Mérida; henequen.

Tepalcatepec (tāpälkätäpěk'), town (pop. 2,721), Michoacán, W central Mexico, on Tepalcatepec R. and 65 mi. SW of Uruapan; rice, sugar, fruit.

Tepalcatepec River, in Jalisco and Michoacán, W Mexico, rises in mts. SW of Jiquilpan near Jalisco-Michoacán border, flows c.150 mi. S and E to the Río de las Balsas (Guerrero border) 25 mi. S of La Huacana. Hydroelectric project.

Tepalcingo (tāpälsēng'gō), town (pop. 3,076), Morelos, central Mexico, 33 mi. SE of Cuernavaca; agr. center (rice, sugar cane, fruit, vegetables).

Tepames (tāpä'mēs), town (pop. 1,413), Colima, W Mexico, 12 mi. SSE of Colima; corn, rice, sugar cane, tobacco, coffee, fruit, livestock.

Tepanco (tāpäng'kō), officially Tepanco de López, town (pop. 971), Puebla, central Mexico, 13 mi. NW of Tehuacán; corn, sugar cane, fruit, livestock.

Tepango or **Tepango de Rodríguez** (tāpäng'gō dā rōdrē'gēs), town (pop. 1,892), Puebla, central Mexico, in Sierra Madre Oriental, 10 mi. NE of Zacatlán; coffee, tobacco, corn, sugar cane, fruit.

Tepatepec (tāpätäpěk'), town (pop. 2,382), Hidalgo, central Mexico, 25 mi. NW of Pachuca; corn, beans, potatoes, maguey, livestock.

Tepatitlán de Morelos (tāpätētlän' dā mōrā'lōs), city (pop. 8,894), Jalisco, central Mexico, 40 mi. ENE of Guadalajara; agr. center (corn, beans, vegetables, stock).

Tepatlán (tāpätlän'), officially San Felipe Tepatlán, town (pop. 820), Pueblo, central Mexico, in Sierra Madre Oriental, 17 mi. ESE of Huauchinango; sugar cane, coffee, fruit.

Tepatlaxco (tāpätlä'skō). **1** Officially Tepatlaxco de Hidalgo, town (pop. 4,037), Puebla, central Mexico, on central plateau, 16 mi. E of Puebla; agr. center (grain, maguey, livestock). **2** Town (pop. 568), Veracruz, E Mexico, in Sierra Madre Oriental, 13 mi. NE of Córdoba; fruit.

Tepe, Turkey: see KARAKOCAN.

Tepeaca (tāpää'kä), city (pop. 3,963), Puebla, central Mexico, on central plateau, on railroad and 21 mi. ESE of Puebla; alt. 7,359 ft. Maguey-growing and -processing (pulque) center; fruit (pears, apples, nuts, etc.), cereals, vegetables. Marble and onyx deposits near by. Has picturesque old churches, ruins of early colonial fortified convent.

Tepeapulco (tāpääpōōl'kō), town (pop. 1,299), Hidalgo, central Mexico, 28 mi. SE of Pachuca; maguey.

Tepechitlán (tāpāchētlän'), town (pop. 1,065), Zacatecas, N central Mexico, 4 mi. S of Tlaltenango; grain, fruit, sugar cane, vegetables, livestock.

Tepecoacuilco (tāpākwäkwēl'kō), officially Tepecoacuilco de Trujano, town (pop. 2,439), Guerrero, SW Mexico, on N slopes of Sierra Madre del Sur, 6 mi. SE of Iguala; alt. 3,297 ft. Cereals, sugar cane, fruit, forest products (rubber, resin, vanilla).

Tepecoyo (tāpäkoi'ō), town (pop. 2,678), La Libertad dept., SW Salvador, in coastal range, 11 mi. W of Nueva San Salvador; coffee, balsam of Peru extraction.

Tepe Gawra (tě'pā gourä') [Kurdish, =great mound], locality, Mosul prov., N Iraq, 15 mi. NE of Mosul. Important excavations, begun here in 1927 and continued for many years, have unearthed 26 levels of anc. cities. At the 12th level (c.4000 B.C.) was found a complex architectural layout of buildings, some of them whitewashed.

Tepehuacán (tāpāwäkän'), officially Tepehuacán de Guerrero, town (pop. 804), Hidalgo, central Mexico, in foothills of Sierra Madre Oriental, 23 mi. ESE of Jacala; corn, tobacco, sugar cane, fruit.

Tepehuanes (tāpäwä'nēs), officially Santa Catarina de Tepehuanes, town (pop. 1,230), Durango, N Mexico, in Sierra Madre Occidental, 28 mi. NW of Santiago Papasquiaro; alt. 5,866 ft. Rail terminus; mining (silver, gold, lead, copper).

Tepeji, Puebla, Mexico: see TEPEXI.

Tepeji del Río (tāpā'hē děl rē'ō), town (pop. 5,815), Hidalgo, central Mexico, 40 mi. WSW of Pachuca; agr. center (cereals, cotton, fruit, vegetables, stock); cotton, flour mills.

Tepelenë (tāpälā'nů) or **Tepelena** (–nä), Ital. *Tepeleni*, town (1945 pop. 383), S Albania, on Vijosë R. and 30 mi. ESE Valona, strategic road center. Ruins of Turkish fortress. Coal (at Gusmar) and iron deposits near by. Situated on site of anc. Antigonea, it developed into an important commercial center which flourished under Ali Pasha (b. here). Declined as result of Balkan Wars and 1920 earthquake.

Tepemaxalco (tāpāmäsäl'kō), officially San Felipe Tepemaxalco, town (pop. 290), Puebla, central Mexico, 17 mi. SW of Atlixco; corn, wheat, sugar.

Tepeojuma (tāpāōhōō'mä), town (pop. 856), Puebla, central Mexico, on railroad and 13 mi. SSW of Atlixco; cereals, sugar cane, livestock.

Tepepan or **Tepepam** (tāpāpän', –päm'), town (pop. 1,811), Federal Dist., central Mexico, adjoining Xochimilco, 13 mi. S of Mexico city; cereals, vegetables, fruit, stock.

Tepetitán (tāpätētän'), town (pop. 657), Tabasco, SE Mexico, on affluent of Grijalva R. and 38 mi. ESE of Villahermosa; corn, fruit.

Tepetitla (–tēt'lä), town (pop. 2,030), Tlaxcala, central Mexico, on Puebla border, 15 mi. NW of Puebla; cereals, maguey, alfalfa, stock. Sometimes Lardizábal.

Tepetitlán (–tētlän'), town (pop. 604), Hidalgo, central Mexico, 45 mi. W of Pachuca; alt. 6,561 ft.; corn, maguey, livestock.

Tepetlán (tāpātlän'), town (pop. 696), Veracruz, E Mexico, in Sierra Madre Oriental, 13 mi. NE of Jalapa; coffee.

Tepetlaoxtoc (–loustōk'), officially Tepetlaoxtoc de Hidalgo, town (pop. 1,763), Mexico state, central Mexico, 23 mi. NE of Mexico city; cereals, stock.

Tepetlixpa (–tlē'spä), town (pop. 3,266), Mexico state, central Mexico, 35 mi. SE of Mexico city; agr. center (cereals, fruit, livestock).

Tepetongo (–tōng'gō), town (pop. 844), Zacatecas, N central Mexico, 45 mi. WSW of Zacatecas; alt. 7,250 ft.; cereals, vegetables, livestock.

Tepetzala (–tsä'lä), officially Santa Isabel Tepetzala, town (pop. 1,543), Puebla, central Mexico, 19 mi. ENE of Puebla; grain, maguey, livestock.

Tepetzintla (–tsēn'tlä). **1** Town (pop. 566), Puebla, central Mexico, 9 mi. E of Zacatlán; cereals, fruit. **2** Town (pop. 1,312), Veracruz, S Mexico, in Sierra Madre Oriental foothills, 32 mi. NW of Tuxpan; corn, sugar cane, coffee, fruit. Petroleum wells near by.

Tepexco (tāpě'skō), town (pop. 662), Puebla, central Mexico, 15 mi. WNW of Matamoros; corn, sugar cane, fruit.

Tepexi (tāpā'hē), officially Tepexi de Rodríguez, town (pop. 1,683), Puebla, central Mexico, on central plateau, 37 mi. SE of Puebla; alt. 5,741 ft. Sugar cane, stock. Sometimes Tepeji.

Tepexpan (tůpěsh'pän, Sp. tāpās'pän), officially Santa Cruz Tepexpan, town (pop. 2,455), Mexico state, central Mexico, 35 mi. NW of Mexico city; cereals, livestock. Here, in the Valley of Mexico, a skull and skeleton of an anc. primitive man was unearthed in 1947.

Tepeyahualco (tāpěyäwäl'kō). **1** Town (pop. 1,101), Puebla, central Mexico, on railroad and 38 mi. W of Jalapa; alt. 7,621 ft.; corn, maguey. **2** Officially Tepeyahualco Cuauhtémoc, town (pop. 626), Puebla, central Mexico, 27 mi. SE of Puebla; cereals, beans.

Tepeyanco (tāpěyäng'kō), officially San Francisco Tepeyanco, town (pop. 1,174), Tlaxcala, central Mexico, 5 mi. S of Tlaxcala; cereals, maguey, stock. Thermal springs near by.

Tepezalá (tāpāsälä'), town (pop. 1,429), Aguascalientes, N central Mexico, on railroad and 25 mi. NNE of Aguascalientes; silver and copper mining; stock raising.

Tepic (tāpēk'), city (pop. 17,547), ⊙ Nayarit, W Mexico, at foot of extinct Sangangüey volcano (7,716 ft.), on W plateau of Sierra Madre Occidental, on railroad and 120 mi. NW of Guadalajara, 415 mi. NW of Mexico city; 21°31'N 104°54'W; alt. 3,123 ft. Commercial, processing, and agr. center (coffee, sugar cane, rice, corn, tobacco, beans, fruit, vegetables, cattle, hogs); tanneries, cotton gins, tobacco factories, distilleries (vegetable oil), rice mills, sugar refineries. Airport, radio station. Tepic was occupied by Cortés; it still retains its old colonial character because of its long isolation before advent of the railroad. Colorful Indian market. Has cathedral, municipal palace. Vast Aguirre sugar plantations near by. Waterfall and resort 3 mi. N.

Te-p'ing, China: see TEHPING.

Tepla or **Mesto Tepla** (myě'stô tě'plä), Czech *Město Teplá*, Ger. *Stadt Tepl* (shtät" tě'pŭl), town (pop. 1,169), W Bohemia, Czechoslovakia, on railroad and 28 mi. NW of Pilsen. Klaster Tepla (klä'shtěr těp'lä), Czech *Klášter Teplá*, village (pop. 324) just SE of town, has monastery with fine library.

Teplaya Gora (tyô"plŭ gŭrä'), town (1932 pop. estimate 2,400), E Molotov oblast, Russian SFSR, on Koiva R. and 45 mi. ENE (under jurisdiction) of Chusovoi, on railroad; iron foundry; charcoal burning. Precious stone deposits near by.

Teplice or **Teplice-Sanov** (tě'plĭtsě-shä'nôf), Czech *Teplice-Šanov*, Ger. *Teplitz* or *Teplitz-Schönau* (tě'plĭts-shû'nou), city (pop. 22,783), NW Bohemia, Czechoslovakia, in NE foothills of the Erzgebirge, 10 mi. W of Usti nad Labem; rail junction; industrial center; mfg. (glass, porcelain, ceramics, firebricks, cement, clothing, knit goods, hats, paper, artificial flowers), jute processing. Peat and lignite mining in vicinity. Noted health resort with radioactive thermal springs (82°–115°F.) known in Celtic and Roman times, and picturesque castle. Urban area (pop. 45,183) includes industrial town of TRNOVANY (E). The famous encounter bet. Goethe and Beethoven took place (1812) in Teplice.

Teplice nad Metuji (näd' mě"tōōyĭ), Czech *Teplice nad Metují*, Ger. *Wekelsdorf* (vä'kŭlzdôrf), town (pop. 842), NE Bohemia, Czechoslovakia, in the Sudetes, 19 mi. NE of Dvur Kralove; rail junction; noted mtn. excursion center, especially to Adrspach (ä'důrshspäkh), Czech *Adršpach*, 4 mi. NW.

Teplik (tyě'plyĭk), town (1926 pop. 7,011), E Vinnitsa oblast, Ukrainian SSR, 22 mi. WSW of Uman; metalworks.

Teplitz Bay (tyě'plyĭts), inlet on W shore of Rudolf Isl., Franz Josef Land, Russian SFSR, in Arctic Ocean; 81°48'N 57°50'E. Site of govt. observation station.

Teploklyuchenka (tyě"plŭklyōō'chĭn-kŭ), village, NE Issyk-Kul oblast, Kirghiz SSR, 6 mi. E of Przhevalsk; wheat; metalworks.

Teplovka (tyô'plŭfkŭ), village (1939 pop. over 500), SW Chkalov oblast, Russian SFSR, on right tributary of Ural R. and 22 mi. NNE of Uralsk; metalworking; wheat, livestock. Until c.1940, Teply.

Teploye (tyô'plŭyŭ), village (1926 pop. 1,062), S Tula oblast, Russian SFSR, 40 mi. S of Tula; wheat, rubber-bearing plants.

Teply, Russian SFSR: see TEPLOVKA.

Teply Klyuch, Russian SFSR: see KLYUCHEVSK.

Teply Stan, Russian SFSR: see SECHENOVO.

Tepoca, Cape (tāpō'kä), rocky headland on Gulf of California, Sonora, NW Mexico, opposite (N of) Tiburón Isl. 90 mi. WNW of Hermosillo; 29°22'N 112°27'W, towered over by Tepoca Peak (1,857 ft.).

Teposcolula (tāpōskōlōō'lä), town (pop. 1,818), Oaxaca, S Mexico, on Inter-American Highway, in Sierra Madre del Sur, and 18 mi. WNW of Nochixtlán; alt. 7,070 ft. Cereals, coffee, sugar cane, fruit, livestock.

Tepoto (täpō'tō), 2 coral islands in Tuamotu group, Fr. Oceania, S Pacific; one is in RAEVSKI ISLANDS, the other in DISAPPOINTMENT ISLANDS.

Tepotzotlán (tāpōtsōtlän'), town (pop. 1,378), Mexico state, central Mexico, on central plateau, 20 mi. NNW of Mexico city; grain, maguey, livestock. Old church and monastery, founded 1584 by Jesuits, now is a natl. monument; decorated with pictures by famous Mex. artists.

Tepoztlán (tāpōstlän'), town (pop. 3,230), Morelos, central Mexico, on railroad and 12 mi. NE of Cuernavaca; alt. 7,565 ft.; sugar cane, fruit, vegetables. Picturesque Aztec village; has 16th-cent. monastery. Tepozteco pyramid is near by.

Te Puke (tē" pōō'kē), borough (pop. 1,144), N N. Isl., New Zealand, near Bay of Plenty, 105 mi. SE of Auckland; corn, sheep, dairy products.

Tepupa (tāpōō'pä), town (pop. 552), Sonora, NW Mexico, on Moctezuma R. (near its confluence with the Yaqui), and 75 mi. E of Hermosillo; corn, wheat, beans, cattle.

Tequendama Falls (tākěndä'mä), Cundinamarca dept., central Colombia, on Bogotá (or Funza) R., in Cordillera Oriental, and 15 mi. W of Bogotá. A rock-walled gorge set in amphitheater of forest-clad hills, it drops 482 ft. A popular tourist site, reached by rail from Bogotá. Hydroelectric station near by.

Teques, Los, Venezuela: see LOS TEQUES.

Tequesquetengo, Lake (tākäskātěng'gō) (□ 48), Morelos, central Mexico, 4 mi. N of Jojutla; popular fishing and hunting resort.

Tequexquipan (tākäskē'pän), town (pop. 2,665), Mexico state, central Mexico, 27 mi. SW of Toluca; cereals, stock.

Tequila (tākē'lä). **1** City (pop. 4,728), Jalisco, W Mexico, on railroad and 35 mi. WNW of Guadalajara; alt. 3,986 ft.; maguey- and banana-growing center; tequila mfg. **2** Town, Veracruz, Mexico: see ROA BÁRCENA.

Tequisquiapan (tākēskyä'pän), town (pop. 1,648), Querétaro, central Mexico, on affluent of Moctezuma R. and 33 mi. E of Querétaro; alt. 6,204 ft. Grain, alfalfa, beans, livestock. Hydroelectric plant near by.

Tequixquiac (tākēskyäk'), town (pop. 3,732), Mexico state, central Mexico, on central plateau, on railroad and 33 mi. N of Mexico city; agr. center (cereals, maguey, fruit, stock). Site of tunnel linking Cuautitlán R., and thus L. Texcoco and L. Zumpango, with Pánuco R. system.

Ter, river, Spain: see TER RIVER.

Téra (tě'rä), town (pop. c.4,300), SW Niger territory, Fr. West Africa, near Upper Volta border, 100 mi. WNW of Niamey; stock raising (cattle, goats, sheep); subsistence crops.

Teradomari (tärä'dō-mä'rē), town (pop. 13,023), Niigata prefecture, central Honshu, Japan, on Sea of Japan, 11 mi. W of Sanjo; rice growing, fishing. Mineral springs.

Terai or **Tarai** (both: tŭrī'), N India and S Nepal, undulating, partly marshy land N of N plains of India, below S Himalayan foothills; has dispersed sabai-grass tracts. Notoriously unhealthy, area is gradually being cultivated (oilseeds, rice, wheat, barley, corn, jute), with a concentration on sugar cane around Gorakhpur dist. (NE Uttar Pradesh).

Interspersed with the Terai is the Bhabar, a region of gravel and shingle supporting dense sal forests intermixed with sissoo and cotton trees. E part of Terai called EASTERN and WESTERN DUARS. In Nepal, inhabited mainly by Tharus.

Teraino (tärī'nō), town (pop. 6,935), Ishikawa prefecture, central Honshu, Japan, 3 mi. NE of Komatsu, in rice-growing area; mfg. (silk textiles, pottery).

Teramo (tĕ'rämô), province (□ 752; pop. 249,532), Abruzzi e Molise, S central Italy; ⊙ Teramo. Mtn. and hill terrain with Gran Sasso d'Italia in SW; extends E to Adriatic Sea; watered by Vomano and Tordino rivers. Agr. (cereals, grapes, potatoes, olives, fruit); livestock raising (sheep, cattle). Mfg. at Giulianova, Teramo, and Atri. Area reduced in 1927 to help form Pescara prov.

Teramo, town (pop. 16,229), ⊙ Teramo prov., Abruzzi e Molise, S central Italy, on Tordino R. and 15 mi. SSE of Ascoli Piceno; 42°39'N 13°42'E. Rail terminus; agr. center; mfg. (macaroni, licorice, woolen textiles, hats, furniture). Bishopric. Has Romanesque cathedral (begun 12th cent.; restored in 14th cent.) and remains of Roman amphitheater.

Terán (tärän'), town (pop. 1,685), Chiapas, S Mexico, 3 mi. W of Tuxtla; cereals, sugar cane, tobacco, fruit, stock.

Terang (tŭrăng'), town (pop. 2,204), SW Victoria, Australia, 115 mi. WSW of Melbourne; rail junction; dairying, agr. (flax) center.

Terao (tärou'), village (1930 pop. 169), Chiloé prov., S Chile, on E coast of Chiloé Isl., 17 mi. SE of Castro; potatoes; fishing, lumbering.

Ter Apel (tĕr ä'pŭl), town (pop. 2,697), Groningen prov., NE Netherlands, 11 mi. SE of Stadskanaal; potato-flour-milling and dairying center; hide-processing; peat production. Near by is 13th-cent. monastery.

Terascos, Sierra de los (syĕ'rä dā lōs tärä'skōs), mountain range in W Michoacán, W Mexico, W and NW of Uruapan; forms part of W-E volcanic belt of central Mexico; c.25 mi. long NE–SW. Newly erupted volcano PARICUTÍN is in S.

Terasho, Japan: see KONAN.

Teratsu (tärä'tsōō) or **Terazu** (-zōō), town (pop. 6,004), Aichi prefecture, central Honshu, Japan, 12 mi. SW of Okazaki; agr. (rice, wheat, watermelons); raw silk; poultry.

Terauchi, Japan: see AKITA, city.

Terazu, Japan: see TERATSU.

Terborg (tĕrbôrkh'), town (pop. 2,246), Gelderland prov., E Netherlands, on Old Ijssel R. and 20 mi. ESE of Arnhem; iron foundries; enamelware; cattle market.

Terbuny (tyĭrbōō'nē), town (1939 pop. over 500), NE Kursk oblast, Russian SFSR, 33 mi. SSW of Yelets; flour mill.

Tercan (tĕrjän'), village (pop. 1,551), Erzincan prov., E central Turkey, 50 mi. E of Erzincan; grain. Formerly Mamahatun.

Terceira Island (tĕrsā'rŭ), easternmost (□ 153; 1950 pop. 61,029) of the central Azores, in the Atlantic, 25 mi. ENE of São Jorge Isl.; ANGRA DO HEROÍSMO (38°39'N 27°13'W), its chief city and port, is on S shore. Of volcanic origin, it rises to 3,356 ft. in the Caldeira de Santa Bárbara; 18 mi. long, 11 mi. wide. Steep coast line, rugged interior (volcanic cones, basalt plateaus). Agr.: wheat, corn, sweet potatoes, pineapples, bananas, wine. Cattle raising. Lajes (or Lagens) air base near NE coast. Administratively part of Angra do Heroísmo dist.

Tercero, Río (rē'ō tĕrsä'rō), river, rises in Sierra de Comechingones, W central Córdoba prov., Argentina, flows E 150 mi., past Río Tercero town, Villa María, and Bell Ville joining the Río Cuarto (here called the Saladillo) to form CARCARAÑA RIVER, which flows to the Paraná. Dam (finished 1934) on its upper reaches furnishes hydroelectric power and irrigation.

Tercero Abajo, Argentina: see VILLA MARÍA.

Tercero Arriba, Argentina: see OLIVA.

Terdal (tär'dŭl), town (pop. 7,295), Bijapur dist., S Bombay, India, 50 mi. SW of Bijapur; market center for millet, cotton, peanuts, wheat; handicraft cloth weaving. Has 12th-cent. Jain temples. Sometimes spelled Tordal.

Terdoppio River (tĕrdôp'pyô), Lombardy, N Italy, rises near S end of Lago Maggiore, 5 mi. SW of Sesto Calende; flows c.60 mi. S, bet. Agogna and Ticino rivers, through the Lomellina, past Gambolò and Tromello, to Po R. 8 mi. SW of Pavia; partly canalized.

Terebovlya (tyĕrĭbôv'lyŭ), city (1931 pop. 7,840), central Ternopol oblast, Ukrainian SSR, 17 mi. SSE of Ternopol; agr. center; cereal processing; red-sandstone quarrying, brick mfg. Hog raising near by. Has mus., old church, ruins of castle. An old Pol. town, frequently assaulted by Tatars; scene of defeat (1675) of Turks by Poles. Passed to Austria (1772); reverted to Poland (1919); ceded to USSR in 1945. Until 1944, called Trembovlya, Pol. *Trembowla* (trĕmbôv'lä).

Teregova (tĕrĕgô'vä), village (pop. 3,706), Severin prov., SW Rumania, on Timis R., on railroad and 40 mi. SE of Lugoj; tourist center on W slopes of the Transylvanian Alps; also flour milling, nickel mining, stone quarrying.

Terek (tyĕ'rĭk), former oblast of Russia, in Northern Caucasus; ⊙ was Vladikavkaz. Coextensive with Terek R. basin, it was reorganized (1921) as a govt. and passed 1924 to Northern CAUCASUS Territory.

Terek, town (1948 pop. over 2,000), E Kabardian Autonomous SSR, Russian SFSR, on Terek R., on railroad (Murtazovo station) and 25 mi. E of Nalchik; metalworks. Just W, across Terek R., are starch-processing plant and flour mill of Aleksandrovskaya (1926 pop. 2,296).

Terekhovka (tyĕrĭkhôf'kŭ), town (1939 pop. over 500), SE Gomel oblast, Belorussian SSR, 19 mi. SE of Gomel; flax processing.

Terekli-Mekteb (tyĕrĭklyē"-myĭktyĕp'), village (1939 pop. over 500), central Grozny oblast, Russian SFSR, on dry Caspian steppe, 45 mi. NW of Kizlyar; sheep raising.

Terek Range (tyĕ'rĭk), N outlier of the central Greater Caucasus, Russian SFSR; forms right watershed of Terek R., W of Grozny; rises to 3,050 ft. Oil-bearing area.

Terek River, N Caucasus, Russian SFSR, rises on Georgian side of the central Greater Caucasus in glaciers W of Mt. Kazbek, flows NNW, through Daryal Gorge in N front range, past Dzaudzhikau and Elkhotovo, E, past Mozdok and Shelkovskaya, and NE, forming 60-mi.-wide swampy delta mouth on Caspian Sea below Kizlyar; 367 mi. long. Its main delta arms are the New Terek (S), flowing to Agrakhan Gulf of Caspian Sea, and the Old Terek, entering the Caspian at Krainovka. Used for irrigation in lower course, where levees contain the aggraded river bed. Receives Malka (left) and Sunzha (right) rivers. Upper valley is used by Georgian Military Road.

Teremno (tyĭryĕm'nŭ), village (1939 pop. over 500), SE Volyn oblast, Ukrainian SSR, 4 mi. ENE of Lutsk; grain, livestock.

Terempa, Indonesia: see ANAMBAS ISLANDS.

Terena (tĭrā'nŭ), town (pop. 856), Évora dist., S central Portugal, 28 mi. E of Évora, in grain-growing region. Has many medieval bldgs.

Terenga or **Teren'ga** (tyĭryĕn'yŭgŭ), village (1926 pop. 3,168), E Ulyanovsk oblast, Russian SFSR, 40 mi. S of Ulyanovsk, in forested grain area; woodworking, distilling.

Teren-Uzyak or **Teren'-Uzyak** (tyĭryĕn'yŭ-ōōzyäk'), village (1948 pop. over 2,000), central Kzyl-Orda oblast, Kazakh SSR, on the Syr Darya, on Trans-Caspian RR and 28 mi. NW of Kzyl-Orda; rice-growing area.

Teresa (tārä'sä), town (1939 pop. 862; 1948 municipality pop. 3,356), Rizal prov., S Luzon, Philippines, 15 mi. E of Manila; marble quarrying.

Teresa Cristina, Brazil: see RESERVA.

Teresa de Cofrentes (tārā'sä dhā kōfrĕn'tĕs), town (pop. 1,843), Valencia prov., E Spain, 30 mi. WNW of Játiva; olive-oil processing, flour milling; lumbering. Wine, fruit in area.

Teresén (tārāsĕn'), town (pop. 764), Monagas state, NE Venezuela, in coastal range, 38 mi. NW of Maturín; coffee, tobacco, corn, livestock.

Teresina (tĭrĭzē'nŭ), city (1950 pop. 53,425), ⊙ Piauí, NE Brazil, on right bank of Parnaíba R. at influx of Poti R., opposite Timon (Maranhão), and 200 mi. SE of São Luís; 5°5'S 42°50'W. Agr. processing and trade center of middle Parnaíba valley, with cotton and sugar mills, distilleries, soap factories, and sawmills. Ships cattle, hides and skins (from Piauí uplands), rice, cereals, and cotton. Healthy climate because of inland location. City is S terminus of railroad to São Luís (Maranhão) via Itapecuru valley. Has faculty of law. Airport. Built near site of old Poti, city became ⊙ Piauí prov. in 1852. Formerly spelled Therezina, Theresina, or Terezina.

Teresópolis (tĭrĭzô'pōōlēs), city (pop. 9,747), central Rio de Janeiro state, Brazil, near crest of the great escarpment (Serra dos Orgãos), 35 mi. NNE of Rio; alt. 2,950 ft. Popular summer resort (healthy upland climate) towered over by sheer mtn. peaks (especially the Dedo de Deus). Flower growing; vegetables shipped to capital. Fruit preserving; mfg. of flour products, furniture. Numerous fine villas and estates amidst lush vegetation. Linked to Rio by railroad and by scenic modern highway via Petrópolis. Named (1890) after former Empress Theresa Christina. Old spelling, Therezopolis.

Terespol (tĕrĕ'spôl), town (pop. 2,301), Lublin prov., E Poland, on Bug R. (USSR border) opposite Brest, on Warsaw-Moscow RR; frontier station; cement mfg., flour milling. Also called Terespol nad Bugiem.

Teressa Island (tŭrĕ'sŭ), island of the Nicobars, in E Bay of Bengal, 80 mi. NNW of Great Nicobar.

Teresva (tyĭryĕs'vŭ), Hung. *Taracköz* (tŭ'rŭtskŭz"), village (1941 pop. 3,348), S Transcarpathian Oblast, Ukrainian SSR, on Tissa R. (Rum. frontier) and 11 mi. WNW of Sighet (Rumania); rail junction.

Terevinto (tārävēn'tō), town (pop. c.1,400), Santa Cruz dept., central Bolivia, 17 mi. WNW of Santa Cruz; sugar cane, rice, corn.

Terewah, Lake (□ 55), N New South Wales, Australia, 340 mi. NW of Newcastle; 19 mi. long, 6 mi. wide; shallow. Sometimes called Narran L.

Terezin (tĕ'rĕzēn), Czech *Terezín*, Ger. *Theresienstadt* (tärā'zēŭnshtät"), town (pop. 1,446), N Bohemia, Czechoslovakia, on Ohre R., on railroad and 11 mi. SSE of Usti nad Labem; furniture and knitwear mfg. Founded as fortress under Maria Theresa; later became military arsenal and camp. In Second World War, under Ger. occupation of Czechoslovakia in early 1940s, a notorious concentration camp (primarily for Eastern Jews) was located here.

Terezina, Brazil: see TERESINA.

Terglou, peak, Yugoslavia: see TRIGLAV.

Tergnier (tĕrnyā'), town (pop. 3,370), Aisne dept., N France, on Saint-Quentin Canal, opposite Fargniers, and 13 mi. S of Saint-Quentin; rail junction; large iron foundry, sugar refinery, hosiery mill. Leveled, 1917–18, in First World War; since rebuilt on modern plan. Damaged again in Second World War.

Ter Goes, Netherlands: see GOES.

Ter Gouw, Netherlands: see GOUDA.

Terhagen (tĕrhä'khŭn), town (pop. 3,801), Antwerp prov., N Belgium, on Rupel R. and 10 mi. S of Antwerp; brick-mfg. center. Formerly spelled Terhaegen.

Terhulpen, Belgium: see HULPE, LA.

Teriberka (tyĕrēbyĕr'kŭ), town (1939 pop. over 2,000), N Murmansk oblast, Russian SFSR, on Barents Sea, on Kola Peninsula, at mouth of small Teriberka R., 55 mi. ENE of Murmansk; fish canning, metalworking.

Terijoki, Russian SFSR: see ZELENOGORSK.

Terim, Aden: see TARIM.

Terinam Tso or **Terinam Tsho** (tĕ'rēnäm tsō'), Chinese *T'ieh-li-nan-mu Hu* (tyĕ'lē'nän'mōō'hōō'), lake in central Tibet, 350 mi. WNW of Lhasa; 31°N 85°45'E.

Terlano (tĕrlä'nô), Ger. *Terlan*, village (pop. 599), Bolzano prov., Trentino–Alto Adige, N Italy, near the Adige, 5 mi. NW of Bolzano. Noted for its white wine. Lead mines near by.

Terlingua (tûrlĭng'gwŭ), village, Brewster co., extreme W Texas, in the Big Bend, c.70 mi. S of Alpine; quicksilver mines (now inactive). S is scenic Santa Elena Canyon of the Rio Grande, in BIG BEND NATIONAL PARK.

Terlizzi (tĕrlē'tsē), town (pop. 21,085), Bari prov., Apulia, S Italy, 6 mi. SSW of Molfetta; ceramics mfg. center.

Terlton (tûrl'tŭn), town (pop. 122), Pawnee co., N Okla., 28 mi. W of Tulsa, in agr. area.

Termales (tĕrmä'lĕs) or **Ruiz** (rōōēs'), spa (pop. 233), Caldas dept., W central Colombia, at NW foot of Nevado del Ruiz, 12 mi. SE of Manizales; alt. c.11,480 ft.; health resort with sulphur springs.

Termas de Chillán (tĕr'mäs dā chĭyän'), village (1930 pop. 83), Ñuble prov., S central Chile, in the Andes (alt. 5,715 ft.), at W foot of Nevados de Chillán, 35 mi. SE of Chillán; health resort with noted sulphur springs. Sometimes Baños de Chillán or Baños Termales.

Termas de Jahuel, Chile: see JAHUEL.

Termas del Río Hondo (dĕl rē'ō ōn'dō) or **Las Termas** (läs), village (1947 pop. 4,759), W Santiago del Estero prov., Argentina, on the Salí R. (Río Dulce) and 40 mi. NW of Santiago del Estero, on railroad; watering place and agr. center (wheat, corn, oats, alfalfa, livestock). Its warm sulphur springs, long known to the Indians, are frequented by tourists.

Termas de Puyehue (dā pōōyā'wā), village (1930 pop. 105), Osorno prov., S central Chile, on E shore of L. Puyehue, in Chilean lake dist., 50 mi. ESE of Osorno; health resort with well-known thermal springs; alpine scenery.

Termas de Río Blanco, Chile: see RÍO BLANCO.

Termas de Tolhuaca, Chile: see TOLHUACA.

Terme (tĕrmĕ'), anc. *Thermodon*, village (pop. 2,993), Samsun prov., N Turkey, Black Sea port 34 mi. E of Samsun; corn.

Termeno (tĕrmā'nô), Ger. *Tramin*, village (pop. 2,299), Bolzano prov., Trentino–Alto Adige, N Italy, near the Adige, 12 mi. SSW of Bolzano.

Termens (tĕr'mĕns), town (pop. 1,511), Lérida prov., NE Spain, on the Segre and 10 mi. NE of Lérida; agr. trade (livestock, cereals, sugar beets, wine, olive oil).

Termez (tyĭrmyĕs'), city (1933 pop. estimate 25,000), ⊙ Surkhan-Darya oblast, Uzbek SSR, near the Amu Darya (Afghanistan border), at mouth of the Surkhan Darya, on Kagan-Stalinabad RR and 300 mi. SSW of Tashkent; 37°15'N 67°17'E. Cotton ginning (long-staple fiber), metalworking, food processing, textile milling, rug weaving. One of hottest cities of USSR (max. 132°F.). Site of several anc. tombs, Buddhist monastery, 9th-cent. mausoleum. Flourished in antiquity. Its port, on the Amu Darya, is Pakhta-Gisar.

Termignon (tĕrmēnyō'), village (pop. 351), Savoie dept., SE France, in upper Maurienne valley, 3 mi. W of Lanslebourg; hydroelectric plant on Arc R.; asbestos quarries.

Terminal Island, S Calif., artificial island (c.6 mi. long) in LOS ANGELES HARBOR, connected by drawbridge to Wilmington, by ferry to San Pedro. Here are Fish Harbor (1,200 fishing vessels), fish canneries (tuna, sardines, mackerel) and by-products plants; shipyards; a federal prison; meteorological station; and a navy seaplane base. Residents are chiefly fishermen.

Termini Imerese (tĕr'mēnē ēmĕrā'zĕ), anc. *Thermae Himerenses*, town (pop. 20,467), Palermo prov., N Sicily, port on Tyrrhenian Sea, 20 mi. SE of Palermo, in citrus-fruit and grape region; sulphur refining, metal working, boat building, cotton milling; macaroni, tanning extracts. Resort, with warm mineral springs and baths. Has cathedral, mus. of antiquities, and some Roman ruins, including an aqueduct. Outpost of Himera and a famed watering place; established as town by Carthaginians in 407 B.C., following their destruction of Himera, whose inhabitants sought refuge here. Taken by Romans 252 B.C. during First Punic War.

Términos, Laguna de (lägōō'nä dā tĕr'mēnōs), lagoon, inlet of the Gulf of Campeche, in Campeche, SE Mexico, on SW Yucatan Peninsula; 45 mi. long, 12–15 mi. wide. CARMEN ISLAND is across its entrance. Receives Palizada and Candelaria rivers.

Terminus Dam, Calif.: see KAWEAH RIVER.

Termoli (tĕr'mōlē), town (pop. 6,573), Campobasso prov., Abruzzi e Molise, S central Italy, port on the Adriatic, 17 mi. ESE of Vasto; fishing center; mfg. (furniture, macaroni). Bishopric. Has 12th-cent. cathedral and ruins of 13th-cent. castle. Badly damaged (1943–44) in Second World War by air bombing and fighting.

Termonbarry (tûrmŭnbă'rē), agr. village (district pop. 519), E Co. Roscommon, Ireland, on the Shannon, 5 mi. W of Longford; E terminus of the Royal Canal.

Termonde, Belgium: see DENDERMONDE.

Termunterzijl (tĕr'mûntûrzīl'), town (pop. 243) and port, Groningen prov., NE Netherlands, on Eems R. estuary and 6 mi. ESE of Delfzijl; shipping, shrimp fishing. Sometimes spelled Termunterzyl.

Ternate (tĕrnä'tē), volcanic island (□ 41; pop. 13,022), N Moluccas, Indonesia, in Molucca Sea, 18 mi. W of Halmahera; 0°48'N 127°20'E; 10 mi. long, 8 mi. wide; rises to 5,627 ft. in center of isl. Densely wooded (ebony, teak, rattan, gum). Agr. (rice, sago, coffee), fishing. Chief town is Ternate (pop. 7,126), on E coast; important transit port for New Guinea and Halmahera, exporting teak, ebony, rattan, copra, spices, bird skins. Formerly town was ⊙ sultanate of Ternate, important in Moluccan history from 12th to 17th cent. Isl. was first in Moluccas to accept Islam, introduced in 15th cent. In 1522 the Portuguese built fort here which fell 1574 to the hostile natives; Christian centers in Moluccas were soon destroyed. Sir Francis Drake visited isl. in 1579, and was followed by other Englishmen. First Du. settlement was made 1599, and Du. sovereignty established 1683.

Ternberg (tĕrn'bĕrk), town (pop. 4,015), SE Upper Austria, on Enns R. and 7 mi. S of Steyr; power station.

Ternei or **Terney** (tyĭrnyā'), town (1948 pop. over 2,000), Maritime Territory, Russian SFSR, port on Sea of Japan, 270 mi. NNE of Vladivostok; fish canning.

Terneuzen (tĕrnû'zŭn), town (pop. 9,492), Zeeland prov., SW Netherlands, on Flanders mainland 13 mi. SE of Flushing and on the Western Scheldt, at N end of Ghent-Terneuzen Canal; a free port for Belgium. Coke ovens; fertilizer mfg., shipbuilding; fruit market. Sometimes called Neuzen.

Terni (tĕr'nē), province (□ 826; pop. 191,559), Umbria, central Italy; ⊙ Terni. Hilly terrain, watered by Tiber, Nera, and Paglia rivers. Chiefly agr. (cereals, fodder, grapes, olives, sugar beets) and stock raising (sheep, cattle). Cement mfg. is widespread. Hydroelectric plant near Montoro. Mfg. at Terni (iron and steel), Orvieto, Narni, and Amelia. Formed 1927 from Perugia prov.

Terni, anc. *Interamna Nahars*, city (pop. 37,295), ⊙ Terni prov., Umbria, central Italy, on Nera R. and 46 mi. NNE of Rome; 42°33'N 12°39'E. Rail junction; industrial center; iron- and steelworks, arms and munitions factories, chemical plants, tanneries; mfg. of locomotives, automobile chassis, turbines, furniture, soap, glass, macaroni. Its famous waterfalls (Cascata delle Marmore), 4 mi. SE, descend 525 ft. in 3 falls, furnishing water power; they were formed when the Romans connected (272 B.C.) Velino R. with the Nera. Bishopric. Has Roman remains (amphitheater), medieval churches and palaces. Roman emperor Tacitus b. here. Badly damaged in Second World War by air bombing (1943–44).

Ternitz (tĕrn'ĭts), town (pop. 8,418), SE Lower Austria, on Schwarza R. and 2 mi. W of Neunkirchen; iron- and steelworks, paper mills.

Ternopol or **Ternopol'** (tûrnō'pŭl, Rus. tyĭrnô'pŭl), oblast (□ 5,300; 1946 pop. estimate 1,500,000), W Ukrainian SSR; ⊙ Ternopol. In central part of Volyn-Podolian Upland; bordered by Kremenets Hills (N); bounded S by Dniester R., E by Zbruch R. Drained by left tributaries of the Dniester (Zolotaya Lipa, Strypa, Seret, Zbruch) and by upper Goryn R. Has fertile black-earth soils; humid continental climate (short summers). Mineral resources include lignite (Zolochev, Kremenets), phosphorite (S), peat and chalk (Kremenets Hills). Extensive agr. (wheat, rye, barley, tobacco, sunflowers); winegrowing (near Zaleshchiki); cattle, hog, and horse raising; beekeeping. Industries based on agr. (food processing and preserving, tanning, distilling); stone quarrying, brickmaking. Light mfg. in main urban centers (Ternopol, Kremenets, Chortkov). Formed (1939) out of parts of Pol. Tarnopol and Wolyn provs., following Soviet occupation of E Poland; held by Germany (1941–44); ceded to USSR in 1945.

Ternopol or **Ternopol'**, city (1931 pop. 35,831), ⊙ Ternopol oblast, Ukrainian SSR, in Volyn-Podolian Upland, on Seret R. (here forms artificial lake) and 75 mi. ESE of Lvov; 49°33'N 25°36'E. Rail junction (3 rail lines), airport; agr.-trading (cereals, eggs) and -processing (grain, sugar beets, fruit, tobacco) center; distilling (liquor, vinegar, beer); mfg. of agr. machinery, cement, chalk, candles, soap; sawmilling. Stone quarry near by. Has technical schools, mus., several churches and monasteries, including 15th-cent. synagogue and old castle transformed into church. Founded 1540 by Pol. hetman Jan Tarnowski, fortified and developed as commercial town. Severely damaged during Confederation of Bar (1770); passed to Austria (1772) and became a noted horse-trading center. Captured by Russians during First World War and assaulted by Austro-Germans (1915). Reverted to Poland (1919); scene of Pol.-Soviet battles (1920); ceded to USSR in 1945. Jewish pop. largely exterminated during Second World War. Until 1944 called Tarnopol (tärnô'pôl), its Pol. name.

Ternovka (tyĭrnôf'kŭ). **1** Village (1926 pop. 3,380), central Penza oblast, Russian SFSR, 5 mi. S of Penza; truck produce, orchards. **2** Village (1926 pop. 2,300), central Saratov oblast, Russian SFSR, on left bank of Volga R., opposite Krasny Tekstilshchik and 15 mi. SSW of Engels; wheat, tobacco. **3** Village (1926 pop. 2,890), E Voronezh oblast, Russian SFSR, 25 mi. NW of Borisoglebsk; flour milling, metalworking.

Ternovsk, Russian SFSR: see KAGANOVICH, city, Moscow oblast.

Ternovskoye, Russian SFSR: see TRUNOVSKOYE.

Teror (tärôr'), town (pop. 1,436; commune pop. 9,049), Grand Canary, Canary Isls., 8 mi. WSW of Las Palmas; chick-peas, sweet peas, potatoes, cereals, fruit, livestock; timber. Starch mfg. Popular resort, with medicinal springs. Has church with shrine of Virgin del Pino, isl.'s patron saint.

Terowie (tûrou'ē), village (pop. 574), S South Australia, 50 mi. E of Port Pirie; wheat, wool.

Terpeniye, Cape (tyĭrpâ'nyēŭ), Jap. *Kita-shiretoko-misaki*, cape on E coast of Sakhalin, Russian SFSR, at end of long, narrow Terpeniye Peninsula; 48°38'N 144°45'E. Forms E side of Terpeniye Gulf.

Terpeniye Gulf, Jap. *Taraika-wan*, inlet of Sea of Okhotsk on E coast of Sakhalin, Russian SFSR; bounded E by Terpeniye Peninsula; 85 mi. wide. Ports are Poronaisk and Makarov.

Terpne or **Terpni** (tĕrpnē'), village (pop. 2,663), Serrai nome, Macedonia, Greece, just NW of Nigrita. Formerly called Tserpista or Cherpista.

Terque (tĕr'kā), town (pop. 1,308), Almería prov., S Spain, 14 mi. NNW of Almería; cereals, fruit; ships grapes.

Terra Alta, town (pop. 1,649), Preston co., N W.Va., near Md. line, 24 mi. SE of Morgantown. Near by are Terra Alta L. (resort) and a state tuberculosis sanatorium. Inc. 1890.

Térraba, Río Grande de, Costa Rica: see DIQUÍS RIVER.

Terra Bella, village (pop. c.300), Tulare co., S central Calif., 7 mi. S of Porterville; packs fruit, truck; cans olives.

Terrabona (tĕräbō'nä), town (1950 pop. 996), Matagalpa dept., W central Nicaragua, 15 mi. S of Matagalpa; sugar, corn, beans, rice, plantains.

Terrace, village (pop. 355), W B.C., on Skeena R. and 70 mi. ENE of Prince Rupert; lumbering, brick making, furniture mfg., mixed farming. Gold and silver mined near by.

Terrace, Pa.: see WEST MIFFLIN.

Terrace Park, village (pop. 1,265), Hamilton co., extreme SW Ohio, on Little Miami R. and 12 mi. E of downtown Cincinnati; residential. Settled 1791, inc. 1893.

Terracina (tĕr-rächē'nä), anc. *Anxur*, town (pop. 15,642), Latina prov., Latium, S central Italy, port on Gulf of Gaeta, 60 mi. SE of Rome; bathing resort; fishing; wine making, food canning. Limestone quarries near by. Bishopric. Has Roman ruins (Temple of Venus, amphitheater, baths) and walled medieval area. In the old Forum, with its well-preserved pavement, stands the cathedral (remodeled 17th cent.). Badly damaged by air and naval bombing (1943–44) in Second World War.

Terrak, Norway: see BINDALSEIDET.

Terral (tĕ'rŭl), town (pop. 616), Jefferson co., S Okla., 32 mi. E of Wichita Falls (Texas), and on Red R. (Texas line); cotton ginning.

Terralba (tĕr-räl'bä), town (pop. 7,028), Cagliari prov., W Sardinia, 13 mi. S of Oristano, in the Campidano.

Terranora (tĕ"rŭnô'rŭ), village (pop. 257), NE New South Wales, Australia, on Tweed R., near its mouth, and 70 mi. S of Brisbane; drydock, govt. wharf.

Terranova, Gulf of (tĕr"ränô'vä), inlet of Tyrrhenian Sea, in NE Sardinia, S of Golfo degli Aranci; 5 mi. wide, 7 mi. deep; fisheries (sea mussels, oysters). Chief port, Olbia.

Terra Nova, Lake (tĕ'rŭ nō'vŭ) (□ 10), SE N.F., on Terra Nova R., 35 mi. SSE of Gander; 8 mi. long, up to 3 mi. wide. At E end is settlement of Terra Nova (pop. 99).

Terranova di Sibari (tĕr-ränô'vä dē sē'bärē), town (pop. 3,776), Cosenza prov., Calabria, S Italy, near Crati R., 13 mi. SE of Castrovillari, in agr. (cereals, fruit), stock-raising region. Near by is site of anc. SYBARIS.

Terranova di Sicilia, Sicily: see GELA.

Terranova Pausania, Sardinia: see OLBIA.

Terra Nova River, SE N.F., flows 70 mi. NE, through several lakes, including L. St. John and Terra Nova L., to Bonavista Bay 30 mi. SE of Gander.

Terranova Sappo Minulio, Italy: see TAURIANOVA.

Terranuova Bracciolini (tĕrränwô'vä brät-chôlē'nē), town (pop. 2,091), Arezzo prov., Tuscany, central Italy, 2 mi. N of Montevarchi; alcohol distillery, paper mill, cotton dyeworks, nail and macaroni factories.

Terras do Bouro (tĕ'rŭsh dōō bō'rōō), town, Braga dist., N Portugal, 12 mi. NE of Braga; corn, beans.

Terrasini Favarotta (tĕr"räzē'nē fävärôt'tä) or **Terrasini,** town (pop. 6,401), Palermo prov., NW Sicily, port on Gulf of Castellammare and 15 mi. WNW of Palermo.

Terrasson (tĕräsō'), town (pop. 2,860), Dordogne dept., SW France, on the Vézère and 11 mi. W of Brive-la-Gaillarde; glass mill (bottles); food preserving (truffles, fruits, early vegetables), shoe mfg. Tourist center. Has 15th-cent. church.

Terrebonne (târbôn'), county (□ 782; pop. 46,864), S Que., on the St. Lawrence, NW of Montreal; ⊙ St. Jérôme.

Terrebonne, town (pop. 2,209), S Que., on Mille Îles R. and 12 mi. NNW of Montreal; tobacco processing, woodworking, mfg. of shoes, fiber products, agr. implements. Inc. 1860. Has commercial col.

Terrebonne (tĕ'rŭbōn"), parish (□ 1,391; pop. 43,328), SE La.; ⊙ Houma. On Gulf of Mexico (S) and bounded partly E by small Bayou Pointe au Chien, W by Atchafalaya R.; swampy coast is indented by Atchafalaya, Caillou, and Terrebonne bays. Crossed by Gulf Intracoastal Waterway; drained by Grand Caillou, Du Large, Terrebonne, and Black bayous; includes several lakes. Canning and shipping of sea food, vegetables; oil wells; sugar and lumber milling; agr., fur trapping, hunting, fishing. Formed 1822.

Terrebonne, Bayou (bī'ō), SE La., rises in Lafourche parish, flows c.55 mi. S, past Houma (head of navigation), to head of Terrebonne Bay; lower course partly canalized; intersects Gulf Intracoastal Waterway at Houma.

Terrebonne Bay, Terrebonne parish, SE La., shallow inlet of the Gulf of Mexico, c.60 mi. SSW of New Orleans; c.12 mi. long N–S. Oil, gas wells in SE part. Adjoins Timbalier Bay (E), L. Pelto (W). Oyster beds; fishing.

Terre-de-Bas (târ-dû-bä'), islet (□ 3.65; pop. 1,319), Les Saintes isls., Guadeloupe dept., Fr. West Indies, just W of Terre-de-Haut, 11 mi. SSE of Basse-Terre city; 15°52'N 61°38'W. Fishing, stock raising; mfg. of charcoal. Sometimes called Terre-d'en-Bas or Terre-du-Bas. A smaller islet of that name is in the Petite Terre group 27 mi. ESE of Pointe-à-Pitre, Guadeloupe.

Terre-de-Haut (târ-dō'), islet (□ 1.75; pop. 1,039), Les Saintes isls., Guadeloupe dept., Fr. West Indies, just E of Terre-de-Bas, 12 mi. SE of Basse-Terre city; 15°52'N 61°35'W. Fishing, stock raising; mfg. of charcoal. Sometimes called Terre-d'en-Haut or Terre-du-Haut. A smaller islet of that name is in the Petite Terre group 27 mi. ESE of Pointe-à-Pitre, Guadeloupe.

Terre Haute (tĕ'rŭ hōt', tĕ'rē hŭt'), city (pop. 64,214), ⊙ Vigo co., W Ind., on plateau above the Wabash and c.70 mi. WSW of Indianapolis; commercial, industrial, and banking center for wide coal-mining and agr. area; hq. for mining companies. Mfg.: brick, tile, paint, coke by-products, steel and other metal products, glass, paper and pasteboard containers, clothing, pharmaceuticals, liquor, food products. U.S. ordnance depot and chemical plant. Clay pits near by. Seat of Rose Polytechnic Inst. and a state teachers col. Near by are St. Mary-of-the-Woods Col. (at St. Mary-of-the-Woods, c.6 mi. NW) and a Federal penitentiary. Points of interest: war memorial (including a stadium) in memory of soldiers of World War I; Dresser House, birthplace of Theodore Dreiser and Paul Dresser (who is also commemorated by Dresser Memorial Park). Eugene V. Debs was b. here. Indian burial mounds in vicinity. Settled c.1811, platted 1816, inc. 1853.

Terre Hill (tĕ'rŭ), borough (pop. 1,000), Lancaster co., SE Pa., 15 mi. SSW of Reading.

Terreiro da Luta (tĕrā'rōō dä lōō'tŭ), height (alt. 3,300 ft.) on Madeira, overlooking Funchal (3 mi. S); mtn. terminus of rack-and-pinion railway. Hotel, panorama.

Terrell (tĕ'rŭl). **1** County (□ 329; pop. 14,314), SW Ga.; ⊙ Dawson. Bounded NE by Kinchafoonee R., and SW by Ichawaynochaway Creek.

Coastal plain agr. (cotton, corn, fruit, peanuts) and timber area; mfg. at Dawson. Formed 1856. **2** County (□ 2,388; pop. 3,189), extreme W Texas; ⊙ Sanderson. Broken high plateau area (alt. 1,300–3,600 ft.), bounded S by the Rio Grande (Mex. border), partly on E by Pecos R. Ranching (sheep, goats; some cattle, horses); hunting. Formed 1905.

Terrell, city (pop. 11,544), Kaufman co., NE Texas, 28 mi. E of Dallas; trade, processing center in rich blackland agr. area (cotton, wheat, dairy products); cotton ginning, cottonseed-oil, lumber, and flour milling, mfg. of milk products and other foods, brooms, mattresses, machinery. Seat of Texas Military Col. and a state mental hosp. Settled c.1860, laid out 1872, inc. 1881.

Terrell Hills, city (pop. 2,708), Bexar co., S central Texas, NE suburb of San Antonio; flour milling, cotton ginning, cottonseed-oil milling. Inc. 1939.

Terrenate or **San Nicolás Terrenate** (sän nēkōläs' tĕränä'tā), town (pop. 947), Tlaxcala, central Mexico, 23 mi. NE of Tlaxcala; maguey center.

Terre-Neuve (tĕr-nûv'), town (1950 census pop. 773), Artibonite dept., NW Haiti, in the small Terre-Neuve range, 13 mi. NNW of Gonaïves. Copper mines in cotton- and fruitgrowing region. Also iron, gold, lead, zinc, silver deposits.

Terrenoire (tĕrnwär'), town (pop. 3,169), Loire dept., SE central France, 2.5 mi. E of Saint-Étienne; steel mills; metalworking (small arms, precision tools, kitchen stoves), mfg. of rayon, biscuits, perfumes.

Terre Noire Creek (tûr" nôr'), SW Ark., rises W of Arkadelphia, flows c.45 mi. SE to Little Missouri R. 2 mi. above its junction with Ouachita R.

Terrer (tĕrĕr'), village (pop. 1,651), Saragossa prov., NE Spain, on Jalón R. and 4 mi. WSW of Calatayud; sugar refinery, flour mills; cereals, wine, truck produce.

Terre Rouge (târ' rōōzh'), village (pop. 2,173), N Mauritius, 3 mi. NE of Port Louis; rail junction; sugar cane.

Terrier-Rouge (tĕryā-rōōzh'), town (1950 census pop. 2,032), Nord dept., N Haiti, on Plaine du Nord, 17 mi. ESE of Cap-Haïtien; sisal, fruit.

Terril, town (pop. 425), Dickinson co., NW Iowa, 14 mi. NE of Spencer, in stock and grain area.

Terrill, Mount (11,530 ft.), in Fish Lake Plateau, S central Utah, 24 mi. E of Richfield.

Terrinches (tĕrēn'chĕs), town (pop. 1,700), Ciudad Real prov., S central Spain, near Albacete prov. border, 31 mi. ESE of Valdepeñas; cereals, olives, potatoes, grapes, livestock.

Territet, Swtizerland: see MONTREUX.

Territoires du Sud, Algeria and Tunisia: see SOUTHERN TERRITORIES.

Ter River (tĕr), in Gerona and Barcelona provs., NE Spain, in Catalonia, rises on S slopes of the E Pyrenees above Camprodón, flows S, past Ripoll and Manlleu, then E, through Gerona plain, to the Mediterranean (Gulf of Rosas) 19 mi. ENE of Gerona; 105 mi. long. Receives the Fresser (right). Hydroelectric plants (at Ripoll, Manlleu, El Pastoral) supply Catalonian industry.

Terror, Mount (10,750 ft.), Antarctica, extinct volcano on Ross Isl., in Ross Sea off Victoria Land, 20 naut. mi. E of Mt. Erebus; 77°30'S 168°40'E. Discovered 1841 by Sir James Ross.

Terry, county (□ 898; pop. 13,107), NW Texas; ⊙ Brownfield. On Llano Estacado, here crossed by intermittent Sulphur Springs Creek and Sulphur Draw; alt. 3,200–3,600 ft. Agr., especially grain sorghums; also corn, peanuts, cotton, peas, alfalfa, fruit, truck; dairying, poultry, livestock (cattle, hogs). Oil, natural-gas wells; sodium sulphate, driller's clay production. Formed 1876.

Terry. 1 Town (pop. 497), Hinds co., W Miss., 15 mi. SSW of Jackson, near Pearl R.; truck farming. **2** Town (pop. 1,191), ⊙ Prairie co., E Mont., on Yellowstone R. and 40 mi. NE of Miles City; shipping point for grain and livestock. Founded 1883, inc. 1912.

Terry Peak (7,070 ft.), W S.Dak., near Lead, in Black Hills.

Terrytown, town (pop. 228), Scotts Bluff co., W Nebr.

Terryville, Conn.: see PLYMOUTH.

Ters-Ashchibulak, reservoir, USSR: see ASSA RIVER, Kazakh SSR.

Terschelling (tĕrskhĕ'lĭng), island (□ 37; pop. 3,544), one of West Frisian Isls., Friesland prov., NW Netherlands, bet. North Sea and the Waddenzee; separated by the Boomkensdiep from Vlieland isl. (SW), by the Borndiep from Ameland isl. (E); 17 mi. long, 3 mi. wide. N protected by dunes, S by heavy dike. Agr., fishing, cattle raising. Brandaris lighthouse, on W shore, a landmark. Chief village, Westterschelling. Ferry to Harlingen.

Tersishan, Lake (tĕrsĭs-hän') (□ 16), central Turkey, 55 mi. NNE of Konya; 8 mi. long, 2 mi. wide.

Terskei Ala-Tau or **Terskey Ala-Tau** (tyĭrskyä' ŭlä"-tou'), range of Tien Shan mountain system in Kirghiz SSR; extends from the peak Khan-Tengri 225 mi. W to Chu R.; rises to 16,440 ft. The lake Issyk-Kul lies N.

Tertenia (tĕrtä'nyä), village (pop. 2,379), Nuoro prov., SE Sardinia, 40 mi. NNE of Cagliari; barite deposits.

Terter, city, Azerbaijan SSR: see MIR-BASHIR.

Terter River (tyĭrtyĕr'), W Azerbaijan SSR, rises in Karabakh Upland near Armenian border, flows c.90 mi. generally ENE, past Istisu, Kelbadzhar, Mir-Bashir, and Barda, to Kura R. 14 mi. SE of Yevlakh. Used for irrigation. Hydroelectric station at Madagiz.

Tertre (târt'rü), town (pop. 4,488), Hainaut prov., SW Belgium, 6 mi. W of Mons; coal-mining center; coke plants; mfg. (coal-tar chemicals, ceramics). Gas pipeline leads to Antwerp.

Tertry (tĕrtrē'), village (pop. 169), Somme dept., N France, 8 mi. SE of Péronne. Here, in 687, Pepin of Héristal defeated king of Neustria. Formerly spelled Testry.

Teruel (tĕrwĕl'), province (□ 5,713; pop. 232,064), E Spain, in Aragon; ⊙ Teruel. Generally mountainous with small plain in N, and Iberian Mts. in SW. Mostly barren, with some fertile valleys and irrigated areas; drained by Jiloca, Guadalope, and Turia rivers. Rich iron and coal mines (Sierra Menera in Iberian Mts.), some sulphur, zinc, and manganese deposits; clay and gypsum quarries. Agr. products: sugar beets and wine (N), olive oil, cereals, hemp, saffron, fruit, livestock (especially sheep). Has poor communications, practically no industries. Chief towns: Teruel, Alcañiz, Híjar.

Teruel, city (pop. 14,377), ⊙ Teruel prov., E Spain, in Aragon, on left bank of Turia R. and 75 mi. NW of Valencia, in barren plateau region; 40°21'N 1°7'W. Agr. trade center (hemp, sugar beets, olive oil, cereals), with some industries (producing calcium carbide, resins, soap, rubber shoes, tiles, chocolate, flour products, plaster). Episcopal see. Remains of old walls and narrow streets give it a medieval aspect. Its 16th-cent. cathedral, Gothic church of St. Peter, several Mudejar towers, and imposing 2-storied aqueduct (16th cent.) with 90 arches—all were severely damaged in bitter Sp. civil war fighting, during which city changed hands 3 times (1937–38).

Tervakoski (tĕr'väkōs"kē), village in Janakkala commune (pop. 11,357), Häme co., S Finland, in lake region, 14 mi. SSE of Hämeenlinna; paper.

Tervel (tĕrvĕl'). **1** Village (pop. 1,781), Stalin dist., NE Bulgaria, in S Dobruja, 25 mi. NE of Tolbukhin; grain, sheep. In Rumania (1913–40) called Curt-Bunar. **2** Village (pop. 3,427), Yambol dist., SE Bulgaria, 9 mi. S of Yambol; grain, tobacco. Formerly Pandaklii.

Terzhola (tûr-zhô'lä), village (1939 pop. over 2,000), W Georgian SSR, 7 mi. NW of Zestafoni.

Terzigno (tĕrtsē'nyô), town (pop. 4,320) Napoli prov., Campania, S Italy, at E foot of Vesuvius, 5 mi. NNE of Torre Annunziata; cotton and hemp mills, sausage factory.

Tes, river, Mongolia and USSR: see TES RIVER.

Tesanj, Teshan, or **Teshan'** (all: tĕ'shänyü), Serbo-Croatian *Tešanj*, village (pop. 2,894), N central Bosnia, Yugoslavia, 9 mi. SSW of Doboj; center of plum-growing region.

Teschen (tĕ'shün), Czech *Těšín* (tyĕ'shēn), Pol. *Cieszyn* (chĕ'shĭn), territory (□ c.850) and city, a former principality now partly in S Poland and partly in E Silesia, Czechoslovakia. Noted for its coal mines (Karvina), iron-ore deposits, and concentration of modern rail lines. Long an object of dispute, it became a principality within duchy of Silesia, and passed (1526), with Bohemia, to the Hapsburgs; remained in Austrian Silesia until 1919. Divided by Conference of Ambassadors (Paris; 1920) along Olse R., with W section, including Karvina coal basin, town of Bohumin, and W suburb (CESKY TESIN) of CIESZYN, awarded to Czechoslovakia; E section, with most of city of Cieszyn and adjoining area, was given to Poland. After Munich Pact (1938) Poland seized Czech portion; whole territory was subsequently inc. (1939) into Germany. In 1945, it returned to its pre-Munich status. Production of iron in Teschen region dates from Roman times.

Teschen, town, Poland: see CIESZYN.

Tescott, city (pop. 412), Ottawa co., central Kansas, on Saline R. and 17 mi. NW of Salina; livestock, grain.

Tesechoacán, Mexico: see VILLA AZUETA.

Tesha (tyĕ'shŭ), town (1946 pop. over 500), SW Gorki oblast, Russian SFSR, 15 mi. NE of Kulebaki; sawmilling.

Teshan, Yugoslavia: see TESANJ.

Teshi (tĕ'shē), town, S Gold Coast colony, on Gulf of Guinea, 10 mi. ENE of Accra; fishing.

Teshikaga, Japan: see DESHIKAGA.

Teshio (tāshē'ō), town (pop. 8,804), N Hokkaido, Japan, on Sea of Japan, at mouth of Teshio R., 37 mi. S of Wakkanai; agr. (rice, potatoes, soybeans), lumbering.

Teshio River, Jap. *Teshio-gawa*, second longest river of Hokkaido, Japan; rises in mts. 30 mi. NE of Asahigawa, flows NNW, past Nayoro and Piuka, and SSW to Sea of Japan at Teshio; 188 mi. long. Drains mountainous, forested area.

Tesin, Czechoslovakia and Poland: see TESCHEN; CIESZYN.

Tesina River, Italy: see ASTICO RIVER.

Tesistán (tāsēstän'), town (pop. 1,367), Jalisco, central Mexico, 12 mi. NW of Guadalajara; grain, peanuts, sugar cane, fruit, livestock.

Teslic or **Teslich** (both: tĕ'slĭch), Serbo-Croatian *Teslić*, village (pop. 3,236), N Bosnia, Yugoslavia, on Usora R., on railroad and 15 mi. SW of Doboj; brown-coal mine; ironworks; lumber milling, wood cracking. Vrucica or Vruchitsa, Serbo-Croatian *Vrućica*, health resort, is 2 mi. S.

Teslin (tĕz'lĭn, tĕs'–), Indian village, S Yukon, near B.C. border, on Teslin L., 90 mi. ESE of Whitehorse and on Alaska Highway; 60°10'N 132°44'W; fur-trading post; airfield, radio and weather station, Royal Canadian Mounted Police post.

Teslin Lake (□ c.200), NW B.C. and S Yukon, 65 mi. ESE of Whitehorse; c.80 mi. long, 1–3 mi. wide. On E shore is Teslin village. Drains N into Lewes R. by Teslin R. (120 mi. long); receives Nisutlin R.

Tesovo-Netylski or **Tesovo-Netyl'skiy** (tyĕ'sŭvŭ-nyĭtĭl'skē), town (1939 pop. over 500), NW Novgorod oblast, Russian SFSR, on railroad (Rogavka station) and 30 mi. NNW of Novgorod; sawmilling.

Tes River (tĕs), Mongolian *Tesin Gol* (tĕ'sēn gōl'), Tuvinian *Tes Khem* (khĕm), NW Mongolian People's Republic, rises in the N Khangai Mts. 65 mi. SW of Muren, flows 353 mi. W, through USSR's Tuva Autonomous Oblast, passing near Samagaltai, then forming part of USSR-Mongolia line, and into lake Ubsa Nor.

Tessala Mountains (tĕsälä'), range of the Tell Atlas in Oran dept., NW Algeria, extending c.40 mi. SW-NE bet. the Oran Sebkha (N) and the plain of Sidi-bel-Abbès (S). Highest peak, Djebel Tessala (3,480 ft.).

Tessaoua (tĕsä'wä), town (pop. c.4,000), S Niger territory, Fr. West Africa, near Nigeria border, 65 mi. W of Zinder; peanuts, millet, livestock. Tannery; airstrip.

Tessel, Netherlands: see TEXEL.

Tessé-la-Madeleine, France: see BAGNOLES-DE-L'ORNE.

Tessenderlo (tĕsĕn'dûrlō"), town (pop. 8,116), Limburg prov., NE Belgium, 6 mi. NNE of Diest; pyrites processing, mfg. of sulphuric acid, superphosphates. Formerly spelled Tessenderloo.

Tessenei (tĕsĕnā'), town (pop. 1,850), Agordat div., W Eritrea, near Anglo-Egyptian Sudan border, on Gash R. and 85 mi. WSW of Agordat; road junction; alt. c.1,920 ft. Industrial and agr. center; cotton ginning, cottonseed-oil extraction, soap mfg., andropogon distilling (for perfume). Collecting station for gum arabic. Gash R., dammed here, irrigates fertile plain growing cotton, durum wheat, dom palms, tobacco, and coffee. Water shared with neighboring Sudan according to Agreement of Khartoum (1925). Following Br. occupation (1941) in Second World War, a spur of the Sudan railroad was built from Kassala (30 mi. NW) to Tessenei.

Tessin (tĕsēn'), town (pop. 4,530), Mecklenburg, N Germany, on the Recknitz and 14 mi. ESE of Rostock; agr. market (grain, sugar beets, potatoes, stock).

Tessin, Switzerland: see TICINO.

Tessville, Ill.: see LINCOLNWOOD.

Tessy-sur-Vire (tĕsē'-sür-vēr'), village (pop. 623), Manche dept., NW France, on the Vire and 10 mi. S of Saint-Lô; horse raising, sawmilling. Captured (July, 1944) by Americans in Saint-Lô offensive of Second World War.

Teste, La, or **La Teste-de-Buch** (lä tĕst'-dü-büsh'), town (pop. 5,965), Gironde dept., SW France, on S shore of Arcachon Basin, 31 mi. WSW of Bordeaux; fishing and fish canning, turpentine mfg. Ostreiculture.

Testigos, Los (lōs tĕstē'gōs), small Caribbean island group and a federal dependency of Venezuela, 50 mi. NE of Margarita Isl.; 11°23'N 63°7'W.

Testour (tĕstōōr'), village, Tunis dist., N Tunisia, on the Medjerda near influx of Siliana R. and 12 mi. ENE of Teboursouk; olive groves. Handicraft mfg. by Moors who settled here in 17th cent. Houses have slanted, hollow-tiled roofs. Near by are ruins of Aïn-Tounga (anc. *Thignica*).

Test River, Hampshire, England, rises 7 mi. W of Basingstoke, flows 30 mi. W and S to Southampton Water at Southampton. Receives Anton R. 4 mi. S of Andover.

Tesu, district, Uganda: see SOROTI.

Tesuque (tüsōō'kē), pueblo (□ 26.5), Santa Fe co., N central N.Mex. Tesuque village (1948 pop. 162) is in Sangre de Cristo Mts., 7 mi. N of Santa Fe; alt. c.6,400 ft. Crafts are pottery making and painting. Feast day occurs Nov. 12. Village discovered 1540 by Coronado expedition, settled at present site c.1700.

Tet (tāt), Hung. *Tét*, town (pop. 4,358), Györ-Moson co., NW Hungary, 12 mi. SSW of Györ; wheat, corn, peaches; cattle, horses. Poet Karoly Kisfaludy b. here.

Tetachuck Lake (tĕ'tüchŭk") (18 mi. long, 1–2 mi. wide), W central B.C., in Coast Mts., in Tweedsmuir Park, 120 mi. WSW of Prince George, E of Eutsuk L. Drains E into Nechako R.

Tétange (tātäzh'), town (pop. 2,408), S Luxembourg, 3 mi. ESE of Esch-sur-Alzette; iron mining; mfg. of railroad and mining equipment, shoes.

Tetbury, former urban district (1931 pop. 2,237), S Gloucester, England, 16 mi. S of Gloucester; agr. market.

Tete (tĕ'tā), town (1940 pop. 2,733), ⊙ Tete dist. (□ 38,768; pop. 419,147), Manica and Sofala prov., NW Mozambique, on the Zambezi (head of lower-course navigation) and 250 mi. NNW of Beira; 16°8'S 33°35'E. Center of colony's chief mining region. Coal mined at near-by Moatize is shipped downstream from Benga (just SE). Gold is washed in streams near Nyasaland and Northern Rhodesia border (N and NW). Uranium and asbestos deposits discovered in dist. 1947. Branch railroad from Mutarara (130 mi. SE) to reach Tete in early 1950s. Town also ships cattle, skins, cotton. Founded 1531 by Portuguese, it has a mid-16th-cent. church.

Tetecala (tātākä'lä), city (pop. 1,892), Morelos, central Mexico, 17 mi. SW of Cuernavaca; alt. 3,294 ft.; coconut growing. Anc. Indian town. Xochicalco (sōchēkäl'kō) pyramid and ruins of old fortified city are near by.

Tetela (tātā'lä), officially Tetela de Ocampo, town (pop. 707), Puebla, central Mexico, 13 mi. SE of Zacatlán; corn, sugar cane, fruit. Gold and silver mining since pre-Columbian days.

Tetela del Volcán (dĕl vōlkän'), town (pop. 1,770), Morelos, central Mexico, at SW foot of Popocatepetl, on railroad and 20 mi. W of Atlixco; corn, sugar cane, fruit, livestock.

Tetelcingo (tātĕlsĕng'gō), town (pop. 1,313), Morelos, central Mexico, 5 mi. NE of Cuautla; sugar, fruit, stock.

Teteles (tātā'lĕs), town (pop. 652), Puebla, central Mexico, 6 mi. WNW of Teziutlán; coffee, fruit, sugar cane.

Tetepango (tātāpäng'gō), town (pop. 1,861), Hidalgo, central Mexico, on railroad and 28 mi. W of Pachuca; alt. 7,086 ft.; cereals, fruit, vegetables, stock.

Teterboro (tē'tûr-), borough (pop. 28), Bergen co., NE N.J., 5 mi. E of Passaic; makes aircraft parts and equipment; large freight airport here is administered by Port of New York Authority. Named Bendix 1937, renamed Teterboro 1943.

Teterev River (tyĕ'tyĭryĭf), NW Ukrainian SSR, rises WSW of Berdichev in Volyn-Podolian Upland, flows 210 mi. generally NE, past Zhitomir, Radomyshl, and Ivankov (head of navigation), to Dnieper R. 35 mi. N of Kiev.

Teterow (tā'tŭrō), town (pop. 9,612), Mecklenburg, N Germany, on small Teterow L. (drained by a headstream of Peene R.), 16 mi. E of Güstrow; machinery mfg., sugar refining, fruit processing and canning; agr. market (grain, sugar beets, fruit, potatoes, stock). Has 13th-cent. church and 2 old town gates.

Teteven (tĕ'tĕvĕn), city (pop. 4,701), Pleven dist., N Bulgaria, health resort on Beli Vit R. (headstream of the Vit) and 40 mi. SSW of Pleven; agr. and woodworking center; furniture mfg., veneering, tanning; fruitgrowing and preserving. Has woodworking school.

Teteven Mountains, N central Bulgaria, part of central Balkan Mts., S of Teteven; rise to 7,112 ft. in Vezhen peak. Crossed by Zlatitsa Pass. Vit R. rises in N slopes (covered by beech forests). Sometimes called Zlatitsa Mts.

Tetiaroa (tātēärō'ä), uninhabited atoll (1,600 acres) Windward group, Society Isls., Fr. Oceania, S Pacific, 25 mi. N of Tahiti; consists of 13 islets covered with coconut groves.

Tetipac (tātēpäk'), town (pop. 581), Guerrero, SW Mexico, on S slope of central plateau, 7 mi. NNW of Taxco; alt. 5,462 ft.; cereals, sugar cane, fruit.

Tetir (tātēr'), inland village (pop. 564), Fuerteventura, Canary Isls., 5 mi. WNW of Puerto de Cabras; cereals, vegetables, fruit.

Tetiyev (tyĭtyē'ŭf), town (1939 pop. over 2,000), SW Kiev oblast, Ukrainian SSR, 35 mi. SW of Belaya Tserkov; metalworks. Pop. largely Jewish until Second World War.

Tetiz (tātēs'), town (pop. 1,373), Yucatan, SE Mexico, 20 mi. W of Mérida; rail terminus; henequen growing.

Tetla or **Santiago Tetla** (säntyä'gō tāt'lä), town (pop. 2,505), Tlaxcala, central Mexico, 3 mi. NE of Apizaco; corn, wheat, barley, alfalfa, beans, maguey, stock.

Tetlanohca (tātlänō'kä), officially San Francisco Tetlanohca, town (pop. 2,071), Tlaxcala, central Mexico, at W foot of Malinche volcano, 15 mi. NNE of Puebla; grain, alfalfa, livestock.

Tetlatlahuca (tātlätläōō'kä), officially Santa Isabel Tetlatlahuca, town (pop. 1,381), Tlaxcala, central Mexico, 15 mi. NNW of Puebla; cereals, stock.

Tetlin (tĕt'lĭn), village (pop. 73), E Alaska, near upper Tanana R., 30 mi. SE of Tanacross; 63°9'N 142°31'W; center of native trapping reserve. School.

Tetnuld or **Tetnul'd** (tyĭtnōōlt'), peak (15,922 ft.) in main range of the central Greater Caucasus, on Russian SFSR–Georgian SSR border, 12 mi. E of Mestia.

Teton (tē'tŏn). **1** County (□ 459; pop. 3,204), E Idaho; ⊙ Driggs. Plateau area bordering on Wyo. and including irrigated valley of Teton R. Dairying, agr. (potatoes, dry beans, sugar beets). Part of Targhee Natl. Forest in SW. Formed 1915. **2** County (□ 2,294; pop. 7,232), N central Mont.; ⊙ Choteau. Irrigated agr. region drained by Teton R.; crossed in W by Lewis and Clark Natl. Forest. Grain, livestock. Pishkun Bird Reservation and Reservoir in SW. Formed 1893. **3** County (□ 2,815; pop. 2,593), NW Wyo.; ⊙ Jackson. Grain, livestock area, bordering on Idaho and Yellowstone Natl. Park; watered by Snake R. and Jackson L. Coal. Includes Jackson Hole, Grand Teton Natl. Park, and parts of Teton Natl. Forest and Teton Range. Formed 1921.

Teton, village (pop. 463), Fremont co., E Idaho, 5 mi. S of St. Anthony and on Teton R.; alt. 5,004 ft.; peas, beans, potatoes.

Tetonia (tētō'nēŭ), town (pop. 232), Teton co., E Idaho, 6 mi. N of Driggs.

Teton Pass, Wyo.: see TETON RANGE.

Teton Range (tē'tŏn), branch of Rocky Mts., mainly in NW Wyo., with some outliers in SE Idaho, just S of Yellowstone Natl. Park and W of Jackson L. and Snake R. Grand Teton (13,766 ft.) is highest point in range, much of which lies within GRAND TETON NATIONAL PARK. Elkhorn Peak (10,040 ft.) is in Idaho. Teton Pass (8,429 ft.) and Phillips Pass (10,700 ft.) are just S of park, in Wyo. Range includes part of Targhee Natl. Forest. Was frequented in 1st half of 19th cent. by fur traders.

Teton River. **1** In NW Mont., rises in several branches in Continental Divide, flows 143 mi. E, past Choteau, to Marias R. just above its influx into Missouri R. NE of Fort Benton. Bynum Reservoir, on branch of main stream, is unit in irrigation system. **2** In NW Wyo. and E Idaho, rises in 2 forks near Teton Pass in S Teton Range, joining near Victor, Idaho; flows N and W to Henrys Fork W of Rexburg; c.60 mi. long, including longer fork.

Tetovo (tĕ'tôvô), village (pop. 4,546), Ruse dist., NE Bulgaria, 16 mi. E of Ruse; wheat, rye, sunflowers.

Tetovo, Turkish *Kalkandelen*, town (pop. 16,919), NW Macedonia, Yugoslavia, on narrow-gauge railroad and 25 mi. W of Skoplje; trade center of the lower Polog; handicraft (pottery). Abandoned silver and lead mine. Apples, beans, chestnuts grown in vicinity. Starting point for mtn. climbing and skiing on near-by Sar Mts. Has painted mosque and picturesque former Turkish houses.

Tetragona, Mount (tĕ"trŭgō'nŭ) (4,511 ft.), NE Labrador, near head of Seven Islands Bay; 59°18'N 63°55'W.

Tetri-Tskaro (tyĭtrē'-tskŭrô'), village (1932 pop. estimate 810), S Georgian SSR, 20 mi. SW of Tiflis; grain, livestock. Manganese deposits near by. Until c.1945, Agbulakh.

Têt River (tĕt), Pyrénées-Orientales dept., S France, rises near Pic de Carlitte in the Pyrenees, flows 75 mi. ENE, through the CONFLENT valley, past Mont-Louis, Prades, and Perpignan, to the Gulf of Lion 9 mi. below Perpignan. Flash floods cause great damage.

Tetschen, Czechoslovakia: see DECIN.

Tetsugen, Korea: see CHORWON.

Tetsunishi, Manchuria, see MUKDEN.

Tetsuzan, Korea: see CHOLSAN.

Tettau (tĕ'tou), village (pop. 1,811), Upper Franconia, N Bavaria, Germany, 13 mi. SW of Saalfeld; rail terminus; glass.

Tettenborn (tĕ'tŭnbôrn), village (pop. 1,213), in former Prussian Saxony prov., W Germany, after 1945 in Lower Saxony, 11 mi. NE of Nordhausen; woodworking.

Tettenhall, residential urban district (1931 pop. 5,769; 1951 census 7,742), SW Stafford, England, 2 mi. NW of Wolverhampton. Has 14th-cent. church built on site of 10th-cent. church.

Tettnang (tĕt'näng), town (pop. 5,025), S Württemberg, Germany, after 1945 in Württemberg-Hohenzollern, 5.5 mi. ENE of Friedrichshafen; hops trade.

Te-tu, Manchuria: see TEHTU.

Tetuán (tātwän'), city (pop. 93,658), ⊙ Spanish Morocco, on the small Río Martín at S foot of Mt. Dersa, 29 mi. SE of Tangier, amidst subtropical gardens and olive groves; 35°34'N 5°22'W. Residence of Sp. high commissioner and of Khalifa (the highest native official appointed by sultan of Morocco, who resides at Rabat, Fr. Morocco). Linked by narrow-gauge railroad with Río Martín (6 mi. NE), its port on the Mediterranean, and with Ceuta (23 mi. N). Airfield. Here are concentrated most of the Sp. protectorate's industries: cabinetmaking, printing, fish canning, mfg. of tobacco products, matches, soap, building materials, textiles, flour products. There is a well-developed handicraft industry and active trade in livestock, grain, truck produce, and, especially, citrus fruit. Overlooked by its *casbah* (1st built 1286), Tetuán is a city of fountains and of mosques, with terraced white houses amidst luxuriant vegetation. City has a noted school for native arts, an archaeological mus., and a radio transmitter. Dating from beginning of 14th cent., Tetuán was an early corsair stronghold. Rebuilt 1492 by Jewish refugees from Portugal, it became an important commercial center. Captured 1860 by Spaniards under O'Donnell. Permanently occupied by them in 1915. Tetuán is also capital of Yebala territory (□ 1,173; 1945 pop. 234,409), an administrative subdivision of the protectorate. In 1945, c.⅕ of pop. of Tetuán was Spanish; there were 7,628 Jews.

Tetuán de las Victorias, Spain: see CHAMARTÍN.

Tetulia River, E Pakistan: see DAKHIN SHAHBAZPUR ISLAND.

Tetyukhe (tyĭtyōō'khyĕ'), town (1947 pop. over 10,000), E Maritime Territory, Russian SFSR, on small Tetyukhe R., 20 mi. inland from Sea of Japan coast and 220 mi. NE of Vladivostok; mining of complex ores (lead, zinc, tin, cadmium). Linked by railroad with its port **Tetyukhe-Pristan** or **Tetyukhe-Pristan'** (1947 pop. over 2,000), 22 mi. SE; site of refinery.

Tetyushi (tyĭtyōō'shē), city (1938 pop. 8,500); SW Tatar Autonomous SSR, Russian SFSR, on right bank of Volga R. (landing) and 45 mi. NNE of Ulyanovsk; grain-trading center; flour milling, metalworking; fruitgrowing, fisheries. Founded in 1578.

Teublitz (toi'blĭts), village (pop. 2,535), Upper Palatinate, E central Bavaria, Germany, near the Nab, 14 mi. N of Regensburg; rye, wheat, potatoes, cattle.

Teuchern (toi'khûrn), town (pop. 6,985), in former Prussian Saxony prov., central Germany, after 1945 in Saxony-Anhalt, 7 mi. SE of Weissenfels; lignite mining.

Teuchira, Cyrenaica: see TOCRA.

Teuchitlán (tĕōōchētlän'), town (pop. 1,727), Jalisco, W Mexico, 32 mi. W of Guadalajara; corn, wheat, sugar cane, fruit, vegetables.

Teuco River, Argentina: see BERMEJO RIVER.

Teufelsbrücke, Switzerland: see DEVIL'S BRIDGE.

Teufen (toi'fŭn), town (pop. 4,062), Appenzell Ausser Rhoden half-canton, NE Switzerland, 3 mi. S of St. Gall; embroideries, cotton textiles, clothes; woodworking.

Teufenbach (toif'ŭnbäkh), village (pop. 627), Styria, central Austria, near Mur R., 14 mi. W of Judenburg; summer resort (alt. 2,490 ft.).

Teukchan, Formosa: see SINCHU.

Teulada (tĕōōlä'dä), village (pop. 3,665), Cagliari prov., SW Sardinia, 25 mi. SW of Cagliari, in fruit- (oranges, lemons) and herb-growing area; iron deposits; domestic ceramics, embroidery.

Teulada (tĕōōlä'dhä), town (pop. 1,740), Alicante prov., E Spain, 20 mi. SE of Gandía; olive-oil processing; ships raisins and almonds.

Teulada, Cape (tĕōōlä'dä), southernmost point of Sardinia; 38°51'N 8°39'E. Tunny fisheries; white marble.

Téul de González Ortega (tā'ōōl dā gōnsä'lĕs ôrtä'gä) or **San Juan Bautista del Téul** (sän whän' boutē'stä dĕl), town (pop. 2,425), Zacatecas, N central Mexico, on interior plateau, 23 mi. SSW of Tlaltenango; agr. center (grain, sugar cane, fruit, livestock).

Teulon (tū'lŏn), village (pop. 580), SE Man., 35 mi. N of Winnipeg; dairying; grain.

Teupitz (toi'pĭts), town (pop. 1,550), Brandenburg, E Germany, on small Teupitz L., 11 mi. S of Königs Wusterhausen; potatoes, livestock. Has insane asylum.

Teustepe (tĕōōstā'pä), town (1950 pop. 517), Boaco dept., central Nicaragua, on upper Malacatoya R. and 12 mi. WSW of Boaco; livestock, dairying; some agr.

Teutendorf (toi'tŭndôrf), village (pop. 284), Mecklenburg, N Germany, 12 mi. E of Rostock. Friedrich von Flotow b. here.

Teutoburg Forest (toi'tōbōōrk"), Ger. *Teutoburger Wald* (toi'tōbōōr"gŭr vält'), narrow range of the Weser Mts., NW Germany, extends c.60 mi. NW-SE bet. Bevergern and Bad Lippspringe; rises to 1,465 ft. (S of Detmold). Forested slopes; woodworking. On a hill near Detmold is the Hermannsdenkmal, a monument commemorating the battle of the Teutoburg Forest (A.D. 9), in which German tribes, led by Arminius (or Hermann), decisively defeated the Romans under Varus.

Teutopolis (tūtō'pŭlĭs, tōō-), village (pop. 919), Effingham co., SE central Ill., 3 mi. E of Effingham, in agr. area. Seat of St. Joseph's Seminary.

Teutschenthal, Germany: see UNTERTEUTSCHENTHAL.

Tevaram or **Thevaram** (tāvä'rŭm), town (pop. 8,803), Madura dist., S Madras, India, 9 mi. SW of Bodinayakkanur, in Kambam Valley; cardamom, bamboo in Cardamom Hills (W); grain, coconut palms, mangoes.

Tevarya, Israel: see TIBERIAS.

Tevel (tĕ'vĕl), town (pop. 2,516), Tolna co., SW central Hungary, 13 mi. WNW of Szekszard; potatoes, cattle.

Tevere, Italy: see TIBER RIVER.

Teverone River, Italy: see ANIENE RIVER.

Teversal (tûr'sŭl), village and parish (pop. 946), W Nottingham, England, 4 mi. W of Mansfield; coal mining. Has church of Norman origin.

Teviotdale, Scotland: see TEVIOT RIVER.

Teviothead (tĕv'yŭt-hĕd, tĕv'-), agr. village and parish (pop. 353), W Roxburgh, Scotland, on Teviot R. near its source, and 9 mi. SW of Hawick.

Teviot River (tĕv'yŭt, tĕv'-), Roxburgh, Scotland, rises SW of Teviothead, on Dumfries border, flows 37 mi. NE, past Teviothead and Hawick, to the Tweed at Kelso. Its valley, of noted scenic beauty, is called Teviotdale.

Tevriz (tyĭvrēs'), village (1948 pop. over 10,000), NW Omsk oblast, Russian SFSR, on Irtysh R.

(landing) and 85 mi. NW of Tara, in agr. area (flax); lumbering.

Te Waewae Bay (tē″ wī′wī), inlet of Tasman Sea, S S.Isl., New Zealand; 18 mi. E-W, 10 mi. N-S; merges with Foveaux Strait (SE). Receives Waiau R. Orepuki is on E shore.

Tewfiq, Port, Egypt: see PORT TAUFIQ.

Tewkesbury (tūks′bûrē), municipal borough (1931 pop. 4,352; 1951 census 5,292), N Gloucester, England, on the Severn (crossed by a Telford bridge) at mouth of the Avon, 10 mi. NNE of Gloucester; agr. market, with agr.-machinery works and flour mills. Notable church built 1123; there are many old timbered houses. Dramatic festivals are held here, in continuation of the Tewkesbury Festival Plays begun in 17th cent. Just S is "Bloody Meadow," site of final defeat (1471) of Lancastrians in War of the Roses. Monastery founded here c.715, was refounded in 12th cent., and became one of richest Benedictine monasteries in England.

Tewkesbury (tūks′bûrē), village (pop. 119), N Tasmania, 75 mi. WNW of Launceston; flax, potatoes. Agr. experiment station.

Tewksbury, residential town (pop. 7,505), Middlesex co., NE Mass., 5 mi. ESE of Lowell. Settled 1637, inc. 1734. Includes part of Silver Lake village.

Texada Island (tĕksā′dŭ) (□ 118), in Strait of Georgia, SW B.C., 50 mi. NW of Vancouver; separated from mainland by Malaspina Strait; 31 mi. long, 4 mi. wide; rises to 2,892 ft. Limestone quarrying; copper and gold mining. Vanada and Blubber Bay are main settlements.

Texarkana (tĕk″särkă′nŭ), dual city (pop. 40,628), Bowie co., NE Texas, and ⊙ Miller co., NW Ark., astride state line near Red R., c.60 mi. NNW of Shreveport, La. Pop. in Texas, 24,753; in Ark., 15,875; has 2 municipal govts. Railroad center, with shops; shipping, processing, mfg. center for livestock, dairying, agr. region (cotton); mfg. (clay products, creosoted wood and other lumber products, caskets, fertilizer, feed, cottonseed oil, food products, refined sulphur and lead, clothing). U.S. ordnance works near. Settled 1873 on site of Indian village. Indian mounds near by.

Texarkana Reservoir, Texas: see SULPHUR RIVER.

Texas, village (pop. 858), SE Queensland, Australia, 145 mi. SW of Brisbane and on Dumaresq R., on New South Wales border; rail terminus in tobacco-growing area.

Texas (tĕk′sŭs), state (land □ 263,644; with inland waters □ 267,339; 1950 pop. 7,711,194; 1940 pop. 6,414,824), S and SW U.S., bordered S by Mexico, W by N.Mex., N by Okla., NE by Ark., E by La. and Gulf of Mexico; 1st in area, 6th in pop.; admitted 1845 as 28th state; ⊙ Austin. Comprising almost $^1/_{11}$ of the nation's total area, the "Lone Star State" extends 770 mi. bet. Texhoma (N) and Brownsville (S) and 760 mi. bet. Orange (E) and El Paso (W). The Rio Grande flows c.1,300 mi. along the entire Mexican boundary, while the Red R. defines most of the Okla. line and the Sabine R. most of the La. line. Texas varies considerably in topography and climate and may be roughly divided into coast plain (E, S), interior lowlands (N center), high plains (Panhandle, W, S center), and basin and range country (far W). Its 625-mi. coast line (tidewater) is characterized by long barrier beaches (e.g., Padre Isl.), behind which are lagoons (e.g., Laguna Madre), bays (e.g., Galveston, Matagorda, Aransas), and some marshland. Extending 150–250 mi. inland to a line running through L. Texoma, Fort Worth, Temple, Austin, San Antonio, and Del Rio is the Gulf coastal plain, developed on sands, clays, and marls, and rising gradually to 650–950 ft. in the W. Drained (E–W) by the Sabine, Trinity, Brazos, Colorado, and Nueces rivers, the coast plain sweeps N from arid sand plains along the Rio Grande to a series of in-facing escarpments (cuestas) and intervening prairie and timber belts. Along the W border (from San Antonio to Red R. valley) is the black prairie belt, a rich agr. land of black limestone soils. E Texas consists of low, sandy hills and rolling plains, extensively timbered. W of Dallas, bet. Waco and the Red R., is a transition zone bet. coast plain and interior lowlands, comprising the Grand Prairie, flanked by the Eastern and Western Cross Timbers. W of Waco is an upland area of limestone formations, strongly eroded, and dominated by several flat-topped hills. Extending S from central Okla. are the interior lowlands, rolling prairie land (c.1,000–2,500 ft.), marked by occasional resistant limestone and sandstone escarpments, and drained by headstreams of Red and Brazos rivers; the section is bounded S by the Callahan Divide, a chain of mesas and buttes standing 400–600 ft. above the plain. In the Panhandle and W is the High Plains section of the Great Plains, known, S of the Canadian R., as the LLANO ESTACADO or Staked Plain, a semiarid, treeless, almost level expanse (alt. 2,500–4,000 ft., S–N), bordered on the E by the irregular Cap Rock escarpment, which forms the "break of the plains." A SE extension of the High Plains is the EDWARDS PLATEAU (alt. 1,000–3,000 ft.), another resistant limestone formation, its margins well dissected, especially S and E, where the Balcones Escarpment overlooks the coast plain. In central Texas, largely in Llano and Burnet counties, is a rugged area of exposed crystalline rocks, sometimes called the Central Mineral Region. The Edwards Plateau is cut off from its W part—Stockton Plateau—by the deep canyon of the Pecos R., which flows SE from N.Mex. to the Rio Grande above Del Rio. Elsewhere the trans-Pecos country consists of an elevated region, crossed NW–SE by a series of mtn. ranges and basin valleys. The E group of mts., linking the Rockies with Mexico's Sierra Madre Oriental, include the Sacramento Mts., rising to 8,751 ft. in Guadalupe Peak (state's highest point) in the Guadalupe Mts., Davis Mts. (Mt. Livermore, 8,382 ft.), Santiago Mts., and, in the Big Bend country, the Chisos Mts. Bet. this group and the Rio Grande to the W are block ranges (e.g., Franklin, Hueco, Quitman mts.) and broad basins (e.g., Diablo Bolson, Hueco Basin) of interior drainage. Texas' climate is humid subtropical in the E half of the state, dry continental throughout the Panhandle, with desert conditions in the trans-Pecos section. Mean annual precipitation is 30 inches for the entire state, ranging from 56 inches along the lower Sabine to less than 10 inches in the far W. Snowfall on the High Plains and in some mtn. areas averages 20 inches yearly. Mean Jan. temperatures of Houston (E), Amarillo (N), and El Paso (W) are, respectively, 54°F., 33°F., and 45°F.; mean July temp. 83°F., 77°F., and 82°F.; annual rainfall 46 inches, 21 inches, and 8 inches. The growing season varies from 180 days in the N Panhandle to 300 days in the far S. Native vegetation consists of grassland in the coastal, black, and Grand prairie belts and over most of the N central and high plains; pine forest in the E, including the valuable longleaf and loblolly pine; oak-hickory in the inner coast plain and Cross Timbers; desert grasses (chiefly mesquite) in the S coast plain, S High Plains, and the trans-Pecos basins; piñon-juniper woodland on Edwards Plateau and the far W mtn. ranges; and creosote bush along the Pecos and Rio Grande. Some 36,500,000 acres are classified as forest land, of which 10,750,000 acres are commercially exploitable; natl. forest reserves comprise 1,714,000 acres. Although only c.17% of the total area is under cultivation, the state ranks 2d to Calif. in crop value. Farm acreage is 141,000,000, most of which is range and pasture land, only 27,500,000 acres being in crops. Texas is an important producer of cotton (ranks 1st), winter wheat, corn, grain sorghums (ranks 1st), oats, hay, peanuts, rice, barley, truck crops, fruit, and pecans. It leads in number of cattle (8,500,000), sheep (6,700,000), horses (360,000), and goats (3,250,000). Large-scale commercial and mechanized farming dominates, the state having by far the most farms of over 1,000 acres; it also has the most farms of under 30 acres. Migratory labor is considerable. The heaviest concentrations of cotton (principal cash crop) are in the black prairie belt, around Corpus Christi, in the NE, and in places on the High Plains; the yield per acre is below the natl. average. Corn is the chief feed-grain crop in the E, but W of the 25-inch rainfall line grain sorghums predominate. About 75% of the wheat is raised in the N Panhandle; oats are grown in the N central and central parts; hay mainly in N center. Texas' rice crop (2d to La.'s) is confined to the level, easily irrigated lands along the Gulf coast bet. the lower Colorado and Sabine rivers. The W Cross Timbers is the major peanut-producing area. Most of the state's c.2,500,000 acres of irrigated land is devoted to commercial vegetable growing, chiefly potatoes, tomatoes, onions, cabbage, spinach, carrots, beets, beans, and watermelons. Noted truck areas are the lower Rio Grande valley (Brownsville-McAllen), Corpus Christi section, Laredo, Winter Garden (bet. San Antonio and Eagle Pass), and the region just S of San Antonio. The state's fruit crop includes peaches (mostly NE), apples, pears, grapes, berries, and figs, as well as the important citrus production (oranges, grapefruit) of the irrigated lower Rio Grande dist. Pecans (in which Texas usually ranks 1st) are produced along the middle Colorado, Brazos, and Trinity rivers. Tyler, in Smith co. (NE), is famous for its rose-growing industry. Cattle—widely distributed throughout the state—are raised primarily for beef, though in the NE there is emphasis on dairying. Huge ranches are located on the W High Plains, the N central plains, and the Gulf coast prairies (including 1,000,000-acre King Ranch, largest in U.S.). Sheep- and goat-grazing areas center on the Edwards and Stockton plateaus. Texas is the leading wool producer and from its Angora goats comes c.90% of the country's mohair clip. Hogs are kept on farms mostly in the corn-growing E half of the state. Poultry raising is important, Texas usually ranking 1st in number of turkeys and 2d or 3d in chickens. In bay and coastal waters shrimp, oysters, sea trout, red fish, drumfish, red snapper, flounder, and Spanish mackerel are caught in quantity. Texas leads all states in value of mineral production. Almost ⅔ of the value comes from petroleum, extensively developed on the High Plains (E of Amarillo, N and S of Midland), N central plains (W of Wichita Falls, E of Abilene), in the NE (near Tyler), and throughout the Gulf coast plain. Annual production is c.40% of U.S. output, and reserves are estimated as over 50% of U.S. total. The largest refineries are along the Gulf coast at Houston, Baytown, Port Arthur, Beaumont, Texas City, and Corpus Christi. Texas is also the principal producer of natural gas, found in all petroleum areas, with an especially heavy concentration in the N Panhandle around Amarillo; high-pressure pipe lines carry the gas to the West, Midwest, and Northeast. The Amarillo dist. supplies c.90% of the country's helium, while near-by Hutchinson, Moore, and Gray counties produce most of the carbon black. Natural gasoline and liquefied petroleum gases are important products. About ¾ of U.S. native sulphur is found in Wharton, Brazoria, and Fort Bend counties on the Gulf coast, and there are extensive salt deposits throughout the W High Plains (bedded deposits) and coastal plain (salt domes, worked in Van Zandt, Harris, and Anderson counties). Considerable amounts of sand and gravel, clay products, fuller's earth, graphite (Burnet co.), limestone, granite, sandstone, gypsum, and native asphalt are produced. Some bituminous coal (N center) is mined and large lignite deposits underlie the inner coastal plain. E Texas iron ores (mostly limonite) are utilized by a blast furnace near Daingerfield. Mercury (at Terlingua) and silver are obtained in the Big Bend country. Magnesium (state's production ranks 1st) is recovered from sea water at Freeport; magnesite (from Llano co.) is calcined for fertilizer. Industrially, Texas is primarily a processor of raw materials, both mineral and agr. Petroleum refining is by far the leading industry. The availability of cheap natural gas has been largely responsible for zinc smelting in the Panhandle area, copper refining at El Paso, tin smelting at Texas City, and antimony smelting at Laredo, as well as for the important chemical industry along the Gulf coast at Port Neches, Port Arthur, Beaumont, Houston, Texas City, Brazosport (industrial area including Freeport and Velasco), and Corpus Christi. There is an aluminum plant near Port Lavaca. Meat packing, centering in Fort Worth, ranks 2d in product value. Other important items are cottonseed products, flour, bread, canned vegetables and fruit, dairy and poultry products, oilfield machinery, lumber products, paper (at Lufkin and Houston), textiles, clothing (notably at Dallas), cement, and leather goods; also printing and publishing, airplane mfg., and shipbuilding. The major ports (exporting mainly petroleum products, cotton, wheat) are Houston, Port Arthur, Galveston, Texas City, Corpus Christi, and Beaumont, most of which are joined by feeder canals to the Gulf Intracoastal Waterway, which extends from Orange to Brownsville. HOUSTON, linked to Galveston Bay by Houston Ship Channel, is state's largest city, the principal U.S. cotton outlet, and an important oil, commercial, and industrial center. Large inland cities are DALLAS, SAN ANTONIO, FORT WORTH, AUSTIN, EL PASO, Waco, Amarillo, Lubbock, Wichita Falls, San Angelo, and Laredo. Texas ranks 1st in main-line railroad mileage and has several large airports, including U.S. Air Force bases at San Antonio, Fort Worth, and El Paso. Chief recreational areas consist of a few Gulf resorts (fishing), several dude ranches, state parks, and some of the wilder tracts (hunting) W of the Pecos, such as in Big Bend Natl. Park. Leading educational institutions are Univ. of Texas (at Austin), Baylor Univ. (at Waco), Southern Methodist Univ. (at Dallas), Univ. of Houston, Rice Inst., and Texas State Univ. for Negroes (all at Houston), Agr. and Mechanical Col. of Texas (at College Station), Texas Christian Univ. (at Fort Worth), Texas Technological Col. (at Lubbock), and Hardin-Simmons Univ. (at Abilene). In the 16th cent. the region was inhabited mainly by the Caddo (E, center) and Karankawa (coast) Indians. Later the Apaches and Comanches ruled over the W parts. The coastal section was early known to the Spanish through the exploration of de Pineda (1519) and the shipwrecked de Vaca (1528–35), while the gold-seeking Coronado crossed the High Plains in 1541–42. The French, under La Salle, made an unsuccessful attempt at colonization at Matagorda Bay (1685). However, a mission was founded in 1681 or 1682 at Ysleta (extreme W) by refugees from the Pueblo revolt in N.Mex., and in 1690, on the Neches R. near the present Weches (E), the Mission San Francisco de los Tejas (after the Tejas or Texas Indians) was established. Later settlements were Nacogdoches (1716), San Antonio (1718), and Goliad (1749). American interest in E Texas increased after the Louisiana Purchase, when several filibustering expeditions were undertaken; but all American claims to the area were officially renounced by the 1819 treaty with Spain. In 1823, land along the Brazos R. was settled by Americans under Stephen Austin, who had received a grant from the newly-independent Mexican govt. Soon other American colonies were founded. Discontent with Mexican rule, highlighted by such incidents as the Fredonian rebellion, brought strong demands for civil rights. Hostilities broke out in 1835 at Gonzales and the Texas Revolution was on. The fall of the heroically-defended Alamo was redeemed by Sam Houston's decisive victory in the battle of San Jacinto, after which the Mexican dictator, Santa Anna, recognized Texas' independence (1836). A Comanche uprising was quelled in 1840. Most Texans favored annexation to the U.S., but such a step was opposed by anti-slavery forces in the North, and it wasn't until 1845 that the 9-year old republic was admitted to the Union as a state. This act was largely responsible for the Mexican War (1846–48), precipitated by the famous "American blood on American soil" skirmish in the disputed area bet. the Nueces and Rio Grande rivers. By Treaty of Guadalupe Hidalgo, Mexico gave up claims to Texas, whose S and W boundaries were fixed along the Rio Grande (Texan claims to N.Mex. territory were relinquished in 1850). The opening of the plains region was furthered by the erection of federal forts (as protection against Indians), such as those along the stage coach trail from Fort Smith (Ark.) to Fort Bliss near El Paso. Texas sided with the South during the Civil War and suffered the lawlessness and corruption of the Reconstruction era (1865–70). As the railroads pushed back the frontier, settlement increased rapidly. From the open ranges and, later, from great fenced ranches cowboys drove cattle over the Chisholm and Western trails to Kansas railheads and the grasslands farther N. The development of cotton and wheat farming was also notable. The rich strike at Spindletop near Beaumont in 1901 was the 1st of a succession of spectacular oil discoveries throughout Texas, which have dominated the state's economic life in the 20th cent. Industrial output (especially in chemicals) was enormously increased during the Second World War. See also articles on the cities, towns, geographic features, and the 254 counties: ANDERSON, ANDREWS, ANGELINA, ARANSAS, ARCHER, ARMSTRONG, ATASCOSA, AUSTIN, BAILEY, BANDERA, BASTROP, BAYLOR, BEE, BELL, BEXAR, BLANCO, BORDEN, BOSQUE, BOWIE, BRAZORIA, BRAZOS, BREWSTER, BRISCOE, BROOKS, BROWN, BURLESON, BURNET, CALDWELL, CALHOUN, CALLAHAN, CAMERON, CAMP, CARSON, CASS, CASTRO, CHAMBERS, CHEROKEE, CHILDRESS, CLAY, COCHRAN, COKE, COLEMAN, COLLIN, COLLINGSWORTH, COLORADO, COMAL, COMANCHE, CONCHO, COOKE, CORYELL, COTTLE, CRANE, CROCKETT, CROSBY, CULBERSON, DALLAM, DALLAS, DAWSON, DEAF SMITH, DELTA, DENTON, DE WITT, DICKENS, DIMMIT, DONLEY, DUVAL, EASTLAND, ECTOR, EDWARDS, ELLIS, EL PASO, ERATH, FALLS, FANNIN, FAYETTE, FISHER, FLOYD, FOARD, FORT BEND, FRANKLIN, FREESTONE, FRIO, GAINES, GALVESTON, GARZA, GILLESPIE, GLASSCOCK, GOLIAD, GONZALES, GRAY, GRAYSON, GREGG, GRIMES, GUADALUPE, HALE, HALL, HAMILTON, HANSFORD, HARDEMAN, HARDIN, HARRIS, HARRISON, HARTLEY, HASKELL, HAYS, HEMPHILL, HENDERSON, HIDALGO, HILL, HOCKLEY, HOOD, HOPKINS, HOUSTON, HOWARD, HUDSPETH, HUNT, HUTCHINSON, IRION, JACK, JACKSON, JASPER, JEFF DAVIS, JEFFERSON, JIM HOGG, JIM WELLS, JOHNSON, JONES, KARNES, KAUFMAN, KENDALL, KENEDY, KENT, KERR, KIMBLE, KING, KINNEY, KLEBERG, KNOX, LAMAR, LAMB, LAMPASAS, LA SALLE, LAVACA, LEE, LEON, LIBERTY, LIMESTONE, LIPSCOMB, LIVE OAK, LLANO, LOVING, LUBBOCK, LYNN, MCCULLOCH, MCLENNAN, MCMULLEN, MADISON, MARION, MARTIN, MASON, MATAGORDA, MAVERICK, MEDINA, MENARD, MIDLAND, MILAM, MILLS, MITCHELL, MONTAGUE, MONTGOMERY, MOORE, MORRIS, MOTLEY NACOGDOCHES, NAVARRO, NEWTON, NOLAN, NUECES, OCHILTREE, OLDHAM, ORANGE, PALO PINTO, PANOLA, PARKER, PARMER, PECOS, POLK, POTTER, PRESIDIO, RAINS, RANDALL, REAGAN, REAL, RED RIVER, REEVES, REFUGIO, ROBERTS, ROBERTSON, ROCKWALL, RUNNELS, RUSK, SABINE, SAN AUGUSTINE, SAN JACINTO, SAN PATRICIO, SAN SABA, SCHLEICHER, SCURRY, SHACKELFORD, SHELBY, SHERMAN, SMITH, SOMERVELL, STARR, STEPHENS, STERLING, STONEWALL, SUTTON, SWISHER, TARRANT, TAYLOR, TERRELL, TERRY, THROCKMORTON, TITUS, TOM GREEN, TRAVIS, TRINITY, TYLER, UPSHUR, UPTON, UVALDE, VAL VERDE, VAN ZANDT, VICTORIA, WALKER, WALLER, WARD, WASHINGTON, WEBB, WHARTON, WHEELER, WICHITA, WILBARGER, WILLACY, WILLIAMSON, WILSON, WINKLER, WISE, WOOD, YOAKUM, YOUNG, ZAPATA, ZAVALA

Texas. 1 County (□ 1,183; pop. 18,992), S central Mo.; ⊙ Houston. In the Ozarks; dairy and poultry region, corn, wheat, hay; pine, oak timber; barite deposits. Part of Mark Twain Natl. Forest here. Formed 1845. **2** County (□ 2,056; pop. 14,235), extreme NW Okla.; ⊙ Guymon. In high plains of the Panhandle; bounded N by Kansas, S by Texas; intersected by North Canadian R. and small Coldwater and Goff creeks. Agr. (wheat, grain, sorghums; dairy products; livestock, poultry). Some mfg. at Guymon and Optima. Oil and gas wells. Formed 1907.

Texas City, industrial city (pop. 16,620), Galveston co., S Texas, across Galveston Bay 6 mi. NNW of Galveston. Deepwater port, on channel connecting with those to Houston (NW), to Galveston, and to the Gulf of Mexico; ships petroleum products, chemicals, sulphur, cotton, grain, metals. Has huge tin smelter, chemical industry (alcohol, ether, sulphuric acid, ethylene, styrene mfg.), oil refineries. Inc. 1912. Expanded greatly in Second World War; large area rebuilt after explosions and fires (April, 1947) which caused great loss of life and property damage.

Texcalac or **Santa María Texcalac** (sän'tä märē'ä tĕskäläk'), town (pop. 1,926), Tlaxcala, central Mexico, 3 mi. E of Apizaco; cereals, maguey, beans, stock.

Texcaltitlán or **Santiago Texcaltitlán** (säntyä'gō tĕskältētlän'), town (pop. 3,732), Mexico state, central Mexico, 31 mi. SW of Toluca; sugar cane, cereals, coffee, stock.

Texcalyacac (–yäkäk'), officially San Mateo Texcalyacac, town (pop. 1,417), Mexico state, central Mexico, 15 mi. SE of Toluca; cereals, livestock.

Texcatepec (–tāpĕk'). **1** Town (pop. 1,064), Hidalgo, central Mexico, 35 mi. WNW of Pachuca; corn, beans, fruit, stock. Another town named Texcatepec is 40 mi. NE of Pachuca. **2** Town (pop. 305), Veracruz, E Mexico, 65 mi. WSW of Tuxpan; corn, fruit.

Texcoco (tĕskō'kō), officially Texcoco de Mora, city (pop. 5,437), Mexico state, central Mexico, on central plateau, near L. Texcoco, on railroad and 18 mi. ENE of Mexico city; alt. 7,392 ft. Mfg. (woolen textiles and yarn, glassware) and agr. center (maguey, cereals, livestock); caustic soda and potash plant. Anc. capital of an Aztec kingdom, it was then the 2d most important town of Mexico and long a cultural center. Many archaeological remains (pyramids, temples, etc.). Has a 16th-cent. church. Summer palace of King Netzahualcoyotl was situated on Texcotzingo Hill, 5 mi. E. Texcotzingo ruins are 7 mi. E. Also spelled Tezcuco.

Texcoco, Lake, in Federal Dist. and Mexico state, central Mexico, 2½ mi. E of Mexico city. Largest of the lakes in the plateau depression called the Valley of Mexico, it has been receding constantly and is now mostly nitrous desert since its outlet, the Cuautitlán, drains it, via canal and Tequixquiac tunnel, to Pánuco R. system.

Texcotzingo, Mexico: see TEXCOCO.

Texel (tĕ'sŭl), largest and southernmost island (□ 64; pop. 9,401) of West Frisian Isls., North Holland prov., NW Netherlands, bet. North Sea and the Waddenzee; separated by the Marsdiep from Helder on mainland, by the Eierlandschegat from Vlieland isl.; 15 mi. long, 6 mi. wide. Diluvial sands and gravel with boulder clay; dunes on W coast; dikes along E coast. Eierland (or Eijerland) polder (NE), drained c.1835, is large breeding ground for sea birds. Sheep raising, sheep-cheese mfg. Chief villages are Burg or Den Burg (pop. 2,888) and its port of Oudeschild (pop. 775), in SE part of isl. Ferry from Oudeschild to Helder. Sometimes spelled Tessel.

Texhoma (tĕks-hō'mů), town (pop. 1,763), Texas co., NW Okla., and Sherman co., extreme N Texas, 80 mi. N of Amarillo, on state line; pop. in Okla. 1,464, in Texas, 299. Shipping point in grain, cattle area.

Texhuacán (tĕshwäkän'), town (pop. 1,105), Veracruz, E Mexico, in Sierra Madre Oriental, 20 mi. SSW of Córdoba; coffee, fruit.

Texico (tĕk'sĭkō), town (pop. 691), Curry co., E N.Mex., on Texas line, 7 mi. E of Clovis, contiguous to Farwell, Texas; trade center for ranching region. On boundary bet. Central and Mountain time zones.

Texíguat (tāhē'gwät), town (pop. 950), El Paraíso dept., S Honduras, on Texíguat R. (right affluent of the Choluteca) and 22 mi. SW of Yuscarán; grain, beans, coffee, sugar cane.

Texing (tĕk'sĭng), village (pop. 546), central Lower Austria, 17 mi. SW of Sankt Pölten.

Texistepec (tāhēstāpĕk'), town (pop. 2,714), Veracruz, SE Mexico, on Isthmus of Tehuantepec, 20 mi. SW of Minatitlán; sugar cane, coffee, fruit.

Texistepeque (tāksēstāpā'kā), city (pop. 1,057), Santa Ana dept., W Salvador, 10 mi. NNE of Santa Ana; grain, fruit, livestock. Just S is rail junction of Texis Junction.

Texline, town (pop. 437), Dallam co., extreme N Texas, on high plains of the Panhandle, 35 mi. NW of Dalhart, at N.Mex. line; shipping point for grain, cattle region.

Texmelucan (tĕsmälōō'kän), officially San Martín Texmelucan, city (pop. 7,572), Puebla, central Mexico, on railroad, on Inter-American Highway and 22 mi. NW of Puebla; alt. 7,473 ft. Processing (cotton mills, flour mills, wine and liquor distilleries) and agr. center (corn, wheat, maguey, cotton, livestock). Has Franciscan and Carmelite convents.

Texola (tĕksō'lů), town (pop. 265), Beckham co., W Okla., near Texas line, 15 mi. E of Shamrock, Texas; cotton, broomcorn.

Texoloc (tähōlōk'), officially San Damián Texoloc, town (pop. 1,711), Tlaxcala, central Mexico, 4 mi. SW of Tlaxcala; cereals, maguey, beans, stock.

Texoma, Lake, Texas and Okla.: see DENISON DAM.

Texon (tĕk'sŏn), village (pop. c.1,100), Reagan co., W Texas, 75 mi. WSW of San Angelo; hq. for oil field.

Teya (tĕ'yä), town (pop. 1,465), Yucatan, SE Mexico, 38 mi. E of Mérida; henequen.

Teyá (tää'), town (pop. 1,302), Barcelona prov., NE Spain, 11 mi. NE of Barcelona. Wine, hazelnuts, vegetables in area.

Teyahalee Peak, N.C.: see SNOWBIRD MOUNTAINS.

Te-yang, China: see TEHYANG.

Teyateyaneng (tĕyätĕyä'nĕng), village, ⊙ Teyateyaneng dist. (pop. 57,553, with absent laborers 64,836), NW Basutoland, on main N–S road and 19 mi. NE of Maseru. Dist. formerly called Berea.

Teyde, Pico de, Canary Isls.: see TEIDE, PICO DE.

Teye River, Sierra Leone: see JONG RIVER.

Teykovo, Russian SFSR: see TEIKOVO.

Teza River (tyĕ'zŭ), Ivanovo oblast, Russian SFSR, rises E of Privolzhsk, flows c.70 mi. S, past Shuya (head of navigation), to Klyazma R. SW of Yuzha.

Tezcuco, Mexico: see TEXCOCO.

Teziutlán (tāsūtlän'), city (pop. 8,386), Puebla, central Mexico, on plateau, near Veracruz border, on railroad and 75 mi. NE of Puebla; alt. 6,575 ft. Trade, agr. (coffee, tobacco, sugar cane, corn, apples, pears, plums, oranges), and mfg. (cigars, ceramics, brushes, leather goods) center. Airfield. Copper mines near by. Picturesque anc. town.

Tezontepec (tāsŏntāpĕk'). **1** Town (pop. 2,071), Hidalgo, central Mexico, on railroad and 20 mi. SSW of Pachuca; grain, maguey, livestock. **2** Officially Tezontepec de Aldama, town (pop. 5,207), Hidalgo, central Mexico, on Tula R. and 36 mi. W of Pachuca; agr. center (corn, wheat, maguey, beans, fruit, livestock).

Tezoyuca (tāsoiōō'kä), town (pop. 1,348), Mexico state, central Mexico, 20 mi. NE of Mexico city; maguey, cereals, livestock.

Tezpur (täz'pŏŏr), town (pop. 11,879), ⊙ Darrang dist., N central Assam, India, in Brahmaputra valley, on the Brahmaputra and 92 mi. NE of Shillong; rail spur terminus, airport; trades in tea, rice, rape and mustard, sugar cane, jute; tea processing. Was ⊙ div. of anc. Pal kingdom (A.D. c.1000); has 10th-cent. carvings, sculptures, and temple ruins.

Tezzeron Lake (tĕ'zŭrŏn) (□ 24), central B.C., 10 mi. NE of Stuart L., 50 mi. NNW of Vanderhoof; 14 mi. long, 2–4 mi. wide. Drains into Stuart L.

Thaba Bosiu (tä'bä bōsē'ōō), village and mission station, Maseru dist., NW Basutoland, 12 mi. E of Maseru. After defeating Matabele here (1831), Chief Moshesh founded Basuto nation and made his hq. here. Later village was scene of defeat of Boers under Wepener. Treaty of Thaba Bosiu (1866) ceded part of Basutoland to Orange Free State.

Thabantshonyana (tä'bän-chōnyä'nä), highest peak (11,425 ft.) in the Drakensberg, in Basutoland, just W of Natal border (U. of So. Afr.), c.75 mi. SSW of Ladysmith; 29°28'S 29°16'E. Highest peak in Africa S of Kilimanjaro, its height was determined in 1951.

Thaba Putsua Range (pōōtsōō'ä), central Basutoland, extends 50 mi. NE–SW; rises to 10,157 ft.

Thabarie, Palestine: see TIBERIAS.

Thabaung (thŭboun'), village, Bassein dist., Lower Burma, on Bassein R. and 18 mi. N of Bassein.

Thabazimbi (thäbäzēm'bē), town (pop. 3,696), W Transvaal, U. of So. Afr., near Limpopo R., 95 mi. NW of Pretoria; rail terminus; iron-mining center.

Thabeikkyin (dhŭbāk'chĭn'), village, Katha dist., Upper Burma, port on left bank of Irrawaddy R. and 65 mi. N of Mandalay, in defile; shipping point for Mogok ruby mines (linked by road).

Tha Bo (tä'bô'), village (1937 pop. 5,964), Nongkhai prov., NE Thailand, on right bank of Mekong R. (Laos line) opposite (6 mi. SSW of) Vientiane.

Thabor, Mont (mō täbôr'), peak (10,440 ft.) of the Cottian Alps, in Savoie dept., SE France, near Ital. border, 8 mi. SW of Modane. Until 1947, peak formed Fr.-Ital. border.

Thabraca, Tunisia: see TABARKA.

Thab Sakae, Thailand: see THAP SAKAE.

Thabt, Jabal al-, Egypt: see THEBT, GEBEL EL.

Thachap Kangri (tä'chăp käng'grē) or **Thachhab Gangri** (tä'chăb găng'grē), peak (20,970 ft.) on Chang Tang plateau, NW Tibet, at 33°28'N 82°15'E.

Thacher Island, NE Mass., just off E side of Cape Ann; ½ mi. long; 42°38'N 70°35'W. Cape Ann lighthouse here.

Tha Chin, town, Thailand: see SAMUTSAKHON.

Tha Chin River (tä' chēn'), right delta arm of Chao Phraya R., S Thailand, branches off above Chainat, flows 170 mi. S, past Suphanburi (head of navigation) to Gulf of Siam at Samutsakhon (also called Tha Chin). Canalized in lower course, it is linked by canals with the Chao Phraya proper (E) and the Mae Khlong (W). Also called Suphanburi R.

Thackerville, town (pop. 178), Love co., S Okla., 10 mi. S of Marietta, within bend of Red R.; cotton ginning. L. Texoma is just E.

Thagaste, Algeria: see SOUK-AHRAS.

Thaibinh (tī'bĭng'), town (1936 pop. 6,000), ⊙ Thaibinh prov. (□ 600; 1943 pop. 1,139,800), N Vietnam, in Tonkin, in Red R. delta, 55 mi. SE of Hanoi; agr. (rice, tobacco, cotton, sugar cane, sericulture); distillery.

Thaibinh River, Vietnam: see CAU, SONG.

Thailand (tī'lănd), Thai *Muang Thai,* officially *Prathet Thai* [=kingdom of the Thai], or **Siam**

(sīăm'), Thai *Sayam*, independent constitutional kingdom (□ 196,861; 1947 pop. 17,324,291) of SE Asia, in the Indochinese and Malay peninsulas; ⊙ BANGKOK (Krung Thep). Long known as Siam, it changed its name to Thailand in 1939, to Siam in 1945, and once more to Thailand in 1949. Situated on N and W shores of Gulf of Siam, it is bounded S by Malaya (along Kalakhiri Range), W by Andaman Sea and Burma (along Tenasserim and Thanon Thong Chai ranges, the Salween R., and Daen Lao Range), NE and E by Laos (along Luang Prabang Range and Mekong R.), and SE by Cambodia (along Dangrek and Cardamom mts.). Closed off by these peripheral mts., Thailand is drained by, in addition to the Salween and Mekong frontier streams, the great Chao Phraya R. (Mae Nam or Menam), which flows entirely within Thai territory. The tropical monsoon climate of Thailand consists generally of a rainy season (SW monsoon; May–Oct.), a cool, dry season (NE monsoon; Oct.–Feb.), and a hot, dry season (March–May). Geographically, Thailand falls into 4 main divisions: N highlands, central basin of Chao Phraya R., E Korat Plateau, and S peninsular Thailand. The N highlands, consisting of parallel limestone ranges (Thanon Thong Chai, Khun Tan, Phi Pan Nam) and the deeply cut valleys of the 4 headstreams (Ping, Wang, Yom, Nan rivers) of the Chao Phraya, oriented N–S, rise to 8,452 ft. in Inthanon Peak. They are covered with monsoon (teak) and evergreen forests; here elephants are domesticated and rice, tobacco, sugar cane (refining at Lampang and Uttaradit), and lac are the leading agr. products. Chiangmai is center of teak trade and N rail terminus. The densely settled, central alluvial flood plain of the Chao Phraya and the lesser Mae Klong and Bang Pakong rivers is the economic heart of the country, and its great rice-producing region. It is crossed by a multitude of river channels and irrigation canals. Secondary crops in this important hinterland of Bangkok are corn, sesame, sugar palms, coconuts (Samutsongkhram), and pepper (Chanthaburi). In the isolated Korat Plateau, underlain by horizontal sandstone and shale, erratic rainfall and indifferent soils handicap agr. (rice, corn, cotton, tobacco; sericulture) and place greater emphasis on the rearing of cattle, hogs, buffaloes, and horses. The Korat Plateau is served by rail lines linking the large centers of Nakhon Ratchasima (Korat), Ubon, and Udon. Narrow, elongated peninsular Thailand (S) extends across the Isthmus of Kra onto the N Malay Peninsula where it borders on Malaya. It is divided by the central, tin-bearing Phuket and Sithammarat ranges into E coast (rain maximum: Oct.–Feb.) and W coast (rain maximum: May–Oct.) tracts. Tin, Thailand's leading mineral product (mined at Phuket, Phangnga, Ranong, and Yala), coconuts, and rubber are the leading local export items. Tungsten (in association with tin), lead, and coal are also mined. Other peninsular centers are Songkhla, Pattani, and Suratthani. Mineral resources elsewhere in Thailand include semiprecious stones (Chanthaburi, Bo Phloi, Chiang Khong), silver, gold (To Mo, Bang Saphan, Lomsak, Wattana Nakhon), iron (Ta Khli), copper (Chanthuk), petroleum (Fang), saltpeter, and sulphur. Marine and fresh-water fisheries furnish salt fish, an important food staple and export item. Aside from river and coastwise navigation, railroads constitute the chief means of transportation. The rail net links Bangkok with Chiangmai, with the Korat Plateau, with Pnompenh (Cambodia) via Aranyaprathet, and with Malaya (via Padang Besar and Sungei Golok) and is supplemented by short feeder highways. Air transportation radiates from Don Muang, Bangkok's airport. Foreign trade passes mainly through the ports of Bangkok (rice, teak), Phuket (tin), and Songkhla (rubber); textiles, machines, autos, petroleum, and steel products are imported. The Buddhist Thai people proper (Siamese) and the related Lao, speaking an Indochinese language and using an alphabet probably derived from the Cambodian, constitute nearly 90% of pop. The chief minorities are: the Chinese (6%), settled mainly in port cities and active in industry, trade, and mining; the Moslem Malays (3%), on Malay Peninsula and offshore isls., who engage in agr. and fishing; the Cambodians and Annamese; and the Shans and Burmese. Administratively, Thailand falls into 71 provs. (*changwat*), subdivided into dists. (*amphoe*) and communes (*tambon*). Like other countries of SE Asia, Thailand was peopled through successive migrations from central Asia into territory inhabited by primitive Negrito tribes. When the original migrants reached the central plain of Thailand, they came in contact with Indian culture, and Hinduized city-states were founded. These came (A.D. c.1000) under the sway of the Mon incursions from Burma and the power of the rising Khmer empire. The Thai, who originated in SW China and had penetrated after 6th–7th cent. into the present N Thailand, formed the first truly Thai state at Sukhothai in 1257, following the expulsion of the Khmers from the upper Chao Phraya basin. The Khmer power was entirely broken in middle 14th cent. and, with the decline of Sukhothai, the center of Thai rule passed (c.1350) to AYUTTHAYA. During the Ayutthaya period, Thailand expanded (14th–15th cents.) at expense of Lao states (N) and Cambodia (E) and established close contact with Europeans during 17th cent., but declined as result of indecisive wars with the Burmese, who destroyed Ayutthaya in 1767. The restored Thai state, after brief residence at Thonburi, set up its capital (1782) at Bangkok. The late 19th cent. saw progressive Thai modernization under an absolute monarchy, chiefly under Mongkut (1851–68) and Chulalongkorn (1868–1910). Although Thailand was forced to surrender Laos (1893, 1904), parts of Cambodia (1904, 1907) and its suzerainty over N Malay states of Perlis, Kedah, Kelantan, and Trengganu (1909), it managed to remain an independent buffer state bet. the rising colonialism of France in Indochina, and of England in Malaya and Burma. A constitution was granted, 1932. During Second World War, Thailand sided with Japan and temporarily (1941–46) annexed portions (□ 26,750) of Laos and Cambodia, as well as (1943–46) the N Malayan states and the Burmese Shan states of Kengtung and Mongpan.

Thainguyen (tī'ngōōyĕn'), town (1936 pop. 6,000), ⊙ Thainguyen prov. (□ 1,350; 1943 pop. 153,500), N Vietnam, in Tonkin, port on the Song Cau and 40 mi. N of Hanoi; center of mining region; coal (Phanme), zinc (Langhit), magnetite and limonite.

Tha Kham, Thailand: see SURATTHANI.

Thakhek (tä'kĕk'), town, ⊙ Khammouane (or Cammon) prov. (□ 10,200; 1947 pop. 104,000), central Laos, on left bank of Mekong R. (Thailand line), opposite Nakhon Phanom, and 140 mi. ESE of Vientiane; linked by highway via Tanap with Vinh (central Vietnam). Agr.: cardamoms; pigs, cattle (hides, horns), poultry raising. Tin mining near Pak Hin Boun, 18 mi. NW.

Thakurdwara (täkōōrdvä'rŭ), town (pop. 6,220), Moradabad dist., N central Uttar Pradesh, India, 24 mi. N of Moradabad; wheat, rice, pearl millet, sugar cane. Founded 18th cent. Plundered (1805) by Pindaris.

Thakurgaon (tä'kōōrgoun), village, Dinajpur dist., NW East Bengal, E Pakistan, on tributary of the Mahananda and 30 mi. NNW of Dinajpur; rice, jute, sugar cane, rape and mustard. Noted annual fairs at Nekmard (12 mi. WSW) and Alawakhawa (10 mi. NW) villages.

Thal (täl), town (pop. 2,130), Thuringia, central Germany, in Thuringian Forest, 5 mi. SE of Eisenach; steel milling. Climatic health resort.

Thal (tŭl), village, Kohat dist., central North-West Frontier Prov., W Pakistan, on Kurram R. and 55 mi. WSW of Kohat; rail terminus; control post for Afghan traveling merchants.

Thal, desolate tract in Sind-Sagar Doab, W Punjab, W Pakistan; from Salt Range (60 mi. wide here) extends 170 mi. S, narrowing to a point SW of Muzaffargarh. Mainly treeless and sandy, with scanty rainfall; often called a desert. Scattered pasturage for sheep and camels; sparse pop. (largely Jat tribes). Canal irrigation project (headworks on Indus R. below Kalabagh) under construction.

Thal (täl), town (pop. 3,764), St. Gall canton, NE Switzerland, 9 mi. ENE of St. Gall, near the Alter Rhein and Austrian border; metalworking, cement works; silk textiles.

Thala (tälä'), town (pop. 1,671), Kasserine dist., W Tunisia, 28 mi. N of Kasserine; olive trees, esparto grass, horses. Scene of fighting during Tunisian campaign (1943) of Second World War. Former ⊙ Kasserine dist.

Thalang (tälăng'), village (1937 pop. 1,874), on Phuket isl., S Thailand, 10 mi. N of Phuket town; tin mining.

Thalang, island, Thailand: see PHUKET, island.

Thale (tä'lŭ), town (pop. 18,082), in former Prussian Saxony prov., central Germany, after 1945 in Saxony-Anhalt, at N foot of the lower Harz, on the Bode and 6 mi. SW of Quedlinburg, in lignite-mining region; mfg. (steel products, machinery, enamelware). Tourist resort.

Thaleischweiler (täl"ĭsh'vī"lŭr), village (pop. 2,256), Rhenish Palatinate, W Germany, 5 mi. N of Pirmasens; rye, potatoes.

Thale Sap (tŭlä' säp') or **Thale Luang** (lōō'ŭng), coastal lagoon on E coast of Malay Peninsula, S Thailand, bet. Phatthalung and Songkhla (S), where it connects with Gulf of Siam; 50 mi. long, up to 15 mi. wide. Studded with forested isls., it lies in fertile rice-growing dist. and abounds in fish. Sometimes spelled Tale Sap.

Thalgau (täl'gou), town (pop. 2,802), Salzburg, W Austria, 13 mi. ENE of Salzburg; mfg. of chemicals.

Thalheim (täl'hīm), SE suburb (pop. 3,113), of Wels, central Upper Austria.

Thalheim, town (pop. 9,502), Saxony, E central Germany, at N foot of the Erzgebirge, 10 mi. SSW of Chemnitz; hosiery-knitting center; leather mfg.

Thalj, Jabal al-, Lebanon: see HERMON, MOUNT.

Thalwil (täl'vēl), town (pop. 7,965), Zurich canton, N Switzerland, on L. of Zurich and 6 mi. S of Zurich; silk mills.

Thamaing (thŭmīn'), town (pop. 5,645), Insein dist., Lower Burma, on railroad and 7 mi. NNW of Rangoon; cotton-milling center; site of govt. spinning and weaving mill (completed 1950).

Thame (tām), urban district (1931 pop. 3,012; 1951 census 3,585), SE Oxfordshire, England, on the Thame and 9 mi. SW of Aylesbury; agr. market. Has 13th-cent. church and grammar school founded 1558, attended by John Hampden. Hampden, mortally wounded at battle of CHALGROVE, was brought to Thame, where he died.

Thame River (tām), in Buckingham and Oxford, England, rises just N of Aylesbury, flows 40 mi. SW, past Thame, to the Thames just S of Dorchester.

Thames (tĕmz), borough (pop. 4,200) and port, ⊙ Thames co. (□ 419; pop. 2,314), N N.Isl., New Zealand, 50 mi. SE of Auckland, at mouth of Thames R., and on Firth of Thames; iron foundries. Exports frozen fish, gold. School of mines. Thames borough is in, but independent of, Thames co.

Thames, Firth of, SE arm of Hauraki Gulf, N N.Isl., New Zealand; 22 mi. long, 10 mi. wide; receives Thames R. Thames on SE shore.

Thames Ditton, England: see ESHER.

Thamesford (tĕmz'fŭrd), village (pop. estimate 500), S Ont., on Middle Thames R. and 12 mi. ENE of London; dairying, farming.

Thames Haven, England: see STANFORD-LE-HOPE.

Thames River (tĕmz), S Ont., rises NNW of Woodstock, flows 160 mi. SW, past Woodstock, London, and Chatham, to L. St. Clair 15 mi. WSW of Chatham. Navigable below Chatham. Near Oxford was fought (1813) the battle of the Thames, in which the Americans defeated British-Indian force; Indian chief Tecumseh was killed here.

Thames River, anc. *Tamesis*, principal river of England, rises on E slope of Cotswold Hills, Gloucester, in 4 headstreams: Thames or Isis (rises at Thames Head, 3 mi. WSW of Cirencester), Churn R. (rises at Seven Springs, 4 mi. SSE of Cheltenham; 16 mi. long), Coln R. (rises 5 mi. ESE of Cheltenham; 20 mi. long), and Leach R. (rises 10 mi. ENE of Cirencester; 15 mi. long). Churn R. joins the Thames at Cricklade; Coln R. and Leach R. join it near Lechlade. From here river follows winding course E, bounding parts of counties of Gloucester, Wiltshire, Oxford, Berkshire, Buckingham, Surrey, Middlesex, Kent, and Essex. It flows past Oxford, Abingdon, Reading, Maidenhead, Windsor, Staines, Chertsey, Kingston-on-Thames, Brentford, London, Gravesend, Tilbury, and Southend-on-Sea, to North Sea at The Nore. From Lechlade to The Nore it is 210 mi. long; navigable for barges below Lechlade, for ships to 800 tons below London Bridge, and for ocean-going vessels below Tilbury. Thames receives Kennet, Loddon, Wey, Mole, Thame, Darent, Medway, Windrush, Cherwell, Lea, and Roding rivers. It is joined by several canals, including Oxford, Thames and Severn, and Grand Junction. Above Oxford river is also called the Isis. It is tidal to Teddington; below this point it is under jurisdiction of Port of London Authority, established in 1909. Port of London proper extends bet. London Bridge (river is 900 ft. wide here) and Blackwall; this section of the Thames is called The Pool. In London river is crossed by 15 bridges, chief among which are London Bridge, Westminster Bridge (built 1750, rebuilt 1862), Waterloo Bridge (built 1817, rebuilt 1935), and Tower Bridge (built 1894). River is controlled by Thames Conservancy Board, set up in 1857. In upper reaches the Thames valley is broad, flat basin; it becomes narrow at Goring Gap, where it divides Chiltern Hills from North Downs. Below this gap valley again becomes broad basin. In anc. times much of riparian land was marshy fen. In Middle Ages upper Thames valley was prosperous region; site of many religious houses. Because of absence of industries here the Thames is not an important transportation route above London and is chiefly noted for scenic beauty, angling, and boating (annual Henley regatta is rowed on the Thames). Below London there are numerous industrial towns, served by Thames-borne shipping.

Thames River, N N.Isl., New Zealand, rises W of L. Rotorua, flows 90 mi. N, past Te Aroha, to Firth of Thames of Hauraki Gulf; port of Thames at mouth. One of chief sources of dominion's fish supply. Sometimes called Waihou R.

Thames River (thāmz, tĕmz), E Conn., estuary receiving Yantic and Shetucket rivers at Norwich (head of navigation); flows 15 mi. S to Long Isl. Sound at New London, whose harbor it forms. Extensive flood-control works in Thames drainage basin. Yale-Harvard boat races held on the Thames since 1878.

Thamesville (tĕmz'vĭl), village (pop. 828), S Ont., on Thames R. and 16 mi. NE of Chatham; dairying, lumbering, brick and tile mfg.

Thamesville (thāmz'vĭl), village (pop. 5,518), New London co., SE Conn., on Thames R. and 2 mi. S of Norwich.

Thamsbrück (täms'brük), town (pop. 1,560), in former Prussian Saxony prov., central Germany, after 1945 in Thuringia, on the Unstrut and 9 mi. SE of Mühlhausen; vegetables, tobacco, grain, stock.

Thamshamn (täms'hämŭn), village in Orkanger canton, Sor-Trondelag co., central Norway, port on Orkdal Fjord (inlet of Trondheim Fjord), 2 mi. NE of Orkanger village; industrial center, and terminus of railroad from Lokken, whose pyrite mines feed the copper smelters of Thamshamn. Produces pure sulphur and rich copper matte. Frequently spelled Thamshavn.

Thamugadi, Algeria: see TIMGAD.

Than, India: see THANGADH.

Thana (tä'nŭ), district (□ 3,834; pop. 997,859), W Bombay, India, partly (SW section) on N Salsette Isl.; ⊙ Thana. Bordered W by Arabian Sea, E by Western Ghats; comprises N Konkan region; drained by several mtn. streams and (S) by Ulhas R. Rice and cotton milling, handicraft cloth weaving. Coastal strip grows sugar cane, plantains, betel leaf; fishing centers (pomfrets, jewfish, Bombay duck) at Bassein, Agashi, Palghar, and Dahanu. Trade and industries mainly SW, at Thana, Kalyan, and Bhiwandi. In 16th–17th cent., Portuguese set up trading posts along coast; area under Mahrattas in early-18th cent. Original dist. (□ 3,526; 1941 pop. 932,733) was enlarged by inc. (1949) of former Gujarat state of Jawhar. Pop. 64% Hindu, 29% tribal, 5% Moslem, 4% Christian.

Thana, town (pop. 29,751), ⊙ Thana dist., W Bombay, India, on NE Salsette Isl., 20 mi. NE of Bombay city center, on Thana Creek (connects Ulhas R. and Bombay Harbour); trade center for rice, cloth fabrics, betel leaf, sugar cane; cotton milling, mfg. of woolen cloth, matches, ice, bone fertilizer. Important Port. trading post in 16th–17th cent.

Thana Bhawan (tä'nŭ bä'vŭn), town (pop. 9,407), Muzaffarnagar dist., N Uttar Pradesh, India, 19 mi. WNW of Muzaffarnagar; wheat, gram, sugar cane, oilseeds. Has 17th-cent. mosques and tombs.

Thana Creek, S distributary of Ulhas R., W central Bombay, India, flows 15 mi. S past Thana, bet. Salsette Isl. (W) and mainland (E), into Bombay Harbour.

Thana Devli (tä'nŭ dāv'lē), former Western Kathiawar state (□ 117; pop. 18,748) of Western India States agency; merged 1948 with Saurashtra. Also called Amarnagar.

Thana Ghazi (tä'nŭ gä'zē), village, E Rajasthan, India, 20 mi. SW of Alwar; millet, gram, barley.

Thanatpin (thŭnät'pĭn), village, Pegu dist., Lower Burma, 6 mi. SE of Pegu, on Thongwa-Pegu RR and on Pegu-Sittang canal.

Thanbyuzayat (thän-byōō-zŭyät'), village, Amherst dist., Lower Burma, in Tenasserim, on Moulmein-Ye RR and 35 mi. S of Moulmein. In 1943 Jap. army built a railroad from here to Ban Pong, Thailand, using Allied prisoners. Rubber plantations.

Thandaung (thändoung', thŭdoun'), village, Toungoo dist., Lower Burma, 20 mi. NE of Toungoo; tea plantations in hills.

Thandla (tänd'lŭ), village, W Madhya Bharat, India, 36 mi. SW of Ratlam; corn, millet, cotton; cotton ginning.

Thane, fishing village (pop. 58), SE Alaska, on Gastineau Channel 5 mi. SE of Juneau.

Thanesar (tänā'sŭr), town (pop. 6,574), Karnal dist., E Punjab, India, 21 mi. NNW of Karnal, 1 mi. NW of Kurukshetra; wheat, maize, gram; pilgrimage site. Very old town; early ⊙ Harsha (early-7th cent. A.D.); sacked 1014 by Mahmud of Ghazni.

Thanet, Isle of (thă'nĭt), island (10 mi. long, 5 mi. wide) forming NE tip of Kent, England, bounded by the Thames estuary, the Channel, and branches of the Stour. Main towns are the resorts of Margate, Ramsgate, and Broadstairs. Isl. was occupied by Romans, whose fort guarded the entrance to former Wantsume channel (now dried up). Has rocky coast line, but inland area is level agr. land. At NE end is NORTH FORELAND, with lighthouse.

Thangadh (tän'gŭd) or **Than,** village, N Saurashtra, India, 32 mi. WSW of Wadhwan; rail junction; mfg. (pottery, bolts, nuts). A sacred site, associated with legends of Hindu mythology.

Thang Lha, pass, Tibet: see TANG PASS.

Thanglha Range, China: see TANGLHA RANGE.

Thanhhoa (tä'nyŭ-hwä'), town, ⊙ Thanhhoa prov. (□ 4,900; 1943 pop. 1,127,200), N central Vietnam, in former Annam, on railroad and 80 mi. S of Hanoi; agr. center; cotton, jute, tung oil, castor beans, cinnamon; cattle market. Sawmill, paper and match mills at Hamrong (NE). Citadel built 1804. Held after 1946 by the Vietminh.

Thanhthuy (tä'nyŭ-twē'), town, Hagiang prov., N Vietnam, on Clear R. and China frontier, 10 mi. NW of Hagiang.

Thani, Thailand: see SUKHOTHAI.

Thanjinath (tŭn'jēnät), village, Khasi and Jaintia Hills dist., W Assam, India, in Khasi Hills; 19 mi. S of Shillong; rice, cotton. Coal deposits near by.

Thann (tän), town (pop. 5,779), Haut-Rhin dept., E France, on the Thur at SE foot of the Vosges, and 12 mi. WNW of Mulhouse; industrial center; large chemical works, foundries (textile machinery), and boilerworks. Mfg. of alcohol and cotton goods. Winegrowing in area. Its remarkable Gothic 14th–16th-cent. church damaged in Second World War.

Thannhausen (tän'hou"zŭn), village (pop. 3,118), Swabia, SW Bavaria, Germany, on Mindel R. and 20 mi. WSW of Augsburg; meat processing, brewing, tanning. Has 2 mineral springs. Chartered c.1348.

Thanon Thong Chai Range, Burma-Thailand: see TANEN TAUNGGYI RANGE.

Thaon-les-Vosges (tāō'-lā-vōzh'), town (pop. 7,484), Vosges dept., E France, on Moselle R. and Canal de l'Est, 5 mi. N of Épinal; textile bleaching and dyeing works.

Thapsacus, Syria: see DIBSE.

Thap Sakae (täp' sŭkă'), village (1937 pop. 3,414), Prachuabkhirikhan prov., S Thailand, on W coast of Gulf of Siam, on railroad and 25 mi. SSW of Prachuabkhirikhan; tin-mining center. Also spelled Thab Sakae.

Thapsus, Tunisia: see TEBOULBA.

Thara (tŭr'ŭ), village, Banas Kantha dist., N Bombay, India, 45 mi. WSW of Palanpur; millet, wheat. Was ⊙ former Western India state (□ 78; pop. 12,339) of Thara; state inc. 1949 into Banas Kantha dist.

Tharad (tŭräd'), village, Banas Kantha dist., N Bombay, India, 55 mi. WNW of Palanpur; millet. Was ⊙ former Western India state (□ 126; pop. 62,157) of Tharad; state inc. 1949 into Banas Kantha dist.

Tharamangalam, India: see TARAMANGALAM.

Tharandt (tä'ränt), town (pop. 4,559), Saxony, E central Germany, on Wild Weisseritz R. and 8 mi. SW of Dresden; mfg. of machinery, cameras; woodworking. Has forestry school and experimental station, founded 1816. Hydroelectric power station near by.

Thar Desert (tär, tŭr) or **Indian Desert,** extensive sandy waste in NW India and W Pakistan, bet. Sutlej and Indus valleys (W), Aravalli Range (E), Rann of Cutch (SW), and Punjab plains (NE); c.500 mi. long, 300 mi. wide. Includes large area of W Rajasthan and S Punjab (India) and Bahawalpur and Khairpur states and E Sind (W Pakistan). Largely an arid, desolate region of shifting sand dunes, occasional scrub brush, and isolated rock outcrops. Annual rainfall average below 10 in.; Luni R. (SE) is only sizable natural watercourse; irrigation canals have partly reclaimed N and W edges for agr. Sparsely populated and predominantly pastoral (camel, sheep, and goat breeding); caravans trade in hides, wool, salt, blankets, felts. Jodhpur, Bikaner, Jaisalmer, Sardarshahr, Barmer, and Umarkot are chief towns.

Thargomindah (thär"gōmĭn'dŭ), village, S Queensland, Australia, 185 mi. SW of Charleville; cattle.

Tharoch (tŭrōch'), village, SE Himachal Pradesh, India, in W Kumaun Himalayas, 32 mi. ESE of Simla. Was ⊙ former princely state of Tharoch (□ 70; pop. 5,363) of Punjab Hill States, India; since 1948, state merged with Himachal Pradesh.

Thar Parkar (tŭr' pär'kŭr), district (□ 13,649; 1951 pop. 734,000), SE Sind, W Pakistan; ⊙ Umarkot. On SW edge Thar Desert; bounded S by Rann of Cutch; W area irrigated by Eastern Nara Canal and branches. Agr. (millet, cotton, wheat, rice); cotton ginning, handicraft mfg. (cloth, woolen blankets, camel fittings), rice husking, embroidering. Large deposits of natural salt occur on edge of desert, with works in SW corner and SE of Khipro. Chief towns: Mirpur Khas, Umarkot. Formerly called Thar and Parkar, names given to desert and to extreme SE hilly section.

Tharrawaddy (thă"rŭwô'dē, thärä'wädē', Burmese thä'yäwŭdē"), central district (□ 2,784; 1941 pop. 593,909), Pegu div., Lower Burma, bet. Irrawaddy R. and the Pegu Yoma; ⊙ Tharrawaddy. Drained by Myitmaka (Hlaing) R. and served by Rangoon-Prome RR. Rice fields in plain; extensive teak forests (govt. reserves) on W slopes of Pegu Yoma. Pop. is 90% Burmese, 5% Karen.

Tharrawaddy, town (pop. 7,131), ⊙ Tharrawaddy dist., Lower Burma, on Rangoon-Prome RR and 65 mi. NNW of Rangoon.

Tharrawaw (thärŭwô', Burmese thäyŭwô'), village, Tharrawaddy dist., Lower Burma, on left bank of Irrawaddy R. (opposite Henzada; rail ferry) and 80 mi. NW of Rangoon, on rail spur from Letpadan.

Tharsa, India: see NAGPUR, city.

Tharsis (tär'sēs), mining village (pop. 3,242), Huelva prov., SW Spain, in the Sierra Morena, 25 mi. NNW of Huelva (linked by rail); copper-mining center. Iron, manganese, and iron-copper pyrite mines in vicinity. Sometimes identified as the biblical Tarshish, it was known to Phoenicians and Romans for its rich deposits.

Tha Rua (tä' rŭ'ŭ), village (1937 pop. 3,079), Ayutthaya prov., S Thailand, on Pa Sak R., on railroad, and 20 mi. NNE of Ayutthaya; junction for Phra Phuttabat (shrine); iron smelter. Rama VI Barrage on Pa Sak R. feeds extensive canal system. Sometimes spelled Tarua.

Tha Saan, Thailand: see BANG PAKONG.

Thasos (thā'sŏs, Gr. thä'sôs), Lat. *Thasus*, Greek island (□ 170; pop. 13,829) in N Aegean Sea, off Mesta R. mouth, 15 mi. SE of Kavalla and separated from mainland by 4-mi.-wide Thasos Strait; belongs to Kavalla nome, Macedonia; of circular shape, 15 mi. in diameter; rises to 3,947 ft. in Mt. Ypsarion (Ipsarion). Agr. (olive oil, wine), lumbering, sheep and goat raising. Fisheries; lead-zinc mining on SW shore; marble quarries. Chief town is Thasos or Limen (Limin; pop. 1,493), on N coast. In anc. times known for its gold mines, 1st exploited by the Phoenicians; settled either 708 B.C. or c.680 B.C. by colonists from Paros (among them the poet Archilochus), who founded a school of sculpture here. In 5th cent. B.C. isl. passed to Persians under Mardonius and later to Athens against whose rule it staged 2 revolts (465–63, 411 B.C.). The 5th cent. Gr. painter Polygnotus was b. here. From Athens, Thasos passed to Macedonia and, after 1462, to Turkey; administered 1841–1908 by Egypt. Returned to Greece, 1913. Sometimes spelled Thassos.

Thasra (täs'rŭ), village (pop. 5,179), Kaira dist., N Bombay, India, 34 mi. E of Kaira; local agr. market; cotton ginning.

Thatcham, town and parish (pop. 3,230), S Berkshire, England, near Kennet R., 3 mi. E of Newbury; agr. market. Has 15th-cent. church and chantry.

Thatch Cay (kā, kē), islet (286.8 acres; alt. 482 ft.), U.S. Virgin Isls., off NE shore of St. Thomas Isl., at N entrance of Pillsbury Sound, 5 mi. E of Charlotte Amalie; 18°22'N 64°51'W.

Thatcher. 1 Town (pop. 1,284), Graham co., E Ariz., on Gila R. and 3 mi. WNW of Safford in irrigated agr. area. Seat of jr. col. Gila Mts. are N, Pinaleno Mts. S. Founded 1881 by Mormons. **2** Village (pop. c.150), Las Animas co., S Colo., 35 mi. NE of Trinidad; alt. c.5,400 ft. Helium deposits here.

Thathiengarpet or **Thathiyangarpet** (tŭtĭyŭng'gŭrpĕt), town (pop. 7,684), Trichinopoly dist., S Madras, India, 27 mi. NW of Trichinopoly; cotton weaving. Magnetite deposits in Pachaimalai Hills (N). Sometimes spelled Tattayyangarpettai and Tattaiyangarpettai.

Thatkhe (tät'khā'), town, Langson prov., N Vietnam, 35 mi. NW of Langson, near China border; trading center (rice, corn, cotton, tobacco, cloth).

Thaton (thŭtōn'), district (□ 4,872; 1941 pop. 592,638), Tenasserim div., Lower Burma; ⊙ Thaton. Bet. Sittang R. estuary (W) and Thaungyin R. (Thailand frontier; E), astride lower Salween R. Has largest plain (rice, tobacco) in Tenasserim, bounded E by Dawna Range, drained by Bilin, Salween, and Hlaingbwe rivers. Tungsten mines. Served by coastal Pegu-Martaban RR. Pop. is 55% Karen, 25% Burmese, 12% Mon.

Thaton, town (pop. 16,851), ⊙ Thaton dist., Lower Burma, on Pegu-Martaban RR and 35 mi. NNW of Moulmein; has laterite pagoda. Founded 534 B.C.; was early Mon capital, but declined as political power after founding of Pegu; remained a great center of Buddhism until 11th cent. when it was conquered by Burmese under Anawratha.

That Phanom (tät' pŭnōm'), village (1937 pop. 7,877), Nakhon Phanom prov., E Thailand, on right bank of Mekong R. (Laos line) and 34 mi. S of Nakhon Phanom; religious pilgrimage center; has 16th-cent. shrine with venerated Buddha relic. Also spelled That Panom and Dhatu Pnom.

Thatto Heath, England: see SAINT HELENS.

Thau, Étang de (ātā' dŭ tō'), lagoon (□ 30) on the Gulf of Lion, in Hérault dept., S France, c.15 mi. SW of Montpellier; 12 mi. long, 3 mi. wide. Average depth: 16 ft. At Sète (on narrow tongue of land which separates lagoon from the sea) the Étang de Thau has canalized outlet (.5 mi. long). Terminus of Canal du MIDI and RHONE-SÈTE CANAL.

Thaungdut (thoungdōōt'), village, Upper Chindwin dist., Upper Burma, on right bank of Chindwin R. and 15 mi. NNW of Paungbyin. Was (until 1947) ⊙ Shan state of Hsawnghsup.

Thaungyin River (thoung-jĭn'), Thai *Mae Muai*, on Burma-Thailand border, flows 180 mi. along E foot of Dawna Range, past Myawaddy and Mae Sot, to Salween R. 90 mi. N of Moulmein.

Tha Uthen (tä' ōōtān'), village (1937 pop. 6,425), Nakhon Phanom prov., NE Thailand, on right bank of Mekong R. (Laos line) opposite Pak Hin Boun, 18 mi. NW of Nakhon Phanom. Sometimes spelled Tauden.

Thawville, village (pop. 267), Iroquois co., E Ill., 32 mi. SSW of Kankakee, in rich agr. area.

Thaxted, town and parish (pop. 1,610), NW Essex, England, on Chelmer R. and 10 mi. NE of Bishop's Stortford; agr. market. Has 15th-cent. church and 17th-cent. guildhall.

Thaya River, Czechoslovakia and Austria: see DYJE RIVER.

Thayer (thâr), county (□ 577; pop. 10,563), SE Nebr.; ⊙ Hebron. Agr. area bounded S by Kansas; drained by Little Blue R. Grain, livestock, dairy and poultry produce. Formed 1871.

Thayer. 1 Village (pop. 695), Sangamon co., central Ill., 18 mi. SSW of Springfield, in agr. and bituminous-coal area. **2** Town (pop. 152), Union co., S Iowa, 16 mi. E of Creston; livestock, grain. **3** City (pop. 423), Neosho co., SE Kansas, 13 mi. S of Chanute, in diversified-farming area. Coal and shale mines, gas and oil wells near by. **4** City (pop. 1,639), Oregon co., S Mo., on Spring R. and 23 mi. SE of West Plains; ships lumber, dairy products. Inc. 1890. **5** Village (pop. 90), York co., SE central Nebr., 10 mi. NNE of York and on branch of Big Blue R.

Thayetchaung (thŭyĕt"choun'), village, Tavoy dist., Lower Burma, in Tenasserim, on Tavoy R. estuary and 15 mi. S of Tavoy.

Thayetmyo (-myō'), S district (□ 4,626; 1941 pop. 297,434) of Magwe div., Upper Burma; ⊙ Thayetmyo. Astride Irrawaddy R., bet. the Arakan

Yoma and Pegu Yoma, in dry zone (annual rainfall 45 in.). Extensive teak forests (govt. reserves); cotton-growing region; tobacco. Oil (at Minhla), coal, limestone. Served by Irrawaddy steamers. Although administratively in Upper Burma, it is one of the historical Lower Burma dists.

Thayetmyo, town (pop. 9,279), ⊙ Thayetmyo dist., Upper Burma, on right bank of Irrawaddy R. (opposite Allanmyo) and 35 mi. N of Prome. Cement-milling center (limestone quarries, S); gold and silver carving. Founded 1306. Rose to importance (1853) as Br. cantonment after 2d Anglo-Burmese War.

Thayettabin, Burma: see MAHAMUNI.

Thayne, village (pop. 229), Lincoln co., W Wyo., on Salt R., near Idaho line, and 14 mi. N of Afton, in Star Valley; alt. 5,790 ft. Dairy products, grain, livestock.

Thayngen (tĭng'ŭn), town (pop. 2,254), Schaffhausen canton, N Switzerland, N of the Rhine, on Biber R. and 5 mi. N of Schaffhausen, near Ger. border; limestone, cement, tiles; canning, paper products, flour.

Thazi (thä'zē'), village, Meiktila dist., Upper Burma, on Rangoon-Mandalay RR and 80 mi. S of Mandalay; rail junction (workshops) in millet and sesame area.

Thealka (thēăl'kē), mining village (1940 pop. 818), Johnson co., E Ky., on Levisa Fork and 45 mi. SSW of Huntington, W.Va.; bituminous coal.

Thebarton (thĕ'bûrtŭn), W suburb (pop. 14,585) of Adelaide, SE South Australia; agr. center.

Theben, Czechoslovakia: see DEVIN.

Thebes (thēbz), city of anc. Egypt. LUXOR, KARNAK, and QURNA, on both banks of the Nile c.450 mi. S of Cairo, now occupy parts of its site, which is famous for its vast and beautiful ruined temples, obelisks, colossal statues, and tombs, including that of Tut-ankh-amen. The city developed at a very early date from a cluster of villages but remained obscure until a Theban family established the XI dynasty (c.2160 B.C.). It rapidly became prominent as the royal residence of XVIII, XIX, and XX dynasties (1600–1200 B.C.) and was seat of worship of the god Amon. It was the reservoir for the immense wealth of the New Empire, but as the empire began to decay and the locus of power to shift to the Nile delta, Thebes went into decline. It was sacked 661 B.C. by the Assyrians (an event referred to in the Bible, where city is called No) and by the Romans (29 B.C.); by 20 B.C. Strabo reported only a few scattered villages. Though great damage has been done to the ruins, they are still among the most splendid in the world, and the anc. city has been the scene of much important archaeological work. The fame of the city had reached the Greeks of Homer's day and it appears as the city of a "hundred gates" in the *Iliad;* the later Greeks called it *Diospolis* (city of Zeus).

Thebes, Gr. *Thevai* or *Thivai* (both: thē'vā), city (pop. 12,428), Boeotia nome, E central Greece, on railroad and 30 mi. NW of Athens; 38°21'N 23°19'E. Trade in wheat, olive oil, wine, tobacco, cotton. Silk milling and dyeing. One of the leading cities of anc. Greece, Thebes was traditionally founded by Cadmus, for whom the acropolis (Cadmea) was named. Historically Thebes was settled before 1,000 B.C. by the Boeotians; it rapidly became one of their leading towns and headed (6th cent. B.C.) the Boeotian League. Hostility to Athens dated from Athenian collaboration with Plataea after 519 B.C. Thebes sided (480–479) with Persians against Greeks, and with Sparta in Peloponnesian War, but joined Athens in Corinthian War. During its hegemony (379–362) under Pelopidas and Epaminondas, Thebes broke the Spartan power at Leuctra (371 B.C.). Thebes joined Athens against Philip of Macedon and shared defeat at Chaeronea (338 B.C.). Thebes was destroyed 336 B.C. by Alexander the Great. Pindar b. here. The rebuilt city had some commercial importance in Middle Ages.

Thebes, village (pop. 541), Alexander co., extreme S Ill., on the Mississippi and 21 mi. NW of Cairo.

The Bight, town (pop. 401), central Bahama Isls., on central Cat Isl., 135 mi. ESE of Nassau; 24°19'N 75°23'W. Produces sisal, corn, potatoes, fruit.

The Brill, Netherlands: see BRIELLE.

Thebt, Gebel el, Gebel eth Thebt (both: gĕ'bĕl ĕth-thĕbt'), or **Jabal al-Thabt** (jĕ'bĕl ĕth-thĕbt'), peak (8,000 ft.), Sinai Peninsula, NE Egypt, 18 mi. SSE of Gebel Katherina.

The Dalles (dălz), city (pop. 7,676), ⊙ Wasco co., N Oregon, on S bank of Columbia R. (Wash. line), 190 mi. above river mouth, and 70 mi. E of Portland; trade center and busy inland port (reached by ocean-going steamers of c.8,000 tons) in grain, fruit, and livestock (cattle, sheep) area; flour and lumber milling; canneries, salmon fisheries, railroad repair shops. Rapids in river gorge are circumvented here by canal (8.5 mi. long, 8 ft. deep), built 1908–15, and BONNEVILLE DAM, c.40 mi. downstream, is by-passed by locks (completed 1937). Seat of Eastern Oregon State Tuberculosis Hosp. A mission here (1838–47) was replaced by a fort around which grew a settlement (c.1852); inc. 1857.

Thedaw, Burma: see WUNDWIN.

The Dells, Wis.: see DELLS OF THE WISCONSIN.

Thedford (thĕd'fûrd), village (pop. 623), S Ont., 30 mi. ENE of Sarnia; sawmilling, flax milling. Limestone quarried near by.

Thedford, village (pop. 275), ⊙ Thomas co., central Nebr., 60 mi. N of North Platte and on Middle Loup R.; livestock, grain. Near by is Halsey Div. of Nebr. Natl. Forest.

Thedinghausen (tā"dĭng-hou'zŭn), village (pop. 2,458), in Brunswick exclave, NW Germany, after 1945 Lower Saxony, near left bank of the Weser, 13 mi. SE of Bremen; chemicals, furniture, flour products.

Theel River (tāl), central Saar, rises 7 mi. WNW of St. Wendel, flows 13 mi. generally SW, past Lebach, to Prims R. 3 mi. WSW of Lebach.

The Forks, plantation (pop. 45), Somerset co., W central Maine, at confluence of Dead and Kennebec rivers, c.45 mi. above Norridgewock; hunting, fishing area.

The Glen, resort village, Warren co., E N.Y., in the Adirondacks, on the Hudson and 21 mi. NNW of Glens Falls.

Thegon (thĕ'gōn), village, Prome dist., Lower Burma, 17 mi. SE of Prome, on railroad to Rangoon.

The Hague, Netherlands: see HAGUE, THE.

The Hummocks, R.I.: see ISLAND PARK.

Theil, Le (lù tā'), village (pop. 786), Orne dept., NW France, on the Huisne and 7 mi. SW of Nogent-le-Rotrou; cigarette paper mfg., cider distilling. Also called Le Theil-sur-Huisne.

Theissen (tī'sŭn), village (pop. 4,050), in former Prussian Saxony prov., central Germany, after 1945 in Saxony-Anhalt, 3 mi. NW of Zeitz; lignite mining; power station.

Theiss River: see TISZA RIVER.

Thélepte (tālĕpt'), village, Kasserine dist., W Tunisia, on railroad and 17 mi. SW of Kasserine; railroad shops. Airfield. Roman ruins.

Thelj, Jebel eth, Lebanon: see HERMON, MOUNT.

Thelon Game Sanctuary (□ 15,000), E Mackenzie and W Keewatin districts, Northwest Territories, on upper Thelon R., bet. Aberdeen L. (E) and Artillery L., 50 mi. NE of Fort Reliance. Largest musk-ox herd on North American mainland.

Thelon River, Northwest Territories, rises in E Mackenzie Dist. E of Great Slave L., flows generally NE through Thelon Game Sanctuary to Keewatin Dist. boundary, thence E through Aberdeen and Schultz lakes to Baker L. (opening on Chesterfield Inlet); c.550 mi. long. Receives Dubawnt R.

The Maldens and Coombe or **Malden and Coombe** (môl'-, kōōm'), residential municipal borough (1931 pop. 23,405; 1951 census 45,559), N Surrey, England, c.10 mi. SW of London. Includes residential town of New Malden (pop. 20,120), with knitting mills, printworks, and mfg. of phonograph records and electrical equipment. Malden is in S, and Coombe in N.

Themar (tā'mär), town (pop. 3,978), Thuringia, central Germany, at S foot of Thuringian Forest, on the Werra and 10 mi. ESE of Meiningen; woodworking. Has 15th-cent. church, 17th-cent. town hall, and medieval town walls.

Themi, Nepal: see THIMI.

Themina, Greece: see PHYMAINA.

Then Arkadu, India: see SOUTH ARCOT.

The Narrows, village, Md.: see NARROWS PARK.

Thénezay (tānzā'), village (pop. 839), Deux-Sèvres dept., W France, 11 mi. ENE of Parthenay; horse breeding.

Theni, India: see ALLINAGARAM.

Thenon (tŭnō'), village (pop. 729), Dordogne dept., SW France, 17 mi. ESE of Périgueux; goose liver and truffle processing, mfg. (cement, furniture).

Theodore, village (pop. 386), E central Queensland, Australia, on Dawson R. and 115 mi. SSW of Rockhampton; terminus of railroad from Rockhampton; cotton.

Theodore, agr. village (pop. 329), SE central Sask., near Whitesand R., 25 mi. NW of Yorkton.

Theodore Roosevelt National Memorial Park (□ 91.1), along Little Missouri R. in W N.Dak. Includes 3 sections: in the Badlands along Little Missouri R. in McKenzie co., S of Watford City; site of Theodore Roosevelt's Elkhorn Ranch hq., in Billings co. 5 mi. N of Medora; and an area of petrified forest at Medora. Established 1947 in commemoration of Theodore Roosevelt's interest in development of the West.

Theodoro River, Brazil: see ROOSEVELT RIVER.

Theodosia, Russian SFSR: see FEODOSIYA.

Theodosiopolis, Turkey: see ERZURUM, city.

Théodule: see MATTERHORN.

Theophilo Ottoni, Brazil: see TEÓFILO OTONI.

The Pas (päz, pä), town (pop. 3,102), W Man., on Saskatchewan R. and 320 mi. NW of Winnipeg; 53°49'N 101°15'W; trade center for mining (gold, silver, zinc, copper) and fur-trapping region. Outfitting point for Beaver and Herb lakes region. Airfield. Became important c.1920 as starting point of railroad to Churchill.

The Plains. 1 Village (pop. 1,004, with adjacent Hocking), Athens co., SE Ohio, on Hocking R., just N of Athens. **2** Town (pop. 405), Fauquier co., N Va., near Little R., 10 mi. N of Warrenton, in dairying, agr. area.

Thera or **Thira** (both: thēr'ŭ), formerly *Santorin* (săntûrĭn') or *Santorini* (säntôrē'nē), southernmost island (□ 31; pop. 9,704) of the Cyclades, Greece, in Aegean Sea, S of Ios; 36°25'N 25°30'E. Forming portion of a volcanic crater, Thera is crescent-shaped, 12 mi. long and 3 mi. wide; it rises to 1,858 ft. in the Prophet Elias. It is noted for the Santorin earth, a volcanic tuff used in making hydraulic cement. It produces a famous wine, as well as cotton, wheat, barley, tobacco, and vegetables. Main town, Thera (pop. 1,831), is on W shore. Scene of many volcanic eruptions (the latest severe one in 1866). Settled by Laconian Dorians before 9th cent. B.C., Thera was cofounder (with Crete) of Cyrene, anc. ⊙ Cyrenaica, in 631 B.C. Became tributary to Athens in 427 B.C. Since Middle Ages, when it was under Venetian duchy of Naxos and, after 1537, under Turks, it was known, until recently, as Santorin or Santorini, for its patron saint, St. Irene. Prehistoric remains and ruins from the classical period have been excavated.

Thérain River (tārē'), Oise dept., N France, rises S of Formerie, flows c.50 mi. SE, past Beauvais, Mouy, and Montataire, to the Oise below Creil.

The Range, village, Gwelo prov., E central Southern Rhodesia, in Mashonaland, 9 mi. E of Enkeldoorn. Hq. of native commissioner.

Therasia or **Thirasia** (thērā'shù, Gr. thērùsē'ù), Aegean island (□ 4; pop. 600) in the Cyclades, Greece, off NW end of Thera isl., with which it forms remains of anc. volcanic crater; 36°25'N 25°20'E; 3 mi. long, 1 mi. wide; cotton, grapes.

Theresa. 1 (thùrē'sù) Village (pop. 925), Jefferson co., N N.Y., on Indian R. and 18 mi. NNE of Watertown; paper milling. Lakes (resorts) near by. **2** (thùrē'sù) Village (pop. 461), Dodge co., E Wis., on Rock R. and 18 mi. S of Fond du Lac; cannery, brewery.

Thérèse Island (tārĕs'), one of the Seychelles, off W coast of Mahé Isl., 5 mi. SW of Victoria; 4°40'S 55°24'E; 1 mi. long, ½ mi. wide.

Theresienstadt, Czechoslovakia: see TEREZIN.

Theresina, Brazil: see TERESINA.

Theresiopel, Yugoslavia: see SUBOTICA.

Therezina, Brazil: see TERESINA.

Therezopolis, Brazil: see TERESÓPOLIS.

Therma, Greece: see SALONIKA, city.

Therma, N.Mex.: see EAGLE NEST.

Thermae Himerenses, Sicily: see TERMINI IMERESE.

Thermaic Gulf, Thermaicus Sinus, Thermaikos Kolpos, Greece: see SALONIKA, GULF OF.

Thermal, village (pop. c.950), Riverside co., S Calif., in Coachella Valley, 23 mi. SE of Palm Springs.

Thermal Springs District, New Zealand: see HOT SPRINGS DISTRICT.

Therme or **Thermi** (both: thĕr'mē), town (pop. 3,472), Salonika nome, central Macedonia, Greece, 6 mi. SE of Salonika, on Chalcidice peninsula; site of Salonika airport, aviation and agr. colleges. Formerly called Sedes or Sedhes.

Thermia, Greece: see KYTHNOS.

Thermodon, Turkey: see TERME.

Thermon (thĕr'môn), anc. *Thermum,* village (pop. 2,665), Acarnania nome, W central Greece, 19 mi. NE of Missolonghi, on E shore of L. Trichonis; oats; olive oil; wine; livestock. Formerly called Kephalovryson or Kefalovrison. The anc. Thermum (destroyed 218 B.C. by Philip V of Macedon) was the religious and political center of the Aetolian League. The site, with traces of an anc. temple of Apollo, was excavated 1897–99.

Thermopolis (thûrmŏ'pùlĭs), town (pop. 2,870), ⊙ Hot Springs co., N central Wyo., on Bighorn R. and 110 mi. NW of Casper; alt. 4,326 ft. Resort and trade center in livestock, sugar-beet, and grain region; oil refinery. Oil fields, coal and sulphur mines near by. Mineral hot springs in vicinity taken over by state as Hot Springs State Park. Founded 1897.

Thermopylae (thûrmŏ'pĭlē), Gr. *Thermopylai* or *Thermopilai* (both: thĕrmôpē'lā) [=hot gates], pass in E central Greece, bet. Kallidromon massif and Malian Gulf, 9 mi. SE of Lamia. Here Leonidas, king of Sparta, at the head of 300 Spartans and 700 Thespians, lost (480 B.C.) a heroic battle against the Persians under Xerxes. Here in 279 B.C. the Greeks held back the Gauls under Brennus, who ultimately broke through. In 191 B.C. Antiochus III of Syria was defeated here by the Romans.

Thermum, Greece: see THERMON.

The Rock, village (pop. 861), S New South Wales, Australia, 115 mi. W of Canberra; rail junction; sheep, agr.

The Rock, town (pop. 147), Upson co., W central Ga., 7 mi. NE of Thomaston.

Thesalia, spa, Ecuador: see MACHACHI.

Thespiae (thĕs'pĭ-ē), chief city of anc. S Boeotia, Greece, 8 mi. WSW of Thebes, near E foot of the Zagora section of the Helicon. Thespiae was represented at the stand of Thermopylae (480 B.C.) and at Plataea (479 B.C.). It sided with Sparta against Thebes after 382 B.C. and remained important until Roman times. Eros and the Muses were worshipped here. On site is modern village of Thespiai (pop. 1,427), formerly Eremokastron.

Thesprotia (thĕsprô'tē'ù), nome (□ 615; pop. 56,734), S Epirus, Greece; ⊙ Egoumenitsa. Bounded N by Albania, W by Strait of Corfu, S by Acheron R., and E by W foothills of Pindus system, it is drained by Thyamis R. (N). **Agr.:** barley, corn, almonds; olive oil; lumbering. Main centers are Egoumenitsa, Philiates, Paramythia, Margaritіon, and Parga. Formed in middle 1930s.

Thessalon (thĕ'sùlŏn), town (pop. 1,316), S central Ont., on L. Huron, 40 mi. ESE of Sault Ste. Marie, opposite Drummond Isl., in farming, dairying, fishing, lumbering area.

Thessalonica, Thessalonike, or **Thessaloniki,** Greece: see SALONIKA.

Thessaly (thĕ'sùlē), Gr. *Thessalia* (thĕsùlē'ù), division (□ 5,907; pop. 589,280) of N central Greece; ⊙ Larissa. Situated bet. Epirus (W) and the Aegean Sea (E), bet. Macedonia (N) and central Greece (S), Thessaly consists mainly of the fertile Trikkala and Larissa lowlands, bounded on all sides by mts. These are the Othrys (S), the main Pindus system (W), the Chasia, Kamvounia, and Olympus mts. (N), and the Ossa and Pelion, which bar access to the Aegean. The main passes leading into Thessaly are the Metsovon gap in the Pindus, Petra Pass and the Vale of Tempe on either side of the Olympus, and the pass across the Othrys from Lamia. The lowlands are drained by the Peneus R. and its affluents (Titaresios, Enipeus rivers) and contains (E) L. Voiveis. The Magnesia peninsula (SE) encloses the vast Gulf of Volos. Situated in the lee of the Pindus barrier, Thessaly receives only 20 in. of annual rainfall, mainly during the winter. It is one of Greece's leading wheat-growing regions, producing also tobacco, olives, vegetables, and citrus fruit. Chromite is mined E of Pharsala. Industry is centered at Larissa and Volos, the only major port. These cities, as well as the lesser centers of Trikkala, Karditsa, and Kalambaka, are served by the main Salonika–Athens RR and a narrow-gauge system based on Volos. The Thessalians, an Aeolian tribe, entered the region from the NW before 1000 B.C. The Thessalian cities became oligarchal, the greatest families being the Aleudae at Larissa and the Scopadae at Crannon. Thessaly was allied to the Persians in 480 B.C. but remained neutral in Peloponnesian War. After Jason, tyrant of Pherae, briefly united Thessaly in 374 B.C., the region passed 344 B.C. to Philip II of Macedon. It became 146 B.C. part of the Roman prov. of Macedonia and later a separate prov. It received a large Walachian immigration in early Middle Ages, fell to the Turks c.1400, and became part of Greece in 1881, except for extreme N portion that remained under Turkish rule until 1913. It is divided administratively into the nomes of KARDITSA, LARISSA, MAGNESIA (which includes most of the Northern Sporades), and TRIKKALA.

Thetford, municipal borough (1931 pop. 4,098; 1951 census 4,445), S Norfolk, England, on Little Ouse R., at mouth of the small Thet, and 12 mi. N of Bury St. Edmunds; agr. market. Site of anc. camp of Castle Hill (100 ft. high, 1,000 ft. in circumference), one of largest earthworks in Great Britain. There are a ruined Cluniac priory (founded 1104), a mus. in 15th-cent. house, three 14th-cent. churches, and a number of other old bldgs. Town important in Saxon and Danish times and for a time was capital of the kings and bishops of East Anglia. Thomas Paine b. here. Just W is extensive wood and health area of Thetford Warren.

Thetford, town (pop. 1,046), Orange co., E Vt., on the Connecticut and 30 mi. SE of Barre, in agr. area. Settled 1764.

Thetford Mines, city (pop. 12,716), S Que., 50 mi. S of Quebec; asbestos-mining center; jute-bag mfg., dairying. Chromium, feldspar are also mined. Developed after asbestos deposits were discovered here, 1876.

Thetideion or **Thetidhion** (both: thĕtē'dhēôn), village (1928 pop. 200), Larissa nome, SE Thessaly, Greece, 7 mi. NE of Pharsala; chromite mining. Formerly called Alchani or Alkhani.

Theunissen (tûnĭ'sùn), town (pop. 3,109), central Orange Free State, U. of So. Afr., 60 mi. NE of Bloemfontein; alt. 4,638 ft.; rail junction; grain, stock. Diamond mines near by.

Theusing, Czechoslovakia: see TOUZIM.

Theux (tû), town (pop. 5,332), Liége prov., E Belgium, 5 mi. SSW of Verviers; wool spinning and weaving. Has church with 15th-cent. frescoes. Just E is agr. village of Franchimont (frăshēmō'), a medieval stronghold; has ruins of 14th-cent. castle.

Thevai, Greece: see THEBES.

The Vale, Guernsey, Channel Isls.: see VALE.

Thevaram, India: see TEVARAM.

Thevenard, village and port (pop. 323), S South Australia, on Denial Bay of Great Australian Bight and 220 mi. NW of Port Lincoln, on spur of Port Lincoln–Penong RR; exports wheat, wool.

Theveste, Algeria: see TEBESSA.

The Weirs, resort village, Belknap co., central N.H., N suburb of Laconia, at head of Winnipesaukee R. (outlet of L. Winnipesaukee), on site of anc. Indian village and fish weirs. Steamer terminus, boat yards.

Theydon (thā'dùn), village, Salisbury prov., E Southern Rhodesia, in Mashonaland, on railroad and 10 mi. E of Marandellas; alt. 5,279 ft. Tobacco, peanuts, citrus fruit, dairy products.

Theydon Bois (boiz'), residential town and parish (pop. 1,504), SW Essex, England, 2 mi. S of Epping.

Thèze (tĕz), village (pop. 261), Basses-Pyrénées dept., SW France, 12 mi. N of Pau; winegrowing, hog raising.

Thiais (tēā'), town (pop. 8,049), Seine dept., N central France, a SSE suburb of Paris, 6 mi. from Notre Dame Cathedral, just W of Choisy-le-Roe; mfg. (cartons, radio sets, ink, hats). Has large new Parisian cemetery. Scene of fighting in 1870.

Thiaki, Greece: see ITHACA.

Thiamis River, Greece: see THYAMIS RIVER.

Thian Shan, China and USSR: see TIEN SHAN.

Thiant (tyā'), town (pop. 2,387), Nord dept., N France, on Escaut R. and 5 mi. SW of Valenciennes; hardware mfg.

Thiaucourt (tyōkōōr'), village (pop. 995), Meurthe-et-Moselle dept., NE France, 9 mi. WNW of Pont-à-Mousson; noted vineyards. Captured by Americans in Sept., 1918. Site of Saint-Mihiel American Cemetery. Near-by Regniéville and Remenauville were completely destroyed in First World War.

Thibar (tēbär'), agr. village, Teboursouk dist., N central Tunisia, 9 mi. WNW of Teboursouk.

Thiberville (tēbĕrvēl'), village (pop. 844), Eure dept., NW France, 7 mi. NW of Bernay; ribbon weaving, cider distilling.

Thibodaux (tĭ'bùdō), town (pop. 7,730), ⊙ Lafourche parish, SE La., on Bayou Lafourche and 45 mi. WSW of New Orleans; commercial center for oil and agr. area (sugar cane, vegetables, grain; dairy products). Sugar milling; mfg. of machinery, farm implements, metal products, brooms, brick. Oil fields near by. Laid out c.1820, inc. 1838. Chief Justice White b. near by.

Thiéblemont-Farémont (tyāblùmō'-fārāmō'), village (pop. 230), Marne dept., N France, 7 mi. ESE of Vitry-le-François.

Thiede-Steterburg (tē'dù-shtā'tùrbōōrk), NE residential district of WATENSTEDT-SALZGITTER, NW Germany.

Thief River, rises in Thief L. (□ 11; 5 mi. long, 3 mi. wide), NW Minn., flows 37 mi. SSW, through marshy area, to Red Lake R. at city of Thief River Falls.

Thief River Falls, city (pop. 6,926), ⊙ Pennington co., NW Minn., on Red Lake R., at mouth of Thief R., and c.75 mi. NW of Bemidji; commercial center and shipping point for grain, livestock, poultry area; dairy products.

Thiel, Netherlands: see TIEL.

Thièle Canal (tyĕl) or **Zihl Canal** (tsēl), W Switzerland, connects N end of L. of Neuchâtel with L. Biel; 5 mi. long; constructed (1878) along old bed of **Thièle** (or **Zihl**) **River.** Lower course of Orbe R., which enters S end of L. of Neuchâtel at Yverdon, is also called Thièle R.

Thielen-Saint-Jacques, Belgian Congo: see KANDA-KANDA.

Thielrode, Belgium: see TIELRODE.

Thielson, Mount (thēl'sùn, tēl'–) (9,178 ft.), SW central Oregon, peak in Cascade Range, c.15 mi. N of Crater L.

Thielt, Belgium: see TIELT.

Thiene (tyā'nĕ), town (pop. 8,840), Vicenza prov., Veneto, N Italy, 12 mi. N of Vicenza. Rail junction; industrial center; silk, cotton, woolen, and hemp mills, foundries, mfg. (shoes, hats, buttons, cheese, paper, saddles, liquor, marmalade). Has 15th-cent. palace with frescoes by Paolo Veronese.

Thiensville (thēnz'vĭl), village (pop. 897), Ozaukee co., E Wis., on Milwaukee R. and 13 mi. N of Milwaukee, in dairy and farm area; boatbuilding, shoe mfg. Silver-fox farms. Seat of Evangelical Lutheran Theological Seminary. Victor L. Berger lived in near-by Mequon.

Thiepval (tyĕpväl'), village (pop. 32), Somme dept., N France, 4 mi. NNE of Albert. Scene of heavy fighting in battle of the Somme (1916). Site of Br. First World War memorial.

Thiérache (tyārăsh'), old district of Picardy, N France, now in Aisne dept.; ⊙ was Vervins.

Thieralplistock (tēr'älplē-shtôk'), peak (11,109 ft.) in Bernese Alps, S central Switzerland, 11 mi. SE of Meiringen.

Thiers (tyâr), town (pop. 11,180), Puy-de-Dôme dept., central France, 23 mi. ENE of Clermont-Ferrand; leading cutlery-mfg. center. Also produces umbrella handles, watch springs, plastics. Picturesquely terraced above deep Durolle R. Romanesque church of St. Genès has fragments of mosaics dating from Merovingian times.

Thiersheim (tērs'hīm), village (pop. 1,780), Upper Franconia, NE Bavaria, Germany, in the Fichtelgebirge, 6 mi. S of Selb; textile mfg., metal- and woodworking; lumber, paper, and flour milling; brewing, tanning.

Thiersville (tyârvēl'), village (pop. 1,739), Oran dept., NW Algeria, on railroad and 10 mi. S of Mascara; woodworking, winegrowing.

Thierville-sur-Meuse (sür-mûz'), village (pop. 1,710), Meuse dept., NE France, on left bank of the Meuse and 2 mi. NW of Verdun; cheese; rabbit-skin processing.

Thiès (tyĕs), town (pop. c.34,800, of which c.2,100 are Europeans), W Senegal, Fr. West Africa, rail junction 35 mi. E of Dakar; trading and agr. center (peanuts, millet, rice, manioc, potatoes, bananas, mangoes, tangerines, pineapples; livestock). Meat packing; military airfield. Alumina phosphate deposits near by.

Thiesi (tyā'zē), village (pop. 3,399), Sassari prov., NW Sardinia, 16 mi. SSE of Sassari. Sometimes spelled Tiesi.

Thieu (tyû), town (pop. 2,225), Hainaut prov., SW Belgium, on Canal du Centre and 7 mi. ENE of Mons; Portland cement.

Thiézac (tyāzäk'), village (pop. 506), Cantal dept., S central France, in Massif du Cantal, on the Cère and 13 mi. NE of Aurillac; mfg. of blue cheese.

Thika (tē'kä), town (pop. c.4,000), S central Kenya, on railroad and 25 mi. NE of Nairobi; alt. 4,943 ft.; coffee and sisal center; mfg. (wattle extract, metal containers, safety matches, native garments).

Thil (tēl), town (pop. 2,302), Meurthe-et-Moselle dept., NE France, 7 mi. ESE of Longwy; iron mining.

Thillot, Le (lù tēyō'), town (pop. 2,650), Vosges dept., E France, on upper Moselle R. and 13 mi. SE of Remiremont, in the central Vosges; mfg. of belts and cord, tanning, cotton milling.

Thimble Islands, S Conn., group of many small isls. in Long Isl. Sound, SE of Branford; hotels, summer homes.

Thimi (tē'mē), town, central Nepal, in Nepal Valley, 4 mi. ESE of Katmandu; pottery mfg. Formerly spelled Themi.

Thimister (tēmēstâr'), village (pop. 2,095), Liége prov., E Belgium, 4 mi. N of Verviers; mfg. of apple cider.

Thingangyun (thĭng-găn'jōōn"), town (pop. 7,984), Insein dist., Lower Burma, on Rangoon-Mandalay RR and 5 mi. NE of Rangoon.

Thingeyjar (thĕng'gā"är), Icelandic *Þingeyjar,* county [Icelandic *sýsla*] (pop. 5,750), NE Iceland; ⊙ Husavik. In coastal region bet. Eyja Fjord (W) and Langanes peninsula (E). Generally low, rising toward S and along Eyja Fjord; drained by Skjalfandafljot R. Sheep and goat raising, fishing.

Thingeyri or **Thingeyri i Dyrafirdi** (thĕng'gā"rē ē dē'räfĭr"dhē), Icelandic *Þingeyri í Dýrafirði,* fishing village (pop. 310), Isafjardar co., NW Iceland, on Vestfjarda Peninsula, on Dyra Fjord (18-mi.-long inlet of Denmark Strait), 17 mi. SW of Isafjordur.

Thingvallavatn (thĕng'gvät"lävä"tùn), Icelandic *Þingvallavatn,* lake (□ 46), SW Iceland, 20 mi. E of Reykjavik; 9 mi. long, 2–6 mi. wide; c.350 ft. deep. Drained S by short Sog R. into Olfusa R. Historical locality of Thingvellir on N shore.

Thingvellir (thĕng'gvĕt"lĭr), Icelandic *Þingvellir,* locality, Arne co., SW Iceland, on N shore of Thingvallavatn, 25 mi. ENE of Reykjavik. Icelandic republic founded here (A.D. 930); meeting place (930–1798) of the Althing (parliament). Independent republic of Iceland proclaimed here, June 17, 1944. Surrounded by volcanic hills, site has noted lava formations.

Thingvold, Norway: see TINGVOLL.

Thio (tē'ō), village (pop. 550), Massawa div., SE Eritrea, fishing port on Red Sea, 120 mi. SE of Massawa; 14°40'N 40°57'E.

Thio (tyō), village (dist. pop. 2,802), E New Caledonia, 45 mi. NNW of Nouméa; nickel mines; agr. products, livestock.

Thionville (tyōvēl'), Ger. *Diedenhofen* (dē'dùnhōfùn), town (pop. 15,195), Moselle dept., NE France, port on the Moselle, near Luxembourg border, and 17 mi. N of Metz; industrial and communications center in iron-mining dist. Heavy metallurgy (blast furnaces, forges, steel rolling mills, aluminum and copper foundries); mfg. of railroad equipment, kitchen ranges, plumbing equipment, fertilizer, cement, lubricating oils. Formerly fortified, it remains a garrison town. Seized (1643) from its Sp. garrison by Louis II of Condé; defended (1815) by General Hugo (Victor Hugo's father); scene (1870) of Prussian victory over Fr. Marshal Bazaine. Suffered some damage in Second World War.

Thira, Greece: see THERA.

Thirasia, Greece: see THERASIA.

Third Connecticut Lake, N.H.: see CONNECTICUT LAKES.

Thirlmere, lake in the Lake District, S Cumberland, England, 4 mi. SE of Keswick; 3 mi. long, ¼ mi. wide. The lake is a source of water for Manchester, with which it is connected by a 100-mi.-long aqueduct built 1894. Its level has been raised by construction of a dam.

Thiron (tērō'), village (pop. 310), Eure-et-Loir dept., NW central France, in the Perche hills, 8 mi. E of Nogent-le-Rotrou; livestock.

Thirsk (thûrsk), town and parish (pop. 2,658), North Riding, N central Yorkshire, England, on a tributary of Swale R. and 10 mi. NE of Ripon; agr. market; flour mills and agr.-machinery works. Has 15th-cent. church and remains of Norman castle. Site of racecourse.

Thirumangalam, India: see TIRUMANGALAM.

Thiruvanaikoil, India: see SRIRANGAM, city.

Thiruvella, India: see TIRUVALLA.

Thisselt, Belgium: see TISSELT.

Thisted (tē'stĕdh), amt (□ 686; 1950 pop. 88,091), N Jutland, Denmark; comprises Thy or Ty (both: tü) (W peninsula of Jutland N of Lim Fjord),

Mors isl., other small isls.; ⊙ Thisted. Thy peninsula is low, wooded region; chalk and limestone quarries. Mors isl. is more fertile. Chief cities: Nykobing, Thisted.

Thisted, city (1950 pop. 9,155), ⊙ Thisted amt, N Jutland, Denmark, on Lim Fjord, 45 mi. W of Aalborg; 56°57'N 8°32'E. Machinery and textile mfg.; shipbuilding. Has 13th-cent. church.

Thistil Fjord (thĭ'stŭl), Icelandic *Þistilfjörður* (thĭ'-stĭlfyûr"dhür), inlet (25 mi. long, 40 mi. wide at mouth) of Greenland Sea, NE Iceland, bet. Melrakkasletta and Langanes peninsulas; 66°20'N 15°25'W. Raufarhofn and Thorshofn, fishing villages, are on fjord.

Thistle, Md.: see ILCHESTER.

Thistle Island (□ 15; pop. 6), South Australia, in Indian Ocean, at entrance to Spencer Gulf, 6 mi. off S coast of Eyre Peninsula; 9 mi. long, 2 mi. wide; rises to 772 ft. Rugged; limestone cliffs; livestock, barley.

Thithia or **Cicia** (both: dhēdhē'ä), limestone island (□ 13; pop. 750), Lau group, Fiji, SW Pacific; 4 mi. long; copra.

Thivai, Greece: see THEBES.

Thiverval (tēvĕrväl'), village (pop. 166), Seine-et-Oise dept., N central France, 10 mi. WNW of Versailles. Natl. agr. college at near-by Grignon.

Thiviers (tēvyā'), town (pop. 2,397), Dordogne dept., SW France, 19 mi. NE of Périgueux; paper and cement mills; mfg. (tools, slippers); goose liver and truffle processing.

Thizy (tēzē'), town (pop. 3,391), Rhône dept., E central France, in the Monts du Beaujolais, 12 mi. E of Roanne; cotton-weaving center (chiefly shirts).

Thjorsa (thyōrs'ou"), Icelandic *Þjórsá*, river, central and SW Iceland, rises on central plateau NE of Hofsjokull, flows c.125 mi. SW to Atlantic 8 mi. ESE of Stokkseyri.

Thoen (tŭn), village (1937 pop. 5,192), Lampang prov., N Thailand, on Wang R. and 50 mi. SSW of Lampang; gold mining.

Thog Daurakpa, Tibet: see THOK DAURAKPA.

Thog Jalung, Tibet: see THOK JALUNG.

Thoiras, France: see LASALLE.

Thoissey (twäsā'), village (pop. 993), Ain dept., E France, river port near the Saône (canal), 9 mi. S of Mâcon; wicker-furniture, hosiery mfg., tanning.

Thok Daurakpa (tōk' dou'räkpä) or **Thog Daurakpa** (tōg'), Chinese *Tui-la-k'o-p'a* (twā'lä'kŭ'pä'), town, central Tibet, on Chang Tang plateau, 290 mi. NW of Shigatse; 32°10'N 85°20'E. Gold mines.

Thok Jalung (tōk' jä'lōōng) or **Thog Jalung** (tōg'), Chinese *Cha-lun* (jä'lōōn'), town, W central Tibet, in Aling Kangri range, 85 mi. NE of Gartok; alt. 16,330 ft. Gold mines; trades in wool, barley, salt).

Tholen or **Tolen** (both: tō'lŭn), island, Zeeland prov., SW Netherlands, NW of Bergen op Zoom; bounded by the Eendgracht (N, E), the Mastgat (NW), the Eastern Scheldt (S, SW); 11 mi. long, 6 mi. wide. Agr. (root vegetables, sugar beets, potatoes, wheat, oats); oyster culture. Chief town, Tholen (pop. 2,909), 4.5 mi. NW of Bergen op Zoom; anchovy-fishing center. Isl. flooded in Second World War.

Tholey (tō'lī), village (pop. 1,570), NE Saar, 7 mi. W of St. Wendel; stock, grain. Founded as Roman settlement, formerly site of 7th-cent. Benedictine abbey, of which early-Gothic church remains. Many Roman relics in vicinity.

Tholy, Le (lŭ tôlē'), village (pop. 292), Vosges dept., E France, 9 mi. NE of Remiremont; cheese mfg., linen milling.

Thomar, Portugal: see TOMAR.

Thomas. 1 County (□ 540; pop. 33,932), S Ga.; ⊙ THOMASVILLE. Bounded S by Fla. line; drained by Ochlockonee and Aucilla rivers. Coastal plain agr. (cotton, tobacco, corn, melons, pecans, peanuts, livestock) and forestry (lumber, naval stores) area. Formed 1825. **2** County (□ 1,070; pop. 7,572), NW Kansas; ⊙ Colby. Rolling plain, drained by headstreams of Solomon and Saline rivers. Grain, livestock. Formed 1885. **3** County (□ 716; pop. 1,206), central Nebr.; ⊙ Thedford. Agr. area drained by Middle Loup and Dismal rivers; much of Halsey Div. of Nebr. Natl. Forest in E. Livestock, grain. Formed 1825.

Thomas. 1 Town (pop. 1,171), Custer co., W Okla., 19 mi. NE of Clinton, in agr. area (wheat, cotton, sweet potatoes; dairy products; livestock); cotton ginning, sweet-potato canning; ships sweet-potato seedlings. Platted 1902. **2** City (pop. 1,146), Tucker co., NE W.Va., 10 mi. ENE of Parsons, near Md. line; trade center for coal-mining and agr. region. Blackwater Falls State Park is near by. Founded 1884.

Thomas, Fort, Ky.: see FORT THOMAS.

Thomasboro, village (pop. 330), Champaign co., E Ill., 9 mi. NNE of Champaign, in agr. area.

Thomas Point, Md.: see SOUTH RIVER.

Thomasroith (tō'märoit), village, SW central Upper Austria, 19 mi. WSW of Wels, in Hausruck Mts.; rail terminus. Lignite mining.

Thomaston. 1 Town (pop. 1,027), Marengo co., W Ala., c.20 mi. SE of Demopolis; lumber. **2** Town (pop. 4,896), Litchfield co., W Conn., on Naugatuck R. and 8 mi. N of Waterbury; clock-making center since early 19th cent.; glass and metal products, machinery; agr. (dairy products, truck, fruit). Settled 1728, set off from Plymouth 1875. **3** City (pop. 6,580), ⊙ Upson co., W central Ga., 38 mi. W of Macon; textile center in agr. (cotton, peaches) and livestock area; mfg. (tire cord, fabric, sheeting, boxes, lumber); ships peaches. Inc. 1825. **4** Town (pop. 2,810), including Thomaston village (pop. 2,398), Knox co., S Maine, with small port at head of St. George R. inlet, just SW of Rockland; cement plant. State prison. "Montpelier," home of Henry Knox, is restored. Trading post c.1630, fort 1719, inc. 1777. **5** Residential suburban village (pop. 2,045), Nassau co., SE N.Y., on NW Long Isl., just SE of Great Neck village. Inc. 1931.

Thomastown, Gaelic *Baile Mhic Anndáin*, town (pop. 806), central Co. Kilkenny, Ireland, on the Nore and 10 mi. SSE of Kilkenny; agr. market (cattle; barley, potatoes). Site of Thomastown Castle.

Thomasville. 1 Town (pop. 2,425), Clarke co., SW Ala., 55 mi. SW of Selma; lumber milling, cotton ginning, cooperage. Founded 1887. **2** City (pop. 14,424), ⊙ Thomas co., S Ga., 32 mi. NNE of Tallahassee, Fla., near Ochlockonee R. Market and processing center for farm and timber region; mfg. of cotton thread, clothing, boxes, lumber; fruit and vegetable canning and packing, meat packing, peanut processing, silica-sand mining; railroad shops. Winter resort; large estates and gardens near by. Founded 1826. **3** City (pop. 11,154), Davidson co., central N.C., 6 mi. SW of High Point; mfg. center known for its chairs; furniture factories, lumber, cotton, and hosiery mills. Inc. 1852.

Thomazeau (tômäzō'), town (1950 pop. 910), Ouest dept., S Haiti, on Cul-de-Sac plain, 18 mi. ENE of Port-au-Prince; sugar cane, cotton.

Thomazina, Brazil: see TOMAZINA.

Thomery (tômrē'), village (pop. 1,378), Seine-et-Marne dept., N central France, on left bank of the Seine and 4 mi. E of Fontainebleau; noted for its grapes.

Thomonde (tômōd'), village (1950 pop. 1,183), Artibonite dept., E central Haiti, 9 mi. SSE of Hinche; sugar cane.

Thompson. 1 Textile town (pop. 5,585), Windham co., extreme NE Conn., on R.I. and Mass. lines, on Quinebaug R. and 4 mi. NE of Putnam. Includes mill villages of Mechanicsville, Wilsonville, Grosvenor Dale, and North Grosvenor Dale (pop. 2,232). Thompson village has early 19th-cent. houses. Quaddick Reservoir here. Settled 1707, set off from Killingly 1785. **2** Town (pop. 698), Winnebago co., N Iowa, 10 mi. NW of Forest City; creamery. **3** Village (pop. 270), Grand Forks co., E N.Dak., 11 mi. S of Grand Forks, in potato-growing area. **4** Village (pop. 1,158, with adjacent Tower Hill), Fayette co., SW Pa., 10 mi. NW of Uniontown. **5** Borough (pop. 320), Susquehanna co., NE Pa., 7 mi. SE of Susquehanna.

Thompson, Lake, Kingsbury co., E S.Dak., SE of De Smet; 3 mi. long, 2 mi. wide.

Thompson Cone, N.Mex.: see MIMBRES MOUNTAINS.

Thompson Falls, town (pop. 851), ⊙ Sanders co., NW Mont., on the Clark Fork and 80 mi. NW of Missoula; lead, silver mines; hay, potatoes, timber. Near-by dam on the Clark Fork used to produce hydroelectric power.

Thompson Island, E Mass., in Boston Bay SSE of downtown Boston; c.1 mi. long.

Thompson Lake, village, S Mackenzie Dist., Northwest Territories, on small Thompson L., 30 mi. ENE of Yellowknife; gold mining.

Thompson Lake, SW Maine, E of Otisfield; c.9 mi. long; drains N, past Oxford, into Little Androscoggin R.; resorts.

Thompson Peak. 1 In Calif.: see KLAMATH MOUNTAINS. **2** In N central N.Mex., in Sangre de Cristo Mts., 8 mi. E of Santa Fe; 10,546 ft.

Thompson River, S B.C., formed at Kamloops by the North Thompson and South Thompson rivers; flows W and S to Fraser R. at Lytton. North Thompson R. rises in the Rockies in Thompson Icefield on slope of Mt. Sir John Thompson, flows S, past Blue River, and SW to Kamloops. South Thompson R. issues from Shuswap L., flows SW to Kamloops. Thompson R. is 304 mi. long to head of North Thompson R. Discovered 1808 by Simon Fraser.

Thompson River, S Iowa and N Mo., rises near Greenfield, Iowa, flows c.175 mi. SE and S to Grand R. near Chillicothe, Mo.

Thompsons Creek or **Thompson Creek,** SE Miss., rises in N Wayne co., flows c.50 mi. generally S to Leaf R. c.8 mi. E of New Augusta.

Thompson's Falls, Kenya: see THOMSON'S FALLS.

Thompson's River, NW Mont., rises in Thompson Lakes (small chain c.10 mi. long, ½ mi. wide), flows c.50 mi. S, past Cabinet Mts., to the Clark Fork near Thompson Falls town.

Thompsontown, agr. borough (pop. 486), Juniata co., central Pa., 17 mi. E of Lewistown; flour, shirts; sawmills.

Thompsonville. 1 Village, Conn.: see ENFIELD. **2** Village (pop. 530), Franklin co., S Ill., 17 mi. ENE of Herrin, in bituminous-coal, agr. area. **3** Village (pop. 313), Benzie co., NW Mich., on Betsie R. and 24 mi. SW of Traverse City; wood products.

Thomson. 1 City (pop. 3,489), ⊙ McDuffie co., E Ga., 28 mi. W of Augusta; rayon-weaving and wood-working center. Gold mines near by. Inc. 1854. **2** Village (pop. 559), Carroll co., NW Ill., near the Mississippi, 9 mi. NNE of Clinton (Iowa), in rich agr. area. Hunting near by. **3** Village (pop. 170), Carlton co., E Minn., on St. Louis R., near Wis. line, and 16 mi. WSW of Duluth; grain, potatoes. Jay Cook State Park is near by.

Thomson's Falls, town (pop. c.2,000), W central Kenya, on Laikipia Plateau E of Great Rift Valley, 30 mi. NNE of Nakuru; alt. 7,680 ft.; rail spur terminus and resort, in farming dist. (coffee, wheat, tea, corn). Falls are 243 ft. high. Also spelled Thompson's Falls.

Thonburi (tôn'bōōrē'), city (1947 pop. 167,046), ⊙ Thonburi prov. (□ 142; 1947 pop. 289,352), S Thailand, right-bank portion of BANGKOK conurbation, on Chao Phraya R. opposite Bangkok proper; terminus (Bangkok Noi station) of railroad to Malaya; industrial center; saw- and rice mills along river front. Arsenal, naval col. Fruit gardening on outskirts. The original site of Bangkok, Thonburi was (1767–82) temporary ⊙ Thailand following fall of Ayutthaya and prior to founding of new Bangkok on left bank.

Thônes (tōn), village (pop. 1,398), Haute-Savoie dept., SE France, on the Fier and 10 mi. E of Annecy, in the Bornes (Savoy Pre-Alps); alt. 2,054 ft. Winter-sports resort. Woodworking, cheese and hosiery mfg.

Thongwa (thōn'gwä"), town (pop. 10,546), Hanthawaddy dist., Lower Burma, 25 mi. E of Rangoon; head of railroad to Pegu. Center of rice-growing area; fisheries. Was ⊙ former Thongwa dist. until its dissolution (1903).

Thonon-les-Bains (tônō'-lā-bē'), town (pop. 11,267), Haute-Savoie dept., SE France, on a height overlooking S shore of L. of Geneva, 20 mi. NE of Geneva; health resort with alkaline springs; aluminum works; mfg. (flour products, pottery, clocks, hypodermic needles), woodworking. Important lumber and cheese trade. Has natl. piscicultural establishment. Connected by funicular railway with Rives, its small port. Former ⊙ Chablais.

Thonotosassa (thŭnō'tŭsä"sŭ), village (1940 pop. 515), Hillsborough co., W Fla., 12 mi. ENE of Tampa, on small L. Thonotosassa. Peat mining near by.

Thonze (thōn"zĕ'), town (pop. 7,962), Tharrawaddy dist., Pegu div., central Lower Burma, on Rangoon-Prome RR and 3 mi. S of Tharrawaddy.

Thor, town (pop. 271), Humboldt co., N central Iowa, 15 mi. NNE of Fort Dodge.

Thor, Le (lŭ tôr'), village (pop. 1,245), Vaucluse dept., SE France, 9 mi. E of Avignon; winegrowing, fruit shipping. Has church built c.1200.

Thor, Mount (9,673 ft.), SE B.C., in Monashee Mts., 28 mi. S of Revelstoke; 50°36'N 118°5'W.

Thorburn, village (pop. estimate 700), N N.S., 6 mi. ESE of New Glasgow; coal mining.

Thordsen, Cape (thôrd'sŭn, Nor. tōr'sŭn), on N shore of Is Fjord, central West Spitsbergen, Spitsbergen group, bet. mouth of Nord Fjord (W) and Bille Fjord (E), 15 mi. N of Longyear City; 78° 27'N 15°30'E. Mining of phosphate deposits begun by Swedes, 1872–73; later discontinued. Site (1882–83) of Swedish observation station during 1st International Polar Year.

Thorenburg, Rumania: see TURDA, town.

Thorenc (tôrăk'), health resort, Alpes-Maritimes dept., SE France, in Provence Alps, 11 mi. NNW of Grasse; alt. 4,100 ft. Sanatoriums.

Thorens-Glières (tôrā'-glēâr'), village (pop. 290), Haute-Savoie dept., SE France, in the Bornes (Savoy Pre-Alps), 9 mi. NE of Annecy; cheese mfg. St. Francis of Sales b. here. Until 1947, called Thorens.

Thoré River (tôrā'), in Tarn dept., S France, rises SW of Saint-Pons (Hérault dept.), flows 35 mi. W, through textile-mfg. region (Labastide-Rouairoux, Mazamet, Labruguière) to the Agout 2 mi. SW of Castres.

Thorhild, village (pop. estimate 300), central Alta., 45 mi. NNE of Edmonton; coal mining; wheat, dairying.

Thorigny or **Thorigny-sur-Marne** (tôrēnyē'-sür-märn'), town (pop. 2,598), Seine-et-Marne dept., N central France, on right bank of Marne R., opposite Lagny, and 17 mi. E of Paris; foundries.

Thorisvatn (thō'rĭsvä"tŭn), Icelandic *Þórisvatn*, lake (□ c.27), S central Iceland; 65°16'N 18°53'W. It is 8 mi. long. Drains N into Pjorsa R.

Thorn or **Torn** (both: tôrn), village (pop. 1,930), Limburg prov., SE Netherlands, 7 mi. WSW of Roermond, on Belg. border; brickworks.

Thorn, Poland: see TORUN.

Thornaby-on-Tees (thôr'nŭbē, tēz), municipal borough (1931 pop. 21,233; 1951 census 23,413), North Riding, N Yorkshire, England, 3 mi. WSW of Middlesbrough and on Tees R. opposite Stockton; steel milling, shipbuilding, mfg. of concrete.

Thornapple River, S central and SW Mich., rises SW of Lansing in Eaton co., flows c.80 mi. NW, past Vermontville, Nashville, Hastings, and Middleville, to Grand R. 9 mi. E of Grand Rapids.

Thornbrough Channel (17 mi. long, 1–3 mi. wide), SW B.C., W entrance of Howe Sound from Strait of Georgia, separates Gambier Isl. (E) and W shore of Howe Sound. Port Mellon, Gibsons Landing, and Hopkins Landing are on W shore.

Thornburg. 1 Town (pop. 138), Keokuk co., SE Iowa, 20 mi. NE of Oskaloosa; livestock, grain. 2 Borough (pop. 335), Allegheny co., SW Pa., just W of Pittsburgh.

Thornbury, town (pop. 838), S Ont., on Nottawasaga Bay, inlet of Georgian Bay, 24 mi. E of Owen Sound; apple packing, flour milling, brick and tile mfg.

Thornbury, town and parish (pop. 2,645), SW Gloucester, England, 11 mi. NNE of Bristol; agr. market. Has early 16th-cent. castle (incomplete) built by duke of Buckingham.

Thorncliffe, town in ECCLESFIELD parish, West Riding, S Yorkshire, England, 6 mi. N of Sheffield; steel center (blast furnaces, rolling mill, foundries); chemical works and iron mines.

Thorndale, town (pop. 855), Milam co., central Texas, 40 mi. NE of Austin; trade point in cotton, corn, grain area; cotton processing; ships mineral salts (wells near by). Settled 1880, inc. 1929.

Thorndike. 1 Town (pop. 534), Waldo co., S Maine, 15 mi. NW of Belfast, in agr., recreational area. 2 Village, Mass.: see PALMER.

Thorne, town and parish (pop. 14,606), West Riding, S Yorkshire, England, on Don R. and 9 mi. NE of Doncaster; coal-mining center. Has church dating from 12th cent.

Thorne, village (pop. 37), Rolette co., N N.Dak., 17 mi. SW of Rolla.

Thorne Centre, village, SW Que., 40 mi. NW of Ottawa; mica mining.

Thorney, town and parish (pop. 2,119), in Isle of Ely, N Cambridge, England, 6 mi. ENE of Peterborough; agr. market. Has ruins of 12th-cent. abbey; abbey church rebuilt 1638. In late 11th cent. Hereward the Wake made a stand here against William the Conqueror.

Thorney Island, England: see CHICHESTER HARBOUR.

Thornhill, village (pop. estimate 850), S Ont., 12 mi. N of Toronto; dairying, truck gardening.

Thornhill, England: see DEWSBURY.

Thornhill. 1 Town (pop. 1,044) in Morton parish (pop. 1,661), W Dumfries, Scotland, on Nith R. and 14 mi. NW of Dumfries; agr. market; ham and bacon curing. Has natural history mus. and 18th-cent. market cross. Near by are several anc. castles. On Nith R., 2 mi. N, is agr. village of Carronbridge. 2 Agr. village, S Perthshire, Scotland, 7 mi. W of Dunblane, near Doune.

Thorn Hill, suburb (pop. 1,753) of Frankfort, Franklin co., N central Ky.

Thornliebank (thôrn″lēbăngk′), S industrial suburb of Glasgow, Scotland, in Eastwood parish.

Thornloe (thôrn′lō), village (pop. 145), E Ont., 16 mi. NNW of Haileybury, in lumbering and mining region (gold, silver, cobalt).

Thornton, Yorkshire, England: see BRADFORD.

Thornton, town in Markinch parish, central Fifeshire, Scotland, 6 mi. WSW of Leven; coal mining.

Thornton. 1 Village (1940 pop. 636), Calhoun co., S Ark., 24 mi. NE of Camden, in agr. and timber area. 2 Village (pop. 1,217), Cook co., NE Ill., S suburb of Chicago; makes limestone products. Inc. 1900. 3 Town (pop. 441), Cerro Gordo co., N Iowa, 17 mi. SSW of Mason City, in agr. area. 4 Town (pop. 460), Grafton co., central N.H., on Pemigewasset R. and 9 mi. N of Plymouth; agr., summer colony. 5 Village, R.I.: see JOHNSTON. 6 Town (pop. 623), Limestone co., E central Texas, 33 mi. ESE of Waco; trade point in cotton, timber area; lumber milling.

Thornton Cleveleys (klēv′līz), urban district (1931 pop. 10,152; 1951 census 15,437), W Lancashire, England. Includes market town of Thornton, 3 mi. S of Fleetwood, and, just W, on Irish Sea, market town and seaside resort of Cleveleys.

Thornton Heath, England: see CROYDON.

Thornton-le-Moors, village and parish (pop. 166), NW of Cheshire, England, 5 mi. NNE of Chester; mfg. of petroleum chemicals. Has 17th-cent. mansion of Elton Hall and 16th-cent. church.

Thornton River, N Va., rises in the Blue Ridge in Rappahannock co., flows c.40 mi. generally SE to Rappahannock R. 9 mi. NE of Culpeper.

Thorntown, town (pop. 1,380), Boone co., central Ind., on Sugar Creek and 18 mi. ENE of Crawfordsville, in livestock and grain area; livestock serums; poultry hatcheries. Settled 1830.

Thornville, village (pop. 432), Perry co., central Ohio, 11 mi. S of Newark, in agr. area.

Thornwood, residential village (1940 pop. 1,347), Westchester co., SE N.Y., just S of Pleasantville; marble products.

Thorofare, N.J.: see PAULSBORO.

Thorold (thô′rōld, -rŭld, thŭ′-), town (pop. 5,305), S Ont., on Welland Ship Canal and 4 mi. SE of St. Catherines; paper, pulp, and lumber mills, abrasives works.

Thoronet, Le (lù tôrōnā′), village (pop. 224), Var dept., SE France, near the Argens, 10 mi. SW of Draguignan; bauxite mining.

Thorp, city (pop. 1,383), Clark co., central Wis. 36 mi. ENE of Eau Claire, in dairying region; makes cheese, evaporated milk; sawmill; nurseries. Inc. as village in 1893, as city in 1948.

Thorpe, residential town and parish (pop. 1,280), NW Surrey, England, 2 mi. SSE of Egham. Has 14th-cent. church.

Thorpe, village (pop. 1,362), McDowell co., S W.Va., 7 mi. SE of Welch; bituminous-coal area.

Thorsby (thôrz′bē), village (pop. estimate 300), central Alta., near North Saskatchewan R., 32 mi. SW of Edmonton; coal mining.

Thorsby, town (pop. 828), Chilton co., central Ala., 6 mi. NW of Clanton, in fruit and cotton area; lumber. Seat of Thorsby Inst.

Thorshavn (tôrs″houn′), Faeroese *Tórshavn*, city (pop. 4,390) and port, ⊙ Faeroe Isls., on SE Stromo isl., on Nolso Fjord; 62°1′N 6°46′W. Seafaring, fishing; commercial center for Faeroes. Settlement probably dates from 10th cent.

Thorshofn (thōrs′hû″pùn), Icelandic *Þórshöfn*, fishing village (pop. 357), Thingeyjar co., NE Iceland, at base of Langanes peninsula, on SE shore of Thistil Fjord; 66°12′N 15°20′W.

Thorvald Nilson Mountains (thôr′vôld nĭl′sùn), massif (c.13,000 ft.) of Queen Maud Range, Antarctica; 86°20′S 158°W. Discovered 1911 by Amundsen.

Thorvik, Norway: see TORVIK.

Thotnot (tôt′nôt′), town, Longxuyen prov., S Vietnam, on Bassac R., in Mekong delta, 10 mi. SE of Longxuyen; rice mill, distillery.

Thottayam or **Thottiam** (tō′tŭyŭm), town (pop. 7,202), Trichinopoly dist., S Madras, India, on Cauvery R. and 26 mi. WNW of Trichinopoly; rice, plantain. Seasonal temple-festival market. Sometimes spelled Tottiyam.

Thouarcé (tōōärsā′), village (pop. 627), Maine-et-Loire dept., W France, on the Layon and 14 mi. S of Angers; winegrowing center; liqueur distilling. Lignite deposits near by.

Thouars (tōōär′), town (pop. 9,865), Deux-Sèvres dept., W France, on the Thouet and 21 mi. SSW of Saumur; road and railroad center, livestock market; meat preserving, mfg. (flour products, casein, paints). Has two 12th–15th-cent. churches and a castle atop a rock overlooking the river. Its feudal lords adhered to English cause throughout Hundred Years War. Damaged in Second World War.

Thouet River (tōōā′), Deux-Sèvres and Maine-et-Loire depts., W France, rises in Gâtine hills 3 mi. W of Secondigny, flows 70 mi. N, past Parthenay, Airvault, Thouars, and Montreuil-Bellay (head of navigation), to the Loire near Saumur. Receives the Argenton (left) and the Dive (right).

Thoune, town, Switzerland: see THUN.

Thourotte (tōōrôt′), town (pop. 2,393), Oise dept., N France, on the Oise and its lateral canal, and 5 mi. NE of Compiègne; mirror and asphalt works.

Thourout, Belgium: see TORHOUT.

Thousand Island Park, N.Y.: see WELLESLEY ISLAND.

Thousand Islands, group of over 1,500 small isls. in a widening of the St. Lawrence at the outlet of L. Ontario, near Kingston, Ont., some belonging to Canada, some to U.S., and some to individuals. Group includes isls. of: Amherst, Wolfe, Howe, Simcoe, Grenadier (Ont.); Grindstone, Wells, and Carleton (N.Y.). Popular and beautiful summer resort. On Ont. mainland and several Canadian isls. is St. Lawrence Isls. Natl. Park (189 acres; established 1914).

Thousand Islands, Du. *Duizend Eilanden* (doi′zùnd ī′ländùn), group of c.100 coral islets of Indonesia, in Java Sea, off NW coast of Java, 40 mi. NNW of Jakarta; 5°35′S 106°33′E; only about 5 isls. are inhabited. Coconuts and fish are main products.

Thousand Islands International Bridge, links U.S. and Canada, spanning the St. Lawrence bet. Collins Landing, N.Y., and vicinity of Gananoque, Ont. Consists of 2 main suspension structures, 3 smaller bridges, and roadways across Wellesley and Hill isls.; total length, c.6½ mi. Completed 1938.

Thousand Lake Mountain, Utah: see FISH LAKE PLATEAU.

Thousand Oaks, village (pop. 1,243), Ventura co., S Calif., 25 mi. ESE of Ventura.

Thousand Palms, resort village (pop. c.200), Riverside co., S Calif., 8 mi. ESE of Palm Springs, in Coachella Valley.

Thousand Temples, The, Indonesia: see CHANDI SEWU.

Thrace (thrās), anc. *Thracia* (thrā′sēù), Bulg. *Trakiya* (träkē′yä), Gr. *Thrake* or *Thraki* (both: thrä′kē), region of SE Europe, of varying extent at different periods. In earliest times, it was considered bounded N by the Danube, E by Black Sea, S by Sea of Marmara and Aegean Sea, and SW by Macedonia along the Rhodope Mts., and drained by Maritsa R. in what is still known as the Thracian Plain. The region was settled by tribes akin to the Illyrians. Greek colonies established along its shores includes Abdera, Aenus (Enos), Byzantium (later Constantinople and Istanbul), Apollonia (Sozopol), and Tomi (Constanta). The Roman prov. of Thrace (created A.D. 46), with chief centers at Serdica (Sofia), Philippopolis (Plovdiv), and Adrianople (Edirne), extended only N to the Balkan Mts., the N section bet. the Balkans and the Danube being included in Lower Moesia. Following the Barbarian invasions, this N section passed (7th cent.) to Bulgarians; the S (Byzantine) part went to Turks in 1361. The entire region was controlled (1453–1878) by Ottoman Empire and considered part of Rumelia. Following the separation (1878) of Bulgaria and autonomous Eastern Rumelia (both were merged, 1885), the political meaning of the term Thrace became restricted to then remaining Turkish (S) Thrace, which was further carved up after the Balkan Wars (1912–13). According to 1913 treaties of Bucharest (bet. Bulgaria and Greece) and of Constantinople (bet. Bulgaria and Turkey), W Thrace (bet. Mesta and Maritsa rivers) passed to Bulgaria and E Thrace (E of the Maritsa) to Turkey. Bulgaria also obtained (1913) a small area on the Black Sea around Malko Tirnovo. The Maritsa line was slightly modified (1915) by the Sofia treaty. Following the First World War, the Bulg. hold on W Thrace was restricted by the Treaty of Neuilly (1919) to the N mtn. half in the Rhodopes, corresponding to the Arda R. valley; Greece received the S remainder of W Thrace on the Aegean coast. E Thrace, up to the Catalca (Chatalja) line, was also adjudged to Greece by the Treaty of Sèvres (1920; never in effect) which was, however, nullified by the Conference of Lausanne (1923), which left E Thrace to Turkey, separated by Maritsa R. from Greek Thrace. Turkish Thrace, without separate administrative status, corresponds to TURKEY in Europe and contains the provs. of Adrianople (Edirne), Kirklareli, Tekirdag, and European sections of Istanbul and Canakkale provs. Greek Thrace constitutes the major administrative division of Thrace (□ 3,315; pop. 359,923; ⊙ Komotine), formerly called Western Thrace [Gr. *Dytike Thrake* or *Dhitiki Thraki*], divided into the nomes of HEVROS, RHODOPE, and XANTHE. Thrace is largely agricultural, producing tobacco, wheat, silk, cotton, olive oil and fruit.

Thracian Chersonese, Turkey: see GALLIPOLI PENINSULA.

Thracian Plain, Bulg. *Trakiyska Nizina*, in central Bulgaria, bordered by Sredna Gora, outlier of Balkan Mts. (N), Rhodope Mts. (S), and Tundzha R. (E); drained by Maritsa R. Includes basins of Plovdiv, Stara Zagora, and Khaskovo.

Thracian Sea, Greece: see AEGEAN SEA.

Thracica, Chersonesus, Turkey: see GALLIPOLI PENINSULA.

Thrall (thrôl), town (pop. 585), Williamson co., central Texas, 34 mi. NE of Austin, in farm area (cotton, corn, truck). Had oil booms (1925, 1930).

Thrapston, town and parish (pop. 1,679), E Northampton, England, on Nene R. and 8 mi. E of Kettering; agr. market; metalworking. Has 13th–14th-cent. church and 17th-cent. bridge.

Threapland, England: see BOTHEL AND THREAPLAND.

Three Brothers, Fr. *Trois Frères* (trwä′ frâr′), uninhabited islands (□ 345 acres) of Chagos Archipelago in Indian Ocean, a dependency of Mauritius; 6°9′S 71°35′E.

Three Cities, name applied to 3 old adjacent towns, SENGLEA, COSPICUA, and VITTORIOSA (total pop. 11,394), SE Malta, across Grand Harbour from Valletta.

Three Forks, village, S B.C., in Selkirk Mts., near Slocan L., 35 mi. N of Nelson; silver, lead, zinc mining.

Three Forks, town (pop. 1,114), Gallatin co., SW Mont., near point at which Gallatin R. joins Jefferson and Madison rivers to form Missouri R., 30 mi. NW of Bozeman; grain, livestock. Site of town was once visited by Lewis and Clark.

Three Hills, town (pop. estimate 1,000), S Alta., 30 mi. NW of Drumheller; coal mining; grain elevators, stock.

Three Kings Islands, uninhabited group (□ c.3) of 3 rocky islets in S Pacific, 40 mi. WNW of N.Isl., New Zealand; largest is 1.5 mi. long; bird sanctuary.

Three Lakes, resort village (pop. c.500), Oneida co., N Wis., 15 mi. NE of Rhinelander, in lake region; lumbering, submarginal farming.

Three Oaks, village (pop. 1,572), Berrien co., extreme SW Mich., 20 mi. NW of South Bend (Ind.), in area growing fruit, corn, wheat; mfg. (lingerie, braid). Has mus. containing Indian and historic relics. Settled 1850, inc. 1867.

Three Pagodas Pass (alt. 925 ft.), on Burma-Thailand line, in the Tenasserim Yoma, 100 mi. SE of Moulmein, on chief route linking the two countries. During Second World War, Thanbyuzayat–Ban Pong RR was built by Japanese through the pass.

Three Point, mining village, Harlan co., SE Ky., in the Cumberlands, 28 mi. ENE of Middlesboro; bituminous coal.

Three Points, Cape, SW Gold Coast, on Gulf of Guinea, 25 mi. WSW of Takoradi; 4°44′N 2°4′W; lighthouse.

Three Rivers, Que.: see TROIS RIVIÈRES.

Three Rivers. 1 Village, Tulare co., central Calif., on Kaweah R. and 22 mi. ENE of Visalia, in Sierra Nevada foothills; hq. for Kings Canyon and Sequoia natl. parks (E). 2 Village, Mass.: see PALMER. 3 City (pop. 6,785), St. Joseph co., SW Mich., 25 mi. S of Kalamazoo, and on St. Joseph R. near influx of short Portage and Rocky rivers. Trade and industrial center for farm area; mfg. (railroad equipment, stokers, machinery, paper products, clothing); nursery. Has remains of Indian village sites and garden beds. A Fr. trading post and Jesuit mission were located here in 17th cent. Settled 1829; inc. as village 1855, as city 1895. **4** Hamlet, Otero co., S central N.Mex., just W of Sierra Blanca, 30 mi. NNW of Alamogordo; alt. c.4,550 ft. Trading and railroad-loading point in livestock region. Mescalero Indian Reservation is just E. **5** Town (pop. 2,026), Live Oak co., S Texas, 28 mi. W of Beeville and on Frio R. just below influx of Atascosa R. and just above mouth of the Frio on the Nueces; a trade center in agr., cattle-ranching, oil- and gas-producing area; oil refinery, creamery, glass and tile plants. Inc. 1927.

Three Saints Bay, small inlet, SE Kodiak Isl., S Alaska, on Gulf of Alaska, W of Sitkalidak Isl., 60 mi. SW of Kodiak; 57°8′N 153°30′W; site of Russian settlement in Alaska, established 1784 by Grigorii Shelekhov (Gregory Shelekov) and named after one of his ships; moved to Kodiak, 1792. Now site of Old Harbor village.

Three Sisters, 3 peaks of Cascade Range, central Oregon, W of Bend. They are North Sister (10,094 ft.), Middle Sister (10,053 ft.), and South Sister (10,354 ft.). Large glaciers on all 3.

Three Sisters, The, mountain (9,744 ft.), SW Alta., near B.C. border, in Rocky Mts., on SE edge of Banff Natl. Park, 15 mi. SE of Banff.

Three Springs, borough (pop. 417), Huntingdon co., S central Pa., 14 mi. SSW of Mount Union.

Three Villages, name applied to ATTARD, BALZAN, and LIJA (total pop. 7,067), central Malta, c.3 mi. W of Valletta, in orange-growing dist.

Throckley, England: see NEWBURN.

Throckmorton (thrŏk′môrtun), county (□ 913; pop. 3,618), N Texas; ⊙ Throckmorton. Drained by Brazos R. and its Clear Fork. Agr. (wheat, cotton, grain sorghums, oats, some fruit and truck); livestock (mainly cattle; some sheep, hogs, poultry); some dairying. Oil wells. Formed 1858.

Throckmorton, town (pop. 1,320), ⊙ Throckmorton co., N Texas, c.60 mi. SW of Wichita Falls; trade, shipping center in oil, cattle, agr. (wheat, cotton, poultry) area. Settled before 1880, inc. 1917.

Throgs Neck (thrŏgz), SE N.Y., peninsula in the Bronx borough of New York city, marking N side of mouth of East R. on Long Island Sound. Lighthouse at its tip (40°48′N 73°47′W). Here is U.S. Fort Schuyler, seat of N.Y. State Maritime Col.

Thromö, Norway: see TROMOY.

Throop (trōōp, thrōōp), anthracite-mining borough (pop. 5,861), Lackawanna co., NE Pa., on Lackawanna R. and 3 mi. NE of Scranton.

Throston, England: see HARTLEPOOL.

Thrupp, agr. village and parish (pop. 1,254), central Gloucester, England, on Frome R. just SE of Stroud.

Thrussington, town and parish (pop. 522), NE Leicester, England, on Wreak R. and 8 mi. NE of Leicester; shoe industry. Has 14th-cent. church.

Thrybergh (thrī′bûr, –bûrû), town and parish (pop. 3,876), West Riding, S Yorkshire, England, 3 mi. NE of Rotherham; coal mining.

Thuanan (twŭn′ăn′), village, Thuathien prov., central Vietnam, seaside resort on South China Sea, 5 mi. NE of Hue.

Thuathien, province, Vietnam: see HUE.

Thubursicum Numidarum, Algeria: see KHEMISSA.

Thudaumot (tōō′zou′mōt′), town, ⊙ Thudaumot prov. (□ 2,000; 1943 pop. 230,600), S Vietnam, on Saigon-Locninh RR and 15 mi. N of Saigon; timber-trading center; rice, rubber, sugar cane, castor beans. School of applied arts. Military barracks.

Thuduc (tōō′ dōōk′), town, Giadinh prov., S Vietnam, on railroad and 10 mi. NE of Saigon; rice. Railroad workshops at Dian, 4 mi. N.

Thueyts (tüā′), village (pop. 524), Ardèche dept., S France, on the Ardèche and 9 mi. WNW of Aubenas, in the Monts du Vivarais; silk throwing, fruit shipping. Small spa at Neyrac-les-Bains (2 mi. E).

Thugga, Tunisia: see DOUGGA.

Thuile, La (lä twēl′), village (pop. 287), Val d'Aosta region, NW Italy, on Little St. Bernard road, 5 mi. NE of pass; customs station; iron- and steelworks. Resort (alt. 4,726 ft.), with mineral springs. Anthracite mines near by. Called Porta Littoria c.1938–45.

Thuillies (twēyē′), village (pop. 1,797), Hainaut prov., S Belgium, 9 mi. SW of Charleroi, in sugar-beet area.

Thuin (twē), town (pop. 5,736), Hainaut prov., S Belgium, on Sambre R. and 9 mi. SW of Charleroi; barge building.

Thuir (twēr′), town (pop. 2,926), Pyrénées-Orientales dept., S France, at foot of E Pyrenees, 8 mi. SW of Perpignan, in winegrowing area; produces apéritifs, pottery.

Thule (thū′lē, thōō′lē), name given by the ancients to the most northerly land of Europe. It was an island discovered and described (c.310 B.C.) by Pytheas and variously identified with Jutland, Iceland, Norway, and Mainland isl. in the Shetlands. From it was derived the phrase "Ultima Thule," used figuratively to denote the most distant goal of human endeavor or a land remote beyond all reckoning.

Thule (tōō′lû), settlement (pop. 123), ⊙ Thule colony dist. (pop. 322), NW Greenland, on S shore of Wolstenholme Fjord, inlet of N Baffin Bay; 76°33′N 68°47′W. Walrus and polar-bear hunting center; airfield, meteorological and radio station, hosp., trading post. Noted for its pure Eskimo pop., the last group of which migrated here from Ellesmere and Devon isls., Canada, bet. 1862 and 1866, it has given its name to anthropological term Thule culture. Settlement founded (1910) by Knud Rasmussen; was private trading station until later taken over by Greenland administration. Base of Rasmussen's 5 Thule expeditions (1912–24).

Thum (tōōm), town (pop. 4,276), Saxony, E central Germany, in the Erzgebirge, 11 mi. S of Chemnitz; hosiery knitting, machinery mfg.

Thumeir, Ath, or **Ath Thumair,** or **Al-Thumayr** (all: ăth-thōōmär′), village, ⊙ Qutaibi tribal area, Western Aden Protectorate, 50 mi. NNW of Aden; 13°31′N 44°52′E. Sometimes spelled At Tamer.

Thun, Fr. *Thoune* (both: tōōn), town (1950 pop. 24,135), Bern, central Switzerland, on NW shore of L. of Thun, on Aar R. and 17 mi. SSE of Bern; year-round resort. Metal products (aluminum, copper), watches, clothes, flour; printing. Zähringen-Kyburg castle (12th cent.), Scherzligen church (12th cent.), town hall (16th cent.), parish church.

Thun, Lake of, Ger. *Thunersee* (tōō′nûrzā), Bern canton, central Switzerland; 10 mi. long, □ 18, alt. 1,830 ft., max. depth 712 ft. Aar R. enters lake at SE, connecting it with L. of Brienz, and leaves at NW, near Thun; Kander R. enters lake at NW. Situated in Bernese Alps, it is popular among tourists; several resorts lie on its shores (e.g., Spiez, Gunten, Oberhofen). Thun (NW) is main town.

Thunder Bay, district (□ 52,471; pop. 85,200), W Ont., on L. Superior and L. Nipigon; ⊙ Port Arthur.

Thunder Bay, inlet (32 mi. long, 13 mi. wide at mouth) on NW shore of L. Superior, W Ont. On W shore are Port Arthur and Fort William. Receives Kaministikwia R.

Thunder Bay River, NE Mich., rises near Atlanta in Montmorency co., flows generally E c.60 mi., through forest and farm area, past Hillman, to Thunder Bay (an inlet of L. Huron) at Alpena. Furnishes power. Chief tributaries are North Branch (c.40 mi. long), Lower South Branch (c.20 mi. long), and Upper South Branch (c.30 mi. long).

Thunderbolt, resort town (pop. 1,238), Chatham co., E Ga., just E of Savannah, near the Atlantic; fishing.

Thunder Lake, Cass co., N central Minn., 27 mi. SW of Grand Rapids, in state forest; 3 mi. long, 2 mi. wide. Resorts.

Thundersley, England: see BENFLEET.

Thunersee, Switzerland: see THUN, LAKE OF.

Thüngen (tüng′ûn), village (pop. 1,398), Lower Franconia, NW Bavaria, Germany, 10 mi. NNW of Würzburg; brewing; fruitgrowing (pears, plums). Has castle dating from 2d half of 16th cent.

Thung Song, Thailand: see CHA MAI.

Thuong, Song, Vietnam: see PHULANGTHUONG.

Thurcroft, town and parish (pop. 5,463), West Riding, S Yorkshire, England, 5 mi. SE of Rotherham; coal mining.

Thurgau (tōōr′gou), Fr. *Thurgovie* (türgôvē′), canton (□ 388; 1950 pop. 149,360), NE Switzerland; on N is the Rhine, on N and NE is L. Constance; ⊙ Frauenfeld. Fertile area (cereals, wine, cattle) drained by the Thur; numerous orchards, some gardens. Metal products, textiles, clothes, foodstuffs produced; woodworking. Pop. German speaking and largely Protestant. Became a canton in 1803.

Thüringer Saale, Germany: see SAALE RIVER.

Thuringia (thyōōrĭn′jû, thōō–), Ger. *Thüringen* (tü′rĭng-ûn), state (□ 6,022; 1946 pop. 2,927,497), central Germany; ⊙ WEIMAR. Bordered by Bavaria (S), Hesse (W), Lower Saxony (NW), Saxony-Anhalt (NE), and Saxony (E). Predominantly hilly, traversed NW-SE by THURINGIAN FOREST. Drained by Thuringian Saale, Werra, and White Elster rivers. Fertile region; grain, vegetables, fruit (JENA), sugar beets. Highly industrialized; textile-milling centers in E (APOLDA, GERA, GREIZ); important industrial hubs are ERFURT, GOTHA (railroad cars), Jena (optical instruments, glass), MÜHLHAUSEN (locomotive repair shops), NORDHAUSEN, and SONNEBERG; SCHMALKALDEN, SUHL, and ZELLA-MEHLIS are metalworking centers. Thuringian toys and glassware are world-renowned. There are numerous resorts: BAD SALZUNGEN, EISENACH, OBERHOF. The home of the Germanic Thuringians, region was conquered (6th–8th cent.) by the Franks and Christianized by St. Boniface. In 11th cent., the landgraves of Thuringia emerged as powerful princes of the Holy Roman Empire. After death (1227) of last landgrave, succession to Thuringia was long disputed, but major part eventually fell to house of Wettin, i.e., to margraves of Meissen, who in 1423 became electors of SAXONY. At division of Wettin lands (1485), most of the Thuringian territories came to Ernestine branch. In 16th cent., Thuringia was a center of the Reformation. Under the Ernestines, Thuringia split into several duchies (see SAXE-ALTENBURG, SAXE-COBURG, SAXE-GOTHA, SAXE-MEININGEN, SAXE-WEIMAR) which underwent numerous territorial redivisions in the course of their history. The states joined the German Empire in 1871; their rulers were expelled in 1918. The state of Thuringia (□ 4,541; 1939 pop. 1,743,624) was formed in 1920 under Weimar Republic through incorporation of Saxe-Coburg-Gotha (less city of Coburg, which joined Bavaria), Saxe-Altenburg, Saxe-Meiningen, Saxe-Weimar-Eisenach, and the principalities of REUSS, SCHWARZBURG-RUDOLSTADT, and SCHWARZBURG-SONDERSHAUSEN. Thuringia was greatly devastated in Second World War. After 1945, it was placed in Soviet occupation zone; it inc. many former Prussian enclaves and border areas, notably Erfurt. In 1949, Thuringia became one of the states of the German Democratic Republic (East German state).

Thuringian Forest, Ger. *Thüringer Wald* (tü′rĭng-ûr vält′), forested mountain range, central Germany, extends c.80 mi. SE-NW bet. the upper Werra and the Thuringian Saale; rises to 3,222 ft. in the Beerberg; second-highest peak is the Inselsberg (3,005 ft.). S outlier is called Franconian Forest. Noted for its scenic beauty; numerous resorts (Eisenach, Friedrichroda, Giessübel, Oberhof). Wood carving and toymaking (centered at Sonneberg) are chief home industries; glass and china mfg. is important (Ilmenau). Other mfg. centers are Schmalkalden, Suhl, and Zella-Mehlis. Slate quarrying at Lehesten. Werra and Ilm rivers rise here. Was iron-mining center until 16th cent.; small deposits of high-grade iron ore still worked in SW. Uranium-ore prospecting was begun after Second World War.

Thuringian Saale, Germany: see SAALE RIVER.

Thurles (thûr′lûs), Gaelic *Dúrla Éile*, urban district (pop. 6,011), central Co. Tipperary, Ireland, on Suir R. and 24 mi. NNW of Clonmel; agr. market (sugar beets, potatoes); sugar refineries; hunting and fishing center; site of racecourse. It is seat of R.C. archbishop of Cashel, with modern cathedral. Has 12th-cent. castle. In 1174 Donal O'Brien and Roderick O'Connor here defeated Strongbow. Near by is abbey of Holycross.

Thurlow Dam (thûr′lō), E Ala., in Tallapoosa R., at Tallassee. Privately built power dam (62 ft. high, 1,846 ft. long) completed 1931. Formerly known as Lower Tallassee Dam.

Thurlow Islands (thûr′lō) (□ 72), SW B.C., group of 2 isls. at N end of Discovery Passage, bet. Strait of Georgia and Queen Charlotte Strait NW of Sonora Isl., 26 mi. NNW of Campbell River. West Thurlow Isl. is 12 mi. long, 2–3 mi. wide; at E end is Blind Channel fishing village. East Thurlow Isl. is 11 mi. long, 4–6 mi. wide; N end is Thurlow or Shoal Bay, a gold-mining village.

Thurlstone, former urban district (1931 pop. 2,640), West Riding, S Yorkshire, England, 12 mi. NW of Sheffield; woolen milling. Inc. 1938 in Penistone.

Thurman. 1 Town (pop. 284), Fremont co., extreme SW Iowa, 30 mi. S of Council Bluffs; limestone quarries. **2** Village (pop. 142), Gallia co., S Ohio, 15 mi. WNW of Gallipolis, in agr. area. Also called Centerville.

Thurmaston, residential former urban district (1931 pop. 3,723), central Leicester, England, 3 mi. NNE of Leicester. Has ruins of 13th-cent. chapel.

Thurmond, town (pop. 219), Fayette co., S central W.Va., 13 mi. NNE of Beckley, in coal-mining and agr. region.

Thurmont, town (pop. 1,676), Frederick co., N Md., at E base of the Blue Ridge and 15 mi. N of Frederick, in agr. area; makes shoes; goldfish raising. Catoctin Recreational Demonstration Area is just W. Settled 1751.

Thurn Pass (tōōrn) (alt. 4,175 ft.), in Kitzbühel Alps, W Austria, connects Tyrol and Salzburg.

Thurnscoe (thûrns′kō), former urban district (1931 pop. 10,548), West Riding, S Yorkshire, England, 8 mi. N of Rotherham; coal mining. Inc. 1937 in Dearne.

Thur River (tür), Haut-Rhin dept., E France, rises in the high Vosges above Saint-Amarin, flows SE, past Thann and Cernay, thence NW, forming several distributaries which reach the Ill bet. Mulhouse and Colmar; c.30 mi. long.

Thur River (tōōr), NE Switzerland, rises in Churfirsten range of St. Gall canton, flows 78 mi. N and W, past Bischofszell, through Thurgau canton, to the Rhine 7 mi. S of Schaffhausen.

Thurrock, urban district (1951 census pop. 81,634), S Essex, England, c.20 mi. E of London; formed 1936 out of GRAYS THURROCK, PURFLEET, TILBURY, and other areas.

Thursday Island (pop. 944), in Torres Strait 15 mi. NW of Cape York Peninsula, Queensland, Australia, surrounded by Prince of Wales, Horn, and Hammond isls.; 1.5 mi. long, 1 mi. wide; rises to 375 ft. Partially wooded; pearl shell, trepangs. Chief town, Port Kennedy. Became (1912) a municipality of Queensland.

Thurso (thûr′sō), village (pop. 1,295), SW Que., on Ottawa R. and 24 mi. ENE of Ottawa; lumbering, dairying, stock raising.

Thurso, burgh (1931 pop. 2,946; 1951 census 3,203), N Caithness, Scotland, on Thurso Bay of the Atlantic, at mouth of Thurso R., 19 mi. NW of Wick; 58°36′N 3°32′W; agr. market and port, exporting Caithness flagstones; woolen milling.

Northernmost burgh on Scottish mainland. Has 16th-cent. church, many 17th-cent. houses, and mus. Near by are ruins of anc. bishop's palace. In Middle Ages Thurso was chief port for trade bet. Scotland and Scandinavia.

Thurso River, Caithness, Scotland, rises 5 mi. WSW of Watten, flows 27 mi. NE and N, past Halkirk, to the Atlantic at Thurso.

Thurston. 1 County (□ 390; pop. 8,590), NE Nebr.; ⊙ Pender. Farm area bounded E by Missouri R. and Iowa; drained by Logan Creek. Winnebago Indian Reservation in E, Omaha Indian Reservation in SE. Feed, livestock, grain. Formed 1889. **2** County (□ 719; pop. 44,884), W Wash.; ⊙ OLYMPIA, the state capital. Bounded NE by Nisqually R., N by Puget Sound; includes Nisqually Indian Reservation and part of Snoqualmie Natl. Forest. Lumber, coal; oysters, livestock, fruit, nuts, dairy products, poultry. Formed 1852.

Thurston. 1 Village (pop. 156), Thurston co., NE Nebr., 5 mi. N of Pender and on Logan Creek. **2** Village (pop. 454), Fairfield co., central Ohio, 24 mi. ESE of Newark, in stock-raising and farming area.

Thurstonland and Farnley Tyas, former urban district (1931 pop. 3,981), West Riding, SW Yorkshire, England. Here are woolen-milling towns of Thurstonland, 4 mi. S of Huddersfield, and Farnley Tyas, 3 mi. SE of Huddersfield. Inc. 1938 in Kirkburton.

Thurston Peninsula, Antarctica, bet. Bellingshausen Sea and Amundsen Sea; terminates in Cape Flying Fish (71°20′S 98°W). Discovered 1940 by R. E. Byrd.

Thury-Harcourt (türē'-ärkōōr'), village (pop. 614), Calvados dept., NW France, on the Orne and 14 mi. SSW of Caen; resort in hedgerow country, heavily damaged during Normandy campaign (1944) of Second World War.

Thurzo, Czechoslovakia: see GELNICA.

Thusis (tōō'zĭs), circle (pop. 3,911) and town (pop. 1,400), Grisons canton, E Switzerland; town is on Hinterrhein R. and 11 mi. SSW of Chur, at N end of Splügen Road.

Thvedestrand, Norway: see TVEDESTRAND.

Thwart Island (□ 11), E N.F., in the Bay of Exploits, inlet of Notre Dame Bay, 30 mi. SW of Twillingate; 6 mi. long, 3 mi. wide; 49°19′N 55°12′W.

Thy, Denmark: see THISTED, amt.

Thyamis River or **Thiamis River** (both: thē'ŭmĭs), in S Epirus, Greece, rises in the Merope on Albanian line 15 mi. W of Konitsa, flows 60 mi. S and W to Strait of Corfu, in delta 7 mi. NW of Egoumenitsa. Hydroelectric plant. Unsuccessfully proposed (1878) at Berlin as N limit of Greece. Formerly called Kalamas.

Thyatira, Turkey: see AKHISAR.

Thyboron, Denmark: see TYBORON.

Thy-le-Château (tē-lü-shätō'), town (pop. 1,593), Namur prov., S Belgium, 9 mi. S of Charleroi; metal foundries; metal-utensil mfg.

Thynias, Turkey: see IGNEADA.

Thyrsus River, Sardinia: see TIRSO RIVER.

Thysdrus, Tunisia: see DJEM, EL-.

Thysville (tĭsvēl'), town (1948 pop. 6,198), Leopoldville prov., W Belgian Congo, on railroad and 130 mi. ENE of Boma; commercial center with large railroad workshops; sugar mfg. for export. Also has tourist facilities and is known as a resort (alt. 2,308 ft.). R.C. and Baptist missions; hosp. for Europeans; airport.

Tiabaya (tyäbī'ä), city (pop. 2,162), Arequipa dept., S Peru, on Chili R. (irrigation) and 5 mi. SW of Arequipa; alfalfa, potatoes, sugar cane, grain, vegetables.

Tiacevo, Ukrainian SSR: see TYACHEVO.

Tiahuanaco or **Tiahuanacu** (tēäwänä'kō), town (pop. c.15,500), La Paz dept., W Bolivia, near L. Titicaca, 38 mi. WSW of La Paz, on La Paz–Guaqui RR. Near by is anc. ruined city (alt. 12,645 ft.) of Tiahuanaco, one of major archaeological sites of South America and seat of a pre-Inca civilization thought to have been either Colla or Aymará. Impressive artistic remains include a monolithic gateway (Puerta del Sol).

Tia Juana, Mexico: see TIJUANA.

Tía Juana (tē'ä hwä'nä), town (pop. 830), Zulia state, NW Venezuela, on NE shore of L. Maracaibo, 11 mi. SE of Cabimas; petroleum drilling; oil field extends into lake.

Tiana (tyä'nä), village (pop. 1,318), Barcelona prov., NE Spain, 9 mi. NE of Barcelona; cotton-fabric mfg.; agr. trade (wine, vegetables).

Tianeti (tyĕŭnyĕ'tyē), village (1932 pop. estimate 1,460), NE Georgian SSR, on Iora R. and 25 mi. NNE of Tiflis; road junction in forest area; grain, livestock.

Tianguá (tyăng-gwä'), city (pop. 2,196), NW Ceará, Brazil, in Serra Grande, near Piauí border, 40 mi. W of Sobral; coffee, tobacco, sugar, stock.

Tianguismanalco (tyäng-gēzmänäl'kō), town (pop. 1,658), Puebla, central Mexico, 18 mi. WSW of Puebla; corn, wheat, sugar cane, fruit.

Tianguistenco (tyäng-gēstĕng'kō), officially Tianguistenco de Galeana, town (pop. 2,129), Mexico state, central Mexico, 13 mi. SE of Toluca; cereals, stock; dairying.

Tianguistengo (–gō), town (pop. 1,049), Hidalgo, central Mexico, 13 mi. NE of Metztitlán; alt. 5,534 ft.; corn, beans, fruit, cotton, vegetables.

Tian Shan, China and USSR: see TIEN SHAN.

Tiaong (tyäông'), town (1939 pop. 2,529; 1948 municipality pop. 26,454), Quezon prov., S Luzon, Philippines, on railroad and 20 mi. W of Lucena; agr. center (coconuts, rice).

Tiaret (tyärĕt'), city (pop. 22,344), Oran dept., N Algeria, in the S Tell at edge of the High Plateaus (S), on railroad and 110 mi. ESE of Oran; 35°23′N 1°20′E; alt. 3,870 ft. Road junction at entrance to a pass across the Tell Atlas to Relizane (NW) and to the coast. Commercial center for fertile agr. dist. (called the Sersou Plateau) extending E into Alger dept. along S foot of the Ouarsenis Massif. Trade in cereals, cattle, sheep, and wool. Occupied in Roman times. Seat of a Moslem sect after 8th cent. A.D. Taken by French in 1843, and completely rebuilt.

Tiarno (tyär'nô), village (pop. 1,353), Trento prov., Trentino-Alto Adige, N Italy, 7 mi. W of Riva; toymaking.

Tiaroye (tyärō'yā), village, W Senegal, Fr. West Africa, on Cape Verde peninsula and 9 mi. NE of Dakar. Fisheries. Military camp.

Tías (tē'äs), village (pop. 934), Lanzarote, Canary Isls., 5 mi. W of Arrecife; potatoes, chick-peas, peas, lentils, cereals, fruit, grapes, livestock. Stone quarrying.

Tiassalé (tyäsä'lā), town (pop. 1,700), S Ivory coast, Fr. West Africa, on right bank of Bandama R. near its union with Nzi R., and 70 mi. WNW of Abidjan; coffee, cacao, palm kernels, hardwood.

Tiba, Japan: see CHIBA, city.

Tibagi (tēbúzhē'), city (pop. 1,364), E central Paraná, Brazil, on Tibagi R. and 45 mi. NNW of Ponta Grossa; sawmilling, agr. processing (rice, sugar cane, corn, tapioca, lard). In diamond zone. Monte Alegre (15 mi. NNW) has state's largest pulp and paper mill. Formerly spelled Tibagy.

Tibagi River, E Paraná, Brazil, rises 40 mi. W of Curitiba, flows c.270 mi. NNW to the Paranapanema 30 mi. N of Londrina. Interrupted by falls, one of which (Mauá) generates power for Monte Alegre paper mill. Diamond washings in middle course. Formerly spelled Tibagy.

Tibagy, Brazil: see TIBAGI.

Tiban, Wadi (wă'dē tĭbăn'), coastal stream of Western Aden Protectorate, rises in Yemen near Taiz, flows 60 mi. SSE, past Lahej, to Aden Bay at Hiswa. Used for irrigation in lower course.

Tibás, San Juan de, Costa Rica: see SAN JUAN.

Tibati (tēbä'tē), village, Adamaoua region, N central Fr. Cameroons, 95 mi. SW of N'Gaoundéré; native trade center (salt, manioc, spices); communications point; stock raising.

Tibbermore, Scotland: see PERTH, burgh.

Tiberias (tībē'rēŭs), Hebrew *Tevarya* or *Tebarya*, Arabic *Tabariya*, residential town (1946 pop. estimate 11,810; 1949 pop. estimate 7,700), NE Israel, Lower Galilee, on W shore of Sea of Galilee, 30 mi. E of Haifa; 695 ft. below sea level; noted health resort with medicinal hot springs; commercial center of Lower Galilee. Has tombs of Maimonides, Rabbi Akiba ben Joseph, and Rabbi Johanan ben Zaccai. Remains of 18th-cent. fortifications. Electric power station. Founded c.20 B.C. by Herod Antipas, named for Emperor Tiberius. Fortified by Josephus Flavius Tiberias, became a center of Jewish life in Palestine after destruction of Second Temple. Was seat of the Sanhedrin; the Mishna (A.D. c.200) and the Jerusalem Talmud (A.D. c.400) were completed here. At time of Crusades, the town, then called *Thabarie*, was occupied and fortified under Godfrey of Bouillon; became ⊙ principality of Galilee. Captured (1187) by Saladin. Attempt (1560) by duke of Naxos to resettle Jews here on large scale failed. Town was heavily damaged by earthquakes in 1837 and 1927, and by destructive flood May, 1934. Largely evacuated by Arab pop. in 1948.

Tiberias, Lake, Palestine: see GALILEE, SEA OF.

Tiber River (tī'bŭr), Ital. *Tevere* (tā'vĕrĕ), anc. *Tiberis*, central Italy, rises in Etruscan Apennines on Monte Fumaiolo at alt. of 4,160 ft., flows generally S, across small E corner of Tuscany, through Umbria and part of Latium, past Città di Castello, Umbertide, Orte, Rome, and Ostia, to Tyrrhenian Sea, which it enters in 2 mouths, the chief (S) 17 mi. SE of Rome and the other (N) at near-by Fiumicino, from which it is navigable 21 mi. to Rome; total length, 251 mi. Principal tributaries: Nera and Aniene (left) and Paglia (right) rivers. Connected with Arno R. by Paglia R. and CHIANA watercourse. Receives waters of lakes Albano and Vico.

Tibesti Massif (tĭbĕ'stē, tēbĕstē') (□ c.38,600), highest mountain group of the Sahara and of Fr. Equatorial Africa, largely in NW Chad territory, partly in Libya and Fr. West Africa; extends SE–NW c.300 mi. in length and 175 mi. in width to NW of Largeau (Faya); rises to 11,204 ft. in Emi Koussi volcano. Extremely rugged and of volcanic origin, its rocks have been fantastically shaped by intense wind erosion. Because of a favorable rainfall, dates, vegetables, barley, hard wheat, millet, corn, watermelons, and tobacco are grown in a few fertile oases; camels, asses, sheep, and goats are raised. Its semi-nomadic pop. includes Tibus and Arabs. Tibesti Massif was 1st explored by Gustav Nachtigal in 1869.

Tibet (tĭbĕt'), Chinese *Sitsang* or *Hsi-tsang*, Tibetan *Bodyul*, country of central Asia and, since 1951, an autonomous province (□ 560,000; pop. 3,000,000) of SW China; ⊙ Lhasa. It is bounded N by Sinkiang along the Kunlun mts.; NE by Tsinghai along Tanglha Range; E by Tibetan Autonomous Dist. of Sikang prov. along upper Yangtze (Kinsha) R.; S by India's Assam state, by Bhutan, Sikkim, and Nepal, and by India's Uttar Pradesh, Himachal Pradesh, and Punjab states; and W by Ladakh dist. of Kashmir. With an average elevation of 13–15,000 ft., Tibet is the highest region of the world, consisting essentially of a vast high plateau situated bet. the Kunlun mts. (N) and the Himalayas (S). The N stony desert section of the plateau—Chang Tang—is separated by the Trans-Himalayas from the S latitudinal river valleys of the upper Brahmaputra, Indus, and Sutlej rivers. Tibet, which is also traversed (E) by the canyon-encased longitudinal upper courses of the Salween and Mekong rivers and extends to the upper Yangtze, thus gives rise to many of S and E Asia's mightiest rivers. Among its numerous lakes (many saline) are Nam Tso (the largest), and the sacred Manasarowar and Rakas. The Cretaceous and Jurassic sediments of the plateau contain few minerals; the principal deposits are gold (Thok Jalung, Thok Daurakpa), iron pyrites, salt, soda, and borax. Having essentially a highland climate varying with elevation and exposure, Tibet is characterized by large diurnal and annual temp. ranges, almost rainless summers (1–3 inches), and only light snow in winter. These climatic extremes increase toward N and NW, where the Chang Tang has no trees or shrubs and only a sparse short-grass cover. Conditions permitting some agr. development exist only in the river valleys of S Tibet, where the SW summer monsoon penetrates somewhat through the Himalayan barrier and gives a brief, warm rainy season (May–Sept.). Here settled pop. and economy are concentrated, growing barley (Tibet's staple crop), wheat, peas, and beans, and engaging in handicraft industries (metalworking, weaving, pottery making, wood carving, mfg. of religious articles). The nomadic element of Tibetan pop. raises chiefly yaks (which, with the kiang and the musk deer, are the characteristic animals of the Tibetan high plateau). Sheep, long-haired goats, ponies, and mules also form an important part of the Tibetan pastoral economy, producing wool, woolen cloth, felt, yak's hair, hides, butter, cheese, and dried meat. Tibet's pop., a distinct Mongolian type, is of the Lamaist religion, which is derived from the Mahayana form of Buddhism. The Tibetan language is the main representative of the Tibeto-Burman group and employs an alphabet of the Nagari type. About 10% of the pop. are celibate lamas living in c.3,000 monasteries, including the trio of Drepung, Sera, and Ganden near Lhasa, and Tashi Lumpo near Shigatse. The lamas belong to 3 sects: the dominant celibate Yellow Hats (*Gelukpa or Gelugpa*), whose succession depends upon direct reincarnation; the older but now secondary Red Hats, in whose hierarchy son succeeds father; and the Bon sect, a combination of pre-Buddhist shamanistic practices and Buddhist infusions. Tibet's principal urban centers are Lhasa, Shigatse, and Gyangtse, on or near the Brahmaputra in S; Chamdo in E; and Gartok in W. Transportation is restricted to mule caravans along narrow, stony tracks winding through abrupt river gorges or across the wind-swept plateau. Trade is mainly with Tsinghai (via Nagchu), Sikang (via Chamdo), India (via Yatung and Kalimpong), and Kashmir (via Gartok and Leh). Tibet's only motor route connects Chamdo and Lhasa. In return for its wool, yak's hair, hides, and musk, Tibet imports brick tea, cotton goods, and household ware. Traditionally, Tibet has been (since 17th cent.) a theocracy, under the supreme spiritual and temporal rule of the Dalai [Mongol,=all-embracing] Lama as head of the Lamaist religion, with the Panchen Lama of Tashi Lumpo being 2d in importance. The Dalai Lama is assisted by a council (*kashag*) of 4 ministers (*shapes*), and occasionally receives the advice of a natl. assembly (*tsongdu*) consisting of Tibet's leading monastery and lay officials. He is considered to be the reincarnation of the deity Avalokita, while the Panchen Lama is regarded as the reincarnation of the deity Amitabha. Succession of the 2 grand lamas depends upon direct reincarnation, as the spirits of the deceased lamas pass into some newborn infant. The proper boy is discovered after a usually long search and identified by a series of tests. Emerging out of an obscure history, whose beginning is thought to have been in Ladakh, Tibet flourished in 7th cent. A.D. as an independent kingdom with capital at Lhasa. This kingdom was associated with early syncretic Buddhism fashioned (8th cent.) by the scholar Padma Sambhava into the beginnings of the Lamaist branch. Following an internal breakup (9th cent.) of Tibet and an anticlerical reaction (10th cent.) under the king Langdharma, Lamaism, then dominated by the

Red Hat order, underwent (11th cent.) a great reform movement led by the Indian monk Atisa. He sought to eliminate the last pre-Buddhist shamanistic Bon practices and enforce celibacy. In 13th cent., Tibet fell under Mongol influence, which was to last until 18th cent. In 1270, Kublai Khan, emperor of China, recognized the head of the SAKYA sect as primate of the Lamaist faith and the supreme secular authority in Tibet; this ceased in 1340. In a 2d great reform movement, the lama Tsong-kha-pa (Tsongkapa) reorganized (early-15th cent.) Atisa's sect and founded the Yellow Hat (*Gelukpa*) sect and its 1st lamasery, Ganden. From the Yellow Hats have issued the 2 main lines of Tibetan pontifical succession in modern Tibet—the grand lamas of Lhasa and of Tashi Lumpo. In 17th cent., the ruling Mongol prince bestowed supreme temporal and spiritual control of all Tibet upon the 5th grand lama of Lhasa, who ruled 1640–80 and acquired the title of Dalai Lama. At the same time, the head abbot of Tashi Lumpo lamasery, known variously as Panchen Lama, Panchen Rimpoche, or Tashi Lama, assumed a position 2d only to that of the Dalai Lama. In 1720, the Manchu dynasty of China replaced Mongol rule over Tibet and was represented at Lhasa by 2 officials (ambans); China thereafter claimed suzerainty—often merely nominal. During 18th cent., British authorities in India attempted to establish relations with Lhasa, but the Gurkha war (1792) with Tibet brought an abrupt halt to the *approchement*. Jesuits and Capuchins had visited Tibet in 17th and 18th cent., but throughout 19th cent. Tibet maintained its traditional seclusion. Meanwhile, Ladakh (W) was lost to the Dogra rulers of Kashmir, Nepal gained trade privileges after the Gurkha war (1854–56), and Sikkim was detached (1890) by Britain. In 1893 Britain succeeded in obtaining a trading post at Yatung, but continued Tibetan interference led (1904) to the Younghusband military expedition to Lhasa, which enforced the granting of trading posts at Yatung, Gyangtse, and Gartok. Subsequently, Britain recognized (1906, 1907) China's suzerainty over Tibet. However, after Peking's military expedition reached (1910) Lhasa, the Tibetans were able, with the overthrow (1911) of the Manchu dynasty, to expel (1912) the Chinese and assert their independence. This led Britain to seek a more precise definition of Tibet's status. At a conference (1913–14) of British, Tibetans, and Chinese at Simla, while Tibet was tentatively confirmed under Chinese suzerainty and divided into an inner Tibet (E), to be inc. into China, and an outer autonomous Tibet (W), Chinese disagreement with the limits of inner Tibet (roughly coextensive with the E Tibetan prov. of KHAM) precluded Peking's ratification of the Simla agreement, and undivided Tibet remained *de facto* independent, with the 13th Dalai Lama favoring Britain in exterior relations. In 1922, Lhasa was reached by telegraph from India. In 1924, the pro-Chinese 9th Panchen Lama fled to China, where he died in 1937. After the death (1933) of the 13th Dalai Lama, Tibet gradually drifted back into the Chinese orbit, and a Kuomintang mission (1934–49) was received in Lhasa; but an Indian mission arrived in 1936. The 14th (Chinese-born) Dalai Lama was installed in 1939–40 and assumed full powers (1950) after a 10-year regency. The problem, however, of the succession of the 10th Panchen Lama, with rival candidates supported by Tibet and China, was one of the excuses for the Chinese Communist invasion (Oct., 1950) of Tibet, in which Chamdo and Gartok were initially occupied. By a Tibetan-Chinese agreement (May, 1951), Tibet became a "national autonomous prov." of China under the traditional rule of the Dalai Lama and the Chinese (KUMBUM) candidate for Panchen Lama, but under the actual control of a Chinese military-administrative commission. Historically, Tibet falls into the provs. of Ngari (W), Tsang (W central), Wei (E central), and Kham (E). After its independence (1912), it was divided into 13 smaller provs. and 50-odd dists., which, like their hq., are known as *dzong*.

Tibetan Autonomous District, autonomous division (□ 60,000; pop. 700,000) of Sikang prov., SW China; ⊙ Kangting. Formed 1950, it comprises northern and western ⅔ of Sikang prov. bet. upper Yangtze R. (W) and Luting (E). Pop. is ⅘ Tibetan, and also includes Chinese, Yi, and Chinese Moslems. Main centers are Kangting, Paan, and Kantse.

Tibiri (tēbē'rē), village, S Niger territory, Fr. West Africa, near Nigeria border, 130 mi. W of Zinder and 5 mi. NW of Maradi; peanuts; livestock.

Tiblemont (tēblümō'), village, W Que., 26 mi. NE of Val d'Or; gold mining.

Tibnin (tĭbnēn'), Fr. *Tibnine* or *Tebneen*, village (pop. 1,787), S Lebanon, 25 mi. S of Saida; sericulture, cereals, tobacco.

Tibro (tē'brōō"), village (pop. 2,766), Skaraborg co., S Sweden, near Tida R., 13 mi. E of Skovde; furniture works.

Tibshelf, town and parish (pop. 3,500), E Derby, England, 6 mi. E of Mansfield; coal mining. Church has 15th-cent. tower.

Tibur, Italy: see TIVOLI.

Tiburi-sima, Japan: see CHIBURI-SHIMA.

Tiburon (tēbürō'), town (1950 pop. 884), Sud dept., SW Haiti, at SW extremity of Tiburon Peninsula, 45 mi. WNW of Les Cayes; lumbering.

Tiburon (tĭ'bûrŏn), village (pop. c.350), Marin co., W Calif., at tip of Tiburon Peninsula (c.4 mi. long) on W San Francisco Bay, 5 mi. N of San Francisco water front; rail terminus; railroad shops. Bathing, boating, fishing. Calif. Nautical School for training of merchant marine officers is near by.

Tiburón, Cape (tēbōōrōn'), Caribbean headland on Colombia-Panama border, on Gulf of Darien at W gate of Gulf of Urabá; 8°41'N 77°21'W.

Tiburón Island (□ 458), in Gulf of California, just off W coast of Sonora, Mexico, 75 mi. W of Hermosillo; c.30 mi. long, c.18 mi. wide; rises to 3,996 ft.; 29°N 112°30'W. Inhabited by savage Seri tribes.

Tiburon Peninsula (tēbürō'), SW Haiti, bet. Gulf of Gonaïves (N) and the Caribbean (S); 140 mi. long, traversed by the Massif de la Hotte. Port-au-Prince is at its base. Along its coast are a number of ports—Jérémie, Les Cayes, Jacmel, Petit-Goâve—which ship the products of the fertile region (sugar cane, coffee, cacao, cotton, tropical fruit).

Ticaco (tēkä'kō), town (pop. 1,141), Tacna dept., S Peru, in Cordillera Occidental, on tributary of Sama R. and 2 mi. NNW of Tarata.

Ticao Island (tēkä'ō, tēkou') (□ 129; 1939 pop. 29,797), Masbate prov., Philippines, just E of Masbate isl. across Masbate Passage, separated from SE Luzon by Ticao Pass; 27 mi. long, 1–8 mi. wide. Rice and coconut growing. Chief centers, SAN FERNANDO and SAN JACINTO, are on E coast.

Ticao Pass, strait in the Philippines, bet. Ticao Isl. and SE part of Luzon, merges NW with Burias Pass, SE with Samar Sea and San Bernardino Strait; c.30 mi. long, 11 mi. wide.

Ticapampa (tēkäpäm'pä), town (pop. 737), Ancash dept., W central Peru, on E slopes of Cordillera Negra of the Andes, on road, and 18 mi. SSE of Huarás; zinc, lead, silver mining.

Ticcio, Ethiopia: see TICHO.

Tice, village (pop. 1,133), Lee co., SW Fla., 4 mi. NE of Fort Myers.

Ticehurst, town and parish (pop. 2,650), NE Sussex, England, 9 mi. NNW of Battle; agr. market. Has 13th-cent. church.

Ticha Orlice River (tyĭ'khä ôr'lĭtsĕ), Ger. *Stille Adler* (shtĭ'lū äd'lūr), E Bohemia, Czechoslovakia, rises 2 mi. SSW of Kraliky on Bohemia-Moravia border, flows c.65 mi. W in broad curve, past Usti nad Orlici and Chocen, joining Divocha Orlice R. 1 mi. above Tyniste nad Orlici to form Orlice R.

Ticha River, Bulgaria: see KAMCHIYA RIVER.

Tichau, Poland: see TYCHY.

Tichitt or **Tichit** (tēshēt'), village, E Mauritania, Fr. West Africa, oasis in W Sahara, on caravan trail to Fr. Sudan, 480 mi. ENE of Saint-Louis, Senegal; millet, dates, livestock.

Tichlá (tēchlä'), Saharan outpost and well, S Río de Oro, Sp. West Africa; 21°36'N 14°53'W.

Ticho (tĭ'chō), Ital. *Ticcio*, village (pop. 1,000), Arusi prov., S central Ethiopia, near Mt. Badda, 33 mi. E of Asselle, in cereal-growing and cattle-raising region.

Ticino (tēchē'nō), Fr. *Tessin* (tĕsē'), Ger. *Tessin* (tĕsēn'), canton (□ 1,086; 1950 pop. 175,520), S Switzerland; ⊙ Bellinzona. Pop. Italian speaking and Catholic. Embraces Ticino and Maggia river valleys, part of Lago Maggiore, and L. of Lugano. Largely mountainous, covered with pastures and forests; ADULA and SAINT GOTTHARD mts. rise in N. Vineyards, tobacco and maize fields in the valleys. Resorts include LOCARNO and LUGANO. Well-developed hydroelectric system extends along Ticino R. The industry, largely in S, produces mainly metal products, tobacco, chemicals; also woodworking, printing establishments.

Ticino River, anc. *Ticinus*, Switzerland and N Italy, rises in Switzerland S of Pizzo Rotondo, 11 mi. WSW of Airolo; flows 154 mi. generally S, through Ticino canton and Lago Maggiore, into Italy (here forming boundary bet. Lombardy and Piedmont), to Po R. 3.5 mi. SSE of Pavia, principal town on its banks. Navigable below Lago Maggiore. Forms Valle Levantina in upper course. In lower course, used to irrigate over 190,000 acres, mostly in Lombardy. E terminus of Cavour Canal. On its banks was fought (218 B.C.) one of 1st battles of Second Punic War (battle of the Ticino), in which Carthaginians under Hannibal defeated Romans led by Scipio.

Ticinum, Italy: see PAVIA, city.

Tickem (tēkĕm'), village, W Chad territory, Fr. Equatorial Africa, near swamps of Tickem and Fr. Cameroons border, 50 mi. SW of Bongor; large experimental plantations for African staples (millet, sorgo, corn, manioc). Also spelled Tekem.

Tickfaw River, in Miss. and La., rises in extreme SW Miss., flows S c.105 mi., through SE La., to L. Maurepas at N end; partly navigable.

Tickhill, urban district (1931 pop. 2,297; 1951 census 2,550), West Riding, S Yorkshire, England, 6 mi. S of Doncaster; stone quarrying; mfg. of concrete and quartzite. Has church built 1360 and remains of 11th-cent. castle.

Ticonderoga (tī"kŏndūrō'gū), resort village (pop. 3,517), Essex co., NE N.Y., at falls on outlet of L. George (water power), 38 mi. N of Glens Falls; graphite mining; pencil mfg.; also lumber and paper milling, furniture mfg. Here is Hq. House of N.Y. State Historical Association. Settled in 17th cent.; inc. 1889. Here and at CROWN POINT were fought several battles of the French and Indian War. Near by is Fort Ticonderoga (restored), built by the French in 1755 and 1st called Fort Carillon; renamed after capture (1759) by British and colonial troops under Sir Jeffrey Amherst. In the Revolution, fort was taken (May 10, 1775) by Ethan Allen's Green Mountain Boys and troops under Arnold. Evacuated by Americans, it was occupied by Burgoyne in Saratoga campaign, and again held by British troops in 1780.

Ticuantepe (tēkwäntā'pā), village, Managua dept., SW Nicaragua, 10 mi. SSE of Managua; coffee, corn, beans.

Ticul (tēkōōl'), town (pop. 9,034), Yucatan, SE Mexico, 40 mi. S of Mérida; rail junction; agr. center (henequen, sugar cane, corn, tropical fruit, timber). Has fine colonial buildings. Famous UXMAL Maya ruins are 12 mi. W.

Ticumán (tēkōōmän'), town (pop. 1,193), Morelos, central Mexico, on railroad and 13 mi. SE of Cuernavaca; rice, sugar cane, fruit, vegetables.

Tidaholm (tē"dähôlm'), city (pop. 5,797), Skaraborg co., S central Sweden, on Tida R. and 30 mi. NNW of Jonkoping; textile and lumber milling, metalworking; mfg. of matches, furniture. Inc. as town 1895; as city 1910.

Tidan (tē'dän"), village (pop. 605), Skaraborg co., S central Sweden, on Tida R. and 12 mi. SE of Mariestad; woolen, paper milling; woodworking.

Tida River, Swedish *Tidan* (tē'dän"), SW Sweden, rises W of Jonkoping, flows 100 mi. generally N, past Tidaholm, to L. Vaner at Mariestad.

Tiddim (tĭ'dĭm"), village, N.Chin Hills dist., Upper Burma, near Manipur (India) line, 40 mi. WNW of Kalewa, on road to Imphal; alt. 5,667 ft. In Second World War, briefly held (1944) by Japanese in Manipur campaign.

Tidenham (tĭ'dùnùm), town and parish (pop. 3,147), W Gloucester, England, near Severn R., 2 mi. NE of Chepstow; agr. market. Has 14th-cent. church.

Tideswell (tĭdz'wĕl, tĭd'zùl), town and parish (pop. 1,933), NW Derby, England, 6 mi. ENE of Buxton; cotton milling; former lead-mining center. Has 14th-cent. church, called Cathedral of the Peak.

Tidewater, W.Va.: see VIVIAN.

Tidiguin (tēdhē'gēn), highest peak (8,060 ft.) of the Rif Mts., central Sp. Morocco, 40 mi. SW of Villa Sanjurjo. Snow-covered in winter. Cedar forests on slope.

Tidikelt (tēdēkĕlt'), group of oases, Saharan Oases territory, central Algeria, a SE continuation of the Touat oases, bet. 1°E and 2°30'E, at 27°N. Dates are chief export product. Principal oases: In-Salah, Tit, Aoulef (airfield).

Tidioute (tĭ'dēōōt"), borough (pop. 998), Warren co., NW Pa., 17 mi. SW of Warren and on Allegheny R.; machine shops; agr.

Tidjikja or **Tidjikdja** (tējĕkjä'), town (pop. c.5,700), S central Mauritania, Fr. West Africa, oasis in low Tagant massif of the Sahara, on caravan trail to Fr. Sudan and 370 mi. ENE of Saint-Louis; dates, millet, henna, melons, beans, livestock. Rug mfg.

Tidone River (tēdō'nĕ), N central Italy, rises in Ligurian Apennines 6 mi. E of Varzi, flows 25 mi. generally NNE, past Pianello Val Tidone, to Po R. 8 mi. WNW of Piacenza.

Tidore (tēdō'rē), island (□ 45; pop. 18,360), N Moluccas, Indonesia, in Molucca Sea, 7 mi. W of Halmahera, just S of Ternate; 1°40'N 127°25'E; 9 mi. long, 7 mi. wide; densely wooded and mountainous, rising to 5,676 ft. (volcanic peak). Chief products: spices, timber, rattan, copra, rice, coffee. Port. missionary influence was strong here in 16th cent.; Portuguese fort was built 1578. There were Sp. settlements here 1606–63. The Dutch established 1st settlement 1605 and won sovereignty rights 1667.

Tidworth, England: see NORTH TIDWORTH.

Tiébissou (tyĕbē'sōō), village (pop. c.600), S central Ivory Coast, Fr. West Africa, 36 mi. SSW of Bouako; coffee, cacao, tobacco, yams.

Tiedemann, Mount, or **Mount Teidemann** (tēd'mùn) (12,000 ft.), SW B.C., in Coast Mts., 170 mi. NW of Vancouver, just N of Mt. Waddington.

Tiedra (tyā'dhrä), town (pop. 1,508), Valladolid prov., N central Spain, 20 mi. SW of Medina de Ríoseco; lumbering; sheep, cereals, wine.

Tiefencastel or **Tiefenkastel** (tē'fùnkäs'tùl), town (pop. 270), Grisons canton, E Switzerland, on Albula R. and 7 mi. ESE of Thusis.

Tiefenort (tē'fùnôrt), town (pop. 4,575), Thuringia, central Germany, on the Werra and 12 mi. SW of Eisenach; potash mining; woodworking.

Tiefenstein, W Germany: see IDAR-OBERSTEIN.

Tiefurt (tē'fōōrt), NE suburb of Weimar, Thuringia, central Germany, on Ilm R. Castle (18th cent.) here was summer residence of the Duchess Anna Amalia; numerous literary associations (Goethe, Herder, Wieland).

Tiegenhof, Poland: see NOWY DWOR, Gdansk prov.

Tiehli or **T'ieh-li** (tyĕ'lē'), town, ⊙ Tiehli co. (pop. 27,702), SE Heilungkiang prov., Manchuria, on railroad and 100 mi. NE of Harbin, near Sungkiang line; coal mining; gypsum deposits; soybeans, millet, kaoliang, corn, wheat, hemp, tobacco. Called Tiehshanpao until 1915.

T'ieh-li-nan-mu Hu, Tibet: see TERINAM TSO.

Tiehling or **T'ieh-ling** (tyĕ'lĭng') [Chinese,=iron range], town (1938 pop. 48,972), ⊙ Tiehling co. (1946 pop. 375,732), NE Liaosi prov., Manchuria, on left bank of Liao R. and 40 mi. NE of Mukden, and on South Manchuria RR; agr. and textile-milling center; mfg. of cotton goods, flour, soybean products. Dates from Ming dynasty. Named for iron deposits near by.

Tiehshan. 1 Town, Hupeh prov., China: see TAYEH. **2** or **T'ieh-shan,** mining locality, Shantung prov., China: see KINLINGCHEN.

Tiehshanpao, Manchuria: see TIEHLI.

Tiel (tēl), town (pop. 13,650), Gelderland prov., central Netherlands, on Waal R. and 21 mi. WSW of Arnhem; center of fruitgrowing dist.; preserves, jams; mfg. (chemicals, furniture, metalware, bicycles). Horticultural school (nurseries). Town chartered 1200; trade center and port in Middle Ages and member of Hanseatic League. Formerly also spelled Thiel.

Tielmes (tyĕl'mĕs), town (pop. 1,626), Madrid prov., central Spain, on Tajuña R., on railroad and 23 mi. SE of Madrid; olives, grapes, livestock. Alcohol distilling, olive-oil pressing, mfg. of soap.

Tielrode (tēl'rōdŭ), agr. village (pop. 2,545), East Flanders prov., N Belgium, 18 mi. E of Ghent, near Scheldt R. Formerly spelled Thielrode.

Tielt (tēlt), town (pop. 13,016), West Flanders prov., W Belgium, 9 mi. ENE of Roulers; agr. and poultry market. In early stages of First World War, Ger. hq. on Flanders front. Formerly spelled Thielt.

Tiemblo, El (ĕl tyĕm'blō), town (pop. 3,352), Ávila prov., central Spain, near Alberche R., in fertile valley of the Sierra de Gredos, 20 mi. SE of Ávila; lumbering and agr. center (fruit, grapes, vegetables, livestock); flour milling, naval-stores mfg. Hydroelectric plant. Near by (S) are ruins of anc. Hieronymite monastery, where pact was signed (1468) declaring Isabella heir to Castilian throne. Also in vicinity are famed Toros de Guisando, prehistoric sculptures.

Tien or **T'ien,** province, China: see YUNNAN.

Tienchang or **T'ien-ch'ang** (tyĕn'chäng'), town, ⊙ Tienchang co. (pop. 231,615), N Anhwei prov., China, near Kiangsu line, 40 mi. NNE of Nanking, SW of Kaoyu L.; rice, wheat, beans, kaoliang, corn.

T'ien-chia-an, China: see TIENKIAAN.

Tien-chiang, China: see TIENKIANG.

Tienchen or **T'ien-chen** (tyĕn'jŭn'), town, ⊙ Tienchen co. (pop. 110,604), SW Chahar prov., China, 50 mi. NE of Tatung, near railroad; soap mfg.; millet, kaoliang. Until 1949 in Shansi.

Tien Chih (dyĕ' jû'), lake in E central Yunnan prov., China; 25 mi. long, 7 mi. wide; drains N into Yangtze R.; alt. over 5,500 ft. Kunming is on N shore, Kunyang on SW shore. Steamer service; fisheries. Sometimes called Tien Hu or Kunyang Hu.

T'ien-ching, China: see TIENTSIN.

Tienchu or **T'ien-chu** (tyĕn'jōō'), town (pop. 2,393), ⊙ Tienchu co. (pop. 129,543), easternmost Kweichow prov., China, near Hunan line, 40 mi. ESE of Chenyüan; cotton textiles, embroideries; rice, wheat, millet, beans. Gold washing near by.

Tienchüan or **T'ien-ch'üan** (tyĕn'chüăn'), town, ⊙ Tienchüan co. (pop. 82,482), E Sikang prov., China, 45 mi. E of Kangting and on highway from Szechwan; tea-growing center; medicinal herbs. Until 1938 in Szechwan.

Tienchung or **T'ien-chung** (both: tyĕn'jŏŏng'), Jap. *Tanaka* (tänä'kä), town (1935 pop. 5,558), W central Formosa, 15 mi. SSE of Changhwa and on railroad; rice, sweet potatoes, tobacco, livestock.

Tienchwangtai or **T'ien-chuang-t'ai** (both: tyĕn'jwäng'tī'), town, S Liaosi prov., Manchuria, on lower Liao R. (Liaotung line) and 13 mi. NW of Yingkow; was lower Liao R. port for Newchwang, prior to port's transfer (1836) to Yingkow.

Tienen, Belgium: see TIRLEMONT.

Tiengen (tĕng'ŭn), village (pop. 3,888), S Baden, Germany, at S foot of Black Forest, on the Wutach and 3 mi. ENE of Waldshut; large transformer station; cotton mfg., metalworking. Has baroque church.

Tienho or **T'ien-ho** (tyĕn'hŭ'), town, ⊙ Tienho co. (pop. 75,217), N Kwangsi prov., China, 50 mi. NW of Liuchow; rice, wheat, beans. Sulphur deposits near by.

T'ien-hsi, China: see TIENSI.

Tien Hu, China: se TIEN CHIH.

Tienkiaan or **T'ien-chia-an** (both: tyĕn'jyä'än'), village, N central Anhwei prov., China, on Hwai R. and 30 mi. SW of Pengpu, at foot of the Shunkeng Shan; coal-shipping point; terminus of Hwainan RR from Yüki.

Tienkiang or **Tien-chiang** (both: dyĕn'jyäng'), town (pop. 18,034), ⊙ Tienkiang co. (pop. 230,956), E Szechwan prov., China, 70 mi. NE of Chungking city; rice, sweet potatoes, millet, wheat, indigo, tea.

Tienmen or **T'ien-men** (tyĕn'mŭn'), town (pop. 25,888), ⊙ Tienmen co. (pop. 749,644), S central Hupeh prov., China, 60 mi. W of Hankow; silk and cotton weaving; rice, wheat, beans.

Tienmu Mountains, Chinese *T'ien-mu Shan* (tyĕn'mōō' shän'), NW Chekiang prov., China, on Anhwei border; rise to 5,075 ft. 45 mi. W of Hangchow.

Tieno or **T'ien-o** (tyĕn'-ŭ'), town, ⊙ Tieno co. (pop. 44,363), NW Kwangsi prov., China, 60 mi. NE of Lingyün and on Hungshui R. (Kweichow line); rice, wheat, millet, sweet potatoes.

Tienpai, China: see TINPAK.

Tienpao or **T'ien-pao** (tyĕn'bou'), town, ⊙ Tienpao co. (pop. 143,221), W Kwangsi prov., China, 35 mi. SSE of Poseh; wheat, millet. Gold mines, antimony deposits near by. Until 1913 called Chenan.

Tienpaoshan, Manchuria: see LAOTOWKOW.

Tienshan or **T'ien-shan** (tyĕn'shän'), town, ⊙ Tienshan co. (pop. 9,611), S Inner Mongolian Autonomous Region, Manchuria, 95 mi. W of Tungliao, in Jooda league. Founded 1927; in Jehol until 1949.

Tien Shan or **T'ien Shan** (tyĕn' shän'), Rus. *Tyan-Shan* or *Tyan'-Shan'* (tyän') [Chinese,=Celestial Mountains], one of the great mountain systems of Aisa, in China and USSR, separating in part Russian and Chinese Turkestan. It extends 1,500 mi. generally WSW-ENE, from the Kyzyl-Kum desert of Soviet Central Asia to the China-Mongolia line (43°N 96°E) at W edge of the Gobi. Its highest, glaciated section, on China-USSR border, includes Pobeda [=victory] Peak (24,406 ft.) and the Khan Tengri (22,949 ft.; regarded as the highest point until the discovery of Pobeda Peak in 1943). Of simple structure in the E, where it separates the Dzungaria and Tarim basins of China's Sinkiang prov., the Tien Shan separates into numerous branches (W), which reach their greatest complexity within KIRGHIZIA. The principal offshoots are (from N to S) the Saur and Tarbagatai ranges near L. Zaisan, the Dzungarian Ala-Tau and the Borokhoro Range N of the Ili R., the Trans-Ili Ala-Tau and the Terskei Ala-Tau (which enclose the Issyk-Kul lake basin), the Kirghiz Range, and the Talas Ala-Tau. The Chatkal, Fergana, and Alai ranges enclose the Fergana Valley. The southwesternmost outliers—the parallel Turkestan, Zeravshan, and Gissar ranges—are sometimes considered part of the Pamir-Alai mtn. system, although the Kyzyl-Su—Surkhab—Vakhsh river course is commonly regarded as the boundary bet. the 2 systems. Because of the dryness of the climate, the snow line in the Tien Shan is generally above 11,000 ft. Among the main rivers rising here are the Syr Darya, Chu, and Ili rivers. Mtn. system was formerly also spelled Tian Shan and Thian Shan.

Tienshengkang (dyĕn'shŭng'gäng') or **Tien-sheng-chiang** (–jyäng), N Kiangsu prov., China, port on Yangtze R. and 7 mi. W of Nantung; match mfg.

Tienshihfu, Manchuria: see PENKI.

Tienshui or **T'ien-shui** (tyĕn'shwā), town (1947 pop. estimate 50,000), ⊙ Tienshui co. (1947 pop. 292,981), SE Kansu prov., on Lunghai RR, on Wei R. and 150 mi. SE of Lanchow; tobacco center; winemaking; furniture, lacquer, match, and cotton-textile mfg. Wheat, beans, rice. Coal mines, gold deposits near by. Until 1913 called Tsinchow.

Tiensi or **T'ien-hsi** (both: tyĕn'shē'), town, ⊙ Tiensi co. (pop. 47,095), W Kwangsi prov., China, 45 mi. NW of Poseh; wheat, millet, beans. Until 1936 called Lucheng.

Tientai or **T'ien-t'ai** (tyĕn'tī'), town (pop. 18,294), ⊙ Tientai co. (pop. 253,830), E Chekiang prov., China, on tributary of Ling R., S of Tientai Mts., and 20 mi. NNW of Linhai; Brahman-bead carving, mfg. of paper umbrellas; tea, sesame, rice, wheat. Coal mines near by.

Tientai Mountains, Chinese *T'ien-t'ai Shan* (shän'), E Chekiang prov., China, rising to 4,101 ft. 50 mi. SW of Ningpo. Have noted Buddhist temple.

Tientsin (tĭn'sĭn, tyĕn'jĭn') or **T'ien-ching** (tyĕn'jĭng'), city (1946 pop. 1,707,670; 1947 pop. 1,686,543), NE Hopeh prov., China, Yellow Sea port 70 mi. SE of Peking; 39°8'N 117°12'E. Leading transportation and industrial center of N China, situated on Pai R. (here called Hai R.) and 30 mi. from Gulf of Chihli, at confluence of several navigable tributaries, including the Grand Canal. A major rail hub with lines to Peking, Mukden, and Pukow (opposite Nanking), it is an important mfg. city, producing cotton goods, woolens, camel's-hair fabrics, leather articles, matches, glass, bricks, and processed foods. There are iron- and steelworks. The port is not accessible to ocean-going vessels, which anchor off Taku Bar, and transship goods at Tientsin's outer ports of Tangku and Taku, at mouth of Pai R. Tientsin exports hog bristles, furs, skins, wool, and vegetable oil from N China and the Inner Mongolian provs. Seat of Nankai and Peiyang univs., teachers col., and colleges of engineering and commerce. Of little significance until the mid-19th cent., Tientsin was occupied (1858 and 1860) by the British and French and was opened in 1861 to foreign trade. Concessions were granted, beginning in 1860, to Britain, Belgium, France, Italy, Japan, and Russia, along Pai R. SE of the old walled Chinese city. It was the scene of severe fighting (1900) during the Boxer Rebellion and was jointly occupied by foreign troops. After the uprising, the turreted city wall was razed and the city reconstructed along modern lines. During Sino-Japanese War, it was held (1937–45) by the Japanese. Passed 1949 to Communist control. Became an independent municipality under provincial jurisdiction in 1930 and under the central govt. in 1935. The seat of Tientsin co. (1935 pop. 426,603) was moved (1935) from here to Sienshuiku, 12 mi. SE, thereafter also called Tientsin.

Tientu or **Tien-t'u** (dyĕn'tōō'), town, S Hainan, Kwangtung prov., China, 12 mi. N of Yülin; iron-mining center, linked by rail with Yülin. Developed by Japanese during Second World War.

Tientung or **T'ien-tung** (tyĕn'dŏŏng'), town, ⊙ Tientung co. (pop. 114,690), W Kwangsi prov., China, 40 mi. SE of Poseh and on Yü R.; commercial center; cotton-textile and paper mfg.; rice, beans, bamboo. Gold mines, antimony deposits near by. Until 1936 called Enlung.

Tienyang or **T'ien-yang** (tyĕn'yäng'), town, ⊙ Tienyang co. (pop. 135,292), W Kwangsi prov., China, 18 mi. SE of Poseh and on Sün R.; tung-oil processing; grain, sugar cane. Gold mines, antimony deposits near by. Called Napo until 1936, when co. ⊙ was transferred here from Fengyi, 3 mi. E.

Tienyen (tyĕn'yĕn'), town, Haininh prov., N Vietnam, at mouth of Tienyen R. and 105 mi. ENE of Hanoi, on Tienyen Bay of Gulf of Tonkin; coal, pyrite, and quartz deposits near by.

Tiercé (tyĕrsā'), village (pop. 724), Maine-et-Loire dept., W France, near Sarthe R., 10 mi. NNE of Angers; dairying. Slate quarries near by.

Tiergarten (tēr'gär"tŭn), residential district (1939 pop. 213,572; 1946 pop. 110,620), W central Berlin, Germany, on the Spree. Includes the Tiergarten, a park (c.630 acres), until 18th cent. a deer preserve. Before Second World War, the Tiergartenstrasse, skirting S edge of park, was known as center of Berlin's diplomatic quarter, and the Bendlerstrasse was site of war ministry. After 1945 in British sector.

Tiermas (tyĕr'mäs), town (pop. 489), Saragossa prov., NE Spain, on Aragon R. and 30 mi. W of Jaca, in grain-growing region; noted spa with thermal springs.

Tierp (tē'ĕrp"), town (pop. 1,853), Uppsala co., E Sweden, 25 mi. SE of Gavle; foundries, shoe factories; metal- and woodworking. Has old church with 15th-cent. paintings.

Tierra Amarilla (tyĕ'rä ämärē'yä), town (pop. 1,086), Atacama prov., N Chile, on Copiapó R. (irrigation), on railroad and 10 mi. SSE of Copiapó; agr. center (corn, alfalfa, clover, subtropical fruit). Copper deposits near by.

Tierra Amarilla (tēē'rŭ ămŭrĭ'lŭ), village (1940 pop. 787), ⊙ Rio Arriba co., N N.Mex., near San Juan Mts. and Colo. line, 80 mi. NNW of Santa Fe; alt. c.7,460 ft.; livestock, grain, poultry, potatoes. Coal mines in vicinity. El Vado Dam and Reservoir are 13 mi. SW, Carson Natl. Forest E.

Tierra Azul (tyĕ'rä äsōōl'), village, Boaco dept., central Nicaragua, 21 mi. NE of Boaco; coffee; livestock.

Tierra Blanca (tyĕ'rä bläng'kä), village (pop. 2,164), Cartago prov., central Costa Rica, on SW slopes of Irazú volcano, 3 mi. NE of Cartago, in dairying area.

Tierra Blanca, city (pop. 7,255), Veracruz, E Mexico, in Gulf lowland, 55 mi. SSW of Veracruz. Rail junction; agr. center situated amid rich jungle vegetation; coffee, sugar cane, bananas, palms (coyol).

Tierra Blanca, town (pop. 399), Loreto dept., E Peru, on Ucayali R. and 60 mi. NNW of Contamana; bananas, yucca, sugar cane. Founded as a mission in mid-19th cent.

Tierra Blanca Creek (tĕr'ŭ blăng'kŭ), extreme N Texas, rises in intermittent streams in the Panhandle near N.Mex. line, flows c.70 mi. generally E to join Palo Duro Creek near Canyon to form Prairie Dog Town Fork of Red R. Dam near Canyon forms Buffalo L. (5 mi. long; capacity c.18,000 acre-ft.), a recreation center; also called L. Umbarger (ŭm'bärgŭr).

Tierra Bomba Island (tyĕ'rä bōm'bä), off Caribbean coast of Bolívar dept., N Colombia, forms W shore of Bay of Cartagena, bet. Boca Grande and Boca Chica; 5 mi. long, c.3 mi. wide.

Tierra de Barros (dhä bä'rōs), fertile plain in Estremadura, Badajoz prov., W Spain, SE of Badajoz. Almendralejo is its center. Produces chiefly grapes, olives, cereals.

Tierra de Campos (käm'pōs), region of N central Spain, including large part of Palencia prov. and small area of Valladolid prov., irrigated by Canal of Castile and by Pisuerga R. and its affluents. Called the "granary of Castile" because of its rich crops of cereals. Palencia and Medina de Ríoseco are chief centers.

Tierra del Fuego (dĕl fwā'gō) [Sp.,=fire land], archipelago (□ 27,476; pop. c.10,000), at S tip of South America, separated from mainland by Strait of Magellan and bounded E by the Atlantic, S by the Antarctic waters, and W by the Pacific; bet. 52°27'–55°59'S and 65°–74°45'W. Sometimes considered part of Patagonia. Consists of: one large isl. (□ c.18,000; 250 mi. NW–SE, 280 mi. E–W along S coast), called sometimes simply Tierra del Fuego or Great Isl. (Sp. *Isla Grande*) and, formerly, King Charles South Land; 5 smaller but sizable isls. (Navarino Island, Hoste Island, Clarence Island, Santa Inés Island, and Desolation Island; Staten Island, off SE coast across Le Maire Strait, is sometimes considered to be part of the archipelago); and numerous small islands, islets, and rocks separated by many inlets and channels. At S extremity is Horn Isl., on which is Cape Horn. The main system of the Andes carries through W part of the group, rising to Mt. Sarmiento (7,500 ft.) and Mt. Darwin (7,005 ft.); the Patagonian plateau extends into the E part of the group, notably on the main large isl. The archipelago is a bleak, desolate region, with frequent high winds and much rainfall (snow on the mts.), but the climate, though wet, is not too rigorous; coastal areas receive little snow, though inland there are low July temperatures. Cattle and sheep are bred, there is some agr. (cereals), mining (gold, coal), oil production (Springhill), and lumbering. Most of the pop. is on the main large isl. The aborigines (called Fuegians), extremely primitive, are of 3 tribes: Onas, Alikulufs, and Yahgans. The isls. were discovered 1520 by Magellan but were not well surveyed until 19th cent. The archipelago is divided bet. Chile and Argentina by a line through the main large isl. from Cape Espíritu Santo (N) on Strait of Magellan to Beagle Channel (S) along 68°36′38″ longitude, giving Argentina the E part (□ 7,750) of the main isl. (along with Staten Isl.), and Chile the rest of the archipelago; 3 small isls. (Pictón, Lennox, and Nueva) at mouth of Beagle Channel S of the main isl. are disputed. The Chilean part forms Tierra del Fuego dept. (⊙ Porvenir) of Magallanes prov. (which see); the Argentine section constitutes, along with Staten Isl., the **Territory of Tierra del Fuego** (□ 7,996; pop. 5,045), ⊙ Ushuaia. In the Argentine territory (set up 1884 and administered by a high-ranking naval officer) sheep raising predominates. Among its little-exploited mineral resources are gold in its rivers and beach sands (San Sebastián), large quantities of guano on its coast; also lignite, peat, copper, zinc, nickel and iron ores. Fishing (whales, seals, mackerel, sardines) along its coast. Rich in timber (pine, cypress, oak, etc.). Rural industries: lumbering, gold washing, mining, dairying. Meat packing at Río Grande, fish canneries and sawmills at Ushuaia. Trading in wool, meat, fur (nutria, seal), and lumber.

Tierra del Vino (vē′nō), region of NW Spain, S of Duero (Douro) R., mostly in SE Zamora and partly in S Valladolid provs. Owes its name to the excellent wine produced from its extensive vineyards; grows also cereals, fruit, vegetables. Toro and Medina del Campo are chief towns.

Tierra Nueva (nwā′vä), town (pop. 1,420), San Luis Potosí, N central Mexico, 45 mi. SE of San Luis Potosí; corn, cotton, beans, fruit, livestock.

Tierras Morenas (tyĕ′räs mōrā′näs), village (pop. 2,047), Guanacaste prov., NW Costa Rica, 8 mi. NNW of Tilarán; coffee, corn, beans, sugar cane, livestock.

Tierra Vieja Mountains, Texas: see Sierra Vieja.

Tie Siding, village (pop. c.50), Albany co., SE Wyo., just W of Laramie Mts., 16 mi. SSE of Laramie; alt. c.7,800 ft. Supply point in ranching region.

Tiétar River (tyā′tär), W Spain, rises in the Sierra de Gredos, flows WSW, forming border bet. Ávila and Toledo provs., then traverses Cáceres prov. to join the Tagus 14 mi. SSE of Plasencia; c.100 mi. long. Irrigation reservoir.

Tietê (tyĭtā′), city (pop. 6,771), S central São Paulo, Brazil, on Tietê R. and 30 mi. NNW of Sorocaba; rail-spur terminus. Weaving, distilling; coffee, rice, and dairy-products processing, viticulture; cotton.

Tietê River, São Paulo, Brazil, rises in the Serra do Mar 12 mi. from the Atlantic and 45 mi. NE of Santos, flows over 500 mi. NW bisecting São Paulo state, past Mogi das Cruzes, São Paulo city, and Tietê, to the Paraná at 20°37′S 51°32′W. Receives the Piracicaba (right), Sorocaba (left). Because of numerous rapids and falls (harnessed for power near Itu and Avanhandava), it is navigable only in short sections. Its valley is mostly low and unhealthful, but near São Paulo city it has been drained and canalized, thus reducing flood hazards. The great Santo Amaro reservoirs S of São Paulo, which feed the Cubatão hydroelectric plant, are located on the Tietê's upper tirbutaries. The Tietê valley was one of the chief routes of penetration used by pioneers and prospectors (*bandeirantes*) in 17th–18th cent. The fertile watersheds N and S of the Tietê in central and W São Paulo have been settled by pioneer farmers since First World War.

Tieton (tī′ŭtŭn), town (pop. 620), Yakima co., S Wash., in the Cascades near Tieton R., 15 mi. NW of Yakima.

Tieton Dam, S Wash., irrigation storage dam (completed 1925; c.230 ft. high), in Cascade Range, c.30 mi. W of Yakima; it forms **Tieton Reservoir,** 6 mi. long, from which **Tieton River** flows c.30 mi. ENE to Naches R. above Naches.

Tiferdine, Djebel (jĕ′bĕl tĕfĕrdēn′), peak (12,370 ft.) of the High Atlas in central Fr. Morocco, 28 mi. SE of Azilal. Seasonally snow-covered; 31°38′N 6°15′W.

Tiffin. 1 Town (pop. 256), Johnson co., E Iowa, 8 mi. WNW of Iowa City, in agr. area. **2** City (pop. 18,952), ⊙ Seneca co., N Ohio, c.40 mi. SSE of Toledo and on Sandusky R.; mfg. of glassware, electrical products, machinery, pottery, clothing, wire, furniture, egg dyes; cold-storage plant; poultry hatcheries. Clay pits, limestone quarries. Heidelberg Col. and an orphanage are here. Founded c.1820.

Tiffin River, in Mich. and Ohio, rises in SE Mich., flows c.75 mi. S, past Hudson and Morenci, and into NW Ohio, past Stryker, to Maumee R. at Defiance.

Tiflet (tēflĕt′), town (pop. 3,110), Rabat region, NW Fr. Morocco, 30 mi. ESE of Rabat; agr. trade home industry (rugs, palm-fiber articles). Iron mined here before Second World War. Also spelled Tiflèt.

Tiflis (tĭ′flĭs, Rus. tyĭflyēs′), Georgian *Tbilisi* (ŭtbĭlyē′sē) [from Georgian *tbili*,=warm], city (1939 pop. 519,175), ⊙ Georgian SSR, on Kura R., at end of its upper valley, on railroad and 285 mi. WNW of Baku, 1,000 mi. SSE of Moscow; 41°42′N 44°48′E. Transcaucasian transportation hub (Naftlug junction); economic and cultural center at S end of Georgian Military Road. Railroad shops; mfg. of lathes, oil drills, textile, tea, and winemaking machinery, electrical goods, ceramics, footwear, clothing, textiles (silk and woolen goods, knitwear); woodworking (furniture, musical instruments); tobacco, food, and wine processing. Has 7th-cent. Zion cathedral (seat of patriarch of Georgian Orthodox Church), 6th-cent. St. David church (with Griboyedov tomb) in David's Mt. park (NW; funicular railway), 13th-cent. Metskh church (now art mus.) overlooking the Kura, and ruins of old fortress. Numerous educational and cultural institutions: Georgian acad. of sciences (1941), state univ. (1918), polytechnic, pedagogic, medical, and art schools, opera, Rustaveli theater and botanic gardens. City lies in terraced, basin-like Kura R. valley (alt. 1,300–2,100 ft.), hemmed in by spurs of the Greater Caucasus (E) and Lesser Caucasus (SW) and exposed to N and NW winds. Extends 10 mi. (NW-SE; 2–4 mi. wide) along both banks of the Kura; includes old central Asiatic section (crooked streets, bazaar) at site of old hot sulphur baths (which gave city its name), and Rus. section (N and S) with wide thoroughfares (Rustaveli boulevard), gardens, and modern bldgs. (govt. house, Marx-Engels-Lenin Inst.). Zemo-Avchala hydroelectric station (8 mi. N) supplies city with power. Metallurgical center of Rustavi is 20 mi. SE. Located on natural route bet. Black and Caspian seas. Tiflis was 1st mentioned at end of 4th cent. and became (5th cent.) ⊙ Georgia. Destroyed and rebuilt many times following raids by Huns, Khazars, Persians, Byzantines, Arabs, Mongols, and Turks, Tiflis flourished (12th–13th cent.) during height of Georgian expansion. Last sacked (1795) by Persians; passed (1800–01) to Russia and became ⊙ Tiflis govt. Its development during 19th cent. was speeded after construction (1871) of Baku-Batum RR. Became ⊙ Menshevik govt. (1917–21), then ⊙ Georgian SSR. Was ⊙ former Transcaucasian Soviet Federated Socialist Republic (1921–36). Its name was officially changed (1936) from Rus. Tiflis to Georgian Tbilisi. City underwent reconstruction and urban modernization in late 1930s. It was at Tiflis that Stalin studied theology and entered the revolutionary movement.

Tiflisskaya, Russian SFSR: see Tbilisskaya.

Tift, county (□ 266; pop. 22,645), S central Ga.; ⊙ Tifton. Coastal plain agr. (tobacco, cotton, corn, peanuts, livestock) and timber area intersected by Little R.; mfg. at Tifton. Formed 1905.

Tifton, city (pop. 6,831), ⊙ Tift co., S central Ga., 39 mi. ESE of Albany; tobacco market and processing center; mfg. (yarns, cottonseed oil, fertilizer, brick); peanut shelling; ships vegetable plants. State jr. col. and agr. experiment station here. Settled 1872, inc. 1890.

Tiganesti (tsēgŭnĕsht′), Rum. *Ţigăneşti*. **1** Village (pop. 890), Bucharest prov., S Rumania, on Ialomita R. and 20 mi. N of Bucharest; corn cultivation. Site of 18th-cent. monastery specializing in production of hand-woven materials and embroideries. **2** Village (pop. 5,239), Teleorman prov., S Rumania, on railroad and 5 mi. S of Alexandria; agr. center. Has 18th-cent. church.

Taganion, Greece: see Teganion.

Tigaon (tēgä′ōn, tēgoun′), town (1939 pop. 1,441; 1948 municipality pop. 16,912), Camarines Sur prov., SE Luzon, Philippines, 21 mi. E of Naga, near Lagonoy Gulf; agr. center (rice, abacá, corn).

Tigara, Alaska: see Point Hope.

Tigard (tī′gûrd), village (1940 pop. 1,095), Washington co., NW Oregon, 10 mi. SW of Portland in dairying and truck-farming area; mattresses.

Tigasaki, Japan: see Chigasaki.

Tigatto (tēgä′tō), town (1939 pop. 6,256) in Davao city, Davao prov., SE central Mindanao, Philippines, just NW of Davao proper.

Tigbauan (tēgbä′wän), town (1939 pop. 4,257; 1948 municipality pop. 19,603), Iloilo prov., S Panay isl., Philippines, near Panay Gulf, 14 mi. W of Iloilo; agr. center (rice, coconuts, sugar).

Tiger, resort town (pop. 269), Rabun co., extreme NE Ga., in Blue Ridge Mts., 3 mi. SSW of Clayton.

Tiger Hill, India: see Coonoor; Darjeeling, town.

Tiger River, S.C.: see Tyger River.

Tigerton, village (pop. 827), Shawano co., E central Wis., 32 mi. SE of Wausau; sawmilling, vegetable canning, cheese making. Near by is a park on the dells of Embarrass R.

Tigerville, mining village, Greenville co., NW S.C., in foothills of the Blue Ridge, 14 mi. N of Greenville; vermiculite. Seat of jr. col.

Tigh (tī), island (pop. 10), Inner Hebrides, Inverness, Scotland, just N of Raasay; 1 mi. long, ½ mi. wide.

Tighina, Moldavian SSR: see Bendery.

Tighnabruaich (tīnŭbrōō′ŭkh), seaside resort, S Argyll, Scotland, on the Kyles of Bute, 9 mi. NW of Rothesay.

Tigieglo (tējĕ′lyō), village, in the Upper Juba, S central Ital. Somaliland, on road and 45 mi. E of Hodur; durra growing, leopard hunting, wood carving (spears, arrows). Has fort.

Tigil or **Tigil′** (tyĭgĕl′), village (1939 pop. over 500), SW Koryak Natl. Okrug, Kamchatka oblast, Khabarovsk Territory, Russian SFSR, 105 mi. S of Palana, in reindeer-raising area.

Tigiria (tĭg′ĭryŭ), village, Cuttack dist., E Orissa, India, 22 mi. W of Cuttack. Was ⊙ former princely state of Tigiria (□ 46; pop. 26,331) in Orissa States, along left bank of Mahanadi R.; state inc. 1949 into Cuttack dist.

Tignall (tĭg′nŭl), town (pop. 502), Wilkes co., NE Ga., 19 mi. SSE of Elberton.

Tignes (tē′nyŭ), village (pop. 199), Savoie dept., SE France, on upper Isère R. and 12 mi. SE of Bourg-Saint Maurice, on Col de l'Iseran road bet. Graian Alps (E) and Massif de la Vanoise (W); alt. 5,443. Resort; winter sports. Tignes L. (alt. 6,840 ft.; 2 mi. SW) is at foot of Mont Pourri; Lac de la Sassière (alt. 7,972 ft.; 4 mi. E) is at foot of the Grande-Sassière.

Tignish (tĭgnĭsh′, tĭg′nĭsh), village (pop. estimate 500), NW P.E.I., on the Gulf of St. Lawrence, 40 mi. NNW of Summerside, and at N terminus of the isl. railroad; fishing center and tourist resort.

Tigranocerta, Turkey: see Siirt, town.

Tigre (tē′grā) or **Las Conchas** (läs kōn′chās), city (pop. 24,283), ⊙ Las Conchas dist. (□ 73; pop. 35,906), in Greater Buenos Aires, Argentina, at confluence of Las Conchas and Luján rivers (affluents of the Paraná delta), 18 mi. NW of Buenos Aires. Partly located on an isl. separated from adjoining San Fernando (SE) by canal, it is a popular resort. Also produces apples, oranges, peaches, and plums for Buenos Aires market.

Tigre or **Tigré** (tĭg′rā, tĭgrā′), province (□ c.26,000), N Ethiopia, bordering on Eritrea; ⊙ Makale. Consists partly of Danakil desert (E) and largely of mountainous highlands (4,500–8,000 ft. high) rising to 11,279 ft. in Mt. Alaji. Situated bet. Gash (here called Mareb), Takkaze, and Tsellari rivers, and drained by Ererti, Gheva, and Weri rivers; contains lakes Ashangi and Egogi Bad. Pop. speaks Tigriña and Afar. Agr. (cereals, coffee, legumes, honey, cotton) and stock raising (cattle, donkeys, goats). Salt extracting and potash mining (Dallol) in Danakil desert. Gold deposits S of Aksum. Trade centers: Aduwa (formerly its capital), Makale, Adigrat, Hauzein. Crossed (N–S) by roads through highlands. Its dynasty at Aksum ruled (1st–6th cent.) much of Ethiopia.

Tigre, El, Venezuela: see El Tigre.

Tigre Island (tē′grā), principal island in Gulf of Fonseca, in Valle dept., S Honduras. Volcanic in origin; forms perfect cone 3 mi. across at base; rises to 2,490 ft. Port of Amapala is on NW shore.

Tigre River, Loreto dept., NE Peru, rises in E outliers of the Andes E of Puyo (Ecuador), flows c.360 mi. SE to Marañón R. (Amazon basin) 37 mi. W of Nauta. Along its course are virgin tropical forests. Good navigability during flood season. Main affluent, Corrientes.

Tigre River, NE Venezuela, rises NNW of El Tigre (Anzoátegui state), flows c.170 mi. E and NE, through llanos of Monagas state, joining Morichal Largo R. before emptying into the Caño Mánamo (arm of Orinoco R. delta).

Tigres Bay (tē′grĭsh), inlet of the Atlantic, off SW Angola, 100 mi. SSW of Mossâmedes. Village of Baía dos Tigres on peninsula sheltering bay. Also called Great Fish Bay.

Tigrinna (tēgrĭn′nä), village (1950 pop. 1,659), W Tripolitania, Libya, on the plateau Gebel Nefusa, 2 mi. S of Garian, in agr. (tobacco, barley, olives) and livestock region; weaving (carpets, barracans). Has troglodyte dwellings. Italian agr. settlement established here in 1930s. Sometimes spelled Tegrinna.

Tigris River (tī′grĭs), Arabic *Dijla* (dĭj′lŭ), Turkish *Dicle* (dĕj′lă), biblical *Hiddekil* (hĭ′dĕkĕl), a great river (c.1,150 mi. long) of SW Asia. Rising in Kurdistan in E central Turkey in L. Golcuk, a mountain lake 15 mi. SE of Elazig, it flows SE for 280 mi. in Turkey, passing Maden, Diyarbakir, and

Bismil, and forms a small section (c.20 mi.) of the Syrian border before entering Iraq. Here it continues SE, roughly paralleling the Euphrates, and passing Mosul, Samarra, and Kut al Imara, to join with the Euphrates at Al Qurna, 40 mi. NW of Basra, forming the Shatt al Arab, a 120-mi. section of the joint stream which flows to the head of the Persian Gulf. Though shorter than the Euphrates, it is much swifter and of greater volume, receiving numerous tributaries from the E (particularly in Iraq), the most important being the Great Zab, Little Zab, and the Diyala (the last 2 rising in Iran). In its lower course it is connected by means of a number of semipermanent natural waterways, or canals, with the Euphrates; one of these is the Shatt al Gharraf, which branches off at Kut. The Tigris is navigable by shallow-draught steamers upstream to Baghdad, and beyond Baghdad to Mosul by smaller boats in the high-water season. Rafts are used above Mosul for downstream traffic. The Tigris furnishes much of the water which irrigates Mesopotamia, the birthplace of the great anc. civilizations, and along its banks are the ruins or sites of the anc. cities: Nineveh (opposite Mosul), Seleucia, Ashur, Ctesiphon, Calah.

Tigrovoi or **Tigrovoy** (tyēgrŭvoi'), town (1948 pop. over 500), S Maritime Territory, Russian SFSR, on branch of Trans-Siberian RR and 12 mi. NW (under jurisdiction) of Suchan; sawmilling.

Tiguabos (tēgwä'bōs), town (pop. 1,148), Oriente prov., E Cuba, 11 mi. NW of Guantánamo, in sugar-growing region.

Tigüipa (tēgwē'pä), village, Chuquisaca dept., SE Bolivia, on E slopes of Serranía de Aguaragüe and 26 mi. N of Villa Montes, on road; oil fields.

Tigullio, Golfo, Italy: see Rapallo.

Tigvariak Island (tĭgvâr'ēăk) (2 mi. long, 1 mi. wide; 1939 pop. 15), NE Alaska, in Arctic Ocean, 51 mi. ESE of Beechey Point; 70°13'N 147°10'W; fishing; primitive Eskimo culture.

Tigyaing (tē'jĭng), village, Katha dist., Upper Burma, on right bank of Irrawaddy R. and 30 mi. SSW of Katha.

Tigzirt-sur-Mer (tēgzērt'-sür-mâr'), anc. *Iomnium*, village (pop. 494), Alger dept., N central Algeria, in Great Kabylia, on the Mediterranean, 13 mi. NNE of Tizi-Ouzou. Ruins of Roman temple (2d cent. A.D.) and of early Christian basilica.

Tih, El, Et Tih, or **Al-Tih** (all: ĕt-tē'), desert plateau in central Sinai Peninsula, NE Egypt, bet. N coastal plain and mts.

Tihama or **Tihamah** (tĭhă'mŭ), coastal plain on Red Sea (W) coast of Arabian Peninsula, extending from Gulf of Aqaba (N) to the strait Bab el Mandeb (S), through Hejaz, Asir, and Yemen. It is widest bet. 20° and 24°N, where it forms a natural gateway to central Arabia in the Mecca-Medina area. An arid belt, interrupted only by a few agr. oases, the Tihama rises in E to the abrupt escarpment of the W edge of the tilted Arabian shelf. Sometimes spelled Tehama.

Tihany (tĭ'hŏnyŭ), resort town (pop. 1,027), Veszprem co., W central Hungary, on E shore of Tihany Peninsula (which juts into L. Balaton) and 12 mi. S of Veszprem. Near by is 11th-cent. Benedictine abbey with tomb of Andrew I. At one spot on peninsula is a celebrated echo.

Tihosuco (tēōsōō'kō), town (pop. 512), Quintana Roo, SE Mexico, on Yucatan Peninsula, near Yucatan border, 95 mi. SE of Mérida; chicle, henequen, tropical wood.

Tihran, Iran: see Tiran.

Ti-hua, China: see Urumchi.

Tihuatlán (tēwätlän'), town (pop. 1,943), Veracruz, E Mexico, in Sierra Madre Oriental foothills, 19 mi. SSW of Tuxpan; corn, sugar cane, coffee, fruit.

Tihwa, China: see Urumchi.

Tiinsk (tyēnsk'), village (1926 pop. 3,622), NE Ulyanovsk oblast, Russian SFSR, 12 mi. NNE of Melekess; grain, sunflowers.

Tijara (tĭjä'rŭ), town (pop. 7,380), E Rajasthan, India, 29 mi. NNE of Alwar; market center for millet, gram, cotton; handicraft cloth weaving, coarse paper mfg.

Tijarafe (tēhärä'fā), village (pop. 54; commune pop. 2,937), Palma, Canary Isls., 11 mi. W of Santa Cruz de la Palma, in agr. region (cereals, almonds, bananas, grapes, fruit, livestock). Lumbering; cheese processing. Maritime grotto near by.

Tijesno, Yugoslavia: see Murter Island.

Tíjola (tē'hōlä), city (pop. 2,604), Almería prov., S Spain, on Almanzora R. and 35 mi. N of Almería; flour mills; ships grapes. Agr. trade (cereals, olive oil, fruit, livestock). Copper mines near by.

Tijuana (tēwhä'nä), town (pop. 16,486), Northern Territory, Lower California (which became a new state on Dec. 20, 1951), NW Mexico, at U.S. border, on Tijuana R. (irrigation), on railroad and 12 mi. SE of San Diego (Calif.). Popular resort; noted for race tracks and gambling casinos in Agua Caliente (ä'gwä kälyĕn'tā), its SE district; became famous in prohibition era as wide-open town. Also an agr. center (cotton, cereals, fruit, vegetables). Formerly called Tia Juana. Rodríguez Dam, on the Tijuana, is near by.

Tijuana River, short stream in Lower California, NW Mexico, near U.S. border SE of San Diego; empties into the Pacific just over the line in U.S. Rodríguez Dam (completed c.1936), SE of Tijuana, impounds river for irrigation purposes.

Tijuca, Pico da (pē'kōō dä tēzhōō'kŭ), mountain (3,350 ft.) in Federal Dist. of Brazil, 8 mi. WSW of center of Rio de Janeiro. Excursion spot.

Tijucas (tēzhōō'kŭs), city (pop. 4,614), E Santa Catarina, Brazil, port on Tijucas bay (inlet of the Atlantic), 25 mi. N of Florianópolis; ships rice, sugar, timber.

Tikahau (tēkähä'ōō) or **Tikehau** (tēkāhä'ōō), atoll (pop. 375), N Tuamotu Isls., Fr. Oceania, S Pacific; 15°S 148°10'W. Formerly Krusenstern Isl.

Tikaitnagar (tĭkīt'nŭgŭr), town (pop. 3,279), Bara Banki dist., central Uttar Pradesh, India, 23 mi. E of Nawabganj; trades in rice, gram, wheat, oilseeds, sugar cane. Founded 1784.

Tikal (tēkäl'), site of Mayan ruins in Petén dept., N Guatemala, 27 mi. NE of Flores. Remains, thought to date from largest and perhaps oldest of Mayan cities, include a 229-ft.-high structure.

Tikam Batu (tēkäm'bä'tōō), village (pop. 549), SW Kedah, Malaya, near Muda R. (Penang line), 5 mi. SW of Sungei Patani; rubber, tapioca.

Tikamgarh (tē'kŭmgŭr), town (pop. 16,112), ⊙ Tikamgarh dist., W Vindhya Pradesh, India, 155 mi. W of Rewa; market center for millet, wheat, timber, ghee; flour milling, handicraft cloth weaving; sawmill. Stud farm near by. Was ⊙ former Central India state of Orchha. Formerly also called Tehri.

Tikang, China: see Taochung.

Tikari, India: see Tekari.

Tikehau, Tuamotu Isls.: see Tikahau.

Tikhaya Bay (tyē'khĭŭ), inlet on NW shore of Hooker Isl., Franz Josef Land, Russian SFSR, in Arctic Ocean; 80°20'N 52°48'E. Site of govt. observation and supply station (established 1929).

Tikhaya Sosna River (sŭsnä'), SW European Russian SFSR, rises E of Volokonovka, flows 80 mi. generally NE, past Budennoye, Alekseyevka (Voronezh oblast), and Ostrogozhsk, to Don R. just E of Korotoyak.

Tikhiye Gory, Russian SFSR: see Bondyuzhski.

Tikhonkaya, Russian SFSR: see Birobidzhan.

Tikhonovka, Russian SFSR: see Pozharskoye.

Tikhoretsk (tyĕkhŭryĕtsk'), city (1946 pop. 34,700), NE Krasnodar Territory, Russian SFSR, 95 mi. SSE of Rostov; rail junction; grain center; flour mills, grain elevators, metalworks, locomotive repair shops. Became city in 1926.

Tikhvin (tyĕkh'vēn), city (1939 pop. 16,400), SE Leningrad oblast, Russian SFSR, on Tikhvinka R. and 115 mi. ESE of Leningrad; alunite processing, sawmilling, woodworking center; metalworks, flour mill. Extensive bauxite mines at Boksitogorsk (SE). Known since end of 14th cent., it became trading center on Volga-Onega route. Temporarily occupied by Swedes (1611) and, during Second World War, by Germans (1941). Chartered 1724. Rimsky-Korsakov b. here.

Tikhvin Canal, in Leningrad oblast, Russian SFSR, connects upper course of Tikhvinka River with Sominka R., a left affluent of Chagodoshcha R., in area of Yefimovskaya; forms part of Tikhvin canal system (developed in late-18th cent.; now in disuse) connecting Volga R. at Shcherbakov with Neva R. and Leningrad over 570-mi. route.

Tikhvinka River (tyĕkh'vēn-kŭ), Leningrad oblast, Russian SFSR, rises in swampy lake region near Yefimovskaya, flows 95 mi. generally NW, past Tikhvin, to Syas R. 13 mi. W of Tikhvin. Forms part of Tikhvin canal system; connected with Sominka R., a left affluent of Chagodoshcha R., by Tikhvin Canal.

Tikikluk (tĭkĭk'lŏŏk), village (pop. 48), N Alaska, S of Barrow; 70°30'N 157°W. Sometimes spelled Tikigiluk.

Tikkakoski (tĭk'käkōs"kē), village in Jyväskylä rural commune (pop. 19,929), Vaasa co., S central Finland, in lake region, 11 mi. NNW of Jyväskylä; metalworking.

Tiko (chĕkō), town (pop. 11,010), S Br. Cameroons, administered as part of Eastern Provinces of Nigeria, port on Bimbia R., off Gulf of Guinea, and 12 mi. ENE of Victoria; exports palm oil and kernels, bananas, cacao, hardwood. Airport.

Tikonko (tēkông'kō), town (pop. 961), South-Western Prov., S central Sierra Leone, 7 mi. SSW of Bo; road junction; palm oil and kernels, cacao, coffee. United Methodist mission.

Tikrit (tĭkrēt'), village, Baghdad prov., N central Iraq, on the Tigris and 100 mi. NNW of Baghdad. Saladin (1137?–93) b. here. Sometimes spelled Tekrit.

Tiksi (tyĭksē'), town (1939 pop. over 500), N Yakut Autonomous SSR, Russian SFSR, port on Tiksi Bay (small W inlet of Buor-Khaya Bay), 300 mi. NNW of Verkhoyansk; arctic observation post; supply point on Arctic Sea route. On S side of Tiksi Bay is Cape Kosisty or Cape Kosistyy; site of airfield.

Tikugo River, Japan: see Chikugo River.

Tikuho, Japan: see Chikuho.

Tikves or **Tikvesh** (both: tēk'vĕsh), Serbo-Croatian *Tikveš*, fertile valley in Macedonia, Yugoslavia, extending along Vardar R. from Demir Gate c.20 mi. NW. Wine and cotton growing. Kavadarci is only town.

Tikwah, gold mine in Essequibo co., W central Br. Guiana, on small affluent of the Mazaruni near its mouth, and 12 mi. WSW of Issano.

Tila (tē'lä), town (pop. 1,165), Chiapas, S Mexico, 45 mi. NE of San Cristóbal de las Casas; cereals, fruit.

Tiladummati Atoll (tĭlŭdŏŏm'mŭtē), N group (pop. 12,212) of Maldive Isls., in Indian Ocean, bet. 6°30'N and 7°N, 310 mi. WSW of Cape Comorin (India); coconuts, breadfruit.

Tilakwada (tĭl'ŭkwädŭ), village (pop. 2,308), Baroda dist., N Bombay, India, on Narbada R. and 33 mi. SE of Baroda; local market for cotton, millet, timber. Sometimes spelled Tilakvada.

Tilantongo (tēläntŏng'gō), town (pop. 476), Oaxaca, S Mexico, in Sierra Madre del Sur, 40 mi. WNW of Oaxaca; cereals, sugar cane, fruit. Archaeological remains.

Tilapa (tēlä'pä). **1** Town (pop. 1,922), Mexico state, central Mexico, at N foot of Nevado de Toluca, 5 mi. S of Toluca; cereals, fruit, livestock. **2** Town (pop. 1,090), Puebla, central Mexico, 5 mi. W of Matamoros; corn, sugar cane, fruit.

Tilapa River, SW Guatemala, rises on W slope of volcano Santa María, flows c.50 mi. S and W, past Caballo Blanco, and S forming Quezaltenango-Retalhuleu dept. border, to the Pacific 2 mi. SE of Ocós. Not navigable. Called Ocosito R. in upper course.

Tilarán (tēlärän'), town (1950 pop. 1,117), Guanacaste prov., NW Costa Rica, on road from Cañas to Guatuso Lowland, and 8 mi. WNW of Cañas; agr. and livestock center; coffee, sugar cane, beans, manioc.

Tilarán Mountains, section of continental divide in NW Costa Rica, extends c.40 mi. SE from L. Arenal; rises to c.6,000 ft. Abangares gold fields are at S foot.

Tilburg (tĭl'bûrkh), city (pop. 114,312), North Brabant prov., S Netherlands, on Wilhelmina Canal and 13 mi. E of Breda; rail junction; center of textile industry (wool weaving, mfg. of clothing, textile machinery, dyes); railroad equipment, strawboard; leather tanneries; machine shops. Electric power station; textile research center. Grew rapidly from small village during 19th cent.

Tilbury (tĭl'bē"rē, tĭl'bûrē), town (pop. 2,155), S Ont., 16 mi. SW of Chatham; mfg. of automobile bodies, bricks, tiles.

Tilbury, former urban district (1931 pop. 16,825), S Essex, England, on N bank of the Thames and 22 mi. E of London, opposite Gravesend; 51°27'N 0°22'E; extensive docks are included in Port of London and are terminus of several passenger shipping lines. Industries include shoe mfg. Tilbury Fort, begun under Henry VIII, was later rebuilt and strengthened. In 1588 Queen Elizabeth held celebrated review here when Spanish Armada threatened England. Present docks, begun 1886, were heavily bombed in Second World War. Tilbury urban dist. was inc. (1936) in Thurrock.

Tilcara (tēlkä'rä), town (pop. estimate 500), ⊙ Tilcara dept. (□ 780; 1947 pop. 6,082), central Jujuy prov., Argentina, on railroad, on the Río Grande de Jujuy and 45 mi. NNW of Jujuy; corn, alfalfa, wheat, fruit, livestock; flour milling. Hydroelectric plant. Has colonial church. Ruins of old Inca forts near by.

Tilcara, Sierra de (syĕ'rä dā), subandean mountain range in central Jujuy prov., Argentina, N of Jujuy; 45 mi. long; rises to c.14,000 ft.

Tilcoco or **Quinta de Tilcoco** (kēn'tä dā tēlkō'kō), village (1930 pop. 209), O'Higgins prov., central Chile, 17 mi. SW of Rancagua, in agr. area (grain, wine, fruit, potatoes, livestock).

Tilden. **1** Village (pop. 906), Randolph co., SW Ill., 37 mi. SE of East St. Louis, in agr. and bituminous-coal-mining area. **2** City (pop. 1,033), Antelope and Madison counties, NE central Nebr., 22 mi. W of Norfolk and on Elkhorn R.; livestock, dairy and poultry produce, grain. **3** Village (pop. c.500), ⊙ McMullen co., S Texas, on Frio R. and c.40 mi. E of Cotulla.

Tilden, Fort, N.Y.: see Rockaway Peninsula.

Tileagd (tē'lyägd"), Hung. *Mezőtileagd* (mĕ'zûtē"-lĕŏkt), village (pop. 3,437), Bihor prov., W Rumania, in Crisana, on Rapid Körös R., on railroad, and 12 mi. E of Oradea in dist. noted for its handicraft industries (weaving, embroidery, wood carving); produces ceramics, gypsum, railroad ties; refines petroleum. Asphalt quarrying near by. In Hungary, 1940–45.

Tilff (tĭlf), town (pop. 4,625), Liége prov., E Belgium, on Ourthe R. and 5 mi. S of Liége; steel-rolling mills, zinc processing.

Tilghman Island (tĭl'mŭn), low, sandy isl. (c.4 mi. long, 1½ mi. wide), Talbot co., E Md., in Chesapeake Bay on N side of mouth of Choptank R.; separated from mainland by narrow channel (bridged). Center of large fishing, oystering, and crabbing industry; resort for anglers and duck hunters. Villages are Tilghman (pop. c.1,000) and Avalon (ă'vŭlŏn) at N end, Fairbank at S end. Seafood and vegetables are packed at Tilghman.

Tilhar (tĭl'hŭr), town (pop. 19,256), Shahjahanpur dist., central Uttar Pradesh, India, 12 mi. WNW of Shahjahanpur; trades in wheat, rice, gram, oilseeds, sugar cane. Founded 16th cent.

Tilichiki (tyĭlyĭchēkē'), village (1926 pop. 164), NE Koryak Natl. Okrug, Kamchatka oblast, Khabarovsk Territory, Russian SFSR, at head of Korf Bay of Bering Sea, 225 mi. NE of Palana. Town of KORF is 10 mi. SE.

Tiligulo-Berezanka (tyĭlyĕgōō'lŭ-byĕrĭzän'kŭ), village (1939 pop. over 500), SW Nikolayev oblast, Ukrainian SSR, 27 mi. WSW of Nikolayev; cotton, wheat.

Tilin (tē'lĭn), village, Pakokku dist., Upper Burma, on road and 70 mi. WNW of Pakokku, at S end of Myittha R. valley.

Tilisarao (tēlēsärou'), town (pop. estimate 1,500), NE San Luis prov., Argentina, on railroad and 70 mi. NNE of Mercedes; agr. center (wheat, corn, alfalfa, livestock; dairying). Granite and kaolin deposits near by.

Tilissos, Crete: see TYLISSOS.

Tiliuín (tēlēwēn'), village, Ifni territory, NW Africa, on the Asaca (Fr. Morocco border) and 24 mi. S of Sidi Ifni; 29°2'N 10°14'W. Barley, sheep; some irrigation agr. (alfalfa, corn, tomatoes). Airfield.

Tillabéry or **Tillabéri** (tēläbĕ'rē), town (pop. c.1,000), SW Niger territory, Fr. West Africa, landing on left bank of the Niger and 55 mi. NW of Niamey, linked by rail. Exports mutton and beef to Nigeria. Grows millet, rice, manioc, onions, melons.

Tillamook (tĭ'lùmŏŏk), county (□ 1,115; pop. 18,606), NW Oregon; ⊙ Tillamook. Bounded W by Pacific Ocean; drained in N by Nehalem R. Dairying, logging; fisheries. Formed 1853.

Tillamook, city (pop. 3,685), ⊙ Tillamook co., NW Oregon, near coast, at head of Tillamook Bay, 55 mi. W of Portland; dairy center; flour and lumber milling, fisheries. Known as Lincoln, then Hoquarton, and finally (1885) Tillamook; inc. 1891. Has co. historical mus.

Tillamook Head, NW Oregon, high promontory (c.1,200 ft.) 18 mi. SW of Astoria; lighthouse on isl. offshore.

Tillar (tĭ'lùr), town (pop. 239), Drew co., SE Ark., 7 mi. NW of McGehee, near Bayou Bartholomew.

Tillatoba (tĭlùtō'bù), village (pop. 127), Yalobusha co., N central Miss., 15 mi. NNW of Grenada.

Tillberga (tĭl'bĕr"yä), village (pop. 1,066), Vastmanland co., central Sweden, 6 mi. NE of Vasteras; rail junction; metalworking.

Tille River (tē), Côte-d'Or dept., E central France, rises in the Plateau of Langres 4 mi. NE of Grancey-le-Château, flows c.45 mi. SSE to the Saône below Auxonne.

Tillery, Lake, W central N.C., backed up in Pee Dee R. by hydroelectric dam 10 mi. SE of Albemarle; c.15 mi. long. State park here.

Tilleur (tĭyûr'), town (pop. 6,418), Liége prov., E Belgium, 3 mi. SW of Liége, near Meuse R.; blast furnaces, chemical works.

Tilley, village (pop. 192), SE Alta., 50 mi. NW of Medicine Hat; wheat, stock.

Tillicoultry (tĭlĭkōō'trē), burgh (1931 pop. 2,953; 1951 census 3,818), Clackmannan, Scotland, near Devon R., 3 mi. NE of Alloa; woolen (tartan) milling, paper making. Near by are coal mines. Burgh includes Devonside, on Devon R.

Tillman, county (□ 861; pop. 17,598), SW Okla.; ⊙ Frederick. Bounded S by Red R. (here forming Texas line), and W by its North Fork; also drained by the Deep Red Run. Agr. area (cotton, grain, livestock, poultry; dairy products). Mfg. at Frederick and Grandfield. Sand and gravel pits; some oil wells, refineries. Formed 1907.

Till River, Northumberland, England, rises on The Cheviot in Cheviot Hills, flows 32 mi. N and NW, past Wooler and Flodden, to the Tweed 3 mi. NE of Coldstream.

Tillsonburg (tĭl'sùnbûrg), town (pop. 4,002), S Ont., 24 mi. ENE of St. Thomas; mfg. of machinery, agr. implements, bricks, shoes; lumbering, tobacco processing; in tobacco and fruit region.

Tilly-sur-Seulles (tēyē'-sür-sûl'), village (pop. 421), Calvados dept., NW France, on the Seulles and 12 mi. W of Caen. Heavily damaged (Normandy campaign; June-July, 1944) in Second World War.

Tilos, Greece: see TELOS.

Tilsit, former East Prussia: see SOVETSK, Kaliningrad oblast, RSFSR.

Tiltil (tēltēl'), village (1930 pop. 218), Santiago prov., central Chile, on railroad and 28 mi. NW of Santiago, in agr. area (alfalfa, wheat, fruit, wine, cattle).

Tilton. **1** Town (pop. 100), Whitfield co., NW Ga., 8 mi. SSE of Dalton and on Conasauga R. **2** Village (pop. 1,638), Vermilion co., E Ill., just S of Danville, in agr. and bituminous-coal area. Inc. 1884. **3** Town (pop. 2,085), including Tilton village (pop. 1,127), Belknap co., central N.H., 15 mi. N of Concord and on Winnipesaukee R. (opposite Northfield, with which its interests are bound), near the Merrimack; textiles. Seat of Tilton School for boys. In Sanbornton, as Sanbornton Bridge, until inc. 1869.

Tiltonsville or **Tiltonville**, village (pop. 2,202), Jefferson co., E Ohio, on Ohio R. and 8 mi. N of Wheeling, W.Va.; concrete blocks, lumber. Called Grover until 1930.

Tiltonville, Ohio: see TILTONSVILLE.

Tilt River, Perthshire, Scotland, issues from the small Loch Tilt (alt. 1,653 ft.) in the Grampians 13 mi. NE of Blair Atholl, flows 16 mi. SW, through Glentilt, to Garry R. at Blair Atholl.

Tilwana or **Tilwanah** (tĭlwä'nù), village (pop. 5,389), Minufiya prov., Lower Egypt, 7 mi. SE of Minuf; cereals, cotton, flax.

Tim (tyēm), agr. town (1926 pop. 2,028), N central Kursk oblast, Russian SFSR, 40 mi. E of Kursk; wheat, sunflowers.

Tima, Egypt: see TEMA.

Timagami or **Temagami** (tĭmŏ'gùmē), village (pop. estimate 500), E central Ont., at E end of L. Timagami, 27 mi. SSW of Haileybury; gold and iron mining, lumbering.

Timagami, Lake (□ 90), E central Ont., 30 mi. SW of Haileybury. Irregular in shape, deeply indented by several bays, it is 30 mi. long, 20 mi. wide; contains numerous isls. Drains E into Montreal R.

Timahoe (tĭ"mùhōō'), Gaelic *Tigh Mochue*, village, central Co. Laoighis, Ireland, 7 mi. SE of Port Laoighise; peat-digging center. Has 9th- or 10th-cent. round tower.

Timaná (tēmänä'), town (pop. 2,713), Huila dept., S central Colombia, on upper Magdalena R., on highway N to Neiva, and 11 mi. NE of Pitalito; alt. 3,379 ft. Rice, coffee, cacao; horse and mule breeding. Produces laurel wax and Panama hats.

Timan Ridge (tyēmän'), Rus. *Timanskiy Kryazh*, upland in N European Russian SFSR, bet. basins of Vychegda and Mezen (W) and Pechora (E) rivers; extends from upper reaches of Vychegda R. 350 mi. NNW to Chesha Bay and is continued on Kanin Peninsula; rises to 2,020 ft.

Timarni, India: see TIMURNI.

Timaru (tĭmùrōō'), borough (pop. 18,305; metropolitan Timaru 19,596) and port, ⊙ Levels co. (□ 263; pop. 4,257), E S.Isl., New Zealand, on Canterbury Bight, 95 mi. SW of Christchurch; grain center; rail junction. Exports frozen foods. Airport near by. Timaru is in, but independent of, Levels co.

Timashevo (tyēmä'shĭvŭ), town (1926 pop. 5,073), E central Kuibyshev oblast, Russian SFSR, on Greater Kinel R. and 23 mi. ENE of Kinel, on rail spur; sugar-refining center.

Timashevskaya (-shĭfskīŭ), village (1926 pop. 12,143), E Krasnodar Territory, Russian SFSR, 40 mi. N of Krasnodar; rail junction; flour milling, metalworking, bast-fiber processing (sunn and ambary hemp). Sometimes spelled Timoshevskaya.

Timau (tēmou'), town, Central Prov., S central Kenya, on road and 12 mi. NE of Nanyuki, at N foot of Mt. Kenya; coffee, sisal, wheat, corn.

Timavo River, Yugoslavia and Free Territory of Trieste: see REKA, river.

Timbakion, Crete: see TYMBAKION.

Timbalier Bay (tămbùlyā'), SE La., shallow inlet of the Gulf of Mexico, c.55 mi. SSW of New Orleans; c.14 mi. long. Oil and gas wells; oyster beds; fishing. Adjoins Terrebonne Bay (W), L. Raccourci (N); Timbalier and East Timbalier isls. are bet. bay and Gulf.

Timbalier Island, SE La., barrier island (c.7 mi. long), bet. Timbalier Bay (N) and the Gulf of Mexico (S), c.65 mi. SSW of New Orleans. Timbalier lighthouse (29°3'N 90°22'W) is offshore. Near-by East Timbalier Isl. (c.2 mi. long) is bird refuge.

Timbaúba (tēmbäōō'bù), city (pop. 8,532), E Pernambuco, NE Brazil, near Paraíba border, on railroad and 50 mi. NW of Recife; sugar-milling center. Ships tobacco, livestock.

Timbédra (tēmbā'drä), village, SE Mauritania, Fr. West Africa, in the Sahara, 245 mi. N of Bamako, Fr. Sudan; trades in gum arabic. School for sons of Moorish chieftains.

Timberlake, village (pop. 236), Lake co., NE Ohio, on L. Erie, c.18 mi. NE of Cleveland.

Timber Lake, city (pop. 552), ⊙ Dewey co., N central S.Dak., 80 mi. NNW of Pierre; trading point for farming region; grain, dairy products, livestock, poultry.

Timber Mountain, Nev.: see GRANT RANGE.

Timbersbrook, town, in Congleton urban dist., E Cheshire, England; textile printing.

Timberville, town (pop. 271), Rockingham co., NW Va., in Shenandoah Valley, 14 mi. NNE of Harrisonburg, apple canning.

Timbío (tēmbē'ō), town (pop. 2,138), Cauca dept., SW Colombia, on Pasto-Popayán highway, on W slopes of Cordillera Central, and 8 mi. SSW of Popayán; coffee, tobacco, sugar cane, cacao, fique, fruit, livestock.

Timbiquí (tēmbēkē'), village (pop. 251), Cauca dept., SW Colombia, in Pacific lowlands, 14 mi. NE of Guapi; gold- and platinum-placer mines.

Timbiras (tēmbē'rùs), city (pop. 727), N central Maranhão, Brazil, on Itapecuru R., on São Luís–Teresina RR and 14 mi. NNW of Codó; tobacco. Until 1944, Monte Alegre.

Timblin, borough (pop. 327), Jefferson co., W central Pa., 12 mi. W of Punxsutawney.

Timbó (tēmbô'), city (pop. 1,386), E Santa Catarina, Brazil, in Itajaí Açu valley, 15 mi. WNW of Blumenau, in fertile area of diversified farming.

Timbo (tēm'bō), village, W central Fr. Guinea, Fr. West Africa, 25 mi. NE of Mamou; bananas, peanuts, rubber. Rail station at Beauvois, 7 mi. SSE.

Timboroa (tēmbōrō'ä), village, Rift Valley prov., W Kenya, at W edge of Great Rift Valley, 15 mi. WSW of Eldama Ravine; alt. 9,009 ft.; hardwood industry. Highest point (9,150 ft.) on Kenya-Uganda RR is just N.

Timbuktu (tĭm"bŭktōō'), Fr. *Tombouctou* (tōbōōk-tōō'), town (pop. c.7,000), central Fr. Sudan, Fr. West Africa, near left bank of the Niger, in upper-Niger depression, center of caravan trade on trans-Saharan road to Algeria and Morocco, and 430 mi. NE of Bamako; 16°47'N 3°W. Deals in salt and other products of the region (gum, rice, millet, wheat; livestock, hides). Airfield. Settled 1087, it flourished as a center of commerce for Negro tribes. Its fame as a mart for slaves and gold spread to Europe, and it was one of the chief centers of Moslem culture in W Sudan. Its prosperity was destroyed by a Moroccan army that crossed the Sahara and took it in 1591. After 1800 it changed hands frequently, its trade was destroyed after abolition of slavery, and it was little more than a vast ruin when the French seized it in 1893. There remain forts and several mosques. Its port Kabara adjoins S. Also spelled Timbuctoo.

Timbun Mata (tēmbōōn' mä'tù), island (18 mi. long, 1–6 mi. wide) belonging to Br. North Borneo, in Darvel Bay, 80 mi. SSE of Sandakan; sago, copra; fishing.

Time, Norway: see KVERNALAND.

Time, village (pop. 57), Pike co., W Ill., 28 mi. WSW of Jacksonville, in agr. area.

Timelkam (tĭm'ùlkäm), town (pop. 3,023), S central Upper Austria, 2 mi. W of Vöcklabruck; has cattle market.

Timer-Tau, Russian SFSR: see TEMIR-TAU, Kemerovo oblast.

Timessa (tēmĕ'sä) or **Tmessa** (tmĕ'sä), village (pop. 223), central Fezzan, Libya, 90 mi. SE of Sebha, in a Saharan oasis; date growing.

Timewell, Ill.: see MOUND STATION.

Timfi, Greece: see TYMPHE.

Timfors (tēm'fôrs", –fôsh"), village (pop. 555), Kronoberg co., S Sweden, on Laga R. and 20 mi. E of Laholm; paper milling.

Timfristos, Greece: see TYMPHRESTOS.

Timgad (tēmgäd'), anc. *Thamugadi*, ruined city of NE Algeria, in Constantine dept., 17 mi. ESE of Batna, at N foot of the Aurès massif. Called the Pompeii of N Africa, because of extensive remains of Roman city and colony founded here A.D. 100 by Trajan. Destroyed by native tribes in 7th cent., town was forgotten until excavations were undertaken in 1881. Ruins include Trajan's triumphal arch, a capitol, several baths with mosaic floors, a theater (seating c.3,500), a library, and a forum.

Timimoun (tēmēmōōn'), village (pop. 5,683) and Saharan oasis, in Aïn-Sefra territory, W central Algeria, at S edge of the Great Western Erg, on El-Goléa–Adrar auto track, 180 mi. SW of El-Goléa; 29°15'N 0°15'E. Belongs to the Gourara group of oases; date palms; goats, camels.

Timiris, Cape, Fr. West Africa: see MIRIK, CAPE.

Timiryazevo (tyēmĭryä'zyĭvŭ), village (1939 pop. 1,589), N Kaliningrad oblast, Russian SFSR, on narrow-gauge railroad and 11 mi. W of Sovetsk, in swampy, wooded dist. Until 1945, in East Prussia and called Neukirch (noi'kĭrkh).

Timiryazevski or **Timiryazevskiy** (–zyĭfskē), town (1940 pop. over 500), SE Tomsk oblast, Russian SFSR, on left bank of Tom R. and 4 mi. SW of Tomsk. Until 1940, called Novaya Eushta.

Timis, Rumania: see PREDEAL.

Timiskaming (tùmĭ'skùmĭng), district (□ 5,896; pop. 50,604), E central Ont., on L. Timiskaming and on Que. border; ⊙ Haileybury.

Timiskaming, town (pop. 2,168), SW Que., on S part of L. Timiskaming, 33 mi. NE of North Bay, in dairying, stock-raising, mining (gold, silver, cobalt, arsenic) region. Also spelled Temiskaming and Témiscamingue. Inc. 1920; originally called Kipawa. Just S are the Long Sault Rapids.

Timiskaming, Lake (□ 110), SW Que. and E Ont., expansion of Ottawa R., extending 62 mi. bet. Timiskaming (SSE) and New Liskeard (NNW), 1–10 mi. wide; alt. 589 ft. In N part are several isls.; on NW shore is Haileybury, with adjoining mining region.

Timisoara (tēmēsh-wä'rä), Rum. *Timişoara*, Hung. *Temesvár* (tĕ'mĕshvär), city (1948 pop. 111,987), ⊙ Timisoara prov., W Rumania, in Banat, on Bega Canal and 75 mi. NE of Belgrade, 250 mi. NW of Bucharest; 45°45'N 21°14'E. Major industrial and commercial center and rail hub. Produces woolen and cotton textiles, electrical appliances, rolling stock, pianos, hardware, silverware, chemicals, pharmaceuticals, paints and varnishes, rubber and clay products, footwear, gloves, hats, metal furniture, liquor, confectionery, printed matter, tobacco, foodstuffs, bells. Timisoara is seat of R.C. and Orthodox bishops. City consists of inner town formerly surrounded by ramparts (now made into boulevards), and outlying suburbs; municipal airport is to N. Educational institutions include a polytechnical inst. (1920), the Univ. of the West (1945), artillery school, commercial and fine-arts academies, deaf-mute institute. Timisoara is also known for numerous recreation facilities, notably the beaches along the canal. Most notable architectural features are: 18th-cent. R.C. church with leaning tower built by Fischer von Erlach; 15th-cent. Hunyadi Castle (now barracks) reconstructed in 1856 after 1849 bombardment; 18th-cent. R.C. episcopal residences; several 18th-cent. churches; an 18th-cent. Moorish-style synagogue; 18th-cent. town hall; municipal theater. An old Roman settlement later occupied by the Avars, Timisoara and adjacent area (duchy) came under Magyar domination (896) and was formally attached to Hungary (1010). Janos Hunyadi resided here (15th cent.) as the ban of Banat. From 1552 on, city was held by the Turks until its deliverance (1716) by Eugene of Savoy. Under the Austrian rule Ger. colonists were recruited for settlement within fortified walls. Siege by Hung. revolutionaries (1849) lasted 3 months. Industrial development, greatly fostered by proximity of iron deposits, dates from mid-19th cent. Though occupied by Serbia after First World War, it was finally awarded to Rumania (1919). The foreign element (Hungarians 30,630; Germans 16,139) is still dominant in its economic life.

Timis Pass, Rumania: see Predeal Pass.

Timis River (tē'mēsh), Rum. *Timiş*, Hung. *Temes* (tĕ'mĕsh), Serbo-Croatian *Tamiš* (tä'mēsh), in W Rumania and NE Yugoslavia, rises in SW part of Transylvania Alps 12 mi. SE of Resita, flows SE to Teregova, thence W in a wide northward curve, past Caransebes and Lugoj, across Yugoslav border, and past Boka and Orlovat to the Danube at Pancevo, just E of Belgrade; c.200 mi. long. Its left tributary, Barsava R. [Rum. *Bârsava*, Hung. *Berzava*, Serbo-Croatian *Brzava*] is canalized in lower course for c.30 mi., forming so-called Timis Canal.

Timken, city (pop. 138), Rush co., central Kansas, on Walnut Creek and 8 mi. ESE of La Crosse; wheat, livestock. Gas and oil fields near by.

Timkovichi (tyĭmkô'vĕchē), village (1926 pop. 2,699), W Bobruisk oblast, Belorussian SSR, 25 mi. W of Slutsk; food products. Former rail terminus (until 1939) near Pol. border.

Timmancherla, India: see Guntakal.

Timmendorfer Strand (tĭ'mŭndôr"fŭr shtränt'), commune (pop. 10,572), in Schleswig-Holstein, NW Germany, 10 mi. NE of Lübeck; Baltic seaside resort extending c.5 mi. along Lübeck Bay. Until 1937 in Oldenburg.

Timmernabben (tĭ'mŭrnä"bŭn), fishing village (pop. 562), Kalmar co., SE Sweden, on Kalmar Sound of the Baltic, 20 mi. N of Kalmar; pottery works; seaside resort.

Timmins, town (pop. 28,790), E central Ont., on Mattagami R., at mouth of Mountjoy R., and 130 mi. NNW of Sudbury; commercial center for Porcupine gold-mining region (discovered 1909), with gold mines, paper, pulp, lumber mills, breweries. Peat is worked near by.

Timmonsville, town (pop. 2,001), Florence co., E central S.C., 11 mi. SW of Florence, in agr. and dairying area (tobacco, cotton, cattle, truck); textiles, lumber.

Timnath, town (pop. 177), Larimer co., N Colo., on Cache la Poudre R., in lake region, and 6 mi. SE of Fort Collins; alt. 4,875 ft.

Timok, oblast, Yugoslavia: see Zajecar.

Timok River (tē'môk), E Serbia, Yugoslavia, formed by junction of the Crna Reka (or Crni Timok) and Beli Timok River just NE of Zajecar; flows c.50 mi. NNE, along Bulg. border, to the Danube 7 mi. E of Negotin. Timok Basin, Serbo-Croatian *Timočki Basen*, extends along its 2 headstreams; high-grade bituminous coal. Zajecar-Negotin RR follows entire course.

Timoleague (tĭ"mŭlēg'), Gaelic *Tigh Molaga*, town (pop. 281), S Co. Cork, Ireland, on Courtmacsherry Bay, 7 mi. SSW of Bandon; agr. market (dairying; oats, potatoes). Has remains of 14th-cent. Franciscan abbey, once noted for its Spanish wines, on site of 7th-cent. church built by St. Molaga.

Timon (tē'mō), city (pop. 1,937), E Maranhão, Brazil, on left bank of Parnaíba R. (Piauí border), opposite Teresina (bridge), and on short spur of São Luís–Teresina RR; processing center for babassu oil and carnauba wax; sugar milling, alcohol distilling. Founded as Cajazeiras; called Flores until 1944.

Timonium (tĭmō'nēŭm), village (pop. c.250), Baltimore co., N Md., c.10 mi. N of downtown Baltimore.

Timor (tē'môr, tī'–), largest and easternmost island (□ 13,071; pop. c.800,000), of the Lesser Sundas, part belonging to Indonesia, part to Portugal, bet. the Savu and Banda seas in N and Timor Sea in S, 525 mi. NW of Darwin, Australia; 8°19'–10°22'S 123°28'–127°18'E; long, narrow, 300 mi. long, 10–60 mi. wide. Isl. is almost wholly mountainous, rising to 9,678 ft. at Mt. Ramelau in central area. Maximum summer temp. in coastal areas is 95°F. Jan.–March is rainy season; mean annual rainfall 58 in. There are sandalwood, coconut, and eucalyptus trees. Among wild animals are the marsupials called cuscus, monkeys, deer, civet cats, snakes, and crocodiles. The natives (of Malay and Papuan stock) are predominantly Christian. The Portuguese settled here c.1520. Coming in 1613, the Dutch became bitter rivals of the Portuguese, and succeeded (1618) in taking possession of W end of isl. Isl. was under Br. rule 1811–16. Border bet. Du. and Port. territories was settled by treaty of 1859, and confirmed in treaty of 1904 which finally became effective in 1914. In Second World War isl. was occupied early in 1942 by the Japanese. The colony of **Portuguese Timor** (□ 7,383; 1940 pop. 438,350) comprises E half of isl. and its exclave Oe-Cusse in Indonesian section; includes offshore isls. of Atauro and Jaco; chief port and ⊙ Dili. Principal products are copra, tobacco, coffee, and sandalwood. Before the area became (1926) an independent colony, it was governed from Macao. **Indonesian Timor** (□ 5,765; 1930 pop. 350,064) comprises W half of isl.; ⊙ Kupang. Chief products: sandalwood, copra, cattle, hides, ponies. Fishing is important. The area (formerly known as Dutch Timor and Netherlands Timor) became part of Du.-sponsored state of East Indonesia when it was created Dec., 1946; became Indonesian territory in 1950.

Timorlaut or **Timor Laoet,** Indonesia: see Tanimbar Islands.

Timor Sea, arm of Indian Ocean, bet. Timor and N coast of Australia, merges with Arafura Sea (NE); c.300 mi. wide.

Timoshevskaya, Russian SFSR: see Timashevskaya.

Timote, Arroyo (äroi'ō tēmō'tä), river, Florida dept., S central Uruguay, rises in the Cuchilla Grande Principal 5 mi. NNE of Cerro Colorado, flows 50 mi. NW to the Yí 28 mi. E of Durazno.

Timotes (tēmō'tēs), town (pop. 1,775), Mérida state, W Venezuela, in Andean spur, on N side of Mucuchíes (or Timotes) Pass, on transandine highway, on Motatán R., and 39 mi. NE of Mérida; alt. 6,614 ft. Wheat, fruit; cattle raising. Known for dairy products; flour milling. Mica deposits near by.

Timotes Pass, Venezuela: see Mucuchíes Pass.

Timpanogos, Mount (tĭmpŭnō'gŭs), highest peak (12,008 ft.) in Wasatch Range, N central Utah, 10 mi. N of Provo. Timpanogos Cave Natl. Monument is on NW slope.

Timpanogos Cave National Monument (250 acres; established 1922), N central Utah, on NW slope of Mt. Timpanogos and 22 mi. SSE of Salt Lake City. Series of 3 connected chambers, notable for their lining of crystal filigree (pink and white) and variety of tints exhibited by stalactite, stalagmite, and helictite formations. The Great Heart of Timpanogos is large stalactite resembling a human heart.

Timpas Creek (tĭm'pŭs), SE Colo., rises in several branches in SW Otero co., flows 54 mi. NE to Arkansas R. W of La Junta. Intermittent in upper half of course.

Timperley, town and parish (pop. 7,080), N Cheshire, England, 2 mi. NE of Altrincham; metal-working, mfg. of electrical equipment.

Timpson, village (pop. 1,455), Shelby co., E Texas, near Attoyac Bayou, c.45 mi. S of Marshall; ships truck; lumber milling, cotton ginning, vegetable canning. Natural gas, lignite produced near by.

Timsah, Lake (tĭm'sä), NE Egypt, 40 mi. NNW of Suez; c.2 mi. wide (E–W), 3 mi. long; crossed by Suez Canal. Ismailia on NW shore.

Timsbury, agr. village and parish (pop. 1,464), NE Somerset, England, 3 mi. NW of Radstock; limestone quarrying.

Timucuy (tēmōōkwē'), town (pop. 1,212), Yucatan, SE Mexico, 12 mi. SSE of Mérida; henequen.

Timur (tyēmōōr'), village (1948 pop. over 2,000), central South Kazakhstan oblast, Kazakh SSR, on Trans-Caspian RR and 30 mi. SSE of Turkestan, in cotton area. Near by is 14th-cent. burial mound.

Timurni (tĭmōōr'nē) or **Timarni** (tĭmŭr'nē), town (pop. 4,951), Hoshangabad dist., W Madhya Pradesh, India, 8 mi. ENE of Harda; wheat, cotton, millet, oilseeds. Sawmilling near by. Dense teak and sal forests (S).

Timusi (tēmōō'sē), town (pop. c.3,700), La Paz dept., W Bolivia, in Cordillera Real, 9 mi. ENE of Carabuco; *oca*, potatoes, barley.

Tina (tī'nŭ), town (pop. 224), Carroll co., NW central Mo., 13 mi. N of Carrollton.

Tina, El, Et Tina, or **Al-Tinah** (all: ĕt-tē'nŭ), village (1937 pop. 107), Canal Governorate, NE Egypt, on Suez Canal, on Cairo–Port Said RR, and 15 mi. S of Port Said. It is located on the old Pelusiac branch of the Nile, and on the Bay of Pelusium, which is often called Tina Bay.

Tina, Monte (mōn'tā tē'nä), **Loma Tina** (lō'mä), or **Alto Bandera** (äl'tō bändā'rä), peak, S central Dominican Republic, in the Cordillera Central, 55 mi. WNW of Ciudad Trujillo; 18°45'N 70°42'W. Long considered highest peak (10,301 ft.) in the West Indies, it is sometimes said to be only 9,281 ft., 2d to Pico Trujillo, to NW.

Tina, Plain of (tē'nŭ), or **Plain of Pelusium** (pĭlōō'-shēŭm), NW Sinai Peninsula, NE Egypt, extends E from Suez Canal along Bay of Pelusium. Ruins of Pelusium here.

Tinaca Point (tēnä'kä), S tip of Mindanao, Philippines, on Sarangani Strait; 5°33'N 125°19'E.

Tinaco (tēnä'kō), town (pop. 1,282), Cojedes state, N Venezuela, on Tinaco R. and 11 mi. ENE of San Carlos; sugar cane, corn, yucca, cattle.

Tinaco River, Cojedes state, N Venezuela, rises in coastal range E of Bejuma (Carabobo state), flows c.100 mi. S, past Tinaquillo and Tinaco, to Tirgua R. 10 mi. NW of El Baúl.

Tinaga Island, Philippines: see Calagua Islands.

Tinago (tēnägō'), town (1939 pop. 5,791) in San Isidro municipality, NW Leyte, Philippines, on Visayan Sea, 50 mi. WNW of Tacloban; agr. center (sugar cane, rice).

Tinajas (tēnä'häs), town (pop. 1,327), Cuenca prov., E central Spain, 30 mi. NW of Cuenca; olives, cereals, anise. Cotton milling.

Tinajas Altas Mountains (äl'täs), in extreme SW corner of Ariz., E of Yuma Desert, SE of Yuma. Extends into Mexico.

Tinajillas Pass (tēnähē'yäs), in the Andes of Azuay prov., S Ecuador, on Pan American Highway, and 21 mi. S of Cuenca; alt. 11,489 ft.

Tinajo (tēnä'hō), village (pop. 785), Lanzarote, Canary Isls., 10 mi. NW of Arrecife; grapes, cereals, fruit, onions, garlic, tomatoes, goats, sheep. Flour mills; saltworks.

Tinambac (tēnämbäk'), town (1939 pop. 1,749; 1948 municipality pop. 14,103), Camarines Sur prov., SE Luzon, Philippines, on San Miguel Bay, 17 mi. NE of Naga; agr. center (rice, abacá, corn).

Tinaquillo (tēnäkē'yō), town (pop. 3,935), Cojedes state, N Venezuela, on S slope of coastal range, on Tinaco R. and 29 mi. SW of Valencia; agr. center (coffee, sugar cane, corn, cattle). Asbestos plant works near-by deposits.

Tinca (tēng'kä), Hung. *Tenke* (tĕng'kĕ), village (pop. 4,100), Bihor prov., W Rumania, on Black Körös R., on railroad, 20 mi. S of Oradea; health resort with mineral springs.

Tin Can Island, Tonga: see Niuafoo.

Tinchebray (tēshbrā'), town (pop. 1,949), Orne dept., NW France, 9 mi. SE of Vire; hardware-mfg. center (agr. tools, locks, traps); chocolate mfg., textile printing.

Tin City, village, W Alaska, W Seward Peninsula, on Bering Strait, 6 mi. SE of Wales, 100 mi. NW of Nome; tin mining.

Tinco (tēng'kō), village (pop. 235), Ancash dept., W central Peru, on E slopes of Cordillera Negra, just NW of Carhuás; thermal springs in agr. region (cereals, potatoes).

Tindall (tĭn'dŭl), town (pop. 102), Grundy co., N Mo., on Weldon R. and 6 mi. N of Trenton.

Tindari, Cape (tēn'därē), or **Cape Tindaro** (tēn'-därō), point on NE coast of Sicily, on Gulf of Patti, 4 mi. ENE of Patti; 38°9'N 15°3'E. Site of anc. Tyndaris.

Tindharia (tĭndär'yŭ), village, Darjeeling dist., N West Bengal, India, 14 mi. SSE of Darjeeling; railroad shops; tea, rice, corn, cardamom, oranges.

Tindivanam (tĭn'dĭvŭnŭm), town (pop. 18,177), South Arcot dist., E Madras, India, 70 mi. SW of Madras; road and trade center; exports rice, textiles, cashew nuts, peanut oil. Industrial school. Granite quarries near by.

Tindja (tēnjä'), village, Bizerte dist., N Tunisia, 9 mi. SW of Bizerte, on an isthmus bet. L. of Bizerte (E) and L. Achkel (W); fishing, citrus growing.

Tindouf (tēndōōf'), village (pop. 1,412) and Saharan oasis, Aïn-Sefra territory, westernmost Algeria, near Sp. Sahara border, on Agadir (Fr. Morocco)–Dakar (Fr. West Africa) desert track; 27°40'N 8°8'W. Airfield.

Tinée River (tēnā'), Alpes-Maritimes dept., SE France, rises in Maritime Alps near Ital. border, flows 40 mi. SSE in high valley, past Saint-Étienne-de-Tinée, to the Var 5 mi. ESE of Villars-sur-Var. Hydroelectric plants.

Tinemaha Reservoir, Calif.: see Owens River.

Tineo (tēnē'ō), town (pop. 1,308), Oviedo prov., NW Spain, 30 mi. W of Oviedo; agr. trade center (livestock, cereals, wine, fruit); lumbering. Coal mines in area.

Tinerhir (tēngēr'), village and oasis, Marrakesh region, S central Fr. Morocco, on S slope of the High Atlas, 70 mi. SW of Ksar es Souk; 31°31'N 5°32'W. Date palms. Military post.

Tines, Les (lā tēn'), Alpine village of Haute-Savoie dept., SE France, resort in Chamonix valley, 3 mi. NNE of Chamonix, at foot of the Mer de Glace; alt. 3,553 ft. Winter sports.

Tinfoss, Norway: see Tinnfoss.

Ting, China: see Han River.

Tingambato (tĭng-gämbä'tō), town (pop. 2,768), Michoacán, central Mexico, 9 mi. ENE of Uruapan; sugar cane, coffee, cereals, fruit.

Tingan (dĭng'än'), town, ⊙ Tingan co. (pop. 191,415), N Hainan, Kwangtung prov., China, on Nantu R. and 22 mi. S of Kiungshan; sugar cane, peanuts; vegetable-oil extracting. Iron deposits near by.

Ting Chiang, China: see Han River.

Ting-chieh, Tibet: see Tingkye.

Tingchow. **1** Town, Fukien prov., China: see Changting. **2** Town, Hopeh prov., China: see Tinghsien.

Tingfan, China: see Hweishui.

Tingha (tĭng'gŭ), town (pop. 1,534), N New South Wales, Australia, 205 mi. NNW of Newcastle; tin-mining center.

Tinghai (dĭng'hī'), town (pop. 17,086), ⊙ Tinghai co. (pop. 442,620), NE Chekiang prov., China, port on S shore of Chusan isl. in Hangchow Bay,

35 mi. ENE of Ninghsien; naval base; fisheries, saltworks. Tinghai co. is almost coextensive with Chusan Archipelago.

Tinghing or **Ting-hsing** (both: dĭng'shĭng'), town, ⊙ Tinghing co. (pop. 221,861), N central Hopeh prov., China, 35 mi. NE of Paoting and on Peking-Hankow RR; cotton weaving, paper mfg.; wheat, sesame.

Ting-hsi, China: see TINGSI.

Ting-hsiang, China: see TINGSIANG.

Tinghsien (dĭng'shyĕn'), town, ⊙ Tinghsien co. (pop. 445,474), W Hopeh prov., China, 35 mi. SW of Paoting and on Peking-Hankow RR; cotton, wheat, rice, millet, corn, poultry. Agr. experiment station. Until 1913 called Tingchow.

Ting-hsin, China: see TINGSIN.

Ting-hsing, China: see TINGHING.

Tingi Hills (tĭng'gē), NE Sierra Leone, c.20 mi. NE of Sefadu; c.10 mi. long; rise to 6,080 ft.

Tingis, N Africa: see TANGIER.

Ting-jih, Tibet: see TINGRI.

Ting Kiang, China: see HAN RIVER.

Tingkow, China: see TENGKOW.

Tingkye (tĭng'kyĕ), Chinese *Ting-chieh* (dĭng' jyĕ'), town [Tibetan *dzong*], S Tibet, 85 mi. SW of Shigatse; alt. 13,800 ft. Sometimes spelled Tengkye.

Tinglev (tĭng'lĕv), town (pop. 1,364), Tonder amt, S Jutland, Denmark, 15 mi. E of Tonder; rail junction; cement and machinery mfg.

Tingley, town (pop. 333), Ringgold co., S Iowa, 16 mi. SSE of Creston, in agr. area.

Tingnan (dĭng'nän'), town (pop. 7,857), ⊙ Tingnan co. (pop. 71,244), S Kiangsi prov., China, in Kiulien Mts., on Kwangtung line, 90 mi. S of Kanchow; rice, ramie. The name Tingnan was formerly applied to a town 8 mi. SW which is now known as old Tingnan. Present Tingnan was called Siali until it became co. ⊙ in 1928.

Tingo (tĕng'gō), spa, Pichincha prov., N central Ecuador, in the Andes, at S foot of the Cerro Ilaló, 7 mi. SE of Quito, in fertile Chillos Valley; popular resort for Quito residents; mineral springs. Situated in grain-growing region. Also mfg. of textile goods and tobacco products.

Tingo, village (pop. 248), Arequipa dept., S Peru, on Chili R., 3 mi. SSW of Arequipa; popular resort.

Tingo de Saposoa (dā säpōsō'ä), town (pop. 676), San Martín dept., N central Peru, landing on Huallaga R. and 16 mi. SE of Saposoa, for which it is the port.

Tingo María (märē'ä), town (pop. 668), Huánuco dept., central Peru, on W slopes of Cordillera Oriental, in the tropics, landing at confluence of Monzón R. and Huallaga R., 60 mi. NNE of Huánuco, on highway to Pucallpa (Loreto dept.). Colonization center; lumbering; model farm for rubber cultivation; coca, tobacco, food crops, cattle. Tourist resort.

Tingpien (dĭng'byĕn'), town, ⊙ Tingpien co. (pop. 28,503), northwesternmost Shensi prov., China, 115 mi. NW of Yenan, at Great Wall (Suiyuan line); wheat, millet, beans.

Tingri (tĭng'grē), Chinese *Ting-jih* (dĭng'rŭ'), town [Tibetan *dzong*], S Tibet, in N Nepal Himalayas (alt. 14,250 ft.), on Katmandu-Lhasa trade route and 145 mi. WSW of Shigatse; barley. Lead mine and hot spring (N).

Ting River, China: see HAN RIVER.

Tingsi or **Ting-hsi** (both: dĭng'shē'), town, ⊙ Tingsi co. (pop. 108,856), SE Kansu prov., China, 60 mi. SE of Lanchow; licorice, wheat, millet, beans; sheep raising. Until 1914 called Anting.

Tingsiang or **Ting-hsiang** (both: dĭng'shyäng'). **1** Town, ⊙ Tingsiang co. (pop. 121,460), N Shansi prov., China, on upper Huto R. and 50 mi. NNE of Taiyüan, on rail spur; wheat, corn. **2** Town, ⊙ Tingsiang co. (pop. 5,603), SW Sikang prov., China, 90 mi. SSE of Paan, near Yunnan line; wheat, beans. Called Sangpiling until 1913.

Tingsin or **Ting-hsin** (both: dĭng'shĭn'), town, ⊙ Tingsin co. (pop. 13,228), NW Kansu prov., China, 75 mi. NE of Kiuchüan, where the Hei and Peita rivers join to form the Etsin Gol, at S edge of the Gobi· alt. 4 067 ft. Until 1928 called Maomu.

Tingsryd (tĭngs'rüd"), town (pop. 1,050), Kronoberg co., S Sweden, on small Tik L., Swedish *Tiken* (tē'kŭn), 25 mi. SSE of Vaxjo; health resort; sawmilling, furniture mfg.

Tingstad (tĭng'städ"), residential village (pop. 1,596), Goteborg och Bohus co., SW Sweden, on Gota R., just N of Goteborg.

Tingtao or **Ting-t'ao** (dĭng'tou'), town, ⊙ Tingtao co. (pop. 217,449), S Pingyuan prov., China, 14 mi. SE of Hotseh; cotton-weaving center; wheat, millet, kaoliang, fruit. Until 1949 in Shantung prov.

Tinguá, Serra do (sĕ'rŭ dŏŏ tēng-gwä'), a spur of the Serra do Mar, in central Rio de Janeiro state, Brazil, SW of Petrópolis; rises to 5,400 ft. Source of Rio's water supply.

Tingüindín (tĭng-gwēndēn'), officially Tingüindín de Argándar, town (pop. 2,897), Michoacán, central Mexico, 20 mi. SW of Zamora; sugar cane, tobacco, fruit, stock.

Tinguiririca River (tĭng-gērērē'kä), central Chile, rises in the Andes at foot of Tinguiririca Volcano, flows c.110 mi. NW, past San Fernando, to join Cachapoal R. 3 mi. WSW of Las Cabras, forming Rapel R. Used for irrigation.

Tinguiririca Volcano, Andean peak (14,100 ft.), Colchagua prov., central Chile, near Argentina border, 40 mi. SE of San Fernando; 34°49'S 70°22'W. Sulphur deposits.

Tingvalla, Sweden: see KARLSTAD.

Tingvoll (tĭng'vôl), village (pop. 680; canton pop. 3,531), More og Romsdal co., W Norway, on E shore of Sunndals Fjord, 19 mi. SE of Kristiansund; textile factories. Has medieval stone church; sanatorium for the tubercular. Formerly spelled Tingvold or Thingvold. Name Tingvoll Fjord sometimes applied to outer section of Sunndals Fjord.

Tingwick (tĭng'wĭk), village (pop. estimate 500), S Que., 8 mi. N of Asbestos; asbestos mining.

Tingyüan (dĭng'yüăn'). **1** Town, ⊙ Tingyüan co. (pop. 396,326), N Anhwei prov., China, 50 mi. NNE of Hofei; rice, wheat, kaoliang, corn, tobacco. **2** Town, Shensi prov., China: see CHENPA. **3** Town, Szechwan prov., China: see WUSHENG. **4** Town, Yunnan prov., China: see MOWTING.

Tingyüanying (dĭng'yüăn'yĭng'), village, in Ningsia section of Inner Mongolia, China, 45 mi. WNW of Yinchwan, across Alashan Mts.; chief trade center of Alashan Mongols. Formerly called Wangyeh, Tzehu. Near by stood Halachar, ⊙ Tangut kingdom (c.1000–1227), conquered by Jenghiz Khan.

Tinhbien (tĭng'byĕn'), town, Chaudoc prov., S Vietnam, on Vinhte Canal (Cambodia line) and 13 mi. SW of Hatien.

Tinhtuc (tĭng'tŏŏk'), village, Caobang prov., N Vietnam, in Piaouac Range, 25 mi. W of Caobang; tin and tungsten mines.

Tinian (tĭ'nēŭn, tēnēän'), island (□ 39), Saipan dist., S Marianas Isls., W Pacific, c.3 mi. SW of Saipan; 11 mi. long, 4.5 mi. wide; rises to 150 ft. Composed of madrepore limestone; phosphate deposits worked by transient laborers. Port is Sunharon Roads on W coast. Site of anc. stone columns. In Second World War, isl. (site of Jap. airfield) was taken, 1944, by U.S. forces. Leper colony established here in 1948.

Tinibras, Mont (mō tēnēbrä'), summit (9,944 ft.) of Maritime Alps, on Fr.-Ital. border, 3 mi. NE of Saint-Étienne-de-Tinée.

Tinicum Island (tĭn'ĭkŭm), SE Pa., in Delaware R. just SW of Philadelphia, off Essington; separated from mainland by creeks and marshes. First permanent European settlement in Pa., founded as ⊙ NEW SWEDEN, was made here in 1643.

Tinker Air Force Base, Okla.: see OKLAHOMA CITY.

Tinkisso River (tĭngkē'sō), Fr. Guinea, W Fr. West Africa, rises in S outliers of the Fouta Djallon mts., E of Mamou, flows c.250 mi. NNE and E, past Dabola, to the Niger just S of Siguiri. Alluvial gold deposits.

Tin Lake, Norway: see TINN LAKE.

Tinley Park, village (pop. 2,326), Cook co., NE Ill., SW suburb of Chicago, 15 mi. E of Joliet; some mfg. (waterproofing compound, poultry equipment); agr. (soybeans, corn, oats). Inc. 1892.

Tinmouth (tĭn'mŭth), town (pop. 248), Rutland co., W Vt., on Clarendon R. and 12 mi. S of Rutland; dairy products.

Tinn, canton, Norway: see RJUKAN.

Tinnanpo, Korea: see CHINNAMPO.

Tinne River (tĭ'nŭ), Telemark co., S Norway, flows from S end of Tinn L. c.25 mi. SE, past Arlifoss, Gronvollfoss, Svelgfoss, and Tinnfoss (hydroelectric plants), to Heddal L. at Notodden.

Tinnevelly (tĭnŭvĕ'lē), since 1948 officially **Tirunelveli** (tĭ"rŏŏnĕl'vĕlē), southernmost district (□ 4,342; pop. 2,244,543) of Madras, India; ⊙ Palamcottah. Bordered E by Gulf of Mannar, SE by Indian Ocean, W by Western Ghats. Lowland (drained by Tambraparni R.) includes cotton soil (N), alluvial valleys (center), red sands (S) with sand hills (up to 219 ft.) along SE coast. Mainly agr., with cotton (N), palmyra (S), rice along rivers, sesame, sunn hemp (jute substitute), grain. Industry based on agr. products: cotton milling, palmyra processing, tanning. Pearl and chank fishing, fish curing along coast (saltworks). PAPANASAM hydroelectric works furnish power to main industrial centers of Tinnevelly-Palamcottah-Melapalaiyam urban complex, Ambasamudram, Tenkasi, Koilpatti, main port of Tuticorin. Health resort at Kuttalam. Dist. was scene of early labors of St. Francis Xavier.

Tinnevelly, since 1948 officially **Tirunelveli**, city (pop. 60,676), Tinnevelly dist., S Madras, India, on Tambraparni R. opposite Palamcottah (bridge) and 85 mi. SSW of Madura; sugar refineries; cotton textiles, palmyra products; trade in timber from Shencottah (Travancore). Important mission station. Has col. Sivaite temple.

Tinnfoss (tĭn'fôs), falls on Tinne R., Telemark co., S Norway, 1 mi. N of Notodden; hydroelectric plant for paper factory. Sometimes spelled Tinfoss.

Tinnis, Egypt: see TENNIS.

Tinn Lake (tĭn), Nor *Tinnsjø*, Telemark co., S Norway, c.50 mi. NNW of Skien, 20 mi. NNW of Notodden; □ 17; 23 mi. long; alt. 623 ft. From railhead at Mael, on W shore at mouth of the Mana, ferry connects with railhead at Tinnoset, on S shore, where Tinne R. leaves the lake. Sometimes spelled Tin.

Tinogasta (tēnōgä'stä), town (pop. 2,176), ⊙ Tinogasta dept. (□ 11,855; pop. 16,609), S central Catamarca prov., Argentina, on the Río Colorado or Abaucán R. (irrigation) and 115 mi. WNW of Catamarca; alt. c.4,000 ft. Rail terminus and agr. center (alfalfa, corn, wine, fruit, cotton, olives, vegetables, livestock). Tin and coal mines near by. Earthquake zone.

Tinoñgan (tēnô'nyŭgän), town (1939 pop. 6,857) in Isabela municipality, Negros Occidental prov., W central Negros isl., Philippines, 11 mi. E of Binalbagan; agr. center (rice, sugar cane).

Tinos, Greece: see TENOS.

Tiñosa, La (lä tēnyō'sä), village (pop. 425), Lanzarote, Canary Isls., minor port on fine Atlantic bay, 10 mi. WSW of Arrecife; ships fruit. Fishing. Sometimes called Puerto Tiñosa.

Tiñoso, Cape (–sō), on the Mediterranean, in Murcia prov., SE Spain, 10 mi. SW of Cartagena; 37°33'N 1°6'W.

Tinpak (dĕn'bäk'), Mandarin *Tienpai* (dyĕn'bī'), town (pop. 4,606), ⊙ Tinpak co. (pop. 348,886), SW Kwangtung prov., China, port on S.China Sea, 65 mi. ENE of Chankiang; wheat, rice; fisheries. Tungsten mining near by.

Tinquipaya (tĭngkēpī'ä), town (pop. 12,400), Potosí dept., W central Bolivia, in E outlier of Eastern Cordillera of the Andes, 27 mi. NNW of Potosí; grain, livestock.

Tinsley, town (pop. 20,253) in Sheffield county borough, West Riding, S Yorkshire, England, just NE of Sheffield; steel-rolling mills, coal mining.

Tinsman, town (pop. 118), Calhoun co., S Ark., 34 mi. NNE of El Dorado.

Tinsukia (tĭn'sŏŏkyŭ), town (pop. 8,338), Lakhimpur dist., NE Assam, India, in Brahmaputra valley, 31 mi. E of Dibrugarh; rail junction; tea, rice, jute, sugar cane, rape and mustard; tea processing; tin-can factory. Extensive tea gardens near by.

Tinta (tēn'tä), town (pop. 1,653), Cuzco dept., S Peru, on Vilcanota R., on railroad and 55 mi. SE of Cuzco, in agr. region (grain, potatoes); cobalt and iron deposits; alt. 11,394 ft. Site of Inca remains.

Tintagel (tĭntă'jŭl), agr. village and parish (pop. 1,234), N Cornwall, England, 5 mi. NW of Camelford. Just NW, on the Atlantic, is promontory of Tintagel Head, site of remains of Tintagel Castle, legendary birthplace of King Arthur. Has Norman church and ruins of Saxon forts.

Tintah, village (pop. 235), Traverse co., W Minn., 17 mi. NE of Wheaton, in grain area.

Tintea (tsēn'tyä), Rum. *Ţintea*, village (pop. 2,452), Prahova prov., S central Rumania, 9 mi. NNW of Ploesti; oil and natural-gas production.

Tinténiac (tētānyäk'), agr. village (pop. 825), Ille-et-Vilaine dept., W France, on Ille-Rance Canal and 15 mi. NNW of Rennes.

Tintern Abbey (tĭn'tŭrn, –tûrn), beautiful ruins in Monmouth, England, on the Wye and 4 mi. N of Chepstow. Tintern Abbey was founded 1131 by Walter de Clare for Cistercians; present remains date mainly from 13th and 14th cent. Subject of poem by Wordsworth.

Tintigny (tētēnyē'), village (pop. 1,115), Luxembourg prov., SE Belgium, in the Ardennes, on Semois R. and 13 mi. W of Arlon; pig market.

Tintín (tēntēn'), village (pop. c.3,800), Cochabamba dept., central Boliva, 9 mi. SW of Mizque, on highway from Cochabamba to Sucre and to Santa Cruz; alt. 7,054 ft.; corn, potatoes; livestock. Terminus of railroad from Cochabamba (extension projected to Santa Cruz) and of oil pipe line from Camiri. Also written Tín-Tín.

Tintina (tēntē'nä), town (pop. estimate 1,000), ⊙ Moreno dept. (□ c.6,000; 1947 pop. 35,749), N central Santiago del Estero prov., Argentina, on railroad and 110 mi. NE of Santiago del Estero; agr. center (corn, alfalfa, livestock). Airport.

Tintinara (tĭntĭnă'rŭ), village, SE South Australia, 105 mi. SE of Adelaide and on railroad; sheep.

Tinto (chĕn'tō), town (pop. 363), in Br. Cameroons, administered as part of Eastern Provinces of Nigeria, on upper Cross R. and 25 mi. SE of Mamfe; road junction; cacao, bananas, palm oil and kernels.

Tinto, Río, Honduras: see SICO RIVER.

Tinto, Río (tēn'tō), river in Huelva prov., SW Spain, rises near the famous mines of Ríotinto, flows c.60 mi. S and SW, past Moguer and Palos, to join Odiel R. 3 mi. below Huelva near the Atlantic. Not navigable.

Tinto Hills (tĭn'tō), range in central Lanark, Scotland, extending 5 mi. E-W bet. Douglas Water (W) and the Clyde (E); highest peak is Tinto (2,335 ft.), 8 mi. SE of Lanark.

Tinui (tĭnōō'ē), township (pop. 254), ⊙ Castlepoint co. (□ 203; pop. 522), S N.Isl., New Zealand, 75 mi. NE of Wellington; sheep.

Tinum (tēnōōm'), town (pop. 1,360), Yucatan, SE Mexico, 12 mi. NW of Valladolid; henequen, sugar cane, corn, timber. Maya ruins are near by. Sometimes spelled Tinún.

Tinyahuarco, Peru: see FUNDICIÓN DE TINYAHUARCO.

Tin-Zaouaten (tĕn'-zäwätĕn') or **Fort Pierre Bordes** (fôr pyâr' bôrd'), Saharan outpost in southernmost Algeria, on Fr. West Africa border, in rugged Tassili n' Ahaggar plateau region, 330 mi. NNE of Gao (Fr. Sudan); 19°58'N 2°50'E.

Tioga (tīō'gŭ). **1** County (□ 525; pop. 30,166), S N.Y., bounded S by Pa. line; ⊙ Owego. Dairying area, with diversified mfg. especially at Owego; also poultry raising, grain growing. Intersected by Susquehanna R., and drained by Cayuta, Catatonk, and Owego creeks. Formed 1791. **2** County (□ 1,150; pop. 35,474), N Pa.; ⊙ Wellsboro. Agr. and timber area; drained E by Tioga R., W by Pine Creek; bounded N by N.Y. Mfg. (metal and electrical products, leather); bituminous coal, natural gas; agr. (maple sugar, buckwheat, hay, dairying); recreation. Formed 1804.

Tioga. 1 Village (pop. 338), Rapides parish, central La., 5 mi. N of Alexandria; trade center for near-by U.S. veterans hosp.; veneer products. **2** Village (pop. 456), Williams co., NW N.Dak., 36 mi. NE of Williston. **3** Agr. borough (pop. 544), Tioga co., N Pa., on Tioga R. and 20 mi. SW of Elmira, N.Y.; grist mill. **4** Town (pop. 529), Grayson co., N Texas, 22 mi. SW of Sherman; resort, with mineral wells; dairying.

Tioga Center, resort village, Tioga co., S N.Y., on the Susquehanna and 23 mi. E of Elmira.

Tioga Pass, E Calif., highway pass (alt. 9,946 ft.) across the Sierra Nevada, just W of Mono L.; E gateway to Yosemite Natl. Park.

Tioga River, in Pa. and N.Y., rises in W Bradford co., N Pa., flows 55 mi. NW, past Blossburg and Mansfield, into N.Y., where it joins Cohocton R. to form the Chemung at Painted Post.

Tioman (tēōmän'), island (□ 53; pop. 657) in South China Sea, Pahang, Malaya, 35 mi. off Endau (Johore); 13 mi. long, 2–8 mi. wide; rises 3,383 ft.

Tione di Trento (tyō'nĕ dē trĕn'tô), town (pop. 1,853), Trento prov., Trentino–Alto Adige, N Italy, on Sarca R. and 19 mi. W of Trent; foundry, shoe and furniture factories.

Tionesta (tīūnĕ'stů). **1** Lumber-milling village (pop. c.800), Modoc co., NE Calif., c.40 mi. WNW of Alturas. **2** Borough (pop. 728), ⊙ Forest co., NW Pa., 14 mi. ENE of Oil City and on Allegheny R., at mouth of Tionesta Creek (c.60 mi. long). Flood-control dam on creek; state fish hatchery. Lumber, flour; gas, oil; dairying.

Tior, Indonesia: see WATUBELA ISLANDS.

Tioughnioga River (tīūnō'gů, tīôf"nēō'gů, tēŏk" nēō'gů), central N.Y., rises in SW Madison co., flows SW, past Cortland, then generally SSE to Chenango R. at Chenango Forks; c.70 mi. long. At Cortland, main stream (sometimes called East Branch above this point) receives West Branch (c.15 mi. long).

Tipasa (tēpäzä'), village (pop. 717), Alger dept., N central Algeria, on the Mediterranean 37 mi. WSW of Algiers; vineyards, citrus groves. Near-by is the bathing resort of Chenoua-Plage. Of Punic origin, Tipasa was made a Roman commune in 1st cent. A.D. Anc. ruins include Thermae, a fountain, and a vast early Christian cemetery. The well-known mausoleum (inaccurately called the Tomb of the Christian Woman) of a Mauretanian royal family is 6 mi. E, atop a coastal hill. Formerly spelled Tipaza.

Tiphsah, Syria: see DIBSE.

Tipitapa (tēpētä'pä), town (1950 pop. 1,400), Managua dept., SW Nicaragua, on Inter-American Highway, on Tipitapa R., at its efflux from L. Managua, and 14 mi. ENE of Managua; road center; tourist resort; trades in livestock and agr. products. Brick and tile mfg. Thermal baths. Here a peace pact was signed (1927) bet. U.S. and Moncada, leader of Nicaraguan liberal revolutionaries.

Tipitapa River, SW Nicaragua, issues from SE end of L. Managua at Tipitapa, forming falls (dry in summer); flows 20 mi. SE to L. Nicaragua, forming Tisma Lagoon in lower course.

Tippah (tĭ'pů), county (□ 464; pop. 17,522), N Miss., bordering N on Tenn.; ⊙ Ripley. Drained by a headstream of Hatchie R., by Tallahatchie R., and by Small Tippah Creek. Agr. (cotton, corn); pine timber. Formed 1836.

Tipp City, village (pop. 3,304), Miami co., W Ohio, 13 mi. N of Dayton and on Great Miami R.; canned foods, pulp and paper products, furniture, motor vehicles, metal products, glassware. Formerly Tippecanoe City.

Tippecanoe (tĭ"pùkůnōō'), county (□ 501; pop. 74,473), W central Ind.; ⊙ Lafayette. Intersected by the Wabash; also drained by Tippecanoe R. and Wildcat Creek. Rich agr. area (grain, livestock). Diversified mfg., railroad shops, packing plants at Lafayette. Bituminous-coal mines. Formed 1826.

Tippecanoe City, Ohio: see TIPP CITY.

Tippecanoe River, Ind., rises in NW Whitley co., flows NW, through several lakes, then generally W, past Monterey, and SW to the Wabash 8 mi. NE of Lafayette; 166 mi. long. Power dams impound Freeman and Shafer lakes (resorts) in lower course. Battle of Tippecanoe (1811) on site of present Battle Ground town ended in Gen. W. H. Harrison's victory over Indians.

Tippera (tĭp'ůrů), district (□ 2,531; pop. 3,860,139), SE East Bengal, E Pakistan; ⊙ Comilla. Bounded NE by Assam (India), E by Tripura, W by Meghna R.; drained by tributaries of the Meghna. Alluvial soil (marshes in N); rice, jute, oilseeds, sugar cane, tobacco, betel leaves. Major jute-pressing centers at Chandpur and Akhaura; mfg. of chemicals, matches, bricks, plywood, electrical supplies, bell metal, brassware, soap, ice; fertilizer factory at Brahmanbaria; general-engineering factory at Comilla; oilseed and flour milling, tea processing, metal casting. Part of Tripura until 1833, when inc. into Mogul empire; ceded 1765 to English. Part of former Br. Bengal prov., India, until inc. 1947 into new Pakistan prov. of East Bengal, following creation of Pakistan.

Tipperary (tĭ"pùrâ'rē), Gaelic *Thiobrad Árann*, county (□ 1,642.6; pop. 136,014), Munster, S Ireland; ⊙ Clonmel. Bounded by cos. Waterford (S), Cork (SW), Limerick (W), Clare and Galway (NW), Offaly (N), Laoighis (NE), and Kilkenny (E). Drained by the Shannon, Lough Dergy, Suir R., and their tributaries. Surface mountainous on borders (rises to 3,018 ft. on Galty More), sloping toward central fertile Golden Valley of Suir R. Agr. is chief occupation; dairying is important; main crops are potatoes, beets. Salmon fisheries. Industries include sugar refining, woolen milling, tanning, malting, bacon and ham curing, food canning. Besides Clonmel, other towns are Tipperary, Cashel, Cahir, Thurles, Nenagh, Templemore, Carrick-on-Suir, and Roscrea. In anc. times co. was divided bet. kingdoms of Thomond (N) and Ormond (S); later Cashel became ⊙ kingdom of Munster. There are many notable castle ruins and remains of ecclesiastical bldgs. (Cashel, Clonmel, Holycross).

Tipperary, Gaelic *Tiobraid Árann*, urban district (pop. 5,267), W Co. Tipperary, Ireland, 21 mi. WNW of Clonmel; agr. market in dairying region, with processing of dairy products. There are ruins of gateway to friary founded under Henry III. Town was site of castle (no remains) of King John and was center of the Land League agitation.

Tippermuir, Scotland: see PERTH, burgh.

Tipton, municipal borough (1931 pop. 35,814; 1951 census 39,382) in the Black Country, S Stafford, England, 5 mi. SSE of Wolverhampton; steelworking; mfg. of boilers, asphalt, electrical equipment, machinery, chemicals, soap, bottles, sausages; bacon and ham curing and packing. The 1st steam engine built by James Watt is exhibited here. The borough includes industrial towns of Dudley (S; in Worcester), Dudley Port (SE; pop. 5,357), and Horseley Heath (SE; pop. 5,134).

Tipton. 1 County (□ 261; pop. 15,566), central Ind.; ⊙ Tipton. Agr. area (corn, wheat, hogs, cattle); timber. Mfg. at Tipton. Drained by Cicero Creek, small Turkey Creek, and South Fork of Wildcat Creek. Formed 1844. **2** County (□ 458; pop. 29,782), W Tenn.; ⊙ Covington. Bounded W by the Mississippi, N by Hatchie R. Predominantly cotton-growing and livestock-raising area; cotton processing at Covington. Formed 1823.

Tipton. 1 City (pop. 5,633), ⊙ Tipton co., central Ind., on Cicero Creek and 15 mi. SSE of Kokomo, in agr. area (grain, livestock); mfg. (machinery, furniture, piston rings, canned goods, livestock supplies, cigars, chemicals, brooms); timber. Laid out 1845. **2** City (pop. 2,633), ⊙ Cedar co., E Iowa, 22 mi. ENE of Iowa City; mfg. (feed, beverages, wood products); limestone quarries. Inc. 1857. **3** City (pop. 246), Mitchell co., N central Kansas, 21 mi. SW of Beloit; grain, livestock. **4** City (pop. 1,234), Moniteau co., central Mo., 12 mi. W of California; agr.; garment factory. State industrial home for Negro girls. Laid out 1858. **5** Town (pop. 1,172), Tillman co., SW Okla., near North Fork of Red R., 10 mi. NW of Frederick, in agr. area (cotton, alfalfa, corn, grain; dairy products); cotton ginning, oil refining. Organized 1910.

Tipton, Mount (7,364 ft.), W Ariz., highest peak in Cerbat Mts., c.25 mi. N of Kingman.

Tiptonville, town (pop. 1,953), ⊙ Lake co., NW Tenn., on Reelfoot L., 22 mi. NNW of Dyersburg; center of recreation area (hunting, fishing, bathing); agr., lumbering, mfg. of cottonseed products, soybean oil, concrete blocks.

Tiptur (tĭptōōr'), town (pop. 7,513), Tumkur dist., central Mysore, India, 40 mi. W of Tumkur; trades in coconuts, coir products (rope, sacks), grain, biris; hand-loom cotton and woolen weaving.

Tipuani (tēpwä'nē), village (pop. c.1,400), La Paz dept., W Bolivia, on Tipuani R. and 45 mi. ENE of Sorata, in tropical lowlands; gold mining.

Tipuani River, La Paz dept., W Bolivia, rises in Cordillera de La Paz 15 mi. NE of Sorata, flows c.40 mi. NE, past Tipuani, to Mapiri R. at Guanay. Gold placers along course.

Tiputini River (tēpōōtē'nē), Napo-Pastaza prov., NE Ecuador, minor right affluent (c.120 mi. long) of Napo R., which it joins 20 mi. NW of Nueva Rocafuerte. Tiputini airfield is at its mouth. Sometimes spelled Tiputine.

Tiquicheo (tēkēchä'ō), town (pop. 603), Michoacán, central Mexico, 14 mi. NE of Huetamo; rice, sugar cane, fruit.

Tiquina (tēkē'nä), village (pop. c.6,360), La Paz dept., W Bolivia, port on Strait of Tiquina of L. Titicaca and 50 mi. WNW of La Paz; tourist resort. Consists of 2 sections, San Pablo (N of strait) and San Pedro (S).

Tiquina, Strait of, in L. Titicaca, W Bolivia, bet. Copacabana Peninsula (W) and Achacachi Peninsula (E); connects L. Chucuito (NW) and L. Uinamarca (SE); ¾–7 mi. wide, 10 mi. long. Tiquina village lies at SE end.

Tiquipaya (tēkēpī'ä), town (pop. c.5,300), Cochabamba dept., central Bolivia, on S slopes of Cordillera de Cochabamba, 6 mi. NW of Cochabamba; wheat, barley, potatoes, corn; cattle.

Tiquisate or **Pueblo Nuevo Tiquisate** (pwĕ'blō nwā'vō tēkēsä'tā), town (1950 pop. 3,226), Escuintla dept., S Guatemala, on branch of Nahualate R. and 20 mi. SE of Mazatenango; center of major banana-growing area, developed in 1940s. Another Tiquisate (pop. 5,572) is 20 mi. SSW, on the Pacific, at mouth of Madre Vieja R.

Tirach Mir, W Pakistan: see TIRICH MIR.

Tiradentes (tē"rūdĕn'tĭs), city (pop. 1,198), S Minas Gerais, Brazil, on railroad and 6 mi. ENE of São João del Rei. Has fine colonial cathedral containing an early-18th-cent. organ.

Tirah (tē'rů), tribal region, W North-West Frontier Prov., W Pakistan, in S spurs of Safed Koh Range, S of Khyber Pass. Inhabited by nominally independent Afridi tribes.

Tiran or **Tihran** (tērän'), village (1946 pop. estimate 4,300), Tenth Prov., in Isfahan, W central Iran, 30 mi. W of Isfahan; grain, cotton.

Tiran, Japan: see CHIRAN.

Tirana or **Tiranë** (both: tērä'nů), city (1945 pop. 59,887), ⊙ Albania, centrally located in fertile plain, 19 mi. E of its port, Durazzo, with which it is linked by railroad and highway; 41°20'N 19°28'E. Leading industrial and commercial center of Albania; mfg. of cotton textiles, soap, alcohol, cigarettes; flour milling, dairying; power station. A modern city with wide thoroughfares, Tirana is centered on Scanderbeg Square (govt. buildings; Etehem Bey mosque, built 1791–1819), which is adjoined NW by the Bazaar. Near by is the old 17th-cent. mosque with tomb of Suleiman Pasha. City has univ., teachers and agr. colleges, music and art schools. Founded in early 17th cent. by Turkish general Suleiman Pasha and originally named Teheran, for a Turkish victory in Persia. After its selection (1920) as Albania's capital, it expanded greatly and was developed along modern urban lines. A new residential city was built under Italian rule (1939–43) in S suburbs and after Second World War an industrial section (textile mill) was developed on W outskirts.

Tiran Island (tērän'), in Red Sea, at entrance to Gulf of Aqaba, N Hejaz, Saudi Arabia; 10 mi. long, 5 mi. wide.

Tirano (tērä'nô), town (pop. 3,867), Sondrio prov., Lombardy, N Italy, in the Valtellina, on Adda R. and 15 mi. ENE of Sondrio. Rail and road center, near junction of Bernina, Splügen, and Selvio routes to Switzerland; lumber, silk, soap, macaroni, wine. Hydroelectric plant. Near by is pilgrimage church of Madonna di Tirano, built 1503–33.

Tirap (tĭräp'), tribal frontier tract (□ c.2,000; pop. c.6,000) of NE Assam, India, on undefined Burma border, NE of Naga Hills; 27°30'N, bet. 96° and 97°E. Separated (1950) from Sadiya frontier tract; ⊙ Margherita.

Tiraque (tērä'kä), town (pop. 7,800), Cochabamba dept., central Bolivia, in Cordillera de Cochabamba, 30 mi. E of Cochabamba, on branch of Cochabamba–Santa Cruz highway; alt. 10,564 ft.; corn, potatoes, barley. Another Tiraque (pop. 2,700; sometimes called Tiraque Chico or Tiraquecito) is 8 mi. N of Totora.

Tiraspol or **Tiraspol'** (tyērůspôl'), city (1939 pop. 43,000), SE Moldavian SSR, in Bessarabia, on left bank of Dniester R. and 40 mi. ESE of Kishinev; one of leading fruit- and vegetable-canning centers of USSR; fruit juices, marmalade, wine; flour and oilseed milling, tanning, shoe mfg.; machine shops. Teachers and agr. colleges. Founded 1793. Was ⊙ Moldavian Autonomous SSR (1930–40).

Tirat Shalom or **Tirath Shalom** (both: tērät' shälōm'), residential settlement (pop. 350), W Israel, in Judaean Plain, 3 mi. WNW of Rehovot, in citrus-growing region. Founded 1930.

Tirat Tsvi (Tsevi) or **Tirat Zvi** (both: tsvē'), settlement (pop. 300), NE Israel, near border of Jordan, in the Jordan valley, 6 mi. SSE of Beisan; sausage mfg.; banana growing, fish breeding. Founded 1937; attacked (1948) by Arab invaders. Sometimes spelled Tirath Tsvi (Tsevi) or Tirath Zvi.

Tirau (tē'rou), township (pop. 569), ⊙ Matamata co. (□ 930; pop. 12,139), N N.Isl., New Zealand, 95 mi. SE of Auckland; sheep, dairy products.

Tire (tĭrĕ'), town (pop. 21,953), Smyrna prov., W Turkey, rail terminus near Kucuk Menderes R., 40 mi. SE of Smyrna; emery, antimony, arsenic; tobacco, olives, figs, grain. Sometimes spelled Tireh.

Tirebolu (tĭrĕ'bôlōō), anc. *Tripolis*, village (pop. 4,923), Giresun prov., N Turkey, port on Black Sea near mouth of Harsit R., 22 mi. ENE of Giresun, 48 mi. W of Trebizond; copper, manganese, zinc; hazelnuts, corn, millet. Sometimes spelled Tireboli.

Tiree, Scotland: see TYREE.

Tirgua River (tēr'gwä) or **San Carlos River** (sän kär'lōs), N Venezuela, rises in coastal range at Bejuma (Carabobo state), flows c.110 mi. S and SSE, past San Carlos, to Cojedes R. at El Baúl. Receives Tinaco R.

Tirhut (tĭr'ōōt), division (□ 12,594; pop. 11,959,827) of Bihar, India; ⊙ Muzaffarpur. Comprises 4 dists.: CHAMPARAN, SARAN, MUZAFFARPUR, DARBHANGA.

Tirich Mir (tē'rĭch mēr'), highest mountain (25,263 ft.) in the Hindu Kush, in Chitral state, N North-West Frontier Prov., W Pakistan, 155 mi. N of Peshawar. Sometimes spelled Tirach Mir.

Tirig (tērēg'), town (pop. 1,131), Castellón de la Plana prov., E Spain, 18 mi. WSW of Vinaroz; olive-oil processing; wine, wheat, beans.

Tiriolo (tērēô'lô), town (pop. 2,917), Catanzaro prov., Calabria, S Italy, 5 mi. WNW of Catanzaro; cement mfg.; domestic weaving.

Tirlemont (tērlmō'), Flemish *Tienen* (tē'nŭn), town (pop. 22,428), Brabant prov., central Belgium, 11 mi. ESE of Louvain; beet-sugar refining center; leather tanning, beer brewing; agr. market. Has 13th–15th-cent. church of Notre Dame du Lac. Subject to repeated sieges and pillages in Middle Ages; saw final actions of Belgian war of independence (1831).

Tirlyanski or **Tirlyanskiy** (tyĭrlyän'skē), town (1939 pop. over 10,000), E Bashkir Autonomous SSR, Russian SFSR, in the S Urals, on railroad and 20 mi. NNE (under jurisdiction) of Beloretsk. Metallurgical center, based on Komarovo-Zigazinski and local iron deposits; blast furnace; steel and rolling mills. Quartz and talc deposits near by.

Tirman (tērmän'), village (pop. 698), Oran dept., NW Algeria, in the Tell Atlas, 22 mi. SSE of Sidi-bel-Abbès; livestock raising.

Tirnavos, Greece: see TYRNAVOS.

Tirnoular, Fr. India: see TIRUNALLAR.

Tirnovo (tŭr'nôvô). **1** City, Burgas dist., Bulgaria: see MALKO TIRNOVO. **2** City (pop. 16,182), Gorna Oryakhovitsa dist., N Bulgaria, on Yantra R. and 60 mi. ESE of Pleven; agr. center; textile milling, tanning, dyeing, flour products. Has teachers col., technical schools, several monuments, and ruins of 12th-cent. churches, 16th-cent. mosque, medieval fortress and castle. Seat of Eastern Orthodox metropolite. Became ⊙ 2d Bulg. Kingdom proclaimed here 1186. Developed as commercial center under Turkish rule (1393–1877). Bulg. constitution drafted here (1879) and independence of Bulgaria declared (1908) by Tsar Ferdinand. Sometimes spelled Trnovo.

Tiro (tī'rō), village (pop. 335), Crawford co., N central Ohio, 15 mi. NW of Mansfield, in agr. and timber area.

Tirodi (tĭrō'dē), village, Balaghat dist., central Madhya Pradesh, India, 21 mi. N of Tumsar; rail spur terminus serving near-by manganese mines.

Tirol, Austria: see TYROL.

Tiros (tē'rōōs), city (pop. 1,682), W Minas Gerais, Brazil, 55 mi. SE of Patos de Minas; diamonds found here.

Tiroubouvané, Fr. India: see MANDAGADIPPATTU.

Tirpol, Afghanistan: see TIRPUL.

Tirpul or **Tirpol** (tĭr'pōōl), town (pop. 8,000), Herat prov., NW Afghanistan, just SE of Kohsan, 55 mi. WNW of Herat, and on right bank of the Hari Rud; alt. 2,460 ft.; center of Afghanistan's chief oil field.

Tirrukovail, Ceylon: see TIRUKOVIL.

Tirsa (tĭr'sä), village (pop. 7,835), Faiyum prov., Upper Egypt, 8 mi. N of Faiyum; cotton, cereals, sugar cane, fruits.

Tirschenreuth (tĭr'shŭnroit), town (pop. 7,496), Upper Palatinate, NE Bavaria, Germany, in Bohemian Forest, on the Waldnab and 16 mi. NNE of Weiden; mfg. of porcelain, glass, cloth, meat products; tanning. Has mid-17th-cent. church. Chartered 1364. Kaolin quarried in area.

Tirschtiegel, Poland: see TRZCIEL.

Tirso, Lake (tēr'sô), one of the largest Italian reservoirs (□ 8.5), in Cagliari prov., central Sardinia, 23 mi. SW of Nuoro; 13.5 mi. long, up to 3 mi. wide. Formed on Tirso R. by Tirso Dam (up to 197 ft. high; built 1918–23) at Santa Chiara d'Ula (S end), center of Sardinian hydroelectric system. Receives Taloro R. Also called L. Omodeo.

Tirso River, anc. *Thyrsus*, central Sardinia, chief river of isl.; rises on plateau W of Buddusò, flows 93 mi. SW, through L. TIRSO, to Gulf of Oristano 3 mi. WSW of Oristano. Major hydroelectric source; irrigates Oristano plain; fisheries. Receives Flumineddu R.

Tirthahalli (tēr'tŭhŭlē), town (pop. 5,226), Shimoga dist., NW Mysore, India, on Tunga R. (headstream of the Tungabhadra) and 28 mi. SW of Shimoga; tile mfg., sawmilling, handicraft sandalwood carving; local trade in rice, betel nuts, chili.

Tiru-Anantapuram, India: see TRIVANDRUM.

Tirubhuvane, Fr. India: see MANDAGADIPPATTU.

Tiruchendur or **Tiruchchendur** (both: tĭrōōchăn'dōōr), town (pop. 11,110), Tinnevelly dist., S Madras, India, port on Gulf of Mannar, 35 mi. ESE of Tinnevelly; rail terminus. Has Sivaite temple.

Tiruchengodu (–chĕng'gōdōō), town (pop. 15,516), Salem dist., S central Madras, India, 27 mi. SW of Salem; cotton-milling center (mills powered by Mettur hydroelectric plant). Isolated peak (1,923 ft.) just NW; corundum deposits; Sivaite temple with 10th-cent. Chola inscriptions here. Sometimes spelled Tiruchengode.

Tiruchirapalli, India: see TRICHINOPOLY.

Tirukandayur, India: see TIRUR.

Tirukattupalli or **Tirukkattuppalli** (tĭrōōkăt'tōōp-pŭl-lē), town (pop. 5,609), Tanjore dist., SE Madras, India, on arm of Cauvery R. delta and 13 mi. WNW of Tanjore; rice milling.

Tirukkalikkunram (–kŭlĭkōōn'rŭm), town (pop. 9,505), Chingleput dist., E Madras, India, 35 mi. SSW of Madras; pilgrimage center (Sivaite and Vishnuite). Anc. temple has great bathing tank; feeding of birds by priests is a daily ritual. Famous rock-cut temples (Seven Pagodas) 9 mi. E, at Mahabalipuram, on Bay of Bengal. Early Du. settlement of Sadras (founded 1647; finally ceded to English in 1824) is 8 mi. SE, on coast. Sometimes spelled Tirukalikundram. Also called Pakshitirtham.

Tirukkoyilur or **Tirukoilur** (both: –kō'yĭlōōr), town (pop. 14,800), South Arcot dist., SE Madras, India, on Ponnaiyar R. and 40 mi. NW of Cuddalore; rice and sugar milling.

Tirukovil or **Tirrukovail** (–kō'vĭl), village (pop. 1,022), Eastern Prov., Ceylon, on E coast, 42 mi. SSE of Batticaloa. Anc. Hindu pilgrimage site. Also spelled Tirukkovil.

Tirukurungudi, India: see NANGUNERI.

Tirumakudal Narsipur (tĭrōōmŭkōō'dŭl nŭr'sĭpōōr), town (pop. 3,587), Mysore dist., S Mysore, India, on Cauvery R., at Kabbani R. mouth, and 17 mi. ESE of Mysore city center, in silk-growing area; silk milling, hand-loom silk and cotton weaving; sugar-cane market. Also spelled Tirumakudlu Narsipur.

Tirumala, hill, India: see TIRUPATI.

Tirumalaivasal, India: see TIRUMULAIVASAL.

Tirumalarajanpatnam or **Tirumalrayapatnam** (–mŭlŭrä'jŭnpŭtnŭm), Fr. *Grand' Aldée* or *Grande Aldée* (grãdäldā'), town (commune pop. 9,477), Karikal settlement, Fr. India, 3 mi. S of Karikal. Also spelled Tirumalrayanpattinam.

Tirumangalam or **Thirumangalam** (both: –mŭng'gŭlŭm), town (pop. 11,111), Madura dist., S Madras, India, 11 mi. SW of Madura, in cotton area; trade center for agr. products, timber from Palni Hills (NW) and Sirumalai Hills (N); cotton pressing; fabric dyeing. Marble quarry 8 mi. N, at Kokkulam.

Tirumayam (–mŭyŭm'), town (pop. 4,752), Trichinopoly dist., S Madras, India, 10 mi. SW of Pudukkottai; rice, millet, peanuts.

Tirumulaivasal or **Tirumullaivasal** (–mōōlĭvä'sŭl), town (pop. 6,113), Tanjore dist., SE Madras, India, port on Coromandel Coast of Bay of Bengal, 30 mi. N of Negapatam; exports rice. Formerly spelled Tirumulavasal and Tirumullavasal; also spelled Tirumalaivasal.

Tirunallar (tĭ'rōōnŭlär), Fr. *Tirnoular* (tērnōōlär'), town (commune pop. 14,632), Karikal settlement, Fr. India, 3 mi. W of Karikal. Also Tirunalar.

Tirunelveli, India: see TINNEVELLY.

Tiruparankundram, India: see TIRUPPARANKUNDRAM.

Tirupati (tĭ'rōōpŭtē), city (pop. 20,143), Chittoor dist., central Madras, India, in a valley of Eastern Ghats, 35 mi. NNE of Chittoor; noted handicrafts (silk weaving, wood carving, brassware); rice and oilseed milling. Famous anc. shrines (mainly Sivaite) on sacred hill of Tirumala, just NW; scene of large pilgrimages. Renigunta, rail and road junction, is 6 mi. E.

Tirupattur, India: see TIRUPPATTUR.

Tirupparankundram or **Tiruparankundram** (tĭ"rōōpŭrŭngkōōn'drŭm), town (pop. 5,702), Madura dist., S Madras, India, 4 mi. SW of Madura; temple-festival trade center. Also spelled Tiruparankunram.

Tiruppattur or **Tirupattur** (both: tĭr"ōōpŭt-tōōr'), **1** City (pop. 23,008), North Arcot dist., E central Madras, India, on railroad and 50 mi. SW of Vellore; trade center in agr. area for products (tanbark, tamarind, nux vomica, hemp narcotics) of Javadi Hills (E). Industrial school. Junction of rail spur to road center of Krishnagiri, 23 mi. W. Jalarpet, 5 mi. N, is rail junction for line to Bangalore via Kolar (gold fields). **2** Town (pop. 12,911), Ramnad dist., S Madras, India, 35 mi. NE of Madura; road center; trades in cotton fabrics and agr. products (chiefly peanuts).

Tiruppur or **Tirupur** (tĭ'rōōpōōr), city (pop. 33,099), Coimbatore dist., SW Madras, India, on Noyil R. and 28 mi. ENE of Coimbatore; major cotton-trade and -milling center; rice milling. Training center for revival of village hand spinning and weaving (khaddar). Market for cattle-breeding center of Kangayam, 16 mi. ESE. Corundum mining near by.

Tiruppuvanam or **Tirupuvanam** (both: tĭrōōp'-ōōvŭnŭm), town (pop. 8,151), Ramnad dist., S Madras, India, on Vaigai R. and 11 mi. SE of Madura; betel farms.

Tirur (tĭrōōr'), town (pop 9,489), Malabar dist., SW Madras, India, 25 mi. SSE of Calicut; coir retting. Linked with port of Ponnani by transport canal. Also called Tirukandayur or Trikkandiyur.

Tiruttani (tĭrōō'tŭnē), town (pop. 7,197), Chittoor dist., central Madras, India, 35 mi. E of Chittoor; rice milling; sugar cane, tamarind. Sivaite temple on near-by hill is place of pilgrimage.

Tiruturaipundi or **Tirutturaipundi** (both: tĭr"ōōtōō-rĭpōōn'dē), town (pop. 8,071), Tanjore dist., SE Madras, India, in Cauvery R. delta, 21 mi. SW of Negapatam; rail junction; rice, tobacco, coconut palms.

Tiruvadamarudur or **Tiruvadaimarudur** (tĭrōōvŭdĭ'-mŭrōōdōōr), town (pop. 11,683), Tanjore dist., SE Madras, India, on Cauvery R. and 4 mi. NE of Kumbakonam, in rice, betel, and plantain area. Sivaite temple (Chola inscriptions). Experimental farm 2 mi. NE.

Tiruvadanai (–vä'dänī), village, Ramnad dist., S Madras, India, 8 mi. WNW of Tondi, in palmyra-growing area.

Tiruvadi (–vä'dē), town (pop. 9,302), Tanjore dist., SE Madras, India, in Cauvery R. delta and 6 mi. NNW of Tanjore; pith-carving of temple models; brass and copper vessels. Hindu place of pilgrimage. Also spelled Trivadi.

Tiruvalla (–vŭ'lŭ), city (pop. 18,002), W central Travancore, India, 35 mi. N of Quilon; coir rope and mats, tiles; rice milling, cashew-nut processing. Also spelled Thiruvella.

Tiruvallur (tĭ'rōōvŭlōōr), town (pop. 12,700), Chingleput dist., E Madras, India, 25 mi. WNW of Madras; road center; rice milling, mfg. of stoneware vessels. Vishnuite and Sivaite temples attract many pilgrims. Sometimes spelled Trivellore.

Tiruvalur, India: see TIRUVARUR.

Tiruvanaikkaval, India: see SRIRANGAM, city.

Tiruvannamalai (tĭr'ōōvŭn-nä'mŭlī), city (pop. 33,575), North Arcot dist., E central Madras, India, 50 mi. S of Vellore; road and trade center; exports rice, peanuts, millet, and products (sandalwood, tanbark, nux vomica, hemp narcotics) of Javadi Hills (NW). Annual cattle fair. Isolated peak (just NW; 2,682 ft.) has large Sivaite temple, near which was the retreat (*ashram*) of Sri Ramana Maharshi, noted religious recluse (d. here 1950). Was strategic 18th-cent. military post.

Tiruvarur (tĭrōōvä'rōōr) or **Tiruvalur** (–vä'lōōr), city (pop. 22,275), Tanjore dist., SE Madras, India, in Cauvery R. delta, 14 mi. W of Negapatam; road center; rail junction; rice milling. Sivaite temple is noted place of pilgrimage.

Tiruvattiyur. 1 Town, Chingleput dist., Madras, India: see TIRUVOTTIYUR. **2** Village, North Arcot district, Madras, India: see TIRUVETIPURAM.

Tiruvetipuram or **Tiruvettipuram** (–vĕt'tĭpōōrŭm), town (pop., including village of Tiruvattiyur, 12,522), North Arcot dist., E central Madras, India, on Cheyyar R. and 33 mi. SE of Vellore; cotton and silk weaving. Name Tiruvattiyur or Tiruvattur often refers to town of Tiruvetipuram.

Tiruvottiyur (–vŏ'tĭyōōr), town (pop. 13,909), Chingleput dist., E Madras, India, outer suburb of Madras, on Coromandel Coast of Bay of Bengal, 10 mi. N of city center; match-mfg. center; mfg. of abrasives, tanning, rice milling; cattle trade (milch cows). Also spelled Tiruvattiyur.

Tiruvur (–vōōr'), village, Kistna dist., NE Madras, India, 40 mi. N of Bezwada; rice, chili, peanuts. Sometimes spelled Tiruvuru.

Tirwa (tĭr'vŭ), town (pop. 2,421), Farrukhabad dist., central Uttar Pradesh, India, 10 mi. SW of Kanauj; wheat, gram, jowar, rice. Also called Ganj Tirwa.

Tiryns (tĭr'ĭnz), anc. town in Argolis and Corinthia nome, NE Peloponnesus, Greece, 2.5 mi. N of Nauplia, near Argos. Excavations (1884–85) by Schliemann and Dörpfeld uncovered extensive Cyclopean ruins, including massive walls and pre-Homeric palace. In Gr. mythology, Tiryns was founded by Proetus, a brother of king Acrisius of Argos, was ruled by Perseus, and was birthplace of Hercules. The city flourished 11th–10th cent. B.C. and was destroyed (468 B.C.) by Argos. Just S is modern village of Tiryns or Tirins (pop. 240), site of agr. school.

Tisa, river: see TISZA RIVER.

Tisaiyanvilai, Tisaiyanvillai, or **Tisayanvilai** (tĭsī'-yŭnvĭlī), town (pop. 10,303), Tinnevelly dist., S Madras, India, 31 mi. SE of Tinnevelly; palmyra products. Also spelled Tisianvillai.

Tisa River: see TISZA RIVER.

Tisbury, town and parish (pop. 1,387), S Wiltshire, England, 7 mi. NE of Shaftesbury; agr. market in dairying region. Has 13th–15th-cent. church and remains of castle.

Tisbury, town (pop. 1,930), Dukes co., SE Mass., on N Martha's Vineyard, 20 mi. SE of New Bedford; summer resort; fishing. Includes VINEYARD HAVEN village and West Chop village, on headland (with lighthouse) at W side of entrance to harbor of Vineyard Haven. Settled 1660, inc. 1671.

Tiscapa, Lake (tēskä'pä), small crater lake (□ 1), SW Nicaragua, in S outskirts of Managua. Presidential palace is on Tiscapa Hill on NW shore.

Tischnowitz, Czechoslovakia: see TISNOV.

Tisdale (tĭz'dāl, –dŭl), town (pop. 1,469), central Sask., 75 mi. ESE of Prince Albert; grain elevators, flour and lumber mills.

Tishkovka (tyĕsh'kŭfkŭ), village (1926 pop. 8,188), W Kirovograd oblast, Ukrainian SSR, 37 mi. ESE of Uman; metalworks.

Tishomingo (tĭ-shŭmĭng'gō), county (□ 451; pop. 15,544), extreme NE Miss.; ⊙ Iuka. Borders E on Ala., N on Tenn.; on NE is Pickwick Landing

Reservoir, impounded by dam in Tennessee R. Hilly, rising to 806 ft. in Woodall Mtn. (highest point in state), and drained by tributaries of Tennessee and Tombigbee rivers. Farming area (cotton, corn, sweet potatoes, hogs); lumbering. Mfg. of clay and wood products. Clay, sandstone, limestone, phosphorus, and bauxite deposits. Formed 1836.

Tishomingo. **1** Village (pop. 335), Tishomingo co., extreme NE Miss., 12 mi. S of Iuka; lumber milling. Clay, sandstone, phosphorus-rock, and bauxite deposits near by. **2** City (pop. 2,325), ⊙ Johnston co., S Okla., 24 mi. NW of Durant, and on L. Texoma; trade center for agr. area; concrete, lumber, sand and gravel. Murray State School of Agr. and a U.S. fish hatchery are here. Settled 1850; was chief city of the Chickasaw Indians (⊙ Chickasaw Nation) after c.1855.

Tisianvillai, India: see TISAIYANVILAI.

Tiskilwa (tĭ'skĭl"wŭ), village (pop. 962), Bureau co., N Ill., on Bureau Creek and 6 mi. SSW of Princeton, in agr. and bituminous-coal area; mfg. (dairy products, feed, tile).

Tisma (tēz'mä), town (1950 pop. 792), Masaya dept., SW Nicaragua, 10 mi. NNE of Masaya, on Tisma Lagoon (formed by Tipitapa R.), in livestock area.

Tisma Lagoon, SW Nicaragua, formed by Tipitapa R.; 6 mi. long, 2 mi. wide. Connects with Genízaro Lagoon (SE; 7 mi. long, 1½ mi. wide), which is separated from L. Nicaragua by narrow isthmus.

Tismana (tēzmä'nä), village (pop. 794), Gorj prov., SW Rumania, in S foothills of the Transylvanian Alps, 16 mi. WNW of Targu-Jiu; site of picturesque monastery (14th–16th-cent.) and climatic resort (1,706 ft.).

Tisnov (tyĭsh'nôf), Czech *Tišnov*, Ger. *Tischnowitz* (tĭsh'nōvĭts), town (pop. 4,587), W Moravia, Czechoslovakia, on Svratka R., on railroad and 13 mi. NNW of Brno; health resort (alt. 885 ft.) in Bohemian-Moravian Heights; textile and paper mfg. Noted 13th-cent. monastery is just NW.

Tisovec (tyĭ'sôvĕts), Ger. *Theissholz* (tīs'hôlts), Hung. *Tiszolc* (tĭ'sôlts), village (pop. 3,988), S Slovakia, Czechoslovakia, in Slovak Ore Mts., 37 mi. E of Banska Bystrica; terminus of cogwheel line from Brezno nad Hronom; large ironworks; woodworking. Ruins of former Hussite stronghold of Muran are 7 mi. E.

Tissa (tēsä'), agr. village, Fez region, N central Fr. Morocco, 24 mi. NE of Fez; olive groves.

Tissamaharama (tĭs"ŭmŭhŭrä'mŭ), anc. *Mahagama* or *Magama*, village (pop., including surrounding villages, 4,908), Southern Prov., Ceylon, 16 mi. NE of Hambantota; rice and coconut plantations; vegetables (largely tomatoes). One of anc. ruined cities of Ceylon; was ⊙ Singhalese kingdom, c.3d cent. B.C. Extensive Buddhist ruins include large stupas, temples, pillars, and sculptures; Buddhist pilgrimage center. Anc. irrigation tanks, here, restored 1897. Also called Tissa.

Tissa River: see TISZA RIVER.

Tisselt (tĭ'sûlt), town (pop. 2,558), Antwerp prov., N central Belgium, near Willebroek Canal, 5 mi. W of Mechlin; mfg. (drainage pipes). Formerly spelled Thisselt.

Tissington, agr. village and parish (pop. 250), W Derby, England, 4 mi. N of Ashbourne. Known for old custom of dressing the wells on Maundy Thursday, celebrating fact that village wells aided surrounding country during Black Death epidemic.

Tisso (tĭ'sû), Dan. *Tissø*, lake (3 mi. long, 2 mi. wide), W Zealand, Denmark, in Holbaek amt, 17 mi. SW of Holbaek.

Tissuari Island (tĭswä'rĭ), in W Goa dist., Portuguese, India, bounded W by Arabian Sea and separated from mainland by small rivers; 11 mi. long (E-W), 3–10 mi. wide. Rice, betel and cashew nuts, mangoes; salt drying; fishing. On N shore are Pangim and Goa.

Tista (tē'stŭ), village, Rangpur dist., N East Bengal, E Pakistan, on Tista R. (rail bridge) opposite Kaunia; rail junction (terminus of rail spur to Kurigram); soap mfg.

Tista River, in N India and E Pakistan, formed in the Himalayas by confluence of Lachen Chu and Lachung Chu rivers at Chuntang, Sikkim; flows S past Rangpo and Kalimpong, and SSE past Jalpaiguri and Mekhliganj, into E Pakistan, past Kaunia, to the Brahmaputra 10 mi. NE of Gaibanda; length, c.250 mi. In upper course, divides Nepal (W) and Assam (E) Himalayas.

Tisul or **Tisul'** (tyēsōōl'), village (1926 pop. 3,925), NE Kemerovo oblast, Russian SFSR, 45 mi. SE of Mariinsk, in agr. area; metalworks.

Tisza, river: see TISZA RIVER.

Tiszabura (tĭ'sŏbōōrŏ), town (pop. 2,831), Jasz-Nagykun-Szolnok co., E central Hungary, on Tisza R. and 10 mi. NW of Kunhegyes; wheat, rye, hogs, sheep.

Tiszacsege (tĭ'sŏ-chĕgĕ), town (pop. 6,307), Hajdu co., E Hungary, on Tisza R. and 16 mi. W of Hajdubószörmeny; fishing; wheat, corn, sheep, cattle.

Tiszadada (tĭ'sŏdŏdŏ), town (pop. 3,334), Szabolcs co., NE Hungary, on Tisza R. and 23 mi. WNW of Nyiregyhaza; fishing; agr. (potatoes, corn, hogs).

Tiszaderzs (tĭ'sŏdĕrzh), town (pop. 3,308), Jasz-Nagykun-Szolnok co., central Hungary, near Tisza R., 9 mi. SW of Tiszafüred; potatoes, rye, cattle; vineyards.

Tiszadob (tĭ'sŏdôb), town (pop. 4,279), Szabolcs co., NE Hungary, on Tisza R. and 27 mi. W of Nyiregyhaza; fishing; agr. (wheat, corn, hogs).

Tiszaeszlar (tĭ'sŏĕslär), Hung. *Tiszaeszlár*, town (pop. 3,754), Szabolcs co., NE Hungary, on Tisza R. and 15 mi. NW of Nyiregyhaza; fishing; agr. (corn, potatoes, cattle).

Tiszaföldvar (tĭ'sŏfûl"dvär), Hung. *Tiszaföldvár*, town (pop. 12,097), Jasz-Nagykun-Szolnok co., E central Hungary, near the Tisza, 13 mi. SSE of Szolnok; brickworks, basket weaving.

Tiszafüred (tĭ'sŏfürĕd), town (pop. 10,666), Heves co., N Hungary, near Tisza R., 40 mi. W of Debrecen; rail center; flour mills, distilleries, fisheries; agr. experiment station (wheat).

Tiszakarad (tĭ'sŏkŏräd), Hung. *Tiszakarád*, town (pop. 4,694), Zemplen co., NE Hungary, on Tisza R. and 14 mi. S of Satoraljaujhely; grain, potatoes, cattle.

Tiszakürt (tĭ'sŏkürt), town (pop. 5,249), Jasz-Nagykun-Szolnok co., E central Hungary, on Tisza R. and 12 mi. E of Kecskemet; river port; fishing.

Tiszalök (tĭ'sŏlûk), town (pop. 5,633), Szabolcs co., NE Hungary, on Tisza R. and 16 mi. WNW of Nyiregyhaza; rail junction; tile-, brickworks; fishing. Dam, hydroelectric plant, irrigation barrage.

Tiszaluc (tĭ'sŏlōōts), Hung. *Tiszalúc*, town (pop. 3,618), Zemplen co., NE Hungary, near Tisza R., 13 mi. ESE of Miskolc; flour mills; wheat, corn, hogs.

Tiszanana (tĭ'sŏnänŏ), Hung. *Tiszanána*, town (pop. 4,905), Heves co., N Hungary, 12 mi. ESE of Heves; agr.

Tiszapüspöki (tĭ'sŏpüsh-pûkē), town (pop. 2,478), Jasz-Nagykun-Szolnok co., E central Hungary, near Tisza R., 6 mi. ENE of Szolnok; wheat, tobacco, cattle, poultry.

Tisza River (tĭ'sŭ, Hung. tĭ'sŏ), Ger. *Theiss* (tīs), Czech, Rumanian, and Serbo-Croatian *Tisa* (tē'sä), Rus. *Tissa* (tĭ'sŭ), longest Danube tributary (c.800 mi.) in E Europe. Formed 2 mi. above RAKHOV in W Ukrainian SSR by 2 headstreams, the Black Tisza (right) and the White Tisza (left), that rise at about 6,000 ft. in the NW Carpathians. After short southward course, it turns W to skirt, past SIGHET and KHUST, the Ukraino-Rumanian border, and enters the Great Hungarian Plain (where it is used for irrigation), flowing generally SW past TOKAJ to SZOLNOK, whence it flows S once more, paralleling the Danube in many windings and meanders (largely canalized). Below SZEGED it continues S into the fertile Vojvodina lowland of Yugoslavia and joins the Danube c.25 mi. NNW of Belgrade. An irregular river of great water volume (spring and summer floods), the Tisza has to be controlled by dikes. It is navigable for light-draught vessels for c.450 mi.; its middle and lower course from Szolnok downstream is of good navigability for freight; passenger traffic from SENTA (Yugoslavia). The river is known for its fisheries; it is also extensively used for logging. Principal affluents are the SOMES RIVER, KÖRÖS RIVER, and MURES RIVER (left). The Tisza is joined by canal with Timisoara (Rumania) and is additionally linked with the Danube (Becej-Bezdan) through Danube-Tisza Canal near its mouth in Yugoslavia. Another canal to the Danube was begun 1950 in Hungary bet. Ujkecske and Dunaharaszti.

Tiszaroff (tĭ'sŏrôf), town (pop. 5,530), Jasz-Nagykun-Szolnok co., E central Hungary, on Tisza R. and 9 mi. WNW of Kunhegyes; flour mill, distillery; agr.

Tiszasüly (tĭ'sŏ-shüĭ), town (pop. 3,268), Jasz-Nagykun-Szolnok co., E central Hungary, on Tisza R. and 11 mi. E of Jaszladany; sawmill; agr.

Tiszaszentimre (tĭ'sŏsĕntĭm"rĕ), town (pop. 3,839), Jasz-Nagykun-Szolnok co., E central Hungary, 15 mi. NW of Karcag; wheat, corn, hogs, sheep.

Tiszaujlak, Ukrainian SSR: see VYLOK.

Tiszavarkony (tĭ'sŏvärkônyû), Hung. *Tiszavárkony*, town (pop. 2,131), Jasz-Nagykun-Szolnok co., E central Hungary, on Tisza R. and 8 mi. S of Szolnok; river port.

Tiszolc, Czechoslovakia: see TISOVEC.

Tit (tēt), oasis, Saharan Oases territory, central Algeria, one of the Tidikelt group of oases, 65 mi. WSW of In-Salah; 26°57'N 1°30'E. Date palms.

Titabar (tĭtä'bŭr), village, Sibsagar dist., E central Assam, India, 12 mi. S of Jorhat; rail junction; tea, rice, rape and mustard; tea processing. Sericulture and rice research stations.

Titagarh (tĭt'ägŭr), town (pop. 57,416), 24-Parganas dist., SE West Bengal, India, on the Hooghly and 12 mi. N of Calcutta city center; jute and paper milling, mfg. of glass, tea and textile machinery. Also spelled Tittagarh.

Titan, Russian SFSR: see MAGNITKA.

Titano, Mount: see SAN MARINO.

Titao, China: see LINTAO.

Tita Peninsula, Japan: see CHITA PENINSULA.

Tit-Ara or **Tit-Ary** (tyĕt"-ŭrä', –ŭrē'), town (1943 pop. over 500), N Yakut Autonomous SSR, Russian SFSR, at head of Lena R. delta, 80 mi. N of Bulun; fish canning.

Titaresios River or **Titarisios River** (both: tētärē'sēôs), in N Thessaly, Greece, rises in Kamvounia Mts., flows 35 mi. S and SE to Peneus R. below Larissa. Sometimes called Xerias or Xirias. The upper course is known as Sarantaporos (Sarandaporos) or Voulgaris.

Titchfield, town and parish (pop. 2,366), S Hampshire, England, 8 mi. NW of Portsmouth; agr. market, with tanning industry. Has remains of 13th-cent. Premonstratensian abbey; 15th-cent. church includes Saxon relics. Charles I was arrested here (1647).

Titchfield, Jamaica: see PORT ANTONIO.

Titel (tē'tĕl), village (pop. 5,427), Vojvodina, N Serbia, Yugoslavia, port on Tisa R., opposite Knicanin, on railroad and 29 mi. NNW of Belgrade, in the Backa.

Titeri or **Titteri** (tĕtrē'), range of the Tell Atlas, in Alger dept., N central Algeria, extends c.50 mi. WSW-ENE bet. Boghari and Aumale at N edge of the High Plateaus. Rises to 5,940 ft. in the Djebel Dira overlooking Aumale.

Titesti (tĕtĕsht'), Rum. *Titeşti*, village (pop. 851), Valcea prov., S central Rumania, in the Transylvanian Alps, 24 mi. NW of Curtea-de-Arges.

Tithwal (tĭtväl'), village, Muzaffarabad dist., W Kashmir, in NW Pir Panjal Range, on Kishanganga R. and 18 mi. E of Muzaffarabad; corn, rice, wheat, barley. Also spelled Titwal.

Titi (tē'tē), town (pop. 1,550), N Negri Sembilan, Malaya, 21 mi. NNE of Seremban; tin mining.

Titicaca, Lake (tētēkä'kä), largest lake (□ 3,200) of South America and highest (12,507 ft.) large lake of the world, in SE Peru and W Bolivia; 110 mi. long, 35 mi. wide, c.700 ft. deep. Consists of 2 sections connected by Strait of Tiquina: L. Chucuito (NW; 85 mi. long, 35 mi. wide) and L. Uinamarca (SE; 15 mi. long, 35 mi. wide). Major transportation artery bet. Peru and Bolivia, with international steamer service connecting Puno and Guaqui. Other important coastal towns are, in Bolivia: Puerto Acosta, Achacachi, Puerto Pérez, Desaguadero, Copacabana; in Peru: Juli, Pomata, Yunguyo. The lake includes isls. of Titicaca and Coati, with archaeological remains. Receives, in Bolivia, Suches R.; in Peru, Ilave, Coata, and Ramis rivers. Outlet: Desaguadero R. The name Titicaca is sometimes applied only to L. Chucuito.

Titicaca Island in L. Titicaca, W Bolivia, off Copacabana Peninsula, 9 mi. NNW of Copacabana; 7 mi. long, 2 mi. wide; archaeological site of Inca and pre-Inca civilizations. Also called Isla del Sol [Sp., =island of the sun].

Titi Islands, New Zealand: see MUTTON BIRD ISLANDS.

Titiribí (tētērēbē'), town (pop. 2,925), Antioquia dept., NW central Colombia, on W slopes of Cordillera Central, 21 mi. SW of Medellín; alt. 5,092 ft. Gold and coal mining; agr. (coffee, sugar cane, corn, yucca, beans, bananas, stock).

Titisee (tē'tēzā"), lake (□ .5), S Baden, Germany, in Black Forest, 15 mi. SE of Freiburg; 1 mi. long, ½ mi. wide, 131 ft. deep; alt. 2,785 ft. Drained by the Wutach. Noted climatic health resort and winter-sports and tourist center of Titisee (pop. 1,503) is at NE tip.

Titlagarh (tĭt'lŭgŭr), town (pop. 5,652), Bolangir dist., W Orissa, India, 37 mi. SSW of Bolangir; mfg. of graphite crucibles, emery powder, valve-grinding paste. Sometimes spelled Titilagarh.

Titlis (tĭt'lĭs), peak (10,639 ft.) in Alps of the Four Forest Cantons, central Switzerland, 3 mi. SSE of Engelberg.

Titograd (tē'tōgrăd, tē'tôgrät), town (pop. 12,206), ⊙ Montenegro, Yugoslavia, N of L. Scutari, on Moraca R., at short Ribnica R. mouth, on narrow-gauge railroad and 185 mi. SSW of Belgrade, in Zeta lowland. Trade and highway center of Montenegro; airfield; tobacco and cigarette mfg. Cotton experiment station. The Duklja, anc. *Dioclea*, a castle where Emperor Diocletian allegedly was born, stands N of town. In Middle Ages, called Ribnica; birthplace of 12th-cent. Serbian ruler Stephen Nemanja; leading city of Montenegro until Turkish occupation in 15th cent. Returned (1878) to Montenegro. Completely damaged in Second World War, it was rapidly rebuilt. Until c.1945, called Podgorica or Podgoritsa.

Titonka (tĭtŏng'kŭ), town (pop. 589), Kossuth co., N Iowa, 14 mi. NE of Algona; feed milling.

Titova Korenica (tē'tôvä kôrĕ'nĭtsä), village (pop. 1,457), W Croatia, Yugoslavia, at W foot of the Pljesevica, 21 mi. NE of Gospic, near Bosnia border. Until c.1945, called Korenica.

Titovka (tyē'tŭfkŭ), village, NW Murmansk oblast, Russian SFSR, on bay of Motovka Gulf, at mouth of Titovka R. (50 mi. long), 45 mi. NW of Murmansk; fisheries.

Titovo Uzice or **Titovo Uzhitse** (tē'tôvô ōō'zhĭtsĕ), Serbo-Croatian *Titovo Užice*, town (pop. 11,266), ⊙ Titovo Uzice oblast (formed 1949), W Serbia, Yugoslavia, on railroad and 70 mi. SSW of Belgrade; trade center for stock-raising region; munitions industry, meat packing. Hydroelectric plant. Chromium deposits, apple growing in vicinity. Manganese mining, c.30–40 mi. S of town. Until 1947, called Uzice or Uzhitse.

Titov Veles (tē'tôv vĕ'lĕs), Turkish *Köprülü* or *Köprili*, town (pop. 14,866), Macedonia, Yugoslavia, on Vardar R. and 26 mi. SSE of Skoplje. Rail and road junction; trade center for agr. region (fruit, vegetables, truck gardening, sericulture); poppy-oil and opium industry; handicraft (pottery making). Has cloister, Roman guardhouse, castle ruins. First mentioned in 216 B.C. Until c.1945 called Veles.

Titran, Norway: see FROYA.

Ti Tree Point (tē), village (pop. 70), ⊙ Weber co. (□ 118; pop. 317), S N.Isl., New Zealand, 70 mi. SSW of Napier, in fertile valley; sheep raising.

Titron (tĭtrōn′), town (pop. 4,042), Saharanpur dist., N Uttar Pradesh, India, 25 mi. SW of Saharanpur; wheat, rice, rape and mustard, gram, corn.

Tittabawassee River (tĭ″tŭbŭwŏ′sē), E central Mich., rises in SW Ogemaw co. flows c.75 mi. S and E, past Midland, to join the Shiawassee to form the Saginaw R. just SW of Saginaw. Short West and East branches join main stream near its head.

Tittagarh, India: see TITAGARH.

Titteri, Algeria: see TITERI.

Titterstone Clee Hill, England: see CLEE HILLS.

Tittmann, Mount (11,000 ft.), S Alaska, in St. Elias Mts., 120 mi. NW of Yakutat; 61°8′N 141°14′W.

Tittmoning (tĭt′mō″nĭng), town (pop. 2,296), Upper Bavaria, Germany, on the Salzach and 15 mi. NNE of Traunstein, on Austrian border; rail terminus; textile mfg., metalworking, lumber milling, printing. Has partly preserved medieval walls; also 15th–17th-cent. former castle of archbishops of Salzburg.

Titu (tē′tōō), village (pop. 908), Bucharest prov., S central Rumania, 11 mi. ESE of Gaesti; rail junction.

Titule (tētōō′lā), town, Eastern Prov., N Belgian Congo, on Congo-Nile highway and 60 mi. NE of Buta; rail terminus and trading center in cotton-producing area; cotton ginning. R.C. mission.

Titus (tī′tŭs), county (□ 418; pop. 17,302), NE Texas; ⊙ Mount Pleasant. Bounded N by Sulphur R., S by Cypress Bayou; drained by White Oak Bayou. Forested area (pine, oak; lumbering), with agr. (cotton, sweet potatoes, peanuts, corn, fruit, truck), dairying, livestock (cattle, sheep, hogs, horses). Large oil production; also natural gas, asphalt, clay. Mfg., oil refining, farm-products processing at Mt. Pleasant. Formed 1846.

Titusville (tī′tŭsvĭl). **1** City (pop. 2,604), ⊙ Brevard co., central Fla., 35 mi. E of Orlando and on Indian R. lagoon; citrus-fruit shipping point, and resort; boat yards. Inc. 1886 as town, reincorporated 1909. **2** City (pop. 8,923), Crawford co., NW Pa., on Oil Creek and 40 mi. SE of Erie; mfg. (machinery, tools, metal products); milk, buckwheat, potatoes. Near-by Drake Well Memorial Park marks site of 1st successful oil well (1859) in U.S.; city grew in oil boom of 1860s; its last oil refinery closed in 1950. Settled 1796, laid out 1809, inc. as borough 1847, as city 1866.

Titwal, Kashmir: see TITHWAL.

Tiugsá (tēōōgsä′), village, Ifni territory, NW Africa, 11 mi. E of Sidi Ifni; 29°23′N 10°W. Barley, sheep. Argan trees.

Tiumen, Russian SFSR: see TYUMEN.

Tiuquilemu (tyōōkēlā′mōō), town (pop. 1,082), Ñuble prov., S central Chile, 5 mi. N of San Carlos. Sometimes spelled Tiuquilemo.

Tivaouane (tēväwä′nā), town (pop. c.7,100), W Senegal, Fr. West Africa, on railroad and 45 mi. ENE of Dakar; peanut-growing center; livestock.

Tivat (tē′vät), Ital. *Teodo* (tĕŏ′dô), village, SW Montenegro, Yugoslavia, on E shore of Bay of Tivat (S inlet of Gulf of Kotor), 4 mi. W of Kotor. Naval base with arsenal and several miles of quays. Wine- and fruitgrowing in vicinity. Until 1921, in Dalmatia.

Tivat, Bay of, Yugoslavia: see KOTOR, GULF OF.

Tivenys (tēvä′nēs), town (pop. 1,366), Tarragona prov., NE Spain, near the Ebro, 6 mi. N of Tortosa; olive-oil processing; trades in wine, almonds, hazelnuts, fruit.

Tiverton (tĭ′vûrtŭn), village (pop. 282), S Ont., near L. Huron, 8 mi. NNE of Kincardine; dairying.

Tiverton, municipal borough (1931 pop. 9,610; 1951 census 10,869), E central Devon, England, on Exe R. and 13 mi. N of Exeter; lace mfg., silk milling, limestone and sandstone quarrying; agr. market. Has Blundell's school, founded 1604; 15th-cent. church; and remains of castle built 1106.

Tiverton, town (pop. 5,659), Newport co., SE R.I., on Sakonnet R. and 18 mi. SE of Providence, in residential, resort, farming, fishing area. Includes villages of North Tiverton (1940 pop. 1,893; makes textiles) and Tiverton Four Corners. Inc. 1692 as a Mass. town, annexed to R.I. 1746.

Tividale, town (pop. 3,758), in Rowley Regis municipal borough, S Stafford, England; machinery, machine tools.

Tivisa (tēvē′sä), town (pop. 1,934), Tarragona prov., NE Spain, 16 mi. E of Gandesa; wax and soap mfg., olive-oil and wine processing; lumbering.

Tivoli (tĭ′vŭlē, It. tē′vôlē), anc. *Tibur*, town (pop. 16,886), Roma prov., Latium, central Italy, on Aniene R. and 17 mi. ENE of Rome, beautifully situated on a ridge amidst olive groves. Paper-milling center; mfg. (hardware, shoes, soap, glass, macaroni). Travertine quarries near by. Bishopric. Noted for its waterfalls, which supply power to large hydroelectric plant below the town, and for the Renaissance Villa d'Este with its terraced gardens. Has cathedral with 12th-cent. Romanesque campanile, ruins of anc. Roman villas, notably that of Hadrian, and a well-preserved temple (Temple of Vesta), now a church. Severely damaged by air bombing (1943–44) in Second World War.

Tivoli, village (pop. 753), Dutchess co., SE N.Y., just SE of Saugerties, across the Hudson.

Tivon or **Tiv'on** (both: tēv-ōn′), residential settlement, NW Israel, bet. Zebulun Valley and Plain of Jezreel, near SE slope of Mt. Carmel, near Kishon R., 9 mi. SE of Haifa; garden suburb and tourist resort. Founded 1947.

Tiwi (tēwē′), village, E Oman, on Gulf of Oman, 70 mi. SE of Muscat, at foot of Eastern Hajar hill country; fishing; dates, fruit. Sometimes spelled Taiwi and Teiwi.

Tiwi (tē′wē), town (1939 pop. 1,222; 1948 municipality pop. 14,350), Albay prov., SE Luzon, Philippines, on Lagonoy Gulf, 22 mi. N of Legaspi; abacá, rice, coconuts.

Tixán (tēksän′), village, Chimborazo prov., central Ecuador, in the Andes, on Guayaquil-Quito RR and 4 mi. NE of Alausí; sulphur mining. Hydroelectric plant.

Tixcacalcupul (tēskäkälkōōpōōl′), town (pop. 775), Yucatan, SE Mexico, 11 mi. SSE of Valladolid; henequen, tropical woods, fruit.

Tixkokob (tēskōkōb′), town (pop. 2,758), Yucatan, SE Mexico, 14 mi. E of Mérida; rail junction in henequen-growing region.

Tixmeuac (tēsmĕwäk′), town (pop. 1,340), Yucatan, SE Mexico, 11 mi. E of Tekax; henequen, sugar cane, fruit, timber.

Tixpéual (tēspā′wäl), town (pop. 985), Yucatan, SE Mexico, 11 mi. E of Mérida; henequen. Sometimes Tixpehual.

Tixtla (tēs′lä), officially Tixtla de Guerrero, city (pop. 6,130), Guerrero, SW Mexico, in Sierra Madre del Sur, 5 mi. NE of Chilpancingo; alt. 4,527 ft. Agr. center (cereals, sugar cane, tobacco, coffee, fruit); lumbering. Former ⊙ Guerrero. Birthplace of revolutionary leader Vicente Guerrero. Mex. patriot Morelos y Pavón won victory here over Sp. royalists (1811).

Tixtlancingo (tēslänsĕng′gō), town (pop. 1,687), Guerrero, SW Mexico, in Pacific lowland, 17 mi. NNW of Acapulco; rice, sugar, fruit, livestock.

Tizapán (tēsäpän′), town (pop. 8,424), Federal Dist., central Mexico, 10 mi. SSW of Mexico city; residential suburb in fruitgrowing region.

Tizapán el Alto (ĕl äl′tō), town (pop. 1,905), Jalisco, central Mexico, on S shore of L. Chapala, 40 mi. SE of Guadalajara; cereals, vegetables, fruit, stock.

Tizard Bank (tĭ′zûrd), Chinese *Tsingho* or *Ching-ho* (both: jĭng′hŭ′), Chinese dependency in S.China Sea; 10°15′N 114°20′E; c.30 mi. long (E–W), c.8 mi. wide. Consists of a lagoon bordered by reefs that are dry at low water. Includes ITU ABA ISLAND.

Tizayuca (tēsīōō′kä), town (pop. 3,033), Hidalgo, central Mexico, on railroad, on Inter-American Highway and 27 mi. SW of Pachuca; agr. center (cereals, beans, maguey, stock).

Tizgui Remtz (tēdh′gē rĕmth′), oasis, Southern Protectorate of Morocco, Sp. West Africa, near left bank of the Uad Dráa; 28°20′N 9°25′W. Date palms.

Tizi (tēzē′), village (pop. 1,091), Oran dept., NW Algeria, 7 mi. SW of Mascara; rail junction; wine-growing, sheep raising.

Tizimín (tēsēmēn′), town (pop. 6,687), Yucatan, SE Mexico, 95 mi. E of Mérida; rail terminus; agr. center (henequen, chicle, corn, fruit); tropical wood.

Tizi n' Talghemt (tēzēn′ tälgĕmt′), pass (alt. 6,440 ft.) across the High Atlas in central Fr. Morocco, connecting upper Moulouya valley at Midelt (N) with Oued Ziz valley at Ksar-es-Souk (S); has road.

Tizi n' Test (tĕst′), pass (alt. 7,300 ft.) across the High Atlas, in SW Fr. Morocco, providing access from the Haouz lowland (around Marrakesh; N) to the Sous plain (around Taroudant; S). Marrakesh-Agadir road uses Oued N'Fis gorge for N ascent. Lead and zinc mines just NE of pass.

Tizi n' Tichka (tēshkä′), pass (alt. 8,464 ft.) across the High Atlas, in SW central Fr. Morocco, on road from Marrakesh (NW) to Ouarzazate (SE).

Tizi-Ouzou (tēzē′-ōōzōō′), town (pop. 4,700), Alger dept., N central Algeria, in Great Kabylia, 55 mi. E of Algiers; rail terminus; regional commercial center with important fig-processing and olive-oil industry.

Tiziwa, town, Japan: see CHIJIWA.

Tiziwa Bay, Japan: see TACHIBANA BAY.

Tiznados River (tēsnä′dōs), Guárico state, central Venezuela, rises S of L. Valencia, flows c.150 mi. S to Portuguesa R. 4 mi. NNW of La Unión (Barinas state). Lower course navigable for small craft.

Tiznit (tēznēt′), town (pop. 6,476), Agadir frontier region, SW Fr. Morocco, near the Atlantic and N border of Ifni enclave (Spanish), 50 mi. S of Agadir; 29°44′N 9°43′W. S road terminus and head of trans-Saharan track to Mauritania (Fr. West Africa); commercial and military center of region (extending S to the Oued Dra) not pacified by French until 1934. Irrigated orchards and date palms; vegetables, barley. Iron deposits in Tachilla and Ouarzemine ranges (c.15 mi. NE). Founded 1882.

Tizu, Japan: see CHIZU.

Tizzana (tētsä′nä), village (pop. 147), Pistoia prov., Tuscany, central Italy, 8 mi. SSE of Pistoia.

Tjandi Sewoe, Indonesia: see CHANDI SEWU.

Tjareme, Mount, Indonesia: see CHAREMAI, MOUNT.

Tjeldoy (tyĕl′ûü), Nor. *Tjeldøy*, island (□ 72; pop. 806) in Ofot Fjord, Nordland co., N Norway, 25 mi. W of Narvik; 13 mi. long, 8 mi. wide. Separated from mainland (E) and from Hinnoy (W and N) by narrow straits. Fishing, agr.

Tjepoe, Indonesia: see CHEPU.

Tjerebon, Indonesia: see CHERIBON.

Tjiamis, Indonesia: see CHIAMIS.

Tjiandjoer or **Tjiandjur**, Indonesia: see CHIANJUR.

Tjilatjap, Indonesia: see CHILACHAP.

Tjiledoeg or **Tjiledug**, Indonesia: see CHILEDUG.

Tjimahi, Indonesia: see CHIMAHI.

Tjirebon, Indonesia: see CHERIBON.

Tjitarum River, Indonesia: see CHITARUM RIVER.

Tjolling, Norway: see ULA.

Tjombal, Indonesia: see CHOMBAL.

Tjorn (chûrn), Swedish *Tjörn*, island (□ 54; pop. 8,735), SW Sweden, in the Skagerrak at N entrance to the Kattegat, 20 mi. NW of Goteborg, just S of Orust isl.; separated from mainland by 2-mi.-wide channel. Isl. is 10 mi. long (NE–SW), 3–8 mi. wide. Kyrkesund (W) is chief fishing village; also several fishing ports and seaside resorts. Fish curing and canning.

Tjotta (tyût′tä), Nor. *Tjøtta*, village (pop. 160; canton pop. 2,395), Nordland co., N central Norway, on Tjotta isl. (□ 4; pop. 246) in North Sea, 20 mi. W of Mosjoen; zinc and lead mining.

Tkibuli (ŭtkēbōō′lyē), city (1944 pop. 10,100), W Georgian SSR, 15 mi. NE of Kutasi; rail terminus; bituminous coal-mining center. Until 1940s, spelled Tkvibuli.

Tkvarcheli (ŭtkvŭrchē′lyē), city (1942 pop. 10,018), SE Abkhaz Autonomous SSR, Georgian SSR, on rail spur (Kvezani station) from Ochemchiri and 35 mi. ESE of Sukhumi; bituminous coal-mining center; power plant. Includes Akarmara (E). Coking-coal deposits known since 1881; opened for exploitation 1935.

Tkvibuli, Georgian SSR: see TKIBULI.

Tlachichilco (tlächēchēl′kō), town (pop. 599), Veracruz, E Mexico, in Sierra Madre Oriental, 25 mi. S of Chicontepec; corn, coffee.

Tlachichuca (–chōō′kä), town (pop. 2,200), Puebla, central Mexico, at NW foot of Pico de Orizaba, on railroad and 9 mi. NNE of Serdán; alt. 8,397 ft.; cereals, maguey, stock.

Tlacoachixtlahuaca (tläkwächēsläwä′kä), town (pop. 1,338), Guerrero, SW Mexico, on S slope of Sierra Madre del Sur, 13 mi. NE of Ometepec; fruit.

Tlacochahuaya (tläkōchäwī′ä), officially San Jerónimo Tlacochahuaya, town, Oaxaca, S Mexico, in Sierra Madre del Sur, 10 mi. SE of Oaxaca; fruit, stock. Has pre-Columbian ruins with notable carvings; municipal palace, 16th-cent. church, 17th-cent. convent.

Tlacojalpan (–häl′pän), town (pop. 1,633), Veracruz, SE Mexico, on Papaloápam R. and 15 mi. SW of Cosamaloapan; sugar cane, bananas.

Tlacolula (–lōō′lä), officially Tlacolula de Matamoros, city (pop. 5,297), Oaxaca, S Mexico, in Sierra Madre del Sur, 18 mi. SE of Oaxaca; alt. 5,249 ft. Rail terminus; mining (gold, silver, lead, copper) and agr. (cereals, sugar cane, coffee, tobacco, fruit, livestock) center. Market center, known for colorful display. Has 16th-cent. parish church, and 6,600-yard aqueduct, finished 1846. Indian town dates from 1250; settled 1560 by Spanish.

Tlacolulan (–län), town (pop. 765), Veracruz, E Mexico, in Sierra Madre Oriental, 11 mi. NNW of Jalapa; corn, coffee, fruit.

Tlacotalpan (–täl′pän), city (pop. 4,939), Veracruz, SE Mexico, in Sotavento lowlands, on Papaloápam R. and 32 mi. WNW of San Andrés Tuxtla; agr. center (coconuts, sugar cane, coffee, bananas, cattle). Anc. Indian post. Site of Amer. defeat (1847) in Mexican War.

Tlacotepec (–tāpĕk′). **1** Town (pop. 1,580), Guerrero, SW Mexico, in Sierra Madre del Sur, 33 mi. WNW of Chilpancingo; alt. 5,249 ft.; sugar cane, coffee, tobacco, fruit. **2** Town (pop. 3,695), Mexico state, central Mexico, 6 mi. S of Toluca; agr. center (grain, livestock); dairying. **3** Town (pop. 2,345), Michoacán, central Mexico, 3 mi. NW of El Oro; cereals, livestock. **4** Town (pop. 1,005), Puebla, central Mexico, 23 mi. NW of Tehuacán; alt. 6,480 ft.; corn, sugar cane, palms, livestock. **5** Officially Tlacotepec de Mejía, town (pop. 1,593), Veracruz, E Mexico, in Sierra Madre Oriental, 8 mi. ENE of Huatusco; corn, coffee, fruit.

Tlacotepec, Cerro, mountain (10,594 ft.) in Guerrero, SW Mexico, in Sierra Madre del Sur, just SE of Cerro Teotepec, 38 mi. NNW of Acapulco, 25 mi. SSW of Tlacotepec.

Tlacotepec de Díaz (dā dē′äs), town (pop. 565), Puebla, central Mexico, 35 mi. E of Tehuacán; rice, fruit, stock.

Tlacotlapilco (–tläpēl'kō), town (pop. 2,720), Hidalgo, central Mexico, on Tula R. and 37 mi. NW of Pachuca; agr. center (corn, wheat, beans, maguey, fruit, stock).

Tlacoyalco (tläkoiäl'kō), officially San Marcos Tlacoyalco, town (pop. 1,945), Puebla, central Mexico, 20 mi. NW of Tehuacán; corn, sugar cane, stock.

Tlacuilotepec (tläkwēlōtāpĕk'), town (pop. 1,218), Puebla, central Mexico, 10 mi. N of Huauchinango; alt. 4,330 ft.; coffee, sugar cane, fruit.

Tláhuac (tlä'wäk), town (pop. 3,296), Federal Dist., central Mexico, 15 mi. SE of Mexico city; cereals, fruit, vegetables, livestock.

Tlahualilo de Zaragoza (tläwälē'lō dā särägō'sä) or **Zaragoza,** town (pop. 2,949), Durango, N Mexico, in irrigated area, 40 mi. N of Torreón; alt. 3,599 ft. Rail junction; agr. center (cotton, grain, fruit, vegetables, sugar cane).

Tlahuapan (tläwä'pän"), officially Santa Rita Tlahuapan, town (pop. 1,507), Puebla, central Mexico, 30 mi. NW of Puebla; cereals, beans, maguey.

Tlahuelilpa (tläwälēl'pä), officially Tlahuelilpa de Ocampo, town (pop. 1,920), Hidalgo, central Mexico, 33 mi. W of Pachuca; cereals, beans, cotton, fruit, stock.

Tlaixpan (tlīspän'). **1** Officially San Miguel Tlaixpan, town (pop. 1,552), Mexico state, central Mexico, 3 mi. E of Texcoco; cereals, maguey, livestock. **2** Officially San Mateo Tlaixpan, town (pop. 1,674), Puebla, central Mexico, 32 mi. ESE of Puebla; cereals, maguey.

Tlajomulco (tlähōmōōl'kō), officially Tlajomulco de Zúñiga, town (pop. 3,425), Jalisco, W Mexico, on railroad and 15 mi. SSW of Guadalajara; wheat-growing center; corn, chick-peas, beans, fruit, stock.

Tlalamac (tlälämäk'), officially San Andrés Tlalamac, town (pop. 1,974), Mexico state, central Mexico, at W foot of Popocatepetl, 40 mi. SE of Mexico city; cereals, fruit, stock.

Tlalancaleca (tlälängkälä'kä), officially San Matías Tlalancaleca, town (pop. 2,890), Puebla, central Mexico, 27 mi. NW of Puebla; cereals, maguey.

Tlalchapa (tlälchä'pä), town (pop. 1,660), Guerrero, SW Mexico, in Río de las Balsas valley, 15 mi. ENE of Altamirano; cereals, sugar, cotton, fruit.

Tlalcuapan (tlälkwä'pän), officially San Pedro Tlalcuapan, town (pop. 1,516), Tlaxcala, central Mexico, at W foot of Malinche volcano, 5 mi. ESE of Tlaxcala; grain, alfalfa, stock.

Tlalixcoyan (tlälēskoi'än), town (pop. 1,058), Veracruz, E Mexico, 28 mi. S of Veracruz; coffee, fruit, stock.

Tlalixtaquilla (tlälēstäkē'yä), town (pop. 1,564), Guerrero, SW Mexico, in Sierra Madre del Sur, near Oaxaca border, 14 mi. SE of Tlapa; cereals, fruit, stock.

Tlalmanalco (tlälmänäl'kō), officially Tlalmanalco de Velázquez, town (pop. 2,479), Mexico state, central Mexico, on railroad and 28 mi. SE of Mexico city; cereals, vegetables, livestock; paper mfg. Has old Franciscan convent with frescoes.

Tlalnelhuayocan (tlälnĕlwīō'kän), town (pop. 428), Veracruz, E Mexico, 4 mi. NW of Jalapa; coffee.

Tlalnepantla (tlälnāpän'tlä). **1** Officially Tlalnepantla de Galeana, town (pop. 4,389), Mexico state, central Mexico, 8 mi. NNW of Mexico city; rail junction; mfg. and dairying center. Mercury, antimony, and tin smelters; cement plant. Agr. processing industries. Anc. city; founded by Otomi Indians, later conquered by the Aztecs. Its Spanish colonial church was begun 1583. Tenayuca and Santa Cecilia pyramids, outstanding Aztec monuments, are near by (E). **2** City (pop. 1,024), Morelos, central Mexico, 17 mi. ENE of Cuernavaca; peach-growing center; sugar cane, vegetables, livestock.

Tlalpan or **Tlalpam** (tlälpän', –päm'), city (pop. 10,436), Federal Dist., central Mexico, 10 mi. S of Mexico city; resort and residential suburb on NW slopes of extinct Cerro Ajusco volcano, with orchards, picturesque fountains. Textile- and paper-milling center. Has church of San Agustín de las Cuevas (1532). Anc. Aztec city. Famous Cuicuilco pyramid, 1½ mi. W, considered oldest man-made structure on the continent, is estimated to be 9–10,000 years old; originally measured 396 ft. in diameter and 60 ft. in height, now is partly covered by an old lava flow.

Tlaltelulco (tläĺtälōōl'kō), officially La Magdalena Tlaltelulco, town (pop. 2,380), Tlaxcala, central Mexico, 4 mi. SE of Tlaxcala; grain, alfalfa, maguey, stock.

Tlaltempan (tlältĕm'pän), officially Santa Catarina Tlaltempan, town (pop. 1,369), Puebla, central Mexico, 30 mi. S of Puebla; corn, sugar cane, fruit.

Tlaltenango (tläĺtänäng'gō). **1** Town (pop. 1,938), Puebla, central Mexico, 13 mi. NW of Puebla; grain, maguey, fruit. **2** Town (pop. 4,627), Zacatecas, N central Mexico, on interior plateau, 80 mi. SW of Zacatecas; alt. 5,653 ft.; agr. center (grain, fruit, tobacco, sugar cane, livestock).

Tlaltenco or **Tlaltengo** (tläĺtĕng'kō, –gō), town (pop. 2,711), Federal Dist., central Mexico, 12 mi. SE of Mexico city; cereals, fruit, vegetables, stock.

Tlaltetela (tläĺtātä'lä) or **Axocuapan** (ähōkwä'pän), town (pop. 1,059), Veracruz, E Mexico, in Sierra Madre Oriental, 22 mi. S of Jalapa; coffee, fruit. Sometimes Tlaltetela Axocuapan.

Tlaltizapán (tläĺtēsäpän'). **1** Officially San Pedro Tlaltizapán, town (pop. 1,999), Mexico state, central Mexico, 14 mi. SE of Toluca; cereals, livestock. **2** Town (pop. 1,966), Morelos, central Mexico, on railroad and 17 mi. SSE of Cuernavaca; rice, wheat, sugar cane, coffee, fruit, stock.

Tlanalapan (tlänälä'pän). **1** Town (pop. 1,515), Hidalgo, central Mexico, 25 mi. SE of Pachuca; cereals, maguey, livestock. **2** Officially San Rafael Tlanalapan, town (pop. 2,169), Puebla, central Mexico, 24 mi. NW of Puebla; cereals, maguey, livestock.

Tlanchinol (tlänchēnōl'), town (pop. 693), Hidalgo, central Mexico, 19 mi. SW of Huejutla; alt. 5,213 ft.; cereals, sugar cane, tobacco, fruit.

Tlanepantla (tlänāpän'tlä), town (pop. 1,492), Puebla, central Mexico, 25 mi. SE of Puebla; cereals, vegetables.

Tlanisco (tlänē'skō), officially San Pedro Tlanisco, town (pop. 1,589), Mexico state, central Mexico, 13 mi. S of Toluca; cereals, livestock.

Tlaola (tläō'lä), town (pop. 760), Puebla, central Mexico, 8 mi. ESE of Huauchinango; alt. 5,256 ft.; corn, sugar cane, fruit.

Tlapa (tlä'pä), city (pop. 2,976), Guerrero, SW Mexico, in Sierra Madre del Sur, 60 mi. E of Chilpancingo; cereals, sugar cane, fruit, forest products (resin, rubber, vanilla).

Tlapacoyan (tläpäkoi'än). **1** Town (pop. 870), Puebla, central Mexico, 12 mi. ESE of Huauchinango; sugar cane, coffee, fruit. **2** Town (pop. 3,953), Veracruz, E Mexico, in Sierra Madre Oriental, 37 mi. NW of Jalapa; agr. center (corn, sugar cane, coffee, tobacco, fruit).

Tlapanalá (–nälä'), town (pop. 902), Puebla, central Mexico, 17 mi. SSW of Atlixco; cereals, sugar cane, stock.

Tlapehuala (tläpäwä'lä), town (pop. 2,393), Guerrero, SW Mexico, on Río de las Balsas R. and 11 mi. SE of Altamirano; sugar cane, tobacco, coffee, cotton, fruit, cereals, forest products (resin, rubber, vanilla).

Tlapujahua (tläpōōhä'wä), officially Tlapujahua de Rayón, town (pop. 5,385), Michoacán, central Mexico, on central plateau, 3 mi. W of El Oro; silver, gold, lead, copper, tin mining.

Tlaquepaque or **San Pedro Tlaquepaque** (sän pā'drō tläkäpä'kä), town (pop. 11,486), Jalisco, central Mexico, on central plateau, 5 mi. S of Guadalajara; rail junction; agr. center (wheat, corn, peanuts, sugar cane, tobacco, vegetables, fruit); summer resort.

Tlaquilpa (tläkēl'pä), town (pop. 1,479), Veracruz, E Mexico, in Sierra Madre Oriental, 17 mi. S of Orizaba; coffee, corn, fruit. Sometimes Tlaquilpan.

Tlaquiltenango (tläkēltänäng'gō), town (pop. 2,518), Morelos, central Mexico, on railroad and 20 mi. SSE of Cuernavaca; rice, sugar, fruit, vegetables.

Tlatlauquitepec (tlätloukē"täpĕk'). **1** Town (pop. 1,366), Puebla, central Mexico, 9 mi. WNW of Teziutlán; corn, coffee, sugar cane, fruit, vegetables. Oil deposits near by. **2** Officially La Magdalena Tlatlauquitepec, town (pop. 406), Puebla, central Mexico, 21 mi. SSE of Puebla; cereals, livestock.

Tlatlaya (tlätlī'ä), town (pop. 515), Mexico state, central Mexico, 26 mi. SW of Sultepec; sugar cane, fruit; silver and gold deposits.

Tlaxcala (tläskä'lä), state (□ 1,555; 1940 pop. 224,063; 1950 pop. 282,495), central Mexico; ⊙ Tlaxcala. The smallest state in the republic, it is almost completely surrounded by Puebla, only bounded W by Mexico state and NW by Hidalgo. It is a mountainous region (average alt. c.7,000 ft.), largely on the central plateau (W), the S being dominated by the Malinche volcano. Climate is cool and dry, with more rain in the Malinche area. The coal, silver, and gold deposits are thus far unexploited. Primarily an agr. state; its most important crop is maguey, from which the native liquor pulque is distilled; produces also corn, wheat, barley, alfalfa, beans, peas; contains good pasture for stock raising (cattle, sheep, goats). Apizaco and Tlaxcala are processing centers. The present state comprises roughly the same territory as the pre-Sp. nation of the Tlaxcalan Indians, who held out against the Aztecs but were defeated (1519) by Cortés and became his allies.

Tlaxcala, officially Tlaxcala de Xicohténcatl, city (pop. 3,261), ⊙ Tlaxcala, central Mexico, on central plateau, 60 mi. ESE of Mexico city; alt. c.7,500 ft.; 19°18'N 98°14'W. Rail terminus; agr. center (corn, wheat, barley, alfalfa, beans, livestock); rayon and cotton mills; mfg. of shoes, pulque. Anc. capital of Tlaxcalan Indian kingdom conquered 1519 by Cortés, who founded here (1521) the oldest Christian church in the Americas, the still preserved San Francisco. The city was largely destroyed by a flood (1701). The Ocotlán sanctuary, one of Mexico's most famous shrines, is on Cerro de Ocotlán, a hill near by. Numerous ruins in vicinity.

Tlaxcalancingo, Mexico: see TLAZCALANCINGO.

Tlaxcalilla (tläskälē'yä), town (pop. 1,512), Hidalgo, central Mexico, 12 mi. E of San Juan del Río; grain, beans, fruit, maguey, livestock.

Tlaxco (tlä'skō). **1** Town (pop. 1,119), Puebla, central Mexico, 18 mi. N of Huauchinango; coffee, sugar cane, tobacco, fruit. **2** Officially Tlaxco de Morelos, city (pop. 3,504), Tlaxcala, central Mexico, on central plateau, 40 mi. N of Puebla; alt. 8,018 ft. Rail terminus; maguey-growing and -processing center.

Tlaxcoapan (tläskwä'pän), town (pop. 2,447), Hidalgo, central Mexico, on railroad and 32 mi. W of Pachuca; alt. 6,827 ft.; cereals, cotton, fruit, tobacco, stock; flour mills.

Tlaxiaca (tlähēä'kä), officially San Agustín Tlaxiaca, town (pop. 2,523), Hidalgo, central Mexico, on railroad and 10 mi. W of Pachuca; cereals, beans, maguey, stock.

Tlaxiaco (–kō), town (pop. 6,604), Oaxaca, S Mexico, in Sierra Madre del Sur, 65 mi. WNW of Oaxaca; alt. 6,758. Agr. center (cereals, sugar cane, fruit, livestock); antimony mining; coal and iron deposits.

Tlaxmalac (tläsmäläk'), town (pop. 1,533), Guerrero, SW Mexico, 8 mi. E of Iguala; cereals, sugar cane, fruit.

Tlayacapan (tlīäkä'pän), town (pop. 1,743), Morelos, central Mexico, 17 mi. ENE of Cuernavaca; sugar cane, fruit, vegetables, livestock.

Tlazala (tläsä'lä), officially Santiago Tlazala, town (pop. 2,115), Mexico state, central Mexico, 18 mi. NW of Mexico city; cereals, livestock.

Tlazazalca (tläsäsäl'kä), town (pop. 1,632), Michoacán, central Mexico, 15 mi. E of Zamora; cereals, fruit, stock.

Tlazcalancingo (tläskälänsēng'gō), town (pop. 1,929), Puebla, central Mexico, 5 mi. W of Puebla; cereals, fruit, livestock. Sometimes Tlaxcalancingo.

Tlell (tŭlĕl'), village, W B.C., on E Graham Isl., on Hecate Strait, at mouth of Tlell R., 30 mi. SSE of Massett; lumbering, stock raising.

Tlemcen (tlĕmsĕn'), city (pop. 50,272), Oran dept., NW Algeria, in the Tell, at N foot of Tlemcen Mts., 70 mi. SW of Oran, near Morocco border; 34°51'N 1°18'W. Old Arab city noted for its handicraft industries (especially oriental rugs, brassware) and for the architectural remains (mosques, minarets, walls) of its medieval splendor as ⊙ Arab sultanate. Situated in a well-watered high basin (2,500 ft.) receiving c.27 in. of annual rainfall, city is surrounded by orchards (hence old Roman name of *Pomaria*), vineyards, olive groves, and wheat fields. Linked by rail with Oujda (Fr. Morocco; W), Oran, and by a spur with Béni-Saf, its port on the Mediterranean. Trade in region's agr. produce, wool, sheep, and horses. Mfg. of flour products, hosiery, footwear, combs, furniture; olive-oil and palm-fiber processing, sugar refining. Despite Fr. occupation since 1842, Tlemcen has remained a native Moslem community (with important Jewish minority). Sometimes spelled Tlemsen.

Tlemcen Mountains, range of the Tell Atlas, in Oran dept., NW Algeria, extend c.50 mi. NE from Fr. Morocco border S of Tlemcen city. Rise to 6,047 ft. in the Djebel Tenouchfi (or Tnouchfi) at edge of the High Plateaus. Winegrowing on N slopes.

Tlilapan (tlēlä'pän), town (pop. 416), Veracruz, E Mexico, 6 mi. E of Orizaba; coffee, fruit.

Tlumach (tlōō'mŭch), Pol. *Tłumacz* (twōō'mäch), city (1931 pop. 6,836), central Stanislav oblast, Ukrainian SSR, on right tributary of the Dniester and 14 mi. ESE of Stanislav; rail spur terminus; flour milling, distilling. Has old palace. Passed from Poland to Austria (1772); reverted to Poland (1919); ceded to USSR in 1945.

Tluste, Ukrainian SSR: see TOLSTOYE.

Tlyanchi-Tamak (tlyŭnchē"-tŭmäk'), village (1939 pop. over 2,000), E Tatar Autonomous SSR, Russian SFSR, 27 mi. SW of Menzelinsk; grain, livestock.

Tlyarata (tlyŭrŭtä'), village (1948 pop. over 500), SW Dagestan Autonomous SSR, Russian SFSR, in the E Greater Caucasus, on the upper Avar Koisu and 35 mi. SW of Khunzakh; grain, sheep. Pop. largely Avar. Sometimes spelled Tlyarota.

Tmessa, Fezzan: see TIMESSA.

Tmolus, Mount, Turkey: see BOZ DAG.

Tnouchfi, Djebel, Algeria: see TLEMCEN MOUNTAINS.

To, China: see TO RIVER.

Toa, Cuchillas de (kōō'chē'yäs dā tō'ä), range, Oriente prov., E Cuba, 20 mi. W of Baracoa; extends 30 mi. NW from Toa R. to Sagua de Tánamo R.; rises to over 2,200 ft. Yields timber. Sometimes called Cuchillas de Toar.

Toa Alta (tō'ä äl'tä), town (pop. 1,397), N Puerto Rico, 10 mi. SW of San Juan, in agr. region (sugar cane, fruit). Heavily damaged by 1938 fire.

Toa Baja (tō'ä bä'hä), town (pop. 1,824), N Puerto Rico, on La Plata R., on railroad and 9 mi. W of San Juan, in agr. region (fruit, sugar cane, cattle). Founded 1511. Has one of oldest churches in Puerto Rico. A candied-fruit factory is near by.

Toabré (twäbrā'), village (pop. 443), Coclé prov., central Panama, 9 mi. NNE of Penonomé; rice, corn, beans, sugar cane, livestock.

Toango, Br. Cameroons: see TOUNGO.

Toano Mountains (tō'ünō) (6–9,000 ft.), NE Nev., in E Elko co., near Utah line; Western Pacific RR cuts the range at Silver Zone Pass (5,940 ft.), 75 mi. E of Elko. Sometimes spelled Toana.

Toar, Cuchillas de, Cuba: see TOA, CUCHILLAS DE.

Toa River (tō'ä), Oriente prov., E Cuba, rises at S foot of the Cuchillas de Toa, flows c.50 mi. E to coast 4 mi. NNW of Baracoa.

Toas Island (tō'äs), islet of Zulia state, NW Venezuela, in Tablazo Bay, bet. Gulf of Venezuela and L. Maracaibo. EL TORO is on it.

Toast, village (pop. 1,401), Surray co., NW N.C., just W of Mt. Airy.

Toay (tō-ī'), town (1947 pop. 3,020), ⊙ Toay dept. (pop. 6,540), E central La Pampa prov., Argentina, on railroad and 7 mi. SW of Santa Rosa; alfalfa, wheat, oats, corn, livestock; sawmills.

Toba (tō'bä), town (pop. 11,223), Mie prefecture, S Honshu, Japan, port on S shore of Ise Bay, 8 mi. E of Uji-yamada; fishing center. Pearl culture, with women divers working mainly off the shores of near-by Suga-jima.

Toba, Lake (tō'bä) (□ 488), N central Sumatra, Indonesia, 45 mi. S of Medan; alt. 2,985 ft.; 55 mi. long, 18 mi. wide. Drained by Asahan R. Central part of lake is nearly filled by large isl. of Samosir (□ 205; 27 mi. long, 12 mi. wide), linked with W shore of lake by narrow isthmus; stock raising, fishing. This region, peopled by the Batak or Battak, is a non-Moslem enclave in Sumatra; S of L. Toba the Batak are Protestants, N of it animists.

Tobacco River. 1 In E central Mich., rises near Farwell in Clare co., flows generally E c.40 mi., past Clare and Beaverton, to Tittabawassee R. in N Midland co. **2** In NW Mont., rises in Lincoln co., flows c.35 mi. NW, past Whitefish Range, to Kootenai R. near Eureka and British Columbia line.

Tobacco Root Mountains, range of Rocky Mts. in SW Mont., rise N of Virginia City; extend N to Jefferson R. Highest peaks: Ward Peak (10,267 ft.), Branham Peaks (10,420 ft.), Granite Peak (10,575 ft.). Silver, lead, and gold mines here.

Tobago (tŭbā'gō, tō–), island (□ 116.24; pop. 27,161), ward of Trinidad and Tobago crown colony, B.W.I., in the Atlantic, 22 mi. NNE of Galera Point (Trinidad); ⊙ Scarborough. Extends 26 mi. NW-SE bet. 11°20'N 60°32'W and 11°8'N 60°50'W; up to 7½ mi. wide. Pleasant tropical climate, with mean annual temp. 80°F., and dry season Dec.-June. Has several fine anchorages and is crossed by a low ridge rising to 1,890 ft. The fertile isl.'s main products are cacao, coconuts and copra, lime oil, sugar cane, rubber, vegetables, coconut fibers, tobacco, poultry and livestock, which are exported to Trinidad. Its extensive virgin forests abound in hardwood. The isl. is also a noted tourist resort linked by vessels with Port of Spain. Its airport Crown Point is near SW tip. Originally called Tapuago by native Indians, it was discovered in 1498 by Columbus on his 3d voyage. It was found to be uninhabited by 1596. Early settlers were Dutchmen from Zeeland (1632), though an unsuccessful attempt at colonization was made from Barbados (1618). Possession of the isl. shifted frequently bet. the colonial powers, but has remained British since 1814. It was amalgamated with Trinidad in 1888, forming the colony of Trinidad and Tobago, of which it was declared a ward (divided into 7 parishes) 10 years later.

Toba-Kakar Range (tō'bŭ-kä'kŭr), NE Baluchistan, W Pakistan; from Gumal R. extends c.250 mi. SW, parallel to Afghanistan border; c.20 mi. wide. Several peaks over 8,000 ft., including Kand (10,955 ft.) and Sakir (10,519 ft.) in center. Watered (center, SW) by the upper Pishin Lora and (center, NE) by tributaries of Zhob R. Limestone ridges, with deposits of chromite and asbestos (center). Khojak Pass (rail tunnel; alt. c.7,450 ft.) is in SW section, 9 mi. SE of Chaman.

Tobarra (tōvä'rä), town (pop. 7,615), Albacete prov., SE central Spain, in Murcia, agr. trade center 6 mi. N of Hellín; chemical mfg., flour- and sawmilling, vegetable canning, olive-oil processing. Ships hemp, wine, fruit. Iron mines near by.

Tobas, Argentina: see EL ZAPALLAR.

Tobata (tōbä'tä), city (1940 pop. 84,260; 1947 pop. 68,083), Fukuoka prefecture, N Kyushu, Japan, on Hibiki Sea, 33 mi. NE of Fukuoka, adjacent to Yawata (SW) and Kokura (SE). Coal-loading port; industrial center; govt.-owned steel mills, coke ovens; also mfg. of refined sugar, cotton thread, plate glass, alcohol. Heavily bombed (1945) in Second World War.

Toba Tek Singh (tō'bŭ tāk' sĭng), town (pop. 6,666), Lyallpur dist., E central Punjab, W Pakistan, 50 mi. SW of Lyallpur; local market (wheat, cotton, gram, ghee); cotton ginning, hand-loom weaving.

Tobatí (tōbätē'), town (dist. pop. 7,985), La Cordillera dept., S central Paraguay, 38 mi. E of Asunción; lumbering and agr. center (tobacco, fruit, cotton, livestock). Also a resort set in picturesque landscape. Known for its fine colonial church. Founded 1536. Kaolin deposits near by.

Töb Aymag, Mongolia: see CENTRAL AIMAK.

Tobe (tō'bā), town (pop. 6,467), Ehime prefecture, NW Shikoku, Japan, just S of Matsuyama; agr. center (rice, soybeans, oranges, pears); pottery making. Industrial school.

Tobercurry, Ireland: see TUBBERCURRY.

Tobermore (tŭ"bŭrmôr'), town (pop. 353), S Co. Londonderry, Northern Ireland, 12 mi. SE of Dungiven; agr. market (flax, oats, potatoes).

Tobermory (tōbŭrmô'rē), burgh (1931 pop. 722; 1951 census 692), on N coast of Mull isl., Argyll, Scotland, on the Sound of Mull, 27 mi. NW of Oban; fishing port and seaside resort; whisky distillery. Surroundings are noted for scenic beauty. Harbor is sheltered by small Calve Isl. (1 mi. long).

Tobetsu (tō'bātsōō), town (pop. 16,220), W Hokkaido, Japan, 10 mi. NE of Sapporo; oil-field center.

Tobi (tō'bē), coral island (pop. 141), Palau dist., westernmost of W Caroline Isls., W Pacific, 104 mi. SW of Merir; 3°1'N 131°11'E; c.1 mi. long, ½ mi. wide; coconut palms.

Tobias (tŭbī'ŭs), village (pop. 240), Saline co., SE Nebr., 20 mi. WSW of Wilber; livestock, grain, poultry produce.

Tobias Barreto (tōōbē'ŭs bŭrĕ'tōō), city (pop. 2,191), S Sergipe, NE Brazil, on Bahia border, 70 mi. WSW of Aracaju; livestock market; manioc, cereals. Until 1944, called Campos.

Tobin, Mount, Nev.: see SONOMA RANGE.

Tobique River (tōbēk'), NE N.B., rises at foot of Mt. Carleton, flows c.100 mi. SW to St. John R. at Andover.

Toblach, Italy: see DOBBIACO.

Tobol (tŭbôl'), town (1945 pop. over 500), NW Kustanai oblast, Kazakh SSR, on S.Siberian RR, on Tobol R. and 50 mi. SW of Kustanai.

Tobol River, in N Kazakh SSR and SW Siberian Russian SFSR, rises in N Mugodzhar Hills SW of Dzhetygara; flows 1,042 mi. NNE, past Kustanai, Kurgan, and Yalutorovsk, to Irtysh R. at Tobolsk. Receives Ui, Iset, Tura, and Tavda rivers (left). Navigable below mouth of Tura R.; at high water, to Uporovo, below Yalutorovsk.

Tobolsk or **Tobol'sk** (tŭbôlsk'), city (1939 pop 32,200), S Tyumen oblast, Russian SFSR, in W Siberia, on Irtysh R., at mouth of Tobol R., and 120 mi. NE of Tyumen; shipbuilding, sawmilling, fur- and fish-marketing. Bone-carving handicrafts. Site of a kremlin (library, govt. archives; now a mus.) and monument (1839) to Yermak, Rus. conqueror of Siberia. Has Siberian historical mus., theater (est. 1797). Founded 1587 near site of former Tatar capital, SIBIR; became first administrative and commercial center of W Siberia until transfer (1824) of govt. seat to Omsk; then became ⊙ Tobolsk govt. (see TYUMEN oblast); declined following construction of Trans-Siberian RR. Tsar Nicholas II and family exiled here (1917–18).

Tobón (tōbōn'), extinct volcano (5,905 ft.), El Progreso dept., E central Guatemala, 9 mi. SE of El Progreso.

Toboso (tōbō'sō), town (1939 pop. 6,396) in Escalante municipality, Negros Occidental prov., NE Negros isl., Philippines, on Tañon Strait, 28 mi. ENE of Bacolod; agr. center (rice, sugar cane).

Toboso, El (ĕl tōvō'sō), town (pop. 2,714), Toledo prov., central Spain, in New Castile, in upper La Mancha, 14 mi. NE of Alcázar de San Juan, 60 mi. ESE of Toledo, in agr. region (cereals, vegetables, anise, saffron, grapes, olives, garlic, almonds; wool, sheep). Alcohol and liquor distilling, cheese processing, earthen-jar mfg. Silicate gravel deposits. The town is famous as the supposed home of Dulcinea del Tobosa, heroine of Cervantes' *Don Quixote*.

Tobruk (tōbrŏŏk', tō'brŏŏk), Ital. *Tobruch*, town (pop. 4,130), E Cyrenaica, Libya, port on Mediterranean Sea, on coastal highway and 90 mi. SE of Derna; flour mill, liquor distillery, soap factory. Has airport at El Adem. Occupied by Italians in 1911. Strongly fortified and a major supply port, it was scene of fierce fighting in Second World War. Taken by Australians on Jan. 22, 1941. Later isolated and besieged by Rommel's forces for more than 8 months until relieved Dec. 10, 1941. With Rommel's 2d great offensive it fell (June 21, 1942) in a one-day assault with surrender of some 25,000 troops. Recaptured by British late in 1942 after the Alamein offensive.

Toby, Mount (10,537 ft.), SE B.C., in Selkirk Mts., 60 mi. NE of Nelson; 50°13'N 116°33'W.

Tocache Nuevo (tōkä'chä nwā'vō) or **Tocache,** town (pop. 348), San Martín dept., N central Peru, landing on Huallaga R., in E outliers of the Andes, and 120 mi. S of Tarapoto, 50 mi. NE of Huacrachuco. Sometimes Tocachi.

Tocaima (tōkī'mä), town (pop. 3,727), Cundinamarca dept., central Colombia, in W foothills of Cordillera Oriental, on Bogotá R., on railroad and 16 mi. NE of Girardot; health resort with noted thermal springs.

Tocantinópolis (tōōkäntēnō'pōōlēs), city (pop. 2,388), N Goiás, N central Brazil, on left bank of Tocantins R. (Maranhão border) and 70 mi. N of Carolina (Maranhão); corn, sugar, tobacco, coffee shipped on small river craft. Until 1944, called Boa Vista.

Tocantins River (tōōkätēns'), right tributary of the Amazon, in N central and N Brazil, rises in S central Goiás (N of Goiânia) in several headstreams (Almas, Uru, Maranhão), flows N bisecting Goiás state, past Pôrto Nacional and Pedro Afonso, forming Goiás-Maranhão border below Carolina, and, after receiving the Araguaia (its chief tributary) it traverses Pará state, entering Pará R. (S distributary of Amazon delta) 50 mi. SW of Belém (here river is 8 mi. wide). Total length, 1,640 mi. Interrupted by numerous rapids, its upper course is navigable for small craft above Carolina, and again bet. Imperatriz and São João do Araguaia. Regular navigation on lower course begins at Tucuruí, which is to be linked to São João do Araguaia by a railroad (under construction) circumventing rapids in that stretch. Diamond washings in Marabá and Carolina area. Babassu palms line upper course. The Tocantins receives the Araguaia (left), and Paraña, Somno, and Manuel Alves Grande rivers (right).

Toccoa (tŏ'kōŭ), city (pop. 6,781), ⊙ Stephens co., NE Ga., c.40 mi. N of Athens, near S.C. line. Industrial center; road-building and farm machinery, dyed yarns, clothing, sheeting, furniture, caskets, metal houses. Near by are Toccoa Falls (186 ft. high). Inc. 1875.

Toccoa, Lake, Ga.: see BLUE RIDGE DAM.

Toccoa River, Ga.: see OCOEE RIVER.

Tocco da Casauria (tôk'kô dä käzou'rēä), town (pop. 4,093), Pescara prov., Abruzzi e Molise, S central Italy, near Pescara R., 5 mi. NE of Popoli. Oil wells near by.

Toccopola (tŏ"kŭpō'lŭ), town (pop. 262), Pontotoc co., N Miss., 13 mi. W of Pontotoc, in agr., dairying, and timber area.

Toce River (tô'chĕ), in Piedmont, N Italy, rises in Lepontine Alps 24 mi. N of Domodossola, flows 45 mi. S to Lago Maggiore, 3 mi. NE of Gravellona Toce. Receives outlet stream of L. of Orta. Chief affluent, Anza R. Also spelled Tosa. Toce Falls (c.500 ft. high) are on upper reaches, at 46°24'N 8°25'E.

Tochapan (tōchä'pän), town (pop. 2,245), Puebla, central Mexico, 40 mi. SW of Puebla; cereals, maguey, livestock.

T'o Chiang, China: see TO RIVER.

Tochigi (tō'chĭgē), prefecture (□ 2,485; 1940 pop. 1,206,657; 1947 pop. 1,534,311), central Honshu, Japan; ⊙ UTSUNOMIYA. Mountainous W area is part of Nikko Natl. Park. Numerous small streams (tributaries of Tone R.) drain its many fertile plains producing rice, wheat, tobacco. Extensive production of silk cocoons and textiles; mining of coal, copper, gold, silver. Principal centers: Utsunomiya, Tochigi, ASHIKAGA, SANO, NIKKO, ASHIO.

Tochigi, city (1940 pop. 31,195; 1947 pop. 42,553), Tochigi prefecture, central Honshu, Japan, 15 mi. SW of Utsunomiya; mfg. (rope, soybean paste), woodworking. In 1884, ⊙ prefecture was shifted from Tochigi to Utsunomiya. Sometimes spelled Totigi.

Tochimilco (tōchēmēl'kō), town (pop. 2,192), Puebla, central Mexico, on railroad and 26 mi. WSW of Puebla; cereals, sugar cane, vegetables.

Tochio (tōchē'ō), town (pop. 10,695), Niigata prefecture, central Honshu, Japan, 8 mi. ENE of Nagaoka, in rice-growing area; silk and rayon textiles.

Tochtepec (tōchtāpĕk'), town (pop. 1,243), Puebla, central Mexico, 30 mi. SE of Puebla; cereals, vegetables.

Tocina (tō-thē'nä), town (pop. 4,067), Seville prov., SW Spain, near the Guadalquivir, on railroad and 20 mi. NE of Seville; cereals, olives, sugar beets, livestock. Near by is sugar mill (Los Rosales suburb).

Tocksfors (tŭks"fôrs', –fôsh'), Swedish *Töcksfors*, village (pop. 570), Varmland co., W Sweden, near Norwegian border, at N end of Fox L., 25 mi. WSW of Arvika; pulp and lumber mills.

Tocnik, castle, Czechoslovakia: see ZEBRAK.

Toco (tō'kō), town (pop. c.6,200), Cochabamba dept., central Bolivia, on S slopes of Cordillera de Cochabamba, on railroad and 2 mi. SSE of Cliza; corn, wheat, potatoes.

Toco or **El Toco** (ĕl), village (1930 pop. 338), Antofagasta prov., N Chile, on railroad, on Loa R. and 40 mi. E of Tocopilla; nitrate mining.

Toco (tō'kō), village, NE Trinidad, B.W.I., 2 mi. W of Galera Point, 40 mi. ENE of Port of Spain, in coconut-growing region. Fishing; fine beaches. Has emergency landing field. The community was studied by Melville J. Herskovits (*Trinidad Village*, 1947).

Tocoa (tōkō'ä), town (pop. 582), Colón dept., N Honduras, on Aguán R., on railroad and 18 mi. SSW of Trujillo; commercial center; rice, sugar cane, bananas.

Tocomechí (tōkōmächē'), village (pop. c.1,000), Santa Cruz dept., central Bolivia, 7 mi. NE of Warnes; sugar cane.

Toconao (tōkōnou'), village (1930 pop. 439), Antofagasta prov., N Chile, oasis on Andean plateau of the Atacama Desert, near E edge of the Salar de Atacama, 75 mi. SE of Calama; agr. center (alfalfa, corn, potatoes, wine) in picturesque setting of woods and cascades.

Toconey (tōkōnā'), village (1930 pop. 144), Maule prov., central Chile, on Maule R. and 25 mi. W of

Talca, in agr. area (wheat, potatoes, lentils, wine). Sometimes Toconei.

Tocópero (tōkō'pärō), town (pop. 577), Falcón state, NW Venezuela, in Caribbean lowlands, 29 mi. ENE of Coro; divi-divi. Petroleum deposits near by.

Tocopilla (tōkōpē'yä), town (pop. 15,516), ⊙ Tocopilla dept. (□ 6,141; pop. 33,124), Antofagasta prov., N Chile, port on the Pacific, 110 mi. N of Antofagasta; 22°5'S. Rail terminus, shipping and mining center. Exports nitrates, iodine and copper ores. Supplies electric power to inland mining camps, notably Chuquicamata. Has copper smelters. Airport. Port for deep-sea fishing.

Tocorpuri, Cerro de (sĕ'rō dā tōkōrpōō'rē), Andean peak (22,162 ft.) on Bolivia-Chile border; 22°26'S.

Tocos (tō'kōōsh), dam on upper Piraí R., SW Rio de Janeiro state, Brazil, near Itaverá. Its reservoir (alt. 1,470 ft.) is connected by tunnel with Ribeirão das Lajes reservoir (alt. 1,410 ft.).

Tocqueville (tôkvēl'), village (pop. 2,741), Constantine dept., NE Algeria, on N slope of Hodna Mts., 27 mi. SW of Sétif; rail-spur terminus; phosphate-mining center. Mine at Djebel M'Zaïta, just S.

Tocra (tō'krä), anc. *Teuchira* or *Tauchira*, and, later, *Arsinoë*, town (pop. 908), W Cyrenaica, Libya, near Mediterranean Sea, on coastal highway and 40 mi. NE of Benghazi; dates, figs, grapes. An important Greek and later Roman colony, it has ruins of anc. walls and bldgs. Scene of fighting (1941–42) bet. Axis and British in Second World War.

Tocumbo (tōkōōm'bō), town (pop. 1,589), Michoacán, central Mexico, on small lake, 25 mi. SW of Zamora; corn, sugar cane, fruit, livestock.

Tocumen (tōkōō'mĕn) or **Tocumén** (tōkōōmĕn'), village (pop. 41) and airport, central Panama, on Inter-American Highway and 12 mi. NE of Panama city. Developed in 1940s.

Tocumwal (tō'kŭmwôl), town (pop. 1,341), S New South Wales, on Murray R. and 140 mi. NNE of Melbourne, near Victoria border; sheep and agr. center.

Tocuyito (tōkōōyē'tō), town (pop. 1,455), Carabobo state, N Venezuela, 9 mi. SW of Valencia; coffee, corn, sugar cane, cacao.

Tocuyo or **El Tocuyo** (ĕl tōkōō'yō), town (pop. 5,417), Lara state, NW Venezuela, on upper Tocuyo R., on N slopes of Andean spur, on transandine highway and 38 mi. SW of Barquisimeto, agr. center (coffee, sugar cane, corn, wheat, cacao, tobacco, stock); henequen-bag factories. Old colonial town, founded 1545. Frequented by tourists.

Tocuyo de la Costa (dā lä kō'stä), town (pop. 2,243), Falcón state, NW Venezuela, on lower Tocuyo R. (2½ mi. from its mouth on the Caribbean) and 45 mi. NNW of Puerto Cabello, in fertile agr. region (sugar cane, cacao, corn, divi-divi).

Tocuyo River, in Lara and Falcón states, NW Venezuela, rises in Andean spur S of Humocaro Alto, flows N through Segovia Highlands, past Tocuyo, to Siquisique, then E, through coastal lowlands, to the Caribbean 3 mi. E of Tocuyo de la Costa; c.200 mi. long. Its upper valley is generally arid, but around Carora there are well-watered cattle plains. Lower course navigable for small craft.

Toda (tō'dä), town (pop. 12,026), Saitama prefecture, central Honshu, Japan, just W of Kawaguchi, in agr. area (rice, wheat); cotton textiles.

Toda Bhim (tō'dŭ bēm'), town (pop. 5,841), E Rajasthan, India, 60 mi. E of Jaipur; wheat, millet, barley.

Todalen, Norway: see Stangvik.

Toda Rai Singh (tō'dŭ rī' sĭng'), town (pop. 5,702), E central Rajasthan, India, 65 mi. SSW of Jaipur; local trade in millet, cotton, gram.

Todd. 1 County (□ 376; pop. 12,890), S Ky.; ⊙ Elkton. Bounded S by Tenn.; drained by Pond R., Elk and West forks of Red R. Rolling agr. area (dark tobacco, corn, wheat, hogs, cattle, fruit); timber, stone quarries. Some mfg. (especially wood products). Includes Blue and Gray State Park (near Elkton) and Jefferson State Monument at Fairview. Formed 1819. **2** County (□ 947; pop. 25,420), W central Minn.; ⊙ Long Prairie. Agr. area watered by Long Prairie R. L. Osakis is in SW. Dairy products, livestock, grain; deposits of marl and peat. Formed 1855. **3** County (□ 1,388; pop. 4,758), S S.Dak., on Nebr. line; unorganized and attached to Tripp co. for judicial purposes; includes all of closed area of Rosebud Indian Reservation; drained by South Fork White R. Formed 1909.

Todd, town (pop. 89), Ashe and Watauga counties, NW N.C., 8 mi. NNE of Boone.

Toddington, town and parish (pop. 2,500), S Bedford, England, 4 mi. N of Dunstable; agr. market. Has 14th–15th-cent. church.

Todd Island, islet, S Franklin Dist., Northwest Territories, in Simpson Strait, off Booth Point, S King William Isl.; 68°27'N 96°27'W. Graves and other relics of Franklin expedition (1847–48) were found here by Hall (1861–65).

Toddville, fishing village, Dorchester co., E Md., near Fishing Bay 19 mi. S of Cambridge; packs crabs, oysters.

Todgarh (tōd'gŭr), village, SW Ajmer state, India, 65 mi. SSW of Ajmer, in Aravalli Range; corn, wheat, barley, poppies.

Todi (tô'dē), anc. *Tuder*, town (pop. 3,820), Perugia prov., Umbria, central Italy, on hill near the Tiber, 23 mi. S of Perugia; machinery (agr., wine), wrought-iron articles, cutlery, furniture, soap. Bishopric. Has anc. walls and other Etruscan, Roman, and medieval remains, several 13th-cent. palaces, old cathedral, fine Renaissance church of the Consolation (begun 1508), and church of San Fortunato (13th–15th cent.) with tomb of Jacopone da Todi, who was b. here.

Tödi (tû'dē) or **Piz Rusein** (pēts' rōōzīn'), highest peak (11,886 ft.) of Glarus Alps, E central Switzerland, 8 mi. SSW of Linthal on the Glarus-Grisons line. Kleiner Tödi (9,829 ft.) is just W.

Todmorden (tŏd'mûrdŭn, tŏd'môr–), municipal borough (1931 pop. 22,222; 1951 census 19,072), West Riding, SW Yorkshire, England, on Calder R., on Rochdale Canal, 8 mi. SE of Burnley; cotton milling, mfg. of textile machinery, chemicals. In municipal borough are cotton-milling towns of Walsden (S) and Cornholme (NW).

Todor Ikonomov (tô'dôr ēkônô'môf), village (pop. 3,122), Kolarovgrad dist., NE Bulgaria, in SW Dobruja, 20 mi. N of Novi Pazar; rail terminus; sheep raising, lumbering.

Todos los Santos, Lake (tō'dōs lōs sän'tōs) (□ 50), Llanquihue prov., S central Chile, near Argentina line, in Chilean lake dist., separated from L. Llanquihue by Osorno Volcano, 35 mi. NE of Puerto Montt; 20 mi. long. Drains into Reloncaví Sound via Petrohué R. Famed for its beauty, it is bounded by wooded slopes and snow-covered volcanoes. It has many islets and branches. Popular tourist resort; lumbering, fishing.

Todos os Santos Bay (tō'dōōz ōōs sän'tōōs) [Port.,= All Saints Bay], sheltered inlet of the Atlantic, Bahia, E Brazil; 25 mi. long, 20 mi. wide; entrance (S) commanded by city of Salvador (E) and Itaparica Isl. (W). Receives Paraguaçu R. Fertile lowland surrounding it is called Recôncavo. Oil field recently developed along E shore (bet. Lobato and Candeias). Discovered 1501 by Amerigo Vespucci.

Todos Santos (tō'dōs sän'tōs), port, Cochabamba dept., central Bolivia, on Chaparé R. and 80 mi. ENE of Cochabamba, with which it is connected by road; river-navigation center in tropical lowlands; agr. (sugar cane, rice, bananas). Sometimes called Puerto Todos Santos.

Todos Santos or **Todos Santos Cuchumatán** (kōōchōōmätän'), town (1950 pop. 1,533), Huehuetenango dept., W Guatemala, on W slopes of Cuchumatanes Mts., 17 mi. NNW of Huehuetenango; alt. 8,041 ft.; pottery, woolen and cotton textiles.

Todos Santos, town (pop. 1,831), Southern Territory, Lower California, NW Mexico, on Pacific coast, 50 mi. S of La Paz; sugar cane, fruit.

Todos Santos Islands, 2 barren rocks (□ ½) on Pacific coast of NW Lower California, Mexico, at entrance to Todos Santos Bay, 10 mi. SW of Ensenada; 31°48'N 116°48'W. Guano deposits.

Todtnau (tōt'nou), village (pop. 2,220), S Baden, Germany, in Black Forest, at SW foot of the Feldberg, 12 mi. SSE of Freiburg; rail terminus; brush and textile mfg., metal- and woodworking, paper milling. Climatic health resort and winter-sports center (alt. 2,162 ft.). First mentioned in 12th cent. Was silver-mining center in 14th cent.

Toeangkoe, Indonesia: see Banyak Islands.

Toeban, Indonesia: see Tuban.

Toei, Korea: see Tongyong.

Toekangbesi Islands, Indonesia: see Tukangbesi Islands.

Toeloengagoeng, Indonesia: see Tulungagung.

Toen, Formosa: see Taoyüan.

Toetoes Bay (toi'toiz), inlet of Foveaux Strait, S S.Isl., New Zealand, E of Bluff; 16 mi. E-W, 5 mi. N-S. Receives Mataura R.

Tofane, Le (lĕ tôfä'nĕ), group of 3 adjacent peaks in the Dolomites, Belluno prov., N Italy, 4 mi. W of Cortina d'Ampezzo. Chief summit is 10,640 ft. high; has small glaciers. Scene of fighting in First World War bet. Austrians and Italians.

Tofield (tō'fēld), town (pop. 608), central Alta., near Beaverhill L., 25 mi. NNE of Camrose; rail junction; coal mining, mixed farming.

Tofino (tŭfē'nō), village (pop. 246), SW B.C., on W central Vancouver Isl., on Clayoquot Sound, 50 mi. W of Port Alberni; 49°8'N 125°55'W; sawmilling, gold mining. Opposite are Vargas and Meares isls.

Tofo, El, Chile: see El Tofo.

Toftevag, Norway: see Halsnoy.

Toftlund (tôft'lōōn), town (pop. 1,585), Haderslev amt, S Jutland, Denmark, 17 mi. WSW of Haderslev; margarine, flour.

Tofua (tōfōō'ä), uninhabited island (□ 21), largest of Haabai group, central Tonga, S Pacific; rises to 1,700 ft. Crater lake in active volcano.

Toga, New Hebrides: see Torres Islands.

Togane (tō'gänā), town (pop. 13,348), Chiba prefecture, central Honshu, Japan, on N central Chiba Peninsula, 14 mi. ESE of Chiba; collection center for rice, raw silk.

Togchhen, Tibet: see Tokchen.

Toggenburg (tô'gŭnbōōrk), valley extending generally along upper Thur R., NE Switzerland; consists of dists. of Alt-Toggenburg (pop. 12,596), Neu-Toggenburg (pop. 11,634), Ober-Toggenburg (pop. 11,025), and Unter-Toggenburg (pop. 23,088), all in St. Gall canton. Territory was governed by counts of Toggenburg until 15th cent., when it passed to St. Gall. Quarrels bet. Protestants of Toggenburg and abbot of St. Gall served as pretext for War of the Toggenburg (18th cent.). Textile production, dairy farming, and livestock breeding (Upper Toggenburg); summer resorts, skiing centers.

Togi (tō'gē), town (pop. 2,957), Ishikawa prefecture, central Honshu, Japan, on W Noto Peninsula, on Sea of Japan, 15 mi. NW of Nanao; rice, raw silk.

Togiak (tō'gēăk), Eskimo village (pop. 101), SW Alaska, at head of Togiak Bay inlet (12 mi. long, 18 mi. wide at mouth) of Bristol Bay, 70 mi. W of Dillingham; fishing.

Togian Islands (tōgyän'), small group (pop. 10,827), Indonesia, in Gulf of Tomini indenting N Celebes; 0°20'S 122°E; comprise Batudaka or Batoedaka (both: bätōōdä'kŭ; pop. 1,086; 18 mi. long, 8 mi. wide), Togian (pop. 4,362; 13 mi. long, 7 mi. wide), Talata Ko (tŭlä'tŭkō'; 10 mi. long, 5 mi. wide), and Una Una or Oenaoena (both: ōō"nä ōō'nä; pop. 3,523; 6 mi. in diameter, with active volcano, c.1,500 ft. high). Chief product is copra. Sometimes called Schildpad Isls.

Töging (tû'gĭng), village (pop. 6,576), Upper Bavaria, Germany, on the Inn and 3 mi. E of Mühldorf; hydroelectric-power station; aluminum plant; printing.

Togo: see Togoland.

Togo (tō'gō), village (pop. 263), SE Sask., on Man. border, 40 mi. ENE of Yorkton; mixed farming.

Togo (tō'gō'), town (pop. 4,903), Fukuoka prefecture, N Kyushu, Japan, 16 mi. NNE of Fukuoka; rice, wheat, barley.

Togo, Lake (tō'gō), coastal lagoon (c.7 mi. long, 3 mi. wide), S Fr. Togoland, just NW of Anécho; communicates with mouth of Mono R. Receives small Haho and Sio rivers.

Togochi (tōgō'chē), town (pop. 6,634), Hiroshima prefecture, SW Honshu, Japan, 18 mi. NW of Hiroshima; rice-growing, stock-raising center.

Togoland (tō'gōlănd") or **Togo** (tō'gō), former German protectorate (□ c.35,000), W Africa, on Gulf of Guinea (bet. 1°14'E and 1°45'E), bounded by Gold Coast (W) and Dahomey of Fr. West Africa (E). Ger. influence in area was formally recognized, 1885–86, by British and French, and N frontiers were fixed 1897–99. Occupied (1914) by British and French during First World War and divided provisionally into Br. (W) and Fr. (E) spheres. In 1922 the 2 parts of Togoland were placed by the League of Nations under Br. and Fr. mandates. In 1946 Togoland was placed by the U.N. under Br. and Fr. trusteeship. **British Togoland** (□ 13,040; 1948 pop. 378,666), in the W and inland, has been administered (since 1923) as part of the Gold Coast. Ho dist., the S section of Br. Togoland, is administered as part of Gold Coast colony, while the N section, which includes entire Krachi dist. (⊙ Kete-Krachi) and parts of other dists., is administered by the Northern Territories. Br. Togoland, a long narrow strip bet. 6°20'N and 11°N and without a coast line, is bounded W by Daka and Volta rivers and drained by Oti R. It includes rain forest (S) and open savanna (N). Main forest products are cacao (centers at Kpandu, Hohoe, Wora Wora), coffee, palm oil and kernels, hardwood, rubber. N section produces shea nuts and raises cattle. Fishing in Volta R. Main food crops are rice, millet, beans, yams, cassava, corn. Local handicraft industries include weaving of cotton (grown in S section), mfg. of bricks, tiles, baskets, mats, pottery. Pop. is largely Ewe (S) and Dagomba (N). Main centers (linked by N-S road) are Ho and Kpandu (S), Kete-Krachi and Yendi (N). **French Togoland** (□ c.21,500; 1947 pop. estimate c.944,500), along the coast and on E, is a narrow strip of land bet. 6°N and 11°N stretching 35 mi. along the Slave Coast and 330 mi. N into interior; ⊙ Lomé. Borders N on Upper Volta, E on Dahomey. The littoral, covered by rain forest, is fringed by coastal lagoons, among them L. Togo. There are no good harbors. The central section is traversed NNE-SSW by hilly Togo Mts. (rise to c.3,500 ft.), outliers of the Atakora Mts. of Dahomey. Its N lowland is in the savanna zone of the Sudan. Mono R. crosses entire territory N-S. The Oti R. forms part of NW boundary with Br. Togoland. Climate is equatorial-humid, with 2 alternating dry and wet seasons. Lower Togoland, the most important part, yields forest products (hardwood, palms, gum) and principal export crops, such as cacao, palm kernels, palm oil, cotton, copra, kapok. The interior uplands grow coffee and cacao; peanuts and livestock in N. Subsistence crops include corn, rice, manioc, tubers, beans. Industries are negligible apart from some cotton ginning and kapok processing, vegetable-oil extracting, and native handicrafts (leather, metal-work, plaited goods, textiles). Chromium, gold, and lead deposits have been reported. Leading port and commercial center is Lomé, from which railroads lead to interior (Blitta, Palimé) and along coast to

Anécho, the 2d port (roadstead). Other centers are Klouto, Atakpamé, and Sokodé. Racially the densely populated Negro region offers a diverse picture, with Hamitic strains prominent in N, Ewe and Mina tribes in S.

Toguchin (tŭgōōchĕn'), city (1945 pop. 14,200), E Novosibirsk oblast, Russian SFSR, on Inya R., on branch of Trans-Siberian RR and 60 mi. E of Novosibirsk, in agr. area; hemp- and flax-milling center. Coal mining. Industrialized after c.1935.

Togul (tŭgōōl'), village (1926 pop. 3,428), NE Altai Territory, Russian SFSR, near Chumysh R., 90 mi. E of Barnaul, in agr. area.

Togur (tŭgōōr'), town (1939 pop. over 500), central Tomsk oblast, Russian SFSR, 5 mi. NW of Kolpashevo; sawmilling.

Togura, Japan: see TOKURA.

Togus, Maine: see CHELSEA.

Togus Pond, Kennebec co., S Maine, lake (1.5 mi. long) just E of Augusta; source of small **Togus River**, which flows 7 mi. SW to the Kennebec.

Togwotee Pass, Wyo.: see WIND RIVER RANGE.

Tohak Lake (50 mi. long, 3–12 mi. wide), central Keewatin Dist., Northwest Territories, N of Baker L.; 65°13'N 96°15'W. Drains SE into Chesterfield Inlet.

Tohakum Peak, Nev.: see LAKE RANGE.

Tohana (tōhä'nŭ), town (pop. 8,950), Hissar dist., S Punjab, India, 39 mi. NNE of Hissar; local market for millet, gram, cotton.

Tohen (tōhĕn'), village (pop. 400), in the Mijirtein, N Ital. Somaliland, port on Indian Ocean, near Cape Guardafui, 40 mi. ESE of Alula; fishing; mother of pearl, tunny; date growing.

Tohma River (tōmä'), central Turkey, rises 35 mi. S of Sivas, flows 122 mi. E, past Gurun and Darende, to the Euphrates 13 mi. NNE of Malatya.

Tohoku, Japan: see HONSHU.

Tohopekaliga Lake (tŭhō"pŭkŭlī'gŭ), Osceola co., central Fla., 18 mi. S of Orlando; c.11 mi. long, 2–5 mi. wide. Kissimmee city is at N end. Lake is joined by Kissimmee R. (rising here) to Hatchineha L. (S); and connected by canal with East Tohopekaliga L. (c.5 mi. in diameter), just NE.

Toi, Formosa: see TOWWEI.

Toi (tō'ē) or **Doi** (dō'ē), town (pop. 7,594), Shizuoka prefecture, central Honshu, Japan, on W Izu Peninsula, on Suruga Bay, 23 mi. ESE of Shizuoka; mining (gold, silver), lumbering, fishing. Hot springs.

Toi, Cape, Jap. *Toi-misaki*, in Miyazaki prefecture, SE Kyushu, Japan; E point of Ariake Bay; 31°22'N 131°21'E.

Toide (tōē'dä), town (pop. 5,833), Toyama prefecture, central Honshu, Japan, 5 mi. SSW of Takaoka, in rice-growing area; textiles, patent medicines.

Toijala (toi'yälä), town (pop. 5,604), Häme co., SW Finland, in lake region, 20 mi. S of Tampere; rail junction; glassworks.

Toishan (toi'sän'), Mandarin *T'ai-shan* (tī'shän'), town (pop. 6,864), ⊙ Toishan co. (pop. 748,513), S Kwangtung prov., China, 65 mi. SW of Canton; rail junction. Tungsten and bismuth mining near by. Its declining agr. has caused much emigration. Until 1914 called Sunning.

Toi-Tyube or **Toy-Tyube** (toi-työōbyĕ'), village (1926 pop. 2,453), N Tashkent oblast, Uzbek SSR, 15 mi. S of Tashkent; cotton; dairying, vegetable processing.

Toiyabe Range (toiyä'bē), central Nev., in Nye and Lander cos., extends N-S along E bank of Reese R., through part of Toiyabe Natl. Forest. Mt. Callahan (10,203 ft.) is in N, Arc Dome (11,775 ft.) in S. Austin is mining and ranching center in W foothills.

Tojo (tō'-jō'), town (pop. 7,515), Hiroshima prefecture, SW Honshu, Japan, 29 mi. NNW of Fukuyama; commercial center for agr., dairying area; sake, soy sauce, charcoal.

Tojosen-ko, Korea: see TONGSONGCHON RIVER.

Tok (tôk), highest mountain (2,827 ft.) of the Brdy, S Bohemia, Czechoslovakia, WNW of Pribram.

Toka (tō'kä), town (pop. 13,575), Niigata prefecture, central Honshu, Japan, 20 mi. SE of Kashiwazaki; silk textiles, charcoal; livestock.

Tokachi-dake (tōkä'chē-dä"kä), volcanic peak (6,814 ft.), central Hokkaido, Japan, 30 mi. SE of Asahigawa. Long thought to be extinct, it erupted in 1926.

Tokachi River, Jap. *Tokachi-gawa*, S central Hokkaido, Japan, rises in mts. 35 mi. SE of Asahigawa, flows S, ESE, past Memuro, Obihiro, and Ikeda, and SSE to the Pacific at Otsu; 122 mi. long. Swamps and peat bogs along lower course. Sometimes spelled Tokati.

Tokai (tōkī'), village (pop. 1,047), N Kedah, Malaya, on railroad and 6 mi. SSE of Alor Star; rice.

Tokaichi (tōkī'chē), town (pop. 11,532), Hiroshima prefecture, SW Honshu, Japan, 37 mi. NE of Hiroshima; commercial center for livestock and agr. area (rice, wheat); raw silk.

Tokaj or **Tokay** (both: tōkā', tō'kā, Hung. tô'koi), town (pop. 5,903), Zemplen co., NE Hungary, at E foot of Mt. Tokaj and at junction of Bodrog and Tisza rivers, 19 mi. NW of Nyiregyhaza. Home of well-known Tokay wine, from grapes grown on slopes of the HEGYALJA. Mfg. (chemicals, matches, cognac); lumber mills.

Tokaj, Mount, NE Hungary, peak (1,692 ft.) of Tokaj-Eperjes Mts.; wine center of Tokaj at E foot.

Tokaj-Eperjes Mountains (–ĕ'pĕryĕsh"), volcanic outlier of the Carpathians, in E Slovakia and NE Hungary, extending 60 mi. N-S bet. Hernad and Bodrog rivers. Consists of Slovak section (N), known as Presov (prĕ'shôf) Mts., rising to 3,583 ft. 11 mi. ESE of Presov (Hung. *Eperjes*), and a lower Hung. section known as Tokaj Mts., on whose E slope lies the Hegyalja winegrowing dist.

To-kan, pass, Bhutan: see DONGA LA.

Tokar (tō'kär), town, Kassala prov., NE Anglo-Egyptian Sudan, near Red Sea, 40 mi. SSE of Port Sudan, in area irrigated by Barka R.; major cotton center; millet, corn, fruits; livestock. Its port is Trinkitat (linked by rail). Road leads SE to Karora on Eritrea border. Two battles took place here (1884) during Mahdi wars.

Tokara-gunto (tōkä'rägōōn'tō), volcanic island group (1950 pop. 2,938) of Amami-gunto, Ryukyu Islands, bet. E.China Sea (W) and Philippine Sea (E), 80 mi. S of Kyushu; comprises 8 isls. and scattered islets. Largest isls. are Nakano-shima (6 mi. long; pop. 1,039) and Suwanose-shima (5 mi. long, 3.5 mi. wide); surrounded by coral reefs. Both have active volcanoes. Fishing. Formerly sometimes called Shichi-to; also called Jitsu-to or Jitto.

Tokarevka (tŭkä'ryĭfkŭ). **1** Town (1939 pop. over 500), NE Karaganda oblast, Kazakh SSR, on Nura R., near railroad (Nurinskaya station), and 17 mi. N of Karaganda; cattle. **2** Village (1926 pop. 1,472), SW Tambov oblast, Russian SFSR, 50 mi. SSW of Tambov; flour-milling center; metalworks.

Tokashiki-shima (tōkä'shĭkē-shĭmä), volcanic island (□ 10; 1950 pop. 1,194) of Kerama-retto, Okinawa Isls., in Ryukyu Islands, in East China Sea, 15 mi. W of Okinawa; 6 mi. long, 2 mi. wide. Mountainous, forested. Sweet potatoes, sugar cane.

Tokat (tôkät'), prov. (□ 4,322; 1950 pop. 387,456), N central Turkey; ⊙ Tokat. Bordered N by Canik Mts.; drained by Yesil Irmak and Kizil Irmak. Antimony, marble, lignite mines. Tobacco, sugar beets, opium, legumes, dye plants, grain.

Tokat, town (1950 pop. 21,700), ⊙ Tokat prov., N central Turkey, on the Yesil Irmak, 45 mi. NNW of Sivas; copper refinery, handling copper from the Maden mines; mfg. of leather goods, tiles; antimony, lignite, marble near by. Wheat, vetch, dye plants, tobacco, opium.

Tokati River, Japan: see TOKACHI RIVER.

Tokatsu, Japan: see MASUDA, Shimane prefecture.

Tokay, Hungary: see TOKAJ.

Tokchen (tōk'chĕn) or **Togchhen** (tōg'chĕn), Chinese *T'o-k'o-ch'eng* (tô'kŭ'chŭng'), town, SW Tibet, near Manasarowar L., on main Leh-Lhasa trade route and 105 mi. SE of Gartok; alt. 15,700 ft.

Tokchon (tŭk'chŭn'), Jap. *Tokusen*, township (1944 pop. 15,711), S.Pyongan prov., N Korea, on Taedong R. and 60 mi. NNE of Pyongyang; stock raising, lumbering.

Tok Cut-off (tōk), highway in E Alaska, extends 136 mi. SW from Alaska Highway at Tok Junction, 11 mi. ESE of Tanacross, to Richardson Highway just N of Gulkana; provides short-cut to Valdez, connects with Glenn Highway (to Anchorage) S of Gulkana. Serves Slana, Chistochina, Gakona.

Toke (tō'kā), town (pop. 6,531), Chiba prefecture, central Honshu, Japan, on N central Chiba Peninsula, 10 mi. SE of Chiba; rice, raw silk, poultry.

Tokelau (tōkĕlä'ōō), coral island group (□ c.6; pop. 1,388), S Pacific, c.300 mi. N of Western Samoa; 9°S 172°W. Composed of 3 atolls, ATAFU, NUKUNONO, FAKAOFO. Discovered 1765 by British, placed 1926 under administration of Western Samoa (Apia is Tokelau port of entry) as part of N.Z. mandate. Natives of Polynesian stock. Chief export, copra. Also called Union Isls.

Toke River (tō'kŭ). **1** In Telemark co., S Norway, issues from small lake NW of Kragero, flows 10 mi. SE to the Skagerrak at Kragero; several falls furnish power for lumber mills and hydroelectric plants. **2** In Telemark co., S Norway, flows from Totak lake 20 mi. S to Bandak lake; 292-ft. falls.

Tőketerebes, Czechoslovakia: see TREBISOV.

Tokewanna Peak, Utah: see UINTA MOUNTAINS.

Toki (tō'kē), town (pop. 6,378), Gifu prefecture, central Honshu, Japan, 6 mi. E of Tajimi, in agr. area (rice, wheat); pottery, raw silk.

To Kiang, China: see TO RIVER.

Tokio, Japan: see TOKYO.

Tokitsu (tōkē'tsōō), town (pop. 7,999), Gifu prefecture, central Honshu, Japan, 4 mi. ENE of Tajimi; pottery making; agr. (rice, wheat).

Tokiwa (tōkē'wä), town (pop. 6,248), Fukushima prefecture, N central Honshu, Japan, 15 mi. ENE of Koriyama; tobacco, rice, silk cocoons.

Tok Junction (tōk), village (pop. 131), SE Alaska, at junction of Alaska Highway and Tok Cut-off to Richardson Highway, 11 mi. ESE of Tanacross; trapping; supply point.

Tokko (tŭkô'), village, S Yakut Autonomous SSR, Russian SFSR, on Tokko R. (right affluent of the Chara) and 110 mi. SSW of Olekminsk; 59°9'N 119°39'E; lumbering, trapping.

Toklat (tō'klăt), village (1939 pop. 16), central Alaska, on Kantishna R. and 40 mi. W of Nenana; trapping; supply point for prospectors in Kantishna dist.

Tokmak, Turkey: see ESME.

Tokmak (tŭkmäk'), city (1939 pop. 19,431), N Frunze oblast, Kirghiz SSR, in Chu valley, on railroad and 35 mi. E of Frunze, in agr. area (sugar beets, fruit); auto repair shops; metalworking, wool washing, tanning, processing of fiber plants. Sugar refinery at adjoining Oktyabrski.

Toko, Formosa: see TUNGKANG.

T'o-k'o-ch'eng, Tibet: see TOKCHEN.

Tokod (tô'kôd), town (pop. 6,379), Komarom-Esztergom co., N Hungary, 7 mi. SW of Esztergom; glass mfg. Lignite mines near by.

Tököl (tû'kûl), town (pop. 6,722), Pest-Pilis-Solt-Kiskun co., N central Hungary, on Csepel Isl. in the Danube and 14 mi. SSW of Budapest; wheat, corn, cattle, poultry.

Tokoname (tōkō'nämā), town (pop. 13,696), Aichi prefecture, central Honshu, Japan, on W Chita Peninsula, port on Ise Bay, 5 mi. W of Handa; ceramic center.

Tokorozawa (tōkō'-rō'zäwä), town (pop. 40,616), Saitama prefecture, central Honshu, Japan, 8 mi. NW of Musashino; agr. center (rice, wheat, sweet potatoes); cotton textiles.

Tokosun, China: see TOKSUN.

Tokotan (tŭkŭtän'), chief village on Urup Isl., S Kuriles, Russian SFSR, on W (Sea of Okhotsk) coast; 45°52'N 149°48'E; fox farm; fisheries.

Tokoto or **T'o-k'o-t'o** (tô'kŭ'tô'), town (pop. 10,911), ⊙ Tokoto co. (pop. 86,833), SE central Suiyuan prov., China, 45 mi. SW of Kweisui, near Yellow R., on E edge of irrigation dist.; millet, wheat, rice, licorice, cattle. Its port Hokow (just S) is downstream head of navigation on Yellow R.

Tok River (tôk), Chkalov oblast, Russian SFSR, rises 13 mi. W of Bulanovo, flows 130 mi. W, past Grachevka, to Samara R. just E of Buzuluk.

Toksun or **Toqsun** (tōksün'), Chinese *Tokosun* or *T'o-k'o-hsün* (both: tŭ'kŭshün'), town, ⊙ Toksun co. (pop. 25,634), E central Sinkiang prov., China, at W edge of Turfan depression, 85 mi. SE of Urumchi; road junction for highways N and S of the Tien Shan; cotton textiles; sericulture; grain, fruit, vegetables, saltworks and coal mines near by.

Toktogul, Kirghiz SSR: see MUZTOR.

Tokuno-shima (tōkōō'nō-shĭmä), island (□ 98; 1950 pop. 53,333) of isl. group Amami-gunto, in Ryukyu Islands, bet. East China Sea (W) and Philippine Sea (E), 25 mi. SW of Amami-O-shima; 16 mi. long, 8 mi. wide; hilly; fertile (sugar cane, sweet potatoes, raw silk). Chief town, Kametsu (SE).

Tokura (tōkōō'rä) or **Togura** (–gōō'rä), town (pop. 4,949), Nagano prefecture, central Honshu, Japan, 8 mi. NW of Ueda; rice, wheat, raw silk. Hot springs.

Tokusen, Korea: see TOKCHON.

Tokushima (tōkōō'shĭmä), prefecture [Jap. *ken*] (□ 1,600; 1940 pop. 718,717; 1947 pop. 854,811), E Shikoku, Japan; ⊙ Tokushima. Bounded NE by Harima Sea (E section of Inland Sea), E by Kii Channel, SE by Philippine Sea. Includes offshore isls. of OGE-SHIMA and SHIMADA-SHIMA. Mountainous; rises to 6,414 ft. at Mt. Tsurugi, 2d highest peak of Shikoku. Extensive forested and agr. area, drained by Yoshino R. Widespread cultivation of tobacco, fruit (oranges, pears), rice, wheat, soybeans. Livestock raising in interior. Principal products: raw silk, cotton textiles, woodwork, charcoal, dolls, camellia oil, fans. Many of coastal towns are fishing ports; others are saltmaking centers. Tokushima is chief mfg. center.

Tokushima, city (1940 pop. 119,581; 1947 pop. 103,320), ⊙ Tokushima prefecture, E Shikoku, Japan, on Kii Channel, near mouth of Yoshino R., 70 mi. SW of Osaka; 34°4'N 134°33'E. Transportation and mfg. center; cotton textiles, woodworking, machinery, sake, *tabi*. The port of Tokushima includes wharves (for small ships only) at the city itself and at the more important outer port at KOMATSUJIMA. Site of feudal castle. Puppet shows are given here annually. Includes (since 1937) former towns of Kamona and Kamo. Bombed (1945) in Second World War.

Tokuyama (tōkōō'yämŭ), city (1940 pop. 38,419; 1947 pop. 79,001), Yamaguchi prefecture, SW Honshu, Japan, port on inlet of Suo Sea, 20 mi. ESE of Yamaguchi; commercial center for large agr. area (rice, wheat, tobacco); stockyards. Produces coal briquettes, bottles, yarn, soy sauce. Exports grain, livestock. Since early 1940s, includes former towns of Tonda, Kushigahama, and Fukugawa.

Tokyo (tō'kyō), city (□ 221; 1940 pop. 6,778,804; 1947 pop. 4,177,548; 1950 pop. 6,275,190), ⊙ Japan, in central Honshu, on Kwanto plain, on NW shore of Tokyo Bay and on small Sumida R., 250 mi. ENE of Osaka; 35°41'N 139°45'E. One of the 5 largest cities of the world. Financial, industrial, and cultural center; focal point of large urban belt including Kawasaki and Yokohama. Originally, because of its shallow harbor, Tokyo used Yokohama as its outport, but improvements made possible the use of Tokyo harbor by large ships. In 1941 the ports of Tokyo and Yokohama were combined under the name Keihin, with Tokyo handling domestic trade primarily. City is divided into 23 wards [Jap. *ku*]; until 1947 there were 35 wards. Administrative and residential areas are W, factory dists. generally E of Sumida R. Just E of Imperial Palace and Diet bldgs. are financial and business dists. with Marunouchi and Ginza as principal streets. Has shipyards, automobile plants, engineering works, chemical plants, and textile mills. Principal academic institutions are Tokyo Univ. (founded 1869; for a time it was called Tokyo Imperial Univ.), Waseda Univ. (1882), Rikkyo or St. Paul's Univ. (1883), Inst. of Chemical and Physical Research (1917), Tokyo Women's Medical Col. (1900), and Keio-Gijuku Univ. (1867). Yasukuni-jinja is Shinto shrine dedicated to war dead; has mausoleums of Tokugawa shoguns. Tokyo founded in 12th cent. as small village called Yedo (also spelled Yeddo and Edo). Its rise dates from 1603, when it became hq. of Ieyasu, founder of Tokugawa shogunate. With restoration of imperial power in 1868, it became imperial ⊙, succeeding Kyoto, and was renamed Tokyo [Jap., =eastern capital], in contradistinction to Saikyo [Jap., =western capital] which was alternate name for Kyoto. Earthquake of 1923 destroyed nearly half of city. In Second World War, Tokyo was 1st bombed in April, 1942, by bombers led by Gen. James Doolittle. Greater Tokyo (□828; 1940 pop. 7,354,971; 1947 pop. 5,000,777) includes city of Tokyo, surrounding communities, and isl. group Izu-shichito S of Sagami Sea. Sometimes spelled Tokio.

Tokyo Bay, Jap. *Tokyo-wan* and *Tokyo-kaiwan*, inlet of Philippine Sea, central Honshu, Japan, bet. Miura and Chiba peninsulas; connected with Sagami Sea (SW) by Uraga Strait; 30 mi. long, 20 mi. wide. On its W shore are Tokyo and Yokohama. Formerly called Yedo Bay.

Tol, Caroline Isls.: see TRUK.

Tola, river, Mongolia: see TOLA RIVER.

Tola (tō'lä), town (1950 pop. 653), Rivas dept., SW Nicaragua, 7 mi. W of Rivas; grain.

Tolaga Bay (tōlä'gŭ), township (pop. 354), ⊙ Uawa co. (□ 256; pop. 1,503), E N.Isl., New Zealand, 25 mi. NNE of Gisborne, on W shore of Tolaga bay (1.5 mi. wide); sheep, corn.

Tolamba, W Pakistan: see TALAMBA.

Tolar (tō'lür), town (pop. 338), Hood co., N central Texas, c.40 mi. SW of Fort Worth, in agr. area; ships petrified wood.

Tola River or **Tuula River** (both: tō'lä, tōō'lä), N Mongolian People's Republic, rises on S slopes of Kentei Mts. 70 mi. NE of Ulan Bator, flows 437 mi. SW, past Ulan Bator, and NW, to Orkhon R. 120 mi. NW of Ulan Bator. Freezes Nov.-April.

Tolba River (tŭlbä'), S Yakut Autonomous SSR, Russian SFSR, rises on W Aldan Plateau, flows c.200 mi. N and NE to Lena R. 100 mi. E of Olekminsk. Oil deposits in lower course.

Tolbazy (tŭlbä'zē), village (1948 pop. over 2,000), central Bashkir Autonomous SSR, Russian SFSR, 30 mi. N of Sterlitamak; wheat, oats, livestock.

Tolbukhin (tôlbōō'khĭn), city (pop. 31,049), Stalin dist., NE Bulgaria, in S Dobruja, 26 mi. N of Stalin (Varna); agr. and commercial center; food processing (flour, oilseeds, meat), cotton and woolen milling, metal industries. Customs rail station. Metal-shaping school. Under Turkish rule (until 1878) called Haji-Oglu-Bazarjik, later, in Bulgaria, Bazarjik (Bazardzhik). In Rumania (1913–40), it was, as Bazargic, ⊙ Caliacra dept.(□ 1,737; 1930 pop. 166,911). The modern Bulg. name was Dobrich until city was renamed (1949) for Soviet general who took it (1944) during Second World War.

Tolbukhino (tŭlbōō'khēnŭ), village (1926 pop. 805), E Yaroslavl oblast, Russian SFSR, 18 mi. NNE of Yaroslavl; flax, wheat. Until 1950, Davydkovo.

Tolcayuca (tōlkīōō'kä), town (pop. 1,952), Hidalgo, central Mexico, 19 mi. SW of Pachuca; grain, beans, maguey, stock.

Tolchester Beach (tŏl'chĕ"stŭr), summer-resort village, Kent co., E Md., on the Eastern Shore, 21 mi. E of Baltimore, across Chesapeake Bay (summer steamer service); bathing, fishing; amusement park. Near by is monument marking site of skirmish in War of 1812.

Tolcsva (tôlch'vŏ), town (pop. 2,845), Zemplen co., NE Hungary, on E slope of Tokaj Mts., 26 mi. NNW of Nyiregyhaza; fruit preserves; grapes, apples, pears.

Toldos, Los, Argentina: see LOS TOLDOS.

Told Point, England: see REDCAR.

Tolé (tōlā'), village (pop. 536), Chiriquí prov., W Panama, in Pacific lowland, 50 mi. ESE of David, near Inter-American Highway; trading center; lumbering, stock raising.

Toledo (tŭlē'dō, Sp. tōlā'dhō), town (pop. c.5,700), Oruro dept., W Bolivia, in the Altiplano, 25 mi. SW of Oruro; alt. 12,152 ft.; annual agr. fair.

Toledo, southernmost district (□ 2,125, including 6 sq. mi. of cays; pop. 6,403) of Br. Honduras; ⊙ Punta Gorda. Coastal plain with mountainous interior (Maya Mts.). Drained by Sarstoon and Moho rivers. Agr. (sugar cane, rice, coconuts, bananas), lumbering; sugar milling, sawmilling. Coastal boat service. Principal centers are Punta Gorda, San Antonio, Toledo, and Monkey River.

Toledo or **Toledo Settlement**, village (pop. 771), Toledo dist., S Br. Honduras, 2 mi. NW of Punta Gorda; sugar cane, bananas, timber; sugar- and sawmilling. Amer. settlement colonized 1868 by immigrants from U.S.

Toledo, town (1939 pop. 2,737; 1948 municipality pop. 39,225), central Cebu isl., Philippines, small port on Tañon Strait, 18 mi. WNW of Cebu city; agr. center (corn, coconuts). Ferry service to San Carlos. Oil deposits in vicinity.

Toledo, province (□ 5,925; pop. 480,008), central Spain, in New Castile; ⊙ Toledo. Bounded N by the Sierra de Gredos (Ávila prov.) and S by the Montes de Toledo (Ciudad Real prov.), it borders N and NE on Madrid prov., E on Cuenca prov., W on Cáceres prov., and SW on Badajoz prov. Crossed E-W by the Tagus. Climate is generally dry and extreme, i.e., cold winters, hot summers. The W section is mountainous, E section forms part of upper La Mancha. Fertile La Sagra plain, in N, is watered by Alberche R. Picturesque La Jara mtn. region extends W into Estremadura. Stock raising (chiefly goats and sheep) takes lead over agr. Main crops include wheat, barley, olives, grapes, saffron, chick-peas, beans, anise, fruit. Among mineral resources, some phosphate, graphite, iron, lead, salt, kaolin, lime, clay, and building material are exploited. Foremost processing industries are flour milling, olive-oil extracting, alcohol distilling, wine making. Also textile and cement mills, potteries, dairy plants, tanneries, foundries. Talavera de la Reina is known for its ceramics, while Toledo has long been famed for its mfg. of arms and marzipan. Other important towns are Ocaña, Mora, Consuegra. N and NW sections of the prov. fell, after bitter fighting, to the Nationalist forces in 1st year (1936) of Sp. civil war; the rest held out until last phase of hostilities.

Toledo, anc. *Toletum*, city (pop. 27,427, with suburbs 34,592), ⊙ Toledo prov., central Spain, in New Castile, on right bank of the Tagus (crossed by old arched bridges Alcántara and San Martín), and 40 mi. SSW of Madrid (linked by railroad and highway); 39°52'N 40°1'W. One of Spain's historically and architecturally most notable cities, summing up all that is typically Spanish, and recording incomparably the country's past political, religious, and cultural events. Though economically decayed, Toledo still manufactures its famed sabers and firearms, ceramics, silk and woolen textiles, religious ornaments, and its well-known marzipan —all only reminders of more prosperous days. There are a few minor processing industries based on produce of the fertile surrounding valley. The city is built on slopes of a high granite hill which is almost entirely encircled by a bend of the Tagus. With tortuous, steep streets, it has a medieval character remindful of Andalusia and North Africa because of the dominant Moorish features. As Spain's oldest archbishopric (its archbishop is primate of Spain), it has a magnificent cathedral (begun 1226), which is a combination of Mudejar, Gothic, plateresque, Churrigueresque, and neoclassic styles. The interior contains ornate chapels and great artistic riches, such as El Greco's *Expolio*. Perhaps the most famous painting by El Greco, *The Burial of the Count of Orgaz*, is treasured in Santo Tomé church. El Greco's house is a mus. His famous *View of Toledo* is in Metropolitan Mus., N.Y. Among the many fine religious bldgs. are San Juan de los Reyes in flamboyant Gothic style, old Santo Cristo de la Cruz chapel, the former Tránsito synagogue (14th cent.), and San Leocadia basilica. Of the secular edifices, the most celebrated is the alcazar, a 16th-cent. palace of Charles V, built on city's highest point, long a military acad. and frequently damaged, most tellingly during long siege (1936) of Sp. civil war. Noteworthy also are the Mudejar palace of King Pedro I, art school, archaeological mus., 16th-cent. Hospital of Talavera, and the Taller del Moro ("Moor's workshop"). The imposing walls include the Mudejar gate Puerta del Sol. At Zacodover square all of Toledo's life converges. Outside the city proper are its railroad station, bull ring, Roman remains, famous Fábrica de Armas (arms factory), and San Servando castle across the river. Of Celtiberian origin, Toledo became a Roman colony and later the Visigothic capital, which achieved prominence because of the numerous church councils held here, leading (589) to abjuration of Arianism. It was captured (712) by the Moors and became, after dissolution of the caliphate of Córdoba, capital of independent kingdom, under which trade and culture flourished. Toledo was taken (1085) by Alfonso VI and remained anc. ⊙ Spain until Philip II definitely removed (1561) his court to Madrid. The city suffered severely during War of Spanish Succession (1701–14). It was occupied (1808–14) by the French. With the exception of its alcazar, Toledo remained at beginning of Sp. civil war in Loyalist hands until Gen. Varela entered (Sept., 1936) the city.

Toledo. 1 Village (pop. 905), ⊙ Cumberland co., SE central Ill., 15 mi. SSE of Mattoon, in agr. area; makes brooms, shoes. **2** Town (pop. 2,106), ⊙ Tama co., central Iowa, near Iowa R., 17 mi. ESE of Marshalltown; corn cannery, button factory. State Juvenile Home here. Indian sanatorium near by. Inc. 1866. **3** City (□ 41; pop. 303,616), ⊙ Lucas co., NW Ohio, on harbor on Maumee R. just above its mouth on Maumee Bay of L. Erie, c.95 mi. W of Cleveland; a principal Great Lakes port, and hub of great railroad network; lake vessels load soft coal (for which Toledo is one of world's principal ports), oil (brought here by pipe lines), farm products, manufactured goods; iron ore is principal incoming cargo. Port of entry. Important industries are shipbuilding, oil refining, and mfg. of automobiles, automobile parts, glass, electrical equipment; also makes steel, pig iron, foundry and machine-shop products, cement, tools, precision instruments, paints, chemicals, textiles, paper, and food products. Army ordnance depot here. City's downtown dist. lies W of the Maumee, and is connected with E Toledo by several bridges; to W and SW are residential sections and suburbs (Maumee, Rossford, Perrysburg, Sylvania, Ottawa Hills). Along both banks of river are miles of railroad tracks, railroad yards, coal and ore docks, warehouses, and factories; on W bank are Bay View Park near L. Erie, site of a U.S. naval armory, and the Zoological Park. Has a notable art mus., a R.C. cathedral, a state hosp. for the insane. State memorials mark sites of Fort Meigs and near-by scene of battle of Fallen Timbers (1794). Seat of Univ. of Toledo and of Mary Manse Col. for women. Settled 1817 as Port Lawrence on site of Fort Industry (1794); consolidated with Vistula as Toledo in 1833; inc. 1837. Gave its name to bloodless Toledo War (1835–36), the Ohio-Mich. dispute over boundary in this region. Opening of Wabash and Erie Canal and Miami and Erie Canal in 1840s, coming of railroads, development of Ohio coal fields, tapping of gas and oil deposits in 19th century, and establishment of Libbey glassworks in 1880s marked steps in Toledo's commercial and industrial development. **4** City (pop. 2,323), ⊙ Lincoln co., W Oregon, on Yaquina R., near Yaquina Bay, and 30 mi. W of Corvallis; lumber-milling center in fruit, truck, and dairying area; lumber and paper products. Founded c.1868, inc. 1905. **5** Town (pop. 602), Lewis co., SW Wash., 16 mi. SSE of Chehalis and on Cowlitz R.; logging, dairying.

Toledo (tōlā'dhō), town (pop. 1,200), Canelones dept., S Uruguay, rail junction 11 mi. NNE of Montevideo, in stock-raising and agr. region (grain, wine).

Toledo, Montes de (mōn'tĕs dhā tōlā'dhō), rugged range in central Spain, along Toledo–Ciudad Real prov. border, extends c.70 mi. E-W though continued by smaller ranges in Estremadura (W) and New Castile (E). Forms watershed bet. the Tagus (N) and Guadiana (S); rises to c.5,000 ft. Also called Cordillera Oretana.

Tolemaide, Cyrenaica: see TOLMETA.

Tolen, Netherlands: see THOLEN.

Tolentino (tôlĕntē'nô), town (pop. 5,710), Macerata prov., The Marches, central Italy, on Chienti R. and 11 mi. SW of Macerata. Mfg. center; tanneries, paper mills, foundry; bicycles, agr. tools, electrical equipment. Bishopric. Has 13th-cent. walls and cathedral. Treaty signed here in 1797 bet. Pope Pius VI and Bonaparte. Near by, in 1815, Murat defeated by Austrians.

Toletum, Spain: see TOLEDO, city.

Tolfa (tôl'fä), town (pop. 4,534), Roma prov., Latium, central Italy, 9 mi. ENE of Civitavecchia. Situated in volcanic **Tolfa Hills**, which contain deposits of alum (mined here and at near-by Allumiere), mercury, iron, lead, and zinc.

Tolga (tôlgä'), village (pop. 6,870), Touggourt territory, NE Algeria, oasis in the Ziban region of the N Sahara, terminus of rail spur 22 mi. SW of Biskra; date palms watered by artesian wells. Ruins of Byzantine fort; large mosque.

Tolga (tôl'gä), agr. village and canton (pop. 2,047), Hedmark co., E Norway, on Glomma R. and 15 mi. SW of Roros; formerly pyrite-mining and -smelting center.

Tolhuaca (tōlwä'kä), village (1930 pop. 29), Malleco prov., S central Chile, on slopes of the Andes, at NW foot of Tolhuaca Volcano (9,120 ft.), 60 mi. SE of Angol; alt. 3,935 ft.; thermal springs. L. Malleco is 3 mi. W. Sometimes called Termas de Tolhuaca.

Tolima (tōlē'mä), department (□ 8,876; 1938 pop. 547,796; 1950 estimate 747,140), W central Colombia; ⊙ Ibagué. Extends along Magdalena valley, flanked N-S by Cordillera Oriental (E), Cordillera Central (W). Includes the snow-capped volcanic peaks Nevado del Ruiz, Nevado del Tolima (W), and Nevado del Huila (S). Climate ranges from tropical in Magdalena valley to cool in uplands. Among mineral resources are gold (Ibagué, Santa Isabel, Líbano), silver, copper, mercury, sulphur, coal, petroleum. Mainly a stock-grazing and coffeegrowing region, its other crops are corn, rice, wheat, tobacco, sugar cane, yucca, bananas, cotton, potatoes, cacao, vegetables. Processing industries are centered at Ibagué, Honda, Líbano, Armero. Railroad shops at Espinal. Sugar refining at Ambalema. Honda is a landing on the Magdalena, serving as transshipment point for river and rail traffic.

Tolima, Nevado del (nävä'dō dĕl), Andean volcano (18,438 ft.) in Tolima dept., W central Colombia, in Cordillera Central, just E of Nevado Quindío, 17 mi. NNW of Ibagué. On its lower slopes coffee is grown extensively. Erupted 1829.

Tolimán (tōlēmän'), inactive volcano (10,344 ft.), Sololá dept., SW central Guatemala, near L. Atitlán, 3 mi. SW of San Lucas. Last erupted 1852.

Tolimán. 1 Town (pop. 2,937), Jalisco, W Mexico, in W outliers of Sierra Madre Occidental, 30 mi. SE of Autlán; agr. center (grain, vegetables, sugar cane, cotton, fruit). **2** City (pop. 2,105), Querétaro, central Mexico, on central plateau, 35 mi. NE of Querétaro; alt. 5,649 ft. Known for opal mines. Antimony mining. Agr. center (grain, sugar cane, cotton, tobacco, fruit, livestock).

Toling (tō'lĭng) or **Töling** (tû'lĭng), Chinese *T'o-lin* (tō'lĭn'), town, SW Tibet, in SE Zaskar Range of Kumaun Himalayas, on the Sutlej and 37 mi. SW of Gartok; alt. 12,200 ft. Large lamasery. Sometimes called Tolingmath and spelled Totling.

Tolkemit, Poland: see TOLMICKO.

Tolland (tŏ'lŭnd, tō'–), county (□ 416; pop. 44,709), NE Conn., on Mass. line; ⊙ Rockville. Mfg. (textiles, lumber, thread, wood products, buttons, paper goods), agr. (dairy products, poultry, truck, potatoes, tobacco, fruit). Resorts on lakes. Has several state forests. Drained by Willimantic, Hockanum, Scantic, and Hop rivers. Constituted 1785.

Tolland. 1 Town (pop. 1,659), Tolland co., NE Conn., on Willimantic R. and 18 mi. NE of Hartford, in hilly agr. area; dairying. Shenipsit L. is W. Settled and inc. 1715. **2** Agr. town (pop. 107), Hampden co., SW Mass., 23 mi. W of Springfield. State forest here.

Tollarp (tôl'ärp"), village (pop. 820), Kristianstad co., S Sweden, 10 mi. SW of Kristianstad; metalworking, food canning, chocolate mfg.

Tollegno (tôl-lā'nyō), village (pop. 1,840), Vercelli prov., Piedmont, N Italy, 2 mi. N of Biella; woolen mills.

Tollense Lake (tô'lŭnzŭ), Ger. *Tollensesee* (–zā"), lake (□ 6.7), Mecklenburg, N Germany, just SW of Neubrandenburg; 7 mi. long, 1–2 mi. wide, greatest depth 111 ft., average depth 57 ft. Traversed by Tollense R.

Tollense River, N Germany, rises 4 mi. S of Penzlin, flows 50 mi. generally N, through Tollense L. and past Neubrandenburg, to the Peene at Demmin.

Tollesbury (tōlz'–), town and parish (pop. 1,694), E Essex, England, near Blackwater R. estuary, 7 mi. ENE of Maldon; agr. market and fishing port. Near by are noted oyster beds. Church is partly pre-Norman.

Tolleson (tŏ'lŭsŭn), town (pop. 3,042), Maricopa co., S central Ariz., 10 mi. W of Phoenix, in irrigated Salt R. valley. Settled 1911, inc. 1929.

Tolley, village (pop. 248), Renville co., N N.Dak., 14 mi. W of Mohall.

Tollose (tû'lûsŭ), Dan. *Tølløse*, town (pop. 1,223), Holbaek amt, Zealand, Denmark, 7 mi. S of Holbaek; dairy plant; mfg. (briquettes, bricks).

Tollygunge (tŏl'ēgŭnj), town (pop. 58,594), 24-Parganas dist., SE West Bengal, India, 4.5 mi. S of Calcutta city center; mfg. of chemicals, paint, bricks, soap, rubber goods; general engineering factories, silk mill, tannery. Jute research laboratory (founded 1938).

Tolly's Nullah (tŏl'ēz nŏŏl'lä), canal in Calcutta municipality and 24-Parganas dist., West Bengal, India; from the Hooghly at Kidderpore extends 18 mi. S and E to river arm of Ganges Delta 8 mi. NNE of Baruipur; part of Calcutta and Eastern Canals system. Opened 1777.

Tolmachevo (tŭlmä'chĭvŭ), town (1926 pop. 904), SW Leningrad oblast, Russian SFSR, 8 mi. N of Luga; sawmilling center.

Tolmachi (tŭlmŭchē'), village (1939 pop. over 500), central Kalinin oblast, Russian SFSR, 22 mi. NNE of Likhoslavl; flax.

Tolmein, Yugoslavia: see TOLMIN.

Tolmeta (tōlmā'tä), Ital. *Tolemaide*, anc. *Ptolemais*, village (pop. 350), W Cyrenaica, Libya, port on Mediterranean Sea, 15 mi. NE of Barce. Was the port of anc. Barca (Barce) and an important city of Cyrenaica; flourished until 4th–5th cent. A.D. Has Greek and Roman remains. Also spelled Tolmeita and Tolmetta.

Tolmezzo (tôlmĕ'tsô), town (pop. 3,164), Udine prov., Friuli–Venezia Giulia, NE Italy, at S foot of Carnic Alps, near Tagliamento R., 25 mi. NNW of Udine; paper, cement, skis, hosiery. Has mus. Noted for its high annual rainfall, which averages 88 inches.

Tolmicko (tôlmēts'kô), Ger. *Tolkemit* (tôl'kŭmĭt), town (1939 pop. 3,875; 1946 pop. 972) in East Prussia, after 1945 in Gdansk prov., N Poland, on Vistula Lagoon, 12 mi. NNE of Elbing; fishing.

Tolmin (tôl'mĭn), Ital. *Tolmino* (tôlmē'nô), Ger. *Tolmein* (tôl'mīn), village (pop. 1,695), W Slovenia, Yugoslavia, on Isonzo R., on railroad and 38 mi. W of Ljubljana. Until 1947, in Italy.

Tolna (tôl'nŏ), county (□ 1,390; pop. 273,154), W central Hungary; ⊙ Szekszard. Hilly except in river valleys; drained by Danube, Sarviz, and Sio rivers and by Sio and Kapos canals. Main agr. products: wheat, corn, potatoes, wine; barley, hemp, beans also grown; hogs, sheep, ducks, geese. Extensive truck farming (paprika, honey); silk cocoons. Industry, mainly flour mills, distilleries, at Szekszard, Ujdombovar, Bonyhad, Paks.

Tolna, town (pop. 8,314), Tolna co., SW central Hungary, on arm of the Danube and 6 mi. NE of Szekszard; market center; wool and silk mills, distillery, brickworks. Agr., dairy farming in area.

Tolna (tŭl'nŭ), village (pop. 281), Nelson co., E central N.Dak., 29 mi. SE of Devils Lake.

Tolnanemedi (tôl'nŏnä"mĕdē), Hung. *Tolnanémedi*, town (pop. 2,478), Tolna co., W central Hungary, on Kapos Canal and 22 mi. NNW of Szekszard; thread, paint; agr.

Tolo, Gulf of (tō'lō), large inlet (100 mi. N–S, 10–100 mi. E-W) of Molucca Sea, Indonesia, indenting E coast of Celebes, connected with Molucca Passage (NE) by Peleng Strait (6–12 mi. wide). Banggai Archipelago is at NE side of entrance. Also called Tomori Bay.

Tolochin (tŭlô'chĭn), town (1926 pop. 3,615), SW Vitebsk oblast, Belorussian SSR, 31 mi. WSW of Orsha; flax processing, sawmilling; fruit and vegetable farms. Until c.1940, Tolochino.

Tolong (tōlông'), town (1939 pop. 2,257; 1948 municipality pop. 10,608), Negros Oriental prov., S Negros isl., Philippines, on Sulu Sea, 35 mi. W of Dumaguete; agr. center (corn, coconuts, sugar).

Tolono (tŭlō'nō, tō–), village (pop. 1,065), Champaign co., E Ill., 8 mi. S of Champaign, in agr. area. Marker on site where Lincoln last spoke (1861) to the people of Ill., on his way to Washington.

Tolosa, Argentina: see LA PLATA.

Tolosa, France: see TOULOUSE.

Tolosa (tŏŏlō'zŭ), village (pop. 1,845), Portalegre dist., central Portugal, 18 mi. NW of Portalegre; grain, olives, sheep; cork-oak forests.

Tolosa (tōlō'sä), town (pop. 10,114), Guipúzcoa prov., N Spain, in the Basque Provs., 14 mi. SSW of San Sebastián; commercial and industrial center with many paper mills; metalworking (machinery, hardware). Also mfg. of woolen and silk textiles, berets, cider, candy; tanning and hemp processing. Ships chestnuts. Has church of Santa María and 12th-cent. armory. Was old ⊙ Guipúzcoa prov.

Tolovana (tō"lŭvă'nŭ), village (1939 pop. 28), central Alaska, on Tanana R. and 30 mi. NW of Nenana; placer gold mining.

Tolox (tōlōks'), town (pop. 2,650), Málaga prov., S Spain, on affluent of the Guadalhorce and 27 mi. W of Málaga; spa in agr. region (cereals, olives, grapes, raisins, figs, oranges, esparto, livestock); olive-oil pressing, flour milling, liquor distilling. Tolox or Torrecilla peak (c.6,300 ft.) is 5 mi. W.

Tolstoy (tŏl'stoi), town (pop. 180), Potter co., N central S.Dak., 22 mi. NE of Gettysburg.

Tolstoye (tŭlstoi'ŭ), town (1931 pop. 3,600), S Ternopol oblast, Ukrainian SSR, on left tributary of the Dniester and 11 mi. SSW of Chortkov; flour milling, brickmaking; stone quarrying. Until 1944, called Tluste, Pol. *Tłuste* (twŏŏ'stĕ).

Tolt (tōlt), town (pop. 446), King co., W central Wash., on Snoqualmie R. and 20 mi. E of Seattle, in agr. region.

Toltén (tōltĕn'), town (pop. 1,014), Cautín prov., S central Chile, near mouth of Toltén R., 3 mi. inland from the Pacific, 50 mi. SW of Temuco; resort and agr. center (wheat, barley, potatoes, livestock); flour milling, dairying.

Toltén River, Cautín prov., S central Chile, rises in L. Villarrica, flows c.80 mi. NW and W, past Pitrufquén and Toltén, to the Pacific 3 mi. SSW of Toltén; navigable c.12 mi. for small craft.

Tolú (tōlŏŏ'), town (pop. 4,969), Bolívar dept., N Colombia, port on Gulf of Morrosquillo of Caribbean Sea, 65 mi. S of Cartagena; outlet for produce of the agr. and stock-raising savannas; also forest products (tolu balsam).

Toluca (tōlŏŏ'kä), officially Toluca de Lerdo, city (pop. 43,429), ⊙ Mexico state, central Mexico, in Toluca Valley of central plateau, at foot of Nevado de Toluca, 37 mi. WSW of Mexico city; 19°17'N 99°40'W; alt. 8,661 ft. Rail junction; summer resort; mfg. and agr. center (cereals, fruit, livestock). Silver, gold, lead, and copper mines. Power plants, flour and textile mills, lumberyards, brewery, food canneries, tanneries, printing press; mfg. of chocolate, sweets, tile, brushes, cigars. Indian handicrafts; native market. Airfield. Has govt. palace, state mus., El Calvario shrine.

Toluca (tŭlŏŏ'kŭ, tō–), city (pop. 1,419), Marshall co., N central Ill., 32 mi. NE of Peoria, in agr. area; mfg. (clothing, feed). Inc. 1894.

Toluca, Nevado de (nävä'dō dā tōlŏŏ'kä), Aztec *Cinantécatl* or *Zinantécatl*, extinct volcano (15,020 ft.), Mexico state, Mexico, 13 mi. SSW of Toluca; 19°6'N 99°46'W. Has deep crater lakes.

Toluca Lake (tŭlŏŏ'kŭ), suburb of LOS ANGELES city, Los Angeles co., S Calif., in San Fernando Valley, bet. Burbank (NE) and Universal City. Small Toluca L. here.

Toluca Valley, Mexico state, central Mexico, basin of the large central plateau, W of Valley of Mexico, with TOLUCA at its center; alt. over 8,600 ft. Densely populated area; carries on intensive dairy farming. Gold mining at El Oro.

Tolun (dô'lŏŏn'), Mongolian *Dolon* or *Dolonnor* (dōlōn'nōr'), town, ⊙ Tolun co. (pop. 19,570), NE Chahar prov., China, on highway and 120 mi. NE of Kalgan; trade center in stock-raising dist.; wool weaving, tanning. Noted for its brassware (bells). Has lamasery dating from 1694, for which it was formerly called Lamamiao. Former summer residence of Kublai Khan is at Shangtu or Shangtuho, 10 mi. NW, on upper Lwan R.

Tolve (tôl'vĕ), town (pop. 4,879), Potenza prov., Basilicata, S Italy, 12 mi. ENE of Potenza; wine, olive oil, dairy products.

Tölz, Bad, Germany: see BAD TÖLZ.

Tom, river, Russian SFSR: see TOM RIVER.

Tom, Mount (1,202 ft.), W central Mass., just N of Holyoke. Highest point of Mt. Tom Range, which lies mostly within Mt. Tom state reservation (1,800 acres); hiking and ski trails, campgrounds. Mount Tom village is just N, in Easthampton town.

Toma, La, Argentina: see CUATRO DE JUNIO.

Toma, La, Dominican Republic: see LA TOMA.

Toma, La, Ecuador: see LOJA, city.

Tomabal (tōmäbäl'), village (pop. 236), Libertad dept., NW Peru, in W foothills of Cordillera Occidental, 5 mi. NNE of Virú; rail terminus; sugar cane, rice. Also Tomaval.

Tomah (tō'mŭ), city (pop. 4,760), Monroe co., W central Wis., on branch of Lemonweir R. and 38 mi. ENE of La Crosse, in dairy and livestock region; processes lumber, dairy products; railroad shops. Inc. 1883.

Tomahawk, city (pop. 3,534), Lincoln co., N Wis., on Wisconsin R. and 36 mi. N of Wausau, in wooded lake-resort region; paper milling, furniture mfg. It is state hq. for forest-fire protection. Platted 1887, inc. 1891.

Tomakomai (tōmä'-kō'mī), town (pop. 30,760), SW Hokkaido, Japan, on the Pacific, 40 mi. NE of Muroran; major paper-milling center; lumbering, fishing. Oil field near by.

Tomakovka (tŭmä'kŭfkŭ), village (1926 pop. 11,820), S Dnepropetrovsk oblast, Ukrainian SSR, 17 mi. W of Zaporozhe; dairy plant, flour mill.

Tomales Bay (tōmä'lĭs), narrow inlet of Pacific Ocean, extending into NW Marin co., W Calif.; c.14 mi. long, 1 mi. wide. Tomales village (pop. c.450) is c.2 mi. inland, near mouth of bay; dairying; resort.

Tomanivi, Fiji: see VICTORIA, MOUNT.

Tomar (tŏŏmär'), city (pop. 6,246), Santarém dist., Ribatejo prov., central Portugal, 29 mi. NNE of Santarém; noted for magnificent convent-castle of the Knights Templars, overlooking city from hill just W. Though 1st castle was built in 12th cent. to withstand Moorish assault (culminating in the defense of the city in 1190), most of the present bldgs. date from 16th cent. Other fine ecclesiastical structures include the churches of São João Baptista (1510) and Santa Maria dos Olivais (13th–15th cent.). Today a minor industrial center, Tomar has textile and paper mills, alcohol distillery, sawmills, and plants processing cork and resins. City's importance dates from 14th–16th cent., when it was seat of Knightly Order of Christ. Here, in 1581, Philip II of Spain was proclaimed king of Portugal, though he had ascended the throne in 1580. Formerly spelled Thomar.

Tomares (tōmä'rĕs), town (pop. 2,311), Seville prov., SW Spain, 3 mi. W of Seville (linked by tramways); cereals, olives.

Tomari (tōmä'rē), town (pop. 7,637), Toyama prefecture, central Honshu, Japan, on E shore of Toyama Bay, 27 mi. NE of Toyama, in rice-growing area; textiles, sake.

Tomari. 1 (tōmä'rē) Village, Kuriles, Sakhalin oblast, Russian SFSR: see GOLOVNINO. **2** (tŭmä'-rē) City (1940 pop. 11,381), S Sakhalin, Russian SFSR, port on Sea of Japan, on W coast railroad and 65 mi. NW of Yuzhno-Sakhalinsk; mfg. (pulp, paper, wood alcohol); fish canning. Coal-mining research station for Ugolny mine (E). Under Jap. rule (1905–45), called Tomarioru (tōmärēō'rōō).

Tomarikishi, Russian SFSR: see VAKHRUSHEV.

Tomarioru, Russian SFSR: see TOMARI, Sakhalin.

Tomaros (tô'mŭrôs), W outlying mountain of Pindus system, S Epirus, Greece; rises to 6,475 ft. 13 mi. S of Ioannina. Also called Olytsikas or Olitsikas.

Tomarovka (tŭmä'rŭfkŭ), village (1926 pop. 9,596), S Kursk oblast, Russian SFSR, on Vorskla R. and 15 mi. WNW of Belgorod; sugar beets.

Tomasaki, Mount, Utah: see LA SAL MOUNTAINS.

Tomás Barrón (tōmäs' bärōn'), village (pop. c.4,700), Oruro dept., W Bolivia, in the Altiplano, near Desaguadero R., c.35 mi. NW of Oruro, on La Paz–Oruro RR; alt. 12,490 ft.; barley, potatoes, sheep. Shipping point for mines in Cordillera de Tres Cruces (N). Until early 1940s, Eucaliptus.

Tomás Gomensoro (tōmäs' gōmĕnsō'rō), town (pop. 2,000), Artigas dept., NW Uruguay, on railroad and 15 mi. SE of Bella Unión; shipping point (cattle, horses; grain).

Tomashev, Poland: see TOMASZOW, Lodz prov.

Tomashevka (tŭmä'shĭfkŭ), Pol. *Tomaszówka* (tômäshŏŏf'kä), town (1939 pop. over 500), SW Brest oblast, Belorussian SSR, on Bug R., opposite Wlodawa (Poland), on railroad and 37 mi. S of Brest; flour milling, sawmilling, brick mfg.

Tomashov, Poland: see TOMASZOW, Lublin prov.

Tomashpol or **Tomashpol'** (tŭmăsh'pŭl), town (1926 pop. 5,985), S Vinnitsa oblast, Ukrainian SSR, 33 mi. E of Mogilev-Podolski; sugar refining.

Tomás Laranjeira, Brazil: see PÔRTO GUAÍRA.

Tomaszow (tômä'shŏŏf), Pol. *Tomaszów*, Rus. *Tomashev* (tŭmä'shĭf). **1** or **Tomaszow Mazowiecki** (mäzôvyĕts'kē), city (pop. 30,255), Lodz prov., central Poland, port on Pilica R. and 29 mi. SE of Lodz; ironworks; mfg. of woolen, artificial silk, agr. tools, bricks; tanning, sawmilling, brewing, flour milling. Was small factory settlement (pop. 30) in 1822. Also called Tomaszow Rawski. **2** or **Tomaszow Lubelski** (lŏŏbĕl'skē), Rus. *Tomashov* (–shŭf), town (pop. 7,338), Lublin prov., E Poland, on Solokija R. and 20 mi. SSE of Zamosc; flour milling, sugar refining, sawmilling, mfg. of candy, vegetable oil. Before Second World War, pop. was 50% Jewish. Also called Tomaszow Ordynachi or Tomaszow Zamojski.

Tomaszowka, Belorussian SSR: see TOMASHEVKA.

Tomaszow-Lvov Ridge, Poland and Ukrainian SSR: see ROZTOCZE.

Tomatlán (tōmätlän'). **1** Town (pop. 741), Jalisco, W Mexico, in lowland near Pacific coast, 60 mi. WNW of Autlán; sugar cane, cotton, rice, bananas. **2** or **Buenavista Tomatlán** (bwānävē'stä), town (pop. 927), Michoacán, W Mexico, 16 mi. W of Apatzingán; rice, fruit, sugar cane. **3** Town (pop. 1,411), Veracruz, E Mexico, at E foot of Pico de Orizaba, on railroad and 12 mi. NNW of Córdoba; coffee, sugar cane, fruit.

Tomaval, Peru: see TOMABAL.

Tomave (tōmä'vā), town (pop. c.6,100), Potosí dept., SW Bolivia, in Cordillera de Chichas, on road and 30 mi. NE of Uyuni; corn, fruit.

Tomayapo (tōmīä'pō), town (pop. c.700), Tarija dept., S Bolivia, 28 mi. NW of Tarija; corn.

Tomazina (tŏŏmŏozē'nŭ), city (pop. 872), NE Paraná, Brazil, on the Rio das Cinzas, on railroad and 80 mi. ESE of Londrina; hog raising, lard and cornmeal processing, wine making. Coal deposits. Formerly spelled Thomazina.

Tombador, Serra do (sĕ'rŭ dŏŏ tōmbŭdôr'), low range in N central Mato Grosso, Brazil, separating courses of upper Juruena and Arinos rivers (above their confluence) in lat. 11°–13°S.

Tomball (tŏm"bôl'), town (pop. 1,065), Harris co., S Texas, 28 mi. NW of Houston, in oil, timber, agr. area; sawmill. Inc. 1935.

Tom Bean, town (pop. 286), Grayson co., N Texas, 11 mi. SE of Sherman, in agr. area.

Tombelaine (tōbŭlĕn'), granite islet in Bay of Saint-Michel of English Channel, off coast of Manche dept., NW France, 2 mi. N of Mont-Saint-Michel. Accessible from Genêts (2 mi. NE) across sands at low tide.

Tombigbee River (tŏmbĭg'bē), in NE Miss. and W Ala., formed by confluence of West and East forks near Amory, Miss., flows SSE, past Aberdeen and Columbus, Miss., to Demopolis, Ala. (where it receives Black Warrior R.), then S to junction with Alabama R., forming Mobile R. 30 mi. N of Mobile Bay (45 mi., river distance); 384 mi. long; from farthest headstream (525 mi. above mouth), drains □ 19,500. East Fork (rising in Prentiss co.) is sometimes called Tombigbee R. Main stream not extensively navigable above Demopolis. Work was begun 1950 on lock and dam at Demopolis as units in 260-mi. waterway (Tombigbee Canal) to follow the upper Tombigbee and extend to Pickwick Landing Reservoir in Tennessee R., at a point N of Iuka, Miss. Locks and dams in lower course and in Black Warrior R. make navigation possible along Mobile, Tombigbee, and Black Warrior rivers from city of Mobile to Birmingham area. Shipments of sugar, manganese, phosphates, paper products, fuel oil, and chemicals proceed upstream; iron and steel products, coal, coke, cement, lime, and cotton are delivered downstream.

Tomblaine (tōblĕn'), SE suburb (pop. 2,397) of Nancy, Meurthe-et-Moselle dept., NE France, on right bank of the Meurthe; flannel mfg. Agr. school.

Tombolo (tôm'bôlô), village (pop. 2,656), Padova prov., Veneto, N Italy, 2 mi. E of Cittadella; silk mills.

Tombos (tōm'bŏŏs), city (pop. 2,504), SE Minas Gerais, Brazil, on Rio de Janeiro border, on railroad and 12 mi. S of Carangola; coffee, rice; mica deposits.

Tombouctou, Fr. West Africa: see TIMBUKTU.

Tombstone, city (pop. 910), Cochise co., SE Ariz., 40 mi. NW of Douglas; alt. 4,539 ft. Old mining town which boomed in 1880s (when it had pop. of c.7,000); laid out 1879 and named by Ed Schieffelin, prospector who discovered here some of richest gold mines in Ariz. Its principal mine filled with water in 1909. Lead, gold, and silver are still mined, but tourist trade is main industry. Inc. 1881; ⊙ Cochise co., 1881–1931.

Tomé (tōmā'), town (pop. 10,722), ⊙ Tomé dept. (□ 433; pop. 34,455), Concepción prov., S central Chile, on Concepción Bay, on railroad and 15 mi. NNE of Concepción. Port, commercial and industrial center (coal mining, textile and flour milling, sugar refining, distilling); beach resort; vineyards. Ships timber from Ñuble prov.; also coal and grain. Suffered in 1939 earthquake.

Tome (tō'mā), town (pop. 10,680), Miyagi prefecture, N Honshu, Japan, on Kitakami R. and 15 mi. N of Ishinomaki; agr. (rice, soybeans, potatoes, tobacco); horse breeding.

Tomea (tōmä'ŭ), island (□ 18; pop. 12,208), Tukangbesi Isls., Indonesia, bet. Flores and Molucca seas, 30 mi. SE of Wangiwangi; 5°45'S 123°57'E; 8 mi. long, 4 mi. wide; generally low. Fishing, agr. (coconuts, sago).

Tomeco (tōmā'kō), village (1930 pop. 332), Concepción prov., S central Chile, 25 mi. ESE of Concepción; wheat, corn, beans, lentils, wine, sheep.

Tomelilla (tōō'mŭlĭ"lä), town (pop. 3,237), Kristianstad co., S Sweden, 10 mi. NNE of Ystad; rail junction; agr. center (grain, potatoes, sugar beets, stock). Has art mus.

Tomelloso (tōmĕlyō'sō), city (pop. 28,462), Ciudad Real prov., S central Spain, in New Castile, near the Alto Guadiana, 50 mi. ENE of Ciudad Real. Linked by rail with Madrid and Córdoba. One of Spain's leading viticultural centers, known for its cognac and sweet wine (vermouth, *mistela*). The surrounding region of La Mancha also produces aromatic plants, cereals, livestock. Mfg. of cement products, leather goods, cheese, sausages. Has fine 16th-cent. church. Medicinal springs.

Tom Green, county (□ 1,543; pop. 58,929), W Texas; ⊙ SAN ANGELO. On N Edwards Plateau; alt. c.1,700–2,600 ft.; drained by North, Middle, and South Concho rivers, here joining to form Concho R. Mainly ranching region (sheep, goats, cattle); agr. (cotton, oats, wheat, grain sorghums, fruit, pecans, truck), dairying, poultry raising. Oil wells; clay, sand, limestone. Hunting, fishing; tourist trade. Formed 1874.

Tomhannock Reservoir, lake in Rennselaer co., E N.Y., 11 mi. NNE of Troy; c.6 mi. long; fed by small streams.

Tomie (tōmē'ä), town (pop. 14,442) on Fukae-shima of isl. group Goto-retto, Nagasaki prefecture, Japan, on SE coast; chief town of isl.; agr. center (rice, wheat, sweet potatoes). Fishing.

Tomiku (tōmē'kōō), town (pop. 5,992), Oita prefecture, NE Kyushu, Japan, on E Kunisaki Peninsula, 25 mi. N of Oita; rice, wheat, barley, charcoal.

Tomina, province, Bolivia: see PADILLA.

Tomina (tōmē'nä), town (pop. 4,020), Chuquisaca dept., S central Bolivia, 12 mi. NW of Padilla; corn, potatoes, wheat. Sometimes called Villa Tomina.

Tomina (tô'mĕnä), village (pop. 5,914), NW Bosnia, Yugoslavia, 5 mi. SE of Sanski Most.

Tomini, Gulf of (tōmē'nē), large inlet of Molucca Passage, Indonesia, indenting E coast of Celebes, separating long NE peninsula from E peninsula; 260 mi. E-W, 60–130 mi. N-S. Contains Togian Isls. Also called Gulf of Gorontalo.

Tomioka (tōmē'ōkä). **1** Town (pop. 17,547), Gumma prefecture, central Honshu, Japan, 8 mi. SW of Takasaki, in agr. area (rice, wheat); textile mills. **2** Town (pop. 6,632), Fukushima prefecture, central Honshu, Japan, on the Pacific, 21 mi. NNE of Taira; rice, silk cocoons; fishing. **3** Town (pop. 4,389) on Shimo-jima of Amakusa Isls., Kumamoto prefecture, Japan, on NW coast of isl., 22 mi. N of Ushibuka; seaside resort. Has biological lab. of Kyushu Imperial Univ. **4** Town, Shizuoka prefecture, Japan: see FUJIMIYA. **5** Town (pop. 9,183), Tokushima prefecture, E Shikoku, Japan, 12 mi. SE of Tokushima; agr. center (rice, wheat, truck).

Tomis, Rumania: see CONSTANTA, city.

Tomishima (tōmē'shĭmä), town (pop. 24,567), Miyazaki prefecture, E Kyushu, Japan, on Hyuga Sea, 11 mi. S of Nobeoka; agr. center (rice, wheat); textiles, lumber, livestock. Formed (1937) by combining adjacent towns of Tomitaka and Hososhima.

Tomislavgrad, Yugoslavia: see DUVNO.

Tomisuhara, Japan: see YOKKAICHI, Mie prefecture.

Tomita, Japan: see YOKKAICHI, Mie prefecture.

Tomitaka, Japan: see TOMISHIMA.

Tomkins Cove, village (1940 pop. 684), Rockland co., SE N.Y., 4 mi. SW of Peekskill, across the Hudson; stone quarrying. Bear Mtn. section of Palisades Interstate Park is just N.

Tomlinson Run State Park, W.Va.: see CHESTER.

Tomlishorn, Switzerland: see PILATUS.

Tommerup (tô'mŭrŏŏp), town (pop. 1,157), Odense amt, Denmark, on Fyn isl. and 9 mi. SW of Odense; malt, furniture, textiles.

Tom Miller Dam, S central Texas, in the Colorado just W of Austin; 1,530 ft. long; for power, flood control. A reconstruction (completed 1940) of dam built 1915, made useless by floods. Also called Austin Dam. Impounds L. Austin (capacity 21,500 acre-ft.).

Tommot (tŭmôt'), city (1941 pop. 2,800), in SE Yakut Autonomous SSR, Russian SFSR, on Aldan R. (head of navigation) and 40 mi. NE of Aldan, on Yakutsk-Never highway; gold mining. Became city in 1923; center of Aldan gold basin until rise of Aldan city in 1930s.

Tomo (tō'mō), town (pop. 18,117), Hiroshima prefecture, SW Honshu, Japan, port on Hiuchi Sea, 7 mi. S of Fukuyama; sake-producing center; ironware, canned fish. Port for excursion steamers of Inland Sea; forms W boundary of Inland Sea Natl. Park. Includes scenic isl. of Sensui-jima (1 mi. long, ½ mi. wide) just E of town.

To Mo (tô' mô'), village (1937 pop. 679), Narathiwat prov., S Thailand, on Malay Peninsula, 35 mi. S of Narathiwat, near the Sungei Golok (Malaya line); gold mining.

Tomochi (tōmō'chē), town (pop. 8,446), Kumamoto prefecture, W Kyushu, Japan, 16 mi. SE of Kumamoto; rail terminus; rice, raw silk, lumber.

Tomolasta, Cerro (sĕ'rō tōmōlä'stä), pampean peak (6,681 ft.), highest of the Sierra de San Luis, N San Luis prov., Argentina, 38 mi. NNE of San Luis.

Tomon-ko, Korea and Manchuria: see TUMEN RIVER.

Tomooku (tōmō'kōō), town (pop. 2,645), Tokushima prefecture, E Shikoku, Japan, on Philippine Sea, 35 mi. SSW of Tokushima; fishing center. Formed 1923 by combining villages of Tomoura and Okuura. Sometimes called Tomoura.

Tomor or **Tomori,** Albania: see TOMORR.

Tomori Bay, Indonesia: see TOLO, GULF OF.

Tomo River (tō'mō), Vichada commissary, E Colombia, rises at Meta intendancy line S of Orocué, flows c.400 mi. in meandering course ENE, through uninhabited llano lowlands, to Orinoco R. 60 mi. SSW of Puerto Carreño.

Tömörkeny (tû'mûrkānyû), Hung. *Tömörkény*, town (pop. 3,809), Csongrad co., S Hungary, 9 mi. SW of Csongrad; market center; wheat, corn, cattle.

Tomorr (tô'môr) or **Tomorri** (tô'môrē), highest mountain range in central Albania, extends c.30 mi. NNW-SSE bet. Devoll and Osum rivers; rises to 7,933 ft. in Tomorr peak, 11 mi. E of Berat, which offers panoramic view over great part of Albania. Another peak (Abbas Ali or Abas Ali; c.7,870 ft.; 5 mi. S) is site of Abbas Ali monastery, a noted Bektashi (Moslem sect) pilgrimage center. Also spelled Tomor or Tomori.

Tömös Pass, Rumania: see PREDEAL PASS.

Tomoura, Japan: see TOMOOKU.

Tompa (tôm'pŏ), town (pop. 5,715), Bacs-Bodrog co., S Hungary, 15 mi. S of Kiskunhalas; wheat, corn, cattle, hogs.

Tompkins, village (pop. 440), SW Sask., in the Cypress Hills, 32 mi. ENE of Maple Creek; wheat, livestock.

Tompkins, county (□ 491; pop. 59,122), W central N.Y.; ⊙ Ithaca. Includes S end of Cayuga L. (resorts) and Taughannock Falls State Park. Dairying and farming area (grain, poultry, fruit). Mfg. at Ithaca. Formed 1817.

Tompkinsville. 1 Town (pop. 1,859), ⊙ Monroe co., S Ky., near Tenn. line and Dale Hollow Reservoir, 24 mi. SSE of Glasgow; agr. (corn, wheat, burley tobacco, livestock); makes smoking pipes and other wood products, soft drinks; flour milling. In nearby Old Mulkey Meeting House State Park is oldest (1798) log meeting house in Ky. **2** A port and industrial section of Richmond borough of New York city, SE N.Y., on NE Staten Isl., just S of St. George; mfg. (clothing, chemicals, electrical equipment).

Tompo (tŭmpô'), village, E central Yakut Autonomous SSR, Russian SFSR, on Tompo R. (affluent of the Aldan), 230 mi. NE of Yakutsk; trade post.

Tomra, Norway: see VESTNES.

Tom River or **Tom' River** (tôm), in Kemerovo and Tomsk oblasts, Russian SFSR, rises in the Kuznetsk Ala-Tau, flows 440 mi. W and N, through Kuznetsk Basin, past Stalinsk (head of navigation), Kemerovo, and Tomsk, to Ob R. 30 mi. NNW of Tomsk. Chief tributaries: Mras-Su, Usa, and Kondoma rivers.

Toms Brook, town (pop. 256), Shenandoah co., NW Va., near North Fork of Shenandoah R., 4 mi. SW of Strasburg; lime.

Tomsk (tŏmsk, Rus. tômsk), oblast (□ 121,400; 1946 pop. estimate c.600,000), Russian SFSR, in W central Siberia; ⊙ Tomsk. Drained by middle Ob R. and its tributaries (Chulym, Ket, Tym, and Vasyugan rivers). Except for extreme SE, it comprises vast flatland (VASYUGANYE) covered by thick forests and marshes, which form great inland seas in the spring; continental climate. Partial swamp drainage along main rivers has created agr. areas, chiefly for grain and dairy farming. Pop. (Russians in SE, Khanty in NW, Evenki in E) also engaged in fur trapping, fishing, lumbering (sawmilling at KOLPASHEVO, Mogochin). Navigation developing with drainage of swampy river beds. Chief city is TOMSK, an important cultural center. Formed 1944 out of Novosibirsk oblast, absorbing former (1932–44) Narym okrug.

Tomsk, city (1939 pop. 141,215), ⊙ Tomsk oblast, Russian SFSR, on spur of Trans-Siberian RR, on Tom R. and 125 mi. NE of Novosibirsk, 1,800 mi. E of Moscow; 56°30'N 84°57'E. Industrial and cultural center in W Siberia; mfg. (electric motors, ballbearings, rubber goods, pencils, matches, light bulbs), agr. processing (flour, tobacco, alcohol, meat, vegetable oil). Has univ. (1888), polytechnic institute (1900), medical and teachers colleges, electrotechnical and rail-transportation schools, library, botanic gardens. Located on right bank of Tom R., Tomsk is adjoined (1604) by lumber port of Cheremoshniki. Founded 1604 by Boris Godunov; developed rapidly as an important trading post; became in 19th cent. the leading city of Siberia.

By-passed by Trans-Siberian RR (c.40 mi. SE), Tomsk lost its leadership after 1900, 1st to Omsk, later to Novosibirsk; continues to be the educational center of Siberia. Was ⊙ Tomsk govt. until 1925; became (1944) ⊙ Tomsk oblast.

Toms River, village (pop. 2,517), ⊙ Ocean co., E N.J., on Toms R., near Barnegat Bay, and 20 mi. SSE of Freehold; fishing center; clay, timber; fruit, poultry. Co. mus. and several 18th-cent. bldgs. here. A Revolutionary privateering port; burned (1782) by Loyalists and British.

Toms River, N.J., rises in N Ocean co., flows 19 mi. SE and E, past Toms River village (head of navigation), to Barnegat Bay; broadens into tidal inlet in lower 5 mi. Resorts, fishing villages around mouth.

Tonacatepeque (tōnäkätāpā'kā), city (pop. 4,219), San Salvador dept., central Salvador, 7 mi. NE of San Salvador; market center; mfg. (cotton goods, clothing); coffee, livestock.

Tonalá (tōnälä'). **1** City (pop. 6,379), Chiapas, S Mexico, in Pacific lowland, on railroad and 60 mi. SW of Tuxtla; processing and agr. center (rice, sugar cane, cacao, tobacco, coffee, fruit, livestock); tanning; salt mining; forest industry. Airfield. **2** Town (pop. 3,126), Jalisco, central Mexico, 8 mi. ESE of Guadalajara; agr. center (grain, sugar cane, tobacco, vegetables, fruit); native potteries. **3** Town (pop. 1,246), Oaxaca, S Mexico, in Sierra Madre del Sur, 18 mi. WSW of Huajuápan; alt. 4,429 ft.; potteries.

Tonalá River, SE Mexico, rises in N foothills of Sierra Madre on Isthmus of Tehuantepec, flows in its entire length of c.100 mi. NW along Veracruz-Tabasco border to Gulf of Campeche 20 mi. ENE of Coatzacoalcos. Called Pedegral R. in upper course.

Tonalea (tōnūlē'ū), village, Coconino co., N Ariz., in Hopi Indian Reservation, 90 mi. N of Winslow. Navajo Natl. Monument is N.

Tonale Pass (tōnä'lē) (alt. 6,178 ft.), on border bet. Lombardy and Trentino–Alto Adige, N Italy, in Rhaetian Alps, bet. Ortles (N) and Adamello (S) groups, 3 mi. E of Ponte di Legno. Crossed by road bet. Edolo and Malè. Formerly on Austro-Ital. border; scene of fighting in First World War.

Tonan, Formosa: see TOWNAN.

Tonantins (tōōnäntēns'), town (pop. 459), W Amazonas, Brazil, on left bank of the Amazon, 100 mi. NE of São Paulo de Olivença; rubber, Brazil nuts.

Tonara (tōnä'rä), village (pop. 3,362), Nuoro prov., central Sardinia, 22 mi. SSW of Nuoro.

Tonasket (tŭnă'skĭt), town (pop. 957), Okanogan co., N Wash., 24 mi. NNE of Okanogan and on Okanogan R.; apples, livestock; gold, silver, lead.

Tonatico (tōnätē'kō), officially San Gaspar Tonatico, town (pop. 1,855), Mexico state, central Mexico, 35 mi. S of Toluca; sugar cane, fruit, coffee, stock.

Tonawanda (tŏnuwŏn'dŭ), industrial city (pop. 14,617), Erie co., W N.Y., 7 mi. N of Buffalo, and on Niagara R. at terminus of the Barge Canal, here following Tonawanda Creek; canal- and lake-shipping, commercial, and railroad center. Mfg. of chemicals, paper and metal products, hardware, furniture, heaters, office and amusement equipment, machinery, wood and lumber products, lenses, paints; oil refining. Tonawanda Indian Reservation is E. Organized 1836, inc. 1903.

Tonawanda Creek, W N.Y., rises in W Wyoming co., flows c.90 mi. N, NW, and W, past Batavia and through Tonawanda Indian Reservation, to Niagara R. at Tonawanda. Partly canalized as a section of N.Y. State Barge Canal.

Tonaya (tōnī'ä), town (pop. 1,870), Jalisco, W Mexico, in W outliers of Sierra Madre Occidental, 23 mi. E of Autlán; grain, sugar cane, tobacco, fruit.

Tonayán (tōnīän'), town (pop. 649), Veracruz, E Mexico, in Sierra Madre Oriental, 11 mi. N of Jalapa; corn, fruit.

Tonbridge (tŭn'–), urban district (1931 pop. 16,333; 1951 census 19,239), W Kent, England, on Medway R. and 4 mi. N of Tunbridge Wells; agr. market; mfg. of chemicals, paper, agr. machinery. "Tunbridge ware," wooden mosaics, is also made. Has partly-Norman church, 1553 school, and ruins of moated Norman castle.

Tocontín (tōngkōntēn'), village, Francisco Morazán dept., S central Honduras, 3 mi. S of Tegucigalpa. Site of Tegucigalpa airport; military aviation school.

Tonda (tōn'dä). **1** Town (pop. 7,748), Osaka prefecture, S Honshu, Japan, 2 mi. WSW of Takatsuki; agr. center (rice, wheat); sake, straw products. **2** Town, Yamaguchi prefecture, Japan: see TOKUYAMA.

Tondabayashi (tōn"däbä'yäshē), town (pop. 29,783), Osaka prefecture, S Honshu, Japan, 12 mi. SSE of Osaka; commercial center for agr. area (tobacco, fruit, truck); mfg. (cotton textiles, sake).

Tondano (tōndä'nō), town (pop. 15,007), NE Celebes, Indonesia, at N end of L. Tondano (□ 17.8; 8 mi. long, 4 mi. wide), 13 mi. SSE of Menado; 1°18'N 124°53'E; trade center for region producing copra, coffee, sugar cane, ebony, nutmeg. Near by are high waterfalls.

Tondela (tōndā'lŭ), town (pop. 1,521), Viseu dist., N central Portugal, on railroad and 13 mi. SW of Viseu, in fruitgrowing area (oranges, grapes, apples); paper- and sawmilling.

Tonder (tû'nûr), Dan. *Tønder*, amt (□ 505; 1950 pop. 41,998), SW Jutland, Denmark; ⊙ Tonder. Area is low, flat, sometimes marshy; livestock, agr. After 1864 in Germany until 1920 plebiscite.

Tonder, Dan. *Tønder*, Ger. *Tondern*, city (1950 pop. 7,031), ⊙ Tonder amt, S Jutland, Denmark, 65 mi. SW of Odense, on Ger. border (customs station); 54°56'N 8°52'E. Brewing, mfg. of margarine, automobile bodies; meat packing. City dates from 13th cent. After 1864 in Germany until 1920 plebiscite.

Tondi (tōn'dē), town (pop. 8,289; 70% Moslem), Ramnad dist., S Madras, India, port on Palk Strait, 29 mi. NNE of Ramnad. Saltworks on coast, 3 mi. NNE.

Tondiarpet, India: see MADRAS, city.

Tone River, Somerset, England, rises on E edge of Exmoor, 7 mi. SW of Watchet, flows 29 mi. S and NE, past Wellington and Taunton, to Parrett R. at Isle of Athelney.

Tone River (tō'nā), Jap. *Tone-gawa*, central Honshu, Japan, rises in mts. in Gumma prefecture, 35 mi. N of Maebashi; flows S and SE (forming boundary bet. Chiba and Ibaraki prefectures), past Toride and Sawara, to the Pacific at Choshi; 230 mi. long. Its lower course is connected with a series of lagoons; tidal estuary is 10 mi. long, 1 mi. wide. Hydroelectric plants in upper course.

Tong, England: see BRADFORD.

Tong (toung), village, Sontay prov., N Vietnam, 2 mi. SW of Sontay; military training center; airport.

Tonga (tông'gä), village, Upper Nile prov., S central Anglo-Egyptian Sudan, on left bank of the White Nile, E of L. No, on road and 40 mi. W of Malakal; cotton shipping. R.C. mission.

Tonga (tŏng'gŭ, tông'ä), island group (□ 250; 1948 pop. 45,558) and Br. protected state, S Pacific, 2,000 mi. NE of Sydney; 15°45'–22°20'S 175°45'–176°12'W. Comprises c.150 coral and volcanic isls. in 3 main groups: TONGATABU (largest, seat of Nukualofa, ⊙ Tongan kingdom), VAVAU, HAABAI. Outlying N isls. are NIUATOBUTABU, TAFAHI, NIUAFOO. Coconut palms, tree ferns; rats, bats, some snakes. Range of temp.: 53°–93°F. Polynesian natives. Compulsory primary education; 2 boys' secondary schools. Chief export is copra. Discovered 1616 by the Dutch; visited 1773 by Cook, who named group Friendly Isls. English missionaries arrived 1797. Constitutional monarchy established 1862, group came 1900 under Br. protection. Sometimes called Friendly Isls.

Tongaat (tông'gät), town (pop. 5,536), E Natal, U. of So. Afr., near Indian Ocean, 20 mi. NNE of Durban; agr. (sugar, tobacco, Kaffir corn, mealies).

Tonga Deep, ocean depth (30,131 ft.) of South Pacific Ocean, E of Tonga Isls. and N of Kermadec Deep; discovered 1895.

Tongala (tŏng-gă'lŭ), village (pop. 848), N Victoria, Australia, 105 mi. N of Melbourne; livestock; cheese factory.

Tongaland, U. of So. Afr.: see ZULULAND.

Tonganoxie (tŏng'gŭnŏk'sē), city (pop. 1,138), Leavenworth co., NE Kansas, 24 mi. W of Kansas City, Kansas; trade center for general-farming area; dairy products. Coal mining, rock quarrying in vicinity. State park near by. Inc. 1871.

Tongareva: see PENRHYN.

Tongariro (tŏng-gŭrē'rōō), active volcanic peak (6,458 ft.) in Tongariro Natl. Park, central N.Isl., New Zealand; hot springs on slopes, blue lake on summit.

Tongariro National Park (□ 234), central N.Isl., New Zealand, near L. Taupo. Its volcanic mts. include RUAPEHU, highest peak of N.Isl., as well as TONGARIRO and NGAURUHOE. Lava deserts.

Tongass National Forest (tŏng'gŭs) (□ 25,860), S Alaska, bet. S slope of St. Elias Mts. and the Pacific coast bet. Yakutat Bay and Dry Bay.

Tongatabu (tông'ätä'bōō), coral island group (pop. 16,234), S Tonga, S Pacific; 21°14'S 175°W; includes Eua, Tongatabu (largest, most populous isl. of Tonga), and several islets. Nukualofa, ⊙ Tongatabu group and of Tongan kingdom, is on Tongatabu. Sometimes spelled Tongatapu.

Tongcho (tông'chô'), Jap. *Toso*, town (1944 pop. 12,433), Kangwon prov., central Korea, N of 38°N, on Sea of Japan, 50 mi. ENE of Chunchon; fishing.

Tonge, England: see BOLTON.

Tongeren, Belgium: see TONGRES.

Tongerloo-Saint-Norbert, Belgian Congo: see IBEMBO.

Tongjoson-man, Korea: see EAST KOREA BAY.

Tongka or **Tongkah,** Thailand: see PHUKET, town.

Tongking, Vietnam: see TONKIN.

Tongoa, New Hebrides: see SHEPHERD ISLANDS.

Tongoy or **Tongoi** (tōng-goi'), village (pop. 384), Coquimbo prov., N central Chile, minor port on Tongoy Bay of the Pacific, 28 mi. SW of La Serena; copper smelting. Rail line to Ovalle and Tamaya.

Tongquil Island (tôngkēl') (□ 18.9; 1939 pop. 776), in Samales Group, Sulu prov., Philippines, at NE end of Sulu Archipelago, 25 mi. S of Basilan Isl. Tungkil municipal dist. (1948 pop. 3,673) embraces the whole Samales Group.

Tongres (tō'grŭ), Flemish *Tongeren* (tông'ŭrŭn), town (pop. 13,721), Limburg prov., NE Belgium, 11 mi. NNW of Liége; rail junction; market center for fruitgrowing area (apples, cherries, plums). Has 12th-cent. church with 10th-cent. cloisters. Important center in Roman times; led a revolt against Rome in 54 B.C. Anc. ⊙ Germanic Tungri tribe. Destroyed by Salian Franks in 4th cent., by Attila in 451, and by Normans in 881.

Tongres-Sainte-Marie, Belgian Congo: see RUTSHURU.

Tongsa (tông'sä) or **Trongsa** (trông'shä), fortified town [Bhutanese *dzong*], central Bhutan, on Tongsa R. and 40 mi. ESE of Punakha. Former hq. of E Bhutan and of last Tongsa governor, who became (1907) 1st hereditary maharaja of Bhutan.

Tongsang, China: see TUNGSHAN, Fukien prov.

Tongsa River, central Bhutan, rises in main range of W Assam Himalayas, on glacier of Kangri peak; flows S past Tongsa, and SSE to Manas R. at 26°52'N 90°57'E; c.100 mi. long. Also called Mangde Chu.

Tongsongchon River (tông'sŭng'chŭn'), Jap. *Tojo-sen-ko*, Korean *Tongsongchon-gang*, S.Hamgyong prov., N Korea, formed by several small streams rising in mtn. range N of Hamhung, flows SW, turning SE past Hamhung, to E.Korea Bay at Hungham; c.50 mi. long. Called Songchon R. in upper course.

Tongue, agr. village and parish (pop. 1,184), N Sutherland, Scotland, on Kyle of Tongue (sea inlet 9 mi. long, 5 mi. wide at mouth), and 33 mi. WSW of Thurso. Has ruins of Castle Bharruich or Varrich. In mouth of Kyle of Tongue is Roan Isl.

Tongue of the Ocean, deep Atlantic channel, central Bahama Isls., on E edge of the Great Bahama Bank; extends c.100 mi. S from New Providence Isl. along E coast of Andros Isl.

Tongue River. 1 In N.Dak., rises in Cavalier co., flows E and N 100 mi., past Cavalier, to Pembina R. near Pembina. **2** In N Wyo. and SE Mont., rises in Bighorn Mts. near Sheridan, Wyo.; flows 265 mi. NE, through Tongue River Indian Reservation, to Yellowstone R. at Miles City, Mont.

Tongyong (tông'yŭng'), Jap. *Toei*, town (1946 pop. 41,627), S.Kyongsang prov., S Korea, port on Korea Strait, opposite Koje Isl., 40 mi. SW of Pusan; fishing and mfg. center. Fish processing, rice refining, rope making. Artisan industries: textiles, lacquer ware, woodwork. There are boatyards. Exports salted fish and fish oil.

Tonhil, Mongolia: see TONKHIL.

Tonica (tŏ'nĭkŭ), village (pop. 585), La Salle co., N Ill., 8 mi. S of La Salle; dairy products, livestock, poultry.

Tónichi (tō'nēchē), town (pop. 583), Sonora, NW Mexico, on Yaqui R. and 95 mi. ESE of Hermosillo; rail terminus; fruit, cereals, lumber. Hot springs near by.

Tonila (tōnē'lä), town (pop. 2,453), Jalisco, W Mexico, at SE foot of Colima volcano, 22 mi. SSW of Guzmán; alt. 4,105 ft.; agr. center (corn, sugar cane, tobacco, fruit).

Tonilita (tōnēlē'tä), village (pop. 267), Jalisco, W Mexico, on railroad and 24 mi. S of Guzmán; hydroelectric plant; lumbering.

Tonj (tōnj), town (pop. 1,100), Bahr el Ghazal prov., S Anglo-Egyptian Sudan, on Tonj R. (a non-navigable tributary of L. Ambadi) and 55 mi. SE of Wau; cotton, peanuts, sesame, corn, durra; livestock.

Tonj River, S Anglo-Egyptian Sudan, rises on Nile-Congo watershed at Uganda border, flows over 300 mi. NNE, past Tonj and into the SUDD swamps, joining Jur R. in L. Ambadi to form the BAHR EL GHAZAL. Nonnavigable. Floods July-March. Also called Ibba in upper course.

Tonk (tôngk), former princely state (□ 2,543); pop. 353,687) in Rajputana States, India; ⊙ was Tonk. Consisted of 6 detached areas in Rajputana and Central India, acquired by Pathan chieftain bet. 1798 and 1817. In 1948, merged with union of Rajasthan.

Tonk, city (pop. 38,650), ⊙ Tonk dist., E Rajasthan, India, 50 mi. S of Jaipur, near Banas R.; agr. market (millet, wheat, gram); cotton weaving, wool carding; felt handicrafts. Was ⊙ former Rajputana state of Tonk.

Tonka Bay, village (pop. 899), Hennepin co., E Minn., on small peninsula in L. Minnetonka, 17 mi. W of Minneapolis.

Tonkawa (tŏng'kŭwô), city (pop. 3,643), Kay co., N Okla., 13 mi. W of Ponca City, and on Salt Fork of Arkansas R.; oil refining; mfg. of concrete blocks, feed, cereals, dairy products; cotton ginning. Oil and natural-gas wells. Seat of Northern Okla. Jr. Col. Settled 1893, inc. 1894.

Tonkhil or **Tonhil** (both: tông'khēl), village, Gobi Altai aimak, W Mongolian People's Republic, 170 mi. SW of Uliassutai.

Tonkin, Tongking, or **Tonking** (tŏn'kĭn, tŏng'kĭng), Fr. *Tonkin* (tōkē'), former Fr. protectorate (□ 44,670; 1943 pop. 9,851,200) in N Indochina, constituting (after 1945–46) N VIETNAM; ⊙ Hanoi. Bounded N by the Chinese Kwangtung, Kwangsi, and Yunnan provs., SW by Laos, S by Annam, and SE by Gulf of Tonkin; consists mainly of dissected, steep-walled highlands (rising to 10,308 ft. in the Fansipan), which enclose the combined delta of the Song Cau and Red River, the heart of Tonkin. Here are most of Annamese pop. (85% of total), the great rice fields (occasionally modernized by irrigation works), and the cities of Hanoi and Haiphong where industry and trade are concentrated. The mtn. regions are sparsely peopled by non-Annamese groups (mainly Thai tribes, Muang, and the Chinese groups of Man and Miao); their economy is given over chiefly to subsistence farming and fishing. Besides rice, the important crops in Tonkin are corn, vegetables, cotton, and raw silk. Rice milling, textile mfg. (Namdinh), and alcohol distilling are the chief processing industries. Tonkin has the only important coal fields of Indochina, in the Quangyen basin at Hongay, Campha, and Uongbi, and on Kebao Isl. Zinc (at Chodien), tin (in Piaouac Range), and tungsten are also mined. The area is served by railroads radiating from Hanoi to Kunming (China) and Dongdang (on Chinese border), as well as to Haiphong, the leading port. In early times part of China, Tonkin was (after A.D. 939) the original Annamese state, which expanded (1472) with the annexation of Champa. After the dynastic division (16th cent.) of the Annamese lands, the northern territories (Tonkin proper and the N Annamese provs. of Thanhhoa, Nghean, and Hatinh) were ruled (until 1788) by the Le dynasty from the city of Tonkin (modern Hanoi), whose name came to be applied by Europeans to entire region. Following disorders in late 18th cent., Tonkin was brought (1802) under the rule of the restored Annamese Nguyen line of Hue. The French first penetrated into Tonkin in 1866 to open the Red River to Fr. trade; a Fr. military expedition followed (1873), imposing its protectorate (1874), but became involved (1882–85) in war with China which claimed suzerainty over Tonkin. The Fr. protectorate over Tonkin was finally accepted (1884–85) by Annam and China, and Tonkin joined (1887) the Union of Indochina. After Second World War, Tonkin was the seat of the Vietminh revolt and became part (1945–46) of Vietnam.

Tonkin, Gulf of, NW arm of South China Sea, bounded W by Tonkin (N Vietnam), N by China's Kwangtung prov., and E by Luichow Peninsula and Hainan Isl. (separated by Hainan Strait); 300 mi. long, 150 mi. wide. Receives the Red R. Main ports are Benthuy and Haiphong in Vietnam, Pakhoi in China.

Tonkino (tŭnkē'nŭ), village (1926 pop. 1,006), NE Gorki oblast, Russian SFSR, 20 mi. SSW of Shakhunya; flax.

Tonkolili, Sierra Leone: see MABONTO.

Tonle Sap (tônlä' säp') [Cambodian,=fresh-water lake] or **Great Lake,** Fr. *Grand Lac* (grā'läk'), Annamese *Bienhoa* (byĕn'hwä'), central Cambodia; natural flood reservoir (□ c.1,000 at low water) of the lower Mekong, with which it is connected by the Tonle Sap R. (70 mi. long) joining the Mekong at Pnompenh (forming the confluence known as QUATRE BRAS). At high water (June–Nov.), the lake receives the flood waters of the Mekong, inundates surrounding forest area (□ 2,500), and increases in depth from 3–10 ft. (dry season) to 30–40 ft. At low-water stage, the flow of the Tonle Sap R. is reversed (toward the Mekong) and the lake is largely reduced to a shallow, reed-choked swamp with narrow water channels. During the floods, the lake constitutes an important navigation route enabling vessels of 12-ft. draught to navigate up the swollen tributaries to Kompong Thom, Siemreap, Battambang, and Pursat. During low water (Dec.–May), silting at lake outlet restricts navigation to the Tonle Sap R. bet. Pnompenh and Kompong Chhang. The inundated forests provide excellent breeding ground for fish, which are the basis of Cambodia's economic activity during low-water stage. The lake is a residual maritime gulf barred from the sea by the sediments of the Mekong R.

Tonna, Wales: see ABERDULAIS.

Tonnay-Boutonne (tônā'-bōōtôn'), village (pop. 561), Charente-Maritime dept., W France, on the Boutonne and 12 mi. E of Rochefort; dairying.

Tonnay-Charente (–shärät'), town (pop. 2,547), Charente-Maritime dept., W France, port on the Charente and 3 mi. E of Rochefort; head of navigation for ocean-going vessels; fertilizer mfg. (imported phosphates), zinc smelting, brandy distilling.

Tonnegrande (tôn-grād'), town (commune pop. 89), N Fr. Guiana, on small Cayenne R., near the coast, and 13 mi. SW of Cayenne; sugar cane, manioc, tropical fruit.

Tonneins (tônē'), town (pop. 4,527), Lot-et-Garonne dept., SW France, on the Garonne and 11 mi. SE of Marmande; tobacco-growing center; mfg. of shoes, chemicals, flour-milling equipment; printing, fruit shipping. Was a Huguenot stronghold.

Tonnerre (tônâr'), town (pop. 3,802), Yonne dept., N central France, on Armançon R. and Burgundy Canal, and 19 mi. ENE of Auxerre; agr. market; foundry; mfg. (building material, beeswax, furniture). Has 13th-cent. hosp. Damaged in Second World War.

Tönning (tû'nĭng), town (pop. 6,018), in Schleswig-Holstein, NW Germany, on Eiderstedt peninsula, harbor on Eider R. near its mouth on the North Sea, and 12 mi. SW of Husum; boatbuilding; mfg. of chemicals, building materials, rope, flour products; woodworking. Has Romanesque-Gothic church with baroque tower. First mentioned 1186. Chartered 1590. Was fortress, 1644–1714. Center of cattle-export trade to England until 1900.

Tönnisstein, Bad, Germany: see BURGBROHL.

Tono (tō'nō'), town (pop. 9,503), Iwate prefecture, N Honshu, Japan, 19 mi. WNW of Kamaishi; rice, soybeans, millet, potatoes.

Tonopah (tō'nŭpä, tōnŭpä'), village (pop. 1,375), ⊙ Nye co., S central Nev., c.170 mi. SE of Reno; alt. 6,033 ft.; supply point in mining (gold, silver), livestock, and grain area. Settled 1900, when rich silver deposits were discovered.

Tonosho (tōnōshō'), largest town and port (pop. 7,885) on Shodo-shima, Kagawa prefecture, Japan, on W peninsula of isl., in agr. area (wheat, sweet potatoes). Exports cotton thread, tobacco, soy sauce. Sometimes called Tosho.

Tonosí (tōnōsē'), town (pop. 378), Los Santos prov., S central Panama, in Pacific lowland, on Tonosí R. (35-mi.-long coastal stream) and 26 mi. SW of Las Tablas; bananas, livestock.

Tonoyama, Japan: see HIRAKATA, Osaka prefecture.

Tonsberg (tŭns'bărg", –băr"), Nor. *Tønsberg,* city (pop. 11,883), ⊙ Vestfold co., SE Norway, port at head of Tonsberg Fjord, 45 mi. S of Oslo; 59°16'N 10°25'E. Rail junction and shipping and whaling center, with shipyards, machine shops, and mfg. of paper, rope, shoes, oilskin, butter, beer. Noted for silverware made here. Has naval col., co. mus. First mentioned in 871, it is Norway's oldest city, and was of considerable importance in Middle ages. Destroyed by fire in 1536, it did not recover its commercial position until late 18th cent. Whaling boom in mid-19th cent. increased its prosperity. Site of ruins of anc. Tunsberghus castle. Near by are anc. royal grave mounds; at OSEBERG, 3 mi. NE, anc. viking ship was excavated.

Tonsberg Fjord, Nor. *Tønsbergfjord,* inlet (16 mi. long) of Oslo Fjord, SE Norway, bet. mainland and a group of isls., of which Notteroy is the largest. The fjord is c.4 mi. wide at mouth, narrowing to c.½ mi. at head, where Tonsberg city lies. A narrow, 3-mi.-long strait (Stein or Sten Canal) connects N end with Oslo Fjord.

Tonshayevo (tŭnshī'ŭvŭ), village, NE Gorki oblast, Russian SFSR, rear railroad, 13 mi. ENE of Shakhunya; flax.

Tons River (tŏns). **1** N (left) tributary of the Ganges, in Uttar Pradesh, India, formed on Ganges Plain by confluence of 2 headstreams 5 mi. WNW of Akbarpur, flows c.150 mi. SE, past Akbarpur, Jalalpur, Azamgarh, Muhammadabad, and Mau, to the Ganges just W of Ballia. **2** S (right) tributary of the Ganges, in central India, rises in Vindhya Range in S Vindhya Pradesh c.15 mi. N of Katni (Murwara), flows c.175 mi. NE to the Ganges 17 mi. SE of Allahabad.

Tonstad (tōn'stä), village (pop. 180; canton pop. 699), Vest-Agder co., S Norway, on the Sira, on N shore of Sirdal L., 27 mi. N of Flekkefjord. Molybdenum deposits near by.

Tontal, Sierra del (syĕ'rä dĕl tōntäl'), subandean range in S San Juan prov., Argentina, W of San Juan; extends c.50 mi. N–S; rises to c.13,500 ft.

Tontitown (tŏn'tētoun"), town (pop. 203), Washington co., NW Ark., 8 mi. NNW of Fayetteville, in the Ozarks; winegrowing.

Tonto Basin (tŏn'tō), valley in central Ariz., extends S from Mogollon Rim, bet. Mazatzal Mts. and Sierra Ancha, to Salt R. Used for livestock grazing and fruit and potato culture. Drained by Tonto Creek, which rises in Mogollon Rim and flows c.45 mi. S to Roosevelt Reservoir in Salt R.

Tontogany (tŏntŏ'gŭnē), village (pop. 368), Wood co., NW Ohio, 5 mi. WNW of Bowling Green.

Tonto National Monument (tŏn'tō) (1,120 acres; established 1907), in SE central Ariz., just S of Roosevelt Reservoir, 60 mi. E of Phoenix; includes 2 large, well-preserved masonry dwellings built (probably in 14th cent.) by Indians in caves of quartzite cliff. Inhabitants practiced irrigated farming in Salt R. valley and produced polychromatic pottery and cotton cloth.

Tonwarghar (tōn'vŭrgär) or **Morena** (mō'rānŭ), district, N Madhya Bharat, India; ⊙ Morena.

Tony, village (pop. 182), Rusk co., N Wis., 5 mi. ENE of Ladysmith; dairy products, cheese boxes.

Tonypandy, Wales: see RHONDDA.

Toodyay, town (pop. 610), SW Western Australia, 45 mi. NE of Perth and on Avon R.; orchards, vineyards.

Tooele (tōōĭ'lŭ), county (□ 6,911; pop. 14,636), NW Utah; ⊙ Tooele. Mining and grazing area bordering on Nev. Includes Stansbury Mts. and part of Wasatch Natl. Forest in E, part of Great Salt L. in NE, and much of Great Salt Lake Desert in W. Copper, lead, zinc; livestock. Formed 1850.

Tooele, city (pop. 7,269), ⊙ Tooele co., NW central Utah, 25 mi. SW of Salt Lake City, S of Great Salt L.; alt. 4,923 ft. Rail and trade center for mining, grazing, and agr. area (wheat, alfalfa, sugar beets). Smelts ore from mines (silver, lead, copper) in vicinity. Settled c.1850. Proving ground of U.S. Chemical Warfare Service. Tunnel (built 1937–42; more than 4 mi. long) extends E through Oquirrh Mts. to mines in Bingham Canyon.

Toole (tōōl), county (□ 1,965; pop. 6,867), N Mont.; ⊙ Shelby. Agr. region bordering on Alta.; drained S by Marias R. Grain, livestock; petroleum, natural gas. Formed 1914.

Toombs (tōōmz), county (□ 369; pop. 17,382), E central Ga.; ⊙ Lyons. Bounded S by Altamaha R., NE by Ohoopee R. Coastal plain agr. area (cotton, corn, peanuts, tobacco, cattle, hogs); mfg. at Vidalia and Lyons. Formed 1905.

Toomevara or **Toomyvara** (both: tōō"mĭvă'rŭ, tōō"mŭ–), Gaelic *Tuaim Ui Mheádhra,* town (pop. 266), N Co. Tipperary, Ireland, 7 mi. E of Nenagh; agr. market (dairying; potatoes, beets).

Toomsboro, town (pop. 711), Wilkinson co., central Ga., 32 mi. E of Macon; sawmilling.

Toone, town (pop. 231), Hardeman co., SW Tenn., 20 mi. S of Jackson, in timber, agr. area.

Toowoomba (tŭwōōm'bŭ), city (pop. 33,290), SE Queensland, Australia, 65 mi. W of Brisbane; commercial center of Darling Downs; summer resort; alt. 2,000 ft. Produces wool, wheat, dairy foods. Coal mines and Ravensbourne Natl. Park near by.

Topanfalva, Rumania: see CAMPENI.

Topanga (tōpăng'gŭ), resort village, Los Angeles co., S Calif., in Santa Monica Mts., 8 mi. NW of Santa Monica. Intermittent Topanga Creek flows S, through Topanga Canyon (followed by highway across mts.), to the Pacific at Topanga Beach.

To-p'a-t'e-la, Tibet: see DOBTRA.

Topawewa, Ceylon: see POLONNARUWA.

Topaz Lake, in W Nev. and E Calif., artificial body of water on West Walker R.; irrigation.

Topchikha (tŭpchē'khŭ), village (1939 pop. over 2,000), central Altai Territory, Russian SFSR, on Turksib RR and 45 mi. SW of Barnaul; metalworks.

Topdalselv, Norway: see TOVDAL RIVER.

Topeka (tŭpē'kŭ). **1** Village (pop. 72), Mason co., central Ill., 22 mi. SW of Pekin, in agr. area. **2** Town (pop. 557), Lagrange co., NE Ind., 24 mi. ESE of Elkhart, in agr. area. **3** City (pop. 78,791), ⊙ Kansas and Shawnee co., NE Kansas, on Kansas R. and c.55 mi. W of Kansas City; 39°3'N 95°40'W; alt. 886 ft. Third largest city in state; trade and industrial center for rich agr. area. There are large railroad repair shops; publishing, printing, and wholesale houses; and insurance firms. Chief industries are flour milling, food packing (meat, poultry, eggs), and dairying. Manufactures also include foundry products, tires, tents and awnings, clothing, medicine. Laid out 1854 on Oregon Trail by Free Staters from Lawrence (Kansas), and from New England; inc. 1857. Short-lived Free State constitution was signed here in 1855. City became state capital in 1861, when Kansas was admitted to Union. Important factor in growth was construction of Atchison, Topeka, and Santa Fe RR (promoted by C. K. Holliday; completed from Topeka to Atchison by 1872). Has state hosp. for insane, reform school, vocational school for Negroes (1895), several business colleges, and Washburn Municipal Univ. of Topeka (coeducational; 1865). Mus. and library of Kansas Historical Society, Mulvane Art Mus., Grace Church Cathedral (Protestant Episcopal), and state library are here. City contains a municipal airport, an attractive park system, and 2 bridges across Kansas R., one of them (completed 1938) being 4,400 ft. long. State capitol (1903) is modeled after the natl. capitol. Severe damage was done here by great flood of July, 1951.

Topia (tō'pyä), mining settlement (pop. 45), Durango, N Mexico, on W slopes of Sierra Madre Occidental, 55 mi. NE of Culiacán; alt. 5,577 ft.; silver, gold, copper mining.

Topilejo (tōpēlā'hō), town (pop. 2,129), Federal Dist., central Mexico, 13 mi. S of Mexico city; cereals, fruit, livestock.

Topinabee (tŏ'pŭnŭbē), resort village (pop. c.250), Cheboygan co., N Mich., 13 mi. SSW of Cheboygan, on SW shore of Mullett L.

Topki (tôp'kē), city (1940 pop. over 24,000), NW Kemerovo oblast, Russian SFSR, on branch of Trans-Siberian RR and 20 mi. WSW of Kemerovo (linked by railroad); truck produce, metalworks, railroad shops; handles coal, lumber, construction materials.

Topla, Bay of, Yugoslavia: see KOTOR, GULF OF.

Topla River (tôp'lyä), Slovak *Topl'a,* Hung. *Tapoly* (tŏ'poi), E Slovakia, Czechoslovakia, rises in E spur of the High Tatra c.20 mi. NW of Presov, flows E past Bardejov, and SSE to Ondava R. 5 mi. NE of Secovce; c.70 mi. long.

Toplet (tô'plĕts), Rum. *Topleţ,* village (pop. 1,981), Severin prov., SW Rumania, on railroad and 6 mi. N of Orsova; foundries produce agr. equipment, pig iron, drums, and tin plate.

Toplica River or **Toplitsa River** (both: tô'plĕtsä), S Serbia, Yugoslavia, rises in the Kapaonik, flows c.70 mi. E, past Kursumlija and Prokuplje, to Southern Morava R. 8 mi. SSW of Nis. Lower course followed by railroad.

Toplice (tô'plĕtsĕ), **Toplice pri Novem Mestu** (prē nô'vĕm mĕ'stō), or **Dolenjske Toplice** (dô'-lĕnyŭskĕ), Ger. *Töpliz* (tû'plĭts), village, S Slovenia, Yugoslavia, near Krka R., 6 mi. WSW of Novo Mesto; terminus of rail spur to Novo Mesto. Health resort with mineral waters. Founded in 16th cent. Until 1918, in Carniola.

Toplita or **Toplicza** (tô'plētzä), Rum. *Toplița*, Hung. *Marosheviz* (mŏ'rōsh-hā"vēz), village (pop. 9,095), Mures prov., central Rumania, in Transylvania, in W foothills of the Moldavian Carpathians, on Mures R., on railroad and 32 mi. NE of Targu-Mures; trading center and popular summer resort (alt. 2,133 ft.) with mineral springs and baths. Base for excursions into picturesque mts. near by. In Hungary, 1940–45.

Topo (tō'pō), fishing village, Angra do Heroísmo dist., central Azores, at E tip of São Jorge Isl., 30 mi. WSW of Angra do Heroísmo (on Terceira Isl.); 38°33'N 27°46'W.

Topo, Pico (pē'kōō), volcano (5,358 ft.) on Pico Isl., central Azores, overlooking town of Lajes do Pico; 38°26'N 28°14'W.

Topo Chico (tō'pō chē'kō), village (pop. 783), Nuevo León, N Mexico, in foothills of Sierra Madre Oriental, 4 mi. NW of Monterrey; thermal springs; bathing resort.

Topock (tō'pŏk), village (pop. c.100), Mohave co., W Ariz., on Havasu L. (forming part of Calif. line) and 40 mi. SW of Kingman. Topock Bridge (592 ft. long) crosses Colorado R. to Calif.; inspection station.

Topola (tôpô'lä). **1** Village, central Serbia, Yugoslavia, 40 mi. S of Belgrade, in the Sumadija. Has tower of former fortress and church with fine iconostasis. On near-by hill is church in Serbo-Byzantine style, built entirely of white marble and noted for fine mosaics decorating its interior; has tombs of Karageorge and kings Alexander I and Peter I. Former royal villa and royal vineyards (with model farm) in vicinity. Topola was center of Serbian insurrection of 1804 and a residence of Karageorge. **2** or **Backa Topola** or **Bachka Topola** (both: bäch'-kä), Serbo-Croatian *Bačka Topola*, Hung. *Topolya* (tô'pôyŏ), village (pop. 14,177), Vojvodina, N Serbia, Yugoslavia, on railroad and 20 mi. S of Subotica, in the Backa; mineral waters; flour milling. Winegrowing in vicinity.

Topolcany (tô'pôlchänĭ), Slov. *Topol'čany*, Hung. *Nagytapolcsány* (nŏ'dyŭtŏ'pôlchänyŭ), town (pop. 8,580), W Slovakia, Czechoslovakia, on Nitra R., on railroad, and 17 mi. N of Nitra; sugar refining, distilling, woodworking, leather-goods mfg.

Topolcianky (tô'pôltsyän-kĭ), Slovak *Topol'cianky*, Hung. *Kistapolcsány* (kĭsh'tŏ'pôlchänyŭ), village (pop. 2,096), SW Slovakia, Czechoslovakia, 16 mi. ENE of Nitra, in winegrowing area; rail terminus. Has 16th-cent. church. Its castle is a summer residence of Czechoslovak president.

Topolev Mys (tô'pŭlyĭf), village (1926 pop. 1,523), S East Kazakhstan oblast, Kazakh SSR, on SE L. Zaisan, 40 mi. NW of Zaisan; lake port.

Topoliane or **Topoliani**, Greece: see CHRYSOS.

Topolnitsa River (tôpôlnē'tsä), W central Bulgaria, rises in central Sredna Gora 4 mi. SW of Koprivshtitsa, flows 96 mi. S in an arc, past Koprivshtitsa, through Zlatitsa Basin, to Maritsa R. 2 mi. W of Pazardzhik. Separates central and Ikhtiman sections of Sredna Gora. Has gold-carrying sand.

Topolnoye Lake, Russian SFSR: see KULUNDA STEPPE.

Topolobampo (tōpōlōbäm'pō), town (pop. 598), Sinaloa, NW Mexico, port inlet of Gulf of California, 8 mi. S of Los Mochis; rail terminus in Río del Fuerte irrigation area producing corn, sugar cane, chick-peas, fruit, vegetables; fishing.

Topolog (tô'pôlôg), village (pop. 2,566), Constanta prov., SE Rumania, 16 mi. W of Babadag. Altan-Tepe copper-pyrite works are c.10 mi. ESE.

Topoloveni (tôpôlôvān'), village (pop. 1,129), Arges prov., S central Rumania, 32 mi. S of Campulung; extensive orchards and vineyards; wine production, trade in prunes.

Topolovgrad (tôpô'lôvgrät), city (pop. 6,591) Yambol dist., SE Bulgaria, on N slope of Sakar Mts. 28 mi. SSW of Yambol; agr. center in tobacco and vineyard area; sericulture, truck produce. Until 1934, Kavaklii.

Topolov Pass (tô'pô'lôf), S Bulgaria, in NE Rhodope Mts., 12 mi. SE of Asenovgrad, on road bet. Plovdiv and Arda R. valley.

Topolsica (tôpôl'shĭtsä), Slovenian *Topolšica*, Ger. *Topolschitz* (tô'pôlshĭts), village, N Slovenia, Yugoslavia, 2 mi. NNW of Sostanj; health resort. Until 1918, in Styria.

Topolya, Yugoslavia: see TOPOLA, Vojvodina, Serbia.

Topornino, Russian SFSR: see KUSHNARENKOVO.

Topozero (tôp'ô"zyĭrŭ), Finnish *Tuoppajärvi* (tōō'ôp-päyăr"vē), lake (□ c.350), N Karelo-Finnish SSR, 100 mi. NW of Belomorsk; 45 mi. long, 15 mi. wide, 185 ft. deep; drains NW through Kovda R. Kestenga on N shore.

Toppenish (tŏ'pŭnĭsh), city (pop. 5,265), Yakima co., S Wash., 18 mi. SSE of Yakima, in Yakima Indian Reservation; potatoes, hay, sugar beets, fruit; food-processing plants. Inc. 1907.

Topputturai, India: see VEDARANNIYAM, town.

Toprakkale (tôpräk'kälĕ"), village (pop. 584), Seyhan prov., S Turkey, 5 mi. W of Osmaniye; rail junction.

Topsail, village (pop. 672), SE N.F., on SE side of Conception Bay, NE Avalon Peninsula, 10 mi. WSW of St. John's; fishing port, seaside resort; site of hydroelectric plant.

Topsfield. 1 Village, Washington co., E Maine, 28 mi. NW of Calais, in hunting, fishing area. **2** Town (pop. 1,412), Essex co., NE Mass., 8 mi. NNW of Salem; chalk; sand and gravel deposits. Has 17th-cent. house. Settled c.1635, inc. 1648.

Topsham (tŏp'sŭm), town and parish (pop. 3,437), SE Devon, England, on Exe R. estuary and 4 mi. SE of Exeter; agr. market, yachting port. Important seaport until late 17th cent.

Topsham. 1 (tŏp'sŭm) Town (pop. 2,626), including Topsham village (pop. 1,569), Sagadahoc co., SW Maine, on the Androscoggin (water power) opposite Brunswick; paper milling, mining and grinding of feldspar. Settled c.1730, inc. 1764. Includes village of Pejepscot. **2** (tŏp'sŭm, tō'shŭm) Town (pop. 733), Orange co., E Vt., on Waits R. and 14 mi. ESE of Barre.

Topton, borough (pop. 1,572), Berks co., E central Pa., 16 mi. NE of Reading. Founded 1859, inc. 1875.

Topusko (tô'pōōskô), village, N Croatia, Yugoslavia, on Glina R. and 6 mi. WSW of Glina, near Bosnia border; health resort (known since Roman times) with warm mineral springs. Iron mine; blast furnace.

Toqsun, China: see TOKSUN.

Toquema Range (tŭkē'mŭ), central Nev., largely in Nye co.; extends N–S bet. Toiyabe Range (W) and Monitor Range (E), in part of Toiyabe Natl. Forest. Highest point is Mt. Jefferson (11,807 ft.), 54 mi. NNE of Tonopah. Bald Mtn. (9,275 ft.) is in S, Wildcat Peak (10,534 ft.) in N. Sometimes spelled Toquima.

Toquerville (tūkâr'vĭl), town (pop. 219), Washington co., SW Utah, 20 mi. NE of St. George; fruit. Zion Natl. Monument is E.

Toquima Range, Nev.: see Toquema Range.

Tor, Manchuria: see TAO RIVER.

Tor (tôr), **El Tor, Et Tor** (both: ĕt-tōr'), or **Al-Tur** (ĕt-tōōr'), town, NE Egypt, near S tip of Sinai Peninsula, on Gulf of Suez, 50 mi. NW of Ras Muhammad. Has quarantine station.

Tor, Jebel et, Palestine: see GERIZIM, MOUNT.

Tora (tō'rä), village, Eastern Prov., NE Belgian Congo, on left bank of Kibali R. and 32 mi. NNW of Watsa; gold-mining center; rice processing.

Torahime (tōrä'hēmä), town (pop. 6,733), Shiga prefecture, S Honshu, Japan, just N of Nagahama; rice.

Tora-Khem (tŭrä"-khyĕm'), village, NE Tuva Autonomous Oblast, Russian SFSR, on the Greater Yenisei and 100 mi. NE of Kyzyl; gold mining, fur trading.

Tor al Baha (tōr' äl bä'hū), village, Subeihi tribal area, Western Aden Protectorate, 55 mi. NW of Aden, on road to Yemen and near Yemen border; center of administration for E Subeihi area; radio station.

Toral de los Vados (tōräl' dhā lōs vä'dhōs), village (pop. 1,475), Leon prov., NW Spain, on Sil R. and 10 mi. W of Ponferrada; cement mfg.; lumbering, stock raising; cereals, wine, nuts.

Torano (tôrä'nô), village (pop. 1,678), Massa e Carrara prov., Tuscany, central Italy, just N of Carrara; firearms mfg.

Torata (tōrä'tä), town (pop. 437), Moquegua dept., S Peru, on W slopes of Cordillera Occidental, on affluent of Moquegua R. and 17 mi. ENE of Moquegua; alt. 7,218 ft. Grain, wine, fruit.

Toraya (tōrī'ä), town (pop. 876), Apurímac dept., S central Peru, in the Andes, 40 mi. SW of Abancay; grain, stock.

Torbali (tôrbälŭ'), Turkish *Torbalı*, village (pop. 4,851), Smyrna prov., W Turkey, on railroad and 21 mi. SSE of Smyrna; emery, iron, manganese; tobacco, wheat.

Torbat, for names in Iran beginning thus: see under TURBAT.

Torbay (tôr'bā), town (pop. 1,419), SE N.F., on NE coast of Avalon Peninsula, 7 mi. NNW of St. John's; 47°40'N 52°45'W; fishing port, with mink farms. In Second World War, Canadian air base was established here.

Tor Bay, inlet (5 mi. long, 10 mi. wide at entrance) of the Atlantic, E N.S., 12 mi. SE of Guysborough.

Tor Bay, inlet of the English Channel, S Devon, England, bet. the promontories Hope's Nose and Berry Head; 4 mi. wide, 4 mi. long; shelters Torquay (N), Paignton, and Brixham (S). Has good anchorage for ocean-going ships.

Torbeck (tôrbĕk'), agr. town (1950 census pop. 958), Sud dept., SW Haiti, on SW coast of Tiburon Peninsula, 5 mi. SW of Les Cayes; bananas, sugar cane.

Torbeyevo (tŭrbyā'ŭvŭ), town (1948 pop. over 2,000), SW Mordvinian Autonomous SSR, Russian SFSR, on railroad and 70 mi. W of Ruzayevka, in grain-growing area; flour milling, distilling.

Torbole (tôr'bôlĕ), village (pop. 863), Trento prov., Trentino–Alto Adige, N Italy, port at NE end of Lago di Garda, near mouth of Sarca R., 2 mi. SE of Riva. Resort; fish hatchery.

Torc, Lough, Ireland: see KILLARNEY, LAKES OF.

Torcello (tôrchĕl'lô), island in Lagoon of Venice, 6 mi. NE of Venice, N Italy. Once a flourishing town; has ruins of cathedral of Santa Maria Assunta (founded 641; rebuilt 864 and 1008) and 12th-cent. church of Santa Fosca.

Torchiarolo (tôrkyärô'lô), village (pop. 2,457), Brindisi prov., Apulia, S Italy, 12 mi. SSE of Brindisi.

Torchin (tôr'chĭn), Pol. *Torczyn* (tôr'chĭn), town (1931 pop. 3,210), S central Volyn oblast, Ukrainian SSR, 15 mi. W of Lutsk; flour milling.

Torch Keys, Fla.: see FLORIDA KEYS.

Torch Lake. 1 In Antrim co., NW Mich., c.17 mi. NE of Traverse City, separated from Grand Traverse Bay and Elk L. (W) by narrow neck of land; c.17 mi. long, 2 mi. wide. Resorts, parks are on shores; yacht racing. Joined by passage to Round L. (S). **2** In Houghton co., NW Upper Peninsula, Mich., on Keweenaw Peninsula c.5 mi. ENE of Houghton; c.6 mi. long, 1½ mi. wide. Lake Linden village is on N shore. Channel leads S from lake into KEWEENAW WATERWAY.

Torcola, island, Yugoslavia: see SCEDRO ISLAND.

Torczyn, Ukrainian SSR: see TORCHIN.

Torda, Rumania: see TURDA, town.

Tordal, India: see TERDAL.

Tordehumos (tôr-dhāōō'mōs), town (pop. 1,381), Valladolid prov., N central Spain, 8 mi. SW of Medina de Ríoseco; horse breeding; cereals, vegetables, wine.

Tordera (tôr-dhā'rä), town (pop. 1,613), Barcelona prov., NE Spain, 12 mi. NE of Arenys de Mar; cork processing; mfg. of knit goods, hats, cotton cloth; flour- and sawmilling; sparkling wine.

Tordesillas (tôr-dhāsē'lyäs), town (pop. 3,700), Valladolid prov., N central Spain, in Leon, on Duero (Douro) R. and 18 mi. SW of Valladolid; mfg. of brandy, chocolate, flour products; cereals, wine, livestock. Has monastery of Santa Clara, with Moorish patios and baths; medieval castle, the residence of Queen Joanna the Mad; and church of San Antolín, with notable tombs. Treaty signed here (1494) bet. Spain and Portugal established new demarcation line for colonial expansion. Irrigation canal near by.

Tordesilos (–sē'lōs), village (pop. 611), Guadalajara prov., central Spain, near Teruel prov. border, 19 mi. SE of Molina; cereals, vegetables, potatoes, livestock; flour milling.

Tordillo, Argentina: see GENERAL CONESA.

Tordino River (tôrdē'nô), S central Italy, rises in the Apennines in Monti della Laga, 6 mi. E of Amatrice; flows 35 mi. E, past Teramo, to the Adriatic near Giulianova.

Tore (tû'rŭ), Swedish *Töre*, village (pop. 1,484) Norrbotten co., NE Sweden, on small inlet of Gul. of Bothnia, 25 mi. NE of Lulea; sawmilling, wallboard mfg. Includes Torefors (tû"rŭfôrs', –fōsh'), Swedish *Törefors*, village.

Toreboda (tû"rŭbōō'dä), Swedish *Töreboda*, town (pop. 3,341), Skaraborg co., S central Sweden, on Gota Canal and 12 mi. E of Mariestad; metalworking.

Torefors, Sweden: see TORE.

Torei or **Torey** (tŭryā'), village (1948 pop. over 500), S Buryat-Mongol Autonomous SSR, Russian SFSR, on Dzhida R. and 300 mi. SW of Ulan-Ude; grain, livestock.

Torekov (tōō'rŭkōōv"), fishing village (pop. 419), Kristianstad co., SW Sweden, on the Kattegat, 15 mi. NW of Angelholm; seaside resort.

Torelló or **San Felíu de Torelló** (sän fālē'ōō dhā tōrĕlyō'), town (pop. 4,232), Barcelona prov., NE Spain, on Ter R. and 8 mi. N of Vich; wood turning, cotton spinning, metal stamping. Cereals, vegetables, livestock, lumber in area.

Toreno (tōrā'nō), town (pop. 1,157), Leon prov., NW Spain, on Sil R. and 12 mi. NNE of Ponferrada; flour mills; ships chestnuts, beans, fruit. Coal mines and iron deposits near by.

Torey, Russian SFSR: see TOREI.

Torgau (tôr'gou), town (pop. 18,455), in former Prussian Saxony prov., central Germany, after 1945 in Saxony-Anhalt, port on the Elbe and 30 mi. NE of Leipzig; mfg. of chemicals, glass, agr. machinery, pottery, bricks; metalworking, vegetable-oil pressing. Has late-Gothic church with grave of Luther's wife, Katharina von Bora; and 16th-cent. Hartenfels castle, a former residence of electors of Saxony. First mentioned 973; chartered 1288. Torgau League of Protestant princes formed 1526; its constitution (*Torgau Articles*) was written (1530) by Luther and published here. In Thirty Years War, scene (1631) of important council of war, under Gustavus Adolphus, which decided future Protestant action and policy. Near by Frederick the Great defeated (Nov., 1760) Austrians under Daun. Captured by French in 1811; passed to Prussia in 1815. At close of Second World War, U.S. and Soviet troops made 1st contact on the Elbe near by, on April 27, 1945.

Torgelow (tôr'gŭlō), town (pop. 10,066), in former Prussian Pomerania prov., N Germany, after 1945 in Mecklenburg, on Uecker R. and 25 mi. NW of Stettin; metalworking, machinery and chemical mfg.; agr. market (grain, potatoes, sugar beets, stock).

Torget (tôr'gû), island (□ 7; pop. 442) in the North Sea, Nordland co., N central Norway, just offshore, 40 mi. SW of Mosjoen; rises to 853 ft. in Torghatten mtn., which is pierced by a natural tunnel formed by ocean erosion. Sometimes called Torgoy, Nor. *Torgøy*.

Torghondi or **Torghundi** (tōrgōn'dē), frontier post, Herat prov., NW Afghanistan, on USSR border, opposite Kushka, 60 mi. N of Herat. Also called Qara Tepe or Kara Tepe.

Torgiano (tôrjä'nô), village (pop. 680), Perugia prov., Umbria, central Italy, near the Tiber, 6 mi. SSE of Perugia; mfg. of agr. tools.

Torgovy, Russian SFSR: see SALSK.

Torgoy, Norway: see TORGET.

Torhout (tôr'hout), town (pop. 12,237), West Flanders prov., W Belgium, 12 mi. SSW of Bruges; agr. and horse market. Formerly spelled Thourout.

Tori or **Tori-Bossito** (tō'rē-bōsē'tō), village, S Dahomey, Fr. West Africa, 32 mi. W of Porto-Novo; palm kernels, palm oil, copra, corn.

Toride (tōrē'dā), town (pop. 10,515), Ibaraki prefecture, central Honshu, Japan, port on Tone R. and 20 mi. NNW of Chiba, in agr. area; rail junction; cotton textiles, vinegar.

Tori Fatehpur (tō'rē fŭ'tāpŏŏr), village, Jhansi dist., S Uttar Pradesh, India, 35 mi. E of Jhansi. Was ⊙ former petty state of Tori Fatehpur (□ 27; pop. 6,269) of Central India agency; in 1948, state merged with Vindhya Pradesh; in 1950, inc. into Jhansi dist. of Uttar Pradesh.

Torigny-sur-Vire (tōrēnyē'-sür-vēr'), village (pop. 1,628), Manche dept., NW France, 8 mi. SE of Saint-Lô; dairying, cattle raising. Has a 16th-cent. castle (now town hall). Heavily damaged in Second World War.

Toriimatsu, Japan: see KASUGAI.

Torija (tōrē'hä), town (pop. 698), Guadalajara prov., central Spain, 10 mi. NE of Guadalajara; wheat, barley, vetch, chick-peas, olives, sheep. Has remains of castle of Knights Templars.

Toriñana, Cape (tōrēnyä'nä), or **Cape Touriñán** (tōrēnyän'), on Atlantic coast of Galicia, in La Coruña prov., NW Spain, 50 mi. WSW of La Coruña; 43°3'N 9°18'W. Westernmost point of Spain, though Cape Finisterre (S), generally considered the westernmost, is at about same longitude.

Torino (tôrē'nô), province (□ 2,636; pop. 1,312,324), Piedmont, NW Italy; ⊙ Turin. Drained by the Po and its many affluents, including Dora Riparia, Orco, and Dora Baltea rivers. Consists of Po plain (E) encircled by Cottian and Graian Alps (W), which rise to over 9,000 ft. Agr. (cereals, fodder, hemp, vegetables, fruit) chiefly in well-irrigated Po plain. Livestock raising (cattle, sheep) widespread. Mines at Perosa Argentina (graphite, talc), Usseglio (cobalt, nickle, asbestos), and Traversella (copper, iron). Hydroelectric plants, chiefly in Dora Riparia R. valley. Mfg. at Turin, Pinerolo, Ivrea, Chieri. Famous resorts include Claviere, Sestriere, Ceresole Reale, and Bardonecchia. Has important rail and highway routes with France via Val di Susa. In 1927, Aosta prov. was detached; its S portion (□ 578) reverted to Torino prov. in 1945, when Aosta prov. became autonomous region of Val d'Aosta. Torino prov. lost territory (□ 58) to France (1947) in Mont Cenis, Montgenèvre, Mont Thabor, and Mont Chaberton regions.

Torino, city, Italy: see TURIN.

Torino (tŭrē'nō), village (pop. 9), Will co., NE Ill.

Tori-shima (tōrē'-shĭmä), southernmost island (□ 1.7) of isl. group Izu-shichito, Greater Tokyo, Japan, in Philippine Sea, 150 mi. S of Hachijo-jima; 1.5 mi. in diameter. Rises to 1,516 ft. at Mt. Asahi (active volcano). Eruption in 1939 caused inhabitants to leave. Formerly sometimes called Ponafidin, St. Peters, Fonafidin.

Torit (tōrēt'), town (pop. 3,500), Equatoria prov., S Anglo-Egyptian Sudan, N of Imatong Mts., on road and 75 mi. SE of Juba. R.C. mission with technical school.

Toritto (tôrēt'tô), town (pop. 6,900), Bari prov., Apulia, S Italy, 13 mi. SW of Bari; wine, olive oil.

To River (tō), Chinese *To Kiang* or *T'o Chiang* (both: tŭ' jyäng'), Szechwan prov., China, rises N of Chengtu in several headstreams (some connected with Chengtu plain canals), flows c.300 mi. SSE, past Kienyang (head of navigation), Tzechung, and Fushun, to Yangtze R. at Luhsien. Sometimes called Chung Kiang or Lu Ho.

Toriya (tōrē'yä), town (pop. 6,437), Ishikawa prefecture, central Honshu, Japan, just SW of Nanao, in rice-growing area; rayon and silk textiles.

Torja, Rumania: see TURIA.

Torkham (tōr'khŭm), village, Eastern Prov., E Afghanistan, 40 mi. ESE of Jalalabad, at W end of Khyber Pass; frontier post on Pakistan line opposite Landi Khana (rail terminus).

Torkman, Iran: see TURKMAN.

Torkovichi (tôr'kŭvēchē), town (1948 pop. over 2,000), S Leningrad oblast, Russian SFSR, on Oredezh R. and 20 mi. ENE of Luga; glassworking center.

Tormentine, Cape (tôr'mŭntĭn), most easterly point of N.B., on Northumberland Strait opposite Prince Edward Isl., 50 mi. E of Moncton; 46°6'N 63°46'W. Settlement of Cape Tormentine (pop. estimate c.125) is lobster-fishing port and rail terminal. Railroad and automobile ferry to Port Borden, P.E.I.

Tormes River (tôr'mĕs), in Ávila and Salamanca provs., W Spain, rises on N slopes of the Sierra de Gredos 30 mi. SW of Ávila, flows 176 mi. generally NW, past Salamanca, to the Duero (Douro) near Fermoselle at Port. frontier. For last 20 mi. of its course, it forms border bet. Salamanca and Zamora provs. Hydroelectric power plant 12 mi. SSW of Alba de Tormes and 2 dams below Salamanca.

Tormosin (tŭrmŭsēn'), village (1948 pop. over 2,000), SW Stalingrad oblast, Russian SFSR, 23 mi. SW of Nizhne-Chirskaya; wheat, mustard, cotton.

Torn, Netherlands: see THORN.

Torna, Czechoslovakia: see TURNA.

Tornacuxtla (tôrnäkōō'slä), town (pop. 1,438), Hidalgo, central Mexico, 9 mi. WNW of Pachuca; cereals, maguey, stock.

Tornado Mountain (10,169 ft.), on Alta.-B.C. border, in Rocky Mts., 40 mi. NE of Fernie.

Tornala, Czechoslovakia: see SAFARIKOVO.

Tornavacas (tôrnävä'käs), town (pop. 1,953), Cáceres prov., W Spain, 10 mi. SSE of Béjar; stock raising; chestnuts, wine.

Tornea, Finland: see TORNIO.

Torne Lake, Swedish *Torneträsk* (tôr'nŭtrĕsk") (□ 124), Lapland, N Sweden, near Norwegian border, 30 mi. NW of Kiruna; 40 mi. long (WNW-ESE), 1-6 mi. wide; max. depth 538 ft. Drained ESE by Torne R. Several Lapp camps on shore; also Abisko, tourist resort (SW).

Torne River, Swedish *Torne älv* (tôr"nŭ ĕlv'), Finnish *Torniojoki* (tôr'nēōyō"kē), in Lapland, N Sweden and N Finland, issues from L. Torne, flows SE past Pajala to Swedish-Finnish border, thence flows S along border past Overtornea and Tornio to Gulf of Bothnia at Haparanda; 250 mi. long. Important logging route. Chief tributary is Muonio R. (mōō'ônyō), Swedish *Muonio älv*, Finnish *Muoniojoki*, which rises in Lapland near meeting point of Norwegian, Swedish, and Finnish borders, flows 180 mi. generally SSE, forming border bet. Sweden and Finland, to Torne R. 4 mi. SE of Pajala. The Muonio-Torne is 354 mi. long.

Tornesch (tôrn'ĕsh), village (pop. 5,570), in Schleswig-Holstein, NW Germany, 5 mi. SE of Elmshorn; chemicals, leather goods, toys; woodworking.

Tor Ness (tôr"nĕs'), SW tip of Hoy isl., Orkneys, Scotland; lighthouse (58°47 N 3°17'W); considered NW boundary of Pentland Firth.

Torngat Mountains, N Labrador, northernmost range of the Laurentian Plateau, extending 120 mi. N-S (58°30'-60°20'N) bet. the Atlantic and Que. border; rises to 5,500 ft. on Cirque Mtn.

Tornio (tōr'nēō), Swedish *Torneå* (tōr'nŭō"), city (pop. 3,409), Lapi co., NW Finland, on small isl. in Tornio or Torne R. (Swedish border; bridge) near its mouth on Gulf of Bothnia, opposite Haparanda (Sweden), 15 mi. NW of Kemi; rail junction; leather mfg., brewing, salmon fishing; lumber trade. Has 17th-cent. church, mus. Inc. 1621; ceded (1809) by Sweden. In First and Second World wars, important transit point for refugees, wounded, and prisoners of war.

Torniojoki, Finland and Sweden: see TORNE RIVER.

Torno, El (ĕl tôr'nō), village (pop. 1,701), Cáceres prov., W Spain, 11 mi. NE of Plasencia; olive-oil processing; stock raising; wine, potatoes, fruit.

Tornova, Rumania: see TARNOVA.

Tornquist, town (pop. 2,745), ⊙ Tornquist dist. (□ 1,603; pop. 9,146), SW Buenos Aires prov., Argentina, on Sauce Chico R. and 45 mi. N of Bahía Blanca, in agr. zone (grain, sheep, cattle).

Tornyospalca (tôr'nyôsh-pältsŏ), Hung. *Tornyospálca*, town (pop. 3,244), Szabolcs co., NE Hungary, 30 mi. NE of Nyiregyhaza; potatoes, beans, tobacco; cattle, hogs.

Toro or **El Toro** (ĕl tō'rō), village (1930 pop. 5), Coquimbo prov., N central Chile, in the Andes, 75 mi. E of La Serena; thermal springs containing arsenic.

Toro, town (pop. 3,102), Valle del Cauca dept., W Colombia, in Cauca valley, 15 mi. SW of Cartago; agr. center (coffee, tobacco, sugar cane, fruit, cereals, stock).

Toro, rapids, Nicaragua: see SAN JUAN RIVER.

Toro, town, Bauchi prov., Northern Provinces, E central Nigeria, on Bauchi Plateau, 15 mi. NE of Jos; tin mining; dairying. Native teachers training school.

Toro, city (pop. 7,881), Zamora prov., NW Spain, in Leon, on Duero (Douro) R. and 19 mi. E of Zamora; agr. trade center (wine, fruit, cereals, vegetables). Food processing, brandy distilling, flour- and sawmilling, tanning, cotton-cloth mfg. Has 12th-cent. Romanesque church, 18th-cent. town hall, fine clock tower, and bridge spanning the Duero. Here in 1476 Ferdinand and Isabella defeated Charles V of Portugal, who was supporting the partisans of Juana la Beltraneja.

Toro, district, Uganda: see FORT PORTAL.

Toro, Russian SFSR: see SHAKHTERSK.

Toro, El (ĕl), highest hill (1,107 ft.) of Minorca, Balearic Isls., 10 mi. NW of Mahón.

Toro, El, Venezuela: see EL TORO.

Toro, Lake, Argentina: see POZUELOS, LAKE.

Toro, Lake (tô'rō) (18 mi. long, 15 mi. wide), S Que., in the Laurentians, 90 mi. N of Montreal; alt. 1,178 ft. Drains into St. Maurice R.

Toro, Lake (tō'rō), or **Lake Maravilla** (märävē'yä), Magallanes prov., S Chile, 30 mi. NNW of Puerto Natales, bounded by snow-capped Patagonian peaks; 22 mi. long.

Toro Amarillo (tō'rō ämärē'yō), village, Limón prov., Costa Rica, 1.5 mi. W of Guápiles; railhead on line from Limón.

Toro Gorge, Japan: see KUMANO RIVER.

Törökbalint (tû'rûgbälĭnt), Hung. *Törökbálint*, town (pop. 5,176), Pest-Pilis-Solt-Kiskun co., N central Hungary, in Buda Mts., 9 mi. SW of Budapest; summer resort; grapes, apples, pears.

Törökbecse, Yugoslavia: see VOLOSINOVO.

Törökkanizsa, Yugoslavia: see NOVI KNEZEVAC.

Törökszentmiklos (tû'rûksĕntmĭ"klôsh), Hung. *Törökszentmiklós*, town (pop. 30,145), Jasz-Nagykun-Szolnok co., E central Hungary, 10 mi. E of Szolnok; machine mfg., flour mills; corn, wheat, horses, sheep.

Toroku, Formosa: see TOWLIU.

Toronaic Gulf (tōrōnā'ĭk) or **Gulf of Kassandra** (kŭsăn'drŭ), anc. *Toronaicus Sinus*, arm of Aegean Sea, bet. Kassandra and Sithonia prongs of Chalcidice peninsula, Greek Macedonia; over 30 mi. long, up to 15 mi. wide. Named for anc. Torone, on SE shore.

Toro Negro River (tō'rō nā'grō), central Puerto Rico, rises in the Cordillera Central NW of Villalba, flows c.25 mi. N to the Manatí. There are 2 hydroelectric plants (completed in 1929 and 1937) along its upper course.

Torontalgyülvesz, Rumania: see GIULVAZ.

Torontalvasarhely, Yugoslavia: see DEBELJACA.

Toronto (tŭrŏn'tō), city (pop. 667,457), ⊙ Ontario prov. and York co., S Ont., on N shore of L. Ontario, at mouth of Humber R., 200 mi. NE of Detroit; 43°40'N 79°23'W. Second-largest city of Canada; commercial, financial, and industrial center. It is lake port, with a good harbor and extensive dock installations. Business center of Ont. mining industry, with mining and stock exchanges. Industrial establishments include railroad shops, automobile and farm-machinery plants, and other metalworks; meat packing, printing and publishing, shipbuilding, processing of foodstuffs. Average temp. range is from 10°F. (Jan.) to 70°F. (July); mean annual rainfall is 26.7 inches, snowfall 59.2 inches. City is laid out on gentle slope at foot of an escarpment. It has numerous tall modern bldgs. Toronto Univ., founded (1827) as King's Col., has several affiliated cols. and professional schools; attached are an observatory, the Connaught Laboratories, Royal Ontario Mus., Toronto General Hosp., Conservatory of Music, and School of Architecture. Among noted Toronto bldgs. are University Col.; Osgoode Hall; the Bank of Commerce; Royal York Hotel; and Casa Loma, on high ground above city, formerly private mansion, now public property. Seat of Anglican and R.C. archbishops, city has St. James's (Anglican) and St. Michael's (R.C.) cathedrals, and several hundred churches. There are numerous parks, including Riverdale and High parks, 3 zoological gardens, bathing beaches, amusement and exhibition grounds; since 1912 Toronto has been scene of annual Canadian National Exhibition. First mentioned on 1656 map, Toronto early became fur-trade center. In late 17th cent. a Sulpician settlement was established here, and in 1749 a fort was built by the French. It was destroyed (1759) by its garrison and site was occupied by the British. Settlement by United Empire Loyalists began 1793 under Governor Simcoe; town was named York, and became ⊙ Upper Canada (1796). Legislature 1st met here 1797. In War of 1812 it was twice captured by the Americans, and govt. bldgs. were destroyed. Inc. as city 1834, its name was again changed to Toronto. It became a center of 1837 separatist rebellion. Act of Union (1840) removed ⊙ to Kingston; Toronto again became ⊙ Upper Canada in 1849 and of Ontario in 1867. City's chief suburbs are New Toronto, Weston, Mimico, Danforth, Islington, and Downsview. Municipal airport is at Malton; there is a seaplane base on L. Ontario. Hydroelectric power is supplied by Niagara Falls.

Toronto. 1 Town (pop. 165), Clinton co., E Iowa, on Wapsipinicon R. and 29 mi. NNW of Davenport. **2** City (pop. 600), Woodson co., SE Kansas, on Verdigris R. and 28 mi. WSW of Iola, in livestock, grain, and oil area. Near by is the site of Toronto Reservoir, for flood control and water conservation on the Verdigris. **3** City (pop. 7,253), Jefferson co., E Ohio, 7 mi. N of Steubenville and on Ohio R.; steel products, clay products, glass, paper, machinery, dairy products. Laid out 1818. **4** Town (pop. 322), Deuel co., E S.Dak., 13 mi. S of Clear Lake.

Toronto, Lake (tōrōn'tō) (□ 95; alt. 4,320 ft.), Chihuahua, N Mexico, c.20 mi. SW of Camargo, on Conchos R., which enters W and leaves E; 23 mi. long. Hydroelectric plants near by.

Toronto Island (tŭrŏn'tō), islet, S Ont., in L. Ontario, just S of Toronto, within narrow spit of land that forms Toronto harbor.

Toronto Junction, former city, S Ont., merged 1909 with Toronto.

Toropalca (tōrōpäl'kä), town (pop. c.4,300), Potosí dept., S Bolivia, on headstream of Tumusla R. and 32 mi. N of Cotagaita, in agr. area; corn, potatoes are grown.

Toro Peak, Calif.: see SANTA ROSA MOUNTAINS.

Toropets (tŭrŭpyĕts'), city (1926 pop. 10,733), E central Velikiye Luki oblast, Russian SFSR, 40 mi. ENE of Velikiye Luki; distilling center; food processing. Teachers col. dates from 1167; former ⊙ principality. Passed (14th cent.) to Lithuania and (late-15th cent.) to Muscovy.

Toro Point, naval radio direction finder station, Cristobal dist., N Panama Canal Zone, at NW gate of Limon Bay of the Caribbean adjoining Fort Sherman (S), 3 mi. WNW of Colón. Lighthouse.

Toro River (tō'rō), Salta prov., Argentina, flows S 100 mi. to join Guachipas R. just E of Coronel Moldes, forming Pasaje or Juramento R., the upper part of the Río Salado.

Tororo (tōrō'rō), town, Eastern Prov., SE Uganda, 25 mi. S of Mbale; alt. 3,862 ft. Rail junction (branch line to Soroti). Has large cement plant (built 1949). Trade in cotton, corn, millet, sweet potatoes, bananas. Limestone quarries just S. Apatite mined at Busumbu (N).

Toros (tôrôs'), village (pop. 4,007), Pleven dist., N Bulgaria, on Vit R. and 9 mi. SE of Lukovit; flour milling; livestock, truck.

Toros Daglari (tôrôs' dälärŭ') or **Toros Mountains,** Turkish *Toros Dağları*, Turkish name for the TAURUS MOUNTAINS which extend along Mediterranean S coast of Asia Minor. In its E section, in one of its subranges called Bolkar Mts., is the **Toros Dagi** (tôrôs' däŭ), Turkish *Toros Dağı*, a group rising to 11,762 ft. in Medetsiz Dag or Mededsiz Dag.

Torotoro (tōrōtō'rō), town (pop. c.2,800), Potosí dept., W central Bolivia, near Caine R., 17 mi. ENE of San Pedro; potatoes, corn, *oca*. Sometimes Toro Toro.

Torpenhow and Whitrigg (trŭpĕ'nŭ, tôrpĕ'nō), parish (pop. 292), W Cumberland, England. Includes dairying village of Torpenhow, 6 mi. SSW of Wigton, with church dating from Norman times; and granite quarrying village of Whitrigg, 7 mi. SSW of Wigton.

Torphichen (tôrfĭ'kŭn), agr. village and parish (pop. 4,175), central West Lothian, Scotland, 2 mi. N of Bathgate. Has remains of 12th-cent. preceptory church and hosp. of Knights Templars.

Torphins, Scotland: see KINCARDINE O'NEIL.

Torpoint, urban district (1931 pop. 3,975; 1951 census 5,852), SE Cornwall, England, on Tamar R. estuary (here called Hamoaze), opposite Devonport, and 3 mi. W of Plymouth; agr. market in dairying area; oil-storage installations.

Torpsbruk (tôrps'brük"), village (pop. 232), Kronoberg co., S Sweden, on Morrum R. and 13 mi. NW of Vaxjo; lumbering, sawmilling.

Torquay (tôr'kwā), village (pop. 287), SE Sask., 23 mi. W of Estevan; mixed farming.

Torquay (tôr'kē'), municipal borough (1931 pop. 46,165; 1951 census 53,216), S Devon, England, bet. Tor Bay and Babbacombe Bay of the Channel, 19 mi. S of Exeter; important seaside resort and fishing and yachting port, with mfg. of pottery, terra cotta, pharmaceuticals; metalworking, marble polishing. Known for its mild climate, charm, and historical interest. Has remains of Tor Abbey (founded 1196) and of 12th-cent. St. Michael's Chapel (near by). The "Spanish barn" was reputed refuge of survivors of the Armada. Has mus. of natural history and is seat of South Devon Technical Col. Near by is Kent's Cavern, where prehistoric remains have been found. Municipal borough includes resort towns of Babbacombe (NE; pop. 5,280) and Cockington (W; pop. 4,770).

Torquay, Tasmania: see DEVONPORT.

Torquemada (tôrkämä'dhä), town (pop. 2,587), Palencia prov., N central Spain, on Pisuerga R. and 12 mi. ENE of Palencia; tanning and flour milling; livestock, cereals, wine, truck produce. Gypsum quarries near by. Tomás de Torquemada's family took its name and title from the town.

Torralba (tôräl'vä), town (pop. 939), Cuenca prov., E central Spain, in Serranía de Cuenca, 18 mi. NNW of Cuenca; olives, cereals, saffron, cherries, livestock; flour milling.

Torralba de Calatrava (dhā käläträ'vä), town (pop. 5,168), Ciudad Real prov., S central Spain, 9 mi. E of Ciudad Real; processing and agr. center (olives, grapes, barley, potatoes, livestock). Olive-oil extracting, alcohol distilling, sawmilling, vegetable canning; mfg. of soft drinks, sandals, plaited goods. Limekilns.

Torralba de Oropesa (ōrōpä'sä), town (pop. 804), Toledo prov., central Spain, 17 mi. W of Talavera de la Reina; olives, cereals, grapes.

Torrance, village in Campsie parish, S Stirling, Scotland, 3 mi. W of Kirkintilloch; coal mining.

Torrance (tŏ'rŭns), county (□ 3,340; pop. 8,012), central N.Mex.; ⊙ Estancia. Agr. (grain, beans) and livestock area, watered by Laguna del Perro. Parts of Cibola and Lincoln natl. forests in W and S, respectively; Manzano Range in W. Formed 1903.

Torrance, industrial and residential city (pop. 22,241), Los Angeles co., S Calif., c.15 mi. S of downtown Los Angeles, near Los Angeles Harbor; steel mill, oil wells and refineries, railroad shops; mfg. of oil-field machinery, brick, tile, plumbing equipment, building materials, food products. Flower growing (greenhouses). Established 1911 as planned city; inc. 1921.

Torrão (tôrã'ō), town (pop. 3,449), Setúbal dist., S central Portugal, 40 mi. SE of Setúbal; agr. trade (rice, grain, sheep); cork shipping.

Torre Alháquime (tô'rā älä'kēmā), town (pop. 957), Cádiz prov., SW Spain, on affluent of the Guadalete and 12 mi. NNW of Ronda; olive-oil pressing, flour milling; gypsum quarrying.

Torre Annunziata (tôr'rĕ än-nōōntsyä'tä), city (pop. 38,606), Napoli prov., Campania, S Italy, port on Bay of Naples, at S foot of Vesuvius, 12 mi. SE of Naples. Macaroni and firearms mfg. center; iron- and steelworks (machinery), packing box factories, cotton, hemp, and lumber mills. Exports macaroni, wine, pozzuolana. Destroyed by eruption of Vesuvius in 1631.

Torrebelvicino (tôr"rĕbĕlvēchē'nō), village (pop. 1,549), Vicenza prov., Veneto, N Italy, 2 mi. W of Schio, in foothills of Monti Lessini; woolen mills. Zinc mine near by.

Torreblanca (tôräbläng'kä), town (pop. 3,147), Castellón de la Plana prov., E Spain, 20 mi. NE of Castellón de la Plana; olive-oil processing; fruit shipping (muscat grapes, oranges, almonds); wine, cereals.

Torreblascopedro (tô"räväskōpā'dhrō), town (pop. 2,667), Jaén prov., S Spain, 6 mi. S of Linares; olive-oil processing; cereals, livestock.

Torrecampo (tôrākäm'pō), town (pop. 3,994), Córdoba prov., S Spain, 12 mi. NE of Pozoblanco; agr. center (olive oil, cereals, sheep, hogs).

Torre-Cardela (tô'rā-kär-dhā'lä), town (pop. 2,009), Granada prov., S Spain, 18 mi. NW of Guadix; cereals, livestock.

Torrecilla, peak, Spain: see TOLOX.

Torrecilla de la Orden (tôrā-thē'lyä dhā lä ôr'dhĕn), town (pop. 1,361), Valladolid prov., N central Spain, 18 mi. WSW of Medina del Campo; livestock market; cereals, vegetables, wine.

Torrecilla del Pinar (dhĕl pēnär'), town (pop. 909), Segovia prov., central Spain, 29 mi. N of Segovia; grain- and winegrowing.

Torrecilla en Cameros (ĕn kämä'rōs), town (pop. 1,487), Logroño prov., N Spain, 17 mi. SW of Logroño; furniture mfg.; vegetables, fruit, livestock; lumber. Mineral springs near by.

Torrecillas de la Tiesa (-lyäs dhā lä tyā'sä), town (pop. 2,317), Cáceres prov., W Spain, 11 mi. NE of Trujillo; cereals, livestock.

Torre das Vargens (tō'rĭ däsh vär'zhĕnsh), village (pop. 470), Portalegre dist., central Portugal, 24 mi. W of Portalegre; rail junction.

Torre de Don Miguel (tô'rā dhā dhōn mēgĕl'), town (pop. 1,594), Cáceres prov., W Spain, 30 mi. NW of Plasencia; olive-oil processing; fruit, livestock.

Torre de Esteban Hambran, La (lä tō'rā dhā ĕstā'vän äm'brän), town (pop. 1,830), Toledo prov., central Spain, 33 mi. SW of Madrid; grapes, cereals, olives, fruit, livestock. Olive-oil pressing, liquor and alcohol distilling, sawmilling.

Torre de Juan Abad (hwän' ävädh'), town (pop. 3,906), Ciudad Real prov., S central Spain, in New Castile, 21 mi. SE of Valdepeñas; cereals, grapes, olives, livestock. Olive-oil extracting, alcohol distilling, tile mfg.

Torre del Campo (dhĕl käm'pō), town (pop. 9,457), Jaén prov., S Spain, 6 mi. W of Jaén; olive-oil production. Mfg. of bonnets, hose, soap, pork sausage; brandy and liqueur distilling. Horse breeding. Cereals. Gypsum quarries near by. Has anc. castle.

Torre del Español (ĕspänyōl'), village (pop. 1,124), Tarragona prov., NE Spain, 14 mi. NE of Gandesa; olive-oil processing; wine, almonds, fruit.

Torre del Greco (tôr'rĕ dĕl grā'kō), city (pop. 37,052), Napoli prov., Campania, S Italy, port on Bay of Naples, at SW foot of Vesuvius, 7 mi. SE of Naples; bathing resort. Noted for its coral-working industry, dating from 16th cent.; macaroni mfg., lava quarrying, fishing. Repeatedly damaged by earthquakes and eruptions; built on lava stream of 1631 which destroyed much of the older town.

Torre del Mar (tô'rā dhĕl mär'), town (pop. 3,832), Málaga prov., S Spain, minor Mediterranean port serving Vélez-Málaga (2½ mi. N), on railroad and 17 mi. E of Málaga; fishing; sugar milling; mfg. of salted fish, liquor, soap. Bathing beaches.

Torredembarra (tôrā-dhĕmbä'rä), town (pop. 1,740), Tarragona prov., NE Spain, fishing port on the Mediterranean, and 8 mi. ENE of Tarragona; mfg. of electric cables, cotton and silk ribbons; trades in olive oil, wine, hemp, hazelnuts. On nearby hill is Roman triumphal arch (2d cent. A.D.).

Torre de Miguel Sesmero (tô'rā dhā mēgĕl' sāzmā'rō), town (pop. 2,197), Badajoz prov., W Spain, 20 mi. SE of Badajoz; cereals, olives, grapes; olive-oil pressing; stock raising.

Tôrre de Moncorvo (tō'rĭ dĭ mōng-kôr'vōō), town (pop. 2,544), Bragança dist., N Portugal, 45 mi. SSW of Bragança, near influx of Sabôr R. into the Douro; winegrowing; grain, olives, potatoes. Has ruined castle.

Torre de' Passeri (tôr'rĕ dĕpäs'sĕrē), town (pop. 4,091), Pescara prov., Abruzzi e Molise, S central Italy, near Pescara R., 7 mi. NE of Popoli; mfg. of agr. tools.

Torre de Santa María (tô'rā dhā sän'tä märē'ä), village (pop. 1,428), Cáceres prov., W Spain, 21 mi. SE of Cáceres; olive oil, wine, stock.

Torredonjimeno (tôrā-dhōn-hēmā'nō), city (pop. 14,274), Juén prov., S Spain, on fertile plain, 10 mi. W of Jaén; olive-oil production center. Homespun-cloth and soap mfg., brandy distilling; bell foundry. Ships aniseed. Cereals, wine, livestock in area. Limestone quarries.

Torrefarrera (tô"räfärä'rä), village (pop. 1,104), Lérida prov., NE Spain, 4 mi. N of Lérida; cereals, sugar beets, cherries, olives.

Torregrosa (tôrägrō'sä), village (pop. 2,310), Lérida prov., NE Spain, 11 mi. ESE of Lérida, and on fertile Urgel plain; olive-oil processing; sheep raising; cereals, almonds.

Torreira (tôrā'rŭ), fishing village (pop. 1,392), Aveiro dist., N central Portugal, 9 mi. NNW of Aveiro, on sand bar bet. Aveiro lagoon and open Atlantic; resort.

Torrejoncillo (tôrāhōn-thē'lyō), village (pop. 5,076), Cáceres prov., W Spain, 30 mi. N of Cáceres; mfg. of woolen textiles, knit goods, footwear; meat and olive-oil processing; cereals, wine.

Torrejoncillo del Rey (dhĕl rā'), town (pop. 1,875), Cuenca prov., E central Spain, 24 mi. W of Cuenca; cereals, grapes, olives, vegetables; cheese making.

Torrejón de Ardoz (tôrāhōn' dā ärdōth'), town (pop. 2,691), Madrid prov., central Spain, on railroad and 11 mi. E of Madrid; cereals, cattle, sheep. New international airport.

Torrejón de Velasco (vālä'skō), town (pop. 1,241), Madrid prov., central Spain, 17 mi. S of Madrid; cereals, olives, grapes, sheep. Olive pressing, wine making, dairying.

Torrejón el Rubio (ĕl rōō'vyō), town (pop. 1,484), Cáceres prov., W Spain, 19 mi. SSE of Plasencia; cereals, livestock.

Torrelaguna (tô"rälägōō'nä), town (pop. 2,146), Madrid prov., central Spain, in New Castile, near Jarama R. (Isabel II Canal), 30 mi. NNE of Madrid; cereals, olives, grapes, sheep, goats. Flour milling; mfg. of soft drinks, plaster, tiles.

Torrelavega (tô"rälävā'gä), city (pop. 9,428), Santander prov., N Spain, in Old Castile, 14 mi. SW of Santander, in fertile area; commercial, industrial, and road center. Chemical works (dyes, sulphuric acid, caustic soda, soap, rubber tires); food industries (processed meat, dairy products, candy); other mfg. (rayon, knit goods, shoes, cordage, furniture). Lumbering, cattle raising. Iron, lead, calamine mines in vicinity. Parochial church has statue of Christ sculptured by Cano. Town was founded in 14th cent.

Torrella de' Lombardi (tôr-rĕl'lä dĕlômbär'dē), village (pop. 1,602), Avellino prov., Campania, S Italy, near headwaters of Ofanto R., 17 mi. ENE of Avellino; hosiery factories.

Torrellas (tôrĕ'lyäs) or **Puig Mayor** (pōōch' mīôr'), highest peak (4,741 ft.) of Majorca, Balearic Isls., 18 mi. NNE of Palma.

Torrelobatón (tô"rälōvätōn'), town (pop. 1,117), Valladolid prov., N central Spain, 16 mi. W of Valladolid; cereals, livestock; lumber.

Torremaggiore (tôr"rĕmäd-jō'rĕ), town (pop. 15,100), Foggia prov., Apulia, S Italy, 5 mi. W of San Severo; mfg. of agr. machinery; wine making.

Torremayor (tôrämīôr'), town (pop. 904), Badajoz prov., W Spain, near the Guadalete, 10 mi. W of Mérida; cereals, olives, vegetables, stock.

Torremegía (tôrämāhē'ä), town (pop. 1,698), Badajoz prov., W Spain, on railroad and 9 mi. S of Mérida; olives, cereals, grapes, sheep, hogs.

Torremocha (tôrāmō'chä), town (pop. 2,863), Cáceres prov., W Spain, 14 mi. SE of Cáceres; meat processing, flour milling, olive pressing; wool trade. Cereals, wine.

Torremolinos (tôrāmōlē'nōs), resort town (pop. 2,203), Málaga prov., S Spain, on the Mediterranean, 7 mi. SW of Málaga (linked by railroad).

Torrens, Lake (tŏ'rĕnz), salt lake (□ 2,230), S central South Australia, 90 mi. N of Port Pirie; 120 mi. long, 40 mi. wide; partly dry in summer.

Torrens Island, South Australia, in Gulf St. Vincent, forms E shore of inlet leading to inner harbor of Port Adelaide; 3.5 mi. long, 2 mi. wide; low, sandy. Reserve for native flora.

Torrens River, SE South Australia, rises in Mt. Lofty Ranges, flows 50 mi. WSW, past Gilberton, Adelaide, and Hindmarsh, to Gulf St. Vincent at Henley and Grange.

Torrente (tôrĕn'tä), city (pop. 12,781), Valencia prov., E Spain, 5 mi. SW of Valencia, in rich truck-farming area. Mfg. of footwear, ceramics, soap, wax, buttons, cotton and silk textiles; food processing (chocolate, condensed milk, vegetables, olive and cottonseed oil), flour milling. Trades in cereals, wine, livestock.

Torrente de Cinca (dhā thĭng'kä), village (pop. 1,251), Huesca prov., NE Spain, on Cinca R. and 3 mi. S of Fraga; sheep raising; olives, wine, almonds, figs. Coal mines near by.

Torrenueva (tôränwā'vä), town (pop. 5,018), Ciudad Real prov., S central Spain, in New Castile, 7 mi. S of Valdepeñas; agr. center (cereals, grapes, olives). Olive-oil pressing, vegetable canning; antimony mining.

Torreón (tōrāōn'), city (pop. 75,796), Coahuila, N Mexico, on Nazas R. and 200 mi. W of Monterrey; the metropolis of fruitful LAGUNA DISTRICT; commercial, industrial, trade center. Situated on broad, flat, alluvial basin (alt. 3,730 ft.) broken by scattered ranges of barren mts. Has grown rapidly as industrial modern city since its founding in 1893. Connected by important rail lines with Chihuahua, Monterrey, Zacatecas, Durango. Located in most important cotton-growing section in Mexico, wheat being another major crop. Torreón is also a center for near-by mining areas (silver, zinc, copper, lead, arsenic). Industries include: smelters, cotton and textile mills, flour mills, vegetable-oil plants, chemical plants, breweries, wineries. Hydroelectric station, airport. Has fine govt. bldgs. Across Nazas R., in Durango, are Gómez Palacio and Ciudad Lerdo.

Torreon (tŏrēōn'), village (1940 pop. 615), Torrance co., central N.Mex., just E of Manzano Range, 14 mi. WSW of Estancia, in ranching, agr. area; alt. c.7,000 ft. Pueblo ruins here. Part of Cibola Natl. Forest just W, Mosca Peak 8 mi. NW.

Torreorgaz (tôrāôrgäth'), town (pop. 2,014), Cáceres prov., W Spain, 10 mi. SE of Cáceres; flour mills; potatoes, cereals.

Torre Orsaia (tôr'rĕ ôrsä'yä), village (pop. 1,928), Salerno prov., Campania, S Italy, 9 mi. WNW of Sapri.

Torre Orsina (tôr'rĕ ôrsē'nä), village (pop. 438), Terni prov., Umbria, central Italy, on Nera R. and 4 mi. E of Terni; mfg. of agr. tools.

Torre Pellice (tôr'rĕ pĕl'lēchĕ), town (pop. 3,267), Torino prov., Piedmont, NW Italy, on Pellice R. (left affluent of upper Po R.) and 7 mi. SW of Pinerolo, in grape-growing, stock-raising region; rail terminus; powdered milk, locks. Resort. Was chief settlement of the Waldenses.

Torreperogil (tôrāpārōhēl'), town (pop. 9,590), Jaén prov., S Spain, near the Guadalquivir, 5 mi. ENE of Úbeda; agr. trade center. Olive-oil and meat processing, alcohol and brandy distilling, flour milling, soap and footwear mfg. Cereals, wine, livestock, lumber in area.

Tôrres (tô'rĭsh), city (pop. 1,394), northernmost Rio Grande do Sul, Brazil, port on the Atlantic, 100 mi. NE of Pôrto Alegre; brandy distilling.

Torres (tô'rĕs), town (pop. 4,306), Jaén prov., S Spain, 16 mi. E of Jaén; olive-oil processing, flour milling, soap mfg. Cereals, wine, vegetables, lumber in area.

Torres, Cape (tô'rĕs), headland on Bay of Biscay, in Oviedo prov., N Spain, 3 mi. NW of Gijón; 43°37'N 5°44'W.

Torresandino (tôrāsändē'nō), town (pop. 1,152), Burgos prov., N Spain, 9 mi. N of Roa; cereals, potatoes, sugar beets, grapes, stock.

Torre Santa Susanna (tôr'rĕ sän'tä sōōzän'nä), town (pop. 5,882), Brindisi prov., Apulia, S Italy, 16 mi. SW of Brindisi; wine, olive oil, cheese.

Torres de Berrellén (tô'rĕs dhä bĕrĕlyĕn'), town (pop. 1,507), Saragossa prov., NE Spain, near the Ebro, 12 mi. NW of Saragossa; sugar beets, alfalfa, fruit (melons).

Torres de Cotillas (kōtē'lyäs), town (pop. 2,223), Murcia prov., SE Spain, 7 mi. WNW of Murcia; fruit canning, olive-oil processing; pepper, truck produce, cereals.

Torres de la Alameda (lä älämä'dhä), town (pop. 983), Madrid prov., central Spain, 17 mi. E of Madrid; olives, grain, grapes, livestock. Sulphur springs.

Torres de Segre (sĕ'grä), town (pop. 1,348), Lérida prov., NE Spain, on Segre R. and 8 mi. SW of Lérida; sheep, sugar beets, wine, olive oil.

Torres Islands (tô'rĭz), northernmost group (pop. 150) of New Hebrides, SW Pacific, 60 mi. N of Espiritu Santo; comprise Hiu (largest isl., 10 mi. long), Tegua, Toga, Lo. Polynesian natives.

Tôrres Novas (tô'rĭsh nô'vŭsh), town (pop. 6,303), Santarém dist., central Portugal, 18 mi. NNE of Santarém; textile-milling center; alcohol distilling, mfg. (scales, pottery, glue). Just E is junction of rail lines from Oporto (N) and Spain (E) to Lisbon.

Torres Strait (tô'rĭz, –rĭs), channel bet. S coast of New Guinea and N coast of Cape York Peninsula, Australia; connects Arafura Sea with Coral Sea; 95 mi. wide. Endeavour Strait (SW) leads into Gulf of Carpentaria, and Great Northeast Channel (NE) into Gulf of Papua of Coral Sea. Contains many isls.; Prince of Wales Isl., largest. Discovered 1606 by Torres, Sp. navigator.

Tôrres Vedras (tô'rĭsh vā'drŭsh), town (pop. 4,762), Lisboa dist., W central Portugal, on railroad and 27 mi. N of Lisbon; important winegrowing center. Mfg. (ceramics, gunpowder, cordage). Recaptured from Moors in 1148. Until 16th cent. it was frequently a royal residence. Hq. of Wellington's defense system for Lisbon in Peninsular War (1810).

Torretta (tôr-rĕt'tä), village (pop. 3,409), Palermo prov., NW Sicily, 7 mi. W of Palermo.

Torrevieja (tôrävyā'hä), city (pop. 9,019), Alicante prov., E Spain, fishing port on the Mediterranean, 30 mi. SSW of Alicante; terminus of branch railroad from Dolores. Exports quantities of salt from lagoons near by. Boatbuilding, sail mfg.; also salted fish, soap, tiles, furniture, canned fruit. Olive oil, wine, truck produce in area. Bathing resort.

Torrey, town (pop. 241), Wayne co., S central Utah, 15 mi. ESE of Loa and on Fremont R.; alt. 7,000 ft.; agr., livestock. Capitol Reef Natl. Monument is just E.

Torrey Mountain, Mont.: see PIONEER MOUNTAINS.

Torreys Peak (14,264 ft.), central Colo., in Front Range, c.45 mi. W of Denver.

Torricella Peligna (tôr-rēchĕl'lä pĕlē'nyä), town (pop. 2,075), Chieti prov., Abruzzi e Molise, S central Italy, 16 mi. SSW of Lanciano.

Torricella Sicura (sēkōō'rä), village (pop. 743), Teramo prov., Abruzzi e Molise, S central Italy, 2 mi. W of Teramo; cementworks.

Torrico (tôrē'kō), town (pop. 1,747), Toledo prov., central Spain, 22 mi. WSW of Talavera de la Reina; cereals, olives, grapes, livestock.

Torridal River, Norway: see OTRA RIVER.

Torridge River, Devon, England, rises 7 mi. SE of Hartland, flows 40 mi. SE and NW, past Torrington and Bideford, to Barnstaple Bay of the Bristol Channel near Appledore. Receives Okement R.

Torridon, Loch (lŏkh tŏ'rĭdŭn), sea inlet, W Ross and Cromarty, Scotland, extending 13 mi. inland from the Inner Sound, bet. Loch Maree (N) and Loch Carron (S); 4 mi. wide at mouth. E section is called Upper Loch Torridon.

Torriglia (tôr-rē'lyä), village (pop. 973), Genova prov., Liguria, N Italy, near headwaters of Scrivia R., 14 mi. NE of Genoa, in cattle-raising, cereal-growing region; resort (alt. 2,592 ft.).

Torrijo de la Cañada (tôrē'hō dhä lä känyä'dhä), village (pop. 1,627), Saragossa prov., NE Spain, 14 mi. NW of Calatayud; flour mills; cereals, fruit, wine. Some coal and iron mines and limestone quarries near by.

Torrijo del Campo (dhĕl käm'pō), village (pop. 1,479), Teruel prov., E Spain, on the Jiloca and 35 mi. NNW of Teruel; cereals, saffron, sheep.

Torrijos (tôrē'hōs), town (pop. 3,875), Toledo prov., central Spain, in New Castile, on Madrid-Cáceres RR and 16 mi. WNW of Toledo; agr. center (cereals, grapes, olives, vegetables, livestock). Lumbering, flour milling, dairying; mfg. of chocolate, meat products. Anc. town, with fine collegiate church, convent, and palace of counts of Altamira; remains of old walls, fortifications.

Torrington (tŏ'rĭngtŭn). **1** Industrial city (pop. 27,820), coextensive with Torrington town, Litchfield co., NW Conn., on the Naugatuck and 22 mi. W of Hartford. Brass and metal products center since early 19th cent.; sports equipment, hardware, textiles, tools, machinery, needles, electrical equipment, lumber, brushes. Site of John Brown's birthplace is marked; post office murals commemorate him. State forest here. Settled c.1735, town inc. 1740, city inc. 1923. **2** Town (pop. 3,247), ⊙ Goshen co., SE Wyo., on N.Platte R., near Nebr. line, and 75 mi. NNE of Cheyenne; alt. 4,100 ft. Trade center for mining and irrigated agr. region; sugar beets, livestock, grain, beans, potatoes; food processing (beet sugar, meat and dairy products). Oil wells, coal mines in vicinity. Hq. of soil-conservation project. Fossil beds near by.

Torrinha (tôrē'nyŭ), city (pop. 1,718), central São Paulo, Brazil, on railroad and 40 mi. WNW of Piracicaba; coffee, rice, cattle.

Torrita di Siena (tôr-rē'tä dē syā'nä), village (pop. 755), Siena prov., Tuscany, central Italy, 5 mi. N of Montepulciano; cement works, alcohol distillery. Lignite mines near by. Enclosed by 16th-cent. walls; has 14th-cent. church.

Torroella de Montgrí (tôrōĕ'lyä dhä mōntgrē'), town (pop. 3,090), Gerona prov., NE Spain, 16 mi. NE of Gerona, 3 mi. from the Mediterranean, near Ter R.; agr. trade center (olive oil, wine, cereals, livestock). Montgrí hill, above town, is crowned by 13th-cent. fortress, formerly royal palace of kings of Aragon.

Torrox (tôrôks'), town (pop. 5,215), Málaga prov., S Spain, near the Mediterranean, 26 mi. E of Málaga; agr. center situated on fertile plain surrounded by coastal hills; sugar cane, grapes, raisins, olives, oranges, figs, almonds, truck produce. Sugar and flour milling, liquor distilling, olive-oil processing. Torrox Point is 2 mi. S.

Torrubia del Campo (tôrōō'vyä dhĕl käm'pō), town (pop. 1,311), Cuenca prov., E central Spain, 35 mi. E of Aranjuez; cheese making, olive-oil pressing; grain, wine, sheep. Limekilns.

Torry, Scotland: see ABERDEEN.

Torryburn, town and parish (pop. 1,910), SW Fifeshire, Scotland, on the Firth of Forth, 4 mi. WSW of Dunfermline; coal-shipping port; coal mines.

Torsa River (tōr'sŭ), in Tibet, Bhutan, India, and E Pakistan, rises in W Assam Himalayas in SE Tibet, in headstreams (1 flows through Chumbi Valley) joining near Yatung; flows S (in Tibet and Bhutan called Amo Chu), past Yatung and Chumbi, and generally SSE, through Bhutan, past Dorkha, across NE West Bengal (India), past Cooch Behar, into East Bengal (Pakistan), to the Brahmaputra 14 mi. WSW of Dhubri; length, c.200 mi. A right arm, Dharla R., branches off W of Cooch Behar, flowing S to JALDHAKA RIVER. Right arm of Raidak R. joins the Torsa 18 mi. SE of Cooch Behar; Torsa R. also called Raidak or Dudhkumar below this confluence.

Torsas (tōōrs'ōs"), Swedish *Torsås*, village (pop. 618), Kalmar co., SE Sweden, near Kalmar Sound of the Baltic, 20 mi. NE of Karlskrona; furniture mfg., woodworking.

Torsby (tōōrs'bü"), village (pop. 1,102), Varmland co., W Sweden, at N end of L. Fryk, 35 mi. NNW of Arvika; sawmilling, woodworking.

Torshalla (tôrs-hĕ'lä), Swedish *Torshälla*, city (pop. 2,221), Sodermanland co., E Sweden, on short river draining L. Hjalmar into L. Malar, near its mouth on L. Malar, 4 mi. NNW of Eskilstuna; metalworking, flour milling. Has 13th-cent. mills, 15th-cent. church with noted paintings, and 18th-cent. town hall. Dating from pagan times, originally called Torshag; chartered 1317. In Middle Ages, trade center rivaling Eskilstuna.

Torshavn, Faeroe Isls.: see THORSHAVN.

Torshiz, Iran: see KASHMAR.

Torslanda, Sweden: see GOTEBORG.

Tortkovac or **Tortkovats** (both: tôrt'kôväts), mountain (4,277 ft.) in Dinaric Alps, central Bosnia, Yugoslavia, 10 mi. NE of Zenica.

Tortola (tôrtō'lŭ), island (□ 21; pop. 5,421), main island of the Br. Virgin Isls., Lesser Antilles, bet. St. John (SSW) and Virgin Gorda (E); on it is Road Town (18°26'N 64°32'W), ⊙ presidency. Irregularly shaped, the rugged isl. is c.12 mi. long, 3 mi. wide, rises to 1,781 ft. (Mt. Sage). Stock raising is its mainstay; also produces fruit, vegetables, sugar cane, and charcoal, which are exported to St. Thomas Isl. and Puerto Rico. First settled by Du. buccaneers (1648).

Tórtola de Henares (tôr'tōlä dhä ānä'rĕs), town (pop. 725), Guadalajara prov., central Spain, 5 mi. N of Guadalajara; cereals, grapes, olives, esparto, livestock; apiculture.

Tórtoles de Esgueva (tôr'tōlĕs dhä ĕzgwä'vä), town (pop. 1,181), Burgos prov., N Spain, 9 mi. NNW of Roa; wheat, potatoes, chick-peas, tubers, fruit, sheep, goats. Mfg. of woolen goods. Has Benedictine col.

Tortolì (tôrtōlē'), village (pop. 2,449), seat of commune of Arbatax di Tortolì, Nuoro prov., E Sardinia, 32 mi. SE of Nuoro; corkworking, pottery making. Its port is Arbatax, 3 mi. E, on Tyrrhenian Sea.

Tortona (tôrtō'nä), anc. *Dertona*, town (pop. 13,250), Alessandria prov., Piedmont, N Italy, on Scrivia R. and 12 mi. E of Alessandria, in cereal- and forage-growing region. Rail junction; industrial center; mfg. (truck chassis, agr. machinery, silk, paper, lime, bricks), wine distilleries. Bishopric. Has cathedral (1584) and 9th-cent. church (rebuilt 13th cent.). Guelph stronghold; destroyed by Frederick Barbarossa in 1155. Near by are ruins of citadel dismantled by Napoleon in 1801, after battle of Marengo.

Tortorici (tôrtorē'chē), village (pop. 2,680) and commune (pop. 11,398), Messina prov., NE Sicily, in Nebrodi Mts., 13 mi. NW of Randazzo, in nut-growing region.

Torto River (tôr'tô), N Sicily, rises in Madonie Mts. W of Valledolmo, flows 30 mi. generally N, along W edge of Madonie Mts., to Tyrrhenian Sea 4 mi. E of Termini Imerese.

Tortosa (tôrtō'sä), anc. *Dertosa*, city (pop. 11,951), Tarragona prov., NE Spain, port on the Ebro and 40 mi. SW of Tarragona, on fertile coastal plain near rice-growing Ebro delta; head of ocean navigation. A leading olive-oil processing and shipping center. Mfg. of chemical fertilizer, soap, pharmaceuticals, cement, hats, knitwear, liqueur, chocolate; rice-, flour-, and sawmilling. Trades in wines, hazelnuts, fruit. Episcopal see. Has a 14th-cent. Gothic cathedral (on site of anc. mosque) with baroque additions; remains of a medieval castle; and a Renaissance palace. Ebro seismological observatory is 1 mi. NW. Tortosa flourished in 2d cent. B.C. under Romans, and again in 8th cent. under Moors, who began construction of irrigation canals. Freed 1148 by Christians, it later repulsed another Moorish attack, chiefly through heroism of its women.

Tortosa, Syria: see TARTUS.

Tortosa, Cape, headland, Tarragona prov., NE Spain, on the Mediterranean, at NE tip of Ebro delta, on Buda Isl., 20 mi. ESE of Tortosa; 40°40'N 0°56'E.

Tortosendo (tôrtōōzān'dōō), town (pop. 2,939), Castelo Branco dist., central Portugal, on railroad and 4 mi. SSW of Covilhã; wool textile-milling center.

Tortue, Île de la, Haiti: see TORTUGA ISLAND.

Tortuera (tôrtwā'rä), town (pop. 724), Guadalajara prov., central Spain, 10 mi. NNE of Molina; grain, sheep. Has airport (N).

Tortuga (tôrtōō'gŭ), village (pop. 176), W central Trinidad, B.W.I., 8 mi. NE of San Fernando, in cacao-growing region. Its Notre Dame de Montserrat has shrine of Black Virgin.

Tortuga Island (tôrtōō'gŭ, –tū'gŭ, Sp. –tōō'gä) [Sp.,=turtle], locally *Île de la Tortue* (ēl dü lä tôrtü'), island (□ 70; 1950 census pop. 12,494) off NW Haiti (to which it belongs), 6 mi. N of Port-de-Paix; 23 mi. long, c.3 mi. wide. Bananas and subsistence crops are grown. Notorious as early rendezvous of Fr. and English privateers who in 17th cent. from here began incursions of the main isl. and scourged the Caribbean.

Tortuga Island (□ 2½), in Gulf of California, off E coast of Lower California, NW Mexico, 25 mi. NE of Santa Rosalía; 3 mi. long, 2 mi. wide; rocky, uninhabited; rises to 1,016 ft.

Tortuga Island, federal dependency of Venezuela, in the Caribbean, 55 mi. W of Margarita Isl., 110 mi. ENE of Caracas; 15 mi. long, 6 mi. wide. Uninhabited because of lack of fresh water; has a salt lake. Semiwild goats graze upon it. Named for the numerous turtles on its coast.
Tortugas, village, N.Mex.: see LAS CRUCES.
Tortugas, island, Fla.: see DRY TORTUGAS.
Tortuguero Lagoon (tôrtōōgā'rō) (c.3 mi. long), N Puerto Rico, near the ocean. The Tortuguero U.S. army camp is on its S shore.
Tortuguero River, NE Costa Rica, rises at N foot of the volcano Turrialba near Guápiles, flows 55 mi. NE, through swampy Tortuguero flood plain, to the Caribbean at Tortuguero Bay, small coastal trade port, 50 mi. NW of Limón.
Tortum (tôrtōōm'), village (pop. 1,635), Erzurum prov., NE Turkey, 32 mi. NNE of Erzurum; wheat, barley.
Torul (tôrōōl'), village (pop. 1,615), Gumusane prov., NE Turkey, on Harsit R. and 12 mi. NW of Gumusane; copper deposits. Formerly Ardasa.
Torun (tô'rōōnyŏŏ), Pol. *Toruń*, Ger. *Thorn* (tôrn), city (1946 pop. 68,085; 1950 estimate c.80,000), Bydgoszcz prov., N central Poland, port on the Vistula, near Drweca R. mouth, on a crossing from the Kujawy to Chelmno lake area, and 26 mi. ESE of Bydgoszcz. Rail junction; industrial center; mfg. of machinery, tools, armature, furniture, chemicals, textiles, cartons, roofing materials; sawmilling, distilling; trades in swine, lumber, grain. Has univ.; several Gothic bldgs. Following founding (1231) of its castle by Teutonic Knights, Torun immediately became an important trade center; chartered 1333. Treaties (1411, 1466) of Torun forced Teutonic Knights to become vassals of Pol. kings. Synods of Pol. and Lith. Protestants (1595) and of Pol. Protestants and Catholics (1645) held here. Peak of development (Pol. trade routes leading to the sea joined here) reached in early-17th cent., when its pop. (30,000) equaled that of Warsaw; suffered heavily during Swedish invasions. A religious incident here (1724) caused Russia and Prussia to guarantee rights of religious minorities in Poland. Pop. fell to 5,000 during partitions in late-18th cent. Included in Germany 1793–1807, 1815–1918, and 1939–45. A frontier fortress at end of 19th cent.; was (1919–39) ⊙ Pomorze prov. During Second World War, Ger. administrative hq.; suffered relatively little damage. Copernicus b. here.
Torup (tōō'rŭp"), village (pop. 443), Halland co., SW Sweden, on Nissa R. and 20 mi. NNE of Halmstad; rail junction; hydroelectric station; grain, flax, sugar beets.
Torva or **Tyrva,** Est. *Tõrva* (all: tûr'vä), town (pop. 2,599), S Estonia, 15 mi. NNW of Valga, in flax area.
Torvastad (tôr'västä), canton (pop. 2,343), Rogaland co., SW Norway, on NW shore of Karmoy, SSW of Haugesund; fisheries; produces herring meal and oil.
Torvik (tor'vēk, –vĭk), village in Eid canton (pop. 499), More og Romsdal co., W Norway, 2 mi. from Romsdal Fjord, 16 mi. SE of Molde. Formerly spelled Thorvik. Near-by Skotthamar (formerly called Skothammeren) was scene of 1612 battle.
Tory Island (tô'rē), Gaelic *Torach*, island (3 mi. long, 1 mi. wide) in the Atlantic, off NW coast of Co. Donegal, Ireland, 9 mi. NNE of Bloody Foreland. Has ruins of church, monastery, and round tower, possibly dating from time of St. Columba. According to legend isl. was in anc. times peopled by the Fomorians, a race of giants. It retains many anc. laws. Fishing is carried on. At W end of isl. is lighthouse (55°16'N 8°15'W).
Torysa River (tô'rĭsä), Hung. *Tarca* (tŏr'tsŏ), in E central and S Slovakia, Czechoslovakia, rises in E spur of the High Tatra 5 mi. NE of Levoca, flows c.80 mi. E and SSE, past Sabinov and Presov, to Hornad R. 6 mi. SE of Kosice.
Törzburg, Rumania: see BRAN.
Torzhok (tŭrzhôk'), city (1926 pop. 14,449; 1939 pop. 31,800), central Kalinin oblast, Russian SFSR, on Tvertsa R. (head of navigation) and 35 mi. WNW of Kalinin; road hub; center of tanning and footwear industries; flax processing; gold-embroidery handicrafts. Has ruins of old underground fortifications, regional and art mus. Flax-growing research institute. Dates from 1130; developed on Novgorod-Suzdal border; sacked 1238 by Mongols; passed 1478 to Moscow.
Tosa, river, Italy: see TOCE RIVER.
Tosa (tō'sä), former province in S Shikoku, Japan; now Kochi prefecture.
Tosa Bay, Jap. *Tosa-wan*, inlet of Philippine Sea, Kochi prefecture, S Shikoku, Japan, bet. Ashizuri Point (W) and Muroto Point (E); 75 mi. long, 35 mi. wide. Kochi (chief port of S coast) is in N.
Tosa-kure, Japan: see KURE, Kochi prefecture.
Tosa River, Italy: see TOCE RIVER.
Tosa-saga, Japan: see SAGA, Kochi prefecture.
Tosa-yamada, Japan: see YAMADA, Kochi prefecture.
Toscana, Italy: see TUSCANY.
Toscanella, Italy: see TUSCANIA.
Toscas, Las, Argentina: see LAS TOSCAS.
Toscas, Las, Uruguay: see LAS TOSCAS.
Toscolano (tôskôlä'nô), village (pop. 1,843), Brescia prov., Lombardy, N Italy, on W shore of Lago di Garda, 21 mi. NE of Brescia; paper mills, hosiery factory.
Tosei, Formosa: see TUNGSHIH.
Toseki, Formosa: see TUNGSHIH.
Toshi-jima (tōshē'jĭmä), island (□ 3; pop. 4,247), Mie prefecture, Japan, in Ise Bay (inlet of Philippine Sea), just NE of Toba; 4 mi. long, 1 mi. wide; hilly, fertile. Fishing.
Toshima (tō'shĭmä), town (pop. 4,521) on Awajishima, Hyogo prefecture, Japan, on Harima Sea, 14 mi. NNE of Sumoto; fishing port; rice, wheat, fruit.
To-shima (tō'shĭmä), island (□ 1.5; pop. 409) of isl. group Izu-shichito, Greater Tokyo, Japan, in Philippine Sea, 12 mi. SSW of O-shima; roughly circular, 1.5 mi. in diameter; rises to 1,664 ft. Fishing, farming.
Toshimoe, Russian SFSR: see KASATKA.
Toshkovski or **Toshkovskiy** (tŭshkôf'skē), town (1926 pop. 909), W Voroshilovgrad oblast, Ukrainian SSR, in the Donbas, 14 mi. NE of Popasnaya; coal mines.
Tosho, Japan: see TONOSHO.
Tosia, Turkey: see TOSYA.
Tosna River (tô'snŭ), central Leningrad oblast, Russian SFSR, rises in marshy lake region NE of Torkovichi, flows 50 mi. N, past Tosno, to Neva R. near Otradnoye.
Tosno (tô'snŭ), town (1940 pop. 13,000), central Leningrad oblast, Russian SFSR, on Tosna R. and 35 mi. SE of Leningrad; rail junction; sawmilling, mfg. of autobus bodies.
Toso, Korea: see TONGCHO.
Tossa (tō'sä), town (pop. 1,153), Gerona prov., NE Spain, fishing port and bathing resort on the Mediterranean, and 19 mi. SSE of Gerona. Cork processing; agr. trade (olive oil, wine, cereals, potatoes). Has Roman remains.
Tossignano (tôs-sēnyä'nô), village (pop. 515), Bologna prov., Emilia-Romagna, N central Italy, near Santerno R., 8 mi. SW of Imola; lime- and cementworks.
Töss River (tûs), N Switzerland, rises 3 mi. NNE of Wald, flows 36 mi. NW, past Winterthur, to the Rhine 12 mi. N of Zurich.
Tost, Poland: see TOSZEK.
Tostado (tōstä'dō), town (pop. estimate 2,000), ⊙ Nueve de Julio dept. (□ 6,270; 1947 census 19,494), NW Santa Fe prov., Argentina, on railroad and 85 mi. NW of San Cristóbal; agr. center (corn, wheat, alfalfa, cotton, livestock); flour.
Tostedt (tō'shtĕt), village (pop. 3,562), in former Prussian prov. of Hanover, NW Germany, after 1945 in Lower Saxony, 22 mi. SW of Hamburg; mfg. of household goods, food processing.
Toston (tŏ'stŭn), village (pop. c.200), Broadwater co., W central Mont., on Missouri R. and 40 mi. SE of Helena, in irrigated grain and livestock region.
Tostón Point (tōstōn'), NW headland of Fuerteventura, Canary Isls., 17 mi. NW of Puerto de Cabras; 28°43'N 14°1'W.
Tosu (tō'sōō), town (pop. 16,142), Saga prefecture, N central Kyushu, Japan, 4 mi. N of Kurume; rail junction; commercial center for agr. area (rice, grain, vegetables); cotton mills, sake brewery.
Tosya (tōsyä'), town (1950 pop. 11,591), Kastamonu prov., N Turkey, near Devrez R., 28 mi. SSE of Kastamonu; rice mill. Also spelled Tosia.
Toszeg (tō'sĕg), Hung. *Tószeg*, town (pop. 4,672), Jasz-Nagykun-Szolnok co., E central Hungary, 5 mi. S of Szolnok; corn, tobacco, cattle, hogs.
Toszek (tō'shĕk), Ger. *Tost* (tôst), town (1939 pop. 3,625; 1946 pop. 2,620) in Upper Silesia, after 1945 in Katowice prov., S Poland, 13 mi. NNW of Gleiwitz (Gliwice), in coal-mining region; agr. market (grain, potatoes, livestock). Has remains of old castle, rebuilt 17th cent.
Tota, Laguna de (lägōō'nä dā tō'tä), lake (□ 21; alt. 9,892 ft.) in Boyacá dept., central Colombia, in E Cordillera Oriental, 10 mi. S of Sogamoso; 7 mi. long, c.2 mi. wide. One of the country's largest inland lakes, towered over by mts., it is a popular tourist resort known for its extraordinary beauty. Used for irrigation. Outlet: Upía R., affluent of the Meta.
Totak (tō'täk), lake (□ 15), Telemark co., S Norway, 65 mi. NW of Skien; 16 mi. long, c.2 mi. wide, 820 ft. deep; alt. 2,247 ft. Drained by Toke R., which flows S to Bandak lake.
Totalán (tōtälän'), town (pop. 831), Málaga prov., S Spain, near coast, 7 mi. E of Málaga; olives, oranges, almonds, carobs, livestock.
Totana (tōtä'nä), city (pop. 10,368), Murcia prov., SE Spain, 25 mi. SW of Murcia; agr. trade center in fertile dist. yielding oranges and other fruit, cereals, almonds, vegetables. Mfg. of ceramics, printer's ink, linen, footwear, tiles, plaster; olive-oil processing, flour milling, fruit canning.
Totapola (tōtŭpō'lŭ), peak (7,741 ft.) in S central Ceylon, on Horton Plains, 10 mi. SSE of Nuwara Eliya. Also spelled Totupola.
Totatiche (tōtätē'chā), town (pop. 1,612), Jalisco, W Mexico, near Zacatecas border, 18 mi. SW of Colotlán; alt. 5,807 ft.; grain, alfalfa, stock.
Totecacinte, Honduras and Nicaragua: see TEOTECACINTE.
Toteng (tō'tĕng), village, Ngamiland dist., N Bechuanaland Protectorate, at E end of L. Ngami, 260 mi. SE of Bulawayo, 40 mi. SW of Maun, in Batawana native reserve; road junction. Sometimes spelled Totin.
Totenkopf, Germany: see KAISERSTUHL.
Tôtes (tōt), agr. village (pop. 673), Seine-Inférieure dept., N France, 16 mi. N of Rouen; apples.
Totes Gebirge (tō'tŭs gŭbĭr'gŭ), mountain range in the Salzkammergut of W central Austria, on border of Styria and Upper Austria; extends 35 mi. W of Pyhrn Pass. Rises to 8,245 ft. in the Grosser Priel. Resorts of Altaussee and Grundlsee (with their lakes) at S foot.
Totigi, Japan: see TOCHIGI, city.
Totimehuacán (tōtēmäwäkän'), town (pop. 1,441), Puebla, central Mexico, 6 mi. S of Puebla; grain, beans, fruit, stock.
Totin, Bechuanaland Protectorate: see TOTENG.
Totis, Hungary: see TATA.
Totkomlos (tōt'kômlōsh), Hung. *Tótkomlós*, town (pop. 10,993), Bekes co., SE Hungary, 19 mi. E of Hodmezövasarhely; flour mill; agr., cattle raising.
Totland, town and parish (pop. 1,488), W Isle of Wight, Hampshire, England, on The Solent, 12 mi. WSW of Cowes; seaside resort, with beach at foot of high cliffs.
Totling, Tibet: see TOLING.
Totma or **Tot'ma** (tôt'yŭmŭ), city (1944 pop. 10,000), central Vologda oblast, Russian SFSR, on Sukhona R. and 110 mi. ENE of Vologda; sawmilling, flax processing, metalworking. Salt springs near by. Chartered 1539.
Totnes (tŏt'nĭs), municipal borough (1931 pop. 4,526; 1951 census 5,534), S Devon, England, on Dart R. and 7 mi. NW of Dartmouth; agr. market. Has noted Tudor houses, ruins of Norman castle, 16th-cent. guildhall, 15th-cent. church. There are remains of anc. walls and 2 town gates.
Totness (tōt'nĕs), town (pop. 1,081), ⊙ Coronie dist. (□ 578; pop. 4,563), N Du. Guiana, on the coast, 80 mi. W of Paramaribo; coconut growing.
Totocuitlapilco (tōtōkwētläpēl'kō), officially San Miguel Totocuitlapilco, town (pop. 1,688), Mexico state, central Mexico, 7 mi. SE of Toluca; cereals, stock.
Totogalpa (tōtōgäl'pä), town (1950 pop. 461), Madríz dept., NW Nicaragua, 8 mi. NE of Somoto; mfg. (hats, mats).
Totolac or **San Juan Totolac** (sän hwän' tōtōläk'), town (pop. 1,154), Tlaxaca, central Mexico, 2 mi. W of Tlaxcala; grain, maguey, alfalfa, livestock.
Totolapa (tōtōlä'pä), town (pop. 855), Chiapas, S Mexico, at S foot of Sierra de Hueytepec, 10 mi. SSW of San Cristóbal de las Casas; cereals, fruit, stock.
Totolapan (–pän), town (pop. 999), Morelos, central Mexico, 22 mi. ENE of Cuernavaca; sugar cane, fruit, stock.
Totoltepec (tōtōltāpĕk'), officially Totoltepec de Guerrero, town (pop. 961), Puebla, central Mexico, 13 mi. ENE of Acatlán; cereals, sugar cane, stock.
Totomi (tōtō'mē), former province in central Honshu, Japan; now part of Shizuoka prefecture.
Totonicapán (tōtōnēkäpän'), department (□ 410; 1950 pop. 96,641), W central Guatemala; ⊙ Totonicapán. In W highlands; highest dept. of Guatemala; drained by headstreams of Chixoy R. (N) and Samalá R. (SW). Mainly agr. (corn, wheat, beans, fodder grasses); sheep raising. Flour milling is main industry; home handicraft produces textiles, furniture, and pottery. Main centers: Totonicapán, San Cristóbal. Formerly spelled Totonicapam.
Totonicapán, city (1950 pop. 9,492), ⊙ Totonicapán dept., W central Guatemala, on Inter-American Highway and 12 mi. ENE of Quezaltenango; 14°54'N 91°21'W; alt. 8,215 ft. Market and textile center; cotton and woolen milling; home handicraft (pottery, furniture, leather goods). Sulphur springs. Site of 1817 Indian revolt.
Totora (tōtō'rä). **1** City (pop. c.14,500), ⊙ Carrasco (until c.1925 Totora) prov., Cochabamba dept., central Bolivia, on S slopes of Cordillera de Cochabamba and 70 mi. ESE of Cochabamba, on Cochabamba–Santa Cruz highway; alt. 8,540 ft. Coca cultivation; corn, wheat, potatoes. **2** Town (pop. c.3,500), Oruro dept., W Bolivia, in the Altiplano, 65 mi. WNW of Oruro; alt. 13,323 ft.; potatoes, alpaca.
Totora, Cordillera de (kôrdĭyā'rä dā), Andean range in W San Juan prov., Argentina, E spur of the Andes, 20 mi. WNW of Calingasta; curves c.30 mi. W–E; rises to c.17,500 ft.
Totoral, Argentina: see VILLA GENERAL MITRE.
Totoral (tōtōräl'), village (pop. c.980), Oruro dept., W Bolivia, at S end of Serranía de Achacollo, 10 mi. SSE of Poopó; alt. 15,489 ft.; tin-mining center.
Totoralillo (tōtōrälē'yō), village (1930 pop. 25), Atacama prov., N central Chile, on Copiapó R. (irrigation), on railroad, and 20 mi. SSE of Copiapó, in copper-mining area; alfalfa, corn, goats.
Totoras (tōtō'räs), town (pop. estimate 3,000), S central Santa Fe prov., Argentina, 40 mi. NW of Rosario; corn, flax, wheat, vegetables, potatoes, cattle, hogs; dairying; grain elevators.

Tototlán (tōtōtlän'), town (pop. 4,125), Jalisco, central Mexico, 37 mi. ESE of Guadalajara; wheat-growing center.

Totowa (tō'tůwů), residential borough (pop. 6,045), Passaic co., NE N.J., W suburb of Paterson; metal products, burial vaults. Inc. 1898.

Totoya (tōtō'yä), limestone island (□ 11; pop. 672), Lau group, Fiji, SW Pacific; crescent-shaped, 1 mi. wide; copra.

Totskoye (tôt'skůyů), village (1926 pop. 6,371), W Chkalov oblast, Russian SFSR, on Samara R., on railroad and 25 mi. SE of Buzuluk; metalworking; wheat, livestock.

Totsuka, Japan: see YOKOHAMA.

Totsu River, Japan: see KUMANO RIVER.

Totten, Fort, N.Y.: see BAYSIDE.

Totten Coast, part of Wilkes Land, Antarctica, on Indian Ocean, bet. Sabrina Coast and Banzare Coast; c.120°E. Discovered 1840 by Charles Wilkes, U.S. explorer.

Tottenham (tŏ'tůnům), village (pop. 367), central New South Wales, Australia, 250 mi. WNW of Sydney; rail terminus; copper-mining center.

Tottenham, village (pop. 561), S Ont., 30 mi. NW of Toronto; dairying, grain.

Tottenham (tŏt'nům, tŏ'tůnům), residential municipal borough (1931 pop. 157,772; 1951 census 126,921), Middlesex, England, N suburb of London. Its history dates from Danish times. There are a cross dating from c.1600, ruins of All Hallows Church (dates from 11th cent.), and 16th-cent. Bruce Castle, built on site of manor house belonging to Robert Bruce's father. Sir Rowland Hill had a school here. In the borough (S) is residential area of Stamford Hill.

Tottenville, SE N.Y., a residential section of Richmond borough of New York city, on S tip of Staten Isl., across Arthur Kill (bridged) from Perth Amboy, N.J.; mfg. (clothing, pottery, tools, metal products); fishing.

Tottington, urban district (1931 pop. 6,532; 1951 census 5,824), SE Lancashire, England, 3 mi. NW of Bury; cotton and rayon milling. Has 18th-cent. church. In urban dist. is cotton-milling village (pop. 587) of Hawkshaw.

Tottiyam, India: see THOTTAYAM.

Totton, England: see ELING.

Tottori (tōt-tō'rē), prefecture [Jap. *ken*] (□ 1,347; 1940 pop. 484,390; 1947 pop. 587,606), S Honshu, Japan; ⊙ Tottori, its chief port. Bounded N by Sea of Japan, NW by lagoon Naka-no-umi. Generally mountainous terrain, drained by several small streams. Radioactive hot springs at Misasa. Extensive stock raising and lumbering; also fishing. Agr. (rice, wheat, pears, persimmons, tobacco); mfg. (cotton textiles, sake, soy sauce, tissue paper, pottery). Chief centers: Tottori, YONAGO.

Tottori. 1 Town (pop. 12,100), SE Hokkaido, Japan, on the Pacific, 3 mi. NE of Kushiro; paper milling. **2** City (1940 pop. 49,261; 1947 pop. 57,218), ⊙ Tottori prefecture, S Honshu, Japan, port on Sea of Japan, at mouth of short Sendai R., 80 mi. NW of Kobe. Mfg. center (lacquer ware, tissue paper, ornamental coral, sake); spinning mills; woodworking. Dairying, stock raising; fishery. Exports raw silk, fruit (persimmons, grapes). Has agr. experiment station, agr. school. Hot springs.

Totupola, peak, Ceylon: see TOTAPOLA.

Tototla (tōtōōt'lä), town (pop. 956), Veracruz, E Mexico, in Sierra Madre Oriental, 4 mi. N of Huatusco; fruit.

Tou- or **T'ou-**, for Chinese names beginning thus and not found here: see under Tow-.

Touat (twät), group of Saharan oases in Aïn-Sefra territory, W central Algeria, along Colomb-Béchar–Gao (Fr. West Africa) auto track and caravan route; fed by underground streams. Date palms, tobacco, henna. Chief oasis, Adrar. It is adjoined by the Gourara (NNE) and Tidikelt (SE) oases.

Touba (tōō'bä), village (pop. c.1,300), W Ivory Coast, Fr. West Africa, 70 mi. WNW of Séguéla; coffee, palm kernels, cotton, rice, yams, manioc.

Touba, village, W Senegal, Fr. West Africa, rail terminus 105 mi. ENE of Dakar, in peanut-growing region. Site of pilgrimage to grave of Amadou Bamba, founder of Mouride sect.

Toubkal, Djebel (jĕ'bĕl tōōbkäl'), highest peak (13,665 ft.) of the High Atlas, SW central Fr. Morocco, and culminating point of the Atlas Mts. of French North Africa, 40 mi. S of Marrakesh. Seasonally snow-covered; winter-sport resort area; 31°4'N 7°55'W.

Touchet (tōō-shĕt'), village, Walla Walla co., SE Wash., 16 mi. W of Walla Walla, at junction of Touchet and Walla Walla rivers; grain, livestock, poultry.

Touchet River, SE Wash., rises in Umatilla Natl. Forest; flows c.85 mi. NW, W, and S, past Dayton and Waitsburg, to Walla Walla R. at Touchet.

Toucy (tōōsē'), village (pop. 1,520), Yonne dept., N central France, on Ouanne R. and 14 mi. WSW of Auxerre; road junction; woodworking, bicycle assembling, ocher processing. Larousse b. here.

Toufflers (tōōflârs'), town (pop. 1,999), Nord dept., N France, 4 mi. SE of Roubaix; customhouse on Belg. border opposite Templeuve; mfg. (baby carriages, biscuits).

Tougaloo (tōōgůlōō'), village, Hinds co., W Miss., 7 mi. NNE of Jackson. Seat of Tougaloo Col. (Negro; Congregationalist; founded 1867).

Tougan (tōōgän'), town (pop. c.3,500), W Upper Volta, Fr. West Africa, 110 mi. NW of Ouagadougou. Trades in region's agr. produce (peanuts, cotton, sesame, spices, tobacco, kapok, shea-nut butter, millet, corn, fruit); cattle raising; cotton ginning. R.C. mission.

Touggourt (tōōg-gōōrt'), military territory (□ 52,094; 1948 pop. 284,940), of E Algeria, northeasternmost of the SOUTHERN TERRITORIES, in the Sahara; ⊙ Touggourt. Bounded by Constantine dept. (N), Alger dept. (NW), and Tunisia (E). In SE, it touches on the Fezzan, near Ghadames. The Chott Melrhir (saline lake) is in NE. Central and S part of territory covered by sand dunes of the Great Eastern Erg. Railroad from Constantine penetrates territory at Biskra and reaches Touggourt. Chief oases are those of the Souf (center, El-Oued) and Oued Rhir (center, Touggourt) groups, well known for their Deglet Nur dates. The Ziban region (just S of Biskra) also contains several oases (Sidi-Okba, Tolga).

Touggourt, town (pop. 14,704), ⊙ Touggourt territory, E Algeria, chief of the Oued Rhir Saharan oases, 120 mi. S of Biskra; 33°7'N 6°5'E. S terminus of railroad from Philippeville (260 mi. NNE on the Mediterranean), via Constantine and Biskra; head of trans-Saharan auto track to Djanet (southeasternmost Algeria). A leading date-shipping center. Oasis, fed by artesian waters, grows date palms, cereals, and some vegetables. Important trade in wool, sheep, goats, and handicraft products. Occupied by French 1854. Fr. garrison wiped out in unsuccessful 1871 uprising. Also spelled Tuggurt.

Tougué (tōōgā'), town (pop. c.7,200), N Fr. Guinea, Fr. West Africa, in Fouta Djallon mts., 75 mi. ENE of Labé; cattle-raising and agr. trade center (rubber, honey, beeswax, rice).

Touïl, Oued, Algeria: see CHÉLIFF RIVER.

Touïla, Djebel, Algeria: see AMOUR, DJEBEL.

Touïla, Djebel (jĕ'bĕl twēlä'), mountain (alt. 2,182 ft.) in Kairouan dist., central Tunisia, 27 mi. SW of Kairouan. Lead and zinc mines. Sidi-Saad (4 mi. SE) is nearest railroad station.

Touille (tōō'yů), village (pop. 149), Haute-Garonne dept., S France, on the Salat and 13 mi. E of Saint-Gaudens; metalworks.

Touisset, Mass.: see SWANSEA.

Toujane (tōōzhän'), village, Southern Territories, SE Tunisia, in the Matmata range, 28 mi. S of Gabès; nomadic grazing.

Toukoto (tōōkō'tō), village, S Fr. Sudan, Fr. West Africa, on Dakar-Niger RR and 140 mi. WNW of Bamako. Railroad shops.

Toul (tōōl), anc. *Tullum*, town (pop. 8,971), Meurthe-et-Moselle dept., NE France, on Moselle R., at junction of Marne-Rhine Canal and Canal de l'Est, and 13 mi. W of Nancy; mfg. (porcelain, household equipment, furniture), wine and brandy trade. Old town, enclosed by 17th-cent. fortifications, seriously damaged in Second World War, including 13th–14th cent. church of Saint-Gengoult (with cloister) and 13th–15th-cent. former cathedral. An episcopal see from 5th cent. until Fr. Revolution; in Middle Ages a free imperial city ruled by its bishops. Seized by Henry II of France in 1552; French possession confirmed in 1648; fortified by Vauban. Toul capitulated to Germans in 1870 after 6-week siege. In First World War remained in Allied hands, but was heavily shelled.

Toulepleu (tōōlplû'), village (pop. c.1,300), W Ivory Coast, Fr. West Africa, near Liberia border, 80 mi. SW of Man; coffee, rice, kola nuts.

Toulon (tōōlŏn', Fr. tōōlō'), anc. *Telo Martius*, city (pop. 116,141), Var dept., SE France, port on the Mediterranean, at foot of Mont Faron, 29 mi. ESE of Marseilles; 43°7'N 5°56'E. Chief Fr. naval base, on sheltered roadstead (consisting of outer and inner bays separated by breakwater 1 mi. long) surrounded by fortified heights. Metal and armament works connected with naval arsenal (heavily damaged). Produces chemicals (calcium carbide, dyes, varnishes), footwear (chiefly cork soles), furniture, clothing, flour products. Petroleum refining, tanning, brewing. Important shipyards at La Seyne-sur-Mer (3 mi. SW). Fortified by Vauban in 17th cent., Toulon's chief defense installations are at La Mourillon (guarding NE entrance to inner bay), on SAINT-MANDRIER PENINSULA, atop Mont Faron, and along E approaches to outer bay. Dating from pre-Roman times, Toulon became episcopal see in 6th cent., but remained unimportant throughout Middle Ages. With Provence it became French in 1481, and its growth was stimulated by Henry IV. Surrendered to English by royalists in 1793; recaptured later that year by French after a siege in which young Bonaparte distinguished himself. In Nov., 1942, as Germans were proceeding to occupy Toulon following Allied landings in North Africa, French fleet (immobilized here since 1940) was scuttled to avoid its capture by Axis powers. Made a Ger. submarine base, Toulon was heavily bombed in 1943–44. A primary target of Allied invasion of S France (Aug., 1944), taken within a week of initial landings.

Toulon (tōōlŏn', tōō'lŏn), city (pop. 1,173), ⊙ Stark co., N central Ill., 10 mi. SSE of Kewanee, in agr. and bituminous-coal area; corn, oats, wheat, livestock, poultry; mfg. (cheese, cement blocks, monuments). Inc. 1859.

Toulon-sur-Arroux (tōōlō'-sür-ärōō'), agr. village village (pop. 1,229), Saône-et-Loire dept., E central France, 15 mi. SW of Le Creusot and on Arroux R. (spanned by 16th-cent. bridge).

Toulouse (tōōlōōz'), anc. *Tolosa*, city (pop. 225,854), ⊙ Haute-Garonne dept., S France, in Languedoc, on the Garonne, at junction of Garonne Lateral Canal and Canal du Midi, and 380 mi. S of Paris; 43°36'N 1°27'E. One of France's leading commercial and cultural centers. Has chemical fertilizer, airplane, and machinery plants. Important hosiery and shoe industry. Flour milling, printing, canning, paper milling, and mfg. of glassware, perfumes, and tin cans. Central market for Aquitaine Basin agr. output (grains, fruits, vegetables, livestock). Site of the large 11th–12th-cent. Romanesque basilica of Saint-Sernin, with tomb of St. Thomas Aquinas; 13th-cent. Gothic Jacobin church; Gothic cathedral of Saint-Étienne (12th–15th cent.); 18th-cent. *capitole* (town hall); and many fine 16th–17th-cent. Renaissance bldgs., such as the Assézat mansion. The old quarter has been left intact since 18th cent. There are noteworthy museums of painting, sculpture, and natural history. Its univ. (2d oldest of France) was established 1230. The Académie des Jeux Floraux has also existed since 13th cent. The nodality of Toulouse increased rapidly with the development of railroad and road transportation and the city's pop. has doubled since 1870, bringing about considerable suburban growth. An important city even before the Roman conquest, Toulouse became an episcopal see in 4th cent. and later an archdiocese. Was ⊙ of Visigoths (419–507); of the Carolingian kingdom of Aquitaine (781–843); and of a powerful separate countship, which in 12th cent. included most of Languedoc and part of Guienne and Provence. Attracting the best troubadours, it became center of southern French literature. In 1271 the countship passed to the French crown, but Toulouse, governed by elected magistrates and enjoying special privileges, remained virtually independent until 1790. In 1814 Soult made an unsuccessful stand against Wellington at Toulouse. During Second World War the city's industrial dist. was damaged.

Toumbista, Greece: see NEOS SKOPOS.

Tummo, Fezzan: see TUMMO.

Toumodi (tōōmō'dē), village (pop. c.800), S central Ivory Coast, Fr. West Africa, 110 mi. NW of Abidjan; cacao, coffee, cotton, palm kernels, palm oil. Protestant mission.

Toungo (chōäng'gō), town, S Br. Cameroons, administered as part of Adamawa prov. of Nigeria, on E slopes of Shebshi Mts., on road and 70 mi. SSW of Yola; peanuts, sesame, rice, cotton; cattle raising. Sometimes spelled Toango.

Toungoo (toung'gōō), N district (□ 6,457; pop. 474,858), Pegu div., Lower Burma, astride Sittang R., bet. Pegu Yoma (W) and Karenni hills (E); ⊙ Toungoo. Extensive rice cultivation on central plain; teak forests in hills; coffee and sugar cane (mill at Zeyawaddy). Served by Rangoon-Mandalay RR. Burman stronghold (13th cent.) against Shans and Mons and seat of Toungoo dynasty. Formerly spelled Taungu and Toungu. Until Second World War in Tenasserim div.

Toungoo, town (pop. 23,223), ⊙ Toungoo dist., Lower Burma, on Rangoon-Mandalay RR and 150 mi. N of Rangoon; 18°57'N 96°26'E. Rice and saw-milling center. From late 13th cent. it was center of one of the 3 chief states of Burma; in 16th cent. it preceded Pegu as ⊙ united Burmese kingdom.

Touques River (tōōk), in Orne and Calvados depts., NW France, rises in Perche hills above Gacé, flows 67 mi. N, past Lisieux (head of navigation) and Pont-l'Évêque, to the Channel at Trouville-Deauville. Its picturesque valley is lined with fine apple orchards.

Touquet-Paris-Plage, Le (lů tōōkā'-pärē-pläzh'), town (pop. 3,178), Pas-de-Calais dept., N France, fashionable beach resort on Channel coast, 14 mi. S of Boulogne, at mouth of Canche R. Heavily damaged in Second World War.

Touraine (tōōrān', Fr. tōōrĕn'), old province of W central France; ⊙ Tours; now forms Indre-et-Loire and part of Indre depts. Traversed by the broad valley of the Loire (Val de Touraine) and its important tributaries, the Cher, Indre, and Vienne. Because of the fertility of its valleys, the prov. has been called "the garden of France." It is also famous for its châteaux (Amboise, Chenonceaux, Chinon, Azay-le-Rideau). Touraine takes its name from a Gallic tribe, the Turones. Conquered c.507 by Clovis. In 10th cent. the countship of Tours passed to counts of Blois, who ceded it (11th cent.) to counts of Anjou. Taken by the English in 1152, Touraine was recaptured (1204) by Philip II of France, and definitively incorporated into royal domain by Henry III. A Protestant stronghold, it suffered economically from revocation of Edict of Nantes. In 1790, Touraine was broken up into present depts.

Tourane (tōōrän'), city (1943 pop. 50,900), Quangnam prov., central Vietnam, in Annam, port and naval base on S shore of Bay of Tourane of South China Sea, on railroad and 50 mi. SE of Hue; soap mfg., cotton and silk spinning. Cham antiquities mus. Airport and seaplane base. Originally ceded to France by Annam in 1787. Captured by France 1858 and became Fr. concession outside of Annam protectorate.

Tourcham (tōōrchäm'), village, Ninhthuan prov., central Vietnam, rail station (3 mi. NW) of Phanrang, on Saigon-Hanoi RR; junction for Dalat branch; remains of Cham tower shrines.

Tourcoing (tōōrkwē'), city (pop. 73,772), Nord dept., N France, near Belg. border, 8 mi. NE of Lille; with ROUBAIX (its twin city just SSE), it produces 80% of France's woolen textiles (carding, combing, spinning, weaving, dyeing, and finishing; mfg. of clothing, hosiery, upholstery fabrics and rugs); cotton and flax spinning, tanning. Together with suburbs forms part of important Lille-Roubaix-Tourcoing industrial conurbation (pop. c.600,000). Occupied by Germans in First World War.

Tour-d'Aigues, La (lä tōōr-dĕg'), village (pop. 1,262), Vaucluse dept., SE France, 13 mi. SE of Apt; fruit- and winegrowing. Has ruined 16th-cent. castle.

Tour-de-Carol, La, France: see LATOUR-DE-CAROL.

Tour-de-Peilz, La (lä tōōr-dů-pěls'), town (pop. 4,481), Vaud canton, W Switzerland, on L. Geneva, adjacent to and ESE of Vevey. Medieval castle, park with numerous residences.

Tour-du-Pin, La (–dü-pē'), town (pop. 3,748), Isère dept., SE France, on the Bourbre and 29 mi. NNW of Grenoble; mfg. (clothing, silk fabrics, chocolate, shoes, hosiery, and biscuits). Paper milling near by. Poultry raising in area. Its 19th-cent. church preserves 16th-cent. tryptich. Seat of medieval barony.

Touriñán, Cape, Spain: see TORIÑANA, CAPE.

Tourlaville (tōōrlävēl'), E suburb (pop. 1,700) of Cherbourg, Manche dept., NW France; ships fruit, vegetables; dairying.

Tourmalet (tōōrmälā'), pass in central Pyrenees, Hautes-Pyrénées dept., SW France, near Pic du Midi de Bigorre, 10 mi. S of Bagnères-de-Bigorre; alt. 6,936 ft. Connects Luz (Gave de Pau valley) and Campan (upper Adour valley). Highest point on scenic Pyrenees road.

Tournai or **Tournay** (both: tōōrnā'), Flemish *Doornik* or *Doornijk* (dōr'nĭk), town (pop. 32,507), Hainaut prov., SW Belgium, on Scheldt R. and 27 mi. WNW of Mons, near Fr. border. Rail junction; carpet-mfg. center; cement, stone, and chalk quarrying; leather tanning, printing, brewing, millinery mfg. Has 11th-cent. cathedral and belfry, 14th-cent. bridge, 15th-cent. tower of Henry VIII, 17th-cent. cloth hall, and numerous medieval bldgs. Relay post in Roman times; Frankish possession until 840, when it was attached to Flanders. Became Fr. crown domain in 1188; captured by Henry VIII of England in 1513; sold to France in 1518. Tournai was taken (1521) by Charles V and attached to the Netherlands; taken (1667) by Louis XIV, who created a parliament here; taken (1745) by Louis XV. In 18th cent. was major center of carpet and china mfg.

Tournan-en-Brie (tōōrnä'-ä-brē'), town (pop. 1,911), Seine-et-Marne dept., N central France, 20 mi. ESE of Paris; agr. market. Damaged in Second World War.

Tournay, Belgium: see TOURNAI.

Tournay (tōōrnā'), village (pop. 892), Hautes-Pyrénées dept., SW France, 9 mi. ESE of Tarbes; winegrowing, cattle and horse raising.

Tourneppe, Belgium: see DWORP.

Tournon (tōōrnō'), town (pop. 4,615), Ardèche dept., S France, on right bank of Rhone R., near mouth of the Doux, and 10 mi. NNW of Valence; hosiery and chemical mfg., silk dyeing. Wine and fruit commerce. Also called Tournon-sur-Rhône.

Tournon-d'Agenais (–däzhůnä'), village (pop. 254), Lot-et-Garonne dept., SW France, 14 mi. E of Villeneuve-sur-Lot; plums, wheat.

Tournon-Saint-Martin (–sē-märtē'), (pop. 782), Indre dept., central France, on Creuse R. and 9 mi. NW of Le Blanc; dairying.

Tournon-sur-Rhône, France: see TOURNON.

Tournus (tōōrnü'), town (pop. 4,470), Saône-et-Loire dept., E central France, port on right bank of Saône R. and 15 mi. SSE of Chalon-sur-Saône; metallurgical center (aluminum reducing, mfg. of heating and electrical equipment). Produces varnishes, cosmetics, and glucose. Site of remarkable church of Saint-Philibert (10th–12th cent.) and remains of an abbey. Damaged during Second World War. Painter Greuze b. here.

Touros (tō'rōōs), city (pop. 1,437), E Rio Grande do Norte, NE Brazil, port on the Atlantic, 45 mi. NNW of Natal; sugar, cotton. Lighthouse (NW) at tip of Brazilian bulge.

Tourouvre (tōōrōō'vrů), village (pop. 537), Orne dept., NW France, in the Perche hills, 7 mi. NE of Mortagne; sawmilling, horse raising. Sent many emigrants to Canada in 17th cent.

Tours (tōōrz, tōōr, Fr. tōōr), anc. *Caesarodunum*, later *Urbs Turonum*, city (pop. 76,207), ⊙ Indre-et-Loire dept., W central France, on a tongue of land bet. the Loire and the Cher above their confluence and 125 mi. SW of Paris; important regional transportation and commercial center with trade in wine, brandy, fruit preserves, grain; manufactures include agr. machinery, railroad and electrical equipment, pharmaceuticals, chemical fertilizer, silk and leather goods, ribbons, china, and pottery; distilling, printing and publishing. Surrounded by the celebrated castles of the Loire valley, Tours attracts numerous tourists. Has 12th–16th-cent. Gothic cathedral with fine façade and stained-glass windows; 17th–18th-cent. archiepiscopal palace occupied by mus. of fine arts; old square lined with 15th-cent. gabled houses; and the new basilica of St. Martin containing the saint's tomb. Just outside the city center are the Château of Plessis-lès-Tours (2 mi. W) where Louis XI lived and died and which is now a medical institute, and the abbey of Marmoutier (3 mi. ENE), founded by St. Martin. Tours is connected with its residential suburbs of Saint-Cyr and Saint-Symphorien by fine 18th-cent. stone bridge (heavily damaged 1942–44) over the Loire. Known as the Caesarodunum of the Romans, the city passed to the Visigoths (5th cent.) and to the Franks (6th cent.); in 732 Charles Martel defeated the Saracens in a battle N of Poitiers, but sometimes called the battle of Tours. During the Middle Ages it became a center of learning and the seat of an archbishop. Louis XI established silk manufactories in Tours, but after the revocation of the Edict of Nantes, the city (a Huguenot stronghold during Wars of Religion) suffered a prolonged economic decline. Only since the advent of railroads has Tours assumed its present importance as a hub of commerce and transport. Seat of French govt. during siege of Paris (1870). In First World War chief supply base of the American Expeditionary Forces. In Second World War 20% of city was destroyed or heavily damaged, including house where Balzac was born.

Tour Saillère (tōōr säyâr'), peak (10,571 ft.) in Pennine Alps, SW Switzerland, 7 mi. WNW of Martigny-Ville.

Tours-sur-Marne (tōōr-sür-märn'), village (pop. 735), Marne dept., N France, on the Marne and its lateral canal, 8 mi. E of Épernay; winegrowing (champagne).

Tourves (tōōrv), village (pop. 1,150), Var dept., SE France, in Lower Provence Alps, 7 mi. W of Brignoles; bauxite mining; tanning.

Toury (tōōrē'), village (pop. 1,797), Eure-et-Loir dept., N central France, in the Beauce, 20 mi. N of Orléans; sugar-beet distilling; livestock feed mfg.

Tousen (tō'shěnyů), Czech *Toušeň*, village (pop. 1,448), N central Bohemia, Czechoslovakia, on Elbe R., on railroad and 14 mi. ENE of Prague; health resort with mineral springs.

Touskov or **Mesto Touskov** (myĕ'stô tōsh'kôf), Czech *Město Touškov*, Ger. *Tuschkau* (tōōsh'kou), town (pop. 1,212), W Bohemia, Czechoslovakia, on Mze R., on railroad and 6 mi. WNW of Pilsen.

Toutle River (tōō'tůl), SW Wash., rises in Spirit L. in Columbia Natl. Forest, flows c.60 mi. W to Cowlitz R. above Castle Rock. Receives South Fork (c.30 mi. long) near Toutle village.

Toutry (tōōtrē'), agr. village (pop. 350), Côte-d'Or dept., E central France, on Serein R. and 10 mi. E of Avallon; tool-making machines made at Montzeron near by.

Touvet, Le (lů tōōvā'), village (pop. 678), Isère dept., SE France, in GRÉSIVAUDAN valley, 15 mi. NE of Grenoble, at foot of Grande Chartreuse massif; glove mfg.

Touvre River (tōō'vrů), Charente dept., W France, rises near Magnac-sur-Touvre in 3 spectacular springs fed by waters diverted from Tardoire and Bandiat rivers, flows 6 mi. W, past Ruelle, into the Charente above Angoulême. Powers paper mills.

Touws River (tōz), Afrikaans *Touwsrivier* (tōs"-rĭfěr'), town (pop. 2,411), SW Cape Prov., U of So. Afr., on Touws R. and 40 mi. ENE of Worcester, at foot of the Wittebergen mts.; rail junction; agr. center (fruit, grain, tobacco).

Touz, in Azerbaijani names: see TAUZ.

Touzim (tō'zhĭm), Czech *Toužim*, Ger. *Theusing* (toi'zing), town (pop. 884), W Bohemia, Czechoslovakia, on railroad and 12 mi. SSE of Carlsbad.

Tovacov (tô'váchôf), Czech *Tovačov*, village (pop. 2,525), central Bohemia, Czechoslovakia, on Morava R. and 11 mi. S of Olomouc; rail terminus; agr. center (barley, oats, sugar beets, wheat). Has picturesque castle.

Tovar (tōvär'), town (pop. 4,173), Mérida state, W Venezuela, in Andean spur, on transandine highway, on affluent of Chama R. and 45 mi. WSW of Mérida; commercial town in fertile agr. valley (sugar, corn, coffee, cacao, tobacco, vegetables).

Tovarkovo, Russian SFSR: see KAGANOVICH, Tula oblast.

Tovarnik (tô'värnĭk), village, N Yugoslavia, on railroad and 18 mi. ESE of Vinkovci, on Serbia-Croatia border.

Tovaros, Hungary: see TATA.

Tovdal River (tōv'däl), Nor. *Tovdalselv*, sometimes *Topdalselv*, Aust-Agder co., S Norway, rises in the highlands E of the Setesdal, flows SW, traversing Herefoss L. and forming many rapids and falls, into Tovdal Fjord, an inlet of the Skagerrak at Kristiansand. Length, 90 mi.

Tové (tō'vā), village, S Fr. Togoland, on railroad and 36 mi. NW of Lomé; palm oil, coffee.

Tovil-Dara, Tadzhik SSR: see TAVIL-DARA.

Tövis, Rumania: see TEIUS.

Tovsala, Finland: see TAIVASSALO.

Towada, Lake (tōwä'dä), Jap. *Towada-ko* (□ 25), N Honshu, Japan, in Aomori and Akita prefectures, 21 mi. ESE of Hirosaki, in mtn. area; 6 mi. long, 5 mi. wide. Contains pine-clad islets; trout fishing. Lake is central feature of Towada Natl. Park (□ 165).

Towanda (tůwŏn'dů, tō–). **1** Village (pop. 400), McLean co., central Ill., 6 mi. NE of Bloomington, in rich agr. area. **2** City (pop. 417), Butler co., S Kansas, 17 mi. ENE of Wichita, in cattle and grain region. Oil wells near by. **3** Borough (pop. 4,069), ⊙ Bradford co., NE Pa., 29 mi. SE of Elmira, N.Y., and on Susquehanna R.; electrical products, textiles; agr. Settled 1794, laid out 1812 as Meansville, inc. and renamed 1828.

Towang (tō'wäng), Tibetan *Mön Tawang* (mûn' täwäng'), village, Balipara frontier tract, N Assam, India, in central Assam Himalayas, near Tibet and Bhutan borders, 60 mi. NNW of Udalguri, on India-Tibet trade route.

Toward Point (tou'ůrd), promontory on the Firth of Clyde, at E entrance to the Kyles of Bute, SE Argyll, Scotland, 7 mi. SSW of Dunoon; lighthouse (55°54'N 4°56'W). Near by is 19th-cent. Castle Toward, adjoining ruins of an earlier structure.

Towcester (tou'stůr), town and parish (pop. 2,252), S Northampton, England, on Tove R. and 9 mi. SSW of Northampton; shoe mfg.; agr. market. Has 14th-cent. church and 15th-cent. chantry house. Site of the Roman station *Lactodorum*, on Watling Street.

Tower, city (pop. 773), St. Louis co., NE Minn., on S shore of Vermilion L., at W end of Vermilion iron range, in Superior Natl. Forest, 24 mi. NNE of Virginia; resort in iron-mining and truck-farming region. First iron mines at Vermilion L. opened here 1884. The Vermilion L. Indian Reservation is just W.

Tower City. **1** Village (pop. 292), Cass co., E N. Dak., 40 mi. W of Fargo; grain, livestock, dairy products. **2** Borough (pop. 2,054), Schuylkill co., E central Pa., 19 mi. WSW of Pottsville; anthracite; clothing. Laid out 1868, inc. 1892.

Tower Falls, Wyo.: see YELLOWSTONE NATIONAL PARK.

Tower Hill. **1** Village (pop. 784), Shelby co., central Ill., 30 mi. S of Decatur, in bituminous-coal and farm area; grain milling. **2** Village (pop. 1,158, with adjacent Thompson), Fayette co., SW Pa., 10 mi. NW of Uniontown.

Tower Island, Antarctica, 10 naut. mi. off NW coast of Palmer Peninsula, in the South Pacific; 63°33'S 59°50'W. Discovered 1821 by Edward Bransfield, Br. explorer.

Tower Island, Galápagos: see GENOVESA ISLAND.

Towers Mountain (7,600 ft.), in Bradshaw Mts., central Ariz., 22 mi. SSE of Prescott.

Towie (tou'ē), village and parish (pop. 569), W Aberdeen, Scotland, on Don R. and 5 mi. E of Strathdon; woolen milling. Ruins of anc. castle.

Tow Law (tou' lô'), urban district (1931 pop. 3,559; 1951 census 3,186), W central Durham, England, 10 mi. W of Durham; steel milling.

Towliu or **Tou-liu** (both: dō'lyō'), Jap. *Toroku* (tōrō'kōō), town (1935 pop. 9,578), W central Formosa, 17 mi. NNE of Kiayi and on railroad; sugar-milling center; pineapple cannery; sweet potatoes, vegetables; lumber, bamboo, charcoal.

Townan or **Tou-nan** (both: dō'nän'), Jap. *Tonan* (tō'nän), town (1935 pop. 4,659), W central Formosa, 14 mi. N of Kiayi and on railroad; mfg. (tiles, soy sauce, noodles).

Town and Country, town (pop. 162), St. Louis co., E Mo.

Town Creek, town (pop. 763), Lawrence co., NW Ala., near L. Wilson (in Tennessee R.), 17 mi. SE of Florence.

Towner, county (□ 1,044; pop. 6,360), N N.Dak., bordering on Manitoba; ⊙ Cando. Prairie, watered by creeks and streams. Grain refining, dairy produce, livestock, poultry. Formed 1883.

Towner, city (pop. 955), ⊙ McHenry co., N central N.Dak., 41 mi. E of Minot and on Souris R. Hay, cattle shipping; diversified farming; dairy products, poultry, grain.

Townhill, village, SW Fifeshire, Scotland, 2 mi. N of Dunfermline; coal mining.

Towns, county (□ 172; pop. 4,803), NE Ga., on N.C. line; ⊙ Hiawassee. In Chattahoochee Natl. Forest and the Blue Ridge, rising to 4,784 ft. in BRASSTOWN BALD; drained by Hiwassee R., forming Chatuge Reservoir (N). Farm (corn, hay, potatoes, fruit, livestock), lumber, and resort area. Formed 1856.

Towns, town (pop. 96), Telfair co., S central Ga., 9 mi. ESE of McRae and on Little Ocmulgee R.

Townsend (toun'zůnd). **1** Town (pop. 441), New Castle co., N central Del., 5 mi. S of Wilmington; canning, shipping of farm products. **2** Agr. town (pop. 2,817), Middlesex co., N Mass., 9 mi. NE of Fitchburg, near N.H. line; cooperage, woolens;

granite, timber. Settled 1676, inc. 1732. Includes village of Townsend Harbor. **3** Town (pop. 1,316), ⊙ Broadwater co., W central Mont., on Missouri R. and 30 mi. SE of Helena; gold and silver mines; dairy products, grain, sugar beets, livestock, timber. Founded 1883, inc. 1895. **4** Resort town (pop. 328), Blount co., E Tenn., on Little R. and 23 mi. SSE of Knoxville, near Great Smoky Mts. Natl. Park.

Townsend, Mount (7,260 ft.), SE New South Wales, Australia, near Mt. KOSCIUSKO, in Muniong Range of Australian Alps. Discovered by Count Strzelecki, a Pole, and called Mt. Kosciusko when it was thought to be the highest Australian peak. Later, the name was shifted to a near-by peak, found to be higher.

Townsend Harbor, Mass.: see TOWNSEND.

Townsends Inlet, SE N.J., navigable passage (bridged) entering Intracoastal Waterway and Townsends Sound from the Atlantic, 2.5 mi. S of Sea Isle City. Townsends Inlet village (resort), on S Ludlam Beach, is just N of inlet; to NW, sheltered from ocean by barrier beaches, is **Townsends Sound** (c.2.5 mi. long), with Intracoastal Waterway passing along E edge.

Townshend (toun'zŭnd), town (pop. 584), including Townshend village (pop. 178), Windham co., SE Vt., on West R. and 14 mi. NNW of Brattleboro; wood products, printing. Townshend State Forest here.

Townshend Island (toun'zĕnd) (□ 32), in Coral Sea just off E coast of Queensland, Australia; forms NE shore of Shoalwater Bay; 9 mi. long, 5 mi. wide; rises to 475 ft. Cape Townshend, its N extremity (22°12'S 150°30'E), forms NE side of entrance to Shoalwater Bay. Sheep-raising.

Townsville, city (pop. 34,109), E Queensland, Australia, on Cleveland Bay and 690 mi. NW of Brisbane, on slopes of Castle Hill; 19°16'S 146°50'E. Second port of state; sheep-raising and mining center; exports wool, hides, meat, cobalt, copper, sugar. Founded 1868 with gold rush at Ravenswood.

Townsville, town (pop. 219), Vance co., N N.C., 12 mi. N of Henderson, near Va. line.

Townville, borough (pop. 351), Crawford co., NW Pa., 14 mi. E of Meadville.

Towoeti, Lake, Indonesia: see TOWUTI, LAKE.

Towshan or **Tou-shan** (both: dō'shän'), town, S Kwangtung prov., China, 14 mi. S of Toishan; rail terminus; commercial center.

Towson (tou'sŭn), industrial and residential suburb (1940 pop. 10,606) of Baltimore, ⊙ Baltimore co. (since 1854), N Md., bet. Loch Raven Reservoir (NE) and L. Roland (SW), 7 mi. N of downtown Baltimore. Large plants produce electric tools, aircraft radio equipment, scientific instruments. Seat of a state tuberculosis hosp. (opened 1896) and a state teachers col. Hampton Natl. Historic Site (43.3 acres; established 1948), containing one of the great Georgian Colonial mansions (built c.1790) of America, and the new campus of Goucher Col. are near by.

Towtaokow or **T'ou-tao-kou** (both: tō'dou'gō'), village, SE Kirin prov., Manchuria, on rail spur and 20 mi. SW of Yenki; coal mining.

Towton Field (tou'tŭn), West Riding, central Yorkshire, England, 2 mi. S of Tadcaster. Here forces of Edward IV defeated the Lancastrians in 1461.

Towuti, Lake, or **Lake Towoeti** (both: tōwōō'tē), central Celebes, Indonesia, at base of SE peninsula, 45 mi. S of Kolonodale; 30 mi. long.

Towwei or **Tou-wei** (both: dō'wā'), Jap. *Toi* (tō'ē), town (1935 pop. 3,360), N Formosa, on E coast, 8 mi. NE of Ilan and on railroad; tea, rice, fruit, livestock; rice milling, mfg. of wood and bamboo products. Has 18th-cent. Buddhist temples.

Towyn (tou'ĭn), urban district (1931 pop. 3,802; 1951 census 4,491), SW Merioneth, Wales, on Cardigan Bay of Irish Sea, 12 mi. N of Aberystwyth; seaside resort, with medicinal spring (St. Cadvan's Well); woolen milling. Urban dist. includes town (pop. 1,203) of Aberdovey, Welsh *Aberdyfi* (both: ăbûrdŭ'vē), on Cardigan Bay at mouth of Dovey R., 3 mi. SSE of Towyn; seaside resort, with leather tanneries.

Towy River (tŭ'wē), Cardigan and Carmarthen, Wales, rises 8 mi. E of Tregaron, flows 65 mi. SW, past Llandovery, Llandilo, Carmarthen, and Llanstephan, to Carmarthen Bay of Irish Sea just S of Llanstephan.

Toxaway (tŏk'sŭwā), textile-mill village (pop. 2,397, with adjacent Riverside Mills), Anderson co., NW S.C., adjacent to Anderson.

Toxey, town (pop. 251), Choctaw co., SW Ala., 14 mi. S of Butler.

Toya, Lake (tō'yä), Jap. *Toya-ko* (□ 27), SW Hokkaido, Japan, near NE shore of Uchiura Bay, 15 mi. NNW of Muroran; roughly circular, 7 mi. in diameter; wooded islet in center.

Toyah (toi'yŭ), town (pop. 409), Reeves co., extreme W Texas, 19 mi. SW of Pecos; shipping point in ranching area (cattle, sheep).

Toyama (tōyä'mä), prefecture [Jap. *ken*] (□ 1,644; 1940 pop. 822,569; 1947 pop. 979,229), central Honshu, Japan; ⊙ Toyama. Bounded N by Toyama Bay (inlet of Sea of Japan); large coastal plain with extensive rice fields. Mountainous interior, rising to 9,950 ft. at Mt. Tate. Drained by Jintsu and Kurobe rivers. Making of patent medicines is major industry. Other products: textiles, bronze and lacquer ware. Chief centers: Toyama, TAKAOKA.

Toyama, city (1940 pop. 127,859; 1947 pop. 137,818), ⊙ Toyama prefecture, central Honshu, Japan, on S shore of Toyama Bay, at mouth of Jintsu R., 110 mi. NNE of Nagoya; 36°41'N 137°13'E. Principal center of patent-medicine industry in Japan; aluminum ware, textiles, dolls; woodworking. Bombed (1945) in Second World War. Includes (since early 1940s) former towns of Shinjo and Higashi-iwase.

Toyama Bay, Jap. *Toyama-wan*, inlet of Sea of Japan, central Honshu, Japan, sheltered W by Noto Peninsula; Nagate Point forms NW side of entrance; 40 mi. long, 40 mi. wide. Toyama is on N shore, Nanao on W inlet containing Noto-shima.

Toyohama (tōyō'hämŭ). **1** Town (pop. 8,723), Aichi prefecture, central Honshu, Japan, on SE Chita Peninsula, on Ise Bay, 13 mi. S of Handa; fishing center; pottery, cotton textiles. **2** Town (pop. 6,484), Kagawa prefecture, N Shikoku, Japan, on Hiuchi Sea, 17 mi. SW of Marugame; fishing center; textiles, shell buttons.

Toyohara, Formosa: see FENGYÜAN.

Toyohara, Russian SFSR: see YUZHNO-SAKHALINSK.

Toyohashi (tōyō'hä'shē), city (1940 pop. 142,716; 1947 pop. 129,355), Aichi prefecture, central Honshu, Japan, on Atsumi Bay, at base of Atsumi Peninsula, 40 mi. SE of Osaka; mfg. center; cotton-textile mills, metal- and woodworking factories, food-processing plants. Agr., sericulture, and marine experiment stations. Bombed (1945) in Second World War.

Toyohira (tōyō'hērä), town (pop. 26,054), W Hokkaido, Japan, just SE of Sapporo; agr. (rice, wheat, soybeans), stock raising, lumbering. Hot springs near by.

Toyokawa (tōyō'käwŭ), city (1940 pop. 11,369; 1947 pop. 55,036), Aichi prefecture, central Honshu, Japan, 37 mi. SE of Nagoya; cotton milling; raw silk, poultry. Includes (since early 1940s) former towns of Ushikubo (1940 pop. 7,187) and Ko or Kofu (1940 pop. 6,568).

Toyoma (tōyō'mä), town (pop. 4,886), Fukushima prefecture, central Honshu, Japan, on the Pacific, 6 mi. SE of Taira; rice, charcoal; fishing.

Toyomi (tōyō'mē), town (pop. 7,657), Chiba prefecture, central Honshu, Japan, on E Chiba Peninsula, 6 mi. SE of Togane; agr., poultry raising, fishing; cotton textiles. Sometimes called Toyoumi.

Toyonaka (tōyō'näkŭ), city (1940 pop. 45,013; 1947 pop. 76,314), Osaka prefecture, S Honshu, Japan, 10 mi. N of Osaka; residential; rice, wheat, flowers.

Toyooka (tōyō'kä). **1** Town (pop. 21,694), Hyogo prefecture, S Honshu, Japan, 34 mi. E of Tottori; commercial center for agr. area (rice, wheat); raw silk. **2** Town (pop. 5,150), Oita prefecture, NE Kyushu, Japan, on Beppu Bay, 10 mi. NW of Oita; rice, wheat, barley; charcoal. **3** Town (pop. 11,506), Saitama prefecture, central Honshu, Japan, 8 mi. SW of Kawagoe; textiles, processed tea.

Toyoshina (tōyō'shĭnä), town (pop. 7,924), Nagano prefecture, central Honshu, Japan, 6 mi. NW of Matsumoto; rice, raw silk; spinning.

Toyoumi, Japan: see TOYOMI.

Toyoura (tōyō'rä). **1** Agr. town (pop. 11,007), SW Hokkaido, Japan, on Uchiura Bay, 23 mi. NW of Muroran. **2** Town (pop. 4,323), Ibaraki prefecture, central Honshu, Japan, on the Pacific, 4 mi. NE of Hitachi; fishing; summer resort.

Toy-Tyube, Uzbek SSR: see TOI-TYUBE.

Tozaki, Point (tōzä'kē), Jap. *Tozaki-hana*, SE Kyushu, Japan, in Philippine Sea, at S end of Hyuga Sea; 31°40'N 130°E.

Tozeur (tôzûr'), town and oasis (pop. 12,464), ⊙ Tozeur dist. (pop. 44,970), SW Tunisia, at NW edge of the Chott Djerid, 110 mi. W of Gabès; 33°55'N 8°9' E. Rail terminus and chief center of the Bled-el-Djerid group of oases; date growing and shipping; olives, vegetables. Handicraft wool spinning and mfg. of blankets, rugs, silk goods. Saltworks. Airfield. Desert track to El-Oued (Algeria).

Tpig (tŭpēk'), village, S Dagestan Autonomous SSR, Russian SFSR, in the E Greater Caucasus, 31 mi. WNW of Kasumkent; hardy grain, livestock. Dist. inhabited by Aguls, one of mtn. tribes of Dagestan.

Traben-Trarbach (trä'bŭn-trär'bäkh), town (pop. 5,390), in former Prussian Rhine Prov., W Germany, after 1945 in Rhineland-Palatinate, on the Mosel and 18 mi. NNW of Idar-Oberstein; wine. Traben and Trarbach were united in 1904.

Trabia (trä'byä), village (pop. 4,740), Palermo prov., N Sicily, port on Tyrrhenian Sea and 2 mi. W of Termini Imerese.

Trabzon, Turkey: see TREBIZOND.

Tracadie (trä'kŭdē). **1** Village (pop. estimate 200), NE N.S., on George Bay, 16 mi. E of Antigonish; fishing port. Acadian French settlement. Has Trappist monastery (1825). **2** Fishing village, N central P.E.I., on Tracadie Bay, 12 mi. NE of Charlottetown.

Trachenberg, Poland: see ZMIGROD.

Tracy. 1 City (pop. 8,410), San Joaquin co., central Calif., 18 mi. SW of Stockton; dairy products, beet sugar, feed; packs fruit, vegetables. Has railroad shops, and a pumping plant of Central Valley project. Inc. 1910. **2** City (pop. 3,020), Lyon co., SW Minn., 17 mi. SSE of Marshall; agr. trading center, with railroad repair shops, for grain and livestock area; dairy products, beverages. Settled 1872, inc. as city 1893. **3** Town (pop. 201), Platte co., W Mo., on Little Platte R. opposite Platte City.

Tracy City, resort town (pop. 1,414), Grundy co., SE central Tenn., in the Cumberlands, 30 mi. WNW of Chattanooga, in timber and coal region; makes handles. Inc. since 1940.

Tracy-le-Mont (träsē'-lŭ-mō'), village (pop. 1,049), Oise dept., N France, 9 mi. NE of Compiègne; woodworking, brush mfg.

Tradate (trädä'tē), town (pop. 4,716), Varese prov., Lombardy, N Italy, 8 mi. SSE of Varese; mfg. (silk textiles, plastics, motorcycles, bicycles). Seminary near by.

Trade Town, town, Grand Bassa co., S Liberia, on Atlantic Ocean, 15 mi. SE of Buchanan; palm oil and kernels, cassava, rice.

Tradewater River, W Ky., rises in N Christian co., flows c.110 mi. generally NW, past Dawson Springs, to Ohio R. 5 mi. SW of Sturgis.

Trading Bay (10 mi. long, 30 mi. wide), S Alaska, on W shore of Cook Inlet, 60 mi. WSW of Anchorage; 60°55'N 151°33'W; receives Chakachatna R.

Traena (trăn'ä), islet in North Sea, Nordland co., N central Norway, near Arctic Circle, 60 mi. W of Mo. Site of caves where remains of prehistoric habitation were found.

Traer (trâr), town (pop. 1,627), Tama co., central Iowa, near Wolf Creek, 23 mi. SSW of Waterloo; mfg. of wood, dairy, and meat products. State park near by. Inc. 1875.

Traeth Bach, Wales: see DWYRYD RIVER.

Trafalgar (trŭfăl'gŭr, –făl'–), town (pop. 439), Johnson co., central Ind., 25 mi. S of Indianapolis, in agr. area.

Trafalgar, Cape (trŭfăl'gŭr), Latin *Junonis Promontorium*, headland on Atlantic coast of SW Spain, in Cádiz prov., at W entrance to Strait of Gibraltar and 28 mi. SE of Cádiz; 36°11'N 6°2'W. Off the cape was fought (Oct. 21, 1805) the famous naval battle in which Nelson, though fatally wounded, won victory over Fr. and Sp. fleets.

Trafaria (trŭfŭrē'ŭ), village (pop. 1,716), Setúbal dist., S central Portugal, near mouth of Tagus R. (S bank), 4 mi. SW of Lisbon; fish processing, mfg. of explosives.

Trafford. 1 Town (pop. 551), Jefferson co., N central Ala., 20 mi. N of Birmingham. **2** Borough (pop. 3,965), Westmoreland and Allegheny counties, SW Pa., ESE suburb of Pittsburgh; mfg. of electrical insulation. Inc. 1904.

Trafford Park, industrial area, SE Lancashire, England, on Manchester Ship Canal in S part of county borough of Salford; petroleum refining; mfg. (machinery, petroleum products, paint, soap, concrete, asbestos cement, wood products). The area was laid out in early 1930s as an experiment in industrial planning to encourage the foundation of industries other than Lancashire's traditional textile industry, hard hit by shrinking markets.

Trafoi (träfoi'), village (pop. 182), Bolzano prov., Trentino–Alto Adige, N Italy, on Stelvio Pass road, 8 mi. NE of Bormio; health resort (alt. 5,062 ft.) at N foot of Ortles mtn. group.

Traful (träfōōl'), village (pop. estimate 300), SW Neuquén natl. territory, Argentina, on L. Traful, in Argentine lake dist., and 35 mi. SSW of San Martín de los Andes; resort and stock-raising center; sawmills.

Traful, Lake (□ 27; alt. c.2,600 ft.), in the Andes, SW Neuquén natl. territory, Argentina, in Argentine lake dist., N of L. Nahuel Huapí; 20 mi. long, 1–3 mi. wide. On S bank is resort village of Traful. Outlet: Traful R., affluent of Limay R.

Tragacete (trägä-thā'tā), town (pop. 740), Cuenca prov., E central Spain, in Serranía de Cuenca, on headstream of the Júcar and 24 mi. NE of Cuenca; cereals, beans, potatoes, honey, wool, sheep, goats. Dairying, lumbering, saltworking.

Traghen (trägĕn'), walled village (pop. 822), central Fezzan, Libya, 30 mi. E of Murzuk, in a Saharan oasis (dates, cereals, vegetables). Has anc. fort.

Tragwein (träg'vīn), town (pop. 2,505), NE Upper Austria, 15 mi. ENE of Linz, N of the Danube; brewery.

Traian (träyän'), village (pop. 1,402), Galati prov., SE Rumania, 12 mi. WSW of Braila.

Traiguén (trīgĕn'), town (pop. 8,828), ⊙ Traiguén dept. (□ 834; pop. 36,281), Malleco prov., S central Chile, 32 mi. S of Angol; rail terminus and agr. center (wheat, oats, potatoes, fruit). Flour mills, sawmills; furniture mfg.

Traiguén Island, Chile: see CHONOS ARCHIPELAGO.

Traiguera (trīgā'rä), town (pop. 2,069), Castellón de la Plana prov., E Spain, 9 mi. WNW of Vinaroz; olive oil, wine, almonds.

Trail, city (pop. 9,392), SE B.C., near Wash. border, on Columbia R. and 100 mi. N of Spokane; metal-smelting center (silver, lead, zinc, gold, copper) in mining region; mfg. of sulphuric acid, fertilizer.

Trail Creek, town (pop. 817), La Porte co., NW Ind., just E of Michigan City.

Trail Island, Greenland: see TRAILL ISLAND.

Traill, county (□ 861; pop. 11,359), E N.Dak.; ⊙ Hillsboro. Agr. area bounded E by Red River of the North; drained by Goose R. Wheat processing, dairy products, livestock, turkeys. Formed 1875.

Traill Island (trāl) (70 mi. long, 25 mi. wide), in King Oscar Archipelago, E Greenland, in Greenland Sea; 72°35′N 23°20′W. Forms NE shore of King Oscar Fjord, just S of Geographical Society Isl. Generally mountainous, it is low and level in N and central parts; rises to 6,180 ft. Sometimes spelled Trail.

Trail of the Lonesome Pine, SW Va. and SE Ky., name sometimes applied to scenic route (mainly following Ky. Highway 15 and U.S. Highway 23) across the Cumberlands in Ky. and the Appalachians in Va., through region described in John Fox's novel *The Trail of the Lonesome Pine.* Route extends SE from Wolfe co., E central Ky., crossing Pine Mtn. at Pound Gap, thence S and SW into Lee co., SW Va.

Trainer, borough (pop. 2,001), Delaware co., SE Pa., on Delaware R. just below Chester; oil refining.

Traipu (trīpōō′), city (pop. 1,622), central Alagoas, NE Brazil, landing on left bank of lower São Francisco R. 36 mi. NW of Penedo; ships sugar, lumber.

Traisen (trī′zůn), town (pop. 3,004), central Lower Austria, on Traisen R. and 11 mi. S of Sankt Pölten; rail junction; ironworks.

Traisen River, central Lower Austria, rises near Sankt Aegyd am Neuwalde, flows 50 mi. N, past Sankt Pölten, to the Danube 7 mi. E of Krems an der Donau.

Traiskirchen (trīs′kĭrkhůn), town (pop. 5,930), E Lower Austria, 3 mi. E of Baden; rubber mfg., flour mills; vineyards.

Traismauer (trīs′mour), town (pop. 3,134), central Lower Austria, on Traisen R. and 8 mi. SE of Krems. Anc. Roman settlement.

Trait, Le (lů trā′), town (pop. 3,572), Seine-Inférieure dept., N France, on right bank of Seine R. and 13 mi. WNW of Rouen; large shipbuilding yards. Damaged in Second World War.

Trajano de Morais (trůzhä′nōō dĭ môrīs′), city (pop. 728), E central Rio de Janeiro state, Brazil, on railroad and 30 mi. ENE of Nova Friburgo; coffee.

Trajan's Wall (trā′jůnz), remains of Roman fortifications in Constanta prov., Rumania, extending from the great bend of the Danube 4 mi. SSW of Cernavoda to the Black Sea at Tomi near Constanta. It was erected under Trajan (1st-2d cent. A.D.) to protect Lower Moesia against invaders from the N. Another wall, also called Trajan's Wall, was constructed further N, from Prut R. to the Black Sea.

Trakai or **Trakay** (trä′kī), Ger. *Traken,* Pol. and Rus. *Troki,* city (1931 pop. 2,637), SE Lithuania, on S shore of small lake, 14 mi. WSW of Vilna; cement and flour mills, brickworks. Ruins of castle near by. In Rus. Vilna govt. until it passed (1921) to Poland; to Lithuania in 1939.

Trakiya, Bulgaria and Greece: see THRACE.

Tralee (trůlē′, trā-), Gaelic *Tráighlí,* urban district (pop. 9,990), ⊙ Co. Kerry, Ireland, in W part of co., on Lee R. near its mouth on Tralee Bay, and 160 mi. SW of Dublin, 60 mi. WNW of Cork; 52°16′N 9°42′W; seaport, linked with Tralee Bay at Blennerville by 1-mi.-long ship canal. Industries include mfg. of agr. implements, shoes, hosiery, furniture, toys, cattle feed. Copper is mined in vicinity. Tralee was hq. of the Desmonds, who had castle here. In 1643 and 1691 town was burned by inhabitants upon approach of English forces. In 13th cent. town was site of Dominican monastery.

Tralleborg, Sweden: see TRELLEBORG.

Tralles, Turkey: see AYDIN, town.

Trallwm, Wales: see WELSHPOOL.

Tramagal (trůmůgäl′), town (pop. 2,164), Santarém dist., central Portugal, on left bank of Tagus R. and 3 mi. SW of Abrantes; concrete mfg.

Tramandaí (trůmändäē′), town (pop. 749), NE Rio Grande do Sul, Brazil, bathing resort on the Atlantic, 65 mi. E of Pôrto Alegre; hotels, casino. Old spelling, Tramandahy.

Tramayes (trämā′), village (pop. 517), Saône-et-Loire dept., E central France, 11 mi. W of Mâcon; cattle.

Tramelan-Dessous (trämůlã-důsōō′) and **Tramelan-Dessus** (trämůlã důsü′), adjacent towns (total pop. 4,524), Bern canton, NW Switzerland, 9 mi. NW of Biel; watches, metalworking.

Tramin, Italy: see TERMENO.

Trammel, Lake, W Texas, impounded by dam in small Sweetwater Creek (a S tributary of Clear Fork of Brazos R.), 6 mi. S of Sweetwater; c.1 mi. long.

Trammel Fork of Drake Creek, Tenn., Ky.: see DRAKE CREEK.

Tramore (trůmôr′), Gaelic *Tráigh Mhór,* town (pop. 2,379), SE Co. Waterford, Ireland, on Tramore Bay, 7 mi. SSW of Waterford; fishing port and resort; racecourse.

Tramping Lake, village (pop. 202), W Sask., 50 mi. SW of North Battleford; wheat.

Tramutola (trämōō′tôlä), village (pop. 2,928), Potenza prov., Basilicata, S Italy, 23 mi. S of Potenza. Limestone quarries and lignite deposits near by.

Tramy (trä′mē′), village, Quangnam prov., central Vietnam, in Annamese Cordillera, 38 mi. SSW of Faifo; cinnamon-growing center.

Tranas (trän′ōs″), Swedish *Tranås,* city (1950 pop. 13,809), Jonkoping co., S Sweden, near Somme L., 35 mi. NE of Jonkoping; furniture mfg., woolen milling, fur processing, metalworking; health resort with mineral springs. Inc. as town 1882; as city 1919.

Trancas (träng′käs), town (pop. estimate 1,000), ⊙ Trancas dept. (□ c.1,500; 1947 pop. 9,957), N Tucumán prov., Argentina, on railroad and 43 mi. NNW of Tucumán, in agr. area (corn, alfalfa, sugar cane, livestock).

Trancoso (trängkō′sō), village (pop. 2,264), Zacatecas, N central Mexico, 14 mi. SE of Zacatecas; cereals, vegetables, maguey, livestock.

Trancoso (trãng-kō′zōō), town (pop. 1,381), Guarda dist., N central Portugal, 16 mi. NNW of Guarda. Preserves medieval ramparts and 13th-cent. church. Scene of Port. victory over Spaniards in 1385.

Tranebjaerg (trä′nůbyĕr), town (pop. 771), Holbaek amt, Zealand, Denmark, on central Samso isl. and 45 mi. WNW of Holbaek; furs; mfg. (margarine, machinery).

Tranemo (trä′nůmōō″), village (pop. 1,062), Alvsborg co., SW Sweden, 20 mi. SE of Boras; hosiery mills.

Tranent (trůnĕnt′), burgh (1931 pop. 4,526; 1951 census 5,639), W East Lothian, Scotland, 7 mi. W of Haddington; coal mining.

Trang (träng), town (1947 pop. 8,622), ⊙ Trang prov. (□ 1,922; 1947 pop. 148,591), S Thailand, in Malay Peninsula, on railroad and 70 mi. ENE of Songkhla, on Trang R. (short coastal stream flowing to Andaman Sea at Kantang); linked by road with Phatthalung; tin and coal mining near by. Large Chinese pop.

Trangan, Indonesia: see ARU ISLANDS.

Trangbang (träng′bäng′), town (1936 pop. 8,039), Tayninh prov., S Vietnam, on Saigon-Pnompenh highway and 30 mi. NW of Saigon; tobacco and rubber plantations.

Trangbom (träng′bŏm′), village, Bienhoa prov., S Vietnam, on Saigon-Hanoi RR and 25 mi. NE of Saigon; lumbering center; forestry research station.

Trangsund, Russian SFSR: see VYSOTSK, Leningrad oblast.

Trangsviken (trôngs′vē″kůn), Swedish *Trångsviken,* village (pop. 382), Jamtland co., NW central Sweden, at NW end of Stor L., 20 mi. NW of Ostersund; limestone quarries, sawmills.

Trani (trä′nē), anc. *Turenum,* town (pop. 29,962), Bari prov., Apulia, S Italy, port on the Adriatic, 8 mi. ESE of Barletta. Noted for its wine. Bell foundry; stone-cutting. Quarry near by. Archbishopric. Has Romanesque cathedral, 13th-cent. castle, several palaces. Achieved great prosperity during the Crusades and again in 15th–16th cent. Its *ordinamenta maris* (1063) probably 1st medieval maritime code.

Tranninh, province, Laos: see XIENGKHOUANG.

Tranninh Plateau (trän′nĭng′), N Laos, at N end of Annamese Cordillera, extends (c.40 mi. wide, c.30 mi. long) E of Luang Prabang; alt. c.3,900–4,600 ft. Its red clay and sandstone hills are deeply cut by valleys of small streams, lined with oak and pine forests. Chief town is Xiengkhouang. Mineral deposits (gold, tin, tungsten, precious stones); hot springs. Crossed by Luang Prabang–Vinh road.

Tranquebar (trăng′kůbär), Tamil *Tarangampadi* (tůrŭng′gŭmpůdē), town (pop. 11,111), Tanjore dist., SE Madras, India, port on Coromandel Coast of Bay of Bengal, 18 mi. N of Negapatam, near N border of Fr. settlement of Karikal. Rail terminus; exports agr. products of Cauvery R. delta; salt factory. Site of 1st Protestant mission in India (1706). Under Danes from 1620 (except for English occupation, 1801–14) until sold 1845 to English.

Tranqueras (trängkā′räs), town (pop. 3,200), Rivera dept., NE Uruguay, on Tacuarembó R., on railroad and 20 mi. SSW of Rivera; road junction; livestock, grain, vegetables.

Tranqui Island (träng′kē) (□ 35; pop. 1,516), just off SE coast of Chiloé Isl., S Chile, 30 mi. SSE of Castro; 43°S; 15 mi. long, c.3 mi. wide.

Trans-Alai Range or **Trans-Alay Range** (trăns″-ălī′, trănz″-), Rus. *Zaalaiski Khrebet,* branch of Pamir-Alai mtn. system, extends c.125 mi. W from USSR-China border, along Kirghiz-Tadzhik SSR border; forms N border of the Pamir; rises to 23,382 ft. in Lenin Peak (formerly Mt. Kaufman), first climbed in 1928. Osh-Khorog highway crosses at Kyzyl-Art Pass (alt. 14,045 ft.). The Kyzyl-Su, in Alai Valley, separates it from ALAI RANGE.

Transalpine Gaul, France: see GAUL; FRANCE.

Transandine Railway, narrow-gauge section across the Andes bet. Mendoza (Argentina) and Los Andes (Chile) of the transcontinental railroad from Buenos Aires on the Atlantic to Valparaiso on the Pacific. Partly cog-line (6.7 mi.), it passes through a c.2-mi.-long tunnel underneath Uspallata Pass (at S foot of the Aconcagua) at an altitude of 10,468 ft. The international boundary runs roughly across tunnel's center. Distance from the border to Mendoza is 111 mi., from border to Los Andes 44 mi. The railroad was inaugurated in May, 1910. Service was, however, interrupted several times, particularly by destructions caused by glacial flood in 1934 on the Argentina side; reopened 1944. Because of the great hazards of this line (it is also snowbound for many months), other transandine rail links have been constructed. Most important of these is the c.550-mi.-long Transandine RR of the North (opened 1948) from Salta (N Argentina) via Socompa Pass (12,657 ft.) to Antofagasta (N Chile). An alternate link across the lower S Andes from Zapala in Neuquén natl. territory of S Argentina via Pino Hachado Pass is under consideration. There are also several railroads across the main W cordillera of the Andes in Bolivia and the Pacific-coast countries.

Transbaikalia (trăns″bīkä′lyů, trănz″-), Rus. *Zabaikalye* or *Zabaykal′ye,* region of SE Siberian Russian SFSR, bet. L. Baikal (W) and upper Amur R. (E), on Mongolian frontier. Includes BURYAT-MONGOL AUTONOMOUS SSR and CHITA oblast.

Transcarpathian Oblast (trănz″kärpā′thēůn), Rus. Zakarpatskaya Oblast, administrative division (□ 5,000; 1947 pop. estimate 900,000) of W Ukrainian SSR; ⊙ Uzhgorod. Bet. the central Carpathians (Beshchady, Gorgany, Chernagora) and upper Tissa R.; bounded S by Rumania, SW by Hungary, W by Czechoslovakia, NW by Poland. Forests (mainly oak and beech) occupy half of area; sheep grazing in subalpine meadows. Salt mining (Solotvino); lignite and low-grade iron deposits. Agr., with corn, wheat, oats, wine, fruit, tobacco (S), potatoes and rye (on mtn. slopes). Lumbering, woodworking, wood cracking important in mts. Flour milling, handicrafts (leather, baskets, embroidery) are chief rural industries. Oblast is linked with rest of Ukraine by Uzhok, Veretski, and Yablonitsa passes (roads, railroads). Pop. (now largely of Ukrainian stock) was formerly very mixed and included Magyars, Jews, Slovaks, and Germans. Main centers: Uzhgorod, Mukachevo, Khust, Beregovo. Originally part of Hungary, the region was given (1918) to Czechoslovakia and confirmed by the Trianon Treaty (1920). While in Czechoslovakia the area constituted a prov. variously known as Ruthenia, Carpathian Ruthenia, Carpathian Russia, or Subcarpathian Ruthenia [Czech *Podkarpatská Rus*]. Following Munich Pact, Hungary annexed (1938) a S border strip of the region, including the main cities. Remaining territory, temporarily an autonomous unit (Carpatho-Ukraine, Czech. *Karpatská Ukraina;* ⊙ Khust) within Czechoslovakia, was annexed (1939) by Hungary and made an autonomous dist. (Carpathia, Hung. *Kárpátalja;* extraterritorial ⊙ at Uzhgorod). The region was occupied (1944) by Soviet troops and was returned briefly to Czechoslovakia, who ceded the whole area to USSR in 1945.

Transcaspian Oblast (trăns″-kăs′pēůn, trănz″-), former administrative division of Rus. Turkestan, roughly coextensive with present Turkmen SSR; ⊙ was Ashkhabad. Made a govt. in 1917, became (1922) part of Turkestan Autonomous SSR and renamed Turkmen Oblast. Abolished in 1924 when area became part of Turkmen SSR.

Trans-Caspian Railroad, major rail link of Soviet Central Asia, linking Krasnovodsk on Caspian Sea and Chkalov in S Urals region. Built from 1880 to 1905, the line describes a wide arc, passing through (or near) Ashkhabad, Bukhara, Samarkand, Tashkent, Kyzyl-Orda, Aralsk (at N tip of Aral Sea), and Aktyubinsk. Its principal branch lines lead to Kushka, Kungrad, Stalinabad, and the Fergana Valley. At Arys, it connects with the Turkestan-Siberia RR. Taking advantage of oases at the foot of the central Asian ranges, the railroad skirts the deserts of Kara-Kum and Kyzyl-Kum.

Transcaucasia, USSR: see CAUCASUS.

Transcona (trănskō′nů), town (pop. 6,132), SE Man., 7 mi. E of Winnipeg; railroad center with large shops, creosoting plant, grain elevators.

Transdanubia, Hungary: see DUNANTUL.

Trans-Himalayas (hĭmä′lůyůz, hĭmůlā′ůz), ill-defined mountain area, S Tibet, separated from CHANG TANG plateau (N) by ALING KANGRI range, from the Himalayas (S) by Brahmaputra R.; bordered SW by KAILAS RANGE, SE by NYENCHEN TANGLHA range; 600 mi. long, 140 mi. wide in center, narrowing to 20 mi. at E and W ends. Forms watershed bet. Bay of Bengal (S) and enclosed drainage depression (N). There is no marked crest line or central alignment and no division by rivers as in the great Himalayas; passes are generally higher (average alt., 17,500 ft.; Ding La, at 19,308 ft., is highest). Discovered 1906 and named by Sven Hedin.

Trans-Ili Ala-Tau (trăns″-ēlē′ ä′lä tou′), Rus. *Zailiski Ala-Tau, Zailiiski Ala-Tau,* or *Zailiyskiy Ala-Tau,* range of Tien Shan mtn. system, in Alma-Ata oblast, Kazakh SSR, on Kirghiz SSR border; extends W from Chilik R. to Chu-Ili Mts.; rises to 16,027 ft. in Talgar peak. Intensive irrigated agr. (mainly orchards) on N slopes, site of Alma-Ata.

Transilvania, Rumania: see TRANSYLVANIA.

Transinne (trăsēn′), village (pop. 425), Luxembourg prov., SE Belgium, 9 mi. NW of Libramont, in the Ardennes; kaolin-earth quarrying.

Trânsito (trän'sētō), town (pop. estimate 1,500), E central Córdoba prov., Argentina, 60 mi. E of Córdoba; wheat, flax, corn, livestock; mfg. of electrical goods.

Trânsito or **El Trânsito** (ĕl), village (1930 pop. 322), Atacama prov., N central Chile, on affluent of Huasco R., on W slope of the Andes, and 35 mi. SE of Vallenar, in agr. area (corn, alfalfa, wine, goats), at an Andean pass, the Paso del Inca.

Trânsito, El, Honduras: see NACAOME.

Trânsito, El, Salvador: see EL TRÁNSITO.

Trânsito Island, Chile: see CHONOS ARCHIPELAGO.

Trans-Jordan or **Transjordania:** see JORDAN.

Trans-Juba, Ital. Somaliland: see JUBALAND.

Transkei (trănskā', träns–), district (□ 2,504; total pop. 256,028; native pop. 253,307) of the TRANSKEIAN TERRITORIES, E Cape Prov., U. of So. Afr., bounded by Great Kei R. (SW), Tembuland (NW, N, and NE), and Indian Ocean (E); center near 32°5'S 28°10'E; ⊙ Butterworth. Dairying, stock raising, wool production are chief occupations. Largely a native reserve, dist. adopted council system of administration 1895, when Transkei General Council was established.

Transkeian Territories (trănskī'ŭn, –kā'ŭn, träns–), division (□ 16,554; total pop. 1,279,922; native pop. 1,250,811) of E Cape Prov., U. of So. Afr., extends bet. Great Kei R. (S), Indian Ocean (E), and Natal Prov. and Basutoland borders (N); ⊙ Umtata. Includes districts of Transkei (consisting of Fingoland and Galekaland regions and Idutywa Reserve), Tembuland (including Bomvanaland), Griqualand East, and Pondoland. Greater part of division consists of native reserve (□ c.13,000); stock raising, wool production, grain growing are chief activities. Much labor for the Witwatersrand mines is recruited here. Division was formerly part of KAFFRARIA region. Native councils were established in several parts of present territory and united (1895) in Transkei General Council; council system expanded until, with adherence of Pondoland (1930), the United Transkeian Territories General Council was set up to govern present area.

Transleithania (trăns'lēthā'nēŭ), formerly part of Austria-Hungary E of Leitha R., an area now in Hungary. The area W of Leitha R.—Cisleithania—is now in Austria.

Transnistria (trănsnĭ'strēŭ), former Rumanian administrative division organized (1941–43) in occupied Ukrainian SSR, bet. Dniester and Southern Bug rivers; ⊙ was Odessa. Used for exiled Jewish pop. of Rumania.

Trans-Nzoia, district, Kenya: see KITALE.

Transoxiana (trăns"ŏksēā'nŭ) or **Sogdiana** (sŏg'dēă'nŭ), anc. region of central Asia, across (N of) the Amu Darya (anc. *Oxus*) and extending to the Syr Darya; chief cities were Samarkand and Bukhara. Conquered 329 B.C. by Alexander the Great, it fell (7th cent. A.D.) to the Arabs and was a center of Islamic culture until 9th cent. Controlled (13th-15th cents.) by the Mongols, later by the Uzbeks and emirs of Bukhara. Anc. Sogdian was an Iranian language written in an Aramaic script.

Transpadane Republic, Italy: see CISALPINE REPUBLIC.

Transquaking River (trăn'skwā"kĭng), Dorchester co., E Md., on the Eastern Shore, rises just S of Secretary, flows c.25 mi. S through muskrat-trapping marshes to head of Fishing Bay.

Trans-Siberian Railroad, major rail line of Asiatic USSR, linking European Russia with the Pacific coast; 4,600 mi. long, bet. Chelyabinsk and Vladivostok. Built 1892–1905, the original line ran generally E through Omsk, Novosibirsk, Krasnoyarsk, Irkutsk, Chita, and, as the Chinese Eastern RR, through Manchuria, to Vladivostok. During the First World War an all-Russian link was completed bet. Chita and Vladivostok, following the Amur and Ussuri rivers. The opening of the railroad was of tremendous consequence in the history of Siberia, opening it up to settlement and industrialization.

Transvaal (trănsväl', trănz–, Afrikaans tränsfäl') [across the Vaal river], province (□ 110,450; pop. 4,283,038), NE U. of So. Afr., bounded by Natal and Orange Free State across Vaal R. (S), Cape Prov. (SW), Bechuanaland Protectorate (W), Southern Rhodesia across Limpopo R. (N), Mozambique (E), and Swaziland (SE); ⊙ Pretoria. Surface, part of the Northern Karroo, is generally high veld country, 3–4,000 ft. high, broken (S) by high ridge of the WITWATERSRAND, rising to c.6,000 ft. Drakensberg range extends in to SE part of prov.; other ranges rising above general plateau level are Zoutpansberg, Magaliesberg, and Strydpoort mts. Main streams are Vaal, Limpopo, Crocodile, Magalakwin, and Komati rivers. In NE part of prov. is Kruger Natl. Park. Ranching, stock raising, agr.; products include wool, hides, skins, wheat, corn, citrus and deciduous fruit, tobacco, vegetables, wattles. Gold mining, centered on the Witwatersrand (which produces a large part of the world's gold), is chief industry; other mineral resources include diamonds, coal, iron, chrome, nickel, copper, asbestos, cryolite, platinum. Among mfg. industries are iron and steel milling (Vereeniging, Pretoria), mfg. of cement, leather, machinery, chemicals, explosives. Johannesburg is largest city of the Union; other important towns are Germiston, Springs, Nigel, Vereeniging, Heidelberg, Roodepoort-Maraisburg, Randfontein, Potchefstroom, Pietersburg, Witbank, Krugersdorp, Klerksdorp. Prov. settled by Boer Voortrekkers from Cape Colony beginning 1835; native Matabele were driven out and Andries Pretorius was appointed (1848) commandant of Boer settlers. Under Sand River Convention (1852) Great Britain recognized the independence of Transvaal, which in 1853 became the South African Republic, led by Martinus Pretorius. Transvaal was annexed (1877) by Great Britain, but after a meeting at Paardekraal, Dec., 1880, followed by armed rising, and the defeat of the British in several engagements, 1880–81, self-govt. was restored 1881. Paul Kruger elected president 1883. Witwatersrand gold field proclaimed 1886, followed by great influx of prospectors from the Cape, England, and other countries. Refusal of political rights to *Uitlanders* [foreigners] led to abortive Jameson Raid (1895–96) and later to South African War (1899–1902). After Treaty of Vereeniging (May 31, 1902) Transvaal became British crown colony. Self-govt. introduced 1907; Transvaal became prov. of U. of So. Afr. 1910.

Transylvania (trănsĭlvā'nyŭ) [Latin, =beyond the woods], Rum. *Transilvania* or *Ardeal* (ärdĕäl'), Ger. *Siebenbürgen* (zē'bŭnbür"gŭn), Hung. *Erdély* (ĕr'dā), historic province (□ 24,009; 1948 pop. 3,420,829) of central Rumania; chief city, Cluj. It is separated in S from Walachia by the Transylvanian Alps, in E from Moldavia and Bukovina by the Moldavian Carpathians. Banat, Crisana, and Maramures lie along its SW, W, and N borders, with the Apuseni Mts. penetrating inland from W. The interior is a plateau (mean alt. 1,000–1,600 ft.) traversed NE–SW by Mures R. E and S sections are drained by Olt. R., NW section by Somes R. Mures and Somes valleys provide the 2 main openings into the Alföld plain. Continental climate, with long and severe winters in mountains. Economically and culturally, it is the most advanced region in Rumania. Natural resources: lignite deposits in Jiu R. valley; large reserves of methane; iron, manganese, precious metals, lead, sulphur, some copper, and salt; also abundant mineral springs. Much of Rumanian metallurgical and chemical industries is concentrated here (Hunedoara, Stalin, Cluj, and Sibiu provs.). Mfg. of textiles, food processing, and lumbering are developed as well. Stock raising is important (cattle and horses; Merino sheep, buffaloes, hogs). Forage crops, cereals, potatoes, flax, and sugar beets are principal crops, and the vineyards and orchards are notable. Chief cities are Cluj, Stalin (Brasov), and Sibiu. Rural pop. is predominantly Rumanian (Walachian), while Magyar and German elements (c.⅓ of total pop.) are large, constituting the majority in some towns. Rumanians belong to Orthodox faith, most of Hungarians to R.C. and Unitarian churches; Germans are Protestants. A distinct branch of Magyar stock are the Szeklers, former frontier-guards settled in foothills of the Carpathians. There are also some Gypsies, Jews, and descendants of 17th-cent. Armenians who are today fairly Magyarized. Anciently a part of Roman Dacia (established A.D. 107 by Trajan), the territory was overrun after late 3d cent. A.D. by Germanic, Mongol, and Slavonic tribes, and incorporated in 11th cent. into the domain of Hungarian crown by Ladislaus I, as a principality under a local voivode. In 12th-13th cent. Saxon colonists, invited by the kings of Hungary, built the first 7 fortified towns (present Sibiu, Cluj, Stalin, Bistrita, Medias, Sebes, and Sighisoara), which were granted the title of royal free cities. Transylvanian diets constituted of representatives of Magyars, Szeklers, and Germans met as early as 1229; no political rights were recognized for the peasant majority of Walachians or Vlachs (later called Rumanians) until 1848. Mongol and Turkish invasions ravaged the country in 13th cent. After defeat of Louis II by the Turks at Mohacs (1526), Transylvanian princes gradually cut loose from Hungary and became tributary to the Sultan. Reformation movement brought about the conversion of previously all-catholic Magyars and Germans to Calvinist, Lutheran, and Unitarian faiths. Michael the Brave united briefly (1593–1601) Transylvania, Moldavia, and Walachia. Under Gabriel Bethlen (1613–29) and George Rakoczy (1631–48), Transylvania achieved its "Golden Age" and was considered the main bulwark of Protestantism in E Europe. Following Turkish collapse before Vienna (1683), the territory was placed under the Hapsburg Leopold I by the treaties of Vienna (1686) and Blaj (1687), recognized by Turkey at the peace of Karlovci (1699). Transylvania came then under direct administration of Vienna. Resistance of some Magyar factions continued, however, until the peace of Satu-Mare (1711). Transylvania was proclaimed a grand principality in 1765. Walachian or Rumanian demands for political rights were rejected by the Diet (1790–91). When a wave of Magyar nationalism swept the country demanding reunion with Hungary, Rumanians swore fealty to the Hapsburgs at Blaj (1848) and supported Austro-Russian troops against Magyar revolutionaries after proclamation of union by the Diet at Cluj. Austrian constitution of 1851 abolished Saxon privileges and reduced the country to a Hapsburg crownland. Through the *Ausgleich* of 1867, Transylvania became again an integral part of Hungary and was dominated by Magyar racial policy until 1918. National council of Rumanians of Transylvania was established at Arad following First World War and a convention assembled at Alba-Iulia (1918) to proclaim solidarity with Rumania. Final incorporation into Rumanian state was effected by Treaty of Trianon (1920). During interwar years considerable controversy prevailed among local nationalities. The N part (□ 17,040; pop. c.2,700,000) of Transylvania was reannexed by Hungary briefly (1940–45). The name Transylvania is sometimes extended to include Banat and Crisana-Maramures.

Transylvania, county (□ 379; pop. 15,194), W N.C., on S.C. line; ⊙ Brevard. Blue Ridge area, partly in Pisgah Natl. Forest, in W; drained by French Broad R. Farming (vegetables, hay, corn), dairying, poultry raising, timber (oak, poplar, chestnut, hemlock); sawmilling; resort region; mfg. at Brevard and Pisgah Forest. Formed 1861.

Transylvanian Alps (–nēŭn), Rum. *Carpaţii Meridionali* (kärpäts'-mĕrēdyônäl'), Hung. *Déli-Kárpátok* (dā'lē-kär'pätôk) or *Erdélyi-Havasok* (ĕr'-dāyē-hŏ'vŏshôk), S section of the Carpathians in central and SW Rumania, extending c.170 mi. in length and 25–40 mi. in width bet. the upper valley of Prahova R. (E) and the Danube at the Iron Gates (W), forming most of Walachia-Transylvania border. Rise to 8,361 ft. in Negoi and 8,344 ft. in Moldoveanu peaks, both in the Fagaras Mts. It is broken into number of crystalline massifs (FAGARAS, BUCEGI, VULCAN, RETEZAT, GODEANU, TARCU) having a typical alpine topography but no permanent snow cover. Traces of former glaciation abound (cirques, lakes, moraines). Resources include coal and iron ore deposits in the Banat, major lignite seams in the upper Jiu valley. Extensive forests; subalpine meadows support large sheep-grazing industry. Communication channels are provided by the narrow gorges of Olt and Jiu rivers and the passes of Bran, Turnu Rosu, Surduc, and Porta Orientalis. Arges, Dambovita, Ialomita, and Jiu rivers rise here.

Traon (trä'-ōn'), town, Cantho prov., S Vietnam, port on Bassac R. and 10 mi. SE of Cantho; rice.

Trapani (trä'pänē), province (□ 968; pop. 375,169), W Sicily; ⊙ Trapani. Hilly terrain, rising to 3,742 ft. at Monte Sparagio; drained by small rivers. Agr.: vineyards (W coast), wheat (center), citrus fruit (NW), olives; sheep raising in NW. Tunny fisheries in Egadi Isls., off W coast. Saltworks. Limestone, sandstone, gypsum. Anc. ruins at Segesta, Selinus, Motya.

Trapani, anc. *Drepanum,* city (pop. 52,661), ⊙ Trapani prov., W Sicily, on Mediterranean Sea, 46 mi. W of Palermo; 38°1'N 12°31'E. Salt-shipping port; canned tunny fish, Marsala wine, alcohol, macaroni; soap, glass; working of coral, marble, wood. Power station. Extensive saltworks (S). During First Punic War, important Carthaginian naval station. Bishopric. Has cathedral (damaged in Second World War), church (founded 1332; remodeled 1760), convent, castle, palaces (Palazzo Staiti destroyed, Palazzo Riccio badly damaged in Second World War), archaeological mus. (damaged in Second World War), technical and nautical institute. Heavily bombed 1943.

Trapezus, Turkey: see TREBIZOND, city.

Trapiche (träpē'chā), town (pop. estimate 500), N San Luis prov., Argentina, at SE foot of Sierra de San Luis, 18 mi. NE of San Luis; resort, stock-raising, and mining center (copper, nickel, sulphur, mica deposits near by).

Trappe (trăp). **1** Town (pop. 325), Talbot co., E Md., 6 mi. NNE of Cambridge; vegetable canneries. Historic homes in vicinity include Hampden (1665); The Wilderness, with boxwood gardens; Saulsbury House (1663); and Crosidore, birthplace of John Dickinson. **2** Borough (pop. 773), Montgomery co., SE Pa., 9 mi. NW of Norristown. Oldest Lutheran church (1743) in America here.

Trapper Peak, Mont.: see BITTERROOT RANGE.

Trappes (trăp), town (pop. 2,438), Seine-et-Oise dept., N central France, 6 mi. WSW of Versailles; sawmilling. Damaged in Second World War. Ruined abbey of Port-Royal-des-Champs (founded 1204; hq. of Jansenists; razed 1710) is 3 mi. SSE.

Trappist, Ky.: see GETHSEMANE.

Trappstadt (träp'shtät), village (pop. 761), Lower Franconia, N Bavaria, Germany, 17 mi. WNW of Coburg; grain, cattle.

Traquair (trŭkwâr'), agr. village and parish (pop. 551), E Peebles, Scotland, just S of Innerleithen. Traquair House is noted 17th-cent. mansion.

Traralgon (trŭrăl'gŭn), town (pop. 4,384), S Victoria, Australia, 90 mi. ESE of Melbourne; rail junction; livestock.

Trarbach, Germany: see TRABEN-TRARBACH.

Traryd (trä'rüd"), village (pop. 550), Kronoberg co., S Sweden, on Laga R. and 19 mi. SSW of Ljungby; ironworks, hydroelectric station.

Tras (träs), village (pop. 415), W Pahang, Malaya, in central Malayan range, 4 mi. SW of Raub; rubber collecting.

Trashi Bhup Tso or **Trashi Phub Tsho** (both: trä'shē pōōb tsō), Chinese *T'a-shih-pu Hu* (tä'shü'bōō' hōō'), lake in central Tibet, 400 mi. NW of Lhasa; 32°10'N 84°55'E.

Trashi Cho, Bhutan: see TASHI CHHO.

Trashi Lhümpo, Tibet: see TASHI LUMPO.

Trashi Phub Tsho, Tibet: see TRASHI BHUP TSO.

Trasierra (träsyĕ'rä), town (pop. 1,150), Badajoz prov., W Spain, 3 mi. S of Llerena; cereals, olives, sheep, goats.

Trasimeno, Lake (träzēmā'nô), or **Lake of Perugia** (pûrōō'jēŭ) (□ 50), Umbria, central Italy, 10 mi. W of Perugia; circular, 10 mi. in diameter; max. depth 20 ft.; alt. 850 ft. Contains 3 islets. Has artificial subterranean outlet (SE; opened 1898) to an affluent of the Tiber. On its shores Hannibal defeated (217 B.C.) Romans under Flaminius.

Traskanda, Finland: see JÄRVENPÄÄ.

Traskwood, town (pop. 199), Saline co., central Ark., 9 mi. SSW of Benton.

Traslovslage (trĕs'lŭfs"lä"gŭ), Swedish *Träslövsläge*, fishing village (pop. 721), Halland co., SW Sweden, on the Kattegat, 3 mi. S of Varberg.

Trás os Montes (träz ōōsh mōn'tĭsh), village, Malange prov., N central Angola, 100 mi. SW of Vila Henrique de Carvalho. Formerly Cucumbi.

Trás-os-Montes, former province (□ 4,163; 1940 pop. 502,347), northeasternmost Portugal; old ⊙ Bragança. It contained Bragança and Vila Real dists. Bounded by Spain (N and E) and by the Douro (S). Along right bank of Douro R. is Portugal's renowned winegrowing region (port wine). Prov. was part of county of Portugal before Moors had been expelled from territory S of the Douro. In 1936, prov. was superseded by larger Trás-os-Montes e Alto Douro prov. Formerly spelled Traz-os-Montes.

Trás-os-Montes e Alto Douro (ē äl'tōō dō'rōō), province (□ 4,569; 1940 pop. 592,079), northernmost Portugal, formed 1936 from old Trás-os-Montes prov. and N part of old Beira prov.; ⊙ Vila Real. It contains Bragança and Vila Real dists., and small sections of Guarda and Viseu dists. Cities: Bragança, Vila Real, Miranda do Douro, Chaves, Lamego.

Traspinedo (träspēnä'dhō), town (pop. 1,319), Valladolid prov., N central Spain, near the Duero (Douro), 14 mi. ESE of Valladolid; cereals, sugar beets, chicory; pine wood.

Trastenik (trŭstĕnēk'). **1** Village (pop. 6,370), Pleven dist., N Bulgaria, 11 mi. NW of Pleven; flour milling; livestock, legumes, oil-bearing plants. Formerly Marashki Trastenik. **2** Village (pop. 4,412), Ruse dist., NE Bulgaria, 12 mi. SSW of Ruse; sugar beets, sunflowers, truck.

Trat (trät), town (1947 pop. 2,366), ⊙ Trat prov. (□ 1,076; 1947 pop. 44,819), SE Thailand, near Gulf of Siam, 210 mi. SE of Bangkok, on road from Chachoengsao and near Cambodia line; rice, pepper, coconuts. Held by Fr. troops, 1904–07. Also spelled Krat.

Tratayén, Argentina: see AÑELO.

Trattendorf, Germany: see SPREMBERG.

Traû, Yugoslavia: see TROGIR.

Trauíra, island, Brazil: see MARACAÇUMÉ RIVER.

Traun (troun), town (pop. 9,296), central Upper Austria, on Traun R. and 6 mi. S of Linz; textiles.

Traun, Lake, Ger. *Traunsee* (troun'zā) or *Gmundner See* (gŭmōōn'dŭnŭrzā), lake (□ 10), S Upper Austria, in the Salzkammergut, 35 mi. E of Salzburg; 8 mi. long, 1–2 mi. wide, max. depth 645 ft., alt. 1,384 ft. Traversed by Traun R. The Traunstein towers on E shore. Among resorts on the lake are Gmunden at N, Ebensee at S tip.

Traun River, Upper Austria, rises in the Totes Gebirge near Bad Aussee, NE of Obertraun; flows 80 mi. N, through the Salzkammergut, past Wels, to the Danube 3 mi. SE of Linz. Traverses lakes of Hallstatt and Traun; passes resort towns of Bad Ischl, Ebensee, and Gmunden. Navigable in parts by small craft. Hydroelectric plant at the Traunfall, N of Steyremühl.

Traunstein (troun'shtīn), peak (5,546 ft.) of the Salzkammergut, in S Upper Austria; rises almost perpendicularly on E shore of L. Traun.

Traunstein, city (1950 pop. 14,467), Upper Bavaria, Germany, at N foot of the Salzburg Alps, on the Traun and 24 mi. E of Rosenheim; rail junction; saltworks; textile and paint mfg., metalworking, printing, lumber and paper milling, brewing. Summer resort (alt. 1,906 ft.), with salt and mud baths. Has late-17th-cent. church. Chartered 1311.

Trautenau, Czechoslovakia: see TRUTNOV.

Travagliato (trävälyä'tô), town (pop. 5,102), Brescia prov., Lombardy, N Italy, 7 mi. W of Brescia; mfg. (hosiery, silk textiles, bakery machinery).

Travancore (tră'vŭnkôr, trăvŭnkôr'), locally *Tiruvankur* or *Tiruvalumkodi*, administrative division (□ 7,662; 1941 pop. 6,070,018; 1948 pop. estimate 6,502,000) of TRAVANCORE-COCHIN, India; ⊙ Trivandrum. Lies bet. MALABAR COAST of Arabian Sea (W) and crest of S section of Western Ghats (E, on Madras border) and includes Cape Comorin (S, on Indian Ocean). Coastal lowlands (10–20 mi. wide; have noted lagoon-canal network), alluvial central plains (30–40 mi. wide), and highlands (average alt. c.7,000 ft.; rise to 8,841 ft. in Anai Mudi peak) are drained by many streams, notably Periyar R. (forms PERIYAR LAKE). Travancore has tropical monsoon climate, annual mean temp. varying little from 80°F.; annual rainfall 80–100 in.; short dry season (Jan.–March). Rice is important in all areas except higher mtn. ranges; dense coconut, palmyra, and areca groves in coastal lowlands (experimental jute growing since 1948); mangoes, jack, tamarind, cassava, peanuts, cashew nuts, in central plains. In the Ghats (mainly in Anaimalai and Cardamom hills) are extensive tea, coffee, cardamom, pepper, and rubber plantations; teak, ebony, blackwood, and bamboo tracts; turmeric and other spices; elephants, leopards, and bison. Numerous fishing villages along coast. Travancore's beach sands contain rich deposits of ilmenite, monazite, rutile, and zircon; since 1920s, Travancore has been world's leading producer of ilmenite; India's Atomic Energy Commission began construction (1950) of plant at Alwaye to process monazite (formerly used mainly for mfg. of gas-light mantles) for thorium. Varied industries, powered by Pallivasal hydroelectric works at MUNNAR, include copra, aluminum, rubber, and tea processing, rice, cassava, and cashew-nut milling, mfg. of coir products (rope and mats), cotton and silk textiles, glass, tiles and pottery, plywood, paper, matches, and chemical fertilizer. Principal cities are Trivandrum (has Univ. of Travancore), Alleppey, Nagercoil, Quilon (major port), Kottayam, Alwaye, Shencottah. Madras port of COCHIN (on NW coast; connected by lagoon-canal system with Quilon) serves Travancore's variegated hinterland. Quilon and Trivandrum (airport) are linked by rail via Ariankavu pass in the Ghats with Tenkasi junction in Madras. From early Christian era, region was part of the domains of the Chera dynasties and had flourishing trade with Rome and China; allegedly evangelized by St. Thomas the Apostle. Vijayanagar kingdom held the region from 1534 until its downfall in 1565. First Br. settlement established 1684 at Anjengo. In mid-18th cent., descendants of the Chera kings unified warring successor kingdoms of the Vijayanagars, and Travancore became a staunch ally of the British in their wars with the Mysore sultans, Hyder Ali and Tippoo Sahib; formal treaty concluded 1795. As a princely state, it was known for its comparatively high degree of literacy (48% in 1941) and progressive government (had legislative council and equal franchise for women). Many cultural patterns of Travancore—matrilineal descent, elaborate and rigid caste system—are common to the rest of KERALA. In 1949, state merged with Cochin to form Travancore-Cochin.

Travancore-Cochin (kō'chĭn'), constituent state (□ 9,155; 1951 census pop. 9,265,157), SW India; ⊙ Trivandrum. Bordered W by Malabar Coast of Arabian Sea and entirely surrounded on its land side by Madras. Formed 1949 by merger of MADRAS STATES of TRAVANCORE and COCHIN; enclaves exchanged 1950 with Madras. One of most densely populated areas in India (over 800 persons per sq. mi.); pop. comprises Hindus (60%), Christians (30%), and Moslems (10%). Main languages are Malayalam (spoken by over 90% of pop.), Tamil, Telugu, and Kanarese.

Travancore Hills, India: see CARDAMOM HILLS.

Travassac, France: see DONZENAC.

Travedona (trävĕdô'nä), village (pop. 1,211), Varese prov., Lombardy, N Italy, 8 mi. W of Varese; mfg. (linen goods).

Travelers Rest, village, Greenville co., NW S.C., 8 mi. N of Greenville, in foothills of the Blue Ridge; textiles, insulating material.

Travemünde (trä"vümün'dŭ), outer suburb of Lübeck, NW Germany, at mouth of Trave R. estuary on Lübeck Bay of the Baltic, 10 mi. NE of Lübeck city center; popular seaside resort with fishing harbor and airport. First mentioned 1219, it was acquired by Lübeck in 1329 as a harbor. Lost its importance as Lübeck's outer harbor after regulation (in late-19th cent.) of Trave estuary. Inc. 1913 into city of Lübeck.

Traventhal (trä'vŭntäl), village (pop. 655), in Schleswig-Holstein, NW Germany, on the Trave and 3 mi. S of Bad Segeberg; stud. Peace of Traventhal (1700) was concluded here bet. Sweden and Denmark. Formerly sometimes Travendal.

Trave River (trä'vŭ), NW Germany, rises 5 mi. S of Eutin, flows 65 mi. SW, S, and E, past Bad Oldesloe (head of barge navigation), to Lübeck, where it forms a 15-mi.-long estuary (navigable for small ocean-going craft) which reaches Lübeck Bay of the Baltic at Travemünde. Receives Elbe-Trave Canal at Lübeck.

Travers (trävär'), town (pop. 1,653), Neuchâtel canton, W Switzerland, in Val de Travers, a valley of upper Areuse R. Asphalt deposits bet. Travers and Couvet. Fleurier is largest town in valley.

Traverse (tră'vŭrs), county (□ 572; pop. 8,053), W Minn.; ⊙ Wheaton. Agr. area bordering S.Dak. and N.Dak., bounded W by L. Traverse and Bois de Sioux R.; watered by Mustinka R. Corn, oats, barley. Formed 1862.

Traverse, Cape, on S coast of P.E.I., at narrowest point of Northumberland Strait, 3 mi. SE of Port Borden and 9 mi. NE of Cape Tormentine, N.B.; 46°13'N 63°40'W.

Traverse, Lake, S.Dak. and Minn.; 26 mi. long, 3 mi. wide at widest point; forms part of boundary bet. S.Dak. and Minn. and is source of Bois de Sioux R. Traverse–Bois de Sioux Dam at N end. Drained in NE by Mustinka R., Minn.

Traverse City, city (pop. 16,974), ⊙ Grand Traverse co., NW Mich., at head of West Arm of Grand Traverse Bay of L. Michigan, 37 mi. NW of Cadillac, in orchard and farm region (cherries, apples, potatoes). Mfg. (sprayers, farm tools, wood products, furniture, baskets, metal caskets, foundry products, leather goods, canned foods, corn and potato products, dairy products); fisheries. City's annual natl. cherry festival and near-by lakes attract tourists. Settled 1847; inc. as village 1881, as city 1895. Indian relics remain in vicinity; a state park is just E.

Traversella (trävĕrsĕl'lä), village (pop. 369), Torino prov., Piedmont, NW Italy, 7 mi. NW of Ivrea. Copper and iron mines near by.

Traversetolo (trävĕrsā'tôlô), town (pop. 1,167), Parma prov., Emilia-Romagna, N central Italy, 11 mi. SSE of Parma; clocks.

Travinh (trä'vĭng'), town, ⊙ Travinh prov. (□ 700; 1943 pop. 285,600), S Vietnam, in Cochin China, port on Mekong delta arm, 65 mi. SSW of Saigon; rice cultivation; distilling. Airport.

Travis (tră'vĭs), county (□ 1,015; pop. 160,980), S central Texas; ⊙ AUSTIN, ⊙ Texas, seat of Univ. of Texas, and commercial center. Crossed SW-NE by Balcones Escarpment; drained by Colorado R. (power, flood-control dams). Agr. (cotton, grain sorghums, corn, oats, forage, potatoes, peaches, pecans) in E and SE; also dairying, poultry raising. Ranching (goats, sheep, cattle) in hilly W and NW; mohair, wool marketed. Clay, limestone. Mfg., processing at Austin. Recreational areas among lakes, hills of W. Formed 1840.

Travis, SE N.Y., a residential section of Richmond borough of New York city, on W Staten Isl., near Arthur Kill. Co. airport is just W.

Travis, Fort, Texas: see GALVESTON.

Travis, Lake, Texas: see MARSHALL FORD DAM.

Travis Air Force Base, Calif.: see FAIRFIELD.

Travnik (träv'nĭk), town (pop. 8,132), central Bosnia, Yugoslavia, on Lasva R., on railroad and 45 mi. NW of Sarajevo, at S foot of Vlasic Mts.; tobacco and leather processing, dairying. Hydroelectric plant on Lasva R. Fortress (built by King Tvrtko II), Jesuit monastery and col. First mentioned in 1479. Was Turkish ⊙ Bosnia (1555–88; 1638–1851) until its transfer to Sarajevo.

Trawden, urban district (1931 pop. 2,549; 1951 census 2,114), NE Lancashire, England, near Yorkshire boundary just ESE of Colne; cotton milling.

Trawsfynydd (trousvŭ'nĭdh), town and parish (pop. 1,557), NW Merioneth, Wales, 9 mi. E of Portmadoc; agr. market, on edge of artificial reservoir (c.1300 acres) of power company.

Trazegnies (träzĕnyē'), town (pop. 7,107), Hainaut prov., S central Belgium, 7 mi. NW of Charleroi; coal mining.

Traz-os-Montes, Portugal: see TRÁS-OS-MONTES.

Trbiz, Italy: see TARVISIO.

Trbovlje (tŭrbôv'lyĕ), Ger. *Trifail* (trĭf'īl), village (pop. 13,743), central Slovenia, Yugoslavia, near Sava R. 27 mi. ENE of Ljubljana, near Zagreb-Trieste RR; brown-coal mine (largest in Yugoslavia); cement plant. Until 1918, in Styria.

Treadway Lake, Cass co., W central Ill., bayou lake (c.8 mi. long) along Illinois R., extending NE from Beardstown.

Treadwell, village (1939 pop. 13), SE Alaska, on Douglas Isl., just SE of Douglas; mining settlement, largely abandoned. The gold mines here, once among the richest in Alaska, operated from 1881 to 1917, when a cave-in halted operations.

Trealaw, Wales: see RHONDDA.

Treasure, county (□ 984; pop. 1,402), S central Mont.; ⊙ Hysham. Agr. area drained by Yellowstone R. Grain, livestock. Formed 1919.

Treasure Island, town (pop. 75), Pinellas co., W Fla., near St. Petersburg. Sometimes Treasure Island City.

Treasure Island, W Calif., artificial island (400 acres) in San Francisco Bay, just N of Yerba Buena Isl. (causeway connection). Constructed as site of Golden Gate International Exposition (1939–40); became U.S. naval base in 1941.

Treasure Mountain, peak (13,442 ft.) in Rocky Mts., Gunnison co., W central Colo.

Treasury Islands, coral group, Solomon Isls., SW Pacific, 25 mi. SE of Bougainville. Comprise Mono (6 mi. in diameter), Stirling Isl. (3 mi. long, 1 mi. wide), and a few smaller islets. Blanche Harbor (2 mi. wide) is bet. Mono and Stirling. In Second World War, isls. (site of Jap. base) were taken (1943) by U.S. forces.

Treat's Island, Maine: see LUBEC.

Trebbia River (trĕb'byä), anc. *Trebia*, N central Italy, rises in Ligurian Apennines 15 mi. NE of Genoa, near Torriglia; flows 70 mi. NNE, past Bobbio, to Po R. near Piacenza. On its banks Hannibal defeated the Romans in 218 B.C. and in

1799 French were defeated by Russo-Austrian army.

Trebbin (trĕ'bĭn), town (pop. 4,554), Brandenburg, E Germany, 15 mi. SE of Potsdam; stone quarrying; woodworking, printing. Before Second World War, a center for glider training.

Trebechovice pod Orebem (tŭrzhĕ'bĕkhôvĭtsĕ pôd' ô"rĕbĕm), Czech *Třebechovice pod Orebem*, Ger. *Hohenbruck* (hō'ŭnbrŏŏk), town (pop. 4,117), E Bohemia, Czechoslovakia, on Orlice R., on railroad, and 8 mi. E of Hradec Kralove; mfg. of leather goods.

Trebenice (tŭrzhĕ'bĕnyĭtsĕ), Czech *Třebenice*, Ger. *Trebenitz* (trā'bŭnĭts), village (pop. 1,467), N Bohemia, Czechoslovakia, on railroad and 14 mi. SSW of Usti nad Lebem; fruit canning. Deposits of Bohemian garnets in vicinity.

Trebevic or **Trebevich** (both: trĕbĕ'vĭch), Serbo-Croatian *Trebević*, mountain in Dinaric Alps, SE Bosnia, Yugoslavia; c.10 mi. long; highest point (5,343 ft.) is 3 mi. SSE of Sarajevo.

Trebic (tŭrzhĕ'bĕch), Czech *Třebíč*, Ger. *Trebitsch* (trā'bĭch), town (pop. 15,622), W Moravia, Czechoslovakia, on Jihlava R., on railroad and 33 mi. W of Brno; noted for tanning and leather industry producing shoes, boots, and gloves. Has remarkable 13th-cent. Romanesque-Gothic basilica.

Trebinje (trĕ'bĕnyĕ), town (pop. 3,296), S Herzegovina, Yugoslavia, on Trebisnica R., on railroad and 13 mi. ENE of Dubrovnik, at E edge of Popovo Plain; road junction; center of tobacco-growing, wood-carving region. Has 11th-cent. monastery (several Serbian rulers buried here) and well-preserved oriental quarters. Formerly Orthodox Eastern bishopric.

Trebisacce (trĕbēsät'chĕ), village (pop. 1,734), Cosenza prov., Calabria, S Italy, on Gulf of Taranto, 18 mi. WNW of Castrovillari; bathing resort; cement mfg.; fishing.

Trebisnica River or **Trebishnitsa River** (both: trĕ'bĭshnĕtsä), Serbo-Croatian *Trebišnica*, Herzegovina, Yugoslavia, rises near Bileca, flows c.60 mi. S and WNW, past Trebinje, through Popovo Plain, disappearing underground 13 mi. SE of Metkovic. Bjelasica mtn. lies along its right bank; railroad follows its entire course.

Trebisov (trĕ'bĭshôf), Slovak *Trebišov*, Hung. *Tőketerebes* (tû'kĕtĕrĕbĕsh), town (pop. 6,676), SE Slovakia, Czechoslovakia, 23 mi. ESE of Kosice, in fertile agr. dist. (wheat, sugar beets, corn); rail junction; sugar refining.

Trebizond (trĕ'bĭzŏnd), Turkish *Trabzon* (träbzôn'), prov. (□ 1,753; 1950 pop. 419,148), NE Turkey, on Black Sea; ⊙ Trebizond. Bordered S by Trebizond and Rize Mts. Copper and lead in Harsit R. valley, iron in S. Fine forests; corn, potatoes, tobacco, apples, pears, plums, citrus fruit; wool. Salt-water fishing.

Trebizond, Turkish *Trabzon*, anc. *Trapezus*, city (1950 pop. 33,969), ⊙ Trebizond prov., NE Turkey, port on Black Sea, 110 mi. NW of Erzurum; 40°55'N 39°50'E. Market for tobacco, corn, hazel nuts, filberts flour, beans, eggs. Its port was modernized, 1945–49. It was anciently a Greek colony founded by Sinope, later became ⊙ Roman prov. of Pontus Cappadocia, and still later ⊙ Empire of Trebizond (1204–1461). It was long head of the historic trade route to Persia, notably to Tabriz.

Trebizond Mountains, Turkish *Trabzon*, NE Turkey, extend 50 mi. WNW-ESE bet. Black Sea and Harsit R.; rise to 10,660 ft. in Kemer Dag.

Treblinka (trĕblĭng'kä), village, Warszawa prov., E central Poland, on railroad and 5 mi. S of Malkinia, across Bug R. During Second World War, site of Ger. extermination camp.

Trebnitz, Poland: see TRZEBNICA.

Trebnje (trĕb'nyĕ), Ger. *Treffen* (trĕ'fŭn), village (pop. 1,935), S Slovenia, Yugoslavia, 11 mi. NW of Novo Mesto; rail junction. Until 1918, in Carniola.

Trébol, El, Argentina: see EL TRÉBOL.

Trebon (tŭrzhĕ'bônyŭ), Czech *Třeboň*, Ger. *Wittingau* (vĭ'tĭng-gou), town (pop. 4,172), S Bohemia, Czechoslovakia, on railroad and 13 mi. ENE of Budweis, in pond and lake region; center of fresh-water fishing industry (carp, tench, pike), mostly for export. Major fish pond (□ 2.8) of Rozmberk is 2 mi. N. Local castle contains noted archives.

Trebsen (trĕp'sŭn), town (pop. 3,045, Saxony, E central Germany, on the Mulde and 5 mi. NNE of Grimma, in lignite-mining region.

Trebujena (trāvōōhā'nä), town (pop. 4,684), Cádiz prov., SW Spain, in marshy lowland, 13 mi. N of Jerez; cereals, grapes and wine, olives, stock. Has pier (c.3 mi. N) on Guadalquivir R., where ships on way to Seville call.

Trebur (trā'bōōr), village (pop. 3,170), S Hesse, W Germany, in former Starkenburg prov., 11 mi. WNW of Darmstadt; grain. An anc. settlement, it was a royal domain and, until 12th cent., scene of several diets. Passed to counts of Katzenellenbogen in 1249, to Hesse in 1479. Formerly also spelled Tribur.

Trebushany (tryĕbōōshä'nē), Czech *Trebušany*, Hung. *Trebusafejérpatak*, village (1941 pop. 2,648), E Transcarpathian Oblast, Ukrainian SSR, on Tissa R. (Rum. border), on railroad and 10 mi. S of Rakhov.

Trebusice, Czechoslovakia: see KOMORANY.

Trecastagni (trĕkästä'nyē), village (pop. 3,104), Catania prov., E Sicily, on SE slope of Mt. Etna, 5 mi. W of Acireale; alcohol distillery, soap mfg.

Trecate (trĕkä'tĕ), town (pop. 9,117), Novara prov., Piedmont, N Italy, near Ticino R., 6 mi. ESE of Novara, in rice-growing, cattle-raising region; cotton mills.

Trecenta (trĕchĕn'tä), village (pop. 1,466), Rovigo prov., Veneto, N Italy, on Tartaro R. and 16 mi. WSW of Rovigo.

Tred Avon River (trĕd" ă'vŭn), E Md., irregular estuary (c.12 mi. long) entering Choptank R. in central Talbot co., on the Eastern Shore; navigable to just below Easton.

Tredegar (trĭdē'gŭr), urban district (1931 pop. 23,192; 1951 census 20,375), W Monmouth, England, on Sirhowy R. and 20 mi. N of Cardiff; tinplate-mfg. and coal-mining center. In urban dist. (N) is town of Sirhowy (pop. 6,361).

Treebeek (trā'bāk), town (pop. 3,283), Limburg prov., SE Netherlands, 4 mi. NNW of Heerlen; knitting mills, here, erected by state mines administration to provide employment for miners' families.

Treece, city (pop. 378), Cherokee co., extreme SE Kansas, at Okla. line, 19 mi. W of Joplin, Mo. Zinc and lead mines in vicinity.

Tree Island, China: see AMPHITRITE GROUP.

Treeton, town and parish (pop. 2,175), West Riding, S Yorkshire, England, 3 mi. S of Rotherham; coal mining. Has 13th-cent. church.

Trefaldwyn, Wales: see MONTGOMERY.

Treffen (trĕ'fŭn), town (pop. 2,948), Carinthia, S Austria, 4 mi. N of Villach; summer resort.

Treffen, Yugoslavia: see TREBNJE.

Treffort (trĕfôr'), village (pop. 530), Ain dept., E France, on W slope of Revermont range, 8 mi. NE of Bourg; cheese.

Treffurt (trĕ'fōōrt), town (pop. 3,612), in former Prussian Saxony prov., central Germany, after 1945 in Thuringia, on the Werra and 11 mi. WSW of Mühlhausen, opposite Heldra, in cherry-growing region; cigar mfg., woodworking; stone quarrying. Has 13th-cent. church, and remains of anc. Normannstein castle.

Treforest, Wales: see PONTYPRIDD.

Trefriw (trĕv'rū), town and parish (pop. 723), E Caernarvon, Wales, on Conway R. and 9 mi. S of Conway; woolen milling, granite quarrying. Just N is spa of Trefriw Wells, with chalybeate springs.

Tref-y-clawdd, Wales: see KNIGHTON.

Tregaron (trĭgă'rŭn), town in parish of Caron is Clawdd (kăr'ŭn ĕs kloudh') (pop. 1,296), central Cardigan, Wales, on Teifi R. and 10 mi. NE of Lampeter; agr. market at S edge of largest British peat moor. Town is of anc. origin. On Teifi R., 3 mi. SW, is site of Roman station.

Trego (trē'gō), county (□ 901; pop. 5,868), W central Kansas; ⊙ Wakeeney. Prairie region, drained in N by Saline R., in S by Smoky Hill R. Grain, livestock. Formed 1879.

Treguaco or **Trehuaco** (both: trāwä'kō), village (1930 pop. 448), Ñuble prov., S central Chile, on Itata R. and 35 mi. WNW of Chillán, in agr. area (wheat, wine, corn, lentils, potatoes, livestock); lumbering.

Tréguier (trāgyā'), Breton *Landreger*, town (pop. 2,572), Côtes-du-Nord dept., W France, fishing port on narrow estuary of Jaudy and Guindy rivers, 11 mi. ENE of Lannion; agr. trade (potatoes, early vegetables). Formerly an episcopal see; noted for its 14th–15th-cent. cathedral built of granite, and for its 15th-cent. cloister. Ernest Renan b. here.

Treharris (trēhă'rĭs), town (pop. 8,504) in Merthyr Tydfil county borough, NE Glamorgan, Wales, on Taff R.; coal mining.

Treherbert, Wales: see RHONDDA.

Treherne (trŭhûrn'), village (pop. estimate 550), S Man., 30 mi. SW of Portage la Prairie, at N end of Pembina Mts.; oil and gas wells, flour mills.

Trehuaco, Chile: see TREGUACO.

Treia (trā'yä), town (pop. 1,765), Macerata prov., The Marches, central Italy, 7 mi. W of Macerata; macaroni mfg. Bishopric.

Treider Aa, Latvia: see GAUJA RIVER.

Treig, Loch (lŏkh trēg'), lake, S Inverness, Scotland, at foot of Ben Nevis, 15 mi. E of Fort William; 6 mi. long, 1 mi. wide. Drains into Spean R. Water-tunnel connections with Loch Linnhe at Fort William and with reservoir just W of Loch Laggan are part of LOCHABER hydroelectric system.

Treignac (trĕnyäk'), village (pop. 1,514), Corrèze dept., S central France, in Monts de Monédières, on the Vézère and 19 mi. N of Tulle; fruitgrowing and preserving, flour milling, wool spinning. Picturesque old quarter with 15th-cent. church and bridge.

Treinta y Tres (trān'tä ē trās'), department (□ 3,683; pop. 68,850), E central Uruguay; ⊙ Treinta y Tres. Bounded E by Brazil (L. Mirim), W by the Cuchilla Grande Principal, NE by Tacuarí R., SE by Cebollatí R. Drained by Olimar R. Chiefly agr.: wheat, corn, oats, linseed; cattle and sheep raising. Main centers: Treinta y Tres, General Enrique Martínez, Vergara. Dept. was formed 1884.

Treinta y Tres, city (pop. 18,500), ⊙ Treinta y Tres dept., E central Uruguay, on the Olimar Grande R., on railroad and highway, and 150 mi. NE of Montevideo; 33°19'S 54°27'W. Commercial center in stock-raising (cattle, sheep) and agr. area (wheat, corn, oats, linseed). Airport.

Tre Island (trā), Vietnam island in South China Sea, off Nhatrang; 8 mi. long, 3 mi. wide; rises to 1,509 ft.

Treixedo (trāshā'dōō), village (pop. 1,090), Viseu dist., N Portugal, on railroad and 19 mi. SW of Viseu; wine, olives, rye.

Treize-Arbres, Les, France: see SALÈVE, MONT.

Trekanten (trā'kän"tŭn), village (pop. 632), Kalmar co., SE Sweden, 10 mi. W of Kalmar; sawmills.

Trekhrechye or **Trekhrech'ye** (tryôkh"ryĕch'yĭ) [Rus.,=three rivers], agr. district of the Barga, N Inner Mongolian Autonomous Region, Manchuria; main village, Nalemutu (Dragotsenka). Situated bet. the Gan, Derbul, and Haul rivers (3 right tributaries of the Argun, for which the dist. is named), Trekhrechye was colonized (late-19th cent.) by Russians who constitute 80% of total pop. of c.10,000. Grain (wheat, rye, oats), flax, and hemp are the main products.

Trelandsfoss (trā'länsfôs), waterfall (79 ft.) on Kvina R., Vest-Agder co., S Norway, 12 mi. ENE of Flekkefjord; hydroelectric plant.

Trelawney (trĭlô'nē), village, Salisbury prov., Southern Rhodesia, in Mashonaland, on railroad and 20 mi. SE of Sinoia; tobacco-growing center.

Trelawny (trĭlô'nē), parish (□ 352.55; pop. 47,535), Cornwall co., W central and N Jamaica; ⊙ Falmouth. A semiarid region with limestone hills and plateaus, bounded S by the Cockpit Country. Watered by Martha Brae R. Along the coast were, in colonial times, large sugar estates; with their decline the parish lost much of its importance. Main products, apart from sugar cane, are coffee, bananas, ginger, pimento, honey, rum, dyewood; mules.

Trélazé (trāläzā'), town (pop. 5,945), Maine-et-Loire dept., W France, 5 mi. ESE of Angers; chief slate-quarrying center of France; match factory.

Trelech a'r Bettws (trĕlākh'-är-bĕ'tōōs), agr. village and parish (pop. 1,056), W Carmarthen, Wales, 7 mi. NW of Carmarthen.

Trelew (trĕlyōō'), town (1947 pop. 5,878), E Chubut natl. territory, Argentina, on Chubut R. and 10 mi. WNW of Rawson; rail junction, commercial and agr. center. Sawmills, limekiln, brewery; dairy industry. Agr.: alfalfa, wheat, potatoes, fruit; sheep raising. Trout and salmon fishing. Has natl. col., theaters. One of the most important towns in Patagonia, it was founded 1888 and 1st settled by Welshmen.

Trelleborg (trĕ"lŭbôr'yŭ), southernmost city (1950 pop. 17,126) of Sweden, Malmohus co., 17 mi. SSE of Malmo; 55°22'N 13°10'E. Baltic seaport, terminus of train ferries to Sassnitz, Germany, and Odra, Poland; rail junction. Sugar refineries, glass and rubber works, lumber mills; mechanical industries. Has 13th-cent. church (rebuilt in 19th cent.). First mentioned (1167) as *Trälaborg*, city was a herring-fishing center in Middle Ages. Also spelled Tralleborg, Swedish *Trälleborg*.

Trélon (trā'lõ'), town (pop. 2,772), Nord dept., N France, 9 mi. SE of Avesnes; glassworks, tanneries.

Tremadoc, Wales: see PORTMADOC.

Trembesh, Bulgaria; see POLSKI TRAMBESH.

Tremblade, La (lä trāblăd'), town (pop. 3,467), Charente-Maritime dept., W France, near mouth of Seudre R., 15 mi. SSW of Rochefort; important oyster beds; mfg. (vinegar, baskets).

Tremblant, Mount (trĕm'blŭnt), **Mont Tremblant** (mõ trāblā'), or **Trembling Mountain,** peak (3,150 ft.), SW Que., in the Laurentians, 70 mi. NW of Montreal in Montagne Tremblante Park, a popular ski resort. At its foot is Trembling L. or L. de la Montagne Tremblante (7 mi. long).

Trembles, Les (lā trā'blŭ), village (pop. 671), Oran dept., NW Algeria, on the Mékerra, on railroad and 9 mi. NE of Sidi-bel-Abbès; wine, cereals.

Trembleur (trāblûr'), town (pop. 2,164), Liége prov., E Belgium, 7 mi. NE of Liége; coal mining.

Trembleur Lake (□ 45), central B.C., N of Stewart L., 75 mi. E of Smithers; 20 mi. long, 2–3 mi. wide. Drains SE into Stuart L.

Trembowla, Ukrainian SSR: see TEREBOVLYA.

Tremedal, Brazil: see MONTE AZUL, Minas Gerais.

Tremembé (trĭmĭmbĕ'), city (pop. 2,113), SE São Paulo, Brazil, on Paraíba R., on railroad and 5 mi NNE of Taubaté; oil-shale extracting and distilling; dairying.

Tremessen, Poland: see TRZEMESZNO.

Tremezzo (trĕmĕ'tsô), village (pop. 374), Como prov., Lombardy, N Italy, port on W shore of L. Como, 14 mi. NNE of Como; resort with many villas and gardens. In near-by hamlet of Giulino di Messegra, Mussolini and several other leading fascists were executed on April 28, 1945.

Tremiti Islands (trā'mētē) (□ 1.2; pop. 407), anc. *Diomedeae Insulae*, Foggia prov., S Italy, in Adriatic Sea, c.15 mi. N of Gargano promontory. Chief isls. are San Domino (largest; 1.5 mi. long), San Nicola, and Caprara. Agr. (cereals, grapes, olives, figs); fishing. Pianosa isl. is 14 mi. NE.

Tremont (trē'mŏnt). **1** Village (pop. 1,138), Tazewell co., central Ill., 13 mi. SSE of Peoria, in agr.

and bituminous-coal area. **2** Fishing, resort town (pop. 1,115), Hancock co., S Maine, on S Mt. Desert Isl. Inc. 1848. **3** Borough (pop. 2,102), Schuylkill co., E central Pa., 10 mi. WSW of Pottsville; anthracite; clothing. Laid out 1844, inc. 1866.

Tremont City, village (pop. 396), Clark co., W central Ohio, 6 mi. NW of Springfield, near Mad R.

Tremonton (trē'mŭntŭn), city (pop. 1,662), Box Elder co., N Utah, on Malad R. and 18 mi. W of Logan; alt. c.4,320 ft.; processing point in sugar-beet and grain area; dairy products, feed, canned foods, turkeys. Laid out 1903, inc. 1906.

Tremor (trämôr'), anthracite-mining area, Leon prov., NW Spain, 20 mi. NW of Astorga; crossed by small Tremor and Baeza rivers. Folgoso de la Ribera (pop. 588) and Igueña (pop. 316) are chief towns.

Tremosna (tûrzhĕ'môshnä), Czech *Třemošná,* village (pop. 3,176), W Bohemia, Czechoslovakia, on railroad and 5 mi. N of Pilsen; kaolin and fire-clay quarrying.

Tremp (trĕmp), city (pop. 3,459), Lérida prov., NE Spain, in Catalonia, on Noguera Pallaresa R. and 40 mi. NNE of Lérida, near S end of Tremp or Talarn reservoir and hydroelectric plant. Cement mfg.; sheep raising; agr. trade (wine, olive oil, sugar beets, cereals). Some coal deposits near by.

Trempealeau (trĕm'pŭlō), county (□ 739; pop. 23,730), W Wis.; ⊙ Whitehall. Bounded partly on W by Trempealeau R., SW by wooded bluffs along the Mississippi, SE by Black R.; drained by Buffalo, Black, and Trempealeau rivers. Dairying, stock raising, farming area; tobacco, grain, poultry; some timber. Processing of farm products. Includes Perrot State Park. Formed 1854.

Trempealeau, village (pop. 645), Trempealeau co., W Wis., on the Mississippi and 16 mi. NNW of La Crosse, in hilly area. Trempealeau Bluffs, Perrot State Park, Indian mounds, and site of old French fort are near by.

Trempealeau River, W Wis., rises in Jackson co., flows W, past Whitehall, then SW, past Arcadia, to the Mississippi just E of Winona, Minn.; c.70 mi. long.

Trempen, Russian SFSR: see NOVOSTROYEVO.

Trémuson (trāmüzō'), village (pop. 182), Côtes-du-Nord dept., W France, 4 mi. W of Saint-Brieuc; lead-zinc mining and processing.

Trenche River (trĕsh), central Que., rises in Laurentian Plateau 50 mi. W of L. St. John, flows 75 mi. S to the Saint Maurice 22 mi. N of La Tuque. Hydroelectric plant (completed 1950) at Trenche near junction with the Saint Maurice.

Trencianska Tepla (trĕn'chĕänskä tyĕ'plä), Slovak *Trenčianská Teplá,* Hung. *Hőlak* (hû'lŏk), village (pop. 3,194), W Slovakia, Czechoslovakia, 5 mi. NE of Trencin; rail junction. Has 19th-cent. castle.

Trencianske Teplice (-skĕ tyĕ'plĭtsĕ), Slovak *Trenčianske Teplice,* Hung. *Trencsenteplic* (trĕn'chĕntĕplĭts), town (pop. 2,414), W Slovakia, Czechoslovakia, 6 mi. ENE of Trencin; rail terminus; popular health resort amidst extensive forests, with radioactive mud baths and sulphurous thermal springs (96°–107°F.); alt. 1,300 ft. Of legendary foundation, it became known in Roman times; was private property until 1909.

Trencin (trĕn'chĭn), Slovak *Trenčin,* Ger. *Trentschin* (trĕn'chĭn), Hung. *Trencsén* (trĕn'chān), town (pop. 12,380), W Slovakia, Czechoslovakia, on Vah R. and 67 mi. NE of Bratislava, in wheat, barley, and potato region; rail junction; trade center; mfg. (woolen textiles, clothing, liquor, medicines, glass, starch, margarine), woodworking. Has remains of 14th-cent. fortress, 14th-cent. church.

Trendelburg (trĕn'dŭlbŏŏrk), town (pop. 1,502), in former Prussian prov. of Hesse-Nassau, W Germany, after 1945 in Hesse, on the Diemel and 5 mi. NNE of Hofgeismar; woodworking.

Trenel (trānĕl'), town (pop. estimate 2,000), ⊙ Trenel dept. (pop. 7,405), NE La Pampa prov., Argentina, on railroad and 20 mi. W of General Pico; grain, livestock center; flour milling.

Trenewydd, Wales: see NEWTOWN.

Trengalek, Indonesia: see TRENGGALEK.

Trengereid (trĕng'ūr-ād), village (pop. 169) in Haus canton, Hordaland co., SW Norway, on Sor Fjord, on railroad and 11 mi. ENE of Bergen; industrial center; limestone quarrying; mfg. of lime, cellulose; smelting. Quarries and factories also at Risnes (S).

Trenggalek (trĕng-gälĕk'), town (pop. 8,571), E Java, Indonesia, 70 mi. SE of Solo; trade center for agr. area (rice, corn, peanuts, tobacco, tea, rubber, cinchona bark); pottery making. Also spelled Trengalek.

Trengganu (trĕng-gä'nōō), state (□ 5,050; pop. 225,996), NE Malaya, on South China Sea; ⊙ Kuala Trengganu. Bounded by Kelantan (W) and Pahang (SW), it is drained by Trengganu (center) and Kemaman (S) rivers. The narrow coastal belt (dunes, swamps) is backed by agr. river valleys, and further inland by jungle-covered mts. rising to 4,978 ft. in the Gunong Lawit. Climate conditioned by NE monsoon (Nov.–March). Rice, rubber, coconuts, and betel nuts are the leading agr. products; fisheries and forestry (sawmilling at Chukai and Kuala Dungan). Iron, tin, tungsten, and manganese mining, chiefly near Chukai and Kuala Dungan. Mfg.: silk sarongs, cotton fabrics, boat building. Pop. (90% Malay, 7% Chinese) is concentrated in coastal belt where the leading centers (Kuala Trengganu, Chukai, Kuala Dungan, Kuala Besut) are linked by coastwise vessels and coastal road. Subject to Srivijaya kingdom of Palembang, Trengganu passed (14th cent.) to Javanese rule. The present Sultan's ruling house (dating from 1701) paid tribute to Siam after 1776, until all their rights passed (1909) to Great Britain and it became one of the unfederated Malay states. After Second World War, when it was annexed (1943–45) by Thailand, it joined the Federation of Malaya.

Trengganu, town, Malaya: see KUALA TRENGGANU.

Trengganu River, chief river of Trengganu, NE Malaya, rises near Kelantan border, flows 100 mi. SE and NE, past Kuala Brang, to South China Sea at Kuala Trengganu.

Trenque Lauquén (trĕng'kā loukĕn'), city (pop. 10,671), ⊙ Trenque Lauquén dist. (□ 2,127; pop. 26,131), W Buenos Aires prov., Argentina, 195 mi. N of Bahía Blanca; agr. center; dairying (cheese, butter), flour milling, meat packing.

Trent, Ital. *Trento,* anc. *Tridentum,* city (pop. 37,290), ⊙ Trentino–Alto Adige and Trento prov., N Italy, on Adige R. and 45 mi. N of Verona, on route to Brenner Pass, 70 mi. NNE; 46°5'N 11°9'E. Rail junction; mfg. (electric motors, foundry products, chemicals, dyes, tar, cement, glass, wine, alcohol, macaroni). Archbishopric. Has 12th-cent. Romanesque church (bomb damage repaired), cathedral (11th–16th cent.), 16th-cent. municipal palace, a famous bronze statue of Dante, and notable Romanesque and Renaissance bldgs. The famous Council of Trent met here 1545–63 in church of Santa Maria Maggiore (built 1520–23). Trent was the seat of a Lombard duchy (6th cent.) and of a Frankish march (8th cent.). To safeguard their road into Italy the emperors invested (12th cent.) the bishops of Trent with temporal powers over a sizeable territory. The prince-bishops ruled, except for a few short intervals, until 1802, when the bishopric was secularized and became part of Tyrol; the episcopal residence was the Castello del Buon Consiglio (13th cent.; enlarged 1528). Trent having always been Italian in language and culture, there developed a strong movement for its union with Italy; this was achieved in 1919 by the Treaty of St. Germain. In Second World War suffered heavy damage from air bombing (1940–45).

Trent. 1 Town (pop. 213), Moody co., E S.Dak., 10 mi. S of Flandreau and on Big Sioux R. **2** Town (pop. 296), Taylor co., W central Texas, 22 mi. W of Abilene, in cotton, cattle area.

Trent Canal, S Ont., system of navigation bet. Bay of Quinte of L. Ontario at Trenton (S) and Georgian Bay of L. Huron (N); comprises Trent R. to Rice L., thence passes through a series of rivers, lakes (including Kawartha lakes), and artificial channels, to L. Simcoe, then by Severn R. to Georgian Bay. The system, c.220 mi. long, is primarily a source of water power and is of little navigational importance.

Trentino–Alto Adige (trĕntē'nō–äl'tô ä'dējĕ), autonomous region (□ 5,252; pop. 669,029), N Italy; ⊙ Trent. Borders Austria and Switzerland (N), Lombardy (W), and Veneto (E). Alpine terrain with high mtn. ranges, including Eastern Alps (N), Dolomites (E), Ortles and Adamello groups (W), and many picturesque valleys. Comprises German- and Italian-speaking provs. of BOLZANO (the Alto Adige) and TRENTO (the Trentino), formerly part of Austrian Tyrol. Passed to Italy after First World War. Called Venezia Tridentina until 1947, when it became an autonomous region, granting official recognition to its mixed population, particularly the German majority in Bolzano prov.

Trento (trĕn'tô), province (□ c.2,160; pop. c.369,030), TRENTINO–ALTO ADIGE, N Italy; ⊙ TRENT. Alpine terrain with 75% of area over 3,000 ft. Has high mtn. ranges (Dolomites, Ortles, Adamello) and picturesque valleys (Val di Sole, Val Lagarina, Val di Fiemme, Valsugana). Drained by Adige, Brenta, Sarca, and Noce rivers. Includes N part of Lago di Garda. Agr. (cereals, fodder, grapes, fruit). Tobacco raising in Val Lagarina; olive growing around Lago di Garda. Stock raising (cattle, goats, swine). Forestry. Hydroelectric power well developed, with major plants at Riva, Mezzocorona, and Marlengo. Marble quarries at Brentonico. Mines at Mollaro (bituminous schist) and Darzo (barite). Noted as tourist region; many resorts (Riva, Arco, Predazzo). Mfg. at Trent, Rovereto, Riva. Formerly part of Austrian Tyrol; passed to Italy after First World War; became a prov. in 1927. In 1948 reduced by loss of German-speaking communes (□ c.355; pop. c.22,280) to Bolzano prov. (N).

Trento, city, Italy: see TRENT.

Trentola (trĕn'tôlä), town (pop. 4,248), Caserta prov., Campania, S Italy, 1 mi. W of Aversa, in agr. region (cereals, hemp, fruit).

Trenton. 1 Town (pop. 2,699), N N.S., on East R. just N of New Glasgow; mfg. of railroad cars, steel products. **2** Town (pop. 8,323), SE Ont., on Bay of Quinte, at mouth of Trent R., at S end of Trent Canal and 11 mi. WSW of Belleville; woolen, paper, and flour milling; mfg. of machinery, clothing, silverware.

Trenton. 1 City (pop. 904), ⊙ Gilchrist co., N Fla., 30 mi. W of Gainesville; lumbering, farming. **2** Town (pop. 755), ⊙ Dade co., extreme NW Ga., 16 mi. SW of Chattanooga, Tenn., at foot of Lookout Mtn.; mfg. (lumber, hosiery). **3** City (pop. 1,432), Clinton co., SW Ill., 25 mi. E of East St. Louis, in agr. region (corn, wheat, livestock, poultry); dairy products, flour, beverages. Inc. 1865. **4** Town (pop. 577), Todd co., S Ky., near Tenn. line, 16 mi. SE of Hopkinsville, in agr. area. **5** Town (pop. 358), Hancock co., S Maine, at mouth of Union R., 30 mi. E of Belfast, in fishing, resort area. **6** Village (pop. 6,222), Wayne co., SE Mich., 15 mi. SSW of downtown Detroit and on Detroit R., opposite Grosse Isle. Farm trade center and port. Mfg. (chemicals, metal products, boats); oil refining; limestone quarrying. Dairy, truck, and poultry farming. Settled 1816, on site of Indian village; inc. 1855. **7** City (pop. 6,157), ⊙ Grundy co., N Mo., on Thompson R. and 20 mi. N of Chillicothe; rail center, with railroad shops; grain and livestock market; food-processing plants; coal. Has jr. col. Crowder State Park near by. Ruskin Col. (a socialist experiment) here 1897–1905. Laid out 1841. **8** Village (pop. 1,239), ⊙ Hitchcock co., S Nebr., 22 mi. W of McCook and on Republican R.; grain, livestock, dairy and poultry produce. **9** City (pop. 128,009), ⊙ N.J. and Mercer co., W N.J., on the Delaware, and at head of navigation, c.30 mi. above Camden; 40°14'N 74°45'W; alt. c.40 ft. Mfg. (wire rope, cables, structural steel, pottery, rubber goods, airplane and auto equipment, steam turbines, hardware, cigars, porcelain, clothing, paper, linoleum, asbestos fabrics, home appliances, metal products). Has state teachers col. (1855), Rider Col., a jr. col., state prison, and other state institutions. Settled 1679 by Friends; became ⊙ N.J. 1790; inc. as city 1792; adopted commission govt. in 1911 and again in 1939; under municipal manager system 1935–39. Revolutionary battle of Trenton (1776) is commemorated by 155-ft. granite monument (1893) topped by statue of Washington; Washington's Delaware R. crossing point (c.8 mi. N) is a state park. City grew as commercial center after development of water power and canal and railroad construction; Roebling wire-rope works came 1848, pottery making began c.1850, and by 1860 there were many industries. Points of interest: golden-domed capitol (1792); capitol annex (1931; with state library and mus.); First World War memorial building (1932); barracks built 1758, now restored as mus.; Friends' meetinghouse (1739); Bloomsbury Court (c.1719), city's oldest house, home of William Trent, who bought land here in 1714 and aided growth of settlement. "Bow Hill" was home of Annette Savage, mistress of Joseph Bonaparte. Fitch's operation of a steamboat on the Delaware (1786) is commemorated by a stone. Controversial discoveries of evidences of glacial man were made near Trenton in 1872 by Dr. C. C. Abbott. Annual farm show (January) and state fair (September) held here. Zebulon Pike b. in Lamberton, now part of Trenton. **10** Village (pop. 331), Oneida co., central N.Y., 13 mi. N of Utica, in limestone-producing area. Post office name is Barneveld (bär'nŭvĕld", –vŭl). Near by in Steuben Memorial Park is grave of Baron von Steuben. **11** Town (pop. 469), ⊙ Jones co., SE N.C., 15 mi. SE of Kinston and on Trent R.; sawmilling. **12** Village (pop. 987), Butler co., SW Ohio, 4 mi. WSW of Middletown; metal stamping. **13** Town (pop. 296), Edgefield co., W S.C., 7 mi. ESE of Edgefield; fertilizer. **14** City (pop. 3,868), ⊙ Gibson co., NW Tenn., on North Fork of Forked Deer R. and 25 mi. E of Dyersburg, in cotton-, strawberry-, and cabbage-growing area; makes textiles, cottonseed products; lumber milling. **15** Town (pop. 603), Fannin co., NE Texas, 13 mi. SW of Bonham; shipping point in agr. area (cotton, corn, onions). **16** Town (pop. 451), Cache co., N Utah, 16 mi. NNW of Logan; alt. 4,461 ft.; irrigated grain fields.

Trenton Falls, N.Y.: see WEST CANADA CREEK.

Trent River, SE Ont., issues from Rice L., flows in a winding course E and S, past Campbellford, to Bay of Quinte at Trenton; 150 mi. long. Forms part of Trent Canal system, which links Georgian Bay and L. Ontario.

Trent River, third-longest stream (170 mi.; the Thames and the Severn are longer) in England, rises on Biddulph Moor, Stafford, 4 mi. ESE of Congleton, flows SE past Stoke-on-Trent and the Potteries, through Staffordshire, turning NE at Derby line, past Burton-on-Trent and into Nottinghamshire, passing Nottingham and Newark, and finally into Lincolnshire, passing Gainsborough and the Isle of Axholme, to junction with the Ouse 14 mi. W of Hull, forming the Humber. In its lower course is a high tidal bore. Chief tributaries are the Sow, Tame, Dove, Soar, Devon, and Idle rivers. It is navigable for barges below Burton-on-Trent; canal connections (principally the Trent and Mersey Canal) make it an important inland waterway.

Trent River, SE N.C., formed by junction of small creeks in Jones co.; flows c.80 mi. ENE past Trenton and Pollocksville, to Neuse R. at New Bern.

Trentschin, Czechoslovakia: see TRENCIN.
Treorky, Wales: see RHONDDA.
Trepassey Bay (trùpă'sē), inlet (10 mi. long, 15 mi. wide at entrance) of the Atlantic, SE N.F., on S coast of Avalon Peninsula, 65 mi. SSW of St. John's; 46°40'N 53°22'W. At head is fishing village of Trepassey (pop. 541).
Trepca or **Trepcha** (both: trĕp'chä), Serbo-Croatian *Trepča*, mine, S Serbia, Yugoslavia, 3 mi. NE of Mitrovica, at S foot of the Kopaonik, in the Kosovo. Produces lead, zinc, silver, and pyrite; one of largest of its kind in Europe. Linked by 8-mi.-long aerial ropeway with ZVECAN.
Tréport, Le (lù trāpôr'), town (pop. 4,795), Seine-Inférieure dept., N France, on English Channel at mouth of Bresle R., opposite Mers-les-Bains, and 16 mi. NE of Dieppe; fishing port and beach resort; fruit and vegetable shipping, lingerie mfg. Suffered much damage in Second World War.
Treptow (trāp'tō). **1** District (1939 pop. 118,159; 1946 pop. 108,035), SE Berlin, Germany, on the Spree and 5 mi. SE of city center. Electrical-equipment mfg. center; pharmaceutical works. Includes Johannisthal section (airport). After 1945 in Soviet sector. **2** or **Treptow an der Tollense,** Pomerania, Germany: see ALTENTREPTOW.
Treptow or **Treptow an der Rega,** Poland: see TRZEBIATOW.
Trepuzzi (trĕpōō'tsē), town (pop. 7,766), Lecce prov., Apulia, S Italy, 6 mi. NW of Lecce; olive oil, wine.
Trequanda (trĕkwän'dä), village (pop. 551), Siena prov., Tuscany, central Italy, 19 mi. SE of Siena; pottery making; quarrying. Has castle, and 13th-cent. church with paintings by Sodoma.
Treriksroys (trā"rēksrü'ūs), Nor. *Treriksrøys*, Swedish *Treriksröset* (trā"rēksrü'sùt), Finnish *Kolmen Vallakunnan Kivi* (kōl'mĕn väl'täkōōn"nän kĭ'vē) [=three countries' cairn], locality in Lapland where borders of Norway, Sweden, and Finland meet, 60 mi. SE of Tromso; 69°2'N 20°32'E. It is also northernmost point of Sweden.
Tres Árboles (trās är'bōlĕs), village (pop. 400), Río Negro dept., W Uruguay, in the Cuchilla de Haedo, 27 mi. NNW of Paso de los Toros, 80 mi. E of Paysandú; rail junction.
Tres Arroyos (trās' äroi'ōs), city (pop. 29,479), ⊙ Tres Arroyos dist. (□ 2,484; pop. 53,183), S Buenos Aires prov., Argentina, 110 mi. ENE of Bahía Blanca; commercial and agr. center in livestock, grain area; dairying, flour milling; mfg. of ceramics, sweets, furniture. Has natl. col.
Três Barras (trās bä'rùs), town (pop. 1,947), N Santa Catarina, Brazil, on the Rio Negro (Paraná border), on railroad and 32 mi. W of Mafra; sawmilling center.
Três Barras, Rio das, Mato Grosso, Brazil: see SÃO MANUEL RIVER.
Tres Bocas (trās bō'käs), village, Paysandú dept., NW Uruguay, 50 mi. NE of Paysandú; road junction in cattle-raising area.
Tresckow (trĕ'skō), village (pop. 1,250), Carbon co., E central Pa., 2 mi. S of Hazleton, in anthracite region.
Tresco (trĕ'skō), island (962 acres; pop. 248) of SCILLY ISLANDS, Cornwall, England, 3 mi. NNW of St. Mary's. Abbey Gardens have subtropical plants. Site of Cromwell's castle.
Três Corações (trās kōōrüsō'ĭs), city (pop. 7,141), S Minas Gerais, Brazil, on the Rio Verde and 50 mi. NNE of Itajubá; rail junction; one of state's principal livestock markets.
Trescore Balneario (trĕskô'rĕ bälnĕä'rēō), village (pop. 2,503), Bergamo prov., Lombardy, N Italy, 8 mi. E of Bergamo; mineral spa with sulphur baths; mfg. (silk, buttons).
Tres Cruces (trās' krōō'sĕs), village (pop. estimate 500), N central Jujuy prov., Argentina, on railroad and 90 mi. NNW of Jujuy; stock-raising and zinc-mining center.
Tres Cruces, village, Artigas dept., NW Uruguay, on railroad and road, and 20 mi. W of Artigas, near the Arroyo Tres Cruces Grande; cereals, cattle, sheep.
Tres Cruces, Cerro (sĕ'rō), Andean peak (10,640 ft.) on Ecuador-Peru border, in Cordillera del Cóndor, 55 mi. SSE of Loja.
Tres Cruces, Cerro, peak (10,308 ft.) in Chiapas, S Mexico, in main range of Sierra Madre, 15 mi. NW of Motozintla.
Tres Cruces, Cordillera de (kôrdĭyä'rä dā), Aymará *Quimza Cruz* or *Quimsa Cruz*, part of Eastern Cordillera of the Andes, W Bolivia; extends 30 mi. from La Paz R. (NW) to Ichoca (SE); rises to over 18,000 ft. Rich mining region (tin, tungsten, antimony, lead, silver), with main mines at Araca (NW), Caracoles, Monte Blanco, and Colquiri (SE). Name is sometimes applied to 90-mi. sec. of Eastern Cordillera extending SE to point ENE of Oruro.
Tres Cruces, Nevados (nāvä'dōs), Andean volcanic mountains on Argentina-Chile border, 30 mi. WSW of Cerro Incahuasi; 27°5'S. Peaks rise to 21,720 ft., 20,853 ft., and 19,780 ft.
Tres Cruces Grande, Arroyo (äroi'ō, grän'dā), river, Artigas dept., NW Uruguay, rises in NW foothills of the Cuchilla de Belén 20 mi. SE of Tres Cruces, flows 60 mi. NW to Cuareim R.
Tres Días (trās dē'äs), mountain (4,094 ft.), S central Puerto Rico, in the Cordillera Central and Toro Negro unit of the Caribbean Natl. Forest, 10 mi. NE of Ponce.
Tresenda (trĕzĕn'dä), village (pop. 335), Sondrio prov., Lombardy, N Italy, on Adda R. and 10 mi. E of Sondrio.
Tres Esquinas (trās ĕskē'näs), village, Caquetá commissary, S Colombia, on Caquetá R. at mouth of Orteguaza R., and 65 mi. SSE of Florencia; forest products (rubber, balata gum, resins).
Tres Fjord, Norway: see MOLDE FJORD.
Tres Forcas, Cape (trās' fôr'käs), Fr. *Cap des Trois Fourches* (kăp' dā trwä' fōōrsh'), headland on the Mediterranean coast of Sp. Morocco, 10 mi. N of Melilla; 35°27'N 2°58'W; lighthouse.
Tres Hermanas Mountains (trās ĕrmä'näs), SW N. Mex., in Luna co., near Mexico line; rises to 5,805 ft. Gold, silver, copper, and onyx are mined.
Tres Hermanos (trās ĕrmä'nōs), village, Guanacaste prov., NW Costa Rica, 2 mi. NNW of La Sierra. Gold mining.
Tresigallo (trĕzēgäl'lō), village (pop. 915), Ferrara prov., Emilia-Romagna, N central Italy, 14 mi. E of Ferrara; agr. machinery factory.
Tre Signori (trĕ sēnyō'rē), 3 peaks in N Italy. **1 Corno dei Tre Signori** (11,020 ft.), at S end of Ortles group, at junction of Brescia, Sondrio, and Trento provs., 12 mi. SE of Bormio. Has several glaciers. **2 Pizzo dei Tre Signori** (8,379 ft.), in Bergamasque Alps, at junction of Bergamo, Como, and Sondrio provs., 13 mi. NNE of Lecco. **3 Pizzo dei Tre Signori,** on Austro-Ital. border: see DREIHERRNSPITZE.
Tres Isletas (trās' ēslā'täs), town (pop. estimate 1,500), central Chaco natl. territory, Argentina, 25 mi. N of Presidencia Roque Sáenz Peña; lumbering and agr. center (cotton, corn, sunflowers, livestock); sawmills, cotton gins.
Tresjuncos (trās-hōōng'kōs), town (pop. 1,571), Cuenca prov., E central Spain, 10 mi. NNW of Belmonte; cereals, vegetables, olives, grapes, sheep.
Treska River (trĕs'kä), W Macedonia, Yugoslavia, rises near the Stogovo, 12 mi. SE of Debar; flows E past Kicevo and Brod Makedonski, and N to Vardar R. near Skoplje; c.75 mi. long. The POREC lies along its middle course. Hydroelectric plant supplies electricity to Skoplje. Also called Jehlovac R., Serbo-Croatian *Jehlovačka Reka*, as headstream, Golema Reka in upper course, and Velika Reka in middle course.
Treskavica or **Treskavitsa** (both: trĕ'skävētsä), mountain in Dinaric Alps, Yugoslavia, on Bosnia-Herzegovina line; c.10 mi. long; highest point (6,849 ft.) is 8 mi. NW of Kalinovik.
Três Lagoas (trās lùgō'ùs), city (pop. 5,154), SE Mato Grosso, Brazil, near Paraná R. (São Paulo border), on São Paulo–Corumbá RR and 190 mi. E of Campo Grande; cattle-shipping and meat-packing center. Airfield.
Tres Lagos (trās lä'gōs), village (pop. estimate 200), W Santa Cruz natl. territory, Argentina, in foothills, 140 mi. WNW of Santa Cruz; sheep-raising center; also alfalfa, horses, cattle. Resort on route to lakes San Martín (NW), Viedma (W), Argentino (SW). Airport.
Tres Lomas (trās lō'mäs), town (pop. 3,848), W Buenos Aires prov., Argentina, 35 mi. SSW of Trenque Lauquén; rail junction and agr. center (wheat, alfalfa, rye, cattle).
Tres Marías Islands or **Las Tres Marías** (läs trās märē'äs), archipelago (□ c.100), W Mexico, c.60 mi. off Pacific coast of Nayarit, bet. 21°14' and 21°40'N. The lofty and rugged group consists of 3 major isls.: María Cleófas (märē'ä klāō'fäs) (□ 8.7) in S, María Magdalena (mägdälā'nä) (□ 32.5) in center, and María Madre (mä'drā) (□ 56; c. 11 mi. long), the largest, in N. Situated just NNW of María Madre is small San Juanito Isl. (sän whänē'tō) (□ 3.4; 3 mi. long). On María Madre the Mex. govt. maintains penal colony and lighthouse; isl. rises to 2,011 ft. Otherwise isls. are, because of lack of water, uninhabited. They contain some guano and salt deposits, and maguey and lumber.
Tres Montes Gulf (trās mōn'tĕs), N inlet of Gulf of Peñas in SW Taitao Peninsula, Aysén prov., S Chile; bounded W by **Tres Montes Peninsula** (SW part of Taitao Peninsula), whose S tip is Point Tres Montes (46°59'S 75°26'W).
Tres Morros, Alto de (äl'tō dā trās mô'rōs), Andean massif (c.12,150 ft.) in N Cordillera Central of Antioquia dept., N central Colombia, 75 mi. NW of Medellín.
Tresnuraghes (trĕznōōrä'gĕs), village (pop. 2,262), Nuoro prov., W Sardinia, 14 mi. W of Macomer; domestic embroidery and netting.
Tres Picos (trās pē'kōs), highest point (4,200 ft.) of the Sierra de la Ventana, SW Buenos Aires prov., Argentina, 45 mi. NNE of Bahía Blanca.
Tres Piedras (trās pēä'dräs), village (pop. c.150), Taos co., N N.Mex., 28 mi. NW of Taos in S foothills of San Juan Mts.; alt. c.8,000 ft.; livestock, grain, potatoes.
Três Pontas (trās pōn'tùs), city (pop. 5,116), S Minas Gerais, Brazil, 12 mi. NNE of Varginha; coffee- and sugar-growing.
Tres Porteñas (trās pōrtā'nyäs), town (pop. estimate 500), N Mendoza prov., Argentina, in Mendoza R. valley (irrigation area), 25 mi. E of Mendoza; rail terminus; farming center (wine, alfalfa, corn, livestock; apiculture), wine and vinegar making, dried-fruit processing.
Tres Puentes (trās pwĕn'täs), village (1930 pop. 46), Magallanes prov., S Chile, N suburb of Punta Arenas, on Strait of Magellan; meat packing. Petroleum wells near by.
Tres Puntas, Cabo (kä'bō trās pōōn'täs), Atlantic cape in S Comodoro Rivadavia military zone, Argentina, at S edge of Gulf of San Jorge, 38 mi. N of Puerto Deseado; 47°6'S 65°52'W.
Tres Puntas, Cabo de (dā), low wooded headland of Guatemala, on Caribbean Sea; separates Bay of Amatique (SW) and Gulf of Honduras (NE); 15°58'N 88°37'W. Also called Cape Manabique.
Três Rios (trās rē'ōōs), city (pop. 10,285), N Rio de Janeiro state, Brazil, on Paraíba R. above influx of the Paraibuna, and 55 mi. N of Rio; import and rail center near Minas Gerais border; cotton milling, mfg. of soap and chemicals, distilling, rice processing, dairying. Until 1943, city was called Entre Rios.
Tres Ríos (trās rē'ōs) or **La Unión** (lä ōōnyōn'), town (1950 pop. 1,916), Cartago prov., Costa Rica, on Inter-American Highway, on railroad and 5 mi. WNW of Cartago; important coffee center. Summer resort.
Trest (tùrzhĕ'shtyù), Czech *Třešť*, Ger. *Triesch* (trēsh), town (pop. 4,424), W Moravia, Czechoslovakia, in Bohemian-Moravian Heights, on railroad and 9 mi. SSW of Jihlava; textile and cheese production, mfg. of furniture, matches.
Trestenberg, Rumania: see TASNAD.
Tres Valles (trās vä'yĕs), village (pop. 1,371), Veracruz, SE Mexico, in Gulf lowland, 19 mi. SE of Tierra Blanca; rail junction; banana and mango growing.
Tres Vírgenes, Las (läs trās vēr'hĕnĕs), volcanic massif in Lower California, Mexico, near coast of Gulf of California, 25 mi. NW of Santa Rosalía; rises to 6,545 ft. Last erupted 1746.
Tres Zapotes (säpō'tĕs), village (pop. 1,003), SE Veracruz, E Mexico, 15 mi. W of San Andrés Tuxtla. Pre-Maya monument dating from 291 B.C. was found here (1939) near a colossal stone head.
Trets (trā), town (pop. 2,122), Bouches-du-Rhône dept., SE France, near the Arc, 13 mi. ESE of Aix-en-Provence, in lignite-mining area. Preserves parts of town walls.
Tretten (trĕt'tùn), village (pop. 252) in Oyer (Nor. *Øyer*) canton (pop. 3,671), Opland co., S central Norway, in the Gudbrandsdal, on Lagen R., on railroad and 14 mi. NNW of Lillehammer; casein mfg.; agr., stock raising. In Second World War, scene (April, 1940) of engagement bet. Anglo-Norwegian and German forces.
Tretyakovo or **Tret'yakovo** (tryĕtyŭkô'vù), village (1939 pop. over 500), S Altai Territory, Russian SFSR, on railroad and 50 mi. SE of Rubtsovsk.
Treuburg, Poland: see OLECKO.
Treuchtlingen (troikht'lĭng-ùn), town (pop. 5,221), Middle Franconia, W central Bavaria, Germany, on the Altmühl and 6 mi. SW of Weissenburg; rail junction; textile and pottery mfg., brewing, flour and lumber milling. Limestone quarries in area.
Treuddyn, Wales: see TRYDDYN.
Treuen (troi'ùn), town (pop. 9,030), Saxony, E central Germany, at NW foot of the Erzgebirge, 8 mi. ENE of Plauen; textile milling (cotton, wool, silk); mfg. of rope, musical instruments.
Treuenbrietzen (troi"ùnbrē'tsùn), town (pop. 8,569), Brandenburg, E Germany, 25 mi. SSW of Potsdam; metalworking; market gardening. Has two 13th-cent. churches.
Treuer River, Australia: see MACUMBA RIVER.
Treungen, Norway: see NISSEDAL.
Treutlen (trōōt'lĭn), county (□ 194; pop. 6,522), E central Ga.; ⊙ Soperton. Bounded SW by Oconee R. Coastal plain agr. (tobacco, corn, peanuts, livestock) and naval-stores area. Formed 1917.
Trevélez (trāvā'lĕth), village (pop. 1,401), Granada prov., S Spain, in the Sierra Nevada at foot of the Mulhacén, 22 mi. SE of Granada; noted for its cured hams. Stock raising, lumbering; chestnuts, nuts, potatoes. Trout fishing. Mineral springs. Iron and copper mining near by.
Trevelín (trävälēn'), village (pop. estimate 800), W Chubut natl. territory, Argentina, 10 mi. SW of Esquel; resort and trade center in Andean valley; agr. (wheat, oats, alfalfa, sheep, cattle), lumbering, dairying. Los Alerces natl. park, comprising lakes, waterfalls, and forests, is near by.
Tréveray (trāvrā'), village (pop. 617), Meuse dept., NE France, on the Ornain and Marne-Rhine Canal, 15 mi. SE of Bar-le-Duc; iron foundry.
Trèves (trĕv), village (pop. 176), Gard dept., S France, near the Causse Noir, 12 mi. WNW of Le Vigan; lumbering.
Treves, Germany: see TRIER.
Treveskyn (trĭvĕ'skĭn), village (pop. 1,854, with adjacent Morgan), Allegheny co., W Pa., 11 mi. SW of downtown Pittsburgh. Post Office name is Cuddy.
Trevi (trā'vē), village (pop. 1,092), Perugia prov., Umbria, central Italy, 6 mi. SSE of Foligno; mfg. of agr. tools.

Treviana (trāvyä'nä), town (pop. 1,102), Logroño prov., N Spain, 10 mi. SW of Miranda de Ebro; cereals, wine, livestock; lumber.

Trévières (trāvyâr'), village (pop. 503), Calvados dept., NW France, on the Aure and 9 mi. WNW of Bayeux; dairying.

Treviglio (trĕvē'lyô), town (pop. 13,818), Bergamo prov., Lombardy, N Italy, in fertile plain bet. Serio and Adda rivers, 20 mi. ENE of Milan. Rail junction; agr. and industrial center; foundries, silk and woolen mills, alcohol distillery; mfg. (pianos, organs, glassware, buttons, celluloid, fertilizer).

Trevilians (trůvĭl'yůnz), village, Louisa co., central Va., 22 mi. E of Charlottesville. In Civil War, a Confederate victory (called battle of Trevilian Station) was won here in June, 1864.

Treviño (trāvē'nyō), town (pop. 354), Burgos prov., N Spain, 8 mi. SSW of Vitoria; main settlement in the Condado de Treviño (pop. 3,729), an enclave in Álava prov. Grain growing; flour milling. The region also produces potatoes, fruit, timber, resins, livestock. Mineral springs (Cucho) and stone quarries near by.

Treviso (trĭvē'zōō), town (pop. 131), SE Santa Catarina, Brazil, 8 mi. W of Urussanga; coal deposits.

Treviso (trĕvē'zô), province (□ 956; pop. 570,566), Veneto, N Italy; ⊙ Treviso. Consists of fertile Venetian plain (70% of area) and hills (N), including the Montello. Irrigated by Piave, Livenza, Musone, and Sile rivers. Agr. (cereals, grapes, raw silk, sugar beets, tobacco); stock raising (cattle, horses). Mfg. at Treviso, Vittorio Veneto, Castelfranco Veneto, and Montebelluna.

Treviso, anc. *Tarvisium*, city (pop. 43,949), ⊙ Treviso prov., Veneto, N Italy, in center of fertile Venetian plain, on Sile R. and 16 mi. NNW of Venice; 45°40'N 12°15'E. Rail and road center; foundries; mfg. of agr. machinery, wax, brushes; paper and rice mills; ceramic, electric, and printing industries. Bishopric. Has cathedral (badly damaged in 1944) with works by Titian and Bordone, who was b. here, and church of Santa Maria Maddalena with paintings by Veronese. An old town with narrow, winding streets, canals, 15th- and 16th-cent. houses. In early Middle Ages seat of a Lombard duchy. Held by Venice, 1339–1796. Passed to French in 1797, to Austria in 1848. Bombed in First and Second World Wars. In severe raids of 1944–45, many bldgs. were destroyed or badly damaged; worst raid (1944) cost over 2,000 lives.

Trevorton (trĕ'vůrtůn), village (pop. 2,545), Northumberland co., E central Pa., 5 mi. W of Shamokin, in anthracite region.

Trévoux (trāvōō'), town (pop. 2,374), Ain dept., E France, on left bank of Saône R. and 13 mi. NNW of Lyons; screw-plate and drawplate-mfg. center. Gold and silver filigreeing, industrial diamond cutting, condenser mfg. Has ruins of medieval castle, and a 17th-cent. assembly hall. Was ⊙ of Dombes dist. until 16th cent.

Treynor (trā'nůr), town (pop. 247), Pottawattamie co., SW Iowa, 14 mi. ESE of Council Bluffs.

Treysa (trī'zä), town (pop. 6,899), in former Prussian prov. of Hesse-Nassau, W Germany, after 1945 in Hesse, 19 mi. ENE of Marburg; rail junction; lumber milling. Has 14th-cent. church.

Trézel (trāzĕl'), town (pop. 4,936), Oran dept., N Algeria, 16 mi. SE of Tiaret, on fertile Sersou Plateau; agr. trade (cereals, wine, esparto; horses, sheep; wool).

Trezevant (trĕ'zĭvůnt), town (pop. 765), Carroll co., NW Tenn., 11 mi. W of Huntingdon, in farm area.

Trezzo sull'Adda (trĕ'tsô sōōl-läd'dä), town (pop. 5,489), Milano prov., Lombardy, N Italy, on Adda R. and 19 mi. NE of Milan; textiles, ironworks. Has ruined Visconti castle.

Trhove Sviny (tŭr'hôvā svĭ'nĭ), Czech *Trhové Sviny*, Ger. *Schweinitz* (shvīn'ĭts), town (pop. 2,458), S Bohemia, Czechoslovakia, on railroad and 12 mi. SE of Budweis, in oat- and rye-growing region; livestock market.

Triabunna, town (pop. 330), E Tasmania, 39 mi. NE of Hobart and on inlet of Tasman Sea; coal mines, freestone quarries; orchards.

Triadelphia (trīůdĕl'fēů), town (pop. 741), Ohio co., W.Va., 5 mi. E of Wheeling.

Triaditsa, Bulgaria: see SOFIA, city.

Triaga (trēägä'), village, Sfax dist., E Tunisia, 27 mi. WNW of Sfax; olives, wool fats.

Trialet Range (trēůlyĕt'), N range of the Lesser Caucasus, in central Georgian SSR; extends c.80 mi. bet. Tiflis (E) and Akhaltsikhe (W); rises to 9,350 ft. Crossed by Borzhomi-Akhalkalaki road. Forms divide bet. Khram (S) and Kura rivers.

Triana (trēä'nō), SW section of Seville, Seville prov., Spain, on right bank of the Guadalquivir; chiefly a working-class dist.; known for its pottery.

Trianda, Greece: see TRIANTA.

Tria Nesia or **Tria Nisia** (both: trē'ä nē'sēů), 3 islets in the Dodecanese, Greece, SE of Syrnai; 36°17'N 26°45'E.

Triang (trēäng'), village (pop. 917), S central Pahang, Malaya, on E coast railroad and 14 mi. S of Temerloh; rubber plantations.

Triangle, village (pop. 1,585, with near-by Dumfries), Prince William co., N Va., near the Potomac, 30 mi. SW of Washington

Triangle, The, tribal region of Kachin State, Upper Burma, bet. Mali and Nmai rivers (headstreams of the Irrawaddy); 100 mi. long, 30 mi. wide. Pop. is Kachin.

Triangles, The, reef (c.12 mi. long) of several islets in Gulf of Mexico, 115 mi. W of Celestún, Yucatan. Lighthouse at 20°58'N 92°20'W.

Triângulo Mineiro (trēäng'gōōlōō mēnä'rōō), triangle-shaped region of W Minas Gerais, Brazil, bet. Paranaíba R. (N; Goiás border) and the Rio Grande (S; São Paulo border); important cattle-raising area. Collecting centers for cattle shipment to São Paulo are at Uberaba and Uberlândia. Diamond washings in tributaries of the Rio Grande.

Tria Nisia, Greece: see TRIA NESIA.

Trianon (trēänõ'), 2 small châteaux in the park of Versailles, Seine-et-Oise dept., N central France, 11 mi. WSW of Paris. The Grand Trianon was built (1687) by Mansart as a retreat for Louis XIV. The Petit Trianon, built for Louis XV by Gabriel, was favorite residence of Marie Antoinette who had rustic cottages built near by. Here the peace treaty with Hungary was signed in 1920.

Trianta or **Trianda** (both: trēän'dů), town (pop. 2,096), Rhodes isl., Greece, on NW shore, 4 mi. SW of Rhodes. On site of anc. Ialysus (īă'lĭsůs), a leading city of Rhodes and a member of the Dorian Hexapolis.

Triassic Lowland, E U.S.: see APPALACHIAN MOUNTAINS.

Triaucourt-en-Argonne (trēōkōōr'-änärgôn'), village (pop. 426), Meuse dept., NE France, on S slope of the Argonne, 11 mi. SE of Sainte-Menehould; cheese mfg. Until 1947, called Triaucourt.

Tribbey, mining village (1940 pop. 622), Perry co., SE Ky., in Cumberland foothills, 5 mi. NE of Hazard; bituminous coal.

Tribeni, India: see ALLAHABAD, city; HOOGHLY, town.

Tribeni Canal (trĭbā'nē), irrigation canal in Champaran dist., NW Bihar, India; from left bank of Gandak R. extends 62 mi. SE to point 6 mi. NE of Bettiah; in drought area, now extensively cultivated (rice, wheat, barley, sugar); opened 1909.

Triberg (trē'bĕrk), town (pop. 4,380), S Baden, Germany, in Black Forest, on the Gutach (waterfall 525 ft.) and 12 mi. WNW of Villingen; watch-making industry; metal- and woodworking. Noted climatic health resort and winter-sports center (alt. 2,132 ft.-2,296 ft.). Has 18th-cent. pilgrimage church.

Tribes Hill, village (1940 pop. 647), Montgomery co., E central N.Y., on Mohawk R. and 5 mi. W of Amsterdam.

Triborough Bridge (trī'bůrů), in New York city, SE N.Y., system of 4 vehicular bridges and an elevated highway, spanning East and Harlem rivers and connecting Manhattan, the Bronx, and Queens boroughs. Passes over Randalls and Wards isls. in East R.; 17½ mi. long, including approaches. Built 1929–36.

Tribsees (trĭp'zās), town (pop. 4,932), in former Prussian Pomerania prov., N Germany, after 1945 in Mecklenburg, 20 mi. SW of Stralsund; agr. market (grain, sugar beets, potatoes, stock).

Tribune, city (pop. 1,010), ⊙ Greeley co., W Kansas, 55 mi. NW of Garden City; grain, livestock.

Tribur, Germany: see TREBUR.

Tricao Malal (trēkou' mälăl'), town (pop. estimate 600), N Neuquén natl. territory, Argentina, 20 mi. N of Chos Malal, in Andean foothills; wheat, alfalfa, livestock; flour milling.

Tricarico (trēkä'rēkô), town (pop. 7,865), Matera prov., Basilicata, S Italy, 18 mi. E of Potenza; agr. trade center (cereals, grapes, olives, livestock); macaroni, wine. Bishopric. Has cathedral, 17th-cent. castle, and old walls.

Tricase (trēkä'zĕ), town (pop. 6,124), Lecce prov., Apulia, S Italy, 13 mi. SSE of Maglie; agr. center (olives, grapes, figs, citrus fruit, tobacco); hemp milling.

Tricastin (trēkästē'), region in SW Drôme and NW Vaucluse depts., SE France, along left bank of Rhone R., bet. Montélimar (N), Nyons (E), and Orange (S); ⊙ Saint-Paul-Trois-Châteaux; fruits, vegetables, truffles, olives.

Tricca, Greece: see TRIKKALA.

Tricesimo (trēchā'zēmô), village (pop. 2,033), Udine prov., Friuli–Venezia Giulia, NE Italy, 6 mi. N of Udine.

Trichinopoly (trĭchĭnŏp'ůlē), since 1949 officially **Tiruchirapalli** (tĭr"ōōchĭrŭpŭl'lē), district (□ 5,514; pop. 2,632,439), S Madras, India; ⊙ Trichinopoly. Drained by Cauvery R.; Pachaimalai Hills (magnetite mines) in N. Agr.: cotton, rice, millet, oilseeds (sesame, peanuts). Main towns: Trichinopoly, Karur, Golden Rock, Srirangam. Original dist. (□ 4,329; 1941 pop. 2,194,091) was enlarged 1948 by inc. of Madras State of Pudukkottai. Also called Tiruchi.

Trichinopoly, since 1949 officially **Tiruchirapalli**, city (pop. 159,566), ⊙ Trichinopoly dist., S Madras, India, on Cauvery R. and 180 mi. SW of Madras. Rail and road center in agr. area; airport; cotton milling, cigar mfg., tanning; gold and silver filigree. St. Joseph's Col., Bishop Heber's Col., National Col. Locomotive and railway-car works in SE suburb of Golden Rock. Gypsum, limestone, and mica workings near by. Area of ruined 17th-cent. fort in N part of city includes steep granite rock (273 ft.; crowned by 17th-cent. Dravidian temple). Was ⊙ successive Tamil kingdoms (10th-17th cent.). Site of 18th-cent. battles bet. Indian powers, French, and English until ceded to English by Nawabs of Arcot in 1801. Also called Tiruchi.

Trichonis, Lake, or **Lake Trikhonis** (both: trēkhônēs') (□ 37.4), in Acarnania nome, W central Greece, bet. Arakynthos and Panaitolikon massifs, 10 mi. NNE of Missolonghi; 12 mi. long, 3 mi. wide. Fisheries. Drains (W) via L. Lysimachia into Achelous R. Formerly called L. Agrinion and L. Vrachori (Vrakhori).

Trichur (trĭchōōr'), city (pop. 57,524), central Cochin, India, 37 mi. N of Ernakulam; cotton-milling center; cotton textiles, coir products (rope, mats), copra; rice and oilseed milling, soap mfg., sawmilling. Has col. Cotton mills, tileworks in suburb of Pudukad, 5 mi. S.

Tricorner Knob (6,150 ft.), W N.C., peak of Great Smoky Mts., 15 mi. E of Gatlinburg, Tenn.

Tricorno, peak, Yugoslavia: see TRIGLAV.

Trident, village, Gallatin co., SW Mont., on Missouri R. near its origin, 30 mi. NW of Bozeman; cement.

Trident Park (10,141 ft.), SE B.C., in Selkirk Mts., on W edge of Hamber Provincial Park, 60 mi. N of Revelstoke; 51°53'N 118°8'W.

Tridentum, Italy: see TRENT.

Trie (trē), village (pop. 934), Hautes-Pyrénées dept., SW France, on Lannemezan Plateau, 13 mi. S of Mirande; livestock market; wool combing, wood-working.

Trieben (trē'bůn), village (pop. 1,857), Styria, central Austria, 24 mi. NW of Knittelfeld; processes magnesite.

Triebes (trē'bůs), town (pop. 5,316), Thuringia, central Germany, 9 mi. WNW of Greiz; textile milling.

Triel-sur-Seine (trēĕl'-sür-sĕn'), town (pop. 2,856), Seine-et-Oise dept., N central France, on right bank of Seine R. and 6 mi. SSW of Pontoise; metal-works; truck gardening.

Trier (trēr) or **Treves** (trēvz), Fr. *Trèves* (trĕv), anc. *Augusta Treverorum*, city (1939 pop. 88,150; 1946 pop. 63,420; 1950 pop. 74,709), in former Prussian Rhine Prov., W Germany, after 1945 in Rhineland-Palatinate, on the Moselle (Mosel) and 75 mi. WSW of Mainz, near Luxembourg line; 49°46'N 6°39'E. The main center of the Moselle wine region, it is also a rail junction and has steel-rolling mills and mfg. of textiles, leather goods, tobacco; brewing, distilling. Has played an important part in history since Roman times, and has retained more Roman monuments than any other Ger. city. Founded by Augustus, Treves was ⊙ Roman prov. of Belgica and later of prefecture of Gaul. Named for the Treveri, a people of E Gaul. Under Roman Empire, Trier reached a pop. of c.50,000 and was a major commercial center with large wine trade. Was frequent residence of the Western emperors from c.295 until its capture (early 5th cent.) by the Franks. An episcopal see since 4th cent., it was made an archiepiscopal see in 815. The archbishops of Trier became powerful temporal princes whose territories extended along both sides of the Saar and Moselle and across the Rhine. They ranked 2d among the spiritual electors of the Holy Roman Empire. Trier flourished as a commercial and cultural center. Seat of a univ. from 1473 until its occupation by the French in 1797. Archbishopric of Trier was secularized and was formally ceded to France in 1801. The Congress of Vienna (1814–15) awarded Trier to Prussia. Again became R.C. episcopal see in 1821; pop. is predominantly Catholic. It was occupied by the French after the First World War and suffered considerable damage in the Second World War; captured by U.S. forces March, 1945; later placed in Fr. occupation zone. The chief Roman monuments escaped war damage. These are the Porta Nigra (an imposing and well-preserved fortified gate), the amphitheater, and the imperial baths. Destroyed were: Romanesque chapel, 3 Gothic houses, all museums (the collections were saved). Heavily damaged were: Gothic church of Our Lady, a gem of 13th-cent. Ger. architecture; baroque electoral palace and Kesselstatt palace. The celebrated Romanesque cathedral, also heavily damaged, embodies part of a 4th-cent. basilica; its chief treasure is the Holy Coat of Treves, supposed to be the seamless coat of Jesus. The rare exhibitions (e.g., 1844, 1891, and 1933) of the relic have been the occasions of huge pilgrimages. Trier has theological seminary (founded 1773); school of viticulture. Karl Marx b. here.

Triesch, Czechoslovakia: see TREST.

Triesen (trē'zůn), village (pop. 1,192), Liechtenstein, near the Rhine, 3 mi. S of Vaduz; cattle raising, mfg. of cotton goods.

Triesenberg (trē'zůnbĕrk), village (pop. 1,075), Liechtenstein, 2.5 mi. SSE of Vaduz, scattered on mtn. slope bet. 2,500 and 5,000 ft.; stock raising, weaving.

Trieste (trēĕst', Ital. trēĕ'stā), Slovenian *Trst* (tûrst), Ger. *Triest*, anc. *Tergeste*, city (1936 pop. 248,379), ⊙ Free Territory of Trieste, beautifully situated on Gulf of Trieste at head of the Adriatic, 70 mi. ENE of Venice; 45°39'N 13°46'E. A leading

Mediterranean outlet and entrepôt for Central Europe, and major industrial center, with extensive shipyards, iron- and steelworks (mfg. of ship plates), coal-gas plant, petroleum refineries, mfg. of marine engines, cranes, jute cloth and sacks, garments, pasta, cognac, beer, soap, cigarette paper, paints and varnishes. Seat of large insurance companies. Annual fair. Its port, extending 8 mi. along the Gulf of Trieste and the industrial waterfront of its inlet, Muggia Bay (S), was 1st developed 1867–83; includes 3 distinct basins, old free port (N), new free port (S), and customs port (center). ZAULE industrial port was developed after Second World War. Situated at the foot of the Karst, the city is dominated by San Giusto hill, crowned by 15th-cent. castle, cathedral (dating partly from 6th cent.), war memorials, and Roman relics. The old city of narrow winding streets (with Roman amphitheater) extends down the hill to large waterfront square, Piazza dell'Unità, flanked by city hall, zone govt. offices (former Austrian and Ital. govt. palace), and shipping offices. Trieste has univ. (1924) and several museums (Roman antiquities, modern art, applied arts, marine fauna). A prosperous Roman colony, Trieste developed by 1295 into a free commune, which passed (1382) under Austrian control. A free port after 1719, the city grew greatly after c.1800, becoming the only Austrian seaport and a natural outlet for Central Europe. In 1867 it was made an Austrian crownland (□ 37; 1910 pop. 229,510) and ⊙ Küstenland. A center of Ital. irredentism, it was annexed (1919) to Italy and became ⊙ Trieste prov. (□ 494; 1936 pop. 351,595) of Venezia Giulia; its economic prosperity declined. During Second World War, city was heavily bombed (1944). Made (1947) ⊙ Free Territory of Trieste and placed under Anglo-American administration.

Trieste, Free Territory of, free state (□ 285; 1949 pop. estimate 380,000), under protection of United Nations Security Council, S central Europe, on NE Adriatic Sea. Bounded on land side by Yugoslavia, except for 2-mi.-long common frontier with Italy (extreme NW), the Free Territory includes city of Trieste and Adriatic coastal strip of NW Istria, 30 mi. long and varying in width from 2 mi. at Duino (N) to 15 mi. (S). Physiographically, it consists of the edge of the unproductive Karst (N), a belt of sandstone hills (center), and a lower karstic plateau (bauxite deposits; S). Climate is of Mediterranean type along coast and lower valleys; at higher altitudes colder winters and heavier year-round rainfall prevail. The territory lies in the path of the infamous bora, a violent, cold northeaster. Agr. in infertile Karst (N) is restricted to small-scale cultivation of potatoes, hay, beans, and rye, in marked contrast to intensive, commercialized farming (S) of fresh vegetables, fruit (cherries, peaches), olives, and vineyards. Dairy cattle and sheep are raised. The Adriatic off the Trieste coast is a rich fishing zone, extensively exploited from southern ports (canning, boatbuilding) of Isola, Capodistria, Pirano, and Cittanova. Modern large-scale industry (shipbuilding, steel milling, oil refining) on the basis of imported raw materials is restricted to city of Trieste, a leading shipping and insurance center. Rural industry processes canned goods, wine, and cognac. Marble quarried at Aurisina, salt produced near Portorose. N section of territory is served by Paris-Milan-Belgrade RR and trunk highways; agr. south relies exclusively on road transport. Pop. largely Italian (70%; mainly in larger urban centers); Slovenian and Croatian minorities in rural areas. Area belonged to Austria from 1382 to 1919, and, as part of VENEZIA GIULIA, to Italy from 1919 until 1947, when the Free Territory was set up by Ital. peace treaty. Pending appointment by the Security Council of a territorial governor (on whose selection agreement could not be reached by the great powers), the Free Territory was divided into 2 zones (separated by so-called Morgan Line) under Anglo-American (N) and Yugoslav (S) administration. Anglo-American Zone or Zone "A" (□ 86; 1949 pop. estimate 310,000; ⊙ Trieste) includes industrial city of Trieste and unproductive rural areas of the Karst, with lesser towns of Muggia, Duino, and Aurisina. Local govt. in the 6 communes is headed by the appointed zone president; Italian is the official language, although Slovanian is permitted as a 2d language in Slovenian-majority communes. Yugoslav Zone or Zone "B" (□ 199; 1949 pop. estimate 70,000; ⊙ Capodistria) includes the important S agr. section of the Free Territory, with the towns of Capodistria, Pirano, and Buie. For local govt. purposes, this zone has been constituted as the administrative region of Istra (Serbo-Croatian,=Istria), headed by an elected people's committee; Italian, Slovenian, and Croatian are official languages.

Trieste, Gulf of, NE inlet of Gulf of Venice, at head of the Adriatic, bet. Cape Salvore (NW Istria) and mouth of the Tagliamento; 20 mi. wide. Receives Isonzo R.; contains Grado Isl. Chief ports: Trieste, Monfalcone, Capodistria.

Triesting River (trēs'tĭng), E Lower Austria, rises on Schöpfl mtn., flows 35 mi. E, past Berndorf, and N to Schwechat R. just SW of Schwechat.

Trieux (trēû'), town (pop. 2,049), Meurthe-et-Moselle dept., NE France, 6 mi. N of Briey; iron mines.

Trieux River, Côtes-du-Nord dept., W France, rises in Armorican Massif 5 mi. NW of Corlay, flows 45 mi. N, past Guingamp and Pontrieux (head of navigation), to English Channel opposite Bréhat isl.

Trifail, Yugoslavia: see TRBOVLJE.

Triftern (trĭf'tûrn), village (pop. 3,207), Lower Bavaria, Germany, 4 mi. SE of Pfarrkirchen; oats, rye, cattle, hogs.

Trifush, Albania: see TROPOJË.

Trigal (trēgäl'), town (pop. c.3,200), Santa Cruz dept., central Bolivia, in E foothills of Cordillera de Cochabamba, 15 mi. NNW of Valle Grande; tobacco plantations.

Trigg, county (□ 466; pop. 9,683), SW Ky.; ⊙ Cadiz. Bounded S by Tenn., W by Kentucky Reservoir (Tennessee R.); drained by Cumberland and Little rivers. Gently rolling agr. area (dark tobacco, wheat, corn, livestock); limestone quarries; timber. Includes part of Kentucky Woodlands Wildlife Refuge. Formed 1820.

Triggiano (trēd-jä'nô), town (pop. 13,047), Bari prov., Apulia, S Italy, 5 mi. SE of Bari; trades in wine, olive oil, almonds, fruit.

Triglav (trē'gläf, trĭ'–), Ital. *Tricorno* (trēkôr'nô), highest peak (c.9,395 ft.) of Julian Alps and highest in Yugoslavia, in NW Slovenia, 40 mi. NW of Ljubljana. Until 1947, on Yugoslav–Ital. frontier. View includes part of Adriatic Sea. Formerly also Terglou (tĕr'glōō).

Trignac (trēnyäk'), town (pop. 2,402), Loire-Inférieure dept., W France, 3 mi. N of Saint-Nazaire; metallurgical center (foundries, rolling mills) supplying Saint-Nazaire shipyards. Damaged in Second World War.

Trigno River (trē'nyô), S central Italy, rises in the Apennines 12 mi. N of Isernia, flows 52 mi. SW and NE to the Adriatic 6 mi. SE of Vasto. Forms part of Chieti-Campobasso prov. boundary.

Trigo Mountains (trē'gō), Yuma co., SW Ariz., near Colorado R. (Calif. line); rise to 2,767 ft. N extension is Dome Rock Range.

Trigueros (trēgā'rōs), town (pop. 5,877), Huelva prov., SW Spain, on railroad and 10 mi. NE of Huelva; agr. trading and processing (olives, grapes, cereals, chick-peas, almonds, livestock). Mfg. of shoes, tiles, bottle corks; sawmilling.

Trikala, Greece: see TRIKKALA.

Trikeri, Greece: see TRIKKERI.

Trikhonis, Lake, Greece: see TRICHONIS, LAKE.

Trikkala or **Trikala** (both: trē'kûlû), nome (□ 1,328; pop. 120,184), W Thessaly, Greece; ⊙ Trikkala. Bounded W by Pindus system and N by Chasia Mts., it is drained by upper Peneus R. and includes part of Trikkala lowland (SE). Agr.: corn, vegetables, olives, almonds, wheat; livestock, dairy products. Main centers are Trikkala and Kalambaka, served by narrow-gauge railroad from Volos.

Trikkala or **Trikala,** anc. *Tricca,* city coextensive with **Trikka** or **Trika** dist. (1951 pop. 27,890), ⊙ Trikkala nome, W Thessaly, Greece, on narrow-gauge railroad and 35 mi. W of Larissa (linked by highway); processing of agr. and dairy products (corn, olives, cheese, eggs). Winter residence of Walachian shepherds from Pindus and Chasia Mts. Bishopric. An anc. center of worship of Asclepius (remains of temple), it was (14th-16th cents.) ⊙ Thessaly under Serbian rule and under Turks, who called it Thirhala. Passed 1881 to Greece. Bombed in Second World War.

Trikkandiyur, India: see TIRUR.

Trikkeri or **Trikeri** (both: trē'kĕrē), town (pop. 1,986), Magnesia nome, SE Thessaly, Greece, 20 mi. SSE of Volos, on extremity of Magnesia peninsula, forming Gulf of Volos. The **Strait of Trikkeri** (W), separating the peninsula from the Thessalian mainland, is entrance to Gulf of Volos.

Trikomo (trē'kômō), village (pop. 2,081), Famagusta dist., E Cyprus, 30 mi. ENE of Nicosia; wheat, barley, citrus fruit, olives; sheep, cattle.

Trillo (trē'lyō), town (pop. 822), Guadalajara prov., central Spain, in New Castile, on the Tagus and 30 mi. ENE of Guadalajara. Noted spa in picturesque valley, with fine garden and cascades. Lumbering, vegetable growing, sheep raising, gypsum quarrying. Baños de Carlos III are just across river.

Trim, Gaelic *Baile Átha Truim,* urban district (pop. 1,383), ⊙ Co. Meath, Ireland, in S central part of co., on the Boyne and 25 mi. NW of Dublin; agr. market (cattle, horses; potatoes), with paper mills. It has remains of King John's Castle, founded 1173 by Hugh de Lacy and scene of imprisonment of Henry of Lancaster (later Henry IV). Yellow Steeple, a ruined 13th-cent. tower, marks site of abbey reputedly founded 432 by St. Patrick. Of anc. town walls 2 gates remain. Talbot's Castle (1415) became school. Tower of parish church dates from 1449. In vicinity are remains of 13th-cent. Dominican abbey, Abbey of SS. Peter and Paul (founded 1206), and remains of Scurlogstown Castle (1080), with 2 round towers.

Trimbach (trĭm'bäkh), town (pop. 4,112), Solothurn canton, N Switzerland, near Olten; aluminum, foodstuffs; woodworking.

Trimbak (trĭm'bŭk), town (pop. 4,261), Nasik dist., central Bombay, India, in Western Ghats, 18 mi. SW of Nasik; Hindu pilgrimage center (annual festival fair). Godavari R. rises 1 mi. S. Sometimes spelled Trimbuk.

Trimble, county (□ 146; pop. 5,148), N Ky.; ⊙ Bedford. Bounded W and N by Ohio R. (Ind. line); drained by Little Kentucky R. Gently rolling upland agr. area (burley tobacco, grain, livestock), in outer Bluegrass region. Timber. Stone quarries. Formed 1837.

Trimble. 1 Town (pop. 141), Clinton co., NW Mo., 25 mi. SE of St. Joseph. **2** Village (pop. 566), Athens co., SE Ohio, 10 mi. N of Athens, and on small Sunday Creek, in coal-mining area. **3** Town (pop. 674), on Dyer-Obion co. line, NW Tenn., 16 mi. NE of Dyersburg, in timber and farm area.

Trimountain, village (pop. 1,360, with adjacent Painesdale), Houghton co., NW Upper Peninsula, Mich., 6 mi. SW of Houghton, on Keweenaw Peninsula.

Trimulgherry, India: see SECUNDERABAD.

Trin (trŭn), city (pop. 2,165), Sofia dist., W Bulgaria, at S foot of Rui Mts., on Yerma R. and 35 mi. WNW of Sofia; agr. center in Znepole (znĕ'pôlĕ) Basin (□ 21; rye, hemp, livestock, truck). Has technical school. Linked with Leskovac (Yugoslavia) by road across Rui Mts. Gold mining in near-by Mislovshtitsa (pop. 552), pottery in Busintsi (pop. 492). Also spelled Trn.

Trinacria, Sicily: see SICILY.

Trinchera (trĭnchâ'rû), village (pop. c.200), Las Animas co., S Colo., 27 mi. ESE of Trinidad, near N.Mex. line; alt. 5,741 ft.; livestock-shipping point.

Trinchera Creek, S Colo., rises in Sangre de Cristo Mts., flows c.50 mi. W, past Fort Garland, to the Rio Grande 12 mi. SSE of Alamosa. Small reservoirs, SE and SW of Fort Garland, are formed by 2 dams in stream.

Trinchera Peak, Colo.: see SANGRE DE CRISTO MOUNTAINS.

Trincheras, Las, Venezuela: see LAS TRINCHERAS.

Trincomalee (trĭng"kûmûlē'), town (pop. 29,146), ⊙ Eastern Prov. and Trincomalee dist. (□ 1,165; pop., 68,635), Ceylon, on NE coast, on promontory in N Koddiyar Bay overlooking a N inlet of the bay (Trincomalee Inner Harbour; one of finest natural harbors in the world), 145 mi. NE of Colombo; 84°32'N 81°13'E. Rail terminus; vegetable gardens, rice and coconut plantations. Meteorological observatory. On promontory at E of town is Fort Frederick (built 1676 by Dutch) on site of anc. Sivaite Temple of a Thousand Columns, built by Tamils and destroyed 1622 by Portuguese; N of fort is Sami or Swamy Rock, a Hindu pilgrimage center. Town was an early Tamil settlement; occupied by Portuguese in 17th cent.; captured 1639 by Dutch; 1673 by French; recaptured 1674 by Dutch; taken 1782 by English; restored to Dutch by French in 1783; captured 1795 by English; formally ceded to English in 1802. Formerly a hq. of Br. fleet. In Second World War, chief Br. naval base in the East following fall of Singapore; bombed 1942 by Japanese. Seaplane base at China Bay, small W inlet of Inner Harbour. Foul Point is 6 mi. ESE of town; lighthouse. Noted hot springs 5 mi. NW, at Kanniyai.

Trindade (trēndä'dĭ), city (pop. 1,953), S Goiás, central Brazil, just NW of Goiânia; rutile deposits.

Trindade, volcanic island (□ 4) in South Atlantic Ocean, c.700 mi. E of Vitória (Espírito Santo), Brazil; rises to above 2,000 ft. Braz. possession; 20°31'S 29°20'W. Sometimes Trinidad.

Trindade, village, São Tomé e Príncipe, on São Tomé Isl., 5 mi. SW of São Tomé (linked by rail); cacao, coffee.

Trinec (tûrzhĭ'nĕts), Czech *Třinec,* town (pop. 6,615; urban commune pop. 14,716), E Silesia, Czechoslovakia, on Olse R., on railroad and 20 mi. SE of Ostrava, near Pol. border; large blast furnaces and ironworks fed by regional iron mines and Ostrava-Karvina coal. Lime kilns at Dolni Listna (dôl'nyē lĕsht'nä), Czech *Dolní Lištna,* just E. First ironworks established in 1839.

Tring, residential urban district (1931 pop. 4,364; 1951 census 5,018), W Hertford, England. Has wooden market house (1750) and 15th-cent. church. Near by is Tring Park, former seat of Rothschild family, with Wren mansion and zoological mus.

Tring Jonction (zhōksyō'), village (pop. 288), S Que., 33 mi. SSE of Quebec; dairying, pig raising.

Trinidad (trĭ'nĭdăd), island (□ 1,863.82; pop. 530,276), Trinidad and Tobago crown colony, B.W.I., in the Atlantic, 10 mi. off Venezuela coast; ⊙ Port of Spain. Lies just N of the Orinoco delta, borders W on the Gulf of Paria; separated from Venezuela by narrow channels: Dragon's Mouth (NW) and Serpent's Mouth (S); situated 350 mi. E of Caracas and 600 mi. SE of San Juan, Puerto Rico. Southernmost and largest of the Lesser Antilles, of roughly square shape with 2 peninsulas (NW and SW) jutting into the Gulf of Paria, it extends bet. 10°2'–10°50'N and 60°55'–61°56'W; average length 50 mi. N-S, average width 37 mi. Has humid, tropical climate, in path of NE trade winds. Mean annual temp. 76°F.; main rainy period June-Dec., rainfall varying bet. 50-120 inches. The isl. is free from hurricanes. Trinidad belongs geologically to the South American continent. Generally low and level, crossed E-W by 3 ranges of hills rising in Mt. Aripo (N) to 3,085 ft. Watered by numerous unnavigable rivers, among them the Caroni and Ortoire. Swamps adjoin most of isl.'s indented coastline, which has many fine beaches (bathing, fishing) and provides good anchorage on the Gulf of Paria. Still covered largely by virgin forests. Its best-known landmark is the Pitch Lake near La Brea (SW), a vast seepage of natural asphalt now covering c.114 acres. In the same W region (Pointe-à-Pierre), and in S and center, are large petroleum deposits, the chief source of income. Among the agr. products yielded by the fertile soil are cacao, coconuts, copra, sugar cane, coffee, citrus fruit, and tonka beans, which are exported, as are rum, bitters, lime oil, timber. Fishing along the coast (tarpon, cavalla, kingfish, mackerel, snappers, groupers). Deer, ducks, wild hogs, armadillos abound. Largest city, leading commercial center, and a major Caribbean port is Port of Spain; the Piarco airport is 12 mi. ESE of it. Petroleum is shipped through the oil-refining centers of San Fernando and Pointe-à-Pierre. Trinidad ranks high as a winter resort, noted for its fine beaches and equable climate. The isl., called by aboriginal Indians Iere (Land of the Humming Bird), was discovered by Columbus on July 31, 1498. The Spanish made only feeble attempts at colonization. Sir Walter Raleigh destroyed the anc. capital, San José de Oruña (now St. Joseph), in 1595. Trinidad was raided by the Dutch (1640) and the French (1677 and 1690). Spain opened the isl. to foreign R.C. settlers in 1783; this led to a large influx of Fr. refugees from Haiti. Trinidad was surrendered to Great Britain in 1797, which was confirmed by a treaty of 1802. After 1845, East Indian immigrants were introduced. Several naval and army air bases (total □ 56) were leased in 1940 to the U.S. for 99 years, though they were not established until 1941; largest in NW and N. The colony was granted universal suffrage in 1945. The white pop. is chiefly composed of English, Portuguese, French, and Spanish. About ⅓ are of East Indian descent, and there are several thousand Chinese, but the Negro element predominates. English is generally spoken. Trinidad is divided into 8 counties and 3 municipalities (Port of Spain, San Fernando, and Arima).

Trinidad (trĭ'nĭdăd, Sp. trēnēdädh'), S suburb (pop. estimate 14,000) of San Juan, S San Juan prov., Argentina, on railroad; wine making, flour milling.

Trinidad. 1 City (1949 pop. estimate 10,400), ⊙ Beni dept. and Cercado prov., NE Bolivia, near Mamoré R., 250 mi. ENE of La Paz, in the llanos; 14°47'S 64°38'W. River transportation center; airport. Connected by road with its port, Puerto Ballivián, c.5 mi. WNW, on an arm of Mamoré R.; surrounding streams sometimes inundate the city. Commercial center for agr. products (sugar cane, rice, cotton), cattle, furs, valuable feathers; sugar refining, alcohol distilling. Has cathedral, one of few massive buildings of durable material, and govt. house. City founded 1556 by Spanish explorers; removed 6 years later from its original location on Mamoré R. to its present site. A mission was founded by Jesuits in 1687; in 1821 city was made capital of prov., becoming capital of dept. in 1856. Formerly of some importance, it declined considerably; is again growing in importance because of its air and river transportation facilities, which make it possible to export products of surrounding regions. **2** Village, Pando dept., N Bolivia, on Madre de Dios R. and 25 mi. WSW of Riberalta; rubber.

Trinidad, island, Brazil: TRINDADE.

Trinidad, city (pop. 15,453), Las Villas prov., central Cuba, at S foot of the Potrerillo (Sierra de Trinidad), on railroad and 45 mi. S of Santa Clara, 3 mi. N of its port Casilda. Trading and processing center for rich agr. region (sugar cane, coffee, cacao, tobacco, honey, beeswax, cattle). Sawmilling (tropical woods), dairying, mfg. of cigars and cigarettes. Airfield. A picturesque colonial city, founded 1514 by Diego de Velázquez, its fine architecture testifies to former prosperity. Also popular with tourists for its cool climate and mtn. scenery. Gold, copper, and amianthus deposits near by. The sugar central of Trinidad is 8 mi. E.

Trinidad. 1 Town (pop. 2,028), Copán dept., W Honduras, 13 mi. N of Santa Rosa; trade center in tobacco area. **2** City (pop. 1,439), Santa Bárbara dept., W Honduras, near Ulúa R., 15 mi. NNE of Santa Bárbara; commercial center in coffee area; sugar cane, grain, livestock. Founded 1794.

Trinidad. 1 NE residential suburb (pop. 15,219) of Asunción, Paraguay, on Paraguay R.; liquor distilleries. Botanical garden. Church of Holy Trinity with anc. Jesuit altar. Sometimes Santísima Trinidad. **2** Town (dist. pop., including JESÚS, 16,777) Itapúa dept., SE Paraguay, 17 mi. NNE of Encarnación; maté center; lumbering, viticulture. Founded 1706 as Jesuit mission. Has fine old ruined church.

Trinidad, Philippines: see LA TRINIDAD.

Trinidad. 1 Town (pop. 188), Humboldt co., NW Calif., on the coast, 17 mi. N of Eureka; redwood mill. Near by is Trinidad Head, a promontory 400 ft. high, with lighthouse. **2** City (pop. 12,204), ⊙ Las Animas co., S Colo., on Purgatoire R., just E of Sangre de Cristo Mts., and 75 mi. S of Pueblo, near N.Mex. line; alt. 5,999 ft. Rail, shipping, and industrial center for coal-mining, dairying, and livestock region; sugar beets, beans, grain; mfg. (candy, bricks, tiles, household and mechanical appliances, beverages). Settled 1859 on Santa Fe Trail near Raton Pass, inc. 1876. City grew with development of coal mines which supply smelters in Pueblo. Kit Carson Mus. and statue here. Annual rodeo. Part of San Isabel Natl. Forest near by. **3** Village (pop. c.750), Henderson co., E Texas, on the Trinity and 22 mi. ENE of Corsicana; lignite mines; large power plant.

Trinidad, city (pop. 15,700), ⊙ Flores dept., SW central Uruguay, in the Cuchilla Porongos (a N outlier of the Cuchilla Grande Inferior), on rail branch from Durazno, and 100 mi. NNW of Montevideo (connected by highway). Dairies; agr. products (wheat, corn, linseed, oats, fruit); viticulture; cattle and sheep raising. Has municipal bldg., parochial church, public schools. Airport. Also called Porongos.

Trinidad, La, Argentina: see VILLA LA TRINIDAD.

Trinidad, Sierra de (syĕ'rä dā), mountain range, Las Villas prov., central Cuba, just N of Trinidad; rises in the Pico Potrerillo to 3,205 ft. On its slopes fruit and sugar cane are grown. Has sand quarries. The Sierra de San Juan adjoins W.

Trinidad and Tobago (tōbā'gō, tō–), crown colony (□ 1,980.06; pop. 557,970), B.W.I., in the Atlantic just off Venezuela; ⊙ Port of Spain. Comprises the 2 southernmost isls. of the Lesser Antilles: TRINIDAD and TOBAGO, and a number of small islets near Venezuela coast (Orinoco delta). Tobago was amalgamated with Trinidad in 1888, becoming a ward of the latter in 1898.

Trinidad Gulf, inlet of the Pacific, S Chile, bet. Mornington Isl. (N) and Madre de Dios Isl. (S).

Trinidad Head, Calif.: see TRINIDAD.

Trinidad Island (□ 64), in Bahía Blanca (bay), SW Buenos Aires prov., Argentina, 25 mi. SE of Bahía Blanca city; 15 mi. long, 5 mi. wide.

Trinidad Peninsula, Antarctica: see LOUIS PHILIPPE PENINSULA.

Trinil (trē'nĭl), village, S central Java, Indonesia, on Solo R. and 40 mi. ENE of Solo (Surakarta), at NE foot of Mt. Lawu. Skull cap, femur, and some teeth of Java man (*Pithecanthropus erectus*) were found here (1891–92) by E. Dubois; additional parts were found after 1936. At Ngandong, 6 mi. downstream, skulls of a more advanced fossil type (Solo man or *Homo soloensis*) were found beginning in 1931.

Trinitapoli (trēnētä'pôlē), town (pop. 11,805), Foggia prov., Apulia, S Italy, 29 mi. ESE of Foggia; wine, olive oil; soap mfg. Saltworks of Margherita di Savoia just E.

Trinitaria, La, Mexico: see LA TRINITARIA.

Trinité (trēnētā'), town (pop. 1,900), E Martinique, minor port 11 mi. NE of Fort-de-France; trades in agr. produce (sugar cane, pineapples); sugar milling, rum distilling. Sometimes La Trinité.

Trinité, La, Jersey, Channel Isls.: see TRINITY.

Trinité-Porhoët, La (lä trēnētā'-pôrôĕt'), village (pop. 646), Morbihan dept., W France, 13 mi. NW of Ploërmel; woodworking.

Trinity, village (pop. 369), SE N.F., on NW side of Trinity Bay, on railroad and 40 mi. NNW of Carbonear; fishing port.

Trinity, Fr. *La Trinité* (lä trēnētā'), agr. village and parish (1945 pop. 1,467), Jersey, Channel Isls., 4 mi. N of St. Helier.

Trinity. 1 County (□ 3,191; pop. 5,087), N Calif.; ⊙ Weaverville. Mtn. area, mostly within Klamath Mts., with Coast Ranges in SW; rises to 9,038 ft. at Mt. Eddy, 8,936 ft. at Thompson Peak. In N is Salmon-Trinity Alps primitive area; in S is a reserve of wilderness lands. Drained by Trinity, Eel, and Mad rivers. Much of co. is within Trinity, Shasta, and Mendocino natl. forests. Gold mining (since gold rush days); also sand and gravel, silver, manganese. Great timber stands (mostly fir; also pine, cedar). Stock raising (cattle, sheep), dairying, some farming (chiefly hay). Mtn. scenery, camping, hiking attract vacationers. Formed 1850. **2** County (□ 704; pop. 10,040), E Texas; ⊙ Groveton. Bounded SW by Trinity R., NE by Neches R. Includes part of Davy Crockett Natl. Forest. Wooded area (lumbering is chief industry); also livestock (cattle, hogs, poultry, sheep), some agr. (cotton, corn, peanuts, sugar cane, forage crops). Clay, fuller's earth mining. Formed 1850.

Trinity. 1 Town (pop. 342), Morgan co., N Ala., near Wheeler Reservoir (in Tennessee R.), 5 mi. W of Decatur. **2** Town (pop. 764), Randolph co., central N.C., 4 mi. S of High Point. **3** City (pop. 2,054), Trinity co., E Texas, near the Trinity, 18 mi. NE of Huntsville; rail, trade, processing center in petroleum, pine, cotton, truck area; lumber milling. Settled c.1873, inc. 1903.

Trinity Alps, Calif.: see KLAMATH MOUNTAINS.

Trinity Bay, bight of Coral Sea, NE Queensland, Australia, bet. Cape Tribulation (N) and Cape Grafton (SE); sheltered by Great Barrier Reef; connected with open sea by Trinity Opening; 65 mi. wide. Port of Cairns on S shore, Port Douglas on NW shore.

Trinity Bay, inlet (80 mi. long, 20 mi. wide at entrance) of the Atlantic, SE N.F., bet. NW coast of Avalon Peninsula and the mainland, 40 mi. WNW of St. John's. On shore of bay are several fishing settlements and fish canneries.

Trinity Bay, Texas: see GALVESTON BAY.

Trinity Cape, SE central Que., on the Saguenay, 30 mi. above its mouth and 36 mi. ESE of Chicoutimi; 1,500 ft. high. Just ESE is Eternity Cape.

Trinity Island (15 naut. mi. long, 13 naut. mi. wide), Antarctica, off NW coast of Palmer Peninsula, in the South Pacific; 63°45'S 60°40'W. Discovered 1902 by Otto Nordenskjöld, Swedish explorer.

Trinity Islands, group of 2 small isls. (Sitkinak Isl., Tugidak Isl.), S Alaska, in Gulf of Alaska, S of Kodiak Isl.; 56°32'N 154°25'W; uninhabited except for occasional trappers and prospectors.

Trinity Mountains, Calif.: see KLAMATH MOUNTAINS.

Trinity Opening, deep channel of Coral Sea, breaking through Great Barrier Reef off NE coast of Queensland, Australia, and leading into Trinity Bay (site of Cairns); c.30 mi. long, 6–11 mi. wide.

Trinity Peninsula, Antarctica: see PALMER PENINSULA; LOUIS PHILIPPE PENINSULA.

Trinity Pond, lake (6 mi. long, 1 mi. wide), E N.F., 20 mi. SW of Bonavista. Drains into Trinity Bay.

Trinity Range (5,000–7,500 ft.), NW Nev., largely in Pershing co., W of Lovelock and Humboldt R.

Trinity River. 1 In NW Calif., rises in NE Trinity co., flows 130 mi. in a semicircle SW and NW, through Klamath Mts., to Klamath R. 36 mi. NE of Eureka. Principal tributary is 50-mi.-long South Fork, which rises in SE Trinity co., flows NW. Since gold rush days, when the Trinity and its tributaries were scenes of great activity, much gold has been removed by placer and hydraulic mining. **2** In Texas, rises in 3 main forks in N Texas: West Fork receives Clear Fork at Fort Worth, then joins Elm Fork at Dallas to form the Trinity, flowing thence c.510 mi. generally SSE to Trinity Bay, NE arm of Galveston Bay. Navigable for shallow-draft vessels to Liberty, c.40 mi. above mouth. East Fork (c.110 mi. long) rises in Grayson co., flows generally S to main stream c.30 mi. SSE of Dallas. West Fork (c.150 mi. long) rises in intermittent streams S of Wichita Falls, flows SE to Fort Worth, thence E to Dallas; in it are BRIDGEPORT, EAGLE MOUNTAIN, and WORTH lakes. Clear Fork rises in Parker co., flows SE, then NE, to West Fork; c.60 mi. long. Elm Fork rises in E Montague co., flows E to Gainesville, then S to West Fork; c.100 mi. long. River system has projects for flood control, irrigation, and water supply to cities (including Dallas, Fort Worth). Lavon Reservoir (capacity 423,400 acre-ft.) is in East Fork, Benbrook Reservoir (capacity 258,630 acre-ft.) is in Clear Fork, L. Dallas (impounded 1926 by Garza Dam) and site of Garza-Little Elm Reservoir (projected capacity 1,016,200 acre-ft.) are in Elm Fork. Grapevine Reservoir (capacity c.534,000 acre-ft.) is c.20 mi. NW of Dallas on Denton Creek, a tributary of Elm Fork.

Trinity Ville or **Trinityville,** town (pop. 1,420), St. Thomas parish, SE Jamaica, at S foot of Blue Mts., 18 mi. E of Kingston, in fruitgrowing region (coconuts, bananas, sugar cane, coffee).

Trinkitat (trĭng'kĭtät), village, Kassala prov., NE Anglo-Egyptian Sudan, on bay (protected by coral reefs) of Red Sea, 70 mi. SSE of Port Sudan; minor cotton-shipping center. Sambuk-trade with ports on Arabian shore of Red Sea. Connected with Tokar (18 mi. S) by a light railroad.

Trino (trē'nô), town (pop. 8,638), Vercelli prov., Piedmont, N Italy, near Po R., 11 mi. SSW of Vercelli, in irrigated region (rice, wheat); mfg. (rice-mill machinery, cement).

Trintange (trĭntäzh'), village (pop. 131), SE Luxembourg, 4 mi. WNW of Remich; cherry-growing center.

Triolet (trēôlā'), village (pop. 5,200), N Mauritius, on road, 4 mi. NNW of Pamplemousses; sugar cane.

Trion (trī'ŏn), town (pop. 3,028), Chattooga co., NW Ga., 22 mi. NNW of Rome and on Chattooga R.; textile mfg. center. Settled 1847, inc. 1863.

Trionto, Cape (trēôn'tô), on W shore of Gulf of Taranto, S Italy, 7 mi. ENE of Rossano; 38°37'N 16°46'E. At mouth of **Trionto River,** which rises in La Sila mts. 5 mi. ESE of Acri, flows 25 mi. E and N to the Gulf.

Triora (trēô'rä), village (pop. 623), Imperia prov., Liguria, NW Italy, on Taggio R. and 12 mi. N of San Remo; wine. Slate quarries near by.

Triphylia (trĭfĭ'lēŭ, trĕfēlē'ŭ), region of W Peloponnesus, Greece, S of Alpheus R.

Triplett, town (pop. 301), Chariton co., N central Mo., near Grand R., 6 mi. NNW of Brunswick, in agr. area.

Triplicane, India: see MADRAS, city.

Triplicane River, India: see COOUM RIVER.

Tripoli (trĭ'pūlē), anc. *Tripolis*, Arabic *Tarabulus el Sham, Tarabulus esh Sham*, or *Tarabulus al-Sham* (all: tärä'bŏŏlŏŏs ĕsh-shăm'), city (1946 pop. 59,001, with suburbs 86,371), ⊙ North Lebanon prov., Lebanon, seaport on the Mediterranean, 40 mi. NNE of Beirut; 34°26'N 35°51'E. Shipping, trading, and processing center, with rail lines to Beirut and Homs (Syria), and terminus of the oil pipe line from Kirkuk (Iraq). Has oil refinery, cotton gins, soapworks. Exports oil, silk, soap, citrus fruit, wool. Sponge fishing. The anc. city was probably founded after 700 B.C.; became capital of the Phoenician federation of Tyre, Sidon, and Aradus. Flourished under the Seleucids and Romans. Captured A.D. 638 by the Arabs. Taken 1109 by Crusaders after a long siege, in which the great library was destroyed. Sacked 1289 by sultan of Egypt and later rebuilt. Of the anc. city only some massive walls, towers, and a castle remain.

Tripoli, anc. *Oea,* Arabic *Tarabulus el Gharb* or *Tarabulus al-Gharb* (both: tärä'bōōlōōs ĕl gärb'), largest city (1950 pop. 144,616) and ⊙ LIBYA (after Jan. 1, 1952, Benghazi, too, became a ⊙) and Tripolitania, port on the central Mediterranean, 215 mi. SSW of Malta, 400 mi. W of Benghazi; 32°52'N 13°12'E. Administrative and commercial center of Libya, situated on a rocky promontory with a semi-artificial harbor (E), amidst a coastal oasis (□ c.20; 3½ mi. wide). Linked by trunk coastal highway with all major centers of Tripolitania and Cyrenaica, and by shorter roads with settlements in the Gefara and Gebel Nefusa regions just S. Railroad to Zuara (W) and Garian (S). Exports esparto grass, hides, dates, salt, sponges, henna, carpets. Mfg. of tobacco products, soap, building materials; alcohol distilling, flour milling, olive-oil pressing, tanning; sponge and tunny fishing; artisan metalworking, carpet weaving. Has old quarter (at promontory's base), partly enclosed by old walls, and modern European section (S and SE) with hotels, theaters, modern thoroughfares and stores. The massive old castle (probably 1st built in Roman times) is the chief landmark. There are several mosques. An arch of Marcus Aurelius is the most noteworthy Roman ruin. An early Tyrian colony (7th cent.? B.C.), it was later dominated by Rome, Vandals (5th cent. A.D.), Byzantines (6th cent.), and Arabs (7th–16th cent.). Under Turkish rule (1551–1911) was stronghold of pirates who terrorized the Mediterranean, especially in 16th–17th cent., and were fought (1801–05) by the U.S. marines. Occupied by Italians in 1911 and became capital of Libya. An important Axis base in Second World War, it was bombed (1940–42) and taken by British in 1943. Airport at Mellaha (5 mi. E) was leased 1948 to U.S. as an air base (Wheelus Field).

Tripoli (trĭpō'lē, trĭ'pūlē), town (pop. 1,124), Bremer co., NE Iowa, near Wapsipinicon R., 21 mi. N of Waterloo; food cannery. Sand and gravel pits near by. Settled 1850, inc. 1894.

Tripolis (trē'pôlĭs), city (pop. 14,961), ⊙ Arcadia nome, central Peloponnesus, Greece, on E slopes of Maenalon mts., 60 mi. SE of Patras; commercial and transportation (road-rail) center; textile milling, tanning, woodworking, cheese processing. Trades in wheat, potatoes, tobacco. Summer resort. Founded c.1467 in area of anc. cities of Mantinea and Tegea, it was seat of Turkish pashas of Morea. Destroyed 1825 during Gr. war of independence. Formerly called Tripolitza.

Tripolis, Lebanon: see TRIPOLI.

Tripolis, LIBYA: see TRIPOLITANIA.

Tripolis, Turkey: see TIREBOLU.

Tripolitania (trĭ"pŭlĭtā'nēŭ), anc. *Tripolis,* W division (□ c.100,000; 1947 pop. estimate 806,000) of LIBYA, on the central Mediterranean; ⊙ TRIPOLI. Bounded by CYRENAICA (E), FEZZAN (S), and Tunisia (W). Almost entirely within the Sahara, which here virtually touches the Mediterranean coast, Tripolitania has little cultivable land. A coastal strip extending from Tunisian border to Gulf of Sidra contains a string of oases where most of the sedentary pop. is concentrated. Tripoli is the only deep-water port along the straight coastline. S of the coastal belt is the arid, sandy Gefara plain which, in S, rises to the Gebel Nefusa plateau. Further S, the Hammada el Hamra rock expanse is already part of the Sahara proper. The Gebel es-Soda range rises to c.2,700 ft. in SE. Drainage is limited to intermittent wadis. Yearly rainfall is less than 4 in. through most of territory; the Tripoli-Misurata coastal oases and the Gebel Nefusa plateau around Garian receive 10–15 in. of rain. Barley, wheat, olives, dates, almonds, vegetables are grown in the oases. Irrigated agr. settlements established in late 1930s by Italians produce some market and forage crops. Nomadic stock raising (goats, sheep, camels) is principal occupation of Berber and Arab pop. Minor mineral resources include salt (Pisida, Tripoli) and alabaster (Azizia). Tunny and sponge fisheries. Industry (olive-oil pressing, flour milling, esparto-grass processing, distilling) is concentrated in Tripoli. Handicraft industries include carpet weaving, metal- and leatherworking, pottery mfg. Coastal highway links chief towns (Tripoli, Homs, Misurata) and leads into Cyrenaica. Other roads and desert tracks link coast with Giofra oases, the Fezzan, and the Gebel Nefusa region. Short rail lines (95 mi.) serve Tripoli, Zuara, Azizia, and Garian. Pop. is over 90% Moslem; in 1947, there remained 44,419 Italians and 28,606 Jews. Coastal area was colonized after 7th cent. B.C. by Phoenicians who founded the 3 cities of Oea (Tripoli), Sabratha, and Leptis Magna. It subsequently passed to Carthage, Rome (145 B.C.–A.D. 450; 1st called Regio Cyrtica; later, as a Roman prov., Tripolitania), the Vandals (5th cent.), and the Byzantine Empire. Conquered by Moslems in 7th cent., it was successively ruled by Arab and Berber dynasties. While nominally under Turkish domination from mid-16th cent. until 1912, it became a virtually autonomous pashalik in early 18th cent. As one of the Barbary States, it engaged in piracy and fought the U.S. (1801–5). Ceded to Italy in 1911–12, it became W division of Ital. colony of Libya. Penetration and pacification of the interior was not completed until 1920s. Captured by British in 1943, and under Br. military administration since Second World War. Wheelus air base (near Tripoli) leased to U.S. in 1948. Under the U.N. decision of 1949, Tripolitania is one of the constituent units (Cyrenaica and Fezzan are the others) of an independent federal kingdom of Libya established by 1952.

Tripolitza, Greece: see TRIPOLIS.

Tripp, county (□ 1,620; pop. 9,139), S S.Dak., on Nebr. line; ⊙ Winner. Agr. area bounded N by White R. and watered by several creeks and artificial lakes. Dairy products, livestock, poultry, grain. Formed 1893.

Tripp, city (pop. 913), Hutchinson co., SE S.Dak., 33 mi. S of Mitchell; dairy products, grain, livestock, poultry. Co. fair takes place here annually.

Tripp Lake, SW Maine, resort lake (c.2.5 mi. long) in Androscoggin co., near Poland.

Triptis (trĭp'tĭs), town (pop. 4,147), Thuringia, central Germany, on Orla R. and 14 mi. SW of Gera; china mfg.

Tripunittura or **Trippunittura** (trĭpōōnĭ'tōōrŭ), town (pop. 12,606), SW Cochin, India, residential suburb (5 mi. SE) of Ernakulam. It is site of Sanskrit Col.

Tripura (trĭp'ōōrŭ), centrally ruled state (□ 4,049; 1951 pop. 649,930), NE India; ⊙ Agartala. Bounded N, W, and S by E Pakistan, E by Assam; mainly hill region (sal and bamboo tracts) of 4 parallel ranges S of Surma Valley; drained by tributaries of Barak (upper Surma) and Meghna rivers. Crops: rice, cotton, tea, mustard, jute, tobacco, sugar cane. Main trade center, Agartala. Early-16th-cent. Hindu temple (pilgrimage center) at Radhakishorepur. Formerly a princely state in Bengal States of Eastern States agency; inc. 1949 into India and placed under administration of chief commissioner appointed by govt. of India. Pop. 70% Hindu, 23% Moslem, 6% tribal (including Chakmas). Sometimes called Hill Tippera.

Trisanna River (trēzä'nä), Tyrol, W Austria, rises on the Dreiländerspitze, flows c.20 mi. NE, through the Paznauntal, joining Rosanna R., with which it flows (as Sanna R.) 4 mi. E to Inn R. at Landeck.

Trischen (trĭ'shŭn), uninhabited North Sea island (□ 3) of North Frisian group, NW Germany, 6 mi. off Schleswig-Holstein coast. Inhabited c.1500. Following re-formation (1850) of isl., permanent settlement was unsuccessfully attempted in early-20th cent.

Trisching (trĭ'shĭng), village (pop. 510), Upper Palatinate, E Bavaria, Germany, 9 mi. E of Amberg; lignite mining.

Tristan da Cunha (trĭ'stăn dŭ kōōn'yŭ), principal island (□ 40; 1945 pop. 230) of Tristan da Cunha group, a dependency (since 1938) of St. Helena colony, in the S Atlantic, roughly halfway bet. South Africa and South America, c.1,800 mi. W of Cape Town and 1,600 mi. SSW of St. Helena; 37°6'S 12°15'W. Main settlement, Edinburgh. Mountainous isl. (7 mi. long, 6 mi. wide) rises in an extinct volcano to 7,640 ft. At the summit is a crater lake. Only a small section in NW is cultivated, yielding mostly potatoes. Some fruit (apples, peaches) are grown and livestock (sheep, cattle, poultry) are raised. Fishing is plentiful. Native juniper trees supply wood. Isl. was 1st sighted by the Portuguese in 1506. Occupied by a Br. military force after arrival (1815) of exiled Napoleon in St. Helena. Garrison was withdrawn in 1817, though a few stayed behind, later joined by shipwrecked sailors. During Second World War the isl. became (1942) a Br. meteorological and radio station. A South African company obtained (1948) rights to establish fishing and canning industry. The Tristan da Cunha Isls. include other tiny uninhabited islets: GOUGH ISLAND, INACCESSIBLE ISLAND, NIGHTINGALE ISLANDS, and a few rocks.

Triste Gulf (trē'stā), inlet of the Caribbean in N Venezuela; Tucacas, Puerto Cabello are its ports.

Trisul ((trĭsōōl'), peak (23,360 ft.) in SE Kumaun Himalayas, in Garhwal dist., NW Uttar Pradesh, India, 11 mi. SW of Nanda Devi mtn.

Trisuli River (trĭsōō'lē), in S Tibet and central Nepal, rises in N Nepal Himalayas NW of Jongka, Tibet; flows S past Jongka and Kyerong, into Nepal, and W joining Kali Gandaki R. 55 mi. W of Katmandu to form GANDAK RIVER; total length, c.150 mi. Formerly called Trisulganga.

Trith-Saint-Léger (trēt-sē-lā-zhā'), town (pop. 3,229), Nord dept., N France, on left bank of Escaut R. and 3 mi. SSW of Valenciennes; forges and rolling mills.

Tritle, Mount (trĭ'tŭl) (7,793 ft.), Yavapai co., central Ariz., N of Bradshaw Mts., 8 mi. S of Prescott.

Triton (trē'tôn), town, Chaudoc prov., S Vietnam, in marshy region, 20 mi. SSW of Chaudoc; pottery works. Cambodian pagodas.

Triton Island (trī'tŭn) (□ 7.5; pop. 350), E N.F., in Notre Dame Bay, 40 mi. WSW of Twillingate; 7 mi. long, 2 mi. wide, 49°31'N 55°40'W; fishing.

Triton Island, Chinese *Chungkien* or *Chung-chien* (both: jōōng'jyĕn'), southwesternmost of the Paracel Isl., China, in S.China Sea, c.100 mi. SW of Woody Isl.; 15°47'N 111°14'E. Fisheries.

Trittau (trĭ'tou), village (pop. 4,760), in Schleswig-Holstein, NW Germany, 16 mi. ENE of Hamburg; mfg. of textiles, woodworking. Summer resort.

Triumph. 1 Village (1940 pop. 509), Plaquemines parish, extreme SE La., on W bank (levee) of the Mississippi and 55 mi. SE of New Orleans, in the delta; citrus-fruit growing; orange wine. Near by are old Fort Jackson (1815) and Fort St. Philip (1795), which figured in Confederate defense of New Orleans (1862). **2** Village (pop. 561), Martin co., S Minn., 15 mi. WNW of Fairmont, in grain, livestock, and poultry area; dairy products. Small lakes near by.

Triumpho. 1 City, Alagoas, Brazil: see IGREJA NOVA. **2** City, Pernambuco, Brazil: see TRIUNFO. **3** City, Rio Grande do Sul, Brazil: see BOM JESUS DO TRIUNFO.

Triunfo (trēōōm'fōō). **1** City (pop. 2,327), central Pernambuco, NE Brazil, in hill range on Paraíba border, 60 mi. WNW of Sertânia; alt. 3,200 ft. Cotton and coffee market. Formerly spelled Triumpho. **2** City, Rio Grande do Sul, Brazil: see BOM JESUS DO TRIUNFO.

Triunfo, Mexico: see EL TRIUNFO.

Triunfo, El, Honduras: see EL TRIUNFO.

Triunfo, El, Salvador: see PUERTO EL TRIUNFO.

Trivadi, India: see TIRUVADI.

Trivandrum (trĭvŭn'drōōm), locally *Tiru-Ananta-puram* (tĭ'rōō-ŭnŭn'tŭpōōrŭm), city (pop. 128,365), ⊙ Travancore-Cochin and Travancore administrative division, India, on Malabar Coast of Arabian Sea, 50 mi. NW of Cape Comorin, 780 mi. SSE of Bombay; 8°29'N 76°58'E. Road center; rail terminus; airport. Malayalam cultural center. Mfg. of cotton and silk textiles, rubber and ebonite goods, plywood, coir rope and mats, copra, pharmaceuticals, soap; palmyra-sugar milling, processing of monazite and ilmenite. Univ. of Travancore, technical (textile chemistry), arts, and Sanskrit cols. Mus., observatory. Old fort contains early-18th-cent. temple to Vishnu, which attracts many pilgrims. City is residence of maharaja (*rajpramukh*) of Travancore-Cochin. Noted handicraft ivory and wood carving.

Trivellore, India: see TIRUVALLUR.

Trivento (trēvĕn'tô), town (pop. 2,611), Campobasso prov., Abruzzi e Molise, S central Italy, near Trigno R., 16 mi. NNW of Campobasso; woolen mills. Bishopric. Near by are ruins of anc. Terventum.

Trivières (trēvyâr'), town (pop. 3,859), Hainaut prov., S Belgium, 9 mi. E of Mons; coal mining.

Trivigno (trēvē'nyô), village (pop. 1,657), Potenza prov., Basilicata, S Italy, 11 mi. ESE of Potenza; wine, dairy and meat products.

Trjevna, Bulgaria: see TRYAVNA.

Trmice (tûr'mĭtsĕ), Ger. *Türmitz* (tûr'mĭts), town (pop. 5,070), NW Bohemia, Czechoslovakia, 7 mi. E of Teplice, in urban area of Usti nad Labem; rail junction.

Trn, Bulgaria: see TRIN.

Trnava (tŭr'nävä), Ger. *Tyrnau* (tĭr'nou), Hung. *Nagyszombat* (nŏ'dyŭsôm'bŏt), city (pop. 24,226), W Slovakia, Czechoslovakia, 27 mi. NE of Bratislava, in fertile agr. region. Rail junction (repair shops); ironworks; noted for local development of agr. industries (making of high-quality malt, food processing, sugar refining, fertilizer mfg.). R.C. bishopric; former seat of Jesuit univ. Has 16th-cent. tower, medieval cathedral, 18th-cent. town hall. Founded in 6th–7th cent., it has been regarded since Middle Ages as cultural center of Slovak Catholicism; in Hussite hands in 1439. Transferred from Hungary (1920) by treaty of Trianon. Yearly pilgrims' meetings held here.

Trnovany (tŭr'nôvänĭ), Ger. *Turn* (tōōrn), town (pop. 11,555), NW Bohemia, Czechoslovakia, 8 mi. W of Usti nad Labem, in urban area of Teplice; metallurgical industry; textile and hosiery mfg., food processing.

Trnovo, Bulgaria: see TIRNOVO.

Troad, Asia Minor: see TROAS; TROY.

Troarn (trôärn'), village (pop. 587), Calvados dept., NW France, on marshy Dives R. and 8 mi. E of Caen; cider distilling, horse raising.

Troas (trō'ăs). **1** or **the Troad** (trō'ăd), the region about anc. TROY on NW coast of Asia Minor (present-day Turkey), watered by the Scamander and the Simoïs and crossed by Mt. Ida. Scene of the events of the *Iliad* and an anc. center of Aegean civilization. Archaeologists have uncovered here a wealth of antiquities. **2** or **Alexandria Troas,** anc. Greek city of Mysia, on NW coast of Asia Minor (present-day Turkey), opposite isl. of Tenedos and c.15 mi. S of site of anc. Troy; an important city under the Greeks and Romans, who thought it was on the site of Troy. The Bible mentions it. Few remains.

Trobajo del Camino (trōvä'hō dhĕl kämē'nō), village (pop. 2,150), Leon prov., NW Spain, just WNW of Leon; brewery, flour mills; ceramics, dairy products; meat processing.

Trobriand Islands (trō'brēŭnd, -ănd"), small volcanic group, Territory of Papua, SW Pacific, 95 mi. SE of New Guinea; 8°38'S 151°4'E; comprise KIRIWINA (main isl.) and many small isls. Isls. produce yams, pearl shell, pearls, sea cucumbers. Anc. stone formations found 1936. In Second World War, made Allied base (1943).

Trochu (trō'shōō), village (pop. 515), S central Alta., 55 mi. NE of Calgary; coal mining; grain elevators.

Trodday, island, Inner Hebrides, Inverness, Scotland, just off N end of Skye; 57°41'N 6°18'W.

Troense (trōn'sù), town (pop. 644) and port, Svendborg amt, Denmark, on NE Taasinge isl. and 2 mi. SE of Svendborg.

Troezen (trē'zĕn), anc. city in Peloponnesus, Greece, on Argolis Peninsula, 30 mi. ESE of Nauplia. Founded by Ionians, it is the home of Theseus. Ruins include temples, market place. Modern village of Troizen or Troizin (pop. 656), of Attica nome, was formerly called Damala.

Trofaiach (trōfī'äkh), town (pop. 5,693), Styria, SE central Austria, 5 mi. NW of Leoben; summer resort, baths.

Trofarello (trôfärĕl'lô), village (pop. 2,832), Torino prov., Piedmont, NW Italy, 6 mi. S of Turin; rail junction.

Trofimovsk (trŭfē'mŭfsk), town (1943 pop. over 500), N Yakut Autonomous SSR, Russian SFSR, on Trofim branch of Lena R. delta mouth, 140 mi. N of Bulun; fish canning.

Trogen (trō'gŭn), town (pop. 1,669), NE Switzerland, 4 mi. ESE of St. Gall; alternate ⊙ Appenzell Ausser Rhoden half-canton.

Trogir (trô'gēr), Ital. *Traù* (träōō'), village, S Croatia, Yugoslavia, on Adriatic Sea, 9 mi. W of Split, in Dalmatia, on both Ciovo Isl., Serbo-Croatian *Čiovo*, Ital. *Bua*, and the mainland, separated by narrow channel (bridged). Seaside resort. Marble in vicinity. R.C. bishopric since 10th cent. Has 13th-cent. cathedral, 15th-cent. town hall and castles, Renaissance loggia, palaces. Anc. Gr. colony; later ruled by Romans, Serbs, Hungarians, Venetians, and Austrians.

Troglav, peak, Yugoslavia: see DINARA.

Tröglitz (trûk'lĭts), town (pop. 4,248), in former Prussian Saxony prov., central Germany, after 1945 in Saxony-Anhalt, 2 mi. NE of Zeitz; lignite mining; synthetic-oil plant. Heavily bombed in Second World War.

Troia (trô'yä), town (pop. 7,037), Foggia prov., Apulia, S Italy, 14 mi. SW of Foggia; mfg. of agr. machinery. Bishopric. Has cathedral (founded 1093).

Troina (trôē'nä), town (pop. 12,024), Enna prov., NE central Sicily, 23 mi. NE of Enna, in stock-raising region. Has mus. Badly damaged (1943) in Second World War.

Trois-Bassins, Les (lā trwä'-bäsē'), town and commune (pop. 3,609), near W coast of Réunion isl., on road and 19 mi. NW of Saint-Pierre; sugar cane, coffee, grain.

Troisdorf (trois'dôrf), town (pop. 11,679), in former Prussian Rhine Prov., W Germany, after 1945 in North Rhine-Westphalia, 2 mi. NW of Siegburg; rail junction; mfg. of plastics and celluloid. Site, during Second World War, of large propellant-explosives plant.

Trois-Épis, Les, France: see TURCKHEIM.

Trois-Évêchés, Pic des, France: see BLANCHE, MONTAGNE DE LA.

Trois-Fontaines (trwä-fōtĕn'), Ger. *Dreibrunnen* (drī'brōō"nŭn), village (pop. 957), Moselle dept., NE France, on NW slopes of the Vosges, 6 mi. SE of Sarrebourg; makes optical glass, watch crystals.

Trois Frères, in Indian Ocean: see THREE BROTHERS.

Trois-Ilets (trwäzēlā'), town (pop. 939), SW Martinique, on Fort-de-France Bay, opposite Fort-de-France (5 mi. SSE); coffee and sugar growing; limekiln; sugar milling, rum distilling. Empress Josephine b. here (June 23, 1763).

Trois-Marabouts (trwä'-märäbōō'), village (pop. 704), Oran dept., NW Algeria, 3 mi. WNW of Aïn-Témouchent; wine, olives.

Trois-Moûtiers, Les (lā trwä-mōōtyā'), village (pop. 396), Vienne dept., W central France, 5 mi. NW of Loudun; dairying. Megalithic monuments near by.

Trois Pistoles (trwä pēstōl'), town (pop. 2,176), SE Que., on the St. Lawrence and 27 mi. NE of Rivière du Loup; lumbering, pulp milling; in dairying region.

Trois-Ponts (trwä-pō'), village, Liége prov., E Belgium, in N Ardennes, 8 mi. WSW of Malmédy, near Amblève R.; rail junction. Commune center of Fosse-lez-Stavelot (pop. 1,134) is 2 mi. SW.

Trois Rivières (trwä rēvyâr') or **Three Rivers**, city (pop. 42,007), S Que., on the St. Lawrence, at mouth of St. Maurice R., and 80 mi. NE of Montreal; pulp, paper, cotton-milling center, with grain elevators, foundries, lumbering, woodworking, dairying, mfg. of clothing, shoes. Iron oxides and ochres are mined in region. Has R.C. cathedral and prov. technical col.; site of mineral springs. Hydroelectric power is supplied from Shawinigan Falls. Founded 1634 by Champlain, it was major port in French times.

Trois-Rivières, town (commune pop. 9,922), S Basse-Terre isl., Guadeloupe, minor port 4 mi. ESE of Basse-Terre city; coffee, cacao, vanilla.

Trois Rivières, Les (lā), river, N Haiti, rises in the Massif du Nord SE of Plaisance, flows c.65 mi. NW to the Atlantic at Port-de-Paix. Nonnavigable.

Troisvierges (trwävyârzh'), Ger. *Ulflingen* (ōōlf'lĭng-ŭn), town (pop. 1,192), N Luxembourg, in the Ardennes, 11 mi. NNE of Wiltz; frontier station near Belg. border; market center for agr. area (rye, oats, wheat, potatoes, cattle).

Troitsk (trô'yĭtsk), city (1939 pop. 46,700), E Chelyabinsk oblast, Russian SFSR, in W Siberia, on Ui R., on railroad (just N of Zolotaya Sopka junction) and 70 mi. SSE of Chelyabinsk. Agr. center for adjacent steppeland; processing of hides, meat, animal and vegetable fats; mfg. of shoes, felt boots, saddles, soap; metalworking, flour milling; grain storage. Has veterinary col., regional mus., and old churches. Founded 1743 as stronghold; chartered 1784.

Troitski or **Troitskiy** (trô'yĭtskē). **1** Town (1926 pop. 1,034), S central Moscow oblast, Russian SFSR, 10 mi. WNW of Podolsk; woolen milling. **2** Town (1940 pop. estimate 6,000), SE Sverdlovsk oblast, Russian SFSR, on Trans-Siberian RR (Peklevskaya station) and 3 mi. N of Talitsa; woolen and felt mfg. center; flour milling, sawmilling; grain storage. Until 1928, Peklevskaya.

Troitsko-Khartsyzsk (-skŭ-khŭrtsĭsk'), town (1939 pop. over 500), E Stalino oblast, Ukrainian SSR, in the Donbas, on railroad (Skosyrskaya station) and 7 mi. SE of Khartsyszk; coal mines.

Troitsko-Pechorsk (-pyĭchôrsk'), village (1926 pop. 558), SE Komi Autonomous SSR, Russian SFSR, on Pechora R. (landing) and 185 mi. ENE of Syktyvkar (linked by road); agr., fur trapping. Petroleum deposits. Formerly called Troitsko-Pechorskoye.

Troitskosavsk, Russian SFSR: see KYAKHTA.

Troitsko-Sergiyevskaya Lavra, Russian SFSR: see ZAGORSK.

Troitskoye (trô'yĭtskŭyŭ). **1** Town (1926 pop. 5,260), central Altai Territory, Russian SFSR, on railroad (Bolshaya Rechka station) and 45 mi. SE of Barnaul; metalworks. **2** Village (1939 pop. over 500), W Astrakhan oblast, Russian SFSR, 7 mi. N of Stepnoi; cattle, horses; wheat, mustard. **3** Village (1926 pop. 3,177), N Chkalov oblast, Russian SFSR, 65 mi. NE of Chkalov; wheat, sunflowers, livestock. Formerly called Troitsk. **4** Village (1939 pop. over 500), NW Chkalov oblast, Russian SFSR, on Lesser Kinel R. and 23 mi. SE of Buguruslan; wheat, sunflowers, livestock. **5** Village (1926 pop. 2,171), N Kemerovo oblast, Russian SFSR, 34 mi. E of Anzhero-Sudzhensk, in agr. area. **6** Village (1939 pop. over 500), S Khabarovsk Territory, Russian SFSR, on Amur R. (landing) and 90 mi. NNE of Khabarovsk; fisheries. Fish-processing plants near by. Pop. is largely Nanai (formerly called Golds). **7** Village, Sverdlovsk oblast, Russian SFSR: see BOGDANOVICH. **8** Village (1926 pop. 5,819), central Odessa oblast, Ukrainian SSR, 38 mi. SE of Balta; metalworks, flour mill. **9** Village (1939 pop. over 2,000), NW Voroshilovgrad oblast, Ukrainian SSR, 50 mi. NNW of Starobelsk; sunflower-oil press.

Trojan, Bulgaria: see TROYAN.

Troki, Lithuania: see TRAKAI.

Troldheimen, Norway: see TROLLHEIMEN.

Troldtinder, Norway: see TROLLTINDER.

Trollhattan (trôl'hĕ'tän), Swedish *Trollhättan*, city (1950 pop. 24,264), Alvsborg co., SW Sweden, on Gota R., near L. Vaner, 40 mi. NNE of Goteborg. River here drops 108 ft. in 6 falls; water power is used for one of Sweden's largest hydroelectric plants (state-owned), supplying cities, railroads, and industries in S part of country. Falls bypassed by navigation canal. Industries include locomotive, machinery, and chemical works, steel, cotton, and cellulose mills. Inc. 1916 as city.

Trollheimen (trôl'hāmŭn) [Nor.,=gnomes' home], mountains in Sor-Trondelag co. and More og Romsdal co., central Norway, extending from Sunndals Fjord (W) to Gaula valley (E), and passing into the Dovrefjell (S); rise to 5,540 ft. in the Snota (45 mi. ESE of Kristiansund) and 5,386 ft. in the Trollhetta (8 mi. E of the Snota). Formerly spelled Troldheimen.

Trolltinder (trôl'tĭn-nŭr) [Nor.,=gnomes' peaks], mountains (5,850 ft.) in More og Romsdal co., W Norway, on S side of the Romsdal, 16 mi. SSE of Andalsnes. Peaks include Kongen (the king), Dronningen (the queen), and Bispen (the bishop). Subject of many legends. Sometimes spelled Troldtinder.

Trombay (trŏmbā'), village, W central Bombay, India, 10 mi. NE of Bombay city center, at mouth of Thana Creek; salt pans; ferry here to Elephanta Isl. (S) in Bombay Harbour.

Trombetas River (trōmbā'tŭs), NW Para, Brazil, rises on S slope of the Serra Acaraí near Br. Guiana border, flows 470 mi. generally S to the Amazon above Óbidos. Navigable in middle course only. Chief tributary, Erepecuru R. (left).

Tromello (trômĕl'lô), village (pop. 3,041), Pavia prov., Lombardy, N Italy, on Terdoppio R. and 14 mi. WNW of Pavia, in the Lomellina.

Tromen Volcano (trō'mĕn), subandean peak (13,000–13,500 ft.) in N Neuquén natl. territory, Argentina, 13 mi. SW of Buta Ranquil; 37°9'S. Inactive since 1882.

Trommald (trŭ'môld"), village (pop. 117), Crow Wing co., central Minn., near Mississippi R., 14 mi. NE of Brainerd. Iron mines near by in Cuyuna iron range.

Tromoy (trôm'ûü), Nor. *Tromøy*, island (□ 11; pop. 2,656) in the Skagerrak, Aust-Agder co., S Norway, just SE of Arendal; 7 mi. long, 3 mi. wide. Agr., including fruit cultivation; fishing. Shipyards at Pusnes village. Has 13th-cent. stone church. Formerly spelled Thromö and Tromö.

Trompia, Val (väl trôm'pyä), valley of upper Mella R., Brescia prov., Lombardy, N Italy; extends c.25 mi. N of Brescia. Rich in minerals (iron, lead, barite, fluorite). Cattle raising and sawmilling in N; agr. (wheat, corn) in S.

Trompsburg (trômps'bûrkh), town (pop. 1,706), SW Orange Free State, U. of So. Afr., 70 mi. SSW of Bloemfontein; alt. 4,712 ft.; grain, stock. Formerly Jagersfontein Road.

Troms (trôms), county [Nor. *fylke*] (□ 10,071; pop. 113,722), N Norway; ⊙ Tromso. Extends bet. the Norwegian Sea (W) and Finland and Sweden (E); bounded NE by Finnmark co. and S by Nordland co. Coast line is rugged and indented by numerous mtn.-lined fjords, including Lyngen Fjord. Senja, Kvaloy, and Ringvassoy are its largest isls., and the N isls. of the Vesteralen group lie within co. Industries are chiefly based on the important fisheries. Iron is mined on Bjarkoy and adjacent isls. and in Salangen region. Lapps form part of pop.

Tromsdalen (trôms'dälŭn), village (pop. 749) in Tromsoysund canton, Troms co., N Norway, on Tromso Sound, opposite Tromsoy (ferry), 2 mi. E of Tromso city. Summer camp of Swedish Lapps. Formerly called Storsteinnes.

Tromso (trôms'û), Nor. *Tromsø*, city (pop. 10,990), ⊙ Troms co., N Norway, on E Tromsoy, an isl. on Tromso Sound of Norwegian Sea, just off the mainland, 95 mi. NNE of Narvik; 69°39'N 18°58'E. Seaport; center for Arctic fisheries and sealing; chief port for shipping to Spitsbergen and Jan Mayen. Has fish-freezing, filleting, fish-oil, and cold-storage plants; margarine mfg., brewing. Seaplane base; site of geophysical observatory. Sun does not set here bet. May 1st and July 23d. Mean temp. range from 25°F. (Feb.) to 52°F. (July); average annual rainfall 41.2 inches. Mission settlement founded here in 13th cent.; town grew in late 18th cent. and for some time had important trade with Russia. In Second World War, it was last seat (April–June, 1940) of Norwegian govt. before its evacuation to England. German battleship *Tirpitz* sunk here by R.A.F. in Second World War. Just SSW is suburb of Tromsoysund.

Tromsoy (trôms'ûü), Nor. *Tromsøy*, wooded island (□ 8; pop. 14,452) in Tromso Sound of Norwegian Sea, Troms co., N Norway, just off the mainland. TROMSO city is on E coast. Important fisheries.

Tromsoysund (trôms'ûüsōōn), Nor. *Tromsøysund*, village (pop. 2,683; canton pop. 10,360), Troms co., N Norway, on Tromsoy; SSW suburb of Tromso; fishing, fish canning. Also called Tromsoya (trôms'ûyä), Nor. *Tromsøya*.

Trona (trō'nŭ), village (pop. 2,450), San Bernardino co., S Calif., in Mojave Desert, c.115 mi. N of San Bernardino; processing plant extracts potash from Searles L., a large playa.

Tronador, Monte (mōn'tā trōnädōr'), Andean peak (c.11,200 ft.) on Argentina-Chile border, 30 mi. W of San Carlos de Bariloche (Río Negro); 41°10'S 71°55'W. Has a number of waterfalls and glaciers, and overlooks L. Nahuel Huapí. Its main peak is in Chile. At N foot is Pérez Rosales Pass.

Tronçais, Forêt de (fôrĕ' dŭ trōsā'), forest (□ 40), in Allier dept., central France, E of the Cher and c.12 mi. SE of Saint-Amand-Montrond; provides wood for veneer and furniture making. Supplied charcoal for early 19th-cent. heavy industry at Montluçon.

Tronche, La (lä trōsh'), NE suburb (pop. 4,420) of Grenoble, Isère dept., SE France, on right bank of the Isère; hospitals.

Tronchiennes, Belgium: see DRONGEN.

Trondelag (trŭn'nŭläg), Nor. *Trøndelag*, region in central Norway, bet. North Sea and Swedish border, around Trondheim Fjord; divided into NORD-TRONDELAG and SOR-TRONDELAG counties.

Trondenes (trôn'nŭnās), village (pop. 177; canton pop. 4,045), Troms co., N Norway, on E Hinnoy of Vesteralen group, 2 mi. NNE of Harstad. Has fortified stone church (c.1250).

Trondheim (trôn'hām), city (pop. 57,128), ⊙ Sor-Trondelag co., W Norway, on S shore of Trondheim Fjord, at mouth of short Nid R. (hydroelectric plants), 250 mi. N of Oslo; 63°26'N 10°25'E. Major seaport, ice-free the year round; has extensive trade with Great Britain and the Continent; terminus of railroads from Oslo, Ostersund, and Stockholm, and Nordland co.; seaplane base and airport (E). Fishing center, with shipyards, cold-storage plants, fish canneries; textile mills, plants processing iron alloys, wire, margarine, soap, paint; metalworking. Exports metals (from mines at Roros, Folldal, Lokken), cellulose, paper, fish, cod-liver oil. Noted for its large cathedral, founded 1075 (to house grave of St. Olaf), enlarged after 1153, rebuilt (1872–1906) in blue soapstone; scene of coronation of Norwegian kings. City has medieval bishops' palace, 13th-cent. Church of Our Lady, 17th-cent. Kristiansten (formerly Christiansten) fortress, and large 18th-cent. wooden royal mansion. Seat of Royal Norwegian Society of Sciences (founded 1760), technical col., teachers col., several museums, and art gall. Port is protected by Munkholm islet, Nor. *Munkholmen*, with 17th-cent. fortifications on site of a 12th-cent. Benedictine monastery. In 9th cent., Harold III (Harold Fairhair) established his court at Lade, now ENE suburb. In 997, Olaf I Tryggvason made site of present city his ⊙ and built church; here the Norwegian kings were elected. City of Nidaros was established (1016) here by St. Olaf and rapidly became a place of pilgrimage and Norway's largest and wealthiest city, with extensive trade with N Norway and the Lofoten Isls. Bishopric founded here in 1153. Its importance declined with rise of Hanseatic League. With introduction of the Reformation, shrine of St. Olaf was carried away (1564) to Denmark. At about the same time, city of Nidaros was renamed Trondhjem (trôn'yĕm). Visited by destructive fires at frequent intervals, city was repeatedly rebuilt. Its economic importance grew again with coming of the railroad; line to Oslo completed in 1877, connected with Swedish network in 1881; direct line to Oslo (Dovre RR) completed in 1921. Name was changed (1930) to Nidaros (nē'därōs, –rōōs), but after protests from inhabitants it reassumed (1931) its old name, spelling being changed to Trondheim. Sometimes spelled Drontheim.

Trondheim Channel, Nor. *Trondheimsleden* or *Trondheimsleida*, sound (50 mi. long, 3–5 mi. wide) of North Sea, W Norway, bet. Hitra and Smola isls. (N) and mainland (S).

Trondheim Fjord, Nor. *Trondheimsfjord*, inlet (c.80 mi. long, 2–15 mi. wide) of the North Sea extending deep into N Norway; it is considered the natural boundary bet. N and S Norway. Trondheim city and Levanger are on S shore. Extends several arms: Orkdal Fjord (SW), Strinda Fjord (E), and Asen Fjord, Nor. *Åsenfjord* (NE). Tributary valleys form one of Norway's most fertile agr. regions.

Trondhjem, Norway: see TRONDHEIM.

Trondra (trŏn'drü), island (pop. 91) of the Shetlands, Scotland, off SW coast of Mainland isl., just S of Scalloway, whose harbor it protects; 2½ mi. long, 1 mi. wide.

Trones, Norway: see VERDAL.

Trong (trŏŏng), village (pop. 624), NW Perak, Malaya, 10 mi. S of Taiping; rubber.

Trongsa, Bhutan: see TONGSA, town.

Tronoh (trōnō'), town (pop. 3,024), central Perak, Malaya, on slopes of Kledang Range, 14 mi. SW of Ipoh; a tin-mining center of Kinta Valley.

Tronto River (trôn'tô), central Italy, rises in the Apennines on Monti della Laga, SE of Amatrice; flows N, past Arquata del Tronto, and E, past Acquasanta and Ascoli Piceno, to the Adriatic 4 mi. SSE of San Benedetto del Tronto; 58 mi. long. Used for hydroelectric power.

Tronzano Vercellese (trôntsä'nô vĕrchĕl-lā'zĕ), village (pop. 2,699), Vercelli prov., Piedmont, N Italy, 12 mi. W of Vercelli; casein.

Troodos Mountain (trô'ôdhôs), highest peak (6,406 ft.) of Cyprus, in isl.'s S range—customarily called OLYMPUS MOUNTAINS—33 mi. SW of Nicosia. Snow-covered (Nov.–May), it is a favorite resort area, especially in summer, when the govt. resides here at Troodos village (pop., including adjacent Pano PLATRES, 502; alt. c.5,500 ft.). Commands fine view across the isl., and to Turkey and Lebanon. Asbestos quarries and chromite mines at its foot. Sometimes also called Mt. Olympus.

Troon, burgh (1931 pop. 8,544; 1951 census 10,061), W Ayrshire, Scotland, on Firth of Clyde, 6 mi. N of Ayr; coal-shipping port and seaside resort; mfg. of colliery equipment. At harbor entrance is lighthouse (55°33'N 4°42'W). In Firth of Clyde, off Troon, is LADY ISLE.

Tropea (trôpā'ä), anc. *Trapeia*, town (pop. 5,400), Catanzaro prov., Calabria, S Italy, fishing port on Tyrrhenian Sea, 11 mi. W of Vibo Valentia. Bishopric. Has 12th-cent. cathedral (restored).

Trophy Mountain (9,000 ft.), S B.C., in Cariboo Mts., 80 mi. NNE of Kamloops; 51°47'N 119°48'W.

Tropic, town (pop. 483), Garfield co., S Utah, 22 mi. SE of Panguitch; cattle, sheep. Bryce Canyon Natl. Park just W.

Tropojë (trôpô'yü) or **Tropoja** (trôpô'yä), village (1930 pop. 216), N Albania, near Yugoslav border, 25 mi. NW of Kukës, in North Albanian Alps. Sometimes called Trifush.

Troppau, Czechoslovakia: see OPAVA.

Trosa (trōō'sä"), city (pop. 1,132), Sodermanland co., E Sweden, on bay of the Baltic, 20 mi. ENE of Nykoping; resort. Founded in 17th cent.; destroyed (1719) by Russians. Near by is royal summer palace of Tullgarn, built in 18th cent. on site of 13th-cent. castle.

Trosky, castle, Czechoslovakia: see BOHEMIAN PARADISE.

Trosky, village (pop. 140), Pipestone co., SW Minn., near S.Dak. line, 8 mi. SSE of Pipestone, in grain and potato area.

Trosna (trô'snŭ), village (1926 pop. 2,193), SW Orel oblast, Russian SFSR, 36 mi. SSW of Orel, on Orel-Kursk highway; hemp.

Trossachs (trŏ'săks), short wooded valley bet. Loch Katrine and Loch Achray, SW Perthshire, Scotland, 8 mi. W of Callander, overlooked by Ben Venue and Ben A'an. It is associated with Scott's *The Lady of the Lake* and *Rob Roy*.

Trossingen (trô'sĭng-ŭn), town (pop. 6,427), S Württemberg, Germany, after 1945 in Württemberg-Hohenzollern, in Swabian Jura, 5 mi. E of Schwenningen; mfg. of musical instruments (accordions, harmonicas); paper milling.

Trostan (trŏ'stŭn), mountain (1,817 ft.), N central Co. Antrim, Northern Ireland, 4 mi. WSW of Cushendall.

Trostberg (trôst'bĕrk), town (pop. 5,526), Upper Bavaria, Germany, on the Alz and 12 mi. NNW of Traunstein; chemicals (carbide, nitrogen); paper milling, printing, leatherworking, textile mfg. Has late-15th-cent. church. Chartered 1457.

Trostyanets (trŭstyŭnyĕts'). **1** Village (1939 pop. over 500), E Lvov oblast, Ukrainian SSR, 6 mi. E of Zolochev; lignite mining. **2** City (1948 pop. over 10,000), SE Sumy oblast, Ukrainian SSR, 32 mi. S of Sumy; sugar refining, distilling, flour milling, mfg. (furniture, medical equipment). **3** Town (1926 pop. 1,329), SE Vinnitsa oblast, Ukrainian SSR, 20 mi. SE of Tulchin; distilling, metalworking.

Trotsk. 1 City, Kuibyshev oblast, Russian SFSR: see CHAPAYEVSK. **2** City, Leningrad oblast, Russian SFSR: see GATCHINA.

Trotter, village (pop. 1,127), Fayette co., SW Pa., 10 mi. NE of Uniontown.

Trotwood, village (pop. 1,066), Montgomery co., W Ohio, 5 mi. WNW of Dayton.

Trou (trōō), town (1950 census pop. 2,918), Nord dept., N Haiti, 16 mi. ESE of Cap-Haïtien, in agr. region (tobacco, sugar cane, sisal, fruit). Sometimes Le Trou.

Troublesome Peak (11,500 ft.), in Rocky Mts., Grand co., N Colo.

Trouin (trōōē'), village, Ouest dept., S Haiti, 23 mi. WSW of Port-au-Prince; coffeegrowing.

Troup (trōōp), county (□ 447; pop. 49,841), W Ga.; ⊙ La Grange. Bounded W by Ala. line; drained by Chattahoochee R. Piedmont agr. (cotton, corn, truck, fruit, livestock) and timber area; textile mfg. at La Grange, Hogansville, and West Point. Formed 1826.

Troup, city (pop. 1,539), on Cherokee-Smith co. line, E Texas, 16 mi. SE of Tyler; oil refining, brick making; cans, ships tomatoes; nurseries.

Trousdale (trouz'dāl), county (□ 116; pop. 5,520), N Tenn.; ⊙ Hartsville. Bounded S by Cumberland R. Livestock, tobacco, corn, grain. Formed 1870.

Trousers Lake (□ 3.1; 4 mi. long, 2 mi. wide), N central N.B., 35 mi. E of Grand Falls.

Troussey (trōōsā'), village (pop. 351), Meuse dept., NE France, on the Meuse and 6 mi. SE of Commercy; junction of Marne-Rhine Canal and Canal de l'Est. Stone quarries.

Trout Creek, town (pop. 370), SE central Ont., 24 mi. S of North Bay; lumbering.

Trout Creek Pass, 9,346 ft., at S end of Park Range, central Colo., 26 mi. SE of Leadville; crossed by highway.

Troutdale. 1 Town (pop. 514), Multnomah co., NW Oregon, 11 mi. E of Portland; aluminum, truck. **2** Town (pop. 250), Grayson co., SW Va., in the Blue Ridge, 11 mi. SSE of Marion.

Trout Hall, town (pop. 1,000), Clarendon parish, central Jamaica, on Minho R., on May Pen–Frankfield RR and 15 mi. NW of May Pen, in fruitgrowing region.

Trout Lake (□ 156), NW Ont., in Patricia dist., 90 mi. NW of Sioux Lookout; 17 mi. long, 14 mi. wide. Drains S into English R.

Trout Lake, village (pop. c.350), Chippewa co., E Upper Peninsula, Mich., 27 mi. NW of St. Ignace, on Trout L. (c.3 mi. long). Trade center for resort and hunting area.

Trout Lake. 1 In Itasca co., N central Minn., at W end of Mesabi iron range, 6 mi. ENE of Grand Rapids; 4.5 mi. long, 1 mi. wide. Large ore-washing plant is on lake. Iron-mining villages of Bovey and Coleraine are on N shore. **2** In Vilas co., N Wis., 20 mi. NW of Eagle River city, in wooded resort area; 4 mi. long, 2 mi. wide.

Troutman or **Troutmans,** town (pop. 613), Iredell co., W central N.C., 5 mi. S of Statesville; mfg. of clothing, furniture.

Trout Peak, Wyo.: see ABSAROKA RANGE.

Trout Run, village, Lycoming co., N central Pa., 11 mi. N of Williamsport, in hunting, fishing, lumbering area.

Trout River, village, S Que., frontier point on N.Y. border, 10 mi. SE of Huntingdon; dairying.

Troutville. 1 Borough (pop. 223), Clearfield co., W central Pa., 7 mi. SSW of Du Bois. **2** Village, Va.: see FINCASTLE.

Trouville or **Trouville-sur-Mer** (trōōvēl'-sür-mâr'), town (pop. 6,781), Calvados dept., NW France, on the Channel at mouth of Touques R., opposite DEAUVILLE, and 9 mi. S of Le Havre; popular bathing resort with casino, boardwalk, and numerous hotels. Fishing industry; also paint and varnish mfg.

Trowbridge (trō'brĭj, trou'–), urban district (1931 pop. 12,011; 1951 census 13,844), W Wiltshire, England, 8 mi. ESE of Bath; agr. market; mfg. (leather, woolens), bacon and ham curing, brewing. Parish church (13th cent.) contains tomb of George Crabbe, rector here from 1814 until his death. Has 16th-cent. town hall. Town has been center of West of England broadcloth industry since 14th cent.

Trowutta, village (pop. 238), NW Tasmania, 110 mi. WNW of Launceston; dairying and agr. center; sawmills.

Troy, classical *Troia* (trō'yù) or *Troja* (trō'jù) and *Ilion* (ĭ'lēŏn) or *Ilium* (ĭ'lēŭm), anc. city of Asia Minor made famous by the Trojan War. Its site is almost universally accepted as the mound now named Hissarlik, in Asiatic Turkey, on the Kucuk Menderes R. (anc. Scamander) 4 mi. SE of the mouth of the Dardanelles. The site was identified by Heinrich Schliemann, who made the 1st excavations (1871–82); Dörpfeld made further excavations, and 9 successive cities were found to have occupied the site, from the Neolithic to the Roman period. The most recent investigations identify Homeric Troy with the 7th stratum. The Troy of the Trojan War (perhaps c.1200 B.C.) was a Phrygian city in the center of a region known as TROAS. The legend of the Trojan War is told in the *Iliad* and the *Aeneid* and serves as the background for the *Odyssey*.

Troy. 1 City (pop. 8,555), ⊙ Pike co., SE Ala., near Conecuh R., 45 mi. SE of Montgomery; trade center for cotton, peanut, and corn area in Black Belt; mfg. (wood products, shirts, fertilizer); peanuts and peanut oil, cottonseed oil. Settled 1824, inc. 1843. Has state teachers col. **2** Village (pop. 531), Latah co., N Idaho, 10 mi. E of Moscow; lumber milling, firebrick mfg. Clay deposits near by. **3** City (pop. 1,260), Madison co., SW Ill., 16 mi. ENE of East St. Louis, in bituminous-coal and agr. area (corn, wheat; dairy products; poultry, livestock); brassworks, pump factory. Settled as Columbia 1814, renamed Troy 1819; inc. as city 1892. **4** Town (pop. 537), Perry co., S Ind., on the Ohio at mouth of small Anderson R., and 3 mi. NNW of Tell City, in agr. and bituminous-coal area. **5** City (pop. 977), ⊙ Doniphan co., extreme NE Kansas, 13 mi. W of St. Joseph, Mo.; shipping center for applegrowing region; vinegar mfg. Apple Blossom Festival takes place here annually in Aug. Indian mounds have been excavated near by. Founded 1855, inc. 1860. **6** Town (pop. 553), Waldo co., S Maine, 19 mi. NW of Belfast, in agr., recreational area. **7** City (pop. 1,738), ⊙ Lincoln co., E Mo., near Cuivre R., 30 mi. NW of St. Charles; cattle, poultry, grain; coal. Federal-state recreation project near by. Laid out c.1819. **8** Town (pop. 770), Lincoln co., NW Mont., 17 mi. W of Libby and on Kootenai R., near Idaho line; railroad div.; trading point for silver-mining region in near-by Cabinet Mts. **9** Town (pop. 1,360), Cheshire co., SW N.H., 9 mi. SE of Keene, near Mt. Monadnock; textiles. Settled 1762, inc. 1815. **10** City (pop. 72,311), ⊙ Rensselaer co., E N.Y., on E bank of the Hudson, just N of Albany, and opposite influx of Mohawk R.; port, commercial and industrial center, near junction with the Hudson of the Erie and Champlain divisions of the N.Y. State Barge Canal. Known for its shirt- and collar-making industry; also produces other clothing, valves, fire hydrants, machinery, brushes, abrasives, surveying instruments, aircraft and auto parts. Seat of Rensselaer Polytechnic Inst., Russell Sage Col., and Emma Willard School for girls. Here in early-19th cent. lived Samuel Wilson, said to be original of natl. figure "Uncle Sam." Laid out 1786, inc. 1816, on site included in patroon grant given to Kiliaen Van Rensselaer in 17th cent. by Dutch West India Company. **11** Town (pop. 2,213), ⊙ Montgomery co., central N.C., 40 mi. S of High Point; agr. trade center; mfg. of cotton goods, hosiery, furniture; sawmilling. Inc. 1879. **12** City (pop. 10,661), ⊙ Miami co., W Ohio, 18 mi. N of Dayton and on Great Miami R.; mfg. of machinery, airplanes, furniture, electrical goods, pulp and paper products, air compressors; meat-packing plant. Gravel pits. Settled c.1807, inc. 1818. **13** Borough (pop. 1,371), Bradford co., N Pa., 21 mi. S of Elmira, N.Y.; dairying; metal and leather products, boats. Settled 1793, inc. c.1844. **14** Town (pop. 242), Greenwood co., W S.C., 16 mi. SSW of Greenwood; lumber. **15** Town (pop. 593), Obion co., NW Tenn., 8 mi. SW of Union City, in cotton and livestock area. **16** Town (pop. 1,786), Orleans co., N Vt., on Missisquoi R. and 12 mi. WSW of Newport, on Que. line; dairying, wood products. Includes North Troy village (pop. 1,057), a port of entry. Granted 1792, organized 1802. Fortified against smugglers in War of 1812. **17** Town (1940 pop. 133), Gilmer co., central W.Va., on the Little Kanawha, 16 mi. W of Weston.

Troya, Cerro (sĕ'rō troi'ä), Andean peak (11,485 ft.) on Colombia-Ecuador border, 5 mi. S of Tulcán; 0°44'N 77°41'W.

Troyan (trôyän'), city (pop. 5,223), Pleven dist., N central Bulgaria, on N slope of Troyan Mts., on Beli Osam R. (headstream of the Osam) and 36 mi. S of Pleven. Health resort; rail terminus; woodworking center; mfg. (furniture, leather clothing, shoes, woolen cloth, jam), plum-brandy distilling; sawmilling, veneering, brick- and tileworks, pottery. School of ceramics. Summer resort (Troyan monastery; pop. 56) is 5 mi. SE. Sometimes spelled Trojan. **Troyan Mountains**, part of central Balkan Mts., are S of Troyan; rise to 7,104 ft. in Ambaritsa peak; headwaters of Osam R. rise on N slopes. Crossed by **Troyan Pass** (alt. 5,038 ft.), 9 mi. S of Troyan; highway links Troyan and Karlovo.

Troyanov (trŭyä'nŭf), town (1926 pop. 5,151), S Zhitomir oblast, Ukrainian SSR, 12 mi. SSW of Zhitomir; sawmilling.

Troyekurovo (trŭyĭkōō'rŭvŭ), village (1926 pop. 1,188), SW Ryazan oblast, Russian SFSR, 17 mi. NW of Chaplygin; rail junction; coarse grain, wheat, tobacco.

Troyes (trwä), anc. *Augustobona*, city (pop. 53,521), ⊙ Aube dept., NE central France, on the braided Seine, on its lateral canal, and 55 mi. ESE of Paris; 48°18'N 4°4'E. Major textile and commercial center with hosiery (rayon, nylon) and cotton mills; mfg. (textile machinery, sewing needles, mirrors, fertilizer, cartons); flour milling, cloth bleaching and dyeing. Has many fine Gothic and Renaissance churches (including 13th-16th-cent. cathedral of Saint-Pierre), noted for their stained glass windows, a number of old wooden houses, mus., and library. A Roman town, it became seat of a bishop in 4th cent. and later ⊙ Champagne. Its medieval fairs were of such importance that they set standards for all of Europe (the troy weight survives). Troyes became an art center in 15th cent. (schools of sculpture and glass painting). Its prosperity suffered from revocation of Edict of Nantes. City, including most churches, damaged in Second World War. Chrestien de Troyes and Pope Urban IV b. here.

Troy Grove, village (pop. 258), La Salle co., N Ill., on Little Vermilion R. and 14 mi. NW of Ottawa. Has state monument to James Butler "Wild Bill" Hickok, b. here.

Troyon (trwäyō'), village (pop. 306), Meuse dept., NE France, on the Meuse and Canal de l'Est, 9 mi. NNW of Saint-Mihiel. Fr. resistance at nearby Troyon fort saved Verdun from encirclement in First World War.

Troy Peak, Nev.: see Grant Range.

Trozza, Djebel, Tunisia: see Ala, El-.

Trsice (tŭr'shĭtsĕ), Czech *Tršice*, village (pop. 1,055), E central Moravia, Czechoslovakia, 8 mi. SE of Olomouc; known for its hops.

Trstena (tŭr'styĕnä), Slovak *Trstená*, town (pop. 2,468), N Slovakia, Czechoslovakia, on railroad and 23 mi. NE of Ruzomberok; lumbering.

Trstenik (tûrstĕ'nĭk), village (pop. 2,139), central Serbia, Yugoslavia, on the Western Morava, on railroad and 17 mi. W of Krusevac; millstone quarrying; winegrowing, tobacco raising.

Trsteno (tûrstĕ'nô), Ital. *Cannosa* (kän-nō'zä), resort village, S Croatia, Yugoslavia, on Adriatic Sea, 8 mi. NW of Dubrovnik, in Dalmatia.

Trub (trōōp), town (pop. 2,173), Bern canton, central Switzerland, on the stream Trubbach and 20 mi. E of Bern; farming.

Trubchevsk (trōōpchĕfsk'), city (1926 pop. 11,085), S Bryansk oblast, Russian SFSR, on Desna R. and 50 mi. SW of Bryansk, in hemp-growing dist.; vegetable drying, hemp milling. Has 16th-cent. cathedral. Chartered 1185.

Trubetchino (trōōbyĕ'chĭnŭ), village (1939 pop. over 2,000), SW Ryazan oblast, Russian SFSR, 20 mi. ESE of Lebedyan; wheat, sugar beets, rubber-bearing plants.

Trubia (trōō'vyä), town (pop. 742), Oviedo prov., NW Spain, 6 mi. W of Oviedo, and on Nalón R.; noted since 18th cent. for its armaments industry; now site of govt. arms factory (chiefly cannons).

Truchas (trōō'chŭs), village (1940 pop. 694), Rio Arriba co., N N.Mex., near Rio Grande, in Sangre de Cristo Mts., 25 mi. NNE of Santa Fe; alt. 7,622 ft. Trading point in grain and livestock area. Presbyterian church and mission training school here. Santa Fe Natl. Forest near by. North Truchas Peak 11 mi. ESE.

Truchas, 3 peaks in N N.Mex., in Sangre de Cristo Mts., c.25 mi. NE of Santa Fe. All are over 13,000 ft. high, and one of them, North Truchas, was thought until recent surveys to be 13,306 ft., highest in the state; it is now known to be c.13,110 ft.; Wheeler Peak (13,151 ft.) is highest in N.Mex.

Truchtersheim (trüktĕrzĕm', Ger. trōōkh'tûrs-hīm), village (pop. 684), Bas-Rhin dept., E France, 9 mi. NW of Strasbourg.

Trucial Oman, Trucial 'Oman, or **Trucial 'Uman** (all: ō'măn, ōmän'), region (□ 6,000; 1951 pop. estimate 40,000) on E coast of Arabian Peninsula, extending along the **Trucial Coast**, a 350-mi. section of Persian Gulf littoral bet. the Oman Promontory and the base of Qatar peninsula (W). Consists largely of the 7 constituent **Trucial Sheikdoms** of Abu Dhabi, Ajman, Dibai, Kalba, Ras al Khaima, Sharja, and Umm al Qaiwain, bound by truces concluded with Great Britain, which is represented by political agent at Sharja. The region includes the low coastal belt bet. the Persian Gulf and the interior sands of the Rub' al Khali; it becomes hilly only in its E section, in the spinal range of the Oman Promontory, where the sheikdom capitals and pop. are concentrated. Area has a dry desert climate with 5 inches of annual precipitation. Pop. consists of tribal Arabs, 10% nomadic and largely of Sunni Moslem sect. Pearling, fishing, and some agr. (dates, grain, vegetables) by well irrigation are the chief activities. Petroleum exploration was begun in 1950. Formerly notorious for piracy, the region was once known as Pirate Coast. Following hostilities against the British East India Company, the 1st truce was signed in 1820 bet. Britain and the sheiks of Abu Dhabi, Ajman, Dibai, Sharja, and Umm al Qaiwain. This truce was made perpetual in 1853, and in 1892 the trucial sheiks agreed not to enter into agreements with countries other than Great Britain. The 5 original Trucial Sheikdoms were later joined by Ras al Khaima (1919) and Kalba (1937).

Truckee (trŭ'kē), village (pop. 1,025), Nevada co., E Calif., on Truckee R., in the Sierra Nevada, at E end of Donner Pass, 25 mi. SW of Reno, Nev.; alt. 5,820 ft. Winter-sports center. L. Tahoe is 10 mi. S, Donner L. is just W.

Truckee Pass (alt. c.5,800 ft.), E Calif., in the Sierra Nevada near Truckee (Nevada co.). An emigrant trail ran through pass.

Truckee River, in E Calif. and W Nev., rises in L. Tahoe (on state line), flows c.120 mi. generally NE, past Truckee, Calif., and Reno, Nev., to S end of Pyramid L. With installations on Carson River, furnishes water for Newlands irrigation project, which serves 87,500 acres around Fallon, Nev. Small dam at Truckee's source regulates passage of water from lake; diversion dam in Nev., 20 mi. E of Reno, turns part of flow into Truckee Canal, extending 31 mi. E, past Fernley, to N tip of Lahontan Reservoir in Carson R. Little Truckee River is most important tributary; supplies irrigation water to Truckee storage project.

Trud (trōōt), village (pop. 3,198), Plovdiv dist., S central Bulgaria, 6 mi. N of Plovdiv; livestock, grain, sugar beets. Formerly Klimentina.

Trud (trōōt), town (1947 pop. over 500), W Kalinin oblast, Russian SFSR, 20 mi. S of Bologoye; glassworks.

Trudarmeisk or **Trudarmeysk** (trōōdŭrmyäsk'), village (1945 pop. over 500), W Kemerovo oblast, Russian SFSR, on railroad and 15 mi. NW of Kiselevsk, in Kuznetsk Basin.

Trudfront (trōōdfrônt'), town (1939 pop. over 500), E Astrakhan oblast, Russian SFSR, on Bakhtemir arm of Volga R. delta mouth and 35 mi. SSW of Astrakhan; fish-processing center.

Trudovaya, Ukrainian SSR: see Rumyantsevo, Stalino oblast.

Trudovoye (trōōdŭvoi'ŭ), town (1943 pop. over 500), S Maritime Territory, Russian SFSR, on Trans-Siberian RR, 7 mi. SW (under jurisdiction) of Artem; lignite mining.

Truedstorp, Sweden: see Skromberga.

Truel, Le, France: see Saint-Rome-de-Tarn.

Truesdail or **Truesdale**, town (pop. 235), Warren co., E central Mo., adjacent to Warrenton.

Truesdale, town (pop. 158), Buena Vista co., NW Iowa, 6 mi. N of Storm Lake.

Trugberg (trōōk'bĕrk), peak (12,914 ft.) in Bernese Alps, S central Switzerland, 12 mi. SSE of Interlaken.

Trujillanos (trōōhĕlyä'nōs), town (pop. 966), Badajoz prov., W Spain, 4 mi. ENE of Mérida; cereals, vegetables, olives, fruit, livestock.

Trujillo (trōōhē'yō), town (pop. 2,486), Valle del Cauca dept., W Colombia, in Cordillera Occidental, 11 mi. WNW of Tuluá; tobacco, sugar cane, coffee, cacao, cereals, cattle.

Trujillo, province (□ 1,491; 1935 pop. 100,147; 1950 pop. 160,345), E central Dominican Republic, on the Caribbean; ⊙ San Cristóbal. Mostly mountainous, especially in W section, bounded N by outliers of the Cordillera Central. Important coffee- and rice-growing region; also cacao, tobacco, sugar cane, corn, fruit, livestock. Copper deposits, mined in colonial era. Prov. set up 1934.

Trujillo, city (pop. 2,957), ⊙ Colón dept., N Honduras, Caribbean port on Trujillo Bay (5 mi. wide; sheltered N by Cape Honduras), 130 mi. E of Puerto Cortés; 15°55'N 85°59'W. Commercial center in agr. and livestock region; exports bananas, coconuts, mahogany, hides. Has many Sp. colonial bldgs. Founded 1525; became 1st ⊙ of Sp. colonial prov. of Honduras; flourished in early 17th cent. Was bishop's see (1531–1561) until its removal to Comayagua. Sacked 1643 by Du. pirates; remained in ruins until 1787, when it was resettled by Galicians. Largely replaced since c.1920 by new port of Puerto Castilla. Formerly spelled Truxillo.

Trujillo, city (pop. 38,961), ⊙ Libertad dept. and Trujillo prov. (□ 2,506; pop. 123,006), NW Peru, on coastal plain, on Pan American Highway, and 8 mi. NNW of its port Salaverry (connected by railroad), 300 mi. NNW of Lima; 8°7'S 79°2'W. Third largest city in Peru, it is an important commercial, industrial, and road center in irrigated sugar-cane and rice area. Food industries (rice, noodle, chocolate, confectionery); brewing, tanning, mfg. of cocaine, soap, wax, candles, textiles; machine and railroad shops. Airport. Tourist resort. Bishopric. Has a cathedral, several old churches and colonial mansions, univ. Founded 1534 by Diego de Almagro. A city wall (of which traces remain) was built 1617 to ward off attacks by English pirates. City was partly destroyed by earthquakes in 17th and 18th cent. The ruins of Chan Chan are 4 mi. W.

Trujillo (trōōhē'lyō), city (pop. 5,771; commune pop. 13,753), Cáceres prov., W Spain, in Estremadura, 26 mi. E of Cáceres; agr.-trade and road center; meat and cheese processing, flour milling, soap and knitwear mfg. Cereals and livestock in area. Mineral springs. Has some Roman remains, Moorish castle restored by French, 15th-cent. Gothic church of Santa María, and church of Santa María de la Concepción with Pizarro's tomb. Francisco Pizarro and several other conquistadors b. here built fine mansions with wealth amassed in South America.

Trujillo, (trōōhē'yō), state (□ 2,860; 1941 pop. 264,270; 1950 census 284,583), W Venezuela, on L. Maracaibo; ⊙ Trujillo. Mostly mountainous, traversed SW–NE by Andean spur culminating in Teta de Niquitao (13,143 ft.). Drained by Motatán R. Climate varies: humid-tropical near L. Maracaibo, semitropical in densely inhabited uplands, cool with year-round rains in high Andean areas. Mineral resources include petroleum deposits, near Escuque and Betijoque. Virgin forests, covering half the state, yield fine construction timber. Principally an agr. region; produces coffee on its lower slopes, also sugar cane, cacao, tobacco, corn, yuca; in higher uplands wheat, barley and potatoes are grown. In lowland llanos, cattle are raised. Trujillo and Valera are trading and processing centers.

Trujillo, city (1941 pop. 6,954; 1950 census 11,794), ⊙ Trujillo state, W Venezuela, in Andean spur, on transandine highway and 70 mi. NE of Mérida, 250 mi. WSW of Caracas; 9°23'N 70°26'W; alt. c.2,600 ft. Has semitropical climate. Market center in agr. region (cacao, coffee, corn, sugar cane, tobacco, fruit); flour mills, ice plants. Founded 1556. From here Simón Bolívar issued (1813) his Decree of Trujillo, committing himself to a "fight to the death."

Trujillo, Pico (pē'kō), peak (10,115 ft.), central Dominican Republic, in the Cordillera Central, 35 mi. SW of Santiago; 19°3'N 70°58'W. Sometimes considered highest elevation in the West Indies, though Monte Tina, to SE, is said to be 10,301 ft.

Trujillo Alto (äl'tō), town (pop. 1,082), E Puerto Rico, on Loíza R. and 11 mi. SE of San Juan; agr. center (sugar, tobacco); truck gardening, dairying. Settled in early 19th cent. by settlers from Canary Isls. Plastics factory near by. Gypsum deposits in vicinity.

Trujillo City, Dominican Republic: see Ciudad Trujillo.

Trujillo Valdez or **Trujillo Valdés** (both: väldĕs'), province (□ 717; 1935 pop. 59,119; 1950 pop. 81,351), S Dominican Republic, on the Caribbean; ⊙ Baní. Mountainous, semiarid region in outliers of the Cordillera Central and Sierra de Ocoa. Has fertile, irrigated areas, where coffee, rice, sugar cane, and fruit are grown. San José de Ocoa is known for its tobacco. Has coal deposits. Salt is worked at small Calderas Bay.

Trujillo Valdez, town, Dominican Republic: see José Trujillo Valdez.

Truk (trŭk, trōōk), island group (□ 39; pop. 9,510), E Caroline Isls., W Pacific, 7°25'N 151°47'E. Cluster of 57 volcanic isls., surrounded by atoll reef, with c.40 fairly large coral isls. Major volcanic isls. are Tol (□ 9, rising to 1,483 ft.), Moen (□ 8.5), Fefan (□ 5.5), Dublon (□ 3.7, rising to 1,168 ft.), Udot (□ 1.9), Uman (□ 1.7). Kuop, 2 mi. S, is generally considered one of Truk isls. Produces copra, dried bonito. In Second World War, group was site of Jap. naval base. Truk dist. (□ 49; pop. 14,618) includes East Fayu, Etal, Losap, Lukunor, Murilo, Nama, Namoluk, Namonuito, Nomwin, Pulap, Pulusuk, Puluwat, Satawan. Formerly Hogolu.

Trumag (trōōmäg'), village (1930 pop. 341), Osorno prov., S central Chile, inland river port on the Río Bueno (Valdivia prov. border) and 15 mi. N of Osorno; ships wool, timber, lard.

Truman, village (pop. 1,106), Martin co., S Minn., 12 mi. N of Fairmont, in grain, livestock area; dairy products, feed.

Trumann, city (pop. 3,744), Poinsett co., NE Ark., 15 mi. SE of Jonesboro, in agr. (cotton, corn, hay) and timber area; large woodworking plant.

Trumansburg, village (pop. 1,479), Tompkins co., W central N.Y., in Finger Lakes region, 10 mi. NW of Ithaca, near Cayuga L.; food processing, mfg. of metal products. Agr. (poultry, fruit, grain). Annual fair held here. Settled 1792, inc. 1865.

Trumbauersville (trŭm'bou"ûrzvĭl"), borough (pop. 838), Bucks co., SE Pa., 3 mi. SW of Quakertown.

Trumbayung Chu, river, Tibet: see NYANG CHU.

Trumbull (trŭm'bŏŏl), county (□ 630; pop. 158,915), NE Ohio; ⊙ Warren. Bounded E by Pa. line; drained by Mahoning and Grand rivers and Mosquito and Pymatuning creeks. Includes Mosquito Creek Reservoir. Agr. area (livestock, dairy products, clover, grain). Mfg. (especially steel milling) at Warren, Niles, and Girard, industrial suburbs of Youngstown. Sand and gravel pits. Formed 1800.

Trumbull. 1 Town (pop. 8,641), Fairfield co., SW Conn., on Poquonock R., just N of Bridgeport; includes villages of Nichols (pop. 1,171) and Long Hill (1940 pop. 1,897). Settled c.1690, inc. 1797. **2** Village (pop. 150), Adams and Clay counties, S Nebr., 9 mi. NE of Hastings, near Platte R.

Trumbull, Mount (8,028 ft.), NW Ariz., c.70 mi. SW of Kanab, Utah.

Trumelet (trümlā'), village (pop. 1,772), Oran dept., N Algeria, on fertile Sersou Plateau at S edge of the Tell Atlas, 10 mi. ENE of Tiaret; European farms grow cereals

Trümmelbach (trü'mŭlbäkh), stream in Bernese Alps, S central Switzerland, tributary of White Lütschine R.; noted for its falls (950 ft.) of 5 cascades S of Lauterbrunnen.

Trumpington, residential town and parish (pop. 1,183), S Cambridge, England, on Cam R. and 2 mi. S of Cambridge. Site of Chaucer's mill, mentioned in poems of Tennyson and Rupert Brooke.

Trun (trũ), village (pop. 1,109), Orne dept., NW France, on the Dives and 7 mi. NNE of Argentan; cattle market; footwear mfg. Stubbornly defended (1944) by Germans withdrawing from Argentan-Falaise pocket in Second World War.

Trundle, village (pop. 807), central New South Wales, Australia, 220 mi. WNW of Sydney; sheep, agr.

Trungkhanhphu (trōōng'khä'nyŏŏfōō'), town, Caobang prov., N Vietnam, 21 mi. NE of Caobang, near China frontier; road center.

Trunovskoye (trōōnôf'skŭyŭ), village (1926 pop. 16,168), NW Stavropol Territory, Russian SFSR, 31 mi. NNE of Stavropol; flour mill, metalworks; wheat, sunflowers, castor beans. Until 1936, Ternovskoye.

Truro (trōōr'ō), town (pop. 10,272), central N.S., near head of Cobequid Bay of the Bay of Fundy, 50 mi. NNE of Halifax; railroad center; mfg. of clothing, machinery; lumbering, metalworking, printing. Site of agr. col. First settled by Acadians; originally named Cobequid. Inc. 1765.

Truro, municipal borough (1931 pop. 11,064; 1951 census 12,851), W Cornwall, England, at confluence of Kenwyn R. and Allen R. (here forming Truro R.), at head of Falmouth harbor, 8 mi. N of Falmouth; port and tourist center; metal- and woodworking. In 1876 it became cathedral city of a Cornish bishopric. Has modern cathedral in Early English style. Formerly important tin-mining center, with Stannary courts (miners' own courts). There is mus. of Cornish exhibits.

Truro. 1 Town (pop. 354), Madison co., S central Iowa, near South R., 29 mi. SSW of Des Moines, in agr. area. **2** Town (pop. 661), Barnstable co., SE Mass., near N tip of Cape Cod, 8 mi. SSE of Provincetown; summer resort; artist colony. Formerly thriving port and fishing center. Includes North Truro village; fish-freezing plant; site of Cape Cod or Highland Light (1st installed 1797), one of most powerful on Atlantic coast; also has naval radio and coast guard stations. South Truro village is resort. Settled 1700, inc. 1709.

Truro Shoal, China: see MACCLESFIELD BANK.

Truscott (trŭs'kŭt), village (pop. c.500), Knox co., N Texas, near North Fork of Wichita R., c.75 mi. W of Wichita Falls; shipping point in cattle-ranching, cotton, and grain region.

Trusina (trōō'sĕnä), mountain (3,769 ft.) in Dinaric Alps, S Herzegovina, Yugoslavia, 8 mi. S of Nevesinje.

Truskavets (trōōskŭvyĕts'), Pol. *Truskawiec* (trōōskä'vyĕts), city (1931 pop. 2,280), central Drogobych oblast, Ukrainian SSR, on N slope of E Beskids, 5 mi. S of Drogobych; rail spur terminus; noted health resort with mineral springs; lumber.

Truskmore (trŭskmôr'), mountain (2,113 ft.) on borders of Co. Leitrim and Co. Sligo, Ireland, 8 mi. NE of Sligo.

Trusovo, Russian SFSR: see ASTRAKHAN, city.

Trussville, town (pop. 1,575), Jefferson co., N central Ala., 15 mi. NE of Birmingham; lumber. Cahaba Village, a Federal subsistence homestead, is here. Alabama Boys Industrial School near by. Inc. since 1940.

Trusthorpe, England: see MABLETHORPE AND SUTTON.

Trust Territory of the Pacific Islands: see PACIFIC ISLANDS, TRUST TERRITORY OF THE.

Truth or Consequences, town (pop. 4,563), ⊙ Sierra co., SW N.Mex., on Rio Grande, E of Black Range, and 105 mi. NNW of El Paso, Texas; alt. c.4,200 ft. Health resort with hot mineral springs; trade center in livestock, agr. area. Hosp. for treatment of poliomyelitis here. Annual regatta on near-by Elephant Butte Reservoir. Caballo Reservoir is just S. Formerly Hot Springs.

Trutnov (trōōt'nôf), Ger. *Trautenau* (trou'tŭnou), town (pop. 12,201), NE Bohemia, Czechoslovakia, in foothills of the Riesengebirge, 10 mi. NNE of Dvur Kralove; rail junction; center of Bohemian linen industry; mfg. of jute rugs, bags, glassware. Flax grown in vicinity both for fiber production and seed. Has 18th-cent. churches, arcades. Anthracite deposits near by.

Truxillo, Honduras: see TRUJILLO.

Truxton, village (pop. c.500), Cortland co., central N.Y., on Tioughnioga R. and 11 mi. NE of Cortland; food products.

Truyère River (trüyâr'), in Lozère, Cantal, and Aveyron depts., S central France, rises in Montagnes de la Margeride 5 mi. SW of Grandrieu, flows 100 mi. N and SW in canyon bet. Massif du Cantal (N) and Monts d'Aubrac (S), to the Lot at Entraygues. Spanned by Garabit viaduct near RUINES. Important hydroelectric installations at BROMMAT.

Trwyn y Gader, Wales: see CARMEL HEAD.

Tryavna (tryäv'nä), city (pop. 4,298), Gorna Oryakhovitsa dist., N central Bulgaria, on N slope of Tryavna mts., 8 mi. E of Gabrovo; mfg. (woolen and cotton textiles, furniture, marmalade), fruit canning; horticulture. Has school of carpentry, monument to Bulg. poet Petko Slaveikov. Buildings (19th cent. churches, wooden houses) reflect town's past activity as a woodcarving center under Turkish rule. Sometimes spelled Trjevna. **Tryavna Mountains,** part of central Balkan Mts., are S of Tryavna; lignite mines. Crossed by **Tryavna Pass,** 7 mi. SSE of Tryavna, with ¾-mi.-long railroad tunnel.

Tryddyn or **Treuddyn** (both: trĭ'dhĭn), town and parish (pop. 1,243), Flint, Wales, 7 mi. NW of Wrexham; coal mining.

Trylandsfoss (trü'länsfôs), waterfall on small river at its influx into the Audna, Vest-Agder co., S Norway, 22 mi. WNW of Kristiansand; hydroelectric plant.

Tryon (trī'ŏn", trī'ŭn). **1** Village (pop. c.150), ⊙ McPherson co., W central Nebr., 30 mi. NNW of North Platte; grain, livestock, poultry produce. **2** Town (pop. 1,985), Polk co., W N.C., at S.C. line, 15 mi. SE of Hendersonville, in the Blue Ridge foothills; year-round resort; textile mills; domestic weaving and woodworking. Inc. 1885. **3** Town (pop. 285), Lincoln co., central Okla., 17 mi. SSE of Stillwater; cotton ginning.

Tryphena, New Zealand: see GREAT BARRIER ISLAND.

Trysil River, Norway: see KLAR RIVER, Sweden.

Trzcianka (chŭchän'kä), Ger. *Schönlanke* (shûn"-läng'kŭ), town (1939 pop. 9,618; 1946 pop. 4,482) in Pomerania, after 1945 in Poznan prov., NW Poland, 15 mi. WSW of Schneidemühl (Pila); furniture mfg., sawmilling. Has 16th-cent. church. Chartered 1836. Until 1938, in former Prussian prov. of Grenzmark Posen–Westpreussen. In Second World War, c.40% destroyed.

Trzciel (chŭchĕl'), Ger. *Tirschtiegel* (tĭrsh'tē"gŭl), town (1939 pop. 2,218; 1946 pop. 1,239) in Brandenburg, after 1945 in Zielona Gora prov., W Poland, on Obra R. and 18 mi. NE of Swiebodzin; agr. market (grain, potatoes, livestock). Grew around 14th-cent. castle; chartered 17th cent. Until 1939, Ger. frontier point on Pol. border.

Trzcinsko Zdroj (chŭchē'nyŭskô zdrōō'ē), Pol. *Trzcińsko Zdrój*, Ger. *Bad Schönfliess in Neumark* (bät" shûn'flēs ĭn noi'märk), town (1939 pop. 2,659; 1946 pop. 1,366), in Brandenburg, after 1945 in Szczecin prov., NW Poland, on small lake, 25 mi. N of Küstrin (Kostrzyn); health resort. Chartered 1281.

Trzebiatow (chĕbyä'tōōf), Pol. *Trzebiatów*, Ger. *Treptow* or *Treptow an der Rega* (trĕp'tō än dĕr rā'gä), town (1939 pop. 10,883; 1946 pop. 5,995) in Pomerania, after 1945 in Szczecin prov., NW Poland, on the Rega, near its mouth, and 40 mi. W of Köslin (Koszalin); agr. market (grain, sugar beets, potatoes, livestock); mfg. (furniture, bricks, leather. Chartered 1277; later joined Hanseatic League. In 1534, parliament here introduced Reformation into Pomerania.

Trzebinia (chĕbē'nyä), town (pop. 4,140), Krakow prov., S Poland, 22 mi. WNW of Cracow; rail junction; metallurgical, chemical, and food industries; 2 coal mines, stone quarry; zinc smelter, petroleum refineries, limekilns. Zinc and lead deposits near by.

Trzebnica (chĕbnē'tsä), Ger. *Trebnitz* (trāb'nĭts), town (1939 pop. 8,500; 1946 pop. 3,170) in Lower Silesia, after 1945 in Wroclaw prov., SW Poland, 13 mi. N of Breslau (Wroclaw); health resort. Heavily damaged (c.80% destroyed) in Second World War. Has 13th-cent. church of former Cistercian convent, founded 1203, secularized 1810.

Trzemeszno (chĕmĕsh'nô), Ger. *Tremessen* (trā'-mĕ"sŭn), town pop. 4,779), Bydgoszcz prov., W central Poland, on railroad and 25 mi. SW of Inowroclaw; brewing, flour milling, furniture mfg.

Trzic (tŭr'zhĭch), Slovenian *Tržič*, Ger. *Neumarktl* (noi'märktŭl), village, N Slovenia, Yugoslavia, at S foot of the Karawanken, on Kranj-Klagenfurt road and 24 mi. NNW of Ljubljana; terminus of railroad to Kranj. Leather, paper, woolen textile, fur, and light metallurgical industries. Summer resort; winter sports. Until 1918, in Carniola.

Tsabong (tsä'bông), village, ⊙ Kgalagadi dist., SW Bechuanaland Protectorate, near U. of So. Afr. border, in Kalahari Desert, near Molopo R., 200 mi. W of Mafeking; camel-police and radio station. Sometimes spelled Tsabon.

Tsageri (tsŭgyĕ'rē), town (1932 pop. estimate, 2,120), N Georgian SSR, 27 mi. N of Kutaisi, in silk and winegrowing area; grain, livestock.

Tsagli, Greece: see ERETRIA.

Tsagveri (tsŭgvĕ'rē), town (1926 pop. 596), central Georgian SSR, in pine forest, 5 mi. E of Borzhomi (linked by narrow-gauge railroad); health resort (mineral springs); alt. 3,385 ft.

Tsaidam (tsī'däm'), salt-marsh depression in N central Tsinghai prov., China, W of lake Koko Nor, bet. W branches of the Kunlun system; 300 mi. long (WNW-ESE), 100 mi. wide; mean alt. 9,000 ft. Frozen 8 months of the year.

Tsakir (tsŭkēr'), village (1948 pop. over 2,000), SW Buryat-Mongol Autonomous SSR, Russian SFSR, on Dzhida R. and 14 mi. NE of Gorodok; sawmilling, gold mining.

Tsala Apopka Lake (tŭsä'lŭ ŭpŏp'kŭ) (c.16 mi. long), E Citrus co., central Fla., c.55 mi. NNE of Tampa; shallow and largely overgrown with water lilies, it has many isls. and very irregular shore; has outlets into swamplands (E) which are drained by Withlacoochee R.

Tsalapitsa (tsäläpē'tsä), village (pop. 6,350), Plovdiv dist., S central Bulgaria, 8 mi. WNW of Plovdiv; rice, vineyards, fruit, truck.

Tsalendzhikha (tsŭlyĭnjĕ'khŭ), village (1932 pop. estimate 1,600), W Georgian SSR, 12 mi. NE of Zugdidi; tea, tung oil.

Tsali, Greece: see MOUNTZINOS.

Tsalka (tsäl'kŭ), village (1939 pop. over 2,000), S Georgian SSR, 35 mi. W of Tiflis and on Khram R., which here forms reservoir (12 mi. long, 2.5 mi. wide) for Khram hydroelectric station at MOLOTOVO (S); dairying, potatoes, wheat.

Tsamanda, Mount, Greece-Albania: see TSAMANTA, MOUNT.

Tsamanta, Mount or **Mount Tsamanda** (both: tsämän'dä) (5,924 ft.), on Albanian-Greek border, in Epirus, 23 mi. SE of Argyrokastron; 39°46'N 20°22'E. Also called Murgana or Mourgana.

Tsamkong, China: see CHANKIANG.

Tsana, lake, Ethiopia: see TANA.

Tsane (tsä'nä), village, Kgalagadi dist., Bechuanaland Protectorate, in Kalahari Desert, 260 mi. NW of Mafeking; 24°5'S 21°55'E.

Tsang, China: see TSANG RIVER.

Tsang (tsäng), Chinese *Hou-tsang* (hō'dzäng') [=posterior Tibet], W central historical province of Tibet; main town, Shigatse.

Ts'ang-ch'i, China: see TSANGKI.

Tsanghsien or **Ts'ang-hsien** (tsäng'shyĕn'), town, ⊙ Tsanghsien co. (pop. 448, 029), E Hopeh prov., China, 60 mi. SSW of Tientsin and on Tientsin-Pukow RR; salt-producing center; straw plait, hides, agr. products. Until 1913, Tsangchow.

Tsangki or **Ts'ang-ch'i** (both: tsäng'chē'), town (pop. 26,203), ⊙ Tsangki co. (pop. 250,662), N Szechwan prov., China, 10 mi. N of Langchung and on left bank of Kialing R.; rice, sweet potatoes, wheat, millet, beans, indigo.

Tsangkow or **Ts'ang-k'ou** (both: tsäng'kō'), industrial town, E Shantung prov., China, on Kiaochow Bay, 10 mi. N of Tsingtao, and on Tsingtao-Tsinan RR; site of Tsingtao airport.

Tsangne La, Tibet and China: see TANG PASS.

Tsangpo River, Tibet: see BRAHMAPUTRA RIVER.

Tsang River (dzäng), Mandarin *Chang Kiang* (*Chiang*) (jäng' jyäng') or *Chang Shui* (shwā), left headstream of Kan R., in SW Kiangsi prov., China, rises on Hunan line, flows 100 mi. E, past Shangyiu, joining Kung R. at Kanchow to form Kan R.

Tsangwu, China: see WUCHOW.

Tsangyüan or **Ts'ang-yüan** (tsäng'yüän'), village, ⊙ Tsangyüan dist. (pop. 15,739), SW Yunnan prov., China, 60 mi. SW of Mienning, on Burma border; timber, rice, millet, beans, rapeseed.

Tsan-huang, China: see TSANHWANG.

Tsanhwang or **Tsan-huang** (both: dzän'hwäng'), town, ⊙ Tsanhwang co. (pop. 88,630), SW Hopeh prov., China, 30 mi. S of Shihkiachwang, near Peking-Hankow RR; wheat, kaoliang, millet, beans.

Tsanta, China: see LIENSHAN, Yunnan prov.

Tsao-ch'iang, China: see TSAOKIANG.

Tsaochow, China: see HOTSEH.

Tsaochwang or **Tsao-chuang** (both: dzou'jwäng'), town, SW Shantung prov., China, 7 mi. N of Yihsien and on spur of Tientsin-Pukow RR; coal-mining center.

Tsaohsien or **Ts'ao-hsien** (tsou'shyĕn'), town, ⊙ Tsaohsien co. (pop. 617,002), S Pingyuan prov., China, 30 mi. SSE of Hotseh, near Honan line; cotton weaving; peanuts, wheat, pears. Until 1949 in Shantung prov.

Tsaokiang or **Tsao-ch'iang** (both: dzou'chyäng'), town, ⊙ Tsaokiang co. (pop. 280,689), SW Hopeh prov., China, 32 mi. W of Tehchow; cotton, felt, wool, grain.

Tsaoshan or **Ts'ao-shan** (both: tsou'shän'), Jap. *Sozan* (sō'zän), village, N Formosa, 7 mi. NNE of Taipei, on S slope of the Tatun Shan; noted health resort.

Tsaotun or **Ts'ao-t'un** (both: tsou'tōōn'), Jap. *Soton* (sō'tōn), town (1935 pop. 5,724), W central Formosa, 11 mi. S of Taichung and on railroad; banana center; rice, sugar cane, livestock.

Tsaoyang (dzou'yäng'), town (pop. 25,506), ⊙ Tsaoyang co. (pop. 286,442), N Hupeh prov., China, near Honan line, 40 mi. ENE of Siangyang; cotton-growing center; rice, wheat, ramie, beans, medicinal herbs.

Tsar, Mount (11,232 ft.), SE B.C., near Alta. border, in Rocky Mts., in Hamber Provincial Park, 55 mi. SSE of Jasper; 52°6'N 117°48'W.

Tsaratanana (tsärätänä'nü), town, Majunga prov., N central Madagascar, 120 mi. SE of Majunga; cattle market; gold mining in vicinity.

Tsaratanana Massif, mtn. region, N Madagascar, c.50 mi. wide, 110 mi. long; rises to 9,450 ft., highest point in Madagascar.

Tsarekonstantinovka, Ukrainian SSR: see KUIBYSHEVO, Zaporozhe oblast.

Tsareva-livada (tsä'rĕvä-lĭvä'dä), village (pop. 589), Gorna Oryakhovitsa dist., N central Bulgaria, on N slope of Tryavna Mts., 3 mi. S of Dryanovo; summer resort; rail junction; fruit, truck, winegrowing.

Tsarevo (tsä'rĕvô), city (pop. 1,896), Burgas dist., SE Bulgaria, port on Black Sea, 30 mi. SE of Burgas; lumber and charcoal exports. Until 1934, Vasiliko; name changed from Tsarevo to Michurin in 1950.

Tsarevokokshaisk, Russian SFSR: see IOSHKAR-OLA.

Tsarevosanchursk, Russian SFSR: see SANCHURSK.

Tsarevo Selo, Yugoslavia: see CAREVO SELO.

Tsaribrod, Yugoslavia: see DIMITROVGRAD.

Tsarichanka (tsŭrĕchän'kŭ), agr. town (1926 pop. 5,847), NW Dnepropetrovsk oblast, Ukrainian SSR, on Orel R. and 35 mi. NW of Dnepropetrovsk; light mfg.

Tsaritsyn, Russian SFSR: see STALINGRAD, city.

Tsaritsyno, Russian SFSR: see LENINO, Moscow oblast.

Tsar Kaloyan (tsär' kälôyän'), village (pop. 5,829), Ruse dist., NE Bulgaria. 19 mi. SE of Ruse; wheat, rye, sunflowers. Formerly Torlak.

Tsar Krum (tsär' krōōm'), village (pop. 469), Kolarovgrad dist., E Bulgaria, on Golyama Kamchiya R., at mouth of Vrana R., and 5 mi. S of Kolarovgrad; rail junction; swine raising; fruit, truck. Formerly Chatali.

Tsarsko-selo (tsär'skô-sĕ'lô), village (pop. 4,067), Plovdiv dist., S central Bulgaria, 2 mi. N of Parvomai; vineyards, cotton, tobacco. Formerly Chikardzhii.

Tsarskoye Selo, Russian SFSR: see PUSHKIN.

Tsavo (tsä'vō), town, Coast Prov., SE Kenya, near Athi R., on railroad and 27 mi. N of Voi; 3°S 38°28'E; coffee, tea, sisal, corn; dairy farming. Graphite deposits. Airfield. Tsavo Natl. Park (□ c.7,000), just NW, is a game reserve (elephants, gazelles, zebras, giraffes).

Tsa-yü, Tibet: see RIMA.

Tsazin, Yugoslavia: see CAZIN.

Tschaslau, Czechoslovakia: see CASLAV.

Tschenstochau, Poland: see CZESTOCHOWA.

Tschernembl, Yugoslavia: see CRNOMELJ.

Tschirnau, Poland: see CZERNINA.

Tschuapa River (chwä'pä), central Belgian Congo, rises 15 mi. SE of Katako Kombe, flows NW past Moma, Bondo, and Ikela, and W past Bokungu to join Lomela R. just W of Boende, forming the Busira; 600 mi. long. Navigable for 435 mi. downstream from Moma.

Tsebrikovo (tsĕ'brĕkŭvŭ), village (1926 pop. 2,408), W Odessa oblast, Ukrainian SSR, 55 mi. NNW of Odessa; winery.

Tsechow, China: see TSINCHENG.

Tsehheng or **Ts'e-heng** (tsŭ'hŭng'), town (pop. 1,005), ⊙ Tsehheng co. (pop. 53,462), SW Kweichow prov., China, 55 mi. E of Hingi, near Kwangsi line; alt. 3,342 ft.; grain. Mercury deposits near by.

Tsehleh, China: see CHIRA.

Tsehpu, China: see POSGAM.

Tsekhanov, Poland: see CIECHANOW.

Tsekhanovets, Poland: see CIECHANOWIEC.

Tsekhotsinek, Poland: see CIECHOCINEK.

Tselfat, Fr. Morocco: see PETITJEAN.

Tselina (tsĭlyē'nŭ), village (1926 pop. 2,214), S Rostov oblast, Russian SFSR, on railroad and 25 mi. W of Salsk; wheat, cotton, livestock.

Tsellari River (tsĕ'lärē), NE Ethiopia, rises on Mt. Abuna Josef, flows c.115 mi. NW to Takkaze R. 25 mi. E of Mt. Ras Dashan.

Ts'e-lo, China: see CHIRA.

Tsemah (tsĕmä'), settlement, Lower Galilee, NE Israel, near Syrian border, at S end of Sea of Galilee, on railroad and 6 mi. SE of Tiberias. Founded 1949 on site of village of Samakh, abandoned by Arab pop., 1948.

Tsementny or **Tsementnyy** (tsĭmyĕnt'nē). **1** Town (1926 pop. 2,204), N Bryansk oblast, Russian SFSR, 13 mi. N of Bryansk; cement-making center; power plant. **2** Town (1935 pop. over 500), W central Sverdlovsk oblast, Russian SFSR, 4 mi. SSW of Nevyansk, near railroad (Shurala junction); cement making.

Ts'en-ch'i, China: see SHUMKAI.

Tseng, river, China: see TSENG RIVER.

Tseng-ch'eng, China: see TSENGSHING.

Tseng River (dzŭng), Chinese *Tseng Kiang* or *Tseng Chiang* (both: dzŭng'jyäng'), S central Kwangtung prov., China, rises N of Lungmoon, flows 70 mi. S, past Lungmoon and Tsengshing, to East R. delta near Sheklung.

Tsengshing (dzĕng'shĭng'), Mandarin *Tseng-ch'eng* (dzŭng'chŭng'), town (pop. 6,379), ⊙ Tsengshing co. (pop. 275,471), S Kwangtung prov., China, on the Tseng and 37 mi. ENE of Canton; known for its litchi nuts. Gold mining.

Tsengwen River (tsŭng'wŭn'), Jap. *Sobun* (sō'bōōn), W central Formosa, rises in the Ali Shan, flows 85 mi. SW of Formosa Strait 9 mi. NW of Tainan.

Tsenkung or **Ts'en-kung** (tsŭn'gōōng'), town (pop. 1,608), ⊙ Tsenkung co. (pop. 74,088), E Kweichow prov., China, near Hunan line, 20 mi. NNE of Chenyüan; paper and inkstone making; embroideries; rice, wheat, beans. Saltworks near by. Until 1913 called Szechow, and 1913–30, Szehsien.

Tsenovo (tsĕ'nôvô), village (pop. 3,469), Ruse dist., NE Bulgaria, on Yantra R. and 7 mi. NNW of Byala; livestock, grain, sunflowers. Formerly Chanshovo.

Tsentralno-Bokovskoi or **Tsentral'no-Bokovskoy** (tsĭntrăl'nŭ-bŭkŭfskoi'), town (1939 pop. over 500), S Voroshilovgrad oblast, Ukrainian SSR, in the Donbas, just N of Bokovo-Antratsit; anthracite mines.

Tsentralny or **Tsentral'nyy** (tsĭntrăl'nē), town (1939 pop. over 2,000), E central Kemerovo oblast, Russian SFSR, 70 mi. SSW of Tyazhin; gold mining.

Tse-p'u, China: see POSGAM.

Tser, Yugoslavia: see CER.

Tserpista, Greece: see TERPNI.

Tservenka, Yugoslavia: see CRVENKA.

Tsesarevich Aleksei Island, Russian SFSR: see MALY TAIMYR ISLAND.

Tsesis, Latvia: see CESIS.

Tsetame, India: see CHUNTANG.

Tsetinye, Yugoslavia: see CETINJE.

Tsetsen Khan, Mongolia: see UNDUR KHAN.

Tsetserlik or **Tsetserlig** (tsĕ'tsĕrlĕkh), town (pop. over 2,000), ⊙ North Khangai aimak, central Mongolian People's Republic, on highway and 250 mi. W of Ulan Bator, in NE Khangai Mts. Formerly seat of a monastery.

Tsévié (tsĕ'vyā), village, S Fr. Togoland, on railroad and 20 mi. N of Lomé; agr. trade; cacao, palm oil and kernels, cotton. R.C. and Protestant missions.

Tsfat, Israel: see SAFAD.

Tshala (chä'lä), village, Kasai prov., S Belgian Congo, on Lubilash R. and 75 mi. SSW of Kabinda; 2 large hydroelectric power plants supply energy to diamond fields of Bushimaie R.

Tshaninagongo, E central Africa: see NYIRAGONGO.

Tshela (chĕ'lä), village, Leopoldville prov., W Belgian Congo, near the Cabinda border, 55 mi. N of Boma; rail terminus and center of trade with Cabinda and Fr. Equatorial Africa. Also agr. center with palm mills, rubber and cacao plantations. Large hosp.

Tshibinda or **Tshibinda-Mulungu** (chēbēn'dä-mōōlōōng'gōō), village, Kivu prov., E Belgian Congo, 17 mi. NNW of Costermansville; center of agr. research, with coffee, tea, cinchona, aleurite, and aromatic-plant plantations. Sometimes called Mulungu or Mulungu-Tshibinda.

Tshikapa (chēkä'pä), village (1948 pop. 5,440), Kasai prov., S Belgian Congo, on right bank of Kasai R. opposite mouth of the Tshikapa (Chicapa) and 200 mi. SW of Lusambo; leading center of diamond-mining operations, employing c.14,000 workers. Gravels of the rivers are worked. First diamond was discovered in vicinity in 1907. Steamboat landing; airport. Has large hospitals for Europeans and natives, trade schools. Protestant mission.

Tshikapa River, Angola and Belgian Congo: see CHICAPA RIVER.

Tshilenge (chēlĕng'gä), village, Kasai prov., S Belgian Congo, on Lubilash R. and 45 mi. W of Kabinda; center of Baluba tribe; cotton growing.

Tshilongo (chēlông'gō), village, Katanga prov., SE Belgian Congo, on railroad and 55 mi. NW of Jadotville, in cattle-raising region.

Tshimbamba (chēmbäm'bä), village, Leopoldville prov., W Belgian Congo, on N side of the mouth of Congo R. (Angola border) and 25 mi. WSW of Boma; center of native trade; palm-oil milling.

Tshimbane (chēmbä'nā), village, Leopoldville prov., W Belgian Congo, on left bank of Kwilu R. and 140 mi. SSE of Inongo; palm-oil milling, sawmilling, cattle raising.

Tshofa (chō'fä), village, Kasai prov., central Belgian Congo, on Lomami R. and 80 mi. NE of Kabinda; cotton ginning.

Tshuapa, district, Belgian Congo: see BOENDE.

Tsi (tsē), village, Eastern Prov., NE Belgian Congo 28 mi. NNE of Kilo-Mines; gold mining, gold processing.

Tsian or **Chi-an** (both: jē'än'), town, ⊙ Tsian co. (pop. 123,371), S Liaotung prov., Manchuria, on right bank of Yalu R. (Korea border), opposite Manpojin, and 40 mi. SSE of Tunghwa, on railroad; gold and copper mining. Formerly called Tungkow.

Tsianglo or **Chiang-lo** (both: jyäng'lŭ'), town (pop. 6,099), ⊙ Tsianglo co. (pop. 71,594), NW Fukien prov., China, 45 mi. WNW of Nanping and on tributary of Min R.; rice, sweet potatoes, rapeseed.

Tsiaoki or **Chiao-ch'i** (both: jyou'chē'), Jap. *Shokei* (shō'kā), town (1935 pop. 1,466), N Formosa, near E coast, 5 mi. N of Ilan and on railroad; health resort (hot springs); rice milling, brick and tile mfg., hat- and ropemaking. Agr.: rice, soybeans, fruit, livestock.

Tsiaotso or **Chiao-tso** (both: chyou'dzô'), town, SW Pingyuan prov., China, on railroad and 30 mi. WSW of Sinsiang; coal-mining center.

Tsibritsa River (tsĭbrē'tsä), NW Bulgaria, rises WNW of Mikhailovgrad in outlier of W Balkan Mts., flows 52 mi. NE, past Valchedrama, to the Danube at Dolni Tsibar. Also called Tsibar R.

Tsienan or **Ch'ien-an** (both: chyĕn'än'), town, ⊙ Tsienan co. (pop. 480,248), NE Hopeh prov., China, 40 mi. NE of Tangshan, and on Lwan R., near Great Wall (Jehol line); kaoliang, millet.

Tsienkiang or **Ch'ien-chiang** (both: chyĕn'jyäng'). **1** Town (pop. 21,732), ⊙ Tsienkiang co. (pop. 254,077), S central Hupeh prov., China, 40 mi. E of Kiangling and on Han R.; cotton and silk weaving; millet, wheat, rice, medicinal herbs. **2** Town, Kwangsi prov., China: see TSINKONG.

Tsienshan or **Ch'ien-shan** (both: chyĕn'shän'), town, ⊙ Tsienshan co. (pop. 265,319), N Anhwei prov., China, 25 mi. WNW of Anking, SE of Tapieh Mts.; rice, wheat, tea, lacquer, tung oil; vegetable-tallow processing (soap, candles), papermaking.

Tsientang River or **Chientang River** (both: jyĕn'däng'), Chinese *Tsientang Kiang* or *Ch'ien-t'ang Chiang* (both: jyäng), Chekiang prov., China, rises in 2 main branches (main W branch flows past Chühsien and lesser E branch past Kinhwa) which join at Lanchi, flows NNE, past Kienteh (where it receives Sinan R. from Anhwei), Tunglu, and Fuyang, and into HANGCHOW BAY below Hangchow. Total length, including main W headstream, 285 mi. Navigable below Kienteh for small vessels. Also called Fuchun in lower course.

Tsiho or **Ch'i-ho** (both: chē'hŭ'), town, ⊙ Tsiho co. (pop. 288,486), NW Shantung prov., China, 13 mi. WNW of Tsinan and on Yellow R.; jujubes, millet, peanuts, medicinal herbs.

Tsihombe, Madagascar: see TSIOMBE.

Tsiki, China: see CHIKI.

Tsikiotsing, China: see CHIKURTING.

Tsilma River or **Tsil'ma River** (both: tsē'lyŭmŭ), in N Komi Autonomous SSR, Russian SFSR, rises in Timan Ridge, flows c.125 mi. N and E to Pechora R. at Ust-Tsilma.

Tsimei or **Chi-mei** (both: jē'mā'), town, SE Fukien prov., China, 8 mi. N of Amoy, on inlet of Formosa Strait; site of Tsimei acad.

Tsimlyanskaya (tsēmlyän'skīŭ), village (1926 pop. 3,112), E Rostov oblast, Russian SFSR, on right bank of Don R. and 95 mi. E of Shakhty; flour milling, food processing; wheat, cotton, vineyards. In 1930s, also spelled Tsymlyanskaya.

Tsimo or **Chi-mo** (both: jē'mŭ'), town, ⊙ Tsimo co. (pop. 719,643), E Shantung prov., China, 25 mi. NNE of Tsingtao; grain, peanuts, grapes, poultry.

Tsimova, Greece: see AREOPOLIS.

Tsimpsean Peninsula (sĭmp-shēăn'), W B.C., in Prince Rupert region, extends 36 mi. NW into Chatham Sound from mouth of Skeena R. to mouth of Portland Inlet, separated from mainland by Work Channel (30 mi. long, 1 mi. wide); 12 mi. wide at base. Off W coast are Digby, Kaien (on which is Prince Rupert), and Smith isls. Rises to 3,350 ft. Port Simpson village is in N. Sometimes spelled Tsimshian Peninsula.

Tsin. 1 Province, China: see SHANSI. **2** or **Ts'in,** province, China: see SHENSI.

Tsin, river, China: see TSIN RIVER.

Tsinan. 1 or **Ch'in-an** (both: chĭn'än'), town, ⊙ Tsinan co. (pop. 225,564), SE Kansu prov., China, 20 mi. NW of Tienshui; tobacco processing, cotton and ramie weaving; wheat, rice, beans. **2** or **Chinan** (both: jē'nän'), city (1946 pop. 591,490; 1947 pop. 574,781), ⊙ Shantung prov., E China, near Yellow R., 220 mi. S of Peking; 36°41'N 117°E. Junction (railroad shops) of Tientsin-Pukow RR and of railroad to Tsingtao; industrial center; flour and oilseed milling, cotton weaving; mfg. of flour and egg products, matches, cement, ceramics, paper. It is connected by navigable canal and Siaoching R. with Gulf of Chihli, S of Yellow R. delta. Traditionally known for its silk goods and imitation precious stones. Seat of Cheloo univ. City consists of old walled town (E) with scenic Taming L., and modern commercial suburb (W) extending to Yellow R. bank suburb of Lokow (N). An anc. city dating from 6th cent. A.D., it flourished after 11th cent., and became ⊙ Shantung under the Ming dynasty. It was opened to foreign trade in 1906, and linked by railroad with Tsingtao. Occupied 1928 and 1937–45 by Japanese. Passed 1948 to Communist control. An independent municipality since 1930, it was ⊙ Licheng co. until transfer (1935) of co. seat to Wangshejenchwang, thereafter called LICHENG.

Tsinandali or **Tsinondali** (tsĭnŭndä'lyē), village (1939 pop. over 500), E Georgian SSR, in Kakhetia, on railroad and 6 mi. ESE of Telavi; major winemaking center.

Tsincheng or **Chin-ch'eng** (both: jĭn'chŭng'), town, ⊙ Tsincheng co. (pop. 298,019), SE Shansi prov., China, 45 mi. S of Changchih, near S end of Taihang Mts., in agr. area (rice, wheat); one of the earliest ironworking centers of China, near coal and iron mines. Called Tsechow until 1912.

Tsinchow. 1 Town, Hopeh prov., China: see TSINHSIEN. **2** Town, Kansu prov., China: see TIENSHUI. **3** Town, Shansi prov., China: see TSINHSIEN.

Tsingan or **Ching-an**, China (both: jĭng'än'). **1** Town, Heilungkiang prov., Manchuria, China: see TAOAN. **2** Town (pop. 6,222), ⊙ Tsingan co. (pop. 48,905), NW Kiangsi prov., China, 27 mi. NW of Nanchang rice, hemp.

Tsingchen or **Ch'ing-chen** (both: chĭng'jŭn'), town (pop. 10,166), ⊙ Tsingchen co. (pop. 110,841), central Kweichow prov., China, 15 mi. W of Kweiyang and on main road to Yunnan; alt. 4,085 ft.; tobacco processing; rice, wheat, millet, kaoliang, fruit. Iron mines, bauxite deposits near by.

Tsingcheng, China: see KAOTSING.

Tsingchengchen, China: see NANTSING.

Tsingchow. 1 Town, Hunan prov., China: see TSINGHSIEN. **2** Town, Shantung prov., China: see YITU.

Tsingchwan or **Ch'ing-ch'uan** (both: chĭng'chwän'), town (pop. 9,203), ⊙ Tsingchwan co. (pop. 55,066), NW Szechwan prov., China, 20 mi. E of Pingwu, near Kansu line; tobacco, indigo, rice, wheat.

Tsingelion (tsĭng-gĕ'lēōn), SW mountain spur of Alibotush Mts., in Gr. Macedonia, E of Struma R. near Bulg. line; rises to 4,246 ft. 18 mi. NNW of Serrai. Sometimes called Angistron.

Tsingfeng or **Ch'ing-feng** (both: chĭng'fŭng'), town, ⊙ Tsingfeng co. (pop. 340,678), N Pingyuan prov., China, on main road and 45 mi. ESE of Anyang; wheat, millet, kaoliang, beans. Until 1949 in Hopeh prov.

Tsinghai, Chinghai, or **Ch'ing-hai** (all: chĭng'hī'), or **Koko Nor** (kōkō nōr') [all mean "blue sea"], province (□ 250,000; pop. 1,200,000) of NW China; ⊙ Sining. Bounded E and NE by Kansu, NW by Sinkiang, SW by Tibet, S by Sikang, and SE by Szechwan, Tsinghai is largely a high, barren plateau forming the NE part of the Tibetan highlands (average alt. 10,000 ft.). It lies in the E section of the Kunlun mtn. system and contains its outliers, notably the Nan Shan, the Amne Machin, and Bayan Kara Mts. Bet. these lofty ranges are (N) the Tsaidam, salt-marsh depression (frozen 8 months of the year) and the lake Koko Nor (Tsing Hai), for which the prov. is named. In the precipitous mtn. gorges of the south rise some of Asia's greatest streams, the Yellow, Yangtze, and Mekong rivers, whose upper reaches are within tens of miles of each other. Mineral resources (gold; coal at Weiyüan; silver, lead, zinc, gypsum) are hardly exploited. The chief economic area and the most thickly settled part is the Sining R. valley (in extreme NE), adjoining Kansu prov., of which it was a part until 1928. Here grain (corn, millet, sorghum), rhubarb, and potatoes are grown. Elsewhere, nomadic grazing is the main occupation, and the chief exports are wool and hides. Pop. is Moslem Chinese in extreme NE (Sining area) and speaks N Mandarin Chinese dialect; it is West Mongolian in Tsaidam, and Tibetan in S. The noted KUMBUM lamasery is at Hwangchung. Tsinghai prov. is crossed by caravan routes leading from Lanchow via Sining to Jyekundo and Chamdo (S) and to Lhasa (SW), and by a lesser route to Sinkiang (W). Historically the Amdo section of Tibet, the region came (early-16th cent.) under the rule of the Southern Mongols. Under Chinese (Manchu) domination after 1724, it was administered as a dependency from Sining (Kansu prov.). In 1928, the Sining area was detached from Kansu and Tsinghai became a prov. of China.

Tsinghai or **Ching-hai** (both: jĭng'hī'), town, ⊙ Tsinghai co. (pop. 212,620), E central Hopeh prov., China, 20 mi. SW of Tientsin, and on Tientsin-Pukow RR and Grand Canal; wheat, kaoliang, millet.

Tsing Hai, lake, China: see KOKO NOR.

Tsingho. 1 or **Ch'ing-ho** (both: chĭng'hŭ'), town, ⊙ Tsingho co. (pop. 173,218), SW Hopeh prov., China, 45 mi. SW of Tehchow; cotton, corn, beans, kaoliang. **2** or **Ching-ho** (jĭng'hŭ'), town, ⊙ Tsingho co. (pop. 11,810), N Sinkiang prov., China, on highway N of the Tien Shan, near L. Ebi Nor, 90 mi. NE of Kashgar; salt-producing center; magnesium salts. **3** or **Ch'ing-ho** (chĭng'hŭ'), town, ⊙ Tsingho co. (pop. 5,164), NE Sinkiang prov., China, in the Altai Mts., on Mongolian border, 200 mi. NNE of Kitai.

Tsingho Bank, China: see TIZARD BANK.

Tsinghsien. 1 or **Ch'ing-hsien** (both: chĭng'shyĕn'), town, ⊙ Tsinghsien co. (pop. 267,647), E Hopeh prov., China, 45 mi. SW of Tientsin and on Tientsin-Pukow RR; winegrowing; cotton, wheat, millet. **2** or **Ching-hsien** (jĭng'shyĕn'), town, ⊙ Tsinghsien co. (pop. 80,276), SW Hunan prov., China, near Kweichow line, 50 mi. S of Chihkiang; timber. tea, hemp, rice. Gold mining. Until 1913 called Tsingchow.

Tsinghwa or **Ching-hua** (both: jĭng'hwä'). **1** Town, Pingyuan prov., China: see POAI. **2** Town (pop. 783), ⊙ Tsinghwa co. (pop. 11,503), NW Szechwan prov., China, 90 mi. N of Kangting, near Sikang border, in mtn. region; gold placers.

Tsingkang or **Ch'ing-kang** (both: chĭng'gäng'), town, ⊙ Tsingkang co. (pop. 223,130), S Heilungkiang prov., Manchuria, 60 mi. NNW of Harbin; soybeans, kaoliang, rye, millet, corn. Formerly called Tsoshukang.

Tsingki, China: see HANYÜAN.

Tsingkiang. 1 or **Ch'ing-chiang** (both: chĭng'jyäng'), town (pop. 22,567), ⊙ Tsingkiang co. (pop. 164,064), N central Kiangsi prov., China, on railroad and 55 mi. SW of Nanchang, on Yüan R. near Kan R. confluence; commercial center; cotton, rice, oranges. Until 1912 called Linkiang. **2** or **Ching-chiang** (both: jĭng'jyäng'), town (pop. 28,530), ⊙ Tsingkiang co. (pop. 381,615), S Kiangsu prov., China, 50 mi. ESE of Chinkiang, across Yangtze R.; cotton spinning and weaving; rice, wheat, beans. **3** or **Ch'ing-chiang** (chĭng'jyäng'), town, Kweichow prov., China: see KIENHO. **4** or **Ching-chiang** (jĭng'jyäng'), town, Yunnan prov., China: see SUIKIANG.

Tsingkiangpu, China: see HWAIYIN.

Tsingkien or **Ch'ing-chien** (both: chĭng'jyĕn'), town, ⊙ Tsingkien co. (pop. 89,049), NE Shensi prov., China, 45 mi. NE of Yenan, in mtn. region; millet, wheat, kaoliang, melons.

Tsingkow or **Ch'ing-k'ou** (both: chĭng'kō'), town, SW Shantung prov., China, 20 mi. NW of Lienyün, on Yellow Sea; once an active port, it has been superseded by modern Lienyün.

Tsingling Mountains, China: see TSINLING MOUNTAINS.

Tsingliu or **Ch'ing-liu** (both: chĭng'lyō'), town (pop. 2,412), ⊙ Tsingliu co. (pop. 55,287), W Fukien prov., China, 45 mi. NE of Changting and on Sha R. (tributary of Min R.); rice, sugar cane, beans. Coal mining near by.

Tsinglo or **Ching-lo** (both: jĭng'lô'), town, ⊙ Tsinglo co. (pop. 103,759), N Shansi prov., China, 50 mi. NW of Taiyüan; millet, wheat, beans, kaoliang.

Tsinglung or **Ch'ing-lung** (both: chĭng'lŏŏng'). **1** Town (pop. 9,151), ⊙ Tsinglung co. (pop. 56,511), SW Kweichow prov., China, 50 mi SW of Anshun and on main road to Yunnan; alt. 1,607 ft.; grain. Formerly Annan. **2** Town, ⊙ Tsinglung co. (pop. 216,539), SE Jehol prov., Manchuria, China, 65 mi. NE of Tangshan, beyond Great Wall; kaoliang, millet, corn. Originally called Tachangtze, it was later (1933–49) called Tushan. Town was in Hopeh prov. until 1949.

Tsingmai (chĭng'mī', Cantonese chĭng'män'), Mandarin *Ch'eng-mai* (chŭng'mī'), town, ⊙ Tsingmai co. (pop. 152,680), N Hainan, Kwangtung prov., China, on branch of Nantu R. and 30 mi. SW of Kiungshan; betel nuts, sesame, sugar cane, rice, duck eggs; oil extracting. The name Tsingmai formerly applied to town (now called Old Tsingmai) 20 mi. NE, on coast. Present Tsingmai was called Kimkang or Kamkong until made co. seat.

Tsingning or **Ching-ning** (both: jĭng'nĭng'), town, ⊙ Tsingning co. (pop. 139,684), SE Kansu prov., China, 70 mi. N of Tienshui; match mfg., tobacco processing, wheat.

Tsingpien or **Ching-pien** (both: jĭng'byĕn'). **1** Town, ⊙ Tsingpien co. (pop. 9,589), NW Shensi prov., China, 70 mi. NW of Yenan, at Great Wall (Suiyuan line); rice, wheat, peanuts. **2** Town, Yunnan prov., China: see PINGPIEN.

Tsingping or **Ch'ing-p'ing** (both: chĭng'pĭng'). **1** Town, ⊙ Tsingping co., SE Jehol prov., Manchuria, China, 100 mi. E of Chengteh; agr. products. Called Mangniuyingtze until 1947, and Lingnan, 1947–49. **2** Town, Kweichow prov., China. see LUSHAN. **3** Town, ⊙ Tsingping co. (pop. 161,758), northeasternmost Pingyuan prov., China, 50 mi. W of Tsinan; cotton weaving; peanuts, melons. Until 1949 in Shantung prov.

Tsingpu or **Ch'ing-p'u** (both: chĭng'pōō'), town (1935 pop. 95,617), ⊙ Tsingpu co. (1946 pop. 270,832), S Kiangsu prov., China, 23 mi. WSW of Shanghai; oil pressing; rice, wheat, beans. Lake fisheries near by.

Tsingshen or **Ch'ing-shen** (both: chĭng'shŭn'), town (pop. 6,729), ⊙ Tsingshen co. (pop. 116,149), W Szechwan, China, 20 mi. NNE of Loshan and on right bank of Min R.; tea and tobacco processing; rice, sugar cane, wheat, beans.

Tsingshih or **Ching-shih** (both: jĭng'shû'), town, N Hunan prov., China, port on Li R. and 7 mi. E of Lihsien; commercial center of Li R. valley; exports hemp, tung oil, tea oil.

Tsingshui or **Ch'ing-shui** (both: chĭng'shwā'), town, ⊙ Tsingshui co. (pop. 106,399), SE Kansu prov., China, 20 mi. NE of Tienshui; tobacco processing; wheat, rice, beans.

Tsingshui, Chingshui, or **Ch'ing-shui** (all: chĭng'shwā'), Jap. *Kiyomizu* (kēyō'mēzōō), town (1935 pop. 8,445), W central Formosa, near W coast, 11 mi. NW of Taichung, and on railroad; home industry (hatmaking; pottery, wood products); rice, livestock; fishing.

Tsingshuiho or **Ch'ing-shui-ho** (both: chĭng'shwā'hŭ'), town (pop. 7,065), ⊙ Tsingshuiho co. (pop. 27,969), E Suiyuan prov., China, near Shansi line, 60 mi. S of Kweisui, at Great Wall, near Yellow R.; cattle raising; grain, licorice.

Tsingsi or **Ching-hsi** (both: jĭng'shē'), town, ⊙ Tsingsi co. (pop. 244,558), SW Kwangsi prov., China, 50 mi. S of Poseh, near Vietnam line; rice, wheat, millet, corn. Antimony deposits near by. Until 1913 called Kweishun.

Tsingsing or **Ching-hsing** (both: jĭng'shĭng'), town, ⊙ Tsingsing co. (pop. 201,552), SW Hopeh prov., China, near Shansi line, 25 mi. W of Shihkiachwang, on rail spur; major coal-mining center.

Tsingtao or **Ch'ing-tao** (both: tsĭng'tou', chĭng'dou'), city (1946 pop. 759,057; 1947 pop. 787,722), E Shantung prov., China, Yellow Sea port at entrance of Kiaochow Bay, 190 mi. ESE of Tsinan, 260 mi. SE of Peking; 36°4'N 120°19'E. Head of railroad to Tsinan (railroad shops); industrial and shipping center; mfg. of cotton and silk goods, leather, machinery, soap, cement, acids, matches, egg products; flour and oilseed milling. One of China's leading Yellow Sea ports and a naval base, Tsingtao has a sheltered deepwater harbor on Kiaochow Bay, equipped with modern loading facilities. Airport at Tsangkow (N). Seat of Shantung univ. Popular climatic and beach resort. Until late-19th cent. a fishing village, it was fortified in 1891 and passed in 1898 to Germany as part of the Kiaochow lease. Under Ger. rule, Tsingtao developed rapidly as a modern city. It was captured by Japanese in 1914 and remained under Jap. rule until its return to China in 1922. During Sino-Japanese War, city was held (1938–45) by the Japanese and later was a U.S. naval base until invested (1949) by the Communists. It became an independent municipality in 1929.

Tsingteh or **Ching-te** (both: jĭng'dŭ'), town, ⊙ Tsingteh co. (pop. 63,141), S Anhwei prov., China, 45 mi. SSW of Süancheng, in Hwang Mts.; rice, wheat, corn, silk.

Tsingtien or **Ch'ing-t'ien** (both: chĭng'tyĕn'), town (pop. 6,612), ⊙ Tsingtien co. (pop. 255,753), S Chekiang prov., China, 24 mi. WNW of Wenchow and on Wu R. (head of launch navigation); soapstone quarries; tung oil, tea, fruit, rice.

Tsingyang or **Ch'ing-yang** (both: chĭng'yäng'), town, ⊙ Tsingyang co. (pop. 113,677), S Anhwei prov , China, 45 mi. ENE of Anking; rice, tung oil, silk.

Tsingyü or **Ching-yü** (both: jĭng'yü'), town, ⊙ Tsingyü co. (pop. 22,583), NE Liaotung prov., Manchuria, 50 mi. ESE of Hailung; soybeans, kaoliang. Called Mengkiang until 1949.

Tsingyüan. 1 or **Ch'ing-yüan** (chĭng'yüan'), city, Hopeh prov., China: see PAOTING. **2** or **Ching-yüan** (jĭng'yüăn'), town, ⊙ Tsingyüan co. (pop. 76,425), SE Kansu prov., China, 55 mi. NE of Lanchow and on Yellow R.; tobacco processing; wheat. Coal mines, saltworks. **3** or **Ch'ing-yüan** (chĭng'yüăn'), town, ⊙ Tsingyüan co. (pop. 130,160), N central Liaotung prov., Manchuria, China, 80 mi. ENE of Mukden and on railroad; gold mining; wheat, beans, kaoliang, millet. Until 1929 called Pakiachen. **4** or **Ch'ing-yüan** (chĭng'yüăn'), town, ⊙ Tsingyüan co. (pop. 78,520), central Shansi prov., China, 20 mi. SW of Taiyüan; beans, kaoliang, wheat. **5** (jĭng'yüăn') or **Ching-yen** (jĭng'yĕn'), town (pop. 15,492), ⊙ Tsingyüan co. (pop. 169,752), SW Szechwan prov., China, 20 mi. NE of Loshan; rice, sweet potatoes, millet, wheat, beans. Saltworks near by.

Tsingyün (chĭng'yün'), Mandarin *Ch'ing-yüan* (chĭng'yüăn'), town (pop. 20,265), ⊙ Tsingyün co. (pop. 557,563), central Kwangtung prov., China, on North R. and 45 mi. NNW of Canton; sericulture; exports silkworm eggs.

Tsinhsien. 1 or **Chin-hsien** (jĭn'shyĕn'), town, ⊙ Tsinhsien co. (pop. 196,976), SW Hopeh prov., China, 30 mi. E of Shihkiachwang and on railroad; cotton, wheat, beans, kaoliang. Until 1913 called Tsinchow. **2** or **Ch'in-hsien** (chĭn'shyĕn'), town, ⊙ Tsinhsien co. (pop. 116,329), SE Shansi prov., China, on railroad and 45 mi. NNW of Changchih; cotton weaving, tanning; winegrowing; rice, wheat cattle. Until 1912 called Tsinchow.

Tsining or **Chi-ning** (both: jē'nĭng'). **1** City (1936 pop. estimate 150,000), W Shantung prov., China, on rail spur and 16 mi. SW of Tzeyang, and on Grand Canal, near Pingyuan line; industrial center; iron- and copperworks; cotton weaving, match mfg. Trades in wheat, beans, kaoliang. **2** Town (pop. 18,886), ⊙ Tsining co. (pop. 100,901), E Suiyuan prov., China, 75 mi. E of Kweisui and on railroad; road hub and commercial center; cattle raising; oats, wheat. Saltworks and coal mines near by. Called Pingtichüan until 1922. Was in Shansi until 1914, and in Chahar, 1914–28. Near by are the hq. of the right wing of the Mongolian Chahar league. **3** Town, ⊙ Tsining co., SE Sungkiang prov., Manchuria, on Muling R. and 85 mi. NE of Mutankiang; rail junction.

Tsinkiang or **Chin-chiang** (both: jĭn'jyäng'), town (pop. 120,655), ⊙ Tsinkiang co. (pop. 591,677), SE Fukien prov., China, 45 mi. NE of Amoy, on inlet of Formosa Strait; major commercial center; rice, wheat, sugar cane, sweet potatoes. Dating from the T'ang dynasty (A.D. 618–906), it has been identified with Zaiton (Zaitun or Zayton), whence Marco Polo embarked on his return voyage. One of leading ports on Fukien coast until closed by sandbanks and supplanted (19th cent.) by Amoy.

Its maritime trade now passes through the port of ANHAI, 20 mi. SSW. Tsinkiang was called Chüanchow until 1913.

Tsinkong (tsĕn'gông'), Mandarin *Tsienkiang* or *Ch'ien-chiang* (both: chyĕn'jyäng'), town, ⊙ Tsinkong co. (pop. 114, 326), central Kwangsi prov., China, on Hungshui R. and 50 mi. SSW of Liuchow, and on road to Nanning; cotton textiles; rice, wheat, peanuts. Coal mines, bauxite near by.

Tsinling Mountains (chĭn'lĭng'), Chinese *Ch'in-ling Shan* (chĭn'lĭng' shän'), E outlier of the Kunlun system in S Shensi prov., China, bet. Wei (N) and Han (S) rivers; range rises to over 12,000 ft. in the Taipai Shan, 75 mi. WSW of Sian. A major natural obstacle, the Tsinling system is precipitous on N (Wei R.) side and has a gradual S slope. It is a climatic barrier and separates the N loess lands from the S forest soils. Historically, it has checked the advance of the Mongols and has separated (19th cent.) the Moslem and Taiping rebellion areas. Sometimes erroneously spelled Tsingling.

Tsinondali, Georgian SSR: see TSINANDALI.

Tsin River or **Chin River**, Chinese *Tsin Shui* or *Ch'in Shui* (both: chĭn' shwā'), in SE Shansi and W Pingyuan provs., China, rises in Taiyo Mts., flows c.200 mi. SSE, past Chinyüan, Tsinyang, and Wuchih, to Yellow R. on Honan line.

Tsinshui or **Ch'in-shui** (both: chĭn'shwā'), town, ⊙ Tsinshui co. (pop. 116,373), S Shansi prov., China, 55 mi. SW of Changchih; millet, kaoliang, beans. Coal mining near by.

Tsin Shui, river, China: see TSIN RIVER.

Tsinsien or **Chin-hsien** (both: jĭn'shyĕn'), town (pop. 5,095), ⊙ Tsinsien co. (pop. 168,754), N central Kiangsi prov., China, on S shore of Poyang L., on Chekiang-Kiangsi RR and 30 mi. SE of Nanchang; rice, cotton, wheat, millet. Coal mining.

Tsintsar or **Tsintser**, mountain, Yugoslavia: see CINCAR.

Tsinyang or **Ch'in-yang** (both: chĭn'yäng'), town, ⊙ Tsinyang co. (pop. 315,285), SW Pingyuan prov., China, on Tsin R. and 50 mi. WSW of Sinsiang; rail terminus; center for production of medicinal herbs (*tihwang*). An anc. city, dating from 5th cent. A.D., it has been largely superseded by modern commercial town of Poai. Called Hwaiking until 1913, it was in Honan prov. prior to 1949.

Tsinyün or **Chin-yün** (both: jĭn'yün'), town (pop. 4,632), ⊙ Tsinyün co. (pop. 199,260), S central Chekiang prov., China, 40 mi. SE of Kinhwa; mfg. of paper; tung oil, timber, rice, wheat.

Tsiombe (tsēyōōmb') or **Tsihombe** (tsēhōōm'bā), village, Tuléar prov., S Madagascar, near S coast, 95 mi. WSW of Fort-Dauphin; mica mining; cattle raising. R.C. and Protestant missions.

Tsipa River (tsĕ'pŭ), NE Buryat-Mongol Autonomous SSR, Russian SFSR, rises on Vitim Plateau, flows 268 mi. generally NE, past Tsipikan, to Vitim R. below Kalakan.

Tsipiana, Greece: see NESTANE.

Tsipikan (tsĭpĕkän'), town (1939 pop. over 2,000), N Buryat-Mongol Autonomous SSR, Russian SFSR, on Tsipa R. and 315 mi. NE of Ulan-Ude; center of Vitim Plateau gold-mining dist.

Tsipori or **Tzippori** (both: tsēpōrē'), agr. settlement, Lower Galilee, N Israel, 4 mi. NNW of Nazareth. Founded 1949 on site of village of Saffuriya (säfōōrē'yä), abandoned (1948) by Arab pop. In Roman times site of important town of *Diocaesaria* or *Sepphoris;* later for some time seat of the Sanhedrin. Called Sephorie during Crusades, it was held by Knights Templars and was army assembly center. Ruins of 12th-cent. church extant.

Tsipya or **Tsip'ya** (tsēpyä'), village (1939 pop. over 500), NW Tatar Autonomous SSR, Russian SFSR, 15 mi. W of Malmyzh; grain, livestock.

Tsiribihina River (tsērēbēhē'nŭ), W Madagascar, formed by several large headstreams c.10 mi. SW of Miandrivazo, meanders W past Belo-sur-Tsiribihina to Mozambique Channel; total length, including Mania headstream, c.325 mi. Navigable for ships below Serinam (30 mi.) and for shallow-draught boats for 130 mi. below Miandrivazo. Rice grown in its valley.

Tsiroanomandidy (tsērwänōōmändē'dē), town, Tananarive prov., W central Madagascar, 95 mi. W of Tananarive; climatic resort and native market (cattle, coffee, pulse).

Tsishan or **Chi-shan** (both: jē'shän'), town, ⊙ Tsishan co. (pop. 110,984), SW Shansi prov., China, on Fen R. and 45 mi. SW of Linfen; rice, wheat, cotton, millet, fruit.

Tsisia or **Ch'i-hsia** (both: chē'shyä'), town, ⊙ Tsisia co. (pop. 332,600), E Shantung prov., China, 35 mi. SW of Chefoo; silk weaving; peanuts, grain.

Tsiteli-Tskaro (tsētyĕ'lyē-tskŭrô'), town (1939 pop. over 2,000), SE Georgian SSR, on Shiraki Steppe, 70 mi. ESE of Tiflis, in livestock zone; metalworks; grain, sunflowers. Mirzaani oil field is SE.

Tsitsi or **Chi-chi** (both: jē'jē'), Jap. *Shushu* (shōō'shōō), town (1935 pop. 2,550), W central Formosa, on Choshui R. and 22 mi. SSE of Taichung city, on railroad; rice milling, pottery mfg.; bananas, rice, sugar cane, fruit.

Tsitsihar (tsē'tsē'här', chē'chē'här'), Chinese *Ch'i-ch'i-ha-erh* (chē'chē'här'), city (1947 pop. 174,675), ⊙ Heilungkiang prov., Manchuria, and ⊙ but independent of Lungkiang co. (1947 pop. 278,846), port on Nonni R. (head of navigation), on branch of Chinese Eastern RR, and 170 mi. NW of Harbin; 47°22'N 123°57'E. Major administrative and trade center; 2d-largest city of N Manchuria (after Harbin); flour and soybean milling, tobacco processing, distilling, match mfg.; chemical and auto assembly plants. Arsenal, army barracks. With its near-by railroad stations of ANGANGKI and FULARKI, it is the transportation center of the Nonni valley. Founded 1691 as a Chinese fortress among Mongol nomadic tribes, it developed largely in spread-out Mongolian pattern around the small, walled Chinese inner city. The industrial and railroad settlement developed in E outskirts. Tsitsihar was an early ⊙ Heilungkiang prov., became in Manchukuo the ⊙ Lungkiang prov. (1934–46), and was later ⊙ Nunkiang prov. (1946–49). It was officially called Lungkiang from 1913 until it became an independent municipality in 1947. City's former Chinese name was Pukwei.

Tsitung or **Ch'i-tung** (both: chē'dōōng), town, ⊙ Tsitung co. (pop. 131,266), NW Shantung prov., China, 40 mi. NE of Tsinan, near Yellow R.; cotton weaving; peanuts, wheat, millet.

Tsivil or **Tsivil'** (tsēvēl'), name of 2 rivers in Chuvash Autonomous SSR, Russian SFSR. **Greater Tsivil River**, Rus. *Bolshoi Tsivil*, rises N of Shumerlya, flows c.90 mi. NE, past Kalinino and Tsivilsk, to the Volga 5 mi. W of Mariinski Posad. Receives **Lesser Tsivil River**, Rus. *Maly Tsivil* (right; 50 mi. long), at Tsivilsk.

Tsivilsk or **Tsivil'sk** (tsēvēlsk'), city (1931 pop. 2,999), NE central Chuvash Autonomous SSR, Russian SFSR, on Greater Tsivil R., at mouth of the Lesser Tsivil, and 21 mi. SSE of Cheboksary, in wheat area; agr. center; flour milling, starch mfg. Founded 1584.

Tsivory (tsēvōō'rē), village, Tuléar prov., S Madagascar, 85 mi. NW of Fort-Dauphin; mica mining. Protestant mission.

Tsiyang or **Chi-yang** (both: jē'yäng'), town, ⊙ Tsiyang co. (pop. 284,891), N Shantung prov., China, on Yellow R. and 25 mi. NNE of Tsinan; peanuts, jujubes, millet, kaoliang.

Tsiyüan or **Chi-yüan** (both: jē'yüän'), town, ⊙ Tsiyüan co. (pop. 334,018), southwesternmost Pingyuan prov., China, 70 mi. WSW of Sinsiang, near Shansi line; cotton weaving; millet, wheat, kaoliang, beans. Until 1949 in Honan prov.

Tskhaltubo (tsŭkhŭltōōbô'), town (1939 pop. over 500), W Georgian SSR, on rail spur and 8 mi. NW of Kutaisi; health resort (hot radioactive springs).

Tskhinval or **Tskhinvali**, Georgian SSR: see STALINIR.

Tsna River (tsnä), central European Russian SFSR, rises NW of Rzhaksa, flows 250 mi. N, past Kotovsk, Tambov (head of navigation; c.160 mi. above mouth), Morshansk, and Sasovo, to Moksha R. N of Sasovo. Formerly navigable only in spring; canalized to Tambov after Second World War. Carries lumber, vegetables, grain.

Tsnori (tsnô'rē), town (1939 pop. over 500), E Georgian SSR, in Kakhetia, 60 mi. E of Tiflis; rail terminus (Tsnoris-Tskhali station); vineyards, tobacco.

Tso, China: see LI RIVER, Kwangsi prov.

Tso Chiang, China: see LI RIVER, Kwangsi prov.

Tsochow, China: see TSOHSIEN.

Tsochüan or **Tso-ch'üan** (dzô'chüän'), town, ⊙ Tsochüan co. (pop. 71,396), E Shansi prov., China, near Hopeh line, 65 mi. SE of Taiyüan; medicinal herbs, indigo; cattle raising. Until 1912 called Liaochow; later, 1912–49, Liaohsien.

Tsofit or **Tzofit** (both: tsōfēt'), settlement (pop. 250), W Israel, in Plain of Sharon, 5 mi. ENE of Herzliya; citriculture, mixed farming. Founded 1933. Also spelled Zofit; sometimes called Tzofim.

Tsohsien (dzwô'shyĕn'), town, ⊙ Tsohsien co. (pop. 30,762), SW Kwangsi prov., China, 13 mi. N of Tsungshan; agr. products. Until 1912, Tsochow.

Tso Kiang, China: see LI RIVER, Kwangsi prov.

Tsomoling, Tibet: see LHASA.

Tsomo Tretung (tsō'mō trĕ'tōōng), lake (□ 40), S Tibet, 70 mi. SW of Shigatse; alt. 13,700 ft.

Tsona (tsō'nä), Chinese *Ch'u-na* (chōō'nä'), town [Tibetan *dzong*], S Tibet, in central Assam Himalayas, on India-Tibet trade route (via Bum La pass), and 125 mi. SSE of Lhasa.

Tso River, China: see LI RIVER, Kwangsi prov.

Tsoshui (dzô'shwā'), town (pop. 2,415), ⊙ Tsoshui co. (pop. 26,976), S Shensi prov., China, 40 mi. S of Sian, in Tsinling mtn. region; wheat, millet, beans, kaoliang. Until 1914, Siaoyi.

Tsoshukang, Manchuria: see TSINGKANG.

Tsouka, Mount, Albania-Greece: see MAKRYKAMBOS, MOUNT.

Tsoukalio Lagoon (tsōōkälēō') (□ 8.5), in Arta nome, S Epirus, Greece, 10 mi. SW of Arta, on N shore of Gulf of Arta; 5 mi. long, 2 mi. wide; fisheries.

Tsowhsien or **Tsou-hsien** (both: dzō'shyĕn'), town, ⊙ Tsowhsien co. (pop. 365,430), SW Shantung prov., China, 12 mi. SE of Tzeyang and on Tientsin-Pukow RR; ramie and silk weaving; kaoliang, peanuts, medicinal herbs. Birthplace of Chinese sage Mencius (372–289 B.C.).

Tsowping or **Tsou-p'ing** (both: dzō'pĭng'), town, ⊙ Tsowping co. (pop. 174,836), NW Shantung prov., China, 40 mi. ENE of Tsinan; straw plait; melons, peanuts, wheat.

Tsoying (dzô'yĭng'), Jap. *Saei* (sä'ā), town, S Formosa, on W coast, 3 mi. NNW of Kaohiung; naval station.

Tsrar Sharif (tsrär' shŭrēf') or **Charar Sharif** (chŭrär'), town (pop. 4,037), Baramula dist., W central Kashmir, 15 mi. S of Srinagar; rice, corn, wheat, oilseeds. Has mosque, tomb of Moslem saint.

Tsrmnitsa, region, Yugoslavia: see CRMNICA.

Tsrna; Tsrni [Serbo-Croatian, = black], in Yugoslav names: see CRNA; CRNI.

Tsrno Yezero, Yugoslavia: see DURMITOR.

Tsrnya, Yugoslavia: see CRNJA.

Tsrvan Mountains, Yugoslavia: see CRVANJ MOUNTAINS.

Tsu (tsōō), city (1940 pop. 68,625; 1947 pop. 68,662), ⊙ Mie prefecture, S Honshu, Japan, on W shore of Ise Bay, 35 mi. SW of Nagoya; commercial and mfg. center (cotton textiles, flour, wood products, soy sauce). Has feudal castle and several old temples. Bombed (1945) in Second World War. Sometimes spelled Tu.

Tsubaki (tsōōbä'kē), town (pop. 6,287), Tokushima prefecture, E Shikoku, Japan, on small peninsula in Kii Channel, 18 mi. SSE of Tokushima; camellia oil. Fishing.

Tsubame (tsōōbä'mā), town (pop. 19,983), Niigata prefecture, central Honshu, Japan, 3 mi. NW of Sanjo; makes copperware. Ski resort. Sometimes spelled Tubame.

Tsubata (tsōōbä'tä), town (pop. 4,330), Ishikawa prefecture, central Honshu, Japan, 9 mi. NE of Kanazawa, in rice-growing area; rail junction; silk textiles, mulberry wine.

Tsubetsu (tsōōbā'tsōō), town (pop. 12,784), E Hokkaido, Japan, 20 mi. SW of Abashiri; rice growing, lumbering.

Tsuchisawa, Japan: see TSUCHIZAWA.

Tsuchiura (tsōōchē'ōōrä), city (1940 pop. 31,000; 1947 pop. 53,298), Ibaraki prefecture, central Honshu, Japan, on W arm of lake Kasumi-ga-ura, 25 mi. SW of Mito, in rice-growing area; mfg. (silk yarn, soy sauce, woodwork). Includes (since early 1940s) former town of Manabe (1940 pop. 5,251). Sometimes spelled Tutiura.

Tsuchiyama (tsōōchē'yämŭ), town (pop. 4,518), Shiga prefecture, S Honshu, Japan, 20 mi. W of Yokkaichi, in agr. area (rice, wheat, tea); lumber, charcoal.

Tsuchizakiminato, Japan: see AKITA, city.

Tsuchizawa (tsōōchē'zäwŭ) or **Tsuchisawa** (-säwŭ), town (pop. 5,855), Iwate prefecture, N Honshu, Japan, 6 mi. E of Hanamaki; agr. (rice, soybeans), livestock; paper milling, weaving. Until early 1940s, called Junikabura.

Tsuda (tsōō'dä). **1** Town (pop. 2,751), Hiroshima prefecture, SW Honshu, Japan, 16 mi. W of Hiroshima; agr. center; sake, soy sauce. Horse breeding. **2** Town (pop. 7,739), Kagawa prefecture, N Shikoku, Japan, on Harima Sea, 12 mi. ESE of Takamatsu; agr. center (rice, sweet potatoes, tobacco, radishes). Sometimes spelled Tuda. **3** Town (pop. 8,844), Osaka prefecture, S Honshu, Japan, 15 mi. NE of Osaka, in agr. area; flour milling.

Tsudakhar (tsōōdŭkhär'), village (1939 pop. over 500), central Dagestan Autonomous SSR, Russian SFSR, in Gimri Range, 10 mi. SW of Levashi, in fruitgrowing area; fruit canning. Pop. largely Darghin.

Tsudanuma (tsōōdä'nōōmä), town (pop. 21,913), Chiba prefecture, central Honshu, Japan, just NW of Makuhari, in agr. area; flour mills, canneries; poultry raising.

Tsüen- or **Ts'üen-**, for Chinese names beginning thus and not found here: see under CHÜAN-.

Tsugaru Strait (tsōōgä'rōō), Jap. *Tsugaru-kaikyo*, channel of Japan bet. Honshu (S) and Hokkaido (N); connects Sea of Japan (W) with the Pacific (E); 15–25 mi. wide. Hakodate on N shore. Strait is connected with Aomori and Mutsu bays of Honshu by Tairadate Strait (5 mi. wide). Sometimes spelled Tugaru.

Tsugawa (tsōōgä'wä), town (pop. 5,243), Niigata prefecture, central Honshu, Japan, 15 mi. E of Muramatsu; lumber; woodworking, sake brewing.

Tsuge (tsōō'gā), town (pop. 4,921), Mie prefecture, S Honshu, Japan, 18 mi. NW of Tsu; rice, raw silk, poultry raising. Until early 1940s, called Higashitsuge.

Tsugitaka-yama, Formosa: see SYLVIA, MOUNT.

Tsuida, Japan: see SHIIDA.

Tsuji (tsōō'jē), town (pop. 5,368), Tokushima prefecture, N Shikoku, Japan, 39 mi. W of Tokushima; agr. center (rice, wheat, tobacco); raw silk.

Tsukechi (tsōōkā'chē), town (pop. 8,145), Gifu prefecture, central Honshu, Japan, 25 mi. WNW of Iida, in rice-growing area; pottery, silk textiles, raw silk.

Tsukidate (tsōōkē'dätä). **1** Town (pop. 5,277), Fukushima prefecture, N Honshu, Japan, 8 mi. E of Fukushima; rice, soybeans, silk cocoons. **2** Town (pop. 7,646), Miyagi prefecture, N Honshu, Japan, 6 mi. ESE of Wakayanagi; rice, silk cocoons.

Tsukinoki (tso͞okĕ′nōkĕ), town (pop. 11,217), Miyagi prefecture, N Honshu, Japan, on Abukuma R. and 13 mi. SSW of Sendai; agr. (rice, wheat), raw-silk culture; horse breeding.

Tsukuba (tso͞oko͞o′bä), town (pop. 4,449), Ibaraki prefecture, central Honshu, Japan, 11 mi. NW of Tsuchiura; rice, oranges.

Tsukumi (tso͞oko͞o′mē), town (pop. 21,731), Oita prefecture, E Kyushu, Japan, on inlet of Hoyo Strait, 18 mi. SE of Oita; agr. (rice, wheat, oranges) and mfg. center (woodworking, cement, limestone). Sometimes spelled Tukumi.

Tsulukidze (tso͞olo͞okē′dzĭ), city (1926 pop. 9,026), W Georgian SSR, 15 mi. WNW of Kutaisi; silk-spinning center; sawmilling, tea processing, dairying. Until 1936, Khoni.

Tsuma (tso͞o′mä), town (pop. 13,139), Miyazaki prefecture, E Kyushu, Japan, 13 mi. N of Miyazaki; agr. center (rice, wheat); raw silk, lumber. Sometimes spelled Tuma.

Tsumagi (tso͞omä′gē) or **Tsumaki** (-mä′kē), town (pop. 5,502), Gifu prefecture, central Honshu, Japan, 4 mi. SE of Tajimi; pottery making.

Tsuman or **Tsuman′** (tso͞o′mŭnyŭ), Pol. *Cumań* (tso͞o′mänyŭ), town (1939 pop. over 500), E Volyn oblast, Ukrainian SSR, on left tributary of Goryn R. and 25 mi. ENE of Lutsk; grain, potatoes; lumbering.

Tsumeb (tso͞o′mĕb), town, N South-West Africa, 35 mi. NE of Grootfontein; alt. 4,230 ft.; rail terminus; mining and smelting center (copper, lead, zinc, cadmium). Airfield.

Ts′ung-chiang, China: see TSUNGKIANG.

Tsungfa (tso͝ong′fä′), Mandarin *Ts′ung-hua* (tso͝ong′-hwä), town (pop. 1,017), ⊙ Tsungfa co. (pop. 137,871), central Kwangtung prov., China, 35 mi. NE of Canton; rice, wheat, peanuts, tobacco. Tungsten, tin, molybdenum mines near by.

Tsungjen or **Ch′ung-jen** (both: cho͝ong′rŭn′), town (pop. 13,348), ⊙ Tsungjen co. (pop. 107,154), central Kiangsi prov., China, 60 mi. S of Nanchang; rice, ramie, wheat, beans; mfg. of bamboo paper. Coal and kaolin deposits near by.

Tsungkiang or **Ts′ung-chiang** (both: cho͝ong′jyäng′), town (pop. 1,499), ⊙ Tsungkiang co. (pop. 94,567), SE Kweichow prov., China, 20 mi. SE of Jungkiang, at Kwangsi line; embroideries; wheat, millet, tobacco. Sulphur deposits, asbestos quarry near by. Until 1941 called Pingmei.

Tsungli or **Ch′ung-li** (both: cho͝ong′lē′), town, ⊙ Tsungli co. (pop. 84,574), NE central Chabar prov., China, 25 mi. NE of Kalgan; cattle raising; agr. products.

Tsungming or **Ch′ung-ming** (both: cho͝ong′mĭng′), island (□ 275; pop. 423,459) in estuary of Yangtze R., Kiangsu prov., China; 40 mi. long, 8 mi. wide. Sugar cane, rice, wheat, beans, corn, rapeseed, cotton. On S shore lies Tsungming town (pop. 26,311), with cotton-weaving industry. Isl. appeared as a sandbank in A.D. 629; was settled after 1277.

Tsungning or **Ch′ung-ning** (both: cho͝ong′nĭng′), town (pop. 12,379), ⊙ Tsungning co. (pop. 91,347), W Szechwan prov., China, 24 mi. NW of Chengtu, on Chengtu plain; rice, wheat, sweet potatoes, rapeseed.

Tsungshan or **Ch′ung-shan** (both: cho͝ong′shän′), town, ⊙ Tsungshan co. (pop. 63,739), SW Kwangsi prov., China, 50 mi. SW of Nanning and on Li R.; peanut-oil processing; grain, beans, sugar cane. Until 1913 called Taiping.

Tsungsin or **Ch′ung-hsin** (both; cho͝ong′shĭn′), town, ⊙ Tsungsin co. (pop. 31,285), SE Kansu prov., China, 15 mi. SW of Kingchwan, near Shensi border; kaoliang, millet.

Tsungteh or **Ch′ung-te** (both: cho͝ong′dŭ′), town (pop. 10,139), ⊙ Tsungteh co. (pop. 188,429), N Chekiang prov., China, 25 mi. NE of Hangchow and on Grand Canal; silk textiles; rice, wheat. Until 1914 called Shihmen.

Tsungyang or **Ch′ung-yang** (both: cho͝ong′yäng′), town (pop. 13,438), ⊙ Tsungyang co. (pop. 132,-231), SE Hupeh prov., China, near Hunan-Anhwei line, 50 mi. E of Yoyang (Hunan prov.); tea-growing center. Coal mining near by.

Tsungyi, Chungyi, or **Ch′ung-i** (all: cho͝ong′yē′), town (pop. 6,763), ⊙ Tsungyi co. (pop. 84,673), SW Kiangsi prov., China, 27 mi. WSW of Kanchow; rice, wheat, cotton. Tungsten, tin, gold mining.

Tsunhwa or **Tsun-hua** (dzo͝on′hwä′), town, ⊙ Tsunhwa co. (pop. 361,216), NE Hopeh prov., China, 40 mi. NNW of Tangshan, near Great Wall (Jehol line); cotton, grain, furs.

Tsun-i, China: see TSUNYI.

Tsuno (tso͞o′nō), town (pop. 15,171), Miyazaki prefecture, E Kyushu, Japan, on Hyuga Sea, 25 mi. NNE of Miyazaki; agr. and fishing center; rice, lumber, livestock. Sometimes spelled Tuno.

Tsuno-shima (tso͞onō′-shĭmä), island (□ 2; pop. 1,996), Yamaguchi prefecture, Japan, in Sea of Japan just off SW coast of Honshu, 12 mi. NNW of Kogushi; 2.5 mi. long, 1 mi. wide; hilly. Fishing.

Tsunozu (tso͞onō′zo͞o), town (pop. 3,751), Shimane prefecture, SW Honshu, Japan, on Sea of Japan, 9 mi. NE of Hamada; fishing; rice, raw silk; sake, soy sauce.

Tsuntang, India: see CHUNTANG.

Tsunyi or **Tsun-i** (both: dzo͝on′yē′), town (pop. 65,924), ⊙ Tsunyi co. (pop. 545,806), N Kweichow prov., China, 75 mi. N of Kweiyang and on main road to Szechwan; alt. 2,723 ft.; trades in wild silk; cotton and silk textiles; paper and pottery mfg. Winegrowing; mushrooms, rice, wheat, millet, beans. Had officer-training school in Second World War.

Turashima (tso͞orä′shĭmä) or **Tsurajima** (-jĭmä), town (pop. 22,191), Okayama prefecture, SW Honshu, Japan, on Hiuchi Sea, 12 mi. WSW of Okayama; agr. center (rice, wheat, grapes); textiles, raw silk. Sometimes spelled Turasima.

Tsurib (tso͞orĕp′), village, S central Dagestan Autonomous SSR, Russian SFSR, in the E Greater Caucasus, 12 mi. SSW of Gunib; grain, stock; lumbering. Charoda village just N. Pop. largely Avar.

Tsur Moshe or **Tzur Moshe** (both: tso͞or′mōshā′), settlement (pop. 225), W Israel, in Plain of Sharon, 4 mi. SE of Natanya; farming. Founded 1937.

Tsuro, Japan: see MUROTOZAKI.

Tsuruda, Japan: see TSURUTA.

Tsuruga (tso͞oro͞o′gä), city (1940 pop. 31,346; 1947 pop. 28,268), Fukui prefecture, S Honshu, Japan, port on SE inlet of Wakasa Bay, 50 mi. NNE of Kyoto. Rail junction; important port; steamer connection with Vladivostok. Mfg. center (textiles, dyes, pottery); fishery. Exports textiles, cement, pottery, beer, dyes. Sometimes Turuga.

Tsurugi (tso͞oro͞o′gē), town (pop. 5,767), Ishikawa prefecture, central Honshu, Japan, 8 mi. SSW of Kanazawa; commercial center for agr. area (tobacco, rice); mfg. (silk textiles, sake).

Tsurugi, Mount, Jap. *Tsurugi-zan,* second highest peak (6,414 ft.) of Shikoku, Japan, in Tokushima prefecture, 13 mi. S of Anabuki. Buddhist temple, Shinto shrine on slopes. Sometimes Turugi.

Tsurumai (tso͞oro͞o′mī), town (pop. 4,215), Chiba prefecture, central Honshu, Japan, on central Chiba Peninsula, 10 mi. W of Ichinomiya; rice, wheat, raw silk.

Tsurumi, Cape (tso͞oro͞o′mē), Jap. *Tsurumi-saki,* Oita prefecture, E Kyushu, Japan, on Hoyo Strait; 32°56′N 132°5′E.

Tsurumi, Mount, Jap. *Tsurumi-dake,* volcanic peak (5,200 ft.), Oita prefecture, NE Kyushu, Japan, 4 mi. W of Beppu; densely forested slopes. Sometimes spelled Turumi.

Tsuruoka (tso͞oro͞o′ôkä), city (1940 pop. 35,986; 1947 pop. 42,792), Yamagata prefecture, N Honshu, Japan, 43 mi. NW of Yamagata; mfg. (silk textiles, lacquer ware), metalworking. Hot springs near by. Sometimes spelled Turuoka.

Tsurusaki (tso͞oro͞o′-sä′kē), town (pop. 17,256), Oita prefecture, E Kyushu, Japan, 5 mi. E of Oita, on S shore of Beppu Bay; commercial center in rice-growing area.

Tsuruta (tso͞oro͞o′tä) or **Tsuruda** (-dä), town (pop. 7,617), Aomori prefecture, N Honshu, Japan, 11 mi. N of Hirosaki; rice, apples.

Tsushi (tso͞o′shē), town (pop. 4,612) on Awaji-shima, Hyogo prefecture, Japan, on Harima Sea, 8 mi. NW of Sumoto; rice, wheat, raw silk, fruit. Fishing.

Tsushima (tso͞o′shĭmä), town (pop. 31,737), Aichi prefecture, central Honshu, Japan, 11 mi. W of Nagoya; woolen mills.

Tsushima, island (□ 271; pop. 57,482, including offshore islets), Nagasaki prefecture, Japan, bet. Korea Strait and Tsushima Strait, 60 mi. NW of Kyushu; 45 mi. long, 10 mi. wide. Larger N portion is separated at high tide from S part. Rocky, arid; rises to 2,168 ft. Fisheries. Chief town, Izuhara. In Russo-Japanese War, Rus. fleet was destroyed (1905) near here. Sometimes spelled Tusima.

Tsushima Current: see JAPAN CURRENT.

Tsushima Strait, Jap. *Tsushima-kaikyo,* strait connecting Sea of Japan (N) and East China Sea (S), bet. Tsushima (W) and many small isls. (E); c.60 mi. long, 40 mi. wide. In Russo-Japanese War, scene of major Jap. victory (1905) over Rus. fleet. Tsushima Strait is sometimes considered part of Korea Strait.

Tsusho, Formosa: see TUNGSIAO.

Tsutani, Japan: see TSUYA.

Tsutung, Formosa: see CHUTUNG.

Tsuwang or **Ch′u-wang** (both: cho͞o′wäng′), town, N Pingyuan prov., China, on Hopeh line, 75 mi. NE of Sinsiang, and on Wei R.; rail terminus. Also called Tsuwangchen.

Tsuwano (tso͞owä′nō), town (pop. 6,530), Shimane prefecture, SW Honshu, Japan, 25 mi. NE of Yamaguchi; mfg. (tissue paper, sake, soy sauce); bamboo, raw silk, grain. Sometimes spelled Tuwano.

Tsuya (tso͞o′yä) or **Tsutani** (tso͞otä′nē), town (pop. 7,339), Miyagi prefecture, N Honshu, Japan, on the Pacific, 9 mi. SW of Kesennuma; mining (gold, silver, copper). Until late 1930s, called Mitake.

Tsuyama (tso͞oyä′mä), city (1940 pop. 35,111; 1947 pop. 51,642), Okayama prefecture, SW Honshu, Japan, 28 mi. NNE of Okayama; rail junction; commercial and distribution center; spinning mills, woodworking factory, tissue-paper mill. Produces also bamboo ware, sake, agr. products (rice, sweet potatoes, persimmons, watermelons). Ships raw silk, grain, fruit, lumber, charcoal Has sericulture experiment station. Sometimes spelled Tuyama.

Tsuyazaki (tso͞oyä′-zä′kē), town (pop. 8,337), Fukuoka prefecture, N Kyushu, Japan, port on Genkai Sea, 14 mi. NNE of Fukuoka; rice, wheat, barley. Exports sake.

Tsuyung (tso͞o′yo͞ong′) or **Ch′u-hsiung** (cho͞o′-shüng′), town, ⊙ Tsuyung co. (pop. 103,578), central Yunnan prov., China, on Burma Road and 70 mi. W of Kunming; alt. 6,251 ft.; cotton and silk textiles; rice, wheat, millet, beans.

Tsuzawa (tso͞ozä′wä), town (pop. 3,166), Toyama prefecture, central Honshu, Japan, 14 mi. ENE of Kanazawa, in rice-growing area; raw silk, medicines.

Tsymlyanskaya, Russian SFSR: see TSIMLYANSKAYA.

Tsyp-Navolok, Russian SFSR: see RYBACHI PENINSULA.

Tsyurupinsk (tsyo͞oro͞opēnsk′), town (1939 pop. over 10,000), SW Kherson oblast, Ukrainian SSR, 5 mi. E of Kherson, across Dnieper R. (landing); terminus of railroad from Dzhankoi; woodworking, furniture mfg. Formerly called Aleshki.

Tsyurupy, Imeni (ē′mĭnyē tsyo͞oro͞o′pē), town (1939 pop. over 500), E central Moscow oblast, Russian SFSR, 6 mi. NNE of Vinogradovo; cotton textiles, flour mill. Until 1935, Vanilovo.

Tu, Japan: see TSU.

Tu, Nam, Burma: see MYITNGE RIVER.

Tua, Tanjung, Indonesia: see HOG POINT.

Tualatin (twä′lŭtĭn), city (pop. 248), Washington co., NW Oregon, on Tualatin R. and 10 mi. SW of Portland.

Tualatin River, NW Oregon, rises W of Portland, flows N, then E past Hillsboro, and SE to Willamette R. above Oregon City; c.60 mi. long. Valley is important nut-producing area (filberts, walnuts).

Tuam (tū′ŭm), Gaelic *Tuaim,* town (pop. 3,868), N Co. Galway, Ireland, 19 mi. NNE of Galway; agr. market (beets, potatoes; sheep), with sugar refineries. It is seat of R.C. archbishop (see was founded in 6th cent. by St. Jarlath) and of Protestant bishop. Protestant cathedral was founded c.1130 by Thurlough O'Connor. There is Gothic R.C. cathedral, 12th-cent. Cross of Tuam, and St. Jarlath's R.C. Col. Near by are remains of round tower.

Tuamotu Islands (to͞o′ämō′to͞o) or **Low Archipelago,** coral group (□ 330; pop. 5,127), FRENCH ESTABLISHMENTS IN OCEANIA, S Pacific, c.300 mi. S of Marquesas Isls.; 15°–21°30′S 135°40′–149°40′W. Comprise 80 atolls in 1,300-mi. chain; ⊙ Papeete in Tahiti, Society Isls. Small, flat isls.; RANGIROA is largest, FAKARAVA most important. Isls. have coconut, pandanus, and breadfruit trees; produce pearl shell, copra. Discovered 1606 by the Spanish, annexed 1881 by France. Part of group is governed with GAMBIER ISLANDS. Formerly Paumotu or Dangerous Archipelago.

Tuan (do͞o′än′), town, ⊙ Tuan co. (pop. 267,160), NW central Kwangsi prov., China, 75 mi. WSW of Liuchow, near Hungshui R.; paper-milling center; cotton-textile mfg., tobacco processing; rice, wheat, bans, cattle.

Tuan, Tanjong, Malaya: see RACHADO, CAPE.

Tuanaka, Tuamotu Isls.: see RAEVSKI ISLANDS.

Tuangku, Indonesia: see BANYAK ISLANDS.

Tuapeka, New Zealand: see LAWRENCE.

Tuapse (to͞oŭpsyĕ′), city (1939 pop. c.29,600), S Krasnodar Territory, Russian SFSR, major petroleum port on Black Sea, 60 mi. S of Krasnodar, on coastal railroad; terminus of pipe lines from Grozny and Maikop oil fields; petroleum-refining center, shipbuilding, metalworking, food processing, brewing. Exports petroleum products, grain. Seaside resort; orchards, vineyards. Founded 1838 as Rus. fortress of Velyaminovski; became a city (renamed Tuapse) in 1896; developed as commercial center.

Tua River (to͞o′ŭ), in Bragança dist., N Portugal, rises near Sp. border, flows c.70 mi. SSW to the Douro near Carrazeda de Anciãis.

Tuar-Kyr (to͞oär″-kĭr′), village, NW Ashkhabad oblast, Turkmen SSR, 130 mi. ENE of Krasnovodsk, near Kara-Bogaz-Gol gulf; coal deposits.

Tuas (to͞oäs′), village (pop. 727), at SW tip of Singapore isl., 14 mi. W of Singapore; rubber, pineapples.

Tuasivi (to͞oäsē′vē), town, E coast of SAVAII, Western Samoa; hq. of resident commissioner; site of govt. hosp.

Tuath, Loch, Scotland: see MULL.

Tuath, Loch A, Scotland: see BROAD BAY.

Tubabao Island (to͞obäbä′ō, –bou′) (1939 pop. 1,336), Samar prov., Philippines, in Leyte Gulf, nearly connected to narrow SE peninsula of Samar isl.; shelters Guiuan (U.S. naval base); 2 mi. long. Coconuts.

Tubac, Ariz.: see NOGALES.

Tuba City, village (pop. c.150), Coconino co., N Ariz., 65 mi. NNE of Flagstaff; administration and trading point in Navajo Indian Reservation.

Tubai, Society Isls.: see MOTU ITI.

Tubala or **Tubalah** (to͞o′bälŭ), village and oasis, Quaiti state, Eastern Aden Protectorate, 4 mi. N of Shihr and on road to the Wadi Hadhramaut; date gardens; source of Shihr water supply; hot sulphur springs.

Tuban or **Toeban** (both: to͞obän′), town (pop. 23,285), NE Java, Indonesia, fishing port on Java Sea, 50 mi. WNW of Surabaya; 6°54′S 112°4′E;

trade center for rice- and corn-growing region. Has large Chinese colony. Formerly opium-smuggling center.

Túbano, Dominican Republic: see PADRE LAS CASAS.

Tubará (tōōbärä'), town (pop. 2,375), Atlántico dept., N Colombia, in Caribbean lowlands, 16 mi. SW of Barranquilla; cotton growing, oil drilling.

Tubarão (tōōbŭrā'ō), city (pop. 6,830), SE Santa Catarina, Brazil, on coastal plain, 65 mi. SSW of Florianópolis; center of important coal-mining region. Coal mined at near-by Araranguá, Criciúma, Urussanga, and Lauro Müller is beneficiated here, then taken by rail to ports of Laguna (14 mi. E) and Imbituba (25 mi. NE), whence it is shipped to Volta Redonda steel mill (Rio de Janeiro). Graphite deposits. Meat packing; distilling.

Tuba River (tōō'bŭ), S Krasnoyarsk Territory, Russian SFSR, formed by union of Kizir (160 mi. long) and Amyl (116 mi. long) rivers; flows 76 mi. W, past Kuragino, to Yenisei R. 18 mi. below Minusinsk.

Tub Aymag, Mongolia: see CENTRAL AIMAK.

Tubayq, Al-, Jordan: see TUBEIQ, EL.

Tubbercurry or **Tobercurry** (both: tŭ″bûrkûr'ē), Gaelic *Tobar an Choire*, town (pop. 880), S Co. Sligo, Ireland, 19 mi. SW of Sligo; agr. market (cattle, potatoes).

Tubbergen (tŭ'bĕr-khŭn), town (pop. 1,083), Overijssel prov., E Netherlands, 6 mi. NE of Almelo, near Ger. border; textile dyeing; dairy products.

Tubeiq, El, Et Tubeiq, or **Al-Tubayq** (all: ĕt-tōōbāk'), hilly region of SE Jordan, on Saudi Arabia frontier; rises to 3,986 ft.

Tubeke, Belgium: see TUBIZE.

Tubhar (tōōb'här), village (pop. 10,061), Faiyum prov., Upper Egypt, 8 mi. W of Faiyum; cotton, cereals, sugar cane, fruits.

Tubigon (tōōbē'gōn), town (1939 pop. 1,114; 1948 municipality pop. 23,344), NW Bohol isl., Philippines, on Bohol Strait, 23 mi. NNE of Tagbilaran; agr. center (rice, coconuts).

Tubilla del Agua (tōōvē'lyä dhĕl ä'gwä), town (pop. 221), Burgos prov., N Spain, 25 mi. N of Burgos, in agr. region (cereals, vegetables, potatoes, nuts, honey, livestock). Has Byzantine church.

Tübingen (tü'bĭng-ŭn), city (pop. 34,345), S Württemberg, Germany, after 1945 ⊙ Württemberg-Hohenzollern, on the Neckar and 18 mi. SSW of Stuttgart; 48°31'N 9°3'E. A cultural center, it is also a rail junction and has mfg. of textiles (cotton, wool, blankets), clothing, machinery, electric motors, precision instruments, furniture, shoes. Printing. Medieval aspect of old town is dominated by late-Gothic church of St. George; the castle, 1st mentioned in 11th cent., was renovated in Renaissance style. Has 15th–16th-cent. city hall. The noted univ. (founded 1477), where Melanchthon taught, now has many scientific institutes. Its theological faculty, led by F. C. Baur, was famous in 19th cent. Town was chartered c.1200, sold to Württemberg 1342, and became its 2d capital in mid-15th cent. Ludwig Uhland b. here.

Tubinski or **Tubinskiy** (tōō'bĭnskē), town (1939 pop. 6,800), SE Bashkir Autonomous SSR, Russian SFSR, in the S Urals, 22 mi. NNW of Baimak; gold, copper mining. Formerly Tubinski Rudnik.

Tubize (tübēz'), Flemish *Tubeke* (tü'bā'kŭ), town (pop. 9,337), Brabant prov., central Belgium, 3 mi. SSW of Hal, and on Charleroi-Brussels Canal; locomotive-mfg. center; machine mfg.; artificial silk.

Tubong (tōō'bông'), town, Khanhhoa prov., S central Vietnam, on Bengoi Bay and railroad, 37 mi. NNE of Nhatrang.

Tubuai Islands (tōōbōōī') or **Austral Islands** (ô'strŭl), volcanic group, FRENCH ESTABLISHMENTS IN OCEANIA, S Pacific, c.330 mi. S of Society Isls.; 21°45'–23°50'S 147°40'–154°30'W. Consist of 4 isls. (RIMATARA, RURUTU, RAIVAVAE, TUBUAI) and 1 uninhabited atoll (MARIA ISLAND). Tubuai, largest isl. (□ 17; pop. 1,006), is 6 mi. long, rises to 1,309 ft.; its chief town is Mataura, Isl. was discovered 1777 by Capt. Cook, annexed 1880 by France. Group is fertile and mountainous; has pandanus, ironwood, coconut trees, livestock; produces coffee, arrowroot, some copra. Polynesian natives. Tubuai Isls. Administration (□ 115; pop. 3,921) also governs RAPA (c.325 mi. SE of Tubuai group) and uninhabited BASS ISLES.

Tubuai Manu, Society Isls.: see MAIAO.

Tubuñgan (tōōbōō'nyŭgän), town (1939 pop. 2006; 1948 municipality pop. 10,464), Iloilo prov., S Panay isl., Philippines, 18 mi. WNW of Iloilo; agr. center (rice, sugar cane).

Tuburan (tōōbōō'rän), town (1939 pop. 3,364; 1948 municipality pop. 53,654), N Cebu isl., Philippines, on Tañon Strait, 30 mi. NNW of Cebu city; agr. center (corn, coconuts).

Tubutama (tōōbōōtä'mä), town (pop. 347), Sonora, NW Mexico, on Altar (affluent of Magdalena) R. and 45 mi. SW of Nogales; wheat, corn, beans, cotton, sugar cane.

Tucabaca, Bolivia: see TUCAVACA.

Tucacas (tōōkä'käs), town (pop. 2,523), Falcón state, NW Venezuela, Caribbean port on Triste Gulf, 27 mi. NW of Puerto Cabello; rail terminus (linked with Barquisimeto). Exports copper ore from Aroa (Yaracuy); also cacao, coffee, goatskins.

Tucannon River (tūkă'nŭn), SE Wash., rises in Umatilla Natl. Forest, flows c.70 mi. generally NW to Snake R. near mouth of Palouse R.

Tucano (tōōkä'nōō), city (pop. 1,748), NE Bahia, Brazil, near Itapicuru R., 50 mi. N of Serrinha; caroa fibers, wool, rice.

Tucapau, S.C.: see STARTEX.

Tucapel (tōōkäpĕl'), village (1930 pop. 578), Ñuble prov., S central Chile, 55 mi. SSE of Chillán; wheat, corn, wine, livestock.

Tucavaca (tōōkävä'kä), village, Santa Cruz dept., E Bolivia, on Tucavaca R. and 75 mi. WNW of Puerto Suárez. Also spelled Tucabaca.

Tucavaca River, Santa Cruz dept., E Bolivia, rises in Serranía de Sunsas 15 mi. NW of San Juan, flows 130 mi. SE, past Tucavaca, joining San Rafael R. c.3 mi. S of Tucavaca to form the Otuquis. Also spelled Tucabaca.

Tuchan (tüshã'), village (pop. 1,086), Aude dept., S France, in the Corbières, 16 mi. NW of Perpignan; winegrowing.

Tuchang or **Tu-ch'ang** (dōō'chäng'), town (pop. 3,003), ⊙ Tuchang co. (pop. 201,081), N Kiangsi prov., China, 45 mi. SSE of Kiukiang, on N shore of Poyang L.; rice, cotton, ramie, indigo.

Tuchel, Poland: see TUCHOLA.

Tu-ch'eng, China: see DOSING.

Tuchin (tōō'chĭn), Pol. *Tuczyn* (tōō'chĭn), village (1931 pop. 2,940), central Rovno oblast, Ukrainian SSR, on Goryn R. and 14 mi. ENE of Rovno; flour milling, tanning, meat preserving, weaving.

Tuchkovo (tōōch'kŭvŭ), town (1940 pop. estimate 3,700), W central Moscow oblast, Russian SFSR, on Moskva R. and 45 mi. WSW of Moscow; brickworks.

Tuchola (tōō-khô'lä), Ger. *Tuchel* (tōō'khŭl), town (pop. 5,750), Bydgoszcz prov., N Poland, 33 mi. N of Bydgoszcz, near Brda R.; rail junction; mfg. of bricks, furniture, machinery; brewing, sawmilling, distilling. **Tuchola Forests,** Pol. *Bory Tucholskie* (bô'rĭ tōō-khôl'skyĕ), lie N, bet. Brda and Vistula rivers; mostly pines, with some oak, beech; long in use.

Tuchow (tōō'khōōf), Pol. *Tuchów*, town (pop. 3,026), Krakow prov., S Poland, on Biala R., on railroad and 9 mi. S of Tarnow; flour milling. Iron-ore deposits just E.

Tuckahoe (tŭ'kŭhō). **1** Village (pop. c.1,000), Cape May co., S N.J., on Tuckahoe R. and 18 mi. WSW of Atlantic City; cans, ships tomatoes. Hunting, fishing near by. Settled by Quakers before 1700. **2** Residential village (pop. 5,991), Westchester co., SE N.Y., just E of Yonkers and N of Bronxville, in New York city metropolitan area; marble quarrying; mfg. (stucco, clothing, chemicals). Settled 1684, inc. 1903.

Tuckahoe Creek, E Md., on the Eastern Shore, rises just SE of Templeville, flows c.45 mi. generally SSW, forming Queen Annes-Caroline and Talbot-Caroline co. lines, to Choptank R. 6 mi. SW of Denton.

Tuckahoe River, S N.J., rises in SW Atlantic co., flows c.25 mi. S and E, past Tuckahoe (head of navigation), through Great Cedar Swamp, to Great Egg Harbor Bay S of Great Egg Harbor R. mouth.

Tuckasegee River (tŭkŭsē'gē), W N.C., rises in the Blue Ridge W of Brevard, flows 50 mi. NW past Cullowhee, Whittier, and Bryson City, to Little Tennessee R. (Fontana Reservoir) near Bryson City. Sometimes Tuckaseigee R Glenville Dam (150 ft. high, 900 ft. long; for power; completed 1941) on small West Fork of Tuckasegee R. is 22 mi. SW of Bryson City; forms Glenville Reservoir (5 mi. long, 1 mi. wide; also known as Glenville L.).

Tucker, county (□ 421; pop. 10,600), NE W.Va., at base of Eastern Panhandle; ⊙ Parsons. On Allegheny Plateau, with Laurel Ridge along W border; drained by Cheat R. Most of co. is in Monongahela Natl. Forest. Blackwater Falls State Park is here. Coal mining; lumbering; agr. (livestock, dairy products, fruit), limestone quarrying. Some industry at Parsons. Formed 1856.

Tucker, village (pop. 1,474), De Kalb co., NW central Ga., 12 mi. ENE of Atlanta.

Tucker Island, SE N.J., sandy barrier isl. (c.2 mi. long) bet. Great Bay and the Atlantic, and bet. Beach Haven Inlet (N) and Little Egg Inlet (S); seaward side is called Tucker Beach.

Tuckerman, town (pop. 1,253), Jackson co., NE Ark., 30 mi. WSW of Jonesboro, in agr. area (cotton, corn, rice).

Tuckerman Ravine, N.H.: see WASHINGTON, MOUNT.

Tuckernuck Island, Nantucket co., SE Mass., in the Atlantic just W of Nantucket Isl.; separated from Martha's Vineyard (NW) by Muskeget Channel; c.5 mi. long.

Tucker's Town, Bermuda, part of SE Bermuda Isl., in St. George's parish.

Tuckerton, resort borough (pop. 1,332), Ocean co., SE N.J., near Little Egg Harbor, 16 mi. N of Atlantic City, at head of navigation of short Tuckerton Creek; boatyards, fishing. A marine radio-transmitting station is near by. Settled c.1700, inc. 1901. Important 18th-cent. port; raided by British, 1778.

Tuckshuck, Alaska: see TAKSHAK.

Tuckum, Latvia: see TUKUMS.

Tucquegnieux (tüknyĕü'), town (pop. 3,476), Meurthe-et-Moselle dept., NE France, 5 mi. NNW of Briey; iron mining.

Tucson (tōō'sŏn, tōōsŏn'), city (pop. 45,454), ⊙ Pima co., SE Ariz., c.110 mi. SE of Phoenix, S of Santa Catalina Mts., E of Tucson Mts.; alt. c.2,390 ft.; 2d-largest city in state. Rail center (large repair shops of Southern Pacific here); distributing point for mineral, livestock, irrigated agr. area. Produces flour; manufactures bricks and tiles, electronic equipment, iron products, paint, and plumbing materials. Has mild dry climate and is tourist and health resort, with many sanitariums and hospitals. Seat of Univ. of Ariz. (1891), state school for deaf and blind, state mus., U.S. mining, botanical, and agr. experiment stations. Near by are Davis-Monthan Air Force Base, Saguaro Natl. Monument, bldgs. of San Xavier del Bac mission (consecrated 1797; considered finest mission architecture in Southwest), and ruins of Pueblo villages. Fiesta and rodeo take place in Feb. Settled c.1695 by Spaniards; site of San Xavier mission (c.1700) amd presidio (1776); city inc. 1871. Part of Gadsden Purchase (1853); territorial ⊙ 1867–77. Growth stimulated by arrival of railroad (1880) and by discovery of silver at Tombstone and copper at Bisbee. Copper, silver, and gold mines are now in vicinity.

Tucson Mountains, W of Tucson, SE Ariz.; Amole Peak (4,683 ft.) is a landmark.

Tucuche, El (ĕl tūkōō'chē), peak (3,072 ft.), N Trinidad, B.W.I., 9 mi. NE of Port of Spain.

Tucumán (tōōkōōmän'), province (□ 10,425; pop. 593,371), NW Argentina; ⊙ Tucumán. Located in outliers of the Andes, bordered W by Catamarca prov., it slopes from the western ranges to Santiago del Estero prov. (E). Drained by the Río Salí or Dulce and by Santa María or Cajón R., which, with their many affluents, are used for hydroelectric power and irrigation. In lower, populated parts, climate is humid and warm. Mineral resources (iron ore, manganese, copper, lead, sodium, lime, mica, in hills near Tucumán city) of prov. are little exploited. Agr.: sugar cane (grown extensively), corn, alfalfa, wheat; tobacco (SW), rice (S center), citrus (S), peanuts (center and NE), cotton (center), olives (center and S). Stock raising (cattle, sheep, mules, hogs, horses), especially in N. Lumbering (walnut, quebracho, cedar, laurel, etc.) in center and NE. Sugar refining, alcohol distilling, dairying, flour milling, chemical mfg., meat packing, food canning; some mfg. of cement, ceramics, and textiles.

Tucumán, city (pop. 192,156), ⊙ Tucumán prov. and Tucumán dept. (□ c.110; 1947 pop. 202,693), NW Argentina, on the Río Salí or Dulce, on railroad, and 665 mi. NW of Buenos Aires; alt. 1,385 ft.; 26°51'S 65°13'W. Agr., lumbering, and industrial center. Sugar refineries, alcohol distilleries, grain mills, sawmills; mfg. of citrus extracts, frozen meat, dairy products, beer, lime, cement, ceramics, matches, textile goods, canned food. Trade in products of a large agr. area producing sugar, corn, alfalfa, rice, tobacco, fruit, livestock. Has administrative bldgs., govt. palace with adjoining mus., San Francisco church with statue of St. Francis of Assisi, cathedral, univ., seismographic station, libraries, and theaters. An old colonial town, it was founded in 1565 as San Miguel de Tucumán and moved 1580 to its present site. On September 24, 1812, Gen. Belgrano here defeated the Sp. royalists. The congress of the United Provinces of Río de la Plata met in Tucumán on July 9, 1816, to proclaim their independence.

Tucumcari (tōō'kŭmkă"rē), city (pop. 8,419), ⊙ Quay co., E N.Mex., near Canadian R. and Texas line, c.165 mi. E of Albuquerque. Railroad div. point, with repair shops; trade and cattle-shipping center in irrigated grain region. Hq. of Tucumcari irrigation project here. Conchas Dam, Reservoir, and State Park are 30 mi. WNW. City inc. 1908. Growth followed arrival (1901) of railroad.

Túcume (tōō'kōōmā), town (pop. 1,449), Lambayeque dept., NW Peru, on coastal plain, on Pan-American Highway and 13 mi. N of Lambayeque; rice milling; also cotton cultivation.

Tucupido (tōōkōōpē'dō), town (pop. 2,541), Guárico state, N central Venezuela, in llanos 17 mi. ENE of Valle de la Pascua; cattle grazing.

Tucupita (–tä), town (1941 pop. 3,399; 1950 census 8,546), ⊙ Delta Amacuro territory, NE Venezuela, landing on the Caño Mánamo (arm of Orinoco R. delta) and 120 mi. NE of Ciudad Bolívar, 350 mi. ESE of Caracas; 9°4'N 62°3'W. In agr. region (corn, bananas, cacao, sugar cane, tobacco). Founded c.1885.

Tucupita, Caño (kä'nyō), central arm of Orinoco R. delta, Delta Amacuro territory, NE Venezuela; branches off from the Caño Mánamo at Tucupita, flows c.55 mi. NE to the Caño Macareo.

Tucurú or **San Miguel Tucurú** (sän mēgĕl' tōōkōōrōō'), town (1950 pop. 376), Alta Verapaz dept., central Guatemala, on Polochic R. and 17 mi. SE of Cobán; market center; bananas, coffee.

Tucuruí (tōōkōōrwē'), city (pop. 620), E Pará, Brazil, head of navigation on left bank of Tocantins R. and 165 mi. SSW of Belém. N terminus of railroad (partially completed) circumventing Tocantins R. rapids to São João do Araguaia. Airport. Until 1944, Alcobaça.

Tucutí (to͞oko͞otē′), village (pop. 397), Darién prov., E Panama, on Tucutí R. (left affluent of the Tuira, c.60 mi. long) and 30 mi. SSE of La Palma; lumbering; stock raising; corn, rice, beans.

Tuczno (to͞och′nō), Ger. *Tütz* (tüts), town (1939 pop. 2,748; 1946 pop. 1,647) in Pomerania, after 1945 in Koszalin prov., NW Poland, on small lake, 25 mi. W of Schneidemühl (Pila); grain, sugar beets, potatoes, livestock. Until 1938, in former Prussian prov. of Grenzmark Posen-Westpreussen.

Tuczyn, Ukrainian SSR: see TUCHIN.

Tuda, Japan: see TSUDA, Kagawa prefecture.

Tudashk or **Tudeshk** (to͞odĕshk′), village, Tenth Prov., in Isfahan, W central Iran, 60 mi. E of Isfahan and on Isfahan-Yezd road; opium, cotton, grain. Also known as Tudasht or Tudesht.

Tuddal, Norway: see SAULAND.

Tudela (to͞o-dhā′lä), anc. *Tutela*, city (pop. 12,873), Navarre prov., N Spain, on the Ebro (crossed by arched Roman bridge) and 50 mi. NW of Saragossa; industrial and communications center. Sugar mill, canneries (vegetables); mfg. of cement, alcohol, soap, potassium salts, licorice extracts, tiles, shoes, chocolate, beet sugar. Trades in wine, sugar beets cereals, livestock. Episcopal see, 1844–51; now belongs to Tarazona bishopric. Among the anc. city's distinguished bldgs. is its superb 12th-cent. Santa María cathedral (now collegiate church), built in Romanesque-Gothic transitional style and noted for its fine portals.

Tudela de Duero (dhĕl dhwā′rō), town (pop. 3,464), Valladolid prov., N central Spain, on the Duero (Douro) and 8 mi. ESE of Valladolid; agr. trade center (wine, cereals, vegetables, sugar beets).

Tudelilla (to͞o-dhālē′lyä), town (pop. 1,384), Logroño prov., N Spain, 8 mi. W of Calahorra; wine, olive oil, cereals, livestock.

Tudeshk, Iran: see TUDASHK.

Tudor-Vladimirescu I (to͞o′dôr-vlädēmērĕsk′), SW suburb (1948 pop. 58,081) of Bucharest, in Bucharest municipality, S Rumania.

Tudor Vladimirescu II, outer SW rural suburb (1948 pop. 4,920) of Bucharest, Bucharest prov., S Rumania, on right bank of Dambovita R.

Tudun Wada (to͞odo͞on′ wädä′), town (pop. 3,132), Kano prov., Northern Provinces, N Nigeria, 55 mi. SSW of Kano; road center in tin-mining region; cotton, peanuts, millet; cattle, skins.

Tuéjar (twā′här), town (pop. 2,147), Valencia prov., E Spain, 26 mi. WNW of Liria; flour mills; wine, olive oil; lumber. Gypsum quarries near by.

Tuensang (to͞o′ĕn′säng), village, ⊙ Naga Tribal Area, E Assam, India, in Naga Hills, 45 mi. S of Nazira.

Tufanganj (to͞ofän′gŭnj), town (pop. 1,412), Cooch Behar dist., NE West Bengal, India, on Raidak R. and 14 mi. E of Cooch Behar; rice, jute, tobacco, oilseeds, sugar cane.

Tuffé (tüfā′), village (pop. 615), Sarthe dept., W France, 17 mi. ENE of Le Mans; foundries.

Tüffer, Yugoslavia: see LASKO.

Tufo (to͞o′fō), village (pop. 1,387), Avellino prov., Campania, S Italy, 7 mi. N of Avellino. Sulphur mines near by.

Tuftonboro, town (pop. 697), Carroll co., E N.H., on E L. Winnipesaukee and 18 mi. NE of Laconia. Includes Melvin Village (summer resort) and Mirror Lake village on small Mirror L.

Tug [Somali,=river], for names beginning thus and not found here, see under following part of name.

Tugaloo River (tŭ′gŭlo͞o, to͞o′gŭlō), NE Ga. and NW S.C., formed SE of Tallulah Falls, Ga., by junction of Chattooga and Tallulah rivers; flows 45 mi. SE, along Ga.-S.C. line, joining Seneca R. 13 mi. WSW of Anderson, S.C., to form Savannah R. Has 2 dams in upper course.

Tugaru Strait, Japan: see TSUGARU STRAIT.

Tugaske (tŭgă′skē), village (pop. 201), S Sask., 50 mi. NW of Moose Jaw; grain elevators.

Tugela River (to͞ogā′lŭ), Natal, U. of So. Afr., rises on Basutoland border, on Mont-aux-Sources in Drakensberg range, flows c.300 mi. E, through deep gorge, falling c.2,800 ft. in a series of falls, past Bergville and Colenso, to Indian Ocean 25 mi. S of Eshowe. Receives Klip and Buffalo rivers. Lower course forms S border of Zululand.

Tug Fork, river, W.Va., Ky., and Va., rises in McDowell co., S W.Va., flows 154 mi. generally NW, past Welch and Williamson, W.Va., along Ky.-W.Va. line, to Louisa, Ky., here joining Levisa Fork to form Big Sandy R. Partially navigable by means of dams and locks.

Tuggerah, Lake (tŭgĕ′rŭ), lagoon (□ 29), E New South Wales, Australia, opening into the Pacific 38 mi. NNE of Sydney; 10 mi. long, 4 mi. wide; summer resort.

Tuggurt, Algeria: see TOUGGOURT.

Tughlakabad, India: see DELHI, state.

Tuglie (to͞o′lyĕ), town (pop. 5,879), Lecce prov., Apulia, S Italy, 7 mi. ENE of Gallipoli; wine, olive oil.

Tugolesski Bor or **Tugolesskiy Bor** (to͞ogŭlyĕ′skē bôr″), town (1939 pop. over 500), E Moscow oblast, Russian SFSR, 5 mi. E (under jurisdiction) of Shatura; peat works.

Tugolukovo (to͞ogŭlo͞o′kŭvŭ), village (1926 pop. 4,987), S Tambov oblast, Russian SFSR, 50 mi. SSE of Tambov; wheat, sunflowers.

Tugssâk or **Tugssâq** (both: to͞okhshäk′), hunting settlement (pop. 55), Upernavik dist., W Greenland, on islet in Baffin Bay, 20 mi. N of Upernavik; 73°4′N 56°8′W.

Tuguegarao (to͞ogägärä′ō, –rou′), town (1939 pop. 10,281; 1948 municipality pop. 29,083), ⊙ Cagayan prov., N Luzon, Philippines, on Cagayan R. and 110 mi. NE of Baguio; 17°35′N 121°45′E. Trade center for agr. area (tobacco, rice). Airfield.

Tugulym (to͞ogo͞olĭm′), village (1948 pop. over 2,000), SE Sverdlovsk oblast, Russian SFSR, on Trans-Siberian RR and 33 mi. WSW of Tyumen; food processing, lumbering.

Tug Wajale (to͞og′wäjä′lā), village, W Br. Somaliland, on Ethiopian border, 50 mi. W of Hargeisa; camels, sheep, goats.

Tuhshan or **Tushan** (both: do͞o′shän′), town (pop. 11,640), ⊙ Tuhshan co. (pop. 125,607), S Kweichow prov., China, 70 mi. SE of Kweiyang and on railroad; alt. 3,271 ft.; cotton weaving, papermaking; rice, wheat, tobacco, millet. Antimony deposits near by.

Tuichi River (twē′chē), La Paz dept., NW Bolivia; formed by confluence of Pelechuco and Queara rivers c.3 mi. W of Pata; flows c.110 mi. NE and SE, past San José de Uchupiamomas, to Beni R. 9 mi. S of Rurrenabaque. Petroleum deposits along course.

Tuikao Shan, Formosa: see ALI SHAN.

Tui-la-k'o-p'a, Tibet: see THOK DAURAKPA.

Tuim (to͞oēm′), town (1945 pop. over 500), NW Khakass Autonomous Oblast, Krasnoyarsk Territory, Russian SFSR, on railroad and 75 mi. NW of Abakan; sawmilling.

Tuimazy or **Tuymazy** (to͞oēmä′zē), town (1948 pop. over 2,000), W Bashkir Autonomous SSR, Russian SFSR, on right tributary of Ik R., on railroad and 15 mi. NE of Oktyabrski (oil center), in Tuimazy oil field; flour milling, meat packing.

Tuineje (twēnā′hā), village (pop. 354), Fuerteventura, Canary Isls., 17 mi. SW of Puerto de Cabras; potatoes, corn, alfalfa, fruit, cochineal, tomatoes; wool. Limekilns, flour mills.

Tuin Gol or **Tüyin Gol** (tü′yēn gōl′), river in W central Mongolian People's Republic, rises on S slopes of the Khangai Mts. 50 mi. SW of Tsetserlik, flows 150 mi. S to lake Orok Nor in Gobi desert.

Tuira River or **Tuyra River** (twē′rä), longest (125 mi.) river of Panama, in Darien prov., rises in Darien highlands S of El Real, flows SE and then N, past Pinogana, El Real, and Chepigana, to San Miguel Gulf of the Pacific, forming 4-mi.-wide estuary (Puerto Darién) at La Palma. Navigable for 80 mi. above mouth. Receives the Chucunaque (right) near El Real. Basin is inhabited by Choco Indians.

Tuís (twēs), town (pop. 5,430), Cartago prov., central Costa Rica, on Tuís R. (right affluent of Reventazón R.) and 7 mi. SE of Turrialba; coffee center.

Tuisarkan or **Tuyserkan** (to͞oēsĕrkän′), town, Fifth Prov., in Malayer, W central Iran, 17 mi. S of Hamadan, on reverse slope of the Alwand; grain, fruit, tobacco, opium.

Tuitul, Cerro (sĕ′rō twētōol′), Andean peak (17,280 ft.) in W Salta prov., Argentina, 50 mi. W of San Antonio de los Cobres; 24°10′S.

Tujunga (tŭhŭng′gŭ), former city, Los Angeles co., S Calif., in San Fernando Valley, at base of San Gabriel Mts.; residential. Annexed 1932 by LOS ANGELES city. Tujunga (or Big Tujunga) Canyon, a recreational area, is N.

Tujunga Creek or **Big Tujunga Creek**, S Calif., a flood-time tributary of Los Angeles R., rises in San Gabriel Mts. N of Mt. Wilson, flows W and SW, through Tujunga or Big Tujunga Canyon (recreational area), and across San Fernando Valley, to Los Angeles R. Wide gravel bed of lower course, generally dry, is called Tujunga Wash. Flood-control works include Big Tujunga No. 1 Dam (251 ft. high, 800 ft. long; completed 1931), on upper course; Hansen Dam (122 ft. high, 10,509 ft. long; completed 1940), on lower course.

Tukan (to͞okän′), town (1939 pop. over 2,000), central Bashkir Autonomous SSR, Russian SFSR, in the S Urals, on S.Siberian RR and 40 mi. WSW of Beloretsk; mining center in Komarovo-Zigazinski iron dist.

Tukangbesi Islands or **Toekangbesi Islands** (both: to͞okängbĕ′sē), Indonesia, bet. Flores and Molucca seas, 20 mi. E of Buton across Buton Passage; 5°38′S 123°30′E. Comprise WANGIWANGI, TOMEA, BINONGKO, KALEDUPA, and many islets. Isls. are generally level. Fishing, agr. (coconuts, sago).

Tukh (to͞okh), **Tukh el Malaq**, or **Tukh al-Malaq** (both: ĕl mălăk′), village (pop. 10,064), Qalyubiya prov., Lower Egypt, on Cairo-Alexandria RR and 7 mi. SSE of Benha; cotton, flax, cereals, fruits.

Tukh Dalaka or **Tukh Dalakah** (dă′lăkŭ), town (pop. 11,279), Minufiya prov., Lower Egypt, 3 mi. SW of Tala; cereals, cotton, flax.

Tuklung (to͝ok′lo͝ong), village (pop. 30), SW Alaska, near Dillingham.

Tuktoyaktuk, Northwest Territories: see PORT BRABANT.

Tuk-Tuk, Northwest Territories: see PORT BRABANT.

Tukumi, Japan: see TSUKUMI.

Tukums (to͞o′ko͞oms), Ger. *Tuckum*, city (pop. 8,144), N Latvia, in Zemgale, 35 mi. W of Riga; rail junction; agr. market (grain, fodder); sawmilling, dairying, flour milling; mfg. of leather goods, rope woolens, concrete products. Has castle ruins.

Tukuyu (to͞oko͞o′yo͞o), town, Southern Highlands prov., S Tanganyika, in densely populated dist., 30 mi. SSE of Mbeya; tea, wheat, coffee, tobacco, pyrethrum; livestock. Called Neu-Langenburg under Ger. rule.

Tukwila (tŭk″wĭ′lŭ), town (pop. 800), King co., W central Wash., near Tacoma.

Tula (to͞o′lä). **1** Officially Tula de Allende, town (pop. 3,386), Hidalgo, central Mexico, on central plateau, on Tula R. and 45 mi. NNW of Mexico city, 40 mi. W of Pachuca; alt. 6,771 ft. Rail junction; agr. center (cereals, beans, sugar cane, cotton, livestock); cotton and flour mills; lime kilns. Once capital of the Toltecs; contains some anc. remains and colonial relics. Jasso cement factory is 4 mi. SE. **2** City (pop. 4,588), Tamaulipas, NE Mexico, on interior plateau, 65 mi. SW of Ciudad Victoria; alt. 3,848 ft.; agr. center (cereals, livestock, mescal); flour milling, tanning.

Tula (to͞o′lŭ), oblast (□ 9,300; 1946 pop. estimate 1,500,000) in W central European Russian SFSR; ⊙ Tula. In NE Central Russian Upland, in transition zone bet. forest and wooded steppe; leached black earth; bounded (NW) by Oka R.; rainfall and tree density decrease toward SE. Minerals include lignite of Moscow Basin, iron ore, marble, refractory clays, gypsum, gravel. Basic crops: coarse grain (W), wheat (E), potatoes (center); also sugar beets (SE), rubber-bearing plants (S), flax (W center), truck produce (around Tula). Lignite mining (Shchekino, Bolokhovo, Kaganovich, Bogoroditsk), iron mining (Kireyevka, Ogarevka). Metallurgical works (near Tula), extensive ironworks, synthetic-rubber mfg. (Yefremov), flour milling, distilling, sugar refining. Formed 1937 out of Moscow oblast.

Tula, city (1939 pop. 272,404), ⊙ Tula oblast, Russian SFSR, on Upa R. and 105 mi. S of Moscow; 54°12′N 37°37′E. Rail hub in Moscow lignite basin, metalworking center; mfg. (samovars, locks, arms, agr. machinery, ironware, clothing goods), tanning, flour milling, sugar refining. Metallurgical works at Kosaya Gora (S) and Novotulski (E). Old kremlin (1521) is in center of city, surrounded by quadrangular turreted wall. It was restored in 1950. Has art and agr. mus., institutes of pedagogy and mechanical engineering. Founded 12th cent. as outpost of Ryazan on Upa R. isl., chartered 1380. Suffered repeated Tatar and Lithuanian attacks (14th–15th cent.). After 1503, became S fortress of Moscow domain; developed into arms-mfg. center in 17th cent. Peter the Great built 1st ironworks (1701) and 1st arms factory (1712). Increased industrial development in 19th cent. Was ⊙ Tula govt. until 1929. During Second World War, Tula withstood close siege (1941) by Germans in Moscow campaign.

Tula (to͞o′lŭ), village (1940 pop. 158), Lafayette co., N Miss., 13 mi. SE of Oxford, in agr. and timber area.

Tulagi (to͞olä′gē), volcanic island, Solomon Isls., SW Pacific, 2 mi. S of Florida across Tulagi Harbor; 3 mi. in circumference; former ⊙ protectorate. Site of chief Chinese settlement in group. In Second World War, Tulagi, occupied early 1942 by Japanese, was the scene (Aug. 7, 1942), along with GUADALCANAL, of Allied attack.

Tulahuén (to͞oläwĕn′), village (1930 pop. 1,078), Coquimbo prov., N central Chile, 40 mi. SE of Ovalle; copper-mining center.

Tulainyo Lake (to͞olŭn′yō), E Calif., tiny lake (alt. over 12,020 ft.) just N of Mt. Whitney, in the Sierra Nevada; one of highest in U.S.

Tulak (to͞olŭk′), town (pop. over 2,000), Herat prov., NW Afghanistan, 90 mi. ESE of Herat, in W outliers of the Hindu Kush. Pop.: Persian-speaking Taimanis. Also spelled Telek.

Tulalip (tŭlă′lĭp, to͞o–), village (pop. c.100), Skagit co., NW Wash., on Puget Sound just NW of Everett; Indian Agency hq. for Tulalip and other nearby Indian reservations.

Tulamba, W Pakistan: see TALAMBA.

Tulameen (tŭ″lŭmēn′), village, S B.C., in Cascade Mts., on Tulameen R. at mouth of Otter Creek, and 55 mi. W of Penticton; coal mining.

Tulan (do͞o′län′), town, ⊙ Tulan co. (pop. 40,000), E central Tsinghai prov., China, 130 mi. W of Sining; road junction on trade routes to Tibet and Sinkiang; salt-producing center; livestock, camels. Until 1931 called Silikow.

Tulancingo (to͞olänsēng′gō), city (pop. 12,552), Hidalgo, central Mexico, on central plateau, 24 mi. E of Pachuca; alt. 7,290 ft. Rail junction; agr. center (corn, wheat, vegetables, maguey, livestock); dairying, flour and textile milling. Airfield.

Tulare (to͞olâ′rē, to͞olâr′), county (□ 4,845; pop. 149,264), central Calif.; ⊙ Visalia. Extends E from San Joaquin Valley to crest of the Sierra Nevada; Mt. WHITNEY (14,495 ft.), highest point in U.S., is on E boundary. Includes SEQUOIA NATIONAL PARK, parts of Kings Canyon Natl. Park, and Inyo and Sequoia natl. forests. Tule River and Strathmore Indian reservations are in co. Drained by Kaweah, St. Johns, Tule, and Kern rivers. Citrus fruit (grown in thermal belt), long-staple cotton, grapes, deciduous fruit, alfalfa, grain, truck, olives; stock and poultry raising, dairying. Lumbering (pine, fir); working of sand and gravel, tungsten, clay deposits; marble and granite quarries; natural-gas wells. Farm-produce packing, processing, and shipping (at Visalia, Tulare, Porterville, Lindsay, Exeter, Woodlake, Dinuba); lumber milling. Formed 1852.

Tulare. 1 (to͞olâ'rē, to͞olâr') City (pop. 12,445), Tulare co., S central Calif., in San Joaquin Valley, 45 mi. SE of Fresno; rail junction; shipping and processing center; creameries, cheese and dried-milk plants, cotton gins, fruit canneries, packing plants. Co. fairgrounds here. Founded 1872, inc. 1888. 2 (to͞olâr') Town (pop. 212), Spink co., E central S.Dak., 10 mi. S of Redfield; trade center for farming area.

Tulare Lake (to͞olâ'rē, to͞olâr'), Kings co., S central Calif., virtually dry lake basin in San Joaquin Valley, S of Hanford; waters of Kings, Kaweah, and Kern rivers, now diverted upstream for irrigation, reach it only in unusually wet seasons. Also fed by Tule R. Lake (part of whose bed is now farm land) was once c.50 mi. long, c.35 mi. wide. Slough connects it with Buena Vista L. (55 mi. SSE).

Tula River (to͞o"lä), central Mexico, rises NW of Mexico city, flows c.100 mi. N and NW, past Tula, Mixquiahuala, and Ixmiquilpan, to Moctezuma R. at Querétaro border, 9 mi. SW of Zimapán.

Tularosa (to͞olu̇rō'su̇, -zu̇), village (pop. 1,642), Otero co., S N.Mex., just W of Sacramento Mts., 12 mi. NNW of Alamogordo; alt. 4,514 ft. Trade and livestock-shipping point; lumber, cotton. Platted 1862. Mescalero Indian Reservation and part of Lincoln Natl. Forest near by.

Tularosa Basin, desert plain in S N.Mex. and W Texas; from the Rio Grande near El Paso extends c.130 mi. N bet. Franklin, Organ, San Andres mts. (W) and Hueco and Sacramento mts. (E); 20–40 mi. wide. Contains large alkali flat and remarkable gypsum dunes of WHITE SANDS NATIONAL MONUMENT.

Tularosa Mountains, W N.Mex., in Catron co., just E of Tularosa R., near Ariz. line, within Apache Natl. Forest. Highest point, Eagle Peak (9,802 ft.).

Tularosa River, W N.Mex., rises in several forks in Catron co., flows c.40 mi. SW, past Tularosa Mts., to San Francisco R. just S of Reserve. Drains part of Apache Natl. Forest.

Tulatovo, Russian SFSR: see IRISTON.

Tulbagh (tŭl'bäkh), town (pop. 1,206), SW Cape Prov., U. of So. Afr., 25 mi. NNW of Wellington; winegrowing center. Scene of noted flower shows; has mus. and old church. First settled 1699. Drostdy village, 3 mi. NNE, has large wineries.

Tulcán (to͞olkän'), town (1950 pop. 10,658), ⊙ Carchi prov., N Ecuador, in the Andes, on Pan-American Highway, near Colombia border (6 mi. W of Ipiales), and 90 mi. NE of Quito; 0°49'N 77°43'W; alt. c.9,000 ft. Trading, cattle-raising, and agr. center (cereals, sugar cane, coffee); tanning, dairying, mfg. of woolen goods (carpets, ponchos). Customhouse. An old Indian city, it was severely damaged by 1923 earthquake. Thermal springs near by. On Colombia border, 3 mi. N, is natural Rumichaca bridge, across which passes Pan American Highway.

Tulcea (to͝ol'chä), town (1948 pop. 21,642), Galati prov., SE Rumania, in Dobruja, on Sfantu-Gheorghe arm of the Danube delta, 40 mi. ESE of Galati; rail terminus, fishing center, and important inland port, trading in grain, livestock, animal products, and wine. Woodworking, tobacco processing, flour milling, sulphuric acid and cordage mfg. Limestone, marble, and granite quarrying in near-by Tulcea hills. Non-Rumanian nationals represent c.30% of pop.

Tulchin or **Tul'chin** (to͞olchĕn'), city (1926 pop. 17,391), S central Vinnitsa oblast, Ukrainian SSR, 40 mi. SSE of Vinnitsa; clothing and leather industries; fruit canning. Main Decembrist revolutionary center (1825).

Tulcingo (to͞olsĕng'gō), town (pop. 1,881), Puebla, central Mexico, 40 mi. S of Matamoros; corn, sugar cane, fruit, stock.

Tule, Mexico: see SANTA MARÍA DEL TULE.

Tule, El, Mexico: see EL TULE.

Tuléar (to͞oläär'), province (□ 75,210; 1948 pop. 848,300), W and S Madagascar; ⊙ Tuléar. Drained by Tsiribihina, Mangoky, and Onilahy rivers. Region of dry plateaus noted for cattle raising and pulse production (beans, lima beans, dry peas). Corn, rice (under irrigation), castor beans, sisal, raphia are also grown. There are valuable coal deposits (in Sakoa R. basin); mica, copper, and some gold. Lumbering is active in SE. Fisheries. Main centers: Tuléar, Fort-Dauphin, Morondava.

Tuléar, town (1948 pop. 15,654), ⊙ Tuléar prov., SW Madagascar, on Mozambique Channel at N end of St. Augustin Bay, 400 mi. SW of Tananarive; 23°20'S 43°45'E. Main seaport of SW coast, shipping pulse, corn, rice, castor beans, peanuts, sisal, raphia. Also exports mother-of-pearl, tortoise shell and edible sea molluscs (for China). Sisal processing. Its agr. station experiments with fodder, cotton, and fruit trees; there is also a large livestock-breeding farm. R.C. and Protestant missions. Seaplane base.

Tule Creek (to͞o'lē), NW Texas, formed on Llano Estacado W of Tulia by intermittent headstreams, flows c.45 mi. E and NE to Prairie Dog Town Fork of Red R.; lower course of c.15 mi. is through scenic Tule Canyon, gorge cut in Cap Rock escarpment by stream's descent from high plains.

Tuleiken or **Tuleyken** (to͞olyäkyĕn'), village (1939 pop. over 500), NE Osh oblast, Kirghiz SSR, near Osh; cotton.

Tulelake (to͞o"lēläk'), city (pop. 1,028), Siskiyou co., N Calif., 25 mi. SE of Klamath Falls, Oregon; center of reclamation project. In Second World War, a relocation camp for evacuated Japanese-Americans was near by. Lava Beds Natl. Monument and Tule L. (site of waterfowl refuge) are S. Inc. 1937.

Tule Lake (to͞o'lē), NE Siskiyou co., N Calif., near Oregon line; has variable area. Receives Lost R. (N). Used for storage of irrigation water for surrounding region which is undergoing reclamation. U.S. waterfowl refuge (c.37,000 acres) is here. Tulelake city is just N, Lava Beds Natl. Monument just S.

Tulemayarvi (to͞o'lyĭmīŭrvē), Finnish *Tulemajärvi*, lake in SW Karelo-Finnish SSR, 65 mi. W of Petrozavodsk; 5 mi. long, 2 mi. wide. Iron deposits on shore.

Tule River (to͞o'lē), S central Calif., formed in the Sierra Nevada E of Porterville by its North and Middle forks, flows c.50 mi. SW and W into Tulare L. Site of planned Success Reservoir (for flood control) of CENTRAL VALLEY project.

Tuleyken, Kirghiz SSR: see TULEIKEN.

Tulghes (to͞ol'gĕsh), Rum. *Tulgheș*, Hung. *Gyergyótölgyes* (dyĕr'dyōtŭl"dyĕsh), village (pop. 4,526), Bacau prov., E central Rumania, in the Moldavian Carpathians, 31 mi. N of Mercurea-Ciuc. In Hungary, 1940–45.

Tulh Pass, Aden: see TALH PASS.

Tuli (to͞o'lē), village, Bulawayo prov., S Southern Rhodesia, in Matabeleland, near Buchunaland Protectorate border, on Shashi R. and 65 mi. SSW of West Nicholson; cattle, sheep, goats; corn. Coal deposits. A Br. base in occupation (1890s) of Southern Rhodesia and in 1896 Matabele rebellion. Formerly called Fort Tuli.

Tulia (to͞o'lēu̇), city (pop. 3,222), ⊙ Swisher co., NW Texas, on Llano Estacado, 25 mi. N of Plainview; market, processing, and shipping center for wheat, cotton, dairying, and cattle region; cotton ginning, cheese mfg. Tule Canyon is near. Settled 1890, inc. 1909.

Tulik Volcano, Alaska: see UMNAK ISLAND.

Tuliszkow (to͞olēsh'ko͞of), Pol. *Tuliszków*, Rus. *Tulishkov* (to͞olēsh'ku̇f), town (pop. 2,128), Poznan prov., central Poland, 9 mi. WNW of Turek; distilling, flour milling.

Tuljapur (to͞ol'jäpo͝or), town (pop. 7,109), Osmanabad dist., W Hyderabad state, India, 11 mi. S of Osmanabad; road center; agr. market (wheat, millet, cotton, rice). Hindu place of pilgrimage.

Tulkarm (to͞ol'kärm), town (1946 pop. estimate 8,860) of Palestine, after 1948 in W Jordan, on Israeli border, on W slope of Samarian Hills, at E edge of Plain of Sharon, 20 mi. NE of Tel Aviv; rail junction.

Tulla (tŭ'lu̇), Gaelic *Tulach*, town (pop. 470), E central Co. Clare, Ireland, 10 mi. E of Ennis; agr. market (dairying, cattle raising; grain, potatoes).

Tulla, Loch, Scotland: see ORCHY RIVER.

Tullaghoge or **Tullyhogue** (both: tŭ"lu̇hōg'), agr. village (district pop. 950), NE Co. Tyrone, Northern Ireland, 3 mi. S of Cookstown; flax, potatoes, oats; cattle. Site of great rath; former residence of the O'Hagans, Justiciars of Tyrone. Each O'Neill chief of Ulster was inaugurated here; in 1602 the inauguration stone was destroyed by Lord Mountjoy.

Tullahassee (tŭ"lu̇hă'sē), town (pop. 209), Wagoner co., E Okla., 7 mi. NW of Muskogee, near Arkansas R.; cotton ginning.

Tullahoma (tŭlu̇hō'mu̇), town (pop. 7,562), Coffee co., central Tenn., 55 mi. NW of Chattanooga, in timber and farm area; mfg. of shoes, baseballs, bedspreads, clothing, wood and leather products, cheese. State vocational school for girls near by. U.S. Air Force's huge Arnold Engineering Development Center was begun here, 1951. Settled 1850; inc. 1852. Captured (1863) by Federal troops in Civil War.

Tullamore (tŭ"lu̇môr'), village (pop. 326), central New South Wales, Australia, 230 mi. WNW of Sydney; tin mines.

Tullamore, Gaelic *Tulach Mhór*, urban district (pop. 5,897), ⊙ Co. Offaly, Ireland, in central part of co., on the Grand Canal and 50 mi. W of Dublin; woolen milling, alcohol distilling; agr. market (barley, potatoes; cattle). Near by is Durrow, with abbey founded 553 by St. Columba.

Tulle (tül), town (pop. 14,744), ⊙ Corrèze dept., S central France, 45 mi. SSE of Limoges; road center. Has natl. factory of firearms. Produces accordions, wooden toys, woolens, brushes, food preserves, tanning extracts. Antimony deposits near by. Has given its name to tulle material first produced here. Old town extends for 1½ mi. along gorge of Corrèze R. and is dominated by modern administrative bldgs. and schools on N slope. Has 12th–14th-cent. cathedral with enamel paintings.

Tullgarn, palace, Sweden: see TROSA.

Tulliallan, Scotland: see KINCARDINE, Fifeshire.

Tullibody (tŭ"lĭbŏ'dē), village in Alloa parish, Clackmannan, Scotland, near Devon R.; leather tanning.

Tullinge (tŭ'lĭng-u̇), residential village (pop. 2,053), Stockholm co., E Sweden, 11 mi. SW of Stockholm; tourist resort.

Tullins (tülē'), town (pop. 3,039), Isère dept., SE France, near the Isère, 14 mi. NW of Grenoble; market center in chestnut-growing area. Industrial suburb of Fures (1 mi. NNE) has paper mills, edge-tool factories.

Tulln (to͞oln), anc. *Comagena*, town (pop. 5,354), central Lower Austria, on the Danube and 14 mi. WNW of Vienna. Was Roman settlement, river port. Has anc. church, airport.

Tulloch Dam, Calif.: see STANISLAUS RIVER.

Tulloch Point (tŭ'lŭk), S extremity of King William Isl., S Franklin Dist., Northwest Territories, on Simpson Strait, opposite Adelaide Peninsula; 68°27'N 97°5'W.

Tullos (tŭ'lu̇s), town (pop. 732), La Salle parish, central La., 36 mi. N of Alexandria, near Bayou Castor; center for oil field near by; agr. (truck, cotton, corn, potatoes); timber.

Tullow (tŭ'lō), Gaelic *Tulach Ó bhFéidhlim*, town (pop. 1,674), NE Co. Carlow, Ireland, on Slaney R. and 8 mi. ESE of Carlow; agr. market (sheep; wheat, potatoes, beets). Anc. cross is relic of priory.

Tullum, France: see TOUL.

Tully (tŭ'lē), town (pop. 2,068), NE Queensland, Australia, 75 mi. SSE of Cairns; sugar-producing center.

Tully, resort village (pop. 744), Onondaga co., central N.Y., near Big L. (c.2 mi. long), 18 mi. S of Syracuse; mfg. (dairy and food products, cheese boxes). Agr. (poultry, potatoes, cabbage, hay).

Tullyhogue, Northern Ireland: see TULLAGHOGE.

Tullytown, borough (pop. 648), Bucks co., SE Pa., 6 mi. SW of Trenton, N.J., and on Delaware R. Near by is "Pennsbury," restored home of William Penn.

Tuloma River (to͞o'lu̇mŭ), W Murmansk oblast, Russian SFSR, leaves lake Notozero (35 mi. long; receives Lotta and Nota rivers), flows 40 mi. NE to Kola Gulf at Murmashi (site of Tuloma hydroelectric station).

Tulovo (to͞o'lôvô), village (pop. 1,169), Stara Zagora dist., central Bulgaria, in Kazanlik Basin, 9 mi. ESE of Kazanlik; rail junction; horticulture (roses, mint), grain, truck produce; chestnut and mulberry groves.

Tulsa (tŭl'su̇), county (□ 572; pop. 251,686), NE Okla.; ⊙ TULSA. Intersected by Arkansas R. and Bird Creek. Stock raising, agr. (dairy products; poultry, corn, grain, truck, pecans, fruit, cotton). Mfg. at Tulsa. Important oil and gas production, oil refining; some coal mining. Formed 1907.

Tulsa, city (pop. 182,740), ⊙ Tulsa co., NE Okla., on Arkansas R. (bridges) 15 mi. E of mouth of the Cimarron, and 100 mi. NE of Oklahoma City; 36°9'N 95°59'W; alt. c.800 ft. State's 2d largest city. Known as the "oil capital of the world," Tulsa is an administrative, financial, supply, and distribution center for the oil industry of the mid-continent region, with hq. of many major oil firms and pipe-line operators, huge refineries; center of production and distribution of oil-field equipment; hub of pipe lines carrying oil and natural gas from Texas, La., and Okla. to cities of N and E U.S. Also produces machinery; iron, steel, and brass products; glass, aircraft, automotive parts, furniture, chemicals, textiles, plastics, paint, brick and tile, clothing, packed meat and other food products. A maintenance center for airline equipment. Surrounding region has oil and natural-gas fields, farms (fruit, cotton, corn, grain, vegetables; dairy products), cattle ranches, strip coal mines. Near-by industrial towns are Sand Springs and Sapulpa. Seat of Univ. of Tulsa, Spartan Col. of Aeronautical Engineering; also has an art gall., state fairgrounds, and bldgs. of the International Petroleum Exposition (biennial). Mohawk Park (recreation) is near by. Tulsa region was 1st settled in mid-19th cent. by Indian immigrants of the Five Civilized Tribes; town was founded in 1880 as railroad depot, and inc. in 1896. Greatest growth came after discovery of oil in 1901.

Tulsequah (tŭl"su̇kwä'), village, NW B.C., on Alaska border, on Taku R. and 40 mi. NE of Juneau; gold mining.

Tulsipur (to͞ol'sēpo͝or), town (pop. 7,245), Gonda dist., NE Uttar Pradesh, India, 16 mi. NE of Balrampur; sugar processing; rice, wheat, gram, sugar cane. Sometimes called Tulshipur.

Tulskaya or **Tul'skaya** (to͞ol'skīŭ), village (1926 pop. 1,825), S central Krasnodar Territory, Russian SFSR, on Belaya R. and 7 mi. SSE of Maikop; tobacco, orchards.

Tultepec (to͞oltäpĕk'), town (pop. 2,566), Mexico state, central Mexico, 17 mi. N of Mexico city; grain, maguey, stock.

Tultitlán (to͞oltētlän'), officially Tultitlán de Mariano Escobedo, town (pop. 2,730), Mexico state, central Mexico, 15 mi. N of Mexico city; grain, maguey, stock.

Tuluá (to͞olwä'), town (pop. 12,017), Valle del Cauca dept., W Colombia, in Cauca valley, on railroad and highway, and 55 mi. NE of Cali; trading and agr. center (tobacco, coffee, cacao, sugar, cattle).

T'u-lu-fan, China: see TURFAN.

Tuluksak (tōōlōōk'săk), Eskimo village (pop. 116), W Alaska, on lower Kuskokwim R. and 35 mi. NE of Bethel; supply point for trappers.

Tulumba or **Villa Tulumba** (vē'yä tōōlōōm'bä), village (pop. estimate 800), ⊙ Tulumba dept. (□ c.3,000; pop. 19,176), N Córdoba prov., Argentina, 70 mi. N of Córdoba; tourist resort and stock-raising center.

Tulum Valley (tōōlōōm'), central San Juan prov., Argentina, bet. Sierra de Villicún and Sierra del Pie de Palo, extends NNE from San Juan, in irrigation area (wine, grain, fruit).

Tulun (tōōlōōn'), city (1940 pop. estimate 30,000), SW Irkutsk oblast, Russian SFSR, on Trans-Siberian RR, on Iya R. and 220 mi. NW of Irkutsk; linked by highway with Ust-Kut (on Lena R.). Industrial center; sawmilling, linen mfg.; distillery, meat plant. Has noted grain-selection station; teachers col.

Tulung, India: see CHUNGTANG.

Tulungagung or **Toeloengagoeng** (both: tōōlōōng"-ägōōng'), town (pop. 31,767), SE Java, Indonesia, on tributary of Brantas R., 80 mi. ESE of Solo; 8°3'S 111°54'E; trade center for agr. area (sugar, copra, rice, corn, tobacco, tea, cinchona bark, rubber); textile works. Marble quarries near by.

Tulyehualco (tōōlyāwäl'kō), town (pop. 2,820), Federal Dist., central Mexico, 15 mi. SSE of Mexico city; cereal, fruit, vegetables, livestock.

Tuma, Japan: see TSUMA.

Tuma (tōō'mŭ), town (1948 pop. over 2,000), N Ryazan oblast, Russian SFSR, 50 mi. NE of Ryazan; woodworking.

Tumacacori National Monument (tōō"mŭkă'kŭrē) (10 acres; established 1908), S Ariz., near Mex. line, 48 mi. S of Tucson. Here is R.C. mission church built by Franciscans at Pima Indian village visited (1691) by Father Kino. Dedicated 1822, abandoned after 1827, upon secularization of missions. Mus. has historical exhibits.

Tumac-Humac Mountains, Guianas-Brazil: see TUMUC-HUMAC MOUNTAINS.

Tumaco (tōōmä'kō), city (pop. 9,671), Nariño dept., SW Colombia, port on the Pacific, built on small isl. off coast, 110 mi. WNW of Pasto; 1°49'N 78°46'W. Colombia's leading Pacific port after Buenaventura, with a rail line running inland to meet the Pasto highway at El Diviso, it is a trading center in an unhealthy, torrid climate. Exports coffee, cacao, tobacco, vegetables, tagua nuts, rubber, copper and gold dust; has pearl fisheries, saltworks. Customhouse, airport. Badly damaged by 1947 fire.

Tumaco Road, inlet of the Pacific in Nariño dept., SW Colombia, a bay (22 mi. long, 12 mi. wide at its entrance) surrounded by tropical forested lowlands. Port of Tumaco is on isl. near SW gate.

Tumán (tōōmän'), village (pop. 3,302), Lambayeque dept., NW Peru, on coastal plain, on Taimi Canal (irrigation), on railroad and 10 mi. E of Chiclayo; sugar-producing center; sugar milling, distilling.

Tuman-gang, Korea-Manchuria: see TUMEN RIVER.

Tumanovo (tōōmä'nŭvŭ), village (1926 pop. 175), NE Smolensk oblast, Russian SFSR, 21 mi. NE of Vyazma; peat works.

Tumanyan (tōōmŭnyän'), village (1939 pop. over 500), N Armenian SSR, on railroad and 10 mi. S of Alaverdi; fireproof clays.

Tuma River (tōō'mä), central Nicaragua, rises near San Rafael del Norte in Cordillera Dariense, flows c.150 mi. E to Río Grande 21 mi. W of La Cruz. Navigable for small vessels.

Tumatumari, village and falls in central Br. Guiana, on Potaro R. 9 mi. W of its mouth; linked by road with Wismar-Rockstone RR, on lower Essequibo R. In diamond- and gold-bearing region.

Tumba (tōōm'bä), village, Leopoldville prov., W Belgian Congo, near railroad, 110 mi. ENE of Boma; trading center for native produce (manioc, plantain, bananas, yams); cattle raising. R.C. mission with small seminary and trade schools.

Tumba (tōōm'bä), peak (6,166 ft.) in Belasica mts., on Greek-Yugoslav-Bulg. border, 15 mi. WSW of Petrich, Bulgaria.

Tumba (tŭm'bä"), village (pop. 1,092), Stockholm co., E Sweden, 12 mi. SW of Stockholm. Paper mill, established 1755 by the Riksbank (national bank), makes paper for Swedish banknotes.

Tumba, Lake (tōōm'bä) (□ 193), W Belgian Congo, E of Congo R. and 75 mi. NNW of L. Leopold II; 25 mi. long, 18 mi. wide, 6–20 ft. deep. Empties into the Congo by Irebu channel just opposite influx of the Ubangi. Shallow, with low shores. Navigable for river steamers.

Tumbaco (tōōmbä'kō), village, Pichincha prov., N central Ecuador, in the Andes, on Quito-Ibarra RR and 8 mi. E of Quito; fruit, cereals, sugar cane. Near by are the Cunuc-Yacu thermal springs.

Tumbador or **El Tumbador** (ĕl tōōmbädōr'), town (1950 pop. 655), San Marcos dept., SW Guatemala, in Pacific piedmont, 11 mi. NNW of Coatepeque; coffee, sugar cane, grain, livestock.

Tumbalá (tōōmbälä'), town (pop. 441), Chiapas, S Mexico, in spur of Sierra Madre, 45 mi. NNE of San Cristóbal de las Casas; alt. 5,164 ft.; cereals, fruit.

Tumbarumba (tŭm"bŭrŭm'bŭ), town (pop. 1,196), S New South Wales, Australia, 75 mi. WSW of Canberra; rail terminus; sheep.

Tumbatu Island (tōōmbä'tōō), in Indian Ocean, Zanzibar protectorate, off NW coast of Zanzibar isl.; opposite Mkokotoni; 6 mi. long, 2 mi. wide. Copra, corn, cassava, sweet potatoes; fishing. Ruins of medieval Persian settlement in SE.

Tumbaya (tōōmbī'ä), town (pop. estimate 500), ⊙ Tumbaya dept. (□ c.1,400; 1947 pop. 4,367), SW Jujuy prov., Argentina, on the Río Grande de Jujuy, on railroad and 26 mi. NW of Jujuy; agr. center (corn, alfalfa, wine, livestock); flour milling.

Tumbayung Chu, river, Tibet: see NYANG CHU.

Tumbes (tōōm'bĕs), department (□ 1,591; pop. 26,473), NW Peru; ⊙ Tumbes. Bordered by Ecuador (N and E) and the Pacific (W); drained by Zarumilla and Tumbes rivers. Primarily a plain, reaching E to Andean foothills. Has occasional rainfall, unlike the generally dry conditions on coastal plain. Main Peruvian tobacco dist.; cotton, rice; cattle and goat raising; fisheries. Charcoal burning (San Pedro de los Incas), salt extraction (Zarumilla), and petroleum refining (Zorritos) are main industries. Crossed by Pan American Highway; served by railroad bet. Tumbes and Puerto Pizarro. Tumbes was first constituted as a littoral prov. in 1901 and became a dept. in 1942. Sometimes Túmbez.

Tumbes, city (pop. 6,355), ⊙ Tumbes dept. and Tumbes prov. (formed 1942), NW Peru, on coastal plain, on Tumbes R., on Pan American Highway and 630 mi. NNW of Lima; 3°34'S 80°28'W. Road junction, connected by railroad with Puerto Pizarro; airport. Tobacco center; cotton, rice; charcoal burning, rice milling. Tourist resort. Here in 1532 Pizarro began his conquest of Peru. Tumbes developed considerably after Peru-Ecuador conflict through trade with Ecuadorian border towns. Became city in 1942. Sometimes Túmbez.

Tumbes River, in Peru and Ecuador, rises as the Puyango or Puango in S Ecuador, flows c.110 mi. W and N, in mid-course along international line, and past Tumbes (Peru), to the Pacific in the Gulf of Guayaquil, 4 mi. W of Puerto Pizarro. Navigable for small craft. Formerly spelled Túmbez.

Tumbotino (tōōm'bŏtyĕnŭ), town (1939 pop. over 2,000), W Gorki oblast, Russian SFSR, 3 mi. NW of Pavlovo, across Oka R.; metalworking center.

Tumby Bay (tŭm'bē), village (pop. 596), S South Australia, on SE Eyre Peninsula, 28 mi. NNE of Port Lincoln and on Tumby Bay (formerly Harvey Bay) of Spencer Gulf; wheat, talc; jetty.

Tumen or **T'u-men** (tōō'mŭn'), town (1938 pop. 26,306), E Kirin prov., Manchuria, on railroad and 20 mi. E of Yenki, on Tumen R. (Korea line); frontier station and lumber center; sawmilling.

Tumen River, Chinese *Tumen Kiang* or *T'u-men Chiang* (both: tōō'mŭn' jyäng'), Jap. *Tomon-ko* (tōmōn'kō'), Korean *Tuman-gang* (tōōmän'gäng'), river on Korea-Manchuria line, rises on E slopes of Changpai mtn., flows NE along international border, past Musan and Hoeryong, turns E and SE at Tumen, and empties into Sea of Japan, forming Korea-USSR line near mouth; 324 mi. long. Unnavigable except in lower reaches, it drains lumbering and coal-mining area. Frozen Nov.–March.

Tumeremo (tōōmärä'mō), town (pop. 2,621), Bolívar state, SE Venezuela, 23 mi. E of El Callao, 160 mi. ESE of Ciudad Bolívar; 7°14'N 61°26'W; gold-mining center. Airfield.

Tumilat, Wadi (wă'dē tōōmē'lăt), narrow valley, NE Egypt, running E-W (30°33'N) through the Arabian Desert bet. the Damietta branch of the Nile and the Suez Canal. In anc. times it carried a small Red Sea–Nile canal, and in the valley Ramses II built the treasure city of Tell el Maskhuta near ABU SUWEIR. Today the Ismailia Canal and the Cairo–Ismailia RR follow its course.

Tumindao Island (tōōmēndä'ō, –dou') (□ 6.9; pop. c.3,000), Sulu prov., Philippines, in Sibutu Group of Sulu Archipelago, just W of Sibutu.

Tuminkatti (tōōm'ĭnkŭt"tē), town (pop. 5,188), Dharwar dist., S Bombay, India, 14 mi. S of Ranibennur; chili, cotton, millet, peanuts. Also spelled Tumminkatti or Tamminkatti.

Tumkur (tōōmkōōr'), district (□ 4,084; pop. 953,877), E central Mysore, India; ⊙ Tumkur. On Deccan Plateau; drained (S) by Shimsha R. Agr.: coconuts, betel nuts, tobacco, oilseeds (peanuts, castor beans), millet, rice; silk growing in center, S, and E. Sheep and goat raising, hand-loom weaving, biri mfg., gold- and blacksmithing. Manganese mined in W, granite and corundum in E hills (sandalwood plantations, lac cultivation). Chief towns: Tumkur, Chiknayakanhalli, Gubbi, Kunigal (horse-breeding farm).

Tumkur, town (pop. 21,893), ⊙ Tumkur dist., central Mysore, India, 80 mi. NNE of Mysore; road center; rice milling, tobacco curing, goldsmithing, mfg. of biris, wooden furniture, bricks, tiles; handicrafts (brass vessels, glass bangles, coir rope and sacks). Betel nut farming. Science Col. (affiliated with Univ. of Mysore). Picturesque resort on Devarayadurga hill (alt. c.3,900 ft.), 8 mi. E.

Tumlong (tōōm'lông'), village, E Sikkim, India, 7 mi. N of Gangtok, in extreme W Assam Himalayas; corn, rice, pulse. Buddhist monastery near by.

Tummel River (tŭ'mŭl), Perthshire, Scotland, issues from E end of Loch Rannoch, flows 29 mi. E and SE, through Loch Tummel (4 mi. long), past Pitlochry, to the Tay just SE of Logierait. Receives Garry R.

Tumminkatti, India: see TUMINKATTI.

Tummo or **Toummo** (tōōm'mō), water hole, S Fezzan, Libya, on Fr. West Africa border, 160 mi. S of Gatrun. On route to L. Chad.

Tumpat (tōōm'pät'), town (pop. 4,335), N Kelantan, Malaya, South China Sea port at mouth of Kelantan R., 7 mi. NW of Kota Bharu, near Thailand line; rail terminus and coastwise port of call; saw- and rice milling; copra warehouse. During Second World War, Jap. troops landed here, Dec. 1941.

Tumsar (tōōm'sŭr), town (pop. 13,266), Bhandara dist., central Madhya Pradesh, India, 16 mi. NNE of Bhandara, on rail spur serving manganese mines (N); agr. market; rice milling, wheelmaking.

Tumu (tōō'mōō), town, Northern Territories, N Gold Coast, 65 mi. ENE of Lawra, near Fr. West Africa border, on road; shea nuts, durra, yams; cattle, skins.

Tumuc-Humac Mountains (tōōmōōk' ōōmäk', tōō'-mōōk-ōō'mäk), in Brazil *Serra de Tumucumaque* (sĕ'rŭ dĭ tōōmōōkōōmä'kĭ), range of N South America, on border bet. Brazil and Du. and Fr. Guiana, extending c.180 mi. E–W in lat. 2°N, forming E continuation of the Serra Acaraí and N watershed of Amazon basin. Rises to c.2,800 ft. Sometimes Tumac-Humac.

Tumus, Russian SFSR: see BYKOVSKI.

Tumusla River (tōōmōō'slä), Potosí dept., S Bolivia, rises in several branches in Cordillera de los Frailes, flows 45 mi. SE, past Tumusla, joining Cotagaita R. c.15 mi. W of Palca Grande. The combined stream, which is sometimes considered (down to the influx of the Cinti) to be the Tumusla and sometimes the Cotagaita, flows E and S, joining the San Juan just below Villa Abecia to form PILAYA RIVER.

Tumut (tŭ'mŭt), town (pop. 2,725), S New South Wales, Australia, 50 mi. W of Canberra; rail terminus; sheep center; dairy plant; chromite. Yarrangobilly limestone caves are 33 mi. SE.

Tumutuk (tōōmōōtōōk'), village (1948 pop. over 2,000), E Tatar Autonomous SSR, Russian SFSR, on Ik R. and 39 mi. NNE of Bugulma; wheat, livestock.

Tumwater (tŭm'wôtŭr), town (pop. 2,725), Thurston co., W Wash., just S of Olympia and on Deschutes R. Founded 1845 as 1st American settlement in Puget Sound area. Sometimes considered the end of the Oregon Trail.

Tun, Iran: see FIRDAUS.

Tuna (tōō'nä) or **Düna** (dü'nä), Chinese *T'u-na* (tōō'nä'), village, S Tibet, on main India-Lhasa trade route, 18 mi. NNE of Phari; alt. 14,723 ft.

Tunadal (tü'nädäl"), village (pop. 723), Vasternorrland co., E central Sweden, on small inlet of Gulf of Bothnia, opposite Alno isl., 3 mi. NE of Sundsvall; sawmilling, woodworking.

Tunapui (tōōnä'pwē), town (pop. 1,114), Sucre state, NE Venezuela, 10 mi. SE of Carúpano; cacao growing.

Tunapuna (tōō'nŭpōō'n"), town (pop. 7,328), NW Trinidad, B.W.I., on railroad and 9 mi. E of Port of Spain; sugar center. Its inhabitants are predominantly Indian.

Tunari (tōō'nä'rē) peak (17,060 ft.) in Cordillera de Cochabamba, central Bolivia, 15 mi. WNW of Cochabamba.

Tunas, Victoria de las, Cuba: see VICTORIA DE LAS TUNAS.

Tunas de Zaza (tōō'näs dā sä'sä), village (pop. 475), Las Villas prov., central Cuba, Caribbean port for Sancti-Spíritus (20 mi. N; linked by rail), with fine harbor at mouth of Zaza R. Ships chiefly sugar cane and lumber; also tobacco, honey, and beeswax. Sometimes called Zaza.

Tunb Island (tōō'nŭb), in Persian Gulf, belonging to Sharja sheikdom of Trucial Oman; 26°15'N 55°18'E; 2 mi. across.

Tunbridge, town (pop. 774), Orange co., E Vt., on First Branch of White R. and 20 mi. S of Barre; lumber, dairy products. Annual co. "World's Fair."

Tunbridge Wells (tŭn'brĭj, tŭm'–), municipal borough (1931 pop. 35,365; 1951 census 38,397), SW Kent, England, 15 mi. SW of Maidstone; a "Royal Borough," it was once a fashionable spa. Chalybeate springs were discovered here 1606; subsequently noted visitors (among them Henrietta Maria, Catherine of Braganza, Queen Anne, Dr. Johnson, Garrick, Richardson, "Beau" Nash, and Thackeray) established resort as social center. There is a promenade, called Pantiles, lined by a colonnade and lime trees. Near by are curious sandstone formations. The town's industries include brick- and tileworks and biscuit bakeries. "Tunbridge" wooden mosaics are also noted. Also called Royal Tunbridge Wells.

Tunca River, Turkey and Bulgaria: see TUNDZHA RIVER.

Tunceli (tōōn"jĕlē'), province (□ 3,229; 1950 pop. 105,663), E central Turkey; ⊙ Cemiskezek. Bordered N by Munzur and Mercan Mts., SE by Peri R., S by Murat R., SW by Euphrates R.; also drained by Munzur R. Tin and copper E of Hozat. Formerly Dersim.

T'un-ch'i, China: see TUNKI.
Tundja River, Bulgaria and Turkey: see TUNDZHA RIVER.
Tundla (tōōnd'lŭ), town (pop. 7,318), Agra dist., W Uttar Pradesh, India, 14 mi. W of Agra; rail junction; pearl millet, gram, wheat, barley, oilseeds.
Tunduma (tōōndōō'mä), road center, Southern Highlands prov., SW Tanganyika, 50 mi. SW of Mbeya; customs post on Northern Rhodesia border.
Tunduru (tōōndōō'rōō), town, Southern Prov., SE Tanganyika, on road and 175 mi. WSW of Lindi, near Mozambique border; agr. trade center; tobacco, peanuts, rice, corn, sesame; livestock.
Tundzha River (tōōn'jŏŏ), Turkish *Tunca* (tōōnjä'), in Bulgaria and European Turkey, rises in Central Balkan Mts. on S foot of Boter Peak, flows 206 mi. E and S, past Yambol and Yelkhovo, to the Maritsa at Adrianople (Edirne), Turkey. Sometimes spelled Tunja and Tundja.
Tune, Norway: see GREAKER.
Tunes (tōō'nĭsh), village (pop. 200), Faro dist., S Portugal, 20 mi. WNW of Faro; rail junction; pottery mfg.
Tunes, Tunisia: see TUNIS.
Tung, China: see EAST RIVER.
Tunga (dōōng'ä'), town, ⊙ Tunga co. (pop. 328,830), NE Pingyuan prov., China, 50 mi. SW of Tsinan, near Yellow R. and Shantung line; wheat, millet, peanuts. Until 1949 in Shantung prov.
Tungabhadra River (tōōng"găbŭ'drŭ), chief tributary of Kistna R., S India; c.400 mi. long. Formed at Kudali (7 mi. NE of Shimoga) by union of 2 headstreams (Tunga and Bhadra rivers) rising in Western Ghats in NW Mysore; flows c.180 mi. generally NNE, forming Mysore-Bombay and Bombay-Madras borders, then for c.220 mi. NE and E along Hyderabad-Madras border, past Gangawati, Alampur, and Kurnool, to right bank of Kistna R. 16 mi. NE of Kurnool; confluence forms rich agr. area (□ c.2,000; oilseeds, rice, tobacco) in Hyderabad. Navigable by coracle for c.200 mi. above mouth. Dammed for irrigation and hydroelectricity near Hospet; project was begun 1948. Main tributary, Hagari R.
Tungan. 1 or **T'ung-an** (tōōng'än'), town (pop. 6,963), ⊙ Tungan co. (pop. 211,159), S Fukien prov., China, 20 mi. NNE of Amoy, on inlet of Formosa Strait; sugar cane, rice, wheat, sweet potatoes, peanuts. Former port, supplanted by Amoy. 2 (dōōng'än') Town, Hopeh prov., China: see ANTZE. 3 (dōōng'än') Town, ⊙ Tungan co. (pop. 234,087), S Hunan prov., China, on Kwangsi line, on railroad and 25 mi. WNW of Lingling; rice, wheat, beans. Antimony mining (N). 4 (dōōng'än') Town, Kwangtung prov., China: see WANFOW. 5 (dōōng'än') Town, Sungkiang prov., Manchuria, China: see MISHAN. 6 or **T'ung-an** (tōōng'än'), town, Szechwan prov., China: see TUNGNAN.
Tunga River (tōōng'gŭ), left headstream of the Tungabhadra, in NW Mysore, India, rises in Western Ghats near Mysore-Madras border, flows c.75 mi. generally NE past Sringeri, Tirthahalli, and Shimoga, joining Bhadra R. at Kudali (7 mi. NE of Shimoga) to form Tungabhadra R.
Tungchang, China: see LIAOCHENG.
Tungcheng. 1 or **T'ung-ch'eng** (tōōng'chŭng'), town, ⊙ Tungcheng co. (pop. 899,453), N Anhwei prov., China, in Tapieh Mts., 60 mi. SSW of Hofei, in tobacco-growing region; rice, cotton, hemp, tung oil, silk. 2 or **T'ung-ch'eng** (tōōng'-chŭng'), town (pop. 11,094), ⊙ Tungcheng co. (pop. 175,738), SE Hupeh prov., China, near Hunan-Anhwei line, 45 mi. ESE of Yoyang (Hunan prov.); rice, hemp. 3 or **T'ung-cheng** (tōōng'jŭng'), town, ⊙ Tungcheng co. (pop. 48,878), SW Kwangsi prov., China, 30 mi. W of Nanning; sugar processing; rice, millet, bamboo, timber. Until 1914 called Yungkang.
T'ung-chiang, town, China: see TUNGKIANG.
Tung Chiang, river, China: see EAST RIVER.
Tung-chiang, Formosa: see TUNGKANG.
Tungchow. 1 Town, Hopeh prov., China: see TUNGHSIEN. 2 Town, Kiangsu prov., China: see NANTUNG. 3 Town, Shensi prov., China: see TALI.
Tungchwan. 1 or **T'ung-ch'uan** (tōōng'chwän'), town, ⊙ Tungchwan co. (pop. 59,950), central Shensi prov., China, 55 mi. NNE of Sian; terminus of spur of Lunghai RR; coal-mining center; pottery mfg. Until 1946 called Tungkwan or Tungkwan North. 2 or **T'ung-ch'uan** (tōōng'chwän'), town, Szechwan prov., China: see SANTAI. 3 or **Tung-ch'uan** (dōōng'chwän'), town, Yunnan prov., China: see HWEITSEH.
Tungefoss (tōōng'ŭfôs), waterfall (43 ft.) on Mandal R., Vest-Agder co., S Norway, 28 mi. NW of Kristiansand; hydroelectric plant.
Tungfeng (dōōng'fŭng'), town, ⊙ Tungfeng co., (pop. 274,829), N Liaotung prov., Manchuria, 70 mi. ESE of Szeping and on railroad; coal mining; basalt quarry; flour and soybean-oil milling; brick and tile plants. Hemp, tobacco; sericulture. Until 1914 called Tungping.
Tung Hai: see EAST CHINA SEA.
Tunghai or **T'ung-hai** (tōōng'hī'). 1 City, Shantung prov., China: see SINHAI. 2 Town, ⊙ Tunghai co. (pop. 51,568), SE central Yunnan prov., China, 60 mi. S of Kunming, on small lake; alt. 6,073 ft.; rice, wheat, millet, beans.
Tunghai (dōōng'hī'), island of SW Kwangtung prov., China, in Kwangchow Bay of S.China Sea, forming part of CHANKIANG municipality.
Tunghiang or **T'ung-hsiang** (both tōōng'shyäng'), town (pop. 10,958), ⊙ Tunghiang co. (pop. 148,411), N Chekiang prov., China, 34 mi. NE of Hangchow, near Grand Canal; silk, cotton, tobacco, rice, wheat.
Tunghing (dōōng'hĭng'), Mandarin *Tung-hsing* (dōōng'shĭng'), town SW Kwangtung prov., China, on China Vietnam border, opposite Moncay, 27 mi. SW of Fangcheng; commercial center.
Tungho or **T'ung-ho** (tōōng'hŭ'), town, ⊙ Tungho co. (pop. 98,000), W Sungkiang prov., Manchuria, 110 mi. ENE of Harbin and on left bank of Sungari R.; soybeans, barley, rye, tobacco, timber. Until 1914 called Tatung.
T'ung-hsiang, Chekiang prov., China: see TUNGHIANG.
Tung-hsiang, Kiangsi prov., China: see TUNGSIANG.
Tunghsiao, Formosa: see TUNGSIAO.
Tunghsien or **T'ung-hsien** (tōōng'shyĕn'), town, ⊙ Tunghsien co. (pop. 307,294), N Hopeh prov., China, on Pai R. and 12 mi. E of Peking, and on railroad and highway; wheat, cotton, millet, chestnuts. Until 1913 called Tungchow, it was formerly Peking's river port.
T'ung-hsin, China: see TUNGSIN.
Tung-hsing, China: see TUNGHING.
T'ung-hsü, China: see TUNGSÜ.
Tunghwa or **T'ung-hua** (tōōng'hwä'), city (1947 pop. 80,058), ⊙ but independent of Tunghwa co. (1946 pop. 254,573), NE Liaotung prov., Manchuria, on railroad and 125 mi. E of Mukden; center of Tungpientao mining region. Coal, iron-ore, and limestone mining near by. Match mfg. Agr.: soybeans, kaoliang, rice, tobacco. Developed greatly under Manchukuo rule, when it was (1937–43) ⊙ Tunghwa prov. (□ 12,240; 1940 pop. 982,387). Under Nationalist rule (1946–49), it was ⊙ Antung prov. (□ 24,045; pop. 3,341,908).
Tungi (tōōng'gē), village, Dacca dist., E central East Bengal, E Pakistan, 13 mi. N of Dacca; rail junction (spur to Bhairab Bazar).
Tungjen or **T'ung-jen** (tōōng'rŭn'). 1 Town (pop. 11,430), ⊙ Tungjen co. (pop. 112,940), NE Kweichow prov., China, 50 mi. ESE of Szenan, at Hunan line; tung oil, tea oil, hides, embroidered goods; medicinal herbs, grain. Mercury mines, lead deposits. Until 1913, the name Tungjen was applied to KIANGKOW (18 mi. E). 2 Town, ⊙ Tungjen co. (pop. 2,138), E Tsinghai prov., China, 70 mi. S of Sining; cattle raising; agr. products. Until 1934 called Lungwusze.
Tungkang (dōōng'gäng') or **Tung-chiang** (–jyäng'), Jap. *Toko* (tō'kō), town, S Formosa, fishing port on W coast, 15 mi. S of Pingtung, at mouth of Lower Tanshui R.; sugar milling, fish processing. Seaplane landing and naval anchorage. Was once a flourishing port and trade center.
Tungken, Manchuria: see HAILUN.
Tungkiang or **T'ung-chiang** (both: tōōng'jyäng'). 1 Town, NE Sungkiang prov., Manchuria, China, 115 mi. NE of Kiamusze, and on Sungari R. just above its mouth on Amur R. Called Lahasusu, Chinese *Linkiang*, until 1913. 2 Town (pop. 10,794), ⊙ Tungkiang co. (pop. 172,120), NE Szechwan prov., China, 45 mi. NNW of Tahsien, near Shensi border, in mtn. region; mushroom-collecting center; rice, wheat, indigo, tobacco.
Tung Kiang, river, China: see EAST RIVER.
Tungkil, Philippines: see TONGQUIL ISLAND.
Tungkow, Manchuria: see TSIAN.
Tungku (dōōng'gōō'), town (pop. 10,288), ⊙ Tungku co. (pop. 51,135), NW Kiangsi prov., China, on Hunan line, 38 mi. SW of Siushui, at source of Siu R.; rice, tea. Gold deposits. Hot springs (S).
Tungkun (dōōng'gōōn'), Mandarin *Tung-kuan* (dōōng'gwän'), town (pop. 63,767), ⊙ Tungkun co. (pop. 644,910), S Kwangtung prov., China, on S arm of East R. delta, 32 mi. ESE of Canton; rush weaving (mats); sugar cane, bananas. Tin mining near by.
Tungkwan. 1 or **T'ung-kuan** (tōōng'gwän'), town (pop. 18,629), ⊙ Tungkwan co. (pop. 55,350), E Shensi prov., China, at Honan border, on Lunghai RR, on Yellow R. bend (Shansi line), opposite rail terminus of Fenglingtu, and 80 mi. E of Sian; commercial center; mfg. of tinware; melons, fruit. 2 or **Tungkwan North**, town, Shensi prov., China: see TUNGCHWAN.
Tungkwang or **Tung-kuang** (both: dōōng'gwäng'), town, ⊙ Tungkwang co. (pop. 282,408), NW Shantung prov., China, 35 mi. NNE of Tehchow and on Tientsin-Pukow RR; cotton, oilseed, wheat, millet. Until 1949 in Hopeh prov.
Tunglan (dōōng'län'), town, ⊙ Tunglan co. (pop. 116,934), NW Kwangsi prov., China, 65 mi. NE of Poseh and on Hungshui R.; tung-oil and tea-oil processing, cotton-textile mfg.; rice, wheat.
Tungliang or **T'ung-liang** (tōōng'lyäng'), town (pop. 9,816), ⊙ Tungliang co. (pop. 404,636), S central Szechwan prov., China, 40 mi. NW of Chungking city; paper milling; rice, sugar cane, wheat, rapeseed, beans. Coal and iron mines near by.
Tungliao or **T'ung-liao** (tōōng'lyou'), town, ⊙ Tungliao co. (pop. 227,500), SE Inner Mongolian Autonomous Region, Manchuria, on Liao R., on railroad and 110 mi. WNW of Szeping; Chinese agr. center. Called Paiyintailai until 1908.
Tungling or **T'ung-ling** (tōōng'lĭng'), town, ⊙ Tungling co. (pop. 162,861), S Anhwei prov., China, 45 mi. NE of Anking and on Yangtze R.; silkgrowing center; rice, wheat, beans; fisheries. Copper mining at the Tungkwan Shan, just SE.
Tungliu (dōōng'lyō'), town, ⊙ Tungliu co. (pop. 24,330), S Anhwei prov., China, on Yangtze R. and 24 mi. SSW of Anking, on Kiangsi line; rice, cotton, wheat, rapeseed, silk.
Tunglo or **T'ung-lo** (both: tōōng'lô'), Jap. *Dora* (dō'rä), town (1935 pop. 3,717), NW Formosa, 5 mi. S of Miaoli and on railroad; rice, sugar cane, sweet potatoes, bananas, oranges.
Tunglu or **T'ung-lu** (tōōng'lōō'), town (pop. 5,273), ⊙ Tunglu co. (pop. 110,295), NW Chekiang prov., China, 45 mi. SW of Hangchow and on Tsientang R.; papermaking; tung oil, indigo, tobacco, lacquer. Lime quarries.
Tungming (dōōng'mĭng'), town, ⊙ Tungming co. (pop. 216,419), S Pingyuan prov., China, near Yellow R., 70 mi. E of Sinsiang; wheat, millet, kaoliang, beans. Until 1949 in Hopeh prov.
Tungnafellsjokull (tōōng'näfĕ"tŭlsyû"kŭtŭl), Icelandic *Tungnafellsjökull*, glacier, central Iceland; rises to 4,665 ft. at 64°45'N 17°59'W.
Tungnan or **T'ung-nan** (tōōng'nän'), town (pop. 10,562), ⊙ Tungnan co. (pop. 280,267), central Szechwan prov., China, 30 mi. WNW of Hochwan and on right bank of Fow R.; cotton textiles; tobacco processing; rice, sugar cane, sweet potatoes, wheat. Until 1914, Tungan.
Tungning (dōōng'nĭng'), town, ⊙ Tungning co. (pop. 39,825), S Sungkiang prov., Manchuria, on Suifun R. and 90 mi. ESE of Mutankiang, on USSR line; gold and coal mining. Formerly Sanchakow.
Tungokochen (tōōn-gŭkŭchĕn'), village, W Chita oblast, Russian SFSR, 135 mi. NE of Chita; lumbering.
Tungon, China: see WANFOW.
Tungpeh. 1 or **Tungpei**, or **T'ung-pei** (all: tōōng'-bā'), town, ⊙ Tungpeh co. (pop. 37,961), NE central Heilungkiang prov., Manchuria, China, 160 mi., N of Harbin and on railroad; kaoliang, corn, millet, soybeans. 2 or **T'ung-pai** (tōōng'bī'), town, ⊙ Tungpeh co. (pop. 114,178), S Honan prov., China, on Hupeh line, 40 mi. WNW of Sinyang; silk weaving, tung-oil and lacquer processing; rice, wheat, beans. The Tungpeh Mts. are a hill range on Honan-Hupeh border.
Tungpientao (dōōng'byĕn'dou'), mining district in NE Liaotung prov., Manchuria, on Yalu R. (Korea line); main centers are Tunghwa and Linkiang. Site of rich coal and iron mines, dolomite deposits.
Tungpin, Manchuria: see YENSHOW.
Tungping or **Tung-p'ing** (both: dōōng'pĭng'). 1 Town, Liaotung prov., Manchuria, China: see TUNGFENG. 2 Town, ⊙ Tungping co. (pop. 413,725), W Shantung prov., China, on Grand Canal (Pingyuan line) and 60 mi. SW of Tsinan, on small Tungping L.; cotton, grain.
Tungpu or **T'ung-p'u**, Tibet: see RANGSUM.
Tungsha, China: see PRATAS ISLAND.
Tungshan. 1 (dōōng'shän') Main town (pop. 19,870) of Tungshan isl. (pop. 81,209) in Formosa Strait, S Fukien prov., China, 60 mi. SW of Amoy; sweet potatoes, wheat, rice; food processing. Sometimes spelled Tongsang. The isl. shelters (W) Tungshan Bay (or Chaoan Bay). 2 or **T'ung-shan** (tōōng'-shän'), town (pop. 9,107), ⊙ Tungshan co. (pop. 54,446), SE Hupeh prov., China, 65 mi. SSE of Hankow; tea-growing center; hemp weaving, vegetable-oil processing, paper mfg. 3 or **T'ung-shan** (tōōng'shän'), city, Shantung prov., China: see SÜCHOW.
Tungshek, Formosa: see TUNGSHIH.
Tungsheng (dōōng'shŭng'), town (pop. 5,589), ⊙ Tungsheng co. (pop. 26,916), S central Suiyuan prov., China, 50 mi. S of Paotow, in Ordos Desert; cattle raising; grain, licorice.
Tungshih (dōōng'shû'). 1 Jap. *Tosei* (tō'sā) Town (1935 pop. 11,510), W central Formosa, 12 mi. NE of Taichung; rice, bananas, pineapples, oranges, sugar cane; lumber. 2 Jap. *Toseki* (tō'sākē) Town, W central Formosa, minor port on W coast, 19 mi. W of Kiayi; exports salt, glass jars, honey. Sometimes spelled Tungshek.
Tungsiang or **Tung-hsiang** (both: dōōng'shyäng'). 1 Town (pop. 4,773), ⊙ Tungsiang co. (pop. 127,106), central Kiangsi prov., China, 50 mi. SE of Nanchang and on Chekiang-Kiangsi RR; rice, cotton. 2 Town, Szechwan prov., China: see SÜANHAN.
Tungsiao, Tunghsiao, or **T'ung-hsiao** (all: tōōng'-shyou'), Jap. *Tsusho* (tsōō'shō), town (1935 pop. 3,250), NW Formosa, on W coast, 10 mi. SW of Miaoli, and on railroad; rice, sugar cane, tea, livestock.
Tungsin or **T'ung-hsin** (both: tōōng'shĭn'), town (pop. 2,933), ⊙ Tungsin co. (pop. 25,734), SE Ningsia prov., China, 105 mi. S of Yinchwan, on Kansu border; millet, kaoliang. Gypsum quarrying.
Tung Song, Thailand: see CHA MAI.
Tungsten, village, Boulder co., N central Colo., on branch of Boulder Creek, in Front Range, and 30 mi. WNW of Denver; alt. 7,800 ft.; tungsten mines.

Tungsü or **T'ung-hsü** (both: tŏŏng'shü'), town, ⊙ Tungsü co. (pop. 139,107), N Honan prov., China, 25 mi. SSE of Kaifeng; rice, wheat, beans, millet.

Tungtai or **Tung-t'ai** (dŏŏng'tī'), town, ⊙ Tungtai co. (1946 pop. 1,186,140), N Kiangsu prov., China, 60 mi. NE of Yangchow; rice, wheat, beans, kaoliang, cotton.

Tungtao or **T'ung-tao** (tŏŏng'dou'), town, ⊙ Tungtao co. (pop. 27,784), SW Hunan prov., China, near Kwangsi-Kweichow line, 70 mi. SSW of Chihkiang; tung oil, tea, corn, rice. Gold deposits.

Tungteh or **T'ung-te** (both: tŏŏng'dŭ'), town, ⊙ Tungteh co. (pop. 35,000), SE Tsinghai prov., China, 170 mi. S of Sining and on upper Yellow R. Until 1931 called Lakiashih.

Tungting Lake, Chinese *Tung-t'ing Hu* (dŏŏng'tĭng' hōō'), shallow lake (□ 1,450, at low water), one of largest in China, in N Hunan prov., serving as natural overflow reservoir for Yangtze R. (N), with which it is connected by several channels, chiefly the YOYANG canal. During the summer, the lake receives the flood waters of the Yangtze and nearly triples in size, reaching max. dimensions of 80 mi. (E–W) and 45 mi. (N–S). During the winter, it is reduced to a muddy plain. Its shores are low and marshy, and the few lake-side towns—Nanhsien and Ansiang in N; Hanshow and Yüankiang in S—are protected by embankments. The lake is gradually filling up as a result of sedimentation. It receives the combined Siang-Tzu delta (S), and Yüan and Li rivers (W). Region surrounding the lake is one of China's leading rice producers.

Tungtsichen, Manchuria: see LINTIEN.

Tungtze or **T'ung-tzu** (both: tŏŏng'dzŭ'), town (pop. 13,160), ⊙ Tungtze co. (pop. 258,001), N Kweichow prov., China, 30 mi. N of Tsunyi and on main road to Szechwan; alt. 3,041 ft.; cotton weaving, papermaking; timber, grain. Coal mines, manganese deposits.

Tungurahua (tōōng-gōōrä'wä), province (□ 1,462; 1950 pop. 184,726), central Ecuador, in the Andes; ⊙ Ambato. Mountainous prov. N of Chimborazo peak, and including the snow-capped volcanoes Tungurahua and Carihuairazo. Watered by Patate and Chambo rivers, headstreams of the Pastaza. Frequently shaken by earthquakes. It has a temperate climate; main rains Dec.–April. The region is noted for its fruit (apples, pears, peaches, strawberries, citrus, grapes); also grows barley, corn, wheat, sugar cane, potatoes, vegetables, cinchona. Some cattle and sheep raising. Ambato, a leading commercial center, has processing industries. Baños, gateway to the Amazon basin, is a spa. Area was severely hit by earthquake of 1949.

Tungurahua, Andean volcano (16,512 ft.), Tungurahua prov., central Ecuador, 19 mi. SE of Ambato, with Baños at its N foot; 1°26'S 78°26'W. Quiescent from 1773 to 1886, when it devastated Baños, it is now fairly dormant, though emitting vapors.

Tunguska Basin (tŏŏn-gōō'skŭ), large unexploited coal basin (□ c.400,000) of E Siberian Russian SFSR, bet. Yenisei and Lena rivers; drained by Angara (Upper Tunguska), Stony (Middle) Tunguska, and Lower Tunguska rivers. Estimated reserves, 440 billion tons.

Tunguska River, Russian SFSR: see ANGARA RIVER; LOWER TUNGUSKA RIVER; STONY TUNGUSKA RIVER.

Tunguu (tŏŏng-gōō'), town, central Zanzibar, on road and 10 mi. ESE of Zanzibar town; copra; livestock.

Tungwei or **T'ung-wei** (tŏŏng'wā'), town, ⊙ Tungwei co. (pop. 174,692), SE Kansu prov., China, 50 mi. NW of Tienshui; grain, licorice.

Tungyang (dŏŏng'yäng'), town (pop. 9,727), ⊙ Tungyang co. (pop. 437,094), central Chekiang prov., China, 35 mi. ENE of Kinhwa and on tributary of Tsientang R.; hams, fruit, rice, wheat, medicinal herbs.

Tunhwa or **Tun-hua** (dŏŏn'hwä'), town, ⊙ Tunhwa co. (pop. 125,624), E central Kirin prov., Manchuria, on Mutan R. and 90 mi. ESE of Kirin, and on railroad; lumbering center; wood-pulp, flour and soybean milling.

Tunhwang or **Tun-huang** (dŏŏn'hwäng'), town, ⊙ Tunhwang co. (pop. 33,013), northwesternmost Kansu prov., China, 70 mi. WSW of Ansi, and on anc. Silk Road (near former Jade Gate). Oil and gold deposits near by. Chinese scriptures and paintings of Tang dynasty (A.D. 618–906) were found (1900) in stone caves near by.

Tuni (tŏŏ'nē), town (pop. 13,060), East Godavari dist., NE Madras, India, 35 mi. NNE of Cocanada; agr. market; rice milling; oilseeds, sugar cane.

Tunía (tōōnē'ä), town (pop. 1,508), Cauca dept., SW Colombia, on Popayán-Manizales highway, on slopes of Cordillera Central, and 19 mi. NNE of Popayán; alt. 5,561 ft.; coffee, tobacco, sugar cane, stock.

Tunica (tū'nĭkŭ, tōō'–), county (□ 458; pop. 21,664), NW Miss.; ⊙ Tunica. Bounded NW and W by Mississippi R., here forming Ark. line; and partly bounded E by Coldwater R. Rich agr. area (cotton, corn). Cotton ginning, cottonseed processing, lumber milling. Formed 1836.

Tunica, town (pop. 1,354), ⊙ Tunica co., NW Miss., near Mississippi R., 35 mi. SSW of Memphis, Tenn.; trade center for agr. area (cotton, corn); mfg. of cottonseed products, lumber milling.

Tunis (tū'nĭs), anc. *Tunes*, city (1946 pop. 364,593; 1936 pop. 219,578), ⊙ Tunisia, seaport at W end of shallow L. of Tunis (inlet of Gulf of Tunis), strategically located near narrowest part of Mediterranean Sea, 150 mi. from W tip of Sicily, and 400 mi. E of Algiers; 36°48'N 10°12'E. Situated on a hilly isthmus bet. L. of Tunis and Sedjoumi salt flat (SW), city is linked with its outport of LA GOULETTE, at lake's outlet (6 mi. ENE), by a channel (for ships drawing 20 ft.) and a causeway (electric trolley) across the lake. Tunis is chief commercial, industrial, and transport center of the French protectorate; seat of the bey of Tunis and of Fr. resident-general; and a mecca for tourists. From here and from La Goulette, phosphates, iron ore, Mediterranean fruits, dates, olive oil, esparto (for European paper mills), sponges, native carpets and pottery are exported. Mfg. is concentrated in S dists. and in SE suburbs of Djebel-Djelloud and Mégrine. Here are superphosphate and allied chemical works; fruit-canning, preserving, and drying plants; wineries and distilleries, flour mills, olive-oil and soap factories. Explosives (for mining), perfumes, footwear, and hosiery are also produced, and there are varied metalworks, including railroad repair shops. Saltworks near by. Tunis is E terminus of standard-gauge railroad which crosses French North Africa from Marrakesh (Fr. Morocco). A narrow-gauge line continues S to Sousse, Sfax, and Gabès along Tunisia's E coast, and inland to the phosphate-mining region of Gafsa and to the iron, lead, zinc, and phosphate area S of Le Kef near Algerian border. El-Aouina international airport is 5 mi. NE. Seaplane base at Khéreddine near La Goulette. Tunis has a Mediterranean subtropical climate (yearly average temp. 64°F.), with Saharan influences (sirocco) in summer months. Rainfall (annual average 15 inches), concentrated in winter, shows marked variations from year to year. Modern Tunis was laid out along a regular pattern bet. the lake and the old Moslem quarter, which, contained within its old walls and virtually untouched by European influences, is a maze of narrow, crooked streets (mostly impassable to vehicles) and dark covered passageways. Two mosques, extensive bazaars, and the *casbah* (renovated; now a barracks) are of special note. There is a Moslem univ. Tunis still receives part of its water supply from Zaghouan area (30 mi. S) via anc. Roman aqueduct. The outskirts of Tunis include residential Le Bardo (W; noted mus.); La Marsa (10 mi. NE), with beylical palace and resident general's summer residence; Maxula-Radès, a bathing resort on S shore of Gulf of Tunis; and the remains of anc. CARTHAGE (9 mi. NE). Of Phoenician origin, Tunis, probably older than Carthage, was eclipsed by Carthage during its early history. Under the Aglabite dynasty (13th cent.), city replaced Kairouan as capital and became a leading trade center with Europe and the Levant. Turks, who captured Tunis 1533, were temporarily (1535–69, 1573–74) dislodged by Spaniards. After 1591, Turkish governors were practically independent and city throve as a pirate center. French occupation (1881) was formalized by treaty of Le Bardo. In Second World War, Tunis, held by the Axis from Nov., 1942 to May 7, 1943, was the base for their final stand in N Africa. The deepening of Tunis–La Goulette channel and improvement of port installations are important postwar projects. Of city's 1946 pop., 66,422 were Fr. citizens and 46,629 Italians. Moslem majority was growing rapidly. City is ⊙ Tunis suburban dist. (□ 1,104; pop. 239,173, not including Tunis city).

Tunis, Gulf of, semi-circular inlet of the central Mediterranean off N Tunisia, bounded by Cape Bon Peninsula (E) and by headland of Sidi Ali el Mekki (W); 30 mi. long, 40 mi. wide. Receives Medjerda R. At La Goulette (near head of gulf) is entrance to L. of Tunis.

Tunis, Lake of, shallow coastal lagoon of Tunisia, closed off from the Gulf of Tunis (Mediterranean Sea) by a narrow bar, pierced at La Goulette; 6 mi. long, 4 mi. wide. City of Tunis (at W end) is linked with La Goulette by a deep-sea channel (depth, 24.5 ft.) and causeway running lengthwise across lake. Medjerda R. formerly entered the sea here. Also called El Bahira.

Tunisia (tūnē'zhŭ, tūnĭ'shŭ), Fr. *Tunisie* (tünēzē'), French protectorate (□ c.48,300; pop. 3,230,952), N Africa, since 1946 an associated state of the Fr. Union; ⊙ TUNIS. Washed by the Mediterranean on N and E; bounded W by Algeria, SE by Libya. Its long and irregular coast line has many good harbor sites. The Cape BON peninsula pointing toward Sicily (90 mi. NE) controls the narrows which link the E and W basins of the Mediterranean; flanking it are 2 large embayments, the Gulf of Tunis and the Gulf of Hammamet. The Gulf of Gabès, which indents SE coast, contains KERKENNAH and DJERBA isls. In N Tunisia, bet. the coast and the Medjerda valley, run the E spurs of the Tell Atlas, a relatively inaccessible region of folded ranges and dense oak forests. S of the Medjerda (Tunisia's main stream), a series of broken ranges, outliers of Algeria's Saharan Atlas, run SW–NE along Cape Bon peninsula, rising to 5,066 ft. in the Djebel Chambi. The arid plateau which extends southward merges with the Sahara in the latitude of the shotts; these shallow salt lakes (Djerid, Rharsa, Fedjedj) form a continuous E–W depression across S central Tunisia from Algerian border to the Gulf of Gabès. The southern 2/5 of the country lies wholly within the Sahara. N Tunisia has a Mediterranean climate with winter rainfall (15–20 in. average; up to 40 in. in Tell Atlas) and dry, hot summers. Precipitation decreases toward S and W. Less than 1/4 of country's surface is arable. Agr. is concentrated in fertile Medjerda valley (granary of Tunisia), in the coastal belt E and S of Tunis, and in scattered irrigated mtn. valleys and oases of the interior. Wheat and barley are chief crops; extensive olive groves are strung out along the E coast (Sahel) bet. gulfs of Hammamet and Gabès; wine, citrus fruit, market vegetables, tobacco, and perfume flowers are grown SE of Tunis and in Cape Bon peninsula; dates, from the BLED-EL-JERID oases, are exported. Pastures occupy almost 1/2 of productive land; sheep and goats, raised under a semi-nomadic grazing system, far outnumber beef and dairy animals. The oak and Aleppo pine forests yield cork, pitprops, and fuel wood. There are tunny and sponge fisheries off the E coast. Tunisia has important but little-diversified mineral resources. Phosphate rock (mined in GAFSA dist., shipped from Sfax and Tunis) is country's leading export product. Iron and lead are mined near Algerian border S of Le Kef; zinc has been of increasing importance since Second World War; lignite is found on Cape Bon peninsula. Petroleum exploration was begun 1949 in Tunis area, and the exploitation of potash deposits near the Chott Djerid is under consideration. An important hydroelectric project was under construction (1950) on the Medjerda and its tributary, the Mellègue, in NW Tunisia. Although the greatest number of industrial plants (olive-oil mills) are still hand-operated, Tunisia's light industries have been undergoing rapid modernization; they include mfg. of soap, perfume, fruit juices, canned fish and vegetables; processing of dates; quarrying and mfg. of building materials. Among new installations are a superphosphate plant near Sfax, an olive-oil refinery at Mégrine (suburb of Tunis), and a factory making aluminum goods. Handicraft industries (carpets, clothing, leather goods, metal and wooden articles, dyes, embroidery, pottery, artistic ceramics) are the principal source of income of the urban Moslem pop. and an important export item, together with minerals, esparto grass (for European paper mills), and olive oil. Tunisia has 1,350 mi. of railroads; only the trunk line from Tunis and Bizerte to Algeria and Morocco is of standard gauge; narrow-gauge lines run S of Tunis along the E coast to Gabès, with spurs from Sousse and Sfax leading inland to the mining dists. and to the Tozeur oasis. There are c.5,000 mi. of improved roads, and an international airport at El-Aouina, outside of Tunis. Tunis, with its outport of LA GOULETTE, is country's principal commercial and shipping center; BIZERTE is chiefly a naval base; Sousse, Sfax, and Gabès are E coast ports. Inland centers include the Moslem holy city of KAIROUAN, the mining town of Gafsa, and the agr. centers of Béja and Mateur. In addition to the Arabic-speaking Moslem majority, there were, in 1946, 70,971 native Jews, 143,977 French, 84,935 Italians, and 6,459 Maltese; bet. 1936 and 1946, the non-European pop. increased by c.25%, the European pop. by 12%. The coast of Tunisia, early settled by Phoenicians, passed to CARTHAGE in 6th cent. B.C. A Roman prov. from 2d cent. B.C., it became a rich wheat- and olive-growing region; numerous ruins remain from that period. Held by Vandals (5th cent.) and Byzantines (6th cent.). Conquered (7th cent.) by Arabs, who founded Kairouan. The Berber pop. was converted to Islam, and in a 2d wave of Arab conquest (11th cent.) it received a large admixture of Arab stock and culture. Coastal points were briefly held by Normans of Sicily in 12th cent. Tunisia attained its greatest power under the Berber Hafsid dynasty (1228–1574). During the last years of the Hafsids, Spain seized several coastal cities, but was ousted (1574–79) by Turks. Under its Turkish governors, the beys, country attained virtual independence, and as one of the Barbary States, it became a pirate stronghold. The present Hussein dynasty of hereditary beys was established 1705. Heavy debts contracted by the beys led (1869) to Fr., Br., and Ital. economic intervention. After a period of Fr.-Ital. rivalry, France occupied country in 1881; with the treaty of Le Bardo (1881), implemented by La Marsa convention of 1883, the bey accepted the protectorate under a Fr. resident-general. Italy's long-standing claim to Tunisia, based chiefly on the large number of its nationals residing there, became more insistent shortly before Second World War. After the fall of France (1940) Tunisia remained loyal to Vichy govt. Late in 1942, with the Germans driven W across Egypt and Libya and with Allied landings in Algeria, Tunisia became the focus of the N African campaign; the Mareth line, Kasserine and Faïd passes, and Medjez-el-Bab, are among the places made famous by the war. In May, 1943, the last Axis forces in N Africa surrendered on Cape Bon peninsula; the bey of Tunis was deposed by Gen. Giraud. After the war, reconstruction and agr. development proceeded rapidly. Surging nationalist agitation for independence was somewhat allayed by the death in exile (1948) of the deposed bey. Tunisia has a dual govt. One, deriving from Fr. sovereignty, is headed by the resident-general and by appointed civil inspectors (*contrôleurs civils*) for the country's 21 administrative dists.; the other, deriving from Tunisian sovereignty, includes a council of ministers (with Fr. advisors) and local consultative assemblies; the beylic decree is the legislative instrument. Southern Territories are under military rule.

Tunis Mills (tū'nĭs, to͞o'–), village, Talbot co., E Md., on the Eastern Shore 18 mi. NNW of Cambridge, and on inlet of Miles R. Historic old estates in vicinity.

Tunja (to͞on'hä), city (pop. 16,597), ⊙ Boyacá dept., central Colombia, on Pan American Highway, in a high valley of Cordillera Oriental, on railroad and 80 mi. NE of Bogotá; 5°32'N 73°22'W; alt. 9,252 ft. Communication, commercial, and agr. center (cereals, sugar cane, potatoes, fruit, stock); active trade with the llano cattle country; mfg. of woolen and cotton goods, soap, flour. Emerald and coal mines, and mineral springs are near by. Bishopric. Has fine parks, colonial bldgs., churches. An old city, it was founded 1539 by the Spanish on site of the Chibcha Indian capital, Hunsa. Declared itself independent from Spain in 1811 and served as base for Bolívar's liberating operations (1819), thus contributing to the victory at Boyacá.

Tunjang (to͞onjäng'), village (pop. 482), N Kedah, Malaya, on railroad 10 mi. N of Alor Star; rice.

Tunja River, Bulgaria and Turkey: see Tundzha River.

Tunkás (to͞ongkäs'), town (pop. 1,606), Yucatan, SE Mexico, 18 mi. E of Izamal; henequen, sugar cane, corn.

Tunkhannock (tŭngk-hă'nŭk), residential borough (pop. 2,170), ⊙ Wyoming co., NE Pa., 17 mi. WNW of Scranton and on Susquehanna R.; clothing mfg.; agr.; flagstone quarrying. Settled 1775, inc. 1841.

Tunki or **T'un-ch'i** (both: to͞on'chē'), city, S Anhwei prov., China, 115 mi. S of Wuhu, near Kiangsi line; major tea-producing center, known for the Keemun variety (named for near-by Kimen). Became independent municipality in 1949.

Tunliu or **T'un-liu** (to͞on'lyō'), town, ⊙ Tunliu co. (pop. 123,231), SE Shansi prov., China, 15 mi. NW of Changchih, in winegrowing area; vinegar distilling, flour milling; rice, wheat, kaoliang, corn. Coal mines near by.

Tunnel Hill, town (1940 pop. 255), Whitfield co., NW Ga., 6 mi. NW of Dalton, in agr. area.

Tunnelhill, borough (pop. 535), Cambria co., SW central Pa., just E of Gallitzin.

Tunnelton, town (pop. 544), Preston co., N W.Va., 16 mi. ENE of Grafton.

Tunn Lake (to͞on), Nor. *Tunnsjø*, lake (□ 38), Nord-Trondelag co., central Norway; contains several isls. Tunnsjoen (to͞on'shûŭn) (Nor. *Tunnsjøen*) village, on SE shore, is 40 mi. NE of Grong.

Tuno (to͞o'nû), Dan. *Tunø*, island (□ 1.3; pop. 243), Denmark, in the Kattegat, 2.5 mi. W of Samso.

Tuno, Japan: see Tsuno.

Tunstall (tŭn'stŭl). **1** Town and parish (pop. 6,024), NE Durham, England, 2 mi. S of Sunderland; coal mining. **2** Town, Stafford, England: see Stoke-on-Trent.

Tuntange (tütäzh'), Ger. *Tuntingen* (to͞on'tĭng-ŭn), village (pop. 349), W Luxembourg, 9 mi. NW of Luxembourg city; chalk quarrying; agr. (apples, potatoes, wheat, oats).

Tunungayualuk Island (12 mi. long, 11 mi. wide), just off E Labrador; 56°4'N 61°4'W.

Tunuyán (to͞ono͞oyän'), town (pop. estimate 1,200), ⊙ Tunuyán dept. (□ 1,260; 1947 pop. 20,563), central Mendoza prov., Argentina, on Tunuyán R. (irrigation area), on railroad and 50 mi. S of Mendoza; lumbering and agr. center (potatoes, wine, fruit, livestock); sawmilling, wine making. Irrigation dam and hydroelectric station.

Tunuyán, Sierra del, Argentina: see Guayquerías del Tunuyán, Sierra.

Tunuyán River, Mendoza prov., Argentina, rises on Tupungato peak near Chile line, flows S, E, and NE, past Tunuyán and Rivadavia, turns SE and flows past Santa Rosa to swamps (S of L. Bebedero), out of which flows the Río Salado; c.250 mi. long. Used for irrigation and hydroelectric power.

Tuoi-Khaya or **Tuoy-Khaya** (to͞o-oi″-khŭyä'), village (1948 pop. over 500), SW Yakut Autonomous SSR, Russian SFSR, on Chona R. (right affluent of Vilyui R.) and 320 mi. WNW of Olekminsk.

Tuolluvaara, Sweden: see Kiruna.

Tuolumne (to͞o-ŏ'lŭmē), county (□ 2,275; pop. 12,584), central and E Calif.; ⊙ Sonora. In the Sierra Nevada, here crossed by Sonora Pass. E part of co. is within Yosemite National Park. Includes part of Stanislaus Natl. Forest. Drained by Tuolumne and Stanislaus rivers (hydroelectric, irrigation, water-supply projects). W portion is in Mother Lode country; Sonora, Jamestown, and Columbia are survivors among once-roaring gold camps. Lumbering (pine, fir, cedar); gold mining (quartz mines); marble, limestone, sand and gravel quarrying. Many campgrounds, lakes and streams (trout fishing), hiking trails, winter-sports facilities. Cattle grazing, some farming (fruit, hay), poultry raising. Formed 1850.

Tuolumne, village (pop. 1,284) Tuolumne co., central Calif., in the Sierra Nevada, c.55 mi. E of Stockton; lumbering center in Mother Lode gold-mining country. Indian reservation near by.

Tuolumne Meadows, Calif.: see Yosemite National Park.

Tuolumne River, central Calif., rises in Yosemite National Park in Tuolumne co., flows c.110 mi. W to San Joaquin R. 10 mi. W of Modesto. In Yosemite region are river's Grand Canyon and Hetch Hetchy Valley and reservoir. In SW Tuolumne co. is Don Pedro Dam (284 ft. high, 1,040 ft. long; completed 1923 for irrigation and power), impounding Don Pedro Reservoir (c.10 mi. long). Farther downstream are offstream Modesto and Turlock reservoirs, both fed by the Tuolumne, used for irrigation.

Tupã (to͞opä'), city (pop. 2,704), W São Paulo, Brazil, on watershed bet. Tietê (N) and Peixe (S) rivers, 38 mi. WNW of Marília; temporary rail terminus (as of 1948), in expanding zone of pioneer agr. settlements; sawmilling, cotton ginning, coffee and rice processing; sericulture.

Tupaceretã, Brazil: see Tupanciretã.

Tupaciguara (to͞opŭsē″gwŭrä'), city (pop. 3,047), westernmost Minas Gerais, Brazil, in the Triângulo Mineiro, 30 mi. NW of Uberlândia; cattle-raising center. Diamond washings. Formerly spelled Tupacyguara.

Tupai, Society Isls.: see Motu Iti.

Tupambaé (to͞opämbäā'), town (pop. 1,800), Cerro Largo dept., NE Uruguay, in the Cuchilla Grande Principal, on railroad and 45 mi. SW of Melo; wheat, corn, oats, sheep, cattle.

Tupanciretã (to͞opä″sĕrĭtä'), city (pop. 3,688), central Rio Grande do Sul, Brazil, on railroad and 40 mi. N of Santa Maria; agr. trade center (cereals, maté, fruit); beef jerking. Has govt. wheat experiment station. Founded 18th cent. as Jesuit mission. Until 1938, Tupaceretã (old spelling, Tupaceretan).

Tupátaro (to͞opä'tärō), town (pop. 1,828), Michoacán, central Mexico, 10 mi. NW of El Oro; cereals, livestock.

Tupelo (to͞o'pŭlō, tū'–). **1** Town (pop. 188), Jackson co., NE Ark., 15 mi. S of Newport. **2** City (pop. 11,527), ⊙ Lee co., NE Miss., 55 mi. NNW of Columbus; trade, processing, and shipping center for cotton, dairying, and timber area; mfg. of clothing, lighting fixtures, brick, cottonseed and dairy products, lumber, fertilizer; cattle market (meat packing); cotton gins and compress. A U.S. fish hatchery is here. Just W is Tupelo Natl. Battlefield Site (1 acre; established 1929), where, in 1864, Confederate troops under Stephen D. Lee and Nathan Bedford Forrest made an unsuccessful attempt to advance on Sherman's line of communications. Tombigbee State Park and Ackia Battleground National Monument are near by. **3** Town (pop. 277), Coal co., S central Okla., 20 mi. SE of Ada.

Tupichev (to͞opē'chĭf), village (1926 pop. 2,988), NW Chernigov oblast, Ukrainian SSR, 20 mi. NNE of Chernigov; flax processing.

Tupigachi (to͞opēgä'chē), town, Pichincha prov., N central Ecuador, in the Andes, 37 mi. ENE of Quito, in agr. region (cereals, potatoes, stock).

Tupik (to͞o'pĭk), village (1948 pop. over 500), NE Chita oblast, Russian SFSR, on Tungir R. (right affluent of Olekma R.), and 50 mi. N of Mogocha, in gold-mining area.

Tupiza (to͞opē'sä), city (pop. c.9,400), ⊙ Sud Chichas or Sur Chichas prov., Potosí dept., SW Bolivia, on Tupiza R. (branch of San Juan R.) and 125 mi. S of Potosí, on Villazón-Uyuni RR. Important commercial and mineral trade center; orchards, corn; railroad shops; flour mill.

Tupper or **Tupper Creek,** village (pop. estimate 250), E B.C., on Alta. border, 19 mi. SSE of Dawson Creek; lumbering, grain, stock.

Tupper Lake, resort village (pop. 5,441), Franklin co., N N.Y., in the Adirondacks, 17 mi. SE of Saranac Lake village, near Tupper L. (□ c.6; 8 mi. long; sometimes called Big Tupper L.); woodworking (wooden dishes, flooring). A U.S. veterans' tuberculosis hosp. is near by. Little Tupper L. (□ c.4; c.5 mi. long) is 12 mi. SSW. Settled 1890, inc. 1902.

Tupton, agr. parish (pop. 1,948), NE central Derby, England. Includes villages of New Tupton, 3 mi. S of Chesterfield and, just S, Old Tupton.

Tupuaemanu, Society Isls.: see Maiao.

Tupungatito (to͞opo͞ong-gätē'tō), Andean peak (18,500 ft.) on Argentina-Chile border, just SW of Tupungato peak; 33°24'S. Sometimes called Bravard, name also given to peak (18,865 ft.) just SE.

Tupungato (to͞opo͞ong-gä'tō), town (pop. estimate 1,000), ⊙ Tupungato dept. (□ 950; 1947 census pop. 7,628), NW Mendoza prov., Argentina, 40 mi. SW of Mendoza; alt. 3,495 ft. Agr. (potatoes, grain, wine, fruit) and lumbering center; sawmills. Oil wells near by. Founded 1609 by Jesuits.

Tupungato, Andean peak (21,490 ft.) on Argentina-Chile border, 50 mi. SSE of the Aconcagua; 33°22'S. First climbed 1897 by Zurbriggen and Vines of the FitzGerald expedition. At N foot is a pass (15,594 ft.).

Tuque, La (lä tŭk'), town (pop. 7,919), S Que., on St. Maurice R. and 80 mi. N of Trois Rivières; pulp-milling center, mfg. of hosiery, furniture. Hydroelectric station.

Túquerres (to͞o'kĕrĕs), town (pop. 4,324), Nariño dept., SW Colombia, on high plateau of the Andes, on El Diviso–Pasto highway and 25 mi. WSW of Pasto; alt. 10,183 ft. Cattle-raising and gold-mining center. In earthquake zone.

Tur, Al-, Egypt: see Tor.

Tur, Jebel et, Palestine: see Gerizim, Mount.

Tura or **Turah** (to͞o'rŭ), village (pop. 18,175), Giza prov., Upper Egypt, on Cairo-Helwan RR, and 8 mi. SSE of Cairo city center. In vicinity there are large quarries used both in anc. and modern times. Just S is one of largest cement factories in Egypt.

Tura (to͞o'rō), town (pop. 7,043), Pest-Pilis-Solt-Kiskun co., N central Hungary, 25 mi. ENE of Budapest; flour mills; vineyards, wheat, cattle, horses.

Tura (to͞o'rŭ), village, ⊙ Garo Hills dist., W Assam, India, in Garo Hills, 105 mi. W of Shillong; trades in rice, cotton, mustard, jute.

Tura (to͞orä'), town (1948 pop. over 2,000), ⊙ Evenki Natl. Okrug, Krasnoyarsk Territory, Russian SFSR, on Lower Tunguska R. and 600 mi. NE of Krasnoyarsk; 64°10'N 99°55'E. Trading point; radio station. Until 1938, Turinskaya Kultbaza.

Tura, river, Russian SFSR: see Tura River.

Turaba, Wadi, or **Wadi Turabah** (wă'dē to͞orä'bä), valley in W Nejd, Saudi Arabia, E of Mecca; chief towns are Turaba (120 mi. E of Mecca) and Khurma or Khurmah (150 mi. ENE of Mecca).

Turah, Egypt: see Tura.

Turaif or **Turayf** (to͞orīf'), settlement, northernmost Saudi Arabia, near Jordan border, 125 mi. NW of Jauf; 31°35'N 38°30'E. Oil-pumping station on pipe line from Abqaiq to Saida. Formerly called Hibar.

Turaiyur (to͞orīyo͞or'), town (pop. 15,713), Trichinopoly dist., S Madras, India, 23 mi. NNW of Trichinopoly; trade center in grain and cotton area. Magnetite deposits in Pachaimalai Hills (N).

Turan (to͞orän'), desert lowland of Soviet Central Asia, S and SE of Aral Sea. The Amu Darya and Syr Darya divide it into the Kara-Kum desert (SW), the Kyzyl-Kum desert (center), and the Aral Kara-Kum (N). The region has very little precipitation and is sparsely populated, except in the oases along the 2 major rivers, where cotton, fruit, and rice are grown. Sheep are raised in the desert.

Turan, city (1945 pop. over 1,000), N Tuva Autonomous Oblast, Russian SFSR, on Kyzyl-Minusinsk highway and 40 mi. NNW of Kyzyl; trading center; flour milling.

Turano River (to͞orä'nô), central Italy, rises in the Apennines 9 mi. SW of Avezzano, flows c.50 mi. NW, past Rocca Sinibalda, to Velino R. 4 mi. NW of Rieti. In upper course, forms boundary bet. Aquila and Roma provs.

Turany (to͞o'rănĭ). **1** Village, S Moravia, Czechoslovakia: see Brno. **2** or **Turany nad Vahom** (năd'vä″hôm), Hung. *Nagyturány* (nŏ'dyŭto͞o″-rănyŭ), village (pop. 2,458), N Slovakia, Czechoslovakia, on Vah R., on railroad and 15 mi. SE of Zilina; woodworking industry (notably construction materials).

Tura River (to͞orä'), SW Siberian Russian SFSR, rises in the central Urals c.15 mi. WNW of Kushva, flows E and N, past Verkhnyaya Tura, Nizhnyaya Tura, and Malomalsk, generally E, past Verkhoturye, SE, past Lenskoye, Turinsk, Turinskaya Sloboda, and Tyumen, and E to Tobol R. 50 mi. E of Tyumen; length, c.625 mi. Spring navigation up to Verkhoturye; regular navigation below Turinsk; lumber floating. Receives Tagil, Nitsa, Pyshma (right), Is and Aktai (left) rivers.

Turasima, Japan: see Tsurashima.

Turawa (to͞orä'vä), village in Upper Silesia, after 1945 in Opole prov., S Poland, 8 mi. NE of Oppeln (Opole) and on Mala Panew R. (irrigation dam and reservoir).

Turayf, Saudi Arabia: see Turaif.

Turba or **Turbah** (to͞or'bŭ), village, Taiz prov., SW Yemen, on southwesternmost point of Arabian Peninsula, 100 mi. W of Aden, at Aden Protectorate border.

Turbaco (to͞orbä'kō), town (pop. 8,977), Bolívar dept., N Colombia, on railroad and 10 mi. SE of Cartagena; agr. center (cereals, sugar cane, fruit, stock). Noted for the score of tiny mud volcanoes (c.35 ft. high) near by erupting at regular intervals, twice a minute.

Turbacz, peak, Poland: see Gorce.

Turbaná (to͞orbänä'), town (pop. 3,571), Bolívar dept., N Colombia, in Caribbean lowlands, 13 mi. SSE of Cartagena; sugar, tobacco, rice, fruit, livestock.

Turbat (to͞or'bŭt), village, ⊙ Makran state, SW Baluchistan, W Pakistan, on Dasht (Kech) R. and 250 mi. WNW of Karachi; dates, wheat; palm-mat weaving.

Turbat-i-Haidari or **Torbat-e-Heydari** (both: tōr-bät'ĕ-hādärē'), town (1940 pop. 23,816), Ninth Prov., in Khurasan, NE Iran, 75 mi. SSW of Meshed and on Meshed-Zahidan road; alt. 4,480 ft. Trade center; sugar beets, grain, opium, saffron; produces wool, silk; beet-sugar refinery. Formerly prosperous town, devastated by famine (1870s). Named for Haidar, 12th-cent. mystic buried here. Sometimes spelled Torbat-Heydariyeh.

Turbat-i-Jam or **Torbat-e-Jam** (–jäm'), town (1939 pop. 8,870), Ninth Prov., in Khurasan, NE Iran, on highway to Herat and 90 mi. SE of Meshed, and on small Jam R. (left tributary of the Hari Rud); grain, fruit. Named for Jam, 11th-cent. mystic poet buried near by. Also called Turbat-i-Shaikh-Jam or Torbat-i-Sheykh-Jam.

Turbe (tōōr'bĕ), village (pop. 5,907), central Bosnia, Yugoslavia, 5 mi. W of Travnik.

Turbenthal (tōōr'bûntäl), town (pop 2,401), Zurich canton, N Switzerland, on Töss R. and 7 mi SE of Winterthur; cotton and woolen textiles.

Turbeville (tûr'bĕvĭl), town (pop. 271), Clarendon co., E central S.C., 19 mi. E of Sumter, in tobacco-growing area.

Turbie, La (lä türbē'), village (pop. 891), Alpes-Maritimes dept., SE France, 7 mi. ENE of Nice, on the Grande Corniche of Fr. Riviera overlooking Monaco and Monte-Carlo; alt. 1,598 ft. Has Roman trophy to Augustus (built 5th cent.). Slightly damaged in Second World War. Mont-Agel (3,805 ft.), a fortified peak, rises 2 mi. NE.

Turbigo (tōōrbē'gô), town (pop 3,719), Milano prov., Lombardy, N Italy, on Ticino R. and 8 mi. NE of Novara; tanning center; machinery factories; hydroelectric plant.

Turbio, El, Argentina: see EL TURBIO.

Turbio, Río, Chile: see ELQUI RIVER.

Turbio, Rio (rē'ō tōōr'byō), river in Guanajuato, central Mexico, rises N of León in Sierra Madre Occidental, flows c.100 mi. S, past San Francisco del Rincón and Manuel Doblado, to Lerma R. 12 mi. SE of Pénjamo.

Turbo (tōōr'bō), town (pop. 1,097), Antioquia dept., NW Colombia, minor port on Gulf of Urabá (Caribbean Sea), and 150 mi. NW of Medellín, 180 mi. SSW of Cartagena, in rice- and fruitgrowing region Airfield. Oil deposits near by.

Turbo (tōōr'bō), town, Rift Valley prov., W Kenya, on railroad and 20 mi. WNW of Eldoret; alt 5,933 ft. Coffee, tea, sisal, corn.

Turbotville, borough (pop. 518), Northumberland co., E central Pa., 16 mi. N of Sunbury.

Turbov (tōōr'bûf), village (1926 pop. 3,140), N Vinnitsa oblast, Ukrainian SSR, 13 mi. NE of Vinnitsa; sugar refinery; kaolin.

Turchin, peak, Yugoslavia: see RUDOKA.

Turchino, Passo del (päs'sô dĕl tōōrkē'nô), pass (alt. 1,745 ft.) in Ligurian Apennines, N Italy, 11 mi. NW of Genoa. Crossed by road bet. Voltri and Ovada; penetrated by railroad tunnel (4 mi. long) bet. Genoa and Ovada.

Turcianske Teplice (tōōr'chĕänskĕ tyĕ'plĭtsĕ), Slovak *Turčianske Teplice*, town (pop. 647), W central Slovakia, Czechoslovakia, on SW slopes of the Greater Fatra, on railroad and 25 mi. SSE of Zilina; health resort (alt. 1,699 ft.) with thermal (98°–109°F.) and radioactive springs. Until 1945, called Stubnianske Teplice (stōōb'nyänskĕ), Slovak *Štubnianske Teplice*, Hung. *Stubnyafürdo*.

Turciansky Svaty Martin (–skĭ svä'tĭ mär'tyĭn), Slovak *Turčiansky Svätý Martin*, Hung. *Turócszentmárton* (tōō'rōts-sĕntmär'tôn), town (pop. 10,637), NW Slovakia, Czechoslovakia, on railroad and 14 mi. SE of Zilina; noted for paper milling and woodworking (cellulose, bentwood furniture, matches, lumber, packing materials); knit goods, baskets. Former cultural center and cradle of Slovak independence movement. Has 13th-cent. church with 12th-cent. sacristy, Slovak Natl. Mus. with extensive ethnographic collections. Union of Czech and Slovak lands was proclaimed here, 1918.

Turcin, peak, Yugoslavia: see RUDOKA.

Turckheim (türkĕm'), Ger. *Türkheim* (türk'hīm), town (pop. 2,431), Haut-Rhin dept., E France, on the Fecht, at E foot of the Vosges, and 4 mi. W of Colmar; noted for its white wine. Paper milling, wax and polish mfg. Near by, Turenne defeated imperialists in 1675. Les Trois-Épis (2 mi. WNW; alt. 2,263 ft.) is a favorite resort (panorama over Alsace lowland) and pilgrimage point.

Turco (tōōr'kō), town (pop. 1,900), Oruro dept., W Bolivia, in the Altiplano, on Turco R. (branch of Lauca R.) and c.75 mi. WSW of Oruro; alt. 12,745 ft.; potatoes, alpaca.

Turda (tōōr'dä), Ger. *Thorenburg* (tō'rûnbōōrk), Hung. *Torda* (tôr'dŏ), town (1948 pop. 25,905), Cluj prov., NW central Rumania, in Transylvania, on Aries R., on railroad and 190 mi. NW of Bucharest, 15 mi. SE of Cluj; industrial center based on methane supply from Sarmasel (pipe line built in 1914). Has important chemical works, silica and cement mills. Produces machinery, furniture, china, glass, bricks, pottery, leather goods, beer, confectionery; processes asphalt. There are salt mines and a salt lake with bathing facilities in the vicinity. Notable features include 15th-cent. R.C. church, 15th-cent. Reformed church with Gothic portal, historic palace of princes participating in the Transylvanian diets, extensive Roman remains. Originally a Dacia city, later a Roman colony, Turda was repeatedly burned and sacked by Michael the Brave and the Turks.

Turdera (tōōrdā'rä), town (pop. estimate 6,000), in Greater Buenos Aires, Argentina, adjoining Temperley, 12 mi. SSW of Buenos Aires; agr. (corn, alfalfa, livestock), mfg. (shoes, brushes, textiles).

Turégano (tōōrā'gänō), town (pop. 1,469), Segovia prov., central Spain, in Old Castile, 16 mi N of Segovia. Historic, walled Castilian town with a noted medieval castle. In agr. region (cereals, chick-peas, grapes, livestock). Lumbering. Flour milling, chocolate mfg.; limekiln. Livestock fairs. Was once owned by bishops of Segovia.

Turek (too'rĕk), town (pop. 7,179), Poznan prov., central Poland, 25 mi. NE of Kalisz; rail spur terminus; weaving, flour milling, sawmilling, brewing, tanning.

Turén, Venezuela: see VILLA BRUZUAL.

Turenne (türĕn'), village (pop. 1,457), Oran dept., NW Algeria, on railroad and 13 mi. WSW of Tlemcen; winegrowing, olive-oil pressing.

Turfan (tōōrfän'), Chinese *T'u-lu-fan* (tōō'lōōfän'), town, ⊙ Turfan co. (pop. 60,303), E Sinkiang prov., China, 100 mi SE of Urumchi; cotton- and wine-growing center; sericulture; cotton weaving, paper mfg. It is the chief town of the Turfan depression, the lowest point (940 ft. below sea level) of the Asiatic continent, at S foot of the Bogdo Ola mts The depression (sometimes called Lukchun depression) was a center of an Indo-Iranian civilization (A.D. 200–400), later absorbed by the Uigurs, who had their capital here (9th-13th cent.). Archaeological finds made in 1900s include much Nestorian literature and the bulk of the extant Manichaean literature.

Turgai or **Turgay** (tōōrgī'). **1** Town (1945 pop over 500), E Akmolinsk oblast, Kazakh SSR, 70 mi. NE of Akmolinsk; antimony mine. **2** Village (1939 pop. over 2,000), SW Kustanai oblast, Kazakh SSR, on Turgai R. and 240 mi. S of Kustanai; cattle breeding. Founded 1845 in Rus. conquest of Kazakhstan.

Turgai Gates or **Turgay Gates**, lake-filled elongated depression in Kustanai oblast, Kazakh SSR, joining Turan Lowland and W. Siberian Plain; separate the S Urals (W) and Kazakh Hills (E). Principal lakes (from S to N): Sary-Kopa. Ak-Suat, Sary-Muin, Kushmurun

Turgai River or **Turgay River**, in Kustanai and Aktyubinsk oblasts, Kazakh SSR, formed by junction of the Sary-Turgai (rising in W Kazakh Hills) and the Kara-Turgai (rising in Ulu-Tau range), 25 mi. NE of Turgai; flows c.140 mi. SW, past Turgai, through dry steppe and salt-lake region, to Irgiz R. 50 mi. SE of Irgiz

Turgel, Estonia: see TURI.

Turginovo (tōōrgē'nûvŭ), village (1939 pop. over 500), S Kalinin oblast, Russian SFSR, near W end of Volga Reservoir, 23 mi. S of Kalinin; flax.

Turgot (türgō'), village (pop 1,590), Oran dept., NW Algeria, 9 mi. N of Aïn-Témouchent; wine.

Turgoyak (tōōrgŭyäk'), town (1926 pop. 2,108), W central Chelyabinsk oblast, Russian SFSR, on Miass R. and 12 mi. N of Miass; gold mining.

Turgutlu (tōōrgōōtlōō'), town (1950 pop. 25,139), Manisa prov., W Turkey, on railroad near Gediz R. and 30 mi. ENE of Smyrna; lignite; cotton, tobacco, wheat, barley. Noted for melons which are known by the town's former name, Kassaba or Kasaba (sometimes spelled Cassaba) (käsä'bä).

Turhal (tōōrhäl'), town (pop 8,110), Tokat prov., N central Turkey, on railroad, on the Yesil Irmak, and 25 mi. WNW of Tokat; important sugar refinery. Sometimes Turkhal

Turi or **Tyuri**, Est. *Türi* (all· tü'rē), Ger. *Turgel*, city (pop. 2,903), central Estonia, on Parnu R. and 50 mi. SE of Tallinn; rail junction; paper-milling center; brickworks

Turi (tōō'rē), town (pop. 7,731), Bari prov., Apulia, S Italy, 17 mi. SSE of Bari; wine, olive oil.

Turi (tōō'rē), village Rift Valley prov., W Kenya, on railroad and 25 mi. W of Nakuru; coffee, tea, wheat, corn.

Turí, Vega de (vā'gä dā tōōrē'), grazing dist. in Antofagasta prov., N Chile, at W foot of the Andes, 45 mi. ENE of Calama; stock raising (llama, vicuña, alpaca); hot springs. Ruins of pre-Sp. city near by.

Turia (tōō'ryä), Hung. *Torja* (tôr'yŏ), village (pop. 4,391), Stalin prov., central Rumania, in Transylvania, 5 mi. NW of Targu-Sacuesc; summer resort (alt. 3,084 ft.) with alkaline and carbonic springs and mud baths; sulphur deposits near by. In Hungary, 1940–45.

Turiaçu (tōōryŭsōō'), city (pop. 1,011), northernmost Maranhão, Brazil, at mouth of Turiaçu R. on the Atlantic, 90 mi. NW of São Luís; gold found in Turiaçu R. and in interfleuve extending to Gurupi R. Airfield. Formerly spelled Turiassú and Tury-Assú.

Turiaçu River, N Maranhão, Brazil, rises near 4°S 46°30'W, flows over 200 mi. NNE, past Santa Helena (head of navigation), to the Atlantic below Turiaçu. Alluvial gold washings along its course.

Turiamo (tōōryä'mō), village, Aragua state, N Venezuela, port on inlet of the Caribbean, 10 mi. E of Puerto Cabello, NW of Maracay (connected by highway); cacao-growing region. Its excellent natural harbor is being improved.

Turia River (tōō'ryä) or **Guadalaviar River** (gwädhälävyär'), in Teruel and Valencia provs., E Spain, rises in the Montes Universales near Albarracín, flows 150 mi. generally SE, past Teruel and Valencia, to the Mediterranean at Villanueva del Grao. Feeds 8 irrigation canals in the plain of Valencia, which owes to river its extraordinary fertility. Falls (500 ft.) near Chulilla.

Turiassú, Brazil: see TURIAÇU.

Turicato (tōōrēkä'tō), town (pop. 496), Michoacán, central Mexico, 8 mi. SSE of Tacámbaro; cereals, fruit, sugar cane.

Turiguanó Island (tōōrēgwänō') (15 mi. long, 6 mi. wide), off Camagüey prov., E Cuba, 9 mi. N of Morón. Bounded by Leche Lagoon (S), it is linked with main isl. through tidal marshes.

Turiisk, Ukrainian SSR: see TURISK.

Turin (tōō'rĭn, tyōō'–), Ital. *Torino* (tôrē'nô), anc. *Taurasia*, Roman *Augusta Taurinorum*, city (pop. 608,211; commune pop. 629,115), NW Italy, ⊙ Piedmont and Torino prov., on Po R., at mouth of the Dora Riparia, and 80 mi. WSW of Milan, on fertile plain bounded W by Cottian and Graian Alps; 45°4'N 7°40'E. Fourth largest city of Italy and one of the country's chief industrial and transportation centers. Leads in mfg. of automobiles (Fiat and Lancia plants produce 85% of national total), clothing, leather goods, caramels, chocolates, and vermouth. Other major products include airplane motors, aluminum, hats, glass, paper, rubber, plastics, furniture, radios, porcelain, publications, food products, tobacco, matches, and fertilizers. Has large power stations served by hydroelectric plants of Dora Riparia and Orco rivers. Bishopric since c.415; became archbishopric in 1510. Religious buildings include Renaissance cathedral of San Giovanni Battista (1492–98), Waldensian church (1850–53), seminary (damaged), and, on near-by hill, basilica of Superga (1717–31), long the royal burial church. Among its famous palaces are Palazzo Madama (damage restored; used 1848–60 by Sardinian senate); Palazzo Reale (1646–58; damaged), containing one of finest weapons collections of Europe and formerly residence of king of Sardinia; and Palazzo Carignano (1680; damaged), birthplace (1820) of Victor Emmanuel II, used by Sardinian chamber of deputies (1848–59), Ital. parliament (1861–64), and now a mus. In Palazzo Carignano, kingdom of Italy proclaimed Mar. 14, 1861. One of chief monuments is Mole Antonelliana, started 1863 as a synagogue and completed 1878–90 by the city as mus. (Museo del Risorgimento Italiano) dedicated to Victor Emmanuel II. Educational institutions include univ. founded 1404 (building dates from 1713; war damage being restored); acad. of science (1783), housed in former Jesuit col. (1679; damaged), and containing a famous Egyptian mus.; schools of paleography (1872), obstetrics, and trade. Across the Po is a public garden (damaged) containing botanical garden and royal chateau (now a polytechnic institute). A major recreational center is the 70,000-seat stadium (1911), one of the largest in Europe. Turin was the capital of the Taurini; became a Roman colony under Augustus; passed to house of Savoy (c.1280); occupied by French 1536–62; withstood a 117-day siege in 1706 during War of the Spanish Succession, when French were defeated by Eugene of Savoy. In 1720, Turin became capital of kingdom of Sardinia, and in 19th cent. was the political and intellectual center of the Risorgimento, which established kingdom of Italy. Turin served as its capital until 1864. In Second World War, Turin's industrial and military importance made it a prime aerial target. Bombed 105 times bet. June, 1940, and April, 1945; several thousand people were killed or seriously injured, numerous houses were destroyed, and 31 churches and 67 palaces were damaged.

Turin. 1 Town (pop. 185), Coweta co., W Ga., 10 mi. ESE of Newnan; sawmilling. **2** Town (pop. 160), Monona co., W Iowa, 6 mi. E of Onawa, in agr. area. **3** (also tū'rĭn) Village (pop. 273), Lewis co., N central N.Y., on Black R. and 12 mi. SSE of Lowville, in timber area.

Turinsk (tōōrēn'sk), city (1926 pop. 4,493; 1945 pop. estimate 13,000), E central Sverdlovsk oblast, Russian SFSR, port on Tura R., on railroad and 60 mi. W of Tavda; major lumber-milling center; mfg. (matches, cellulose), tanning. Founded 1607; developed in 17th cent. as trade center on route to Siberia. Declined following southward shift of Siberian colonization. Lumber industry developed during Second World War.

Turinskaya Kultbaza, Russian SFSR: see TURA.

Turinskaya Sloboda (tōōrēn'skŭ slŭbŭdä'), village (1926 pop. 2,286), SE Sverdlovsk oblast, Russian SFSR, on Tura R. (landing) and 40 mi. SE of Turinsk; wheat, livestock.

Turinski or **Turinski Rudnik**, Russian SFSR: see KRASNOTURINSK.

Turi Rog or **Turiy Rog** (tōō'rē rôk"), village (1939 pop. over 500), SW Maritime Territory, Russian SFSR, near Manchurian border, on NW shore of

L. Khanka, 100 mi. N of Voroshilov; terminus of spur (from Manzovka) of Trans-Siberian RR.

Turís (tōōrēs'), town (pop. 3,981), Valencia prov., E Spain, 19 mi. WSW of Valencia; makes guitars; olive-oil processing; wine, cereals.

Turisk, Turiisk, or **Turiysk** (tōōrēsk'), Pol. *Turzysk* (tōō'zhĭsk), town (1931 pop. 1,500), central Volyn oblast, Ukrainian SSR, on Turya R. and 11 mi. SW of Kovel; flour- and sawmilling.

Turja River, Ukrainian SSR: see TURYA RIVER.

Türje (tür'yĕ), town (pop. 2,433), Zala co., W Hungary, 16 mi. NE of Zalaegerszeg; rail junction; grain, vineyards, cattle.

Turka (tōōr'kŭ), city (1931 pop. 10,145), SW Drogobych oblast, Ukrainian SSR, in the Beshchady, near Stry R., 25 mi. SW of Drogobych; agr.-processing center (flour, fruit, vegetables), lumbering; stone quarry. Has wooden Ruthenian churches. Passed from Poland to Austria (1772); reverted to Poland (1919); ceded to USSR in 1945.

Turkana, Kenya: see LODWAR.

Turkana Escarpment (tōōrkä'nŭ), steeply-sloped upland on Uganda-Kenya border, bet. Mt. Zulia (N) and Mt. Moroto (S); rises to over 4,000 ft.

Turkeli, Turkey: see AVSA ISLAND.

Turkestan or **Turkistan** (tûrkĭstăn', -stän', Rus. tōōrkyĭstän'), vast region of central Asia, inhabited by Turkic-speaking peoples, extending from the Caspian Sea (W) to the Gobi (E), separated by the Tien Shan and the Pamir into Western (Russian) Turkestan and Eastern (Chinese) Turkestan. A small section of N Afghanistan, with the towns of Andkhui and Mazar-i-Sharif, is commonly included in Turkestan. **Russian Turkestan** consists essentially of the deserts Kara-Kum and Kyzyl-Kum, which constitute the *Turan* lowland, W of the Tien Shan and Pamir-Alai mtn. systems. The Syr Darya and the Amu Darya are its main rivers. Following the Mongol conquest (late-13th cent.), W Turkestan became part of the Jagatai domain. It was conquered (late-14th cent.) by Tamerlane, and his successors, the Timurids, controlled the region through the 15th cent. Later arose the Uzbek khanates of Khiva, Bukhara, and Kokand. Following its conquest by the Russians (2d half of 19th cent.), W Turkestan was constituted as the Rus. governor-generalship of Turkestan (including the oblasts of Samarkand, Fergana, Syr-Darya, Semirechye, and the Transcaspian Oblast) and the protected khanates of Khiva and Bukhara. After the Bolshevik revolution, W Turkestan existed briefly as an autonomous SSR (1922–24) and, as a result of the reshuffling of internal boundaries along ethnic lines, was divided among the newly created Kazakh, Kirghiz, Tadzhik, Turkmen and Uzbek SSRs (see separate articles). **Chinese Turkestan** consists, properly speaking, only of the Tarim basin S of the Tien Shan. It is, however, commonly applied to the entire territory included in China's SINKIANG prov., which also includes Dzungaria, N of the Tien Shan.

Turkestan, city (1939 pop 54,000, including BORISOVKA), central South Kazakhstan oblast, Kazakh SSR, near Trans-Caspian RR, 95 mi. NW of Chimkent, in agr. area (cotton, lucerne, wheat); cotton-ginning center; metalworks. Has 14th-cent. mosque built during Tamerlane's reign. Site of anc. cities of Yasy and Hazrat. Fell to Russians in 1864.

Turkestan Range, branch of Tien Shan mountain system, W Tadzhik SSR, extends c.200 mi. W from Alai Range, along N watershed of Zeravshan R.; rises to 13,800 ft. Crossed by Leninabad-Stalinabad highway. Sometimes considered part of Pamir-Alai system.

Turkestan-Siberia Railroad, commonly abbreviated **Turksib,** major trunk line in SW Asiatic USSR, linking Siberia and Central Asia. Built 1927–30, it runs from Novosibirsk (junction with Trans-Siberian RR), past Barnaul, Semipalatinsk, Alma-Ata, and Chimkent, to Arys (N of Tashkent), at junction with Trans-Caspian RR. Carrying mainly grain from Siberia and cotton from Central Asia, it spurred the economic development of large sections of the SE Kazakh SSR. Spurs carry the lead of Tekeli, the phosphate of Chulak-Tau, and the coal of Lenger.

Turkeve (tōōr'kĕvĕ), Hung. *Túrkeve,* city (pop. 13,806), Jasz-Nagykun-Szolnok co., E central Hungary, 9 mi. NE of Mezötur; brickworks.

Turkey, Turkish *Türkiye* (tür"kēyĕ'), republic (□ 296,185; 1950 pop. 20,934,670), Asia Minor and SE Europe; ⊙ ANKARA. Its European section is separated from Asia Minor by one of the world's most strategic waterways, the narrow c.200-mi. E-W channel through the BOSPORUS, the Sea of MARMARA, and the DARDANELLES, linking the landlocked Black Sea with the Aegean Sea of the Mediterranean. Turkey in Asia or ANATOLIA (□ 287,117; 1950 pop. 19,308,441), 97% of the total area, is an enormous rectangle washed by Black Sea (N), Aegean Sea (W), and Mediterranean Sea (S). Its S boundary in the E is with Syria and Iraq, and it borders E on Iran, the Armenian SSR, and Georgian SSR. Turkey in Europe (□ 9,068; 1950 pop. 1,626,229) comprises Eastern THRACE and is bounded by the Black Sea (E), Bulgaria (N), Greece along Maritsa R. (W), and the Aegean Sea (SW). Almost all the isls. off the deeply indented Aegean coast of Asia Minor now belong to Greece. The country lies approximately bet. 36°–42°N and 26°–45°E. It is administratively divided into provinces (Turkish *il;* formerly called *vilayet*), usually named after their chief cities. Some of the older regional names relating to ethnic minorities are still in use; thus, NE Asiatic Turkey forms part of ARMENIA (principally Trebizond, Erzurum, and Kars provs.), which overlaps sections of KURDISTAN, roughly around L. VAN and near Iraqi border. CILICIA (SE) lies bet. the Mediterranean and Taurus Mts. Anatolia itself refers either to all of Asia Minor or only the elevated interior plateau, which the Turks consider their heartland, symbolized by the removal of the capital from cosmopolitan ISTANBUL (formerly Constantinople) to Ankara in the rugged uplands. Turkey in Europe is a land of rolling hills, largely forested in E, and in its W section agr. productive, watered by Ergene R., affluent of the Maritsa. The pop. is concentrated around Edirne (ADRIANOPLE) and Istanbul. Asiatic Turkey has fertile, partly wooded coastal strips—about 75 mi. wide—backed by steep ranges that form an almost continuous rim around the vast, steppe-like uplands (average alt. over 2,500 ft.). Highest among those ranges are the TAURUS MOUNTAINS and Anti-Taurus in the S, rising in the ALA DAG to 12,251 ft. Along the Black Sea is the Pontic system (e.g., KURE MOUNTAINS, IGLAZ MOUNTAINS). In NE and E these diverse ridges join towards the USSR and Iran in the tumbled mass of the Armenian highlands, culminating near international line in the famous Mt. ARARAT (16,945 ft.), the country's highest peak. There are several large lakes, notably the saline L. Van (E) and L. TUZ (center). Turkey has numerous rivers, but none of them are navigable. In the E rise the EUPHRATES RIVER (with its principal affluent, MURAT RIVER) and the TIGRIS RIVER. Longest river entirely in Turkey is the KIZIL IRMAK, which flows in a wide sweep to the Black Sea. Other streams draining the plateau are the Seyhan and Ceyhan rivers, which traverse the major alluvial Cilician plains and fall into the Gulf of ISKENDERUN. The Gediz and BUYUK MENDERES (the Maeander) flow W to the Aegean. The great hydroelectric potential is as yet untapped, though projects on Sakarya, Gediz, and Euphrates rivers are planned. The climatic pattern follows closely the varied relief. The Anatolian plateau is semi-arid (deserts occur in SE) and winters are harsh, with frequent snowfalls; summers are hot and dry. Where irrigation is practiced, the land is fertile. Ankara, at an elevation of 2,910 ft., has an average temp of 53.4°F. Only the marginal lowlands of the W and S coast have an equable Mediterranean type of climate. While the rainfall is here about 20–30 inches, it increases to c.100 inches in the semitropical E part of the Black Sea belt, where tea is cultivated. The generally mild Bosporus and Thrace have occasional cold winds and rain all year round. Istanbul has an annual mean of 57.5°F. Though metallurgy was developed in Anatolia earlier than almost anywhere else on the globe, mining is today only of secondary importance, still hampered by insufficient communications. There are, however, high-grade deposits of various minerals. Local needs are met by the large coal fields along the Black Sea around ZONGULDAK and EREGLI; excellent coal is also found near the Dardanelles and in SMYRNA and KONYA regions. In meerschaum (chiefly mined near ESKISEHIR), emery, and, particularly, chromium (Fethiye, Eskisehir), Turkey is one of the world's leading producers. There are iron deposits in Buyuk Menderes and Sakarya valleys, and in the Cilician plains; large copper deposits on upper Tigris at ERGANI. Petroleum has been struck near Iraqi border. Among other mineral resources are manganese, mercury, antimony, sulphur, asbestos. Minor deposits of nickel, tin, zinc, cobalt, platinum, silver, gold, arsenic, phosphate, alabaster, borax are known to exist. Turkey is predominantly an agr. and pastoral country (about ⅔ of the people are rural), yet only 20% of the generally fertile soil is under cultivation, since irrigation has hardly been developed; c.14% of the area is covered by forests; over half is grazing land. Wheat and barley are the leading crops, followed by other cereals—rye, corn, rice, millet, canary seed. All these crops, like cotton (SE), grapes, apples, soybeans, sunflowers, and sugar beets, are grown for local consumption. The country is far better known for its commercial crops, principally tobacco, grown both in European and Asiatic lowlands; SAMSUN and BAFRA on the Black Sea are the chief centers. Turkey's raisins, figs (Smyrna region), and opium (from the poppy seeds grown in AFYONKARAHISAR and KONYA provs.) are held in high esteem. Other agr. products exported include olives and olive oil, valonia (for tanning), filberts, walnuts, flax, hemp, sesame, vegetable dyes, licorice root, spices. Sericulture is centered at BURSA, also a well-known spa. However, economically the people depend much more on livestock as a source of income. Cattle, water buffaloes, oxen, horses, sheep, goats, asses, camels, mules are grazed extensively. Animals, skins, hides, dairy products, and eggs are shipped, besides large quantities of fine mohair wool from the renowned Angora goats. Fishing is profitable, particularly in the Bosporus. Turkish industries are on the whole of recent origin and are still in the initial stage of development. The 5-year plan inaugurated in 1934 made great strides. Owing to a lack of private enterprise and of foreign capital, more than a half of the new plants—as well as most public utilities—are state-owned. Turkey now makes textiles, glass, paper, chemicals, cement, household utensils, sugar, and food products. The mfg. of tobacco goods, rugs, and carpets (ISPARTA, UHAK, BERGAMA) has a long tradition. Large iron- and steelworks were established at KARABUK. The country still depends largely on imports of machinery, vehicles, petroleum products, pharmaceuticals, and dyes. By far the leading centers of private industrial enterprise are Istanbul and Smyrna (site of an international fair). They are also the leading ports, followed by MERSIN, Iskenderun (formerly Alexandretta), and Samsun. Minor ports are TREBIZOND, GIRESUN (center for hazelnut trade), SINOP, IZMIT, ANTALYA. Ankara, which has soared since 1920s to 2d place among the country's cities, has important state-owned factories (cement, textiles) and is the seat of a univ. Two other universities are at Istanbul, still Turkey's financial and commercial capital, and a picturesque, polyglot city. ADANA (S), the 4th city, in fertile delta near Mediterranean coast, is a flourishing textile and agr. center. Apart from Ankara there are few large cities on the plateau; among those with more than 50,000 inhabitants are Eskisehir (railroad repair shops, aircraft assembly plant), KAYSERI (textile mills, workshops), Konya (old ⊙ Seljuk Turkish kingdom), GAZIANTEP, and Erzurum. The new Turkey has embarked upon an ambitious road and communication program. A 10-year plan improved the sparse railroad net (now about 4,750 mi.) and highways. There is a government-owned merchant marine. The main provincial centers are linked by airlines. Through the Orient Express Turkey is connected with South and Western Europe. Another express establishes a link with Syria, Iraq (the BAGHDAD RAILWAY), Lebanon, Israel, and Egypt. Owing to the large-scale massacres and emigration of Armenians in the late-19th cent. and early 20th cent., and owing to the forced emigration of the Greeks and Bulgarians after 1923, Turkey lost some of its most progressive elements, particularly in commerce, but has gained in homogeneity; 86% of the people are now Turkish-speaking. There is complete separation of church and state, but the vast majority are nominally Sunnite Moslems. Kurds are the largest ethnic minority (c.9%), though Moslems by religion. The Jews, Greek Orthodox, and Armenian Christians are chief religious minorities. There are small groups of Lazis (NE) and Circassians (S). In 1920s about 500,000 Turks were repatriated from Greece. About 1% speak Arabic. The Turks themselves, although they regard the Osmalis or Ottomans—who came from Central Asia—as their ancestors, are racially as diverse as any nation. Turkey has since the dawn of history occupied a key position on the world's crossroads. It saw the flowering of the great Greek and Roman periods and the early development of Christianity. The names of its great old cities testify to its age-long importance: TROY, EPHESUS, ANTIOCH, TARSUS, PERGAMUM, SARDIS, MILETUS. Many races left their imprint—among the earliest the Hittites (2000–1200 B.C.). Many empires controlled through it the approaches to the Middle East, and—until the Sp. and Port. discoveries—the commercial land routes to the Far East. While Anatolia is one of the oldest inhabited regions in the world, the history of Turkey as a national state began only with the collapse (1918) of the OTTOMAN EMPIRE, that—as an heir to the Byzantine Empire (Constantinople was conquered 1453)—held at one time all of the Balkans and SE Europe as far as Vienna; the Near East including present day Syria, Lebanon, Palestine, and Arabia; and North Africa including Egypt, Tripolitania, Tunis, and Algeria. This empire declined after 18th cent. In the nationalistic movements of the 19th cent. and early 20th cent., most of the territories in Europe achieved their independence, but the Ottoman Empire was dealt its death blow after the First World War, in which Turkey had sided with the Central Powers. By the Treaty of Sèvres (1920) it was reduced to the N half of the Anatolian peninsula and a narrow neutralized and Allied-occupied zone of the Straits. The humiliating terms aroused nationalistic Young Turks who rallied under the leadership of Kemal Pasha, later known as Kemal Ataturk. They waged a successful offensive against the Allies in S Anatolia and concluded (1921) a treaty of friendship with Soviet Russia. A complete rout of the Greek invaders led (1922) to Turkish capture of Smyrna. The Treaty of Lausanne (1923) established the present boundaries of Turkey, except for the disputed region of the sanjak of ALEXANDRETTA (Hatay prov.), which was ceded by France only in 1939. Turkey was to exercise full sovereign rights over its entire territory except for the zone of the Straits, which was to remain demilitarized; this last restriction was lifted in 1936

(Montreux Convention). Turkey was formally proclaimed a republic in Oct., 1923, with Kemal Ataturk as president. The caliphate was abolished in 1924, and in the same year a constitution was promulgated. Despite a parliament and universal suffrage (extended to women in 1934), Kemal emerged as virtual dictator. Turkey underwent an unparalleled transformation from a backward, feudal monarchy to a cohesive, westernized republic. The religious, social, and cultural bases of Turkish society, as well as its political and economic structure were changed. Religious orders and polygamy were abolished, and the wearing of the traditional fez was forbidden. Turkey adopted the Latin alphabet and the Swiss civil code. Primary education and civil marriage were made compulsory. Religious rebellions by the Kurds were put down. In the economic field, Turkish policy under Kemal aimed at obtaining economic self-sufficiency. After the unique population exchanges among Turkey, Greece, and Bulgaria, the republic sought friendly relations with all its neighbors. Entered the League of Nations in 1932, joined (1934) the Balkan Pact, and concluded (1936) a non-aggression pact with Iraq, Iran, and Afghanistan. Ismet Inonu, who succeeded Ataturk as president in 1938, observed initially a neutral policy during the Second World War, although Turkey received lend-lease aid from the U.S. after 1941. Turkey declared war on Germany and Japan only in Jan., 1945, and joined the United Nations one month later. Relations with Russia became more strained after the USSR denounced (1945) its friendship pact with Turkey and demanded joint control of the Straits. In 1947 Turkey became one of the recipients of U.S. assistance under the Truman Doctrine. The post-war years saw a relaxation of state capitalism in favor of free enterprise and an increasing democratization, culminating in 1950 election of the democratic opposition leader Celal Bayar to succeed Inonu. Turkey is divided into the following 63 provs.: ADRIANOPLE (Edirne), AFYONKARAHISAR, AGRI, AMASYA, ANKARA, ANTALYA, AYDIN, BALIKESIR, BILECIK, BINGOL, BITLIS, BOLU, BURDUR, BURSA, CANAKKALE, CANKIRI, CORUH, CORUM, DENIZLI, DIYARBAKIR, ELAZIG, ERZINCAN, ERZURUM, ESKISEHIR, GAZIANTEP, GIRESUN, GUMUSANE, HAKARI, HATAY, ICEL, ISTANBUL, ISPARTA, KARS, KASTAMONU, KAYSERI, KIRKLARELI, KIRSEHIR, KOCAELI, KONYA, KUTAHYA, MALATYA, MANISA, MARAS, MARDIN, MUGLA, MUS, NYGDE, ORDU, RIZE, SAMSUN, SEYHAN, SIIRT, SINOP, SIVAS, SMYRNA, TEKIRDAG, TOKAT, TREBIZOND, TUNCELI, URFA, VAN, YOZGAT, ZONGULDAK.

Turkey. 1 Town (pop. 223), Sampson co., S central N.C., 8 mi. E of Clinton; market for peppers. **2** City (pop. 1,005), Hall co., NW Texas, just below Cap Rock escarpment, c.40 mi. W of Childress, in agr. area (cotton, grain sorghums, cattle); marketing and shipping center, with grain elevators, cotton gins and compresses.

Turkey Creek, N Okla., rises in Alfalfa co., flows c.65 mi. SSE, past Lahoma and Drummond, to Cimarron R. c.8 mi. N of Kingfisher.

Turkey Point, Md.: see ELK NECK.

Turkey River, NE Iowa, rises in Howard co., flows 135 mi. SE, past Elkader, to Mississippi R. 6 mi. SSE of Guttenberg. Receives Volga R. at Garber.

Turkhal, Turkey: see TURHAL.

Türkheim, France: see TURCKHEIM.

Türkheim (tŭrk'hīm), village (pop. 4,033), Swabia, SW Bavaria, Germany, on the Wertach and 7 mi. ENE of Mindelheim; rail junction; dairying, tanning.

Turki (tōōr'kē), village (1926 pop. 7,650), W Saratov oblast, Russian SFSR, on Khoper R., on rail spur and 10 mi. WNW of Arkadak; flour milling; wheat, fruit.

Türkismühle (tür'kĭsmü'lù), village (pop. 527), NE Saar, 8 mi. NNW of St. Wendel; frontier station near Ger. border; rail junction. Stock, poultry, grain. Formerly part of Prussian Rhine Prov.; annexed to Saar in 1947.

Turkistan, China and USSR: see TURKESTAN.

Turkman or **Torkman** (both: tōrkmän'), formerly **Turkmanchai** (tōōrkmänchī'), village, Fourth Prov., in Azerbaijan, NW Iran, 20 mi. NW of Mianeh and on road to Tabriz. By the treaty signed here in 1828, Persia ceded Erivan and Nakhichevan sections of Armenia to Russia.

Turkmen Canal (tûrk'mĕn), navigation and irrigation trunk canal, Turkmen SSR, extending from the Amu Darya at Takhia-Tash headworks 680 mi. SW through the dry Uzboi arm in the Kara-Kum desert to Krasnovodsk on Caspian Sea. Construction project (begun 1951) includes 3 dams and hydroelectric stations (total capacity, 100,000 kw)—one at Takhia-Tash and two on the canal proper; a net of irrigation canals in SW Turkmen SSR, in Amu Darya delta, and in Kara-Kum desert; and aqueducts supplying the large urban centers of the SW Turkmen SSR.

Turkmen Dagi (türkmĕn' däü), Turkish *Türkmen Daği*, peak (6,000 ft.), W central Turkey, 20 mi. ENE of Kutahya.

Turkmenia (tûrkmē'nēŭ), **Turkmenistan** (tûrk"-mĕnĭstăn', –stän', Rus. tōōrkmyĕ"nyĭstän'), or **Turkmen Soviet Socialist Republic** (tûrk'mĕn), constituent republic (□ 187,200; 1947 pop. estimate 1,170,000) of the USSR, in Central Asia; ⊙ Ashkhabad. Bounded by Caspian Sea (W), Kazakh and Uzbek SSR (in part along the Amu Darya; N, NE), and Afghanistan and Iran (along the Kopet Dagh; S). Essentially a desert lowland (the Kara-Kum occupies 90% of total area); has a mid-lat. desert and steppe climate, with mean temp. of 25°–30° F. (Jan.) and 82°–90° F. (July). Yearly precipitation, 4–8 in.; 16 in. in mts. Pop. is concentrated in oases at foot of the Kopet Dagh and along Tedzhen, Murgab, and Amu Darya rivers; consists of Turkmen (72%; a Turkic people of Sunni Moslem religion), Uzbeks (11%), and Russians (8%). Administratively, republic falls into 4 oblasts: ASHKHABAD, CHARDZHOU, MARY, TASHAUZ. Basic economic activity in the desert is raising of karakul sheep, fat-tailed sheep, and camels. Agr. (in irrigated oases): cotton (short-staple along the Amu Darya, long-staple in Murgab oasis); dry subtropical crops (guayule, sesame, millet, sweet potatoes, dates, palms, figs, sugar cane) in Atrek R. valley; sericulture, vineyards, orchards, melons (Chardzhou area). Irrigation aided by construction (in 1950s) of Tedzhen reservoir and navigable Turkmen Canal. Industry based on mineral resources: petroleum (Nebit-Dag, Cheleken), ozocerite, iodine, bromine (Cheleken), Glauber's salt (Kara-Bogaz-Gol), sulphur (Serny Zavod, Darvaza), lignite (W), potash (SE). Fisheries along Caspian Sea, with canneries at Kizyl-Kup, Kuuli-Mayak, and Kianly. Chief industrial centers (along Trans-Caspian RR) are Krasnovodsk, Ashkhabad, Tedzhen, Mary, and Chardzhou. Principal exports: cotton, fruit, silk, karakul, rugs, petroleum. The Turkmen (also known as Turkomans) first appeared in the region under Arab rule (8th–9th cent.) and, under Seljuk Turks, ruled Margiana (⊙ Merv) until the coming (13th cent.) of the Mongols. After the fall (15th cent.) of Tamerlane's empire, the Turkmen came under Uzbek domination, and after c.1800 under Khiva khanate. Conquered (1869–85) by Russia, region was inc. into Transcaspian Oblast of Rus. Turkestan. Turkmen SSR was formed (1924) and made a constituent republic out of Turkmen oblast of temporary Turkestan Autonomous SSR and parts of Khorezm and Bukhara SSRs.

Turkmen-Kala (tōōrkmyĕn"-kŭlä'), town (1939 pop. over 500), central Mary oblast, Turkmen SSR, on Murgab oasis, 28 mi. ESE of Mary; cotton.

Turkmen Soviet Socialist Republic: see TURKMENIA.

Turk Mine, village, Bulawayo prov., SW central Southern Rhodesia, in Matabeleland, on road and 32 mi. NNE of Bulawayo; gold mining.

Turks and Caicos Islands (kī'kōs, kī'kŭs), archipelago (□ 201.7; 1943 pop. 6,138; 1947 estimate 8,929), B.W.I.; ⊙ Grand Turk. Geographically the SE continuation of the Bahamas, they are politically a dependency of Jamaica (c.350 mi. to SW). Consist of 2 groups of small islets and cays, TURKS ISLANDS and CAICOS ISLANDS, separated by Turks Island Passage. Situated N of Windward Passage (bet. Cuba and Haiti), just below the Tropic of Cancer; extend bet. 21°–22°N and 71°–72°30'W. Include about 30 isls., of which only 8 are inhabited. Largest isl. is Middle Caicos or Grand Caicos. Salt panning is the principal industry. The archipelago has an equable, healthy climate because of constant trade winds; average temp. c.80°F.; 31.7 in. rainfall. Struck by severe hurricanes in 1925, 1928, and 1945. Some activity in sponge and fibers; lobster fishing. The inhabitants are mostly colored. The isls. were discovered 1512 by Ponce de León. Uninhabited until 1678, when Bermudians established salt-panning industry. The French attacked the isls. in 1753 and 1764. Occupied by British in 1766, and placed under Bahama govt. in 1799. Annexed to Jamaica in 1873.

Turksib, USSR: see TURKESTAN-SIBERIA RAILROAD.

Turks Island Passage, c.20-mi.-wide channel in the Caribbean, separating Caicos Isls. (W) from Turks Isls. (E), at about 21°40'N 71°W.

Turks Islands, E group of TURKS AND CAICOS ISLANDS, B.W.I., dependency of Jamaica, 135 mi. NNW of Cap-Haïtien (Haiti), separated from Caicos Isls. by Turks Island Passage; bet. 21°10'–21°31'N and 71°5'–71°15'W. Isls. consist of Grand Turk (pop. 1,668) and Salt Cay (pop. 420) and some smaller islets. On Grand Turk is the capital of the dependency. Main industry is salt panning; also sponge fishing, fiber growing, lobster canning.

Turku (tōōr'kōō), Swedish *Åbo* (ō'bōō), city (pop. 99,272), ⊙ Turku-Pori co., SW Finland, on Gulf of Bothnia, at mouth of Aura R., 100 mi. WNW of Helsinki; 60°27'N 22°16'E. Seaport, kept ice-free the year round, terminus of mail steamers from Stockholm; rail junction; airport at Artukainen (W). Industrial and cultural center, with shipyards; steel, lumber, flour, woolen, cotton, and hosiery mills; machinery, tobacco, and pottery works; sugar refinery, distillery. Second-largest and oldest city of Finland; seat of Lutheran archbishop; site of Swedish (1918) and Finnish (1922) univ. Has cathedral (completed 1290); 13th-cent. castle, enlarged in 16th cent.; Greek-Orthodox church (1846); nautical school, housed in former observatory; historical, biological, and art mus. City is seat of several learned societies. Growing up around a medieval castle, Turku was ⊙ Finland until 1812. Chartered (1525) by Gustavus Vasa of Sweden. Seat of national univ., from 1640 to 1827, when city was virtually destroyed by fire; univ. reopened (1828) in Helsinki. Under Treaty of Abo (1743) Sweden ceded part of SE Finland to Russia. City suffered heavy damage by Russian bombing during Finnish-Russian War (1939–40) and during Second World War.

Turku-Pori (tōōr'kōō-pō'rē), Swedish *Åbo-Björneborg* (ō'bōō-byûr'nùbôr"yù), county [Finnish *lääni*] (□ 8,499; including water area, □ 8,885; pop. 623,169), SW Finland; ⊙ Turku. On Gulf of Bothnia, it has deeply indented coast line, protected by innumerable skerries. Surface is low and level, dotted with numerous small lakes; drained by Kokemäki, Aura, and several smaller rivers. Agr. (rye, oats, barley, sugar beets, potatoes), stock raising, and dairying are important. Fishing. Limestone and granite quarries, mines (copper, zinc, lead, silver, and gold). Industries include lumbering, timber processing, and woodworking, metalworking and refining (copper, nickel), textile milling, tanning. Considerable part of coastal pop. is Swedish-speaking. Cities are Turku, Pori, Rauma, Uusikaupunki, and Naantali.

Turkwell River, NW Kenya, rises on NE slopes of Mt. Elgon, flows c.200 mi. NNE, past Kacheliba and Lodwar, to L. Rudolf.

Turkyany (tōōrkyä'nē), town (1939 pop. over 2,000) in Azizbekov dist. of Greater Baku, Azerbaijan SSR, on S shore of Apsheron Peninsula, 20 mi. E of Baku; seaside resort.

Turleque (tōōrlā'kā), town (pop. 2,099), Toledo prov., central Spain, 29 mi. SE of Toledo; cereals, saffron, olives, grapes, stock.

Turley, village (1940 pop. 606), Tulsa co., NE Okla., 6 mi. N of Tulsa; oil refining.

Turlock (tûr'lŏk), city (pop. 6,235), Stanislaus co., central Calif., in San Joaquin Valley, 13 mi. SE of Modesto; trade and shipping center of Turlock irrigation project (begun 1887), using Tuolumne R.; melons, other truck, alfalfa, fruit, grain, dairy products, poultry. Inc. 1908.

Turlock Reservoir, Calif.: see TUOLUMNE RIVER.

Turlough (tûr'lŏkh), Gaelic *Turlach*, agr. village (district pop. 1,013), central Co. Mayo, Ireland, on Castlebar R. and 4 mi. NE of Castlebar; cattle, potatoes. There is anc. round tower.

Turmantas (tōōr'mäntäs), Pol. *Turmont*, village, NE Lithuania, on Latvian border opposite Zemgale, on railroad and 12 mi. S of Daugavpils; Pol.-Latvian customs station (1921–39).

Turmequé (tōōrmākā'), town (pop. 662), Boyacá dept., central Colombia, in Cordillera Oriental, 18 mi. SSW of Tunja; alt. 7,887 ft. Wheat, corn, fique; mfg. (fique bags, footwear). Founded 1537 on site of anc. Indian settlement.

Turmero (tōōrmā'rō), town (pop. 4,142), Aragua state, N Venezuela, on railroad and highway, E of L. Valencia, and 9 mi. E of Maracay; agr. center (coffee, cacao, sugar cane, corn, fruit, cattle).

Türmitz, Czechoslovakia: see TRMICE.

Turna or **Turna nad Bodvou** (tōōr'nä näd' bôd"vō), Hung. *Torna* (tôr'nŏ), village (pop. 1,462), S Slovakia, Czechoslovakia, on railroad, on Bodva R. and 19 mi. WSW of Kosice. Has picturesque 13th-cent. cathedral and castle ruins.

Turnagain Arm, S Alaska, NE arm (50 mi. long, 2–13 mi. wide) of Cook Inlet, on N side of Kenai Peninsula, 15 mi. S of Anchorage. Named 1778 by Capt. James Cook.

Turnau, Czechoslovakia: see TURNOV.

Turnberry, resort village in Kirkoswald parish, S Ayrshire, Scotland, on Firth of Clyde, 5 mi. N of Girvan; noted golfing center. Just N is promontory of Turnberry Point (55°20'N 4°52'W) with ruins of Turnberry Castle, reputed birthplace of Robert Bruce.

Turneffe Island (tûrnĕf'), in Caribbean Sea, in Belize dist., Br. Honduras, 20 mi. E of Belize; 23 mi. long, 3–7 mi. wide. Coconuts; fisheries. At high tide S extremity of cay breaks into several small isls. enclosing a lagoon.

Turner. 1 County (□ 293; pop. 10,479), S central Ga.; ⊙ Ashburn. Drained by Little and Alapaha rivers. Coastal plain agr. (peanuts, pecans, cotton, corn, melons) and forestry (lumber, naval stores) area. Formed 1905. **2** County (□ 611; pop. 12,100), SE S.Dak.; ⊙ Parker. Rich agr. area drained by branches of Vermillion R. Livestock, dairy products, grain, poultry. Formed 1871.

Turner. 1 Village (1940 pop. 788), Wyandotte co., NE Kansas, on Kansas R.; SW suburb of Kansas City, Kansas. **2** Town (pop. 1,712), Androscoggin co., SW Maine, on the Androscoggin and 20 mi. N of Auburn; agr.; fruit canning and shipping; lumber mills. Includes Turner Center village, long known for dairying. Settled c.1773, inc. 1786. **3** Village (pop. 193), Arenac co., E Mich., 38 mi. N of Bay City, near Au Gres R., in farm area. **4** Village (pop. c.200), Blaine co., N Mont., port of entry near Sask. line, 40 mi. NNW of Malta. **5** City (pop. 610), Marion co., NW Oregon, 7 mi. SE of Salem.

Turner Air Force Base, Ga.: see ALBANY.
Turner Center, Maine: see TURNER.
Turner Falls, Okla.: see ARBUCKLE MOUNTAINS.
Turners Falls, Mass.: see MONTAGUE.
Turner's Peninsula, low tongue of land on S coast of Sierra Leone; extends c.80 mi. from Liberian border WNW to Shebar Strait, bet. Atlantic Ocean (S) and Waanje and Kittam rivers (N); up to 4 mi. wide. Mangrove swamps. An early slave-trading area; ceded (1825) to the Crown.
Turners Station, town (pop. 89), Henry co., N Ky., 22 mi. SW of Warsaw, in Bluegrass region.
Turner Valley, village (pop. 1,157), SW Alta., at foot of Rocky Mts., on Sheep R. and 27 mi. SSW of Calgary; center of major oil and natural-gas area, extending c.10 mi. N and S from village. Oil refineries; gas pipe lines to Calgary, Lethbridge, and other S Alta. towns. Production began 1914.
Turnerville, village (pop. 1,048), Iberville parish, S La.
Turney, town (pop. 152), Clinton co., NW Mo., 28 mi. SE of St. Joseph.
Turnhout (tûr'nout, tûrnout'), town (pop. 32,429), Antwerp prov., N Belgium, at junction of Antwerp-Turnhout Canal and Canal d'Embranchement, 24 mi. ENE of Antwerp; market center for agr. area; mfg. (bricks, Portland cement, paper, lace). Former castle of dukes of Brabant is now Palace of Justice.
Türnich (tür'nĭkh), village (pop. 10,231), in former Prussian Rhine Prov., W Germany, after 1945 in North Rhine-Westphalia, on canalized Erft and 10 mi. WSW of Cologne, in lignite-mining region.
Türnitz (tür'nĭts), town (pop. 2,774), S Lower Austria, 20 mi. SSW of Sankt Pölten; rail terminal; scythes, cutlery.
Turnov (tŏŏr'nôf), Ger. *Turnau* (tŏŏr'nou), town (pop. 8,425), N Bohemia, Czechoslovakia, on Jizera R. and 13 mi. SSE of Liberec; rail junction; popular summer resort (Bohemian Paradise near by). Noted precious and semi-precious stone-cutting industry; gem-cutters' trade school; intensive production of synthetic gems. Also mfg. of cotton textiles, ready-made garments. Has 16th-cent. town hall, 17th-cent. Franciscan monastery, research institute for precious stones. Bohemian garnets, amethysts, and agates found in Kozakov mtn., 5 mi. ENE.
Turnu-Magurele (tŏŏr'nŏŏ-mŭgŏŏrā'lĕ), Rum. *Turnu-Măgurele,* town (1948 pop. 11,493), Teleorman prov., S Rumania, in Walachia, on left bank of the Danube opposite Nikopol (Bulgaria), near mouth of Olt R., and 80 mi. SW of Bucharest; rail terminus and inland port with brisk trade in livestock and grain. Fishing. Mfg. of furniture, soap, and candles; tanning, flour milling. Anc. Roman camp; has ruins of 14th-cent. fortress. Danube boats lay up here in winter.
Turnu Rosu Pass (rô'shŏŏ), Rum. *Turnu Roşu,* Ger. *Roter Turm* (rō'tùr tŏŏrm') [=red tower], defile (alt. 1,198 ft.) cut by Olt R. through the Transylvanian Alps, W of Fagaras Mts.; c.7 mi. long; railroad and highway corridor and major communications channel bet. Transylvania and Walachia. Site of historic fortress, and noted battleground in wars against the Turks and in 1916.
Turnu-Severin (–sĕvĕrēn'), anc. *Drubeta,* town (1948 pop. 31,296), Gorj prov., SW Rumania, in Walachia, on left bank of the Danube (Yugoslav border) below the Iron Gates, on railroad and 160 mi. W of Bucharest; inland port and industrial center. Brisk trade in livestock, grain, lumber, fruit; important shipyards for construction and repair of river craft, notably oil tankers; railroad repair shops; aircraft mfg.; marine arsenal. Produces alcohol, beer, flour, confectionery, hats, furniture, terra cotta. Known for its extensive rose gardens. Surrounding vineyards are noted for their white wine. There are remains of the anc. Roman city, Severus' tower (A.D. 222–235), medieval churches and fortress. Mus. has archaeological and ethnographical collections. Stone pillars of famous Trajan's Bridge (A.D. 103) across the Danube are still to be seen near by at low water.
Turo (tŏŏ'rū), Dan. *Turø,* island (□ 2.9; pop. 1,511), Denmark, ½ mi. from S shore of Fyn isl., separated from Taasinge isl. (SW) by Svendborg Sound; fishing, seafaring.
Turochak (tŏŏrŭchăk'), village (1948 pop. over 2,000), NE Gorno-Altai Autonomous oblast, Altai Territory, Russian SFSR, 50 mi. ENE of Gorno-Altaisk and on Biya R. (head of navigation); gold and manganese mining; power plant.
Turocszentmarton, Czechoslovakia: see TURCIANSKY SVATY MARTIN.
Turon, city (pop. 632), Reno co., S central Kansas, 30 mi. WSW of Hutchinson, in wheat area. Oil wells near by.
Turopolje (tŏŏ'rôpô"lyĕ), plain in N Croatia, Yugoslavia, bet. Sava and lower Kupa rivers. Village of Turopolje is 14 mi. SSE of Zagreb.
Turov (tŏŏ'rŭf), town (1926 pop. 5,393), W Polesye oblast, Belorussian SSR, on Pripet R. and 65 mi. W of Mozyr, near former Pol. border; sawmilling.
Turquino, Pico (pē'kō tŏŏrkē'nō), highest peak (6,560 ft.) of Cuba, in the Sierra Maestra, in Oriente prov., 65 mi. W of Santiago de Cuba; 19°59'N 76°50'W.
Turre (tŏŏ'rā), town (pop. 1,753), Almería prov., S Spain, 17 mi. SSE of Huércal-Overa; olive-oil processing, flour milling; almonds, cereals, esparto, grapes.
Turrell (tûrl, tŭ'rŭl), town (pop. 670), Crittenden co., E Ark., 21 mi. NW of Memphis (Tenn.), in cotton-growing area.
Turriaco (tŏŏr-rēä'kō), village (pop. 1,936), Gorizia prov., Friuli–Venezia Giulia, NE Italy, near Isonzo R., 4 mi. ENE of Monfalcone.
Turrialba (tŏŏryäl'bä), city (1950 pop. 5,449), Cartago prov., central Costa Rica, on branch of Inter-American Highway, on Turrialba R. (small affluent of the Reventazón), at SE foot of Turrialba volcano, on railroad and 15 mi. NE of Cartago. Important commercial center; coffee, sugar cane, corn, bananas, livestock. Seat of Inter-American Inst. of Agr. Sciences.
Turrialba, volcano (10,974 ft.) in the Cordillera Central, central Costa Rica, 8 mi. NW of Turrialba; 10°02'N 83°45'W.
Turriers (türēā'), village (pop. 145), Basses-Alpes dept., SE France, in Provence Alps, 12 mi. SSE of Gap.
Turriff (tûr'ĭf), burgh (1931 pop. 2,298; 1951 census 2,994), N Aberdeen, Scotland, near Deveron R., 10 mi. SSE of Banff; agr. market, with agr. machinery works. Has 16th-cent. remains of old church dating from c.7th cent.
Turris Libisonis, Sardinia: see PORTO TORRES.
Turrubares, San Pablo de, Costa Rica: see SAN PABLO.
Turrúcares (tŏŏrŏŏ'kärĕs), village, Alajuela prov., W central Costa Rica, on railroad and 11 mi. SW of Alajuela, in Turrúcares plain (a major grain-growing belt); corn, beans, rice, sugar cane, fruit, fodder crops.
Turshiz, Iran: see KASHMAR.
Tursi (tŏŏr'sē), town (pop. 3,127), Matera prov., Basilicata, S Italy, 11 mi. SSW of Pisticci, in agr. (cereals, fruit, cotton) and stock-raising region. Bishopric.
Turta, Mongolia: see TURTU.
Turtkul or **Turtkul'** (tŏŏrtkŏŏl'), city (1939 pop. 19,600), S Kara-Kalpak Autonomous SSR, Uzbek SSR, on the Amu Darya and 95 mi. SE of Nukus; cotton ginning, food processing, light mfg. Until c.1920, called Petro-Aleksandrovsk; former (to 1939) ⊙ Kara-Kalpak Autonomous SSR.
Turtle Bay, SE N.Y., a dist. of E Manhattan borough of New York city, along East R. N of 42d St. Site of United Nations' hq.
Turtle Creek, borough (pop. 12,363), Allegheny co., SW Pa., industrial E suburb of Pittsburgh; bituminous coal; cement blocks, electrical equipment. Trading post near here c.1750. Settled c.1765, inc. 1892.
Turtle Creek, S Wis., rises in small lake N of Delavan in Walworth co., flows S to Delavan, then SW to Rock R. at Beloit; c.35 mi. long.
Turtleford, village (pop. 273), W Sask., 50 mi. NW of North Battleford; wheat, oats.
Turtle Islands (□ 1.2; 1948 pop. 449), small group of rocks and islets in Sulu prov., Philippines, 10 mi. off NE coast of Borneo, c.125 mi. NW of S tip of Sulu Archipelago; 6°10'N 118°10'E.
Turtle Islands, group of islands belonging to Sierra Leone, in the Atlantic off W point of Sherbro Isl., off mouth of Sherbro R., 60 mi. SSE of Freetown. Historically part of the colony; administered under South-Western Prov. of the protectorate. Used in fishing season.
Turtle Lake. 1 City (pop. 839), McLean co., central N.Dak., 50 mi. N of Bismarck, near Turtle L.; ships cattle, coal, grain; dairy products. **2** Village (pop. 696), Barron co., NW Wis., 21 mi. WSW of Rice Lake, in wooded lake-resort area; dairy products, canned peas, snowplows.
Turtle Lake, Itasca co., N central Minn., in state forest, 26 mi. NNW of Grand Rapids; 4.5 mi. long, 2 mi. wide. Has fishing resorts. Drains through small stream into Bowstring L.
Turtle Mountains, in N N.Dak. and S Manitoba, plateau 2,000 ft. above sea level, 3–400 ft. above surrounding country; extends 20 mi. N-S, 40 mi. E-W. It has timber, numerous lakes, and small deposits of low-grade manganese. Turtle Mtn. Indian Reservation is in valley on SE border of plateau.
Turtle River, village (pop. 57), Beltrami co., N Minn., 10 mi. NNE of Bemidji, in lake and forest region; grain.
Turtmann (tŏŏrt'män), Fr. *Tourtemagne* (tŏŏrtŭmä'nyŭ), village (pop. 637), Valais canton, S Switzerland, on stream Turtmannbach near its confluence with the Rhone, and 8 mi. E of Sierre; hydroelectric plant.
Turton, urban district (1931 pop. 11,847; 1951 census 10,951), S central Lancashire, England, 4 mi. N of Bolton; cotton and rayon milling. Near by is prehistoric stone circle, and a manor house dating from 15th cent. In urban dist. (W) is paper-milling village of Belmont, site of Bolton reservoir, and cotton-milling towns of Bradshaw and Bromley Cross.
Turton, town (pop. 201), Spink co., NE central S.Dak., 24 mi. ENE of Redfield; trading point for farming area.
Turtu or **Turta** (tŏŏr'tŭ), village, Khubsugul aimak, NW Mongolian People's Republic, landing at N end of L. Khubsugul, on highway and 170 mi. WSW of Irkutsk, near USSR line; freight transshipment point on USSR-Mongolia trade route.
Turtucaia, Bulgaria: see TUTRAKAN.
Turuga, Japan: see TSURUGA.
Turugart Pass (tŏŏrŏŏgärt') (alt. 12,155 ft.), in the Kokshaal-Tau section of the Tien Shan system, on USSR-China border, just S of lake Chatyr-Kul, on Kashgar-Naryn (Kirghiz SSR) trade route.
Turugi, Mount, Japan: see TSURUGI, MOUNT.
Turukhan River (tŏŏrŏŏkhän'), N Krasnoyarsk Territory, Russian SFSR, rises near Arctic Circle 80 mi. SSW of Igarka, flows 320 mi. S and E to Yenisei R. opposite Staroturukhansk.
Turukhansk (–khänsk'), village (1940 pop. over 3,000), N Krasnoyarsk Territory, Russian SFSR, on Yenisei R., at mouth of Lower Tunguska R., and 125 mi. SSE of Igarka. Formerly Monastyrskoye, later (briefly in 1920s) Novoturukhansk, and finally Turukhansk. Near by (12 mi. NW), near confluence of Turukhan and Yenisei rivers, is hamlet of Staroturukhansk, founded 1607 as Novaya Mangazeya (Rus.,=new Mangazeya), which succeeded (c.1670) old Mangazeya as fur center of NW Siberia; it was later renamed Turukhansk and became administrative seat of the old Turukhansk dist. of the Yeniseisk govt. and a center of tsarist penal colonies. This administrative center was moved c.1920 to the site of Monastyrskoye, which eventually took the name of Turukhansk.
Turumi, Mount, Japan: see TSURUMI, MOUNT.
Turumiquire, Cerro (sĕ'rō tŏŏrŏŏmēkē'rā), peak (8,517 ft.), NE Venezuela, on Sucre–Monagas border, 32 mi. SE of Cumaná.
Turuntayevo (tŏŏrŏŏntī'ŭvŭ), village (1948 pop. over 500), S Buryat-Mongol Autonomous SSR, Russian SFSR, 30 mi. N of Ulan-Ude; lumbering.
Turuoka, Japan: see TSURUOKA.
Turuvekere (tŏŏrŏŏvĕ'kĕrĕ), town (pop. 2,678), Tumkur dist., central Mysore, India, 32 mi. WSW of Tumkur; rice, coconuts, tobacco; handicrafts (coir mats, woolen blankets, biris).
Turya River or **Tur'ya River** (tŏŏr'yŭ), Pol. *Turja* (tŏŏr'yä), Volyn oblast, Ukrainian SSR, rises W of Torchin in Volyn-Podolian Upland, flows 110 mi. NW and N, past Turisk and Kovel, to Pripet R. 15 mi. NE of Ratno.
Tury-Assú, Brazil: see TURIAÇU.
Turzovka (tŏŏr'zôfkä), Hung. *Turzófalva* (tŏŏr'zōfŏlvŏ), town (9,341), NW Slovakia, Czechoslovakia, on railroad and 12 mi. NNW of Zilina; lumbering.
Turzysk, Ukrainian SSR: see TURIYSK.
Tus, Iran: see MESHED.
Tusa (tŏŏ'zä), village (pop. 4,965), Messina prov., N Sicily, near Tyrrhenian coast, 13 mi. ESE of Cefalù. Near by are ruins (2 mi. in circumference) of Halaesa or Alaesa, founded 403 B.C.
Tusby, Finland: see TUUSULA.
Tuscaloosa (tŭskùlŏŏ'sù), county (□ 1,340; pop. 94,092), W central Ala.; ⊙ Tuscaloosa. Coastal plain drained by Black Warrior, Sipsey, and North rivers. Cotton, corn, timber, bees; coal, iron. Mfg. at Tuscaloosa. Formed 1818.
Tuscaloosa, city (pop. 46,396), ⊙ Tuscaloosa co., W central Ala., on left bank of Black Warrior R. and 50 mi. SW of Birmingham, near fall line. Trade and educational center, with boat connections; mfg. (paper, cotton products, rubber tires, phenol, bakery products), woodworking, dairying, oil refining; synthetic resin. Coal mines and rock quarries near by. Seat of Univ. of Ala. and Negro jr. col. Has fine ante-bellum homes and state hosp. for insane. Founded after Creek revolt of 1813. Grew as plantation center; state ⊙ 1826–46.
Tuscambia River (tŭskăm'bēŭ), Miss. and Tenn., rises near Boonesville in Prentiss co., NE Miss.; flows c.50 mi. N and NW into SW Tenn., to Hatchie R. 6 mi. E of Middleton; largely canalized.
Tuscan Apennines, Italy: see ETRUSCAN APENNINES.
Tuscan Archipelago (tŭ'skùn), island group (□ c.115; pop. c.33,000), Italy, in Tyrrhenian Sea, bet. coast of Tuscany and Corsica. Comprises isls. of ELBA, CAPRAIA, PIANOSA, MONTE CRISTO, and GORGONA, belonging to Livorno prov., GIGLIO and GIANNUTRI, belonging to Grosseto prov., and several islets. Represents part of sunken mtn. range. Iron mining (Elba), agr. (grapes, fruit), and fishing (tunny, sardines) are chief occupations.
Tuscania (tŏŏskä'nyä), town (pop. 5,260), Viterbo prov., Latium, central Italy, near Marta R., 12 mi. W of Viterbo; paper mfg. Etruscan tombs near by. Called Toscanella until 1911.
Tuscany (tŭ'skùnē), Ital. *Toscana* (tôskä'nä), region (□ 8,876; pop. 2,978,013), central Italy; ⊙ Florence. Bordered by Emilia-Romagna (N), Liguria (NW), Latium (S), The Marches and Umbria (E), Ligurian and Tyrrhenian seas (W). Comprises 9 provs.: AREZZO, FIRENZE, GROSSETO, LIVORNO, LUCCA, MASSA E CARRARA, PISA, PISTOIA, SIENA. Includes TUSCAN ARCHIPELAGO, of which ELBA is largest isl. Extends c.170 mi. S from Etruscan Apennines and c.100 mi. E from Ligurian Sea. Area 90% hilly and mountainous, with narrow coastal plain and river valleys, notably the Val d'Arno. Arno R. and its tributaries, Sieve, Pesa, Elsa, and Era rivers, drain N third of area. Other major rivers: Om-

brone, Cecina, upper Tiber. Forests (chestnut, conifer, oak) cover 36% of region; leading chestnut producer of Italy. Maritime climate, ranging to continental in interior. Rainfall chiefly in autumn and winter; scarce in summer. Malaria, formerly widespread in the MAREMMA (S), has largely disappeared through land reclamation projects. Agr. (wheat, olives, grapes, mushrooms, flowers) is chief activity; noted for its wine (Chianti) and olive oil. Stock raising (sheep, cattle) and fishing also carried on. Rich in minerals, producing 90% of Italy's iron ore (Elba), most of its mercury (Monte Amiata) and boric acid (Maremma); copper and iron pyrite (Gavorrano, Montieri), manganese (Monte Argentario), magnesite, lignite (Val d'Arno, Roccastrada, Gavorrano). Its Carrara marble (Apuane Alps) is famous throughout the world. Chief industries: iron and steel (Florence, Follonica, Leghorn, Piombino, Portoferraio), textiles (Prato, Lucca), precision instruments (Florence), shipbuilding (Leghorn), airplane mfg. (Marina di Pisa), ceramics, glass, furniture (Cascina), straw hats (Signa). Tuscany includes large part of anc. Etruria and contains valuable Etruscan remains. Conquered by Romans (3d cent. B.C.); later became Lombard duchy. Most cities became free communes in 11th–12th cent. and some (Pisa, Lucca, Siena, Florence) developed into strong republics. Florence chief power in 14th–15th cent. In late Middle Ages and throughout the Renaissance, Tuscany was a center of arts and learning. Formed a grand duchy from 1569 until 1860, with few interruptions. United with Italy in 1861. In Second World War, heavy fighting and numerous air raids (1943–44) left few of its towns completely undamaged.

Tuscarawas (tŭskůrô'wůs), county (□ 571; pop. 70,320), E Ohio; ⊙ New Philadelphia. Intersected by Tuscarawas R., Stillwater Creek, and small Sugar, Sandy, and Conotton creeks. Includes part of Atwood Reservoir. Agr. (livestock; dairy products; grain); mfg. at New Philadelphia, Dover, and Newcomerstown; coal mines, clay pits. Formed 1808.

Tuscarawas, village (pop. 700), Tuscarawas co., E Ohio, 7 mi. SSE of New Philadelphia, in coal-mining area; clay products.

Tuscarawas River, E and central Ohio, rises in Summit co. in NE Ohio, flows generally S through Stark and Tuscarawas counties, then W to unite with the Walhonding at Coshocton to form the Muskingum; c.125 mi. long. Flood-control reservoir at Dover, on main stream; Tappan, Piedmont, Clendening, Leesville, Atwood reservoirs are on tributaries.

Tuscarora (tŭskůrô'rů). **1** Old mining camp (pop. c.100), Elko co., NE Nev., bet. Tuscarora Mts. (W), Independence Mts. (E), 40 mi. NNW of Elko. In 1870s and '80s, as chief camp of rich silver and gold dist., had pop. of several thousand. **2** Village (1940 pop. 766), Schuylkill co., E central Pa., 4 mi. SW of Tamaqua, in anthracite region.

Tuscarora Deep, ocean depth (27,929 ft.) of North Pacific Ocean, at N end of Japan Trench, off Kurile Isls.; 44°55'N 152°26'E. Discovered in 1874 by the *U.S.S. Tuscarora,* it was considered the greatest ocean depth until early 20th cent.

Tuscarora Mountain, S Pa., NE-SW ridge (1,500–1,900 ft.) of the Appalachians; runs from N end of Cove Mtn. near Md. border NE c.70 mi. along borders bet. Fulton, Huntingdon, and Juniata counties (W) and Franklin and Percy counties (E), to Juniata R. opposite Millerstown.

Tuschen, village (pop. 802), Essequibo co., N Br. Guiana, on right bank of Essequibo R. estuary, on railroad and 14 mi. WNW of Georgetown; sugar plantations.

Tuschkau, Czechoslovakia: see TOUSKOV.

Tuscola (tŭskō'lů), county (□ 816; pop. 38,258), E Mich.; ⊙ Caro. Bounded NW by Saginaw Bay; drained by Cass R. and its affluents. Agr. (sugar beets, beans, grain, potatoes, fruit, livestock; dairy products); coal mining; fisheries. State game refuge in co. Organized 1850.

Tuscola. 1 City (pop. 2,960), ⊙ Douglas co., E central Ill., 20 mi. S of Champaign; mfg. (brooms, wood products); agr. (corn, wheat; dairy products; livestock, poultry). Platted 1857, inc. 1861. **2** Town (pop. 497), Taylor co., W central Texas, 16 mi. S of Abilene, in cotton, cattle area. L. Abilene recreation area (state park; fishing, resort) is c.5 mi. W.

Tusculum, Italy: see FRASCATI.

Tuscumbia (tŭskŭm'bēů). **1** City (pop. 6,734), ⊙ Colbert co., NW Ala., on left bank of Tennessee R. and 95 mi. NW of Birmingham, just S of Sheffield; cotton and rubber products, lumber, fertilizer. Settled c.1815. Helen Keller b. here. Industries stimulated by construction of Wilson Dam (5 mi. NE) and development of TVA. **2** Town (pop. 221), ⊙ Miller co., central Mo., on Osage R. and 11 mi. SE of Eldon; resort; agr.; barite mines.

Tushan. 1 Town, Jehol prov., Manchuria, China: see TSINGLUNG. **2** Town, Kweichow prov., China: see TUHSHAN.

Tushar Mountains (tŭ'shůr), in Fishlake Natl. Forest, Piute and Beaver counties, SW central Utah; extend S from Pavant Mts. along W bank of Sevier R. Chief peaks: Circleville Mtn. (11,276 ft.), Mt. BELKNAP (12,139 ft.), and DELANO PEAK (12,173 ft.).

Tushin, Poland: see TUSZYN.

Tushino (tōō'shĭnů), city (1939 pop. 24,600), central Moscow oblast, Russian SFSR, adjoining (NW of) Moscow, on left bank of Moskva R.; textile milling, mfg. (trolley busses, conveyor machinery). Site of main Moscow military airport. Was hq. (1608–10) of the 2d false Dimitri, pretender to Rus. throne. Became city in 1938.

Tusima, Japan: see TSUSHIMA.

Tuskar Rock, islet in St. George's Channel, off SW coast of Co. Wexford, Ireland, 7 mi. ENE of Carnsore Point; lighthouse (52°12'N 6°12'W).

Tuskegee (tŭskē'gē), city (pop. 6,712), ⊙ Macon co., E Ala., 40 mi. E of Montgomery, in cotton, corn, potato area; lumber, cottonseed oil, fertilizer. Seat of U.S. Negro veterans hosp. and Tuskegee Inst., noted Negro school of which Booker T. Washington was principal. Settled early 19th cent., inc. 1843.

Tusnad (tōōsh'näd), Rum. *Tuşnad,* Hung. *Tusnadfürdő* (tōōzh'nŏtfür"dů), village (pop. 724), Stalin prov., E central Rumania, on Olt R., on railroad and 14 mi. SSE of Mercurea-Ciuc; summer and winter-sports resort (alt. 2,165 ft.) in W foothills of the Moldavian Carpathians, with ferruginous and carbonic springs and baths; flour milling, stone quarrying. In Hungary, 1940–45.

Tussey Mountain (tŭ'sē), NE-SW ridge (1,900–2,200 ft.) of the Appalachian system, S and central Pa., running c.95 mi. NE from point in S Bedford co. near Pa.-Md. border to S part of Centre co., forming part of border bet. Blair and Huntingdon counties; sandstone.

Tussvik, Norway: see TUSVIK.

Tustin (tŭ'stĭn). **1** City (pop. 1,143), Orange co., S Calif., 3 mi. E of Santa Ana; packs citrus fruit. **2** Village (pop. 229), Osceola co., central Mich., 10 mi. SSW of Cadillac and on small South Branch of Manistee R.

Tustna (tōōst'nä), island (□ 34; pop. 1,100), in North Sea, More og Romsdal co., W Norway, 7 mi. ENE of Kristiansund; 13 mi. long, 6 mi. wide; hilly and sparsely wooded. Formerly called Tusteren.

Tustumena Lake (tŭ"stůmē'nů) (23 mi. long, 2–7 mi. wide), S Alaska, on W Kenai Peninsula, 40 mi. W of Seward; game hunting, fishing.

Tusvik (tōōs'vēk, –vĭk), village in Sykkylven canton, More og Romsdal co., W Norway, on S shore of Stor Fjord, 10 mi. ESE of Alesund; furniture mfg. Sometimes spelled Tussvik.

Tuszyn (tōō'shĭn), Rus. *Tushin* (tōō'shĭn), town (pop. 3,696), Lodz prov., central Poland, 11 mi. SSE of Lodz; flour milling.

Tutak (tōōtäk'), village (pop. 809), Agri prov., E Turkey, on Murat R. and 20 mi. SW of Karakose

Tutayev (tōōtī'ůf), city (1945 pop. 26,100), central Yaroslavl oblast, Russian SFSR, on Volga R. and 21 mi. NW of Yaroslavl; linen-milling center; sheepskins, woolen goods, lumber products. Has 17th-cent. cathedrals and a monastery. Until early 1920s, called Romanov-Borisoglebsk for its 2 sections separated by Volga R.

Tutbury, village and parish (pop. 2,003), E Stafford, England, on Dove R. and 4 mi. NNW of Burton-on-Trent; agr. market in dairying region; milk processing and canning. Former site of pre-Norman castle (dismantled during Civil War), where Mary Queen of Scots was a prisoner. Has 15th-cent. inn.

Tutela, Spain: see TUDELA.

Tutela Heights, Ont.: see BRANTFORD.

Tuticorin (tōōtĭkŏrĭn'), Tamil *Tuttukkudi* (tōōt'-tōōk-kōōdĭ), city (pop. 75,614), Tinnevelly dist., S Madras, India, port on Gulf of Mannar, 75 mi. S of Madura. Rail terminus (steamer route to Colombo); cotton-milling and trading center; exports raw cotton, cotton goods, palmyra products, coffee, tea, rice, chilis; fish-drying industry. Jesuit mission. Saltworks N and S of city. Harbor protected by long sandspit of Hare Isl. (E). Founded c.1540 by Portuguese; held (1658–1825, except for brief periods of control by English and by Nizams of Hyderabad) by Dutch, who established lucrative pearl trade; passed to English in 1825.

Tutin (tōō'tĭn), village (pop. 4,563), W Serbia, Yugoslavia, 14 mi. SW of Novi Pazar, near Montenegro border, in the Sanjak.

Tutiura, Japan: see TSUCHIURA.

Tutóia (tōōtô'yů), city (pop. 2,518), NE Maranhão, Brazil, port on the Atlantic at mouth of Parnaíba R., and 140 mi. ESE of São Luís; 2°43'S 42°18'W. Ships cotton, rice, gums and oils, timber, hides and skins. Diatomite mined near by. Formerly spelled Tutoya.

Tutong (tōōtông'), town, in W section of Brunei, NW Borneo, on small Tutong R. (35 mi. long) and 20 mi. WSW of Brunei town; lumbering, agr. (cassava, sago), stock raising, fishing.

Tutoya, Brazil: see TUTÓIA.

Tutrakan (tōō'träkän), Rum. *Turtucaia,* city (pop. 7,203), Ruse dist., NE Bulgaria, in S Dobruja, port on right bank of the Danube (Rum. border), opposite Oltenita, and 34 mi. ENE of Ruse; exports grain; fisheries. In Rumania (1913–40).

Tuttle. 1 Village (pop. 368), Kidder co., central N.Dak., 20 mi. N of Steele. **2** Town (pop. 715), Grady co., central Okla., 21 mi. SW of Oklahoma City, in agr. area (cotton, wheat, alfalfa, livestock); cotton ginning.

Tuttle Lake, in Martin co., S Minn., and Emmet co., NW Iowa, 10 mi. SSW of Fairmont, Minn.; 7 mi. long, 1 mi. wide. Fed and drained by East Des Moines R. State park is on S shore of lake, in Iowa.

Tuttlingen (tŭt'lĭng-ůn), town (pop. 18,438), S Württemberg, Germany, after 1945 in Württemberg-Hohenzollern, in Swabian Jura, on the Danube and 21 mi. NNE of Schaffhausen; rail junction; noted for its surgical instruments; also mfg. of shoes, tanning, paper milling. Repeatedly destroyed during wars. Above town is the ruined castle Honburg.

Tutuila (tōōtōōē'lä), island (□ c.40; pop. 15,556), largest in American SAMOA, S Pacific; 14°17'S 170°41'W; harbor at PAGOPAGO; rugged in E, fertile plain in SW, Matafao Peak (2,141 ft.) near center. Ceded 1900 to U.S., and put under Navy Dept. for use as naval station. Privately owned land, as in all American Samoa. Copra is chief product.

Tutule or **San Pedro de Tutule** (sän pā'drō dā tōōtōō'lā), town (pop. 791), La Paz dept., SW Honduras, 14 mi. W of La Paz; commercial center; coffee, sugar cane, grain.

Tutun (tōōtōōn'), village (pop. 10,224), Faiyum prov., Upper Egypt, 12 mi. SSW of Faiyum; cotton, cereals, sugar cane, fruits.

Tutupaca Volcano (tōōtōōpä'kä), Andean peak (19,048 ft.) on Moquegua-Tacna dept. border, S Peru, 55 mi. ENE of Moquegua.

Tutwiler (tŭt'wīlůr), town (pop. 939), Tallahatchie co., NW central Miss., 15 mi. SSE of Clarksdale; rail junction in cotton region.

Tütz, Poland: see TUCZNO.

Tutzing (tōō'tsĭng), village (pop. 4,343), Upper Bavaria, Germany, on W shore of the Starnberger See, 7 mi. SSW of Starnberg; rail junction; mfg. (wrist cameras, textiles, chemicals); resort.

Tuula River, Mongolia: see TOLA RIVER.

Tuusniemi (tōōs'nē"ĕmē), village (commune pop. 7,111), Kuopio co., S central Finland, on lake of Saimaa system, 25 mi. ESE of Kuopio; asbestos mining.

Tuusula (tōō'sōōlä), Swedish *Tusby* (tüs'bü"), residential village (commune pop. 16,079), Uusimaa co., S Finland, on 5-mi.-long L. Tuusula, Finnish *Tuusulanjärvi* (tōō'sōōlänyăr"vē), 14 mi. N of Helsinki, in lumbering region.

Tuva Autonomous Oblast or **Tuvinian Autonomous Oblast** (tōō'vů), administrative division (□ 66,100; 1946 pop. estimate 150,000) of S Siberian Russian SFSR; ⊙ Kyzyl. Along upper reaches of Yenisei R., bet. Sayan Mts. (N) and Tannu-Ola Range (S; Mongolian border). Dry continental climate with long, snowless winters (average Jan. temp. –25°F.). Grain farming (irrigation in dry Khemchik R. lowlands) and livestock raising (cattle, sheep, horses) on W and central steppes; hunting, lumbering, reindeer raising (E) in forested mts. Gold, coal (near Kyzyl), salt, asbestos, and copper mining. Tanning, sheepskin mfg., sawmilling. Chief centers: Kyzyl (center of road network), Chadan, Shagonar, Turan. Pop. 75% Tuvinian (a Turkic ethnic group), 25% Russian. Formerly known as Uryankhai Territory, part of Chinese Empire; Russian protectorate (1912–21); declared independent (1921) as Tannu-Tuva (after 1934, simply Tuva) People's Republic; inc. (1944) into USSR.

Tuwaiq, Jabal, or **Jabal Tuwayq** (jă'băl tōōwĭk'), mountain range (3,545 ft.) of S central Nejd, Saudi Arabia, at c.46°E bet. 21° and 26°N; rises in a scarp of Jurassic limestone 800 ft. above central plateau (W). It contains some of the most populated dists. of Nejd.

Tuwairij, Iraq: see HINDIYA.

Tuwano, Japan: see TSUWANO.

Tuwayq, Jabal, Saudi Arabia: see TUWAIQ, JABAL.

Tuwayrij or **Tuwayriq,** Iraq: see HINDIYA.

Tuxcacuesco (tōōskäkwĕ'skō), town (pop. 1,074), Jalisco, W Mexico, 21 mi. ESE of Autlán; grain, sugar cane, fruit, tobacco.

Tuxcueca (tōōskwā'kä), town (pop. 965), Jalisco, central Mexico, on S shore of L. Chapala, 36 mi. SSE of Guadalajara; grain, beans, fruit, livestock.

Tuxedo Lake, N.Y.: see TUXEDO PARK.

Tuxedo Park (tŭksē'dō), residential village (1940 pop. 1,651), Orange co., SE N.Y., on Ramapo R. and Tuxedo L. (c.1½ mi. long), in the Ramapos, 6 mi. NW of Suffern. Tuxedo Park colony here, a private residential development begun (1886) by Pierre Lorillard, became known for its sports and social functions; in 1941, plans were made to open colony to inexpensive homes.

Tuxer Alps (tōōk'sůr), group of Eastern Alps in Tyrol, W Austria, bet. Sill, Inn, and Ziller rivers, adjoining Stubai Alps (W) and Kitzbühel Alps (NE); main range (S) extends 20 mi. NE from Brenner Pass, rising to 11,414 ft. in the Olperer. Many pastures in lower N range. Just S are Zillertal Alps.

Tuxford, town and parish (pop. 1,239), N central Nottingham, England, 11 mi. NNW of Newark. Has 14th-cent. church.

Tuxpan (tōōkspän'). **1** Town (pop. 6,763), Jalisco, W Mexico, on interior plateau, on railroad and 11

mi. SE of Guzmán; alt. 4,000 ft. Agr. center (corn, sugar cane, fruit, livestock). Largely populated by Indians of Aztec origin. **2** Town (pop. 1,848), Michoacán, central Mexico, 11 mi. SSE of Hidalgo; corn, sugar cane, beans, fruit, livestock. **3** Town (pop. 10,315), Nayarit, W Mexico, on Pacific coastal plain, on San Pedro R. (sometimes called Tuxpan R.), and 40 mi. NW of Tepic; processing and agr. center (corn, cotton, sugar cane, tobacco, beans, tomatoes, bananas). **4** or **Tuxpam,** city (pop. 13,381), Veracruz, E Mexico, on Tuxpan R. (7 mi. from its mouth on the Gulf) and 100 mi. NNW of Jalapa; oil-pumping and -loading station, with petroleum wells. Exports timber, chicle, rubber, vanilla, dyewood, hides. Tanning, lumbering, liquor distilling. Tropical agr. dist.; produces bananas, zapupe and pita plants (for cordage fibers). Radio station, airfield.

Tuxpan River. 1 or **Coahuayana River** (kwäwīä'nä), W Mexico, rises in Sierra Madre Occidental in Jalisco NE of Guzmán, flows c.110 mi. SW and S, past Tuxpan and Tonilita, and along Colima–Michoacán border, to the Pacific 6 mi. NNW of San Juan de Lima Point. **2** or **Tuxpam River,** Veracruz, E Mexico, rises in Sierra Madre Oriental near Hidalgo–Veracruz border N of Apulco, flows c.100 mi. NE and E to Gulf of Mexico at Tuxpan. Navigable for smaller ships c.35 mi. upstream. Called Pantepec R. in upper course. **3** River, W Mexico: see SAN PEDRO RIVER.

Tuxtepec (tōōstäpěk'). **1** Officially San Juan Tuxtepec, town (pop. 1,697), Mexico state, central Mexico, 40 mi. NW of Mexico city; cereals, maguey, fruit, livestock. **2** Town (pop. 4,912), Oaxaca, S Mexico, on Tuxtepec R., in Gulf lowland, and 75 mi. S of Veracruz; agr. center (cereals, sugar cane, fruit, coffee, livestock); tanneries, lumber mills.

Tuxtepec River, Oaxaca, S Mexico, rises on Mixtecapán plateau (Sierra Madre del Sur) SE of Nochixtlán, flows c.120 mi. N, E, and NNE, past Cuicatlán and Tuxtepec, to PAPALOÁPAM RIVER at Veracruz border 4 mi. N of Tuxtepec. Navigable in lowlands. Called Quiotepec R. in middle course.

Tuxtilla (tōōstē'yä), town (pop. 1,053), Veracruz, SE Mexico, on Papaloápam R. and 11 mi. SW of Cosamaloapan; sugar cane, bananas.

Tuxtla or **Tuxtla Gutiérrez** (tōō'slä gōōtyě'rěs), city (pop. 15,883), ⊙ Chiapas, S Mexico, in Chiapas Valley, at foot of Sierra Madre, on Inter-American Highway, and 450 mi. ESE of Mexico city; alt. 1,804 ft.; 16°46'N 93°7'W. Trading, lumbering, processing, and agr. center (corn, cotton, cacao, coffee, tobacco, sugar cane, henequen, tropical fruit, cattle, horses); lumber mills, tanneries; mfg. (cigars, shoes, leatherware, soap). Radio station, airfield. Has archaeological mus. State capital since 1891.

Tuxtla Chico (chē'kō), town (pop. 2,824), Chiapas, S Mexico, in Pacific lowland, on Inter-American Highway, near Guatemala border, 7 mi. ENE of Tapachula; coffee, cacao, sugar cane, fruit, stock.

Tuxtla Gutiérrez, Mexico: see TUXTLA.

Tuxtlas, Los, Mexico: see SAN ANDRÉS TUXTLA.

Tuxtla Volcano or **San Martín Tuxtla Volcano** (sän märtēn' tōō'slä) (5,085 ft.), Veracruz, SE Mexico, 8 mi. N of San Andrés Tuxtla. Last erupted 1793; fairly dormant since then, although it emits smoke.

Túy (tōō'ē), city (pop. 2,871), Pontevedra prov., NW Spain, in Galicia, on hill above Miño R., opposite Port. town of Valença, 14 mi. SSE of Vigo; customs station; flour- and sawmills; agr. trade (livestock, wine, cereals, flax). Episcopal see. Has imposing, fortress-like Romanesque cathedral (12th cent.; largely restored), and several churches and convents. One of oldest Galician towns, it was occupied by Romans; capital of the Suevi (6th cent.) and of Visigothic King Witiza (early 8th cent.); taken soon after by Moors; liberated by Christians (12th cent.); played important role in wars bet. Castile and Portugal.

Tuyama, Japan: see TSUYAMA.

Tuya-Muyun, Kirghiz SSR: see TYUYA-MUYUN.

Tuyenquang (tōō'yěn'kwäng'), town (1936 pop. 6,000), ⊙ Tuyenquang prov. (□ 2,300; 1943 pop. 83,600), N Vietnam, in Tonkin, on Clear R. (head of navigation) and 70 mi. NW of Hanoi; lignite, zinc, and iron mines. Forest produce: gums, resins, bamboo, rattan. Agr. and sericulture experiment station.

Tuyhoa (twē'hwä'), town, Phuyen prov., S central Vietnam, at mouth of the Song Ba, on railroad and 26 mi. S of Songcau, in sugar-cane dist.; sugar refinery. Has 4th-cent. Cham towers.

Tüyin Gol, Mongolia: see TUIN GOL.

Tuymazy, Russian SFSR: see TUIMAZY.

Tuyra River, Panama: see TUIRA RIVER.

Tuy River (twē), N Venezuela, rises in coastal range of Aragua state N of La Victoria, flows c.125 mi. E, past El Consejo (Aragua state), Cúa, Ocumare, and Santa Teresa (all in Miranda state), to the Caribbean 10 mi. SE of Higuerote. Navigable for small craft. In its fertile valley grow sugar cane, coffee, cacao, rice, corn, fruit, and hardwood.

Tuyserkan, Iran: see TUISARKAN.

Tuyuk (tōōyōōk'), village, NE Osh oblast, Kirghiz SSR, 28 mi. E of Uzgen; site of extensive coal deposits (Uzgen coal basin).

Tuyün (dōō'yün'), town (pop. 14,998), ⊙ Tuyün co. (pop. 116,313), S Kweichow prov., China, 55 mi. ESE of Kweiyang and on railroad; alt. 2,382 ft.; cotton weaving, papermaking, pottery mfg.; rice, wheat, millet, tea, tobacco.

Tuz, Lake (tōōz) (□ 626), central Turkey, 65 mi. NE of Konya; 50 mi. long, 32 mi. wide; alt. 2,950 ft. Yields quantities of salt.

Tuzamapan (tōōsämä'pän), officially Tuzamapan de Galeana, town (pop. 1,310), Puebla, central Mexico, 32 mi. ESE of Huauchinango; coffee, sugar cane, tobacco, fruit.

Tuzantán (tōōsäntän'), town (pop. 991), Chiapas, S Mexico, in Pacific lowland, 3 mi. E of Huixtla; coffee, sugar cane, lemons, livestock.

Tuzantla (tōōsän'tlä), town (pop. 988), Michoacán, central Mexico, 30 mi. SSW of Zitácuaro; cereals, sugar cane, fruit.

Tuzha (tōō'zhŭ), village, SW Kirov oblast, Russian SFSR, 21 mi. N of Yaransk; flax.

Tuzigoot National Monument (tōō'zĭgōōt) (42.67 acres; established 1939), central Ariz., on Verde R. opposite Clarkdale, and 30 mi. NE of Prescott. Ruins (excavated and restored 1933–34) of large pre-Columbian Indian pueblo (500 ft. long, 100 ft. wide), built on limestone ridge. Occupied A.D. 1000–1400; reached max. size in late 13th cent. Mus. in monument area.

Tuz Khurmatli (tōōz khōōrmät'lē), town, Kirkuk prov., NE Iraq, on railroad and 40 mi. SSE of Kirkuk; wheat, barley, sheep raising. Sometimes called Tuz Khurmatu (khōōrmä'tōō).

Tuzla (tōōz'lä) [Turkish,=salt], city (pop. 28,916), ⊙ Tuzla oblast (formed 1949), NE Bosnia, Yugoslavia, 50 mi. N of Sarajevo, at W foot of the Majevica. Center of Tuzla lignite area (mines at Kreka and Ugljevik) and of Tuzla petroleum field, believed to contain oil (1st discovered 1896; probably associated with local salt deposits) and natural gas in considerable quantities. In center of a salt dist. (called *Salinas* in Roman period, *Soli* in Serbian periods), with wells operated since Roman times. Orthodox Eastern bishopric. Bituminous coal in the MAJEVICA. Plum growing, mineral springs in vicinity. Consists of Donja (lower) Tuzla and Gornja (upper) Tuzla. Suburb of Simin Han or Simin Khan, terminus of railroad to Doboj, has saltworks (built 1884) and stone quarry.

Tuzla, Lake (tōōzlä') (□ 7), central Turkey, 25 mi. NE of Kayseri; 5 mi. long; alt. 3,630 ft.

Tuzla Island (tōō'zlŭ), former sandspit of Taman Peninsula, in Kerch Strait, Krasnodar Territory, Russian SFSR, 6 mi. SE of Kerch; 2½ mi. long, ¼ mi. wide. Fisheries. Separated (c.1930) from mainland.

Tuzluca (tōōzlōōjä'), village (pop. 2,577), Kars prov., NE Turkey, near Aras R. (USSR line), 50 mi. SE of Kars; grain.

Tuzly (tōōzlē'), Rum. *Tuzla* (tōō'zlä), village (1941 pop. 2,433), E Izmail oblast, Ukrainian SSR, 25 mi. SW of Belgorod-Dnestrovski, on Burnas Lagoon of Black Sea; seaside resort; mud baths.

Tvaaker (tvō'ō"kůr), Swedish *Tvååker*, village (pop. 694), Halland co., SW Sweden, near the Kattegat, 6 mi. SE of Varberg; grain, flax, sugar beets.

Tvarditsa (tvärdē'tsä), village (pop. 3,596), Stara Zagora dist., E central Bulgaria, on S slope of Yelena Mts., 15 mi. NNW of Nova Zagora; horticulture (roses, mint), livestock. Bituminous coal deposits in mts. (N). Linked with Yelena (N) by road through **Tvarditsa Pass** (alt. 3,585 ft.); also called Yelena-Tvarditsa Pass.

Tvarditsa Mountains, Bulgaria: see YELENA MOUNTAINS.

Tvedestrand (tvā'důsträn), town (pop. 1,038), Aust-Agder co., S Norway, on an inlet of the Skagerrak, 13 mi. NNE of Arendal; flourishing shipbuilding center until the steamship era. Has paper mills; exports wood pulp. The Nes manor house, home of Jacob Aall, is a natl. monument. Formerly spelled Thvedestrand.

Tver, Russian SFSR: see KALININ, city.

Tvertsa River (tvyĭrtsä'), Kalinin oblast, Russian SFSR, rises in Valdai Hills near Vyshni Volochek, flows S, past Torzhok (head of navigation), and E to the Volga at Kalinin; 115 mi. long. Connected by VYSHNEVOLOTSK Canal with MSTA RIVER (N), forming section of obsolete Vyshnevolotsk canal system, whose reconstruction will make river navigable in entire course.

Twain Harte, resort hamlet, Tuolumne co., central Calif., in the Sierra Nevada, c.60 mi. ENE of Stockton; winter sports.

Twanshantze, Manchuria: see JAOHO.

Twante (twäntä'), village, Hanthawaddy div., Lower Burma, on Twante Canal and 15 mi. WSW of Rangoon; glazed pottery.

Twante Canal, Lower Burma, links Rangoon R. at Rangoon with lower Irrawaddy R.; 22 mi. long. Used by Irrawaddy steamers. Originally built 1883, enlarged 1915 and 1935.

Twapia (twä'pyä), township (pop. 1,006), Western Prov., NW Northern Rhodesia, 4 mi. W of Ndola; tobacco, wheat, corn; market gardening.

Twardogora (tvärdōgōō'rä), Pol. *Twardogóra*, Ger. *Festenberg* (fě'stůnběrk), town (1939 pop. 3,861; 1946 pop. 1,828) in Lower Silesia, after 1945 in Wroclaw prov., SW Poland, 25 mi. NE of Breslau (Wroclaw); agr. market (grain, potatoes, livestock); woodworking. After 1945, briefly called Twarda Gora, Pol. *Twarda Góra*.

Tweed, village (pop. 1,343), SE Ont., on Stoco L., 22 mi. N of Belleville; mfg. of steel products, leather, bricks; woodworking, flour milling. Asbestos and actinolite mined near by.

Tweeddale, Scotland: see PEEBLES, county.

Tweed Heads, town (pop. 2,066), NE New South Wales, Australia, on Queensland border adjacent to Coolangatta, at mouth of Tweed R., and 70 mi. S of Brisbane; seaside resort; agr., dairy products.

Tweed Island (2 mi. long, 1 mi. wide), W N.F., on N side of the Bay of Islands, 27 mi. NW of Corner Brook; 49°14'N 58°22'W.

Tweedmouth, England: see BERWICK-UPON-TWEED.

Tweed River, NE New South Wales, Australia, rises in McPherson Range, flows 50 mi. E, past Murwillumbah and Condong, to the Pacific at Tweed Heads. Wharf and drydock at Terranora, near entrance.

Tweed River (97 mi. long), mainly in SE Scotland, partly in England, rises at Tweed's Well, 6 mi. NNW of Moffat, at foot of Hart Fell, in Peebles uplands, near sources of the Clyde and the Annan; flows E through Peebles, Selkirk, and Roxburgh, then NE bet. Berwick and Northumberland, forming part of boundary bet. England and Scotland, to the North Sea at Berwick-on-Tweed. On its course are Dryburgh Abbey, Kelso, and Coldstream. Receives Ettrick Water, Gala Water, Leader Water, Teviot R., and Whiteadder Water. There are important salmon fisheries. Navigable only for few miles in its tidal section. Peebles co. is also called Tweeddale.

Tweedsmuir (twēdz'mūr), agr. village and parish (pop. 177), SW Peebles, Scotland, on the Tweed and 9 mi. SE of Biggar. Remains of anc. Celtic camps near by.

Tweedsmuir Park (□ 5,400), W central B.C., 120 mi. WSW of Prince George, on E slope of Coast Mts. Has several peaks over 7,000 ft. high and numerous lakes, largest of which are Eutsuk, Whitesail, Tahtsa, and Tetachuck. Ootsa L. is on N boundary of park.

Tweed's Well, spring, source of the Tweed, in SW Peebles, Scotland, at foot of Hart Fell, 6 mi. NNW of Moffat.

Tweedvale, village, SE South Australia, 17 mi. E of Adelaide; woolen mills.

Tweeling, town (pop. 1,264), E Orange Free State, U. of So. Afr., 50 mi. NNE of Bethlehem; alt. 5,279 ft.; grain, stock.

Twello (twě'lō), village (pop. 1,409), Gelderland prov., E central Netherlands, 6 mi. ENE of Apeldoorn; meat processing. Sometimes spelled Tweloo.

Twelve Bens, The, Ireland: see BENNA BEOLA.

Twelve Mile House, Alaska: see BIRCH CREEK.

Twelve Pins, The, Ireland: see BENNA BEOLA.

Twelve Pole Creek, W W.Va., formed at Wayne by junction of East Fork (c.45 mi. long) and West Fork (c.50 mi. long), both rising in Mingo co. and flowing generally NW; flows 29 mi. N and NW to Ohio R. just E of Ceredo.

Twente, De (dů twěn'tů), region in SE part of Overijssel prov., E Netherlands, comprising towns of Enschede, Hengelo, Almelo, and Oldenzaal. Important center of textile industry; also dyeing, bleaching, textile-machinery mfg.; agr. (fruit, vegetables, potatoes); dairying center. Formerly constituted a co. (⊙ Oldenzaal). Sometimes spelled De Twenthe.

Twente Canal, E Netherlands, extends 32 mi. E–W, bet. IJssel R. 2 mi. NNW of Zutphen and Enschede; serves Lochem, Goor, Delden, and Hengelo. Joined at Hengelo by branch (7 mi. long) to Oldenzaal. Carries coal for textile industry's power plants. Sometimes called Twente-Rhine Canal.

Twenty-four Parganas or **24-Parganas** (pŭr'gŭnŭz), district (□ c.4,000; pop. c.3,620,000), SE West Bengal, India, in Ganges Delta; ⊙ Alipore. Bounded W by Hooghly R., E by E Pakistan; drained by river arms of the Ganges Delta; Sundarbans in S. Alluvial soil (rice, jute, pulse, potatoes, betel leaves, mustard, sugar cane); extensive swamps; salt-water lake just E of Calcutta, slowly filling with silt of tidal channels. Heavily industrialized area extends along the Hooghly from Budge-Budge to N limit of dist. Major Indian jute-milling and chemical-mfg. center; cotton and rice milling, mfg. of matches, glass, soap, cement, silk cloth. Main towns: Garden Reach, South Suburban, Tollygunge, Titagarh, Baranagar; Bhatpara is only city. Noted bathing festival and large annual fair on Sagar Is. Ruins of 18th-cent. fort at Garulia; Kali temple at Dakhineswar, associated with Ramakrishna. Name of dist. derived from number of fiscal divisions in Zamindari of Calcutta ceded (1757) to English by nawab of Bengal. Barrackpore figured in Sepoy rebellions of 1824 and 1857. Original dist. (□ 3,696; 1941 pop. 3,536,386) was enlarged 1947 by inc. of SW portion of Jessore dist. following creation of Pakistan. Until 1947, NE area (□ 320; pop. 133,104) of Bangaon and Gaighata was in Jessore dist.

Twentynine Palms, oasis village (pop. 1,022), San Bernardino co., S Calif., 70 mi. E of San Bernardino, in Mojave Desert; health resort. Hq. for Joshua Tree Natl. Monument (just S). Railroad station is Palm Springs.

Twickenham (twĭ'kŭnŭm, twĭk'nŭm), residential municipal borough (1931 pop. 39,906; 1951 census 105,645), Middlesex, England, on the Thames and 11 mi. WSW of London; mfg. of electrical equipment, asphalt, chemicals, pharmaceuticals. Rugby football matches bet. Oxford and Cambridge are played here. Twickenham was residence of Alexander Pope, who is buried here, and of Tennyson, Dickens, and Fielding. Near by was Horace Walpole's "Strawberry Hill" estate. Orleans House was for some time residence of Louis Philippe. In 1937 Hampton and Teddington became part of Twickenham.

Twiggs, county (□ 365; pop. 8,308), central Ga.; ⊙ Jeffersonville. Bounded W by Ocmulgee R. Coastal plain agr. (cotton, corn, grain, pecans, peaches) and kaolin-mining area. Formed 1809.

Twila (twī'lŭ), mining village (1940 pop. 980), Harlan co., SE Ky., in the Cumberlands, 20 mi. ENE of Middlesboro; bituminous coal.

Twilight, borough (pop. 318), Washington co., SW Pa., just S of Charleroi.

Twillingate, village (pop. 921) on NE coast of Twillingate Isl., E N.F., 170 mi. NW of St. John's; 49°40'N 54°46'W; fishing port, with lobster- and salmon-canning plants. Has lighthouse, hosp., and govt. bait depot. Lumbering near by.

Twillingate Island (□ 12; pop. 2,093), E N.F., in Notre Dame Bay, 40 mi. ESE of Cape St. John; 7 mi. long, up to 4 mi. wide; 49°40'N 54°46'W. Twillingate, chief settlement, is on NE coast. Lobster and salmon fishing and lumbering are chief occupations.

Twin Bridges, town (pop. 497), Madison co., SW Mont., 33 mi. SSE of Butte. State orphans' home here. Beaverhead R. in Jefferson R. system unites with Ruby R. just S of town, joining Big Hole R. just N to form Jefferson R.

Twin Brooks, town (pop. 113), Grant co., NE S.Dak., 7 mi. W of Milbank.

Twin Buttes (būts), a double-coned peak, E Ariz., 14 mi. E of Holbrook; higher butte is 5,685 ft.

Twin City, city (pop. 1,018), Emanuel co., E central Ga., 11 mi. E of Swainsboro; mfg. (clothing, lumber). Inc. 1924 as a consolidation of Graymont and Summit.

Twin Falls, county (□ 1,942; pop. 40,979), S Idaho; ⊙ Twin Falls. Livestock and dairying area bordering on Nev. and bounded N by Snake R. Irrigated regions are in N, along Snake R., and in SW, along Salmon Falls Creek. Potatoes, dry beans, sugar beets, onions, flax, apples. Includes part of Snake River Plain in N, mtn. region in S. Formed 1907.

Twin Falls, city (pop. 17,600), ⊙ Twin Falls co., S Idaho, near Snake R., c.115 mi. SE of Boise; alt. 3,492 ft. Processing and shipping center for dairying, agr., and stock-raising area; canned fruit, dairy and meat products, flour, beet sugar, beverages; mfg. of overalls, cement pipe, farm machinery. Laid out 1903, inc. as village 1905, as city 1907. Founded as trading point for large, private irrigation project that has been praised as model of land reclamation. Includes 2 areas (totaling c.360,000 acres) N and S of river. Principal crops are fruits, vegetables, sugar beets, grains. Near-by point of interest is Twin Falls, in 500-ft. gorge of Snake R. Flow of S falls has been diverted for generation of hydroelectric power; N falls are c.125 ft. high. Twin Falls–Jerome Bridge crosses river 2.5 mi. N of city.

Twining, village (pop. 196), Arenac co., E Mich., 35 mi. N of Bay City, in farm area.

Twin Islands, SE Keewatin Dist., Northwest Territories, group (□ 55) of 2 small isls. in James Bay, NE of Akimiski Isl.; 53°10'N 80°10'W. Game sanctuary.

Twin Lakes. 1 Village (pop. 6,733, with adjacent Delmar), Santa Cruz co., W Calif., on Monterey Bay, just E of Santa Cruz. **2** Village (pop. c.50), Lake co., central Colo., in Sawatch Mts., 12 mi. SSW of Leadville, just NW of Twin Lakes Reservoir; alt. 9,015 ft.; fishing resort. Near by is Twin Lakes Tunnel, extending c.4 mi. through Sawatch Mts., in Continental Divide, and conducting water from Roaring Fork R. through reservoir to Arkansas R. Mt. Elbert is 4 mi. NW of village. **3** Resort, Conn.: see SALISBURY. **4** Resort village (pop. c.50), Lowndes co., S Ga., 10 mi. SSE of Valdosta and on two small lakes. **5** Village (pop. 637), Kenosha co., extreme SE Wis., 10 mi. ESE of Lake Geneva, near Ill. line, in lake-resort and farm area; summer resort.

Twin Lakes. 1 Two linked lakes (each c.4 mi. long) in Penobscot co., central Maine, 6 mi. W of Millinocket. Receive West Branch of Penobscot R. from Pemadumcook L. (N). **2** Lakes in Mich.: see LEWISTON.

Twin Mountain, village, N.H.: see CARROLL, town.

Twin Mountain, peak, Oregon: see ELKHORN RIDGE.

Twin Oaks, town (pop. 81), St. Louis co., E Mo., near the Meramec, 15 mi. W of St. Louis.

Twin Peak (8,887 ft.), E Calif., in the Sierra Nevada, just W of L. Tahoe.

Twin Peaks, Idaho: see SALMON RIVER MOUNTAINS.

Twins, The, mountain (12,085), SW Alta., near B.C. border, in Rocky Mts., on S edge of Jasper Natl. Park, 50 mi. SE of Jasper.

Twin Sisters, Colo.; see FRONT RANGE.

Twin Valley, village (pop. 899), Norman co., NW Minn., on Wild Rice R. and 12 mi. ESE of Ada, in agr. area; dairy products.

Twisp, town (pop. 776), Okanogan co., N Wash., 25 mi. W of Okanogan and on Methow R.; gold, silver, dairy products, lumber. W of the town is **Twisp Pass** (alt. 6,066 ft.), which joins Cascade Pass (alt. 5,392 ft.) to traverse Cascade Range.

Twistringen (tvĭs'trĭng-ŭn), village (pop. 5,509), in former Prussian prov. of Hanover, NW Germany, after 1945 in Lower Saxony, 20 mi. SW of Bremen; grain, cattle.

Two Buttes (būts), town (pop. 121), Baca co., SE Colo., 16 mi. NE of Springfield; alt. 4,075 ft. Near-by reservoir used for irrigation.

Twodot (tōō'dŏt"), village (pop. c.100), Wheatland co., central Mont., on Musselshell R. and 10 mi. W of Harlowton. Power substation here, controlling current for electric railroad.

Twofold Bay, inlet of Tasman Sea, SE New South Wales, Australia; 4 mi. long, 3.5 mi. wide; Eden on N shore. Formerly site of whaling station.

Two Harbors, city (pop. 4,400), ⊙ Lake co., NE Minn., on L. Superior and 25 mi. NE of Duluth, in dairying and truck-farming area. Resort; shipping center for iron ore from Mesabi and Vermilion iron ranges; railroad repair shops. Settled 1882, inc. as village 1888, as city 1907. Grew as lumber- and ore-shipping point. U.S. coast guard base is here. Huge docks are prominent feature of city.

Two Hills, village (pop. 289), E Alta., on the small Vermilion Lakes, near North Saskatchewan R., 45 mi. NW of Vermilion; cereal-food mfg., mixed farming; grain, stock.

Two Islets, group of 2 islets off E N.F., 35 mi. E of Fogo Isl.; 49°45'N 53°14'W. Together with Funk Isl., just E, they were the last breeding grounds of the now extinct great auk.

Two Mountains, Lake of the (□ 63), S Que., expansion of the Ottawa R., extends 24 mi. bet. Rigaud and Jesus Isl., 1–6 mi. wide. Contains Île Bizard. Drains NE into the St. Lawrence by Mille Îles and Prairies rivers.

Two Rivers, city (pop. 10,243), Manitowoc co., E Wis., at base of Door Peninsula, on L. Michigan, at mouth of small Twin R., 6 mi. NE of Manitowoc; commercial fishing port and industrial center (aluminum ware, electrical appliances, machinery, woodwork, chemicals, woolen goods); cheese-processing plants, breweries. Point Beach State Forest is near by. Inc. 1878.

Two Rivers, stream in Kittson co., NW Minn., formed by confluence of Middle Fork (30 mi. long) and South Fork (50 mi. long) near Hallock, flows 30 mi. W to Red River of the North on N.Dak. line. Receives North Fork (40 mi. long) 7 mi. W of Hallock. Two Rivers State Park is on South Fork near Bronson. Forks flow W through marshy area.

Two Sicilies, The, former kingdom in S Italy and Sicily. Consisted of kingdoms of Sicily and Naples, which were frequently reunited after Norman conquest (1061–91). Became part of Holy Roman Empire under Hohenstaufen dynasty, notably under Frederick II (1197–1250), when it was a center of classic and Arabic learning. Alfonso V of Aragon styled (1442) himself King of the Two Sicilies. Officially merged (1816) by Ferdinand IV of Naples (Ferdinand III of Sicily). Fell (1860) to Garibaldi, and was thus inc. into Kingdom of Italy.

Two Wells, village (pop. 277), SE South Australia, 23 mi. N of Adelaide; agr. center.

Twyford (twī'fŭrd). **1** Town and parish (pop. 1,392), E Berkshire, England, on Loddon R. and 5 mi. ENE of Reading; agr. market. Has 13th-cent. church and 17th-cent. almshouses. **2** Town and parish (pop. 2,212), central Hampshire, England, on Itchen R. and 3 mi. S of Winchester; agr. market. Here Alexander Pope attended school, and Benjamin Franklin wrote part of his autobiography.

Twynholm (twī'nŭm), agr. village and parish (pop. 720), S Kirkcudbright, Scotland, 2 mi. NW of Kirkcudbright. On the Dee, 2 mi. E, is village of Cumstoun (kŭm'stŭn), with remains of anc. castle.

Ty, Denmark: see THISTED, amt.

Tyachevo (tyä'chĭvŭ), Czech *Tačovo* or *Tiačevo* (tä'chôvô, tyä'chĕ–), Hung. *Técső* (tā'chû), town (1941 pop. 10,131), S Transcarpathian Oblast, Ukrainian SSR, on Tissa R. (Rum. border), on railroad and 50 mi. SE of Mukachevo; fruit-growing center (notably apples and prunes); distilling, preserving.

Tyamagondlu (tyä'mŭgŏndlōō), town (pop. 4,154), Bangalore dist., central Mysore, India, 25 mi. NW of Bangalore; trades in rice, grain, tobacco. Also spelled Tyamagondal.

Tyana (tī'ŭnŭ), anc. town of Cappadocia, S central Asia Minor (now in Turkey), 15 mi. SSW of Nigde, at N foot of the Taurus. Inc. into Roman Empire A.D. 272. Apollonius of Tyana b. here. Extensive ruins.

Tyan-Shan, China and USSR: see TIEN SHAN.

Tyan-Shan or **Tyan'-Shan'** (tyän-shän'yŭ), oblast (□ 21,200; 1946 pop. estimate 125,000), central Kirghiz SSR; ⊙ Naryn. In Tien Shan mtn. area; bounded N by Terskei Ala-Tau and Kirghiz Range, E by Fergana Range, S by Kokshaal-Tau (China-USSR border). Drained by Naryn R. Agr. (wheat) in mtn. valley; livestock raising (cattle, sheep, horses). Tungsten, gold mining. Crossed by Frunze-Naryn-Osh highway. Pop. mainly Kirghiz. Formed 1939.

Tyao River (tŭyō'), right headstream of Kaladan R. on India-Burma border, rises in NE Lushai Hills, flows 93 mi. S along frontier, joins Boinu R. to form Kaladan R. 23 mi. ESE of Lungleh.

Tyasmin River (tyäsmēn'), central Ukrainian SSR, rises NNW of Kirovograd, flows N past Smela, and E past Chigirin and Novo-Georgiyevsk (port) to Dnieper R. just W of Kremenchug; 100 mi. long.

Tyatino (tyä'tyĭnŭ), fishing village on Kunashir Isl., S Kuriles, Russian SFSR, on NE coast, at S foot of Tyatya [Jap. *Chacha*] volcano (5,978 ft.), 25 mi. NE of Yuzhno-Kurilsk. Under Jap. rule (until 1945), called Chinomiji (chēnō'mējē).

Tyaya, Japan: see CHAYA.

Tyazhin (tyä'zhĭn), village (1948 pop. over 2,000), NE Kemerovo oblast, Russian SFSR, on Trans-Siberian RR and 35 mi. E of Mariinsk, in agr. area; dairying. Rail station for upper Kiya R. gold-mining dist.

Tybee Island, one of the Sea Isls., in Chatham co., SE Ga., just off the coast, 15 mi. ESE of Savannah, at mouth of Savannah R.; c.4 mi. long, 3 mi. wide; connected to mainland by causeway. Has lighthouse (32°1'N 80°51'W) and U.S. Fort Screven at N end; Savannah Beach (sometimes called Tybee) at S end. Little Tybee Isl. is just S.

Tyboron (tü'bôrŭn), Dan. *Tyborøn*, town (pop. 1,400) with adjacent fishing port, Thisted amt, N Jutland, Denmark, at W entrance to Lim Fjord, 25 mi. SW of Thisted. Also spelled Thyboron.

Tyburn, town, England: see CASTLE BROMWICH.

Tyburn (tī'bûrn), short subterranean river in W London, England, which gave its name to the gallows that stood at Marble Arch, at junction of Edgware Road and Oxford Street until 1783, when place of executions was moved to Newgate prison. Among those hanged at Tyburn were Perkin Warbeck and John Sheppard.

Tychy (tĭ'khĭ), Ger. *Tichau* (tĭ'khou), residential town (1946 commune pop. 12,056), Katowice prov., S Poland, 10 mi. S of Katowice. Developed greatly, c.1950, as residential city for 80,000 industrial workers in Katowice and Chorz›w.

Tycocktow, China: see TAIKOKTOW.

Tyczyn (tĭ'chĭn), town (pop. 2,209), Rzeszow prov., SE Poland, 5 mi. S of Rzeszow.

Tydal (tü'däl), village and canton (pop. 799), Sor-Trondelag co., central Norway, on Nea (Nid) R. and 35 mi. N of Roros, near mts. (E) which rise to 5,800 ft. Lumbering, animal husbandry near by.

Tydd Saint Giles (tĭd' sŭnt jĭlz'), agr. village and parish (pop. 937), in Isle of Ely, N Cambridge, England, 6 mi. N of Wisbech; fruit growing. Has 13th-cent. church.

Tyee (tīē'), village, SE Alaska, on S tip of Admiralty Isl., 22 mi. W of Kake across Frederick Sound; fishing; cannery.

Tygart River (tī'gŭrt), central W.Va., rises in S Randolph co., flows N past Elkins, and generally NNW past Grafton, joining the West Fork at Fairmont to form Monongahela R.; c.130 mi. long. Near Grafton is Tygart R. Dam (1,921 ft. long, in 3 sections 207–230 ft. high above stream bed; completed 1938; for flood control and future power production). Its reservoir (capacity 287,600 acre-ft.) is surrounded by state park. Near Fairmont are scenic Valley Falls, in a gorge.

Tygarts Creek (tī'gŭrts), NE Ky., rises in Carter co., flows c.90 mi. generally NNE, past Olive Hill, to Ohio R. near Fullerton.

Tygda (tĭgdä'), village (1939 pop. over 2,000), Amur oblast, Russian SFSR, on Trans-Siberian RR and 115 mi. ESE of Skovorodino; junction for highway to Zeya gold fields.

Tygerberg (tī'khŭrbĕrkh), mountain (7,060 ft.), S Cape Prov., U. of So. Afr., 20 mi. NNE of Oudtshoorn; 33°20'S 22°15'E; highest peak of Great Swartberg range.

Tyger River, NW S.C., formed S of Spartanburg by several branches rising in the Blue Ridge; flows c.45 mi. SE to Broad R. opposite Shelton. Also spelled Tiger R.

Tyin Lake (tü'ĭn) (□ 13.5), Opland co., S central Norway, at S foot of Jotunheim Mts., 75 mi. W of Lillehammer; alt. 3,537 ft. It is 10 mi. long, 1–2 mi. wide; drains W into Sogne Fjord via Tya R.

Tyko, Finland: see TEIJO.

Tykocin (tĭkō'tsēn), Rus. *Tykotsin* (tĭkō'tsyĭn), town (pop. 1,712), Bialystok prov., NE Poland, on Narew R. and 17 mi. WNW of Bialystok; tanning, flour milling.

Tyldesley (tĭlz'lē), formerly Tyldesley with Shakerley, urban district (1931 pop. 14,846; 1951 census 18,096), S Lancashire, England, 5 mi. SSW of Bolton; coal mining, cotton spinning. Includes (ESE) rayon-spinning and coal-mining town of Boothstown.

Tyler. 1 County (□ 927; pop. 11,292), E Texas; ⊙ Woodville. Bounded N and E by Neches R. Lumbering (pine, hardwoods) is important; also agr. (corn, cotton, vegetables, sugar cane), some livestock, dairying. Some oil produced. Hunting, fishing. Formed 1846. **2** County (□ 256; pop. 10,535), NW W.Va.; ⊙ Middlebourne. Bounded NW by Ohio R. (Ohio line); drained by Middle Island Creek. Oil and natural-gas wells; agr. (livestock, dairy products, tobacco, grain, truck); some industry (including petroleum processing) at Sistersville. Formed 1814.

Tyler. **1** Suburb (pop. 1,053, with near-by Woodlawn) of Paducah, McCracken co., SW Ky. There is also a hamlet called Tyler in Fulton co. **2** Village (pop. 1,121), Lincoln co., SW Minn., 21 mi. NE of Pipestone; agr. trading point in livestock and poultry area; dairy products, cement blocks, tile. Settled 1879. **3** City (pop. 38,968), ⊙ Smith co., E Texas, c.90 mi. ESE of Dallas. Transportation (rail, highway) focus, in rich agr. area (especially truck); known for its large rose-growing industry. On edge of great East Texas oil field, it is refining center, administrative hq. for oil companies. Railroad shops, diversified mfg. (cottonseed oil, peanut products, canned foods, glass, foundry and machine-shop products, furnaces, wood products, mattresses, clothing); limestone quarries. Seat of Tyler Jr. Col., Texas Col., and Butler Col. Has large municipal rose garden; state fish hatchery near. Founded 1846.

Tyler, Fort, N.Y.: see GARDINERS ISLAND.

Tylerton, Md.: see SMITH ISLAND.

Tylertown, town (pop. 1,331), ⊙ Walthall co., S Miss., 21 mi. ESE of McComb, near La. line, in agr. and timber area; cotton ginning, lumber milling, clothing mfg.

Tylicz Pass (tĭ'lēch), Pol. *Przełęcz Tylicka* (pshĕ'wĕch tĭlĕts'kä), Slovak *Průsmyk Tylićský* (prōōs'mĭk tĭ'lĭch-skē), pass (alt. 2,257 ft.) in the Beskids, 7 mi. SE of Krynica, Poland; road leads SE to Bardejov, Czechoslovakia.

Tylissos or **Tilissos** (both: tē'lĭsôs), anc. *Tylissus*, village (pop. 1,505), Herakleion nome, central Crete, 8 mi. SW of Candia; raisins, potatoes, wheat, olive oil. Excavations revealed important remains of Minoan period, including statues and scriptures.

Tylos: see BAHREIN.

Tylovai or **Tylovay** (tĭlŭvī'), village (1939 pop. over 500), E Udmurt Autonomous SSR, Russian SFSR, 32 mi. NNW of Votkinsk; wheat, flax, livestock.

Tylus: see BAHREIN.

Tymbakion or **Timbakion** (both: tĭmbä'kēôn), town (pop. 2,455), Herakleion nome, central Crete, small port on Gulf of Mesara, 30 mi. SSW of Candia; chief town of Mesara lowland; wheat, barley, olives, citrus fruits, olive oil.

Tymovskoye (tĭmôf'skŭyŭ), village (1948 pop. over 10,000), central N Sakhalin, Russian SFSR, on Tym R., on road and 21 mi. E of Aleksandrovsk, in agr. area; sawmill. Until 1949, Derbinskoye.

Tymphe or **Timfi** (both: tĭm'fē), mountain massif (8,192 ft.) in central Pindus system, S Epirus, Greece, S of upper Aoos R. in area of Konitsa. Sometimes called Gamela (Gamila) and Vradeton (Vradheton) for individual peaks.

Tymphrestos or **Timfristos** (both: tĭmfrĭstôs'), mountain massif at S end of Pindus system, in Eurytania nome, central Greece; rises to 8,595 ft. 3 mi. NE of Karpenesion. Also called Velouchi or Veloukhi.

Tym River (tĭm). **1** In W Krasnoyarsk Territory and N Tomsk oblast, Russian SFSR, rises in marshes 125 mi. W of Yartsevo, flows 400 mi. WSW, past Napas, to Ob R. 60 mi. NW of Narym. **2** or **Tym' River,** in N Sakhalin, Russian SFSR, rises in E range of Sakhalin Isl., E of Tymovskoye; flows c.120 mi. SW and N, through central agr. valley, to Sea of Okhotsk at Nogliki.

Tyndall, village (pop. estimate 300), SE Man., 24 mi. NE of Winnipeg; dairying; grain.

Tyndall city (pop. 1,292), ⊙ Bon Homme co., SE S.Dak., 70 mi. SW of Sioux Falls; trade center for agr. area; grain, livestock, dairy products, poultry. Municipal power plant is here. Founded 1879.

Tyndall, Mount (14,025 ft.), E Calif., in the Sierra Nevada, 6 mi. NNW of Mt. Whitney and on E boundary of Sequoia Natl. Park.

Tyndall Air Force Base, Fla.: see PANAMA CITY.

Tyndaris (tĭn'dŭrĭs), ancient Greek colony on NE coast of Sicily, founded by Dionysius I in 396 B.C.; allied with Timoleon, it aided Romans during Punic Wars. Attained great power; during Christian period, became bishopric. Its ruins, on Cape Tindari, 4 mi. ENE of Patti, include Greek town walls, Roman gymnasium and theater.

Tyndrum (tĭndrŭm'), resort village, SW Perthshire, Scotland, at foot of Ben Lui, on Argyll border, 9 mi. N of Ardlui. Former lead-mining center.

Tyndynskiy (tĭndĭn'skē), town (1939 pop. over 2,000), NW Amur oblast, Russian SFSR, on spur of Trans-Siberian RR, on Never-Yakutsk highway, and 90 mi. N of Skovorodino. Gold fields near by.

Tynec nad Labem (tē'nĕts näd' lä"bĕm), Czech *Týnec nad Labem*, village (pop. 1,756), E Bohemia, Czechoslovakia, on Elbe R., on railroad and 8 mi. NNE of Kutna Hora; summer resort with 18th-cent. castle (now a hotel).

Tynec nad Sazavou (sä"zävō), Czech *Týnec nad Sázavou*, village (pop. 1,146), S central Bohemia, Czechoslovakia, on Sazava R., on railroad and 5 mi. NW of Benesov; machine works; barley.

Tynemouth (tĭn'mŭth, tĭn'-), county borough (1931 pop. 64,922; 1951 census 66,544) and seaport, SE Northumberland, England, on North Sea at mouth of the Tyne, 8 mi. ENE of Newcastle-upon-Tyne; 55°1'N 1°26'W; shipbuilding center; coal-shipping and fishing port. Has ruins of 14th-cent. castle and of 12th-cent. priory built on site of 7th-cent. Saxon priory founded by the Northumbrian king Edwin. One of the churches dates from 12th cent. In county borough are coal-mining town of North Shields (W), with shipbuilding, metallurgical, chemical, and glass industries, and Cullercoats (N), on North Sea, with marine radio station.

Tyne River (tīn), N England, formed 2 mi. NW of Hexham (in Northumberland) by confluence of the South Tyne (rises on Cross Fell in Cumberland, flows 33 mi. N and E) and the North Tyne (rises in S Cheviot Hills, flows 32 mi. SE); from the confluence, the Tyne flows 30 mi. E, past Blaydon, Newcastle-upon-Tyne, Gateshead, Wallsend, Hebburn, Jarrow, and South Shields, to North Sea at Tynemouth; in the last 18 mi. it forms boundary bet. Northumberland and Durham. Navigable for ocean-going ships below Newcastle; this sector is lined by almost continuous dock and industrial works (ironworking, shipbuilding, coal mining).

Tyne River, Midlothian and East Lothian, Scotland, rises 3 mi. S of Borthwick, flows 28 mi. NE, past Pencaitland, Haddington, and East Linton, to North Sea 4 mi. W of Dunbar.

Tyneside, major industrial area of Durham and Northumberland, England, along both banks of the lower Tyne, comprising Newcastle-upon-Tyne, Gateshead, Wallsend, Hebburn, Jarrow, South Shields, and Tynemouth. Chief industries are shipbuilding, coal mining, and shipping; also machinery works and iron and steel foundries.

Tynewydd, Wales: see RHONDDA.

Tyngsboro or **Tyngsborough** (both: tĭngz'bŭrō), town (pop. 2,059), Middlesex co., NE Mass., on Merrimack R. and 6 mi. WNW of Lowell; lumber, building materials. Settled c.1660, inc. 1809.

Tyniste nad Orlici (tē'nyĭshtyĕ näd' ôr"lĭtsē), Czech *Týniště nad Orlicí*, village (pop. 3,208), E Bohemia, Czechoslovakia, near junction of headstreams of Orlice R., 12 mi. SE of Hradec Kralove; rail junction; mfg. of furniture and carpets.

Tyn nad Vltavou (tĭn näd' vŭl"tävō), Czech *Týn nad Vltavou*, Ger. *Moldautein* (môl'doutīn), town (pop. 3,523), S Bohemia, Czechoslovakia, on Vltava R., near Luznice R. mouth, and 17 mi. NNW of Budweis, in barley and oats region; rail terminus; lumber trade; barge building.

Tynset (tün'sŭt), village (pop. 715; canton pop. 4,097), Hedmark co., E Norway, on Glomma R., on railroad and 30 mi. SW of Roros, in pyrite-mining region. Has 18th-cent. church.

Tyonek (tīō'nĭk), village (pop. 132), S Alaska, on NW shore of Cook Inlet, 45 mi. WSW of Anchorage; fishing. School.

Tyosen: see KOREA.

Tyosi, Japan: see CHOSHI.

Tyras, city, Ukrainian SSR: see BELGOROD-DNESTROVSKI.

Tyras River, USSR: see DNIESTER RIVER.

Tyre (tīr), Arabic *Sur* (sōōr), *El Sur*, or *Es Sur* (both: ĕs-sōōr'), Fr. *Tyr* or *Sour*, Hebrew *Zor* (tsōr), Lat. *Tyrus*, one of the great cities of the anc. world and an important center of Phoenician civilization. Its site, the present-day town (pop. 9,455) of Sur, is in Lebanon, on a tiny peninsula on the Mediterranean, 45 mi. SSW of Beirut and 23 mi. SSW of Saida (Sidon). It was built on an isl. just off the mainland, but the accretion of sand around a mole built by Alexander the Great to facilitate his siege of the city (333–332 B.C.) has formed a causeway ½ mi. wide. The date of Tyre's founding is uncertain and may antedate the 2d millenium B.C.; at any rate, by 1400 B.C. it was a flourishing city and began to eclipse the older port of Sidon. The maritime supremacy of Tyre was established by 1100 B.C., by which date its seamen seem to have sailed past the Gates of Hercules (Gibraltar) and to have colonized Utica and Gades. Tyrians founded Carthage in 9th cent. B.C. Tyre was famous for its industries, such as textile manufacture, and particularly for the purple Tyrian dye. It fell continually under foreign rule but maintained its importance through many centuries. It was taken by the Assyrians, Babylonians, and Persians, and recovered quickly from the sack by Alexander. In 64 B.C. it became part of the Roman Empire. Christianity was introduced early, and a splendid cathedral, of which there are remains, was built in 4th cent. A.D. After the rise of Islam, Tyre came under Moslem rule and continued to be important down into the Middle Ages. It fell to the Crusaders in 1124 and was destroyed in 1291, when the Moslems retook it; it never recovered. Most of the ruins date from the Crusades; any left by the Phoenicians are underneath the present town. Tyre is frequently mentioned in the Bible.

Tyree or **Tiree** (tīrē'), island (□ 29.5, including Skerryvore; pop. 1,448) of the Inner Hebrides, Argyll, Scotland, 2 mi. SW of Coll, 15 mi. W of Mull; 12 mi. long, up to 6 mi. wide; rises to 460 ft. Near village of Scarinish (S) is an airfield. Chief occupations are crofting and quarrying of pink marble; isl. is noted for its horses.

Tyret or **Tyret'** (tĭrĕt'yŭ), village (1926 pop. 867), S Irkutsk oblast, Russian SFSR, on Trans-Siberian RR and 50 mi. NW of Cheremkhovo; junction of highway to Zhigalovo. Alabaster deposits.

Tyrie (tīrē'), agr. village and parish (pop. 2,195), N Aberdeen, Scotland, 5 mi. SW of Fraserburgh. Parish includes NEW PITSLIGO.

Tyri Fjord (tü'rē), lake (□ 51), Buskerud co., SE Norway, 15 mi. W of Oslo; 20 mi. long, 1–8 mi. wide, up to 922 ft. deep. Fed (N) by Begna R. and waters of Rands Fjord; drains SW into Drammen R. SE arm (7 mi. long) is called Hols Fjord.

Tyringe (tü'rĭng-ŭ), village (pop. 2,749), Kristianstad co., S Sweden, 7 mi. W of Hassleholm; mfg. of tools, furniture, food products. Tourist resort, with sanitarium.

Tyringham (tēr'ĭng-ŭm), town (pop. 235), Berkshire co., SW Mass., in the Berkshires, 14 mi. S of Pittsfield.

Tyrisevä, Russian SFSR: see USHKOVO.

Tyristrand (tü'rĭsträn), village and canton (pop. 1,503), Buskerud co., SE Norway, on Tyri Fjord, on railroad and 8 mi. SW of Honefoss; agr., lumbering. Paper- and sawmilling at Skjerdalen (shăr'dälŭn) village, just NE; sometimes spelled Skjaerdalen.

Tyrnau, Czechoslovakia: see TRNAVA.

Tyrnavos or **Tirnavos** (both: tĭr'nŭvôs), town (pop. 7,018), Larissa nome, central Thessaly, Greece, on highway and 10 mi. NW of Larissa, on Titaresios R.; trade center for silk, wheat, vegetables, legumes, livestock, dairy. Alcohol distillery.

Tyrnovo (tĭrnô'vŭ), Rum. *Târnova* (tŭrnô'vä), village (1941 pop. 2,000), N Moldavian SSR, on railroad and 30 mi. NNW of Beltsy; wheat, sunflowers.

Tyrny-Auz (tĭrnē"-ŭōōs'), town (1939 pop. over 500), SW Kabardian Autonomous SSR, Russian SFSR, in the central Greater Caucasus, on Baksan R. and 35 mi. WSW of Nalchik; tungsten- and molybdenum-mining center. Developed in late 1930s.

Tyro (tī'rō), city (pop. 279), Montgomery co., SE Kansas, near Okla. line, 11 mi. W of Coffeyville, in stock-raising and agr. region. Oil and gas fields here.

Tyrol or **Tirol** (both: tĭ'rŭl, tĭrōl', Ger. tērōl'), autonomous prov. [*Bundesland*] (including East Tyrol □ 4,884; 1951 pop. 426,499), W Austria, bordering Germany (N), Salzburg and Carinthia (E), Italy (S), and Vorarlberg (W); ⊙ Innsbruck. Wholly mountainous, it is noted for scenic beauty of its Alps: W—part of Rhaetian Alps and Arlberg region; N—Bavarian and Salzburg Alps; E—Kitzbühel Alps; S—Zillertal and Ötztal Alps; center—Tuxer and Stubai Alps. Brenner Pass is in S. Traversed (SW–NE) by the Inn. Pop. engaged mainly in subsistence farming, cattle raising (dairy products), and forestry; wheat and rye raised along the Inn. Industry (textiles, cellulose) centers in Innsbruck, Landeck, and Kufstein. Tyrolese glass paintings are well known. Salt mined in large quantities near Solbad Hall. Active tourist trade. Tyrol formed part of anc. Rhaetia, conquered by Romans in 15 B.C. Invaded in 6th cent. by Teutonic tribes. N portion (present Tyrol) was divided into petty countships, later united under counts of Tyrol and deeded (1363) to the Hapsburgs. Large parts of S Tyrol (now in Italy) were ruled by bishops of TRENT and bishops of Brixen (see BRESSANONE) from 11th cent. until early 19th cent., when the bishoprics were secularized and fell to Austria. Treaty of Pressburg (1805) awarded all of Tyrol to Napoleon's ally, Bavaria. At resumption of war bet. Austria and France in 1809, Tyrolean peasants, led by Andreas Hofer, rose in revolt and were crushed only by numerical superiority of Fr. and Bavarian troops. Napoleon attached S Tyrol to Italy in 1810, but the Congress of Vienna (1815) restored both parts to Austria. The Treaty of Saint-Germain (1919) awarded S Tyrol (the predominantly Ger.-speaking prov. of BOLZANO and the predominantly Italian prov. of TRENTO) to Italy. This cession resulted in separation of **East Tyrol,** Ger. *Osttirol* (ôst'tērōl"), SE part (□ 780; pop. 37,779) of present Tyrol, cut off by Salzburg-Ital. corridor. Mountainous with Hohe Tauern on N; drained by the Drau; ⊙ Lienz. In 1945 Tyrol was placed in French, East Tyrol in Br. occupation zone.

Tyrol Alps, Austria: see BAVARIAN ALPS.

Tyrone (tĭrōn'), county (□ 1,218; 1937 pop. 127,586; 1951 census 132,049), Ulster, W Northern Ireland; ⊙ Omagh. Bounded by cos. Monaghan (S) and Donegal (W), Ireland; cos. Fermanagh (SW), Londonderry (N), and Armagh (SE); and by Lough Neagh (E). Drained by Mourne and Blackwater rivers and their tributaries. Surface is generally hilly, rising to Sperrin Mts. in NE. Coal deposits in E and SE; marble and red sandstone are quarried. Main agr. occupations are raising of oats, flax, and potatoes, grazing of cattle, and dairying. Leading industries are linen and woolen milling, tanning, mfg. of hosiery, thread, rope, fish nets, soap. Towns are Omagh, Dungannon, Coalisland, Cookstown, Clogher, and Augher. Co. was center of earldom of Tyrone, held by the O'Neills; Dungannon was their chief stronghold. There are remains of early castles and abbeys.

Tyrone (tīrōn', tĭ-). **1** Town (pop. 156), Fayette co., W central Ga., 13 mi. ENE of Newnan. **2** Village (pop. c.250), Grant co., SW N.Mex., 9 mi. SW of Silver City near Ariz. line; alt. c.5,900 ft.; health resort. Big Burro Mts. are SW in part of Gila Natl. Forest. Mining was formerly important. **3** Town (pop. 261), Texas co., extreme NW Okla., near Kansas line, 30 mi. NE of Guymon. **4** Borough (pop. 8,214), Blair co., central Pa., 15 mi. NE of Altoona and on Little Juniata R.; shipping center; mfg. (paper, metal products); agr. Laid out c.1850, inc. 1857.

Tyronza (tĭrŏn'zŭ), town (pop. 656), Poinsett co., NE Ark., 29 mi. SE of Jonesboro, in agr. area.

Tyrrell (tĭ'rŭl), county (□ 399; pop. 5,048), NE N.C.; ⊙ Columbia. Bounded N by Albemarle Sound, E by Alligator R. Forested and swampy tidewater area; farming (corn, soybeans), sawmilling, fishing. Formed 1729.

Tyrrell, Lake (tĭ'rŭl), salt lake (□ 67), NW Victoria, Australia, 200 mi. NW of Melbourne; 14 mi. long, 7 mi. wide; usually dry.

Tyrrell, Mount (9,610 ft.), SE B.C., in Selkirk Mts., 50 mi. NNE of Nelson; 50°2'N 116°45'W.

Tyrrhenian Sea (tĭrē'nēŭn), arm of Mediterranean Sea bet. W coast of Italy and isls. of Corsica, Sardinia, and Sicily. Connects with Ligurian Sea (NW) in Tuscan Archipelago and with Ionian Sea (SE) via Strait of Messina. Chief arms: Bay of Naples and gulfs of Gaeta, Salerno, Policastro, and Sant'Eufemia. Principal ports: Naples, Palermo, and Civitavecchia.

Tyrus, Lebanon: see TYRE.

Tyrva, Estonia: see TORVA.

Tysfjord, canton, Norway: see KJOPSVIK.

Tys Fjord (tüs), inlet (30 mi. long, 2–9 mi. wide) of Vest Fjord, Nordland co., N Norway, 30 mi. WSW of Narvik. Hellemo Fjord (15 mi. long) is S arm. Fishing.

Tysmenitsa (tĭsmyĕ'nyĭtsŭ), Pol. *Tyśmienica* (tĭshmyĕnyĕ'tsä), town (1931 pop. 7,257), E Stanislav oblast, Ukrainian SSR, on right tributary of the Bystritsa and 6 mi. E of Stanislav; agr. processing (cereals, hides, vegetables), dairying; brick mfg. Has 17th-cent. monastery, several old churches. An old Ruthenian settlement, known since 12th cent.; passed to Poland in 1340; chartered in 1513; developed as trade center. Subjected to several Tatar and Turkish invasions (15th–17th cent.). Passed to Austria (1772), reverted to Poland (1919); ceded to USSR in 1945.

Tysmienica River (tĭshmyĕnē'tsä), Pol. *Tyśmienica*, Rus. *Tysmenitsa* or *Tys'menitsa* (both: tĭshyŭmyĭnyĕ'tsŭ), Lublin prov., E Poland, rises 19 mi. NE of Lublin, flows NNW, past Ostrow Lubelski, and SW, past Kock, to Wieprz R. just SSW of Kock; 45 mi. long.

Tysnesoy (tüs'näs-ûü), Nor. *Tysnesøy*, island (□ 77; pop. 3,187) bet. Bjorna and Hardanger fjords, Hordaland co., SW Norway, 25 mi. S of Bergen; 12 mi. long, 8 mi. wide; agr., lumber milling. Constitutes most of Tysnes canton (pop. 4,009). Godoysund (gōd'ûüsōōn) (Nor. *Godøysund*) village, on N shore, is a summer resort.

Tyson, Vt.: see PLYMOUTH.

Tysons Corner or **Tysons Crossroads**, village (pop. 1,674), Fairfax co., N Va., near Vienna.

Tysse (tüs'sŭ), village (pop. 321) in Samnanger canton (pop. 2,440), Hordaland co., SW Norway, at head of 20-mi. Samnanger Fjord (a NE branch of Bjorna Fjord), 16 mi. E of Bergen; hydroelectric plant; spinning, hose knitting.

Tyssedal (tüs'sŭdäl), village (pop. 1,402) in Odda canton, Hordaland co., SW Norway, on Sor Fjord (branch of Hardanger Fjord), 4 mi. N of Odda; farming and fruitgrowing; produces aluminum.

Tytärsaari, Russian SFSR: see TYUTYARSAARI.

Tythegston Higher, Wales: see LALESTON.

Ty Ty (tĭ'tĭ"), town (pop. 478), Tift co., S central Ga., 8 mi. W of Tifton.

Tyubu-sangaku National Park, Japan: see CHUBU-SANGAKU NATIONAL PARK.

Tyukalinsk (tyōōkŭlyĕnsk'), city (1948 pop. over 10,000), W central Omsk oblast, Russian SFSR, 75 mi. NW of Omsk; agr. center; metalworks; dairying, flour milling, mfg. of felt boots.

Tyukhtet (tyōōkhtyĕt'), village (1948 pop. over 2,000), SW Krasnoyarsk Territory, Russian SFSR, 50 mi. NW of Achinsk.

Tyukod (tyō'kôd), town (pop. 3,537), Szatmar-Bereg co., NE Hungary, 15 mi. WNW of Satu-Mare, Rumania; tobacco, potatoes, corn, cattle, hogs.

Tyuleni Island or **Tyuleniy Island** (tyōōlyĕ'nē) [Rus.,=seal], Jap. *Kaihyo-to* (kīhyō'-tō'), islet in Sea of Okhotsk, 11 mi. off Cape Terpeniye, S Sakhalin, Russian SFSR; 48°30'N 144°38'E.

Tyulkubas or **Tyul'kubas** (tyōōlkōōbäs'), town (1948 pop. over 2,000), SE South Kazakhstan oblast, Kazakh SSR, on Turksib RR and 35 mi. ENE of Chimkent.

Tyulyachi (tyōōlyŭchē'), village (1948 pop. over 2,000), NW central Tatar Autonomous SSR, Russian SFSR, 20 mi. SE of Arsk; grain, legumes, livestock.

Tyumen or **Tyumen'** (tyōōmĕn'yŭ), oblast (□ 526,300; 1946 pop. estimate 900,000) in W Siberian Russian SFSR; ⊙ Tyumen. On W. Siberian Plain; drained by Irtysh and Ob rivers. Includes (N) KHANTY-MANSI NATIONAL OKRUG and YAMAL-NENETS NATIONAL OKRUG. S section (80% of pop., 10% of area) is crossed by Trans-Siberian RR (site of main cities: Tyumen, Yalutorovsk, Ishim), has agr. (wheat) and cattle raising (wool, meat) on steppe, grain and dairy farming on wooded steppe, lumbering and fur trapping in forest region. In natl. okrugs (N), hunting (furs), fishing, reindeer breeding are important. First section of Siberia conquered by Russians (16th cent.); until 1923 included in Tobolsk (later renamed Tyumen) govt. Formed 1944 out of major part of Omsk oblast. Sometimes spelled Tiumen.

Tyumen or **Tyumen'**, city (1939 pop. 75,537), ⊙ Tyumen oblast, Russian SFSR, port on Tura R., on Trans-Siberian RR and 180 mi. E of Sverdlovsk, 1,050 mi. E of Moscow; 57°8'N 65°25'E. Industrial center; sawmilling (matches, plywood), shipbuilding, tanning; mfg. of sheepskins, felt boots; food processing (meat, flour), woolen milling. River-rail freight (largely lumber) transfer point. Has remains of fortress wall. Founded 1586, the oldest Rus. town in Siberia. Former terminus of Perm (now Molotov)-Tyumen RR; until construction of Trans-Siberian RR, Tyumen was "gateway to Siberia." Sometimes spelled Tiumen.

Tyumentsevo (–myĕn'tsyĭvŭ), village (1926 pop. 4,916), N Altai Territory, Russian SFSR, on E Kulunda Steppe, 90 mi. W of Barnaul; dairy farms.

Tyup (tyōōp), village (1939 pop. over 2,000), NE Issyk-Kul oblast, Kirghiz SSR, on NE shore of Issyk-Kul (lake), at mouth of Tyup R., 18 mi. N of Przhevalsk; wheat. Formerly Preobrazhenskoye.

Tyup River, NE Issyk-Kul oblast, Kirghiz SSR, rises in the Terskei Ala-Tau, flows c.60 mi. N and W to Issyk-Kul (lake) at Tyup. Coal in upper reaches (Dzhargalan).

Tyuri, Estonia: see TURI.

Tyurisevya, Russian SFSR: see USHKOVO.

Tyurya-Kurgan (tyōōryä"-kōōrgän'), village (1926 pop. 1,260), S Namangan oblast, Uzbek SSR, on railroad and 8 mi. WSW of Namangan; cotton; metalworks.

Tyutyarsaari (tyōō'tyŭrsŭä"rē), Finnish *Tytärsaari* (tü'tärsärē), island in Gulf of Finland, in Leningrad oblast, Russian SFSR, 105 mi. W of Leningrad, 27 mi. off Estonian coast. In Finland until 1940.

Tyuya-Muyun or **Tuya-Muyun** (tyōōyä"-mōōyōōn'), village, N Osh oblast, Kirghiz SSR, 15 mi. SW of Osh, in wheat and orchard area. Vanadium and uranium ores.

Tyuzenzi, Lake, Japan: see CHUZENJI, LAKE.

Tyvrov (tĭv'rŭf), town (1926 pop. 3,419), central Vinnitsa oblast, Ukrainian SSR, on the Southern Bug and 15 mi. S of Vinnitsa; food processing.

Tywardreath (tĭwûrdrĕth'), agr. village and parish (pop. 2,617), central Cornwall, England, near St. Austell Bay of the Channel, 5 mi. ENE of St. Austell. Church dates from 15th cent.

Tzarácua Falls (tsärä'kwä), Michoacán, central Mexico, on affluent of Tepalcatepec R., 4 mi. SW of Uruapan.

Tzechow. 1 Town, Hopeh prov., China: see TZEHSIEN. **2** Town, Szechwan prov., China: see TZECHUNG.

Tzechung or **Tzu-chung** (both: dzŭ'jōōng'). **1** Town, Hupeh prov., China: see ICHENG. **2** Town (pop. 55,662), ⊙ Tzechung co. (pop. 705,638), SW central Szechwan prov., China, on railroad to Chungking city, on left bank of To R. and 75 mi. SE of Chengtu; major sugar-milling center; match mfg.; rice, wheat, sweet potatoes, beans, oranges. Oil deposits and saltworks near by. Until 1913 called Tzechow.

Tzechwan or **Tzu-ch'uan** (both: dzŭ'chwän'), town, ⊙ Tzechwan co. (pop. 340,852), N central Shantung prov., China, 50 mi. E of Tsinan and on spur of Tsingtao-Tsinan RR; bauxite- and coal-mining center; pottery mfg.

Tzehing or **Tzu-hsing** (both: dzŭ'shĭng'), town, ⊙ Tzehing co. (pop. 123,354), SE Hunan prov., China, 25 mi. NE of Chenhsien; rice, wheat, tea, hemp. Tungsten, coal, sulphur, zinc, and arsenic found near by. Until 1914 called Hingning.

Tzehsien or **Tz'u-hsien** (both: tsŭ'shyĕn'), town, ⊙ Tzehsien co. (pop. 107,825), SW Hopeh prov., China, 50 mi. S of Singtai and on Peking-Hankow RR; coal-mining center; porcelain mfg. Until 1913 called Tzechow.

Tzehu, China: see TINGYÜANYING.

Tzekam (jē'gŭm'), Mandarin *Tzu-chin* (dzŭ'jĭn'), town (pop. 6,313), ⊙ Tzekam co. (pop. 204,726), E Kwangtung prov., China, 65 mi. NE of Waiyeung; rice, wheat, sugar cane, oranges. Until 1914 called Wingon.

Tzekao Shan, Formosa: see SYLVIA, MOUNT.

Tzeki. 1 or **Tz'u-ch'i** (tsŭ'chē'), town (pop. 17,577), ⊙ Tzeki co. (pop. 267,161), NE Chekiang prov., China, 10 mi. NW of Ningpo and on railroad; rice, wheat, beans, bamboo shoots. **2** or **Tzu-ch'i** (dzŭ'chē'), town (pop. 4,652), ⊙ Tzeki co. (pop. 29,171), E Kiangsi prov., China, 35 mi. ENE of Nanchang; rice, cotton. Graphite deposits. Until 1914, Luki.

Tzekiang, China: see KAIYANG.

Tzekung or **Tzu-kung** (both: dzŭ'gōōng'), city (1948 pop. 223,327), SW Szechwan prov., China, 110 mi. W of Chungking city; major oil and natural-gas center; important saltworks. Municipality was formed in 1942 by union of Tzeliutsing and Kungtsing (5 mi. WSW).

Tzekwei or **Tzu-kuei** (both: dzŭ'gwā'), town (pop. 18,448), ⊙ Tzekwei co. (pop. 217,898), W Hupeh prov., China, near Szechwan line, on left bank of Yangtze R. (gorges) and 40 mi. WNW of Ichang, in rice-growing region. Coal deposits near by. Until 1912 called Kweichow.

Tzeli or **Tz'u-li** (both: tsŭ'lē'), town, ⊙ Tzeli co. (pop. 376,344), NW Hunan prov., China, on Li R. and 40 mi. NW of Changteh. Sulphur, arsenic found near by.

Tzeliutsing, China: see TZEKUNG.

Tzetung or **Tzu-t'ung** (both: dzŭ'tōōng'), town (pop. 13,129), ⊙ Tzetung co. (pop. 168,690), NW Szechwan prov., China, 36 mi. N of Santai; rice, sweet potatoes, wheat. Iron deposits near by.

Tzeyang or **Tzu-yang** (both: dzŭ'yäng'). **1** Town, ⊙ Tzeyang co. (pop. 224,486), SW Shantung prov., China, 75 mi. S of Tsinan and on Tientsin-Pukow RR; silk-weaving center; wheat, peanuts, millet, beans. Until 1913 called Yenchow. **2** Town (pop. 3,746), ⊙ Tzeyang co. (pop. 89,154), S Shensi prov., China, 35 mi. NW of Ankang, near Han R.; tea-growing center; grain. **3** Town (pop. 10,148), ⊙ Tzeyang co. (pop. 540,958), W Szechwan prov., China, on railroad to Chungking city, on right bank of To R. and 50 mi. SE of Chengtu; sugar-milling center; rice, sweet potatoes, wheat, beans.

Tzeya River, China: see HUTO RIVER.

Tzeyüan or **Tzu-yüan** (both: dzŭ'yüän'), town, ⊙ Tzeyüan co. (pop. 69,633), NW Kwangsi prov., China, 65 mi. NNE of Kweilin; rice, wheat, cotton, peanuts. Until 1936 called Siyen.

Tzeyün or **Tzu-yün** (both: dzŭ'yün'), town (pop. 3,426), ⊙ Tzeyün co. (pop. 68,189), S Kweichow prov., China, 65 mi. SSW of Kweiyang; embroidered goods; ramie, tea, rice, wheat. Until 1913 called Kweihwa.

Tzia, Greece: see KEA.

Tzicuilán (tsēkwēlän'), town (pop. 2,653), Puebla, central Mexico, 29 mi. ESE of Huauchinango; corn, coffee, sugar cane, fruit.

Tzimol (tsēmōl'), town (pop. 2,363), Chiapas, S Mexico, adjoins Comitán; fruit, cotton, sugar, corn.

Tzinacapan (tsēnäkä'pän), town (pop. 2,093), Puebla, central Mexico, 27 mi. SE of Huauchinango; corn, sugar, fruit.

Tzintzuntzan (tsēnt"sōōntsän'), city (pop. 1,077), Michoacán, central Mexico, on E shore of L. Pátzcuaro, 26 mi. WSW of Morelia; anc. ⊙ Tarascan empire, with many ruins and stone idols in vicinity. Sometimes Zintzuntzan.

Tzippori, Israel: see TSIPORI.

Tzitzio (tsēt'syō), town (pop. 521), Michoacàn, central Mexico, 15 mi. SE of Morelia; corn, beans, livestock. Sometimes Zitzio.

Tzofim or **Tzofit**, Israel: see TSOFIT.

Tzompantepec (tsōmpäntäpĕk'), officially San Salvador Tzompantepec, town (pop. 508), Tlaxcala, central Mexico, 10 mi. NE of Tlaxcala; cereals, maguey, livestock.

Tzoumagia or **Tzoumayia**, Greece: see HERAKLEIA.

Tzoumerka (dzōōmĕr'kŭ), massif in central Pindus system, S Epirus, Greece, bet. Arachthos and Achelous rivers; rises to 7,837 ft. 20 mi. SE of Ioannina. Also called Athamanika.

Tzu-, for Chinese names beginning thus and not found here: see under TZE-.

Tzu, river, China: see TZU RIVER.

Tzucacab (tsōōkäkäb'), town (pop. 1,784), Yucatan, SE Mexico, 19 mi. SE of Tekax; henequen, fruit, timber.

Tzu-ch'i or **Tz'u-ch'i**, China: see TZEKI.

Tzu-chin, China: see TZEKAM.

Tzu-ch'uan, China: see TZECHWAN.

Tzu-hsing, China: see TZEHING.

Tzunjuyú, Guatemala: see PANAJACHEL.

Tzu River, Chinese *Tzu Shui* (dzŭ'shwā'), central Hunan prov., China, rises on Kwangsi line, flows 460 mi. N and NE, past Shaoyang, Sinhwa, and Yiyang, to Tungting L. at Yüankiang, forming common delta with Siang R. (E). Traverses rich antimony-mining region; navigation impeded by rapids.

Tzur Moshe, Israel: see TSUR MOSHE.

Tzu Shui, China: see TZU RIVER.

U

Ü, Tibet: see WEI.
Uaca, Ethiopia: see WAKA.
Uaddan (wăd-dăn'), Saharan oasis (1950 pop. 2,500), SE Tripolitania, Libya, near Fezzan border, on road and 13 mi. ENE of Hun; dates, figs, barley; camel breeding.
Ua Huka (ōō'ä hōō'kä) or **Uahuka**, volcanic island (pop. 190), Marquesas Isls., Fr. Oceania, S Pacific, c.25 mi. W of Nuku Hiva; 7.5 mi. long, 5 mi. wide; rises to 2,430 ft. Mountainous; barren coast line. Formerly Washington Isl.
Ualan, Caroline Isls.: see KUSAIE.
Ualdia, Ethiopia: see WALDIA.
Ualual, Ethiopia: see WAL WAL.
Uanle Uen (wän'lä wĕn'), town (pop. 1,400), in the Benadir, S Ital. Somaliland, on road and 50 mi. NW of Mogadishu, in agr. (durra, corn) and livestock region.
Ua Pou (ōōä pōō'), volcanic island (pop. 685), Marquesas Isls., Fr. Oceania, S Pacific, c.30 mi. S of Nuku Hiva; 9 mi. long, 5 mi. wide. Its mtn. range rises to c.4,040 ft. Sometimes spelled Uapu. Former names: Adams Isl., Trevennen Isl.
Uardere, Ethiopia: see WARDERE.
Uasin Gishu Plateau (ōōä'sĭn gē'shōō), tableland along W rim of Great Rift Valley, in W Kenya, W of Elgeyo Escarpment; 90 mi. long, 30 mi. wide; alt. 5,000–8,000 ft. Its center is Eldoret. Wheat, corn, coffee, livestock. Many South African settlers.
Uatumã River (wŏŏtōōmä'), E Amazonas, Brazil, rises in S outliers of the Guiana Highlands, flows c.250 mi. SE to the Amazon (left bank) above Urucará.
Uaupés (woupĕs'), city (pop. 433), NW Amazonas, Brazil, on left bank of the Rio Negro just below influx of Uaupés R., and 500 mi. NW of Manaus; 0°7'S 67°6'W. Sweet potatoes. Brazil nuts, rubber, hardwood. Has anc. fort. Until 1944, called São Gabriel.
Uaupés River, in SE Colombia and NW Brazil, rises in Vaupés commissary (Colombia) in E foothills of the Andes, flows ESE, entering Amazonas (Brazil) below Mitú, to the Rio Negro just above Uaupés. Length, 500 mi. Interrupted by numerous rapids. Spelled Vaupés in Colombia. Also called the Cayari or Caiari.
Uawa, New Zealand: see TOLAGA BAY.
Uaxactún (wäkh-äktōōn'), village (pop. 70), Petén dept., N Guatemala, 37 mi. NNE of Flores; airfield for chicle shipments. Site of extensive Mayan ruins, discovered 1916.
Uayma (wī'mä), town (pop. 975), Yucatan, SE Mexico, 8 mi. NW of Valladolid; corn, henequen, sugar cane.
Ub (ōōp), village (pop. 2,402), W Serbia, Yugoslavia, 16 mi. NE of Valjevo.
Ubá (ōōbä'), city (pop. 10,911), SE Minas Gerais, Brazil, at E end of the Serra da Mantiqueira, 50 mi. NE of Juiz de Fora; rail junction; agr. trade center (coffee, tobacco, sugar); mfg. of flour products, furniture. Deposits of asbestos and radioactive minerals. Has school of pharmacy and dentistry.
Übach-Palenberg (ü'bäkh-pä'lŏŏnbĕrk), village (pop. 14,020), in former Prussian Rhine Prov., W Germany, after 1945 in North Rhine-Westphalia, near Dutch border, 10 mi. N of Aachen. Formed 1935 through incorporation of Frelenberg, Scherpenseel, Übach, and Palenberg (with Carolingian chapel).
Ubagai (ōōbägī'), town (pop. 7,246), Tochigi prefecture, central Honshu, Japan, 10 mi. E of Utsunomiya; rice, tobacco.
Ubagan River (ōōbŏŏgän'), NE Kustanai oblast, Kazakh SSR, rises in W Kazakh Hills, flows c.200 mi. N, through L. Kushmurun (formerly L. Ubagan), to Tobol R. near Zverinogolovskoye.
Ubaíra (ōōbäē'rŏŏ), city (pop. 2,093), E Bahia, Brazil, on railroad and 50 mi. WSW of Nazaré; ships sugar, coffee, tobacco, cattle, skins. Marble quarries. Until 1944, called Areia.
Ubaitaba (ōōbītä'bŏŏ), city (pop. 2,181), E Bahia, Brazil, on the Rio de Contas and 45 mi. NNW of Ilhéus, in cacao-growing area. Until 1944, called Itapira.
Ubajara (ōōbŏŏzhä'rŏŏ), city (pop. 1,265), NW Ceará, Brazil, in Serra Grande, on Piauí border, 40 mi. SW of Sobral; sugar, coffee. Kaolin deposits.
Ubajay (ōōbähī'), town (pop. estimate 800), E Entre Ríos prov., Argentina, on railroad and 33 mi. SSW of Concordia; wheat, flax, corn, livestock.
Ubal (ōōbäl'), village, Hodeida prov., W Yemen, 37 mi. E of Hodeida; road junction in coffeegrowing dist., where motor road (built 1930s) to Sana leaves former main route via Manakha. Also spelled Abal and Obal.
Ubangi River (ūbăng'gē, ōōbäng'gē), Fr. *Oubangui* (ōōbägē'), major tributary of the Congo in N and W central Africa, formed by the union of Uele and Bomu rivers on Belgian Congo–Fr. Equatorial Africa border, flows W and NW along the border past Banzyville and Pandu, then turns S and flows past Bangui, still separating Belgian Congo and Fr. Equatorial Africa, to join the Congo opposite Irebu, 60 mi. SW of Coquilhatville. Length, c.660 mi.; with the Uele, c.1,400 mi. Receives Lua and Giri rivers (left), Koto R. (right). Navigable for c.100 mi. in upper course bet. Yakoma and Banzyville, and for c.375 mi. in lower course (numerous isls.) downstream from Bangui. Middle course is obstructed by rapids. Confluence of Uele and Bomu was explored in 1884; thorough hydrographic survey of entire course was carried out by French expedition, 1910–11.
Ubangi-Shari (–shä'rē), Fr. *Oubangui-Chari* (–shärē'), French overseas territory (□ 238,220; 1950 pop. 1,071,800), central Fr. Equatorial Africa; ⊙ Bangui. Bounded S by Belgian Congo along Ubangi and Bomu rivers, E by Anglo-Egyptian Sudan, W by Fr. Cameroons; adjoins N on Chad territory, SW on Middle Congo territory. Drained by tributaries of the Ubangi and by headstreams of Shari R. On NW fringe of central African plateau, it is largely park-savanna country with forest galleries along chief streams; S of Bangui are dense forests; toward the Anglo-Egyptian Sudan is semidesert area. Tropical climate; rainy season March–Dec. Produces coffee and cotton for shipment to France; has several gold and diamond fields (in SW) and exports fine carbonados. Secondary crops include sisal, groundnuts, millet, sorghum, pulse. Wild rubber, palm products, beeswax are gathered. Some livestock. Has good road net. Bangui is main center; other towns include Berberati and Bambari. After 1890, the area was visited by Fr. explorers and border arrangements were made (1893–94) with Congo Free State and Cameroons. It became part of Fr. Equatorial Africa in 1910, when it also included Chad colony (and was called Ubangi-Shari-Chad); lost Chad colony 1920. In 1946, when it acquired territorial status (with representation in Fr. parliament), a strip of territory in N was transferred to Chad.
Ubaredmet (ōōbŭrydmyĕt'), town (1948 pop. over 2,000), NW East Kazakhstan oblast, Kazakh SSR, 45 mi. NNW of Ust-Kamenogorsk; tungsten and tin mining.
Ubari (ōōbä'rē), Fr. *Oubari*, walled village (pop. 243), central Fezzan, Libya, on road and 110 mi. WSW of Sebha, in a Saharan oasis (date growing); caravan center. Has mosque, ruined Turkish fort.
Ubaté (ōōbätā'), town (pop. 2,682), Cundinamarca dept., central Colombia, in Cordillera Oriental, 50 mi. NNE of Bogotá; alt. 9,186 ft. Textile milling; agr. (wheat, potatoes, fruit, livestock). Zinc deposits near by.
Ubatuba (ōōbŏŏtōō'bŏŏ), city (pop. 1,052), SE São Paulo, Brazil, port on small bay of the Atlantic, at foot of the Serra do Mar, 40 mi. SE of Taubaté; sugar, fruit.
Ubay (ōō'bī), town (1939 pop. 1,731; 1948 municipality pop. 29,961), NE Bohol isl., Philippines, on Camotes Sea, 50 mi. NE of Tagbilaran; agr. center (rice, coconuts).
Ubaye River (übī'), Basses-Alpes dept., SE France, rises at foot of the Aiguille de Chambeyron near Ital. border, flows 50 mi. generally W, through picturesque Alpine valley, past Barcelonnette, to the Durance 7 mi. below Savines. Followed by road to Maddalena Pass.
Ube (ōō'bä), city (1940 pop. 100,680; 1947 pop. 108,728), Yamaguchi prefecture, SW Honshu, Japan, 18 mi. E of Shimonoseki, across Suo Sea (W section of Inland Sea); coal-mining center; cement, cotton yarn, fertilizer, magnesium. Bombed (1945) in Second World War.
Úbeda (ōō'vä-dhä), city (pop. 29,336), Jaén prov., S Spain, in Andalusia, 30 mi. NE of Jaén; alt. 2,500 ft.; olive-oil production center also making olive-pressing equipment. Esparto processing, metal founding, tanning, liqueur and brandy distilling, flour- and sawmilling; other mfg. includes soap, tiles, knitwear, hats, furniture, sausage. Trades in esparto, wine, cereals, and livestock. Has anc. walls, several churches in 16th-cent. Renaissance style, a church tower, and several fine mansions including the towered Casa de las Torres. Was originally an Iberian settlement and still retains its Iberian name.
Ubehebe Crater, Calif.: see DEATH VALLEY NATIONAL MONUMENT.
Ubekendt Island (ōō'bŏŏkĕnt) (20 mi. long, 3–15 mi. wide), W Greenland, in inlet of Baffin Bay, bet. Karrats Fjord (N) and Umanak Fjord (S), 40 mi. NW of Umanak; 71°10'N 53°40'W. Separated from Upernavik Isl. (E) by Igdlorssuit Sound (15 mi. long, 7 mi. wide). Generally hilly, rises to 3,773 ft. Igdlorssuit settlement on E coast. Sometimes spelled Ubekyendt.
Uberaba (ōōbĭrä'bŏŏ), city (1950 pop. 43,915), W Minas Gerais, Brazil, near São Paulo line, 260 mi. W of Belo Horizonte; 19°46'S 47°56'W; alt. 2,500 ft. Center of important stock-raising dist. (Triângulo Mineiro), linked by rail with São Paulo city, Belo Horizonte, and Anápolis (Goiás). Chief industries are meat processing, sugar and cotton milling, lime mfg. Yearly stock fair noted for fine breed of zebu cattle. Increasing commercial prosperity followed NW advance of agr. frontier from São Paulo. Airfield.
Uberaba, Lake (Sp. ōōbärä'bä), on Bolivia-Brazil border, 95 mi. N of Puerto Suárez; 10 mi. long, 5 mi. wide. Receives several affluents; connected with L. GAIBA (S) by the Canal Pedro II, which forms small sector of Bolivia-Brazil border, and by a second outlet in Brazilian territory.
Übergossene Alm (übŭrgô'sŭnŭ älm'), range of Salzburg Alps, W Austria, extending 10 mi. W from the river Salzach; rises to 9,639 ft. in the Hochkönig. Iron ore mined near Werfen at NE foot.
Überherrn, Saar: see BISTEN.
Überhofen, Saar: see RIEGELSBERG.
Überkingen, Bad, Germany: see BAD ÜBERKINGEN.
Uberlândia (ōōbĕrlän'dyŏŏ), city (1950 pop. 36,467), W Minas Gerais, Brazil, in Triângulo Mineiro, on São Paulo–Goiás RR and 60 mi. NNW of Uberaba; cattle-raising and -shipping center, with meat-drying plants. Airfield. Advancing agr. frontier has increased city's commercial importance.
Überlingen (ü'bŭrlĭng"ŭn), town (pop. 7,809), S Baden, Germany, on the Überlinger See (a branch of L. of Constance), 7 mi. N of Constance; steamer station; mfg. of chemicals and machinery; metal- and woodworking, lumber milling. Winegrowing. Resort with mineral spring. Has 14th-cent. church, 15th-cent. town hall. Was imperial city.
Überlinger See: see CONSTANCE, LAKE.
Ubiaja (ōōbyä'jä), town (pop. 6,034), Benin prov., Western Provinces, S Nigeria, 60 mi. ENE of Benin City; agr. trade center; palm oil and kernels, hardwood, rubber, kola nuts. Lignite deposits.
Übigau (ü'bēgou), town (pop. 3,312), in former Prussian Saxony prov., central Germany, after 1945 in Saxony-Anhalt, near the Black Elster, 13 mi. E of Torgau; grain, potatoes, livestock.
Ubin, Pulau (pōōlou' ōōbĭn'), island (pop. 1,456) off NE Singapore isl., in Johore Strait; 1°25'N 103°57'E; 4.5 mi. long. Granite quarries.
Ubinas (ōōbē'näs), town (pop. 485), Moquegua dept., S Peru, at S foot of Ubinas Volcano, 25 mi. N of Omate; grain, livestock.
Ubinas Volcano, Andean peak (17,390 ft.) on Moquegua-Arequipa dept. border, S Peru, just NE of Nevado de Pichu Pichu; 16°25'S 70°54'W.
Ubinskoye (ōōbēn'skŭyŭ), village (1939 pop. over 2,000), central Novosibirsk oblast, Russian SFSR, on Trans-Siberian RR and 50 mi. E of Barabinsk; dairy farming.
Ubinskoye Lake (□ 216), central Novosibirsk oblast, Russian SFSR, in E Baraba Steppe, 5 mi. N of Ubinskoye; 28 mi. long, 10 mi. wide; well stocked with fish.
Ubirama, Brazil: see LENÇÓIS PAULISTA.
Ubly (ŭ'blē), village (pop. 743), Huron co., E Mich., 17 mi. SW of Harbor Beach, and on North Branch of Cass R., in farm area (grain, potatoes, beans, livestock).
Ubon (ōō'bôn'), officially **Ubonratchthani** or **Ubonratchathani** (ōō'bôn'rä'chätä'nē), town (1947 pop. 9,690), ⊙ Ubon prov. (□ 8,947; 1947 pop. 850,526), E Thailand, in Korat Plateau, on left bank of Mun R. below mouth of Chi R., 310 mi. ENE of Bangkok and on railroad; trading center, linked by road with Mekong R. at Pakse (Laos); rice, cotton, tobacco, lac; weaving; hog and cattle raising. Developed greatly after construction (c.1930) of railroad from Bangkok. Sometimes spelled Ubol.
Ubrique (ōōvrē'kä), town (pop. 6,863), Cádiz prov., SW Spain, in spur of the Cordillera Penibética, 15 mi. WSW of Ronda. Noted for its leather industry, it also produces woolen goods, hats, soap, plaster. Jasper and lime quarrying; flour milling; lumbering. Situated in agr. region (cereals, vegetables, livestock). Has sulphur springs.
Ubrug or **Oebroeg** (both: ōōbrōōg'), village in Preanger region, SW Java, Indonesia, at foot of Mt. Pangrango, on short Chichatik R. and 25 mi. S of Bogor; important hydroelectric station.
Ubsa Nor, Ubsa Nur, or **Ubsa Nuur** (all: ōōb'sä nōr', nōōr'), aimak (□ 31,300; pop. 50,000), W Mongolian People's Republic; ⊙ Ulankom. Bounded N by Tuva Autonomous Oblast of Russian SFSR, it rises to 13,504 ft. in Kharkira peak and contains (center) the semi-desert lake depression of Ubsa Nor and Kirgis Nor. Pop. (West Mongols, Tuvinians, Khotons) engages in stock grazing and primitive agr.
Ubsa Nor, Ubsa Nur, or **Ubsa Nuur,** largest salt lake (□ 1,290) of Mongolian People's Republic, on USSR (Tuva Autonomous Oblast) border; max. dimensions: 52 mi. long, 49 mi. wide; alt. 2,438 ft. Heavily mineralized, the lake contains chiefly sodium sulphate and chloride and magnesium chloride. It occupies a semi-desert depression and receives Tes R.
Ubur Khangai, Mongolia: see SOUTH KHANGAI.
Ubur Khangaün, Mongolia: see ARBAI KHERE.
Ucacha (ōōkä'chä), town (pop. 2,763), S central Córdoba prov., Argentina, 30 mi. NW of La Car-

lota; cereals, flax, alfalfa, vegetables, livestock; dairying.

Ucayali, province, Peru: see CONTAMANA.

Ucayali River (ōōkīä'lē), E Peru, one of the Amazon's main headstreams, formed by union of Apurímac (Tambo) and Urubamba rivers at 11° 17'S 73°47'W, flows c.1,000 mi. N, past Masisea, Pucallpa, and Contamana, joining Marañón R. to form the Amazon 55 mi. SSW of Iquitos at 4°30'S 73°27'W. Navigable in its entire length for small craft; vessels drawing 5 ft. can reach mouth of Pachitea R., c.675 mi. from Iquitos. Main affluents are Pachitea (left), Tapiche (right). The Ucayali was 1st discovered 1641 by Franciscan monk Illescas. First map of it was made 1700.

Uccle (ü'klü), Flemish *Ukkel* (û'kûl), S suburb (pop. 56,910) of Brussels, Brabant prov., central Belgium; mfg. of textiles, metals, wood and food products. Site of Belgian royal observatory (50°47'56"N 4°21'45"E).

Uch (ōōch), town (pop. 3,110), Bahawalpur state, W Pakistan, 38 mi. WSW of Bahawalpur; dates, wheat; hand-loom weaving. Annual festival fair. Known also as Uch-i-Sharif or Uch Sharif, it was a center of Moslem learning in Middle Ages.

Uch-Adzhi (ōōch"-ŭjē'), town (1939 pop. over 500), NE Mary oblast, Turkmen SSR, on Kara-Kum desert, on Trans-Caspian RR and 60 mi. NE of Mary. Junction of rail spur to Chamchakly, 20 mi. ESE; site of extensive saksaul wood plantations.

Uchaly (ōōchŭlē'), village (1948 pop. over 2,000), E Bashkir Autonomous SSR, Russian SFSR, 50 mi. NE of Beloretsk, on small lake; wheat, livestock. Jasper deposits near by (NNE).

Uch-Aral (ōōch"-ŭräl'), village (1939 pop. over 2,000), NE Taldy-Kurgan oblast, Kazakh SSR, W of Ala-Kul (lake), 150 mi. NE of Taldy-Kurgan; irrigated agr. (wheat).

Ucha River (ōō'chŭ), Moscow oblast, Russian SFSR, rises on Klin Dmitrov Ridge N of Krasnaya Polyana, flows 30 mi. E, past Pushkino, to Klyazma R. below Ivanteyevka. Middle course is crossed by Moscow Canal, which forms Pyalovo and Ucha reservoirs (hydroelectric plants) W of Pushkino.

Uchigo (ōō'chĭgō), town (pop. 33,185), Fukushima prefecture, central Honshu, Japan, just SW of Taira, 35 mi. SE of Koriyama; coal-mining center.

Uchi Lake, village, NW Ont., in Patricia dist., on Uchi L. (4 mi. long), 75 mi. NNW of Sioux Lookout; gold mining.

Uchimchak (ōōchĭmchăk'), village, NW Talas oblast, Kirghiz SSR, 30 mi. SW of Talas; arsenic mining.

Uchino (ōōchĭnō'), town (pop. 9,642), Niigata prefecture, central Honshu, Japan, 8 mi. SW of Niigata; rice growing.

Uchinoko (ōōchĭnō'kō), town (pop. 6,280), Ehime prefecture, NW Shikoku, Japan, 21 mi. SSW of Matsuyama; rail terminus; commercial center for agr. area; spinning mill, sawmill. Sometimes spelled Utinoko.

Uchinomaki (ōōchĭnō'mäkē), town (pop. 6,992), Kumamoto prefecture, central Kyushu, Japan, 22 mi. NE of Kumamoto; health resort (alkaline hot springs); rice, lumber, charcoal, tea. Sometimes spelled Utinomaki.

Uchinoura (ōōchĭnō'rä), town (pop. 10,800), Kagoshima prefecture, SE Kyushu, Japan, on E Osumi Peninsula, on Ariake Bay and 37 mi. SE of Kagoshima; commercial center in agr. and forested area; rice, raw silk, lumber, livestock. Fishing. Sometimes spelled Utinoura.

Uchiumi, Japan: see UTSUMI.

Uchiura Bay (ōōchē'ōōrä), Jap. *Uchiura-wan*, crescent-shaped inlet of the Pacific, SW Hokkaido, Japan; 35 mi. long, 30 mi. wide. Muroran is at SE entrance. Sometimes called Volcano Bay; formerly sometimes called Iburi Bay.

Uch-Kupryuk, Uzbek SSR: see MOLOTOVO, Fergana oblast.

Uch-Kurgan (ōōch"-kōōrgän'). **1** Village, Osh oblast, Kirghiz SSR: see MOLOTOVABAD. **2** Village (1926 pop. 4,422), E Namangan oblast, Uzbek SSR, on Naryn R., on railroad and 20 mi. ENE of Namangan; junction of rail spur to Tashkumyr; E terminus of Great Fergana Canal; cotton ginning.

Uch-Kzyl (ōōch-ksĭl'), village (1939 pop. over 2,000), S Surkhan-Darya oblast, on Kagan-Stalinabad RR and 8 mi. NNW of Termez; oil field. Also spelled Uch-Kizil.

Uchôa (ōōshō'ū), city (pop. 2,110), NW São Paulo, Brazil, on railroad and 16 mi. SE of São José do Rio Prêto; coffee, cattle. Formerly Ignacio Uchoa and Inácio Uchôa.

Uchterek (ōōchtyĕ'rĭk), village (1948 pop. over 2,000), NE Dzhalal-Abad oblast, Kirghiz SSR, on Naryn R. and 55 mi. N of Dzhalal-Abad; cotton.

Uch Turfan (ōōch' tōōrfän'), Chinese *Wushih* (wōō'shû'), town, ⊙ Uch Turfan co. (pop. 78,734), SW Sinkiang prov., China, 50 mi. W of Aksu, and on Bedel Pass road to USSR; cotton textiles; sericulture; cattle raising.

Ucka (ōōch kä), Serbo-Croatian *Učka*, Ital. *Monte Maggiore* (môn'tĕ mäd-jō'rĕ), highest peak (4,580 ft.) of Istria, NW Croatia, Yugoslavia, in the Cicarija, in Dinaric Alps, 11 mi. WSW of Rijeka (Fiume). Tourist excursions here from near-by Opatija.

Uckange (ükäzh'), Ger. *Uckingen* (ōō'kĭng-ŭn), town (pop. 2,885), Moselle dept., NE France, on left bank of Moselle R. and 4 mi. S of Thionville; blast furnaces, brewery.

Ückermünde, Germany: see UECKERMÜNDE.

Ücker River, Germany: see UECKER RIVER.

Uckfield, former urban district (1931 pop. 3,555), E central Sussex, England, 8 mi. NNE of Lewes; agr. market, with shoe mfg. Has 15th-cent. church.

Uckingen, France: see UCKANGE.

Uclés (ōōklās'), town (pop. 3,517), Cuenca prov., E central Spain, 40 mi. W of Cuenca; agr. center (grain, grapes, sheep). Town is known for its fortress-like monastery (founded by Santiago order), later a Jesuit col. Here Moors defeated (1108) the "Seven Counts" for whom it is named.

Ucluelet (ūklōō'lĭt), village (pop. estimate 350), SW B.C., on SW Vancouver Isl., on Ucluelet Inlet (5 mi. long) of Barkley Sound, 22 mi. SE of Tofino; fishing, farming. Port of entry.

Ucon (ū'kŏn), village (pop. 356), Bonneville co., SE Idaho, 8 mi. NNE of Idaho Falls; alt. 4,801 ft.

Ucria (ōōkrē'ä), village (pop. 3,748), Messina prov., NE Sicily, in Nebrodi Mts., 8 mi. SW of Patti.

Ucú (ōōkōō'), town (pop. 585), Yucatan, SE Mexico, 9 mi. NW of Mérida; henequen.

Uda (ōō'dä), town (pop. 4,718), Nara prefecture, S Honshu, Japan, 17 mi. SSE of Nara; rice, raw silk. Mercury mining.

Udai, river, Ukrainian SSR: see UDAI RIVER.

Udaipur (ōōdī'pōōr). **1** Former princely state (□ 1,045; pop. 118,331) of Chhattisgarh States, India; ⊙ was Dharmjaygarh. Since 1948, inc. into Raigarh dist. of Madhya Pradesh. **2** or **Mewar** (mā'vär), former princely state (□ 13,170; pop. 1,926,698) of Rajputana States, India; ⊙ was Udaipur. Maharanas of Mewar (Sesodia clan) have traditionally ranked highest among Rajput princes. Established c.8th cent. A.D., with ⊙ at CHITOR. Made long, courageous resistance to Moslem invaders. In 1568, ⊙ moved to Udaipur city. Mahratta raids in late-18th and early-19th cent.; treaty with British in 1818. In 1948, merged with union of Rajasthan. Formerly sometimes spelled Oodeypore or Odeypore.

Udaipur. 1 City (pop. 59,648), ⊙ Udaipur dist., S Rajasthan, India, 210 mi. SW of Jaipur, in SE Aravalli Range; agr. market center (corn, wheat, millet, cotton); mfg. of rubber stamps, embroideries; handicraft cloth weaving; asbestos and clay factory. Has col., fine palace. Rail terminus is 3 mi. E. On W edge of city is beautiful Pichola L., with its 2 small isls. (marble palaces), one of which was refuge for Shah Jahan while in revolt against his father, Jahangir. Founded c.1560; became ⊙ state in 1568, after sack of Chitor. Formerly sometimes spelled Oodeypore or Odeypore. Just E is village of Ahar, where stand cenotaphs of many chiefs of Mewar. **2** Town (pop. 7,510), NE Rajasthan, India, 22 mi. ENE of Sikar, in N Aravalli Range; local agr. market (barley, wheat, millet). **3** Village, Tripura, India: see RADHAKISHOREPUR.

Udaipura (ōōdī'pōōrŭ), town (pop. 2,870), E Bhopal state, India, 70 mi. ESE of Bhopal; local agr. market (wheat, cotton, oilseeds).

Udaipur Garhi (ōōdī'pōōr gŭr'hē) or **Udaipur,** town, SE Nepal, in Mahabarat Lekh range, 90 mi. SE of Katmandu; alt. 4,561 ft. Nepalese military station; fort.

Udai River or **Uday River** (ōōdī'), in N central Ukrainian SSR, rises just N of Ichnya, flows 130 mi. SSE, past Priluki, Ladan, and Piryatin, to Sula R. just above Lubny.

Udaiyarpalaiyam or **Udaiyarpalayam** (both: ōōdī"-yŭrpä'lŭyŭm), town (pop. 7,920), Trichinopoly dist., S Madras, India, 45 mi. NE of Trichinopoly; timber (acacias), tanning bark; peanut- and castor-oil extraction, cotton weaving.

Udalguri (ōōdŭl'gōōrē), village, Darrang dist., NW Assam, India, in Brahmaputra valley, 43 mi. WNW of Tezpur; S terminus of shortest trade route from India to Lhasa, Tibet; rice, tea, rape and mustard; mfg. of brass utensils. Large annual fair attended by Tibetans.

Udall (ū'däl"), city (pop. 410), Cowley co., SE Kansas, 23 mi. SSE of Wichita, in grain and cattle area. Oil fields near by.

Udamalpet (ōōdŭmŭl'pĕt), city (pop. 17,791), Coimbatore dist., SW Madras, India, 35 mi. SSE of Coimbatore; cotton-milling and trade center in cotton and sugar-cane area. Road leads through Anaimalai Hills (S) to Travancore-Cochin, serving sandalwood, coffee, and tea plantations. Also spelled Udumalpet.

Udangudi (ōōdŭng'gōōdē), town (pop. 13,184), Tinnevelly dist., S Madras, India, 31 mi. SE of Tinnevelly; betel farms; palmyra. Formerly also Udankudi.

Uda River (ōōdä'). **1** In central Buryat-Mongol Autonomous SSR, Russian SFSR, rises in Yablonovy Range, flows 252 mi. W, past Khorinskoye, to Selenga R. at Ulan-Ude. Receives Kurba (right) R. **2** In Irkutsk oblast and Krasnoyarsk Territory, Russian SFSR: see CHUNA RIVER. **3** In Khabarovsk Territory, Russian SFSR, rises in spur of E Stanovoi Range, flows c.330 mi. ENE to Sea of Okhotsk at Chumikan. Receives Maya R. (left)

Udarny or **Udarnyy** (ōōdär'nē), town (1947 pop. over 500), S Sakhalin, Russian SFSR, 5 mi. NE of Uglegorsk; coal mining. Under Jap. rule (1905–45), called Taihei (tī'hā').

Uday, Udaya, or **Udayadhani,** Thailand: see UTHAITHANI.

Uday, river, Ukrainian SSR: see UDAI RIVER.

Udayagiri (ōōdŭ'yŭgĭrē), village, Nellore dist., E central Madras, India, 55 mi. NW of Nellore; oilseeds, millet. Garnet quarries near by.

Udayagiri, hill, India: see BHILSA, KHANDGIRI.

Udayapur (ōōd'ŭyŭpōōr), village, SE Madhya Bharat, India, 29 mi. NNE of Bhilsa; wheat. Has finely carved 11th-cent. temple, Moslem ruins with inscriptions.

Udaypur, Tripura, India: see RADHAKISHOREPUR.

Uday River, Ukrainian SSR: see UDAI RIVER.

Udbina (ōōd'bēnä), village, W Croatia, Yugoslavia, 20 mi. E of Gospic; local trade center.

Udde, Mongolia: see DZAMYN UDE.

Uddeholm (ŭ'dŭhôlm"), village (pop. 473), Varmland co., SW central Sweden, in Bergslag region, on small tributary of Klar R., 30 mi. NW of Filipstad; seat of one of Sweden's major iron-mining and lumbering concerns.

Uddevalla (ŭ'dŭvä"lä), city (1950 pop. 24,922), Goteborg och Bohus co., SW Sweden, on By Fjord, Swedish *Byfiord* (bü'fyôrd"), inlet of the Skagerrak, 45 mi. N of Goteborg; rail junction; textile and paper milling, wood- and metalworking, stone quarrying, match mfg. Inc. 1498; suffered destruction in Danish-Swedish wars.

Uddingston, town in Bothwell parish, N Lanark, Scotland, on the Clyde and 2 mi. NNW of Bothwell; coal mining, iron founding, and mfg. of agr. machinery.

Udd Island, Russian SFSR: see CHKALOV ISLAND.

Uddjaur, Lake (ŭd'your"), expansion (□ 92) of Skellefte R., Lapland, N Sweden, 100 mi. W of Boden; 30 mi. long, 1–6 mi. wide. Connected with lakes Hornavan (NW) and Storavan (SE).

Ude, Mongolia: see DZAMYN UDE.

Udell (ūdĕl', ū'dĕl), town (pop. 96), Appanoose co., S Iowa, near source of Fox R., 8 mi. ENE of Centerville, in bituminous-coal-mining area.

Uden (ü'dŭn), town (pop. 4,644), North Brabant prov., E central Netherlands, 13 mi. ESE of 's Hertogenbosch; cattle market; synthetic fertilizer.

Udenhout (ü'dŭnhout), agr. village (pop. 2,853), North Brabant prov., S Netherlands, 5 mi. NNE of Tilburg.

Udgir (ōōdgēr'), town (pop. 11,238), Bidar dist., W central Hyderabad state, India, on railroad and 45 mi. NNW of Bidar; road center; cotton ginning; millet, oilseeds, rice, tobacco. Has 15th-cent. fort.

Udhampur (ōōdäm'pōōr), district (□ 908; pop. 113,013), Jammu prov., SW Kashmir; ⊙ Udhampur. In S Punjab Himalayas; drained by Chenab R. Agr. (corn, wheat, barley, rice, oilseeds, gram); extensive fruit orchards. Main towns: Udhampur, Ramnagar. Original dist. (□ 5,070; 1941 pop. 294,217) reduced in late 1940s to form new dist. of Doda. Prevailing mother tongue, Dogri.

Udhampur, town (pop. 4,666), ⊙ Udhampur dist., SW Kashmir, in S Punjab Himalayas, 20 mi. NE of Jammu; trades in corn, wheat, barley, fruit. Palace. Founded 19th cent.

Udi (ōō'dē), town, Onitsha prov., Eastern Provinces, S Nigeria, 10 mi. SSW of Enugu; coal mining.

Udine (ōō'dēnē), province (□ 2,766; pop. 721,670), FRIULI-VENEZIA GIULIA, NE Italy, bordering on Austria and Yugoslavia (N), and the Adriatic; ⊙ Udine. Terrain ranges from Carnic Alps in N to extensive plain in S. Watered by Tagliamento, Livenza, Fella, and Degano rivers. Agr. (cereals, raw silk, grapes, tobacco); cattle raising; forestry. Zinc and lead mines at Cave del Predil. Mfg. at Pordenone, Udine, Cividale del Friuli, Gemona del Friuli, and Sacile. Officially called Friuli prov. from 1923 to c.1945.

Udine, city (pop. 54,638), ⊙ Friuli-Venezia Giulia and Udine prov., NE Italy, 65 mi. NE of Venice, on an extensive plain; 46°3'N 13°14'E. Industrial and transportation center; mfg. (automobile chassis, machinery, aluminum, cotton and hemp textiles, furniture, glass, macaroni, paper, pharmaceuticals, cement). Archbishopric. Has cathedral consecrated 1335 (damaged by bombs), 16th-cent. archiepiscopal palace with frescoes by Tiepolo, town hall (1448–56), clock tower (1527), and Renaissance fountain. Castle, former seat of patriarchs and Venetian governors, stands in center on a hill; rebuilt starting 1517. In 13th cent. capital of patriarchs of Aquileia; in 1420 conquered by Venice. Passed to Austrians in 1797 by Treaty of Campo Formio; united with Italy 1866. Hq. of Ital. army 1915–17. Bombed (1944–45) in Second World War.

Udipi (ōō'dĭpē), city (pop. 18,043), South Kanara dist., W Madras, India, near Malabar Coast of Arabian Sea, 34 mi. N of Mangalore; rice and sugar milling, fish curing (sardines, mackerel), sandal-oil distilling. Tile factory 3 mi. W, at small port of Malpe; lighthouse; fishery.

Udjung, Indonesia: see SURABAYA.

Udmurt Autonomous Soviet Socialist Republic (ōōd'mōōrt), administrative division (□ 16,300; 1939 pop. 1,220,007) of E central European Russian SFSR; ⊙ Izhevsk. In highlands bet. Kama and Vyatka rivers; drained by Izh, Kilmez, and Cheptsa rivers. Humid continental climate (short summers). Scattered quartz sand, limestone, and peat deposits. Extensive agr., with flax (center, N), rye, oats, potatoes, wheat (SE); livestock (S, W). Industries based on agr. (flax processing, tanning, food processing and preserving), timber (lumber floating, sawmilling), and mineral resources (glass and brick mfg.). Iron smelting and heavy mfg. (Izhevsk, Votkinsk); light mfg. (Sarapul, Glazov, Mozhga). Pop. 52% Udmurts, 43% Russians, 2% Tatars. The Udmurts (formerly called Votyak or Votiak) are a Finnic group of Rus. culture and Greek Orthodox religion; dominated (13th–15th cent.) by the Golden Horde; colonized (16th cent.) by Russians. Area became Votyak Autonomous Oblast in 1920; renamed Udmurt in 1932; gained present status in 1934. Was part of Nizhegorod (Gorki) territory (1929–36).

Udny (ŭd′nē), agr. village and parish (pop. 1,475), E Aberdeen, Scotland, 5 mi. E of Old Meldrum. Modern Udny Castle incorporates remains of earlier structure.

Udo (ōō′dō), village (pop. 3,327), Miyazaki prefecture, SE Kyushu, Japan, on Philippine Sea, 19 mi. S of Miyazaki; rice, lumber. Fishing. Seat of natl. shrine dedicated to father of Jimmu, 1st emperor of Japan.

Udobnaya (ōōdôb′nīŭ), village (1926 pop. 7,752), SE Krasnodar Territory, Russian SFSR, in N foothill of the Greater Caucasus, on Urup R. and 60 mi. SSE of Armavir, on road to Cherkessk; flour mill; wheat, sunflowers, sunn and ambary hemp.

Udomlya (ōō′dŭmlyŭ), village (1948 pop. over 2,000), N Kalinin oblast, Russian SFSR, 35 mi. E of Bologoye; peat works, sawmill.

Udon or **Udonthani** (ōō′dôn′tä′nē′), town (1947 pop. 11,995), ⊙ Udon prov. (□ 4,598; 1947 pop. 382,564), NE Thailand, 300 mi. NE of Bangkok; communications center of N Korat Plateau; rail terminus; projected extensions to Mekong R. (Laos line) at Khonkaen and Nakhon Phanom; rice, cotton, sugar cane, sericulture, lac. Also spelled Udorn, Utara and Uttara. Local name, Mak Khaeng.

Udong, Cambodia: see OUDONG.

Udorn, Thailand: see UDON.

Udot, Caroline Isls.: see TRUK.

Udumalpet, India: see UDAMALPET.

Udych (ōō′dĭch), village (1926 pop. 801), SE Vinnitsa oblast, Ukrainian SSR, 15 mi. WSW of Uman; sugar mill.

Udzhary (ōōjä′rē), city (1948 pop. over 2,000), central Azerbaijan SSR, rail station (9 mi. SSW) of Geokchai; cotton-ginning center; sericulture.

Uea, Wallis Isls.: see UVEA.

Uebi Scebeli, Ethiopia and Ital. Somaliland: see SHEBELI, WEBI.

Ueckermünde or **Ückermünde** (both: ü″kŭrmün′dŭ), town (pop. 11,177), in former Prussian Pomerania prov., N Germany, after 1945 in Mecklenburg, fishing port on Uecker R. just above its mouth on Stettin Lagoon, and 30 mi. NW of Stettin; agr. market (grain, potatoes, sugar beets, stock); brick- and tileworks. In peat region.

Uecker River or **Ücker River** (both: ü′kŭr), N Germany, rises c.10 mi. SSW of Prenzlau, flows 64 mi. N, through small Upper and Lower Uecker lakes, past Prenzlau, Pasewalk, and Torgelow, to Stettin Lagoon just N of Ueckermünde. Navigable in lower course. Formerly sometimes Üker.

Ueda (ōōä′dä). **1** Town (pop. 9,115), Fukushima prefecture, central Honshu, Japan, on the Pacific, 11 mi. SW of Taira; mulberry and rice fields. **2** City (1940 pop. 35,069; 1947 pop. 41,773), Nagano prefecture, central Honshu, Japan, on Shinano R. and 18 mi. SSE of Nagano; sericulture center; spinning mills. Hot-springs resorts near by.

Uegit (wĕgēt′), village, in the Upper Juba, SW Ital. Somaliland, 55 mi. NW of Isha Baidoa; water hole. Its wells are inhabited by blind fish.

Uehling (ū′lĭng), village (pop. 250), Dodge co., E Nebr., 20 mi. N of Fremont and on Logan Creek.

Ueki (ōōä′kē). **1** Town (pop. 4,793), Fukuoka prefecture, N Kyushu, Japan, 8 mi. SW of Yawata; coal mining. **2** Town (pop. 2,216), Kumamoto prefecture, W Kyushu, Japan, 6 mi. N of Kumamoto; lumber (pine).

Uele, district, Belgian Congo: see BUTA.

Uelen (ōōyĭlyĕn′), village (1948 pop. over 500), NE Chukchi Natl. Okrug, Kamchatka oblast, Khabarovsk Territory, Russian SFSR, near Cape Dezhnev, 380 mi. ENE of Anadyr; govt. arctic station; trading post, airfield.

Uele River (wĕ′lä), main headstream of Ubangi R., in NE and N Belgian Congo; rises as the Kibali on the Congo-Nile divide 27 mi. W of Mahagi, flows c.180 mi. N and NW, past Tora, to Dungu where it receives Dungu R. and becomes the Uele, flowing in a meandering course W, past Niangara, Bambili, and Bondo, to join Bomu R. at Yakoma, forming the Ubangi; total length, c.700 mi. Receives Bomokandi R. Uele R. drains a major cotton-producing area; Kibali R. region is noted for its extensive goldfields. Upper course of Uele was discovered (1870) by Schweinfurth; confluence with Bomu R. was explored in 1884. Also spelled Welle.

Uelkal or **Velkal** (ōōyĭlkäl′, vyĭl–), village (1948 pop. over 500), E Chukchi Natl. Okrug, Kamchatka oblast, Khabarovsk Territory, Russian SFSR, on Anadyr Gulf of Bering Sea, 110 mi. NE of Anadyr; airfield, trading post.

Uelzen or **Ülzen** (both: ül′tsŭn), town (pop. 20,614), in former Prussian prov. of Hanover, NW Germany, after 1945 in Lower Saxony, on the Ilmenau and 21 mi. SSE of Lüneburg; rail center and transshipment point; repair shops. Mfg. of agr. machinery, electrical motors, concrete structures, asbestos, garments; food processing (sugar, cheese, preserves, beer, spirits). Has Gothic church, priory, and Holy Ghost chapel. First mentioned 972. Chartered 1270. Scene (April, 1945) of heavy fighting in Second World War.

Ueno (ōōā′nō). **1** Town (pop. 15,152), Aichi prefecture, central Honshu, Japan, on NE shore of Ise Bay, just S of Nagoya; agr. center (rice, wheat); raw silk, textiles; poultry. **2** City (1940 pop. 20,780; 1947 pop. 39,373), Mie prefecture, S Honshu, Japan, 40 mi. E of Osaka; mfg. center (Panama hats, umbrellas, sake, soy sauce, drugs, wood products); raw silk, terra cotta.

Uenohara (ōōā′-nō′härŭ), town (pop. 8,735), Yamanashi prefecture, central Honshu, Japan, 13 mi. W of Hachioji; rice, raw silk.

Uenzerich (wĕnzĕrēk′), Fr. *Ouenzerig* or *Ouenzeriq*, village (pop. 1,150), central Fezzan, Libya, on road and 65 mi. WNW of Sebha, in a Saharan oasis; dates, cereals, vegetables.

Uerdingen, Germany: see KREFELD.

Ueschinen (ü′shēnŭn), valley in Bernese Alps SW central Switzerland, 10 mi. N of Leuk; alt. 5,000–6,500 ft.

Uetendorf (ü′tŭndôrf), town (pop. 2,185), Bern canton, W central Switzerland, 3 mi. NW of Thun; flour.

Uetersen, Germany: see ÜTERSEN.

Uetikon (ü′tĭkôn), town (pop. 2,174), Zurich canton, N Switzerland, 10 mi. SE of Zurich; chemicals.

Ufa (ōōfä′), city (1939 pop. 245,863), ⊙ Bashkir Autonomous SSR, Russian SFSR, on right bank of the Belaya, at Ufa R. mouth, and 715 mi. E of Moscow; 54°44′N 55°56′E. River port (grain and lumber exports); rail junction (3 lines); industrial center; mfg. (airplanes, mining machinery, cables, typewriters, clothing, shoes, leather goods), food processing (flour, meat, dairy products), cotton milling; clay refractory. Gypsum and limestone deposits on banks of Belaya R. Cultural center of Bashkirs; aviation, medical, agr., and teachers colleges, research institutes. Has revolutionary, regional, and art museums, noted old cathedral, Palace of Labor and Art, and monument to Lenin. City includes Dema (since 1944; rail junction; locomotive and car repair shops) and Kirzhak (port on left bank of Belaya R.; shipyards), and adjoins CHERNIKOVSK (NE industrial suburb until 1944). Founded 1586 as Rus. stronghold. Became commercial center of trade route to Siberia; developed following building of Samara (now Kuibyshev)-Zlatoust RR (1888). Was ⊙ Ufa govt. until 1919; ⊙ Bashkir Autonomous SSR since 1922. Rus. writer Aksakov b. here, 1791.

Ufa River (ōōfä′), E European Russian SFSR, rises on N slope of the S Urals, in small lake just E of Karabash; flows NNW past Nyazepetrovsk, and SSW past Krasnoufimsk, Sarana, Karaidel (head of navigation), and Krasny Klyuch, to Belaya R. at Ufa; length, 599 mi. Navigable for c.300 mi.; used for lumber floating for c.500 mi. Receives Bisert and Tyui (right), Ai and Yuryuzan (left) rivers; all used for lumber floating.

Ufenau, Switzerland: see ZURICH, LAKE OF.

Uffculme (ŭf′kŭm), town and parish (pop. 1,672), E Devon, England, on Culme R. and 7 mi. E of Tiverton; agr. market; woolen mills. Has 13th-cent. church.

Uffenheim (ōō′fŭnhīm), town (pop. 3,919), Middle Franconia, W Bavaria, Germany, 9 mi. WNW of Windsheim; machinery mfg., woodworking, brewing, lumber and flour milling. Portions of medieval walls and towers still stand. Chartered c.1349. Limestone quarries in area.

Uffington, England: see WHITE HORSE VALE.

Ufipa Plateau (ōōfē′pä), SW Tanganyika, bet. lakes Tanganyika and Rukwa; rises to 6,000 ft. Coal deposits. Main town, Sumbawanga.

Ufra (ōōfrä′), town (1939 pop. over 500), W Ashkhabad oblast, Turkmen SSR, on Krasnovodsk Gulf, 4 mi. E (under jurisdiction) of Krasnovodsk; fisheries.

Ugalla River, Tanganyika: see MALAGARASI RIVER.

Uganda (ūgăn′dŭ), British protectorate (□ 93,981, including 13,689 sq. mi. of lakes; pop. 4,937,712), E central Africa, N of L. Victoria; ⊙ Entebbe. Bounded N by Anglo-Egyptian Sudan, E by Kenya, S by Tanganyika (N section of L. Victoria, with Sese isls., belongs to Uganda), SW by Ruanda-Urundi and W by Belgian Congo. Situated in E African plateau, territory is crossed by W Great Rift Valley which, along W frontier, forms a deep trench occupied by lakes Albert, Edward, and George. Outstanding mts. rising above the savanna-covered tableland (3–6,000 ft. high) are RUWENZORI (16,795 ft.), bet. lakes Albert and Edward, volcanic Mt. ELGON (14,178 ft.), along Kenya border, and the northernmost peaks of volcanic VIRUNGA range (SW). Uganda is drained by the headwaters of the White Nile; the VICTORIA NILE issues from L. Victoria, descends Ripon Falls and Owen Falls, crosses swampy, many-armed L. KYOGA, and enters L. Albert below MURCHISON FALLS; the Albert Nile, leaving L. Albert just W of Victoria Nile's influx, flows N entering Anglo-Egyptian Sudan at Nimule. Most of Uganda's rainfall is concentrated in 2 rainy seasons (March-May, Sept.-Nov.) and averages 40–55 in. a year. Higher figures are recorded in central lakes area, lower ones in NE highlands. Temperatures, decreasing with alt., show little seasonal variation; mean yearly temp. at Entebbe 71°F.; diurnal range c.20°F. Game, especially the elephant and the buffalo, is found everywhere; crocodiles and hippopotami abound in rivers and along marshy lake shores. Much of Uganda's soil is fertile; chief commercial crops are cotton, coffee, sugar, tobacco, tea, rubber, sisal. Principal native food crops are bananas, millet, sweet potatoes; corn, rice, chilies, yams, peanuts, and some wheat are also grown. Most of pop. is engaged in agr., except for semi-nomadic pastoral tribes in drier NE. Cotton lint and cottonseed, which represent over 60% of exports, are grown entirely by natives. European estates grow coffee, rubber, and tea. Territory has diversified mineral deposits (gold, tin, tungsten, mica, copper, tantalite-columbite, phosphates) but only tin (at Kikagati and Mwirasandu) and apatite (near Tororo) are commercially exploited. Cotton ginning, sugar milling, alcohol distilling, coffee curing, and cigarette mfg. are only important industries. A cement plant was completed at Tororo in 1949. Power from OWEN FALLS hydroelectric plant (begun 1949 in conjunction with a dam for long-range storage of Nile waters in L. Victoria) is planned to spur industrial development. Principal commercial centers are Kampala (terminus of railroad from Mombasa, Kenya) and Jinja. Entebbe, the capital, is only a residential town for Br. officials. Soroti (near E end of L. Kyoga) is terminus of rail spur from Tororo. There are 2,500 mi. of all-weather roads; airports at Kampala and Entebbe. Both L. Victoria and L. Albert have steamship service. The Victoria Nile is navigated in L. Kyoga section bet. Namasagali and Masindi Port; the Albert Nile is navigable throughout its length in Uganda. The African pop. is divided into 4 groups, the Bantu (majority), Nilotic, Nilo-hamitic, and Sudanian tribes. The chief native language is Luganda (spoken by inhabitants of Kingdom of Buganda); Swahili is widely understood. In 1948, there were 7,565 Europeans (including 4,020 Polish refugees) and 33,856 Indians in Uganda. John Speke (1862), Samuel Baker (1864), and Henry Stanley (1875) were among 1st Europeans to explore the region, thus discovering the source of the Nile. Anglican missionaries arrived in 1877 and were followed in 1879 by Fr. Catholic missionaries. Following a period of civil strife fostered by religious factions, Arab traders and native Moslems destroyed the missions (1888) and briefly held the comparatively civilized native Kingdom of Buganda. By Anglo-Ger. agreement of 1890, Uganda came under Br. influence and Lord Lugard brought the Baganda (inhabitants of Buganda) under control of Br. East Africa Co. Br. protectorate over Buganda was proclaimed in 1894, and to it were added (1896) several adjoining regions, thus forming present area of Uganda. Territory is ruled by an appointed governor with the aid of an executive and a legislative council. It is administratively divided into 4 provs.: Eastern (⊙ Jinja), Northern (⊙ Gulu), Western (⊙ Masindi), and Buganda (⊙ Kampala; under terms of Uganda Agreement of 1900, Buganda has a self-governing native administration headed by the Kabaka or king). The technical services (railroads, mail, customs, statistical services, etc.) of Uganda are coordinated with those of neighboring Tanganyika and Kenya under an administrative body called the East Africa High Commission (established 1948), composed of the governors of the 3 territories; administrative hq. are at Nairobi.

Ugarchin (ōōgŭrchĕn′), village (pop. 8,035), Pleven dist., N Bulgaria, 15 mi. W of Lovech; cattle market; flour milling; dairying, truck gardening.

Ugarit (ōōgŭrēt′), anc. city, ⊙ Ugarit kingdom, W Syria, on whose site is modern locality of Ras Shamra, just N of Latakia. The remains, discovered c.1930, have yielded valuable historical information. The anc. city dates from at least 5th millennium B.C.

Ugaro (ōōgä′rō), village, Agordat div., W Eritrea, near Gash R., 30 mi. SW of Barentu; chief gold-mining center of Eritrea; has gold-ore-treatment plant.

Ugarteche (ōōgärtā′chā), town (pop. estimate 600), N Mendoza prov., Argentina, on railroad and 23 mi. S of Mendoza, in irrigated area (potatoes, corn, wheat, alfalfa, wine, fruit, livestock); wine making, sawmilling.

Ugashik (ūgă′shĭk), village (pop. 46), SW Alaska, on Alaska Peninsula, on Ugashik R. and 6 mi. E of Pilot Point; fishing; fish cannery.

Ugborough (ŭg'bŭrŭ), town and parish (pop. 1,845), S Devon, England, 12 mi. E of Plymouth; agr. market. Has 14th-cent. church.

Ugento (o͞ojĕn'tô), town (pop. 5,114), Lecce prov., Apulia, S Italy, 13 mi. SE of Gallipoli; wine, olive oil. Bishopric.

Ugie (ū'gē), village (pop. 1,708), E Cape Prov., U. of So. Afr., in Griqualand East dist. of the Transkeain Territories, in Drakensberg range, 40 mi. NW of Umtata; stock, grain.

Ugie River, Aberdeen, Scotland, rises SW of New Aberdour, flows 21 mi. SE to the North Sea just N of Peterhead.

Ugíjar (o͞ohē'här), city (pop. 2,077), Granada prov., S Spain, in Alpujarras region, 24 mi. SSE of Guadix; silk spinning center. Olive-oil processing; stock raising, lumbering; cereals, oranges, figs, honey. Gold and quicksilver mining near by. Scene of a Moriscos rising (1568).

Ugine or **Ugines** (üzhēn'), town (pop. 4,232), Savoie dept., SE France, near the Arly, 6 mi. N of Albertville, in Savoy Alps; steel-milling center (electric furnaces).

Uglegorsk (o͞oglyĭgôrsk'), city (1940 pop. 35,115), S Sakhalin, Russian SFSR, on Tatar Strait, 125 mi. S of Aleksandrovsk; coal-mining center; pulp and paper mill, brickworks. Coal mining at Udarny (NE). Under Jap. rule (1905–45), called Esutoru (ĕso͞otō'ro͞o).

Ugleuralsk, Russian SFSR: see POLOVINKA.

Uglezavodsk (o͞oglyĭzŭvôdsk'), town, S Sakhalin, Russian SFSR, near E coast, in Naiba R. valley, near Bykov; coal mining. Under Japanese rule (1905–45) called Higashi-naibuchi.

Uglezhzheniye [Rus.,=charcoal burning], Russian SFSR: see SEROV; FILKINO.

Ugliano, island, Yugoslavia: see ULJAN ISLAND.

Uglich (o͞o'glyĭch), city (1945 pop. over 20,000), W Yaroslavl oblast, Russian SFSR, port on Volga R. and 55 mi. W of Yaroslavl; rail terminus; food-processing (cheese), woolen milling; paper- and sawmilling. Large hydroelectric station (completed 1941) with reservoir (SW). Castle (built 1481–83), where Dmitri, son of Ivan the Terrible, allegedly was murdered (1591), is now a mus. Has church of Holy Dmitri (1692) and 14th-cent. monastery. City dates from 1148; became ⊙ principality, which passed 1364 to Moscow; flourished in late-16th cent. (pop. c.40,000); declined after destruction (1609) by Poles. **Uglich Upland** lies SE of Uglich, bet. Volga R. and L. Nero; rises to 660 ft.

Ugljevik or **Uglyevik** (o͞o'glyĕvĭk), lignite-mining center in NE Bosnia, Yugoslavia, 18 mi. NE of Tuzla.

Uglovka (o͞o'glŭfkŭ), town (1926 pop. 794), E Novgorod oblast, Russian SFSR, 17 mi. SW of Borovichi; rail junction; limestone and peat works.

Uglovoye (o͞oglŭvoi'ŭ), town (1943 pop. over 500), SW Maritime Territory, Russian SFSR, on Trans-Siberian RR, 6 mi. SW (under jurisdiction) of Artem; lignite mining.

Uglovskoye (o͞o'glŭfskŭyŭ), village (1948 pop. over 500), W Altai Territory, Russian SFSR, on small L. Lyapunikha and 45 mi. WSW of Rubtsovsk, in agr. area.

Ugodski Zavod or **Ugodskiy Zavod** (o͞ogôt'skē zŭvôt'), village (1939 pop. over 500), NE Kaluga oblast, Russian SFSR, 11 mi. E of Maloyaroslavets; metalworks.

Ugolnaya or **Ugol'naya** (o͞o'gŭlnŭ), rail station, S Maritime Territory, Russian SFSR, 15 mi. N of Vladivostok; junction of Trans-Siberian RR and branch line to Suchan and Nakhodka.

Ugolny or **Ugol'nyy** (o͞o'gŭlnē). **1** Town (1946 pop. over 500), SE Chukchi Natl. Okrug, Kamchatka oblast, Khabarovsk Territory, Russian SFSR, on Anadyr Gulf, 135 mi. SSE of Anadyr; coal mining. **2** Town (1947 pop. over 500), S Sakhalin, Russian SFSR, on slope of W range, 7 mi. E of Tomari; coal mining. Under Jap. rule (1905–45), called Taiei. **3** Town, Sverdlovsk oblast, Russian SFSR: see KARPINSK.

Ugolnye Kopi, Russian SFSR: see KOPEISK.

Ugra River (o͞ogrä'), W central European Russian SFSR, rises in Smolensk-Moscow Upland SE of Yelnya, flows c.230 mi. generally E, past Yukhnov, to Oka R. 5 mi. W of Kaluga.

Ugwashi Uku, Nigeria: see OGWASHI UKU.

Uh, river, Ukrainian SSR and Czechoslovakia: see UZH RIVER, Transcarpathian Oblast.

Uharie River (ūwô'rē), central N.C., rises in short headstreams joining S of High Point, flows c.60 mi. S to Pee Dee R. SE of Badin, bet. Badin and Tillery lakes. Sometimes spelled Uwharrie.

Uherske Hradiste (o͞o'hĕrskā hrä'dĭshtyĕ), Czech *Uherské Hradiště*, Ger. *Ungarisch-Hradisch* (o͞ong'-gärĭsh-hrä'dĭsh), town (pop. 7,617; urban commune pop. 16,202), E Moravia, Czechoslovakia, on left bank of Morava R., on railroad and 14 mi. SW of Gottwaldov. Agr., trade, and cultural center of MORAVIAN SLOVAKIA; sugar, malt, confectionery, soap; woodworking. Horse and cattle fairs held here. Has 17th-cent. Franciscan abbey, old town hall with spire, new town hall with noted frescoes, well-known ethnographic mus. Founded 1257.

Uhersky Brod (-skē brôt″), Czech *Uherský Brod*, Ger. *Ungarisch Brod* (o͞ong'gärĭsh brōt″), town (pop. 6,457), E Moravia, Czechoslovakia, 13 mi. S of Gottwaldov; rail junction; agr. trade center of MORAVIAN SLOVAKIA. Has noted ethnographic mus. J. A. Comenius b. here.

Uhersky Ostroh (ô'strô), Czech *Uherský Ostroh*, Ger. *Ungarisch-Ostra* (o͞ong'gärĭsh-ô'strä), town (pop. 766; commune pop. 4,269), E Moravia, Czechoslovakia, on Morava R., on railroad and 20 mi. SW of Gottwaldov; agr. trade center (wheat, barley, sugar beets, potatoes). Former fort against Magyar incursions. Picturesque Moravian-Slovakian fairs held near by in summer display wealth of regional folklore.

Uhingen (o͞o'ĭng-ŭn), village (pop. 5,405), N Württemberg, Germany, after 1945 in Württemberg-Baden, on the Fils and 3 mi. W of Göppingen; grain, cattle.

Uhlava River (o͞o'lävä), Czech *Úhlava*, SW Bohemia, Czechoslovakia, rises in Bohemian Forest 4 mi. NNW of Zelezna Ruda, flows c.45 mi. generally N, past Nyrsko, to Radbuza R. in S outskirts of Pilsen.

Ühlfeld (ül'fĕlt), village (pop. 1,240), Middle Franconia, W Bavaria, Germany, on the Aisch and 9 mi. NE of Neustadt; beer.

Uhlirske Janovice (o͞o'hlĕrshskā yä'nôvĭtsĕ), Czech *Uhlířské Janovice*, town (pop. 1,853), central Bohemia, Czechoslovakia, on railroad and 10 mi. SW of Kutna Hora; sugar beets, wheat, potatoes.

Uhl River (o͞ol), in NE Punjab and N central Himachal Pradesh, India, rises in SE Punjab Himalayas, 17 mi. ENE of Palampur; flows c.55 mi. SSE to Beas R. 4 mi. E of Mandi. Dam 3 mi. NNE of Jogindarnagar supplies town's hydroelectric plant.

Uhrichsville (yo͞o'rĭksvĭl), city (pop. 6,614), Tuscarawas co., E Ohio, 8 mi. SE of New Philadelphia and on Stillwater Creek; makes sewer pipe, pottery, china, brick, cigars; coal mining. Settled 1804; platted 1833; inc. 1921 as city.

Uhrineves (o͞o'hŭrzhĕnyĕvĕs), Czech *Uhříněves*, village (pop. 4,581), E central Bohemia, Czechoslovakia, on railroad and 9 mi. SE of Prague; sugar beets, wheat, potatoes. Large botanical gardens at near-by Pruhonice (pro͞o'hônyĭtsĕ), Czech *Průhonice*.

Uhrovec, Czechoslovakia: see BANOVCE NAD BEBRAVOU.

Ui, river, Russian SFSR: see UI RIVER.

Ui, Tibet: see WEI.

Uichi or **Uychi** (o͞o″ēchē'), village (1939 pop. over 2,000), E Namangan oblast, Uzbek SSR, 8 mi. ENE of Namangan; cotton; metalworks.

Uíge or **Uíje** (wē'zhā), town (pop. 1,474), ⊙ Congo prov. and Uíge dist. (pop. 263,279), NW Angola, 150 mi. NE of Luanda; alt. c.3,000 ft. Coffee center. Also produces almonds, raffia, beans. Prov. ⊙ transferred here 1946 from Luanda.

Uigursai or **Uygursay** (o͞o″ēgo͞orsī'), mining town (1947 pop. over 500), SW Namangan oblast, Uzbek SSR, on short river Uigur-Sai (tributary of the Syr Darya), near Pap.

Uíje, Angola: see UÍGE.

Uijongbu (o͞o'ē'jŭng'bo͞o'), Jap. *Giseifu*, town (1949 pop. 21,816). Kyonggi prov., central Korea, S of 38°N, 12 mi. NNE of Seoul; agr. center (soy beans, millet).

Uiju (o͞o'ē'jo͞o'), Jap. *Gishu*, township (1944 pop. 27,378), N.Pyongan prov., N Korea, on Yalu R. and 9 mi. NE of Sinuiju, in gold-mining and agr. area (rice, wheat, soy beans); cotton textiles. Provincial ⊙ until 1923, supplanted by Sinuiju.

Uil (o͞oēl'), village (1948 pop. over 2,000), W Aktyubinsk oblast, Kazakh SSR, on Uil R. (intermittent steppe stream) and 140 mi. SW of Aktyubinsk, in petroleum area; dairying. Gypsum quarries near by.

Uinamarca, Lake (wēnämär'kä), or **Lake Uinaimarca** (wēnī–), SE part (□ 15 mi. long, 35 mi. wide) of L. TITICACA, in SE Peru and W Bolivia. Also Huañamarca, Wuiñaimarca, Wiñaymarca, Winamarca.

Uinkaret Plateau (ū″ĭng'kărĕt″), Mohave co., NW Ariz., extends c.50 mi. N from Colorado R. bet. Kanab and Shivwits plateaus. Mt. TRUMBULL (8,028 ft.) and Mt. EMMA (7,698 ft.) are in S.

Uinskoye (o͞oēn'skŭyŭ), village (1948 pop. over 2,000), SE Molotov oblast, Russian SFSR, 50 mi. SE of Osa; flax processing, lumbering; livestock.

Uinta (ūĭn'tŭ), county (□ 2,070; pop. 7,331), SW Wyo.; ⊙ Evanston. Livestock, grain region, bounded S and W by Utah; watered by branches of Green R. Coal, oil. Foothills of Uinta Mts. in S. Formed 1869.

Uintah (ūĭn'tŭ), county (□ 4,420; pop. 10,300), NE Utah; ⊙ Vernal. Mtn. and plateau area crossed by Green R., bordering on Colo. Part of Dinosaur Natl. Monument in NE, of Ashley Natl. Forest in NW. Livestock; oil, asphalt. Formed 1850.

Uintah, town (pop. 317), Weber co., N Utah, 5 mi. SE of Ogden.

Uinta Mountains (ūĭn'tŭ), range of Rocky Mts. in NE Utah and SW Wyo.; extend E from Wasatch Range through sections of Wasatch and Ashley natl. forests. Chief peaks: Marsh Peak (12,219 ft.), Hayden Peak (12,473 ft.), Tokewanna Peak (13,173 ft.), Mt. Lovenia (13,227 ft.), Gilbert Peak (13,422 ft.), Mt. Emmons (13,428 ft.), and KINGS PEAK (13,498 ft.), highest point in state. Range includes High Uintas Primitive Area (□ 381) set aside (1931) by U.S. Forest Service. Bear R. rises near Hayden Peak.

Uinta River, E Utah, rises near Mt. Emmons in Uinta Mts., flows c.50 mi. generally SE to Duchesne R. 20 mi. SW of Vernal.

Uioara-de-Sus (o͞oyo͞oä'rä-dā-so͞os'), Hung. *Felsőmarosújvár* (fĕl'shûmôrôsho͞o″ēvär), village (pop. 1,131), Cluj prov., central Rumania, on Mures R. and 25 mi. NNW of Alba-Iulia; mfg. of chemicals.

Ui River or **Uy River** (o͞o'ē), SW Siberian Russian SFSR, rises on E slope of the S Urals, NNE of Iremel mtn.; flows SE past Uiskoye, and generally ENE past Troitsk and Karakulskoye, to Tobol R. just E of Ust-Uiskoye; c.250 mi. long. Receives Toguzak (right) and Uvelka (left) rivers.

Uiskoye or **Uyskoye** (o͞o'ēskŭyŭ), village (1939 pop. over 2,000), W Chelyabinsk oblast, Russian SFSR, on Ui R. and 30 mi. W of Plast; dairying; grain, livestock. Regional mus. Gold placers near by.

Uisong (o͞o'ē'sŭng'), Jap. *Gijo*, town (1949 pop. 20,182), N.Kyongsang prov., S Korea, 34 mi. NNE of Taegu; agr. (rice, soy beans, cotton, ramie, tobacco), gold and copper mining.

Uist, North, and **South Uist** (ū'ĭst, o͞o'ĭst), islands of Outer Hebrides, Scotland: see NORTH UIST and SOUTH UIST. The term The Uists is sometimes used to refer collectively to North Uist, South Uist, and Benbecula.

Uitenhage (oi'tŭnhä″khŭ), town (pop. 26,520), S Cape Prov., U. of So. Afr., on Zwartkops R. and 17 mi. NW of Port Elizabeth; auto assembly, woolen milling and processing, railroad workshops, tire mfg. Site of Dower Memorial Training School; botanical gardens. Airport. Founded 1804.

Uitgeest (oit'khāst), village (pop. 3,927), North Holland prov., NW Netherlands, on Alkmaar L. and 8 mi. NW of Zaandam; mfg. (wood, dairy products, milk sugar), cattle raising, flower growing.

Uithoorn (oit'hōrn), town (pop. 2,380), North Holland prov., W Netherlands, on Amstel R. and 11 mi. SSW of Amsterdam; mfg. (coal-tar products, upholstering materials), meat packing.

Uithuizen (oit'hoiz″ŭn), town (pop. 3,353), Groningen prov., N Netherlands, 14 mi. NNE of Groningen; drainage pipes, cement blocks, mustard.

Uitkijk (oit'kīk), village, Surinam dist., N Du. Guiana, on Saramacca R. and 13 mi. WSW of Paramaribo, in coffee and rice region.

Ujae (o͞ojī'), atoll (pop. 243), Ralik Chain, Kwajalein dist., Marshall Isls., W central Pacific, 120 mi. W of Kwajalein; 30 mi. long; 14 islets. Sometimes spelled Uyae.

Ujain, India: see UJJAIN.

Ujarad, Rumania: see ARADUL-NOU.

Ujarasugssuk (o͞oyäräso͞okh'sho͞ok), fishing and hunting settlement (pop. 65), Ritenbenk dist., W Greenland, on E Disko isl., on the Vaigat, 30 mi. WNW of Ritenbenk; 69°52'N 52°26'W.

Ujarrás or **Ujarraz,** Costa Rica: see PARAÍSO.

Ujazd (o͞o'yäst), Ger. *Bischofstal* (bĭ'shôfs-täl), town (1939 pop. 2,196; 1946 pop. 2,986) in Upper Silesia, after 1945 in Opole prov., S Poland, on Klodnica R. (Gliwice Canal) and 16 mi. WNW of Gleiwitz (Gliwice); agr. market (grain, potatoes, livestock). Church (pilgrimage center). Until 1936, called Ujest.

Ujbanya, Czechoslovakia: see NOVA BANA.

Ujdombovar (o͞o'ĭdômbôvär), Hung. *Újdombóvár*, town (pop. 5,568), Tolna co., SW central Hungary, just E of Dombovar; woolen mills, vegetable canneries, distilleries, lumberyards.

Ujegyhaz, Rumania: see NOCHRICH.

Ujelang (o͞o'jĕläng'), atoll (pop. 136), Kwajalein dist., Ralik Chain, Marshall Isls., W central Pacific, 430 mi. WNW of Kwajalein; 9°46'N 160°59'E; 11 mi. long, 3 mi. wide; 32 islets. Captured 1944 by U.S. forces. Bikini natives, moved here in 1947 from Rongerik, were moved again in 1949 to KILI. Formerly Providence Isl. Sometimes considered to be one of Caroline Isls.

Ujest, Poland: see UJAZD.

Ujfeherto (o͞o'ĭfĕhärtō), Hung. *Újfehértó*, town (pop. 15,154), Szabolcs co., NE Hungary, 11 mi. S of Nyiregyhaza; distilleries, flour mills; wheat, tobacco, potatoes, peaches, apples; cattle, sheep.

Ujgradiska, Yugoslavia: see NOVA GRADISKA.

Ujhani (o͞ojä'nē), town (pop. 11,955), Budaun dist., central Uttar Pradesh, India, 8 mi. WSW of Budaun; cotton milling, sugar refining; wheat, pearl millet, mustard, barley, gram. Rohilla mosque.

Ujhartyan (o͞o'ĭhôrtyän), Hung. *Újhartyán*, town (pop. 5,530), Pest-Pilis-Solt-Kiskun co., central Hungary, 25 mi. SE of Budapest; grain, clover, cattle, hogs.

Ujhely, Hungary: see SATORALJAUJHELY.

Uji (o͞o'jē). **1** Town (pop. 13,110), Kyoto prefecture, S Honshu, Japan, on Uji R. (middle course of Yodo R.) and 8 mi. S of Kyoto, just W of Higashi-uji; fashionable resort; known for green tea. Fishing (with cormorants). Hydroelectric plant near by. Has monastery Byodo-in (11th cent.), known for its central pavilion called Phoenix Hall. Sometimes spelled Uzi. **2** Town, Kyoto prefecture, Japan: see HIGASHI-UJI.

Ujiie (o͞ojē'ā), town (pop. 14,026), Tochigi prefecture, central Honshu, Japan, 10 mi. NE of Utsunomiya; rice, wheat, silk cocoons; agr. implements.

Ujiji (o͞ojē'jē), town (pop. c.10,000) Western Prov., W Tanganyika, small port on L. Tanganyika, 4 mi. SE of Kigoma; 4°55'S 29°40'E. Fishing and trade center; rice milling. An Arab slave and ivory trade center until end of 19th cent.; later supplanted by KIGOMA. Here on Nov. 10, 1871, under a mango tree, replaced since 1946 by a monument, Stanley successfully ended his search for Livingstone.

Uji River, Japan: see YODO RIVER.

Ujitsu, Formosa: see WUJIH.

Uji-yamada (o͞o'jē-yä'mädä), city (1940 pop. 52,555; 1947 pop. 65,970), Mie prefecture, S Honshu, Japan, on SW shore of Ise Bay, 45 mi. SSW of Nagoya; important religious center. Produces cotton textiles, umbrellas, tobacco. Site of shrines of Ise (collectively called Daijingu), one of which is dedicated to Amaterasu-o-mikami, "divine ancestress" of imperial family. Has univ. (Jingu kogaku-kan), mus. of antiquities, and mus. of agr. Includes (since early 1940s) former town of Kamiyashiro (1940 pop. 2,754). Bombed (1945) in Second World War. Sometimes spelled Uzi-yamada.

Ujjain (o͞ojīn', o͞o'jīn), city (pop., including Madhavnagar and cantonment areas, 81,272), ⊙ Ujjain dist., W central Madhya Bharat, India, on Malwa plateau, on Sipra R. and 32 mi. NNW of Indore. One of 7 sacred cities of Hindus; rail junction; trade center (grain, textiles, cotton, opium); cotton ginning and milling, dyeing, oilseed milling, handloom weaving, mfg. of hosiery, ice, confectioneries, strawboard, batteries; metal- and tileworks, distillery. A famous pilgrimage center. Ujjain holds several festival fairs, including (every 12th year) Kumbh Mela. Lies on 1st meridian of old Hindu geographers (23°10'N 75°46'E); remains of observatory, built c.1730, are just S. One of oldest sites in India; was ⊙ anc. Aryan kingdom of Avanti and later of many Malwa dynasties; ruled A.D. c.400 by Chandra Gupta II (Vikramaditya). Captured by Delhi sultan Altamsh in 1235, by Khiljis in 1305, and by Moguls c.1570. Was ⊙ Gwalior from c.1750 to 1810, when Lashkar was founded. Sometimes spelled Ujain.

Ujkecske (o͞o'ĭkăch-kĕ), Hung. *Újkécske*, town (pop. 10,381), Pest-Pilis-Solt-Kiskun co., central Hungary, on the Tisza and 19 mi. E of Kecskemet; river port; lumber, flour mills; grain, paprika, tobacco, cattle, poultry.

Ujkigyos (o͞o'ĭkēdyōsh), Hung. *Újkígyós*, town (pop. 6,194), Bekes co., SE Hungary, 7 mi. SSW of Bekescsaba; flour mills; grain, tobacco, sheep.

Ujlak, Yugoslavia: see ILOK.

Ujleta (o͞o'ĭlātŏ), Hung. *Újléta*, town (pop. 2,278), Bihar co., E Hungary, 12 mi. ESE of Debrecen; corn, dairy farming.

Ujmoldova, Rumania: see MOLDOVA-NOUA.

Ujpest (o͞o'ĭpĕsht), Hung. *Újpest*, Ger. *Neu-Pest*, city (pop. 76,001), Pest-Pilis-Solt-Kiskun co., N central Hungary, on the Danube and 5 mi. N of Budapest city center; rail center. Agr. chemical experiment station. Mfg. of boats, chemicals, cosmetics, pharmaceuticals, textiles (cotton, wool, hemp, flax), electrical appliances, leather goods, glass, furniture, candy; tanneries. Extensive wine cellars.

Ujristan or **Ajrestan** (ŭj'rĭstän"), village, Kandahar prov., S central Afghanistan, in outliers of the Hindu Kush, 110 mi. N of Kandahar.

Ujscie (o͞o'ēshchĕ), Pol. *Ujście*, Ger. *Usch* (o͞osh), town (1946 pop. 1,643), Poznan prov., W Poland, on Notec R. and 7 mi. S of Schneidemühl (Pila); glassworking, mfg. of agr. machinery.

Ujszasz (o͞o'ĭsäs), Hung. *Újszász*, town (pop. 5,468), Jasz-Nagykun-Szolnok co., central Hungary, on the Zagyva and 9 mi. NNW of Szolnok; rail center; corn, cattle.

Ujszentanna, Rumania: see SFANTA-ANA.

Ujtatrafüred, Czechoslovakia: see NOVY SMOKOVEC.

Ujué (o͞ohwā'), town (pop. 1,279), Navarre prov., N Spain, 10 mi. ESE of Tafalla; cereals, wine.

Ujungbatu, Indonesia: see BANYAK ISLANDS.

Ujvidek, Yugoslavia: see NOVI SAD.

Ukasiksalik Island (6 mi. long, up to 9 mi. wide), E Labrador, at entrance of Davis Inlet (pop. 120); 55°53'N 60°53'W.

Ukaturaka (o͝okätōo͞rä'kä), village, Equator Prov., NW Belgian Congo, on Ukuturaka Isl. in Congo R., 95 mi. WSW of Lisala; steamboat landing and trading post; palm products.

Ukawa (o͞o'käwä), town (pop. 5,497), Ishikawa prefecture, central Honshu, Japan, on E Noto Peninsula, on Toyama Bay, 16 mi. NNE of Nanao; lumbering.

'Ukaykah, Iraq: see 'AKAIKA.

Ukerewe, lake, Africa: see VICTORIA, LAKE.

Ukerewe Island (o͝okĕrā'wā), largest island in L. Victoria, in Tanganyika, N of Mwanza and on N side of Speke Gulf; 30 mi. long, 10 mi. wide.

Üker River, Germany: see UECKER RIVER.

Ukholovo (o͞o'khŭlŭvŭ), village (1926 pop. 3,339), S Ryazan oblast, Russian SFSR, 18 mi. ENE of Ryazhsk; metalworks.

Ukhra, India: see RANIGANJ.

Ukhrul (o͝okro͞ol'), village, Manipur, NE India, 34 mi. NE of Imphal; rice, mustard, sugar cane. Figured in Jap. invasion of India in 1944.

Ukhta. 1 (o͝okh'tŭ), Finnish *Uhtua* (o͞o'to͞oä), village (1948 pop. over 2,000), W central Karelo-Finnish SSR, on Middle Kuito L., 105 mi. WNW of Kem (linked by road); woodworking, sawmilling. **2** (o͝okhtä') City (1939 pop. over 10,000), central Komi Autonomous SSR, Russian SFSR, on Ukhta R. (left affluent of Izhma R.) near its mouth, on N.Pechora RR and 160 mi. NE of Syktyvkar; 63°45'N 53°40'E. Center of petroleum fields developed during Second World War; refinery. Called Chib-Yu until 1939; became city in 1943.

Ukhtomskaya, Russian SFSR: see LYUBERTSY.

Ukiah (ūkī'ŭ), city (pop. 6,120), ⊙ Mendocino co., NW Calif., c.55 mi. NNW of Santa Rosa and on Russian R., trade and shipping center for region producing pears, prunes, grapes, hops, livestock; makes fiberboard. Seat of an international latitude observatory and a fish hatchery. Near by are a state hosp., carbonated springs (resorts), and propagating gardens for native plants. Inc. 1876.

Ukivok, Alaska: see KING ISLAND.

Ukkel, Belgium: see UCCLE.

Ukmerge (o͝ok"mĕrgā'), Lith. *Ukmergė*, Pol. *Wilkomierz*, Rus. *Vilkomir*, city (pop. 12,376), E central Lithuania, on Sventoji R. and 40 mi. NE of Kaunas; rail spur terminus; machine shops; mfg. of shoes, vegetable oils, glazed tile; sawmilling (prefabricated houses), brewing, flour milling. Dates from 10th cent.; in Rus. Kovno govt. until 1920.

Ukraine (ū'krān, ūkrān') or **Ukrainian Soviet Socialist Republic** (ūkrā'nēŭn), Rus. *Ukraina* (o͝okrĭē'nŭ, o͝okrī'nŭ), constituent republic (□ 222,600; 1947 pop. estimate 40,500,000) of SW European USSR; ⊙ Kiev. The 2d-largest Soviet republic in pop. and in economic potentialities. Borders SW and W on Rumania, Moldavian SSR, Hungary, Czechoslovakia, and Poland, NW on Belorussian SSR, and NE and E on Russian SFSR. Bounded (S) by Sea of Azov, Crimea, and Black Sea. Largely a steppe lowland, rising to Donets Ridge (SE), Volyn-Podolian Upland (W), and reaching in extreme W to the Carpathians; drained by the Dnieper and its affluents (Pripet, Desna, Sula, Psel, Vorskla rivers), the Southern Bug, the Dniester, and the Northern Donets (an affluent of the Don). Climate varies from moderate humid continental (NW) to mid-lat. dry steppe (SE) types. Mean temp., 14°–27° F. (Jan.), 67°–73° F. (July); yearly precipitation, 12–20 in. The Ukraine falls into 3 major vegetation zones: mixed forests of Polesye lowland (NW), with podsols and considerable marshiness; wooded steppe (center), with black-earth soils; and true steppe (S), with fertile black-earth soils merging (E) with chestnut soils. Chief mineral resources are coking coal and anthracite of DONETS BASIN, lignite, peat, iron ore (KRIVOI ROG), manganese (NIKOPOL), petroleum, natural gas, ozocerite, and potash in Carpathian foothills, salt, mercury, limestone, and fire clays in Donets Basin. Pop. consists mainly of Ukrainians (80%; Slavic group of Rus. culture, with some Pol. influence, and of Greek-Orthodox and Uniate religion). Minorities are Russians (9%), Jews, and Poles. Administratively divided until 1925 into govts., *uyezds*, and volosts; then (1925–32) into okrugs and *raions* (*rayons*); since 1932 into oblasts and *raions*. Since, 1944, it comprises 25 oblasts: CHERNIGOV, CHERNOVTSY, DNEPROPETROVSK, DROGOBYCH, IZMAIL, KAMENETS-PODOLSKI, KHARKOV, KHERSON, KIEV, KIROVOGRAD, LVOV, NIKOLAYEV, ODESSA, POLTAVA, ROVNO, STALINO, STANISLAV, SUMY, TERNOPOL, TRANSCARPATHIAN OBLAST, VINNITSA, VOLYN, VOROSHILOVGRAD, ZAPOROZHE, ZHITOMIR. One of the chief coal and steel regions of the USSR, the Ukraine produces iron and steel (at Stalino, Makeyevka, Zhdanov, Kerch in Crimea, Zaporozhe, Dnepropetrovsk), heavy machinery (at Kramatorsk, Kharkov), chemicals (acids, soda, fertilizer, aniline dyes), agr. products (sugar, flour, tobacco, alcohol, vegetable oils, canned goods). Power stations operate on water power (DNEPROGES) and coal dust (SHTERGRES, ZUGRES). The Ukraine falls into distinct agr. regions: rye, oats, buckwheat, potatoes, tobacco, fodder crops, dairy farming in the wooded Polesye; sugar beets, winter wheat, barley, legumes, dairy and beef cattle, hogs in the wooded steppe; wheat, barley, corn, millet, sunflowers, melons, fruit, vineyards, beef cattle, sheep, and hogs in the drier steppe; alpine dairy farming, corn, orchards, beekeeping in the Carpathians. Chief industrial centers (served by dense rail and highway network) are Kiev, Kharkov, Odessa, Dnepropetrovsk, Stalino, Lvov, Zaporozhe, Makeyevka, Zhdanov, and Voroshilovgrad. The Dnieper is the main navigable river; Odessa, Nikolayev, Kherson, and Zhdanov the chief seaports. NW wooded portion of the present Ukraine formed part of Kievan Russia (9th–11th cent. A.D.), while its S steppes were visited after 1000 B.C. by successive westward migration waves (Scythians, Goths, Huns, Petchenegs), which culminated in 13th-cent. Tatar invasion. In 14th cent. most of the Ukraine came under Lith. rule and, after Union of Lublin (1569), under Pol. rule, while Crimean Tatar khanate controlled the S central steppes. The Ukrainians (Little Russians or Ruthenians) developed as a separate ethnic group after 14th–15th cent. and were 1st organized politically and militarily (17th cent.) as Zaporozhe Cossacks, who revolted against the Poles and formed a vassal Muscovite state in 1654. Russia annexed the left bank Ukraine (E of the Dnieper) and Kiev in 1667 and the right-bank sections in 2d and 3d Pol. partitions (1793, 1795). S steppes passed (1733–91) to Russia from Turks. Ukrainian SSR was first proclaimed in Dec., 1917, and, following Ger. occupation and brief counter-revolutionary regimes, was confirmed in Dec., 1919; joined the USSR in 1922. A major theater of war during Second World War, it was held (1941–44) by Germans. Since 1939, its area has been enlarged by annexation of SE Poland (1939; including Lvov, Stanislav, Drogobych, Ternopol, Rovno, and Lutsk), N BUKOVINA and N and S parts of BESSARABIA (1940), and Transcarpathian Oblast (1945). Moldavian Autonomous SSR (created 1924) was separated (1940) from the Ukraine to form Moldavian SSR (see MOLDAVIA). Formerly also called Little Russia. The Ukraine was admitted to the United Nations in 1945 as an independent nation.

Ukrainian Canal, USSR: see SOUTH UKRAINIAN CANAL.

Ukrepleniye Kommunizma, Russian SFSR: see IVANISHCHI.

Ukrina River (o͞o'krēnä), N Bosnia, Yugoslavia, formed by junction of 2 branches 8 mi. SSE of Prnjavor; flows c.40 mi. N, past Derventa, to Sava R. near Bosanski Brod.

Uksyanskoye (o͝oksyän'skŭyŭ), village (1926 pop. 2,349), NW Kurgan oblast, Russian SFSR, 20 mi. S of Dalmatovo; metalworks.

Uku-shima (o͝oko͞o'shĭmä), northernmost isl. (□ 10; pop. 11,401) of isl. group Goto-retto, Nagasaki prefecture, Japan, in E.China Sea, 25 mi. W of Kyushu; 33°16'N 129°7'E; 5 mi. long, 3.5 mi. wide; hilly. Fishing. Chief town, Taira. Sometimes called Uku.

Ukuwela (o͝oko͝ov'ĕlŭ), village (pop., including nearby villages, 1,077), Central Prov., Ceylon, in Matale Valley, 3.5 mi. S of Matale; cacao works; trades in tea, rubber, cacao, rice.

Ula, India: see BIRNAGAR.

Ula (o͞o'lä), village (pop. 101) in Tjolling (Nor. *Tjølling*) canton (pop. 4,475), Vestfold co., SE Norway, on the Skagerrak, 6 mi. ESE of Larvik. At foot of hills which rise to 380 ft., it is a popular summer resort; 2 mi. NE is Kjerringsvik (chăr'-rĭngsvĕk), village, another resort. Canton has several flour- and sawmills, machine shop, and boat yards.

'Ula, Al, Saudi Arabia: see 'ALA, EL.

Ulaan Baatar, Mongolia: see ULAN BATOR.

Ulaan Goom, Mongolia: see ULANKOM.

Ulaan Nuur, Mongolia: see ULAN NOR.

Uladulla (u"lŭdŭ'lŭ), municipality (pop. 1,844), SE New South Wales, Australia, 75 mi. E of Canberra, on coast; dairying center; summer resort.

Ulai, Iran: see KARUN RIVER.

Ulala, Russian SFSR: see GORNO-ALTAISK, city.

Ulan Bator (o͞o'län bä'tōr) or **Ulaan Baatar** (bä'tär) (=red hero), city (pop. 70,000), ⊙ Mongolian People's Republic, in, but independent of, Central Aimak, on right bank of Tola R. and 280 mi. S of Ulan-Ude (USSR; linked by railroad since 1949); alt. 4,300 ft.; 47°55'N 106°53'E. Political, cultural, and economic center of Outer Mongolia, situated in a valley at foot of the Bogdo Ula, which rises 3,000 ft. above the city. Most of the city's industry is concentrated (since 1934) in the so-called industrial combine, producing woolen cloth, felt, sheepskins, saddles and harnesses, shoes, and knitwear. There are also large woolwashing and meat-packing plants, power plant, auto repair shops; brick, tile, and lumber mills; brewery and distillery. Coal is mined at Nalaikha, 20 mi. SE. Ulan Bator is the country's transportation hub, from which highways radiate to Choibalsan, Kalgan, Dalan Dzadagad, Tsetserlik, and Kobdo. It is linked by air with Ulan-Ude and Mongolian aimak centers. The city has univ. (1942), printing plant; and library with Mongolian, Tibetan, and Chinese manuscripts. Originally city was centered at the monastery section and the residence of the Living Buddha (Mongolia's former spiritual leader), now the natl. mus. It now focuses on the central Sukhe Bator square (with equestrian statue of the Mongolian revolutionary leader, who died in 1923), traversed by main E–W thoroughfare and adjoined by city's main govt. and public bldgs. Trade is transacted mainly in the former Chinese commerical section (on E outskirts); industry is concentrated in new left-bank section. Founded 1649 as a monastery town, the city later developed as a trading center on the tea route bet. Russia and China, particularly after the establishment there of Russian and Chinese firms in 1860s. Here autonomous Mongolia was 1st proclaimed in 1911. After First World War, the city was (1921) the hq. of the Russian counterrevolutionary army of Baron von Ungern-Sternberg. Until 1924, Ulan Bator was known to foreigners as Urga (Örgöö,=palace), to Mongolians as Da Khure (Da Hüryee,=great monastery), and to Chinese as Kulun (K'u-lun).

Ulanchap, China: see OLANCHAB.

Ulan-Erge, Russian SFSR: see KRASNOYE, Astrakhan oblast.

Ulangom, Mongolia: see ULANKOM.

Ulan Hoto (o͞olän′ hōtō′) [Mongol,=red city], Chinese *Wu-lan-hao-t'e,* city (pop. c.10,000), ⊙ Inner Mongolian Autonomous Region, Manchuria, on Tao R., on railroad, and 225 mi. W of Harbin; 46°5′N 122°1′E. Administrative center and hq. of Mongolian Khingan league; has lamasery. Was ⊙ South Hsingan prov. in Manchukuo. Called Wang-yehmiao until 1949, when it became ⊙ Inner Mongolian Autonomous Region.

Ulankom, Ulangom, or **Ulaan Goom** (all: o͞o′läng-gōm), town (pop. over 2,000), ⊙ Ubsa Nor aimak, W Mongolian People's Republic, near SW shore of lake Ubsa Nor, 140 mi. N of Kobdo; road junction.

Ulan Nor, Ulan Nur, or **Ulaan Nuur** (all: nōr′, no͞or′), intermittent lake (□ 65, when filled) in S central Mongolian People's Republic, 75 mi. NW of Dalan Dzadagad, in Gobi desert. Receives the Ongin Gol.

Ulanov (o͞olä′nŭf), town (1926 pop. 2,841), NW Vinnitsa oblast, Ukrainian SSR, 35 mi. NNW of Vinnitsa; metalworks; light mfg.

Ulanovski or **Ulanovskiy** (-skē), town (1948 pop. over 500), E Tula oblast, Russian SFSR, 1 mi. S of Bolokhovo, in Moscow Basin; lignite mining. Until 1948, Ulanovka.

Ulan-Ude (o͞olän′-o͞odĕ′) [Mongolian,=red Uda], city (1926 pop. 28,918; 1939 pop. 129,417; 1946 pop. estimate 150,000; 80% Russian, 20% Buryat-Mongol), ⊙ Buryat-Mongol Autonomous SSR, Russian SFSR, on Selenga R., at mouth of the Uda, on Trans-Siberian RR and 50 mi. E of L. Baikal, 2,750 mi. ESE of Moscow; 51°49′N 107°35′E. Industrial center; locomotive and car building, sawmilling, mfg. of woolen textiles, glass, meat packing, sugar milling. River port; major transportation center (junction for railroad to Naushki on Mongolian frontier, and for highway to Ulan-Bator). Seat of agr. and teachers col., hospitals, tuberculosis sanatorium. Founded 1666; place of exile until it became, c.1780, a city; 1st called Udinsk, later Verkhneudinsk. Developed rapidly as commercial center at junction of trade routes from Irkutsk to Kyakhta and Nerchinsk. Gold boom in 1840s–60s and building of Trans-Siberian RR furthered its growth. Here the Far Eastern Republic was 1st proclaimed, 1920; in 1923, city became ⊙ Buryat-Mongol Autonomous SSR. Renamed (c.1935) Ulan-Ude.

Ulapara or **Ullapara** (o͞olä′pärŭ), village, Pabna dist., central East Bengal, E Pakistan, on tributary of the Atrai and 18 mi. SW of Sirajganj; trades in rice, jute, oilseeds.

Ulapes (o͞olä′pĕs), village (pop. estimate 400), ⊙ San Martín (or General San Martín) dept. (□ 1,900; 1947 pop. 3,924), SE La Rioja prov., Argentina, at NE foot of Sierra de Ulapes (a short pampean mtn. range), 70 mi. WNW of Villa Dolores (Córdoba prov.); agr. center (corn, alfalfa, wine, goats, cattle).

Ulawan (o͞olä′wän′), highest mountain (7,546 ft.) of New Britain, Bismarck Archipelago, SW Pacific, near Gazelle Peninsula. Sometimes called The Father.

Ulba or **Ul'ba** (o͞olbä′), town (1939 pop. over 10,000), N East Kazakhstan oblast, Kazakh SSR, in Altai Mts., on Ulba R., on railroad (Ulbastroi station) and 40 mi. NE of Ust-Kamenogorsk; large hydro-electric plant.

Ulba River or **Ul'ba River,** East Kazakhstan oblast, Kazakh SSR, rises in Ivanov Range of Altai Mts., flows 100 mi. SW, past Ulba (hydroelectric plant) to Irtysh R. at Ust-Kamenogorsk.

Ulbo, Yugoslavia: see OLIB ISLAND.

Ulcinj (o͞ol′tsĭnyŭ), Ital. *Dulcigno* (do͞olchē′nyō), village, S Montenegro, Yugoslavia, on Adriatic coast, near Albania border, 35 mi. S of Titograd; shallow-water seaport; summer bathing resort. Castle ruins. One of main Yugoslav centers of sea-salt production near by. Passed (1421) to Venice; under Turkish rule (1571–1878); in Ital. Albania (1941–44).

Ulcumayo (o͞olko͞omī′ō), town (pop. 1,065), Junín dept., central Peru, in Cordillera Central, 12 mi. NNE of Junín; potatoes, grain. Copper and silver mining near by.

Ulea (o͞olä′ä), town (pop. 1,125), Murcia prov., SE Spain, on Segura R. and 15 mi. NW of Murcia; esparto-rope mfg.; lemon and orange groves. Segura falls (hydroelectric plant) 3 mi. NNW.

Uleaborg, Finland: see OULU.

Uleai, Caroline Isls.: see WOLEAI.

Ule älv, Finland: see OULU RIVER.

Uleelhöe, Indonesia: see ULE-LUE.

Ulefoss (o͞o′lŭfôs), village (pop. 1,448) in Holla canton (pop. 4,296), Telemark co., S Norway, 14 mi. WNW of Skien, on W shore of Nor L., at E terminus of BANDAK-NORSJA CANAL. Falls here furnish power for hydroelectric plant, sawmill, ironworks. Also cash-register mfg. Niobium and apatite mining. Has agr. school. At Fen village, 2 mi. SE, is iron mine.

Ulegei, Ulegey, or **Ölögey** (all: ŭ′lŭgā), town, ⊙ Bayan Ulegei aimak, W Mongolian People's Republic, on Chuya highway and 100 mi. NW of Kobdo, and on Kobdo R.

Uleila (o͞olā′lŭ) or **Awlaylah** (oulā′lŭ), village (pop. 9,461), Daqahliya prov., Lower Egypt, 6 mi. E of Mit Ghamr; cotton, cereals.

Ule-Lue, Uleelhöe, or **Oeleëlheuë** (o͞olā″lo͞o′ā, o͞olŭlŭ′ā), village (dist. pop. 626), extreme NW Sumatra, Indonesia, on Indian Ocean, at mouth of Achin R., 3 mi. W of Kutaraja; rail terminus; port for Kutaraja, shipping copra and pepper. Formerly spelled Olehleh.

Ulen (ū′lŭn). **1** Town (pop. 83), Boone co., central Ind., just N of Lebanon, in agr. area. **2** Village (pop. 525), Clay co., W Minn., on small affluent of Wild Rice R. and 29 mi. NE of Fargo, N.Dak., in grain, livestock, poultry area; dairy products.

Ule träsk, Finland: see OULU, LAKE.

Ulety (o͞olyô′tē), village (1948 pop. over 2,000), SW Chita oblast, Russian SFSR, on Ingoda R. and 65 mi. SW of Chita; wheat, dairying, lumbering.

Ulfborg (o͞olf′bôr), town (pop. 1,195), Ringkobing amt, W Jutland, Denmark, 13 mi. N of Ringkobing; machine shops.

Ulflingen, Luxembourg: see TROISVIERGES.

Ulfsteen, Norway: see ULSTEINVIK.

Ulft (ûlft), town (pop. 4,224), Gelderland prov., E Netherlands, on Old IJssel R. and 21 mi. ESE of Arnhem, near Ger. border; iron foundry; enamelware mfg.

Ulhas River (o͞ol′hŭs), W Bombay, India, rises in W Western Ghats, E of Khopoli; flows N and W, past Kalyan, to Arabian Sea at Bassein; c.80 mi. long. Separates N and NE Salsette Isl. from mainland. In lower course, known as Bassein Creek. Its left distributary, Thana Creek, flows S, bet. Salsette Isl. and mainland, into Bombay Harbour.

Ulianovsk, Russian SFSR: see ULYANOVSK.

Uliaser Islands or **Oeliaser Islands** (both: o͞olyä′sĕr), group (□ 193; pop. 40,395), S Moluccas, Indonesia, in Banda Sea, near Amboina, just off SW coast of Ceram. Comprise HARUKU (largest), SAPARUA, NUSALAUT. Isls. are generally low and fertile, producing coconuts, cloves, sago. Has hot springs. Cannibalism was formerly practiced here.

Uliassutai or **Ulyaasatay** (o͞ol′yäsätī″), since 1928 officially **Dzhibkhalantu** or **Jibhalanta** (jĕb′khäläntä) [Mongolian,=magnificent (city)], city (pop. c.5,000), ⊙ Dzabkhan aimak, W central Mongolian People's Republic, 470 mi. W of Ulan Bator and on Uliassutai R. (minor right tributary of Dzabkhan R.); 47°45′N 96°49′E. Major commercial center of W Khangai Mts. area; wool, hides, fur; processing of agr. and livestock products. Developed in 18th cent. as Chinese fortress and administrative center of Mongolia.

Ulieta, Society Isls.: see RAIATEA.

Ulila (o͞o′lēlä), village (commune pop. 1,205), E central Estonia, 10 mi. W of Tartu; peat-fed power plant, serving Tartu city.

Ulindi River (o͞olēn′dē), E tributary of the Lualaba, in E Belgian Congo, formed by several headstreams 35 mi. SW of Costermansville, flows c.260 mi. W and NW, past Shabunda and Kalima-Kingombe, to Lualaba R. 18 mi. S of Lowa village. Together with Elila R. it drains an important gold- and tin-mining area.

Uling (o͞olĕng′, o͞o′lĕng), village (1939 pop. 1,381), in Naga municipality, central Cebu isl., Philippines, 14 mi. WSW of Cebu city; coal mining, marble quarrying.

Ulithi (o͞olē′thē, -tē, ūlē′thē) or **Uluthi** (-lo͞o′-), atoll (pop. 402), Yap dist., W Caroline Isls., W Pacific, 85 mi. ENE of Yap; 19 mi. long, 10 mi. wide. Mogmog (c.½ mi. long) is chief islet. Isolated isl. of Falalop (c.½ mi. long) is 1 mi. NE of main atoll. In Second World War, site of Jap. seaplane base; taken (1944) without opposition, it became large U.S. naval base. Site of radio beacon.

Uliveto Terme (o͞olēvä′tô tĕr′mĕ), village (pop. 1,352), Pisa prov., Tuscany, central Italy, on the Arno and 6 mi. E of Pisa; resort with mineral waters; wax and glycerin industries.

Uljan Island (o͞olyän′), Ital. *Ugliano* (o͞olyä′nô), Dalmatian island (□ 20) in Adriatic Sea, W Croatia, Yugoslavia. Chief villages, Preko (3 mi. SW of Zadar) and Uljan (6 mi. E of Zadar), on E coast. Winegrowing, fishing.

Ulla (o͞o′lŭ), town (1926 pop. 2,187), W Vitebsk oblast, Belorussian SSR, on Western Dvina R., at mouth of Ulla R., and 30 mi. W of Vitebsk; sawmilling.

Ullal, India: see MANGALORE.

Ullapara, E Pakistan: see ULAPARA.

Ullapool (ŭ′lŭpo͞ol), town in Lochbroom parish, NW Ross and Cromarty, Scotland, on E shore of Loch Broom, 45 mi. NW of Inverness; 57°52′N 5°15′W; fishing port; woolen mills.

Ulla River (o͞o′lyä), Galicia, NW Spain, rises in Galician Mts. in Lugo prov. 10 mi. NNW of Chantada, flows 70 mi. W, forming boundary bet. Pontevedra and La Coruña provs., to Arosa Bay of the Atlantic, below Padrón.

Ulla River (o͞o′lŭ), N Belorussian SSR, rises in lakes SW of Lepel, flows E, past Lepel and Chashniki, and N to Western Dvina R. at Ulla; c.80 mi. long. Upper course linked to Berezina R.

Ulla-Ulla (o͞o′yä-o͞o′yä), village, La Paz dept., W Bolivia, 34 mi. N of Puerto Acosta, on road; customs station near Peru border.

Ulldecona (o͞oldäkō′nä), town (pop. 4,305), Tarragona prov., NE Spain, 16 mi. S of Tortosa; mfg. of soap, brushes, liqueurs, shoe polish; sawmilling, olive-oil and meat processing. Trades in wine, fruit, cereals.

Ullensaker, Norway: see GARDERMOEN.

Ullensvang, Norway: see ESPE.

Ulleval (o͞ol′lŭvôl), Nor. *Ullevål,* residential garden suburb (pop. 8,288) of Oslo, SE Norway, 2 mi. N of city center. Has large municipal hosp. Until 1948, in Akershus co. Sometimes spelled Ullevaal.

Ullin (ŭ′lĭn), village (pop. 773), Pulaski co., extreme S Ill., 19 mi. N of Cairo, in agr. area.

Üllö (ül′lû), Hung. *Üllő,* town (pop. 7,277), Pest-Pilis-Solt-Kiskun co., N central Hungary, 15 mi. SE of Budapest; distilleries, flour mills.

Ulloa (o͞oyō′ä), town (pop. 2,110), Valle del Cauca dept., W Colombia, in Cauca valley, 30 mi. SW of Manizales; sugar cane, tobacco, coffee, cereals, fruit, stock.

Ulloma (o͞oyō′mä), town (pop. c.3,700), La Paz dept., W Bolivia, in the Altiplano, on Desaguadero R. and 24 mi. S of Corocoro; alpaca and sheep raising.

Ullstein, Norway: see ULSTEINVIK.

Ullswater (ŭlz′-), picturesque lake (□ c.3), 2d largest in England, in the Lake District, on Cumberland and Westmorland border, 5 mi. SW of Penrith; 7½ mi. long, ½ mi. wide. Divided into 3 reaches; 4 small isls. are in N end. Near by is the waterfall of Aira Force and, just W, Gowbarrow, a natl. park since 1910.

Ullún (o͞oyo͞on′), town (pop. estimate 500), ⊙ Ullún dept. (□ c.950; pop. estimate 4,000), S San Juan prov., Argentina, on San Juan R. (irrigation area) and 12 mi. WNW of San Juan, in fruit- and winegrowing area.

Ullung Island (o͞ol′lo͝ong′), Korean *Ullung-do,* Jap. *Utsuryo-to* (□ 28; 1946 pop. 13,244), N.Kyongsang prov., Korea, in Sea of Japan, 140 mi. E of Samchok (on E coast of mainland); roughly circular, 6 mi. in diameter; volcanic, hilly. Fishing, silk-cocoon production, agr. (potatoes, soy beans).

Ulm (o͞olm), city (1939 pop. 74,387; 1946 pop. 58,087; 1950 pop. 69,941), Württemberg, Germany, after 1945 in Württemberg-Baden, on left bank of the Danube (which here becomes navigable), opposite mouth of the Iller, and 44 mi. SE of Stuttgart; 48°24′N 10°E. Rail hub; diversified-mfg. center; iron and brass foundries; iron and steel construction. Produces vehicles; building, brewing, and agr. machinery; safes, stoves, metalware. Also precision instruments (radio parts, tower clocks), switch gears, heating pads, textiles (cotton, linen, surgical dressings, hats), clothing. Food processing (dairy products, noodles, fruit juices, beer). Head of projected canal connecting the Danube and the Neckar (at Plochingen). Second World War destruction (about 65%) included most of old dist. with its historic bldgs.; noted Protestant Münster, started 1377, and after Cologne Cathedral Germany's largest Gothic church, escaped damage. Ulm was 1st mentioned as royal domain in 854. A flourishing commercial center, it became a free imperial city in 14th cent. and was one of the most powerful cities of the Holy Roman Empire. Accepted Reformation c.1530; declined after religious wars. Deeply in debt, Ulm and its possessions passed to Bavaria in 1802; territory on left bank of Danube was ceded to Württemberg in 1810, Bavaria erecting NEU-ULM (connected by 2 bridges) on right bank. Ulm rapidly developed as border city; was important port as head of Danube navigation (for floats) until 1897. Fell to U.S. and Fr. troops in April, 1945. Einstein b. here. Sometimes called Ulm an der Donau.

Ulm (ŭlm). **1** Town (pop. 131), Prairie co., E central Ark., 8 mi. NE of Stuttgart. **2** Village (pop. c.100), Cascade co., W central Mont., on Missouri R. and 10 mi. SW of Great Falls; grain-shipping.

Ulmarra (ŭlmă′rŭ), municipality (pop. 1,633), NE New South Wales, Australia, on Clarence R. and 150 mi. S of Brisbane; dairying center; bananas, timber.

Ulmer, Mount (ŭl′mŭr), highest peak (12,500 ft.) of Sentinel Mts., Ellsworth Highland, Antarctica; 77°30′S 86°W. Discovered 1935 by Ellsworth.

Ulmerfeld (o͞ol′mŭrfĕlt), village (pop. 706), W Lower Austria, on Ybbs R. and 4 mi. SW of Amstetten; paper mill.

Ulmers, town (pop. 139), Allendale co., SW S.C., 35 mi. SSW of Orangeburg.

Ulricehamn (ŭl″rēsähä′mŭn, ŭlrē″sä-), city (pop. 6,882), Alvsborg co., S Sweden, at N end of L. Asund, Swedish *Åsunden* (ōs′ŭn″dŭn) (8 mi. long, 1 mi. wide), 30 mi. W of Jonkoping; rail junction; health resort, with large sanitarium. Textile milling, woodworking, clothing mfg. Has 17th-cent. church and 18th-cent. town hall. Founded in 14th cent.; chartered 1604. Until 1741 called Bogesund.

Ulrichsberg (o͞ol′rĭkhsbĕrk), town (pop. 2,929), N Upper Austria, on Grosse Mühl R. and 34 mi. NW of Linz, near Czechoslovak line; potatoes, rye.

Ulriksfors (ŭl″rĭksfôrs′, -fôsh′), village (pop. 466), Jamtland co., N central Sweden, on expansion of Vangel R., Swedish *Vängelälven* (vĕng′ŭlĕl″vŭn), tributary of Angerman R., 50 mi. NE of Ostersund; rail junction; pulp mills, sulphite works.

Ulsan (o͞ol′sän′), Jap. *Urusan,* town (1949 pop. 24,375), S.Kyongsang prov., S Korea, 33 mi. NNE of Pusan; coal-mining and agr. center. Near by are whaling stations where whales are processed.

Ulsta, Scotland: see YELL.

Ulsteinvik (o͞ol'stänvēk), village (pop. 1,306) in Ulstein (sometimes spelled Ulfsteen, Ullstein, or Ulvsten) canton (pop. 2,835), More og Romsdal co., W Norway, port on W shore of Hareid isl., 13 mi. SW of Alesund; furniture mfg.

Ulster (ŭl'stůr), northernmost province (□ 8,331; 1946 census pop. in Ireland 263,887; 1951 census pop. in Northern Ireland 1,370,709) of Ireland. Six of its counties—Antrim, Armagh, Down, Fermanagh, Londonderry, Tyrone—are in Northern Ireland; 3—Cavan, Donegal, Monaghan—in Ireland. Many inhabitants are of English or Scottish descent.

Ulster, county (□ 1,143; pop. 92,621), SE N.Y.; ⊙ Kingston. Bounded E by the Hudson; situated mainly in the Catskills; also includes N part of the Shawangunk range and part of the highlands of the Hudson. Drained by Wallkill R., and by Rondout, Esopus, and other creeks. Ashokan Reservoir is in co. Summer-resort area; has several small lakes (Mohonk, Minnewaska, others). Dairying, farming (fruit, truck, potatoes), poultry raising. Mfg. at Kingston and Marlboro. Formed 1683.

Ulster Canal, Ireland and Northern Ireland, extends 48 mi. SW-NE bet. Upper Lough Erne, Co. Fermanagh, Northern Ireland, and Blackwater R. 7 mi. NW of Armagh; enters Ireland just SW of Clones, serves Clones and Monaghan, Co. Monaghan, Ireland, re-enters Northern Ireland 7 mi. WSW of Armagh.

Ulster Heights, resort village, Ulster co., SE N.Y., in the Catskills, 6 mi. NW of Ellenville. Lakes near by.

Ulster Spring, town (pop. 1,700), Trelawny parish, W central Jamaica, 30 mi. NW of May Pen; tropical fruit, spices, stock.

Última Esperanza, department, Chile: see PUERTO NATALES.

Última Esperanza Strait (o͞ol'tēmä ĕspärän'sä), sound on Patagonian coast of Magallanes prov., S Chile, joining Almirante Montt Gulf at Puerto Natales (SE); 40 mi. long, c.3 mi. wide.

Ulu (o͞o'lo͞o), village, Central Prov., S central Kenya, on railroad and 22 mi. SSW of Machakos; sisal, rubber, coffee, wheat, corn.

Ulúa River (o͞olo͞o'ä), W Honduras, rises E of Marcala in Sierra de Guajiquiro, flows c.200 mi. N, past Masaguara, through area of Jesús de Otoro (here called Río Grande de Otoro) and Santa Bárbara, into Sula Valley, past Pimienta and Protección, to Gulf of Honduras 15 mi. ENE of Puerto Cortés. Receives Jaitique (outlet of L. Yojoa) and Comayagua rivers (right), Jicatuyo R. (left). Navigable in Sula Valley.

Ulu Bedok (o͞o'lo͞o bůdôk'), village (pop. 3,291), E Singapore isl., 5 mi. ENE of Singapore; rubber, coconuts.

Ulu Bernam (o͞o'lo͞o bůrnäm'), village (pop. 1,147), N Selangor, Malaya, on Bernam R. (Perak line) opposite Tanjong Malim, 40 mi. NNE of Kuala Lumpur; rubber.

Uluborlu (o͞olo͞o'bôrlo͞o), village (pop. 4,341), Isparta prov., W central Turkey, 22 mi. N of Isparta; wheat, barley, vetch.

Ulu Dag (o͞olo͞o' dä), Turkish *Ulu Dağ*, anc. *Olympus*, peak (8,179 ft.), NW Turkey, 9 mi. SE of Bursa. Copper and coal on NW slopes.

Ulughchat (o͞olo͞okchät'), Chinese *Wukia* or *Wu-ch'ia* (both: wo͞o'chyä'), formerly *Wulukokiati* (wo͞o'lo͞o'kŭchyä'tē), town, ⊙ Ulughchat co. (pop. 13,157), SW Sinkiang prov., China, 9 mi. WNW of Kashgar, and on road to USSR border crossing at Irkestan; cattle raising; wheat, cotton.

Ulugh Muztagh (o͞o'lo͞og mo͞oz'täg), Chinese *Wu-lu-mu-ssu-t'a-ko* (wo͞o'lo͞o'mo͞o'sŭ'tä'gŭ'), highest peak (25,340 ft.) of the Kunlun mts., on undefined NE Tibet–SE Sinkiang prov. (China) border, at 36°25'N 87°25'E. Until discovery of the Ulugh Muztagh, the MUZTAGH was regarded as the culminating point.

Uluguru Mountains (o͞olo͞ogo͞o'ro͞o), mtn. block (c.5,000 ft.), E Tanganyika, 110 mi. W of Dar es Salaam; mica mines; uranium, graphite deposits; gold placers. Town of Morogoro at N foot.

Ulukhanlu, Armenian SSR: see ZANGIBASAR.

Ulukhe River (o͞olo͞okhĕ'), Maritime Territory, Russian SFSR, rises in S Sikhote Alin Range, flows 165 mi. N, past Chuguyevka, joining Daubikhe R. SE of Kirovski to form Ussuri R.

Ulukisla (o͞olo͞o"kŭshlä"), Turkish *Ulukışla*, village (pop. 4,266), Nigde prov., S central Turkey, on railroad and 32 mi. SSW of Nigde; lead deposits.

Ulu Langat (o͞o'lo͞o läng"ät'), village (pop. 570), E Selangor, Malaya, 8 mi. ESE of Kuala Lumpur; rice, rubber, timber.

Ulundi (o͞olo͞on'dē), agr. village, Zululand, central Natal, U. of So. Afr., 40 mi. N of Eshowe; scene (July 3, 1879) of final battle of Zulu War, where chief Cetewayo's forces were decisively defeated.

Ulundurpet (o͞olo͞on'do͞orpĕt), town (pop. 11,726), South Arcot dist., SE Madras, India, 32 mi. WSW of Cuddalore; rice, peanuts, sesame, millet. Formerly called Kiranur and Ulundurpettai.

Ulüngor Nor, China: see ULYUNGUR NOR.

Ulus (o͞olo͞os'), village (pop. 632), Zonguldak prov., N Turkey, 45 mi. ENE of Zonguldak; coal mines; grain, flax, hemp.

Ulutau (o͞olo͞otou'), village, NW Karaganda oblast, Kazakh SSR, in Ulu-Tau range, 55 mi. N of Karsakpay; copper and gold deposits. Founded 1846 as Rus. military post, Ulutavski.

Ulu-Tau, range in W Karaganda oblast, Kazakh SSR, W of Kazakh Hills; rises to 3,730 ft.; extensive copper, manganese, iron, and coal deposits.

Ulu-Telyak (o͞olo͞o"-tyĭlyäk'), village (1926 pop. 560), NE Bashkir Autonomous SSR, Russian SFSR, on railroad and 44 mi. ENE of Ufa; lumber.

Uluthi, Caroline Isls.: see ULITHI.

Ulu Yam (o͞o'lo͞o yäm'), village, NE Selangor, Malaya, on railroad and 21 mi. N of Kuala Lumpur, in rubber dist. Tin-mining village of **Ulu Yam Bharu** (pop. 846) is 2 mi. SE.

Ulva (ŭl'vů), island (pop. 25) of the Inner Hebrides, Argyll, Scotland, on W coast of Mull, from which it is separated by narrow Sound of Ulva and Loch Tuath; 5 mi. long, up to 3 mi. wide; rises to 1,025 ft. Has notable basaltic formations.

Ulverston (ŭl'vůrstůn), urban district (1931 pop. 9,234; 1951 census 10,076), N Lancashire, England, on Furness peninsula 8 mi. NE of Barrow-in-Furness; steel production, leather tanning, paper milling, metalworking, mfg. of electrical appliances. Limestone quarrying near by. Has Quaker meetinghouse with 1541 Bible, and church of 12th-cent. origin.

Ulverstone (ŭl'vůrstůn), town and port (pop. 3,432), N Tasmania, 55 mi. WNW of Launceston and on Bass Strait, at mouth of Leven R.; agr. center; dehydrated vegetables, butter; grain, fruit, cattle.

Ulvik (o͞ol'vēk, –vĭk), village and canton (pop. 1,517), Hordaland co., SW Norway, on a branch of Hardanger Fjord, 55 mi. E of Bergen; summer resort. FINSE is in canton.

Ulvila (o͞ol'vĭlä), Swedish *Ulvsby* (ŭlfs'bü"), village (commune pop. 6,216), Turku-Pori co., SW Finland, on Kokemäki R. and 4 mi. SE of Pori; tanneries. Has 14th-cent. church. Original site of Pori city.

Ulvsten, Norway: see ULSTEINVIK.

Ulvsund, strait, Denmark: see SMAALANDSFARVAND.

Ulyaasatay, Mongolia: see ULIASSUTAI.

Ulyanovka or **Ul'yanovka** (o͞olyä'nŭfkŭ). **1** Town (1926 pop. 3,732), central Leningrad oblast, Russian SFSR, 26 mi. SE of Leningrad. Formerly Sablino; renamed 1923 for Lenin (Ulyanov). **2** Town, Odessa oblast, Ukrainian SSR: see GRUSHKA. **3** Village (1926 pop. 5,109), central Sumy oblast, Ukrainian SSR, 21 mi. WNW of Sumy; sugar refining.

Ulyanovo or **Ul'yanovo** (–nůvů), village (1926 pop. 3,043), SE Kaluga oblast, Russian SFSR, 28 mi. SSE of Sukhinichi; hemp processing. Until 1938, called Plokhino.

Ulyanovsk or **Ul'yanovsk** (–nŭfsk), oblast (□ 14,400; 1946 pop. estimate 1,200,000) in E central European Russian SFSR; ⊙ Ulyanovsk. In middle Volga R. valley; drained by Greater Cheremshan, Sviyaga, Barysh, Syzran, and Inza rivers. Humid continental climate (short summers). Mineral resources: marl, tripoli, phosphorite, quartz sand, oil shale, peat. Extensive agr., with wheat, rye, oats, barley, orchards; coriander (N), sunflowers (S, NE) potatoes and legumes (W, NW), hemp (near Inza); livestock. Industries based on agr. (woolen and hemp milling, food processing, tanning), lumber (wood cracking, sawmilling, paper mfg., lumbering), and minerals (marl quarrying, peat digging, tripoli-brick mfg.). Machine mfg. (Ulyanovsk), cement making (Sengilei), light mfg. and agr. processing (Inza, Melekess). Served by Ryazan-Kuibyshev and Inza-Ufa railroads. Formed 1943 out of W part of Kuibyshev oblast. Sometimes spelled Ulianovsk.

Ulyanovsk or **Ul'yanovsk,** city (1939 pop. 102,106), ⊙ Ulyanovsk oblast, Russian SFSR, on narrow watershed bet. right bank of the Volga and right bank of Sviyaga R., 425 mi. ESE of Moscow; 54°19'N 48°23'E. Major port; commercial and industrial center; mfg. (trucks, lathes, precision instruments, building materials), agr. processing (grain, meat, potatoes, fruit, hops), sawmilling. Power plant (N suburb), based on local oil shale. Teachers and agr. colleges. Has mus. of Rus. novelist Ivan Goncharov (b. here 1812), historical and art museums, old cathedral and nunnery, 18th-cent. churches, and several monuments. Extensive parks adjoin Volga waterfront (E; projected funicular railway from port to city). Founded 1648 as Rus. stronghold; assaulted by Cossack rebels under Stenka Razin in 1670; chartered 1796. Formerly called Simbirsk; renamed 1924 for Lenin (Vladimir I. Ulyanov), b. here 1870. His former home is now a nat. mus. Was ⊙ Ulyanovsk (Simbirsk) govt. prior to 1928.

Ulyanovskoye or **Ul'yanovskoye** (o͞olyä'nŭfskŭyů), village (1947 pop. over 500), S Sakhalin, Russian SFSR, on Aniva Gulf, 33 mi. SSW of Aniva; fisheries. Under Jap. rule (1905–45), called Dorokawa.

Ulysses (ūlĭ'sēz). **1** City (pop. 2,243), ⊙ Grant co., SW Kansas, on North Fork Cimarron R. and 35 mi. SW of Garden City, in grain area; carbon black. Inc. 1921. **2** Village (pop. 374), Butler co., E Nebr., 32 mi. NW of Lincoln and on Big Blue R.; grain.

Ulyungur Nor or **Ulüngor Nor** (both: o͞olüng-gōr' nōr'), Chinese *Pu-lun-t'o Hai* (bo͞o'lo͞on'tŭ hī'), salt lake in northernmost Sinkiang prov., China, in the Dzungaria, 185 mi. ENE of Chuguchak. Town of Bulun Tokhoi is near by.

Ülzen, Germany: see UELZEN.

Ulzio (o͞ol'tsyô), village (pop. 841), Torino prov., Piedmont, NW Italy, on Dora Riparia R. and 13 mi. SW of Susa, in cereal-growing, livestock-raising region; resort (alt. 3,575 ft.). Has sawmill. Gypsum and slate quarries near by. Until 1937, Oulx.

Um, in Arabic names beginning thus and not found here: see UMM.

Umago (o͞o'mägō), Slovenian *Umag* (o͞o'mäg), village (pop. 2,398), S Free Territory of Trieste, fishing port on the Adriatic, 18 mi. SW of Trieste; fish canning. Bauxite deposits (E). Placed 1947 under Yugoslav administration.

Umaisha (o͞omī'shä), town (pop. 2,552), Benue prov., Northern Provinces, central Nigeria, on Benue R. and 50 mi. SW of Nasarawa; shea-nut processing; cassava, durra, yams.

Umaknak Island, Alaska: see AMAKNAK ISLAND.

Umala (o͞omä'lä), town (pop. c.10,600), La Paz dept., W Bolivia, in the Altiplano, 16 mi. W of Sicasica; alt. 12,211 ft.

Umaltinski or **Umal'tinskiy** (o͞omŭltyēn'skē), town (1942 pop. over 500), SW Khabarovsk Territory, Russian SFSR, on Umalta R. (right branch of Bureya R.) and 180 mi. WNW of Komsomolsk; molybdenum- and tungsten-mining center. Until 1942, Polovinka.

Uman, Caroline Isls.: see TRUK.

Umán (o͞omän'), town (pop. 3,679), Yucatan, SE Mexico, 10 mi. SW of Mérida; rail junction; henequen-growing center.

Uman or **Uman'** (o͞o'mŭnyů), city (1926 pop. 44,812), SW Kiev oblast, Ukrainian SSR, 115 mi. S of Kiev; rail terminus; agr. center; food processing (flour milling, distilling, meat packing); metalworking, mfg. of clothing, shoes; kaolin quarries. Agr. and teachers colleges. Founded in early-17th cent.; became seat of Count Potocki and known as one of most beautiful cities of W Ukraine. Scene of bloody Cossack revolt (1768) resulting in murder of 18,000 Polish and Jewish inhabitants. Passed 1793 to Russia. In Second World War, held (1941–43) by Germans.

Umanak (o͞o'mänäk), town (pop. 394), ⊙ Umanak dist. (pop. 1,477), W Greenland, on small isl. in Umanak Fjord; 70°40'N 52°8'W. Fishing and hunting base; meteorological and radio station, hosp., sanitarium. Founded 1763.

Umanak Fjord, inlet (100 mi. long, 15–30 mi. wide) of Baffin Bay, W Greenland; 71°N 52°30'W. Nugssuak peninsula forms S shore; Ubekendt and Upernavik isls. (N) separate it from Karrats Fjord. Several branches extend to edge of inland icecap and receive extensive glaciers; QARAJAQ ICE FJORD is southernmost arm. Fjord contains several mountainous isls. Marble quarries at Marmorilik (E).

Umangi, Belgian Congo: see LISALA.

Umango, Sierra de (syĕ'rä dā o͞omäng'gō), subandean range in W La Rioja prov., Argentina, W of Villa Castelli; extends c.30 mi. NE-SW; rises to c.15,000 ft.

Umanskaya, Russian SFSR: see LENINGRADSKAYA.

Umaria (o͞omŭr'yŭ), town (pop. 6,842), S Vindhya Pradesh, India, 75 mi. SSW of Rewa; markets grain, timber; mfg. of shellac, paperboard. Coal mines near by.

Umarkhed (o͞omŭrkād'), town (pop. 8,978), Yeotmal dist., SW Madhya Pradesh, India, 60 mi. SSW of Yeotmal; cotton ginning.

Umarkot (o͞om'ŭrkōt), town (pop. 4,275), ⊙ Thar Parkar dist., SE Sind, W Pakistan, on W edge of Thar Desert, 175 mi. ENE of Karachi; market center (millet, cotton, cattle); exports ghee, tobacco, grain, dried fruit; handicraft cloth weaving. A medieval Rajput fort; noted as refuge of exiled Humayun and birthplace (1542) of Akbar.

Umasi La, pass, Kashmir: see SUMJAM.

Umatac (o͞omä'täk), coast town (pop. 387) and municipality (pop. 580), SW Guam; cattle grazing.

Umatilla (ūmŭtĭ'lŭ), county (□ 3,231; pop. 41,703), NE Oregon; ⊙ Pendleton. Agr. area bordering on Wash., bounded NW by Columbia R., drained by Umatilla R. Wheat, livestock. Blue Mts. are in E and S, in Umatilla Natl. Forest. Umatilla Indian Reservation is near Pendleton. Formed 1862.

Umatilla. 1 Town (pop. 1,312), Lake co., central Fla., 31 mi. NNW of Orlando; ships citrus fruit. Has home for crippled children. Settled 1862. **2** City (pop. 883), Umatilla co., N Oregon, c.30 mi. NW of Pendleton and on Umatilla R. where it joins Columbia R.

Umatilla Dam, Oregon: see MCNARY DAM.

Umatilla River, N Oregon, rises in Blue Mts. in Umatilla co., flows W, past Pendleton, then NW to Columbia R. at Umatilla; c.85 mi. long. Cold Springs Dam (117 ft. high, 3,450 ft. long; completed 1908), on small affluent and 6 mi. E of Hermiston, forms Cold Springs Reservoir (2.5 mi. long; capacity 50,000 acre-ft.).

'Umayrah, Khawr, Aden: see KHOR 'UMEIRA.

Umbagog Lake, Maine and N.H.: see RANGELEY LAKES.

Umballa, India: see AMBALA, district.

Umbarger, Lake, Texas: see TIERRA BLANCA CREEK.

Umbazooksus Lake, Piscataquis co., N central Maine, 50 mi. NNE of Greenville, in wilderness recreational area; 3.5 mi. long, 1 mi. wide. Joined by stream to Chesuncook L.

Umbeluzi River (o͞ombĕlo͞o'zē), SE Africa, rises in Swaziland on E slope of the Drakensberg near Mbabane, flows E into Mozambique at Goba, thence to Delagoa Bay of Indian Ocean at Lourenço Marques; length, over 100 mi.

Umbertide (o͞ombĕr'tĕdĕ), town (pop. 2,866), Perugia prov., Umbria, central Italy, on the Tiber and 14 mi. NNW of Perugia; flour mills, tobacco factory, bricks, ceramics. Church of Santa Croce has work by L. Signorelli.

Umbilin, Indonesia: see OMBILIN.

Umboi, Bismark Archipelago: see ROOKE ISLAND.

Umbozero (o͞omb'ô"zyĭrŭ), lake (□ c.200) in central Murmansk oblast, Russian SFSR, on Kola Peninsula, 13 mi. E of Kirovsk; 30 mi. long, 10 mi. wide, 250 ft. deep; empties S through Umba R. (80 mi. long) into Kandalaksha Bay of White Sea at Umba, just W of Lesnoi. Village of Umbozero on SE shore of lake.

Umbrete (o͞ombrā'tā), town (pop. 2,897), Seville prov., SW Spain, 9 mi. W of Seville; olives, grain, and grapes are processed here.

Umbría or **Puerto Umbría** (pwĕr'tō o͞ombrē'ä), village, Putumayo commissary, S Colombia, landing on affluent of upper Putumayo R. and 19 mi. SSE of Mocoa. Some tropical forest products (rubber, balata gum, resins, fine wood).

Umbria (ŭm'brēŭ), region (□ 3,270; pop. 722,544), central Italy; ⊙ Perugia. Bordered by Tuscany (NW), Lazio (SW), and The Marches (E). Comprises provs. of PERUGIA and TERNI. Crossed by the Apennines and upper Tiber R. valley. Contains L. Trasimeno (W). Mainly agr. (cereals, wine, olive oil, fruit; some sugar beets and tobacco). Major hydroelectric plants are centered about Terni. Chief industries include food products, woolen and cotton textiles, chemicals, cement, ceramics, iron- and steelworks (Terni). The anc. Umbrians (one of parent stocks of Ital. people) were conquered by Romans in 3d cent. B.C. After a period of local autonomy and petty tyrants (from 12th to mid-16th cent.), passed largely under direct papal rule. The Umbrian school of painting flourished in 15th–16th cent., with such masters as Pinturicchio and Perugino.

Umbuzeiro (o͞ombo͞ozā'ro͞o), city (pop. 918), E Paraíba, NE Brazil, on Pernambuco border, 18 mi. NW of Limoeiro; cotton, sugar, beans.

Umcari or **Umchari** (both: o͞omchä'rē), Serbo-Croatian *Umčari*, village, N central Serbia, Yugoslavia, on railroad and 21 mi. SSE of Belgrade.

Umea (ü'mŭō"), Swedish *Umeå*, city (1950 pop. 17,113), ⊙ Vasterbotten co., NE Sweden, on Ume R., near Gulf of Bothnia, and 320 mi. NNE of Stockholm; 63°50'N 20°15'E. Seaport, shipping timber and tar; mfg. of machinery, furniture; woodworking, lumber and pulp milling. Inc. 1622 as city. Burned (1720) by Russians, and occupied (1809) by them. City rebuilt after fire, 1888.

'Umeira, Khor, Aden: see KHOR 'UMEIRA.

Um el 'Amad, Jordan: see UMM EL 'AMAD.

Umerdjim, Syria: see UMM ER REJIM.

Ume River, Swedish *Ume älv* (ü'mŭ ĕlv'), Lapland, N Sweden, rises on Norwegian border SE of Mo, flows 285 mi. SE, through Storuma L., over several falls (power stations), past Stensele, Lycksele, Vannas, and Umea, to Gulf of Bothnia at Holmsund. Receives Vindel R. Important logging route; salmon fishing.

Umfolozi River (o͞om"fōlō'zē), in Zululand, Natal, U. of So.Afr., rises in 2 headstreams (White and Black Umfolozi rivers), flows c.100 mi. E through sugar-cane dist. to Indian Ocean 120 mi. NE of Durban.

Umfuli River (o͞omfo͞o'lē), N central Southern Rhodesia, rises 25 mi. SW of Marandellas, flows 150 mi. WNW, past Beatrice and Seigneury Drift, joining Umniati R. 55 mi. W of Sinoia to form Sanyati R.

Umgeni River (o͞omgā'nē), E Natal, U. of So. Afr., rises on SE slope of the Drakensberg S of Mooi River, flows 150 mi. in a winding course generally SE, past HOWICK (noted falls), to Indian Ocean in N part of Durban city. Lower course forms Valley of a Thousand Hills, fertile fruitgrowing region.

Umguza River (o͞omgo͞o'zä), W central Southern Rhodesia, rises SE of Bulawayo, flows 90 mi. NW, past Sawmills, to Gwaai R. 19 mi. WNW of Sawmills. Teak and mahogany logging.

Umi (o͞o'mē), town (pop. 20,005), Fukuoka prefecture, N Kyushu, Japan, 6 mi. E of Fukuoka; coal-mining center.

Umiat (o͞o'mēăt), village, N Alaska, on Colville R. and 170 mi. SE of Barrow; 69°23'N 152°10'W; airfield, radio station; trapping, hunting region.

Umingan (o͞omēng'än, -gän), town (1939 pop. 2,937; 1948 municipality pop. 29,729), Pangasinan prov., central Luzon, Philippines, 35 mi. ESE of Dagupan; agr. center (rice, copra, corn).

Umka (o͞om'kä), village, N central Serbia, Yugoslavia, on the Sava, on railroad and 12 mi. SW of Belgrade.

Umkomaas (o͞omkō'mäs), town (pop. 1,283), SE Natal, U. of So. Afr., on Indian Ocean at mouth of Umkomaas R., 30 mi. SSW of Durban; popular resort.

Umkumute (o͞om"ko͞omo͞o'tē), village (pop. 99), SW Alaska, near Bethel.

Umlejh, Saudi Arabia: see UMM LAJJ.

Umma (ŭ'mŭ), anc. Sumerian city, S Mesopotamia, whose site is in SE central Iraq, in Diwaniya prov., 50 mi. NNW of Nasiriya, NE of site of Erech. Flourished in 3d millennium B.C.

Umm al-'Amad, Jordan: see UMM EL 'AMAD.

Umm al-Ba'rur, Iraq: see SHAMIYA, ASH.

Umm al Qaiwain or **Umm al-Qaywayn** (o͞om' ăl kīwīn'), sheikdom (□ 200; pop. 2,000) of TRUCIAL OMAN, extending along 15-mi. section of Trucial Coast of Persian Gulf bet. sheikdoms of Ajman and Ras al Khaima. Consisting of Umm al Qaiwain town (18 mi. NE of Sharja) and environs, it includes date-palm oasis of Falq Al 'Ali (fălk' ăl' ălē'), 16 mi. SE of Umm al Qaiwain town.

Umm al-Rajam, Syria: see UMM ER REJIM.

Ummanz (o͞o'mänts), Baltic island (□ 7.6; pop. 541), N Germany, just W of Rügen isl., of which it formed part until recent times; 5 mi. long, 2–3 mi. wide. Fishing.

Umm Bugmah, Egypt: see ABU ZENIMA.

Umm el 'Amad or **Umm al-'Amad** (both: o͞om ĕl ämăd'), village (pop. c.300), N central Jordan, 12 mi. SSW of Amman; wheat, barley. Sometimes spelled Um el 'Amad.

Umm er Rejim, Umm el Rejim, or **Umm al-Rajam** (all: o͞om'mĕr-rĕ'jĭm), Fr. *Umerdjim*, town, Aleppo prov., NW Syria, on railroad and 45 mi. SSW of Aleppo; cotton, cereals.

Umm er Rzam (-zäm') or **Umm er Rzem** (-zĕm'), village (pop. 1,600), E Cyrenaica, Libya, near Mediterranean Sea, on highway and 25 mi. SE of Derna; sheep, goats; barley, dates.

Ummerstadt (o͞o'mŭr-shtät"), town (pop. 1,070), Thuringia, central Germany, on the Rodach and 7 mi. W of Coburg; woodworking.

Umm Hajar (o͞om häjär'), Ital. *Om Ager* or *Om Hager*, village (pop. 1,300), Agordat div., W Eritrea, near Ethiopian and Anglo-Egyptian Sudan borders, above Setit R., 50 mi. S of Tessenei; alt. c.1,800 ft.; cotton ginning.

Umm Huweitat or **Umm Huwaytat** (o͞om ho͝owā'tät), village (pop. 647), Red Sea Frontier Prov., E Egypt, 20 mi. SW of Safaga; phosphate mining.

Umm Keddada (o͞om' kĕd-dä'dŭ), village, Darfur prov., W Anglo-Egyptian Sudan, on road and 90 mi. E of El Fasher; gum arabic; livestock. Police post.

Umm Lajj (o͞om' lăj'), village, N Hejaz, Saudi Arabia, minor Red Sea port 280 mi. NW of Jidda; 25°1'N 37°16'E. Coastal trade; fisheries; date groves. Sometimes spelled Omlouj and Umlejh.

Umm Nasan or **Umm Na'san** (o͞om' năsän'), uninhabited island of Bahrein archipelago, in Persian Gulf, off NW coast of Bahrein proper; 4 mi. long, 2½ mi. wide.

Umm Ruwaba (ro͞owă'bŭ), town (pop. 9,450), Kordofan prov., central Anglo-Egyptian Sudan, on railroad and 75 mi. ESE of El Obeid; agr. and trade center; cotton, gum arabic, sesame, peanuts, corn, durra; livestock.

Umm Said or **Umm Sa'id** (o͞om' säēd'), oil-loading terminal on E shore of Qatar peninsula, 25 mi. SSE of Doha; linked by pipe line with producing field at DUKHAN.

Umm Shomer, Gebel (gĕ'bel o͞om' shō'mĕr), **Jebel Umm Shomar** (jĕ'bĕl), or **Jabal Umm Shumar** (jĕ'bĕl o͞om' sho͞o'mĕr), peak (8,484 ft.), Sinai Peninsula, NE Egypt, 11 mi. SSW of Gebel Katherina; 2d highest point of Sinai Peninsula.

Umnak Island (o͞om'năk) (83 mi. long, 2–18 mi. wide), Fox Isls., Aleutian Isls., SW Alaska, 5 mi. W of Unalaska Isl.; 53°11'N 168°25'W; rises to 7,236 ft. on Mt. Vsevidof (SW). Native settlement at Nikolski. Sheep ranching (introduced 1923) and fox farming are main activities; herds of reindeer. In Second World War army and air bases were established; native herdsmen were evacuated and sheep stocks perished. New herds were introduced 1944. Tulik Volcano, 4,103 ft. high (E), erupted June 4, 1945.

Umniati River (o͞omnyä'tē), central Southern Rhodesia, rises 25 mi. NE of Enkeldoorn, flows 225 mi. WNW and N, joining Umfuli R. 55 mi. W of Sinoia to form Sanyati R.

Umpire, town (pop. 83), Howard co., SW Ark., 26 mi. NNW of Nashville.

Umpqua River (ŭmp'kwŭ), W Oregon, formed through confluence, near Roseburg, of N.Umpqua R. (100 mi. long) and S.Umpqua R. (95 mi. long), which rise (E) in Cascade Range; flows 111 mi. N and W to Pacific Ocean near Reedsport. N branch drains part of Umpqua Natl. Forest. Livestock, grain, fruit, and garden truck in river basin.

Umrala (o͞omrä'lŭ), town (pop. 3,444), E Saurashtra, India, 22 mi. WNW of Bhaunagar; agr. (cotton, millet, sugar cane).

Umrer (o͞omrär'), town (pop. 19,361), Nagpur dist., central Madhya Pradesh, India, 25 mi. SE of Nagpur; agr. trade center (wheat, millet, cotton, oilseeds); cotton ginning. Sal and satinwood in near-by forests.

Umreth (o͞om'rät), town (pop. 16,949), Kaira dist., N Bombay, India, 28 mi. E of Kaira; trades in rice, millet, wheat, cloth fabrics; cotton ginning, match mfg.

Umri (o͞om'rē), town (pop. 5,325), Nander dist., N Hyderabad state, India, 22 mi. ESE of Nander; cotton ginning; agr. market (chiefly millet, wheat).

Umsaskis Lake, Aroostook co., N Maine, 65 mi. WSW of Presque Isle; joined by Allagash R. to Churchill and Long lakes; 5 mi. long.

Umsweswe (o͞omswĕs'wā), village, Salisbury prov., central Southern Rhodesia, in Mashonaland, on railroad 11 mi. SW of Gatooma; gold mining.

Umta (o͞om'tŭ), town (pop. 5,179), Mehsana dist., N Bombay, India, 16 mi. N of Mehsana; local grain market (millet, wheat).

Umtali (o͞omtä'lē), province (□ 14,483; pop. c.300,000), E Southern Rhodesia, in Mashonaland; ⊙ Umtali. Bounded E by Mozambique. Lies in high veld (4–6,000 ft.) in N, in middle veld (2–4,000 ft.) in S. Inyanga and Chimanimani mts. along E frontier rise above 8,500 ft. Chief crops: tobacco, corn, deciduous fruit (in Inyanga dist.), citrus. Livestock ranches (especially in Bikita dist.). Important gold mines at Penhalonga. Copper (Headlands), corundum (Rusape), lead and tungsten (Odzi) also mined. Chief centers are along Beira-Salisbury RR. European pop. (1946), 8,827. Prov. formed c.1948.

Umtali, city (pop. 9,737), ⊙ Umtali prov., E Southern Rhodesia, in Mashonaland, 135 mi. SE of Salisbury; alt. 3,672 ft. Commercial center; frontier station on Mozambique border, on railroad from Beira; rail workshops; mfg. (industrial alcohol, dehydrated vegetables, jams, flour products, clothing), lumber milling. Shipping point for Penhalonga gold mines. Agr. (tobacco, corn, citrus fruit), dairy products. Developed after construction (1899) of Salisbury-Beira RR.

Umtata (o͞omtä'tŭ), town (pop. 7,340), E Cape Prov., ⊙ TRANSKEIAN TERRITORIES and Tembuland dist., U. of So. Afr., on Umtata R. and 110 mi. NNE of East London; rail terminus. Judicial center of Native Territories and seat of United Transkeian Territories General Council; center of stock-raising, wool-producing, grain-growing region. Has Anglican cathedral. Umtata Falls are 2 mi. SE.

Umuahia (o͞omä'hēä), town (pop. 1,712), Owerri prov., Eastern Provinces, S Nigeria, on railroad and 26 mi. NNE of Aba; road center; palm oil and kernels, kola nuts. Has hosp., govt. training school, agr. education center.

Umuni Gobi, Mongolia: see SOUTH GOBI.

Umvukwe Range (o͞omvo͞o'kwā), N Southern Rhodesia, extends c.100 mi. N from Hunyani R. (35 mi. W of Salisbury); rises to 5,731 ft. Forms N section of great norite dike; major chrome-mining dist., with chief centers at Darwendale, Maryland, and Kildonan.

Umvuma (o͞omvo͞o'mä), town (pop. 1,061), Gwelo prov., central Southern Rhodesia, in Mashonaland, on railroad and 50 mi. ENE of Gwelo; alt. 4,540 ft. Farming center; tobacco, wheat, dairy products, citrus fruit, livestock. Has R.C. mission. Until middle 1920s, a copper-mining center; site of Falcon mine.

Umzimhlava River (o͞omzĭmlyä'vŭ), Transkeian Territories, E Cape Prov., U. of So. Afr., rises in the Drakensberg N of Kokstad, flows 150 mi. in a winding course generally S, past Kokstad, to Umzimvubu R. 35 mi. NNW of Port St. Johns.

Umzimkulu River (o͞omzĭmko͞o'lo͞o), S Natal, U. of So. Afr., rises in the Drakensberg on Basutoland border S of Mokhotlong, flows 200 mi. in a winding course SE to Indian Ocean at Port Shepstone. Mid-course forms part of Cape Prov.–Natal border.

Umzimvubu River (o͞omzĭmvo͞o'bo͞o), Transkeian Territories, E Cape Prov., U. of So. Afr., rises in the Drakensberg near junction of Cape Prov., Natal, and Basutoland borders, flows c.300 mi. in a winding course generally S to Indian Ocean at Port St. Johns. Receives Umzimhlava R.

Umzingwane River (o͞omzĭng-gwä'nā), S Southern Rhodesia, rises in high veld S of Bulawayo, flows 200 mi. generally SSE, past West Nicholson, to Limpopo R. just W of Beitbridge.

Umzinto (o͞omzĭn'tō), town (pop. 3,123), SE Natal, U. of So. Afr., near Indian Ocean, 40 mi. SW of Durban; sugar-growing center.

Una, Brazil: see IBIÚNA.

Una (o͞o'nŭ). **1** Town (pop. 5,394), Hoshiarpur dist., N central Punjab, India, on tributary of Sutlej R. and 21 mi. ESE of Hoshiarpur; local market for wheat, corn, timber. **2** Town (pop. 9,847), S Saurashtra, India, 60 mi. SE of Junagarh; markets grain, cotton, coconuts; hand-loom weaving.

Una (o͞o'nŭ), village, NW Archangel oblast, Russian SFSR, on Onega Peninsula, 70 mi. W of Archangel; lumbering.

Unac River or **Unats River** (both: o͞o'näts), W Bosnia, Yugoslavia, rises at N foot of Sator Mts., flows c.40 mi. NNW, past Drvar, to Una R. 14 mi. WSW of Petrovac.

Unadilla (ŭnŭdĭ'lŭ). **1** Town (pop. 1,098), Dooly co., central Ga., 39 mi. S of Macon, in farm (cotton, peanuts, corn) area; feed, sawmilling. **2** Village (pop. 216), Otoe co., SE Nebr., 23 mi. ESE of Lincoln and on Little Nemaha R. **3** Village (pop. 1,317), Otsego co., central N.Y., on Susquehanna

R. at mouth of Unadilla R., and 35 mi. NE of Binghamton, in farming and dairying area; mfg. (silos, farm equipment, road machinery, furniture, cutlery). Settled 1790, inc. 1827.

Unadilla River, central N.Y., rises in S Herkimer co., flows c.60 mi. SW and S, past West Winfield, to Susquehanna R. at Unadilla.

Unaí (ōōnäē'), city (pop. 631), NW Minas Gerais, Brazil, near Goiás border, 60 mi. N of Paracatu; cattle raising. Formerly spelled Unahy.

Unai Pass (ōōnī') (alt. 10,525 ft.), in S outlier of the Hindu Kush, E central Afghanistan, 50 mi. W of Kabul and on road to Panjao and Herat; links Kabul and Helmand river valleys.

'Unaiza, Saudi Arabia: see ANAIZA.

Unaka Mountains (ūnă'kü, ū'nükü), SE U.S., name often applied to a SW division (2–6,000 ft.) of the Appalachians running NE–SW along Tenn.–N.C. line and extending into Va. and Ga., bet. Great Appalachian Valley (NW) and the BLUE RIDGE escarpment (SE). Reach highest elevations in GREAT SMOKY MOUNTAINS; also include IRON MOUNTAINS and Unicoi, Chilhowee, Stone, Bald, and Holston ranges. Natl. forests (chiefly Cherokee, Pisgah, and Nantahala) cover most of range. Name sometimes restricted to mts. in Unicoi-Carter counties, Tenn., and Avery-Mitchell counties, N.C., bet. Nolichucky and Doe rivers; rise to 5,258 ft. in Unaka Mtn., c.5 mi. E of Erwin, Tenn., on state line.

Unalakleet (ūnūlŭklēt'), village (pop. 462), W Alaska, on E shore of Norton Sound, at mouth of Unalakleet R., 150 mi. ESE of Nome; 63°52'N 160°47'W; fishing, trapping, reindeer herding, gold mining. Has native school, Swedish Lutheran mission; airfield; radio station. Coal mining near by.

Unalaska (ŭ"nŭlă'skü, ōō"–), village (pop. 171), on N shore of Unalaska Isl., Aleutian Isls., SW Alaska, 3 mi. S of Dutch Harbor. Home base of Coast Guard in Bering Sea area. Has Greek Orthodox church, public school, and Methodist native school. Fishing, fish canning; supply point for trappers and fishermen. Established in 1760s by Russian fur traders.

Unalaska Island (30 mi. long, 6–30 mi. wide), Fox Isls., Aleutian Isls., SW Alaska, just E of Umnak Isl.; 53°34'N 166°55'W; rises to 6,680 ft. on Makushin Volcano (NE). Mountainous, treeless, and foggy. Native Aleuts live in main settlements of Kashega and Unalaska. Fishing, trapping, and fish processing are principal activities. Discovered 1741 by Bering, it became center of Russian fur trade in Alaska after trading post had been established (1759) by Stepan Golotov; later superseded by Kodiak. Aleut rising (1762) was bloodily suppressed by Russians. When United States entered Second World War native Aleuts were evacuated, repatriated 1945. Unalaska Bay (NE) contains small Amaknak Isl., site of DUTCH HARBOR.

Unao (ōōnou'), since 1948 officially **Unnao**, district (□ 1,788; pop. 959,542), central Uttar Pradesh, India; ⊙ Unao. On Ganges Plain; bounded S by the Ganges; irrigated by Sarda Canal. Agr. (wheat, barley, rice, gram, oilseeds, millets, corn, sugar cane, cotton); mango and mahua groves. Main towns: Unao, Maurawan, Purwa, Safipur.

Unao, since 1948 officially **Unnao**, town (pop. 20,107), ⊙ Unao dist., central Uttar Pradesh, India, 11 mi. NNE of Cawnpore; rail and road junction; trades in grains, oilseeds, sugar cane, cotton. Founded 8th cent. Bone-meal processing at village of Magarwara, 4 mi. SW.

Unare Lagoon (ōōnä'rä) (□ c.23), Anzoátegui state, NE Venezuela, separated from the Caribbean by narrow bar (on which El Hatillo is situated), 35 mi. W of Barcelona; 15 mi. long, up to 3 mi. wide. Receives Unare R.

Unare River, NE Venezuela, rises W of Pariaguán, flows c.120 mi. NW and N, in upper course along Guárico–Anzoátegui border, past Onoto and Clarines (Anzoátegui state), to the Caribbean at E end of Unare Lagoon, 35 mi. W of Barcelona. Navigable for small craft during rainy season.

Una River (ōō'nä), W Yugoslavia, rises 12 mi. E of Gracac, flows 159 mi. generally NE, past Bihac, Krupa, Novi town, and Dubica town, to Sava R. opposite Jasenovac. Navigable for 43 mi. Middle course followed by railroad; lower course constitutes Bosnia-Croatia border. Receives Unac and Sana rivers.

Unats River, Yugoslavia: see UNAC RIVER.

Una Una, Indonesia: see TOGIAN ISLANDS.

Unava (ōōnä'vŭ), town (pop. 13,866), Mehsana dist., N Bombay, India, 20 mi. S of Mehsana; agr. (millet, pulse, wheat, oilseeds). Has shrine to Moslem saint (large Moslem pop.).

'Unayzah, Saudi Arabia: see ANAIZA.

'Unayzah, Jabal, SW Asia: see 'ANEIZA, JEBEL.

Uncanoonuc Mountains (ŭngkŭnōō'nŭk), Hillsboro co., S N.H., twin peaks near Goffstown, WNW of Manchester; ski trails. Alt. of N peak, 1,320 ft.; S peak (1,321 ft.) has summit railway.

Uncastillo (ōōng-kästē'lyō), town (pop. 3,031), Saragossa prov., N Spain, 33 mi. NE of Tudela; flour mills; trades in cereals and sheep.

Uncasville, Conn.: see MONTVILLE.

Unchahra (ōōn'chärŭ), town (pop. 6,128), S central Vindhya Pradesh, India, 14 mi. S of Satna; trades in grain, building stone, cloth fabrics, oilseeds. Until 1720, was ⊙ former Nagod state. Also spelled Unchehra.

Uncía (ōōnsē'ä), city (pop. c.8,600), ⊙ Bustillo prov., Potosí dept., W central Bolivia, on E slopes of Cordillera de Azanaques, 48 mi. SE of Oruro; terminus of rail branch from Machacamarca; alt. 12,864 ft. A major tin-mining center gradually being replaced by new CATAVI mines, 4 mi. N.

Uncompahgre Peak (ŭn-kŭmpä'grē) (14,306 ft.), in San Juan Mts., SW central Colo., 12 mi. ENE of Ouray.

Uncompahgre Plateau, SW Colo., tableland extending c.60 mi. NW–SE, bet. San Miguel and Gunnison rivers; rises to 10,338 ft. in SE tip. Lies within part of Uncompahgre Natl. Forest.

Uncompahgre River, SW Colo., rises in San Juan Mts. S of Ouray, flows c.75 mi. NNW, past Montrose, to Gunnison R. at Delta. River valley produces hay, fruit, vegetables. Has 6 small irrigation dams; supplementary water brought from Gunnison R. by Gunnison Tunnel.

Und, Lake, Swedish *Unden* (ŭn'dŭn) (9 mi. long, 1–6 mi. wide), S central Sweden, 14 mi. WSW of Askersund. Drains S into L. Vatter.

Undalselv, Norway: see AUDNA RIVER.

Undavalle, India: see BEZWADA.

Underhill, town (pop. 698), Chittenden co., NW Vt., in Green Mts., 15 mi. E of Burlington; resorts; flour and feed milling. Includes part of Mt. Mansfield State Forest.

Underwood. **1** Town (pop. 278), Pottawattamie co., SW Iowa, on Mosquito Creek and 12 mi. NE of Council Bluffs; apiary. **2** Village (pop. 336), Otter Tail co., W Minn., on North Turtle L., 10 mi. E of Fergus Falls; dairy products. **3** Village (pop. 1,061), McLean co., central N.Dak., 48 mi. NNW of Bismarck; coal mines, diversified farming.

Undi (ōōn'dē), town (pop. 7,531), West Godavari dist., NE Madras, India, in Godavari R. delta, on rail branch and 24 mi. ESE of Ellore; rice milling; oilseeds, tobacco, sugar cane. Fish processing (prawn from Colair L.) 5 mi. W, at village of Akid or Akividu.

Undol, Russian SFSR: see LAKINSKI.

Undory (ōōndô'rē), village (1926 pop. 2,043), N Ulyanovsk oblast, Russian SFSR, on right bank of the Volga (landing) and 21 mi. N of Ulyanovsk; grain, orchards. Phosphorite and oil-shale deposits near by.

Undur Khan or **Öndör Haan** (both: ûn'dûr khän'), town (pop. over 2,000), ⊙ Kentei aimak, E central Mongolian People's Republic, on Kerulen R. and 180 mi. E of Ulan Bator; highway and trading center; coal mining. Until 1931, called Tsetsen Khan.

Unea, Bismarck Archipelago: see VITU ISLANDS.

Unebi (ōōnā'bē), town (pop. 11,383), Nara prefecture, S Honshu, Japan, 14 mi. S of Nara; agr. center (rice, wheat); raw silk, medicine.

Unecha (ōōnyĕ'chŭ), city (1939 pop. over 10,000), W central Bryansk oblast, Russian SFSR, 75 mi. WSW of Bryansk; rail junction; railroad shops, flour mills. Became city in 1940.

Unegytei or **Unegytey** (ōōnyĕgĭtyā'), village (1948 pop. over 2,000), central Buryat-Mongol Autonomous SSR, Russian SFSR, 45 mi. NE of Ulan-Ude, near Kurba R.; livestock, lumbering.

'Uneiza, Jordan: see 'INAZA.

Uneyev, Poland: see UNIEJOW.

Unfederated Malay States: see MALAYA.

Ung, river, Ukrainian SSR and Czechoslovakia: see UZH RIVER, Transcarpathian Oblast.

Unga (ŭng'gŭ), village (pop. 107), on SE Unga Isl., Shumagin Isls., SW Alaska; 55°11'N 160°30'W; cod-fishing center. It was an otter-fishing station under Russians. Scene of extensive gold-mining activity c.1900.

Unga Island (ŭng'gŭ) (20 mi. long, 11–14 mi. wide; 1939 pop. 231), largest of Shumagin Isls., SW Alaska, off SW Alaska Peninsula; 55°16'N 160°41'W; rises to 2,270 ft.; cod fishing and canning. Unga village on SE.

Ungar, Indonesia: see KARIMUN ISLANDS.

Ungaran or **Oengaran** (both: ōōng"ärän'), town (pop. 6,345), central Java, Indonesia, 10 mi. S of Semarang, at foot of volcanic Mt. Ungaran (6,726 ft.); trade center for agr. area (sugar, rice, rubber, cassava). Has fort built in 1786.

Ungarie, village (pop. 367), S central New South Wales, Australia, 165 mi. NW of Canberra; rail junction; hardwood timber, sheep, wheat.

Ungarisch-Altenburg, Hungary: see MOSONMAGYAROVAR.

Ungarisch-Brod, Czechoslovakia: see UHERSKY BROD.

Ungarisch-Hradisch, Czechoslovakia: see UHERSKE HRADISTE.

Ungarisch-Ostra, Czechoslovakia: see UHERSKY OSTROH.

Ungava (ŭng-gä'vŭ, –gä'vŭ), **New Quebec** (kwēbĕk', kwŭ–), or **Nouveau Québec** (nōōvō' kābĕk'), district (□ 239,780; pop. 3,067) of N Que., extending S from Ungava Bay, including Que. part of Labrador. It formerly included the whole peninsula of Labrador and was originally under the Hudson's Bay Co.; made part of the Northwest Territories in 1869, it became a separate district in 1895, bounded E by the strip of Labrador belonging to Newfoundland. In 1912 it was added to Que. prov. and in 1927 its boundary with Labrador was established. Drained by Kaniapiskau, Koksoak, Whale, and Larch rivers. Comprises a high plateau which forms watershed bet. the St. Lawrence and Hudson Bay. Region contains immense iron deposits; exploitation has begun in BURNT CREEK CAMP area, on Que.-Labrador border, in S part of dist. Plans for development include hydroelectric power project on upper Kaniapiskau R., and railroad to Sept Îles. District includes settlement of Fort Chimo and Crystal I air base.

Ungava Bay, inlet (200 mi. long, 160 mi. wide at mouth) of Hudson Strait, N Que. Mouth of bay is bet. N end of Labrador peninsula (E) and Cape Hopes Advance (W). In it is Akpatok Isl. Receives Payne, Leaf, Koksoak, Whale, and George rivers. Hopes Advance Bay (20 mi. long) is W arm.

Ungava Peninsula, N Que., 400 mi. long, 350 mi. wide, bet. Ungava Bay (E) and Hudson Bay (W), bordering on Hudson Strait (N). Generally hilly, peninsula rises to c.1,500 ft. and is studded with lakes, largest of which is Payne L., drained by Payne R. Base of peninsula is N limit of wooded country.

Ungeny (ōōngyĕ'mē), Rum. *Ungheni* (ōōngĕn'), city (1941 pop. 2,671), W Moldavian SSR, on Prut R. (Rum. border), on main Kiev-Bucharest RR and 10 mi. E of Jassy; rail junction; Soviet-Rumanian customs station. Rum. village of Ungheni or Ungheni-Prut (1941 pop. 625) is just across Prut R.; towns on both banks were formerly in Rumania.

Unggi (ōōng'gē), Jap. *Yuki*, town (1944 pop. 20,882), N.Hamgyong prov., N Korea, on Sea of Japan, 10 mi. NNE of Najin, with which it is connected by tunnel; northernmost port of Korea. Has deep, natural harbor; port was opened 1921. Marine products and livestock are chief exports.

Ungheni, Moldavian SSR: see UNGENY.

Ungkung (wông'gông'), Mandarin *Huang-kang* (hwäng'gäng'), town, E Kwangtung prov., China, on small Ungkung R., near Challum Bay, 30 mi. NE of Swatow; communications center near Fukien prov. border.

Unguja Ukuu (ōōng-gōō'jä ōōkōō') village, on W coast of Zanzibar, 17 mi. SSE of Zanzibar town; copra, corn, sweet potatoes; fishing. Anc. ⊙ Zanzibar, reduced by Portuguese and Arabs in 16th and 17th cents.

Ungvar, Ukrainian SSR: see UZHGOROD.

Unhais da Serra (ōōnyīsh' dä sĕ'rŭ), village (pop. 1,367), Castelo Branco dist., central Portugal, on SE slope of Serra da Estrêla, 6 mi. WSW of Covilhã; wool milling. Has radioactive hot springs.

Unhel (ōōnhāl'), town (pop. 3,407), W Madhya Bharat, India, 17 mi. NW of Ujjain; cotton gins.

Unhost (ōōn'hôshtyŭ), Czech *Unhošt'*, Ger. *Unhoscht* (ōōn'hôsht), town (pop. 3,063), central Bohemia, Czechoslovakia, on railroad and 13 mi. W of Prague. Has 14th-cent. church, old monuments. Recreation center of Nouzov, with mineral springs, is 2 mi. SW.

Uni (ōō'nyē), village (1926 pop. 127), E Kirov oblast, Russian SFSR, 50 mi. SSE of Zuyevka; road hub; flax processing.

União (ōōnyā'ō). **1** City, Ceará, Brazil: see JAGUARUANA. **2** City (pop. 3,246), N central Piauí, Brazil, landing on right bank of Parnaíba R. (Maranhão border) and 35 mi. N of Teresina; ships cotton, rice, cattle, babassu nuts.

União da Vitória (dä vētô'ryŭ), city (pop. 3,782), S Paraná, Brazil, downstream end of navigation on Iguassú R. (Santa Catarina border), opposite Pôrto União, and 125 mi. SW of Curitiba; rail junction; livestock and agr.-trade center (hogs, skins, grain); tanning, woodworking. Formerly spelled União da Victoria.

União dos Palmares (dōōs pŭlmä'rĭs), city (pop. 6,102), E Alagoas, NE Brazil, on railroad and 37 mi. NW of Maceió; cotton-growing center; vegetable-oil processing (cottonseed, coconut, castor bean); ships hides, tobacco, alcohol. Here a revolt of Negro slaves was suppressed in 1650. Until 1944, called União.

Uniara (ōōnyä'rŭ), town (pop. 4,785), E Rajasthan, India, 70 mi. SSE of Jaipur; wheat, millet, gram, cotton.

Unicoi (ū'nĭkoi), county (□ 185; pop. 15,886), NE Tenn.; ⊙ Erwin. Mtn. region, with Bald Mts. partly along N.C. line (SW, S); drained by Nolichucky R. Includes part of Cherokee Natl. Forest. Lumbering, agr. (tobacco, fruit, corn, hay), livestock raising; some industry at Erwin. Formed 1875.

Unicoi, village (1940 pop. 522), Unicoi co., NE Tenn., 9 mi. S of Johnson City, in scenic mtn. region near N.C. line.

Unicoi Mountains, range of the Appalachians along Tenn.–N.C. line, SW of Great Smoky Mts. Natl. Park, bet. Little Tennessee and Hiwassee rivers. Includes Hooper Bald (5,600 ft.), 10 mi. W of Robbinsville, N.C., and Haw Knob (5,472 ft.), 2 mi. farther W, on state line; Snowbird Mts. are an E extension. Situated in Cherokee and Nantahala natl. forests; sometimes considered a range of Unaka Mts.

Unicov (ōō'nyĭchôf), Czech *Uničov*, Ger. *Mährisch-Neustadt* (mâ'rĭsh-noi'shtät), town (pop. 3,063), N central Moravia, Czechoslovakia, on railroad and 13 mi. NNW of Olomouc; oats, barley, wheat.

Unie, island, Yugoslavia: see UNIJE ISLAND.

Unieh, Turkey: see UNYE.

Uniejow (ōōnyĕ'yōōf), Pol. *Uniejów*, Rus. *Uneyev* (ōōnyā'yĭf), town (1946 pop. 2,074), Poznan prov., central Poland, on the Warta and 32 mi. NW of Lodz; flour milling, brick mfg., oil processing.

Unieux (ünyû'), town (pop. 4,584), Loire dept., SE central France, near influx of Ondaine R. into the Loire, 6.5 mi. WSW of Saint-Étienne; steel mills.

Unije Island (ōō'nēyĕ), Ital. *Unie* (ōōn'yĕ), NW Croatia, Yugoslavia, in N Adriatic Sea, off NW coast of Losinj Isl.; 6 mi. long, 2 mi. wide. Chief village, Unije, is 25 mi. SE of Pula.

Unimak (ōō'nĭmăk), village (1939 pop. 88), on SW Unimak Isl., Aleutian Isls., SW Alaska, 80 mi. ENE of Dutch Harbor; 54°35'N 164°7'W; fishing, trapping.

Unimak Island (70 mi. long, 17–30 mi. wide), Fox Isls., NE Aleutian Isls., nearest to Alaska Peninsula, SW Alaska, 70 mi. ENE of Dutch Harbor; 54°24'–55°N 163°3'–164°56'W. Mountainous surface rises to active SHISHALDIN VOLCANO (center), scene of several eruptions in recent years; less active POGROMNI VOLCANO (W). Main villages: Unimak (SW), False Pass (E). Isl. is game sanctuary; native Aleuts are trappers and fishermen; there are salmon canneries.

Unimak Pass, sea passage (20-30 mi. wide) in NE Aleutian Isls., bet. Unimak Isl. (NE) and Krenitzin Isls. (SW), SW Alaska, bet. N Pacific and Bering Sea; 54°20'N 164°50'W; easternmost navigation channel through Aleutian Isls.

Unión, department, Argentina: see BELL VILLE.

Unión (ōōnyōn'), village (pop. estimate 400), ⊙ Mitre (or General Mitre) dept. (□ 1,220; 1947 census 4,742), SE Santiago del Estero prov., Argentina, 115 mi. SE of Loreto, in agr. area (corn, alfalfa, livestock).

Union, village (pop. 677), S Mauritius, on railroad and 2 mi. NE of Souillac; sugar milling, alcohol distilling.

Unión (ōōnyōn'), town (dist. pop. 2,820), San Pedro dept., central Paraguay, 80 mi. NE of Asunción; stock-raising center; tanneries.

Union (ū'nyŭn). **1** County (□ 1,052; pop. 49,686), S Ark.; ⊙ El Dorado. Bounded S by La. line and NE and E by Ouachita R. Oil center of state (drilling, refining, mfg. of petroleum products). Agr. (fruit, peanuts, sweet potatoes, corn, cotton, livestock). Formed 1829. **2** County (□ 240; pop. 8,906), N Fla.; ⊙ Lake Butler. Flatwoods area with several small lakes. Farming (corn, vegetables, peanuts), cattle raising, forestry (lumber, naval stores). Formed 1921. **3** County (□ 319; pop. 7,318), N Ga., on N.C. line; ⊙ Blairsville. In the Blue Ridge, largely in Chattahoochee Natl. Forest; drained by NOTTELY RIVER (dam and reservoir in N). BRASSTOWN BALD (4,784 ft.) in E. Farm (hay, corn, potatoes, livestock), lumber, and resort area. Formed 1832. **4** County (□ 414; pop. 20,500), S Ill.; ⊙ Jonesboro. Bounded W by Mississippi R. and at extreme NW corner by Big Muddy R.; drained by Cache R. Agr. area (wheat, corn, fruit, truck, poultry; dairy products), with some mfg. (wood products, machinery, flour, shoes, monuments). Limestone, granite, marble quarries. Includes part of Shawnee Natl. Forest. Formed 1818. **5** County (□ 168; pop. 6,412), E Ind.; ⊙ Liberty. Bounded E by Ohio line; drained by East Fork of Whitewater R. Farming (grain, hogs), dairying. Some mfg. at Liberty. Formed 1821. **6** County (□ 426; pop. 15,651), S Iowa; ⊙ Creston. Rolling prairie agr. area (hogs, cattle, poultry, corn, oats) drained by Little Platte, Grand, and Thompson rivers; bituminous-coal deposits. Formed 1851. **7** County (□ 343; pop. 14,893), W Ky.; ⊙ Morganfield. Bounded W by Ohio R. (Ill. and Ind. line), SW by Tradewater R. Rolling upland agr. area (livestock, corn, wheat, hay, tobacco). Bituminous coal mines, sand and gravel pits. Some mfg. at Uniontown, Sturgis, Morganfield. Formed 1811. **8** Parish (□ 906; pop. 19,141), N La.; ⊙ Farmerville. Bounded N by Ark., E by Ouachita R.; drained by Bayou D'Arbonne. Contains large natural-gas field. Agr. (corn, cotton, hay, peanuts, sweet potatoes, soybeans). Cotton ginning, lumber milling. Formed 1839. **9** County (□ 422; pop. 20,262), N Miss.; ⊙ New Albany. Drained by Tallahatchie R. and tributaries. Includes part of Holly Springs Natl. Forest. Agr. (cotton, corn, sorghum, fruit, poultry), dairying; timber. Some mfg., including farm-products processing, at New Albany. Formed 1870. **10** County (□ 103; pop. 398,138), NE N.J., bounded NW by Passaic R. and E by Newark Bay and Arthur Kill; ⊙ Elizabeth. Industrial, residential area, with many commuter's communities; mfg. (chemicals, clothing, machinery, trucks, home appliances, radio, aircraft and auto parts, tools, motors, concrete and stone products, pharmaceuticals, plastics, rubber goods, paint, paper products); truck farming, dairying. Drained by Rahway R. Formed 1857. **11** County (□ 3,817; pop. 7,372), extreme NE N.Mex.; ⊙ Clayton. Livestock-grazing and grain area; watered N by headwaters of North Canadian and Cimarron rivers; borders on Texas, Okla., and Colo. Most of co. is high plateau (5–6,000 ft.). Capulin Natl. Monument in NW. Formed 1893. **12** County (□ 645; pop. 42,034), S N.C.; ⊙ Monroe. Bounded S and SW by S.C., NE by Rocky R. Piedmont farming (cotton, corn, hay), dairying, and saw-milling area; mfg. at Monroe. Formed 1842. **13** County (□ 434; pop. 20,687), central Ohio; ⊙ Marysville. Drained by Darby Creek, and small Mill and Rush creeks. Agr. area (livestock, dairy products, grain, poultry); mfg. at Marysville; limestone quarries, sand and gravel pits. Formed 1820. **14** County (□ 2,032; pop. 17,962), NE Oregon; ⊙ La Grande. Mtn. area crossed by Grande Ronde R. Livestock, wheat, lumber. Part of Whitman Natl. Forest is in SE, part of Umatilla Natl. Forest in N. Blue Mts. extend throughout most of co. Formed 1864. **15** County (□ 318; pop. 23,150), central Pa.; ⊙ Lewisburg. Agr. area; bounded E by West Branch of Susquehanna R.; forested recreation area in W part. Dairying, grist-mill products; furniture, textiles, lumber; limestone. Formed 1813. **16** County (□ 515; pop. 31,334), N S.C.; ⊙ Union. Bounded N by Pacolet R., S by Enoree R., E by Broad R.; drained by Tyger R. Includes part of Sumter Natl. Forest. Mainly agr. (cotton, corn, sweet potatoes), with some mfg., chiefly at Union. Formed 1785. **17** County (□ 454; pop. 10,792), SE S.Dak., bordering on Iowa and Nebr.; ⊙ Elk Point. Agr. area bounded E by Big Sioux R. and Iowa, S by Missouri R. Dairy products, livestock, poultry, grain. Formed 1862. **18** County (□ 212; pop. 8,670), NE Tenn.; ⊙ Maynardville. Bounded NW by Powell R.; crossed by Clinch R., here forming part of Norris Reservoir. Partly mountainous; traversed by ridges of the Appalachians. Agr. (tobacco, fruit, livestock). Formed 1850.

Union. **1** Town (pop. 261), Tolland co., NE Conn., on Mass. line, 8 mi. SW of Southbridge, Mass.; agr., lumbering. Includes Mashapaug village, near 800-acre Mashapaug Pond (resort); state forests. **2** Village (pop. 435), McHenry co., NE Ill., on Kishwaukee R. and 18 mi. NW of Elgin, in dairying and agr. area. **3** Town (pop. 490), Hardin co., central Iowa, near Iowa R., 8 mi. S of Eldora; rendering works. **4** Town (pop. 1,085), Knox co., S Maine, on St. George R. just NW of Rockland; agr.; wood and metal products. Settled 1774, inc. 1786. **5** Town (pop. 1,559), on Neshoba-Newton co. line, E central Miss., 29 mi. WNW of Meridian, in agr., timber, and dairying area; shirt mfg., lumber and cottonseed-products milling. **6** City (pop. 2,917), ⊙ Franklin co., E central Mo., near Missouri R., 42 mi. W of St. Louis; farm trade center; produces flour, shoes; lead, coal mines. Laid out 1826. **7** Village (pop. 277), Cass co., SE Nebr., 30 mi. S of Omaha, near Missouri R., in orchard region. **8** Village, N.H.: see WAKEFIELD. **9** Town, Hudson co., N.J.: see UNION CITY. **10** Township (pop. 38,004), Union co., NE N.J., 6 mi. SW of Newark; mfg. (machinery, paint, metal and concrete products, chemicals, pharmaceuticals, musical instruments, food products, plastics); truck, dairy products; nurseries. Settled 1747 from Conn. as Connecticut Farms, inc. 1808. Its church and other buildings burned in Revolution. **11** Town (1940 pop. 306), Hertford co., NE N.C., 3 mi. NNW of Ahoskie. **12** Village (pop. 370), Montgomery co., W Ohio, 11 mi. NW of Dayton and on Stillwater R. **13** or **Union City**, town (pop. 301), Canadian co., central Okla., 23 mi. WSW of Oklahoma City; cotton ginning; ships grain. **14** City (pop. 1,307), Union co., NE Oregon, on branch of Grande Ronde R., 14 mi. SE of La Grande, and near Wallowa Mts.; alt. 2,789 ft.; trade center for livestock, fruit, and grain area; lumber milling, dairying. Livestock experiment station of Oregon State Col. is here. Founded 1862, inc. 1878. **15** City (pop. 9,730), ⊙ Union co., N S.C., 25 mi. SE of Spartanburg; mfg. town in agr. area; textiles, lumber, printing, cottonseed products, foundry and machine-shop products, bakery products. Fine old houses in vicinity. Settled 1791. **16** Town (pop. 300), ⊙ Monroe co., SE W.Va., 18 mi. ESE of Hinton; lumbering, flour milling.

Unión (ōōnyōn'), N industrial section of Montevideo, S Uruguay.

Union, Cape, NE Ellesmere Isl., NE Franklin Dist., Northwest Territories, on the Lincoln Sea of the Arctic Ocean, at entrance of Robeson Channel; 82°13'N 61°7'W.

Unión, La, in Latin America: see LA UNIÓN.

Unión, La. **1** City, San Marcos dept., Guatemala: see SAN MARCOS, city. **2** Town, Zacapa dept., Guatemala: see LA UNION.

Unión, La, province, Peru: see COTAHUASI.

Unión, La (lä ōōnyōn'), city (pop. 7,207), Murcia prov., SE Spain, mining center 6 mi. E of Cartagena (joined by branch railroad). Products of its rich lead-silver ore, zinc, and iron-manganese mines are exported through its Mediterranean port of Portman (pop. 1,159); 3 mi. SE. Lead and iron foundries; zinc-processing plant. City was created (1869) from union of 2 old communities of Garbanzal and Herrería; hence its name. Frequent pop. changes according to fluctuations in world lead market.

Union, Lake (ū'nyŭn), W central Wash., in heart of Seattle, linked to Puget Sound and L. Washington by ship canal; wharves, drydocks, shipyards.

Union, Mount, peak (7,971 ft.), Yavapai co., central Ariz., 10 mi. SSE of Prescott.

Unión, Villa, Mexico: see VILLA UNIÓN, Sinaloa.

Unión Bay, Argentina: see ANEGADA BAY.

Union Bay, village (pop. estimate 500), SW B.C., on E Vancouver Isl., on Strait of Georgia, opposite Denman Isl., 10 mi. SE of Courtenay; cod and lumbering port.

Union Beach, borough (pop. 3,636), Monmouth co., E N.J., on Raritan Bay and 7 mi. SE of Perth Amboy. Inc. 1925.

Union Bleachery, village (pop. 9,337, with adjacent Sans Souci), Greenville co., NW S.C., adjacent to Greenville; textile-finishing plant.

Union Bridge, town (pop. 840), Carroll co., N Md., 17 mi. NE of Frederick, in agr. area; railroad shops, clothing factories, cement works.

Union Center, village (pop. 261), Juneau co., central Wis., on Baraboo R. and 30 mi. NW of Baraboo, in dairying region.

Union City. **1** Village, Conn.: see NAUGATUCK. **2** City (pop. 1,490), Fulton co., NW central Ga., 16 mi. SW of Atlanta, in farm area. **3** City (pop. 5,194), in E Ind. and W Ohio, 30 mi. E of Muncie; pop. in Randolph co., Ind., is 3,572; pop. in Darke co., Ohio, is 1,622. Ships agr. products and livestock; mfg. (bus bodies, automobile parts, furniture, luggage, flour, canned foods, dairy equipment). **4** Village (pop. 1,564), Branch and Calhoun counties, S Mich., 17 mi. S of Battle Creek, at confluence of Coldwater and St. Joseph rivers, in agr. and dairying area; makes food products. Indian mounds in vicinity. Settled 1830, inc. 1866. **5** City (pop. 55,537), Hudson co., NE N.J., just N of Hoboken; mfg. (embroideries, silk, soap, lamps, toilet preparations, clothing, handbags, paper products). Since 1914, passion play *Veronica's Veil* has been presented here annually during Lent, under auspices of Holy Family Church. Inc. 1925 after consolidation of West Hoboken and Union towns. **6** Town, Okla.: see UNION. **7** Borough (pop. 3,911), Erie co., NW Pa., 19 mi. SE of Erie; mfg. (furniture, wood products, powdered milk); potatoes, cabbage, buckwheat. Growth stimulated by oil boom of 1860s. Settled c.1785, inc. 1863. **8** City (pop. 7,665), ⊙ Obion co., NW Tenn., near Ky. line, 33 mi. NNE of Dyersburg; trade, processing, shipping center in cotton, grain, corn, livestock-raising area; mfg. of shoes, shirts, dairy products; lumbering, meat packing. Reelfoot L. is 15 mi. W. Platted 1854; inc. 1861.

Uniondale, town (pop. 2,028), S Cape Prov., U. of So. Afr., in Outeniqua Mts., 55 mi. E of Oudtshoorn; grain, fruit, tobacco. Gold diggings near by.

Union Dale, borough (pop. 350), Susquehanna co., NE Pa., 10 mi. N of Carbondale.

Uniondale. **1** Town (pop. 293), Wells co., E Ind., 19 mi. SSW of Fort Wayne, in agr. area. **2** Residential village (1940 pop. 1,104), Nassau co., SE N.Y., near Hempstead.

Unión de Reyes (ōōnyōn' dā rĕ'yĕs), town (pop. 5,503), Matanzas prov., W Cuba, rail junction 17 mi. S of Matanzas, in agr. region (sugar cane, livestock); foundries. Near by is the sugar central Santo Domingo.

Unión de San Antonio (sän äntō'nyō), city (pop. 2,167), Jalisco, central Mexico, 20 mi. W of León; corn, wheat, beans, livestock.

Unión de Tula (tōō'lä), town (pop. 3,933), Jalisco, W Mexico, 40 mi. SSW of Ameca; alt. 4,367 ft.; agr. center (grain, sugar cane, cotton, tobacco, fruit).

Union Gap (ū'nyŭn), town (pop. 1,766), Yakima co., S Wash., just S of Yakima and on Yakima R., in irrigated agr. region.

Union Grove, village (pop. 1,358), Racine co., SE Wis., 12 mi. WSW of Racine, in farm area; mfg. (brick, feed, sauerkraut, evaporated milk, radio parts, metal products, canned foods).

Union Hall or **Unionhall**, Gaelic *Bréantráigh*, town (pop. 151), SW Co. Cork, Ireland, on small inlet of the Atlantic, 5 mi. E of Skibbereen; fishing port, seaside resort. Dean Swift stayed here 1723 and celebrated area in poem.

Union Hill, village (pop. 138), Kankakee co., NE Ill., 15 mi. W of Kankakee.

Union Island, islet (□ 4.4; pop. 1,252), S Grenadines, dependency of St. Vincent, B.W.I., 40 mi. SSW of Kingstown; 12°35'N 61°25'W. Cotton growing.

Union Islands: see TOKELAU.

Unión Juárez (ōōnyōn' hwä'rĕs), town (pop. 583), Chiapas, S Mexico, at SE foot of Tacaná volcano, on Guatemala border, 17 mi. NE of Tapachula; alt. 4,153 ft.; coffee.

Union Lake, N.J.: see MAURICE RIVER.

Union Mills, village (pop. c.225), Carroll co., N Md., 35 mi. NW of Baltimore; vegetable cannery. Flour mill, erected 1796, still operates.

Union of Malaya: see MALAYA.

Union of South Africa: see SOUTH AFRICA, UNION OF.

Union of Soviet Socialist Republics (USSR), Rus. *Soyuz Sovetskikh Sotsialisticheskikh Respublik*

(SSSR), or **Soviet Union,** Rus. *Sovetskiy Soyuz,* federal state (□ c.8,600,000; 1950 pop. estimate 201,300,000) in E Europe and N and W central Asia; ⊙ Moscow (*Moskva*). Comprises 16 union republics: the RUSSIAN SOVIET FEDERATED SOCIALIST REPUBLIC, the largest and most populous, extending through Europe and Asia; KARELIA, ESTONIA, LATVIA, LITHUANIA, BELORUSSIA, UKRAINE, and MOLDAVIA, along the W border of the European USSR; GEORGIA, ARMENIA, and AZERBAIJAN, in Transcaucasia; KAZAKHSTAN, TURKMENIA, UZBEKISTAN, TADZHIKISTAN, and KIRGHIZIA, in Central Asia. The conventional geographic boundary bet. the European and Asiatic USSR follows the Ural Mts., the Ural R., and, bet. the Caspian and Black seas, the crest of the Greater Caucasus. For statistical purposes, however, the Urals and Transcaucasia are commonly included in the USSR in Europe (□ 2,110,600; 1950 pop. estimate 162,900,000), while Siberia (Asiatic part of the Russian SFSR) and the 5 republics of Central Asia constitute the USSR in Asia (□ 6,460,000; 1950 pop. 38,400,000). Covering one sixth of the earth's inhabited land area (i.e., excluding Antarctica), the USSR is the world's largest state and ranks third (after China and India) in population. It extends from the Baltic Sea at 20°E nearly half way around the world to the Bering Strait at 170°W, and from the Arctic Ocean at Cape Chelyuskin (77°44'N) to Kushka (35°N) on the Afghanistan frontier. It is bounded in Europe by Norway and Finland, and S of the Baltic Sea by Poland, Czechoslovakia, Hungary, and Rumania; in Asia, by Turkey and Iran bet. the Black and Caspian seas, and E of the Caspian by Iran, Afghanistan, China's Sinkiang prov., the Mongolian People's Republic, Manchuria, and Korea. Its Pacific shores are washed by the Sea of Japan, the Sea of Okhotsk, and Bering Sea; its Arctic shores by the Chukchi, East Siberian, Laptev, Kara, and Barents seas. In broad geographic terms, the USSR is a lowland, divided by the low Urals into the East European plain (W) and West Siberian plain (E), rising E toward the Central Siberian Plateau and the highlands of the Far East. This vast area of low and medium elevation is ringed along the S margins by the high ranges of the Carpathians, the Crimea, the Caucasus, the Kopet Dagh, the Tien Shan and Pamir-Alai systems, and the Altai and Sayan mts. The highest point of the USSR, Stalin Peak (24,590 ft.), is in the Pamir-Alai system; in Europe, Mt. Elbrus (18,481 ft.), in the Caucasus, is the highest. At the other extreme is the Batyr (or Karagiye) Depression, near the Caspian Sea, which reaches 433 ft. below sea level. The USSR is drained by some of the longest rivers in the world and contains some of the largest lakes. The European USSR is drained by the Volga, Ural, Dnieper, Don, and Northern Dvina rivers; the Asiatic part by the Ob-Irtysh, Lena, Amur, Amu Darya, and Yenisei. Among the lakes are, in addition to the Caspian Sea, lakes Ladoga and Onega in Europe and the Aral Sea and lakes Baikal and Balkhash in Asia. The country's climate is of the continental type, with the severity increasing from W to E as the moderating influence of the Atlantic Ocean decreases. The world's cold pole is in the Verkhoyansk-Oimyakon area of NE Siberia. Special climatic regions are in the Soviet Far East (Pacific monsoons), in the S CRIMEA (Mediterranean), and in TRANSCAUCASIA (humid subtropical). With the exception of the highlands, the USSR falls into latitudinal vegetation and soil zones: the tundra, along the Arctic shore—10% of total area; the coniferous forest (taiga) and the lesser mixed forests with podsolized soils—50% of total area; the black-earth steppe, largely under cultivation—12% of total area; and the semi-desert and desert with brown and gray soils in Central Asia—18% of total area. The tremendous natural resources of the USSR make it vitually self-sufficient. The leading minerals are coal, oil, oil shale, iron, manganese, copper, lead-zinc, salt, potash, and gold. Coal is found in the Donets, KUZNETSK, and Moscow basins, and at KARAGANDA, VORKUTA, and CHEREMKHOVO, with the remote Tunguska and Lena basins so far largely unexploited. Petroleum is produced in the Caucasus at BAKU, GROZNY, and MAIKOP, in the Second Baku (bet. the Volga and the Urals), and in the EMBA and UKHTA areas; oil shale in Estonia and in the middle Volga region. The leading iron deposits are those of KRIVOI ROG, KERCH, MAGNITOGORSK, and the Kursk magnetic anomaly. Manganese, of which the USSR is the world's leading producer, is mined at NIKOPOL and CHIATURA. Copper (in the Urals and Kazakhstan) and lead-zinc ores (in Kazakhstan) are the chief non-ferrous metals. Salt (ARTEMOVSK, L. BASKUNCHAK) and potash (SOLIKAMSK) form the basis of a major chemical industry, while gold is found mainly in the Aldan and Kolyma basins of E Siberia. The chief deficiencies are in tin, rubber, and other tropical crops (coffee, bananas). The leading exports are furs, timber, fish and caviar, manganese and chromium. The Soviet regime has transformed the USSR from a primarily agricultural to a primarily industrial state; industrial production was 42.1% of the total in 1913 and 85.7% in 1940. Wheat (in the Ukraine, the Kuban and trans-Volga steppes, and in SW Siberia) and cotton (in Central Asia) are the chief crops. Secondary agr. products are sugar beets, flax, hemp, and sunflowers. Industry is scattered throughout the USSR, with special concentration in the Moscow and Leningrad areas, the DONETS BASIN, and the Urals. The largest cities are Moscow, LENINGRAD, GORKI, and KUIBYSHEV in the European Russian SFSR; KIEV, KHARKOV, and ODESSA in the Ukraine; Baku and TIFLIS (Tbilisi) in Transcaucasia; SVERDLOVSK and CHELYABINSK in the Urals; TASHKENT in Central Asia; and NOVOSIBIRSK and OMSK in Siberia. Although the USSR has access to many seas, most of them are ice-bound a great part of the year. The only ice-free ports are on the Black Sea (notably Odessa), KALININGRAD and LIEPAJA on the Baltic, MURMANSK on the Barents Sea, and VLADIVOSTOK on the Sea of Japan. Other large ports are ARCHANGEL, Leningrad, and RIGA. The country's rail net (wide-gauge, unlike that of other European countries) is dense in Europe, but is limited in Asia to the Trans-Siberian, South Siberian, Trans-Caspian, and Turkestan-Siberia lines and spurs. River and canal navigation plays an important part, particularly in Europe. Pop. is densest in middle reaches of the European USSR, in the mixed forest and steppe zone, along the Trans-Siberian RR in Siberia, and in the oases of Central Asia. It is sparsest in N Siberia and the deserts of Central Asia. The industrialization of the country has produced a great increase in urban pop. from 17.9% in 1926 to 32.8% in 1939. The USSR is a multinational state. The leading ethnic and linguistic groups are: the Slavs—Russians (50% of total pop.), Ukrainians (15%), Belorussians (5%); the Turkic peoples—Uzbeks (2.5%), Tatars (2%), Kazakhs (1.5%), Azerbaijani Turks (1%); the Ugro-Finnic peoples—Mordvinians, Estonians, Udmurts, Mari. Separate groups are the Latvians and Lithuanians, the Georgians, the Armenians, Jews, and Moldavians, all of which number more than 1% of total pop. Slavs thus comprise nearly ¾ of USSR's pop., a situation reflected by the political, economic, and cultural leadership of the Russian people in particular. The territory of the USSR is organized into national autonomous units and administrative-economic regions. Separate ethnic groups are constituted into autonomous units ranging from a union republic (the highest category), through autonomous republic, autonomous oblast, national okrug, and national rayon, to the national village council. Homogeneous ethnic areas are in turn divided into oblasts or territories [Rus. *krai* or *kray*], rayons, and village councils. Urban centers, in accordance with their pop. and economic importance, may be towns (properly called workers settlements or city-type settlements) and cities of varying categories, which may be directly subordinate to the rayon, the oblast, or territory, or even directly to the republic. For the history of RUSSIA up to 1917, see that article. Under the leadership of Lenin the USSR emerged from the Russian Revolution of 1917 as the political successor of the Russian Empire. The USSR was the 1st country to adopt Marxism or Communism as the basis of its social, political, and economic constitution. Following a period of civil war, complicated by foreign intervention and by war (1920) with Poland, the USSR was formally created (1922) by union of the Russian and Transcaucasian SFSRs and the Ukrainian and Belorussian SSRs. The principles of the dictatorship of the proletariat and of the public ownership of the land and of the means of production, originally proclaimed in 1917, continued to form the basis of the constitutions of 1924 and, later, 1936. Initial difficulties in socialization of the country led to the temporary expedient of the relaxed New Economic Policy (NEP). During this mildly capitalist period, which helped to put the war-devasted Soviet economy back on its feet, Lenin died (1924). Of the 2 main protagonists in the struggle for leadership of the state—Stalin and Trotsky—Stalin emerged victorious. Although Stalin's plan called for a more gradual transformation of society than Trotsky's, with emphasis on the USSR, the Soviet Union continued to guide the Communist parties abroad, while at home a completely planned economy succeeded the NEP program. In a series of five-year plans (1928–33, 1933–38, 1938–42), industrialization of the economy was speeded to a spectacular degree, with the production of basic machinery and capital equipment stressed at the expense of consumer goods. The kulaks (well-to-do farmers) were "liquidated" and agr. was organized into collective and state farms. As a corollary of these developments, state control increased over all political, social, and cultural aspects of Soviet life. In a series of trials (1935–39) deviationist elements were purged and a monolithic unity was thus achieved on the eve of the Second World War. Soviet foreign relations, long hampered by mutual distrust of the nations of Europe and Asia, had been carried out by Chicherin and later by Litvinov, who brought about U.S. recognition in 1933 and Soviet admission into the League of Nations in 1934. The Western nations' failure to accept the Soviet's active role in the containment of Germany in the late 1930s brought about an abrupt shift in Soviet foreign policy under the leadership of Molotov. This led to the nonaggression pact with Germany in Aug., 1939, and territorial annexations (1939–40) in FINLAND (following a local war, 1939–40), the 3 Baltic States, E Poland, N BUKOVINA, and BESSARABIA. In June, 1941, came the attack by Germany, in which Rumania, Finland, Hungary, Slovakia, and Italy joined. By the end of 1941, Axis troops had overrun the W European USSR with c.40% of total pop. and stood along the line Leningrad-Moscow-Rostov. A Soviet counter-drive saved Moscow, but in the summer of 1942, the Germans drove to Stalingrad and into the Caucasus. A major Soviet counter-attack developed and drove the Axis troops steadily westward (1943 and 1944) until final victory in Europe in May, 1945. In accordance with previous understandings with the Western Allies, the USSR joined (Aug. 9, 1945) the final phase of the war against Japan, occupying Manchuria, N Korea, S Sakhalin, and the Kurile Isls. Wartime cooperation bet. the USSR and the West ceased soon after the armistice, and relations bet. the USSR and the U.S.—the two chief post-war powers—became increasingly strained. Friction became particularly acute over the fate of jointly occupied countries (Germany, Austria, Korea) and in the halls of the United Nations. Domestically, a post-war five-year plan (1946–50) was primarily concerned with reconstruction of war-damaged areas. During the Second World War, the USSR had absorbed (1944) the Tuva People's Republic. After the War, the Soviet Union annexed the Petsamo (PECHENGA) dist. from Finland, the N half of East Prussia (KALININGRAD oblast) from Germany, the Carpatho-Ukraine (TRANSCARPATHIAN OBLAST) from Czechoslovakia, and S SAKHALIN and the KURILE ISLANDS from Japan. In addition, the Soviet Union acquired naval base leases in the PORKKALA area of Finland and the Kwantung (PORT ARTHUR) dist. of Manchuria. For further information, see the separate articles on the various components of the Soviet Union and on the cities, towns, and geographic features.

Union Pass, Wyo.: see WIND RIVER RANGE.

Union Point, town (pop. 1,724), Greene co., NE central Ga., 6 mi. ENE of Greensboro; mills (hosiery, yarn, lumber).

Union River, S Maine, rises in N Hancock co., flows c.30 mi. S through Graham L., past Ellsworth (falls here), to mouth at **Union River Bay,** 8-mi. inlet of Blue Hill Bay.

Union Springs. 1 City (pop. 3,232), ⊙ Bullock co., SE Ala., 38 mi. SE of Montgomery, in the Black Belt; farm trade center; lumber, cotton products, fertilizer; dairying. Settled 1836. **2** Village (pop. 957), Cayuga co., W central N.Y., on E shore of Cayuga L., 8 mi. SW of Auburn; summer resort; some mfg. (salt blocks, thermometers); dairy products, truck.

Union Star, town (pop. 373), De Kalb co., NW Mo., 20 mi. NE of St. Joseph; agr.

Uniontown. 1 Town (pop. 1,798), Perry co., W central Ala., 30 mi. W of Selma; cord, yarn, and twine, lumber, dairy products. Settled early 19th cent. **2** City (pop. 232), Bourbon co., SE Kansas, 15 mi. W of Fort Scott, in dairying and general-farming region. **3** City (pop. 1,054), Union co., W Ky., on the Ohio and 19 mi. W of Henderson, in agr. and bituminous-coal area; makes bricks, tiles; grain elevator. Settled c.1810; inc. 1840. **4** Village (pop. 232), Muskingum co., central Ohio, 9 mi. SW of Zanesville, in limestone and coal area. Post office name is East Fultonham. **5** Borough (pop. 323), Dauphin co., E central Pa., on Mahantango Creek and 26 mi. N of Harrisburg. Post office is Pillow. **6** City (pop. 20,471), ⊙ Fayette co., SW Pa., 40 mi. SSE of Pittsburgh; bituminous coal; coke, metal products, clothing, beverages, dairy products; lumber; limestone. Fort Necessity Natl. Battlefield Site is near by; Gen. Braddock buried near fort. Gen. George C. Marshall b. here. Settled c.1767, inc. as borough 1796, as city 1916. **7** Village (pop. 1,280), Northumberland co., E central Pa. **8** Town (pop. 254), Whitman co., SE Wash., near Idaho line, 10 mi. NNW of Lewiston, Idaho; wheat, livestock, dairy products.

Unionville, village (pop. estimate 550), S Ont., 16 mi. NNE of Toronto; dairying, truck gardening.

Unionville. 1 Village, Conn.: see FARMINGTON. **2** Village (pop. 2,770, with adjoining Phillipsburg), Tift co., S Ga., near Tifton. **3** Town (pop. 204), Appanoose co., S Iowa, 20 mi. SW of Ottumwa, in agr. area. **4** Village (pop. 531), Tuscola co., E Mich., 21 mi. ENE of Bay City, near Saginaw Bay, in farm area; fisheries; coal mines; grain elevators. **5** City (pop. 2,050), ⊙ Putnam co., N Mo., 29 mi. NW of Kirksville; agr., coal, clay. Inc. c.1855. **6** Village (pop. 454), Orange co., SE N.Y., near N.J. line, 9 mi. SE of Port Jervis; mfg. (labels, pulp, paper); summer resort. **7** Town (pop. 124), Union co., S N.C., 10 mi. NNE of Monroe. **8** Borough (pop. 341), Centre co., central Pa., 5 mi. W of Bellefonte. Post office is Fleming.

Unionville Center, village (pop. 237), Union co., central Ohio, 22 mi. WNW of Columbus.

Uniopolis (ūnēŏ'pŭlĭs), village (pop. 271), Auglaize co., W Ohio, 10 mi. S of Lima, in agr. area.

United Khasi and Jaintia Hills, India: see KHASI AND JAINTIA HILLS.

United Kingdom of Great Britain and Northern Ireland, kingdom (□ 94,279; 1931 pop. 46,180,870; 1951 census pop. 50,211,602) in the British Isles; ⊙ LONDON. Its constituent parts are GREAT BRITAIN (ENGLAND, SCOTLAND, and WALES) and NORTHERN IRELAND. Legislative power is vested in bicameral Parliament, consisting of an elected House of Commons (lower chamber) and a House of Lords (upper chamber) made up of all members of the hereditary peerage. Executive power is vested in a govt. headed by a prime minister and responsible to Parliament. Parliamentary legislation requires royal assent, which in practice is never withheld. Power of the House of Lords has been reduced by successive statutes; the lords cannot veto bills originating in the Commons, and themselves cannot originate finance bills. While all constituent parts of the United Kingdom are represented in Parliament, Northern Ireland, the Isle of Man, and the Channel Isls. also have legislatures of their own, whose power is limited to legislation of a purely local character. The body of acts of Parliament forms the United Kingdom's constitution, which is thus a flexible and dynamic concept. Parliamentary elections are based upon universal suffrage and must be held at least every 5 years, except under special circumstances. The official title of United Kingdom of Great Britain and Ireland dates from union (1800) bet. Great Britain and Ireland; no change was made after creation (1922) of Irish Free State, but in 1927 the present title was adopted. It did not, however, gain widespread usage until after Second World War. Full title is frequently abbreviated to United Kingdom or U.K.

United Provinces or **United Provinces of Agra and Oudh**, India: see UTTAR PRADESH; AGRA; OUDH.

United States, republic (land only □ 2,977,128; with inland waters but without □ c.60,400 of Great Lakes surface □ 3,022,387; 1950 pop. 150,697,361; 1940 pop. 131,669,275; all figures excluding territories and possessions) of North America; ⊙ Washington, in Dist. of Columbia. The United States together with □ 597,236 of territories and possessions has □ 3,619,623; 1950 pop. 153,694,423; 1940 pop. 134,265,231. Continental U.S. consists of 48 states (see table at end of this article) and a federal dist. U.S. territories include ALASKA, on North American continent; PUERTO RICO and the VIRGIN ISLANDS OF THE UNITED STATES, in the West Indies; several isls. in the Pacific—HAWAIIAN ISLANDS (Territory of Hawaii), GUAM, American SAMOA, WAKE ISLAND, MIDWAY, CANTON ISLAND, ENDERBURY ISLAND, and a few others. The U.S. holds the PANAMA CANAL ZONE under perpetual lease from the govt. of Panama, and has trusteeship under the UN of the Caroline, Marshall, and Marianas isl. chains. It occupied other Pacific isls.—among them the Ryukyu Isls. and the Bonin Isls.—after the Second World War. Continental U.S. extends from the Pacific to the Atlantic, bounded N by Canada (3,986.8-mi. boundary, partly along the Great Lakes) and S by Mexico (2,013-mi. boundary). Westernmost point is Cape Alava, Wash. (48°10'N 124°44'W), easternmost point is West Quoddy Head, Maine (44°49'N 66°57'W), northernmost point is the Northwest Angle in Lake of the Woods, Minn. (49°23'N 95°9'W), southernmost mainland point is Cape Sable, Fla. (25°7'N 81°5'W). Extreme measurement E–W is 2,807 mi., N–S 1,598 mi. Coast line totals 11,936 mi. (5,565 mi. along the Atlantic, 2,730 mi. along the Pacific, 3,641 mi. along the Gulf of Mexico). Country is divided into 4 time zones, with a 3-hr. difference bet. the Pacific and Eastern zones. Physiographically, the United States may be divided into 6 broad divisions; from E to W are the Atlantic coastal plain (continued as Gulf coastal plain along Gulf of Mexico); the Appalachian highlands; the immense interior plains; the Rocky Mts. belt; the intermontane basins and plateaus W of the Rockies; and the mts. and valleys of the Pacific borderland. A 7th division, part of the Laurentian Plateau of Canada, dips into U.S. in the Great Lakes region. The Atlantic coastal plain begins on N with Cape Cod and Long Isl., widens S of New York, and eventually becomes a broad sandy belt which includes all of Fla., and meets the wide Gulf coastal plain in Ga. Atlantic and Gulf coasts are essentially coast lines of submergence, with numerous embayments, sandspits (e.g., Cape Cod, Sandy Hook), and barrier beaches backed by lagoons. The NE coast has many fine bays, but from the great capes (Fear, Lookout, Hatteras) of the N.C. coast southward, large bays are few. Principal feature of Gulf of Mexico coast is the great delta of the Mississippi, thrusting SE from New Orleans. Much of coast is fringed by marshlands, barrier beaches, and countless lagoons and waterways. W of the Atlantic coastal plain is the PIEDMONT, the transition zone bordering W on the APPALACHIAN MOUNTAINS, which extend from the St. Lawrence on NE to Ala. on SW, where they meet the Gulf plain. The Appalachians (and the ADIRONDACK MOUNTAINS of N.Y., which are geologically related to the Laurentian Plateau rather than to the Appalachian system) include all of the chief E highlands. Mt. Washington (6,288 ft.) is highest point in New England; the Black Mts. (N.C.) rise to 6,684 ft. at Mt. Mitchell, highest point in E North America. The Appalachian Plateau W of the mts. includes the Cumberland and Allegheny plateaus and their fringing highlands. The GREAT LAKES (□ 94,710, of which □ c.60,400 are in U.S.) lie along the Can. border from N.Y. to Minn.; a S extension of the Laurentian Plateau (in Minn., Wis., and the Upper Peninsula of Mich.) partially embraces L. Superior. W and S of the Great Lakes, extending from the Appalachians to the Rockies and meeting the Gulf coastal plain on S are the great central or interior plains (alt. c.500–1,000 ft.), drained (except for basin in the Dakotas and Minn. of the N-flowing Red R.) by the great Missouri-Mississippi system. Above the GREAT PLAINS—which slope E from the base of the Rockies—rises a single highland area, the BLACK HILLS. In the S, and W of the Mississippi, rise the OZARK MOUNTAINS and OUACHITA MOUNTAINS. W of the Great Plains, the ROCKY MOUNTAINS sweep into the NW U.S. from Canada and extend into N N.Mex., whence connecting ranges continue S to link the Rockies with the Sierra Madre of Mexico. The Rocky Mtn. system within U.S. is broken by high basins (such as the Wyoming Basin and Laramie Plains) and plateaus. Highest peak of the Rockies (in Colo.) is Mt. Elbert, 14,431 ft. W of the Rockies is the great, arid region of basin-and-range country and plateaus which separates the E and W belts of the cordillera. In N are the volcanic Columbia Plateau (Wash., Oregon, S Idaho) drained by the COLUMBIA RIVER; W of the Southern Rockies the enormous COLORADO PLATEAU is drained by the COLORADO RIVER and its tributaries, while the midsection is occupied by the GREAT BASIN, a region of interior drainage containing the GREAT SALT LAKE and large desert or near-desert tracts, including DEATH VALLEY, lowest point (280 ft. below sea level) on the continent. Westernmost prov. of the U.S. is the system of mts. (actually 2 belts of differing geologic history) bet. the intermontane region and the Pacific. The CASCADE RANGE extends from B.C. into Wash. and across Oregon into N Calif., whence it is continued S by the towering SIERRA NEVADA, extending for most of length of Calif. and including Mt. WHITNEY, 14,495 ft., highest point in U.S. W of the Cascades, rising from the Pacific from NW Wash. to S Calif., are the COAST RANGES, bordered only occasionally by coastal plains and often rising steeply above the ocean. The W coast, a coast line of emergence, has few isls. (except in Puget Sound) and few good harbors besides PUGET SOUND (N), SAN FRANCISCO BAY (Calif.). Lowlands lie about Puget Sound and along river valleys of Oregon; chief Calif. lowlands are the great CENTRAL VALLEY and the Los Angeles basin of S Calif. The vast MISSOURI RIVER-MISSISSIPPI RIVER system drains almost all of the interior plains, except for the Great Lakes basin on NE, the RIO GRANDE basin (including part of Mexico) on SW, and most of the Gulf coastal plain, much of which drains directly into the Gulf. Principal affluents of the Missouri are the Yellowstone, Niobrara, Platte, and Kansas rivers; Mississippi tributaries are led in importance by the Ohio, and also include the Tennessee, the Cumberland, the Wabash, the Arkansas (with its tributaries the Cimarron and the Canadian), and the Red. The Great Lakes drain to the Atlantic through the SAINT LAWRENCE RIVER (Canada and N.Y.). The E slope of the Appalachians and the E coastal region drain to the Atlantic; principal rivers are the Penobscot, Kennebec, Merrimack, Connecticut, Hudson, Delaware, Susquehanna, Potomac, James, Pee Dee, Santee, Savannah, Saint Johns. W of the Cascades and the Sierra Nevada, principal rivers are the Willamette, Columbia, SACRAMENTO, San Joaquin rivers. The United States, with its enormous expanse and varied topography, contains a number of climatic regions. E of about the 100th meridian (which marks the approximate boundary bet. the more humid E and the generally drier W) are 3 broad E–W climatic zones. Northernmost, from E N.Dak. across center of the Great Lakes region and into New England, has a humid-continental climate, with 20 to 40 inches of rainfall (increasing toward E), with occasional areas of more precipitation, and Jan. normal temperatures bet. −5°F. and −20°F., July normal temps. from 50°F. to 68°F. The 2d zone, the warm-summer continental belt, passes across S tip of L. Michigan on N, extends S to latitude of St. Louis, and continues to E coast to include Middle Atlantic states; it has generally more rainfall and higher temp. (Jan. normal bet. 14°F. and 30°F., July bet. 68°F. and c.80°F.). An extension of the humid-continental belt invades this zone along crest of the Appalachians. Southernmost belt of the E portion is classified as humid subtropical, with warm summers (July 68°F. to c.85°F. except for cooler coastal strips) and mild winters (Jan. 30°F. to 70°F., N–S) and generally more abundant rainfall (to 80 inches along the Gulf). The S tip of Fla. is in the tropical rainy belt, with 80-inch rainfall. From the 100th meridian W, the Great Plains and the lowlands of the Rockies have a steppe climate, with sparse rainfall (10–20 inches), cold to cool winters (Jan., −4°F. to 14°F. in N, to 30°F. in S) and generally hot summers, modified locally by alt. Temps. and precipitation in the Rockies vary with alt. and exposure, as they do in the Cascades and the Sierra Nevada farther W; precipitation ranges from under 10 inches in the arid lowlands to hundreds of inches of snowfall on the higher crests. The Coast Ranges, the W slope of the Sierra Nevada, and the Cascades receive the rainfall carried by the moisture-laden westerly winds, and thus account for the aridity of the intermontane region, where there is generally less than 10 inches of rainfall; here temp. range, according to alt., is from 14°F. in Jan. to over 90°F. in July. The mild marine-climate belt extends along the W coast as far S as N Calif.; here Jan. normal temp. range is from 50°F. to 68°F. in S and 14°F. to 32°F. in N (July normal is bet. c.50°F. and c.70°F. in both N and S); 40 to over 100 inches of rainfall support heavy vegetation. About ¼ of the U.S. is in forest, of which the trees of only slightly more than 200,000,000 acres are classified as saw timber. The Northwest (including N Idaho, W Mont.) has c.40% of the remaining merchantable timber, chiefly Douglas fir, ponderosa and sugar pine, western hemlock, red and Port Orford cedar; the pine belt of the SE and S accounts for much of the remaining softwood saw-timber stands, while hardwoods (deciduous forests) make up less than 20% of available timber reserves. Despite maintenance of c.180,000,000 acres of natl. forests and similar preserves, the rate of cut and destruction exceeds that of tree growth, and the remaining stands of virgin timber promise to go the way of the great North Woods forests (Mich., Wis., Minn.), logged off in last half of 19th cent., and the northeastern forests, whose large timber was gone by end of 19th cent., and the great central hardwood forest, cleared to make way for agr. Growing seasons, determined by elevation as well as latitude, vary widely. Along the Gulf and SE coasts and in Fla. season is upwards of 240 days; this belt is succeeded by NE–SW belts of progressively shorter growing periods until the 150-day zone is reached, across N.Mex., SE Colo., Nebr., Iowa, S Wis., and thence along the S Great Lakes into S New England. N New England, the N Great Lakes, and the N central plains have a 120-day (or less) season; it is less than 90 days in the Rockies and W high plateaus, about 120 days in the W intermontane lowlands, and 200 days or over in much of the W, including a 240-day belt in S Calif. Year-round agr. is practiced in irrigated regions (such as Calif.'s Imperial Valley) of the Southwest. The United States' share of the wheat belts of North America, its great livestock ranges on the W plains (cattle, sheep) and the Gulf coast (cattle), the rich Corn Belt (whose produce largely goes into fattening livestock, especially hogs), and its many productive specialized areas (dairy products, fruits, vegetables) make it one of world's ranking food-producing nations. In addition, the U.S. leads the world in the production of cotton and tobacco. Leading crops for the nation are wheat, corn, oats, barley, sorghums, rye, buckwheat, rice, flaxseed, cotton, tobacco, hay, soybeans, peanuts, potatoes and sweet potatoes, beans and peas, sugar cane, sugar beets, citrus and other fruits, nuts, vegetables in enormous variety, and table, wine, and raisin grapes. Important states in the production of wheat and other grains are Kansas, Mont., the Dakotas, Nebr., Okla., Wash., Oregon, Ohio, Texas, Colo., Ill., Mo., Ind., Mich., Idaho. The Corn Belt crosses the Middle Western states S of the Great Lakes, which are bordered by one of the most important dairy-farming belts, extending E and NE into New England. The Cotton Belt is in the S and SE; of recent years, Texas, N.Mex., Ariz., and Calif. have grown in importance as cotton-growing states, in addition to Miss., Ark., Ala., S.C., Ga., La., N.C., Tenn., Mo., and Okla. The subtropical Gulf coast region produces rice, sugar cane, citrus, other fruits, and truck crops. The Atlantic coastal plain is an important area for truck crops, peanuts, poultry, and fruit; the Piedmont produces tobacco, cotton, fruit, and livestock, as well as general crops. Leading tobacco-growing states are N.C., Ky., Va., Tenn., S.C., Ga., Pa., Wis., and Md. The Great Plains, parts of the Gulf Coast (especially in Texas), the arid lands of the W and SW, and the ranges of the Rocky Mtn. region are important for livestock grazing. Irrigated agr. (more than 20,000,000 acres in U.S., of which half were in the Rocky Mtn. region, c.⅓ in the Pacific states) has been fostered by an enormous program of reclamation (also important for hydroelectric power) which includes such dams as Grand Coulee (Wash.), Hungry Horse (Mont.), Shasta and Friant (Calif.). Fruit regions include the E Cascade region of Wash. and Oregon, many parts of Calif., the citrus-fruit belts in Ariz., the Rio Grande valley of Texas, Fla., and the Mississippi delta (La.); an important fruit belt lies along the Great Lakes. Maine and New York have large potato acreages, as does Idaho.

Truck-farming areas are found near all sizable cities, but those notable for their extent and for long-range shipments are principally in Calif., Ariz., Texas (Rio Grande valley), Fla., and the SE Atlantic coastal plain. The South has developed many specialty-crop regions to replace the former one-crop type of farm economy. A chronic agr. problem of the U.S. is the loss (estimated at up to ½) of soil fertility due to overcropping and improper farming methods. Erosion (estimated to affect seriously nearly 300,000,000 acres) and soil depletion are being combatted by Federal and state-sponsored programs. Overstocking has seriously affected most of the nation's rangeland as well, and, together with deforestation, has added to the menace of floods on the major rivers. About 70% of U.S. farm production is from family-size farms, while c.20% is from large-scale mechanized farms. The mineral resources of the U.S. are generally ranked 1st among those of the world. It produces more than ⅓ of world's coal (chiefly bituminous and anthracite), and more than 60% of the world's petroleum, as well as enormous quantities of natural gas, important as industrial and domestic fuel, and an important amount of helium (Texas). Coal reserves include enormous beds of lignite and sub-bituminous coal (in W). Of strategic minerals, the U.S. is richest in iron ore (of which it has huge reserves of low-grade ore, less of the richer ores), zinc, copper, and lead; it produces varying proportions of its requirements of magnesium, molybdenum, uranium, vanadium, phosphate rock, sulphur, bauxite, salt, fluorspar, nitrates, quicksilver, potash, limestone, cement rock, and borates. Gold and silver are abundant as well, and building stone (marble, slate, granite) are quarried. Principal bituminous coal fields are in the Appalachians (which also contain the anthracite field of E Pa.) and the central plains, (Ill., Ind., Iowa, Mo., Nebr., Okla., Kansas); lesser deposits are in N.Mex., Ariz., Colo., Utah, Mont., Wyo., Colo., Utah, N.Mex., Texas, Wash., Oregon, and Calif. Petroleum and natural gas are produced along the Gulf coast (where wells have also been driven in coastal waters), in the lower Mississippi valley, the Appalachian plateau, the mid-continent area centering on Okla. and Kansas, in E Texas, the Rocky Mtn. and N Great Plains region (especially Wyo., Mont., N.Dak.), and the S Central Valley and S coastal region of Calif. Iron comes chiefly from the great iron ranges (chiefly in Minn., Mich.) of the L. Superior region and from the S Appalachians (Birmingham dist.). Copper mining is important in the Upper Peninsula of Mich. (less than formerly), the Butte region of Mont., and from Utah, Ariz., N.Mex., Colo., Nev., Calif., Wash., and Oregon. U.S. lead-producing dists. are in Coeur d'Alene region of Idaho, Bingham dist. of Utah, the Tri-State region of Kansas, SW Mo., and Okla.; zinc comes from Tri-State region, Coeur d'Alene dist., and E Tenn.; silver from Mont., Idaho, Nev., Ariz.; gold from Calif., Utah, Idaho, Nev., Ariz., Mont., Colo., S.Dak., Wash., Ore., and N.Mex. Fisheries are a valuable resource for food fish, shell fish, and varieties used for oil and fertilizer. Great wealth in raw materials, fuel and power resources (coal, petroleum, natural gas, water power), transportation facilities, and manpower have made the U.S. the leading manufacturing nation of the globe. The most important mfg. belt extends from New England and the Middle Atlantic states as far S as the Potomac, and W across the lower Great Lakes to the upper Mississippi valley. Here are the great iron and steel centers—the Chicago-Gary area, the Pittsburgh-Youngstown dist., and others, the great concentration of automobile plants in Detroit and its environs, and many other metal-using industries. The greatly diversified manufacturing dists. of the great urban centers and of the New England industrial towns produce textiles, shoes, and a wide variety of light-industry products requiring precision and skill. Within this belt are most of the ranking industrial centers—New York, Chicago, Detroit, Philadelphia, Boston, Pittsburgh, Cleveland, Buffalo, Bridgeport, Milwaukee, Baltimore, Cincinnati, Providence, and Youngstown. Outside of this NE region, the most important mfg. dists. are those of St. Louis, Kansas City, Indianapolis, Richmond, Winston-Salem, Birmingham, New Orleans, Memphis, Omaha, Minneapolis, the Seattle-Tacoma region, Portland (Oregon), San Francisco, and Los Angeles. The steel industry in recent years has spread W (to Geneva, Utah; Pittsburg and Fontana, Calif.) and SE (to vicinity of Philadelphia and Baltimore) from its long-established centers. The development of hydroelectric projects has attracted electrometallurgical plants to such areas as the South (Tenn., N.C., Texas, Ala.) and the Pacific Northwest (Wash., Oregon). Available power and raw materials have stimulated growth of the South's textile (cotton, synthetic fibers) industries to supplement its other chief industries—the processing of farm products, handling of tobacco (Richmond, Winston-Salem, Durham), and furniture mfg. (in the Piedmont). The development of Gulf Coast resources—petroleum, sulphur, salt; and magnesium from sea water—has given rise to important chemical and metallurgical industries. Meat packing has developed to an enormous industry in such cities as Chicago, Kansas City, Omaha, and Fort Worth, at transportation crossroads bet. the livestock ranges and the large markets of the E; similarly, flour milling has been established at such centers as Minneapolis, Buffalo, and Kansas City, the farm-machinery industry has concentrated in the Middle West, and metal-refining and smelting centers have developed in the W. The U.S. has many active seaports, led by New York, Philadelphia, Baltimore, Hampton Roads, Boston, on the E coast; Houston and New Orleans, on the Gulf; Los Angeles, San Francisco, Portland, and Seattle, on the Pacific. The nation's railroad network (heaviest in the E) totals more than 225,000 mi. of main-line track. Principal inland navigation is on the Great Lakes and the Mississippi, connected with Great Lakes by Illinois Waterway. The Intracoastal Waterway and the N.Y. State Barge Canal are the largest U.S. canal systems. The U.S. has scores of natl. parks, monuments, and historic sites; among its scenic and recreational regions are Grand Canyon, Yellowstone, Grand Teton, Rocky Mountain, Yosemite, Sequoia, Lassen Volcanic, and Mount Rainier natl. parks and Death Valley Natl. Monument in the W; in the E are Niagara Falls (continent's largest cataract), and Great Smoky Mountains, Shenandoah, Acadia, and Everglades natl. parks. Spain, England, and France were chief nations to establish colonies in the present U.S., although the Netherlands (New Netherland, in what later became N.Y. and N.J.) and Sweden (New Sweden, where parts of Pa., N.J., and Del. are now) also established settlements. First permanent European settlement in present U.S. was made by Spaniards in 1565, at St. Augustine, Fla. From New France (present Canada), French influence spread through the Great Lakes area and down the Mississippi to the colony of Louisiana. British settlements were made on the Atlantic coast, beginning with Jamestown (Va.) in 1607; the Plymouth colony (New England) was established 1620. After the American Revolution (1765–83), the 13 former Br. colonies (Mass., N.H., Conn., R.I., N.Y., N.J., Pa., Del., Md., Va., N.C., S.C., and Ga.) became the 1st states, and others were soon added under the Ordinance of 1787, which set up territorial govt. for the NORTHWEST TERRITORY and established a method of admitting new states to the union. By Treaty of Paris (1783), the U.S. acquired dominion over the entire region from the Atlantic to the Mississippi and from the Great Lakes and Canada on the N to the Sp. possessions in Fla. and along the Gulf of Mexico on the S. By the Louisiana Purchase (1803) from France, a vast region including much of present La. and extending far N and NW to an indefinite boundary along the Rockies was acquired. Fla. was purchased in 1819; the Webster-Ashburton Treaty (1842) settled much of the boundary bet. NE U.S. and Canada. Texas was annexed 1845. Upper Calif. (present Calif.) and N.Mex. (including most of present Ariz. and N.Mex., all of Utah and Nev., and parts of Colo. and Wyo.) were acquired from Mexico by the Treaty of Guadalupe Hidalgo (1848), which also established much of Mex. boundary. Gadsden Purchase (1853–54) added to the U.S. a strip of land in present Ariz. and N.Mex., and setted the remainder of the boundary. Under a treaty (1846) with England, an area (mostly present Wash. and Oregon) was acquired as Oregon Territory (established 1848); this treaty also established the westernmost portion of the Can. boundary (along 49th parallel); from the Rockies E to Lake of the Woods, this boundary had been settled in 1818. Alaska was purchased (1867) from the Russians; Puerto Rico and the Philippine Isls. were acquired (1898) as the result of the Spanish-American War (the Philippines became a commonwealth in 1945 and independent in 1946), and Hawaii was annexed the same year. In terms of area, the U.S. covered □ 867,980 in 1790, □ 1,685,865 in 1810, □ 2,973,965 in 1860. See articles on the cities, towns, geographic features, and the 48 states:

State	Land area (sq. mi.)	1950 pop.	Year admitted
Alabama	51,078	3,061,743	1819
Arizona	113,580	749,587	1912
Arkansas	52,725	1,909,511	1836
California	156,803	10,586,223	1850
Colorado	103,967	1,325,089	1876
Connecticut	4,899	2,007,280	1788
Delaware	1,978	318,085	1787
District of Columbia	61	802,178	1791
Florida	54,262	2,771,305	1845
Georgia	58,518	3,444,578	1788
Idaho	82,808	588,637	1890
Illinois	55,947	8,712,176	1818
Indiana	36,205	3,934,224	1816
Iowa	55,986	2,621,073	1846
Kansas	82,113	1,905,299	1861
Kentucky	40,109	2,944,806	1792
Louisiana	45,177	2,683,516	1812
Maine	31,040	915,774	1820
Maryland	9,887	2,343,001	1788
Massachusetts	7,907	4,690,514	1788
Michigan	57,022	6,371,766	1837
Minnesota	80,009	2,982,483	1858
Mississippi	47,420	2,178,914	1817
Missouri	69,270	3,954,653	1821
Montana	146,316	591,024	1889
Nebraska	76,653	1,325,510	1867
Nevada	109,802	160,083	1864
New Hampshire	9,024	533,242	1788
New Jersey	7,522	4,835,329	1787
New Mexico	121,511	681,187	1912
New York	47,929	14,830,192	1788
North Carolina	49,142	4,061,929	1789
North Dakota	70,054	619,636	1889
Ohio	41,122	7,946,627	1803
Oklahoma	69,283	2,233,351	1907
Oregon	96,350	1,521,341	1859
Pennsylvania	45,045	10,498,012	1787
Rhode Island	1,058	791,896	1790
South Carolina	30,594	2,117,027	1788
South Dakota	76,536	652,740	1889
Tennessee	41,961	3,291,718	1796
Texas	263,644	7,711,194	1845
Utah	82,346	688,862	1896
Vermont	9,278	377,747	1791
Virginia	39,899	3,318,680	1788
Washington	66,977	2,378,963	1889
West Virginia	24,090	2,005,552	1863
Wisconsin	54,715	3,434,575	1848
Wyoming	97,506	290,529	1890

United States Range, N Ellesmere Isl., NE Franklin Dist., Northwest Territories, extends c.250 mi. WSW-ENE across N part of isl. (the region called Grant Land), from Nansen Sound to the Lincoln Sea of the Arctic Ocean, in lat. 82°N; rises to over 11,000 ft.

Unity, town (pop. 817), W Sask., 45 mi. SW of North Battleford; natural-gas and salt production, dairying, flour milling; grain, stock.

Unity. 1 Resort town (pop. 1,014), Waldo co., S Maine, on Unity Pond and 18 mi. NW of Belfast; agr.; lumbering. **2** Town (pop. 653), Sullivan co., SW N.H., 38 mi. WNW of Concord. **3** Village (pop. 355), on Clark-Marathon co. line, central Wis., 35 mi. WSW of Wausau, in dairying and farming area.

Unity Pond, Waldo co., S Maine, near Unity, 20 mi. NW of Belfast; 4 mi. long, 1.5 mi. wide. Noted for fishing.

Universal, town (pop. 479), Vermillion co., W Ind., 12 mi. NNW of Terre Haute, in agr. and bituminous-coal area.

Universal City, unincorporated suburb surrounded by LOS ANGELES city, Los Angeles co., S Calif., just SW of Burbank; motion-picture studio here.

Universales, Montes (mōn'tēs ōōnēvĕrsä'lēs), mountain range, Teruel prov., E Spain, extending from Teruel to Cuenca prov. border, and forming with near-by Sierra de Albarracín a watershed where rise Tagus, Júcar, Turia, and Jiloca rivers. Average alt. 4,000 ft.

University, Miss.: see OXFORD.

University City, city (pop. 39,892), St. Louis co., E Mo., near Mississippi R., suburb W of St. Louis. Inc. 1906.

University Heights. 1 Town (pop. 446), Johnson co., E Iowa, suburb of Iowa City. **2** A residential section of W Bronx borough of New York city, SE N.Y., opposite N Manhattan. A division of New York Univ. and the Edgar Allen Poe cottage are here. **3** City (pop. 11,566), Cuyahoga co., N Ohio, an E suburb of Cleveland. Seat of John Carroll Univ. Inc. 1908 as Idlewood, renamed 1925.

University Park. 1 Town (pop. 457), Mahaska co., S central Iowa, adjacent to Oskaloosa. Kletzing Col. is here. **2** Town (pop. 2,205), Prince Georges co., central Md., NE of Washington. Inc. 1936. **3** City (pop. 24,275), Dallas co., N Texas, N residential suburb of Dallas. Seat of Southern Methodist Univ. Settled 1914, inc. 1924.

Unjha (ōōn'jŭ), town (pop. 13,216), Mehsana dist., N Bombay, India, 12 mi. N of Mehsana; trades in millet, wheat, oilseeds; hand-loom weaving, oilseed milling. Formerly spelled Unza.

Unley (ŭn'lē), S residential suburb (pop. 44,164) of Adelaide, SE South Australia; agr. center.

Unna (ōō'nä), town (pop. 23,007), in former Prussian prov. of Westphalia, W Germany, after 1945 in North Rhine-Westphalia, in the Ruhr, 10 mi. E of Dortmund; coal-mining center; steel plants, wire mills, brassworks. Has 14th-cent. castle and church; remains of 13th-cent. town walls. Founded by Charlemagne.

Unnao, India: see UNAO.

Unnichchai (ōōn-nĭch'ī), village (pop. 217), Eastern Prov., Ceylon, 12 mi. SW of Batticaloa; rice plantations. Land development (□ 30) planned. Just W is Unnichchai Tank (2.5 mi. long, 2 mi. wide), a large irrigation lake.

Uno, Japan: see TAMANO.

Unomachi, Japan: see UWA.

Unquillo (ōōngkē'yō), town (pop. 3,700), N central Córdoba prov., Argentina, in hills, 14 mi. NNW of Córdoba; resort, rail terminus, and agr. center; granite quarrying, stock raising, dairying.

Unruhstadt, Poland: see KARGOWA.

Unseburg (ŏŏn'zŭbŏŏrk), village (pop. 2,678), in former Prussian Saxony prov., central Germany, after 1945 in Saxony-Anhalt, 16 mi. SSW of Magdeburg; lignite and potash mining.

Unshin River, Co. Sligo, Ireland, flows 11 mi. from Lough Arrow NNW to Ballysadare Bay at Ballysadare.

Unst (ŭnst), island (□ 46.6, including UYEA and MUCKLE FLUGGA isls.; pop. 1,247), northernmost large isl. of the Shetlands, Scotland, just NE of N end of Yell isl., from which it is separated by Bluemull Sound; 12 mi. long, 6 mi. wide; rises to 935 ft. Deeply indented and hilly. Chief villages: Baltasound, on E coast, fishing and fish-curing center, with hosiery-knitting industry; and fishing port of Haroldswick, on NE coast of isl. Unst is noted for its fine wool. There are many Pictish and Norse remains. NW extremity of isl. is Herma Ness, promontory rising to 675 ft.; 60°50'N 0°52'W.

Unstone, town and parish (pop. 2,411), N Derby, England, 7 mi. S of Sheffield; coal mining.

Unstrut River (ŏŏn'shtrōōt), central Germany, rises at SW edge of the Eichsfeld just NW of Dingelstädt, flows c.115 mi. generally E, past Dingelstädt, Mühlhausen, Sömmerda, Artern, Rossleben, and Freyburg, to the Thuringian Saale 2 mi. N of Naumburg. Receives Gera (left), Wipper and Helme (right) rivers.

Unsworth, village and parish (pop. 2,461), SE Lancashire, England, 3 mi. SSE of Bury; cotton and woolen milling.

Unta Dhura, pass, Tibet-India border: see ANTA DHURA.

Unteraar Glacier, Switzerland: see AAR RIVER.

Unterägeri (ŏŏn'tûrä'gûrē), town (pop. 2,969), Zug canton, N central Switzerland, at efflux of Lorze R. from the Aegerisee, 4 mi. SE of Zug; cotton textiles.

Unterammergau (ŏŏn"tûrä'mûrgou"), village (pop. 1,459), Upper Bavaria, Germany, in Bavarian Alps, on the Ammer and 9 mi. NNW of Garmisch-Partenkirchen; abrasive-stone quarrying and grinding; wood carving.

Unterdrauburg, Yugoslavia: see DRAVOGRAD.

Unterföhring (ŏŏn"tûrfû'rĭng), village (pop. 2,358), Upper Bavaria, Germany, on the Isar and 5 mi. NNE of Munich; tanning, lumber milling.

Unterfranken, Germany: see LOWER FRANCONIA.

Untergrombach (ŏŏn"tûrgrôm'bäkh), village (pop. 3,539), N Baden, Germany, after 1945 in Württemberg-Baden, 3.5 mi. S of Bruchsal; mfg. of cigars and cigarettes.

Unterhaching (ŏŏn"tûrhä'khĭng), village (pop. 8,033), Upper Bavaria, Germany, 6 mi. SSE of Munich; mfg. of chemicals, glass; woodworking.

Unterheinriet (ŏŏn"tûrhīn'rēt), village (pop. 1,050), N Württemberg, Germany, after 1945 in Württemberg-Baden, 6 mi. SE of Heilbronn; cigar mfg.

Unterkochen (ŏŏn'tûrkô"khŭn), village (pop. 4,365), N Württemberg, Germany, after 1945 in Württemberg-Baden, on the Kocher and 2 mi. SE of Aalen; grain.

Unterlahn, Germany: see DIEZ.

Unterloitsch, Yugoslavia: see DOLENJI LOGATEC.

Unterlüss (ŏŏn'tûrlüs), village (pop. 2,923), in former Prussian prov. of Hanover, NW Germany, after 1945 in Lower Saxony, 17 mi. NE of Celle; kieselguhr quarrying.

Untermünstertal (ŏŏn"tûrmün'stûrtäl"), village (pop. 2,088), S Baden, Germany, in Black Forest, 10 mi. SSW of Freiburg; silk mfg., woodworking.

Unteröwisheim (ŏŏn"tûrû'vĭs-hīm"), town (pop. 2,514), N Baden, Germany, after 1945 in Württemberg-Baden, on the Kraichbach and 3.5 mi. NW of Bruchsal; mfg. of cigars and cigarettes.

Untersberg (ŏŏn'tûrsbĕrk), peak (6,473 ft.) in the Salzburg Alps, on Austro-German border, 5 mi. SSW of Salzburg; numerous caves. Marble quarries at Bischofswiesen (S foot). According to legend, Charlemagne still dwells in the Untersberg, waiting to liberate Germany in her hour of greatest need.

Untersee (ŏŏn'tûrzā"), lake (□ 24), on German-Swiss border, a branch of L. CONSTANCE, with which it is connected by 2-mi.-long-stretch of the Rhine; length c.10 mi., width c.3 mi.; average depth 92 ft., greatest depth 151 ft.; alt. 1,296 ft. A narrow peninsula below Radolfzell (NW shore) divides it into 2 branches, the Zeller See and the Gnaden See. The Rhine leaves it at Stein (Switzerland). Isl. of Reichenau (Germany) is SE of Radolfzell.

Unterseen (ŏŏn'tûrzā'ŭn), town (pop. 3,107), Bern canton, central Switzerland, on Aar R. opposite Interlaken; woodworking.

Untertaunus, Germany: see BAD SCHWALBACH.

Unterteutschenthal (ŏŏn"tûrtoi'chŭntäl"), village (pop. 3,372), in former Prussian Saxony prov., central Germany, after 1945 in Saxony-Anhalt, 7 mi. WSW of Halle; potash and lignite mining; magnesium production. Railroad station called Teutschenthal.

Untertürkheim (ŏŏn"tûrtürk'hīm"), E suburb of Stuttgart, Germany, on right bank of the Neckar, 3 mi. E of city center; car and truck mfg.

Untervalden, Russian SFSR: see PODLESNOYE.

Unterwalden (ŏŏn'tûrväl"dŭn), Fr. *Unterwald* (ŏŏn'tûrvält), canton, central Switzerland, consisting of OBWALDEN and NIDWALDEN half-cantons. Pop. German speaking and Catholic. In 1291 Unterwalden formed with the cantons of Uri and Schwyz a league which became the nucleus of the Swiss Confederation. With Lucerne, these cantons became the Four Forest Cantons.

Unterwalden, Russian SFSR: see PODLESNOYE.

Unterwasser (ŏŏn'tûrvä"sûr), resort (alt. 3,000 ft.), St. Gall canton, NE Switzerland, on the Thur and 5 mi. N of Wallenstadt, bet. the Churfirsten and the Säntis; winter sports.

Unterwellenborn-Röblitz (ŏŏn"tûrvĕ'lŭnbôrn-rû'-blĭts), town (pop. 2,959), Thuringia, central Germany, near the Thuringian Saale, 4 mi. E of Saalfeld; metallurgical center; site of Maxhütte steelworks, producing pig iron, ingot, and rolled-steel products on basis of near-by Schmiedefeld and Kamsdorf iron mines. Developed considerably after Second World War.

Unterwesterwald, Germany: see MONTABAUR.

Unterwiesenthal, Germany: see OBERWIESENTHAL.

Untsukul or **Untsukul'** (ōōntsōōkōōl'), village (1926 pop. 2,315), central Dagestan Autonomous SSR, Russian SFSR, on the Avar Koisu and 18 mi. WSW of Buinaksk; fruit canning; orchards, grain. Pop. largely Avar. Sometimes spelled Untsukuli.

Unuma (ōōnōō'mä), town (pop. 8,868), Gifu prefecture, central Honshu, Japan, on Kiso R. and 10 mi. E of Gifu; building-stone quarrying; agr. (rice, sweet potatoes, raw silk).

Unwin, Mount (10,723 ft.), W Alta., near B.C. border, in Rocky Mts., in Jasper Natl. Park, 30 mi. SE of Jasper, overlooking Maligne L.

Unye (ünyĕ'), Turkish *Ünye*, town (pop. 6,382), Ordu prov., N Turkey, port on Black Sea, 32 mi. WNW of Ordu; millet, sugar beets; zinc and copper near by. Sometimes Unieh.

Unza, India: see UNJHA.

Unzen National Park (ōōnzĕn') (□ 50), Nagasaki prefecture, W Kyushu, Japan, on central Shimabara Peninsula; alt. 2,400 ft. Site of health resort known for sulphide hot springs. Mts. in central part rise to 4,460 ft. at Mt. Unzen.

Unzha River (ōōn'zhŭ), central European Russian SFSR, rises in 2 headstreams (Yuza and Kema rivers) in the Northern Uvals, WSW of Nikolsk; flows 340 mi. generally S, through rich timber region, past Kologriv, Manturovo (Kostroma oblast), and Makaryev, to the Volga opposite Yuryevets. Navigable for 140 mi.; timber floating. Receives Neya R. (right).

Unzmarkt (ōōnts'märkt), village (pop. 878), Styria, central Austria, on Mur R. and 10 mi. WNW of Judenburg; rail junction; steelworks, lumberyards, summer and winter resort.

Uolchitte, Ethiopia: see WALKITE.

Uondo, Ethiopia: see WANDO.

Uongbi (wŭng'bē'), town, Quangyen prov., N Vietnam, 16 mi. ESE of Dongtrieu; coal-mining center. Its loading port is Port Redon.

Uota, Ethiopia: see WOTA.

Uotsuri-shima, Japan: see SENKAKU-GUNTO.

Uozaki (ōō-ō'zäkē), town (pop. 12,198), Hyogo prefecture, S Honshu, Japan, on Osaka Bay, bet. Kobe (SW) and Mikage (NE); sake brewing, fishing.

Uozu (ōō-ō'zōō), town (pop. 15,535), Toyama prefecture, central Honshu, Japan, on E shore of Toyama Bay, 13 mi. NE of Toyama; mfg. (textiles, patent medicines). Fishery.

Upala (ōōpä'lä), village, Alajuela prov., N Costa Rica, in tropical Guatuso Lowland, 24 mi. SSW of San Carlos (Nicaragua); stock raising, lumbering; cacao, ipecac root.

Upanda, Serra (sĕ'rŭ ōōpän'dŭ), W edge of Angola's central plateau, in Benguela prov., overlooking coastal lowland. Rises to 8,071 ft. N of Vila Mariano Machado.

Upa River (ōō'pŭ), Tula oblast, Russian SFSR, rises NW of Volovo in Central Russian Upland, flows in tortuous course N and W, past Tula, S and W, past Krapivna and Odoyevo, to Oka R. 6 mi. SE of Chekalin; 150 mi. long.

Upata (ōōpä'tä), town (pop. 4,120), Bolívar state, E Venezuela, in outliers of Guiana Highlands, on highway to San Félix and 80 mi. E of Ciudad Bolívar, in cattle-raising region. Gold mines near by.

Upemba, Lake (ōōpĕm'bä), expansion (□ c.190) of Lualaba R. in SE Belgian Congo, S of L. Kisale; 16 mi. long, 18 mi. wide. Swampy and overgrown with papyrus. Its E shore is in Upemba Natl. Park.

Upemba National Park (□ 748; established 1939), in Katanga prov., SE Belgian Congo; extends E of the Lualaba and SE of L. Kisale and L. Upemba. Includes park-like savanna sections with fauna of zebras, peccaries, buffaloes, and antelopes; also papyrus swamps, abode of crocodiles and hippopotami.

Upernavik (ōōpĕr'nävĭk) or **Upernivik** (–nĭvĭk), settlement (pop. 321), ⊙ Upernavik dist. (pop. 1,443), W Greenland, on islet in Baffin Bay; 72°47'N 56°10'W. Sealing and whaling base, meteorological and radio station, hosp. Founded 1772. Graphite deposits near by. On Kaersorssuak isl. (S) are noted bird cliffs. On Kingigtok isl. (NNW) 14th-cent. stone with runic inscription was found.

Upernavik Ice Fjord or **Upernivik Ice Fjord,** Dan. *Upernavik Isfjord* or *Upernivik Isfjord,* inlet (30 mi. long, 3–15 mi. wide) of Baffin Bay, W Greenland; 72°55'N 55°10'W. Extends ESE to edge of inland icecap, receiving large glacier noted for rapid rate of flow and of calving.

Upernavik Island or **Upernivik Island** (17 mi. long, 5–17 mi. wide), W Greenland, bet. Umanak Fjord (S) and Karrats Fjord (N); 71°17'N 52°50'W. Separated from mainland (E) by narrow channel, from Ubekendt Isl. (W) by 7-mi.-wide Igdlorssuit Sound. Rises to 6,893 ft.

Uphall (ŭp-hôl'), town and parish (pop. 11,119), E West Lothian, Scotland, 6 mi. ENE of Bathgate; shale-oil mining and refining center. Parish includes BROXBURN.

Upham (ŭ'pŭm), city (pop. 403), McHenry co., N N.Dak., 22 mi. NW of Towner.

Upholland (ŭp-hŏ'lŭnd), urban district (1931 pop. 5,605; 1951 census 6,314), SW Lancashire, England, 4 mi. W of Wigan; mfg. of bricks and tiles; market for dairy-farming and agr. region. Has ruins of 14th-cent. priory and unfinished 14th-cent. church, now inc. in modern church.

Upice (ōō'pĭtsĕ), Czech *Úpice*, Ger. *Eipel* (ī'pĕl), town (pop. 5,498), NE Bohemia, Czechoslovakia, on railroad and 10 mi. NE of Dvur Kralove; mfg. linen, jute textiles.

Upington, town (pop. 10,154), NW Cape Prov., U. of So. Afr., on Orange R. and 220 mi. W of Kimberley; 28°27'S 21°15'E; rail junction on main line to South-West Africa; agr. center (grain, fruit, Karakul sheep); copper mining. Tungsten, scheelite, wolframite deposits in region. Site of agr. experiment station. Airport.

Upland. 1 City (pop. 9,203), San Bernardino co., S Calif., midway bet. Los Angeles and San Bernardino and adjacent to Ontario (S); packs citrus fruit. San Antonio Peak is just N. Inc. 1906. **2** Town (pop. 1,565), Grant co., E central Ind., 11 mi. ESE of Marion, in agr. area; lumber milling; mfg. of canned goods, gloves. Seat of Taylor Univ. **3** Village (pop. 251), Franklin co., S Nebr., 32 mi. SW of Hastings. **4** Borough (pop. 4,081), Delaware co., SE Pa., just NW of Chester. Inc. 1869.

Uplands, England: see STROUD.

Uplands, village, Central Prov., S central Kenya, on railroad and 20 mi. NW of Nairobi; bacon mfg.; sisal, wheat, coffee, corn; vegetable gardening, dairying.

Uplands Park, town (pop. 563), St. Louis co., E Mo.

Upleta (ōōplä'tŭ), town (pop. 16,291), W central Saurashtra, India, 50 mi. SW of Rajkot; agr. market (peanuts, millet, cotton, gram, wheat); oilseed milling, cotton ginning, hand-loom weaving. Formerly in Gondal state.

Uplyme (ŭplīm'), town and parish (pop. 1,005), E Devon, England, just NW of Lyme Regis; agr. market. Has 14th-cent. church.

Upminster, residential town and parish (pop. 5,732), SW Essex, England, 4 mi. ESE of Romford.

Upolu (ōōpō'lōō'), volcanic island (□ 430; pop. 42,764), Western SAMOA, S Pacific, under N.Z. mandate, c.10 mi. SE of Savaii; 2d largest but most important and most populous isl. of Samoa; chief town is Apia, ⊙ Territory of Western Samoa. Has mtn. range with highest peak Vaaifetu (3,608 ft.), craters, crater lakes; fertile lowlands. Produces cacao, rubber, bananas, coconuts. Saluafata, on N coast, is U.S. naval station. VAILIMA, home of Robert Louis Stevenson, is near Mt. Vaea.

Upolu Point, Hawaii, T.H., N extremity of isl., on Kohala Peninsula; 20°16'N 155°51'W.

Upornaya (ōōpôr'nīŭ), village (1926 pop. 9,545), SE Krasnodar Territory, Russian SFSR, in N foothill of the Greater Caucasus, 24 mi. SE of Labinsk; wheat, sunflowers, sunn and ambary hemp, essential oils.

Uporovo (ōōpô'rŭvŭ), village (1939 pop. over 500), SW Tyumen oblast, Russian SFSR, on Tobol R. (head of navigation) and 20 mi. S of Yalutorovsk, in agr. area; grain, livestock.

Upoto, Belgian Congo: see LISALA.

Upper, in Rus. names: see also VERKHNE-, VERKHNEYE, VERKNNI, VERKHNIYE, VERKHNYAYA.

Upper Alps, France: see HAUTES-ALPES.

Upper Ammonoosuc River (ămŭnōō'sŭk), Coos co., N N.H., rises just N of Presidential Range, flows c.35 mi. N and W to Connecticut R. near Northumberland, c.50 mi. above junction of AMMONOOSUC RIVER with the Connecticut at Woodsville.

Upper Angara River (äng"gärä'), Rus. *Verkhnyaya Angara* (vyĕrkh'nyŭ), NW Buryat-Mongol Autonomous SSR, Russian SFSR, rises in Vitim-Baikal divide, flows 250 mi. SW to L. Baikal (outlet: ANGARA RIVER), forming small delta mouth near Nizhne-Angarsk. Navigable in lower course.

Upper Arlington, city (pop. 9,024), Franklin co., central Ohio, suburb 5 mi. WNW of Columbus.

Upper Arrow Lake, B.C.: see ARROW LAKES.

Upper Aulaqi, Aden: see AULAQI.

Upper Austria, Ger. *Oberösterreich* (ō'bûrû"stûrīkh"), autonomous prov. [*Bundesland*] (□ 4,625; 1951 pop. 1,107,562), N Austria, bordering Germany (W), Czechoslovakia (N), Lower Austria (E), Styria and Salzburg (S); ⊙ Linz. Predominantly hilly region at N base of Eastern Alps, with Hausruck Mts. (SW center), and large part of SALZKAMMERGUT resort area (S). Drained by Danube, Inn (Ger. border), Enns, and Traun rivers. Extensive forests. Chiefly agr.: all cereals (except corn), potatoes, cattle, poultry; fruit and wine (E and N). Industry (metalworking, textiles, chemicals) centers in Linz, Wels, Steyr, and Ebensee. Lignite mined in HAUSRUCK MOUNTAINS; salt produced in the Salzkammergut. Bad Ischl is chief resort. Created duchy and given to dukes of Austria in 1156. In 1945 region N of the Danube was placed in Soviet, region S of the Danube in U.S. occupation zone.

Upper Avon River, England: see AVON RIVER.

Upper Bann River, Northern Ireland: see BANN RIVER.

Upper Bavaria (bůvâ′rēů), Ger. *Oberbayern* (ō′bůrbī′ůrn), administrative division [Ger. *Regierungsbezirk*] (□ 6,308; 1946 pop. 2,349,797; 1950 pop. 2,453,882) of S BAVARIA, Germany; ⊙ Munich. Bounded S and E by Austria; N by Lower Bavaria, Upper Palatinate, and Middle Franconia; W by Swabia. Includes (S) the Salzburg Alps and Bavarian Alps (with the Zugspitze, Germany's highest mtn.), favorite tourist regions with many resorts (Bad Reichenhall, Berchtesgaden, Garmisch-Partenkirchen, Oberammergau); numerous lakes. Drained by Inn, Isar, and Lech rivers (right tributaries of the Danube). Agr. (wheat, rye) in N; cattle raising in S. Industries (metals, chemicals, beer) at Munich, Freising, Ingolstadt, and Rosenheim. Lignite mining at Hausham, Peissenberg, Peiting, and Penzberg; salt deposits at Bad Reichenhall and Berchtesgaden; petroleum wells around Tegernsee.

Upper Bay, N.Y. and N.J.: see NEW YORK BAY.

Upper Beeding, agr. village and parish (pop. 1,103), central Sussex, England, on Adur R. and 6 mi. NE of Worthing; cementworks. Church has Norman tower and includes fragments of anc. Benedictine priory.

Upper Bingham, Utah: see BINGHAM CANYON.

Upper Brookville, village (pop. 469), Nassau co., SE N.Y., on NW Long Isl., 3 mi. ESE of Glen Cove, in summer-resort area.

Upper Buchanan, Liberia: see BUCHANAN.

Upper Burma: see BURMA.

Upper Canada: see ONTARIO.

Upper Chateaugay Lake, N.Y.: see CHATEAUGAY LAKE.

Upper Chindwin (chĭn′dwĭn′), district (□ 6,889; 1941 pop. 209,575) of Sagaing div., Upper Burma, at Manipur (India) border; ⊙ Mawlaik. Astride upper Chindwin R., bounded W by Kabaw Valley and N by Naga Hills. Annual rainfall, 67 in. Agr.: rice, sesame, beans; teak forests. Served by Chindwin steamers and by India-Burma route via Tamu. Pop. is 47% Burmese, 44% Shan (Thai).

Upper Cormorant Lake, Minn.: see CORMORANT LAKE.

Upper Darby, urban township (pop. 84,951), Delaware co., SE Pa., suburb just SW of Philadelphia; in 2 sections, separated by Lansdowne borough; mainly residential, with some mfg. (aircraft parts, plastic, wood, and rubber products, furniture, communications equipment). Includes villages of Upper Darby (1940 pop. 1,798, with adjacent Fernwood), Highland Park (1940 pop. 7,778), Bywood (1940 pop. 6,678), and part of Drexel Hill (partly in HAVERFORD township). Inc. 1907.

Upper Fairmount, village (pop. c.500), Somerset co., SE Md., near Big Annemessex R. 21 mi. SSW of Salisbury; fishing, truck farming.

Upper Falls of Yellowstone River, Wyo.: see YELLOWSTONE NATIONAL PARK.

Upper Fox River, Wis.: see FOX RIVER.

Upper Franconia (frăngkō′nēů), Ger. *Oberfranken* (ō′bůrfrăng′kůn), administrative division [Ger. *Regierungsbezirk*] (□ 2,897; 1946 pop. 1,076,438; 1950 pop. 1,113,835) of NE Bavaria; ⊙ Bayreuth. Bounded by Thuringia (N), Saxony (NE), Czechoslovakia and Upper Palatinate (E), Middle Franconia (S), and Lower Franconia (W). Hilly, forested region, including Franconian Jura (SW), Franconian Forest (N), and the Fichtelgebirge (NE); drained by Main, Pegnitz, and Saxonian Saale rivers. Industries centered at Bamberg (cotton, electrotechnical goods), Hof (textiles), Selb (Rosenthal porcelain), Coburg (auto bodies, machine tools), Kulmbach (malt mfg., brewing), and Neustadt (toys). Cattle raising; some agr. (rye, barley, cabbage, hops). Pop. predominantly Protestant. The area is part of old historic region of FRANCONIA.

Upper Galilee, Israel: see GALILEE.

Upper Ganges Canal, India: see GANGES CANALS.

Upper Garonne, France: see HAUTE-GARONNE.

Upper Gull Lake, Minn.: see GULL LAKE.

Upper Hesse (hĕ′sē, hĕs), Ger. *Oberhessen* (ō′bůrhĕ′sůn), former province (□ 1,269; 1939 pop. 351,735) of Hesse (see HESSE-DARMSTADT), W Germany; ⊙ was Giessen. Surrounded by former Prussian prov. of Hesse-Nassau. Hilly region drained by Nidda and Ohm rivers. Industry concentrated at Giessen. Prov. abolished 1945.

Upper Hutt (hŭt), borough (pop. 5,494), S N.Isl., New Zealand, 20 mi. NE of Wellington; summer resort; agr. center.

Upper Iowa River, rises in Mower co., SE Minn., flows ESE into NE Iowa, at Chester, then generally E, past Decorah, to Mississippi R. at Lansing; 160 mi. long.

Upper Jay, resort village, Essex co., NE N.Y., in the Adirondacks, 12 mi. ENE of Lake Placid village.

Upper Juba (jōō′bä), region, SW Ital. Somaliland, bordering on Ethiopia (N) and Kenya (W). Hot, semi-arid plain rising to 1,500 ft. in Hodur plateau (N center). Watered by Juba R. Agr. (durra, corn); pastoralism (cattle, goats, sheep, camels). Chief centers: Isha Baidoa, Hodur, Bur Acaba, Lugh Ferrandi, Bardera.

Upper Katanga, Belgian Congo: see ELISABETHVILLE.

Upper Klamath Lake (klă′můth), large, fresh-water lake in Klamath co., S Oregon, extending N from city of Klamath Falls and bordering (NE) on Klamath Indian Reservation; 20 mi. long, 8 mi. wide. Receives Williamson R. in N, drains (S) through Link R. and L. Ewauna into Klamath R. Used for irrigation; site of waterfowl refuge. N arm is Agency L.

Upper Kundysh River, Russian SFSR: see GREATER KUNDYSH RIVER.

Upper Lake MacNean, Ireland: see MACNEAN, UPPER LAKE.

Upper Langwith, town and parish (pop. 2,416), NE Derby, England, 5 mi. N of Mansfield; coal mining. Has church dating from 12th cent.

Upper Largo or **Kirkton of Largo**, town in Largo parish, E Fifeshire, Scotland, near the Firth of Forth, 3 mi. NE of Leven; agr. market, golfing resort.

Upper Loire, France: see HAUTE-LOIRE.

Upper Lomami, Belgian Congo: see KAMINA.

Upper Lusatia, Germany: see LUSATIA.

Upper Marlboro (märl′bůrů), town (pop. 702), ⊙ Prince Georges co. (since 1732), central Md., 15 mi. ESE of Washington; tobacco market. Agr. substation of Univ. of Md. here. Near by is Northampton estate, with gardens laid out 1788.

Upper Marne, France: see HAUTE-MARNE.

Upper Matecumbe Key, Fla.: see FLORIDA KEYS.

Upper Merwede River, Du. *Boven Merwede* (bō′vů mĕr′vādů), SW Netherlands; formed by junction of Maas and Waal rivers at Woudrichem; flows 5.5 mi. W, past Gorinchem, forking into Lower Merwede R. and New Merwede R. 4.5 mi. W of Gorinchem. Entire length navigable.

Upper Mesa Falls, E Idaho, cascade (more than 100 ft. high) in a fork of Snake R., 8 mi. NE of Ashton. Downstream are Lower Mesa Falls, about half as high.

Uppermill, England: see SADDLEWORTH.

Upper Mitton, England: see STOURPORT-ON-SEVERN.

Upper Montclair, N.J.: see MONTCLAIR.

Upper Narrows Dam; **Upper Narrows Reservoir**, Calif.: see YUBA RIVER.

Upper Nile, province (□ 92,270; 1948 pop. estimate 742,933), S central Anglo-Egyptian Sudan, bordered E by Ethiopia; ⊙ Malakal. A level alluvial grassland with intermittent well-wooded areas and swamp forests in S. Drained by the Bahr el Jebel and Sobat R. Important stock-raising region (cattle, sheep, goats); native fishing; some agr. (peanuts, corn, durra); hardwoods. Largely populated by Nilotic Shilluk and Nuer tribes. Main centers are Malakal and Nasir. Gambela, in W Ethiopia, is a trading post under Upper Nile prov. administration.

Upper Norwood, England: see CROYDON.

Upper Nyack (nī′ăk″), village (pop. 1,195), Rockland co., SE N.Y., on W bank of the Hudson, just N of Nyack.

Upper Palatinate (půlă′tĭnĭt″), Ger. *Oberpfalz* (ō′bůrpfälts′), administrative district [Ger. *Regierungsbezirk*] (□ 3,724; 1946 pop. 888,522; 1950 pop. 896,520) of E Bavaria, Germany; ⊙ Regensburg. Borders Czechoslovakia (E), Lower Bavaria (S), Upper Bavaria (SW), Middle Franconia (W), and Upper Franconia (NW, N). Hilly region, including Bohemian Forest (E) and the Fichtelgebirge (N); drained by Danube, Altmühl, Nab, and Regen rivers. Lignite- and iron-ore-mining, with iron industry in Amberg, Schwandorf, and Sulzbach-Rosenberg region; glass and porcelain mfg. in Bohemian Forest (Weiden, Tirschenreuth); kaolin quarried near Schnaittenbach. Regensburg is important communications center. Includes historic Upper PALATINATE region, Regensburg and its former territories, and several petty principalities; dist. was constituted in 1837.

Upper Pohatcong Mountain, N.J.: see POHATCONG MOUNTAIN.

Upper Pyrenees, France: see HAUTES-PYRÉNÉES.

Upper Red Lake, Minn.: see RED LAKE.

Upper Red Rock Lake, Mont.: see RED ROCK LAKES.

Upper Rhine, France: see HAUT-RHIN.

Upper Rice Lake, Clearwater co., NW central Minn., 20 mi. WSW of Bemidji; 2 mi. long. Source of Wild Rice R.

Upper Richardson Lake, Maine: see RANGELEY LAKES.

Upper River, division (□ 790; pop. 47,387) of E Gambia; ⊙ Basse. Extends along 75-mi. section of Gambia R. Produces peanuts, beeswax, hides and skins. Ferry crossings at Basse and Fatoto, chief centers. Has Anglican and R.C. mission schools. Pop. is largely Fulah.

Upper Saddle River, borough (pop. 706), Bergen co., NE N.J., on small Saddle R. and 4 mi. W of Pearl River, N.Y.

Upper Saint Regis Lake, N.Y.: see SAINT REGIS RIVER.

Upper Sandusky (sůndŭ′skē, săn–), village (pop. 4,397), ⊙ Wyandot co., N central Ohio, 17 mi. NNW of Marion, and on Sandusky R., in agr. area; machinery, metal and clay products, brick, auto parts, steam pumps, stokers; creameries, poultry hatcheries, greenhouses. Limestone quarries. Wyandot Natl. Mus. of Indian and pioneer relics is here. Laid out 1843.

Upper Saône, France: see HAUTE-SAÔNE.

Upper Saranac Lake, N.Y.: see SARANAC LAKES.

Upper Savoy, France: see HAUTE-SAVOIE.

Upper Senegal and Niger, former name for FRENCH SUDAN, Fr. West Africa.

Upper Sheikh (shāk), town, central Br. Somaliland, in Ogo highland, on road and 40 mi. NNW of Burao; camels, sheep, goats. Airfield. Govt. boarding school. With near-by (NW) Lower Sheikh, it is also known as Sheikh.

Upper Silesia, province, Germany: see SILESIA.

Upper Sind Frontier (sĭnd), district (□ 1,969; 1951 pop. 347,000), N Sind, W Pakistan; ⊙ Jacobabad. A hot, dry tract, irrigated by canals, including North Western Canal (W) of Sukkur Barrage system; bordered E by Indus R. Agr. (millet, rice, gram, wheat); handicraft work (woolen carpets, embroidered shoes, saddlebags, palm mats and baskets). Before Br. occupation of N Baluchistan in late-19th cent., area constituted a military frontier, with cantonment at Jacobabad.

Upper Swinford, England: see STOURBRIDGE.

Upper Tallassee Dam, Ala.: see YATES DAM.

Upper Topa, W Pakistan: see MURREE.

Upper Tunguska River, Russian SFSR: see ANGARA RIVER.

Upper Volta (vŏl′tů), Fr. *Haute-Volta*, French overseas territory (□ c.113,100; pop. c.3,037,000), central Fr. West Africa; ⊙ OUAGADOUGOU. Borders N and W on Fr. Sudan, SW on Ivory Coast, S on Gold Coast and Fr. Togoland, SE on Dahomey, E on Niger territory. A wooded savanna land of Sudanese vegetation. Climate is almost equatorial, with a rainfall of up to 60 in. in S sections. In the territory rise the Black and White Volta rivers. It is foremost a stock-raising (goats, sheep, cattle) region, where tsetse flies hardly occur. Principal crops for export are peanuts, shea nuts, sesame. Cotton and sisal plantations are increasing. Subsistence crops include millet, corn, rice, beans, sweet potatoes, manioc. Vegetable-oil extracting, shea-nut butter mfg.; native handicraft (metal and leather goods). Among leading towns are Ouagadougou, Bobo-Dioulasso (until recently terminus of railroad from Abidjan), Koudougou, Ouahigouya, Tenkodogo, Fada. It is served by good roads. France made the native (Mossi) kingdom of Ouagadougou a protectorate in 1897; later Upper Volta became part of a French colony, and was created a separate colony in 1919. In 1932 it was partitioned among Fr. Sudan, Niger, and Fr. Ivory Coast, but was reconstituted in 1947 and given representation in the French parliament.

Upper Yafa, Aden: see YAFA.

Upper Yosemite Fall, Calif.: see YOSEMITE NATIONAL PARK.

Uppinangadi, India: see PUTTUR, South Kanara dist.

Uppingham (ŭ′pĭng-ům), town and parish (pop. 1,703), Rutland, England, 6 mi. S of Oakham; agr. market. Site of famous public school founded 1587. Has 14th-cent. church.

Uppland (ŭp′lănd), province [Swedish *landskap*] (□ 5,004; pop. 798,590), E Sweden, on Gulf of Bothnia and on the Baltic. Included in Uppsala co., E part of Vastmanland co., and N part of Stockholm co., with part of Stockholm city.

Upplandsbodarne (ŭp″läntsbōō′därnů), village (pop. 1,757), Uppsala co., E Sweden, on Dal R., near its mouth on Gulf of Bothnia, 10 mi. ESE of Gavle; sawmilling; grain, potatoes, stock.

Uppsala (ŭp′sůlů, Swed. ŭp′sä″lä), county [Swedish *län*] (□ 2,055; 1950 pop. 154,791), E central Sweden; ⊙ Uppsala. Bet. L. Malar (S) and Gulf of Bothnia and Dal R. (N); comprises W part of Uppland prov. Low level surface drained by Fyris R.; agr. (grain, potatoes), stock raising, and dairying are important. Major iron deposits in Dannemora region. There are several iron- and steelworks. Sawmilling near mouth of Dal R.; major hydroelectric plant at Alvkarleby. Cities are Uppsala and Enkoping. Sometimes spelled Upsala.

Uppsala, city (1950 pop. 63,072), ⊙ Uppsala co., E Sweden, on Fyris R. and 40 mi. NNW of Stockholm; 59°52′N 17°38′E. Cultural and educational center; site of oldest Swedish univ. (founded 1477 during regency of Sten Sture the Elder); seat of Lutheran primate of Sweden. The univ. has ranked among the world's greatest universities since its reorganization in 1595. In the cathedral (1260–1435) are tombs of Gustavus I, Linnaeus, Swedenborg, and of other Swedish notables; until recent times Swedish kings were crowned here. Other noted bldgs. include vast univ. library, with many invaluable manuscripts, among them the *Codex argenteus* of Ulfilas; 16th-cent. castle, baroque archbishops' palace, Victoria Mus., and Linnaean Mus., and bldg. of Royal Society of Sciences. Seat of several publishing houses; other industries include mfg. of bicycles, pianos; flour milling, metalworking. City, originally called *Östra Aros* (ûs'trä"ä'rôs"), grew up near Old Uppsala (see GAMLA UPPSALA), now a small village, but which in 9th cent. was pagan ⊙ of Sweden; it declined in early 13th cent. The archiepiscopal see was established here in 1270, and Uppsala acquired considerable importance in 14th and 15th cent. Sometimes spelled Upsala.

Upsala (ŭpsä'lü), village (pop. 366), Morrison co., central Minn., on small affluent of Mississippi R. and 15 mi. SW of Little Falls, in agr. area; dairy products.

Upshur (ŭp'shûr). **1** County (□ 589; pop. 20,822), NE Texas; ⊙ Gilmer. Partly bounded S by Sabine R.; drained by Cypress and Little Cypress bayous. Partly wooded (mainly pine; extensive lumbering); large oil production (in East Texas field); also natural gas, clay, lignite, iron ore. Agr. (especially sweet potatoes; also truck, fruit, peanuts, forage crops, cotton), livestock (cattle, poultry, hogs), some dairying. Formed 1846. **2** County (□ 352; pop. 19,242), central W.Va.; ⊙ Buckhannon. On Allegheny Plateau; drained by Buckhannon R. Agr. (livestock, fruit, tobacco); bituminous-coal mines, natural-gas wells; timber. Industry at Buckhannon. Includes part of new Audra State Park. Formed 1851.

Upson, county (□ 333; pop. 25,078), W central Ga.; ⊙ Thomaston. Bounded W and S by Flint R. Piedmont peach-raising area; agr. (cotton, corn, truck, livestock); textile mfg. at Thomaston and Silvertown. Formed 1824.

Upstart, Cape, E Queensland, Australia, in Coral Sea; forms E side of entrance to Upstart Bay; 19°42'S 147°45'E. Composed of granite; rises to 2,420 ft.

Upton, village (pop. 735), S Que., 12 mi. E of St. Hyacinthe; dairying, stock raising.

Upton, town and parish (pop. 1,011), West Riding, S Yorkshire, England, 6 mi. SSE of Pontefract; coal mining.

Upton, county (□ 1,312; pop. 5,307), W Texas; ⊙ Rankin. High prairies in N and E; Castle and King mts. in SW; co. alt., 2,500–3,000 ft. Ranching region (chiefly sheep; some goats, cattle), with oil, natural-gas wells; no agr. Produces clay, potash, salt. Formed 1887.

Upton. 1 Town (pop. 383), Hardin and Larue counties, central Ky., 15 mi. S of Elizabethtown, in stock-raising and limestone-quarrying area. **2** Town (pop. 105), Oxford co., W Maine, on Umbagog L. and 24 mi. WNW of Rumford, in hunting, fishing area. **3** Town (pop. 2,656), Worcester co., S central Mass., 13 mi. SE of Worcester; dairying, truck; millinery, lumber. Settled 1728, inc. 1735. Includes village of West Upton (1940 pop. 691). **4** Town (pop. 951), Weston co., NE Wyo., just W of Black Hills, 27 mi. NW of Newcastle; alt. c.4,230 ft. Shipping point for bentonite in livestock, grain, turkey-raising area; chemicals, lumber.

Upton, Camp, N.Y.: see YAPHANK.

Upton-upon-Severn, town and parish (pop. 1,968), S Worcester, England, on Severn R. and 9 mi. S of Worcester; agr. market. Has 14th-cent. church.

Upwell, town and parish (pop. 1,621), in Isle of Ely, N Cambridge, England, 5 mi. SSE of Wisbech, in fruitgrowing region.

'Uqayr, Al, Saudi Arabia: see OQAIR.

Uqsor, El, or **El Uqsur**, Egypt: see LUXOR.

Ur (ŭr, ûr), the biblical **Ur of the Chaldees**, anc. city of Sumer, S Mesopotamia, whose site is in SE Iraq, in Muntafiq prov., 11 mi. SW of Nasiriya (on the Euphrates), near the Baghdad-Basra RR. An important city of Sumerian culture and identified in the Bible as the home of Abraham, it dates from remotest antiquity and disappeared from historical records some time in 4th cent. B.C.; eventually its site was covered with sand and forgotten. Excavation in 19th and early 20th cent. yielded important archaeological discoveries. A place existed here before a great flood—perhaps the biblical flood—and it was a flourishing place by 3500 B.C.; its 1st dynasty of kings (c.3200) inherited a rich culture from the past. Ur was captured (c.2800) by Sargon. A new dynasty was established (c.2300) under Ur-Nammu (Ur-Engur), who built the great ziggurat which stood, covered with sand, for centuries. The mound, standing out above the desert land—and called by the Arabs Tall al Muqaiyir [hill of pitch], also spelled Muqayyar, Mukayyar, Mugheir, Mughayyar, etc.—led to the rediscovery of the city. Ur continued as a great commercial city on the Euphrates. It fell to the Elamites and later to Babylon and was destroyed and rebuilt throughout the years by various kings and conquerors, including Nebuchadnezzar in 6th cent. B.C. About the middle of 6th cent. B.C., Ur went into a decline from which it never recovered. A record dated 324 B.C. mentions it (by another name), but its existence as a great city was already forgotten. The Euphrates, which was the source of its wealth, probably also, by changing its course, caused the city's final decline.

Urabá, Gulf of (ōōräbä'), inlet of the Caribbean in NW Colombia, bounded W by Chocó dept. and E by Antioquia dept.; the S part of Gulf of Darien. Its mouth is c.25 mi. wide bet. Cape Tiburón (Panama border) and Caribana Point; extends S c.50 mi. Receives Atrato R. In a region with an unhealthy, tropical climate, it is surrounded by marshy, forested lowlands, largely undeveloped, but on which thrive sugar cane, cotton, coffee, rubber, fruit, fiber plants, livestock. Petroleum deposits have been discovered. Main settlement is port of Turbo (Antioquia).

Ura Bay, Russian SFSR: see URA-GUBA.

Uracas, Marianas Isls.: see PAJAROS.

Urach (ōō'räkh), town (pop. 6,204), S Württemberg, Germany, after 1945 in Württemberg-Hohenzollern, in Swabian Jura, 8 mi. E of Reutlingen; mfg. of cotton, pumps, automobile parts; woodworking, meat processing. Summer resort. Has 15th-cent. castle and church. Founded in 12th cent. Chartered c.1260. Ruins of fortress Hohenurach on near-by hill.

Urachiche (ōōrächē'chā), town (pop. 2,175), Yaracuy state, N Venezuela, in coastal range, 22 mi. ENE of Barquisimeto, in agr. region (cacao, sugar cane, coffee, corn, fruit, stock).

Uracoa (ōōräkō'ä), town (pop. 1,319), Monagas state, NE Venezuela, on Uracoa R., in lower Orinoco basin, and 75 mi. SE of Maturín; cattle raising.

Uradome (ōōrä'dōmā), town (pop. 3,696), Tottori prefecture, S Honshu, Japan, on Sea of Japan, 8 mi. NE of Tottori; seaside resort; rice, raw silk. Fishery. Pine-covered islets near its shore. Sometimes called Uratomi.

Uraga, town, Japan: see YOKOSUKA, Kanagawa prefecture.

Uraga Strait (ōōrä'gä), Jap. *Uraga-kaikyo*, central Honshu, Japan, connects Sagami Sea with Tokyo Bay, bet. Miura Peninsula (W) and Chiba Peninsula (E); 15 mi. long, 6–9 mi. wide. Yokosuka (naval base) is on W shore.

Ura-Guba (ōōrä"-gōōbä) [Rus.,=Ura bay], village, NW Murmansk oblast, Russian SFSR, on Ura Bay of Barents Sea and 23 mi. NNW of Murmansk; agr., fishing.

Urai, Formosa: see WULAI.

Urakawa (ōōrä'käwü). **1** Town (pop. 12,384), S Hokkaido, Japan, fishing port on the Pacific, 55 mi. SSW of Obihiro; agr., stock raising, lumbering. **2** Town (pop. 5,838), Shizuoka prefecture, central Honshu, Japan, 13 mi. NNW of Futamata; rice, tea, raw silk, charcoal.

Ural, river, USSR: see URAL RIVER.

Uralets (ōōrä'lyĭts), town (1939 pop. over 2,000), W Sverdlovsk oblast, Russian SFSR, in the central Urals, 8 mi. ENE of Visim, on rail spur from Nizhni Tagil; gold and platinum placers. Called Krasny Ural until 1933.

Uralla (yōōră'lü), municipality (pop. 1,186), E New South Wales, Australia, 160 mi. NNW of Newcastle; gold-mining center; orchards.

Uralmedstroi, Russian SFSR: see KRASNOURALSK.

Ural Mountains (yōō'rŭl, Rus. ōōräl'), mountain system of USSR, forming the traditional physiographic boundary bet. Europe and Asia and separating the East European plain (W) from the West Siberian plain (E). Of low average elevation (seldom exceeding 6,000 ft.), the Urals extend c.1,300 mi. N–S along 60°E from the Arctic Ocean to the bend of Ural R. The Pai-Khoi (N) and Mugodzhar mts. (S) are tectonic prolongations of the Urals proper. These are commonly divided into the Northern Urals (N of 61°N), the Central Urals (bet. 61° and 55°N), and the Southern Urals (bet. 55° and 51°N). The **Northern Urals** rise in a rocky, treeless chain amidst the tundra, extend S from the hill Konstantinov Kamen (1,480 ft.; 68°30'N), and are sometimes called the Polar Urals in their northernmost (lower) section. Bet. 65°30'N and 64°N the Urals attain their greatest height, in 2 parallel ranges (the watershed being the lower eastern range) rising in Naroda (or Narodnaya) peak to 6,184 ft. Small glaciers were discovered here (1929–33). Other peaks of the Northern Urals are the Sablya, the Telpos-Iz, and the Isherim (the southernmost; 61°N). The **Central Urals** rise to 5,154 ft. in the Konzhakovski Kamen at their N end, but are considerably lower in the S, where low passes are common, descending to 1,345 ft. in the Trans-Siberian RR gap W of Sverdlovsk. At Yurma mtn. begin the **Southern Urals**, which, unlike the N sections, consist of several parallel ranges, reaching a combined width of c.100 mi. and rising to 5,377 ft. in the Yaman-Tau and to 5,197 ft. in the Iremel. The Urals are a major watershed bet. the Pechora and Volga basins (W) and the Ob-Irtysh basin (E), giving rise on their gradual W slopes to the Usa, Pechora, Vishera, Belaya, and Ural rivers, on the abrupt E slopes to the Sosva, Tura, Iset, Miass, and Tobol rivers. Constituting a considerable climatic barrier, the Urals contribute to the great continentality of Siberia in barring access to the moderating air masses of Atlantic origin. The Urals are densely forested, conifers predominating in N and on E (Siberian) slopes and deciduous trees on W (European) slopes. The mts. form one of the most highly mineralized regions of the USSR, the chief minerals being iron (Magnitnaya, Blagodat, Lebyazhye, and Vysokaya mts.), manganese, nickel, chrome, copper (Krasnouralsk, Kirovgrad, Karabash, Mednogorsk), platinum and gold, bauxite (Severouralsk, Kamensk-Uralski), asbestos, precious stones, coal (Kizel, Kopeisk), potash (Solikamsk), and petroleum (Ishimbai, Krasnokamsk). The folding of the Urals took place as part of the Hercynian orogenesis in the late Paleozoic period and was accompanied (mainly in E) by faulting and igneous intrusions (origin of chief metallic deposits). The mts. were peneplained in the Mezozoic and again uplifted in more recent times. The Rus. fur hunters of Novgorod 1st reached the Northern Urals in 12th cent. Industry was introduced here (16th cent.) by the salt-trading Stroganov family, which sponsored the military expedition (1581) of Yermak into Siberia, the 1st organized Rus. penetration beyond the Urals. Charcoal metallurgy based on iron and copper mining (begun in late 17th cent.) flourished under Peter the Great, but lost its initial preeminence with the development (late 18th cent.) of coke metallurgy and was eclipsed (1890s) by the Donbas and other Ukrainian industrial dists. Since the 1930s, the Urals have again become a leading industrial region of the USSR. Constituted after the Bolshevik Revolution as the Ural Oblast (1923–34), the Urals are divided administratively (since 1938) into the oblasts of Sverdlovsk, Molotov, Chelyabinsk, and Chkalov, and the Bashkir and Udmurt Autonomous SSRs.

Uralneft, Russian SFSR: see VERKHNE-CHUSOVSKIYE GORODKI.

Uralo-Kavkaz (ōōrä'lü-kŭfkäs'), town (1926 pop. 538), SE Voroshilovgrad oblast, Ukrainian SSR, in the Donbas, 4 mi. NE of Krasnodon; coal mines.

Uralo-Klyuchi (ōōrä'lō klyōō'chē), town (1949 pop. over 500), W Irkutsk oblast, Russian SFSR, near Taishet.

Ural River (yōō'rŭl, Rus. ōōräl'), in SE European Russian SFSR and NW Kazakh SSR, rises in the S Urals c.25 mi. NE of Iremel mtn., flows S past Verkhne-Uralsk, Magnitogorsk, and Orsk, generally W past Novo-Troitsk, Chkalov, Ilek, and Uralsk, and S through dry steppe, past Inderborski, Kulagino, and Guryev, to Caspian Sea 10 mi. SW of Guryev, forming small delta mouth; 1,574 mi. long. Navigable 910 mi. to Chkalov (northbound shipments include petroleum and fish; southbound, grain and livestock). Dammed at Magnitogorsk and above Orsk. Has extensive fisheries; major source of water supply for W Kazakh steppe. Receives Sakmara, Chagan, Kushum (right), and Kumak, Or, Ilek, Utva (left) rivers. Sometimes considered as border line bet. Europe and Asia. Until 1775, called Yaik R.

Uralsk or **Ural'sk** (yōōrälsk', Rus. ōōrälsk'), city (1939 pop. 66,201), ⊙ West Kazakhstan oblast, Kazakh SSR, on Ural R., on railroad and 230 mi. E of Saratov, 1,300 mi. NW of Alma-Ata; 51°10'N 51°20'E. Center of agr. area; meat packing, wool washing, tanning, flour milling; mfg. of mother-of-pearl. Teachers col. Founded c.1613–22; until 1775, called Yaitski Gorodok.

Urambo (ōōräm'bō), village, Western Prov., W Tanganyika, on railroad and 50 mi. W of Tabora; center of peanut-growing scheme (ground 1st cleared 1947).

Uramir, Tadzhik SSR: see RAMIT.

Uran (ōōr'ŭn), town (pop. 5,794), Kolaba dist., W Bombay, India, 9 mi. SE of Bombay; saltworks, distillery. Mfg. of tiles and abrasives 2 mi. NW, at Mora.

Urana, village (pop. 444), S New South Wales, Australia, 160 mi. W of Canberra; coal-mining center; wheat, sheep.

Urania (ūrā'nēü), village (pop. 1,004), La Salle parish, central La., 40 mi. N of Alexandria, in timber and oil-producing area; mills lumber, creosoted products, pulpwood, paper, wood alcohol. A Yale Univ. forestry camp is here.

Uraricoera River (ōōrürēkwĕ'rü), Rio Branco territory, northernmost Brazil, one of the headstreams of the Rio BRANCO, rises in the Serra Pacaraima at Venezuela border, flows c.300 mi. E to a junction with the Tacutú 20 mi. above Boa Vista to form the Rio Branco. Not navigable.

Urartu: see ARARAT, MOUNT, Turkey.

Uras (ōō'räs), village (pop. 2,913), Cagliari prov., W Sardinia, 15 mi. SSE of Oristano.

Uratomi, Japan: see URADOME.

Ura-Tyube (ōōrä"-tyōōbyĕ'), city (1932 pop. estimate 24,300), central Leninabad oblast, Tadzhik SSR, on Stalinabad-Leninabad highway, on N slope of Turkestan Range, and 40 mi. SW of Leninabad, in wheat and grape area; wine-producing center; fruit canning; camel-wool processing. Breeding of mtn. horses. Fell to Russians (1866). Was ⊙ former Ura-Tyube oblast (1945–47).

Uravakonda (ōōrŭvŭkōn'dŭ), town (pop. 11,125), Anantapur dist., NW Madras, India, 30 mi. NW of Anantapur; hand-loom cotton weaving. Gold mines 10 mi. ESE.

Uravan (yōō'rŭvăn), village (pop. c.800), Montrose co., W Colo., on San Miguel R. and c.45 mi. WSW of Montrose; alt. c.5,000 ft. Uranium and vanadium processed here.

Urawa (ōōrä'wä), city (1940 pop. 59,671; 1947 pop. 106,176), ⊙ Saitama prefecture, central Honshu, Japan, adjacent to Omiya (N), on Ara R. and 15 mi. NNW of Tokyo; principally residential. Includes (since early 1940s) former town of Mutsuji (1940 pop. 7,884).

Urayasu (ōōrä'-yä'sōō). **1** Town (pop. 14,659), Chiba prefecture, central Honshu, Japan, on N shore of Tokyo Bay, adjacent to Tokyo (W); rice growing, fishing. **2** Town (pop. 4,826), Tottori prefecture, S Honshu, Japan, on Sea of Japan, 22 mi. ENE of Yonago; rice, raw silk. Formed in early 1940s by combining villages of Ozuka, Ichise, and Isezaki.

Uraz (ōō'räs), Ger. *Auras* (ou'räs), town (1939 pop. 1,673; 1946 pop. 806) in Lower Silesia, after 1945 in Wroclaw prov., SW Poland, on the Oder and 12 mi. NW of Breslau (Wroclaw); agr. market (grain, sugar beets, potatoes, stock).

Urazovka (ōōrä'zŭfkŭ), Tatar village (1926 pop. 1,768), SE Gorki oblast, Russian SFSR, 11 mi. SE of Sergach; wheat.

Urazovo (–zŭvŭ), village (1926 pop. 12,748), SE Kursk oblast, Russian SFSR, on Oskol R. and 8 mi. SSW of Valuiki; flour milling; chalk quarrying.

Urbach, France: see FOUDAY.

Urbain (ûrbān'), village (pop. 57), Franklin co., S Ill., 10 mi. N of Herrin, in bituminous-coal and agr. area.

Urbakh, Russian SFSR: see PUSHKINO, Saratov oblast.

Urbana (ûrbă'nŭ). **1** City (pop. 22,834), ⊙ Champaign co.,E Ill., adjoining CHAMPAIGN city, with which it is closely tied economically and socially. Seat of Univ. of Ill. Trade center in rich farm area; railroad shops; mfg. of scientific instruments, seed, disinfectants, cigars, paint. Crystal Lake Park is here. Settled 1822, inc. 1833. Lincoln spoke here (1854) against the Kansas-Nebraska Bill. **2** Town (pop. 414), Benton co., E central Iowa, near Cedar R., 20 mi. NNW of Cedar Rapids. **3** Town (pop. 359), Dallas co., SW central Mo., 14 mi. NNW of Buffalo. **4** City (pop. 9,335), ⊙ Champaign co., W central Ohio, 13 mi. NNE of Springfield, in rich farming and stock-raising area; mfg. of paper, metal products, tools, food products, railroad equipment, screens; gravel pits; fruit-packing house. Has a jr. col. Ohio Caverns are 10 mi. N. Laid out 1805, inc. 1868.

Urbana, La, Venezuela: see LA URBANA.

Urbancrest, village (pop. 823), Franklin co., central Ohio, a SW suburb of Columbus.

Urbandale. **1** Town (pop. 1,777), Polk co., central Iowa, W suburb of Des Moines. Settled 1901, inc. 1917. **2** Town (pop. 35), Randolph co., N central Mo., just S of Moberly.

Urbania (ōōrbä'nyä), town (pop. 2,789), Pesaro e Urbino prov., The Marches, central Italy, on Metauro R. and 7 mi. SW of Urbino; pottery mfg. Bishopric, with seminary. Noted in 16th cent. for its majolica. Badly damaged by air bombing (1944) in Second World War.

Urbank, village (pop. 162), Ottertail co., W Minn., 30 mi. SE of Fergus Falls.

Urbanna (ûrbă'nŭ), town (pop. 505), Middlesex co., E Va., on short Urbanna Creek (navigable) near the Rappahannock and 14 mi. ENE of West Point; packs, ships seafood; summer resort.

Urbano Santos (ōōrbä'nŏŏ sän'tŏŏs), city (pop. 833), NE Maranhão, Brazil, 95 mi. SE of São Luís; cotton, sugar, babassu nuts.

Urbeis, France: see ORBEY.

Urbina (ōōrbē'nä), rail station in central Ecuador, on Tungurahua-Chimborazo prov. border, in the Andes, 17 mi. SSW of Ambato; highest point (11,800 ft.) on Guayaquil-Quito RR.

Urbino (ōōrbē'nô), town (pop. 5,459), Pesaro e Urbino prov., The Marches, central Italy, 19 mi. SW of Pesaro; silk textiles, majolica, cutlery, bricks, wrought iron. Archbishopric. Has cathedral (rebuilt 1789–1801), 14th-cent. church of San Francesco, small university (founded 1671), and early Renaissance ducal palace housing Natl. Gall. of the Marches (mus., picture gall., historical and topographical dept.). Flourished under Montefeltro family (12th–16th cent.) and under the dukes Della Rovere (1508–1626). Became an art center noted for its school of painting (15th–17th cent.) and its majolica. Raphael b. here.

Urbión, Sierra de (syĕ'rä dhā ōōrvyōn'), small massif of central plateau (Meseta), in Old Castile, N central Spain, on Soria-Logroño prov. border, 20 mi. NE of Soria. Rises to 7,310 ft.; near its peak is the source of the Duero (Douro). A lagoon, drained by affluent of the Ebro, is on its N slope.

Urbisaglia (ōōrbēsä'lyä), village (pop. 831), Macerata prov., The Marches, central Italy, 8 mi. SSW of Macerata; silk mill. Near by are ruins (theater, amphitheater) of anc. *Urbs Salvia*.

Urbs Vetus, Italy: see ORVIETO.

Urcos (ōōr'kōs), town (pop. 2,328), ⊙ Quisipicanchi prov. (□ 2,516; enumerated pop. 59,879, plus estimated 8,000 Indians), Cuzco dept., S central Peru, on Vilcanota R., on railroad and 27 mi. SE of Cuzco; alfalfa, grain, livestock; woolen mill. Archaeological remains.

Urcuquí (ōōrkōōkē'), village, Imbabura prov., N Ecuador, in the Andes, 9 mi. NW of Ibarra; sugar refining.

Urda (ōōr'dhä), town (pop. 5,406), Toledo prov., central Spain, 35 mi. SSE of Toledo; agr. center (cereals, carobs, grapes, olives, saffron, livestock); apiculture. Alcohol distilling, flour milling, cheese processing; marble quarrying. Mfg. of tiles and leather goods.

Urda (ōōrdä'), village (1926 pop. 4,282), W West Kazakhstan oblast, Kazakh SSR, 130 mi. E of Stalingrad, in livestock-breeding area (cattle, camels, horses). Was ⊙ former Bukei govt. (1917–25).

Urdalsknud, Norway: see RUVEN MOUNTAINS.

Urdaneta (ōōrdhänā'tä), town (1939 pop. 3,276; 1948 municipality pop. 35,811), Pangasinan prov., central Luzon, Philippines, 16 mi. ESE of Dagupan, near Agno R.; agr. center (rice, copra, corn).

Urdinarrain (ōōrdēnärīn'), town (pop. estimate 1,500), S central Entre Ríos prov., Argentina, on railroad and 32 mi. NW of Gualeguaychú; agr. center (grain, livestock); tannery.

Ürdingen, Germany: see KREFELD.

Urdos (ürdôs'), village (pop. 176), Basses-Pyrénées dept., SW France, on the Gave d'Aspe, in Aspe valley of W Pyrenees, 22 mi. S of Oloron-Sainte-Marie, and 5 mi. NNW of Somport pass (Sp. border); customhouse; 3 hydroelectric plants near by. Portalet state prison, 1 mi. N.

Urdos, Port d', France and Spain: see SOMPORT.

Urdzhar (ōōrjär'), village (1939 pop. over 2,000), SE Semipalatinsk oblast, Kazakh SSR, on Urdzhar R. (influx of the Ala-Kul) and 80 mi. SE of Ayaguz (joined by highway); irrigated agr. (wheat, opium); sheep breeding.

Ure, Norway: see STAMSUND.

Urechye or **Urech'ye** (ōōryĕ'chyĭ), town (1926 pop. 2,055), W central Bobruisk oblast, Belorussian SSR, 15 mi. ESE of Slutsk; wood cracking, food processing.

Uren or **Uren'** (ōōrĕn'yŭ), village (1926 pop. 1,149), N central Gorki oblast, Russian SFSR, on railroad and 27 mi. S of Vetluga; flax processing.

Ureña (ōōrā'nyä), town (1950 pop. 840), ⊙ Pérez Zeledón canton, San José prov., S central Costa Rica, 6 mi. NW of El General; rice, corn, beans, tobacco; poultry and stock raising; lumbering. Until 1931 called San Isidro.

Ureña, town (pop. 1,658), Táchira state, W Venezuela, near Colombia border, 19 mi. NW of San Cristóbal; grain, fruit, stock. Agua Caliente thermal springs are 1½ mi. E.

Ureparpara, New Hebrides: see BANKS ISLANDS.

Ure River (ūr), Yorkshire, England, rises in the Pennines 16 mi. NW of Hawes, flows 50 mi. E and SE, past Hawes, Askrigg, Ripon, and Boroughbridge, to junction with Swale R. 12 mi. NW of York, forming the Ouse. Sometimes called Yore.

Ures (ōō'rĕs), city (pop. 2,981), Sonora, NW Mexico, on Sonora R. and 40 mi. NE of Hermosillo; agr. center (wheat, corn, beans, livestock).

Ureshino (ōōrā'shĭnō), town (pop. 14,017), Saga prefecture, W Kyushu, Japan, on S central Hizen Peninsula, 16 mi. ESE of Sasebo; agr. center (rice, tea). Alkaline hot springs.

Urfa (ōōrfä'), province (□ 7,998; 1950 pop. 295,734), S Turkey; ⊙ Urfa. Bordered W by Euphrates R., S by Syria. Agr. (grain, canary-grass, lentils, vetch, hemp, onions).

Urfa, anc. *Edessa* (ĭdĕ'sŭ, ē–), city (1950 pop. 37,456). ⊙ Urfa prov., S Turkey, 85 mi. SSE of Malatya, 30 mi. from Syrian line; 37°5'N 38°42'E. Center in agr. area (wheat, barley, hemp, vetch); tobacco factory. A very anc. city, Edessa is in Arabic tradition associated with Abraham. Known as Arrhoe at time of Alexander the Great; ⊙ independent kingdom of Osroene, 137 B.C.–A.D. 216. Christian church established here early in 3d cent.; became seat of numerous monasteries. Later fell to Moslems; taken (1097) by the Crusaders and became ⊙ Latin principality until 1144, when it fell to Moslems. Permanently taken by Turks in 1637. There are remains of old castle and walls. In late 19th cent. many Christians (mostly Armenians) massacred here. Formerly also spelled Orfa.

Urfahr, Austria: see LINZ.

Urft River (ōōrft), W Germany, rises on the Eifel, flows c.30 mi. N and NW to the Roer, 5 mi. WNW of Gemünd. Large reservoir (completed 1903) is 1 mi. W of Gemünd.

Urga, Mongolia: see ULAN BATOR.

Urgal River, Russian SFSR: see SREDNI URGAL.

Urgel, city, Spain: see SEO DE URGEL.

Urgel Canal (ōōrhĕl'), Lérida prov., NE Spain, runs from Segre R. near Pons, winding 46 mi. SW through Urgel plain, to the Segre at Lérida. With many secondary canals, it is used for irrigation.

Urgench (ōōrgyĕnch'), city (1939 pop. over 10,000), ⊙ Khorezm oblast, Uzbek SSR, on Khiva oasis, on railroad and 18 mi. NE of Khiva, 445 mi. W of Tashkent; 41°34'N 60°37'E. Cotton ginning, cottonseed-oil extracting, food processing, metalworking. Teachers col. Named for anc. Urgench (modern KUNYA-URGENCH); called Novy Urgench or Novo-Urgench [Rus.,=new Urgench] until 1937. Superseded Khiva as local center after 1932.

Urgnano (ōōrnyä'nô), village (pop. 3,601), Bergamo prov., Lombardy, N Italy, near Serio R., 7 mi. S of Bergamo; agr. center.

Urgun or **Orgun** (ōōrgōōn'), town, Southern Prov., E Afghanistan, 50 mi. S of Gardez, near Pakistan line, in lumbering area (pine).

Urgup (ürgüp'), Turkish *Ürgüp* or *Ürküp*, village (pop. 4,468), Kayseri prov., central Turkey, 32 mi. WSW of Kayseri; grain, legumes, potatoes, onions, sugar beets.

Urgut (ōōrgōōt'), town (1932 pop. estimate 18,400), E Samarkand oblast, Uzbek SSR, 22 mi. SE of Samarkand; cotton-milling center.

Uri (ōō'rē), town (pop. 1,281), Muzaffarabad dist., W Kashmir, in NW Pir Panjal Range, on Jhelum R. and 38 mi. SE of Muzaffarabad; corn, rice, wheat, oilseeds. Scene of fighting in 1947, during India-Pakistan struggle for control. Ochre deposits NW, lead deposits E. Sometimes called Pirasthan.

Uri (ōō'rē), canton (□ 415; 1950 pop. 28,569), central Switzerland, its least populated canton; ⊙ Altdorf. Pop. German speaking and Catholic. It extends along upper Reuss R., with some cultivated fields, meadows, and forests in the valley; its lower mtn. slopes, covered with pastures, rise to Alpine peaks and glaciers (SAINT GOTTHARD in S). Resorts in mts. and on L. of Lucerne. Hydroelectric plants along the Reuss. Industrial center, Altdorf. The scene of the William Tell legend, Uri in 1291 formed with Schwyz and Unterwalden the league which became the nucleus of Switzerland. With Lucerne, these cantons became known as the Four Forest Cantons.

Uri, Lake of, Switzerland: see LUCERNE, LAKE OF.

Uriage, France: see SAINT-MARTIN-D'URIAGE.

Uriah (yōōrī'ŭ), village (1940 pop. 711), Monroe co., SW Ala., 45 mi. NE of Mobile; naval stores.

Uriangato (ōōryäng-gä'tō), town (pop. 5,201), Guanajuato, central Mexico, 37 mi. SW of Celaya; alt. 5,800 ft.; agr. center (corn, wheat, sugar cane, vegetables, fruit, stock).

Uribante River (ōōrēbän'tä), W Venezuela, rises in Andean spur near San Cristóbal (Táchira state), flows c.150 mi. E, along Barinas–Apure border, joining Sarare R. 4 mi. NNE of Guadualito to form Apure R.

Uribia (ōōrē'byä), town (pop. 304), ⊙ Guajira commissary, N Colombia, on interior lowlands, on isthmus of Guajira peninsula, 50 mi. E of Ríohacha, 500 mi. NNE of Bogotá. Divi-divi gathering; tannery. Airfield. Founded c.1930 as ⊙ Guajira commissary. Petroleum wells near by.

Uriburu (ōōrēbōōr'ōō), village (pop. estimate 1,000), E La Pampa natl. territory, Argentina, on railroad and 25 mi. ENE of Santa Rosa; wheat, alfalfa, corn, sheep, cattle.

Urica (ōōrē'kä), town (pop. 481), Anzoátegui state, NE Venezuela, 55 mi. SE of Barcelona; cotton, corn, cattle.

Urich (yōō'rĭk), agr. city (pop. 400), Henry co., W central Mo., near South Grand R., 14 mi. WNW of Clinton.

Uriconium, England: see WROXETER.

Urie River (ōō'rē), Aberdeen, Scotland, rises 4 mi. SE of Huntly, flows 19 mi. SE, past Inverurie, to Don R. just S of Inverurie. Sometimes spelled Ury.

Urigam, India: see KOLAR GOLD FIELDS.

Urim (ōōrēm'), agr. settlement (pop. 120), S Israel, in the Negev, 18 mi. WSW of Beersheba. Founded 1946.

Uriondo (ōōryōn'dō), town (pop. c.3,100), ⊙ Avilés or Avilez prov., Tarija dept., S Bolivia, 13 mi. SSE of Tarija; wheat, potatoes. Until c.1945, Concepción.

Urique (ōōrē'kä), town (pop. 308), Chihuahua, N Mexico, in Sierra Madre Occidental, on Urique R. (affluent of the Río Verde) and 150 mi. SW of Chihuahua; alt. 5,245 ft.; copper mining.

Urique River, Chihuahua, NW Mexico, rises in Sierra Madre Occidental, flows c.120 mi. NW and S, past Urique, joining the Río Verde near Sinaloa border to form the Río del FUERTE.

Urireo (ōōrērā'ō), village (pop. 2,557), Guanajuato, central Mexico, 21 mi. S of Celaya; cereals, alfalfa, sugar cane, potatoes, fruit, vegetables. Cooperative settlement.

Uri-Rotstock, Switzerland: see ROTSTOCK.

Uritsk (ōōrētsk'), city (1939 pop. over 10,000), central Leningrad oblast, Russian SFSR, at Ligovo station, 8 mi. SW of Leningrad; metal and clothing industries. Residential section. Until 1925, called Ligovo. During the Second World War, it was an advanced Ger. position in the long siege of Leningrad (1941–44).

Uritski or **Uritskiy** (ōōrēt'skē), town (1939 pop. over 10,000), NE Bryansk oblast, Russian SFSR, N suburb of Bryansk, at Maltsevskaya station; ironworking center.

Uritskoye (–skŭyŭ), village (1948 pop. over 2,000), NE Kustanai oblast, Kazakh SSR, 75 mi. ENE of Kustanai; cattle; metalworks. Until 1923 called Vsekhsyatskoye.

Uritsura (ōōrē'tsōōrä) or **Urizura** (–zōōrä), town (pop. 4,947), Ibaraki prefecture, central Honshu, Japan, 8 mi. N of Mito; rice growing.

Urjala, Finland: see NUUTAJÄRVI.

Urk (ûrk), former island (200 acres; pop. 4,455) in the IJsselmeer, North Holland prov., N central Netherlands, 24 mi. ESE of Enkhuizen; now part of North East Polder; 1 mi. long, ½ mi. wide. Fishing, cattle raising; ice mfg.

Urkarakh (ōōrkŭräkh'), village (1926 pop. 2,376), E central Dagestan Autonomous SSR, Russian SFSR, near SE end of Gimry Range, 35 mi. WNW of Derbent; grain, sheep.

Urkut (o͝or'ko͞ot), Hung. *Úrkút*, mining town (pop. 1,683), Veszprem co., NW central Hungary, in Bakony Mts., 12 mi. W of Veszprem; manganese.

Urla (o͝orlä'), town (pop. 10,206), Smyrna prov., W Turkey, near S shore of Gulf of Smyrna, 23 mi. WSW of Smyrna; zinc, iron, emery, gold; tobacco, raisins.

Urlati (o͝orläts'), Rum. *Urlaţi*, town (1948 pop. 6,555), Prahova prov., S central Rumania, in Walachia, 11 mi. ENE of Ploesti; oil and natural-gas center; petroleum refining. Also trade in wine, fruit, plum brandy, livestock. Has church with fine frescoes, art mus.

Urman (o͞ormän'), town (1937 pop. over 500), NE Bashkir Autonomous SSR, Russian SFSR, on railroad and 40 mi. ENE of Ufa; lumbering.

Urmar, Tanda, India: see TANDA-URMAR.

Urmary (o͞ormä'rē), town (1939 pop. over 2,000), E Chuvash Autonomous SSR, Russian SFSR, on railroad and 20 mi. ENE of Kanash; woodworking, flour milling; limestone quarrying.

Urmia, town, Iran: see RIZAIYEH.

Urmia, Lake (o͝or'mēŭ), or **Lake Rizaiyeh** (rĕzäēyĕ'), Persian *Daryacheh-i- Urumiyeh* (däryächĕ'ē-o͞oro͞omēyĕ'), *-i-Rizaiyeh*, or *-i-Shahi* (-ĕshähē'), largest lake (□ 1,500–2,300) of Iran, in Azerbaijan, bet. Tabriz and Turkish frontier; 90 mi. long (N–S), 30 mi. wide; alt. 4,000 ft. Shallow (to 20 ft. deep) and saline (23%), it has no outlet and receives the Talkheh (E) and Zarineh (S) rivers. Steamers connect main lake port and rail terminus of Sharifkaneh (NE) with Gelma Khaneh, landing of Rizaiyeh. Lake level fluctuates bet. low summer stage, and high winter stage when river-mouth marshes are flooded. Contains rocky, circular Shahi Isl. (10 mi. across), connected with the mainland at low water; and small Sheep Isls. (S).

Urmiri (o͞ormē'rē). **1** Village, La Paz dept., Bolivia: see SAPAHAQUI. **2** Town (pop. c.2,800), Oruro dept., W Bolivia, at S end of Serranía de Achacollo, 15 mi. SSE of Poopó; alt. 12,150 ft.; mineral springs.

Urmston (ûrmz'tŭn), urban district (1931 pop. 9,284; 1951 census 39,233), SE Lancashire, England, 5 mi. WSW of Manchester; metalworking, flour milling; mfg. of paint.

Urnaes, Norway: see ORNES.

Urnäsch (o͝or'nĕsh), town (pop. 2,481), Appenzell Ausser Rhoden half-canton, NE Switzerland, 5 mi. S of Herisau; textiles, knit goods, flour. Has 17th-cent. church.

Urnen, Switzerland: see NIEDERURNEN.

Urnersee, Switzerland: LUCERNE, LAKE OF.

Urnes, Norway: see ORNES.

Uromi (o͞orô'mē), town, Benin prov., Western Provinces, Nigeria, 5 mi. NNW of Ubiaja; palm oil and kernels, hardwood, rubber, kola nuts, cotton.

Uronarti (o͞orōnär'tē), Arabic *Gezira el Melik* or *Jazırat al-Malik* [=king's island], rocky island in the Nile, N Anglo-Egyptian Sudan, 37 mi. SW of Wadi Halfa. Has ruins of fortress of Middle Empire (2100–1700 B.C.).

Urosevac or **Uroshevats** (both: o͞o'rôshĕväts), Serbo-Croatian *Uroševac*, village (pop. 6,709), S Serbia, Yugoslavia, on railroad and 20 mi. S of Pristina, in the Kosovo.

Urozhainoye or **Urozhaynoye** (o͞orŭzhī'nŭyŭ), village (1939 pop. over 500), NE Kabardian Autonomous SSR, Russian SFSR, on right bank of Terek R. and 11 mi. ESE of Prokhladny, in hemp-growing area; metalworks, flour mill; orchards.

Urpeth, town and parish (pop. 3,127), N Durham, England, 2 mi. NNW of Chester-le-Street; coal mining.

Urquhart (ûr'khŭrt), agr. village in Urquhart and Logie-Wester parish (pop. 1,792), SE Ross and Cromarty, Scotland, on Cromarty Firth, 2 mi. E of Dingwall.

Urquhart and Glenmoriston (glĕnmŏ'rĭstŭn) parish (pop. 1,488), N central Inverness, Scotland. Includes STRONE.

Urquiza (o͞orkē'sä), town (pop. estimate 1,200), central Entre Ríos prov., Argentina, on railroad and 45 mi. NW of Concepción del Uruguay; agr. (grain, livestock) and dairy center.

Urr (ûr), agr. village and parish (pop. 4,032, including Dalbeattie burgh), E Kirkcudbright, Scotland, on Urr Water and 4 mi. ENE of Castle Douglas. Near by is Mote of Urr, Saxon or early Norman fortification.

Urrao (o͞orä'ō), town (pop. 3,707), Antioquia dept., NW central Colombia, in valley of Cordillera Occidental, 40 mi. W of Medellín; alt. 6,188 ft. Agr. area (coffee, stock); lumbering, dairying (known for its cheese). Airfield. Founded 1845. Gold placer mines near by.

Urray (ŭ'rā), agr. village and parish (pop. 1,826), SE Ross and Cromarty, Scotland, on Orrin R. and 5 mi. SW of Dingwall. Parish includes MUIR-OF-ORD.

Urr Water (ûr), river, Kirkcudbright, Scotland, rises 8 mi. ENE of Dalry, flows 27 mi. SE, past Urr and Dalbeattie, to Solway Firth 6 mi. S of Dalbeattie.

Ursatyevskaya or **Ursat'yevskaya** (o͞orsä'tyĭfskīŭ), town (1932 pop. estimate 4,600), S Tashkent oblast, Uzbek SSR, on Trans-Caspian RR, at junction of branch to Kokand and Andizhan, and 75 mi. S of Tashkent; rail workshops; metalworks.

Urserental (o͝or'sŭrŭntäl"), valley of the upper Reuss, in S Uri canton, central Switzerland, SW of Andermatt.

Urshelski or **Urshel'skiy** (o͞orshĕl'skē), town (1926 pop. 3,230), S Vladimir oblast, Russian SFSR, on rail spur and 18 mi. WNW of Gus-Khrustalny; glassworking center; woodworking.

Ursina (ûrsī'nŭ), borough (pop. 334), Somerset co., SW Pa., 18 mi. SW of Somerset.

Ursk (o͞orsk), town (1948 pop. over 10,000), W Kemerovo oblast, Russian SFSR, 25 mi. NW of Guryevsk, on Salair Ridge; gold placers.

Úrsulo Galván (o͞or'so͞olō gälvän'), town (pop. 1,349), Veracruz, E Mexico, in Gulf lowland, 38 mi. SE of Jalapa; corn, fruit, livestock.

Ursus (o͞or'so͞os), industrial suburb of Warsaw, Warszawa prov., E central Poland, 6 mi. WSW of city center; large tractor plant.

Urswick (ûrz'wĭk, ûr'zĭk), parish (pop. 1,074), N Lancashire, England, on Furness peninsula. Includes sheep-raising and agr. villages of Great Urswick, 2 mi. SSW of Ulverston, and Little Urswick, 3 mi. SSW of Ulverston. Bet. the 2 villages is 13th-cent. church.

Uruáchic (o͞orwä'chĕk), mining settlement (pop. 395), Chihuahua, N Mexico, in Sierra Madre Occidental, 150 mi. WSW of Chihuahua; gold, silver, lead, copper, manganese mining.

Uruaçu (o͞orwŭso͞o'), city (pop. 820), central Goiás, central Brazil, 130 mi. N of Goiânia; a leading rock-crystal-mining region with extensive reserves. Until 1944, called Santana (formerly spelled Sant' Anna).

Uruapan (o͞orwä'pän), officially Uruapan del Progreso, city (pop. 20,583), Michoacán, W central Mexico, on central plateau, 60 mi. WSW of Morelia; alt. 5,285 ft. Rail terminus; agr. center in rich semitropical area producing coffee, rice, corn, wheat, sugar cane, and tropical fruit; forest products (resins). Lumbering, rice milling, liquor and alcohol distilling, vegetable-oil extracting; mfg. of shawls, ceramics, sweets, lemon citrates. Noted for Tarascan Indian lacquer ware. Airfield. Serves as base for tourists visiting PARICUTÍN volcano and impressive Tlaráracua waterfalls near by. The city was founded 1540 by Franciscan friar Juan de San Miguel.

Urubamba (o͞oro͞obäm'bä), city (pop. 3,866), ⊙ Urubamba prov. (□ 397; pop. 32,830), Cuzco dept., S central Peru, at SE foot of Cordillera Vilcabamba, on Urubamba R. and 21 mi. NNW of Cuzco; alt. 9,350 ft. Rail terminus in agr. region (cereals, potatoes); flour-milling and mining (gold, silver, copper) center.

Urubamba River, Cuzco dept., S and S central Peru, rises as Vilcanota R. at S foot of the Nudo de Vilcanota on Cuzco–Puno dept. border, flows c.450 mi. NW, N, and WNW, through Andean ranges, past Sicuani, Urcos, Urubamba, Machupicchu, and Quillabamba, to join the Apurímac (here called the Tambo) in forming the Ucayali at 11°17'S 73°47'W. The Urubamba is used for irrigation in its high Andean valley, the most populated region of Cuzco dept. It passes through steep gorges, forming many rapids. The Vilcanota was the sacred river of the Incas.

Urubichá (o͞oro͞obēchä'), village (pop. c.600), Santa Cruz dept., E central Bolivia, 85 mi. NW of Concepción; cotton. A Franciscan mission until 1938.

Urubu-Pungá Falls (o͞oro͞obo͞o'-po͞ong-gä'), on upper Paraná R., S central Brazil, on Mato Grosso–São Paulo border, 7 mi. above influx of Tietê R. Height: 33 ft. Just below is head of uninterrupted navigation to Guaíra Falls on Paraguay border.

Uruburetama (o͞oro͞obo͞orĭtä'mŭ), city (pop. 2,039), N Ceará, Brazil, in Uruburetama hills, 70 mi. W of Fortaleza; cotton, coffee, sugar. Kaolin deposits. Formerly called São João de Uruburetama.

Urubu River (o͞oro͞obo͞o'), E Amazonas, Brazil, enters the Amazon (left bank) below Itacoatiara after a SE course of c.160 mi.

Urucanga, Brazil: see URUSSANGA.

Urucará (o͞oro͞okŭrä'), city (pop. 372), E Amazonas, Brazil, on left bank of the Amazon and 70 mi. NE of Itacoatiara; rubber, Brazil nuts, manioc, copaiba oil.

Urucú, Brazil: see CARLOS CHAGAS.

Uruçuí (o͞oro͞oswē'), city (pop. 1,524), SW Piauí, Brazil, port on right bank of Parnaíba R. (Maranhão border), opposite Benedito Leite, and 110 mi. WSW of Floriano; ships hides and skins, cotton, gunpowder (made from local nitrate deposits). Airfield. Formerly spelled Urussuhy.

Urucuia River (o͞oro͞oko͞o'yŭ), NW Minas Gerais, Brazil, rises in the Serra Geral de Goiás, flows 180 mi. S and E to the São Francisco (left bank) above São Francisco (city). Navigable in lower course.

Urucum, Morro do, Brazil: see CORUMBÁ, Mato Grosso.

Urucurituba (o͞oro͞oko͞orĕto͞o'bŭ), city (pop. 417), E Amazonas, Brazil, near right bank of Amazon R., 170 mi. ENE of Manaus; rubber, guarana, hardwood.

Uruguaiana (o͞oro͞ogwīä'nŭ), city (1950 pop. 33,272), SW Rio Grande do Sul, Brazil, port on Uruguay R. (Argentine border), opposite Paso de los Libres, and 35 mi. W of Pôrto Alegre; 29°46'S 57°6'W. Livestock center with meat-processing and by-products industries (candles, soap); mfg. of tobacco products, perfumes; tanning, leatherworking. Port of entry. Linked by rail with Pôrto Alegre and Uruguay. Airfield. International bridge across the Uruguay inagurated 1945. Founded by Jesuit missionaries; occupied by Paraguayan troops in 1865. Formerly spelled Uruguayana.

Uruguay (yo͞o'rŭgwā, -gwī, Sp. o͞oro͞ogwī'), republic (□ 72,152; pop. 2,202,936), SE South America, on the Atlantic; ⊙ MONTEVIDEO. Smallest and one of the most progressive of South American nations. On the S it extends along the Río de la Plata to the Uruguay R. (navigable to SALTO), which separates it from Argentina. Brazil is on N and NE. Uruguay lies roughly bet. 30°–35°S and 53°–58°30'W. It consists largely of rolling grassland, a continuation of the Argentinian "Wet Pampa," broken by minor ridges from the Brazilian Highlands, which rise in Cuchilla GRANDE PRINCIPAL to c.1,600 ft. The low Cuchilla de SANTA ANA stretches along Brazil line. Numerous rivers flow slowly through wooded valleys to the Río de la Plata system and the large coastal lagoon L. MIRIM (E). The longest inland river, Río NEGRO, on its way to Uruguay R. traverses the country's center, where it now forms the extensive Río Negro reservoir (RINCÓN DEL BONETE or Embalse del Río Negro) and hydroelectric project. Along the coast, frequently disrupted by lagoons, stretches an alluvial plain fringed E of Montevideo by a string of renowned beach resorts (e.g., ATLÁNTIDA, PIRIÁPOLIS, PUNTA DEL ESTE). Wholly within the temperate zone, Uruguay has a healthful, equable climate with moderate seasonal changes. While frosts are practically unknown, occasional droughts occur. Winter is the principal rainy season. The fertile soil is well suited to all kinds of cultivation, but 60% of the land is exclusively devoted to pasturage, based on natural forage. Stock raising, chiefly of cattle and sheep, provides animal produce constituting about 95% of all exports. Leading export is wool (c.40% of exports), followed by salted, canned, and frozen meat (from the many *frigoríficos*), leather, hides, bristles, fats, bones, and agr. produce. Crops, predominantly grown in coastal depts., are wheat, corn, flaxseed, oats, citrus, grapes, peaches, pears, birdseed, manioc, tobacco. Mineral resources are negligible and unimportant, but there are some deposits of coal, silver, copper, lead, manganese, and building materials. Apart from the processing of animal products, wine making, brewing, flour milling, and textile milling are important, though an increasing amount of commodities is manufactured in Montevideo. Montevideo is the chief port, seat of the only univ., and administrative and social center, with about ⅓ of the country's entire pop.; it handles the bulk of all foreign trade. Imports consist of petroleum, coal, vehicles, machinery, textile yarn and fibers, sugar, and mate. Montevideo is connected by ferry with Buenos Aires (130 mi. W across the Río de la Plata). International airport just E at Carrasco. Among other ports are Salto, PAYSANDÚ, FRAY BENTOS (a meat-packing center), MERCEDES, and COLONIA. The inland towns play only a secondary part. It is because of Uruguay's position, 1st as an isolated area bet. the nuclei of Spanish and Portuguese settlement, then as a buffer bet. contending Argentine and Brazilian nationalism, that it became an independent state. The aborigines, the fierce Charrúa Indians, after long resistance, were absorbed into the Sp. and Port. populations so that in N Uruguay today is found most of the mestizo element, about 10% of the total. Most of the people, concentrated in the S, are of European descent, Spanish and Italian predominating; there are almost no Negroes or pure Indians. The European discovery of the region called by the Spanish *Banda Oriental* [Sp.,= east bank, i.e., of the Uruguay and the Río de la Plata] is closely linked with that of the Río de la Plata. Although this estuary was explored in early 16th cent. successively by Amerigo Vespucci, Juan Díaz de Solís, and Sebastian Cabot, it was not until 1624 that the Spaniards established their 1st permanent settlement, at Soriano. Montevideo was founded in 1726. From early colonial days Uruguay was claimed by both the Portuguese (who set up Colonia) and the Spanish. In 1717 the Portuguese fortified a hill at present Montevideo. The Spaniards drove them out (1724) and from then until the wars of independence controlled the *Banda Oriental*. There grew up on the pampa, an admirable grazing country, an independent and hardy class, the *gaucho*. It was the *gaucho* who fought for independence, and the tradition of the *gaucho*, his personal loyalties and rivalries, that kept the nation in a state of almost continuous anarchy for three quarters of a century after independence was won. In 1776 the *Banda Oriental* was inc. into the viceroyalty of La Plata, but was occupied (1820) by Brazilian forces during the Argentine struggle for independence, in spite of the efforts of the liberator José Gervasio Artigas. Five years later the "Thirty-three Immortals" under Lavalleja declared Uruguay independent, and in 1827 Brazil was defeated at ITUZAINGÓ. Uruguay emerged as a buffer state bet. Argentina and Brazil, recognized by foreign powers in 1828. Internal political strife and civil war lasted all through 19th cent. With the rise (1904) of the liberal statesman Batlle y Ordóñez to the presidency Uruguay's politics became stabilized. While the country prospered materially, Batlle embarked, particularly during his 2d administration, on a generous social program, which has become a model for all South America. Uruguay entered the Second World War in 1945, and joined the U.N. soon after. Uruguay's modest but progressive industrial development, the expansion of its communications and utilities, and its stable economic and political life have attracted increasing amounts of foreign capital. Uruguay continued to be, after the Second World War, the most economically healthy country of South America. For further information, see separate articles on cities, towns, physical features, and the following departments: ARTIGAS, CANELONES, CERRO LARGO, COLONIA, DURAZNO, FLORES, FLORIDA, LAVALLEJA, MALDONADO, MONTEVIDEO, PAYSANDÚ, RÍO NEGRO, RIVERA, ROCHA, SALTO, SAN JOSÉ, SORIANO, TACUAREMBÓ, TREINTA Y TRES.

Uruguay, Argentina: see CONCEPCIÓN DEL URUGUAY.

Uruguayana, Brazil, see URUGUAIANA.

Uruguay River, South America, rises in coastal range of S Brazil, flows in a wide arc W, SW, S, along Brazil-Argentina and Uruguay-Argentina border, joining PARANÁ RIVER above Buenos Aires to form the Río de la PLATA; length c.1,000 mi. Its principal headstream, the Pelotas, rises only 40 mi. from the Atlantic on W slope of the Serra do Mar (Brazil), and forms Santa Catarina–Rio Grande do Sul line. After receiving the Canoas and Peixe rivers (right), it assumes the name of Uruguay, and forms Brazil-Argentina border below influx of the Pepiri Guaçu, and then, veering SW, it passes Santo Tomé, Argentina (head of upper-course navigation) and Uruguaiana (Brazil). After the influx of Quaraí R. just above Monte Caseros (Argentina) and Bella Unión (Uruguay), navigation on the Uruguay is interrupted by rapids as far as Salto (Uruguay). Here (at Salto Grande falls) is a hydroelectric project jointly operated by Uruguay and Argentina. Lower course is navigable for ocean vessels to Concepción del Uruguay (Argentina) and Paysandú (Uruguay), c.130 mi. above its mouth, and for smaller ships to Concordia (Argentina) and Salto, c.190 mi. From Fray Bentos (where it is 6 mi. wide), river widens to 9 mi. at its mouth. Major tributaries are: left—Ijuí, Ibicuí, Quaraí (Cuareim), Arapey, Río Negro; right—Aguapey, Miriñay. The Uruguay's importance as a traffic artery is less than that of the Paraná, because of rapids in mid-course and lack of navigable tributaries.

Uruk, Iraq: see ERECH.

Urukthapel (ōōrōōk'tăpĕl), coral island, Palau group, W Carolina Isls., W Pacific, 6 mi. SW of Babelthuap; c.10 mi. long; rises to 587 ft.

Urumchi (ōōrōōmchē'), Chinese *Tihwa* or *Ti-hua* (both: dē'hwä'), city (1947 pop. 69,991), ⊙ Sinkiang prov., NW China, in the Dzungaria, 1,500 mi. WNW of Peking, 300 mi. E of Kuldja; 43°48'N 87°35'E. Located on N slope of the Tien Shan, Urumchi is a political and commercial center at junction of caravan routes from USSR, Lanchow (Kansu prov.), and Kashgar. It has flour-milling, paper-mfg., oilseed-pressing, tanning, and printing industries. Seat of Sinkiang col. Became independent municipality in 1945. Sometimes Urumtsi.

Urumea River (ōōrōōmā'ä), in Navarre and Guipúzcoa provs., N Spain, rises in E spurs of the Cantabrian Mts. in Navarre prov., flows 27 mi. NNW to Bay of Biscay at San Sebastián.

Urumiyeh, Iran: see RIZAIYEH.

Urum-Jenikoi, Bulgaria: see BALGAROVO.

Urundi, division, Ruanda-Urundi: see KITEGA; RUANDA-URUNDI.

Urungwe, district, Southern Rhodesia: see MIAMI.

Urun Islampur (ōōr'ōōn ĭslăm'pōōr), town (pop. 12,359), Satara South dist., S Bombay, India, 22 mi. NW of Sangli; market center for millet, peanuts, wheat, rice; hand-loom weaving. Sometimes called Islampur.

Urupês (ōōrōōpĕs'), city (pop. 2,303), N São Paulo, Brazil, 20 mi. W of Catanduva; macaroni, meat, coffee, rice, corn. Until 1944, Mundo Novo.

Urup Island (ōōrōōp'), Jap. *Uruppu-to* (ōōrōōp'-pō-tō'), fourth-largest (□ 581) of Kurile Isls., Russian SFSR, in S section of main group; separated from Brouton Isl. and the Black Brothers (N) by Urup Strait, from Iturup Isl. (S) by Friz (Vries) Strait; 45°55'N 149°55'E; 75 mi. long, 12 mi. wide. Consists of 4 connected volcanic groups, rising to 4,350 ft. Main village, Tokotan, on W coast. Fox farming, fishing, sulphur mining; hot springs.

Urup River, in the N Caucasus, Russian SFSR, rises in the W Greater Caucasus, flows c.90 mi. NNW, past Pregradnaya, Otradnaya, and Sovetskaya (Krasnodar Territory), to Kuban R. at Armavir.

Urupskaya, Russian SFSR: see SOVETSKAYA, Krasnodar Territory.

Urup Strait (ōōrōōp'), Jap. *Minami-uruppu-suido* (mēnä'mē-ōōrōōp'pō-sōōē'dō), in S main Kurile Isls. chain, Russian SFSR; separates Brouton Isl. and the Chernye Bratya (N) and Urup Isl. (S); 17 mi. wide.

Urusan, Korea: see ULSAN.

Urus-Martan, Russian SFSR: see KRASNOARMEISKOYE, Grozny oblast.

Urussanga (ōōrōōsăng'gŭ), city (pop. 716), SE Santa Catarina, Brazil, on railroad and 35 mi. W of Laguna; coal mines. Founded 1878 by Italians. Also spelled Uruçanga.

Urussu (ōōrōōsōō'), town (1939 pop. over 500), SE Tatar Autonomous SSR, Russian SFSR, near Ik R., 9 mi. NNW of Oktyabrski (connected by rail and pipe line), in Tuimazy oil field; rail junction.

Urussuhy, Brazil: see URUÇUÍ.

Urutukan, Russian SFSR: see OROTUKAN.

Uryankhai Territory: see TUVA AUTONOMOUS OBLAST, Russian SFSR.

Ury River, Scotland: see URIE RIVER.

Uryu, Russian SFSR: see KIRILLOVO.

Uryupinsk (ōōryōōpēnsk'), city (1926 pop. 14,409), NW Stalingrad oblast, Russian SFSR, on Khoper R. and 37 mi. S of Borisoglebsk, on rail spur; major agr.-processing center; flour milling, meat packing, canning, sunflower-oil extraction; agr.-machine mfg. Agr. col. Became city in 1929.

Urzhum (ōōrzhōōm'), city (1926 pop. 5,696), SE Kirov oblast, Russian SFSR, near Vyatka R., 100 mi. SSE of Kirov; metalworks. Founded 1554 as fortress under Ivan the Terrible; chartered 1584. S. M. Kirov b. here.

Urziceni (ōōrzēchān'), town (1948 pop. 4,425), Ialomita prov., SE Rumania, on Ialomita R. and 50 mi. NW of Calarasi; rail junction; mfg. of candles and copperware, flour milling. Tobacco and experimental cotton plantations near by.

Us (üs), village (pop. 612), Seine-et-Oise dept., N central France, 6 mi. NW of Pontoise; sugar milling, cork mfg.

Usa (ōō'sä). **1** Town, Kochi prefecture, Japan: see SHIN-USA. **2** Town (pop. 5,317), Oita prefecture, N Kyushu, Japan, 24 mi. NW of Oita; rail junction; rice-growing center; produces *ame* (rice jelly). Has 8th-cent. shrine containing natl. treasures. Airfield. Bombed (1945) in Second World War.

Usa (ōōsä'), town (1948 pop. over 2,000), E Kemerovo oblast, Russian SFSR, in the Kuznetsk Ala-Tau, on upper Usa R. and 70 mi. ENE of Stalinsk; manganese mining.

Usagre (ōōsä'grā), town (pop. 3,264), Badajoz prov., W Spain, 15 mi. ESE of Zafra; lumbering, stock raising, agr. (cereals, olives, tubers, grapes).

Usak or **Ushak** (both: ōō-shäk'), Turk. *Uşak*, town (1950 pop. 19,946), Kutahya prov., W Turkey, on railroad and 60 mi. SSW of Kutahya, 125 mi. E of Smyrna; noted for carpet mfg.; important sugar factory. Agr. area (valonia, vetch, barley, wheat, millet, sugar beets, cotton).

Usakos (ōōsä'kōs), town (pop. 2,366), W South-West Africa, 100 mi. WNW of Windhoek, 17 mi. WSW of Karibib; rail junction with locomotive and machine shops. Tourmaline deposits near by.

Usambara Mountains (ōōsämbä'rä), NE Tanganyika, NW of Tanga, bet. Kenya border and Pangani R.; rise to 8,400 ft. Important sisal-producing region, with main centers at Korogwe and Lushoto; coffee and tung plantations; cinchona. Mica deposits.

Usa River (ōōsä'). **1** In Kemerovo oblast, Russian SFSR, rises in the Kuznetsk Ala-Tau, flows 70 mi. SW, past Usa, to Tom R. Large iron and manganese deposits found along its course. **2** In Komi Autonomous SSR, Russian SFSR, rises in the N Urals at c.67°50'N, flows 420 mi. SW, past Sangorodok and Abez, to Pechora R. at Ust-Usa. Navigable May-Oct. below Sangorodok. Receives Vorkuta R. (right) and the Kos-Yu (left). **3** In Kuibyshev oblast, Russian SFSR: see SAMARA BEND.

Usch, Poland: see UJSCIE.

Uscilug, Ukrainian SSR: see USTILUG.

Uscio (ōō'shō), village (pop. 976), Genova prov., Liguria, N Italy, 5 mi. NW of Rapallo; slate-quarrying center.

Used (ōōsādh'), village (pop. 1,370), Saragossa prov., NE Spain, 8 mi. SW of Daroca; cereals, saffron, sheep.

Usedom (ōō'zŭdôm), Pol. *Uznam* (ōōz'näm), Baltic island (□ 172) in former Prussian Pomerania prov., E Germany, after 1945 divided bet. Mecklenburg (W part; □ 136.8; pop. 38,086) and Szczecin prov., NW Poland (E part; □ 35; pop. 5,771); border extends N–S just W of Swinemünde. Isl. separated from mainland (W) by Peene estuary (bridges) and (S) by Stettin Lagoon, from Wolin isl. (E) by the narrow Swine; 32 mi. long, 1–15 mi. wide; irregular in shape, with even, sandy NE shoreline; elsewhere coast is indented. Lowland, partly wooded; several lakes. Tourist trade and fisheries are important; grain, potatoes, livestock are chief agr. products. Heringsdorf, Ahlbeck, Bansin (seaside resorts), and Usedom town are main centers in Ger. part of isl.; Swinemünde is chief town and seaport in Pol. part. During Second World War, main Ger. guided-missile research and testing station at Peenemünde (NW). In Thirty Years War, Gustavus Adolphus occupied isl. in 1630; awarded (1648) to Sweden under Treaty of Westphalia; passed to Prussia in 1720.

Usedom, town (pop. 2,562) in former Prussian Pomerania prov., E Germany, after 1945 in Mecklenburg, on SW Usedom isl., on small inlet of Stettin Lagoon, 10 mi. E of Anklam; agr. market (grain, potatoes, livestock). Has late-Gothic church and town gate.

Usehat (ōōsä'hŭt), town (pop. 2,548), Budaun dist., central Uttar Pradesh, India, on tributary of the Ganges and 7 mi. SSE of Kakrala; wheat, pearl millet, mustard, barley, rice.

Useko, Tanganyika: see MABAMA.

Useldange (üzŭldäzh'), town (pop. 538), W central Luxembourg, 5 mi. E of Redange; leather tanning and mfg., liquor distilling, paints, varnishes.

Useless Bay, Sp. *Bahía Inútil* (bäē'ä ēnōō'tēl), inlet on W (Chilean) coast of main isl. of Tierra del Fuego, on Strait of Magellan; 40 mi. long, 17 mi. wide at mouth. Caleta Josefina on N shore.

Useras (ōōsā'räs), town (pop. 1,098), Castellón de la Plana prov., E Spain, 14 mi. NW of Castellón de la Plana; olive-oil processing, flour milling; wine, figs, almonds.

Usetsu (ōōsā'tsōō) or **Uzetsu** (ōōzā'tsōō), town (pop. 7,566), Ishikawa prefecture, central Honshu, Japan, on E Noto Peninsula, on Toyama Bay, 20 mi. NNE of Nanao; fishing. Sometimes called Ushutsu.

Usha (ōōshä'), agr. settlement (pop. 250), NW Israel, in Zebulun Valley, 7 mi. E of Haifa. Modern village founded 1936 on site of anc. fortified city of Usha which, after destruction of Second Temple, was for some time ⊙ Jewish Palestine and seat of the Sanhedrin.

Ushachi (ōōshä'chē), town (1948 pop. over 2,000), SE Polotsk oblast, Belorussian SSR, 22 mi. SSW of Polotsk; dairy farming.

Ushak, Turkey: see USAK.

Ushakov Island (ōōshŭkôf'), in Kara Sea of Arctic Ocean, 175 mi. W of Komsomolets Isl. of Severnaya Zemlya archipelago, in Krasnoyarsk Territory, Russian SFSR; 80°50'N 79°30'E. Named for Soviet explorer.

Ushaktal (ōōshäktäl'), Chinese *Hoshe* or *Hoshih* (both: hŭ'shŭ'), town, ⊙ Ushaktal co. (pop. 3,303), E central Sinkiang prov., China, 35 mi. NE of Kara Shahr; 42°13'N 87°E. Sericulture; grain. Copper mines, saltworks near by.

Ushant (ŭ'shŭnt), Fr. *Ouessant* (wĕsä'), Breton *Enez Eusa*, anc. *Uxantis* (pop. 2,223), island (westernmost point of France) in the Atlantic off W tip of Brittany, 26 mi. WNW of Brest, administratively in Finistère dept.; 5 mi. long, 2 mi wide; rock-bound and barren. Port of Lampaul, on SW side; fishing. Lighthouse, 48°28'N 5°3'W. Near by, naval battles were fought bet. French and English in 1778 and 1794.

Ushaw Moor, England: see BEARPARK.

Ushba (ōōshbä'), peak (15,410 ft.) in main range of the central Greater Caucasus, NW Georgian SSR, 8 mi. NW of Mestia.

Ushda, W Pakistan: see USTA MUHAMMAD.

Ushibuka (ōōshĭbōō'kä), chief town and port (pop. 17,097), on S tip of Shimo-jima of Amakusa Isls., Kumamoto prefecture, Japan, on E.China Sea; fishing center. Exports fish, coal, lumber, charcoal. Sometimes spelled Usibuka.

Ushiku (ōō'shĭkōō), town (pop. 6,379), Chiba prefecture, central Honshu, Japan, on central Chiba Peninsula, 8 mi. SSE of Goi; rice, wheat, raw silk; poultry raising.

Ushikubo, Japan: see TOYOKAWA.

Ushimado (ōōshĭmä'dō), town (pop. 6,551), Okayama prefecture, SW Honshu, Japan, port on Harima Sea, 13 mi. E of Okayama; agr. center (rice, wheat, peppermint); raw silk, sake. Exports pears, watermelons.

Ushiro, Russian SFSR: see ORLOVO.

Ushishir Islands (ōōshē'shĭr), Jap. *Ushishiru-to* (ōōshē'shĭrōō-tō'), group (□ 4) of 2 islands in central main Kurile Isls. chain, Russian SFSR; separated from Rasshua Isl. (N) by Sredni Strait, from Ketoi Isl. (S) by Rikord Strait; 47°32'N 152°50' E; hot springs. Fox farming; wild-life reserve.

Ushizu (ōōshē'zōō), town (pop. 5,868), Saga prefecture, NW Kyushu, Japan, on E Hizen Peninsula, 5 mi. W of Saga; rice, wheat, raw silk. Sometimes spelled Usizu.

Ushkar, Kashmir: see BARAMULA, town.

Ushkovo (ōōsh'kŭvŭ), village, N Leningrad oblast, Russian SFSR, 4 mi. NW of Zelenogorsk, on Gulf of Finland; rail junction and seaside resort. Called Tyrisevä (Tyurisevya) in Finland (until 1940) and, until 1948, in USSR.

Ushnuiyeh or **Oshnuiyeh** (both: ōshnōōēyĕ'), town (1940 pop. estimate 8,000), Fourth Prov., in Azerbaijan, NW Iran, 35 mi. S of Rizaiyeh, in agr. and pastoral area; grain, tobacco growing; sheep raising; rugmaking.

Ushomir (ōōshō'mēr), village (1926 pop. 2,524), N central Zhitomir oblast, Ukrainian SSR, 9 mi. SW of Korosten and on Uzh R., in wooded area; clothing handicrafts.

Ush-Tobe (ōōsh-tŭbyĕ'), town (1939 pop. over 10,000), central Taldy-Kurgan oblast, Kazakh SSR, on Turksib RR, on river Kara-Tal and 25 mi. NW of Taldy-Kurgan; irrigated agr. (rice); meat packing. Developed in 1930s; formerly Ush-Tyube.

Ushuaia (ōōswī'ä), village (1947 pop. 2,006), ⊙ Tierra del Fuego natl. territory and Ushuaia dept., Argentina, chief settlement of the Argentine part of Tierra del Fuego, and port on Beagle Channel, 1,450 mi. SSW of Buenos Aires, 160 mi. SE of Punta Arenas (Chile); 54°49'S 68°20'W. The southernmost town in the world. Sheep-raising, lumbering, and fish-canning center. Has penal settlement with several workshops. Airport. Formerly a Protestant mission, it was founded 1884. Known for its impressive scenery. In 1948 a pioneer settlement of Ital. immigrants was founded near by.

Ushumun (ōōshōōmōōn'), town (1926 pop. 825), S Amur oblast, Russian SFSR, on Trans-Siberian RR and 135 mi. ESE of Skovorodino; junction of railroad to Amur R.

Ushutsu, Japan: see USETSU.

Usia (ōōs'yŭ), town (pop. 8,466), Ghazipur dist., E Uttar Pradesh, India, 13 mi. SE of Ghazipur; rice, barley, gram, oilseeds.

Usiacurí (ōōsyäkōōrē'), town (pop. 2,902), Atlántico dept., N Colombia, in Caribbean lowlands, 22 mi. SW of Barranquilla; popular spa, with thermal waters, in cotton-growing area; mfg. of Panama hats. Sulphur, magnesite, gypsum, and petroleum deposits near by.

Usibelli (ōōsĭbĕ'lē), village (pop. 28), central Alaska, near Nenana.

Usibuka, Japan: see USHIBUKA.

Usilampatti (ōōsĭlŭm'pŭt-tē), town (pop. 11,745), Madura dist., S Madras, India, 23 mi. W of Madura, in cotton area; agr. products, bamboo, timber from Palni Hills (NW) and Sirumalai Hills (NE). Agr. school.

Usingen (ōō'zĭng-ŭn), town (pop. 3,109), in former Prussian prov. of Hesse-Nassau, W Germany, after 1945 in Hesse, 9 mi. W of Bad Nauheim; metal smelting, mfg. of aluminum powder.

Usizu, Japan: see USHIZU.

Usk (ŭsk), urban district (1931 pop. 1,315; 1951 census 1,612), central Monmouth, England, on Usk R. and 9 mi. NNE of Newport; agr. market. Has remains (mostly 13th cent.) of castle dating from Norman times and of small palace. Church (12th–15th cent.) was part of Benedictine convent. Site of Roman station.

Uskok Mountains, Yugoslavia: see ZUMBERAK MOUNTAINS.

Uskoplje (ōōskô'plyĕ), hamlet, on Dalmatia-Herzegovina border, Yugoslavia, 3 mi. NE of Dubrovnik; narrow-gauge rail junction.

Usk River (ŭsk), Welsh *Wysg* (ōō'ĭsk), Wales and England, rises 7 mi. SSE of Llandovery, flows 60 mi. E and SE, past Brecknock, Crickhowell, Abergavenny, Usk, and Caerleon, to Bristol Channel at Newport. The river is noted for its associations with King Arthur, and also for its beauty and its good fishing.

Usku or **Osku** (both: ōskōō'), village, Third Prov., in Azerbaijan, NW Iran, 16 mi. WSW of Tabriz; local trade center.

Üsküb, Yugoslavia: see SKOPLJE.

Uskudama, Turkey: see ADRIANOPLE, city.

Uskudar (ōōskōōdär'), **Scutari**, or **Skutari** (both: skōō'tŭrē), Turkish *Üsküdar*, anc. *Chrysopolis*, city (pop. 60,722), Istanbul prov., NW Turkey, at S entrance of the Bosporus, on the Asiatic side opposite Istanbul proper, of which it constitutes a part; mfg. and commercial suburb, with fine gardens, mosques, and a notable cemetery. During Crimean War it was base (1854–56) of British Army and site of the military hospital made famous by the work of Florence Nightingale.

Uslar (ōōs'lär), town (pop. 6,207), in former Prussian prov. of Hanover, W Germany, after 1945 in Lower Saxony, 16 mi. NW of Göttingen; metalworking; mfg. of furniture, textile ornaments, tobacco; brewing, distilling.

Uslava River (ōō'slävä), Czech *Úslava*, W Bohemia, Czechoslovakia, formed in S foothills of the Brdy by junction of 2 headstreams just NE of Nepomuk; flows c.30 mi. NW, past Blovice, through Pilsen, to Berounka R. just NNE of city.

Usman or **Usman'** (ōō'smŭnyŭ), city (pop. 13,456), NW Voronezh oblast, Russian SFSR, 33 mi. NE of Voronezh; tobacco-processing center; meat packing, flour milling. Founded 1646 as Rus. fortress on steppe border.

Usmanabad, India: see OSMANABAD.

Usmun (ōōsmōōn'), town (1948 pop. over 2,000), SE Yakut Autonomous SSR, Russian SFSR, 19 mi. S of Aldan, on Yakutsk-Never highway; gold mines.

Usmyn or **Usmyn'** (ōōsmĭn'yŭ), village (1926 pop. 135), S Velikiye Luki oblast, Russian SFSR, 18 mi. N of Velizh; flax.

Usoi, Tadzhik SSR: see SAREZ LAKE.

Usoke (ōōsō'kä), village, Western Prov., W central Tanganyika, on railroad and 30 mi. W of Tabora; corn, millet, mushrooms.

Usolskaya, Russian SFSR: see BEREZNIKI.

Usolye or **Usol'ye** (ōōsô'lyĭ). **1** officially **Usolye-Sibirskoye** or **Usol'ye-Sibirskoye** (–sēbēr'skŭyŭ), city (1939 pop. over 10,000), SE Irkutsk oblast, Russian SFSR, on Angara R., on Trans-Siberian RR (Angara station) and 45 mi NW of Irkutsk. Salt-mining center; sawmilling (matches produced), tanning. Extensive salt mines and petroleum deposits to N. Health resort near by. **2** City (1926 pop. 8,974), central Molotov oblast, Russian SFSR, on right bank of Kama R., opposite Berezniki, and 15 mi. SSW of Solikamsk; salt-mining and -processing center; chemical works; textile mfg., sawmilling, meat packing. Has old cathedral. Formerly also called Usolye-Solikamskoye; was center of Rus. chemical industry prior to First World War. Superseded in 1930s by new industrial city of BEREZNIKI, with which it was temporarily inc. (1932–40).

Usora, suburb, Yugoslavia: see DOBOJ.

Usora River (ōōsô'rä), N Bosnia, Yugoslavia, rises 12 mi. SE of Kotor Varos, flows c.50 mi. NE, past Teslic, to Bosna R. 2 mi. S of Doboj. Called Velika Usora in upper course. Receives Mala Usora R. (right).

Uspallata (ōōspäyä'tä), town (pop. estimate 400), NW Mendoza prov., Argentina, at W foot of Sierra de los Paramillos, on Transandine RR, on Mendoza R. and 45 mi. ENE of Uspallata Pass, 35 mi. NW of Mendoza; alt. 5,743 ft. Tourist resort, farming and mining (copper, zinc) center. Agr. (potatoes, alfalfa, barley, livestock). Oil wells near by. San Martín's armies camped at Uspallata. Darwin visited here in 1835.

Uspallata, Sierra de, Argentina: see PARAMILLOS, SIERRA DE LOS.

Uspallata Pass, La Cumbre (lä kōōm'brā), or **Bermejo Pass** (bĕrmā'hō), pass (c.12,650 ft.) across the Andes, on Argentina-Chile border, at S foot of the ACONCAGUA, bet. Mendoza, Argentina, and Santiago, Chile; 32°50'S 70°4'W. In 1817 San Martín sent part of his army through the pass to fight Sp. royalists in Chilean War of Independence. In 1887 was begun the Transandine RR (narrow gauge, partly cog), which pierces the mts. through a 2-mi. tunnel under the pass at alt. of 10,468 ft.; opened 1910, it connects Valparaiso (Chile) and Mendoza (Argentina). In the pass is the statue Christ of the Andes (Cristo Redentor), dedicated March 13, 1904, and commemorating a series of peace and boundary settlements bet. Chile and Argentina. Puente del Inca and Las Cuevas are at Argentine end, Portillo at Chilean end of pass.

Uspantán or **San Miguel Uspantán** (sän mēgĕl' ōōspäntän'), town (1950, 1,199), Quiché dept., W central Guatemala, in E outlier of Cuchumatanes Mts., 17 mi. ENE of Sacapulas; alt. 6,033 ft.; coffee, sugar cane, corn, livestock.

Uspenka (ōōspyĕn'kŭ). **1** Village (1939 pop. over 500), E Pavlodar oblast, Kazakh SSR, 45 mi. NE of Pavlodar; cattle breeding. **2** Town, Maritime Territory, Russian SFSR: see KIROVSKI, Maritime Territory. **3** Town (1926 pop. 3,680), S Voroshilovgrad oblast, Ukrainian SSR, in the Donbas, 12 mi. SSW of Voroshilovgrad; coal mines.

Uspenovka, Russian SFSR: see KIROVSKI, Maritime Territory.

Uspenskaya, Russian SFSR: see USPENSKOYE, Krasnodar Territory.

Uspenski or **Uspenskiy** (ōōspyĕn'skē), town (1948 pop. over 2,000), central Karaganda oblast, Kazakh SSR, on railroad (Neldy station) and 80 mi. S of Karaganda. Copper and iron deposits near by. One of oldest copper mines in Kazakh SSR, established in 19th cent.; supplied old copper smelter at Spasski Zavod, 60 mi. NNE.

Uspenskoye (–skŭyŭ). **1** Village (1926 pop. 8,758), SE Krasnodar Territory, Russian SFSR, on left bank of Kuban R. and 16 mi. SE of Armavir; flour mill; dairying, quarrying. Sometimes called Uspenskaya. Another Uspenskaya (1926 pop. 13,405) is 50 mi. N of Armavir, in wheat area. **2** Village, Tatar Autonomous SSR, Russian SFSR; see BOLGARY.

Usquepaug or **Usquepaugh** (both: ŭs'kwĭpôg), village in Richmond and South Kingstown towns, Washington co., S central R.I., on Queen R. and 24 mi. SSW of Providence, in agr. area.

Usquepaug River, R.I.: see QUEEN RIVER.

Usquil (ōōskēl'), city (pop. 1,921), Libertad dept., NW Peru, in Cordillera Occidental, 11 mi. ENE of Otusco; wheat, coca, coffee.

Ussat or **Ussat-les-Bains** (üsä'-lā-bē'), village (pop. 113), Ariège dept., S France, in central Pyrenees, on Ariège R. and 9 mi. S of Foix; resort with mineral springs.

Usseglio (ōō-sā'lyô), village (pop. 217), Torino prov., Piedmont, NW Italy, 11 mi. NE of Susa; resort (alt. 4,169 ft.). Has major hydroelectric plant. Cobalt, nickle, asbestos mines near by.

Ussel (üsĕl'), town (pop. 5,893), Corrèze dept., S central France, on S slopes of Plateau of Millevaches, 33 mi. NE of Tulle; road and market center; aluminum foundry; mfg. (notebooks, furniture, meat preserves, candles). Sawmilling. Has 15th–16th-cent. houses with oriels.

USSR: see UNION OF SOVIET SOCIALIST REPUBLICS.

Ussuri, oblast, Russian SFSR: see MARINE TERRITORY.

Ussuri, rail station, Russian SFSR: see LESOZAVODSK.

Ussuri Bay or **Ussuri Gulf** (ōōsōō'rē), inlet of Peter the Great Bay of Sea of Japan, Russian SFSR, E of Muravyev-Amurski Peninsula; c.30 mi. wide at mouth, 35 mi. long. Shkotovo is on N shore.

Ussuri River, Chinese *Wu-su-li* (wōō'sōō'lē), on Manchuria-USSR border, rises in S Sikhote-Alin Range in 2 branches (the Ulukhe and the Daubikhe), flows N along international line, past Lesozavodsk (head of navigation), Iman (opposite Hulin), and Bikin (opposite Jaoho), to Amur R. in 2 arms at Fuyüan and Khabarovsk. (The isl. bet. the 2 arms is disputed by USSR and China.) Total length, 365 mi.; including the Ulukhe, 530 mi.; and including the Daubikhe, 540 mi. Receives Iman, Bikin, and Khor rivers (right); Sungacha (outlet of L. Khanka) and Muling rivers (left). An important waterway used for logging; and frozen Nov.–April.

Ussurka (ōōsōōr'kŭ), town (1948 pop. over 500), W Maritime Territory, Russian SFSR, 125 mi. NNE of Voroshilov, near Trans-Siberian RR; health resort; mineral (carbonic, chalybeate) springs.

Ussy (üsē'), village (pop. 216), Calvados dept., NW France, 5 mi. NW of Falaise; tree nurseries.

Ust-Abakan or **Ust'-Abakan** (ōōst"-ŭbŭkän'), town (1939 pop. over 500), E Khakass Autonomous Oblast, Krasnoyarsk Territory, Russian SFSR, on Yenisei R., below mouth of Abakan R., and 10 mi. NE of Abakan; lumber milling, ship repair yards.

Ust-Abakanskoye, Russian SFSR: see ABAKAN.

Ust-Alekseyevo or **Ust'-Alekseyevo** (ōōst"-ŭlyĭksyā'-ŭvŭ), village, E Vologda oblast, Russian SFSR, on Yug R. and 23 mi. SSE of Veliki Ustyug; flax processing. Also called Ust-Alekseyevskoye.

Usta Muhammad (ōōs'tŭ mōōhŭm'mŭd), town (pop. 1,925), Sibi dist., E Baluchistan, W Pakistan, on S Kachi plain, 95 mi. SSE of Sibi; wheat, millet, pulse. Sulphur-ore deposits (NE). Also called Usta or Ushda.

Ust-Apuka, Russian SFSR: see OLYUTORSKOYE.

Ustaritz (üstärēts'), village (pop. 976), Basses-Pyrénées dept., SW France, on Nive R. and 6 mi. S of Bayonne; beret mfg., flour milling, dairying.

Ust-Barguzin or **Ust'-Barguzin** (ōōst"-bŭrgōōzēn'), town (1948 pop. over 2,000), W Buryat-Mongol Autonomous SSR, Russian SFSR, port on L. Baikal, at mouth of Barguzin R., 125 mi. NNE of Ulan-Ude; fish canning.

Ust-Belaya or **Ust'-Belaya** (ōōst-byĕ'lŭ), village (1948 pop. over 500), E central Chukchi Natl. Okrug, Kamchatka oblast, Khabarovsk Territory, Russian SFSR, on Anadyr R., opposite mouth of Belaya R., and 135 mi. WNW of Anadyr; reindeer farm; govt. arctic station, trading post, airfield.

Ust-Belokalitvenskaya, Russian SFSR: see BELAYA KALITVA.

Ust-Bolsheretsk or **Ust'-Bol'sheretsk** (ōōst"-bŭlshĭ-ryĕtsk'), village (1947 pop. over 2,000), Kamchatka oblast, Khabarovsk Territory, Russian SFSR, fishing port on S Kamchatka Peninsula, on Sea of Okhotsk, at mouth of Bolshaya R., 100 mi. WSW of Petropavlovsk; fish canneries.

Ust-Borovaya, Russian SFSR: see BOROVSK, Molotov oblast.

Ust-Bukhtarma or **Ust'-Bukhtarma** (ōōst"-bōōkhtŭr-mä'), village (1948 pop. over 2,000), central East Kazakhstan oblast, Kazakh SSR, on Irtysh R., at mouth of the Bukhtarma, and 50 mi. SE of Ust-Kamenogorsk; cattle breeding. Formerly Bukhtarminsk.

Ust-Buzulukskaya or **Ust'-Buzulukskaya** (ōōst"-bōōzōōlōōk'skŭ), village (1939 pop. over 500), NW Stalingrad oblast, Russian SFSR, on Khoper R., opposite Buzuluk R. mouth, and 30 mi. SW of Novo-Annenski; metalworks; wheat, sunflowers. Until c.1940, Ust-Buzulutskaya.

Ust-Charyshskaya Pristan or **Ust'-Charyshskaya Pristan'** (ōōst-chŭrĭsh'skŭ prē'stŭnyŭ), village (1926 pop. 7,244), central Altai Territory, Russian SFSR, on Ob R., below mouth of Charysh R., and 37 mi. E of Aleisk; river port; flour mill.

Ust-Dvinsk, Latvia: see DAUGAVGRIVA.

Ust-Dzhegutinskaya or **Ust'-Dzhegutinskaya** (ōōst-jĭgōō'tyĭnskŭ), village (1926 pop. 4,990), SE Stavropol Territory, Russian SFSR, in N foothills of the Greater Caucasus, on Kuban R. and 11 mi. SSW of Cherkessk, in agr. (wheat, corn) and livestock area. Terminus of rail line from Nevinnomyssk and N end of Sukhumi Military Road. Until 1943, in Karachai Autonomous Oblast.

Ustek (ōō'shtyĕk), Czech *Úštěk*, Ger. *Auscha* (ou'-shä), town (pop. 1,329), N Bohemia, Czechoslovakia, 14 mi. SE of Usti nad Labem; rail junction; trade in hops. Health station of Jelec (yĕ'lets) is 3 mi. NW, just outside of village of Levin (lĕ'vēn), Czech *Levín*; peat baths, ferruginous springs.

Uster (ōō'stŭr), town (pop. 10,547), Zurich canton, N Switzerland, 9 mi. ESE of Zurich; bicycles, cotton textiles, knit goods, beer. Medieval castle.

Ust-Garevaya, Russian SFSR: see DOBRYANKA, Molotov oblast.

Ustica (ōō'stēkä), volcanic island (□ 3; pop. 1,141) in Tyrrhenian Sea off NW Sicily, 40 mi. NNW of Palermo, in Palermo prov.; 38°42'N 13°11'E. Rises to 784 ft. in center; agr. (grapes, wheat, legumes), fishing.

Ustilug (ōōstyē'lōōk), Pol. *Uścilug* (ōōshchē'wōōk), city (1931 pop. 4,771), W Volyn oblast, Ukrainian SSR on Bug R. (Pol. border) and 7 mi. W of Vladimir-Volynski; agr. processing (grain, vegetable oils), distilling, sawmilling, brick mfg., hatmaking; lumber exports. Allegedly founded before 12th cent.; scene of defeat (1431) of Lithuanians and Tatars by Pol. king Wladislaw II Jagiello. Passed to Russia (1795); reverted to Poland (1921); ceded to USSR in 1945.

Usti nad Labem (ōō'styĕ näd' lä"bĕm), Czech *Ústí nad Labem*, Ger. *Aussig* (ou'sĭkh), city (pop. 34,410), ⊙ Usti prov. (□ 1,600; pop. 622,747), NW Bohemia, Czechoslovakia, port on W bank of Elbe R. and 45 mi. NNW of Prague; 50°40'N 14°2'E. Export center in coal-mining region; rail junction; industrial hub of NW Bohemia; chemical works (notably synthetic nitrogen installations), ironworks, oil refinery; mfg. of food products, soap, candles, electrical goods, rubber articles, varnishes, textiles. Exports include fruit, sugar, cement. Has medieval and Renaissance churches, museums. Founded in 13th cent. Urban area (pop. 56,328) includes town of TRMICE (SW) and STREKOV (SSE). Just SW begins the important lignite basin and highly industrialized area of Most-Chomutov.

Usti nad Orlici (ôr"lĭtsĭ), Czech *Ústí nad Orlicí*, Ger. *Wildenschwert* (vĭl'dŭnshvĕrt), town (pop. 8,093), E Bohemia, Czechoslovakia, on Ticha Orlice R. and 28 mi. W of Pardubice, in oat-growing region; rail junction; intensive textile (cotton, woolen) and leather (notably driving belts and other industrial products) mfg.

Ustinovka (ōōstyē'nŭfkŭ), village (1926 pop. 6,031), S Kirovograd oblast, Ukrainian SSR, 40 mi. SSE of Kirovograd; metalworks, flour mill.

Ustipraca or **Ustipracha** (both: ōōstēprä'chä), Serbo-Croatian *Ustiprača* [=mouth of the Praca], village, SE Bosnia, Yugoslavia, on Drina R., at Praca R. mouth, and 9 mi. SSE of Rogatica; rail junction.

Ust-Ishim or **Ust'-Ishim** (ōōst-ēshēm'), village (1948 pop. over 2,000), NW Omsk oblast, Russian SFSR, on Irtysh R. (landing), at mouth of Ishim R., and 110 mi. ESE of Tobolsk, in agr. area.

Ust-Izhora or **Ust'-Izhora** (ōōst-ēzhô'rŭ), town (1939 pop. over 2,000), central Leningrad oblast, Russian SFSR, on Neva R., at mouth of the Izhora, and 13 mi. SE of Leningrad; brickworking, sawmilling. Here Alexander Nevski defeated the Swedes (1240).

Ustka (ōōst'kä), Ger. *Stolpmünde* (shtôlp"mün'dŭ), town (1939 pop. 4,783; 1946 pop. 2,807) in Pomerania, after 1945 in Koszalin prov., NW Poland, on the Baltic, at Slupia R. mouth, 11 mi. NW of Stolp (Slupsk); fishing port; fish canning and smoking. Chartered after 1945.

Ust-Kachka or **Ust'-Kachka** (ōōst-käch'kŭ) village (1939 pop. under 500), central Molotov oblast, Russian SFSR, on left bank of Kama R. and 5 mi. S of Krasnokamsk; health resort (sulphur and bromine springs) developed after 1945.

Ust-Kalmanka or **Ust'-Kalmanka** (ōōst-kŭlmän'kŭ), village (1939 pop. over 2,000), central Altai Territory, Russian SFSR, on Charysh R. and 33 mi. SE of Aleisk; dairy farming.

Ust-Kamchatsk or **Ust'-Kamchatsk** (ōōst-kŭmchätsk'), village (1939 pop. over 500), Kamchatka oblast, Khabarovsk Territory, Russian SFSR, port on the Pacific, at mouth of Kamchatka R., 265 mi. NNE of Petropavlovsk, on E Kamchatka Peninsula; fisheries.

Ust-Kamenogorsk or **Ust'-Kamenogorsk** (ōōst"-kŭmyĭnŭgôrsk'), city (1926 pop. 13,908), ⊙ East Kazakhstan oblast, Kazakh SSR, on Irtysh R., at mouth of Ulba R., on railroad (Zashchita station) and 105 mi. ESE of Semipalatinsk, 510 mi. NE of Alma-Ata; 50°N 82°35' E. Industrial center in W Altai Mts.; zinc smelting, mfg. of mining equipment, vegetable-oil pressing, metalworking, tanning, distilling. Irtysh R. hydroelectric station at Ablaketka (SE). Founded 1720 as Rus. military frontier post; formerly called Zashchita.

Ust-Kan or **Ust'-Kan** (ōōst-kän'), village (1926 pop. 558), W Gorno-Altai Autonomous Oblast, Altai Territory, Russian SFSR, on Charysh R. and 90 mi. SW of Gorno-Altaisk, in livestock-raising area.

Ust-Karsk or **Ust'-Karsk** (ōōst-kärsk), town (1939 pop. over 2,000), E Chita oblast, Russian SFSR, on Shilka River and 55 mi. NE of Sretensk; gold mines.

Ust-Katav or **Ust'-Katav** (ōōst-kŭtäv'), city (1939 pop. over 10,000), W Chelyabinsk oblast, Russian SFSR, in the S Urals, on Yuryuzan R., on railroad and 60 mi. WSW of Zlatoust; railroad stock and streetcar mfg. center. Bauxite and marl deposits near by. Founded 1759; became city in 1942. Formerly called Ust-Katavski Zavod.

Ust-Kishert or **Ust'-Kishert'** (ōōst-kēshĕrt'yŭ), village (1932 pop. estimate 3,400), SE Molotov oblast, Russian SFSR, near Sylva R., on railroad (Kishert station) and 12 mi. ESE of Kungur; hemp milling; wheat, flax, clover, livestock. Refractory-clay deposits near by.

Ust-Koksa or **Ust'-Koksa** (ōōst-kŭksä'), village (1926 pop. 360), SW Gorno-Altai Autonomous Oblast, Altai Territory, Russian SFSR, on Katun R. and 115 mi. S of Gorno-Altaisk; dairy farming.

Ust-Kozhva, Russian SFSR: see KOZHVA.

Ust-Kulom or **Ust'-Kulom** (ōōst-kōōlôm'), village (1926 pop. 2,479), S Komi Autonomous SSR, Russian SFSR, on Vychegda R. (head of May–Nov. navigation) and 90 mi. E of Syktyvkar (linked by road); flax; fur trapping.

Ust-Kureika or **Ust'-Kureyka** (ōōst-kōōrā'kŭ), village, N Krasnoyarsk Territory, Russian SFSR, on Yenisei R., at mouth of Kureika R., and 70 mi. SSE of Igarka, on Arctic Circle; river port.

Ust-Kut or **Ust'-Kut** (ōōst-kōōt'), town (1939 pop. over 2,000), N Irkutsk oblast, Russian SFSR, on Lena R. (head of navigation) and 310 mi. N of Irkutsk; river-road transshipment center, on highways, from Tulun and Irkutsk. Salt deposits.

Ust-Kyakhta or **Ust'-Kyakhta** (ōōst-kyäkh'tŭ), village, S Buryat-Mongol Autonomous SSR, Russian SFSR, port on Selenga R. and 110 mi. SSW of Ulan-Ude; flour milling. Important transshipment point in 18th and 19th cent. for Kyakhta trade.

Ust-Labinskaya or **Ust'-Labinskaya** (ōōst-lä'-bĭnskīŭ), village (1926 pop. 19,856), central Krasnodar Territory, Russian SFSR, on Kuban R. (head of navigation), at mouth of Laba R., and 35 mi. ENE of Krasnodar; agr. center; flour and sunflower-oil mills; sugar beets.

Ust-Luga or **Ust'-Luga** (ōōst-lōōgä'), village (1939 pop. over 500), W Leningrad oblast, Russian SFSR, on Luga Bay, at mouth of Luga R., 21 mi. NNW of Kingisepp; fish canning, sawmilling.

Ust-Maya or **Ust'-Maya** (ōōst-mī'ŭ), village (1948 pop. over 2,000), SE Yakut Autonomous SSR, Russian SFSR, on Aldan R., at mouth of Maya R., and 190 mi. ESE of Yakutsk; river port.

Ust-Medveditskaya, Russian SFSR: see SERAFIMOVICH.

Ust-Nera or **Ust'-Nera** (ōōst-nyĭrä'), village, E Yakut Autonomous SSR, Russian SFSR, on Indigirka R., at mouth of the Nera (right affluent), and 95 mi. N of Oimyakon; power station.

Ust-Niman or **Ust'-Niman** (ōōst-nyĭmän'), village, SW Khabarovsk Territory, Russian SFSR, on Bureya R., at mouth of short Niman R., and 310 mi. ENE of Blagoveshchensk, on spur of Trans-Siberian RR, in Bureya coal basin.

Ust-Nytva, Russian SFSR: see NYTVA.

Ust-Olenek or **Ust'-Olenek** (ōōst-ŭlyĭnyôk'), village (1948 pop. over 500), NW Yakut Autonomous SSR, Russian SFSR, on Laptev Sea, at mouth of Olenek R., and 200 mi. E of Nordvik; reindeer raising. Coal deposits near by.

Ust-Orda or **Ust'-Orda** (ōōst-ŭrdä'), a Buryat-Mongol national okrug (□ 8,000; 1946 pop. estimate 100,000) in SE Irkutsk oblast, Russian SFSR; ⊙ Ust-Ordynski. Extends E from Trans-Siberian RR to L. Baikal, N of Irkutsk. Agr. area (dairy farming), livestock raising (horses, cattle, pigs); some coal mining (near Cheremkhovo), lumbering (35% of area is wooded). Until 1937, part of Buryat-Mongol Autonomous SSR.

Ust-Ordynski or **Ust'-Ordynskiy** (ōōst-ŭrdĭn'skē), town (1948 pop. over 2,000), ⊙ Ust-Orda Buryat-Mongol Natl. Okrug, SE Irkutsk oblast, Russian SFSR, on Irkutsk-Kachuga road, 40 mi. NNE of Irkutsk; dairy products. Until 1941, called Ust-Orda.

Ustovo (ōō'stôvô), city (pop. 2,010), Plovdiv dist., S Bulgaria, in SE Rhodope Mts., on left branch of Arda R. and 5 mi. E of Smolyan; market center (tobacco, potatoes, rye, livestock); carpet mfg.

Ust-Port or **Ust'-Port** (ōōst-pôrt'), village, W Taimyr Natl. Okrug, Krasnoyarsk Territory, Russian SFSR, N of Arctic Circle, on Yenisei R. 45 mi. WNW of Dudinka; fish-canning plant. Formerly Ust-Yeniseiski Port.

Ust-Pozhva, Russian SFSR: see POZHVA.

Ustrumca or **Ustrumdja,** Yugoslavia: see STRUMICA, town.

Ustrzyki Dolne (ōōst-zhē'kē dôl'nĕ), city (1931 pop. 3,964), Rzeszow prov., SE Poland, near Ukrainian border, on Strvyazh R. and 28 mi. WSW of Sambor; petroleum refinery; sawmilling, distilling. In USSR (1939–51) called Nizhniye Ustriki. Surrounding area (□ 185) was acquired (1951) from Drogobych oblast, Ukrainian SSR.

Ust-Srednikan or **Ust'-Srednikan** (ōōst"-srĕdnyĭ-kän'), village (1948 pop. over 500), N Khabarovsk Territory, Russian SFSR, 200 mi. N of Magadan (linked by highway); gold mines. Sometimes called Srednikan.

Ust-Sysolsk, Russian SFSR: see SYKTYVKAR.

Ust-Taimyra or **Ust'-Taymyra** (ōōst-tīmĭ'rŭ) settlement, N Taimyr Natl. Okrug, Krasnoyarsk Territory, Russian SFSR, at mouth of Taimyra R., 76°15'N 99°E. Govt. observation post.

Ust-Tarka or **Ust'-Tarka** (ōōst-tŭrkä'), village (1939 pop. over 500), W Novosibirsk oblast, Russian SFSR, on Om R. and 25 mi. NNW of Tatarsk; dairy farming. Formerly called Kushagi.

Ust-Taskan, Russian SFSR: see TASKAN RIVER.

Ust-Tsilma or **Ust'-Tsil'ma** (ōōst-tsēlmä'), village (1926 pop. 3,264), N Komi Autonomous SSR, Russian SFSR, on Pechora R. (landing), opposite mouth of Tsilma R., and 130 mi. NNW of Ukhta; chamois-leather factory; airfield.

Ust-Uda or **Ust'-Uda** (ōōst-ōōdä'), village (1948 pop. over 2,000), S Irkutsk oblast, Russian SFSR, on Angara R. and 90 mi. N of Cheremkhovo; sawmilling.

Ust-Uiskoye or **Ust'-Uyskoye** (ōōst-ōō'ēskŭyŭ), village (1926 pop. 4,195), SW Kurgan oblast, Russian SFSR, near Kazakh SSR border, on Ui R., near its confluence with the Tobol, and 70 mi. SSE of Shumikha; flour mill, dairy plant.

Ust-Ulagan or **Ust'-Ulagan** (ōōst"-ōōlŭgän'), village (1948 pop. over 500), E Gorno-Altai Autonomous Oblast, Altai Territory, Russian SFSR, on Bashkaus R. (inlet of Teletskoye L.) and 125 mi. SE of Gorno-Altaisk.

Ustun Tagh, China: see ALTYN TAGH.

Ust-Urt or **Ust'-Urt** (ōōst-ōōrt'), desert plateau (□ 62,000) in Guryev oblast, Kazakh SSR, and in Kara-Kalpak Autonomous SSR, Uzbek SSR; bet. Caspian and Aral seas; alt. c.600–800 ft.; rises in escarpments above surrounding plain. Semi-nomadic livestock raising (sheep, goats, camels).

Ust-Usa or **Ust'-Usa** (ōōst-ōōsä'), village (1948 pop. over 2,000), N Komi Autonomous SSR, Russian SFSR, on Pechora R. (landing), at mouth of Usa R., and 220 mi. WSW of Vorkuta; meat (game, fowl) packing, sawmilling; reindeer raising.

Ust-Vashka, Russian SFSR: see LESHUKONSKOYE.

Ust-Vorkuta, Russian SFSR: see SANGORODOK.

Ust-Voya or **Ust'-Voya** (ōōst-voi'ŭ), village, E Komi Autonomous SSR, Russian SFSR, on Pechora R. and 130 mi. NE of Ukhta; grindstone works.

Ust-Vym or **Ust'-Vym'** (ōōst-vĭm'), village (1926 pop. 918), W Komi Autonomous SSR, Russian SFSR, on Vychegda R. (landing), at mouth of Vym R., and 40 mi. NNW of Syktyvkar; flax.

Ust-Yansk or **Ust'-Yansk** (ōōst-yänsk'), village, N Yakut Autonomous SSR, Russian SFSR, on lower Yana R. and 10 mi. N of Kazachye; trading post; reindeer raising; radio station. Fossil mammoth ivory excavations.

Ustye or **Ust'ye** (ōōst'yĭ), town (1939 pop. over 2,000), central Vologda oblast, Russian SFSR, on Kubeno L., 28 mi. NNW of Vologda, at mouth of Kubena R.; sawmilling; glassworks; clothing mill.

Ust-Yeniseiski Port, Russian SFSR: see UST-PORT.

Ustyug Veliki, Russian SFSR: see VELIKI USTYUG.

Ustyuzhna (ōō'styōōzhnŭ), city (1926 pop. 5,195), SW Vologda oblast, Russian SFSR, on Mologa R. and 55 mi. WSW of Cherepovets; distilling center; flax processing, flour milling. Chartered 1340.

Ust-Zyryanka, Russian SFSR: see BEREZNIKI.

Usuda (ōōsōō'dä), town (pop. 4,848), Nagano prefecture, central Honshu, Japan, 19 mi. SE of Ueda; rice, livestock, raw silk.

Usui (ōōsōō'ē), town (pop. 4,373), Chiba prefecture, central Honshu, Japan, 3 mi. WNW of Sakura, in forested area; raw silk.

Usukhchai or **Usukhchay** (ōōsōōkh-chī'), village (1930 pop. over 500), S Dagestan Autonomous SSR, Russian SFSR, in the E Greater Caucasus, on Samur R. and 50 mi. SW of Derbent; irrigated orchards. Pop. largely Lezghian.

Usuki (ōō'sōōkē), town (pop. 26,792), Oita prefecture, E Kyushu, Japan, port on Hoyo Strait, 13 mi. SE of Oita; sawmills; charcoal. Exports lumber, bamboo articles. Near-by stone cliffs have anc. carvings of images of Buddha.

Usulután (ōōsōōlōōtän'), department (□ 1,291; pop. 188,584), E Salvador, on the Pacific; ⊙ Usulután. Bounded W by Lempa R.; crossed E-W by coastal range (volcanoes Tecapa, Jucuapa, Usulután); includes Jiquilisco Bay (S). One of Salvador's most fertile depts.; produces grain, tropical fruit, coffee, sugar cane. Main centers: Usulután, Jiquilisco (S), Jucuapa, Santiago de María, Berlín (N). Crossed by railroad and Inter-American Highway. Formed 1865.

Usulután, city (pop. 9,590), ⊙ Usulután dept., SE Salvador, at S foot of volcano Usulután, on railroad and road, 55 mi. ESE of San Salvador; alt. 230 ft.; 13°20'N 88°26'W. Commercial center on Pacific coastal plain; grain, coffee, sugar cane, fruit; hardwood lumbering.

Usumacinta River (ōōsōōmäsēn'tä), in Guatemala and Mexico; formed by confluence of Pasión R. and Chixoy R. (rising in Guatemala) at Mexican border; forms part of international line and meanders NW c. 350 mi. into Chiapas and Tabasco, past Tenosique, Balancán, Emiliano Zapata, and Jonuta, to the Gulf of Campeche 10 mi. S of Alvaro Obregón. Above its mouth its main arm unites with the Grijalva. Length, with the Chixoy, c.600 mi. Other arms near its mouth include San Pedro y San Pablo and Palizada rivers, the latter flowing into the Laguna de Terminos. Navigable for c.300 mi., the Usumacinta is used for floating logs and shipping chicle.

Usumbura (ōōsōōmbōō'rä, Fr. ōōzōōmbōōrä'), town (1949 pop. 17,701), ⊙ RUANDA-URUNDI, in W Urundi, at NE extremity of L. Tanganyika, opposite Uvira, in cotton-growing region; 3°26'S 29°15'E. Chief port of Ruanda-Urundi, exporting mainly cotton, coffee, derris, hides; commercial center, air communications point. Mfg. of pharmaceuticals, native canoes, nets; fishing, fish processing. Has R.C. and Protestant missions and schools, hospitals for Europeans and natives, airport with customs station, large military camp. Germans established here the 1st military camp of Ruanda-Urundi, in 1899.

Usva or **Us'va** (ōōs'vŭ), town (1948 pop. over 2,000), E central Molotov oblast, Russian SFSR, on Usva R. and 10 mi. S of Gubakha, on railroad; mining center in Kizel bituminous-coal basin.

Usva River or **Us'va River,** Molotov oblast, Russian SFSR, rises in the central Urals NW of Kosya, flows c.120 mi. SW and S, past Usva, to Chusovaya R. at Chusovoi; lumber floating.

Usvyaty (o͞osvyä'tē), village (1948 pop. over 2,000), S Velikiye Luki oblast, Russian SFSR, on small L. Usvyaty, 35 mi. SE of Nevel; dairying, distilling.

Usworth Colliery, England: see WASHINGTON.

Usyaty (o͞osyä'tē), N suburb of Prokopyevsk, Kemerovo oblast, Russian SFSR, in Kuznetsk Basin; metalworks.

Utah (ū'tô", ū'tä"), state (land □ 82,346; with inland waters □ 84,916; 1950 pop. 688,862; 1940 pop. 550,310), W U.S., bordered W by Nev., N by Idaho, NE by Wyo., E by Colo., S by Ariz.; 10th in area, 38th in pop.; admitted 1896 as 45th state; ⊙ Salt Lake City. The "Mormon State" or the "Beehive State" extends 345 mi. N–S, 275 mi. E–W. Mtn. ranges, desert basins, broad tablelands, deep canyons, and irrigated river valleys comprise Utah's varied topography. A series of broken mtn. ridges and plateaus extends roughly N–S through the center of the state, forming the boundary bet. the Colorado Plateau (E) and the Great Basin (W). This central highland strip begins in the WASATCH RANGE (a spur of the Rockies) in the N, which rises to 12,008 ft. in Mt. Timpanogos, and continues southward in Wasatch Plateau, Pavant Mts., Tushar Mts., Aquarius Plateau, and Markagunt and Paunsaugunt plateaus, whose S edges form the scenic Pink Cliffs. In this section, drained by Bear R. (N) and by Jordan, Sevier, and Virgin rivers (S), are the bulk of the state's pop. and all its large cities. In NE Utah the Uinta Mts. (with an E-W axis) rise to 13,227 ft. in Kings Peak, highest point in the state. S of the Uintas, in E Utah, lies the Colorado Plateau, carved by wind and water into such prominent features as the Tavaputs Plateau with its S escarpment—the Book Cliffs, the splendid gorges of the COLORADO RIVER and GREEN RIVER, the domed Henry, La Sal, and Abajo mts., and many remarkable natural bridges, multi-colored sandstone cliffs, and isolated buttes and mesas. In W Utah, which consists of the E part of the Great Basin, are GREAT SALT LAKE DESERT and the noted GREAT SALT LAKE, largest inland body of salt water in the Western Hemisphere. This lake and UTAH LAKE and SEVIER LAKE to the S are remnants of prehistoric L. BONNEVILLE, whose receding waters left well-preserved terraces along the W base of the Wasatch Range, where Ogden, Salt Lake City, Provo, and other cities now stand. W Utah, a drab region of extensive salt flats, desert plains, and block mts., has no drainage outlet to the sea. The state (average alt. c.6,000 ft.) has a very dry continental climate of the steppe and desert variety; precipitation—less than 5 in. in the Great Basin—is heaviest in the N mts. Salt Lake City has mean temp. of 26°F. in Jan. and 77°F. in July, with an annual average rainfall of 14 in. and c.45 in. of snow. About 72% of the land area, including almost 9,000,000 acres of natl. forests, is in Federal ownership. Total farm land is over 10,000,000 acres, divided among some 26,000 farms. Cattle and, especially, sheep are raised throughout the state, and wool, sheep, and lambs are important exports. Soil erosion is severe. Only c.3% of the land is arable and most of this is under irrigation; chief irrigation projects are located in Sanpete Valley and on PROVO RIVER, Clarkston Creek, and Strawberry R. Wheat, hay, alfalfa, sugar beets, oats, barley, potatoes, truck crops, peaches, and apples are the principal crops; much of the grain is grown for fodder. The majority of crop farms are in N and N central Utah, especially in the valleys just W of the Wasatch Range. Turkey and dairy farming are also carried on in this region. There are agr.-processing plants (flour, sugar, canned food) in Logan, Smithfield, Brigham City, Ogden, Provo, Spanish Fork, and Cedar City. Commercially valuable forests (chiefly pine, spruce, fir) amount to some 1,500,000 acres, but, since they are difficult of access and far from markets, the state imports almost all of its lumber. Utah, whose mineral wealth is main source of income, is a leading producer of copper and of lead, silver, zinc, and gold and has important reserves of bituminous coal, iron ore, salt, potash, phosphate rock, gypsum, alunite and natural gas. Chief mining dists. are in vicinity of Bingham Canyon (large open-pit copper mine), Park City, and Eureka; smelters at Salt Lake City, Midvale, Garfield (cobalt refinery), Murray, and Tooele. Most of the ore (in raw or semi-finished state) is shipped to refining and mfg. centers outside of Utah. There are oil refineries at Salt Lake City and Logan, a large steel plant at Geneva (near Provo), iron foundries at Provo and Salt Lake City, and processing plants for the uranium and vanadium ores mined in the SE. Salt Lake City, the state's largest city, is a major transportation, commercial, and financial center of the Rocky Mtn. region. Efforts have been made to increase the tourist industry. Among the many recreational areas and scenic attractions are ZION NATIONAL PARK, BRYCE CANYON NATIONAL PARK, CEDAR BREAKS NATIONAL MONUMENT, Natural Bridges, Rainbow Bridge, and Arches natl. monuments, and the popular resorts of SALTAIR (on Great Salt L.), Alta and Brighton (skiing), and Ogden Canyon. Colorful SW Utah is often used as a location by motion-picture producers; Bonneville Salt Flats in Great Salt L. Desert is a famous automobile speedway. Leading educational institutions are Univ. of Utah (at Salt Lake City), Brigham Young Univ. (at Provo), and Utah State Agr. Col. (at Logan). Archaeologists have discovered in caves and cliff dwellings in Utah evidence of a prehistoric culture. When Spanish missionaries explored the area in 1776 it was occupied by Ute, Paiute, and Shoshone Indians. From 1820 to 1840 came the fur trappers, including Gen. William Ashley, Jim Bridger (credited with the discovery of Great Salt L.), and Jedediah Smith. The 1st real settlement of the country, however, was by the Mormons, who, having trekked overland from Mo. and Ill. to escape religious persecution, arrived in Salt Lake valley in July, 1847; under the leadership of Brigham Young, they founded Salt Lake City and established several closely-knit, self-sufficient, agr. communities; they were the 1st to undertake irrigation on a large scale in the U.S. Until 1848, when it was ceded (by Treaty of Guadalupe Hidalgo) to the U.S., Utah was part of Mexico; in 1850 it was organized as a territory. Before this, however, the Mormons attempted to set up their own state (Deseret) but Congress refused to recognize it. In the next few years the colonists suffered from grasshopper plagues, Indian disturbances (1853–54 and 1865–68), and opposition by the Federal govt., which almost resulted in a clash with U.S. troops (1857). Although the Mormons concentrated on agr. and only essential consumer manufactures, with the advent of non-Mormon settlers (called Gentiles by the Mormons) and the completion of the transcontinental railroad at Promontory in 1869, extensive mining operations and stock raising became important. In response to public opinion in the East, Congress rejected several Mormon petitions for statehood and passed legislation aimed at stamping out the Mormon practice of polygamy; in the enforcement of these acts by Federal officials in Utah civil liberties were often infringed. However, when, in 1890, the Mormon church officially renounced polygamy, tension was eased and statehood for Utah followed 6 years later. Since then struggles bet. Mormons and anti-Mormons have become rare and polygamy is now almost non-existent. The Mormons, who comprise c.75% of all church members, live mostly in the N central part of the state. Problems facing modern Utah's economy arise from high freight rates, distant markets, and the lack of additional agr. land. See also articles on the cities, towns, geographic features, and the 29 counties: BEAVER, BOX ELDER, CACHE, CARBON, DAGGETT, DAVIS, DUCHESNE, EMERY, GARFIELD, GRAND, IRON, JUAB, KANE, MILLARD, MORGAN, PIUTE, RICH, SALT LAKE, SAN JUAN, SANPETE, SEVIER, SUMMIT, TOOELE, UINTAH, UTAH, WASATCH, WASHINGTON, WAYNE, WEBER.

Utah, county (□ 1,998; pop. 81,912), N central Utah; ⊙ Provo. Irrigated agr. area drained by Utah L. and tributaries. Part of Wasatch Range is in E, including Mt. Timpanogos and Timpanogos Cave Natl. Monument. Agr. (livestock, hay, sugar beets, truck), mining (iron, copper, silver, lead, zinc). Mfg. at Provo. Formed 1850.

Utah Beach, section of Normandy coast, Manche dept., NW France, bet. Saint-Marcouf (N) and mouth of Vire R. (S), N and NE of Carentan, where units of American First Army landed on June 6, 1944, in invasion of France.

Utah Lake (□ 150), in Utah co., N central Utah, c.30 mi. S of Salt Lake City, just W of Provo; 23 mi. long, 8 mi. wide. Largest fresh-water lake in state. Drains through Jordan R. into Great Salt L. and is remnant of prehistoric L. Bonneville. Tributaries are Spanish Fork and Provo R. Used for irrigation, as storage reservoir.

Utan (o͞ot'ŭn), village (pop. 3,160), Thana dist., W Bombay, India, on NW Salsette Isl., 14 mi. NW of Thana; fish curing (pomfrets, jewfish), salt drying. Lighthouse 2 mi. N.

Utangan River, India: see BANGANGA RIVER.

Utan Melintang, Malaya: see HUTAN MELINTANG.

Utansjo (ū'tän-shû"), Swedish *Utansjö*, village (pop. 573), Vasternorrland co., E central Sweden, on Gulf of Bothnia at mouth of Angerman R., 10 mi. N of Harnosand; pulp and cellulose mills.

Utara, Thailand: see UDON.

Utaradit, Thailand: see UTTARADIT.

Utashinai (o͞otä'shĭnī'), town (pop. 42,080), W central Hokkaido, Japan, 23 mi. SW of Asahigawa; coal-mining center.

'Utaybah, Al-, Syria: see 'ATEIBE, EL.

Utazu (o͞otä'zo͞o), town (pop. 7,771), Kagawa prefecture, N Shikoku, Japan, on Hiuchi Sea, just W of Sakaide; major saltmaking center.

Utcubamba River (o͞otko͞obäm'bä), Amazonas dept., N Peru, rises S of Chachapoyas, flows c.130 mi. NW to Marañón R. 10 mi. N of Bagua.

Ute (ūt), town (pop. 563), Monona co., W Iowa, 20 mi. E of Onawa, in stock and grain area.

Utebo (o͞otā'vō), village (pop. 1,536), Saragossa prov., NE Spain, near the Ebro, 7 mi. NW of Saragossa; meat processing; metalworks.

Utelle (ütĕl'), village (pop. 162), Alpes-Maritimes dept., SE France, above the Vésubie and 15 mi. N of Nice.

Utena or **Utyana** (o͞o'tä"nä), Rus. *Utsyany*, city (pop. 6,276), E Lithuania, on road and 80 mi. NE of Kaunas; mfg. (shoes, starches, flour), sawmilling. In Rus. Kovno govt. until 1920.

Ute Pass (ūt) (7,600 ft.), central Colo., in Front Range, just N of Pikes Peak. Used in latter half of 19th cent. by miners on way to gold fields of Cripple Creek and Leadville. Now crossed by highway.

Ute Peak (ūt). **1** Peak in Colo.: see WILLIAMS RIVER MOUNTAINS. **2** Outlying peak (10,151 ft.) of Sangre de Cristo Mts., N N.Mex., near Colo. line, 8 mi. WSW of Costilla.

Ütersen (ü'tûrzŭn), town (pop. 13,991), in Schleswig-Holstein, NW Germany, harbor on short navigable tributary of Elbe estuary, 17 mi. NW of Hamburg; center for Ger. rose growing; mfg. of artificial fertilizer, pharmaceuticals, cellulose, machinery, textiles, furniture, leather goods. Cement works; flour and paper mills. Former Cistercian nunnery (founded 1235) now houses Protestant sisterhood. Chartered 1870. Also spelled Uetersen.

Utete (o͞otē'tā), town, Eastern Prov., E Tanganyika, on Rufiji R. and 90 mi. SSW of Dar es Salaam (linked by road); cotton, sisal, copra. Airfield.

Utevka (o͞otyĕf'kŭ), village (1926 pop. 5,097), E Kuibyshev oblast, Russian SFSR, near Samara R., 26 mi. SE of Kinel; wheat, sunflowers; cattle, sheep.

Uthaithani (o͞otī'tä'nē'), town (1947 pop. 7,364), ⊙ Uthaithani prov. (□ 2,442; 1947 pop. 104,852), central Thailand, near Chao Phraya R., 115 mi. N of Bangkok, in rice-growing region. Also called Uthai, Uday, Udaya, or Udayadhani.

Uthamapalayam, India: see UTTAMAPALAIYAM.

Uthina, Tunisia: see OUDNA.

Utiariti (o͞otyo͞orētē'), town, NW Mato Grosso, Brazil, on tributary of Juruena R. and 200 mi. NW of Cuiabá; rubber gathering. Airfield. Formerly spelled Utiarity.

Utica (ū'tĭkŭ), anc. city of North Africa, 20 mi. NW of anc. Carthage and 18 mi. N of modern Tunis (N Tunisia), near marshy mouth of the Medjerda (anc. *Bagradas*). Traditionally founded by Phoenicians from Tyre c.1100 B.C., it was 2d in importance to Carthage, which was founded some 2 centuries later. It allied itself with Rome against Carthage in the 3d Punic War, and upon destruction of Carthage was made ⊙ Roman prov. of Africa. Here Cato the Younger committed suicide (46 B.C.) after being defeated by Caesar in battle of Thapsus. In 3d cent. A.D. Utica became an episcopal see. Fell to the Vandals (439), was captured by the Byzantines (534), and was finally destroyed by the Arabs (c.700). Excavations of the ruins, now 6 mi. inland, have yielded an amphitheater, baths, and fortifications.

Utica (o͞o'tēkä), town (pop. 1,478), Cundinamarca dept., central Colombia, in W foothills of Cordillera Oriental, on railroad and 17 mi. E of Honda; sugar cane, tobacco, bananas, yucca.

Utica (ū'tĭkŭ). **1** Village, Ill.: see NORTH UTICA. **2** City (pop. 365), Ness co., W central Kansas, 20 mi. NW of Ness City, in grain and livestock region; grain milling. **3** City (pop. 1,196), Macomb co., SE Mich., 20 mi. N of Detroit and on Clinton R., in dairy and truck area; flour mill. Ships rhubarb. State park near by. Settled 1817; inc. as village 1838, as city 1931. **4** Village (pop. 194), Winona co., SE Minn., near Mississippi R., 17 mi. W of Winona; dairy products. **5** Town (pop. 824), Hinds co., W Miss., 29 mi. WSW of Jackson; cotton ginning, sawmilling. **6** Village (pop. c.50), Judith Basin co., central Mont., on Judith R. and 32 mi. WSW of Lewistown. Silver, lead, gold, sapphires, and zinc are mined in near-by Little Belt Mts. **7** Village (pop. 550), Seward co., SE Nebr., 32 mi. W of Lincoln; grain. **8** City (pop. 101,531), a ⊙ Oneida co., central N.Y., on Mohawk R. and the Barge Canal, and c.45 mi. E of Syracuse; commercial and industrial center, in rich farming and dairying region; port of entry; large textile industry (knit goods, sheets and pillowcases, cotton cloth). Also makes firearms, heating equipment, machinery, electronic equipment, furniture, paper and wood products. N.Y. Masonic Home and Hosp., and a state mental hosp. (oldest in N.Y.) are here. Historical collections associated with co. are in Oneida Historical Bldg. Has an art inst. and mus. Its many parks have facilities for summer and winter sports. Large Welsh pop. holds annual eisteddfod. First settled permanently after the Revolution, on site of earlier settlement wiped out by Indian-Tory raid. Inc. as village in 1798, as city in 1832. Coming of the Erie and other canals brought industrial growth and many immigrants after 1825; 1st railroad was completed in 1836. Textile industry began in 1840s. **9** Village (pop. 1,510), Licking co., central Ohio, 12 mi. N of Newark and on North Fork of Licking R., in rich agr. area; rural trade center; fertilizer, feed. **10** Borough (pop. 264), Venango co., NW Pa., 7 mi. WNW of Franklin and on French Creek. **11** Town (pop. 84), Yankton co., SE S.Dak., 10 mi. NNW of Yankton; trading point for farming region.

Utiel (o͞otyĕl'), city (pop. 9,512), Valencia prov., E Spain, 46 mi. W of Valencia; wine-production center; alcohol and brandy distilling, olive pressing; mfg. of resin products, tiles, wax, soap, nougats. Agr. trade (cereals, livestock).

Utik Lake (ū′tĭk) (24 mi. long, 5 mi. wide), NE central Man.; 55°17′N 95°55′W. Drains NE into Hayes R.

Utila Island (ōōtē′lä), westernmost island (pop. 1,124) in Bay Islands dept., N Honduras, in Caribbean Sea, 20 mi. NNW of La Ceiba; 8 mi. long, 3 mi. wide; in hurricane zone. Produces chiefly coconuts. Town of Utila (pop. 974) is on SE shore.

Utinga (ōōtēng′gù), industrial SE suburb of São Paulo city, in São Paulo state, SE Brazil, on São Paulo-Santos RR, just NW of Santo André, and 8 mi. from São Paulo city center; metalworks (machinery, structural shapes), meat-packing plants.

Utinoko, Japan: see UCHINOKO.

Utinomaki, Japan: see UCHINOMAKI.

Utinoura, Japan: see UCHINOURA.

Utirik (ōō′tĭrĭk), atoll (pop. 164), Ratak Chain, Kwajalein dist., Marshall Isls., W central Pacific, 215 mi. NE of Kwajalein; triangular reef with base 10 mi. wide.

Utkinski Zavod, Russian SFSR: see STAROUTKINSK.

Utmanzai (ōōt′mŭnzī), town (pop. 10,129), Peshawar dist., central North-West Frontier Prov., W Pakistan, on Swat R. and 15 mi. NE of Peshawar; agr. market (corn, wheat, barley); handicrafts (cloth weaving, felt mats). Sometimes spelled Uttmanzai.

Utnur (ōōtnōōr′), village (pop. 1,401), Adilabad dist., NE Hyderabad state, India, 25 mi. SE of Adilabad; rice, oilseeds.

Uto (ōō′tō), town (pop. 6,981), Kumamoto prefecture, W Kyushu, Japan, 8 mi. SSW of Kumamoto; rail junction; commercial center for agr. area (rice, wheat); sake, raw silk. Site of feudal castle.

Utopia, Lake (□ 5.3; 5 mi. long, 2 mi. wide), SW N.B., 3 mi. NE of St. George; drains into Magaguadavic R.

Utorgosh (ōōtôr′gŭsh), town (1939 pop. over 500), W Novgorod oblast, Russian SFSR, 40 mi. WSW of Novgorod; flax processing.

Utowana Lake (ūtùwä′nù), Hamilton co., NE central N.Y., in the Adirondacks, 3 mi. SW of Blue Mountain Lake village; c.2½ mi. long. Joined by streams to Raquette L. (W), and to small Eagle L. and thence to Blue Mountain L. (E).

Utra (ōōt′rä), suburb of Joensuu, Kuopio co., SE Finland, on Pieli R. and 4 mi. E of city; log-sorting station.

Utracán, Argentina: see GENERAL ACHA.

Utraula (ōōtrou′lŭ), town (pop. 8,112), Gonda dist., NE Uttar Pradesh, India, 16 mi. ESE of Balrampur; rice milling; rice, wheat, gram, corn, sugar.

Utrecht (ū′trĕkt, Du. ü′trĕkht), province (□ 501.9; pop. 549,566), central Netherlands; ⊙ Utrecht. Bounded by the Ijsselmeer and North Holland prov. (N), South Holland prov. (W), Lek R. (S), Gelderland prov. (E). Mainly low-lying country, rising in E where Gelderland heaths overlap prov. boundary. Drained by Lower Rhine, Lek, and Vecht rivers, with lake area (Loosdrechtsche Plassen) N. Extensive growing of green and root vegetables; dairying; fruitgrowing in SW. Mfg. and processing industries concentrated in Utrecht and Amersfoort areas. Chief towns: Amersfoort, Zeist. In Middle Ages prov. was episcopal territory, ruled by archbishop of Utrecht under protection of Holy Roman Empire; came progressively under influence of Holland. In 1527 prov. sold to Charles V; became (1579) one of Seven United Provinces, signatories of Union of Utrecht.

Utrecht, city (pop. 185,246), ⊙ Utrecht prov., central Netherlands, on Merwede Canal and 21 mi. SE of Amsterdam, at junction of the Old Rhine and the Crooked Rhine; 52°7′N 5°5′E. Major rail junction (hq. of Netherlands railroads), with repair shops; metal-rolling mills (steel, aluminum); mfg. of machinery, wood products, asphalt, radios, electric bulbs, cotton and kapok products, food products, edible fats, fertilizer. Financial center, with a number of insurance companies and the natl. mint. An old city with many sunken canals. Has univ. (founded 1636), 14th-cent. cathedral, many examples of modern architecture. Seat of R.C. archbishop of the Netherlands. A Rhine R. crossing in Roman times, called *Trajectum ad Rhenum;* became (696) a bishopric; granted town charter (1122) by Emperor Henry V. Bishop Henry of Bavaria ceded temporal power (1527) to Emperor Charles V. Archbishopric (created 1559) suppressed 1580; revived 1851. Residence of many early Ger. emperors. Revolted against Spain, 1577; became hq. of anti-Spanish Union of Utrecht (1579), resulting in formation of United Provinces. Treaty of Utrecht (1713) ended War of Spanish Succession.

Utrecht (Afrikaans ü′trĕkh), town (pop. 3,770), NW Natal, U. of So. Afr., on Dorps R. and 25 mi. ENE of Newcastle; rail terminus; coal mining; center of stock-raising, wool-producing, fruitgrowing region. Founded 1852, it later became ⊙ a small Boer republic; inc. in Transvaal 1868, ceded to Natal 1903.

Utrechtsche Vecht River, Netherlands: see VECHT RIVER.

Utrera (ōōtrā′rä), city (pop. 26,654), Seville prov., S Spain, in Andalusia, 18 mi. SE of Seville; rail junction, trading and processing center in one of Spain's most fertile regions (olives, cotton, fruit, vegetables, grapes, grain, rice, livestock). Busy city, surrounded by plantations and pastures. Industries include olive-oil pressing, food canning, flour milling, liquor distilling, tanning, textile milling; mfg. of margarine, cooking fats, soap, plaster, and refined sulphur. A city of predominantly Moorish character, it contains ornate mansions and fine religious bldgs., such as parochial church of Santa María (with 18th-cent. tower) and Santiago church; also has noted Salesian col. Above city are ruins of a Moorish castle. Just NE (c.1 mi.) is a grandiose convent famed for its shrine to the Virgin. Utrera was, during early Christian centuries, a bishopric.

Utrillas (ōōtrē′lyäs), town (pop. 1,171), Teruel prov., E Spain, 35 mi. NNE of Teruel; cereals, saffron. Bituminous-coal mines near by.

Utsayantha, Mount, N.Y.: see STAMFORD.

Utsjoki (ōōts′yō″kē), village (commune pop. 924), Lapi co., Norway, on Kevu R., near its mouth on Tana R., 70 mi. W of Kirkenes; Lapp trade center.

Utsumi (ōōtsōō′mē) or **Uchiumi** (ōōchē′ōōmē), town (pop. 7,991), Aichi prefecture, central Honshu, Japan, on S Chiba Peninsula, on Ise Bay, 12 mi. SSW of Handa; agr. (rice, sweet potatoes), fishing; raw silk.

Utsunomiya (ōōtsōōnō′mēä), city (1940 pop. 87,868; 1947 pop. 97,075), ⊙ Tochigi prefecture, central Honshu, Japan, 60 mi. N of Tokyo; rail junction; tourist resort; tobacco processing. Has anc. Buddhist temple. Became ⊙ prefecture in 1884, succeeding Tochigi. Sometimes spelled Utunomiya.

Utsuryo-to, Korea: see ULLUNG ISLAND.

Utsyany, Lithuania: see UTENA.

Uttamapalaiyam or **Uthamapalayam** (both: ōōt″-ŭmŭpä′līyŭm), town (pop. 11,474), Madura dist., S Madras, India, 6 mi. NNE of Cumbum, in Kambam Valley; rice, sesame, tamarind. Also spelled Uttamapalayam.

Uttara, Thailand: see UDON.

Uttaradit (ōōt′trä′rŭdĭt′), town (1947 pop. 5,494), ⊙ Uttaradit prov. (□ 2,983; 1947 pop. 170,844), N Thailand, on Bangkok-Chiangmai RR, on Nan R., and 270 mi. N of Bangkok; sugar refinery; rice, tobacco, fruit, teak. Phra Then shrine (4 mi. SW) is center of yearly pilgrimage. Also spelled Utaradit.

Uttaramerur or **Uttiramerur** (ōō′tŭrŭmĕrōōr), town (pop. 12,134), Chingleput dist., E Madras, India, 15 mi. SSE of Conjeeveram; rice and oilseed milling.

Uttarpara (ōōt″tŭrpä′rŭ), town (pop. 13,610), Hooghly dist., S West Bengal, India, on the Hooghly and 6 mi. N of Calcutta city center; chemical and bone-meal mfg. Col., large public library.

Uttar Pradesh (ōōtŭr prŭdāsh′), constituent state (□ 112,523; 1941 pop., based on adjusted 1950 boundaries, c.56,500,000; 1951 census pop. 63,254,118), N India; ⊙ Allahabad. Bounded N and NE by Tibet (boundary undefined) and Nepal, E by Bihar, and (as Uttar Pradesh curves SE–NW) by Vindhya Pradesh (bet. 2 narrow prongs of Uttar Pradesh reaching S to Madhya Pradesh), Madhya Bharat, Rajasthan, Indian Punjab (Delhi is on S portion of Punjab-Uttar Pradesh border), and Himachal Pradesh. Lies mainly S of the Himalayas, in upper basin of GANGES RIVER, whose main tributaries in Uttar Pradesh, JUMNA RIVER (right) and GOGRA RIVER and GUMTI RIVER (left), form great alluvial doabs in E half of state; crossed in NW dists. of Almora, Dehra Dun, Garhwal, Naini Tal, and Tehri by KUMAUN HIMALAYAS (rise to 25,447 ft. and 25,645 ft. in Kamet and NANDA DEVI mountains) and the longitudinal valleys (*duns*) of SIWALIK RANGE; plains along state's irregular S border are broken by N offshoots of VINDHYA RANGE and its N branch (KAIMUR HILLS) and are drained by Betwa, Ken, Son, and Tons rivers (all affluents of the Jumna). Greater part of state (Ganges plain) slopes gradually S and SE from the marshy Terai below the Himalayas; overall climate is tropical savanna, with annual rainfall averaging 37–40 in. (W–E) and mean temp. ranging from 60°F. in Dec. to 90°F. in May. Plains area produces large quantities of barley, gram, linseed, wheat (mainly in Ganges-Jumna Doab), corn, rape and mustard, and rice, also cotton, millet, tobacco, and jute; most important sugar-growing area of India is in W. About ¾ state's pop. depends directly on agr.; double cropping is important and is assisted by state's many irrigation works, notably Agra, Betwa, Ganges, and Sarda canals—especially necessary in W areas; projects on Nayar, Rampanga, and Rihand rivers to furnish additional irrigation and hydroelectric power. Uttar Pradesh has over 30,000,000 head of cattle—used primarily as draft animals, although dairy farming is more prevalent than in most Indian states; best grazing in Kaimur Hills. Forests (total □ c.6,000; mainly in Kumaun Himalayas) contain valuable timber (deodar, sal, Khair). State's mineral resources are insignificant, but some coal is found in SE dists. and copper in Almora dist. Industry is mainly based on agr.; Uttar Pradesh is India's major sugar-milling state and also processes cotton, rice, flour, oilseeds, jute, and tobacco. Other industries include glass, silk (Benares is famous for its silk saris), paper, chemical fertilizer, power alcohol, leather goods, and cutlery. Cawnpore, with its great modern wool and cotton mills and leather factories, is state's leading mfg. town. Noted handicrafts include wool, cotton, and silk weaving, glass blowing, brass and lacquerware, and pottery. Principal cities are CAWNPORE, LUCKNOW, AGRA, BENARES, ALLAHABAD, Bareilly, Meerut, Moradabad, Aligarh, Saharanpur, Shahjahanpur, and Jhansi. Trade centers are well served by rail and road nets; airports at Allahabad, Benares, Cawnpore, and Lucknow. Pop. (density averages 520 persons per sq. mi.; almost 1,000 in E Ganges valley) is over 87% rural, was only 8% literate in 1941, and consists mainly of Hindus (84%) and Moslems (15%). Hindi is spoken by over 80% of the pop. and Urdu by almost 20%; Hindustani (dialect composed of both languages), the lingua franca of India, is largely spoken here. State has 5 universities—at Agra, Aligarh, Allahabad, Benares, and Lucknow. Other institutions include Armed Forces Academy and Forest Research Inst. at Dehra (or Dehra Dun), Central Drug Research Inst. at Lucknow, Central Building Research Inst. at Roorkee. Agr. research at Allahabad and Saharanpur. Noted hill resorts include NAINI TAL (summer hq. of state govt.) and MUSSOORIE. The course of the Ganges is studded with some of the most sacred Hindu pilgrimage centers in India, notably Allahabad, Benares, Hardwar, Badrinath, and Devaprayag (the last 2 are on Alaknanda and Bhagirathi rivers—headstreams of the Ganges). Numerous places of archaeological and historical interest—Agra (site of the Taj Mahal), AJODHYA, FATEHPUR SIKRI, KASIA, KANAUJ, MEERUT, MUTTRA, and SARNATH—testify to region's varied cultural background. Area of present state was scene of the great Hindu epics, the MAHABHARATA and the RAMAYANA. Buddhism spread over the region from Bihar during Asokan empire (250 B.C.), but Brahmanism revived 4th–7th cent. A.D. under the Guptas and Harsha. Rajput clans (7th–13th cent.) gave way to Delhi sultans (13th–14th cent.), who were succeeded by Afghans under Sher Shah (mid 16th cent.) and Mogul empire (17th cent.). As the Mogul control declined in 18th cent., the plains became a major battlefield of the struggle bet. the English, the Mahrattas, and other Indian powers for supremacy in India. Mogul AGRA Province, geographically equivalent to major portion of present state, was annexed by East India Co. during late 18th and early 19th cent. as part of BENGAL presidency; joined with OUDH in 1877 (Agra Prov. and Oudh were overrun by rebel forces during Sepoy Rebellion of 1857–58), and the union was named United Provinces of Agra and Oudh in 1902. In 1937, it was constituted an autonomous prov., commonly called merely United Provinces (in 1941: □ 106,247; pop. 55,020,617). Enlarged 1949 by inc. of former princely states (total □ 6,276; 1941 pop. 1,325,839) of Benares, Rampur, and Tehri and again in 1950 by transfer of several detached enclaves (total □ c.1,000; 1941 pop. c.200,000) from Vindhya Pradesh. Name changed to Uttar Pradesh when it became (1950) a constituent state of the republic of India. State comprises 50 dists.: Agra, Aligarh, Allahabad, Almora, Azamgarh, Bahraich, Ballia, Banda, Barabanki, Bareilly, Basti, Benares, Bijnor, Budaun, Bulandshahr, Cawnpore, Dehra Dun, Etah, Etawah, Farrukhabad, Fatehpur, Fyzabad, Garhwal, Ghazipur, Gonda, Gorakhpur, Hamirpur, Hardoi, Jalaun, Jaunpur, Jhansi, Kheri, Lucknow, Mainpuri, Meerut, Mirzapur, Moradabad, Muttra, Muzaffarnagar, Naini Tal, Partabgarh, Pilibhit, Rae Bareli, Rampur, Saharanpur, Shahjahanpur, Sitapur, Sultanpur, Tehri, and Unao.

Utti (ōōt′tē), Swedish *Uttis* (ŭ′tĭs), village in Valkeala commune (pop. 14,916), Kymi co., SE Finland, in lake region, 9 mi. E of Kouvola; scene (1789) of Swedish victory under Gustavus III over Russians.

Uttiramerur, India: see UTTARAMERUR.

Uttis, Finland: see UTTI.

Uttmanzai, W Pakistan: see UTMANZAI.

Uttoxeter (ŭtŏk′sĭtûr, ŭtŏk′–, ŭk′sĭtûr), urban district (1931 pop. 5,909; 1951 census 7,440), E Stafford, England, 11 mi. NW of Burton-on-Trent; milk processing and canning, mfg. of biscuits and agr. machinery; dairy market. Has church with tower dating from 14th cent. Samuel Johnson's father had a bookstall here.

Utuado (ōōtwä′dō), town (pop. 9,693), W central Puerto Rico, on N slopes of the Cordillera Central, 14 mi. S of Arecibo; coffee-trading center; tobacco processing; tree nursery. Adjoining E is the large Toro Negro unit of the Caribbean Natl. Forest. Numerous caves with ethnological and paleontological remains near by.

Utukok River, NW Alaska, rises in Brooks Range near 68°33′N 161°7′W, flows c.200 mi. generally N to Arctic Ocean at 70°8′N 162°13′W. Utukok settlement at mouth.

Utunomiya, Japan: see UTSUNOMIYA.

Utupua (ōōtōōpōō′ä), volcanic island, Santa Cruz Isls., Solomon Isls., SW Pacific, 60 mi. SE of Ndeni; 15 mi. long, 10 mi. wide.

Utvaer, Norway: see SOLUND ISLANDS.

Utyana, Lithuania: see UTENA.

Ütze (ü′tsù), village (pop. 5,019), in former Prussian prov. of Hanover, W Germany, after 1945 in Lower Saxony, 10 mi. N of Peine; woodworking.

Utzenstorf (ōōt'sŭnstôrf"), town (pop. 2,344), canton, NW Switzerland, 5 mi. S of Soloth paper, leather, flour.

Uudenmaa, county, Finland: see Uusimaa.

Uuras, Russian SFSR: see Vysotsk, Lenin oblast.

Uusikaarlepyy, Finland: see Nykarleby.

Uusikaupunki (ōō'sĭkou"pōōngkē), Swedish N (nü'städ"), city (pop. 4,099), Turku-Pori co Finland, on Gulf of Bothnia, 35 mi. NW of T port, shipping granite and timber; rail term Granite-quarrying center, with shipyards, m shops. Has 17th-cent. church. Founded Treaty of Nystad (1721) ended Northern W

Uusimaa (ōō'sĭmä"), Swedish *Nyland* (nü county [Finnish *lääni*] (□ 3,788; including area, □ 4,076; pop. 641,266), S Finland; ⊙ sinki. On Gulf of Finland, it has indented line. Surface is low and level, rising towa Drained by several short streams. Agr. (ryc sugar beets, barley, potatoes), stock raisin dairying are carried on. Granite and lim quarries. Lumbering, timber-processing, and working industries are important; other inc (chiefly in Helsinki region) are textile metalworking; mfg. of cement, ceramics, gla chinery. Fishing. Cities are Helsinki, Lovisa, Ekenas, and Hango. Co. includes kala defense region and naval base, leased to USSR. Majority of pop. is Swedish-s (except in Helsinki). With the Finnish ger the word county, the name Uusimaa h Uudenma (ōō'dĕnmä").

Uva (ōōvä'), town (1948 pop. over 2,000), Udmurt Autonomous SSR, Russian SFSR WNW of Izhevsk; rail spur terminus; lur

Uva Basin (ōōv'ŭ), E extension of Ceyl Country, SE central Ceylon; c.25 mi. lo mi. wide; average alt., 3,000 ft.; average 50 in. Highest point, 9-pointed peak 6,679 ft.) of Namunukula, is 6 mi. SE of also spelled Namanakula and Nam Unique in Ceylon for its covering of g (*patanas*) instead of forests. Main towns: Bandarawela.

Uvac River or **Uvats River** (both: ōō' Serbia, Yugoslavia, rises 8 mi. WSW of flows c.70 mi. NW to Lim R. 2 mi. NW of Forms 2-mi.-long Serbia-Croatia border its mouth.

Uvalda (ūväl'dŭ), town (pop. 511), Montgo E central Ga., 14 mi. SSW of Vidalia.

Uvalde (ūväl'dē), county (□ 1,588; pop. 5), SW Texas; ⊙ Uvalde. Crossed E-W by Escarpment, dividing hilly N (part of rds Plateau) from S plains; drained by Nue rio, Leona, and Sabinal rivers. Ranching ally goats, sheep; also cattle); mohair, woo ped; extensive bee keeping, some irrigated a ick, fruit). Asphalt mines. Hills, canyons, -fed streams attract tourists; hunting. For 1850.

Uvalde, city (pop. 8,674), ⊙ Uvalde co., exas, c.80 mi. WSW of San Antonio; trade, m center for ranching region (especially goats; attle, sheep), with some irrigated agr. (spina ships mohair, wool, cattle, pecans, honey, asph ourist trade (scenic mts., canyons to N). Sea outh-west Jr. Col. John N. Garner's home is U.S. fish hatchery on Frio R. is near. Foun 1854, inc. as town 1886, as city 1921.

Uvaly (ōō'välĭ), Czech *Úvaly*, village (p 1,706), E central Bohemia, Czechoslovakia, 1. E of Prague; wheat, sugar beets, potatoes.

Uvaly, Russian SFSR: see Northe Uvals; Vyatka Uval.

Uva Province (ōōv'ŭ), administrati division (□ 3,277; pop., including estate pop., 303), SE Ceylon; ⊙ Badulla. Bounded NW by Mahaweli Ganda, SW by the Walawe Ganda a Basin and Lunugala Ridge, parts of Ceylon H Country, in W area. Largely agr.; tea, rice, rubber plantations; vegetables, fruit. Main to s: Badulla, Bandarawela. Projected dam and wer plant at Inginiyagala. Pilgrimage centers at tnuwara and Kataragama. Has Diyaluma F s. Part of prov. was principality of Kandyan k dom until occupied, early-19th cent., by Engli Scene of revolt 1817 against English. Pop. mai Kandyan Singhalese and Indian Tamil. Create 1886.

Uvarovichi (ōōvä'rŭvĭchē), town (192 op. 1,662), central Gomel oblast, Belorussian R, 17 mi. NW of Gomel; metalworks.

Uvarovka (ōōvä'rŭfkŭ), village (1939 p. over 500), W Moscow oblast, Russian SFSR, 5 mi. W of Mozhaisk; flax.

Uvarovo (-rŭvŭ), village (1926 pop 11,581), SE Tambov oblast, Russian SFSR, or orona R. and 55 mi. SE of Tambov; sunflower oil.

Uvat (ōōvät'), village (1926 pop. 3), S Tyumen oblast, Russian SFSR, on Irtysh R. and 65 mi. N of Tobolsk; grain, livestock.

Uvats River, Yugoslavia: see Uvac River.

Uvdal (ōōv'däl), village and canton (pop. 1,318), Buskerud co., S Norway, at E foot of the Hardangervidda, near head of the Numedal, 50 mi. W of Honefoss; livestock. Formerly called Opdal.

Uvea (ōōvā'ä), Fr. *Ouvéa*, coral island (pop. c.2,300), northernmost of Loyalty Isls., SW Pacific, 30 mi. of Lifu; 20°32'S 166°35'E; 23 mi. long, 3.5 mi. lagoon formed by W coast and 2 rows of Most fertile of group; coconuts. Produces a. Chief town, Fayahoué. Formerly Halgan. volcanic island (pop. 4,765), Wallis Islands, Pacific, 250 mi. W of Samoa; 13°17'S 176°10'W; i. long, 4 mi. wide; rises to 479 ft. Site of tautu, ⊙ protectorate. Extinct crater. Only abited isl. of group. Sometimes called Uea.

ski or **Uvel'skiy** (ōōvĕl'skē), town (1948 pop. 2,000), central Chelyabinsk oblast, Russian SR, on railroad (Nizhne-Uvelskaya station) and mi. NNW of Troitsk; refractory-clay quarrying. airying and flour milling 4 mi. W, at Nizhnevelskoye (1939 pop. over 500).

nza (ōōvĕn'zä), town, Western Prov., W Tanganka, on Malagarasi R., on railroad and 55 mi. SE of Kigoma; salt-mining center.

ira (ōōvē'rä), town (1948 pop. 600), Kivu prov., Belgian Congo, on NW shore of L. Tanganyika, n railroad and 65 mi. SSE of Costermansville; erminus of lake navigation and commercial center; customs station. Cotton ginning. Has R.C. and Protestant missions and research institute for study of trypanosomiasis in Ruzizi area. Kalundu (kälōōn'dōō), Uvira's port on the Tanganyika, is an important transshipment point and head of railroad to Kamaniola. Cotton, wheat, and corn are grown in the region and cattle are raised.

Uvita, La, village, Costa Rica: see La Uvita.

Uvita, La (lä ōōvē'tä), small coral island in Caribbean Sea, off port of Limón, Costa Rica. Quarantine station; lighthouse; 10°N 83°1'W.

Uvkusigssat (ōōfkōōsĭkh'shät), fishing and hunting settlement (pop. 66), Umanak dist., W Greenland, at mouth of Ingnerit, 25-mi.-long E arm of Umanak Fjord, 30 mi. NNE of Umanak; 71°4'N 51°53'W.

Uvkusigssat Fjord, Greenland: see Karrats Fjord.

Uvod River or **Uvod' River** (ōōvôt'yŭ), central European Russian SFSR, rises near Pistsovo, flows c.85 mi. S, past Ivanovo and Kokhma, to Klyazma R. just E of Kovrov.

Uwa (ōō'wä), town (pop. 8,661), Ehime prefecture, W Shikoku, Japan, 36 mi. SSW of Matsuyama; agr. and stock-breeding center. Agr. school. Sometimes called Unomachi (official name until 1889).

Uwajima (ōōwä'jĭmä), city (1940 pop. 52,101; 1947 pop. 52,108), Ehime prefecture, W Shikoku, Japan, port on Hoyo Strait, 45 mi. SSW of Matsuyama; rail junction; mfg. center (cotton textiles, paper, machinery, sake, soy sauce). Exports raw silk, rice, fish. Bombed (1945) in Second World War.

Uweinat, Gebel (gĕ'bĕl ōō'wīnăt), peak (6,256 ft.) on Egypt-Anglo-Egyptian Sudan-Libya border, in Libyan Desert; c.21°45'N 25'E.

Uwet (hōō'wĕt), town, Calabar prov., Eastern Provinces, SE Nigeria, on Calabar R. and 23 mi. NNW of Calabar; hardwood, rubber, palm oil and kernels, cacao, kola nuts. Monazite deposits.

Uwharrie River, N.C.: see Uharie River.

Uxbridge (ŭks'brĭj), town (pop. 1,406), S Ont., 35 mi. NNE of Toronto; wool, flour, grist milling; dairying.

Uxbridge, residential urban district (1931 pop. 31,880; 1951 census 55,944), Middlesex, England, on Colne R. and 16 mi. W of London; mfg. of electrical equipment and agr. machinery. Site of "Treaty House" where Charles I held indecisive negotiations with Parliamentarians in 1645. Has 15th-cent. church, 13th-cent. Moor Hall mansion, and 16th-cent. inn. In urban dist. are residential areas of Cowley, Harefield (site of sanitarium), Hillingdon, and Ickenham.

Uxbridge, town (pop. 7,007), Worcester co., S Mass., on Blackstone R. and 16 mi. SE of Worcester; mfg. (worsteds, woolens); dairying, truck. Settled 1662, inc. 1727.

Uxküll, Latvia: see Ikskile.

Uxmal (ōōzmäl', ōōsh-), ruined Maya city in Yucatan, SE Mexico, 40 mi. S of Mérida. Rivals Chichén Itzá as one of continent's most remarkable archaeological sites, being noted for its austere, classic style and balanced ornaments of rare grandeur. Its structures include so-called Governor's Palace, Turtle House, House of the Dwarf, Nunnery, etc. Believed to have been founded as an aristocratic center in 10th cent. by the Tutul Xiu family, a Maya nation; it was abandoned 1441.

Uy, river, Russian SFSR: see Ui River.

Uyae, Marshall Isls.: see Ujae.

Uyak Bay (ōō'yăk), S Alaska, W Kodiak Isl., inlet (35 mi. long, 1–5 mi. wide) of Shelikof Strait, 60 mi. WSW of Kodiak. Uyak fishing village and cannery on W shore.

Uyar (ōōyär'), city (1939 pop. over 10,000), SE Krasnoyarsk Territory, Russian SFSR, on Trans-Siberian RR and 60 mi. ESE of Krasnoyarsk; meat packing. Kaolin deposits. Formerly Klyukvenny.

Uychi, Uzbek SSR: see Uichi.

Uyea (yōō'ŭ). **1** Islet of the Shetlands, Scotland, just off NW extremity of Mainland isl.; 1 mi. long; rises to 231 ft. Noted for good grazing land; there is some copper ore. **2** Islet (pop. 12) of the Shetlands, Scotland, just S of Unst; 2 mi. long, 1 mi. wide; rises to 163 ft.

Uyedineniye Island (ōōyĭdyĭnyē'nyēŭ) [Rus.,=solitude], in Kara Sea of Arctic Ocean, 185 mi. off NW Taimyr Peninsula, Krasnoyarsk Territory, Russian SFSR; 77°30'N 82°15'E. Govt. observation post. Also called Lonely Isl.

Uygursay, Uzbek SSR: see Uigursai.

Uyo (ōōyô), town (pop. 743), Calabar prov., Eastern Provinces, SE Nigeria, 28 mi. WNW of Calabar; road center; palm oil and kernels, cacao, kola nuts. Teachers col., oil-palm research station.

Uy River, Russian SFSR: see Ui River.

Uyskoye, Russian SFSR: see Uiskoye.

'Uyun or **'Uyun al Qasim** (ōōyōōn' ăl kä'sĕm'), town and oasis, Qasim prov. of Nejd, Saudi Arabia, 24 mi. NW of Buraida; grain (sorghum, wheat), dates, vegetables; stock raising. Sometimes 'Ayun.

Uyuni (ōōyōō'nē), city (pop. c.5,900), ⊙ Quijarro (until c.1930 called Porco) prov., Potosí dept., SW Bolivia, in the Altiplano, 170 mi. S of Oruro; alt. 12,037 ft. Junction of railroads from Antofagasta (Chile), Villazón (Bolivia-Argentina border), and Oruro; important trading and mining center; customs house, airport. Silver mines of Pulacayo and Huanchaca near by. Salar de Uyuni is W. City founded 1890 and developed rapidly. Has large Slav and Syrian colony. Cold climate due to its exposed location.

Uyuni, Salar de (sälär'dā), largest salt flat of Bolivia, Potosí dept., SW Bolivia, in the Altiplano, 20 mi. W of Uyuni; 90 mi. long, 75 mi. wide; alt. 12,073 ft. Receives Río Grande de Lípez (SE). On shore are Salinas de Garci Mendoza (N), Colcha "K" (S), and Llica (NW), connected by roads which cross the Salar. Separated from Salar de Coipasa (N) by Cordillera de Llica.

Uyu River (ōō'yōō), in Upper Burma, rises S of Hukawng Valley, flows 150 mi. SW to Chindwin R. below Homalin. Jade mines in upper course at Lonkin and Tawmaw.

Uzair, Al, Iraq: see 'Azair, Al.

Uzaka, Japan: see Nenaka.

Uza Srbija, republic, Yugoslavia: see Serbia.

'Uzayr, Al-, Iraq: see 'Azair, Al.

Uzbekistan (ōōz"bĕkĭstăn', -stän', ŭz"-, Rus. ōōzbyĕkĭstän') or **Uzbek Soviet Socialist Republic** (ōōz'bĕk, ōōzbĕk', ŭz-, Rus. ōōzbyĕk'), constituent republic (□ 157,300; 1947 pop. estimate 6,000,000) of the USSR, in Central Asia; ⊙ Tashkent. Bounded by Turkmen SSR (SW), Kazakh SSR (N), Kirghiz and Tadzhik SSR (E), and Afghanistan (along short stretch of the Amu Darya; S). Economically the most developed Soviet Central Asian republic. Includes Kara-Kalpak Autonomous SSR, and falls administratively into 9 oblasts: Andizhan, Bukhara, Fergana, Kashka Darya, Khorezm, Namangan, Samarkand, Surkhan Darya, and Tashkent. Situated largely in Kyzyl-Kum desert (W) and in fertile piedmont loess lowland (E), with spurs of Tien Shan mtn. system only at its periphery (E). Although the Amu Darya (which irrigates the Khorezm oasis) and the Syr Darya (Golodnaya Step irrigation) pass in part through Uzbek territory, its principal oases are irrigated by lesser streams: Fergana Valley by tributaries of the Syr Darya, linked by Fergana Canal; Tashkent oasis by Chirchik and Angren rivers; Samarkand and Bukhara oases by the Zeravshan; Kashka Darya and Surkhan Darya oases by their homonymous streams. Dry continental climate; mean temp., 27°F. (Jan.), 77°–86°F. (July). Yearly precipitation, 3 in. (in desert) to 24 in. (in foothills). Pop. consists of Uzbeks (76%), Kara-Kalpaks, Tadzhiks, Russians, Bukhara Jews, and Armenians. Uzbekistan leads in Soviet irrigated agr. and is principal producer of cotton, rice, and silk. American cotton (in rotation with lucerne) is most commonly grown, with some Egyptian long-staple in hot Surkhan Darya valley (Termez). Other crops are sesame, yellow tobacco, sugar beets (Yangi-Yul), fruit (apricots, peaches, grapes, melons). Karakul sheep, goats, camels, mules, and donkeys are chief livestock types. Industrial phase of economy is based on mineral resources (petroleum near Andizhan and at Chimion and Khaudag, coal at Angren, copper at Almalyk, sulphur, ozocerite, tungsten, molybdenum, and marble), electro-chemical industry (Chirchik), textile milling (cotton at Tashkent and Fergana; silk at Margelan; wool), metallurgy (Begovat), mfg. of agr. machinery (Tashkent), and dry-agr. processing (rice milling, fruit canning and drying, wine making). Main urban centers are Tashkent, Samarkand, and Bukhara. Principal exports are cotton, cottonseed oil, silk, dried fruit, karakul, wine. The Uzbeks (or Uzbegs), a Turkic ethnic group of Persian culture and Sunni Moslem religion, were formerly called Sarts. They developed out of the merger of nomad and sedentary peoples under the Golden Horde, from one of whose chiefs, Uzbeg Khan, they received their name. During 16th cent., they conquered the former empire of Tamerlane, but split up into separate khanates, notably those of Khiva, Bukhara, and Kokand, which fell (1865–76) to Russia. Formed (1924) as a constituent republic within the USSR out of parts of Turkestan Autonomous SSR and Khorezm and Bukhara SSRs, Uzbekistan at first included Tadzhik Autonomous SSR, which became a separate constituent republic of the Soviet Union in 1929.

Uzboi or **Uzboy** (ōōzboi′), dry river bed in W Ashkhabad oblast, Turkmen SSR; from area SSW of Aral Sea it runs c.300 mi. S and SW, through Kara-Kum desert, bet. Greater Balkhan and lesser Balkhan ranges, towards Caspian Sea. Believed to be former course of the Amu Darya connecting Aral and Caspian Seas.

Uzda (ōōzdä′), town (1926 pop. 2,498), SW Minsk oblast, Belorussian SSR. 33 mi. SSW of Minsk; agr. products.

Uzel (üzĕl′), village (pop. 680), Côtes-du-Nord dept., W France, 17 mi. SSW of Saint-Brieuc; linen weaving. Also called Uzel-près-l'Oust.

Uzen or **Uzen'** (ōōzyĕn′yŭ), name of 2 steppe rivers in Saratov oblast (Russian SFSR) and West Kazakhstan oblast (Kazakh SSR). **Greater Uzen River**, Rus. *Bolshoi Uzen*, rises in the Obshchi Syrt S of Pugachev, flows 370 mi. S and SSE, past Novouzensk, Aleksandrov-Gai, and Furmanovo, to salt lake in Caspian Lowland E of Novaya Kazanka. **Lesser Uzen River** Rus. *Maly Uzen*, rises S of Yershov, flows (parallel to and W of the Greater Uzen) S, past Piterka, and SSE, past Kaztalovka, to small lake just SE of Novaya Kazanka; 260 mi. long.

Uzerche (üzârsh′), town (pop. 2,603), Corrèze dept., S central France, above gorge of Vézère R. and 15 mi. NW of Tulle; road center and livestock market; paper milling, tanning, flour milling. Of Gallo-Roman origin, it preserves several stately 15th–16th-cent. houses with oriels.

Uzès (üzĕs′), town (pop. 3,482), Gard dept., S France, in the Garrigues, 12 mi. N of Nîmes; produces pottery, licorice, and olive-oil; olive preserving, fruit and wheat shipping. Has former cathedral (17th cent.) with noteworthy cylindrical tower, and a 12th–14th-cent. palace of the dukes of Uzès. Episcopal see 5th cent. to 1790.

Uzès-le-Duc (-lü-dük′), agr. village (pop. 1,365), Oran dept., NW Algeria, near the Mina, 31 mi. ENE of Mascara; rail junction.

Uzetsu, Japan: see USETSU.

Uzgen (ōōzgyĕn′), city (1939 pop. 13,120), NE Osh oblast, Kirghiz SSR, on the Kara Darya, on rail-

road and 30 mi. NE of Osh; cotton; metalworks. Center of coal basin (E) with mining at TUYUK and KARA-TYUBE. Once an active livestock-trading center; declined economically until reached by railroad in late 1940s, whereupon began the development of the coal basin.

Uzha Srbiya, republic, Yugoslavia: see SERBIA.

Uzhgorod (ōōzh′gŭrŭt), Czech *Užhorod* (ōōsh′-hôrôt), Hung. *Ungvár* (ōōng′gvär), city (1941 pop. 35,250), ⊙ Transcarpathian Oblast, Ukrainian SSR, on Uzh R., near Czech border, 165 mi. ENE of Budapest, 380 mi. WSW of Kiev; 48°40′N 22°18′E. Economic and cultural center; rail junction; airport; important woodworking (notably furniture) industry; processing of margarine, alcohol, liquors; flour milling, metalworking; brick kilns. Hydroelectric power station. Has univ. (1945). Medieval castle fortress, 16th-cent. palace, colorful Russian Orthodox church here. City dates from 13th cent. A town of Austria-Hungary, it passed 1920 to Czechoslovakia, 1938 to Hungary, and 1945 to USSR.

Uzhitse, Yugoslavia: see TITOVO UZICE.

Uzhok Pass (ōō′zhŭk), Czech *Užok* (ōō′zhôk), Pol. *Użok* (ōō′zhôk), Hung. *Uzsok* (ōō′zhôk), pass (alt. 2,876 ft.), in SW Ukrainian SSR, in Beshchady Mts., 34 mi. NE of Uzhgorod; important rail and highway corridor. Uzh R. rises here.

Uzhorod, Ukrainian SSR: see UZHGOROD.

Uzh River (ōōzh), Czech *Už* or *Uh* (ōōsh, ōō), Hung. *Ung* (ōōng). **1** In W Transcarpathian Oblast, Ukrainian SSR, and SE Slovakia, Czechoslovakia; rises just SE of Uzhok Pass, flows c.70 mi. generally SW, past Uzhgorod, to Laborec R. 11 mi. SSE of Michalovce, Czechoslovakia. **2** In N Ukrainian SSR, rises E of Novograd-Volynski in Pripet Marshes, flows c.125 mi. E, past Korosten and Kaganovichi Pervye (head of navigation), to Pripet R. at Chernobyl.

Uzhur (ōō-zhōōr′), town (1948 pop. over 10,000), SW Krasnoyarsk Territory, Russian SFSR, 120 mi. WSW of Krasnoyarsk and on Achinsk-Abakan RR; ceramic and metal industries.

Uzi, Japan: see UJI.

goslavia: see TITOVO UZICE.
in), village (1926 pop. 5,954), central
st, Ukrainian SSR, 13 mi. E of Belaya
sugar refining.
ska: see OUZINKIE.
a, Japan: see UJI-YAMADA.
(ōōzlŭvī′ŭ), city (1940 pop. 20,851),
v oblast, Russian SFSR, 7 mi. SSW of
sk; rail junction; metalworking, food
. Lignite mines near by. Became city in
ring Second World War, briefly held
Germans in Moscow campaign.
-voi′ŭ), village (1939 pop. 643), E Kali-
blast, Russian SFSR, 10 mi. NW of
sk. Until 1945, in East Prussia and called
rg (rou′tŏŏnberk″).
ōts′näkh), town (pop. 2,487), St. Gall
Switzerland, on stream Steinerbach and
of Rapperswil; cotton and silk textiles.
cent. nunnery.
U nd, E Germany and Poland: see USE-

U inian SSR: see UZHOK PASS.
U ania: see OZUN.
U ainian SSR: see UZHOK PASS.
U **Ozuakoli** (ōōzwä′kōlē), town, Owerri
stern Provinces, S Nigeria, on railroad
NW of Bende; market center; palm oil
s. Leper settlement.
U (ōōzōōn″-ŭgäch′), village (1939 pop.
), SW Alma-Ata oblast, Kazakh SSR,
s-Ili Ala-Tau, 32 mi. W of Alma-Ata, in
gr. area (wheat, tobacco, garden fruit);
ng.
Uz (ōōzōōn′kûprü), Turkish *Uzunköprü*,
to pop. 12,059), Adrianople prov., Turkey
in on Ergene R., on railroad 28 mi. SSE
of ple; market center (wheat, rye, rice).
S ite in area. Sometimes spelled Uzun
K
Uzv zerland: see OBERUZWIL.
Uzz zä′nô), village (pop. 216), Pistoia prov.,
Tu entral Italy, 1 mi. E of Pescia; paper
mi dry.

V

Vaagaamo, Norway: see VAGAMO.

Vaago (vô′wû), Dan. *Vaagø*, Faeroese *Vágar*, island (□ 69; pop. 2,256) of the W Faeroe Isls.; c.14 mi. long, 7 mi. wide. Terrain high in NW; highest point 2,368 ft. In S is Sorvaag L. (c.4 mi. long, ½ mi. wide; Dan. *Sørvaag*, Faeroese *Sörvágs*), largest in the Faeroes. W coast is cut by Sørvaag Fjord (6 mi. long). Fishing, sheep raising.

Vaagsoy, Norway: see VAGSOY.

Vaaifetu (vä′ĭfä′tōō), peak (3,608 ft.), Upolu, Western Samoa, 9 mi. SE of Apia.

Vaajakoski (vä′yäkōs″kē), village in Jyväskylä rural commune (pop. 19,929), Vaasa co., S central Finland, on small lake near N end of L. Päijänne, 5 mi. E of Jyväskylä; paper milling, woodworking; mfg. of matches, clothing.

Vaalbank Dam (väl′băngk, Afrikaans fäl′bängk), Orange Free State and Transvaal, U. of So. Afr., on Vaal R., 50 mi. SSE of Johannesburg, 20 mi. SE of Vereeniging, at NW end of irrigation reservoir (□ 63). Near by is Deneysville, seaplane base for Johannesburg.

Vaaldam, U. of So. Afr.: see DENEYSVILLE.

Vaale, Norway: see VALE.

Vaalebru, Norway: see RINGEBU.

Vaal River (väl), U. of So. Afr., rises in SE Transvaal near Swaziland border N of Ermelo, flows SW to Standerton, thence W and WSW, forming border bet. Transvaal and Orange Free State, through extensive Vaalbank Dam irrigation works, past Vereeniging and Barkly West, crossing into Cape Prov., to Orange R. 7 mi. WSW of Kimberley; c.750 mi. long. Receives Wilge, Hartz, and several smaller rivers.

Vaals (väls), town (pop. 5,956), Limburg prov., SE Netherlands, 3 mi. W of Aachen (Germany), on Ger. border; mfg. (needles, woolens, cement, tobacco products); chalk quarrying. The Vaalserberg, highest point (1,056 ft.) in the Netherlands, is 1 mi. S, at junction of Netherlands, Belg., and Ger. frontiers.

Vaasa, Swedish *Vasa* (both: vä′sä), county [Finnish *lääni*] (□ 15,061; including water area, □ 16,011; pop. 608,320), W Finland; ⊙ Vaasa. On Gulf of Bothnia, it has indented coast line, protected by several small isls. Surface is low and level near coast, rises toward E (lake region). Drained by Lapua, Pyhä, and several smaller rivers. Generally wooded, co. has important lumbering and timber-processing industry. Feldspar and limestone quarries. Mfg. industries in coastal cities; Jakobstad is a center of tobacco-processing industry. Considerable part of pop. is Swedish-speaking. Cities are Vaasa, Jyväskylä, Kokkola, Jakobstad, Nykarleby, Kasko, and Kristinestad.

Vaasa, Swedish *Vasa*, city (pop. 33,993), ⊙ Vaasa co., W Finland, on inlet of Gulf of Bothnia, 220 mi. NW of Helsinki; 63°8′N 21°42′E. Seaport, shipping timber and wood products, with regular steamer lines to Sweden; rail terminus; airport. Fisheries. Lumber, cotton, hosiery, and flour mills, sugar refineries, large bakeries, motor and soap works. Almost half of pop. is Swedish-speaking. Many modern bldgs. include Ostrobothnian historical mus. and city library. Founded 1606, inc. 1611, city was rebuilt closer to sea after destructive fire (1852) and renamed Nikolainkaupunki or Nikolaistad (until 1918). During Finnish war of independence (1918) ⊙ White Finland.

Vaassen or **Vasen** (both: vä′sŭn), town (pop. 5,931), Gelderland prov., E central Netherlands, 5 mi. N of Apeldoorn; metal foil, chemicals, ink, lacquer, soap powder, cigars, wooden shoes, coconut-fiber mats; iron foundry.

Vabkent (vŭpkyĕnt′), village (1926 pop. 1,825), S Bukhara oblast, Uzbek SSR, 18 mi. N of Bukhara; cotton; metalworks.

Vabre (vä′brŭ), village (pop. 991), Tarn dept., S France, in the Monts de Lacaune, 11 mi. NE of Castres; textile milling.

Vac (väts), Hung. *Vác*, Ger. *Waitzen*, city (pop. 22,130), Pest-Pilis-Solt-Kiskun co., N central Hungary, on the Danube and 19 mi. N of Budapest; rail junction, river port; market center. Mfg. (zinc plates, photographic supplies, radiators, surveying instruments, furniture, buttons, textiles, shoes, soap, candles); distilleries, flour mills, cement works. Bishopric; 18th-cent. cathedral, episcopal palace, R.C. acad. Large prison. Summer resort. Formerly spelled Vacz or Vacs.

Vaca Diez, Bolivia: see RIBERALTA.

Vaca Guzmán (bä′kä gōōsmän′), town (pop. c. 2,000), ⊙ Luis Calvo prov., Chuquisaca dept., SE Bolivia, on Camiri-Tintín oil pipe line, 20 mi. NW of Camiri; straw hat mfg., tobacco, corn, sugar cane, fruit. Until c.1945, Muyupampa.

Vaca Key, Fla.: see FLORIDA KEYS.

Vacaria (vŭkŭrē′ŭ), city (pop. 4,189), NE Rio Grande do Sul, Brazil, in the Serra Geral, 50 mi. NNE of Caxias do Sul; wheat, clover, tobacco; cattle and horse raising. Formerly spelled Vaccaria.

Vacas (bä′käs), town (pop. c.8,100), Cochabamba dept., central Bolivia, in Cordillera de Cochabamba, on road and 15 mi. E of Arani; barley, corn, potatoes.

Vacas, Las, Chile: see LAS VACAS.

Vacaville (vă′kŭvĭl, vä′–), town (pop. 3,169), Solano co., W central Calif., 30 mi. WSW of Sacramento; fruit processing and shipping. Founded 1850, inc. 1892.

Vaccarès, Étang de, France: see CAMARGUE.

Vaccaria, Brazil: see VACARIA.

Vacha (fä′khä), town (pop. 4,383), Thuringia, cent many, at N foot of Rhön Mts., on the Wer 17 mi. SW of Eisenach, opposite Philippsthal; (machinery, electrical equipment); stone ying. Has remains of medieval walls.

Vacha hŭ), town (1939 pop. over 500), SW Gork st, Russian SFSR, 16 mi. SW of Pavl etalworking center.

Vacha (vŭ′chä), S central Bulgaria, formed just evin by confluence of streams rising in W Rh Mts.; flows 75 mi. N, past Devin and Krich Maritsa R. 7 mi. W of Plovdiv. Sometimes d Vicha. Formerly called Krichim R.

Vache, (ēl ä väsh′), Caribbean island (□ 20), off SW ti, 7 mi. SSE of Les Cayes; 8 mi. long, c.2 mi. . Cotton, citrus fruit, cattle. Chromite deposi so spelled Île à Vaches.

Vachi (ē′), village, S Dagestan Autonomous SSR, R n SFSR, in the E Greater Caucasus, 15 mi. SS Kumukh; hardy grain, sheep. Pop. largely , one of Dagestan mtn. tribes.

Vacoas ō′ŭs), residential town (pop. 10,756), W cent Mauritius, in central plateau, on railroad an ½ mi. NW of Curepipe. Sugar milling and dis g at Réunion (just S). The Mare aux Vacoas rvoir (4 mi. S) supplies drinking water to Plain Wilhems residential dist., irrigates W coast ca elds and feeds Tamarin R. hydroelectric station.

Vacs or **V** Hungary: see VAC.

Vad (väd) llage (pop. 447), Kopparberg co., central Swe , on Kolback R. and 5 mi. WNW of Fagersta wmilling, woodworking.

Vad (vät), lage (1926 pop. 1,685), S Gorki oblast, Russian SR, 17 mi. NE of Arzamas; wheat, hemp.

Vada (vä′ village (pop. 1,279), Livorno prov., Tuscany, tral Italy, 16 mi. SSE of Leghorn, on coast of L rian Sea; sulphur oils.

Vada Arka India: see NORTH ARCOT.

Vadagaon, lia: see WADGAON, Kolhapur dist.

Vadakku Viyur (vŭdŭk′kōō vŭl-lēyōōr′), town (pop. 8,845 Tinnevelly dist., S Madras, India, 25 mi. SSW of innevelly, in grain area. Also called Vallioor.

Vadakku Viravanallur, India: see VIRAVANALLUR.

Vadali (vŭdä), town (pop. 5,450), Sabar Kantha dist., N Bombay, India, 24 mi. NNE of Himatnagar; wheat, rie, millet; pottery mfg.

Vadavar Canal (vä′dŭvär), Tanjore dist., SE Madras, India, exends from Vennar R. c.30 mi. generally SE, serving area SE of Tanjore, around Mannargudi.

Vader (vā′dûr), town (pop. 426), Lewis co., SW Wash., 15 mi. N of Kelso; agr.

Vadgaon (vŭd′goun). **1** Town, Kolhapur district, Bombay, India: see WADGAON. **2** Village (pop. 1,803), Poona dist., central Bombay, India, 22 mi.

NW of Poona; local market for millet, gur, wheat. Scene of Mahratta victory (1779) over British. Sometimes spelled Wadgaon.

Vadheim, Norway: see HOYANGER.

Vadi, India: see SAVANTVADI, town.

Vadia (väd'yŭ), former Western Kathiawar state (□ 90; pop. 16,818) of Western India States agency; merged 1948 with Saurashtra. Sometimes called Wadia.

Vadigenhalli (vŭ'dĭgĕnhŭlē), town (pop. 4,607), Bangalore dist., E Mysore, India, 25 mi. NE of Bangalore; trades in cotton, tobacco.

Vadillo de la Sierra (bä-dhē'lyō dhä lä syĕ'rä), town (pop. 881), Ávila prov., central Spain, 23 mi. W of Ávila; stock raising; flour milling.

Vadinsk (vä'dyĭnsk), village (1926 pop. 9,958), NW Penza oblast, Russian SFSR, 28 mi. WNW of Nizhni Lomov, in grain area; potatoes, legumes, hemp. Was a 16th-cent. fortress. Until c.1940, Kerensk.

Vadnagar (vŭd'nŭgŭr), town (pop. 13,550), Mehsana dist., N Bombay, India, 20 mi. NE of Mehsana; trade center for millet, pulse, wheat, oilseeds; handicraft cloth weaving, dyeing, printing. Has fine Hindu gateway.

Vadocondes (bä"dhōkōn'dĕs), town (pop. 997), Burgos prov., N Spain, on the Douro (Duero) and 7 mi. E of Aranda de Duero.

Vado Ligure (vä'dō lē'gōōrĕ), anc. *Vada Sabatia*, town (pop. 4,979), Savona prov., Liguria, NW Italy, port on Gulf of Genoa and 3 mi. SW of Savona, in cherry- and peach-growing region. Industrial center: iron- and steelworks; railroad shops; shipyards; petroleum refinery, coke and ammonia plants, porcelain factory. Quartz quarry near by.

Vadonville (vädōvēl'), village (pop. 295), Meuse dept., NE France, on the Canal de l'Est and 4 mi. NW of Commercy; rail junction; foundry.

Vadso (väts'ü), Nor. *Vadsø*, city (pop. 2,107), ⊙ Finnmark co., N Norway, on N side of mouth of Varanger Fjord, 150 mi. ENE of Hammerfest, 110 mi. NW of Murmansk; 70°4'N 29°47'E. Fishing center; fish-oil and guano processing; trades in reindeer skins and meat. City center destroyed in Second World War. Has considerable Finnish pop.

Vadstena (väd'stä"nä, väs'tā"nä), city (pop. 3,129), Ostergotland co., S central Sweden, on NE shore of L. Vatter, 25 mi. W of Linkoping; lake port (on Gota Canal route); lace-making center; popular tourist resort. Its cloister (founded c.1370 by St. Bridget of Sweden; secularized 1595) gave town great religious importance and made it center of pilgrimages. Has castle built 1545 by Gustavus Vasa; 15th-cent. town hall.

Vaduj (vŭdōōj'), village (pop. 5,505), Satara North dist., central Bombay, India, 32 mi. ESE of Satara; agr. market (millet, wheat).

Vadului-Voda or **Vaduluy-Voda** (vŭdōōlōō"ē-vŭdä'), Rum. *Vadu-lui-Vodă* (vä'dōō-lōō'ē-vō'dŭ), village (1941 pop. 1,103), E central Moldavian SSR, on Dniester R. and 12 mi. ENE of Kishinev; orchards, vineyards. Site of projected hydroelectric dam on the Dniester linked by navigable canal with Kishinev.

Vaduri (vädōōr') or **Vadurile** (vädōō'rĭlyĕ), village, Bacau prov., NE Rumania, in Moldavia, on Bistrita R. and 7 mi. W of Piatra-Neamt; lumber-milling center.

Vaduz (vädōōts'), town (pop. 2,041), ⊙ principality of Liechtenstein, near the Rhine (Swiss border), 22 mi. SSE of Saint Gall (Switzerland) and 8 mi. SW of Feldkirch (Austria), in agr. region (corn, wheat, potatoes, wine, cattle). Mfg. of cotton goods. Residence of ruling prince. Over it towers castle (rebuilt in 16th cent., after being destroyed by Swiss); Three Sisters peak in background.

Vaenga, Russian SFSR: see VAYENGA.

Vaerdal River, Norway: VERDAL RIVER.

Vaeroy (vâr'üü), Nor. *Værøy*, island (□ 6; pop. 1,145) in North Sea, one of the Lofoten Isls., Nordland co., N Norway, 10 mi. S of Moskenesoy, 55 mi. WNW of Bodo; fishing, fowling; summer resort. Vaeroy village is in N.

Vafio, Greece: see VAPHIO.

Vag, river, Czechoslovakia: see VAH RIVER.

Vaga, Tunisia: see BÉJA.

Vagagno, Monte, Yugoslavia: see VELEBIT MOUNTAINS.

Vagai or **Vagay** (vŭgī'). **1** Town (1948 pop. over 500), S Tyumen oblast, Russian SFSR, on Trans-Siberian RR, on upper Vagai R. and 40 mi. ESE of Yalutorovsk; dairying. **2** Village (1939 pop. over 500), S Tyumen oblast, Russian SFSR, on Irtysh R., at mouth of Vagai R., and 35 mi. SE of Tobolsk, in agr. area (flax, grain, livestock).

Vagai River or **Vagay River**, S Tyumen oblast, Russian SFSR, rises near Trans-Siberian RR, flows 170 mi. N, past Aromashevo, through densely populated valley, to Irtysh R. at Vagai village. Yermak, 16th-cent. conqueror of Siberia, was killed near its mouth.

Vagamo (vô'gômô), Nor. *Vågåmo*, village (pop. 442) in Vaga (Nor. *Vågå*) canton (pop. 3,740), Opland co., S central Norway, on Otta R. at E end of Vagavatn expansion, 70 mi. NW of Lillehammer; dairying, lumbering; steatite quarry. Sometimes spelled Vaagaamo.

Vagan, canton, Norway: see KABELVAG.

Vaganjski Vrh, Yugoslavia: see VELEBIT MOUNTAINS.

Vagar, Faeroe Isls.: see VAAGO.

Vaga River (vä'gŭ), in N European Russian SFSR, rises W of Totma (Vologda oblast), flows 330 mi. NNE, past Verkhovazhye, Velsk (Archangel oblast), and Shenkursk, to Northern Dvina R. SE of Semenovskoye. Navigable for 235 mi. below Velsk. Important trade route in 14th–15th cent.

Vagarshapat, Armenian SSR: see ECHMIADZIN.

Vagay, Russian SFSR: see VAGAI.

Vagbeszterce, Czechoslovakia: see POVAZSKA BYSTRICA.

Vagen, Norway: see BERGEN.

Vaggeryd (vä'gürüd"), village (pop. 1,773), Jonkoping co., S Sweden, on Laga R. and 19 mi. S of Jonkoping; rail junction; furniture mfg., pulp milling.

Vaghia, Greece: see VAGIA.

Vaghodia (vŭgōd'yŭ), town (pop. 4,025), Baroda dist., N Bombay, India, 12 mi. E of Baroda; market center for cotton, oilseeds, rice, millet.

Vagia or **Vayia** (both: vä'yēä), town (pop. 3,327), Boeotia nome, E central Greece, 7 mi. W of Thebes; livestock raising. Also spelled Vaghia.

Vagney (vänyā'), village (pop. 945), Vosges dept., E France, on Moselotte R. and 6 mi. E of Remiremont, in the Vosges; granite quarrying.

Vagonoremont (vŭgō"nŭrĭmônt'), town (1926 pop. 919), central Moscow oblast, Russian SFSR, on railroad (Lianozovo station) and 10 mi. NNW of Moscow; railroad shops, brickworks.

Vagonozavod, Russian SFSR: see NIZHNI TAGIL.

Vagos (vä'gōōsh), town (pop. 2,027), Aveiro dist., N central Portugal, 6 mi. SSW of Aveiro; mfg. (chinaware, footwear).

Vagra (vä'grŭ), village, Broach dist., N Bombay, India, 13 mi. NW of Broach; local market for millet; wheat; cotton ginning.

Vag River, Czechoslovakia: see VAH RIVER.

Vagsoy (vôks'üü), Nor. *Vågsøy*, island (□ 24; pop. 3,480) in North Sea, Sogn og Fjordane co., W Norway, N of Nord Fjord mouth, separated from mainland by narrow strait, 24 mi. N of Floro; 7 mi. long, 5 mi. wide; fishing. At Maloy (môl'üü) (Nor. *Måløy*, sometimes *Maaløy*, formerly *Moldøy*) village (pop. 1,805), in Sor-Vagsoy canton (pop. 2,837), at SE tip, there is canning of fish and lobsters. Isl. sometimes spelled Vaagsoy.

Vagthus Point (väg'thŭs), headland, S St. Croix Isl., U.S. Virgin Isls., 3 mi. S of Christiansted; 17°42'N 64°43'W.

Vagujhely, Czechoslovakia: see NOVE MESTO NAD VAHOM.

Vahanga, Tuamotu Isls.: see ACTAEON ISLANDS.

Vah River (vä), Slovak *Váh*, Ger. *Waag* (väk), Hung. *Vág* (väg), W Slovakia, Czechoslovakia, formed on N slope of the Low Tatra 22 mi. WSW of Poprad by union of Biely Vah R. (Slovak *Biely Váh*), rising on Krivan Peak in the High Tatra, and the Cierny Vah R. (Slovak *Cierny Váh*), rising on Kralova Hola peak in the Low Tatra; flows W, past Liptovsky Svaty Mikulas, Ruzomberok, and Zilina, in a narrow gorge through the Lesser Fatra, then SSW, past Trencin, and S, past Piestany, across the Little Alföld, to the Danube at Komarno; 245 mi. long. Receives Orava and Little Danube rivers (right), Nitra R. (left). Dammed in middle course, near Puchov.

Vaiano (väyä'nô), village (pop. 2,039), Firenze prov., Tuscany, central Italy, 6 mi. N of Prato; woolen mill.

Vaico River (vī'kō'), short stream of Cochin China, in S Vietnam, formed E of Tanan by 2 long headstreams rising in Cambodia, flows 30 mi. E to the Dongnai-Saigon delta. The West Vaico flows 120 mi. SE, past Soairieng, through the Plaine des Joncs, past Gobacchien (head of navigation), and Tanan; the East Vaico flows 120 mi. SSE and is navigable by 5-ft.-draught vessels to area of Tayninh.

Vaida-Guba, Russian SFSR: see RYBACHI PENINSULA.

Vaiden (vä'dŭn), town (pop. 583), a ⊙ Carroll co., central Miss., 27 mi. ESE of Greenwood, in cotton and timber region.

Vaidisvarankovil, India: see VAITHISVARANKOIL.

Vaigach Island or **Vaygach Island** (vīgäch') (□ 1,430), in Arctic Ocean bet. Barents (W) and Kara (E) seas; forms part of Nenets Natl. Okrug, Archangel oblast, Russian SFSR; separated from Novaya Zemlya (N) by strait Karskiye Vorota, from mainland (S) by strait Yugorski Shar; 60 mi. long, 30 mi. wide; tundra, hilly in center. Nenets (formerly called Samoyed) pop. engaged in fishing, seal hunting, reindeer raising. Govt. observation stations at Varnek (S coast; site of lead mine) and at Vaigach, near the N cape Bolvanski Nos.

Vaigai River (vī'gī), in Madura and Ramnad dists., S Madras, India, rises on N Kottai Malai peak in Western Ghats, flows NNE through fertile agr. Kambam Valley, and SE past Solavandan, Madura, and Paramagudi to Palk Bay of Palk Strait 11 mi. ESE of Ramnad; 165 mi. long. Irrigation canals (length of main channel, c.45 mi.) of PERIYAR LAKE project begin at Peranai Dam, 8 mi. WNW of Solavandan and run E through sugarcane and rice area. Receives Suruli R. (left).

Vaigat (vī'gät), strait (90 mi. long, 6–15 mi. wide), W Greenland, extends NW–SE bet. Baffin Bay and head of Disko Bay; 70°10'N 53°W. Separates Disko isl. (SW) and Nugssuak peninsula (NE).

Vaihingen (fī'ĭng-ŭn). **1** Town (pop. 4,552), N Württemberg, Germany, after 1945 in Württemberg-Baden, on the Enz and 8 mi. WSW of Bietigheim; grain, cattle. Has 16th-cent. castle. **2** SW suburb of Stuttgart, N Württemberg, Germany, after 1945 in Württemberg-Baden, 5 mi. SW of city center. Inc. 1942 into Stuttgart.

Vaijapur (vī'jäpōōr), town (pop. 8,507), Aurangabad dist., NW Hyderabad state, India, 40 mi. W of Aurangabad; road center; cotton, millet, wheat, oilseeds; match mfg. Sometimes spelled Vijapur.

Vaikam (vī'kŭm), city (pop. 15,246), NW Travancore, India, on navigable lagoon, 15 mi. NNW of Kottayam; rice milling, cashew-nut and cassava processing; coir mats and rope, brassware.

Vail, town (pop. 532), Crawford co., W Iowa, 17 mi. W of Carroll, in agr. area.

Vaila (vā'lŭ), island (pop. 5) of the Shetlands, Scotland, off W coast of Mainland isl. across Vaila Sound, 11 mi. WNW of Scalloway; 1½ mi. long, 1 mi. wide; rises to 264 ft. Lighthouse (60°12'N 1°33'W).

Vailate (vēlä'tē), village (pop. 2,677), Cremona prov., Lombardy, N Italy, 20 mi. E of Milan; mfg. of mill machinery.

Vailima (vīlē'mä), estate, home of Robert Louis Stevenson on Upolu, Western Samoa, where he lived for 5 years. His tomb is on summit of near-by Mt. Vaea.

Vailly (väyē'), village (pop. 1,623), Aisne dept., N France, on Aisne R. (canalized) and 9 mi. ENE of Soissons; livestock market. Also called Vailly-sur-Aisne.

Vailly-sur-Sauldre (-sür-sō'drŭ), village (pop. 605), Cher dept., central France, on Grande Sauldre R. and 14 mi. WNW of Cosne; livestock and fruit market; woodworking.

Vail Pass, Colo.: see GORE RANGE.

Vainikkala (vī'nĭk-kä"lä), village in Ylämaa commune (pop. 3,259), Kymi co., SE Finland, 25 mi. SSE of Lappeenranta; frontier station on USSR border, 20 mi. NW of Vyborg, on Helsinki-Leningrad main line.

Vairag (vī'räg), town (pop. 4,713), Sholapur dist., E Bombay, India, 13 mi. SSE of Barsi; market center for cotton, peanuts, millet.

Vaires-sur-Marne (vâr-sür-märn'), town (pop. 5,281), Seine-et-Marne dept., N central France, on right bank of Marne R. (canalized) and 14 mi. E of Paris; mfg. (building materials, hardware).

Vair River (vâr), Vosges dept., E France, rises in the Monts Faucilles near Vittel, flows c.25 mi. NNW to the Meuse below Coussey.

Vaisali, India: see LALGANJ, Muzaffarpur dist.

Vaison-la-Romaine (väzō'-lä-rômĕn'), anc. *Vasio*, town (pop. 2,188), Vaucluse dept., SE France, on the Ouvèze and 13 mi. N of Carpentras; mfg. (agr. and viticultural instruments, electrical appliances, cartons, flour products). Modern town, on right bank, occupies site of Roman resort; medieval city on rocky left bank. Roman ruins include a theater, bridge, and a villa. Among medieval bldgs. are 12th-cent. Romanesque church, cloister and chapel. Episcopal see from 4th cent. to 1790. Town was center of Fr. underground resistance in the Second World War.

Vaithisvarankoil or **Vaitheeswarankoil** (vītēs"-vŭrŭngkō'ĭl), town (pop. 3,882), Tanjore dist., SE Madras, India, in Cauvery R. delta, 7 mi. NNE of Mayavaram; rice, plantain, mangoes. Formerly spelled Vaidisvarankovil.

Vaitolahti, Russian SFSR: see RYBACHI PENINSULA.

Vaitupu (vītōō'pōō), atoll (□ 2.1; pop. 728), central Ellice Isls., SW Pacific; 7°30'S 178°42'E; copra. Site of govt. school.

Vaivara or **Vayvara** (vī'värä), rail junction in NE Estonia, 15 mi. W of Narva; rail spur to Vivikond oil-shale mine. Sillamae refinery is 1 mi. N. Vaivara village is 3 mi. E, on railroad.

Vaja (vä'ä"), Swedish *Väja*, village (pop. 2,274), Vasternorrland co., E central Sweden, on Angerman R. estuary and 25 mi. NNW of Harnosand; lumber, pulp, and paper mills. Includes Dynas (dü'nĕs"), Swed. *Dynäs*, village.

Vajdahunyad, Rumania: see HUNEDOARA, town.

Vajern (vä'ürn), Swedish *Väjern*, village (pop. 258), Goteborg och Bohus co., SW Sweden, on the Skagerrak, 9 mi. NW of Lysekil; stone quarrying.

Vajnory (vī'nôrĭ), Hung. *Pozsonyszőllős* (pô'-zhônyŭsŭl"lŭsh), town (pop. 2,640), SW Slovakia, Czechoslovakia, on railroad and 6 mi. NE of Bratislava; site of municipal airport for Bratislava.

Vakarel (väkärĕl'), village (pop. 2,940), Sofia dist., W central Bulgaria, in Ikhtiman Sredna Gora, 10 mi. NNW of Ikhtiman; sheep, hardy grain. Site of major Sofia radio transmitter. **Vakarel Pass** (alt. 2,696 ft.), just S of Vakarel, on highway to Plovdiv, separates Sofia and Ikhtiman basins.

Vakfikebir (väkfŭ'kĕbĭr"), Turkish *Vakfıkebir*, village (pop. 1,341), Trebizond prov., NE Turkey, port on Black Sea 22 mi. W of Trebizond; corn, wheat, potatoes, sugar beets. Formerly Buyukliman.

Vakh, Russian SFSR: see VAKH RIVER.

Vakhan (vŭkhän'), village, SW Gorno-Badakhshan Autonomous Oblast, Tadzhik SSR, in the Pamir, on Panj R., at junction of Pamir and Vakhan rivers, and 55 mi. SE of Khorog; wheat. Mineral springs. Until c.1935, Zung.

Vakh River (väkh), E Khanty-Mansi Natl. Okrug, Tyumen oblast, Russian SFSR, rises in Ob-Yenisei divide, flows 560 mi. W, past Laryak, to Ob R. 110 mi. E of Surgut. Part of former trade route from the Ob to the Yenisei.

Vakhrushev (vŭkrōō'shĭf), town (1940 pop. 5,137), S Sakhalin, Russian SFSR, on E coast railroad and 18 mi. SSW of Poronaisk; coal mining. Under Jap. rule (1905–45), called Tomarikishi (tōmä'rēkĭshē).

Vakhrushi (–shē), town (1939 pop. over 2,000), N central Kirov oblast, Russian SFSR, on Slobodskoi rail spur and 12 mi. NE of Kirov; shoe mfg.

Vakhsh (väkhsh), town (1941 pop. over 500), S Stalinabad oblast, Tadzhik SSR, in Vakhsh valley, 5 mi. NW of Kurgan-Tyube, in long-staple-cotton dist.; cotton ginning.

Vakhsh River, a headstream of the Amu Darya, S Tadzhik SSR; formed by junction of SURKHAB RIVER and OBI-KHINGOU RIVER near Komsomolabad; flows c.200 mi. SW, past Komsomolabad and Nurek, through rich Vakhsh valley (cotton, subtropical crops; irrigated by Vakhsh canal system) centered at Kurgan-Tyube, joining Panj R. on Afghanistan border 18 mi. SW of Nizhni Pyandzh to form the AMU DARYA.

Vakhshstroi or **Vakhshstroy** (vŭkhsh-stroi'), town (1939 pop. over 500), S Stalinabad oblast, Tadzhik SSR, in Vakhsh valley, 9 mi. SSE of Kurgan-Tyube, in long-staple-cotton dist.; irrigation canal installations. Hydroelectric station.

Vakhtan (vŭkhtän'), town (1939 pop. over 2,000), NE Gorki oblast, Russian SFSR, on rail spur and 30 mi. ENE of Vetluga; sawmilling, wood cracking (rosins)

Vaksdal (väks'däl), village (pop 917) in Bruvik canton, Hordaland co., SW Norway, on Sor Fjord, on railroad and 16 mi. ENE of Bergen; mfg. of furniture, flour.

Vaku (vä'kōō), village, Leopoldville prov., W Belgian Congo, 40 mi. NNE of Boma; palm-oil milling, rubber plantations. R. C. mission.

Val (väl), Hung. *Vál*, town (pop. 2,778), Fejer co., N central Hungary, 16 mi. NE of Szekesfehervar; corn, sheep, horses.

Vala (vŭl'ŭ), town (pop 4,665), E Saurashtra, India, 19 mi. WNW of Bhaunagar; local agr. market (millet, wheat, cotton); cotton ginning. Close by is very old site of *Vallabhipur*, where strong dynasty ruled from c.480 to 790; visited c.640 by Hsüan-tsang; coins, copper plates, and terra-cotta images have been found among ruins. Vala was ⊙ former Eastern Kathiawar state of Vala (□ 190; pop. 16,197) of Western India States agency; state merged 1948 with Saurashtra.

Valaam Island (vä'lŭäm), Finnish *Valamo* (vä'lämô) (□ 10), in N L. Ladoga, SW Karelo-Finnish SSR, 23 mi. SSE of Sortavala (boat connection); 5 mi. long, 4 mi. wide; rises to 200 ft. Site of noted Greek Orthodox monastery (founded 992); mainly 19th-cent. bldgs. In Finland, 1918–40.

Valabgonda, India: see ZAFARGARH.

Valachia, province, Rumania: see WALACHIA.

Valadares (vŭlŭdä'rĭsh), S suburb (pop. 3,410) of Oporto, Pôrto dist., N Portugal, on railroad to Aveiro, near the Atlantic.

Valado dos Frades (vŭlä'dōō dōōsh frä'dĭsh), village (pop. 1,807), Leiria dist., W central Portugal, on railroad and 2 mi. SE of Nazaré; processing of forest products.

Valais (välā'), Ger. *Wallis* (vä'lĭs), canton (□ 2,021; 1950 pop. 158,227), S Switzerland, in upper Rhone valley from its source to its influx into L. Geneva; ⊙ Sion. In the valleys of the Rhone and its tributaries there are meadows and fertile fields (cereals), with some orchards, gardens, and vineyards (wine making) along the Rhone; lower mtn. slopes become covered with forests, then pastures (stock raising). Nearly half the cantonal area, entirely unproductive, includes high peaks and glaciers of the (N) Bernese and (S) Pennine Alps. Some of Switzerland's highest peaks (Matterhorn, Dufourspitze, Dom, Weisshorn) form the cantonal frontier, which includes Fr. and Ital. borders. Valais has a well-developed hydroelectric system (highest capacity plant at Chandoline). Numerous resorts and winter sports centers (largest, ZERMATT). Mfg. chiefly metal products and chemicals; some coal mining, wool production. Pop. mainly French speaking and Catholic. Taken by Romans in 57 B.C., Valais later passed to Burgundians and Franks. It was a canton of the Helvetic Republic (1802), a Fr. département (1810), and, finally, a Swiss canton (1815).

Valais Alps, Switzerland: see PENNINE ALPS.

Valaksa, Greece: see VALAXA.

Valam (vä'lŭm), town (pop. 5,010), Mehsana dist., N Bombay, India, 9 mi. NNE of Mehsana; agr. market (millet).

Valamaz (vŭlŭmäs'), town (1939 pop. over 2,000), W Udmurt Autonomous SSR, Russian SFSR, 60 mi. NW of Izhevsk; lumbering; livestock. Quartz sand deposits near by. Glassworks, porcelain mfg. at Valamazski Zavod (1926 pop. 1,173), 5 mi. NE.

Valamo Island, Karelo-Finnish SSR: see VALAAM ISLAND.

Valandovo (vä'ländôvô), village, Macedonia, Yugoslavia, near Vardar R., 8 mi. SSW of Strumica, near Gr. border; local trade center in sericulture region. Chromium mine near by.

Val-André, Le, France: see PLÉNEUF.

Valangiman or **Valangaman** (vŭlŭng'gŭmŭn), town (pop. 5,770), Tanjore dist., SE Madras, India, on arm of Cauvery R. delta and 5 mi. S of Kumbakonam; rice, plantain, coconut palms.

Valarpattanam, India: see CANNANORE, city.

Valasske Klobouky (vä'lăshskä klô'bōkĭ), Czech *Valašské Klobouky*, Ger. *Wallachisch Klobauk* (vä'läkhĭsh klô'bouk), town (pop. 2,525), E Moravia, Czechoslovakia, on railroad and 16 mi. ESE of Gottwaldov; slipper mfg. Lysa Pass is 5 mi. NE.

Valasske Mezirici (mĕ'zĭrzhēchē), Czech *Valašské Meziříčí*, Ger. *Wallachisch Meseritsch* (vä'läkhĭsh mä'zŭrĭch), town (pop. 8,513), E Moravia, Czechoslovakia, at junction of Horni Becva and Dolni Becva rivers, in W foothills of the Beskids, 22 mi. NNE of Gottwaldov; rail hub; hat-mfg. center; furniture, glass. Has woodworking trade school.

Valatie (vŭlā'shŭ), village (pop. 1,225), Columbia co., SE N.Y., on Kinderhook Creek and 13 mi. NNE of Hudson, in dairying, poultry raising, and applegrowing region. Inc. 1856.

Valavanur (vŭlŭvŭnōōr'), town (pop. 7,112), South Arcot dist., E Madras, India, 6 mi. ESE of Villupuram, near border of Fr. settlement of Pondicherry; rice, cassava.

Valaxa (väläk'sŭ), uninhabited island (□ 1.7) in Aegean Sea, Euboea nome, Greece, ½ mi. off E coast of isl. of Skyros; 3 mi. long, 1 mi. wide. Sometimes spelled Valaksa.

Val Barette (väl bărĕt'), village (pop. 489), SW Que., on small L. Gauvin, in the Laurentians, 8 mi. ESE of Mont Laurier; dairying.

Valberg, France: see GUILLAUMES.

Valberg (vŏl'bĕr"yŭ), Swedish *Vålberg*, village (pop. 1,288), Varmland co., W Sweden, on Nor R. and 10 mi. W of Karlstad; sawmilling, woodworking. Includes villages of Stora Barum (stōō'rä bō'rŭm"), Swedish *Stora Bårum*, and Alvenas (ĕl'vŭnĕs"), Swedish *Älvenäs*.

Valbonnais (välbônā'), village (pop. 285), Isère dept., SE France, in Dauphiné Alps, near Bonne R. (tributary of Drac R.), 22 mi. SSE of Grenoble; cheese mfg.; orchards.

Val Brillant (väl brēlā'), village (pop. 953), SE Que., on L. Matapedia, 22 mi. SSW of Matane; dairying, lumbering.

Valbrona (välbrô'nä), village (pop. 1,131), Como prov., Lombardy, N Italy, near L. Lecco, 5 mi. WNW of Lecco; cutlery, silk textiles, machinery.

Valcartier or **Valcartier Village** (välkärtyā'), village (pop. estimate 800), S Que., 15 mi. WNW of Quebec; dairying. Near by is militia training camp.

Valcea, Rumania: see RAMNICU-VALCEA.

Valcele (vŭl'chĕlĕ), Rum. *Vâlcele*, Hung. *Előpatak* (ĕ'lŭpŏtŏk), village (pop. 709), Stalin prov., central Rumania, on W slopes of the Carpathians and 5 mi. W of Sfantu-Gheorghe; health resort (alt. 2,113 ft.) with alkaline and ferruginous springs and mud baths; bottling of mineral waters; trout fishing. In Hungary, 1940–45.

Valchedarma, Bulgaria: see VALCHEDRAMA.

Valchedrama (vŭlchĕdrŭ'mä), village (pop. 8,068), Vidin dist., NW Bulgaria, on Tsibritsa R. and 13 mi. SE of Lom; flour milling; fruit, truck, winegrowing, livestock. Formerly Valchedarma.

Valcheta (bälchā'tä), village (pop. estimate 900), ⊙ Valcheta dept., E central Río Negro natl. territory, Argentina, on railroad and 75 mi. W of San Antonio Oeste; agr. (sugar beets, potatoes, fruit, wine, sheep, cattle), lead mining.

Valchi-tran (vŭl'chē-trŭn') village (pop. 3,930), Pleven dist., N Bulgaria, 13 mi. ESE of Pleven; grain, legumes, oil-bearing plants.

Valcour Island (välkŏŏr'), Clinton co., NE N.Y., island in L. Champlain, 5 mi. SSE of Plattsburg; c.2 mi. long. Valcour village is near by, on N.Y. shore. One of 1st naval engagements in the Revolution was fought here (1776) bet. British fleet and American ships under Benedict Arnold.

Valcourt (välkŏŏr'), village (pop. 360), S Que., 20 mi. ENE of Granby; dairying center; lumbering.

Valcov, Ukrainian SSR: see VILKOVO.

Valdagno (väldä'nyô), town (pop. 6,081), Vicenza prov., Veneto, N Italy, 14 mi. NW of Vicenza, in Monti Lessini. Woolen center; mfg. (textile machinery, hydraulic presses, liquor). Lignite mines, marble and barite quarries near by.

Valdahon (väldäô'), village (pop. 787), Doubs dept., E France, 16 mi. ESE of Besançon; beer, dairy produce. Military camp near by.

Valdai or **Valday** (väldī', Rus. vŭldī'), city (1926 pop. 5,772), SE Novgorod oblast, Russian SFSR, 80 mi. SE of Novgorod, on L. Valdai (□ 15); knitting mill; dairying, metalworking. Formerly famed for making of bells. Chartered 1770.

Valdai Hills or **Valdai Uplands**, Rus. *Valdayskaya Vozvyshennost*, moraine region in W European Russian SFSR; extend c.300 mi. SW–NE; form watershed of western Dvina, Volga, and L. Ilmen basins; rise to 1,053 ft. at Mt. Kammenik, W of L. Seliger. Consists of parallel Vyshnevolotsk (SE), Ostashkov, and Valdai (NW) ridges, separated by lake-filled depressions. Principal lakes: L. Valdai, L. Seliger, L. Peno, L. Volgo.

Val-d'Ajol, Le (lŭ väl-dăzhôl'), town (pop. 2,206), Vosges dept., E France, on SW slope of the Vosges, 8 mi. SW of Remiremont; cotton milling, metalworking.

Val d'Aosta (väl däô'stä), autonomous region (□ 1,260; pop. 83,455), NW Italy; ⊙ Aosta. Borders Switzerland (N), Piedmont (E and S), and France (W). Largely French-speaking. Comprises valley of upper Dora Baltea R. (the Val d'Aosta, which extends generally NW–SE bet. Mont Blanc and Pont-Saint-Martin), and its tributary valleys, including Gressoney, Val de Cogne, and Valtournanche. Enclosed by Pennine Alps (N) and Graian Alps (S and W); along its borders are Grand Combin, Matterhorn, and Monte Rosa (N), and Gran Paradiso (SW). Agr. (cereals, grapes, potatoes) in valleys; stock (cattle, goats). Hydroelectric plants in Val d'Aosta, Gressoney, and Valtournanche. Mining at Cogne (iron), La Thuile (anthracite), Champdepraz (copper), and Brusson (gold). Mfg. at Aosta, Châtillon, Pont-Saint-Martin, and Verres. Many celebrated resorts, including Châtillon, Courmayeur, Gressoney, and Valtournanche. Has roads leading to Switzerland via Great St. Bernard Pass and to France via Little St. Bernard Pass. Formerly Aosta prov. (□ 1,838), the region became (Sept., 1945) Val d'Aosta region, independent of Piedmont, a free zone outside Ital. customs barrier, and S portion (□ 578) was returned to Torino prov., from which Aosta prov. had been formed in 1927.

Valdaracete (bäldärä-thā'tā), town (pop. 1,333), Madrid prov., central Spain, 30 mi. ESE of Madrid; olives, grapes, cereals, esparto, livestock. Wine making, olive-oil pressing.

Val d'Arno, Italy: see ARNO RIVER.

Val David (väl dävēd'), village (pop. estimate 750), S Que., in the Laurentians, on North R. and 4 mi. ESE of Ste. Agathe des Monts; dairying; ski resort.

Valdealgorfa (bäl-dhäälgôr'fä), village (pop. 1,558), Teruel prov., E Spain, 8 mi. SE of Alcañiz; olive-oil processing; cereals, wine, fruit.

Valdeazogues (bäl-dhää-thō'gĕs), mercury mines in Ciudad Real prov., S central Spain, near PUERTOLLANO.

Valdecaballeros (bäl-dhäkävälyā'rōs), town (pop. 1,529), Badajoz prov., W Spain, 9 mi. NE of Herrera del Duque; lumbering, stock raising, growing and processing of olives and grain.

Valdecabras (–kä'vräs), village (pop. 365), Cuenca prov., E central Spain, 8 mi. NE of Cuenca; potatoes, fruit, cereals, livestock; timber. Known for near-by Ciudad Encantada ("enchanted city"), a unique group of quaintly shaped rocks, resembling a city.

Valdecarros (–kä'rōs), village (pop. 1,047), Salamanca prov., W Spain, 19 mi. SE of Salamanca; cereals.

Val de Chiana, Italy: see CHIANA.

Valdefuentes (–fwĕn'tĕs), town (pop. 2,754), Cáceres prov., W Spain, 20 mi. SE of Cáceres; olive oil, wine, cereals.

Valdeganga (–gäng'gä), town (pop. 2,697), Albacete prov., SE central Spain, 14 mi. NE of Albacete; wool spinning, wine processing; hemp, cereals, saffron. Gypsum quarries near by.

Valdelacasa de Tajo (–läkä'sä dhā tä'hō), village (pop. 2,197), Cáceres prov., W Spain, 28 mi. SW of Talavera de la Reina; stock raising; cereals, olive oil, vegetables.

Valdelaguna (–lägōō'nä), town (pop. 829), Madrid prov., central Spain, 24 mi. SE of Madrid; cereals, grapes, olives, sugar beets, potatoes.

Valdelarco (–lär'kō), town (pop. 765), Huelva prov., SW Spain, in Sierra Morena, 8 mi. WNW of Aracena; olives, cork, chestnuts, livestock; timber.

Valdemanco del Esteras (–mäng'kō dhĕl ĕstä'räs), town (pop. 684), Ciudad Real prov., S central Spain, on Badajoz prov. border, 50 mi. W of Ciudad Real; cereals, olives, livestock; timber.

Valdemarpils (väl'dĕmärpēls), Lettish *Valdemārpils*, Ger. *Sassmacken*, city (pop. 1,135), NW Latvia, in Kurzeme, 8 mi. N of Talsi, in potato-growing area.

Valdemarsvik (väl"dămärsvēk'), town (pop. 3,035), Ostergotland co., SE Sweden, at head of Valdemar Bay, Swedish *Valdemarsvik*, 10-mi.-long inlet of the Baltic, 30 mi. SE of Norrkoping; seaport, with shipyards, sawmills, tanneries.

Valdemorillo (bäl-dhämōrē'lyō), town (pop. 1,429), Madrid prov., central Spain, 20 mi. W of Madrid; cereals, grapes, forage, livestock; apiculture. Limekilns; mfg. of glassware and porcelain ware, pottery, crystal, chocolate. Clay quarrying. Mineral springs.

Valdemoro (bäl-dhämō'rōs), town (pop. 2,713), Madrid prov., central Spain, 15 mi. S of Madrid; cereals, olives, grapes, sheep. Gypsum quarrying; plaster mfg., olive-oil pressing.

Valdemoro-Sierra (—syĕ'rä), town (pop. 960), Cuenca prov., E central Spain, in the Serranía de Cuenca, 19 mi. E of Cuenca; cereals, honey, livestock; apiculture; flour milling; salt mining. Iron deposits. Hydroelectric plant.

Valdenoceda (–nō-thä'dhä), village (pop. 1,507), Burgos prov., N Spain, on the Ebro and 38 mi. N of Burgos; cereals. fruit, potatoes, livestock; timber. Rayon factory; dairy products.

Valdeobispo (–ōvē'spō), village (pop. 1,118), Cáceres prov., W Spain, 9 mi. WNW of Plasencia; olive oil, cereals, livestock.

Valdeolivas (–ōlē'väs), town (pop. 1,373), Cuenca prov., E central Spain, 35 mi. NW of Cuenca; olive-oil center; also grapes and livestock.

Valdepeñas (–pä'nyäs). **1** City (pop. 29,891), Ciudad Real prov., S central Spain, in New Castile, on Javalón R., on railroad and 32 mi. ESE of Ciudad Real. Active commercial and viticultural center on La Mancha plain, celebrated for its fine wines. The fertile region also produces olives, saffron, livestock. Among its other industries are vinegar, liquor, and alcohol distilling, olive-oil extracting, cheese processing, tanning; mfg. of sulphur, tartaric acid, lime, ceramics, cement articles, soft drinks, woolen goods. Has sumptuous parochial church and palace of marquis of Santa Cruz. **2** or **Valdepeñas de Jaén** (dhā häĕn'), city (pop. 5,977), Jaén prov., S Spain, in mountainous dist., 12 mi. S of Jaén; olive-oil and cheese processing, flour milling; mfg. of willow articles, flower extracts, soap. Ships nuts. Lumber, livestock, cereals. Coal and red-marble deposits.

Valdepeñas de la Sierra (dhā lä syĕ'rä), town (pop. 694), Guadalajara prov., central Spain, 22 mi. NW of Guadalajara; lumbering, stock raising, grain- and winegrowing.

Valderaduey River (–ärä-dhwä') or **Araduey River** (ärä-dhwä'), NW Spain, rises in Leon prov. 20 mi. NNE of Sahagún, flows 110 mi. SSW, through Leon, Valladolid, and Zamora provs., to the Duero (Douro) 2 mi. above Zamora.

Valderas (bäl-dhä'räs), town (pop. 3,186), Leon prov., NW Spain, 38 mi. SSE of Leon; agr. trade center (livestock; lumber; cereals, wine); tanning, brandy distilling, flour milling.

Valderiès (väldĕrēä'), agr. village (pop. 198), Tarn dept., S France, 7 mi. NNE of Albi.

Valderrama (bäldĕrä'mä), town (1939 pop. 1,722; 1948 municipality pop. 9,388), Antique prov., W Panay isl., Philippines, 31 mi. NW of Iloilo; rice-growing center. Chrome-ore deposits.

Valderrobres (bäl-dhärō'vrĕs), town (pop. 2,061), Teruel prov., E Spain, 20 mi. SE of Alcañiz; paper mfg., olive-oil processing, flour milling. Wine, cereals, lumber, livestock in area. Fine town hall.

Valderrueda (bäl-dhärwä'dhä), town (pop. 405), Leon prov., NW Spain, 36 mi. ENE of Leon, in rich coal-mining area. Mineral springs near by.

Valders (vôl'dūrz), village (pop. 560), Manitowoc co., E Wis., 11 mi. W of Manitowoc; dairy products, canned vegetables, cement blocks. Thorstein Veblen was b. here.

Valdés, Ecuador: see VALDEZ.

Valdés, Lo, Chile: see LO VALDÉS.

Val de Santo Domingo (bäl' dhā sän'tō dōmĭng'gō), town (pop. 1,590), Toledo prov., central Spain, 20 mi. NW of Toledo; cereals, grapes, olives, onions, potatoes; olive-oil pressing, tile mfg.

Valdese (vŭl'dēs, –dēz), town (pop. 2,730), Burke co., W central N.C., 6 mi. E of Morganton, near Rhodhiss L.; hosiery-mfg. center; cotton mills. Farm colony started here in 1893 by Waldensians from Cottian Alps, N Italy. Inc. 1921.

Valdes Island (väl'dĕs) (□ 9), SW B.C., Gulf Isls., in Strait of Georgia bet. Gabriola Isl. (NW) and Galiano Isl. (SE), 25 mi. SW of Vancouver; 10 mi. long, 1 mi. wide; farming, lumbering.

Valdés Peninsula (bäldĕs'), on Atlantic Ocean in NE Chubut natl. territory, Argentina, bet. San Matías Gulf and Golfo Nuevo; joined to mainland by 5-mi.-wide isthmus; 55 mi. N–S, 35 mi. W–E. Puerto Pirámides in W on Golfo Nuevo. Sheep raising. Salt beds in S central part.

Valdestillas (bäl-dhĕstē'lyäs), town (pop. 1,205), Valladolid prov., N central Spain, 12 mi. SSW of Valladolid; chemical-fertilizer mfg.; sugar beets, wine, cattle. Summer resort.

Valdetorres (bäl-dhātō'rĕs), town (pop. 1,207), Badajoz prov., W Spain, near Guadiana R., on Madrid-Badajoz RR and 15 mi. E of Mérida; cereals, olives, livestock.

Valdetorres de Jarama (dhā härä'mä), town (pop. 881), Madrid prov., central Spain, near the Jarama, 21 mi. NNE of Madrid; cereals, grapes, olives, livestock. Mfg. of tiles.

Val de Travers, Switzerland: see TRAVERS.

Valdeverdeja (bäl-dhāvĕr-dhä'hä), town (pop. 4,571), Toledo prov., central Spain, near the Tagus, 25 mi. WSW of Talavera de la Reina; agr. center (cereals, grapes, olives, livestock); apiculture. Olive-oil presses, potteries.

Valdevimbre (–vēm'brä), town (pop. 1,103), Leon prov., NW Spain, 13 mi. SSW of Leon; brandy distilling; lumber, livestock, wine, cereals.

Valdez (văldēz'), town (pop. 560), S Alaska, on Valdez Arm of Prince William Sound, 120 mi. E of Anchorage; 61°7'N 146°16'W; supply center for gold-mining and fur-farming region; outfitting point for big-game hunting; fishing and fish processing. Has excellent ice-free harbor, seaplane base, airfield; S terminus of Richardson Highway to Fairbanks. Established 1898 as port for Yukon gold fields, obviating transit through Canada. Harbor was explored and named by Spaniards, 1790.

Valdez (bäldĕs') or **Limones** (lēmō'nĕs), town (1950 pop. 2,870), Esmeraldas prov., N Ecuador, minor Pacific port on offshore isl. in Santiago R. estuary, 45 mi. ENE of Esmeraldas, in region of tropical lowland forests (mangrove, tagua nuts, bananas, coco). Sometimes Valdés.

Valdez (văldēz'), village (1940 pop. 682), Las Animas co., S Colo., on Purgatoire R. and 11 mi. WSW of Trinidad; alt. 6,000 ft.; coal mining.

Valdez Arm (văldēz'), S Alaska, inlet (28 mi. long, 3 mi. wide) of Prince William Sound; 60°58'N 146°49'W; extends NE to Valdez. Upper part called Port Valdez.

Valdieri (väldyā'rē), village (pop. 983), Cuneo prov., Piedmont, NW Italy, on branch of Stura di Demonte R. and 11 mi. SW of Cuneo. Marble, slate quarries near by. Terme di Valdieri (alt. 4,416 ft.) is 8 mi. SW; resort with numerous hot sulphur springs (up to 153°F.); point of ascent for near-by Punta Argentera.

Valdigna d'Aosta, Italy: see MORGEX.

Valdilecha (bäl-dhēlā'chä), town (pop. 1,547), Madrid prov., central Spain, 22 mi. ESE of Madrid; grapes, olives, cereals, sheep; lumbering; vegetable canning, alcohol distilling.

Val-d'Isère (väl-dēzâr'), village (pop. 148), Savoie dept., SE France, on upper Isère R. and 12 mi. NNE of Lanslebourg, bet. Graian Alps (E) and Massif de la Vanoise (W); alt. 6,037 ft. Winter-sports and summer resort. Col d'Iseran 3 mi. SE.

Valdivia (bäldē'vyä), province (□ 8,083; 1940 pop. 191,642; 1949 estimate 217,573), S central Chile; ⊙ Valdivia. Situated bet. the Andes and the Pacific, it includes part of the Chilean lake dist. resort area (lakes Calafquén, Panguipulli, Riñihue, Ranco, Pirehueico) and a number of volcanic peaks. Drained by the Río Bueno and Calle-Calle (or Valdivia) R. Has temperate, moist climate. One of Chile's most important cattle areas; also hogs and sheep. Agr.: wheat, barley, potatoes, apples. Its major ports are Valdivia and CORRAL. The prov. is rich in timber and is noted for freshwater fishing (salmon, trout) in its lakes and brooks. Settled in early colonial days, it was site of battles in Indian wars and in struggle for independence.

Valdivia, city (1940 pop. 34,496; 1949 estimate 31,674), ⊙ Valdivia prov. and Valdivia dept. (□ 4,517; 1940 pop. 126,940), S central Chile, at union of Calle-Calle and Cruces rivers (here forming the Valdivia, which flows 11 mi. to the Pacific at the port of Corral; site of steel plant), 450 mi. SSW of Santiago; 39°48'S 73°17'W. Rail terminus, major inland port, resort, gateway to Chilean lake dist., and commercial, agr., and industrial center An outlet for rich S central Chilean territory, it exports coal, timber, wax, cereals, cordage, leather and woolen goods. Mfg.: tanneries, shoe factories, sugar refineries, breweries, large shipyards, flour mills, textile mills, sawmills; vegetable fibers, metal products. In agr. area (cereals, potatoes, apples, livestock). A progressive town with fine modern bldgs., it was founded 1552 by Pedro de Valdivia. Admiral Cochrane in service of Chilean independents captured it in 1820 from Spaniards. A large influx of Ger. immigrants in middle of 19th cent. contributed to city's development and character.

Valdivia, town (pop. 977), Antioquia dept., NW central Colombia, in Cauca valley, 16 mi. N of Yarumal; alt. 3,937 ft. Trading post in agr. region (corn, sugar cane, coffee, yucca, fruit, stock). Gold mines near by. Has port on Cauca R., 4 mi. N.

Valdivia de Paine (bäldē'vyä dā pān'), town (pop. 1,069), Santiago prov., central Chile, 16 mi. SW of Buin, on Maipo R.

Valdivia River, Chile: see CALLE-CALLE RIVER.

Valdivieso, Sierra (syĕ'rä bäldēvyā'sō), Patagonian range in S part of main isl. of Tierra del Fuego, Chile and Argentina, extends c.25 mi. WNW-ESE across international boundary N and NW of Ushuaia bet. L. Fagnano (N) and Beagle Channel (S); rises to c.5,000 ft.

Valdobbiadene (väldôb-byä'dĕnĕ), town (pop. 3,384), Treviso prov., Veneto, N Italy, near Piave R., 20 mi. NW of Treviso; alcohol distillery, silk mill, hosiery factory, metalworks mfg. (stoves, wine). Has 14th-cent. church (remodeled 17th–18th cent.). Fortunatus, who became bishop of Poitiers, b. here in 530.

Valdoie (väldwä'), N suburb (pop. 3,295) of Belfort, Territory of Belfort, E France; electrical equipment mfg., woolen and cotton milling.

Val d'Or (väl dôr'), town (pop. 4,385), W Que., near L. Blouin, 60 mi. ESE of Rouyn; mining center (gold, copper, zinc, lead, molybdenum), dairying, lumbering, agr. (grain, oats, potatoes). Inc. 1935. Just S is Bourlamaque. Airfield.

Valdorf (fäl'dôrf), village (pop. 6,736), in former Prussian prov. of Westphalia, NW Germany, after 1945 in North Rhine-Westphalia, 7 mi. E of Herford; mud baths.

Val-d'Osne, France: see OSNE-LE-VAL.

Valdosta (văldŏ'stŭ), city (pop. 20,046), ⊙ Lowndes co., S Ga., c.65 mi. ENE of Tallahassee, Fla., in lake region near Fla. line; market, processing, and shipping center for timber, tobacco, and agr. area; mfg. of naval stores, lumber, veneer, boxes, cigars, cottonseed oil, feed, pecan and metal products; tobacco stemming and redrying, vegetable canning, creosoting; railroad shops. Ga. State Woman's Col., Emory Jr. Col., and Moody Air Force Base here. Founded 1860.

Valdres (väl'drŭs), region and administrative district (□ 2,089; pop. 19,080), Opland co., S central Norway, on E slope of the Hemsedalsfjell; drained by upper Begna R. Surface is rugged and mountainous; there are important slate quarries. Stock raising is chief agr. occupation. Fagernes village, 40 mi. W of Lillehammer, is center of region. Until opening (1909) of Oslo-Bergen RR, the Valdres was one of chief trade routes bet. SE and W Norway.

Valduggia (väldōōd'jä), village (pop. 511), Vercelli prov., Piedmont, N Italy, 3 mi. E of Borgosesia; foundries.

Vale or **The Vale**, agr. village and parish (1931 pop. 5,279), Guernsey, Channel Isls., on N coast of isl., 4 mi. N of St. Peter Port. Has early-Norman church.

Vale (vô'lŭ), Nor. *Våle*, village and canton (pop. 2,841), Vestfold co., SE Norway, 5 mi. SW of Holmestrand; flour- and sawmills, tannery, cement works. Sometimes spelled Vaale.

Vale (vä'lyĭ), village (1939 pop. over 500), SW Georgian SSR, 5 mi. WSW of Akhaltsikhe, near Turkish border; rail terminus in lignite-mining area.

Vale (vāl), town (pop. 1,518), ⊙ Malheur co., E Oregon, on Malheur R. and c.55 mi. NW of Boise, Idaho; alt. 2,243 ft.; trade center for sugar-beet, livestock, and potato area. Has medicinal hot springs (serving sanitarium) and stone quarry. Chief town of Vale irrigation project (established 1928; includes 32,000 acres in vicinity of Vale and uses water from MALHEUR RIVER and its NORTH FORK). OWYHEE DAM is 24 mi. S. Settled 1864, inc. 1889.

Valea-Dosului (vä'lĕä-dô'sōōlōōē), Hung. *Nagyompoly* (nŏ'dyômpoi), village (pop. 1,026), Hunedoara prov., central Rumania, in Apuseni Mts., 20 mi. WNW of Alba-Iulia; gold and mercury mining.

Valea-lui-Mihai (vä'lĕä-lōōē-mēkhī), Hung. *Érmihályfalva* (âr'mēhoifŏl"vŏ), village (pop. 9,136), Bihor prov., NW Rumania, 18 mi. SW of Carei; rail junction near Hung. border; mfg. of alcohol, cart wheels.

Valea-Lunga (vä'lĕä-lōōng'gŭ), Rum. *Valea-Lungă*, Ger. *Langenthal* (läng'ūntäl), Hung. *Hosszuászó* (hôsh'sōōäsō), village (pop. 1,819), Sibiu prov., central Rumania, on railroad and 6 mi. SE of Blaj.

Valea-Mare (vä'lĕä-mä'rā), village (pop. 525), Arges prov., S central Rumania, 14 mi. SW of Targoviste.

Valea-Viseului (vä'lĕä-vēshä'ōōlōōē), Rum. *Valea-Vişeului*, Hung. *Visóvölgy* (vē'shōvûldyû), village (pop. 1,109), Baia-Mare prov., NW Rumania, on USSR border, on Tisa R., on railroad and 10 mi. E of Sighet; tourist center. In Hungary, 1940–45.

Valea-Voevozilor (vä'lĕä-vōĕvōzēlôr') or **Valea-Voevozi** (–vō'zē), E suburb (pop. 1,593) of Targoviste, Prahova prov., S central Rumania; mfg. of ceramics; woodworking.

Valebru, Norway: see RINGEBU.

Vale de Cambra (vä'lĭ dĭ kăm'brŭ), town (pop. 779), Aveiro dist., N central Portugal, 20 mi. NE of Aveiro; resort; wool milling.

Vale de Espinho (vä'lĭ dĕshpē'nyōō), village (pop 2,115), Guarda dist., N central Portugal, near Sp. border, 25 mi. SE of Guarda; rye, potatoes, wheat, olives, wine.

Vale de Prazeres (vä'lĭ dĭ prŭzä'rĭsh), village (pop. 1,531), Castelo Branco dist., central Portugal, on railroad and 20 mi. N of Castelo Branco; grain, corn, olives, beans; oak woods.

Vale de Santarém (vä'lĭ dĭ săntŭrān'), village (pop. 1,611), Santarém dist., central Portugal, on railroad and 4 mi. SW of Santarém; olive-oil pressing.

Vale de Vargo (vä'lĭ dĭ vär'gōō), village (pop. 1,637), Beja dist., S Portugal, near Sp. border, 25 mi. E of Beja; grain, olive oil, sheep.

Vale do Paraíso (vä'lĭ dōō pŭrŭē'zōō), village (pop. 1,056), Lisboa dist., central Portugal, 14 mi. SW of Santarém; wine, oranges, olives.

Valeggio sul Mincio (välā'jô sōōl mēn'chô), village (pop. 2,103), Verona prov., Veneto, N Italy, on Mincio R. and 14 mi. SW of Verona, in sericulture region; agr. tools.

Valegotsulovo, Ukrainian SSR: see DOLINSKOYE.

Valen, Isle (vă'lĭn), island (□ 3.5; pop. 147), SE N.F., in Placentia Bay, 22 mi. NW of Argentia; 3 mi. long, 2 mi. wide; 47°30'N 54°23'W. Fishing.

Valença (vŭlĕn'sŭ). **1** City (pop. 9,636), E Bahia, Brazil, on small Una R., near the Atlantic, and 22 mi. SSW of Nazaré; industrial center: metal founding, textile milling, distilling. Ships coffee, tobacco, cacao, fish. Hydroelectric plant. **2** City, Piauí, Brazil: see VALENÇA DO PIAUÍ. **3** City, Rio de Janeiro, Brazil: see MARQUÊS DE VALENÇA.

Valença or **Valença do Minho** (dōō mē'nyōō), town (pop. 1,706), Viana do Castelo dist., northernmost Portugal, on left bank of Minho R., opposite Túy (Spain), and 25 mi. NNE of Viana do Castelo; customs station at 2-storied internatl. road and railroad bridge across the Minho. Mfg. (chocolate, textiles). Surrounded by perfectly preserved 17th-cent. ramparts.

Valença do Piauí (dōō pyou-ē'), city (pop. 1,264), central Piauí, Brazil, 50 mi. NNE of Oeiras (connected by road); grows sugar cane; sawmilling, cattle raising; copper mining. Nitrate deposits 20 mi. NE. Until 1944, called Valença; and, 1944–48, Berlengas.

Valençay (välăsā'), village (pop. 1,612), Indre dept., central France, 25 mi. NNW of Châteauroux; winegrowing. Has sumptuous 16th-17th-cent. Renaissance château in which Ferdinand VII of Spain was confined (1808–14) by Napoleon and which later became the property of Talleyrand.

Valence (välăs'). **1** Town (pop. 34,249), ⊙ Drôme dept., SE France, on a terrace overlooking left bank of Rhone R. and 55 mi. S of Lyons; commercial center for Rhone valley fruits and olives and Côtes-du-Rhône wines. Mfg. (flour products, cartons, footwear, furniture, silk fabrics). Has 11th-12th-cent. Romanesque cathedral, faithfully restored in 17th cent. Old ⊙ of duchy of Valentinois (a dependency of Dauphiné) which Louis XII conferred (1498) upon Cesare Borgia. Seriously damaged in Second World War. **2** or **Valence-sur-Baïse** (-sür-bäēz'), village (pop. 625), Gers dept., SW France, on Baïse R. and 5 mi. S of Condom; brandy distilling, flour milling. **3** or **Valence-d'Agen** (-däzhä'), town (pop. 2,505), Tarn-et-Garonne dept., SW France, on Garonne Lateral Canal and 12 mi. WNW of Castelsarrasin; agr. market (fruits, poultry); dairying, distilling, food preserving, furniture mfg.

Valence-d'Albigeois (välăs'-dälbēzhwä'), village (pop. 601), Tarn dept., S France, in the Ségala, 14 mi. ENE of Albi; wheat and corn growing, dairying.

Valencia, Ireland: see VALENTIA.

Valencia (vůlĕn'shů, Sp. bälĕn'thyä), town (1939 pop. 1,139; 1948 municipality pop. 15,289), S Bohol isl., Philippines, on Mindanao Sea, 25 mi. E of Tagbilaran; agr. center (rice, coconuts).

Valencia (vůlĕn'shů, Sp. bälĕn'thyä), region (□ 8,998; pop. 2,176,670) and former kingdom, E Spain, on the Mediterranean, comprising provs. of (N–S) CASTELLÓN DE LA PLANA, Valencia, and ALICANTE. Bounded by Catalonia (N), Aragon and New Castile (W), Murcia (S and W). Covered (W) by various mtn. ranges generally sloping to narrow alluvial coastal plain of great fertility called "garden of Spain." Irrigation works and intensive system of cultivation started here by Moors. Densely populated coast contrasts with some barren areas of interior. Chief rivers: Turia, Júcar, Segura. Coast forms 2 wide gulfs (Gulf of Valencia; Gulf of Alicante), separated by promontory (Cape Nao). Warm climate, pleasant along coast. Agr. products: citrus and other fruit, vegetables, dates (Elche), rice (Albufera lagoon), olive oil, wine, vegetable fibers, tobacco; processing industries. Sericulture, carried on since anc. times, has declined. Some fishing on S coast. Marble, gypsum, and limestone quarries; saltworks (Torrevieja). Non-agr. industries (less developed in Castellón de la Plana prov.) include metalworking (Sagunto, Valencia), and mfg. of textiles, chemicals, cement, paper (Alcoy), pottery (Valencia), footwear, furniture, candy. Good communications. Exports agr. products (especially the famous Valencia oranges). There are prehistoric remains of old Iberian towns; colonized by Greeks and Carthaginians; occupied by Romans and Visigoths. Fell to Moors (8th cent.), under whom Valencia became (1022) independent emirate; city and dist. of Valencia was ruled (1094-99) by the Cid. Independence restored (1146); kingdom was conquered (1238–52) by James I of Aragon, but preserved its political privileges until 18th cent. It attained economic and artistic eminence in 15th-16th cent.; declined after the expulsion (1609) of the Moriscos. Has had new economic revival in 20th cent.

Valencia, province (□ 4,155; pop. 1,256,633), E Spain, in Valencia, on the Mediterranean; ⊙ Valencia. Bordered on W and NW by irregular ranges forming edge of central plateau and sloping E to coastal plain (max. width 15 mi.). On the low, sandy coast is the Albufera lagoon. Watered by Turia and Júcar rivers. Mountainous region is mostly rough and arid (sheep raising, lumbering); hilly dist. has olive groves and vineyards; green coastal plain is one of richest agr. areas of Spain, having little rainfall but being crossed by countless irrigation canals (fed by the Turia and the Júcar), several of them dating from Moorish times. The plain is covered with fruit orchards, vegetable gardens, mulberry and olive groves, and rice fields (S); produces also tobacco, peanuts, flowers, honey, hemp, saffron. Citrus fruit, table grapes, onions supply a world-wide market. Sericulture is important. Gypsum, cement, clay, marble quarries; some unexploited mineral deposits. Metalworking (in Sagunto and Valencia); food processing (flour, olive oil, wine, canned fruit and vegetables, honey); mfg. of cement, ceramics, chemicals, textiles, footwear, furniture, burlap. Chief cities: Valencia, Alcira, Játiva, Gandía, Sagunto.

Valencia, city (pop. 409,670), ⊙ Valencia prov. and region, E Spain, on Turia (Guadalaviar) R., on fertile irrigated plain near the Mediterranean, 200 mi. ESE of Madrid; 39°29'N 0°22'W. Third largest city of Spain; agr., industrial, and communications center. Its seaport of Villanueva del Grao (2 mi. E), at mouth of the Turia, exports oranges and other fruit, rice, vegetables, olive oil, and wine. Bathing resorts near by. Valencia's varied industries, greatly developed in recent times, include shipyards, metalworks (railroad and electric equipment, machinery, hardware), coke ovens, oil refinery, chemical works, match and tobacco factories, textile mills (silk, rayon, linen), breweries. Other mfg.: cement, paper, furniture, colored tiles and pottery, toys, musical instruments, perfumes and cosmetics. Agr. processing: vegetable oils, rice, fruit, vegetables, meat; distilling (brandy and liqueur). Specialty products (ladies' fans, laces, embroideries) also exported. City has gay, picturesque aspect, with blue-and-white-tiled domes of churches; has narrow, busy streets in old town, and fine avenues, gardens, and promenades in new dist. Seat of archbishop, of univ. (confirmed c. 1500 by Pope Alexander VI), and of art school (founded 1680). Of old walls, only 2 gates (14th cent. on Roman foundations) remain. Gothic cathedral called La Seo (13th-15th cent.), rich in works of art (damaged in 1936), has detached octagonal Miguelete bell tower (152 ft.). In near-by Plaza de la Constitución meets the *Tribunal de las Aguas*, which has settled, since 10th cent., disputes connected with irrigation of garden region around city. Also notable are churches of San Martín (14th cent.; baroque additions), San Nicolás, and San Andrés (both originally mosques), 15th-cent. Gothic *Lonja* (Silk Exchange), the Colegio del Patriarca and the Audiencia (both Renaissance; 16th cent.), and several baroque mansions. Univ. has library with hundreds of incunabula. Citadel built by Charles V is now a barracks. Important collection of paintings, especially of Valencian school (16th-17th cent.) housed in Colegio de San Carlos. Botanical garden, with subtropical plants, and picturesque flower market are famous. The Glorieta is a fine pleasure ground. The fiestas of Valencia were long celebrated. City first mentioned (138 B.C.) under Romans, taken by Visigoths (5th cent. A.D.), and by Moors (8th cent.), under whom it was seat of independent kingdom; held by the Cid (1094–99); retaken by Moors, liberated (1238) by Christians, under whom it had its great commercial and cultural development; declined with expulsion of Moors (1609). In 19th and 20th cent. it has had a new economic revival. In Sp. civil war, seat (1936–37) of Loyalist govt.

Valencia (vůlĕn'shů), village (pop. 1,132), N Trinidad, B.W.I., just E of U.S. army base, 20 mi. E of Port of Spain; sawmilling.

Valencia, county (□ 5,637; pop. 22,481), W N.Mex.; ⊙ Los Lunas. Livestock-grazing and agr. region; watered by Rio Puerco and San Jose R.; borders on Ariz. Grain, fruit, truck products. Zuni and San Mateo mts. are in N, parts of Cibola Natl. Forest in NW and N, El Morro Natl. Monument in W. Pueblo Indian areas in E, part of Zuni Indian Reservation in W. Formed 1852.

Valencia, borough (pop. 298), Butler co., W Pa., 16 mi. N of Pittsburgh.

Valencia (bälĕn'syä), city (1941 pop. 53,938; 1950 census 85,243), ⊙ Carabobo state, N Venezuela, in valley of coastal range, near W shore of L. Valencia, 20 mi. S of its port Puerto Cabello on the Caribbean, 75 mi. WSW of Caracas (linked by railroad and highway); 10°11'N 68°W; alt. 1,568 ft. Venezuela's 4th largest city, situated in its leading agr. region (principally sugar cane and cotton; also cacao, coconuts, coffee, corn, fruit, cattle), it is a distributing, trading, and mfg. center. Frequented by tourists for its pleasant semitropical climate. Industries include textile milling, tanning, sugar refining, meat packing, brewing, sawmilling, lime and marble quarrying; mfg. of tobacco products, leather goods, cement, straw hats, soap, vegetable oil, dairy products, furniture. Airport. Bishopric. Has higher institutions of learning, a natl. col., cathedral, public market, central plaza, a monument to Bolívar with highest obelisk in South America. Old colonial city, founded 1555, it twice served as capital (1812 and 1830), but the disease-laden marshes of L. Valencia caused the seat of govt. to be moved to Caracas. Here met the congress (1830) which declared Venezuela's independence from Gran Colombia.

Valencia, Lake (□ c.125; alt. 1,362 ft.), N Venezuela, in Carabobo and Aragua states, in basin of coastal range just E of Valencia and 50 mi. WSW of Caracas; 18 mi. long (W–E), up to 10 mi. wide. Second only to L. Maracaibo, it is the largest interior fresh-water lake of Venezuela, situated in fertile agr. region (cotton, sugar cane, tobacco, corn, coffee, fruit, cattle). Near Maracay, on NE shore, is a natl. airport for hydroplanes. Among its many affluents is Aragua R. (E). Once bordered by marshes, the lake is now a popular resort with a healthy climate. Formerly also Tacarigua.

Valencia de Alcántara (bälĕn'thyä dhä älkän'tärä), town (pop. 6,904), Cáceres prov., W Spain, in Estremadura, 48 mi. W of Cáceres, near Port. line; Sp. customs station on railroad to Portugal; agr. trade center (cereals, fruit, wine, livestock; lumber). Mfg. of furniture, soap, cheese; cork processing, flour- and sawmilling, olive pressing. Has 14th-cent. church. After liberation (1221) from Moorish rule, belonged to Knights of Alcántara; was important stronghold in Sp.-Port. wars.

Valencia de Don Juan (dhōn' hwän'), town (pop. 3,558), Leon prov., NW Spain, on Esla R. and 22 mi. SSE of Leon; agr. trade center (cereals, wine, livestock; lumber); brandy distilleries, flour mills. Marble quarries near by. Of its anc. fortifications, city walls still remain. In council held here (1050), the basis of Castilian privileges was laid.

Valencia de las Torres (läs tô'rĕs), town (pop. 2,410), Badajoz prov., W Spain, 11 mi. N of Llerena; cereals, olives, grapes, sheep.

Valencia del Barrial, Spain: see VALENCIA DEL VENTOSO.

Valencia del Mombuey (dhĕl mōmbwā') or **Valencita** (bälĕn-thē'tä), town (pop. 2,107), Badajoz prov., W Spain, near Port. border, 19 mi. W of Jerez de los Caballeros; acorns, olives, cereals, livestock; timber.

Valencia del Ventoso (vĕntō'sō) or **Valencia del Barrial** (bäryäl'), town (pop. 5,157), Badajoz prov., W Spain, 9 mi. W of Fuente de Cantos; agr. center (cereals, chick-peas, olives, livestock).

Valenciana or **La Valenciana** (lä, bälĕnsyä'nä), former silver-mining village, Guanajuato, central Mexico, just N of Guanajuato; was noted for extremely large production.

Valenciennes (välăsyĕn'), town (pop. 37,716), Nord dept., N France, on the Escaut (canalized) and 28 mi. SE of Lille; industrial and transportation center near Belg. border, in coal-mining basin (important mines in suburban Anzin); foundries, forges, rolling mills (steel tubing), machine shops (mining and heating equipment, bicycles). Famous lace industry (which died out in 19th cent.) has been revived. Mfg. of rayon, hosiery, cambric handkerchief and trimmings. Other mfg. (starch, soap, chicory, beer, industrial oils, tiles, glass). A leading beet-sugar processing and trading center. Has school of fine arts (founded 1782) and former Jesuit col. (now a lycée) which contains library. Important town of medieval Hainaut. Passed definitively to France in 1678. Its industrial establishments were wrecked during First World War occupation. Town center was destroyed in Second World War. Emperor Baldwin I, Froissart, and Watteau b. here.

Valencina, officially Valencina del Alcor (bälĕnthē'nä dhĕl älkôr'), town (pop. 1,865), Seville prov., SW Spain, 5 mi. W of Seville; olives, cereals, grapes; liquor distilling.

Valencita, Spain: see VALENCIA DEL MOMBUEY.

Valeni (vŭlān'), Rum. *Văleni*. **1** or **Valeni-de-Munte** or **Valenii-de-Munte** (-dā-mōōn'tĕ), town (1948 pop. 4,554), Prahova prov., S central Rumania, in Walachia, on railroad and 17 mi. N of Ploesti; popular summer resort and cultural center. Printing, dye mfg., tanning. Seat of a much-frequented summer univ. Has 17th-cent. monastery, several times destroyed by earthquakes and finally restored in 1809, 19th-cent. church, school for missionaries, religious art mus. Founded in 15th cent., Valeni was formerly an important trading center. Noted Cheia and Suzana monasteries lie respectively 14 and 18 mi. NNW. **2** Village (pop. 4,049), Teleorman prov., S Rumania, 24 mi. SE of Slatina; vineyards, orchards.

Valensole (välăsôl'), village (pop. 1,168), Basses-Alpes dept., SE France, on tableland in Provence Alps, 22 mi. SW of Digne; perfume mfg., truffle canning.

Valentano (välĕntä'nô), village (pop. 2,877), Viterbo prov., Latium, central Italy, near L. Bolsena, 18 mi. NW of Viterbo. Has castle.

Valentia or **Valencia** (vůlĕn'shēů), Gaelic *Dairbhre*, island (6,504 acres; pop. c.1,200; 7 mi. long, 2 mi. wide), Co. Kerry, Ireland, in Dingle Bay 1 mi. off the coast, 35 mi. SW of Tralee. It is E terminal of several transatlantic cables, 1st of which was laid by the *Great Eastern* in 1865 from Trinity Bay, Newfoundland. There is also a radio station. At NE end of isl. is fishing port and resort of Knightstown, formerly seat of the Knights of Kerry. Isl. was formerly known for its slate quarries. The harbor is an anchorage for fishing vessels.

Valentigney (välătēnyā'), town (pop. 4,235), Doubs dept., E France, 4 mi. SSE of Montbéliard and part of its industrial dist., on the Doubs; tool making; metalworks.

Valentin (vůlyĭntyĕn'), town (1944 pop. over 500), SE Maritime Territory, Russian SFSR, on Sea of Japan, 120 mi. ENE of Vladivostok; fish canning.

Valentín Alsina (bälĕntēn' älsē'nä), town (pop. estimate 25,000) in S Greater Buenos Aires, Argentina, separated from Federal Dist. by Riachuelo R.; industrial, residential center. Wire, textiles, shoes, stockings, ceramics, chemicals, paper, nails; tin foundries, meat-packing and dairying plants, sawmills.

Valentine. **1** Village (pop. c.100), Mohave co., NW Ariz., near Grand Wash Cliffs, 26 mi. NE of Kingman. Truxton Canyon Agency is here, serving as hq. for Camp Verde, Havasupai, Hualpai, and Yavapai Indian reservations. **2** City (pop. 2,700), ⊙ Cherry co., N Nebr., 120 mi. E of Chadron and on Niobrara R., near S.Dak. line; livestock, grain, dairy and poultry produce. Near by are state fish hatchery, agr. experiment station, site of Fort Niobrara, and Niobrara game reserve. Settled 1882. **3** Town (pop. 510), Jeff Davis co., extreme W Texas, 33 mi. NW of Marfa; alt. 4,431 ft.; trading, shipping point in livestock region.

Valenza (välĕn'tsä), town (pop. 8,084), Alessandria prov., Piedmont, N Italy, on Po R. and 7 mi. N of Alessandria, in cereal- and forage-growing region; clothing industry; gold- and silverworking, shoemaking.

Valenzano (välĕnzä'nō), town (pop. 6,113), Apulia, S Italy, 6 mi. S of Bari; wine, olive oil.

Valenzuela (bälĕnswā'lä), town (dist pop. 7,806), La Cordillera dept., S central Paraguay, in Cordillera de los Altos, 55 mi. ESE of Asunción; agr. center (oranges, livestock).

Valenzuela (bälĕn-thwā'lä), town (pop. 3,346), Córdoba prov., S Spain, 13 mi. NE of Baena; olive-oil processing, plaster mfg., flour milling. Cereals, fruit, vegetables, livestock. Gypsum quarries.

Valenzuela de Calatrava (dhā kälāträ'vä), town (pop. 1,796), Ciudad Real prov., S central Spain, 13 mi. SE of Ciudad Real; olives, cereals, grapes, sheep. Mfg. of silk lace.

Valera (bälā'rä), city (pop. 10,553), Trujillo state, W Venezuela, on transandine highway, on Motatán R., in Andean spur, and 12 mi. WSW of Trujillo. Largest city in state and leading commercial center, in agr. region (sugar cane, cacao, coffee, fruit, grain); trade in coffee; flour milling. Airport. Has notable Gothic cathedral.

Valera de Abajo (bälā'rä dhā ävä'hō), town (pop. 1,467), Cuenca prov., E central Spain, 20 mi. S of Cuenca; grain, saffron, grapes, sheep, goats. Lumbering, flour milling, gypsum quarrying.

Valera de Arriba (ärē'vä), town (pop. 922), Cuenca prov., E central Spain, 18 mi. S of Cuenca; saffron, grapes, potatoes, livestock; flour milling.

Valeria (vůlēr'ēů), town (pop. 57), Jasper co., central Iowa, 18 mi. ENE of Des Moines.

Valerianovsk (vŭlyĕrēä'nůfsk), town (1933 pop. over 500), W Sverdlovsk oblast, Russian SFSR, in the central Urals, on short left tributary of Tura R. and 6 mi. SW of Is; gold placers; magnetite and titanium deposits.

Valerian Way (vůlēr'ēůn), anc. Roman road extending from Tibur (Tivoli) to Aternum (Pescara) and beyond.

Valérien, Mont (mõ välārēē'), hill (alt. 532 ft.) in Seine dept., N central France, just W of Suresnes and 6 mi. from center of Paris. Fortified 1841, it was an important defensive position during siege of Paris, 1870–71.

Valetta, Malta: see VALLETTA.

Valette-du-Var, La (lä välĕt'-dü-vär'), ENE suburb (pop. 3,205) of Toulon, Var dept., SE France.

Valga (väl'gä), Latvian *Valka* (väl'kä), Ger. *Walk*, Rus. *Valk* (both: välk), Estonia-Latvian border city, on main Tallinn-Riga RR and 90 mi. NE of Riga, 125 mi. SSE of Tallinn. Estonian *Valga* (pop. 10,842), a rail junction (repair shops) with brewing and lumber industry (sawmilling, furniture mfg.), adjoins Latvian *Valka* (S; pop. 3,268), a rail junction and sawmilling center. Originally in Rus. govt. of Livonia; disputed after First World War and divided bet. Estonia and Latvia.

Valgodemar or **Valgaudemar** (both: välgōdmär'), high valley of little Séveraisse R. in Hautes-Alpes dept., SE France, extending from the Drac near Saint-Firmin c.15 mi. ENE into the Massif du Pelvoux. La Chapelle-en-Valgodemar (alt. 3,444 ft.) at foot of Pic d'Olan is center for alpinists.

Valgorge (välgôrzh'), village (pop. 156), Ardèche dept., S France, 13 mi. WSW of Aubenas; sheep and cattle raising.

Valguarnera or **Valguarnera Caropepe** (välgwärnā'-rä kärōpā'pē), town (pop. 13,228), Enna prov., central Sicily, 8 mi. SE of Enna, in grape- and olive-growing region; macaroni. Sulphur mines near by.

Valhalla (vălhă'lů), residential village (1940 pop. 2,139), Westchester co., SE N.Y., just N of White Plains, at S end of Kensico Reservoir.

Valias (välē'äs) or **Valiasi** (välē'äsē), village (1930 pop. 322), central Albania, 7 mi. NW of Tirana, in Ishm R. valley.

Valiente Peninsula (bälyĕn'tā), on Caribbean coast of W Panama, forming E side of Chiriquí Lagoon; 20 mi. long, 4 mi. wide.

Valier (vůlēr'). **1** Village (pop. 808), Franklin co., S Ill., 15 mi. N of Herrin, in bituminous-coal-mining and agr. area. **2** Town (pop. 710), Pondera co., N Mont., on L. Frances and 17 mi. NW of Conrad, in irrigated region; livestock, dairy products, grain, sugar beets.

Valinco, Gulf of (välēng'kō), in the Mediterranean off SW coast of Corsica, c.18 mi SSE of Ajaccio; 14 mi. wide, 12 mi. deep. Bounded by Capo di Muro (N) and Cape Senetosa (S). Near its head is port of Propriano.

Valinhos, Brazil: see GUARAÚNA.

Valira River (bälē'rä), in Andorra and NE Spain, rises in several headstreams in the central Pyrenees, flows 25 mi. SW, through main Andorra valley, past Andorra la Vella, to Segre R. at Seo de Urgel. Also spelled Balira.

Val Jalbert (väl zhälbâr'), village (pop. 29), S central Que., on S shore of L. St. John, at mouth of Ouiatchouan R., 5 mi. SE of Roberval; lumbering. Near by are 236-ft. waterfalls.

Valjevo or **Valyevo** (vä'lyĕvô), town (pop. 16,620), W Serbia, Yugoslavia, 45 mi. SW of Belgrade; rail terminus; center of plum- and apple-growing region; mfg. of agr. machinery. Magnesite deposits. Cattle raising in vicinity.

Val-Joyeux, Le, France: see VILLEPREUX.

Valjunquera (bälhōōng-kā'rä), village (pop. 1,121), Teruel prov., E Spain, 11 mi. SE of Alcañiz; mfg. of soap, sulphur carbide; olive-oil processing. Has churrigueresque church.

Valk, Estonia and Latvia: see VALGA.

Valka, Latvia: see VALGA.

Valkeakoski (väl'kääkōs"kē), town (pop. 10,173), Häme co., SW Finland, in lake region, 18 mi. SE of Tampere; rail terminus; pulp, cellulose, and paper mills, machine shops.

Valkeala (väl'käälä), village (commune pop. 14,916), Kymi co., SE Finland, in lake region, 6 mi. NE of Kouvola; lumbering region.

Valkenburg (väl'kůnbůrkh), town (pop. 4,489), Limburg prov., SE Netherlands, 6 mi. E of Maastricht; tourist center with many parks and grottoes; chalk quarries; leather goods. Ruined 13th-cent. castle. Sometimes spelled Valkenberg.

Valkenswaard (väl'kůnsvärt), village (pop. 11,071), North Brabant prov., S Netherlands, 6 mi. S of Eindhoven, near Belg. frontier; mfg. (cigars, farm wagons).

Valki (väl'kē), city (1939 pop. over 10,000), W Kharkov oblast, Ukrainian SSR, 28 mi. WSW of Kharkov; dairying, fruit canning, flour milling, metalworking.

Valkom (väl'kōm), village in Perna commune (pop. 8,286), Uusimaa co., S Finland, on bay of Gulf of Finland, 3 mi. S of Lovisa; timber-shipping port, rail terminus.

Valla (vä'lä"), village (pop. 1,058), Sodermanland co., E Sweden, 5 mi. ENE of Katrineholm; wood- and metalworking, flour milling.

Vallabhipur, India: see VALA, town.

Vallada (bälyä'dhä), town (pop. 2,327), Valencia prov., E Spain, 11 mi. SW of Játiva; olive-oil processing, basket mfg.; wine, cereals, oranges. Gypsum quarries near by.

Valladolid (bäyädōlēdh'). **1** City, Michoacán, Mexico: see MORELIA. **2** City (pop. 6,402), Yucatan, SE Mexico, 90 mi. ESE of Mérida; rail terminus; agr. center (henequen, corn, beans, cotton, sugar cane, coffee, fruit; timber). Historic colonial town with fine bldgs. Point of departure for CHICHÉN ITZÁ ruins. Site of bloody uprising (1847).

Valladolid (välůdō'lĭd, -dŏlĭd', Sp. bä"yädhōlēdh', bäl"yä-), town (1939 pop. 2,795; 1948 municipality pop. 13,393), Negros Occidental prov., W Negros isl., Philippines, 17 mi. SW of Bacolod; agr. center (rice, sugar cane).

Valladolid (välůdŏlĭd', Sp. bälyä-dhōlēdh'), province (□ 3,222; pop. 332,526), N central Spain, in Leon; ⊙ Valladolid. Consists of tableland (part of central Sp. plateau) crossed by some hill ranges. Drained by the Duero (Douro) and its tributaries (Pisuerga, Esgueva, Eresma, Adaja). Has some very fertile dists. (Tierra de Campos, Tierra del Vino) and river valleys yielding cereals, wine, fruit, vegetables, flax, and sugar beets; stock raising (mainly sheep). Lumbering. Mineral resources are scarce (salt, iron, sulphur). Of the prov.'s once-flourishing commercial and industrial life little has remained; the wool industry barely survives in a few towns (coarse cloth and blankets). Agr. processing (flour, wine, dairy products, meat), tanning; other mfg.: candy, ceramics, leather goods, liqueurs. Poor communications. Valladolid city is the only industrial center (railroad equipment); other towns: Medina del Campo, Nava del Rey, Peñafiel. The city of Valladolid was once ⊙ Castile, and therefore the prov. of Valladolid is sometimes considered part of Old Castile; in modern times, however, it has generally been placed in Leon.

Valladolid, city (pop. 111,253), ⊙ Valladolid prov., N central Spain, on fertile plain, on left bank of Pisuerga R. at influx of Esgueva R. and the Canal of Castile, and 100 mi. NW of Madrid; 41°39'N 4°44'W. Communications and industrial center, and one of chief grain markets of Spain. Has railroad shops and metalworks (railroad equipment, engines, hardware), chemical works (fertilizers, glues, resins, inks), tanneries, breweries, flour and sugar mills; mfg. of footwear, knit goods, cotton textiles, burlap, gloves, ceramics, pianos, wax, and liqueurs. Archbishopric; and seat of univ. (founded 1346). The arcaded Plaza Mayor is center of city life. Among numerous works of art are late-Renaissance cathedral (16th–17th cent.), and churches of Santa María Antigua (12th cent.; Romanesque), of San Pablo (13th cent.; later restored) with richly ornamented façade, and of Santa Ana with paintings by Goya. An art mus. is housed in the plateresque Colegio de Santa Cruz; while the Colegio de San Gregorio (15th cent.), with its adorned Gothic façade and fine cloisters, contains the municipal offices. The 14th-cent. Colegio de San Benito stands on site of old alcazar. Other notable landmarks are baroque univ. bldg., monument to Columbus (who died here), old royal palace, and house where Cervantes lived (1603–06). Of obscure origin, the city derived its name from Moorish *Belad Ulid*. After its liberation from Moors (10th cent.), it received many privileges and was favorite residence of kings of Castile (14th–15th cent.) and scene of festivals and brilliant tournaments. Ferdinand and Isabella were married here (1469). After reaching its peak of prosperity in 16th cent. (Philip II was b. here), it shared with Toledo the residency of Sp. royalty and declined with the transfer of ⊙ Castile to Madrid in 1561. It was again ⊙ Spain briefly in 1600–06. City is now generally placed in the historic region of Leon. Has had economic revival since 19th cent.

Vallam (vŭl'lŭm), town (pop. 8,076), Tanjore dist., SE Madras, India, 7 mi. SW of Tanjore; crystal ornaments and eyeglasses; mortar and stucco mfg. Quarries near by (laterite, limestone, quartz).

Vallauris (välōrēs'), town (pop. 3,924), Alpes-Maritimes dept., SE France, near the Mediterranean, 9 mi. SE of Grasse; grows flowers and extracts essential oils, produces culinary and artistic pottery.

Vallay (vă'lā), island (pop. 19), Outer Hebrides, Inverness, Scotland, just off N coast of North Uist; 3 mi. long, 1 mi. wide.

Valldemosa (bäl-dhāmō'sä), town (pop. 1,277), Majorca, Balearic Isls., 9 mi. N of Palma. Resort in picturesque setting, with Moorish alcazar and an old charterhouse (founded 1399) in which Chopin spent a winter with George Sand. The Miramar retreat, built by an Austrian archduke amid the isl.'s finest scenery, is 2 mi. N; in Middle Ages it was site of a linguistic acad.

Vall de Uxó (bäl'dhā ōō-shō'), city (pop. 9,612), Castellón de la Plana prov., E Spain, 15 mi. SW of Castellón de la Plana; hemp and cork processing, basketmaking, olive pressing, flour milling; other mfg.: footwear, chemicals (bleaches, dyes, pharmaceuticals). Ships fruit (oranges, dried figs). Barite mines and kaolin quarries.

Valle, Colombia: see VALLE DEL CAUCA.

Valle (bä'yā), department (□ 815; 1950 pop. 71,884), S Honduras, on Gulf of Fonseca; ⊙ Nacaome. Bounded W by Goascarán R. (Salvador border); drained by Nacaome R.; contains S hill outliers of the Andes and a broad coastal lowland. Agr. (corn, beans, rice, cotton, henequen). Saltworks, mangrove swamps, and fisheries along coast. Gold and silver mining at El Tránsito, near Nacaome. Main centers: Nacaome, Goascarán, San Lorenzo (served by Inter-American Highway), port of Amapala on Tigre Isl. Formed 1893 out of Choluteca and La Paz depts.

Valle (väl'lů). **1** Village and canton (pop. 1,021), Aust-Agder co., S Norway, on Otra R. and 75 mi. N of Kristiansand; tourist center in the heart of the Setesdal. **2** Village, Vest-Agder co., Norway: see SOR-AUDNEDAL.

Valle, El, Mexico: see VALLE DE JUÁREZ.

Valle, El, Venezuela: see EL VALLE.

Valle, Río del (rē'ō dĕl bä'yā), river in SE Catamarca prov., Argentina, rises in Sierra de Ambato 20 mi. N of La Puerta, flows c.85 mi. S, past La Puerta, Piedra Blanca, San Isidro, and Catamarca, losing itself 25 mi. S of Catamarca in Capayán dept. Irrigates the area of Piedra Blanca, where fruit, cotton, and alfalfa are grown. Hydroelectric power station and dam on its course.

Valleberga, Sweden: see SKROMBERGA.

Vallecas (bälyā'käs), town (pop. 4,214), Madrid prov., central Spain, on railroad and 4 mi. SE of Madrid, in agr. region. Gravel and gypsum quarrying. Mfg. of plaster, cement articles, acids, fertilizers, meat products. Iron foundry. Bet. Vallecas and the capital extends the new suburb Puente de Vallecas or Nueva Numancia.

Vallecillo (bäyäsē'yō), town (pop. 461), Nuevo León, N Mexico, on Inter-American Highway and 70 mi. NNE of Monterrey; sugar cane, cotton, cactus fibers.

Vallecito, Cerro (sĕ'rō bäyäsē'tō), Andean volcano (20,075 ft.) in W Catamarca prov., Argentina, near Chile border, just SE of Cerro Colorados.

Vallecito Dam, Colo.: see LOS PINOS RIVER.

Valle de Abdalagís (bä'lyā dhā äv-dhälähēs'), town (pop. 2,960), Málaga prov., S Spain, at S foot of the Sierra de Abdalagís, 20 mi. NW of Málaga; cereals, olives, tubers, almonds, chickpeas; flour milling, olive-oil processing.

Valle de Allende, Mexico: see ALLENDE, Chihuahua.

Valle de Ángeles (bä'yā dā än'hēlĕs), town (pop. 801), Francisco Morazán dept., S central Honduras; 11 mi. ENE of Tegucigalpa; alt. 4,167 ft. Flower gardens; wheat, coffee, fruit.

Valle de Banderas (bä'yā dā bändä'räs), town (pop. 1,361), Nayarit, W Mexico, near Banderas Bay, 55 mi. SSW of Tepic; corn, cotton, sugar cane, rice, tobacco, tomatoes, bananas.

Valle de Bravo (bä'yā dā brä'vō), city (pop. 3,956), Mexico state, central Mexico, 32 mi. W of Toluca; cereals, fruit, livestock; dairying. Site of Ixtapantongo hydroelectric plant.

Valle de Guadalupe (bä'yā dā gwädälōō'pā), town (pop. 1,010), Jalisco, central Mexico, 24 mi. SW of San Juan de los Lagos; grain, beans, livestock.

Valle de Guanape (bä'yä dā gwänä'pā), town (pop. 1,219), Anzoátegui state, N Venezuela, 70 mi. WSW of Barcelona; coconuts, cotton, sugar cane, corn, stock.

Valle de Juárez (bä'yä dā whä'rĕs), town (pop. 1,060), Jalisco, central Mexico, 45 mi. E of Sayula; corn, wheat, beans, fruit, livestock. Sometimes El Valle.

Valle de la Pascua (bä'yä dā lä päs'kwä), town (pop. 6,703), Guárico state, N central Venezuela, in llanos 110 mi. SE of Caracas; cattle-grazing center; dairy products.

Valle de la Serena (dhā lä sārā'nä), town (pop. 4,003), Badajoz prov., W Spain, 13 mi. W of Castuera; agr. center (cereals, grain, hogs, sheep); flour, dairy products.

Valle de las Zapatas (bä'yä dā läs säpä'täs), village, León dept., W Nicaragua, on upper Estero Real and 20 mi. NE of León; gold and silver mining.

Valle del Cauca (bä'yä dĕl kou'kä) or **Valle**, department (□ 8,085; 1938 pop. 613,230; 1950 estimate 1,007,020), W Colombia, on the Pacific; ⊙ Cali. Crossed N–S by Cordillera Occidental (W) and Cordillera Central (E), which flank the Cauca valley, it is mainly mountainous, apart from sparsely inhabited coastal lowlands and San Juan R. delta. Climate is hot and humid all year round on the coast, semitropical with 2 annual rainy seasons in fertile Cauca valley. Rich in silver, gold, and platinum, mined near Buenaventura, Bugalagrande, Dagua, Palmira, Sevilla; coal near Cali, Buga, Yumbo. Its rich soil yields sugar cane, coffee, tobacco, yucca, cotton, cacao, bananas, rice, corn, vegetables. Extensive cattle raising. Processing industries are at Buga, Buenaventura, Cartago, and Palmira; and, on a large scale, at Cali, Colombia's 4th city, the leading commercial and industrial center of the western region. Buenaventura is the country's main Pacific port.

Valle de Matamoros (dhā mätämō'rōs), town (pop. 2,467), Badajoz prov., W Spain, 3 mi. N of Jerez de los Caballeros; olives, chestnuts, cereals, vegetables, livestock.

Valle de Santa Ana (sän'tä ä'nä), town (pop. 1,983), Badajoz prov., W Spain, 3 mi. N of Jerez de los Caballeros; cereals, olives, fruit, vegetables, livestock.

Valle de Santiago (säntyä'gō), city (pop. 12,278), Guanajuato, central Mexico, on central plateau, in Lerma R. basin, 45 mi. S of Guanajuato; alt. 5,623 ft. Agr. center (grain, sweet potatoes, fruit, livestock); shoe mfg., lumber milling. Crater lakes near by.

Valle de Zaragoza (särägō'sä), town (pop. 825), Chihuahua, N Mexico, on Conchos R., near L. Toronto, and 85 mi. SSE of Chihuahua; corn, cotton, tobacco, sugar cane, livestock; lumbering.

Valledolmo (väl"lĕdôl'mô), town (pop. 6,873), Palermo prov., central Sicily, in Madonie Mts., near headwaters of Torto R., 18 mi. SSE of Termini Imerese.

Valledupar (bäyädōōpär'), town (pop. 3,339), Magdalena dept., N Colombia, at SE foot of Sierra Nevada de Santa Marta, on affluent of César R. and 80 mi. SSW of Ríohacha; agr. center (corn, coffee, ginger, livestock). Cattle research station, airfield.

Valledupar, Serranía de (sĕränē'ä dā), Andean range on Colombia-Venezuela border, a N part of Cordillera Oriental, E of Sierra Nevada de Santa Marta; c.45 mi. long NE–SW bet. 10°50' and 10°15'N. Together with Serranía de los Motilones (S) and Montes de Oca (N), it forms Sierra de Perijá.

Vallée Jonction (välā' zhōksyō'), **Valley Junction, or L'Enfant Jésus** (läfā' zhäzü'), village (pop. 1,175), S Que., on Chaudière R. and 35 mi. SSE of Quebec; railroad center; shoe mfg., dairying.

Valle Fértil, department, Argentina: see SAN AGUSTÍN, San Juan prov.

Valle Fértil, Sierra de (syĕ'rä dā bä'yä fĕr'tēl), pampean range in E San Juan prov., Argentina, along La Rioja prov. border, extends c.70 mi. NW from San Agustín; rises to c.8,000 ft.

Valle Grande, department, Argentina: see PAMPICHUELA.

Valle Grande (bä'yä grän'dā), city (pop. c.11,100), ⊙ Valle Grande prov., Santa Cruz dept., central Bolivia, in E foothills of Cordillera de Cochabamba, 80 mi. SW of Santa Cruz; road junction, airport; trade center for agr. area (corn, potatoes, barley).

Vallegrande, Yugoslavia: see VELALUKA.

Valle Grande Mountains (vī'ū grŏn'dä, grăn'dē), N N.Mex., NW of Santa Fe, W of the Rio Grande; extend N–S from Jemez Creek to Rio Chama. Range surrounds Valle Grande, enormous crater (□ c.180; alt. 9,000 ft.). Range also known as Jemez Mts. Prominent points: Cerro Pelado (sĕ'rō pīlä'dō) (10,115 ft.); Redondo Peak (11,254 ft.); Chicoma Peak (11,950 ft.), highest point in range. Los Alamos is just SE.

Valle Hermoso (bä'yä ĕrmō'sō), town (pop. 2,091), NW Córdoba prov., Argentina, 27 mi. NW of Córdoba; resort in N Córdoba hills; cattle-raising center; lime factory. Has old Jesuit church. Hydroelectric station on Cosquín R. here.

Vallehermoso (bälyäĕrmō'sō), town (pop. 983; commune pop. 7,369), Gomera, Canary Isls., 12 mi. NW of San Sebastián; wheat, tomatoes, potatoes, tobacco, bananas, grapes, cattle; fishing; wine making, flour milling.

Vallehermoso (bä"yäĕrmō'sō, bäl"yä–), town (1939 pop. 4,778; 1948 municipality pop. 22,119), Negros Oriental prov., E Negros isl., Philippines, on Tañon Strait, 33 mi. ENE of Binalbagan; agr. center (corn, coconuts, sugar cane, tobacco).

Valle Hermoso Pass (bä'yä ĕrmō'sō) (11,529 ft.), in the Andes, on Argentina-Chile border; 32° 22'S.

Vallejo (vŭlā'ō, vŭlā'hō), city (pop. 26,038), Solano co., W Calif., on San Pablo Bay at mouth of Napa R., and N of Oakland; on Mare Isl. (reached by causeway) is U.S. navy yard, established 1854 by David G. Farragut. Port; processing and commercial center; flour and lumber milling, meat packing, dairying. Vallejo Col. (jr.) is here. Carquinez Bridge across Carquinez Strait is just SE. Founded by and named for Gen. M. G. Vallejo; ⊙ Calif. during 1851–54. Inc. 1866. Influx of workers for great naval shipyards doubled city's pop. in Second World War.

Vallelado (bälyälä'dhō), town (pop. 976), Segovia prov., central Spain, 23 mi. SE of Valladolid; grain, grapes, chicory, garlic, sugar beets, livestock. Plaster mfg.

Valle Lomellina (väl'lĕ lōmĕl-lē'nä), village (pop. 1,810), Pavia prov., Lombardy, N Italy, 24 mi. W of Pavia; mfg. (harmoniums, harmonicas).

Vallelunga Pratameno (väl"lĕlōōng'gä prätämā'nô), village (pop. 6,129), Caltanissetta prov., central Sicily, 18 mi. NW of Caltanissetta.

Vallemaggia (väl"lĕmäd'jä), district (pop. 4,047), Ticino canton, S Switzerland; watered by Maggia R. Val Lavizzara and Valle Maggia, valleys, extend along upper and lower courses, respectively, of Maggia R.

Valle María (bä'yä märē'ä), town (pop. estimate 700), W Entre Ríos prov., Argentina, 18 mi. S of Paraná, in agr. area (grain, livestock, poultry).

Valle Mosso (väl'lĕ mōs'sō), village (pop. 1,590), Vercelli prov., Piedmont, N Italy, 6 mi. NE of Biella; woolen and cotton mills, textile machinery, electric motors, saddles.

Valle Nacional (bä'yä näsyōnäl'), town (pop. 1,191), Oaxaca, S Mexico, in valley on N slopes of Sierra Madre del Sur, 25 mi. SW of Tuxtepec; in coffee and tobacco dist.

Vallenar (bäyänär'), town (pop. 8,472), ⊙ Huasco dept. (□ 5,650; pop. 22,374), Atacama prov., N central Chile, 100 mi. NNE of La Serena, 85 mi. SSW of Copiapó; 28°35'S 70°45'W. Rail junction; copper-mining (mines at Algarrobo, Domeyko) and agr. center noted for its wines. Also fruit, alfalfa, goats. Gold and silver deposits near by. Airport. Its port is Huasco. Heavily damaged in 1922 earthquake.

Vallendar (fä'lŭndär), town (pop. 6,040), in former Prussian Rhine Prov., W Germany, after 1945 in Rhineland-Palatinate, on right bank of the Rhine and 2 mi. N of Coblenz; pottery works.

Vallentigny (välätēnyē'), village (pop. 313), Aube dept., NE central France, 16 mi. NNW of Bar-sur-Aube; sauerkraut processing and shipping.

Vallentuna (vä'lŭntü"nä), village (pop. 1,310), Stockholm co., E Sweden, 15 mi. N of Stockholm; brick mfg. Has medieval church. Runic stone (11th cent.) found here. Includes Ballsta (bĕl'stä"), Swedish *Bällsta*, village.

Valleraugue (välŭrōg'), village (pop. 529), Gard dept., S France, on upper Hérault R. and 6 mi. N of Le Vigan, at foot of Mont Aigoual; silk spinning.

Valleroy (välŭrwä'), town (pop. 2,088), Meurthe-et-Moselle dept., NE France, 3 mi. S of Briey, near Orne R.; iron mining.

Valles or **Ciudad de Valles** (syōōdädh' dā vä'yĕs), city (pop. 7,240), San Luis Potosí, E Mexico, in fertile Gulf dist., on railroad, on Inter-American Highway and 75 mi. WSW of Tampico; agr. center (coffee, tobacco, sugar cane, cereals, fruit, cattle). Taninul (tänēnōōl') sulphur spas are 7 mi. E.

Vallescure, France: see SAINT-RAPHAËL.

Valleseco (bälyäsā'kō), town (pop. 623; commune pop. 4,727), Grand Canary, Canary Isls., 18 mi. WSW of Las Palmas; cereals, apples, potatoes, chestnuts; milk, cheese. Popular resort. Flour milling; stock raising.

Vallespir (välŭspēr'), valley of upper Tech R., Pyrénées-Orientales dept., S France, bet. Massif du Canigou (N) and main range of E Pyrenees (S). Grows rye and potatoes near its head (Prats-de-Mollo area); apple and cherry orchards and cork oaks are in lower reaches bet. Arles-sur-Tech and Céret (chief town). Has noted resorts (Amélie-les-Bains, Le Boulou) and hydroelectric installations.

Vallet (välā'), village (pop. 1,193), Loire-Inférieure dept., W France, 14 mi. ESE of Nantes; wine-growing.

Valletta or **Valetta** (vŭlĕ'tŭ), city (pop. 18,666), ⊙ Malta, major Br. naval base and Mediterranean port of call on isl.'s SE coast, roughly halfway bet. Gibraltar and Suez, 135 mi. SW of Syracuse and 250 mi. ESE of Tunis. Built on outer section of narrow, precipitous peninsula of Mt. Sceberras (c.1½ mi. long, ¾ mi. wide) terminating in Fort St. Elmo and flanked by 2 deep harbors, MARSAMUSCETTO HARBOUR (W) and GRAND HARBOUR (E). The administrative, cultural, and commercial center of the colony. Dockyards line both harbors. Attracts tourists because of its outstanding architectural treasures and a fine, equable climate. Many of its bldgs. were severely damaged by Second World War air raids. The picturesque city of white limestone is cut by steep and narrow streets, though the principal thoroughfares are wide. Notable are the Palace of the Grand Masters (now governor's residence) and the Conventual Church (co-cathedral) of St. John, both not too seriously damaged; the fine St. Mary of Damascus church (1576), destroyed; the city's earliest bldg., Victory Church, unharmed. Of the celebrated *auberges*—hostels built for the different nationalities (*Langues*) of the Order of The Knights of Malta (Knights Hospitalers or Knights of St. John)—perhaps the finest, Auberge de Castille, is practically intact; the Auberge de France was destroyed; the Auberge d'Italie suffered severely. The many fine collections were saved, however. City has a univ. (1769), the Royal Malta Library with archives of the order, graceful Manoel Theatre (built 1731, among Europe's oldest). Valletta was founded by the grand master Jean Parisot de la Vallette to celebrate the 1565 naval victory over the Turks. Became ⊙ in 1570. Surrendered to Napoleon in 1798. Revolted soon after and shut up Fr. garrison in city's ramparts until taken by the British in 1800. In June, 1940, 1st Axis bombs were dropped on the dockyard. Violent air attacks continued into 1943. Italian fleet capitulated here Sept., 1943.

Valle Viejo, Argentina: see SAN ISIDRO, Catamarca.

Valley. **1** County (□ 3,719; pop. 4,270), central Idaho; ⊙ Cascade. Mtn. and plateau area bounded E by Middle Fork of Salmon R., and drained by North Fork of Payette R. Stock raising, lumbering, dairying, agr. (timothy, clover, rye), quicksilver, tungsten mining. Includes much of Salmon R. primitive area and parts of Idaho and Payette natl. forests. Formed 1917. **2** County (□ 5,082; pop. 11,353), NE Mont.; ⊙ Glasgow. Irrigated agr. area bordering Sask.; bounded S by Missouri R. and Fort Peck Reservoir; drained by Milk R. Grain, livestock. Part of Fort Peck Indian Reservation in E. Formed 1893. **3** County (□ 570; pop. 7,252), central Nebr.; ⊙ Ord. Agr. region drained by N.Loup and Middle Loup rivers. Livestock, grain, dairy and poultry produce. Formed 1873.

Valley, village (pop. 1,113), Douglas co., E Nebr., 20 mi. W of Omaha and on Platte R.; resort; dairying, feed, grain, stock.

Valley, The, village, central Anguilla, B.W.I.; 18°13'N 63°4'W; sea-island cotton.

Valley Center, city (pop. 854), Sedgwick co., S central Kansas, on Little Arkansas R. and 10 mi. N of Wichita, in wheat region; grain storage. Oil and gas wells near by.

Valley City, city (pop. 6,851), ⊙ Barnes co., SE N.Dak., 60 mi. W of Fargo and on Sheyenne R.; flour milling, dairy products, grain. State teachers col. Settled 1872, inc. 1883.

Valley Falls. **1** City (pop. 1,139), Jefferson co., NE Kansas, on Delaware R. and 24 mi. NNE of Topeka; flour milling, dairying, poultry packing, bottling. Laid out 1855; inc. as village 1869, as city 1871. **2** Village (pop. 555), Rensselaer co., E N.Y., on Hoosic R. and 13 mi. NNE of Troy, in dairying and grain-growing area. **3** Industrial village (1940 pop. 5,412), administrative center of Cumberland town, Providence co., NE R.I., on Blackstone R. and 5 mi. N of Providence; textiles, upholstery goods, curtains, yarn, metal and wire products.

Valleyfield or **Salaberry de Valleyfield**, city (pop. 17,052), S Que., at E end of L. St. Francis, 35 mi. SW of Montreal; W terminal of Beauharnois Canal; cotton- and silk-milling center; distilling, dairying, mfg. of chemicals, bronze powder, asbestos, felt. Has seminary. Near by is hydroelectric station.

Valley Forge, village, Chester co., SE Pa., 3 mi. SE of Phoenixville and on Schuylkill R. Near by is Valley Forge State Park, scene of Washington's winter encampment 1777–78.

Valley Grove, village (1940 pop. 1,196), Ohio co., NW W.Va., in Northern Panhandle, 8 mi. ENE of Wheeling, near Pa. line.

Valley Head, town (pop. 418), De Kalb co., NE Ala., 45 mi. NNE of Gadsden, near Ga. line; shipping point for farm produce; lumber.

Valley Junction, Que.: see VALLÉE JONCTION.

Valley Junction, Iowa: see WEST DES MOINES.

Valley Mills, town (pop. 1,037), Bosque co., central Texas, on Bosque R. and 21 mi. WNW of Waco, in farm area.

Valley of Ten Thousand Smokes, region (□ 72), S Alaska, in KATMAI NATIONAL MONUMENT, 8 mi. NW of Katmai Volcano; 58°20'N 155°15'W; 15 mi. long, 7 mi. wide. Punctured by thousands of small volcanoes (fumaroles), created by eruption of Katmai Volcano (1912), emitting jets of steam. In time, as valley floor cools, this will become a geyser field.

Valley Park, city (pop. 2,956), St. Louis co., E Mo., on Meramec R., bet. Mississippi and Missouri rivers, and 15 mi. WSW of St. Louis.

Valley Springs. **1** Village (pop. c.200), Calaveras co., central Calif., in Sierra Nevada foothills, 30 mi. NE of Stockton; rail point for much of co. **2** Town (pop. 389), Minnehaha co., SE S.Dak., 13 mi. E of Sioux Falls, near Minn. line, and on branch of Big Sioux R.

Valley Stream, residential village (pop. 26,854), Nassau co., SE N.Y., on SW Long Isl., 6 mi. SE of Jamaica; mfg. (clothing, furniture, wood products, machinery, synthetic jewels, airplanes and parts). Agr. (dairy products; poultry, truck, vegetables). Near by is Valley Stream State Park (107 acres), with recreational facilities. Inc. 1925.

Valley View. 1 Village (pop. 998), Cuyahoga co., N Ohio, a SE suburb of Cleveland, on Cuyahoga R. **2** or **Valleyview,** village (pop. 611), Franklin co., central Ohio, a W suburb of Columbus. **3** Village (pop. 1,618), Schuylkill co., E central Pa., 18 mi. N of Pottsville. **4** Village (pop. c.700), Cooke co., N Texas, 9 mi. S of Gainesville, near Elm Fork of Trinity R.; farm trade point.

Valliant (văl'yůnt), town (pop. 661), McCurtain co., extreme SE Okla., 23 mi. E of Hugo, in agr. and lumbering area; cotton ginning.

Vallière or **Vallières** (both: vălyĕr'), town (1950 census pop. 364), Nord dept., NE Haiti, at source of the Grande Rivière du Nord, 28 mi. SE of Cap-Haïtien; rice, coffee, timber.

Vallinkoski (väl'lĭn-kōs"kē), village, Kymi co., SE Finland, on Vuoksi R. (rapids) and 2 mi. S of Imatra, frontier station in USSR border, opposite Svetogorsk; hydroelectric station.

Vallioor, India: see VADAKKU VALLIYUR.

Vallirana (bälyērä'nä), village (pop. 1,199), Barcelona prov., NE Spain, 13 mi. W of Barcelona; mfg. (cement, cotton and silk fabrics); agr. trade. Lead mines; limestone, marble, and gypsum quarries.

Vallo della Lucania (väl'lô dĕl'lä lōōkä'nyä), town (pop. 2,967), Salerno prov., Campania, S Italy, 27 mi. WNW of Sapri. Bishopric.

Valloire (välwär'), village (pop. 143), Savoie dept., SE France, resort in Dauphiné Alps, near Maurienne valley, 9 mi. SE of Saint-Jean-de-Maurienne; alt. 4,692 ft. Winter sports. On road (*route des Alpes*) to Col du Galibier, 8 mi. S.

Vallombrosa (väl-lômbrô'zä), village, Firenze prov., Tuscany, central Italy, in Etruscan Apennines, on NW slope of the Pratomagno, 15 mi. ESE of Florence. Resort (alt. 4,000 ft.), with noted 11th-cent. Benedictine abbey which served as school of forestry, 1866–1914.

Vallon (välō'), village (pop. 1,078), Ardèche dept., S France, 14 mi. S of Aubenas; distilling. In near-by gorge (15 mi. long) of the Ardèche are stalactite caverns and a natural bridge (Pont d'Arc).

Vallorbe (välôrb'), town (pop. 3,592), Vaud canton, W Switzerland, on Orbe R., at Fr. border, and 18 mi. NW of Lausanne; customs station. Metal products (drills, saws, files), chemicals. La Dernier hydroelectric plant is SW.

Vallorcine (välôrsēn'), Alpine resort (pop. 55), Haute-Savoie dept., SE France, at N foot of Mont Blanc massif, customs station near Swiss border, 8 mi. NNE of Chamonix; transfer point on Saint-Gervais-les-Bains–Martigny-Ville RR.

Vallouise (välwēz'), village (pop. 283), Hautes-Alpes dept., SE France, in a wild valley of Massif du Pelvoux, 8 mi. SW of Briançon; alt. 3,829 ft. Barrelmaking. Slate quarries.

Valls (bäls), city (pop. 9,948), Tarragona prov., NE Spain, in Catalonia, 12 mi. N of Tarragona, in irrigated valley; industrial and commercial center. Produces cotton and woolen fabrics, knit and leather goods, chemicals (sulphur fertilizer, tartaric acid), liqueurs, alcohol; olive-oil processing, tanning, sawmilling. Trades in wine, livestock, cereals, almonds, hazelnuts.

Vallvik (väl'vēk"), village (pop. 870), Gavleborg co., E central Sweden, on Gulf of Bothnia, near mouth of Ljusna R., 8 mi. SSE of Soderhamn; pulp mills, sulphite works.

Valmadrera (välmädrā'rä), village (pop. 3,243), Como prov., Lombardy, N Italy, 2 mi. W of Lecco; paper lace, hardware.

Val Marie (văl mărē'), village (pop. 301), S Sask., near Mont. border, 70 mi. S of Swift Current; wheat, livestock.

Valmaseda (bälmäsä'dhä), town (pop. 3,641), Vizcaya prov., N Spain, 15 mi. WSW of Bilbao; metalworks (cutlery); woolen mill. Agr. trade (*chacolí* wine, vegetables, potatoes, livestock).

Valmead, village (pop. 1,524), Caldwell co., W central N.C., just N of Lenoir.

Valmeyer (văl'mīr), village (pop. 656), Monroe co., SW Ill., 24 mi. SSW of East St. Louis, in agr. area.

Valmiera or **Valmera** (väl'myĕrä), Ger. *Wolmar* (vôl'mär), Rus. (until 1917) *Volmar* or *Vol'mar*, city (pop. 8,482), N Latvia, in Vidzeme on Gauja R. and 65 mi. NE of Riga; rail junction; commercial and agr. center; flax and woolen milling, tanning, sawmilling, brick mfg., brewing; slaughterhouse. Has castle ruins.

Valmojado (bälmōhä'dhō), town (pop. 1,934), Toledo prov., central Spain, 25 mi. SW of Madrid; cereals, grapes, olives, sheep. Sawmilling, olive-oil extracting.

Valmont (välmō'), agr. village (pop. 482), Seine-Inférieure dept., N France, 25 mi. NE of Le Havre.

Valmontone (välmôntô'nĕ), town (pop. 5,489), Roma prov., Latium, central Italy, 10 mi. NE of Velletri. Largely destroyed in Second World War.

Val Morin (väl môrē'), village (pop. estimate 300), S Que., in the Laurentians, on North R. and 5 mi. SW of Ste. Agathe des Monts; dairying; ski resort.

Valmy (välmē'), village (pop. 1,383), Oran dept., NW Algeria, at E edge of the Oran Sebkha; saltworks.

Valmy (välmē'), village (pop. 284), Marne dept., N France, 6 mi. W of Sainte-Menehould; slaked-lime factory. Two monuments commemorate Fr. victory over Prussians in 1792.

Valognes (välô'nyů), town (pop. 2,997), Manche dept., NW France, in center of Cotentin Peninsula, 11 mi. SE of Cherbourg; egg- and poultry-shipping center. Heavily damaged during Allied drive for Cherbourg (June, 1944) in Second World War.

Valois (välwä'), village (pop. estimate 400), S Que., SW Montreal Isl., on L. St. Louis, 10 mi. SW of Montreal; dairying, truck gardening.

Valois (välwä'), old district of N France, now in SE Oise and SW Aisne depts.; historical ⊙ was Crépy-en-Valois.

Valona (vůlō'nů), Albanian: Gheg *Vlonë* (vůlô'nů) or *Vlona* (vůlô'nä), Tosk *Vlorë* (vůlô'rů) or *Vlora* (vůlô'rä), anc. *Aulon*, city (1945 pop. 14,640), SW Albania, port on Bay of Valona, 70 mi. SSW of Tirana; 40°28'N 19°30'E. Major commercial center, trading mainly in olives and olive oil; soap mfg., dairying. Airport. Port installations (connected by road with city, 1.5 mi. inland) include Valona port proper, with general cargo and bitumen piers, and Krionero anchorage [Albanian *Uj të ftohtë*,=cold water; 1.5 mi. S], with lighthouse and petroleum pier (linked by pipe line with Kucovë oilfield). A bishopric in 5th cent., Valona figured in struggle (11th–12th cents.) bet. Normans of Sicily and Byzantines, passed 1345 to Serbs, later to Venice until it was occupied (1464) by the Turks, who held it (except for brief Venetian rule, 1690–91) until Balkan Wars. Here an independent Albania was proclaimed (1912). During First World War, it was held (1914–20) by Italians and made a naval base (later transferred to Saseno isl.). Formerly also called Avlona.

Valona, Bay of, Albanian *Gji i Vlonës* (dyē' ē vůlô'nůs), sheltered inlet of Strait of Otranto, in SW Albania, bet. 2 prongs (Acroceraunia and Lungara) of Ceraunian Mts.; 15 mi. long, 6 mi. wide. An important military harbor at entrance to the Adriatic, it has a naval base on SASENO isl. (off its mouth). Valona port is on E shore.

Valongo (vŏolông'gōō), town (pop. 1,914), Pôrto dist., N Portugal, on railroad and 6 mi. ENE of Oporto; antimony mines, slate quarries.

Válor (vä'lôr), town (pop. 1,341), Granada prov., S Spain, 21 mi. SSE of Guadix; vegetables, grapes, wine; lumber. Mineral springs. Played notable role in Moriscos' bloody rising (1568–70).

Valoria la Buena (bälô'ryä lä bwā'nä), town (pop. 1,049), Valladolid prov., N central Spain, 14 mi. NE of Valladolid; wine, cereals, sugar beets, fruit. Gypsum quarries.

Valpaços (vŭlpä'sōōsh), town (pop. 1,867), Vila Real dist., N Portugal, 32 mi. NE of Vila Real; rye, potatoes; sheep and goat raising.

Valparaíba, Brazil: see CACHOEIRA PAULISTA.

Valparaíso (vŭlpůräē'zōō), city (pop. 3,469), NW São Paulo, Brazil, on fertile watershed bet. Tietê (N) and Aguapeí (S) rivers, on railroad and 28 mi. W of Araçatuba; agr.-processing center (coffee, manioc, rice, cotton); stock raising, beekeeping.

Valparaiso (vălpůrī'zō), Sp. *Valparaíso* (bälpäräē'sō), province (□ 1,860; 1940 pop. 425,065; 1949 estimate 522,273), central Chile, on the Pacific; ⊙ Valparaiso. Consists of low hills and rich fertile valleys, particularly valley of Aconcagua R. Grows wine, fruit, cereals, alfalfa, vegetables, and hemp on large scale. Cattle raising throughout prov.; goats in dry N area. Fisheries along coast. Copper, silver, gold, and some lime in the hills. Mining, flour milling, wine making, distilling, food canning. Large sugar and petroleum refineries at Valparaiso, its great port. Its beaches, particularly those of VIÑA DEL MAR, are popular resorts. Easter Isl. and Juan Fernández Isls. are part of prov.

Valparaiso, Sp. *Valparaíso* city (1940 pop. 209,945; 1949 estimate 182,689), ⊙ Valparaiso prov. and Valparaiso dept. (□ 1,101; 1940 pop. 343,848), central Chile, on the Pacific (Valparaiso Bay), and 60 mi. WNW of Santiago; 33°2'S 71°40'W. Second largest city of Chile and the most important port on W coast of South America, it is the trade and mfg. center for a rich agr. area (wine, fruit, grain, livestock), terminus of the Transandine RR to Argentina, and a major fishing and whaling station. As outlet for Chile's central valley, it handles half of country's imports and large volume of its exports. Mfg.: metal products, sugar, chemicals, petroleum products, pharmaceuticals, paint, textiles, shoes and other leather goods, enamelware, vegetable oils, confectioneries, beer, cement. Its institutions of higher learning include: univ. of technology, a Catholic univ., mining and art schools, naval acad. The city is built along the curve of a bay and climbs steep hills which bound it like an amphitheater. In NW is the port, protected by breakwaters, with old colonial bldgs. Almendral, in the SE part, along the water front, is the commercial section. Los Cerros, the residential section, on slopes overlooking the bay, is reached by funiculars. Has fine parks and boulevards. Among its churches are the colonial La Matriz and a new cathedral. With a mild climate, Valparaiso attracts numerous tourists to its beaches (e.g., Playa Ancha and Torpederas), particularly to the near-by suburb of VIÑA DEL MAR. Site of Valparaiso was discovered 1536 and a settlement was later established by Pedro de Valdivia. It experienced raids by buccaneers during the colonial period. After its great development had begun under the Chilean republic, it suffered a merciless naval bombardment in 1866 by the Spanish, and several earthquakes, the most severe in 1906, when the city was leveled. Rebuilt in modern fashion, it continued to develop rapidly.

Valparaíso (bälpäräē'sō), town (pop. 1,968), Antioquia dept., NW central Colombia, on E slopes of Cordillera Occidental, near Cauca R., 45 mi. S of Medellín; alt. 4,508 ft. Agr. (coffee, corn, sugar cane, stock) and lumbering center (carob, cedar, oak, walnut); also vanilla and other forest products.

Valparaíso, town (pop. 3,952), Zacatecas, N central Mexico, on interior plateau, 70 mi. ENE of Zacatecas; alt. 6,397 ft.; agr. center (corn, wheat, chick-peas, alfalfa, chili, stock).

Valparaiso (vălpůrā'zō). **1** Resort city (pop. 1,047), Okaloosa co., NW Fla., on Choctawhatchee Bay, c.45 mi. ENE of Pensacola. Eglin Air Force Base is just SW. **2** City (pop. 12,028), ⊙ Porter co., NW Ind., 18 mi. ESE of Gary, in dairy and poultry area; mfg. (magnets, machine parts, agr. implements, ball and rubber bearings, castings, fiber products, furniture, paint, varnish, feed, electrical insulation). Seat of Valparaiso Univ. Settled 1834, inc. 1865. **3** Village (pop. 392), Saunders co., E Nebr., 20 mi. NNW of Lincoln; feed, grain, livestock.

Valpoi (välpoi'), town, N Goa dist., Portuguese India, 21 mi. ENE of Pangim; market center for timber (teak, blackwood), rice; sawmills.

Valpovo (väl'pôvô), village (pop. 3,811), NE Croatia, Yugoslavia, on railroad and 14 mi. NW of Osijek, near the Drava (Hung. border), in Slavonia; local trade center. Castle.

Valréas (välrääs'), town (pop. 3,773), Vaucluse dept., SE France, 19 mi. NNE of Orange, center of an enclave (c.9 mi. long, 7 mi. wide; pop. 7,669) within Drôme dept. Carton-mfg. center. Trade in wines, olive oil, truffles, fruits. A papal city, 1317–1562. Has 12th-cent. church and a ruined 14th-cent. castle.

Val-Saint-Lambert (väl-sē-läbär'), town, Liége prov., E Belgium, on Meuse R. and 5 mi. WSW of Liége; center of crystal and glass industry.

Val Saint Michel (väl sē mē-shĕl'), town (pop. 316), S Que., 10 mi. W of Quebec; dairying; vegetables, poultry.

Valsayn (văl'sān), govt. stock farm, NW Trinidad, B.W.I., just S of St. Joseph. Here last Sp. governor signed treaty of capitulation (1797).

Valsequillo de Gran Canaria (bälsākē'lyō dhā grän' känä'ryä), village (pop. 358), Grand Canary, Canary Isls., 9 mi. SW of Las Palmas; barley, wheat, corn, fruit, grapes; flour milling, wine making. Mineral springs.

Vals-les-Bains (väl-lā-bē'), town (pop. 2,669), Ardèche dept., S France, in gorge of Volane R. (small tributary of the Ardèche), 4 mi. NNW of Aubenas; noted spa with thermal establishment. Its mineral waters are bottled and shipped.

Valsoyfjord (väls'ůüfyôr"), Nor. *Valsøyfjord*, village and canton (pop. 1,422), More og Romsdal co., W Norway, on a 5-mi. fjord, 23 mi. E of Kristiansund; agr., and fisheries. At village of Valsoybotn (–bôtůn) (Nor. *Valsøybotn*), 5 mi. ESE, at head of fjord: lumber milling, carpentering, cement casting.

Vals-près-Le-Puy (väl-prĕ-lů-pwē'), SW suburb (pop. 600) of Le Puy, Haute-Loire dept., S central France; lacemaking. Has theological seminary.

Valsugana (välsōōgä'nä), valley of upper Brenta R., N Italy; extends from Pergine Valsugana E to confluence of Cismon R. with the Brenta. Contains lakes Caldonazzo and Levico. Agr. (corn, raw silk, fruit), livestock raising, forestry. Has resorts (Levico, Roncegno) frequented by tourists. Chief center, Borgo.

Valtellina (vältĕl-lē'nä), valley (□ c.1,020) of upper Adda R., in Sondrio prov., Lombardy, N Italy, bet. Rhaetian Alps (N) and Bergamasque Alps (S); extends c.70 mi. E and NE from L. Como to Ortles mtn. group. Forestry, cattle and sheep raising, agr. (rye, corn, grapes). Many hydroelectric plants (Grossotto, Morbegno, Bormio, Lovero Valtellino) and resorts. Chief towns: Sondrio, Tirano, Bormio.

Valtice (väl'tyĭtsĕ), Ger. *Feldsberg* (fĕlts'bĕrk), village (pop. 2,938), S Moravia, Czechoslovakia, on railroad and 6 mi. W of Breclav, on Austrian border, in wheat and grape region; makes sparkling wine. Has castle. Inc. into Czechoslovakia in 1919.

Valtierra (bältyĕ'rä), town (pop. 2,724), Navarre prov., N Spain, near the Ebro, 10 mi. N of Tudela; sugar beets, cereals, olive oil.

Valtierrilla (bältyĕrē'yä), town (pop. 2,233), Guanajuato, central Mexico, on Lerma R. and 5 mi. SE of Salamanca; grain, sugar cane, vegetables, fruit, stock.

Valtournanche (vältōōrnăsh′), village (pop. 283), Val d'Aosta region, NW Italy, 18 mi. NE of Aosta; resort (alt. 5,000 ft.). Lies in the Valtournanche (scenic valley of Pennine Alps), which extends 17 mi. S from slopes of the Matterhorn to Val d'Aosta; watered by a small affluent of Dora Baltea R. Hydroelectric plants.

Valuiki or **Valuyki** (vŭlōō′ēkkē), city (1926 pop. 10,243), SE Kursk oblast, Russian SFSR, on Oskol R. and 125 mi. SE of Kursk; rail junction; mfg. of agr. machinery; flour milling, sunflower-oil extraction, distilling. Founded 1593 as one of southernmost fortified outposts of Moscow. During Second World War, held (1942–43) by Germans.

Valvasone (välväzô′nĕ), village (pop. 1,421), Udine prov., Friuli-Venezia Giulia, NE Italy, 18 mi. WSW of Udine.

Valvedditturai, Ceylon: see POINT PEDRO, town.

Valverde (bälvĕr′dhā), town (pop. 1,680), chief settlement of HIERRO, Canary Isls., 115 mi. WSW of Santa Cruz de Tenerife; 27°46′N 17°57′W. Exports cereals, wine, potatoes, fruit. Stock raising; flour milling.

Valverde, town (1950 pop. 6,600), Santiago prov., NW Dominican Republic, in fertile Cibao region, 25 mi. WNW of Santiago; rice-growing and -milling center. Lumbering and gold washing in vicinity.

Val Verde (văl vûr′dē), county (□ 3,242; pop. 16,635), SW Texas; ⊙ Del Rio. Partly on Edwards Plateau; bounded SW and S by the Rio Grande (Mex. border), drained by Pecos R. and Devils R. (power dams). A leading Texas sheep-raising co.; goat ranches also important; some cattle and horse breeding. Irrigated agr. in Rio Grande valley: alfalfa, fruit (especially grapes), truck. Hunting, fishing in Devils and Walk lakes. Formed 1885.

Valverde de Burguillos (bälvĕr′dhā dhā bōōrgē′lyōs), town (pop. 1,051), Badajoz prov., W Spain, 13 mi. E of Jerez de los Caballeros; olive and grain growing; flour milling.

Valverde de Júcar (hōō′kär), town (pop. 3,028), Cuenca prov., E central Spain, on Madrid-Valencia highway, and 25 mi. S of Cuenca; agr. center (cereals, grapes, olives, livestock). Olive-oil pressing, flour milling.

Valverde de la Vera (lä vā′rä), town (pop. 1,203), Cáceres prov., W Spain, 33 mi. ENE of Plasencia; olive oil, wine, pepper.

Valverde del Camino (dhĕl kämē′nō), city (pop. 10,678), Huelva prov., SW Spain, in Andalusia, on railroad and 24 mi. NNE of Huelva; mining (copper and iron pyrites), processing, and stock-raising center in agr. region (grapes, wheat, barley, chickpeas). Sawmilling, flour milling, liquor distilling; mfg. of shoes, furniture, textile goods, bottle corks.

Valverde de Leganés (lāgänās′), town (pop. 4,086), Badajoz prov., W Spain, 14 mi. S of Badajoz; agr. center (cereals, olives, livestock); olive-oil pressing, flour milling; mfg. of soft drinks and tiles.

Valverde del Fresno (frĕ′snō), town (pop. 3,637), Cáceres prov., W Spain, near Port. border, 30 mi. SW of Ciudad Rodrigo; mfg. of woolen blankets and soap, olive-oil processing; cereals, livestock.

Valverde de Llerena (dhā lyārā′nä), town (pop. 2,537), Badajoz prov., W Spain, 10 mi. E of Llerena; grain, olives, grapes, livestock.

Valverde del Majano (dhĕl mähä′nō), town (pop. 973), Segovia prov., central Spain, 5 mi. W of Segovia; cereals, vegetables, livestock; mfg. of meat products, flour milling.

Valverde de Mérida (dhā mā′rē-dhä), town (pop. 1,557), Badajoz prov., W Spain, 6 mi. E of Mérida; cereals, hogs, sheep; flour milling, olive-oil processing.

Valverde Island, Chile: see CHONOS ARCHIPELAGO.

Valyevo, Yugoslavia: see VALJEVO.

Vama (vä′mä), town (1948 pop. 4,580), Suceava prov., N Rumania, on Moldava R. and 7 mi. NE of Campulung; rail junction and summer resort. Also mfg. of bricks and cardboard; limestone quarrying; lumbering. Has noted 18th-cent. commemorative cross. Known since 1409.

Vamberk (väm′bĕrk), village (pop. 3,112), E Bohemia, Czechoslovakia, on railroad and 29 mi. SE of Hradec Kralove; smoked-meat industry; mfg. of electrodes, lace making.

Vamdrup (väm′drŏop), town (pop. 2,069), Ribe amt, E central Jutland, Denmark, 32 mi. ESE of Esbjerg; rail junction; mfg. (furniture, automobile bodies).

Vammala (väm′mälä), town (pop. 1,124), Turku-Pori co., SW Finland, on Kokemä R. (rapids) and 30 mi. WNW of Tampere, in lumbering region. Has church (c.1400).

Vamospercs (vä′môsh-pārch), Hung. *Vámospércs*, town (pop. 5,244), Hajdu co., E Hungary, 8 mi. E of Debrecen; wheat, paprika, cattle, horses.

Vampula (väm′pōōlä), village (commune pop. 3,850), Turku-Pori co., SW Finland, 40 mi. NNE of Turku; limestone quarries.

Vamsadhara River (vŭmsŭdä′rŭ), in S Orissa and NE Madras, India, rises in Eastern Ghats, SE of Bhawanipatna, flows S past Gunupur, and E to Bay of Bengal ENE of Chicacole; c.150 mi. long.

Van (vän), province (□ 6,857; 1950 pop. 143,949), SE Turkey, in Armenia; ⊙ Van. Bordered W by L. Van, E by Iran. Drained by Buhtan R. Coal; rye, apples. Pop. largely Kurd.

Van, town (1950 pop. 13,471), ⊙ Van prov., SE Turkey, near E shore of L. Van, 150 mi. SE of Erzurum, 175 mi. ENE of Diyarbakir; alt. 5,659 ft.; 38°32′N 43°18′E. Trade center for wheat-growing area. An anc. center of Armenian civilization; the so-called "Vannic inscriptions" have been found here. Its old citadel dates back to 8th cent. B.C. In 1895–96, scene of massacres of Armenians.

Van, town (pop. 610), Van Zandt co., NE Texas, 23 mi. NW of Tyler; oil-field center.

Van, Lake (□ 1,453), salt lake, E Turkey, in Armenia, 65 mi. SW of Mt. Ararat and extending to within 35 mi. of the Iranian line; 75 mi. long, 50 mi. wide; alt. 5,640 ft. Has no outlet. On its shores, notably at town of Van, developed the anc. Armenian civilization.

Vanadium (vùnā′dēùm). **1** Hamlet, San Miguel co., SW Colo., on San Miguel R., in NW foothills of San Juan Mts., and 8 mi. WNW of Telluride; alt. 7,650 ft. Vanadium deposits here. **2** Village (pop. c.150), Grant co., SW N.Mex., in foothills of Pinos Altos Mts., 10 mi. E of Silver City; alt. c.6,000 ft.; silver, lead, copper, zinc mined here. Railroad station is called Hanover Junction.

Van Alstyne (văn ăl′stīn), town (pop. 1,649), Grayson co., N Texas, 15 mi. S of Sherman; rail point in cotton area; cotton processing.

Vananda (vùnăn′dù), village, SW B.C., on N Texada Isl., port on Malaspina Strait, 20 mi. ENE of Courtenay across Strait of Georgia; copper, gold, silver mining; limestone quarrying.

Vananda, village (pop. c.100), Rosebud co., E central Mont., on small branch of Yellowstone R. and 18 mi. NW of Forsyth; supply point in livestock region.

Vanavara (vŭnùvŭrä′), village (1948 pop. over 500), S Evenki Natl. Okrug, Krasnoyarsk Territory, Russian SFSR, 270 mi. SSE of Tura and on Stony Tunguska R.

Van Buren (văn byōō′rùn). **1** County (□ 714; pop. 9,687), N central Ark.; ⊙ Clinton. Drained by Middle Fork of Little Red R. Agr. (corn, cotton, hay, livestock); timber. Part of Ozark Natl. Forest in SW. Formed 1833. **2** County (□ 487; pop. 11,007), SE Iowa, on Mo. line; ⊙ Keosauqua. Prairie agr. area (hogs, cattle, poultry, corn, soybeans, hay) drained by Des Moines and Fox rivers. Bituminous-coal mines, limestone quarries. Has state parks. Formed 1836. **3** County (□ 607; pop. 39,184), SW Mich.; ⊙ Paw Paw. Bounded W by L. Michigan; drained by Paw Paw and Black rivers. Fruitgrowing region (especially apples, peaches; also cherries, strawberries, grapes); truck, livestock, dairy products. Mfg. at South Haven and Paw Paw. Resorts; fisheries, nurseries. Organized 1837. **4** County (□ 255; pop. 3,985), central Tenn.; ⊙ Spencer. Bounded N by Caney Fork of Cumberland R.; hilly region in the Cumberlands. Livestock raising, some farming, lumbering. Formed 1840.

Van Buren. **1** City (pop. 6,413), ⊙ Crawford co., NW Ark., on Arkansas R. and 5 mi. NE of Fort Smith; ships agr. produce (strawberries, cotton, truck, dairy products); zinc smelting; railroad shops. Hardwood timber, natural-gas wells in region. U.S. soil-conservation project near by. Settled 1818, laid out c.1838, inc. 1843. **2** Town (pop. 815), Grant co., E central Ind., 11 mi. ENE of Marion, in agr. area. **3** Town (pop. 5,094), including Van Buren village (pop. 3,732), Aroostook co., NE Maine, on St. John R. and 22 mi. N of Caribou, in lumbering and potato-growing area. Pulp mills; port of entry; trade center. Includes Keegan village (1940 pop. 832). Inc. 1881. **4** Resort town (pop. 708), ⊙ Carter co., S Mo., in the Ozarks, on Current R. and 38 mi. NW of Poplar Bluff; lumber products. State park near by.

Vanburen or **Van Buren**, village (pop. 308), Hancock co., NW Ohio, 7 mi. N of Findlay. Van Buren State Park is near by.

Vance (văns), county (□ 269; pop. 32,101), N N.C.; ⊙ Henderson. Bounded N by Va., SW by Tar R. Piedmont tobacco and timber area; important tungsten deposits (mined near Henderson); textile mfg., sawmilling. Formed 1881.

Vance, town (pop. 106), Orangeburg co., S central S.C., 25 mi. E of Orangeburg, near L. Marion.

Vance Air Force Base, Okla.: see ENID.

Vanceboro (văns′bŭrù, –bŭrō). **1** Town (pop. 497), Washington co., E Maine, on Spednik L. and St. Croix R. and 28 mi. NNW of Calais; port of entry; hunting, fishing, lumbering. **2** Town (pop. 753), Craven co., E N.C., 15 mi. NNW of New Bern; sawmilling.

Vanceburg, town (pop. 1,528), ⊙ Lewis co., NE Ky., on left bank (levee) of the Ohio and 18 mi. SW of Portsmouth, Ohio, in agr. area (dairy products, livestock, truck); mfg. of shoes, railroad ties, cooperage products; flour milling. Old covered bridge near by. Settled c.1796; inc. 1827.

Vanch (vänch), village (1939 pop. over 500), W Gorno-Badakhshan Autonomous Oblast, Tadzhik SSR, on Vanch R. and 60 mi. N of Khorog; wheat, cattle.

Vanch River, Tadzhik SSR, rises in branch of Fedchenko Glacier, flows c.60 mi. SW, past Vanch, to Panj R. 8 mi. SW of Vanch. Gold placers in upper course.

Vancouver (vănkōō′vùr), city (pop. 275,353), SW B.C., near Wash. border, with a fine natural harbor on Burrard Inlet of the Strait of Georgia, opposite Vancouver Isl.; 49°17′N 123°7′W. Largest city of W Canada and 3d-largest city of the Dominion, commercial center for B.C., and chief Canadian port on the Pacific, open the year round. There are extensive dock and grain-elevator facilities; shipping services link city with Victoria, Seattle, and other U.S., Alaskan, Far Eastern, Australian, and New Zealand ports. Exports include grain, lumber, fish, metals, and minerals. Vancouver is W terminal of Canadian Pacific and Canadian National RRs. Tourist center. Industries include shipbuilding, fish canning, lumbering; mfg. of steel products, furniture. Site of Univ. of British Columbia, with agr. col., whose new bldgs. are at the growing residential suburb of Point Grey (W), on the Strait of Georgia. Among notable features is Stanley Park (900 acres), with zoo and extensive gardens. Vancouver's mean temp. ranges from 36°F. (Jan.) to 63°F. (July and Aug.); average annual rainfall, 57.4 inches. First settlement, founded here c.1875 and named Granville, was reached by Canadian Pacific RR in 1886; inc. the same year and named after Capt. George Vancouver, who had entered Burrard Inlet in 1792 aboard the *Discovery*. City's suburbs include West Vancouver and Burnaby. Adjoining Vancouver are the cities of North Vancouver, opposite, on N side of Burrard Inlet (bridge, ferry), forming part of the Vancouver harbor system, and New Westminster.

Vancouver, city (pop. 41,664), ⊙ Clark co., SW Wash., on Columbia R. opposite Portland, Oregon, connected by bridge; 45°38′N 122°41′W. Important port, shipping grain, lumber; mfg. (food, paper, textile products). Permanent military post (Vancouver Barracks) and airport, plus development of the aircraft industry, doubled its pop. during Second World War. Power from near-by Bonneville Dam aids in aluminum production. Several historic monuments, 2 state homes, and Clark Col. are here. Founded 1825 by the Hudson's Bay Company, it is the oldest settlement in the state; became a U.S. possession 1846; inc. 1857. Fort Vancouver Natl. Monument (65 acres; authorized 1948) includes site of hq. depot of Hudson's Bay Company and old Fort Vancouver (forerunner of Vancouver Barracks), which was early seat of military and political authority and the trading center of vast Pacific Northwest.

Vancouver, Cape, W Alaska, on Bering Sea, at N end of Etolin Strait, W extremity of Nelson Isl., opposite Nunivak Isl.; 60°37′N 165°14′W.

Vancouver, Mount (15,700 ft.), on Yukon-Alaska border, in St. Elias Mts., 160 mi. W of Whitehorse, on SE edge of Seward Glacier; 60°20′N 139°41′W.

Vancouver Island, Canada, largest island (□ 13,049; pop. 147,262, including adjacent isls. 150,407) off W coast of North America, part of British Columbia, separated from mainland by Queen Charlotte Strait and Johnstone Strait (NE), the Strait of Georgia (SE), Haro Strait (S), and Juan de Fuca Strait (SW); 285 mi. long, 30–80 mi. wide. E coastline is generally even; W coast is deeply indented by Barkley, Clayoquot, Nootka, Kyuquot, and Quatsino sounds. Generally mountainous, isl. is structurally part of the Coast Mts. of B.C. and of the Olympic Mts. of Wash.; Golden Hinde (7,219 ft.), in Strathcona Provincial Park in central part of isl., is highest peak. Other high mts. are Mt. Elkhorn (7,200 ft.) and Victoria Peak (7,095 ft.). There are numerous lakes; largest are Cowichan, Great Central, Kennedy, Buttle, and Nimpkish lakes. In climate the isl. resembles Wash. and Ore. W of the Cascades, being influenced by warm moist Pacific winds. Heavily wooded, isl. has important lumbering industry. Coal, gold, and copper are mined; in coastal areas dairying and fruitgrowing are carried on. Fishing (salmon, herring, halibut) and fish canning are important. VICTORIA, ⊙ B.C., is largest city and trade center of Vancouver Isl. Other cities are NANAIMO, ALBERNI, Port Alberni, Courtenay, Cumberland, Duncan, and Ladysmith. Esquimalt, near Victoria, is important naval base; Bamfield (SW) is chief Canadian transpacific cable terminal. Isl. was 1st visited by Capt. James Cook (1778) and was surveyed (1792) by Capt. George Vancouver. John Meares built fort at Nootka Sound in 1788; it was seized by the Spaniards in 1789, but under Nootka Convention of 1790 Spain relinquished her exclusive claim to the N Pacific Coast of North America, and Spanish colony at Nootka was abandoned, 1795. Treaty of Washington, 1846 (the Oregon Treaty), confirmed British sovereignty over Vancouver Isl., and region was granted to the Hudson's Bay Co. with view to colonization. Vancouver Isl. became a crown colony in 1849 and was united with mainland colony of B.C. in 1866.

Vancsod (vän′chôd), Hung. *Váncsod*, town (pop. 2,245), Bihar co., E Hungary, 5 mi. E of Berettyoujfalu; grain, cattle.

Vandalia (văndā′lēù). **1** City (pop. 5,471), Fayette co., S central Ill., on Kaskaskia R. and 29 mi. N of Centralia, in agr. and oil-producing area; corn, wheat, dairy products, poultry, livestock; shoe and roofing factories; poultry hatchery. Inc. 1821; was

2d ⊙ Ill. (1820–39). Lincoln and Douglas served in legislature here. Points of interest: old capitol (1836), preserved as state memorial; old Presbyterian church; Lincoln collection in library. State penal farm is near by. **2** Village (pop. 360), Cass co., SW Mich., 31 mi. SSW of Kalamazoo, in farm area. Elk are raised here for sale to parks and zoos. **3** City (pop. 2,624), Audrain co., NE central Mo., 23 mi. ENE of Mexico; grain, fruit, cattle, poultry; fire-clay products, dresses; coal. Inc. 1874. **4** Village (pop. 927), Montgomery co., W Ohio, near Great Miami R., 9 mi. N of Dayton.

Vandemere (vănʹdůmēr), fishing town (pop. 475), Pamlico co., E N.C., 22 mi. ENE of New Bern, on inlet of Pamlico Sound; small cannery.

Vanderbijl Park or **Van der Byl** (both: vănʹdůrbĭl, Afrikaans făn dûr bĭlʹ), town (pop. 2,120), S Transvaal, U. of So. Afr., near Orange Free State border, near Vaal R., 5 mi. W of Vereeniging; steel center (blast furnaces, rolling mills); machinery works. Steelworks built 1941; town site laid out 1946.

Vanderbilt. 1 Village (pop. 410), Otsego co., N Mich., 21 mi. SE of Petoskey, in fishing and hunting area; sawmills. **2** Borough (pop. 937), Fayette co., SW Pa., 4 mi. WNW of Connellsburg.

Vanderburgh, county (□ 241; pop. 160,422), SW Ind.; ⊙ EVANSVILLE. Bounded S by Ohio R., here forming Ky. line; drained by small Pigeon Creek. Agr. (winter wheat, hogs, soybeans, corn); bituminous-coal mining. Extensive mfg. at Evansville, shipping and industrial center for SW Ind. Formed 1818.

Vandercook, village (pop. 3,190), Jackson co., S Mich., just S of Jackson.

Vandergrift, borough (pop. 9,524), Westmoreland co., W central Pa., 24 mi. NE of Pittsburgh and on Kiskiminetas R.; mfg. (sheet steel, machinery, gloves); bituminous coal; agr. Laid out 1895, inc. 1897.

Vanderhoof, village (pop. 350), central B.C., on Nechako R. and 50 mi. W of Prince George; cattle-shipping center and distributing point for the Nechako valley mixed-farming area; dairying.

Vanderlin Island, Australia: see SIR EDWARD PELLEW ISLANDS.

Van Deusenville, Mass.: see GREAT BARRINGTON.

Van Diemen Gulf (văn dēʹmůn), arm of Timor Sea; bounded N by Cobourg Peninsula, E and S by N coast of Northern Territory, Australia, W by Melville Isl.; 90 mi. long, 50 mi. wide. Outlets: Clarence Strait (W), Dundas Strait (N). Receives South Alligator R.

Van Diemen's Land: see TASMANIA.

Van Diemen Strait, Japan: see OSUMI STRAIT.

Vandiola (bändyōʹlä), village, Cochabamba dept., central Bolivia, on N slopes of Cordillera de Cochabamba, 65 mi. ENE of Cochabamba; subtropical agr. products (fruits, cacao, coca).

Vandiver (vănʹdůvůr), village (pop. c.350), Shelby co., central Ala., 17 mi. E of Birmingham; farming, lumbering. School and camp for delinquent youths near by.

Vandling, borough (pop. 722), Lackawanna co., NE Pa., 18 mi. NNE of Scranton and on the Lackawanna R.

Vandoeuvre-lès-Nancy (vādûʹvrů-lā-nāsēʹ), S residential suburb (pop. 5,147) of Nancy, Meurthe-et-Moselle dept., NE France; vinegar mfg.

Vandra or **Vyandra,** Est. *Vändra* (all: vănʹdrä), town (pop. 938), W central Estonia, on rail spur and 27 mi. NE of Parnu; mfg. (wood pulp, glass).

Vandsburg, Poland: see WIECBORK.

Vanduser (văndōōʹzůr), town (pop. 281), Scott co., SE Mo., in Mississippi flood plain, 10 mi. NW of Sikeston.

Van Dyke, village (1940 pop. 9,513), Macomb co., SE Mich., suburb just N of Detroit.

Vanegas (bänäʹgäs), town (pop. 1,633), San Luis Potosí, N central Mexico, on interior plateau, 25 mi. NW of Matehuala; alt. 5,660 ft. Rail junction; cereals, maguey. Silver, gold, and copper deposits near by.

Vaner, Lake, or **Lake Vener,** Swedish *Vänern* (vĕʹnůrn), largest lake (□ 2,141) of Sweden, in SW part of country, and 3d-largest lake of Europe; extends 90 mi. NE–SW bet. Vanersborg and Karlstad. Other cities on shore are Lidkoping, Mariestad, Kristinehamn, and Amal. It is 5–46 mi. wide; up to 321 ft. deep. Drained SW by Gota R.; receives Klar, Tida, Let, By, and Nor rivers. Forms part of Gota Canal route. S part of lake is also called L. Dalbo, Swedish *Dalbosjön* (dälʹbōō-shûn″).

Vanersborg (vĕ″nůrsbôrʹyů), Swed. *Vänersborg,* city (1950 pop. 15,655), ⊙ Alvsborg co., SW Sweden, at SW end of L. Vaner, at outlet of Gota R., 50 mi. NNE of Goteborg; 58°22′N 12°20′E. Rail junction, inland port; mfg. of clothing, electrical equipment, bricks, matches, shoes, machinery. Has ornithological mus. Inc. 1642 as city. Suffered severe fires, 1777 and 1834. Developed rapidly in 19th cent. after opening of Gota Canal.

Van Ettan Lake, Mich.: see PINE RIVER, NE Mich.

Van Etten, village (pop. 504), Chemung co., S N.Y., near Cayuta Creek, 15 mi. NE of Elmira, in agr. area.

Vanga (văngʹgä), town, Coast prov., SE Kenya, small port on Indian Ocean, on Tanganyika line 50 mi. SW of Mombasa; fisheries. Formerly spelled Wanga.

Vangaindrano (văng-gändrăʹnōō), town, Fianarantsoa prov., SE Madagascar, near Indian Ocean coast, 135 mi. SSE of Fianarantsoa; cattle market. R.C. and Protestant missions.

Vange (vănj), town and parish (pop. 2,300), S Essex, England, 10 mi. E of Southend-on-Sea; agr. market.

Vangia (vänʹzhäʹ), town, Khanhhoa prov., S central Vietnam, on Bengoi Bay and railroad, 32 mi. N of Nhatrang.

Vangou, Russian SFSR: see LAZO, village.

Vangsnes (vängsʹnās), peninsula and village in Balestrand canton, Sogn og Fjordane co., W Norway, on S shore of Sogne Fjord, 60 mi. SE of Floro. On the point of the peninsula is a large statue of the saga hero Frithjof, erected 1913 by Wilhelm II of Germany.

Vanguard, village (pop. 285), S Sask., on Noteken Creek and 35 mi. SE of Swift Current; wheat, stock.

Vanguardia (bänggwärʹdyä), military post (Fortín Vanguardia), Santa Cruz dept., E Bolivia, 50 mi. SSW of Puerto Suárez, near Brazil border.

Vangunu (vängʹōōnōō), volcanic island, New Georgia group, Solomon Isls., SW Pacific, 2 mi. SE of main isl. of New Georgia; c.15 mi. long, 10 mi. wide.

Van Hoevenberg, Mount, N.Y.: see LAKE PLACID.

Van Hook, village (pop. 380), Mountrail co., central N.Dak., 26 mi. S of Stanley; trading point; co-operative creamery.

Van Horn (vănʹ hôrn), town (pop. 1,161), ⊙ Culberson co., extreme W Texas, in mtn. region, c.110 mi. SE of El Paso; alt. 4,010 ft. Highway junction; shipping, trade center for scenic cattle- and sheep-ranching region; tourist trade. Inc. after 1940.

Van Horne (văn hôrnʹ), town (pop. 511), Benton co., E central Iowa, 21 mi. W of Cedar Rapids, in agr. area.

Van Horn Mountains (vănʹ hôrn), extreme W Texas, range extending c.25 mi. S from region S of Van Horn; highest point, 5,786 ft.

Van Houten (văn houʹtůn), village (1940 pop. 542), Colfax co., NE N.Mex., 10 mi. SW of Raton, near Colo. line; alt. c.6,700 ft.; coal mining.

Vani (väʹnyē), village (1932 pop. estimate 2,040), W Georgian SSR, near Rion R., 12 mi. SE of Samtredia; wineries; corn, livestock.

Vanikoro (vänēkôʹrō), volcanic island, Santa Cruz Isls., Solomon Isls., SW Pacific, 75 mi. SE of Ndeni; 30 mi. long, 10 mi. wide; copra, kauri pine (sawmilling).

Vanilovo, Russian SFSR: see TSYURUPY, IMENI.

Vaniyambadi or **Vaniambadi** (both: vä″nĭyŭmbäʹ-dē), city (pop. 31,281), North Arcot dist., central Madras, India, on Palar R., and 39 mi. WSW of Vellore, in agr. area; trades in products (tanbark, nux vomica, hemp narcotics) of Javadi Hills (E); hides and skins; tannery. Islamiah Col.

Vanju-Mare (vûnzh-mäʹrĕ), Rum. *Vânju-Mare,* agr. village (pop. 2,771), Gorj prov., SW Rumania, 15 mi. SSE of Turnu-Severin.

Vankaner, India: see WANKANER.

Vankarem, Cape (vŭn-kůryĕmʹ), on N coast of Chukchi Peninsula, NE Siberian Russian SFSR; 67°47′N 175°43′W. Govt. arctic station, trading post, airfield.

Vankleek Hill (vănklēkʹ), town (pop. 1,435), SE Ont., 50 mi. E of Ottawa; lumbering, pump mfg., dairying.

Van Lear, town (pop. 1,096), Johnson co., E Ky., near Levisa Fork, 45 mi. SSW of Huntington, W. Va., in agr., coal-mining, and oil-producing region of the Cumberlands.

Vanleer, town (pop. 243), Dickson co., N central Tenn., 40 mi. W of Nashville, in timber and farm area; makes handles.

Vanlue (vănʹlōō″, văn″lōōʹ), village (pop. 365), Hancock co., NW Ohio, 9 mi. ESE of Findlay, in agr. region.

Van Meter, town (pop. 364), Dallas co., central Iowa, on Raccoon R. near mouth of South Raccoon R., and 18 mi. W of Des Moines, in agr. area.

Van Mijen Fjord (vänʹ mēʹyůn), Nor. *Van Mijenfjorden,* E arm (40 mi. long, 1–10 mi. wide) of Bell Sound, SW West Spitsbergen, Spitsbergen group; 77°48′N 14°40°–17°E. Mouth protected by Akseloya (Nor. *Akseløya*), islet. Sveagruva coal-mining settlement on NE shore. Mts. at head rise to over 3,000 ft.

Van Mountains (vän), E Turkey, S and SE of L. Van, extend E to Iranian frontier and S to Buhtan R.; rise to 12,300 ft. in Baset Dag.

Vanna, town (pop. 145), Hart co., NE Ga., 11 mi. SW of Hartwell.

Vannas (vĕnʹnĕs″), Swedish *Vännäs,* town (pop. 2,482), Vasterbotten co., NE central Sweden, on Ume R. and 17 mi. WNW of Umea; rail junction; metalworking, lumber and flour milling; charcoal.

Vannasby (vĕ″nĕsbüʹ), Swedish *Vännäsby,* village (pop. 829), Vasterbotten co., NE central Sweden, on Ume R. at mouth of Vindel R., and 14 mi. WNW of Umea; woodworking, shoe mfg.

Vannes (vän), anc. *Civitas Venetorum,* Breton *Guened,* town (pop. 23,510), ⊙ Morbihan dept., W France, port on Gulf of Morbihan, 45 mi. SW of Rennes; commercial and road center; mfg. (linen goods, lace, rope, metalware), boatbuilding, leatherworking, printing. Dating from pre-Roman times (stronghold of Veneti in 1st cent. B.C.), Vannes is center of a region noted for its megalithic monuments (especially at Carnac and Locmariaquer), and has a fine mus. of Celtic and Roman antiquities. Has a 13th-cent. cathedral and medieval ramparts enclosing inner city. Here in 1532 Brittany was united with French crown.

Vannes-le-Châtel (vän-lů-shätĕlʹ), village (pop. 277), Meurthe-et-Moselle dept., NE France, 10 mi. SSW of Toul; glassworks.

Vanni, Ceylon: see WANNI.

Van Norden, Lake, Calif.: see YUBA RIVER.

Vannovka (väʹnůfků), village (1948 pop. over 2,000), SE South-Kazakhstan oblast, Kazakh SSR, 43 mi. ENE of Chimkent; irrigated agr. (wheat).

Vannovski or **Vannovskiy** (väʹnůfskē), town (1939 pop. over 500), E Fergana oblast, Uzbek SSR, on railroad and 12 mi. WNW of Fergana; petroleum-refining center, serving Chimion and Andizhan oil fields.

Van Nuys (văn nīzʹ), suburban community, Los Angeles co., S Calif., part (since 1915) of Los ANGELES city, in San Fernando Valley, 15 mi. NW of downtown Los Angeles; municipal govt. branch offices for the valley are here. Automobile assembly and aircraft plants. In Birmingham section (W) is U.S. veterans' hosp.

Vanoise, Massif de la (mäsēfʹ dů lä vänwäzʹ), high mountain group of Savoy Alps, Savoie dept., SE France, bounded (N) by Doron de Bozel R. valley and (S) by Maurienne valley. Rises to 12,668 ft. at the Grande-Casse and to 12,018 ft. at the Grande-Motte. Glaciers.

Vanosa, India: see DARYAPUR.

Vanoua Lava, New Hebrides: see VANUA LAVA.

Vanport, village (1940 pop. 705), Beaver co., W Pa., on Ohio R. just WSW of Beaver; mfg. of firebricks; sand, gravel.

Vanport City, village (1948 pop. estimate 18,500), NW Oregon, just N of Portland, on the Columbia opposite Vancouver, Wash. Built 1942–43 to house shipyard workers (during Second World War had pop. of 42,000), after 1945 it became a low-cost housing project. On May 30, 1948, the town was submerged when flood waters breached the Columbia embankment, causing some loss of life and great destruction.

Van Rhynsdorp (vän rīnsʹdôrp), town (pop. 1,597), W Cape Prov., U. of So. Afr., 60 mi. W of Calvinia; stock (sheep, goats, horses), grain, feed crops; dairying.

Vans, Les (lā vãʹ), village (pop. 1,075), Ardèche dept., S France, near the Chassezac, 19 mi. N of Alès, at foot of the Cévennes; market (cherries, chestnuts, hides, silk).

Vansbro (vänsʹbrōō″), village (pop. 1,387), Kopparberg co., central Sweden, on West Dal R. at mouth of short Van R., Swedish *Vanån* (vänʹōn), and 40 mi. NW of Ludvika; rail junction; mfg. of chemicals; metalworking, sawmilling. Ostra Vansbro (ûsʹträ), Swedish *Östra Vansbro,* village (pop. 1,198), 2 mi. E, has sawmilling, woodworking; it includes villages of Saltvik (sältʹvēk″) and Dalasagen (däʹläsō″gůn), Swedish *Dalasågen.*

Vanscuro, Cima (chēʹmä vänskōōʹrō), Ger. *Pfannspitze* (pfänʹshpĭtsů), peak (8,786 ft.) in Carnic Alps, on Austro-Ital. border, 5 mi. NE of Monte Croce di Comelico Pass.

Vansittart Island (vănsĭʹtůrt) (47 mi. long, 6–16 mi. wide), SE Franklin Dist., Northwest Territories, in Foxe Channel, just off S Melville Peninsula; 65°55′N 84°5′W.

Van Starkenborgh Canal (vän stärʹkůnbôrkh) or **Omsnijding Canal** (ōmʹsnīdĭng), Groningen prov., N Netherlands; extends 10 mi. SSE–NNW, bet. the HOENDIEP at Noordhornerga (8 mi. WNW of Groningen) and EEMS CANAL 1.5 mi. ENE of Groningen.

Van Tassell, town (pop. 34), Niobrara co., E Wyo., on Niobrara R., near Nebr. line, and 20 mi. ESE of Lusk; alt. 4,736 ft.

Vanthli (vŭntʹlē), town (pop. 11,613), S Saurashtra, India, 9 mi. WSW of Junagarh; agr. (cotton, millet, oilseeds); handicraft metalware. Taken (c.1748) for short time by Mahrattas. Sometimes spelled Vanthali.

Vanua Balavu, Fiji: see VANUA MBALAVU.

Vanua Lava (vänōōʹä läʹvä), Fr. *Vanoua Lava,* volcanic island (pop. 430), largest of Banks Isls., New Hebrides, SW Pacific, 75 mi. NNE of Espiritu Santo; 15 mi. long, 10 mi. wide. Mangrove forests; sulphur deposits.

Vanua Levu (vänōōʹä lāʹvōō), volcanic island (□ 2,137; pop. 39,958), 2d largest of Fiji isls., SW Pacific, 20 mi. NE of Viti Levu; 110 mi. long; Lambasa is chief town. Mtn. range rises to Mt. Thurston (3,139 ft.); contains hot springs. Natewa Bay indents E coast; E peninsula connected to rest of isl. by isthmus 2.5 mi. wide. Near isthmus is salt lake 3 mi. in circumference. Largest river Ndreketi; Savusavu and Wainunu bays on S coast. Gold, sugar, rice, copra. Formerly Sandalwood Isl.

Vanua Mbalavu or **Vanua Balavu** (both: vänōōʹä ŭmbäläʹvōō), largest island (□ 21; pop. 1,446) of

Lau group, Fiji, SW Pacific; 17 mi. long; rises to 930 ft.; limestone. Lomaloma chief port and town; copra.

Vanves (väv), town (pop. 20,458), Seine dept., N central France, just SSW of Paris, 3 mi. from Notre Dame Cathedral, bet. Issy-les-Moulineaux (W) and Malakoff (E); metalworks; mfg. (footwear, flags, clocks), woodworking. Has 15th-cent. church and the Lycée Michelet.

Van Wert (văn wûrt′), county (□ 409; pop. 26,971), W Ohio; ⊙ Van Wert. Bounded W by Ind. line; drained by Little Auglaize R. and headwaters of Auglaize R. Diversified farming (corn, wheat, oats, livestock, poultry); mfg. at Van Wert; limestone quarries, clay pits; nurseries. Formed 1837.

Van Wert. 1 Town (1940 pop. 311), Polk co., NW Ga., just S of Rockmart. **2** Town (pop. 318), Decatur co., S Iowa, 11 mi. S of Osceola, in livestock area. **3** City (pop. 10,364), ⊙ Van Wert co., W Ohio, 26 mi. WNW of Lima; trade center and rail junction in diversified-farming area. Mfg.: paperboard containers, overalls, cigars, tile, food products, and woodworking machinery. Holds annual Peony Festival (June); has peony nurseries. Marsh Foundation School for underprivileged children is here. Settled 1835, inc. 1848.

Vanyen (vän′yĕn′), town, Sonla prov., N Vietnam, on Black R. and 70 mi. W of Hanoi; coal mining.

Van Zandt (văn zănt′), county (□ 855; pop. 22,593), NE Texas; ⊙ Canton. Bounded NE by Sabine R., partly E by Neches R. Rich diversified agr., livestock area, with large oil, salt, natural-gas production. Cotton, corn, grains, legumes, sweet potatoes, fruit, truck, pecans; nursery stock (especially roses); extensive dairying, poultry and livestock raising (cattle, hogs, sheep). Formed 1848.

Vaour (väōōr′), village (pop. 180), Tarn dept., S France, in the Causses, 20 mi. NW of Albi; sheep raising.

Vapenny Podol (vä′pĕnē pô′dôl), Czech *Vápenný Podol*, village (pop. 482), E Bohemia, Czechoslovakia, 7 mi. SW of Chrudim; rail terminus; footwear mfg. Chrudimka R. is dammed 3 mi. S, at village of Sec (sĕch), Czech *Seč*.

Vaphio or **Vafio** (vä′fyō), locality, Laconia, Greece, on Eurotas R. and 5 mi. S of Sparta. The Vaphio cups of finely ornamented gold, found (1889) in a tomb, date from Minoan times (c.1500 B.C.).

Vapi (wä′pē′), town, Saravane prov., S Laos, on the Se Done and 33 mi. W of Saravane.

Vapincum, France: see GAP.

Vapnyarka (vŭpnyär′kŭ), town (1948 pop. over 10,000), S Vinnitsa oblast, Ukrainian SSR, 40 mi. E of Mogilev-Podolski; rail junction; metalworks, dairy plant.

Var (vär), department (□ 2,325; pop. 370,688), in Provence, SE France, on the Mediterranean; ⊙ Draguignan. Occupied by S outliers of Provence Alps, including granitic coastal massifs of Estérel and Monts des Maures. Drained by the Argens. Rocky and indented coastline (bays of Toulon, Hyères, Saint-Tropez, capes Camarat, Lardier, Bénat, Cépet) forms part (E of Hyères) of Fr. Riviera. Îles d'Hyères off-shore. Winegrowing area with olive and mulberry groves, and large cork-oak forests in coastal hills. Other agr. crops: cherries, strawberries, tobacco. Dept. has important bauxite deposits in Brignoles area. Principal industries: shipbuilding and naval armaments (Toulon, La Seyne-sur-Mer, Saint-Tropez), cork processing, olive-oil mfg. Chief towns are TOULON, Hyères, Fréjus, Saint-Raphaël. Formed in 1790, dept. lost Grasse dist. to Alpes-Maritimes dept. in 1860, so that Var R. (after which it is named) no longer traverses it. Along its coastline Allies invaded S France (Aug., 1944) in Second World War.

Var, river, France: see VAR RIVER.

Vara (vä′rä″), town (pop. 2,462), Skaraborg co., S central Sweden, 25 mi. E of Trollhattan; rail junction; brick mfg.

Vara Blanca (bä′rä bläng′kä), village, Heredia prov., central Costa Rica, in the Desengaño, on NE slopes of Barba volcano, near source of Sarapiquí R., 10 mi. NNW of Heredia. Dairying; fruit, fodder crops.

Vara de Rey (bä′rä dhä rā′), town (pop. 1,819), Cuenca prov., E central Spain, 38 mi. NW of Albacete; saffron, cereals, olives, esparto, grapes, potatoes, livestock.

Varadero (bärädä′rō), town (pop. 2,050), Matanzas prov., W Cuba, popular seaside resort near base of Hicacos Peninsula, 22 mi. ENE of Matanzas. Has fine large beaches (Playa Varadero, Playa Azul) along peninsula. Fishing, boating.

Varades (värād′), village (pop. 765), Loire-Inférieure dept., W France, on Loire R. and 23 mi. WSW of Angers; winegrowing. Sanatoriums.

Varaita River (värī′tä), NW Italy, rises in Cottian Alps on Monte Viso, flows 55 mi. E and N to Po R. near Pancalieri. Furnishes power to hydroelectric plants at Casteldelfino, Sampeire, and Brossasco.

Varaklani or **Varaklyany** (vä′räklănē), Lettish *Varakļani*, Ger. *Warklany*, city (pop. 1,661), E central Latvia, in Latgale, 24 mi. W of Rezekne; rye, flax.

Varallo (väräl′lô), town (pop. 3,642), Vercelli prov., Piedmont, N Italy, on Sesia R. and 7 mi. N of Borgosesia, in irrigated region (rice, cereals); rail terminus; metal products, cotton textiles, paper, plastics. Gold mines near by. Resort. Has convent, school of applied arts, mus., picture gall. In the churches of Santa Maria della Grazie and San Gaudenzio are works by Gaudenzio Ferrari. On near-by hill, the Sacro Monte, is a 15th-cent. sanctuary with a church (1649) and 43 chapels, including 3 with frescoes by Ferrari. Formerly called Varallo Sesia.

Varamin, Iran: see VERAMIN.

Varanasi, India: see BENARES, city.

Varangaon (vŭr′ŭngoun), town (pop. 7,012), East Khandesh dist., NE Bombay, India, 22 mi. E of Jalgaon; local trade center (cotton, millet); cotton ginning.

Varanger Fjord (väräng′ŭr), Nor. *Varangeren Fjord*, inlet (60 mi. long, 3–35 mi. wide) of Barents Sea of Arctic Ocean, Finnmark co., NE Norway. Vadso city is on N shore. Bok Fjord is S arm; receives Pasvik R. at its head at Kirkenes.

Varangéville (värāzhāvēl′), town (pop. 3,873), Meurthe-et-Moselle dept., NE France, on Meurthe R. and Marne-Rhine Canal, opposite Saint-Nicolas, and 7 mi. SE of Nancy; salt-mining center; chemical works (soda).

Varanno, Czechoslovakia: see VRANOV.

Varano, Lago di (lä′gô dē värä′nô), shallow lagoon (□ 23) on N coast of Gargano promontory, S Italy; separated from the Adriatic by a sand bar (canals in E and W); 7 mi. long, 5 mi. wide; fishing.

Vara River (vä′rä), N Italy, rises in Ligurian Apennines 10 mi. NNE of Chiavari, flows 35 mi. SE, past Varese Ligure, to Magra R. near Vezzano Ligure.

Varas (bä′räs). **1** Town (pop. 1,229), Aconcagua prov., central Chile, on Ligua R. just NE of La Ligua, in agr. area (beans, potatoes, oats). Copper deposits near by. An old pre-Columbian Indian settlement. **2** Suburb (pop. 1,229) of La Ligua, Aconcagua prov., N central Chile.

Varasd, Yugoslavia: see VARAZDIN.

Varatec, Rumania: see BALTATESTI.

Varazdin (väräzh′dĭn), Serbo-Croatian *Varaždin*, Ger. *Warasdin*, Hung. *Varasd* (vŏ′rŏsht), town (pop. 17,176), N Croatia, Yugoslavia, on Drava R. and 38 mi. NNE of Zagreb. Rail junction; trade center in winegrowing region; mfg. (woolen textiles, clothes, furniture). Has old churches and castle with mus. Chartered in 1209. Lignite mining near by (SW). Varazdinske Toplice (–dĭnskĕ tôp′lĭtsĕ), Serbo-Croatian *Varaždinske Toplice* [=hot baths of Varazdin], 8 mi. SSE of Varazdin, is health resort with radioactive sulphur springs; called *Aquae Jasae* by Romans.

Varazze (värä′tsĕ), town (pop. 7,055), Savona prov., Liguria, NW Italy, port on Gulf of Genoa and 18 mi. W of Genoa, in orange-growing region; shipyards, cotton and paper mills, tanneries. Resort of Riviera di Ponente.

Varbak (vûrbäk′), village (pop. 1,812), Kolarovgrad dist., E Bulgaria, in Deliorman upland, 8 mi. N of Kolarovgrad; horse-raising center. Formerly Kabinyuk-syuyutlyu.

Varberg (vär′bĕr″yû), city (1950 pop. 12,524), Halland co., SW Sweden, on the Kattegat, 40 mi. S of Goteborg; seaport; seaside and health resort, with mud baths. Bicycle and shoe mfg., linen milling, metalworking. Has 13th-cent. castle and historical mus. Scene of many actions in Danish-Swedish wars.

Varbitsa Mountains (vûrbē′tsä), E central Bulgaria, 25-mi. section of E Balkan Mts., E of Kotel Mts.; rise to 3,370 ft. Crossed by *Varbitsa Pass* (alt. 2,556 ft.), 20 mi. SSE of Omortag, on highway to Karnobat (SSE). Sometimes spelled Vrbica or Vrbitza.

Varbovka (vûrbôf′kä), village (pop. 2,905), Gorna Oryakhovitsa dist., N Bulgaria, 15 mi. NNE of Sevliyevo; fruit and truck gardening, livestock.

Varcar Vakuf, Yugoslavia: see MRKONJIC GRAD.

Varciorova (vûrchôrô′vä), Rum. *Vârciorova*, village (pop. 449), Gorj prov., SW Rumania, on left bank of the Danube, on railroad and 11 mi. WNW of Turnu-Severin; mfg. of brushes and lime.

Vardal, Norway: see NYGARD.

Vardaman (vär′dûmŭn), town (pop. 686), Calhoun co., N central Miss., 36 mi. E of Grenada, near Yalobusha R.; lumber mills.

Vardar River (vär′dûr), Gr. *Axios* (äksēôs′), Lat. *Axius*, main river of Macedonia, in S Yugoslavia and NE Greece; rises in S Shar Mts. 4 mi. SW of Gostivar, flows NNE past Gostivar, and SE past Skoplje, Titov Veles, and Djevdjelija, and into Greece to Gulf of Salonika in delta 5–15 mi. WSW of Salonika; c.230 mi. long. Canalized in lower course. Receives Treska R. and the Crna Reka (right) and the Lepenac, Pcinja, and Bregalnica rivers (left). Cotton, rice, wine, and vegetables are produced in its valley.

Varde (vär′dû), city (pop. 8,118), Ribe amt, W Jutland, Denmark, 10 mi. N of Esbjerg; rail junction; mfg. (steel, machinery); hydroelectric plant.

Vardena, Greece: see PHALAKRON.

Vardhousia, Greece: see VARDOUSIA.

Vardo (vōrd′û″), Swedish *Vårdö*, fishing village (commune pop. 699), Aland co., SW Finland, on Vardo isl. (4 mi. long, 2 mi. wide), one of Aland group, on inlet of Gulf of Bothnia, 18 mi. ENE of Mariehamn.

Vardo (värd′û), Nor. *Vardø*, city (pop. 3,104), Finnmark co., NE Norway, on Vardoy (värd′ûü) (Nor. *Vardøy*), isl. (□ 1.4), just off the coast in Barents Sea of Arctic Ocean, 170 mi. E of Hammerfest, 110 mi. NW of Murmansk; 70°22′N 31°8′E. Fishing center, with port ice-free the year round; trades in fish products. Heavily damaged in Second World War. Vardohus fortress established on isl. in 1307. Town inc. 1787. Nansen started here in 1893 on polar expedition on the *Fram*; returned to Vardo in 1896. Formerly a center of trade with Russia and Finland.

Vardousia or **Vardhousia** (both: värdhōō′sēû), anc. *Corax*, massif in W central Greece, rises to 7,709 ft. 18 mi. NW of Amphissa. Also spelled Vardusia.

Varedo (värā′dô), town (pop. 3,452), Milano prov., Lombardy, N Italy, 9 mi. N of Milan; furniture mfg. center.

Varegovo (vär′yĭgŭvŭ), town (1939 pop. over 2,000), central Yaroslavl oblast, Russian SFSR, 23 mi. NW of Yaroslavl; peat-working center.

Varel (fä′rûl), town (pop. 12,085), in Oldenburg, NW Germany, after 1945 in Lower Saxony, in East Friesland, near North Sea, 17 mi. N of Oldenburg city; rail junction; foundry; mfg. of machinery, textiles (cotton, wool), cosmetics, soap, pipe tobacco; mfg. of fruit juices. Brickworks. Has 13th-cent church.

Varella, Cape (värĕlä′), easternmost point of Vietnam, on South China Sea; 12°53′N 109°27′E.

Varel-Land, Germany: see LANGENDAMM.

Varena (värā′nä), Lith. *Varėna*, Pol. and Rus. *Orany*, city (pop. c.2,000), S Lithuania, on railroad and 40 mi. SW of Vilna; summer resort. In Rus. Vilna govt. until 1920. City was divided (1920–39), town proper being located in Lithuania and railroad station (3 mi. SSE) in Poland.

Varenikovskaya (vŭrĕ′nyĭkŭfskīŭ), village (1926 pop. 8,155), W Krasnodar Territory, Russian SFSR, on lower Kuban R. (landing) and 16 mi. SE of Temryuk, on branch railroad to Taman; flour mill; cotton, wheat.

Varenna (värĕn′nä), resort village (pop. 593), Como prov., Lombardy, N Italy, port on E shore of L. Como. 12 mi. NNW of Lecco; silk industry. Marine biological institute. Marble quarries near.

Varenne River (värĕn′), Orne and Mayenne depts., W France, rises 11 mi. NNE of Domfront, flows 30 mi. S, past Domfront and Ambrières, to the Mayenne 8 mi. above town of Mayenne.

Varennes (värĕn′), village (pop. 781), S Que., on the St. Lawrence and 14 mi. NNE of Montreal; truck gardening, dairying; mineral springs.

Varennes or **Varennes-en-Argonne** (–zänärgôn′), village (pop. 609), Meuse dept., NE France, on Aire R. and 16 mi. WNW of Verdun; sawmilling. Here Louis XVI and Marie Antoinette were arrested (1791) while attempting to flee France in disguise. Village badly damaged in First World War.

Varennes-sur-Allier (–sür-älyā′), town (pop. 2,159), Allier dept., central France, near the Allier, 13 mi. N of Vichy; woodworking center; produces syrup flavors, vegetable oils, sparkling wines.

Varennes-sur-Amance (–ämäs′), agr. village (pop. 500), Haute-Marne dept., NE France, 14 mi. ENE of Langres.

Vares or **Varesh** (both: vä′rĕsh), Serbo-Croatian *Vareš*, village (pop. 2,303), E central Bosnia, Yugoslavia, 21 mi N of Sarajevo, on rail spur. Iron and manganese mines; 2 blast furnaces (pig iron) and foundry (cast-iron products).

Varese (värā′zĕ), province (□ 463; pop. 396,232), Lombardy, N Italy; ⊙ Varese. Borders Swiss canton of Ticino on N. Largely mountainous rising to 5,321 ft. in N, and hilly. Drained by Olona R. Contains several lakes, including L. of Varese and parts of Lago Maggiore and L. of Lugano. Smallest prov. of Lombardy and after Milano prov., the most industrialized. Cotton milling and mfg. (textile machinery, bicycles, motorcycles, airplanes) are leading industries. Centers at Varese, Busto Arsizio, Gallarate, Saronno, Somma Lombardo, and Sesto Calende. Agr. (cereals, fodder, raw silk, grapes); cattle and sheep raising. Limestone, clay, and marble quarries. Formed 1927 from Milano and Como provs.

Varese, city (pop. 23,348), ⊙ Varese prov., Lombardy, N Italy, in Alpine foothills near L. of Varese, 30 mi. NNW of Milan; 45°49′N 8°50′E. Rail junction; tourist and industrial center; airplane (Macchi) and automobile plants, foundries, silk mills, breweries, tanneries, shoe and luggage factories; mfg. of machinery, motorcycles, bicycles, bells, furniture, glass, candy, salami. Has many villas, basilica (1580–1615), and 18th-cent. palace with mus. of prehistoric and Roman antiquities. Atop near-by hill is a church originally founded by St. Ambrose in 6th cent. On the road leading to the pilgrim shrine are fifteen 17th-cent. chapels, symbolizing the mystery of the Rosary. Became capital of prov. in 1927.

Varese, Lake of (□ 6), in Varese prov., Lombardy, N Italy, 3 mi. W of Varese; 5 mi. long, 2.5 mi. wide; alt. 781 ft., max. depth 85 ft. Discharges into Lago Maggiore, 4 mi. W.

Varese Ligure (lē′gōōrĕ), village (pop. 898), La Spezia prov., Liguria, N Italy, on Vara R. and 14 mi. NE of Chiavari, in cereal and cattle region.

Varfolomeyevka (vŭrfŭlŭmyā'ŭfkŭ), village (1939 pop. over 500), S Maritime Territory, Russian SFSR, near Daubikhe R., 40 mi. ESE of Spassk-Dalni, in agr. area (grain, soybeans). Terminus of spur (from Manzovka) of Trans-Siberian RR. Coal deposits near by.
Vargarda (vôr'gōr"dä), Swedish *Vårgårda*, village (pop. 1,480), Alvsborg co., SW Sweden, on Save R. and 12 mi. NE of Alingsas; flour mills, brickworks.
Vargashi (vŭrgŭshē'), town (1948 pop over 2,000), E central Kurgan oblast, Russian SFSR, on Trans-Siberian RR and 20 mi. E of Kurgan; flour mill.
Vargas Island (vär'gŭs), (□ 11; 5 mi. long, 2–5 mi. wide), SW B.C., in Clayoquot Sound off W Vancouver Isl., 50 mi. W of Port Alberni. Yarksis Indian village is in E.
Vargem Grande (vär'zhĕm grän'dĭ). **1** City (pop. 759), N Maranhão, Brazil, 85 mi. SSE of São Luís; cotton, babassu nuts, carnauba wax. Roads to Itapecuru Mirim and Brejo. **2** City, São Paulo, Brazil: see VARGEM GRANDE DO SUL.
Vargem Grande do Sul (dōō sōōl'), city (pop. 3,721), E São Paulo, Brazil, 12 mi. NNW of São João da Boa Vista; rail-spur terminus; dairy products (butter, cheese); coffee, rice, sugar cane. Until 1944, Vargem Grande.
Varginha (vŭrzhē'nyŭ), city (pop. 10,954), S Minas Gerais, Brazil, on the Rio Verde, on railroad and 80 mi. SW of São João del Rei; coffeegrowing center; also ships sugar cane, cereals, dairy products.
Vargon (vär'yŭn"), Swedish *Vargön*, village (pop. 2,410), Alvsborg co., SW Sweden, on Gota R. near L. Vaner, and 3 mi. SE of Vanersborg; paper mills, sulphite works, foundries; hydroelectric station.
Varhely, Rumania: see SARMIZEGETUZA.
Variav (vär'yŭv), town (pop. 2,867), Surat dist., N Bombay, India, 4 mi. N of Surat; millet, sugar cane. Sometimes spelled Variad.
Varignana (värēnyä'nä), village (pop. 305), Bologna prov., Emilia-Romagna, N central Italy, 10 mi. SE of Bologna; lime- and cementworks.
Varilhes (värēl'), village (pop. 1,150), Ariège dept., S France, on Ariège R. and 5 mi. S of Pamiers; sawmilling, cereal- and winegrowing. Several hydroelectric plants near by.
Varillas, Las, Argentina: see LAS VARILLAS.
Varin (vä'rēn), Slovak *Varín*, Hung. *Várna* (vär'-nŏ), village (pop. 1,895), NW Slovakia, Czechoslovakia, on Vah R., on railroad and 6 mi. ESE of Zilina; limestone quarrying.
Varina (vŭrī'nŭ) town (pop. 144), Pocahontas co., N central Iowa, 38 mi. WNW of Fort Dodge.
Varka, Poland: see WARKA.
Varkaus (vär'kous), town (pop. 16,858), Kuopio co., SE Finland, on lake of Saimaa system, 40 mi. S of Kuopio; lumber, plywood, pulp, and paper mills, shipyards, machine shops, foundries.
Varkenshoek, Indonesia: see HOG POINT.
Varmdo, Swedish *Värmdö* (vĕrmd'ŭ"), island (□ 135; pop. 10,544) in Baltic, E Sweden, 10 mi. E of Stockholm. Irregular in shape, it is 14 mi. long, 4–14 mi. wide, with deeply indented coastline. Gustavsberg is chief town; also several popular seaside resorts.
Varmezö, Rumania: see BUCIUMI.
Varmland (vĕrm'länd), Swedish *Värmland*, county [Swedish *län*] (□ 7,426; 1950 pop. 280,149). W Sweden; ⊙ Karlstad. Comprises greatest part of Varmland province [Swedish *landskap*] (□ 7,718; pop. 310,272). Bet. Norwegian border and N shore of L. Vaner; includes W part of Bergslagen region. Forested; drained by Klar, Nor, and By rivers. Among many lakes are L. Fryk, L. Leland, and Glaf Fjord. Iron mining and smelting, steel, lumber, paper, and pulp milling are chief industries. Cities are Karlstad, Kristinehamn (industrial center) Arvika, Filipstad. Sometimes Vermland.
Varna, Bulgaria: see STALIN.
Varna (vär'nŭ), village (1932 pop. estimate 3,300), SE Chelyabinsk oblast, Russian SFSR, 55 mi. SSW of Troitsk, on railroad (Tamerlan station); dairying; meat preserving. Chromite deposits near by.
Varna, village (pop. 400), Marshall co., N central Ill., 19 mi. S of Spring Valley, in agr. area.
Varnado (vär'nŭdō, värnŭdō'), village (pop. 306), Washington parish, SE La., 70 mi. NE of New Orleans, near Pearl R.; lumber milling.
Varnamo (vĕr'nämōō"), Swedish *Värnamo*, city (1950 pop. 11,394), Jonkoping co., S Sweden, on Laga R. 40 mi. S of Jonkoping; rail junction; mfg. of furniture, wire, wheel spokes, rubber products, bricks; paper milling. Inc. 1920 as city.
Varnavino (vŭrnä'vēnŭ), village (1948 pop. over 2,000), N Gorki oblast, Russian SFSR on Vetluga R. and 40 mi. SSW of Vetluga; flax. Formerly called Varnavin.
Varner, town (pop. 3), Lincoln co., SE Ark., 25 mi. ESE of Pine Bluff, in agr. area. State prison farm near.
Varnous (värnōōs'). **1** Mountain range in Yugoslavia and Greece: see BABA. **2** Peak in Baba range on Yugoslav-Greek border 10 mi. NW of Phlorina. Also called Garvani.
Varnsdorf (värnz'dôrf), Ger. *Warnsdorf* (värnz'-dôrf), town (pop. 15,661), N Bohemia, Czechoslovakia, on Ger. border opposite Gross Schönau and 31 mi. NE of Usti nad Labem; rail junction; iron foundries; mfg. (silks, cottons, velvets, linen, footwear, industrial leather goods, hosiery, cutlery, needles, dyes), fur processing, woodworking. Has 18th-cent. St. Peter and Paul church with fine paintings. After Second World War, pop. greatly reduced through departure of Ger. nationals.
Varnville, town (pop. 1,180), Hampton co., SW S.C., just SE of Hampton; turpentine.
Varosha, S section of FAMAGUSTA, E Cyprus.
Varoslöd (vä'rôsh-lûd), Hung. *Városlőd*, town (pop. 1,885), Veszprem co., NW central Hungary, on Torna R. and 13 mi. WNW of Veszprem; mfg. (porcelain, faïence).
Varosszalonak, Austria: see STADTSCHLAINING.
Varpalota (vär'pŏlôtŏ), Hung. *Várpalota*, town (pop. 8,807), Veszprem co., NW central Hungary, on SE slope of Bakony Mts., 11 mi. W of Szekesfehervar. Lignite-mining center; mfg. of nitrate fertilizer, soap, vegetable oil, starch.
Varreddes (värĕd'), village (pop. 795), Seine-et-Marne dept., N central France, on the Marne and 4 mi. NE of Meaux. Near by is American First World War memorial.
Var River (vär), Alpes-Maritimes dept., SE France, rises in Maritime Alps 14 mi. SE of Barcelonnette, flows 84 mi. generally SSE, past Puget-Théniers, to the Mediterranean 4 mi. SW of Nice. Receives the Loup (right), the Tinée and Vésubie (left). Not navigable.
Vars, Col de (kôl dŭ vär'), pass (alt. 6,926 ft.) in the Chaîne du Parpaillon, SE France, Dauphiné Alps, on Hautes-Alpes–Basses Alpes dept. border, 11 mi. NNE of Barcelonnette. On Guillestre-Barcelonnette road (*route des Alpes*). Winter sports.
Varshava, Poland: see WARSAW.
Varshets (vŭrshĕts'), village (pop. 2,605), Vratsa dist., NW Bulgaria, 9 mi. ESE of Berkovitsa; sheep raising. Summer resort with mineral springs.
Varta, Poland: see WARTA, town, Lodz prov.
Varta River, Poland: see WARTA RIVER.
Vartashen (vŭrtŭshĕn'), village (1948 pop. over 10,000), N Azerbaijan SSR, on S slope of Greater Caucasus, 15 mi. SE of Nukha; tobacco, rice.
Vartej, India: see BHAUNAGAR, city.
Vartejeni, Moldavian SSR: see VERTYUZHANY.
Vartholomion (värthôlŏmēôn'), town (pop. 3,473), Elis nome, W Peloponnesus, Greece, on Peneus R. and 18 mi. NW of Pyrgos; rail junction; Zante currants, figs, wheat, wine, livestock. Sometimes called Vartholomio.
Varto (värtô'), village (pop. 899), Mus prov., E Turkey, 31 mi. N of Mus; wheat. Formerly Gumgum.
Vartoapele-de-Sus or **Vartoape-de-Sus** (vûrtwä'pĕl-dā-sōōs'), Rum. *Vârtoapele-de-Sus*, village (pop. 2,101), Teleorman prov., S Rumania, 11 mi NE of Rosiorii-de-Vede; orchards.
Värtsilä (värt'sĭlä), village (commune pop. 1,634), Kuopio co., SE Finland, near USSR border, 40 mi. SE of Joensuu; steel mill, foundry, machine shop, nail plant.
Värtsilä, Karelo-Finnish SSR: see VYARTSILYA.
Varttirayiruppu, India: see WATRAP.
Varushanad Hills (vŭrōō'shŭnäd), E spur of S Western Ghats, SW Madras, India, partly on Madura-Ramnad dist. line; extend c.30 mi. NE from Kottai Malai peak (6,624 ft.); up to 20 mi. wide. Teak, eucalyptus, ivory on forested S plateau; bamboo, turmeric, hides and skins. A NE extension, the Andipatti Hills, extends to a point 25 mi. SW of Dindigul.
Varva, Sweden: see HILLEBYN.
Varva (vär'vŭ), agr. town (1926 pop. 3,484), SE Chernigov oblast, Ukrainian SSR, 15 mi. ESE of Priluki; grain.
Varvara (värvä'rä), village (pop. 2,218), Plovdiv dist., W central Bulgaria, at N foot of W Rhodope Mts., 10 mi. WSW of Pazardzhik; rail junction; vineyards, fruit, truck, livestock. Has mineral baths.
Varvaropolye, Ukrainian SSR: see PERVOMAISK, Voroshilovgrad oblast.
Varvarovka (vŭrvä'rŭfkŭ), town (1926 pop. 2,841), S Nikolayev oblast, Ukrainian SSR, just NW of Nikolayev, across Dnieper R.
Várzea Alegre (vär'zēŭ ălā'grĭ), city (pop 2,495), S Ceará, Brazil, 26 mi. N of Crato; cotton, sugar, livestock.
Várzea Grande (grăn'dĭ), city (pop. 1,291), central Mato Grosso, Brazil, on right bank of Cuiabá R., opposite Cuiabá.
Varzi (värtsē), village (pop. 2,142), Pavia prov., Lombardy, N Italy, 15 mi. SE of Voghera. Commercial center for agr. (rice, grapes, cereals) area; bicycle factory.
Varzob (vŭrzôp'), village (1939 pop. over 500), N Stalinabad oblast, Tadzhik SSR, on Stalinabad-Leninabad highway, on Varzob R., and 12 mi. N of Stalinabad; wheat, cattle. Until c.1935, Obi-Dzhuk.
Varzob River, Tadzhik SSR, rises on S slope of Gissar Range, flows c.50 mi. S, past Varzob, to Dyushambinka R. (right tributary of Kafirnigan R). Site of hydroelectric plants serving Stalinabad.
Varzy (värzē'), village (pop. 1,081), Nièvre dept., central France, 9 mi. SW of Clamecy; horses, cattle. Has 14th-cent. church containing fine triptych.
Vas (vŏsh), county (□ 1,262; pop. 237,306), W Hungary; ⊙ Szombathely. Hilly region, mts. in W; heavily forested in SW; drained by Raba and Gyöngyös rivers. Main industrial centers (SZOMBATHELY, Körmend, Köszeg, Sarvar, Szentgotthard) have textile and flour mills, machinery works. Agr. (wheat, potatoes, clover), dairy farming in NE, hogs; fruit (plums, apples, pears). Once a Roman stronghold; declined in importance during Middle Ages; rose again to prominence in 17th cent., when wars fought here against Turks. Large Ger. pop. in W. Formerly the co. included a small region (PREKMURJE), now in Yugoslavia.
Vas (väs), village (pop. 493), Belluno prov., Veneto, N Italy, 6 mi. S of Feltre, in Piave R. valley; paper mills.
Vasa, Finland: see VAASA.
Vasa Barris River (vä'zŭ bä'rēs), in Bahia and Sergipe, NE Brazil, rises in Brazilian plateau, flows c.220 mi. SE to the Atlantic below São Cristóvão. Intermittent-flowing, with periodic floods. Rice plantations in lower valley.
Vasarosnameny (vä'shärôsh-nŏ"mānyŭ), Hung. *Vásárosnamény*, town (pop. 3,754), Szatmar-Bereg co., NE Hungary, on the Tisza and 30 mi. ENE of Nyiregyhaza; brickworks, flour mills.
Vasas (vŏ'shŏsh), town (pop. 2,735), Baranya co., S Hungary, in Mecsek Mts., 6 mi. NE of Pecs; coal mines.
Vasavad (vŭsä'vŭd), town (pop. 5,776), central Saurashtra, India, 36 mi. SSE of Rajkot; cotton, millet. Was ⊙ former petty state of Vasavad; state merged 1948 with Saurashtra. Sometimes spelled Vaswad.
Vasby (vĕs'bü"), Swedish *Väsby*, residential village (pop. 1,399), Stockholm co., E Sweden, 14 mi. NNW of Stockholm. Has 18th-cent. castle.
Vascau (väshkŭ'ōō), Rum. *Vașcău*, Hung. *Vaskoh* (vŏsh'kôkh), village (pop. 1,371), Bihor prov., W Rumania, on Black Körös R. and 46 mi. SE of Oradea; rail terminus and sawmilling center; iron and manganese mining, marble quarrying.
Vascauti, Ukrainian SSR: see VASHKOVTSY.
Vasco da Gama, Portuguese India: see MORMUGÃO.
Vascongadas, Spain: see BASQUE PROVINCES.
Vasen, Netherlands: see VAASSEN.
Vashkovtsy (vŭshkôf'tsē), Rum. *Vășcăuți* (vŭshkŭ-ōōts'), town (1941 pop. 5,916), W Chernovtsy oblast, Ukrainian SSR, in N Bukovina, on Cheremosh R., on railroad and 20 mi. WNW of Chernovtsy; flour milling, distilling.
Vashon Island (vă'shŏn"), Wash., in Puget Sound, just N of Tacoma; 13 mi. long. Includes villages of Burton and Vashon (hothouse flowers and vegetables); site of state park.
Vasht, Iran: see KHASH.
Vasilevichi (vŭsē'lyĭvēchē), village (1926 pop. over 2,000), E Polesye oblast, Belorussian SSR, 28 mi. NE of Mozyr; peat works. Rail junction.
Vasilevo, Russian SFSR: see CHKALOVSK.
Vasilika (vŭsēlĭkä'), town (pop. 3,414), Salonika nome, Macedonia, Greece, on Chalcidice peninsula 15 mi. SE of Salonika; wheat, cotton, silk.
Vasiliko, Bulgaria: see TSAREVO.
Vasilikon (vŭsēlĭkôn'). **1** Town (pop. 2,216), W Euboea, Greece, 5 mi. SE of Chalcis; wheat, wine stock raising (sheep, goats). **2** Town, Peloponnesus, Greece: see SICYON.
Vasilishki (vŭsē'lyĭshkē), Pol. *Wasiliszki* (väsēlyēsh'-kē), town (1939 pop. over 2,000), N Grodno oblast Belorussian SSR, 20 mi. WSW of Lida; flour milling, lumbering.
Vasilkov, Poland: see WASILKOW.
Vasilkov or **Vasil'kov** (vŭsēlkôf'), city (1926 pop. 21,322), W central Kiev oblast, Ukrainian SSR, 20 mi. SSW of Kiev; tanning center; machine mfg. flour milling. Decembrist revolutionary center (1825).
Vasilkovka or **Vasil'kovka** (–kŭ), village (1926 pop. 10,894), SE Dnepropetrovsk oblast, Ukrainian SSR, on Volchya R. and 45 mi. ESE of Dnepropetrovsk; dairying, food processing.
Vasilsursk or **Vasil'sursk** (–sōōrsk), town (1926 pop. 3,389), E Gorki oblast, Russian SFSR, on Volga R., at mouth of the Sura, and 75 mi. ESE of Gorki; woodworking.
Vasilyevka or **Vasil'yevka** (vŭsē'lyĭfkŭ), town (1948 pop. over 10,000), W central Zaporozhe oblast, Ukrainian SSR, 25 mi. S of Zaporozhe; flour dairy products; metalworks.
Vasilyevo or **Vasil'yevo** (–lyĭvŭ), town (1939 pop 10,200), W Tatar Autonomous SSR, Russian SFSR, on left bank of the Volga, opposite Sviyaga R. mouth, and 15 mi. W of Kazan; sawmilling, glassworking center. Developed in 1930s.
Vasilyevski Mokh or **Vasil'yevskiy Mokh** (–lyĭfskē môkh"), town (1939 pop. over 500), S Kalinin oblast, Russian SFSR, on rail spur and 10 mi. N of Kalinin; peat-working center.
Vasio, France: see VAISON-LA-ROMAINE.
Vasiova, Rumania: see BOCSA-MONTANA.
Vasishchevo (vŭsē'shchĭvŭ), town (1926 pop. 3,055). N central Kharkov oblast, Ukrainian SSR, 12 mi. SSE of Kharkov; truck.
Vasishta Godavari River, India: see GODAVARI RIVER.
Vasishtanadi River, India: see VELLAR RIVER.
Vasiss (vŭsēs'), village (1948 pop. over 500), NE Omsk oblast, Russian SFSR, 40 mi. NE of Tara, in agr. area (flax).

Vasknarva (väsk'närvä), village, NE Estonia, landing on L. Peipus, at outlet of Narva R., 30 mi. SW of Narva.

Vaskoh, Rumania: see VASCAU.

Vaskut (vŏsh'kōōt), Hung. *Vaskút,* town (pop. 4,705), Bacs-Bodrog co., S Hungary, 5 mi. SSE of Baja; grain, paprika, cattle.

Vaslui (väslōō'ē), town (1948 pop. 13,738), Barlad prov., E Rumania, in Moldavia, on Barlad R., on railroad, and 175 mi. NNE of Bucharest; trading center (grain, livestock, hides); mfg. of bricks, tiles, edible oils, oil cake. Founded in 15th cent. Has 15th-cent. church recently restored, remains of a palace of Stephen the Great. Occupied (1944) by USSR army.

Vaso (vä'sō), town (pop. 9,567), Kaira dist., N Bombay, India, 8 mi. SSE of Kaira; market center for millet, tobacco, pulse; calico printing; copper and brass utensils.

Vasquez Mountains (vă'skŭs), N central Colo., in Front Range; extend N–S bet. Williams and Fraser rivers; include part of Continental Divide. Chief peaks: Byers Peak (12,778 ft.) and Vasquez Peak (12,800 ft.), c.45 mi. W of Denver.

Vásquez Territory (bä'skĕs), oil-bearing region of central Colombia, extreme W Boyacá dept., bordering W on Magdalena R. along Velásquez R., c.100 mi. NNW of Bogotá.

Vass (văs), town (pop. 757), Moore co., central N.C., 8 mi. NE of Southern Pines; mfg. of textiles, furniture.

Vassalboro or **Vassalborough** (văs'ŭlbŭrŭ), town (pop. 2,261), Kennebec co., SW Maine, on the Kennebec and 10 mi. above Augusta. Seat of Oak Grove, Friends' girls' preparatory school. Textiles made at North Vassalboro. Settled c.1760, inc. 1771.

Vassan (väsä'), village, W Que., near L. la Motte, 11 mi. NW of Val d'Or; gold, molybdenum, bismuth mining.

Vassar (vă'sŭr), city (pop. 2,530), Tuscola co., E Mich., 18 mi. ESE of Saginaw and on Cass R.; mfg. of auto parts; agr. (potatoes, grain, beans). Settled 1849, inc. 1871 as village, as city 1945.

Vassen (vä'sŭn), residential village (pop. 868), Norrbotten co., NE Sweden, on small inlet of Gulf of Bothnia, at mouth of Kalix R., just SE of Kalix.

Vassouras (vŏosō'rŭs), city (pop. 4,833), W central Rio de Janeiro state, Brazil, near Paraíba R., on railroad and 45 mi. NW of Rio; dairying center; textile milling, rice processing, mfg. of tobacco products and vegetable oil. Kaolin is quarried near by.

Vassy (väsē'). **1** Village (pop. 693), Calvados dept., NW France, in Normandy Hills, 10 mi. E of Vire; cider distilling. **2** Town, Haute-Marne dept., France: see WASSY.

Vastan, Turkey: see GEVAS.

Vasteras (vĕs"tŭrōs'), Swedish *Västerås,* city (1950 pop. 59,990), ⊙ Vastmanland co., E central Sweden, on NW shore of L. Malar, at mouth of Svart R., 55 mi. WNW of Stockholm; 59°37'N 16°32'E. Lake port; a center of Swedish electrical industry (mfg. of motors, generators, locomotives, appliances); iron, steel, and glass works, lumber mills. Hydroelectric plant. Seat of Lutheran bishop. Has 13th-cent. cathedral, on site of 11th-cent. church; 12th-cent. castle (later rebuilt), and noted episcopal library. Trade and cultural center in Middle Ages, it was scene of several parliaments, notably the Vasteras Recess (1527), which introduced Reformation in Sweden and put church under state control, and the parliament which here adopted (1544) law of succession to the throne. Formerly spelled Vesteras, Swedish *Vesterås.*

Vasterbotten (vĕs'tŭrbô"tŭn), Swedish *Västerbotten,* county [Swed. *län*] (□ 22,837; 1950 pop. 231,740), N Sweden; ⊙ Umea. Bet. Gulf of Bothnia and Norwegian border, it comprises Vasterbotten province [Swedish *landskap*] (□ 7,169; pop. 148,141), in E part of co., and parts of Angermanland and Lappland provs. Low undulating surface (E) rises toward wooded mts. on Norwegian border, with peaks over 5,000 ft. high. Drained by Angerman, Vindel, Ume, Skellefte and several smaller rivers. Agr. (rye, oats), stock raising, dairying, and lumbering are important. Rich metal mines at Boliden and Kristineberg. Chief industries are lumber and pulp milling, woodworking, metal smelting (Ronnskar), tar and charcoal mfg. Cities are Umea (chief port), Skelleftea, and Lycksele (Lapp trading center). Formerly spelled Vesterbotten.

Vasterdalalven, Sweden: see DAL RIVER.

Vastergotland (vĕs'tŭryŭt"lănd), Swedish *Västergötland,* province [Swedish *landskap*] (□ 6,801; pop. 877,357), SW Sweden, on the Skagerrak. Included in Skaraborg co., S part of Alvsborg co., and S part of Goteborg och Bohus co. Formerly spelled Vestergotland.

Vasternorrland (vĕs'tŭrnôr"lănd), Swedish *Västernorrland,* county [Swedish *län*] (□ 9,924; 1950 pop. 283,620), NE central Sweden; ⊙ Harnosand. On Gulf of Bothnia, it comprises Medelpad prov. (S) and S part of Angerman prov. (N). Highland region with low level coastal strip; drained by Ljunga, Indal, Angerman, and several smaller rivers. One of Sweden's greatest lumbering regions, co. has important sawmilling, woodworking, pulp, cellulose, and wood-chemicals industries. Aluminum milling at Kubikenborg. Cities are Sundsvall, Harnosand, Solleftea, and Ornskoldsvik. Formerly spelled Vesternorrland.

Vastervik (vĕs'tŭrvēk"), Swed. *Västervik,* city (1950 pop. 15,741), Kalmar co., SE Sweden, on Gamleby Bay, Swedish *Gamlebyviken,* 15-mi.-long inlet of the Baltic, 60 mi. SSE of Norrkoping; 57°45'N 16°38'E. Seaport, with shipyards; stone quarrying; mfg. of matches, machinery, glass, furniture. Has town hall (1793) and remains of 13th-cent. castle. Known since 13th cent., city was trade center in 16th and 17th cent. Suffered heavily in Danish-Swedish wars. Port grew rapidly in 19th cent. Formerly spelled Vestervik.

Vastmanland (vĕst'mänlănd"), Swed. *Västmanland,* county [Swedish *län*] (□ 2,611; 1950 pop. 203,803), central Sweden; ⊙ Vasteras. Extends N from L. Malar, includes SW part of Uppland prov. and E part of Vastmanland prov. [Swedish *landskap*] (□ 3,458; pop. 210,539). Fertile lowland in SE part of co. (market gardening, dairying), rising to hilly Bergslagen mining region (N). Drained by Kolback, Arboga, and several smaller rivers. Iron mining, centered on Fagersta, is chief industry. Copper, lead, feldspar are also mined. Mfg. of heavy electrical equipment (Vasteras), tool steel (Fagersta); steel milling, woodworking, lumbering are important. Cities are Vasteras, Fagersta, Koping, Arboga, and Sala. Formerly spelled Vestmanland.

Vasto (väs'tô), anc. *Histonium,* town (pop. 10,964), Chieti prov., Abruzzi e Molise, S central Italy, near Adriatic Sea, 36 mi. SE of Pescara. Agr. center; olive oil, wine, citrus fruit, cereals, macaroni. Bishopric. Has cathedral, 16th-cent. palace, and mus. Called Istonio c 1937–47.

Vasudevanallur (väsōōdā"vŭnŭl'lōōr'), town (pop. 12,134), Tinnevelly dist., S Madras, India, 21 mi. NNE of Tenkasi; grain; cotton weaving.

Vasvar (vŏsh'vär), Hung. *Vasvár,* Ger. *Eisenburg,* town (pop. 4,477), Vas co., W Hungary, 15 mi. SE of Szombathely; potatoes, wheat, hogs.

Vaswad, India: see VASAVAD.

Vasyugan (vŭsyōōgän'), village, SW Tomsk oblast, Russian SFSR, on Vasyugan R. and 120 mi. WNW of Narym. Formerly Vasyuganskoye. Novy Vasyugan, village (1948 pop. over 500), is on upper Vasyugan R. and 180 mi. W of Narym.

Vasyugan River, W Tomsk oblast, Russian SFSR, rises in VASYUGANYE marshes, flows NW, N, past Novy Vasyugan, and E, past Vasyugan, to Ob R. near Kargasok; 625 mi. long. Navigable below Novy Vasyugan.

Vasyuganskoye, Russian SFSR: see VASYUGAN.

Vasyuganye or **Vasyugan'ye** (-gä'nyŭ), marshy region (□ 23,200) in Novosibirsk and Tomsk oblasts, Russian SFSR, of W.Siberian Plain, bet. Irtysh and Ob river basins; forested, swampy, low plain with occasional ridges; drained by Vasyugan R. Turns into large inland sea during spring floods. Pop. (mainly Khanty) engaged in hunting, fishing.

Vatan (vätä'), village (pop. 1,653), Indre dept., central France, 12 mi. NW of Issoudun; road junction; makes linen goods.

Vaté, New Hebrides: see EFATE.

Vaternish Point (wô'tŭrnĭsh), NW headland of Isle of Skye, Scotland; 57°34'N 6°39'W.

Vatersay (vä'tŭrsā), island (pop. 240), Outer Hebrides, Inverness, Scotland, just S of Barra; 3 mi. long, 2½ mi. wide; rises to 624 ft.

Vathi or **Vathy** (both: vä́thē'). **1** Town, Ithaca isl., Greece: see ITHACA, town. **2** Town, Meganisi isl., Greece: see MEGANESI. **3** Town, Samos isl., Greece: see VATHY.

Vathia, Greece: see AMARYNTHOS.

Vathi Avlidhos, Greece: see VATHY AULIDOS.

Vathy or **Vathi** (both: väthē'), town (pop. 5,052), on NE shore of Samos isl., Greece; 37°45'N 26°59'E; trade in wine, tobacco, olive oil, figs, carobs. Cigarette mfg. Just N, on Vathy Bay, is town of LIMEN VATHEOS, the capital of Samos nome.

Vathy Aulidos or **Vathi Avlidhos** (both: ävlē'dhôs), village (pop. 2,011), Boeotia nome, E central Greece, on S Gulf of Euboea, on railroad and 4 mi. S of Chalcis; wine; wheat; fisheries. On site of anc. AULIS.

Vatican City (vă'tĭkŭn), sovereign papal state (□ 108.7 acres; pop. c.1,000), enclave of Rome, W central Italy. The Pope is absolute ruler, represented by a secretary of state. Situated mainly along W bank of the Tiber, W of Castel Sant' Angelo, and including papal residence, papal church, and some adjoining offices. In its SE corner is the piazza of St. Peter's Church, surrounded by colonnades serving as entrance to St. Peter's. N of the piazza is a quadrangular area containing a few streets of administrative bldgs. and Belvedere Park, which is adjoined by the pontifical palaces (with famous art collections and library), the Vatican proper. Beyond the palaces lie the Vatican Gardens, making up half of the area of the little state, which is bounded on W and S by Leonine Wall. The Vatican enjoys extraterritorial rights over certain important basilicas, churches, and other bldgs. in Rome, among them the Lateran (the 1st-ranking church of R.C. Church), St. Mary Major, the palace of San Callisto, and the papal summer villa Castel Gandolfo some miles from Rome. There are also a railroad and radio station, the Pontifical Gregorian Univ. (opened 1930); independent mail and currency. Vatican City was set up (1929) through Lateran Treaty, ending conflict bet. Pope and Ital. govt. over occupation of Papal States and seizure of Rome in 1870.

Vaticano, Cape (vätēkä'nô), Calabria, S Italy, at N end of Gulf of Gioia, 8 mi. NW of Nicotera; 38°37'N 15°50'E; lighthouse.

Vatika, Greece: see NEAPOLIS.

Vatili (vätēlē'), village (pop. 2,249), Famagusta dist., E Cyprus, 17 mi. E of Nicosia; wheat, barley, almonds, olives; sheep, cattle. An irrigation reservoir is near by.

Vatnajokull (vät'näyû"kütŭl), Icelandic *Vatnajökull,* glacier region (□ 3,200), SE Iceland; 63°55'–64°50'N 15°10'–18°10'W. Huge icefield, 90 mi. long (ENE–WSW), up to 60 mi. wide. Contains several active volcanoes, including Grimsvatn. Generally 2,000 ft. high, it rises to 6,952 ft. on Hvannadalshnjukur (S), highest peak of Iceland.

Vatomandry (vätōōmän'drē), town, Tamatave prov., E Madagascar, on coast and Canal des Pangalanes, 35 mi. SSW of Tamatave; small seaport and trading center, specializing in coffee and raphia. Graphite mining and treating, hardwood lumbering. Hosp., trade school. One of the oldest centers of European colonization in Madagascar.

Vatonta, Greece: see NEA ARTAKE.

Vatra-Dornei (vä'trä-dôr'nā), town (pop. 7,078), Suceava prov., N Rumania, on Bistrita R., on railroad, and 15 mi. SSW of Campulung; reputed health and winter-sports resort (with mineral springs) in the E Carpathians; alt. 2,631 ft. Also manganese mining; lumbering; furniture and brick mfg. Has 17th-cent. church. Has been known as spa since 18th cent. Sometimes called Dorna-Vatra.

Vattalkundu, India: see BATLAGUNDU.

Vatter, Lake, Swedish *Vättern* (vĕ'tŭrn), 2d-largest lake (□ 733) of Sweden, in S central part of country; extends 80 mi. NNE–SSW bet. Jonkoping and Askersund. Other cities on shore are Motala, Vadstena, Huskvarna, Hjo, and Karlsborg. It is up to 16 mi. wide; 390 ft. deep. Drained E into Baltic by Motala R.; forms part of Gota Canal route. Noted for its dangerous currents and its mirages, lake contains (S) Visingso, Swedish *Visingsö* (vē'sĭngs-û"), island (□ 9.5; pop. 1,029), site of prehistoric burial ground, and 17th-cent. castle and church. Formerly spelled L. Vetter, Swedish *Vettern.*

Vatukoula (vä'tōōkō-ōō'lä), town (pop. 3,457), N Viti Levu, Fiji, 55 mi. NW of Suva; gold mining.

Vatu Lele (vä'tōō lā'lā), volcanic island (□ 12; pop. 395), Fiji, SW Pacific, 20 mi. S of Viti Levu; 8 mi. long; bananas.

Vaubecourt (vōbkōōr'), village (pop. 364), Meuse dept., NE France, on the Aisne and 12 mi. N of Bar-le-Duc; hogs.

Vauclin (vōklē'), town (pop. 2,122), SE Martinique, on the Atlantic, at E foot of Vauclin volcano, 15 mi. ESE of Fort-de-France, in coffee and sugar region. Sometimes Le Vauclin.

Vaucluse (vōklōōz'), municipality (pop. 9,138), E New South Wales, Australia, at S side of entrance to Port Jackson; residential suburb of Sydney.

Vaucluse (vōklüz'), department (□ 1,381; pop. 249,838), in Provence, SE France; ⊙ Avignon. Bounded by the Rhone (W) and by the Durance (S), it lies within fertile Rhone valley, its E part penetrated by parallel outliers of the Provence Alps (Mont Ventoux, Monts de Vaucluse, Montagne du Lubéron). Drained by Aygues, Ouvèze, Sorgue and Coulon rivers. A leading agr. dept. reputed for its wines (*Côtes-du-Rhône*), and diversified fruit (apricots, peaches, melons, almonds, strawberries) shipped throughout France. Cultivation of olive and mulberry trees, tobacco and lavender are also important. Millet is widely grown. Several ocher quarries in Apt area. Industry, though diversified (chemicals, paper, pottery, brooms, textiles), is on a small scale, except for fruit and vegetable preserving, which is chief activity of Cavaillon, Carpentras, and Pertuis. AVIGNON, the papal city, and Orange, with Roman relics, are tourist centers. Formed 1793, dept. includes former Comtat Venaissin, principality of Orange, and papal state of Avignon. Canton of Valréas, administratively in Vaucluse dept., forms enclave in Drôme dept.

Vaucluse, village, Vaucluse dept., France: see FONTAINE-DE-VAUCLUSE.

Vaucluse (vōklōōz'), village (1940 pop. 507), Aiken co., W S.C., 6 mi. NW of Aiken; cotton milling.

Vaucluse, Monts de (mõ dü vōklüz'), outlying range of Provence Alps, in Vaucluse dept., SE France, overlooking Rhone lowland E of Avignon. Extends 25 mi. E–W, paralleled by Mont Ventoux (10 mi. N) and Montagne du Lubéron (10 mi. S). Rises to 4,075 ft.

Vaucouleurs (vōkōōlûr'), town (pop. 2,452), Meuse dept., NE France, on left bank of the Meuse and 12 mi. SSE of Commercy; iron foundries; mfg. of flannel goods, beer, lime. Here, in 1428–29, Joan of Arc prevailed upon Robert de Baudricourt (town's governor) to send her with an escort to the Dauphin (later Charles VII) at Chinon.

Vaucresson (vōkrĕsō′), town (pop. 3,227), Seine-et-Oise dept., N central France, a W suburb of Paris, 9 mi. from Notre Dame Cathedral. Stud.
Vaud (vō), Ger. *Waadt* (vät), canton (□ 1,239; 1950 pop. 376,707), W Switzerland; ⊙ Lausanne. Woods in the Jura (W), meadows and fertile fields (center), pastures (livestock) in the Alps (SE), and vineyards (wine) on N shores of L. Geneva (S). Numerous resorts are on L. Geneva (MONTREUX and LAUSANNE), on L. of Neuchâtel (YVERDON), and in the Alps (largest, LEYSIN). Metal- and woodworking, printing; watchmaking in W. Pop. mainly French speaking and Protestant. Conquered 58 B.C. by Romans, Vaud later passed to Franks and Burgundians. Joined Swiss Confederation in 1803.
Vaudreuil (vōdrōōl′, Fr. vōdrû′ē), county (□ 201; pop. 13,170), S Que., on Ont. border and on Ottawa R.; ⊙ Vaudreuil.
Vaudreuil, village (pop. 506), ⊙ Vaudreuil co., S Que., on S side of L. of the Two Mountains, 24 mi. SW of Montreal; truck gardening; resort.
Vaudrevange (vōdrůvãzh′), town (pop. 3,976), W Saar, near Fr. border and Saar R., 2 mi. NW of Saarlouis; ceramics mfg. (since 1788). Was ⊙ Fr. *bailliage d'Allemagne* (later Sarre prov.) from 1661 until replaced by Saarlouis after 1680. Name changed in 1945 from Wallerfangen to its early Fr. name.
Vaughan (vôn), town (pop. 181), Warren co., N N.C., 9 mi. E of Warrenton.
Vaughn (vôn), village (pop. 1,356), Guadalupe co., central N.Mex., 38 mi. SW of Santa Rosa; shipping point for wool, livestock. Settled 1905, inc. 1916.
Vaugirard (vōzhērär′), a SW district of Paris, France, on left bank of the Seine, constituting the 15th *arrondissement*. Has grounds of Paris Fair.
Vaugneray (vōnyůrā′), village (pop. 750), Rhône dept., E central France, in the Monts du Lyonnais, 8 mi. W of Lyons; hosiery and cheese mfg.
Vaujours (vō-zhōōr′), town (pop. 2,624), Seine-et-Oise dept., N central France, an outer ENE suburb of Paris, 12 mi. from Notre Dame Cathedral, on Ourcq Canal just NE of Livry-Gargan; mfg. of kitchen ranges.
Vaulry (vōrē′), village (pop. 119), Haute-Vienne dept., W central France, 7 mi. SSE of Bellac; tin and wolfram deposits.
Vaulx-en-Velin (vō-ã-vůlē′), E suburb of Lyons, Rhône dept., E central France, N of Villeurbanne; site of modern rayon plant with adjoining workers' settlement named *Cité de la Société du textile artificiel* (pop. 2,019).
Vaulx-lez-Tournai (vō-lā-tōōrnā′), village (pop. 1,668), Hainaut prov., W Belgium, on Scheldt R. and 2 mi. SE of Tournai; cement quarrying.
Vaupés (boupĕs′), commissary (□ 57,857; 1938 pop. 7,767; 1950 estimate 7,850), SE Colombia; ⊙ Mitú. Bordering E on Venezuela and Brazil, bounded N by Guaviare R., S by Apaporis R., E by Guainía R. or Río Negro, SE by Papury R. and Taraíra R. Its vast expanses of forested lowlands are crossed by Vaupés and Inírida rivers, all belonging to the Amazon system. Has tropical, humid climate. An undeveloped region populated largely by Indians, it exports some of its rich forest products (e.g., rubber, balata gum).
Vaupés River, Colombia: see UAUPÉS RIVER, Brazil.
Vauvert (vōvâr′), town (pop. 2,798), Gard dept., S France, 11 mi. SSW of Nîmes; distilling. Wine and cereal trade.
Vaux (vō). **1** Hamlet in Aisne dept., N France, 2 mi. W of Château-Thierry. Point of furthest Ger. advance on road to Paris, 1918, in First World War. Carried by Americans (June, 1918). **2** Fort, Meuse dept., NE France, 4.5 mi. NE of Verdun, hotly contested in battle for Verdun (March–June, 1916) during First World War. **3** Castle, France: see MELUN.
Vaux, Mount (vō) (10,891 ft.), SE B.C., in Rocky Mts., in Yoho Natl. Park, 40 mi. W of Banff.
Vauxhall (vŏks′hôl), village (pop. estimate 250), S Alta., 40 mi. NE of Lethbridge; wheat.
Vauxhall (vŏks′hôl′, vŏk′sôl), district of Lambeth metropolitan borough, London, England, on S bank of the Thames (here crossed by Vauxhall Bridge), 1.5 mi. S of Charing Cross. Site of important gasworks. It is named for the former Vauxhall Gardens, opened as amusement center c.1660, 1st known as New Spring Gardens and mentioned by Pepys and several English dramatists. The gardens were closed 1859.
Vaux-lès-Saint-Claude (vō-lā-sē-klōd′), village (pop. 399), Jura dept., E France, on the Bienne and 7 mi. WSW of Saint-Claude, in the central Jura; wood turning, pipe mfg.
Vaux-sur-Chevremont (vō-sür-shĕvrůmō′), town (pop. 4,731), Liége prov., E Belgium, SE suburb of Liége. Basilica is object of pilgrimage.
Vauzelles (vōzĕl′), workers' residential community (pop. 2,461), Nièvre dept., central France, 4 mi. N of Nevers, in metallurgical dist.
Vav (väv), village, Banas Kantha dist., N Bombay, India, 60 mi. WNW of Palanpur; millet. Was ⊙ former Western India state (□ 759; pop. 24,673) of Vav; state inc. 1949 into Banas Kantha dist. Village and state also spelled Wao.
Vavau (vävou′), coral island group (pop. 8,199), N Tonga, S Pacific; 18°40′S 174°W. Largest and only important isl. is Vavau; c.10 mi. long; rises to 450 ft.; isl. is port of entry and site of Neiafu, ⊙ Vavau group. Known for beautiful caves. Formerly Mayorga.
Vavdos or **Vavdhos** (both: väv′dhôs), village (pop. 1,385), Chalcidice nome, Macedonia, Greece, 7 mi. NW of Polygyros; chrome and magnesite mining.
Vavilovo, Russian SFSR: see ASHA.
Vavincourt (vävĕkōōr′), village (pop. 407), Meuse dept., NE France, 4 mi. NNE of Bar-le-Duc; cattle.
Vavitu, Tubuai Isls.: see RAIVAVAE.
Vavoua (vä′vwä), village (pop. c.600), W central Ivory Coast, Fr. West Africa, 32 mi. N of Daloa; coffee, cacao, palm kernels.
Vavozh (vŭvôsh′), village (1948 pop. over 2,000), W Udmurt Autonomous SSR, Russian SFSR, 47 mi. W of Izhevsk; wheat, rye, oats, livestock. Limestone deposits near by.
Vavul Mala, peak, India: see WYNAAD.
Vavuniya (vŭv′ōōnĭyŭ), town (pop. 1,082), ⊙ Vavuniya (formerly Mullaitivu) dist. (□ 1,155; pop., including estate pop., 23,276), Northern Prov., Ceylon, 28 mi. NNE of Anuradhapura; road junction; timber center; rice plantations.
Vaxholm (väks′hôlm″), residential city (pop. 2,969), Stockholm co., E Sweden, on isl. (2 mi. long, 1 mi. wide) of same name in the Baltic, 11 mi. ENE of Stockholm; seaside resort. On islet, just E, is 17th-cent. fortress.
Vaxjo (vĕk′shû″), Swedish *Växjö*, city (1950 pop. 20,104), ⊙ Kronoberg co., S Sweden, 110 mi. NE of Malmo; 56°53′N 14°49′E. Rail junction; commercial center; paper mills, mechanical works; mfg. of matches, furniture. Seat of Lutheran bishop. Its 11th-cent. cathedral was, according to tradition, founded by St. Sigfrid. Has historical mus. Chartered 1342, city was trade center of Smaland prov. in Middle Ages. Tegnér was a bishop of Vaxjo and died here. Sometimes called Vexio. On Helga L., Swedish *Helgasjön* (hĕl′gä-shûn″) (8 mi. long, 1–5 mi. wide), 2 mi. N, is ruin of 16th-cent. Kronoberg castle.
Vaya-koi, Bulgaria: see DOLNO YEZEROVO.
Vayalpad (vŭyŭl′pŭd), village, Chittoor dist., central Madras, India, 45 mi. NW of Chittoor; peanuts, rice, sugar cane. Dyewood (red sanders) in near-by forested hills.
Vayenga (vŭyĕn′gŭ), town (1948 pop. over 500), NW Murmansk oblast, Russian SFSR, on Kola Gulf, 12 mi. NE of Murmansk; fishing port; naval flotilla station. Also spelled Vaenga.
Vaygach Island, Russian SFSR: see VAIGACH ISLAND.
Vayia, Greece: see VAGIA.
Vaynor, agr. village and parish (pop. 3,163), S Brecknock, Wales, 3 mi. N of Merthyr Tydfil; stone quarrying.
Vayrac (väräk′), village (pop. 732), Lot dept., SW France, near the Dordogne, 16 mi. SSE of Brive-la-Gaillarde.
Vayvara, Estonia: see VAIVARA.
Vazec (vä′zhĕts), Slovak *Važec*, Hung. *Vázec* (vä′zĕts), village (pop. 2,747), N Slovakia, Czechoslovakia, in the High Tatra, on Biely Vah R., on railroad and 31 mi. E of Ruzomberok; lumbering, lace making. Noted for colorful regional costumes. Stalactite caverns near by. Destroyed by great forest fire in 1930; later rebuilt.
Vazovgrad, Bulgaria: see SOPOT.
Vazzola (vätsô′lä), village (pop. 1,263), Treviso prov., Veneto, N Italy, 14 mi. NNE of Treviso; alcohol distilleries.
Vcheraishe or **Vcherayshe** (fchĭrī′shĭ), village (1926 pop. 3,777), SE Zhitomir oblast, Ukrainian SSR, 25 mi. E of Berdichev; sugar beets.
Veadeiros, Chapada dos (shŭpä′dŭ dōōs vēädā′rōōs), mountain range of E central Goiás, central Brazil, NNW of Formosa. Highest peak, 5,505 ft. Rock crystals found here. Wheat grown on slopes.
Veauche, France: see SAINT-GALMIER.
Veazie (vē′zē), town (pop. 776), Penobscot co., S Maine, on the Penobscot just above Bangor; Maine's 1st railroad built here, 1836.
Veberod (vā′bůrûd″), Swedish *Veberöd*, village (pop. 756), Malmohus co., S Sweden, 10 mi. ESE of Lund; brick making; grain, sugar beets, potatoes, stock.
Veblen (vĕ′blůn), city (pop. 476), Marshall co., NE S.Dak., 23 mi. ENE of Britton; dairy products, livestock, grain.
Veblungsnes, Norway: see ANDALSNES.
Vecchiano (vĕk-kyä′nô), town (pop. 3,091), Pisa prov., Tuscany, central Italy, on Serchio R. and 5 mi. N of Pisa; agr. center (wine, olive oil, cereals, fruit, vegetables).
Vechel, Netherlands: see VEGHEL.
Vechelde (fĕ-khĕl′dů), village (pop. 2,145), in Brunswick, NW Germany, after 1945 in Lower Saxony, 6 mi. W of Brunswick, in sugar-beet region; food processing (sugar, canned goods), metalworking
Vechigen (vĕ′khĭgůn), town (pop. 2,803), Bern canton, W central Switzerland, 5 mi. E of Bern.
Vechta (fĕkh′tä), town (pop. 12,621), in Oldenburg, NW Germany, after 1945 in Lower Saxony, 32 mi. NNE of Osnabrück; mfg. of cigars. Has Gothic church.
Vecht River (vĕkht), Ger. *Vechte* (fĕkh′tů), in NW Germany and E Netherlands, rises near Billerbeck, flows generally NNW, past Nordhorn (head of navigation), turns W before entering the Netherlands (at Laar), then continues past Hardenberg, Ommen, and Dalfsen to the Zwartewater 3 mi. N of Zwolle. Length c.100 mi. At Nordhorn it is joined with Ems R. (Dortmund-Ems Canal) through short Ems-Vechte Canal.
Vecht River, central Netherlands, branches from the Old Rhine at Utrecht, flows 23 mi. N, past Maarssen, Breukelen, Vreeland, Weesp, and Muiden, to the Ijsselmeer just N of Muiden. Entire length navigable. Also called Utrechtsche Vecht R.
Vecinal Rivera, Uruguay: see RIVERA, city.
Vecoux (vůkōō′), village (pop. 458), Vosges dept., E France, on Moselle R. and 3 mi. SSE of Remiremont; thread mfg.
Vecses (vĕ′chāsh), Hung. *Vecsés*, town (pop. 18,491), Pest-Pilis-Solt-Kiskun co., N central Hungary, 11 mi. SE of Budapest; flour mills. Summer resort.
Vectis, England: see WIGHT, ISLE OF.
Vedano Olona (vĕdä′nô ôlô′nä), village (pop. 3,029), Varese prov., Lombardy, N Italy, 4 mi. SE of Varese; tannery; furniture and comb factories.
Vedaranniyam (vādä″rŭn-nĭyŭm′), town (pop. 14,508), Tanjore dist., SE Madras, India, at NE end of Vedaranniyam Swamp, 27 mi. S of Negapatam, in tobacco area; saltworks. Also spelled Vedaraniam and Vedaranayam. Port of Topputturai is 2 mi. N, rail station of Agastyampalli is 1 mi. S. Projected port of Point Calimere is 7 mi. SSW; rail terminus. **Vedaranniyam Canal** leaves Bay of Bengal at Topputturai, extends c.35 mi. N, through coastal tobacco areas, to Negapatam; also serves Vedaranniyam saltworks; receives Vennar R.
Vedaranniyam Swamp, salt flats along Palk Strait, in Tanjore dist., SE Madras, India; extends c.30 mi. bet. ports of Point Calimere (E) and Adirampatnam (W); 1–5 mi. wide. Inundation twice yearly leaves thick salt deposit; saltworks; lignite deposits; mangrove tracts.
Vedavati River, India: see HAGARI RIVER.
Vedbaek (vĕdh′bĕk), town (pop. 1,444), Copenhagen amt, NE Zealand, Denmark, on the Oresund and 12 mi. N of Copenhagen; truck produce, orchards.
Vedder Crossing, village, SW B.C., near Wash. border, 5 mi. SSW of Chilliwack; dairying; stock, fruit, vegetables.
Vedelago (vĕdĕlä′gô), village (pop. 1,244), Treviso prov., Veneto, N Italy, 11 mi. W of Treviso; silk mill.
Vedène (vůdĕn′), village (pop. 1,433), Vaucluse dept., SE France, 5 mi. NE of Avignon; chemical- and brickworks.
Vedeno (vĭdyô′nů), village (1930 pop. over 500), W Dagestan Autonomous SSR, Russian SFSR, on N slope of Andi Range, on Grozny-Botlikh road and 32 mi. S of Grozny; livestock raising; lumber. Until 1944, in Chechen-Ingush Autonomous SSR.
Vedevag (vā′důvôg″), Swedish *Vedevåg*, village (pop. 844), Orebro co., S central Sweden, on Hork R. and 4 mi. SSE of Lindesberg; iron, paint, lacquer, and brick works, sawmills.
Vedi (vyĭdyē′), village (1939 pop. over 500), S Armenian SSR, 21 mi. SE of Erivan; distilling (wines, brandies). Until c.1935, Beyuk-Vedi or Biyuk-Vedi.
Vedia (bādh′yä), town (pop. 3,605), ⊙ Leandro N. Alem dist. (□ 6,191; pop. 16,955), N Buenos Aires prov., Argentina, 34 mi .WNW of Junín; agr. center (wheat, corn, livestock; dairying).
Vedlozero (vĕd′lō″zyĭrŭ), village, S Karelo-Finnish SSR, on small lake Vedlozero, 50 mi. WSW of Petrozavodsk; grain.
Vedmork, Norway: see VEMORK.
Vedoy, Norway: see VEOY.
Vedrin (vůdrē′), town (pop. 2,632), Namur prov., S central Belgium, 3 mi. N of Namur; pyrites processing; mfg. of sulphuric acid.
Vedsten, Norway: see SARPSBORG.
Vedum (vā′dŭm″), village (pop. 501), Skaraborg co., SW Sweden, 19 mi. W of Falkoping; grain, stock.
Veedersburg, town (pop. 1,719), Fountain co., W Ind., near the Wabash, and 21 mi. WNW of Crawfordsville; agr. (livestock, grain, poultry); condensed milk, brick; bituminous-coal mines.
Veendam (vān′däm), town (pop. 6,245), Groningen prov., NE Netherlands, 7 mi. WSW of Winschoten; peat production center; mfg. (machinery, paper, strawboard, buttons, shoes, stockings), sawmills; flour growing.
Veenendaal (vā′nůndäl), town (pop. 7,719), Utrecht prov., central Netherlands, 19 mi. ESE of Utrecht; artificial-silk, wool, and cotton mills; egg, honey, and wool markets.
Veere or **Vere** (both: vā′rů), town (pop. 845), Zeeland prov., SW Netherlands, on Walcheren isl., on the Veersche Gat and 4 mi. NE of Middelburg; fishing port; frequented by artists. Has many 15th- and 16th-cent. buildings. Town since 1358; from 15th cent. until 1795 center of extensive wool trade with Scotland. Occupied 1813 by French. Important port until beginning of 19th cent. Residence (1497–99) of Erasmus.

Veersche Gat (vär'skhů kät'), SW Netherlands, North Sea inlet (7.5 mi. long) extending SE–NW, bet. Walcheren isl. (W) and North Beveland isl. (E), to dike connecting Walcheren isl. (W) and South Beveland (E).

Vefsna River (věfs'nä), Nordland co., N central Norway, rises on E edge of the Borgefjell on Swedish border, flows 100 mi. in a winding course generally NW, to Vefsn Fjord at Mosjoen. Forms numerous waterfalls.

Vefsn Fjord (věf'sŭn), inlet (c.30 mi. long) of the North Sea in Nordland co., N central Norway; receives Vefsna R. at Mosjoen.

Vega (vā'gä), island (□ 63; pop. 1,753) in North Sea, Nordland co., N central Norway, 35 mi. SW of Mosjoen; 10 mi. long, 7 mi. wide. Fishing, agr. Formerly called Vegen.

Vega (vā'gů), town (pop. 620), ⊙ Oldham co., extreme N Texas, in plains of the Panhandle, 35 mi. W of Amarillo; trade, shipping point for cattle and grain region.

Vega, La, in Latin America: see LA VEGA.

Vega Alta (bā'gä äl'tä), town (pop. 3,492), N Puerto Rico, on railroad and 14 mi. WSW of San Juan; citrus-fruit center; sugar milling, tobacco stripping, mfg. of cigars. Tool factory near by.

Vegaarshei, Norway: see VEGARSHEI.

Vega Baja (bā'gä bä'hä), town (pop. 5,536), N Puerto Rico, on railroad and 17 mi. W of San Juan; citrus-fruit and sugar-cane center; also pineapples, corn, vegetables, stock; mfg. of cigars, gloves, china, rugs. Airport 3 mi. NW. Just NE is the San Vicente sugar mill. Popular beaches are near by on the coast.

Vega de Alatorre (bā'gä dā älätō'rā), town (pop. 1,055), Veracruz, E Mexico, in Gulf lowland, 14 mi. E of Misantla; corn, coffee, tobacco.

Vega de Arure, Canary Isls.: see ARURE.

Vegadeo (bāgä-dhā'ō), town (pop. 2,212), Oviedo prov., NW Spain, on Eo R. and 6 mi. S of Ribadeo; agr. trade center (cereals, livestock; lumber); metalworking, tanning; salmon fishing. Iron mines near by.

Vega de San Mateo (bā'gä dhā sän' mätā'ō), resort village (pop. 1,450), Grand Canary, Canary Isls., 10 mi. SW of Las Palmas. Sometimes San Mateo.

Vega Island (vē'gů), Antarctica, off NE coast of Palmer Peninsula, just N of Ross Isl., in the South Pacific; 63°48'S 57°20'W; 20 naut. mi. long, 7 naut. mi. wide. Discovered 1902 by Otto Nordenskjöld, Swedish explorer.

Veganzones (bāgän-thō'nĕs), town (pop. 648), Segovia prov., central Spain, 19 mi. N of Segovia; grain growing.

Vega Real, La, valley, Dominican Republic: see LA VEGA REAL.

Vegarshei (vä'gôrs-hā), Nor. *Vegårshei,* village and canton (pop. 1,911), Aust-Agder co., S Norway, on Vegars L. (□ 34), on railroad and 20 mi. N of Arendal. Has co. school. Rutile was mined here. Sometimes spelled Vegaarshei.

Vegas or Las Vegas (läs vā'gäs), town (pop. 1,393), Havana prov., W Cuba, 37 mi. SE of Havana; sugar cane, vegetables, cattle.

Vegen, Norway: see VEGA.

Vegesack (fā'gůzäk), section (since 1939) of Bremen, Germany, on right bank of the Weser at mouth of Hamme R., and 10 mi. NW of Bremen city center.

Veghel or **Vechel** (both: vä'khůl), town (pop. 6,144), North Brabant prov., SE central Netherlands, on Aa R. and the Zuid-Willemsvaart and 11 mi. SE of 's Hertogenbosch; synthetic fertilizer, ironware, jute bags, linen.

Veglia, Yugoslavia: see KRK; KRK ISLAND.

Veglie (vä'lyě), town (pop. 6,016), Lecce prov., Apulia, S Italy, 11 mi. WSW of Lecce, in agr. (olives, grapes, tobacco)- and stock-raising region.

Vegoritis, Lake (věgôrē'tĭs), anc. *Bigoritis* (□ 25), in Greek Macedonia, bet. Vermion (S) and Voras (N) massifs, 18 mi. E of Phlorina; 10 mi. long, 3 mi. wide; fisheries. Arnissa is on NE shore. Also called L. Ostrovon.

Vegreville (vē'grůvĭl), town (pop. 1,563), central Alta., on Vermilion R. and 60 mi. E of Edmonton; distributing center for rich farming region; grain, dairying, mixed farming, stock.

Veguellina de Órbigo (bāgělyē'nä dhä ôr'vēgō), village (pop. 1,532), Leon prov., NW Spain, 19 mi. SW of Leon; linen mfg.; sugar and flour mills; agr. trade (cereals, vegetables, sugar beets).

Végueta (bā'gātä), town (pop. 1,461), Lima dept., W central Peru, on coastal plain, E of Végueta Point on the Pacific, 6 mi. NNW of Huacho (connected by highway), in cotton-growing area.

Veguitas (bāgē'täs), town (pop. 2,377), Oriente prov., E Cuba, on Central Highway, on railroad and 13 mi. E of Manzanillo; sugar cane, tobacco, fruit, cattle.

Vegusdal (vä'gōōsdäl), village and canton (pop. 827), Aust-Agder co., S Norway, 27 mi. N of Kristiansand, in lake region; agr., lumbering. Formerly spelled Veigusdal.

Vehkalahti, Finland: see HAMINA.

Vehmaa (vě'mä", věkh'mä"), Swedish *Vehmo* (vā'mōō), village commune (pop. 4,644), Turku-Pori co., SW Finland, 13 mi. SE of Uusikaupunki; granite quarries.

Vehoa or **Vihowa** (both: vĭhō'ŭ), town (pop. 3,781), Dera Ghazi Khan dist., SW Punjab, W Pakistan, 75 mi. NNW of Dera Ghazi Khan; wheat, millet, dates; sheep breeding. Sometimes spelled Vihoa.

Veidelevka or **Veydelevka** (vyādyĭlyĕf'kŭ), village (1926 pop. 4,151), SW Voronezh oblast, Russian SFSR, 15 mi. ESE of Valuiki; flour mill.

Veigusdal, Norway: see VEGUSDAL.

Veigy-Foncenex (vā-zhē'-fōsůněks'), commune (pop. 531), Haute-Savoie dept., SE France, near S shore of L. Geneva, 7 mi. NE of Geneva; customs station of Veigy on Swiss border.

Veii (vēē'), anc. city (circumference c.5 mi.) of Etruria, central Italy, 10 mi. NW of Rome. One of the most powerful Etruscan cities, it was constantly at war with Rome until it fell (396 B.C.) to Camillus. There are Etruscan and Roman ruins, including tombs.

Veimarn or **Veymarn** (vyāmärn'), village (pop. over 500), W Leningrad oblast, Russian SFSR, 7 mi. E of Kingisepp; rail junction; limestone works, oil-shale deposits.

Veinticinco de Mayo. **1** Department, Río Negro natl. territory, Argentina: see MAQUINCHAO. **2** Department, San Juan prov., Argentina: see VILLA SANTA ROSA.

Veinticinco de Mayo or **25 de Mayo** (bāntēsēng'kō dā mī'ō), city (pop. 10,182), ⊙ Veinticinco de Mayo dist. (□ 1,841; pop. 42,197), N central Buenos Aires prov., Argentina, 40 mi. SSW of Chivilcoy; agr. center (grain, livestock); dairying, flour milling, meat packing, tanning. Founded 1837.

Veintiocho de Marzo, Argentina: see AÑATUYA.

Veintisiete de Abril or **27 de Abril** (bāntēsyā'tā dā āvrēl'), village (dist. pop. 4,692), Guanacaste prov., NW Costa Rica, 10 mi. W of Santa Cruz; stock raising; corn, rice, beans.

Veiros (vā'rōōsh), village (pop. 2,418), Évora dist., S central Portugal, 9 mi. NE of Estremoz; grain milling, oil pressing, sheep raising.

Veisivi, Dents de, Switzerland: see DENTS DE VEISIVI.

Veitsch (fīch), town (pop. 3,967), Styria, E central Austria, 8 mi. W of Mürzzuschlag; magnesite mined near by.

Vejbystrand (vā"büstränd'), fishing village (pop. 581), Kristianstad co., SW Sweden, on Skalder Bay of the Kattegat, 6 mi. NNW of Angelholm; seaside resort.

Vejen (vě'yůn), town (pop. 3,664), Ribe amt, S central Jutland, Denmark, 26 mi. E of Esbjerg; rail junction; mfg. (margarine, asphalt paper).

Vejer de la Frontera (bāhěr' dhā lä frōntā'rä), city (pop. 8,709), Cádiz prov., SW Spain, on small Barbate R., near the Atlantic, and 28 mi. SE of Cádiz; agr. center (cereals, grapes, oranges, vegetables, livestock); wine and liquor distilling; fishing. Sometimes spelled Veger.

Vejgaard (vī'gôr), town (pop. 10,052), residential E suburb of Aalborg, Aalborg amt, N Jutland, Denmark.

Vejle (vī'lů), amt (□ 907; pop. 201,113), E Jutland, Denmark, including Hjarno isl.; ⊙ Vejle. Fertile soil in E part; vegetable and dairy farming, cattle breeding. Other cities: Kolding, Fredericia.

Vejle, city (pop. 29,448) and port, ⊙ Vejle amt, E Jutland, Denmark, on Vejle Fjord and 40 mi. SSW of Aarhus; commercial and industrial center, rail junction, with good harbor. Iron foundry, mfg. (hardware, candy, machinery, textiles), dairy plant, meat cannery, fisheries. City dates from Middle Ages.

Vejle Fjord (13 mi. long), E Jutland, Denmark, inlet of the Little Belt. Vejle city at head.

Vejprty (vā'pŭrtĭ), Ger. *Weipert* (vī'pěrt), town (pop. 5,476), W Bohemia, Czechoslovakia, in the Erzgebirge, on railroad and 20 mi. NNE of Carlsbad, on Ger. border opposite Jöhstadt; mfg. of artificial silk, stockings, lace, cloth buttons; munitions industry.

Vejsnaes Bay, Denmark: see MARSTAL BAY.

Vekil-Bazar or **Vekil'-Bazar** (vyĭkēl"-bŭzär'), village, central Mary oblast, Turkmen SSR, on Murgab oasis, 10 mi. NE of Mary; cotton.

Vela (bā'lä), town (pop. 2,635), S central Buenos Aires prov., Argentina, 20 mi. W of Tandil; stock raising, dairying.

Vela, Cabo de la (kä'bō dā lä), headland on Caribbean coast of NW Guajira peninsula, N Colombia; 12°13'N 72°10'W.

Vela, La, Venezuela: see LA VELA.

Velada (bālä'dhä), town (pop. 1,990), Toledo prov., central Spain, 7 mi. W of Talavera de la Reina; cereals, grapes, olives, cork, timber, livestock. Stone quarrying.

Velaluka (välälōō'kä), Ital. *Vallegrande* (vällěgrän'dě), village, S Croatia, Yugoslavia, on W coast of Korcula Isl., on Adriatic Sea, 22 mi. W of Korcula, in Dalmatia; resort; fishing, fish canning.

Velanai (vä'lŭnī), island (pop. 18,263) in Northern Prov., Ceylon; separated from Jaffna Peninsula by Jaffna Lagoon; 13 mi. long; 5 mi. wide. Extensive rice plantations; coconut and palmyra palms, vegetables. Main settlement, Kayts. Ferry to Karaitivu (N) and Punkudutivu (S) isls.

Velanganni, India: see NEGAPATAM.

Velarde (vůlär'dē), village (1940 pop. 885, with near-by Lyden village), Rio Arriba co., N N.Mex., on Rio Grande, just W of Sangre de Cristo Mts., and 33 mi. N of Santa Fe; alt. 5,600 ft. Trading point for agr. area; fruit, chili, truck. Part of Carson Natl. Forest, Picuris Pueblo Indian village near by.

Velardeña (bālärdā'nyä), mining settlement (pop. 2,581), Durango, N Mexico, on railroad and 40 mi. SSW of Torreón; gold, silver, lead, copper mining.

Velas (vě'lůsh), town (pop. 1,016), Angra do Heroísmo dist., central Azores, near W tip of São JORGE ISLAND, 25 mi. NE of Horta (on Faial Isl.); 38°41'N 28°13'W; whaling, dairying.

Velasco, Bolivia: see SAN IGNACIO, Santa Cruz.

Velasco, Cuba: see VELAZCO.

Velasco (vůlă'skō), city (pop. 2,260), Brazoria co., S Texas, opposite FREEPORT at mouth of Brazos R., in Brazosport industrial area; chemical mfg., extraction of magnesium from sea water; fishing. Settled in early 1820s; scene of battle (1832) bet. Texans and Mexicans, and signing (1836) of treaty ending Texas Revolution. Grew (especially after 1940) in Freeport boom. Inc. after 1940.

Velasco, Sierra de (syě'rä dā vālä'skō), subandean mountain range in central La Rioja prov., Argentina, bet. Chilecito and La Rioja; extends c.100 mi. S from Catamarca prov. border, forming E wall of Famatina Valley; rises to c.13,000 ft. Coal deposits.

Velásquez River (bāläs'kěs), small E affluent of the Magdalena, W Boyacá dept., central Colombia, in oil-bearing Vásquez Territory.

Velay (vůlā'), region of S central France, in the Massif Central, bet. Montagnes de la Margeride (W) and Monts du Vivarais (E), occupying W and central Haute-Loire dept.; Le Puy is chief city. The volcanic Monts du Velay, extending c.30 mi. from Allègre (N) to Langogne (S), separate the upper Loire and Allier rivers. They rise to 4,669 ft. The basin of Le Puy (center) is agr. (rye, lentils); the arid granitic plateau (E) has summer pastures. Named after the Vellaves, a Gallic tribe, Velay was a medieval countship under suzerainty of counts of Toulouse and later of English rulers of Aquitaine. After Hundred Years' War it became part of Languedoc prov. and was inc. into Haute-Loire dept. in 1790.

Velayos (bälī'ōs), town (pop. 832), Ávila prov., central Spain, on railroad and 13 mi. N of Ávila; grain, beans, chick-peas, sheep.

Velazco or **Velasco** (both: bālä'skō), town (pop. 1,776), Oriente prov., E Cuba, on railroad and 14 mi. NW of Holguín; sugar cane, tobacco, fruit, cattle.

Velázquez (bālä'skěs), town (pop. 2,000), Rocha dept., SE Uruguay, 30 mi. N of Rocha, in stock-raising region (cattle, sheep).

Velbazh Pass (věl'bäsh) (alt. 3,877 ft.), on Bulgaro-Yugoslav border, on NE slope of Osogov Mts., just W of Gyuyeshevo (Bulgaria). Carries main highway bet. Kyustendil (Bulgaria) and Kriva Palanka (Yugoslavia).

Velbert (fěl'bůrt), town (pop. 36,200), in former Prussian Rhine Prov., W Germany, after 1945 in North Rhine-Westphalia, in the Ruhr, 8 mi. S of Essen; metalworking center (locks; fittings for vehicles, ships, furniture, windows). First mentioned in 9th cent. Developed industrially after 1880.

Velburg (fěl'bōōrk), town (pop. 1,932), Upper Palatinate, central Bavaria, Germany, 10 mi. ESE of Neumarkt; brewing. Limestone quarries in area. Just NE is large stalactite cave.

Velbuzhd, Bulgaria: see KYUSTENDIL.

Veld or **Veldt** (both: vělt, fělt) [Du.,=field], interior plateau region of the Union of South Africa and of Southern Rhodesia, particularly the elevated, undulating grasslands of TRANSVAAL and ORANGE FREE STATE, which were settled by the Boers on their great trek. Of paleozoic *karoo* formation, the Veld comprises territory of varying elevation: the Low Veld (500–2,000 ft.), the Middle Veld (2–4,000 ft.), and the High Veld, sometimes also called NORTHERN KAROO (4–6,000 ft.). According to vegetation, another, less customary, typology distinguishes bet. Tree Veld, Bush Veld, and Grass Veld, which roughly correspond to the above-stated 3 subdivisions. The Veld as a whole is well-suited to grazing, but cereals and potatoes are also widely grown. It is rich in all kinds of minerals, especially gold in WITWATERSRAND section of High Veld, centering on JOHANNESBURG.

Velda, town (pop. 480), St. Louis co., E Mo., W of St. Louis.

Velda Village Hills, town (pop. 1,527), St. Louis co., E Mo., just W of St. Louis. Inc. since 1940.

Velden (fěl'dŭn). **1** Village (pop. 3,233), Lower Bavaria, Germany, on the Great Vils and 7 mi. SW of Vilsbiburg; machine shops; brewing, woodworking. **2** Town (pop. 1,051), Middle Franconia, N central Bavaria, Germany, on the Pegnitz and 8 mi. NNE of Hersbruck; brewing, flour milling. Hops, horse-radish. Has Gothic church with renovated (1724–29) interior. Chartered 1376.

Velden am Wörthersee (äm vûrt'ůrzā), village (pop. 2,498), Carinthia, S Austria, on W shore of the Wörthersee and 9 mi. E of Villach; furniture mfg.; meteorological station; summer resort. Has 16th-cent. château.

Veldes; Veldeser See, Yugoslavia: see BLED LAKE.

Veldhoven (vĕlt'hōvŭn), village (pop. 3,184), North Brabant prov., S Netherlands, 4 mi. SW of Eindhoven; linen mfg.

Velebit Mountains (vĕlĕ'bĕt), Ital. *Alpi Bebie* (äl'pē bĕb'yĕ), in Dinaric Alps, W Croatia, Yugoslavia, partly in Dalmatia; extend c.100 mi. along Adriatic Sea. Highest peaks: Vaganjski Vrh, Ital. *Monte Vagagno* (5,766 ft.; 13 mi. S of Gospic); Rajinac (5,432 ft.; 27 mi. NW of Gospic). Mts. rise steeply from coast; crossed by a few winding roads. The narrow Velebit Channel, Serbo-Croatian *Podgorski Kanal* or *Planinski Kanal*, Ital. *Canale della Morlacca*, of Adriatic Sea extends c.80 mi. along W foot of mts.; separates mainland from near-by isls.

Velehrad (vä'lĕhrät), village (pop. 1,018), E Moravia, Czechoslovakia, 4 mi. NW of Uherske Hradiste. Well-known pilgrimage center with primitive 13th-cent. church, destroyed several times by fire and again rebuilt. Great regional fairs held here in summer.

Veleka River (vĕ'lĭkŭ), Turkish *Velika* (vĕlĭkä'), in European Turkey and SE Bulgaria, rises in Turkey in Istranca (Strandzha) Mts. 18 mi. W of Malko-Tirnovo, flows 55 mi. E, mostly in Bulgaria, to Black Sea just S of Akhtopol.

Velence (vĕ'lĕntsĕ), town (pop. 3,016), Fejer co., W central Hungary, on N shore of L. Velence and 10 mi. ENE of Szekesfehervar; champagne mfg.; truck farming (grapes, cattle, poultry, eggs).

Velence, Lake, Fejer co., W central Hungary, 6 mi. E of Szekesfehervar; 5 mi. long, c.1 mi. wide, 5 ft. deep; fish. Town of Velence on N shore.

Velenje (vĕ'lĕnyĕ), Ger. *Wöllan* (vûl'än), village, N Slovenia, Yugoslavia, on railroad 12 mi. NW of Celje; lignite mine; power plant. Castle ruins. Until 1918, in Styria.

Veles, Yugoslavia: see TITOV VELES.

Velestinon (vĕlĕstē'nôn), anc. *Pherae* (fē'rē), town (pop. 2,984), Magnesia nome, SE Thessaly, Greece, 10 mi. W of Volos; rail junction. The anc. Pherae, on its site, was home of mythical Admetus. It flourished (early 4th cent. B.C.) when its tyrants (notably Jason, c.370 B.C.) rivaled the power of Larissa for the control of Thessaly.

Veleta (bālā'tä), second highest peak (11,128 ft.) of the Sierra Nevada, in Granada prov., S Spain, 16 mi. SE of Granada. Copper deposits.

Veletma or **Velet'ma** (vyĕlyĭtmä'), town (1939 pop. over 500), SW Gorki oblast, Russian SFSR, on Veletma R. (right tributary of the Oka) and 6 mi. SSW of Kulebaki.

Vélez (bā'lĕs), town (pop. 2,996), Santander dept., N central Colombia, in W Cordillera Oriental, on Tunja–Puerto Berrío road, and 31 mi. NNE of Chiquinquirá; alt. 7,119 ft. Agr. center (sugar cane, coffee, tobacco, corn, wheat, rice, fruit, cattle, hogs); mfg. (food preserves, clothing, footwear). Sericultural school. Copper and coal deposits near.

Vélez Blanco (bā'lĕth bläng'kō), town (pop. 2,251), Almería prov., S Spain, 3 mi. NNW of Vélez Rubio; olive presses, flour mills. Agr. trade (cereals, fruit, livestock; lumber). Marble quarries near by. Lead and copper mining. Dominated by hill topped by 16th-cent. castle.

Vélez de Benaudalla (bā'lĕth dhā bänou-dhä'lyä), town (pop. 2,756), Granada prov., S Spain, 6 mi. N of Motril; olive-oil processing, flour milling. Almonds and corn. Lead mines.

Vélez de la Gomera, Peñón de, Spain: see PEÑÓN DE VÉLEZ DE LA GOMERA.

Vélez-Málaga (bā'lĕth-mä'lägä) city (pop. 10,813), Málaga prov., S Spain, in Andalusia, on coastal plain (*vega*), on Vélez R., on railroad and 17 mi. E of Málaga. Served by its Mediterranean landing TORRE DEL MAR, 2½ mi. S. Trading, processing, and agr. center (raisins, grapes, almonds, oranges, lemons, sugar cane, olives, livestock); sugar milling, olive-oil processing, liquor distilling, tanning; limekilns; mfg. of soap. The anc. city, of Phoenecian origin, has an old church and ruins of a Moorish castle. Vélez-Málaga was a bishopric for 3 cent., being succeeded by Málaga. Damaged by 1884 earthquake.

Velez Mountains or **Velezh Mountains** (vĕ'lĕsh), Serbo-Croatian *Velež Planina*, in Dinaric Alps, central Herzegovina, Yugoslavia, along left bank of lower Neretva R.; c.10 mi. long N–S. Highest peak, Botin (6,458 ft.), is 10 mi. E of Mostar.

Vélez Rubio (bā'lĕth rōō'vyō), town (pop. 5,235), Almería prov., S Spain, in Andalusia, 60 mi. NNE of Almería; olive-oil processing, flour milling, chocolate mfg., wool spinning. Agr. trade (cereals, wine, fruit); lumbering, stock raising. Mineral spring. Stalactite cave near by.

Vélez Sarsfield, Argentina: see TAMA.

Velgiya or **Vel'giya** (vyĕl'gēŭ), town (1939 pop. over 500), E Novgorod oblast, Russian SFSR, 3 mi. E of Borovichi; paper mill.

Velhartice (vĕl'härtyĭtsĕ), village (pop. 559), SW Bohemia, Czechoslovakia, on railroad and 10 mi. SSE of Klatovy; summer resort noted for trout fishing; hide processing. Has 13th-cent. castle, partly rebuilt in 17th cent.

Velhas, Rio das (rē'ōō däs vĕ'lyŭs). **1** River in central Minas Gerais, Brazil, rises on W slope of the Serra do Espinhaço just N of Ouro Prêto, flows c.500 mi. NNW in a tortuous course across central plateau, past Sabará and Santa Luzia, to the São Francisco (right bank) at Guaicuí (below Pirapora). Navigable bet. rapids. Iron, gold, fluorspar, and semiprecious-stone deposits in valley. **2** River in the Triângulo Mineiro of W Minas Gerais, Brazil, flows c.200 mi. NW to the Paranaíba (left bank) 40 mi. NNW of Uberlândia. Diamond washings.

Velichovsky, Czechoslovakia: see JAROMER.

Velika (vĕ'lĭkä), village, N Croatia, Yugoslavia, 9 mi. N of Pozega, at S foot of the Papuk, in Slavonia; rail terminus; health resort.

Velika Cvrstnica or **Velika Chvrstnitsa** (chvŭrst'nĭtsä), Serbo-Croatian *Velika Čvrstnica*, mountain in Dinaric Alps, NW Herzegovina, Yugoslavia, W of Neretva R. Highest point (7,308 ft.) is 11 mi. WSW of Jablanica. Mala Cvrstnica extends SE.

Velika Gorica (gô'rĭtsä), village (pop. 2,015), N Croatia, Yugoslavia, on railroad and 8 mi. SSE of Zagreb; lumbering. Mala Gorica village lies just S.

Velika Kapela (kä'pĕlä), mountain range in Dinaric Alps, NW Croatia, Yugoslavia; continued SE by Mala Kapela; ranges extend c.50 mi. NW–SE; highest point, Bijela Lasica (5,028 ft.), is 13 mi. W of Ogulin. Large forests.

Velika Kikinda, Yugoslavia: see KIKINDA.

Velika Kladusa or **Velika Kladusha** (both: klä'dōōshä), Serbo-Croatian *Velika Kladuša*, village (pop. 4,102), NW Bosnia, Yugoslavia, 14 mi. N of Cazin, near Croatia border. Mala Kladusa is SSE.

Velika Ljubisnja or **Velika Lyubishnya** (lyōō'bĭshnyä), Serbo-Croatian *Velika Ljubišnja*, mountain in Dinaric Alps, N Montenegro, Yugoslavia, bet. Tara and Cotina rivers; highest point (7,341 ft.) is 12 mi. N of Zabljak. The Mala Ljubisnja (6,530 ft.) is ENE of the peak.

Velika Morava River, Yugoslavia: see MORAVA RIVER.

Velika Plana, Yugoslavia: see PLANA.

Velika Plazenica or **Velika Plazhenitsa** (plä'zhĕnĭtsä), Serbo-Croatian *Velika Plaženica*, mountain in Dinaric Alps, SE Bosnia, Yugoslavia; highest point (5,792 ft.) is 12 mi. W of Bugojno. Mala Plazenica (5,104 ft.) rises 2 mi. S of the peak.

Velika Reka, river, Yugoslavia: see TRESKA RIVER.

Velika River, Bulgaria-Turkey: see VELEKA RIVER.

Velikaya (vĭlyē'kĭŭ) [Rus.,=GREAT, LARGE, BIG], in Rus. names: see also VELIKI, VELIKIYE, VELIKO- [Rus. combining form], VELIKOYE.

Velikaya, river, Russian SFSR: see VELIKAYA RIVER.

Velikaya Bagachka (bŭgäch'kŭ), town (1926 pop. 3,267), central Poltava oblast, Ukrainian SSR, on Psel R. and 38 mi. WNW of Poltava; flour milling.

Velikaya Guba (gōōbä'), village (1926 pop. 171), S Karelo-Finnish SSR, on L. Onega, 40 mi. NE of Petrozavodsk; grain.

Velikaya Mikhailovka or **Velikaya Mikhaylovka** (mēkhī'lŭfkŭ), village (1932 pop. estimate 1,550), W Odessa oblast, Ukrainian SSR, 55 mi. NW of Odessa; winery, flour mill. Until 1945, Grosulovo.

Velikaya River, W European Russian SFSR, rises in Bezhanitsy Upland NE of Pustoshka, flows 265 mi. W and N, past Opochka, Ostrov, and Pskov, to L. Pskov, forming small delta mouth. Navigable (April–Nov.) below Pskov.

Velike Lasce (vĕ'lĭkĕ läsh'chĕ), Slovenian *Velike Lašče*, village, S Slovenia, Yugoslavia, on railroad and 17 mi. S of Ljubljana.

Veliki or **Velikiy** [Rus.,=GREAT, LARGE, BIG], in Rus. names: see also VELIKAYA, VELIKIYE, VELIKO- [Rus. combining form], VELIKOYE.

Veliki Beckerek, Yugoslavia: see ZRENJANIN.

Veliki Berezny or **Velikiy Bereznyy** (vĭlyē'kē bĭryôz'nē), Czech *Velké Berezne* (vĕl'kā bĕ'rĕznĕ), Hung. *Nagyberezna* (nŏ'dyŭbĕ'rĕznŏ), village (1941 pop. 4,032), NW Transcarpathian Oblast, Ukrainian SSR, on Uzh R., on railroad and 20 mi. NNE of Uzhgorod.

Veliki Bochkov or **Velikiy Bochkov** (bŭchkôf'), Czech *Velký Bočkov*, Hung. *Nagybocsko* (nŏdyŭbôch"kô), Rum. *Bocicoiul-Mare* (bôchēkō' yōōl mä'rā), village (1941 pop. 7,426), S Transcarpathian Oblast, Ukrainian SSR, on right bank of Tissa R. (Rum. border) and 36 mi. SE of Khust; wood cracking. Rail station is across Tissa R., on Rum. (left) bank. A town of Austria-Hungary which passed 1920 to Czechoslovakia, 1938 to Hungary, and 1945 to USSR.

Veliki Burluk or **Velikiy Burluk** (bōōrlōōk'), village (1926 pop. 6,917), NE Kharkov oblast, Ukrainian SSR, 25 mi. NNW of Kupyansk; flour mill, metalworks. Also called Bolshoi Burluk.

Veliki Drvenik Island (vĕ'lĭkē drĕv'nĭk), Ital. *Zirona Grande* (zērô'nä grän'dĕ), Dalmatian island in Adriatic Sea, S Croatia, Yugoslavia, c.15 mi. WSW of Split; 3 mi. long. Mali Drvenik Isl., Ital. *Zirona Piccola*, is just W.

Veliki Glubochek or **Velikiy Glubochek** (vĭlyē'kē glōōbô'chĭk), village (1939 pop. over 500), central Ternopol oblast, Ukrainian SSR, on Seret R. and 5 mi. NNW of Ternopol; wheat, barley, tobacco. Until 1944, called Glubochek Veliki, Pol. *Huboczek Wielki* (hwōōbô'chĕk vyĕl'kē).

Veliki Repen, Free Territory of Trieste: see MONRUPINO.

Veliki Trnovac or **Veliki Trnovats** (both: vĕ'lĭkē tŭr'nôväts), village pop. 5,203), S Serbia, Yugoslavia, 10 mi. SW of Vranje, just NW of Bujanovac.

Veliki Ustyug or **Velikiy Ustyug** (vĭlyē'kē ōō'styōōk), city (1926 pop. 19,171), NE Vologda oblast, Russian SFSR, on Sukhona R., opposite mouth of the Yug, on Sharya-Kotlas road and 35 mi. SSW of Kotlas; hog-bristle products, alcohol; metalworks, shipyards, clothing and food industries. Has 17th-cent. Troitse-Gledin monastery and cathedral, regional mus. Founded (10th cent.) at confluence of Sukhona-Yug rivers; moved (13th cent.) 3 mi. upstream to present site; became (16th-17th cent.) flourishing trade center of NE Russia. Handicraft industries (silver- and woodworking, carving, embroidery) in vicinity. Sometimes called Ustyug Veliki. Was ⊙ Northern Dvina govt. (1918–29).

Velikiye [Rus.,=GREAT, LARGE, BIG], in Rus. names: see also VELIKAYA, VELIKI, VELIKO- [Rus. combining form], VELIKOYE.

Velikiye Borki (vĭlyē'kēŭ bôr'kē), village (1939 pop. over 500), central Ternopol oblast, Ukrainian SSR, 7 mi. ESE of Ternopol; rail junction; wheat, barley, tobacco. Until 1944, called Borki Velikiye, Pol. *Borki Wielkie* (bôr'kē vyĕl'kyĕ).

Velikiye Dederkaly (dyĕdyĭrkä'lē), Pol. *Dederkaly*, town (1939 pop. over 500), N Ternopol oblast, Ukrainian SSR, 16 mi. ESE of Kremenets; grain, livestock.

Velikiye Krynki (krĭn'kē), village (1939 pop. over 2,000), S central Poltava oblast, Ukrainian SSR, 26 mi. N of Kremenchug; metalworks.

Velikiye Luki (lōō'kē), oblast (□ 17,300; 1946 pop. estimate 900,000) in W European Russian SFSR; ⊙ Velikiye Luki. In lake-studded moraine region; Valdai Hills (E); drained by upper western Dvina, Lovat, and Velikaya rivers. Sandy and clayey soils; extensive forests (E). Chief crops: flax, potatoes, fodder; dairy cattle and hogs extensively raised. Lignite mining (Nelidovo, Andreapol). Industry based on agr. (flax processing, distilling, dairying) and lumber (sawmilling at Kholm, Nelidovo, Zapadnaya Dvina, Peno). Handicraft industries produce carts, sleds, and wagon wheels. Chief industrial centers: Velikiye Luki, Nevel. Formed 1944 out of Kalinin oblast.

Velikiye Luki, city (1926 pop. 20,771), ⊙ Velikiye Luki oblast, Russian SFSR, on Lovat R. and 260 mi. W of Moscow; 56°21'N 30°31'E. Rail junction; industrial center; railway-car repair, garment mfg., dairying, flour milling, distilling, brickworking. Dates from mid-12th cent.; controlled successively by Novgorod, Lithuania, and (late-15th cent.) by Moscow. Captured (1580) by Bathory; destroyed by fire in early-17th cent. Chartered 1770. During Second World War, held (1941–43) by Germans.

Velikiye Mosty (mŭstĭ'), city (1931 pop. 4,348), N central Lvov oblast, Ukrainian SSR, 27 mi. NNE of Lvov; agr. processing (cereals), sawmilling. Until 1941, called Mosty Velikiye, Pol. *Mosty Wielkie* (mô'stĭ vyĕl'kyĕ).

Veliko- [Rus. combining form,=GREAT, LARGE, BIG], in Rus. names: see also VELIKAYA, VELIKI, VELIKIYE, VELIKAYE.

Veliko-Alekseyevski or **Veliko-Alekseyevskiy** (vĭlyē'kŭ-ŭlyĭksyā'ŭfskē), town (1947 pop. over 500), N Tashkent oblast, Uzbek SSR, on Trans-Caspian RR and 45 mi. WSW of Tashkent; rubber-bearing plants.

Velikodvorski or **Velikodvorskiy** (vĭlyē"kŭdvôr'skē), town (1926 pop. 2,441), S Vladimir oblast, Russian SFSR, 25 mi. S of Gus-Khrustalny; glassworks.

Veliko Gradiste, Yugoslavia: see GRADISTE, E Serbia.

Velikoknyazheskoye (–knyä'zhĭskŭyŭ), village (1939 pop. over 2,000), W Stavropol Territory, Russian SFSR, near Kuban R., 6 mi. WNW of Nevinnomyssk; metalworks.

Veliko-Mikhailovka or **Veliko-Mikhaylovka** (–mēkhī'lŭfkŭ), village (1926 pop. 10,456), SE Kursk oblast, Russian SFSR, 45 mi. ENE of Belgorod; wheat, sunflowers.

Velikooktyabrski or **Velikooktyabr'skiy** (–ŭktyä'bŭrskē), town (1926 pop. 244), W Kalinin oblast, Russian SFSR, 6 mi. SE of Firovo; glassworks. Until 1941, Pokrovskoye.

Veliko-Polovetskoye (vĭlyē"kŭ-pŭlŭvyĕt'skŭyŭ), village (1926 pop. 4,344), W Kiev oblast, Ukrainian SSR, 10 mi. WNW of Belaya Tserkov; sugar beets.

Veliko-Rakovetskaya (–rä'kŭvyĕtskĭŭ), Czech *Velký Rakovec* (vĕl'kē rä'kôvĕts), Hung. *Nagyrákóc* (nŏ'dyŭrä"kōts), village (1941 pop. 4,218), S central Transcarpathian Oblast, Ukrainian SSR, 9 mi. NW of Khust; lignite mining.

Velikoye [Rus.,=GREAT, LARGE, BIG], in Rus. names: see also VELIKAYA, VELIKI, VELIKIYE, VELIKO–.

Velilla de Guardo (bālē'lyä dhā gwär'dhō), village (pop. 1,032), Palencia prov., N central Spain, on Carrión R. and 42 mi. ENE of Leon; lumber, livestock. Trout fishing. Anthracite and bituminous-coal mines, marble and granite quarries near by.

Velilla de San Antonio (sän' äntō'nyō), town (pop. 909), Madrid prov., central Spain, on Jarama R. and 11 mi. ESE of Madrid; olives, cereals, grapes, truck.

Velille (bālē'yā), town (pop. 250), Cuzco dept., S Peru, in Cordillera Occidental, 70 mi. S of Cuzco; grain, stock; gold washing; mfg. of woolen goods.

Veli Losinj, Yugoslavia: see Losinj Island.

Velindre, Wales: see Llangeler.

Vélines (vālēn'), village (pop. 309), Dordogne dept., SW France, near Dordogne R., 17 mi. ESE of Libourne, in winegrowing area.

Vélingara (vělĭng-gä'rä), town (pop. c.700), S Senegal, Fr. West Africa, near Br. Gambia, 150 mi. ENE of Ziguinchor; lumbering.

Velingrad (vě'lĭn-grät), city (8,352), Plovdiv dist., SW Bulgaria, on Chepino R. and 21 mi. SW of Pazardzhik; major health resort (thermal springs); sawmilling (wood products, turpentine); truck, flax. Formed 1949 by union of former villages of Chepino and Ladzhene.

Velino River (vělē'nô), central Italy, rises in the Apennines 10 mi. SSE of Norcia, flows SSW, past Antrodoco, W, past Cittaducale and Rieti, and NW to Nera R. 4 mi. E of Terni; 55 mi. long. Its famous falls, Cascata delle Marmore, furnish power for industries of Terni.

Velistsikhe (vělyĭstsē'khyĭ), village (1926 pop. 5,934), E Georgian SSR, in Kakhetia, near Alazan R., 16 mi. SE of Telavi; vineyards.

Velizh (vyĭlyēsh'), city (1926 pop. 10,510), NW Smolensk oblast, Russian SFSR, on Western Dvina R. and 65 mi. NW of Smolensk; sawmilling center; woodworking, dairying, tanning. Founded 1536 as fortress; fought over by Poland and Russia; annexed 1772 by Russia.

Velizhany (vyĭlyĭzhä'nē), village (1939 pop. over 500), SW Tyumen oblast, Russian SFSR, 30 mi. N of Tyumen, in agr. area (grain, livestock).

Vélizy-Villacoublay (vālēzē'-vēläkōōblā'), outer SW suburb (pop. 3,642) of Paris, Seine-et-Oise dept., N central France, 9 mi. SW of Notre Dame Cathedral; has airport, aircraft shops, and military installations.

Velka, Czechoslovakia: see Poprad, town.

Velka Bites (věl'kä bē'těsh), Czech *Velká Bíteš*, Ger. *Gross-Bitesch* (grôs-bē'těsh), town (pop. 1,714), W Moravia, Czechoslovakia, 18 mi. WNW of Brno; oats.

Velka Bytca, Czechoslovakia: see Bytca.

Velka Destna (děsht'nä), Czech *Velká Deštná*, Ger. *Deschnaer Kuppe* (děsh'nāūr kŏŏ'pū), highest mountain (3,655 ft.) of the Adlergebirge, on Czechoslovak-Pol. border, 15 mi. SW of Glatz (Klodzko), Poland.

Velka Fatra, mountains, Czechoslovakia: see Greater Fatra.

Velka Javorina (yä'vôrzhĭnä), Slovak *Velká Javořina*, mountain (3,175 ft.) in the White Carpathians, Czechoslovakia, on Moravia-Slovakia border, 16 mi. E of Straznice.

Velkal, Russian SFSR: see Uelkal.

Velke Berezne, Ukraine: see Veliki Berezny.

Velke Kapusany (věl'kā kä'pŏŏshänĭ), Slovak *Vel'ké Kapušany*, Hung. *Nagykapos* (nŏ'dyŭkŏ"pôsh), town (pop. 2,371), E Slovakia, Czechoslovakia, on railroad and 48 mi. SE of Presov; wheat, sugar beets, grapes. Held by Hungary, 1938–45.

Velke Karlovice (kär'lôvĭtsě), Czech *Velké Karlovice*, Ger. *Karlowitz* (kär'lōvĭts), village (pop. 3,167), E Moravia, Czechoslovakia, on Horni Becva R. and 30 mi. ENE of Gottwaldov; rail terminus; scenic year-round resort in the Beskids; lumbering, linen making.

Velke Losiny (lô'sĭnĭ), Czech *Velké Losiny*, village (pop. 1,941) N Moravia, Czechoslovakia, in the Jeseniky, on railroad and 6 mi. NNE of Sumperk; health resort (alt. 1,350 ft.) with sulphur and peat baths.

Velke Mezirici (mě'zĭrzhēchē), Czech *Velké Meziříčí*, Ger. *Gross-Meseritsch* (grôs-mā'zūrĭch), town (pop. 6,217), W Moravia, Czechoslovakia, 29 mi. WNW of Brno; rail terminus; tanning center; mfg. of footwear, glue. Has Gothic church, castle with art collections. Fish ponds in vicinity.

Velke Popovice, Czechoslovakia: see Jilove.

Velke Zernoseky (zhěr'nôsěkĭ), Czech *Velké Žernoseky*, village (pop. 575), N Bohemia, Czechoslovakia, on railroad, on Elbe R. and 8 mi. S of Usti nad Labem; noted for winemaking. Just across the Elbe is twin village of Male Zernoseky (mä'lā), Czech *Malé Žernoseky*.

Velky Bockov, Ukrainian SSR: see Veliki Bochkov.

Velky Meder, Czechoslovakia: see Calovo.

Velky Ostrov Zitny, Czechoslovakia: see Schütt.

Velky Rakovec, Ukrainian SSR: see Veliko-Rakovetskaya.

Vella Lavella (vě'lä lävě'lä), volcanic island, Solomon Isls., SW Pacific, 225 mi. NW of Guadalcanal; 7°43'S 156°40'E; 25 mi. long, 10 mi. wide; copra. In Second World War, U.S. defeated Japan in naval battle of Vella Lavella (1943).

Vellalur (vě'lŭlŏŏr), town (pop. 9,816), Coimbatore dist., SW Madras, India, on Noyil R. and 4 mi. ESE of Coimbatore; cotton milling; betel farms.

Vellar River (vě'lär), S Madras, India, rises in SW Kalrayan Hills, flows c.110 mi. generally E, past Attur, Pennadam, and Bhuvanagiri, to Coromandel Coast of Bay of Bengal at Porto Novo. In upper course, sometimes also called Vasishtanadi. Name Vellar sometimes applied to Vennar R. (S).

Vellberg (fěl'běrk), town (pop. 1,287), N Württemberg, Germany, after 1945 in Württemberg-Baden, 6.5 mi. ESE of Schwäbisch Hall; grain, cattle. Has medieval fortifications.

Velleia (věl-lā'yä), village (pop. 469), Piacenza prov., Emilia-Romagna, N central Italy, 19 mi. S of Piacenza; oil wells. Once a Ligurian, later a Roman, town. Its ruins (Roman amphitheater, temple, forum) excavated 1760–76; now included in a provincial park.

Vellés, La (lä vělyěs'), village (pop. 1,136), Salamanca prov., W Spain, 10 mi. NE of Salamanca; cereals, vegetables.

Velletri (věl-lā'trē), anc. *Velitrae*, town (pop. 20,419), Roma prov., Latium, central Italy, in Alban Hills, 21 mi. SE of Rome; rail junction; noted wine-making center; agr. machinery, furniture. Bishopric. Of Volscian origin; fell to Romans in 338 B.C.

Vellinge (vě'lĭng-ů), village (pop. 1,123), Malmohus co., S Sweden, 10 mi. S of Malmo; rail junction; brick making, tanning; mechanical workshops.

Vellisca (bělyē'skä), town (pop. 918), Cuenca prov., E central Spain, 50 mi. ESE of Madrid; cereals, olives, livestock; apiculture.

Vellón, El (ěl vělyōn'), town (pop. 834), Madrid prov., central Spain, 25 mi. N of Madrid; cereals, grapes, livestock; flour milling.

Vellore (vŭlôr'), Tamil *Velluru* (věl'lŏŏrŏŏ), city (pop. 71,502), ⊙ North Arcot dist., E central Madras, India, on Palar R. and 75 mi. WSW of Madras; trade center in agr. area (rice, peanuts, sugar cane, cotton); biri-mfg. and flower-gardening center; exports products (sandalwood, tanbark, nux vomica, hemp narcotics) of Javadi Hills (SW). Vellore Christian Medical Col. (outgrowth of Missionary Medical Col. for Women) is medical and psychiatric research center; industrial schools. Vijayanagar fort (noted specimen of military architecture) contains Dravidian temple; a strategic military base during 18th-cent. struggle bet. French and English for dominance in India. Rail junction of Katpadi is 4 mi. N, across river (rail bridge).

Velluda, Sierra (syě'rä běyōō'dä), Andean range in Bío-Bío prov., S central Chile, on SW bank of L. Laja 50 mi. E of Los Angeles; extends c.15 mi. SE to Argentina border; rises to 11,745 ft.

Velma, village (pop. c.500), Stephens co., S Okla., 16 mi. E of Duncan, near Wildhorse Creek; oil field.

Velobriga, Portugal: see Viana do Castelo, city.

Velouchi, Greece: see Tymphrestos.

Veloukhi, Greece: see Tymphrestos.

Velpur (väl'pŏŏr), town (pop. 10,030), West Godavari dist., NE Madras, India, in Godavari R. delta, 37 mi. E of Ellore; rice and oilseed milling; tobacco, sugar cane. Sometimes spelled Velpuru.

Velsen or **Velzen** (both: věl'zŭn), town (commune pop. 41,329), North Holland prov., W Netherlands, on North Sea Canal and 2 mi. E of Ijmuiden; major center of steel industry; blast furnaces, coke ovens; paper mills. Includes town of Ijmuiden. Nitrogen plant 1 mi. W. Considerable destruction in Second World War.

Velsk or **Vel'sk** (vyělsk), city (1926 pop. 3,499), SW Archangel oblast, Russian SFSR, on railroad, on Vaga R. and 150 mi. W of Kotlas; food processing, dairying (butter). Wood-distillation plants near by. Chartered 1780.

Velten (fěl'tůn), town (pop. 10,301), Brandenburg, E Germany, near the Havel, 15 mi. NW of Berlin; clay quarrying; metalworking; mfg. of tiled stoves, machine tools, chemicals, linoleum.

Veltrusy (věl'trŏŏsĭ), village (pop. 1,883), central Bohemia, Czechoslovakia, on Vltava R., on railroad and 13 mi. NNW of Prague. Has old chapel. Across the Vltava is a large park, laid out in 18th cent., noted for its statues and pavilions.

Veluwe (vā'lüvů), region of Gelderland prov., central Netherlands; bounded by Utrecht prov. (W), the Ijsselmeer (N), Ijssel R. (E), the Lower Rhine (S); heathland, partly wooded, and (E) a plateau rising to 300 ft. Silver-fox breeding, beekeeping, tourist resorts. Chief towns: Apeldoorn, Ede, Harderwijk.

Velva, city (pop. 1,170), McHenry co., central N. Dak., 21 mi. SE of Minot and on Souris R. Lignite mines; diversified farming; grain, livestock, poultry. Laid out 1891, inc. 1905.

Velvary (věl'värĭ), Ger. *Welwarn* (věl'värn), town (pop. 2,169), N central Bohemia, Czechoslovakia, 16 mi. NNW of Prague, in coal-mining region; rail terminus; foundries produce solders, nonferrous scrap and alloy elements.

Velvendos (vělvěndhôs'), town (pop. 3,614), Kozane nome, Macedonia, Greece, 15 mi. ESE of Kozane, at foot of Pieria massif; tobacco, wine, livestock; lumber. Hydroelectric plant on Aliakmon R., NW.

Velyun, Poland: see Wielun.

Velzen, Netherlands: see Velsen.

Vemalwada (vā"mŭlvä'dŭ), town (pop. 6,640), Karimnagar dist., E central Hyderabad state, India, 17 mi. W of Karimnagar; rice, oilseeds.

Vembadi Shola (vām'bŭdē shō'lŭ), peak (8,221 ft.) in S Madras, India, in Palni Hills (S spur of Western Ghats), 50 mi. WNW of Madura, 5 mi. WSW of Kodaikanal.

Vemend (vā'mānd), Hung. *Véménd*, town (pop. 2,479), Baranya co., S Hungary, 12 mi. NW of Mohacs; wheat, corn, hemp, cattle, hogs.

Vementry (vě'mŭntrē), island of the Shetlands, Scotland, on S side of St. Magnus Bay, just off Mainland isl., 4 mi. NW of Aith; separated from Muckle Roe isl. (N) by Swarbacks Minn; 2 mi. long, 2 mi. wide; rises to 298 ft.

Vemork (vā'môrk), village (pop., with adjoining Froystul, 199), Telemark co., S Norway, on the Mana and 2 mi. W of Rjukan; site of Rjukan heavy-water plant. Also spelled Vedmork.

Vempalle (věm'pŭlě), town (pop. 6,629), Cuddapah dist., central Madras, India, 26 mi. WSW of Cuddapah; peanut milling; rice, turmeric. Limestone quarries, asbestos workings near by.

Ven (vān), island (□ 2.9; pop. 852), Malmohus co., S Sweden, in the Oresund, near Danish line, 5 mi. NW of Landskrona, SE of Helsingor; 55°54'N 12°42'E. It is 2.5 mi. long, 1 mi. wide. Has 13th-cent. church. Isl. was granted (1576) by Denmark to the astronomer Tycho Brahe, who built Uranienborg castle (1576–80) and Stjarneborg observatory (1584; slight remains). In 19th cent. isl. was royal hunting ground. It is reputed site (c.1000) of naval battle of Svoldern. Sometimes spelled Hven.

Venaco (věnä'kô), village (pop. 1,542), central Corsica, 5 mi. SSE of Corte; marble quarries.

Venadillo (bānädē'yō), town (pop. 2,659), Tolima dept., W central Colombia, in Magdalena valley, 30 mi. NE of Ibagué, in agr. region (rice, yucca, bananas, coffee, cattle). Petroleum deposits near.

Venado (bānä'dō), town (pop. 2,011), San Luis Potosí, N central Mexico, on interior plateau, 55 mi. N of San Luis Potosí; alt. 5,740 ft. Agr. center (wheat, corn, beans, cotton). Agr. experiment station. Rail station is 4 mi. E.

Venado Island, Monagas state, NE Venezuela, in Gulf of Paria, just off the coast at mouth of Guanipa R.; 6 mi. long, c.1½ mi. wide.

Venado Tuerto (twěr'tō), city (1947 pop. census 15,814), SW Santa Fe prov., Argentina, 95 mi. SW of Rosario; agr. center (corn, wheat, flour, flax, sunflowers, livestock; apiculture). Mfg.: frozen meat, dairy products, malt, flour, cement articles, insecticides.

Venafro (věnä'frô), anc. *Venafrum*, town (pop. 4,225), Campobasso prov., Abruzzi e Molise, S central Italy, near Volturno R., 12 mi. SW of Isernia; macaroni, olive oil. Bishopric. Has Roman ruins, medieval castle. Near by is Fr. military cemetery with c.3,200 dead of Second World War.

Venaissin or **Comtat Venaissin** (kōtä' vůnāsě'), former papal possession (1274–1791) in Provence, SE France, consisting of territory around Avignon on left bank of the Rhone. Annexed to France after a plebiscite, it was incorporated in Vaucluse dept. Old ⊙ Carpentras.

Venâncio Aires (vĭnä'syŏŏ ī'rĭs), city (pop. 2,254), central Rio Grande do Sul, Brazil, 16 mi. NE of Santa Cruz do Sul; potatoes, fruit, tobacco. Agates and amethysts found near by. Old spelling, Venancio Ayres.

Venango (vĭnăng'gō), county (□ 675; pop. 65,328), NW Pa.; ⊙ Franklin. Oil-producing region drained by Allegheny R. Drake Well Memorial Park near Titusville marks site of 1st successful oil well, 1859. Mfg. (petroleum products, oil-well supplies and machinery, metal products, bottles, railroad supplies); dairy products; sandstone, natural gas. Oil City is its industrial center. Formed 1800.

Venango. **1** Village (pop. 233), Perkins co., S Nebr., 18 mi. WSW of Grant, at Colo. line. **2** Borough (pop. 359), Crawford co., NW Pa., 10 mi. N of Meadville and on French Creek.

Venarey (vůnārā'), town (pop. 3,010), Côte-d'Or dept., E central France, on Burgundy Canal and 8 mi. SE of Montbard; important railroad yards and cheese factory at Les Laumes-d'Alésia (lā lōm-dälāzyä'), 1 mi. NE.

Venaria Reale (věnä'rēä rěä'lě), town (pop. 8,395), Torino prov., Piedmont, NW Italy, 5 mi. N of Turin, in irrigated region (fodder, wheat, corn); rayon center.

Vénasque (vānäsk'), Sp. *Benasque* (bänä'skā), narrow pass (alt. 8,032 ft.) in the central Pyrenees N of the Maladetta, on Franco-Spanish border, 7 mi. SSE of Luchon (Fr.); inaccessible by road.

Vencac or **Venchats** (both: věn'chäts), Serbo-Croatian *Venčac*, mountain (2,158 ft.) in central Serbia, Yugoslavia, 3 mi. S of Arandjelovac, in the Sumadija. Marble quarrying.

Vence (vãs), town (pop. 3,897), Alpes-Maritimes dept., SE France, in Provence Alps, 8 mi. WNW of Nice; health resort noted for its mild climate. Fig growing. Its Romanesque church (cathedral until 1790) was begun in 12th cent.

Venceslau Braz or **Wenceslau Braz** (both: vĕnsĭslou' bräzh'), city (pop. 1,201), NE Paraná, Brazil, 110 mi. NNW of Curitiba; rail junction; mfg. of pottery and mattresses, metalworking, cotton ginning, rice milling. Coal mines and clay quarries in vicinity.

Venchats, mountain, Yugoslavia: see Vencac.

Vencsellö (věn'chěl'lû), Hung. *Vencsellő*, town (pop. 3,554), Szabolcs co., NE Hungary, near the Tisza, 17 mi. NNW of Nyiregyhaza; potatoes, rye, cattle, hogs.

Vendas Novas (vān'dŭsh nô'vŭsh), town (pop. 3,272), Évora dist., S central Portugal, 25 mi. NE of Setúbal; rail junction; cork-processing center; flour milling. Has artillery school.

Vendée (vädā'), department (□ 2,709; pop. 393,787), W France, formed of part of old Poitou prov.;

⊙ La Roche-sur-Yon. Generally level region on Bay of Biscay, with marshy coastal areas (Marais Breton, Marais Poitevin) and low hills in NE. Drained by the Sèvre Nantaise, the Sèvre Niortaise, and its tributary the Vendée (which gave the dept. its name). It includes the offshore isls. of Noirmoutier and Yeu. The dept. is predominantly agr. (wheat, vegetables, fruit and wine), and one of France's ranking cattle-raising districts. Fishing in isls. Principal towns: La Roche-sur-Yon, Fontenay-le-Comte, and Les Sables-d'Olonne, a popular bathing resort. In French Revolution, the Vendée was at the center of a peasant uprising (Wars of the Vendée, 1793–95) against the Revolutionary government which spread to adjoining regions of Poitou, Anjou, and Brittany, and led to fierce battles bet. Royalists and Republicans. Fontenay-le-Comte was dept.'s ⊙ 1790–1806.

Vendée River, Vendée dept., W France, rises 6 mi. E of La Châtaigneraie, flows 45 mi. past Fontenay-le-Comte, and joins the Sèvre Niortaise in the Marais Poitevin, 7 mi. from the Bay of Biscay.

Vendelso (vĕn'dŭlsû"), Swedish *Vendelsö*, residential village (pop. 2,675), Stockholm co., E Sweden, on small lake, 9 mi. SSE of Stockholm; metalworking.

Vendeuvre-sur-Barse (vādû'vrü-sür-bärs'), village (pop. 1,529), Aube dept., NE central France, 11 mi. W of Bar-sur-Aube; mfg. (agr. machinery, hosiery); religious statuettes made.

Vendin-le-Vieil (vādē-lü-vyā'), town (pop. 3,626), Pas-de-Calais dept., N France, on Haute-Deûle Canal and 4 mi. NNE of Lens, in coal-mining area.

Vendôme (vādōm'), town (pop. 7,907), Loir-et-Cher dept., N central France, on Loir R. and 19 mi. NW of Blois; road and rail hub and glove-mfg. center; wood carving, tanning, printing, bookbinding, food preserving, and pottery mfg. Noted for Gothic church of La Trinité with 12th cent. detached belfry, and for its 11th-cent. castle, the stronghold of the counts (later dukes) of Vendôme. Duchy (⊙ Vendôme) was united with crown by Henry IV in 1589. Town suffered during Wars of Religion. Occupied by Germans in 1870. Louis I de Condé and Marshal Rochambeau b. here.

Vendrell (bĕndrāl'), town (pop. 4,046), Tarragona prov., NE Spain, 16 mi. ENE of Tarragona, and on winegrowing plain near the Mediterranean; road center. Mfg. of fertilizer, flour products, liqueurs, nougats and other candy, rope; olive-oil processing, flour milling. Trades in wine, cereals, vegetables. Has lofty bell tower surmounted by revolving figure.

Vendsyssel (vĕn'süsŭl), agricultural region of N Jutland, Denmark, N of Lim Fjord, on the Kattegat, mostly in Hjorring amt. Central part, called *Højvendsyssel*, is hilly, reaching 446 ft.

Vendurutti, island, India: see COCHIN, city.

Venecia (bānā'syä), town (pop. 1,990), Antioquia dept., NW central Colombia, in Cauca valley, 23 mi. SW of Medellín; coffee, corn, sugar cane, yucca, fruit, livestock. Coal mines, lime and gypsum deposits are near by.

Venedocia (vĕnŭdō'shŭ), village (pop. 170), Van Wert co., W Ohio, 8 mi. SE of Van Wert, near Little Auglaize R.

Venedy (vĕ'nŭdē), village (pop. 149), Washington co., SW Ill., 28 mi. WSW of Centralia, in agr. and bituminous-coal area.

Vener, Lake, Sweden: see VANER, LAKE.

Venetie (vŭnē'tē, vē'nŭtī), village (pop. 81), N central Alaska, on Chandalar R. at mouth of East Chandalar R., and 60 mi. NW of Fort Yukon; placer gold mining.

Veneto (vā'nātô) or **Venetia** (vŭnē'shŭ), region (□ 7,098; pop. 3,566,136), N and NE Italy; ⊙ Venice. Bordered by Lombardy (W), Trentino-Alto Adige (N), Emilia-Romagna (S), Friuli-Venezia Giulia, Austria, and the Adriatic (E). Comprises 7 provs.: BELLUNO, PADOVA, ROVIGO, TREVISO, VENEZIA, VERONA, VICENZA. In S a fertile plain extends E and NE from Mincio and Po rivers to the Adriatic, bounded N by mtn. area lying bet. Lago di Garda (SW) and Austria (NE) and including Monte Baldo, Monti Lessini, Asiago plateau, Dolomites, and Carnic Alps. Watered by Po, Adige, Brenta, Piave, and Livenza rivers, which empty into the Adriatic. Climate ranges from maritime type (S) to Alpine (N). Predominantly agr.; a leading producer of Italy's cereals, raw silk, potatoes, sugar beets, hemp, grapes, and tobacco. Apples and pears are widely grown. Truck gardening and fishing (Chioggia) important along Adriatic coast. Livestock raising. Forestry and tourism in the Alps. Has well-developed hydroelectric power industry. Quarries in Monti Lessini (marble) and Euganean Hills (trachyte). Mining at Agordo (copper), Schio (lead, kaolin), Torrebelvicino (zinc), Valdagno (lignite). Industry at Porto Marghera (oil refining, zinc smelting), Padua (machinery), Treviso (foundries), Vittorio Veneto (automobiles, textiles), Vicenza (iron and steel), Schio (wool), Verona, Bassano. Anciently the home of the Veneti; came under Romans (2d cent B.C.), who made Aquileia ⊙ region forming part of Venetia. Suffered heavily during barbaric invasions. Towns began to acquire importance in 10th cent.; later became free communes. Gradually the Republic of Venice grew supreme, conquering most of its neighbors by early 15th cent. After fall of Venice (1797), Veneto passed to Austria. In 1866, through Italy's participation in the Austro-Prussian War, it was awarded to Italy. Formerly included Udine prov., which was detached after Second World War to help form Friuli-Venezia Giulia. Sometimes called Venezia Euganea.

Venev (vĕnyôf'), city (1926 pop. 5,941), NE Tula oblast, Russian SFSR, 28 mi. ENE of Tula; clothing mfg., food processing. Founded c.1400. During Second World War, briefly held (1941) by Germans in Moscow campaign.

Venezia (vĕnā'tsēä), province (□ 949; pop. 629,137), Veneto, N Italy; ⊙ Venice. Bounded E by the Adriatic; consists of natural and reclaimed lowland bet. Tagliamento (NE) and Adige (SW) rivers. Traversed by lower courses of Piave, Livenza, Brenta, and Sile rivers. Agr. (sugar beets, cereals, fruit, vegetables); cattle raising; fishing (Chioggia, Pellestrina). Resorts, including the famous Lido. Mfg. at Porto Marghera, San Donà di Piave, and Mira.

Venezia, city, Italy: see VENICE.

Venezia Euganea, Italy: see VENETO.

Venezia Giulia (jū'lyä), former region (□ 3,356; 1936 pop. 977,257) of NE Italy. Comprised provs. of Carnaro (Fiume), Gorizia, Istria (Pola), Trieste, and Zara. By 1947 treaty of peace Italy retained part (□ 180; 1948 pop. c.140,000) of Gorizia prov. (which was included in Friuli-Venezia Giulia). The Free Territory of Trieste was formed from another small area (□ 285; 1949 pop. c.380,000) and Yugoslavia the rest (□ 2,891; pop. c.500,000).

Venezia Tridentina, Italy: see TRENTINO-ALTO ADIGE.

Venezuela (vĕnŭzwā'lŭ, -wē'lŭ, Sp. bānāswā'lä), republic (□ 352,141; 1941 pop. 3,850,771, plus c.100,000 Indians; 1950 census 4,985,716, plus c.100,000 Indians), N South America; ⊙ CARACAS. It has a long (c.1,750 mi.), irregular coast line on the Caribbean and extends c.650 mi. S from about 12°N to within a degree of the equator. There are 4 main geographic regions—the GUIANA HIGHLANDS, the Orinoco basin, the coastal lowlands, and the mts. of the north. Colombia borders Venezuela on W and SW, where the Cordillera Oriental of the Colombian Andes sends off spurs which enclose the Maracaibo basin and then skirt the coast. Br. Guiana (E) and Brazil (SE and S) share the Guiana Highlands, whose ranges (e.g., PACARAIMA and PARIMA) follow the international line; the 3 countries converge at Mt. RORAIMA (9,219 ft.). In the far south, Venezuela thrusts into the Amazon basin, with which the ORINOCO RIVER is linked by the CASIQUIARE RIVER. MARGARITA ISLAND and adjacent islets, comprising the state of Nueva Esparta, are off its NE coast. Roughly 4/5 of the country is drained by the Orinoco, N of which are the vast, wet, hot plains called the LLANOS. Rising in the Guiana Highlands, the Orinoco turns in a wide semicircle NW, N, and E around the great mtn. mass towards the ocean, where it forms a large, swampy delta, opposite the British isl. of Trinidad. It receives other large rivers, such as Guaviare, Meta, Apure, Caura, and Caroní. It is navigable c.1,000 mi. upstream to PUERTO AYACUCHO, below Apures and Maipures rapids. The llanos region is, apart from the delta jungles, predominantly savanna, where cattle grazing has long been the chief activity, with its staunch herdsmen, the *llaneros*, playing a colorful part in the nation's history. During the rainy season (April–Oct.) there are great floods, and the herds are driven to the N uplands to be fattened and slaughtered. A few subsistence crops (corn, beans, cassava, rice, and cotton) are grown. The once-important gathering of egret plumes has declined. Principal trading center for the llanos, and, indeed for the entire underdeveloped transandean section, is CIUDAD BOLÍVAR, a port for sea-going vessels c.260 mi. up the Orinoco from the ocean, shipping cattle, hides, and the forest products (balata, chicle, tonka beans, vanilla, divi-divi, cedar, mahogany, medicinal plants, indigo, etc.) of the Guiana Highlands. Ciudad Bolívar is linked by airline with the country's leading cities. A highway from SOLEDAD across the Orinoco leads to PUERTO DE LA CRUZ. The Guiana Highlands, covering more than ½ of Venezuela, are even less developed than the llanos. The densely forested tableland, of great geological antiquity and still largely unexplored, is dissected by deep valleys, down which gush some of the world's highest waterfalls (e.g., ANGEL FALL). Rich in minerals, the highlands yield gold (EL CALLAO, GUASIPATI, TUMEREMO) and diamonds (SANTA ELENA). Iron mines, chiefly concentrated S of SAN FÉLIX in the IMATACA range (EL PAO, CERRO BOLÍVAR) have recently been built up by American interests. Ore is shipped from PALUA down the Orinoco and transshipped from the new port of PUERTO DE HIERRO on PARIA PENINSULA. All mineral resources are, however, overshadowed by petroleum, which, as the lifeblood of Venezuela's economy, makes up at least 90% of the nation's exports and is the principal source of revenue. Venezuela is the world's largest exporter of petroleum and is 2d only to the U.S. in production of crude petroleum. Apart from some wells in NE, such as CARIPITO near the San Juan R., petroleum comes from the fabulously rich MARACAIBO basin. The torrid lowland region around shallow, bottle-necked L. Maracaibo is arid in the goat-grazing N, while sugar cane, cacao, and subsistence crops are raised in alluvial S along navigable CATATUMBO RIVER and its tributary, the ZULIA RIVER. Coconut palms (for copra) are grown at the narrows. Most of the oil fields and refineries (e.g., CABIMAS, LAGUNILLAS, SAN LORENZO, MENE GRANDE, BACHAQUERO) are on the E shore. Maracaibo, at the lake's entrance (NW), 2d city of the republic, is the export center for the industry; it also ships coffee (from Cúcuta in Colombia), cacao, sugar, hides, and hardwood. Petroleum is loaded here on lighters making for WILLEMSTAD (Curaçao) and ARUBA, Du. West Indies. Some petroleum is now refined on PARAGUANÁ PENINSULA (LAS PIEDRAS, PUNTA CARDÓN) and transferred to transoceanic tankers. Although the Maracaibo region is at present the economically most valuable section of Venezuela, most of the pop. lives in the cool mtn. backbone, the Caribbean or Venezuelan highlands, where virtually all social, agr., and mfg. activities are carried on. Here are, except for Maracaibo, the major cities, with ports at foot of the abruptly rising mts. The Andean ranges form several separate ridges. The highest, SIERRA NEVADA DE MÉRIDA, turns NE from Colombian line near SAN CRISTÓBAL to BARQUISIMETO, rising in LA COLUMNA (or Bolívar) peak to 16,411 ft. It is continued E by the SEGOVIA HIGHLANDS, followed by parallel coastal and interior ranges, bet. which lie fertile intramontane basins (VALENCIA with L. Valencia and CARACAS VALLEY). A far eastern spur reaches onward into N Trinidad. As in all Andean countries, climate and vegetation here depend chiefly upon altitude, with which the scant precipitation increases. Rainy season May–Nov. In the low *tierra caliente* (up to c.2,000 ft.) are grown cacao, bananas, corn, rice; in the *tierra templada* (c.2,000–c.6,000 ft.), is the coffee belt, while sugar cane, cotton, tobacco are also grown; in the *tierra fría* (c.6,000–c.10,000 ft.) is grown wheat; and in the windswept *páramos* beyond, there are stock grazing and potato growing. Coffee, the principal commercial crop of the country, is shipped from PUERTO CABELLO and LA GUAIRA, the country's principal port, connected with Caracas by 23-mi.-long steep highway and railroad. Other exports are corn, gold, cattle, hides, and skins. Through La Guaira pass the bulk of imports (machinery, vehicles, metal goods, food and beverages, textiles, chemicals). At Valencia and MARACAY are important dairy and meat-packing plants. The highlands' chief consumer industry, cotton textile milling, is centered at Caracas, which also manufactures clothing, rubber goods, cement, cigarettes, leather articles, etc. It is the focal point for the nation's social and commercial life, and seat of a univ. (other universities are at Mérida and Maracaibo). Caracas is joined by a transandean branch of the Pan American Highway with the major highland cities. Along the Caribbean coast and around Margarita Isl. (now known for its magnesite deposits) there is fishing for pearls, red snappers, mackerel, tuna, herring, sardines. An estimated 20% of the pop. lives on fish. The highland region has scattered coal deposits and some asbestos, mica, copper, tin, and salt. Fish canning and other processing industries are also prominent in CUMANÁ, considered the oldest (1521) permanent Sp. settlement on the continent. At base of Paraguaná Peninsula is CORO (founded 1527), the 1st colonial capital. The Sp. conquistadores who followed the voyages of Columbus (1498) and Ojeda (1499), struck by the native villages built on stilts on L. Maracaibo, called the new land Venezuela ("little Venice"). Early expeditions were undertaken by Germans (Alfinger, Speyer, Federmann) employed by the Welser banking house, which had acquired a concession from Charles V. Politically the region became (1718) a part of the viceroyalty of New Granada (present Colombia) and was made temporarily a separate captaincy-general in 1731. During 18th cent. the Venezuelan coast line was frequently attacked by buccaneers and the ports did a thriving smuggling business with the English. A 1st attempt (1797) to set up a republic was unsuccessful, as was that of Francisco de Miranda (1811–12), who was soon joined by the most famous of all South American liberators, Simón Bolívar, a native of Caracas. In 1813 Bolívar freed most of the territory, only to lose it the following year. He established (1817) republican hq. at Angostura (later Ciudad Bolívar), but Venezuela was not freed until the victory at CARABOBO (1821). The union of Greater Colombia (*Gran Colombia*), which included present-day Venezuela, Colombia, Ecuador, and Panama, fell apart when Venezuela under Bolívar's lieutenant Páez seceded (1830). The nation was to be controlled by successive oligarchies. Personalism, with but few exceptions, was the rule. A brief liberal regime under Juan Falcón created (1864) the United States of Venezuela. Among the *caudillos* were the Monagas brothers and Guzmán Blanco. The Venezuelan

Boundary Dispute led (1899) to loss of territory to Br. Guiana. During the ruthless dictatorship of Juan Vicente Gómez (1908–35) the country achieved great prosperity due to the development (begun 1918) of its petroleum fields. In 1945 Venezuela declared war on the Axis powers. A junta, headed by Rómulo Betancourt, gained control the same year and promulgated (1947) a new constitution providing for presidential election by popular vote. First to be elected was the prominent novelist Rómulo Gallegos was was removed (Nov., 1948) only a few months after his inauguration by a military coup d'état. A merchant fleet jointly owned by Colombia, Ecuador, and Venezuela was set up and the Quito Charter (1948) promised to establish closer ties bet. the former members of the Greater Colombia confederacy. The Venezuelan pop. consists of c.70% mestizos, c.10% each of Indians and whites, and c.5% each of mulattoes and *zambos*. For further information see separate articles on cities, regions, physical features, and the following territorial units: the 20 states of ANZOÁTEGUI, APURE, ARAGUA, BARINAS, BOLÍVAR, CARABOBO, COJEDES, FALCÓN, GUÁRICO, LARA, MÉRIDA, MIRANDA, MONAGAS, NUEVA ESPARTA, PORTUGUESA, SUCRE, TÁCHIRA, TRUJILLO, YARACUY, and ZULIA; and the 2 territories AMAZONAS and DELTA AMACURO; the scattered offshore isls. are included in a federal dependency.

Venezuela, Gulf of, inlet of the Caribbean in Venezuela and Colombia; bounded by Guajira peninsula (W) and Paraguaná Peninsula (E); communicates S, through Tablazo Bay and a narrow channel, with L. MARACAIBO. Extends N-S c.75 mi.; extreme width (W-E) 150 mi., including Gulf of Coro (E). Sometimes called Gulf of Maracaibo.

Vengerovo (vyĕn′gĭrŭvŭ), village (1939 pop. over 2,000), W Novosibirsk oblast, Russian SFSR, on Tartas R., near its confluence with the Om, and 25 mi. N of Chany; flour milling, dairying.

Vengetinder, Norway: see VENJETINDER.

Vengrov, Poland: see WEGROW.

Vengurla (vāng′gŏŏrlŭ), town (pop., including suburban area, 21,663), Ratnagiri dist., S Bombay, India, port on Arabian Sea, 85 mi. SSE of Ratnagiri, in the Konkan; trade center for coconuts, mangoes, myrobalans, coir, molasses; cashew-nut processing, betel farming, fish curing (mackerel, sardines, catfish). Lighthouse (NW). Saltworks and shark-oil extraction 4 mi. NW, at Shiroda. Vengurla settled 1638 by Dutch; later a pirate stronghold; ceded 1812 to British.

Venialbo (bānyäl′vō), town (pop. 1,625), Zamora prov., NW Spain, 14 mi. SE of Zamora; sawmilling; wine, cereals, livestock.

Veniaminof Crater (vĕnēä′mĭnŏf), active volcano (8,400 ft.), SW Alaska, on Alaska Peninsula, 40 mi. WSW of Chignik; 56°12′N 159°22′W; glaciers cover upper slopes. Erupted June, 1939.

Venice (vĕ′nĭs), Ital. *Venezia*, city (pop. 170,830), ⊙ Veneto and Venezia prov., N Italy, within Lagoon of Venice (□ 212; 25 mi. long, average width 10 mi.) in NW corner of Gulf of Venice (N part of the Adriatic); 45°26′N 12°20′E. Built on 118 small isls. connected with mainland (2.5 mi. W) by railroad and modern highway bridge. Bet. isls. run 160 canals crossed by c.400 bridges. Gondolas and other boats form chief means of conveyance. City produces art objects, jewelry, cotton and silk textiles, flour; large printing and publishing trade. Most of industry and commerce is centered at its port, PORTO MARGHERA. Chief artery of traffic is the Grand Canal (2 mi. long, 18 ft. deep, average width 228 ft.), which curves through Venice from Piazza San Marco to the railway station. On both sides rise innumerable Romanesque, Gothic, and Renaissance palaces (12th-18th cent.), including Ca' d'Oro (now a mus.), Ca' Pesaro (houses modern art mus.), 15th-cent. Ca' Foscari (now the School of Commerce), and Ca' Rezzonico. Piazza San Marco with the adjoining Piazzetta is the heart of Venice. Here are church of San Marco, dedicated in 830 to patron saint of Venice, Doge's palace, Bridge of Sighs (Ital. *Ponte dei Sospiri;* built 1595–1605), Procuratie palaces, and 16th-cent. library. Other important bldgs. include: Acad. of Fine Arts with a collection of Venetian masters, Scuola di San Rocco with frescoes by Tintoretto, and arsenal (founded 1104). Among the numerous churches are the Frari with paintings by Titian, SS. Giovanni e Paolo (13th–15th cent.), 17th-cent. Santa Maria della Salute, and San Salvatore (1506–1663) with an *Annunciation* by Titian. The 15th-cent. equestrian statue of Bartolomeo Colleoni by Verrocchio is celebrated. Among the great architects who helped beautify Venice are Andrea Palladio, Scarpagnino, Sansovino, and members of the Lombardo family. The Venetian school of art flourished in 15th and 16th cent.; great painters include Fra Bartolommeo, the Bellini, Crivelli, Giorgione, Jacopo Palma, Sebastiano Del Piombo, Paul Veronese, Titian, and Tintoretto. The printers John of Speyer, Nicholas Jenson, and Aldus Manutius worked in Venice, which was long one of the printing and publishing centers of Europe. The history of Venice began in 5th cent. when refugees, fleeing before Teutonic invaders, settled on the isls. These communities were organized (697) under a doge, and being favorably situated for handling trade bet. East and West, became a strong maritime, commercial, and political power which extended her rule over Dalmatia (997) and began building her Eastern Empire. During the Crusades, Venice took strategic points in the Peloponnesus, Aegean Sea (especially Crete), and Constantinople (1402) under Doge Enrico Dandolo. Defeated Genoa in 1380 after a long rivalry. Republic attained height of her success in world commerce in 14th and early 15th cent. Lost most of her overseas possessions in 16th and 17th cent.; in 1797 occupied by Napoleon. United with Kingdom of Italy in 1866.

Venice. 1 Beach resort (with amusement dist.) and residential section of Los ANGELES city, Los Angeles co., S Calif., along Santa Monica Bay, just S of Santa Monica. Oil field (1930); oil refinery. Annexed 1925 by Los Angeles. **2** Resort city (pop. 727), Sarasota co., SW Fla., 18 mi. S of Sarasota, on Gulf coast; rail terminus; ships cucumbers. Florida Medical Center and Kentucky Military Inst. are here. **3** Industrial city (pop. 6,226), Madison co., SW Ill., on the Mississippi (bridged to St. Louis), N of East St. Louis; steel mills. Settled 1804, platted 1841; inc. as village in 1873, as city in 1897. **4** Village, Plaquemines parish, extreme SE La., 65 mi. SE of New Orleans, in the delta; levees protecting W bank of the Mississippi end near here. Fur trapping, hunting, fishing.

Venice, Gulf of, N section of the Adriatic, bet. Istria and Po R. delta; 50–60 mi. wide; receives Po, Adige, Piave, and Tagliamento rivers. Venice is on NW shore (lagoons), Rovinj and Pula on Istrian coast. Gulf of Trieste is NE inlet.

Vénissieux (vānēsyû′), suburb (pop. 15,006) of Lyons, Rhône dept., E central France, 5 mi. SSE of city center; glass- and metalworks, textile mills. Damaged in Second World War.

Venjetinder (vĕn′yŭtĭn-nŭr), mountains (6,549 ft.) of the Dovrefjell, More og Romsdal co., W Norway, on N side of the Romsdal, 20 mi. SE of Andalsnes. Sometimes spelled Vengetinder.

Venkatagiri (vĕng′kŭtŭgĭrē), town (pop. 16,408), Nellore dist., E central Madras, India, 40 mi. SW of Nellore; oilseed milling, tanning; rice, millet, cashew. Dyewood (red sanders), satinwood in Eastern Ghats (W).

Venkatapuram (vĕng′kŭtŭpŏŏrŭm), village, East Godavari dist., NE Madras, India, on Godavari R. and 120 mi. NW of Rajahmundry; rice, oilseeds. Teak, sal, bamboo in near-by forests. Also called Venkatapur.

Venlo (vĕn′lō), town (pop. 26,822; commune pop. 41,566), Limburg prov., SE Netherlands, on Maas R. and 15 mi. NNE of Roermond; rail junction, frontier station near Ger. border; lumber mills; mfg. (woodwork, furniture, machine tools, chemicals, soap, electric bulbs, optical instruments, umbrellas, religious ornaments); vegetable, fruit, and egg market. Has 15th-cent. Gothic church, 16th-cent. town hall (*Stadhuis*), 17th-cent. *Oudemannenhuis* (old men's house). Damaged (1944) in Second World War. Sometimes spelled Venloo.

Vennachar, Loch (lŏkh vĕ′nŭkh-ŭr), lake (4 mi. long, ¾ mi. wide; 111 ft. deep), SW Perthshire, Scotland, W of Callander; drained by Teith R.

Vennar River (vĕ′när), arm of Cauvery R., in Tanjore dist., S Madras, India; from the Grand Anicut (regulating dams) flows E, past Tanjore, and SE to Vedaranniyam Canal 15 mi. S of Negapatam; 90 mi. long; has several distributaries in SE Cauvery delta; source of Vadavar Canal. Sometimes called Vellar, also name of a river which enters Bay of Bengal at Porto Novo, 50 mi. N of Negapatam.

Vennesla, Norway: see VIKELAND.

Veno (vā′nû), Dan. *Venø*, island (□ 2.5; pop. 193) in W Lim Fjord, N Jutland, Denmark, SW of Salling peninsula; 5 mi. long, .5–1.5 mi. wide; highest point, 89 ft. In center is Veno town, with church and school.

Venosa (vĕnô′zä), anc. *Venusia*, town (pop. 10,885), Potenza prov., Basilicata, S Italy, 22 mi. N of Potenza; agr. trade center; cereals, wine, olive oil, vegetables. Bishopric. Has Benedictine abbey (11th cent.; restored) containing tomb of Robert Guiscard and 15th-cent. castle. Jewish catacombs near by. Horace b. here.

Venosta, Val (väl vĕnô′stä), valley of upper Adige R., N Italy, extending from Passo di Resia S and E to Merano. Agr., livestock raising, forestry. Marble quarries at Lasa and Morter. Chief centers: Glorenza, Silandro, Malles Venosta.

Venoste, Alpi, Italy and Austria: see ÖTZTAL ALPS.

Venray or **Venraij** (both: vĕn′rī″), town (pop. 5,356), Limburg prov., E Netherlands, 13 mi. NW of Venlo; leather goods, strawboard, cardboard, coffee, cigars; lumber mills; cattle raising, agr. Also spelled Venrai and Venraai.

Venta, La, Mexico: see LA VENTA.

Venta Belgarum, England: see WINCHESTER.

Venta de Baños (bĕn′tä dhä bä′nyōs), town (pop. 4,326), Palencia prov., N central Spain, rail junction 7 mi. SSE of Palencia; sugar mill; agr. trade (cereals, wine, vegetables). Mineral springs near.

Venta del Moro (dhĕl mō′rō), town (pop. 1,352), Valencia prov., E Spain, 14 mi. W of Requena; olive-oil processing, flour milling.

Venta Icenorum, England: see NORWICH.

Ventana, Sierra de la (syĕ′rä dā lä bĕntä′nä), mountain range in SW Buenos Aires prov., Argentina, extends 30 mi. SE from Tornquist, rising to 4,200 ft. at Tres Picos. Remnant of tertiary mtn. formation. Quartzite quarries.

Ventanas (bĕntä′näs), village, Los Ríos prov., W central Ecuador, on highway to Guayaquil, on tributary of Guayas R. and 28 mi. ENE of Vinces, in fertile agr. region (cacao, rice, sugar cane, tropical fruit); rice milling.

Venta River (vĕn′tä), Ger. *Windau*, in Lithuania and Latvia, rises in hills SE of Telsiai, Lithuania; flows E, NNW past Kursenai, and NNW past Kuldiga, Latvia (head of navigation), to Baltic Sea at Ventspils; length, 215 mi. Timber floating. Connected with Dubysa R. in upper course by 25-mi. canal.

Ventas or **Ventas del Espíritu Santo** (bĕn′täs dhĕl ĕspē′rētōō sän′tō), E residential suburb of Madrid, Madrid prov., central Spain.

Ventas con Peña Aguilera, Las (läs, kōm pā′nyä ägēlā′rä), town (pop. 2,957), Toledo prov., central Spain, 21 mi. SSW of Toledo; grain growing, stock raising, cheese processing, lumbering, granite quarrying. Has remains of anc. castle.

Venta Silurum, England: see CAERWENT.

Ventavon (vätävō′), village (pop. 120), Hautes-Alpes dept., SE France, 12 mi. NNW of Sisteron. Hydroelectric plant on Durance R. near by.

Ventersburg (fĕn′tŭrsbûrkh″), town (pop. 2,123), central Orange Free State, U. of So. Afr., 30 mi. S of Kroonstad; grain, stock; grain elevator.

Ventersdorp (–dôrp″), town (pop. 3,516), SW Transvaal, U. of So. Afr., on Schoon Spruit R. and 30 mi. NW of Potchefstroom; agr. center (corn, stock); grain elevator.

Venterspost (vĕn′tŭrzpōst″, fĕn′tŭrs–), town (pop. 11,763), S Transvaal, U. of So. Afr., on W Witwatersrand, 9 mi. SW of Randfontein; gold mining.

Venthon (vätō′), village (pop. 133), Savoie dept., SE France, on the Doron de Beaufort and 2 mi. NNE of Albertville; aluminum and carborundum works.

Ventilla (bĕntē′yä), town (pop. c.4,000), Cochabamba dept., central Bolivia, in Cordillera de Cochabamba, on railroad and 32 mi. ENE of Oruro; corn, vegetables.

Ventimiglia (vĕntēmē′lyä), Fr. *Vintimille* (vĕtēmē′), town (pop. 11,216), Imperia prov., Liguria, NW Italy, port on Gulf of Genoa, at mouth of Roya R. and 18 mi. ENE of Nice; customs station near Fr. border; important international railroad station. Noted flower market. Bishopric. Has 12th-cent. cathedral (restored 1875–77), ruined Genoese fort, mus. of Roman antiquities. Roman ruins (theater, fountain, tombs) near by. Near village of Grimaldi, 3 mi. W, are: the caverns (damaged in Second World War) where prehistoric remains of Cro-Magnon man have been found; a mus.; and the famous Hanbury Gardens containing c.6,000 plants of every latitude.

Ventimiglia di Sicilia (dē sēchē′lyä), village (pop. 4,534), Palermo prov., N Sicily, 8 mi. SW of Termini Imerese; macaroni.

Ventnor (vĕnt′nŭr), urban district (1931 pop. 5,114; 1951 census 7,308), on S coast of Isle of Wight, Hampshire, England, on the Channel, 8 mi. SSE of Newport; seaside and health resort, with pier. Town is built on cliff-side terraces. Because of the good air and mild climate, there are many hosps. and tuberculosis sanitaria. Just ENE is village of Bonchurch, where Swinburne is buried. Just E is high headland of Dunnose.

Ventnor or **Ventnor City,** resort city (pop. 8,158), Atlantic co., SE N.J., on Absecon Beach just SW of Atlantic City. Inc. 1903.

Ventosa, La (lä vĕntō′sä), town (pop. 1,019), Cuenca prov., E central Spain, 19 mi. WNW of Cuenca; olives, cereals, saffron, grapes, livestock; olive-oil pressing, flour milling.

Ventotene Island (vĕntôtā′nĕ) (□ 5; pop. 1,379), in PONTINE ISLANDS, in Tyrrhenian Sea, off central Italy, bet. isls. of Ponza and Ischia, 35 mi. SE of Monte Circeo; 2 mi. long, 5 mi. wide; rises to 456 ft. (S). Chief port, Ventotene (pop. 888); fishing. Islet of Santo Stefano (pop. 368) is 1 mi. E.

Ventoux, Mont (mō vätōō′), outlying ridge of the Provence Alps, in Vaucluse dept., SE France, overlooking Rhone valley (W), c.28 mi. NE of Avignon. Extends 15 mi. E–W with steep N slopes. Rises to 6,273 ft. Connected by series of hills with parallel Monts de Vaucluse (c.10 mi. S). Observatory and winter sports station at summit.

Ventry, Gaelic *Ceann Trágha*, fishing village, W Co. Kerry, Ireland, on an inlet of Dingle Bay, 4 mi. W of Dingle. Region was last part of Ireland to be evacuated by Danes.

Ventspils (vänts′pĕls), Ger. *Windau* (vĭn′dou), Rus. (until 1917) *Vindava* (vēndä′vä), city (pop. 15,671), NW Latvia, in Kurzeme, major ice-free Baltic port at mouth of Venta R., 100 mi. WNW of Riga; 57°24′N 21°34′E. Third-largest Latvian port; exports timber, grain, flax, hemp, butter. Rail junction (repair yards); sawmilling center; fisheries; mfg. (foundry products, woolens, leather goods, rope, glass, bricks, soap, starch, flour). Summer resort (bathing beach). Port consists of outer harbor (protected by moles) and 8-mi.-long commercial harbor along lower Venta R. Has 13th-cent. castle. City chartered 1343; developed in 19th cent. as major Rus. grain port.

Ventuari River (bĕntwä'rē), Amazonas territory, S Venezuela, rises on Bolívar state border at about 4°30'N 64°35'W, flows 285 mi. W and SW to Orinoco R. in a wide delta 40 mi. E of San Fernando de Atabapo. Good navigability for large stretches.

Ventura (vĕntōō'rū), county (□ 1,857; pop. 114,647), S Calif.; ⊙ Ventura. Mainly mountainous; chief agr. land is wide delta of Santa Clara R., here entering the Pacific. Also drained by Ventura and Cuyama rivers. Includes some of Santa Barbara Isls. Mt. Pinos (in N) is 8,831 ft. Includes part of Los Padres Natl. Forest. A leading Calif. co. in lemon growing; also produces other citrus fruit, lima beans, walnuts, sugar beets, truck. Cattle grazing, some dairying, poultry raising. Oil and natural-gas fields, refineries. Santa Paula, Ventura (old mission here), Oxnard, Fillmore are agr. processing, packing, and shipping centers. Formed 1873.

Ventura. 1 Officially **San Buenaventura** (săn bwānūvĕntōō'rū), city (pop. 16,534), ⊙ Ventura co., S Calif., on the coast, 65 mi. NW of Los Angeles, bet. mouths of Santa Clara R. and short Ventura R.; oil-shipping (railroad, coastwise vessels) and -refining point in agr. area (lima beans, lemons, walnuts), with oil fields. San Buenaventura Mission (bldgs. are restorations) was established here by Junípero Serra in 1782. Seat of jr. col. Has good beach. Inc. 1866. **2** Resort village (pop. c.200), Cerro Gordo co., N Iowa, near Clear Lake.

Venturia (vĕntōō'rēū), village (pop. 190), McIntosh co., S N.Dak., 9 mi. WSW of Ashley, near S.Dak. line.

Venú, Dominican Republic: see VERAGUA.

Venus. 1 Resort, S.C.: see MOUNTAIN LAKE. **2** Town (pop. 357), Johnson co., N central Texas, 25 mi. SSE of Fort Worth, in agr. area; cotton ginning; feed.

Venusia, Italy: see VENOSA.

Venus Point, northernmost point of Tahiti, Society Isls., S Pacific; 17°29'S 149°30'W; site of scientific observation of Venus made 1769 by members of British Royal Society.

Venustiano Carranza (bānōōstyä'nō kärän'sä). **1** City (pop. 3,982), Chiapas, S Mexico, in Sierra Madre, 45 mi. SE of Tuxtla; cereals, sugar cane, tobacco, fruit, livestock. San Bartolomé until 1934. **2** Officially Ciudad Venustiano Carranza, city (pop. 3,254), Jalisco, W Mexico, on interior plateau, 13 mi. SE of Sayula; alt. 4,354 ft. Agr. center (grain, beans, sugar cane, fruit, livestock). Formerly San Gabriel. **3** Town (pop. 4,123), Michoacán, central Mexico, on central plateau, 19 mi. SE of Ocotlán; agr. center (cereals, vegetables, fruit, livestock). Formerly San Pedro Caro.

Venyukovski or **Venyukovskiy** (vĕnyōōkôf'skē), town (1941 pop. over 500), S central Moscow Oblast, Russian SFSR, 3 mi. NW of Lopasnya; machine shops.

Venzone (vĕntsô'nē), village (pop. 1,346), Udine prov., Friuli–Venezia Giulia, NE Italy, on Tagliamento R. and 4 mi. N of Gemona del Friuli; silk mills. Has 14th-cent. cathedral, palace (1410; largely destroyed in Second World War).

Veoy (vā'ûü), Nor. *Veøy*, island (□ 1; pop. 2) in Romsdal Fjord, More og Romsdal co., W Norway, 10 mi. ESE of Molde; formerly joined to Sekken isl. (W). Contains pagan worship ground, early Christian churchyard, medieval royal residence, stone church. Formerly called Vedoy. Veoy canton (pop. 2,369) embraces Sekken isl. and part of the mainland.

Vep (vāp), Hung. *Vép*, town (pop. 2,994), Vas co., W Hungary, 5 mi. E of Szombathely; wheat, honey, truck farming.

Vepery, India: see MADRAS, city.

Vepsh River, Poland: see WIEPRZ RIVER.

Vera (bā'rä) or **Jobson**, town (pop. estimate 4,000), ⊙ Vera dept. (□ 7,000; 1947 pop. 34,595), N Santa Fe prov., Argentina, on railroad and 85 mi. NE of San Cristóbal; commercial and agr. center (flax, cotton, corn, sunflowers, livestock); meat packing.

Vera, city (pop. 3,753), Almería prov., S Spain, 10 mi. SE of Huércal-Overa; mfg. of artificial flowers; esparto processing. Agr. trade (cereals, oranges, grapes, vegetables). Iron mine. Liberated in 1488 from Moors by the Catholic Kings, who granted wide privileges. Destroyed in 1518 by earthquake; rebuilt by Charles V.

Vera (vēr'ū), town (pop. 164), Washington co., NE Okla., 20 mi. NNE of Tulsa; trading point for farming and stock-raising area.

Verá, Laguna, Paraguay: see YPOÁ, LAKE.

Vera Cruz (vĕ'rū krōōzh), city (pop. 5,784), W central São Paulo, Brazil, on railroad and 5 mi. E of Marília, in zone of pioneer agr. settlements; cotton, coffee, rice, grain, livestock.

Veracruz (bäräkrōōs'), town (pop. 862), Copán dept., W Honduras, 6 mi. NE of Santa Rosa; tobacco, grain. Tobacco school.

Veracruz (vĕrūkrōōz', Sp. bäräkrōōs'), state (□ 27,759; 1940 pop. 1,619,338; 1950 pop. 2,057,175), E Mexico; ⊙ Jalapa. Stretches c.430 mi. along the Gulf of Mexico from Tamaulipas (Tamesí R.) in N to Tabasco (Tonalá, or Pedegral, R.) in S; includes the N part of the Isthmus of Tehuantepec. Extending inland from 30 to 100 mi., Veracruz rises westward from a tropical coastal plain to temperate valleys and highlands of Sierra Madre Oriental. Bordered W by San Luis Potosí, Hidalgo, Puebla, Oaxaca. The Pico de Orizaba, Mexico's highest peak is on Puebla border. Several large lagoons, including the Tamiahua and Alvarado, indent the coastline. Veracruz is drained by Pánuco, Tamesí, Tuxpan, Papaloápam, San Juan, and Coatzacoalcos rivers. Climate is hot and humid on the coast, subtropical to temperate in the uplands. Petroleum is found along the entire E coast, with main wells at Pánuco, Villa Cuauhtémoc, Alamo, Chapopotla, Tepetzintla, Moloacán, Coatzacoalcos, Minatitlán, Coatzintla, and Amatlantepetl. Predominantly an agr. state; its main crops include coffee, sugar cane, tobacco, cereals, beans, citrus fruit, bananas, pineapples, coconuts, maguey, vanilla, cotton, cacao. Córdoba is especially noted for its coffee, San Andrés Tuxtla for its tobacco. Stock raising (cattle, hogs) is carried on mainly in the lowlands of La Huasteca (N) and Sotavento (SE). State's extensive tropical forests yield dyewood, hardwood, chicle, rubber, resin, and orchids. Orizaba, a resort, is also one of Mexico's most important textile-milling centers, and with Jalapa, Córdoba, and Tuxpan possesses various processing industries (coffee roasting, flour milling, sugar refining, cigar making, tanning, alcohol distilling). City of Veracruz is, with Tampico, one of Mexico's 2 leading ports. In pre-Columbian times Veracruz was populated by Indians of Totonac and Huastec stock, who antedated the Aztecs; there are a number of archaeological remains. The coast was discovered 1518 by Juan de Grijalva. One year later, Cortés landed at José Cardel (Antigua Veracruz). Veracruz became a state in 1824.

Veracruz, officially Veracruz Llave, city (pop. 71,720), Veracruz, E Mexico, major port on Gulf of Mexico, 200 mi. E of Mexico city; 19°12'N 96°8'W. Rivals Tampico as Mexico's most important port. Railhead; shipping, trading, and processing center in fertile reclaimed agr. area (coffee, tropical fruit, tobacco, livestock). Has fine docks and warehouses; exports coffee, chicle, hides, vanilla, dyewood, tobacco. Mfg.: cement, vegetable oil, chocolate, cigars, chemicals, soap, liquor and wine, vinegar, forest products; lumber mills, tanneries, flour and textile mills. Radio stations, airfield, naval school. The city has fine beaches and fishing grounds. The old fortress of San Juan de Ulúa (sän whän' dā ōōlōō'ä), on an islet 1 mi. from the mainland, was the last stronghold of the Spanish until their expulsion (1821). Isla de los Sacrificios (3 mi. SE), another isl. near by, is alleged to have been the site of Aztec human sacrifices. Veracruz was founded near by in 1520, after 1st landing of Cortés, on April 17, 1519; its present location was selected in 1599. The city was looted by pirates in 1653 and 1712, and was captured by the French in 1838 and 1861 and by U.S. forces under General Winfield Scott in 1847. U.S. naval forces landed here briefly in 1914, an incident that led to severing of diplomatic relations.

Vera Cruz (vēr'ū krōōz'), town (pop. 143), Wells co., E Ind., on the Wabash and 6 mi. SE of Bluffton, in agr. area.

Vera de Bidasoa (bā'rä dhā bē-dhäsō'ä), town (pop. 1,646), Navarre prov., N Spain, on Bidassoa R. and 6 mi. SE of Irún; iron- and steelworks. Iron, lead, and silver mines near by.

Veragua (bārä'gwä), village (1935 pop. 2,847), Espaillat prov., N Dominican Republic, near coast, 27 mi. ENE of Santiago; cacao, rice, coffee. Formerly Venú.

Veraguas (bārä'gwäs), province (□ 4,635; 1950 pop. 107,209) of W central Panama; ⊙ Santiago. Extending across entire isthmus from Mosquito Gulf of the Caribbean Sea to the Pacific (S), it is traversed by the continental divide (Veraguas Mts., rising to over 6,000 ft.) and includes Coiba Isl. of the Pacific and W Azuero Peninsula. Agr. (coffee, sugar cane, corn, rice), stock raising, lumbering. Gold mining. Magnesium, zinc, mercury, lead, iron, and precious-stone deposits. Woodworking. Crossed by Inter-American Highway. Main centers are Santiago and Soná. Formed originally in 1719, when it covered entire W section of Panama.

Veramin or **Varamin** (both: värämēn'), town, Second Prov., in Teheran, N Iran, 28 mi. SSE of Teheran and on railroad to Meshed; center of agr. plain irrigated by the river Jaj Rud; grain, sugar beets, cotton, opium, fruit (grapes, figs), truck produce. Sugar refinery, paper mill; rug weaving.

Veranopolis (vĭrūnô'pōōlēs), city (pop. 1,879), NE Rio Grande do Sul, Brazil, near Taquari R., 75 mi. NNW of Pôrto Alegre; winegrowing. Has wheat experiment station. Center of Italian immigrant settlements established 1870–90. Until 1944, called Alfredo Chaves.

Verapaz, Guatemala: see ALTA VERAPAZ; BAJA VERAPAZ.

Veraval (vārä'vŭl), town (pop. 30,275), S Saurashtra, India, port on Arabian Sea, on Kathiawar peninsula, 42 mi. S of Junagarh; trades in timber, cotton, oilseeds, millet, coconuts; cotton ginning, oilseed milling, mfg. of matches, textile bobbins, bone fertilizer; sawmills; fishing (chiefly Bombay duck) off coast. Lighthouse (S). Formerly in Junagarh state.

Verba (vyĕr'bŭ), Pol. *Werba* (vĕr'bä), village (1939 pop. over 500), S Rovno oblast, Ukrainian SSR, on Ikva R. and 13 mi. SSW of Dubno; grain, truck; sawmilling.

Verbania (vĕrbä'nyä), commune (pop. 13,649), Novara prov., Piedmont, N Italy, bordering on Lago Maggiore. Chief towns, INTRA and PALLANZA. Formed c.1938.

Verbano, Lago, Italy: see MAGGIORE, LAGO.

Verbasz, Yugoslavia: see VRBAS.

Verbenico, Yugoslavia: see VRBNIK.

Verberie (vârbürē'), village (pop. 1,899), Oise dept., N France, on left bank of the Oise and 9 mi. SW of Compiègne; woodworking. Has 13th–15th-cent. church.

Verbicaro (vĕrbēkä'rô), town (pop. 5,493), Cosenza prov., Calabria, S Italy, 16 mi. WSW of Castrovillari, in grape-growing region.

Verbilki (vyĭrbēl'kē), town (1926 pop. 2,600), N Moscow oblast, Russian SFSR, 12 mi. N of Dmitrov; porcelain works.

Verblyud, rail station, Russian SFSR: see ZERNOVOI.

Verblyud (vyĭrblyōōt'), laccolithic mountain (2,959 ft.) of the N Caucasus foothills, Russian SFSR, 13 mi. NW of Pyatigorsk.

Verbovski or **Verbovskiy** (vyĭrbôf'skē), town (1944 pop. over 500), SE Vladimir oblast, Russian SFSR, just SW of Murom.

Vercel (vĕrsĕl'), village (pop. 770), Doubs dept., E France, in the central Jura, 18 mi. ESE of Besançon; cheese.

Vercelli (vĕrchĕl'lē), province (□ 1,157; pop. 366,146), Piedmont, N Italy; ⊙ Vercelli. Mtn. terrain in N, including Pennine Alps which rise to over 9,000 ft. Highly irrigated plains in S, watered by CAVOUR CANAL and Dora Baltea and Sesia rivers. A major rice region of Piedmont; also wheat, corn, grapes. Livestock raising (cattle, horses, swine). Gold mining near Alagna Valsesia and Varallo. Has highly industrialized piedmont region (woolen, cotton, and paper mills) extending from Biella NE to Borgosesia. Important rice market at Vercelli. Formed 1927 from Novara prov.

Vercelli, anc. *Vercellae*, city (pop. 32,397), ⊙ Vercelli prov., Piedmont, N Italy, on Sesia R. and 40 mi. NE of Turin, in irrigated region (rice, cereals); 45°19'N 8°25'E. Rail junction; a major rice market of Italy; rice and flour milling, sugar refining; macaroni products; textile factories (rayon, cotton, woolen); shoe mfg.; fertilizer plants; machinery (agr., rice mill). Bishopric from 4th cent. to 1817, when it was made archbishopric. Has basilica of Sant'Andrea (1219–27), cathedral (rebuilt 16th cent.), church of San Cristoforo (with frescoes by Gaudenzio Ferrari), school of obstetrics, mus. with paintings by Sodoma (Giovanni Antonio Bazzi) who was born here and, with Ferrari, headed its famous 16th-cent. school of painting. In cathedral library is the Vercelli Book or Codex Vercellensis, an 11th-cent. Anglo-Saxon MS containing religious poems, notably *Elene* by Cynewulf, and homilies. Became capital in 1927. Plain S of Vercelli generally designated as RAUDIAN FIELDS.

Vercenik Dag (vĕrchĕnĭk' dä), Turkish *Verçenik Dağ*, peak (12,175 ft.), NE Turkey, in Rize Mts., 32 mi. SE of Rize.

Verchères (vĕr-shâr'), county (□ 199; pop. 14,214), S Que., on the St. Lawrence and on Richelieu R.; ⊙ Verchères.

Verchères, village (pop. 906), ⊙ Verchères co., S Que., on the St. Lawrence and 20 mi. NNE of Montreal; food canning, boat building; resort. Opposite, in the St. Lawrence, is Verchères Isl. Fort Verchères was defended (1692) by Madeleine de Verchères against the Iroquois.

Verchères Island (8 mi. long, 1 mi. wide), S Que., in the St. Lawrence, 20 mi. NE of Montreal.

Vercors (vĕrkôr'), Jurassic limestone massif of the Dauphiné Pre-Alps, in Isère and Drôme depts., SE France, extending c.35 mi. N–S, from Isère R. valley near Grenoble to Drôme R. valley near Die. Separated from high Alps (E) by Drac R. Rises to 7,697 ft. at Grand-Veymont peak. Forest cover at lower altitudes. Villard-de-Lans is chief resort. Its E escarpment overlooking the Drac is called Montagnes de Lans.

Verda, mining village (pop. 1,446), Harlan co., SE Ky., in the Cumberlands, on Clover Fork of Cumberland R. and 32 mi. NE of Middlesboro; bituminous coal.

Verdadero, El, Spain: see MOTRIL.

Verdal (văr'däl), village (pop. 2,084; canton pop. 8,162), Nord-Trondelag co., central Norway, on Trondheim Fjord at mouth of Verdal R., on railroad and 7 mi. NE of Levanger; agr., lumber milling, quarrying. Sanatorium for the tubercular, 2 mi. NNW. Lumber milling at Trones (trō'nās) village (pop. 130), 2 mi. NW. STIKLESTAD village is in canton.

Verdal River, Nor. *Verdalselv*, Nord-Trondelag co., central Norway, issues from small lake near Swedish border 31 mi. ESE of Steinkjer, flows 45 mi. W to Trondheim Fjord at Verdal. Has caused catastrophic landslides (notably in 1892). Sometimes spelled Vaerdal.

Verde, Cape (vûrd, vûr'dē), or **Cape Vert** (vâr), peninsula forming westernmost part of Africa, on Atlantic coast of Senegal, Fr. West Africa, with city and port of Dakar on S shore; c.20 mi. long (E–W), up to 7 mi. wide. At its W tip is Cape Almadies, 14°45'N 17°33'W.

Verde, El, Mexico: see EL VERDE, Sinaloa.

Verde, La, Argentina: see LA VERDE.

Verde, Rio (rē'ōō vĕr'dĭ). **1** River in SE Mato Grosso, Brazil, rises in the Serra das Araras, flows c.200 mi. SE to the Paraná (right bank) 30 mi. SSW of Três Lagoas. Not navigable. **2** River in S Minas Gerais, Brazil, rises in the Serra da Mantiqueira near São Paulo border, flows c.100 mi. NNW, past Pouso Alto and Três Corações, to the Sapucaí-Guaçu below Varginha. Navigable.

Verde, Rio (rē'ōō vĕr'dĭ), Sp. *Río Verde* (rē'ō vĕr'dā), river on Brazil-Bolivia border near 14°S, a left tributary (c.50 mi. long) of the Guaporé.

Verde, Río (rē'ō bĕr'dhā). **1** River, Chihuahua, NW Mexico, rises in Sierra Madre Occidental at Durango border, flows c.175 mi. NW, joining Urique R. near Sinaloa border to form the Río del FUERTE. **2** River, Jalisco, Mexico: see SAN PEDRO RIVER. **3** River, Oaxaca, Mexico: see ATOYAC RIVER. **4** River, San Luis Potosí, N central and NE Mexico, rises in Sierra Madre Oriental NE of San Luis Potosí, flows c.120 mi. SE, past San Nicolás Tolentino and Río Verde city, to Santa María R. (headstream of the Pánuco) 15 mi. E of Aquismón.

Verde, Río, river in the Paraguayan Chaco, flows c.150 mi. E along Presidente Hayes–Boquerón dept. border to Paraguay R. 25 mi. NW of Concepción; not navigable.

Verde Island (vûr'dē, vûrd, Sp. bĕr'dhā) (□ 6.5; 1939 pop. 2,974), Batangas prov., Philippines, in Verde Isl. Passage, off S coast of Luzon, 12 mi. S of Batangas town; 3 mi. long; rises to 1,309 ft. Fishing. Included in Batangas municipality.

Verde Island Passage, strait in the Philippines, bet. SW coast of Luzon and Mindoro isl., connecting Tablas Strait with S.China Sea; 8–20 mi. wide. Contains Maricaban and Verde isls.

Verdel (vûrdĕl'), village (pop. 142), Knox co., NE Nebr., 70 mi. NW of Norfolk and on Ponca Creek, near Missouri R.

Verdello (vĕrdĕl'lô), village (pop. 2,806), Bergamo prov., Lombardy, N Italy, 6 mi. SSW of Bergamo.

Verden (fâr'dûn), town (pop. 16,700) in former Prussian prov. of Hanover, NW Germany, after 1945 in Lower Saxony, on the Aller and 21 mi. SE of Bremen; mfg. of machinery, precision instruments, chemicals, furniture, tobacco products, feed; food processing (flour, spirits, beverages, canned goods), dyeing, woodworking, printing. Has Gothic cathedral. Bishopric, founded by Charlemagne, passed in 1648 as secularized duchy to Sweden. Ceded 1719 to Hanover.

Verden (vûr'dûn), town (pop. 508), Grady co., central Okla., 8 mi. WNW of Chickasha, and on Washita R., in agr. area.

Verde River (vĕr'dē, vûr'dē), central Ariz., rises c.30 mi. SE of Seligman, flows c.190 mi. generally S, past Clarkdale and Cottonwood, to Salt R. 25 mi. ENE of Phoenix. BARTLETT DAM holds its waters for irrigation. Valley has many remains of early Indian civilizations, at Montezuma Castle and Tuzigoot natl. monuments and other places.

Verdigre (vûr'dûgrē), village (pop. 570), Knox co., NE Nebr., 50 mi. NW of Norfolk, near Missouri R.; dairy and poultry produce, livestock, grain.

Verdigris River (vûr'dûgrēs), in SE Kansas and NE Okla., rises in Chase co. in Kansas SW of Emporia, flows SSE, past Toronto and Altoona, then S, past Neodesha, Independence, and Coffeyville, entering Okla. in Nowata co., and joining Arkansas R. 5 mi. NE of Muskogee; 351 mi. long. Drains farming and stock-raising area. Gas and oil wells, and deposits of limestone, clay, and shale in river basin. Chief tributaries: Caney, Fall, and Elk rivers. Plan to improve main stream for navigation, from point near Catoosa (Okla.) to mouth, is being considered by U.S. Army Engineers. Near Toronto and Neodesha (Kansas) and Oologah (Okla.) are sites of flood-control reservoirs.

Verdon. 1 Village (pop. 366), Richardson co., SE Nebr., 8 mi. NW of Falls City, near Missouri R. **2** Town (pop. 34), Brown co., NE S.Dak., 25 mi. SE of Aberdeen.

Verdon River (vĕrdō'), Basses-Alpes dept., SE France, rises in Provence Alps 6 mi. SW of Barcelonnette, flows 110 mi. generally SW, past Castellane, through a mighty canyon (12 mi. long; tourist attraction) to the Durance 8 mi. S of Manosque.

Verdon-sur-Mer, Le (lù vĕrdō'-sür-mâr'), village (pop. 1,163), Gironde dept., SW France, on the Gironde, at its mouth on Bay of Biscay, opposite Royan, 55 mi. NNW of Bordeaux; railroad terminal and port for Bordeaux for passenger liners. Severely damaged during Second World War.

Verdú (bĕr-dhōō'), town (pop. 1,619), Lérida prov., NE Spain, 7 mi. SW of Cervera; pottery mfg., olive-oil processing; wine, cereals, fruit.

Verdugo City (vûrdōō'gō), residential village (1940 pop. 1,273), Los Angeles co., S Calif., in foothills of San Gabriel Mts., c.10 mi. N of downtown Los Angeles.

Verdugo Hills, Calif.: see GLENDALE.

Verdun (vûrdŭn', Fr. vĕrdû'), residential city (pop. 67,349), S Que., on S shore of Montreal Isl., on the St. Lawrence, opposite Nun's Isl.; S suburb of Montreal.

Verdun or **Verdun-sur-Meuse** (vûrdŭn', Fr. vĕrdû'-sür-mûz'), anc. *Verodunum,* fortified town (pop. 12,948), Meuse dept., NE France, in Lorraine, on Meuse R. and Canal de l'Est, and 36 mi. W of Metz; strategic communications center at E approaches of Paris Basin; mfg. (dragées, alcohol, lingerie, furniture). Episcopal see since 4th cent. By Treaty of Verdun Charlemagne's empire was partitioned (843) among 3 sons of Emperor Louis I. Verdun was one of 3 bishoprics (with Metz and Toul) which Henry II acquired (1552) for France from Holy Roman Empire. After 1871, it became chief Fr. fortress, facing German-held Metz, and was surrounded by a ring of defenses in depth. Scene of longest and bloodiest battle (1 million men killed) of First World War. Fiercest combats took place around Forts Douaumont and Vaux, Hill 304, and Hill Le Mort-Homme. Although Falkenhayn's attack (Feb. 21, 1916) carried Germans to within 3.5 mi. of Verdun proper, desperate Fr. resistance ("They shall not pass") under Pétain and Nivelle succeeded in repulsing all assaults. British Somme offensive (July, 1916) relieved immediate pressure on Verdun, and by Dec., 1916, most of ground lost had been recovered. Virtually destroyed, Verdun was rebuilt after Armistice. In Second World War, it was easily captured by Germans in 1940, and by Americans in 1944. Its 11th-cent. Romanesque cathedral and other bldgs. were damaged once again. Verdun battlefield, including military cemeteries, war memorials, battle sites, and supply routes ("Sacred Road" to Bar-le-Duc), forms a much-visited national sanctuary.

Verdun, W.Va.: see VERDUNVILLE.

Verdun-sur-Garonne (-gärôn'), village (pop. 1,027), Tarn-et-Garonne dept., SW France, on the Garonne and 13 mi. SSW of Montauban; cereals, fruits, vegetables (gherkins).

Verdun-sur-le-Doubs (-lù-dōō'), village (pop. 1,045), Saône-et-Loire dept., E central France, at mouth of the Doubs on Saône R., and 11 mi. NE of Chalon-sur-Saône; cattle, poultry.

Verdun-sur-Meuse, France: see VERDUN.

Verdunville (vûr'dûnvĭl) or **Verdun** (vûr'dûn), mining village (pop. 2,941, with adjacent Mudfork or Mud Junction), Logan co., SW W.Va., just W of Logan.

Vere, Netherlands: see VEERE.

Verecski Pass, Ukrainian SSR: see VERETSKI PASS.

Vereda Nueva (bārā'dä nwā'vä), town (pop. 1,838), Havana prov., W Cuba, 22 mi. SW of Havana, in agr. region (tobacco, sugar cane, vegetables).

Vereeniging (fûrē'nĭkhĭng) [Du.,=union], town (pop. 40,490), S Transvaal, U. of So. Afr., on Orange Free State border, on Vaal R. (bridge) and 35 mi. S of Johannesburg; alt. 4,750 ft.; steel center (rolling mills, blast furnaces) in largest coal-mining region of the Union; mfg. of liquid fuel, fire bricks, agr. machinery, corn products; sawmilling. Govt. pasture research station near by. Airfield. Founded 1892, it became municipality 1905. Treaty of Vereeniging (May 31, 1902) ended South African War.

Veregin, Sask.: see VERIGIN.

Vereide (văr'ădù), village in Gloppen canton (pop. 3,779), Sogn og Fjordane co., W Norway, on Gloppen Fjord (an arm of Nord Fjord), 40 mi. ENE of Floro. Has stone church mentioned as early as 1303. Formerly spelled Vereid and Verejde. Sandane (formerly spelled Sandene) village (pop. 784), 3 mi. SE, is woolen-milling and tourist center.

Vereker Banks, China: see PRATAS ISLAND.

Verendrye National Monument (vĕ'rùndrē) (253 acres; established 1917), NW N.Dak., adjoining Sanish, on the Missouri; honors Pierre de la Vérendrye, who 1st explored (c.1738) what is now N.Dak., and his 2 sons, who visited area in 1742.

Vere Plain (vēr), S lowland region of Clarendon parish, S Jamaica, along mouth of Minho R., W continuation of Liguanea Plain. In the irrigated area, sugar cane is largely cultivated. Formerly a parish with Alley as ⊙.

Veresegyhaz (vĕr'ĕ-shĕdyùhäz), Hung. *Veresegyház,* town (pop. 5,663), Pest-Pilis-Solt-Kiskun co., N central Hungary, 14 mi. NE of Budapest; truck gardening. Summer resort.

Vereshchagino (vyĕrĭshchä'gĭnŭ), city (1939 pop. over 10,000), W Molotov oblast, Russian SFSR, on railroad and 60 mi. W of Molotov; mfg. center; metalworking, hemp milling, knitwear mfg., food processing. Called Krasnoye Vereshchagino in 1920s. Sawmilling 10 mi. SW, at Borodulino.

Verespatak, Rumania: see ROSIA-MONTANA.

Veretiya, Russian SFSR: see BEREZNIKI.

Veretski Pass or **Veretskiy Pass** (vĭryĕt'skē), Czech *Verecki,* Hung. *Verecski,* pass (alt. 2,763 ft.) in the Carpathians, SW Ukrainian SSR, bet. Beshchady and Gorgany mts., 20 mi. SW of Skole; rail and highway corridor. Also called Mukachevo Pass (mōōkä'chĭvŭ).

Vereya (vyĕrăyä'). **1** City (1926 pop. 3,357), SW Moscow oblast, Russian SFSR, on Protva R. 13 mi. SSE of Mozhaisk; shoe mfg., linen milling, dairying. Chartered 1381. **2** Town (1939 pop. over 500), E Moscow oblast, Russian SFSR, 15 mi. from Orekhovo-Zuyevo.

Verfeil (vĕrfā'), agr. village (pop. 488), Haute-Garonne dept., S France, 12 mi. ENE of Toulouse; livestock raising.

Verga, Cape (vûr'gù), headland on coast of Fr. Guinea, Fr. West Africa, 70 mi. NW of Conakry; 10°12'N 14°28'W.

Vergara (bĕrgä'rä), town (pop. 4,081), Guipúzcoa prov., N Spain, 16 mi. W of Tolosa; cotton-textile center. Also mfg. of dyes, sandals, candy; meat processing, flour milling. Convention concluded here (1839) between generals Espartero and Maroto ended 1st Carlist war.

Vergara, town (pop. 3,000), Treinta y Tres dept., E central Uruguay, on railroad and road, and 32 mi. NE of Treinta y Tres; road junction; local trade and administrative center. Wheat, corn, linseed, cattle and sheep.

Vergara River, in Malleco and Bío-Bío provs., S central Chile, formed near Angol by union of Rehue and Malleco rivers, flows c.25 mi. N to the Bío-Bío at Nacimiento.

Vergas (vûr'gùs), village (pop. 301), Otter Tail co., W Minn., 30 mi. NNE of Fergus Falls, in lake region; dairy products.

Vergato (vĕrgä'tō), town (pop. 1,702), Bologna prov., Emilia-Romagna, N central Italy, on Reno R. and 18 mi. SW of Bologna; jute mill.

Vergel, Brazil: see BOM JARDIM, Rio de Janeiro.

Vergel (bĕrhĕl'), village (pop. 2,262), Alicante prov., E Spain, 13 mi. SE of Gandía; olive-oil processing; raisins, almonds, oranges and other fruit. Mineral springs.

Vergemoli (vĕrjä'môlē), village (pop. 342), Lucca prov., Tuscany, central Italy, 4 mi. SSW of Castelnuovo di Garfagnana; iron mining.

Vergennes (vûrjĕnz'). **1** Village (pop. 312), Jackson co., SW Ill., 17 mi. WNW of Herrin, in agr. region. **2** City (pop. 1,736), Addison co., W Vt., on Otter Creek, near L. Champlain, and 21 mi. S of Burlington; trade center for dairying, resort region; hardware. State industrial school here. Settled 1766, set off 1788, city inc. 1794; region disputed by claimants of N.H. and N.Y. grants before Revolution. Macdonough's fleet built here in War of 1812. Anc. Indian implements excavated here, 1937.

Verges (bĕr'hĕs), town (pop. 1,160), Gerona prov., NE Spain, near Ter R., 13 mi. NE of Gerona, in irrigated agr. area (cereals, beetroot, wine, fruit); olive-oil processing. Has medieval castle.

Vergt (vâr), village (pop. 788), Dordogne dept., SW France, 11 mi. S of Périgueux; woodworking.

Veria, Greece: see VEROIA.

Verigin or **Veregin** (both: vĕ'rùgĭn), agr. village (pop. 248), E Sask., 8 mi. W of Kamsack.

Verín (bārēn'), town (pop. 2,562), Orense prov., NW Spain, on Támega R. and 34 mi. SE of Orense; customs station near Port. border; popular watering place. Trades in wine, cereals, fruit, livestock. Tin mining near by.

Verinag, Kashmir: see VERNAG.

Verissimo River (vĕrē'sēmōō), S Goiás, central Brazil, right tributary of Paranaíba R. Length, c.60 mi. Diamond washings.

Verka (vār'kŭ), village, Amritsar dist., W Punjab, India, suburb (4 mi. NE) of Amritsar; mfg. of electrical apparatus, paints, turpentine, woolen and silk goods, condiments.

Verkh-Chebula (vyĕrkh"-chĕbōōlä'), village (1926 pop. 2,616), NE Kemerovo oblast, Russian SFSR, 10 mi. SSW of Mariinsk, in agr. area; metalworks.

Verkh-Irmen or **Verkh-Irmen'** (-ĕrmyĕn'yù), village (1939 pop. over 2,000), SE Novosibirsk oblast, Russian SFSR, 35 mi. SSW of Novosibirsk.

Verkhne- [Rus. combining form,=UPPER], in Rus. names: see also VERKHNEYE, VERKHNI, VERKHNIYE, VERKHNYAYA.

Verkhne-Avzyano-Petrovsk, Russian SFSR: see VERKHNI AVZYAN.

Verkhne-Bakanski or **Verkhne-Bakanskiy** (vyĕrkh"-nyĭ-bŭkän'skē), town (1926 pop. 2,898), W Krasnodar Territory, Russian SFSR, in NW outlier of the Greater Caucasus, on railroad and 10 mi. NW of Novorossisk; cement making.

Verkhne-Berezovski or **Verkhne-Berezovskiy** (-byĕrĭzôf'skē), town (1945 pop. over 500), NW East Kazakhstan oblast, Kazakh SSR, 35 mi. NW of Ust-Kamenogorsk; copper, lead-zinc mining.

Verkhne-Chusovskiye Gorodki (-chōōsŭfskē'ù gŭrŭtkē'), town (1932 pop. estimate 7,500), E central Molotov oblast, Russian SFSR, on right bank of Chusovaya R. and 25 mi. WSW of Chusovoi, on rail spur (Uralneft station); petroleum extracting and refining. Mineral springs (iodine and bromide content). Small-scale oil production began in 1929. Formerly also called Chusovskiye Gorodki.

Verkhne-Dneprovsk (vyĕrkh"nyĭ-dŭnyĭprôfsk'), town (1926 pop. 5,907), W Dnepropetrovsk oblast, Ukrainian SSR, on Dnieper R. and 35 mi. WNW of Dnepropetrovsk; metalworking, food industries (mainly flour milling).

Verkhne-Imbatskoye (-ēmbăt'skŭyù), village, N Krasnoyarsk Territory, Russian SFSR, on Yenisei

R. and 300 mi. S of Igarka; river port; trading point.

Verkh-Neivinski or **Verkh-Neyvinskiy** (vyĕrkh-nyävĕn'skē), town (1926 pop. 4,057), SW central Sverdlovsk oblast, Russian SFSR, on Tavatui L., on railroad and 15 mi. S of Nevyansk; metalworking, chromite processing. Nickel deposits. Founded 1762 as ironworks; gold- and platinum-mining center in 1920s.

Verkhne-Kamchatsk (vyĕrkh"nyĭ-kŭmchätsk'), village (1948 pop. over 500), Kamchatka oblast, Khabarovsk Territory, Russian SFSR, on S central Kamchatka Peninsula, on Kamchatka R. and 110 mi. NNW of Petropavlovsk, in agr. area. Founded 1697.

Verkhne-Kolymsk, Russian SFSR: see ZYRYANKA.

Verkhne-Kurmoyarskaya (–kōōrmŭyär'skīŭ), village (1939 pop. over 500), SW Stalingrad oblast, Russian SFSR, on left bank of Don R. and 17 mi. NNW of Kotelnikovski; flour mill; wheat, cotton, mustard. Pop. largely Cossack.

Verkhne-Stalinsk (–stä'lyĭnsk), town (1939 pop. over 500), SE Yakut Autonomous SSR, Russian SFSR, 8 mi. SSE of Aldan, on Yakutsk-Never highway; gold mines.

Verkhne-Tarasovka (–tŭrä'sŭfkŭ), village (1926 pop. 2,534), W Rostov oblast, Russian SFSR, on railroad and 14 mi. S of Millerovo; flour milling. Tarasovka, just S, has quartz-sand quarries.

Verkhne-Teploye (vyĕrkh"nyĭ-tyô'plŭyŭ), village (1939 pop. over 500), E central Voroshilovgrad oblast, Ukrainian SSR, 18 mi. NNE of Voroshilovgrad; wheat.

Verkhne-Ubinskoye, Kazakh SSR: see VERKHUBINKA.

Verkhneudinsk, Russian SFSR: see ULAN-UDE.

Verkhne-Uralsk or **Verkhne-Ural'sk** (–ōōrälsk'), city (1926 pop. 10,005), W Chelyabinsk oblast, Russian SFSR, on upper Ural R. and 28 mi. N of Magnitogorsk; agr.-processing center; distilling, tanning, flour milling, dairying, soap mfg. Founded in 1740s as stronghold of Verkhne-Yaitsk; renamed Verkhne-Uralsk and chartered in 1775.

Verkhne-Usinskoye (–ōōsĕn'skŭyŭ), village (1926 pop. 2,242), S Krasnoyarsk Territory, Russian SFSR, in Western Sayan Mts., 110 mi. SE of Minusinsk, near Minusinsk-Kyzyl highway. Gold placers near by.

Verkhne-Vilyuisk or **Verkhne-Vilyuysk** (–vĭlyōō'ēsk), village, SW Yakut Autonomous SSR, Russian SFSR, on Vilyui R. and 45 mi. WSW of Vilyuisk; lignite deposits.

Verkhne-Yarkeyevo (–yŭrkyä'ŭvŭ), village (1926 pop. 785), NW Bashkir Autonomous SSR, Russian SFSR, 80 mi. NW of Ufa; wheat, livestock. Until c.1940, Yarkeyevo.

Verkhneye [Rus.,=UPPER], in Rus. names: see also VERKHNE- [Rus. combining form], VERKHNI, VERKHNIYE, VERKHNYAYA.

Verkhneye (vyĕrkh'nyŭŭ), city (1926 pop. 11,153), W Voroshilovgrad oblast, Ukrainian SSR, in the Donbas, on the Northern Donets and 3 mi. SSE of Lisichansk, on railroad (Pereyezdnaya station); chemical (soda) works; glass mfg. Formerly also called Vyssheye.

Verkhneye Dubrovo (dōōbrô'vŭ), town (1940 pop. over 500), S Sverdlovsk oblast, Russian SFSR, on railroad (Kosulino station) and 9 mi. NE of Aramil; fireproof-brick mfg.; refractory-clay quarrying.

Verkhni or **Verkhniy** [Rus.,=UPPER], in Rus. names: see also VERKHNE- [Rus. combining form], VERKHNEYE, VERKHNIYE, VERKHNYAYA.

Verkhni Avzyan or **Verkhniy Avzyan** (vyĕrkh"nyē ŭvzyän'), town (1926 pop. 7,980), E central Bashkir Autonomous SSR, Russian SFSR, in the S Urals, 47 mi. SW of Beloretsk; mining center in Komarovo-Zigazinski iron dist. Chromite deposits near by. Until 1942, Verkhne-Avzyano-Petrovsk or Verkhne-Avzyano-Petrovski Zavod.

Verkhni Balyklei, Russian SFSR: see GORNY BALYKLEI.

Verkhni Baskunchak or **Verkhniy Baskunchak** (bŭskōōnchäk'), town (1926 pop. 3,381), NE Astrakhan oblast, Russian SFSR, near L. BASKUNCHAK, 140 mi. NNW of Astrakhan; rail junction; salt-shipping center; food processing. Linked by rail spur with Nizhni Baskunchak saltworks.

Verkhni Karachan or **Verkhniy Karachan** (kŭrŭchän'), village (1926 pop. 6,780), E Voronezh oblast, Russian SFSR, 12 mi. WNW of Borisoglebsk; woodworking.

Verkhni Khorog, Tadzhik SSR: see SHUGNAN.

Verkhni Landekh or **Verkhniy Landekh** (lŭndyĕkh'), village (1926 pop. 468), E Ivanovo oblast, Russian SFSR, 45 mi. E of Shuya; garment mfg.

Verkhni Lomov or **Verkhniy Lomov** (lô'mŭf), village (1939 pop. over 500), NW Penza oblast, Russian SFSR, on rail spur and 6 mi. SW of Nizhni Lomov; match mfg.

Verkhni Lyubazh or **Verkhniy Lyubazh** (lyōō'bŭsh), village (1939 pop. over 500), NW Kursk oblast, Russian SFSR, 35 mi. NNW of Kursk; hemp. Until c.1941, Lyubazh.

Verkhni Mamon or **Verkhniy Mamon** (mŭmôn'), village (1926 pop. 9,847), SE Voronezh oblast, Russian SFSR, on Don R. and 37 mi. E of Rossosh; wheat, sunflowers. Large tree nursery near by.

Verkhni Nagolchik or **Verkhniy Nagol'chik** (nŭgôl'chĭk), town (1939 pop. over 500), S Voroshilovgrad oblast, Ukrainian SSR, in the Donbas, 2 mi. S of Bokovo-Antratsit; anthracite mines.

Verkhni Rogachik or **Verkhniy Rogachik** (vyĕrkh"nyē rŭgä'chĭk), village (1926 pop. 12,670), NE Kherson oblast, Ukrainian SSR, 55 mi. NW of Melitopol; dairy farming.

Verkhni Tagil or **Verkhniy Tagil** (tŭgēl'), town (1926 pop. 5,895), SW central Sverdlovsk oblast, Russian SFSR, on small lake formed by upper Tagil R., 5 mi. SW (under jurisdiction) of Kirovgrad. Founded 1716 as ironworks.

Verkhni Talin, Armenian SSR: see TALIN.

Verkhni Ufalei or **Verkhniy Ufaley** (ōōfŭlyä'), city (1926 pop. 12,671), NW Chelyabinsk oblast, Russian SFSR, in the central Urals, on railroad and 75 mi. NW of Chelyabinsk; major nickel-refining center, based on local deposits; metallurgy (largely pig iron); charcoal burning, sawmilling; marble quarrying. Founded 1765; became city in 1940.

Verkhni Uslon or **Verkhniy Uslon** (ōōslôn'), village (1939 pop. over 2,000), NW Tatar Autonomous SSR, Russian SFSR, on right bank of the Volga, opposite Kazan waterfront; summer resort. Flour milling, limestone quarrying near by.

Verkhniye [Rus.,=UPPER], in Rus. names: see also VERKHNE- [Rus. combining form], VERKHNEYE, VERKHNI, VERKHNYAYA.

Verkhniye Kigi (vyĕrkh"nyēŭ kē'gē), village (1926 pop. 2,830), NE Bashkir Autonomous SSR, Russian SFSR, on right tributary of Ai R. and 45 mi. WNW of Zlatoust; lumbering; rye, oats, livestock.

Verkhniye Mully (mōōlē'), village (1939 pop. over 500), S central Molotov oblast, Russian SFSR, 5 mi. SW of Molotov; dairying; truck.

Verkhniye Sergi (syĕr'gē), town (1926 pop. 5,797), SW Sverdlovsk oblast, Russian SFSR, in the central Urals, on Serga R. (right tributary of Ufa R.) and 9 mi. E of Nizhniye Sergi; mfg. (oil-drilling tools), metalworking. Until 1938, Verkhne-Serginski Zavod.

Verkhniye Tatyshly (tŭtĭshlē'), village (1926 pop. 898), N Bashkir Autonomous SSR, Russian SFSR, 65 mi. NNE of Birsk; grain, livestock.

Verkhnyaya [Rus.,=UPPER], in Rus. names: see also VERKHNE- [Rus. combining form], VERKHNEYE, VERKHNI, VERKHNIYE.

Verkhnyaya (vyĕrkh'nyĭŭ), rail junction in W Sverdlovsk oblast, Russian SFSR, 5 mi. NE of Kushva; spurs lead to Verkhnyaya Tura, Krasnouralsk, and Buksina (32 mi. NE; lumbering).

Verkhnyaya Angara River, Russian SFSR: see UPPER ANGARA RIVER.

Verkhnyaya Berezovka (bĭryô'zŭfkŭ), E suburb of Ulan-Ude, Buryat-Mongol Autonomous SSR, Russian SFSR; site of tuberculosis sanatorium.

Verkhnyaya Khava (khä'vŭ), village (1926 pop. 2,478), NW central Voronezh oblast, Russian SFSR, 32 mi. ENE of Voronezh; metalworks.

Verkhnyaya Khortitsa (khôr'tyĭtsŭ), village (1926 pop. 2,604), NW Zaporozhe oblast, Ukrainian SSR, 6 mi. W of Zaporozhe (across Dnieper R.); truck produce. Until 1930s, called Khortitsa.

Verkhnyaya Pyshma (pĭshmä'), city (1935 pop. estimate 10,800), S Sverdlovsk oblast, Russian SFSR, in E foothills of the central Urals, on railroad and 10 mi. N of Sverdlovsk; a major copper-refining center, based on local deposits. Developed as mining center in 1850s. Called Pyshma until 1946, when it became city.

Verkhnyaya Salda (sŭldä'), city (1932 pop. estimate 10,500), W central Sverdlovsk oblast, Russian SFSR, in E foothills of the central Urals, on Salda R. (right tributary of Tagil R.), on railroad and 25 mi. ENE of Nizhni Tagil; metallurgical center (quality steels, steel girders, rails); sawmilling. Asbestos quarrying near by. Developed prior to First World War; became city in 1938. Until 1928, Verkhne-Saldinski Zavod.

Verkhnyaya Sinyachikha (sēnyä'chĭkhŭ), town (1926 pop. 2,272), central Sverdlovsk oblast, Russian SFSR, on railroad and 60 mi. ENE of Nizhni Tagil; metallurgical center (steel, pig iron), based on local iron (Alapayevsk mining dist.), charcoal, limestone. Coal, peat, bauxite deposits near by.

Verkhnyaya Toima or **Verkhnyaya Toyma** (toimä'), village, S Archangel oblast, Russian SFSR, on Northern Dvina R. and 85 mi. NW of Kotlas; grain.

Verkhnyaya Tunguska River, Russian SFSR: see ANGARA RIVER.

Verkhnyaya Tura (tōōrä'), city (1932 pop. estimate 15,200), W Sverdlovsk oblast, Russian SFSR, in E foothills of the central Urals, on small lake formed by upper Tura R., 5 mi. NNE of Kushva, on rail spur; metallurgical center (pig iron); sawmilling, charcoal burning, brick mfg. Developed prior to First World War; became city in 1941. Until c.1928, Verkhne-Turinski Zavod.

Verkholensk (vyĕrkhŭlyĕnsk'), village (1926 pop. 1,530) SE Irkutsk oblast, Russian SFSR, on upper Lena R. (landing) and 15 mi. NW of Kachuga, in agr. area. Founded 1642; before 1924, ⊙ Verkholensk dist. of Irkutsk govt.

Verkhoshizhemye or **Verkhoshizhem'ye** (vyĕr"-khŭshēzhĕ'myĭ), village (1926 pop. 212), central Kirov oblast, Russian SFSR, 45 mi. SW of Kirov; wood processing.

Verkhoturye or **Verkhotur'ye** (vyĕrkhŭtōō'ryĭ), city (1926 pop. 4,689), W central Sverdlovsk oblast, Russian SFSR, on Tura R. and 70 mi. NNE of Nizhni Tagil; sawmilling center; metalworking, food processing. Founded 1598; developed as trade center with customs house on major route to Siberia (17th–18th cent.) Declined following southward shift of Siberian colonization to Yekaterinburg (Sverdlovsk) in 1763. Became city in 1947.

Verkhovazhye or **Verkhovazh'ye** (–vä'zhyĭ), village (1926 pop. 918), N Vologda oblast, Russian SFSR, 23 mi. S of Velsk and on Vaga R.; flax. Formerly called Verkhovazhsk.

Verkhovtsevo (vyĭrkhôf'tsyĭvŭ), town (1939 pop. over 500), W central Dnepropetrovsk oblast, Ukrainian SSR, 17 mi. W of Dneprodzerzhinsk; rail junction; metalworks.

Verkhovye or **Verkhov'ye** (vyĭrkhô'vyĭ), village (1939 pop. over 500), central Orel oblast, Russian SFSR, 45 mi. E of Orel; rail junction; hemp milling. During Second World War, briefly held (1941) by Germans.

Verkhoyansk (vûrkōyănsk', Rus. vyĕrkhŭyänsk'), city (1939 pop. over 500), N Yakut Autonomous SSR, Russian SFSR, N of Arctic Circle, on Yana R. and 385 mi. NNE of Yakutsk; 67°32'N 133°25'E. In earth's coldest area; lowest recorded temp. -92°. Fur-trading. Founded 1638; former exile center.

Verkhoyansk Range, NE Yakut Autonomous SSR, Russian SFSR, arc-shaped range extending from Lena R. delta S, along Lena and Aldan rivers, to Oimyakon Plateau; separates Lena basin from Yana and Indigirka basins; rises to 1,600 ft. (N), 8,000 ft. (SE). Coal, silver, lead, zinc deposits.

Verkhozim (–zēm'), town (1939 pop. over 2,000), E Penza oblast, Russian SFSR, 19 mi. SW of Kuznetsk; woolen milling.

Verkhubinka (–bĕn'kŭ), village (1939 pop. over 2,000), NW East Kazakhstan oblast, Kazakh SSR, 35 mi. N of Ust-Kamenogorsk; cattle breeding. Formerly Verkhne-Ubinskoye.

Vermafoss (văr'mäfôs), waterfall (1,250 ft.) on Rauma R., More og Romsdal co., W Norway, 19 mi. SE of Andalsnes; tourist attraction.

Vermala, Switzerland: see MONTANA.

Vermand (vĕrmã'), village (pop. 730), Aisne dept., N France, 7 mi. WNW of Saint-Quentin. Destroyed in First World War.

Vermandois (vârmădwä'), agr. region and former countship of N France, now in Somme and Aisne depts.; old ⊙ was Saint-Quentin. Annexed c.1200 to Fr. crown by Philip II, ceded (1435) to Burgundy, recovered (1477) by Louis XI, and incorporated into Picardy prov.

Vermejo River (vĕrmā'hō), NE N.Mex., rises in Sangre de Cristo Mts. near Colo. line, flows 58 mi. SE, past Dawson, to Canadian R. at French.

Vermelho, Rio (rē'ōō vĕrmā'lyōō), river of W Goiás, central Brazil, rises SE of Goiás city, flows c.100 mi. NW to the Araguaia at Aruanã. Navigable for small craft. Abandoned gold placers.

Vermelles (vĕrmĕl'), town (pop. 3,734), Pas-de-Calais dept., N France, 6 mi. SE of Béthune; coal and lignite mines. In Br. front lines during First World War.

Vermenton (vĕrmätõ'), village (pop. 1,162), Yonne dept., N central France, on Cure R. and 12 mi. SE of Auxerre; port on branch of Nivernais Canal; Burgundy wines.

Vermilion (vûrmĭl'yŭn), town (pop. 1,630), E Alta., near Sask. border, on Vermilion R. and 100 mi. E of Edmonton; oil production and refining; dairying, lumbering; grain, stock.

Vermilion. 1 County (□ 898; pop. 87,079), E Ill., on Ind. line (E); ⊙ Danville. Drained by Vermilion and Little Vermilion rivers; include L. Vermilion (resort) and Kickapoo State Park. Rich agr. area (corn, oats, soybeans, wheat, truck; dairy products; livestock, poultry); bituminous-coal mining; timber; diversified mfg. Formed 1826. **2** Parish (□ 1,224; pop. 36,929), S La.; ⊙ Abbeville. On the Gulf of Mexico (S), and bounded partly N and NW by Bayou Queue de Tortue, SE by Vermilion Bay; drained by Vermilion R. Crossed by Gulf Intracoastal Waterway. Agr. (especially rice; also cotton, corn, hay, sugar cane, sweet potatoes). Sugar and rice milling, cotton ginning, canning. Oil and gas wells; lumber. Contains White L., in swampy coastal area; also a bird sanctuary. Formed 1844.

Vermilion. 1 Village (pop. 316), Edgar co., E Ill., 6 mi. ESE of Paris, in agr. and bituminous-coal area. Formerly Vermillion. **2** Resort village (pop. 2,214), Erie co., N Ohio, 10 mi. WSW of Lorain, near mouth of Vermilion R. on L. Erie; makes lighting fixtures, handles, food products; fisheries. Settled c.1808.

Vermilion, Lake, E Ill., just N of Danville, impounded by dam across North Fork of Vermilion R.; 4 mi. long, ¼–1 mi. wide; recreational facilities.

Vermilion Bay, village (pop. estimate 100), NW Ont., at N end of Eagle L., 25 mi. W of Dryden; gold mining, lumbering. Airfield.

Vermilion Bay, arm of the Gulf of Mexico in S La., 11 mi. S of New Iberia and at mouth of Vermilion R. (entering at NW); c.22 mi. long NE-SW, 10 mi. wide. Partly cut off from Gulf by Marsh Isl.; adjoins West Cote Blanche Bay (E).

Vermilion Lake (□ 59), St. Louis co., NE Minn., at W end of Vermilion iron range, largely in Superior Natl. Forest, W of Ely; c.35 mi. long, 8 mi. wide. There are many summer resorts; boating, fishing, and bathing. Has N outlet in Vermilion R., hundreds of isls., and extremely irregular shore line. Chippewa Indian Reservation and iron mines (Tower and Soudan) are on S shore. Lake includes Wakemap Bay (7 mi. long, max. width 5 mi.) in W.

Vermilion-on-the-Lake, village (pop. 614), Lorain co., N Ohio, on L. Erie, near Vermilion.

Vermilion Pass (5,376 ft.), in Rocky Mts., on Alta.–B.C. border, 22 mi. W of Banff; 51°9′N 116°7′W. First crossed 1858 by Dr. Hector of the Palliser expedition.

Vermilion Range, iron-mining area (or iron range) in St. Louis co., NE Minn., extends E from E end of Vermilion L. to Ely. Ore discovered (1865) by Eames brothers. First shipment took place 1884, following gold rush that collapsed when assays failed to confirm promised values. Iron ore is shipped to Two Harbors, on L. Superior. Chief mining points are Ely, Tower, and Soudan.

Vermilion River. 1 In E Alta., rises S of Vegreville, winds N and E, past Vegreville, through small Vermilion Lakes, to North Saskatchewan R. 30 mi. NE of Vermilion; 175 mi. long. **2** In S central Que., rises NNE of L. Toro, flows 100 mi. NE to St. Maurice R. 22 mi. NW of La Tuque.

Vermilion River. 1 In E Ill., formed by North and South branches in Livingston co., flows generally NW, past Pontiac and Streator, to Illinois R. at Oglesby, opposite La Salle; c.75 mi. long. **2** In E Ill. and W Ind., formed by Middle Fork and North Fork at Danville; flows 30 mi. E and SE, across Ind. line, to the Wabash N of Cayuga. Middle Fork (c.85 mi. long) rises in Ford co., flows SE. North Fork (c.50 mi. long) rises in Benton co., Ind., flows SW into Ill., thence S. Dam impounds L. Vermilion (4 mi. long; resort) just N of Danville. South (or Salt) Fork (c.70 mi. long) rises in Champaign co., flows S, then ENE, to Middle Fork W of Danville. **3** In S La., formed by small streams S of Opelousas, flows c.72 mi. S, past Lafayette and Abbeville, to Vermilion Bay. Navigable for 49 mi. above mouth; followed by Gulf Intracoastal Waterway for short distance in lower course. **4** In NE Minn., rises in Vermilion L., flows 42 mi. N and ENE, through state forest, to Crane L. near Ont. line. **5** In N Ohio, rises near Greenwich, flows c.30 mi. N, past Wakeman, to L. Erie near Vermilion.

Vermilion Sea, Mexico: see CALIFORNIA, GULF OF.

Vermillion, county (□ 263; pop. 19,723), W Ind.; ⊙ Newport. Bounded W by Ill. line, E by Wabash R.; drained by Vermilion R. Bituminous-coal mining; agr. (grain, fruit, livestock); some timber. Some mfg. at Clinton and Cayuga. Formed 1824.

Vermillion. 1 Village, Ill.: see VERMILION, village. **2** City (pop. 283), Marshall co., NE Kansas, 38 mi. NNE of Manhattan, in grain area. **3** Village (pop. 112), Dakota co., SE Minn., on small affluent of Mississippi R. and 20 mi. SSE of St. Paul, in grain, potato, and livestock area. **4** City (pop. 5,337), ⊙ Clay co., SE S.Dak., 50 mi. SSW of Sioux Falls, near Missouri R., and on Vermillion R.; dairy produce, cattle feed, grain, watermelons, cantaloupes, tomatoes. Univ. of S.Dak. is here. Ft. Vermillion, a fur trading post, was built near by in 1835. City was settled 1859, inc. 1873.

Vermillion River, E S.Dak., rises in several branches in E central S.Dak., flows c.150 mi. S to Missouri R. near Vermillion.

Vermion (vĕr′mēôn), anc. *Bermius*, mountain in Macedonia, Greece, W of Giannitsa lowland, rising to 6,775 ft. 6 mi. W of Naousa.

Vermland, Sweden: see VARMLAND.

Vermondans (vĕrmōdã′), suburb (pop. 437) of Pont-de-Roide, Doubs dept., E France, on Doubs R. and 8 mi. S of Montbéliard; hardware, auto springs, tools.

Vermont (vûrmŏnt′), state (land □ 9,278; with inland waters □ 9,609; 1950 pop. 377,747; 1940 pop. 359,231), NE U.S., in New England, bordered N by Que., E by N.H., S by Mass., W by N.Y.; 42d in area, 45th in pop.; admitted 1791 as 14th state; ⊙ Montpelier. Vt. is 156 mi. N–S, 37–89 mi. E–W. In E, Connecticut R. flows along entire N.H. line, while in W, L. Champlain extends c.100 mi. bet. N.Y. and Vt. It is appropriately named the "Green Mountain State," after the GREEN MOUNTAINS, which traverse the center of the state from Mass. to Canada. This forest-clad range of Pre-Cambrian crystalline rocks rises to 4,393 ft. in Mt. Mansfield (highest point in state), 4,241 ft. in Killington Peak, and 4,083 ft. in Camels Hump. To the W, S of Brandon, are the Taconic Mts., rising to 3,816 ft. in Mt. Equinox, while bordering L. Champlain is a 10–20-mi.-wide lowland broken by a group of low sandstone and dolomite hills. To the E is a series of hills and uplands, descending gradually to the Connecticut valley; isolated mtn. peaks (monadnocks), such as Mt. Ascutney (3,144 ft.), occur in places. The longest streams are Otter Creek, Winooski R., and Lamoille R., all draining into L. Champlain. Evidences of glaciation include numerous small lakes and ponds, boulder-strewn regions, and the drift covering over much of the Champlain valley. Vt.'s climate is humid continental, marked by long winters, short summers, and an annual rainfall of 35–45 inches. Snowfall is heavy, averaging 110–120 inches in the Green Mts. The growing season ranges from 120–150 days in the E and W lowlands to less than 100 days in the central mts. Rutland (S center) has mean temp. of 20°F. in Jan., 69°F. in July, and 37 inches of rainfall. Native forest vegetation is largely maple, hemlock, birch, and beech, except in the Green Mts. (spruce, fir) and Connecticut valley (white pine). There are some 3,820,000 acres of commercial forest land, of which 581,000 acres are natl. forest reserves. Agr., particularly dairying, is the leading occupation. Farm and pasture land comprises c.3,900,000 acres, of which 1,150,000 acres are in crops. Hay, corn (for silage), oats, and potatoes are grown chiefly in the Champlain lowland and Connecticut valley. Apples are produced in several sections. The major dairying areas are in the N and throughout the Champlain lowland; milk production is important, the state supplying much of Boston's and New York's needs. The Morgan work horse is much used, especially on hill farms. Vermont turkeys have a wide market. The state produces c.40% of the country's maple sugar and syrup; St. Johnsbury is a noted center. Lumbering is an important industry, white pine and red spruce being particularly valuable. Vt. has large deposits of high-quality marble and granite, used principally for monumental and building purposes. Marble is quarried in the W part of the state, mainly at Rutland, Proctor, Swanton, Isle La Motte, and Middlebury. Granite is worked on the E slopes of the Green Mts., notably at Barre, the leading granite center in the U.S. Slate is also produced in quantity, at Fair Haven and near-by places. The largest U.S. asbestos deposits are mined in the Eden-Lowell sector (N). Talc (at Waterbury, Rochester, and Johnson) is important, and there are workable deposits of limestone, soapstone, kaolin, and copper (Orange co.). Despite abundant waterpower resources, mfg. is not extensively developed. Principal products are machinery and machine tools, cut stone (monuments, tombstones, etc.), lumber and wood products (pulpwood, furniture, toys), paper, food, and textiles (mostly woolens and worsteds). A few large plants specialize in organs, scales, and window screens. Handicrafts still flourish, especially woodworking, leatherworking, and stone cutting. The state's largest towns are Burlington, Rutland, Barre, Brattleboro, Montpelier, St. Albans, Bennington, St. Johnsbury, Winooski, Newport, and Springfield. Vt.'s fine natural setting makes it a great resort center. In summer, the cool climate, mtn. lakes, and hiking trails (notably Long Trail along the crest of Green Mts.) attract thousands of vacationers, while in winter there are many popular skiing areas, such as Stowe, Manchester, Middlebury, and Woodstock. Univ. of Vt. and State Agr. Col. (at Burlington), Norwich Univ. (at Northfield), Middlebury Col. (at Middlebury), and Bennington Col. (at Bennington) are the leading educational institutions. Samuel de Champlain, who explored L. Champlain in 1609, was the 1st white man in the area. The French attempted to found a military post on Isle La Motte in 1666, but not until 1724, when the Mass. govt. built Fort Dummer near the present site of Brattleboro, was the 1st permanent settlement made in what is now Vt. The region soon became the object of conflicting N.H. and N.Y. claims. Beginning with Bennington in 1749, settlements sprang up under the auspices of Gov. Wentworth of N.H. N.Y., which laid claim to the country as far E as the Connecticut R. by virtue of the Duke of York's charter, declared the N.H. grants void. When an order in council (1764) decided in N.Y.'s favor, it attempted to assert its jurisdiction over the territory. Local resistance to N.Y. authority culminated in the organization (1770–71) of the "Green Mountain Boys" under Ethan Allen. This fighting band distinguished itself during the Revolution at the capture of Fort Ticonderoga (1775) in N.Y. and at the battle of Bennington (1777). In 1777 Vt. declared its independence and adopted a constitution. After much opposition on the part of N.Y., Vt. was finally admitted as a state in 1791, the 1st to be added to the original 13. Montpelier became the ⊙ in 1805. In the War of 1812 there was much smuggling of supplies into Canada, until the battle of Plattsburg (1814) on L. Champlain removed the threat of invasion from the state. Anti-Masonry agitation centered in Vt., and in the 1832 presidential election the state was the only one to cast its votes for the Anti-Masonic candidate. Antislavery sentiment was also strong. St. Albans was the scene of the memorable Confederate bank raid in 1864, and just after the Civil War it figured as a base for Fenian raids into Canada. Predominantly rural and conservative, Vermonters have maintained their allegiance to the Republican party ever since it entered natl. politics in 1856. Native sons Chester A. Arthur and Calvin Coolidge succeeded to the presidency in 1881 and in 1923. See also the articles on cities, towns, geographic features, and the 14 counties: ADDISON, BENNINGTON, CALEDONIA, CHITTENDEN, ESSEX, FRANKLIN, GRAND ISLE, LAMOILLE, ORANGE, ORLEANS, RUTLAND, WASHINGTON, WINDHAM, WINDSOR.

Vermont, village (pop. 940), Fulton co., W central Ill., 28 mi. SW of Canton, in agr. and bituminous-coal area; hardwood timber.

Vermontville, village (pop. 707), Eaton co., S central Mich., 25 mi. SW of Lansing and on Thornapple R., in farm area.

Verna, La (lä vĕr′nä), famous monastery founded by St. Francis of Assisi on Monte della Verna, in Etruscan Apennines, Tuscany, central Italy, 17 mi. NNE of Arezzo. Here the saint received the Stigmata in 1224. Has several 13th-cent. churches and chapels, with Della Robbia terra cottas, in a beautiful forest (damaged 1944–45 in Second World War).

Vernag or **Verinag** (vŭrnäg′), town (pop. 2,219), Anantnag dist., SW central Kashmir, in Vale of Kashmir, 14 mi. SSE of Anantnag; rice, corn, oilseeds, wheat. Jhelum R. rises in a near-by spring (anc. Hindu pilgrimage center) at N foot of Banihal Pass; spring is surrounded by octagonal basin, started c.1610 by Jahangir, who also built the gardens which later became his favorite retreat; has inscriptions of Jahangir and Shah Jehan.

Vernagt Glacier (fûrnäkt′), Tyrol, W Austria, in Ötztal Alps, S of the Wildspitze; noted for rapid movement.

Vernal (vûr′nŭl), city (pop. 2,845), ⊙ Uintah co., NE Utah, on small affluent of Green R. and 125 mi. E of Salt Lake City; alt. 5,315 ft. Trade and processing center for ranching and agr. area; dairy products, flour, leather goods, lumber. Coal mines and petroleum shows near by. Ashley Natl. Forest is N, in Uinta Mts.; Dinosaur Natl. Monument is 12 mi. E. Inc. 1879. Known as Ashley Center until 1893.

Vernal Falls, Calif.: see YOSEMITE NATIONAL PARK.

Vernam Field, U.S. airfield, Clarendon parish, S Jamaica, 6 mi. SW of May Pen, 33 mi. WSW of Kingston.

Vernarède, La (lä vĕrnärĕd′), village (pop. 579), Gard dept., S France, 12 mi. NNW of Alès; coal mining.

Vernayaz (vĕrnäyäs′), village (pop. 987), Valais canton, SW Switzerland, near the Rhone, 3 mi. N of Martigny-Ville; hydroelectric plant. N 1 mi. is Pissevache, a cascade 215 ft. high on short Salanfe R.

Verndale, village (pop. 576), Wadena co., W central Minn., c.40 mi. W of Brainerd dairy products.

Vernes, Norway: see STJORDAL.

Vernet or **Vernet-les-Bains** (vĕrnā′-lā-bē′), village (pop. 1,033), Pyrénées-Orientales dept., S France, at foot of Mont Canigou, 5 mi. SSW of Prades; resort with hot sulphur springs. Fruit and vegetable shipping. Iron mining.

Verneuil or **Verneuil-sur-Avre** (vĕrnû′ē-sür-ä′vrü), town (pop. 3,796), Eure dept., NW France, on the Avre and 22 mi. SSW of Évreux; road and market center in apple-growing area; foundries. Has old Norman houses. Fortified (12th cent.) by Henry I of England. Damaged in Second World War.

Vernier (vĕrnyā′), town (pop. 3,356), Geneva canton, SW Switzerland, on the Rhone and 4 mi. W of Geneva; metalworking, chemicals. Verbois hydroelectric plant is near by.

Vernole (vĕr′nôlĕ), village (pop. 2,342), Lecce prov., Apulia, S Italy, 9 mi. SE of Lecce.

Vernoleninsk, Ukrainian SSR: see NIKOLAYEV, city, Nikolayev oblast.

Vernon, city (pop. 5,209), S B.C., near N end of Okanagan L., 190 mi. ENE of Vancouver; fruit-growing center, with packing and dehydrating plants; woodworking; mfg. of cement, electrical appliances.

Vernon (vĕrnō′), town (pop. 10,033), Eure dept., NW France, port on left bank of Seine R. and 16 mi. ENE of Évreux; road center; mfg. (dynamos, batteries, corrugated paper, footwear, dyes, cement); cider distilling, rubber vulcanizing, hardware mfg. Has 13th–15th-cent. church and a 12th-cent. tower. First meeting-place (1452) of the Estates of Normandy. Town center and suburb of Vernonnet (on right bank of the Seine) heavily damaged in 1940 and in 1944.

Vernon (vĕr′nôn), mountain in Greek Macedonia, bet. the Varnous (N) and Mouriki (S) massifs; rises to 6,982 ft. 9 mi. S of Phlorina. Also called Vitsi.

Vernon (vûr′nŭn). **1** Parish (□ 1,360; pop. 18,974), W La.; ⊙ Leesville. Bounded W by Sabine R., here forming Texas line; drained by Calcasieu R. Includes part of Kisatchie Natl. Forest. Agr. (corn, cotton, hay, sweet potatoes, peanuts) and stock raising. Lumber, naval stores; sand and gravel. Formed 1871. **2** County (□ 838; pop. 22,685), W Mo.; ⊙ Nevada. On Osage R. (N); drained by Little Osage and Marmaton rivers. Agr. (corn, wheat, oats), livestock, poultry; coal and asphalt pits, oil wells. Formed 1851. **3** County (□ 805; pop. 27,906), SW Wis., bounded W by the Mississippi (here forming Iowa and Minn. lines); ⊙ Viroqua. Drained by Kickapoo, Bad Axe, and Baraboo rivers. Dairying, tobacco growing, stock raising; processing of dairy products, lumber, tobacco. Formed 1851.

Vernon. **1** Town (pop. 791), ⊙ Lamar co., W Ala., 48 mi. NW of Tuscaloosa; cotton ginning. **2** Industrial city (pop. 432), Los Angeles co., S Calif., suburb just S of Los Angeles; meat packing (Union Stockyards), brewing, steel mfg., oil refining. Home building not now permitted here. **3** Town (pop. 10,115), Tolland co., N Conn., on Hockanum R. (water power) and 12 mi. NE of Hartford; agr. (dairy products, sweet potatoes, poultry, fruit, tobacco). Includes ROCKVILLE, village of Talcottville (textiles). Settled c.1726, inc. 1808. **4** City (pop. 610), Washington co., NW Fla., on Holmes Creek and 15 mi. SW of Chipley. **5** Village (pop. 243), Marion co., S central Ill., 19 mi. N of Centralia, in agr. area; ships pears, peaches. **6** Town (pop. 480), ⊙ Jennings co., SE Ind., on small Vernon Creek and 20 mi. NW of Madison, in agr. area. **7** Village (pop. 678), Shiawassee co., S central Mich., 18 mi. SW of Flint, in farm area; oil and gas fields. **8** Village (pop. 754), Oneida co., central N.Y., 11 mi. SSW of Rome; canned foods, feed, flour, machinery. **9** City (pop. 12,651), ⊙ Wilbarger co., N Texas, near Pease R., c.45 mi. WNW of Wichita Falls; highway, transportation, commercial center for rich oil and agr. (cotton, cattle, wheat) region; meat packing, cotton and cottonseed processing, flour milling, dairying. Tourist trade. Founded 1880 on Dodge City cattle trail; inc. 1890. **10** Village (pop. c.250), Tooele co., W central Utah, 20 mi. NW of Eureka; alt. 5,511 ft.; agr., ranching. **11** Town (pop. 712), Windham co., extreme SE Vt., on the Connecticut, just below Brattleboro; power dam here.

Vernon Center, village (pop. 344), Blue Earth co., S Minn., on Blue Earth R. and 16 mi. SSW of Mankato, in grain and livestock area; dairy products.

Vernonia (vûrnō'nyů), town (pop. 1,521), Columbia co., NW Oregon, c.35 mi. NW of Portland; lumber center; dairying. Inc. 1891.

Vernon Islands, coral group in Clarence Strait, bet. Melville Isl. and NW coast of Northern Territory, Australia, 8 mi. W of Cape Hotham. Comprise E.Isl. (largest; 5 mi. long), N.W.Isl., S.W.Isl., and several islets. Mangroves, eucalyptus.

Vernoux (vĕrnōō'), village (pop. 1,241), Ardèche dept., S France, 11 mi. N of Privas; silk throwing and spinning; chestnut and walnut trade.

Verny (vĕrnē'), village (pop. 235), Moselle dept., NE France, 8 mi. S of Metz.

Verny, Kazakh SSR: see ALMA-ATA, city.

Vero Beach (vēr'ō), city (pop. 4,746), ⊙ Indian River co., central Fla., 15 mi. N of Fort Pierce and on Indian R. lagoon; major shipping center for citrus fruit; resort. Near by are the noted McKee Jungle Gardens. Founded c.1888, inc. 1919 as Vero, renamed 1925.

Veröce, Yugoslavia: see VIROVITICA.

Verodunum, France: see VERDUN.

Veroia or **Verroia** (both: vĕ'rēů), Macedonian *Ber*, anc. *Berea* or *Beroea* (both: bērē'ů), city (pop. 18,898), ⊙ Hematheia nome, Macedonia, Greece, on railroad and 40 mi. W of Salonika, at E foot of the Vermion; textile-milling center (cotton, wool, silk); trade in wheat, vegetables, watermelons. Hydroelectric plant (N); lignite mining near by. Flourished during Roman era when Paul and Silas preached here (Acts 17.10.). Conquered 1361 by Turks, who called it Karaferia or Karaferieh. Also spelled Veria and Verria.

Verolanuova (vĕrô"länwô'vä), town (pop. 4,604), Brescia prov., Lombardy, N Italy, near Oglio R., 13 mi. NNE of Cremona; silk and wax industries.

Verolavecchia (vĕrô"lävĕk'kyä), village (pop. 2,732), Brescia prov., Lombardy, N Italy, 1 mi. W of Verolanuova; agr. center.

Veroli (vä'rôlē), anc. *Verulae*, town (pop. 2,943), Frosinone prov., Latium, S central Italy, 5 mi. N of Frosinone; matches, sulphur oils. Bishopric.

Verona (vůrō'nů, It. vĕrô'nä), province (□ 1,196; pop. 585,893), Veneto, N Italy; ⊙ Verona. Borders on Lago di Garda (W); mtn. terrain in N, including Monte Baldo and Monti Lessini ranges. Fertile Po plain in S, irrigated by Adige and Tartaro rivers. Agr. (cereals, sugar beets, tobacco, castor beans); livestock (cattle, horses). Quarries (marble, limestone) in Monti Lessini. Mfg. at Verona, Legnago, Bussolengo, Cologna Veneta.

Verona, city (pop. 84,862), ⊙ Verona prov., Veneto, N Italy, on Adige R. and 65 mi. W of Venice; 45°26'N 10°59'E. Commercial center; focal point for Brenner Pass road connecting N Italy and central Europe. Noted for its cereal market. Mfg. (agr. and industrial machinery, paper, pharmaceuticals, plastics, furniture, shoes, rope, (macaroni, flour); large printing trade. Bishopric. Has Roman amphitheater (largest extant after the Coliseum; now used for opera performances), church of San Zeno Maggiore (9th–13th cent.), Romanesque cathedral (12th–15th cent. damaged), Gothic church of Sant'Anastasia, 12th-cent. town hall, and many fine palaces, including 14th-cent. Della Scala palace. Has archaeological and art mus. An important Roman colony; later became seat of a Lombard duchy. In 12th cent. a leading city of the Lombard League and under Francesco (Cangrande) della Scala (13th cent.), reached the peak of its power. In 13th and 14th cent. torn by Guelph and Ghibelline strife symbolized in *Romeo and Juliet*. Fell to Milan in 1387; later ruled by Venice (1405–1797). Was a renowned center of art in 15th and 16th cent., with work by Giocondo, San Micheli, Vittorio Pisano, and Paolo Veronese (all b. here). Held by Austria almost continuously from 1797 to 1866; after 1814 its fortifications were strengthened and city became strongest point of the "Quadrilateral." Joined kingdom of Italy in 1866. In Second World War, heavily bombed (especially 1944–45) with considerable damage to industrial areas, many churches and palaces, and c.7,000 dwellings. The 10 bridges across Adige, including Ponte della Pietra, earliest of all surviving Roman bridges, and Ponte Scaligero (1354; being restored), together with the arsenal, were blown up by Germans in their retreat (April, 1945).

Verona. **1** Village (pop. 205), Grundy co., NE Ill., 30 mi. SW of Joliet, in agr. and bituminous-coal area. **2** Town (pop. 374), Hancock co., S Maine, on Verona Isl. (□ c.6), at mouth of Penobscot R., near Bucksport. **3** Town (pop. 589), Lee co., NE Miss., 4 mi. S of Tupelo, in agr. area. **4** Town (pop. 396), Lawrence co., SW Mo., in the Ozarks, on Spring R. and 32 mi. SW of Springfield; ships strawberries. **5** Borough (pop. 10,921), Essex co., NE N.J., 7 mi. NNW of Newark, near Montclair; mfg. (metal products, brushes, soap, stationery); dairy products. Inc. 1907. **6** Village (pop. 189), La Moure co., SE N.Dak., 11 mi. E of La Moure. **7** Village (pop. 426), on Preble-Montgomery co. line, W Ohio, 20 mi. WNW of Dayton, in agr. area. **8** Borough (pop. 4,325), Allegheny co., SW Pa., NE suburb of Pittsburgh on Allegheny R.; chemicals, railroad equipment. Inc. 1871. **9** Village (pop. 748), Dane co., S Wis., 10 mi. SW of Madison, in dairying region.

Verona Park, village (pop. 1,342), Calhoun co., S Mich.

Verônica (bärō'nĕkä), town (pop. 2,659), E Buenos Aires prov., Argentina, near the Punta Piedras, 25 mi. SSE of Magdalena; fruit, poultry, livestock.

Verovka (vyĕ'rŭfkŭ), town (1939 pop. over 2,000), E Stalino oblast, Ukrainian SSR, in the Donbas, 2 mi. NW of Yenakiyevo; coal mines.

Verpillière, La (lä vĕrpēâr'), village (pop. 1,381), Isère dept., SE France, near the Bourbre, 17 mi. SE of Lyons; metal chroming; agr. equipment mfg. Sugar-beet and winegrowing. Iron deposits near by.

Verplanck (vûrplăngk'), residential village (1940 pop. 1,127), Westchester co., SE N.Y., on E bank of the Hudson and 3 mi. SW of Peekskill; crushed limestone.

Verquin (vĕrkē'), S suburb (pop. 2,400), of Béthune, Pas-de-Calais dept., N France, with important coal mines.

Verran, Norway: see FOLLAFOSS.

Verres (vĕr-rĕs'), village (pop. 2,076), Val d'Aosta region, NW Italy, near Dora Baltea R., 19 mi. ESE of Aosta; ironworks, chemical plant, mills (woolen, rayon). Has medieval castle (built 1360–90; recently restored). Copper, quartz mines near by.

Verret, Lake (vůrĕt'), Assumption parish, SE La., 7 mi. W of Napoleonville; c.10 mi. long; fishing. Canals and bayous join it to other waterways of Atchafalaya R. basin.

Verrettes (vĕrĕt'), agr. town (1950 census pop. 1,541), Artibonite dept., central Haiti, on Artibonite R. and 16 mi. ESE of Saint-Marc, on railroad; coffee, bananas.

Verria, Greece: see VEROIA.

Verrières, Les (lā–), village (pop. 1,191), Neuchâtel canton, W Switzerland, on Fr. border, opposite Verrières-de-Joux, 12 mi. NW of Yverdon in the E Jura; dairying, sawmilling.

Verrières-de-Joux (vĕrēâr' dů zhōō'), village (pop. 372), Doubs dept., E France, on Swiss border, opposite Les Verrières, 4 mi. E of Pontarlier, in the E Jura; clock and bicycle accessories.

Verrières-le-Buisson (-lů-bwēsõ'), town (pop. 2,948), Seine-et-Oise dept., N central France, a SSW suburb of Paris, 8 mi. from Notre Dame Cathedral; toy mfg. Botanical garden. Just NW is the Bois de Verrières.

Ver River, Hertford, England, rises 4 mi. S of Luton, flows 11 mi. SE and S, past St. Albans, to Colne R. 4 mi. NE of Watford.

Verro, Estonia: see VORU.

Verroia, Greece: see VEROIA.

Versailles (vûrsālz', Fr. vĕrsī'), city (pop. 63,114), ⊙ Seine-et-Oise dept., N central France, 11 mi. WSW of Paris; a leading tourist attraction in metropolitan area. Has metalworks and a natl. agr. research station. Laid out on a regular plan, its 3 main avenues converge on the Place d'Armes facing the palace. The huge château, consisting of a central square flanked by 3 wings, represents Fr. 1661–82 classic style at its height. Built by Le Vau, Mansart, and Le Brun, it is famous for its marble court and lavishly decorated interior (notably the gall. of mirrors, royal chambers, galleries containing valuable paintings and sculptures). It has become the model for hundreds of imitations. The park, laid out by Le Nôtre in a symmetrical neo-classical pattern, contains fountains, reservoirs and sculptures, grottoes and numerous decorative structures. NW of the palace are 2 smaller castles, the Grand and Petit Trianon, the latter a favorite residence of Marie Antoinette. The sumptuous water displays for which Versailles was famous during the reigns of Louis XIV and XV were supplied by a huge water machine built at Marley-le-Roi (4 mi. NNW). Versailles was a mere village when, in 1629, Louis XIII built a lodge there. Selected as site of the new palace, it grew into a prosperous administrative and commercial center after Louis XIV moved his court here. Originally built at a staggering cost (which caused general resentment), the palace was remodeled by Louis XV. It witnessed beginnings of French revolution and ceased to be a royal residence in 1790 (when it was replaced by the Tuileries in Paris). Made a natl. monument and mus. by Louis Philippe. Palace was the scene of proclamation of German empire (1871) and of Third French Republic (1875), and was traditionally used for joint meetings of the legislature. Here, in 1919, the peace treaty of Versailles was signed. Armored proving grounds of Fr. army established (1949) at Satory camp (just S).

Versailles (vûrsālz'). **1** Village, Conn.: see SPRAGUE. **2** Town (pop. 472), Brown co., W Ill., near Illinois R., 24 mi. WNW of Jacksonville, in agr. and bituminous-coal area. **3** Town (pop. 886), ⊙ Ripley co., SE Ind., c.40 mi. SE of Shelbyville, in agr. area; limestone quarries. **4** City (pop. 2,760), ⊙ Woodford co., central Ky., 13 mi. W of Lexington, in Bluegrass agr. region (burley tobacco, bluegrass seed, livestock, dairy products, poultry, hemp). Mfg. of whisky, clothing, boats, brooms; flour and feed milling. Seat of Margaret Hall (girls' school). Near by are Pisgah Presbyterian Church (1812), home (built 1784) of father of John Marshall, and "Woodburn" and other noted Bluegrass horse farms. Founded 1792. **5** City (pop. 1,929), ⊙ Morgan co., central Mo., near L. of the Ozarks, 38 mi. WSW of Jefferson City; tourist center, trout fisheries; farm trade; coal, timber. Founded c.1835. **6** Village (pop. 1,812), Darke co., W Ohio, 11 mi. NE of Greenville, in agr. area (poultry, grain, fruit, tobacco, truck); overalls, cement blocks, fertilizer. Settled 1819, inc. 1855. **7** Residential borough (pop. 2,484), Allegheny co., SW Pa., on Youghiogheny R. just above McKeesport; pig iron, railroad equipment. Inc. 1892.

Versalles (bĕrsä'yĕs), town (pop. 1,940), Valle del Cauca dept., W Colombia, in Cordillera Occidental, 24 mi. SW of Cartago; alt. 6,233 ft.; coffee, tobacco, sugar cane, cereals, livestock.

Versalles, N residential section of Matanzas, Matanzas prov., W Cuba.

Versec, Yugoslavia: see VRSAC.

Vershina Darasuna, Russian SFSR: see DARASUN.

Vershino-Shakhtaminski or **Vershino-Shakhtaminskiy** (vyĭrshē"nů-shŭkhtŭmĕn'skē), town (1948 pop. over 500), S Chita oblast, Russian SFSR, in Nerchinsk Range, 28 mi. N of Aleksandrovski Zavod; gold and molybdenum mining.

Vershire (vûr'shēr), town (pop. 284), Orange co., E Vt., on Ompompanoosuc R. and 18 mi. SE of Barre. Abandoned copper mines here produced heavily in late 19th cent.

Versmold (fĕrs'môlt), town (pop. 4,953), in former Prussian prov. of Westphalia, NW Germany, after 1945 in North Rhine-Westphalia, 17 mi. E of Bielefeld; grain; hog raising.

Versoix (vĕrswä'), town (pop. 2,114), Geneva canton, SW Switzerland, on L. Geneva, at mouth of short Versoix R., and 5 mi. N of Geneva; paper, flour, chocolate.

Vers-sur-Selle (vâr-sür-sĕl'), village (pop. 470), Somme dept., N France, 5 mi. SSW of Amiens; forges.

Verstanklahorn (fĕrshtäng"lähôrn'), peak (10,830 ft.) in Silvretta Group of Rhaetian Alps, E Switzerland, E of Klosters.

Ver-sur-Mer (vâr-sür-mâr'), village (pop. 613), Calvados dept., NW France, resort near Channel coast, 9 mi. NE of Bayeux; beach 1 mi. N. Heavily damaged 1944 during Normandy invasion (Br. landing area) in Second World War.

Vert, Cape, Fr. West Africa: see VERDE, CAPE.

Vertaison (vĕrtäzõ'), village (pop. 1,253), Puy-de-Dôme dept., central France, 9 mi. E of Clermont-Ferrand; mfg. of prefabricated houses.

Verte, Île (ēlvârt'), or **Green Island** (8 mi. long, 1 mi. wide) in the St. Lawrence, SE Que., 12 mi. NNE of Rivière du Loup; 48°2'N 69°26'W.

Verteillac (vĕrtĕyäk'), village (pop. 309), Dordogne dept., SW France, 7 mi. N of Ribérac; cattle, truffles. Parchment factory at Saint-Paul-Lizonne, 5 mi. SW.

Verteneglio (vĕrtĕnĕ'lyō), Slovenian *Brtonigla* (bûr'tônĕglä), village (pop. 2,473), S Free Territory of Trieste, 2 mi. SW of Buie. Bauxite deposits (W). Placed 1947 under Yugoslav administration.

Vertentes (vĕrtĕn'tĭs), city (pop. 1,545), E Pernambuco, NE Brazil, on S slope of Serra dos Carirís Velhos, 36 mi. W of Limoeiro; cotton, coffee growing; cattle raising.

Vertes (vär'tĕsh), Hung. *Vértes*, town (pop. 2,683), Bihar co., E Hungary, 14 mi. SE of Debrecen; wheat, hemp, hogs.

Vertes Mountains (vär′tĕsh), Hung. *Vértes,* N central Hungary, extend 25 mi. NE from Mor; average alt. 1,560 ft. Deposits of bauxite (at Gant), lignite (at Tatabanya), limestone (at Felsögalla). SW slope forested. Ruins at Mt. Csoka, Hung. *Csókahegy* and at Mt. Gesztes attract many tourists.

Vertientes or **Central Vertientes** (sĕnträl′ bĕrtyĕn′tĕs), sugar-mill village (pop. 2,676), Camagüey prov., E Cuba, 18 mi. WSW of Camagüey.

Vertova (vĕr′tôvä), village (pop. 3,038), Bergamo prov., Lombardy, N Italy, on Serio R. and 12 mi. NE of Bergamo; cotton and woolen mills.

Vertus (vĕrtü′), town (pop. 2,156), Marne dept., N France, 10 mi. SSE of Épernay; winegrowing center (champagne). Its 12th-cent. church severely damaged in Second World War.

Vertyuzhany (vyĕrtyo͝ozhä′nē), Rum. *Vartejeni* (värtĕzhĕn′), village (1941 pop. 1,887), NE Moldavian SSR, on Dniester R. and 16 mi. SE of Soroki, in fruitgrowing area; flour and oilseed milling.

Verulamium, England: see SAINT ALBANS.

Verushov, Poland: see WIERUSZOW.

Verviers (vĕrvyā′), town (pop. 40,422), Liége prov., E Belgium, on Vesdre R. and 13 mi. E of Liége; wool-combing and weaving center; leather tanning; mfg. (shoes, leatherware, machine tools, felt and wool hats, chocolate).

Vervins (vĕrvē′), town (pop. 2,512), Aisne dept., N France, 22 mi. NE of Laon; agr. trade center. Former ⊙ of Thiérache dist. By treaty signed here in 1598, Philip II of Spain and duke of Savoy recognized Henry IV as king of France.

Verwood, town and parish (pop. 1,605), E Dorset, England, 7 mi. NE of Wimborne Minster; agr. market; pottery works.

Verzasca River (vĕrtsä′skä), stream in Ticino canton, S Switzerland, flowing S to Lago Maggiore.

Verzegnis, Monte (môn′tĕ vĕrtsā′nyēs), peak (6,283 ft.) in S Carnic Alps, N Italy, 6 mi. SW of Tolmezzo.

Verzenay (vĕrznā′), village (pop. 1,193), Marne dept., N France, on NE slope of the Montagne de Reims, 9 mi. SSE of Rheims; winegrowing (champagne).

Verzhbnik, Poland: see WIERZBNIK.

Verzhbolovo, Lithuania: see VIRBALIS.

Verzuolo (vĕrtswô′lô), village (pop. 2,132), Cuneo prov., Piedmont, NW Italy, 3 mi. S of Saluzzo; large paper mill. Has castle dating from 1377.

Verzy (vĕrzē′), village (pop. 922), Marne dept., N France, on E slopes of the Montagne de Reims, 10 mi. SE of Rheims; winegrowing (champagne).

Vescles (vĕ′sklü), village (pop. 94), Jura dept., E France, in the central Jura, 12 mi. WSW of Saint-Claude; hydroelectric plant on the Ain.

Vescovato (vĕskôvä′tô), village (pop. 1,061), NE Corsica, 14 mi. S of Bastia; goat-cheese mfg., winegrowing; limes. Refuge of Murat after his exile from Kingdom of Naples in 1815.

Vescovato, town (pop. 3,092), Cremona prov., Lombardy, N Italy, 8 mi. NW of Cremona; silk mills, brush factories.

Vesdre River (vĕz′drü), Ger. *Weser* (vā′zür), E Belgium, rises on Ger. frontier 8 mi. ESE of Eupen, flows 40 mi. W and NW, past Eupen, Limburg, Verviers, and Pepinster, to Ourthe R. at Angleur. Wool-mfg. centers concentrated along its banks W of Verviers.

Veseli nad Luznici (vĕ′sĕlē näd′ lo͝ozh″nyĭchĕ), Czech *Veselí nad Lužnicí,* Ger. *Frohenbruck* (frō′ůnbro͝ok), town (pop. 1,574), S Bohemia, Czechoslovakia, on Luznice R. and 17 mi. NNE of Budweis; fresh-water fishing; barley and potato growing. Has folk art mus. Across the Luznice is rail center of Mezimosti nad Nezarkou, part of urban area of Veseli.

Veseli nad Moravou (mô″rävō), Czech *Veselí nad Moravou,* Ger. *Wesseli* (vĕ′sĕlē), town (pop. 4,281), SE Moravia, Czechoslovakia, on Morava R., and 23 mi. SW of Gottwaldov, in agr. area (barley, wheat, sugar beets, grapes); rail junction.

Veselinovo (vyĕsĭlyē′nůvů), village (1939 pop. over 500), W Nikolayev oblast, Ukrainian SSR, 15 mi. SSW of Voznesensk; cotton ginning, metalworking.

Veselovskoye (vĕsyĭlôf′skůyů), village (1939 pop. over 2,000), SW Novosibirsk oblast, Russian SFSR, 33 mi. NE of Karasuk; dairy farming.

Veseloye (vĭsyô′lůyů), village (1926 pop. 7,464), W Zaporozhe oblast, Ukrainian SSR, 23 mi. NW of Melitopol; dairying.

Vesely or **Veselyy** (vĭsyô′lē), village (1939 pop. over 500), S Rostov oblast, Russian SFSR, on the Western Manych (earth dam, locks) and 50 mi. ESE of Rostov; flour mill; wheat, sunflowers.

Veshenskaya (vyĕ′shĭnskīů), village (1926 pop. 2,943), NE Rostov oblast, Russian SFSR, on left bank of Don R. and 26 mi. ESE of Kazanskaya; wheat, sunflowers, livestock. Phosphorite deposits. Pop. largely Cossack.

Veshkaima or **Veshkayma** (vyĕshkīmä′), village (1926 pop. 4,050), NW Ulyanovsk oblast, Russian SFSR, 30 mi. NE of Inza; distilling, dairying; grain.

Vesijärvi (vĕ′sĭyär″vē), N suburb and port of Lahti, Häme co., S Finland, at S end of Päijänne lake system.

Vésinet, Le (lů vāzēnā′), town (pop. 12,541), Seine-et-Oise dept., N central France, a residential outer suburb of Paris, 10 mi. WNW of Notre Dame Cathedral, in a Seine R. bend and 2 mi. E of Saint-Germain-en-Laye; mfg. (light metal goods, electrical equipment, fountain pens, optical glass). Lies in a park.

Vesique, Puerto, Peru: see PUERTO SAMANCO.

Vesite, Latvia: see VIESITE.

Vesle River (vāl), Marne and Aisne depts., N France, rises in the Champagne badlands ENE of Châlons-sur-Marne, flows 89 mi. NW, past Rheims and Fismes, to the Aisne 6 mi. E of Soissons. Severe fighting took place along its banks in Aug.-Sept., 1918.

Vesontio, France: see BESANÇON.

Vesotsane, Greece: see XEROPOTAMOS.

Vesoul (vůzo͞ol′), town (pop. 10,744), ⊙ Haute-Saône dept., E France, 28 mi. NNE of Besançon; road center and important agr. market (cattle, grain, dairy produce). Lace and dye mfg. Chapel atop conical La Motte hill (1,483 ft.), just N, was severely damaged during Second World War.

Vesper, village (pop. 342), Wood co., central Wis., 8 mi. NW of Wisconsin Rapids; dairy products, lumber, brick.

Vespolate (vĕspôlä′tĕ), village (pop. 2,283), Novara prov., Piedmont, N Italy, 7 mi. S of Novara; cotton and woolen mills.

Vespucio (bĕspo͞o′syō), town (pop. estimate 500), N Salta prov., Argentina, on railroad and 45 mi. NE of Orán; lumbering and stock-raising center; sawmills. Oil wells near by.

Vesta (bĕ′stä), village, Limón prov., E Costa Rica, on Estrella R. and 19 mi. SSE of Limón; terminus of banana plantation railroad.

Vesta, village (pop. 340), Redwood co., SW Minn., on Redwood R. and 15 mi. W of Redwood Falls, in grain, livestock, poultry area; dairy products.

Vestaburg, village (pop. 1,046), Washington co., SW Pa., on Monongahela R. and 17 mi. SE of Washington.

Vest-Agder (vĕst′äg′dür), county [Nor. *fylke*] (□ 2,815; pop. 93,980), S Norway; ⊙ KRISTIANSAND. Includes highland area bet. Ruven Mts. (N) and the North Sea; traversed by several rivers (notably the Audna, Lygna, Sira, Kvina) flowing S to North Sea and the Skagerrak. Most of co. is wooded, agr. being restricted to lower river valleys and flat peninsulas; active river and sea fishing; molybdenum mines; timber is milled in coastal cities. Fish, lumber, wood products, leather goods, agr. and dairy goods are exported. Pop., concentrated near coast, contains a number of repatriated Norwegian-Americans. Well-developed road net, but only a single railroad (with one branch line). Main centers: Kristiansand, Mandal, Farsund, Flekkefjord. Until 1918, co. (then called *amt*) was named Lister og Mandals.

Vestal, village (pop. c.6,000), Broome co., S N.Y., on the Susquehanna, opposite Endicott, and 7 mi. W of Binghamton; sand, gravel; concrete blocks.

Vestby (vĕst′bü), village (pop. 447; canton pop. 3,711), Akershus co., SE Norway, near E shore of Oslo Fjord narrows, 6 mi. SE of Drobak; fox-fur farming, sawmilling.

Vesteralen (vĕs′tůr-ôlůn), Nor. *Vesterålen,* archipelago (□ c.1,200; pop. c.50,000) in Norwegian Sea, in Nordland and Troms counties, N Norway, WSW of Narvik, and just N of the Lofoten Isls., of which they are sometimes considered a part; 68°16′–69°19′N 14°18′–16°47′E. Includes HINNOY (largest isl. in Norway), Langoy, Andoy, Hadseloy, and several smaller isls. Surrounding waters provide one of Norway's best fishing grounds (cod, haddock, halibut, herring, eels). Sometimes spelled Vesteraalen.

Vesteral Fjord (vĕs′tůr-ŏl), Nor. *Vesterålsfjord,* inlet (18 mi. long, 1–4 mi. wide) of Norwegian Sea on SW coast of Langoy (Vesteralen group), Nordland co., N Norway. Eidsfjord village on SE shore. Sometimes called Eidsfjord.

Vesteras, Sweden: see VASTERAS.

Vesterbotten, Sweden: see VASTERBOTTEN.

Vesterbygd, anc. Norse settlement, Greenland: see GREENLAND.

Vesternorrland, Sweden: see VASTERNORRLAND.

Vestervik, Sweden: see VASTERVIK.

Vestfjarda Peninsula (vĕst′fyär″dhä), Icelandic *Vestfjarða,* NW Iceland, extends 80 mi. NW into Denmark Strait; 65°24′–66°28′N 21°18′–24°32′W. Connected with mainland by 6-mi.-wide isthmus bet. Breidi Fjord and Huna Bay, peninsula widens to 90 mi. in NW part. Mountainous, rising to 3,140 ft.; in NW is Drangajokull, glacier (3,035 ft.). Numerous fjords, largest Isafjardardjup (NW). Isafjordur town is commercial center of region; fishing.

Vest Fjord (vĕst), inlet (100 mi. long) of the North Sea, N Norway, bet. mainland (E) and Lofoten Isls. (W). It is 50 mi. wide at mouth, becomes gradually narrower. Ofot Fjord (ENE) and Tys Fjord (SE) are main arms. Fjord and adjacent waters were scene (1940) of repeated naval action on approaches to Narvik.

Vestfold (vĕst′fôl), county [Nor. *fylke*] (□ 903; pop. 147,555), SE Norway, bordering on W shore of Oslo Fjord; ⊙ Tonsberg. Broken terrain, rising in N to 2,070 ft. Fishing, whaling, agr., dairying, lumbering. Chief cities: Tonsberg, Larvik, Horten, Sandefjord, Holmestrand. Before 1918, co. (then called *amt*) was named Jarlsberg og Larvik.

Vestfossen (vĕst′fôs-sůn), village (pop. 626) in Ovre Eiker (Nor. *Øvre Eiker*) canton (pop. 11,011), Buskerud co., SE Norway, on short Vestfoss R. (falls), on railroad and 12 mi. W of Drammen; wood-pulp and cellulose milling; hydroelectric plant.

Vestmanland, Sweden: see VASTMANLAND.

Vestmannaeyjar (vĕst′mänää″är), group of 14 islands of volcanic origin a few miles off S Iceland, 70 mi. SE of Reykjavik; 63°23′N 20°20′W. Only largest isl., Heimaey (hā′mää″), 3 mi. long, is inhabited; on its NE coast is city of Vestmannaeyjar (pop. 3,548), a fishing port. The other islets are nesting grounds of a variety of waterfowl. Group was raided (1627) by Algerian pirates who burned settlement and carried 250 people into slavery. Group also called Westman Isls.

Vestnes (vĕst′nās), village and canton (pop. 3,506), More og Romsdal co., W Norway, at mouth of Tres Fjord (a S arm of Molde Fjord), 32 mi. ENE of Alesund; agr., and fisheries. Mfg. of clothing at villages of Vike, 3 mi. ESE on opposite shore of fjord, and at Tomra, 6 mi. SW. Formerly spelled Vestnaes.

Vestone (vĕstô′nĕ), village (pop. 1,166), Brescia prov., Lombardy, N Italy, on Chiese R. and 15 mi. NNE of Brescia; ironworks; mfg. (agr. machinery, automatic pencils, metalworking tools).

Vestre Gausdal, Norway: see AULSTAD.

Vestre Jakobselv (vĕs′trů yä′kôps-ĕlv), fishing village (pop. 576) in Nord-Varanger canton (pop. 1,945), Finnmark co., NE Norway, on N shore of Varanger Fjord, 10 mi. WNW of Vadso.

Vestspitsbergen, Spitsbergen: see WEST SPITSBERGEN.

Vestur-Skaftafell (vĕ′stür-skäf′täfĕ″tůl), county [Icelandic *sýsla*] (pop. 1,466), S Iceland; ⊙ Vik i Myrdal. Extends along low coast bet. Myrdalsjokull (W) and Vatnajokull (E), include Dyrholaey, cape at S extremity of Iceland, and Laki volcano. Sheep raising, fishing.

Vestvagoy (vĕst′vôg-ûü), Nor. *Vestvågøy,* island (□ 159; pop. 12,272) in North Sea, one of Lofoten Isls., Nordland co., N Norway, 10 mi. W of Svolvaer; 23 mi. long, 10 mi. wide; rises to 3,064 ft. (W). Chief fishing villages are Ballstad (SW) and Stamsund (S). Sometimes spelled Vestvaago.

Vésubie River (vāzübē′), in Alpes-Maritimes dept., SE France, rises in Maritime Alps near Saint-Martin-Vésubie, flows c.25 mi. S to the Var near Levens. Hydroelectric plants.

Vesunna, France: see PÉRIGUEUX.

Vesuvius (vůso͞o′vēůs), Ital. *Vesuvio* (vĕzo͞o′vyô), only active volcano (alt. 3,891 ft.) on European mainland, in Campania, S Italy, on E shore of Bay of Naples, 8 mi. ESE of Naples; 40°49′N 14°26′E. Rises at 10° angle from the bay to the cone, where the gradient increases to 30°-35°. Descends on N and E sides to the plain, with 3° slope from Monte SOMMA (3,714 ft.), a semicircular ridge which half encircles the cone. Sides deeply scarred by lava flows. Bet. cone and Monte Somma is a deep, steep-walled valley (c.3 mi. long, ⅓ mi. wide), Atrio del Cavallo. On W slope, at 1,995 ft., lies seismological observatory (built 1840–45), reached by road and electric railway from Resina. Railway continues to foot of cone, where a funicular ascends almost to verge of crater (diameter c.2,300 ft.). Base of mtn. has circumference of c.45 mi.; encircled by panoramic railroad. On its fertile, lower slopes (below c.1,950 ft.) are grown grapes of the famous Lachryma Christi wine, citrus fruit, vegetables, nuts. Stock raising also important. Earliest recorded eruption occurred in A.D. 79, destroying Pompeii, Herculaneum, and Stabiae. In 1631 Boscotrecase, Torre Annunziata, Torre del Greco, Resina, and Portici, situated along present panoramic railroad, were destroyed. Subsequent severe eruptions occurred in 1779, 1794, 1822, 1872, 1906, and 1929. The eruption in 1944 destroyed San Sebastiano al Vesuvio. On each occasion the cone was altered, so that the height of mtn. has varied several hundred ft., usually averaging about 4,000 ft.

Vesyegonsk or **Ves'yegonsk** (vĕsyĭgônsk′), town (1926 pop. 3,995), NE Kalinin oblast, Russian SFSR, port on Rybinsk Reservoir, 65 mi. NNE of Bezhetsk; rail-spur terminus; distilling center; linen mill.

Veszprem (vĕsp′rām), Hung. *Veszprém,* county (□ 1,646; pop. 279,749), NW central Hungary; ⊙ Veszprem. Heavily forested Bakony Mts. give way (S) to valley of L. Balaton; drained by Sio and Torna rivers. Extensive agr. (potatoes, corn, rye, flax, sugar beets) in NW; orchards, vineyards near L. Balaton; livestock in mts. Industry at Veszprem, Varpalota, Papa. Manganese and bauxite are mined. Many resorts on L. Balaton (Balatonfüred, Siofok, Tihany).

Veszprem, Hung. *Veszprém,* city (pop. 21,557), ⊙ Veszprem co., W central Hungary, 60 mi. SW of Budapest, on S slope of Bakony Mts.; rail and market center; mfg. (textiles, wine, vegetable oil); brickworks. Truck farming in area. Created bishopric by St. Stephen in 1001; its 14th–16th-cent. cathedral built on foundations erected in 12th cent. Dominican monastery dates from 1221. A tall minaret is memento of Turkish rule. Mus. has ethnographical collection.

Veszpremvarsany (vĕsp'rāmvŏr-shänyŭ), Hung. *Veszprémvarsány*, town (pop. 1,307), Veszprem co., NW Hungary, 20 mi. SE of Györ; rail junction; flour mills.

Vesztö (väs'tû), Hung. *Vésztő*, town (pop. 10,597) Bekes co., SE Hungary, 19 mi. NNE of Bekescsaba; flour mills; wheat, corn, camomile, sheep.

Vetagrande (bātägrän'dā), town (pop. 587), Zacatecas, N central Mexico, on interior plateau, 5 mi. N of Zacatecas; alt. 8,668 ft. Silver mining; lead and copper deposits; maguey, cereals, stock.

Vetapalem or **Vetapalemu** (vā'tŭpŭlĕmōō), town (pop. 12,199), Guntur dist., NE Madras, India, in Kistna R. delta, 37 mi. SSW of Guntur; rice milling, hand-loom cotton weaving; tobacco, palmyra, betel palms.

Veta Pass, La, Colo.: see LA VETA.

Veteran, village (pop. 191), SE Alta., 60 mi. S of Wainwright; grain, mixed farming, dairying.

Veth River, Kashmir: see JHELUM RIVER.

Vetka (vyĕt'kŭ), city (1926 pop. 5,896), E Gomel oblast, Belorussian SSR, on Sozh R. and 13 mi. NE of Gomel; cotton textiles.

Vetlanda (vāt'län"dä), city (pop. 6,022), Jonkoping co., S Sweden, near Em R., 40 mi. SE of Jonkoping; rail junction; woolen milling, match mfg., metal- and woodworking. Scene of important stock fairs. Has 18th-cent. church, mus. Inc. 1920 as city.

Vetluga (vyĭtlōō'gŭ), city (1926 pop. 6,066), N Gorki oblast, Russian SFSR, on Vetluga R. (head of navigation) and 120 mi. NNE of Gorki; lumber center; sawmilling, distilling; wood chemicals (resin distillation). Chartered 1778.

Vetluga River, in central European Russian SFSR, rises E of Leninskoye (Kirov oblast) in the Northern Uvals, flows N, W, and generally S, past Vetluga, Varnavino, Krasnye Baki, and Voskresenskoye (Gorki oblast), to the Volga W of (opposite) Kozmodemyansk; 500 mi. long. Navigable for 220 mi. (lumber, grain).

Vetluzhski or **Vetluzhskiy** (vyĭtlōōsh'skē), town (1948 pop. over 2,000), central Gorki oblast, Russian SFSR, on Vetluga R., just N of Krasnye Baki and 70 mi. NE of Gorki; sawmilling, wood cracking.

Vetovo (vĕ'tôvô), village (pop. 4,981), Ruse dist., NE Bulgaria, 17 mi. ESE of Ruse; wheat, rye, sunflowers.

Vetralla (vĕträl'lä), town (pop. 3,416), Viterbo prov., Latium, central Italy, 7 mi. SSW of Viterbo; flour milling. Has cathedral and 11th-cent. church. Near by is Etruscan necropolis of Norchia. Damaged in Second World War.

Vetren (vĕ'trĕn), village (pop. 6,566), Plovdiv dist., W central Bulgaria, 15 mi. WNW of Pazardzhik; grain, rice, livestock, fruit, truck.

Vetrenka (vyĕt'rĭnkŭ), village (1939 pop. over 500), SW Mogilev oblast, Belorussian SSR, 27 mi. SSE of Mogilev; glass and peat works. Until c.1940, spelled Vetrinka.

Vetrina, Greece: see NEON PETRITSI.

Vetrino (vyĕ'trĭnŭ), village (1948 pop. over 500), central Polotsk oblast, Belorussian SSR, 13 mi. WSW of Polotsk, near former Pol. border; flax processing.

Vetschau (fĕ'chou), town (pop. 4,064), Brandenburg, E Germany, in Lower Lusatia, at SW edge of Spree Forest, 11 mi. W of Cottbus; woolen milling, metalworking.

Vetta d'Italia (vĕt'tä dētä'lyä), Alpine peak (9,550 ft.) and northernmost point (47°5'30"N) of Italy, on Austrian border, at head of Valle Aurina, 16 mi. NE of Campo Tures.

Vetter, Lake, Sweden: see VATTER, LAKE.

Vettisfoss (vĕt'tĭsfôs), waterfall (856 ft.) in Sogn og Fjordane co., W Norway, 27 mi. ENE of Sogndal.

Vettore, Monte (môn'tĕ vĕt-tô'rĕ), highest peak (8,130 ft.) of Monti Sibillini, central Italy, 16 mi. W of Ascoli Piceno.

Vetulonia (vĕtōōlô'nyä), village (pop. 791), Grosseto prov., Tuscany, central Italy, 10 mi. NW of Grosseto. An early Etruscan settlement, from which the Romans took their magisterial insignia: the fasces of the lictors, curule chair, purple toga, and brazen trumpets. Near by are necropolises.

Veules-les-Roses (vûl-lā-rōz'), village (pop. 705), Seine-Inférieure dept., N France, on English Channel, 13 mi. WSW of Dieppe; resort amidst chalk cliffs.

Veune Sai, Cambodia: see VOEUNE SAI.

Veurne, Belgium: see FURNES.

Vevay (vē'vā, vē'vē), town (pop. 1,309), ⊙ Switzerland co., SE Ind., on the Ohio and 15 mi. E of Madison; agr. (grain, livestock, truck, tobacco); dairy products, flour. Settled 1796 by Swiss; laid out 1813. Edward Eggleston was b. here.

Vevce, Yugoslavia: see MEDVODE.

Veve or **Vevi** (both: vĕ'vē), town (pop. 2,450), Phlorina nome, Macedonia, Greece, on railroad and 10 mi. E of Phlorina; lignite mining. Formerly called Banitsa.

Veverska Bityska (vĕ'vĕrskä bē'tĕshkä), Czech *Veverska Bítýška*, village (pop. 2,037), W Moravia, Czechoslovakia, on railroad and 10 mi. NW of Brno; lumbering; oats. Noted 11th-cent. castle of Veveri (vĕ'vĕrzhē), Czech *Veveří*, is 2 mi. SE.

Vevey (vûvā'), Ger. *Vivis* (vē'vĭs), town (1950 pop. 14,182), Vaud canton, W Switzerland, on L. Geneva, at mouth of short Veveyse R., 10 mi. ESE of Lausanne; resort with fine mtn. views. An old town (anc. *Viviscus*), it has a medieval church and a mus. Metal, leather, printing, woodworking industries; mfg. (shoes, tobacco, chocolate, fats). Railways connect it with mtn. resorts to N and E.

Vevi, Greece: see VEVE.

Vexin (vĕksē'), agr. region of NW France, along right bank of the Seine, comprised in NW Seine-et-Oise, SW Oise, and NE Eure depts. Subdivided, by Treaty of Saint-Clair-sur-Epte (911) into Vexin Normand (old ⊙ was Gisors), originally given to Rollo of Normandy, and Vexin Français (⊙ was Pontoise), which remained with Fr. crown.

Vexio, Sweden: see VAXJO.

Veyangoda (vāyŭng-gō'dŭ), village, Western Prov., Ceylon, 20 mi. NE of Colombo; coconut-desiccating factory; trades in coconut, rice, tea, rubber, graphite, vegetables. Near by is 2d-cent. B.C. Buddhist monastery and rock temple.

Veymarn, Russian SFSR: see VEIMARN.

Veynes (vĕn), town (pop. 3,055), Hautes-Alpes dept., SE France, on the Petit-Buëch and 13 mi. WSW of Gap; rail transfer point and shipping center; livestock market with slaughterhouses; mfg. (cement, cork soles). Orchards in area.

Veyras (vārä'), village (pop. 78), Ardèche dept., S France, 2 mi. W of Privas; iron mining.

Veyre-Monton (vâr-mōtō'), village (pop. 218), Puy-de-Dôme dept., central France, in the Limagne, 8 mi. SSE of Clermont-Ferrand; winegrowing. Troglodyte dwellings.

Veyrier-du-Lac (vārēā'-dü-läk'), village (pop. 214), Haute-Savoie dept., SE France, on NE shore of L. of Annecy, 3 mi. SE of Annecy; summer resort. Cable car to Mt. Baron (4,200 ft.; hotel) just E.

Veytaux, Switzerland: see MONTREUX.

Vezdemarbán (bāthdhāmärvän'), village (pop. 2,209), Zamora prov., NW Spain, 9 mi. NNE of Toro; mfg. (cotton and woolen textiles, chocolate).

Vézelay (vāzulā'), village (pop. 360), Yonne dept., N central France, on hill near Cure R., 8 mi. WSW of Avallon. Site of celebrated 12th-cent. abbatial church (Basilique de la Madeleine) restored by Viollet-le-Duc in 19th cent. Here St. Bernard preached 2d Crusade in 1146, and Richard I met Philip Augustus prior to 3d Crusade. Beza b. here.

Vézelise (vāzlēz'), village (pop. 1,158), Meurthe-et-Moselle dept., NE France, 15 mi. SSW of Nancy; brewery. Old town hall hit in Second World War.

Vézénobres (vāzānô'brŭ), village (pop. 543), Gard dept., S France, 6 mi. SSE of Alès; winegrowing, olive-oil pressing. Also spelled Vézenobres.

Vézère River (vāzâr'), Corrèze and Dordogne depts., S central France, rises in Plateau of Millevaches 5 mi. NW of Meymac, flows 119 mi. SW, past Uzerche, Terrasson, and Montignac, to the Dordogne 4 mi. below Le Bugue. Traverses a narrow gorge bet. Uzerche and Allassac; powers hydroelectric plant at Le Saillant. Receives the Corrèze 4 mi. W of Brive-la-Gaillarde.

Vezhen (vĕ'zhĕn), N central Bulgaria, peak (7,112 ft.) in Teteven Mts., 5 mi. NW of Klisura.

Vezins, village, Manche dept., France: see DUCEY.

Vezins-de-Lévézou (vüzē'-dü-lāvāzōō'), village (pop. 163), Aveyron dept., S France, in Lévézou range, 14 mi. NNW of Millau; sheep raising; supplies Roquefort with ewe's milk.

Vezirkopru (vĕzĭr'kûprü), Turkish *Vezirköprü*, town (pop. 5,497), Samsun prov., N Turkey, 45 mi. WSW of Samsun; corn, wheat, cotton.

Vezouze River (vüzōōz'), Meurthe-et-Moselle dept., NE France, rises in NW Vosges above Cirey, flows c.30 mi. W, past Blâmont, to the Meurthe at Lunéville. Also spelled Vezouse.

Vezzano (vĕtsä'nô), village (pop. 667), Trento prov., Trentino–Alto Adige, N Italy, 6 mi. W of Trent; foundry.

Vezzano Ligure (lē'gōōrĕ), village (pop. 1,922), La Spezia prov., Liguria, N Italy, near confluence of Magra and Vara rivers, 4 mi. NE of Spezia, in agr. region (cereals, grapes, olives).

Viacha (byä'chä), city (pop. c.23,200), ⊙ Ingavi prov., La Paz dept., W Bolivia, on high plateau, 16 mi. SW of La Paz; alt. 12,635 ft. Major rail and road center, at junction of lines from Guaqui, Arica (Chile), and Oruro to La Paz; industrial center; cement plant, flour mill, brewery; railroad shops.

Viadana, Belgian Congo: see EGBUNDA.

Viadana (vē"ädä'nä), town (pop. 4,755), Mantova prov., Lombardy, N Italy, on Po R. and 13 mi. NE of Parma; macaroni, alcohol, marmalade, brooms.

Viadène Plateau (vyädĕn'), in S Massif Central, S France, occupies N Aveyron dept.; bounded by the Truyère (N), the Lot (S and SW), and the Monts d'Aubrac (E). Average alt. 3,000 ft. Cattle, sheep. Cheese mfg. and slate quarrying.

Vialar (vyälär'), town (pop. 4,993), Alger dept., N central Algeria, on Sersou Plateau at S edge of the Tell Atlas (Ouarsenis Massif), 32 mi. NE of Tiaret; wheat-growing center.

Viale (byä'lā), town (pop. estimate 1,000), W Entre Ríos prov., Argentina, on railroad and 31 mi. ESE of Paraná; agr. center (flax, grain, cotton, livestock).

Via Mala (vē'ä mä'lä), narrow gorge of Hinterrhein R., S of its confluence with the Albula, in the Alps of Grisons canton, E Switzerland. It is walled by vertical cliffs 1,600 ft. high. The Splügen Road lies above the gorge.

Viamão (vyŭmä'ō), city (pop. 1,493), E Rio Grande do Sul, Brazil, 12 mi. ESE of Pôrto Alegre; rice, fruit, manioc. Has noteworthy old church. One of region's earliest 18th-cent. settlements, it was briefly (1763–73) ⊙ Rio Grande do Sul.

Viamonte (bēämōn'tā), town (pop. estimate 1,000), SE Córdoba prov., Argentina, 95 mi. SSE of Villa María; grain, livestock.

Vian (vīăn'), town (pop. 927), Sequoyah co., E Okla., 28 mi. SE of Muskogee, in agr. area (corn, cotton, alfalfa); cotton ginning, mfg. of handles. Tenkiller Ferry Reservoir is NW.

Viana (vyä'nŭ), city (pop. 3,660), N Maranhão, Brazil, 55 mi. SSW of São Luís; rice, cotton, babassu nuts, timber. Has noted church built by Jesuits. Formerly spelled Vianna.

Viana (byä'nä), city (pop. 2,571), Navarre prov., N Spain, 5 mi. NE of Logroño; olive-oil processing, mfg. of brandy and chocolate. Cereals and sheep in area. Title of prince of Viana was borne in Middle Ages by heir to kingdom of Navarre.

Viana do Alentejo (vyä'nŭ dōō älāntā'zhōō), town (pop. 3,428), Évora dist., S central Portugal, 17 mi. SSW of Évora; pottery mfg., winegrowing. Has church built c.1500 in Manueline style.

Viana do Castelo (kŭshtā'lōō), district (□ 814; pop. 258,596), Minho prov., northernmost Portugal; ⊙ Viana do Castelo. Bounded by the Atlantic (W) and by Spain (N and E), the lower Minho forming part of border. Drained by Lima R. Mountainous in E.

Viana do Castelo, anc. *Velobriga*, city (pop. 13,263), ⊙ Viana do Castelo dist., in Minho prov., northernmost Portugal, port on the Atlantic at mouth of Lima R. and 40 mi. N of Oporto; commercial center with important cod-fish trade (Great Banks fisheries). Mfg. (carpets, cordage, berets, flour products, chocolate). Port wine 1st shipped from here to England in 17th cent. Has several 16th–17th-cent. mansions, and a fort commanding river mouth, built by Philip II.

Vianden (vēän'dŭn) town (pop. 1,045), E Luxembourg, on Our R. and 8 mi. NE of Ettelbruck, at Ger. border; leather tanning and mfg.; market center for agr. (rye, oats) region. Has 13th-cent. church, 9th-cent. castle of Orange-Nassau. Suffered considerable damage in Second World War.

Vianen (vēä'nŭn), town (pop. 2,570), South Holland prov., W central Netherlands, on Lek R. and 7 mi. S of Utrecht, on Merwede Canal; mfg. (barrel hoops, bricks, roofing tiles), woodworking.

Vianna, Brazil: see VIANA.

Vianópolis (vyŭnô'pōōlēs), city (pop. 1,168), S Goiás, central Brazil, on railroad and 40 mi. SE of Anápolis; livestock, tobacco. Airfield. Formerly spelled Viannopolis.

Vianos (byä'nōs), town (pop. 1,553), Albacete prov., SE central Spain, 38 mi. SW of Albacete; livestock, cereals, fruit, vegetables.

Viapori, Finland: see SUOMENLINNA.

Viareggio (vē"ärĕd'jô), city (pop. 30,384), Lucca prov., Tuscany, central Italy, port on Ligurian Sea, 13 mi. WNW of Lucca. Rail junction; popular bathing resort; fishing center; shipyards, mfg. (trams, automobile chassis, elevators, pumps, stoves, glass, hosiery). Shelley's body cremated here after he drowned near Spezia. City damaged in Second World War.

Viar River (byär), SW Spain, rises in the Sierra Morena near Monesterio in Badajoz prov., flows c.50 mi. SSE to the Guadalquivir at Cantillana, 17 mi. NE of Seville. Coal deposits in its upper valley.

Viatka, Russian SFSR: see KIROV, city, Kirov oblast.

Viátor (byä'tôr), village (pop. 2,354), Almería prov., S Spain, 4 mi. NNE of Almería; ships grapes. Cereals, esparto.

Viaur River (vyôr), Aveyron dept., S France, rises in Lévézou range near Vezins-de-Lévézou, flows 96 mi. W, across the Ségala Plateau, to the Aveyron 5 mi. S of Najac. Spanned by viaduct (1,345 ft. long, c.400 ft. high) 4 mi. E of Pampelonne.

Viazac (vyäzäk'), village (pop. 20), Lot dept., SW France, on the Célé and 3 mi. NE of Figeac; coal mining.

Vibank (vī'băngk), village (pop. 263), S Sask., 30 mi. ESE of Regina; wheat.

Vibbard, town (pop. 83), Ray co., NW Mo., 11 mi. NW of Richmond.

Vibble (vĭb'lŭ), residential village (pop. 365), Gotland co., SE Sweden, on NW coast of Gotland isl., suburb of Visby.

Víbora, Bolivia: see MONTERO.

Viborg (vē'bôr), amt (□ 1,178; pop. 155,628), N central Jutland, Denmark; ⊙ Viborg. Comprises area W of Djursland and S of Himmerland; includes Salling peninsula and Fuur isl. in Lim Fjord. Land hilly in S, level in N; highest point, 426 ft. Drained by Guden R. and tributaries. Soil mostly poor, except in N Salling; agr., dairy farming. Chief cities: Viborg, Skive.

Viborg, city (pop. 21,522), ⊙ Viborg amt, N central Jutland, Denmark, on Viborg L. and 37 mi. NW of Aarhus; 56°27'N 9°25'E. Rail, highway junction. Tobacco factories, breweries, textile mills, machine shops. Has restored 12th-cent. cathedral.

Viborg, Russian SFSR: see Vyborg.

Viborg (vī'bûrg), city (pop. 644), Turner co., SE S.Dak., 16 mi. S of Parker; dairy produce, livestock, poultry, grain.

Viborg Lake (vē'bôr), Jutland, Denmark, c.3 mi. long, ½ mi. wide; Viborg city on W shore. Embankment, over which Randers-Viborg highway passes (E–W), divides it.

Vibo Valentia (vē'bô välĕn'tyä), town (pop. 10,073), Catanzaro prov., Calabria, S Italy, near Gulf of Sant'Eufemia, 31 mi. SW of Catanzaro. Agr. trade center (wheat, olive oil, wine, silk); mfg. (wagons, agr. tools, wrought-iron products, pottery); canned tomatoes. Has castle built by Frederick II, cathedral, and mus. of antiquities. Founded as Hipponion by Greeks; later flourished as Roman town of Vibo Valentia; has remains of town walls and temples. Rebuilt in 13th cent., after its destruction by Arabs. Badly damaged by earthquakes in 1783 and 1905. Until 1928 called Monteleone di Calabria.

Vibraye (vēbrē'), village (pop. 1,242), Sarthe dept., W France, 18 mi. S of Nogent-le-Rotrou; mfg. of carved wooden umbrella handles.

Vicálvaro (bēkäl'värō), town (pop. 3,133), Madrid prov., central Spain, 4 mi. E of Madrid, in grain-growing region; cement milling; mfg. of tiles, ceramics, and meat products.

Vicarello (vēkärĕl'lô), village, Roma prov., Latium, central Italy, near L. Bracciano, 23 mi. NW of Rome. Near by are hot mineral springs (baths) and remains of Roman villas.

Vicari (vēkä'rē), village (pop. 4,521), Palermo prov., N central Sicily, 23 mi. SSE of Palermo.

Vicchio (vēk'kyô), village (pop. 1,646), Firenze prov., Tuscany, central Italy, on Sieve R. and 14 mi. NE of Florence, in the Mugello; agr. center. Fra Angelico b. here. Heavily damaged by air bombing (1944) in Second World War.

Vicco (vĭ'kō), village (1940 pop. 645), Perry co., SE Ky., in Cumberland foothills, 8 mi. ESE of Hazard, in bituminous-coal-mining area.

Vicdessos (vēkdĕsō'), village (pop. 571), Ariège dept., S France, in central Pyrenees, on Vicdessos R. (small tributary of the Ariège), and 14 mi. SSW of Foix; iron mines.

Vic-en-Bigorre (vēk-ā-bēgôr'), town (pop. 2,816), Hautes-Pyrénées dept., SW France, 11 mi. N of Tarbes; road junction; canning, woodworking, fruit and vegetable shipping.

Vicência (vēsān'syù), city (pop. 1,761), E Pernambuco, NE Brazil, 40 mi. NE of Recife; sugar, coffee, tobacco; horse raising.

Vicente, Point (vĭsĕn'tē), S Calif., promontory 5 mi. W of San Pedro; lighthouse.

Vicente Guerrero (bēsĕn'tā gĕrā'rō). **1** Town Puebla, Mexico: see Santa María del Monte. **2** Towns in Durango and Tlaxcala, Mexico: see Villa Vicente Guerrero.

Vicente López (lō'pĕs), city (pop. 25,600), ⊙ Vicente López dist. (□ 24; pop. 155,211), in Greater Buenos Aires, Argentina, 9 mi. NW of Buenos Aires; industrial center; textiles, thread, cement articles, locks, custom jewelry. Stock raising. Founded 1905, it was named for the author of the Argentinian natl. anthem.

Vicente Noble (nō'blā) or **Noble**, town (1950 pop. 1,957), Barahona prov., SW Dominican Republic, near the Yaque del Sur, 12 mi. N of Barahona; sugar cane, coffee, hardwood. Until 1943, Alpargatal.

Vicentini (bēsĕntē'nē), village (pop. estimate 1,500), E Chaco natl. territory, Argentina, on railroad (Cacuí station) and 5 mi. NW of Resistencia; vegetable-oil and tannin factories; cotton, oranges, livestock.

Vicenza (vēchĕn'tsä), province (□ 1,051; pop. 559,375), Veneto, N Italy; ⊙ Vicenza. Mtn. and hill terrain (Monti Berici, Monti Lessini, Monte Grappa) occupies 75% of area, enclosing irrigated plain on 3 sides. Watered by Brenta, Astico, and Bacchiglione rivers. Agr. (cereals, grapes, sugar beets, tobacco); cattle raising. Mining at Chiampo (marble), Arzignano (basalt, limestone), Recoaro Terme (barite), Schio (kaolin, lead), Torrebelvicino (zinc), and Valdagno (lignite, marble). Mfg. at Vicenza, Bassano, Schio, and Thiene.

Vicenza, anc. *Vicetia* or *Vicentia*, city (pop. 48,279), ⊙ Vicenza prov., Veneto, N Italy, on Bacchiglione R. and 38 mi. W of Venice; 45°33'N 11°32'E. In corridor bet. Monti Berici and Monti Lessini which serves as natural communication route bet. Lombardy and E Veneto. Rail junction; iron-and steelworks, foundries, mfg. (agr. and textile machinery, automobile chassis, furniture, glass, macaroni), electric and printing industries. Bishopric. Cathedral (13th cent.), with frescoes by Montagna, city's greatest painter, largely destroyed by bombs in 1944. Noted for its 15th–18th-cent. palaces. Birthplace of Palladio, who designed many of its finest bldgs., including the basilica (1549–1614; severely damaged 1945), Teatro Olimpico (1580–83), Rotonda, and Palazzo Chiericati (mus.). Anciently a Roman colony. Under Venice after 1404; held by Austria from 1797 until united (1866) with kingdom of Italy. Heavily bombed (1944–45) in Second World War, with damage or destruction of many of its palaces, churches, and dwellings.

Viceroy, village (pop. 218), S Sask., near Willowbunch L., 30 mi. ESE of Assiniboia, in coal-mining region; wheat.

Vic-Fezensac (vēk-füzĕzäk'), town (pop. 2,275), Gers dept., SW France, 16 mi. NW of Auch; Armagnac brandy-distilling and shipping center; mfg. of ink and office supplies.

Vich (bēk), city (pop. 13,818), Barcelona prov., NE Spain, in Catalonia, 38 mi. N of Barcelona; chief industry is meat processing; also tanning, sawmilling; mfg. of cotton and woolen yarns and cloth, dyes, furniture, tiles, flour, dairy products. Draft-horse breeding. Has remains of Roman temple (1st or 2d cent. A.D.), and a cathedral (11th cent.; largely restored in 19th) with Gothic cloisters. Episcopal palace contains archaeological and art mus. Was important under Romans. Episcopal see since Middle Ages.

Vichada (bēchä'dä), commissary (□ 39,764; 1938 pop. 9,094; 1950 estimate 9,190), E Colombia, bordering N and E on Venezuela; ⊙ Puerto Carreño. Extends W from Orinoco R. to 71°5'W, bet. Meta R. (N) and Guaviare R. (S). Has tropical climate with moderate rainfall. Crossed by Tomo and Vichada rivers, affluents of the Orinoco. An undeveloped, sparsely populated region. Some corn, yucca, and cattle are raised, and forest products (gums, resins, vanilla) are gathered.

Vichada River, E Colombia, rises in Meta intendancy near 4°N 72°W, flows c.400 mi. E in meandering course, through uninhabited llano lowlands of Vichada commissary, to Orinoco R. (Venezuela border) 55 mi. SSW of Puerto Ayacucho. Navigable, but little used.

Vichadero (bēchädā'rō), village, Rivera dept., NE Uruguay, on road, and 80 mi. SE of Rivera; gold placers; agr. products (vegetables, grain); cattle.

Vicha River, Bulgaria: see Vacha River.

Vichayal or **San Felipe de Vichayal** (sän fēlē'pā dā vēchīäl'), town (pop. 1,507), Piura dept., NW Peru, on coastal plain, near Chira R., 15 mi. N of Paita, in irrigated area; cotton, fruit.

Vichten (vĭkh'tùn), village (pop. 409), W central Luxembourg, 6 mi. SSW of Ettelbruck; rose-growing center.

Vichuga (vē'chōōgŭ), city (1926 pop. 24,733), N Ivanovo oblast, Russian SFSR, 38 mi. ENE of Ivanovo; cotton-milling center; linen milling, textile-machinery mfg. Became city in 1920.

Vichuquén (bēchōōkĕn'), village (1930 pop. 524), Curicó prov., central Chile, near the Pacific, 45 mi. WNW of Curicó; agr. (grain, chick-peas, wine, livestock). Salt deposits. Near by is the salt Vichuquén Lagoon (5 mi. long).

Vichy (vē-shē'), anc. *Aquae Calidae*, town (pop. 29,144), Allier dept., central France, in Limagne, on the Allier and 28 mi. NNE of Clermont-Ferrand; one of Europe's leading health resorts, with strongly alkaline springs for liver and stomach ailments. Vichy water is bottled (here and in neighboring Saint-Yorre) and exported on a large scale. Vichy is a luxurious spa made up of hotels, thermal establishments, places of entertainment and parks. Known to the Romans, it was "rediscovered" by Mme de Sévigné and later by Napoleon III who initiated its modern growth. After Fr.–Ger. armistice of 1940, it became the seat of the collaborationist Pétain govt., known as the Vichy govt

Vici (vī'sī), town (pop. 620), Dewey co., W Okla., 21 mi. SSE of Woodward, in agr. (cotton, grain) and stock-raising area; bentonite mining.

Vickerstown, England: see Walney Island.

Vickery, village (pop. c.2,000), Dallas co., NE Texas, a N suburb of Dallas.

Vicksburg. **1** Village (pop. 2,171), Kalamazoo co., SW Mich., 12 mi. SSE of Kalamazoo, near Portage R., in farm area (livestock, grain, peppermint; dairy products); mfg. of paper products. Known for Egyptian lotuses grown near by. Inc. 1871. **2** City (pop. 27,948), ⊙ Warren co., W Miss., on bluffs above Mississippi R. (bridged near by to La.), at mouth of Yazoo R., 40 mi. W of Jackson; state's chief river port; cotton- and cattle-shipping center and lumber market. Mfg. and processing center (cottonseed products, hardwood lumber, wood articles, house trailers, foundry and machine-shop products, clothing); chemical plant (under construction in 1951). Has a jr. col. Hq. of U.S. Mississippi River Commission. U.S. Waterways Experiment Station is near by. City is on site of early-18th-cent. French fort and of Spanish Fort Nogales (1791); came into U.S. possession in 1798. Laid out as town in 1819; inc. 1825. As objective of Grant's Vicksburg campaign, city was besieged for 47 days, surrendering on July 4, 1863. Vicksburg Natl. Military Park (1,323.6 acres; established 1899) includes fortifications, emplacements, and trenches used during siege. Just N of city is Vicksburg Natl. Cemetery (119.8 acres; established 1865), with graves of more than 17,000 Union soldiers killed in campaign.

Vicks Peak, N.Mex.: see San Mateo Mountains, Socorro co.

Vic-le-Comte (vēk-lù-kōt'), village (pop. 1,474), Puy-de-Dôme dept., central France, near the Allier, 7 mi. N of Issoire; hog market; mineral springs. Has 16th-cent. church with stained-glass windows.

Vico (vē'kō), village (pop. 1,092), W Corsica, 17 mi. NNE of Ajaccio; hill resort.

Vico, Lago di (lä'gô dē vē'kô), crater lake (□ 4.6), Latium, central Italy, 6 mi. S of Viterbo; 2.5 mi. long, 2 mi. wide, alt. 1,663 ft., max. depth 164 ft. Has subterranean outlet (SE) to short affluent of the Tiber.

Vico del Gargano (vē'kô dĕl gärgä'nô), town (pop. 7,998), Foggia prov., Apulia, S Italy, on Gargano promontory, 12 mi. W of Vieste; agr. center (olives, grapes, almonds, citrus fruit).

Vico Equense (vē'kô ĕkwĕn'sĕ), town (pop. 2,756), Napoli prov., Campania, S Italy, port on Bay of Naples; 4 mi. SW of Castellammare di Stabia; bathing resort. Limestone quarries near by.

Vicopisano (vē"kôpēsä'nô), village (pop. 760), Pisa prov., Tuscany, central Italy, near the Arno, 9 mi. E of Pisa; soap mfg. Has Pisan church (11th–12th cent.) and remains of anc. fortifications.

Viçosa (vēsô'zù). **1** City (pop. 6,652), central Alagoas, NE Brazil, on railroad and 36 mi. NW of Maceió; ships sugar, cotton, livestock. Sugar mills near by. Called Assembléia, 1944–48. **2** City (pop. 6,326), SE Minas Gerais, Brazil, on railroad and 22 mi. S of Ponte Nova. Has state agr. col. (established 1921).

Viçosa do Ceará (dōō sēürä'), city (pop. 1,999), NW Ceará, Brazil, in the Serra Grande, near Piauí border, 45 mi. SSW of Camocim; ships brandy, coffee, cotton. Copper deposits. Has ruins of 18th-cent. Jesuit mission. Until 1944, called Viçosa.

Vicovaro (vēkôvä'rô), village (pop. 2,700), Roma prov., Latium, central Italy, 6 mi. NE of Tivoli.

Vicovul-de-Sus (vēkô'vōōl-dā-sōōs'), village (pop. 5,055), Suceava prov., N Rumania, on Suceava R., on railroad and 13 mi. WNW of Radauti; agr. center. Twin village of Vicovul-de-Jos (pop. 4,191), with sawmills, is 5 mi. SE.

Vic-sur-Aisne (vēk-sür-ĕn'), agr. village (pop. 827), Aisne dept., N France, on the Aisne and 10 mi. W of Soissons. Successfully held by Fr. army during Ger. 1918 offensive.

Vic-sur-Cère (–sâr'), village (pop. 1,248), Cantal dept., S central France, on SW slope of Massif du Cantal, on Cère R. and 10 mi. ENE of Aurillac; spa with casino; cheese mfg.; quarries near by.

Vic-sur-Seille (–sā'), village (pop. 922), Moselle dept., NE France, on the Seille and 3 mi. SSE of Château-Salins; noted for its red wine. Saltworks in area. Has 15th–16th-cent. church and old houses.

Victor. **1** City (pop. 684), Teller co., central Colo., in Front Range, 10 mi. SSW of Pikes Peak, 20 mi. WSW of Colorado Springs; alt. 9,900 ft. Gold-mining point in Cripple Creek dist. Near-by Gold Coin, Independence, and Portland mines are famous producers of gold. **2** Village (pop. 431), Teton co., SE Idaho, near Wyo. line, 10 mi. S of Driggs; alt. 6,207 ft. Gateway to Grand Teton Natl. Park, Wyo. **3** Town (pop. 741), on Iowa-Poweshiek co. line, E central Iowa, 39 mi. WSW of Cedar Rapids; livestock, grain. **4** Village (pop. c.300), Ravalli co., W Mont., 30 mi. S of Missoula and on Bitterroot R., near Bitterroot Range and Idaho line. **5** Village (pop. 1,066), Ontario co., W central N.Y., 15 mi. SE of Rochester; mfg. (tanks, insulators, food products, canvas goods, flour); gypsum quarries. Agr. (fruit, grain, beans, potatoes). Inc. 1879.

Victor Emmanuel Range, central New Guinea; rises to 11,810 ft.

Víctor Fajardo, province, Peru: see Huancapi.

Victor Harbor, town (pop. 1,798), SE South Australia, 45 mi. S of Adelaide on NW shore of Encounter Bay; principal summer resort of state, with fine beach. Harbor is protected by small Granite Isl. (connected with town by causeway ½ mi. long). Sometimes spelled Victor Harbour.

Victoria (bēktô'ryä). **1** Town (pop. estimate 5,000) in Greater Buenos Aires, Argentina, adjoining San Fernando, 15 mi. NW of Buenos Aires; meat packing and food preserving; poultry farming. Beach resort Punta Chica is on the Río de la Plata near by. **2** City (1947 pop. 17,916), ⊙ Victoria dept. (□ 2,200; 1947 pop. 34,199), SW Entre Ríos prov., Argentina, on Victoria R. and 65 mi. SSE of Paraná; rail terminus; mfg. and agr. center (wheat, flax, corn, vegetables, livestock). Makes buttons, leather, fish oil, ceramics. Lime and sand quarries near by.

Victoria, state (□ 87,884; pop. 2,054,701) of Commonwealth of Australia, in SE part of continent; bounded N by New South Wales, W by South Australia, S by Indian Ocean, Bass Strait, and Tasman Sea; bet. parallels of 34° and 39°S lat., and meridians of 141° and 150°E long.; 493 mi. long E–W, 290 mi. wide N–S, with 980-mi. coastline; ⊙ Melbourne, former ⊙ Commonwealth. Most densely populated, smallest state (excepting Tasmania) of Australia. Outstanding coastal feature is Port Phillip Bay, site of Melbourne. Generally mountainous and fertile, except for dry NW plains. Great Dividing Range, continuing from New

South Wales, crosses Victoria E–W. Mt. Bogong (6,508 ft.; in Australian Alps) is highest peak of Victoria. Murray R. on New South Wales border is used primarily for irrigation, receiving large but intermittent rivers (Campaspe, Loddon, Mitta Mitta rivers). Extensive irrigation projects include several reservoirs; Hume Reservoir on New South Wales border, largest. Lakes are shallow and generally dry; lagoons on SE coast. Temperate climate; mean annual temp., 56°F.; rainfall, 26 in. Snow falls (May-Sept.) on mts. in Australian Alps. Flora and fauna are typically Australian. Victoria, primarily an agr. and sheep-raising state, produces wool, wheat, dairy products, corn, fruits, flax. Coal and some gold are mined. Production of gold (discovered 1851) has declined. Large tourist trade: winter sports in Australian Alps, seaside resorts in Melbourne area. Chief exports: wool, wheat, textiles, butter, gold. Principal ports: PORT MELBOURNE, GEELONG. Other centers: Melbourne, BALLARAT, BENDIGO. Portland, on Portland Bay (SW), was 1st settlement (1834) of Victoria; Melbourne founded 1835. As Port Phillips Dist., the area now known as Victoria became (1836) part of colony of New South Wales, in 1851 a separate colony named Victoria, and in 1901 one of states of Commonwealth of Australia. Melbourne was ⊙ (1901–27) of Commonwealth and was supplanted by Canberra.

Victoria (bĕktôr'yä), village, Pando dept., N Bolivia, on Orton R. and 40 mi. E of Puerto Rico; rubber.

Victoria. 1 City, Alagoas, Brazil: see QUEBRANGULO. **2** For all Brazilian names beginning thus and not found here: see VITÓRIA.

Victoria, town (pop. 7,657, including adjacent Bota), S Br. Cameroons, administered as part of Eastern Provinces of Nigeria, port on Ambas Bay of Gulf of Guinea, at S foot of Cameroon Mtn., 10 mi. S of Buea; exports bananas, cacao, palm oil and kernels, hardwood, rubber Has hosp. Founded 1858 by Baptist missionaries.

Victoria. 1 County (□ 2,074; pop. 16,671), NW N.B., on Maine border; ⊙ Grand Falls. Drained by St. John R. **2** County (□ 1,105; pop. 8,028), NE N.S., in Cape Breton Isl.; ⊙ Baddeck. **3** County (□ 1,348; pop. 25,934), S Ont., on Burnt R.; ⊙ Lindsay.

Victoria. 1 City (pop. 44,068), ⊙ British Columbia, at SE extremity of Vancouver Isl., in SW part of prov., on Juan de Fuca Strait, 55 mi. SSW of Vancouver; 48°25'N 123°22'W. Major port, with shipping services to Vancouver and to U.S. Alaskan, Far Eastern, Australian, and New Zealand ports, has train-ferry connections with mainland. Exports lumber, pulp, cement fruit, fish. Mainly residential in character, Victoria is distributing center for Vancouver Isl. Industries include fish canning, lumbering, paper milling, dairying; mfg of woodworking and mining equipment, furniture, matches, pottery, tools, bricks, tiles; grain elevators and cold-storage plants; deep-sea fishing fleet is based here. Tourist center. Mean temp. ranges from 39°F. (Jan.) to 60°F (July and Aug.); average annual rainfall, 27 inches. Site of col. of arts: near the city are the Dominion Astrophysical Observatory and meteorological observatory (48°24'N 123°19'W). Noted features are bldgs. of Provincial Legislature, overlooking head of harbor, and many beautiful parks, including Beacon Hill Park and Gorge Park. Founded 1843 by Hudson's Bay Co. as fur-trading post named Fort Camosun, it was later renamed Fort Victoria. Town was laid out 1851–52 and named Victoria; inc. 1862. It became ⊙ colony of Vancouver Isl. in 1859 and ⊙ B.C. after the isl. became part of the mainland colony in 1866. Its early development was closely connected with the fur trade and then with the B.C. gold rush, when it became an important base. Suburbs include naval base of ESQUIMALT and Oak Bay. **2** Town (pop. 1,108), SE N.F., on Avalon Peninsula on W shore of Conception Bay, just N of Carbonear; hydroelectric station.

Victoria (bēktō'ryä), town (pop. 9,039), ⊙ Victoria dept. (□ 500; pop. 21,985), Malleco prov., S central Chile, on railroad and 38 mi. S of Angol; agr. center (grain, fruit, cattle); distilling, tanning, textile milling, lumbering. Trade with Argentina.

Victoria, village, W Fr. Guinea, Fr. West Africa, landing on the Rio Nunez (Atlantic estuary), 110 mi. NW of Conakry, 16 mi. WSW of Boké; palm kernels, gum, sesame, rice, peanuts; cattle. Mfg. of boxes.

Victoria, town (pop. 1,436), NW Grenada, B.W.I., on open bay 9 mi. NNE of St. George's; cacao, coconuts. Sometimes called Grand Pauvre.

Victoria, Hong Kong: see HONG KONG.

Victoria, principal town (pop. 6,175), of Gozo, Maltese Isls., 17 mi. NW of Valletta, in fertile region (citrus fruit, vegetables; livestock). Lace and candle mfg. Ruined citadel, cathedral, and other medieval remains. Near by are large troglodyte ruins. Formerly called RABAT, the name also of a town on Malta.

Victoria (bēktō'ryä). **1** Town (pop. 1,408), Guanajuato, central Mexico, 21 mi. SE of San Luis de la Paz; alt. 4,643 ft.; barley. **2** City, Tamaulipas, Mexico: see CIUDAD VICTORIA.

Victoria, North Borneo: see LABUAN.

Victoria, town (1939 pop. 5,610; 1948 municipality pop. 24,398), Tarlac prov., central Luzon, Philippines, on railroad and 8 mi. NE of Tarlac; agr. center (rice, coconuts, sugar cane).

Victoria or **Central Victoria,** locality, NE Puerto Rico, just W of Carolina; sugar mill.

Victoria or **Port Victoria,** town (pop. 9,478), ⊙ Seychelles, in Indian Ocean, port on NE coast of Mahé Isl., 700 mi. NE of N tip of Madagascar; 4°37'S 55°27'E. Administrative, commercial, and shipping center; exports copra, essential oils, cinnamon products, patchouli oil, vanilla, tortoise shell, guano. Fisheries. Victoria harbor, 3 mi. wide, is bet. Mahé Isl. (W) and the Mahé Group. Victoria has R.C. mission, Anglican church, hosp., Carnegie library and mus., botanic garden. Formerly also called Mahé.

Victoria, province (□ 21,028; pop. c.300,000), SE Southern Rhodesia, in Mashonaland; ⊙ Fort Victoria. Lies in low and middle veld (1–4,000 ft.); drained by left tributaries (Nuanetsi, Lundi) of Limpopo R. Mainly savanna grasslands. Stock-raising is leading occupation. Asbestos (near Mashaba), gold, and chrome are mined. Zimbabwe ruins (15 mi. SE of Fort Victoria) attract tourists. European pop. (1946), 3,616. Prov. formed c.1948.

Victoria, town, Southern Rhodesia: see FORT VICTORIA.

Victoria, county (□ 313.49; pop. 87,383, exclusive of San Fernando), SW Trinidad, B.W.I., bordering on the Gulf of Paria.

Victoria, county (□ 893; pop. 31,241), S Texas; ⊙ Victoria. Drained by Guadalupe and San Antonio rivers; touches Lavaca Bay in SE. Cattle-ranching area; also dairying, agr. (corn, cotton, hay, grains), poultry and livestock raising (hogs, sheep). Oil, natural-gas wells; clay, sand, gravel deposits. Formed 1836.

Victoria. 1 Village (pop. 469), Knox co., NW central Ill., 14 mi. ENE of Galesburg, in agr. and bituminous-coal area. **2** City (pop. 988), Ellis co., central Kansas, 9 mi. E of Hays, in agr. region. Small oil fields near by. **3** Village (pop. 302), Carver co., SE central Minn., near L. Minnetonka, 22 mi. WSW of Minneapolis; dairy products. **4** City (pop. 16,126), ⊙ Victoria co., S Texas, on Guadalupe R. and c.100 mi. SE of San Antonio, in area of oil fields, cattle ranches, farms; oil refineries, chemical plant, cotton gins and cottonseed-oil mill, food-processing plants, railroad shops, mfg. of machine-shop and foundry products, concrete products; sand, gravel. Seat of Victoria Col. Military airfields established near by in Second World War. Founded 1824, inc. 1839. **5** Industrial town (pop. 1,607), Lunenburg co., S Va., 50 mi. WSW of Petersburg, in agr., timber area; railroad shops; shoe mfg. Settled 1909; inc. 1916.

Victoria, Ciudad de, Mexico: see DURANGO, city.

Victoria, La, in Latin America: see LA VICTORIA.

Victoria, La (lä vēktō'ryä), town (pop. 1,963), Córdoba prov., S Spain, 15 mi. SSW of Córdoba; olive-oil processing, cereals, livestock.

Victoria, Lake, or **Victoria Nyanza** (nĭăn'zŭ, nē–, nyän'zä), largest lake (□ 26,828) of Africa and 2d-largest fresh-water body in the world (only L. Superior is larger), in Br. East Africa, bet. 0°28'N and 3°S, 31°38'E and 34°53'E; 250 mi. long, 150 mi. wide; c.250 ft. deep; alt. c.3,720 ft. Divided mainly bet. Uganda (N) and Tanganyika (S) along 1°S, with a NE corner (including Kavirondo Gulf) jutting into Kenya. It lies in a high basin bet. E and W branches of the Great Rift Valley (in which lie all of E Africa's other great lakes). Usually considered the principal source of the Nile, which (as the Victoria Nile) issues from it at Jinja over Ripon Falls. Lake receives KAGERA (often taken as the Nile's most remote headstream), Mara, and Nzoia rivers. Has deeply indented shores (Kavirondo and Speke gulfs), and a number of isls. (e.g., Sese, Ukerewe). Steamer service (1,300-ton ships with 7-ft. draft) connects main ports: Jinja, Port Bell, Entebbe (in Uganda), Bukoba, Mwanza, Musoma (in Tanganyika), and Kisumu (in Kenya, hq. steamboat administration). Lake was at one time connected with marshy L. KYOGA (N). Discovered 1858 by John Speke, it was explored more extensively by Stanley in 1875. Originally known as Ukerewe, it was renamed in honor of Queen Victoria. A dam begun 1949 at OWEN FALLS (1.5 mi. below Nile's efflux) for long-range storage of headwaters will raise lake's level by more than 3 ft.

Victoria, Lake. 1 Lake (□ 40), SW New South Wales, Australia, 135 mi. S of Broken Hill, near Victoria border; 9 mi. long, 6 mi. wide; shallow. **2** Lagoon (□ 45), SE Victoria, Australia, 135 mi. E of Melbourne, near Tasman Sea; merges with L. King (NE); joined to L. Wellington (W) by narrow passage; 15 mi. long, 3 mi. wide. Contains mullet, sea perch, bream.

Victoria, Lake, USSR and Afghanistan: see ZOR-KUL.

Victoria, Mount, highest peak (10,018 ft.) of Chin Hills, Upper Burma, 7 mi. WNW of Kanpetlet; 21°15'N 93°55'E.

Victoria, Mount, N central Viti Levu, Fiji, SW Pacific; highest peak (4,341 ft.) of group. Also called Tomanivi.

Victoria, Mount, New Guinea: see OWEN STANLEY RANGE.

Victoria, Sierra de la (syĕ'rä dā lä vēktôr'yä), low mountain range (c.1,600 ft.) in N Misiones natl. territory, Argentina, extends c.45 mi. ESE from Iguassú Falls to Brazilian border.

Victoria, Villa, Mexico: see VILLA VICTORIA.

Victoria Dam, Mich.: see ONTONAGON RIVER.

Victoria de Acentejo, La (lä vēktō'ryä dhā ä-thĕntä'hō), town (pop. 651), Tenerife, Canary Isls., 12 mi. WSW of Santa Cruz de Tenerife; grapes, cereals, fruit; flour milling, crockery mfg.

Victoria de las Tunas or **Las Tunas** (bēktôr'yä dā läs tōō'näs), town (pop. 12,754), Oriente prov., E Cuba, on Central Highway, on railroad and 100 mi. NW of Santiago de Cuba; linked by rail with Manatí (25 mi. N) on N coast. Trading and agr. center (sugar cane, bananas, oranges, cattle, beeswax and honey). Airfield. Marble, iron deposits near by. Scene of fighting in revolutionary war.

Victoria Desert, S belt of Western Australian desert, S of Gibson Desert, E of E.Coolgardie Goldfield, N of Nullarbor Plain; sand dunes, scrub, salt marshes. Also called Great Victoria Desert.

Victoria Falls, township (pop. 709), Bulawayo prov., W Southern Rhodesia, in Matabeleland, on Zambezi R., at Victoria Falls opposite Livingstone (Northern Rhodesia), and 240 mi. NW of Bulawayo, on railroad; alt. 2,993 ft. In game reserve; tourist center for the falls; police post. David Livingstone Memorial here.

Victoria Falls, on the middle Zambezi R., S central Africa, along border of Northern and Southern Rhodesia; 17°57'S 25°51'E. One of the world's great natural wonders, surpassing Niagara Falls in width and height. The most remarkable feature of the falls is that the general level of the country is the same above and below the cataracts, the water descending abruptly into a great fissure which extends over a mile at right angles to the course of the river, is less than 400 ft. wide from the lip of the falls to the lip of the opposite cliffs, and is some 400 ft. deep. The river leaves this coffin-like chasm through a narrow opening (called the "Boiling Pot") in the long wall of perpendicular cliffs opposite the falls. The falls, extending along the entire length (over 1 mi.) of the chasm, are divided into several sections by islets (especially Livingstone and Cataract isls.) at the lip of the precipice. Parts of the falls drop no more than 200 ft., and though estimates of the height of the deepest sections (such as Rainbow Falls, the Eastern Cataract, and the Main Falls) are as high as 420 ft., the maximum drop seems to be something less than 350 ft ; the estimates are further confused by the factors of season (April-June is the flood period) and of depth of the river in the chasm (56 ft. at low water). At the "Boiling Pot," the Zambezi enters a winding canyon (45 mi. long, only 400 ft. wide in spots), spanned just below the falls by a cantilever railroad bridge (650 ft. long, 310 ft. above high-water level; opened 1904; adapted for road traffic in 1930). Bridge links Victoria Falls, town in Southern Rhodesia (just S; hotel) with Livingstone in Northern Rhodesia (7 mi. N). Falls were harnessed for hydroelectric power in 1938, but lack of market prevents enlargement of plant. A game park has been established along N shore. Victoria Falls are a leading tourist attraction. The thick mist produced by the spray and the roar of the falls are noticed miles away. June–Oct. is best visiting season. Victoria Falls were discovered (1855) and first described by David Livingstone, who named them for Queen Victoria

Victoria Fjord, inlet (90 mi. long, 17–24 mi. wide) of Lincoln Sea of Arctic Ocean, N Greenland; 82°N 46°W. Extends SE to edge of inland icecap, where it receives several glaciers; contains several small hilly isls. Forms W boundary of Peary Land region.

Victoria Harbour, village (pop. 1,026), S Ont., on Georgian Bay, 20 mi. NW of Orillia; lumbering.

Victoriahavn, Norway: see NARVIK.

Victoria Island, SW Neuquén natl. territory, Argentina, largest isl. in L. Nahuel Huapí; c.10 mi. long, c.2 mi. wide. Site of forestry research station.

Victoria Island (□ 80,340), SW Franklin Dist., Northwest Territories, in the Arctic Ocean, separated from mainland by Dolphin and Union Strait, Coronation Gulf, Dease Strait, and Queen Maud Gulf; from Banks Isl. (W) by Prince of Wales Strait; from Melville Isl. (N) by Viscount Melville Sound; from Prince of Wales Isl. (E) by McClintock Channel; and from King William Isl. (SE) by Victoria Strait; 68°30'–73°27'N 100°30'–119°5'W. Isl. is 320 mi. long, 170–370 mi. wide; coastline is irregular, deeply indented (SW) by Prince Albert Sound (130 mi. long, 40 mi. wide). Generally hilly, rising to c.3,000 ft. On SE coast is Cambridge Bay (69°7'N 104°47'W), U.S.-Canadian weather station and trading post. Isl. was discovered 1838 by Thomas Simpson, explored 1851 by John Rae.

Victoria Island, Chile: see CHONOS ARCHIPELAGO.

Victoria Island, in Arctic Ocean, W of Franz Josef Land; part of Russian SFSR; 5 mi. long, 1 mi. wide; 80°10'N 37°E.

Victoria Lake (□ 14), SW N.F., on Victoria R., 50 mi. SE of Corner Brook, at foot of Annieopsquotch Mts.; 17 mi. long, 2 mi. wide.

Victoria Land, part of Antarctica S of New Zealand, bounded E by Ross Sea, W by Wilkes Land, bet. 78°S and 70°30′S. Consists of series of snow-covered mts., including Mt. Sabine (9,859 ft.) and Mt. Lister (13,350 ft.). On Ross Isl., just off E coast, is Mt. Erebus (13,202 ft.), an active volcano. Interior of Victoria Land is a high plateau which descends toward NW to Cape Adare (71°17′S 170°15′E). Discovered 1841 by Sir James C. Ross. Formerly also called South Victoria Land. The S magnetic pole, tentatively located here (1909) at 72°25′S 155°16′E, was later relocated on George V Coast at 70°S 148°E.

Victoria Mines, village (pop. estimate 100), NE N.S., on Cape Breton Isl., on Sydney Harbour, 7 mi. N Sydney; coal mining. Near by is Low Point cape.

Victoria Nile, name given to upper section of the Nile in central Uganda; issues from N end of L. Victoria (usually considered the source of the White Nile) at Ripon Falls just W of Jinja, flows 260 mi. generally NW, over Owen Falls, through L. KYOGA, then past Masindi Port and Atura, to N end of L. Albert, where it forms swampy estuary. Lower course is impeded by MURCHISON FALLS. Navigable only in its L. Kyoga course, bet. Namasagali and Masindi Port. There are hydroelectric sites in its falls and rapids (see OWEN FALLS). Formerly also called Somerset Nile.

Victoria Nyanza, Africa: see VICTORIA, LAKE.

Victoria Peak, highest peak (3,681 ft.) of Maya Mts., in Cockscomb spur, central Br. Honduras, 30 mi. SW of Stann Creek.

Victoria Peak (7,095 ft.), SW B.C., central Vancouver Isl., 55 mi. NW of Courtenay.

Victoria Point, southernmost village of Lower Burma, in Mergui dist. of Tenasserim, minor port on Andaman Sea at mouth of Pakchan R. (Thailand border) opposite Ranong and 170 mi. S of Mergui, at Kra Isthmus; tin mining (25 mi. N).

Victoria River, W Northern Territory, Australia, rises in hills 240 mi. W of Powell Creek, flows 350 mi. NE, N, past Victoria River Downs, and W to Queens Channel of Joseph Bonaparte Gulf. Navigable 50 mi. by small steamers, 110 mi. by barges.

Victoria River, headstream of Exploits R., SW N.F., rises W of the Long Range Mts., flows 85 mi. ENE, through Victoria L., to Red Indian L.

Victoria River Downs, settlement, W central Northern Territory, Australia, 270 mi. S of Darwin; sheep; airport.

Victorias (bĕktōr′yäs), town (1939 pop. 8,014; 1948 municipality pop. 27,858), Negros Occidental prov., NW Negros isl., Philippines, near Guimaras Strait, 18 mi. NNE of Bacolod; sugar milling and refining.

Victoria Sea, name sometimes applied to shallow section of Arctic Ocean just NW of Franz Josef Land, Russian SFSR. Formerly called Queen Victoria Sea.

Victoria Strait, S Franklin Dist., Northwest Territories, arm (100 mi. long, 50–80 mi. long) of the Arctic Ocean, near 69°30′N 100°W, bet. Victoria Isl. (W) and King William Isl. (E), connecting Queen Maud Gulf (S) with McClintock Channel (NW) and Franklin Strait (NE). At S entrance are Jenny Lind Isl. and the Royal Geographical Society Isls.

Victoriaville, town (pop. 8,516), S Que., on Nicolet R. and 50 mi. N of Sherbrooke; mfg. of furniture, clothing, bricks, maple products; in dairying, fruitgrowing region.

Victoria West, Afrikaans *Victoria-Wes* (vĕs′), town (pop. 2,535), S central Cape Prov., U. of So. Afr., 75 mi. SW of De Aar; alt. 4,164 ft.; sheep-raising, wool-production center.

Victorica (bĕktōrē′kä), town (pop. estimate 1,200), ⊙ Leventue dept. (pop. 7,841), N central La Pampa prov., Argentina, on railroad and 70 mi. NW of Santa Rosa; alfalfa, corn, livestock; dairying. Airport.

Victor Mills, village (pop. 2,654), Spartanburg co., NW S.C., 12 mi. W of Spartanburg.

Victorville, village (pop. 3,241), San Bernardino co., S Calif., c.30 mi. N of San Bernardino, in irrigated agr., and mining area of Mojave Desert; gold, granite. George Air Force Base here. Dude and cattle ranches near by.

Victory, town (pop. 49), Essex co., NE Vt., on Moose R. and 11 mi. NE of St. Johnsbury; hunting, fishing.

Victory Heights, village (pop. 1,857), Chemung co., S N.Y.

Victory Mills or **Victory,** village (pop. 488), Saratoga co., E N.Y., near the Hudson, 9 mi. E of Saratoga Springs, in dairying area.

Vicuña (bĕkōō′nyä), town (pop. 3,415), ⊙ Elqui dept. (□ 2,924; pop. 16,150), Coquimbo prov., N central Chile, on Elqui R., on railroad and 33 mi. ESE of La Serena; health resort in Andean foothills. Fruitgrowing center. Copper and silver mining; liquor mfg.

Vicuña Mackenna, Argentina: see MACKENNA.

Vida (vē′dä), village (pop. 1,157), Teleorman prov., S Rumania, 35 mi. NW of Giurgiu; rail terminus in wheat, corn, and tobacco region.

Vidago (vēdä′gōō), village (pop. 1,266), Vila Real dist., N Portugal, on railroad and 9 mi. SW of Chaves; spa with mineral springs. Its waters are bottled.

Vidal Gormaz, Cerro (sĕ′rō bēdäl′ gōrmäs′), Andean peak (c.18,000 ft.) on Argentina-Chile border, 70 mi. SW of the Cerro Incahuasi; 27°46′S.

Vidalia (vīdāl′yü, vū–). **1** City (pop. 5,819), Toombs co., E central Ga., c.75 mi. W of Savannah; tobacco market; mfg. of naval stores, lumber, clothing, concrete products; peanut shelling, vegetable canning. **2** Town (pop. 1,641), ⊙ Concordia parish, E central La., on Mississippi R. opposite Natchez (Miss.), in agr. area; lumber milling, cotton ginning. Settled c.1786; moved back from river after building of new levees for flood control in 1939.

Vidal Island (bēdäl′), off Patagonian coast of S Chile, N of Adelaide Isls. and adjoining Contreras Isl. (W); 28 mi. long; uninhabited.

Vidauban (vēdōbā′), town (pop. 2,094), Var dept., SE France, on the Argens and 8 mi. SSW of Draguignan; fruit and vegetable shipping; sericulture.

Vidda, Norway: see HARDANGERVIDDA.

Videbaek (vē′dhûbĕk), town (pop. 1,004), Ringkobing amt, W Jutland, Denmark, 14 mi. E of Ringkobing; textiles, bricks.

Videira (vēdā′rù), city (pop. 1,576), central Santa Catarina, Brazil, on Peixe R., on railroad and 25 mi. NE of Joaçaba; winegrowing, cattle raising. Until 1944, called Perdizes.

Viden, Bulgaria: see KONOVO MOUNTAINS.

Videro (vē′dhûrû), Dan. *Viderø*, Faeroese *Viðoy*, island (□ 16; pop. 383) of the NE Faeroe Isls.; c.9 mi. long, 2 mi. wide. Mountainous; highest point 2,768 ft. Fishing, sheep raising.

Vidette (vĭ′dĕt), village (pop. 159), Burke co., E Ga., 14 mi. WSW of Waynesboro.

Vidho, Greece: see VIDO.

Vidigueira (vēdēgā′rù), town (pop. 4,218), Beja dist., S Portugal, 14 mi. NNE of Beja; winegrowing center; olive-oil pressing, hat mfg.

Vidin (vē′dĭn), city (pop. 18,580), Vidin dist. (formed 1949), NW Bulgaria, port on right bank of the Danube (Rum. border), opposite Calafat (rail ferry) 65 mi. NW of Vratsa. Rail terminus; agr. center (grain exports); porcelain mfg., filigreeing (gold and silver), fruit preserving, wine making; fisheries. Has school of viticulture, ruins of medieval fortress, old churches, mosques, synagogues, monuments. Founded 1st cent. A.D. as Roman fortress of Bononia. Became ⊙ Bulgaria under King Ivan Sratsimir and was then called Bdin. Under Turkish rule, 1393–c.1880, except for Austrian occupation (1683–1690); until 1807 was ⊙ independent Turkish dist. under Osman Pazvantoglu.

Vidnava (vĭd′nävä), Ger. *Weidenau* (vī′dùnou), village (pop. 928), NW Silesia, Czechoslovakia, on railroad 10 mi. N of Jesenik, on Pol. border; oats.

Vido or **Vidho** (both: vē′dhô), island (□ .4; 1928 pop. 97) in Channel of Corfu, Greece, 1 mi. N of Corfu city; 39°39′N 19°54′E; fisheries. Has castle, destroyed (1862) by British. Also called Vidos.

Vidon, Sweden: see SKOGHALL-VIDON.

Vidor (vĭ′dōr), village (pop. 2,136), Orange co., SE Texas, 7 mi. NE of Beaumont.

Vidos, Greece: see VIDO.

Vidourle River (vēdōōrl′), in Gard and Hérault depts., S France, rises in the Cévennes near Saint-Hippolyte-du-Fort, flows 59 mi. SSE, past Sauve, Quissac, and Sommières, to the Gulf of Lion at Le Grau-du-Roi. Subject to flash-floods.

Vidra (vē′drä). **1** Village (pop. 3,500), Bucharest prov., S Rumania, on Arges R., on railroad, and 12 mi. SSE of Bucharest; agr. center; dairying. **2** Village (pop. 1,021), Putna prov., E Rumania, 19 mi. NW of Focsani.

Vid River, Bulgaria: see VIT RIVER.

Vidzeme (vĕd′zāmä) [Lettish, =Livonia], hilly former province (□ 8,907; 1935 pop. 406,247) of N Latvia; ⊙ Riga. Originally ruled by Livonian Knights as part of Livonia; passed in 1561 to Poland-Lithuania, in 1629 to Sweden, and in 1721 to Russia. Formed part of Rus. Livonian govt. until 1920, when it passed to independent Latvia.

Vidzy (vē′dzē), Pol. *Widze* (vē′dzĕ), town (1939 pop. over 500), W Polotsk oblast, Belorussian SSR, near Lithuanian border, 22 mi. NNW of Postavy; rye, flax, potatoes. Has ruins of 15th-cent. church. Old commercial town, largely destroyed during First World War.

Vie, river, France: see VIE RIVER.

Viechtach (fēkh′täkh), village (pop. 4,267), Lower Bavaria, Germany, in Bohemian Forest, on the Black Regen and 20 mi. NE of Straubing; paper mfg.; oil-regenerating plant. Also metal- and woodworking, tanning, brewing. Has early-17th-cent. church. Chartered before 1360. Quartz quarries in area.

Viechtwang (fēkht′väng), town (pop. 4,177), S central Upper Austria, 8 mi. E of Gmunden; scythes.

Viedma, for Argentine names: see also BIEDMA.

Viedma (byādh′mä), town (1947 pop. 4,672), ⊙ Río Negro natl. territory and Adolfo Alsina dept. (1947 pop. 8,225), Argentina, inland port on the navigable Río Negro (irrigation) c.19 mi. above its mouth, and opposite Carmen de Patagones (Buenos Aires prov.), 475 mi. SW of Buenos Aires, on railroad; 40°48′S 63°W. Agr. center (alfalfa, oats, wheat, corn, wine, sheep). Has administrative bldgs., the cathedral Las Mercedes, natl. col., agr. school, seismographic station, theaters, airport.

Viedma, Lake, large fresh-water lake (□ 420; alt. 8,333 ft.) in Patagonian Andes of W Santa Cruz natl. territory, Argentina, 10 mi. SE of the Cerro Fitz Roy (Chile border), 25 mi. N of L. Argentino; c.45 mi. long. Mts. rise sharply around it.

Viège, Switzerland: see VISP.

Vieil-Armand, France: see HARTMANNSWILLERKOPF.

Vieira (vyā′rù), town (pop. 2,246), Leiria dist., W central Portugal, 11 mi. NW of Leiria, amidst country's largest pine forest; glass mfg., cabinet-making. Praia de Vieira (on the Atlantic, 2 mi. W) is a beach resort.

Vieira do Minho (dōō mē′nyōō), town (pop. 663), Braga dist., N Portugal, 15 mi. ENE of Braga, at foot of Serra da Cabreira; sheep raising.

Vieja, Peña (pā′nyä vyā′hä), peak (8,573 ft.) of the Cantabrian Mts., N Spain, in the Picos de Europa massif, on Leon-Santander-Oviedo prov. border, 15 mi. NE of Riaño.

Vieja Mountains, Texas: see SIERRA VIEJA.

Vieja Providencia, Colombia: see OLD PROVIDENCE ISLAND.

Viejas Island (byā′häs), in Independencia Bay of Pacific Ocean, Ica dept., SW Peru, 36 mi. S of Pisco, 4 mi. offshore; 14°17′S 76°11′W; 1 mi. wide, 4 mi. long. Large guano deposits.

Viejo, Cerro el (sĕ′rō ĕl vyā′hō), Andean peak (13,451 ft.) in Cordillera Oriental of Colombia, on Norte de Santander–Santander dept. border, 18 mi. WNW of Pamplona.

Viejo, El, Nicaragua: see EL VIEJO.

Vielau (fē′lou), village (pop. 4,500), Saxony, E central Germany, 4 mi. SE of Zwickau; cotton milling.

Viella (byĕ′lyä), town (pop. 661), Lérida prov., NE Spain, chief center of the Valle de Arán in the central Pyrenees, on Garonne R., 60 mi. WNW of Andorra, near Fr. border; alt. 3,300 ft.; tourist resort. Stock raising; cereals. Mineral springs.

Vielle-Aure (vyĕlōr′), village (pop. 193), Hautes-Pyrénées dept., SW France, near head of Aure Valley in central Pyrenees, 14 mi. W of Bagnères-de-Luchon; sheep and livestock raising. Hydroelectric stations near by.

Vielmur (vyĕlmür′), village (pop. 488), Tarn dept., S France, on Agout R. and 8 mi. W of Castres; wool spinning, flour milling, horse raising.

Vielsalm (vēl′sälm), town (pop. 3,818), Luxembourg prov., E Belgium, in the Ardennes, 8 mi. S of Stavelot; slate quarrying; mfg. (abrasives). Considerable destruction in Second World War (Battle of the Bulge, 1944–45).

Vienenburg (fē′nùnbōōrk), town (pop. 6,671), in Brunswick, NW Germany, after 1941 in Lower Saxony, on the Oker and 7 mi. NE of Goslar, 6 mi. W of Schauen; rail junction; metal- and woodworking, dairying, brewing. Until 1941 in former Prussian prov. of Hanover.

Vienna (vēĕ′nù), Ger. *Wien* (vēn), anc. *Vindobona*, city and autonomous province [Ger. *Bundesland*] (□ 469; 1951 pop. 1,760,784), ⊙ Austria and Lower Austria, on the Danube and the Danube Canal, 320 mi. SSE of Berlin; 48°14′N 16°20′E; alt. 560 ft. Industrial, commercial, communication, and cultural center; rail hub on W Europe-Balkan route. Located in a plain at foot of the WIENER WALD (NW), it is an important inland port (head of navigation for vessels of 1,500 tons). Until 1938 city was divided into 21 dists., 20 of them grouped roughly in 2 rings around the central dist. (*Innere Stadt*): ALSERGRUND, BRIGITTENAU, DÖBLING, FAVORITEN, FLORIDSDORF, FÜNFHAUS, HERNALS, HIETZING, JOSEFSTADT, LANDSTRASSE, LEOPOLDSTADT, MARGARETEN, MARIAHILF, MEIDLING, NEUBAU, OTTAKRING, PENZING, SIMMERING, WÄHRING, WIEDEN. Only Floridsdorf was on left bank of the Danube. In 1938 Penzing and Floridsdorf were enlarged, and 5 new dists. formed through inc. of surrounding towns: GROSSENZERSDORF (on left bank of Danube), MÖDLING, LIESING, KLOSTERNEUBURG (on W slope of the Wiener Wald), and SCHWECHAT (from territory ceded by Lower Austria). N and NW dists. are residential; industry centers on left bank of Danube and in S, with manufactures of machinery, textiles, chemicals, furniture and food products; there are breweries, distilleries, flour mills. Fashion center noted for its luxury products (leather goods, artwork, jewelry). The annual "Wiener Messe," an industrial exhibit, attracts buyers from all over the world. Seat of archbishop. A Celtic settlement, the city became an important military and commercial center; Emperor Marcus Aurelius resided and died here. After withdrawal of the Romans, it rapidly changed hands among the tribes who overran the region. The Magyars gained possession of it early in 10th cent., but Leopold I of Babenberg, who became (976) margrave of the Ostmark, the nucleus of Austria, drove them out. In 1101 the Babenbergs built a fortress on the Kahlenberg. In 1137 construction on Vienna's noted cathedral of St. Stephen was begun; several decades later Henry Jasomirgott, 1st duke of Austria, transferred his residence to the town, made it capital of the duchy, and erected a castle, Am Hof. It grew in commercial importance during the Crusades, and was chartered in 1221. Fortified by Ottokar II of Bohemia in late 13th cent. Came (1278) with duchy of Austria to House of Hapsburg. Occupied by Matthias Corvinus of Hungary in late 15th cent., it was restored to Austria after his death in 1490. The Turks, reaching Vienna for the 1st time 1529, were repulsed after a 3-week siege. The Thirty Years War touched Vienna only in passing. Much more serious was the 2d siege by the Turks (1683). At beginning of 18th cent. a new circle of fortifications was built around the city, including most of the suburbs. Many magnificent bldgs. were erected by the 2 noted architects who had made Vienna their home: Bernhard Fischer von Erlach drew up plans for the Hofburg (the imperial residence), and built the beautiful Karlskirche; Johann von Hildebrandt designed the Belvedere (summer residence of Prince Eugene) and the Kinsky palace; together they planned the Schwarzenberg palace and the winter residence of Prince Eugene. Maria Theresa enlarged the old univ. (founded 1365) and completed the royal summer palace of Schönbrunn, started by her predecessor. Joseph II opened the Prater, a large imperial garden which now contains an amusement park, to the public. Haydn, Mozart, Beethoven, and Schubert lived in Vienna and gave it lasting glory. In 1805 and 1809 the city was occupied by Napoleon. The period which followed the brilliant congress of 1814–15 was enlivened by the waltzes of Joseph Lanner and the Strauss family, the farces of Nestroy, and the comedies of Raimund. Grillparzer, the great dramatist, flourished during these years. The revolution of 1848 forced Metternich to resign and Emperor Ferdinand I to abdicate, but was suppressed under his successor, Francis Joseph, from whose reign the modern city dates. By 1860 the old ramparts about the inner city had been replaced by the noted boulevard, the Ringstrasse, lined with handsome bldgs. and parks. The principal edifices on or near the Ringstrasse are the neo-Gothic Rathaus (city hall); the 2 domed museums of natural history and of art, in Italian Renaissance style and identical in appearance; the Votivkirche, one of the finest of modern Gothic churches; the Houses of Parliament, in Greek style; the Palace of Justice; the noted Opera and the Burgtheater, both in Renaissance style; the Künstlerhaus, with permanent exhibitions of paintings; the Musikverein, containing the conservatory of music; and the Acad. of Art. Bet. 1870–1914 Vienna again flourished as a cultural and scientific center. Rokitansky, the pathologist, and Billroth, the surgeon, worked at the General Hospital; at the same time Freud was developing his theory of psychoanalysis. Vienna attracted Brahms, Bruckner, Mahler, Richard Strauss, and Arnold Schönberg, who gave it another period of musical greatness. Hugo von Hofmannsthal, Arthur Schnitzler, and Jacob Wassermann dominated the literary scene. The First World War hit Vienna hard. Starved and torn by revolution (1918), it suddenly found itself the capital of a small republic which was recognized (1919) by the Treaty of Saint-Germain. In 1921, Vienna became an autonomous province of Austria. The highly successful Social-Democratic city govt. initiated a new program of municipal works. In public housing Vienna set an example to the world. Model apartment houses for workers, notably the tremendous Karl Marx Hof, began to supplant Vienna's tuberculosis-breeding slums. Continued labor unrests during the govt. of the 1930s paved the way for the rise of the Nazis; on March 15, 1938, Adolf Hitler entered Vienna, and Austria was annexed. The large Jewish pop. of the city (115,000 in 1938), centering mainly in Leopoldstadt dist., was reduced to a mere 6,000 by 1945, by the time the Russian army entered Vienna after a 7-day battle in April. Most of the destruction wrought by air attacks has been repaired. In accordance with agreements reached at the Potsdam Conference, Vienna was jointly occupied (1945) by British, French, Russian, and U.S. troops: British—Hietzing, Landstrasse, Margareten, Meidling, Schwechat, Simmering dists; French—Fünfhaus, Mariahilf, Ottakring, Penzing dists.; Russian—Brigittenau, Favoriten, Floridsdorf, Grossenzersdorf, Klosterneuburg, Leopoldstadt, Liesing, Mödling, Wieden dists.; U.S.—Alsergrund, Döbling, Hernals, Josefstadt, Neubau, Währing dists. The central dist. was jointly occupied.

Vienna, village (pop. 260), S Ont., near L. Erie, 22 mi. ESE of St. Thomas; dairying, mixed farming, fruitgrowing.

Vienna, Isère dept., France: see VIENNE, town.

Vienna. 1 (vīĕ'nů) City (pop. 2,202), ⊙ Dooly co., central Ga., 8 mi. N of Cordele; trade and processing center for farm and timber area; mfg. of naval stores, vegetable canning, pecan shelling, sawmilling. Inc. 1841. **2** (vī'ĕ"nů, vīĕ'nů) City (pop. 1,085), ⊙ Johnson co., S Ill., 33 mi. NNE of Cairo, in fruitgrowing region of Ill. Ozarks; wheat, corn, dairy products; timber; wood products. Inc. 1837. **3** (vēĕ'nů) Town (pop. 231), Kennebec co., S Maine, 18 mi. NW of Augusta in agr., resort, lumbering region. **4** (vēĕ'nů) Town (pop. 414), Dorchester co., E Md., 15 mi. ESE of Cambridge and on Nanticoke R. (bridged), in truck-farm area; large power plant; vegetable canneries, lumber mill. Founded c.1705, it was a port of entry 1791–1866. **5** (vēĕ'nů, vīĕ'nů) Town (pop. 471), ⊙ Maries co., central Mo., near Gasconade R., 29 mi. SSE of Jefferson City; agr. **6** Town, Ohio: see SOUTH VIENNA. **7** (vēĕ'nů) Town (pop. 306), Clark co., E central S.Dak., 17 mi. SE of Clark; trading point for farming area. **8** (vēĕ'nů) Town (pop. 2,029), Fairfax co., N Va., 12 mi. W of Washington, D.C., in agr., dairying area. Inc. 1890. **9** (vēĕ'nů) Industrial city (pop. 6,020), Wood co., W W.Va., on the Ohio and 4 mi. N of Parkersburg; mfg. of silk thread, vitrolite, glass; truck farming. Laid out 1774.

Vienne (vyĕn), department (□ 2,720; pop. 313,932), in Poitou, W central France; ⊙ Poitiers. Generally level region bet. Armorican Massif (N) and Massif Central (SE), linking Paris and Aquitaine basins. Drained S–N by the Vienne, its tributary the Clain, and the Gartempe which empties into the Creuse. Chiefly agr. (wheat, barley, potatoes); winegrowing; cattle, mule, and poultry raising. Châtellerault (automatic arms, cutlery) is chief industrial center; historic Poitiers is regional commercial and transportation hub.

Vienne, anc. *Vienna*, town (pop. 19,958), Isère dept., SE France, on left bank of the Rhone and 16 mi. S of Lyons; woolen-mfg. center (clothing, blankets, felt); liqueur distilling, metalworking (paper and textile machinery), shoe mfg. Poultry raising in area. Noted for its Roman remains, many of which are still buried. Temple of Augustus and Livia (c.25 B.C.) rivals the *Maison Carrée* of Nîmes. Also has 12th–16th-cent. church (former cathedral) of St. Maurice, and church of Saint-Pierre (dating partly from 6th cent.) which now contains lapidary mus. Seat of the Allobroges; became a leading city of Roman Gaul and one of earliest archiepiscopal sees (suppressed 1790). Here resided (413–534 and 879–933) several kings of Burgundy. An ecclesiastical council held at Vienne (1311–12) abolished Knights Templars. Town was slightly damaged (1944) during Allied sweep up Rhone valley in Second World War.

Vienne-Haute, France: see HAUTE-VIENNE.

Vienne-le-Château (–lů-shätō'), village (pop. 428), Marne dept., N France, on W slope of the Argonne, 7 mi. N of Sainte-Menehould.

Vienne River, Haute-Vienne, Vienne, and Indre-et-Loire depts., W central France; 230 mi. long. Rises in Plateau of Millevaches 6 mi. W of Sornac (Corrèze dept.), flows W, past Limoges, then N past Confolens, Châtellerault (head of navigation), and Chinon to the Loire 8 mi. SE of Saumur. Lower 35 mi. navigable. Receives Clain (left), Taurion and Creuse rivers (right).

Vientiane (vyĕn-tyän'), city (1936 pop. c.14,000), ⊙ Laos and Vientiane prov. (□ 8,000; 1947 pop. 122,000), on left bank of Mekong R. (Thailand frontier), near Nongkhai (Thailand); 17°57'N 102°34'E. Major commercial center; trade in forest products (hardwoods, gums and resins), lac, cotton and silk goods, brocades, hides. Linked by Mekong R. services with Luang Prabang and Savannakhet. Airport. Extending 3 mi. along the river, it has many pagodas, including the Wat Sisaket (archaeological mus.), the Wat Phra Keo former site of the emerald Buddha taken, 1827, by Siamese), and former royal palace (present govt. bldg.). Anc. ⊙ of one of the 2 Lao kingdoms, it flourished after 16th cent. but declined after being sacked (1827) by Siamese. Passed 1893 to Fr. administration and became ⊙ Laos in 1899.

Viento, Cordillera del (kôrdĭyä'rä dĕl byĕn'tō), Andean mountain range in N Neuquén natl. territory, Argentina, W of Chos Malal, extends c.45 mi. S from the Cerro Domuyo to Neuquén R.; rises to c.10,000 ft. Has silver and coal deposits.

Viento Frío (frē'ō), village (pop. 373), Colón prov., central Panama, on Caribbean Sea, and 4 mi. E of Nombre de Dios; cacao, abacá, coconuts, corn, livestock.

Vieques, town, Puerto Rico: see ISABELA SEGUNDA.

Vieques Island (byā'kĕs) (□ 51; 21 mi. long, c.3 mi. wide; pop. 9,211), belonging to Puerto Rico, 9 mi. E of the main isl.; 18°8'N 65°25'W. Fertile isl., with sugar plantations and pastures. Principal industries: sugar milling, charcoal mfg., dairying. Its main town is Isabela Segunda or Vieques (pop. 3,085), a U.S. naval base on the N coast. Other centers are Puerto Real (SW) and Punta Arenas (NW). Sugar mill at Playa Grande. Isl. was annexed by Puerto Rico in 1854. Sometimes called Crab Isl.

Viereth (fē'rĕt), village (pop. 923), Upper Franconia, N Bavaria, Germany, on the Main (canalized) and 5 mi. NW of Bamberg; hydroelectric station; rye, barley, cattle, hogs.

Vie River (vē). **1** In Calvados dept., NW France, rises above Vimoutiers (Orne dept.), flows c.30 mi. NNW, past Livarot, through marshy Auge Valley, to the Dives 6 mi. above Troarn. **2** In Vendée dept., W France, rises 7 mi. N of La Roche-sur-Yon, flows 35 mi. W into the Bay of Biscay at twin ports of Croix-de-Vie, Saint-Gilles-sur-Vie.

Vierlande (fēr'län"dů), SE suburban region of Hamburg, NW Germany, N of the Elbe. River polder reclaimed in 15th cent. by dikes. Truck farming: early vegetables, tomatoes, fruit, strawberries; flowers (lilies of the valley). Main communes are Altengamme, Curslack (or Kurslak), Kirchwärder, and Neuengamme. Region was inc. 1938 into Hamburg city.

Viernheim (fērn'hīm), village (pop. 14,127), S Hesse, W Germany, in former Starkenburg prov., 6 mi. NE of Mannheim; woodworking; fruit, tobacco.

Vierraden (fēr'rä"důn), town (pop. 1,004), Brandenburg, E Germany, near the West Oder, 3 mi. N of Schwedt; tobacco, vegetables.

Viersen (fēr'zůn), city (1950 pop. 36,832), in former Prussian Rhine Prov., W Germany, after 1945 in North Rhine-Westphalia, on the Niers, just N of München Gladbach (linked by tramway); 51°16'N 6°23'E. Rail junction; textile-mfg. center (velvet, plush, silk; cotton and flax spinning, linen weaving, dyeing). Ironworks; coffee roasting, paper milling. Second World War damage c.45%.

Vierset-Barse (vyĕrsā-bärs'), village (pop. 1,657), Liége prov., E central Belgium, 4 mi. SE of Huy; stone quarrying.

Vierumäki (vē'ĕrōōmă"kē), village in Heinola rural commune (pop. 8,695), Mikkeli co., S Finland, in lake region, 12 mi. NE of Lahti; site of noted physical-education col.

Vierverlaten (vĕr'vůrlä"tůn), town (pop. 343), Groningen prov., N Netherlands, on the Hoendiep and 3 mi. W of Groningen; sugar refining. Railroad station is Hoogkerk-Vierverlaten (pop. 2,613).

Vierville-sur-Mer (vyĕrvēl'sür-mâr'), village (pop. 177), Calvados dept., NW France, resort on English Channel, 11 mi. NW of Bayeux. In Second World War, here Americans landed (Omaha Beach; June 6, 1944) in Normandy invasion.

Vier Waldstätten, die, Switzerland: see FOUR FOREST CANTONS, THE.

Vierwaldstättersee, Switzerland: see LUCERNE, LAKE OF.

Vierzon (vyĕrzõ'), urban district (pop. 24,502), Cher dept., central France, on Berry Canal, at junction of Cher and Yèvre rivers, and 18 mi. NW of Bourges; metallurgical and railroad center; steel mills, iron and aluminum foundries; important glass, agr.-machinery, and porcelain factories; mfg. of chemicals and leather goods. Railyards. In 1938, the industrial communes of Vierzon-Forges, Vierzon-Villages, the workers' residential section of Vierzon-Bourgneuf, and Vierzon-Ville were consolidated into urban dist. of Vierzon. Heavily damaged in Second World War.

Viesca (byĕ'skä), town (pop. 3,370), Coahuila, N Mexico, in irrigated Laguna Dist., 40 mi. ESE of Torreón; alt. 3,585 ft. Rail junction; agr. center (cotton, wheat, corn, wine, vegetables, fruit); silver, lead, copper deposits.

Viesca, Laguna de (lägōō'nä dā), depression in LAGUNA DISTRICT of Coahuila, N Mexico, 5 mi. N of Viesca; c.12 mi. in diameter. Has water only during rainy period, when Aguanaval R. reaches it.

Viesite or **Vesite** (vyĕ'sētā), Lettish *Viesīte*, Ger. *Eckengraf*, city (pop. 1,340), S Latvia, in Zemgale, 15 mi. SW of Jekabpils; rail junction; sawmilling.

Vieste (vyĕs'tĕ), town (pop. 10,203), Foggia prov., Apulia, S Italy, port on Adriatic Sea, on E shore of Gargano promontory, 22 mi. NNE of Manfredonia; bathing resort; fishing, tomato canning; wine, olive oil. Bishopric.

Vietnam (vē-ĕt'näm') [Annamese,=land of the south], republic (□ 127,300; pop. 22,600,000), E Indochina, a state associated with France within the French Union; ⊙ Saigon. Formed 1945–50 by union of the Annamese lands of TONKIN or Backy (N Vietnam), ANNAM or Trungky (central Vietnam and the special administrative dist. of the MOI PLATEAUS), and COCHIN CHINA or Namky (S Vietnam). Situated on the E coast of Indochinese Peninsula, Vietnam borders on China (N), Laos and Cambodia (W), Gulf of Siam (SW), and South China Sea and Gulf of Tonkin (E), extending c.1,200 mi. N-S in an arc for the most part, 40–120 mi. wide. N Vietnam (with its combined delta of the RED RIVER and the Song CAU, bounded by dissected, steep-walled highlands, rising to 10,308 ft. in the Fansipan) and S Vietnam (which consists essentially of the vast MEKONG RIVER delta) are linked by long, narrow central Vietnam (hemmed in bet. the mountainous backbone of the ANNAMESE CORDILLERA and the South China Sea). Besides the great delta-forming Red and Mekong rivers, Vietnam is watered only by the shorter coastal streams (Song BA, Song CA, Song MA) of its central section. Vietnam has a tropical monsoon climate dominated by the South China Sea, though altered by local conditions. While a typical monsoon regime (rains, May–Sept.) and high year-round temperatures (mean of coldest month at Saigon: 79°F.) prevail in S, seasonal changes increase toward the north, with cooler winters and greater year-round precipitation. Vietnam's economy rests on agr. and mining. Intensive small-scale rice culture (occasionally modernized, in Red R. delta, by irrigation works) predominates in Mekong delta (one of world's leading rice-export areas), Red. R., and smaller coastal deltas. In contrast are European rubber, tea, and coffee plantations in basaltic residual red soils of Moi Plateaus and hills at N edge of Mekong delta. Of the secondary subsistence crops most important is corn (some exports); others are sweet potatoes, beans, and manioc, while pepper, coconuts (Mekong delta), and cinnamon (Tramy area) are grown for export. Cotton, mulberry trees (silk), and sugar cane are of lesser importance. Cattle, buffaloes, and poultry are raised, and fish products (dried, salted, or smoked) constitute a major export item. The leading mineral products are coal (most of it anthracite or coking grade) mined in the Quangyen basin (Hongay, Campha, Uongbi; Kebao Isl.) near Haiphong, zinc (at Chodien), tin (in Piaouac Range), lead, antimony, chrome, gold (at Bongmieu), phosphates. Modern industry is limited to rice milling (Cholon) and sugar milling (Hiephoa, Tayninh, Tuyhoa), distilling and mfg. of textiles (Namdinh, Haiphong), cement, ceramics, glass (Haiphong), matches (Benthuy, Hamrong) and paper (Dapcau). In addition to coastwise navigation, the Hanoi-Hue-Saigon RR (and parallel highway) is the chief transportation route, connected at Mytho with Mekong R. navigation and at Hanoi with rail lines to Kunming (China) and Dongdang (on Chinese border). Roads lead from Saigon to Pnompenh, from Vinh to Luang Prabang, and across the low Mugia and Ailao passes of the Annamese Cordillera to Thakhek and Savannakhet (Laos). The principal cities are Saigon-Cholon and Haiphong (both leading ports), Hanoi, Hue, Namdinh, Vinh (with its port, Benthuy), Tourane (naval base), and Quinhon. The chief hill station and summer capital is Dalat in Moi Plateaus. The Annamese (more than 80% of total pop.) are a Mongolian race of Chinese culture, Buddhist religion, and Indochinese language, concentrated in Red R. and Mekong deltas and narrow coastal plains. The principal highland minorities are the Moi (3%; original inhabitants of Indochina), the Muong (related to the Annamese), and the Man and Miao (primitive Chinese groups). There are Cambodians in the Mekong delta near the Cambodian border and Chinese in urban centers, chiefly of S Vietnam. At the close of the Second World War, the republic of Vietnam was first set up (Aug.-Sept., 1945) by the Vietminh party (coalition of nationalist and communist groups resisting the return of Fr. rule) with its capital at Hanoi, and recognized (March, 1946) by France within the limits of Tonkin and coastal Annam (excluding Moi Plateaus). Fr. refusal to permit the accession of Cochin China to the new state and continued landing of Fr. troops led to the outbreak of Franco-Vietminh hostilities in Dec., 1946. Having refused to deal with the Vietminh, France installed Bao Dai (former emperor of Annam) as head of a new French-supported state of Vietnam (including Cochin China), which was finally recognized (1950) by France, the U.S., and Great Britain as an associated state within the French Union. Meanwhile, Vietminh forces, organized as the Democratic Republic of Vietnam recognized by the USSR, Communist China, and other states of Soviet bloc, continued to hold most of the country outside the large urban centers and thickly-settled delta areas.

Vietri di Potenza (vyä′trē dē pôtĕn′tsä), village (pop. 3,046), Potenza prov., Basilicata, S Italy, 16 mi. WSW of Potenza; wine, olive oil, cheese.

Vietri sul Mare (sōōl mä′rĕ), town (pop. 3,903), Salerno prov., Campania, S Italy, port on Gulf of Salerno, 2 mi. W of Salerno; bathing resort; ceramics, glass; cotton and woolen mills, foundry.

Viettri (vyĕt′trē′), town, Phutho prov., N Vietnam, port on Red R. at mouth of Clear R., on Hanoi-Kunming RR, 30 mi. NW of Hanoi; lumbering and trading center; mfg. of wood pulp. Sericulture, fisheries.

Vietz, Poland: see WITNICA.

Vieussan (vyûsä′), village (pop. 116), Hérault dept., S France, in Orb R. gorge and 18 mi. NW of Béziers; manganese mining.

Vieux-Boucau-les-Bains (vyû-bōōkō′-lā-bē′), village (pop. 537), Landes dept., SW France, on Bay of Biscay, 19 mi. WNW of Dax; small bathing resort. Cork mfg.

Vieux-Condé (–kõdā′), town (pop. 8,014), Nord dept., N France, on the Escaut, adjoining Condé-sur-l'Escaut (SE), and 7 mi. NNE of Valenciennes; frontier station near Belg. border; forges and stamping mills, shoe factories, gin distilleries.

Vieux Desert, Lac, Wis. and Mich.: see LAC VIEUX DESERT.

Vieux-Fort (–fôr′), town (commune pop. 1,235), S Basse-Terre isl., Guadeloupe, 3 mi. S of Basse-Terre city; coffee, cacao, vanilla.

Vieux Fort, town (pop. 2,618), S St. Lucia, B.W.I., 19 mi. S of Castries, on fertile plain (sugar cane, coconuts); 13°44′N 60°58′W. Has a sugar *central.* In vicinity was started (1939) the Barbados Land Settlement. A U.S. airport and military base (leased in 1940) adjoins NE.

Vieux Grand Port, Mauritius: see OLD GRAND PORT.

Vieux-Habitants (vyûzäbētä′), town (commune pop. 4,528), SW Basse-Terre isl., Guadeloupe, 5 mi. NNW of Basse-Terre city; coffee, cacao; mfg. of soap.

Vieux-Thann (vyû-tän′), Ger. *Alt Thann* (ält tän′), village (pop. 1,662), Haut-Rhin dept., E France, on the Thur adjoining Thann; mfg. of textile machinery, cotton cloth bleaching.

View, Utah: see PLEASANT VIEW.

View Cove, village (1939 pop. 17), SE Alaska, on E shore of Dall Isl., Alexander Archipelago, 30 mi. S of Craig; limestone quarrying.

Vif (vēf), village (pop. 1,082), Isère dept., SE France, on small tributary of Drac R. and 10 mi. SSW of Grenoble; cementworks; winegrowing.

Vig (vē), town (pop. 716), Holbaek amt, Zealand, Denmark, 10 mi. NNW of Holbaek; clothing, cement, and machinery mfg.

Viga (vē′gä, bē′gä), town (1939 pop. 2,770; 1948 municipality pop. 11,000), E Catanduanes isl., Philippines, 20 mi. NNE of Virac; agr. center (coconuts, hemp).

Vigan (vē′gän, bē′gän), town (1939 pop. 7,465; 1948 municipality pop. 21,067), ⊙ ILOCOS SUR prov., N Luzon, Philippines, 45 mi. SSW of Laoag, near mouth of Abra R. on W coast; trade center for rice-growing area.

Vigan, Le (lŭ-vēgä′), town (pop. 2,962), Gard dept., S France, in the Cévennes, on small tributary of Hérault R. and 25 mi. WSW of Alès; silk spinning, hosiery and glove mfg. Chestnut, olive, and mulberry trees in area.

Vigarano Mainarda (vēgärä′nô mīnär′dä), village (pop. 1,015), Ferrara prov., Emilia-Romagna, N central Italy, 6 mi. W of Ferrara.

Vigário (vēēgär′yōō), village, SW Rio de Janeiro state, Brazil, just E of Piraí. Here the Santana reservoir (alt. 1,191 ft.) of Piraí R. is linked via Vigário reservoir and tunnel with FORÇACAVA power plants.

Vigas, Las, Mexico: see LAS VIGAS.

Vigatto (vēgät′tô), village (pop. 942), Parma prov., Emilia-Romagna, N central Italy, near Parma R., 6 mi. S of Parma; canned tomatoes, sausage.

Vigeois (vē-zhwä′), village (pop. 862), Corrèze dept., S central France, on the Vézère and 14 mi. NW of Tulle; fruits, vegetables.

Vigevano (vējā′vänô), town (pop. 24,609), Pavia prov., Lombardy, N Italy, near Ticino R., 19 mi. SW of Milan. Shoe mfg. center; foundries, textile mills, alcohol distillery, plastics and cutlery factories. Bishopric. Has cathedral, 14th-cent. church, and Visconti castle (enlarged 1492).

Viggbyholm (vĭg″bühôlm′), village (pop. 1,337), Stockholm co., E Sweden, at head of Askrike Fjord, Swedish *Askrikefjärden* (äs′krē″kŭfyâr″dŭn), 15-mi.-long inlet of Baltic, 8 mi. N of Stockholm; metalworking. Seat of boarding school. Has 13th-cent. manor house.

Viggiano (vēd-jä′nô), town (pop. 3,598), Potenza prov., Basilicata, S Italy, 22 mi. SSE of Potenza; wine, dairy and meat products.

Viggiù (vēd-jū′), village (pop. 1,522), Varese prov., Lombardy, N Italy, near L. of Lugano, 5 mi. NE of Varese. Resort (alt. 1,585 ft.); marble working, clock mfg. Marble quarries near by.

Vigia (vēzhē′ŭ). **1** City, Minas Gerais, Brazil: see ALMENARA. **2** City (pop. 6,041), E Pará, Brazil, fishing port on right bank of Pará R. (Amazon delta) and 50 mi. NNE of Belém; ships rubber, cacao, vinegar, fish glue. Old colonial settlement.

Vigía, El, Venezuela: see EL VIGÍA.

Vigía, Punta de la (pōōn′tä dä lä bēhē′ä), cape on S central coast of Cuba, Las Villas prov., at W gate of Cienfuegos Bay, 7 mi. S of Cienfuegos; 22°2′N 80°28′W.

Vigía Chico (bēhē′ä chē′kō), rail terminus, Quintana Roo, SE Mexico, on Yucatan Peninsula, on NW shore of Ascención Bay; port for FELIPE CARRILLO PUERTO 33 mi. SW.

Vigie Beach, St. Lucia, B.W.I.: see CASTRIES.

Vigmostad (vĭg′môstä), agr. village and canton (pop. 700), Vest-Agder co., S Norway, in the Audnedal, on Audna R. and 15 mi. NNW of Mandal, in lumbering region. Formerly called Nord-Audnedal.

Vignanello (vēnyänĕl′lô), town (pop. 5,246), Viterbo prov., Latium, central Italy, 9 mi. ESE of Viterbo, in grape- and olive-growing region.

Vignemale (vēnyůmäl′), highest peak (10,821 ft.) of French Pyrenees, Hautes-Pyrénées dept., SW France, on Sp. border, 23 mi. S of Lourdes.

Vigneulles-lès-Hattonchâtel (vēnyûl′-lā-ätōshätĕl′), village (pop. 516), Meuse dept., NE France, on E slope of the Côtes de Meuse, 10 mi. NE of Saint-Mihiel. Captured 1918 by Americans during battle of Saint-Mihiel salient.

Vigneux-sur-Seine ((vēnyû′-sür-sĕn′), town (pop. 7,555), Seine-et-Oise dept., N central France, on right bank of Seine R. and 11 mi. SSE of Paris; metalworks; mfg. (typewriter ribbons, chemicals).

Vignola (vēnyô′lä), town (pop. 3,294), Modena prov., Emilia-Romagna, N central Italy, on Panaro R. and 12 mi. SSE of Modena; paper, liquor, sausage. G. Barocchio da Vignola b. here.

Vignory (vēnyôrē′), village (pop. 453), Haute-Marne dept., NE France, near Marne R., 12 mi. N of Chaumont; dairying. Has 11th-cent. church.

Vigo (bē′gō), city (pop. 44,188), Pontevedra prov., NW Spain, in Galicia, leading Sp. fishing port and most important city of Pontevedra prov., 80 mi. SSW of La Coruña, picturesquely situated on hill slopes on S shore of Vigo Bay. Excellent natural harbor with shipyards and several piers; naval base; port of call of transatlantic lines. Exports fish, granite, wine, livestock. New economic development dates from c.1900. Fish-processing center (sardines, anchovies, tuna, shellfish); boatbuilding, metalworking; chemical works (fertilizers, paints and varnishes), oil refinery, brewery, cider and wine distilleries; mfg. of cement, glass, canning equipment, soap, porcelain. Granite quarries near by. Consists of old town with steep, winding streets dominated by fortifications of 2 anc. castles, and new quarter with fine avenues and modern bldgs. Characteristic fish market and fine bathing beaches. Sp. galleons loaded with gold and precious stones from New World were in part captured and in part sunk here (1702) by British-Dutch fleet; some treasures are still believed to be lying at bottom of bay, but attempts to recover them have been fruitless.

Vigo (vē′gō, vī′gō), county (□ 415; pop. 105,160), W Ind.; ⊙ TERRE HAUTE. Bounded W by Ill. line; intersected by the Wabash; drained by small Honey Creek. Stock raising, farming (especially wheat); bituminous-coal mining; shale, clay pits. Extensive mfg. at Terre Haute, commercial, banking, and industrial center for large surrounding region. Formed 1818.

Vigo Bay (bē′gō), Sp. *Ría de Vigo,* inlet of Atlantic, Pontevedra prov., NW Spain, on W coast of Galicia; 18 mi. long, 10 mi. (at mouth) to ½ mi. wide. Cies Isls. at entrance; resorts and fishing ports on both shores (Vigo, Bayona, Cangas, Redondela).

Vigodarzere, Italy: see PONTEVIGODARZERE.

Vigolzone (vēgôltsô′nĕ), village (pop. 485), Piacenza prov., Emilia-Romagna, N central Italy, near Nure R., 9 mi. S of Piacenza; paper mill.

Vigone (vēgô′nĕ), village (pop. 2,658), Torino prov., Piedmont, NW Italy, 18 mi. SSW of Turin; perfume.

Vigonovo (vēgônô′vô), village (pop. 230), Venezia prov., Veneto, N Italy, near Brenta R., 7 mi. E of Padua; hosiery mfg.

Vigors, Mount (3,756 ft.), N Western Australia, near Hamersley Range.

Vigry, Ozero, Poland: see WIGRY, LAKE.

Vigsnes, Norway: see VISNES.

Viguzzolo (vēgōōtsô′lô), village (pop. 2,055), Alessandria prov., Piedmont, N Italy, 3 mi. E of Tortona.

Vigy (vē-zhē′), village (pop. 536), Moselle dept., NE France, 8 mi. NE of Metz.

Vihiers (vēā′), village (pop. 1,616), Maine-et-Loire dept., W France, 17 mi. ENE of Cholet; mfg. (pottery, cement pipes, furniture).

Vihowa, W Pakistan: see VEHOA.

Vii (vē′ē″), village (pop. 1,518), Vasternorrland co., E central Sweden, on W coast of Alno isl., 5 mi. NE of Sundsvall; sawmills. Includes Alvik (äl′vēk″) village.

Viiala (vē′älä), village (commune pop. 4,389), Häme co., SW Finland, in lake region, 18 mi. S of Tampere; plywood mills, glassworks, machine shops.

Viipuri, Russian SFSR: see VYBORG.

Viitasaari (vē′täsä″rē), village (commune pop. 12,143), Vaasa co., S central Finland, on L. Keitele, 55 mi. N of Jyväskylä; tourist resort, in lumbering region.

Vijapur (vĭjä′pōōr). **1** Town (pop. 11,061), Mehsana dist., N Bombay, India, 23 mi. E of Mehsana; trade center for millet, wheat, oilseeds, timber; tanning. **2** Town, Hyderabad state, India: see VAIJAPUR.

Vijayadurg (vĭjŭyŭdōōrg), village, Ratnagiri dist., W Bombay, India, port on Arabian Sea, 30 mi. S of Ratnagiri; trades in rice, myrobalans, fish (mackerel, pomfrets); aluminum mfg. A Mahratta pirate retreat in 18th cent.

Vijayanagar (–nŭ″gŭr). **1** Village, Sabar Kantha dist., N Bombay, India, 34 mi. NE of Himatnagar. Was ⊙ former princely state of Vijayanagar (□ 135; pop. 13,942) in Rajputana States, India; from 1924 to early 1940s state was in Western India States agency; then transferred to Rajputana States; since 1949, inc. into Sabar Kantha dist., Bombay. **2** City, Madras, India: see HAMPI.

Vijayapur, India: see BIJAPUR, town.

Vijayavada, India: see BEZWADA.

Vijes (bē′hĕs), town (pop. 2,088), Valle del Cauca dept., W Colombia, on Cauca R. and 19 mi. NNE of Cali; coffee, tobacco, sugar cane, livestock.

Vijnita, Ukrainian SSR: see VIZHNITSA.

Vijosa or **Vijosë,** river, Albania-Greece: see AOOS RIVER.

Vik or **Vik i Myrdal** (vēk′ ē mēr′däl″), Icelandic *Vík í Mýrdal,* fishing village, ⊙ Vestur-Skaftafell and Austur-Skaftafell cos., S Iceland, near S foot of Myrdalsjokull; 63°25′N 19°1′W. Radio beacon. Dyrholaey, S extremity of Iceland, is 3 mi. WSW.

Vik (vēk), village (pop. 260; canton pop. 3,266), Sogn og Fjordane co., W Norway, on S shore of Sogne Fjord, 21 mi. SW of Sogndal; tourist center. Has 12th-cent. stone and stave churches.

Vik, Lake, Swedish *Viken* (vē′kŭn) (17 mi. long, 1–2 mi. wide), S central Sweden, 16 mi. E of Mariestad. Forms part of Gota Canal route; drains SE into L. Vatter.

Vikan, Norway: see HUSTAD.

Vikarabad (vĭkä'räbäd), village (pop. 1,340), Medak dist., central Hyderabad state, India, in enclave within Atraf-i-Balda dist., on Musi R. and 37 mi. W of Hyderabad; rail junction with branch to Parbhani, 150 mi. NNW. Rice and oilseed milling near by. Sometimes spelled Viqarabad.

Vikarbyn (vē'kärbün"), village (pop. 919), Kopparberg co., central Sweden, on E shore of L. Silja, 30 mi. NW of Falun; tourist resort.

Vike, Norway: see VESTNES.

Vikeland (vē'kŭlän), village (pop. 461) in Vennesla canton (pop. 4,643), Vest-Agder co., SW Norway, on Otra R. at a waterfall (63 ft.; hydroelectric plant), and 7 mi. N of Kristiansand; mfg. (cellulose, paper, wallboard).

Viken (vē'kŭn), fishing village (pop. 747), Malmohus co., S Sweden, on the Kattegat, at N end of the Oresund, 8 mi. NNW of Halsingborg; resort.

Vikersund, Norway: see GEITHUS.

Vikhren (vē'khrĕn), highest peak (9,558 ft.) in Pirin Mts., SW Bulgaria, 6 mi. SW of Bansko. Also called Yeltepe.

Viking, village (pop. 526), E Alta., 65 mi. ESE of Edmonton; natural-gas production; dairying, mixed farming, grain.

Viking, village (pop. 130), Marshall co., NW Minn., on fork of Snake R. and 13 mi. NW of Thief River Falls; dairy products.

Vikmanshyttan (vēk'mäns-hü"tän), village (pop. 862), Kopparberg co., central Sweden, 5 mi. W of Hedemora; steel and cellulose mills.

Vikna Islands (vĭk'nä), Nor. *Viknaøyane* (vĭk'näü"-üänü), group of 3 islands (□ 81; pop. 3,024) and several islets in North Sea, Nord-Trondelag co., W Norway, just off mainland, 30 mi. NNW of Namsos. Inner Vikna, Nor. *Indre Vikna,* is chief isl. (□ 29; pop. 1,659); on its E coast is fishing village of Rorvik, Nor. *Rørvik,* 30 mi. N of Namsos. Formerly called Vikten Isls.

Vikramasingapuram (vĭkrŭmŭsĭng'gŭpōōrŭm), town (pop. 18,832), Tinnevelly dist., S Madras, India, on Tambraparni R. and 20 mi. W of Tinnevelly; cotton market; textile mills. Development speeded by PAPANASAM hydroelectric project.

Viksnes, Norway: see VISNES.

Vikten Islands, Norway: see VIKNA ISLANDS.

Viktorovka (vĕk'tŭrŭfkŭ), village (1939 pop. over 500), NW Kustanai oblast, Kazakh SSR, 55 mi. WSW of Kustanai; wheat, cattle.

Viktring (fĭk'trĭng), town (pop. 2,687), Carinthia, S Austria, 3 mi. SW of Klagenfurt; textiles.

Vikulovo (vēkōō'lŭnŭ), village (1948 pop. over 2,000), SE Tyumen oblast, Russian SFSR, on Ishim R. (head of navigation) and 65 mi. NE of Ishim, in agr. area (wheat, dairying).

Vila, New Hebrides: see EFATE.

Vila Armindo Monteiro, Portuguese Timor: see FOHOREM.

Vila Arriaga (vē'lŭ ŭryä'gŭ), town (pop. 933), Huíla prov., SW Angola, on railroad and 15 mi. NW of Sá da Bandeira, at foot of central plateau; cotton- and tobacco-growing center.

Vila Boim (vē'lŭ bō'ēn), village (pop. 2,713), Portalegre dist., central Portugal, 7 mi. W of Elvas; cheese mfg., cork stripping. Has ruined feudal castle.

Vila Cabral (vē'lŭ kŭbräl'), town, Niassa prov., N Mozambique, near L. Nyasa, 140 mi. N of Zomba (Nyasaland); 13°25'S 35°20'E. Cotton, corn, beans. Projected W terminus of railroad from Lumbo (opposite Mozambique city), completed (1950) to Lúrio R. W of Entre Rios. Since 1946, ⊙ Lago dist. (□ 46,224; 1950 pop. 258,104).

Vila Campinho, Brazil: see DOMINGOS MARTINS.

Vilacaya (bēlākī'ä), town (pop. c.4,000), Potosí dept., S central Bolivia, 12 mi. SSW of Puna; potatoes, barley, vegetables.

Vila Chã de Ourique (vē'lŭ shã' dĭ ōrē'kĭ), town (pop. 2,454), Santarém dist., central Portugal, 6 mi. SW of Santarém; wine, olives, fruits.

Vila Coutinho (vē'lŭ kōtēn'yōō), village, Manica and Sofala prov., NW Mozambique, near Nyasaland border, on road and 120 mi. NNE of Tete; agr. trade (corn, beans, manioc, livestock).

Vila da Ponte (vē'lŭ dä pōn'tĭ), town (pop. 329), Huíla prov., S central Angola, on upper Okovanggo R. and 120 mi. SSE of Nova Lisboa; rubber; hides and skins. R.C. mission.

Viladecáns (bēlā-dhākäns'), village (pop. 3,653), Barcelona prov., NE Spain, 9 mi. SW of Barcelona; mfg. of silk fabrics; ships hazelnuts, fruit, cereals.

Vila de Frades (vē'lŭ dĭ frä'dĭsh), town (pop. 1,842), Beja dist., S Portugal, 14 mi. N of Beja; wine, olives, oranges.

Vila de João Belo (vē'lŭ dĭ zhwã'ō bĕ'lōō), town (pop. c.2,700), ⊙ Gaza dist. (□ 33,738); pop. c.657,000), Sul do Save prov., S Mozambique, on Limpopo R. above its mouth on Mozambique Channel and 95 mi. NE of Lourenço Marques; exports sugar, rice, corn. Agr. station. Airfield. Accessible for coastal steamers drawing 8 ft. Linked by rail with Chicomo (50 mi. NE). Formerly called Chai-Chai.

Vila de Ourique, Portuguese Timor: see LACLUBAR.

Vila de Rei (vē'lŭ dĭ rā'), town (pop. 351), Castelo Branco dist., central Portugal, 37 mi. WSW of Castelo Branco; resin extracting.

Vila do Bispo (vē'lŭ dōō bēsh'pōō), town (pop. 835), Faro dist., S Portugal, 13 mi. W of Lagos, near Cape St. Vincent; fisheries along near-by Atlantic coast.

Vila do Conde (kõn'dĭ), town (pop. 5,398), Pôrto dist., N Portugal, on the Atlantic at mouth of Ave R., on railroad and 16 mi. NNW of Oporto; fashionable resort (casino); fishing port; boat building, fish canning, rope mfg. Also produces textiles, chocolates, candles. Has 2 old churches.

Vila do Pôrto (pōr'tōō), town (pop. 1,146), Ponta Delgada dist., E Azores, on SW coast of SANTA MARIA ISLAND, 60 mi. SSE of Ponta Delgada (on São Miguel Isl.); 36°56'N 25°9'W. Fishing port. Fish salting, alcohol distilling, earthenware mfg. Santa Maria airport (transatlantic flights) is just N.

Vilaflor (bēlāflôr'), village (pop. 897), Tenerife, Canary Isls., 32 mi. SW of Santa Cruz de Tenerife; cereals, fruit, wine. Mineral springs.

Vila Flor (vē'lŭ flōr'), town (pop. 1,515), Bragança dist., N Portugal, 30 mi. E of Vila Real; winegrowing; rye, potatoes, almonds.

Vila Fontes (vē'lŭ fōn'tĭsh), village, Manica and Sofala prov., central Mozambique, on right bank of lower Zambezi R. and 140 mi. N of Beira; rail junction (spur to Marromeu) on Trans-Zambezia RR; cotton, sisal.

Vila Franca de Xira (vē'lŭ frăng'kŭ dĭ shē'rŭ), town (pop. 7,645), Lisboa dist., central Portugal, on lower Tagus R. just above its estuary, on railroad and 18 mi. NNE of Lisbon; industrial center (textile mills, tanneries, agr. processing plants). Saltworks in area.

Vila Franca do Campo (dōō kăm'pōō), town (pop. 5,256), Ponta Delgada dist., E Azores, on S shore of São Miguel Isl., 13 mi. E of Ponta Delgada; pineapple-shipping center; chicory drying, earthenware mfg., fish canning. The isl.'s 1st capital, town was destroyed by an earthquake in 1522. Near by (4 mi. N) is the Lagoa do Fogo, a crater lake formed 1563.

Vila General Carmona, Portuguese Timor: see AILEU.

Vila General Machado (vē'lŭ zhĭnĭräl' mŭshä'dōō), town (pop. 2,387), Bié prov., central Angola, on Benguela RR and 45 mi. NE of Silva Pôrto; agr. center (European settlement); 4,800 ft. Radio transmitter. Airfield. Formerly called Camacupa.

Vilagos, Rumania: see SIRIA.

Vila Gouveia (vē'lŭ gōvā'ŭ), village, Manica and Sofala prov., central Mozambique, near Southern Rhodesia border, on road and 170 mi. NW of Beira; cattle raising; corn, beans.

Vila Henrique de Carvalho (vē'lŭ ĕnrē'kĭ dĭ kŭrväl'yōō), town (commune pop. 16,154), ⊙ Lunda dist., Malange prov., NE Angola, on upper Chicapa R. and 257 mi. E of Malange; 9°40'S 20°23'E. Communications center S of Chicapa diamond-washing area. Formerly called Saurimo.

Vilaine River (vēlĕn'), Ille-et-Vilaine and Morbihan depts., W France, rises 12 mi. NE of Vitré, flows 140 mi. generally SW, past Vitré, Rennes, and Redon, to the Bay of Biscay 19 mi. NW of Saint-Nazaire. Receives Ille, Meu, Oust (right) and Don (left) rivers. Navigable for ocean-going fishing vessels to Redon, for river barges to Rennes. Largest river of Brittany, and one of France's longest coastal streams.

Vilaka or **Vilyaka** (vē'lăkä), Lettish *Viļaka,* Ger. *Marienhausen,* city, E Latvia, in Latgale, 35 mi. E of Gulbene, near Russian SFSR border, in flax area.

Vila Luiza (vē'lŭ lwē'zŭ), village, Sul do Save prov., S Mozambique, on Delagoa Bay at mouth of Komati R., 18 mi. N of Lourenço Marques (linked by rail); mfg. of cement, crating; peanuts, cotton, rice, corn. Formerly Marracuene.

Vila Luso (vē'lŭ lōō'zōō), town (pop. 2,821), ⊙ Moxico dist. (pop. 264,580), Bié prov., E central Angola, on Benguela RR and 200 mi. ENE of Silva Pôrto; 11°48'S 19°52'E; alt. 4,300 ft. Agr. trade center (beeswax, rice, wheat, corn, oilseeds). Brick mfg. Airfield. Road to Chicapa R. diamond washings (N). Formerly called Moxico.

Vila Mariano Machado (vē'lŭ mŭryä'nōō mŭshä'dōō), town (pop. 349), Benguela prov., W Angola, on Benguela RR and 90 mi. SE of Lobito; sisal plantations; dairying. Govt. experiment farm. Formerly called Ganda.

Vila Murtinho (vē'lŭ mōōrtē'nyōō), village, W Guaporé territory, W Brazil, at confluence of Beni and Mamoré rivers (here forming Madeira R.), opposite Villa Bella (Bolivia), on Madeira-Mamoré RR and 150 mi. SW of Pôrto Velho.

Vilanculos (vēlăngkōō'lōōsh), village, Sul do Save prov., SE Mozambique, on Mozambique Channel, 130 mi. NNW of Inhambane; fishing center. Harbor sheltered by Bazaruto Isls. offshore.

Vilani or **Vilyany** (vē'lănē), Lettish *Viļāni,* Ger. *Weleny,* city (pop. 1,333), E Latvia, in Latgale, 15 mi. W of Rezekne; rye, flax.

Vila Nogueira de Azeitão (vē'lŭ nōgā'rŭ dĭ äzătã'ō), town (pop. 1,076), Setúbal dist., S central Portugal, 7 mi. W of Setúbal; agr. trade (wine, olives, grain, beans, oranges, rice).

Vila Nova (vē'lŭ nô'vŭ), town (pop. 619), Benguela prov., central Angola, on Benguela RR and 22 mi. ENE of Nova Lisboa; alt. 5,600 ft. Developed c.1920 as agr. settlement.

Vila Nova, Brazil: see NEÓPOLIS.

Vila Nova da Baronia (dä bŭrōōnē'ŭ), town (pop. 1,663), Beja dist., S Portugal, on railroad and 21 mi. NNW of Beja; grain, olives, sheep, cork.

Vila Nova da Barquinha (bŭrkē'nyŭ), town (pop. 1,159), Santarém dist., central Portugal, on right bank of Tagus R. and 20 mi. NNE of Santarém; mfg. (soft drinks, textiles, hardware).

Vila Nova da Cerveira (sĕrvā'rŭ), fortified town (pop. 1,014), Viana do Castelo dist., northernmost Portugal, on left bank of Minho R. (Sp. border) and 17 mi. NNE of Viana do Castelo; textiles, ceramics.

Vila Nova de Anços (dĭ ã'sōōsh), village (pop. 1,334), Coimbra dist., N central Portugal, on railroad and 13 mi. SW of Coimbra; rice growing; pine woods.

Vilanova de Bellpuig (bēlänō'vä dhā bālpōōch'), village (pop. 1,516), Lérida prov., NE Spain, 18 mi. E of Lérida, in irrigated agr. area (cereals, wine, olive oil, sugar beets).

Vila Nova de Famalicão (vē'lŭ nô'vŭ dĭ fŭmŭlĕsã'ō), town (pop. 2,178), Braga dist., N Portugal, on railroad and 10 mi. SSW of Braga; agr. trade. Textile milling, button and clock mfg.

Vila Nova de Fozcôa (fôzh-kō'ŭ), town (pop. 3,326), Guarda dist., N central Portugal, near left bank of Douro R., 40 mi. NNE of Guarda; rope mfg.; vineyards (port wine); olives, figs, almonds, oranges. Also spelled Vila Nova de Foz Côa.

Vila Nova de Gaia (gä'yŭ), S suburb of Oporto, Pôrto dist., Portugal, on left bank of the Douro (bridge; trolleys); here port wine is stored in wine-shipper's lodges (*armazens*). Mfg. of pottery, footwear, textiles; cork processing, distilling. The secularized convent of Nossa Senhora da Serra do Pilar (dating from 16th cent.) is now used as a military barracks.

Vila Nova de Milfontes (mēlfōn'tĭsh), town (pop. 808), Beja dist., S Portugal, fishing port at mouth of Mira R. and 12 mi. NNW of Odemira; sardine canning; seaside resort. Numerous prehistoric finds have been made near by.

Vila Nova de Monsarros (mōsä'rōōsh), village (pop. 1,094), Aveiro dist., N central Portugal, 15 mi. N of Coimbra; olive- and winegrowing.

Vila Nova de Ourém (ōrān'), agr. village (pop. 1,539), Santarém dist., central Portugal, 15 mi. SE of Leiria. Has ruined castle. Fátima, 5 mi. SW, is a pilgrimage center.

Vila Nova de Paiva (pī'vŭ), town (pop. 901), Viseu dist., N central Portugal, 16 mi. NE of Viseu; iron smelting, cheese mfg.

Vila Nova de Portimão, Portugal: see PORTIMÃO.

Vila Nova de Tazem (tä'zān), town (pop. 1,807), Guarda dist., N central Portugal, 16 mi. SE of Viseu; vineyards; dairying, textile milling.

Vila Nova do Seles (dōō sĕ'lĭsh), town (pop. 1,115), Benguela prov., W Angola, on road and 35 mi. SE of Novo Redondo. Formerly called Uco.

Vila Paiva de Andrada (vē'lŭ pī'vŭ dĭ ăndrä'dŭ), village, Manica and Sofala prov., central Mozambique, on road and 95 mi. NNW of Beira.

Vila Pereira de Eça (vē'lŭ pĭrā'rŭ dĭ ĕ'sŭ), town (pop. 460), Huíla prov., S Angola, near South-West Africa border, 210 mi. SE of Sá da Bandeira. Also spelled Vila Pereira d'Eça. Formerly called Ngiva.

Vila Pery (vē'lŭ pĕ'rē), village, Manica and Sofala prov., central Mozambique, on Beira RR and 100 mi. WNW of Beira; agr. trade (cotton, bananas, sisal, tobacco, corn); cattle raising. Hydroelectric plant. Sometimes spelled Vila Peri.

Vila Pouca de Aguiar (vē'lŭ pō'kŭ dĭ ăgyär'), town (pop. 1,541), Vila Real dist., N Portugal, on railroad and 15 mi. NNE of Vila Real; winegrowing; olives, wheat, vegetables.

Vila Praia de Âncora, Portugal: see ÂNCORA.

Vilarandelo (vēlŭrăndā'lōō), village (pop. 1,507), Vila Real dist., N Portugal, on N slope of Serra Padrela, 8 mi. SE of Chaves; winegrowing; olives, figs, oranges.

Vilar de Perdizes (vēlär' dĭ pĕrdē'zĭsh), village (pop. 1,766), Vila Real dist., N Portugal, 12 mi. NW of Chaves, near Sp. border; sheep and goat raising.

Vila Real (vē'lŭ rēäl'), district (□ 1,636; pop. 289,114), in Trás-os-Montes e Alto Douro prov., N Portugal; ⊙ Vila Real. Bounded by Spain (N) and by the Douro (S). Traversed by several mtn. ranges, highest near Sp. border. Vineyards for port wine industry along the Douro and in Corgo R. valley S of Vila Real. Chief shipping center: Pêso da Régua. Chaves is principal town in N.

Vila Real, city (pop. 7,980), ⊙ Vila Real dist., and Trás-os-Montes e Alto Douro prov., N Portugal, on Corgo R., on railroad and 50 mi. ENE of Oporto; center of port wine industry; mfg. of ceramics, buttons, flour products; textile dyeing, tanning. Founded 13th cent. Has medieval church and several 17th-cent. houses in main square.

Vila Real de Santo António (vē'lŭ rēäl' dĭ săn'tōō ăntō'nyōō), town (pop. 5,839), Faro dist., S Portugal, 32 mi. ENE of Faro; port on right bank of Guadiana R. estuary (Spanish border), opposite (2 mi. SW of) Ayamonte; Port. railroad terminus; fishing and canning center. Exports copper shipped down the Guadiana from Mina de São Domingos (via Pomarão). Present town was built 1774 to replace near-by Santo António de Arenilha which had been engulfed by the sea c.1600.

Vilar Formoso (vēlär' fôrmō'zo͞o), village (pop. 577), Guarda dist., N central Portugal, on railroad and 25 mi. E of Guarda; customs station on Sp. border opposite Fuentes de Oñoro.

Vila Robert Williams, town (pop. 3,679), Benguela prov., W central Angola, on Benguela RR and 18 mi. SW of Nova Lisboa; alt. 5,700 ft. First European agr. settlement on central plateau, named c.1930 after founder of Benguela RR. Formerly called Caala.

Vilarrodona (bělärō-dhō'nä), town (pop. 1,386), Tarragona prov., NE Spain, 6 mi. ENE of Valls; liqueur mfg.; agr. trade (wine, olive oil, almonds).

Vilas (vī'lŭs), county (□ 867; pop. 9,363), N Wis., bounded N by Mich.; ⊙ Eagle River. Drained by Wisconsin and Manitowish rivers. Mostly a resort area with woods and numerous lakes (including Lac Vieux Desert and Trout L.). Contains Northern State Forest and Lac du Flambeau Indian Reservation. Lumbering. Formed 1893.

Vilas. 1 Town (pop. 132), Baca co., SE Colo., 10 mi. E of Springfield. **2** Town (pop. 71), Miner co., SE central S.Dak., 4 mi. W of Howard.

Vila Salazar (vē'lŭ sŭlŭzär'), town (pop. 2,105), ⊙ Cuanza-Norte dist. (pop. 160,063), Congo prov., NW Angola, on Luanda-Malange RR and 120 mi. ESE of Luanda; alt. 2,460 ft. Agr. center (coffee, tobacco, sisal). Until 1930s, called Dala Tando.

Vila Salazar (vē'lŭ sŭlŭzär'), town, ⊙ Baucau dist. (□ 618; pop. 51,053), Portuguese Timor, in E Timor, near N coast, 60 mi. E of Dili; trade center for agr. and lumbering area. Ceramics mfg. Has airport. Also called Baucau.

Vilaseca de Solcina (bēläsä'kä dhä sōl-thē'nä), town (pop. 2,461), Tarragona prov., NE Spain, 5 mi. W of Tarragona; olive-oil and meat processing; trades in wine, cereals, almonds, hazelnuts.

Vila Teixeira da Silva (vē'lŭ täshä'rŭ dä sēl'vŭ), town (pop. 4,897), Benguela prov., W central Angola, on Bié Plateau, 40 mi. N of Nova Lisboa; agr. (sisal, corn, beans), cattle raising, fiber processing. Until 1930s called Bailundo.

Vila Vasco da Gama (vē'lŭ vä'sko͝o dä gä'mŭ), village, Manica and Sofala prov., NW Mozambique, near Northern Rhodesia border, 125 mi. NW of Tete; gold placers.

Vila Velha de Ródão (vē'lŭ vě'lyŭ dĭ rô'dāō), town (pop. 528), Castelo Branco dist., central Portugal, head of navigation on Tagus R. below its gorge (Portas de Ródão), on railroad and 16 mi. SW of Castelo Branco; ships olive oil, wine, wool, cork, lumber.

Vila Vende (vē'lŭ vān'dĭ), town (pop. 1,594), Braga dist., N Portugal, 6 mi. N of Braga; agr. trade; sheep raising, lumbering.

Vila Verde (vē'lŭ vĕr'dĭ), village (pop. 1,230), Coimbra dist., N central Portugal, 3 mi. ESE of Figueira da Foz; salt panning.

Vila Verde de Ficalho (dĭ fēkä'lyo͞o), town (pop. 2,158), Beja dist., S Portugal, 32 mi. ESE of Beja; frontier station near Sp. border, on highway opposite Rosal de la Frontera; grain, oil, sheep; pottery making.

Vila Veríssimo Sarmento (vē'lŭ vĭrē'sēmo͞o sŭrmēn'-to͞o), town, Malange prov., NE Angola, near Chicapa R., 100 mi. N of Vila Henrique de Carvalho; rubber, diamonds.

Vila Viçosa (vē'lŭ vēsō'zŭ), town (pop. 4,693), Évora dist., S central Portugal, 30 mi. NE of Évora and 16 mi. SW of Elvas; rail terminus; pottery and soap mfg., oil and winemaking. Marble quarries near by. Has 17th-cent. royal castle. Near town is a walled-in game preserve.

Vila-Vila, Bolivia: see VILLA VISCARRA.

Vilbel (fĭl'bŭl), village (pop. 7,004), central Hesse, W Germany, in former Upper Hesse prov., on the Nidda and 5 mi. NNE of Frankfurt; mineral springs. Has remains of Roman bath.

Vilcabamba (bēlkäbäm'bä), town (pop. 1,324), Pasco dept., central Peru, on N slopes of Nudo de Pasco of the Andes, 20 mi. NW of Cerro de Pasco; alt. 13,953 ft.; grain, livestock.

Vilcabamba, Cordillera (kôrdĭyā'rä), Andean range in Cuzco dept., S central Peru, extends c.160 mi. NW from a point N of Cuzco to 12°S; rises in Cerro Salcantay to 20,551 ft. It is intersected by Urubamba R. and forms E watershed of Apurímac R.

Vilcabamba River or **Oropesa River** (ōrōpā'sä), Apurímac dept., S Peru, rises at SE foot of Cordillera de Huanzo, flows c.100 mi. N to Apurímac R. 28 mi. E of Abancay.

Vilcanota, Cordillera de (kôrdĭyā'rä dā bēlkänō'tä), Andean range in Cuzco dept., S Peru, E of Cuzco city; runs SW from c.13°S, parallel to Cordillera de Carabaya, for c.130 mi. to the **Nudo de Vilcanota** (nō͞o'dō) (17,988 ft.) on Puno dept. border, where, at N end of the Altiplano, the Cordillera Oriental and Cordillera Occidental meet. Toward N the Andes spread out into 3 ranges; cordilleras Oriental, Central, and Occidental.

Vilcanota River, Peru: see URUBAMBA RIVER.

Vilches (bēl'chěs), town (pop. 4,933), Jaén prov., S Spain, at foot of the Sierra Morena, 10 mi. NE of Linares, in rich lead-mining dist. of La Carolina; also iron and tungsten mining. Olive-oil processing, flour- and sawmilling. Stock raising; cereals, vegetables. Parochial church preserves trophies of battle of Navas de Tolosa.

Vilcún (bēlko͞on'), town (pop. 1,942), Cautín prov., S central Chile, on railroad and 20 mi. ENE of Temuco; agr. center (wheat, barley, peas, potatoes, livestock); flour milling, lumbering.

Vildstejn, Czechoslovakia: see SKALNA.

Vileika, oblast, Belorussian SSR: see MOLODECHNO, oblast.

Vileika or **Vileyka** (vĭlyā'kŭ), Pol. *Wilejka* (vēlā'kä), city (1931 pop. 5,595), central Molodechno oblast, Belorussian SSR, on Viliya R. and 12 mi. N of Molodechno; lumber-trading center; flour millings, sawmilling, soap mfg., hatmaking. Passed (1793) from Poland to Russia; reverted (1921) to Poland; ceded to USSR in 1945. Was ⊙ Vileika oblast (1939–44).

Vilgort or **Vil'gort** (vēlgôrt'), village (1948 pop. over 2,000), SW Komi Autonomous SSR, Russian SFSR, 3 mi. SW of Syktyvkar; flax, potatoes.

Vilhelmina (vĭlhělmē'nä), village (pop. 1,320), Vasterbotten co., N Sweden, on upper Angerman R. and 60 mi. W of Lycksele; trade center; woodworking; mfg. of fishing equipment.

Vilhena (vēlyā'nŭ), village, SE Guaporé territory, W Brazil, on Cuiabá-Pôrto Velho telegraph line, and 370 mi. SE of Pôrto Velho.

Viliya River (vē'lĭyä), Lith. *Neris,* Pol. *Wilja,* in Belorussian SSR and Lithuania, rises 8 mi. SW of Begoml, Belorussian SSR; flows 317 mi. generally WNW, past Vileika and Vilna (Lithuania; head of navigation), to Neman R. at Kaunas; logging.

Viljakkala (vĭl'yäk-kä"lä), village (commune pop. 2,802), Turku-Pori co., SW Finland, in lake region, 20 mi. NW of Tampere; copper and gold mines.

Viljandi, Vilyandi, or **Vil'yandi** (all: vēl'yändē), Ger. *Fellin,* city (pop. 11,788), central Estonia, on railroad and 80 mi. SSE of Tallinn; agr. market (rye, flax, dairy products, horses); mfg. (matches, linen textiles); machine shop. Has old castle ruins (former residence of Grand Master of the Knights). Viljandi highland (S) rises to 443 ft. Founded 13th cent. by Livonian Knights; became a Hanseatic town; passed in 1561 to Poland, in 1629 to Sweden; occupied (1710) by Russia and inc. into govt. of Livonia until 1920.

Viljoensdrift (fĭl'yo͞onsdrĭft"), town (pop. 3,316), N Orange Free State, U. of So. Afr., near Transvaal border, near Vaal R. (bridge), 4 mi. S of Vereeniging; alt. 4,762 ft.; coal mining.

Viljoenskroon (fĭl'yo͞onskro͞on"), town (pop. 2,209), N Orange Free State, U. of So. Afr., 35 mi. SSW of Potchefstroom; alt. c.4,400 ft.; grain, stock; in coal-mining region.

Vilkaviskis or **Vilkavishkis** (vēlkävēsh'kēs), Lith. *Vilkaviškis,* Pol. *Wyłkowyszki,* Rus. *Volkovyshki,* city (pop. 8,733), SW Lithuania, 40 mi. WSW of Kaunas; industrial center; mfg. of sheet-metal goods, woolens, knitwear, chemicals; hide dressing, flour milling, tobacco processing, sawmilling. Dates from 17th cent.; passed 1795 to Rus. Poland; in Suvalki govt. until 1920.

Vilkija, Vilkiya, or **Vil'kiya** (vēl'kĭyä), Rus. *Vilki* or *Vil'ki,* town (1929 pop. 1,780), S central Lithuania, on right bank of Neman R. and 17 mi. NW of Kaunas, amid gardens; mfg. (machines, felt goods), sawmilling. Gothic church. In Rus. Kovno govt. until 1920.

Vilkitski Strait, Russian SFSR: see BORIS VILKITSKI STRAIT.

Vilkomir, Lithuania: see UKMERGE.

Vilkovo (vēl'kŭvŭ), Rum. *Vâlcov* (vŭl'kôv), town (1941 pop. 5,075), S Izmail oblast, Ukrainian SSR, 15 mi. E of Kiliya, on Kiliya arm of Danube R. delta, near its mouth; important fishing center (sturgeon); black caviar production.

Villa Abecia (bē'yä äbä'syä), town, ⊙ Sud Cinti or Sur Cinti prov., Chuquisaca dept., S Bolivia, on Cotagaita R., near mouth of San Juan R., and 28 mi. SSW of Camargo, on Sucre-Tarija road; vineyards, corn, orchards. Until c.1945, Camataquí; Villa General Germán Busch until c.1948.

Villa Aberastain, Argentina: see ABERASTAIN.

Villa Acuña (äko͞o'nyä), town (pop. 5,607), Coahuila, N Mexico, on the Rio Grande opposite Del Rio (Texas), 50 mi. NW of Piedras Negras; stock-raising center (cattle, sheep); cereals, candelilla wax, istle fibers.

Villa Adelina (ädälē'nä), town (pop. estimate 3,000) in Greater Buenos Aires, Argentina, 12 mi. NW of Buenos Aires; horticultural center with mfg. (cardboard, ceramics).

Villa Ahumada (äo͞omä'dä), town (pop. 1,844), Chihuahua, N Mexico, on railroad and 80 mi. S of Ciudad Juárez; gold, silver, lead, copper mining.

Villa Alba, Argentina: see GENERAL SAN MARTÍN, town, La Pampa natl. territory.

Villa Alberdi (älběr'dē), town (pop. estimate 2,500), S Tucumán prov., Argentina, 60 mi. SSW of Tucumán; rail junction, lumbering and farming center. Sugar refinery, sawmills, flour mills. Sugar cane, corn, wheat, alfalfa, tobacco, livestock. Mineral waters.

Villa Aldama (äldä'mä), town (pop. 1,328), Veracruz, E Mexico, in Sierra Madre Oriental, 20 mi. WNW of Jalapa; coffee, corn, fruit.

Villa Alegre (älā'grā), town (pop. 1,365), Linares prov., S central Chile, 11 mi. NNW of Linares; agr. center (wheat, corn, chick-peas, beans, wine, livestock); flour milling, dairying, wine making.

Villa Alemana (älämä'nä), town (pop. 5,615), Valparaiso prov., central Chile, on railroad and 15 mi. E of Valparaiso; resort and fruitgrowing center; also grain, vegetables, cattle; horticulture; lumbering.

Villa Allende (äyěn'dā), town (pop. 3,420), N central Córdoba prov., Argentina, in hills, 10 mi. NW of Córdoba; resort; stock raising.

Villa Allende. 1 or **San Fernando** (sän fĕrnän'dō), town (pop. 2,794), Chiapas, S Mexico, in Sierra Madre, 10 mi. NW of Tuxtla; cereals, sugar cane, fruit, livestock. **2** or **Allende,** officially San José Allende, town (pop. 687), Mexico state, central Mexico, 30 mi. W of Toluca; cereals, livestock.

Villa Alta (äl'tä), officially San Ildefonso Villa Alta, town (pop. 676), Oaxaca, S Mexico, 40 mi NE of Oaxaca; cereals, coffee, tobacco, sugar, fruit, stock.

Villa Altagracia (ältägrä'syä), town (1950 pop. 1,988), Trujillo prov., S central Dominican Republic, in foothills of the Cordillera Central, 23 mi. NW of Ciudad Trujillo; rice, coffee, fruit.

Villa Alvarez, Mexico: see ZIMATLÁN.

Villa Alvaro Obregón, Mexico: see VILLA OBREGÓN, Federal Dist.

Villa Ana (ä'nä), town (pop. estimate 800), NE Santa Fe prov., Argentina, on railroad and 45 mi. N of Reconquista; stock-raising and lumbering center; sawmills, tannin factory.

Villa Angela (änhä'lä), town (1947 pop. 7,337), S Chaco natl. territory, Argentina, 60 mi. SSW of Presidencia Roque Sáenz Peña; rail terminus; farming and lumbering center (quebracho, carob, guaiacum, guava), with sawmills, cotton gins. Cotton, spurge, corn, flax, sunflowers, livestock. Airport.

Villa Aroma, Bolivia: see SICASICA.

Villa Atamisqui, Argentina: see ATAMISQUI.

Villa Atuel (ätwěl'), town (pop. estimate 1,000), E central Mendoza prov., Argentina, on railroad, on Atuel R. (irrigation) and 27 mi. SE of San Rafael; fruitgrowing center; alcohol distilleries.

Villa Azueta (äswā'tä) or **Tesechoacán** (täsächwä-kän'), town (pop. 3,761), Veracruz, SE Mexico, in Gulf lowland, 38 mi. SW of San Andrés Tuxtla; agr. center (sugar cane, bananas, stock).

Villaba (bēyä'vä, bělyä'vä), town (1939 pop. 3,262; 1948 municipality pop. 14,092), NW Leyte, Philippines, on Visayan Sea, 40 mi. W of Tacloban; agr. center (rice, sugar cane). Rock asphalt is mined.

Villa Ballester (bē'yä bäyěstěr'), city (pop. estimate 15,000) in Greater Buenos Aires, Argentina, N of San Martín, 12 mi. NW of Buenos Aires; mfg. (aluminum articles, electrical appliances, cables, needles, ceramics, plastics, dairy products).

Villa Basilica (vēl'lä bäsē'lēkä), village (pop. 722), Lucca prov., Tuscany, central Italy, 9 mi. NE of Lucca; paper.

Villabate (vēl"läbä'tě), town (pop. 6,542), Palermo prov., NW Sicily, 5 mi. ESE of Palermo, in citrus-fruit region; soap.

Villa Belgrano (bē'yä bělgrä'nō), town (pop. estimate 500), S Tucumán prov., Argentina, on railroad and 55 mi. SSW of Tucumán; stock-raising and dairying center.

Villa Bella (bě'yä), village (pop. c.100), Beni dept., N Bolivia, port at confluence of Beni and Mamoré rivers (here forming Madeira R.), 60 mi. NE of Riberalta, on Brazil border opposite Vila Murtinho (on Madeira-Mamoré RR), Brazil. Center for rubber export and for imports from Brazil; customs station.

Villa Bella. 1 City, Mato Grosso, Brazil: see MATO GROSSO, city. **2** City, Pernambuco, Brazil: see SERRA TALHADA. **3** City, São Paulo, Brazil: see ILHABELA.

Villa Bella da Imperatriz, Brazil: see PARINTINS.

Villa Bella das Palmeiras, Brazil: see PALMEIRAS, Bahia.

Villa Bens (běl'yä běns), town (pop. 3,503), ⊙ Southern Protectorate of Morocco, Sp. West Africa, at Cape Juby on the Atlantic, 150 mi. E of Las Palmas, Canary Isls. (steamship connection); 27°57'N 12°55'W. Fort; airfield. Occupied by Spaniards since 1916. Until c.1940, ⊙ Sp. Sahara. Until 1950, called Tarfaia or Tarfaya, and formerly also called Cabo Juby or Cabo Yubi.

Villablanca (bělyäbläng'kä), town (pop. 2,035), Huelva prov., SW Spain, 6 mi. NE of Ayamonte; cereals, oranges, figs, grapes.

Villablino (bělyäblē'nō), town (pop. 793), Leon prov., NW Spain, on Sil R. and 32 mi. NE of Ponferrada; coal-mining center (anthracite and bituminous) connected with Ponferrada by mining railroad. Near by are mining villages of Caboalles de Abajo (pop. 1,007) and Villaseca de Laciana (pop. 1,701).

Villabona (bělyävō'nä), town (pop. 1,168), Guipúzcoa prov., N Spain, 4 mi. NNE of Tolosa; mfg. (paper, cotton and woolen textiles).

Villabrágima (bělyävrä'hēmä), town (pop. 1,970), Valladolid prov., N central Spain, 6 mi. SW of Medina de Ríoseco; grain, livestock.

Villa Bruzual (bē'yä bro͞oswäl'), town (pop. 1,077), Portuguesa state, W Venezuela, in llanos, 21 mi. S of Acarigua; cotton, cattle. Sometimes Turén.

Villabruzzi (vēl-läbro͞ot'tsē) or **Villaggio** (vēl-läj'-jō), town (pop. 9,000), in the Benadir, S Ital.

Somaliland, on the Webi Shebeli (dammed here 1923 for irrigation), on road and 50 mi. NNE of Mogadishu; agr. colony (full name Villagio Duca degli Abruzzi) developed after 1920 by duke of Abruzzi. Chief crops: sugar cane, cotton, castor beans, bananas. Industries include sugar refining, alcohol distilling, cotton ginning, oilseed pressing, agave-fiber processing, soap mfg. Has hosp. Formerly terminus of railroad (70 mi. long) from Mogadishu, dismantled and removed to Kenya during Second World War.

Villabuena del Puente (bĕlyävwä′nä dhĕl pwĕn′tä), village (pop. 1,488), Zamora prov., NW Spain, 10 mi. S of Toro; lumber, livestock, cereals, wine.

Villa Bustos (bē′yä bōō′stōs), village (pop. estimate 600), ⊙ Sanagasta dept. (□ 585; 1947 census pop. 1,518), central La Rioja prov., Argentina, at E foot of Sierra de Velasco, 14 mi. NW of La Rioja; wine-growing, stock raising.

Villa Canales (känä′lĕs), town (1950 pop. 1,369), Guatemala dept., S central Guatemala, near E shore of L. Amatitlán, on railroad and 11 mi. S of Guatemala; alt. 3,989 ft. Agr. center (coffee, sugar cane, grain, fodder grasses); cattle raising; lumbering. Until 1921, Pueblo Viejo.

Villa Cañas (kä′nyäs), town (pop. estimate 3,500), S Santa Fe prov., Argentina, 26 mi. SE of Venado Tuerto; agr. (flax, cotton, corn, sunflowers, vegetables; apiculture); flour milling.

Villacañas (bĕlyäkä′nyäs), town (pop. 9,094), Toledo prov., central Spain, in New Castile, on railroad to Andalusia, and 40 mi. ESE of Toledo; processing and agr. center in fertile region of upper La Mancha. Olives, saffron, grapes, cereals, sheep. Olive-oil pressing, alcohol and liquor distilling, wine making, flour milling, cheese processing, woolwashing; mfg. of soap extracts and tiles. Sodium and magnesium sulphate is extracted from near-by salt ponds.

Villacarlos (–kär′lōs), town (pop. 2,325), Minorca, Balearic Isls., just E of Mahón, whose fine bay it adjoins; wheat, vegetables, potatoes, livestock; mfg. of sandals, cloth.

Villacarrillo (–kärē′lyō), city (pop. 11,745), Jaén prov., S Spain, in Andalusia, in mountainous dist., 46 mi. NE of Jaén; agr. trade center. Olive-oil processing, flour milling; soap, chocolate mfg. Cereals, wine, beans, livestock in area. Mineral springs.

Villa Castelli (bē′yä kästĕ′lē), village (pop. estimate 500), ⊙ General Lamadrid dept. (□ 2,335; 1947 census 1,210), central La Rioja prov., Argentina, 90 mi. WNW of La Rioja; stock-raising and flour-milling center.

Villa Castelli (vēl′lä kästĕl′lē), village (pop. 3,373), Brindisi prov., Apulia, S Italy, 15 mi. NE of Taranto; wine, olive oil.

Villacastín (bĕlyäkästēn′), town (pop. 1,424), Segovia prov., central Spain, road junction 19 mi. SW of Segovia; trading and stock raising. Flour milling, tile mfg.

Villach (fĭ′läkh), Slovenian *Beljak*, city (1951 pop. 30,061), Carinthia, S Austria, on Drau R. and 22 mi. W of Klagenfurt; rail and industrial center; ships lumber; iron- and steelworks, mfg. of cellulose, metallic colors, lead products, margarine, artificial coffee, felt hats. Has free trade zones. Belonged to bishopric of Bamberg to mid-18th cent. Has 2 Gothic churches, archaeological mus. in City Hall. Warmbad Villach (värm′bät), with mineral spring, is 2 mi. S, at E foot of Villach Alp.

Villach Alp, small mountain group, Carinthia, S Austria, W of Villach; E spur of Gailtal Alps. Zinc and lead mined on N slope, near Bleiberg. Warmbad Villach, resort, is at E foot. Highest peak, Dobratsch (7,106 ft.).

Villacidro (vēl″lächē′drô), town (pop. 7,683), Cagliari prov., SW Sardinia, 25 mi. NW of Cagliari, in the Campidano; rail terminus; summer resort; alcohol distilling. Eucalyptus plantations (mine timbers, poles) near by, in agr. area (herbs, almonds, olives, grapes, oranges).

Villa Cisneros (bēl′yä thēznä′rōs), town (pop. 86; urban dist. pop. c.1,000), ⊙ Río de Oro, Sp. West Africa, on Villa Cisneros peninsula (Arabic *Dájla*; c.25 mi. long, 3 mi. wide) on the Atlantic coast; 23°42′N 15°57′W. Fisheries. Anchorage in Río de Oro Bay (bet. peninsula and mainland). Airport on Europe–South America route. Radio transmitter; fort. First permanent Sp. settlement on W African coast (1884).

Villa Clara, Cuba: see Santa Clara, city.

Villa Colón (bē′yä kōlōn′), town (pop. estimate 1,500), ⊙ Caucete dept. (□ c.3,000; 1947 pop. 18,252), S San Juan prov., Argentina, in San Juan R. valley (irrigation area), on railroad (Caucete station) and 16 mi. SE of San Juan. Wine, fruit, vegetables; wine making; lime deposits. Irrigation dam near by.

Villa Colón, town (pop. 310), ⊙ Mora canton, San José prov., central Costa Rica, 12 mi. W of San José, in arid dist. Mfg. of mats, brooms, baskets. An old Indian center. Formerly called Pacaca.

Villa Colón, Uruguay: see Colón, Montevideo dept.

Villa Concepción or **Villa Concepción del Tío** (kōnsĕpsyōn′ dĕl tē′ō), town (pop. estimate 1,000), E Córdoba prov., Argentina, on arm of the Río Segundo and 80 mi. E of Córdoba; stock-raising center. Has old colonial bldgs.

Villa Concepción, Paraguay: see Concepción, city.

Villaconejos (bĕlyäkōnā′hōs), town (pop. 2,554), Madrid prov., central Spain, 25 mi. SSE of Madrid, in fertile agr. region (cereals, grapes, olives, potatoes, melons, sheep, goats). Medicinal waters.

Villa Constitución (bē′yä kōnstētōōsyōn′), town (pop. estimate 4,000), ⊙ Constitución dept. (□ 1,225; 1947 pop. 69,121), SE Santa Fe prov., Argentina, port on Paraná R. and 26 mi. SE of Rosario; rail terminus and agr. center (flax, potatoes, wheat, grapes, livestock).

Villa Corona (kōrō′nä), town (pop. 3,017), Jalisco, W Mexico, on L. Atotonilco, 27 mi. SW of Guadalajara; alt. 4,475 ft.; agr. center (grain, beans, alfalfa, sugar cane, fruit, stock).

Villa Coronado (kōrōnä′dō), town (pop. 815), Chihuahua, N Mexico, on Florido R. and 35 mi. ESE of Hidalgo del Parral; cereals, cotton, fruit.

Villa Corzo (kôr′sō), town (pop. 877), Chiapas, S Mexico, 40 mi. SSW of Tuxtla; beans, fruit.

Villacoublay, France: see Vélizy-Villacoublay.

Villa Crespo, Argentina: see Crespo, Entre Ríos.

Villa Cuauhtémoc (kwoutā′mōk). **1** Town (pop. 2,515), Mexico state, central Mexico, 28 mi. W of Mexico city; cereals, livestock. Formerly Otzolotepec. **2** or **Pueblo Viejo** (pwĕ′blō byā′hō), town (pop. 4,271), Veracruz, E Mexico, on Tampico Lagoon, near the Gulf, 3 mi. SE of Tampico; petroleum drilling and refining. Bellavista petroleum-refining plant near by.

Villada (bĕlyä′dhä), town (pop. 2,216), Palencia prov., N central Spain, 28 mi. NW of Palencia; flour milling, candy mfg.; agr. trade (livestock, cereals, vegetables).

Villa da Barra, Brazil: see Manaus.

Villa de Álvarez (bē′yä dā äl′värĕs), town (pop. 2,044), Colima, W Mexico, in W foothills of Sierra Madre Occidental, 2 mi. NW of Colima; alt. 1,839 ft. Agr. center (rice, corn, beans, sugar, tobacco, fruit, stock). Silver deposits near by.

Villa de Cecilia, Mexico: see Ciudad Madero.

Villa de Cos (dā kōs′), town (pop. 1,119), Zacatecas, N central Mexico, 38 mi. NNE of Zacatecas; alt. 6,725 ft.; manganese mining.

Villa de Cura or **Cura** (kōō′rä), town (pop. 8,294), Aragua state, N Venezuela, in valley of coastal range, 17 mi. SE of Maracay, 50 mi. SW of Caracas; agr. center (coffee, cacao, sugar cane, indigo, cotton). Copper deposits near by. Heavily damaged by 1900 earthquake.

Villa de Don Fadrique, La (lä vē′lyä dhā dhōm′ fädhrē′kā), town (pop. 5,105), Toledo prov., central Spain, on railroad and 15 mi. N of Alcázar de San Juan (Ciudad Real prov.). Agr. center on La Mancha plain: saffron, cereals, potatoes, grapes, olives, wool, sheep, goats. Alcohol and liquor distilling, wine making, cheese processing, sawmilling, plaster mfg.

Villa del Campo (bē′lyä dhĕl käm′pō), town (pop. 1,367), Cáceres prov., W Spain, 21 mi. NW of Plasencia; wheat, olive oil, wine.

Villa del Carbón (bē′yä dĕl kärbōn′), town (pop. 1,623), Mexico state, central Mexico, 26 mi. NW of Mexico city; grain, fruit, livestock.

Villa del Cerro, Uruguay: see Cerro.

Villa Delgado (bē′yä dĕlgä′dō), residential town (pop. 7,495), San Salvador dept., S central Salvador, 2.5 mi. NE of San Salvador; pottery making; agr. Formed 1935 by union of 3 adjoining towns of Paleca, Aculhuaca, and San Sebastian.

Villa del Nevoso, Yugoslavia: see Bistrica.

Villa de los Ranchos, Argentina: see Villa del Rosario.

Villa del Prado (bē′lyä dhĕl prä′dhō), town (pop. 2,387), Madrid prov., central Spain, on railroad and 34 mi. WSW of Madrid; grapes, tomatoes, olives, sheep. Noted for white wines. Also liquor distilling, olive-oil pressing, pottery mfg.

Villa del Refugio, Mexico: see Tabasco, town, Zacatecas.

Villa del Río (rē′ō), city (pop. 6,493), Córdoba prov., S Spain, 8 mi. NE of Bujalance; chemical works (carbon disulphide, soap, peanut oils); chocolate mfg., olive-oil processing. Cereals, mules.

Villa del Rosario (bē′yä, rōsä′ryō), town (pop. 4,308), ⊙ Río Segundo dept. (□ c.2,000; pop. 61,342), central Córdoba prov., Argentina, on the Río Segundo and 40 mi. ESE of Córdoba; rail junction; agr. center (wheat, corn, peanuts, alfalfa, livestock); dairy products. Formerly Villa de los Ranchos.

Villa del Salvador (sälvädōr′), town (pop. estimate, including Angaco Norte, 2,000), ⊙ Angaco Norte dept. (□ c.950; 1947 pop. 6,375), S San Juan prov., Argentina, adjoining (NE) Angaco del Norte and 9 mi. NE of San Juan; wine, alfalfa, corn, onions, livestock (goats, mules, horses).

Villa de María (bē′yä dā märē′ä), town (pop. estimate 500), ⊙ Río Seco dept. (□ c.3,900; pop. 13,974), N Córdoba prov., Argentina, on the Río Seco and 110 mi. NNE of Córdoba; livestock center. Called Río Seco until c.1945.

Villa de Reyes (dā rā′ĕs), town (pop. 2,383), San Luis Potosí, N central Mexico, on interior plateau, near Guanajuato border, 25 mi. S of San Luis Potosí; alt. 5,968 ft. Agr. center (grain, fruit, beans, livestock). Its railroad station is 3 mi. NW. Sometimes Reyes.

Villa de San Antonio (sän äntō′nyō), town (pop. 1,159), Comayagua dept., W central Honduras, in Comayagua valley, on road and 10 mi. SSE of Comayagua; commercial center; sugar milling; sugar cane, rice. Sometimes called San Antonio. Archaeological site of Tenampúa is 4 mi. SE.

Villa de San Francisco (fränsē′skō), town (pop. 813), Francisco Morazán dept., S central Honduras, on Choluteca R. and 8 mi. SE of San Juan de Flores; grain, sugar cane, livestock.

Villa de Santa Rita, Argentina: see Catuna.

Villa de Soto (sō′tō) or **Soto**, town (pop. estimate 1,000), NW Córdoba prov., Argentina, 60 mi. NW of Córdoba; stock raising, sawmilling, viticulture.

Villa Diego (dyā′gō), town (pop. estimate 800), SE Santa Fe prov., Argentina, on Paraná R. and 5 mi. S of Rosario, in agr. area (corn, alfalfa, grapes, potatoes).

Villadiego (bĕlyä-dhyā′gō), town (pop. 1,224), Burgos prov., N Spain, 19 mi. NW of Burgos; flour milling, mfg. of bags and tiles; limekiln.

Villa Dolores (bē′yä dōlō′rĕs). **1** City (pop. 14,176), W Córdoba prov., Argentina, on the Río de los Sauces, opposite San Pedro, and 70 mi. SW of Córdoba; trade center for agr. and mineral area. Corn, peanuts, wheat, wine, tobacco, fruit, sheep, cattle. Airport. Tobacco research station. **2** Town, San Luis prov., Argentina: see Concarán.

Villa Domínico (dōmē′nēkō), city (pop. estimate 5,000) in Greater Buenos Aires, Argentina, 5 mi. SE of Buenos Aires; residential and mfg. (tanneries, paper mills, food-preserving plants).

Villadose (vēl″lädô′zē), village (pop. 1,269), Rovigo prov., Veneto, N Italy, 5 mi. E of Rovigo.

Villadossola (vēl″lädôs′sôlä), town (pop. 3,920), Novara prov., Piedmont, N Italy, near Toce R., 4 mi. SSW of Domodossola; foundries, chemical plant, jute mill. Gold mines near by.

Villa Elisa (bē′yä ālē′sä). **1** Town (pop. 3,160), NE Buenos Aires prov., Argentina, 8 mi. NW of La Plata; dairying; truck. **2** Town (pop. estimate 1,500), E Entre Ríos prov., Argentina, on railroad and 16 mi. WNW of Colón; agr. center (grain, poultry, livestock); flour milling, dairying.

Villa Escalante (bē′yä ĕskälän′tä), town (pop. 2,951), Michoacán, central Mexico, 7 mi. SSW of Pátzcuaro; alt. 7,230 ft.; agr. center (cereals, coffee, tropical fruit, sugar cane). Formerly Santa Clara.

Villa Escobedo (ĕskōbā′dō), town (pop. 505), Chihuahua, N Mexico, 5 mi. NW of Hidalgo del Parral; rail terminus; lead and zinc mining; silver and gold deposits.

Villaescusa de Haro (bĕlyä ĕskōō′sä dhā ä′rō), town (pop. 1,226), Cuenca prov., E central Spain, 4 mi. NNE of Belmonte; cereals, grapes, olives, livestock; lumbering; plaster mfg.

Villafáfila (bĕlyäfä′fēlä), town (pop. 1,612), Zamora prov., NW Spain, 12 mi. SSE of Benavente; cereals, wine, fruit. Salt marshes near by.

Villafaniés (–fänyās′), town (pop. 1,560), Castellón de la Plana prov., E Spain, 9 mi. N of Castellón de la Plana; olive-oil processing; lumbering; cereals, wine, fruit.

Villa Federal (bē′yä fādäräl′), town (1947 pop. 9,196), N Entre Ríos prov., Argentina, 55 mi. NW of Concordia; rail junction, agr. center (corn, wheat, flax, cattle, hogs, poultry); flour.

Villafeliche (bĕlyäfālē′chä), town (pop. 1,063), Saragossa prov., NE Spain, 13 mi. SE of Calatayud; agr. center (cereals, sugar beets, wine); mfg. of explosives.

Villa Flores (bē′yä flō′rĕs), town (pop. 3,288), Chiapas, S Mexico, 38 mi. SSW of Tuxtla; agr. center (corn, beans, sugar cane, tropical fruit).

Villa Florida, Paraguay: see Florida.

Villa Franca, Paraguay: see Franca.

Villafranca (bĕlyäfräng′kä), town (pop. 3,028), Navarre prov., N Spain, near Aragon R., 15 mi. NNW of Tudela; agr. center (cereals, truck produce, sugar beets, wine, livestock).

Villafranca de Bonany (dhä bōnänē′), town (pop. 2,118), Majorca, Balearic Isls., 23 mi. E of Palma; cereals, grapes, melons, hogs.

Villafranca de Córdoba (kôr′dhōvä), town (pop. 3,990), Córdoba prov., S Spain, on the Guadalquivir and 14 mi. ENE of Córdoba; olive-oil processing, fruit canning; cereals, livestock.

Villafranca del Bierzo (dhĕl byĕr′thō), town (pop. 2,839), Leon prov., NW Spain, 12 mi. WNW of Ponferrada; terminus of branch railroad from Toral de los Vados, in fertile agr. area (wine, cereals, fruit, chestnuts).

Villafranca de los Barros (dhä lōs bä′rōs), city (pop. 15,002), Badajoz prov., W Spain, in Estremadura, on railroad and 40 mi. SE of Badajoz. Agr. and processing center in fertile Tierra de Barros (cereals, vegetables, olives, grapes, livestock). Mfg. of olive oil, liquor, flour, sweets, meat products, shoes, soap, knives; sulphur; sawmilling. Has Jesuit col.

Villafranca de los Caballeros (kävälyä′rōs), town (pop. 4,913), Toledo prov., central Spain, near Ciudad Real prov. border, 45 mi. SSE of Aranjuez; agr. and processing center. Cereals, olives, grapes, anise, saffron, sheep, mules. Alcohol and liquor distilling, flour milling, cheese processing. Magnesium-sulphate mining. Hydroelectric plant. Thermal springs.

Villafranca del Panadés (dhĕl pänä-dhās'), town (pop. 10,504), Barcelona prov., NE Spain, in Catalonia, 25 mi. W of Barcelona; wine-production center. Also tanning, flour- and sawmilling; mfg. of chemicals (dyes, sulphates, cream of tartar), silk fabrics, cement, soap, liqueurs, flour products. Ships fruit, garlic, hazelnuts. Has medieval palace of Aragonese kings and a largely restored church with 14th-cent. bell tower.

Villafranca de Oria (dhā ō'ryä), town (pop. 4,335), Guipúzcoa prov., N Spain, 8 mi. SW of Tolosa; mfg. of furniture, knitwear, brandy, cider; sawmilling. Agr. trade (chestnuts, apples). Mineral springs.

Villafranca di Verona (vēl"läfräng'kä dē vĕrō'nä), town (pop. 4,986), Verona prov., Veneto, N Italy, 10 mi. SW of Verona, in sericulture region; mfg. (silk textiles, fishing nets). Here in 1859, following decisive battles of Magenta and Solferino, a preliminary Franco-Austrian peace treaty was signed whereby Austria ceded Lombardy to Italy.

Villafranca in Lunigiana (ēn lōōnējä'nä), village (pop. 1,689), Massa e Carrara prov., Tuscany, central Italy, near Magra R., 6 mi. SSE of Pontremoli; tanning extracts, soap.

Villafranca Piemonte (pyĕmôn'tĕ), village (pop. 3,247), Torino prov., Piedmont, NW Italy, near Po R., 22 mi. SSW of Turin, in irrigated cereal, fruit, cattle region; agr. and commercial center. Bet. 1934–50, called Villafranca Sabauda.

Villafrechós (bĕlyäfrächōs'), town (pop. 1,185), Valladolid prov., N central Spain, 10 mi. W of Medina de Ríoseco; cereals, wine, livestock.

Villa Frontado (bē'yä frōntä'dō), town (pop. 692), Sucre state, NE Venezuela, on shore of Gulf of Cariaco, just W of Cariaco, 33 mi. E of Cumaná; coconut growing.

Villa Frontera (frōntä'rä) or **Frontera**, town (pop. 6,035), Coahuila, N Mexico, in E outliers of Sierra Madre Oriental, adjoining Monclova, 115 mi. NW of Monterrey; alt. 1,926 ft. Rail junction; agr. center (cereals, fruit, cattle); flour milling, wax mfg.

Villafruela (bĕlyäfrwä'lä), town (pop. 1,051), Burgos prov., N Spain, 15 mi. N of Roa; cereals, potatoes, sheep.

Villa García (bē'yä gärsē'ä). **1** Town, Nuevo León, Mexico: see GARCÍA. **2** Town (pop. 1,922), Zacatecas, N central Mexico, 55 mi. SE of Zacatecas; mercury-mining center.

Villagarcía (bĕlyägär-thē'ä), town (pop. 5,079), Pontevedra prov., NW Spain, Atlantic seaport on Arosa Bay, and 12 mi. NNW of Pontevedra; exports fish, fish oils, lumber. Fishing and fish-processing center; boatbuilding, metalworking, tanning; mfg. of acetone, candles, ceramics; flour- and sawmilling. Popular bathing resort.

Villagarcía de la Torre (dhā lä tō'rā), town (pop. 3,292), Badajoz prov., W Spain, 5 mi. NW of Llerena; mining (coal, copper) and agr. (olives, cereals, vegetables, stock). Has remains of anc. Moorish castle.

Villagarcía del Llano (dhĕl lyä'nō), town (pop. 1,232), Cuenca prov., E central Spain, 23 mi. N of Albacete; saffron, cereals, grapes, sheep. Exports pine cones.

Villa General Germán Busch, Bolivia: see VILLA ABECIA.

Villa General Mitre (bē'yä hānäräl' mē'trä), town (pop. estimate 1,000), ⊙ Totoral dept. (□ c.1,600; pop. 17,526), N Córdoba prov., Argentina, 50 mi. N of Córdoba; health resort and agr. center; winegrowing, cattle raising. Sometimes called General Mitre.

Villa General Pérez, Bolivia: see VILLA PÉREZ.

Villa General Roca (rō'kä), village (pop. estimate 300), ⊙ Belgrano dept. (□ 2,380; 1947 pop. 8,636), N San Luis prov., Argentina, at W foot of Sierra de San Luis, 50 mi. N of San Luis; stock-raising center.

Village-Neuf (vēläzh'-nûf'), Ger. *Neudorf* (noi'dôrf), town (pop. 2,178), Haut-Rhin dept., E France, on left bank of the Rhine (Ger. border), near Swiss border, 4 mi. NNW of Basel; mfg. of railroad rolling stock; truck gardening.

Village of the Branch, village (pop. 163), Suffolk co., SE N.Y., on central Long Isl., 9 mi. SW of Port Jefferson, in farm area (potatoes, truck).

Villaggio, Ital. Somaliland: see VILLABRUZZI.

Villaggio Duca degli Abruzzi, Ital. Somaliland: see VILLABRUZZI.

Villaggio Mussolini, Sardinia: see ARBOREA.

Villa Gobernador Gálvez (bē'yä gōbĕrnädōr' gäl'vĕs), town (pop. estimate 800), SE Santa Fe prov., Argentina, 5 mi. S of Rosario; rail junction (Coronel Aguirre station) and agr. center (corn, alfalfa, grapes, livestock).

Villa Gonzáles Ortega (gōnsä'lĕs ôrtā'gä), town (pop. 1,637), Zacatecas, N central Mexico, 45 mi. ESE of Zacatecas; grain, maguey, beans, stock. Formerly El Carro.

Villagonzalo (bĕlyägōn-thä'lō), town (pop. 2,125), Badajoz prov., W Spain, on the Guadalete, on railroad and 9 mi. ESE of Mérida; olives, cereals, grapes, livestock. Flour milling, olive-oil pressing.

Villagrán (bēyägrän'). **1** Town (pop. 4,141), Guanajuato, central Mexico, on Lerma R. and 12 mi. W of Celaya, on railroad; agr. center (grain, alfalfa, sugar cane, vegetables, fruit, livestock). Formerly El Guaje. **2** Town (pop. 1,128), Tamaulipas, NE Mexico, at E foot of Sierra Madre Oriental, on Inter-American Highway and 65 mi. NNW of Ciudad Victoria; sugar cane, cereals, livestock.

Villagrande, Italy: see AURONZO.

Villagrande Strisaili (vēl"lägrän'dĕ strēzäē'lē), village (pop. 2,313), Nuoro prov., E Sardinia, 26 mi. SSE of Nuoro; iron mines.

Villa Grove. **1** Village (pop. c.100), Saguache co., S central Colo., on San Luis Creek, bet. foothills of Sawatch and Sangre de Cristo mts., and 15 mi. NE of Saguache; alt. c.7,960 ft.; ranching. **2** City (pop. 2,026), Douglas co., E Ill., on Embarrass R. and 17 mi. SSE of Champaign, in agr. area; cannery, railroad shops; ships grain, fruit. Inc. 1913.

Villa Guardia (vēl'lä gwär'dyä), village (pop. 238), Como prov., Lombardy, N Italy, 4 mi. SW of Como; silk-milling center.

Villaguay (bīyägwī'), town (1947 pop. 16,664), ⊙ Villaguay dept. (□ 2,875; 1947 pop. 56,608), central Entre Ríos prov., Argentina, 90 mi. E of Paraná; rail terminus; agr. center (wheat, oats, corn, alfalfa, wine, citrus fruit, livestock); tanning, tobacco processing. Has natl. col., agr. school, theater.

Villa Guerrero (bē'yä gĕrā'rō). **1** Town (pop. 1,097), Jalisco, W Mexico, 26 mi. SW of Colotlán; corn, wheat, livestock. **2** Town (pop. 2,390), Mexico state, central Mexico, 27 mi. S of Toluca; cereals, sugar cane, fruit, livestock.

Villa Guillermina (gīyĕrmē'nä), town (pop. estimate 1,500), NE Santa Fe prov., Argentina, 65 mi. N of Reconquista; rail junction; lumbering center; sawmilling, tannin processing.

Villa Gustavo A. Madero, Mexico: see GUSTAVO A. MADERO.

Villa Hayes (ä'yĕs), town (dist. pop. 5,124), ⊙ Presidente Hayes dept., central Paraguay, on right bank of Paraguay R., in Chaco region, and 15 mi. NE of Asunción; 25°7'S 57°35'W. Trading and agr. center (sugar cane, alfalfa, corn, cotton); alcohol distilleries, sugar refineries. Founded 1855 by Carlos Antonio López, it was renamed in honor of Amer. President Rutherford B. Hayes, arbiter in boundary dispute bet. Paraguay and Argentina after War of the Triple Alliance (1865–70).

Villahermosa (bēyäĕrmō'sä), town (pop. 1,530), Tolima dept., W central Colombia, at NE foot of Nevado del Ruiz, 30 mi. E of Manizales, in agr. region (potatoes, wheat, corn, coffee, sugar cane, bananas, yucca, stock); alt. 6,749 ft.

Villahermosa (bēyäĕrmō'sä), city (pop. 25,114), ⊙ Tabasco, SE Mexico, on Grijalva R., in Gulf lowland, and 425 mi. ESE of Mexico city; 17°59'N 92°55'W. Distributing, processing, and agr. center (sugar cane, coffee, cacao, tobacco, vanilla, cereals, beans, bananas, rubber); sugar refining, alcohol and liquor distilling, banana processing, cigar making, rice milling, lumbering; mfg. of soap, tile, rum, clothing. Airfield, radio station. Founded 1596, it was named Villahermosa in 1598, became San Juan Bautista in 1826, and Villahermosa once more in 1915.

Villahermosa (bēlyäĕrmō'sä), town (pop. 5,414), Ciudad Real prov., S central Spain, in New Castile, 26 mi. E of Valdepeñas. Agr. center on La Mancha plain (Campo de Montiel); cereals, chick-peas, vetch, truck produce, sheep; apiculture. Lumbering. Flour milling, cheese processing, plaster and tile mfg. Gypsum quarrying.

Villa Hidalgo (bē'yä ēdäl'gō). **1** Town (pop. 538), Durango, N Mexico, 65 mi. SE of Hidalgo del Parral; alt. 5,590 ft.; corn, candelilla, livestock. **2** Town (pop. 2,175), Jalisco, central Mexico, 32 mi. SW of Aguascalientes; corn, wheat, beans, alfalfa, livestock. Formerly Paso de Sotos. **3** Town (pop. 910), San Luis Potosí, N central Mexico, 29 mi. NE of San Luis Potosí; corn, wheat, cotton, maguey. Formerly Iturbide. **4** Town (pop. 869), Zacatecas, N central Mexico, on interior plateau, 50 mi. SW of San Luis Potosí; alt, 7,405 ft. Silver, lead, zinc, arsenic, and antimony mining. Formerly Santa Rita.

Villahoz (bēlyäōth'), town (pop. 1,123), Burgos prov., N Spain, 21 mi. SW of Burgos; cereals, grapes, livestock.

Villa Huidobro (bē'yä wēdō'brō) or **Cañada Verde** (känyä'dä bĕr'dä), town (pop. estimate 2,000), ⊙ General Roca dept. (□ c.5,400; pop. 29,679), S Córdoba prov., Argentina, 120 mi. SSW of Río Cuarto; rail junction; agr. center (grain, flax, alfalfa, livestock).

Villa Ignacio Allende, Mexico: see IGNACIO ALLENDE.

Villa Independencia (bē'yä ēndäpĕndĕn'syä) or **Independencia**, town (pop. estimate 500), S San Juan prov., Argentina, on San Juan R. (irrigation area) and 14 mi. SE of San Juan; winegrowing.

Villaines-la-Juhel (vēlĕn'-lä-zhüĕl'), village (pop. 1,256), Mayenne dept., W France, 16 mi. E of Mayenne; cattle and grain market.

Villa Ingavi (bē'yä ĭng-gä'vē), town, Tarija dept., SE Bolivia, 18 mi. NNE of Yacuiba, on road; fruit, vegetables. Formerly Caiza.

Villa Iris (ē'rēs), town (pop. 2,155), SW Buenos Aires prov., Argentina, near La Pampa natl. territory line, 65 mi. NW of Bahía Blanca; stock raising.

Villa Isabel (ēsäbĕl'), town (1950 pop. 2,860), Monte Cristi prov., NW Dominican Republic, on highway, and 13 mi. SE of Monte Cristi; rice, onions, potatoes. Until 1938, Villa Vásquez.

Villa Jara (hä'rä), town (pop. 1,984), Veracruz, E Mexico, in Sierra Madre Oriental foothills, 15 mi. ENE of Córdoba, on railroad; coffee, fruit. Formerly Paso del Macho.

Villa Jardón, Argentina: see RANCÚL.

Villa Jiménez (hēmā'nĕs), town (pop. 3,356), Michoacán, central Mexico, 40 mi. WNW of Morelia; agr. center (corn, sugar cane, fruit, livestock).

Villajoyosa (bē"lyähoiō'sä), city (pop. 5,429), Alicante prov., E Spain, port on the Mediterranean, and 18 mi. NE of Alicante; fishing, fish salting, boat building, sail mfg. Hemp and esparto processing (fish nets, rope, mats), olive pressing, flour milling. Bathing resort. Has remains of anc. walls.

Villajuán (bēlyähwän'), town (pop. 1,609), Pontevedra prov., NW Spain, Atlantic fishing port and bathing resort on Arosa Bay, and 12 mi. NW of Pontevedra; vineyards.

Villa Juárez (bē'yä hwä'rĕs). **1** Town (pop. 4,797), Puebla, central Mexico, in SE foothills of Sierra Madre Oriental, 10 mi. NE of Huauchinango; agr. center (sugar cane, coffee, tobacco, fruit). **2** Town (pop. 3,418), San Luis Potosí, N central Mexico, on interior plateau, 45 mi. ENE of San Luis Potosí; agr. center (corn, wheat, beans, cotton, maguey). Formerly Carbonera. **3** City, Tamaulipas, Mexico: see CIUDAD MANTE.

Villa Julia Molina, Dominican Republic: see JULIA MOLINA.

Villa Krause (krou'sä), town (pop. estimate 500), S San Juan prov., Argentina, in San Juan R. valley (irrigation area), on railroad, and 4 mi. S of San Juan, in fruit and wine area.

Villa La Angostura (lä äng-gōstō'rä), or **La Angostura**, village (pop. estimate, 500), SW Neuquén natl. territory, Argentina, bet. L. Nahuel Huapí and L. Correntoso, 50 mi. SW of San Martín de los Andes; resort in Argentinian lake dist.; stock raising (sheep, cattle). Formerly Correntoso.

Villa Lagarina (vēl'lä lägärē'nä), village (pop. 668), Trento prov., Trentino–Alto Adige, N Italy, near Adige R., 2 mi. N of Rovereto; sausage factory.

Villa Larroque, Argentina: see LARROQUE.

Villa La Trinidad (bē'yä lä trēnēdädh'), town (pop. estimate 3,000), S Tucumán prov., Argentina, 45 mi. SSW of Tucumán; rail terminus; agr. center (sugar cane, corn, alfalfa, rice, cotton, livestock); sugar refining, alcohol distilling, lumbering. Until c.1945 called La Trinidad.

Villalba (bēyäl'bä), town (pop. 1,511), central Puerto Rico, in the Cordillera Central, 10 mi. NE of Ponce; sugar-milling center. Adjoining N is a demonstration farm of Univ. of Puerto Rico, and the Toro Negro hydroelectric plants.

Villalba (vēl-läl'bä), village (pop. 4,392), Caltanissetta prov., central Sicily, 16 mi. NW of Caltanissetta.

Villalba (bēlyäl'vä). **1** Town (pop. 2,546), Lugo prov., NW Spain, 20 mi. NNW of Lugo; meat and cheese processing, tanning; lumbering. Cereals, chestnuts, potatoes, livestock in area. **2** Town, Madrid prov., Spain: see COLLADO VILLALBA.

Villalba del Alcor (dhĕl älkôr'), town (pop. 4,138), Huelva prov., SW Spain, 27 mi. W of Seville; agr. center (cereals, grapes, olives, hogs). Antimony mining; alcohol distilling.

Villalba de la Sierra (dhā lä syĕ'rä), town (pop. 960), Cuenca prov., E central Spain, on Júcar R. and 12 mi. N of Cuenca; cereals, honey, livestock; apiculture. Flour milling; lumbering.

Villalba de los Alcores (lōs älkō'rĕs), town (pop. 1,033), Valladolid prov., N central Spain, 10 mi. ESE of Medina de Ríoseco; cereals, livestock; lumber.

Villalba de los Barros (bä'rōs), town (pop. 3,196), Badajoz prov., W Spain, in fertile Tierra de Barros, 31 mi. SE of Badajoz; olives, cereals, grapes, livestock. Flour milling, olive-oil pressing.

Villalba del Rey (dhĕl rā'), town (pop. 1,705), Cuenca prov., E central Spain, 34 mi. NW of Cuenca; olives, wheat, sheep.

Villaldama (bēyäldä'mä), city (pop. 2,648), Nuevo León, N Mexico, in N valley of Sierra Madre Oriental, on railroad and 55 mi. NNW of Monterrey; alt. 1,434 ft. Mining (gold, silver, lead) and agr. center (wheat, nuts).

Villalgordo del Júcar (bēlyälgôr'dhō dhĕl hōō'kär), town (pop. 1,886), Albacete prov., SE central Spain, near the Júcar, 8 mi. NE of La Roda; olive-oil processing, flour milling; wine, saffron, truck produce.

Villa Linch, Argentina: see LYNCH.

Villalobos (bēlyälō'vōs), town (pop. 1,030), Zamora prov., NW Spain, 12 mi. ESE of Benavente; cereals, wine, vegetables, livestock.

Villalón de Campos (bēlyälōn' dä käm'pōs), town (pop. 2,993), Valladolid prov., N central Spain, 15 mi. N of Medina de Ríoseco; cheese-trade center; tanning, flour milling, chocolate mfg.; cereals, vegetables, livestock.

Villalonga (bēlyälông'gä), town (pop. 3,158), Valencia prov., E Spain, 6 mi. S of Gandía; paper mfg., olive-oil processing; fruit, almonds, peanuts, honey. Marble quarries near by.

Villa López (bē'yä lō'pĕs), town (pop. 1,312), Chihuahua, N Mexico, on Florido R. and 40 mi. ENE of Hidalgo del Parral; corn, wheat, cotton, tobacco, stock.

Villalpando (bēlyälpän'dō), town (pop. 2,700), Zamora prov., NW Spain, 30 mi. NE of Zamora; flour milling, brandy distilling; lumbering; agr. trade (cereals, vegetables, wine, livestock).

Villalpardo (-pär'dhō), town (pop. 988), Cuenca prov., E central Spain, 35 mi. NNE of Albacete; olives, cereals, grapes, saffron; olive-oil pressing.

Villaluenga (-lwĕng'gä), town (pop. 1,840), Toledo prov., central Spain, on railroad and 12 mi. NW of Toledo; cereals, olives, sheep, cattle. Gravel quarrying; cement mfg. Airfield.

Villaluenga del Rosario (dhĕl rōsä'ryō), town (pop. 501), Cádiz prov., SW Spain, in spur of the Cordillera Penibética, 12 mi. WSW of Ronda; cork, cereals, vegetables, livestock.

Villa Lynch, Argentina: see LYNCH.

Villa Madero (bē'yä mädā'rō). **1** or **Francisco I. Madero** (fränsē'skō ē'), town (pop. 2,810), Durango, N Mexico, on railroad and 33 mi. NE of Durango; agr. center (corn, wheat, cotton, vegetables, fruit). **2** Town (pop. 634), Michoacán, central Mexico, 26 mi. S of Morelia; cereals, fruit, livestock.

Villamagna (vēl"lämä'nyä), village (pop. 729), Chieti prov., Abruzzi e Molise, S central Italy, 4 mi. SE of Chieti; macaroni factory.

Villa Mainero (bē'yä mīnä'rō) or **Mainero,** town (pop. 913), Tamaulipas, NE Mexico, at E foot of Sierra Madre Oriental, 65 mi. NW of Ciudad Victoria; cereals, sugar cane, stock.

Villa Maipú, Argentina: see MAIPÚ, Mendoza prov.

Villamalea (bēlyämälā'ä), town (pop. 2,811), Albacete prov., SE central Spain, 30 mi. NE of Albacete; alcohol distilling, olive-oil processing, sawmilling; saffron, fruit, wine, cereals.

Villamañán (-mänyän'), town (pop. 1,574), Leon prov., NW Spain, 20 mi. S of Leon; brandy distilling; wine, cereals, livestock.

Villamanca River, Argentina: see SALADILLO RÍO, Buenos Aires prov.

Villamanrique (-rē'kä), town (pop. 2,661), Ciudad Real prov., S central Spain, 25 mi. SE of Valdepeñas; cereals, grapes, olives; olive oil, flour.

Villamanrique de la Condesa (dhā lä kōndā'sä), town (pop. 3,105), Seville prov., SW Spain, 20 mi. SW of Seville; agr. center (corn, grapes, olives, livestock; cork, timber; apiculture); sericulture; lumbering.

Villamanrique de Tajo (tä'hō), town (pop. 600), Madrid prov., central Spain, on the Tagus and 33 mi. SE of Madrid; cereals, grapes, fruit, sheep, cattle. The Buenamesón hydroelectric plant is near by.

Villamanta (bēlyämän'tä), town (pop. 746), Madrid prov., central Spain, on railroad and 24 mi. WSW of Madrid; olives, cereals, truck produce, chick-peas; olive-oil pressing.

Villa Mantero (bē'yä mäntā'rō), town (pop. estimate 1,000), E Entre Ríos prov., Argentina, on railroad and 31 mi. WNW of Concepción del Uruguay, in grain and stock area. Formerly Mantero.

Villamar (bēyämär'), town (pop. 3,147), Michoacán, central Mexico, 26 mi. SSE of Ocotlán; cereals, beans, sugar cane, fruit, stock. Formerly Guarachita.

Villamar (vēl-lämär'), village (pop. 2,876), Cagliari prov., S central Sardinia, on Flumini Mannu R. and 28 mi. NNW of Cagliari; rail junction.

Villamarchante (bēlyämärchän'tā), town (pop. 3,865), Valencia prov., E Spain, near Turia R., 15 mi. WNW of Valencia; olive-oil processing, flour milling; wine, cereals, vegetables. Mineral springs. Lime and gypsum quarries near by.

Villa María (bē'yä märē'ä), city (pop. 24,906), ⊙ Tercero Abajo (or General San Martín) dept. (□ c.1,800; pop. 56,001), central Córdoba prov., Argentina, on the Río Tercero and 85 mi. SE of Córdoba. Rail junction; commercial, agr., and industrial center. Mfg.: dairy products, cement products, textiles, food preserves, flour. Agr.: grain growing, stock raising. Fishing. Has natl. col. A dynamite factory is near by.

Villa María, town (pop. 2,654), Caldas dept., W central Colombia, on W slopes of Cordillera Central, on railroad and 3 mi. SSE of Manizales; resort in agr. region (coffee, stock). Sometimes Villamaría.

Villa Mariano y Loza, Argentina: see SOLARI.

Villamartín (bēlyämärtēn'), city (pop. 7,892), Cádiz prov., S Spain, on Guadalete R. and 40 mi. NE of Cádiz; resort and agr. center (grapes, cereals, olives, vegetables, livestock); dairying; fishing, hunting.

Villamarzana (vēl"lämärtsä'nä), village (pop. 1,128), Rovigo prov., Veneto, N Italy, 6 mi. SW of Rovigo; rope factory.

Villa Matamoros (bē'yä mätämō'rōs), town (pop. 1,519), Chihuahua, N Mexico, 13 mi. SSE of Hidalgo del Parral; silver and lead mining. Formerly Las Cuevas or San Isidro de las Cuevas.

Villamayor (bēlyämīôr'), outer suburb (pop. 2,549) of Saragossa, Saragossa prov., NE Spain, 6 mi. NE of city center.

Villamayor de Calatrava (dhā käläträ'vä), town (pop. 2,006), Ciudad Real prov., S central Spain, 18 mi. SW of Ciudad Real; cereals, vegetables, grapes, olives, stock. Lead mining.

Villamayor de Campos (käm'pōs), town (pop. 1,577), Zamora prov., NW Spain, 18 mi. ESE of Benavente; cereals, vegetables, wine.

Villamayor de Santiago (säntyä'gō), town (pop. 4,611), Cuenca prov., E central Spain, 40 mi. SE of Aranjuez; agr. center (cereals, anise, saffron, grapes, olives). Olive-oil pressing, sawmilling, flour milling, cheese making.

Villamblard (vēläblär'), village (pop. 423), Dordogne dept., SW France, 12 mi. N of Bergerac; sawmilling.

Villamediana de Iregua (bēlyämā-dhyä'nä dhā ērā'gwä), town (pop. 1,438), Logroño prov., N Spain, 3 mi. SE of Logroño; olive-oil processing. Wine, cereals, vegetables, lumber in area.

Villa Mercedes, Argentina: see MERCEDES, San Luis.

Villamesías (bēlyämäsē'äs), town (pop. 1,386), Cáceres prov., W Spain, 15 mi. S of Trujillo; olive oil, wine, livestock.

Villamiel (bēlyämyĕl'), town (pop. 1,407), Cáceres prov., W Spain, 31 mi. SW of Ciudad Rodrigo; soap mfg.; olive oil, wine, vegetables.

Villamil (bēyämēl'), village, W Galápagos Isls., Ecuador, minor Pacific port on S Isabela Isl., 100 mi. W of Puerto Baquerizo; 0°58'S 91°1'W. A penal colony is near by.

Villaminaya (bēlyämēnī'ä), village (pop. 832), Toledo prov., central Spain, 13 mi. SE of Toledo; cereals, olives, potatoes, sheep, cattle. Processes olive oil and cheese.

Villaminozzo (vēl"lämēnô'tsō), village (pop. 681), Reggio nell'Emilia prov., Emilia-Romagna, N central Italy, in Etruscan Apennines, 6 mi. SE of Castelnovo ne'Monti.

Villa Montes (bē'yä mōn'tĕs), town (pop. c.5,000), Tarija dept., SE Bolivia, at W edge of the Chaco, on Pilcomayo R. and 80 mi. ENE of Tarija. Road and commercial center in petroleum region, and on route of projected Yacuiba–Santa Cruz RR; trades in tropical products (rice, sugar cane, fruit); cattle. Town created c.1905 by union of former missions of San Antonio and San Francisco. Military base for Chaco war, when its pop. rose to c.20,000.

Villamor de los Escuderos (bēlyämôr' dhā lōs ĕskōō-dhā'rōs), town (pop. 1,149), Zamora prov., NW Spain, 20 mi. SSE of Zamora; wine, cereals, fruit.

Villa Morelos (bē'yä mōrā'lōs). **1** Town (pop. 2,004), Michoacán, central Mexico, 30 mi. NW of Morelia; cereals, fruit, vegetables, livestock. **2** Town (pop. 670), San Luis Potosí, N central Mexico, 21 mi. ENE of San Luis Potosí; alt. 5,295 ft.; corn, beans, cotton. Formerly Armadillo.

Villa Morra (bē'yä mô'rä), E suburb of Asunción, Paraguay.

Villamuelas (bēlyämwā'läs), town (pop. 807), Toledo prov., central Spain, 16 mi. E of Toledo; olives, cereals, grapes; limekilns.

Villamuriel de Cerrato (bēlyämōōryĕl' dhā thĕrä'tō), town (pop. 1,213), Palencia prov., N central Spain, on Carrión R. and 4 mi. S of Palencia; cereals, wine, fruit, sheep.

Villa Nador (bēl'yä nädhôr'), city (pop. 23,817), ⊙ Kert territory (□ 2,362; 1945 pop. 310,576), E Sp. Morocco, port on a lagoon (Mar Chica) of the Mediterranean, on mining railroad and 8 mi. S of Melilla, by which it is commercially overshadowed. Trade in livestock, barley, olives, fruits. Tahuima airfield just S. Beni bu Ifrur iron mines 5 mi. SW. Also called Nador.

Villandraut (vēlädrō'), village (pop. 704), Gironde dept., SW France, on the Ciron and 28 mi. SSE of Bordeaux; dairying, sawmilling. Has ruined castle of Clement V.

Villandry (vēlädrē'), village (pop. 247), Indre-et-Loire dept., W central France, on Cher R. near its influx into the Loire and 9 mi. WSW of Tours. Has 16th-cent. château containing collection of Spanish paintings and Renaissance furniture.

Villanière (vēlänyâr'), village (pop. 317), Aude dept., SW France, 9 mi. N of Carcassonne; gold arsenic, copper mining.

Villano, Cape (bēlyä'nō), on Atlantic coast of Galicia, in La Coruña prov., NW Spain, 42 mi. WSW of La Coruña; 43°9'N 9°12'W. Lighthouse.

Villa Nogués (bē'yä nōgĕs'), village, central Tucumán prov., Argentina, 9 mi. WSW of Tucumán; resort.

Villano River (bīyä'nō), Napo-Pastaza prov., NE Ecuador, rises NE of Puyo, flows c.80 mi. E to Curaray R. near 77°W.

Villanova (vĭl'ūnō'vū), village, Delaware co., SE Pa., 11 mi. NW of Philadelphia. Seat of Villanova Col.

Villanova Monferrato (vēl"länô'vä mônfĕr-rä'tô), village (pop. 2,496), Alessandria prov., Piedmont, N Italy, 3 mi. NNE of Casale Monferrato.

Villanova Monteleone (môn'tĕlĕō'nĕ), village (pop. 4,862), Sassari prov., NW Sardinia, 16 mi. SSW of Sassari.

Villanubla (bēlyänōō'vlä), town (pop. 1,223), Valladolid prov., N central Spain, 7 mi. NW of Valladolid; cereals, vegetables, livestock.

Villa Nueva (bē'yä nwā'vä). **1** Town (pop. 4,016), central Córdoba prov., Argentina, just S of Villa María; wheat, corn, flax, livestock; dairying. **2** or **Villa Nueva de Guaymallén** (dā gwīmäyĕn'), town (pop. estimate 1,000), ⊙ Guaymallén dept. (□ c.70; 1947 pop. 60,952), N Mendoza prov., Argentina, in Mendoza R. valley (irrigation area), 3 mi. ESE of Mendoza; agr. center (wine, fruit, potatoes, alfalfa). Wine, barrels; sawmills.

Villanueva (bēyänwä'vä). **1** Town (pop. 3,879), Bolívar dept., N Colombia, in Caribbean lowlands, 19 mi. E of Cartagena; sugar cane, tobacco, rice, corn, livestock. **2** Town (pop. 3,751), Magdalena dept., N Colombia, at W foot of Serranía de Valledupar near Venezuela border, 65 mi. S of Ríohacha; coffee, corn, livestock; liquor distilling. Gold and coal deposits near by.

Villa Nueva (bē'yä nwā'vä), town (1950 pop. 3,009), Guatemala dept., S central Guatemala, 10 mi. SW of Guatemala; alt. 4,300 ft.; grain; cattle raising; lumbering.

Villanueva or **Villa Nueva,** town (pop. 2,078), Cortés dept., NW Honduras, in Sula Valley, on railroad and 13 mi. S of San Pedro Sula; bananas, sugar cane, grain, livestock.

Villanueva (bēyänwä'vä), city (pop. 4,241), Zacatecas, N central Mexico, on interior plateau, on Juchipila R. and 35 mi. SW of Zacatecas; alt. 6,414 ft. Agr. center (grain, sugar cane, tobacco, vegetables, livestock). Anc. Aztec ruins are at QUEMADA near by.

Villanueva, town (1950 pop. 654), Chinandega dept., W Nicaragua, 38 mi. NE of Chinandega and on Villanueva R. (branch of the Estero Real); road center; corn, beans, rice.

Villanueva de Alcardete (bēlyänwä'vä dhā älkär-dhā'tā), town (pop. 4,043), Toledo prov., central Spain, 40 mi. SE of Aranjuez; agr. center on La Mancha plain (cereals, chick-peas, beans, potatoes, sugar beets, grapes, sheep, goats). Lumbering. Alcohol distilling, flour milling, cheese processing.

Villanueva de Alcolea (dhā älkōlā'ä), town (pop. 1,477), Castellón de la Plana prov., E Spain, 18 mi. NNE of Castellón de la Plana; olive-oil processing; wheat, wine, beans.

Villanueva de Algaidas, Spain: see RINCONA.

Villanueva de Alpicat (älpēkät'), village (pop. 1,341), Lérida prov., NE Spain, 5 mi. NW of Lérida; livestock, olive oil; lumbering.

Villanueva de Arosa (ärō'sä), town (pop. 1,238), Pontevedra prov., NW Spain, Atlantic fishing port on Arosa Bay, 12 mi. NW of Pontevedra; fish processing (anchovies and sardines). Wine, corn, livestock in area.

Villanueva de Bocas (bō'käs), town (pop. 1,068), Toledo prov., central Spain, 21 mi. S of Aranjuez; cereals, grapes, olives.

Villanueva de Castellón (kästĕlyōn'), town (pop. 5,436), Valencia prov., E Spain, 6 mi. N of Játiva; agr. trade center (truck produce, wheat, rice, peanuts); rice milling, furniture and paper mfg.

Villanueva de Córdoba (kôr'dhōvä), town (pop. 15,903), Córdoba prov., S Spain, in Andalusia, on S slope of the Sierra Morena, 13 mi. ESE of Pozoblanco; agr. trade center (cereals, livestock, wine). Olive pressing, flour milling, sirup distilling, peat processing. Bismuth mines.

Villanueva de Gállego (gä'lyāgō), village (pop. 1,779), Saragossa prov., NE Spain, near Gállego R., 8 mi. NNE of Saragossa; flour and paper mills; sugar beets, cereals.

Villanueva de Infantes, Spain: see INFANTES.

Villanueva de la Fuente (lä fwĕn'tā), town (pop. 4,054), Ciudad Real prov., S central Spain, in New Castile, near Albacete prov. border, 38 mi. E of Valdepeñas. Agr. center (cereals, chick-peas, potatoes, fruit, olives, livestock); flour milling; hunting.

Villanueva de la Jara (hä'rä), town (pop. 2,713), Cuenca prov., E central Spain, 31 mi. N of Albacete; olives, cereals, fruit, truck produce, saffron, stock. Lumbering. Alcohol distilling flour milling.

Villanueva de la Reina (rā'nä), town (pop. 3,538), Jaén prov. S Spain, on the Guadalquivir and 17 mi. WSW of Linares; olive-oil processing, flour milling; lumbering, stock raising.

Villanueva del Ariscal (dhĕl ärēskäl'), town (pop. 2,764), Seville prov., SW Spain, 9 mi. W of Seville; olives, grapes, fruit, goats, hogs.

Villanueva del Arzobispo (är-thōvē'spō), city (pop. 10,660) Jaén prov., S Spain, near the Guadalquivir, 6 mi. NE of Villacarrillo; olive-oil production center. Carbon disulphide and soap mfg., flour milling.

Villanueva de las Cruces (dhā läs krōō'thĕs), town (pop. 635), Huelva prov., SW Spain, 26 mi. N of Huelva; acorns, cereals, livestock.

Villanueva de la Serena (dhā lä sārā'nä), town (pop. 16,060), Badajoz prov., W Spain, in Estremadura, near the Guadiana, on railroad and 30 mi. E of Mérida. Processing, trading, and agr. center on fertile plain (cereals, grapes, fruit, wool, livestock). Flour milling, olive pressing, liquor distilling; mfg. of soap, fertilizer, paper bags, cement goods, furniture, chocolate; limekiln, iron foundries. Has Roman remains.

Villanueva de la Sierra (syĕ'rä), town (pop. 1,510), Cáceres prov., W Spain, 21 mi. NW of Plasencia; soap mfg., olive-oil processing; stock raising; cereals, wine.

Villanueva de las Minas (läs mē'näs), coal-mining camp (pop. 9,299), Seville prov., SW Spain, 2½ mi. NW of Villanueva del Río (the commune center) and 24 mi. NE of Seville (linked by rail). Sometimes called Minas de la Reunión.

Villanueva de las Torres (tô'rĕs), town (pop. 1,762), Granada prov., S Spain, 18 mi. NNE of Guadix; cereals, esparto, fruit, vegetables. Mineral springs.
Villanueva de la Vera (lä vä'rä), town (pop. 3,123), Cáceres prov., W Spain, 35 mi. ENE of Plasencia; olive-oil and cheese processing, flour milling; fruit and pepper shipping; stock raising; trout fishing.
Villanueva del Campillo (dhĕl kämpē'lyō), town (pop. 837), Avila prov., central Spain, 26 mi. W of Avila; rye, potatoes, forage, livestock.
Villanueva del Campo (käm'pō), town (pop. 2,503), Zamora prov., NW Spain, 14 mi. E of Benavente; brewery; blanket mfg.; agr. trade (cereals, wine, cattle, sheep).
Villanueva del Conde (kōn'dā), town (pop. 1,110), Salamanca prov., W Spain, 13 mi. NW of Béjar; olive-oil processing, alcohol distilling; lumbering; wine, fruit, vegetables.
Villanueva del Duque (dhōō'kā), town (pop. 3,475), Córdoba prov., S Spain, on S slope of Sierra Morena, 8 mi. W of Pozoblanco; olive-oil processing. Stock raising; cereals, vegetables, wine; lumber. Silver-bearing lead mines.
Villanueva del Fresno (frĕ'snō), town (pop. 6,393), Badajoz prov., W Spain, customs station near Port. border, 37 mi. SSW of Badajoz; processing and agr. center (olives, acorns, herbs, cereals, livestock). Olive-oil pressing, flour milling. Stock raising. Also limekilns; mfg. of soft drinks, tiles.
Villanueva del Grao, El Grao, or **Grao de Valencia** (dhĕl grä'ō, –dhā välĕn'thyä), harbor section of Valencia, Valencia prov., E Spain, adjoined N by Pueblo Nuevo del Mar. Has large artificial port facilities.
Villanueva del Huerva (dhĕl wĕr'vä), town (pop. 1,150), Saragossa prov., NE Spain, 24 mi. SSW of Saragossa; alcohol mfg.; lumbering; wine, cereals.
Villanueva de los Castillejos (dhā lōs kästē'lyōs), town (pop. 2,894), Huelva prov., SW Spain, 25 mi. NW of Huelva; stock raising (hogs, goats, sheep, cattle); liquor distilling, mfg. of hats and buttons; apiculture.
Villanueva del Rey (dhĕl rā'), town (pop. 3,263), Córdoba prov., S Spain, 10 mi. SE of Peñarroya-Pueblonuevo, in bituminous coal-mining dist. Olive-oil processing; cereals, wine, livestock. Argentiferous copper and iron deposits.
Villanueva del Río (rē'ō), town (pop. 972), Seville prov., SW Spain, on the Guadalquivir and 23 mi. NE of Seville; cereals, olives, beetroot, cotton, livestock. NW of it, belonging to same municipality, is VILLANUEVA DE LAS MINAS, a coal-mining center on railroad to Seville.
Villanueva del Río Segura (sägōō'rä), town (pop. 1,287), Murcia prov., SE Spain, on Segura R. and 15 mi. NW of Murcia; citrus groves.
Villanueva del Rosario (dhĕl rōsä'ryō), town (pop. 2,611), Málaga prov., S Spain, near Guadalhorce R., in spur of the Cordillera Penibética, 18 mi. N of Málaga; olives, cereals, livestock; olive-oil pressing, flour milling.
Villanueva del Trabuco (trävōō'kō), town (pop. 2,262), Málaga prov., S Spain, on the Guadalhorce and 21 mi. N of Málaga; olives, cereals, stock; olive-oil pressing, flour milling, charcoal burning.
Villanueva de San Carlos (dhā sän' kär'lōs), town (pop. 1,169), Ciudad Real prov., S central Spain, 24 mi. S of Ciudad Real; cereals, chick-peas, grapes, truck produce, livestock.
Villanueva de San Juan (sän' hwän'), town (pop. 2,508), Seville prov., SW Spain, 13 mi. SSW of Osuna; olives, cereals, livestock; timber.
Villanueva de Tapia (tä'pyä), town (pop. 1,529), Málaga prov., S Spain, 17 mi. NE of Antequera; cereals, grapes, olives.
Villanueva y Geltrú (bēlyänwä'vä ē hĕltrōō'), town (pop. 16,677), Barcelona prov., NE Spain, on the Mediterranean, 25 mi. WSW of Barcelona, in wine-growing area. Cotton milling; mfg. of rubber products, electric cables, metal pipes, cement, dyes, flour products, brandy. Agr. trade (cereals, hazelnuts, fruit). Has anc. castle, art mus.
Villanur, Fr. India: see VILLENOUR.
Villany (vĭl'länyŏŏ), Hung. *Villány*, town (pop. 2,100), Baranya co., S Hungary, at E foot of Villany Mts., 12 mi. SE of Pecs; rail junction; flour mill, wine.
Villany Mountains (vĭl'länyŏŏ), Hung. *Villány*, Baranya co., S Hungary, extend 21 mi. W from Villany; rise to 1,450 ft. Excellent wine grown on slopes. Deposits of bauxite; hot sulphur springs at Harkany.
Villa Obregón (bē'yä ōbrāgōn'). **1** Town (pop. 9,113), Federal Dist., central Mexico, 9 mi. SSW of Mexico city; a residential suburb of the capital (linked by tramways). Situated in fruitgrowing dist. Paper mill; mfg. of pencils, chemicals. Church and monastery of El Carmen (dating from 1615) is fine example of churrigueresque style. Monument to Alvaro Obregón is on site where he was killed. The home of Diego Rivera is opposite San Angel Inn, formerly a 17th-cent. castle. Sometimes called Villa Alvaro Obregón; formerly San Angel. **2** Town (pop. 1,316), Jalisco, central Mexico, 50 mi. NE of Guadalajara; corn, beans, livestock. Formerly Cañadas.
Villa Ocampo (ōkäm'pō), town (pop. estimate 2,000), NE Santa Fe prov., Argentina, 50 mi. NNE of Reconquista; rail junction; processing center in agr. area. Sugar refineries, paper mills, tannery, corn mill. Agr. (cotton, corn, rice, sunflowers, peanuts, livestock). Formerly called Ocampo.
Villa Ocampo, town (pop. 1,800), Durango, N Mexico, on upper Florido R.. near Chihuahua border, and 35 mi. SSE of Hidalgo del Parral; alt. 5,643 ft.; cereals, cotton, stock.
Villaodrid (bēlyou-dhrēdh'), village (pop. 260), Lugo prov., NW Spain, 30 mi. NE of Lugo, in iron-mining area; connected by mining railroad with shipping port of Ribadeo.
Villa Ojo de Agua, Argentina: see OJO DE AGUA.
Villa Oliva, Paraguay: see OLIVA.
Villa Orías, Bolivia: see TARVITA.
Villa Oropeza, Bolivia: see YOTALA.
Villapalacios (bēlyäpälä'thyōs), town (pop. 1,850), Albacete prov., SE central Spain, 48 mi. SW of Albacete; livestock, lumber, olive oil, wine.
Villa Park (vĭ'lŭ), residential village (pop. 8,821), Du Page co., NE Ill., W suburb of Chicago, 17 mi. E of St. Charles; mfg. (fertilizer, beverages). Inc. 1914.
Villa Pérez or **Villa General Pérez** (bē'yä hānäräl' pā'rĕs), town (pop. c.3,800), La Paz dept., W Bolivia, in Eastern Cordillera of the Andes, 28 mi. NNE of Puerto Acosta; alt. c.14,000 ft. Until 1930s, Charazani or Charasani. PUERTO PÉREZ, another town in La Paz dept., was formerly called Villa Pérez.
Villa Pesqueira, Mexico: see PESQUEIRA.
Villa Prat (prät'), town (pop. 1,588), Talca prov., central Chile, on Mataquito R. and 25 mi. NNE of Talca; grain, wine, beans, livestock; flour milling, dairying.
Villa Pucarani, Bolivia: see PUCARANI.
Villaputzu (vēl"läpōōt'sōō), village (pop. 2,847), Cagliari prov., SE Sardinia, near Flumendosa R., 29 mi. NE of Cagliari.
Villaquejida (bēlyäkähē'dhä), town (pop. 1,199), Leon prov., NW Spain, on Esla Canal and 32 mi. S of Leon; cereals, vegetables, fruit, livestock.
Villa Quesada (bē'yä käsä'dä), town (pop. 1,892), Alajuela prov., N central Costa Rica, at NW foot of Poás volcano, 20 mi. NW of Alajuela; commercial center of San Carlos lowland; grain, tobacco, coffee; stock raising, lumbering.
Villa Quilino, Argentina: see QUILINO.
Villa Quinteros (kēntā'rōs), town (pop. estimate 1,000), S central Tucumán prov., Argentina, on railroad and 36 mi. SW of Tucumán; agr. center (sugar cane, corn, rice, livestock); sawmill, sugar refinery.
Villar (bĭyär'), town (pop. c.3,600), Chuquisaca dept., S central Bolivia, 21 mi. S of Padilla; corn, potatoes, ají.
Villaralbo (bēlyäräl'vō), village (pop. 1,218), Zamora prov., NW Spain, on the Duero (Douro) and 4 mi. E of Zamora; brandy distilling, cotton-cloth mfg.; livestock, cereals, wine.
Villaralto (–tō), town (pop. 3,793), Córdoba prov., S Spain, 9 mi. NW of Pozoblanco; sheep and hog raising; cereals, vegetables.
Villarcayo (–kī'ō), town (pop. 1,413), Burgos prov., N Spain, 40 mi. SW of Bilbao; cereals, livestock; timber. Lumbering. Flour milling, mfg. of chocolate and meat products.
Villard, resort village (pop. 288), Pope co., W Minn., 7 mi. NE of Glenwood, in livestock and poultry area; dairy products. Small lakes near by.
Villard-Bonnot (vĭyär'-bônō'), town (pop. 4,820), Isère dept., SE France, on the Isère and 9 mi. NE of Grenoble, in GRÉSIVAUDAN valley. Industrial suburb of BRIGNOUD is 1.5 mi. NNE.
Villard-de-Lans (–dŭ-läs'), town (pop. 1,738), Isère dept., SE France, in the Vercors massif, 12 mi. SW of Grenoble; alt. 3,428 ft. Popular resort and winter-sports station of the Dauphiné Pre-Alps.
Villar de Cañas (bēlyär' dhā kä'nyäs), town (pop. 1,645), Cuenca prov., E central Spain, 31 mi. SW of Cuenca; olives, cereals, grapes, livestock.
Villar de Ciervo (thyĕr'vō), village (pop. 1,224), Salamanca prov., W Spain, near Port. border, 15 mi. NW of Ciudad Rodrigo; flour milling; lumbering; livestock, wine, olive oil, cereals.
Villar de Domingo García (dhōmĭng'gō gär-thē'ä), town (pop. 760), Cuenca prov., E central Spain, 15 mi. NW of Cuenca; cereals, saffron, sheep.
Villar del Arzobispo (dhĕl är-thōvē'spō), town (pop. 3,923), Valencia prov., E Spain, 15 mi. NW of Liria; olive-oil processing, sawmilling, brandy distilling; wine, cereals. Kaolin mines.
Villar del Humo (ōō'mō), town (pop. 1,306), Cuenca prov., E central Spain, 30 mi. ESE of Cuenca; cereals, saffron, honey, grapes, livestock; flour milling.
Villar del Pedroso (pādhrō'sō), village (pop. 1,465), Cáceres prov., W Spain, 26 mi. SW of Talavera de la Reina; flour mills; olive oil, wine, livestock.
Villar del Pozo (pō'thō), town (pop. 343), Ciudad Real prov., S central Spain, 9 mi. S of Ciudad Real; cereals, grapes, olives, forage, stock. Medicinal springs. Iron mining.
Villar del Rey (rā'), town (pop. 3,978), Badajoz prov., W Spain, 18 mi. NNE of Badajoz; cereals, olives, flour, stock.
Villar de Olalla (dhā ōlä'lyä), village (pop. 1,140), Cuenca prov., E central Spain, 5 mi. SW of Cuenca; cereals, truck produce, saffron, grapes, livestock. Plaster mfg.
Villar de Rena (rā'nä), town (pop. 393), Badajoz prov., W Spain, 31 mi. ENE of Almendralejo; grain, olives, grapes.
Villardompardo (bēlyär-dhōmpär'dhō), town (pop. 2,635), Jaén prov., S Spain, 13 mi. WNW of Jaén; olive oil, fruit, cereals.
Villards-d'Heria (vēlär-dārēä'), village (pop. 288), Jura dept., E France, in the central Jura, 7 mi. WNW of Saint-Claude; wood turning, pipe making.
Villareal (bē"yäräal', bēl"yä–), town (1939 pop. 2,888; 1948 municipality pop. 15,094), W Samar isl., Philippines, on Samar Sea, 15 mi. SSE of Catbalogan; agr. center (rice, hemp, coconuts).
Villa Real da Praia Grande, Brazil: see NITERÓI.
Villa Regina (bē'yä rähē'nä), town (1947 pop. 2,152), N Río Negro natl. territory, Argentina, in Río Negro valley (irrigation area), on railroad and 30 mi. E of Fuerte General Roca; processing center in agr. area (alfalfa, tomatoes, wine, pears, apples, plums, cherries; goats, cattle, poultry); wine making, food canning, lumbering.
Villarejo de Fuentes (bēlyärā'hō dhā fwĕn'tĕs), town (pop. 1,923), Cuenca prov., E central Spain, in La Mancha, 35 mi. SW of Cuenca; cereals, vegetables, sheep.
Villarejo del Valle (dhĕl vä'lyä), town (pop. 936), Ávila prov., central Spain, in the Sierra de Gredos, 28 mi. SW of Ávila; grapes, olives, chestnuts, figs, goats. Lumbering.
Villarejo de Salvanés (dhā sälvänās'), town (pop. 3,828), Madrid prov., central Spain, 26 mi. SE of Madrid; agr. center (vegetables, grapes, olives, cereals, truck produce, livestock). Olive-oil pressing, alcohol distilling, cheese processing.
Villares, Los (lōs vēlyä'rĕs), town (pop. 4,236), Jaén prov., S Spain, 6 mi. S of Jaén; agr. center. Olive-oil processing, flour milling; stock raising. Gypsum and stone quarries.
Villares del Saz (bēlyä'rĕs dhĕl säth'), town (pop. 1,540), Cuenca prov., E central Spain, 25 mi. SW of Cuenca; grain, grapes, sheep; flour.
Villargordo (bēlyärgôr'dhō), town (pop. 4,361), Jaén prov., S Spain, near the Guadalquivir, 13 mi. NNE of Jaén; olive-oil processing; sheep, cereals. Iron mining.
Villargordo del Cabriel (dhĕl kävrēĕl'), town (pop. 1,341), Valencia prov., E Spain, 18 mi. WNW of Requena; olive oil, saffron, cereals, wine; sheep raising. Salt mines near by.
Villa Rica, Brazil: see OURO PRÊTO.
Villa Rica (bē'yä rē'kä), village (pop. 24), Pasco dept., central Peru, in Cordillera Oriental, 70 mi. E of Oxapampa; coffee, cacao; lumbering.
Villa Rica (vĭ"lŭ rē'kŭ, vĭ'lŭ rē"kŭ), town (pop. 1,703), Carroll and Douglas cos., W Ga., 31 mi. W of Atlanta; mfg. (clothing, yarn, lumber, cottonseed oil, fertilizer). Settled after discovery of gold here 1826. Inc. 1830.
Villarino, Argentina: see MÉDANOS.
Villarino (bēlyärē'nō), village (pop. 1,864), Salamanca prov., W Spain, near Duero (Douro) R. and Port. border, 48 mi. NW of Salamanca; olive-oil processing, flour milling; wine, cereals, livestock.
Villa Río Hondo, Argentina: see RÍO HONDO.
Villa Rivas, Villa Riva, or **Riva** (bē'yä rē'väs, –vä), town (1950 pop. 910), Duarte prov., E central Dominican Republic, in fertile La Vega Real valley, on Yuna R., on railroad and 24 mi. ESE of San Francisco de Macorís; cacao, rice.
Villa Rivero (rēvā'rō), town (pop. c.8,200), Cochabamba dept., central Bolivia, on S slopes of Cordillera de Cochabamba and 6 mi. SSE of Punata, on road; alt. 9,108 ft.; wheat, potatoes. Until 1900s, Muela.
Villa Robles, Argentina: see ROBLES.
Villarodin-Bourget (vēlärôdē'-bōōrzhā'), commune (pop. 494), Savoie dept., SE France, in Alpine Maurienne valley, on Arc R. and 2 mi. ENE of Modane; electrochemical works.
Villarosa (vēl"lärô'zä), town (pop. 8,700), Enna prov., central Sicily, 6 mi. WNW of Enna, in cereal-growing region. Sulphur mines near by.
Villar Perosa (vēl-lär' pārô'zä), village (pop. 1,260), Torino prov., Piedmont, NW Italy, 6 mi. NW of Pinerolo; ironworks, textile mills.
Villarquemado (bēlyärkämä'dhō), village (pop. 1,521), Teruel prov., E Spain, 14 mi. NW of Teruel; trades in sugar beets, hemp, fruit.
Villarramiel (–rämyĕl') town (pop. 3,189), Palencia prov., N central Spain, 20 mi. WNW of Palencia; tanning, hemp processing, candy mfg.; cereals, livestock, flax.
Villarrasa (–rä'sä), town (pop. 2,702), Huelva prov., SW Spain, on railroad and 20 mi. NE of Huelva; grain, grapes, olives; lumber.
Villarreal (–räal'), city (pop. 16,777), Castellón de la Plana prov., E Spain, in Valencia, 5 mi. SW of Castellón de la Plana, in fertile irrigated Mijares valley. Fruit- and vegetable-shipping center (citrus fruit, melons, almonds, tomatoes, peppers). Mfg. of sandals, hemp and cotton cloth, chemical fertilizers, wax, soap, tiles; olive-oil and wine processing, brandy distilling, sawmilling. Honey in area. Has church with octagonal tower and tiled domes.
Villarreal de Urrechua (dhā ōōrā'chwä), town (pop. 1,860), Guipúzcoa prov., N Spain, 12 mi. WSW of Tolosa; metalworking (hardware, auto accessories). Cereals, chestnuts, livestock in area.

Villarrica, department, Chile: see LONCOCHE.

Villarrica (bēyärē'kä), town (pop. 4,679), Cautín prov., S central Chile, on L. Villarrica at outlet of Toltén R., 45 mi. SE of Temuco; rail terminus, resort and agr. center (grain, livestock); lumbering, flour milling, dairying, fishing. In magnificent scenery facing Villarrica Volcano. One of oldest Chilean towns, founded 1552 as an outpost against Indians.

Villarrica, city (dist. pop. 27,687), ⊙ Guairá dept., S Paraguay, on railroad and 85 mi. ESE of Asunción; 25°44'S 56°27'W. Second largest city of Paraguay. Trading, processing, and agr. center, shipping maté, tobacco, cotton, sugar cane, oranges, wine, cattle, hides. Sawmilling, textile milling, maté processing, flour milling, sugar refining, liquor distilling, cotton ginning, wine making, tanning, shoe mfg. Old colonial town, with cathedral. A shrine draws many pilgrims annually. Founded 1576 on the Paraná, re-established 1682 on present site.

Villarrica, Lake (□ 65), Cautín prov., S central Chile, in Andean foothills, in N part of Chilean lake dist., 40 mi. SE of Temuco; 13 mi. long, c.5 mi. wide. Towered over by Villarrica Volcano and surrounded by pine forests, it is a noted tourist site with resorts of Villarrica and Pucón on its shores. Fishing, yachting.

Villarrica Volcano, Andean peak (9,325 ft.), Cautín prov., S central Chile, on SE bank of L. Villarrica, 60 mi. SE of Temuco. Somewhat active. Winter sports.

Villarrín de Campos (bēlyärēn' dā käm'pōs), town (pop. 1,787), Zamora prov., NW Spain, 20 mi. NNE of Zamora; cereals, wine, sheep.

Villarrobledo (bēlyärōvlā'dhō), city (pop. 18,739), Albacete prov., SE central Spain, in Murcia, 45 mi. NW of Albacete; wine- and cheese-processing and -shipping center. Mfg. of earthen jars, tiles, perfumes, soap, beverages; alcohol distilling, sawmilling. Trades in cereals, saffron, esparto, livestock. The Carlists were defeated here (1836) by Queen Christina's troops.

Villarroya de la Sierra (bēlyäroi'ä dhā lä syĕ'rä), town (pop. 2,041), Saragossa prov., NE Spain, 11 mi. NW of Calatayud; agr. trade (cereals, wine, sugar beets, fruit); lumber.

Villarrubia de los Ojos (bēlyärōō'vyä dhā lōs ō'hōs), town (pop. 7,706), Ciudad Real prov., S central Spain, in New Castile, 24 mi. NE of Ciudad Real. Agr. center on La Mancha plain: hemp, anise, saffron, olives, cereals, fruit, grapes, livestock; apiculture. Olive-oil pressing, liquor and alcohol distilling, flour milling, dairying, plaster mfg. Lime quarrying. Near by (S) are extensive ponds called Ojos del Guadiana.

Villarrubia de Santiago (dhā säntyä'gō), town (pop. 3,559), Toledo prov., central Spain, 35 mi. SE of Madrid; agr. center (cereals, olives, grapes, livestock). Alcohol distilling, cheese processing. Mineral springs.

Villarrubio (–vyō), town (pop. 766), Cuenca prov., E central Spain, 7 mi. SE of Tarancón; olive- and winegrowing, stock raising.

Villars (vēlär'). **1** or **Villars-les-Dombes** (–lā-dōb'), village (pop. 941), Ain dept., E France, in the Dombes dist., 16 mi. SSW of Bourg; fish, cattle, and cereal market. **2** Village (pop. 102), Vaucluse dept., SE France, 4 mi. N of Apt; ocher quarries. Lavender- and winegrowing.

Villars-sur-Ollon (–sür-ôlô'), health resort (alt. 4,120 ft.), Vaud canton, SW Switzerland, above Rhone valley, 15 mi WNW of Sion; winter sports.

Villars-sur-Var (–vär'), village (pop. 496), Alpes-Maritimes dept., SE France, near the Var, 18 mi. NNW of Nice, in Provence Alps; olives.

Villarta (bēlyär'tä), town (pop. 981), Cuenca prov., E central Spain, 33 mi. NNE of Albacete; cereals, grapes, livestock; olive-oil pressing, alcohol distilling.

Villarta de los Montes (dhā lōs mōn'tĕs), town (pop. 2,160), Badajoz prov., W Spain, 14 mi. E of Herrera del Duque; cereals, olives, grapes, livestock. Sanctuary is just W.

Villarta de San Juan (sän' hwän'), town (pop. 2,458), Ciudad Real prov., S central Spain, on combined Gigüela-Záncara R. and 32 mi. NE of Ciudad Real; cereals, potatoes, olives, saffron, cattail, grapes, sheep. Alcohol distilling, cheese making, woolwashing, charcoal burning, plaster mfg.

Villas, Las, province, Cuba: see LAS VILLAS.

Villa Saladillo (bē'yä säläde'yō) or **Saladillo,** village (pop. estimate 500), N central San Luis prov., Argentina, on the Río Quinto and 27 mi. E of San Luis; former ⊙ Pringles dept. Grain, livestock. Has an anc. chapel.

Villasalto (vēl"läsäl'tô), village (pop. 2,250), Cagliari prov., SE Sardinia, 24 mi. NE of Cagliari; antimony smelter. Antimony, arsenic mines near by.

Villasandino (bēlyäsände'nō), town (pop. 943), Burgos prov., N Spain, 21 mi. W of Burgos; grain growing, stock raising (sheep, horses, mules).

Villa San Giovanni (vēl'lä sän jōvän'nē), town (pop. 4,066). Reggio di Calabria prov., Calabria, S Italy, port on Strait of Messina, 7 mi. N of Reggio di Calabria; silk milling; fishing. Ferry service across strait to Messina, 4 mi. SW.

Villa San José (bē'yä sän hōsā'), agr. town (1947 pop. 5,852), E Entre Ríos prov., Argentina, on railroad and 5 mi. WNW of Colón; agr. and meat-packing center; wheat, corn, flax, livestock.

Villa Sanjurjo (bēl'yä sänhōōr'hō), town (pop. 10,770), ⊙ Rif territory (□ 1,342; 1945 pop. 168,533), central Sp. Morocco, port on W shore of Alhucemas Bay (of Mediterranean Sea), 55 mi. W of Melilla; 35°15'N 3°56'W. Sp. protectorate's chief fishing port; canning, saltworking, vegetable-fiber processing, cabinetmaking, mfg. of soap, ceramics. Harbor is sheltered from N winds by a headland (Cabo Nuevo). In 1945, c.½ of town's pop. was Spanish. Sometimes also called Alhucemas. Alhucemas isls. are 3 mi. SE.

Villasanta (vēl"läsän'tä), town (pop. 3,532), Milano prov., Lombardy, N Italy, 2 mi. NE of Monza; mfg. (ribbon, shoes, iceboxes).

Villa Santa Maria (vēl'lä sän'tä märē'ä), town (pop. 2,977), Chieti prov., Abruzzi e Molise, S central Italy, on Sangro R. and 20 mi. S of Lanciano; mfg. (woolen textiles, fireworks, irrigation pumps).

Villa Santa Rosa (bē'yä sän'tä rō'sä), town (pop. estimate 1,000), ⊙ Veinticinco (25) de Mayo dept. (□ c.2,200; 1947 pop. 9,911), S San Juan prov., Argentina, on railroad (Algarrobo Verde station) and 18 mi. SE of San Juan; wine center in San Juan R. valley (irrigation area).

Villa Santina (vēl'lä säntē'nä), village (pop. 1,052), Udine prov., Friuli–Venezia Giulia, NE Italy, near Tagliamento R., 4 mi. W of Tolmezzo; iron foundry.

Villa Sarandí, Uruguay: see SARANDÍ GRANDE.

Villasboas (bēyäsbō'äs), village, Durazno dept., central Uruguay, on railroad and highway, and 12 mi. N of Durazno; wheat, corn, sheep.

Villasbuenas de Gata (bēlyäs vwä'näs dhā gä'tä), town (pop. 1,002), Cáceres prov., W Spain, 31 mi. NW of Plasencia; produces olive oil.

Villaseca de Henares (bēlyäsä'kä dhā änä'rĕs), town (pop. 386), Guadalajara prov., central Spain, 32 mi. NE of Guadalajara; cereals, livestock. Near by is the Matillas portland-cement plant.

Villaseca de Laciana, Spain: see VILLABLINO.

Villaseca de la Sagra (dhā lä sä'grä), town (pop. 1,359), Toledo prov., central Spain, on a canal of the Tagus, and 10 mi. NE of Toledo; grain growing, flour milling; potteries.

Villasequilla or **Villasequilla de Yepes** (bēlyäsäkē'lyä dhā yā'pĕs), town (pop. 1,940), Toledo prov., central Spain, 16 mi. E of Toledo; cereals, sugar beets, potatoes, grapes, olives, livestock.

Villa Serrano (bē'yä sĕrä'nō), town (pop. c.8,980), ⊙ B. Boeto prov., Chuquisaca dept., S Bolivia, 60 mi. E of Sucre; wheat, corn, vegetables. Until 1940s, Pescado.

Villasis (bēyä'sēs, bēlyä'–), town (1939 pop. 3,213; 1948 municipality pop. 23,952), Pangasinan prov., central Luzon, Philippines, 20 mi. SE of Dagupan, near Agno R.; agr. center (rice, copra, corn).

Villa Somoza (bē'yä sōmō'sä). **1** Town (1950 pop. 507), Chontales dept., S Nicaragua, on road and 5 mi. E of Santo Tomás; grain, sugar cane, livestock. Developed in 1940s. **2** Village, León dept., W Nicaragua, on upper Villanueva R. and 4 mi. NNW of El Sauce; terminus of rail branch from León; corn, sesame, beans, livestock.

Villasor (vēl-läsôr'), village (pop. 3,692), Cagliari prov., S Sardinia, near Flumini Mannu R., 14 mi. NNW of Cagliari; mineral spring.

Villa Tejeda (bē'yä tāhā'dä), town (pop. 1,113), Veracruz, E Mexico, in foothills of Sierra Madre Oriental, on railroad and 33 mi. WSW of Veracruz; coffee, sugar cane, fruit. Formerly Camarón.

Villa Tenares, Dominican Republic: see TENARES.

Villatobas (bēlyätō'väs), town (pop. 4,038), Toledo prov., central Spain, in New Castile, 18 mi. SE of Aranjuez; communications point and agr. center in upper La Mancha; cereals, potatoes, olives, grapes, sugar beets, sheep. Alcohol distilling, chocolate and plaster mfg.

Villa Tomina, Bolivia: see TOMINA, town.

Villatoro (bēlyätō'rō), town (pop. 726), Ávila prov., central Spain, 23 mi. WSW of Ávila; fruit, potatoes, beans, sugar beets, carobs, livestock. The Villatoro pass (c.4,450 ft.) is 2 mi. SW.

Villa Tulumba, Argentina: see TULUMBA.

Villaudric (vēlōdrēk'), village (pop. 426), Haute-Garonne dept., S France, 13 mi. SSE of Montauban; winegrowing.

Villa Unión (bē'yä ōōnyōn'), village (pop. estimate 500), ⊙ General Lavalle dept. (□ 3,215; 1947 census 6,661), W La Rioja prov., Argentina, in Famatina Valley, 85 mi. W of La Rioja; stock-raising and coal-mining center.

Villa Unión. **1** Town (pop. 1,932), Coahuila, N Mexico, 32 mi. SW of Piedras Negras (Texas border); cereals, cattle, istle fibers, candelilla wax. **2** Town (pop. 2,936), Durango, N Mexico, 40 mi. ESE of Durango; agr. center (corn, wheat, cotton, sugar cane, vegetables, livestock). **3** Town (pop. 4,002), Sinaloa, NW Mexico, on Presidio R. and 12 mi. E of Mazatlán, on railroad; agr. center (chick-peas, corn, sugar cane, tobacco, cotton, tomatoes, fruit); textile mill, soap works.

Villa Urquiza (bē'yä ōōrkē'sä), village (pop. estimate 600), W Entre Ríos prov., Argentina, port on Paraná R. and 10 mi. NE of Paraná, in agr. area (flax, alfalfa, wheat, livestock; apiculture).

Villava (bēlyä'vä), town (pop. 1,948), Navarre prov., N Spain, 3 mi. NE of Pamplona; olive-oil, brandy mfg.; cereals, wine, livestock.

Villa Vallelonga (vēl'lä väl-lĕlông'gä), village (pop. 1,838), Aquila prov., Abruzzi e Molise, S central Italy, 15 mi. SE of Avezzano; bauxite mining.

Villa Velha, Brazil: see ESPÍRITO SANTO, city.

Villaverde (bēlyävĕr'dhā), town (pop. 2,832, with suburbs 7,981), Madrid prov., central Spain, rail junction 4 mi. S of Madrid, in agr. region (truck produce, cereals, grapes, sheep). Tanning, meat packing; mfg. of ceramics, glassware, cardboard boxes, valves, elevators, precision instruments. Clay quarrying. Medicinal springs.

Villaverde del Río (dhĕl rē'ō), town (pop. 2,467), Seville prov., SW Spain, on right bank of the Guadalquivir and 15 mi. NNE of Seville, in agr. region (cereals, cotton, sugar beets, olives, oranges, tobacco, livestock); fishing.

Villaverla (vēl"lävĕr'lä), village (pop. 1,632), Vicenza prov., Veneto, N Italy, 8 mi. N of Vicenza; alcohol distilling, wine making.

Villavicencio (bīyävēsĕn'syō), village, N Mendoza prov., Argentina, in Sierra de los Paramillos, 27 mi. NNW of Mendoza; health resort, with mineral springs. Old amphitheater used by Indians for ritual purposes is near by.

Villavicencio, town (pop. 6,074), ⊙ Meta intendancy, central Colombia, landing on Guatiquía R. (headstream of the Meta) and 45 mi. SE of Bogotá, on highway at E foot of Cordillera Oriental; 4°8'N 73°37'W. Gateway to vast llano lowlands of Orinoco R. basin. Trading and agr. center (cattle, coffee, bananas, rice); distributes hides, furs (nutria), balata gum, and rubber, and supplies Bogotá with cattle. Airport.

Villa Vicente Guerrero (bē'yä bēsĕn'tā gĕrā'rō). **1** or **General Vicente Guerrero** (hānäräl'), town (pop. 4,980), Durango, N Mexico, on railroad and 50 mi. SE of Durango; agr. center (corn, wheat, sugar cane, cotton, tobacco, vegetables, fruit). Formerly Muleros. **2** Town (pop. 7,652), Tlaxcala, central Mexico, on central plateau, 5 mi. N of Puebla; agr. center (corn, wheat, barley, maguey, alfalfa, beans, livestock); flour milling, pulque distilling. San Pablo del Monte until 1940.

Villaviciosa (bēlyävē-thyō'sä). **1** or **Villaviciosa de Córdoba** (dhā kôr'dhōvä), town (pop. 6,226), Córdoba prov., S Spain, 18 mi. NW of Córdoba; olive pressing, flour milling, brandy distilling, honey and wax processing. Fruit, wine, livestock. Lead mines near by. **2** Town (pop. 2,219), Oviedo prov., NW Spain, fishing port at head of inlet of Bay of Biscay, 22 mi. ENE of Oviedo; cider distilling, mfg. of dairy products, sawmilling; cereals, sugar beets, chestnuts, livestock. Near by is 9th-cent. church of San Salvador de Valdediós.

Villaviciosa de Odón (dhā ōdōn'), town (pop. 1,427), Madrid prov., central Spain, on railroad and 12 mi. WSW of Madrid; wheat, oats, barley, fruit. Near by is a magnificent castle of the dukes of Chinchón built (1583) by Juan de Herrera; here Ferdinand VI died, and Godoy was held prisoner.

Villa Victoria (bēktōr'yä). **1** Town (pop. 794), Mexico state, central Mexico, 25 mi. NW of Toluca; cereals, livestock. Dam near by. **2** Town (pop. 896), Michoacán, W Mexico, 40 mi. SE of Colima; rice, sugar cane, fruit. Formerly Chinicuila.

Villavieja (bēyävyā'hä), village (pop. 990), Huila dept., S central Colombia, on upper Magdalena R., on Neiva–Bogotá RR and 20 mi. NE of Neiva; rice, cacao, stock.

Villavieja (bēlyävyā'hä), town (pop. 2,570), Castellón de la Plana prov., E Spain, 12 mi. SW of Castellón de la Plana; sandal mfg.; olive oil, rice, oranges, wheat. Mineral springs.

Villavieja de Yeltes (dhā yĕl'tĕs), town (pop. 2,308), Salamanca prov., W Spain, 20 mi. NNE of Ciudad Rodrigo; tanning, flour milling; cereals, cattle. Granite quarries.

Villa Viscarra (bē'yä bēskä'rä), town (pop. c.4,200), Cochabamba dept., central Bolivia, 60 mi. SE of Cochabamba; alt. 8,038 ft. Transshipment point on railroad from Cochabamba (extension to Tintín; projected to Santa Cruz) and on highway to Sucre and to Santa Cruz; grain, potatoes; livestock. Until c.1940, Vila-Vila.

Villazón (bēyäsōn'). **1** Village, Chuquisaca dept., SE Bolivia, in the Chaco, 95 mi. NE of Villa Montes, on road. Frontier point for Paraguay, established (1938) in Chaco Peace Conference. **2** Town (pop. c.4,600), Potosí dept., S Bolivia, on Bolivia-Argentina border, on RR from Uyuni, and 45 mi. S of Tupiza, opposite La Quiaca (Argentina); alt. 11,319 ft.; commercial trade center; customs house.

Villé (vēlā'), Ger. *Weiler* (vī'lůr), village (pop. 1,222), Bas-Rhin dept., E France, in the E Vosges, 9 mi. NW of Sélestat; rail-branch terminus. Cotton spinning.

Villebois-Lavalette (vēlbwä'-lävälĕt'), agr. village (pop. 602), Charente dept., W France, 13 mi. SSE of Angoulême. Also spelled Villebois-la-Valette.

Villebon-sur-Yvette (vēlbō'-sür-ēvĕt'), SSW suburban commune (pop. 1,860) of Paris, Seine-et-Oise dept., N central France, 11 mi. from Notre Dame Cathedral. Has Paris radio transmitter.

Villebrumier (vēlbrümyā'), village (pop. 323), Tarn-et-Garonne dept., SW France, on the Tarn and 9 mi. SE of Montauban; cereals, cattle, poultry.

Villecresnes (vēlkrān'), village (pop. 963), Seine-et-Oise dept., N central France, 12 mi. SE of Paris; grows roses. Telegraph receiving station at near-by Bois-d'Auteuil.

Ville-d'Avray (vēl-dävrā'), town (pop. 3,397), Seine-et-Oise dept., N central France, a WSW suburb of Paris, 7 mi. from Notre Dame Cathedral, just W of Sèvres; mfg. of soap, pharmaceuticals.

Villedieu or **Villedieu-les-Poêles** (vēldyû'-lā-pwäl'), town (pop. 3,023), Manche dept., NW France, on the Sienne and 12 mi. NE of Avranches; road center noted for its manufactures of hammered copper utensils and church bells; dairying, cider distilling, wool spinning, salmon and trout fishing. Also spelled Villedieu-les-Poëles.

Villedieu, La (lä vēldyû'), agr. village (pop. 398), Vienne dept., W central France, 8 mi. S of Poitiers. Also called La Villedieu-du-Clain.

Villedieu-sur-Indre (–sür-ē'drů), village (pop. 1,471), Indre dept., central France, on Indre R. and 8 mi. WNW of Châteauroux; porcelain mfg.

Ville-en-Tardenois (vēl-ã-tärdnwä'), agr. village (pop. 372), Marne dept., N France, 12 mi. SW of Rheims.

Villefagnan (vēlfänyã'), village (pop. 677), Charente dept., W France, 6 mi. W of Ruffec; white wines.

Villefort (vēlfôr'), village (pop. 722), Lozère dept., S France, on NE slope of Mont Lozère, 18 mi. ENE of Florac; road center; livestock, fruit market. Lead, zinc deposits near by.

Villefranche (vēlfrãsh'). **1** or **Villefranche-sur-Mer** (–sür-mâr'), Ital. *Villafranca*, town (pop. 3,824), Alpes-Maritimes dept., SE France, on Fr. Riviera, 3 mi. ENE of Nice; noted health resort amidst luxuriant subtropical gardens on deep bay of the Mediterranean (fleet anchorage), sheltered by Cape Ferrat peninsula (E); fishing, yacht building, flower growing. Old town, with steep, often covered, streets and flights of steps; preserves 18th-cent. aspect. Port dominated by 16th-cent. citadel. Slightly damaged in Second World War. **2** or **Villefranche-de-Lauragais** (–dů-lōrāgā'), village (pop. 1,922), Haute-Garonne dept., S France, on the Canal du Midi and 19 mi. SE of Toulouse; market center; meat processing, flour milling, poultry shipping. **3** or **Villefranche-sur-Saône** (–sür-sōn'), town (pop. 19,391), Rhône dept., E central France, near the Saône 17 mi. NNW of Lyons; industrial center with textile mills (work and sport clothes, satins and silk linings, flannels), metalworks (agr. and viticultural machines; foundries), and food-processing plants. Important trade in Beaujolais wines. Was ⊙ Beaujolais.

Villefranche-d'Albigeois (–dälbēzh-wä'), agr. village (pop. 386), Tarn dept., S France, 9 mi. ESE of Albi.

Villefranche-de-Conflent (–dů-kõflã'), village (pop. 482), Pyrénées-Orientales dept., S France, in the CONFLENT valley, on Têt R. and 4 mi. SW of Prades; electrometallurgy. Has 12th–14th-cent. church.

Villefranche-de-Lauragais, France: see VILLEFRANCHE, Haute-Garonne dept.

Villefranche-de-Longchapt (–dů-lõshä'), village (pop. 346), Dordogne dept., SW France, 15 mi. E of Libourne; woodworking, winegrowing.

Villefranche-de-Rouergue (–dů-rōōârg'), town (pop. 7,203), Aveyron dept., S France, on the Aveyron and 27 mi. W of Rodez; road and market center; meat processing, mushroom and vegetable shipping, printing, distilling, smelting. Copper deposits near by. Founded 1252 by counts of Toulouse as a stronghold.

Villefranche-du-Périgord (–dü-pārēgôr'), village (pop. 601), Dordogne dept., SW France, 17 mi. SW of Gourdon; wool and cotton spinning, food canning. Formerly Villefranche-de-Belvès.

Villefranche-sur-Mer, France: see VILLEFRANCHE, Alpes-Maritimes dept.

Villefranche-sur-Saône, France: see VILLEFRANCHE, Rhône dept.

Villefranque (vēlfrãk'), village (pop. 209), Basses-Pyrénées dept., SW France, on Nive R. and 4 mi. SSE of Bayonne; saltworks, tanneries.

Villegaignon Island (vēlgänyõ'), in Guanabara Bay, SE Brazil, just off site of Rio de Janeiro's Santos Dumont airport. Belongs to Federal Dist. On it are naval acad. and old fort. Named for Villegaignon, who in 1555 established a Fr. Huguenot settlement here.

Ville-Gozet, La, France: see MONTLUÇON.

Villejuif (vēl-zhwēf'), town (pop. 23,542), Seine dept., N central France, a residential S suburb of Paris, 4 mi. from Notre Dame Cathedral, just S of Kremlin-Bicêtre; mfg. (glass, tiles, furniture, hats, candy). Has 13th-cent. church.

Ville La Salle, Que.: see LASALLE.

Villel de Mesa (bēlyĕl'dhä mä'sä), town (pop. 766), Guadalajara prov., central Spain, 21 mi. NNW of Molina; beans, cereals, sheep, goats. Lumbering. Flour milling, soap mfg. Lime, gypsum, marble, cement quarrying.

Ville Marie (vēl märē'). **1** Village (pop. 1,001), ⊙ Timiskaming co., W Que., on L. Timiskaming, 70 mi. N of North Bay; dairying, cattle market; in gold-, silver-, copper-mining region. **2** Village, S Que., name of original mission settlement on site of MONTREAL.

Villemomble (vēlmõ'blů), town (pop. 18,617), Seine dept., N central France, an outer ENE suburb of Paris, 7 mi. from Notre Dame Cathedral, just S of Le Raincy; precision metalworks; mfg. (porcelain, custom jewelry, gloves).

Villemontel (vēlmõtĕl'), village (pop. estimate 500), W Que., 12 mi. WNW of Amos; dairying; cattle, grain, potatoes.

Villemur-sur-Tarn (vēlmür'-sür-tärn'), town (pop. 2,192), Haute-Garonne dept., S France, on Tarn R. and 13 mi. SE of Montauban; flour milling, macaroni mfg. Winegrowing.

Villena (bēlyā'nä), city (pop. 14,674), Alicante prov., E Spain, in Valencia, 30 mi. NW of Alicante, on slopes of hill dominated by medieval castle of marquis of Villena; wine-production center. Mfg. of cement pipes, shoes, furniture, soap, tiles, cutlery; alcohol distilling, olive-oil and cheese processing, sawmilling. Fruit orchards in area. Saltworks and gypsum quarries near by. Has 16th-cent. church and several old mansions.

Villenauxe (vēlnōks'), village (pop. 1,720), Aube dept., NE central France, 7 mi. NNE of Nogent-sur-Seine; porcelain mfg. Limestone quarries near.

Villenave-d'Ornon (vēlnäv'-dôrnõ'), S suburb (pop. 8,150) of Bordeaux, SW France, near Garonne R.; foundries, tanneries; mfg. of cement pipes, winegrowing.

Villeneuve or **Villeneuve-d'Aveyron** (vēlnûv'-dävārõ'), village (pop. 595), Aveyron dept., S France, 6 mi. N of Villefranche-de-Rouergue; hosiery mfg.

Villeneuve-de-Berg (vēlnûv'-dů-bâr'), village (pop. 1,028), Ardèche dept., S France, 7 mi. SE of Aubenas; flour milling, saddle and floor-tile mfg.

Villeneuve-de-Marsan (–dů-märsã'), village (pop. 869), Landes dept., SW France, on the Midou (headstream of Midouze R.) and 10 mi. E of Mont-de-Marsan; livestock, corn.

Villeneuve-d'Olmes (–dôlm'), village (pop. 372), Ariège dept., S France, 12 mi. ESE of Foix; woolen milling.

Villeneuve-la-Garenne (–lä-gärĕn'), town (pop. 3,584), Seine dept., N central France, a N suburb of Paris, 5.5 mi. from Notre Dame Cathedral, port on left bank of Seine R., opposite Saint-Denis; boat building, mfg. (pharmaceuticals, perfumes). Sand quarries.

Villeneuve-l'Archevêque (–ärsh-vĕk'), village (pop. 1,347), Yonne dept., N central France, 13 mi. ENE of Sens; chemical fertilizer. Has 12th–16th-cent. church.

Villeneuve-le-Roi (–lů-rwä'), town (pop. 14,766), Seine-et-Oise dept., N central France, an outer SSE suburb of Paris, 9 mi. from Notre Dame Cathedral, on left bank of the Seine; shipbuilding, furniture mfg. Just W is Villeneuve-Orly airport. Just E is garden suburb of La Faisanderie.

Villeneuve-lès-Avignon (–lāzävēnyõ'), town (pop. 3,732), Gard dept., S France, on right bank of Rhone R., opposite Avignon; fruit- and vegetable-shipping center. Produces men's clothing and fruit preserves. Important in 14th cent. during papal residence at Avignon. Damaged in Second World War.

Villeneuve-lès-Béziers (–lā-bāzyā'), village (pop. 1,822), Hérault dept., S France, on the Canal du Midi and 4 mi. SE of Béziers; winegrowing, distilling.

Villeneuve-lès-Maguelonne (–lā-mägůlôn'), village (pop. 1,231), Hérault dept., S France, near lagoon of the Gulf of Lion, 5 mi. S of Montpellier; bauxite mining, winegrowing, truck farming.

Villeneuve-Saint-Georges (–sẽ-zhôrch'), town (pop. 18,279), Seine-et-Oise dept., N central France, an outer SSE suburb of Paris, 9 mi. from Notre Dame Cathedral, on right bank of Seine R. at influx of the Yères; aircraft plant; mfg. (electric batteries, tiles). Has large freight-yard and railroad shops.

Villeneuve-sur-Lot (–sür-lôt'), town (pop. 12,305), Lot-et-Garonne dept., SW France, on the Lot and 15 mi. NNE of Agen; road and important commercial center (prune trade); fruit and vegetable preserving, mfg. of tin cans, hosiery, and footwear. Preserves medieval gate, bridge, and arcades.

Villeneuve-sur-Yonne (–sür-yôn'), town (pop. 3,602), Yonne dept., N central France, on Yonne R. and 8 mi. S of Sens; tarpaulins, surgical instruments, furniture, perfumes; distilling.

Villenour (vēlnōōr'), town (commune pop. 27,991), Pondicherry settlement, Fr. India; suburb of Pondicherry, 5 mi. W of city center. Temple here is place of annual Hindu pilgrimage. Sometimes spelled Villanur.

Villenoy (vēlnwä'), SSW suburb (pop. 1,597) of Meaux, Seine-et-Marne dept., N central France, on right bank of the Marne; sugar milling, alcohol distilling, woodworking. First World War military cemetery.

Villeparisis (vēlpärēzē'), outermost ENE suburb (pop. 5,475) of Paris, Seine-et-Marne dept., N central France, 13 mi. ENE of Notre Dame cathedral; mfg. (paints and varnishes, leather goods).

Ville Parle, India: see ANDHERI.

Ville Platte (vĕl' plăt'), town (pop. 6,633), ⊙ Evangeline parish, S central La., c.45 mi. S of Alexandria; market and processing center for rice, cotton, sugar-cane, and lumber area; mfg. of carbon black, brick, canned foods; moss gins. Oil fields near by. Settled in early-19th cent.

Ville-Pommeroeul (vēl-pômůrůl'), village (pop. 1,015), Hainaut prov., W Belgium, near Condé-Mons Canal, 11 mi. W of Mons; coal mining.

Villepreux (vēlprû'), village (pop. 490), Seine-et-Oise dept., N central France, 5 mi. WNW of Versailles. Agr. school. Magnetic observatory of Le Val-Joyeux just S.

Villeréal (vēlrāäl'), village (pop. 898), Lot-et-Garonne dept., SW France, on the Dropt and 16 mi. N of Villeneuve-sur-Lot; horse breeding, plum growing.

Villers-Bocage (vēlâr'-bôkäzh'). **1** Village (pop. 576), Calvados dept., NW France, 15 mi. SW of Caen; dairying. **2** Agr. village (pop. 629), Somme dept., N France, 7 mi. N of Amiens.

Villers-Bretonneux (–brůtônû'), town (pop. 3,280), Somme dept., N France, 10 mi. E of Amiens; hosiery mfg. Here Australians in gallant stand (April, 1918) blocked Ger. advance on Amiens. Australian memorial unveiled 1938.

Villers-Carbonnel (–kärbônĕl'), village (pop. 252), Somme dept., N France, 4 mi. SSW of Péronne; distilling. Limestone quarries.

Villers-Cotterêts (–kôtůrā'), resort (pop. 3,492), Aisne dept., N France, in a forest (□ 50), 14 mi. SW of Soissons; sawmilling and woodworking center. Its 16th-cent. Renaissance castle built by Francis I is now a house for the aged. Here Allies assembled their forces for offensive of July 18, 1918, in First World War. Dumas *père* b. here.

Villers-devant-Orval, Belgium: see ORVAL.

Villersexel (vēlârsĕksĕl'), village (pop. 865), Haute-Saône dept., E France, on Ognon R. and 10 mi. SSW of Lure; cotton milling. A battlefield in Franco-Prussian War of 1870–71.

Villers-Farlay (vēlâr'-färlā'), village (pop. 506), Jura dept., E France, near Loue R., 14 mi. ESE of Dôle; cheese mfg.

Villers-la-Ville (–lä-vēl'), agr. village (pop. 1,163), Brabant prov., central Belgium, 9 mi. E of Nivelles. Has ruins of 12th-cent abbey.

Villers-le-Gambon (–lů-gäbõ'), village (pop. 732), Namur prov., S Belgium, 3 mi. E of Philippeville; marble.

Villers-le-Lac, Doubs dept., France: see LAC-OU-VILLERS.

Villers-Outréaux (–ōōtrāō'), town (pop. 2,122), Nord dept., N France, 10 mi. SSE of Cambrai; embroidering, lingerie mfg.

Villers-Saint-Paul (–sẽ-pôl'), town (pop. 2,350), Oise dept., N France, near the Oise, 7 mi. NW of Senlis; chemical laboratories.

Villers-sur-Mer (–sür-mâr'), village (pop. 1,462), Calvados dept., NW France, bathing resort on the Channel, 16 mi. NW of Lisieux. Beach area damaged in Second World War.

Villerupt (vēlrü'), town (pop. 5,456), Meurthe-et-Moselle dept., NE France, 8 mi. ESE of Longwy; metallurgical center (blast furnaces, foundries). Iron mines. Heavy industry (steel) also at Micheville (1 mi. NE).

Villerval (vēlĕrväl'), village (pop. 402), Pas-de-Calais dept., N France, 5 mi. S of Lens; coal mining.

Villerville (–vēl'), village (pop. 630), Calvados dept., NW France, beach resort on the Channel, 3 mi. NE of Trouville. Heavily damaged in Second World War.

Ville Saint Pierre or **Saint Pierre** (vēl sẽ pyâr'), residential town (pop. 4,061), S Que., on Montreal Isl., SW suburb of Montreal.

Ville-sous-la-Ferté (vēl-sōō-lä-fĕrtā'), village (pop. 374), Aube dept., NE central France, on Aube R. and 9 mi. SSE of Bar-sur-Aube; measuring devices. Former Cistercian abbey of Clairvaux (klârvō') (founded 1115 by St. Bernard of Clairvaux; suppressed in Fr. Revolution) is 2 mi. N; now houses a penitentiary established under Napoleon.

Ville-sur-Haine, Belgium: see HAVRÉ.

Ville-sur-Saulx (vēl-sür-sō'), village (pop. 316), Meuse dept., NE France, on Saulx R. and 7 mi. SW of Bar-le-Duc; paper mill.

Ville-sur-Tourbe (–tōōrb'), village (pop. 259), Marne dept., N France, 9 mi. NNW of Sainte-Menehould.

Villeta (bēyā'tä), town (pop. 2,269), Cundinamarca dept., central Colombia, in W Cordillera Oriental, on railroad and highway, and 40 mi. NW of Bogotá; alt. 6,043 ft. Coffee- and winegrowing. Gold deposits near by.

Villeta, city (dist. pop. 13,991), Central dept., S Paraguay, port on Paraguay R. (Argentina border) and 16 mi. SSE of Asunción; trading, processing, and agr. center (tobacco, cotton, oranges, cattle); ships fruit. Cotton ginning, tobacco processing, vegetable-oil refining. Has modern bldgs., docks, customhouse. Beach. Near by are sites of battles in the War of the Triple Alliance (1865–70).

Villetaneuse (vēltänûz'), town (pop. 3,066), Seine dept., N central France, an outer N suburb of Paris, 8 mi. from Notre Dame Cathedral, just NNW of Saint-Denis; plaster mfg.

Villette, La (lä vēlĕt'), a NE quarter of Paris, France, comprised in 19th *arrondissement*. Has port on Ourcq Canal. Cattle market and slaughter houses.

Villeurbanne (vēlürbän'), E industrial suburb (pop. 80,193) of Lyons, Rhône dept., E central France; center of Lyons area metallurgical industry. Large chemical and rayon factories. Tanning, dyeing, food processing. Built on a regular plan, it has grown rapidly since Industrial Revolution.

Villeveyrac (vēlvāräk'), village (pop. 1,574), Hérault dept., S France, 8 mi. NNW of Sète; bauxite-mining center. Winegrowing.

Villia (vĭ'lēü), town (pop. 3,151), Attica nome, E central Greece, 25 mi. NW of Athens; summer resort; wine; stock raising (sheep, goats).

Villicún, Sierra de (syĕ'rä dā vēyēkōōn'), subandean range in central San Juan prov., Argentina, extends c.40 mi. N from San Juan; rises to c.6,500 ft.

Villiers (fĭlĕrs'), town (pop. 2,171), NE Orange Free State, U. of So. Afr., on Transvaal border, on Vaal R. (rail and road bridges) and 50 mi. SE Vereeniging; alt. 4,693 ft.; stock, grain.

Villiersdorp (fĭlĕrs'dôrp), town (pop. 1,487), SW Cape Prov., U. of So. Afr., on Zonder End R. and 25 mi. E of Stellenbosch; fruitgrowing center (apples, grapes); grape-jelly making. Site of mill erected by Dutch East India Co.

Villiers-Saint-Georges (vēlyā'-sē-zhôrzh'), agr. village (pop. 873), 8 mi. NE of Provins; mfg. of organic fertilizer.

Villiers-sur-Marne (–sür-märn'), town (pop. 6,991), Seine-et-Oise dept., N central France, a residential ESE suburb of Paris, 9 mi. from Notre Dame Cathedral, near left bank of the Marne.

Villingen or **Villingen im Schwarzwald** (fĭ'lĭng-ün ĭm shvärts'vält), town (pop. 17,458), S Baden, Germany, in Black Forest, on the Brigach and 3 mi. W of Schwenningen; rail junction; a center of Black Forest watchmaking industry; mfg. of machinery, precision instruments, silk; metal- and woodworking. Climatic health resort (alt. 2,310 ft.). An anc. settlement; old town is still partly surrounded by medieval walls. Has early-Gothic and baroque churches; old town hall (1534) and new baroque town hall.

Villisca (vĭlĭ'skü), city (pop. 1,838), Montgomery co., SW Iowa, on Middle Nodaway R. near confluence of West Nodaway R., and 15 mi. ESE of Red Oak; mfg. (dairy products, beverages, feed); ships hogs, cattle. Bituminous-coal mines near by. Inc. 1869.

Villivakkam (vĭlĭvä'kŭm), town (pop. 8,881), Chingleput dist., E Madras, India; suburb (5 mi. WNW) of Madras. Ordnance factory 6 mi. W, at village of Avadi; emigration depot.

Villmanstrand, Finland: see LAPPEENRANTA.

Villmergen (fĭl'mĕrgün), town (pop. 2,619), Aargau canton, N Switzerland, 14 mi. W of Zurich; shoes, chemicals, flour.

Villognon (vēlônyō'), village (pop. 222), Charente dept., W France, near Charente R., 15 mi. NNE of Angoulême; paper milling.

Villora (bēlyō'rä), town (pop. 792), Cuenca prov., E central Spain, 35 mi. SE of Cuenca; grain growing and stock raising.

Villorba (vēl-lôr'bä), village (pop. 1,496), Treviso prov., Veneto, N Italy, 5 mi. N of Treviso; mills (cotton, silk).

Villoria (bēlyô'ryä), town (pop. 1,381), Salamanca prov., W Spain, 15 mi. ENE of Salamanca; sheep; cereals, wine, vegetables.

Villoria de Órbigo (dhā ôr'vēgō), village (pop. 1,111), Leon prov., NW Spain, 19 mi. SW of Leon; cereals, vegetables, sugar beets.

Villoruela (bēlyôrwā'lä), town (pop. 1,036), Salamanca prov., W Spain, 14 mi. ENE of Salamanca; basket mfg.; cereals, wine.

Villupuram (vĭl'lōōpōōrŭm), city (pop. 23,829), South Arcot dist., E Madras, India, 23 mi. NW of Cuddalore, in agr. area; rail junction, with spur to Pondicherry; sugar milling.

Vilm, Lake, Poland: see WIELIM, LAKE.

Vilna (vĭl'nü), village (pop. 322), E central Alta., 65 mi. NE of Edmonton; farming, lumbering.

Vilna (vĭl'nü), **Vilnius, Vilnyus,** or **Vil'nyus** (vĕl'nēōōs), Ger. *Wilna* (vĭl'nä), Pol. *Wilno* (vēl'nô), Rus. *Vilna* or *Vilno* (vēl'nü), city (1931 pop. 196,345), ⊙ Lithuania, on Viliya R. (head of navigation) and 480 mi. WSW of Moscow, 240 mi. NE of Warsaw; 54°40'N 25°18'E. Major cultural, commercial, and industrial center; important rail junction; mfg. of agr. implements, radios, electric motors, fertilizer, bone meal, oils, glycerin, cotton and leather goods, glass; sawmilling (matches, paper, cardboard), tobacco and food processing. Has univ. (founded 1578 by Stephen Bathory), art and teachers colleges, conservatory. Its numerous old churches include classical R.C. cathedral (1387; restored 1801), Gothic church of St. Anne and St. Bernard, and others in Muscovite style. Ostra Brama (an old city gate) has a revered image of the Virgin. Episcopal palace and old city hall (now a theater) are in classic tradition. Located amid picturesque pine-clad hills at confluence of the Viliya and its small left affluent, the Vilnia [Pol. *Wilejka*]; includes once-walled inner city at foot of castle hill (ruins of 14th-cent. castle of Jagellon dynasty) and outlying sections of later construction. Since 1947, city includes E industrial suburb of Nauja Vilnia. Vilna dates from 10th cent.; rose to importance when it became (1323) ⊙ grand duchy of Lithuania and (1416) the metropolis of the Lithuanian Orthodox Eastern Church. Following union (1569) of Poland and Lithuania, its Lithuanian culture was gradually replaced by Polish institutions. Suffered during Russo-Polish wars (1650s); in the 1795 partition of Poland it passed to Russia and became ⊙ Vilna govt. Following First World War, when it was held (1915–18) by Germans, it changed hands repeatedly (1918–20) bet. Soviet troops, Lithuanians, and Poles. Captured (1920) by Pol. free corps; its annexation by Poland in 1922 was confirmed (1923) over the claim of Lithuania, leading to the interruption (until 1938) of diplomatic relations bet. the 2 countries. Occupied (1939) by Soviet troops following new partition of Poland; ceded (1939) to Lithuania and succeeded Kaunas as its capital. Until Second World War, when city was held (1941–44) by Germans, who virtually exterminated the Jews, Vilna had been (since 16th cent.) a leading center of Jewish culture in E Europe.

Vilonia (vīlō'nyü), town (pop. 215), Faulkner co., central Ark., 25 mi. N of Little Rock.

Vilos, Los, Chile: see LOS VILOS.

Vilque Chico (bēl'kā chē'kō), village (pop. 435), Puno dept., SE Peru, port on L. Titicaca, 6 mi. E of Huancané; alt. 12,549 ft.; barley, potatoes, livestock.

Vilsbiburg (fĭls'bē'bōōrk), town (pop. 5,755), Lower Bavaria, Germany, on the Great Vils and 11 mi. SE of Landshut; textile mfg., brewing, food processing, metalworking, printing. Has early-15th-cent. church. Chartered before 1372.

Vilseck (fĭls'ĕk), town (pop. 2,057), Upper Palatinate, N central Bavaria, Germany, on the Vils and 12 mi. N of Amberg; woodworking; grain, livestock. Has early-18th-cent. castle, built on Romanesque foundations, with 13th-cent. watchtower. Chartered in 14th cent.

Vilshofen (fĭls"hō'fün), town (pop. 5,713), Lower Bavaria, Germany, at confluence of Danube and Great Vils rivers, 13 mi. WNW of Passau; textile and machinery mfg., brewing, food processing, printing. Chartered 1192. Granite quarries near.

Vils River (fĭls). **1** In Bavaria, Germany, rises 3 mi. S of Freihung, flows 50 mi. generally S, past Amberg, to the Nab opposite Kallmünz. **2** In Bavaria, Germany: see GREAT VILS RIVER.

Vilters (fĭl'türs), town (pop. 2,029), St. Gall canton, E Switzerland, near the Rhine, 19 mi. E of Glarus; metalworking.

Vilvestre (bēlvĕ'strā), town (pop. 1,479), Salamanca prov., W Spain, near Duero (Douro) R. and Port. border, 37 mi. NNW of Ciudad Rodrigo; rye, livestock; lumber.

Vilviestre del Pinar (bēlvyĕ'strā dhĕl pēnär'), town (pop. 939), Badajoz prov., N Spain, 35 mi. WNW of Soria; cereals, livestock; lumber. Flour milling; naval stores.

Vilvoorde (vĭl'vôrdü), Fr. *Vilvorde* (vēlvôrd'), town (pop. 25,996), Brabant prov., central Belgium, on Willebroek Canal and 6 mi. NNE of Brussels; oil refineries, coke plants, grain elevators, steel foundries; mfg. (cement, food products).

Vilya (vē'lyŭ), town (1926 pop. 2,829), SW Gorki oblast, Russian SFSR, 6 mi. SSE of Vyksa; rail junction; peat and lumber-collecting center.

Vilyaka, Latvia: see VILAKA.

Vilyandi, Estonia: see VILJANDI.

Vilyany, Latvia: see VILANI.

Vilyui Range or **Vilyuy Range** (vēlyōō'ē), NW Yakut Autonomous SSR, Russian SFSR, separates Vilyui and Olenek river basins; rises to 3,300 ft.

Vilyui River or **Vilyuy River,** W Yakut Autonomous SSR, Russian SFSR, rises on Central Siberian plateau, flows 1,512 mi. E, through agr. area, past Suntar (head of navigation), Verkhne-Vilyuisk, and Vilyuisk, to Lena R. 180 mi. NW of Yakutsk. Navigable for c.500 mi.; abounds in fish. Platinum, lignite, gold found along banks.

Vilyuisk or **Vilyuysk** (vēlyōō'ēsk), city (1939 pop. over 2,000), S central Yakut Autonomous SSR, Russian SFSR, on Vilyui R. and 280 mi. NW of Yakutsk; livestock and fur center. Founded 1634; Chernyshevski exiled here, 1871–83.

Vimbodí (bēmbō-dhē'), town (pop. 1,240), Tarragona prov., NE Spain, 6 mi. WNW of Montblanch, in winegrowing area; champagne mfg. Lead and barium-sulphate deposits near by.

Vimeiro (vēmā'rōō), village (pop. 518), Lisboa dist., central Portugal, 32 mi. NNW of Lisbon, and 7 mi. NNW of Tôrres Vedras; mineral springs. Here Wellington decisively defeated (1808) French under Junot in Peninsular War.

Vimercate (vēmĕrkä'tē), town (pop. 5,793), Milano prov., Lombardy, N Italy, 6 mi. ENE of Monza; mfg. (textiles, macaroni, alcohol, glass, glue).

Vimeu (vēmû'), small region in Somme dept., N France, bounded by Somme R. estuary (N), English Channel (W), and Bresle R. (SW). Cattle, horses; apple orchards. Known for locksmithing.

Vimieiro (vēmyā'rōō), village (pop. 1,929), Évora dist., S central Portugal, 18 mi. N of Évora; grain, sheep, cork.

Viminal Hill (vĭ'mĭnül), one of the 7 hills of Rome.

Vimioso (vēmyō'zōō), town (pop. 1,713), Bragança dist., N Portugal, near Sp. border, 20 mi. SE of Bragança; livestock.

Vimmerby (vĭ'mürbü"), city (pop. 4,379), Kalmar co., SE Sweden, 50 mi. S of Linkoping; rail junction, wood- and metalworking, furniture mfg., tanning. Old trade center, chartered in 16th cent.

Vimoutiers (vēmōōtyā'), village (pop. 1,461), Orne dept., NW France, 16 mi. NE of Argentan; Camembert cheese mfg., distilling, cotton and linen weaving. Apple and pear orchards. Heavily damaged (1944) in battle of Argentan-Falaise pocket.

Vimperk (vĭm'pĕrk), Ger. *Winterberg* (vĭn'türbĕrk), town (pop. 2,940), S Bohemia, Czechoslovakia, in Bohemian Forest, on railroad and 15 mi. SSW of Strakonice; specializes in printing multilingual prayer books and calendars; mfg. of paper, fruit juices, linen goods. Has 2 castles, one with 15th-cent. printing shop. Lenora glassworks (raw glass) are 9 mi. SSE, on railroad to Volary.

Vimy (vēmē'), town (pop. 2,623), Pas-de-Calais dept., N France, 6 mi. NNE of Arras; coal and lignite mining, metalworking. Near-by **Vimy Ridge** (476 ft.) was unsuccessfully attacked by French in 1915, and taken by Canadians in April, 1917, after bitter fighting in battle of Arras. A memorial was unveiled here in 1936 to Canadians who fell in First World War.

Vina (vī'nü), town (pop. 313), Franklin co., NW Ala., 32 mi. SW of Tuscumbia, near Miss. line; lumber.

Viña, La, Argentina: see LA VIÑA.

Viña, La, Peru: see LA VIÑA.

Viña del Mar (bē'nyä dĕl mär') [Sp.,=vineyard by the sea], city (1940 pop. 65,916, 1949 estimate 98,156), Valparaiso prov., central Chile, on the Pacific, 4 mi. NE of Valparaiso; large beach resort, as well as an industrial and agr. center (fruit, wine, vegetables). Large sugar and petroleum refineries; also textile mills, alcohol distilleries, chemical plants, vegetable-oil and soap works. In a protected bay, with year-round mild climate, it is one of the most popular resorts in all South America. Has fine parks, luxurious hotels, wide boulevards and plazas; municipal casino, race track, sporting clubs, theaters. Among its many beaches stretching N to Concón are: Recreo, Caleta Abarca, Las Salinas, Reñaca, Montemar. Area was developed after 1875.

Vinadio (vēnä'dyō), village (pop. 724), Cuneo prov., Piedmont, NW Italy, on Stura di Demonte R. and 20 mi. WSW of Cuneo. Terme di Vinadio (alt. 4,352 ft.) is 5 mi. W; resort with hot sulphur springs (108°–154°F.).

Viñales (bēnyä'lĕs), town (pop. 1,400), Pinar del Río prov., W Cuba, 13 mi. N of Pinar del Río; mfg. of cigars; lumbering. Oil, coal, and copper deposits near by. Sulphurous waters at San Vicente (5 mi. N). In vicinity (N) is the Viñales Valley, a tourist site noted for its calcareous formations and fine panoramas.

Vinalesa (bēnälā'sä), N suburb (pop. 1,872) of Valencia, Valencia prov., E Spain, in rich truck-farming area; burlap mfg.; hog raising.

Vinalhaven (vī'nülhāvün), town (pop. 1,427), Knox co., S Maine; resort, fishing center on Vinalhaven Isl. (irregular, 8 mi. long) in Penobscot Bay; granite quarries.

Vinará (bēnärä'), town (pop. estimate 500), W Santiago del Estero prov., Argentina, 45 mi. NW of Santiago del Estero, in fruitgrowing and stock-raising area.

Vinaroz (bēnäröth'), city (pop. 8,267), Castellón de la Plana prov., E Spain, in Valencia, port on the Mediterranean, 24 mi. S of Tortosa; exports wine and fruit. Fishing and fish processing, boatbuilding; mfg. of chemicals, cotton cloth, bonnets, tiles, chocolate, soap; rice milling. Trades in wine, olive oil, truck produce. Summer resort.

Vinay (vēnā'). **1** Village (pop. 1,631), Isère dept., SE France, near the Isère, 16 mi. W of Grenoble, in fertile agr. valley; cheese mfg., woodworking. **2** Village (pop. 254), Marne dept., N France, 4 mi. SW of Épernay; winegrowing (champagne).

Vinça (vēsä'), village (pop. 1,400), Pyrénées-Orientales dept., S France, in lower CONFLENT valley, on Têt R. and 6 mi. ENE of Prades; distilling. Potato and fruit trade.

Vincennes (vēsĕn'), city (pop. 48,851), Seine dept., N central France, just E of Paris, 4 mi. from Notre Dame Cathedral; mfg. (electrical equipment, perfumes, toys, candies, biscuits). Its huge castle and dungeon at N edge of the Bois de Vincennes built in 14th cent. The dungeon was made a state prison in 17th cent. and has had many famous inmates. City has Fr. colonial mus. (established 1935), a First World War mus., and military schools.

Vincennes (vĭnsĕnz'), city (pop. 18,831), ⊙ Knox co., SW Ind., on the Wabash (here forming Ill. line) and 55 mi. S of Terre Haute, in agr., bituminous-coal, and oil area; rail-shipping and mfg. center (glass, farm implements, structural steel, canned and processed foods, paper goods, shoes, flour, florists' supplies). Seat of Vincennes Univ. One of oldest settlements in Ind. A French mission was established here in 1702; fortified by and named for François Margane, sieur de Vincennes (c.1730); town developed around fort. Post was later occupied by the British (1763); Americans under Goerge Rogers Clark captured Vincennes (1779) in the American Revolution. In 1805 an Indian treaty was signed here. Vincennes was ⊙ Indiana Territory, 1800–13. Inc. as borough in 1815, as city in 1856. Surviving historic bldgs. include St. Francis Xavier Cathedral (more than 200 years old), and the old capitol, preserved in a public park. George Rogers Clark Memorial (1932) includes a bridge across the Wabash.

Vincennes, Bois de, France: see BOIS DE VINCENNES.

Vincent, New Zealand: see CLYDE.

Vincent. 1 Town (pop 1,240), Shelby co., central Ala., 25 mi. ESE of Birmingham, near Coosa R.; clothing. Deposits of coal, iron, and limestone in vicinity. **2** Town (pop. 193), Webster co., central Iowa, 10 mi. NE of Fort Dodge, in agr. area. **3** Village (pop. 2,018), Lorain co., N Ohio.

Vincentown (vĭn'sŭntoun″), village (1940 pop. 545), Burlington co., W N.J., 4 mi. SSE of Mt. Holly; makes tomato juice.

Vinces (bēn'sĕs), city (1950 pop. 4,129), Los Ríos prov., W central Ecuador, inland port on Vinces R. (Guayas system), in tropical lowlands, and 45 mi. NNE of Guayaquil; trading center and transshipment point for cacao and other tropical produce (coffee, sugar cane, rice, coconuts, citrus, balsa wood, tagua nuts) shipped to Guayaquil. Fishing, rice milling.

Vinces River, central and W central Ecuador, rises S of Santo Domingo de los Colorados (Pichincha prov.), flows c.150 mi. SSW, past Quevedo and Vinces (Los Ríos prov.), to Guayas R. 21 mi. WSW of Babahoyo. Its middle and lower course is navigable. Waters a fertile lumbering and agr. region (cacao, rice, sugar cane, tropical fruit, balsa wood, tagua nuts).

Vinchiaturo (vĕngkyätōō'rō), village (pop. 1,929), Campobasso prov., Abruzzi e Molise, S central Italy, near the Sella di Vinchiaturo, 6 mi. SSW of Campobasso.

Vinchiaturo, Sella di (sĕl'lä dē), pass (alt. 1,818 ft.) bet. S and central Apennines, S central Italy, 3 mi. S of Vinchiaturo. Rail junction for lines joining Campobasso with Benevento and Isernia.

Vinchina (bēnchē'nä), village (pop. estimate 500), ⊙ General Sarmiento dept. (□ 3,525; 1947 pop. 2,738), N La Rioja prov., Argentina, at N end of Famatina Valley, 95 mi. NW of La Rioja; agr. center (wheat, alfalfa, wine, sheep, goats). Dam near by.

Vinchos (bēn'chōs), town (pop. 2,180), Ayacucho dept., S central Peru, on E slopes of Cordillera Occidental, 10 mi. WSW of Ayacucho; grain, alfalfa, potatoes.

Vinci (vēn'chē), village (pop. 931), Firenze prov., Tuscany, central Italy, 16 mi. W of Florence; macaroni. Has 11th-cent. castle (restored). Leonardo da Vinci b. here.

Vindava, Latvia: see VENTSPILS.

Vindelicia (vĭn″dĕlĭ'shēŭ, –shä), anc. Roman prov. bet. the upper Danube (above the Inn) and the Alps, N of Rhaetia, included mainly in Bavaria. What is now Augsburg was chief city.

Vindeln (vĭn'dŭln), village (pop. 913), Vasterbotten co., N Sweden, on Vindel R. and 30 mi. NW of Umea; grain; dairying. Agr. school.

Vindel River, Swedish *Vindelälven* (vĭn'dŭlĕl'vŭn), Lapland, N Sweden, rises on Norwegian border, E of Mo, flows c.280 mi. SE, past Sorsele, Amsele, and Vindeln, to Ume R. at Vannasby. Logging route; salmon fishing.

Vinderup (vĭ'nŭrŏŏp), town (pop. 1,627), Ringkobing amt, W Jutland, Denmark, 34 mi. NNE of Ringkobing; chemicals.

Vindhya Pradesh (vĭn'dyŭ prŭdāsh'), chief commissioner's state (□ 24,600; 1951 census pop. 3,353,019), central India; ⊙ Rewa. Lies within regions of BUNDEKLHAND and BAGHELKHAND; crossed (E-W) by VINDHYA RANGE. Bordered NE, N, and W by Uttar Pradesh, S and SE by Madhya Pradesh; has enclave (Datia dist.; NW) in Madhya Bharat. Mostly hilly country, drained by Betwa, Dhasan, Ken, Tons, and Son rivers, all of which flow N to Jumna-Ganges basin; annual rainfall averages 40–50 in. Predominantly agr. (wheat, millet, gram, corn, oilseeds, cotton); extensive timber forests (sal, bamboo); big game (tigers, bears, panthers) in jungles. Partly developed mineral resources include limestone, coal, ochre, iron ore, corundum, and diamonds (worked near Panna). Chief towns are Rewa, Datia, Chhatarpur, Satna, and Nowgong. Very backward region, with few roads and railroads and mainly small-scale handicraft industries; literacy is extremely low (c.4%). Sites of historical interest at Bharhut, Khajraho, Amarkantak (pilgrimage center at source of Narbada R.), and Bandhogarh (old Rajput fort). State created 1948 by merger of former CENTRAL INDIA princely states of BUNDELKHAND AGENCY, REWA, and KHANIADHANA (Gwalior Residency). In 1950, several detached enclaves were transferred to Uttar Pradesh, Madhya Bharat, and Madhya Pradesh, and Khaniadhana to Madhya Bharat. State comprises 8 dists.: Chhatarpur, Datia, Panna, Rewa, Sahdol, Satna, Sidhi, Tikamgarh. Main language, Hindi. Pop. 91% Hindu, 6% tribal, 2% Moslem.

Vindhya Range, broken chain of hills, central India, forming S escarpment of central Indian upland, bet. Gangetic basin (N) and Narbada and Son valleys (S); c.675 mi. in length, with average alt. of 1,500–3,000 ft. From Gujarat plain (W) it extends ENE across S Madhya Bharat and Bhopal (forming S edge of Malwa plateau) into N Madhya Pradesh, where it divides into N branch (Kaimur Hills), running N of Son R. through Vindhya Pradesh to Ganges valley in W Bihar, and S branch, running bet. upper reaches of Son and Narbada rivers to junction with Satpura Range in plateau (c.3,400 ft.) of Amarkantak. Range has several N offshoots and gives rise to main Jumna-Ganges right-bank tributaries, including Chambal, Betwa, Ken, and Tons rivers; S slopes drained only by small streams. Composed mainly of sandstone.

Vindobona, Austria: see VIENNA.

Vinegar Hill, elevation (398 ft.), central Co. Wexford, Ireland, just E of Wexford. It was hq. of United Irishmen who, in 1798, from here attacked Enniscorthy and were later defeated here by General Lake.

Vine Grove, town (pop. 1,252), Hardin co., N central Ky., 11 mi. NW of Elizabethtown, in agr. area.

Vineland, village (pop. estimate 500), S Ont., on L. Ontario, 8 mi. W of St. Catharines; apples, stone fruit, grapes, berries.

Vineland, borough (pop. 8,155), Cumberland co., S N.J., 7 mi. N of Millville; market center for agr. region (poultry, fruit); mfg. (glassware, clothing, fireworks, cement blocks, machinery, paper products). State school for backward children (noted for research work), home for feeble-minded women, and state veterans' home here. Founded 1861, inc. 1880.

Vineta, Poland: see WOLIN.

Vineyard Haven (vĭn'yŭrd), village (pop. 1,864) in TISBURY town, Dukes co., SE Mass., on N Martha's Vineyard, 21 mi. SE of New Bedford; summer resort. Steamer connections with Woods Hole. Formerly a whaling, fishing, and saltmaking center; has good harbor on Vineyard Sound. Raided by British in 1778.

Vineyard Sound, SE Mass., separates Martha's Vineyard from Elizabeth Isls. and SW tip of Cape Cod; c.20 mi. long, 3–7 mi. wide.

Vinga (vĕng'gä), village (pop. 4,742), Arad prov., W Rumania, on railroad and 18 mi. N of Timisoara; mfg. of chocolate and candy; truck gardening. Settled by Bulgarians. Formerly Theresiopolis.

Vingaker (vĭng'ō″kŭr), Swedish *Vingåker*, village (pop. 1,983), Sodermanland co., SE central Sweden, 12 mi. W of Katrineholm; agr. market.

Vinh (vĭng), town (1936 pop. 30,000), ⊙ Nghean prov. (□ 6,500; 1943 pop. 1,147,900), N central Vietnam, in Annam, on railroad and 160 mi. S of Hanoi, in fertile and densely populated plain, watered by the Song Ca, on which is its port, BENTHUY; trading center (timber); experimental rice station; railroad shops. Airport. Citadel built 1804.

Vinhais (vēnyīsh'), town (pop. 1,463), Bragança dist., N Portugal, near Sp. border, 13 mi. WNW of Bragança; livestock raising.

Vinhchau (vĭng'chou'), town, Baclieu prov., S Vietnam, on South China Sea coast, 18 mi. E of Baclieu; rice, shrimp fisheries.

Vinhhao (vĭng'hou'), village, Binhthuan prov., S central Vietnam, on South China Sea, on railroad, and 22 mi. SW of Phanrang; mineral springs; sanatorium.

Vinhlong (vĭng'loung'), town (1936 pop. 13,000), ⊙ Vinhlong prov. (□ 400; 1943 pop. 215,400), S Vietnam, in Cochin China, port on arm of Mekong delta, 60 mi. SW of Saigon; rice-growing center; coconuts; sawmilling. Former Khmer dist., passed 1731 to Annamese.

Vinhte Canal (vĭng'tā'), on Cambodia-Vietnam line, linking Chaudoc on Bassac R. (arm of the Mekong) and Hatien (port on Gulf of Siam); 60 mi. long.

Vinhyen (vĭng'yĕn'), town, ⊙ Vinhyen prov. (□ 400; 1943 pop. 296,200), N Vietnam, on Hanoi-Kunming RR and 20 mi. NW of Hanoi; sericulture.

Vinica or **Vinica kraj Varazdina** (vē'nĭtsä krī värazhdē'nä), Serbo-Croatian *Vinica kraj Varaždina*, village, N Croatia, Yugoslavia, near Drava R., 9 mi. W of Varazdin, near Slovenia line; lignite area.

Vining (vī'nĭng). **1** Town (pop. 112), Tama co., central Iowa, 27 mi. E of Marshalltown, in agr. area. **2** City (pop. 168), on Clay-Washington co. line, N Kansas, on Republican R. and 17 mi. E of Concordia; grain, livestock. **3** Village (pop. 180), Otter Tail co., W Minn., near East Battle L., 26 mi. E of Fergus Falls; dairy products.

Vinita (vĭnē'tŭ), city (pop. 5,518), ⊙ Craig co., NE Okla., c.60 mi. NE of Tulsa, in agr. and stock-raising area; mfg. of machinery, metal products, packed meat, dairy products, beverages; cotton ginning. Ships livestock. Coal mining. Has a state mental hosp. Grand River Dam is 12 mi. SE. Founded c.1870.

Vinita Park, town (pop. 1,801), St. Louis co., E Mo. Inc. since 1940.

Vinita Terrace, town (pop. 389), St. Louis co., E Mo.

Vinje (vĭn'yŭ), village and canton (pop. 1,931), Telemark co., S Norway, at foot of the Bykle Mts., 70 mi. NW of Skien; tourist center in cattle-raising, lumbering, fishing, hunting area.

Vinjeora (vĭn'yŭ-ŭ″rä), Nor. *Vinjeøra*, village (pop. 100) in Vinje canton (pop. 604), Sor-Trondelag co., central Norway, 40 mi. E of Kristiansund, at head of a 12-mi.-long fjord; fishing. Agr., and lumber milling near by.

Vinkovci (vēn'kôftsē), Hung. *Vinkovcze* (vĭn'kôftsĕ), town (pop. 15,558), NE Croatia, Yugoslavia, on Bosut R. and 17 mi. S of Osijek, in Slavonia; rail junction on Zagreb-Belgrade RR; local trade center; woodworking. Traces of neolithic culture here. Scene of battle (314) bet. Roman emperors Constantine I and Licinius.

Vinkovtsy or **Vin'kovtsy** (vēn'yŭkŭftsē), town (1939 pop. over 2,000), E Kamenets-Podolski oblast, Ukrainian SSR, 28 mi. SE of Proskurov; fruit canning, distilling.

Vinniki (vē'nyĭkē), Pol. *Winniki* (vēnyē'kē), city (1931 pop. 4,414), central Lvov oblast, Ukrainian SSR, 5 mi. ESE of Lvov; summer resort; tobacco mfg., flour milling.

Vinnitsa (vĭ'nĭtsä, Rus. vē'nyĭtsŭ), oblast (□ 8,000; 1946 pop. estimate 2,300,000), W central Ukrainian SSR, in Volyn-Podolian Upland; ⊙ Vinnitsa. Bounded SW by Dniester R.; drained by the Southern Bug. Chiefly agr., with main crops sugar beets and wheat; fruit orchards, tobacco, and corn in SW. One of principal sugar-beet dists. of the Ukraine; numerous refineries and distilleries. Industry at Vinnitsa, Mogilev-Podolski, and Tulchin, and at rail centers of Zhmerinka and Kazatin. Formed 1932.

Vinnitsa, city (1939 pop. 92,868), ⊙ Vinnitsa oblast, Ukrainian SSR, in Podolia, on the Southern Bug and 120 mi. SW of Kiev; 49°13'N 28°30'E. Agr. center, food processing (flour milling, meat packing, distilling, bakery products); mfg. (machines, instruments, superphosphate, knitwear). Medical and teachers colleges. In 14th cent. under Lithuania; passed in 1569 to Poland, in 1793 to Russia. Pop. 40% Jewish until Second World War, when city was held (1941–43) by Germans.

Vinodelnoye, Russian SFSR: see IPATOVO.

Vinogradets (vē'nôgră″dĕts), village (pop. 3,059), Plovdiv dist., W central Bulgaria, 13 mi. NW of Pazardzhik; winegrowing center; rice, truck produce. Formerly Kara Musal.

Vinogradnoye (vēnŭgräd'nŭyŭ), village (1939 pop. over 500), NW North Ossetian Autonomous SSR, Russian SFSR, 9 mi. WSW of Mozdok (across Terek R.); wine making, flour milling, metalworking. Until 1944 (in Kabardino-Balkar Autonomous SSR), called Gnadenburg.

Vinogradov (vēnŭgrä'dŭf), town (1941 pop. 13,331), S Transcarpathian Oblast, Ukrainian SSR, on railroad and 25 mi. SE of Mukachevo; center of viticulture region; mfg. (furniture, bricks, ceramics, shoes), tobacco processing, woodworking. Has Gothic church, castle ruins. Until c.1947, called Sevlyush [Czech *Sevluš* or *Sevljus;* Hung. *Nagyszöllös*]. A town of Austria-Hungary, it passed 1920 to Czechoslovakia, 1938 to Hungary, and 1945 to USSR.

Vinogradovo (–dŭvŭ), village (1939 pop. over 500), E central Moscow oblast, Russian SFSR, 45 mi. SE of Moscow; dairying.

Vinovo (vēnō'vō), village (pop. 2,156), Torino prov., Piedmont, NW Italy, 9 mi. SSW of Turin; food cannery. Has ceramics industry dating from 16th-17th cent.

Vins, Var dept., France: see VINS-SUR-CALAMY.

Vinslov (vĭns'lŭv″), Swedish *Vinslöv*, town (pop. 1,634), Kristianstad co., S Sweden, 7 mi. SE of Hassleholm; furniture mfg.; light industries. Has 12th-cent. church.

Vins-sur-Calamy (vē-sür-kälämē'), village (pop. 291), Var dept., SE France, in Lower Provence Alps, 5 mi. NE of Brignoles; bauxite mining and processing. Until 1937, Vins.

Vinsteren Lake (vĭn'strŭn), expansion (10 mi. long, 1–2 mi. wide) of Vinstra R., Opland co., S central Norway, at S foot of Jotunheim Mts., 50 mi. WNW of Lillehammer; alt. 3,379 ft.

Vinstra (vĭn'strä), village (pop. 395) in Nord-Fron canton (pop. 5,388), Opland co., S central Norway, in the Gudbrandsdal, on Lagen R., at mouth of Vinstra R., on railroad and 40 mi. NW of Lillehammer; stock raising, dairying; ski resort. Just SE is site of Peer Gynt's hut and grave; hut is now in Maihaugen folk mus. in Lillehammer.

Vinstra River, Opland co., S central Norway, rises on SW slope of the Jotunheim Mts., flows 70 mi. generally E, through Bygdin and Vinsteren lakes, to Lagen R. at Vinstra.

Vintar (vĭntär', Sp. bēntär'), town (1939 pop. 3,059; 1948 municipality pop. 14,882), Ilocos Norte prov., NW Luzon, Philippines, 4 mi. NE of Laoag; rice-growing center.

Vintimille, Italy: see VENTIMIGLIA.

Vinto (bēn'tō), town, Cochabamba dept., central Bolivia, on S slopes of Cordillera de Cochabamba, 10 mi. W of Cochabamba, with which it is connected by tramway; on Ovuro-Cochabamba RR; alt. 7,874 ft.; wheat, corn; lumber. Pairumani, famous country home of Patiño, is near by.

Vinton, county (□ 411; pop. 10,759), S Ohio; ⊙ McArthur. Drained by Raccoon Creek, and small Salt and Little Raccoon creeks. Includes Zaleski State Forest. Agr. area (livestock, grain, fruit);

mfg. at McArthur; coal mines, limestone quarries, oil and gas wells. Formed 1850.

Vinton. 1 City (pop. 4,307), ⊙ Benton co., E central Iowa, on Cedar R. and 22 mi. NW of Cedar Rapids; agr. trade center; vegetable canning, poultry packing. Limestone quarries near by. Has state school for blind. Settled 1839, inc. 1869. 2 Oil town (pop. 2,597), Calcasieu parish, extreme SW La., near Sabine R. and Texas line, 22 mi. W of Lake Charles city. Settled c.1880. 3 Village (pop. 378), Gallia co., S Ohio, 13 mi. NW of Gallipolis, and on Raccoon Creek, in agr. area. 4 Town (pop. 3,629), Roanoke co., SW Va., just E of Roanoke, near Blue Ridge Parkway and Roanoke R. Settled 1797; inc. 1884.

Vintondale, borough (pop. 1,185), Cambria co., SW central Pa., 4 mi. W of Nanty Glo.

Vintul-de-Jos (vēn'tso͝ol-dā-zhôs'), Rum. *Vințul de Jos*, Hung. *Alvinc* (ŏl'vēnts), village (pop. 4,392), Hunedoara prov., central Rumania, on Mures R. and 7 mi. SW of Alba-Iulia; rail junction; nickel and cobalt mining. Has 16th-cent. castle.

Viñuela (bēnūā'lä), town (pop. 638), Málaga prov., S Spain, 16 mi. NE of Málaga; olives, figs, cereals, grapes.

Vinuesa (bēnwā'sä), town (pop. 990), Soria prov., N central Spain, near the Duero (Douro), 18 mi. NW of Soria; resort with mineral springs. Also lumbering, flour milling, stock raising.

Vinukonda (vĭno͝okŏn'dŭ), town (pop. 8,065), Guntur dist., NE Madras, India, 50 mi. WSW of Guntur; cotton ginning, cattle raising; peanuts, chili. Steatite mines near by.

Vinzili (vĭnzē'lyē), town (1948 pop. over 500), SW Tyumen oblast, Russian SFSR, near Tyumen.

Vinzons (vĭnzŏnz', Sp. bēnsōns'), town (1939 pop. 2,897; 1948 municipality pop. 14,455), Camarines Norte prov., SE Luzon, Philippines, 5 mi. NW of Daet; agr. center (coconuts, rice, abacá). Formerly Indan (ēndän').

Viola (vīō'lŭ). 1 Town (pop. 206), Fulton co., N Ark., 9 mi. WNW of Salem. 2 Town (pop. 134), Kent co., central Del., 8 mi. S of Dover, in agr. area. 3 Village (pop. 826), Mercer co., NW Ill., 20 mi. S of Rock Island; agr.; bituminous-coal mines. 4 City (pop. 132), Sedgwick co., S Kansas, 23 mi. SW of Wichita, in wheat region. 5 Town (pop. 223), Warren co., central Tenn., 11 mi. SSW of McMinnville. 6 Village (pop. 785), on Vernon-Richland co. line, SW Wis., on Kickapoo R. and 36 mi. SE of La Crosse, in dairying and stock-raising area.

Violet, village, St. Bernard parish, extreme SE La., 10 mi. ESE of New Orleans and on E bank of the Mississippi; seafood processing. Here is W terminus (lock) of Lake Borgne Canal (Violet Canal), connecting river with L. Borgne (E).

Violeta or **Central Violeta** (sĕnträl' byōlā'tä), sugar-mill village (pop. 1,238), Camagüey prov., E Cuba, on railroad and 17 mi. SE of Morón.

Violet Canal, La.: see LAKE BORGNE CANAL.

Vionville (vyōvēl'), village (pop. 224), Moselle dept., NE France, 11 mi. WSW of Metz. Near by, in battle of Mars-la-Tour–Vionville, French were defeated by Germans in 1870.

Viotá (byōtä'), town (pop. 1,341), Cundinamarca dept., central Colombia, 33 mi. WSW of Bogotá; sugar cane, tobacco, yucca, bananas.

Vipava (vēpä'vä), Ger. *Wippach* (vĭp'äkh), Ital. *Vipacco* (vēpäk'kô), village (1936 pop. 1,224), SW Slovenia, Yugoslavia, 16 mi. NE of Trieste. In Italy until 1947. Situated in fertile valley of **Vipava River,** which rises S of Nanos peak, flows c.30 mi. WNW to Soca R. 4 mi. SW of Gorizia.

Vipiteno (vēpētā'nô), Ger. *Sterzing*, town (pop. 2,312), Bolzano prov., Trentino–Alto Adige, N Italy, on Brenner Pass road, 20 mi. NNE of Merano; resort (alt. 3,109 ft.); beer, agr. machinery. Has picturesque 15th-17th cent. houses, town hall (1468–73), and church with 15th-cent. frescoes.

Viqarabad, India: see VIKARABAD.

Viqueque (vēkā'kā), town, ⊙ Viqueque dist. (□ 797; pop. 41,540), Portuguese Timor, in E Timor; copra, rice, cotton, palm oil; lumbering, cattle raising. Airport.

Vir or **Vir Pazar** (vēr' pä'zär), village (pop. 5,519), SW Montenegro, Yugoslavia, on NW shore of L. Scutari, 16 mi. SSW of Titograd, in the Crmnica; terminus of narrow-gauge railway to Bar; trade in fish, corn, and wine. Vineyards near by.

Virac (vēräk', bēräk'), town (1939 pop. 7,961; 1948 municipality pop. 22,503), ⊙ CATANDUANES prov., Philippines, port on S coast of Catanduanes isl., on Cabugao Bay (small inlet of Philippine Sea), 45 mi. NE of Legaspi; 13°35'N 124°13'E. Trade center for agr. area (coconuts, hemp).

Viraco (bērä'kō), town (pop. 1,280), Arequipa dept., S Peru, at S foot of the Nudo Coropuna, 4 mi. NE of Pampacolca; fruit, grapes, grain, stock. Gold mines near by.

Viradouro (vē"rŭdō'ro͞o), city (pop. 2,609), N São Paulo, Brazil, on railroad and 38 mi. NW of Ribeirão Prêto; dairy products; coffee, sugar cane, tobacco, grain.

Viraghattam (vērŭgŭ'tŭm), town (pop. 7,397), Vizagapatam dist., NE Madras, India, 13 mi. SE of Parvatipuram; rice, oilseeds, sugar cane, jute.

Virajpet (vēräj'pāt) or **Virarajendrapet** (vērŭräjăn'drŭpāt), city (pop. 4,106), S Coorg, India, 16 mi. SSE of Mercara; coffee-shipping center on road to Cannanore port; rice (terrace farming), timber (evergreen), cardamom, oranges. Industrial school.

Viramgam (vĭr'ŭmgäm), town (pop., including suburban area, 27,834), Ahmadabad dist., N Bombay, India, 35 mi. WNW of Ahmadabad; rail junction; trades in cotton, oilseeds; millet, peanuts; cotton ginning and milling, handicraft cloth weaving, oilseed milling; copperware.

Viransehir (vĭrän'shĕhĭr"), Turkish *Viranşehir*. 1 Village, Malatya prov., Turkey: see DOGANSEHIR. 2 Village (pop. 2,962), Urfa prov., S Turkey, 55 mi. E of Urfa; grain.

Virapandi (vē'rŭpŭndē). 1 Village, Madura dist., Madras, India: see KOMBAI. 2 Village, Salem dist., S central Madras, India, 8 mi. SW of Salem. Rail station (Virapandi Road or Ariyanur), just N, is shipping point for magnetite, magnesite, and chromite mines of Kanjamalai hill (just NW) and limestone workings at Sankaridrug.

Virarajendrapet, India: see VIRAJPET.

Viravanallur (vē"rŭvŭnŭl-lo͝or'), town (pop. 16,926), Tinnevelly dist., S Madras, India, 12 mi. WSW of Tinnevelly; cotton-weaving center; silk weaving, lace making. Formerly also called Vadakku Viravanallur.

Virbalis (vērbä'lēs), Ger. *Wirballen*, Pol. *Wierzbołów*, Rus. *Verzhbolovo*, city (pop. 4,702), SW Lithuania, on highway and 10 mi. W of Vilkaviskis; mfg. (machines, chemicals, shoes, furniture, oils, fats); flour milling. Virbalis rail station (at KYBARTAI city, 3 mi. NW) was Russo-German (after 1920, Lithuanian-German) customs station until 1945. Dates from 16th cent.; passed (1795) to Rus. Poland; in Suvalki govt. until 1920.

Virdeis, Finland: see VIRRAT.

Virden (vûr'dŭn), town (pop. 1,597), SW Man., near Assiniboine R., 45 mi. W of Brandon; mixed farming, dairying.

Virden. 1 City (pop. 3,206), Macoupin co., SW central Ill., 21 mi. SSW of Springfield, in agr. and bituminous-coal-mining area; corn, wheat, soybeans; mfg. (concrete blocks, tile). Inc. 1857. 2 Village (pop. 146), Hidalgo co., SW N.Mex., on Gila R., near Ariz. line, and 29 mi. NW of Lordsburg.

Vire (vēr), town (pop. 3,179), Calvados dept., NW France, on hill skirted by Vire R., 21 mi. SSE of Saint-Lô; textile center (woolens); dairying (butter, Camembert cheese), Calvados distilling, electrical equipment mfg. Known for its pork sausages. Blue-granite quarries near by. A strategic road center, Vire was almost leveled during Normandy campaign (June–August, 1944) in Second World War. Term "vaudeville" is derived from entertainment once typical of its valley (old Fr. *Vau de Vire*).

Vire River, Calvados and Manche depts., NW France, rises in Normandy Hills above Vire, flows 73 mi. N, past Saint-Lô, to the Channel just N of Isigny. Receives the Aure (right) and the Douve (left). Near its marshy and silted mouth American troops landed (Utah Beach, Omaha Beach) on June 6, 1944, in Normandy invasion.

Vireux-Molhain (vērû'-môlē'), village (pop. 1,445), Ardennes dept., N France, in the Ardennes, near Belg. border, 6 mi. SW of Givet, on left bank of the Meuse; forges; mfg. of ceramic refractories.

Virgen, La, Costa Rica: see LA VIRGEN.

Virgen del Camino, La (lä vēr'hĕn dhĕl kämē'nō), village (pop. 1,327), Leon prov., NW Spain, 5 mi. SW of Leon; cereals, wine, livestock. Has shrine dedicated to the Virgin. Military airport near by.

Virgen del Pilar, La (dhĕl pēlär'), village (pop. 246), Formentera, Balearic Isls., 18 mi. SSE of Iviza; grain growing; flour milling.

Vírgenes, Cabo, or **Cabo de las Vírgenes** (kä'bō dā läs vēr'hānĕs), headland in SE Santa Cruz natl. territory, Argentina, at SE tip of Argentinian mainland, on N shore of mouth of Strait of Magellan, 4 mi. NE of Point Dungeness; 52°20'S 68°21'W; meteorological station and lighthouse. Platinum deposits near by. Also called Cape Virgins or Cape Virgin.

Vírgenes, Las Tres, Mexico: see TRES VÍRGENES, LAS.

Virgie, mining village (1940 pop. 1,252), Pike co., E Ky., in the Cumberlands, 10 mi. SSW of Pikeville; bituminous coal.

Virgil. 1 City (pop. 354), Greenwood co., SE Kansas, on Verdigris R. and 30 mi. SSE of Emporia; livestock, grain. 2 Town (pop. 124), Beadle co., E central S.Dak., on branch of James R. and 10 mi. SW of Huron.

Virgilina (vûrjĭlī'nŭ), town (pop. 323), Halifax co., S Va., at N.C. line, 34 mi. ESE of Danville.

Virgilio, Italy: see PIETOLE.

Virgin, town (pop. 147), Washington co., SW Utah, 20 mi. ENE of St. George and on Virgin R.; orchards.

Virgin, Cape, Argentina: see VÍRGENES, CABO.

Virginal-Samme (vēr-zhēnäl-säm'), town (pop. 2,188), Brabant prov., central Belgium, 7 mi. S of Hal; mfg. (glass, bricks, paper).

Virgin Gorda (gôr'dŭ), island (pop. 504), Br. Virgin Isls., 8 mi. E of Tortola, 15 mi. S of Anegada; irregularly shaped and mostly flat (10 mi. long, 2 mi. wide). Rises in Virgin Peak (center) to 1,371 ft. Produces livestock, vegetables, charcoal for St. Thomas Isl. Has an abandoned copper mine. Spanish Town is near its S tip.

Virginia, Gaelic *Achadh Lir*, town (pop. 318), SE Co. Cavan, Ireland, on Lough Ramor and 20 mi. NW of An Uaimh; agr. market (cattle, pigs; potatoes). Town dates from colonization of Ulster.

Virginia, state (land □ 39,899; with inland waters □ 40,815; 1950 pop. 3,318,680; 1940 pop. 2,677,773), E U.S., bordered E by Atlantic Ocean, NE by Md. and D.C., NW and W by W.Va., SW by Ky., S by Tenn. and N.C.; 33d in area, 15th in pop.; one of the original 13 states, the 10th to ratify (1788) the Constitution; ⊙ Richmond. Roughly triangular in shape, Va. is 425 mi. E–W (along S border) and 200 mi. N–S at its widest points. Extending up to 100 mi. inland is the Tidewater physiographic prov., part of the Atlantic coastal plain, a low-lying region (rising to 200–300 ft.) of sands, clays, and marls. The coast line is one of submergence; the major streams—Potomac (on Md. line), Rappahannock, York, and James rivers, draining SE to Chesapeake Bay—have deep tidal estuaries, forming the 3 peninsulas of this area. Across Chesapeake Bay, somewhat isolated from the rest of the state, is the Eastern Shore, occupying the lower end (c.65 mi.) of DELMARVA PENINSULA. Marshland covers some coastal dists., e.g., Dismal Swamp in the SE. Running approximately through Arlington, Fredericksburg, Richmond, and Emporia is the fall line, marking the sudden increase in slope from the weaker sediments of the coastal plain to the hard crystalline rocks of the Piedmont upland. This elevated rolling plain (alt. 300–1,000 ft.), whose width ranges from 40 mi. (N) to 165 mi. (S), traverses the center of the state and comprises c.⅓ of its total area. It is broken by several ridges and hills and has areas of Triassic sediments, such as the lowland belt bet. the Potomac and Rappahannock rivers. Flanking the Piedmont on the W is the BLUE RIDGE, extending some 300 mi. NE–SW across the state, widening considerably to the S. It is an anc. mtn. mass of Pre-Cambrian rocks, heavily forested, with some of Va.'s finest scenery, and rising to several 4–5,000-ft. peaks, including White Top Mtn. (5,520 ft.) and Mt. Rogers (5,720 ft.; state's highest point). To the W is valley and ridge country of the Folded Appalachians. The E part of this section is the Great Appalachian Valley, sometimes called the Valley of Va., which is actually divided by knobs and ridges into several valleys, the largest of which is the historic SHENANDOAH VALLEY (N), extending c.150 mi. bet. the James and Potomac rivers and partly divided by Massanutten Mtn. Other prominent Appalachian ridges are North, Shenandoah, Walker, and Clinch mts. To the S the section is drained by the headstreams of the James, Roanoke, New, and Tennessee rivers. Along part of the W border are some of the Allegheny Mts., and in the extreme SW is a small area of the Cumberland Plateau, a well-dissected upland of nearly horizontal carboniferous strata, with an alt. of c.2,500–3,500 ft. Most of Va. has a humid subtropical climate, but continental conditions prevail in the W mtn. regions. Annual rainfall ranges from slightly less than 40 in. in N to over 50 in. in extreme SW. Richmond has mean temp. of 39°F. in Jan., 78°F. in July, and 42 in. of rain; Roanoke has mean temp. of 38°F. in Jan., 76°F. in July, and 41 in. of rain. The growing season averages bet. 220 days S of Norfolk (SE) and 150 days in higher mtn. dists. Native vegetation is largely oak and pine throughout the coast plain and Piedmont, while to the W chestnut oak and yellow poplar predominate; Dismal Swamp has red gum, cypress, and tupelo, and there are areas of maple, beech, and birch in the SW. Commercial forest land comprises 14,350,000 acres, natl. forest reserves some 4,125,000 acres. Lumbering is an important industry. Va. is largely an agr. state, with over 16,000,000 acres in farm and pasture land, of which almost 4,000,000 acres are in crops. Farms are usually small, c.35% being under 30 acres, and there is diversified crop production. General farming predominates, hay, corn, and wheat being the chief crops, with oats, barley, and rye of less importance. Wheat does well in the limestone soils of the Shenandoah Valley, where there are large apple orchards. Apples, as well as peaches, are also grown in the W Piedmont belt. Most of the field crops are used for feeding livestock—cattle, hogs, poultry, and some sheep; dairying is mainly in the N. Horses are bred in the Piedmont. Peanuts are an important crop in the SE, much being fed to hogs, especially around Smithfield, whose hams are well known. E Va., with its sandy soils and mild climate, is an intensive truck-farming area, producing considerable quantities of white potatoes (notably on Eastern Shore), sweet potatoes, peas, beans, spinach, kale, tomatoes, and strawberries. Wythe and Smyth counties (SW) grow a large cabbage crop. Tobacco is the leading cash crop, cultivated in the Piedmont S of the James R. The small cotton acreage is confined to the SE, where the growing season averages 200 days. Chesapeake Bay is a great fishing area, especially for oysters, crabs, and clams; other fish caught in Chesapeake, ocean, and estuarine waters include menhaden, alewives, shad, croaker, mackerel, and striped bass. Bituminous coal is the most important mineral resource, mined (largely by machinery) from almost horizontal seams in the Cumberland Plateau counties in the extreme SW. Some anthracite is produced in the Folded Appalachian section. The Piedmont, Blue Ridge, and Great Appalachian Valley have many limestone, sandstone, and soapstone quarries, while sand, gravel, and clay production is important in the coastal plain. Zinc and some lead are mined in the lower Valley, mainly at Austinville. Titaniferous ilmenite and rutile are worked at Roseland in the central Blue Ridge, and manganese ores are found in Augusta co., and at other places. There are also minor deposits of gypsum, pyrite, mica, copper, and salt. Industrially, Va. is primarily a producer of light consumer goods. Tobacco products, especially cigarettes, are the leading industry, centering at Richmond. Also important are rayon and cotton goods, chemicals, ships and boats, furniture, lumber and wood products, paper, canned fruit and vegetables, packed meat, flour, leather goods, and iron products. Large mfg. centers are RICHMOND, NORFOLK, Roanoke, Portsmouth, Alexandria, Lynchburg, Newport News, Danville, Petersburg, and Hopewell. HAMPTON ROADS, consisting of the ports of Newport News, Norfolk, and Portsmouth, is a major port of entry and leading coal exporter. Principal recreational areas are the beautiful SHENANDOAH NATIONAL PARK, with its 107-mi. Skyline Drive along the crest of the Blue Ridge, Hot Springs and Warm Springs in the W, and Virginia Beach on the Atlantic. Rich in colonial, Revolutionary, and Civil War background, the "Old Dominion" has a wealth of historic estates and battlefields, including Colonial Natl. Historic Park (Jamestown Isl., Williamsburg, Yorktown), Washington's home at Mount Vernon, Jefferson's Monticello, Madison's Montpelier, Arlington Natl. Cemetery, and numerous Civil War battlegrounds. The "Mother of Presidents" gave birth to Washington, Jefferson, Monroe, Madison, Tyler, William Henry Harrison, Taylor, and Wilson, as well as to Patrick Henry, Meriwether Lewis, William Clark, Robert E. Lee, "Stonewall" Jackson, Ellen Glasgow, Willa Cather, and Richard E. Byrd. The leading educational institutions are Col. of William and Mary (at Williamsburg), Univ. of Va. (at Charlottesville), Washington and Lee Univ. (at Lexington), Univ. of Richmond, Va. Military Inst. (at Lexington), Va. Polytechnic Inst. (at Blacksburg), and Sweet Briar Col. (at Sweet Briar). Indian tribes of the Powhatan confederacy (Algonquian) inhabited the tidewater region of what is now Va. in the early 17th cent. Va. was the name at first used for all the land in N.America not held by the French or Spanish. The 1st permanent English settlement in America was at Jamestown, at the mouth of the James R., in 1607—a commercial enterprise, sponsored by the London or Virginia Company. The colonists experienced great hardships, and only the vigorous leadership of John Smith kept the company intact. Tobacco cultivation was introduced (1612), temporary peace made with the Indians, and indentured Negroes were obtained (1619) from a Dutch ship. In 1619 met a representative assembly, the house of burgesses; in 1624 Va. became a royal colony. Indian massacres took place in 1622 and 1644. Dissatisfaction with the trade restrictions imposed by the Navigation Act of 1660 was largely responsible for Bacon's rebellion (1676) against Gov. Berkeley, who ruthlessly suppressed the uprising. The stratification of Va. society began at the turn of the 17th cent. Tobacco raising expanded, settlement pushed westward, and small-scale industries were attempted. The Col. of William and Mary was founded in 1693. An increasing number of Negro slaves were imported to work the Tidewater and Piedmont plantations. Beginning c.1730 the Shenandoah Valley was settled by Germans, Quakers, and Scotch-Irish from Pa., whose hard, primitive life contrasted sharply with the tobacco economy to the E. French advances in the W mtn. regions were ended by the Treaty of Paris (1763). Virginians such as Patrick Henry and Richard Henry Lee were among the leading opponents of Br. colonial policies. Important legislative acts were the Virginia Resolves (1765) and Mason's Bill of Rights (1776). Yorktown was the scene of Cornwallis' surrender (1781), which ended the Revolution. The state played a prominent role in the framing of the Constitution, and 4 of the 1st 5 presidents were from the Old Dominion. Va. ceded its claims to the Northwest Territory by 1784; in 1789 it relinquished territory (later regained) for the creation of the Dist. of Columbia; and in 1792 its W county of Kentucky became a separate state. The Va. coast suffered from the Br. blockade during the War of 1812. While agr. experienced a decline in the E, the farmers of the trans-Blue Ridge section prospered, though complaining of the political domination of Tidewater and Piedmont. The tariff and, especially, slavery were burning issues in the ante-bellum period. In 1861 Va. seceded from the Union and Richmond became the Confederate capital. The counties W of the Appalachians opposed secession and in 1863 were admitted to the Union as the state of West Virginia. Va. was the principal theater of operations during the Civil War, with important engagements being fought at Bull Run, Hampton Roads (*Monitor* vs. *Merrimac*), Antietam, Fredericksburg, Chancellorsville, the Wilderness, and Petersburg; Lee surrendered to Grant at Appomattox. Besides the great physical destruction left by the war, the state experienced the political and social upheavals of the Reconstruction era. Military rule ended in 1870. W.Va.'s refusal to assume part of Va.'s pre-Civil War debt resulted in a protracted legal dispute until 1915, when the U.S. Supreme Court ordered the former to pay its share. Although agr. remained dominant, mfg. of tobacco products and textiles and coal mining grew in importance. Shipbuilding boomed in the First and Second world wars. The state's large Negro minority (almost 25% of total pop.) is concentrated in the urban dists.; voting restrictions and segregation have been legally enforced since 1902. See also articles on the cities, towns, geographic features, and the 100 counties: ACCOMAC, ALBEMARLE, ALLEGHANY, AMELIA, AMHERST, APPOMATTOX, ARLINGTON, AUGUSTA, BATH, BEDFORD, BLAND, BOTETOURT, BRUNSWICK, BUCHANAN, BUCKINGHAM, CAMPBELL, CAROLINE, CARROLL, CHARLES CITY, CHARLOTTE, CHESTERFIELD, CLARKE, CRAIG, CULPEPER, CUMBERLAND, DICKENSON, DINWIDDIE, ELIZABETH CITY, ESSEX, FAIRFAX, FAUQUIER, FLOYD, FLUVANNA, FRANKLIN, FREDERICK, GILES, GLOUCESTER, GOOCHLAND, GRAYSON, GREENE, GREENSVILLE, HALIFAX, HANOVER, HENRICO, HENRY, HIGHLAND, ISLE OF WIGHT, JAMES CITY, KING AND QUEEN, KING GEORGE, KING WILLIAM, LANCASTER, LEE, LOUDOUN, LOUISA, LUNENBURG, MADISON, MATHEWS, MECKLENBURG, MIDDLESEX, MONTGOMERY, NANSEMOND, NELSON, NEW KENT, NORFOLK, NORTHAMPTON, NORTHUMBERLAND, NOTTOWAY, ORANGE, PAGE, PATRICK, PITTSYLVANIA, POWHATAN, PRINCE EDWARD, PRINCE GEORGE, PRINCESS ANNE, PRINCE WILLIAM, PULASKI, RAPPAHANNOCK, RICHMOND, ROANOKE, ROCKBRIDGE, ROCKINGHAM, RUSSELL, SCOTT, SHENANDOAH, SMYTH, SOUTHAMPTON, SPOTSYLVANIA, STAFFORD, SURRY, SUSSEX, TAZEWELL, WARREN, WARWICK, WASHINGTON, WESTMORELAND, WISE, WYTHE, YORK.

Virginia. 1 City (pop. 1,572), ⊙ Cass co., W central Ill., 30 mi. WNW of Springfield, in agr. area; corn, wheat, soybeans, livestock, poultry. Platted 1836; inc. as village in 1842, as city in 1872. **2** City (pop. 12,486), St. Louis co., NE Minn., on Mesabi iron range, in lake and forest region, and c.55 mi. NNW of Duluth; trade center for mining, lake-resort, and farm area; dairy products, beverages. Has open-pit and underground iron mines, ore-processing plant, foundries, and lumber mill. Junior col. is here. Settled before 1883, platted 1892; rebuilt after fires of 1893 and 1900. Grew as lumbering and mining point. **3** Village (pop. 113), Gage co., SE Nebr., 13 mi. E of Beatrice.

Virginia Beach, resort town (pop. 5,390), Princess Anne co., SE Va., on the Atlantic just S of Cape Henry, 17 mi. E of Norfolk; fine beach; fish, oyster industries. Seashore State Park and U.S. Fort Story near by. Inc. 1906.

Virginia City. 1 Town (pop. 323), ⊙ Madison co., SW Mont., on branch of Ruby R. and 55 mi. SE of Butte, in agr. region; timber. Alt. 5,822 ft. First town inc. in Mont. (1864), it was founded in 1863, when gold was discovered here in Alder Gulch, and served as territorial ⊙ (1865–75). Mines no longer productive, but town still used as outfitting point by prospectors. Mus. contains relics of gold-rush period. **2** Village (1940 pop. 952), ⊙ Storey co., W Nev., in Virginia Range, 17 mi. SE of Reno; alt. 6,500 ft.; tourist center in mining (gold, silver) and dairying area. Settled 1859, when discovery (1857) of Comstock Lode (chiefly silver) in near-by Mt. Davidson was made known. Grew with increase in mining operations and had pop. of c.11,000 in 1880. The *Territorial Enterprise* (early newspaper on which Mark Twain worked as reporter) was published here after 1861.

Virginia Falls, SW Mackenzie Dist., Northwest Territories, in Mackenzie Mts., on South Nahanni R. at about 61°25′N 125°35′W; drops 316 ft.

Virginia Gardens, town (pop. 235), Dade co., S Fla.

Virginia Key (c.2 mi. long), northernmost of the Florida Keys, S Fla., 1 mi. S of S tip of Miami Beach; 25°44′N.

Virginia Mountains, W Nev., roughly triangular range E of Reno, bet. Carson R. valley (S) and Pyramid L. (NE). Truckee R. crosses range W–E and divides it into PYRAMID RANGE (N) and Virginia Range (S), more commonly known as Washoe Range. Latter rises to 7,870 ft. in Mt. Davidson (site of COMSTOCK LODE), just W of Virginia City.

Virginia Park, village (pop. 2,747), Ottawa co., SW Mich., near L. Michigan, just SW of Holland.

Virginia Peak (10,530 ft.), in Front Range, Jefferson co., central Colo.

Virginia Range, Nev.: see VIRGINIA MOUNTAINS.

Virginia Water, England: see EGHAM.

Virgin Islands, archipelago of c.100 small islands and cays in the West Indies, c.40 mi. E of Puerto Rico and extending for c.60 mi. bet. Virgin Passage (W) and Anegada Passage (E). They are divided bet. U.S. and Great Britain. Though constituting the westernmost part of the Lesser Antilles, the isls. form a geological unit with Puerto Rico, Vieques, Culebra, and the Greater Antilles. They are of volcanic origin overlaid by limestone. The climate is healthful and tropical, without marked extremes in temp., and relieved by NE trade winds. There are generally 2 dry and 2 wet seasons; hurricanes occur occasionally bet. Aug. and Oct. Also subject to light earthquakes. The group was discovered 1493 by Columbus on his 2d voyage. It was then inhabited by Carib and Arawak Indians, but is now predominantly Negro. The **British Virgin Islands** are a presidency (□ 67; 1946 pop. 6,505) of the Leeward Isls. colony, just E of the U.S. Virgin Isls., and W of Anegada Passage; ⊙ Road Town. They are 60 mi. E of Puerto Rico, bet. 18°20′–18°50′N and 64°15′–64°50′W. Include c.32 isls., among them TORTOLA, ANEGADA, VIRGIN GORDA, Jost Van Dyke, Peter Isl., and Salt Isl. The isls. trade mostly with St. Thomas Isl. and Puerto Rico. Cattle grazing is their mainstay. Also produce sugar cane, sea-island cotton, tobacco, limes, vegetables, coconuts. Fishing and charcoal burning. Tortola was 1st settled by the Dutch (1648), but since 1666 the isls. have been a Br. possession. The **Virgin Islands of the United States** are a territory (□ 132.92; 1940 pop. 24,889; 1950 pop. 26,665) of the U.S.; ⊙ Charlotte Amalie. They lie 40 mi. E of Puerto Rico and are separated from Culebra by Virgin Passage; Br. Virgin Isls. are E. Consist of 65 isls. and islets, of which only the 3 largest, SAINT THOMAS ISLAND and SAINT JOHN ISLAND, and, c.35 mi. S, SAINT CROIX ISLAND, are important; most of the islets are uninhabited. With an average mean temp. of 79°F., the isls. have a remarkably mild climate and are becoming increasingly popular as a winter resort. Though an economic liability and though chiefly of strategic importance, they are fertile, but have only moderate rainfall. Among the products are sugar cane, rum, molasses, alcohol, bay rum, limes, cotton, tomatoes, onions, papayas, mangoes, bananas, and dairy products. The rugged, mountainous isls. provide fine, sheltered harbors. Main ports and trading centers are Charlotte Amalie (St. Thomas), and Christiansted and Frederiksted (St. Croix). Originally colonized by the Dutch; permanent settlements were established by the Danish West Indian Company, 1st on St. Thomas (1672). Great prosperity ensued with introduction (1680) of Negro slaves to work on the sugar estates. In 1754 the isls. became a colony under the Danish crown, known as the Danish West Indies. Held by the British for 10 months in 1801, and again 1807–15. Talks about their acquisition by the U.S. were started in 1867, but only came to a conclusion in 1916, when arrangements were made to purchase them for $25,000,000. Formal possession was taken the following year. Initially administered by naval authorities, they now have a civil governor, and are divided into 2 municipalities: St. Thomas and St. John, and St. Croix. Universal suffrage was introduced in 1936, and steps to increase self-government have been taken. From 1835 until recent years the pop. declined steadily. The racial make-up is 9% white, 69% Negro, and 22% mixed. Danish was for 245 years the official language, though an English patois was generally spoken, as well as a polyglot Danish-Creole dialect.

Virgin Mountains (8,000 ft.), in SE Nev. and NW Ariz., E of Virgin R. and L. Mead, N of Colorado R.

Virginópolis (vērzhēnô′po͝olēs), city (pop. 1,929), E central Minas Gerais, Brazil, 55 mi. W of Governador Valadares; coffee, tobacco; gold panning.

Virgin River, Utah, Ariz., and Nev., formed by confluence of East Fork Virgin R. and North Fork Virgin R. just S of Zion Natl. Park, SW Utah, flows 200 mi. generally SW, across NW corner of Ariz., to L. Mead in SE Nev. Used for irrigation; figs, cotton, and pomegranates grown in valley.

Virgin Passage, Caribbean strait (13 mi. wide), bet. Culebra Isl. of Puerto Rico (W) and St. Thomas Isl. of U.S. Virgin Isls. (E), dotted by many rocks and cays.

Virgins, Cape, Argentina: see VÍRGENES, CABO.

Virgo Harbor, Spitsbergen: see DANSKOYA.

Virieu or **Virieu-sur-Bourbre** (vēryû′-sür-bo͞or′brů), village (pop. 601), Isère dept., SE France, on the Bourbre and 6 mi. SSE of La Tour-du-Pin; distilling, footwear mfg. Medieval castle near by.

Virieu-le-Grand (–lů-grã′), village (pop. 869), Ain dept., E France, at foot of the S Jura, 7 mi. NNW of Belley; morocco-leather mfg.

Virje (vēr′yĕ), village (pop. 5,228), N Croatia, Yugoslavia, 10 mi. SE of Koprivnica, in Slavonia.

Viroflay (vērôflā′), E suburb (pop. 12,241) of Versailles, Seine-et-Oise dept., N central France, 9 mi. WSW of Paris; precision metalworking, mfg. of costume jewelry and perfume.

Viron, Greece: see VYRON.

Viroqua (vīrō′kwů), city (pop. 3,795), ⊙ Vernon co., SW Wis., 26 mi. SE of La Crosse, in dairying and tobacco-growing area; cooperative creamery, tobacco warehouse; timber. Settled 1851, inc. 1885.

Virovitica (vērô'vētētsä), Hung. *Verőcze* (vĕ'rûtsĕ), town (pop. 10,161), N Croatia, Yugoslavia, in the Podravina, 70 mi. E of Zagreb, at E foot of Bilo Gora, in Slavonia. Rail junction; local trade center; lumbering, metal- and brickworking. Several R.C. and Orthodox Eastern churches, monastery, castle.

Vir Pazar, Yugoslavia: see VIR.

Virpur (vēr'po͝or), town, central Saurashtra, India, 10 mi. SW of Gondal. Was ⊙ former Western Kathiawar state of Virpur (□ 66; pop. 8,594) of Western India States agency; state merged 1948 with Saurashtra.

Virrat (vĭr'rät), Swedish *Virdeis* (vĭr'dās"), village (commune pop. 12,428), Vaasa co., W Finland, in lake region, 50 mi. N of Tampere; tourist center; lumbering region.

Virsbo (vĭrs'bo͞o"), village (pop. 851), Vastmanland co., central Sweden, on Kolback R. and 13 mi. SE of Fagersta; metalworking, sawmilling. Has 18th-cent. manor.

Virserum (vĭr'sûrŭm"), village (pop. 1,954), Kalmar co., SE Sweden, 30 mi. W of Oskarshamn; wood- and metalworking, furniture mfg.

Virtaniemi (vĭr'tänē"ĕmē), village in Inari commune (pop. 4,568), Lapi co., NE Finland, on Arctic Highway (Rovaniemi-Pechenga), frontier point on USSR border, 80 mi. SW of Pechenga.

Virtasalmi (vĭr'täsäl"mē), village (commune pop. 3,324), Mikkeli co., SE Finland, in Saimaa lake region, 30 mi. N of Mikkeli; limestone and dolomite quarries.

Virton (vērtō'), town (pop. 3,016), Luxembourg prov., SE Belgium, 15 mi. SW of Arlon; agr. and pig market. Agr. center of St-Mard (pop. 2,267) is 1 mi. S.

Virtsu (vērt'so͞o), village (pop. 85), W Estonia, minor port on Muku Sound of Baltic Sea, 25 mi. S of Haapsalu; rail terminus; connected by ferry with Kuivastu on Muhu isl.

Virtsyarv, Estonia: see VORTSJARV.

Virtud, La, Honduras: see LA VIRTUD.

Virú (bēro͞o'), town (pop. 2,573), Libertad dept., NW Peru, on irrigated coastal plain, on Virú R. and 28 mi. SE of Trujillo, on Pan American Highway; sugar cane, rice.

Viruddhachalam, India: see VRIDDHACHALAM.

Virudhunagar or **Virudunagar** (both: vĭr'o͝odo͝onŭ-gŭr"), city (pop. 34,559), Ramnad dist., S Madras, India, 26 mi. SSW of Madura; rail junction; trade and cotton-pressing center. Formerly called Virudupatti.

Virunga (vēro͝ong'gä), **M'fumbiro, Mfumbiro,** or **Mufumbiro** (mŭfo͞om'bērō, mo͞ofo͞ombē'rō), volcanic range in E central Africa, extending across Albertine Rift on Belgian Congo, Ruanda-Urundi, and Uganda borders, just N and NE of L. Kivu and in S part of Albert Natl. Park. Its E section, composed of 6 main volcanoes, now extinct, runs NE and E, rising to c.14,780 ft. in Mt. Karisimbi and to c.14,600 ft. in Mt. Mikeno. Crater lakes. W section of range comprises 2 large active volcanoes, the Nyiragongo (c.11,400 ft.) and the Nyamlagira (c.10,000 ft.). A 3d, much smaller center of volcanic activity is Rumoka (last eruption in 1912), 7 mi. E of Sake. Upsurgence of the Virunga volcanoes, which blocked northward path of outlets of L. Tanganyika in Pleistocene time, has often been given as the reason for formation of L. Kivu and for reversal of the course of Ruzizi R.; by depriving Nile R. of a considerable water supply, it would have contributed to the drying up of Egypt.

Virú River (bēro͞o'), Libertad dept., NW Peru, rises in Cordillera Occidental of the Andes 5 mi. SW of Quiruvilca, flows 50 mi. SW, past Virú, to the Pacific 9 mi. SW of Virú. Used for irrigation.

Viry (vērē'), village (pop. 505), Jura dept., E France, in the central Jura, 9 mi. SW of Saint-Claude; Gruyère cheese mfg., sawmilling.

Viry-Chatillon (-shätēyō'), town (pop. 8,312), Seine-et-Oise dept., N central France, on left bank of the Seine and 13 mi. S of Paris; mfg. (rubber goods, bottle caps, kitchen furniture, precision machinery, cement); asbestos processing.

Vis, Yugoslavia: see VIS ISLAND.

Visa, Turkey: see VIZE.

Visalia (vĭsā'lyŭ). **1** City (pop. 11,749), ⊙ Tulare co., S central Calif., in San Joaquin Valley, 40 mi. SE of Fresno; trade and processing center for fruitgrowing, farming, and dairying region; ships cotton, dairy products, fruit, nuts, alfalfa, livestock. Seat of Col. of the Sequoias. Founded 1852, inc. 1874. **2** Town (pop. 192), Kenton co., N Ky., on Licking R. and 12 mi. S of Covington.

Visalnagar, India: see VISNAGAR.

Visaltia, Greece: see BISALTIA.

Visayan Islands (vĕsī'ŭn) or **Bisayas** (bēsä'yäs), large group in the Philippines, bet. Luzon (N) and Mindanao (S), bounded E by Philippine Sea and W by Mindoro isl. and Sulu Sea. Include BOHOL, CEBU, LEYTE, MASBATE, NEGROS, PANAY, SAMAR, and many smaller isls. Inhabited mainly by the Visayans, of Malayan stock.

Visayan Sea, Philippines, bet. Leyte (E), Masbate (N), Panay (W), Negros and Cebu (S); leads NW to Sibuyan Sea via Jintotolo Channel, S to Mindanao Sea via Tañon Strait and Camotes Sea.

Visbek (vēs'bĕk), village (commune pop. 6,931), in Oldenburg, NW Germany, after in 1945 Lower Saxony, 7 mi. N of Vechta.

Visby (vĭz'bē, Swed. vēs'bü") or **Wisby** (wĭz'bē, Ger. vĭs'bē), city (1950 pop. 14,770), ⊙ Gotland co., SE Sweden, on W Gotland isl., on the Baltic, 115 mi. S of Stockholm; 57°38'N 18°19'E. Though now it is a popular resort and a busy seaport, ice-free the year round, with sugar refining, metal-working, sawmilling, and cement mfg., it is chiefly significant for its history. In pagan days it was a religious center; in 11th cent. German merchants came to the city, which, usually known as Wisby, became one of the 1st members of the Hanseatic League. The ruins of 10 fine churches and the restored Cathedral of St. Mary (erected 1225) testify to its former wealth. An independent republic, Wisby was commercial center of N Europe, coining its own money and developing an international maritime code. Its decline began in 1280, when Sweden took it; sacked (1361) and conquered (1362) by the Danes, who returned it to Hanseatic League in 1370. For next 2 decades it was a pirate stronghold, while its trade was taken by Lübeck. Passed to Denmark 1570, to Sweden 1645. Not till end of 19th cent. did it begin to recover its trade. It is a Lutheran episcopal see and has 13th-cent. turreted walls, archaeological mus., botanical gardens, many old merchants' houses.

Visconde do Rio Branco (vēskōn'dĭ do͞o rē'o͞o brăng'ko͞o), city (pop. 6,526), SE Minas Gerais, Brazil, on railroad and 60 mi. NE of Juiz de Fora; sugar- and coffeegrowing center. Until 1944, called Rio Branco.

Viscount, village (pop. 291), S central Sask., 45 mi. ESE of Saskatoon; wheat, dairying.

Viscount Melville Sound, arm of the Arctic Ocean, W Franklin Dist., Northwest Territories, large section (250 mi. long, 100 mi. wide) of E–W passage through the Arctic Archipelago, bet. Banks, Victoria, and Prince of Wales isls. (S) and Melville and Bathurst isls. (N), near 74°N 100°–115°W. McClure Strait (W) leads to the Beaufort Sea, Barrow Strait and McClintock Channel lead E and SE. Navigable only under favorable weather conditions. W part of sound was discovered (1850–53) by Sir Robert McClure. Sometimes called Melville Sound.

Visé (vēzā'), Flemish *Wezet* (vā'zŭt), town (pop. 5,094), Liége prov., E Belgium, on Meuse R. and 8 mi. NNE of Liége; frontier station on Netherlands border; mfg. of Portland cement; market center for fruitgrowing region (cherries). Has 16th-cent. town hall, two 17th-cent. churches. Almost entirely destroyed in First World War; rebuilt since.

Visegrad (vĭ'shĕgräd), Hung. *Visegrád*, resort town (pop. 1,670), Pest-Pilis-Solt-Kiskun co., N central Hungary, on the Danube and 20 mi. NNW of Budapest; river port. Ruins of 9th-cent. fortress and 13th-cent. castle on near-by hill.

Visegrad or **Vishegrad** (both: vē'shĕgrät), Serbo-Croatian *Višegrad*, town (pop. 1,796), SE Bosnia, Yugoslavia, on Drina R., on railroad and 40 mi. E of Sarajevo, near Serbia border; local trade center. Chromium near by.

Viseu (vēzā'o͞o), city (pop. 1,171), easternmost Pará, Brazil, on left bank of Gurupi R. estuary (Pará-Maranhão line) and 160 mi. E of Belém; cattle, manioc, corn, medicinal roots. Gold deposits in area. Formerly spelled Vizeu.

Viseu, district (□ 1,933; pop. 465,563), in N central Portugal; ⊙ Viseu. In Beira Alta prov., except for N portion along Douro R. which belongs in part to Trás-os-Montes e Alto Douro prov. (NE) and in part to Douro Litoral prov. (NW). Bounded N by the Douro, S by the Mondego. Traversed by several ranges and by Vouga R. which rises in Serra da Lapa. Vineyards in Lamego area yield famed port wine. Other products: grain, fruit, olives. Lumbering in pine woods; resin extracting. Chief towns are Viseu and Lamego. São Pedro do Sul is a watering place.

Viseu, city (pop. 13,499), ⊙ Viseu dist. and Beira Alta prov., N central Portugal, on a bleak plateau E of the Serra do Caramulo, 50 mi. SE of Oporto; terminus of branch railroad; agr. trade center; textile milling, mfg. of explosives, tanning. Airfield. Episcopal see. Noteworthy are the mus. (with collection of old Port. paintings), the Renaissance cloister, and the cathedral (begun in 12th cent.). Some remains of anc. fortifications. A chapel, just SE, is said to contain tomb of Roderic, last of the Gothic kings. City was founded by Romans. It was captured from the Moors by Ferdinand I of Castile c.1060. Formerly also spelled Vizeu.

Viseul-de-Jos (vēshĕ'o͞ol-dā-zhôs'), Rum. *Vişeul-de-Jos*, Hung. *Alsóvisó* (ŏl'shōvēshō), village (pop. 4,733), Baia-Mare prov., NW Rumania, on railroad 24 mi. SE of Sighet. In Hungary, 1940–45.

Viseul-de-Sus (-so͞os'), Rum. *Vişeul-de-Sus*, Hung. *Felsővisó* (fĕl'shûvē"shō), village (pop. 15,914), Baia-Mare prov., N Rumania, 27 mi. SE of Sighet; rail junction and lumbering center on W slopes of the Carpathians; flour milling, tanning, tannin extracting; stone quarrying. Climatic resort. In Hungary, 1940–45.

Visharam (vĭshä'rŭm), **town** (pop. 13,317; 75% Moslem), North Arcot dist., E central Madras, India, on Palar R. and 10 mi. E of Vellore; rice, sugar cane, mangoes, oranges.

Vishegrad, Yugoslavia: see VISEGRAD.

Vishera River (vē'shĭrŭ). **1** In Molotov oblast, Russian SFSR, rises in the N Urals at 61°40'N, flows S, through coniferous taiga and undeveloped mining region (extensive magnetite, hematite, titanium, and vanadium deposits), generally W, past Krasnovishersk, and S to Kama R. 4 mi. ESE of Kerchevski; c.285 mi. long. Navigable for c.50 mi.; lumber floating for c.270 mi. Projected Kama R. dam, above Solikamsk, will largely improve navigation, which is regular up to Krasnovishersk. Receives Kolva R. (right). Once a part of trade route connecting Pechora and Kama rivers. **2** In Novgorod oblast, Russian SFSR, rises N of Valdai Hills in 2 headstreams, Bolshaya Vishera and Malaya Vishera rivers; flows 40 mi. SW to Volkhov R. NE of Novgorod. Connected with Msta River in lower course by 10-mi.-long Vishera Canal.

Vishnevets (vēshnyĭvyĕts'), Pol. *Wiśniowiec* (vēsh-nyô'vyĕts), village (1931 pop. 4,030), N Ternopol oblast, Ukrainian SSR, on Goryn R. and 13 mi. S of Kremenets; tanning, flour milling, hatmaking; dairying. Has 18th-cent. palace with picture gall., ruins of 14th-cent. palace, old churches. Old residence of Pol. gentry; frequently assaulted (15th–17th cent.) by Tatars and Turks. Passed to Russia (1795); reverted to Poland (1919); ceded to USSR in 1945.

Vishnevka (vēshnyôf'kŭ). **1** Village, SE Akmolinsk oblast, Kazakh SSR, on railroad and 35 mi. SE of Akmolinsk, in cattle area; metalworks. **2** Rum. *Vişineşti* (vēshēnĕsht'), town (1930 pop. 1,347; 1941 pop. 515), SW Moldavian SSR, 8 mi. WNW of Komrat. Founded, after 1812, as Ger. agr. colony; Ger. pop. repatriated (1940).

Vishnya River, Ukrainian SSR and Poland: see WISZNIA RIVER.

Vis Hoek or **Vishoek,** U. of So. Afr.: see FISH HOEK.

Vishtitis, Lithuania: see VISTYTIS.

Visim (vē'sĭm), town (1926 pop. 6,809), W Sverdlovsk oblast, Russian SFSR, in the central Urals, on right tributary of Chusovaya R. and 23 mi. SE of Nizhni Tagil, on rail spur; center of noted gold- and platinum-mining region. Founded 1741; until 1933, Visimo-Shaitanski Zavod.

Visimo-Utkinsk (vē'sĕmŭ-o͞ot'kĭnsk), town (1926 pop. 3,081), W Sverdlovsk oblast, Russian SFSR, in the central Urals, on right tributary of Chusovaya R. and 5 mi. WNW of Visim, on rail spur; gold mining. Founded 1771; until 1946, Visimo-Utkinski Zavod.

Visinesti, Moldavian SSR: see VISHNEVKA.

Visingso, island, Sweden: see VATTER, LAKE.

Vis Island (vēs), Ital. *Lissa* (lēs'sä), Dalmatian isl. (□ 39) in Adriatic Sea, S Croatia, Yugoslavia, 33 mi. SSW of Split. Chief village, Vis, Ital. *Lissa* (pop. 2,727), on N coast. Komiza, Serbo-Croatian *Komiža*, Ital. *Comisa*, seaside resort, on W coast, 5 mi. W of Vis. Winegrowing, fishing, fish canning. Isl. has anc. baths and mosaic pavements, R.C. and Orthodox Eastern churches and monasteries, 2 former Br. forts, fine grotto. Known since 4th cent. B.C. as Gr. colony *Issa*; free and prosperous under Romans; Br. naval and trade base (1808–1815). In 2 naval battles fought off isl., the British defeated the French (1811), and the Austrians defeated the Italians (1866).

Visitación or **Santa María Visitación** (sän'tä märē'ä bēsētäsyōn'), town (1950 pop. 344), Sololá dept., SW central Guatemala, near Nahualate R., 1.5 mi. NW of Santa Clara; alt. 6,929 ft.; basket weaving; corn, beans.

Viskafors (vĭs"käfôrs', -fôsh'), village (pop. 1,888), Alvsborg co., SW Sweden, on Viska R. and 6 mi. SSW of Boras; cotton milling, rubber-products mfg. Includes Svaneholm (svä'nŭhôlm) village.

Viska River, Swedish *Viskan* (vĭs'kän), SW Sweden, rises W of Ulricehamn, flows 80 mi. generally SW, past Boras and Skene, to the Kattegat 7 mi. NNW of Varberg. Has several falls; salmon fishing.

Vislanda (vēs'län"dä), village (pop. 889), Kronoberg co., S Sweden, 15 mi. WSW of Vaxjo; rail junction; aluminum foundry, furniture works.

Visla River, Poland: see VISTULA RIVER.

Vislinskaya Kosa, USSR and Poland: see VISTULA SPIT.

Vislinski Zaliv, USSR and Poland: see VISTULA LAGOON.

Visnagar (vĭs'nŭgŭr), town (pop. 17,227), Mehsana dist., N Bombay, India, 11 mi. NE of Mehsana; trade center for millet, pulse, wheat, oilseeds; handicraft cloth weaving, dyeing; copper and brass products. Has col. Formerly called Visalnagar.

Visnes (vĭs'nās), village (pop. 340) in Avaldsnes canton, Rogaland co., SW Norway, on W shore of Karmoy, 6 mi. NW of Kopervik; copper and zinc mining. Formerly spelled Vigsnes or Viksnes.

Visnja Gora (vēsh'nyä gô'rä), Slovenian *Višnja Gora*, Ger. *Weixelburg* (vĭk'sŭlbo͝ork), village, central Slovenia, Yugoslavia, on railroad and 13 mi. SE of Ljubljana; summer resort, winter sports center. Ruins of Auersperg castle here. Until 1918, in Carniola.

Viso, El (ĕl vē'sō), town (pop. 4,001), Córdoba prov., S Spain, 10 mi. NW of Pozoblanco; flour milling, cheese processing, tile mfg. Stock raising, lumbering; cereals, vegetables, wine. Silver-bearing lead mines.

Viso, Monte (môn'tĕ vē'zô), or **Monviso** (mônvēzō), NW Italy, highest peak (12,602 ft.) of Cottian Alps, near Fr. border, 20 mi. W of Saluzzo. Source of Po R.

Visocica Mountains or **Visochitsa Mountains** (both: vē'sôchētsä), Serbo-Croatian *Visočica Planina*, in Dinaric Alps, N Herzegovina, Yugoslavia, along right bank of upper Neretva R.; c.5 mi. long. Highest peak (6,475 ft.) is 13 mi. ESE of Konjic.

Visocnik or **Visochnik** (both: vē'sôchnĭk), Serbo-Croatian *Visočnik*, mountain (4,107 ft.) in Dinaric Alps, E Bosnia, Yugoslavia, 2 mi. WSW of Han Pijesak.

Viso del Alcor, El (dhĕl älkôr'), town (pop. 9,018), Seville prov., SW Spain, on railroad and 15 mi. E of Seville; processing and agr. center (olives, cereals, oranges, livestock). Sawmilling, flour milling, liquor distilling.

Viso del Marqués (märkās'), town (pop. 5,240), Ciudad Real prov., S central Spain, in New Castile, on N slopes of the Sierra Morena, 18 mi. SW of Valdepeñas. Agr. center (cereals, olives, vegetables, truck produce, fruit, sheep, goats). Olive-oil pressing, cheese processing, food canning.

Visoka Glava (vē'sôkä glä'vä) [Serbo-Croatian,= high head], peak (1,797 ft.) in Dinaric Alps, N Bosnia, Yugoslavia, 16 mi. ENE of Kotor Varos.

Visoko (vē'sôkô), town (pop. 5,816), S Bosnia, Yugoslavia, on Bosna R., on railroad and 15 mi. NW of Sarajevo, in Sarajevo coal area; leather industry; handicrafts. In Middle Ages, a leading town of Bosnia.

Visoko, peak, Yugoslavia: see SELECKA MOUNTAINS.

Visotsani, Greece: see XEROPOTAMOS.

Visovölgy, Rumania: see VALEA-VISEULUI.

Visp (fĭsp), Fr. *Viège* (vyĕzh), town (pop. 2,308), Valais canton, S Switzerland, on Visp R., near its confluence with the Rhone, and 25 mi. E of Sion, in a valley (alt. 2,234 ft.) among high mts. Produces chemicals.

Visp River, S Switzerland; its 2 headstreams, Mattervisp R. and Saaservisp R., rise in Valais canton among high Alpine peaks, near Ital. border, joining S of Stalden (site of Ackersand hydroelectric plant). The Visp flows 5 mi. N to the Rhone.

Visselhövede (fĭ"sŭlhû'vûdû), town (pop. 5,219), in former Prussian prov. of Hanover, NW Germany, after 1945 in Lower Saxony, 11 mi. SE of Rotenburg; rail junction; mfg. of chemicals; woodworking, food processing (canned goods, sugar, dairy products).

Visso (vēs'sô), village (pop. 916), Macerata prov., The Marches, central Italy, on Nera R. and 10 mi. N of Norcia; woolen mill.

Vissoie, Switzerland: see ANNIVIERS, Val d'.

Vissotsani, Greece: see XEROPOTAMOS.

Vista (vĭ'stŭ), village (pop. 1,705), San Diego co., S Calif., 8 mi. E of Oceanside; packs and ships citrus fruit, avocados, truck, flowers, poultry. Seat of Palomar Col.

Vista Alegre (vĕsh'tälä'grĭ), village (pop. 328), Aveiro dist., N central Portugal, 4 mi. SSW of Aveiro; noted for its chinaware. Its 17th-cent. chapel contains Renaissance crypt.

Vista Flores (bē'stä flō'rēs), town (pop. estimate 800), W central Mendoza prov., Argentina, on railroad and 10 mi. SW of Tunuyán, in Tunuyán R. valley (irrigation area); wine, oats, alfalfa, apples, livestock.

Vista Hermosa de Negrete (bē'stä ĕrmō'sä dā nĕgrā'tä), town (pop. 5,548), Michoacán, central Mexico, near Lerma R., on railroad and 20 mi. E of Ocotlán; agr. center (cereals, fruit, vegetables, livestock). Sometimes called El Molino.

Vistalegre (bēstälĕ'grā), NE residential suburb (pop., including section of Ventas, 18,547) of Madrid, Madrid prov., central Spain.

Vistonis, Lake (vĭstônēs'), or **Lake Buru** (bōō'rōō), swampy Aegean coastal lagoon (□ 18), W Thrace, Greece, on border of Xanthe and Rhodope nomes, 11 mi. SE of Xanthe; 7 mi. long, 3 mi. wide. Porto Lago is on isthmus separating the lagoon from Aegean Sea. Fisheries.

Vistritsa River, Greece: see ALIAKMON RIVER.

Vistula Lagoon (vĭs'chōōlŭ), Ger. *Frisches Haff* (frĭ'shŭs häf'), Pol. *Zalew Wiślany* (zä'lĕf vĕshlä'-nĭ), Rus. *Vislinski Zaliv* or *Vislinskiy Zaliv* (both: vĭslēn'skyē zä'lyĭf), coastal inlet (□ 332) of Gulf of Danzig, in East Prussia, after 1945 in N Poland and Kaliningrad oblast, Russian SFSR. Separated from Gulf of Danzig by Vistula Spit and Samland peninsula; c.60 mi. long, 6–11 mi. wide, up to 17 ft. deep; only opening is narrow, dredged Baltisk channel (bet. NE end of Vistula Spit and Samland peninsula; serves shipping to Kaliningrad). Mainland coast is picturesque moraine region rising in terraces from a steep shoreline. Chief coastal towns: Ladushkin and Mamonovo (Russian SFSR), Tolmicko and Fravenberg (Frombork; Poland). Poland-USSR border bisects lagoon 30 mi. SW of Kaliningrad. Receives Nogat R. arm of Vistula delta mouth, and Elbing, Pasleka, and Pregel rivers. Fish, especially eels, abound.

Vistula River, Pol. *Wisła* (vēs'wä), Rus. *Visla* (vyēs'lŭ), Ger. *Weichsel* (vīk'sŭl), longest (678 mi.) river of Poland; rises on N slope of the W Beskids, SSE of Cieszyn, flows NNW past Skoczow, generally ENE past Cracow and Tarnobrzeg, N past Sandomierz and Pulawy, NNW through Warsaw, WNW past Nowy Dwor Mazowiecki, Plock, Wloclawek, and Torun, and N past Grudziadz and Tczew, splitting into several arms, with main arm, the Martwa Wisla [Pol.,=dead Vistula], flowing NW, past Danzig, and N to Gulf of Danzig at Nowy Port. NOGAT RIVER is its E estuary arm. The delta region (□ 602) called Vistula Marsh Lands, Pol. *Zulawy Wiślane*, a drained marshland, is crossed by dikes and drainage canals; its water pumps are driven by numerous windmills. River is navigable for steamers to San R. mouth, for smaller craft to Cracow. Connected with the Oder via Brda R., Bydgoszcz Canal, and Notec and Warta rivers, with Neman R. via Narew and Biebrza rivers, Augustow Canal, and Czarna Hancza (Chernaya Gansha) R., and with Bug R. via Narew R. Main tributaries are (right) Skawa, Raba, Dunajec, Wisloka, San, Wieprz, Narew, and Drweca rivers and (left) Nida, Pilica, Brda, and Wierzyca rivers. Before First World War, in upper course formed part of boundary bet. Austria-Hungary and Rus. Poland; from 1919 to 1939, lower course (N of Grudziadz) formed for c.30 mi. border bet. Polish Corridor and East Prussia. Silesian coal and lumber, logged along lower course, are principal products carried on the Vistula. Before First World War, central course (then in Rus. Poland) was guarded by major fortresses of Deblin, Rus. *Ivangorod*, and Modlin, Rus. *Novogeorgievsk;* during war major battles were fought (1914–15) here and at other crossings of the river.

Vistula Spit, Ger. *Frische Nehrung* (frĭ'shû nā'-rōōng), Pol. *Mierzeja Wiślana* (myĕ-zhĕ'yä vēshlä'-nä), Rus. *Vislinskaya Kosa* (vĭslēn'skŭyŭ kô'sŭ), narrow sandspit in East Prussia, after 1945 in N Poland and Kaliningrad oblast, Russian SFSR, separating Vistula Lagoon (S) from Gulf of Danzig of the Baltic (N); extends NE from mainland 25 mi. E of Danzig; c.35 mi. long, 1–2 mi. wide. Largely reforested; has several small fishing and seaside-resort villages. Poland-USSR border crosses peninsula 16 mi. SW of Baltisk.

Vistytis or **Vishtitis** (vēshtē'tēs), Lith. *Vištytis*, village, SW Lithuania, on N shore of L. Vystitis (□ 7), 13 mi. SSE of Nesterov, near junction of Kaliningrad oblast (Russian SFSR), and Lithuania borders.

Vita (vĭt'ŭ), town (pop. 7,399), Satara South dist., central Bombay, India, 28 mi. N of Sangli; trade center for millet, peanuts, wheat, hemp products.

Vita (vē'tä), village (pop. 5,159), Trapani prov., W Sicily, 11 mi. SW of Alcamo.

Vitali Island (vĭtä'lē, Sp. bētä'lē) (□ 20), Zamboanga prov., Philippines, off E coast of Zamboanga Peninsula, Mindanao, in Sibuguey Bay.

Vitarte (bētär'tā), town (pop. 2,275), Lima dept., W central Peru, on coastal plain, on Rímac R., on Lima–La Oroya RR, on highway, and 6 mi. ENE of Lima; sugar cane, cotton, fodder crops.

Vitebsk (vē'tĕpsk, Rus. vē'tyĭpsk), oblast (□ 7,600; 1946 pop. estimate 800,000), NE Belorussian SSR; ⊙ Vitebsk. In W Smolensk-Moscow Upland; drained by Western Dvina (N) and Dnieper (S) rivers. Forested and agr. region with flax (chief crop), grain; pig and dairy-cattle raising. Truck gardens and orchards near Vitebsk. Rural industries: textile milling, lumbering, sawmilling, glassworking, flax and food processing. Chief urban centers: Vitebsk, Orsha. Large peat-fed power plant (*Belgres*) at Orekhovsk. Formed 1938.

Vitebsk, city (1939 pop. 167,424), ⊙ Vitebsk oblast, Belorussian SSR, on Western Dvina R. and 140 mi. NE of Minsk; 55°12'N 30°12'E. Textile and transportation center; mfg. (apparel, knitwear, linen goods, carpets, agr. machinery, machine tools, eyeglasses, tobacco products); dairying, woodworking (prefabricated houses, furniture), tanning. Has cathedral, monastery (1743), state mus. Veterinary, teachers, and medical colleges. Important since 11th cent.; successively ruled by Lithuania and Poland; acquired (1772) by Russia. Until Second World War, when held (1941–44) by Germans, c.45% of pop. was Jewish.

Vitemolla (vē'tûmû"lä), Swedish *Vitemölla*, fishing village (pop. 273), Kristianstad co., S Sweden, on Hano Bay of the Baltic, 10 mi. NW of Simrishamn; seaside resort.

Viterbo (vētĕrbô'), province (□ 1,391; pop. 234,180), Latium, central Italy; ⊙ Viterbo. On Tyrrhenian Sea; extends E to the Tiber. Volcanic hills cover c.⅔ of area; has crater lakes of Bolsena and Vico. Watered by small streams, including the Marta. Agr. (cereals, grapes, olives) and livestock raising predominate. Quarrying (trachyte, tufa, pozzolana); sulphur mining at Latera. Mfg. at Viterbo.

Viterbo, town (pop. 21,281), ⊙ Viterbo prov., Latium, central Italy, bet. lakes Bolsena and Vico, 40 mi. NNW of Rome; 42°25'N 12°6'E. Rail junction; mfg. (furniture, machinery, agr. tools, pottery, cement, paper, flour, macaroni, olive oil, liquor); foundries. Bishopric. Surrounded by old walls; has 12th-cent. cathedral, several notable churches (11th–13th cent.; damaged) pinnacled papal palace (begun 1266), Renaissance town hall (damaged), and picturesque medieval quarter with 13th–14th-cent. houses and palaces. Warm mineral springs near by used since Etruscan times. A favorite papal residence in 13th cent. and several conclaves were held here. Badly damaged by air bombing (1943–44) in Second World War.

Vithkuq (vĭth'kōōk) or **Vithkuqi** (vĭth'kōōkyē), village (1930 pop. 1,000), SE Albania, 12 mi. SW of Koritsa, on headstream of the Osum; hydroelectric station supplying Koritsa.

Viti: see FIJI.

Vitichi (bētēchē'), town (pop. c.8,500), Potosí dept., S central Bolivia, on Vitichi R. (N branch of the Tumusla) and 50 mi. SE of Potosí; corn, potatoes.

Vitigudino (bētēgōō-dhē'nō), town (pop. 2,511), Salamanca prov., W Spain, 42 mi. W of Salamanca; fertilizer mfg., sawmilling; cereals, livestock.

Viti Levu (vē'tē lā'vōō), largest, most important island (□ 4,010; pop. 176,822) of FIJI, SW Pacific; 17°44'S 178°E; 90 mi. long, 65 mi. wide; seat of Suva, ⊙ Br. colony of Fiji. Mountainous; rises to Mt. Victoria (4,341 ft.), highest in the isls.; many inactive volcanoes. Fertile deltas of Rewa, group's largest river, produce sugar, pineapples, rice, cotton. Best harbor is Suva on SE coast. Sugar is chief export; dairying, gold mining. Sometimes called Naviti Levu.

Vitim (vētyĕm'), village (1948 pop. over 2,000), SW Yakut Autonomous SSR, Russian SFSR, on Lena R., opposite mouth of Vitim R., and 120 mi. NNW of Bodaibo.

Vitim-Olekma (–ŭlyĕk'mŭ), former okrug of Russian SFSR, inhabited chiefly by Evenki. Created 1930; inc. 1937 into Chita oblast. Chief town, Kalakan.

Vitim Plateau, gold-mining area of NE Buryat-Mongol Autonomous SSR, Russian SFSR, bet. Vitim and Barguzin rivers. Main centers: Tsipikan, Bagdarin.

Vitim River, in NE Buryat-Mongol Autonomous SSR and NE Irkutsk oblast, Russian SFSR, rises on Vitim Plateau at 5,530 ft., flows S, NE, N, past Kalakan, and NNW, past Bodaibo and Mama, to the Lena at Vitim; 1,132 mi. long. Navigable below Bodaibo. Forms border bet. Buryat-Mongol Autonomous SSR and Chita oblast in upper (N) course. Receives Bodaibo (right) and Mama (left) rivers.

Vitina, Greece: see VYTINA.

Vitkov (vĭt'kôf), Ger. *Wigstadl* (vĕk'shtä"dŭl), town (2,685), S central Silesia, Czechoslovakia, 25 mi. ENE of Olomouc; silk textiles.

Vitkovice, Czechoslovakia: see OSTRAVA.

Vitor (bētōr'), town (pop. 2,343), Arequipa dept., S Peru, on Vitor R. (irrigation), on W slopes of Cordillera Occidental, on Pan American Highway and 21 mi. W of Arequipa; processing and agr. center (alfalfa, potatoes, grapes, grain, sugar cane, cotton); sugar refining, liquor distilling. Gold mines near by.

Vitória (vētô'ryŭ). **1** City (1950 pop. 51,329), ⊙ Espírito Santo, E Brazil, on inlet of Espírito Santo Bay (Atlantic Ocean) and 260 mi. NE of Rio de Janeiro; 20°18'S 40°20'W. Important coffee port and, since Second World War, Brazil's leading iron-ore shipping center; terminus of Rio Doce valley railroad from Itabira (Minas Gerais) iron mines, and of line from Rio de Janeiro. Other exports are rosewood and monazitic sands exploited locally. City has new blast furnace, and textile and sugar mills, tanneries, and coffee-grinding plants; mfg. of furniture, mirrors, paper bags, and preserves. Vitória was founded in mid-16th cent. on an isl. separated from mainland by channels of Santa Maria R. delta. Chief bldgs. are govt. palace in Fr. Renaissance style, Jesuit monastery, law school, and col. of pharmacy. City has been modernized since 1924. Formerly spelled Victoria. **2** City, Pernambuco, Brazil: see VITÓRIA DE SANTO ANTÃO.

Vitoria (bētô'ryä), city (pop. 44,341), ⊙ Álava prov. (one of the Basque Provs.), N Spain, 30 mi. SE of Bilbao, and on fertile plain; 42°51'N 2°40'W. Processing center, with a productive furniture industry; also has metallurgical works (machinery, explosives), tanneries, sugar refineries, flour- and sawmills, brewery, food-processing plants; other mfg.: shoes, clocks, damasks, knit goods, soap, chocolate, candy. Agr. trade center (sugar beets, cereals, potatoes, fruit). Episcopal see. Has old upper town, partly surrounded by anc. walls, with Gothic cathedral (12th-14th cent.) and 12th-cent. church of San Miguel; and modern lower town containing provincial palace with paintings by Ribera, and town hall. Founded (6th cent.) by the Visigoths. Fortified by the kings of Navarre; passed to Castile in 12th cent. Here, in the Peninsular War, Wellington in a great victory defeated (1813) the French, driving them from Spain.

Vitória da Conquista (vētô'ryŭ dä kõngkē'stŭ), city (pop. 7,682), SE Bahia, Brazil, in the Serra do Periperi, on Rio de Janeiro–Bahia highway, and 130 mi. W of Ilhéus; cattle-raising center; ships sugar, manioc. Rock crystal, amethysts, jade, aquamarines found in area. Until 1944, called Conquista.

Vitória de Santo Antão (dĭ sãn'tōō äntä'ō), city (pop. 12,435), E Pernambuco, NE Brazil, on railroad and 28 mi. WSW of Recife, in fertile agr. region; ships fruit and vegetables, tobacco. Sugar milling, alcohol distilling. Until 1944, called Vitória; formerly spelled Victoria.

Vitória do Alto Parnaíba: see ALTO PARNAÍBA.

Vitória do Mearim (dŏŏ mēärēn'), city (pop. 1,245), N Maranhão, Brazil, on lower Mearim R. and 70 mi. SSW of São Luís, in dist. growing cotton, rice, and sugar. Formerly Victoria do Baixo Mearim; and 1944–48, called Baixo Mearim.

Vitorog (vē'tôrôk), mountain in Dinaric Alps, SW Bosnia, Yugoslavia; highest point, Veliki Vitorog (6,255 ft.), is 11 mi. ENE of Glamoc.

Vitor River (bētōr'), Arequipa dept., S Peru, rises as Chili R. in Cordillera Occidental E of the Nudo de Ampato, flows c.160 mi. SW bet. the volcanic peaks El Misti and Chachani, and past Arequipa, to the Pacific at Quilca, for which its lower course is sometimes named. Used for hydroelectric power and irrigation.

Vitosha Mountains (vē'tôshä), W Bulgaria, extend c.15 mi. E-W bet. Iskar R. and Dimitrovo Basin, c.15 mi. N-S bet. Sofia Basin and Samokov Basin; tourist area. Rise to 7,506 ft. at Cherni-vrakh peak; crossed by railroad and highway at Vladaya Pass. Iron ore (once exploited) and peat deposits; several mineral springs. Include Boyana Falls, used by Sofia as source of water supply.

Vitré (vētrā'), town (pop. 7,390), Ille-et-Vilaine dept., W France, on Vilaine R. and 21 mi. E of Rennes; communication center; mfg. (agr. machinery, metal furniture, hosiery, footwear, furs); distilling, cider making, sawmilling. Has medieval ramparts and gabled wooden houses; 14th-15th-cent. feudal castle, and Flamboyant Gothic church of Notre Dame. Near-by Château des Rochers was home of Mme. de Sévigné.

Vitrey or **Vitrey-sur-Mance** (vētrā'-sür-mäs'), village (pop. 567), Haute-Saône dept., E France, 20 mi. E of Langres; cheese mfg., winegrowing.

Vit River (vēt), N Bulgaria, formed by confluence of Beli Vit and Cherni Vit rivers, which rise in Teteven Mts.; flows 121 mi. N and NNE, past Toros, Dermantsi, Sadovets, and Gulyantsi, to the Danube 2 mi. W of Somovit. Formerly Vid R.

Vitry-en-Artois (vētrē'-änärtwä'), town (pop. 2,853), Pas-de-Calais dept., N France, on canalized Scarpe R. and 5 mi. SW of Douai; metalworking, wire mfg., flour milling.

Vitry-le-François (–lù-fräswä'), town (pop. 7,066), Marne dept., N France, on the Marne above mouth of Saulx R. and 19 mi. SSE of Châlons-sur-Marne, at junction of 3 canals (Marne-Saône, Marne-Rhine, and lateral canal to the Marne); transportation center; metalworking, mfg. (porcelain washroom fixtures, Portland cement, malt). Built by Francis I to replace Vitry-en-Perthois (–ā-pĕrtwä') or Vitry-le-Brûlé (–lù-brülā') (3 mi. NE), which had been burned down in 1142 by Louis VII of France and in 1544 by Emperor Charles V. Hq. of General Joffre early in First World War; changed hands several times during 1st battle of the Marne (1914). Partially destroyed in Second World War.

Vitry-sur-Seine (–sür-sĕn'), city (pop. 43,927), Seine dept., N central France, a SSE suburb of Paris, 5 mi. from Notre Dame Cathedral, near left bank of Seine R.; chemical-mfg. center (soap, pharmaceuticals, lubricants); metalworks, paper mills. Has 12th-14th-cent. Gothic church.

Vitsi, mountain, Greece: see VERNON.

Vittangi, Sweden: see KIRUNA.

Vitteaux (vētō'), village (pop. 886), Côte-d'Or dept., E central France, on Brenne R. and 24 mi. WNW of Dijon; marble quarrying, cattle raising.

Vittel (vētĕl'), town (pop. 3,594), Vosges dept., E France, on N slope of Monts Faucilles, 23 mi. W of Épinal; famous watering place with cold mineral springs; its waters are bottled and exported. Produces Vittel salts and pastilles. Brewery.

Vittingfoss, Norway: see HVITTINGFOSS.

Vittoria (vēt-tô'rēä), town (pop. 34,769), Ragusa prov., SE Sicily, 11 mi. W of Ragusa; power station; a major wine market of isl.; alcohol distillery, mfg. (macaroni, gypsum products). Has cathedral.

Vittorio d'Africa (vēt-tô'rēô dä'frēkä), town (pop. 3,000), in the Benadir, S Ital. Somaliland, 5 mi. W of Merca, at edge of GENALE agr. region; cotton ginning, oil pressing (cottonseed, peanut, castor bean).

Vittoriosa (vēt-tōryō'zä), town (pop. 3,816), SE Malta, one of the "Three Cities" together with COSPICUA (S) and SENGLEA (W), on small peninsula in Grand Harbour, across which lies (N) Valletta. Old fortified town, surrounded by walls. Has dockyards. Severely battered in Second World War air raids. Still standing are the castle of St. Angelo (built 870, renovated 1530), the Palace of the Inquisitors, and most of the 16th-cent. *auberges*. The Victory Tower (1549), parish church St. Lawrence (rebuilt 1681), church of the Dominicans (1650) with 16th-cent. cloister, and almost all other noteworthy edifices were ruined. Vittoriosa was 1st town to be occupied (1530) by the Knights Hospitalers. It put up (1565) a staunch 4-month defense against Turkish attacks. Sometimes called Birgu.

Vittorio Veneto (vā'nĕtô), town (pop. 12,034), Treviso prov., Veneto, N Italy, 21 mi. N of Treviso. Industrial and commercial center; mfg. (automobiles, motorcycles, agr. machinery, furniture); foundry, silk, woolen and paper mills, alcohol distillery. Formed 1866 from adjacent towns of Serravalle and Ceneda. Serravalle has cathedral with altarpiece by Titian, Gothic and Renaissance palaces, including one (1462) with archaeological mus. Industrial Ceneda, a bishopric since 6th cent., has cathedral and 15th-cent. palace. Noted for one of final battles (Oct.-Nov., 1918) of First World War, in which Italians decisively defeated Austrians; led to Austro-Hungarian surrender on Nov. 4.

Vittsjo (vĭt'shû"), Swedish *Vittsjö*, village (pop. 1,001), Kristianstad co., S Sweden, 13 mi. NNW of Hassleholm; sawmilling, furniture mfg.

Vitu Islands (vē'tōō), volcanic group (pop. c.2,900), New Britain dist., Bismarck Archipelago, Territory of New Guinea, 40 mi. N of New Britain; comprise Garove (□ 26), Unea (□ 11), and several smaller isls. Coconut, cacao plantations. Chief copra center of Territory of New Guinea. Landlocked Peter Harbor on Garove. Also Witu Isls.; formerly called French Isls.

Vitulano (vētōōlä'nô), village (pop. 2,636), Benevento prov., Campania, S Italy, 8 mi. WNW of Benevento. Marble quarries near by.

Vityazevka (vē'tyŭzyĭfkŭ), village (1939 pop. over 500), S Kirovograd oblast, Ukrainian SSR, 38 mi. SSW of Kirovograd; wheat, sunflowers.

Vitznau (fĭts'nou), village (pop. 956), Lucerne canton, central Switzerland, on L. of Lucerne, 9 mi. ESE of Lucerne; resort (alt. 1,426 ft.) at W foot of the Vitznauerstock, S of the Rigi.

Vivarais (vēvärā'), region and medieval countship of S France, roughly occupying what is now ARDÈCHE dept. Historical ⊙ was Viviers. Inc. into Languedoc in 1229, preserving some autonomy.

Vivarais, Monts du (mõ dü), mountain range in Ardèche and Loire depts., SE central France, forming part of E escarpment of the Massif Central, extending c.60 mi. from the Mont Lozère (SSW) to the Mont Pilat (NNE). It is continued by the CÉVENNES proper (S) and by the Monts du Lyonnais (N). Chief summits are Mont Mézenc (5,755 ft.) and Mont Gerbier de Jonc (5,089 ft.), from which the Monts du Coiron reach SE to the Rhone. Basalt flows and craters point to volcanic origin. Extensive sheep raising. Chestnut and mulberry trees on SE slopes. Cocoons and raw silk are processed locally for shipment to weaving mills in Lyons–Saint-Étienne area. Central and N part of range sometimes called Chaîne des Boutières.

Vivegnis (vēvùnyē'), town (pop. 2,925), Liége prov., E Belgium, on Meuse R. and 6 mi. NE of Liége; coal mining.

Viver (bēvĕr'), town (pop. 1,768), Castellón de la Plana prov., E Spain, 27 mi. NW of Sagunto; olive-oil processing, flour milling, brandy distilling; wine, potatoes. Mineral springs.

Vivero (bēvā'rō), city (pop. 3,529), Lugo prov., NW Spain, in Galicia, fishing port on inlet of Bay of Biscay, 45 mi. N of Lugo; fish processing, boatbuilding, flour- and sawmilling, chocolate mfg. Mineral springs. Ships iron mined near by.

Viverols (vēvrôl'), village (pop. 383), Puy-de-Dôme dept., central France, in Monts du Forez, 10 mi. SE of Ambert; makes wooden shoes.

Viveros (bēvā'rōs), agr. town (pop. 1,767), Albacete prov., SE central Spain, 34 mi. SW of Albacete.

Vivi (vē'vē), village, Leopoldville prov., W Belgian Congo, on right bank of Congo R. opposite Matadi and 25 mi. E of Boma; ⊙ (1879–86) of the original Congo state. Constitution of Congo Free State was proclaimed here, 1885.

Vivian. 1 Town (pop. 2,426), Caddo parish, extreme NW La., 28 mi. NW of Shreveport, near Texas line; center of oil-producing and -refining area; lumber; agr. Inc. 1904. **2** Village (pop. c.250), Lyman co., S central S.Dak., on branch of Missouri R. and 30 mi. S of Pierre. Experimental farm, substation of state agr. col., is near by. **3** Coal-mining village (pop. 1,820, with near-by Tidewater and Bottom Creek), McDowell co., S W.Va., 5 mi. E of Welch.

Viviate (bēvyä'tā), town (pop. 1,261), Piura dept., NW Peru, on coastal plain, on Chira R., on Paita–Piura RR and 17 mi. NE of Paita, in irrigated area; cotton, fruit.

Vivier-au-Court (vēvyā'-ō-kōōr'), town (pop. 1,929), Ardennes dept., N France, 6 mi. ESE of Mézières; iron foundries.

Viviers (vēvyā'), village (pop. 1,295), Ardèche dept., S France, on right bank of Rhone R. and 6 mi. SSW of Montélimar; food processing, metalworking. Important cementworks at near-by Lafarge. Viviers is seat of a bishop. It was ⊙ of VIVARAIS. Also called Viviers-sur-Rhône.

Viviez (vēvyā'), town (pop. 2,413), Aveyron dept., S France, 10 mi. ESE of Figeac; leading zinc-smelting center (ore imported from Sardinia); chemical mfg. Rolling mills at Penchot, 2 mi. N.

Vivikond (vē'vēkônt), town, NE Estonia, 4 mi. SW of Vaivara junction; oil-shale mining.

Vivis, Switzerland: see VEVEY.

Vivonne (vēvôn'), village (pop. 1,213), Vienne dept., W central France, on the Clain and 11 mi. SSW of Poitiers; poultry shipping. Has ruins of a 12th-16th-cent. castle, the ancestral home of Catherine de Vivonne, Marquise de Rambouillet.

Vivsta-Nas (vĭf'stä-nĕs"), Swedish *Vivsta-Näs*, village (pop. 1,740), Vasternorrland co., E central Sweden, on Klinger Fjord (klĭng'ŭr), Swedish *Klingerfjärden*, 10-mi.-long inlet of Gulf of Bothnia, 7 mi. N of Sundsvall; sawmills.

Viza, Turkey: see VIZE.

Vizagapatam (vĭ'zŭgŭpŭ"tŭm), after 1948 officially **Vizagapatnam** (–pŭt"nŭm), former district (□ 9,107; pop. 3,845,944), NE Madras, India; ⊙ was Vizagapatam. Bordered E by Bay of Bengal; crossed along W border by forested N Eastern Ghats. Agr.: rice, oilseeds (sesame, peanuts), sugar cane, tobacco, sunn hemp (substitute jute), coconuts. Forest produce; timber (sal, teak), bamboo, myrobalan. Manganese mining; jute and sunn-hemp processing. Chief towns: Vizagapatam, Vizianagaram, Anakapalle, Chicacole, Bobbili, Bimlipatam. Area covered □ c.18,980 until 1936, when NW half was separated to form Koraput dist. of newly-created Orissa prov. In 1946, dist. was divided into North and South Vizagapatam dists. with capitals at Vizianagaram and Vizagapatam respectively.

Vizagapatam, since 1949 officially **Vizagapatnam,** city (pop. 70,243), ⊙ South Vizagapatam dist., NE Madras, India, seaport on Bay of Bengal, 380 mi. NE of Madras, 470 mi. SE of Calcutta. Connected by rail with industrial towns of central India; airport; exports manganese, myrobalan, oilseeds. Since 1949 a major shipbuilding center; 1st entirely Indian-made steamer launched here, 1948. Inner harbor and entrance channel opened for ocean-going vessels in 1933; quays specially equipped for loading manganese. Coir industry, distillery, fishery (cold-storage plant). Medical col. For many centuries a commercial port; site of mid-17th-cent. English trading post; occupied 1757 by French; recaptured 1758. N suburb of Waltair (wôl'târ), bathing resort, is seat of Andhra Univ. (founded 1926; removed to Guntur in 1942, when Vizagapatam was bombed by Japanese; returned 1946 to Waltair); tuberculosis sanatorium. Waltair rail junction is 2 mi. W of city center. Dolphin's Nose, headland S of entrance channel, is well-known landmark. Simhachalam village, 5 mi. NW, is pilgrimage center; has Vishnuite temple with 12th-cent. inscriptions.

Vizakna, Rumania: see OCNA-SIBIU.

Vizantea, Rumania: see PANCIU.

Vizara, Nyasaland: see CHINTECHE.

Vizcaíno Island (bēskäē'nō), at confluence of the Río Negro and Uruguay R., SW Uruguay; 3 mi. long, 1 mi. wide.

Vizcaya (bēthkī'ä), often, in English, **Biscay** (bĭs'kā), province (□ 858; pop. 511,135), N Spain, one of the Basque Provs., on the Bay of Biscay; ⊙ BILBAO. Covered by NE spurs of the Cantabrian Mts. sloping to sea; drained by Nervión R.; has rocky, indented coast (inlets of Bilbao and Guernica). An important industrial area and one of the most densely populated provs. in Spain. Rich iron mines (known since anc. times) of Somorrostro dist. and hills on left bank of Nervión R. yield 60% of Spain's iron and furnish raw materials for iron and steel industries developed around Bilbao. Prov. leads Spain in iron and steel production: blast furnaces, coke ovens, steel mills, shipyards, mechanical industries. Also produces chemicals (fertilizers, soap, explosives), paper, textiles, glass, and ceramics. Bilbao is leading Sp. port for iron-ore exports, chiefly to Great Britain. Iron industry of Vizcaya, noted in Middle Ages, developed rapidly in 19th cent. There is abundant rainfall and some agr. is carried on, particularly growing of *chacolí* wine; also some sheep and cattle raising. Important fisheries on coast. The Basques preserve their distinct language and traditions. Chief cities: Bilbao (with industrial suburbs of Baracaldo, Sestao, Basauri, Portugalete), Guernica (symbol of Basque glory), and Durango.

Vize (vĭzĕ'), village (pop. 4,900), Kirklareli prov., Turkey in Europe, 30 mi. ESE of Kirklareli; grain center in forested mtn. region. Some coal near by. Sometimes spelled Viza, Visa.

Vize Island or **Wiese Island** (vē'zù, Rus. vē'zyĭ), in Kara Sea of Arctic Ocean, 210 mi. W of Pioner Isl. of Severnaya Zemlya archipelago, in Krasnoyarsk Territory, Russian SFSR; 79°30'N 77°E. Named for Soviet scientist.

Vizeu, Brazil: see VISEU.

Vizeu, Portugal: see VISEU.

Vizhnitsa (vēsh'nyĭtsŭ), Rum. *Vijniţa* (vēzhnē'tsä), town (1941 pop. 2,495), W Chernovtsy oblast, Ukrainian SSR, in N Bukovina, on Cheremosh R., opposite Kuty, and 35 mi. W of Chernovtsy; lumber-milling center; textile and soap mfg. Pop. largely Guzul.

Vizianagaram or **Vizianagram** (vĭzyŭ'nŭgrŭm), city (pop. 51,749), ⊙ North Vizagapatam dist., NE Madras, India, 29 mi. NNE of Vizagapatam; rail junction; shipping point for sunn-hemp (jute substitute) and jute products (cordage, gunny bags; mills at NE suburb of Nellimarla) and for manganese (mines 13 mi. NE, near Garividi rail station); tannery. Col. (affiliated with Andhra Univ.).

Buddhist archaeological remains at Ramathirtam village, just NE. Saltworks 13 mi. SE, on Bay of Bengal, at Konada village.

Vizille (vēzē′), town (pop. 4,603), Isère dept., SE France, on the Romanche near its influx into Drac R., and 8 mi. SSE of Grenoble, at SW end of Belledonne range (Dauphiné Alps); forges, rolling mill; mfg. of abrasives, cartons, and silk fabrics. Iron deposits near by. Its 17th-cent. château damaged in Second World War.

Vizinga (vēzĭn-gä′), village (1926 pop. 321), SW Komi Autonomous SSR, Russian SFSR, on tributary of Sysola R. and 50 mi. SSW of Syktyvkar; flax, potatoes.

Viziru (vēzē′rōō), village (pop. 5,414), Galati prov., SE Rumania, 20 mi. SSW of Braila; agr. center. Has agr. school, with experimental plantations for medicinal herbs.

Vizmberk, Czechoslovakia: see LOUCNA NAD DESNOU.

Vizovice (vē′zôvĭtsĕ), Ger. *Wisowitz* (vē′zōvĭts), town (3,559), E Moravia, Czechoslovakia, 8 mi. E of Zlin; rail terminus; lumbering.

Vizzavona (vēzävônä′, It. vētsävô′nä), resort of central Corsica, 12 mi. S of Corte, amidst beech and pine woods. Vizzavona Pass (2 mi. SW; alt. 3,812 ft.) is highest point on Ajaccio-Bastia RR.

Vizzini (vētsē′nē), town (pop. 14,326), Catania prov., SE Sicily, 14 mi. ESE of Caltagirone, in cereal- and livestock-raising region; cement. Site of cathedral. Grottoes near by. Damaged by earthquakes of 1542 and 1693.

Vlaardingen (vlär′dĭng-ŭn), town (pop. 43,340), South Holland prov., SW Netherlands, on New Maas R. and 7 mi. W of Rotterdam; major port and fishing center; herring curing; mfg. of synthetic fertilizer, soap, linseed oil, chocolate, candy, sails, blocks, rope, crates, boxes; dairy products, cattle feed.

Vlachov, Czechoslovakia: see ROZNAVA.

Vladaya (vlädī′ä), village (pop. 1,891), Sofia dist., W Bulgaria, on W slope of Vitosha Mts., 7 mi. SW of Sofia; summer resort; livestock, truck. Has old monastery. **Vladaya Pass** (alt. 2,936 ft.), just NW of village, carries railroad and highway bet. Sofia and Dimitrovo.

Vladicin Han or **Vladichin Khan** (vlä′dĭchĭn hän′), Serbo-Croatian *Vladičin Han*, village (pop. 3,400), SE Serbia, Yugoslavia, on the Southern Morava, on railroad and 13 mi. NE of Vranje. Sometimes called Vladicki Han.

Vladikavkaz, Russian SFSR: see DZAUDZHIKAU.

Vladimir (vlä′dĭmĕr, Rus. vlŭdyē′mĭr), oblast (□ 10,350; 1946 pop. estimate 1,350,000) in central European Russian SFSR; ⊙ Vladimir. In low forested area; bounded E by Oka R.; watered by Klyazma R. Includes Opolye, a black-earth region NW of Vladimir, bet. Nerl and Kirzhach rivers. Extensive quartz sand and peat deposits (S). Wheat, tobacco, rubber-bearing plants grown in Opolye, cherries near Vladimir; flax, potatoes. Metalworking and machine mfg. (tractors, auto parts, radio and phonograph equipment, precision instruments, electrical goods) at Vladimir, Kirzhach, Aleksandrov; nonferrous metallurgy (copper alloys) at Kolchugino; textile industries at Vyazniki (linen mills), Vladimir, Sobinka, Karabanovo, Strunino (cotton mills). Well-developed glass- and crystal works (Gus-Khrustalny); sawmilling, paper mfg.; handicraft industries. Formed 1944 out of Ivanovo oblast.

Vladimir, city (1939 pop. 66,761), ⊙ Vladimir oblast, Russian SFSR, on left bank of Klyazma R. and 110 mi. ENE of Moscow; 56°8′N 40°25′E. Rail junction; machine and textile mfg. center; tractors, auto parts, machine tools, precision instruments, phonographs, chemicals (plastic products); cotton milling, distilling, fruit canning (cherries). Has Uspenski (Ascension) cathedral (built 1158–94) with mus. of religious antiquities, Demetrius cathedral (1193–97), Golden Gate (1164) and 12th–13th-cent. monasteries, all built of white stone in original Vladimir-Suzdal style. Historical and revolutionary mus., art gall., teachers col. Founded 1108–16 by Vladimir Monomakh; became principal center of Vladimir (former Rostov-Suzdal) principality; destroyed 1238 by Tatars. Declined in 13th cent. and passed (1364) to Moscow. Regained importance after 18th cent. Was ⊙ Vladimir govt., inc. 1929 into Ivanovo oblast.

Vladimirci or **Vladimirtsi** (both: vlä′dĭmĕrtsē), village (pop. 1,476), W Serbia, Yugoslavia, 11 mi. S of Sabac.

Vladimirets (vlŭdyē′mĭrĭts), Pol. *Włodzimierzec* (vōōōdzēmyĕ′zhĕts), village (1931 pop. 2,940), NW Rovno oblast, Ukrainian SSR, 19 mi. WNW of Sarny; flour milling, distilling, lumbering. Has ruins of medieval palace. Known since 11th cent.

Vladimiro-Aleksandrovskoye (–mĭrŭ-ŭlyĭksän′drŭfskŭyŭ), village (1939 pop. over 500), S Maritime Territory, Russian SFSR, 10 mi. NE of Nakhodka, on branch of Trans-Siberian RR; flour milling; grain, soybeans, rice, perilla.

Vladimirovka (vlŭdyē′mĭrŭfkŭ). **1** Village (1926 pop. 6,778), NE Astrakhan oblast, Russian SFSR, on left bank of the Akhtuba, opposite town of Petropavlovski (1948 pop. over 10,000), and 31 mi. WNW of Nizhni Baskunchak, on railroad; saltworks; food canning; Volga R. shipping point for L. Baskunchak salt. **2** Village (1926 pop. 5,076), E Nikolayev oblast, Ukrainian SSR, 30 mi. SSW of Krivoi Rog; cotton, wheat. **3** Town (1939 pop. over 500), SW Stalino oblast, Ukrainian SSR, 27 mi. SW of Stalino; kaolin and fireproof-clay quarries.

Vladimir-Volynski or **Vladimir-Volynskiy** (vlŭdyē′-mĭr-vŭlĭn′skē), Pol. *Włodzimierz* (vōōōdzē′myĕsh), anc. *Lodomeria*, city (1931 pop. 24,581), W Volyn oblast, Ukrainian SSR, on Lug R. (right tributary of Bug R.) and 45 mi. WNW of Lutsk; rail junction (repair shops); grain-trading center; agr. processing (cereals, vegetable oils, hops); tanning, hatmaking, mfg. of sweets. Has technical school, mus., several historical monuments and old churches. One of oldest Ukrainian settlements; known in 9th cent. as town of Lodomira; allegedly refounded (c.988) by Kievan duke Vladimir I, becoming ⊙ independent duchy of Vladimir. Successively dominated by Kievan Russia, duchy of Galich, Poland, and Lithuania; developed as commercial center. Sacked (1431) by Pol. king Wladislaw II Jagiello; repeatedly assaulted by Tatars, Hungarians, and Cossacks (15th–17th cent.); passed to Russia (1795); declined following rise of Lutsk. A scene of Pol.-Soviet battles (1919–20). Reverted to Poland (1921); ceded to USSR in 1945.

Vladislavov, Lithuania: see NAUMIESTIS.

Vladivostok (vlă″dĭvŏ′stŏk, –vŭstŏk′, Rus. vlŭdyēvŭstôk′) [Rus.,=rule the east], Chinese *Hai-shen-wei* [=trepang bay], city (1939 pop. 206,432; 1946 pop. estimate 300,000), ⊙ Maritime Territory, Russian SFSR, on S tip of Muravyev-Amurski Peninsula, bet. Amur Bay and Golden Horn Bay (inlets of Peter the Great Bay), 4,000 mi. ESE of Moscow, 400 mi. SSW of Khabarovsk; 43°7′N 131°53′E. Terminus of Trans-Siberian RR; chief year-round Soviet port on the Pacific; kept open in winter by icebreakers. Industrial center; shipbuilding, airplane mfg.; meat and fish canning, lumber milling (matches, veneers), food processing (flour, rice, vegetable oils, canned goods). Petroleum tanks, cold-storage and power plants. Has polytechnic institute, maritime acad., teachers col., Pacific Inst. of Fisheries and Oceanography, and other research institutes. Base of fishing, crabbing, and whaling flotillas. Supply point for Soviet Pacific littoral (Sakhalin, Kamchatka, Sea of Okhotsh) and terminus of northern (Arctic) sea route. A major exporting and importing center; ships coal, lumber, vegetable oils and oilcake, fish, furs, and grain. Pop. includes Chinese and Koreans. City center is on NW shore of Golden Horn Bay, just N of quayside rail station, along the Svetlanka, chief traffic artery. City limits include entire MURAVYEV-AMURSKI PENINSULA, with sea and summer resorts (Okeanskaya, Sedanka, Vtoraya Rechka) on Amur Bay, up to 10 mi. NNE of city proper. City also includes RUSSIAN ISLAND, and Popova and Reineke isls. (fish canneries). Golden Horn Bay was discovered 1856; 1st Rus. settlement founded 1860. Vladivostok became city in 1880 and developed rapidly following construction (1890s) of Trans-Siberian RR. Developed as naval base after Rus. loss (1905) of Port Arthur. Important supply port in First World War; occupied (1918–22) by Allies and Japanese. Imported lend-lease supplies during Second World War.

Vladychnoye (vlŭdĭch′nŭyŭ), village (1926 pop. 247), N Yaroslavl oblast, Russian SFSR, 25 mi. NNE of Poshekhonye-Volodarsk; flax.

Vlakfontein (fläk′fôntān″), town (pop. 2,279), SW Transvaal, U. of So. Afr., 30 mi. NW of Rustenburg; nickel-mining center.

Vlakhina Mountains (vlä′khēnä), N section of Males Mts., on Bulgaro-Yugoslav border, just S of Osogov Mts. SW of Gorna Dzhumaya, Bulgaria. Also called Pastusha Mts.

Vlasenica or **Vlasenitsa** (both: vlä′sĕnētsä), village (pop. 3,969), E Bosnia, Yugoslavia, on headstream of Jadar R. (hydroelectric plant) and 34 mi. NE of Sarajevo, at N foot of Javor Mts.; cattle and lumber trade.

Vlasic Mountains or **Vlasich Mountains** (both: vlä′shĭch), Serbo-Croatian *Vlašić Planina*, in Dinaric Alps, central Bosnia, Yugoslavia; extend c.10 mi. E-W, bet. Vrbas and Bosna rivers; highest point, Vlasic (6,294 ft.), is 4 mi. N of Travnik. Sheep raising; cheese making.

Vlasim (vlä′shĭm), Czech *Vlašim*, Ger. *Wlaschim* (vlä′shĭm), town (pop. 5,066), SE Bohemia, Czechoslovakia, on railroad and 24 mi. SW of Kutna Hora, in barley and oat dist.; mfg. of hand-worked footwear. Some gold extracted from near-by Roudny mtn.

Vlasotinci or **Vlasotintsi** (both: vlä′sôtĭntsē), village (pop. 5,153), SE Serbia, Yugoslavia, on Vlasina R. (right tributary of the Southern Morava) and 10 mi. ESE of Leskovac; winegrowing. Sometimes spelled Vlasotince or Vlasotintse.

Vlaste or **Vlasti** (both: vlä′stē), town (pop. 2,527), Kozane nome, Macedonia, Greece, 18 mi. NW of Kozane at SE foot of the Mouriki; lumbering; charcoal; wine. Formerly called Polyneri (Polineri) and Vlatse (Vlatsi).

Vlatse or **Vlatsi**, mountain, Greece: see MOURIKI.

Vleuten (vlû′tŭn) village (pop. 1,627), Utrecht prov., W central Netherlands, 5 mi. W of Utrecht; truck gardening.

Vlieland (vlē′länt), island (□ 12; pop. 629), one of West Frisian Isls., Friesland prov., NW Netherlands, bet. North Sea and the Waddenzee; separated by the Eierlandschegat (S) from Texel isl., by the Boomkensdiep (N) from Terschelling isl.; 13.5 mi. long, 2 mi. wide. Consists of uninhabited sand bar (SW), inhabited dune-ringed main area (NE). Shipping, fishing, potato growing, sheep and goat breeding. Chief village, Oost-Vlieland. Ferry service to Oudeschild (Texel) and to Terschelling.

Vlimmeren (vlĭ′mŭrŭn), agr. village (pop. 1,133), Antwerp prov., NE Belgium, 9 mi. WSW of Turnhout. Of anc. origin, village has 14th-cent. church.

Vlissingen, Netherlands: see FLUSHING.

Vlodava, Poland: see WLODAWA.

Vlodrop (vlō′drôp), town (pop. 783), Limburg prov., SE Netherlands, on Roer R. and 6 mi. SE of Roermond, on Ger. border; coal deposits.

Vloesberg, Belgium: see FLOBECQ.

Vlona or **Vlonë**, Albania: see VALONA.

Vlora or **Vlorë**, Albania: see VALONA.

Vloshchova, Poland: see WLOSZCZOWA.

Vlotho (flō′tō), town (pop. 7,417), in former Prussian prov. of Westphalia, NW Germany, after 1945 in North Rhine-Westphalia, on left bank of the Weser and 8 mi. NE of Herford; cigar mfg.

Vlotslavsk, Poland: see WLOCLAWEK.

Vltava River (vŭl′tävä), Ger. *Moldau* (môl′dou), central Bohemia, Czechoslovakia, formed on E slope of Bohemian Forest, 3 mi. S of Volary, by junction of 2 headstreams; flows SSE and generally N, past Cesky Krumlov, Budweis, and Prague, to Elbe R. opposite Melnik; 267 mi. long. Receives Malse, Luznice, and Sazava (right), and Otava and Berounka (left) rivers. Navigable for steamboats for c.50 mi. in lower course (below Stechovice). Large dams and hydroelectric plants at Stechovice and Vrane.

Vnukovo (vnōō′kŭvŭ), town (1947 pop. over 500), central Moscow oblast, Russian SFSR, 2 mi. SW of Odintsovo; brickworks. One of Moscow's civil airports here.

Vobarno (vôbär′nô), town (pop. 3,193), Brescia prov., Lombardy, N Italy, on Chiese R. and 16 mi. NE of Brescia; rail terminus; iron- and steelworks.

Vocin (vô′chĭn), Serbo-Croatian *Vočin* or *Voćin*, village, N Croatia, Yugoslavia, 15 mi. E of Daruvar, bet. the Papuk and the Crni Vrh, in Slavonia; rail terminus.

Vöcklabruck (vûk′läbrōōk), town (pop. 9,079), S central Upper Austria, 35 mi. SW of Linz; mfg. (textiles, files, paper).

Vöcklamarkt (vûk′lämärkt), town (pop. 3,565), SW central Upper Austria, 8 mi. W of Vöcklabruck.

Vodelée (vōdlā′), village (pop. 235), Namur prov., S Belgium, 9 mi. E of Philippeville, near Fr. border; marble.

Vodena, Greece: see EDESSA.

Vodla River (vôd′lŭ), SE Karelo-Finnish SSR, rises in NE lake Vodlozero, flows c.100 mi. S and W, past Pudozh (head of navigation) to L. Onega at Shala. Frozen Nov.-May. Anc. navigation route from L. Onega to White Sea.

Vodlozero (vôd′lô″zyĭrŭ), lake (□ 190) in SE Karelo-Finnish SSR, 30 mi. N of Pudozh; 20 mi. long, 7 mi. wide; fisheries. Frozen Nov.-May.

Vodnany (vôd′nyänĭ), Czech *Vodňany*, Ger. *Wodnian* (vôd′nyän), town (pop. 4,576), S Bohemia, Czechoslovakia, on railroad and 11 mi. S of Pisek; rye, oats. Lignite mines in vicinity. Has fishing trade school. Chelcic (khĕl′chĭts), Czech *Chelčic*, home town of Petr Chelcicky, 15th-cent. founder of Moravian Church, is 2 mi. S.

Vodnjan (vôd′nyän), Ital. *Dignano d'Istria* (dēnyä′nô dē′strēä), village (1936 pop. 5,428), NW Croatia, Yugoslavia, 7 mi. N of Pula, in S Istria. Cathedral.

Vodny or **Vodnyy** (vôd′nē), town (1944 pop. over 500), central Komi Autonomous SSR, Russian SFSR, on Ukhta R. (left branch of Izhma R.) and 9 mi. WSW of Ukhta, in oil field.

Vodopyanovo or **Vodop'yanovo** (vŭdŭpyä′nŭvŭ), agr. village (1926 pop. 4,641), NW Voronezh oblast, Russian SFSR, on Don R. and 25 mi. W of Lipetsk; quarries. Until 1930s, called Patriarsheye.

Voerde (vôr′dŭ, fôr′dŭ). **1** Village (pop. 10,846), in former Prussian Rhine Prov., W Germany, after 1945 in North Rhine-Westphalia, in the Ruhr, near right bank of the Rhine, 3 mi. NW of Dinslaken, in coal-mining region. **2** Town, Westphalia, Germany: see ENNEPETAL.

Voeune Sai or **Veune Sai** (vû′nä sī′), town, Stungtreng prov., NE Cambodia, 60 mi. NE of Stungtreng. Formerly called Moulapoumok.

Vogan (vōgän′), town, S Fr. Togoland, on road and 23 mi. NE of Lomé; copra, palm oil and kernels.

Vogelberg (fō′gŭlbĕrk), peak (10,559 ft.) in Lepontine Alps, E Switzerland, 9 mi. NNE of Biasca.

Vogelkop (vō′gŭlkôp″), peninsula, extreme NW New Guinea, bounded N by the Pacific, S by Ceram Sea and McCluer Gulf. W by Geelvink Bay; shaped like a bird's head, c.225 mi. E-W, c.135 mi. N-S. Connected to mainland by isthmus c.20 mi. wide. Formerly Berau Peninsula.

Vogenée (vōzhnā'), village (pop. 177), Namur prov., S Belgium, 5 mi. NW of Philippeville; foundries; metal utensils.
Vogesen, France: see VOSGES.
Voghera (vōgā'rä), town (pop. 23,562), Pavia prov., Lombardy, N Italy, 15 mi. SSW of Pavia. Rail junction; agr. market; mfg. center (motors, machinery, refrigerators, cotton and silk textiles, hats, wax, canned foods), foundries. Hydroelectric plant. Has 14th-cent. castle, agr. school.
Voglans (vōglã'), village (pop. 327), Savoie dept., SE France, near S shore of Lac du Bourget, 5 mi. NNW of Chambéry; lignite mining.
Vogtland, Germany: see PLAUEN.
Voh (vō), village (pop. 2,382), W New Caledonia, 145 mi. NW of Nouméa; coffee, livestock; nickel mining.
Vohburg (fō'bŏŏrk), village (pop. 2,229), Upper Bavaria, Germany, on the Danube and 9 mi. E of Ingolstadt; grain, livestock. Has ruined medieval castle.
Vohémar (vōōhämär'), town, Majunga prov., N Madagascar, port on Indian Ocean, 90 mi. SSE of Diégo-Suarez; exports cattle (notably to Réunion and Mauritius), coffee, vanilla, rubber, hardwoods, wax. Copper and amethyst mining, lumbering and cattle raising in vicinity. Has R.C. and Protestant missions. Airport.
Vohenstrauss (fō'ün-shtrous), town (pop. 3,323), Upper Palatinate, E Bavaria, Germany, in Bohemian Forest, 9 mi. SE of Weiden; mfg. (cut glass, chemicals, textiles). Has late-16th-cent. castle.
Vohimasina (vōōhēmäsē'nōō), village, Fianarantsoa prov., E Madagascar, on coast and Canal des Pangalanes, 70 mi. ESE of Fianarantsoa; meat canning, rice processing.
Vohipeno (vōōhēpĕ'nōō), town, Fianarantsoa prov., E Madagascar, on Indian Ocean coast and Canal des Pangalanes, 80 mi. SE of Fianarantsoa; coffee center. R.C. and Protestant missions, hosp. for natives.
Vohma or **Vykhma,** Est. *Võhma* (all: vŭkh'mä), town (pop. 566), central Estonia, 18 mi. N of Viljandi; meat packing.
Vöhrenbach (fû'rŭnbäkh), village (pop. 2,018), S Baden, Germany, in Black Forest, on the Breg and 7 mi. W of Villingen; mfg. of machinery, watches, orchestrions; woodworking, lumber milling. Summer resort and winter-sports center (alt. 2,615 ft.).
Vöhringen (fû'rĭng-ŭn). **1** Village (pop. 6,319), Swabia, SW Bavaria, Germany, on the Iller and 10 mi. SSE of Ulm; metalworking; grain, livestock. **2** Village (pop. 1,498), S Württemberg, Germany, after 1945 in Württemberg-Hohenzollern, 11.5 mi. NNE of Rottweil; shoe mfg.
Vöhrum (fû'rōōm), village (pop. 3,558), in former Prussian prov. of Hanover, NW Germany, after 1945 in Lower Saxony, 2 mi. NW of Peine; food processing.
Vohwinkel (fō'vĭng"kŭl), W section (1925 pop. 16,093) of WUPPERTAL, W Germany, 3 mi. W of Elberfeld (linked by suspension tramway); textile mfg., metalworking. First mentioned in 14th cent. Inc. (1929) with neighboring towns to form city of Wuppertal.
Voi (voi), town (pop. c.3,500), SE Kenya, rail junction for Tanganyika, 90 mi. WNW of Mombasa; alt. 1,834 ft.; 3°25'S 38°40'E; sisal center; coffee, tea, corn; dairy farming. Airfield.
Void (vwä), village (pop. 945), Meuse dept., NE France, on Meuse R. and Marne-Rhine Canal, 5 mi. S of Commercy; cream-cheese mfg. Tree nurseries.
Voidia, Greece: see PANACHAIKON.
Voikka (voik'kä), village in Kuusankoski commune (pop. 17,560), Kymi co., SE Finland, on Kymi R. (rapids) and 5 mi. NNW of Kouvola; pulp, cellulose, and paper mills; hydroelectric station. Until 1949 in Uusimaa co.
Voikovo or **Voykovo** (voi'kŭvŭ), town (1939 pop. over 500), central Stalino oblast, Ukrainian SSR, in the Donbas, just SE of Makeyevka; coal mining.
Voikovski or **Voykovskiy** (voi'kŭfskē), town (1939 pop. over 500), SE Stalino oblast, Ukrainian SSR, in the Donbas, near Kuteinikovo.
Voil, Loch, Scotland: see BALQUHIDDER.
Voila (voi'lä), village (pop. 728), Sibiu prov., central Rumania, on Olt R., on railroad and 7 mi. ESE of Fagaras; noted for its picturesque folkways.
Voinesti (voinĕsht'), Rum. *Voineşti,* village (pop. 1,429), Prahova prov., S central Rumania, on Dambovita R. and 14 mi. NW of Targoviste, in oil region.
Voinilov or **Voynilov** (voinyē'lŭf), Pol. *Wojnilów* (voinyē'wōōf), village (1931 pop. 3,170), N Stanislav oblast, Ukrainian SSR, 16 mi. NNW of Stanislav; mfg. (cement, bricks); pottery. Founded 1552.
Voion (vô'yôn), anc. *Boius,* section of Pindus mtn. system in Greek Macedonia, near Albanian border, where it joins the GRAMMOS; rises to 7,192 ft. 11 mi. SW of Nestorion. The Sarantaporos R. has its source here. The name Grammos is sometimes applied also to the Voion.
Voiotia, Greece: see BOEOTIA.
Voiron (vwärō'), town (pop. 9,847), Isère dept., SE France, in the Pre-Alps just N of Isère R. valley, 14 mi. NNW of Grenoble; center of an industrial dist., with paper and textile (canvas, velvet) mills, specializing in manufacture of loose-leaf ledgers; liqueur (Grande Chartreuse) distilling. Also makes textile machinery, transmission belts, lubricating oils, art prints. Has modern (19th cent.) Gothic church.
Voirons, Les (lā vwärō'), range of Chablais massif (Savoy Pre-Alps), Haute-Savoie dept., SE France, overlooking W end of L. Geneva, c.10 mi. ENE of Geneva; 6 mi. long; rises to 4,875 ft. at the Calvaire or Grand-Signal. Panorama attracts tourists.
Voissant (vwäsã'), village (pop. 60), Isère dept., SE France, on the Guiers and 12 mi. SW of Chambéry; electrometallurgy.
Voitersreuth, Czechoslovakia: see VOJTANOV.
Voiteur (vwätûr'), village (pop. 711), Jura dept., E France, on the Seille and 6 mi. NNE of Lons-le-Saunier; winegrowing (chiefly at Château-Chalon, Lavigny, and Le Vernois near by).
Voitsberg (voits'bĕrk), town (pop. 4,584), Styria, S Austria, 13 mi. W of Graz; mfg. (machines, glass). Has 12th-cent. church, castle; ruins of old fortress near by. Lignite mines, electric-power works in vicinity.
Voiussa River, Albania-Greece: see AOOS RIVER.
Voiveis, Lake, or **Lake Voiviis** (both: voivē-ēs'), anc. *Boebeis* (bēbē'ĭs) (□ 44), lake in E Thessaly, Greece, 9 mi. NW of Volos; 18 mi. long, 2.5 mi. wide. Formerly called L. Kavla.
Voivodina, Yugoslavia: see VOJVODINA.
Voi-Vozh or **Voy-Vozh** (voi'-vŭsh), town (1947 pop. over 500), central Komi Autonomous SSR, Russian SFSR, on N.Pechora RR and 70 mi. NNE of Ukhta.
Vojens (vô'yŭns), town (pop. 1,534), Haderslev amt, SE Jutland, Denmark, 7 mi. W of Haderslev; chemicals, machine shops.
Vojnic (voi'nĭch), Serbo-Croatian *Vojnić,* village (pop. 2,137), NW Croatia, Yugoslavia, 14 mi. SSE of Karlovac, at W foot of Petrova Gora; economic center of the Kordun. Heavily damaged in Second World War.
Vojtanov (voi'tänôf), Ger. *Voitersreuth* (voi'tŭrz-roit), village (pop. 297), NW Bohemia, Czechoslovakia, in the Erzgebirge, 6 mi. NW of Cheb; frontier station on Ger. border, opposite Brambach.
Vojvodina, Voivodina, or **Voyvodina** (all: voi'vôdĭnä), autonomous territory [Serbo-Croatian *pokrajina*] (□ 8,683; pop. 1,661,632), N Serbia, Yugoslavia; ⊙ Novi Sad. Borders on Hungary (N) and Rumania (E); consists of the SREM (SW), the BACKA (NW), and the Yugoslav BANAT (E). Part of the Alföld, it is generally flat, reaching its highest point in FRUSKA GORA. The Danube, Sava (which forms S border), and Tisa are chief rivers. Predominantly agr., with 60% of its land under cultivation. Chief crops are grains (wheat, corn, rye, barley, oats); industrial crops (sugar beets, hemp, hops, sunflowers, rape, chicory, tobacco), vegetables (cabbage, potatoes, paprika), fruit (plums, apples, pears) are also grown; vineyards. Stock raising, particularly of cattle, is also important. Some coal (in FRUSKA GORA), natural gas, construction stone, and clays; mineral waters. Home industry and handicrafts are well developed in the large villages. Food processing (flour and sugar milling, meat and vegetable canning, dairying) is chief industry; also mfg. of textiles (hemp products, linen, cotton, woolen, and silk). Good roads, many railroads, and canals linking navigable rivers stimulate trade. Pop. consists of Serbs, Croats, Hungarians, Rumanians, and Slovaks. Besides NOVI SAD, chief towns are SUBOTICA, ZRENJANIN, SOMBOR, PANCEVO, KIKINDA, SENTA, VRSAC, and MITROVICA. Vojvodina has long been a multinational region. Original Slav pop. settled here in early Middle Ages and was ruled by Hungarians; reinforced after 1690 by influx of Serb refugees from Turkish domination and mixed (18th cent.) with Ger. elements. Autonomous territory was formed in 1946.
Vokhma (vôkh'mŭ), village (1939 pop. over 2,000), NE Kostroma oblast, Russian SFSR, 60 mi. NE of Sharya; dairying, flax.
Volant (vōlănt', vō'lănt), borough (pop. 229), Lawrence co., W Pa., 8 mi. NNE of New Castle; bituminous coal.
Volary (vô'lärĭ), Ger. *Wallern* (vä'lĕrn), town (pop. 2,278), S Bohemia, Czechoslovakia, in Bohemian Forest, on railroad and 24 mi. S of Strakonice; skiing resort. Has lumber trade school.
Volcán, El, Panama: see EL VOLCÁN.
Volcán, Sierra del (syĕ'rä dĕl bōlkän'), subandean range in N San Juan prov., Argentina, extends c.25 mi. N from Rodeo; rises to c.13,000 ft.
Volcano, village (pop. c.300), Amador co., central Calif., old gold rush camp in Sierra Nevada foothills, c.45 mi. E of Sacramento.
Volcano Bay, Japan: see UCHIURA BAY.
Volcano Island, uninhabited island in Batangas prov., Philippines, in L. Taal (tä-äl'), S Luzon, 40 mi. S of Manila; 5 mi. long, 3 mi. wide. In center of isl. is an active volcano, Mt. Taal (984 ft.), with several crater lakes; last erupted 1911.
Volcano Islands, Jap. *Kazan-retto,* island group (□ 11; pop. 1,154), W Pacific, 660 naut. mi. S of Tokyo; 24°47'N 141°20'E; 86-mi. chain of volcanic isls. including IWO JIMA, KITA-IWO-JIMA, MINAMI-IWO-JIMA. Mountainous; highest peak on Minami-iwo-jima. Sugar plantations, sulphur mines. Inhabitants: Japanese, some Koreans and Formosans. Annexed 1887 by Japan and placed under Tokyo prefecture. In Second World War, Iwo Jima was taken by U.S. forces. After the group was surrendered (1945) to the U.S. with Jap. defeat, it was removed from Tokyo's jurisdiction and administered by U.S. along with Bonin and Marcus isls.
Volchanka (vŭlchän'kŭ), town (1947 pop. over 500), N Sverdlovsk oblast, Russian SFSR, on railroad (Lesnaya Volchanka station) and 13 mi. NNW of Krasnoturinsk; rail junction; bituminous-coal mining. Developed during Second World War.
Volchansk (vŭlchänsk'), city (1926 pop. 20,810), N Kharkov oblast, Ukrainian SSR, 35 mi. NE of Kharkov; food processing (sunflower oil, meat, flour), distilling, cotton milling. Archaeological mus.
Volcheyarovka (vŭlchĭyä'rŭfkŭ), town (1939 pop. over 500), W Voroshilovgrad oblast, Ukrainian SSR, in the Donbas, 7 mi. SW of Lisichansk; coal mines.
Volchikha (vŭlchē'khŭ), village (1926 pop. 6,731), SW Altai Territory, Russian SFSR, on S Kulunda Steppe, 50 mi. NW of Rubtsovsk; flour mill.
Volchki (vŭlchkē'), village (1926 pop. over 2,000), W Tambov oblast, Russian SFSR, 35 mi. WSW of Tambov; grain. Also called Volchok or Volchek.
Volchya River or **Volch'ya River** (vôl'chyŭ), E Ukrainian SSR, rises in Donets Ridge NW of Stalino, flows 145 mi. W and NNW, past Pokrovskoye and Vasilovka, to Samara R. below Pavlograd.
Volda (vôl'lä), village (pop. 2,341; canton pop. 4,982), More og Romsdal co., W Norway, on E shore of Volds Fjord, 23 mi. S of Alesund; boatbuilding, iron casting; mfg. of motors, textiles, cement, furniture; lumber milling. Agr. and fishing near by. Formerly called Volden.
Volds Fjord (vôls), Nor. *Voldsfjord* or *Voldenfjord,* inlet of the North Sea in More og Romsdal co., W Norway; entrance (guarded by isls. of Hareid and Gurskoy) is 20 mi. SSW of Alesund; extends SE c.15 mi., forming several branches.
Volendam (vō'lŭndäm), picturesque village (pop. 6,882), North Holland prov., NW Netherlands, on the Ijsselmeer, 11 mi. NNE of Amsterdam; tourist center, attracting artists; mfg. (artificial horsehair for upholstery), duck breeding; declining fishing industry. Ferry to Marken isl. (SE).
Volga (vŏl'gŭ, Rus. vôl'gŭ), town (1926 pop. 2,781), W Yaroslavl oblast, Russian SFSR, on Rybinsk Reservoir, at influx of Volga R., 16 mi. WSW of Shcherbakov; vicuña-cloth mill; vegetable oils.
Volga. 1 (vŏl'gŭ) or **Volga City,** town (pop. 423), Clayton co., NE Iowa, on Volga R. and 21 mi. ENE of Oelwein, in agr. and dairying region. **2** (vŏl'gŭ) City (pop. 578), Brookings co., E S.Dak., 7 mi. W of Brookings, near Big Sioux R.; dairy products, livestock, grain, poultry.
Volga-Don Canal (vŏl'gŭ-dŏn', Rus. vôl'gŭ-dôn'), navigable waterway in Stalingrad oblast, Russian SFSR, bet. Krasnoarmeisk (S suburb of Stalingrad) on the Volga and Kalach on the Don; 63 mi. long. Equipped with 3 dams and reservoirs, the canal rises from the Volga to the watershed via 9 locks and descends to the head of the Tsimlyanskaya Reservoir on the Don via 4 more locks. Work on canal, begun before Second World War, was interrupted by the war, resumed in 1947.
Volga German, in Rus. names: see GERMAN VOLGA.
Volga Hills or **Volga Upland,** heights in E central European USSR, extending along right (W) bank of middle Volga, bet. Gorki and Stalingrad; rise to c.1,000 ft.
Volga Reservoir, Rus. *Volzhskoye Vodokhranilishche,* or **Moscow Sea,** Rus. *Moskovskoye More,* artificial lake (□ 126) on upper Volga R., in S Kalinin oblast, Russian SFSR; extends 40 mi. from Turginovo village ENE to Ivankovo; up to 5 mi. wide. Formed 1937 after completion of dam and hydroelectric station at Ivankovo. Filling of reservoir flooded Korcheva city and 200 villages. Joined to Moskva R. by MOSCOW CANAL.
Volga River, anc. *Ra* or *Rha,* Tatar *Itil,* largest river of Europe, in central European Russian SFSR, and principal navigable water artery of the USSR; rises in the Valdai Hills at alt. of 748 ft.; flows generally E, past Rzhev and Kalinin, through Volga and Rybinsk reservoirs, and past Yaroslavl, Kostroma, and Gorki, turns S at Kazan, and continues past Ulyanovsk, Kuibyshev, Saratov, and Stalingrad to the Caspian, forming a broad delta below Astrakhan. Total length, 2,290 mi., of which almost the entire course (c.2,200 mi.) is navigable. Rising near the village of Volgoverkhovye [Rus.,= Volga source], 25 mi. WNW of Ostashkov (Kalinin oblast), the Volga traverses the upper Volga lakes (Sterzh, Vselug, Peno, Volgo) of moraine origin and at Selizharovo receives the navigable Selizharovka R. (outlet of L. Seliger). Downstream navigation begins at Rzhev and river steamboats ascend to Kalinin at mouth of Tvertsa R. (link in Vyshnevolotsk canal system). Bet. Kalinin and Kimry, the Volga is dammed (since 1937) at Ivankovo, forming the Volga Reservoir (connected by Moscow Canal with Moskva R. at Moscow). Other dams and hydroelectric stations (completed 1941)

are at Uglich and Shcherbakov, the latter forming the vast Rybinsk Reservoir, which receives the Mologa and the Sheksna (links in Tikhvin and Mariinsk canal systems). Below Gorki, where the Volga receives its main right affluent, the Oka, the river becomes considerably wider and is lined on right (W) bank by the bluffs of the Volga Hills which contrast sharply with the low-lying left-bank steppe. Dam sites under construction in 1951 in middle course are at Gorodets (near Gorki), and at Kuibyshev, where the Zhiguli Mts. form the characteristic Samara Bend. Below Stalingrad (dam construction begun 1950), the Volga and its parallel arm, the Akhtuba, form a braided flood plain culminating in the vast fish-rich delta (□ c.2,500) on the Caspian Sea. The chief affluents are, on right, the Oka, Sura, and Sviyaga rivers; on left, the Unzha, Vetluga, Kama, and Samara rivers. No tributaries reach the Volga in the dry steppe below Kamyshin, where the river flows below sea level. Navigation period varies from 200 days (late April-late Nov.) at Shcherbakov to 260 days (early March-middle Dec.) at Astrakhan. A tranquil, regular stream, the Volga has a flood stage in May and June and a low-water stage in late summer when shoals and sand bars somewhat impede navigation. Although the Volga enters the Caspian (a closed sea), it plays a paramount role in the water transportation of the USSR. Its vast basin (⅓ of the European USSR) connects the forested N and the grain-growing SE, the central industrial region and the Urals. The freight turnover, which constitutes ⅓ of total Soviet river freight, includes (upriver) oil, grain, salt, and fish and (downriver) lumber. The Volga, in connection with the Vyshnevolotsk, Tikhvin, and Mariinsk canal systems, ar d the Moscow Canal, links the Caspian Sea with Moscow, the Baltic and the White Seas. The Don-Volga canal at Stalingrad was completed 1951. Although the Volga was mentioned by the anc. Greeks after Ptolemy, little was known about the river until the settlement (7th cent.) of Slavic and Finnic tribes, Bulgars and Khazars, along its course, which became an important trade route linking the capitals of the Volgar Bulgars (Bulgar) and of the Khazars (Itil) with central Asia. The Mongol invasions found the Russians entrenched bet. the upper course of the Volga and the Oka, and extending their control as far as Nizhni Novgorod (present-day Gorki; founded 1221). Here the Russians were held until the 16th cent., when the entire Volga passed to their control with the fall of the Tatar khanates of Kazan (1552) and Astrakhan (1556). The Rus. Volga corridor to the Caspian was the scene of numerous insurrections, notably those of Stenka Razin (1670–71) and Pugachev (1773–74). Following the building of E–W railroads in late 19th cent., the Volga became an important longitudinal link bet. the major rail crossings of Gorki, Kazan, Syzran, and Saratov. A German objective during Second World War, the lower Volga was reached briefly (1942–43) by Ger. troops at Stalingrad.

Volga River (vŏl′gů), NE Iowa, rises in Fayette co., flows c.60 mi. ESE to Turkey R. at Garber.

Volga Upland, Russian SFSR: see VOLGA HILLS.

Volgo, Lake (vôl′gů), southernmost of upper Volga R. lakes, in Kalinin oblast, Russian SFSR; 13 mi. long, 2 mi. wide; connects (W) with L. Peno; empties (E) into Volga R. Selizharovo lignite-mining basin on SE shore.

Volhynia (vŏlĭ′nyů), Rus. *Volyn* (vŭlĭ′nyů), Pol. *Wołyń* (vô′wĭnyů), historical region in NW Ukrainian SSR. Name, derived from extinct city of Volyn on Bug R., is used to designate N part of Volyn-Podolian Upland and adjacent part of Pripet Marshes bounded by Bug R. (W) and central Dnieper R. valley (E). One of oldest Slavic-populated regions in Europe, it was dominated (after 9th cent.) by Kievan Russia. Inc. (11th cent.) into independent duchy of Vladimir; annexed by duchy of Galich, which disintegrated c.1340. Disputed by Poland and Lithuania, it passed (14th cent.) to Lithuania and became (1569) quasi-autonomous Pol. prov.; annexed by Russia following 2d (1793) and 3d (1795) partitions of Poland; became a Rus. govt. (⊙ Zhitomir) until 1925. Its W part reverted to Poland (1921) and inc. into Wolyn prov.; ceded to USSR in 1945. Volhynia comprises mainly VOLYN, ROVNO, and ZHITOMIR oblasts. Urban pop. largely Jewish prior to Second World War.

Volin (vō′lĭn), town (pop. 197), Yankton co., SE S.Dak., 12 mi. ENE of Yankton; farm trading point; livestock, grain.

Volintiri, Moldavian SSR: see VOLONTIROVKA.

Volkach (fôl′kăkh), town (pop. 3,049), Lower Franconia, NW Bavaria, Germany, at junction of Main (canalized) and small Volkach rivers, 14 mi. ENE of Würzburg; winegrowing; brewing, tanning, lumber and flour milling; plums. Town hall was renovated in 16th cent.

Volkenroda (fôl″kůnrō′dä), village, in former Prussian Saxony prov., central Germany, after 1945 in Thuringia, 6 mi. NE of Mühlhausen; potash mining; oil deposits (developed after 1931).

Volkerak, Netherlands: see KRAMMER.

Völkermarkt (föl′kůrmärkt), Slovenian *Velikovec*, town (pop. 3,432), Carinthia, S Austria, on Drau R. and 15 mi. ENE of Klagenfurt; highway junction; brewery; resort. Has 12th-cent. fortress.

Volkhov (vôl′khůf), city (1939 pop. over 10,000), central Leningrad oblast, Russian SFSR, on Volkhov R. and 70 mi. E of Leningrad; rail junction; aluminum-refining center; sawmilling, metalworking. Site of hydroelectric station completed 1926. Originally called Gostinopolye, it was renamed Volkhov 1923, Zvanka 1927, Volkhovstroi 1936, and again Volkhov 1940. During Second World War, briefly held (1941) by Germans.

Volkhov River, NW European Russian SFSR, leaves L. Ilmen near Novgorod, flows 140 mi. NNE, past Novgorod, Kirishi, and Volkhov, to L. Ladoga at Novaya Ladoga. Navigable (April–Nov.) as part of Vyshnevolotsk canal system. Rapids at Pcheva (50 mi. above mouth) and at Volkhov were flooded after construction (1926) of VOLKHOV hydroelectric station and raising of river level. Near L. Ilmen, it is linked with Msta R. by 2 cutoff canals. Important trade route (9th-11th cent.).

Volkhovstroi, Russian SFSR: see VOLKHOV, city.

Völklingen (fûlk′lĭng-ůn), city (pop. 33,570), SW Saar, near Fr. border, on Saar R. at mouth of Rossel R., and 7 mi. WNW of Saarbrücken; rail junction; steel-industry and coal-mining center, with coke ovens; mfg. of machinery, electrical equipment, building materials, cement, shoe polish, knit goods, jam; woodworking. Town dates from 9th cent., when it was property of Frankish kings. Just SW is suburb of Geislautern, where coal and iron industry was introduced in 1585; Napoleon here founded mining school in 1807. W suburb of Wehrden is site of major electric power station.

Volkmarsdorf (vôlk′märsdôrf″), E suburb of Leipzig, Saxony, E central Germany.

Volkmarsen (fôlk′mär″zůn), town (pop. 4,001), in former Prussian prov. of Hesse-Nassau, W Germany, after 1945 in Hesse ,17 mi. WNW of Kassel; grain. Has 13th-cent. church.

Volkovintsy (vôl′kůvĕntsē), village (1926 pop. 3,775), E Kamenets-Podolski oblast, Ukrainian SSR, 33 mi. ESE of Proskurov; sugar beets.

Volkovyshki, Lithuania: see VILKAVISKIS.

Volkovysk (vŭlkůvĭsk′), Pol. *Wołkowysk* (vôwkô′-vĭsk), city (1931 pop. 15,027), S central Grodno oblast, Belorussian SSR, 45 mi. SE of Grodno; rail junction; mfg. center (agr. machinery, cork, cement, pottery, bricks); metalworking, tanning, meat preserving, dairying, distilling, flour milling. Has regional mus. (Bagration house), ruins of 14th-cent. church. Old Rus. settlement, known in 13th cent., successively captured by Lithuanians, Teutonic Knights (1410), and Poles. Developed as agr.-processing center in 16th cent. Burned (1812) during retreat of Napoleon's army. Passed (1795) from Poland to Russia; reverted (1919) to Poland. During Second World War, under administration of East Prussia; Jewish pop. largely exterminated. Ceded to USSR in 1945.

Volksrust (vōlks′rŭst, Afrikaans fôlks′rŭst″), town (pop. 5,979), SE Transvaal, U. of So. Afr., near Natal border, in Drakensberg range, on Buffalo R. and 30 mi. N of Newcastle; alt. 5,429 ft.; rail junction; railroad workshops and depot; agr. center (dairying, stock). Just across Natal border are battle sites (1880–81) of Majuba Hill and Laing's Nek.

Volksstaat Hessen, Germany: see HESSE-DARMSTADT.

Vollenhove (vô′lůnhō″vů), town (pop. 1,918), Overijssel prov., N central Netherlands, on the Ijsselmeer, at E edge of North East Polder, 10 mi. W of Meppel; fishing, fish curing, cattle raising. Has 17th-cent. town hall.

Volmar, Latvia: see VALMIERA.

Volmarstein (fôl′mär-shtīn″), village (pop. 7,542), in former Prussian prov. of Westphalia, W Germany, after 1945 in North Rhine-Westphalia, on the Ruhr and 3 mi. W of Hagen. Has 11th-cent. ruined castle.

Volmerange-les-Mines (vôlmůrăzh′-lā-mēn′), Ger. *Wollmeringen* (vôl′můring-ůn), village (pop. 765), Moselle dept., NE France, near Luxembourg border, opposite Dudelange, 7 mi. NW of Thionville; iron mining.

Volmunster (vôlmŭstâr′), Ger. *Wolmünster* (vōl′-münstůr), village (pop. 181), Moselle dept., NE France, 13 mi. E of Sarreguemines.

Volnay (vôlnā′), village (pop. 460), Côte-d'Or dept., E central France, on SE slope of the Mont d'Or, 3 mi. SW of Beaune; celebrated Burgundy vineyards.

Volnovakha (vŭlnůvä′khů), city (1939 pop. over 10,000), S central Stalino oblast, Ukrainian SSR, 32 mi. SSW of Stalino; rail junction; metalworks, flour mills.

Volo, Greece: see VOLOS.

Voloc, Ukrainian SSR: see VOLOVETS.

Volochanka (vŭlůchän′ků), village, S Taimyr Natl. Okrug, Krasnoyarsk Territory, Russian SFSR, 200 mi. WSW of Khatanga; govt. observation post; airfield.

Volochayevka or **Volochayevka I** (vŭlůchī′ůfků), village (1939 pop. over 500), NE Jewish Autonomous Oblast, Russian SFSR, 25 mi. W of Khabarovsk and on Trans-Siberian RR; rail junction. Sawmilling town of **Volochayevka II** (1939 pop. over 500) is 5 mi. NE, on railroad to Komsomolsk, where it crosses Kur R. Area was scene of decisive Rus. victory over Japanese (1922).

Volochisk (–chēsk′), town (1926 pop. 7,280), W Kamenets-Podolski oblast, Ukrainian SSR, on Zbruch R., opposite Podvolochisk, and 37 mi. WNW of Proskurov; sugar refinery. On Austro-Russian border until 1918; USSR-Poland frontier station (1921–39).

Volodarka (–där′ků), town (1926 pop. 3,588), W Kiev oblast, Ukrainian SSR, on road and 21 mi. SSW of Belaya Tserkov; metalworking, food processing; cotton mill.

Volodarsk (–därsk′), town (1939 pop. over 500), SE Voroshilovgrad oblast, Ukrainian SSR, in the Donbas, 3 mi. NW of Sverdlovsk; coal mines.

Volodarski or **Volodarskiy** (–skē), residential town (1926 pop. 3,960), central Leningrad oblast, Russian SFSR, 11 mi. SW of Leningrad; truck produce. Sergiyevski monastery (founded 1735) is 1 mi. N. Formerly Sergiyevo.

Volodarskoye (–skůyů). **1** Village (1948 pop. over 2,000), W Kokchetav oblast, Kazakh SSR, 50 mi. W of Kokchetav; wheat, cattle. **2** Village (1939 pop. over 2,000), S Stalino oblast, Ukrainian SSR, 12 mi. NW of Zhdanov; machine shops, flour mills.

Volodarsk-Volynski or **Volodarsk-Volynskiy** (–vŭlĭn′skē), town (1926 pop. 4,015), central Zhitomir oblast, Ukrainian SSR, 25 mi. NNW of Zhitomir; flax, buckwheat, potatoes. Originally called Gorosh-ki; merged (1920s) with suburb Kutuzovo and called Kutuzov-Volodarsk; later, until c.1932, Volodarsk.

Volodary (vŭlůdä′rē), town (1939 pop. over 10,000), W Gorki oblast, Russian SFSR, near Oka R., 33 mi. WSW of Gorki; flour milling.

Vologda (vô′lůgdů), oblast (□ 56,900; 1946 pop. estimate 1,500,000), in N central European Russian SFSR; ⊙ Vologda. Served W by Mariinsk canal system, including lake Beloye Ozero, Sheksna R., and Rybinsk Reservoir, and E by basin of Sukhona R.; densely forested (E, NW), with alluvial meadows along rivers. Peat in W section. Main industries based on dairy farming (canned milk, butter), flax growing (linen milling at Vologda, Krasavino), sawmilling (along Kovzha R., at Cherepovets, Ustye, Kharovsk), paper milling and celluloid mfg. (Sokol), wood cracking. Potato and grain raised (W, NE) for distilling industry (Belozersk, Ustyuzhna); glassworking in area of Chagoda. Shipbuilding, fishing on Rybinsk Reservoir. Lace handicraft industries. Main mfg. centers: Vologda, Cherepovets, Sokol, Veliki Ustyug. Served by Leningrad-Kirov and Moscow-Archangel railroads and by waterways of Mariinsk and Northern Dvina canal systems. Formed 1937 out of Northern Oblast.

Vologda, city (1939 pop. 95,194), ⊙ Vologda oblast, Russian SFSR, head of navigation on Vologda R. (87 mi. long; affluent of Sukhona R.), at junction of Leningrad-Kirov and Moscow-Archangel railroads, and 250 mi. NNE of Moscow; 59°14′N 39°53′. Transportation and dairying center; railroad shops, metalworks, agr.-machinery works, sawmills, linen and clothing mills, distilling, food processing. Has teachers col. and dairy institute. Site of kremlin with 18th-cent. bishop's palace (now a mus.), St. Sophia cathedral (16th cent.) in N section of city. Spasso-Priluki monastery (founded 1371), with 16th-cent. cathedral, is in suburb. City dates from 1147; ruled by Novgorod; became ⊙ principality (1397–1481) which then fell to Moscow. Flourished (16th cent.) as trading center under Ivan the Terrible, on route to Archangel and foreign markets. Was ⊙ Vologda govt. (dissolved 1929).

Volokolamsk (vŭlůkůlämsk′), city (1926 pop. 4,442), NW Moscow oblast, Russian SFSR, 65 mi. WNW of Moscow; cotton textiles; clothing goods. Has remains of old fortress, 16th-cent. cathedral. Chartered 1159.

Volokonovka (vŭlůkô′nůfků), village (1926 pop. 6,814), SE Kursk oblast, Russian SFSR, on Oskol R. and 20 mi. NW of Valuiki; sunflower-oil extraction, metalworking; chalk quarrying.

Volomin, Poland: see WOLOMIN.

Volonne (vôlŭn′), village (pop. 662), Basses-Alpes dept., SE France, on the Durance and 11 mi. W of Digne; fruit and vegetable shipping.

Volontirovka (vŭlŭntyērôf′ků), Rum. *Volintiri* (vôlēntēr′), village (1941 pop. 6,225), SE Moldavian SSR, on Ukrainian border, 29 mi. SSE of Bendery; tanning, weaving.

Volos (vô′lôs), city coextensive with **Pagasai** (pägäsā′), municipality (1951 pop. 51,134), ⊙ Magnesia nome, SE Thessaly, Greece, port at head of Gulf of Volos, 100 mi. NNW of Athens; 39°23′N 22°25′E. The principal port of Thessaly and one of the leading Greek cities, Volos is the railhead for the Thessalian narrow-gauge system linking Larissa, Trikkala, and Kalambaka. A commercial and industrial center, it produces textiles, cement, cigarettes, canned goods, and dried fruit. Its leading exports are tobacco, wheat, olive oil, and silk cocoons. Seat of the Gr. metropolitan of Demetrias, it has the church of Hagios Theodoros (built on ruins of Byzantine church), remains of Turkish fortress, and a copy of the *Athena Parthenos* of Phidias. A modern city (developed in 19th cent.), Volos is situated at SW foot of the Pelion, in small coastal plain formerly occupied by 3 anc. cities. Iolcus (probable site just NE of Volos) was the kingdom of the mythical Jason and Medea and the port from which the Argonauts sailed in search of the Golden Fleece. It was succeeded in historical times by Pagasae (ruins just SW; for which the municipality of Volos was named), the port for Pherae, which flourished in 4th cent. Pagasae was depopulated at the time of the founding (290 B.C.) of Demetrias, but revived under Roman rule. Demetrias (ruins just SE) was founded by Demetrius Poliorcetes and was a favorite residence of Macedonian kings until 168 B.C. Known as Gholos under Turkish rule, Volos developed rapidly after 1881, when it passed to Greece. It suffered in an earthquake (1928) and from bombings during the Second World War. It was formerly called Volo.

Volos, Gulf of, Gulf of Pagasai, or **Pagasaean Gulf** (pă″gŭsē′ŭn), Gr. *Pagasetikos* (*Pagasitikos*) *Kolpos* (pägäsē′tĭkôs kôl′pôs), anc. *Sinus Pagasaeus* (păgŭsē′ŭs), large inlet of Aegean Sea, in Thessaly, Greece, bet. Pelion and Othrys mts., nearly closed off by Magnesia peninsula; c.20 mi. wide and long. Its entrance is the Strait of Trikkeri. The port of Volos in on N Shore.

Volosca, Yugoslavia: see OPATIJA.

Voloshino (vŭlô′shĭnŭ), village (1926 pop. 2,728), W Rostov oblast, Russian SFSR, 22 mi. W of Millerovo, on Ukrainian border; metalworks; wheat, sunflowers, livestock.

Voloshinovo, Yugoslavia: see VOLOSINOVO.

Voloshka (vŭlôsh′kŭ), town (1941 pop. over 500), SW Archangel oblast, Russian SFSR, 25 mi. NNW of Konosha, on small affluent of Onega R.

Volosinovo or **Voloshinovo** (both: vô′lôshĭnôvô), Serbo-Croatian *Vološinovo*, village (pop. 14,874), Vojvodina, N Serbia, Yugoslavia, on Tisa R. opposite Becej, on railroad and 27 mi. NE of Novi Sad, in the Banat. Until c.1947, Novi Becej, Hung. *Törökbecse.*

Volosko, Yugoslavia: see OPATIJA.

Volosovo (vô′lŭsŭvŭ), town (1939 pop. over 2,000), W central Leningrad oblast, Russian SFSR, 45 mi. SW of Leningrad; rail junction; marble and dolomite quarries.

Volot (vô′lŭt), town (1939 pop. over 500), W Novgorod oblast, Russian SFSR, 24 mi. W of Staraya Russa; flax processing.

Volovets (vŭlŭvyĕts′), Czech *Volovec* (vô′lôvĕts), Hung. *Volóc* (vô′lōts), village (1941 pop. 2,295), N Transcarpathian Oblast, Ukrainian SSR, on railroad and 30 mi. NE of Mukachevo; trading center. Mineral springs near by.

Volovo (vô′lŭvŭ). **1** Village (1926 pop. 4,562), NE Kursk oblast, Russian SFSR, 29 mi. SSE of Livny; wheat. **2** Village (1948 pop. over 2,000), SE Tula oblast, Russian SFSR, 15 mi. S of Bogoroditsk; rail junction; metalworks. During Second World War, briefly held (1941) by Germans in Moscow campaign. **3** Czech *Volové* (vô′lôvā), Hung. *Ökörmező* (û′kûrmĕzû), village (1941 pop. 5,896), N Transcarpathian Oblast, Ukrainian SSR, 37 mi. ENE of Mukachevo.

Volozhin (vŭlô′zhĭn), Pol. *Wołożyn* (vôwô′zhĭn), city (1931 pop. 5,609), S Molodechno oblast, Belorussian SSR, 31 mi. SSW of Molodechno; wood cracking, tanning, flour milling, mfg. (concrete blocks, bricks). Has old churches and synagogues. Passed (1793) from Poland to Russia; reverted (1921) to Poland; ceded to USSR in 1945.

Volpago del Montello (vôlpä′gô dĕl môntĕl′lô), village (pop. 1,233), Treviso prov., Veneto, N Italy, at S foot of the Montello, 10 mi. NNW of Treviso; silk mill, hosiery factory.

Volpiano (vôlpyä′nô), town (pop. 4,345), Torino prov., Piedmont, NW Italy, 10 mi. NNE of Turin.

Völpke (fülp′kŭ), village (pop. 2,416), in former Prussian Saxony prov., central Germany, after 1945 in Saxony-Anhalt, 7 mi. SE of Helmstedt, opposite Offleben; lignite mining; mineral-wax processing.

Volsinii (vŏlsĭ′nēī), anc. city of Etruria, probably on site of modern ORVIETO, central Italy. A powerful member of the Etruscan League, it was sacked by the Romans in 280 B.C. A 2d Volsinii was built near BOLSENA.

Volsk or **Vol'sk** (vôlsk), city (1939 pop. 55,053), N central Saratov oblast, Russian SFSR, on right bank of Volga R. and 65 mi. NE of Saratov; major cement-making center, in picturesque limestone hills; grain trade; mfg. (machines, river boats, leather goods); canned goods, flour, sunflower oil. Teachers col. Orchards near by. Chartered 1780.

Voltaire (vŏltâr′), village (pop. 72), McHenry co., central N.Dak., 25 mi. SE of Minot.

Voltaire, Cape, NE Western Australia, in Timor Sea; N extremity of peninsula bet. Admiralty Gulf and Montague Sound; 14°15′S 125°36′E.

Volta Mantovana (vôl′tä mäntôvä′nä), village (pop. 1,815), Mantova prov., Lombardy, N Italy, near Mincio R., 13 mi. NNE of Mantua, in agr. region (grapes, mulberry groves). Limekilns.

Volta Redonda (vôl′tŭ rĭdōn′dŭ), town (1940 pop. 1,017; 1950 census 33,110), W Rio de Janeiro state, Brazil, on Paraíba R., on Rio–São Paulo RR and 5 mi. ENE of Barra Mansa, 60 mi. WNW of Rio; Brazil's leading steel-milling center, in operation since 1947. With new facilities being continually added, it comprised (in 1950) a coke plant of 55 ovens, 1 blast furnace, 4 open-hearth furnaces, and finishing mills producing rails, structural steel, steel and tin plate. Plant uses high-grade iron ore and alloys from Minas Gerais, coal from Santa Catarina mixed with imported coking coal, and hydroelectric power generated at Ribeirão das Lages plant (20 mi. SE). Coke-oven by-products are locally processed. Volta Redonda is govt.-operated and has received U.S. financial and technical aid. It is one of the most ambitious industrial projects in South America.

Volta River (vŏl′tŭ), W Africa, main river of Gold Coast, formed 38 mi. NW of Yeji by junction of BLACK VOLTA RIVER (right) and WHITE VOLTA RIVER (left); flows SE past Yeji (normal head of canoe traffic) and Kete Krachi, and S past Senchi and Akuse, to Gulf of Guinea at Ada; c.300 mi. long; with either headstream, c.800 mi. long. Navigable for steam launches to Akuse, c.50 mi. upstream. Receives Pru, Sene, and Afram rivers (right), Daka and Oti rivers (left). Dam and hydroelectric plant projected at Ajena (6 mi. N of Senchi), to improve navigation and provide power for alumina-reduction plant.

Volterra (vôltĕr′rä), town (pop. 11,704), Pisa prov., Tuscany, central Italy, 31 mi. SE of Pisa. Rail terminus; alabaster- and salt-mining center, noted for its alabaster products. Bishopric, with seminary. Once a powerful Etruscan town. Surrounded by well-preserved Etruscan and medieval walls, and with its 10th-cent. cathedral, anc. palaces, and fort (14th–15th cent.; now a prison), it has a marked medieval aspect. Damaged (1944) in Second World War.

Voltri (vôl′trē), town (pop. 6,813), Genova prov., Liguria, N Italy, port on Gulf of Genoa and 9 mi. W of Genoa, within Greater Genoa, in flower-growing region. Industrial center; iron- and steelworks, cotton, jute, and flour mills, shipyards, tanneries, chemical factories. Resort. Once famous for paper mills. Forms W boundary of Greater Genoa.

Volturno River (vôltōōr′nô), chief river (109 mi. long) of S Italy, rises in the Apennines 11 mi. N of Venafro, flows SE and WSW, through Campania, past Capua, to Tyrrhenian Sea 22 mi. NNW of Naples. Chief affluent, Calore R. In 1860 Garibaldi defeated troops of Francis II of the Two Sicilies on its banks. In Second World War, crossed (Oct., 1943) by American troops after heavy fighting.

Volubilis (vŏlū′bĭlĭs), ruined Roman city in N central Fr. Morocco, 12 mi. N of Meknès and just NW of Moulay Idris. Chief inland city of anc. Mauretania Tingitana, its prosperity dated from 1st cent. A.D. Known to Arabs as Oulili, it became ⊙ of Idris I after 788. His son, Idris II, established his residence at Fez, which he founded from here in 808. Among the most noteworthy ruins are a forum, a basilica (2d cent. A.D.), and the arch of Caracalla (erected 217). The mus. contains a bronze dog, one of the finest examples of Roman sculpture.

Volunteer Island, Line Isls.: see STARBUCK ISLAND.

Voluntown (vŏ′lŭntoun″), town (pop. 825), New London co., SE Conn., on R.I. line, 12 mi. ENE of Norwich, in agr., recreational area; state forests here.

Volusia (vŭlōō′shŭ), county (□ 1,115; pop. 74,229), NE Fla., bordered by St. Johns R. (W, partly S) and the Atlantic (E); ⊙ De Land. Lowland area, hilly in W, with many lakes and scattered swamps; contains several lagoons in E, including Halifax R., Hillsborough R., and Mosquito Lagoon. Agr. (citrus fruit, vegetables; dairy products; poultry), forestry (lumber, naval stores), fishing. Tourist resorts along coast. Formed 1854.

Voluyak (vôlōō′yäk), village (pop. 1,410), Sofia dist., W Bulgaria, 6 mi. NW of Sofia; rail junction; grain, livestock, truck.

Volve, Lake, or **Lake Volvi** (both: vôl′vē), anc. *Bolbe* (bŏl′bē), lake (□ 28) in Greek Macedonia, at base of Chalcidice peninsula, 22 mi. E of Salonika; 12 mi. long, 3 mi. wide. Drains E into Strymonic Gulf. Also called Besikion.

Volvic (vôlvēk′), village (pop. 1,346), Puy-de-Dôme dept., central France, in Monts Dôme, 4 mi. WSW of Riom; lava rock (extensively quarried here since 12th-cent.) used for building and tombstones, and shipped to Clermont-Ferrand chemical works. Has school of architecture.

Volyn or **Volyn'** (vŭlĭ′nyŭ), oblast (□ 7,680; 1946 pop. estimate 1,100,000), W Ukrainian SSR, in Volhynia; ⊙ Lutsk. In lowland extending N into Pripet Marshes; includes NW part of Volyn-Podolian Upland; bounded W by Bug R. along Poland-USSR border; drained by Styr R. (SE) and other right tributaries of Pripet R. (Stokhod and Turya rivers). Has swampy prairie soils; loess and black earth (S); humid continental climate (short summers). Extensive agr., with wheat, barley (S), rye, flax, potatoes (N); cattle and horse raising. Industries based on agr. (food processing and preserving, distilling, tanning) and timber (sawmilling, woodworking). Light mfg. in main urban centers (Lutsk, Kovel, Vladimir-Volynski). Formed (1939) out of parts of Pol. Wolyn and Polesie provs., following Soviet occupation of E Poland; held by Germany (1941–44); ceded to USSR in 1945.

Volyne (vô′lĭnyĕ), Czech *Volyně*, town (pop. 2,673), S Bohemia, Czechoslovakia, on railroad and 6 mi. S of Strakonice; makes fertilizers; tanning; trout breeding.

Volyn-Podolian Upland (vŏlĭn′-pōdō′lyŭn), Rus. *Volyno-Podol'skaya Vozvyshennost'*, in W Ukrainian SSR, bet. Dniester and Dnieper rivers; rises (W) to 1,430 ft. Rivers cut narrow gorges through crystalline rock formations; deciduous forests (NW), black-earth steppe (SE).

Volzhsk (vôlsh-sk), city (1939 pop. over 10,000), S Mari Autonomous SSR, Russian SFSR, on left bank of Volga R. (landing), opposite Kozlovka, and 30 mi. WNW of Kazan; sawmilling, woodworking center; mfg. (paper, prefabricated houses). Founded c.1935; called Lopatino until 1940, when it became city.

Vom (vôm), town (pop. 6,924), Plateau Prov., Northern Provinces, central Nigeria, on Bauchi Plateau, 9 mi. SW of Bukuru; tin mining; butter factory; cassava, millet, durra. Farm and livestock experimental stations.

Vomano River (vômä′nô), S central Italy, rises in Gran Sasso d'Italia, just NE of Passo Capannelle, flows 45 mi. ENE, past Montorio al Vomano, to the Adriatic 6 mi. NE of Atri.

Vomp (fômp), village (pop. 1,723), Tyrol, W Austria, near Inn R., 13 mi. ENE of Innsbruck; summer resort; rye, wheat.

Vona, Turkey: see PERSEMBE.

Vona (vō′nŭ), town (pop. 209), Kit Carson co., E Colo., 25 mi. W of Burlington; alt. 4,494 ft.

Vonda (vŏn′dŭ), town (pop. 261), S central Sask., 28 mi. NE of Saskatoon, in agr. area; grain elevators, foundry.

Vondrisel (vôn′drĭshĕl), Slovak *Vondrišel*, Hung. *Merény* (mĕ′rānyŭ), village (pop. 1,829), E central Slovakia, Czechoslovakia, in the Low Tatra, on railroad and 14 mi. NNE of Roznava; iron mining. Health resort (alt. 2,165 ft.) of Cernohorske Kupele (chĕr′nôhôrskä kōō′pĕlĕ), Slovak *Černohorské Kúpele*, is just W.

Vonitsa (vô′nētsŭ), town (pop. 2,153), Acarnania nome, W central Greece, port on S shore of Gulf of Arta, 8 mi. ESE of Preveza; fisheries; livestock (meat, hides, dairy products). Remained under Venice after Turkish conquest (15th cent.) of Greece until 1797, when the French turned it over to the Turks.

Vonjama (vŏn′jŭmä), town, Western Prov., NW Liberia, 25 mi. ENE of Kolahun, near Fr. Guinea border; native leathercraft center; cotton weaving; palm oil and kernels, pineapples. Trade in hides and skins.

Voorburg (vōr′bûrkh), town (pop. 35,547), South Holland prov., W Netherlands, 3 mi. E of The Hague; mfg. (ball bearings, screws, insulating material, dairy and meat-cutting machinery, elevators, cardboard); jam processing. Has Hofwijk Mansion, with mementos of 17th-cent. astronomer Christiaan Huygens. Residence (1663–69) of Spinoza.

Voorheesville (vŏŏ′rēzvĭl), village (pop. 895), Albany co., E N.Y., 8 mi. W of Albany.

Voorne (vōr′nŭ), island, South Holland prov., SW Netherlands, SW of Rotterdam; bounded by North Sea (W), the Haringvliet (SW), Putten isl. (E), Brielsche Maas R. (N); with Putten isl., forms isl. of Voorne-en-Putten. Chief towns: Oostvoorne, Brielle, Hellevoetsluis.

Voorschoten (vōr′skhōtŭn), town (pop. 6,129), South Holland prov., W Netherlands, 7 mi. NE of The Hague; plastics, pottery, silverware.

Voorst (vōrst), village (pop. 971), Gelderland prov., E central Netherlands, 3 mi. NW of Zutphen; cigar-box mfg. Has 13th-cent. Nijenbeek Castle.

Vorarlberg (fôr′ärlbĕrk), autonomous province [Ger. *Bundesland*] (□ 1,004; 1951 pop. 193,715), W Austria, bordering Germany (N), Switzerland (W, S), Liechtenstein (SW), and Tyrol (E); ⊙ Bregenz, on E shore of L. Constance. With the Bregenzerwald (center) and part of the Rhätikon and Silvretta Group (S), it is noted for its beautiful mtn. scenery. The Rhine is W boundary; drained by Ill and Bregenzer Ache rivers. Corn, potatoes, fruit grown in Rhine basin; extensive cattle raising (especially in the MONTAFON), dairy farming. Textiles (Bregenz, Feldkirch, Dornbirn); embroidery produced by artisans. Hydroelectric works along Ill and Bregenzer Ache rivers. Active tourist trade. Was part of Roman prov. of Rhaetia. Acquired piecemeal by Hapsburgs in 14th, 15th, and 16th cent.; became (1523) a crownland, administered by Tyrol. Attempt to join Switzerland as canton after First World War failed. Placed (1945) in Fr. occupation zone.

Voras. 1 Mountain massif on Greek-Yugoslav border: see NIDZE. **2** Its peak on Greek-Yugoslav border: see KAJMAKCALAN.

Vorau (fôr′ou), village (pop. 1,099), Styria, E Austria, 24 mi. SSW of Neunkirchen.

Vorchdorf (fôrkh′dôrf), town (pop. 4,820), S central Upper Austria, 8 mi. NE of Gmunden; tannery.

Vörde, Germany: see ENNEPETAL.

Vörden (fûr′dŭn), town (pop. 1,107), in former Prussian prov. of Westphalia, NW Germany, after 1945 in North Rhine-Westphalia, 7 mi. WNW of Höxter.

Vordernberg (fôr′dŭrnbĕrk), town (pop. 2,704), Styria, central Austria, 9 mi. NNW of Leoben; ironworks.

Vorderrhein River (fôr′dĕr-rīn), a headstream of the Rhine, E Switzerland; rises 3 mi. E of Andermatt, flows 42 mi. ENE, past Disentis and Ilanz, joining the Hinterrhein W of Chur to form the Rhine.

Vorderweissenbach (fôr″dŭrvīs′ŭnbäkh), village (pop. 2,170), N Upper Austria, 18 mi. N of Linz, near Czechoslovak line; potatoes, rye, hogs.

Vordingborg (vôr′dĭngbôr), city (1950 pop. 11,231), Praesto amt, Zealand, Denmark, port on the Masnedsund and 50 mi. SSW of Copenhagen; meat packing, brick and cement mfg. Rail and highway bridge, here, crosses Smaalandsfarvand strait to Falster isl. Site of ruined 12th-cent. castle.

Vordingborg Bay, Denmark: see SMAALANDSFARVAND.

Voreppe (vôrĕp′), village (pop. 1,022), Isère dept., SE France, near the Isère and 9 mi. NNW of Grenoble, bet. Grande Chartreuse (NE) and Vercors (S) massifs of Dauphiné Pre-Alps; cement-works; marble quarries.

Vorey (vôrā′), village (pop. 887), Haute-Loire dept., S central France, on the Loire and 10 mi. N of Le Puy; cloth embroidering, mfg. of barium sulphate.

Vorga (vôr′gŭ), town (1948 pop. over 500), S Smolensk oblast, Russian SFSR, 13 mi. S of Roslavl; glassworks, sawmill.

Voringfoss (vû′ringfôs), Nor. *Vøringfoss*, waterfall (535 ft.) on Hardanger Fjord, Hordaland co., SW Norway, 7 mi. ESE of Eidfjord. Tourist attraction.

Vorkuta (vŭrkōōtä′), city (1945 pop. c.30,000), NE Komi Autonomous SSR, Russian SFSR, on Vorkuta R. (right affluent of Usa R.) and 690 mi. NE of Kotlas, 140 mi. from Kara Sea; 67°30′N 64°E. Major coal-mining center in Pechora basin (reserves, 60 billion tons). Developed during Second World War, after construction (1940) of N. Pechora RR from Kotlas. Satellite mining towns (NE) are Oktyabrski and Gornyatski.

Vormsi (vōrm′sē), Ger. *Worms* (vôrms), island (pop. 2,547) of Estonia, in the Baltic, bet. Hiiumaa isl. and mainland; 10 mi. long, 5 mi. wide; level terrain. Pop. largely Swedish.

Vorobyevka or **Vorob'yevka** (vŭrŭbyä′ŭfkŭ), village (1926 pop. 6,206), E Voronezh oblast, Russian SFSR, 19 mi. SE of Buturlinovka; metalworks; mineral pigments.

Vorokhta (vô′rŭkhtŭ), Pol. *Worochta* (vôrôkh′tä), village (1931 pop. 1,130), S Stanislav oblast, Ukrainian SSR, in East Beskids, in upper Prut R. valley, 27 mi. SW of Kolomyya; noted health resort with mineral springs; lumbering, sheep raising.

Vorona River (vŭrô′nŭ), in S central European Russian SFSR, rises in Volga Hills near Pachelma, meanders 255 mi. SSW, past Kirsanov, to Khoper R. at Borisoglebsk. Not navigable.

Voronet, Rumania: see GURA-HUMORULUI.

Voronezh (vŭrō′nĕsh, Rus. vŭrô′nyĭsh), oblast (□ 26,400; 1946 pop. estimate 3,450,000) in SW European Russian SFSR; ⊙ Voronezh. Black-earth steppe, hilly in SW and level in NE; drained by middle Don R., its affluents, the Voronezh and Bityug, and Khoner R. Main wheat-growing region of black-earth belt, producing chiefly spring wheat, rye, and winter wheat. Major industrial crops are sunflowers (grown throughout wheat area), potatoes, and sugar beets (N). Raising of hogs (N) and sheep (S); horse breeding (Khrenovoye). Agr. production is basis of flour, sunflower-oil, alcohol, starch, and molasses industries. Main industrial centers (Voronezh, Lipetsk) produce iron, machinery, chemicals. Refractory clays, marl, limestone, chalk are chief mineral resources. Formed 1934.

Voronezh. 1 City (1926 pop. 120,017; 1939 pop. 326,836), ⊙ Voronezh oblast, Russian SFSR, on right bank of Voronezh R., 5 mi. above confluence with Don R., and 290 mi. SSE of Moscow; 51°39′N 39°12′E. Major industrial center, producing synthetic rubber, locomotives and railroad cars (at OTROZHKA), aircraft, machinery (agr. implements, excavators, bridging equipment, flour-milling machines, Diesel motors), radio apparatus; agr. processing (flour milling, meat packing, sunflower-oil extraction, fruit and vegetable canning, distilling). Univ. (founded 1803 at Dorpat; moved here in First World War), large agr. institute (in N suburb), medical, teachers, and engineering schools. Has monuments to Peter the Great and to 19th-cent. Rus. poets Koltsov and Nikitin, regional mus., Nikitin mus. Founded 1586 as one of first fortified centers in Don R. steppe; became (1694) shipbuilding site under Peter the Great; later a grain and wool-trading center. Changed hands repeatedly (1917–19) during revolution. Was ⊙ Voronezh govt. (until 1928); later (1928–34) ⊙ Central Black-Earth Oblast. During Second World War, a Ger. advance was stopped here (1942–43) in heavy fighting. 2 Town (1926 pop. 6,778), NW Sumy oblast, Ukrainian SSR, 20 mi. WNW of Glukhov; hemp farming.

Voronezh River, in S central European Russian SFSR, rises ESE of Ryazhsk in 2 headstreams, the Polny Voronezh (left; 100 mi. long) and the Lesny Voronezh (right; 95 mi. long), joining S of Michurinsk; flows 225 mi. S, past Lipetsk, to Don R. below Voronezh city. Navigable in lower course.

Voronok (vŭrŭnôk′), village (1926 pop. 3,683), SW Bryansk oblast, Russian SFSR, 17 mi. SSW of Starodub; coarse grain.

Voronovitsa (–nŭvē′tsŭ), town (1926 pop. 3,835), central Vinnitsa oblast, Ukrainian SSR, 12 mi. SE of Vinnitsa; metalworks.

Voronovo (vô′rŭnŭvŭ), Pol. *Werenów* (vĕrĕ′nŏŏf), town (1931 pop. 1,230), NE Grodno oblast, Belorussian SSR, 18 mi. N of Lida; flour milling, pitch processing, lumbering.

Vorontsovka (vŭrŭntsôf′kŭ). 1 Town (1947 pop. over 500), W Sverdlovsk oblast, Russian SFSR, 8 mi. S (under jurisdiction) of Krasnoturinsk, on rail spur; magnetite-mining center, supplying Serov metallurgy; copper mining. Developed prior to First World War. Until 1947, Vorontsovski Zavod. 2 Village (1926 pop. 9,009), central Voronezh oblast, Russian SFSR, 18 mi. SW of Buturlinovka; wood- and metalworking; flour milling.

Vorontsovo (–tsô′vŭ), village (1939 pop. over 500), S Pskov oblast, Russian SFSR, on railroad (Soshikhino station) and 13 mi. ESE of Ostrov; flax processing.

Vorontsovo-Aleksandrovskoye (–ŭlyĭksän′-drŭfskŭyŭ), village (1926 pop. 12,378), SE Stavropol Territory, Russian SFSR, on Kuma R., on railroad and 32 mi. NE of Georgiyevsk, in winegrowing area; flour milling, wine making.

Voropayevo (vŭrŭpī′ŭvŭ), Pol. *Woropajewo*, village (1939 pop. over 500), W Polotsk oblast, Belorussian SSR, 20 mi. W of Glubokoye; rail junction; sawmilling, glassworking, vegetable canning.

Vörösbereny (vû′rŭzh-bĕ″rānyŭ), Hung. *Vörösberény*, town (pop. 3,743), Veszprem co., W central Hungary, on L. Balaton and 6 mi. SE of Veszprem; wine, corn, cattle, poultry.

Voroshilov (vôrŭshē′lôf, –lôf, vŏ–, Rus. vŭrŭshē′lŭf), city (1939 pop. 70,628), S Maritime Territory, Russian SFSR, on fertile Khanka Plain, on Suifun R. and 45 mi. N of Vladivostok. Rail hub on Trans-Siberian RR, at junction of Chinese Eastern RR. Major food-processing center; soybean products (oil, oilcake, glycerine, soap), sugar, rice, flour, alcohol; sawmilling, brickmaking. Railroad and machine workshops. Founded in 1860s by Rus. colonists; developed rapidly after construction (1890s) of Trans-Siberian RR. Chartered 1898 and called Nikolsk-Ussuriski or Nikol'sk Ussuriyskiy until c.1935; ⊙ former Ussuri oblast (1934–43).

Voroshilova, Imeni, Uzbek SSR: see VOROSHILOVO.

Voroshilovabad (vŭrŭshē′lŭvŭbät′), village, S Stalinabad oblast, Tadzhik SSR, 23 mi. S of Kurgan-Tyube (linked by narrow-gauge railroad); long-staple cotton. Developed in 1930s.

Voroshilovgrad (–lŭfgrät′), oblast (□ 10,300; 1946 pop. estimate 1,800,000), E Ukrainian SSR; ⊙ Voroshilovgrad. Includes fertile Central Russian Uplands (N) and Donets Ridge (S); drained by the Northern Donets and its affluent, Aidar R. Rich agr. area (N) with wheat, sunflower, and sugar-beet production; truck produce (S). S area forms part of highly industrialized and urbanized DONETS BASIN, with chief coal-mining centers at Bokovo-Antratsit, Kadiyevka, Krasnodon, Lisichansk, Rovenki, and Sverdlovsk; steel and mfg. industries at Voroshilovgrad and Voroshilovsk; also chemicals, glass, cement. Dense rail network (S). Formed 1938.

Voroshilovgrad, city (1926 pop. 71,765; 1939 pop. 213,007), ⊙ Voroshilovgrad oblast, Ukrainian SSR, in the Donbas, on Lugan R. (right affluent of the Northern Donets) and 420 mi. ESE of Kiev; 48°34′N 39°17′E. Major locomotive mfg. center; steel-pipe rolling, mfg. (coal-mining machines, machine tools, instruments), enameling, meat packing; food, textiles. Agr. and teachers colleges; metal-working school. Founded in 2d half of 18th cent.; iron foundry (built 1797) supplied Black Sea fleet. City pop. played important role in civil war. Until 1935, called Lugansk. In Second World War, held (1941–43) by Germans.

Voroshilovo (vŭrŭshē′lŭvŭ), village (1926 pop. 3,824), SE Andizhan oblast, Uzbek SSR, on Kirghiz SSR border, just N of Karasu; cotton. Formerly called Karasu and, later (1937–c.1940), Imeni Voroshilova.

Voroshilovsk (vŭrŭshē′lŭfsk). 1 City, Stavropol Territory, Russian SFSR: see STAVROPOL, city. 2 City (1926 pop. 16,040; 1939 pop. 54,794), SW Voroshilovgrad oblast, Ukrainian SSR, in the Donbas, 23 mi. WSW of Voroshilovgrad; iron- and steel-milling center; chemical works. Until c.1935, called Alchevsk. Near by is Parizhskaya Kommuna, coal-mining center.

Voroshilovski or **Voroshilovskiy** (–skē). 1 S suburb (1941 pop. over 500) of Archangel, Archangel oblast, Russian SFSR, on the Northern Dvina, near Isakogorka; sawmilling. 2 Town, Molotov oblast, Russian SFSR: see POLOVINKA, city. 3 Town (1939 pop. over 500), S Voroshilovgrad oblast, Ukrainian SSR, in the Donbas, near Uspenka; coal mines.

Voroshilovskoye (–skŭyŭ), village (1939 pop. over 2,000), N Frunze oblast, Kirghiz SSR, in Chu valley, just E of Frunze; orchards, truck produce. Until 1937, Lebedinovskoye.

Vorotynets (vŭrŭtĭ′nyĭts), village (1926 pop. 3,109), E Gorki oblast, Russian SFSR, 32 mi. E of Lyskovo; flour milling; flax.

Vorovskogo, Imeni (ē′mĭnyĕ vŭrôf′skŭvŭ). 1 Town (1941 pop. over 500), E central Moscow oblast, Russian SFSR, on railroad (Khrapunovo station) and 29 mi. E of Moscow; peat-producing center. Until 1941, called Khrapunovo. 2 Town (1926 pop. 1,173), S Vladimir oblast, Russian SFSR, 16 mi. ENE of Gus-Khrustalny; glassworking.

Vorozhba (vŭrŭzhbä′), town (1926 pop. 1,414), E Sumy oblast, Ukrainian SSR, 30 mi. NW of Sumy; rail junction; metalworks.

Vorpommern, region, Europe: see POMERANIA.

Vorselaar (vôr′sŭlär), town (pop. 4,566), Antwerp prov., NE Belgium, 16 mi. E of Antwerp; agr. market (vegetables, potatoes). Has anc. castle and church.

Vorsfelde (fôrs′fĕl″dŭ), village (pop. 3,291), in Brunswick, NW Germany, after 1945 in Lower Saxony, on Aller R. and Weser-Elbe Canal, and 17 mi. NE of Brunswick, 6 mi. W of Oebisfelde; food processing.

Vorskla River (vôr′sklŭ), in W European USSR, rises SSE of Oboyan in SW Central Russian Upland, flows 260 mi. SSW, past Graivoron, Oposhnya, Poltava, and Kobelyaki, to Dnieper R. 35 mi. SE of Kremenchug.

Vorsma (vôr′smŭ), town (1926 pop. 5,439), W Gorki oblast, Russian SFSR, 7 mi. ENE of Pavlovo; steel-working center; mfg. of surgical instruments (since 1827).

Vorst, Belgium: see FOREST.

Vortsjarv or **Vyrtsyarv,** Est. *Võrtsjärv* (vŭrts′yărv), largest lake (□ 110) of Estonia, in S central hills, 20 mi. W of Tartu; c.20 mi. long, 8 mi. wide, c.20 ft. deep. Traversed N-S by Ema R. Sometimes spelled Virtsyarv.

Voru or **Vyru,** Est. *Võru* (all: vŭ′rōō), Ger. *Werro*, Rus. (until 1917) *Verro* (both: vĕ′rō), city (pop. 5,332), SE Estonia, on railroad and 50 mi. W of Pskov, in flax area; linen milling, sawmilling. Castle ruins. Under Livonian Knights until 1561, when it passed to Poland and later (1629) to Sweden; occupied (1710) by Russia, and inc. into Livonia govt. until 1920.

Vorvads River, Denmark: see GUDEN RIVER.

Vorzel or **Vorzel'** (vŭrzĕl′), town (1926 pop. 1,167), N central Kiev oblast, Ukrainian SSR, on railroad and 17 mi. NW of Kiev.

Vosegus, France: see VOSGES.

Vösendorf (fû′zŭndôrf), town (pop. 3,177), after 1938 in Liesing dist. of Vienna, Austria, 6 mi. S of city center; oil refining; machine mfg.

Vosges (vōzh), department (□ 2,279; pop. 342,315), in Lorraine, E France; ⊙ Épinal. Bounded by crest of the Vosges (E). Occupied by plateau of S Lorraine (center and W). Drained S-N by Moselle (center), Meuse (W), and Meurthe (NE) rivers. Diversified agr. (wheat, beets, potatoes, hemp); orchards. Cheese mfg. (Gérardmer area). Large-scale lumbering in the Vosges. Important granite quarries (Basse-sur-le-Rupt, Senones, Saulxures-sur-Moselotte). Cotton and linen milling carried on throughout the Vosges. Other industries are paper milling, furniture mfg., metal-working. Dept. has several well-known spas: Vittel and Contrexéville (waters bottled and exported), Plombières-les-Bains, Bains-les-Bains, Bussang, and Martigny-les-Bains. Chief towns are Épinal (cotton-weaving center), Saint-Dié (textiles, construction), Remiremont, Gérardmer (linen, cheese), and Mirecourt (stringed musical instruments). After 1871, dept. bordered on Germany. During First World War, front extended across NE section and across the Vosges crests. In Second World War, Germans held Vosges passes in 1944 until outflanked; during their withdrawal, Gérardmer, Saint-Dié, and smaller localities suffered heavy damage.

Vosges or **Vosges Mountains,** Ger. *Vogesen*, anc. *Vosegus* or *Vogesus*, mountain range in E France bet. Alsatian plain (E) and plateau of S Lorraine (W). Pear-shaped, it extends c.120 mi. SSW-NNE from Belfort Gap to Ger. border E of Saar Basin, and is continued in Germany as HARDT MOUNTAINS. Geologically similar to the Black Forest (from which they are separated by the Rhine graben), the Vosges consist of granite (higher Vosges; S) and sandstone formations (N). The gently rounded summits are called *ballons* (Ger. *Belchen*). The slopes (steep in Alsace, gentle in Lorraine) are forested (chiefly by pines) up to c.3,500 ft. The lower E slope is covered with vineyards (Riesling). Highest summits: Ballon de GUEBWILLER (4,672 ft.), Hohneck (4,465 ft.), Ballon d'Alsace (4,100 ft.). Main passes S-N: Bussang (2,398 ft.), Col de la Schlucht (3,737 ft.), Col du Bonhomme (3,113 ft.), SAVERNE GAP (1,086 ft.). The Moselle, Meurthe, and Sarre rise on W slope, the Ill on E slope. Until First World War, when crest formed Franco-Ger. border, no railroads crossed the Vosges. Two lines now form Saint-Dié–Strasbourg and Saint-Dié–Sélestat link, the latter opened 1937. A scenic new road follows crest of S Vosges. U.S. troops occupied the Vosges front in First World War. In 1944, during Second World War, Germans briefly attempted to hold Vosges passes.

Voskopojë (vôskôpô'yû) or **Voskopoja** (-pô'yä), medieval *Moscopolis*, village (1930 pop. 397), SE Albania, 10 mi. W of Koritsa; has numerous ruined 18th-cent. churches. Founded c.1300 by Vlachs, it developed as a leading Gr. economic and cultural center (academy, print shop), flourishing in 18th cent. with an estimated pop. of 40,000. Following its destruction (1768, 1785) by Turks, its pop. abandoned it for Koritsa.

Voskresenovka, Russian SFSR: see MIKOYANOVKA.

Voskresensk (vŭskrĭsyĕnsk'), city (1948 pop. over 10,000), E central Moscow oblast, Russian SFSR, on Moskva R. and 50 mi. SE of Moscow; fertilizer-mfg. center (based on Yegoryevsk phosphorite deposits, E); produces superphosphate, phosphate meal, sulphuric acid. Rail junction (line to Yegoryevsk); railroad shops. Woolen milling at Lopatino (NE). Became city in 1938. Until c.1930, Voskresensk was also the name of another Moscow oblast city, ISTRA.

Voskresenskoye (-syĕn'skŭyŭ). **1** Village (1926 pop. 4,207), SW Bashkir Autonomous SSR, Russian SFSR, 37 mi. SSE of Sterlitamak; sawmilling, lumbering. **2** Village (1926 pop. 2,185), E Gorki oblast, Russian SFSR, on Vetluga R. and 35 mi. E of Semenov; flax, potatoes. **3** Village, Kurgan oblast, Russian SFSR: see KIROVO, village, Kurgan oblast. **4** Village (1939 pop. over 500), SW Ryazan oblast, Russian SFSR, 18 mi. WSW of Dankov; grain, wheat. Formerly called Voskresenskoye-Shilovka. **5** Village (1926 pop. 6,195), central Saratov oblast, Russian SFSR, on right bank of Volga R. (landing) and 25 mi. SW of Volsk; flour milling; wheat, sunflowers. **6** Village (1939 pop. over 500), SW Vologda oblast, Russian SFSR, 20 mi. N of Cherepovets; flax processing, dairying. **7** Village, SW Novosibirsk oblast, Russian SFSR: see ANDREYEVSKOYE.

Vöslau, Austria: see BAD VÖSLAU.

Vosne-Romanée (vōn-rômänā'), village (pop. 536), Côte-d'Or dept., E central France, on E slope of the Côte d'Or, 12 mi. SSW of Dijon; noted Burgundy wines.

Voss (vôs), village (pop. 3,011; canton pop. 9,106), Hordaland co., SW Norway, 40 mi. ENE of Bergen; railroad junction; slate quarries; textile mill. Tourist center. Has Norway's oldest wooden bldgs. (built 1270); folk mus. Village heavily damaged in Second World War. At Vossevangen (sometimes spelled Vossavangen) village, ½ mi. SE, are sanatoriums.

Voss Canal, Germany: see FINOW CANAL.

Vossevangen, Norway: see VOSS.

Vostitsa, Greece: see AIGION.

Vostizza, Greece: see AIGION.

Vostochno-Kazakhstan, oblast, Kazakh SSR: see EAST KAZAKHSTAN.

Vostochno-Sibirskoye More, Russian SFSR: see EAST SIBERIAN SEA.

Vostochny or **Vostochnyy** (vŭstôch'nyē), town (1940 pop. 7,421), S Sakhalin, Russian SFSR, on E coast railroad and 25 mi. S of Makarov; coal mining; fisheries. Under Jap. rule (1905–45), called Motodomari or Mototomari.

Vostok Island (västôk'), uninhabited coral island, Line Isls., S Pacific, 125 mi. W of Caroline Isl.; 10°6'S 152°23'W; ½ mi. long. Discovered 1820 by Russians, claimed by U.S. under Guano Act (1856), now abandoned. Formerly called Stavers Isl.

Voth (vōth), village (1940 pop. 798), Jefferson co., SE Texas, on Neches R. and 8 mi. NW of Beaumont; lumber.

Votiak, Russian SFSR: see UDMURT AUTONOMOUS SOVIET SOCIALIST REPUBLIC.

Votice (vô'tyĭtsĕ), Ger. *Wotitz* (vō'tĭts), town (pop. 1,933), S Bohemia, Czechoslovakia, in NW foothills of Bohemian-Moravian Heights, on railroad and 10 mi. SSW of Benesov; summer resort. Noted for Franciscan abbey with extensive library of 15th- and 16th-cent. volumes; 16th-cent. castle. Several battles of Thirty Years War were fought in vicinity (e.g., at JANKOV).

Votkinsk (vôt'kĭnsk), city (1932 pop. estimate 38,900), E Udmurt Autonomous SSR, Russian SFSR, in W foothills of the central Urals, on small lake formed by right tributary of Kama R., on railroad and 30 mi. NE of Izhevsk. Industrial center; iron smelting, steel casting, mfg. (airplanes, narrow-gauge locomotives, steam boilers, dredgers, agr. machinery, boats, metalware). Founded 1759 (oldest machine works in Urals); destroyed by peasant rebels under Yemelyan Pugachev in 1774. Became city in 1935. Formerly called Votkinski Zavod. Rus. composer Tschaikowsky b. here.

Votorantim (vōōtōōrăntĕn'), town (pop. 5,041), SE São Paulo, Brazil, S suburb of Sorocaba; textile mills.

Vottem (vôtĕm'), agr. village (pop. 6,206), Liége prov., E Belgium, 2 mi. N of Liége.

Votuporanga (vōōtōōpôrăng'gŭ), city, NW São Paulo, Brazil, 45 mi. NW of São José do Rio Prêto; temporary rail terminus (as of 1948) in expanding zone of pioneer settlements; cotton gins.

Votyak, Russian SFSR: see UDMURT AUTONOMOUS SOVIET SOCIALIST REPUBLIC.

Vouga River (vō'gŭ), N central Portugal, rises in Serra da Lapa (NE Viseu dist.), flows 84 mi. WSW, past São Pedro do Sul, to the Atlantic W of Aveiro, where it forms a shallow lagoon (□ 25). A dredged channel across sand bar gives fishing vessels access to Aveiro. Harnessed for hydroelectric power.

Vougeot (vōō-zhō'), village (pop. 192), Côte-d'Or dept., E central France, on E slope of the Côte d'Or, 10 mi. SSW of Dijon; Burgundy wines.

Vouillé (vōōyā'), village (pop. 844), Vienne dept., W central France, 10 mi. WNW of Poitiers. The decisive battle of Vouillé (507), in which Clovis defeated the Visigoths and killed Alaric II, was probably fought at Voulon (20 mi. S).

Voujeaucourt (vōō-zhōkōōr'), SW suburb (pop. 1,832) of Montbéliard, Doubs dept., E France, on Doubs R. and Rhone-Rhine Canal.

Voulgarelion (vōōlgŭrä'lēōn), village (pop. 1,843), Arta nome, S Epirus, Greece, 17 mi. NE of Arta, at foot of the Tzoumerka; olive oil; almonds, pears, peaches. Also spelled Voulgharelion.

Voulgaris River, Greece: see TITARESIOS RIVER.

Vouliagmene or **Vouliagmeni** (both: vōōlyägmä'nē), seaside resort (pop. 694) of Athens, Greece, on Saronic Gulf, 12 mi. SSE of Athens, in metropolitan dist.; sulphur springs, mud baths.

Voulkaria, Lake (vōōlkärēä'), Ionian coastal lagoon (□ 6.1), in Acarnania nome, W central Greece, S of Gulf of Arta, near Vonitsa; 3 mi. long, 2 mi. wide; fisheries.

Voulpaix (vōōpā'), village (pop. 426), Aisne dept., N France, 4 mi. W of Vervins; carton factory.

Voulte-sur-Rhône, La (lä vōōt-sür-rōn'), town (pop. 2,526), Ardèche dept., S France, on right bank of Rhone R. and 10 mi. ENE of Privas; lime- and cementworks, rayon factory. Has 14th–16th-cent. castle and old houses.

Vouneuil-sur-Vienne (vōōnû'ē-sür-vyĕn'), village (pop. 312), Vienne dept., W central France, near Vienne R., 7 mi. S of Châtellerault; winegrowing, cattle raising.

Vouraikos River (both: vōōrĭkôs'), Lat. *Buraicus* (bŭrā'ĭkŭs) in N Peloponnesus, Greece, rises in Erymanthos mts., flows c.25 mi. NE, past Kalavryta, to Gulf of Corinth at Diakopton; site of hydroelectric plants.

Vourinos (vōō'rĭnôs), mountain in Greek Macedonia, rises to 6,122 ft. 10 mi. SW of Kozane. Also called Burono.

Vouri River, Fr. Cameroons: see WOURI RIVER.

Vouvray (vōōvrā'), village (pop. 1,567), Indre-et-Loire dept., W central France, on Loire R. and 5 mi. E of Tours; noted for its sparkling white and rosé wines.

Vouxa, Cape (vōōk'sŭ), or **Cape Gramvousa** (grämvōō'sŭ), NW extremity of Crete, on Aegean Sea, W of gulf of Kisamos; 35°37'N 23°35'E. Sometimes spelled Grabusa.

Vouzela (vōzā'lŭ), town (pop. 1,370), Viseu dist., N Portugal, 11 mi. NW of Viseu; resort on Vouga R. at N foot of wooded Serra do Caramulo. Has 13th-cent. church.

Vouziers (vōōzyā'), town (pop. 2,888), Ardennes dept., N France, on Aisne R. and 25 mi. S of Mézières, at edge of the Argonne; agr. trade center; baggage mfg., basket weaving. Hippolyte Taine b. here.

Voves (vôv), village (pop. 1,369), Eure-et-Loir dept., N central France, in the Beauce, 13 mi. SSE of Chartres; rail junction; chemical, fertilizer mfg.

Voxna River, Swedish *Voxna älv* (vôks'nä ĕlv'), N central Sweden, rises SE of Sveg, flows SE to Edsbyn, then E past Alfta to Ljusna R. at Bollnas; 100 mi. long.

Voyampolka (voi-ŭmpôl'kŭ), village, S Koryak Natl. Okrug, Kamchatka oblast, Khabarovsk Territory, Russian SFSR, near NW coast of Kamchatka Peninsula, 50 mi. SSW of Palana; extensive petroleum fields.

Voyevodskoye (vŭyŭvôt'skŭyŭ), village (1948 pop. over 500), E Altay Territory, Russian SFSR, 22 mi. NE of Bisk, in agr. area.

Voykovo, Ukrainian SSR: see VOIKOVO.

Voykovskiy, Ukrainian SSR: see VOIKOVSKI.

Voynilov, Ukrainian SSR: see VOINILOV.

Voyvodina, Yugoslavia: see VOJVODINA.

Voy-Vozh, Russian SFSR: see VOI-VOZH.

Voza, Col de (kôl dŭ vôzä'), Alpine saddle (alt. 5,948 ft.), Haute-Savoie dept., SE France, 6 mi. NW of Mont Blanc, on rack-and-pinion railway from Saint-Gervais-les-Bains to Bionnassay glacier; hotel; winter sports.

Vozdvizhenskoye (vŭzdvēzhĕn'skŭyŭ), village (1926 pop. 948), E Gorki oblast, Russian SFSR, 45 mi. ENE of Semenov; flax, potatoes.

Vozhayel or **Vozhayel'** (vŭzhŭyĕl'), town (1942 pop. over 500), W Komi Autonomous SSR, Russian SFSR, near N.Pechora RR, 21 mi. NE of Zheleznodorozhny.

Vozhd Proletariata or **Vozhd' Proletariata** (vôzhd'yŭ prŭlyĭtŭrēä'tŭ), town (1939 pop. over 500), E Moscow oblast, Russian SFSR, 11 mi. ENE of Yegoryevsk; cotton milling.

Vozhe, Lake (vô'zhĭ) (□ 170), in N European Russian SFSR, on border of Archangel and Vologda oblasts, 40 mi. WSW of Konosha; 26 mi. long, 9 mi. wide, up to 13 ft. deep; swampy; forested banks. Receives Vozhega R. (E; 85 mi. long). Outlet, Svid R. (N). Sometimes called L. Charonda for Charonda village (on W shore; once a trading center on Onega route).

Vozhega (vô'zhĭgŭ), town (1939 pop. over 2,000), N Vologda oblast, Russian SFSR, on railroad and 85 mi. N of Vologda; lumbering; coarse grain.

Vozhgaly (vôzh'gŭlē), village (1926 pop. 254), central Kirov oblast, Russian SFSR, 34 mi. SE of Kirov; flax processing.

Voznesenka (vŭznyĭsyĕnkŭ), village (1948 pop. over 2,000), N Akmolinsk oblast, Kazakh SSR, 17 mi. SSW of Makinsk, in cattle area; metalworks.

Voznesensk (vŭznyĭsyĕnsk'), city (1926 pop. 21,587), W Nikolayev oblast, Ukrainian SSR, on the Southern Bug (landing) and 50 mi. NW of Nikolayev, in agr. area (wheat, rice); metalworking, fruit and vegetable canning, flour milling, dairying. Passed 1774 to Russia; was ⊙ of a former govt. before its transfer to Kherson.

Voznesenskaya Manufaktura, Russian SFSR: see KRASNOARMEISK, Moscow oblast.

Voznesenskoye (-syĕn'skŭyŭ), village (1926 pop. 2,239), SW Gorki oblast, Russian SFSR, 38 mi. SE of Vyksa; potatoes.

Voznesenye or **Voznesen'ye** (-syĕ'nyĭ). **1** Village (1939 pop. over 500), N Archangel oblast, Russian SFSR, on isl. in Northern Dvina R. delta mouth, 5 mi. WNW of Archangel; fisheries. **2** Town (1926 pop. 2,856), NE Leningrad oblast, Russian SFSR, port on L. Onega, at outlet of Svir R., 65 mi. SE of Petrozavodsk; metalworks.

Vozrozhdeniye Island, Kazakh SSR: see ARAL SEA.

Vraa (vrô), town (pop. 1,736), Hjorring amt, N Jutland, Denmark, 7 mi. S of Hjorring; automobile-body mfg.

Vrable (vrä'blĕ), Slovak *Vráble*, town (pop. 3,148), SW Slovakia, Czechoslovakia, on railroad and 11 mi. ESE of Nitra; wheat, potatoes.

Vrabnitsa (vrŭb'nĭtsä), village (pop. 4,069), Sofia dist., W Bulgaria, just N of Sofia; poultry, dairying, truck.

Vracene, Belgium: see VRASENE.

Vrachesh (vrä'chĕsh), village (pop. 3,995), Sofia dist., W Bulgaria, in Botevgrad Basin, 3 mi. WSW of Botevgrad; dairying, hog raising, fruit, truck.

Vrachneika or **Vrakhneika** (both: vräkhnā'kŭ), town (pop. 1,874), Achaea nome, N Peloponnesus, Greece, on railroad and 6 mi. SSW of Patras; Zante currants, wine, wheat. Formerly called Hagios Vasileios.

Vrachori, town, Greece: see AGRINION.

Vrachori, Lake, Greece: see TRICHONIS, LAKE.

Vradeton or **Vradheton,** Greece: see TYMPHE.

Vrakhneika, Greece: see VRACHNEIKA.

Vrakhori, town, Greece: see AGRINION.

Vrakhori, Lake, Greece: see TRICHONIS, LAKE.

Vra Lake (vrô), Nor. *Vråvatn* or *Vrådalsvatn*, Telemark co., S Norway, 45 mi. W of Skien; 11 mi. long, 1 mi. wide; alt. 804 ft. Short 1-mi. canal (with locks) joins it to Nisser L. (S). Sometimes spelled Vraa.

Vran, range, Yugoslavia: see VRAN MOUNTAINS.

Vrana Lake (vrä'nä), Serbo-Croatian *Vransko Jezero* (vrän'skô yĕ'zĕrô), Ital. *Lago di Vrana* (lä'gô dĕvrä'nä), W Croatia, Yugoslavia, near Adriatic Sea, in Dalmatia; 8 mi. long, 1–2 mi. wide; northernmost point 4 mi. E of Biograd.

Vrana River, Bulgaria: see GOLYAMA KAMCHIYA RIVER.

Vrane, Czechoslovakia: see STECHOVICE.

Vrangelya, Ostrov, Russian SFSR: see WRANGEL ISLAND.

Vrango (vräng'û"), Swedish *Vrangö*, fishing village (pop. 340), Goteborg och Bohus co., SW Sweden, on isl. (585 acres) of same name in the Kattegat, 10 mi. SW of Goteborg.

Vranica Mountains or **Vranitsa Mountains** (both: vrä'nĭtsä), in Dinaric Alps, central Bosnia, Yugoslavia, along right bank of upper Vrbas R.; c.10 mi. long N-S. Highest peak (6,911 ft.) is 8 mi. E of Gornji Vakuf.

Vranje or **Vranye** (both: vrä'nyĕ), town (pop. 12,404), S Serbia, Yugoslavia, on left bank of the Southern Morava, on railroad and 50 mi. S of Nis; metal, textile, shoe, and soap industries. Wine, hemp, and quince grown in vicinity. Under Turkish rule until 1878; held by Bulgaria, 1941–44. Formerly Vranja. **Vranjska Banja, Vranska Banya, or Vran'ska Banya,** health resort, with waters of up to 190°F., is 5 mi. E of town, across river.

Vran Mountains (vrän), in Dinaric Alps, Yugoslavia, on Bosnia-Herzegovina line; c.5-mi. long. Highest point, Veliki Vran (6,803 ft.), is 13 mi. W of Jablanica.

Vranov (vrä'nôf). **1** Ger. *Frain* (frīn), village (pop. 870), S Moravia, Czechoslovakia, on Dyje R. and 12 mi. WNW of Znojmo; recreation center; ceramics industry. A large reservoir with dam and hydroelectric works has been formed just W (upstream) by flooding former site of Bitov (bē'tôf), Czech *Bítov*. **2** Hung. *Varannó* (vŏ'rôn-nō), town (pop. 3,964), E Slovakia, Czechoslovakia, on Topla R. and 21 mi. ESE of Presov; rail junction; wheat trade. Mercury mining at Mernik, 5 mi. NNW. Formed (1946) by union of Vranov nad Toplou and Vranovske Dlhe.

Vranovske Dlhe, Czechoslovakia: see VRANOV, Slovakia.

Vranska Banya, Yugoslavia: see VRANJE.

Vranye, Yugoslavia: see VRANJE.

Vrasene (vräʹsůnů), agr. village (pop. 3,900), East Flanders prov., N Belgium, 4 mi. NNE of St-Nicolas. Formerly spelled Vracene.

Vrashka-chuka Pass (vräshʹkä-chōōʹkä) (alt. 1,165 ft.), on Bulgarian-Yugoslav border, in Babin-nos Mts., 8 mi. WSW of Kula (Bulgaria), on road to Zajecar (Yugoslavia). Coal mines near by. Just S is Vrashka-chuka peak (c.2,200 ft.).

Vratimov (vräʹtyĭmôf), village (pop. 2,609), E Silesia, Czechoslovakia, on Ostravice R., on railroad and 5 mi. SSE of Ostrava; cellulose mfg.

Vratislavice nad Nisou (vräʹtyĭslävĭtsĕ nädʹ nĭʺsō), town (pop. 4,455), N Bohemia, Czechoslovakia, on Lusatian Neisse R., on railroad and 2 mi. SE of Liberec; carpet mfg.

Vratnik Pass (vrätʹnĭk) (alt. 3,590 ft.), E central Bulgaria, 10 mi. N of Sliven, on highway to Yelena (NW); separates central and eastern Balkan mts.

Vratsa (vräʹtsä), city (pop. 19,448), ⊙ Vratsa dist. (formed 1949), NW Bulgaria, on N slope of Vratsa Mts., 36 mi. NNE of Sofia; agr. center for Vratsa lowland (vineyards, mulberry groves); mfg. (silk textiles, carriages, furniture, steel safes). Has teachers col., ironworking and textile institutes, silkworm experiment station. Founded in 15th cent. Until 1945 spelled Vrattsa. Was ⊙ former Vratsa oblast (1934–47).

Vratsa Mountains, NW Bulgaria, part of W Balkan Mts., bet. Vratsa (N) and Iskar R. (S); extend W to Petrokhan Pass. Sparse pastureland. Copper, lead, and zinc deposits.

Vrattsa, Bulgaria: see VRATSA, city.

Vrbanja River or **Vrbanya River** (both: vŭrbäʹnyĕ), N central Bosnia, Yugoslavia, rises 9 mi. N of Travnic, flows c.45 mi. NNW, past Kotor Varos, to Vrbas R. just NE of Banja Luka.

Vrbas (vŭrʹbäs), Hung. *Verbász* (vĕrʹbäsh), village (pop. 15,562), Vojvodina, N Serbia, Yugoslavia, on Danube-Tisa Canal (railroad bridge) and 24 mi. NNW of Novi Sad, in the Backa. Flour milling, mfg. of sugar, molasses, dried beet pulp, matches; beekeeping. Includes Novi Vrbas, Hung. *Ujverbász*, and (across the canal) Stari Vrbas, Hung. *Óverbász*.

Vrbas River, Bosnia, Yugoslavia, rises on Herzegovina border 5 mi. WSW of Fojnica, flows 149 mi. N, past Bugojno, Jajce, and Banja Luka, to Sava R. 10 mi. E of Gradiska. Navigable for 48 mi. Receives Vrbanja R.

Vrbica, Bulgaria: see VARBITSA MOUNTAINS.

Vrbnik (vŭrbʹnĭk), Ital. *Verbenico* (vĕrbāʹnēkô), village, NW Croatia, Yugoslavia, on Krk Isl., on Adriatic Sea, 6 mi. NE of Krk; seaside resort; trade center for winegrowing area. Castle. Earliest monuments with Glagolitic inscriptions found here.

Vrbno (vŭrbʹnô), Ger. *Würbenthal* (vürʹbüntäl), village (pop. 2,327), W Silesia, Czechoslovakia, in the Jeseniky, on Opava R., at confluence of its 3 headstreams, and 37 mi. NNE of Olomouc; rail terminus; jute processing, mfg. of sewing supplies. Scenic health resort (alt. 2,624 ft.) of Karlova Studanka (kärʹlôvä stōōʹdänkä), Czech *Karlova Studánka*, Ger. *Karlsbrunn* (kärlzʹbrōōn), with peat baths and springs, is 5 mi. SSW, at E foot of Praded mtn.

Vrbovec (vŭrʹbôvĕts), village (pop. 3,529), N Croatia, Yugoslavia, 21 mi. E of Zagreb, in Slavonia.

Vrbovsko (vŭrʹbôfskô), village, NW Croatia, Yugoslavia, on Dobra R., on railroad and 10 mi. NNW of Ogulin; local trade center; lumbering, match mfg. Orthodox Eastern monastery 3 mi. S.

Vrchlabi (vŭrʹkhläbē), Czech *Vrchlabí*, Ger. *Hohenelbe* (hōʹünĕlbů), town (pop. 5,992), NE Bohemia, Czechoslovakia, in foothills of the Riesengebirge, on Elbe R. and 26 mi. ESE of Liberec; rail terminus; linen and cotton spinning, paper mills. Has 16th-cent. castle (formerly of counts Czernin), 17th-cent. Augustinian abbey, 18th-cent. town hall.

Vrchoslav, Czechoslovakia: see KRUPKA.

Vrdnik (vŭrdʹnĭk), village, Vojvodina, N Serbia, Yugoslavia, 8 mi. SSW of Novi Sad, in Fruska Gora; rail terminus; brown-coal mine. Deposits of building stone and marble.

Vrede (frēʹdů, vrēd), town (pop. 4,153), E Orange Free State, U. of So. Afr., 60 mi. N of Harrismith; alt. 5,457 ft.; rail terminus; agr. center (corn, wheat, sheep, horses); grain elevator. Was temporary ⊙ Orange Free State Republic for short period following May 20, 1900.

Vredefort (frēʹdůfōōrtʺ), town (pop. 1,762), N Orange Free State, U. of So. Afr., 40 mi. SW of Vereeniging; alt. 4,668 ft.; rail terminus; stock, tobacco, fruit.

Vreden (frāʹdůn), town (pop. 5,310), in former Prussian prov. of Westphalia, NW Germany, after 1945 in North Rhine-Westphalia, 15 mi. SW of Gronau, near Dutch border; grain, cattle.

Vredenburgh (vrēʹdůnbûrg), town (pop. 796), Monroe and Wilcox cos., SW Ala., 45 mi. SSW of Selma; lumber.

Vreed-en-Hoop (vrēdʹůn-hōōpʹ), village (pop. 2,090), ⊙ West Demerara dist., Demerara co., N Br. Guiana, on the Atlantic, on left bank of Demerara R. mouth, opposite Georgetown (linked by ferry); terminus of railroad from Parika (16 mi. W) on Essequibo estuary, in fertile agr. region (sugar cane, rice, stock).

Vreeland (vrāʹlänt), village (pop. 972), Utrecht prov., W central Netherlands, on Vecht R. and 10 mi. NNW of Utrecht, in Loosdrechtsche Plassen lake area, surrounded by clay and fenland; agr., truck gardening, cattle raising, peat digging.

Vreeswijk (vrāʹsvĭk), town (pop. 3,317), Utrecht prov., W central Netherlands, on Merwede Canal and 6 mi. S of Utrecht, at junction of Lek R. and Hollandsche Ijssel R. Shipping center; cattle raising, agr. Sometimes spelled Vreeswyk.

Vretstorp (vrātsʹtôrpʺ), village (pop. 946), Orebro co., S central Sweden, 12 mi. SW of Kumla; metalworking, hosiery knitting, sawmilling.

Vrgin Most or **Vrginmost** (vŭrʹgĭn môstʹ), village (pop. 1,644), Croatia, Yugoslavia, on railroad and 17 mi. SE of Karlovac, at NE foot of Petrova Gora; local trade center.

Vrgorac (vŭrʹgôräts), village, S Croatia, Yugoslavia, 50 mi. ESE of Split, in Dalmatia, near Herzegovina border. Asphalt deposits mined since 1753.

Vrhnika (vŭrkhʹnĭkä), Ger. *Oberlaibach* (ōʹbůrlīʺbäkh), Ital. *Nauporto* (noupōrʹtô), anc. *Nauportus*, village, W Slovenia, Yugoslavia, on Ljubljanica R. and 11 mi. SW of Ljubljana; terminus of rail spur to Ljubljana; local trade center; leather factory. Founded (388 B.C.) by Celts. Until 1918, in Carniola.

Vrhovine (vŭrʹkhôvēnĕ), village, W Croatia, Yugoslavia, on railroad and 21 mi. N of Gospic. Starting point of excursions to PLITVICE LAKES.

Vriddhachalam (vrĭd-däʹchŭlům), town (pop. 8,876), South Arcot dist., SE Madras, India, 33 mi. SW of Cuddalore; rail junction; peanuts, sesame, timber (acacia); cotton ginning and weaving. Early Dravidian temples. Lignite deposits near by. Sometimes spelled Viruddhachalam.

Vridsloselille (vrĭsʹlůsůlĭʺlů), Dan. *Vridsløselille*, town (pop. 1,409), Copenhagen amt, Zealand, Denmark, 10 mi. W of Copenhagen.

Vries (vrēs), town (pop. 911), Drenthe prov., N Netherlands, 6 mi. N of Assen; cattle market; milk-can mfg. Founded in 13th cent. as Frisian colony; may have been site of 8th-cent. church dedicated by Bonifacius. Prehistoric graves. Sometimes spelled Fries.

Vries Island, Japan: see O-SHIMA, Izu-shichito.

Vries Strait, Russian SFSR: see FRIZ STRAIT.

Vriezenveen or **Friezenveen** (v–, frēʹzůnvān), town (pop. 6,017), Overijssel prov., E Netherlands, near Overijssel Canal, 4 mi. NNW of Almelo; wool and cotton weaving and knitting; cement, strawboard.

Vrigne-aux-Bois (vrēʹnyōbwäʹ), town (pop. 2,620), Ardennes dept., N France, at foot of the Ardennes, 5 mi. NW of Sedan; iron, copper, and bronze foundries.

Vrigstad (vrēkʹstäʺ), village (pop. 708), Jonkoping co., S Sweden, 19 mi. NE of Varnamo; agr. market (grain, stock); light industries.

Vrindaban, India: see BRINDABAN.

Vrnjci, Vrntsi, or **Vrnʹtsi** (all: vŭrʹnyůtsē), village, S central Serbia, Yugoslavia, on the Western Morava, on railroad and 22 mi. W of Krusevac; health resort, noted for treatment of internal disorders. Also called Vrnjacka Banja or Vrnyachka Banya, Serbo-Croatian *Vrnjačka Banja*.

Vrontades or **Vrondadhes** (both: vrôndäʹdhĭs), city (pop. 5,711), on Chios isl., Greece, 4 mi. N of Chios city; olive oil, wheat, citrus fruit.

Vrouwen-Parochie, Netherlands: see 'T BILDT.

Vrsac or **Vrshats** (both: vŭrʹshäts), Serbo-Croatian *Vršac*, Ger. *Werschetz* (vĕrʹshĕts), Hung. *Versec* (vĕrʹshĕts), city (pop. 24,571), Vojvodina, NE Serbia, Yugoslavia, 45 mi. ENE of Belgrade, in the Banat. Rail junction (lines to Belgrade, Zrenjanin, Rumania); trade center (meat, wine, fruit); meat packing, mfg. of woolen and felt hats. Winegrowing in vicinity. Vrsac Canal, Serbo-Croatian *Vršački Kanal*, a branch of Timis Canal, is WNW.

Vrsovice (vŭrʹshôvĭtsĕ), Czech *Vršovice*, SE suburb of Prague, Czechoslovakia; workers' homes.

Vrucica, Yugoslavia: see TESLIC.

Vrutky (vrōōtʹkĭ), Slovak *Vrútky*, Hung. *Ruttka* (rōōtʹkô), town (pop. 5,927), NW Slovakia, Czechoslovakia, on Vah R. and 11 mi. SE of Zilina; rail junction (repair shops).

Vryburg (frīʹbûrg, frāʹ–), town (pop. 7,216), ⊙ Bechuanaland dist., NE Cape Prov., U. of So. Afr., near Transvaal border, 130 mi. N of Kimberley; stock center; dairying, malting, bone-meal milling, soap mfg.; site of govt. livestock experimental station. It was ⊙ of former Stellaland republic, a state founded 1883 and proclaimed crown colony (1885) together with Bechuanaland.

Vryheid (fräʹhāt) [Du.,=liberty], town (pop. 7,971), N Natal, U. of So. Afr., 150 mi. N of Durban; coal and iron mining; agr. center (corn, sugar, citrus fruit, tobacco, wattle bark, lumber). Alumina deposits near by; copper formerly mined here. Has Anglican cathedral, seat of bishop of Zululand. Just E is Vryheid East (pop. 1,349). Region ceded (1884) to Boers by Zulu chief Dinizulu; town became ⊙ "New Republic," inc. 1888 in South African Republic; ceded 1902 to Natal.

Vsekhsvyatskoye, Kazakh SSR: see URITSKOYE.

Vselug, Lake (fůsyĕʹlōōg), one of upper Volga lakes, Kalinin oblast, Russian SFSR, bet. lakes Sterzh (N) and Peno; 9 mi. long.

Vsetaty (fůshĕʹtätĭ), Czech *Všetaty*, village (pop. 1,636), N central Bohemia, Czechoslovakia, 16 mi. NNE of Prague; rail junction; truck-farming center (early potatoes, onions, cucumbers).

Vsetin (fůsĕʹtyēn), Czech *Vsetín*, Ger. *Wsetin* (fsāʹtĭn), town (pop. 12,554), E Moravia, Czechoslovakia, in the Beskids, on Horni Becva R., on railroad and 16 mi. NE of Gottwaldov; mfg. of bentwood furniture; noted armaments production.

Vsevidof, Mount (vůsēʹvůdôf) (7,236 ft.), SW Alaska, on W Umnak Isl., Aleutian Isls., 15 mi. NNE of Nikolski; 53°8′N 168°42′W; snow-covered volcano.

Vsevolodo-Vilva or **Vsevolodo-Vilʹva** (fůsyĕʹvůlůdů-vēlʹvů), town (1932 pop. estimate 4,300), E central Molotov oblast, Russian SFSR, on railroad and 15 mi. NW of Kizel; wood cracking, charcoal burning. Developed prior to First World War.

Vsevolozhski or **Vsevolozhskiy** (fůsyĕʹvůlůshskē), residential town (pop. 1,324), N Leningrad oblast, Russian SFSR, 13 mi. NE of Leningrad.

Vskhody (fůskhôʹdē), village (1948 pop. over 2,000), E Smolensk oblast, Russian SFSR, on Ugra R. and 37 mi. S of Vyazma; dairying, flax processing.

Vtoroi Orochen or **Vtoroy Orochen** (ftůroiʹ ŭrůchĕnʹ) town (1948 pop. over 500), SE Yakut Autonomous SSR, Russian SFSR, on Yakutsk-Never highway and 7 mi. S of Aldan; gold mines. Formerly Sredne-Serebrovsk.

Vtorye Levye Lamki or **Vtoryye Levyye Lamki** (ftŭrēʹů lyĕʹvēů lämʹkē) [Rus.,=Levye Lamki No. 2], village (1939 pop. over 2,000), N Tambov oblast, Russian SFSR, at Lamki station, 27 mi. WSW of Morshansk; grain, potatoes.

Vtorye Terbuny or **Vtoryye Terbuny** (tyĭrbōōʹnē), village (1939 pop. over 2,000), NE Kursk oblast, Russian SFSR, 40 mi. NW of Voronezh; wheat, potatoes.

Vuadil or **Vuadilʹ** (vōōůdyēlʹ), village (1926 pop. 5,232), SE Fergana oblast, Uzbek SSR, 15 mi. S of Fergana; cotton.

Vuazi (vwäʹzē), village, Leopoldville prov., W Belgian Congo, near railroad, 140 mi. ENE of Boma. Has experimental station for fruit production; growing of native foodstuffs.

Vuchitrn, Yugoslavia: see VUCITRN.

Vucht, Netherlands: see VUGHT.

Vucitrn or **Vuchitrn** (both: vōōʹchētůrn), Serbo-Croatian *Vučitrn*, village (pop. 5,577), S Serbia, Yugoslavia, on Sitnica R., on railroad and 7 mi. SE of Mitrovica, in the Kosovo.

Vuelta, La, Colombia: see LA VUELTA.

Vuelta Abajo (bwĕlʹtä äbäʹhō), region (c.90 mi. long, 10 mi. wide), Pinar del Río prov., W Cuba, along S piedmont of the Sierra de los Órganos and Sierra del Rosario. Famous for the fine quality of its tobacco, supplying about ½ of the Cuban crop. Main centers are Pinar del Río, San Juan y Martínez, and San Luis. Vuelta Abajo in a wider sense comprises the isl.'s entire region W of the meridian of Havana.

Vuelta del Ombú, Argentina: see GOBERNADOR VIRASORO.

Vueltas or **San Antonio de las Vueltas** (sänʹ äntōʹnyō dā läs bwĕlʹtäs), town (pop. 1,400), Las Villas prov., central Cuba, 15 mi. ENE of Santa Clara, in Remedios tobacco-growing region; also raises sugar cane, fruit, cattle, hogs. Mfg. of cigars. The central of Carmita is 5 mi. W.

Vueltas, Cerro de las (sĕʹrō dā läs), peak (10,128 ft.) in the Cordillera de Talamanca, S central Costa Rica, 3 mi. SE of Copey.

Vught or **Vucht** (both: vůkht), town (pop. 13,784), North Brabant prov., S central Netherlands, 2 mi. S of 's Hertogenbosch; furniture, strawboard; truck gardening. Lunatic asylum. Site of Nazi concentration camp in Second World War.

Vuillafans (vwēyäfäʹ), village (pop. 553), Doubs dept., E France, on the Loue and 15 mi. SE of Besançon, in the central Jura; distilling, sawmilling, nail mfg.

Vuka River (vōōʹkä), NE Croatia, Yugoslavia, in Slavonia; rises 15 mi. NNE of Slavonski Brod, flows c.80 mi. E to the Danube at Vukovar.

Vukovar (vōōkôʹvär), Hung. *Vukovár* (vōōkʹôvär), anc. *Valdasus*, town (pop. 14,813), NE Croatia, Yugoslavia, on the Danube (Serbia border) at mouth of the Vuka, 20 mi. SE of Osijek, in Slavonia. Major trade center and river port; mfg. (textiles, leather goods, flour); fishing. Gardens in vicinity. Has remains of Roman castle. Until 1918, ⊙ Srem.

Vulcan, town (pop. 786), S Alta., 50 mi. SE of Calgary; oil production; grain elevators, flour mills.

Vulcan (vōōlkänʹ). **1** Hung. *Zsilyvajdejvulkán* (zhĕlʹyůvoidĕĭvōōlʺkän), village (pop. 5,959), Hunedoara prov., W central Rumania, in the Transylvanian Alps, on headstream of Jiu R., on railroad and 6 mi. SW of Petraseni; coal-mining center; mfg. of activated carbon and gas masks; rubber processing. **2** Hung. *Szacvolkány* (sŏchʹvôlʺkänyů), village (pop. 2,389), Stalin prov., central Rumania, 8 mi. W of Stalin (Brasov); lignite-mining center; lumbering, flour milling. Has 17th-cent. fortified church. About 50% pop. are Germans.

Vulcan, village (1940 pop. 873), Dickinson co., SW Upper Peninsula, Mich., 10 mi. ESE of Iron Mountain.

Vulcana, Rumania: see Pucioasa.

Vulcanesti, Moldavian SSR: see Vulkaneshty.

Vulcan Island, Territory of New Guinea: see Manam.

Vulcan Mountain, Wyo.: see Sierra Madre.

Vulcan Mountains, section of the Transylvanian Alps, W central Rumania, bet. Oltenia and Transylvania; extend NNE-WSW for c.25 mi. along right bank of upper Jiu R.; rise to 6,133 ft. Extensive forests. Numerous shepherds' settlements noted for ewe-cheese making.

Vulcano (vōōlkä'nō), anc. *Hiera* and *Vulcania,* island (□ 8; pop. 401), southernmost of Lipari Isls., in Tyrrhenian Sea off NE Sicily, 16 mi. NNW of Milazzo; 5 mi. long, 3 mi. wide. Separated from Lipari (N) by channel ½ mi. wide. Consists of volcanoes of Gran Cratere (1,266 ft. high; continuously active within historic times) in center, Monte Aria (1,637 ft. high) in S, and Vulcanello (403 ft. high; erupted in 183 B.C., according to Orosius) in N. Last major eruptions 1888–89. Sometimes spelled Volcano.

Vulcan Pass, Rumania: see Surduc Pass.

Vulkaneshty (vōōlkŭnyĕsh'tē), Rum. *Vulcănești* vōōlkŭnĕsht'), village (1941 pop. 7,401), S Moldavian SSR, on small Kagul R. and 16 mi. SE of Kagul; corn, barley; karakul sheep.

Vulpera, Switzerland: see Tarasp.

Vulture Mountains, Maricopa co., W central Ariz., SW of Wickenburg, W of Hassayampa R.; rise to c.3,000 ft.

Vulturesti (vōōltōōrĕsht'), Rum. *Vulturești,* village (pop. 547), Valcea prov., S Rumania, 18 mi. NNW of Slatina.

Vumba Mountains (vōōm'bä), E Southern Rhodesia, near Mozambique border, just SSE of Umtali; rise to 6,268 ft.

Vungliem (vōōng'lyĕm'), town, Vinhlong prov., S Vietnam, in Mekong delta, 18 mi. SE of Vinhlong; rice center.

Vuoksenniska (vōō'ōksĕn-nĭs"kä), village in Ruokolahti commune (pop. 8,227), Kymi co., SE Finland, near USSR border, at E end of L. Saimaa, near mouth of Vuoksi R., 25 mi. ENE of Lappeenranta; lake port; iron, steel, lumber, and pulp mills.

Vuoksi River (vōō'ōksē), Finland and USSR, issues from L. Saimaa near Vuoksenniska, flows c.100 mi. SE, past Tainionkoski, Svetogorsk, and Kamennogorsk, and through the lakes of the Karelian Isthmus to L. Ladoga in 2 mouths, one at Priozersk and the other 30 mi. SSE of Priozersk. Feeds several hydroelectric plants.

Vuolijoki (vōō'ōlĭyō"kē), village (commune pop. 2,696), Oulu co., central Finland, on SW shore of L. Oulu, 20 mi. W of Kajaani; magnetite and ilmenite deposits.

Vuri River, Fr. Cameroons: see Wouri River.

Vurnary (vōōrnä'rē), town (1948 pop. over 2,000), central Chuvash Autonomous SSR, Russian SFSR, on railroad and 20 mi. W of Kanash; mfg. of phosphorite-based chemicals (deposits near by); food processing.

Vutcani (vōōt'kän), village (pop. 3,531), Galati prov., E Rumania, 14 mi. NW of Falciu; flour milling.

Vuyyuru (vōōyōō'rōō), town (pop. 9,625), Kistna dist., NE Madras, India, in Kistna R. delta, 24 mi. NW of Masulipatam; rice and sugar milling; jaggery. Industrial school. Formerly also spelled Wuyyur.

Vvedenka (vĭdyĕn'kŭ). **1** Village (1926 pop. 2,554), N Kustanai oblast, Kazakh SSR, on Tobol R. and 50 mi. N of Kustanai; wheat, cattle. **2** Town (1926 pop. 2,971), N central Kharkov oblast, Ukrainian SSR, 8 mi. W of Chuguyev, in Kharkov metropolitan area; truck produce.

Vyandra, Estonia: see Vandra.

Vyara (vyä'rŭ), town (pop. 7,151), Surat dist., N Bombay, India, 36 mi. E of Surat; market center for pulse, cotton, rice, millet; cotton ginning.

Vyartsilya (vyär'tsēlyŭ), Finnish *Värsilä* (văr'sĭlä), town (1948 pop. over 500), SW Karelo-Finnish SSR, on Finnish border, on railroad and 30 mi. N of Sortavala; iron smelting, nail mfg.; machine shop. In Finland until 1940.

Vyatka, Russian SFSR: see Kirov, city, Kirov oblast.

Vyatka River (vyät'kŭ), in E central European Russian SFSR, rises S of Omutninsk in W foothills of the central Urals, flows N, SW, past Slobodskoi, Kirov, Khalturin, and Kotelnich, and SSE, past Sovetsk (crossing the Vyatka Uval), Vyatskiye Polyany and Mamadysh, to Kama R. below Mamadysh; 849 mi. long. Frozen Nov.-April; important for lumber floating. Receives Cheptsa and Kilmez rivers (left).

Vyatka Uval (ōōväl'), Rus. *Vyatskiy Uval* (-skē), one of the moraine uplands [Rus. *uvaly*] in E central European Russian SFSR; extends from area N of Kazan c.150 mi. N to Kirov; rises to 1,755 ft.; marl and limestone formations. Vyatka R. breaks through its central section.

Vyatski or **Vyatskiy** (vyät'skē), town (1946 pop. over 500), central Kirov oblast, Russian SFSR, near Kirov; lumber milling.

Vyatskiye Polyany (-skēŭ pŭlyä'nē), city (1948 pop. over 10,000), SE Kirov oblast, Russian SFSR, on railroad, on Vyatka R. and 80 mi. ENE of Kazan; paper milling, flour milling; mfg. of prefabricated houses. Became city in 1942.

Vyazemski or **Vyazemskiy** (vyä'zĭmskē), town (1948 pop. over 10,000), S Khabarovsk Territory, Russian SFSR, on Trans-Siberian RR and 65 mi. S of Khabarovsk; sawmills, metalworks.

Vyazma or **Vyaz'ma** (vyäz'mŭ), city (1926 pop. 20,814), E Smolensk oblast, Russian SFSR, on Vyazma R. (left affluent of the Dnieper; c.50 mi. long) and 135 mi. WSW of Moscow; rail junction; flax mills, oil presses; tanning, metalworking, match mfg.; food products (meat, flour). Has regional mus., mus. of antiquities. Dates from 11th cent.; chartered c.1300; passed 1514 to Moscow from Lithuania.

Vyazniki (vyŭznyĭkē'), city (1926 pop. 17,070), NE Vladimir oblast, Russian SFSR, on Klyazma R. and 65 mi. E of Vladimir; major linen-milling center. Has regional and art mus. Cathedral (1670–74) and monastery are typical of 17th-cent. Rus. architecture. Chartered 1778.

Vyazovaya (vyä'zŭvĭŭ), town (1939 pop. over 2,000), W Chelyabinsk oblast, Russian SFSR, in the S Urals, on Yuryuzan R. and 13 mi. NE of Katav-Ivanovsk; rail junction. Marl and bauxite deposits near by.

Vyazovka (vyä'zŭfkŭ). **1** Village (1939 pop. over 2,000), N Saratov oblast, Russian SFSR, 15 mi. SE of Bazarny Karabulak; metalworks; wheat, sunflowers. Kurilovka, village (1939 pop. over 500) and station, is 6 mi. E. **2** Village (1926 pop. 1,630), central Saratov oblast, Russian SFSR, 20 mi. NW of Saratov; vegetable and fruit processing; wheat, sunflowers. **3** Village (1926 pop. 4,599), N Stalingrad oblast, Russian SFSR, 10 mi. SE of Yelan; flour milling; wheat, sunflowers.

Vyborg (vē'bôrg, Rus. vĭ'bŭrk), Finnish *Viipuri* (vē'pōōrē), Swedish *Viborg* (vē'bôryŭ), city (1944 pop. 56,687), NW Leningrad oblast, Russian SFSR, near Finnish border, port on Vyborg Bay of Gulf of Finland, 70 mi. NW of Leningrad; rail junction; commercial and industrial center; mfg. (agr. machines, electric instruments, furniture, fish nets, woolens, cosmetics, porcelain). Its outer port is Vysotsk. Located on cape and isls. in Vyborg Bay; connected by Saimaa Canal with L. Saimaa. Has 16th-cent. towers, mus. in former 17th-cent. town hall, trade and sawmilling schools. Monrepos Park, a former Rus. estate and holiday spot, is just NW of city. Vyborg developed around Swedish castle built (1293) on small rocky isl.; chartered 1403. An early Hanseatic port; fortified in 15th and 16th cents.; seized (1710) by Peter the Great and ceded (1721) by Sweden to Russia; became part of Finland in 1812. Flourished as trading center in late-19th cent.; became 2d city of Finland prior to its cession to USSR in 1940.

Vychegda River (vĭ'chĭgdŭ), N European Russian SFSR, rises in S Timan Ridge, flows S and generally W, through forested, sparsely settled region, past Ust-Kulom, Storozhevsk, Syktyvkar, Yarensk, and Solvychegodsk, joining the Lesser Northern Dvina at Kotlas to form Northern Dvina R. proper; c.700 mi. long. Navigable May-Nov. for 600 mi. below Ust-Kulom. Receives Vym (right), and Northern Keltma and Sysola (left) rivers. Important waterway (16th cent.) in trade with Siberia.

Vyg, river, Karelo-Finnish SSR: see Vyg River.

Vygoda (vĭ'gŭdŭ), Pol. *Wygoda,* town (1931 pop. 900), W Stanislav oblast, Ukrainian SSR, on Svitsa R. and 5 mi. SW of Dolina; rail spur terminus; sawmilling, lumbering, brick mfg.

Vygonichi (vĭ'gŭnēchē), village (1926 pop. 706), central Bryansk oblast, Russian SFSR, on Desna R. and 15 mi. SW of Bryansk; truck produce.

Vygonovo, Lake (vĭ'gŭnŭvŭ), Pol. *Wygonowo* (□ 10), in Pripet Marshes, W Belorussian SSR, 35 mi. N of Pinsk. Connected with Shchara R. (N) and Oginski Canal (S); forms part of Dnieper-Neman waterway.

Vygozero (vĭg'ô"zyĭrŭ) or **Vyg Lake,** Finnish *Uikujärvi* (ōō'ēkōōyărvē), lake (□ c.200) in E central Karelo-Finnish SSR, bet. L. Onega (S) and Onega Bay of White Sea (N); 45 mi. long, up to 20 mi. wide; 40 ft. deep. Receives Segezha R. (W) and upper Vyg R. (SE). Crossed N-S by White Sea–Baltic Canal. Empties N, through canalized lower Vyg R., into Onega Bay of White Sea. Frozen Oct.-April.

Vyg River (vĭk), Finnish *Uikujoki* (ōō'ēkōōyōkē), E Karelo-Finnish SSR, rises in swampy watershed NE of L. Onega, flows c.150 mi. NW and N, through lake Vygozero, to Onega Bay of White Sea at Belomorsk. Lower canalized course is used by White Sea–Baltic Canal. Frozen Nov.-April.

Vyhne (vĭ'nyĕ), Hung. *Vyhnye,* village (pop. 1,135), S Slovakia, Czechoslovakia, 23 mi. SSW of Banska Bystrica; health resort (alt. 1,016 ft.) with ferruginous, carbonic acid, and peat baths. Sklene Teplice (sklĕ'nyā tyĕ'plĭtsĕ), Slovak *Sklené Teplice,* Hung. *Szklenó Fürdő* (sklĕ'nō für'dû), thermal springs (alt. 1,253 ft.) are 3 mi. NE.

Vykhma, Estonia: see Vohma.

Vyksa (vĭk'sŭ), city (1926 pop. 10,910), SW Gorki oblast, Russian SFSR, 18 mi. SSE of Murom; steel-milling center, based on scrap, Krivoi Rog iron ore, and near-by (S) peat deposits; mfg. of stone crushers. Became city in 1934.

Vylok (vĭ'lŭk), Czech *Výlok,* Hung. *Tiszaújlak,* village (1941 pop. 3,429), S Transcarpathian Oblast, Ukrainian SSR, on railroad, on Tissa R. (Hung. border) and 11 mi. SE of Beregovo.

Vym River or **Vym' River** (vĭm), in Komi Autonomous SSR, Russian SFSR, rises in central Timan Ridge, flows c.250 mi. S, through swampy forest region, past Zheleznodorozhny, to Vychegda R. at Ust-Vym.

Vypolzovo (vĭ'pŭlzŭvŭ), town (1939 pop. over 500), N Kalinin oblast, Russian SFSR, 10 mi. W of Bologoye, on highway.

Vyritsa (vĭ'rētsŭ), town (1926 pop. 2,920), central Leningrad oblast, Russian SFSR, 36 mi. S of Leningrad; sawmilling.

Vyrnwy, Lake (vûr'nōōē), reservoir (1,121 acres) on Vyrnwy R., NW Montgomery, Wales, 8 mi. SSE of Bala; 5 mi. long, ½ mi. wide. Built 1880–90 for Liverpool water supply. At SE end is dam, 1,170 ft. long, 160 ft. high.

Vyrnwy River, Montgomery, Wales, rises S of Bala, flows 35 mi. SE, NE, and finally E to the Severn 10 mi. W of Shrewsbury. On upper course is L. Vyrnwy. Lower sector forms boundary bet. Montgomery, Wales, and Shropshire, England.

Vyron or **Viron** (both: vē'rôn), SE suburb (1951 pop. 31,598) of Athens, Greece, 2.5 mi. from city center.

Vyrtsyarv, Estonia: see Vortsjarv.

Vyru, Estonia: see Voru.

Vysehrad (vĭ'shĕhrät), Czech *Vyšehrad,* S district (pop. 4,168) of Prague, Czechoslovakia, on heights above Vltava R. In its 19th-cent. cemetery are buried Dvorak, Smetana, and Bozena Nemcova. Has 12th-cent. St. Martin's chapel, St. Peter and Paul collegiate church. Important in Bohemian history, Vysehrad flourished in 12th cent.; destroyed during Hussite wars. After Thirty Years War, it was made a fortress (bastions still preserved).

Vyselki (vĭ'syĭlkē), village (1926 pop. 5,228), N central Krasnodar Territory, Russian SFSR, on railroad and 29 mi. SW of Tikhoretsk, in wheat and sugar-beet area; flour milling, metalworking.

Vyshcha (vĭ'shchŭ), town (1940 pop. over 500), SW Mordvinian Autonomous SSR, Russian SFSR, 35 mi. WSW of Bednodemyanovsk; sawmilling.

Vyshegrod, Poland: see Wyszogrod.

Vyshgorod (vĭsh'gŭrŭt), village (1939 pop. over 500), NW Ryazan oblast, Russian SFSR, on Oka R. and 15 mi. SE of Ryazan; truck, fruit, wheat grown in the region.

Vyshka (vĭsh'kŭ), oil village (1939 pop. over 500), W Ashkhabad oblast, Turkmen SSR, 17 mi. SW of Nebit-Dag (linked by railroad).

Vyshkov, Poland: see Wyszkow.

Vyshnevolotsk (vĭsh"nyĭvŭlôtsk'), obsolete canal system in Kalinin oblast, Russian SFSR; 1st artificial waterway (constructed 1709–22) connecting Volga R. and Baltic Sea, bet. Kalinin and L. Ladoga; 540 mi. long. Canal system lost importance in 19th cent. because of construction of Mariinsk and Tikhvin canal systems and of railroads. In recent times only of local significance; reconstruction begun in 1940s. Vyshnevolotsk Canal (c.5 mi. long), part of the system, joins Tvertsa River (S) and Msta River (N) at Vyshni Volochek.

Vyshni Volochek or **Vyshniy Volochek** (vĭsh'nyē vŭlô'chĭk, -lŭchôk'), city (1926 pop. 32,022; 1939 pop. 63,642), W central Kalinin oblast, Russian SFSR, in Valdai Hills, on Vyshnevolotsk Canal (locks) and 70 mi. NW of Kalinin; road-rail junction; cotton-milling center; sawmilling. Teachers col. Glassworks at Krasnomaiski (NW). Passed (1478) from Novgorod to Moscow; chartered in 1770. In 18th cent., an important port on Vyshnevolotsk canal system.

Vyskov (vĭsh'kôf), Czech *Vyškov,* Ger. *Wischau* (vĭ'shou), town (pop. 5,802), central Moravia, Czechoslovakia, on railroad, and 18 mi. NE of Brno; agr. center (oats, sugar beets, barley).

Vysmerzhitse, Poland: see Wysmierzyce.

Vysne Hagy (vĭsh'nā hä'gĭ), Czech *Vyšné Hágy,* Slovak *Vyšnie Hágy* (vĭsh'nyĕ), Ger. *Hoch Hagi* (hōkh hä'gē), Hung. *Felsőhági* (fĕl'shûhä"gē), village, N Slovakia, Czechoslovakia, at S foot of Stalin Peak of the High Tatra, 9 mi. NW of Poprad; health resort (alt. 3,558 ft.) with large sanatorium; part of Vysoke Tatry commune.

Vysne Ruzbachy (rōōzh'bäkhĭ), Czech. *Vyšné Ružbachy,* Slovak *Vyšnie Ružbachy* (vĭsh'nyĕ), Hung. *Felsőzúgó* (fĕl'shûzōō"gō), village (pop. 819), N Slovakia, Czechoslovakia, in E foothills of the High Tatra, 5 mi. W of Stara Lubovna; popular health resort (alt. 2,024 ft.) with carbonated thermal and ferruginous-sulphated cold springs and baths. Twin village of Nizne Ruzbachy, with 15th-cent. church, is just SSE, on Poprad R.

Vysny Medzev, Czechoslovakia: see Nizny Medzev.

Vysny Svidnik, Czechoslovakia: see Svidnik.

Vysocany (vĭ'sôchänĭ), Czech *Vysočany,* NE suburb (pop. 18,266) of Prague, Czechoslovakia, on right bank of Vltava R.; mfg. of industrial and electrical equipment.

Vysochany (vĭsô'chŭnē), village (1926 pop. 888), E Vitebsk oblast, Belorussian SSR, 18 mi. SSE of Vitebsk; linen milling.
Vysokaya (vĭsô'kīŭ), mountain (c.1,300 ft.) of the central Urals, W Sverdlovsk oblast, Russian SFSR, 8 mi. WNW of Nizhni Tagil; magnetite deposits mined since 1721; metallurgical and limestone-crushing works (included within Nizhni Tagil city limits). Supplies metallurgical plants of Nizhni Tagil, Verkhnyaya Salda, and Nizhnyaya Salda.
Vysokaya Gora (gŭrä'), village (1939 pop. over 500), NW Tatar Autonomous SSR, Russian SFSR, 10 mi. NE of Kazan; grain, truck.
Vysoke Myto (vĭ'sôkā mē'tô), Czech (*Vysoké Mýto*, Ger. *Hohenmauth* (hō'ùnmout), town (pop. 7,983), E Bohemia, Czechoslovakia, on railroad and 18 mi. ESE of Pardubice; mfg. of cotton textiles and machinery. Large brick kilns in vicinity. Founded in 1264; still has Gothic church, old belfry, part of medieval fortifications.
Vysoke nad Jizerou (näd'yĭ"zĕrō), Czech *Vysoké nad Jizerou*, Ger. *Hochstadt* (hōkh'shtät), town (pop. 1,037), N Bohemia, Czechoslovakia, at foot of the Riesengebirge, on Jizera R. and 16 mi. ESE of Liberec, in glassmaking dist.
Vysoke Tatry (tä'trĭ), Slovak *Vysoké Tatry*, administrative commune in N Slovakia, Czechoslovakia, consisting of 26 mountain resorts and settlements on SE and NE slopes of the High Tatra. Best-known centers: STRBA LAKE, STARY SMOKOVEC, TATRANSKA LOMNICA.
Vysoke Tatry, mountains, Czechoslovakia and Poland: see TATRA MOUNTAINS.
Vysoki i Zeleny Gai or **Vysokiy i Zelenyy Gay** (vĭsô'kē ē zĕlyô'nē gī'), town (1926 pop. 2,639), N central Kharkov oblast, Ukrainian SSR, 8 mi. SW of Kharkov; truck produce.
Vysokinichi (vĭsô'kēnyĭchē), village (1926 pop. 751), NE Kaluga oblast, Russian SFSR, on Protva R. and 19 mi. ESE of Maloyaroslavets; potatoes, wheat.
Vysokopolye or **Vysokopol'ye** (vĭsŭkŭpô'lyĭ), village (1932 pop. estimate 1,050), NW Kherson oblast, Ukrainian SSR, 15 mi. SSW of Apostolovo; dairying, metalworking.
Vysokovsk (vĭsô'kŭfsk), city (1939 pop. over 10,000), N Moscow oblast, Russian SFSR, 8 mi. W of Klin (linked by rail); cotton-milling center; peat works. Called Vysokovski after 1925, until it became city in 1940.
Vysokoye (vĭsô'kŭyŭ). **1** Pol. *Wysokie* or *Wysokie Litewskie* (vĭsô'kyĕ lyĕtyĕf'skyĕ), city (1931 pop. 2,739), W Brest oblast, Belorussian SSR, 23 mi. NW of Brest, near Pol. border; tanning, mfg. (bricks, soap), flour milling, sawmilling. Has 18th-cent. monastery, old palace, and churches. Passed (1795) from Poland to Russia; reverted (1921) to Poland; ceded to USSR in 1945. **2** Village (1948 pop. over 2,000), S central Kalinin oblast, Russian SFSR, 22 mi. S of Torzhok; flax processing. **3** Town (1939 pop. over 500), NW Tula oblast, Russian SFSR, suburb of Aleksin, across Oka R.; limestone quarries.
Vysotsk (vĭsôtsk'). **1** City (1940 pop. over 2,000), NW Leningrad oblast, Russian SFSR, on Karelian Isthmus, outer deep-water port (8 mi. SW) of Vyborg, on Vyborg Bay; lumber shipping. Called Uuras (ōō'räs), Swedish *Trångsund* (trông'sōōn), while in Finland (until 1940) and, until 1948, in USSR. **2** Pol. *Wysock* (vĭ'sôtsk), village (1939 pop. over 2,000), N Rovno oblast, Ukrainian SSR, in Pripet Marshes, on Goryn R. and 26 mi. N of Sarny; rye, potatoes, flax; lumbering.
Vysshaya Dubechnya (vĭ'shĭŭ dōōbyĕch'nyŭ), village (1939 pop. over 500), E Kiev oblast, Ukrainian SSR, on Desna R. and 20 mi. NNE of Kiev; truck produce.
Vyssheye, Ukrainian SSR: see VERKHNEYE.
Vyssi Brod (vĭ'shē brôt"), Czech *Vyšší Brod*, Ger. *Hohenfurth* (hō'ùnfōōrt), autonomous convent settlement (pop. 1,066), S Bohemia, Czechoslovakia, in SE Bohemian Forest, on Vltava R., on railroad and 13 mi. S of Cesky Krumlov, near Austrian border; some paper mfg. Founded in 13th cent., it is still surrounded by a medieval wall. Has 13th-cent. Gothic church, 14th-cent. cloister, large convent library, noted collection of 14th-cent. paintings, jewels, and arms.
Vytegra (vĭ'tyĭgrŭ), city (1926 pop. 5,090), NW Vologda oblast, Russian SFSR, near L. Onega, on Vytegra R. and 100 mi. ENE of Lodeinoye Pole; metalworks, sawmills, shipyards. Chartered 1773.
Vytegra River, Vologda oblast, Russian SFSR, rises in marshy area near Kovzha L., flows 45 mi. NW to L. Onega 11 mi. below Vytegra; canalized in major part of course. Forms part of Mariinsk canal system; connected with Kovzha R. by Mariinsk Canal (SE) and with Svir R. by Onega Canal (NW).
Vytina or **Vitina** (both: vētē'nŭ), town (pop. 1,392), Arcadia nome, central Peloponnesus, Greece, 16 mi. NW of Tripolis; road center; summer resort (sanatorium); alt. 3,600 ft.
Vyya (vĭ'yŭ), rail junction in W Sverdlovsk oblast, Russian SFSR, 15 mi. SSW of Is; spurs lead to Is and Nizhnyaya Tura.
Vzmorye or **Vzmor'ye** (ŭvzmô'ryŭ). **1** Village (1939 pop. 2,411), W Kaliningrad oblast, Russian SFSR, in pine woods, on N coast of Vistula lagoon, 10 mi. W of Kaliningrad, in former royal elk-hunting ground. Until 1945, in East Prussia and called Grossheidekrug or Grossheydekrug (grōs-hī'dŭkrōōk). **2** Town (1947 pop. over 500), S Sakhalin, Sakhalin oblast, Russian SFSR, on E coast railroad and 40 mi. NNW of Dolinsk; coal mining. While under Japanese rule (1905–45), it was called Shiraura.

W

Wa, states, Burma: see WA STATES.
Wa (wä), town (pop. 2,136), Northern Territories, NW Gold Coast, 115 mi. WNW of Tamale; road center; shea nuts, durra, yams; cattle, skins. Has mosque. Hq. Wa dist.
Waabs (väps), village (pop. 2,526), in Schleswig-Holstein, NW Germany, near the Baltic, 7 mi. NE of Eckernförde; cattle. Has Romanesque church.
Waadt, Switzerland: see VAUD.
Waag River, Czechoslovakia: see VAH RIVER.
Waakirchen (vä'kĭr"khŭn), village (commune pop. 2,875), Upper Bavaria, Germany, on N slope of the Bavarian Alps, 5 mi. E of Bad Tölz; lignite mined at Marienstein (pop. 1,119), 2 mi. S.
Waalhaven, Netherlands: see ROTTERDAM.
Waal River (väl), central Netherlands, arm of the Rhine formed by forking of Rhine R. into Lower Rhine R. and Waal R. near Millingen (8 mi. ENE of Nijmegen); flows 52 mi. W, past Nijmegen, Tiel, and Zaltbommel, joining Maas R. at Woudrichem to form UPPER MERWEDE RIVER. Joined by Maas-Waal Canal 2.5 mi. WNW of Nijmegen.
Waalwijk (väl'vīk), town (pop. 12,548), North Brabant prov., S Netherlands, 10 mi. W of 's Hertogenbosch; leather industry (tanning, shoemaking), chemicals, mfg. of machinery, cardboard. Tanning school. Town chartered 1303. Sometimes spelled Waalwyk.
Waanje River (wä-än'jä), SE Sierra Leone, rises in hills N of Kenema, flows c.130 mi. SW, past Bandajuma and Pujehun, joining Sewa R. 30 mi. ESE of Bonthe to form Kittam R. Lower course forms part of N side of Turner's Peninsula.
Waarschoot (vär'skhōt), town (pop. 7,345), East Flanders prov., NW Belgium, 3 mi. SE of Eekloo; textile industry; agr. market. Formerly spelled Waerschoot.
Waas, Mount, Utah: see LA SAL MOUNTAINS.
Waas, Pays de (pĕē dŭ väs') (formerly spelled Pays de Waes), Flemish *Waasland* (väs'länt) (formerly spelled *Waesland*), anc. dist. of East Flanders prov., Belgium, and of adjoining Zeeland prov., Netherlands; noted for its highly fertile soil. Centered at St-Nicolas (Belgium).
Waasmunster (väs'münstŭr), town (pop. 6,654), East Flanders prov., N Belgium, 5 mi. N of Dendermonde; carpet weaving. Formerly spelled Waesmunster.
Waasten, Belgium: see WARNETON.
Wabamun (wŏ'bŭmŭn), village (pop. estimate 200), central Alta., on Wabamun L. (12 mi. long, 6 mi. wide), 40 mi. W of Edmonton; coal mining, mixed farming, lumbering.
Waban, Mass.: see NEWTON.
Wabana, Lake (wôbă'nŭ), Itasca co., N central Minn., 12 mi. N of Grand Rapids; 4 mi. long, 3 mi. wide. Resorts.
Wabash (wô'băsh). **1** County (□ 221; pop. 14,651), SE Ill.; ⊙ Mount Carmel. Bounded E and S by Wabash R.; drained by Bonpas Creek. Agr. area (livestock, corn, wheat, soybeans). Mfg. (electrical and sports equipment, clothing, flour, paper products). Petroleum, natural gas, bituminous coal. Formed 1824. **2** County (□ 421; pop. 29,047), NE central Ind.; ⊙ Wabash. Agr. area (livestock, soybeans, wheat, corn). Mfg. (especially furniture, store fixtures, wood products, electronic equipment) at Wabash. Drained by Wabash, Eel, Salamonie, and Mississinewa rivers. Formed 1832.
Wabash, city (pop. 10,621), ⊙ Wabash co., NE central Ind., on the Wabash and 40 mi. WSW of Fort Wayne; trade center in agr. area (grain, livestock); mfg. of electronic equipment, furniture, store fixtures, automobile parts, asbestos, paperboard, rubber products, clothing, baking powder, packed meat, lime; machine shops, railroad shops. Settled 1835.
Wabasha (wä'bŭshô), county (□ 521; pop. 16,878), SE Minn.; ⊙ Wabasha. Agr. area bounded E by Mississippi R. and Wis. and drained by Zumbro R. Livestock, dairy products, corn, oats, barley. Formed 1849.
Wabasha, city (pop. 2,468), ⊙ Wabasha co., SE Minn., on Mississippi R. at SE tip of L. Pepin and 30 mi. NW of Winona. Resort; trade and shipping center for diversified-farming area; dairy products, flour, soda water. Platted 1843, inc. 1858. Natl. wildlife refuge near by.
Wabash River (wô'băsh), mainly in Ind. and Ill., rises in Grand L. in W Ohio, flows NW into Ind., then W and SW past Logansport and Lafayette, then S and SW past Terre Haute and Vincennes, forms Ill.-Ind. line for c.200 mi., and reaches the Ohio R. at SW corner of Ind.; 475 mi. long; drains □ 33,150. White R. is largest left-bank tributary; from right come the Little Wabash, Embarrass, Tippecanoe, and Vermilion rivers. Agr. (corn, livestock) is important in its fertile basin, whose cities also include Indianapolis, Muncie, and Kokomo (Ind.), Danville, Champaign, and Urbana (Ill.). Has hydroelectric developments and carries barge traffic (chiefly sand and gravel).
Wabasso (wôbă'sō), village (pop. 693), Redwood co., SW Minn., c.40 mi. WNW of New Ulm, in grain, livestock, poultry area; dairy products.
Wabatawangang Lake (wŏ"pŭtŭwŏng'gŏng", wŏ"bŭtŭ-) or **Sand Lake**, Itasca co., N Minn., in Greater Leech Lake Indian Reservation and Chippewa Natl. Forest, 30 mi. NW of Grand Rapids; 6 mi. long, 2 mi. wide. Has fishing resorts. Fed and drained by Bowstring R.
Wabatongushi Lake (wŏbŭtŏng'gŭshē) (20 mi. long, 3 mi. wide), central Ont., 120 mi. N of Sault Ste. Marie; alt. 1,147 ft. Drained S into L. Superior by Michipicoten R.
Wabaunsee (wŭbôn'sē), county (□ 791; pop. 7,212), E central Kansas; ⊙ Alma. Dissected plain, bounded N by Kansas R. Livestock, grain. Formed 1859.
Wabbaseka (wŏbŭsē'kŭ), town (pop. 375), Jefferson co., central Ark., 15 mi. NE of Pine Bluff; cotton.
Wabek (wä'bĕk), village (pop. 15), Mountrail co., NW central N.Dak., 31 mi. SE of Stanley.
Wabeno (wŏbē'nō), village (pop. with adjacent Soperton 1,002), Forest co., NE Wis., on Oconto R. and 39 mi. ESE of Rhinelander; sawmilling.
Wabi, Formosa: see HOMEI.
Wabigoon Lake (wä'bĭgōōn) (16 mi. long, 7 mi. wide), NW Ont., extends SE from Dryden; drains WNW into English R. On shore are gold mines, soapstone quarries.
Wabrzezno (vŏb-zhĕzh'nô), Pol. *Wąbrzeźno*, Ger. *Briesen* (brē'zŭn), town (pop. 9,320), Bydgoszcz prov., N Poland, 23 mi. NE of Torun; mfg. of bricks, agr. machinery, furniture, chemicals, rubber; flour milling, sawmilling; grain and cattle trade.
Waccamaw River (wŏ'kŭmô), SE N.C. and E S.C., rises in L. Waccamaw (5 mi. long, 3 mi. wide), S N.C., 10 mi. E of Whiteville, flows 140 mi. generally SW to Winyah Bay near Georgetown. Tidal in lower 92 mi.; 12-ft. navigation channel to Conway, 44 mi. above mouth. Intracoastal Waterway follows lower course for c.30 mi.
Wachapreague (wŏ'chŭprēg, wŏ'shŭ-), town (pop. 551), Accomack co., E Va., on small bay joined to the Atlantic by Wachapreague Inlet, 7 mi. S of Accomac; sport-fishing resort.
Wachenheim (vä'khŭnhīm), town (pop. 2,486), Rhenish Palatinate, W Germany, on E slope of Hardt Mts., 2 mi. SE of Bad Dürkheim; sparkling wine. Has ruined castle. Chartered 1341.
Wächtersbach (vĕkh'tŭrsbäkh), town (pop. 2,448), in former Prussian prov. of Hesse-Nassau, W Germany, after 1945 in Hesse, 18 mi. NNE of Hanau; pottery works. Has 16th–17th-cent. castle.
Wachusett Mountain (wôchōō'sĭt) (c.2,000 ft.), solitary peak in N central Mass., c.8 mi. SW of Fitchburg, in state reservation (1,500 acres). Road to summit hotel; campgrounds, ski trails and lodge.
Wachusett Reservoir, central Mass., 11 mi. NNE of Worcester; 8.5 mi. long; impounded in valley of S branch of Nashua R. by Wachusett Dam (208 ft. high, 1,476 ft. long; completed 1906). Receives some of its water, through Quabbin Aqueduct, from QUABBIN RESERVOIR (W). Supplies Boston metropolitan area.
Wacken, Belgium: see WAKKEN.
Wacker, native fishing village, SE Alaska, on SW shore of Revillagigedo Isl., 7 mi. NW of Ketchikan.
Wackersdorf (vä'kŭrsdôrf), village (pop. 2,002), Upper Palatinate, E central Bavaria, Germany, 4 mi. SE of Schwandorf; lignite mining.
Waco (wā'kō). **1** Town (pop. 328), Haralson co., NW Ga., 11 mi. NNW of Carrollton. **2** Town (pop. 177), Jasper co., SW Mo., near Spring R., 12 mi. N of Joplin. **3** Village (pop. 180), York co., SE central Nebr., 7 mi. E of York. **4** Town (pop. 310), Cleveland co., SW N.C., 8 mi. NE of Shelby. **5** City (pop. 84,706), ⊙ McLennan co., E central Texas, on the Brazos just below mouth of the Bosque and c.85 mi. S of Dallas; commercial, distribution, mfg. center for wide blackland agr. region (cotton; also corn, grains, hay, dairy prod-

ucts); an important cotton market; rail, highway focus, with railroad shops; has airport and Connally Air Force Base. Textile and cottonseed-oil mills; mfg. of glass, tires, milk products, clothing, bedding, drugs, machine-shop products, wood products. Seat of Baylor Univ., Paul Quinn Col., and a veterans' hosp. Laid out 1849 on site of Hueco (or Waco) Indian village; inc. 1856. Became cotton center before Civil War; building of suspension bridge (1870; extant) and railroad's coming (1881) stimulated growth. Just W is recreational area around L. Waco, formed 1923 by dam in Bosque R.

Waco, Lake, Texas: see BOSQUE RIVER.

Waconia (wŏkō'nyŭ), city (pop. 1,569), Carver co., S central Minn., on small lake, 27 mi. WSW of Minneapolis, in poultry, livestock, grain area; dairy products, beverages. Inc. 1921.

Wada (wä'dä). **1** Town (pop. 8,683), Akita prefecture, N Honshu, Japan, 7 mi. SE of Akita; rice, charcoal. **2** Town (pop. 4,465), Chiba prefecture, central Honshu, Japan, on SE Chiba Peninsula, on the Pacific, 10 mi. ENE of Tateyama; rice, wheat, lumber.

Wadai (wädī'), Fr. *Ouadī* or *Ouaddaï* (wädī'), former independent sultanate of N central Africa, roughly coextensive with present administrative regions of Ouadaï (□ 50,200; 1950 pop. 473,500; ⊙ Abéché) and Batha (□ 44,025; 1950 pop. 324,600; ⊙ Ati), central and E Chad territory, Fr. Equatorial Africa, at SE fringes of the Sahara, and extending to Darfur (Anglo-Egyptian Sudan). Largely arid steppe with shrub forests in hilly sections, sand dunes and some fertile oases in N. Agr. (livestock, millet, sesame, corn, cotton, indigo); trade in cattle, ivory, coffee, ostrich feathers; native handicrafts (notably cotton weaving). Its Mohammedan pop. comprises Negroes and Arabs. Presumably founded in 16th cent., Wadai sultanate was described by Arab geographers and visited by Gustav Nachtigal (1873). In 17th cent. it was under domination of Darfur, but in 19th cent. it became overlord of Kanem, Baguirmi, and Bornu and was noted as a great slave-raiding state. Senussism was introduced c.1850. At apex of its power, it extended from L. Chad (W) to c.22°E and from Shari R. and Bahr Salamat (S) to c.16°N. Recognized Fr. protectorate (1903); pacified by Fr. troops (1903–13).

Wadayama (wädä'yämŭ), town (pop. 4,700), Hyogo prefecture, S Honshu, Japan, 14 mi. S of Toyooka, in agr. area (rice, wheat), poultry; soy sauce, raw silk. Home industries (woodworking, cutlery).

Wad Ban Naga (wäd' băn nä'gä), village, Northern Prov., Anglo-Egyptian Sudan, on right bank of the Nile, on railroad, and 70 mi. NE of Khartoum. Near by are well-preserved ruins (15 B.C.–A.D. 300) of Nagaa or Naga (22 mi. SE) and Musawarat (18 mi. ESE).

Waddamana (wŏ"dŭmă'nŭ), village (pop. 225), central Tasmania, 60 mi. NNW of Hobart and on Ouse R.; hydroelectric plant; sheep.

Waddenzee (vä'dŭnzā), shallow part of North Sea, bet. West Frisian Isls. and N Netherlands mainland. The Lauwers Zee is its main inlet into Frisian mainland, S of Schiermonnikoog isl. Chief ports: Helder, Harlingen. Until building of IJSSELMEER Dam it formed N part of ZUIDER ZEE.

Waddesdon (wädz'dŭn), agr. village and parish (pop. 1,294), central Buckingham, England, 5 mi. WNW of Aylesbury. Has 14th-cent. church and a Rothschild mansion, whose noted art collection is now in British Mus.

Waddingsveen, Netherlands: see WADDINXVEEN.

Waddington (wŏ'dĭngtŭn), village (pop. 819), St. Lawrence co., N N.Y., port of entry on the St. Lawrence and 17 mi. NE of Ogdensburg; paper milling; ships milk. Summer resort; fishing. Ferry near by to Morrisburg, Ont.

Waddington, Mount (wŏ'–) (13,260 ft.), SW B.C., in Coast Mts., 170 mi. NW of Vancouver; 51°22'N 125°15'W.

Waddinxveen or **Waddingsveen** (both: vä'dĭngksfān), town (pop. 6,060), South Holland prov., W Netherlands, 3 mi. NW of Gouda; mfg. (furniture, varnish, sealing wax, paper, ceramics, cement); limekilns.

Wade. 1 Town (pop. 343), Aroostook co., NE Maine, on the Aroostook and 13 mi. NW of Presque Isle. **2** Town (1940 pop. 380), Cumberland co., central N.C., 10 mi. NE of Fayetteville; sawmilling.

Wadebridge, former urban district (1931 pop. 2,460), central Cornwall, England, on Camel R. (15th-cent. bridge) and 6 mi. NW of Bodmin; agr. market center.

Wadelai (wädĕlī'), ruined village, Northern Prov., NW Uganda, on the Albert Nile c.35 mi. below its efflux from L. Albert. Former military post.

Wadena (wŏdē'nŭ), town (pop. 762), SE central Sask., 75 mi. NW of Yorkton; woodworking; lumber, flour, and grist milling; dairying.

Wadena, county (□ 536; pop. 12,806), W central Minn.; ⊙ Wadena. Agr. area drained by Crow Wing R. Dairy products, livestock; peat deposits. Formed 1858.

Wadena. 1 Town (pop. 316), Fayette co., NE Iowa, on Volga R. and 17 mi. NE of Oelwein. Limestone quarries near by. **2** Village (pop. 3,958), ⊙ Wadena co., W central Minn., on small affluent of Leaf R. and c.45 mi. WNW of Brainerd; agr. trading point in grain, livestock, poultry area; dairy and wood products, beverages. Settled 1871, inc. 1881.

Wädenswil (vā'dŭnsvēl), town (pop. 9,436), Zurich canton, N Switzerland, on L. of Zurich and 11 mi. SSE of Zurich; textiles, metal products, soap, knit goods, beer.

Wadern (vä'dŭrn), village (pop. 1,370), N Saar, 15 mi. ENE of Merzig; stock, grain; construction industry. Formerly part of Prussian Rhine Prov.; annexed to Saar in 1946.

Wadersloh (vä'dŭrslō), village (pop. 5,387), in former Prussian prov. of Westphalia, NW Germany, after 1945 in North Rhine-Westphalia, 6 mi. NW of Lippstadt; pumpernickel; hog raising.

Wadesboro, town (pop. 3,408), ⊙ Anson co., S N.C., 45 mi. SE of Charlotte, near S.C. line; textile center; cotton, hosiery, lumber, cottonseed-oil mills; fertilizer and box factories. Settled c.1785.

Wadgaon (vŭd'goun). **1** Town (pop. 5,003), Kolhapur dist., S Bombay, India, 12 mi. NNE of Kolhapur; millet, peanuts, sugar cane. Also spelled Vadgaon or Vadagaon. **2** Village, Poona district, Bombay, India: see VADGAON.

Wadgassen (vät'gä"sŭn), town (pop. 3,550), SW Saar, near Fr. border, on Saar R. and 3.5 mi. SE of Saarlouis; glass mfg. Formerly site of arms factory, established 1794 to supply Napoleon's forces.

Wadhurst (wŏd'hûrst), town and parish (pop. 3,771), NE Sussex, England, 6 mi. SE of Tunbridge Wells; agr. market, with electrical-equipment works. Has 13th–15th-cent. church. In Middle Ages, important center of iron industry.

Wadhwan (vŭd'vän), former princely state (□ 243; pop. 69,882) of Western India States agency, on Kathiawar peninsula; ⊙ was Wadhwan (since c.1950 called Surendranagar); state merged 1948 with Saurashtra.

Wadhwan, town India: see SURENDRANAGAR.

Wadhwan Camp, town (pop. 18,967), Zalawad dist., NE Saurashtra, India, 3 mi. W of Wadhwan; cotton ginning and milling, copperware mfg. Was former Br. civil station (□ 1) and hq. of Eastern Kathiawar Agency.

Wadi [Arabic,=stream, usually a dry watercourse]: for names beginning thus and not found here, see under main part of name.

Wadi (vä'dē), village (pop. 2,625), Gulbarga dist., W Hyderabad state, India, 22 mi. SSE of Gulbarga. Major rail junction on Bombay-Madras line; branch runs through Hyderabad (100 mi. E) and connects with Calcutta-Madras line at Bezwada (240 mi. ESE). Limestone quarries near by.

Wadia, India: see VADIA.

Wadi el Sir, Wadi es Sir, or **Wadi al-Sir** (all: wă'dē ĕs-sĭr'), village (pop. c.7,000), N central Jordan, 6 mi. W of Amman; vineyards, lumbering; clay and silica quarries.

Wadi Estate (vä'dē), former petty princely state (□ 12; pop. 2,022) in Deccan States, Bombay, India; hq. was at Miraj. Inc. 1949 into Belgaum dist., Bombay.

Wadi Halfa (wä'dē hăl'fŭ, wă'–), city (pop. 12,700), Northern Prov., Anglo-Egyptian Sudan, near Egyptian border, on right bank of the Nile and 440 mi. NNW of Khartoum, just below 2d Cataract; 21°50'N 31°17'E. Northern gateway to the Sudan and terminus of rail line from Khartoum; rail-steamer transfer point for navigation down the Nile; commercial and agr. center: cotton, wheat, barley, corn, fruits, durra; livestock. Antiquities mus. Airport. Consists of old Nubian village (N) and European town (S), with govt. hosp. (quarantine station), official residences, railyards and workshops. On W bank of Nile just SW of Wadi Halfa are ruins (town, temples) of Buhen or Behen, an anc. Egyptian colony dating from Middle Empire (2100–1700 B.C.) and known to have existed until Roman times. Wadi Halfa is ⊙ Halfa dist., a former prov. inc. (1930s) into Northern Prov.

Wadi Marasa, Aden: see MARASA.

Wadi Musa (wă'dē mōō'sŭ), village (pop. c.5,000), S central Jordan, on the Wadi Musa (right affluent of Wadi 'Araba) and 14 mi. NW of Ma'an; wheat, barley, fruit. Just W are important ruins of anc. rock city of Petra, ⊙ of Edomites and sometimes identified with biblical Sela.

Wading River, resort village (pop. c.500), Suffolk co., SE N.Y., near N shore of Long Isl., 11 mi. E of Port Jefferson; duck raising. Just E is Wildwood State Park (395 acres).

Wading River, SE N.J., formed in S Burlington co. by junction of West and East branches; flows c.12 mi. SE to Mullica R. c.8 mi. above its mouth.

Wadley (wŏd'lē). **1** Town (pop. 535), Randolph co., E Ala., on Tallapoosa R. and 40 mi. SSE of Anniston; lumber, clothing. Jr. col. here. **2** Town (pop. 1,624), Jefferson co., E Ga., 18 mi. NNW of Swainsboro, near Ogeechee R.; mfg. (boxes, clothing).

Wadmalaw Island (wŏd'mŭlô), Charleston co., S S.C., one of Sea Isls., 11 mi. SW of Charleston, bet. Edisto and Johns isls.; 11 mi. long, 2–11 mi. wide. Connected by highway bridge to Johns Isl. Rockville village (yachting) is on S shore.

Wad Medani (wäd' mĕdä'nē), city (pop. 57,300), ⊙ Blue Nile prov., E central Anglo-Egyptian Sudan, in the Gezira, on left bank of the Blue Nile S of influx of Rahad R., on railroad, and 110 mi. SE of Khartoum; major cotton center; also wheat, barley, corn, fruits, durra; livestock. Agr. research station.

Wadomari (wädō'märē), largest town (1950 pop. 13,260) on Okinoerabu-shima of isl. group Amami-gunto, in the Ryukyu Islands, on E coast of isl.; agr. and fishing center; sugar cane, sweet potatoes. Formerly sometimes called Watomari.

Wadowice (vädôvē'tsĕ), town (pop. 7,123), Krakow prov., S Poland, on Skawa R. and 23 mi. WSW of Cracow; rail junction; mfg. of cement products, wire, footwear; food processing. In Second World War, under Ger. rule, called Frauenstadt.

Wad Rawa (wäd rä'wŭ), village, Blue Nile prov., E central Anglo-Egyptian Sudan, on left bank of the White Nile (opposite Kamlin) and 60 mi. SE of Khartoum; cotton, wheat, barley, corn, fruits; livestock.

Wadsley Bridge (wŏdz'lē), town in Sheffield county borough, West Riding, S Yorkshire, England, on Don R. and 3 mi. NW of Sheffield; steel milling.

Wadsworth (wŏdz'wûrth), town and parish (pop. 1,550), West Riding, SW Yorkshire, England, 5 mi. WNW of Huddersfield; cotton and woolen milling.

Wadsworth, city (pop. 7,966), Medina co., N Ohio, 11 mi. WSW of downtown Akron, within Akron metropolitan dist.; makes matches, valves, fittings, chemicals, rubber products, brick, tile, window shades, dairy products. Settled 1816, inc. 1866.

Wadsworth, Fort, N.Y.: see STATEN ISLAND.

Waelder (wĕl'dŭr), city (pop. 1,275), Gonzales co., S central Texas, 21 mi. E of Luling; trade, shipping point in cattle, poultry, grain area.

Waenfawr (wĭnvour'), agr. village and parish (pop. 1,260), W Caernarvon, Wales, 4 mi. SE of Caernarvon.

Waereghem, Belgium: see WAREGEM.

Waerschoot, Belgium: see WAARSCHOOT.

Waes, Pays de, Belgium and Netherlands: see WAAS, PAYS DE.

Waesland, Belgium: see WAAS, PAYS DE.

Waesmunster, Belgium: see WAASMUNSTER.

Wafangtien, Manchuria: see FUHSIEN, Liaotung prov.

Wagadugu, Fr. West Africa: see OUAGADOUGOU.

Wagah (vä'gŭ), village, Lahore dist., E Punjab, W Pakistan, 13 mi. E of Lahore, near Indian border; wheat, cotton, gram. In 1947, refugee camp set up here to handle influx of Moslems from N India resulting from communal migrations following partitioning of Punjab.

Wagener (wăg'nŭr), town (pop. 584), Aiken co., W central S.C., 30 mi. SW of Columbia.

Wageningen (vä'khŭnĭng"ŭn), town (pop. 15,059) and port, Gelderland prov., central Netherlands, on the Lower Rhine and 10 mi. W of Arnhem; mfg. of bricks, millstones, tiles, furniture, cigars; woodworking, leather tanning, printing; malt growing. Shipbuilding research station; agr. col. In 19th cent., tobacco-growing center.

Wager Bay, trading post, N central Keewatin Dist., Northwest Territories, at head of Wager Bay, an inlet (110 mi. long) of Roes Welcome Sound; 65°55'N 90°49'W.

Wager Island, Chile: see GUAYANECO ISLANDS.

Wagga Wagga (wŏ'gŭ wŏ'gŭ), municipality (pop. 15,340), S New South Wales, Australia, on Murrumbidgee R. and 100 mi. W of Canberra; rail junction; agr. and dairying center; brickyards. R.C. cathedral.

Wäggital (vĕ'gĕtäl"), valley of the Aa of Schwyz canton, NE central Switzerland. River is dammed, creating the Wäggitalersee, a small (□ 2) lake. Several hydroelectric plants in valley.

Waggoner (wăg'nŭr), village (pop. 239), Montgomery co., S central Ill., 13 mi. N of Litchfield, in agr. and bituminous-coal area.

Waghäusel (väk'hoi"zŭl), village (pop. 298), N Baden, Germany, after 1945 in Württemberg-Baden, 5.5 mi. SE of Speyer; large sugar refinery.

Wagin (wă'gĭn), municipality (pop. 1,139), SW Western Australia, 130 mi. SE of Perth; rail center; wheat, oats.

Wagnelée, Belgium: see CHASSART.

Wagner (wăg'nŭr), city (pop. 1,528), Charles Mix co., SE S.Dak., 23 mi. WNW of Tyndall; farm trading center; dairy products, grain, livestock, poultry.

Wagner, Mount, Wyo.: see SALT RIVER RANGE.

Wagoner (wă'gŭnŭr), county (□ 584; pop. 16,741), E Okla.; ⊙ Wagoner. Bounded S by Arkansas R.; drained by Neosho and Verdigris rivers. Agr. (grain, cotton, corn, livestock, soybeans; dairy products). Processing, mfg. at Wagoner. Oil, natural-gas wells; gasoline plants. Timber. Formed 1907.

Wagoner, city (pop. 4,395), ⊙ Wagoner co., E Okla., 14 mi. N of Muskogee; trade center for agr. area (corn, cotton, wheat); cotton ginning, cottonseed-oil and feed milling; mfg. of brick, clay products, lumber. Oil and natural-gas wells; timber. A mus. with Indian and Civil War relics is here. Anc. Indian mounds are near by. Founded c.1887.

Wagon Mound, village (pop. 1,120), Mora co., NE N.Mex., in SE foothills of Sangre de Cristo Mts.,

40 mi. NE of Las Vegas; alt. c.6,200 ft. Trade center; shipping point for wool, livestock.
Wagon Wheel Gap, village (pop. c.50), Mineral co., SW Colo., on Rio Grande, in San Juan Mts., and 8 mi. SE of Creede; alt. 8,450 ft. Fishing resort with mineral springs.
Wagram, Austria: see DEUTSCH WAGRAM.
Wagram (wā'grŭm), town (pop. 397), Scotland co., S N.C., 9 mi. NE of Laurinburg; peach shipping, lumber milling.
Wagrowiec (vōgrô'vyĕts), Pol. *Wągrowiec*, Ger. *Wongrowitz* (vông'grōvĭts), town (1946 pop. 10,006), Poznan prov., W central Poland, on Welna R. and 30 mi. NNE of Poznan; rail junction; mfg. of cement, machinery, furniture; flour milling, brewing, sawmilling; trades in cattle, produce.
Wagstadt, Czechoslovakia: see BILOVEC.
Wagu (wä'gōō), town (pop, 5,641), Mie prefecture, S Honshu, Japan, on Kumano Sea, 17 mi. SSE of Uji-yamada, on small peninsula; fishing, pearling.
Wag Water River (wăg' wô"tŭr), E central and N Jamaica, rises in foothills of Blue Mts. 9 mi. N of Kingston, flows c.25 mi. N to the Caribbean just W of Annotto Bay. Not navigable. Dammed near its source, providing water for Kingston.
Wah (vä'), village, Attock dist., NW Punjab, W Pakistan, 2 mi. S of Hasan Abdal; hand-loom weaving. Cement works near by.
Waha, Belgium: see MARLOIE.
Wahai or **Wahaai** (both: wähī'), town (dist. pop. 13,436), N Ceram, Indonesia, on Ceram Sea; 2°48'S 129°28'E; chief port of Ceram, shipping copra and resin.
Wahiawa (wä'hēŭwä'), city (pop. 8,369), central Oahu, T.H., 17 mi. NW of Honolulu, on plateau in pineapple area.
Wahiawa New Mill, village (pop. 570), S Kauai, T.H.; sugar plantation.
Wahidi (wăhēdē'), tribal country of Eastern Aden Protectorate, W of the Quaiti state; divided into the sultanates of BALHAF and BIR ALI.
Wahjamega (wä"jŭmē'gŭ), village, Tuscola co., E Mich., 4 mi. SW of Caro, near Cass R. Has state hosp. for epileptic children.
Wahkiakum (wôkī'ŭkŭm), county (□ 269; pop. 3,835), SW Wash.; ⊙ Cathlamet. Bounded S by Columbia R. Fish, lumber, livestock, dairy products, hay, potatoes. Formed 1854.
Wahkon (wŏkän'), resort village (pop. 202), Mille Lacs co., E Minn., on Mille Lacs L., 38 mi. N of Princeton; grain, stock.
Wahlern (vä'lŭrn), town (pop. 4,600), Bern canton, W Switzerland, 9 mi. SSW of Bern. Includes hamlet of Schwarzenburg, with 15th-cent. chapel, 16th-cent. castle; milk.
Wahlershausen (vä"lŭrs-hou'zŭn), suburb (pop. 11,596) of Kassel, W Germany, 3 mi. W of city center. Lignite mining near by. Just W is the noted 18th-cent. castle Wilhelmshöhe, former electoral summer residence, amid beautiful grounds with large artificial ruins and cascades.
Wahlstatt (väl'shtät) or **Legnickie Pole** (lĕgnēts'kyĕ pô'lĕ), village (1939 pop. 1,106) in Lower Silesia, after 1945 in Wroclaw prov., SW Poland, 6 mi. SE of Liegnitz (Legnica). Mongol victory (1241) over Germans and Poles here. Benedictine priory (13th cent.), burned (1641) by Swedes in Thirty Years War, was later rebuilt; became cadet school in 19th cent., attended by Hindenburg, Ludendorff. Near-by BREMBERG was scene (1813) of battle of the Katzbach; Blücher was subsequently created prince of Wahlstatt.
Wahlstedt (väl'shtĕt), village (pop. 1,677), in Schleswig-Holstein, NW Germany, 4 mi. WNW of Bad Segeberg. After 1946 settled by Sudeten German costume jewelry workers.
Wahoo (wähōō'), city (pop. 3,128), ⊙ Saunders co., E Nebr., 27 mi. N of Lincoln, 35 mi. W of Omaha, and on branch of Platte R.; cement products, beverages; dairy and poultry produce, grain. Luther Col. here. City founded 1865.
Wahpeton (wô'pŭtŭn). **1** Town (pop. 127), Dickinson co., NW Iowa, 16 mi. NNW of Spencer. **2** City (pop. 5,125), ⊙ Richland co., SE N.Dak., 45 mi. S of Fargo and on Red River of the North. Flour mills, dairy plants, sheet-iron works. Site of State School of Science and U.S. Indian school. Known as Chahinkapa, 1871–93; inc. 1883.
Wahren (vä'rŭn), industrial suburb of Leipzig, Saxony, E central Germany, 5 mi. ENE of city center.
Wahrenbrück (vä"rŭnbrük'), town (pop. 900), in former Prussian Saxony prov., central Germany, after 1945 in Saxony-Anhalt, on the Black Elster and 3 mi. NW of Bad Liebenwerda; grain, potatoes, livestock.
Währing (vā'rĭng), district (□ 2; pop. 71,250) of Vienna, Austria, 2 mi. NW of city center; observatory.
Wahroonga (wŭrōō̆ng'gŭ), town (pop. 5,355), E New South Wales, 12 mi. NW of Sydney; rail junction; mfg. (cereal foods, beef extract).
Wai (vī), town (pop. 14,893), Satara North dist., W central Bombay, India, on Kistna R. and 18 mi. NNW of Satara; trade center; place of pilgrimage; millet, wheat, mangoes.
Waiakoa (wī'ŭkō'ŭ), village (pop. 520), central Maui, T.H.; tuberculosis sanitarium near by.
Waialeale (wī'ä"lā-ä'lā), peak (5,080 ft.), central Kauai, T.H.; contains WAIMEA CANYON; average yearly rainfall on summit, 476 in. Shares, with CHERRAPUNJI, India, the record of having the world's heaviest rainfall.
Waialua Mill (wīŭlōō'ŭ), town (pop. 2,602), Oahu, T.H., on N coast; sugar mill; beach near by.
Waianae (wī'ŭnī'), village (pop. 1,000), W Oahu, T.H., 31 mi. NW of Honolulu.
Waianae Range, W Oahu, T.H., rises to Mt. Kaala (4,030 ft.).
Waiapu, New Zealand: see WAIPIRO BAY.
Waiau (wī'ou), township (pop. 259), E S.Isl., New Zealand, 65 mi. NNE of Christchurch and on Waiau-uha R.; rail terminus; agr. center.
Waiau River, S S.Isl., New Zealand, rises in L. Manapouri, flows 115 mi. S to Te Waewae Bay of Tasman Sea.
Waiau-uha River (-ōō'ŭ), E S.Isl., New Zealand, rises in Spenser Mts., flows 110 mi. S and E to Pacific Ocean 6 mi. N of Cheviot; trout. Sometimes called Dillon R.
Waiblingen (vīp'lĭng-ŭn), town (pop. 14,064), N Württemberg, Germany, after 1945 in Württemberg-Baden, on the Rems and 5 mi. ENE of Stuttgart; rail junction; auto repair; mfg. of machinery, tools, screws, textiles (silk, knit goods, clothing), furniture. Brickworks. Was royal domain. Chartered c.1250. The Ghibellines derived their name from Waiblingen.
Waibstadt (vīp'shtät), town (pop. 3,194), N Baden, Germany, after 1945 in Württemberg-Baden, 10 mi. E of Wiesloch; chicory, fruit.
Waichow, China: see WAIYEUNG.
Waidbruck, Italy: see PONTE GARDENA.
Waidhofen (vīt'hōfŭn). **1** or **Waidhofen an der Thaya** (än dĕr tä'yä), town (pop. 3,600), NW Lower Austria, on Thaya R. and 14 mi. ENE of Gmünd; textiles, rugs. **2** or **Waidhofen an der Ybbs** (ĭps'), town (pop. 5,592), SW Lower Austria, 17 mi. ESE of Steyr; rail junction; ironworks; mfg. (small tools, cutlery); summer resort.
Waifu (wī'fōō), town (pop. 12,341), Kumamoto prefecture, W central Kyushu, Japan, 13 mi. NNE of Kumamoto; rail terminus; rice-producing center.
Waigeu or **Waigeo** (wīgĕ'ōō), largest island (pop. 2,840) of Raja Ampat Isls., Netherlands New Guinea, 40 mi. W of Vogelkop peninsula (NW New Guinea); 0°13'S 130°50'E; 70 mi. long, 30 mi. wide. Isl. is nearly bisected by narrow Mayalibit Bay. Wooded, mountainous terrain rises to c.3,300 ft.; coastline is generally steep and rocky. Chief products: sago, tortoise shell, trepang. Formerly spelled Waygiou.
Waiheke Island (wīhē'kē), volcanic island, New Zealand, bet. Hauraki Gulf and Tamaki Strait, 7 mi. E of Auckland; 12 mi. long, 6 mi. wide; resort. Wool, Manganese.
Waihemo, New Zealand: see PALMERSTON.
Waihi (wī'hē), borough (pop. 3,756), N N.Isl., New Zealand, 70 mi. SE of Auckland; gold mines, dairy plants. School of mines. Summer resort near by.
Waihou River, New Zealand: see THAMES RIVER.
Waihu Island, Chile: see EASTER ISLAND.
Wai Island, Indonesia: see WE ISLAND.
Waikaia (wīkī'ŭ), township (pop. 196), S S.Isl., New Zealand, 50 mi. NNE of Invercargill; agr. center; gold, oil shale. Formerly Switzers.
Waikapu (wī'kä'pōō), village (pop. 577), central Maui, T.H., near the isthmus.
Waikaremoana, Lake (wī"kŭrēmōä'nŭ), E N.Isl., New Zealand, 50 mi. N of Napier; 12 mi. long, 6 mi. wide, 846 ft. deep; alt. 2,000 ft.; timbered shore.
Waikari (wīkă'rē), township (pop. 338), ⊙ Waipara co. (□ 937; pop. 2,361), E S.Isl., New Zealand, 40 mi. N of Christchurch; agr. center; flour mill.
Waikato, county, New Zealand: see HAMILTON.
Waikato River (wīkă'tō), longest river of New Zealand, rises in L. Taupo on N.Isl., flows 220 mi. NW, past Hamilton, to Tasman Sea 25 mi. S of Manukau Harbour. Navigable 80 mi. from mouth by small steamers to Cambridge. Hydroelectric plants at Arapuni and Horahora.
Waikerie (wī'kŭrē), town (pop. 1,506), SE South Australia, 90 mi. NE of Adelaide and on Murray R.; rail terminus; orchards.
Waikiki (wīkēkē'), beach, Honolulu, T.H.; site of Fort DE RUSSY; aquarium at edge of Kapiolani Park.
Waikohu, New Zealand: see TE KARAKA.
Waikouaiti (wī'kōī'tē), borough (pop. 596), ⊙ Waikouaiti co. (□ 312; pop. 3,782), SE S.Isl., New Zealand, 18 mi. N of Dunedin; agr. center; dairy plant.
Wailuku (wīlōō'kōō), city (pop. 7,424), ⊙ Maui co., N Maui, T.H., 2 mi. W of Kahului; largest town on isl.; tourist center.
Waimairi, New Zealand: see PAPANUI.
Waimakariri River (wī"mäkŭrēr'ē), E central S.Isl., New Zealand, rises in N slopes of S.Alps, flows 93 mi. SE to Pegasus Bay at Kaiapoi, near Banks Peninsula.
Waimanalo (wī'mŭnä'lō), village (pop. 868), Oahu, T.H., on SE coast; sugar mill. **Waimanalo Pali** (pä'lē), a pass through Koolau Range, leads down from Makapuu Point to E seaboard.
Waimarino, New Zealand: see RAETIHI.
Waimate (wīmă'tē), borough (pop. 2,351), ⊙ Waimate co. (□ 1,383; pop. 6,097), E S.Isl., New Zealand, 80 mi. NNE of Dunedin; timber, fruit.
Waimate West, New Zealand: see MANAIA.
Waimea (wīmā'ŭ). **1** Village (pop. 560) with Post Office name of **Kamuela** (kä"mōōä'lŭ), N Hawaii, T.H., on huge (500,000-acre) Parker cattle ranch. **2** Village (pop. 1,646), S Kauai, T.H., on Waimea Bay; early ⊙ isl.; Capt. Cook landed 1778 near by. Sugar plantation; ruins of fort built 1815 by Russian traders.
Waimea, New Zealand: see NELSON, city.
Waimea Canyon, central Kauai, T.H., fissures of WAIALEALE mtn.; 2–3,000 ft. deep, formed and colored like a smaller Grand Canyon of the Colorado; c.10 mi. long, 1 mi. wide. Puukapele mtn. on W edge.
Wainfleet-All-Saints, town and parish (pop. 1,324), Parts of Lindsey, E Lincolnshire, England, 5 mi. SW of Skegness; agr. market, with small port connected with The Wash by the short Wainfleet Haven or Steeping R. Site of Magdalen Col. School, founded 1484.
Wainganga River (wĭngŭng'gŭ), in Madhya Pradesh, India, rises in central Satpura Range W of Seoni; flows N, E, and generally S, through fertile rice lands, past Balaghat, Bhandara, and Pauni, joining Wardha R. 40 mi. SE of Chanda to form Pranhita R., an affluent of the Godavari; 360 mi. long. Navigable in lower course during flood season. Chief tributary, Kanhan R.
Waingapu or **Waingapoe** (both: wĭng'äpōō"), town (pop. 2,217), Sumba, Lesser Sundas, Indonesia, port on N coast of isl., on Savu Sea; ships horses. Has airfield.
Waini River, NW Br. Guiana, rises in forest region of North West Dist. at 7°2'N 59°30'W, flows c.175 mi. N and NW to the Atlantic near Venezuela border in 2-mi.-wide mouth 5 mi. N of Morawhanna. A short natural channel, the navigable Mora Passage, links its mouth with Barima R. just above Morawhanna. Navigable for steamers 77 mi. upstream to junction with Barama R. Waterfalls.
Wainscott, village (pop. c.200), Suffolk co., SE N.Y., on SE Long Isl., 3 mi. E of Bridgehampton, in summer-resort area.
Wainwright, village (pop. 224), NW Alaska, on Chukchi Sea, at mouth of Kuk R., 90 mi. WSW of Barrow; 70°39'N 159°46'W; fishing, reindeer herding. Oil and coal deposits near by. Site of Federal school for Eskimos.
Wainwright, town (pop. 1,261), E Alta., near Sask. border, 120 mi. ESE of Edmonton; oil and natural-gas production; oil refineries, grain elevators, flour mills. Railroad divisional point. Near by is Buffalo Natl. Park.
Wainwright, town (pop. 138), Muskogee co., E Okla., 15 mi. SW of Muskogee.
Waipa, New Zealand: see TE AWAMUTU.
Waipahu (wīpä'hōō), city (pop. 7,169), S Oahu, T.H., 11 mi. NW of Honolulu; sugar mill.
Waipara, New Zealand: see WAIKARI.
Waipawa (wī'päwŭ), borough (pop. 1,169), ⊙ Waipawa co. (□ 524; pop. 3,192), E N.Isl., New Zealand, 35 mi. SW of Napier; sheep-raising area.
Waipiro Bay (wī'pērō), township (pop. 321), ⊙ Waiapu co. (□ 793; pop. 5,982), NE N.Isl., New Zealand, 45 mi. NNE of Gisborne, on Open Bay (7 mi. wide); sheep, dairy products.
Waipukurau (wī'pōōkōōrou'), borough (pop. 2,095), ⊙ Waipukurau co. (□ 121; pop. 1,043), and ⊙ Patangata co. (□ 658; pop. 2,518), E N.Isl., New Zealand, 40 mi. SW of Napier; center of sheep-raising area. Waipukurau borough is independent unit.
Wairarapa South, New Zealand: see CARTERTON.
Wairau River (wīrou'), N S.Isl., New Zealand, rises in Spenser Mts., flows 105 mi. NE to Cloudy Bay of Cook Strait.
Wairewa, New Zealand: see LITTLE RIVER.
Wairio (wī'rēō), township (pop. 200), S S.Isl., New Zealand, 31 mi. NW of Invercargill; rail terminus; coal.
Wairoa (wīrō'ŭ, wī'rō-ŭ), borough (pop. 2,857), ⊙ Wairoa co. (□ 1,373; pop. 7,836), E N.Isl., New Zealand, at mouth of Wairoa R., on N shore of Hawke Bay and 40 mi. NE of Napier; dairy plants. Hot springs near by.
Wairoa River. **1** N N.Isl., New Zealand, rises in hills near Hikurangi, flows 95 mi. SW to Kaipara Harbour of Tasman Sea on W coast. Navigable for 20 mi. below Dargaville by small steamers carrying dairy products; log drives. **2** E N.Isl., New Zealand, rises in hills S of Te Karaka, flows c.50 mi. SSW to Hawke Bay on E coast, 40 mi. NE of Napier.
Waisenberg (vī'zŭnbĕrk), town (pop. 2,822), Carinthia, S Austria, 13 mi. NE of Klagenfurt; wheat, rye, corn, cattle.
Waitaki, county, New Zealand: see OAMARU.
Waitaki River (wītä'kē), E S.Isl., New Zealand, formed by union of Tekapo and Ahuriri rivers; flows 95 mi. SE, past Kurow (hydroelectric plant), to the S Pacific 70 mi. N of Dunedin.
Waitangi, New Zealand: see CHATHAM ISLANDS.
Waitara (wī'tŭrŭ), borough (pop. 2,295), ⊙ Clifton co. (□ 444; pop. 2,492), W N.Isl., New Zealand, on S shore of N.Taranaki Bight and 10 mi. NE of New Plymouth; agr. center.

Waite, town (pop. 117), Washington co., E Maine, 22 mi. NW of Calais, in hunting, fishing area.

Waite Hill, village (pop. 305), Lake co., NE Ohio, c.15 mi. ENE of Cleveland.

Waitemata, county, New Zealand: see AUCKLAND, city.

Waitemata Harbour (wī'tŭmä'tŭ), inlet of Hauraki Gulf, N N.Isl., New Zealand, N harbor of city of AUCKLAND, 5 mi. N of Manukau Harbour on W coast.

Waite Park, village (pop. 1,639), Stearns co., central Minn., on Sauk R. and just W of St. Cloud; grain, livestock, poultry.

Waitomo, county, New Zealand: see TE KUITI.

Waitomo Caves (wītō'mō), W central N.Isl., New Zealand, 100 mi. SSE of Auckland, near Te Kuiti; stalactites and stalagmites.

Waitotara, New Zealand: see WANGANUI.

Waitowshan, Manchuria: see PENKI.

Waitsap (wī'dzäp'), Mandarin *Hui-chi* (hwā'jē), town, ⊙ Waitsap co. (pop. 292,894), easternmost Kwangsi prov., China, near Kwangtung line, 60 mi. NE of Wuchow, and on Sui R.; rice, wheat, beans.

Waitsburg, city (pop. 1,015), Walla Walla co., SE Wash., 18 mi. NE of Walla Walla and on Touchet R.; wheat, fruit, barley, alfalfa; flour milling.

Waitsfield, town (pop. 661), Washington co., W central Vt., on Mad R. and 15 mi. SW of Montpelier; lumber, dairy products. Skiing near by, at Mad R. Glen.

Waits River, E Vt., rises E of Barre, flows c.20 mi. SE to the Connecticut at Bradford.

Waitzen, Hungary: see VAC.

Waiuku (wī'ōō'kōō), town (pop. 948), N N.Isl., New Zealand, 30 mi. S of Auckland and on S arm of Manukau Harbour; rail terminus; stockyards.

Waiyeung (wī'yŭrng'), Mandarin *Hui-yang* (hwā'-yäng'), town (pop. 35,120), ⊙ Waiyeung co. (pop. 566,792), E central Kwangtung prov., China, port on East R. and 75 mi. E of Canton; commercial center; exports rice, wheat, beans, pineapples, peanuts. Tin and tungsten mining near by. Opened to foreign trade in 1902. Until 1912 called Waichow, Weichow, or Hweichow.

Waizenkirchen (vī'tsŭnkĭrkhŭn), town (pop. 3,758), Upper Austria, 20 mi. W of Linz; tannery.

Wajay (wähī'), town (pop. 1,389), Havana prov., W Cuba, 9 mi. SSW of Havana; tobacco, vegetables, fruit. Formerly spelled Guajay.

Wajh, Al, Saudi Arabia: see WEJH.

Wajiki (wä'jĭkē), town (pop. 4,697), Tokushima prefecture, E Shikoku, Japan, 15 mi. SSW of Tokushima; rice, raw silk, lumber, charcoal.

Wajima (wä'jĭmä), town (pop. 15,526), Ishikawa prefecture, central Honshu, Japan, on NW Noto Peninsula, on Sea of Japan, 25 mi. NNW of Nanao; rail terminus; mfg. of lacquer ware; poultry raising. Sometimes spelled Wazima. Includes isl. Hekura-jima (1¼ mi. long, ½ mi. wide) in Sea of Japan, 30 mi. N of town proper; generally flat; uninhabited in winter; fishing.

Wajir (wäjēr'), town, Northern Frontier Prov., NE Kenya, 200 mi. NE of Isiolo; 1°44'N 40°5'E; road junction; stock raising; peanuts, sesame, corn, coffee. Airfield.

Waka or **Waka-sur-Momboyo** (wäkä-sür-mōmbōyō'), village, Equator Prov., W Belgian Congo, on Momboyo R. and 120 mi. ESE of Coquilhatville; steamboat landing and trading post; palms, rice, copal.

Waka (wä'kä), Ital. *Uaca,* village, Kaffa prov., SW Ethiopia, near confluence of Gojab and Omo rivers, 50 mi. SE of Jimma.

Wakaf Bharu (wäkäf' bä'rōō), village (pop. 670), N Kelantan, Malaya, on railroad and left bank of Kelantan R., opposite Kota Bharu.

Wakamatsu (wäkä'mätsōō). **1** City and port (1940 pop. 88,901; 1947 pop. 78,694), Fukuoka prefecture, N Kyushu, Japan, 32 mi. NE of Fukuoka, opposite Yawata and Tobata, across small inlet of Hibiki Sea. Chief coal-loading port of Japan, with large imports of raw material for near-by industrial cities. Exports coal, steel, sugar. Heavily bombed (1945) in Second World War. **2** City (1940 pop. 48,091; 1947 pop. 59,024), Fukushima prefecture, N Honshu, Japan, 35 mi. SW of Fukushima; mfg. (textiles, soy sauce), wood- and metalworking, sake brewing. Capture by imperial forces of castle here ended civil war (1868) on Honshu.

Wakamatsu-shima (–shĭmä), island (□ 16; pop. 6,134, including offshore islets) of isl. group Goto-retto, Nagasaki prefecture, Japan, in E.China Sea, 38 mi. W of Kyushu, just SW of Nakadori-shima; 5 mi. long, 4 mi. wide; hilly. Fishing.

Wakamiya (wäkä'mēyä), town (pop. 4,500), Fukuoka prefecture, N Kyushu, Japan, 16 mi. NE of Fukuoka, near Miyata; rice, wheat, barley, raw silk.

Wakarusa (wăkŭrōō'sŭ), town (pop. 1,143), Elkhart co., N Ind., 16 mi. SE of South Bend, in agr. area (dairy products; grain); ladders, concrete vaults.

Wakarusa River, E Kansas, rises in Shawnee co. SW of Topeka, flows 73 mi. E to Kansas R. at Eudora, 8 mi. E of Lawrence.

Wakasa (wä"kä'sä), former province in S Honshu, Japan; now part of Fukui prefecture.

Wakasa, town (pop. 6,858), Tottori prefecture, S Honshu, Japan, 15 mi. SE of Tottori; rail terminus; agr. and livestock center; rice, wheat, raw silk.

Wakasa Bay, Jap. *Wakasa-wan,* inlet of Sea of Japan, S Honshu, Japan, bet. Kyoga Point (W) and Echizen Point (E); 45 mi. long, 20 mi. wide. Tsuruga and Maizuru on S shore.

Wakasa-takahama, Japan: see TAKAHAMA, Fukui prefecture.

Waka-sur-Maringa (wäkä-sür-märĕng-gä'), village, Equator Prov., W Belgian Congo, on Maringa R. and 140 mi. NE of Coquilhatville; steamboat landing and agr. center; palm-oil milling. R.C. mission.

Wakatipu, Lake (wä'kŭtĭp), S central S.Isl., New Zealand, 90 mi. WNW of Dunedin; □ 112; 52 mi. long, 3 mi. wide, 1,242 ft. deep, alt. 1,016 ft. Queenstown is on N shore, Glenorchy on NE shore. Known for unusual rise and fall of water level. Steamship line from Kingston on SE shore to Glenorchy.

Wakaw (wä'kô, wô'–), village (pop. 659), central Sask., on Wakaw L. (12 mi. long), 40 mi. S of Prince Albert; mixed farming, dairying.

Wakayama (wäkä'yämŭ), prefecture [Jap. *ken*] (□ 1,824; 1940 pop. 865,074; 1947 pop. 959,999), on Kii Peninsula, S Honshu, Japan; ⊙ Wakayama. Bounded W by Kii Channel, S by Philippine Sea, SE by Kumano Sea. Generally mountainous and forested terrain, drained by Kumano R. Extensive lumbering in sparsely populated interior; many fishing ports. Rice, citrus fruit, plums grown in coastal area. Mfg. (principally cotton textiles) at Wakayama. Other centers: SHINGU, KAINAN, TANABE.

Wakayama, city (1940 pop. 195,203; 1947 pop. 171,800), ⊙ Wakayama prefecture, S Honshu, Japan, on W Kii Peninsula, on strait bet. Osaka Bay and Kii Channel, at mouth of small Kino R., 35 mi. SW of Osaka. Rail junction; mfg. center (cotton flannel, dyes, yarn); sake breweries, lumber yards. Has 16th-cent. castle of Hideyoshi. Includes (since early 1940s) former town of Kimiidera.

Wakayanagi (wäkä'-yä'nägē), town (pop. 12,172), Miyagi prefecture, N Honshu, Japan, 26 mi. NNW of Ishinomaki; rice, wheat, silk cocoons. Lignite mining.

Wakde Islands (wäk'tŭ), Netherlands New Guinea, just off N coast of isl., in the Pacific, 120 mi. WNW of Hollandia; 1°56'S 139°1'E. Consist of 2 islets, the larger being Wakde, Insumar, or Insoemoar (both: ĭnsōōmwär') and the smaller Insumanai or Insoemanai (both: ĭnsōōmänī'). In Second World War U.S. troops made surprise landing here 1944.

Wake (wä'kā), town (pop. 2,563), Okayama prefecture, SW Honshu, Japan, 15 mi. NE of Okayama; rice, wheat, persimmons, peppermint; raw silk, sake.

Wake (wāk), county (□ 866; pop. 136,450), central N.C.; ⊙ RALEIGH, the state capital. Piedmont farming (tobacco, cotton) and sawmilling area; drained by Neuse R. Mfg. at Raleigh. Formed 1770.

Wake, city (pop. 1,066), Bowie co., NE Texas, a suburb of Texarkana. Also called Wake Village. Inc. after 1940.

Wakeeney or **WaKeeney** (wŏ'kē"nē), city (pop. 2,446), ⊙ Trego co., W central Kansas, 32 mi. WNW of Hays, bet. Saline and Smoky Hill rivers, in grain and livestock region; dairying. Oil wells near by. Prehistoric fossils have been found in vicinity. Platted 1878, inc. 1880.

Wakefield, village (pop. 275), SW Que., on Gatineau R. and 17 mi. NE of Hull; magnesia, lime mfg., brucite mining.

Wakefield, county borough (1931 pop. 59,122; 1951 census 60,380) and city, ⊙ West Riding, S central Yorkshire, England, on Calder R. and 8 mi. S of Leeds; woolen-milling center (industry dates from 14th cent.); mfg. of machine tools, power presses, light metals, chemicals, shoes, rubber and asbestos products; cattle and agr. market. Has 10th-cent. cross remaining from Saxon church, chantry (c.1350) on Calder bridge, 15th-cent. cathedral with 247-ft. spire, and grammar school (1591). At battle of Wakefield (1460) Richard duke of York was defeated and killed by Lancastrians. In Civil War the city was taken by Fairfax (1643). The Towneley cycle of miracle plays originated here. In county borough is industrial suburb of Sandal (SSE; pop. 5,545), with remains of Sandal Castle, originally built in 7th or 8th cent., and center of 1460 battle.

Wakefield. 1 Suburb (pop. 8,906) of Tucson, Pima co., SE Ariz. **2** City (pop. 591), Clay co., N central Kansas, on Republican R. and 16 mi. NW of Junction City; shipping point in cattle and grain region. **3** Town (pop. 19,633), Middlesex co., E Mass., 10 mi. N of Boston; shoes, dies, knit goods, electrical products, rattan chairs. Settled 1639, inc. 1812. Includes village of Greenwood. **4** City (pop. 3,344), Gogebic co., W Upper Peninsula, Mich., 12 mi. ENE of Ironwood, on Gogebic iron-range. Dairy and truck farming; sawmilling; resort. Settled 1866; inc. as village 1887, as city 1919. **5** City (pop. 1,027), Dixon and Wayne counties, NE Nebr., 30 mi. SW of Sioux City, Iowa, and on Logan Creek; grain. **6** Town (pop. 1,267), Carroll co., E N.H., 9 mi. SSE of Ossipee, E of L. Winnipesaukee; inc. 1774. Includes mill village of Union (wood products, machinery; 1st settled 1770) and Province Lake village (resort), near Province L. (2.5 mi. long) on Maine line. **7** Village (pop., with adjacent Peace Dale, 5,224), administrative center of South Kingstown town, Washington co., S R.I., 27 mi. SSW of Providence; woolen milling. Birthplace of Oliver Hazard Perry is mus. **8** Town (pop. 949), Sussex co., SE Va., 28 mi. SE of Petersburg, in agr. area (peanuts). "Wakefield," George Washington's birthplace, is in Westmoreland co., in GEORGE WASHINGTON BIRTHPLACE NATIONAL MONUMENT.

Wake Forest, town (pop. 3,704), Wake co., central N.C., 15 mi. NNE of Raleigh; seat of Wake Forest Col. (men; 1833). Cotton and lumber mills.

Wake Island, coral atoll and 3 islets, bet. Hawaii and Guam; c.45 mi. long, 2.25 mi. wide; 19°17'N 166°35'E. Discovered 1796 by British, claimed 1900 by U.S., made 1934 U.S. naval reservation and 1935 air-line base for route to Orient. Appropriations made in 1939 for naval air base and submarine base. In Second World War, isl. was attacked by Japanese (Dec. 7, 1941; Dec. 8, Pacific time) and, after heroic defense by a small marine garrison, fell on Dec. 23. Wake Isl. bombed by U.S. forces during 1942–45; Japanese garrison surrendered in Sept., 1945.

Wakema (wä'kĕmä), town (pop. 9,359), Myaungmya dist., Lower Burma, in Irrawaddy delta, 30 mi. ESE of Bassein; steamer landing.

Wakeman, village (pop. 620), Huron co., N Ohio, 11 mi. E of Norwalk and on Vermilion R.

Wakemup Bay, Minn.: see VERMILION LAKE.

Wakenaam Island (□ 19.2; pop. 4,513), Essequibo co., N Br. Guiana, in Essequibo R. estuary on the Atlantic, 20 mi. WNW of Georgetown; c.10 mi. long. Rice, coconut plantations. Among settlements is Zeelandia on NW tip.

Wakenda (wô'kŭndô), town (pop. 255), Carroll co., NW central Mo., near Missouri R., 7 mi. ESE of Carrollton.

Wake Village, Texas: see WAKE.

Wakhaldunga, Nepal: see OKHALDHUNGA.

Wakhan (wăkhän'), panhandle of NE Afghanistan, in Afghan Badakhshan, just S of the Pamir highland. Bounded N by Tadzhik SSR of USSR along Panj and Pamir rivers, E by China's Sinkiang prov., and S by Kashmir and Pakistan along the crest of the Hindu Kush. A wild, mountainous region, it has been a political buffer since the demarcation of the frontier by the Anglo-Russian Pamir Commission of 1895–96. Main village, Qala Panja. Sometimes called Little Pamir. The **Wakhan River,** Pashto *Wakhan Darya* (dŭryä'), flows 100 mi. through the Wakhan from W to E, joining Pamir R. near Qala Panja to form Panj R., one of the headstreams of the Amu Darya.

Wakhjir Pass (wäkh'jĭr) (alt. 16,150 ft.), in the E Hindu Kush, on Afghanistan-China line, at E end of Wakhan panhandle; 37°7'N 74°30'E.

Waki (wä'kē), town (pop. 8,225), Tokushima prefecture, E central Shikoku, Japan, on Yoshino R. and 23 mi. W of Tokushima; agr. and livestock-raising center; rice, wheat, raw silk.

Wakino (wä"kē'nō), town (pop. 4,380), Niigata prefecture, central Honshu, Japan, 5 mi. NW of Nagaoka; agr.; noodles, sake.

Wakita (wŏkē'tŭ), town (pop. 440), Grant co., N Okla., 34 mi. N of Enid, in agr. area (grain, poultry).

Wakkanai (wäk-känī'), town (pop. 29,275), extreme N Hokkaido, Japan, on Soya Bay (inlet of La Pérouse Strait), 120 mi. NNW of Asahigawa; fishing, fish canning. Oil field near by.

Wakken (vä'kŭn), agr. village (pop. 2,661), West Flanders prov., W Belgium, 5 mi. SSE of Tielt. Formerly spelled Wacken.

Wakonda (wŭkŏn'dŭ), town (pop. 454), Clay co., SE S.Dak., 17 mi. NNW of Vermillion; dairy products, livestock, grain.

Wakra or **Wakrah,** Qatar: see WAQRA.

Wakulla (wôkōō'lŭ, wŏkŭ'lŭ), county (□ 614; pop. 5,258), NW Fla., bounded S by Apalachee Bay (Gulf of Mexico) and W by Ochlockonee R.; ⊙ Crawfordville. Lowland area drained by St. Marks and Wakulla rivers. Coast is a natl. wildlife refugee; W interior is part of Apalachicola Natl. Forest. Agr. (cattle, hogs, corn, peanuts, vegetables), forestry (lumber, naval stores), and fishing. Formed 1843.

Wakulla, village, Wakulla co., NW Fla., 15 mi. SSW of Tallahassee. Wakulla Springs, a resort, is 4 mi. W; its large, deep spring is source of Wakulla R., which flows c.10 mi. SE to St. Marks R. at St. Marks.

Wakura, Japan: see TAZURUHAMA.

Wakuya (wäkōō'yä), town (pop. 10,138), Miyagi prefecture, N Honshu, Japan, 13 mi. NW of Ishinomaki; rice, wheat, silk cocoons.

Walachia or **Wallachia** (wŏlā'kēu, wŭ–), Rum. *Valachia* (välä'kyä), historic region (□ 29,575; 1948 pop. 6,709,271), S and SE Rumania. Its early ⊙ was Campulung, its 2d Curtea-de-Arges (14th–15th cent.), and its 3d Targoviste (until 1698); its chief city is Bucharest, ⊙ Rumania. Bounded SW, S, and E by the Danube which separates it from

Yugoslavia, Bulgaria, and Rum. Dobruja; N by the Transylvanian Alps; NE by Moldavia. Olt R. divides it into Muntenia or Greater Walachia (□ 20,270; 1948 pop. 4,991,982) in E, the more advanced economically, and Oltenia or Lesser Walachia (□ 9,305; 1948 pop. 1,717,882) in W. Fertile agr. region with zones of continental and zones of mediterranean climate, producing cereals, leguminous plants, livestock, fruit, and wines. Forestry and sheep grazing are well developed on mountain slopes; fresh-water fishing (sturgeon, carp) is carried on in the Danube and its tributaries. Of outstanding industrial importance are the rich oil fields around Ploesti and the mfg. area of Bucharest. Peasant handicrafts (e.g., weaving of rugs, embroidery) are still common. Principal centers are Bucharest, Ploesti, Braila, Craiova, and Giurgiu. Originally a part of the Roman Dacia (the region has retained elements of its Latin speech despite centuries of invasion and foreign rule), the territory was repeatedly overrun by Tatar and Slavonic tribes after the fall of Rome. Principality of Walachia was established c.1290 by Radu Negru or Rudolf the Black, voivode of Transylvania and vassal of Hungary. Though it secured temporary independence from Hungary (1330–69), it soon fell to the Turks (1387). Save for brief spells of relative autonomy Turkish domination continued till mid-19th cent. Dobruja was annexed in 1411. Michael the Brave led successful campaigns against the Turks and united under his rule (1593–1601) Walachia, Transylvania, and Moldavia. Government by native voivodes came to an end with the beheading of Constantine Brancovan (1714). From 1716 the principality was ruled by the Greek Phanariots of Constantinople. Oltenia was held by Austria (1718) and Russia occupied entire Walachia (1769) until treaty of Kutchuk Kainarji (1774). Russian control and incursions lasted well into 19th cent. Treaty of Adrianople (1829) made Walachia and Moldavia virtual protectorates of Russia though still dependent politically on Turkey. Following Russian occupation of Moldavia (1853) in the Crimean War, the 2 Danubian principalities (as Walachia and Moldavia were called) were guaranteed independence by the Congress of Paris (1856). Final unification of Rumanian state came in 1861.

Walaja, India: see WALAJAPET.

Walajabad (välä'jäbäd), town (pop. 5,486), Chingleput dist., E Madras, India, on Palar R. and 35 mi. SW of Madras; road-metal and building-stone quarrying; rice, coconuts, tamarind. Also called Dandei Sivaram.

Walajapet or **Wallajapet** (välä'yäpĕt), town (pop. 11,048), North Arcot dist., E central Madras, India, on Palar R. and 15 mi. E of Vellore; cotton and silk weaving, peanut-oil extraction. Formerly also called Walaja and Walajanagar.

Walawe Ganga (vŭ'lŭvŭ gŭng'gŭ), river, S Ceylon, rises in S Ceylon Hill Country, flows 83 mi. E and generally SSE to Indian Ocean just S of Ambalantota. Forms Sabaragamura-Uva prov. border in middle course; land reclamation project (□ 40) on lower course.

Walberton (wô'bûrtŭn), agr. village and parish (pop. 1,295), SW Sussex, England, 5 mi. NE of Bognor Regis. Church has anc. font.

Walbridge, village (pop. 1,152), Wood co., NW Ohio, 5 mi. SE of Toledo.

Walbrzych, Poland: see WALDENBURG.

Walcha (wŏl'kŭ), municipality (pop. 1,550), E New South Wales, Australia, 135 mi. N of Newcastle; sheep center.

Walchandnagar, India: see KALAMB.

Walchensee (väl'khŭnzā"), lake (□ 6.33), Upper Bavaria, Germany, in the Bavarian Alps, 38 mi. SSW of Munich; 4 mi. long, 3 mi. wide, 630 ft. deep; alt. 2,631 ft. At N tip is one of Germany's largest hydroelectric plants (built 1918–24).

Walcheren (väl'khŭrŭn), westernmost island (□ 80) of Zeeland prov., SW Netherlands, W of Bergen op Zoom; bounded by North Sea (W, NW), the Veersche Gat and Het Sloe (E), the Western Scheldt (S, SW); 10 mi. long, 11 mi. wide. Grows vegetables, potatoes, sugar beets, fruit, wheat. Linked with South Beveland isl. and mainland by railroad and road causeways. Chief towns: FLUSHING, MIDDELBURG. The North Sea dike was ruptured (1944) in Second World War, resulting in great flood damage to substantial part of isl.

Walcott (wŏl'kŭt, wôl'–). **1** Town (pop. 85), Greene co., NE Ark., 11 mi. W of Paragould. Crowley's Ridge State Park is near by. **2** Town (pop. 480), Scott co., E Iowa, 11 mi. WNW of Davenport; mfg. (farm wagons, hoists).

Walcott, Lake, Idaho: see MINIDOKA DAM.

Walcourt (välkōōr'), agr. village (pop. 1,936), Namur prov., S Belgium, 11 mi. S of Charleroi.

Walcz (vä'ōōch), Pol. *Wałcz*, Ger. *Deutsch Krone* (doich' krō'nŭ), town (1939 pop. 14,941; 1946 pop. 7,816) in Pomerania, after 1945 in Koszalin prov., NW Poland, 14 mi. NW of Schneidemühl (Pila); rail junction; woolen milling, brick mfg., woodworking; cattle market. Chartered 1303 by Ascanian margraves of Brandenburg, who ceded it to Poland in 1368; passed 1772 to Prussia. Formerly called Arnskrone. Until 1938, in former Prussian Grenzmark Posen-Westpreussen prov. In Second World War, c.50% destroyed.

Wald (vält), suburb (1925 pop. 27,443) of Solingen, W Germany, 2 mi. WNW of city center. Inc. 1929 into Solingen.

Wald, town (pop. 6,652), Zurich canton, Switzerland, 19 mi. ESE of Zurich; cotton and silk textiles, chocolate; woodworking.

Waldalgesheim (vält"äl'gŭs-hīm), village (pop. 1,602), in former Prussian Rhine Prov., W Germany, after 1945 in Rhineland-Palatinate, 3 mi. W of Bingen; manganese mining.

Waldau, Russian SFSR: see NIZOVYE.

Waldbredimus (vält-brā'dĭmŭs), village (pop. 177), SE Luxembourg, 8 mi. SE of Luxembourg city; stone quarrying; plums.

Waldbröhl (vält'brŭl), village (pop. 10,767), in former Prussian Rhine Prov., W Germany, after 1945 in North Rhine-Westphalia, 18 mi. W of Siegen; forestry.

Waldeck (väl'dĕk), former principality (□ 433; 1910 pop. 61,707) of W Germany; ⊙ was Arolsen. Hilly forested region, drained by Eder and Diemel rivers. Created in 12th or 13th cent., county of Waldeck was united with county of Pyrmont in late-17th cent. Counts were created princes c.1710. Principality came under Prussian administration in 1867. Declared republic in 1918. Pyrmont was annexed to Prussia (Hanover prov.) in 1922. Following 1929 plebiscite, Waldeck became part of former Prussian prov. of Hesse-Nassau. After 1945, was administrative district [Ger. *Landkreis*] (□ 420; 1946 pop. 89,553) of Hesse; ⊙ Korbach.

Waldeck, town (pop. 1,415), in former Prussian prov. of Hesse-Nassau, W Germany, after 1945 in Hesse, near the Eder reservoir, 9 mi. SE of Korbach; agr. market center. Castle, 1st mentioned 1120, was until 1665 seat of counts of Waldeck. Until 1929 in former Waldeck principality.

Waldegrave Islands, Australia: see INVESTIGATOR ISLANDS.

Walden (wôl'dŭn). **1** Town (pop. 696), ⊙ Jackson co., N Colo., on headstream of N.Platte R., bet. Park Range and Medicine Bow Mts., and 55 mi. SW of Laramie, Wyo., near Wyo. line; alt. 8,300 ft. Supply point in livestock and grain region; coal mines. **2** Village (pop. 4,559), Orange co., SE N.Y., on Wallkill R. and 10 mi. WNW of Newburgh, in dairying and resort area; mfg. (clothing, cutlery, gas and temperature gauges, paper, hatters' fur). Inc. 1855. **3** Town (pop. 481), Caledonia co., NE Vt., 10 mi. W of St. Johnsbury; wood products; agr.

Waldenbuch (väl'dŭnbōōkh), village (pop. 3,030), Württemberg, Germany, after 1945 in Württemberg-Baden, 6 mi. SE of Böblingen; cattle.

Waldenburg (–bōōrk). **1** Town (pop. 6,007), Saxony, E central Germany, on the Zwickauer Mulde and 12 mi. NNE of Zwickau; textile milling and knitting, china mfg. Has old castle, Gothic church, and noted park. **2** Town (pop. 1,218), N Württemberg, Germany, after 1945 in Württemberg-Baden, 19 mi. ENE of Heilbronn; wine. Has ruined castle.

Waldenburg or **Walbrzych** (vä'ōōb-zhĭkh), Pol. *Wałbrzych*, city (1939 pop. 64,136; 1950 estimate 81,260) in Lower Silesia, after 1945 in Wroclaw prov., SW Poland, in N foothills of the Sudetes, 40 mi. SW of Breslau (Wroclaw); 50°46'N 16°18'E. Coal-mining center; mfg. of china, glass, soap, pharmaceuticals; linen, flax, hemp, and jute milling. Mining school. Major power station at Sobiecin, 3 mi. WSW. City largely destroyed in Second World War.

Walden Pond (wôl'dŭn), E Mass., small pond (64 acres), just S of Concord, in Walden Pond state reservation (144 acres). Site of Thoreau's famous cabin (1845) is marked.

Walden Ridge, SE Tenn., a ridge-like portion of Cumberland Plateau, in Appalachian system; from Tennessee R. W of Chattanooga extends c.60 mi. NNE, paralleling Sequatchie R. (W), bet. Sand Mtn. (S) and Crab Orchard Mts. (N). Averages 1–2,000 ft., rising to c.3,000 ft. at N end. Signal Mtn., just NW of Chattanooga, is a spur.

Waldershof (väl'dŭrs-hōf), village (pop. 2,707), Upper Palatinate, NE Bavaria, Germany, in the Fichtelgebirge, 11 mi. WSW of Waldsassen; porcelain mfg. Chartered 1463.

Waldfischbach (vält'fĭshbäkh"), village (pop. 3,227), Rhenish Palatinate, W Germany, 6 mi. NNE of Pirmasens; rye, potatoes.

Waldhausen (vält'houzŭn), town (pop. 2,476), NE Upper Austria, 9 mi. NW of Ybbs, N of the Danube; vineyards.

Waldheim (wôld'hīm), village (pop. 480), S central Sask., 35 mi. N of Saskatoon; mixed farming, dairying. First settled by Mennonites.

Waldheim (vält'hīm), town (pop. 12,271), Saxony, E central Germany, on Zschopau R. (dam) and 6 mi. SW of Döbeln; mfg. of furniture, glass, pharmaceuticals, cigars; woolen milling; serpentine quarrying. Has old castle, now prison.

Waldia (wäl'dēä), Ital. *Ualdia*, town, Wallo prov., NE Ethiopia, near source of Takkaze R., on road and 50 mi. N of Dessye; 11°52'N 39°41'E. Trade center (salt, cereals, mules).

Waldkappel (vält'kä"pŭl), town (pop. 1,422), in former Prussian prov. of Hesse-Nassau, W Germany, after 1945 in Hesse, 8 mi. WSW of Eschwege; textiles.

Waldkirch (vält'kĭrkh"), town (pop. 6,343), S Baden, Germany, in Black Forest at NW foot of the Kandel, on the Elz and 8 mi. NE of Freiburg; mfg. of silk, cotton, paper; leather-, metal-, and woodworking; printing. Summer resort.

Waldkirch, town (pop. 2,434), St. Gall canton, NE Switzerland, 5 mi. NW of St. Gall.

Waldkirchen (–ŭn), village (pop. 5,432), Lower Bavaria, Germany, in Bohemian Forest, 13 mi. NE of Passau; rye, oats, cattle. Chartered c.1285.

Waldmohr (vält'mōr"), village (pop. 2,399), Rhenish Palatinate, W Germany, 10 mi. W of Landstuhl; coal mining.

Waldmünchen (vält'mün"khŭn), town (pop. 5,207), Upper Palatinate, E Bavaria, Germany, in Bohemian Forest, 11 mi. NNE of Cham, near Czechoslovak border; rail terminus; cloth mfg., brewing, woodworking, glass grinding. Has late-19th-cent. church.

Waldnab or **Waldnaab**, Germany: see NAB RIVER.

Waldneukirchen (vält'noi'kĭrkhŭn), town (pop. 2,051), SE central Upper Austria, 8 mi. SW of Steyr; furniture mfg.

Waldniel (vält'nēl"), village (pop. 6,076), in former Prussian Rhine Prov., W Germany, after 1945 in North Rhine-Westphalia, 7 mi. W of München Gladbach; cattle.

Waldo (wôl'dō), county (□ 734; pop. 21,687), S Maine, on Penobscot Bay; ⊙ Belfast. Agr., fishing, resort region. Agr. in inland lake region (apples, potatoes, garden truck), dairying, poultry raising; lumbering, wood products, granite quarrying. Drained by Penobscot, Sebasticook, and Sheepscot rivers. Formed 1827.

Waldo. **1** Town (pop. 1,491), Columbia co., SW Ark., 7 mi. NNW of Magnolia, in cotton and timber area; woodworking, cotton ginning. Founded in 1830s. **2** City (pop. 647), Alachua co., N Fla., 13 mi. NE of Gainesville, in agr. area. **3** City (pop. 216), Russell co., N central Kansas, 16 mi. N of Russell; livestock, grain. **4** Town (pop. 324), Waldo co., S Maine, just NW of Belfast. **5** Village (pop. 356), Marion co., central Ohio, 9 mi. SSE of Marion and on Olentangy R. **6** Village (pop. 367), Sheboygan co., E Wis., on small Onion R. and 12 mi. WSW of Sheboygan, in dairy and farm area; cannery.

Waldoboro (wôl'dŭbŭrŭ), fishing, resort town (pop. 2,536), Lincoln co., SW Maine, 25 mi. SE of Augusta, at head of Medomak R. inlet; button factory; mfg. of electrical goods. Settled 1748 by Germans, inc. 1773.

Waldorf (wŏl'dôrf). **1** Village, Charles co., S Md., 20 mi. SSE of Washington; tobacco market, with large warehouses and processing plants; suburban shopping center. Cedarville State Forest is near by. **2** Village (pop. 266), Waseca co., S Minn., on branch of Cobb R. and 27 mi. NW of Albert Lea; dairy products.

Waldport, city (pop. 689), Lincoln co., W Oregon, on Pacific Ocean at mouth of Alsea R. and 40 mi. WSW of Corvallis; fisheries (salmon, crab, clam); lumber milling, dairying.

Waldron (wôl'drŭn), town and parish (pop. 2,722), E Sussex, England, 5 mi. E of Uckfield; agr. market. Church contains anc. font.

Waldron. **1** Town (pop. 1,292), ⊙ Scott co., W Ark., 38 mi. SSE of Fort Smith, in timber, coal, and farm area; cotton ginning, lumber milling. **2** City (pop. 83), Harper co., S Kansas, at Okla. line, 13 mi. SW of Anthony, in wheat area. **3** Village (pop. 427), Hillsdale co., S Mich., 18 mi. SE of Hillsdale, near Ohio line, in livestock and grain region.

Waldsassen (vält'zä"sŭn), town (pop. 7,665), Upper Palatinate, NE Bavaria, Germany, on S slope of the Fichtelgebirge, 6 mi. SW of Cheb, near Czechoslovak border; mfg. of glass, porcelain, Dutch clinkers; brewing. Has Cistercian abbey, founded 1133. Chartered 1693. Pyrite mines in area.

Waldsee (vält'zā"). **1** Village (pop. 3,107), Rhenish Palatinate, W Germany, 5 mi. N of Speyer; tobacco, corn, sugar beets. **2** Town (pop. 5,087), S Württemberg, Germany, after 1945 in Württemberg-Hohenzollern, 11 mi. NNW of Ravensburg; picturesquely situated bet. 2 small lakes; rail junction; silk weaving. Has late-Gothic church, 15th-cent town hall.

Waldshut (valts'hōōt"), town (pop. 6,968), S Baden, Germany, at S foot of Black Forest, on the Rhine (Swiss border; rail and road bridges) and 26 mi. E of Lörrach; hydroelectric plant. Mfg. of chemicals and textiles; metal- and woodworking.

Waldstätten, die Vier, Switzerland: see FOUR FOREST CANTONS, THE.

Waldstein, Czechoslovakia: see BOHEMIAN PARADISE.

Waldthurn (vält'tōōrn"), village (pop. 1,330), Upper Palatinate, E Bavaria, Germany, in Bohemian Forest, 7 mi. E of Weiden; flour and lumber milling.

Waldwick (wôl'dwĭk), residential borough (pop. 3,963), Bergen co., NE N.J., 7 mi. N of Paterson; mfg. (cinder blocks, upholstery fabrics). Inc. 1919.

Waldzell (vält'tsĕl), village (pop. 2,206), W Upper Austria, 6 mi. SSW of Ried; wheat, cattle.

Walensee, Switzerland: see WALLENSTADT, LAKE OF.

Wales, Welsh *Cymru* (kōōm'rē), region and political division (□ 8,016; 1931 pop. 2,593,332; 1951 census 2,596,986; excluding Monmouthshire: (□ 7,470; 1931 pop. 2,158,374; 1951 census pop. 2,172,339) of Great Britain, a principality and peninsula W of England, with which it has been politically united since 1536. Peninsula is 140 mi. long (N-S); bounded by Bristol Channel (S), St. George's Channel (W), which separates it from Ireland, Irish Sea (N), and England (E). Its coast line is deeply indented by Carmarthen Bay (SW) and Cardigan Bay (W); off NW coast is Anglesey isl., separated from mainland by narrow Menai Strait (rail and road bridges). W extremity of Wales, St. David's Head, is 50 mi. from Irish coast. Almost all of Wales is occupied by central massif of the Cambrian Mts., which run in a general NE-SW direction, with parallel valleys, and rise to 3,560 ft. in Snowdon, highest peak of Great Britain S of Scotland. In S Wales a lesser E-W range, cut by lateral valleys, parallels Bristol Channel coast and rises to 2,906 ft. in the Brecon Beacons. Coastal plains are narrow in S and W; level lowland areas of NW and N Wales include Lleyn Peninsula (Caernarvon), Anglesey, and Dee R. valley (Flintshire). Economic center and center of pop. of the region lies in S Wales, including border co. of Monmouth; here are major coal mines and tinplate works, largely concentrated around coastal cities and ports of Newport, Cardiff, Swansea, Port Talbot, Barry, Llanelly, and Neath; and in the valleys extending N from Bristol Channel; centers here are Rhondda, Ebbw Vale, Merthyr Tydfil, Aberdare, Pontypridd, Caerphilly, Mountain Ash, Abertillery, and Tredegar. Other industries in the region are iron mining, mfg. of chemicals and pottery, and oil refining (Llandarcy). Due to its high degree of industrial specialization this region has always been highly sensitive to economic fluctuations and was, during the depression of the 1930s, the most hard-hit dist. of the British Isles, and was proclaimed a "distressed area." Aided by special legislation, efforts were then made to attract a variety of new light industries; many of these are concentrated on the Treforest trading estate near Cardiff. Chief rivers of S Wales are the Wye, Usk, Taff, Neath, and Tawe. Inland region of Wales is mountainous, bleak, and thinly populated; cattle and sheep raising and dairying are principal occupations here. Region is drained by Severn and Dovey rivers, which rise here. At N slope of central massif is fertile lowland region of N Wales, drained by Clwyd, Dee, and Conway rivers. Here is another important coal-mining region, centered on Wrexham; near by are iron and nonferrous-metal mines. N Welsh coast, on Irish Sea, is site of several popular seaside resorts, among them Llandudno, Colwyn Bay, and Prestatyn, which attract numerous visitors, especially from the Midlands. Mtn. region surrounding Snowdon (NW) is frequented by mountaineers; also in this region are major slate quarries. Principal quarrying centers are Blaenau-Ffestiniog, on SE slope of Snowdon, and Bangor, port on Menai Strait, near N foot of Snowdon. Caernarvon and Bangor are shipping, marketing, and cultural centers of NW Wales. Port of Aberystwyth is market and cultural center of W part of Wales, and popular resort on Cardigan Bay. Pembroke and Milford Haven (SW) are fishing ports. Ports of Fishguard (SW) and Holyhead (on Anglesey) are terminals of mail-ship services to Ireland and serve Rosslare and Dún Laoghaire respectively. Welsh climate is maritime in character; W part of region has cool summers and mild winters; warm summers and cold winters prevail in its E part. Annual precipitation ranges from 40 to 60 inches, rising to 80 inches in the central massif. Much of Welsh cultural life is based on the national institution of the *Eisteddfod*, which has helped to perpetuate the Welsh language and strong interest in choral music. Over 30% of pop. speak Welsh as well as English; under 4% speak Welsh only. Univ. of Wales (inc. 1893) comprises 4 constituent colleges, at Aberystwyth (1872), Cardiff (1883), Bangor (1884), and Swansea (1920). Though Romans penetrated to W coast of Welsh peninsula, their rule left little impress on Wales and did not disturb Welsh rule over great parts of W Britain. Christianity was introduced by Celtic monks, notably St. David, later patron saint of Wales. Anglo-Saxon invasion of England did not, at first, seriously affect Wales, but in time the invaders thrust bet. the present Wales and the body of Welsh people S of the Bristol Channel; while the latter maintained their national identity for several centuries, outside pressure from Mercia and Wessex, as well as Norse raids, eventually led to concentration of Welsh power in the Welsh peninsula, defended (E) by dyke said to have been constructed by King Offa. Marked political division bet. N and S Wales disappeared in late 10th cent., when Hywel Dda (Howel the Good) became king over all the Welsh and introduced a unified law code; he also encouraged activities of the bards, forerunners of later Welsh culture. After 1066, William I of England established a series of earldoms in border region of the Welsh Marshes to protect his kingdom; at the same time continuous pressure was exerted against the Welsh, who resisted with guerilla warfare. In 1093 Anglo-Norman barons penetrated into S part of Glamorgan, but dissension within England soon relaxed pressure on Wales and allowed Welsh princes to gain benefits by taking one side or another in the politics of England. In 11th cent. Welsh culture flourished as anc. legends were collected in written form in the *Mabinogion* and the institution of the *Eisteddfod* was regularized. As English invasion was resumed, Welsh cultural level slowly declined. Henry II of England was repulsed (1165) by Owen Gwynedd of N Wales and Rhys ap Gruffyd of S Wales; subsequently Llewelyn ap Iowerth united both sections of the country and skillfully took part in the troubled English affairs of King John. Llewelyn's grandson, Llewelyn ap Gruffyd, was overthrown (1282) and the conquest of Wales was completed by Edward I. English rule was set up (1284) under Statute of Rhuddlan. To placate the Welsh, Edward had his son, later Edward II, who was b. at Caernarvon Castle, proclaimed (1301) prince of Wales, a title borne from then on by the king's eldest son. English rule led to growth of trade, especially in wool, but in general the Welsh remained restive. In early 15th cent. Owen Glendower led a revolt that was briefly successful; later in 15th cent. Owen Tudor was involved in Wars of the Roses; his grandson ascended (1485) English throne as Henry VII. A policy of assimilation was pursued by the Tudors; Welsh land tenure, laws of inheritance, local govt., and organization of the nobility were anglicized in character and structure. Under Henry VIII the Act of Union (1536) established English as the legal language and abolished all Welsh customary laws at variance with those of England. Standardization of Welsh literary language was aided by translation (1588) of the Bible into Welsh by Bishop William Morgan. Reformation made slow headway in Wales; Catholic sentiment remained strong under Elizabeth and James I, and Wales later supported Charles I. This led to oppressive measures under the Commonwealth. Dissent, with strong Calvinist leaning, subsequently gained over the Established Church in Wales, and clergy assumed the role of leadership of the people. Notable was Griffith Jones who, in 18th cent., pioneered in popular education. Methodist movement, influential from educational as well as from religious viewpoint, grew into Calvinistic Methodist Church, to which majority of Welshmen adhered, and which played important part in fostering a non-political Welsh nationalism. Establishment of Church of England in Wales was major political question in late 19th cent., and in 1914 one of the last acts of Parliament applying to Wales alone disestablished the Church. Since end of 18th cent. industrialization of Wales, especially its S part, had progressed rapidly. Resulting shift of pop. led to considerable Welsh emigration, especially to the United States and to Latin America. Though the largely Welsh co. of Monmouth is technically in England, it is often included in Wales for census taking and other purposes. Administratively, Wales is composed of 12 counties besides Monmouthshire: ANGLESEY, Brecknockshire (BRECKNOCK), Carmarthenshire (CARMARTHEN), Caernarvonshire (CAERNARVON), Cardiganshire (CARDIGAN), Denbighshire (DENBIGH), Flintshire (FLINT), Glamorganshire (GLAMORGAN), Merionethshire (MERIONETH), Montgomeryshire (MONTGOMERY), Pembrokeshire (PEMBROKE), Radnorshire (RADNOR).

Wales, village (pop. 138), at W extremity of Seward Peninsula, W Alaska, on Bering Strait, 110 mi. NW of Nome; supply point. Airstrip.

Wales, village (pop. 1,910), Demerara co., N Br. Guiana, on Demerara R. and 9 mi. SSW of Georgetown; rice, sugar cane, stock.

Wales. 1 Town (pop. 437), Androscoggin co., SW Maine, 9 mi. NE of Lewiston. **2** Agr. town (pop. 497), Hampden co., S Mass., 18 mi. E of Springfield. **3** Village (pop. 235), Cavalier co., NE N.Dak., 15 mi. NW of Langdon. **4** Village (pop. c.100), Giles co., S Tenn., 4 mi. NNW of Pulaski; mines and processes phosphate rock. **5** Town (pop. 179), Sanpete co., central Utah, in irrigated Sanpete Valley, 15 mi. N of Manti; coal. **6** Village (pop. 237), Waukesha co., SE Wis., 23 mi. W of Milwaukee, in dairying and farming area.

Waleska (wûlĕ'skû), town (pop. 385), Cherokee co., NW Ga., 7 mi. NW of Canton.

Walezo (wälĕ'zō), town, central Zanzibar, on road and 3 mi. ENE of Zanzibar town; R.C. mission center; leper settlement and home for the aged.

Walferdange (väl'fûrdäsh'), village (pop. 220), S central Luxembourg, on Alzette R. and 3 mi. N of Luxembourg city; mfg. of electrical equipment, meat canning; rose growing.

Walfish Bay, South-West Africa: see WALVIS BAY.

Walford (wôl'fûrd), town and parish (pop. 1,142), N Hereford, England, on Teme R. and 8 mi. W of Ludlow; agr. market. Church dates from 13th cent.

Walgett (wŏl'gût), village (pop. 1,141), N New South Wales, Australia, 320 mi. NW of Newcastle, at junction of Namoi and Darling or Barwon rivers; rail terminus; sheep center.

Walgreen Coast (wôl'grēn), part of Marie Byrd Land, Antarctica, on Amundsen Sea, W of Thurston Peninsula, in c.105°W. Discovered 1940 by R. E. Byrd.

Walhalla (wôlhă'lù), village, S Victoria, Australia, 80 mi. E of Melbourne; gold mining.

Walhalla (wŏlhă'lù, wôl-). **1** City (pop. 1,463), Pembina co., NE N.Dak., near Can. line, 80 mi. NNW of Grand Forks and on Pembina R. Resort; port of entry; potato-shipping center; dairy produce, livestock, poultry, grain. Founded as trading post and mission 1848, platted 1877, inc. 1885. **2** Town (pop. 3,104), ⊙ Oconee co., NW S.C., 38 mi. W of Greenville, near the Blue Ridge; mfg. (cotton textiles, clothing, mill equipment); cotton, corn, wheat, timber. Summer resort. Founded c.1850. Oconee State Park (1,165 acres; recreational facilities) is c.5 mi. NW.

Walheim (väl'hīm), village (pop. 4,302), in former Prussian Rhine Prov., W Germany, after 1945 in North Rhine-Westphalia, near Belgian border, 6 mi. SE of Aachen; rail junction.

Walhonding River (wŏlhŏn'dĭng), central Ohio, formed by junction of Mohican and Kokosing rivers 16 mi. NW of Coshocton, flows c.20 mi. E, uniting with the Tuscarawas at Coshocton to form the Muskingum. Near Nellie, Mohawk Dam (2,330 ft. long, 111 ft. high above streambed; completed 1937; for flood control) impounds Mohawk Reservoir (capacity 285,000 acre-ft.).

Walhorn (välôrn'), village (pop. 1,152), Liége prov., E Belgium, near Ger. border, 7 mi. SSW of Aachen. Zinc-mining center of Astenet is NNE.

Walikale (wälēkä'lä), village, Kivu prov., E Belgian Congo, on Lowa R. and 50 mi. NW of Costermansville; center of native trade; rice processing. Protestant mission.

Walincourt (välēkōōr'), town (pop. 1,936), Nord dept., N France, 9 mi. SSE of Cambrai; lingerie and lace mfg.

Walk, Estonia and Latvia: see VALGA.

Walk, Lake, Texas: see DEVILS RIVER.

Walkden (wŏg'dûn), town (pop. 6,026) in Worsley urban dist., SE Lancashire, England, 7 mi. NW of Manchester; cotton milling, mfg. of chemicals for textile industry.

Walkenried (väl'kûnrēt"), village (pop. 2,599), in Brunswick, NW Germany, after 1945 in Lower Saxony, at S foot of the lower Harz, 7 mi. ESE of Bad Lauterberg, opposite Ellrich; rail junction; woodworking, food processing. Has large ruined former Cistercian abbey (founded 1127).

Walker, England: see NEWCASTLE-UPON-TYNE.

Walker. 1 County (□ 809; pop. 63,769), NW central Ala.; ⊙ Jasper. Hilly area crossed by Mulberry Fork. Coal mining; cotton, livestock, timber. Formed 1832. **2** County (□ 448; pop. 38,198), NW Ga.; ⊙ LaFayette. Bounded SW by Ala. line. Textile-mfg. and agr. area (cotton, corn, soybeans, hay, dairy products, poultry); coal mining. Includes parts of Chickamauga and Chattanooga Natl. Military Park and Chattahoochee Natl. Forest. Formed 1833. **3** County (□ 786; pop. 20,163), E central Texas; ⊙ Huntsville, processing, shipping center. Bounded NE by Trinity R.; drained by tributaries of the Trinity and the San Jacinto. Includes part of Sam Houston Natl. Forest. Rolling wooded area (pine, hardwood lumbering chief industry); fuller's earth, clay mining; some oil wells. Livestock (cattle, hogs, poultry, some horses, mules), dairying, agr. (cotton, corn, forage crops, legumes, fruit, truck). Hunting, fishing. Formed 1846.

Walker. 1 Town (pop. 549), Linn co., E Iowa, 21 mi. NNW of Cedar Rapids; feed milling. **2** Village (pop. 500), Livingston parish, SE La., 19 mi. E of Baton Rouge; lumber milling. **3** Resort village (pop. 1,192), ⊙ Cass co., N central Minn., on bay of Leech L., in Chippewa Natl. Forest, and c.55 mi. NNW of Brainerd; dairy products. State tuberculosis sanitarium and Greater Leech Lake Indian Reservation are near by. **4** Town (pop. 204), Vernon co., W Mo., near Osage R., 8 mi. NE of Nevada.

Walker Air Force Base, N.Mex.: see ROSWELL.

Walker Bay (12 mi. long, 31 mi. wide at mouth), SW Cape Prov., U. of So. Afr., inlet of the Atlantic, SE of False Bay, 40 mi. SE of Cape Town; extends SE from Cape Hangklip. Hermanus town on shore.

Walkerburn, village, E Peebles, Scotland, on the Tweed and 2 mi. E of Innerleithen; woolen milling.

Walker Lake (24 mi. long, 2-6 mi. wide), in Mineral co., W Nev., E of Wassuk Range, N of Hawthorne; fed by Walker R.; has no outlet. Walker River Indian Reservation here.

Walker Mountain, SW Va., a ridge of the Alleghenies; from point W of Bristol, extends c.110 mi. NE to New R. NW of Radford; rises to 2-3,000 ft.

Walker Pass, S central Calif., pass (alt. c.5,250 ft.) across the S Sierra Nevada, c.60 mi. E of Bakersfield.

Walker River, W Nev., formed in Lyon co. by confluence of East Walker and West Walker rivers 7 mi. S of Yerington, flows 50 mi. N, E, and S, around Wassuk Range, to N end of Walker L. Drains Walker River Indian Reservation. Dam in lower course forms small reservoir.

Walkersville, town (pop. 761), Frederick co., N Md., 6 mi. NNE of Frederick; trade point in agr. area; makes clothing. Near by is Glade Valley Farm (thoroughbreds).

Walkerton, town (pop. 2,679), ⊙ Bruce co., S Ont., on South Saugeen R. and 30 mi. SSW of Owen Sound; metalworking, lumbering, flour milling, dairying; mfg. of dies and castings.

Walkerton, town (pop. 2,102), St. Joseph co., N Ind., 19 mi. SW of South Bend; ships mint, onions, grain.

Walkerville, NE suburb (pop. 4,988) of Adelaide, SE South Australia; agr. center.

Walkerville, E suburb of Windsor, S Ont., on Detroit R., opposite Detroit; mfg. of automobiles, automobile accessories, steel products. Merged 1935 with Windsor.

Walkerville. 1 Village (pop. 233), Oceana co., W Mich., 34 mi. NNE of Muskegon, in orchard and farm area. **2** City (pop. 1,631), Silver Bow co., SW Mont.; N suburb of Butte; alt. 6,360 ft. Copper mines. Settled c.1877, inc. 1891.

Walkite (wăl'kĭtā), Ital. *Uolchitte*, village, Shoa prov., central Ethiopia, in the Gurage dist., 80 mi. NE of Jimma; banana growing.

Wall. 1 Borough (pop. 1,850), Allegheny co., SW Pa., E suburb of Pittsburgh. Inc. 1904. **2** Town (pop. 556), Pennington co., SW central S.Dak., 50 mi. E of Rapid City, near Badlands Natl. Monument; livestock, grain.

Wallabi Islands (wŏ'lubē), coral group in Indian Ocean, largest of HOUTMAN ABROLHOS, 35 mi. off W coast of Western Australia. Consists of W. Wallabi Isl. (largest; 3 mi. long, 1 mi. wide), E. Wallabi Isl., North Isl., several smaller islets and rocks. Tourist resort.

Wallabout Bay, N.Y.: see BROOKLYN.

Wallace, village (pop. estimate 300), W N.S., on Wallace Harbour, small inlet of Northumberland Strait, 30 mi. NNW of Truro; resort. Settled 1784. Simon Newcomb b. here.

Wallace, New Zealand: see OTAUTAU.

Wallace, county (□ 911; pop. 2,508), W Kansas; ⊙ Sharon Springs. Gently sloping to rolling plains region, bordering W on Colo; drained by headstreams of Smoky Hill R. Grazing, agr. (corn, barley, wheat). Highest point (4,135 ft.) in Kansas is in W, on Colo. line. Formed 1888.

Wallace. 1 City (pop. 3,140), ⊙ Shoshone co., N Idaho, 75 mi. E of Spokane, Wash.; alt. 2,729 ft. Trading center for mining, lumbering region in Coeur d'Alene Mts.; smelting, woodworking. Lead, silver, zinc mines near by in Coeur d'Alene mining district. Founded 1884 as Placer Center, inc. 1888 as Wallace. **2** Town (pop. 123), Fountain co., W Ind., 14 mi. WSW of Crawfordsville, in agr. and bituminous-coal area. **3** City (pop. 111), Wallace co., W Kansas, on Smoky Hill R. and 8 mi. E of Sharon Springs. **4** Village (pop. 361), Lincoln co., SW central Nebr., 30 mi. SW of North Platte and on branch of Republican R.; grain, livestock, dairy produce. **5** Town (pop. 1,622), Duplin co., SE N.C., 34 mi. N of Wilmington; strawberry market; sawmilling, crate mfg. State agr. experiment station near by. **6** Town (pop. 188), Codington co., NE S.Dak., 22 mi. NW of Watertown.

Wallaceburg, town (pop. 4,986), S Ont., on Sydenham R. and 16 mi. NW of Chatham; sugar refining, flour milling, lumbering, woodworking, shipbuilding; mfg. of castings, glassware.

Wallace Lake, NW La., flood-control reservoir (capacity 96,200 acre-ft.), 12 mi. S of Shreveport; impounded by dam (completed 1943) in a small W tributary of Red R.

Walaceton, borough (pop. 440), Clearfield co., central Pa., 9 mi. SE of Clearfield.

Wallacetown, Scotland: see AYR.

Wallachia, Rumania: see WALACHIA.

Wallachisch Klobauk, Czechoslovakia: see VALASSKE KLOBOUKY.

Wallachisch Meseritsch, Czechoslovakia: see VALASSKE MEZIRICI.

Wallaga (wä'lägä), province (□ c.25,900), W central Ethiopia, bordering on Anglo-Egyptian Sudan; ⊙ Nakamti. Pop. is largely Galla. Situated bet. Blue Nile and Baro rivers. Mountainous plateau region (4,500–9,000 ft. high) in E; outliers extend W and N and are separated by low plateaus (3,000 ft. high). Rises to 10,830 ft. in Mt. Wallel. Drained by Birbir, Dabus, and Dadessa rivers. Highlands are forested and well watered; river valleys are malarial and infested by tsetse fly. Richest mineral region (gold, platinum) of Ethiopia. Placer mining widespread in central (Yubdo, Nejo) and NW (Beni Shangul dist.) parts. Iron mining at Aira. Chief products: coffee, beeswax, hides, gold. Trade centers: Gambela, Nakamti, Nejo, Saio, Gimbi, and Asosa. Crossed by roads linking the Sudan with Addis Ababa. Sometimes written Wollega and Wallega.

Wallagrass (wŏ'lugrăs), plantation (pop. 1,035), Aroostook co., N Maine, 9 mi. S of Fort Kent and on Fish R., in forest area. Ships potatoes, makes skis. Settled 1820 by Acadians, inc. 1859.

Wallajapet, India: see WALAJAPET.

Walland (wä'lund), resort village, Blount co., E Tenn., on Little R. and 18 mi. SSE of Knoxville, in a gap of Chilhowee Mts.; mineral spring.

Wallangarra (wŏ"lŭn-gă'rŭ), village (pop. 768), SE Queensland, Australia, 120 mi. SW of Brisbane, on New South Wales border; sugar cane, bananas. Sometimes written Wallan-garra.

Wallaroo (wŏlŭroo'), town and port (pop. 2,140), S South Australia, on W Yorke Peninsula, on Wallaroo Bay of Spencer Gulf and 55 mi. SSW of Port Pirie; rail terminus; superphosphate works. Exports wheat, wool. Formerly important copper-mining center.

Wallasey (wôl'ŭsē), residential county borough (1931 pop. 97,626; 1951 census 101,331), NW Cheshire, England, on Mersey R. W of and opposite Liverpool, just W of Birkenhead; has major dock system, forming part of port of Liverpool; mfg. of industrial textiles, metal products, paint, synthetic fertilizer. Includes residential and resort towns of New Brighton, Egremont, Liscard, and Seacombe.

Walla Walla (wä'lu wä'lu), county (□ 1,288; pop. 40,135), SE Wash., on Oregon line; ⊙ Walla Walla. Rich wheat and fruit-growing area; lumbering, food processing. Watered by Snake, Columbia, Touchet, and Walla Walla rivers. Whitman Natl. Monument is near Walla Walla city. Formed 1854.

Walla Walla, city (pop. 24,102), ⊙ Walla Walla co., SE Wash., near Oregon line, 65 mi. SW of Lewiston, Idaho, and on Walla Walla R. Trade and distribution point for rich SE Wash. agr. and lumbering area. Has many canneries and other food-processing plants, and lumber mills. Whitman Col. and mus. are here. Settled c.1859. Walla Walla Col., Fort Walla Walla (now a veterans' hosp.), and a state prison are near by. Whitman Natl. Monument (45.8 acres; established 1940) is 6 mi. W, on site of Wailatpu, religious mission founded by Marcus Whitman and wife, killed (1847) by Cayuse Indians; commemorates Whitmans' devotion to needs and welfare of Indians.

Walla Walla River, NE Oregon–SW Wash., rises in Blue Mts. in Oregon, flows c.60 mi. NW, past Walla Walla, to Columbia R. Its valley is irrigated and dry-farm agr. area.

Wallbottle, England: see NEWBURN.

Walldorf (väl'dôrf). **1** Town (pop. 5,712), N Baden, Germany, after 1945 in Württemberg-Baden, 3 mi. WNW of Wiesloch (linked by tramway); tobacco (cigars, cigarettes) and metal (machinery, aluminum household goods) industries. John Jacob Astor b. here. **2** Village (pop. 5,396), S Hesse, W Germany, in former Starkenburg prov., 10 mi. NNW of Darmstadt.

Walldürn (väl'dürn"), town (pop. 5,812), N Baden, Germany, after 1945 in Württemberg-Baden, in the Odenwald, 14 mi. SE of Wertheim; mfg. (devotional articles, artificial flowers, furniture). Noted pilgrimage place since 1400, with splendid pilgrimage church.

Walled Lake, village (pop. 2,788), Oakland co., SE Mich., 11 mi. SW of Pontiac.

Wallel (wä'lĕl), peak (10,830 ft.) in highlands of W central Ethiopia, 20 mi. N of Saio.

Wallenfels (vä'lunfĕls"), village (pop. 2,791), Upper Franconia, N Bavaria, Germany, 7 mi. ENE of Kronach; lumber and flour milling, brewing, tanning.

Wallenpaupack, Lake (wôlŭnpô'păk), NE Pa., largest body of water (c.11 mi. long, ½ to 1 mi. wide) in Pa. Formed 1926 by hydroelectric dam built on Wallenpaupack Creek near Hawley; its outlet drains into Lackawaxen R. Resort.

Wallensee, Switzerland: see WALLENSTADT, LAKE OF.

Wallensen (vä'lunzun), village (pop. 1,652), in Prussian prov. of Hanover, W Germany, after 1945 in Lower Saxony, 13 mi. SE of Hameln; coal mining.

Wallenstadt (vä'lŭn-shtät), town (pop. 3,235), St. Gall canton, E Switzerland, near E shore of L. of Wallenstadt; cotton textiles, woodworking.

Wallenstadt, Lake of, Ger. *Walensee* or *Wallensee* (both: vä'lunzä), E Switzerland, bordering on cantons of St. Gall and Glarus; 9 mi. long, □ 9, alt. 1,374 ft., max. depth 492 ft. The Churfirsten dominates lake on N, which is less populated than S shore. Linth R. enters lake (SW) through Escher Canal, leaves it (W) through Linth Canal, which flows to L. of Zurich. Seez R. enters lake (E) through Seez Canal. Wallenstadt is main town on lake.

Wallenstadtberg (-bĕrk"), health resort (alt. 2,648 ft.), St. Gall canton, E Switzerland, S of the Churfirsten, near L. of Wallenstadt, 1 mi. NW of Wallenstadt; sanatoria near by.

Waller (wô'lur), county (□ 507; pop. 11,961), S Texas; ⊙ Hempstead. Bounded W by Brazos R.; also drained by tributaries of San Jacinto R. Agr. (especially watermelons, other truck and fruit; also corn, rice, peanuts, hay), livestock (cattle, hogs, sheep, poultry). Natural gas, oil wells. Formed 1873.

Waller, village (pop. 715), Waller co., S Texas, 40 mi. NW of Houston, in rich agr. area.

Wallerawang (wŏ"lurŭwŏng'), town (pop. 603), E New South Wales, Australia, 75 mi. WNW of Sydney; rail junction; mining center (coal, gold).

Wallerfangen, Saar: see VAUDREVANGE.

Wallern, Czechoslovakia: see VOLARY.

Wallers (välâr'), town (pop. 2,354), Nord dept., N France, 6 mi. W of Valenciennes; rail junction; cement, enamelware, plywood mfg.

Wallersee (vä'lurzā), lake (□ 2.5), W central Austria, 7 mi. NNE of Salzburg; 4 mi. long, 1 mi. wide, 38 ft. deep. Resort of Seekirchen at SW tip.

Wallerstein (vä'lur-shtīn), village (pop. 2,100), Swabia, W Bavaria, Germany, 3 mi. NNW of Nördlingen; woodworking. Barley; apiculture. Has early-19th-cent. castle. Chartered 1471.

Wallface Mountain (3,860 ft.), Essex co., NE N.Y., in the Adirondacks, just W of Mt. MacIntyre across Indian Pass, and c.7 mi. WNW of Mt. Marcy. Its E face is 1,300-ft. precipice rising above the pass.

Wallingford (wŏ'lĭngfurd), municipal borough (1931 pop. 2,840; 1951 census 3,514), N Berkshire, England, on the Thames and 12 mi. SE of Oxford; agr. market. There are remains of former ramparts and earthworks attributed to Romano-Norman castle. Has anc. bridge, Norman church (containing tomb of Sir William Blackstone), and 17th-cent. town hall.

Wallingford. 1 Town (pop. 16,976), including Wallingford borough (pop. 11,994), New Haven co., S central Conn., on Quinnipiac R. and 12 mi. NNE of New Haven. Silverware center since 1835; mfg. (metal products, electrical equipment, hardware, tools, plastics, fireworks, clothing, chemicals, cutlery); agr. (fruit, dairy products, poultry). Includes Yalesville village (pop. 1,122). Choate school for boys (1896) is in town. Branch of Oneida Community founded here, 1851. Town inc. 1673, borough inc. 1853. **2** Town (pop. 229), Emmet co., NW Iowa, 6 mi. SSE of Estherville; sand pits. **3** Town (pop. 1,482), Rutland co., W central Vt., on Otter Creek and 10 mi. S of Rutland; farm tools, dairy products. Ice caves near by. Includes East Wallingford village. Chartered 1761, settled 1773.

Wallington, England: see BEDDINGTON AND WALLINGTON.

Wallington, borough (pop. 8,910), Bergen co., NE N.J., just SE of Passaic, near Passaic R.; mfg. (machinery, steel tubing, plastics, paint, curtains, handkerchiefs, embroideries). Inc. 1895.

Wallins Creek, town (pop. 525), Harlan co., SE Ky., in the Cumberlands, on Cumberland R. and 22 mi. NE of Middlesboro, in bituminous-coal and timber region.

Wallis, Switzerland: see VALAIS.

Wallis, village (1940 pop. 815), Austin co., S Texas, near San Bernard R., c.45 mi. WSW of Houston, in cotton, corn area.

Wallis, Lake, lagoon (□ 30), E New South Wales, Australia, opening into the Pacific 65 mi. NE of Newcastle; 11 mi. long, 5 mi. wide; summer resort.

Wallis and Futuna Islands (footoo"nä), Fr. protectorate (□ c.75; pop. 6,770), SW Pacific, a dependency of New Caledonia, 250 mi. W of Samoa; established 1842; comprise 2 small groups, WALLIS ISLANDS and HOORN ISLANDS. Main volcanic isls. are Uvea, Futuna, Alofi; several coral islets. Produce copra, timber.

Wallisellen (vä"lĭsĕ'lun), town (pop. 4,184), Zurich canton, N Switzerland, 4 mi. NNE of Zurich; silk textiles, metal products, foodstuffs, cement, knit goods, chemicals.

Wallis Islands, island group (□ c.40; pop. 4,765), WALLIS AND FUTUNA ISLANDS protectorate, SW Pacific, 250 mi. W of Samoa; 13°17'S 176°10'W. Comprises single volcanic isl. (UVEA) surrounded by uninhabited coral islets on barrier reef. Uvea is site of Matautu, ⊙ protectorate. Polynesian natives. Produces copra, timber. Discovered 1781 by the French; placed 1842 under Fr. protectorate.

Wallkill, village (pop. 1,145), Ulster co., SE N.Y., on Wallkill R. and 10 mi. NW of Newburgh; summer resort; mfg. (clothing, paper boxes).

Wallkill River, NW N.J. and SE N.Y., rises S of Sparta, N.J. (dammed here to form L. Mohawk), flows c.90 mi. N and NE to Rondout Creek SW of Kingston, N.Y., shortly above creek's mouth on the Hudson; has power dams. The Wallkill valley, flanked by ridges of the Appalachians, is part of Great Appalachian Valley, and links the Kittatinny valley (N.J.) with the Hudson R. valley.

Wall Lake, town (pop. 753), Sac co., W Iowa, 18 mi. NW of Carroll; livestock, grain.

Wallo (wä'lō), province (□ 30,400), NE Ethiopia, bordering on Eritrea and Fr. Somaliland; ⊙ Dessye. Consists of DANAKIL desert and AUSSA dist. (E) and of highlands W of Great Rift Valley rising to c.13,745 ft. in Abuna Josef mtn. Situated bet. Takkaze, Blue Nile, Tsellari, and Awash rivers; drained by Golima R. Contains lakes Haik and Ardibbo. Pop. speaks Amharic and Afar. Agr. (cereals, corn, cotton) and stock raising (cattle, horses, mules, goats). Salt extracting in Danakil desert. Trade centers: Dessye, Sakota, Muja, Waldia. DESSYE is center of its communications. Lalibala is the major religious shrine. Sometimes Wollo.

Walloomsac (wulōōm'săk), village, Rensselaer co., E N.Y., on Hoosic R. and 2 mi. NE of Hoosick Falls. Near by is Bennington Battlefield State Park.

Walloomsac River, SW Vt. and E N.Y., rises E of Pownal, Vt., in Green Mts.; flows c.30 mi. N and

W, past Bennington, to Hoosic R. below Hoosick Falls, N.Y.

Walloon Lake (wŭlōōn'), NW Mich., 5 mi. SW of Petoskey; 9 mi. long, 1 mi. wide; fishing, boating, bathing.

Wallowa (wŭlou'ŭ), county (□ 3,178; pop. 7,264), extreme NE Oregon; ⊙ Enterprise. Livestock-grazing and lumbering area bordering on Wash. and Idaho, drained by Wallowa and Grande Ronde rivers. Wallowa Mts. are in S and E, in Wallowa Natl. Forest; part of Umatilla Natl. Forest is in NW. Grand Canyon of the Snake R. extends N-S along E boundary. Formed 1887.

Wallowa, city (pop. 1,055), Wallowa co., NE Oregon, 15 mi. NW of Enterprise and on Wallowa R.; lumber, flour. Inc. 1899.

Wallowa Lake, in Wallowa co., NE Oregon; 3 mi. long, .5 mi. wide; resort; used for irrigation. The **Wallowa Mountains** are in Wallowa Natl. Forest, E of La Grande, W of Grand Canyon of the Snake R. Sacajaewea Peak (10,033 ft.), Sentinel Peak (9,500 ft.), and Eagle Cap (9,675 ft.) are chief elevations. **Wallowa River** rises in Wallowa L., flows c.55 mi. NW, past Enterprise and Wallowa, to Grande Ronde R. 12 mi. NNE of Elgin.

Wallsburg, town (pop. 207), Wasatch co., N central Utah, 10 mi. S of Heber.

Wallsend (wôl'zĕnd"), town (pop. 557), E New South Wales, Australia, 7 mi. WNW of Newcastle, in metropolitan area; coal-mining center.

Wallsend, municipal borough (1931 pop. 44,587; 1951 census 48,645), SE Northumberland, England, on the Tyne and 4 mi. ENE of Newcastle-upon-Tyne; shipbuilding, steel milling, coal mining; chemical industry. E terminus of anc. Roman wall of Hadrian. In municipal borough are towns of Willington (E), with coal mines; Willington Quay (E), port on Tyne R., with chemical industry; and (SW) Howdon.

Wallula (wälōō'lŭ), village (pop. c.150), Walla Walla co., SE Wash., at junction of Walla Walla and Columbia rivers, 28 mi. W of Walla Walla; railroad junction. Early boom town, built near site of old Fort Walla Walla (1817); terminus of one of state's 1st railroads, completed 1875.

Wallum Lake, R.I. and Mass.: see BURRILLVILLE.

Wallwitzhafen (väl"vĭts-hä'fŭn), N suburb of Dessau, central Germany, on the Elbe, at mouth of the Mulde; harbor.

Walmaransstad (väl'märänstät"), town (pop. 3,567), SW Transvaal, U. of So. Afr., on Maquassi Spruit R. and 50 mi. SW of Klerksdorp; alt. 4,513 ft.; diamond digging; iron deposits near by. First European house in Transvaal built here 1822; ruins now historical monument.

Walmer (wôl'–), former urban district (1931 pop. 5,335), E Kent, England, on the Channel just S of Deal; seaside resort. Site of Walmer Castle, built by Henry VIII, official residence of lords warden of the CINQUE PORTS, containing memorials of famous wardens, including William Pitt and duke of Wellington (who died here). Inc. 1935 in Deal.

Walmer, residential town (pop. 14,507), S Cape Prov., U. of So. Afr., on Algoa Bay of the Indian Ocean, SW suburb of Port Elizabeth.

Walmersley cum Shuttleworth, parish (pop. 601), SE Lancashire, England. Includes agr. village of Walmersley, 2 mi. N of Bury, site of Bury reservoir; and cotton-milling village of Shuttleworth, 4 mi. N of Bury.

Walney Island (wôl'nē, wŏl'–), off N Lancashire, England, in Irish Sea, opposite Barrow-in-Furness across small Walney Channel; 8 mi. long, 1 mi. wide. Its industrial (shipbuilding, armaments) village of Vickerstown is linked with Barrow-in-Furness by bridge.

Walnut. 1 Village (pop. 1,093), Bureau co., N Ill., 14 mi. NNW of Princeton; dairy products, grain. **2** Town (pop. 888), Pottawattamie co., SW Iowa, near source of Walnut Creek (hydroelectric plant), 35 mi. ENE of Council Bluffs. **3** City (pop. 534), Crawford co., extreme SE Kansas, 21 mi. NW of Pittsburg, in diversified agr. area; feed milling. **4** Town (pop. 481), Tippah co., N Miss., 22 mi. W of Corinth; lumber milling.

Walnut Canyon National Monument (1,641.6 acres; established 1915), N central Ariz., 8 mi. ESE of Flagstaff. Ruins of more than 300 small, pre-Columbian Indian cliff dwellings built in shallow caves of canyon walls; period of max. occupancy was A.D. 1000–1200.

Walnut Cove, town (pop. 1,132), Stokes co., N N.C., 15 mi. NNE of Winston-Salem; veneer and lumber mills.

Walnut Creek, town (pop. 2,420), Contra Costa co., W Calif., 13 mi. NE of Oakland, in San Ramon valley; residential; ships walnuts. Orchards, walnut groves, chicken ranches. Inc. 1914.

Walnut Creek. 1 In SW Iowa, rises in S Shelby co., flows c.70 mi. S and SE to West Nishnabotna R. 11 mi. W of Shenandoah; used for hydroelectric power. **2** In W central Kansas, formed by confluence of 2 headstreams near Ness City, flows 139 mi. E, past Bazine and Albert, to Arkansas R. 5 mi. E of Great Bend.

Walnut Grove. 1 Town (pop. 222), Etowah co., NE Ala., 17 mi. WNW of Gadsden. **2** Village (pop. c.700), Sacramento co., central Calif., on Sacramento R. and 23 mi. S of Sacramento; cans asparagus, spinach. **3** Town (pop. 121), Walton co., N central Ga., 9 mi. SW of Monroe. **4** Village (pop. 890), Redwood co., SW Minn., near Cottonwood R., c.50 mi. WSW of New Ulm, in grain, livestock, and poultry area; dairy products. **5** Town (pop. 517), Leake co., central Miss., 11 mi. SSE of Carthage. **6** Town (pop. 347), Greene co., SW Mo., in the Ozarks, near Sac R., 20 mi. NW of Springfield.

Walnut Hill, village (pop. 156), Marion co., S Ill., 5 mi. SE of Centralia, in agr., oil, and coal area.

Walnut Log, village, Obion co., NW Tenn., on Reelfoot L., 15 mi. W of Union City; outfitting point for hunters, fishermen.

Walnutport, borough (pop. 1,427), Northampton co., E Pa., on Lehigh R. opposite Slatington. Inc. 1909.

Walnut Ridge, city (pop. 3,106), a ⊙ Lawrence co., NE Ark., 21 mi. NW of Jonesboro, in agr. area (cotton, corn, rice); cotton ginning, sawmilling. Seat of Southern Baptist Col. Inc. 1880.

Walnut River, S Kansas, formed by confluence of several headstreams in NE corner of Butler co., flows SW, past El Dorado, then S, past Augusta and Winfield, to Arkansas R. at Arkansas City; 121 mi. long.

Walnut Springs, city (pop. 626), Bosque co., central Texas, c.50 mi. NW of Waco; trade point in farm area (cotton, grain).

Walpi (wŏl'pē), Hopi Indian pueblo, NE Ariz., atop a mesa in Hopi Indian Reservation, c.65 mi. NNE of Winslow; alt. 6,225 ft. Founded c.1700, it is one of most picturesque pueblos in the Southwest; the Antelope ceremony and the snake dance of the Hopis are held here. Many of its people have moved to new village of Polacca, at foot of mesa.

Walpole (wôl'pōl). **1** Village, Maine: see SOUTH BRISTOL. **2** Town (pop. 9,109), Norfolk co., E Mass., on Neponset R. and 15 mi. SW of Boston; machinery, roofing, textiles, paper, surgical dressings, portable buildings, shingles; sawmill. Settled 1659, set off from Dedham 1724. Includes East Walpole village (1940 pop. 1,601). **3** Town (pop. 2,536), Cheshire co., SW N.H., on the Connecticut and 13 mi. NW of Keene; wood products. Has several fine 18th-cent. houses. Includes residential North Walpole village (1940 pop. 997). Settled 1749, inc. 1752.

Walpole Island (10 mi. long, 4 mi. wide), S Ont., in delta of St. Clair R., on NE shore of L. St. Clair. Consists of marshland and is chiefly inhabited by Indians. Tecumseh's grave is on the reservation here.

Walpole Island, uninhabited coral island (310 acres), SW Pacific, 135 mi. E of New Caledonia, of which it is a dependency; guano.

Walpole Saint Peter, town and parish (pop. 1,676), W Norfolk, England, 8 mi. WSW of King's Lynn; agr. market, with flour mills. Has 15th-cent. church.

Walporzheim, Germany: see AHRWEILER.

Walsall (wôl'sôl, –sŭl), county borough (1931 pop. 103,059; 1951 census 114,514), S Stafford, England, 8 mi. NNW of Birmingham, in the Black Country; 52°31'N 2°W; leather-tanning and mfg. center (machine tools, foundry products, aircraft parts, electrical equipment, pharmaceuticals). Near by are coal and iron mines and limestone quarries. In the borough is town (pop. 8,780) of Bloxwich, with leather-, tile-, and brickworks.

Walsden, England: see TODMORDEN.

Walsenburg (wôl'sŭnbûrg), city (pop. 5,596), ⊙ Huerfano co., S Colo., on Cucharas R., just E of Sangre de Cristo Mts., and 45 mi. S of Pueblo; alt. 6,200 ft. Trade center for livestock, poultry, and grain region; flour, meat, and dairy products, beverages, coal. Laid out and inc. 1873. Grew with development of coal deposits in vicinity. Parts of San Isabel Natl. Forest near by.

Walsh, county (□ 1,287; pop. 18,859), NE N.Dak.; ⊙ Grafton. Rich agr. area drained by Forest and Park rivers; bounded E by Red River of the North. Dairy products, livestock, grain, potatoes. Formed 1881.

Walsh, town (pop. 897), Baca co., SE Colo., 18 mi. E of Springfield.

Walsh, Mount (14,780 ft.), SW Yukon, near Alaska border, in St. Elias Mts., 170 mi. W of Whitehorse; 61°1'N 139°59'W.

Walsheim (väls'hīm), village (pop. 642), SE Saar, 9 mi. ENE of Sarreguemines (France); brewing, woodworking.

Walshville, village (pop. 113), Montgomery co., SW central Ill., 7 mi. S of Litchfield, in agr. and coal area.

Walsingham, England: see LITTLE WALSINGHAM.

Walsingham, Cape (wŏl'sĭng-ŭm), SE Baffin Isl., SE Franklin Dist., Northwest Territories, at tip of Cumberland Peninsula, on Davis Strait; 66°2'N 61°56'W. Discovered by Davis, 1585.

Walsoken, former urban district (1931 pop. 4,058), W Norfolk, England, on Nene R. just NE of Wisbech; agr. market in fruitgrowing region. Has church of Norman origin. Inc. 1934 in Wisbech.

Walsrode (väls"rō'dŭ), town (pop. 12,697), in former Prussian prov. of Hanover, NW Germany, after 1945 in Lower Saxony, 25 mi. NW of Celle; chemicals (pharmaceuticals, cosmetics, dyes), machinery, tools, furniture. Food processing (flour products, canned goods, beverages, spirits), leatherworking. Has Gothic church.

Walstonburg (wŏl'stŭnbûrg), town (pop. 177), Greene co., E central N.C., 16 mi. SE of Wilson.

Walsum (väl'zōōm), town (pop. 23,255), in former Prussian Rhine Prov., W Germany, after 1945 in North Rhine-Westphalia, in the Ruhr, port on right bank of the Rhine and 2 mi. SW of Dinslaken; coal mining; mfg. of artificial fiber.

Waltair, India: see VIZAGAPATAM, city.

Walterboro, town (pop. 4,616), ⊙ Colleton co., S S.C., 45 mi. W of Charleston, in agr. area; tourist and winter resort center; lumber, chemicals, naval stores. Hunting and fishing near by.

Walterganj, India: see BASTI, town.

Walters. 1 Village (pop. 139), Faribault co., S Minn., near Iowa line, 16 mi. W of Albert Lea; dairy products. **2** City (pop. 2,743), ⊙ Cotton co., S Okla., 17 mi. SSE of Lawton, near Cache Creek, in grain, cotton, and livestock area; cotton ginning, poultry packing, dairying. Oil wells near by.

Waltershausen (väl"tŭrs-hou'zŭn), town (pop. 11,558), Thuringia, central Germany, on slope of Thuringian Forest, 8 mi. WSW of Gotha; paper and cardboard milling, woodworking; mfg. of wooden and china dolls, electrical equipment, pipes, rubber products. Climatic health resort. Has 18th-cent. church with 15th-cent. tower; Tenneberg castle, rebuilt in 16th–18th cent.

Walthall (wôl'thôl"), county (□ 403; pop. 15,563), S Miss.; ⊙ Tylertown. Bordered S by La.; drained by the Bogue Chitto. Agr. (cotton, corn), dairying, poultry raising; lumbering. Formed 1910.

Walthall, village (pop. 149), ⊙ Webster co., central Miss., c.50 mi. E of Greenwood.

Waltham. 1 (wôl'thŭm, wôl'thăm") Town (pop. 154), Hancock co., S Maine, on Graham L. and 22 mi. ESE of Bangor. **2** (wôl'thăm", –thŭm) Residential city (pop. 47,187), Middlesex co., E Mass., on Charles R. and 10 mi. W of Boston. Mfg. center, known for its watches and clocks since 1854; precision instruments, machinery, tools, gauges, foundry products, clothing; printing. Seat of Brandeis Univ., Fernald school for mentally handicapped, and large army hosp. Settled 1634, set off from Watertown 1738, inc. as city 1884. Site (1814) of 1st Amer. power loom for cotton mfg. **3** (wôl'tŭm) Village (pop. 212), Mower co., SE Minn., 11 mi. NNE of Austin; dairy products. **4** (wôl'thăm") Town (pop. 193), Addison co., W Vt., on Otter Creek and 24 mi. S of Burlington.

Waltham Abbey, England: see WALTHAM HOLY CROSS.

Waltham Cross (wôl'tŭm, –thŭm), residential town in Cheshunt urban dist., SE Hertford, England, on Lea R. and just W of Waltham Abbey; agr. market. Has one of the 3 remaining Eleanor Crosses (restored).

Waltham Holy Cross (wôl'tŭm, –thŭm), urban district (1931 pop. 7,115; 1951 census 8,197), SW Essex, England. Includes residential town of Waltham Abbey, on the Lea and 4 mi. N of Chingford, at edge of Epping Forest. Has abbey built 1030 to contain miraculous cross found in Somerset; was enlarged (1060) by King Harold (believed to have been buried here). Tower contains whipping post, pillory, and stocks; Norman nave now used as parish church. Just S are gunpowder works. There is mfg. (plastics, nonferrous metals, tiles). Just W is town of WALTHAM CROSS, site of an Eleanor Cross.

Waltham-on-the-Wolds (wôl'tŭm, wōldz'), agr. village and parish (pop. 510), NE Leicester, England, 5 mi. NE of Melton Mowbray; cheese making.

Walthamstow (wôl'thŭmstō), residential and industrial municipal borough (1931 pop. 132,972; 1951 census 121,069), SW Essex, England, on Lea R. and 9 mi. NE of London. Has anc. church, 16th-cent. almshouses, and several 16th-cent. manors. William Morris b. here; Disraeli attended local school. Just W is large London reservoir.

Walthill, village (pop. 958), Thurston co., NE Nebr., 25 mi. S of Sioux City, Iowa, near Missouri R.; dairy produce, livestock, grain.

Walton, Derby, England: see BRAMPTON AND WALTON.

Walton (wôl'tŭn). **1** County (□ 1,046; pop. 14,725), NW Fla., bounded E (partly) by Choctawhatchee R., N by Ala. line, and S by Gulf of Mexico; ⊙ De Funiak Springs. Rolling terrain in N rising to 345 ft. (highest point in state); coastal plain in S along Choctawhatchee Bay and the Gulf; co. is drained by Shoal R. Agr. (corn, peanuts, cotton, poultry, cattle, hogs). Some lumber milling and naval-stores mfg. Has part of Choctawhatchee Natl. Forest in SW. Formed 1824. **2** County (□ 330; pop. 20,230), N central Ga.; ⊙ Monroe. Bounded NE by Apalachee R.; drained by Alcovy R. Piedmont agr. (cotton, corn, grain, sorghum, peaches) and timber area; textile mfg. at Monroe. Formed 1818.

Walton. 1 Town (pop. 837), Cass co., N central Ind., 10 mi. SE of Logansport, in agr. area. **2** City (pop. 220), Harvey co., S central Kansas, 7 mi. NE of Newton, in wheat area. **3** Town (pop. 1,358), Boone co., N Ky., 16 mi. SSW of Covington, in outer Bluegrass agr. area (dairy products, livestock, poultry, burley tobacco, corn); canned goods, feed, wood products. **4** Village (pop. 3,947), Delaware co., S N.Y., in the Catskills, on West Branch of Delaware R. and 40 mi. ENE of Binghamton; summer resort. Mfg.: textiles, feed, machinery, wood products. Blue-stone quarries. Inc. 1851.

Walton and Weybridge, urban district (1931 pop. 25,317; 1951 census 38,091), N Surrey, England. Includes several residential towns. Walton-on-Thames (pop. 17,953), on the Thames and 15 mi. SW of London, has mfg. of lubricants and is site of 15th-cent. church. Weybridge, on the Thames, at mouth of Wey R., has brick- and tileworks. Until 1876 Louis Philippe was buried here. Just S of Weybridge is automobile race track and airfield of Brooklands, with aircraft works. Also in urban dist. are residential areas of Oatlands, just SW of Walton-on-Thames, with remains of castle built by Henry VIII, extended by Inigo Jones, and destroyed by Cromwell; and Hersham, on Mole R. and 2 mi. SE of Walton-on-Thames, with electrical-equipment works.

Walton-le-Dale (-lū-), urban district (1931 pop. 12,720; 1951 census 14,711), W central Lancashire, England, on Ribble R. and 2 mi. SE of Preston; engineering. Was hq. of Cromwell in 1648 before battle for Preston. In 1770 Benjamin Franklin here set up the 1st lightning conductor in England. Has remains of Roman station, and 11th-cent. church. In urban dist. is town of BAMBER BRIDGE.

Walton-le-Soken, England: see WALTON-ON-THE-NAZE.

Walton-on-Thames, England: see WALTON AND WEYBRIDGE.

Walton-on-the-Hill. 1 N suburb of Liverpool, SW Lancashire, England; rubber-mfg. center (tires, footwear, furnishings); mfg. of metal containers, soap, paint. Has church containing a Norman font. **2** Residential town and parish (pop. 1,997), central Surrey, England, 4 mi. S of Epsom. Has 14th-cent. manor house and church dating from 13th cent.

Walton-on-the-Naze or **Walton-le-Soken,** former urban district (1931 pop. 3,071) now in Frinton and Walton urban dist. (1948 pop. estimate 7,943), NE Essex, England, on North Sea, 7 mi. S of Harwich; seaside resort, with long pier. Just NE is headland of The Naze.

Waltonville, village (pop. 459), Jefferson co., S Ill., 9 mi. SW of Mount Vernon, in agr. area.

Walton West, Wales: see BROADHAVEN.

Waltrop (väl'trôp), town (pop. 13,404), in former Prussian prov. of Westphalia, W Germany, after 1945 in North Rhine-Westphalia, in the Ruhr, 8 mi. E of Recklinghausen; truck produce.

Walvis Bay (wôl'vĭs), Afrikaans *Walvisbaai* (-bī'), town (pop. 2,270) in Walvis Bay enclave (□ 374; pop. 2,424), W South-West Africa, on Walvis Bay (6 mi. long, 5 mi. wide) of the Atlantic, 170 mi. WSW of Windhoek; 22°57'S 14°30'E. Enclave forms part of Cape Prov., U. of So. Afr., but has been administered by South-West Africa since 1922. Port, with warehouses and cold-storage plants, serves stock-raising, mining region; fisheries. Rail terminus. Whaling station, 1916–30, it is now repair depot for whaling ships operating in Antarctic. Annexed by Dutch 1792, it became British territory 1878 and was added to Cape Colony. It remained British enclave after Germans annexed South-West Africa in 1892. Sometimes called Walfish Bay.

Wal Wal or **Walwal** (wäl'wäl), Ital. *Ualual*, village, Harar prov., SE Ethiopia, in the Ogaden, 275 mi. SE of Harar, in pastoral region (camels, sheep); water hole with c.360 wells. Scene of armed clash (Dec. 5, 1934), an incident leading to Italo-Ethiopian War (1935–36).

Walworth. 1 County (□ 737; pop. 7,648), N central S.Dak.; ⊙ Selby. Agr. area bounded W by Missouri R. Dairy products, livestock, grain. Formed 1873. **2** County (□ 560; pop. 41,584), SE Wis., bounded S by Ill. line; ⊙ Elkhorn. Drained by Turtle Creek and several other small streams. Resort area with several lakes, notably L. Geneva. Comprises extensive dairying region; also farming, and some mfg. Formed 1836.

Walworth, resort village (pop. 1,137), Walworth co., SE Wis., near L. Geneva, 23 mi. ESE of Janesville, in agr. area (dairy products; poultry, grain); pea cannery.

Walzenhausen (vält'sŭnhou"zŭn), town (pop. 2,408), Appenzell Ausser Rhoden half-canton, NE Switzerland, 10 mi. ENE of St. Gall, near Austrian border; mtn. and health resort; silk textiles, embroideries.

Wamac (wä'măk), city (pop. 1,429), on Washington-Marion-Clinton co. line, S Ill., S suburb of Centralia. Inc. 1916.

Wamar, Indonesia: see ARU ISLANDS.

Wamba (wäm'bä), village, Eastern Prov., NE Belgian Congo, 135 mi. WNW of Irumu; agr. center specializing in cotton growing and production of staples (rice, palm oil, groundnuts) for regional goldfields; cotton ginning. Has R.C. and Protestant missions, medical assistants' school. Seat of vicar apostolic.

Wamba River (wäm'bä), SW Belgian Congo, rises in N Angola near Camaxilo, flows c.375 mi. generally NNW, past Kenge, to Kwango R. 40 mi. SSW of Banningville. Navigable in lower 100 mi.

Wambrechies (vãbrü-shē'), outer N suburb (pop. 3,853) of Lille, Nord dept., N France, on Deûle R. (canalized), in truck-farming dist.; flax spinning, chicory mfg.

Wamego (wômē'gō), city (pop. 1,869), Pottawatomie co., NE Kansas, on Kansas R. and 35 mi. WNW of Topeka, in livestock and grain region; mfg. of snowplows. Has municipally owned utilities. Platted 1866, inc. 1869.

Wami River (wä'mē), E Tanganyika, rises in Tendigo Swamp N of Kilosa, flows 130 mi. NE and E to Zanzibar Channel of Indian Ocean at Sadani.

Wamplers Lake (wŏm'plŭrz), SE Mich., 9 mi. W of Clinton; c.2 mi. long, 1 mi. wide; resort. State park here.

Wampsville (wämps'vĭl), village (pop. 379), ⊙ Madison co., central N.Y., 24 mi. E of Syracuse, in dairying area.

Wampum, borough (pop. 1,090), Lawrence co., W Pa., 8 mi. S of New Castle and on Beaver R.; bituminous coal; cement. Settled 1796, inc. 1876.

Wamsutter (wŏm'sŭ"tŭr), town (pop. 103), Sweetwater co., S Wyo., 65 mi. E of Rock Springs; alt. c.6,700 ft.; wool-shipping point.

Wan, China: see WAN RIVER.

Wana (vä'nŭ), village, hq. of South Waziristan agency, SW North-West Frontier Prov., W Pakistan, in N Sulaiman Range, 160 mi. SW of Peshawar; wheat, corn, barley; fruitgrowing; exports firewood, hides, ghee. Fortified 1849 by British in attempt to check raids of Waziri tribes.

Wanaka, Lake (wänä'kŭ), W central S.Isl., New Zealand, 105 mi. NW of Dunedin; □ 75, 30 mi. long, 5 mi. wide; alt. 960 ft.; contains Pigeon Isl. Source of Clutha R.

Wanakena (wŏnŭkē'nŭ), resort village, St. Lawrence co., N N.Y., 35 mi. ENE of Carthage, in the Adirondacks, at influx of Oswegatchie R. into Cranberry L. State school for forest rangers here.

Wanamassa (wŏnŭmă'sŭ), village (pop. 2,512), Monmouth co., E N.J., near the coast, 1 mi. NW of Asbury Park.

Wanamie (wŏ'nŭmē), village (pop. 1,092), Luzerne co., E central Pa., 10 mi. SW of Wilkes-Barre.

Wanamingo (wŏnŭmĭng'gō), village (pop. 496), Goodhue co., SE Minn., on branch of Zumbro R. and 25 mi. NW of Rochester; corn, oats, barley, potatoes, livestock, poultry.

Wanan (wän'än'), town (pop. 2,699), ⊙ Wanan co. (pop. 93,898), SW Kiangsi prov., China, on Kan R. and 45 mi. SSW of Kian; tungsten and bismuth mining; gold deposits.

Wananish (wŏnă'nĭsh), village (pop. c.300), Columbus co., SE N.C., 4 mi. W of Bolton, near L. Waccamaw; sawmilling, mfg. of tools.

Wanaparti, India: see WANPARTI.

Wanapitei Lake (wänŭpĭ'tē) (10 mi. long, 10 mi. wide), SE central Ont., 16 mi. NE of Sudbury. Drained S by **Wanapitei River** (75 mi. long) into Georgian Bay.

Wanaque (wŏ'nŭkē), borough (pop. 4,222), Passaic co., NE N.J., in the Ramapos, on Wanaque R. and 10 mi. NW of Paterson; includes mfg. villages of HASKELL and MIDVALE. Inc. 1918. Near by is **Wanaque Reservoir** (c.6 mi. long, 1 mi. wide; largest in N.J.), formed by dam in **Wanaque River,** which drains Greenwood L. on N.Y.-N.J. line, and flows c.18 mi. SE and S to Pequannock R. just N of Pompton Plains.

Wanasaba, Indonesia: see WONOSOBO.

Wanbera (wän'bĕrä), village (pop. 700), Gojjam prov., NW Ethiopia, 95 mi. WSW of Dangila, in coffee-growing region; 10°37'N 35°39'E; caravan center.

Wanbi, village, SE South Australia, 100 mi. ENE of Adelaide; rail junction; wheat, wool.

Wancheng or **Wan-ch'eng** (wän'chŭng'), town ⊙ Wancheng co. (pop. 45,506), SW Kwangsi prov., China, 30 mi. N of Tsungshan; rice, wheat, beans, kaoliang, potatoes.

Wanchese (wŏn'chēs"), village (1940 pop. 641), Dare co., E N.C., 5 mi. S of Manteo, on SW end of Roanoke Isl.; shad-fishing and trade center.

Wanchow, China: see MANNING.

Wanchüan or **Wan-ch'üan** (wän'chüän'). **1** City, Chahar prov., China: see KALGAN. **2** Town, ⊙ Wanchüan co. (pop. 74,760), SW Shansi prov., China, 32 mi. NNW of Anyi; cotton weaving; wheat, persimmons, pears, medicinal herbs.

Wanchüan River, Mandarin *Wan-ch'üan Ho* (wän'-chüän' hŭ'), E Hainan, Kwangtung prov., China, rises in center of isl. on N slopes of Wuchi Mts., flows 90 mi. E, past Kachek, to S.China Sea at Lokwei.

Wanda, village (pop. 178), Redwood co., SW Minn., 38 mi. W of New Ulm; dairy products.

Wandel Sea, marginal sea of Arctic Ocean, off NE Greenland, at 82°30'N 10°W.

Wanderer Mine, township (pop. 3,099), Gwelo prov., central Southern Rhodesia, in Matabeleland, 5 mi. NNE of Selukwe; gold-mining center.

Wandiwash (vŭndĭväsh'), town (pop. 9,404), North Arcot dist., central Madras, India, 45 mi. SE of Vellore; road center in agr. area. Ruined fort (just N) was scene, 1760, of decisive English victory over French.

Wando (wän'dō), Ital. *Uondo*, village, Sidamo-Borana prov., S Ethiopia, 11 mi. NW of Hula; road junction.

Wando (wän'dô'), Jap. *Kanto*, town (1949 pop. 15,142), on SE coast of Wan Isl., S.Cholla prov., Korea; fishing.

Wan-do, Korea: see WAN ISLAND.

Wandre (vãdr'ü), town (pop. 6,992), Liège prov., E Belgium, 5 mi. ENE of Liège; coal mining; metal industry.

Wandsbek (vänts'bĕk, -bāk), district (1933 pop. 46,255) of Hamburg, NW Germany, adjoining Eilbeck (W) and Barmbeck (NW) dists.; mfg. of cigarettes and chemicals. In Schleswig-Holstein until inc. 1938 into Hamburg. Matthias Claudius here published (1771–75) the literary journal *Wandsbeker Bote* [="Wandsbek Messenger"].

Wandsworth (wŏndz'wûrth, wŏnz'-), residential metropolitan borough (1931 pop. 353,110; 1951 census 330,328) of London, England, on S bank of the Thames, 4 mi. SW of Charing Cross. Borough includes all or part of districts of Putney, Clapham, Tooting, Balham, and Streatham. Industries include oil processing, paper milling, textile printing, brewing, hat making, dyeing. Wandsworth Prison is near by.

Waneta Lake (wŏnē'tŭ), W central N.Y., in Finger Lakes region, just E of Keuka L.; c.3 mi. long, ½ mi. wide. Connected by streams to Lamoka L. (S) and to Keuka L. Formerly called Little L.

Wanette (wŏnĕt'), town (pop. 594), Pottawatomie co., central Okla., 25 mi. SSW of Shawnee, in agr. area; cotton ginning.

Wanfercée-Baulet (vãfĕrsā-bōlā'), town (pop. 5,861), Hainaut prov., S central Belgium, 8 mi. NE of Charleroi; coal mining.

Wanfow (wän'fou'), Mandarin *Yün-fou* (yün'fō'), town (pop. 2,094), ⊙ Wanfow co. (pop. 293,917), W Kwangtung prov., China, 30 mi. WSW of Koyiu; tin-mining center; rice, wheat, tea, cotton, hemp. Until 1914 called Tungon or Tungan.

Wanfried (vän'frēt), town (pop. 3,660), in former Prussian prov. of Hesse-Nassau, W Germany, after 1945 in Hesse, on the Werra and 5 mi. E of Eschwege; textiles.

Wanga, Belgian Congo: see WATSA.

Wanga, Kenya: see VANGA.

Wanganui (wŏng-gŭnōō'ē) city (pop. 23,842; metropolitan Wanganui 26,462) and port, S N.Isl., New Zealand, 95 mi. N of Wellington, near mouth of Wanganui R.; mfg. (soap, clothing, textiles); exports grain, sheep. Airport in outskirts of city. Opera house, Alexander Mus., Wanganui Collegiate School. Settled 1840. Wanganui is ⊙ Waitotara co. (□ 468; pop. 3,382) and ⊙ Wanganui co. (□ 460; pop. 3,403), but forms independent unit.

Wanganui River, W N.Isl., New Zealand, rises NW of L. Taupo, flows 140 mi. S, past Taumarunui, to Cook Strait 95 mi. N of Wellington; drains agr. land.

Wangaratta (wăng"gŭră'tŭ), municipality (pop. 6,670), N Victoria, Australia, on Ovens R. and 125 mi. NE of Melbourne; rail junction; commercial center in livestock, agr. area; flour and woolen mills. Hydroelectric plant.

Wangata, Belgian Congo: see COQUILHATVILLE.

Wang-chiang, China: see WANGKIANG.

Wangching or **Wang-ch'ing** (wäng'chĭng'), town, ⊙ Wangching co. (pop. 151,700), E Kirin prov., Manchuria, 25 mi. NNE of Yenki; gold and coal deposits; timber; fur, skins and hides.

Wangdu Phodrang (wäng'dōō pô'dräng) or **Wangdu Potrang** (pô'träng), fortified town [Bhutanese *dzong*], W central Bhutan, on the Sankosh and 10 mi. S of Punakha; lamaseries. Founded 1578. Also called Angduphodang.

Wangen or **Wangen im Allgäu** (väng'ŭn ĭm äl'goi), town (pop. 9,538), S Württemberg, Germany, after 1945 in Württemberg-Hohenzollern, in the Allgäu, 12 mi. SE of Ravensburg; mfg. of textiles, artificial fiber; woodworking, dairying (cheese). Market center for surrounding dairy region. Has late-Gothic church, 18th-cent. town hall; and dairy research institute. Chartered 1217; later created free imperial city.

Wangen, town (pop. 2,125), Schwyz canton, NE central Switzerland, near L. of Zurich, 16 mi. NE of Schwyz; cotton textiles. Siebnen hydroelectric plant is S.

Wangen bei Olten (bī ŏl'tŭn), town (pop. 2,117), Solothurn canton, N Switzerland, 1 mi. W of Olten; clothes.

Wangerin, Poland: see WEGORZYNO.

Wangerland, Germany: see HOHENKIRCHEN.

Wangerooge (väng"ŭrō'gŭ), North Sea island (□ 2.7; pop. 1,592) of East Frisian group, Germany, 20 mi. NNW of Wilhelmshaven (steamer connection); 4 mi. long (E-W), 1 mi. wide. Nordseebad Wangerooge (center) is popular seaside resort. Damaged in Second World War.

Wangiwangi (wăng"ēwăng'ē), largest island (□ 60; pop. 16,134) of Tukangbesi Isls., Indonesia, bet. Flores and Molucca seas, 20 mi. E of Buton; 5°20'S 123°35'E; 10 mi. long, 7 mi. wide; generally low. Fishing, agr. (coconuts, sago). Sometimes called Wantji.

Wangka (wäng'kä'), village (1937 pop. 1,100), Kanchanaburi prov., SW Thailand, on Khwae Noi R., on railroad, and 165 mi. NW of Bangkok, near Burma line; gold mining.

Wangkiang or **Wang-chiang** (both: wäng'jyäng'), town, ⊙ Wangkiang co. (pop. 205,280), N Anhwei prov., China, 34 mi. SW of Anking and on Yangtze R.; rice, cotton, wheat, beans, tobacco.

Wangkü, China: see CHANGAN, Shensi prov.

Wangkwei or **Wang-k'uei** (both: wäng'kwā'), town, ⊙ Wangkwei co. (pop. 246,014), S Heilungkiang prov., Manchuria, 70 mi. N of Harbin; soybeans, kaoliang, millet, corn.

Wangmo (wäng'mŭ'), town (pop. 1,930), ⊙ Wangmo co. (pop. 63,302), S Kweichow prov., China, 65 mi. E of Hingi, near Kwangsi line; textiles, embroidered goods; grain. Formerly Wangmu.

Wang River (wäng), one of headstreams of Chao Phraya R., N Thailand, rises in Khyn Tan Range SW of Chiangrai, flows 160 mi. S, past Lampang (head of navigation), to Ping R. 20 mi. N of Tak.

Wangshejenchwang, China: see LICHENG, Shantung prov.

Wangtsang or **Wang-ts'ang** (wäng'tsäng'), town (pop. 14,146), ⊙ Wangtsang co. (pop. 97,072), N Szechwan prov., China, 40 mi. NE of Langchung, in mtn. region; tobacco, rice, sweet potatoes, millet. Until 1941 called Wangtsangpa.

Wangtu (wäng'dōō'), town, ⊙ Wangtu co. (pop. 92,622), W Hopeh prov., China, 20 mi. SW of Paoting and on Peking-Hankow RR; cotton, wheat, kaoliang.

Wangyeh, China: see TINGYÜANYING.

Wangyehmiao, Manchuria: see ULAN HOTO.

Wanhatti (vänhä'tē), village, Marowijne dist., NE Du. Guiana, on Cottica R. and 50 mi. E of Paramaribo; Bush Negro settlement; sugar cane, rice.

Wanhsien. 1 (wän'shyĕn') Town, ⊙ Wanhsien co. (pop. 130,042), W Hopeh prov., China, 20 mi. W of Paoting; cotton, wheat, millet. **2** or **Huanhsien** (hwän'shyĕn'), town, ⊙ Wanhsien co. (pop. 5,770), SE Kansu prov., China, on Wan R. and 32 mi. NNW of Kingyang. Called Chutzuchen until c.1940, when co. seat was moved here from old Wanhsien, 22 mi. NW. **3** (wän'shyĕn') Town (pop. 110,381), ⊙ Wanhsien co. (pop. 857,563), E Szechwan prov., China, 135 mi. NE of Chungking city and on left bank of Yangtze R.; major commercial port, trading in tung oil, tobacco, medicinal herbs, and hog bristles. Produces rice, millet, wheat, beans, sugar cane, oranges. Iron mines and coal deposits near by. Opened to foreign trade in 1902.

Wanhwa, Formosa: see TAIPEI.

Wanie Rukula (wän'yä rōōkōō'lä), village, Eastern Prov., E Belgian Congo, on right bank of Congo R. and 32 mi. SE of Stanleyville; hardwood lumbering; sawmills, palm groves.

Wan Island (wän), Korean *Wan-do*, Jap. *Kan-to* (□ 155; 1946 pop. 106,521), S.Cholla prov., Korea, in Cheju Strait, just off SW coast, 30 mi. SE of Mokpo; 10 mi. long, 5 mi. wide; hilly terrain. Fishing. Largest town is Wando.

Wankai (wäng'kī), village, Upper Nile prov., S central Anglo-Egyptian Sudan, on the Bahr el Ghazal at influx of the Bahr el Arab, and 45 mi. NNE of Mezhra er Req; cotton, corn; livestock. Also called Ghabat el Arab.

Wankaner (väng'känär), town (pop. 17,230), N Saurashtra, India, on Kathiawar peninsula, 23 mi. NNE of Rajkot; rail junction; market center (cotton, millet, ghee, cloth fabrics); cotton ginning and milling, handloom weaving; metalware. Was ⊙ former princely state of Wankaner (□ 417; pop. 54,965) of Western India States agency; state merged 1948 with Saurashtra. Sometimes spelled Vankaner.

Wankang (wän'gäng'), town, ⊙ Wankang co. (pop. 93,136), W Kwangsi prov., China, 55 mi. NE of Poseh; cotton textiles; rice, wheat, corn, millet. Until 1936 called Pama.

Wankendorf (väng'kŭndôrf), village (pop. 2,187), in Schleswig-Holstein, NW Germany, 9 mi. ENE of Neumünster; woodworking.

Wan Kiang, China: see WAN RIVER.

Wankie or **Wankie Colliery,** township (pop. 6,319), Bulawayo prov., W Southern Rhodesia, in Matabeleland, on railroad and 185 mi. NW of Bulawayo; alt. 2,567 ft. Major coal-mining center, with mines here and at Madumabisa and Inyantue; coke ovens, brick kilns. Hq. of native commissioner for Wankie dist. Police post.

Wanks River, Nicaragua: see COCO RIVER.

Wanlin (vālē'), village (pop. 547), Namur prov., SE Belgium, on Lesse R. and 9 mi. SE of Dinant; brick mfg.

Wanlockhead (wŏnlŏk-hĕd'), lead-mining village in Sanquhar parish, NW Dumfries, Scotland, in Lowther Hills, 6 mi. ENE of Sanquhar. Mines were opened in 16th cent. and, together with those at LEADHILLS, just NE in Lanark, have been most productive in Great Britain. Silver is also mined.

Wann (wän), town (pop. 99), Nowata co., NE Okla., 18 mi. NNW of Nowata, near Kansas line.

Wanna (vä'nä), village (pop. 2,756), in former Prussian prov. of Hanover, NW Germany, after 1945 in Lower Saxony, 10 mi. SSE of Cuxhaven; shoe mfg.

Wanne-Eickel (vä'nŭ-ī'kŭl), city (1950 pop. 86,370), in former Prussian prov. of Westphalia, W Germany, after 1945 in North Rhine-Westphalia, in the Ruhr, port on Rhine-Herne Canal and 4 mi. NNW of Bochum city center; rail junction; coal-mining center; mfg. of chemicals (synthetic oil and fuel, nitrates). Formed 1926 through incorporation of Wanne and Eickel.

Wannehorn, Gross, Switzerland: see FIESCHERHÖRNER.

Wanni (vŭn'nē) [Singhalese,=wild country], tract (□ c.2,000) of thick jungle, mostly in Northern Prov., Ceylon; formerly a highly-cultivated area served by extensive irrigation tanks (now largely abandoned). Sometimes spelled Vanni.

Wannien (wän'nyĕn'), town (pop. 8,513), ⊙ Wannien co. (pop. 111,439), NW Kiangsi prov., China, 60 mi. E of Nanchang; rice, cotton, tea, ramie, tobacco.

Wanning, China: see MANNING.

Wannsee (vän'zā"), residential section of Zehlendorf dist., SW Berlin, Germany, on small lake, 11 mi. SW of city center; popular excursion resort. After 1945 in U.S. sector.

Wanparti or **Wanaparti** (both: vŭnpŭr'tē), town (pop. 6,926), Mahbubnagar dist., S Hyderabad state, India, 22 mi. SSW of Mahbubnagar; rice and oilseed milling, biri mfg. Wanparti Road or Wanaparti Road, rail station, is 12 mi. W. Also spelled Wanparthi or Wanaparthi.

Wanping or **Wan-p'ing** (wän'pĭng'), town, ⊙ Wanping co. (pop. 269,109), N Hopeh prov., China, on Yungting R. (here crossed by Marco Polo Bridge), 7 mi. SW of Peking, and on Peking-Hankow RR; wheat, kaoliang, millet. Coal mines near by. Until 1928 called Lukowkiao. Scene (1937) of clash bet. Chinese and Jap. troops that began Sino-Japanese War (1937–45).

Wan River (wän'), Chinese *Wan Kiang, Hwan Kiang,* or *Huan Chiang* (all: hwän' jyäng'), SE Kansu prov., China, rises in Shensi-Kansu-Ningsia border area, flows over 150 mi. S, past Wanhsien, Kingyang, and Ninghsien, to King R. on Shensi line, 90 mi. NW of Sian.

Wansen, Poland: see WIAZOW.

Wansleben (väns'lā"bŭn), village (pop. 4,687), in former Prussian Saxony prov., central Germany, after 1945 in Saxony-Anhalt, 10 mi. W of Halle; potash mining.

Wanstead (wŏn'stĭd, -stĕd), residential former urban district (1931 pop. 19,183) now in Wanstead and Woodford municipal borough (1951 census pop. 61,620), SW Essex, England, on Roding R. and 8 mi. NE of London. Wanstead Park, with heronry and lake, formerly belonged to Wanstead House (18th–19th cent.).

Wantage (wŏn'tĭj), urban district (1931 pop. 3,426; 1951 census 5,089), NW Berkshire, England, 14 mi. SW of Oxford, in White Horse Vale; agr. market. Has 13th-cent. church and anc. grammar school; statue of Alfred the Great, who was b. here.

Wantagh (wŏn'tô"), residential village (1940 pop. 2,780), Nassau co., SE N.Y., on S shore of W Long Isl., 4 mi. ENE of Freeport; mfg. of burial vaults. Causeway leads S to Jones Beach State Park.

Wanting (wän'dĭng'), village, westernmost Yunnan prov., China, 60 mi. SW of Lungling, on Burma border; frontier station on Burma Road.

Wantsai (wän'dzī'), town (pop. 14,523), ⊙ Wantsai co. (pop. 165,076), NW Kiangsi prov., China, 90 mi. SW of Nanchang and on Kin R.; ramie-weaving center; sericulture; mfg. of bamboo and straw paper, cotton weaving, tung-oil and camphor processing. Coal mining; limestone deposits.

Wantzenau, La (lä vätsŭnō'), Ger. *Wanzenau* (vänt'sŭnou), town (pop. 2,641), Bas-Rhin dept., E France, on the Ill near its mouth on the Rhine, and 7 mi. NE of Strasbourg; forges.

Wanyin (wä-nyĭn'), S state (myosaship) (□ 219; pop. 10,238), Southern Shan State, Upper Burma; ⊙ Wanyin, village 25 mi. SSE of Taunggyi, on road to Loikaw.

Wanyüan (wän'yüän'), town (pop. 13,917), ⊙ Wanyüan co. (pop. 152,758), NE Szechwan prov., China, 70 mi. NE of Tahsien, on Shensi border, in mtn. region; mushroom-collecting center; tea and tung-oil processing; tobacco, rice, millet, potatoes, wheat. Until 1914 called Taiping.

Wanze or **Wanze-lez-Huy** (vãz-lā-wē'), town (pop. 1,790), Liége prov., E Belgium, 2 mi. NW of Huy; beet-sugar refining.

Wanzenau, France: see WANTZENAU, LA.

Wanzleben (vänts'lā"bŭn), town (pop. 6,261), in former Prussian Saxony prov., central Germany, after 1945 in Saxony-Anhalt, 10 mi. WSW of Magdeburg; agr. market (sugar beets, grain, vegetables). Just NW are remains of castle 1st mentioned in 9th cent.

Wao, India: see VAV.

Wapakoneta (wŏpŭkŭnĕ'tŭ), city (pop. 5,797), ⊙ Auglaize co., W Ohio, 13 mi. SSW of Lima and on Auglaize R.; mfg. (machinery, toys, furniture, motor vehicles, metal stampings, cigars, apiary equipment). Founded 1833.

Wapanucka (wŏpŭnŭ'kŭ), town (pop. 592), Johnston co., S Okla., 30 mi. SSE of Ada, in farm area; cotton ginning. One of 1st schools of Chickasaw Nation was opened here in 1852.

Wapato (wô'pŭtō), town (pop. 3,185), Yakima co., S Wash., 11 mi. S of Yakima; hay, potatoes, tomatoes. Inc. 1908.

Wapawekka Lake (wôpŭwĕ'kŭ, wŏ–) (30 mi. long, 8 mi. wide), central Sask., at foot of the Wapawekka Hill, 140 mi. NE of Prince Albert. Drains E into Churchill R. through Deschambault L.

Wapella (wŭpĕ'lŭ), town (pop. 467), SE Sask., 16 mi. WNW of Moosomin; grain elevators.

Wapella (wŏpĕ'lŭ), village (pop. 504), De Witt co., central Ill., 18 mi. S of Bloomington, in agr. area.

Wapello (wä'pŭlō), county (□ 437; pop. 47,397), SE Iowa; ⊙ Ottumwa. Prairie agr. area (hogs, cattle, poultry, corn, soybeans, wheat) drained by Des Moines R. and Cedar Creek; bituminous-coal mines. Industry at Ottumwa. Formed 1843.

Wapello, city (pop. 1,755), ⊙ Louisa co., SE Iowa, on Iowa R. and 25 mi. N of Burlington; livestock, grain. Settled 1837, inc. 1856.

Wapi Mountains, Nicaragua: see HUAPI MOUNTAINS.

Wappapello Dam (wä'pŭpĕ"lŭ), SE Mo., 14 mi. N of Poplar Bluff; earthfill dam (77 ft. high, 2,700 long) used for flood control on St. Francis R. It forms **Wappapello Reservoir** (10 mi. long) in Wayne and Butler counties.

Wapping (wŏ'pĭng), district of Stepney metropolitan borough, London, England, on N bank of the Thames, 3 mi. E of Charing Cross; extensive dock installations. Here is end of Thames tunnel to Rotherhithe, built 1825–43 by Brunel.

Wappinger Creek (wŏ'pĭnjŭr), SE N.Y., rises in N Dutchess co., flows c.35 mi. SSW, past Wappingers Falls (water power), to the Hudson 8 mi. S of Poughkeepsie.

Wappingers Falls (–jŭrz), village (pop. 3,490), Dutchess co., SE N.Y., in the Hudson highlands, on Wappinger Creek (water power) near its mouth on the Hudson, and 7 mi. S of Poughkeepsie; mfg. (clothing, textiles, plastic and metal novelties). Society of the Cincinnati founded here in 1783. Inc. 1871.

Wapsa Khani (väp'sŭ kŭn'ē), village, E central Nepal, on the Dudh Kosi (tributary of the Sun Kosi) and 19 mi. NNE of Okhaldhunga; copper mining.

Wapsipinicon River (wăp"sĭpĭ'nĭkŏn), NE and E Iowa, rises on Minn. line NNW of McIntire, flows c.225 mi. SE, past Independence and Anamosa, to Mississippi R. 20 mi. NE of Davenport. Receives Little Wapsipinicon R. (c.40 mi. long) and Buffalo Creek.

Waqra or **Waqrah** (wăk'rŭ), town (pop. 5,000), on E coast of Qatar peninsula, 8 mi. SE of Doha; pearling, fishing. Sometimes Wakra and Wakrah.

Waquoit, Mass.: see FALMOUTH.

War, town (pop. 3,992), McDowell co., S W.Va., on Dry Fork and 11 mi. SSW of Welch, in semi-bituminous-coal-mining and agr. (livestock, fruit, tobacco) region. Inc. 1920.

Wara, Fr. Equatorial Africa: see OUARA.

Warabi (wä"rä'bē), town (pop. 27,964), Saitama prefecture, central Honshu, Japan, bet. Urawa (NW) and Kawaguchi (SE), in rice-growing area; textiles.

Waramaug, Lake, W Conn., resort lake in Warren and Washington towns, 13 mi. SW of Torrington; 3 mi. long. State parks here.

Warangal (vŭrŭng'gŭl), district (□ 7,944; pop. 1,321,838), SE Hyderabad state, India, on Deccan Plateau; ⊙ Warangal. Bounded NE by Godavari R.; mainly lowland with isolated granite outcrops; drained by tributaries of the Godavari. Largely sandy red soil; millet, oilseeds (chiefly peanuts, castor beans), rice, cotton. Bamboo (used in paper mfg.), teak, ebony in thickly forested E half of dist. Trade centers: Warangal (transportation and cotton-milling center), Khammam. Kottagudem (coal-mining center) and Yellandlapad (iron-ore, graphite, mica, and marble quarrying) are in area called Singareni coal field. Part of Hyderabad since beginning (early-18th cent.) of state's formation. Pop. 74% Hindu, 7% Moslem, 3% Christian.

Warangal, city (pop. 92,808), ⊙ Warangal dist., E Hyderabad state, India, 85 mi. NE of Hyderabad. Transportation center; airport; cotton-milling and trade (grain, wool, hides and skins) center; printing, bookbinding; noted hand-woven carpet industry. Industrial school. Experimental farm. Has Hindu temple, built c.1160. Rail junction of Kazipet is 5 mi. SW. Mathwada, 2 mi. SE, is commercial suburb. Warangal Fort, 5 mi. SE, was site of 13th-cent. city. Present city sometimes called Hanamkonda.

Waraseoni or **Wara-Seoni** (both: wä'rä-syō'nē), town (pop. 6,607), Balaghat dist., central Madhya Pradesh, India, 10 mi. WSW of Balaghat; rice, flour, oilseed, and sugar milling.

Waratah (wŏ'rŭtä), NW suburb of Newcastle, New South Wales, Australia; steel mills.

Waratah, town (pop. 511), N central Tasmania, 85 mi. W of Launceston; tin-mining center, with rich mines at near-by Mt. Bischoff.

Waratah Bay, inlet of Bass Strait, S Victoria, Australia, bet. Cape Liptrap (W) and a sandy neck joining Wilson's Promontory to mainland; 8 mi. long, 4 mi. wide.

Warba, village (pop. 125), Itasca co., NE central Minn., on Swan R. and 14 mi. SE of Grand Rapids; grain, potatoes.

Warbleton, agr. village and parish (pop. 1,341), E Sussex, England, 12 mi. N of Eastbourne.

Warblington, former urban district (1931 pop. 4,321), SE Hampshire, England, 7 mi. NE of Portsmouth; agr. market. Inc. 1932 in Havant and Waterloo urban dist. Just E, on Chichester Harbour, is town of Emsworth, with oyster fisheries.

Warboys, town and parish (pop. 1,593), E central Huntingdon, England, 7 mi. NE of Huntingdon; agr. market. Has 13th-cent. church.

Warburg (vär'bo͝ork), town (pop. 10,079), in former Prussian prov. of Westphalia, NW Germany, after 1945 in North Rhine-Westphalia, on the Diemel and 19 mi. NW of Kassel; rail junction. Has 13th-cent. church, 16th-cent. town hall. Was member of Hanseatic League.

Warburton, town (pop. 1,597), S central Victoria, Australia, on Yarra R. and 40 mi. E of Melbourne; rail terminus; mtn. resort; timber.

Warburton, village, Sheikhupura dist., E Punjab, W Pakistan, 14 mi. SSW of Sheikhupura; trades in grain, cotton, oilseeds; rice and oilseed milling, cotton ginning, hand-loom weaving.

Warcha (vär'chŭ), village, Shahpur dist., W central Punjab, W Pakistan, at foot of Salt Range, 45 mi. NW of Sargodha, on rail spur; rock-salt mining. Pottery clay quarried c.6 mi. NNW; gypsum deposits near by.

Warche, Barrage de la, Belgium: see BARRAGE DE LA WARCHE.

Warche River (värsh), SE Belgium, rises in 2 branches on Ger. border 15 mi. E of Malmédy, flows 30 mi. generally W, past Butgenbach, Barrage de la Warche, and Malmédy, to Amblève R. just E of Stavelot. Hydroelectric power stations at Butgenbach and Barrage de la Warche.

Ward. 1 County (□ 2,048; pop. 34,782), N central N.Dak.; ⊙ Minot. Agr. area drained by Souris and Des Lacs rivers. Lignite mines; mfg. in Minot; diversified farming (dairy products, poultry, livestock, wheat). Formed 1885. **2** County (□ 827; pop. 13,346), extreme W Texas; ⊙ Monahans. In Pecos valley; Pecos R. is W and S boundary of co.; alt. c.2,500 ft. Oil and natural-gas fields; ranching (cattle, horses, mules, hogs, sheep), some irrigated agr. (water from Red Bluff L., c.60 mi. WNW of Monahans); cotton, alfalfa, grain sorghums, fruit, truck. Formed 1887.

Ward. 1 Town (pop. 364), Lonoke co., central Ark., 28 mi. NE of Little Rock, in agr. area. **2** Town (pop. 10), Boulder co., N central Colo., in Front Range, 13 mi. WNW of Boulder; alt. 9,250 ft.; gold mining. **3** Town (pop. 122), Saluda co., W central S.C., 40 mi. WSW of Columbia. Sometimes called Wards. **4** Town (pop. 96), Moody co., E S.Dak., 10 mi. NE of Flandreau. **5** Village (pop. 2,055), Kanawha co., W W.Va., 15 mi. SE of Charleston, in coal and oil area.

Wardak River, Afghanistan: see LOGAR RIVER.

Wardang Island, South Australia, in Spencer Gulf of Indian Ocean, 3 mi. off W coast of Yorke Peninsula; shelters Port Victoria (E); 4 mi. long, 2 mi. wide; sandy. Sheep run. Formerly Wauraltree.

Wardell (wärdĕl'), town (pop. 454), Pemiscot co., extreme SE Mo., on Little R., near the Mississippi, and 14 mi. NNW of Caruthersville.

Warden, town (pop. 2,004), E Orange Free State, U. of So. Afr., 30 mi. NNW of Harrismith; alt. 5,289 ft.; rail terminus; grain, stock.

Warden, town (pop. 322), Grant co., E central Wash., 34 mi. SE of Ephrata, in Columbia basin agr. region.

Wardenburg (vär'dŭnbo͝ork), village (commune pop. 8,636), in Oldenburg, NW Germany, after 1945 in Lower Saxony, near Hunte R., 5 mi. S of Oldenburg city, in peat region.

Wardensville, town (pop. 171), Hardy co., NE W. Va., in Eastern Panhandle, on Cacapon R. and 33 mi. SSE of Keyser.

Wardere (wär'dĕrĕ), Ital. *Uardere,* village (pop. 1,200), Harar prov., SE Ethiopia, in the Ogaden, 150 mi. SE of Dagahbur, in pastoral region (camels, sheep); water hole.

Wardha (wär'dŭ, vŭr'dŭ), district (□ 2,435; pop. 519,330), central Madhya Pradesh, India, on Deccan Plateau; ⊙ Wardha. Bordered N and W by Wardha R.; undulating plains, with S outliers of Satpura Range in N; drained by tributaries of the Wardha. In major cotton-growing tract; also produces millet, wheat, and oilseeds (chiefly flax); tamarind, date palms along the Wardha. Timber (teak, sal) in hills (cattle raising). Cotton ginning, oilseed milling, handicraft cloth weaving. Hinganghat, Wardha, and Pulgaon are cotton-milling and agr. trade centers. Pop. 85% Hindu, 10% tribal (mostly Gond), 4% Moslem.

Wardha, town (pop. 28,359), ⊙ Wardha dist., central Madhya Pradesh, India, 40 mi. SW of Nagpur; rail junction; cotton-milling and agr. trade center; oilseed milling; millet, wheat, flax. Seksaria Commerce Col. Section of town called Maganwadi has hq. of All-India Village Industries Assn.; was center of Mahatma Gandhi's activities from 1934 until he established permanent hq. at SEVAGRAM, 4 mi. ESE, in 1936.

Wardha River, Madhya Pradesh, India, rises in central Satpura Range, near Pandhurna; flows c.250 mi. generally SE, through important cotton-growing tract, past Ballalpur (collieries), joining Wainganga R. 40 mi. SE of Chanda, on Hyderabad–Madhya Pradesh border, to form Pranhita R., affluent of the Godavari. Receives Penganga R.

Ward Hunt Island (9 mi. long, 1–3 mi. wide), NE Franklin Dist., Northwest Territories, in the Arctic Ocean, just off N Ellesmere Isl.; 83°5'N 75°W.

Wardle, urban district (1931 pop. 4,793; 1951 census 4,893), SE Lancashire, England, 3 mi. NNE of Rochdale; cotton milling, wool finishing, leather mfg.

Wardle, Mount (9,218 ft.), SE B.C., near Alta. border, in Rocky Mts., in Kootenay Natl. Park, 25 mi. SW of Banff; 50°57'N 116°1'W.

Wardner, city (pop. 772), Shoshone co., N Idaho, just S of Kellogg, in mining (zinc, lead) and smelting dist.

Wards, S.C.: see WARD.

Wardsboro, town (pop. 377), Windham co., SE Vt., 17 mi. NW of Brattleboro; wood products. Partly in Green Mtn. Natl. Forest.

Wards Island (255 acres), in New York city, SE N.Y., in East R. bet. Welfare Isl. (S), Randalls Isl. (N). Crossed by roadway of Triborough Bridge, it is connected with Manhattan by a pedestrian drawbridge (1951) giving access to recreational facilities here.

Wardsville, village (pop. 255), S Ont., on Thames R. and 24 mi. NE of Chatham; fruit.

Ware (wâr), residential urban district (1931 pop. 6,181; 1951 census 8,253), E central Hertford, England, on Lea R. and 3 mi. ENE of Hertford; railroad workshops; mfg. of plastics, paint, pharmaceuticals; brewing. Has 14th-cent. parish church; a priory is relic of 14th-cent. Franciscan monastery. The "Great Bed of Ware," mentioned in *Twelfth Night,* is now in Victoria and Albert Mus. in London.

Ware, county (□ 912; pop. 30,289), SE Ga.; ⊙ Waycross. Bounded S by Fla. line; drained by Satilla R. Coastal plain agr. (tobacco, corn, livestock) and forestry (lumber, naval stores) area. Okefenokee Swamp occupies S part. Founded 1824.

Ware, town (pop. 7,517), including Ware village (pop. 6,217), Hampshire co., central Mass., on Ware R. and 22 mi. W of Worcester; textiles, shoes, lumber products. Settled c.1717, inc. 1761.

Waregem (vä'rŭ-khŭm), town (pop. 13,137), West Flanders prov., W Belgium, 8 mi. NE of Courtrai; textile industry; agr. market. Formerly spelled Waereghem. Flanders Field American Cemetery.

Wareham (wâ'rŭm), municipal borough (1931 pop. 2,058; 1951 census 2,750), S Dorset, England, on Frome R. and 6 mi. WSW of Poole; agr. market. Surrounded by early Br. rampart, reinforced by Romans. Has Saxon church, rebuilt in 13th cent., and Saxon and Norman church containing coffin of Edward the Martyr.

Wareham (wâr'hăm", wâ'rŭm), town (pop. 7,569), Plymouth co., SE Mass., on inlet at head of Buzzards Bay and 14 mi. NE of New Bedford; summer resort. Cranberry and oyster center; nails, boatbuilding. Formerly whaling and shipbuilding. Settled 1678, inc. 1739. Includes resort villages of Onset (pop. 1,674), Point Independence, East Wareham (1940 pop. 708), South Wareham, West Wareham, Swifts Beach.

Warehouse Point, Conn.: see EAST WINDSOR.

Waremme (värĕm'), Flemish *Borgworm* (bôrkh'vôrm), town (pop. 4,986), Liége prov., E Belgium, 15 mi. W of Liége; mfg. (motors, agr. machinery); market center for agr. area.

Waren (vä'rŭn), town (pop. 19,807), Mecklenburg, N Germany, at N tip of Müritz L., 19 mi. NW of Neustrelitz; rail junction; sugar refining, dairying; agr. market (grain, sugar beets, vegetables, potatoes, stock). Fishing; popular tourist and water-sports resort.

Warendorf (vä'rŭndôrf), town (pop. 14,050), in former Prussian prov. of Westphalia, NW Germany, after 1945 in North Rhine-Westphalia, on the Ems and 15 mi. E of Münster; linen weaving. Stud.

Ware River, central Mass., rises in N Worcester co., flows c.45 mi. generally SW, joining Quaboag R. to form Chicopee R. in Palmer town.

Ware Shoals, mill village (pop. 3,032), Greenwood co., NW S.C., on Saluda R. and 15 mi. SW of Laurens; textiles, clothing, cottonseed oil.

Warffum or **Warfum** (both: vär'fŭm), town (pop. 2,458), Groningen prov., N Netherlands, 12 mi. N of Groningen; vegetable canning.

Warfield, town and parish (pop. 2,294), E Berkshire, England, 10 mi. E of Reading; agr. market. Has 14th-cent. church.

Warfield, town (pop. 324), Martin co., E Ky., in Cumberland foothills, on Tug Fork (bridged here to Kermit, W.Va.) and 15 mi. NW of Williamson, W.Va.

Warfum, Netherlands: see WARFFUM.

Wargla, Algeria: see OUARGLA.

Wargrave, town and parish (pop. 2,271), E Berkshire, England, on the Thames at mouth of Loddon R., and 6 mi. NE of Reading; agr. market and resort favored by artists.

Warialda (wŏrēăl'dŭ), town (pop. 1,124), N New South Wales, Australia, 210 mi. SW of Brisbane; sheep; agr. center.

Warin (värēn'), town (pop. 3,652), Mecklenburg, N Germany, on small Warin L., 12 mi. SE of Wismar; agr. market (grain, sugar beets, potatoes, stock).

Waringstown (wâr'ĭngztoun), town (pop. 406), NW Co. Down, Northern Ireland, 3 mi. SE of Lurgan; agr. market (flax, oats, potatoes).

Warka, Iraq: see ERECH.

Warka (vär'kä), Rus. *Varka* (vär'kŭ), town (pop. 3,310), Warszawa prov., E central Poland, on Pilica R., on railroad and 32 mi. S of Warsaw; flour milling, distilling, cement mfg. Battlefields (1656; 1944) near by.

Warken (vär'kŭn), village (pop. 182), central Luxembourg, on Wark R., just W of Ettelbruck; mfg. (agr. machinery, iron products).

Wark River (värk), central Luxembourg, rises 6 mi. W of Ettelbruck, flows 12 mi. E, past Mertzig, Feulen, and Warken, to Alzette R. at Ettelbruck, just above its mouth. Not navigable.

Warkworth, village (pop. estimate 650), SE Ont., on Mill Creek and 26 mi. W of Belleville; dairying, mixed farming.

Warkworth (wôr'kwŭrth), town and parish (pop. 713), E Northumberland, England, on Coquet R. near North Sea, and 6 mi. SE of Alnwick; small seaport. Near by are remains of 12th-15th-cent. Warkworth Castle and of Warkworth Hermitage, mentioned in Percy's *Reliques.* Has Norman church with 12th-cent. tower.

Warkworth, town (pop. 619), ⊙ Rodney co. (□ 477; pop. 5,102), N N.Isl., New Zealand, 32 mi. NNW of Auckland; dairies, orchards, sawmills.

Warlingham, England: see CATERHAM AND WARLINGHAM.

Warmbad (värm'bät), town (pop. 594), E South-West Africa, near Orange R., 140 mi. SSE of Keetmanshoop, 150 mi. W of Upington; Karakul-sheep-raising center. Corundum, fluorspar deposits. First white settlement in South-West Africa established here early in 19th cent., attacked by Hottentots, reopened 1818. Germans erected fort here, 1893.

Warmbad Villach, Austria: see VILLACH.

Warmbaths, Afrikaans *Warmbad* (värm'bät), village (pop. 2,960), central Transvaal, U. of So. Afr., 60 mi. N of Pretoria; popular resort with radio-active medicinal springs. Govt. pasture-research station near by.

Warmbrunn, Bad, Poland: see CIEPLICE SLASKIE ZDROJ.

Warmensteinach (vär"mŭn-shtī'näkh), village (pop. 1,572), Upper Franconia, NE Bavaria, Germany, in the Fichtelgebirge, 10 mi. ENE of Bayreuth; glass mfg. (beads and costume jewelry), lumber milling. Summer and winter resort.

Warmia (wôr'mēŭ), Pol. *Warmja* (vär'myä), Ger. *Ermland* (ĕrm'länt) or *Ermeland* (ĕr'mŭlänt), historic region in East Prussia, after 1945 in Olsztyn prov., NE Poland, extending from Vistula Lagoon inland to upper Lyna R. Became bishopric (1243) under Teutonic Knights, with seat in Braniewo (Braunsberg) until 1350, in Lidzbark Warminski (Heilsberg) until 1772, and then in Frombork (Frauenburg); after 1945, its seat was moved to Allenstein (Olsztyn). Region was ceded in 1466 to Poland by the Teutonic Knights; passed in 1772 to Prussia.

Warmia Canal, Pol. *Kanał Warmińskie* (kä'nou värmē'nyŭskyĕ), Ger. *Oberländischer Kanal* (ō'bŭrlĕn"dĭ-shŭr känäl'), in East Prussia, after 1945 in N Poland; bet. L. Druzno (N) and Drweca R. at Ostroda (S); 87 mi. long.

Warminster, urban district (1931 pop. 5,176; 1951 census pop. 8,236), W Wiltshire, England, near Wylye R., 14 mi. SE of Bath; agr. market, with market gardens, nurseries; bacon and ham curing, cheese making, mfg. (electrical equipment, paint). Has grammar school founded 1707, attended by Dr. Arnold, and 14th-cent. church.

Warmja, region, Poland: see WARMIA.

Warmond (vär'mōnt), town (pop. 3,070), South Holland prov., W Netherlands, 3 mi. N of Leiden; mfg. (bamboo mats, wax products); stone quarry.

Warm Springs. 1 City (pop. 557), Meriwether co., W Ga., c.60 mi. SSW of Atlanta; health resort. Famous Warm Springs Foundation for treatment of poliomyelitis was established here in 1927 by Franklin D. Roosevelt, who gave it his 2,600-acre farm. The "Little White House," Ga. home of Roosevelt and scene of his death, was made a natl. shrine. The springs maintain a constant temp. of c.88°F. and flow at rate of 800 gallons per minute. Near by is Franklin D. Roosevelt State Park (formerly Pine Mtn. State Park), a forested recreational area. **2** Village, Deer Lodge co., SW Mont., on the Clark Fork and 8 mi. ENE of Anaconda. State hosp. for insane, mineral springs here. State game farm and state tuberculosis sanatorium near by. **3** Hamlet, Jefferson co., N central Oregon, on Deschutes R. and 11 mi. NW of Madras; hq. Warm Springs Indian Reservation. **4** Resort village, ⊙ Bath co., W Va., in the Alleghenies, 38 mi. W of Staunton, in recreational area; medicinal springs. Railroad station is Hot Springs.

Warm Springs Dam, Oregon: see MALHEUR RIVER.

Warnant (värnä'), village (pop. 753), Namur prov., S Belgium, 6 mi. NW of Dinant; marble quarrying. Near by are remains of 14th-cent. Château de Montaigle.

Warndt (värnt), forested hill region, SW Saar, extends 10 mi. NW-SE along Fr. border SW of Völklingen; c.5 mi. wide. Rises to 1,033 ft. 7 mi. SW of Völklingen.

Warnemünde (vär"nümün'dü), outport of ROSTOCK N Germany, on Mecklenburg Bay of the Baltic, at mouth of Warnow R. estuary, 7 mi. NNW of Rostock; 54°11'N 12°6'E. Seaport; terminus of train ferry to Gedser, Denmark; popular seaside resort. Woodworking, food-products mfg. Port established in 13th cent. Captured by Soviet troops in May, 1945.

Warner, village (pop. 370), S Alta., near Mont. border, 40 mi. SE of Lethbridge; farming, ranching.

Warner. 1 Resort town (pop. 1,080), Merrimack co., S central N.H., 15 mi. WNW of Concord and on Warner R.; wood products, truck, poultry, dairy products. Ski trails near. Settled c.1740, inc. 1774. Includes resort village of Davisville. **2** Town (pop. 382), Muskogee co., E Okla., 18 mi. S of Muskogee; cotton ginning. Connors State Agr. Col. is here.

Warner, Mount (9,296 ft.), SW B.C., in Coast Mts., 130 mi. N of Vancouver; 51°4'N 123°12'W.

Warner Mountains (c.5–10,000 ft.), in extreme NE Calif. and S Oregon, a N-S range c.85 mi. long, mainly in E Modoc co., Calif. Rise to 9,934 ft. in Eagle Peak near S end. Hunting, fishing, lumbering. Surprise Valley is E.

Warner River, S central N.H., rises W of Bradford, flows c.25 mi. E, past Warner, to Contoocook R. 9 mi. NW of Concord.

Warner Robins, town (pop. 7,986), Houston co., central Ga., 14 mi. S of Macon. Also called Wellston. Inc. after 1940.

Warnes (vär'nës), town (pop. 2,282), N central Buenos Aires prov., Argentina, 15 mi. N of Bragado; hog-raising center; corn, sunflowers, cattle.

Warnes, town (pop. c.2,400), ⊙ Warnes prov., Santa Cruz dept., central Bolivia, 20 mi. N of Santa Cruz, in tropical agr. area (sugar cane, rice, corn, coffee).

Warneton (värnütõ'), Flemish *Waasten* (väs'tün), agr. village (pop. 3,294), West Flanders prov., W Belgium, on Lys R. and 7 mi. SSE of Ypres, on Fr. border.

Warnham (wôr'nüm), agr. village and parish (pop. 1,274), N Sussex, England, 2 mi. NNW of Horsham. In parish (SW) is Field Place, where Shelley was born.

Warninglid, England: see SLAUGHAM.

Warnow River (vär'nō), N Germany, rises 6 mi. N of Parchim, flows 79 mi. W, N, and NE, past Bützow (head of navigation), to Rostock, whence it continues in 7-mi.-long N-S estuary (also called Breitling) to Mecklenburg Bay of the Baltic, at Warnemünde.

Warnsdorf, Czechoslovakia: see VARNSDORF.

Warora (vürō'rü), town (pop. 9,542) Chanda dist., S Madhya Pradesh, India, near Wardha R., 28 mi. NW of Chanda; local cotton-trade center; cotton ginning, oilseed milling; glassworks; rice, millet. Limestone deposits near by.

Warquignies (värkënyē'), town (pop. 1,012), Hainaut prov., SW Belgium, 9 mi. WSW of Mons; coal mining.

Warracknabeal (wŏ"rüknübēl'), town (pop. 2,686), W Victoria, Australia, 180 mi. NW of Melbourne, in wheat-raising area; flour mill, alcohol distillery.

Warr Acres, town (pop. 2,378), Oklahoma co., central Okla., near Oklahoma City.

Warragul (wŏ'rügül), town (pop. 3,536), S Victoria, Australia, 55 mi. SE of Melbourne; dairying center (dairy plants, cheese factory).

Warra Haliu (wä'rä häl'yōō), village, Shoa prov., central Ethiopia, 37 mi. SSW of Dessye, in agr. and livestock region; 39°32'N 10°36'E; alt. 9,422 ft. Caravan center with Coptic churches.

Warraq el 'Arab or **Warraq al-'Arab** (both: wäräk' ĕl-äräb'), village (pop. 12,160), Giza prov., Upper Egypt, 4 mi. NW of Cairo city center.

Warrego River (wŏ'rïgō), E central Australia, rises in Carnavon Range, Queensland; flows 495 mi. SSW, past Augathella, Charleville, and Cunnamulla, to Darling R. SW of Bourke, New South Wales. Angellala and Ward rivers, main tributaries.

Warren, municipality (pop. 1,746), central New South Wales, Australia, on Macquarie R. and 250 mi. NW of Sydney; sheep.

Warren, village (pop. estimate 500), E central Ont., on Veuve R. and 40 mi. W of North Bay; dairying, lumbering, mixed farming.

Warren. 1 County (□ 284; pop. 8,779), E Ga.; ⊙ Warrenton. Bounded W by Ogeechee R. Intersected by the fall line. Agr. (cotton, corn, peas, grain), sawmilling, granite quarrying. Timber. Formed 1793. **2** County (□ 542; pop. 21,981), W Ill.; ⊙ Monmouth. Agr. (livestock, corn, wheat, oats, soybeans, poultry, clover; dairy products). Bituminous coal, clay. Mfg. (farm machinery, pottery, sheet-metal products, furnaces). Drained by Henderson Creek and small Swan Creek. Formed 1825. **3** County (□ 368; pop. 8,535), W Ind.; ⊙ Williamsport. Bounded W by Ill. line, SE by Wabash R. Agr. (corn, oats, soybeans); lumber milling. Formed 1827. **4** County (□ 572; pop. 17,758), S central Iowa; ⊙ Indianola. Prairie agr. area (cattle, hogs, poultry, corn, wheat, oats) drained by North, South, and Middle rivers; bituminous-coal deposits. Has state park. Formed 1846. **5** County (□ 546; pop. 42,758), S Ky.; ⊙ BOWLING GREEN. Bounded N by Green R.; drained by Barren R., Trammel and West forks of Drake Creek. Rolling agr. area (dark tobacco, corn, dairy products, livestock, strawberries, poultry). Limestone and asphalt quarries, oil and gas wells. Varied mfg. at Bowling Green. Formed 1796. **6** County (□ 566; pop. 39,616), W Miss.; ⊙ VICKSBURG. Bounded W by the Mississippi (here the La. line), E and S by Big Black R.; intersected by Yazoo R. Agr. (cotton, corn, livestock); timber. Formed 1809. **7** County (□ 428; pop. 7,666), E central Mo.; ⊙ Warrenton. Bounded S by Missouri R. Agr. (wheat, corn, oats), livestock; coal, clay pits; mfg. at Warrenton. Formed 1833. **8** County (□ 361; pop. 54,374), NW N.J., in hilly region bounded W by Delaware R., SE and E by Musconetcong R.; ⊙ Belvidere. Mfg. (textiles, metal goods); agr. (dairy products, truck, grain). In NW is part of Kittatinny Mtn. ridge (cut by Delaware R. W of Blairstown to form Delaware Water Gap). Includes state forests, Jenny Jump Mtn., and part of Stephens State Park. Drained by Pohatcong and Pequest rivers and Paulins Kill. Formed 1824. **9** County (□ 883; pop. 39,205), E N.Y.; ⊙ Lake George. Situated in the S Adirondacks; bounded E by L. George; drained by the Hudson and by Schroon R. Year-round resort region, with many lakes (Schroon, Brant, Loon, Friends, Luzerne), state parks, dude ranches, hiking and skiing trails. Dairying, poultry and stock raising, some farming (hay, clover), lumbering. Lumber and paper milling, other mfg. at Glens Falls. Formed 1813. **10** County (□ 445; pop. 23,539), N N.C., on Va. line; ⊙ Warrenton. Piedmont agr. (tobacco, cotton, corn) and timber area; drained by Roanoke R. and Fishing Creek. Formed 1779. **11** County (□ 408; pop. 38,505), SW Ohio; ⊙ Lebanon. Intersected by Little Miami R.; also drained by small Todd, Caesar, and Turtle creeks. Includes Fort Ancient State Memorial Park. Agr. area (livestock, grain, fruit, tobacco); mfg. at Franklin, Lebanon, Waynesville; sand and gravel pits. Formed 1803. **12** County (□ 910; pop. 42,698), NW Pa.; ⊙ Warren. Plateau area drained by Allegheny R. Had lumber boom in mid-19th cent. followed by oil boom. Cornplanter Reservation on Allegheny R. in NE part is only Indian settlement in Pa. Oil wells and refineries; mfg. (metal products, glass bottles, furniture); dairy products, potatoes; natural gas. Formed 1800. **13** County (□ 443; pop. 22,271), central Tenn.; ⊙ McMinnville. E portion in the Cumberlands; drained by affluents of Caney Fork of Cumberland R. Great Falls Dam and Reservoir are NE of McMinnville; co. will have part of Center Hill Reservoir. Livestock raising, general farming; some mfg. (chiefly at McMinnville). Marble and granite quarries. Tree nurseries. Formed 1807. **14** County (□ 219; pop. 14,801), N Va.; ⊙ Front Royal. In Shenandoah Valley; Blue Ridge is in E, part of Massanutten Mtn. in W; includes part of Shenandoah Natl. Forest and N end of Skyline Drive in Shenandoah Natl. Park. North and South forks join here to form Shenandoah R. Livestock (especially horses; cattle, sheep, hogs, poultry), dairying, agr. (fruit, corn, wheat, hay). Limestone quarrying. Tourist trade. Mfg. (especially rayon) at Front Royal. Formed 1836.

Warren. 1 Residential village (pop. 2,610), Cochise co., SE Ariz., in Mule Mts., near Mex. line, 4 mi. SE of Bisbee; alt. 5,250 ft. Copper, silver, zinc, and gold mines near by. **2** City (1950 pop. 2,615; 1951 special census pop. 3,704), ⊙ Bradley co., S Ark., c.45 mi. S of Pine Bluff; lumber-milling and woodworking town and cotton market. **3** Town (pop. 437), Litchfield co., W Conn., in Litchfield Hills, 12 mi. WSW of Torrington; agr., resorts. Includes 2 state parks, parts of L. Waramaug (SW) and Shepaug Reservoir (E). **4** Village (pop. 1,378), Jo Daviess co., NW Ill., near Wis. line, 24 mi. NW of Freeport, in agr. area. Tri-county fair held here annually. Apple River Canyon State Park is near by. Settled 1843, inc. 1859. **5** Town (pop. 1,247), Huntington co., NE central Ind., on Salamonie R. and 14 mi. SSE of Huntington, in agr. area (poultry, livestock, soybeans, grain); dairy products, feed, canned tomatoes, baby chicks. **6** Town (pop. 1,576), Knox co., S Maine, just W of Rockland and on St. George R.; agr., textiles, lumber. Settled 1736, inc. 1776. **7** Town (pop. 3,406), including Warren village (pop. 1,550), Worcester co., S central Mass., on Quaboag R. and 20 mi. WSW of Worcester; electric switchboards, power presses, textile printing, knit goods. Settled 1664, inc. as Western 1742, renamed Warren 1834. Includes West Warren village (pop. 1,244). **8** Village (pop. 727), Macomb co., SE Mich., 13 mi. N of downtown Detroit, in suburban mfg. and residential area. Makes trucks, auto parts, electrical products. **9** City (pop. 1,779), ⊙ Marshall co., NW Minn., on Snake R. and 23 mi. NE of Grand Forks, N.Dak., in Red R. valley; dairy products, tow. Settled 1878, inc. 1891. **10** Town (pop. 581), Grafton co., W central N.H., on Baker R. and 15 mi. NW of Plymouth; wood products, mica and granite quarries; winter sports. N.H. state sanitarium near Glencliff village (N). **11** City (pop. 49,856), ⊙ Trumbull co., NE Ohio, 13 mi. NW of Youngstown and on Mahoning R.; commercial, railroad, and mfg. center, with large steel mills and plants producing electrical apparatus, machinery, heating and sprinkling systems, auto parts, tires, commercial gases. Lordstown Ordnance Depot near by. Settled 1799, inc. 1834. **12** Borough (pop. 14,849), ⊙ Warren co., NW Pa., 50 mi. ESE of Erie and on Allegheny R., at mouth of Conewango Creek. Oil refineries; furniture, metal products, medicines; dairying. Hq. for Allegheny Natl. Forest (S). Once a lumbering town; oil boom in 1860. Laid out c.1795, inc. 1832. **13** Resort town (pop. 8,513), Bristol co., E R.I., on Mt. Hope Bay and Warren R. just N of Bristol; mfg. (textiles, slide fasteners, rubber flooring, auto parts, canned sea food), shellfish, truck. Transferred from Mass. to R.I. in 1746, inc. 1747. **14** Town (pop. 498), Washington co., W central Vt., on Mad R. and 19 mi. SW of Montpelier; wood products. Partly in Green Mtn. Natl. Forest.

Warren, Mount, Wyo.: see WIND RIVER RANGE.

Warren Park, town (pop. 336), Marion co., central Ind., E suburb of Indianapolis.

Warrenpoint, urban district (1937 pop. 2,310; 1951 census 2,798), SW Co. Down, Northern Ireland, at head of Carlin Lough, at mouth of Newry R. (terminus of Newry Canal), 6 mi. SE of Newry; seaport for Newry and seaside resort. Near-by Narrowater Castle dates from 1663.

Warren River, Mass. and R.I., formed in SE Mass. near state line by junction of Palmer R. and small stream; flows c.9 mi. S into R.I., widening in lower course to form harbor at Warren, to Narragansett Bay at mouth of Providence R.

Warrensburg. 1 Village (pop. 549), Macon co., central Ill., 7 mi. NW of Decatur; corn cannery; agr. (corn, wheat, soybeans, livestock). **2** City (pop. 6,857), ⊙ Johnson co., W central Mo., near Blackwater R., 50 mi. ESE of Kansas City. Agr. center; garment factory, meat-packing plant; coal mines, clay pits, blue-sandstone quarries. Central Missouri Col.; govt. recreational area near by. Inc. as town 1846, as city 1855. **3** Village (pop. 2,358), Warren co., E N.Y., in the Adirondacks, on Schroon R. near its mouth on the Hudson, and 14 mi. NNW of Glens Falls; trade center in farm and resort area; lumber, paper milling.

Warrensville, town (pop. 120), Ashe co., NW N.C., 29 mi. NW of North Wilkesboro.

Warrensville Heights, village (pop. 4,126), Cuyahoga co., N Ohio, a SE suburb of Cleveland. Inc. 1927.

Warrenton, town (pop. 3,551), NE Cape Prov., U. of So. Afr., near Orange Free State and Transvaal borders, in Griqualand West, on Vaal R. (bridge) and 40 mi. N of Kimberley; diamond mining, agr. (stock, dairying, grain, fruit).

Warrenton. 1 City (pop. 1,442), ⊙ Warren co., E Ga., 38 mi. W of Augusta, in agr. and timber area; sawmilling; granite quarries near by. Inc. as town 1810, as city 1908. **2** City (pop. 1,584), ⊙ Warren co., E central Mo., 35 mi. W of St. Charles. Agr.; mfg. (textiles, sheet metal); coal, clay pits. Jr. col., orphans' home here. Founded early in 19th cent. **3** Town (pop. 1,166), ⊙ Warren co., N N.C., 32 mi. NNW of Rocky Mount, near Va. line; mfg. of cotton yarn, boxes; tobacco processing, lumber milling. Founded 1779. **4** City (pop. 1,896), Clatsop co., extreme NW Oregon, just W of Astoria, at mouth of Columbia R., near Pacific Ocean. Cans razor clams; lumber mill. Point Adams coast guard station and U.S. Fort Stevens near by. Inc. 1899. **5** Town (pop. 1,797), ⊙ Fauquier co., N Va., 34 mi. NW of Fredericksburg, in rich agr. area at foot of the Blue Ridge; horse-breeding, racing, fox-hunting center. Settled 18th cent.; inc. 1810.

Warrenville. 1 Village, Conn.: see ASHFORD. **2** Village (pop. 1,891), Du Page co., NE Ill., 10 mi. NE of Aurora. **3** Village (pop. 1,604), Aiken co., W S.C., 5 mi. W of Aiken; textile milling.

Warri (wô'rē), province (□ 5,987; pop. 414,505), Western Provinces, S Nigeria; ⊙ Warri. In W part of Niger R. delta; rain forest (N), swamp forest (S). Chief forest products: hardwood (sawmilling and plywood mfg. at Sapele), rubber, palm oil and kernels (chief processing centers at Burutu and Koko), cacao, kola nuts. Food crops: yams, cassava, plantains. Pop. is Sobo and Jekri (N), Ijo (S).

Warri, town (pop. 10,726), ⊙ Warri prov., Western Provinces, S Nigeria, in Niger R. delta, 170 mi. ESE of Lagos; 5°32'N 5°44'E. Agr. trade center and river port; palm oil and kernels, hardwood, rubber, cacao, kola nuts. Has hosp., teachers col. Reached via Forcados and Escravos rivers (arms of Niger delta).

Warrick (wŏ'rĭk, wô'–), county (□ 391; pop. 21,527), SW Ind.; ⊙ Boonville. Bounded S by Ohio R., here forming Ky. line; drained by small Pigeon and Little Pigeon creeks. Agr. (livestock, fruit, grain, truck, tobacco), bituminous-coal mining, diversified mfg. Formed 1813.

Warrington (wŏ'rĭngtŭn), county borough (1931 pop. 79,317; 1951 census 80,681), S Lancashire, England, on Mersey R. and 16 mi. E of Liverpool; leather-tanning and mfg. center; cotton spinning and weaving; engineering; mfg. of chemicals, industrial soaps, glass, steel, measuring instruments, dies and gauges. A center of habitation since pre-Roman days, local excavations have yielded early Br. and Roman remains, shown in mus. Has two 18th-cent. churches, a 16th-cent. grammar school, and an acad. (founded in 18th cent.) which was an early center of Unitarianism. In 18th cent. the town was a center of the clock-making industry, later developing in other engineering branches. Site (1757–83) of a school for dissenters, taught for a time by Dr. Priestley. Just E and in county borough is chemical-mfg. town of Paddington.

Warrington, village (pop. 13,570), Escambia co., NW Fla., on Pensacola Bay and 4 mi. WSW of Pensacola.

Warrior, town (pop. 1,384), Jefferson co., N central Ala., c.20 mi. N of Birmingham; coal mining.

Warriormine, village (1940 pop. 1,000), McDowell co., S W.Va., on Dry Fork and 12 mi. SSW of Welch, in coal-mining and agr. area.

Warrior River, Ala.: see BLACK WARRIOR RIVER.

Warrior Run, borough (pop. 1,056), Luzerne co., NE central Pa., 5 mi. SW of Wilkes-Barre. Inc. 1895. Post office is Peely.

Warrnambool (wär'nŭmbōōl), municipality and port (pop. 9,993), SW Victoria, Australia, on Indian Ocean and 140 mi. WSW of Melbourne; commercial center for agr. and sheep-raising area; woolen mills, vegetable-dehydration plants. Exports wool, butter.

Warroad (wô'rōd), resort village (pop. 1,276), Roseau co., NW Minn., on Lake of the Woods, near Man. line, and 21 mi. ENE of Roseau; port of entry; shipping point for fish and lumber. Fish hatcheries and lumber and feldspar mills are here. Settled 1890, inc. 1901.

Warsak (vär'sŭk), village, Khyber agency, central North-West Frontier Prov., W Pakistan, on Kabul R. and 15 mi. NW of Peshawar; irrigation headworks; projected hydroelectric plant.

Warsaw (wôr'sô), Pol. *Warszawa* (vär-shä'vä), Rus. *Varshava* (vŭr-shä'vŭ), Ger. *Warschau* (vär'shou), city (after incorporation of adjacent suburbs in 1951: □ 140, pop. estimate 760,000; before 1951: □ 56, pop. in 1939 c.1,289,000, in 1950 c.650,000), ⊙ Poland and ⊙, but independent of, Warszawa prov., in E central part of country, on both banks of the Vistula; 52°15'N 21°E. Political, commercial, and intellectual center of Poland; transportation hub (railroads; inland port at ZERAN; airport at OKECIE). One of principal centers of Pol. metalworking industry; other industries include mfg. of electrical appliances and bulbs, machine tools, construction materials, precision instruments, tractors (at Ursus; WSW), automobiles (at Zeran), chemicals, clothing; textile milling, printing and publishing, food processing. Has univ. (founded 1818; many times closed and reopened, last in 1945), academies of arts and sciences. Major radio station at Raszyn (SW). Virtually destroyed by Germans in Second World War, city's reconstruction after 1945 was rapid. Two major traffic axes were built; E-W thoroughfare links W part of city with Praga, industrial part of Warsaw on right bank of the Vistula (several bridges rebuilt), and passes through tunnel under the razed Stare Miasto [old city] dist. The Stare Miasto was partly occupied by the ghetto, where monument commemorates Jewish rising of Feb., 1943. The Marszalkowska, one of Warsaw's principal avenues, became part of N-S thoroughfare bet. suburbs of Zoliborz (N) and Mokotow (S). Parliament bldg. (*Sejm*) and city hall were built after 1945. Warsaw also has Saxon Gardens, park in city center, and bldg. of council of ministers. Potocki and Czartoryski palaces, Raczynski palace (houses Pol. Acad. of Arts), and Staszica palace (houses Pol. Acad. of Sciences), formerly private mansions, all date from 18th cent. One of principal railroad centers of Eastern Europe, Warsaw has 4 stations; lines radiate to Moscow, Leningrad, Kiev, Prague, Berlin, and Danzig; E-W main line crosses city center through a tunnel. Chief suburbs of Warsaw are Mokotow (S), with airfield; Wlochy (WSW), Wola (W), Powazki (NW), Marymont and Zoliborz (N), and Grochow (SE). City probably grew around castle built (13th cent.) by a duke of Masovia; became in 15th cent. ⊙ Masovia. After fire (1595) of Cracow, it replaced that city as ⊙ Poland. Captured (1655 and again 1656) by Swedes under Charles X. Successively occupied by Charles XII of Sweden (1702) and Russians (1792, 1794); finally passed (1795) to Prussia. Captured (1806) by Napoleon I, who made it ⊙ grand duchy of Warsaw. Scene (1812) of diet which proclaimed re-establishment of Poland; captured (1813) by Russians, to whom it was awarded (1815) by Congress of Vienna, together with the theoretically independent kingdom of Poland. In 1830, led insurrection against Russian rule, but capitulated (1831) after defeat of insurgents at suburb of Grochow. Became (1917) seat of Ger.-sponsored regency council for Poland and (1919) ⊙ Pol. republic. Successfully defended (1920) by Fr. Marshal Weygand against advancing Russians. Scene (1926) of Pilsudski's military coup. In Second World War, city fell (Sept. 27, 1939) to Germans after stubborn resistance. Jewish ghetto was established (contained c.500,000 persons in 1942); in reprisal for Jewish armed rising (Feb., 1943), Germans razed ghetto and killed c.40,000 Jews who had survived. Upon Warsaw's liberation (Jan., 1945) by Russian troops only 200 Jews were alive. In Aug., 1944, Russians had captured Praga, on E bank of the Vistula, and remained inactive during 63-day battle bet. Pol. underground and Germans. During entire war period, 87% of city proper and 42% of Praga were destroyed. Reconstruction was begun in 1945, when it was decided to retain Warsaw as nat. ⊙, and govt. moved here from Lublin. In 1951 near-by suburbs were absorbed, including Wlochy, Okecie, and Wilanow.

Warsaw. 1 City (pop. 2,002), Hancock co., W Ill., on the Mississippi and 3 mi. SSW of Keokuk (Iowa), in agr. area (corn, wheat, oats, soybeans, livestock, poultry; dairy products); mfg. (buttons, beverages, toilet articles, handbags, barrels, metal matches). Limestone quarries; commercial fisheries. Laid out 1834, inc. 1837. Two forts were established here in 1814. **2** City (pop. 6,625), ⊙ Kosciusko co., N Ind., on Tippecanoe R. and 40 mi. WNW of Fort Wayne; center of lake-resort and agr. region. Mfg. of automotive and aircraft equipment, surgical supplies, castings, furniture, vacuum cleaners, cut glass, flour, milk products; lumber milling. Settled c.1836, inc. 1854. **3** Town (pop. 829), ⊙ Gallatin co., N Ky., on the Ohio and 30 mi. SW of Covington; trade center in outer Bluegrass agr. region; furniture making, lumber milling; nurseries. **4** City (pop. 936), ⊙ Benton co., central Mo., on Osage R., at W end of L. of the Ozarks, and 33 mi. S of Sedalia; fishing, hunting resort. **5** Village (pop. 3,713), ⊙ Wyoming co., W N.Y., 17 mi. S of Batavia; mfg. (elevators, textiles, buttons, canned foods, machinery; paper, metal, and stone products); agr. (grain, vegetables). Settled 1803, inc. 1843. **6** Town (pop. 1,598), Duplin co., SE N.C., 27 mi. SSW of Goldsboro, in truck-farm region. **7** Village (pop. 484), Coshocton co., central Ohio, on Walhonding R. and 8 mi. WNW of Coshocton; molding sand, leather goods, food products. **8** Town (pop. 435), ⊙ Richmond co., E Va., 45 mi. SE of Fredericksburg, near the Rappahannock (bridged to Tappahannock); seafood, dairy products, lumber.

Warshau Lake, Poland: see ROS, LAKE.

Warson Woods, town (pop. 529), St. Louis co., E Mo.

Warsop (wôr'sŭp), urban district (1931 pop. 10,749; 1951 census 10,888), W Nottingham, England, 5 mi. NNE of Mansfield. Includes coal-mining towns of Market Warsop, Church Warsop, Welbeck Colliery Village, and Shirebrook. Market Warsop has Norman church.

Warstade (vär'shtä"dŭ), village (pop. 2,636), in former Prussian prov. of Hanover, NW Germany, after 1945 in Lower Saxony, 14 mi. NW of Stade; metalworking; knitwear.

Warstein (vär'shtīn), town (pop. 7,571), in former Prussian prov. of Westphalia, W Germany, after 1945 in North Rhine-Westphalia, 15 mi. S of Lippstadt; foundries. Iron-ore mining. Stalactite cave near by.

Warszawa (vär-shä'vä), province [Pol. *województwo*] (□ 10,871; pop., excluding Warsaw city, 2,073,776), E central Poland; ⊙ Warsaw. Undulating plain, partly wooded; drained by Vistula, Bug, Narew, Bzura, and Pilica rivers. Includes (NW) part of fertile Kujawy dist. Industries concentrated in Warsaw region (Warsaw, Zyrardow, Grodzisk); other important towns are Plock, Pruszkow, Wlochy, and Otwock (resort). Principal crops are rye, potatoes, oats, wheat, sugar beets, flax; stock raising; forestry. Warsaw city forms autonomous prov. Boundaries of pre-Second World War prov. (□ 11,378; 1931 pop. 2,529,228) were altered by transfer of territory to Lodz, Lublin, and Bydgoszcz provs.; small section (NW) transferred 1950 to Olsztyn prov. Before First World War, formed greater part of Varshava (Warszawa) and Plotsk (Plock) govts. of Rus. Poland.

Warszawa, city, Poland: see WARSAW.

Warta (vär'tä). **1** Rus. *Varta* (vär'tŭ), town (pop. 2,896), Lodz prov., central Poland, on Warta R. and 36 mi. W of Lodz; flour milling, distilling, cement mfg. **2** Town, Wroclaw prov., Poland: see BARDO.

Warta River, Ger. *Warthe* (vär'tŭ), Rus. *Varta* (vär'tŭ), third-longest river (492 mi.) of Poland, rises just E of Zawiercie, flows W past Zawiercie, generally N past Czestochowa, Sieratz, and Kolo, W past Konin and Srem, N past Posnan, and W past Oborniki, Miedzychod, and Landsberg (Gorzow Wielkopolski), to Oder River at Küstrin (Kostrzyn). Navigable below Kolo; joined via Notec R. and Bydgoszcz Canal with the Vistula. Chief tributaries: Ner and Notec (right), Prosna and Obra (left) rivers.

Wartau (vär'tou), town (pop. 3,443), St. Gall canton, E Switzerland, near the Rhine, 4 mi. SSW of Vaduz, Liechtenstein; cotton textiles, embroideries; woodworking.

Wartberg (värt'bĕrk). **1** Town (pop. 2,132), Styria, E central Austria, on Mürz R. and 20 mi. NE of Leoben; agr. machinery mfg. **2** or **Wartberg an der Krems** (än dĕr krĕms'), town (pop. 2,605), SE central Upper Austria, 14 mi. WSW of Steyr; wheat, potatoes.

Wartburg (värt'bōōrk), castle, Thuringia, central Germany, on hill (1,247 ft.) at NW end of Thuringian Forest, just SW of Eisenach. Built c.1070 by a landgrave of Thuringia during wars against Henry IV, it was later enlarged and became meeting place of poets and minnesingers; scene (1207) of well-known song contest (Sängerkrieg), subject of Wagner's opera *Tannhäuser*. Luther, brought to castle in 1521 for his protection after the Diet of Worms, here completed his translation of the New Testament. Scene (1817) of festival of the Burschenschaften, nationalist students' organization.

Wartburg (wôrt'bûrg), village, ⊙ Morgan co., NE central Tenn., 40 mi. WNW of Knoxville, in the Cumberlands.

Wartembork, Poland: see BARCZEWO.

Wartenburg or **Wartenburg an der Elbe** (vär'tŭn-bōōrk än dĕr ĕl'bŭ), village (pop. 1,390), in former Prussian Saxony prov., central Germany, after 1945 in Saxony-Anhalt, near the Elbe, 8 mi. ESE of Wittenberg. Here, in Oct., 1813, the Prussians under Blücher and Yorck defeated the French.

Wartenburg, Poland: see BARCZEWO.

Wartha (vär'tä), village (pop. 204), Thuringia, central Germany, on the Werra and 5 mi. WNW of Eisenach, 13 mi. ENE of Obersuhl (Hesse). After 1945, traffic check point bet. East and West Germany.

Wartha, town, Poland: see BARDO.

Warthbrücken, Poland: see KOLO.

Warthenau, Poland: see ZAWIERCIE.

Warthe River, Poland: see WARTA RIVER.

Warton with Lindeth (wôr'tŭn), parish (pop. 1,694), W Lancashire, England. Includes village of Warton, 8 mi. SE of Blackpool; dairy farming, wheat, potato, and barley growing. Has 15th-cent. church tower, bearing coat of arms of the family of George Washington, some of whose members lived here until early 19th cent. Near is 14th-cent. vicarage.

Wartrace, town (pop. 545), Bedford co., central Tenn., 9 mi. E of Shelbyville.

Warud (vŭrōōd'), town (pop. 10,423), Amraoti dist., W Madhya Pradesh, India, 50 mi. NE of Amraoti; cotton ginning, oilseed milling.

Warwick (wŏ'rĭk), city (pop. 7,129), SE Queensland, Australia, on Condamine R. and 80 mi. SW of Brisbane; rail center in agr. area (wheat, apples).

Warwick, parish (1939 pop. 2,193), SW Bermuda, on Bermuda Isl.

Warwick (wôr'wĭk, wŏ'rĭk), village (pop. 1,504), S Que., 40 mi. N of Sherbrooke; woolen milling, woodworking, mfg. of machinery, plastics.

Warwick or **Warwickshire** (wŏ'rĭk,–shĭr), county (□ 983; 1931 pop. 1,535,007; 1951 census pop. 1,860,874), central England; ⊙ Warwick. Bounded by Worcester (W), Stafford (NW), Leicester (NE), Northampton (E), Oxford (SE), and Gloucester (SW). Undulating terrain, drained by Avon, Tame, Leame, and Anker rivers. Has deposits of coal (N and NE), iron ore, granite, limestone, fire clay. Mineral springs at Leamington. Chief cities are Birmingham and Coventry, where major industries are concentrated (steel milling, mfg. of automobiles and aircraft, machinery and machine tools). Stratford-on-Avon and the Arden region are closely associated with Shakespeare. Site of several Roman camps. Part of kingdom of Mercia in Saxon times.

Warwick. 1 Village and parish (pop. 269), N central Cumberland, England, on Eden R. and 4 mi. E of Carlisle; sheep, cattle. Just E, and within the parish, is village of Warwick Bridge, with woolen mill. **2** Municipal borough (1931 pop. 13,459; 1951 census 15,350), ⊙ Warwickshire, England, in center of co., on the Avon at mouth of the Lea, and 19 mi. SE of Birmingham; light-metals industry; mfg. of agr. machinery, furniture, gelatine; agr. market. Has castle built 915 by Æthelflæd, daughter of King Alfred; of the present structure, Caesar's Tower, 147 ft. high, is oldest part. The Parliamentarians successfully defended the castle in 1642. St. Mary's Church, dating partly from 12th cent., was partially burned in 1694 and rebuilt by William Wilson, a pupil of Wren. Noteworthy also are Beauchamp Chapel (1443–64), Leicester Hosp. (1571), and a Norman crypt in the church. The E and W gates, each with a chapel, remain of the town walls. Walter Savage Landor b. in Warwick. The Warwick Vase, found in Hadrian's villa at Tivoli, is in the castle, along with other famous antiquities and art works.

Warwick (wŏ'rĭk, wô'rĭk), county (□ 71; 1950 pop. 39,875; 1940 pop. 9,248), SE Va.; ⊙ Denbigh. On SW (James R.) shore of peninsula bounded S by Hampton Roads, E by Chesapeake Bay, NE by York R. NEWPORT NEWS is in but independent of co. Residential (for workers in Hampton Roads cities); fisheries; some truck, fruit, and dairy farming. Includes U. S. Fort Eustis. Formed 1634.

Warwick. 1 (wôr′wĭk) Town (pop. 449), Worth co., S central Ga., 12 mi. SW of Cordele; sawmilling. Power dam, 2 mi. NW, in Flint R. forms L. Blackshear (□ c.12.5; c.10 mi. long). 2 (wô′rĭk) Town (pop. 429), Franklin co., N Mass., 15 mi. NE of Greenfield. State forest here. 3 (wôr′wĭk, wŏ′rĭk) Village (pop. 2,674), Orange co., SE N.Y., near N.J. line, 19 mi. ESE of Port Jervis, in fruit- and truck-growing area; resort. State training school for boys here. Settled c.1746, inc. 1867. 4 (wôr′wĭk) Village (pop. 155), Benson co., E central N. Dak., 20 mi. SSE of Devils Lake. 5 (wôr′wĭk, wŏ′rĭk) City (pop. 43,028), Kent co., E central R.I., on Pawtuxet R. and Greenwich and Narragansett bays, and 10 mi. S of Providence. Largely a rural area, with many mfg. villages (cotton, silk, and rayon textiles, metal products); agr. (fruit, dairy products, mushrooms, truck); fisheries; coast resorts. Includes villages of APPONAUG, Buttonwoods, Oakland Beach, Cowesett (kōwē′sĭt), HILLSGROVE, Conimicut (kŭnĭm′ĭkŭt), Hoxsie (site of tuberculosis preventorium), Lakewood, Norwood, Pontiac, Rocky Point, Shawomet (shŭwō′mŭt), and Warwick, and Potowomut Peninsula (S), extending into Greenwich Bay. Settled 1643, inc. as town 1644, as city 1931. Nathanael Greene b. here; Warwick village has 17th-cent. Gov. William Greene house. Textile industry dates from 1794. Goddard Memorial State Park is near by.

Warwick Bridge, England: see WARWICK, Cumberland.

Warwick Neck (wôr′wĭk, wŏ′rĭk), central R.I., peninsula bet. Greenwich Bay (W) and Narragansett Bay (E); residential, resort area. Warwick Point, with lighthouse, is at S end.

Warwickshire, England: see WARWICK, county.

Wasatch (wô′săch″), county (□ 1,194; pop. 5,574), N central Utah; ⊙ Heber. Mtn. area largely within Uinta Natl. Forest. Strawberry R. and Strawberry Reservoir (in S) and Provo R. (in N) are used for irrigation; grain, alfalfa, sugar beets, truck products, fruit. Lead, silver, and zinc mines are in vicinity of Heber. Co. formed 1862.

Wasatch Plateau, central Utah, high tableland at S end of Wasatch Range, largely in Sanpete and Emery counties. Rises to 10,986 ft. in Musinia Peak and to 12,300 ft. in South Tent. Lies within Manti Natl. Forest. Is penetrated by irrigation tunnels conducting water from headstream of San Rafael R., on E, to Sanpete Valley, on W.

Wasatch Range, in Rocky Mts. of Idaho and Utah; extends c.250 mi. S from bend of Bear R., in Bannock co., SE Idaho, past Great Salt L. and Salt Lake City, to mouth of San Pitch R. in Sevier R., central Utah. Rises to 12,008 ft. in Mt. TIMPANOGOS. Includes parts of Wasatch and Uinta natl. forests in Utah and is drained by Weber, Ogden, and Provo rivers. Copper, lead, silver, and gold are mined near Provo and Salt Lake City. Major cities of Utah are on W slope.

Waschbank (väs′bängk), town (pop. 1,858), NW Natal, U. of So. Afr., 13 mi. SE of Dundee; coal mining.

Wasco (wŏ′skō), county (□ 2,387; pop. 15,552), N Oregon; ⊙ The Dalles. Bounded W by Cascade Range and N by Columbia R. and Wash.; drained by Deschutes R. Part of Warm Springs Indian Reservation is in SW. Wheat, fruit, lumber, livestock. Formed 1854.

Wasco. 1 City (pop. 5,592), Kern co., S central Calif., in San Joaquin Valley, 24 mi. NW of Bakersfield; agr. (cotton, fruit, potatoes, grain); dairying. Oil wells near by. Inc. 1945. 2 City (pop. 305), Sherman co., N Oregon, 23 mi. E of The Dalles.

Wasdale, England: see WASTWATER.

Wase (wä′sä), town (pop. 3,224), Adamawa prov., Northern Provinces, E central Nigeria, 35 mi. NE of Shendam; silver and lead mining; cassava, durra.

Waseca (wŏsē′kŭ, wô′–), county (□ 415; pop. 14,957), S Minn.; ⊙ Waseca. Agr. area drained by Le Sueur R. L. Elysian in NW. Livestock, dairy products, corn, oats, barley. Formed 1857.

Waseca, city (pop. 4,927), ⊙ Waseca co., S Minn., on 2 small lakes, 26 mi. ESE of Mankato. Resort; trade center for grain, livestock, poultry area; food processing (dairy products, canned vegetables, beverages), poultry hatcheries. Settled before 1870. Demonstration farm and state univ. experiment station are here.

Wash, The, estuarine inlet of the North Sea in E coast of England, bet. Lincolnshire and Norfolk; 20 mi. long, 15 mi. wide. Receives Witham, Welland, Nene, and Ouse rivers. On The Wash are river ports of King's Lynn and Boston. It is mostly shallow, with low, marshy shores, and sandbanks make navigation hazardous.

Washabaugh (wŏ′shŭbô″), county (□ 1,061; pop. 1,551), SW central S.Dak.; unorganized and attached to Jackson co. for judicial purposes; lies within Pine Ridge Indian Reservation; bounded N by White R. Cattle raising. Formed 1883.

Washago (wŭshä′gō), village (pop. estimate 350), S Ont., on Severn R., at N end of L. Couchiching, 11 mi. NE of Orillia; resort; dairying.

Washakie (wŏ′shŭkē), county (□ 2,262; pop. 7,252), N central Wyo.; ⊙ Worland. Irrigated agr. and oil area; watered by Bighorn R. Sugar beets, beans, livestock. Formed 1911.

Washakie Needles, Wyo.: see ABSAROKA RANGE.

Washakie Pass, Wyo.: see WIND RIVER RANGE.

Washburn, county (□ 816; pop. 11,665), NW Wis.; ⊙ Shell Lake. Drained by Namekagon and Yellow rivers. Wooded terrain with many lakes; summer-resort area. Dairying, poultry farming. Formed 1883.

Washburn. 1 Village (pop. 999), on Woodford-Marshall co. line, central Ill., 22 mi. NE of Peoria, in agr. and bituminous-coal area; makes cheese, feed. 2 Town (pop. 1,913), Aroostook co., NE Maine, on the Aroostook and 10 mi. NW of Presque Isle, in farming, lumbering region. Settled c.1829, inc. 1861. 3 City (pop. 913), ⊙ McLean co., central N.Dak., 38 mi. N of Bismarck and on Missouri R.; coal mines; livestock, dairy products, poultry, wheat, rye, flax. 4 City (pop. 2,070), ⊙ Bayfield co., extreme N Wis., on W shore of Chequamegon Bay of L. Superior, 7 mi. N of Ashland; commercial center for dairying, lumbering, and fruitgrowing area. A ranger station is here. Near by is a state fish hatchery. Founded 1884, inc. 1904.

Washburn Range, U-shaped ridge in Rocky Mts. of Yellowstone Natl. Park, NW Wyo., W of Yellowstone R., in N half of park. Highest point, Mt. Washburn (10,317 ft.). Dunraven Pass (8,859 ft.) crossed by highway.

Washdyke, township (pop. 396), E S.Isl., New Zealand, 3 mi. N of Timaru; linen mill; horse racing.

Washington, urban district (1931 pop. 16,989; 1951 census 17,795), NE Durham, England, near Wear R., 5 mi. W of Sunderland; coal mining; chemical works. In urban dist. (N) is coal-mining town of Usworth Colliery (pop. 4,955).

Washington, state (land □ 66,977; with inland waters □ 68,192; 1950 pop. 2,378,963; 1940 pop. 1,736,191), extreme NW U.S., in the Pacific Northwest; bordered by Pacific Ocean (W), B.C. (N), Idaho (E), and Oregon (S); 19th in area, 23d in pop.; admitted 1889 as 42d state; ⊙ Olympia. The "Evergreen State" or the "Chinook State" averages 330 mi. E–W, 220 mi. N–S. It is a region of bold features, with lofty mtn. ranges (running N–S), fertile river valleys, and dry, treeless plains (E). In NW corner, S of Juan de Fuca Strait, is the Olympic Peninsula, occupied by the Olympic Mts. of the Coast Ranges, rising to 7,954 ft. in Mt. Olympus. Just E is Puget Sound, an inlet of the Pacific extending c.100 mi. inland; it contains numerous bays and isls., including Whidbey Isl. and San Juan Isls. The Puget Sound lowland, which also comprises the broad trough S of the sound, is the state's most densely populated area. It enjoys a temperate marine climate, modified by warm ocean currents, with cool summers and mild winters. Seattle's mean daily temp. ranges from 64°F. in July to 40°F. in Jan.; average annual rainfall 33 in. The seaward slopes of the Olympics have an annual precipitation of c.140 in. (heaviest in U.S.), while the landward slopes average only 17 in. The CASCADE RANGE, which divides Wash. in two, has a width here of 50–100 mi. (S–N) and an average elevation of 6,000–8,000 ft. It is dominated by the volcanic cones of Mt. Rainier (14,408 ft.; highest point in state), Mt. Adams (12,307 ft.), Mt. Baker (10,750 ft.), Glacier Peak (10,436 ft.), and Mt. St. Helens (9,671 ft.). It has a rugged surface, with deep valleys, glacial lakes (largest is L. Chelan), and extensive snow fields. Except for the Okanogan Highlands in the N bet. the Cascades and the Northern Rockies along the Idaho line, the E section of Wash. lies in the N part of the Columbia Plateau, a comparatively level expanse underlain by lava beds and crossed by low ridges and dried-up river channels, such as the Grand Coulee. The Blue Mts. extend into the SE corner of the state. Of major importance to the economic life of Wash. is the COLUMBIA RIVER, which flows across the state from NE to SW to the Pacific; in Wash. it receives the Spokane and Snake rivers (left) and the Okanogan, Wenatchee, and Yakima rivers (right). The climate of E Wash. is mainly the dry continental type, with hot summers and cold winters and an annual rainfall of 10–30 in. Spokane, the metropolis of E Wash., has a mean daily temp. ranging from 70°F. in July to 27°F. in Jan., with a yearly rainfall of c.16 in. About 1/3 of state's area is devoted to agr., with farms varying in size from the small truck farms in the W to the large wheat ranches in the E. In the lowlands W of the Cascades the growing season is 180–200 days, while in the Columbia Plateau it varies (N–S) bet. 100 and 200 days. Wash. ranks 1st in U.S. in apple production and is a leading producer of wheat, pears, prunes, strawberries, peaches, and grapes; dry-field peas, potatoes, hay, and sugar beets are also grown. The fruit dists. are concentrated along the right-bank tributaries of the Columbia, chiefly in the irrigated sections of the Wenatchee, Okanogan, and Yakima river valleys. Truck farming is carried on around the urban centers in the Puget Sound lowland and near Spokane, Walla Walla, and Pasco in the E. Large areas in Kittitas, Yakima, Grant, Adams, and Franklin counties along the Columbia R. system are irrigated crop lands. However, the Big Bend, Palouse, and Snake River dists. of E Wash. are dry-farming areas of the INLAND EMPIRE and produce a rich wheat crop. Dairying, poultry farming, and specialized truck farming (berries, flower bulbs) are centered in W Wash.; cranberries are grown on Pacific coast. Large cattle and sheep ranches are located on E slopes of the Cascades and in other E highland areas. Wash., with c.55% of its area forested, is 2d only to Oregon as the nation's leading lumber-producing state; natl. forests occupy some 10,000,000 acres. Principal species (predominantly softwoods) include Douglas fir, ponderosa pine, hemlock, spruce, white pine, larch, alder, cedar, cottonwood, and maple. Majority of sawmills are in Puget Sound and Pacific coast sections; pulp, paper, and plywood are important by-product industries. Coal, the chief mineral resource, is mined in Kittitas co. and the Puget Sound area; gold, silver, building stone, pottery clay, zinc, and copper deposits are also worked (chiefly in Okanogan Highlands); near Chewelah are large magnesite reserves. Wash. leads the nation in total catch (rivers and coastal waters) of sea foods, including salmon, halibut, tuna, oysters, crabs, cod, sharks, and sablefish. Puget Sound is the center of the marine fishing industry, and its ports are also outfitting points for the vast Alaskan and other N Pacific fisheries. Seattle, the state's largest city, is the world's leading halibut port, with large storage and processing facilities; most other coastal towns also have curing, canning, and oil-extracting plants; Aberdeen and Hoquiam are the chief fishing centers on Pacific coast. Serious depletion of fish resources by unlimited catches, logging operations, stream pollution, and river damming led to regulatory legislation (since 1890) and conservation programs; on the Columbia, at Bonneville and Rock Isl. dams, fish ladders and elevators allow salmon to pass upstream, while hatcheries have been constructed just below the massive Grand Coulee Dam. Although agr., lumbering, fishing, and their by-products are the chief industries, Wash. also has diversified mfg. (chemicals, tin cans, malt liquors, iron and steel products, machinery, light consumer goods; publishing). There are aluminum plants at Longview, Spokane, and Vancouver; aircraft factories at Seattle; shipyards along Puget Sound; smelters at Tacoma; and railroad shops at Spokane, Seattle, Tacoma, Everett, and Pasco. The construction of power dams (notably GRAND COULEE DAM and BONNEVILLE DAM) and the distribution of cheap electricity, as well as the Second World War military requirements, considerably expanded the state's industrial output; Hanford Works near RICHLAND is an atomic energy research and plutonium production center. Water power is an important resource. The Puget Sound lowland is the state's principal industrial and trading area, with a chain of seaport cities (Seattle, Tacoma, Bellingham, Everett, and Olympia), which handle a large amount of Alaskan and Oriental traffic. Spokane is the commercial center of the Inland Empire, with an extensive trade in lumber, minerals, wheat, fruit, and livestock. Wash.'s fine natural setting, particularly its mts., lakes, forests, streams, and ocean coast line, offers excellent opportunities for recreation and sport. Besides the beautiful OLYMPIC NATIONAL PARK and MOUNT RAINIER NATIONAL PARK, there are numerous state parks and other recreational areas with a wealth of scenic grandeur. Educational institutions include Univ. of Wash. (at Seattle), State Col. of Wash. (at Pullman), Col. of Puget Sound (at Tacoma), and Gonzaga Univ. (at Spokane). As early as the 16th cent. the coast of the Pacific Northwest was visited by Sp. and English explorers searching for the Northwest Passage. In the late 18th cent., after a prosperous fur trade had been established by the Hudson's Bay Co., further discoveries were made by Capt. James Cook, George Vancouver, and the American Robert Gray, who discovered the Columbia R. Lewis and Clark, proceeding overland from St. Louis, explored the Snake and lower Columbia rivers in 1805. As rival fur companies and pioneers strove for advantage, the U.S. and Great Britain contended for the Oregon Territory (of which the present Wash. was a part), until the treaty of 1846 fixed the Br.-Amer. boundary along the 49th parallel. The influx of settlers (land and gold seekers, missionaries) was not halted by the Indian wars of the mid-19th cent. Wash. became a territory in 1853 and a state in 1889. The lumbering and fishing industries prospered with the advent of the railroads (1887), and the state's pop. grew rapidly thereafter. During the Alaskan gold rush (1897–99) Seattle was the outfitting point for thousands of prospectors. Agr. gradually assumed importance with large-scale production of wheat and fruit; and in recent years the state has benefitted from the development for power and irrigation purposes of the Columbia R. basin. See also articles on the cities, towns, geographic features, and the 39 counties: ADAMS, ASOTIN, BENTON, CHELAN, CLALLAM, CLARK, COLUMBIA, COWLITZ, DOUGLAS, FERRY, FRANKLIN, GARFIELD, GRANT, GRAYS HARBOR, ISLAND, JEFFERSON, KING, KITSAP, KITTITAS, KLICKITAT, LEWIS, LINCOLN, MASON, OKANOGAN, PACIFIC, PEND OREILLE, PIERCE, SAN JUAN, SKAGIT, SKAMANIA, SNOHOMISH,

SPOKANE, STEVENS, THURSTON, WAHKIAKUM, WALLA WALLA, WHATCOM, WHITMAN, YAKIMA.

Washington, city (□ 70; 1950 pop. 802,178, 1940 pop. 663,091) and ⊙ United States, coextensive with District of Columbia, on left (Md.) bank of the Potomac (Va. line) at head of navigation and tidewater and 35 mi. SW of Baltimore; alt. is from sea level to 420 ft.; 38°53'N 77°W (the Capitol). Congressional acts of 1790 and 1791 established the dist., whose land was granted by Md. (1790) and Va. (1789), and ended rivalry bet. Northern and Southern states for the capital. George Washington selected the site for the "Federal City," which was designed by Pierre L'Enfant and laid out by Andrew Ellicott. Construction was begun on the White House in 1792, on the Capitol the following year; 1st session of Congress to be held in Washington convened there 1800, and Jefferson was 1st President to be inaugurated here. Washington was captured and sacked (1814) by the British in War of 1812; the White House, the Capitol, and most of the other public bldgs. were burned. In Civil War, city was several times threatened with Confederate capture, but never taken. Dist. of Columbia first consisted of corporations of Washington, Georgetown, and Alexandria, and Washington and Alexandria counties. Alexandria was returned to Va. in 1846, leaving only former Md. land in the Dist. Georgetown (settled c.1665, inc. 1789) was inc. in Washington in 1895, when that city and Dist. of Columbia became coextensive. City's early growth was slow, and not until the 20th cent. did it assume an urban aspect. It has been developed according to the L'Enfant plan, which is a gridiron arrangement of streets overlaid by wheel-like patterns of wide avenues radiating from the Capitol and White House, and is today a spacious and dignified city of great white-stone public bldgs., mainly neoclassic in style, with an abundance of shade trees along its thoroughfares, and many fine houses. Extensive parks include Potomac Park, with the Tidal Basin lined with the famed Japanese flowering cherry trees; Rock Creek Park (c.1,800 acres); Anacostia Park (1,100 acres); and the Natl. Zoological Park. Monuments and statues occupy many of the circles and squares (e.g., Du Pont Circle, Mt. Vernon Square) laid out at avenue intersections. City is divided into 4 quarters (Northwest, Northeast, Southeast, and Southwest) by streets radiating from the Capitol, seat of the U.S. govt. and dominating monument of city, in 60-acre grounds on an elevated site (Capitol Hill). The central section of Capitol bldg. (which covers c.3½ acres) is surmounted by a 288-ft. dome and a statue of Liberty and is flanked by 2 wings containing the Senate and House chambers. W from the Capitol extends the Mall, bet. Constitution Ave. on N and Independence Ave. on S. Along it are the Natl. Gallery of Art (with some of world's greatest collections of paintings), Freer Gall. of Art (Far Eastern collections), the old and new Natl. Mus. bldgs., and the Smithsonian Institution. At W end of the Mall, and just N of the Tidal Basin, is the 555-ft. marble shaft of the Washington Monument (dedicated 1885), with observation platform near top; further W near the Potomac is the neoclassic Lincoln Memorial (dedicated 1922), facing the Washington Monument across a long reflecting pool. In the Lincoln Memorial are Daniel Chester French's magnificent figure of Lincoln, murals by Jules Guerin, and inscriptions of the Gettysburg Address and the Second Inaugural Address. On S shore of the Tidal Basin is the Thomas Jefferson Memorial (dedicated 1943), a circular neoclassic structure containing a statue of Jefferson (by Rudulph Evans) and panels inscribed with excerpts from Jefferson's writings. Pennsylvania Ave. leads WNW from the Capitol to the White House grounds, which lie across Constitution Ave. N of Washington Monument. Near the White House are many of the great bldgs. housing govt. depts., the principal hotels, shops, and stores, and many points of interest, including Constitution Hall; Corcoran Gall. of Art; the Pan American Union; the U.S. naval hosp.; the house in which Lincoln died and old Ford's Theater (now a mus.) in which he was shot, both natl. memorials; Blair House, where visiting dignitaries stay; St. John's Church, known as the "Presidents' Church." In the dists. farther N and NW of the White House are the bldgs. of foreign legations and embassies, while the U.S. naval observatory and the uncompleted Washington (or Natl.) Cathedral (officially Cathedral of St. Peter and St. Paul; Protestant Episcopal), one of largest churches in world, are in the extreme NW. The gracious old Georgetown dist. is along the Potomac NW of downtown Washington, from which it is separated by Rock Creek Park. It includes Dumbarton Oaks (estate) where agreement was made (1944) to establish the United Nations. To the E of the White House, in the orbit of the Capitol, are the Senate and House office bldgs.; the Library of Congress (established 1800; natl. library of U.S. and one of largest libraries in the world, which houses the originals of the Declaration of Independence and the Constitution of the U.S.); the noted Folger Shakespeare Memorial Library; the Supreme Court bldg.; the U.S. Botanic Garden; the Natl. Archives; the U.S. Govt. Printing Office; and Union Station. Other points of interest in Washington include Bolling Air Force Base; Anacostia Naval Air Station and a U.S. navy yard along small Anacostia R., which enters the Potomac in S Washington; Walter Reed General Hosp. and the Army's medical school; a natl. soldiers' home; the Natl. War Col.; Brookings Institution; Carnegie Institution; many monuments and historic houses; and Battleground Natl. Cemetery, dating from Civil War. Washington's educational institutions include American Univ. (inc. 1893), Catholic Univ. of America (founded 1884–89), Georgetown Univ. (founded 1789, opened 1791, chartered 1815; oldest R.C. col. in U.S.), George Washington Univ. (chartered 1821), Howard Univ. (chartered 1867), Natl. Univ. (inc. 1869), Trinity Col. (established 1897). Arlington Memorial Bridge crosses the Potomac to ARLINGTON co. (Va.), in which are Arlington Natl. Cemetery, containing the Tomb of the Unknown Soldier, Arlington Memorial Amphitheater, the historic Lee Mansion, and U.S. Fort Myer. The Army's huge Pentagon Bldg. is also just across the river, in Va. Washington Natl. Airport is a short distance S of city, along the Potomac. MOUNT VERNON, home of George Washington and now a natl. shrine, is connected with city by Mt. Vernon Memorial Highway, part of George Washington Memorial Parkway (to be 57 mi. long) planned along Md. and Va. shores of the Potomac. Many of the parks, public monuments, and historic sites of city and its environs are included in the Natl. Capital Parks system of 745 units in D.C., Va., and Md. Numerous Federal agencies, bureaus, and installations are located in suburban Md. and Va. Jan. average temp. is 34°F., July average 77°F. Washington is many cities—as many, perhaps, as there are observers; but, in the main, it is 2 cities: as a metropolis it is like most large American cities, as the nation's capital it has a character all its own. Like all large American cities it has its fine residential areas and its shameful slums; its community social organizations and civic pride; and the usual patterns of work and play. As a border city bet. North and South, Washington has long maintained the traditional Southern attitudes toward Negroes, of whom it has a large community; of recent years considerable progress has been made in the field of race relations. Cultural and intellectual life have been promoted by the many educational institutions, a symphony orchestra (which has had intermittent existence since 1902), and art galleries which contain some of the world's finest collections. But Washington is also unique among the cities of the U.S. in the nature of its basic industry—government—which employs most of its workers, and in the fact that its citizens, as residents of a federal dist., do not have the vote. Annually, millions of tourists visit the city's public bldgs., monuments, the shrines containing its historic documents, and the houses of Congress. Every election year brings changes in the political scene, particularly in the membership of Congress and that of the groups (popularly called "lobbyists") who seek the attention of legislators with the aim of promoting or defeating particular measures or policies. Washington's official, formal social life, governed by protocol, has traditionally been supplemented by the entertainments of unofficial but influential hostesses, some of whom have become famous for the brilliance of their gatherings. However, most of the Washington populace—the corps of govt. workers drawn from every state—lives in a manner which the many annual visitors from every part of the nation recognize as very much like their own.

Washington. 1 County (□ 1,069; pop. 15,612), SW Ala.; ⊙ Chatom. Coastal plain on Miss. line, bounded E by Tombigbee R.; drained by Escatawpa R. Cotton, corn, sheep, timber; naval stores. Formed 1800. **2** County (□ 963; pop. 49,979), NW Ark.; ⊙ FAYETTEVILLE. Bounded W by Okla. line; drained by Illinois and White rivers; situated in Ozark region. Stock and poultry raising, agr. (truck, fruit, grain); dairy products. Mfg. at Fayetteville. Timber; coal. Devils Den State Park is in S. Formed 1828. **3** County (□ 2,525; pop. 7,520), NE Colo.; ⊙ Akron. Agr. area, drained by small branches of South Platte R. Wheat, livestock. Formed 1887. **4** County (□ 597; pop. 11,888), NW Fla., bounded W by Choctawhatchee R.; ⊙ Chipley. Rolling agr. area (corn, peanuts, cotton, vegetables, livestock) with many small lakes; drained by Holmes Creek. Has forest industries (lumber milling, naval-stores mfg.). Formed 1843. **5** County (□ 674; pop. 21,012), E central Ga.; ⊙ Sandersville. Bounded E by Ogeechee R. and W by Oconee R. Coastal plain agr. (cotton, corn, truck, pecans), sawmilling, and kaolin-mining area. Formed 1784. **6** County (□ 1,475; pop. 8,576), W Idaho; ⊙ Weiser. Mtn. area bounded W by Snake R. and Oregon and cut (N–S) by irrigated valley of Weiser R. Stock raising, agr. (hay, sugar beets, fruit, truck), quicksilver mining. Includes part of Weiser Natl. Forest. Formed 1879. **7** County (□ 565; pop. 14,460), SW Ill.; ⊙ Nashville. Bounded N by Kaskaskia R.; drained by Little Muddy R. and Beaucoup Creek. Agr. area (corn, wheat, livestock, fruit, poultry; dairy products), with some mfg. (machinery, flour); also bituminous-coal mining. Formed 1818. **8** County (□ 516; pop. 16,520), S Ind.; ⊙ Salem. Bounded N by Muscatatuck R. and East Fork of White R.; drained by Blue R., Lost R., small Twin Creek. Grain-growing area; stone quarrying; timber. Mfg. at Salem. Formed 1813. **9** County (□ 568; pop. 19,557), SE Iowa; ⊙ Washington. Prairie agr. area (hogs, cattle, poultry, corn, oats, wheat) drained by Skunk and English rivers. Formed 1838. **10** County (□ 891; pop. 12,977), N Kansas; ⊙ Washington. Gently rolling plain, bordering N on Nebr.; drained in E by Little Blue R. Grain, livestock. Formed 1860. **11** County (□ 307; pop. 12,777), central Ky.; ⊙ Springfield. Bounded NW by Beech Fork; drained by several creeks. Includes Lincoln Homestead State Park, near Springfield. Rolling upland agr. area (burley tobacco, livestock, dairy products, poultry, corn, wheat), in Bluegrass region. Some timber. Formed 1792. **12** Parish (□ 665; pop. 38,371), SE La.; ⊙ Franklinton. Bounded N by Miss. line, E by Pearl R., partly W by Tchefuncta R.; drained by the Bogue Chitto. Agr. (cotton, corn, hay, sweet potatoes, peanuts, livestock). Cotton and cottonseed processing, lumber and paper milling, other mfg. at Bogalusa. Has extensive forests, with planned reforestation. Formed 1819. **13** County (□ 2,553; pop. 35,187), most easterly in Maine and U.S., on N.B. line; ⊙ Machias. Agr., blueberry gathering (produces 85% of country's canned supply), lumbering, pulp and paper milling, resorts, hunting, fishing, sardine packing. Drained by St. Croix (on N.B. line), Machias, East Machias, and Dennys rivers. Formed 1789. **14** County (□ 462; pop. 78,886), W Md.; ⊙ Hagerstown. Bounded N by Pa. line, S and SW by the Potomac, here separating Md. from W.Va. and Va.; drained by Antietam, Conococheague, Beaver, and several other creeks. Cumberland Valley (locally Hagerstown Valley) is bordered E by the Blue Ridge (locally called South Mtn. and Elk Ridge), W by Bear Pond Mts. and Sideling Hill. Agr. (corn, wheat, peaches, apples, berries, truck, poultry, dairy products); ornamental fish, aquatic plants are raised. Limestone quarries, sand pits. Diversified mfg., especially at Hagerstown; railroad shops, canneries, grain mills. Excellent hunting, fishing in NW and NE. Includes Antietam battlefield and natl. cemetery (near Sharpsburg); Fort Frederick State Park (W); U.S. Camp Ritchie (active in World War II); and parts of Gathland (SE) and Washington Monument (E) state parks. Formed 1776. **15** County (□ 390; pop. 34,544), E Minn.; ⊙ Stillwater. Agr. area bounded S by Mississippi R., E by St. Croix R. and Wis. Dairy products, livestock, grain, poultry. Food processing and mfg. at Stillwater. Forest L. is in NW. Formed 1849. **16** County (□ 728; pop. 70,504), W Miss.; ⊙ GREENVILLE. Bounded W by the Mississippi (here the Ark. line), partly E by Sunflower R.; intersected by several creeks and bayous. Includes lakes Washington and Lee. Agr. (cotton, alfalfa, truck), dairying; lumbering. Formed 1827. **17** County (□ 760; pop. 14,689), SE central Mo.; ⊙ Potosi. In the Ozarks; drained by Big. R. Agr., especially livestock; lumber, mining region (barite, lead, zinc, iron, granite, limestone). Part of Clark Natl. Forest here. Formed 1813. **18** County (□ 385; pop. 11,511), E Nebr.; ⊙ Blair. Agr. area bounded E by Missouri R. and Iowa. Livestock, grain. Formed 1854. **19** County (□ 837; pop. 47,144), E N.Y.; ⊙ Hudson Falls. Bounded NW by L. George, E by Vt. line, W by the Hudson. Part of L. Champlain is in N. Drained by Batten Kill, and Poultney, Mettawee, and Hoosic rivers; traversed by Champlain division of the Barge Canal. Resorts on small lakes. Farming (potatoes, fruit, corn, oats, poultry); dairying. Timber; slate, limestone quarries. Mfg. at Cambridge, Granville, Greenwich, Hudson Falls, Whitehall. Formed 1772. **20** County (□ 336; pop. 13,180), E N.C.; ⊙ Plymouth. Bounded N by Albemarle Sound; forested (pine, gum) tidewater area; farming (peanuts, tobacco, corn), sawmilling, fishing. Phelps L. in SE. Formed 1799. **21** County (□ 637; pop. 44,407), SE Ohio; ⊙ MARIETTA. Bounded SE by Ohio R., here forming W.Va. line; intersected by Muskingum and Little Muskingum rivers and small Duck Creek. Agr. (livestock; dairy products; fruit, truck); mfg. at Marietta; coal mines, limestone quarries. Formed 1788. **22** County (□ 425; pop. 32,880), NE Okla.; ⊙ Bartlesville. Bounded N by Kansas line; drained by Caney R. Agr. (livestock, truck, grain, poultry; dairy products). Oil and natural-gas fields, and refining; some mfg.; zinc mining and smelting. Formed 1907. **23** County (□ 716; pop. 61,269), NW Oregon; ⊙ Hillsboro. Mtn. area in Coast Range. Agr. (fruit, truck, grain, poultry), dairying, logging. Formed 1843. **24** County (□ 857; pop. 209,628), SW Pa.; ⊙ Washington. Coal-mining and mfg. area; bounded W by W.Va., E by Monongahela R. In dispute bet. Va. and Pa. until 1784. Indian chief Logan driven from area 1774 by Lord Dunmore, governor of Va. George Washington owned land here. Bituminous coal; metal and glass products, dairy products; grain, fruit; oil, gas, limestone. Formed 1781. **25** County (□ 324; pop. 48,542), SW R.I., on Conn. line and Block Isl. Sound; ⊙ South Kingstown. Resorts; mfg. (silk, cotton, rayon, and woolen textiles, thread, yarn, paper-milling machinery, printing presses, furniture, wood products, food products), printing; granite quarries; dairying, agr. (potatoes, corn, fruit, truck, tobacco, poultry). Resorts on Block Isl. Sound and Narragansett Bay. Includes state parks and several lakes. Drained by Wood, Hunt, Queen, and Pawcatuck rivers. Inc. 1729. **26** County, S.Dak.: see SHANNON, county. **27** County (□ 327; pop. 59,971), NE Tenn.; ⊙ Jonesboro, oldest town in state. In Great Appalachian Valley; mtn. ridges in S and SE; bounded NE by Watauga R.; drained by Nolichucky R. Includes part of Cherokee Natl. Forest. Agr. (fruit, tobacco, corn, hay), dairying, livestock raising. Iron ore, lead, zinc, manganese deposits; limestone quarries; hardwood timber. Industry at JOHNSON CITY. Formed 1777 as first co. in Tenn. at request of Watauga Assn. of settlers. **28** County (□ 611; pop. 20,542), S central Texas; ⊙ Brenham. Bounded E by Brazos R., N by Yegua Creek. Rich agr. area (partly in Brazos Valley: cotton, corn, grains, hay, peanuts, fruit, truck, pecans; extensive dairying, poultry raising; also beef cattle, hogs, sheep; beekeeping. Oil, natural-gas wells; some lumbering. Mfg., processing at Brenham. Formed 1836. **29** County (□ 2,425; pop. 9,836), SW Utah; ⊙ St. George. Mtn. area bordering on Nev. and Ariz. and drained by Virgin R. Livestock grazing. Zion Natl. Park and Zion Natl. Monument are in E. Pine Valley Mts. and Dixie Natl. Forest in N. Shivwits Indian Reservation is in SW. Formed 1852. **30** County (□ 708; pop. 42,870), central Vt.; ⊙ Montpelier. Granite-quarrying center of state; marble, talc; dairy products, textiles, wood products, machinery, canned corn, maple sugar; winter sports. Includes part of Green Mtn. Natl. Forest and Camels Hump, one of highest peaks of Green Mts. Drained by Winooski and Mad rivers. Organized 1810. **31** County (□ 579; pop. 37,536), SW Va.; ⊙ Abingdon. In Great Appalachian Valley; bounded S by Tenn.; includes parts of Clinch Mtn. (NW), Iron Mts. (SE); drained by North, Middle, and South forks of Holston R. Includes part of Jefferson Natl. Forest and a section of Appalachian Trail. Livestock-raising and agr. area; also poultry, tobacco, fruit, clover, corn. Processing of farm products, gypsum mining; diversified mfg. at Bristol (adjacent to Bristol, Tenn.). Mtn. resorts. Formed 1776. **32** County (□ 428; pop. 33,902), E Wis.; ⊙ West Bend. Hilly dairying and farming area. Processing of dairy products, canning of fruit and vegetables; other industry at West Bend. Resort lakes; winter sports. Drained by Milwaukee and Menomonee rivers and small Rubicon R. Formed 1836.

Washington. 1 Town (pop. 344), Hempstead co., SW Ark., 9 mi. NW of Hope. One of oldest towns in Ark., settled c.1824; was state capital from 1863 to 1865 and, until 1938, co. seat. **2** Town (pop. 2,227), Litchfield co., W Conn., on Shepaug R. and 16 mi. WNW of Waterbury, in hilly agr. and resort region. Includes villages of New Preston (resort on L. Waramaug), Washington Depot, and Washington. Has state park. Gunnery and Rumsey Hall schools for boys here. Settled 1734, inc. 1779. **3** City (pop. 3,802), ⊙ Wilkes co., NE Ga., c.45 mi. WNW of Augusta, in agr., dairying, and timber region; mfg. (textiles, cottonseed products, lumber). Many old classic-revival houses, including the Robert Toombs house (built 1794–1801; remodeled 1837 by Toombs). Settled 1773, laid out 1780. **4** City (pop. 4,285), Tazewell co., central Ill., 10 mi. E of Peoria; trade center in agr. area (corn, oats, hay); canned foods; timber. Inc. 1857. **5** City (pop. 10,987), ⊙ Daviess co., SW Ind., near West Fork of White R., 19 mi. E of Vincennes, in agr. area (grain, fruit); railroad shops; mfg. of wood products, clothing, flour, beverages, canned goods, toys, concrete blocks, railroad supplies, electric signs. Oil and gas wells, bituminous-coal mines. Settled 1805, laid out 1817. **6** City (pop. 5,902), ⊙ Washington co., SE Iowa, 27 mi. SSW of Iowa City; rail junction; agr. trade center; mfg. (pearl buttons, calendars, concrete pipes, feed, farm-implement accessories). Has a jr. col. Inc. 1864. **7** City (pop. 1,527), ⊙ Washington co., NE Kansas, c.50 mi. NNW of Manhattan; trading and shipping center for grain and livestock region; dairy products. Inc. 1875. **8** Village (pop. c.500), Mason co., NE Ky., 3 mi. SW of Maysville. Laid out on Simon Kenton's land; chartered 1786 by Va. legislature; was ⊙ Mason co. until 1848. An early trade center, town was for a time a chief settlement of Ky.; the *Mirror*, 3d newspaper in Ky., was established here 1797. **9** Town (pop. 1,291), St. Landry parish, S central La., 5 mi. N of Opelousas; cotton ginning, cottonseed and soybean processing, sugar milling, furniture mfg. Settled before 1820, inc. 1836. **10** Agr. town (pop. 722), Knox co., S Maine, 14 mi. NW of Rockland and on Washington Pond, 3-mi.-long lake. **11** Town (pop. 281), Berkshire co., W Mass., 8 mi. SE of Pittsfield. State forest here. **12** Village, Macomb co., SE Mich., 12 mi. NW of Mt. Clemens. Near-by Parke Davis Biological Farm produces serums. **13** Village (pop. c.200), Adams co., SW Miss., 6 mi. E of Natchez. Seat of Jefferson Military Col., founded 1802. In 1802 became ⊙ Mississippi Territory; and during 1817–20 was 1st state ⊙. **14** City (pop. 6,850), Franklin co., E central Mo., on Missouri R. and 40 mi. W of St. Louis; agr. trade and shipping center; produces shoes, clothing, pipes, musical instruments. Settled before 1818, inc. 1841. **15** Village (pop. 55), Washington co., E Nebr., 15 mi. NW of Omaha and on branch of Missouri R. **16** Town (pop. 168), Sullivan co., SW N.H., near Highland L., 18 mi. NNE of Keene. **17** Borough (pop. 4,802), Warren co., NW N.J., 11 mi. NE of Phillipsburg; mfg. (hosiery, clothing, porcelain and brass products); agr. (corn, oats, hay); nursery and dairy products. Settled 1741, inc. 1868. **18** City (pop. 9,698), ⊙ Beaufort co., E N.C., 50 mi. SE of Rocky Mount, at head of Pamlico (Tar) R. estuary; shipping center for farming, fishing, and timber area; lumber milling, fertilizer mfg. Founded before 1776. **19** Village (pop. 322), Guernsey co., E Ohio, 7 mi. E of Cambridge. Also called Old Washington. **20** Town (pop. 292), McClain co., central Okla., 28 mi. S of Oklahoma City; cotton ginning. Oil field near by. **21** Industrial city (pop. 26,280), ⊙ Washington co., SW Pa., 23 mi. SW of Pittsburgh. Glass, metal, and fiber products, bituminous coal, bricks, machinery, chemicals, beverages; meat packing; gas, oil; molybdenum is refined. Washington and Jefferson Col. and Washington Seminary are here. Hq. for Whisky Rebellion, 1791. Settled 1769, laid out 1781, inc. as borough 1810, as city 1924. **22** Industrial village (1940 pop. 1,414), administrative center of Coventry town, Kent co., central R.I., on South Branch of Pawtuxet R. and 12 mi. SSW of Providence; cottons, woolens, laces. **23** Village (pop. c.300), Washington co., S central Texas, on the Brazos and 14 mi. NNE of Brenham. Settled 1821; Texas' declaration of independence from Mexico signed here, March 2, 1836; was ⊙ Texas Republic, 1842. Near by is a state park. Also called Washington-on-the-Brazos. **24** City (pop. 435), Washington co., SW Utah, 5 mi. E of St. George, near Virgin R. **25** Town (pop. 650), Orange co., E central Vt., just SE of Barre; lumber, dairy products. **26** Town (pop. 249), ⊙ Rappahannock co., N Va., in E foothills of the Blue Ridge, 19 mi. W of Warrenton; ships apples. Platted 1749 by George Washington.

Washington, Cape, headland (alt. 1,000 ft.), Antarctica, tip of long peninsula jutting into Ross Sea from Victoria Land; 74°42'S 165°45'E. Discovered 1841 by Sir James C. Ross.

Washington, Fort. 1 Old masonry fortification (since 1946 a unit of Natl. Capital Parks), in Prince Georges co., central Md., on the Potomac and 12 mi. S of Washington. Begun 1814 to replace earlier fort destroyed by British in War of 1812; it was designed in part by Pierre L'Enfant. **2** Old fort site in New York city, N.Y.: see WASHINGTON HEIGHTS.

Washington, Lake. 1 In Washington co., W Miss., oxbow lake (c.7 mi. long) formed by cutoff of the Mississippi, 20 mi. S of Greenville; fishing, duck hunting. **2** In W central Wash., large (c.20 mi. long) fresh-water lake forming E boundary of Seattle; connected to L. Union and Puget Sound by L. Washington Ship Canal (8 mi. long; large locks). It serves as docking, shipbuilding, and repair area. Residential Mercer Isl. (5 mi. long) is connected to E and W shores by L. Washington Bridge (6½ mi. long), part of which is supported by pontoons.

Washington, Mount (6,288 ft.), N N.H., in PRESIDENTIAL RANGE of White Mts. and 23 mi. NNW of Conway. Highest peak in state and in NE U.S.; center of summer and winter resort area, with hotels and meteorological station on summit. Tuckerman Ravine, glacial cirque on SE slope, is noted for scenery and skiing. First ascended by white man 1642; bridle path built 1840, carriage road 1861, cog railroad 1869.

Washington Boro, borough (pop. 483), Lancaster co., SE Pa., 3 mi. SE of Columbia and on the Susquehanna R.

Washington Court House, city (pop. 10,560), ⊙ Fayette co., S central Ohio, c.40 mi. SW of Columbus, and on Paint Creek, in rich stock-raising and farming area; auto and airplane parts, pumps, foodstuffs, fertilizer, showcases; livestock market. Founded c.1810.

Washington Crossing. 1 Village, Mercer co., W N.J., on Delaware R., opposite Washington Crossing, Pa., and 8 mi. NW of Trenton. State park commemorates Washington's crossing of the Delaware (Christmas night, 1776) to capture Trenton. **2** Village, Bucks co., SE Pa., 9 mi. NW of Trenton, N.J., and on Delaware R., opposite Washington Crossing, N.J. Washington and 2,400 troops crossed to N.J. Christmas night, 1776, to capture Trenton from the Hessians. Washington Crossing State Park established 1917.

Washington Depot, Conn.: see WASHINGTON.

Washington Grove, town (pop. 400), Montgomery co., central Md., 19 mi. NNW of Washington.

Washington Harbor, Mich.: see ISLE ROYALE NATIONAL PARK.

Washington Heights, SE N.Y., a residential district of N Manhattan borough of New York city, lying along the Hudson N of 135th St. Includes site of Fort Washington, captured by the British (Nov., 1776) in the Revolution.

Washington Irving Island (3 mi. long), NE Franklin Dist., Northwest Territories, on W side of Kane Basin, off E Ellesmere Isl.; 79°34'N 73°15'W.

Washington Island, atoll (□ 2.8; pop. 158), Line Isls., central Pacific, 70 mi. NW of Fanning Isl.; 4°43'N 160°24'W. Discovered 1798 by U.S.; annexed 1889 by the British, included 1916 in Gilbert and Ellice Isls. colony. Copra company imports labor; no indigenous pop. Formerly called Prospect Isl.

Washington Island (□ c.20), Door co., NE Wis., bet. L. Michigan and Green Bay, just off N tip of Door Peninsula; roughly square-shaped, c.5 mi. in diameter. Generally wooded, with rocky cliffs. Ferry landing at Detroit Harbor on S shore; Jackson Harbor on NE shore is fishing village. French traders visited the isl. in 17th cent. Near-by Rock Isl. (1,000 acres; lighthouse) is privately owned.

Washington Land, region, NW Greenland, on Kennedy Channel, opposite NE Ellesmere Isl., bet. Hall Basin and Petermann Glacier (N) and Kane Basin and Humboldt Glacier (S); 80°35'N 64°W. Largely ice-free, except in N part; interior consists of plateau c.4,000 ft. high. At NW extremity is Cape Morton; 81°12'N 63°40'W.

Washington Park. 1 Residential village (pop. 5,840), St. Clair co., SW Ill., just E of East St. Louis and within St. Louis metropolitan area. Inc. 1917. **2** Town (pop. 421), Beaufort co., E N.C., just SE of Washington.

Washingtons Birthplace, Va.: see GEORGE WASHINGTON BIRTHPLACE NATIONAL MONUMENT.

Washingtonville. 1 Village (pop. 823), Orange co., SE N.Y., 9 mi. SW of Newburgh, in dairying area; wine making. Summer resort. **2** Village (pop. 848), on Columbiana-Mahoning co. line, E Ohio, 4 mi. E of Salem; tools, metal stampings. **3** Borough (pop. 194), Montour co., central Pa., 7 mi. NNW of Danville.

Washinomiya (wäshĭnō'mēä), town (pop. 4,811), Saitama prefecture, central Honshu, Japan, 16 mi. E of Kumagaya; rice, wheat; raw silk.

Washita (wô'shĭtô", wô'–), county (□ 1,009; pop. 17,657), W Okla.; ⊙ Cordell. Intersected by Washita R. and Elk Creek. Agr. (cotton, wheat, sorghums), cattle-raising, and dairying area. Mfg. at Cordell and Sentinel. Formed 1891.

Washita River. 1 In Ark. and La.: see OUACHITA RIVER. **2** In Texas and Okla., rises in Texas Panhandle near Okla. line, flows SE into Okla., thence E and SE, past Cheyenne, Clinton, Mountain View, Anadarko, Chickasha, and Pauls Valley, to L. Texoma W of Tishomingo. Length, c.450 mi., excluding 40-mi. arm of L. Texoma backed up by Denison Dam in Red R. downstream from former mouth of the Washita. Drains □ 8,108. Battle of the Washita (1868), a defeat of Cheyenne Indians by Gen. Custer, took place near Cheyenne. Sometimes spelled Ouachita.

Washizu (wä'shĭzōō), town (pop. 9,249), Shizuoka prefecture, central Honshu, Japan, on W shore of L. Hamana, 10 mi. ESE of Toyohashi; summer resort. Fish hatchery.

Washm (wă'shŭm) or **Woshm** (wô'shŭm), oasis district of central Nejd, Saudi Arabia; chief town, Shaqra.

Washoe (wô'shō), county (□ 6,281; pop. 50,205), NW Nev.; ⊙ Reno. Mtn. area bordering on Calif. and Oregon, irrigated in S along Truckee R. by Truckee storage project. Pyramid L., Pyramid Range, and Pyramid Lake Indian Reservation are in S; small part of L. Tahoe is in SW corner. Smoke Creek Desert and Granite Range are near Gerlach. Livestock grazing. Mining (gold, silver, copper, lead) in vicinity of Reno; mfg. at Reno. Formed 1861.

Washoe, village (pop. c.300), Carbon co., S Mont., just SE of Red Lodge, near Wyo. line, in NE foothills of Absaroka Range; coal mining.

Washoe Lake, W Nev., E of L. Tahoe, 16 mi. S of Reno, at S end of Virginia Range; 3.5 mi. long, 2 mi. wide.

Washoe Range, Nev.: see VIRGINIA MOUNTAINS.

Washougal (wŏshōō'gŭl), town (pop. 1,577), Clark co., SW Wash., 15 mi. E of Vancouver and on Columbia R., at mouth of small Washougal R. (c.35 mi. long). Textiles, clothing, dairy products, poultry, prunes. Settled 1860, inc. 1908.

Washta (wăsh'tŭ), town (pop. 403), Cherokee co., NW Iowa, on Little Sioux R. and 14 mi. SW of Cherokee; wood products; sand and gravel pits.

Washtenaw (wŏsh'tŭnô), county (□ 716; pop 134,606), SE Mich.; ⊙ Ann Arbor. Drained by Huron and Raisin rivers. Agr.; livestock, poultry, grain, corn, beans, sugar beets, alfalfa; dairy products. Mfg. at Ann Arbor, Ypsilanti, and Willow Run. Co. has several small lakes (resorts). Organized 1826.

Washtucna (wŏsh-tŭk'nŭ), town (pop. 316), Adams co., SE Wash., 25 mi. SSE of Ritzville, in Columbia basin agr. region.

Washunga (wŏshŭng'gŭ), town (pop. 91), Kay co., N Okla., 15 mi. ENE of Ponca City, and on Arkansas R.

Wasi (vä'sē), town (pop. 5,392), Osmanabad dist., W Hyderabad state, India, 31 mi. NW of Osmanabad; millet, wheat, cotton.

Wasiliszki, Belorussian SSR: see VASILISHKI.

Wasilkow (väsēl'kōōf), Pol. *Wasilków,* Rus. *Vasilkov* or *Vasil'kov* (both: vŭsē'lyŭkŭf), town (pop. 3,948), Bialystok prov., NE Poland, on Suprasl R. and 5 mi. NNE of Bialystok; mfg. of cloth, boxes; tanning, flour milling, sawmilling.

Wasilla (wäsĭ'lŭ), village (pop. 120), S Alaska, 30 mi. NNE of Anchorage, on Alaska RR and on branch of Glenn Highway; supply center for fur-farming and gold-mining region.

Wasit (wä'sĭt), market town in Upper Aulaqi country, Western Aden Protectorate, 15 mi. NW of Nisab.

Wasitah, Al-, Egypt: see WASTA, EL.

Waskada (wŭskä'dŭ), village (pop. estimate 350), SW Man., 65 mi. SW of Brandon; near N.Dak. and Sask. borders; grain, stock.

Waskatenau (wäskă'tŭnō), village (pop. 258), central Alta., near North Saskatchewan R., 50 mi. NE of Edmonton; wheat, stock.

Waskesiu Lake (wŏskŭsōō') (15 mi. long, 2–6 mi. wide), central Sask., in Prince Albert Natl. Park, 50 mi. NNW of Prince Albert. Drains E into Montreal L. and Churchill R.

Waskom (wăs'kŭm), city (pop. 719), Harrison co., E Texas, 16 mi. E of Marshall, near La. line; oil-field trade point.

Wasmes (väm), town (pop. 15,674), Hainaut prov., SW Belgium, 7 mi. ESE of Tournai; coal mining; coal-shipping center; shoe mfg.

Wasmuel (väzmwĕl'), town (pop. 3,543), Hainaut prov., SW Belgium, 5 mi. W of Mons; faïence.

Wasosz (vō'sôsh), Pol. *Wąsosz,* Ger. *Herrnstadt* (hĕrn'shtät), town (1939 pop. 2,941; 1946 pop. 1,084) in Lower Silesia, after 1945 in Wroclaw prov., W Poland, on Barycz R. and 8 mi. WSW of Rawicz; agr. market (grain, sugar beets, potatoes, livestock); woodworking.

Waspán, Nicaragua: see HUASPÁN.

Waspik (väs'pĭk), village (pop. 1,988), North Brabant prov., S Netherlands, 11 mi. NW of Tilburg; leather tanning, shoe mfg.

Waspuc River, Nicaragua: see HUASPUC RIVER.

Wasquehal (väskäl'), outer SE suburb (pop. 9,831) of Roubaix, Nord dept., N France, 4 mi. NE of Lille; cotton and carded wool spinning, textile dyeing, tanning, petroleum refining. Mfg. of electrical machinery, chemicals, rayon, and furniture.

Wassataquoik Lake (wăsŭtă'kwoik), Piscataquis co., N central Maine, 26 mi. NNW of Millinocket, in Baxter State Park; 1.5 mi. long. Source of **Wassataquoik Stream,** which flows c.18 mi. generally SE to East Branch of Penobscot R.

Wasselonne (väsŭlŭn'), Ger. *Wasselnheim* (väs'-ŭlnhīm), town (pop. 2,943), Bas-Rhin dept., E France, at E foot of the Vosges, 8 mi. SSE of Saverne; cotton spinning, chromium and nickel plating, mfg. (building materials, slippers).

Wassenaar (vä'sŭnär), residential town (pop. 22,250), South Holland prov., W Netherlands, 6 mi. NE of The Hague; flower-bulb growing.

Wassenberg (vä'sŭnbĕrk), village (pop. 3,057), in former Prussian Rhine Prov., W Germany, after 1945 in North Rhine-Westphalia, 7 mi. W of Erkelenz; summer resort.

Wasseralfingen (vä"sŭräl'fĭng-ŭn), village (pop. 7,219), N Württemberg, Germany, after 1945 in Württemberg-Baden, on the Kocher and 2 mi. N of Aalen; ironworks. Iron-ore mining.

Wasserbillig (–bĭl"ĭkh), town (pop. 1,638), E Luxembourg, on Moselle R., at mouth of Sûre R., and 4 mi. NE of Grevenmacher, on Ger. border; mfg. (synthetic fertilizer, cement); dolomite, chalk quarries; rose growing.

Wasserburg or **Wasserburg am Inn** (–bōōrk äm ĭn'), town (pop. 6,127), Upper Bavaria, Germany, on the Inn and 15 mi. NNE of Rosenheim; hydroelectric plant; textile mfg., brewing, printing. Has late Gothic castle, 14th-cent. church with rococo interior, two 15th-cent. churches, and 15th-cent. town hall. Chartered before 1220, it was an important trading center in 14th and 15th cent.

Wasserkuppe (–kōō"pŭ), highest peak (3,117 ft.) of the Rhön Mts., in Hohe Rhön range, W Germany, 4 mi. N of Gersfeld. The Fulda rises here.

Wassertrüdingen (–trü'dĭng-ŭn), town (pop. 2,618), Middle Franconia, W Bavaria, Germany, on the Wörnitz and 13 mi. ESE of Dinkelsbühl; textile mfg., tanning, brewing, flour and lumber milling. Sandstone quarries in area.

Wassigny (väsēnyē'), village (pop. 938), Aisne dept., N France, 18 mi. NE of Saint-Quentin; foundry; chair mfg.

Wassuk Range (wä'sŭk), W Nev., E spur of Sierra Nevada, in Mineral co., just W of Walker L. Rises to 10,516 ft. in Cory Peak and 11,303 ft. in Mt. Grant (highest point), 10 mi. WNW of Hawthorne.

Wassy (väsē'), town (pop. 2,524), Haute-Marne dept., NE France, on Blaise R. and 10 mi. S of Saint-Dizier, on branch of Marne-Saône Canal; foundries, metalworks, mfg. (furniture, morocco leather). Has 11th–16th-cent. church. Scene of celebrated massacre of Wassy (1562), one of incidents leading to Wars of Religion. Also called Wassy-sur-Blaise. Formerly spelled Vassy.

Wasta (wä'stŭ), town (pop. 144), Pennington co., SW central S.Dak., 40 mi. E of Rapid City; trading point for cattle area.

Wasta, El, or **Al-Wasta** (both: ĕl wăs'tŭ), village (pop. 7,311), Beni Suef prov., Upper Egypt, on W bank of the Nile, on Ibrahimiya Canal, railway junction to Faiyum, 50 mi. S of Cairo; cotton ginning, woolen and sugar milling; cotton, cereals, sugar cane.

Wa States (wä), constituency (□ 3,287; 1941 pop. 82,614) of Shan State, Upper Burma, E of Lashio, bet. Salween R. and Chinese Yunnan prov.; bounded S by Manglun state. Mountainous region (mean alt. 6,000 ft.), inhabited by the Was, one of the most primitive peoples of Burma, of Mon-Khmer origin, head-hunters and cultivators (poppy, corn, beans) who live in fortified and mutually hostile villages. Formerly administered directly by the Commissioner of the Federated Shan States; inc. into new Shan State in accordance with 1947 Burma Constitution.

Wastwater or **West Water** (wŏst'–), lake in the Lake District, SW Cumberland, England, 14 mi. SW of Keswick and overlooked by Scafell; deepest lake in England (258 ft.), 3 mi. long, ½ mi. wide. At SW end is agr. village of Wasdale, included in St. Bees parish. The ravine of Wasdale or Wastdale extends 8 mi. from NE end of the lake.

Wasungen (vä'zōōng-ŭn), town (pop. 4,762), Thuringia, central Germany, on Werra R., and 7 mi. NNW of Meiningen, in tobacco-growing region; wood- and metalworking, paper milling, glass and cigar mfg. Has 16th-cent. town hall.

Waswanipi River, Que.: see NOTTAWAY RIVER.

Wataga (wŏtä'gŭ), village (pop. 550), Knox co., NW central Ill., 6 mi. NE of Galesburg, in agr. and bituminous-coal area.

Watampone (wätämpō'nä), town (pop. 2,515), SW Celebes, Indonesia, near Gulf of Boni, 75 mi. NE of Macassar; trade center for corn- and rice-growing region.

Watanoha (wätä'-nō'hä), town (pop. 13,602), Miyagi prefecture, N Honshu, Japan, on Ishinomaki Bay, 3 mi. E of Ishinomaki; fishing, agr.; saltmaking.

Watari (wätä'rē), town (pop. 7,306), Miyagi prefecture, N Honshu, Japan, 6 mi. NE of Kakuda; rice, wheat, silk cocoons.

Watauga (wŏtô'gŭ), county (□ 320; pop. 18,342), NW N.C., on Tenn. line; ⊙ Boone. Blue Ridge area in Yadkin and Pisgah natl. forests; drained by Watauga R. and South Fork of New R. Farming (tobacco, vegetables, corn), stock-raising, sawmilling, and resort region. Formed 1849.

Watauga River, in W N.C. and NE Tenn., rises on Grandfather Mtn. in the Blue Ridge, W N.C.; flows NW into NE Tenn., around S end of Stone Mts., past Elizabethton, across Iron Mts., to South Fork of Holston R. 10 mi. SE of Kingsport; c.75 mi. long. Watauga Dam (318 ft. high, 900 ft. long; completed 1949) is 7 mi. E of Elizabethton; a major TVA dam, for flood control and power. Impounds Watauga Reservoir (□ c.10; capacity 678,800 acre-feet) in Carter and Johnson counties, extending 17 mi. E to N.C. border.

Watchet, urban district (1931 pop. 1,936; 1951 census 2,592), W Somerset, England, on Bridgwater Bay of Bristol Channel and 15 mi. NW of Taunton; small port and seaside resort; paper mills. Has 15th-cent. church.

Watch Hill, resort village (pop. c.500) in Westerly town, Washington co., SW R.I., on Watch Hill Point (extreme SW point of state), on sandy peninsula bet. the Atlantic and Little Narragansett Bay; fishing, yachting; fine beach extends along sandbar to Napatree Point (W). Lighthouse, coast guard station near village.

Watchung (wä"chŭng', wä'chŭng"), borough (pop. 1,818), Somerset co., N central N.J., in Watchung Mts., 16 mi. SW of Newark; stone quarrying. Inc. 1926.

Watchung Mountains or **Orange Mountains,** N central and NE N.J., 2 long low ridges of volcanic origin, mainly in Essex and Somerset counties, curving SW from point SW of Paterson to point N of Somerville; alt. c.400–500 ft. The ridges are also called First Watchung and Second Watchung mts.

Watenstedt-Salzgitter (vä'tŭn-shtĕt-zälts'gĭ"tŭr), city (□ 80; 1939 pop. 45,598; 1946 pop. 93,260; 1950 pop. 100,630), in Brunswick, NW Germany, after 1945 in Lower Saxony, c.15 mi. SW of Brunswick. In 1937 the Ger. govt. founded a company to exploit the rich iron deposits in the area; building of smelters and steel plants began the following year. In 1942 the widely distributed industrial settlements were inc. and Watenstedt-Salzgitter emerged. Consists of separated urban clusters; divided into 7 city dists.: FLACHSTÖCKHEIM, GEBHARDSHAGEN, LEBENSTEDT, LICHTENBERG, Salzgitter, THIEDE-STETERBURG, and Watenstedt. Mfg. of coke, coke by-products, machinery, chemicals, textiles; food canning, sugar refining. Gas produced here supplies most of NW Germany. Watenstedt (E) is site of steel mills and major smelter; connected by 11-mi.-long canal with Weser-Elbe Canal. Iron and potash mined at Salzgitter (S); saline baths. There are oil wells within city limits.

Waterbeach, town and parish (pop. 1,435), central Cambridge, England, on Cam R. and 5 mi. NE of Cambridge; agr. market. Near by are ruins of 12th-cent. abbey and remains of Roman dike.

Waterboro, town (pop. 1,071), York co., SW Maine, 16 mi. NW of Biddeford; leather goods, boxes. Waterboro Center is resort area. Settled 1768, inc. 1787.

Waterbury. 1 Industrial city (pop. 104,477), coextensive with Waterbury town, a ⊙ New Haven co., W Conn., 18 mi. NW of New Haven, bisected by Naugatuck R.; brass center (industry began in mid-18th cent.); mfg. (clocks, hardware, silverware, chemicals, clothing, tools, machinery, automobile parts, lighting fixtures, glassware, plastics, bedding, cigars). Historical society has fine collections here. Town includes Waterville village. Settled in late 17th cent., town inc. 1686, city inc. 1853. **2** Village (pop. 141), Dixon co., NE Nebr., 18 mi. W of Sioux City, Iowa, near Missouri R. **3** Town (pop. 4,276), including Waterbury village (pop. 3,153), Washington co., central Vt., on Winooski R. and 11 mi. NW of Montpelier; wood products, machinery, granite and talc, dairy and maple products, canned corn. State hosp. for insane here. Site of Little River Dam, built after 1927 flood. Chartered 1763, settled 1783.

Waterdown, village (pop. 910), S Ont., 6 mi. N of Hamilton; jam and jelly making, basket weaving, woodworking.

Wateree (wô'tŭrē"), village, Richland co., central S.C., on Wateree R. (bridged) and 25 mi. SE of Columbia. State park c.5 mi. E.

Wateree River, S.C., name given to lower section (c.75 mi. long) of CATAWBA RIVER, bet. Great Falls and junction with the Congaree to form Santee R.; navigable for 58 mi. below Camden. Dammed 8 mi. NNW of Camden to form Wateree Pond (c.15 mi. long); hydroelectric works.

Waterfoot, town in Rawtenstall borough, E Lancashire, England; carpet-weaving center; cotton and woolen milling; shoe mfg.

Waterford, village (pop. 1,342), S Ont., on Lynn R. and 7 mi. N of Simcoe; dairying; fruit, vegetables.

Waterford, Gaelic *Phort Láirge,* county (□ 709.8; pop. 76,108), Munster, SE Ireland; ⊙ Waterford. Bounded by the Atlantic (S), cos. Cork (W), Tipperary and Kilkenny (N), and Wexford (E). Drained by Suir R. and Blackwater R. and their tributaries. Surface is largely hilly or mountainous, rising to 2,504 ft. in Comeragh Mts.; leveling toward E and Suir R. valley. Coastline is low and dangerous to shipping; main inlets are Youghal Harbour, Dungarvan Harbour, Tramore Bay, and Waterford Harbour. Marble, limestone, slate, quartz are quarried; some copper, lead, iron is mined. Dairying, bacon and ham curing, cattle and pig raising are important; sea fisheries. Industries include tanning, tobacco processing, jute milling, brewing, food canning, mfg. of agr. implements, shoes. Besides Waterford, other towns are Dungarvan, Lismore, Dunmore East, and Portlaw. There are anc. historical and ecclesiastical bldgs. at Lismore. Co. has numerous associations with early Danish occupation; it was later part of kingdom of Ormond.

Waterford, Gaelic *Port Láirge,* county borough (pop. 28,269) and city, ⊙ Co. Waterford, Ireland, in E part of co., on Suir R., near its mouth on Waterford Harbour, 85 mi. SSW of Dublin; 52°15'N 7°7'W; important seaport, with shipyards. Cattle, beef, dairy products are chief exports. Industries include jute milling, tobacco and dairy-products processing, food canning, bacon and ham curing, mfg. of agr. implements, shoes, cattle feed. Features of city are fragments of anc. city walls; Reginald's Tower (1003), scene of wedding (1171) of Strongbow and daughter of the king of Leinster; Protestant cathedral (begun 1773 on site of 11th-cent. Sigtryg's church), seat of united Protestant dioceses of Cashel, Emly, Waterford, and Lismore; R.C. cathedral (1793); Blackfriar's Priory (1226); and ruins of Franciscan friary founded 1240. Waterford became Danish settlement c.850; c.1050 Reginald, son of Sigtryg, founded Church of Holy Trinity here. In 1170 Raymond le Gros defeated Danes; in 1171 Strongbow occupied Waterford; and in 1172 Henry II landed here. King John chartered town and established mint. In 1649 Cromwell had to abandon siege of Waterford; in 1650 it was stormed by Ireton. Having sided with James II, Waterford surrendered to William III after battle of the Boyne. In 18th cent. it became famous as glass-making center; by mid-19th cent. trade had died out. Just N of Waterford, across Suir R., is suburb of Ferryden.

Waterford. 1 Village (pop. 1,777), Stanislaus co., central Calif., in San Joaquin Valley, 12 mi. E of Modesto; irrigated farming, fruitgrowing. **2** Town (pop. 9,100), New London co., SE Conn., on Long Isl. Sound, just W of New London; agr.; granite quarrying. State tuberculosis sanatorium for children here. Includes villages of Quaker Hill (pop. 1,260) and Millstone (granite). Settled c.1653, set off from New London 1801. **3** Town (pop. 828), Oxford co., W Maine, 11 mi. SW of Paris; wood products, paper. Birth- and burial place of Artemus Ward. **4** Village (pop. c.400), Oakland co., SE

Mich., 7 mi. NW of Pontiac, in agr. area. Summer camps. **5** Village (pop. 2,968), Saratoga co., E N.Y., on W bank of the Hudson at influx of Mohawk R. (bridged), and on the Barge Canal, just N of Cohoes; mfg. (clothing, machinery, paper, textiles). Inc. 1794. **6** Agr. borough (pop. 1,195), Erie co., NW Pa., 13 mi. SSE of Erie; milk, cabbage, potatoes; resort. Ruins of Fort Le Boeuf, built 1753 by French, here. **7** Town (pop. 468), Caledonia co., NE Vt., on the Connecticut, just E of St. Johnsbury. **8** town (1940 pop. 247), Loudoun co., N Va., 5 mi. NW of Leesburg. **9** Village (pop. 1,100), Racine co., SE Wis., on Fox R., near Tichigan L., and 25 mi. SW of Milwaukee, in agr. area; summer resort.

Waterford Harbour, Ireland, inlet (15 mi. long, up to 4 mi. wide) of the Atlantic, bet. Co. Waterford and Co. Wexford, Ireland, formed by tidal estuary of Suir and Barrow rivers. At entrance are lighthouses at Dunmore East and Hook Head.

Waterford Works or Waterford, village (pop. c.1,500), Camden co., SW N.J., 20 mi. SE of Camden, in orchard and vineyard area. Had 18th-cent. bog-iron mines, 19th-cent. glassworks.

Wateringbury, agr. village and parish (pop. 1,061), central Kent, England, on Medway R. and 5 mi. WSW of Maidstone. Has 13th-cent. church.

Water Island, islet (491 acres) off S St. Thomas Isl., U.S. Virgin Isls., outside St. Thomas Harbor, 1 mi. SW of Charlotte Amalie. On it is Fort Segarra, with installations of U.S. Army Chemical Service moved here 1948 from Panama.

Waterkloof (wô'tŭrklōōf", Afrikaans vä"tŭrklōōf'), residential town (pop. 2,059), S central Transvaal, U. of So. Afr., 5 mi. ESE of Pretoria.

Waterloo, municipality (pop. 11,241), E New South Wales, Australia, 4 mi. S of Sydney, in metropolitan area; mfg. (glass, elevators).

Waterloo (wô"tŭrlōō', Flem. vä'tŭrlō"), town (pop. 7,722), Brabant prov., central Belgium, 9 mi. S of Brussels. Famed for battle (June 18, 1815) 3 mi. SSE, at which British and Prussian forces under duke of Wellington and Blücher defeated the French under Napoleon. Large monument commemorates battle. Near by is village of La Belle-Alliance, after which battle of Waterloo is sometimes called.

Waterloo (wô"tŭrlōō'), county (□ 516; pop. 98,720), S Ont., on Grand R.; ⊙ Kitchener.

Waterloo. 1 Town (pop. 9,025), S Ont., NW suburb of Kitchener; distilling center; flour milling, mfg. of shoes, clothing, buttons, upholstery, furniture, agr. machinery. Waterloo Col. is affiliated with Univ. of Western Ontario. **2** Town (pop. 3,173), ⊙ Shefford co. S Que., 65 mi. ESE of Montreal; mfg. of wire, furniture, skis, plastics, clothing; in dairying and agr. region (apples, potatoes, tomatoes).

Waterloo, town (1931 pop. 2,312), Sierra Leone colony, on Sierra Leone Peninsula, on railroad and 17 mi. SE of Freetown; road junction; kola nuts, ginger, rice. Until 1948, site of main Sierra Leone airfield, now near Lungi. R.C. mission. Founded 1819.

Waterloo (wô'tŭrlōō', wô'tŭrlōō"). **1** Town (pop. 327), Lauderdale co., extreme NW Ala., on Pickwick Landing Reservoir (on Tennessee R.), 24 mi. NW of Florence. **2** City (pop. 2,821), ⊙ Monroe co., SW Ill., 18 mi. S of East St. Louis, in agr. area; flour milling; corn, wheat, livestock, dairy products, poultry. Platted 1818, inc. 1849. **3** Town (pop. 1,414), De Kalb co., NE Ind., on small Cedar Creek and 26 mi. NNE of Fort Wayne; livestock, soybeans; dairy products, canned goods, wood products, flour, feed. **4** City (pop. 65,198), ⊙ Black Hawk co., E central Iowa, on Cedar R. and c.50 mi. NW of Cedar Rapids; industrial, transportation, and agr.- trade center, with farm-machinery and cement-mixer factories, meat-packing and soybean-processing plants, bottling works, creameries, railroad shops. Mfg. also of foundry, concrete, and wood products; caskets, clothes, feed. The noted Dairy Cattle Congress and National Belgian Horse Show are held here annually. Settled as Prairie Rapids 1845; named Waterloo 1851; inc. 1868. **5** Village (pop. 382), Douglas co., E Nebr., 18 mi. W of Omaha and on Elkhorn R., near Platte R.; grain, vine seeds. **6** Village (pop. 4,438), a ⊙ Seneca co., W central N.Y., in Finger Lakes region, on Seneca R., bet. Seneca and Cayuga lakes, and 7 mi. ENE of Geneva; mfg. (auto bodies, condiments, canned foods, stone products). Summer resort. Inc. 1824. **7** Town (pop. 162), Laurens co., NW central S.C., 13 mi. NNE of Greenwood; grain milling. **8** Village (pop. 1,667), Jefferson co., S Wis., on small Waterloo Creek and 21 mi. NE of Madison, in dairying region; malt, shoes, cheese, canned vegetables, dairy products. Inc. 1859.

Waterloo with Seaforth, former urban district (1931 pop. 31,187) now in CROSBY municipal borough, SW Lancashire, England. Includes residential and resort town of Waterloo, on Mersey R. estuary and 5 mi. NNW of Liverpool. Its sunsets were frequently painted by Turner. Residential town of Seaforth is on Mersey R. estuary and 4 mi. NNW of Liverpool.

Watermael-Boitsfort (vätŭrmäl-bwäfôr'), Flemish *Watermaal-Bosvoorde* (formerly Watermaal-Boschvoorde) (vä'tŭrmäl-bōs'vōrdŭ), residential town (pop. 19,940), Brabant prov., central Belgium, SE suburb of Brussels. Here is noted garden-city development; site of racecourse. Has 17th-cent. castle. Neolithic remains have been found near by.

Waterman, village (pop. 750), De Kalb co., N Ill., 24 mi. W of Aurora, in rich agr. area; dairy products, grain, livestock, poultry; feed mill.

Water Mill, resort village, Suffolk co., SE N.Y., on SE Long Isl., 2 mi. NE of Southampton.

Waterproof, town (pop. 1,180), Tensas parish, NE La., 50 mi. SW of Vicksburg (Miss.) and on Mississippi R.; agr. Oil and natural-gas field near by.

Waterschei (vä'tŭr-skhī), town, Limburg prov., NE Belgium, 3 mi. NE of Genk; coal mining. Formerly called Waterscheide.

Waterside, E suburb of Londonderry, Co. Londonderry, Northern Ireland, across Foyle R.

Waterside, town in Dalmellington parish, S central Ayrshire, Scotland, on Doon R. and 3 mi. NW of Dalmellington; coal mining, ironworking.

Watersmeet, village (1940 pop. 537), Gogebic co., W Upper Peninsula, Mich., 29 mi. NW of Iron River city and on Middle Branch of Ontonagon R.; trade center for farm, resort, and hunting area.

Waterton-Glacier International Peace Park, Mont. and Alta.: see GLACIER NATIONAL PARK, WATERTON LAKES NATIONAL PARK.

Waterton Lakes National Park (□ 204), S Alta., on Mont. border, 60 mi. SW of Lethbridge. The Canadian part of Waterton-Glacier International Peace Park, created 1932 by acts of Congress and of Canadian Parliament. Surface is mountainous, rising to 9,600 ft. on Mt. Blakiston. In central part of park are the Waterton lakes; the larger lake (11 mi. long; alt. 4,193) straddles Alta.-Mont. border. Park was established 1895.

Watertown. 1 Town (pop. 10,699), Litchfield co., W Conn., on Naugatuck R., just NW of Waterbury; textiles, thread, machinery, tools, plastic and metal products. Includes Oakville, mfg. village (1940 pop. 4,299). Taft school for boys (1890), state park, state forests here. Set off from Waterbury 1780. **2** Village (pop. 1,473), Columbia co., N Fla., 9 mi. SSW of Lake City, in lumbering area. **3** Residential town (pop. 37,329), Middlesex co., E Mass., on Charles R. and 7 mi. W of Boston; mfg. (rubber footwear and goods, clothing, textiles, tools, electrical equipment, stoves). Has large U.S. arsenal, Perkins Inst. for blind. Settled and inc. 1630. **4** Village (pop. 837), Carver co., S central Minn., on South Fork Crow R. and 29 mi. W of Minneapolis, in livestock, poultry, grain area; dairy products, canned vegetables. **5** Industrial city (pop. 34,350), ⊙ Jefferson co., N N.Y., on Black R. (water power from falls) and 65 mi. N of Syracuse; trade and distribution center for rich dairy area, and a gateway to the Thousand Isls. resort region. Mfg.: air brakes, paper products, plumbing equipment, clothing, silk, thermometers. Seat of Jefferson County Historical Society. Settled c.1800; inc. as village in 1815, as city in 1869. **6** City (pop. 12,699), ⊙ Codington co., E S.Dak., 90 mi. NNW of Sioux Falls and on Big Sioux R., near L. Kampeska; 44°53'N 97°7'W. Railway, distribution, and processing center for large farm area; resort. Cement products, sashes and doors, beverages, meat, poultry, and dairy products, flour, wheat, potatoes. State fish hatchery, municipal airport and power plant are here. Platted 1878. **7** City (pop. 933), Wilson co., N central Tenn., 36 mi. ESE of Nashville; makes hosiery, work shirts, evaporated milk. **8** City (pop. 12,417), on Jefferson-Dodge co. line, SE Wis., on Rock R. and 35 mi. ENE of Madison, in farming and dairying area; goose market. Mfg.: shoes, cutlery, machinery; wood, rubber, and paper products. Northwestern Col. is here. Home (1855–57) of Carl Schurz, whose wife established 1st kindergarten in America here in 1856. Near by is a mus. called Octagon House (c.1849). Settled c.1836, inc. 1853.

Water Valley. 1 Town (pop. 346), Graves co., SW Ky., near Bayou de Chien and Tenn. line, 18 mi. SW of Mayfield; canning plant. **2** City (pop. 3,213), a ⊙ Yalobusha co., N central Miss., 27 mi. NNE of Grenada; cotton, corn, watermelons, lumber, livestock; mfg. of work clothes. Inc. 1858.

Waterville, village (pop. 844), S Que., on Coaticook R. and 8 mi. S of Sherbrooke; dairying, stock raising.

Waterville. 1 Village, Conn.: see WATERBURY. **2** Town (pop. 199), Allamakee co., extreme NE Iowa, 10 mi. ESE of Waukon, in dairy region. Limestone quarries near by. **3** City (pop. 676), Marshall co., NE Kansas, on Little Blue R. and 34 mi. NNW of Manhattan, in grain region; poultry packing. **4** City (pop. 18,287), Kennebec co., S Maine, on W bank of the Kennebec, at Ticonic Falls [named for Indian tribe], and 17 mi. N of Augusta; rail and agr. trade center; paper and textile mills; lumber products. Seat of Colby Col. Redington house (1814) is now a mus. Settled 1754 as part of WINSLOW, across the river; set off as town 1802; city inc. 1883. **5** Village, Mass.: see WINCHENDON. **6** City (pop. 1,627), Le Sueur co., S Minn., on 2 small lakes, 15 mi. WSW of Faribault; resort; trade center for grain, livestock, poultry area; dairy products. Inc. as village 1878, as city 1898. **7** Town (pop. 11), Grafton co., central N.H., on Mad R. in White Mts., 20 mi. W of Conway. Includes Waterville Valley, summer resort and winter-sports center. **8** Village (pop. 1,634), Oneida co., central N.Y., 14 mi. SSW of Utica, in dairying and farming area (beans, peas, hops); mfg. (knit goods, canned foods). George Eastman b. here. Inc. 1871. **9** Village (pop. 1,110), Lucas co., NW Ohio, 14 mi. SW of downtown Toledo, and on Maumee R., in agr. area; limestone quarries, oil and gas wells; nurseries. Glass, metal, rubber products; food products. **10** Town (pop. 409), Lamoille co., N central Vt., on North Branch Lamoille R. and 18 mi. SE of St. Albans, in Green Mts. **11** Town (pop. 1,013), ⊙ Douglas co., central Wash., 18 mi. NE of Wenatchee, in Columbia basin agr. region; grain, livestock; clay, limestone. Founded 1886.

Waterville Dam, W N.C., near Tenn. line, in Pigeon R., 15 mi. NW of Waynesville; power dam (280 ft. high, 870 ft. long; concrete arch type); completed 1930. Impounds reservoir c.5 mi. long.

Waterville Valley, N.H.: see WATERVILLE.

Watervliet (vä'tŭrvlēt'), agr. village (pop. 2,181), East Flanders prov., NW Belgium, 7 mi. NNE of Eekloo, near Netherlands border.

Watervliet (wô'tŭrvlēt', -vŭlēt', wô'tŭrvlēt). **1** City (pop. 1,327), Berrien co., extreme SW Mich., 11 mi. NE of Benton Harbor and on Paw Paw R., in orchard and farm area; Paw Paw L. (resort) is just N. Mfg. (paper, flour, dairy products). Settled in 1830s; inc. as village 1891, as city 1925. **2** Industrial city (pop. 15,197), Albany co., E N.Y., on the Hudson (bridged), opposite Troy, in diversified-farming area. U.S. arsenal here (established in War of 1812). Mfg.: steel castings, abrasives, chemicals, bricks, concrete blocks, lumber, furniture, textiles, brushes. Here is Schuyler house (1666). Here in 1776, Ann Lee headed 1st American community of Shakers. Inc. 1896.

Waterways, Alberta: see FORT MCMURRAY.

Wates (wä'tĕs), town (pop. 7,784), central Java, Indonesia, near S coast, 15 mi. WSW of Jogjakarta; trade center for agr. area (sugar, rice, peanuts, cassava).

Watford, village (pop. 1,076), S Ont., 26 mi. E of Sarnia; lumber and flour milling, wire mfg.

Watford (wŏt'fŭrd), residential municipal borough (1931 pop. 56,805; 1951 census 73,072), SW Hertford, England, on Colne R. and 16 mi. NW of London; paper, chemical, paint, leather, food industries. The 15th-cent. parish church (rebuilt) contains many noteworthy monuments. "Cassiobury," former seat of earls of Essex, is now public park. Town is site of The London Orphan School, founded 1813. In municipal borough (S) is residential dist. of Oxhey (pop. 6,147).

Watford City, village (pop. 1,371), ⊙ McKenzie co., W N.Dak., 28 mi. SE of Williston; railhead and trade center; lignite mines; wheat, livestock, dairy. Became ⊙ 1941. Inc. 1934.

Watford Island (1,000 ft. long, 600 ft. wide), W Bermuda, bet. Somerset and Boaz isls.; connected by road with adjacent isls.

Watford Rural, extensive residential parish (pop. 5,583), SW Hertford, England, surrounding Watford. Includes town of RADLETT.

Watha (wā'thŭ), town (pop. 222), Pender co., SE N.C., 7 mi. NNW of Burgaw.

Wathena (wŏ-thē'nŭ), city (pop. 797), Doniphan co., extreme NE Kansas, on Missouri R. and 6 mi. W of St. Joseph, Mo.; shipping point for fruit (chiefly apples) and general agr. region. Gravel pit, stands of oak and walnut timber in vicinity.

Wath-upon-Dearne (wŏth, wăth; dûrn), urban district (1931 pop. 13,655; 1951 census 13,927), West Riding, S Yorkshire, England, on Dearne R. and 10 mi. NE of Sheffield; coal mining; also produces bottles, soap.

Watkins (wŏt'kĭnz), village (pop. 659), Meeker co., S central Minn., c.60 mi. WNW of Minneapolis, in grain, dairying, truck-farming area; dairy products.

Watkins Glen, resort village (pop. 3,052), ⊙ Schuyler co., W central N.Y., in Finger Lakes fruitgrowing region, at S end of Seneca L., 20 mi. WSW of Ithaca. Watkins Glen State Park, with 2-mi. gorge, mineral springs, and several waterfalls, adjoins. Village is farm trade center, with salt plants, grape-juice processing; sand pits. Flood caused great damage here in 1935. Inc. 1842.

Watkinsville, town (pop. 662), ⊙ Oconee co., NE central Ga., 7 mi. SSW of Athens, in agr. area.

Watlam (wŭt'lŭm'), Mandarin *Yülin* (yü'lĭn'), town (1942 pop. 50,000), ⊙ Watlam co. (1946 pop. 371,225), SE Kwangsi prov., China, 50 mi. S of Kweiping and on Lim R.; road center; cotton textiles; indigo, timber, rice, sweet potatoes. Gold deposits near by.

Watling Island or **Watlings Island,** Bahama Isls.: see SAN SALVADOR ISLAND.

Watling Street (wŏt'lĭng), anc. Roman road in England, linking *Londinium* (London) with *Viroconium* (Wroxeter), passing through *Verulamium* (St. Albans), crossing Fosse Way c.13 mi. SW of Leicester, forming border bet. Warwick and Leicester. Same name is sometimes given to road from Dover to London via Canterbury. Watling Street has been important thoroughfare from early Middle Ages until modern times, and now forms S sector of Great North Road, linking London with Scotland.

Watlington, town and parish (pop. 1,418), SE Oxfordshire, England, 7 mi. S of Thame; agr. market, with mfg. of farm implements. Has market hall dating from 1664 and 14th–15th-cent. church.

Watnam (wŭt'näm'), Mandarin *Yünan* (yü'nän'), town (pop. 2,083), ⊙ Watnam co. (pop. 236,724), W Kwangtung prov., China, 30 mi. SSE of Wuchow, near West R. Tin mining near by. Until 1914 called Saining.

Watoebela Islands, Indonesia: see WATUBELA ISLANDS.

Watoga State Park (wŏtō'gù) (c.10,000 acres), Pocahontas co., E W.Va., 7 mi. S of Marlinton, in the Alleghenies. Forested game refuge and recreational area.

Watomari, Ryukyu Isls.: see WADOMARI.

Watonga (wŭtŏng'gù), city (pop. 3,249), ⊙ Blaine co., W central Okla., c.55 mi. WNW of Oklahoma City, near North Canadian R. in agr. area. Cotton ginning, lumber and grain milling, poultry packing; grain elevators; mfg. of gypsum products, bedding, dairy products. A state park is near by. Settled 1892.

Watonwan (wô'tùnwŏn), county (□ 433; pop. 13,881), S Minn.; ⊙ St. James. Agr. area drained by Watonwan R. Corn, oats, barley, livestock, dairy products, poultry. Formed 1860.

Watonwan River, rises in Cottonwood co., SW Minn., flows 90 mi. E, past Madelia, to Blue Earth R. SW of Mankato.

Watou (vätōō'), agr. village (pop. 3,056), West Flanders prov., W Belgium, 5 mi. W of Poperinge, near Fr. border.

Watrap (vŭt'rŭp), town (pop. 9,416), Ramnad dist., S Madras, India, 9 mi. N of Srivilliputtur, at foot of Varushanad Hills; sheep and cattle raising; tanning. Until early 1920s, Varttirayiruppu.

Watrous (wä'trùs), town (pop. 1,126), S central Sask., near Little Manitou L., 60 mi. ESE of Saskatoon; grain elevators, mixed farming.

Watrous (wŏ'trùs), village (pop. c.400), Mora co., N central N.Mex., on Mora R., at mouth of Sapello Creek, E of Sangre de Cristo Mts., and 20 mi. NE of Las Vegas; alt. 6,413 ft. Trade and lumber-shipping point. Sanitarium and ruins of Fort Union (1851–91) near by.

Watsa (wät'sä), village (1948 pop. 5,122), Eastern Prov., NE Belgian Congo, near Kibali R., 110 mi. NNW of Irumu; alt. 3,608 ft. Center of gold-mining area employing c.11,000 native workers; gold-treating plants at Dubele (2 mi. SW), Arebi (8 mi. S), Wanga (20 mi. W). Chief mines are at MOTO, TORA, and ABIMVA. Power is supplied by N'zoro (ùnzō'rō) or Zoro hydroelectric plant (20 mi. N). Watsa has a Dominican mission with trade schools for natives, hosp. for Europeans. Local activities are coordinated with those of KILO-MINES in one large concern, Watsa sector being commonly designated as Moto sector.

Watseka (wŏtsē'kù), city (pop. 4,235), ⊙ Iroquois co., E Ill., on Iroquois R. at mouth of small Sugar Creek, and 25 mi. SSE of Kankakee, in rich agr. area (corn, oats, wheat, soybeans, livestock, poultry); mfg. (dairy products, soft drinks, batteries). Platted as South Middleport in 1860 on site of an early trading post; renamed 1865; inc. 1867. Henry Bacon b. here.

Watsi Kengo (wät'sē kĕng'gō), village, Equator Prov., NW Belgian Congo, on Salonga R. and 40 mi. S of Boende; terminus of steam navigation; palm-growing area.

Wat Sing (wät'sĭng'), village (1937 pop. 5,764), Chainat prov., central Thailand, on Chao Phraya R. and 9 mi. NW of Chainat. Also spelled Wat Singha.

Watsomba (wätsŏm'bä), village, Umtali prov., E Southern Rhodesia, in Mashonaland, on road and 20 mi. N of Umtali; tobacco, corn, citrus fruit, dairy products.

Watson, town (pop. 444), S central Sask., 26 mi. E of Humboldt; railroad junction; grain elevators.

Watson. 1 Town (pop. 309), Desha co., SE Ark., 20 mi. NNE of McGehee, in agr. area. **2** Village (pop. 288), Effingham co., SE central Ill., 7 mi. S of Effingham, in agr. area. **3** Village (pop. 284), Chippewa co., SW Minn., on Chippewa R., near Minnesota R., and 5 mi. NW of Montevideo, in agr. area. State park in vicinity. **4** Town (pop. 199), Atchison co., NW Mo., 12 mi. W of Tarkio, near mouth of Nishnabotna R. in Missouri R.

Watson Lake, village (pop. estimate 100), S Yukon, near B.C. border, on small Watson L., on branch of Alaska Highway; 60°7'N 128°48'W; trading post; airfield, radio and weather station, Royal Canadian Mounted Police post.

Watsontown, borough (pop. 2,327), Northumberland co., E central Pa., 16 mi. NNW of Sunbury and on West Branch of Susquehanna R.; shale quarries. Laid out 1794, inc. 1867.

Watsonville, city (pop. 11,572), Santa Cruz co., W Calif., 15 mi. E of Santa Cruz, near Monterey Bay; shipping center for Pajaro R. valley (apples; also lettuce, other vegetables, fruit). Apple-processing plants, packing and freezing plants. Beach, mtn. resorts near by. Founded 1851, inc. 1868.

Wattala (vŭt'tùlù), town (pop. 2,205), Western Prov., Ceylon, on the Kelani Ganga and 4 mi. NNE of Colombo city center; vegetables, rice, coconuts. Administered by urban council (pop. 12,419) jointly with Mabole (1.5 mi. NNE) and Peliyagoda (1.5 mi. S).

Wattegama (vŭtĕgä'mù), town (pop. 1,078), Central Prov., Ceylon, on Kandy Plateau, 5 mi. NNE of Kandy; alt. 1,620 ft. Extensive tea, cacao, and rubber plantations; vegetables, rice.

Watten (vätä', Fl. vä'tùn), town (pop. 2,432), Nord dept., N France, on the Aa (canalized) and 6 mi. NNW of Saint-Omer, in polder region; jute spinning, chicory mfg., dairying.

Watten (wŏ'tùn, wä'–), agr. village and parish (pop. 908), E central Caithness, Scotland, at SE end of Loch Watten (3 mi. long, 1 mi. wide), on Wick R., and 8 mi. WNW of Wick.

Wattens (vät'ùns), town (pop. 4,149), Tyrol, W Austria, near Inn R., 9 mi. E of Innsbruck, at foot of Tuxer Alps; paper mill, cut glass mfg.; summer resort.

Wattenscheid (vä'tùn-shīt), city (1950 pop. 67,116), in former Prussian prov. of Westphalia, W Germany, after 1945 in North Rhine-Westphalia, in the Ruhr, bet. Essen (W) and Bochum (E); coal-mining center; mfg. of electrical goods and shoes; metalworking. Chartered 1425.

Wattenwil (vä'tùnvēl), residential town (pop. 2,211), Bern canton, W central Switzerland, on Gürbe Canal and 13 mi. S of Bern. Near by is 16th-cent. castle Burgistein.

Watthana Nakhon (wät'tùnä' näkôn'), village (1937 pop. 2,381), Prachinburi prov., SE Thailand on Bangkok–Pnompenh RR and 12 mi. WNW of Aranyaprathet; gold mining.

Wattignies-la-Victoire (vätēnyē-lä-vēktwär'), village (pop. 168), Nord dept., N France, 7 mi. NE of Avesnes; horse raising. French defeated Austrians here in 1793.

Watton (wŏ'tùn), town and parish (pop. 1,413), central Norfolk, England, 21 mi. WSW of Norwich; agr. market. Has church dating from Norman times. Near by is Wayland Wood, associated with the legend of the "Babes in the Wood."

Wattrelos (vätrùlō'), NE suburb (pop. 26,915) of Roubaix, Nord dept., N France, near Belg. border; wool and cotton textiles, chemicals, leather goods.

Watts, town (pop. 267), Adair co., E Okla., on Illinois R., near Ark. line, and c.50 mi. ENE of Muskogee. Small L. Francis (fishing) is formed here by dam on Illinois R.

Watts Bar Dam, E Tenn., in Tennessee R., 50 mi. NE of Chattanooga, upstream from Chickamauga Dam. Major TVA dam (112 ft. high, 2,960 ft. long; completed 1942); concrete construction, earthfill wing. Designed to aid navigation (has lock 360 ft. long, 60 ft. wide, providing max. life of 70 ft.) and flood control and to supply power. Forms Watts Bar Reservoir (□ 60; 72 mi. long, .5–2 mi. wide; capacity 1,132,000 acre-ft.) in Rhea, Meigs, and Roane counties. Reservoir receives Clinch R. in N arm, near Harriman; includes several small isls.

Wattsburg, borough (pop. 343), Erie co., NW Pa., 15 mi. SE of Erie and on French Creek; butter. Ida M. Tarbell b. near here.

Watt's Dyke, England and Wales: see OFFA'S DYKE.

Watts Island, Va., in Chesapeake Bay bet. Tangier Sound (W) and Pocomoke Sound (E), 11 mi. NW of Onancock; c.2 mi. long. Watts Isl. lighthouse is on Little Watts Isl., just S.

Wattsville or **Watts Mill,** textile village (pop. 1,649), Laurens co., NW central S.C., just NE of Laurens; rayons.

Wattwil (vät'vēl), town (pop. 6,106), St. Gall canton, NE Switzerland, on Thur R. and 16 mi. SW of St. Gall; textiles.

Watubela Islands or **Watoebela Islands** (both: wätōōbĕ'lä), group of S Moluccas, Indonesia, bet. Banda Sea (W) and Arafura Sea (E), 65 mi. SE of Ceram; 4°29'S 131°39'E. Comprise 8 isls., largest being Kasiui or Kasioei (both: käsyōō'ē), 9 mi. long, 2 mi. wide, and Tior (tēōr'), 6 mi. long, 3 mi. wide, rising to 1,234 ft. Isls. are wooded and hilly. Chief products: coconuts, fish.

Watuppa Pond, SE Mass., in Fall River city; 7.5 mi. long.

Watzmann (väts'män), peak (8,901 ft.) of the Salzburg Alps, Upper Bavaria, Germany, 5 mi. SSW of Berchtesgaden; glaciers. Königssee is at E foot.

Wau (wou), town (pop. 6,200), ⊙ Bahr el Ghazal prov., S Anglo-Egyptian Sudan, head of navigation on Jur R. and 650 mi. SSW of Khartoum; agr. and trade center; cotton, peanuts, sesame, corn, durra; livestock. R.C. mission with technical school.

Wau, town, Morobe dist., Territory of New Guinea, NE New Guinea, 30 mi. SW of Salamaua, 150 mi. N of Port Moresby; alt. 3,000 ft.; center of rich gold fields accessible only by air.

Waubaushene (wôbùshēn'), village (pop. estimate 600), S Ont., on Georgian Bay, 18 mi. NW of Orillia; dairying; grain.

Waubay (wôbā'), city (pop. 879), Day co., NE S.Dak., 10 mi. E of Webster, near Blue Dog and Waubay lakes; resort; dairy products, grain, wool.

Waubay Lake, Day co., NE S.Dak.; 9 mi. long, 5 mi. wide at widest point; resort. Cormorant Isl. is in it.

Waubeek (wôbēk'), village (pop. c.150), Linn co., E Iowa, on Wapsipinicon R. and 17 mi. NE of Cedar Rapids. Limestone quarries near by.

Waubesa, Lake (wôbē'sù), one of the Four Lakes, Dane co., S Wis., 4 mi. SE of Madison; connected with L. Monona (N) and L. Kegonsa (SE) by Yahara R.; c.3 mi. long, 1½ mi. wide.

Waubun, village (pop. 426), Mahnomen co., NW Minn., in White Earth Indian Reservation, 10 mi. S of Mahnomen; dairy products. Lake resorts in vicinity.

Wauchope (wô'kùp), town (pop. 1,903), E New South Wales, Australia, on Hastings R. and 125 mi. NE of Newcastle; dairying center. Arsenic ore mined near by.

Wauchula (wôchōō'lù), city (pop. 2,872), ⊙ Hardee co., central Fla., c.45 mi. SE of Tampa, near Peace R.; ships truck (especially strawberries) and citrus fruit; has citrus-fruit canneries; makes boxes. Settled around fort built in Seminole War.

Waucoba Mountain, Calif.: see INYO MOUNTAINS.

Waucoma (wôkō'mù), town (pop. 385), Fayette co., NE Iowa, on Little Turkey R. and 20 mi. SW of Decorah; dairy products, feed. Limestone quarries, sand and gravel pits near by.

Wauconda (wŏkŏn'dù), resort village (pop. 1,173), Lake co., NE Ill., on small Bangs L. and 16 mi. WSW of Waukegan, in dairy and farm area.

Waugoshance Point (wô'gù-shăns), Emmet co., NW Mich., a narrow and irregular peninsula extending c.5 mi. W into L. Michigan, 10 mi. WSW of Mackinaw City. Included in Wilderness State Park. Small Waugoshance Isl. is just offshore.

Waukee (wô'kē), town (pop. 501), Dallas co., central Iowa, 14 mi. W of Des Moines; nurseries.

Waukegan (wôkē'gùn), residential and industrial city (pop. 38,946), ⊙ Lake co., extreme NE Ill., on L. Michigan, 35 mi. NNW of Chicago; air, rail, lake shipping. Mfg.: steel and steel products, asbestos, roofing, pharmaceuticals, chemicals, leather products, auto accessories, hardware, radiators, boilers, sporting goods; tin, iron and brass goods; tools, outboard motors, refrigerators, envelopes, lacquer, candy. Dairy, livestock, poultry, and grain farms and resort areas near by. Settled 1835 as Little Fort near old French stockade on site of an Indian village; inc. as village in 1849.

Waukesha (wô'kĭshô), county (□ 556; pop. 85,901), SE Wis.; ⊙ Waukesha. Hilly dairying and farming area, with many resort lakes. Mfg. at Waukesha and Oconomowoc; processing of dairy products is important throughout co. Includes Cushing Memorial State Park. Drained by Fox and Bark rivers. Formed 1846.

Waukesha, city (pop. 21,233), ⊙ Waukesha co., SE Wis., on Fox R. and 16 mi. W of Milwaukee, in dairying and farming area; mfg. (motors; iron, steel, and aluminum products; farm implements, leather goods, air-conditioning equipment, furniture, dairy products, beer). Health resort noted for mineral springs, whose waters are shipped. Seat of Carroll Col. and industrial school for boys. State tuberculosis sanatorium near by. Alexander W. Randall lived here. Settled c.1834, inc. 1895.

Waukewan, Lake (wô'kĭwŏn), Belknap co., central N.H., resort lake just W of Meredith and L. Winnipesaukee, and 9 mi. NNW of Laconia; 2 mi. long.

Waukomis (wôkō'mĭs), town (pop. 537), Garfield co., N Okla., 8 mi. S of Enid; wheat, livestock, poultry; dairy products.

Waukon (wô'kŭn", wôkŏn'), city (pop. 3,158), ⊙ Allamakee co., extreme NE Iowa, 16 mi. E of Decorah; mfg. (dairy, concrete, and wood products; beverages); livestock shipping. Limestone quarries near by. Has annual corn festival. Settled 1849, inc. 1883.

Waulsort (vôlsôr'), village (pop. 565), Namur prov., S Belgium, on Meuse R. and 5 mi. SSW of Dinant; tourist resort. Has 17th-cent. castle.

Waunakee (wô"nùkē'), village (pop. 1,042), Dane co., S Wis., on tributary of Yahara R. and 8 mi. NNW of Madison, in farming and dairying area; dairy products, canned vegetables.

Wauneta (wŏnē'tù), village (pop. 926), Chase co., S Nebr., 40 mi. WNW of McCook and on Frenchman Creek; grain. Light and power plant is here.

Waun Fach, Wales: see BLACK MOUNTAINS.

Waupaca (wôpă'kù), county (□ 751; pop. 35,056), central Wis.; ⊙ Waupaca. Drained by Wolf and Embarrass rivers. Dairying and general farming area (livestock, potatoes, canning crops); some mfg. Includes chain of lakes. Formed 1851.

Waupaca, city (pop. 3,921), ⊙ Waupaca co., central Wis., on Waupaca R. (tributary of Wolf R.) and 34 mi. W of Appleton, in timber and farm area (potatoes, livestock; dairy products); mfg. (stoves, furnaces, concrete products). Center of lake-resort region. Inc. 1875.

Waupun (wôpŭn'), city (pop. 6,725), on Fond du Lac–Dodge co. line, E central Wis., on Rock R and 17 mi. SW of Fond du Lac, in farm and dairy region; mfg. (vulcanizing machinery, pumps, tanks, brake linings, foundry products, art supplies, shoes, beverages, dairy products, canned vegetables). The state prison and a state hosp. for insane are here. Settled 1838, inc. 1878.

Waurai (wou"rī'), volcanic island (□ 275; 1940 pop. 26,394), largest of the Mauri Group, SW Pacific, 950 naut. mi. W of Nauru; 1°6'S 165°3'E. Port of call for transoceanic lines; airport; trades in copra, pearls, mother-of-pearl, sponges.

Wauraltree Island, Australia: see WARDANG ISLAND.

Wauregan, Conn.: see PLAINFIELD.

Waurika (wŏrē'kŭ, wô–), city (pop. 2,327), ⊙ Jefferson co., S Okla., 23 mi. S of Duncan, and on Beaver Creek; trade center for farm area (livestock, grain, cotton, corn); cotton ginning and compressing; mfg. of farm implements, trailers. Oil and gas wells. Grain elevator, poultry hatchery. Settled c.1890, inc. 1903.

Wausa, village (pop. 708), Knox co., NE Nebr., 60 mi. W of Sioux City, Iowa; dairying, grain, livestock, poultry.

Wausau (wô'sô), city (pop. 30,414), ⊙ Marathon co., central Wis., on Wisconsin R. and 85 mi. WNW of Green Bay; commercial center for important dairying area; mfg. of paper, woodwork, machinery, electrical apparatus, plastics, chemicals. Cheese factories, breweries; granite quarries. Near by is Rib Mtn., known for winter sports. Settled 1839, Wausau grew as a lumber town. Inc. 1872.

Wausaukee (wôsô'kē), resort village (pop. 612), Marinette co., NE Wis., on small Wausaukee R. and 25 mi. NW of Marinette, in lake region; cigar mfg.

Wauseon (wô'sēŏn), village (pop. 3,494), ⊙ Fulton co., NW Ohio, 32 mi. WSW of Toledo, in farming and dairying area; mfg. (electrical apparatus, food products, furniture, auto parts, machinery, construction materials). Settled 1835, inc. 1852.

Waushara (wôshä'rŭ), county (□ 628; pop. 13,920), central Wis.; ⊙ Wautoma. Dairying and farming area (rye, poultry, potatoes); timber. Many small lakes (resorts) and W end of L. Poygan in co. Drained by small White and Pine rivers and Willow Creek. Formed 1851.

Wautoma (wôtō'mŭ), city (pop. 1,376), ⊙ Waushara co., central Wis., near small White R., 37 mi. W of Oshkosh, in farm and timber area; dairy products, pickles, beverages. Summer resort. Inc. as village in 1901, as city in 1940.

Wauwatosa (wôwŭtō'sŭ), industrial city (pop. 33,324), Milwaukee co., SE Wis., adjacent to and W of Milwaukee; mfg. (iron castings, leather and wood products, chemicals, concrete and metal products); stone quarries. Seat of several co. institutions. Settled 1835; inc. as village in 1892, as city in 1897.

Wauzeka (wôzē'kŭ), village (pop. 564), Crawford co., SW Wis., near confluence of Wisconsin and Kickapoo rivers, 13 mi. ENE of Prairie du Chien; makes cheese, cheese boxes, handles.

Wave Hill, settlement (dist. pop. 142), W central Northern Territory, Australia, 340 mi. S of Darwin; cattle; airport.

Waveland. 1 Town (pop. 553), Montgomery co., W Ind., near small Little Raccoon Creek, 34 mi. SSW of Lafayette; ships grain. **2** Resort town (pop. 793), Hancock co., SE Miss., 18 mi. WSW of Gulfport, on Mississippi Sound.

Waveney River, Suffolk and Norfolk, England, rises 7 mi. SW of Diss, flows 50 mi. NE, past Diss, Harleston, Bungay, and Beccles, to confluence with Yare R. at W end of BREYDON WATER, 4 mi. WSW of Yarmouth. Navigable below Bungay. Its lower course passes through The BROADS.

Waver, Belgium: see WAVRE.

Waverley, municipality (pop. 74,800), E New South Wales, Australia, on coast 4 mi. SE of Sydney, in metropolitan area; brass foundries, shoe and furniture factories. Bathing beach on Bondi Bay.

Waverley, village in FARNHAM urban dist., W Surrey, England. At "Moor Park," Sir William Temple's estate, Jonathan Swift lived and met "Stella." There are ruins of a Cistercian abbey, founded 1128.

Waverley, Mass.: see BELMONT.

Waverly. 1 Town (pop. 306), Lee and Chambers counties, E Ala., 12 mi. NW of Opelika; lumber. **2** Village (1940 pop. 540), Polk co., central Fla., 9 mi. S of Haines City; mfg. of fertilizer, insecticides; citrus-fruit packing. **3** City (pop. 1,330), Morgan co., central Ill., 21 mi. SW of Springfield, in agr. area (corn, wheat, oats, livestock). Inc. 1867. **4** City (pop. 5,124), ⊙ Bremer co., NE Iowa, on Cedar R. and 17 mi. NNW of Waterloo; rail junction; processes poultry, dairy products; canneries; mfg. of malt syrup, pharmaceuticals, feed, farm tools, caskets, cement blocks. Seat of Wartburg Col. (coeducational; 1868), with Waverly Mus. (1894); and of a Lutheran orphans' home. Inc. 1859. **5** City (pop. 487), Coffey co., E Kansas, 31 mi. E of Emporia, in livestock and grain area. **6** Town (pop. 345), Union co., W Ky., 16 mi. WSW of Henderson, in agr. and bituminous-coal area. **7** Resort village (pop. 493), Wright co., S central Minn., on small lake and 35 mi. W of Minneapolis, in grain and livestock area; dairy products, beverages. **8** Town (pop. 809), Lafayette co., W central Mo., on Missouri R. and 19 mi. E of Lexington; grain, apples, livestock. **9** Village (pop. 310), Lancaster co., SE Nebr., 12 mi. NE of Lincoln, near Salt Creek of Platte R. **10** Village (pop. 6,037), Tioga co., S N.Y., near Pa. line, on Chemung R. and 16 mi. ESE of Elmira; mfg. (feed, furniture, textiles, clothing, milk cans). Agr. (dairy products; poultry, truck). Inc. 1853. **11** Village (pop. 1,679), ⊙ Pike co., S Ohio, 14 mi. S of Chillicothe and on Scioto R.; market center for agr. area; lumber, wood products, concrete products. Lake White State Park (resort) is near by. Village founded 1829. **12** Town (pop. 1,892), ⊙ Humphreys co., central Tenn., 55 mi. W of Nashville, near Kentucky Reservoir, in timber, livestock-raising, peanut-growing region; makes work shirts, wood products, concrete blocks. Indian mounds near by. Laid out 1836. **13** Town (pop. 1,502), Sussex co., SE Va., near Blackwater R., 21 mi. SE of Petersburg; trade center in agr. area (peanuts, livestock); lumber-milling. Inc. 1892. **14** Town (pop. 120), Spokane co., E Wash., 22 mi. SSE of Spokane, in wheat-growing region.

Waverly Hall, town (pop. 690), Harris co., W Ga., 21 mi. NE of Columbus; textile, wood products.

Wavertree, SE residential district (pop. 30,702) of Liverpool, SW Lancashire, England; mfg. of leather goods; metalworking.

Wavre (väv'rŭ), Flemish *Waver* (vä'vŭr), town (pop. 8,254), Brabant prov., central Belgium, on Dyle R. and 14 mi. SE of Brussels; agr. market.

Wavre-Notre Dame, Belgium: see ONZE LIEVE VROUW-WAVER.

Wavre-Sainte-Catherine, Belgium: see SINT-KATELIJNE-WAVER.

Wavrin (vävrē'), town (pop. 3,023), Nord dept., N France, on Deûle R. and 6 mi. SW of Lille; flour milling, tanning, mfg. (tar, chicory, slippers).

Waw (wô), village, Pegu dist., Lower Burma, on Pegu-Sittang canal, at crossing of Pegu-Martaban RR, and 60 mi. NE of Rangoon.

Wawa (wŏ'wŭ), village (pop. estimate 50), central Ont., near Wawa L. (5 mi. long), 100 mi. NNW of Sault Ste. Marie; iron mining.

Wawaitin Falls (wŭwī'tĭn), waterfalls (126 ft. high), NE Ont., on Mattagami R., at N end of Kenogamissi L., 11 mi. SW of Timmins.

Wawanesa (wŏ"wŭnē'sŭ), village (pop. 423), SW Man., on Souris R. and 21 mi. SE of Brandon, in livestock, mixed-farming area.

Wawa River, Nicaragua: see HUAHUA RIVER.

Wawarsing (wŭwôr'sĭng), resort village, Ulster co., SE N.Y., just W of the Shawangunk range, on Rondout Creek and 3 mi. NE of Ellenville.

Wawasee Lake (wäwŭsē'), N Ind., at Syracuse; c.4 mi. long; largest lake in Ind. Resort center. Fish hatchery.

Wawota (wŭwō'tŭ), village (pop. 291), SE Sask., near Man. border, on Little Pipestone Creek and 23 mi. SW of Moosomin; mixed farming.

Waxahachie (wŏk"sĭhă'chē, wŏk"–), city (pop. 11,204), ⊙ Ellis co., N Texas, 27 mi. S of Dallas; market, processing point in rich blackland agr. region; cotton market; also ships truck, nursery stock; mfg. of clothing, textiles, cottonseed oil, furniture; pecan shelling, honey packing. Seat of Southwestern Bible Inst. Founded 1847, inc. 1871.

Waxell Ridge (wăk'sŭl), S Alaska, uneven expanse of peaks and glaciers in E portion of Chugach Mts., N of Bering Glacier; 60°40'N 143°W.

Waxhaw (wăks'hô), town (pop. 818), Union co., S N.C., 12 mi. SW of Monroe, near S.C. line.

Waya, Fiji: see YASAWA.

Wayah Bald Mountain, W N.C.: see NANTAHALA MOUNTAINS.

Waya Lailai, Fiji: see YASAWA.

Wayaopu, China: see CHANGTZE, Shensi prov.

Waycross (wā'krôs), city (pop. 18,899), ⊙ Ware co., SE Ga., c.75 mi. NW of Jacksonville, Fla., near Satilla R. and N of Okefenokee Swamp; tobacco market and shipping center with railroad shops; mfg. (shoes, boxes, lumber, naval stores). Settled 1818, inc. 1874.

Waygiou, Netherlands New Guinea: see WAIGEU.

Wayland. 1 Town (pop. 600), Henry co., SE Iowa, 14 mi. NNW of Mount Pleasant, in livestock and grain area; metal products. Amish-Mennonite colony here. **2** Mining town (pop. 1,807), Floyd co., E Ky., in Cumberland foothills, 16 mi. W of Pikeville; bituminous coal. Timber, oil, and gas in area. **3** Residential town (pop. 4,407), Middlesex co., E Mass., on Sudbury R. and 15 mi. W of Boston; truck, dairying, poultry. Settled c.1638, inc. 1835. Includes Cochituate village (1940 pop. 952), near Cochituate L. **4** Village (pop. 1,591), Allegan co., SW Mich., 20 mi. S of Grand Rapids, in farm area (onions, corn, hay); mfg. (flour, feed, dairy products, sports equipment). Settled 1836, inc. 1858. **5** Town (pop. 350), Clark co., extreme NE Mo., near Mississippi and Des Moines rivers, 8 mi. ESE of Kahoka. **6** Village (pop. 1,834), Steuben co., W central N.Y., 40 mi. S of Rochester; mfg. (chairs, silk, canned foods); agr. (dairy products; grain, potatoes). Summer resort. Inc. 1877.

Wayland Wood, England: see WATTON.

Waymart, borough (pop. 1,068), Wayne co., NE Pa., 5 mi. E of Carbondale. Has mental hosp. Inc. 1851.

Wayne. 1 County (□ 646; pop. 14,248), SE Ga.; ⊙ Jesup. Bounded NE by Altamaha R., SW by Little Satilla R. Coastal plain agr. (tobacco, cotton, corn, livestock) and forestry (lumber, naval stores) area; textile mfg. at Jesup. Formed 1803. **2** County (□ 715; pop. 20,933), SE Ill.; ⊙ Fairfield. agr. area (livestock, poultry, fruit, corn, wheat, hay, redtop seed). Oil wells. Mfg. (clothing, auto parts, paper boxes). Drained by Little Wabash R. and small Elm Creek. Formed 1819. **3** County (□ 405; pop. 68,566), E Ind.; ⊙ Richmond. Bounded E by Ohio lines; drained by Whitewater R., its East Fork, and other tributaries. Agr. (grain, poultry, livestock; dairy products; flower growing); mfg., especially at Richmond; timber. Formed 1819. **4** County (□ 532; pop. 11,737), S Iowa, on Mo. line (S); ⊙ Corydon. Prairie agr. area (hogs, cattle, poultry, corn, soybeans, oats), with bituminous-coal deposits mined in E and S; drained by a branch of Chariton R. Formed 1846. **5** County (□ 484; pop. 16,475), S Ky.; ⊙ Monticello. In Cumberland foothills; bounded S by Tenn.; crossed by Cumberland R. Hilly agr. area; burley tobacco, grain, livestock. Bituminous-coal mines, oil wells, rock quarries; timber. Includes part of Cumberland Natl. Forest. Formed 1800. **6** County (□ 607; pop. 2,435,235), SE Mich.; ⊙ DETROIT. Bounded E by Detroit R. and lakes St. Clair and Erie; drained by Huron R. and the River Rouge. Detroit and the mfg. cities of its metropolitan area produce most of U.S. automobiles and auto parts. Co. has many residential suburbs of Detroit; has farms (especially truck, stock, and dairy farms) and nurseries. Commercial fishing; salt mining. Formed 1796. **7** County (□ 827; pop. 17,010), SE Miss.; ⊙ Waynesboro. Bordered E by Ala.; drained by Chickasawhay R. and Bucatunna and Thompsons creeks. Includes part of Chickasawhay Natl. Forest. Agr. (cotton, corn), cattle raising; lumbering. Formed 1809. **8** County (□ 777; pop. 10,514), SE Mo.; ⊙ Greenville. In Ozark region; drained by St. Francis and Black rivers. Corn, oats, hay, livestock; oak, pine, hickory timber; granite deposits. Parts of Clark Natl. Forest and Wappapello Dam and Reservoir here. Formed 1818. **9** County (□ 443; pop. 10,129), NE Nebr.; ⊙ Wayne. Farm area drained by Logan Creek. Livestock, grain, dairy and poultry produce. Formed 1870. **10** County (□ 607; pop. 57,323), W N.Y.; ⊙ Lyons. Bounded N by L. Ontario (resorts on lake); drained by Canandaigua Outlet, Clyde R., and small Mud Creek; crossed by Barge Canal. Rich fruit-, truck-, and nut-growing region; diversified mfg. at Lyons, Newark, and Sodus. Also dairy farming. Formed 1823. **11** County (□ 555; pop. 64,267), E central N.C.; ⊙ GOLDSBORO. Coastal plain area, intersected by Neuse R. Farming (tobacco, cotton, corn), sawmilling; mfg. at Goldsboro. Formed 1779. **12** County (□ 561; pop. 58,716), N central Ohio; ⊙ Wooster. Intersected by Killbuck Creek, small Chippewa and Sugar creeks, and Lake Fork of Mohican R. Agr. (livestock, poultry, grain, fruit; dairy products). Mfg. at Wooster and Orrville. Sand and gravel pits; coal mining; oil and gas wells; salt production. Formed 1812. **13** County (□ 744; pop. 28,478), NE Pa.; ⊙ Honesdale. Lake region drained by Lackawaxen R.; bounded E by Delaware R. Separated from anthracite region of Lackawanna co. by Moosic Mtn. on W border. L. Wallenpaupack is on Pike co. border. Farming, fruitgrowing; recreation. Formed 1798. **14** County (□ 741; pop. 13,864), S Tenn.; ⊙ Waynesboro. Bounded S by Ala.; drained by Buffalo R. and tributaries of Tennessee R. Timber, limestone, and iron-ore deposits; lumbering; mfg. of wood products; diversified agr. (corn, cotton, soybeans, livestock). Formed 1817. **15** County (□ 2,489; pop. 2,205), S central Utah; ⊙ Loa. Mtn. and plateau area crossed by Dirty Devil R. and bounded on E by Green R. Capital Reef Natl. Monument is E of Torrey; natl. forest area in W. Agr., livestock. Formed 1892. **16** County (□ 573; pop. 38,696), W W.Va.; ⊙ Wayne. On Allegheny Plateau; bounded W by Tug Fork and Big Sandy R. (Ky. line), N by Ohio R. (Ohio line); drained by Twelve Pole Creek. Agr. (livestock, fruit, tobacco, truck); bituminous-coal mines, oil and natural-gas wells, sand and gravel pits; timber. Industry at Wayne, Kenova, and HUNTINGTON (partly in co.). Formed 1842.

Wayne. 1 Town (pop. 459), Kennebec co., S Maine, on Androscoggin L. and 16 mi. W of Augusta; wood products, toys. **2** Village (pop. 9,409), Wayne co., SE Mich., 18 mi. SW of Detroit and on a branch of the River Rouge; mfg. (aircraft and auto parts, oil and gasoline strainers, foundry products); truck and poultry farming. Settled 1836, inc. 1869. **3** City (pop. 3,595), ⊙ Wayne co., NE Nebr., 37 mi. SW of Sioux City, Iowa, and on branch of Logan Creek; beverages; grain, livestock, dairy and poultry produce. State teachers col. here. Platted 1881. **4** Village (pop. 761), Wood co., NW Ohio, 11 mi. ESE of Bowling Green; eggs, dairy products, grain; oil wells. Until 1931, called Freeport. **5** Town (pop. 501), McClain co., central Okla., near Canadian R., 40 mi. SSE of Oklahoma City; cotton ginning. **6** Residential village, Delaware co., SE Pa., 13 mi. NW of Philadelphia; metal products; crushed stone. **7** Town (pop. 1,257), ⊙ Wayne co., W W.Va., on Twelve Pole Creek and 14 mi. S of Huntington, in bituminous-coal region; makes glass.

Wayne, Fort, Mich.: see DETROIT.

Wayne City, village (pop. 726), Wayne co., SE Ill., 17 mi. E of Mount Vernon, in agr. area.

Waynesboro. 1 City (pop. 4,461), ⊙ Burke co., E Ga., 26 mi. S of Augusta, in cotton-growing area; mfg. (clothing, canned foods, fertilizer, metal products, veneer, furniture, lumber). Laid out 1783, inc. 1812. **2** Town (pop. 3,442), ⊙ Wayne co., SE Miss., 29 mi. E of Laurel, near Chickasawhay R.;

trade center for farming, lumbering, and stock-raising area. **3** Borough (pop. 10,334), Franklin co., S Pa., 50 mi. SW of Harrisburg. Fruitgrowing; mfg. (machinery, metal products, clothing, flour); limestone. Resort center. Occupied 1863 by Confederates. Settled 1798, inc. 1818. **4** City (pop. 1,147), ⊙ Wayne co., S Tenn., 25 mi. WNW of Lawrenceburg, in timber and diversified agr. region; lumbering; wood products. **5** City (pop. 12,357), independent of any co., W central Va., in Shenandoah Valley, on South R. and 11 mi. SE of Staunton; trade and industrial center in apple-growing, dairying region; large rayon plant; also mfg. of furniture, wood products, stoves, textiles, food products, pencils, pipe-organ parts. Girls' preparatory school and jr. col., military school for boys here. S entrance to Skyline Drive near by. Settled 1700; inc. as town 1797, as city 1948, when it was separated from Augusta co. Near here, in March, 1865, Union troops defeated Confederates under Early.

Waynesburg. **1** Village (pop. 1,258), Stark co., E central Ohio, 11 mi. SE of Canton; makes tile, brick, refractories; coal mining. **2** Agr. borough (pop. 5,514), ⊙ Greene co., SW Pa., 40 mi. SSW of Pittsburgh; dairy products, livestock; bituminous coal, sandstone; bricks, flour, timber. Waynesburg Col. here. Laid out 1796, inc. 1816.

Waynesfield, village (pop. 733), Auglaize co., W Ohio, 11 mi. SSE of Lima, in agr. area.

Waynesville. **1** Village (pop. 516), De Witt co., central Ill., 18 mi. SSW of Bloomington, in agr. area. **2** Town (pop. 1,010), ⊙ Pulaski co., central Mo., in Ozarks, near Gasconade R., 26 mi. WSW of Rolla; agr. **3** Resort town (pop. 5,295), ⊙ Haywood co., W N.C., 25 mi. WSW of Asheville, near Great Smoky Mts. Natl. Park (NW). Mfg. (rubber and wood products, shoes). Settled before 1800; inc. 1871. **4** Village (pop. 1,016), Warren co., SW Ohio, 16 mi. SSE of Dayton and on Little Miami R.; food products, cement blocks, lumber. Laid out 1796.

Waynetown, town (pop. 658), Montgomery co., W Ind., 10 mi. WNW of Crawfordsville; lumber, feed, flour, tile, brick; clay pits; timber.

Waynoka (wānō'kŭ), town (pop. 2,018), Woods co., NW Okla., 19 mi. SW of Alva, near Cimarron R.; railroad division point, with repair shops; sand, gravel pits. Settled c.1893, inc. 1910.

Wayzata (wīzĕ'tŭ, wīzā'tŭ), city (pop. 1,791), Hennepin co., E Minn., on L. Minnetonka, 13 mi. W of Minneapolis; trade center for resort and agr. area.

Waziers (väzyā'), NE residential suburb (pop. 9,658) of Douai, Nord dept., N France, in coal-mining basin.

Wazikha or **Wazikhwah** (both: wŭzē'khŭ), town (pop. over 2,000), Kabul prov., E Afghanistan, 100 mi. S of Ghazni, near Pakistan line. Sometimes called Marjan.

Wazima, Japan: see WAJIMA.

Wazirabad (vŭzē'räbäd"), town (pop. 27,079), Gujranwala dist., NE Punjab, W Pakistan, 19 mi. NNW of Gujranwala. Rail junction; trade center; timber depot (logs floated down Chenab R. from Kashmir forests collected here); wheat, rice, millet; mfg. of cutlery, locks, rubber goods, walking sticks, hosiery; cotton ginning, tanning; sawmills, metalworks.

Waziristan (vŭzē'rĭstän), tribal region (□ 5,214; 1951 pop. 264,000), SW North-West Frontier Prov., W Pakistan, in N end of Sulaiman Range; bounded W by Afghanistan (separated by Durand Line), S by Gumal R. A mountainous area with dispersed crops (wheat, corn, barley, millet) and local handicraft industries; exports timber (chiefly pine), firewood, hides, mats, ghee to plains (E); goat and sheep grazing. Among Pathan tribes, Waziris predominate. Border incidents and internal disturbances (late-19th to early-20th cent.) led British to set up police posts and undertake retaliatory measures. Administered as 2 political agencies: **North Waziristan** (1951 pop. 128,000), with hq. at Miram Shah; **South Waziristan** (1951 pop. 136,000), with hq. at Wana.

Wazzan, Fr. Morocco: see OUEZZANE.

Wda River (vŭdä') or **Czarna Woda** (chär'nä vô'dä) [Pol.,=black water], Ger. *Schwarzwasser* (shvärts'vä"sŭr), N Poland, rises 5 mi. SE of Bytow, flows 115 mi. generally SSE, through L. Wdzydze, past Swiecie, to Vistula R. just below Swiecie. Several water locks and hydroelectric plants on lower course.

Wdzydze, Lake (vŭdzĭ'dzĕ), Ger. *Weitsee* (vīt'zā") (□ 5.5), NW Poland, on Bydgoszcz-Gdansk prov. border, 6 mi. S of Koscierzyna; 7 mi. long, branching out into several arms. Wda R. flows through.

We, island, Indonesia: see WE ISLAND.

Weakley (wēk'lē), county (□ 576; pop. 27,962), NW Tenn.; ⊙ Dresden. Bounded N by Ky.; drained by headstreams of Obion R. Tobacco, corn, cotton, livestock, sweet potatoes, fruit; timber; some mfg. at Dresden. Formed 1823.

Weald, The (wēld), region in England, formerly forested, bet. the North Downs and South Downs, in Kent, Surrey, and Sussex. The forests formerly supported an important iron industry, based on locally-mined ores. Region now has grazing and hop and fruit cultivation.

Wealdstone (wēld'stŭn), residential former urban district (1931 pop. 27,019), Middlesex, England, just N of Harrow; mfg. of cameras, photographic equipment, glassware. Inc. 1934 in Harrow.

Weare (wâr, wēr), town (pop. 1,345), Hillsboro co., S N.H., 12 mi. SW of Concord and on Piscataquog R.; agr., wood products, toys. Inc. 1764.

Weare Giffard (wēr' jĭ'fŭrd), village and parish (pop. 297), N Devon, England, on Torridge R. and 4 mi. SSE of Bideford; tourist resort; agr. market in strawberry area. Has 15th-cent. church.

Wear River (wēr), England, rises 12 mi. W of Stanhope, near Cumberland border, flows 65 mi. E and NE through Durham co., past Wolsingham, Bishop Auckland, Durham, and Chester-le-Street, to North Sea at Sunderland. Navigable below Durham.

Weatherby, town (pop. 156), De Kalb co., NW Mo., 33 mi. ENE of St. Joseph.

Weatherford. **1** City (pop. 3,529), Custer co., W Okla., 14 mi. E of Clinton; trade center in agr. area (wheat, cotton); cotton ginning; wood products. Seat of Southwestern Inst. of Technology. Near by is an Indian hosp. Founded 1893. **2** City (pop. 8,093), ⊙ Parker co., N Texas, 27 mi. W of Fort Worth; shipping, market center for rich fruit, truck area (melons; also cotton, grains, pecans, peanuts, cattle); cottonseed and peanut oil milling, pecan shelling, grain milling, mfg. of oil-field equipment, clothing. Seat of a jr. col. and a childrens' home. Founded 1856.

Weatherly, borough (pop. 2,622), Carbon co., E central Pa., 7 mi. E of Hazleton; castings, electrical products, machinery, steel; agr. Inc. 1863.

Weathersby, village (pop. 145), Simpson co., S central Miss., 33 mi. SE of Jackson.

Weathersfield, town (pop. 1,288), Windsor co., SE Vt., on the Connecticut, just below Windsor. Includes villages of Ascutney (near Mt. Ascutney), and Perkinsville (pop. 142). Settled c.1775–80.

Weaubleau (wô'blō), town (pop. 432), Hickory co., central Mo., in the Ozarks, 14 mi. SE of Osceola.

Weaver, town (pop. 743), Calhoun co., E Ala., 7 mi. N of Anniston.

Weaver Mountains, in section of Prescott Natl. Forest, W central Ariz., SW of Prescott; rises to 6,583 ft.

Weaver River, Cheshire, England, rises 10 mi. SSW of Crewe, flows 45 mi. N and NW, past Nantwich, Northwich, and Winsford, to Mersey R. 2 mi. SSW of Runcorn. Receives Dane R. at Northwich; navigable below Winsford.

Weaverville. **1** Village (1940 pop. 739), ⊙ Trinity co., N Calif., in Klamath Mts., near Trinity R., 30 mi. NW of Redding; gold. Hq. for Trinity Natl. Forest. Many bldgs., including a Chinese joss house, date from gold rush days. **2** Resort town (pop. 1,111), Buncombe co., W N.C., 7 mi. N of Asheville; has mineral springs.

Webb, county (□ 3,294; pop. 56,141), SW Texas; ⊙ LAREDO, important U.S.–Mex. border city on the Rio Grande, which forms W and SW boundary of co. Irrigated agr. area in valley of Rio Grande, produces onions, other vegetables, melons; also some corn, hay, peanuts, livestock (poultry, hogs, sheep, goats). Cattle ranching in uplands. Oil, natural-gas wells; clay, coal deposits. Formed 1848.

Webb. **1** Town (pop. 344), Houston co., SE Ala., 7 mi. NE of Dothan. **2** Town (pop. 235), Clay co., NW Iowa, 15 mi. SSE of Spencer, in livestock and grain area. **3** Town (pop. 680), Tallahatchie co., NW central Miss., 31 mi. NNW of Greenwood.

Webb, Lake, Franklin co., W central Maine, near Weld; 4 mi. long. Drains through Webb River c.15 mi. S to the Androscoggin.

Webb City. **1** City (pop. 6,919), Jasper co., SW Mo., near Spring R., just N of Joplin; mfg. (shoes, clothing, explosives), dairy products; gravel pits. Platted 1875. **2** Town (pop. 284), Osage co., N Okla., 26 mi. WNW of Pawhuska, in agr. area; cotton ginning.

Webber, city (pop. 96), Jewell co., N Kansas, 32 mi. NW of Concordia, near Nebr. line, in grain and livestock region.

Webbers Falls, town (pop. 489), Muskogee co., E Okla., 21 mi. SE of Muskogee, and on Arkansas R.; cotton ginning. Site of a flood-control reservoir on the Arkansas is near by.

Webberville, village (pop. 600), Ingham co., S central Mich., 20 mi. ESE of Lansing, in farm area.

Webbe Shibeli, Ethiopia and Ital. Somaliland: see SHEBELI, WEBI.

Webbo, Liberia: see WEBO.

Webbwood, town (pop. 415), SE central Ont., on Spanish R. and 45 mi. WSW of Sudbury; nickel, copper, gold mining; lumbering.

Weber, New Zealand: see TI TREE POINT.

Weber (wē'bŭr), county (□ 549; pop. 83,319), N Utah; ⊙ Ogden. Agr. area drained by Weber and Ogden rivers. Includes small part of Great Salt L. in W and part of Cache Natl. Forest and Wasatch Range in E. Livestock, alfalfa, grain, sugar beets, fruit, and truck produce are raised in irrigated area in vicinity of Ogden (important mfg. and shipping center). Co. formed 1850.

Weber River (wē'bŭr), rises in Uinta Mts. near Hayden Peak, N central Utah, flows W, through deep canyon, then NW past Echo City and Morgan to Ogden, where it joins Ogden R.; the combined stream flows to Bear River Bay in Great Salt L.; c.125 mi. long. Echo Dam (151 ft. high, 1,887 ft. long; completed 1931), on river at Echo, forms Echo Reservoir; used for irrigation in Morgan, Summit, Weber, and Davis counties.

Webi Shebeli, Ethiopia and Ital. Somaliland: see SHEBELI, WEBI.

Webo or **Webbo** (wĕ'bō), town, Eastern Prov., SE Liberia, on Cavalla R. (Ivory Coast border) and 35 mi. NNE of Harper; cacao, coffee, cassava, rice.

Web River or **Webi Gestro** (wĕ'bē jĕ'strō), Ital. *Uebi Gestro*, Harar prov., S Ethiopia, rises in highlands 10 mi. NW of Goba, flows c.325 mi. SE to the Ganale Dorya 10 mi. N of Dolo.

Webster. **1** County (□ 195; pop. 4,081), W Ga.; ⊙ Preston. Coastal plain area intersected by Kinchafoonee R. Agr. (corn, truck, fruit, peanuts, pecans); livestock, sawmilling. Formed 1853. **2** County (□ 718; pop. 44,241), central Iowa; ⊙ Fort Dodge. Prairie agr. area (cattle, hogs, poultry, corn, soybeans, hay) drained by Des Moines R. Contains valuable gypsum bed (mined at Fort Dodge); also coal, clay, sand and gravel. Formed 1851. **3** County (□ 339; pop. 15,555), W Ky.; ⊙ Dixon. Bounded NE by Green R., SW by Tradewater R. Rolling agr. area (livestock, grain, hay, poultry, tobacco, fruit); bituminous coal mines, gas wells; timber. Formed 1860. **4** Parish (□ 626; pop. 35,704), NW La.; ⊙ Minden. On Ark. line (N) and partly bounded E by Black Lake Bayou. Agr. (corn, cotton, hay, peanuts, sweet potatoes). Oil and natural-gas wells and refineries; sand, gravel pits. Cotton ginning, lumber and paper milling. Drained by Bayou Dorcheat (navigable). Part of L. Bistineau is in S. Formed 1871. **5** County (□ 416; pop. 11,607), central Miss.; ⊙ Walthall. Drained by Big Black R. and tributaries of Yalobusha R. Agr. (cotton, lespedeza, corn, poultry); lumbering. Formed 1874. **6** County (□ 590; pop. 15,072), S central Mo.; ⊙ Marshfield. In the Ozarks; drained by James R. and Niangua R. Agr. region (corn, wheat, fruit, tomatoes), livestock; oak timber. Formed 1855. **7** County (□ 575; pop. 7,395), S Nebr.; ⊙ Red Cloud. Agr. area bounded S by Kansas; drained by Republican R. Flour, livestock, grain, dairy and poultry produce. Formed 1871. **8** County (□ 551; pop. 17,888), central W.Va.; ⊙ Addison. On Allegheny Plateau; drained by Elk and Gauley rivers. Partly in Monongahela Natl. Forest. Bituminous-coal mining, agr. (livestock, fruit, tobacco); timber; hunting, fishing. Includes Holly R. State Park. Formed 1860.

Webster. **1** Town (pop. 569), Sumter co., central Fla., 17 mi. SW of Leesburg; ships truck produce. **2** Town (pop. 136), Keokuk co., SE Iowa, 7 mi. N of Sigourney; livestock, grain. **3** Town (pop. 1,212), Androscoggin co., SW Maine, just E of Lewiston; mfg. (textiles, shoes, shoe manufacturers' supplies). Sabattus (sŭbăt'ŭs) village and Sabattus Pond (4 mi. long) are on N edge of town. Settled 1774, set off from Lisbon 1840. **4** Town (pop. 13,194), including Webster village (pop. 12,160), Worcester co., S Mass., on branch of Quinebaug R. and 16 mi. SSW of Worcester, near Conn. line; woolens, shoes, optical goods; dairying, fruit. Settled c.1713, inc. 1832. Includes East Village, resort on L. Chaubunagungamaug. **5** Town (pop. 386), Merrimack co., S central N.H., on Blackwater R. and 12 mi. NW of Concord. Home of Daniel Webster and N.H. orphans' home here. **6** Village (pop. 1,773), Monroe co., W N.Y., near L. Ontario, 10 mi. ENE of Rochester, in fruit- and truck-growing area; mfg. (caskets, vinegar, pectin, canned foods, wood and metal products). Summer resort. Inc. 1905. **7** Town (pop. 142), Jackson co., W N.C., on Tuckasegee R. just S of Sylva. **8** Village (1940 pop. 1,394), Westmoreland co., SW Pa., 19 mi. S of Pittsburgh and on Monongahela R. **9** City (pop. 2,503), ⊙ Day co., NE S.Dak., 48 mi. E of Aberdeen, in lake region. Resort; shipping point for livestock and poultry products; wheat, hogs, dairy products. Co. fair grounds are here. Platted 1880. **10** Resort village (pop. 552), Burnett co., NW Wis., in lake region, 23 mi. WNW of Spooner; dairy products, woodwork.

Webster, Lake, Mass.: see CHAUBUNAGUNGAMAUG, LAKE.

Webster, Mount, N.H.: see PRESIDENTIAL RANGE.

Webster City, city (pop. 7,611), ⊙ Hamilton co., central Iowa, on Boone R. and 17 mi. E of Fort Dodge; rail junction; mfg. and trade center; farm machinery and equipment, washing machines, packed poultry and eggs, dairy products, feed, concrete. Sand and gravel pits near by. Has a jr. col. and a pioneer mus. Settled 1851, inc. 1874.

Webster Groves, city (pop. 23,390), St. Louis co., E Mo., near Mississippi R., just W of St. Louis; petroleum products. Webster Col. (part of St. Louis Univ.), Eden Theological Seminary (Protestant). Inc. 1896.

Webster Lake, N.H.: see FRANKLIN.

Webster Springs or **Addison,** town (pop. 1,313), ⊙ Webster co., central W.Va., on Elk R. and 18 mi. NNE of Richwood; health resort, with mineral springs. Hunting, fishing near by. Inc. 1892 as Addison, still its official name.

Websterville, Vt.: see BARRE.

Weches (wĕ'chĭs), village, Houston co., E Texas, 20 mi. NE of Crockett, in Davy Crockett Natl. Forest. Near by in Mission Park is replica of Mission San Francisco de los Tejas (1690), 1st Sp. mission in E Texas.

Wechsel (vĕk'sŭl), an outlier (5,702 ft.) of Eastern Alps, E Austria, on Styria–Lower Austria border, SE of the Semmering.

Wechselburg (vĕk'zŭlbŏŏrk), village (pop. 1,620), Saxony, E central Germany, on the Zwickauer Mulde and 3 mi. SSW of Rochlitz; agr. market. Of Augustinian monastery of Zschillen (founded 1174), the noted Romanesque church remains.

Wecker (vĕ'kŭr), village (pop. 147), E Luxembourg, on Syre R. and 3 mi. WNW of Grevenmacher; metal casting, mfg. (machine tools, pumps, presses, mining equipment). Just NW is industrial village of Biver (pop. 671).

Weda, Indonesia: see HALMAHERA.

Weddell Sea (wĕ'dŭl,–dĕl), embayment of the South Atlantic in Antarctica, SSE of South America, bet. Palmer Peninsula and Coats Land, in about 70°S 40°W. Discovered 1823 by James Weddell, Br. navigator.

Wedderburn, town (pop. 878), W central Victoria, Australia, 125 mi. NW of Melbourne, in livestock area; eucalyptus oil. Former gold-mining town.

Wedding (vĕ'dĭng), workers' residential district (1939 pop. 325,099; 1946 pop. 234,854), N central Berlin, Germany, on Berlin-Spandau Canal (port). Mfg. (electrical equipment, machinery). After 1945 in French sector.

Wedel (vä'dŭl), town (pop. 14,027), in Schleswig-Holstein, NW Germany, on Elbe estuary, 12 mi. W of Hamburg city center; shipbuilding; petroleum refining; mfg. of optical instruments, chemicals, electrotechnical goods, cigarettes; food processing. Hydroelectric plant. Suburb of Schulau (inc. 1875) has fishing and dredge harbor. Town was damaged in Second World War. Nurseries (fruit trees, berry bushes), asparagus growing, and horticulture in vicinity.

Wedge Island, Australia: see GAMBIER ISLANDS.

Wedgeport, town (pop. 1,327), SW N.S., on the Atlantic, 10 mi. SE of Yarmouth; fishing (noted for its tuna), lumbering. Irish moss center. Until 1909 called Tusket Wedge.

Wedmore, agr. village and parish (pop. 2,382), N central Somerset, England, 7 mi. WNW of Wells. Has 15th-cent. church. In 878 Alfred the Great here signed Peace of Wedmore with Danes.

Wednesbury (wĕnz'bŭrē, wĕj'–), municipal borough (1931 pop. 31,531; 1951 census 34,758), S Stafford, England, 5 mi. SE of Wolverhampton, in the Black Country; steel center (steel casting and rolling, production of bars, nuts, bolts, railroad rolling stock, machinery; mfg. of light metals). Believed to have been site of a temple of Woden (Wotan), for whom town is named. Mentioned as site of a battle bet. Saxons and Britons in 592; in 916 Æthelflæd built a castle here. The Perpendicular church of St. Bartholomew is noteworthy.

Wednesfield (wĕns'fēld, wĕj'–), residential urban district (1931 pop. 9,330; 1951 census 17,422), S Stafford, England, 2 mi. NE of Wolverhampton; chemical and metalworking industries. The town's history goes back to Saxon times.

Wedowee (wīdou'ē), town (pop. 559), ⊙ Randolph co., E Ala., near confluence of Little Tallapoosa and Tallapoosa rivers, 37 mi. ESE of Talladega; cotton ginning.

Wedza (wĕd'zä), village, Salisbury prov., E Southern Rhodesia, in Mashonaland, 30 mi. S of Marandellas; tobacco, peanuts, citrus fruit; livestock. Police post. Gold mining (S) near Sabi R.

Weed, lumber-milling village (pop. 2,739), Siskiyou co., N Calif., at W base of Mt. Shasta, 25 mi. SW of Yreka; also creosotes lumber, makes finished wood products.

Weedon, village (pop. estimate 500), S Que., on St. Francis R. and 30 mi. NE of Sherbrooke; lumbering, dairying.

Weedon Beck, agr. village and parish (pop. 1,753), W Northampton, England, on Nene R. and 8 mi. W of Northampton, on Watling Street, a Roman road. The church is of Norman origin and replaces that of a convent established here in 7th cent.

Weed Patch, village (pop. c.1,200), Kern co., S central Calif., 10 mi. SSE of Bakersfield; cotton, potatoes.

Weedsport, village (pop. 1,588), Cayuga co., W central N.Y., on the Barge Canal and 20 mi. W of Syracuse; mfg. of feed, flour, furniture, typewriters; lumber milling. Agr. (dairy products; poultry, fruit). Inc. 1831.

Weehawken (wē'hô"kŭn, wē"hô'kŭn), township (pop. 14,830), Hudson co., NE N.J., on Hudson R. just N of Hoboken, at W terminus of Lincoln Tunnel; mfg. (restaurant equipment, clothing, caskets, decalcomanias); textile bleaching, dyeing, and finishing. Inc. 1859. "Highwood," the James Gore King estate, was scene (1804) of duel bet. Aaron Burr and Alexander Hamilton; bronze bust of Hamilton, who was fatally wounded, marks site.

Weekapaug (wē'kŭpôg), coast village (pop. c.500) in Westerly town, Washington co., SW R.I., 5 mi. SE of Westerly village.

Weeksbury, mining town (pop. 1,340), Floyd co., SE Ky., in Cumberland foothills, 16 mi. SW of Pikeville; bituminous coal.

Weeks Island (pop. 1,499), one of the Five Isls., in Iberia parish, S La., a salt dome in sea marshes just inland from E shore of Vermilion Bay, 13 mi. S of New Iberia; alt. c.200 ft.; pop. 1,250. Has state's largest rock-salt mine; mfg. of chemicals.

Weeksville, village, Pasquotank co., NE N.C., near Albemarle Sound 6 mi. SSE of Elizabeth City, in agr. area; sawmilling.

Weems, village (1940 pop. 730), Lancaster co., E Va., on the Rappahannock and 45 mi. N of Newport News; fisheries; seafood canning, mfg. of fishing equipment.

Weende (vān'dŭ), village (pop. 5,047), in former Prussian prov. of Hanover, W Germany, after 1945 in Lower Saxony, on the Leine, just N of Göttingen; mfg. of chemicals; leather-, metal-, and woodworking; paper milling.

Weenen (vē'nŭn) [Du.,=weeping], town (pop. 2,828), W Natal, U. of So. Afr., on Bushmans R. and 30 mi. SE of Ladysmith; rail terminus; stock, dairying. One of oldest settlements in Natal, it was founded 1839 by Voortrekkers. Several of their advance parties were attacked and killed in region (1838) by Zulu forces under chief Dingaan.

Weener (vā'nŭr), town (pop. 5,649), in former Prussian prov. of Hanover, NW Germany, after 1945 in Lower Saxony, on left bank of the Ems and 6 mi. SW of Leer; customs station near Dutch border; food processing.

Weenusk (wē'nŭsk), village, N Ont., on Hudson Bay, at mouth of Winisk R.; 55°15'N 85°13'W; Hudson's Bay Co. trading post.

Weeping Water, city (pop. 1,070), Cass co., SE Nebr., 30 mi. E of Lincoln and on Weeping Water Creek, near Missouri R.; stone products; timber, grain, livestock, fruit, poultry products. Near by is experimental fruit farm of Univ. of Nebr. City inc. 1857.

Weeping Water Creek, SE Nebr., rises E of Lincoln, flows c.40 mi. E, past Weeping Water, to Missouri R. near Nebraska City.

Weert or **Weerd** (both: vārt), town (pop. 12,604), Limburg prov., SE Netherlands, 16 mi. SE of Eindhoven and on the Zuid-Willemsvaart, 5 mi. N of Belg. border; mfg. (steel and tinplate products, weighing machines, matches, woolen fabrics, flour, dextrine); lithography, brewing, shipbuilding. Has 15th-cent. church. Near by is only zinc plant in Netherlands.

Weesp (vāsp), town (pop. 7,600), North Holland prov., W central Netherlands, on Vecht R. and 8 mi. SE of Amsterdam; cacao products, pharmaceuticals; dairying, cattle raising.

Weetslade (wēts'lād), former urban district (1931 pop. 7,734), SE Northumberland, England, 6 mi. N of Newcastle-upon-Tyne. Here are coal-mining towns of Annitsford, Dudley, Seaton Burn, and Wideopen. Weetslade inc. (1935) in Seaton Valley.

Weeze (vā'tsŭ), village (pop. 5,325), in former Prussian Rhine Prov., W Germany, after 1945 in North Rhine-Westphalia, in the Ruhr, on the Niers and 4 mi. SSE of Goch.

Weferlingen (vā'fŭrlĭng"ŭn), village (pop. 4,806), in former Prussian Saxony prov., central Germany, after 1945 in Saxony-Anhalt, on the Aller and 15 mi. W of Haldensleben, opposite Grasleben; sugar refining, flour milling; brickworks.

Wegan (wē'gŭn), village (pop. 1,520, with near-by Flat Creek), Walker co., NW central Ala., 18 mi. WNW of Birmingham.

Wegberg (vāk'bĕrk), agr. village (pop. 9,724), in former Prussian Rhine Prov., W Germany, after 1945 in North Rhine-Westphalia, 27 mi. NNE of Aachen. Enlarged 1935 through incorporation of Beeck.

Wegeleben (vā'gŭlā"bŭn), town (pop. 4,749), in former Prussian Saxony prov., central Germany, after 1945 in Saxony-Anhalt, on the Bode and 6 mi. E of Halberstadt; agr. market (sugar beets, grain, vegetables).

Weggis (vĕ'gĭs), town (pop. 2,067), Lucerne canton, central Switzerland, on N shore of L. of Lucerne, at SW foot of the Rigi, 6 mi. ESE of Lucerne; year-round resort.

Weggs, Cape, N Ungava Peninsula, NW Que., on Hudson Strait: 62°28'N 73°43'W.

Weglewo, Poland: see SOBIECIN.

Wegliniec (vĕglē'nyĕts), Pol. *Węgliniec*, Ger. *Kohlfurt* (kōl'fŏŏrt), commune (1939 pop. 2,741; 1946 pop. 3,602) in Lower Silesia, after 1945 in Wroclaw prov., SW Poland, 14 mi. NNE of Görlitz, important rail junction; lignite mining, glass mfg. After 1945, briefly called Kalawsk, Pol. *Kaławsk*.

Wegorapa River, Poland and USSR: see ANGERAPP RIVER.

Wegorzewo (vĕgô-zhĕ'vô), Pol. *Węgorzewo*, Ger. *Angerburg* (äng'ŭrbŏŏrk), town (1939 pop. 10,922; 1946 pop. 1,184) in East Prussia, after 1945 in Olsztyn prov., NE Poland, in Masurian Lakes region, just N of L. Mamry, on Angerapp R. and 30 mi. S of Chernyakhovsk (Insterburg; now in Kaliningrad oblast), near USSR border; rail junction; lake fishing and shipping. Founded 1571 by Teutonic Knights. Almost totally destroyed in Second World War.

Wegorzyno (vĕgô-zhĭ'nô), Pol. *Węgorzyno*, Ger. *Wangerin* (väng'ŭrĭn), town (1939 pop. 3,454; 1946 pop. 348) in Pomerania, after 1945 in Szczecin prov., NW Poland, 25 mi. NE of Stargard; grain, sugar beets, potatoes, livestock; starch mfg.

Wegrow (vĕ'grŏŏf), Pol. *Węgrów*, Rus. *Vengrov* (vĕn'grŭf), town (pop. 5,185), Warszawa prov., E Poland, on Liwiec R. and 45 mi. ENE of Warsaw; tanning, mfg. of cement, shingles, parchment; food processing (flour, cereals, dairy products, vinegar).

Wegscheid (väk'shīt), village (pop. 3,018), Lower Bavaria, Germany, in Bohemian Forest, 15 mi. ENE of Passau, on Austrian border; rail terminus; mfg. (damask, linen, madras muslin, shoes).

Wegstadl, Czechoslovakia: see STETI.

Wehbach, Germany, see KIRCHEN-WEHBACH.

Wehlau, Russian SFSR: see ZNAMENSK.

Wehlen (vā'lŭn), town (pop. 2,149), Saxony, E central Germany, in Saxonian Switzerland, on the Elbe and 4 mi. E of Pirna; agr. market; sandstone quarrying. Climatic health resort. Synthetic-oil plant at suburb of Herrenleithe or Herrenleite (both: hĕ'rŭnlī"tŭ). Bastei, 2 mi. E, is noted tourist spot overlooking the Elbe.

Wehlitz (vā'lĭts), village (pop. 2,002), in former Prussian Saxony prov., central Germany, after 1945 in Saxony-Anhalt, on the White Elster, just WSW of Schkeuditz; lignite mining; paper milling.

Wehr (vâr), village (pop. 4,343), S Baden, Germany, on S slope of Black Forest, 11 mi. E of Lörrach; mfg. (cotton, chemicals, paper). Has ruined castle.

Wehrden (vâr'dŭn), village (pop. 1,064), in former Prussian prov. of Westphalia, NW Germany, after 1945 in North Rhine-Westphalia, on left bank of the Weser and 4 mi. S of Höxter; rail junction.

Wehrden, Saar: see VÖLKLINGEN.

Wei, China: see WEI RIVER.

Wei (wā), **Ui,** or **Ü** (both: ü), Chinese *Ch'ien-tsang* (chyĕn'dzäng') [=anterior Tibet], E central historical province of Tibet; main town, Lhasa.

Weichang or **Wei-ch'ang** (wā'chăng') [Chinese, =hunting park], town, ⊙ Weichang co. (pop. 110,179), W Jehol prov., SW Manchuria, 70 mi. WSW of Chihfeng; lumbering center; wool, hemp. Gold deposits. Located in a former imperial hunting park, old Weichang (25 mi. E) was founded in 1863. Present Weichang was called Chutzeshan until 1931, when co. seat was moved to present site.

Weicheng, China: see KARAKHOTO.

Weichow, town, China: see WAIYEUNG.

Weichow or **Wei-chou** (both: wā'jō'), volcanic island in Gulf of Tonkin, Kwangtung prov., China, 30 mi. S of Pakhoi; 4 mi. long, 3 mi. wide. Fishing port of Weichow is on S shore.

Weichsel River, Poland: see VISTULA RIVER.

Weichwan or **Wei-ch'uan** (both: wā'chwän'), town, ⊙ Weichwan co. (pop. 108,369), N Honan prov., China, 40 mi. SW of Kaifeng; grain.

Weida (vī'dä), town (pop. 13,511), Thuringia, central Germany, on small Weida R. near its mouth on the White Elster, and 8 mi. S of Gera; textile milling (cotton, wool, jute), metalworking; mfg. of carpets, leather, shoes. Has medieval Osterburg castle, town hall (1580), and remains of Romanesque church.

Weiden (vī'dŭn). **1** City (1950 pop. 37,686), Upper Palatinate, E Bavaria, Germany, in Bohemian Forest, on the Waldnab and 31 mi. SE of Bayreuth; 49°41'N 12°10'E. Railroad repair shops; mfg. of glass, porcelain, textiles; printing, woodworking. Has mid-16th-cent. city hall. Chartered before 1270. **2** Village, Rhine Prov., Germany: see BROICHWEIDEN.

Weidenau, Czechoslovakia: see VIDNAVA.

Weidenau (vī'dŭnou), town (pop. 12,718), in former Prussian prov. of Westphalia, W Germany, after 1945 in North Rhine-Westphalia, on the Sieg and 2 mi. N of Siegen, in iron-ore-mining region.

Weidenthal (vī'dŭntäl), village (pop. 1,892), Rhenish Palatinate, W Germany, in Hardt Mts., 8 mi. NW of Neustadt; wine; apricots, peaches.

Weidling (vī'lĭng), town (pop. 2,581), E Lower Austria, suburb of Vienna, near the Danube, 1 mi. SW of Klosterneuburg; summer resort.

Weidman (wīd'mŭn), village (pop. c.350), Isabella co., central Mich., 11 mi. NW of Mt. Pleasant, in agr. area.

Weifang (wā'făng'), city (1934 pop. 82,781), E Shantung prov., China, 30 mi. NW of Tsingtao and on railroad to Tsinan; industrial and coal-mining center, with mines at FANGTZE; cotton and silk weaving, match mfg., flour milling, tobacco processing. As ⊙ Weihsien co. (1946 pop. 647,086), city was called Weihsien until 1949, when it was set up as an independent municipality and renamed Weifang.

Weihai (wā'hī'), until 1949 called **Weihaiwei** (wā'hī'wā'), city (1946 pop. 222,247; 1947 pop. estimate 175,000), NE Shantung prov., China, Yellow Sea port on Weihai Bay, sheltered by Liukung Isl., 140 mi. NE of Tsingtao; commercial center; cotton and silk weaving, oilseed milling; mfg. of rubber goods, matches, soap. A small village until end of 19th cent., it was captured in 1895 by Japanese, who held it until 1898. The city and surrounding area (□ 285) was leased (1898–1930) by China to Great Britain. A neutral zone, including the entire tip of the Shantung peninsula E of c.121°35'E, adjoined the leased area. The

British, who called the city Port Edward, developed the harbor as a coaling station and naval base. During Sino-Japanese War, the port was occupied (1938–45) by the Japanese. It became an independent municipality in 1945.

Wei Ho, China: see WEI RIVER.

Wei-hsi, China: see WEISI.

Weihsien (wā'shyĕn'). **1** Town, ⊙ Weihsien co. (pop. 191,387), SW Hopeh prov., China, 40 mi. E of Singtai; cotton, millet, wheat, kaoliang. **2** City, Shantung prov., China: see WEIFANG.

Wei-hsin, China: see WEISIN.

Weihwei, China: see CHIHSIEN.

Weija, Gold Coast: see DENSU RIVER.

Weikersheim (vī'kŭrs-hīm), town (pop. 2,008), N Württemberg, Germany, after 1945 in Württemberg-Baden, on the Tauber and 5.5 mi. E of Mergentheim; grain. Has Renaissance castle.

Weil (vīl'). **1** or **Weil am Rhein** (äm rīn'), town (pop. 8,792), S Baden, Germany, at S foot of Black Forest, near the Rhine, 2 mi. SSW of Lörrach, on Swiss border; mfg. (textiles, chemicals, machinery). **2** or **Weil im Schönbuch** (ĭm shûn'bōōkh), village (pop. 3,085), N Württemberg, Germany, after 1945 in Württemberg-Baden, 5 mi. SSE of Böblingen; cattle.

Weilburg (vīl'bōōrk), town (pop. 5,882), in former Prussian prov. of Hesse-Nassau, W Germany, after 1945 in Hesse, on the Lahn and 11 mi. NE of Limburg; main town of upper Lahn (Ger. *Oberlahn*) dist.; climatic health resort. Has Renaissance castle.

Weil der Stadt (vīl' dĕr shtät'), town (pop. 3,088), N Württemberg, Germany, after 1945 in Württemberg-Baden, 14 mi. WSW of Stuttgart; cattle. Has 15th-cent. church. Created free imperial city in 13th cent. Kepler b. here. Sometimes spelled Weilderstadt.

Weiler, France: see VILLÉ.

Weilheim (vīl'hīm). **1** Town (pop. 10,717), Upper Bavaria, Germany, on the Ammer and 28 mi. S of Munich; rail junction; metalworking, textile mfg., lumber milling, printing. Has 17th-cent. church. Chartered c.1236. **2** or **Weilheim an der Teck** (än dĕr tĕk'), N Württemberg, Germany, after 1945 in Württemberg-Baden at NE foot of the Teck, 4.5 mi. SE of Kirchheim; grain, cattle.

Weili, China: see KARA KUM.

Weil im Schönbuch, Germany: see WEIL, Württemberg.

Weiltingen (vīl'tĭng-ŭn), village (pop. 1,044), Middle Franconia, W Bavaria, Germany, on the Wörnitz and 6 mi. ESE of Dinkelsbühl; brewing; gypsum, flour, and lumber milling.

Weimar (vī'mär), city (pop. 66,659), ⊙ Thuringia, central Germany, on Ilm R. and 55 mi. WSW of Leipzig, 140 mi. SW of Berlin, in a picturesque country of wooded hills; 50°55'N 29°E. Because of its past role, in early 19th cent., as the cultural center of Germany, Weimar has become symbolic of the most admired qualities in the German nation, just as Potsdam became the symbol of Prussian militarism. Though dating from 10th cent., Weimar was of little importance until 1547, when it became the capital of Wettin dukes of Saxe-Weimar, later (after 1815) grand dukes of Saxe-Weimar-Eisenach. Under Elector John Frederick the Wise, Lucas Cranach the Elder worked here. J. S. Bach was court organist and concert master (1708–17); his sons Karl Philipp Emmanuel and Wilhelm Friedemann were b. here. It was, however, under the dowager duchess Anna Amalia and her son, Charles Augustus, that Weimar reached the peak of its fame as a cultural center. C. M. Wieland at 1st dominated the scene in late 18th cent., but after arrival (1775) of Goethe at the court, Weimar and Goethe became virtually synonymous. Goethe made Weimar the literary mecca of Europe during his lifetime, attracting such men as Herder and Schiller and establishing the Weimar state theater, which saw the 1st performances of most of Goethe's and many of Schiller's plays. Franz Liszt was musical director here, 1848–59, and Wagner's *Lohengrin* had its 1st performance here during Liszt's directorship. In 1919 Weimar was scene of German natl. assembly which created Weimar Republic. Under the Hitler regime, which replaced the Weimar Republic in 1933, the Nazis erected, a few mi. NW of Weimar, a monument to the Germany which Weimar did not symbolize—the concentration camp of Buchenwald. U.S. soldiers entered both Weimar and Buchenwald in April, 1945, but they were replaced by Soviet troops later in the year. Even during its greatest glory Weimar was a quiet small town, and it retains that character. It also has industries, including textile milling, publishing, printing; mfg. of machinery, electrical equipment, musical instruments, glass, tobacco, and paper products. Rail junction. Radio station. Site of meteorological observatory. City's noted features include: city church (rebuilt in 18th cent.), with graves of Lucas Cranach the Elder and Herder; former grand-ducal palace (1790-1803); residences of Schiller and Liszt; Wittums Palace, once residence of Duchess Anna Amalia; graves of Goethe, Schiller, Charlotte von Stein; Goethe-Schiller archives; Nietzsche archives; state theater; and Goethe's residence and his garden cottage (the Gartenhaus). City also has state col. of music; col. of art and architecture. Center of Weimar, damaged in Second World War, has been restored. NE suburb of TIEFURT has many literary associations. At Ehringsdorf (SE) important Stone Age relics were found. BELVEDERE hunting lodge (now mus.) is 2 mi. SSE.

Weimar (wī'mŭr), city (pop. 1,663), Colorado co., S Texas, c.85 mi. W of Houston, in agr. area; cottonseed-oil and feed milling, poultry packing; hatcheries; mfg. of pickles, brooms. Laid out 1873.

Weinan (wā'nän'), town (pop. 80,569), ⊙ Weinan co. (pop. 146,460), SE Shensi prov., China, 40 mi. ENE of Sian, and on Wei R., on Lunghai RR; commercial center; cotton weaving; rice, wheat, ramie.

Weinböhla (vīn"bû'lä), residential town (pop. 10,398), Saxony, E central Germany, 4 mi. E of Meissen; market gardening (asparagus, strawberries).

Weiner (wē'nŭr), town (pop. 644), Poinsett co., NE Ark., 19 mi. SSW of Jonesboro, in agr. area.

Weinert (wī'nŭrt), town (pop. 288), Haskell co., NW central Texas, 60 mi. N of Abilene; rail point in cotton, cattle area.

Weinfelden (vīn'fĕldŭn), town (pop. 5,157), Thurgau canton, N Switzerland, 10 mi. E of Frauenfeld, near Thur R.; shoes, knit goods, beer, flour, pastry, rubber products, cotton textiles; woodworking, printing.

Weingarten (vīn'gär"tŭn). **1** Village (pop. 6,429), N Baden, Germany, after 1945 in Württemberg-Baden, 7 mi. NE of Karlsruhe; paper milling. Vineyards. **2** Village (commune pop. 692), Upper Franconia, N Bavaria, Germany, on the Main and 9 mi. SSE of Coburg. Banz (pop. 110), just SW, has former Benedictine abbey founded c.1700, secularized 1803; occupied by Trappists since 1920. Abbey was completely rebuilt in early 18th cent. Main bldg. has collection of fossils and bones of prehistoric animals, found near by. **3** Town (pop. 10,775), S Württemberg, Germany, after 1945 in Württemberg-Hohenzollern, 2 mi. NNE of Ravensburg; mfg. of machinery. Site of former Benedictine abbey (founded 11th cent.), with baroque church noted for its organ. Chartered 1865.

Weinheim (vīn'hīm), town (pop. 22,876), N Baden, Germany, after 1945 in Württemberg-Baden, on the Bergstrasse, at W foot of the Odenwald, 10 mi. NE of Mannheim; rail junction; leather-working center; mfg. of agr. machinery, rubber tires, brooms, brushes; food processing (noodles, macaroni, pudding powder). Has 16th-cent. town hall. Founded c.500. Property of counts palatine from 13th cent. until 1803. Sometimes called Weinheim an der Bergstrasse (än dĕr bĕrk'shträ"sŭ).

Weining (wā'nĭng'), town (pop. 11,003), ⊙ Weining co. (pop. 178,344), westernmost Kweichow prov., China, 140 mi. W of Kweiyang, near Yunnan border, at hub of highways joining Kweichow and Yunnan; wool-textile mfg., embroidering; wine-growing; grain, timber. Coal mines, lead and copper deposits near by. Projected rail junction.

Weinsberg (vīns'bĕrk), town (pop. 4,751), N Württemberg, Germany, after 1945 in Württemberg-Baden, 3 mi. E of Heilbronn; mfg. of chassis, malt coffee; brickmaking. Has late-Romanesque church; ruined castle. Oecolampadius b. here.

Weipert, Czechoslovakia: see VEJPRTY.

Weir, India: see WER.

Weir (wēr). **1** City (pop. 819), Cherokee co., extreme SE Kansas, 8 mi. SSW of Pittsburg, near Mo. line, in coal-mining and diversified agr. region; mfg. of bricks and tiles. Clay pits in vicinity. **2** Town (pop. 570), Choctaw co., central Miss., 7 mi. WSW of Ackerman.

Weir, Lake, Marion co., N central Fla., 15 mi. SE of Ocala; c.5 mi. long, 3 mi. wide.

Weirgate, village (1940 pop. 1,596), Newton co., E Texas, near Sabine R., c.65 mi. NNE of Beaumont; lumbering.

Wei River. 1 Chinese *Wei Shui* (wā' shwā'), chief right tributary of Yellow R., in NW central China, rises in SE Kansu prov. near Weiyüan, flows 540 mi. E, along N foot of Tsinling Mts., past Lungsi and Tienshui (in Kansu prov.), and into S Shensi prov., past Paoki, Sienyang (near Sian), and Weinan, to Yellow R. bend near Tungkwan. Navigable below Sienyang. Receives King and Lo rivers (left). **2** Chinese *Wei Ho* (wā'hŭ'), river in Pingyuan and Hopeh provs., China, rises in Taihang Mts. on Shansi line, flows 200 mi. NE, past Siuwu, Sinsiang, Chihsien, Taokow (head of navigation), Tsuwang, and Kwantao, to Grand Canal at Lintsing.

Weirs, The, N.H.: see THE WEIRS.

Weirton (wēr'tŭn), steel-making city (pop. 24,005), Hancock and Brooke counties, NW W.Va., in Northern Panhandle, on the Ohio and 25 mi. N of Wheeling; huge integrated steel mills here include one of world's largest tin-plating plants, and others specializing in zinc-coated steel products. Mfg. of chemicals, cement products; coal and clay mining. Grew after 1910 as an uninc. "company town;" became a city 1947, when Weirton, Weirton Heights, Marland Heights, and Hollidays Cove (settled 1776) were consolidated.

Weisenau (vī'zŭnou), SE suburb of Mainz, W Germany, on left bank of the Rhine; portland-cement works.

Weisendorf (–dôrf), village (pop. 1,212), Upper Franconia, N Bavaria, Germany, 8 mi. WNW of Erlangen; grain, hogs.

Weisenheim or **Weisenheim am Sand** (–hīm äm zänt'), village (pop. 3,941), Rhenish Palatinate, W Germany, 5 mi. WSW of Frankenthal; fruit export (apricots, peaches, strawberries).

Weiser (wē'zŭr), city (pop. 3,961), ⊙ Washington co., W Idaho, on Snake R. (here forming Oregon line), at mouth of Weiser R., and 60 mi. NW of Boise; trade and fruit-shipping center for irrigated agr. area (fruit, alfalfa, potatoes, sugar beets, livestock); dairy products, flour, beverages; metal-working. Terminus of North and South Panoramic Highway; hq. Weiser Natl. Forest. Intermountain Inst. (coeducational) is here. Laid out 1877, moved 1 mi. W when fire destroyed original city (1890).

Weiser River, rises in Seven Devils Mts., W Idaho, flows 90 mi. SSW, past Cambridge, to Snake R. at Weiser. Used for irrigation.

Weishih, China: see YÜSHIH.

Wei Shui, China, see WEI RIVER.

Weisi or **Wei-hsi** (both: wā'shē'), town, ⊙ Weisi co. (pop. 30,744), NW Yunnan prov., China, on trade route to Sikang, and 60 mi. WNW of Likiang, near Mekong R.; alt. 7,999 ft.; timber, rice, millet. Iron mines near by.

Weisin or **Wei-hsin** (both: wā'shĭn'), town (pop. 1,330), ⊙ Weisin co. (pop. 72,277), NE Yunnan prov., China, on Szechwan border, 35 mi. SW of Süyung, in mtn. region; rice, millet, wheat. Iron deposits near by.

We Island (wā) (□ 45.6; pop. 8,706), Indonesia, 12 mi. NW of N tip of Sumatra bet. Andaman Sea and Indian Ocean, 14 mi. N of Kutaraja; 5°50'N 95°18'E; 10 mi. long, 8 mi. wide, with deeply indented N coast. Hilly, rising to 2,018 ft. Important primarily as site of SABANG, transit port for NW Sumatra. Also spelled Wai.

Weissandt-Gölzau (vī'sänt-gûl'tsou), village (pop. 1,666), in former Anhalt state, central Germany, after 1945 in Saxony-Anhalt, 11 mi. WNW of Bitterfeld; lignite mining; synthetic-oil plant; power station.

Weisse Elster, Germany: see ELSTER RIVER.

Weissenberg (vī'sŭnbĕrk), town (pop. 1,574), Saxony, E central Germany, in Upper Lusatia, 7 mi. N of Löbau; grain, potatoes, livestock.

Weissenburg, France: see WISSEMBOURG.

Weissenburg or **Weissenburg in Bayern** (–bōōrk ĭn bī'ŭrn), town (1950 pop. 13,806), Middle Franconia, W central Bavaria, Germany, on the Swabian Rezat and 28 mi. S of Nuremberg; gold- and silver-lace mfg., metal- and woodworking, brewing. Hog trade. Parts of Roman fortifications still stand. Has late-Gothic church, 15th-cent. town hall. Founded in 9th cent. on Roman site. Created free imperial city in 1360.

Weissenburg, Rumania: see ALBA-IULIA.

Weissenfels (–fĕls"), city (pop. 50,995), in former Prussian Saxony prov., central Germany, after 1945 in Saxony-Anhalt, on the Saxonian Saale and 20 mi. S of Halle, 20 mi. WSW of Leipzig; 51°12'N 11°59'E. Rail junction; center of lignite-mining region. Shoe-mfg. center; paper milling, sugar refining, metalworking, machinery mfg. Has 16th-cent. courthouse, 17th-cent. castle. On site of anc. Slav settlement. Passed to Prussia in 1815.

Weissenhorn (–hôrn"), town (pop. 5,070), Swabia, W Bavaria, Germany, 10 mi. SE of Ulm; mfg. of machines and precision instruments, brewing, woodworking. Chartered c.1342.

Weissensee (–zā"), lake (□ 2.54) in Carinthia, S Austria, 21 mi. W of Villach, in Gailtal Alps; c.8 mi. long, ½ mi. wide, average depth 118 ft., alt. 3,050 ft. Summer resort of Techendorf (pop. 750) on N shore.

Weissensee. 1 District (1939 pop. 90,277; 1946 pop. 82,017), NE Berlin, Germany, 5 mi. NE of city center. Mfg.: food products, machinery, electrical equipment, radios, rubber products, pharmaceuticals. After 1945 in Soviet sector. **2** Town (pop. 4,535), in former Prussian Saxony prov., central Germany, after 1945 in Thuringia, 15 mi. N of Erfurt; agr. center (grain, tobacco, sugar beets, fruit, livestock); furniture mfg. Has Romanesque castle, Romanesque and Gothic churches.

Weissenstadt (–shtät), town (pop. 3,742), Upper Franconia, NE Bavaria, Germany, in the Fichtelgebirge, on the Eger and 12 mi. SW of Selb; textile mfg., metal- and woodworking. Tin mining; stone cutting. Granite quarries in area.

Weissenstein, Estonia: see PAIDE.

Weissenstein (–shtīn), town (pop. 1,127), N Württemberg, Germany, after 1945 in Württemberg-Baden, 7 mi. N of Geislingen; cattle.

Weissenthurm (–tōōrm), village (pop. 4,359), in former Prussian Rhine Prov., W Germany, after 1945 in Rhineland-Palatinate, on left bank of the Rhine and 6 mi. NW of Coblenz; pumice-stone quarries. At N end of village is a watchtower (1350) which marked the boundaries of electorates of Cologne and Trier.

Weisserberg, Czechoslovakia: see WHITE MOUNTAIN.
Weisser Hirsch (vī'sůr hĭrsh'), E suburb of Dresden, Saxony, E central Germany, on hill overlooking Elbe R.; health resort.
Weisseritz River (vī'sůrĭts), E central Germany, formed just above Hainsberg by Red Weisseritz and Wild Weisseritz rivers, flows 10 mi. NE to the Elbe at Dresden.
Weisser Main, Germany: see WHITE MAIN.
Weisser Regen, Germany: see WHITE REGEN RIVER.
Weisshorn (vīs'hôrn), peak (14,792 ft.), one of highest in Pennine Alps, S Switzerland, 6 mi. N of Zermatt; 1st ascended in 1861. Weisshorn Hütte is SE.
Weisskirchen, Czechoslovakia: see HRANICE.
Weisskirchen (vīs'kĭr"khůn), village (pop. 1,490), N Saar, near Ger. border, 12 mi. NE of Merzig; stock, grain; construction industry. Formerly part of Prussian Rhine Prov.; annexed to Saar in 1946.
Weisskirchen, Yugoslavia: see BELA CRKVA.
Weisskugel (vīs'kōōgůl), Ital. *Palla Bianca* (päl'lä byäng'kä), peak (12,287 ft.) of Ötztal Alps, in Tyrol, on Austro-Ital. border; glaciers.
Weissmies (vīs'mēs), peak (13,209 ft.) in Pennine Alps, S Switzerland, 13 mi. S of Brig, 2 mi. from Ital. border.
Weissnollen (vīs'nôlůn), peak (11,815 ft.) in Alps of the Four Forest Cantons, S central Switzerland, 11 mi. ESE of Meiringen.
Weissport (wīs'pôrt"), borough (pop. 674), Carbon co., E Pa., on Lehigh R. opposite Lehighton.
Weissstein, Poland: see BIALY KAMIEN.
Weisstannental, Switzerland: see SEEZ RIVER.
Weisswasser, Czechoslovakia: see BELA POD BEZDEZEM.
Weisswasser (vīs'vä"sůr), town (pop. 12,490), in former Prussian Lower Silesia prov., E central Germany, after 1945 in Saxony, in Upper Lusatia, 17 mi. S of Forst; lignite-mining, glassmaking, and electric-bulb-mfg. center.
Weistritz River, Poland: see BYSTRZYCA RIVER.
Weitensfeld (vīt'ůnsfĕlt), town (pop. 3,153), Carinthia, S Austria, on Gurk R. and 16 mi. NNW of Klagenfurt; tannery; summer resort.
Weitra (vī'trä), village (pop. 2,038), NW Lower Austria, on Lainsitz R. and 6 mi. SW of Gmünd; mfg. of fustian.
Weitsee, lake, Poland: see WDZYDZE, LAKE.
Weitzekow, Manchuria: see PINHSIEN, Sunkiang.
Weixdorf (vīks'dôrf), residential village (pop. 5,973), Saxony, E central Germany, 8 mi. NNE of Dresden; market gardening.
Weixelburg, Yugoslavia: see VISNJA GORA.
Weiyüan (wā'yüän'). **1** Town, ⊙ Weiyüan co. (pop. 50,147), SE Kansu prov., China, 70 mi. SSE of Lanchow; tobacco processing, cotton weaving. **2** Town (pop. 10,870), ⊙ Weiyüan co. (pop. 356,422), SW Szechwan prov., China, 55 mi. E of Loshan; match mfg.; olives, rice, sugar cane, sweet potatoes, millet, wheat. Coal and iron mining, kaolin quarrying near by. **3** Town, ⊙ Weiyüan co. (pop. 26,491), NE Tsinghai prov., China, 50 mi. NNW of Sining and on Tatung R.; coal-mining center; musk, antlers; mushrooms. Until 1931, Pehtatung. **4** Town, Yunnan prov., China: see KINGKU.
Weiyüanpu, China: see HUCHU.
Weiz (vīts), town (pop. 6,830), Styria, SE Austria, 13 mi. NE of Graz; rail terminus; ironworks. Summer resort.
Wejh or **Al Wajh** (ăl wĕj), town (pop. 5,000), N Hejaz, Saudi Arabia, port on Red Sea, 380 mi. NW of Jidda; 26°15'N 36°27'E. Bedouin trading center on small inlet, Sherm Wejh, a good natural harbor. Sometimes spelled Al Wijh.
Wejherowo (vāhĕrô'vô), Ger. *Neustadt* (noi'shtät), town (1946 pop. 13,407), Gdansk prov., N Poland, 14 mi. WNW of Gdynia; rail junction; mfg. of machinery, furniture, cement, bricks, liqueur, candy; tanning, sawmilling; summer resort.
Wekelsdorf, Czechoslovakia: see TEPLICE NAD METUJI.
Wekusko Lake (wĭkōō'skō) (16 mi. long, 8 mi. wide), W Man., 65 mi. NW of L. Winnipeg. Drains NE into Nelson R. On E shore is Herb Lake village.
Welaka (wēlă'ků), town (pop. 459), Putnam co., N Fla., on St. Johns R., near mouth of Oklawaha R., and 12 mi. S of Palatka; fishing. State fish hatchery and game farm near by.
Welbeck Abbey, seat in Welbeck parish (pop. 12), W Nottingham, England, 8 mi. N of Mansfield. Abbey founded c.1150 by Thomas de Cuckney, became country estate in time of Henry VIII and later seat of the duke of Portland. Present house begun 1604.
Welbeck Colliery Village, England: see WARSOP.
Welborn, village (1940 pop. 913), Wyandotte co., NE Kansas; W suburb of Kansas City, Kansas.
Welch. 1 Town (pop. 483), Craig co., NE Okla., 16 mi. N of Vinita, in farm area; coal mines, natural-gas wells. **2** City (pop. 6,603), ⊙ McDowell co., S W.Va., on Tug Fork and 24 mi. NW of Bluefield; semibituminous-coal-mining center, in Pocahontas coal field; lumber milling, beverage mfg. State hosp. here. Settled 1885; inc. 1894.
Welchpool, N.B.: see CAMPOBELLO ISLAND.
Welcome, village (pop. 712), Martin co., S Minn., 8 mi. W of Fairmont, near Iowa line, in grain, livestock, and poultry area; dairy products. Small lakes near by.
Weld, county (□ 4,004; pop. 67,504), NE Colo.; ⊙ Greeley. Coal-mining and irrigated agr. area, bordering on Wyo. and Nebr.; watered by South Platte R., Cache la Poudre R., Milton L., and Riverside and Empire reservoirs. Sugar beets, beans, livestock. Formed 1861.
Weld, town (pop. 361), Franklin co., W central Maine, on L. Webb and 14 mi. WNW of Farmington. Includes part of Mt. Blue State Park.
Weldaad, village (pop. 203), Berbice co., NE Br. Guiana, near the coast, 38 mi. SE of New Amsterdam; rice, coconuts, sugar cane.
Welden (vĕl'důn), village (pop. 1,741), Swabia, W Bavaria, Germany, 10 mi. NW of Augsburg; grain, livestock. Has Gothic church renovated in baroque style (1732). Chartered 1402.
Weldon. 1 Village (pop. 492), De Witt co., central Ill., 20 mi. NNE of Decatur; corn, oats, beans. **2** Town (pop. 229), Decatur co., S Iowa, 9 mi. S of Osceola, near sources of Weldon and Chariton rivers, in livestock area. **3** Town (pop. 2,295), Halifax co., NE N.C., 5 mi. SE of Roanoke Rapids and on Roanoke R.; lumber and veneer mills, brickworks, tobacco warehouses.
Weldon River, S Iowa and N Mo., rises near Weldon, Iowa, flows c.70 mi. S to Thompson R. near Trenton, Mo.; partly canalized.
Weleetka (wůlē'ků), city (pop. 1,548), Okfuskee co., central Okla., 22 mi. SSW of Okmulgee, and on North Canadian R.; trade center for agr. area (watermelons, cotton, corn, grain); cotton ginning, gasoline mfg., vegetable canning.
Weleri (wělě'rē), town (pop. 8,924), central Java, Indonesia, near Java Sea, 25 mi. W of Semarang; trade center for agr. area (sugar, rice, peanuts, tobacco, coffee, kapok).
Welfare Island (139 acres), in New York city, SE N.Y., in East R. bet. Manhattan and Queens boroughs; crossed by Queensboro Bridge. Site of several city hosps., other municipal institutions. Formerly known as Blackwells Isl., it was once the site of a notorious city workhouse and penitentiary.
Weligama (vā'lĭgůmů), town (pop. 11,916), Southern Prov., Ceylon, on SW coast, 15 mi. ESE of Galle; fishing center; trades in vegetables, rice, coconuts, citronella grass, rubber. Large rock-cut statue of anc. Singhalese king is just W. Alexandrite deposits near by. Seaplane base at Koggala, 7 mi. W.
Welimada (vā'lĭmůdů), town (pop. 585), Uva Prov., S central Ceylon, in Uva Basin, 12 mi. WSW of Badulla; tea processing; rice plantations.
Welkenraedt (vĕl'kůnrät), town (pop. 5,027), Liége prov., E Belgium, 4 mi. NNW of Eupen; ceramics, paving blocks.
Welland (wĕ'lůnd), county (□ 387; pop. 93,836), S Ont., on L. Erie, Niagara R., and N.Y. border; ⊙ Welland.
Welland, city (pop. 12,500), Welland co., S Ont., on Welland R., on Welland Ship Canal, and 20 mi. W of Buffalo; canal port; cotton, steel, cordage mills; foundries, rubber, shoe, and carbide works; center of fruitgrowing region.
Welland River, S Ont., rises S of Hamilton, forms part of Welland Ship Canal, enters Niagara R. at Chippawa. Lower course also called Chippawa.
Welland River, England, rises 7 mi. SW of Market Harborough, flows NE bet. Northampton co. and counties of Leicester and Rutland, entering Lincolnshire and flowing past Spalding to The Wash S of Boston; length, 70 mi.
Welland Ship Canal, S Ont., connecting L. Ontario with L. Erie. Port Weller is at L. Ontario terminal, Port Colborne and Humberstone (4 mi. NNE of St. Catharines) at L. Erie terminal. Serves St. Catharines, Thorold, and Welland. It is 27.6 mi. long with 8 lift locks; overcomes difference in level of 326 ft. and bypasses falls of Niagara R. Completed 1932, it superseded earlier canal, opened 1833. Hydroelectric power.
Wellawaya (vělůvä'yů), village, Uva Prov., SE Ceylon, near the Kirindi Oya, 18 mi. S of Badulla; rice plantations.
Wellenstein (vě'lůn-shtīn), village (pop. 403), SE Luxembourg, near Moselle R., and Ger. border, 2 mi. SW of Remich; grapes.
Welle River, Belgian Congo: see UELE RIVER.
Wellersburg, borough (pop. 369), Somerset co., SW Pa., 7 mi. NW of Cumberland, Md.
Wellesley (wělz'lē), village (pop. c.750), S Ont., on Nith R. and 14 mi. W of Kitchener; woolen knitting, dairying, mixed farming, fruitgrowing.
Wellesley, village, Salisbury prov., NE central Southern Rhodesia, in Mashonaland, on railroad and 30 mi. WNW of Salisbury; tobacco, wheat, corn, citrus fruit, dairy products.
Wellesley, residential town (pop. 20,549), Norfolk co., E Mass., on small L. Waban, 14 mi. WSW of Boston; some mfg. (building supplies, paper boxes, cleaning materials, electric machinery, hosiery). Settled 1660, inc. 1881. Seat of Wellesley Col. and of several preparatory schools and Babson school of business. Includes villages of Wellesley Farms and Wellesley Hills.
Wellesley, Province, Malaya: see PROVINCE WELLESLEY.
Wellesley Farms, Mass.: see WELLESLEY.
Wellesley Hills, Mass.: see WELLESLEY.
Wellesley Island, Jefferson co., N N.Y., one of largest of the Thousand Isls., in the St. Lawrence, at Ont. line, just W of Alexandria Bay; c.7½ mi. long, 1–3 mi. wide. Thousand Island Park village (resort), and Watterson Point and Dewolf Point state parks (camping, bathing, fishing) are here. Isl. is crossed by roadway of Thousand Islands International Bridge, whose spans link it to N.Y. shore and to Hill Isl., Ont. (N). Small Mary Isl. (state park here) is just off NE tip. Formerly Wells Isl.
Wellesley Islands, uninhabited island group in Gulf of Carpentaria, Australia, just off NW coast of Queensland; comprise MORNINGTON ISLAND (largest), Bentinck and Sweers isls., several scattered islets. Rocky, with iron deposits; mangrove forests.
Wellfleet. 1 Town (pop. 1,123), Barnstable co., SE Mass., near N end of Cape Cod, 12 mi. SSE of Provincetown; summer resort; fishing village. Formerly oystering, whaling, and fishing center. Includes South Wellfleet village, with remains of 1st U.S. transatlantic wireless station (1901). Settled c.1720, set off from Eastham 1763. **2** Village (pop. 93), Lincoln co., S central Nebr., 25 mi. S of North Platte and on branch of Republican R.
Wellford, town (pop. 721), Spartanburg co., NW S.C., 9 mi. W of Spartanburg; textiles.
Wellhorn (vĕl'hôrn), peak (10,483 ft.) in Bernese Alps, S central Switzerland, 9 mi. SSE of Brienz. The ridge Welligrat extends N.
Wellingborough, urban district (1931 pop. 21,223; 1951 census 28,220), E central Northampton, England, on Nene R., at mouth of Ise R., 10 mi. NE of Northampton; leather-tanning and shoe-mfg. center, also mfg. of machinery and chemicals for tanning industry, machine tools, clothing; flour milling, iron smelting. Site of public school founded 1595. Has 14th-cent. church. It was formerly known for its chalybeate spring.
Wellingdorf, Germany: see KIEL.
Wellington. 1 Municipality (pop. 4,723), E central New South Wales, Australia, on Macquarie R. and 160 mi. NW of Sydney; gold-mining center; dairy products, wool, wheat. **2** Village, SE South Australia, 55 mi. SE of Adelaide and on NE shore of L. Alexandrina at mouth of Murray R.; dried fruits, dairy products.
Wellington, county (□ 1,019; pop. 59,453), S Ont., on Grand R.; ⊙ Guelph.
Wellington. 1 Village (pop. estimate 400), SW B.C., on SE Vancouver Isl., 4 mi. NW of Nanaimo; coal mining. **2** Village (pop. 1,036), SE Ont., on Wellington Bay of L. Ontario, 13 mi. S of Belleville; resort; dairying; fruit, vegetables.
Wellington. 1 Urban district (1931 pop. 8,186; 1951 census 11,412), central Shropshire, England, 10 mi. E of Shrewsbury; mfg. of machinery, agr. implements, toys, flour. Near by is The WREKIN. In urban dist. is COALBROOKDALE and coal-mining town of Lawley. **2** Urban district (1931 pop. 7,132; 1951 census 7,298), S Somerset, England, on Tone R. and 6 mi. WSW of Taunton, at foot of Black Down Hills; agr. market, with woolen milling, mfg. of asbestos and bricks. Has 15th-cent. church. Duke of Wellington took his title from town; on near-by hill is monument to him.
Wellington, town (pop. 8,372), Nilgiri dist., SW Madras, India, suburb (1.5 mi. NW) of Coonoor; military convalescent station. Formerly called Jakatala. Ordnance depot of Aruvankadu or Aravankadu is just W; cordite mfg.; chemical works (constructed 1949). Army staff col. here.
Wellington, provincial district (□ 10,870; pop. 349,404), S N.Isl., New Zealand; site of Wellington, chief port and ⊙ dominion. Largely mountainous; volcanic mts. in Tongariro Natl. Park. Fertile coastal strip. Chief products: fish, dairy foods, andesite (building stone). Area roughly corresponds to Wellington land dist.
Wellington, city and port (pop. 123,771; metropolitan Wellington 173,520) of New Zealand, on S N.Isl., at head of Wellington harbor (formerly Port Nicholson), on Cook Strait; 41°28'S 174°51'E; ⊙ New Zealand since 1865. Harbor is c.3 mi. wide across mouth, 12 mi. long. Seat of governor-general's residence, houses of Parliament, administration office of Univ. of New Zealand, Victoria Univ. Col. (1897), Natl. Art Gall. (1936), Dominion Mus. (Maori art collection), Anglican cathedral (1938). Railroad center; airport near by. Has auto-assembly plant. Produces fish, andesite (building stone). Exports dairy products, wool, meat, hides. Founded 1840. Wellington is ⊙ Hutt co. (□ 459; pop. 11,524) and ⊙ Makara co. (□ 117; pop. 5,005), but city forms independent unit.
Wellington, town (1931 pop. 1,116), Sierra Leone colony, on Sierra Leone Peninsula, on railroad and 7 mi. ESE of Freetown; sawmilling; cassava, corn.
Wellington, town (pop. 8,199), SW Cape Prov., U. of So. Afr., on Great Berg R. and 40 mi. NE of Cape Town, at foot of Slanghoek Mts., crossed

here by Bain's Kloop Pass leading to Breede R. valley; winegrowing, distilling, fruitgrowing, fruit drying and dehydrating, jam making, flour milling, bacon curing, shoe and leather mfg. Site of Huguenot Univ. Col. (founded 1874 as Huguenot Seminary), a constituent col. of Univ. of South Africa.

Wellington. 1 Town (pop. 541), Larimer co., N Colo., 10 mi. NNE of Fort Collins; alt. 5,000 ft.; supply point; sugar-beets, grain. 2 Village (pop. 300), Iroquois co., E Ill., 28 mi. N of Danville, in rich agr. area. 3 City (pop. 7,747), ⊙ Sumner co., S Kansas, on small affluent of Arkansas R. and 27 mi. S of Wichita; trade and rail center, with railroad repair shops, in wheat region; flour milling. Laid out 1871, inc. 1872. Grew as trading point on Chisholm Trail. Further growth followed development (in early 1930s) of oil fields in vicinity. 4 Town (pop. 636), Jefferson co., N Ky., near Louisville. There is also a village called Wellington in Menifee co. 5 Agr., lumbering town (pop. 252), Piscataquis co., central Maine, 20 mi. SW of Dover-Foxcroft. 6 City (pop. 649), Lafayette co., W central Mo., on Missouri R. and 7 mi. WSW of Lexington. 7 Village (pop. 2,992), Lorain co., N Ohio, 14 mi. S of Elyria, in dairying and grain area; makes castings, trucks, steel products, glass cloth, livestock medicines. 8 City (pop. 3,676), ⊙ Collingsworth co., extreme N Texas, on rolling prairie of the E Panhandle, 30 mi. N of Childress, near Salt Fork of Red R.; trade, shipping, processing center for cotton, grain, poultry, and cattle region; creamery, cotton gins. Inc. 1909. 9 Town (pop. 845), Carbon co., E central Utah, 5 mi. SE of Price; dry ice mfg.

Wellington, Lake, lagoon (□ 54), SE Victoria, Australia, 120 mi. E of Melbourne, near Tasman Sea; joined to L. Victoria (E) by narrow passage; 11 mi. long, 7 mi. wide.

Wellington, Mount, Tasmania: see HOBART.

Wellington Channel, central Franklin Dist., Northwest Territories, arm (120 mi. long, 25–40 mi. wide) of the Arctic Ocean, bet. Cornwallis Isl. (W) and Devon Isl. (E); 75°30′N 93°30′W. Extends N from Barrow Strait; opens WNW on Queens Channel and Penny Strait (total length 80 mi.).

Wellington Island, off Patagonian coast of S Chile, separated by Trinidad Gulf from Madre de Dios Archipelago (S), and from the mainland by narrow channels; bet. 48°37′ and 50°3′S, it is 100 mi. long, c.15–25 mi. wide. Penetrated by many sounds. Wharton Peninsula is a SW arm. Rises to over 3,300 ft. Almost entirely uninhabited.

Wellman, town (pop. 1,071), Washington co., SE Iowa, 20 mi. SW of Iowa City; processed turkeys, feed, concrete. Settled 1879, inc. 1880.

Wellow, agr. village and parish (pop. 1,755), NE Somerset, England 4 mi. S of Bath. Has 14th-cent. church.

Wells, village (pop. estimate 1,250), S central B.C., in Cariboo Mts., 75 mi. SE of Prince George; gold and silver mining.

Wells. 1 Urban district (1931 pop. 2,505; 1951 census 2,592), N Norfolk, England, on Holkham Bay, an inlet of North Sea, 9 mi. N of Fakenham; oyster-fishing port. 2 Municipal borough (1931 pop. 4,381; 1951 census 5,835), E central Somerset, England, 17 mi. S of Bristol, at foot of Mendip Hills; mfg. (paper, brushes, cheese). Site of the magnificent 12th-13th-cent. Cathedral of Bath and Wells, with 15th-cent. woodwork. Cathedral and several other medieval bldgs., including remains of moated bishop's palace, are within medieval walls, forming an ecclesiastical city. There are also 15th-cent. church and 15th-cent. almshouse. Town takes name from wells sacred to St. Andrew. Near by is WOOKEY HOLE.

Wells. 1 County (□ 368; pop. 19,564), E Ind.; ⊙ Bluffton. Agr. area (livestock; dairy products; soybeans, grain); mfg., including farm-products processing; limestone quarrying. Drained by Wabash and Salamonie rivers and small Longlois Creek. Formed 1835. 2 County (□ 1,300; pop. 10,417), formerly known as Gingras co., central N.Dak.; ⊙ Fessenden. Agr. area drained by Sheyenne and James rivers. Dairy products, wheat, barley, rye. Formed 1873.

Wells. 1 Town (pop. 2,321), York co., SW Maine, on the coast and 27 mi. SSW of Portland; includes summer resorts of Wells Beach and OGUNQUIT. Was a center of attack in Indian wars. Settled c.1640, inc. 1653. 2 Village (1940 pop. 793), Delta co., S Upper Peninsula, Mich., 2 mi. N of Escanaba, on Little Bay De Noc; mfg. (wood and concrete products, chemicals). 3 Village (pop. 2,475), Faribault co., S Minn., 20 mi. WNW of Albert Lea; trade center for grain, livestock, poultry area; dairy products, canned corn. Settled before 1870. 4 Town (pop. 947), Elko co., NE Nev., 45 mi. NE of Elko; alt. 5,626 ft. Limestone quarrying; stock, grain, hay. Inc. 1927. East Humboldt Range is SW. 5 Village (pop. c.600), Hamilton co., E central N.Y., in the Adirondacks, on East Branch of Sacandaga R. and 32 mi. N of Amsterdam; logging. 6 Town (pop. 718), Cherokee co., E Texas, 15 mi. NW of Lufkin, in agr. area. 7 Town (pop. 487), Rutland co., W Vt., on L. St. Catharine and N.Y. line, 17 mi. SW of Rutland; slate quarries.

Wells, Mount, Australia: see BURRUNDIE.

Wells, Port, S Alaska, bay (35 mi. long, 1–5 mi. wide) on NE shore of Kenai Peninsula, 60 mi. ESE of Anchorage; opens into Prince William Sound at 60°54′N 148°12′W; placer gold mining in region.

Wells Beach, Maine: see WELLS.

Wellsboro, borough (pop. 4,215), ⊙ Tioga co., N Pa., 37 mi. NNW of Williamsport; glass, wood products, electric-light bulbs, evaporated milk. Settled c.1800, laid out 1806, inc. 1830.

Wellsburg. 1 Town (pop. 744), Grundy co., central Iowa, 30 mi. WSW of Waterloo, in agr. area. 2 Village (pop. 638), Chemung co., S N.Y., on Chemung R. and 7 mi. SE of Elmira, near Pa. line. 3 City (pop. 5,787), ⊙ Brooke co., NW W.Va., in Northern Panhandle, on the Ohio and 15 mi. NNE of Wheeling; mfg. of paper products, glass, cement, sheet-metal cans; coal mines. Platted 1790; chartered 1797.

Wellsford, city (pop. 59), Kiowa co., S Kansas, 16 mi. W of Pratt, in grain and livestock region.

Wells Gray Provincial Park (□ 1,820), E B.C., in Cariboo Mts., 90 mi. N of Kamloops. It rises to over 9,000 ft. Has Hobson, Clearwater, Azure, and Murtle lakes. Hunting, fishing.

Wells Island, N.Y.: see WELLESLEY ISLAND.

Wells River, village (pop. 570), in NEWBURY town, Orange co., E Vt.; paper, printing, dairy products. Wells R. (c.15 mi. long), rising in Groton State Forest, enters the Connecticut here.

Wells Saint Cuthbert Out, agr. parish (pop. 3,426), central Somerset, England, just NE of Wells.

Wellston. 1 Town, Ga.: see WARNER ROBINS. 2 Town (pop. 9,396), St. Louis co., E Mo., suburb W of St. Louis. Inc. since 1940. 3 City (pop. 5,691), Jackson co., S Ohio, 27 mi. SE of Chillicothe; mfg. (machinery, clothing, store fixtures, tools); coal mines; truck gardens. Platted 1874. 4 Town (pop. 643), Lincoln co., central Okla., 28 mi. ENE of Oklahoma City, and on the Deep Fork, in agr. and oil-producing area; cotton ginning, feed milling.

Wellsville. 1 City (pop. 729), Franklin co., E Kansas, 34 mi. SW of Kansas City (Kansas), in stock and grain region; hoe mfg. Oil wells near by. 2 City (pop. 1,519), Montgomery co., E central Mo., near West Fork of Cuivre R., 7 mi. NNW of Montgomery City; grain; brickworks. Laid out 1856. 3 Village (pop. 6,402), Allegany co., W N.Y., on Genesee R. and 21 mi. SW of Hornell, in farming and dairying area; oil-refining center; mfg. of oil-well supplies, turbines, heaters, burial cases, aircraft parts, feed. Summer resort. Site of David A. Howe Library (1937), with mus. and theater. Settled c.1795, inc. 1871. 4 City (pop. 7,854), Columbiana co., E Ohio, on Ohio R. and 17 mi. N of Steubenville; pottery, chinaware, firebrick, clay-working machinery; railroad shops. Founded in late-18th cent. 5 Borough (pop. 309), York co., S Pa., 12 mi. WNW of York. 6 City (pop. 1,241), Cache co., N Utah, on Little Bear R. and 8 mi. SW of Logan; alt. 4,495 ft.; trade and processing center for dairying and irrigated agr. area; condensed milk, flour. Settled 1856 by Mormons, inc. 1866. Hyrum Dam is 3 mi. E. Grouse refuge near by.

Wellwood, village (pop. estimate 150), SW Man., 30 mi. ENE of Brandon; stock, grain.

Welna River (vĕ′ōōnä), Pol. *Wełna*, W Poland, rises 2 mi. ESE of Gniezno, flows N and generally W, past Wagrowiec and Rogozno, to Warta R. at Oborniki; c.60 mi. long.

Welper (vĕl′pŭr), town (pop. 6,952), in former Prussian prov. of Westphalia, W Germany, after 1945 in North Rhine-Westphalia, on the Ruhr and 1.5 mi. NE of Hattingen, in coal- and iron-mining region.

Wels (vĕls), anc. *Ovilava*, city (pop. 36,528), central Upper Austria, on Traun R. and 15 mi. SW of Linz; rail and industrial center, cattle and grain market; mfg. (agr. machinery and implements, food products, earthenware). Large hydroelectric plant; natural gas wells. Founded 15 B.C. as Roman town; later became stronghold against Avars and Magyars. Has municipal mus. with prehistoric and Roman antiquities, Gothic parish church, castle where Emperor Maximilian I died in 1519.

Welsberg, Italy: see MONGUELFO.

Welschap, Netherlands: see EINDHOVEN.

Welscher Belchen, France: see ALSACE, BALLON D'.

Welsh, town (pop. 2,416), Jefferson Davis parish, SW La., 24 mi. E of Lake Charles city, in rice-producing area; rice milling, cotton ginning; mfg. of fertilizer, machine-shop and metal products. Oil field near by. Settled 1880, inc. 1889.

Welshpool, town (pop. 638), SE suburb of Perth, Western Australia; tractors, aluminum and copper ware.

Welshpool, Welsh *Trallwm* (trä′lōōm), municipal borough (1931 pop. 5,639; 1951 census 6,034), E Montgomery, Wales, on Severn R. and 18 mi. WSW of Shrewsbury; agr. market; biscuit factory. Church dates from 14th cent. Formerly flannel-mfg. center. Near by is 12th-cent. Red Castle of earls of Powis or Powys, with galleries, large estate, and deer park. Municipal borough includes districts of Buttington (2 mi. NE; pop. 1,233), Llanerchydol (lă′nĕrkh-ŭdôl′) (W; pop. 1,514), and Guilsfield (N; pop. 1,814).

Welton, town (pop. 93), Clinton co., E Iowa, 25 mi. N of Davenport, in agr. area.

Welungen, Poland: see WIELUN.

Welwarn, Czechoslovakia: see VELVARY.

Welwyn (wĕl′wĭn), agr. village (pop. 249), SE Sask., 14 mi. NNE of Moosomin, near Man. line.

Welwyn (wĕ′lĭn), town and parish (pop. 2,762), central Hertford, England, 8 mi. NE of St. Albans; agr. market; plastics works. Has 13th-cent. church; Edward Young was rector here.

Welwyn Garden City (wĕ′lĭn), residential urban district (1931 pop. 8,586; 1951 census 18,296), central Hertford, England, 7 mi. NE of St. Albans; model residential town, founded 1920 by Sir Ebenezer Howard. There are various light industries, including mfg. of food products, chemicals, pharmaceuticals, plastics, radio receivers. At agr. village of Brocket, 2 mi. W, is Brocket Hall, residence of Lord Melbourne and, later, of Lord Palmerston, who died here.

Welzheim (vĕlts′hīm), town (pop. 4,178), N Württemberg, Germany, after 1945 in Württemberg-Baden, 7 mi. NE of Schorndorf; wine. Site of Roman settlement.

Welzow (vĕl′tsō), town (pop. 7,304), Brandenburg, E Germany, in Lower Lusatia, 9 mi. NE of Senftenberg; lignite mining; glass mfg.

Wem, urban district (1931 pop. 2,157; 1951 census 2,410), N Shropshire, England, 11 mi. N of Shrewsbury; agr. market. Has church with 14th-cent. tower; grammar school founded 1650. Hazlitt spent much of his youth here.

Wema (wĕ′mä), village, Equator Prov., W Belgian Congo, on Tshuapa R. and 60 mi. ESE of Boende; steamboat landing. Rubber plantations near by. Has Protestant mission.

Wembley, village (pop. 237), W Alta., near B.C. border and near Wapiti R., 14 mi. W of Grande Prairie; coal mining, lumbering, mixed farming.

Wembley, residential municipal borough (1931 pop. 48,561; 1951 census 131,369), Middlesex, England, 8 mi. WNW of London; metallurgical and electrical-equipment industries. Has large stadium built for British Empire Exhibition here (1924–25). In the borough are residential areas of Sudbury (W), with chemical industry; Alperton (S), with mfg. of electrical cables, chemicals, pharmaceuticals, and glass; and Kenton (N). In 1934 Wembley absorbed near-by areas, including Kingsbury.

Wemding (vĕm′dĭng), town (pop. 4,130), Swabia, W Bavaria, Germany, 11 mi. NNW of Donauwörth; textile mfg., metalworking. Chartered c.1300. Cold sulphur springs near by.

Wemeldinge (vā′mŭldĭng″ŭ), village (pop. 2,160), Zeeland prov., SW Netherlands, on South Beveland isl. 5 mi. E of Goes, on the Eastern Scheldt, near N end of South Beveland Canal; mfg. (sails, building materials), dairy products.

Weme River, Fr. West Africa: see OUÉMÉ RIVER.

Wemmetsweiler (vĕ′mŭtsvī″lŭr), town (pop. 5,417), E central Saar, 5 mi. WNW of Saarbrücken; coal mining.

Wemyss (wēmz), parish (pop. 26,619, including parts of Leven, and Buckhaven and Methil burghs), central Fifeshire, Scotland. Includes also EAST WEMYSS and COALTOWN OF WEMYSS.

Wenan, China: see SINWEN.

Wenatchee (wĭnă′chē), city (pop. 13,072), ⊙ Chelan co., central Wash., 60 mi. NNE of Yakima and on Columbia R., just below mouth of the Wenatchee. Shipping, processing center of apple-growing region; gateway to recreational areas of eastern Cascade Range; aluminum plant; wheat, lumber, dairy products; clay deposits. Agr. col., agr. experiment station, and a prehistoric Indian carving collection are here. Founded 1888, inc. 1901. **Wenatchee Lake** (5 mi. long), in Cascade Range c.35 mi. NW of Wenatchee, is drained by **Wenatchee River,** flowing c.65 mi. S and SE, past Leavenworth and Cashmere, to Columbia R. above Wenatchee. Used for power. The Wenatchee valley is a chief apple-growing region of Wash.

Wenatchee Mountains, Wash.: see CASCADE RANGE.

Wenceslau Braz, Brazil: see VENCESLAU BRAZ.

Wen-ch'ang, China: see MENCHEONG.

Wenchi (wĕn′chē), town (pop. 3,812), Ashanti, W central Gold Coast, 75 mi. NNW of Kumasi; hardwood, rubber, cacao.

Wen-chiang, China: see WENKIANG.

Wenchow or **Wen-chou** (both: wŭn′jō′), chief city (1948 pop. 156,918) of SE Chekiang prov., China, port on right bank of Wu R. estuary, 15 mi. from E.China Sea, 160 mi. SSE of Hangchow; commercial center of SE Chekiang; mfg. (leather goods, straw mats, paper umbrellas); major timber- and bamboo-shipping point. Its former flourishing tea trade (19th cent.) has declined. Opened to foreign trade in 1876. During Sino-Japanese War, it was briefly held (1944–45) by Japanese. Passed to Communist control in 1949. Wenchow, in 1912, became ⊙ Yungkia co. (1948 pop. 732,447), and in 1949 an independent municipality.

Wenchüan or **Wen-ch'üan** (wŭn′chüăn′). 1 Town, N Inner Mongolian Autonomous Region, Manchuria, on railroad and 130 mi. NW of Ulan Hoto; noted health resort; mineral springs. Also called Halun-Arshan. 2 Town, Sinkiang prov., China: see ARASAN.

Wen-ch'uan, Szechwan prov., China: see WENCHWAN.
Wenchwan or **Wen-ch'uan** (both: wŭn'chwän'), town (pop. 3,540), ⊙ Wenchwan co. (pop. 22,624), NW Szechwan prov., China, 55 mi. NW of Chengtu and on left bank of Min R.; medicinal plants, millet. Marble quarrying, antimony deposits near.
Wendell (wĕn'dŭl). **1** Village (pop. 1,483), Gooding co., S Idaho, 20 mi. NW of Twin Falls; turkeys, bee culture. **2** Town (pop. 342), Franklin co., N Mass., 12 mi. E of Greenfield. State forest here. **3** Village (pop. 284), Grant co., W Minn., on Mustinka R. and 7 mi. WNW of Elbow Lake village; dairy products. **4** Town (pop. 1,253), Wake co., central N.C., 14 mi. E of Raleigh; tobacco market; furniture mfg. Settled c.1890; inc. 1903.
Wendelstein (vĕn'dŭl-shtīn), village (pop. 2,605), Middle Franconia, W central Bavaria, Germany, on Ludwig Canal and 7 mi. SSE of Nuremberg; mfg. of precision instruments, woodworking, brewing; hops, hogs. Has Renaissance town hall.
Wenden (vĕn'dŭn). **1** Village (pop. 2,123), in Brunswick, NW Germany, after 1945 in Lower Saxony, on Weser-Elbe Canal and 4 mi. N of Brunswick, in sugar-beet region. **2** Village (pop. 7,688), in former Prussian prov. of Westphalia, W Germany, after 1945 in North Rhine-Westphalia, 4 mi. S of Olpe; forestry.
Wenden, Latvia: see CESIS.
Wendisch Buchholz, Germany: see MÄRKISCH BUCHHOLZ.
Wendji (wĕn'jē), village, Equator Prov., W Belgian Congo, on left bank of Congo R. and 10 mi. SW of Coquilhatville; boat building and repairing.
Wendlingen (vĕnd'lĭng-ŭn), village (pop. 6,392), N Württemberg, Germany, after 1945 in Württemberg-Baden, 3 mi. NW of Kirchheim; grain, cattle.
Wendover, town and parish (pop. 3,571), central Buckingham, England, at foot of Chiltern Hills, 5 mi. SE of Aylesbury; agr. market. Has 13th-14th-cent. church and manor house associated with John Hampden's family.
Wendover, railroad town, Tooele co., W Utah, 115 mi. W of Salt Lake City, at Nev. line. Near by is Wendover Air Force Base. Bonneville Salt Flats, in Great Salt Lake Desert, are c.10 mi. E.
Wendron, town and parish (pop. 3,314), W Cornwall, England, on Cober R. and 3 mi. NE of Helston; tin mining. Has 14th-cent. church.
Wenduine (wĕn'doinŭ), village (pop. 1,618), West Flanders prov., NW Belgium, on North Sea, 9 mi. NE of Ostend; seaside resort. Formerly spelled Wenduyne.
Wengan (wŭng'än'), town (pop. 5,552), ⊙ Wengan co. (pop. 86,155), E central Kweichow prov., China, 60 mi. NE of Kweiyang; cotton weaving; tobacco products, lacquer, paper, embroidered goods.
Wengen (vĕng'ŭn), year-round resort (alt. 4,190 ft.), Bern canton, S central Switzerland, in Bernese Alps, 6 mi. SSE of Interlaken. **Wengernalp,** a peak (6,156 ft.) 2 mi. S of Wengen, commands a fine view of Jungfrau.
Wengyüan, China: see YUNGYÜN.
Wenham (wĕ'nŭm), residential town (pop. 1,644), Essex co., NE Mass., 5 mi. N of Salem, on small lake. Has old houses. Settled 1635, set off from Salem 1643.
Wen-hsi, China: see WENSI.
Wen-hsiang, China: see WENSIANG.
Wenhsien (wŭn'shyĕn'). **1** Town, ⊙ Wenhsien co. (pop. 90,226), SE Kansu prov., China, near Szechwan border, 33 mi. SW of Wutu; lumbering center; wheat, millet. **2** Town, ⊙ Wenhsien co. (pop. 142,516), SW Pingyuan prov., China, 50 mi. SW of Sinsiang, near Yellow R. (Honan line); cotton weaving; wheat, millet. Until 1949 in Honan prov. Formerly called Chinchengchen.
Wenigenjena (vā'nĭgŭnyä"nä), E suburb of Jena, Thuringia, central Germany, on E bank of the Thuringian Saale. Inn here was frequent summer residence of Goethe (who here wrote the *Erlkönig*) and scene (1815) of founding of the Burschenschaften, nationalist students' organization. Schiller was married in small church here.
Wenkiang or **Wen-chiang** (both: wŭn'jyäng'), town (pop. 19,939), ⊙ Wenkiang co. (pop. 116,915), W Szechwan prov., China, 15 mi. W of Chengtu, on Chengtu plain; rice, wheat, rapeseed, sweet potatoes.
Wenling (wŭn'lĭng'), town (pop. 16,298), ⊙ Wenling co. (pop. 500,379), SE Chekiang prov., China, 35 mi. SE of Linhai, near E. China Sea; rice, wheat, cotton, peanuts. Saltworks near by. Until 1914 called Taiping.
Wenlock, village, N Queensland, Australia, on central Cape York Peninsula, 370 mi. NNW of Cairns; gold mine.
Wenlock, municipal borough (1931 pop. 14,149; 1951 census 15,093), central Shropshire, England, 12 mi. SE of Shrewsbury. Includes agr. market town of Much Wenlock (pop. 2,087), with Elizabethan half-timbered guildhall, and ruins of convent founded c.680, refounded 1080 as a Cluniac priory by Roger de Montgomery. Within Wenlock are coal mines, limestone quarries, iron foundries, pottery- and tileworks. Main towns within municipal borough are Madeley (pop. 7,532), 5 mi. SE of Wellington; Ironbridge, 4 mi. NE of Much Wenlock, with iron bridge (built 1779) over the Severn; Barrow (pop. 1,314), 2 mi. E of Much Wenlock; Broseley (pop. 3,216), 3 mi. ENE of Much Wenlock; and Coalbrookdale, 5 mi. S of Wellington.
Wenona (wĭnō'nŭ). **1** City (pop. 1,005), Marshall co., N central Ill., 12 mi. SSW of Streator, in agr. area; ships grain, soybeans. Inc. 1867. **2** Village, Md.: see DEAL ISLAND.
Wenona Beach, village (pop. 1,295), Bay co., E Mich.
Wenonah (wĭnō'nŭ). **1** Village (pop. 125), Montgomery co., S central Ill., 35 mi. SSE of Springfield, in agr. and bituminous-coal area. **2** Borough (pop. 1,511), Gloucester co., SW N.J., on Mantua Creek and 11 mi. S of Camden. Inc. 1883.
Wenshan (wŭn'shän'), town (pop. 13,464), ⊙ Wenshan co. (pop. 77,331), SE Yunnan prov., China, 150 mi. SE of Kunming; alt. 4,199 ft.; rice, wheat, millet, beans. Silver and iron mines, tungsten deposits near by. Until 1914 called Kaihwa.
Wenshang (wŭn'shäng'), town, ⊙ Wenshang co. (pop. 421,044), W Shantung prov., China, 25 mi. NW of Tzeyang, near Grand Canal (Pingyuan line); wheat, beans, kaoliang.
Wenshui (wŭn'shwā'), town, ⊙ Wenshui co. (pop. 165,148), central Shansi prov., China, 40 mi. SW of Taiyüan; kaoliang, grapes. Coal mines near by.
Wensi or **Wen-hsi** (both: wŭn'shē'), town, ⊙ Wensi co. (pop. 134,501), SW Shansi prov., China, 20 mi. N of Anyi and on railroad; wheat, kaoliang, corn, melons.
Wensiang or **Wen-hsiang** (both: wŭn'shyäng'), town, ⊙ Wensiang co. (pop. 63,921), northwesternmost Honan prov., China, 20 mi. E of Tungkwan and on Lunghai RR; cotton weaving; rice, wheat, beans.
Wensu, China: see KONA SHAHR.
Wensum River, Norfolk, England, rises 6 mi. WSW of Fakenham, flows 30 mi. SE, past Fakenham, to Yare R. just below Norwich.
Wenteng (wŭn'dŭng'), town, ⊙ Wenteng co. (pop. 498,085), easternmost Shantung prov., China, 20 mi. S of Weihai; sericulture; cotton weaving; wheat, beans, millet, kaoliang.
Wentworth, municipality (pop. 2,528), SW New South Wales, Australia, 150 mi. SSE of Broken Hill, at junction of Murray and Darling rivers; sheep center; orchards.
Wentworth, county (□ 458; pop. 206,721), S Ont., at head of L. Ontario; ⊙ Hamilton.
Wentworth, town and parish (pop. 1,729), West Riding, S Yorkshire, England, 7 mi. NNE of Sheffield; coal mining. Site of Wentworth Woodhouse, mansion of Earl Fitzwilliam, located in large park and containing notable art collection.
Wentworth. 1 Town (pop. 212), Newton co., SW Mo., in the Ozarks, 25 mi. E of Joplin. **2** Town (pop. 413), Grafton co., W central N.H., on Baker R. and 13 mi. NNW of Plymouth; state fish hatchery. **3** Village (pop. c.200), ⊙ Rockingham co., N N.C., 7 mi. NW of Reidsville. **4** Town (pop. 270), Lake co., E S.Dak., 8 mi. E of Madison; livestock, grain, dairy produce, poultry.
Wentworth, Lake, Carroll co., E N.H., resort lake near Wolfeboro, just E of L. Winnipesaukee; 4 mi. long. State park.
Wentworth Location, village (pop. c.50), Coos co., NE N.H., at Maine line, on Magalloway R. and 30 mi. NNE of Berlin. Sometimes Wentworths Location.
Wentzville, city (pop. 1,227), St. Charles co., E Mo., 20 mi. W of St. Charles; tobacco center in 1870s.
Wenum (vā'nŭm), village, Gelderland prov., E central Netherlands, 3 mi. N of Apeldoorn; lock mfg.
Weobley (wĕ'blē), town and parish (pop. 625), NW Hereford, England, 10 mi. NW of Hereford; agr. market. Has 14th-cent. church, 16th-cent. Ley House, and some remains of Norman border castle.
Weohyakapka, Lake (wē"hī'kăp'kŭ, wē"ŭhī"ŭ-) (c.4 mi. long, 3 mi. wide), Polk co., central Fla., 10 mi. ESE of Lake Wales, in lake dist.
Wepawaug River (wĕ'pŭwôg"), SW Conn., rises near Woodbridge, flows c.12 mi. SSW to Long Isl. Sound at Milford.
Wepener (vĕ'pŭnŭr), town (pop. 2,920), S Orange Free State, U. of So. Afr., near Basutoland border, near Caledon R., 65 mi. SE of Bloemfontein; alt. 4,718 ft.; distributing center for Basutoland; grain, stock; flour mills.
Wépion (vāpē-ō'), village (pop. 2,760), Namur prov., S central Belgium, on Meuse R. and 3 mi. S of Namur; strawberries.
Wepre, Wales: see CONNAH'S QUAY.
Wer (vār), town (pop. 5,071), E Rajasthan, India, 23 mi. SW of Bharatpur; millet, gram, barley. Sometimes spelled Weir.
Werba, Ukrainian SSR: see VERBA.
Werbellin Lake, Ger. *Werbellinsee* (vĕrbĕ'lĭnzā"), lake (□ 3), Brandenburg, E Germany, just S of Joachimsthal; 7 mi. long, 1 mi. wide, greatest depth 164 ft., average depth 62 ft. Drained SW by short canal into Berlin-Stettin Canal.
Werben (vĕr'bŭn), town (pop. 1,847), in former Prussian Saxony prov., central Germany, after 1945 in Saxony-Anhalt, near the Elbe, 13 mi. SE of Wittenberge; grain, sugar beets, potatoes, livestock. Has late-Gothic church, 15th-cent. town gate. Until 1810, seat of Johannite abbey, founded 1160 by Albert the Bear. Scene (1134) of imperial diet. In Thirty Years War, town was hq. (1631) of Gustavus Adolphus after Tilly's capture of Magdeburg.
Werchter (vĕrkh'tŭr), agr. village (pop. 2,664), Brabant prov., central Belgium, on Dyle R. and 7 mi. N of Louvain; food processing.
Werdau (vâr'dou), town (pop. 27,041), Saxony, E central Germany, on the Pleisse and 6 mi. W of Zwickau; rail junction; cotton-milling center; mfg. of railroad cars, machinery, paper, musical and precision instruments, electrical goods, chemicals.
Werden (vâr'dŭn), industrial district (since 1929) of ESSEN, W Germany, on the Ruhr and 4 mi. S of city center; cloth mfg., paper milling; coal mining. Has 9th-13th-cent. church of former Benedictine abbey (founded c.800).
Werder (vĕr'dŭr), town (pop. 11,310), Brandenburg, E Germany, on the Havel and 5 mi. WSW of Potsdam; fruitgrowing and wine-making center; popular resort. Electrical-equipment mfg.
Werdohl (vĕrdōl'), town (pop. 17,211), in former Prussian prov. of Westphalia, W Germany, after 1945 in North Rhine-Westphalia, on the Lenne and 8 mi. SSE of Iserlohn; rail junction; foundries and metalworks.
Werenow, Belorussian SSR: see VORONOVO.
Werfen (vĕrf'ŭn), town (pop. 3,293), Salzburg, W Austria, at NE foot of Übergossene Alm, on the Salzach and 4 mi. N of Bischofshofen; ironworks, brewery. Iron mined near by.
Weri River (wĕ'rē), Tigre prov., N Ethiopia, rises 5 mi. S of Enticcio, flows c.90 mi. SE and WSW to Takkaze R. 32 mi. SSW of Aksum.
Werl (vĕrl), town (pop. 13,417), in former Prussian prov. of Westphalia, W Germany, after 1945 in North Rhine-Westphalia, 8 mi. W of Soest; saltworks. Resort with saline springs.
Wermelskirchen (vĕr"mŭlskĭr'khŭn), town (pop. 18,868), in former Prussian Rhine Prov., W Germany, after 1945 in North Rhine-Westphalia, 3 mi. S of Remscheid; iron foundries, steel mills; textile mfg. (cotton, silk).
Wernberg (vĕrn'bĕrk), village (pop. 1,064), Upper Palatinate, E Bavaria, Germany, in Bohemian Forest, on the Nab and 9 mi. S of Weiden; glass mfg., woodworking, lumber milling. Has 16th-cent. castle with 13th-cent. watchtower. Chartered bet. 1560-70.
Werne (vĕr'nŭ). **1** or **Werne an der Lippe** (än dĕr lĭ'pŭ), town (pop. 16,592) in former Prussian prov. of Westphalia, NW Germany, after 1945 in North Rhine-Westphalia, on the Lippe and 7 mi. W of Hamm; coal mining. **2** District (since 1929) of Bochum, in former Prussian prov. of Westphalia, W Germany, after 1945 in North Rhine-Westphalia, 4 mi. E of city center; coal mining.
Werner, village (pop. 63), Dunn co., W central N. Dak., 36 mi. NNE of Dickinson and on Spring Creek.
Wernersville, borough (pop. 1,280), Berks co., SE central Pa., 8 mi. W of Reading; limestone; resort. Seat of a unit of Woodstock Col. and Seminary. Founded c.1855.
Werneuchen (vĕr'noi"khŭn), town (pop. 4,218), Brandenburg, E Germany, 16 mi. ENE of Berlin; market gardening.
Wernigerode (vĕr"nĕgŭrō'dŭ), town (pop. 33,800), in former Prussian Saxony prov., central Germany, after 1945 in Saxony-Anhalt, at N foot of the upper Harz, on the Holtemme and 12 mi. WSW of Halberstadt, 40 mi. SW of Magdeburg; 51°49'N 10°48'E. Rail junction; tourist center. Metal- and woodworking, paper milling; mfg. of chemicals, electric motors, leather goods, chocolate. Meteorological observatory. Overlooked by castle (1st mentioned 1213), former seat of princes of Stolberg-Wernigerode. Has Romanesque church, 15th-cent. town hall. Founded in 10th cent.; chartered 1229. Joined Hanseatic League in 1267. Captured (April, 1945) by U. S. troops, later occupied by Soviet forces.
Werra River (vĕ'rä), W Germany, rises in the Thuringian Forest 5 mi. N of Eisfeld, meanders 170 mi. generally N, past Meiningen Eschwege and Bad Sooden-Allendorf, to Münden, where it joins FULDA RIVER to form WESER RIVER. Navigable for small craft in lower course.
Werre River (vĕ'rŭ), NW Germany, rises 6 mi. SE of Detmold, flows 40 mi. N and E, past Herford, to the Weser at Rehme.
Werribee (wĕ'rĭbē), town (pop. 3,146), S Victoria, Australia, 19 mi. WSW of Melbourne, near NW shore of Port Phillip Bay; livestock center; dairy plants, cheese factory. School of Dairy Technology, Dairy Research Inst.
Werris Creek (wĕ'rĭs), town (pop. 2,348), E central New South Wales, Australia, 130 mi. NNW of Newcastle; rail junction; coal-mining center.
Werro, Estonia: see VORU.
Werschetz, Yugoslavia: see VRSAC.
Wertach River (vĕr'täkh), Bavaria, Germany, rises in Allgäu Alps near Austrian border, flows 90 mi. NNE, past Kaufbeuren, to the Lech N of Augsburg.

Werth (vârt), town (pop. 690), in former Prussian prov. of Westphalia, NW Germany, after 1945 in North Rhine-Westphalia, 4 mi. W of Bocholt; cattle.

Wertheim (vârt'hīm), town (pop. 9,368), N Baden, Germany, after 1945 in Württemberg-Baden, on the Main, at mouth of Tauber R., and 18 mi. W of Würzburg; metal (agr. machinery, stoves) and wood (paper, boxes, barrels) industries. Has medieval fortifications; 14th–15th-cent. parish church. Near by is ruined castle, built c.1100.

Werther (vâr'tŭr), town (pop. 3,908), in former Prussian prov. of Westphalia, NW Germany, after 1945 in North Rhine-Westphalia, on N slope of Teutoburg Forest, 6 mi. NW of Bielefeld; woodworking.

Wertingen (vâr'tĭng-ŭn), town (pop. 3,053), Swabia, W Bavaria, Germany, 12 mi. SW of Donauwörth; machinery mfg. Has church with 2 Romanesque towers and Gothic choir.

Wervicq, Belgium: see WERVIK.

Wervicq-Sud (vârvēk-süd'), village (pop. 1,478), Nord dept., N France, on the Lys (Belg. border) opposite Wervik, and 10 mi. N of Lille; thread and yarn spinning, jute bag mfg.

Wervik (vĕr'vĭk), town (pop. 12,282), West Flanders prov., W Belgium, on Lys R. and 4 mi. WSW of Menin, on Fr. border; textile center; tobacco mfg. Has rebuilt church dating from 14th–15th cent. Formerly spelled Wervicq.

Wesel (vā'zŭl), town (1939 pop. 24,632; 1946 pop. 13,262), in former Prussian Rhine Prov., W Germany, after 1945 in North Rhine-Westphalia, in the Ruhr, port on right bank of the Rhine, just below mouth of Lippe R. and Lippe Lateral Canal, and 17 mi. S of Bocholt; rail junction; transshipment point. Iron foundry; mfg. of mine locomotives, machinery, pipes, ceramic plumbing fixtures. Flour milling, dairying. Chartered 1241. Joined Hanseatic League in 1350. Was strongly fortified until 1891. Town was almost pulverized by bombings in Feb., 1945 (total destruction 97%). Scene (March, 1945) of major Allied air-borne action and Rhine crossing in Second World War.

Wesenberg, Estonia: see RAKVERE.

Wesenberg (vā'zŭnbĕrk), town (pop. 3,378), Mecklenburg, N Germany, on small Woblitz L. (expansion of the Havel), 7 mi. SW of Neustrelitz; agr. market (grain, potatoes, stock); woodworking. Has remains of medieval castle.

Weser-Elbe Canal (vā'zŭr-ĕl'bŭ), central Germany, part of Mittelland Canal, extends c.135 mi. E from Ems-Weser Canal at Minden (Weser crossing) to the Elbe at Magdeburg suburb of Rothensee (ship elevator); navigable for 1,000-ton vessels. From Glindenberg, 8 mi. N of Magdeburg, a lateral canal leads to Hohenwarthe (ship elevator; Elbe crossing), where it connects with Ihle Canal.

Weseritz, Czechoslovakia: see BEZDRUZICE.

Weser Mountains, Ger. *Wesergebirge* (vā'zŭrgŭbĭr'-gŭ), low ranges astride Weser R. above Minden, NW Germany, bet. Dortmund-Ems Canal (W) and Hanover city; rise to c.1,700 ft.; include the Deister, Teutoburg Forest, and Wiehen Mts. Crossed by the Weser in the *Porta Westfalica* or *Westfälische Pforte* (vĕst"fā'lĭshŭ pfôr'tŭ), S of Minden. In a narrower sense, Weser Mts. are range extending 20 mi. E of Porta Westfalica.

Wesermünde, Germany: see BREMERHAVEN.

Weser River, Belgium: see VESDRE RIVER.

Weser River (vā'zŭr), one of NW Germany's major rivers, formed at Münden through junction of FULDA RIVER and WERRA RIVER; flows generally N, past Hameln, enters N German lowlands through the Porta Westfalica, continues past Minden and Bremen to North Sea, forming 10-mi.-long estuary below Bremerhaven. Length c.300 mi.; with Werra R., c.470 mi. Chief tributaries: Diemel and Hunte (left) and Aller (right) rivers. Large dams on Diemel and Eder rivers (at Helminghausen and Hemfurth) regulate water supply of the Weser. Navigable for its full length; principal commodities shipped are building materials, fuel, and grain. Deepened (1883–94) below Bremen. Connected with Rhine, Ems, and Elbe rivers through great Mittelland Canal system.

Wesham, England: see MEDLAR WITH WESHAM.

Weskeag River (wĕs'kĕg), Knox co., S Maine, 4-mi. inlet forming harbor of South Thomaston.

Weslaco (wĕs'lĭkō), city (pop. 7,514), Hidalgo co., extreme S Texas, in the lower Rio Grande valley, 35 mi. WNW of Brownsville; a shipping, processing center in irrigated citrus, truck, cotton area; canneries; makes feed, fertilizer, boxes. Seat of a Federal fruit and vegetable laboratory. Inc. 1921.

Wesley (wĕs'lē), village (pop. 1,014), NE Dominica, B.W.I., 20 mi. NNE of Roseau; coconuts, limes.

Wesley. 1 Town (pop. 66), Emanuel co., E central Ga., 7 mi. S of Swainsboro. **2** Town (pop. 509), Kossuth co., N Iowa, 12 mi. E of Algona, in livestock and grain area. **3** Town (pop. 149), Washington co., E Maine, 20 mi. NW of Machias, in blueberry-growing region.

Wesleyville, town (pop. 1,067), E N.F., on N side of Bonavista Bay, 40 mi. NW of Cape Bonavista; fishing port, with lobster canneries; lumbering.

Wesleyville (wĕs'lēvĭl), borough (pop. 3,411), Erie co., NW Pa., just E of Erie; flour, electrical parts; railroad shops. Settled 1797, laid out 1828, inc. 1912.

Wespelaar (vĕs'pŭlär), town (pop. 2,088), Brabant prov., central Belgium, 6 mi. NNW of Louvain; mfg. of electric motors. Formerly Wespelaer.

Wessel, Cape (wĕ'sŭl), N extremity of northeasternmost isl. of Wessel Isls. in Arafura Sea, off Northern Territory, Australia; forms NW end of Gulf of Carpentaria; 10°58'S 136°46'E.

Wesselburen (vĕ'sŭlbōō"rŭn), town (pop. 4,796), in Schleswig-Holstein, NW Germany, 7 mi. WNW of Heide, in the N Dithmarschen; market center (grain, vegetables); canning (sauerkraut). Hebbel b. here. Tulips, begonias, gladioli raised in area.

Wesseling (vĕ'sŭlĭng), village (pop. 9,057), in former Prussian Rhine Prov., W Germany, after 1945 in North Rhine-Westphalia, on left bank of the Rhine (landing) 7 mi. S of Cologne; mfg. of corundum.

Wessel Islands, in Arafura Sea, extending NE in 70-mi. chain from Napier Peninsula, N Northern Territory, Australia; largest isl. 30 mi. long, 7 mi. wide.

Wesselton, village, NE Cape Prov., U. of So. Afr., ESE suburb of Kimberley; diamond mine.

Wessem-Nederweerd Canal (vĕ'sŭm-nā'dŭrvārt) or **Noordervaart** (nōr'dŭrvärt'), Limburg prov., SE Netherlands; extends 11 mi. NW-SE, bet. Maas R. near Wessem (5 mi. WSW of Roermond) and the ZUID-WILLEMSVAART near Nederweerd (3 mi. NE of Weert); completed 1928. Navigable by ships to 600 tons with draught to 6.5 ft.

Wessex (wĕ'sĭks), old Anglo-Saxon kingdom, one of the Heptarchy, in S England. It may have been settled as early as 494 by Saxons under Cerdic on Avon R. in S Wiltshire. In late 6th cent. it annexed scattered Saxon settlements in the Chilterns and expelled Celts from region bet. lower Thames valley and lower Severn. Until end of 8th cent., however, kingdom was overshadowed successively by Kent, Northumbria, and Mercia. In late 7th cent. King Ine consolidated W expansion through Somerset and wrung tribute from Kent; he established a law code and made alliance with the Church. Egbert (802–39) defeated Mercia, forced Northumbria to sue for peace, and annexed Devon, Essex, Sussex, and Kent. Mercia regained independence, 830, and Egbert's successors were occupied in combating increasing Danish raids. With reign of Alfred (871–99?) the Danes were halted and history of Wessex becomes that of England. Alfred's successors gradually gained firm control over all England, including the Danelaw. Æthelred (978–1016), however, could not effectively resist invading Vikings and in 1016 Canute established Danish rule. The Wessex of Thomas Hardy's novels is used to mean mainly Dorsetshire.

Wessington, city (pop. 467), Beadle and Hand counties, E central S.Dak., 25 mi. WNW of Huron and on branch of James R.; farm trading point; livestock, dairy produce, grain, poultry.

Wessington Springs, city (pop. 1,453), ⊙ Jerauld co., SE central S.Dak., 25 mi. SW of Huron; trade and shipping point for extensive agr. area; dairy products, grain, livestock, poultry. Jr. col. is here. City founded 1880.

Wesson. 1 Town (1940 pop. 245), Union co., S Ark., 9 mi. SW of El Dorado, near La. line. **2** Town (pop. 1,235), Copiah co., SW Miss., c.40 mi. SSW of Jackson; truck, dairy products, lumber. Seat of Copiah-Lincoln Jr. Col.

West, for names beginning thus and not found here: see under WESTERN.

West, Western, in Rus. names: see also ZAPADN-.

West. 1 Town (pop. 354), Holmes co., central Miss., 32 mi. SE of Greenwood and on Big Black R. **2** City (pop. 2,130), McLennan co., E central Texas, 17 mi. N of Waco; trade, shipping point in cotton, cattle, truck area; cotton ginning, cottonseed-oil milling. Settled 1878, inc. 1894.

Westacre Junction, village, Bulawayo prov., SW Southern Rhodesia, in Matabeleland, 16 mi. SW of Bulawayo; rail junction for Matopos branch.

West Acton, Mass.: see ACTON.

West Albany (ôl'bŭnē), village (1940 pop. 3,786), Albany co., E N.Y., just NW of downtown Albany.

West Alexander, borough (pop. 466), Washington co., SW Pa., 15 mi. WSW of Washington.

West Alexandria, village (pop. 1,183), Preble co., W Ohio, 18 mi. W of Dayton; livestock, grain, tobacco. Makes machinery, tobacco boxes.

West Alligator River, Australia: see SOUTH ALLIGATOR RIVER.

West Allis, city (pop. 42,959), Milwaukee co., SE Wis., adjacent to and W of Milwaukee; residential and industrial suburb; mfg. (heavy machinery, trucks, motors, iron and steel products, wood products, industrial gases). Inc. 1906.

West Aspetuck River (ă'spĭtŭk"), W Conn., rises in W Litchfield co. E of Kent, flows c.15 mi. generally S, joining East Aspetuck R. just above junction with the Housatonic near New Milford. ASPETUCK RIVER is S, in Fairfield co.

West Atchafalaya Floodway, La.: see ATCHAFALAYA RIVER.

West Auburn, Mass.: see AUBURN.

West Auckland (ôk'lŭnd), town and parish (pop. 4,065), central Durham, England, 3 mi. SW of Bishop Auckland; coal mining.

West Ausdale, village (pop. 1,284), Richland co., N central Ohio.

West Australian Current, cold ocean current in Indian Ocean, part of counterclockwise circulation, flowing N along coast of Western Australia.

West Baden Springs or **West Baden** (bā'dŭn), town (pop. 1,047), Orange co., S Ind., on Lost R. and 22 mi. SSW of Bedford; mineral springs. Seat of West Baden Col., part of Loyola Univ. of Chicago.

West Bainbridge or **Diffie**, village (pop. 1,782), Decatur co., SW Ga., near Bainbridge.

West Barnet, Vt.: see BARNET.

West Barns, village, East Lothian, Scotland, 2 mi. WSW of Dunbar; mfg. of agr. implements.

West Barnstable, Mass.: see BARNSTABLE, town.

West Bath, resort town (pop. 578), Sagadahoc co., SW Maine, just SW of Bath; includes village of Birch Point.

West Baton Rouge (bă'tŭn rōōzh"), parish (□ 201; pop. 11,738), SE central La.; ⊙ Port Allen. Bounded E by the Mississippi. Agr. (sugar cane, corn, hay, cotton); oil, lumber; sugar milling. Formed 1807.

West Battle Lake, Minn.: see BATTLE LAKE.

West Bay, town (pop. 1,866) in Cayman Isls., dependency of Jamaica, on W coast of Grand Cayman isl. Turtle and shark fishing, ropemaking, lumbering (mahogany, cedar, dyewood).

West Bay, England: see BRIDPORT.

West Bay, Texas: see GALVESTON BAY.

West Belmar, village (pop. 2,058), Monmouth co., E N.J., near Belmar.

West Bend. 1 Town (pop. 772), Palo Alto co., NW Iowa, 16 mi. SE of Emmetsburg; feed milling. **2** Industrial city (pop. 6,849), ⊙ Washington co., Wis., on Milwaukee R. and 29 mi. NNW of Milwaukee, in hilly dairying, farming, and stock-raising region; mfg. (aluminum ware, leather products, farm implements, automobile parts, washing machines, wood products, concrete, evaporated milk, canned foods, beer). Settled 1844, inc. 1885.

West Bengal, India: see BENGAL.

West Benson, NW suburb (1940 pop. 1,877) of Omaha, Douglas co., E Nebr., on Missouri R.

West Billings, suburb (pop. 2,049) of Billings, Yellowstone co., S Mont.

West Blocton, town (pop. 1,280), Bibb co., W central Ala., 30 mi. SW of Birmingham; coal mining.

West Boldon, England: see BOLDON COLLIERY.

Westboro. 1 or **Westborough**, town (pop. 7,378), including Westboro village (pop. 3,443), Worcester co., E central Mass., 9 mi E of Worcester; abrasives, shoes, food-processing machinery; apples, peaches, poultry. Eli Whitney b. here. Settled c.1675, inc. 1717. **2** Town (pop. 297), Atchison co., NW Mo., 7 mi. NNE of Tarkio.

West Bountiful, town (pop. 682), Davis co., N Utah, N of Salt Lake City, near Bountiful.

Westbourne, village (pop. estimate 150), S Man., on Whitemud R. and 16 mi. NW of Portage la Prairie; stock, grain.

Westbourne. 1 Suburb, Hampshire, England: see BOURNEMOUTH. **2** Town and parish (pop. 4,123), W Sussex, England, 4 mi. WNW of Chichester; agr. market. Has 15th-cent. church.

Westbourne (wĕs'bŭrn), village (1940 pop. 938), Campbell co., NE Tenn., 19 mi. WSW of Middlesboro, Ky., in bituminous-coal area.

West Boylston, residential town (pop. 2,570), Worcester co., central Mass., on Wachusett Reservoir and 6 mi. N of Worcester. Settled 1642, inc. 1808. Includes village of Oakdale.

West Bradford, town and parish (pop. 323), West Riding, W Yorkshire, England, on Ribble R. and 2 mi. N of Clitheroe; cotton milling.

West Branch. 1 Town (pop. 769), Cedar co., E Iowa, 9 mi. E of Iowa City, in agr. area. Herbert Hoover was b. here in 1874. **2** City (pop. 2,098), ⊙ Ogemaw co., NE central Mich., c.50 mi. NNW of Bay City and on small West Branch of Rifle R., in hunting, fishing, and agr. area (livestock, poultry, potatoes, grain, fruit; dairy products). Oil wells, refineries; flour and feed mills. Annual trout festival held here. Inc. as village 1885, as city 1905.

West Branch, for river names beginning thus: see article on main stream.

West Brewster, Mass.: see BREWSTER.

West Bridgewater, residential town (pop. 4,059), including West Bridgewater village (pop. 1,379), Plymouth co., E Mass., 24 mi. S of Boston, just S of Brockton; agr. (truck, dairying, poultry). Massasoit's deed to settlers is in historical mus. here. Settled 1651, set off from Bridgewater 1822.

West Bridgford, residential urban district (1931 pop. 17,822; 1951 census 24,838), S Nottingham, England, on the Trent just SSE of Nottingham. Has 14th-cent. church.

West Bromwich (brŭ'mĭj), county borough (1931 pop. 81,303; 1951 census 87,985), S Stafford, England, 5 mi. WNW of Birmingham, in the Black Country; coal mining; steel casting, metalworking, chemical, and electrical-engineering industries; forms part of the Birmingham industrial area. Has 16th-cent. Oak House, now town mus., and church of 14th-cent. origin. Sometimes called Bromwich.

Westbrook. 1 Town (pop. 1,549), Middlesex co., S Conn., on Long Isl. Sound and 25 mi. E of New Haven; agr., fishing. Settled c.1664, inc. 1840. **2** City (pop. 12,284), Cumberland co., SW Maine, on Presumpscot R. Industrial W suburb of Portland; mfg. (textiles, paper, machinery). Includes Cumberland Mills and Highland Lake communities. Set off from Falmouth as town 1814, city inc. 1891. **3** Village (pop. 1,017), Cottonwood co., SW Minn., 20 mi. NW of Windom, in diversified-farming area; dairying. **4** Village (pop. c.400), Mitchell co., W Texas, 9 mi. WSW of Colorado City; shipping point in cattle-ranching and agr. region.

West Brookfield, agr. town (pop. 1,674), including West Brookfield village (pop. 1,104), Worcester co., central Mass., on Quaboag R. and 17 mi. W of Worcester. Settled 1664, inc. 1848.

West Brooklyn, village (pop. 194), Lee co., N Ill., 19 mi. ESE of Dixon, in agr. area.

Westbrookville, resort village, Sullivan co., SE N.Y., at foot of the Shawangunk range, 11 mi. NE of Port Jervis; makes blankets.

West Brownsville, borough (pop. 1,610), Washington co., SW Pa., on Monongahela R. opposite Brownsville; bituminous coal; railroad shops. James G. Blaine b. here, 1830. Laid out 1831, inc. c.1852.

West Burke, Vt.: see BURKE.

West Burlington, town (pop. 1,614), Des Moines co., SE Iowa, adjoins Burlington; railroad shops; makes burlap and cotton bags, gunstocks. Has fine Catholic grotto. Founded 1883.

West Burra (bûr'ů), island (pop. 591) of the Shetlands, Scotland, off SW coast of Mainland isl., 2 mi. SW of Scalloway; 6 mi. long, 1 mi. wide. Near NW end is promontory of Fugla Ness, site of lighthouse (60°6'N 1°21'W). Just E of West Burra and connected with it by narrow isthmus is isl. of East Burra (pop. 176), 4 mi. long and 1 mi. wide, separated from Mainland isl. by narrow Clift Sound. The 2 isls. are sometimes called simply Burra.

Westbury, urban district (1931 pop. 4,044; 1951 census 5,264), W Wiltshire, England, 4 mi. SSE of Trowbridge; agr. market; woolen mills, tanneries, iron foundries. Has 15th-cent. church. Just ENE is Westbury White Horse, cut in chalk hill, dating from 1778 and replacing earlier figure.

Westbury, town (pop. 908), N central Tasmania, 17 mi. WSW of Launceston; sheep-raising center.

Westbury, residential village (pop. 7,112), Nassau co., SE N.Y., on W Long Isl., 3 mi. E of Mineola; mfg. (clothing, machinery). Automobile races held here. Settled 1650, inc. 1932.

Westbury-on-Severn, former urban district (1931 pop. 1,746), W central Gloucester, on Severn R. and 8 mi. WSW of Gloucester, in fruitgrowing region. Church dates from c.1300.

Westbury-on-Trym (trĭm), N suburb (pop. 26,602) of Bristol, SW Gloucester, England; leather- and machine-tool works. Has 13th-cent. church on site of 8th-cent. Saxon shrine. Robert Southey lived here.

Westby. 1 Town (pop. 396), Sheridan co., extreme NE Mont., on N.Dak. line, 25 mi. ENE of Plentywood. **2** City (pop. 1,491), Vernon co., SW Wis., 22 mi. SE of La Crosse, in agr. area (tobacco, livestock, poultry; dairy products); has several cooperative enterprises; tobacco warehouses. In region of Coon Creek soil conservation project. Inc. 1920.

West Cache Creek, Okla.: see DEEP RED RUN.

West Caicos (kī'kōs, kī'kůs), uninhabited island (□ 10.4; 8 mi. long, 2 mi. wide), Turks and Caicos Isls., dependency of Jamaica, SSW of Blue Hills isl., on Caicos Passage; 21°40'N 72°30'W.

West Caister, England: see CAISTER-ON-SEA.

West Calder (kôl'důr), town and parish (pop. 6,817), SW Midlothian, Scotland, 15 mi. WSW of Edinburgh; shale-oil mining center.

West Caldwell, borough (pop. 4,666), Essex co., NE N.J., 10 mi. NW of Newark, near Passaic R.; mfg. (paint, clothing, metal products, pharmaceuticals). Inc. 1904.

West Camp, village (1940 pop. 540), Ulster co., SE N.Y., on W bank of the Hudson and 15 mi. N of Kingston, in summer-resort and agr. area.

West Canada Creek, N.Y., rises in lakes of the Adirondacks in central Hamilton co., flows generally SW to Prospect, then SE, past Middleville, to Mohawk R. at Herkimer; c.75 mi. long. Dam 2 mi. E of Prospect impounds Hinckley Reservoir (□ c.5; c.7 mi. long), sometimes called Kuyahoora L. At Trenton Falls (c.12 mi. N of Utica) is a scenic gorge, with several falls supplying power to Utica.

West Cape Howe, SW Western Australia, in Indian Ocean, W of Albany; southernmost point of state; 35°8'S 117°38'E.

West Cape May, borough (pop. 897), Cape May co., extreme S N.J., just W of Cape May city.

West Caroga Lake, N.Y.: see CAROGA LAKE.

West Carroll, parish (□ 356; pop. 17,248), NE La.; ⊙ Oak Grove. Bounded E by Bayou Macon, W by Boeuf R., N by Ark. line. Agr. (cotton, corn, hay, sweet potatoes, seed oats). Oil and natural-gas wells. Lumber milling, cotton ginning. Formed 1877.

West Carrollton, village (pop. 2,876), Montgomery co., W Ohio, on Great Miami R. and 7 mi. SSW of downtown Dayton; paper products. Sand and gravel pits near by.

West Carthage (kär'thĭj), village (pop. 2,000), Jefferson co., N N.Y., on Black R., opposite Carthage, and 15 mi. E of Watertown; paper milling. Inc. 1888.

West Chatham, Mass.: see CHATHAM.

West Cheshire, Conn.: see CHESHIRE.

Westchester (wĕst'chĕ"stůr), county (□ 435; pop. 625,816), SE N.Y.; ⊙ White Plains. Bounded W by the Hudson (here widening into Tappan Zee), S by New York city (of whose metropolitan area it is a part), SE by Long Island Sound and Conn., E by Conn., N by Putnam co. Chiefly a suburban residential region, with industrial and residential cities (e.g., White Plains, Yonkers, Mount Vernon, Peekskill, New Rochelle, Rye). Known for its country estates, hilly woodlands, and lakes (including Kensico Reservoir in Bronx R., reservoirs of Croton R. water-supply system, and Mohegan and Peach lakes). Drained by small Byram, Mianus, and Rippowam rivers. Traversed by chief highways connecting New York city with upstate and New England communities: landscaped parkways (Bronx River, Taconic State, Hutchinson River, Saw Mill River, and Cross County parkways), and historic Albany and Boston post roads. Served by New York, New Haven, and Hartford RR and 3 divisions of New York Central RR. Its shore communities are known for yachting. Many recreational areas and parks throughout co. Horticulture, farming (chiefly truck), dairying, poultry raising. Formed 1683.

West Chester. 1 Town (pop. 218), Washington co., SE Iowa, 7 mi. WNW of Washington. **2** Borough (pop. 15,168), ⊙ Chester co., SE Pa., 24 mi. W of Philadelphia; trade center for agr., dairying area. Metal products, canned goods, machinery, hosiery, lumber. State teachers col. here. Laid out 1786, inc. 1799.

Westchester. 1 Village, Conn.: see COLCHESTER. **2** Village (pop. 4,308), Cook co., NE Ill., W suburb of Chicago.

Westchester Heights, SE N.Y., a residential and industrial section of E central Bronx borough of New York city; railroad yards.

West Chicago, city (pop. 3,973), Du Page co., NE Ill., W of Chicago and 5 mi. E of Geneva, in agr. area; mfg. (portable bldgs., builders' supplies, rare-earth chemicals, gas mantles, lighting fixtures); railroad shops. Inc. 1906.

West Chop, Mass.: see TISBURY.

West City, village (pop. 1,081), Franklin co., S Ill., 7 mi. N of West Frankfort, in bituminous-coal-mining and agr. area. Inc. 1911.

West Claremont, N.H.: see CLAREMONT.

West Clarkston, village (pop. 1,920, with adjacent Highland), Asotin co., extreme SE Wash.

Westcliff, England: see SOUTHEND-ON-SEA.

Westcliffe, town (pop. 390), Custer co., S central Colo., on branch of Arkansas R., bet. Sangre de Cristo and Wet mts., and 45 mi. WSW of Pueblo; alt. 7,800 ft.; grain, livestock, dairy products. Silver, lead mines in vicinity.

West Coast, residency (□ 5,195; 1931 pop. 111,608), Br. North Borneo; ⊙ JESSELTON.

West College Corner, town (pop. 513), Union co., E Ind., on state line, adjacent to College Corner (Ohio) and 17 mi. S of Richmond.

West Columbia. 1 Residential town (pop. 1,543), Lexington co., central S.C., at junction of Broad and Saluda rivers, just SW of Columbia; mfg. (foundry products, mattresses, lumber, bagging, baskets). Renamed 1938 from Brookland or New Brookland. **2** City (pop. 2,100), Brazoria co., S Texas, c.45 mi. SSW of Houston, near Brazos R.; oil center in agr. area (cotton, rice, cattle). Founded 1826; with neighboring East Columbia (pop. c.400), was important in Austin's colony, and briefly (1836) ⊙ Texas Republic. Revived after 20th-cent. oil development; inc. 1938.

West Concord (kŏng'kůrd), village (pop. 770), Dodge co., SE Minn., 24 mi. WNW of Rochester, in grain and livestock area; dairying.

West Conshohocken (kŏn"shůhŏ'kůn), borough (pop. 2,482), Montgomery co., SE Pa., 11 mi. NW of Philadelphia and on Schuylkill R. Settled 1850, inc. 1874.

West Corner Brook, N.F.; see CORNER BROOK.

West Cote Blanche Bay (kōt" blänsh'), arm of the Gulf of Mexico, in St. Mary parish, S La., c.20 mi. S of New Iberia, bet. Marsh Isl. (SW) and marshy mainland coast; c.15 mi. long E-W, 11 mi. wide. Opens into Vermilion Bay (W), East Cote Blanche Bay (SE).

West Covina (kōvē'nů), city (pop. 4,499), Los Angeles co., S Calif., 18 mi. E of Los Angeles, in farm area (citrus fruit, walnuts). Inc. 1923.

West Crossett, town (pop. 289), Ashley co., SE Ark., just W of Crossett.

West Dal River, Sweden: see DAL RIVER.

West Danville. 1 Village (1940 pop. 766), Boyle co., central Ky., just W of Danville, in outer Bluegrass agr. region. **2** Village, Vt.: see DANVILLE.

West Dean, England: see DEAN, FOREST OF.

West Decatur (dēkā'tůr), village (1940 pop. 596), Clearfield co., central Pa., 10 mi. SE of Clearfield; makes firebrick. Also called Blue Ball.

West Demerara (dĕmůrâ'rů), district (□ 2,780; pop. 60,559), Demerara co., N Br. Guiana; ⊙ Vreed-en-Hoop. Drained by Demerara R.

West Dennis, Mass.: see DENNIS.

West De Pere, Wis.: see DE PERE.

West Derby (där'bē), E residential suburb of Liverpool, SW Lancashire, England. Has 18th-cent. mansion of Croxteth Hall and church built by Sir Gilbert Scott.

West Des Moines (dů moin'), city (pop. 5,615), Polk co., central Iowa, suburb of Des Moines; mfg. (cement, foundry products). Inc. 1893 as Valley Junction, renamed 1938.

West Des Moines River, Minn. and Iowa: see DES MOINES RIVER.

West Dinajpur (dĭnäj'po͝or), district (□ c.1,350; pop. c.570,000), N West Bengal, India; ⊙ Balurghat. Bounded E and S by E Pakistan, W by Bihar (India), SW by Mahananda R.; drained by the Atrai. Alluvial soil; rice, jute, barley, rape and mustard, chili. Rice milling at Hilli and Raiganj. Hindu and Moslem ruins at Devikot. Formed 1947 from DINAJPUR dist., following creation of Pakistan.

West Dodge, Nebr.: see BENSON.

West Drayton, England: see YIEWSLEY AND WEST DRAYTON.

West Dundee (dŭndē'), village (pop. 1,948), Kane co., NE Ill., on Fox R. (bridged here), just N of Elgin and c.36 mi. WNW of Chicago, in agr. area (dairy products; livestock). Settled in 1830s; inc. 1887. With EAST DUNDEE, across river, it composes community known as Dundee.

West Easton, borough (pop. 1,368), Northampton co., E Pa., on Lehigh R. just above Easton. Inc. 1890.

West Eaton, resort village, Madison co., central N.Y., 29 mi. SE of Syracuse. Lakes near by.

West Elizabeth, borough (pop. 1,137), Allegheny co., SW Pa., on Monongahela R. just above Clairton. Laid out 1833, inc. 1848.

West Elk Mountains, Colo.: see ELK MOUNTAINS.

West Elkton, village (pop. 297), Preble co., W Ohio, 10 mi. WNW of Middletown, in agr. area.

West Elmira (ĕlmī'rů), village (pop. 3,833), Chemung co., S N.Y., just W of Elmira.

West End, town (pop. 543), Grand Bahama Isl., NW Bahama Isls., port at W tip of the isl., 60 mi. E of West Palm Beach, Fla., and 155 mi. NW of Nassau; 26°11'N 78°58'W. Fishing base; has canning and freezing plant. Contains seaplane anchorage. Damaged by 1947 earthquake. Butlin resort village, opened 1950, is 4 mi. E.

West End, town and parish (pop. 3,050), S Hampshire, England, 4 mi. NE of Southampton; agr. market.

West End. 1 Village (pop. 1,662), Marion co., N central Fla. **2** Village, N.J.: see LONG BRANCH. **3** Village (pop. 1,285), Otsego co., central N.Y., near Oneonta. **4** Village (1940 pop. 609), Moore co., central N.C., 11 mi. WNW of Southern Pines; mfg. of furniture, handkerchiefs.

Westend, suburb (pop. 2,797) of High Point, Guilford co., N central N.C. There is also a hamlet called West End in Moore co.

Westend, St. Croix Isl., U.S. Virgin Isls.: see FREDERIKSTED.

West End Anniston, suburb (pop. 3,228, with near-by Cobb Town) of Anniston, Calhoun co., E Ala.

Westende (vĕ'stĕndů), village (pop. 1,967), West Flanders prov., W Belgium, 8 mi. SW of Ostend, near North Sea; brick mfg. Just N, on North Sea coast, is seaside resort of Westende-Bains.

Westerbork (vĕs'tůrbôrk), town (pop. 1,232), Drenthe prov., NE Netherlands, 11 mi. SSE of Assen; mfg. of surgical bandages. Site of Nazi concentration camp in Second World War.

Westerburg (vĕ'stůrbo͝ork), town (pop. 1,851), in former Prussian prov. of Hesse-Nassau, W Germany, after 1945 in Rhineland-Palatinate, in the Westerwald, 12.5 mi. NNW of Limburg; main town of upper Westerwald (Ger. *Oberwesterwald*) dist. Has 16th-cent. church, 18th-cent. castle.

Westeregeln (vĕ"stůrā'gůln), village (pop. 4,539), in former Prussian Saxony prov., central Germany, after 1945 in Saxony-Anhalt, near the Bode, 9 mi. SE of Oschersleben; lignite and potash mining; chemical mfg. Jewelry and handicrafts industry.

Westerham, town and parish (pop. 3,368), W Kent, England, on Darent R. and 5 mi. W of Sevenoaks; agr. market. Has 14th-cent. church.

Westerholt (vĕ'stůrhôlt), town (pop. 8,408), in former Prussian prov. of Westphalia, W Germany, after 1945 in North Rhine-Westphalia, in the Ruhr, 4 mi. W of Recklinghausen city center; truck produce.

Westerkappeln (vĕ"stůrkä'půln), village (pop. 8,041), in former Prussian prov. of Westphalia, NW Germany, after 1945 in North Rhine-Westphalia, 7 mi. NW of Osnabrück; coal mining.

Westerland (vĕ'stůrlänt), town (pop. 10,115), in Schleswig-Holstein, NW Germany, on Sylt isl.; airport (2 mi. NE), rail terminus; one of Germany's most popular North Sea resorts. Metalworking, weaving. Has casino (since 1949). Site of marine laboratory of Kiel Univ. Chartered 1905.

Westerleigh (wĕ'stůrlē), town and parish (pop. 1,511), SW Gloucester, England, 8 mi. NE of Bristol; agr. market. Has 14th–15th-cent. church.

Westerlo (vĕ'stůrlō), agr. village (pop. 6,251), Antwerp prov., N Belgium, on Grande Nèthe R. and 7 mi. SSE of Herentals. Formerly spelled Westerloo.

Westerlo (wĕ'stûrlō″), resort village, Albany co., E N.Y., in the Catskills, 17 mi. SW of Albany. Lakes near by.

Westerly, town (pop. 12,380), Washington co., SW R.I., on Pawcatuck R. (here forming Conn. line), on Block Isl. Sound and 14 mi. E of New London, Conn.; mfg. (rayon, cotton, and silk textiles, webbing, elastic, fish line, stapling machines, paper-mill machinery, printing presses, furniture, wood products, feed, food products); printing; granite quarries; agr. (poultry, dairy products, truck, potatoes). Its villages include industrial Westerly (pop. 8,415) (on the Pawcatuck, bridged here), BRADFORD, White Rock, part of POTTER HILL, and resorts of WEEKAPAUG, Avondale, MISQUAMICUT, and WATCH HILL (site of lighthouse and coast guard station). Inc. 1669.

Western, for names beginning thus and not found here: see under WEST.

Western, in Rus. names: see also: ZAPADN-.

Western, village (pop. 434), Saline co., SE Nebr., 13 mi. WSW of Wilber; grain, livestock, dairy and poultry produce.

Western Aden Protectorate: see ADEN PROTECTORATE.

Western Arpa-Chai, river, USSR: see ARPA-CHAI.

Western Australia, largest state (□ 975,920; pop. 502,480) of Commonwealth of Australia, W of meridian of 129°E (boundary separating it from South Australia and Northern Territory); bounded NW, W, S by Indian Ocean, NE by Timor Sea; 13°45′–35°8′S 113°9′–129°E; 1,270 mi. N–S, 980 mi. E–W, with 4,350-mi. coastline, comprising ⅓ of Australian continent; ⊙ PERTH. Chief port, FREMANTLE. Swanland (SW corner of state) is the only populous, fertile region, other areas being largely arid and sparsely populated. Central desert comprises Great Sandy, Gibson, and Victoria deserts. More than half of state is composed of gold fields; smallest but most productive is E.Coolgardie Goldfield. Principal mtn. ranges: Darling, King Leopold, Hamersley, Stirling ranges. Highest peak, Mt. Bruce (4,024 ft.). Limestone caves in SW coastal plain, S of Perth. Large lakes in interior are usually dry. Largest rivers (N) are intermittent; principal river, Swan R. (SW). Varied climate: tropical (N), temperate (SW). Wyndham, in hottest area of state, has mean annual temp. of 86°F., rainfall 15 in.; temp. range of Perth, 74°–55°F., rainfall 35 in. Cyclones (Nov.–April) on NW coast. Rich native flora includes karri (*Eucalyptus diversicolor*) and jarrah (*Eucalyptus marginata*), flowering gum (*Eucalyptus ficifolia*), sandalwood, wattle (*Acacia*), desert pea (*Clianthus*). Native fauna: marsupials (kangaroos, wallabies, wombats), dingo (wild dog), emus, cassowaries. Rabbits imported 1788 menaced sheep-raising industry; rabbit-proof fence, 1,000 mi. long, built from N to S coast. Unfertile N and NE regions inhabited largely by aborigines. Wheat and fruit belt in Swanland. Broome is center of pearling industry on N coast. Gold mining in central region; limited sheep raising on N and S coasts. Exports gold, grain, timber, dairy products, pearl shell. First settlement (penal colony established 1826) at Albany; 1st colonial settlement (1829), in Perth-Fremantle area, was called Swan River Settlement. Until 1831, colony was governed by New South Wales; became (1901) state of Commonwealth of Australia.

Western Bug River, USSR and Poland: see BUG RIVER.

Western Desert, Arabic *Al-Sahra' al-Gharbiyah*, part of the Libyan Desert, in W and W central Egypt. Most of its small settled areas are included administratively in a so-called frontier province (□ 73; pop. 68,519; ⊙ MATRUH) of Egypt. Borders E on the Nile valley, N on Mediterranean Sea, W on Cyrenaica (25°E). Its oases are SIWA, BAHARIYA (a separate administrative unit), and FARAFRA. In N is the QATTARA DEPRESSION, which played such an important part, in the Second World War, in the ALAMEIN battle. A railroad runs along the coast from Alexandria to Matruh. Other centers in N are Sidi Barrani and Salum. The S section is sometimes called the Southern Desert.

Western Duars or **Bengal Duars** (dwärz), region (□ 1,862) at foot of W Assam Himalayas, in Jalpaiguri dist., N West Bengal, India; separated from Eastern Duars by Sankosh R.; bounded N by Bhutan, S by Cooch Behar dist.; c.22 mi. wide. Piedmont plain except for extension of W Assam Himalayan foothills (N); Terai soil (extensive tea gardens; rice, mustard, tobacco, jute; sal, sissoo, and bamboo tracts). Copper-ore deposits just W of Buxa Duar. Formally ceded to British by Bhutan in 1866, following Bhutan War. Also spelled Dwars and Dooars.

Western Duck Island (2 mi. long, 2 mi. wide), S central Ont., one of the Manitoulin Isls., in L. Huron 4 mi. S of Manitoulin Isl.; 2 mi. E is Inner Duck Isl. (1 mi. long).

Western Dvina River, USSR and Latvia: see DVINA RIVER.

Western Ghats, India: see GHATS.

Western Grove, town (pop. 184), Newton co., NW Ark., 10 mi. SE of Harrison.

Western Hajar, Oman: see HAJAR.

Western Head, cape, SW N.S., on W shore of Liverpool Bay, 4 mi. SSE of Liverpool; 43°59′N 64°40′W.

Western India States, former political agency (□ 37,894; pop. 4,904,156) in W India, largely on Kathiawar peninsula; hq. were at Rajkot. Comprised princely states of Bhaunagar, Cutch, Dhrangadhra, Dhrol, Gondal, Idar, Jafarabad, Junagarh, Limbdi, Mansa, Morvi, Navanagar, Palitana, Porbandar, Radhanpur, Rajkot, Vijayanagar, Wadhwan, Wankaner, and those of subordinate WESTERN KATHIAWAR AGENCY, EASTERN KATHIAWAR AGENCY, and SABAR KANTHA AGENCY. States were under govt. of Bombay presidency until 1924, when agency was formed, with direct relations with govt. of India. In early 1940s, Idar and Vijayanagar were transferred to Rajputana States agency. In 1944, agency merged with Baroda and Gujarat States to form 1 large agency under govt. of India. In 1948–50, majority of states were merged in SAURASHTRA, Cutch became a chief commissioner's state, and Radhanpur and Sabar Kantha Agency were inc. into dists. of Bombay state.

Western Island (3 mi. long), NE N.F., one of the St. Barbe or Horse Isls., at entrance of White Bay, 22 mi. NW of Cape St. John; 50°12′N 55°51′W.

Western Islands, Scotland: see HEBRIDES.

Western Kathiawar Agency (kä'tĭūwär), subdivision (□ 2,552; pop. 435,858) of former Western India States agency, on Kathiawar peninsula, India; hq. were at Rajkot. Comprised princely states of Bilkha, Jasdan, Jetpur, Khirasra, Kotda Sangani, Malia, Manavadar, Thana Devli, Vadia, Virpur, and numerous petty states. Merged 1948 with Saurashtra.

Western Manych River, Russian SFSR: see MANYCH RIVER.

Western Morava River (mô'rävä), Serbo-Croatian *Zapadna Morava*, W Serbia, Yugoslavia, rises at W foot of the Golija, 9 mi. ENE of Sjenica; flows N past Ivanjica (hydroelectric plant) and Arilje, and WSW past Cacak and Trstenik, joining Southern Morava R. near Stalac to form Morava R.; c.150 mi. long. Receives Ibar and Rasina (right) rivers. Called Moravica R. in upper course. Followed by narrow-gauge railroad in lower course.

Western Oblast, Rus. *Zapadnaya Oblast'* (zä'pŭdnīŭ), former administrative division of W European Russian SFSR; ⊙ was Smolensk. Formed 1929 out of govts. of Bryansk and Smolensk; dissolved 1937 into oblasts of Smolensk and Orel.

Western Port, large inlet of Bass Strait, S Victoria, Australia, 30 mi. SE of Melbourne; separated from Port Phillip Bay by Cape Schanck peninsula. Largely filled by French Isl. (N), Phillip Isl. (S), and numerous shoals. W.Passage is 5 mi. wide at entrance; E.Passage, 1 mi. wide.

Western Port or **Westernport,** town (pop. 3,431), Allegany co., W Md., on North Branch of the Potomac (bridged to Piedmont, W.Va.) in the Alleghenies and 19 mi. SW of Cumberland, in bituminous coal-mining area. Many pre-Revolutionary expeditions into the Ohio country set out from here. Settled c.1790.

Western Province, administrative division (□ 1,432; pop., including estate pop., 1,867,351), SW Ceylon; ⊙ COLOMBO. Bounded W by Indian Ocean; largely lowland, drained by Kelani Ganga and Kalu Ganga rivers. Agr. (tea, rubber, coconuts, rice, vegetables, cinnamon, papaya); coir-rope mfg., mat weaving; fishing. Graphite (center at Migahatenna) and garnet (Pallewella) mining; kaolin deposits N of the Kelani Ganga, silica-sand deposits N of Negombo. Main centers: Colombo, Kalutara, Moratuwa, Negombo, Kotte, Dehiwala, Mt. Lavinia, Panadure. Archaeological remains at SITAWAKA and KELANIYA. Created 1833.

Western Provinces, major administrative division (□ 43,763; pop. 3,417,004) of SW Nigeria, on Gulf of Guinea; ⊙ Ibadan. Bounded E by lower Niger R., W by Dahomey. Includes provs. of ABEOKUTA, BENIN, IJEBU, ONDO, OYO, and WARRI. Situated in equatorial forest belt, with mangrove forest (S) changing N into rain forest, deciduous forest, and savanna; drained by Niger R. delta and Benin and Ogun rivers. Produces cacao, palm oil and kernels, hardwood, rubber, kola nuts. Cotton weaving, indigo dyeing, wood carving, brassworking. Phosphate and lignite deposits. Pop. is largely Yoruba (W), Beni (E), and Ijo (SE). Main centers: large Yoruba towns of Ibadan, Oyo, Ogbomosho, Oshogbo, Abeokuta; Benin City of Beni tribe. Formed 1939 out of W section of Southern Provinces of Nigeria.

Western Rajputana States, India: see RAJPUTANA STATES.

Western Reserve, tract of land in present-day NE Ohio, on S shore of L. Erie, extending from Pa. line to just W of Sandusky, Ohio. Reserved by Conn. for its own settlers when it ceded (1786) to the Federal govt. its rights to other western lands, which became part of the NORTHWEST TERRITORY (1787). The Western Reserve was inc. in the Ohio country of the Northwest Territory in 1800 as Trumbull co., and was later divided into 10 counties of Ohio state.

Western Samoa, Territory of: see SAMOA.

Western Sayan Mountains, Russian SFSR: see SAYAN MOUNTAINS.

Western Scheldt (skĕlt), Du. *Wester Schelde* or *Hont*, estuary of Scheldt R. (3–8 mi. wide), formed at point where Scheldt R. enters the Netherlands from Belgium, 9 mi. SSW of Bergen op Zoom; flows c.45 mi. W, past Terneuzen, Flushing, and Breskens, to North Sea. Separates South Beveland and Walcheren isls. from Flanders mainland.

Western Springs, residential village (pop. 6,364), Cook co., NE Ill., W suburb of Chicago; ships seeds, nursery plants. Inc. 1886.

Western Turkestan, USSR: see TURKESTAN.

Westerplatte (vĕ'stûrplä″tŭ), former fortress, Gdansk prov., N Poland, on small peninsula on Gulf of Danzig of Baltic Sea, 4 mi. N of Danzig city center; built 1694. In Second World War, captured (Sept., 1939) by Germans after siege of Pol. garrison.

Wester Schelde, Netherlands: see WESTERN SCHELDT.

Westerstede (vĕ″stûr-shtā'dŭ), village (commune pop. 15,832), in Oldenburg, NW Germany, after 1945 in Lower Saxony, 14 mi. NW of Oldenburg city; main village of Ammerland dist.; brandy distilling.

Westerville, suburban village (pop. 4,112), Franklin co., central Ohio, 12 mi. NNE of downtown Columbus. Seat of Otterbein Col. Settled c.1810, inc. 1858.

Westerwald (vĕ″stûrvält'), mountain region, W Germany, extending c.50 mi. E of the Rhine, bet. Sieg (N) and Lahn (S) rivers; rises to 2,155 ft. in the Fuchskauten. Densely populated despite harsh climate; extensive pastures. Iron-ore mining in Lahn and Sieg valleys; clay quarrying. Lignite deposits exhausted since 19th cent. Geologically it is considered part of Rhenish Slate Mts.

West Fairlee (fârlē'), town (pop. 363), Orange co., E Vt., on Ompompanoosuc R. and 24 mi. SE of Barre, in agr., lumbering, and resort region; L. Fairlee is SE.

West Fairview, borough (pop. 1,896), Cumberland co., S central Pa., on Susquehanna R. opposite Harrisburg. Laid out 1815.

Westfalen, Germany: see WESTPHALIA.

Westfälische Pforte, Germany: see WESER MOUNTAINS.

West Falkland Island: see FALKLAND ISLANDS.

Westfall, town (pop. 3), Malheur co., E Oregon, 23 mi. W of Vale; alt. 3,002 ft.

West Falmouth, U.S.: see FALMOUTH.

West Fargo (fär'gō), village (pop. 159), Cass co., E N.Dak., 5 mi. W of Fargo; meat packing, agr. distributing point.

West Farmington, village (pop. 579), Trumbull co., NE Ohio, 13 mi. NW of Warren, and on Grand R., in agr. area.

West Fayu (fä'yōō), atoll, Yap dist., W Caroline Isls., W Pacific, 46 mi. NNW of Satawal; c.4 mi. long, 1.5 mi. wide.

West Feliciana (fülĭ″shēănŭ), parish (□ 410; pop. 10,169), SE central La.; ⊙ St. Francisville. Bounded W by Mississippi R., N by Miss. line. Agr. (corn, cotton, hay, sugar cane). Lumber; sand, gravel. Canneries, cotton gins. Formed 1824.

Westfield, village in Torphichen parish, W West Lothian, Scotland, 3 mi. NW of Bathgate; paper milling.

Westfield. 1 Village (pop. 661), Clark co., E Ill., 20 mi. E of Mattoon; corn, wheat, oats, livestock, poultry; oil wells. **2** Town (pop. 849), Hamilton co., central Ind., 19 mi. N of Indianapolis, in agr. area. **3** Town (pop. 172), Plymouth co., NW Iowa, near Big Sioux R., 20 mi. NNW of Sioux City. **4** Town (pop. 557), Aroostook co., NE Maine, on Presquile R. just S of Presque Isle. **5** City (pop. 20,962), Hampden co., SW Mass., on Westfield R. and 7 mi. W of Springfield; foundries, lumber mills, machinery, bicycles, prefabricated houses, paper products; tobacco. Has state teachers col. Settled c.1660, set off from Springfield 1669, inc. as city 1920. **6** Residential town (pop. 21,243), Union co., NE N.J., 11 mi. SW of Newark; mfg. (crushed stone, cinder and concrete products, paint, toys); dairy products. Settled before 1700, inc. 1903. **7** Village (pop. 3,663), Chautauqua co., extreme W N.Y., near L. Erie, 17 mi. SW of Dunkirk, in grape-growing area; large grape-juice industry (since 1896); mfg. of airplane parts, machinery, wood products, feed. Summer resort. Settled 1800, inc. 1833. **8** Borough (pop. 1,357), Tioga co., N Pa., 16 mi. NW of Wellsboro; leather; agr. Inc. 1867. **9** Town (pop. 358), Orleans co., N Vt., on Missisquoi R. and 11 mi. WSW of Newport, in agr. area; wood products. **10** Village (pop. 935), Marquette co., central Wis., on branch of Montello R. (tributary of Fox R.) and 24 mi. N of Portage, in agr. area (potatoes, rye, corn); creamery, flour and feed mills, brewery. Fish hatchery here.

Westfield River, W Mass., rises in Hoosac Range in N Berkshire co., flows c.60 mi. generally SE, through Westfield, to the Connecticut opposite Springfield. Furnishes water power to mfg. towns. Lower course once known as Agawam R. West Branch (c.25 mi. long) and Middle Branch (c.20 mi. long) enter from W in Huntington town, below dam impounding Knightville Reservoir (c.3.5 mi. long).

West Flanders, Flemish *West-Vlaanderen* (vĕst-vlän'dûrŭn), Fr. *Flandre Occidentale* (flä″drŭ ōksēdătăl'), province (□ 1,249; pop. 1,002,904), W Belgium; ⊙ Bruges. Bounded by France (W and S), Hainaut prov. (SE), East Flanders prov. and the Netherlands (E), North Sea (N). Fertile soil, drained by Lys R., Yser R., and numerous minor canals. Produces wheat, oats, potatoes, flax (in Lys R. valley), pigs, cattle; major dairying industry. Numerous tourist resorts and fishing centers along North Sea coast (Ostend, Blankenberge, Knokke). Textile industry (cotton, linen, wool) centered on Courtrai. Other important towns: Ypres, Zeebrugge, Roulers, Izegem. W part of prov. was a combat zone throughout First World War. Prov. mainly Flemish-speaking.

Westford. 1 Village, Conn.: see ASHFORD. **2** Town (pop. 4,262), Middlesex co., NE Mass., 8 mi. SW of Lowell; yarn milling; apples. Settled 1653, set off from Chelmsford 1729. Includes Forge Village (pop. 1,115) and Graniteville (1940 pop. 907). **3** Town (pop. 685), Chittenden co., NW Vt., on Browns R. and 14 mi. NE of Burlington; lumber, maple sugar.

West Fork, town (pop. 351), Washington co., NW Ark., 9 mi. SSW of Fayetteville, in the Ozarks and on small West Fork of White R.; bois d'arc wood.

West Fork, for river names beginning thus and not found here: see the article on the main stream.

West Fork, river, central W.Va., rises in Upshur co., flows c.80 mi. N past Weston and Clarksburg, joining Tygart R. at Fairmont to form Monongahela R.

West Forks, plantation (pop. 108), Somerset co., W central Maine, on the Kennebec, at mouth of Dead R.; hunting, fishing.

West Frankfort (frăngk'fŭrt), city (pop. 11,384), Franklin co., S Ill., 45 mi. SSE of Centralia; trade center in bituminous-coal (large shaft mine), oil, and agr. area; livestock, truck, poultry, fruit. Inc. 1905; annexed Frankfort Heights in 1923.

West Friesland (frēz'lănd, Du. frēs'länt), area of North Holland prov., NW Netherlands; bounded by the Ijsselmeer (N, E), North Holland Canal (W), and a line bet. Alkmaar and Hoorn (S). Chief towns: Helder, Alkmaar, Hoorn, Medemblik. Dairying, cattle raising.

West Frisian Islands, Netherlands: see FRISIAN ISLANDS.

West Gardiner (gärd'nŭr), town (pop. 946), Kennebec co., S Maine, just W of Gardiner, from which set off, 1850.

Westgard Pass, Calif.: see INYO MOUNTAINS.

Westgate, village, S Queensland, Australia, 16 mi. SSW of Charleville; rail junction; sheep.

Westgate. 1 Village (pop. 3,303), Palm Beach co., SE Fla. **2** Town (pop. 226), Fayette co., NE Iowa, 8 mi. NNW of Oelwein, in agr. area.

Westgate-on-Sea, town and parish (pop. 4,554), NE Kent, England, on Isle of Thanet, on Thames estuary, 3 mi. W of Margate; bathing resort.

West Geelong, Australia: see GEELONG.

West Glacier, village (pop. c.150), Flathead co., NW Mont., just S of L. McDonald, on Flathead R. and 25 mi. NE of Kalispell; W entrance to Glacier Natl. Park. Formerly Belton.

West Glens Falls, village (pop. 1,665), Warren co., E N.Y.

West Gloucester, Mass.: see GLOUCESTER.

West Glover, Vt.: see GLOVER.

West Godavari (gōdŭvä'rē), district (□ 2,434; pop. 1,380,088), NE Madras, India; ⊙ Ellore. Lies bet. Eastern Ghats (N) and Bay of Bengal (S); SE portion is in Godavari R. delta. Agr.: rice, millet, oilseeds, sugar cane, tobacco, coconuts. Main towns: Ellore, Bhimavaram, Palakollu. Dist. created 1925 by division of original Kistna dist.

West Greenland Current, cold ocean current in Labrador Sea of North Atlantic Ocean, flowing N along SW coast of Greenland. Formed by merger of East Greenland Current and North Atlantic water off Cape Farewell; one terminal branch flows N through Davis Strait; the other turns W to join the Labrador Current. Carries icebergs.

West Greenville, former town, Greenville co., NW S.C., annexed 1948 by GREENVILLE.

West Greenwich (grĕ'nĭch, grĭ'nĭch), rural town (pop. 847), Kent co., W central R.I., 20 mi. SW of Providence; agr., lumbering, resort area. Includes villages of Escoheag (ĕ'skŭhēg"), Nooseneck (administrative center), Nooseneck Hill, and West Greenwich Center. State forests. Set off from East Greenwich 1741.

West Grinstead (grĭn'stĭd), town and parish (pop. 1,583), central Sussex, England, on Adur R. and 6 mi. S of Horsham; agr. market. Has Norman church and remains of Norman castle.

West Grove, borough (pop. 1,521), Chester co., SE Pa., 16 mi. NW of Wilmington, Del.; hosiery mfg.; mushrooms, roses.

West Guildford, Australia: see BASSENDEAN.

West Gulfport, village (pop. 1,853, with adjacent Landon), Harrison co., SE Miss.

West Hallam (hă'lŭm), town and parish (pop. 1,172), SE Derby, England, 2 mi. W of Ilkeston; coal mining. Has 13th–15th-cent. church.

West Ham, residential and industrial county borough (1931 pop. 294,278; 1951 census 170,987), SW Essex, England, on the Thames and 7 mi. ENE of London; important railroad workshops and locomotive works, docks (part of Port of London), and shipyards. Other industries include mfg. of rubber and jute products, chemicals, soap; flour milling, brewing, distilling.

Westham (wĕ'stŭm), residential town and parish (pop. 2,016), SE Sussex, England, 4 mi. NNE of Eastbourne. Has Norman church.

West Hamlin, town (pop. 793), Lincoln co., W W. Va., on Guyandot R. and 5 mi. W of Hamlin.

Westhampton (wĕst"hămp'tŭn). **1** Town (pop. 452), Hampshire co., W central Mass., 8 mi. W of Northampton. **2** Resort village (1940 pop. 736), Suffolk co., SE N.Y., on S shore of Long Isl., on an inlet of Moriches Bay, 6 mi. S of Riverhead. Just S is Westhampton Beach (pop. 1,087), shore resort; inc. 1928.

Westhampton Beach, N.Y.: see WESTHAMPTON.

West Harbour, borough (pop. 1,995), E S.Isl., New Zealand, on W shore of Otago Harbour; residential suburb of Dunedin.

West Harrison, town (pop. 308), Dearborn co., SE Ind., on Whitewater R. and 32 mi. SSE of Connersville, at state line, contiguous to Harrison, Ohio.

West Hartford, residential town (pop. 44,402), Hartford co., central Conn., adjacent to Hartford; mfg. (metal products, ball bearings, tools, furniture, machinery), tobacco packing; agr. (dairy products, truck, hothouse flowers). Seat of American School for Deaf (1817), St. Joseph Col. and Acad. for women, Hartford Col. Noah Webster b. here. Settled 1679, inc. 1854.

West Hartlepool (härt'lĭ-, här'tŭl-), county borough (1931 pop. 68,135; 1951 census 72,597), E Durham, England, on Hartlepool Bay, an inlet of the North Sea, near HARTLEPOOL, 8 mi. N of Middlesbrough; seaport (founded 1844), exporting chiefly coal, importing timber (pit props); shipbuilding; metal, machinery, paper, and asbestos industries. Town shelled by German cruisers (1914) in First World War. In county borough (S) is residential town of Seaton Carew (pop. 5,314).

West Hartsville, village (pop. 2,287), Darlington co., NE S.C., near Hartsville.

West Harwich, Mass.: see HARWICH.

West Haven. 1 Town (pop. 32,010), New Haven co., S Conn., just SW of New Haven, on New Haven Harbor; mfg. (airplane and gun parts, tires, textiles, machinery, tools, hardware, fertilizer, pipe organs, buckles, beer, concrete blocks); agr. Includes Savin Rock, amusement resort, and Allingtown village (1940 pop. 2,849). Set off from Orange 1921. **2** Town (pop. 232), Rutland co., W Vt., on L. Champlain and 18 mi. W of Rutland; dairy products, lumber.

West Haverstraw (hă'vŭrstrô"), village (pop. 3,099), Rockland co., SE N.Y., near W bank of the Hudson, just NW of Haverstraw; mfg. (clothing, textiles, chemicals). State home for crippled children here. Inc. 1883.

West Hazleton (hā'zŭltŭn), residential borough (pop. 6,988), Luzerne co., E central Pa., just W of Hazleton; paper boxes. Inc. 1889.

West Helena (hĕ'lŭnŭ), city (pop. 6,107), Phillips co., E Ark., 3 mi. WNW of Helena; lumber milling, mfg. of wood products. Founded 1909, inc. 1917.

West Hempstead (hĕm'stĭd), village (1940 pop. 3,384), Nassau co., SE N.Y., on W Long Isl., just W of Hempstead; mfg. (furniture, wood products, machinery); truck gardening, flower growing.

West Herrington, town and parish (pop. 4,037), NE Durham, England, 4 mi. SW of Sunderland; coal mining, stone quarrying.

West Hickory, N.C.: see HICKORY.

West Hill, India: see CALICUT.

West Hill, village (pop. 3,723), N Singapore isl., 11 mi. N of Singapore, just S of naval base area; rubber.

West Hillsboro, village (pop. 1,456), Orange co., N central N.C., near Hillsboro.

West Hoathly or **West Hoathley** (hōthlī', hōth'lē), agr. village and parish (pop. 1,632), N Sussex, England, 4 mi. SSW of East Grinstead, in Ashdown Forest. Has 13th-cent. church and 16th-cent. mansion.

West Hoboken, N.J.: see UNION CITY.

Westhofen (vĕst"hō'fŭn), village (pop. 2,164), Rhenish Hesse, W Germany, 7 mi. NW of Worms; furniture mfg.; brickworks. Sugar beets.

West Hollywood, village (pop. 1,196), Broward co., S Fla., near Hollywood.

West Homestead, borough (pop. 3,257), Allegheny co., SW Pa., adjacent to SE Pittsburgh on Monongahela R.; pig iron, machinery. Inc. 1900.

Westhope, city (pop. 575), Bottineau co., N N.Dak., 26 mi. W of Bottineau; flour refining, grain, livestock, dairy produce. U.S. customs station here.

West Horsley, town and parish (pop. 1,267), central Surrey, England, 6 mi. ENE of Guildford. Has 14th-cent. church.

Westhoughton (wĕstou'tŭn), urban district (1931 pop. 16,018; 1951 census 15,002), S central Lancashire, England, 5 mi. WSW of Bolton; cotton milling, mfg. of chemicals, pharmaceuticals, paint. Scene (1812) of 1st organized Luddite riots.

West Hsingan (shĭng'än'), former province (□ 28,545; 1940 pop. 736,701) of W Manchukuo; ⊙ was Tapanshang. Until 1932 in Jehol, it was formed 1934 out of Hsingan prov.; then it reverted in 1946 to Jehol and passed in 1949 to Inner Mongolian Autonomous Region. It was coextensive with the Mongolian JOODA league.

West Huntsville, village (pop. 8,221), Madison co., N Ala., just SW of Huntsville.

West Hurley (hûr'lē), village (1940 pop. 606), Ulster co., SE N.Y., at E end of Ashodan Reservoir, 6 mi. NW of Kingston, in summer-resort and agr. area.

West Indian Island (5 mi. long, 1 mi. wide), E N.F., in the Atlantic E of Notre Dame Bay, just S of Fogo Isl.; 49°32'N 54°20'W. E is East Indian Isl.

West Indies (ĭn'dēz), sometimes called the Antilles (ăntĭ'lēz), archipelago off Central America, extending in an enormous crescent (c.2,500 mi.) from Florida to the coast of Venezuela, and separating the Atlantic from the Caribbean Sea, which it encloses. The Gulf of Mexico is NW. Strategically located on major sea routes bet. North and South America and in the approach to the Panama Canal. Some 15,000,000 people live in the West Indies. The long isl. chain is situated N of the equator bet. 10°–27°N and 60°–85°W. Generally divided into 3 units: the BAHAMA ISLANDS (a group of c.700 isls. and more than 2,000 rocks and reefs), the Greater ANTILLES (CUBA, JAMAICA, HISPANIOLA, and PUERTO RICO), and the Lesser Antilles or Caribbees (LEEWARD ISLANDS, WINDWARD ISLANDS, TRINIDAD and TOBAGO, BARBADOS, and the Dutch and Venezuelan isls. off N coast of Venezuela). Geologically the isls. represent the remainder of several submerged Andean spurs, which meet in Puerto Rico. Apart from the volcanic ranges, frequently overlaid by sedimentary rock, coral limestone makes up the lower sections, including the numerous keys, reefs, and submarine banks. Volcanic disturbances and hurricanes are common features. While the climate varies considerably, especially with alt., it is semitropical to tropical, tempered by NE trade winds. Mild winters make the West Indies one of the world's favorite resort regions. Because of their great fertility they have become a major producer of sugar cane and tropical fruit. Except for Cuba, Haiti, and the Dominican Republic, all the isls. are owned by foreign powers. The Br. West Indies (sometimes also considered to include Br. Honduras and Br. Guiana, and occasionally Bermuda) comprise the Bahamas, Jamaica (with CAYMAN ISLANDS, and TURKS AND CAICOS ISLANDS), Br. Leeward Isls. colony (a federation of 4 presidencies: ANTIGUA with BARBUDA and REDONDA, SAINT KITTS-NEVIS with ANGUILLA and SOMBRERO, MONTSERRAT, and the Br. VIRGIN ISLANDS), Br. Windward Isls. colony (DOMINICA, SAINT LUCIA, SAINT VINCENT, and GRENADA with the GRENADINES), Trinidad and Tobago, and Barbados. The Du. West Indies (sometimes considered to include Du. Guiana) or CURAÇAO territory, officially now known as Dutch or Netherlands Antilles, consist of 2 widely separated groups in the Lesser Antilles: SABA, SAINT EUSTATIUS, and S half of SAINT MARTIN in the Leewards; and 3 isls. off Venezuela: Curaçao, ARUBA, and BONAIRE. The Fr. West Indies (sometimes considered to include Fr. Guiana) comprise GUADELOUPE with dependencies (DÉSIRADE, Les SAINTES, N part of St. Martin, MARIE-GALANTE, and SAINT-BARTHÉLEMY) and MARTINIQUE. The U.S. holds, since Spanish-American War (1898), Puerto Rico with VIEQUES and adjacent isls., and purchased (1917) from Denmark the 3 Virgin Isls. SAINT THOMAS, SAINT JOHN, and SAINT CROIX (now officially called Virgin Isls. of the U.S., formerly called Danish West Indies). Venezuela owns MARGARITA ISLAND and several smaller offshore islets. Originally inhabited by Arawak and Carib Indians, the archipelago was discovered (Oct., 1492) by Columbus, who made his 1st landfall in the Bahamas (supposedly on San Salvador or Watling Isl.) and erroneously believed he had reached India. Cuba and Hispaniola served as bases for further Sp. exploits on the Amer. mainland. The aboriginal Indians were almost entirely exterminated through plague, harsh treatment, and internecine warfare (notably by the Caribs); and Negro slaves, destined to become a dominant element, were introduced in increasing numbers. As a refuge for smugglers, pirates, and buccaneers since early colonial days, the West Indies have become a byword for swashbuckling adventure. Until early 20th cent. the isls. were a pawn among the imperialistic powers, mainly Spain, England, France, and Holland. The U.S., which entered the scene in late 19th cent., exerts the paramount economic influence. In 1940–41 England leased several naval and air bases to the U.S. for 99 years. Though the colonial possessions have achieved a large measure of representative govt., social and political problems still create high feeling, and the relations bet. the independent republics have been frequently strained. For further information, see articles on the various islands, island groups, cities, and political units.

West Island, Singapore colony: see COCOS ISLANDS.

West Jefferson. 1 Resort town (pop. 871), Ashe co., extreme NW N.C., 26 mi. NW of North Wilkesboro, in the Blue Ridge and Yadkin Natl. Forest; mfg. of hardwood flooring, furniture, cheese. **2** Village (pop. 1,647), Madison co., central Ohio, 15 mi. W of Columbus, in grain-growing area; corn cannery.

West Jordan, town (pop. 2,107), Salt Lake co., N central Utah, on Jordan R. and 12 mi. S of Salt Lake City. Inc. after 1940.

West Kankakee (kăngkŭkē'), village (pop. 2,784), Kankakee co., NE Ill., just W of Kankakee.

Westkapelle (vĕst'käpĕ"lŭ), agr. town (pop. 1,839), Zeeland prov., SW Netherlands, on W coast of Walcheren isl. and 8 mi. NW of Flushing. Important dike and lighthouse here. Dike was destroyed in Second World War, resulting in heavy floods; rebuilt 1946–47.

West Kazakhstan (kä"zäkstän'), Rus. *Zapadno-Kazakhstan*, oblast (□ 60,900; 1946 pop. estimate 300,000), W Kazakh SSR; ⊙ Uralsk. Drained by Ural R., flowing through dry steppe. Agr. developed in N (wheat, millet, mustard plants); livestock (cattle, camels, sheep) raised in SE and SW. Salt deposits (NE), natural-gas wells (SW). Meat and livestock products processed at Uralsk. Rail lines pass through extreme N and extreme W area. Pop.: Kazakhs, Russians. Formed 1932.

West Khandesh (khän'dāsh), district (□ 5,320; pop. 912,214), NE Bombay, India, on NW corner of Deccan Plateau; ⊙ Dhulia. Bordered NE by Satpura Range, NW by Narbada R.; N end of Western Ghats in W; drained by Tapti and Panjhra rivers. Agr. (millet, cotton, wheat, oilseeds); forests (W) yield teak, myrobalan, and blackwood. Cotton ginning at Dhulia, Nandurbar, Shirpur, and Shahada. Under Mahrattas in 18th cent. Formerly joined with East Khandesh in 1 dist. called Khandesh; divided 1906. Pop. 55% Hindu, 39% tribal, 5% Moslem.

West Kilbride (kĭlbrīd'), agr. village and parish (pop. 3,946), NW Ayrshire, Scotland, 4 mi. NNW of Ardrossan. Just W, on Firth of Clyde, is resort of Sea Mill, near Farland Head.

West Kilpatrick, Scotland: see OLD KILPATRICK.

West Kingston, R.I.: see SOUTH KINGSTOWN.

West Kirby, England: see HOYLAKE AND WEST KIRBY.

West Kittanning (kĭtă'nĭng), borough (pop. 910), Armstrong co., W Pa., on Allegheny R., opposite Kittanning, and 35 mi. NE of Pittsburgh.

West Korea Bay, Korea and Manchuria: see KOREA BAY.

West La Crosse, suburb (pop. 1,520) of La Crosse, La Crosse co., W Wis.

West Lafayette. 1 (lă'fēĕt", lă"fēĕt') City (pop. 11,873), Tippecanoe co., W central Ind., on the Wabash (bridged), opposite LAFAYETTE. Has state soldiers' home. Inc. 1924. **2** (lă"fāĕt', lă"fēĕt') Village (pop. 1,346), Coshocton co., central Ohio, 5 mi. E of Coshocton; metal products, novelties. Coal mine near by.

West Lake, Chinese *Si Hu* or *Hsi Hu* (both: shē' hōō'), scenic lake of Hangchow, Chekiang prov., China, outside city's W walls; 2 mi. across. Surrounded by wooded hills, it contains picturesque shrine-topped isls. that attract many visitors.

Westlake. 1 Town (pop. 1,871), Calcasieu parish, SW La., on Calcasieu R. and 3 mi. W of Lake Charles city; oil refining. Inc. since 1940. **2** Village (pop. 4,912), Cuyahoga co., N Ohio, 12 mi. WSW of downtown Cleveland; chemicals. Formerly called Dover Center or Dover.

Westland (vĕst'länt), region of South Holland prov., W Netherlands, extending c.10 mi. SW from The Hague to Hook of Holland; fruit- and vegetable-growing area. Main crops: grapes, peaches, tomatoes, cucumbers, early potatoes. Market centers: Naaldwijk, Poeldijk, Monster.

Westland, provincial district (□ 4,880; pop. 17,007), W S.Isl., New Zealand. Narrow coastal plain; bounded E by Southern Alps. Chief borough is Hokitika, principal port, Greymouth. Site of Tasman Natl. Park, containing Mt. Cook, highest peak of New Zealand. Quartz and gold mines. Area roughly corresponds to Westland land dist.

Westland, county, New Zealand: see HOKITIKA.

West Las Vegas, N.Mex.: see LAS VEGAS.

West Lawn, borough (pop. 2,144), Berks co., SE central Pa., 4 mi. W of Reading. Inc. 1920.

West Lebanon (lĕ'bŭnŭn). **1** Town (pop. 642), Warren co., W Ind., near Ill. line, 29 mi. WSW of Lafayette, in grain area. **2** Village, N.H.: see LEBANON. **3** Village (pop. 2,048), Lebanon co., SE central Pa., just W of Lebanon.

West Leechburg, borough (pop. 1,113), Westmoreland co., W central Pa., on Kiskiminetas R., opposite Leechburg, and 24 mi. NE of Pittsburgh; steel products. Inc. 1928.

West Leesport, borough (pop. 535), Berks co., SE central Pa., 7 mi. NNW of Reading and on Schuylkill R.

West Leipsic (lĭp'sĭk), village (pop. 304), Putnam co., NW Ohio, adjacent to Leipsic and 19 mi. W of Findlay.

West Liberty. 1 Town (pop. 1,866), Muscatine co., SE Iowa, 14 mi. NW of Muscatine, in farming, stock-raising, and dairying area; railroad junction; machine shop. Inc. 1867. **2** Town (pop. 931), ⊙ Morgan co., E Ky., on Licking R. and 40 mi. ESE of Mt. Sterling city; trade center for agr., cannel-coal, oil, gas, and timber area. **3** Village (pop. 1,397), Logan co., W central Ohio, 7 mi. S of Bellefontaine, and on Mad R., in grain, livestock, and dairy area; condensed milk, grain products. Ohio Caverns are near by. **4** Borough (pop. 245), Butler co., W Pa., 13 mi. NW of Butler. **5** Village, Ohio co., NW W.Va., in Northern Panhandle, 9 mi. NE of Wheeling. Seat of West Liberty State Col.

West Lincoln, village (pop. 426), Lancaster co., SE Nebr., NW suburb of Lincoln, on a branch of the Platte R.

West Line, town (pop. 68), Cass co., W Mo., near South Grand R., 14 mi. W of Harrisonville.

West Linga (lĭng'gŭ), islet (1½ mi. long) of the Shetlands, Scotland, just W of Whalsay isl. across 1-mi.-wide Linga Channel.

West Linn, city (pop. 2,945), Clackamas co., NW Oregon, on Willamette R. opposite Oregon City; paper milling. Settled in 1840s, inc. 1913.

West Linton, town and parish (pop. 1,200), N Peebles, Scotland, 10 mi. NW of Peebles; agr. market and resort. Once noted for production of carved tombstones.

West Loch Tarbert (lŏkh tär'bûrt). **1** Sea inlet, Argyll, Scotland: see TARBERT. **2** Sea inlet on W coast of Harris, Lewis with Harris isl., Outer Hebrides, Scotland, extending 10 mi. inland to narrow isthmus at Tarbert which separates it from East Loch Tarbert.

Westlock, village (pop. 854), central Alta., 45 mi. NNW of Edmonton; coal mining; grain elevators, flour mills, dairying, mixed farming.

West Logan, village (pop. 1,652), Logan co., SW W.Va., a suburb of Logan.

West Lomond, Scotland: see LOMOND HILLS.

West Long Branch, borough (pop. 2,739), Monmouth co., E N.J., 2 mi. SW of Long Branch. Settled 1711, inc. 1908. "Shadow Lawn," here, was President Wilson's summer White House.

West Looe, England: see LOOE.

West Lorne, village (pop. 728), S Ont., 25 mi. WSW of St. Thomas; dairying, mixed farming, fruit-growing.

West Los Angeles, Calif.: see SAWTELLE.

West Lothian (lō'dhēŭn), formerly **Linlithgow** (lĭnlĭth'gō) or **Linlithgowshire** (–shĭr), county (□ 120.1; 1931 pop. 81,431; 1951 census 88,576), SE central Scotland, on S shore of Firth of Forth; ⊙ Linlithgow. Bounded by Midlothian (SE), Lanark (W), and Stirling (NW). Drained by Almond and Avon rivers. Surface is hilly in S, sloping toward the Firth of Forth. Soil is highly cultivated; dairying is important. Industries include coal and oil-shale mining and refining, paper milling; iron, limestone, and fireclay are also worked. Besides Linlithgow, other towns are Bo'ness, Bathgate, and South Queensferry. There are prehistoric and Roman remains, including traces of Wall of Antoninus, and several anc. castles.

West Lulworth, agr. village and parish (pop. 1,083), S Dorset, England, on the Channel and 8 mi. SW of Wareham; seaside resort. Near by is Lulworth Cove, narrow and deep inlet of sea, surrounded by high cliffs.

West Lynn, England: see KING'S LYNN.

West Maitland, Australia: see MAITLAND.

West Malling (mô'lĭng), town and parish (pop. 2,373), central Kent, England, 5 mi. WNW of Maidstone; agr. market in fruit-growing region. Has remains of Benedictine abbey, founded 1090, and of Norman keep. Church has Norman tower.

West Malvern, England: see MALVERN.

West Manayunk (mă'nēyŭngk), village (1940 pop. 2,584) in LOWER MERION township, Montgomery co., SE Pa., on Schuylkill R. opposite Manayunk, a part of W Philadelphia.

West Manchester. 1 Village, Mass.: see MANCHESTER. **2** Village (pop. 469), Preble co., W Ohio, 26 mi. WNW of Dayton, in agr. area.

West Mancos River, Colo.: see MANCOS RIVER.

Westman Islands, Iceland: see VESTMANNAEYJAR.

Westmanland, plantation (pop. 77), Aroostook co., NE Maine, on Little Madawaska R. and 22 mi. NW of Presque Isle.

West Mansfield, village (pop. 756), Logan co., W central Ohio, 11 mi. E of Bellefontaine, in agr. area.

West Marion, village (pop. 1,233), McDowell co., W N.C., 2 mi. W of Marion. Post office name, Cross Mill.

West Marsh, England: see GRIMSBY.

West Mayfield, borough (pop. 1,768), Beaver co., W Pa., just NW of Beaver Falls.

Westmeath (wĕst'mēdh), Gaelic *na h-Iarmhidhe*, county (□ 680.6; pop. 54,949), Leinster, central Ireland; ⊙ Mullingar. Bounded by cos. Offaly (S), Roscommon and Longford (W), Cavan (N), and Meath (NE and E). Drained by the Shannon and Brosna rivers, served by Royal Canal. Surface is generally low and level, with bogs in S; center and N have low hills. Many lakes; largest, loughs Ree (on the Shannon), Derravaragh, Ennell, Owel, Lene, and Iron. Limestone is quarried; cattle raising, dairying, potato growing are important. Industries include tweed and cotton milling, alcohol distilling, canvas mfg., flour milling. Athlone is largest town. Auburn or Lissoy is associated with Oliver Goldsmith (*The Deserted Village*). Lakes are popular fishing resorts.

West Medway, Mass.: see MEDWAY.

West Memphis (mĕm'fĭs), city (pop. 9,112), Crittenden co., E Ark., on a bend of the Mississippi (bridged near by) and 8 mi. W of Memphis, Tenn. Cotton and cottonseed processing; soybean and lumber mills, distillery. Founded c.1910 as logging camp, inc. as city 1935.

West Mersea (mûr'–, mär'–), urban district (1931 pop. 2,067; 1951 census 3,001), on Mersea Isl., E Essex, England, on Blackwater R. estuary and 8 mi. S of Colchester; seaside resort and yachting center.

West Miami (mīă'mē, –mŭ), town (pop. 4,043), Dade co., S Fla., near Miami. Inc. since 1940.

West Middlesex, borough (pop. 1,217), Mercer co., W Pa., 10 mi. ENE of Youngstown, Ohio, and on Shenango R.; potatoes. Settled 1821, laid out 1836, inc. 1864.

West Middletown, borough (pop. 268), Washington co., SW Pa., 10 mi. NW of Washington.

West Mifflin, borough (pop. 17,985), Allegheny co., W Pa., in industrial region SE of Pittsburgh and N of McKeesport, across the Monongahela. Inc. 1944. Post office name formerly Terrace.

West Milan, N.H.: see MILAN.

West Milford. 1 Resort village (pop. c.350), Passaic co., N N.J., on Pinecliff L. (c.1½ mi. long), 16 mi. NW of Paterson; building supplies. **2** Town (pop. 401), Harrison co., N W.Va., on the West Fork and 6 mi. SW of Clarksburg.

West Millbury, Mass.: see MILLBURY.

West Millgrove, village (pop. 180), Wood co., NW Ohio, 7 mi. NNW of Fostoria; limestone quarry.

West Milton. 1 Village, Saratoga co., E N.Y., 5 mi. WNW of Ballston Spa. Site of an atomic research laboratory operated by General Electric Company. **2** Village (pop. 2,101), Miami co., W Ohio, 14 mi. SSW of Piqua, and on Stillwater R., in agr. area; mfg. (lightning rods, cement vaults); ships goldfish. Settled 1807, inc. 1835.

West Milwaukee (mĭlwô'kē), village (pop. 5,429), Milwaukee co., SE Wis., just W of Milwaukee; steel castings. Inc. 1906.

West Mineral, city (pop. 349), Cherokee co., extreme SE Kansas, 15 mi. SW of Pittsburg, in coal-mining and diversified agr. region.

Westminster (wĕst'mĭnstûr), city and metropolitan borough (1931 pop. 129,579; 1951 census 98,895) of London, England, on N bank of the Thames, extending just N, W, and S from Charing Cross. It is London's largest and most important borough, containing WHITEHALL, center of govt. offices, Downing Street, residence of prime minister, Westminster Abbey, Westminster Palace (housing Parliament), Buckingham Palace, St. James's Palace, the entertainment and shopping areas of Piccadilly and Regent Street, and the fashionable residential dist. of Mayfair. Westminster Cathedral, designed by John F. Bentley and completed 1903, is senior archiepiscopal see of R.C. Church in England and Wales. Westminster Bridge (completed 1750) was 2d bridge over Thames in London; rebuilt 1862. Westminster School, 1st founded in 14th cent. and reestablished by Queen Elizabeth 1559, is famous public school; among its graduates were Wren, Ben Jonson, Cowper, Dryden, Herbert, Cowley, Southey, Locke, Wesley, Hakluyt, Froude, Gibbon, and Jeremy Bentham. Westminster Hosp. was founded 1719. Westminster Abbey, premier church of Great Britain, faces Westminster Palace across Parliament Square. On site of present church an abbey was built 616 by King Sebert of Essex; it was destroyed by Danes and reerected in 985. Edward the Confessor built new church on this site c.1050; in late 13th cent. it was entirely rebuilt by Henry III and Edward I, and subsequently was enlarged and new bldgs. added. In early 16th cent. Henry VIII added Lady Chapel, and later (1722–40) W towers were built by Wren and Hawkesmore. In latter part of 19th cent. extensive restoration work was done under Sir Gilbert Scott. The abbey has been coronation church of England since crowning of Harold (1066), and here are buried 13 British kings, including Edward the Confessor, and 5 queens. Since 14th cent. famous Englishmen have been buried in the abbey or had their statues erected there; in the Poet's Corner are tombs and memorials of some of the greatest Br. poets, including Chaucer, Dryden, Spenser, Browning, Tennyson; others buried in the abbey include Sir Isaac Newton, Ben Jonson, Darwin, Dickens, Hakluyt. Westminster Palace is home of the Br. Houses of Parliament. Of Perpendicular design, it was built (1840–60) by Sir Charles Barry to replace series of anc. bldgs. almost wholly destroyed (1834) by fire. Original palace bldgs. were constructed by Edward the Confessor. Br. sovereigns lived here until reign of Henry VIII, when residence was transferred to Whitehall. Palace then became meeting place of Houses of Parliament. Westminster Hall, now entrance of palace, is sole remaining part of original structure, and was meeting place of highest English law court; here Richard II was deposed, Charles I sentenced to death, and trials of Sir Thomas More and Warren Hastings held. In 1940–41 air raids, palace suffered serious damage; chamber of the House of Commons was destroyed and that of the House of Lords damaged. In clock tower of palace is Big Ben. See, also, LONDON.

Westminster. 1 Village (pop. 3,131), Orange co., S Calif., 10 mi. E of Long Beach, in farm and citrus-fruit region. **2** Town (pop. 1,686), Adams co., N central Colo., just N of Denver; alt. 5,280 ft. Jr. col. here. **3** City (pop. 6,140), ⊙ Carroll co., N Md., 29 mi. NW of Baltimore, in agr. area; mfg. (clothing, shoes, machinery, tools, whisky); canneries, meat-packing plants. Seat of Western Md. Col. and Westminster Theological Seminary. Was important Union supply base in Civil War. Founded 1764, inc. 1837. **4** Town (pop. 2,768), Worcester co., N Mass., 6 mi. SW of Fitchburg; mfg. (crackers, wood products); dairying. Settled 1737, inc. 1759. Has state park, state forests. **5** Town (pop. 2,219), Oconee co., NW S.C., 45 mi. WSW of Greenville; mfg. (cotton textiles, lumber, fertilizer, patent medicine); poultry, fruit, cotton, corn, wheat. Tourist trade for near-by Blue Ridge. **6** Town (pop. 192), Collin co., N Texas, 20 mi. SSE of Sherman, in agr. area. **7** Town (pop. 1,400), including villages of Westminster (pop. 298) and North Westminster (pop. 404), Windham co., SE Vt., on the Connecticut and 15 mi. N of Brattleboro. Granted 1735 or 1736, regranted 1752, chartered 1772. Scene of violence (1775) over conflicting N.Y. and N.H. jurisdiction. Vt. declared independent state of New Connecticut at convention here (1777). *Vermont Gazette; or, Green Mountain Post Boy*, state's 1st newspaper, issued here (1781).

West Mitchell, town (pop. 112), Mitchell co., N Iowa, adjacent to Mitchell.

West Modesto (mōdĕ'stō), village (pop. 2,038), Stanislaus co., central Calif., near Modesto.

West Monkton, agr. village and parish (pop. 1,207), S central Somerset, England, 3 mi. NE of Taunton. Has 15th-cent. church.

West Monroe (mŭnrō'), city (pop. 10,302), Ouachita parish, NE central La., on Ouachita R., opposite MONROE, in agr. (especially fruit and livestock) area; cottonseed-oil mills, compresses; mfg. of paper, soap, turpentine, wood products, clothing, chemicals, meat products. Founded in 1860s, inc. 1926.

Westmont. 1 Residential suburban village (pop. 3,402), Du Page co., NE Ill., W of Chicago and 17 mi. E of Aurora, in agr. area (truck, poultry, livestock; dairy products). Inc. 1921. **2** Village (1940 pop. 8,170), Camden co., SW N.J., in suburban area, 5 mi. SE of Camden; mfg. of hosiery, cast stone products. **3** Borough (pop. 4,410), Cambria co., SW central Pa., just W of Johnstown.

Westmore, resort town (pop. 210), Orleans co., N Vt., on Willoughby L. and 13 mi. SE of Newport; agr. Includes part of Willoughby State Forest.

Westmoreland (wĕst'mŭrlŭnd), parish (□ 320.39; pop. 90,109), Cornwall co., SW Jamaica; ⊙ Savanna-la-Mar. Occupies, with South Negril Point, westernmost part of the isl.; watered by Cabaritta R. Has fertile plains, producing principally rice, sugar cane, breadfruit, cattle, horses, mules; also coffee, cacao, ginger, annatto, pimento, and logwood. Savanna-la-Mar is its leading port and trading center.

Westmoreland. 1 (wĕst"môr'lŭnd) County (□ 1,025; pop. 313,179), SW Pa.; ⊙ Greensburg. Mining and mfg. region; bounded N by Kiskiminetas and Conemaugh rivers, SW by Monongahela R., partly NW by Allegheny R.; drained by Youghiogheny R. and Loyalhanna Creek. Laurel Hill along SE border. Indian chief Pontiac defeated here 1763; Revolutionary Rattlesnake Flag originated here 1775. Subject of interstate dispute (see HANNASTOWN). Bituminous coal; mfg. (metal products, glass, rubber products); agr. (fruit, grain). Formed 1773. **2** (wĕst'mŭrlŭnd) County (□ 236; pop. 10,148), E Va.; ⊙ Montross. On N shore (Potomac R.) of Northern Neck peninsula; bounded SW by the Rappahannock. Here, on the Potomac, are "Wakefield," birthplace of George Washington, included in George Washington Birthplace Natl. Monument, and "Stratford Hall" (at Stratford), home of Lee family. Agr. (truck, esp. tomatoes; tobacco, hay), livestock, poultry. Fishing, shellfishing; seafood canning. Resorts (notably Colonial Beach). Formed 1653.

Westmoreland (wĕst"môr'lŭnd). **1** City, Calif.: see WESTMORLAND. **2** City (pop. 416), ⊙ Pottawatomie co., NE Kansas, 45 mi. NW of Topeka, in cattle and grain region. State park near by. **3** Town (pop. 789), Cheshire co., SW N.H., on the Connecticut and 9 mi. WNW of Keene; agr. **4** Village (1940 pop. 569), Sumner co., N Tenn., near Ky. line, 16 mi. NE of Gallatin, in strawberry-growing region.

Westmoreland City (wĕst"môr'lŭnd), village (pop. 1,234, with adjacent Biddle), Westmoreland co., SW Pa., 10 mi. E of McKeesport.

Westmorland, county (□ 1,430; pop. 64,486), SE N.B., on Northumberland Strait at Nova Scotia border; ⊙ Dorchester.

Westmorland (wĕst'mŭr-lŭnd), county (□ 789; 1931 pop. 65,408; 1951 census 67,383), NW England; ⊙ Appleby. Bordered by Cumberland (N and NW), Durham (NE), Yorkshire (E), Lancashire (S and W). Mainly mountainous or moorland country, cut by deep valleys, drained by Eden R. and Kent R. Cattle and sheep raising, some dairying; oat, barley, and root-vegetable growing. Its W and NW part is in the LAKE DISTRICT, and there are many small tourist resorts on the principal lakes (Windermere, Ullswater, Grasmere). Some granite and limestone quarrying; mfg. of shoes and woolen textiles (Kendal). Chief towns are Kendal, Windermere, and Ambleside.

Westmorland (wĕst"môr'lŭnd), city (pop. 1,213), Imperial co., S Calif., in IMPERIAL VALLEY, 15 mi. N of El Centro. Inc. 1932. Sometimes spelled Westmoreland.

Westmount (wĕst'mount), residential city (pop. 26,047), S Que., on Montreal Isl., W suburb of Montreal. Inc. 1873; became city 1908.

West Musquash Lake, Maine: see MUSQUASH LAKE.

West Mystic, Conn.: see GROTON.

West Nanticoke (năn'tĭkōk), village (1940 pop. 1,760), Luzerne co., NE central Pa., on Susquehanna R. opposite Nanticoke; meat packing.

West New Boston, Mass.: see SANDISFIELD.

West New Brighton, SE N.Y., a residential section of Richmond borough of New York City, on N Staten Isl., on Kill Van Kull; mfg. of paper and mica products; ship repairing.

West Newbury, agr. town (pop. 1,598), Essex co., NE Mass., on Merrimack R. and 11 mi. NE of Lawrence. Settled 1635, inc. 1820.

West Newton. 1 Village, Mass.: see NEWTON. **2** Borough (pop. 3,619), Westmoreland co., SW Pa., 20 mi. SE of Pittsburgh and on Youghiogheny R.; metal products, lumber, beverages; agr. Indian massacre here, 1763. Laid out 1796, inc. 1842.

West New York, industrial town (pop. 37,683), Hudson co., NE N.J., on Hudson R. just N of Weehawken; radio parts, embroideries, clothing, textiles, leather goods, toys. Settled 1790, inc. 1898.

West Nicholson, village, Bulawayo prov., S Southern Rhodesia, in Matabeleland, 80 mi. SE of Bulawayo; rail terminus; livestock center (cattle, sheep, goats); extraction of beef juices. Gold mining.

West Nishnabotna River, Iowa: see NISHNABOTNA RIVER.

West Nodaway River, Iowa: see NODAWAY RIVER.

West Oder River (ō'dŭr), Ger. *Westoder* (vĕst'-ō"dŭr), Pol. *Odra Zachodnia* (ô'drä zä-khôd'nyä), in Pomerania, after 1945 in E Germany and NW Poland, left arm of lower Oder R., runs bet. Hohensaaten (E Germany) and Stettin; regulated and canalized before 1914; 25 mi. long. Forms part of Berlin-Stettin Canal; at Hohensaaten linked by flight of 4 locks with Hohenzollern Canal.

West Okoboji (ō"kōbō'jē), town (pop. 158), Dickinson co., NW Iowa, summer resort on West Okoboji L. (c.6 mi. long, 1–2 mi. wide), 17 mi. N of Spencer. Several state parks near by.

Weston, town in Interior and Labuan residency, W Br. North Borneo, small port on Brunei Bay, 14 mi. SW of Beaufort; rail terminus; ships rubber. Connected by ferry with Victoria on Labuan isl.

Weston, town (pop. 5,740), S Ont., 6 mi. NW of Toronto; mfg. of motors, bicycles, stoves, hardware, cameras.

Weston. 1 Town and parish (pop. 3,783), NW Cheshire, England, on Mersey R. at mouth of Weaver R., on Manchester Ship Canal, just S of Runcorn; mfg. of chemicals; stone quarrying. Just NW is small port of Weston Point. **2** Agr. village and parish (pop. 1,583), NE Somerset, England, 2 mi. WNW of Bath.

Weston, county (□ 2,408; pop. 6,733), NE Wyo.; ⊙ Newcastle. Agr. area bordering S.Dak. Livestock, grain. Part of Black Hills and Black Hills Natl. Forest in NE. Formed 1890.

Weston. 1 Village (pop. c.500), Las Animas co., S Colo., at junction of N and S forks of Purgatoire R., in E foothills of Sangre de Cristo Mts., 20 mi. W of Trinidad; alt. 6,976 ft.; lumbering, agr. Culebra Peak is 17 mi. W. **2** Residential town (pop. 1,988), Fairfield co., SW Conn., near Saugatuck R., 6 mi. N of Norwalk. Includes part of Georgetown village. Settled c.1670, inc. 1787. **3** Town (pop. 162), Webster co., W Ga., 23 mi. WSW of Americus. **4** Village (pop. 382), Franklin co., SE Idaho, near Utah line, 5 mi. SW of Preston; alt. 4,604 ft.; grain. **5** Agr. town (pop. 248), Aroostook co., E Maine, on Grand L. and 28 mi. S of Houlton. **6** Residential town (pop. 5,026), Middlesex co., E Mass., 12 mi. W of Boston. Regis Col. for women, branches of Boston Col. here. Settled c.1642, set off from Watertown 1713. Includes village of Kendall Green. **7** City (pop. 1,067), Platte co., W Mo., on Missouri R. and 30 mi. NW of Kansas City; tobacco market, flour milling; agr. (wheat, corn). Founded 1837. **8** Village (pop. 345), Saunders co., E Nebr., 25 mi. N of Lincoln, near Wahoo, and on branch of Platte R. **9** Village (pop. 973), Wood co., NW Ohio, 8 mi. WSW of Bowling Green; corn, wheat, hogs; food processing, petroleum refining. **10** City (pop. 679), Umatilla co., NE Oregon, 20 mi. NE of Pendleton. **11** Town (pop. 468), Windsor co., S central Vt., on West R. and 16 mi. W of Springfield; wood products, furniture, sports equipment. Partly in Green Mtn. Natl. Forest. **12** Town (pop. 8,945), ⊙ Lewis co., central W.Va., on the West Fork and 18 mi. SSW of Clarksburg, in agr. (livestock, fruit, tobacco), oil, gas, and timber region; mfg. of hand-blown glass, bricks; lumber milling. State hosp. for insane here. Founded 1818.

Weston Point, England: see WESTON.

Weston-super-Mare (sōō"pŭr-mâr'), municipal borough (1931 pop. 28,554; 1951 census 40,165), N Somerset, England, on Bristol Channel and 20 mi. WSW of Bristol; seaside resort near Mendip Hills; brick, tile, and pottery works. Has golf courses and long esplanade. Near by are Worle Hill or Worlebury Hill (with anc. camp) and bird sanctuary of Brean Down. There is a fine view of the coast of Wales.

Weston Turville, agr. village and parish (pop. 1,040), central Buckingham, England, 3 mi. SE of Aylesbury; duck-raising center. Has 15th-cent. church.

West Orange. 1 Residential town (pop. 28,605), Essex co., NE N.J., 4 mi. NW of Newark; also mfg. (electrical equipment, machinery, metal products, tiles, clothing); stone quarries; poultry, fruit, truck. Set off from Orange 1862, town inc. 1900. Edison established his laboratories and home here, 1887. **2** Village (pop. 2,539), Orange co., SE Texas, just SW of Orange.

West Ossipee, N.H.: see OSSIPEE.

Westover. 1 Village (pop. c.150), Somerset co., SE Md., 18 mi. SSW of Salisbury; ships truck (especially strawberries); tomato cannery. **2** Residential village (1940 pop. 1,172), Broome co., S N.Y., W suburb of Johnson City. **3** Borough (pop. 605), Clearfield co., central Pa., 8 mi. NE of Barnesboro; tannery. **4** Town (pop. 4,318), Monongalia co., N W.Va., just W of Morgantown, in coal, gas, and oil region. Inc. 1911.

Westover Air Force Base, Mass.: see SPRINGFIELD.

Westover Hills. 1 Residential village (1940 pop. 635), New Castle co., N Del.; N suburb of Wilmington. **2** Town (pop. 266), Tarrant co., N Texas, W suburb of Fort Worth.

West Palm Beach, city (pop. 43,162), ⊙ Palm Beach co., SE Fla., c.70 mi. N of Miami, and on L. Worth (lagoon), opposite Palm Beach (connected by bridges); popular winter resort, commercial center, and a port of entry. Mfg.: air-conditioning equipment, prefabricated bldgs., concrete products, mirrors, beverages, preserves. A canal extends from here to L. Okeechobee (c.40 mi. W). The Norton Gall. and School of Art was opened in 1941. City was developed by Henry N. Flagler in 1893; and inc. 1894.

West Park, village, Ulster co., SE N.Y., on W bank of the Hudson and 6 mi. N of Poughkeepsie, in grape-growing and resort area. Home of John Burroughs (restored) is here.

West Parley, agr. village and parish (pop. 1,671), SE Dorset, England, on Stour R. and 5 mi. ESE of Wimborne Minster. Has Norman church.

West Paterson (pă'tŭrsŭn), borough (pop. 3,931), Passaic co., NE N.J., just SW of Paterson. Inc. 1914.

West Pearl River, La.: see PEARL RIVER.

West Pelzer, S.C.: see PELZER.

West Pensacola (pĕnsŭkō'lŭ) or **Brownsville**, suburb of Pensacola, Escambia co., extreme NW Fla.

West Petersburg, fishing village (pop. 39), SE Alaska, on E shore of Kupreanof Isl., across Wrangell Narrows from Petersburg; 56°49'N 132°59'W.

Westphalia (wĕstfāl'yŭ), Ger. *Westfalen* (vĕst"fä'-lŭn), former Prussian province (□ 7,806; 1939 pop. 5,209,401), W Germany, after 1945 included in NORTH RHINE-WESTPHALIA; ⊙ was Münster. Bounded by former Prussian Rhine Prov. (SW, W), the Netherlands (NW), former Prussian provs. of Hanover (N,E) and Hesse-Nassau (SE,S). Hilly in S (Rhenish Slate Mts.), lowlands in N. Drained by Lippe and Ruhr (W), Ems (N), and Weser (NE) rivers. The land consists partly of agr. soil, partly of sandy tracts, moors, and heaths. The Ruhr valley, in W, is part of great Westphalian coal basin and of RUHR dist., one of world's most important industrial regions. It is connected with the Ems by the Dortmund-Ems Canal and with the Elbe by the Mittelland Canal. Coal is mined, and also iron, copper, and zinc. Outside the Ruhr dist., there are important textile industries in N Westphalia, particularly at Bielefeld. Region was part of Saxon lands, which extended from the Elbe almost to the Rhine. Stem duchy of Saxony (founded in 9th cent.) was dissolved 1180; region from then on was contained mainly in dioceses of Münster, Paderborn, Minden, and Osnabrück; area (SE) ruled (until 1803) by archbishops of Cologne was called duchy of Westphalia. Westphalian Circle of Holy Roman Empire was formed c.1500. Napoleonic kingdom of Westphalia (1807–13) consisted of Prussian lands W of the Elbe, Electoral Hesse, Brunswick, and Hanover; it did not include Westphalian territories which (including duchy of Westphalia) came to Prussia at Congress of Vienna and were constituted (1816) into a prov. After capture (1945) by British, Canadian, and U.S. troops, Westphalia was inc. into new state of North Rhine-Westphalia in Br. occupation zone.

Westphalia. 1 Town (pop. 160), Shelby co., W Iowa, near sources of Keg and Silver creeks, 6 mi. NW of Harlan. **2** City (pop. 254), Anderson co., E Kansas, 15 mi. WSW of Garnett, in livestock, grain, and dairy region. **3** Village (pop. 459), Clinton co., S central Mich., 18 mi. NW of Lansing, in farm area. **4** Town (pop. 319), Osage co., central Mo., near Missouri and Osage rivers, 14 mi. SE of Jefferson City.

West Pittsfield, Mass.: see PITTSFIELD.
West Pittston, borough (pop. 7,230), Luzerne co., NE Pa., on Susquehanna R. opposite Pittston; silk mills, machine shop. Inc. 1857.
West Plains. 1 Town, Kansas: see PLAINS. **2** City (pop. 4,918), ⊙ Howell co., S Mo., in the Ozarks, 90 mi. ESE of Springfield; agr. shipping center; livestock market; dairy, grain, lumber products, hog serum. Laid out c.1858.
West Point. 1 Cape at W extremity of P.E.I., on Northumberland Strait, on N side of Egmont Bay, 30 mi. NW of Summerside; 46°37′N 64°23′W; lighthouse. **2** Cape at W extremity of Anticosti Isl., E Que., on the St. Lawrence; 49°52′N 64°31′W; lighthouse, radio beacon.
West Point, NW Tasmania, in Indian Ocean, near Marrawah; 40°57′S 144°39′E; lighthouse.
West Point. 1 Town (pop. 115), White co., central Ark., 7 mi. ESE of Searcy. **2** City (pop. 4,076), Troup co., W Ga., 14 mi. SW of La Grange, at Ala. line, formed here by Chattahoochee R.; textile center; mfg. (towels, yarn, textile machinery); bleaching, dyeing. Inc. 1831. **3** Village (pop. 275), Hancock co., W Ill., 14 mi. SE of Keokuk (Iowa), in agr. and bituminous-coal area. **4** Town (pop. 662), Lee co., SE Iowa, 9 mi. NW of Fort Madison, in livestock area. **5** Town (pop. 1,669), Hardin co., N Ky., on the Ohio, at Salt R. mouth, and 20 mi. SSW of Louisville, in agr. area; brickworks. **6** City (pop. 6,432), ⊙ Clay co., E Miss., 15 mi. WNW of Columbus; cottonseed oil, cheese, lumber, farm implements, packed poultry and meat, textiles, clothing. A jr. col. for Negroes is here. Inc. 1858. **7** City (pop. 2,658), ⊙ Cuming co., E Nebr., 55 mi. NW of Omaha and on Elkhorn R.; farm trade center; feed dairy products, grain. Co. mus. and park here. Inc. 1858. **8** Town (pop. 433), Davis co., N Utah, 10 mi. SW of Ogden, just E of Great Salt L. **9** Industrial and port town (pop. 1,919), King William co., E Va., at confluence of Mattaponi and Pamunkey rivers to form the York and 37 mi. E of Richmond. Rail terminus; pulp milling, mfg. of pickles, wood products; fisheries. Settled 17th cent.; inc. 1870.
West Point, U.S. military reservation (area c.15,000 acres), Orange co., SE N.Y., lying mainly on plateau above W bank of the Hudson, 8 mi. S of Newburgh; seat (since 1802) of U.S. Military Acad. Includes Constitution Isl. in the Hudson. Here were Revolutionary forts guarding the Hudson; Fort Putnam (1778) has been restored. Benedict Arnold's plan to betray West Point to the British (1780) was discovered with capture of Major John André.
West Point, peninsula, SW Maine, on E shore of Casco Bay, near Phippsburg.
West Poland, Maine: see POLAND.
Westport, village (pop. 726), SE Ont., on Upper Rideau L., 30 mi. NNE of Kingston; tanning, woodworking, dairying, boatbuilding; furniture.
Westport, Gaelic *Cathair na Mart,* urban district (pop. 3,240), SW Co. Mayo, Ireland, on Westport Bay, inlet of Clew Bay, 10 mi. WSW of Castlebar; fishing port, with dock installations; agr. market (cattle, potatoes); also mfg. of shoes, shirts, hosiery, thread.
Westport, borough (pop. 4,686) and port, ⊙ Buller co. (□ 1,950; pop. 4,936), on NW coast of S.Isl., New Zealand, 95 mi. SW of Nelson, at mouth of Buller R.; govt.-controlled coal port, coaling station for steamers. Bituminous coal mines at nearby Denniston and Millerton.
Westport. 1 Town (pop. 11,667), Fairfield co., SW Conn., on Long Isl. Sound, at mouth of Saugatuck R., just E of Norwalk. Residential and resort area, with state park, summer theater, artists' and writers' colony; mfg. (cable grip devices, cordage, celluloid, chemicals, soap, toys); agr. (truck, fruit, poultry). Includes villages of Greens Farms (1940 pop. 754) and Saugatuck. Settled 1645–50, inc. 1835. **2** Town (pop. 658), Decatur co., SE central Ind., 27 mi. SSE of Shelbyville, in agr. area. **3** Fishing town (pop. 146), Lincoln co., S Maine, 5 mi. E of Bath and on isl. in Sheepscot R. **4** Resort town (pop. 4,989), Bristol co., SE Mass., 7 mi. SE of Fall River and on short Westport R., near R.I. line. Settled 1670, set off from Dartmouth 1787. Includes villages of Acoaxet (ăkŏk′sĭt), Central Village, Horseneck Beach, Westport Mills (industrial), South Westport, North Westport, and Westport Point (on sheltered S inlet). **5** Village (pop. 96), Pope co., W Minn., on Sauk R. near its source and 12 mi. ENE of Glenwood, in grain area. **6** Town, Mo.: see KANSAS CITY. **7** Resort village (pop. 733), Essex co., NE N.Y., on L. Champlain, 24 mi. N of Ticonderoga; lumber. Annual co. fair and a summer regatta held here. **8** Fishing town (pop. 731), Grays Harbor co., W Wash., at entrance to Grays Harbor, 15 mi. WSW of Aberdeen; summer resort.
Westport Annex, village (1940 pop. 1,789), Johnson co., E Kansas; S suburb of Kansas City, Kansas.
Westport Mills, Mass.: see WESTPORT.
Westport Point, Mass.: see WESTPORT.
West Portsmouth, village (pop. 2,613), Scioto co., S Ohio.
West Prussia (prŭ′shŭ), Ger. *Westpreussen* (vĕst′-proisŭn), former province (in 1914: □ 9,867) of Prussia, NE Germany, extending S from the Baltic, bet. Pomerania (W) and East Prussia (E); ⊙ Danzig. Included region of POMERELIA, which came to Prussia with 1st and 2d partitions (1772 and 1793) of Poland. Prov. as constituted before First World War also included W section of originally East Prussian territory, with cities of Elbing, Marienburg, and Marienwerder. Treaty of Versailles (1919) gave most of West Prussia to Poland (formed Pomorze prov. and Polish Corridor); DANZIG dist. was created a free city. Remaining parts of prov. were divided bet. GRENZMARK POSEN-WEST PRUSSIA prov. (W; inc. 1937 with Pomerania prov.) and East Prussia (E). Whole territory was annexed 1939 to Germany and formed into Danzig–West Prussia prov., Ger. *Danzig-Westpreussen* (in 1943: □ 10,061; ⊙ Danzig). In 1945 placed under Pol. administration. Integrated into Pol. territory, it is included in GDANSK prov. and forms N part of BYDGOSZCZ prov.
West Quoddy Head (kwŏ′dē), E Maine, promontory on Atlantic coast, just SE of Lubec village; easternmost point of continental U.S. Has coast guard station and lighthouse (at 44°49′N 66°57′W).
Westray (wĕ′strā), island (□ 18; pop. 1,269) of the Orkneys, Scotland, 10 mi. NNE of Pomona across Westray Firth; 10 mi. long, 1–5 mi. wide; rises to 557 ft. In N part are ruins of 15th-cent. Noltland Castle and of 12th-cent. church. On Noup Head (NW) is lighthouse (59°20′N 3°5′W). Main occupations are fishing, fish curing, cattle raising, and egg production.
West Reading (rĕ′dĭng), borough (pop. 5,072), Berks co., SE central Pa., on Schuylkill R. opposite Reading; textiles, paper. Founded 1873, inc. 1907.
West Riding, administrative division of Yorkshire, England, covering S and SW part of county. See YORK, county.
West River, Chinese *Si Kiang* or *Hsi Chiang* (both: shē′ jyäng′), chief river of S China, draining vast region W of Canton. It rises in E Yunnan prov. in 2 main branches, the longer HUNGSHUI RIVER (left) and the shorter but navigable YÜ RIVER (right), which flow through W and central Kwangsi prov. and join at Kweiping to form West R. (here called Sün R.). It continues E through E Kwangsi, past Pingnam, Tengyün, and Wuchow, and into W Kwangtung prov., past Fungchün, Koyiu, and Samshui, to South China Sea, forming CANTON RIVER DELTA. A short left arm joins North R. at Samshui and gives rise to waterways forming CANTON RIVER at Canton. The main (right) delta branch forms W side of Canton R. delta and flows S, past Kowkong and Pakkai, to South China Sea W of Macao through several mouths. Navigable for steamers below Wuchow in low-water season, and below Kweiping at high-water. Total length (including Hungshui branch): 1,250 mi. The West R. is called Sün R. bet. Kweiping (formerly Sünchow) and Wuchow, where it receives Kwei R.
West River, SE Vt., rises in Green Mts., near Weston, flows c.50 mi. S and SE, past Newfane, to the Connecticut at Brattleboro.
West Riverside, village (pop. 3,798), Riverside co., S Calif., near Riverside.
West Road River, B.C.: see BLACKWATER RIVER.
West Rockingham (rŏ′kĭng-hăm″), village (pop. 1,438), Richmond co., S N.C., 3 mi. W of Rockingham.
West Roxbury, Mass.: see BOSTON.
Westrozebeke (vĕstrō′zūbā″kŭ), agr. village (pop. 1,919), West Flanders prov., W Belgium, 5 mi. W of Roulers. Formerly spelled Westroosebeke or Westroozebeke.
West Rushville, village (pop. 152), Fairfield co., central Ohio, just W of Rushville and 9 mi. ENE of Lancaster.
West Russell, village (1940 pop. 1,081), Greenup co., NE Ky., near the Ohio, just W of Russell.
West Rutland, town (pop. 2,487), Rutland co., SW central Vt., just W of Rutland, from which it was set off in 1886. Marble quarries, limestone; dairy products.
West Sacramento (săkrŭmĕn′tō), industrial suburb (1940 pop. 1,181), Yolo co., central Calif., on Sacramento R., opposite Sacramento; rice milling.
West Saint Paul, city (pop. 7,955), S suburb of St. Paul, Dakota co., E Minn., on S bank of Mississippi R. Ice cream made here.
West Salem (sā′lŭm). **1** Village (pop. 902), Edwards co., SE Ill., 15 mi. WNW of Mount Carmel; livestock, dairy products, poultry, grain. **2** Village (pop. 860), Wayne co., N central Ohio, 13 mi. NE of Ashland; dairy products, poultry; makes canvas products, buffing wheels. **3** City (1940 pop. 1,490), Polk co., NW Oregon, on Willamette R. opposite Salem; lumbering, fruit processing. **4** Village (pop. 1,376), La Crosse co., W Wis., near La Crosse R., 9 mi. NE of La Crosse, in timber and farm area; dairy products, lumber, canned peas. Hamlin Garland's house is here. Inc. 1893.
West Saltney, Wales: see SANDYCROFT.
West Sand Lake, village (1940 pop. 630), Rensselaer co., E N.Y., 7 mi. SE of Troy, in fruitgrowing area.
West Sanford, village (1940 pop. 611), Seminole co., E central Fla., suburb of Sanford; truck growing.
West Sayan Mountains, Russian SFSR: see SAYAN MOUNTAINS.
West Sayville, village (pop. 1,370), Suffolk co., SE N.Y., on S shore of Long Isl., just W of Sayville, in summer-resort area; mfg. of machinery, sea-food canning.
West Shefford, village (pop. 334), S Que., on Centre Yamaska R. and 7 mi. SSE of Granby; dairying, lumbering.
West Siberian Plain, one of largest plains in the world; extends c.2,000 mi. from Ural Mts. E to the Yenisei, c.1,250 mi. from Kara Sea S to Kazakh Hills; drained by Ob and Irtysh rivers. Includes large swampy regions (VASYUGANYE), steppes (Baraba, Kulunda, Ishim), extensive forests, and tundra.
West Siberian Territory, Rus. *Zapadno-Sibirskiy Kray* (zä′pŭdnô-sĭbēr′skē), former administrative division of W Asiatic Russian SFSR; ⊙ was Novosibirsk. Formed 1930 out of W part of Siberian Territory; dissolved into Omsk oblast (1934), and, later, into Novosibirsk oblast and Altai Territory (1937).
Westside, town (pop. 393), Crawford co., W Iowa, 12 mi. W of Carroll; processed soybeans, feed.
West Sleekburn, England: see BEDLINGTONSHIRE.
West Spanish Peak, Colo.: see SPANISH PEAKS.
West Spitsbergen (spĭts′bûrgŭn), Nor. *Vestspitsbergen,* largest island (□ c.15,000; pop. 1,025) of the SPITSBERGEN group, in Arctic Ocean; 76°34′–80°31′N 10°40′–21°35′E. It is 280 mi. long (N–S), 25–140 mi. wide. Mountainous and largely covered with glaciers, it rises to 5,633 ft. on Mt. Newton (NE), near 79°N 16°30′E. Other high peaks are Hornsundtind (S; 4,692 ft.) and Drygalski Crest (NW; 4,669 ft.). Along W coast are numerous other mts. over 3,000 ft. high. Triangular in shape, isl. has deeply indented coast line; largest inlets are Is Fjord (W) and Wijde Fjord (N). LONGYEAR CITY, on Is Fjord, is chief settlement and ⊙ Norwegian possession of Svalbard. Coal is mined here and at settlements of Sveagruva, Ny-Alesund, and Moskushamn. USSR operates mines at Barentsburg, Grumant City, and Pyramiden. Isl. has been starting point for several North Pole flights, including those of Amundsen and Ellsworth, Byrd and Bennett, and Nobile. During Second World War, isl. was evacuated in 1941, but Norwegian forces were landed in 1942. Most settlements were destroyed (summer, 1943) by German naval forces; later rebuilt.
West Springfield, town (pop. 20,438), Hampden co., SW Mass., on Westfield and Connecticut rivers, opposite Springfield; paper, machinery, smelting, chemicals; truck, dairying. Railroad shops. Settled c.1660, inc. 1774.
West Stafford, Conn.: see STAFFORD.
West Sterling, village (pop. 1,531), Whiteside co., NW Ill.
West Stewartstown, N.H.: see STEWARTSTOWN.
West Stockbridge, resort town (pop. 1,165), Berkshire co., W Mass., 10 mi. SW of Pittsfield, near N.Y. line; agr.; lime kilns. Settled 1766, set off from Stockbridge 1774. Includes village of State Line.
West Summerland Key, Fla.: see FLORIDA KEYS.
West Sunbury, borough (pop. 262), Butler co., W Pa., 10 mi. N of Butler.
West Swanzey, N.H.: see SWANZEY.
West Tanfield, village and parish (pop. 491), North Riding, N central Yorkshire, England, on Ure R. and 6 mi. NNW of Ripon; shoe mfg. Has 14th–15th-cent. church and 15th-cent. gatehouse.
West Tavaputs Plateau (tă′vŭpo͞ots), E Utah, high tableland in Carbon and Duchesne counties; extends W to Wasatch Plateau and is bounded E by Green R. and East Tavaputs Plateau. Rises to 10,047 ft. in Mt. Bartles and to 10,285 ft. in Bruin Peak.
West Telford, Pa.: see TELFORD.
West Terre Haute (tĕ′rŭ hōt′, tĕ′rē hŭt′), city (pop. 3,357), Vigo co., W Ind., across the Wabash, W of Terre Haute. Became city in 1933.
Westterschelling, Netherlands: see TERSCHELLING.
West Thurrock, England: see PURFLEET.
West Tisbury (tĭz′bŭrē), town (pop. 347), Dukes co., SE Mass., on central Martha's Vineyard, 21 mi. SE of New Bedford; agr., fishing, tourist trade. State forest. Settled 1669, inc. 1861. Includes North Tisbury village.
West Torrens, W suburb (pop. 22,570) of Adelaide, SE South Australia.
West Torrington (tŏ′rĭngtŭn), suburb (1940 pop. 505) of Torrington, Goshen co., SE Wyo., on N.Platte R., near Nebr. line.
West Union. 1 City (pop. 2,141), ⊙ Fayette co., NE Iowa, 24 mi. S of Decorah; rail junction; concrete blocks, dairy products, sausage, feed; limestone quarries. State park is SE. Inc. 1857. **2** Village (pop. 100), Todd co., W central Minn., near Sauk R., 15 mi. SE of Alexandria; dairy products. **3** Village (pop. 1,508), ⊙ Adams co., S Ohio, 30 mi. W of Portsmouth, in tobacco and grain area. Laid out 1804. **4** Town (pop. 429), Oconee co., NW S.C., 37 mi. WSW of Greenville; lumber and grain mills; cotton, corn, wheat. **5** Town (pop. 1,341), ⊙ Doddridge co., W W.Va., on Middle Island Creek and 24 mi. W of Clarksburg, in agr. region (livestock, fruit, potatoes, tobacco); lumber milling; gas and oil wells. Inc. 1850.

West Unity, village (pop. 827), Williams co., extreme NW Ohio, 9 mi. NE of Bryan; electrical apparatus, furniture, woolen goods.

West University Place, town (pop. 17,074), Harris co., S Texas, W residential suburb of Houston, absorbed 1948 by Houston.

West Upton, Mass.: see UPTON.

West Vernon, town (1940 pop. 955), Wilbarger co., N Texas, W suburb of Vernon.

Westview, town (pop. estimate 1,500), SW B.C., on the Strait of Georgia, 3 mi. SSE of Powell River; lumbering center.

West View. 1 Residential borough (pop. 7,581), Allegheny co., SW Pa., NW suburb of Pittsburgh. Inc. 1905. **2** Village, Sullivan co., NE Tenn., just N of Kingsport.

Westview, village (pop. 625), Cuyahoga co., N Ohio, 14 mi. SW of downtown Cleveland.

Westville, town (pop. 4,115), N N.S., 5 mi. SW of New Glasgow; coal-mining center.

Westville. 1 Village (pop. 3,196), Vermilion co., E Ill., 4 mi. S of Danville; bituminous-coal mines; agr. (corn, wheat, oats, soybeans, livestock, poultry; dairy products); makes overalls. Platted 1873, inc. 1896. **2** Town (pop. 624), La Porte co., NW Ind., 10 mi. WSW of La Porte, in agr. area. **3** Residential borough (pop. 4,731), Gloucester co., SW N.J., on Delaware R., at mouth of Big Timber Creek, and 5 mi. S of Camden; oil refining, mfg. (clothing, chemicals, cinder blocks, burial vaults). Inc. 1924. **4** Town (pop. 781), Adair co., E Okla., 25 mi. W of Fayetteville (Ark.), near Ark. line; canned foods, flour, feed.

Westville Dam, Mass.: see QUINEBAUG RIVER.

West Virginia, state (land □ 24,090; with inland waters □ 24,181; 1950 pop. 2,005,552; 1940 pop. 1,901,974), E central U.S., bordered by Pa. and Md. (N), Va. (E, S), Ky. (SW), and Ohio (W); 40th in area, 29th in pop.; admitted 1863 as 35th state; ⊙ Charleston. The "Panhandle State" has 2 narrow extensions, the NORTHERN PANHANDLE (bet. Ohio and Pa.) and the EASTERN PANHANDLE (bet. Md. and Va.). Natural boundaries include the Ohio R. (W), Big Sandy and Tug Fork rivers (SW), the Potomac R. and its North Branch (N), and mtn. ridges (E, SE). It has extreme dimensions of c.275 mi. (E-W) and c.245 mi. (N-S). Sometimes called the "Mountain State," W.Va. is mostly hilly and has the highest average alt. (1,500 ft.) of any state E of the Mississippi; SPRUCE KNOB is its loftiest point (4,860 ft.); in the Potomac valley it is 240 ft. Over 80% of the area is included in the ALLEGHENY PLATEAU, beyond whose E escarpment (the Allegheny Front) lies the Eastern Panhandle, a part of the Appalachian ridge and valley country. The Allegheny Plateau here descends westward from the Allegheny mtn. country in a series of parallel, NE-SW ridges. Characteristic of the plateau are narrow valleys and—in the E and center—many gorges, water and wind gaps, falls and rapids. The Eastern Panhandle is a valley and ridge area bounded in the extreme E by the Blue Ridge. The Allegheny Front is the chief watershed, dividing the state's rivers between the Ohio and the Potomac. The plateau drains generally NW through the Kanawha R. system and Guyandot R. (S), the Little Kanawha (center), and Monongahela R. system (N). The Eastern Panhandle drains generally NE through the South Branch of the Potomac, the Cacapon, and Shenandoah rivers. In the river valleys are most of the town sites, all of the major routes for roads and railroads, and almost all of the level land for farms. The Ohio, Kanawha, and Monongahela carry large amounts of barge traffic and, with the Cheat, Tygart, New, and Potomac rivers, furnish hydroelectric power. Along the Ohio are Huntington, the state's largest city, Parkersburg, Moundsville, and Wheeling; Charleston and South Charleston are on the Kanawha; Clarksburg, Fairmont, and Morgantown are on the Monongahela. Although natural lakes are lacking, the state has hundreds of mineral springs, most notably WHITE SULPHUR SPRINGS and BERKELEY SPRINGS. More than 60% of the state is timbered (especially in the E part of the Allegheny Plateau), making the state a leading U.S. producer of hardwood lumber; some of the wood-processing centers are Rainelle, Richwood, Beckley, and Elkins. Important species are walnut, chestnut, oak, yellow poplar, and ash. Softwoods are also present. The climate is humid continental, with hot summers (modified by the alt.) and cold winters, with several feet of snow in the higher parts; average temp. for July is 73°F. and for Jan. 33°F. The annual precipitation ranges generally W-E bet. c.30 and 60 in. and averages 45 in. Most (c.70%) of the population is rural, but the labor force is fairly evenly divided between farming, coal mining, and mfg. Livestock (dairy cattle, poultry, hogs, sheep) and livestock products provide c.70% of the farm income, since the predominantly hilly terrain is more adaptable to grazing than to cultivation. The SE is a bluegrass region and the chief center of the widespread animal husbandry. The best farms are found in the Ohio Valley and in adjacent part of the Allegheny Plateau, and in the Eastern Panhandle. More than 75% of the farm land is used for raising hay and corn; other major crops are apples, peaches, wheat, potatoes, and oats. The Eastern Panhandle is the chief fruit region, with Martinsburg the major shipping center; wheat is also important here. Potato production, like hay and corn, is widespread. Oats are grown in the highlands and Northern Panhandle. There is an important tobacco dist. around Huntington. The state's mining and mfg. industries are closely related. W.Va. is the chief U.S. producer of bituminous coal. Coal underlies more than 2/3 of the state. Based on this coal and on iron ore from Minn. and Mich., W.Va. has become one of the leading states in the mfg. of iron and steel; some of the major metal products are mining and construction machinery, railroad equipment, and hardware. These are chiefly in the Northern Panhandle, with Wheeling as its center; steel mills line the Ohio R. here from Weirton to Benwood. Iron and steel products are also manufactured in Huntington, Parkersburg, Charleston, Clarksburg, and Morgantown. Natural gas and oil are next in importance to coal. The fields begin in the Northern Panhandle and extend S across the state. The availability of cheap natural gas for fuel and large quantities of silica sand has also made W.Va. a chief U.S. producer of glass products. Moundsville, Clarksburg, Charleston, and Fairmont are the major glass centers. Much of the oil is shipped out of the state, although some refining is done along the Ohio. The high-grade clay deposits, especially in the Northern Panhandle, have given rise to many potteries. The large salt brines of the Kanawha Valley are the basis of a great chemical industry producing salt, chlorine, bromine, and sodium compounds. Explosives, ammonia, and synthetic fibers are also manufactured here. The principal towns in the valley besides Charleston and South Charleston are Belle and Nitro. In recent years a large salt deposit has been discovered in the Northern Panhandle. There are deposits of low-grade iron ore in the Eastern Panhandle. After earlier explorations by fur traders and others, the 1st towns, Romney and Shepherdstown, were founded (1762) in the Eastern Panhandle by Virginians. Prior to this the rugged mts. and the French, who claimed the Ohio valley, had proved barriers to English settlement. With the defeat of the French (in the French and Indian Wars) and later (1774) of the Indians, colonization progressed. Other important factors after the Revolution were the opening of the Mississippi (through the Louisiana Purchase), the coming of the steamboat, and the completion (1818) of the National Road from Cumberland, Md., to Wheeling. Although a part of Virginia, the region resented the political domination of the eastern part of the state. The different economies—the subsistence farming of the newer W and the plantation system of the older E—and the physical barriers bet. the 2 sections early created deep-rooted difficulties. John Brown's raid (1859) at Harpers Ferry intensified the sectional conflict over slavery. With the outbreak of the Civil War, the W part broke away from Va. and joined the Union, becoming a separate state in 1863. Late in the 19th cent. W.Va. began an industrial expansion based on its rich mineral resources which has continued to the present time. See also articles on the cities, towns, geographic features, and the 55 counties: BARBOUR, BERKELEY, BOONE, BRAXTON, BROOKE, CABELL, CALHOUN, CLAY, DODDRIDGE, FAYETTE, GILMER, GRANT, GREENBRIER, HAMPSHIRE, HANCOCK, HARDY, HARRISON, JACKSON, JEFFERSON, KANAWHA, LEWIS, LINCOLN, LOGAN, MCDOWELL, MARION, MARSHALL, MASON, MERCER, MINERAL, MINGO, MONONGALIA, MONROE, MORGAN, NICHOLAS, OHIO, PENDLETON, PLEASANTS, POCAHONTAS, PRESTON, PUTNAM, RALEIGH, RANDOLPH, RITCHIE, ROANE, SUMMERS, TAYLOR, TUCKER, TYLER, UPSHUR, WAYNE, WEBSTER, WETZEL, WIRT, WOOD, WYOMING.

West-Vlaanderen, Belgium: see WEST FLANDERS.

West Walker River, in E Calif. and W Nev., rises in the Sierra Nevada NW of Mono L., Calif., flows 60 mi. generally NE into Nev., joining East Walker R. in Lyon co. 7 mi. S of Yerington to form Walker R. Part of flow in upper course is diverted into artificial Topaz L., on state line, and used for irrigation.

West Wallsend (wôl'zĕnd), town (pop. 1,683), E New South Wales, Australia, 12 mi. WNW of Newcastle; coal-mining center.

Westward Ho, village (pop. 808), in Northam urban dist., N Devon, England, on Barnstaple Bay of the Bristol Channel and 2 mi. NW of Bideford; seaside resort. Seat of United Services Col., attended by Kipling. Village is named after Kingsley's novel.

West Wareham, Mass.: see WAREHAM.

West Warren, Mass.: see WARREN.

West Warwick (wôr'wĭk, wŏ'rĭk), industrial town (pop. 19,096), Kent co., central R.I., on Pawtuxet R. and 11 mi. SSW of Providence; mfg. (woolen, cotton, rayon, and silk textiles, lace, yarn, braid; metal products); agr. (poultry, dairy products, truck). Includes villages of ARCTIC, CENTREVILLE, CROMPTON, Natick (textile mills), PHENIX, and RIVER POINT (administrative center). Set off from Warwick and inc. 1913.

West Washington, village (pop. 4,492), Washington co., SW Pa., just W of Washington.

Westwego (wĕstwē'gō), town (pop. 8,328), Jefferson parish, SE La., on W bank (levee) of the Mississippi, opposite New Orleans; port and sea-food-processing center; shipbuilding; mfg. of steel products, wood and textile preservatives, chemicals, alcohol. Oil field near by.

West Wenatchee (wĭnă'chē), village (pop. 2,690), Chelan co., central Wash., near Wenatchee.

West Wickham (wĭ'kŭm), residential town and parish (pop. 6,229), NW Kent, England, 3 mi. SSW of Bromley. Has 15th-cent. church and 15th-cent. mansion of Wickham Court, a residence of Anne Boleyn.

West Wildwood, borough (pop. 237), Cape May co., S N.J., on barrier isl., just W of Wildwood, in resort and agr. area; poultry, truck.

West Willington, Conn.: see WILLINGTON.

West Wind Drift, surface drift current moving E in the oceans in the N and S hemispheres at or about 45°N and S lat. Caused by the prevailing westerlies, it is more specifically identified as the North Pacific Current and North Atlantic Current in N hemisphere.

West Windsor, town (pop. 504), Windsor co., E Vt., just W of Windsor.

West Winfield, village (pop. 832), Herkimer co., central N.Y., 15 mi. S of Utica, and on Unadilla R., in agr. area; summer resort.

West Winter Haven, village (pop. 2,326), Polk co., central Fla., near Winter Haven.

Westwood. 1 Lumber-milling village (pop. 3,618), Lassen co., NE Calif., 20 mi. SW of Susanville; a "company town." **2** W residential section of LOS ANGELES city, Los Angeles co., S Calif., near Beverly Hills (E); here is Univ. of Calif. at Los Angeles. Sometimes called Westwood Hills. **3** City (pop. 1,581), Johnson co., E Kansas, a suburb of Kansas City. Inc. after 1940. **4** Village, Boyd co., NE Ky., near the Ohio, 4 mi. NW of Ashland, in Huntington (W.Va.)-Ashland metropolitan dist. **5** Town (pop. 5,837), Norfolk co., E Mass., 14 mi. SW of Boston. Settled 1640, inc. 1897. Includes Islington village (1940 pop. 687). **6** Residential borough (pop. 6,766), Bergen co., NE N.J., 7 mi. N of Hackensack; truck farming. Inc. 1894. **7** Village (pop. 2,296), Allen co., NW Ohio.

Westwood Hills. 1 Town, Calif.: see WESTWOOD, Los Angeles co. **2** City (pop. 431), Johnson co., E Kansas, a suburb of Kansas City.

Westworth Village, residential village (pop. 529), Tarrant co., N Texas, a W suburb of Fort Worth.

West Wycombe, England: see HIGH WYCOMBE.

West Wyoming (wīō'mĭng), borough (pop. 2,863), Luzerne co., NE central Pa., 5 mi. NNE of Wilkes-Barre. Inc. 1898.

West Yarmouth, Mass.: see YARMOUTH.

West Yellowstone, village (pop. c.300), Gallatin co., SW Mont., just S of Hebgen L., near Idaho and Wyo. lines; tourist trade; W entrance to Yellowstone Natl. Park.

West York, borough (pop. 5,756), York co., S Pa., just W of York; machinery, pottery, hosiery, furniture. Inc. 1905.

West Yuma (yōō'mŭ), village (pop. 4,741), Yuma co., SW Ariz., a suburb of Yuma.

Westzaan (vĕst'sän), town (pop. 3,318), North Holland prov., W Netherlands, 2.5 mi. NW of Zaandam, in Zaanstreek industrial area; mfg. (cacao and flour products, paints, lacquers, paper products), vegetable canning.

Wetar (wĕ"tär'), island (□ 1,400; pop. 2,571), S Moluccas, Indonesia, in Banda Sea, 35 mi. N of NE coast of Timor across Wetar Strait (40 mi. wide); 7°45'S 126°20'E; 80 mi. long, 28 mi. wide. Wooded, mountainous, rises to 4,632 ft. Produces trepang, tortoise shell. Chief settlement is Ilwaki on S coast. Also spelled Wetter.

Wetaskiwin (wĕtă'skŭwĭn), city (pop. 2,645), central Alta., 40 mi. S of Edmonton; railroad junction; coal mining, natural-gas production, lumbering; grain elevators, flour mills, dairying; stock, poultry.

Wete (wĕ'tā), main town (pop. 3,806) of Pemba isl., Zanzibar protectorate, on isl.'s NW coast; clove-growing center. Has hosp.

Wetheral (wĕ'dhŭrŭl), village and parish (pop. 3,324), N Cumberland, England, on Eden R. and 4 mi. ESE of Carlisle; cattle and sheep raising, dairying. Former site of a Benedictine priory founded 1100. Parish includes cattle- and sheep-raising village of Great Corby, just E of Wetheral, wool-milling village of Heads Nook, 2 mi. ENE of Wetheral, and leather-tanning village of Scotby, 3 mi . E of Carlisle.

Wetherby, town and parish (pop. 2,541), West Riding, central Yorkshire, England, on Wharfe R. and 8 mi. SE of Harrogate; agr. market.

Wethersfield (wĕ'dhŭrzfēld). **1** Residential town (pop. 12,533), Hartford co., central Conn., on the Connecticut, just below Hartford; ships seeds, truck. State prison here. Settled 1634 by John Oldham; raided by Pequots, 1637. First ship launched in Conn. built here, 1649. Many 18th-cent. buildings here; damaged by 1936 flood of the Connecticut. **2** Former town, Ill.: see KEWANEE.

Wetlet (wĕt'lĕt"), village, Shwebo dist., Upper Burma, on railroad and 35 mi. NNW of Mandalay.

Wetmore, city (pop. 397), Nemaha co., NE Kansas, 40 mi. N of Topeka; livestock, grain.
Wet Mountains, S central Colo., range of Rocky Mts. in Custer, Fremont, Huerfano, and Pueblo counties; extend SSE from Arkansas R. to Huerfano R. Rise to 12,334 ft. in GREENHORN MOUNTAIN in S tip. Include part of San Isabel Natl. Forest.
Wetonka (wĭtŏng'kŭ), town (pop. 115), McPherson co., N S.Dak., 18 mi. NW of Aberdeen.
Wetter (vĕ'tŭr). **1** Town (pop. 2,482), in former Prussian prov. of Hesse-Nassau, W Germany, after 1945 in Hesse, 6 mi. NNW of Marburg; paper. **2** Town (pop. 11,618), in former Prussian prov. of Westphalia, W Germany, after 1945 in North Rhine-Westphalia, on the Ruhr and 3 mi. NW of Hagen; ironworks.
Wetter, Indonesia: see WETAR.
Wetteren (vĕ'tŭrŭn), town (pop. 19,513), East Flanders prov., NW Belgium, on Scheldt R. and 8 mi. ESE of Ghent; textiles.
Wetterhorn (vĕ'tŭrhôrn), peak (highest of its 3 summits, 12,153 ft.) in Bernese Alps, S central Switzerland, 12 mi. ESE of Interlaken; an imposing mtn. E of Grindelwald and N of the Schreckhorn. First climbed 1844–45.
Wetterhorn Peak (wĕ'–) (14,020 ft.), SW Colo., in San Juan Mts., 9 mi. ENE of Ouray.
Wettersteingebirge (vĕ'tŭrshtīn-gŭbĭr"gŭ), range of the Bavarian Alps, extending 15 mi. W of the Isar (at Scharnitz Pass) along Austro-German border S of Garmisch-Partenkirchen; rises (W) to 9,721 ft. in the Zugspitze, Germany's highest mtn.
Wettin (vĕtēn'), town (pop. 3,539), in former Prussian Saxony prov., central Germany, after 1945 in Saxony-Anhalt, on the Saxonian Saale and 10 mi. NW of Halle; furniture mfg., basket weaving; stone quarrying. Overlooked by 10th-cent. ancestral castle of princes of Wettin, who acquired it c.1000. Sold 1288 to archbishopric of Magdeburg.
Wettingen (vĕ'tĭng-ŭn), town (1950 pop. 11,616), Aargau canton, N Switzerland, on Limmat R., SE of Baden; hydroelectric plant; cotton textiles, shoes. Former abbey bldgs. (founded 1227), church (consecrated 1256).
Wettringen (vĕt'rĭng-ŭn), village (pop. 5,381), in former Prussian prov. of Westphalia, NW Germany, after 1945 in North Rhine-Westphalia, 7 mi. SW of Rheine; pumpernickel; hog raising.
Wetumka (wĭtŭm'kŭ), city (pop. 2,025), Hughes co., central Okla., 25 mi. E of Seminole, in agr. area (cotton, peanuts, watermelons, corn); cotton ginning; mfg. of gasoline, feed, furniture, caskets. Gas wells. Settled by Creek Indians.
Wetumpka (wĭtŭm'kŭ), city (pop. 3,813), ⊙ Elmore co., E central Ala., on Coosa R. and 12 mi. NNE of Montgomery; agr. trade center in cotton, corn, and oat region; woodworking, cotton ginning, cloth mfg. Indian mounds and site of Fort Toulouse are near by. Dam in Coosa R., 5 mi. NNW, is unit in hydroelectric development.
Wetzel (wĕt'sŭl), county (□ 362; pop. 20,154), NW W.Va.; ⊙ New Martinsville. Bounded W by Ohio R. (Ohio line); drained by small Fish and Fishing creeks. Oil and natural-gas wells; agr. (livestock, dairy products, grain, tobacco, truck); sand and gravel pits. Mfg. at New Martinsville. Formed 1846.
Wetzikon (vĕt'sĭkôn), town (pop. 6,719), Zurich canton, N Switzerland, 12 mi. ESE of Zurich; silk and cotton textiles, motorcars, knit goods. Early 17th-cent. castle with finds from prehistoric lake dwellings.
Wetzlar (vĕts'lär), city (pop. 22,530), in former Prussian prov. of Hesse-Nassau, W Germany, after 1945 in Hesse, on the Lahn, at mouth of Dill R., and 8 mi. W of Giessen; 50°33'N 8°30'E. Rail junction; metallurgical center with iron-ore mines in vicinity; blast furnaces, iron foundries (pipes, radiators, boilers, stoves, ovens); high-grade steel. Important optical industry (Leicas, microscopes, binoculars). Other mfg.: machine tools, radios, gloves. Cement works. Noted church of St. Mary (8th–15th cent.; restored 1900–10) was damaged in Second World War. Created free imperial city (1180). Seat (1693–1806) of supreme judiciary [Ger. *Reichskammergericht*] of Holy Roman Empire. With surrounding territory it was an exclave (1815–1932) of former Prussian Rhine Prov. In 1772 Goethe here met Charlotte Buff, whom he immortalized in *Werther*.
Wevelgem (vā'vŭl-khĕm), town (pop. 12,126), West Flanders prov., W Belgium, 3 mi. ENE of Menin, near Lys R.; textile industry; agr. market. Formerly spelled Wevelghem.
Wevelinghofen (vā"fŭlĭng-hō'fŭn), town (pop. 4,234), in former Prussian Rhine Prov., W Germany, after 1945 in North Rhine-Westphalia, on the Erft and 7 mi. SSW of Neuss.
Wewahitchka (wē"wŭhĭch'kŭ), town (pop. 1,289), ⊙ Gulf co., NW Fla., 28 mi. E of Panama City, on Dead L.; ships tupelo honey. Inc. 1925.
Wewak (wē'wăk, wĕ'wăk), town, ⊙ Sepik dist., NE New Guinea, 50 mi. W of mouth of Sepik R., 475 mi. NNW of Port Moresby. Coconut plantations. In Second World War, site of Jap. air base (established 1942) taken 1944 by Allies.
Weweantic River (wē"wēăn'tĭk), Plymouth co., SE Mass., rises in Carver town, flows c.20 mi. generally S, through Wareham town, to Buzzards Bay.
Wewelsfleth (vā'vŭlsflāt"), village (pop. 2,144), in Schleswig-Holstein, NW Germany, on the Stör near its mouth on Elbe estuary, and 7 mi. SW of Itzehoe; flour milling. Has 16th-cent. church.
Wewoka (wŭwō'kŭ, wē–), city (pop. 6,747), ⊙ Seminole co., central Okla., c.60 mi. ESE of Oklahoma City; distribution and shipping point for oil-producing and agr. region (corn, wheat, cotton). Mfg. of petroleum products, carbon black, oil-well supplies, brick, tile, chemicals, dairy products, mattresses, cottonseed-oil products; cotton ginning. L. Wewoka (recreation) is near by. Settled 1902 on site of an Indian village; inc. as town 1907, as city 1925.
Wewoka, Lake, Seminole co., central Okla., 3 mi. N of Wewoka; c.3 mi. long; water supply, recreation.
Wexford, Gaelic *Loch Garman*, county (□ 907.9; pop. 91,855), Leinster, SE Ireland; ⊙ Wexford. Bounded by the Atlantic (S), by cos. Waterford and Kilkenny (W), Carlow (NW), Wicklow (N), and by St. George's Channel (E). Drained by Slaney and Barrow rivers. Surface is mainly level, becoming mountainous in NW, rising to 2,610 ft. on Mt. Leinster. Coastline is low, indented, and dangerous to navigation. Isls. include Saltee Isls. and Tuskar Rock (lighthouse); numerous lightships safeguard navigation. Chief inlets are Waterford Harbour, Bannow Bay, and Wexford Harbour. Carnsore Point is SE extremity of Ireland. Marble, slate, granite are quarried; sea fisheries are important. Agr.: dairying; cattle, poultry; wheat, barley, potatoes, beets. Industries include tanning, woolen milling, brewing, bacon and ham curing, iron founding. Besides Wexford, other towns are Enniscorthy, New Ross, Gorey, Rosslare (port), and Bannow. Co. was 1st in Ireland to be colonized by the English. There are numerous anc. castles and ecclesiastical remains (Enniscorthy, Ferns).
Wexford, Gaelic *Loch Garman*, urban district (pop. 12,296), ⊙ Co. Wexford, Ireland, in E part of co., on Wexford Harbour (inlet of St. George's Channel) at mouth of Slaney R., 70 mi. S of Dublin; 52°20'N 6°28'W; fishing port, accessible to small ships, with dock installations. Industries include iron founding, brewing, bacon and ham curing, mfg. of agr. implements, bicycles, hosiery. Near-by Rosslare has superseded Wexford as seaport. Features of town are: Palace of R.C. bishops of Ferns (cathedral at Enniscorthy); R.C. church, built by Pugin; the old Bull Ring; ruins of 12th-cent. Selsker, St. Selsker, or St. Sepulchre Abbey and of anc. Church of St. Patrick. There are few remains of anc. castles, town walls, and gates. In 9th cent. Danish settlement of *Waesfjord* was established here; it was captured by Diarmid MacMurrough and Anglo-Normans in 1169, and Wexford was scene of signing of 1st Anglo-Irish treaty. In 1649 Cromwell took town, inflicting heavy destruction, and in 1798 it was hq. of the rebels. It was formerly noted for its fairs and tourneys.
Wexford, county (□ 563; pop. 18,628), NW Mich.; ⊙ Cadillac. Intersected by Manistee R., and drained by Clam R. Agr.; livestock, poultry, potatoes, grain, beans, corn; dairy products. Mfg. at Cadillac. Resorts (summer and winter). Part of Manistee Natl. Forest, a state fish hatchery, and a state park are here. Includes lakes Mitchell and Cadillac. Organized 1869.
Weyauwega (wīuwē'gŭ), city (pop. 1,207), Waupaca co., central Wis., on Waupaca R. (tributary of Wolf R.) and 25 mi. W of Appleton; trade center in dairying, and grain- and potato-growing area; dairy products. Settled c.1850, inc. 1939.
Weybridge, England: see WALTON AND WEYBRIDGE.
Weybridge (wā'brĭj), town (pop. 402), Addison co., W Vt., on Otter Creek, just NW of Middlebury. Site of U.S. experimental livestock farm.
Weyburn (wā'bŭrn), city (pop. 7,003), SE Sask., 65 mi. SE of Regina; grain elevators; flour milling, dairying, machinery and brick mfg.
Weyerhauser (wā'ŭrhou"zŭr), village (pop. 331), Rusk co., N Wis., 7 mi. WSW of Ladysmith, in farm area. Was important lumber town in late 1800s.
Weyersheim (vāĕrzĕm', Ger. vī'ŭrs-hīm), town (pop. 2,218), Bas-Rhin dept., E France, on the Zorn and 15 mi. N of Strasbourg; hosiery mfg.
Weymouth (wā'mŭth), village (pop. estimate 850), W N.S., on St. Mary Bay, 18 mi. SW of Digby; fishing, lumbering.
Weymouth, England: see WEYMOUTH AND MELCOMBE REGIS.
Weymouth, town (pop. 32,690), Norfolk co., E Mass., on Hingham Bay (inlet of Boston Bay) and 11 mi. SSE of Boston; shoes, paper boxes, tools, machinery, fertilizer, rubber belting, wool processing, lacquer. Settled 1622, inc. 1635. Includes industrial villages of North Weymouth, East Weymouth, and South Weymouth.
Weymouth, Cape (wā'mŭth), NE Queensland, Australia, in Coral Sea; forms N point of entrance to Lloyd Bay; 12°38'S 143°28'E.
Weymouth and Melcombe Regis (wā'mŭth, mĕl'kŭm rē'jĭs), municipal borough (1931 pop. 22,188; 1951 census 37,097), S Dorset, England, on the Channel, at mouth of the Wey, 7 mi. S of Dorchester; 50°37'N 2°27'W. Seaport, naval anchorage, and seaside resort. Sandsfoot Castle is blockhouse built by Henry VIII. Esplanade has statue of George III, who was frequent visitor here. In 1628 John Endecott sailed from here. In municipal borough are towns of Melcombe Regis (N; pop. 10,576) and Wyke Regis (SW; pop. 5,457). Weymouth is the old town. Just S is Isle of Portland.
Weymouth Fore River, E Mass., an inlet of Hingham Bay (arm of BOSTON BAY) bet. Braintree and Quincy on W and NW and Weymouth on S and E; used for shipping.
Wey River (wā). **1** In Dorset, England, rises 4 mi. SSW of Dorchester, flows 6 mi. SE to the Channel at Weymouth. **2** In Surrey, England, rises in 2 branches (one just W of Alton, Hampshire; the other just W of Haslemere) which join at Farnham; flows NE, past Godalming, Guildford, and Woking, to the Thames at Weybridge; 35 mi. long. Navigable below Godalming.
Wezel (vā'zŭl), town, Antwerp prov., N Belgium, 14 mi. SE of Turnhout; zinc processing, dynamite.
Wezet, Belgium: see VISÉ.
Wezzan, Fr. Morocco: see OUEZZANE.
Whakatane (fă"kŭtä'nē), borough (pop. 2,806), ⊙ Whakatane co. (□ 1,677; pop. 10,311), N N.Isl., New Zealand, 105 mi. N of Napier and on Bay of Plenty, at mouth of Whakatane R.; small harbor; dairy center; paper mills.
Whalan (hwā'lŭn), village (pop. 176), Fillmore co., SE Minn., on Root R. and 9 mi. ENE of Preston; corn, oats, barley, potatoes.
Whaleback, small lighthouse isl., SE N.H., off entrance to Portsmouth harbor.
Whale Island, Labrador: see AVIGALIK ISLAND.
Whale Islands, Norway: see HVAL ISLANDS.
Whale Peak (13,074 ft.), in Front Range, bet. Park and Summit counties, central Colo.
Whale River, N Que., rises N of Michikamau L., near Labrador border, flows 300 mi. N, through several lakes, to Ungava Bay 30 mi. NE of Fort Chimo. There are numerous rapids. Formerly important salmon stream.
Whales, Bay of, Antarctica, indents Ross Shelf Ice at 78°30'S 163°50'W. Base (1911) for Amundsen's dash to South Pole and for later expeditions. Roosevelt Isl. and Little America are just S. Discovered 1908 by Shackleton.
Whale Sound, Dan. *Hval Sund*, inlet (40 mi. long, 10–15 mi. wide) of N Baffin Bay, NW Greenland; 77°15'N 70°30'W. S arm of entrance of Inglefield Gulf, separated from N arm (Murchison Sound) by Northumberland and Herbert isls. S shore was site of Peary's base, 1892 and 1894–95.
Whaley Bridge (hwā'lē), urban district (1951 census 5,365), NW Derby, England, on Goyt R. and 6 mi. NNW of Buxton; cotton milling.
Whaley Lake, Dutchess co., SE N.Y., resort lake (c.1½ mi. long) 3 mi. W of Pawling.
Whalley (hwô'lē), village and parish (pop. 4,012), central Lancashire, England, on Calder R. and 6 mi. NE of Blackburn; cattle raising, dairy farming, agr. Has three 11th-cent. Saxon crosses in churchyard; church has 16th-cent. Flemish bell. Near by, ruins of 13th–15th-cent. Cistercian abbey. Just E is large mental institution.
Whalsay or **Whalsey** (hwôl'sē), island (pop. 900) of the Shetlands, Scotland, off NE coast of Mainland isl., 13 mi. NNE of Lerwick, at entrance to Dury Voe; 6 mi. long, 2 mi. wide; rises to 393 ft. Fishing.
Whalsey, Scotland: see WHALSAY.
Whampoa (hwămpō'ŭ), Mandarin *Huang-pu* (hwăng'bōō), town, S Kwangtung prov., China, on isl. in Canton R., 9 mi. ESE of Canton; commercial center and outer deep-water port for Canton. Mfg. of steel, munitions; shipyards. Site of army and navy acad.
Whangamomona (făng"gŭmōmō'nŭ), township (pop. 184), ⊙ Whangamomona co. (□ 447; pop. 851), W N.Isl., New Zealand, 36 mi. ESE of New Plymouth; agr. center.
Whangarei (făng"gŭrā'), borough (pop. 9,289) and port, ⊙ Whangarei co. (□ 1,046; pop. 11,717), N N.Isl., New Zealand, 80 mi. NNW of Auckland and on NW shore of Whangarei Bay. Exports coal, butter, fruit, wool. Kauri forest near by. Limestone, manganese.
Whangarei Bay, inlet of S Pacific, N N.Isl., New Zealand, on E coast of NW peninsula, N of Hauraki Gulf; 9 mi. E–W, 3 mi. N–S; site of Whangarei.
Whangaroa, county, New Zealand: see KAEO.
Whangaroa (făng-gŭrō'ŭ), township (pop. 83), N N.Isl., New Zealand, 135 mi. NNW of Auckland, on small landlocked harbor 1 mi. wide, 5 mi. long. Exports kauri gum.
Whangpoo River, Hwangpoo River, or **Hwangpu River** (all: hwăng'pōō'), Chinese *Hwangpu Kiang* or *Huang p'u Chiang* (both: jyăng'), river in S Kiangsu prov., China, rises in canal network of Kinshan area, flows 60 mi. NE and N, past Shanghai, to Yangtze R. at Woosung. The oceanward access route to Shanghai, the Whangpoo is a major navigation channel, dredged to a low-tide depth of 28 ft., admitting ocean-going vessels. Its course below Shanghai is lined with wharves, docks, warehouses, and industrial plants.

Wharfe River, Yorkshire, England, rises 7 mi. S of Hawes, flows 60 mi. SE, past Ilkley, Otley, and Tadcaster, to Ouse R. near Cawood.

Wharton, England: see WINSFORD.

Wharton (hwôr'tůn), county (□ 1,079; pop. 36,077), S Texas; ⊙ Wharton. On Gulf coastal plains; drained by Colorado and San Bernard rivers. A leading sulphur-producing area of U.S.; also oil, natural gas. Agr. (rice, cotton, corn, wheat, flax, hay, fruit, truck); cattle ranching; dairying, poultry and livestock raising (hogs, horses, mules, sheep). Hunting, fishing. Formed 1846.

Wharton. 1 Residential borough (pop. 3,853), Morris co., N central N.J., on old Morris Canal and 2 mi. NW of Dover; chemicals; mines iron ore. Inc. 1895. **2** Village (pop. 392), Wyandot co., N central Ohio, 9 mi. W of Upper Sandusky; cannery. **3** City (pop. 4,450), ⊙ Wharton co., S Texas, on Colorado R. and c.55 mi. SW of Houston, in oil- and sulphur-producing, cattle-raising, and agr. area (cotton, vegetables, corn, hay, pecans). Wood products, canned foods, dairy products, cottonseed products, motorboats. Seat of a jr. col. Founded 1847, inc. 1902. **4** Village (pop. 1,631, with adjacent Bim), Boone co., SW W.Va., 13 mi. SE of Madison.

Wharton Deep, ocean depth (21,191 ft.) in Indian Ocean, SE of Cocos Isls.; 19°S 102°E.

Wharton Peninsula, Chile: see WELLINGTON ISLAND.

What Cheer, town (pop. 1,119), Keokuk co., SE Iowa, 17 mi. ENE of Oskaloosa; mfg. (brick, tile, pottery, feed). Clay pits near by. Founded 1865, inc. 1880.

Whatcom (hwŏt'kům), county (□ 2,151; pop. 66,733), NW Wash., on British Columbia line and Puget Sound; ⊙ Bellingham (seaport). Includes Mt. BAKER and Mt. SHUKSAN, in Mt. Baker Natl. Forest, and Lummi Indian Reservation; drained by Baker, Nooksack, and Skagit rivers. Rich agr. region in W (fruit, truck, bulbs, sugar beets, dairy products); salmon, lumber, minerals (gold, silver, coal). Formed 1854.

Whately (hwāt'lē), town (pop. 939), Franklin co., W central Mass., near the Connecticut, 8 mi. N of Northampton; tobacco, onions.

Whatley, village (1940 pop. 640), Clarke co., SW Ala., 5 mi. SE of Grove Hill; farming, lumbering.

Wheatcroft, town (pop. 418), Webster co., W Ky., 23 mi. WNW of Madisonville, in agr., timber, and coal-mining area.

Wheatfield, town (pop. 496), Jasper co., NW Ind., 32 mi. SSE of Gary, in agr. area.

Wheathampstead (hwē'tůmstěd, hwě'tům–), town and parish (pop. 3,062), central Hertford, England, on Lea R. and 5 mi. NNE of St. Albans; agr. market; mfg. of pharmaceuticals. Has 13th-cent. church.

Wheatland, county (□ 1,425; pop. 3,187), central Mont.; ⊙ Harlowton. Agr. region drained by Musselshell R. Livestock, grain. Formed 1917.

Wheatland. 1 Town (pop. 581), Yuba co., N central Calif., 12 mi. SE of Marysville; hops, fruit, hogs, dairy products. **2** Town (pop. 735), Knox co., SW Ind., 11 mi. E of Vincennes; trade center for fruit-growing area. **3** Town (pop. 568), Clinton co., E Iowa, near Wapsipinicon R., 25 mi. NW of Davenport. **4** Town (pop. 299), Hickory co., central Mo., in the Ozarks, 18 mi. SE of Osceola. **5** Borough (pop. 1,402), Mercer co., W Pa., on Shenango R. just S of Farrell. Settled 1812, inc. 1872. **6** Town (pop. 2,286), ⊙ Platte co., SE Wyo., near Laramie R., 65 mi. N of Cheyenne, in irrigated sugar-beet and livestock region; alt. c.4,740 ft. Food processing (beet sugar, dairy products, flour); wool, poultry, timber. Mica quarries in vicinity. Annual rodeo. Near by is Eagle Nest Gap, pass on Oregon Trail. Settled c.1885.

Wheatley (hwēt'lē), village (pop. 785), S Ont., near L. Erie, 8 mi. ENE of Leamington; tobacco, fruit, vegetables.

Wheatley. 1 Former urban district (1931 pop. 1,268), E Oxfordshire, England, 5 mi. E of Oxford; agr. market. Near by are limestone quarries. **2** Suburb, Yorkshire, England: see DONCASTER.

Wheatley, town (pop. 406), St. Francis co., E Ark., 20 mi. WSW of Forrest City, in rice and cotton area.

Wheaton. 1 Residential city (pop. 11,638), ⊙ Du Page co., NE Ill., W of Chicago and 10 mi. E of Geneva, in agr. area (corn, oats, barley); nurseries. Seat of Wheaton Col. Experimental farms are here. Settled in 1830s; platted 1853, inc. 1859. Elbert H. Gary b. here. **2** City (pop. 134), Pottawatomie co., NE Kansas, 45 mi. NW of Topeka; cattle, grain. **3** Village (pop. 1,948), ⊙ Traverse co., W Minn., on Mustinka R., near L. Traverse, and c.40 mi. SW of Fergus Falls, in grain, poultry, and livestock area; dairy products. Settled 1884, inc. 1887. **4** City (pop. 394), Barry co., SW Mo., in the Ozarks, 13 mi. SW of Monett.

Wheeler. 1 County (□ 306; pop. 6,712), SE central Ga.; ⊙ Alamo. Bounded E and N by Oconee R., S by Ocmulgee R., SW by Little Ocmulgee R. Coastal plain agr. (corn, peanuts, melons, fruit) and forestry (naval stores) area. Formed 1912. **2** County (□ 576; pop. 1,526), NE central Nebr.; ⊙ Bartlett. Agr. region drained by Cedar R. Stock, grain. Formed 1877. **3** County (□ 1,707; pop. 3,313), N central Oregon; ⊙ Fossil. Mtn. area crossed by John Day R. Lumber, livestock. Formed 1899. **4** County (□ 916; pop. 10,317), extreme N Texas; ⊙ Wheeler. In E Panhandle, and bounded E by Okla. line; alt. 2,000–2,800 ft. Drained by North Fork of Red. R. Underlaid by E part of huge Panhandle natural-gas and oil field; oil and gas wells; gas refineries, carbon-black plants, clay, caliche, silica, gypsum deposits; agr. (grain sorghums, cotton, fruit, truck, dairy products, cattle, hogs, poultry, horses). Formed 1876.

Wheeler. 1 Village (pop. 178), Jasper co., SE Ill., 12 mi. ESE of Effingham, in agr. area. **2** Village (1940 pop. 850), Valley co., NE Mont., 14 mi. SE of Glasgow and on Fort Peck Reservoir, near Fort Peck Dam and Missouri R., in extensively irrigated region. **3** Town (pop. 291), Tillamook co., NW Oregon, 35 mi. S of Astoria, at mouth of Nehalem R.; lumber, fish. **4** Town (pop. 904), ⊙ Wheeler co., extreme N Texas, in the Panhandle, c.40 mi. ESE of Pampa; a trade center in natural-gas, cotton, fruit, cattle region. **5** Village (pop. 235), Dunn co., W Wis., 11 mi. N of Menomonie, in dairying area.

Wheeler Dam, NW Ala., on Tennessee R., 17 mi. E of Florence, c.15 mi. upstream from Wilson Dam. Major TVA dam (72 ft. high, 6,342 ft. long) completed 1936; concrete construction. Designed to aid navigation (has lock 360 ft. long, 60 ft. wide, providing max. lift of 52 ft.) and flood control and to supply power. Forms Wheeler Reservoir (□ 105; 74 mi. long, 1–3 mi. wide; capacity 1,150,400 acre-ft.; sometimes known as Wheeler L.) in Lawrence, Lauderdale, Limestone, Morgan, Madison, and Marshall counties. Reservoir receives Elk R. in Limestone co. and Flint and Paint Rock rivers in Madison co.; has submerged upper part of MUSCLE SHOALS. Wheeler Natl. Wildlife Refuge is just E of Decatur, on both shores of reservoir.

Wheeler Field, air base of U.S. army, central Oahu, T.H., near S edge of Schofield Barracks; established 1922. Along with PEARL HARBOR, it was bombed by Japanese on Dec. 7, 1941.

Wheeler National Monument, Colo.: see CREEDE.

Wheeler Peak. 1 Peak in Calif.: see SWEETWATER MOUNTAINS. **2** Peak (13,058 ft.) in E Nev., in Snake Range, 36 mi. SE of Ely. Highest point in range, 2d highest in state. Lehman Caves Natl. Monument is on E flank of peak. **3** Peak (13,151 ft.) in N N.Mex., in Sangre de Cristo Mts., 70 mi. NNE of Santa Fe, 13 mi. NE of Taos; highest point in state. Until recent surveys, one of the TRUCHAS peaks was thought to be higher.

Wheelersburg, village (pop. 1,013), Scioto co., S Ohio, on the Ohio, 6 mi. E of Portsmouth.

Wheeling. 1 Village (pop. 916), Cook co., NE Ill., N suburb of Chicago, 8 mi. W of Winnetka. **2** City (pop. 58,891), ⊙ Ohio co., NW W.Va., in Northern Panhandle, on the Ohio (bridged) at Ohio line, and 45 mi. SW of Pittsburgh. Third-largest city (after Huntington and Charleston) in W.Va.; industrial and commercial metropolis of rich Northern Panhandle coal- and gas-producing region; port of entry. Has iron- and steelworks; mfg. of tin plate, sheet-metal products, nails, chinaware, tiles, glass, paper, textiles, clothing, stogies and other tobacco products, food products, medicines, furniture, plastics; railroad shops. Has R.C. cathedral. Military school. Wheeling Isl. (residential) in the Ohio is connected by bridges to Ohio and W.Va. banks. Points of interest in city include marker on site of Fort Henry (1774; originally Fort Fincastle), where one of last skirmishes of the Revolution was fought in 1782, Customhouse (1854), mus., and Oglebay Park (c.750 acres). Settled 1769; chartered 1806; inc. 1836. Became W terminus of Natl. Road in 1818, a port of entry in 1831, and a rail terminus in 1852. As a pro-Unionist center in Civil War, became site of Wheeling Conventions (1861–62) which led to formation of W.Va. from the N and W counties of Va. Was ⊙ W.Va., 1863–70, and again, 1875–85.

Wheelock, town and parish (pop. 756), S central Cheshire, England, 4 mi. NE of Crewe; chemicals, aluminum products.

Wheelock. 1 Village (pop. 101), Williams co., NW N.Dak., 20 mi. NE of Williston. **2** Town (pop. 287), Caledonia co., NE Vt., 12 mi. NW of St. Johnsbury.

Wheelton, agr. village and parish (pop. 1,037), central Lancashire, England, 2 mi. NNE of Chorley.

Wheelwright, town (pop. estimate 2,000), S Santa Fe prov., Argentina, 65 mi. SW of Rosario; rail junction and agr. center (wheat, flax, corn, barley, potatoes, livestock; plant nurseries).

Wheelwright. 1 Mining town (pop. 2,037), Floyd co., SE Ky., in Cumberland foothills, 15 mi. SW of Pikeville; bituminous coal. **2** Village, Mass.: see HARDWICK.

Whelen Springs (hwē'lůn), town (pop. 192), Clark co., S central Ark., 21 mi. SSW of Arkadelphia, near Little Missouri R.

Whetstone, town and parish (pop. 1,403), central Leicester, England, 5 mi. WSW of Leicester; shoe industry.

Whetstone Creek, NE S.Dak., formed by confluence of several forks near Wilmot, flows c.35 mi. SE and E to Minnesota R. just S of Ortonville, Minn. Small dike near mouth diverts part of flow into S end of Big Stone L.

Whetstone Mountains, Cochise co., SE Ariz., N of Fort Huachuca; APACHE PEAK (7,684 ft.) is highest point.

Whickham (hwĭ'kům), urban district (1931 pop. 20,756; 1951 census 23,116), N Durham, England, near Tees R., 3 mi. SW of Newcastle-upon-Tyne; coal mining, ironworking, concrete making. In urban dist. are towns of: Swalwell (N; pop. 4,162), with steel industry; Burnopfield (SW), with coal mines; and Lintzford (SW), with coal mines, metalworks, paper and printers'-ink industries.

Whidbey, Point (hwĭd'bē), on SW Eyre Peninsula, S South Australia, in Great Australian Bight; forms W end of Avoid Bay; 34°35'S 135°7'E.

Whidbey Island, Island co., NW Wash., one of largest (c.40 mi. long) isls. in U.S., in Puget Sound NW of Everett; includes Oak Harbor (naval air base), Coupeville, and Langley towns. At N end is scenic Deception Pass (state park here), a swift tidal strait spanned by bridge (1935) to Fidalgo Isl., which is connected by bridges to mainland.

Whidbey Islands, Australia: see GREAT AUSTRALIAN BIGHT.

Whiddy Island (1,000 acres; 3 mi. long), near head of Bantry Bay, SW Co. Cork, Ireland, just off Bantry town. Has ruins of old castle.

Whigham (hwĭ'gům), town (pop. 471), Grady co., SW Ga., 7 mi. W of Cairo, in farm area; sawmilling.

Whim, village (pop. 1,160), Berbice co., NE Br. Guiana, in Atlantic coastland, 13 mi. E of New Amsterdam; sugar cane, rice.

Whippany (hwĭ'pünē), industrial village (1940 pop. 1,325), Morris co., NE N.J., on Whippany R. and 4 mi. NE of Morristown; mfg. (paper products, rubber and cork goods, tar, metal powder); dairy products.

Whippany River, N N.J., rises W of Morristown, flows c.20 mi. generally ENE, past Morristown and Whippany, to Rockaway R. just above its junction with Passaic R.

Whippingham (hwĭ'pĭng-ům), town and parish (pop. 2,169), on Isle of Wight, Hampshire, England, on Medina R. and just S of East Cowes; agr. market, with plywood works.

Whipsnade, England: see DUNSTABLE.

Whistler, village (1940 pop. 4,159), Mobile co., SW Ala., 5 mi. NW of Mobile. Cedar Creek State Park is near by.

Whiston, village and parish (pop. 5,881), SW Lancashire, England, just SE of Prescot; truck gardening, metalworking.

Whitaker (hwĭ'tůkůr), residential borough (pop. 2,149), Allegheny co., SW Pa., E suburb of Pittsburgh on Monongahela R. Inc. 1906.

Whitakers (hwĭ'tůkůrz), town (pop. 962), Nash and Edgecombe counties, E central N.C., 12 mi. NNE of Rocky Mount, in agr. area.

Whitburn, town and parish (pop. 6,082), NE Durham, England, near the coast 3 mi. N of Sunderland; coal mines, paper mills.

Whitburn, burgh (1931 pop. 2,440; 1951 census 5,232), SW West Lothian, Scotland, 3 mi. SW of Bathgate; coal mining. Burns's daughter is buried here.

Whitby, town (pop. 5,904), ⊙ Ontario co., S Ont., on L. Ontario, 28 mi. NE of Toronto; tanning, lumbering; mfg. of leather goods, hardware, lace; grain elevators. Founded 1836.

Whitby. 1 Town, Cheshire, England: see ELLESMERE PORT. **2** Port and urban district (1931 pop. 11,451; 1951 census 11,668), North Riding, NE Yorkshire, England, port at mouth of Esk R. on North Sea, 16 mi. NNW of Scarborough; 54°29'N 0°36'W; shipbuilding, metalworking; resort and agr. market. Making of jet ornaments is a long-established industry. Chief export is coal. The *Streoneshalh* of Bede, it has ruins of abbey founded 657 by St. Hilda; in 664 the Synod of Whitby was held here. Sacked 867 by Danes, but reestablished 1078 by Benedictines. Capt. Cook served his apprenticeship here, and his ship *Resolution* was built here. Town was residence of the poet Cædmon. Has 13th–16th-cent. parish church and archaeological mus.

Whitchurch (hwĭt'chûrch). **1** Town and parish (pop. 2,461), N Hampshire, England, on Test R. and 12 mi. N of Winchester; mfg. of silk, paper, soap. Has 13th-cent. church. **2** Urban district (1951 census 6,856), N Shropshire, England, 18 mi. N of Shrewsbury; metalworking, cheese processing. The 18th-cent. church contains tomb of John Talbot, 1st earl of Shrewsbury.

Whitchurch. 1 Residential town and parish (pop. 12,733), SE Glamorgan, Wales, 3 mi. NNW of Cardiff. There are remains of Roman walls. **2** Town and parish (pop. 706), W Pembroke, Wales, 3 mi. E of St. David's; woolen milling. Just S, on St. Brides Bay of Irish Channel, is woolen-milling village of Solva.

White. 1 County (□ 1,042; pop. 38,040), central Ark.; ⊙ Searcy. Bounded E by White R.; drained by the Bayou des Arc and intersected by Little Red R. Leads Ark. in strawberry production; also produces cotton, potatoes, vegetables, pecans. Mfg. at Searcy, Judsonia, and Bald Knob. Timber; mineral springs. Formed 1835. **2** County (□ 243; 5,951), NE Ga.; ⊙ Cleveland. Blue Ridge Farm (cotton, corn, hay, potatoes, poultry), lumber, and resort area drained by Chattahoochee R. Chattahoochee Natl. Forest occupies N part. Formed 1857. **3** County (□ 501; pop. 20,935), SE Ill.; ⊙ Carmi. Bounded E by Wabash R.; drained by Little Wabash R. Agr. (wheat, corn, livestock, poultry). Mfg. of clothing, wood products, buttons; dairy-products and food processing. Oil and natural-gas wells. Formed 1815. **4** County (□ 497; pop. 18,042), NW central Ind.; ⊙ Monticello. Partly bounded E by Tippecanoe R.; drained by Tippecanoe R. and by Big Monon and small Little Monon creeks. Agr. area (corn, oats, soybeans); mfg. (dairy and food products, flour, furniture, crushed stone, brick); quarries. Resorts on Shafer and Freeman lakes. Formed 1834. **5** County (□ 385; pop. 16,204), central Tenn.; ⊙ Sparta. In the Cumberlands; bounded (S, W) by Caney Fork. Great Falls Reservoir in SW; also includes part of Center Hill Reservoir site. Coal mining, limestone quarrying, lumbering, livestock raising, agr. (especially tobacco; also corn, hay, vegetables). Formed 1806.

White. 1 Town (pop. 454), Bartow co., NW Ga., 9 mi. NNE of Cartersville; manganese mining. **2** City (pop. 525), Brookings co., E S.Dak., 12 mi. NE of Brookings and on branch of Big Sioux R.; dairy produce, livestock, poultry, grain.

Whiteabbey (hwīt'ă'bē), fishing village (district pop. 2,703), SE Co. Antrim, Northern Ireland, on NW shore of Belfast Lough, 5 mi. NNE of Belfast; seaside resort.

Whiteadder Water, river, East Lothian and Berwick, Scotland, rises in Lammermuir Hills 6 mi. S of Dunbar, flows 34 mi. SE to the Tweed 2 mi. WSW of Berwick-on-Tweed. Receives Blackadder Water.

Whiteash (hwīt'ăsh), village (pop. 204), Williamson co., S Ill., 6 mi. E of Herrin, in bituminous-coal-mining and agr. area.

White Bay, inlet (60 mi. long, 20 mi. wide at entrance) of the Atlantic, NE N.F. At entrance of bay are St. Barbe or Horse Isls. Several fishing settlements on shore of bay.

White Bear Lake, city (pop. 3,646), Ramsey co., E Minn., on W shore of White Bear L., 10 mi. N of St. Paul. Resort and residential suburb of St. Paul in truck-farming area; ice cream, boats. Inc. 1922. Railroad name is White Bear.

White Bear Lake, in Washington and Ramsey counties, E Minn., 10 mi. NNE of St. Paul; 3 mi. long, 2 mi. wide.

White Bluff, town (pop. 506), Dickson co., N central Tenn., 29 mi. W of Nashville, in timber and farm area; sawmilling. Montgomery Bell recreation area is near by.

Whitebreast Creek, S Iowa, rises in Clarke co., flows c.80 mi. E and NE to Des Moines R. 6 mi. NE of Knoxville.

White Carpathian Mountains (kärpā'thēŭn), Czech *Bílé Karpaty* (bē'lā kär'pätĭ), Slovak *Biele Karpaty* (byĕ'lā), range in W Slovakia, Czechoslovakia; extend c.50 mi. NE–SW, along Moravian-Slovakian border, bet. Senica (S) and Lysa Pass (N); rise to 3,175 ft. in Velka Javorina mtn.

White Cart Water, river, Renfrew, Scotland, rises 3 mi. S of Eaglesham, flows 20 mi. N and W, past Cathcart, Paisley, and Inchinnan, to the Clyde just N of Renfrew. Receives Black Cart Water at Inchinnan.

White Castle, town (pop. 1,839), Iberville parish, SE central La., on the Mississippi and 19 mi. S of Baton Rouge, in sugar-cane area; sugar milling, moss ginning.

Whitechapel, London, England: see STEPNEY.

White City. 1 Village (1940 pop. 612), St. Lucie co., SE Fla., just S of Fort Pierce, on Indian R. **2** Village (pop. 275), Macoupin co., SW Ill., 26 mi. ENE of Alton, in agr. and bituminous-coal area. **3** City (pop. 540), Morris co., E central Kansas, 17 mi. SSE of Junction City, in grazing and agr. region; poultry packing.

White Cliffs, village, NW central New South Wales, Australia, 125 mi. NE of Broken Hill; opal mine.

White Cloud. 1 City (pop. 308), Doniphan co., extreme NE Kansas, on Missouri R., near Nebr. line, and 28 mi. NW of St. Joseph, Mo.; apple-growing, general agr. Indian burial mounds and ruins of Indian villages have been found near by. **2** Village (pop. 977), ⊙ Newaygo co. W central Mich., on White R. and 34 mi. NE of Muskegon, in farm area. Dairy products, pickles, lumber. State park just SW.

White Deer, town (pop. 629), Carson co., extreme N Texas, in high plains of the Panhandle, 40 mi. ENE of Amarillo; gas (including helium) and oil wells, grain, cattle, hogs.

White Deer Cave, Chinese *Pailutung* (bī'lōō'dōōng'), site in Lü Shan mountain massif, N Kiangsi prov., China, S of Kiukiang, where 13th-cent. Confucianist philosopher Chu Hsi (Chu Hi) lived and taught.

White Drin River (drēn), Serbo-Croatian *Beli Drim*, Albanian *Drin* (or *Drini*) *i bardhë*, Ital. *Drin Bianco*, right headstream of Drin R., in SW Serbia (Yugoslavia) and N Albania, rises in the Zhljeb N of Pec, flows c.80 mi. S through the Metohija and SW into Albania, joining the Black Drin at Kukës to form the Drin.

White Earth. 1 Indian village (1940 pop. 763), Becker co., W Minn., near White Earth L., in White Earth Indian Reservation, 20 mi. N of Detroit Lakes. Hosp. and mission school are here. Wildlife refuge and state forest in vicinity. **2** Village (pop. 218), Mountrail co., NW N.Dak., 18 mi. W of Stanley and on White Earth R.; small ranches, farms.

White Earth Lake, Becker co., W Minn., in White Earth Indian Reservation, 20 mi. NNE of Detroit Lakes; 2.5 mi. long.

White Earth River, rises in NW N.Dak., flows E and S 60 mi., largely in Mountrail co., to Missouri R.

White Elster River, Germany: see ELSTER RIVER.

Whiteface, town (pop. 579), Cochran co., NW Texas, 16 mi. W of Levelland.

Whiteface Mountain (4,872 ft.), Essex co., NE N.Y., in the Adirondacks, 7 mi. NNE of Lake Placid village. State-developed skiing center here. Highway ascends peak almost to summit, whose meteorological station (established 1937) is reached by elevator.

White Face Peak (11,494 ft.), in Rocky Mts., Grand co., N central Colo.

Whiteface River, formed by confluence of 3 forks in St. Louis co., NE Minn., flows 70 mi. SW, past Meadowlands, to St. Louis R. 6 mi. NE of Floodwood. Passes through Whiteface Reservoir (7 mi. long, 2–3 mi. wide) in upper course and drains part of Superior Natl. Forest.

Whitefield, urban district (1931 pop. 9,107; 1951 census 12,912), SE Lancashire, England, 6 mi. NNW of Manchester; cotton milling.

Whitefield. 1 Agr. town (pop. 1,030), Lincoln co., S Maine, on Sheepscot R. and 12 mi. SE of Augusta. Settled c.1770, inc. 1809. **2** Resort town (pop. 1,677), Coos co., NW N.H., in White Mts., bet. Littleton and Lancaster; winter sports; mfg. (furniture, clothing); dairy products, poultry. Granted 1774, inc. 1804.

Whitefish, city (pop. 3,268), Flathead co., NW Mont., 15 mi. N of Kalispell and on Whitefish L., just S of Whitefish Range; lake resort; railway div. point with repair shops, in lumbering region; sawmills. Inc. 1911.

Whitefish Bay (34 mi. long, 1–10 mi. wide), W Ont., E inlet of L. of the Woods, bounded S by Aulneau Peninsula. Contains numerous islets.

Whitefish Bay, village (pop. 14,665), Milwaukee co., SE Wis., N residential suburb of Milwaukee. Inc. 1892.

Whitefish Bay, in Mich. and Ont., SE arm of L. Superior, traversed by international line; c.30 mi. long NW–SE, 15–34 mi. wide. Peninsula terminating at Whitefish Point is at W side of entrance; here are Whitefish Point village, a lighthouse, lifeguard station, and radio-beacon station. Bay is connected with L. Huron (SE) by St. Marys R.

Whitefish Lake. 1 Lake (□ 11) in Crow Wing co., central Minn., in state forest, 23 mi. N of Brainerd; 7.5 mi. long, 4 mi. wide. Fed and drained by Pine R. Has fishing, boating, bathing resorts. Village of Manhattan Beach on E shore. **2** Lake in Flathead co., NW Mont., 15 mi. N of Kalispell, just S of Whitefish Range; 7 mi. long, 1 mi. wide. Used for recreation. City of Whitefish at S end.

Whitefish Point, Mich.: see WHITEFISH BAY.

Whitefish Range, in Rocky Mts. of NW Mont., rises just N of British Columbia line and W of Flathead R.; extends SE to Whitefish, Mont. Elevations of 6–8,100 ft. Lies partly within Flathead Natl. Forest.

Whitefish River, S Upper Peninsula, Mich., rises in E Marquette co., flows SE into Delta co., then SW to N end of Little Bay De Noc; c.45 mi. long.

White Fox, village (pop. 346), E central Sask., 7 mi. NW of Nipawin; dairying, grain.

Whitefriars, area in ALSATIA district of London, England, N of the Thames, near Fleet Street. Formerly site of Carmelite monastery, founded 1241, dissolved 1538. Privilege of sanctuary attached to monastic precincts was preserved until 1697.

Whitehall, street in City of Westminster, London, England, running parallel to N bank of the Thames, from Trafalgar Square to Parliament Square; site of the principal govt. offices and of the Cenotaph (war memorial by Sir E. L. Lutyens). Off Whitehall are Downing Street, residence of Br. prime ministers, New Scotland Yard, and Horseguards Parade. It was site of Whitehall Palace, residence of archbishops of York from time of Henry III until 1529, when it was acquired by Henry VIII; Henry VIII and Cromwell died here, and Charles I was executed before it. Of the palace, partly destroyed by fire (1619 and 1698), only the banquet hall, rebuilt 1622 by Inigo Jones, remains. It now houses Royal United Service Mus.

White Hall. 1 or **Whitehall,** town (pop. 493), Clarke co., NE central Ga., 4 mi. SSE of Athens; mfg. (cotton textiles, yarn). **2** City (pop. 3,082), Greene co., W central Ill., 22 mi. SSW of Jacksonville; bituminous-coal mines, clay deposits; mfg. (clay products, clothing); agr. (corn, wheat, apples, livestock; dairy products). Here is memorial, designed by Lorado Taft, to Annie Louise Keller, teacher killed saving pupils during tornado in 1927. Founded 1820, inc. 1837.

Whitehall. 1 City (pop. 1,819), Muskegon co., SW Mich., 12 mi. NNW of Muskegon, on White L., in fruitgrowing area near L. Michigan; mfg. (chemicals, woodenware, leather). Resort; yacht racing. Swedish midsummer festival held here. Inc. 1867 as village, as city 1943. **2** Town (pop. 929), Jefferson co., SW Mont., on Jefferson R. and 20 mi. ESE of Butte; gold, silver mines; dairy products, grain, sugar beets, timber. **3** Village (pop. 4,457), Washington co., E N.Y., at S end of L. Champlain, on Champlain division of the Barge Canal and 21 mi. NNE of Glens Falls; summer resort. Railroad shops; silk mills; mfg. of machinery. Settled 1759, inc. 1806. **4** Town, N.C.: see SEVEN SPRINGS. **5** Village (pop. 4,877), Franklin co., central Ohio, a SE suburb of Columbus. Inc. 1947. **6** Borough (pop. 7,342), Allegheny co., SW Pa., 5 mi. S of downtown Pittsburgh. Inc. 1947. **7** City (pop. 1,379), ⊙ Trempealeau co., W Wis., on Trempealeau R. and 32 mi. SSE of Eau Claire, in dairy, poultry, and grain area; trade and shipping center; grain elevators, tobacco warehouse, creamery; cooperage; meat packing. Settled 1855; inc. as village in 1887, as city in 1941.

Whitehaven, port and municipal borough (1931 pop. 21,159; 1951 census 24,624), W Cumberland, England, on Irish Sea at entrance to Solway Firth, 35 mi. SW of Carlisle; coal- and iron-mining center; leather tanning, flour and feed-cake milling. Chief imports are grains, timber, hides, cement; exports are coal, coke, leather, quarry stone. Has two 18th-cent. churches. Formerly a hamlet, Whitehaven grew rapidly with the discovery and exploitation of coal deposits in 17th cent. In 1788 the town was attacked by John Paul Jones.

White Haven, borough (pop. 1,461), Luzerne co., E central Pa., 14 mi. SSE of Wilkes-Barre and on Lehigh R.; explosives, machinery, clothing; dairying. Inc. c.1853.

Whitehaven. 1 Fishing village (pop. c.100), Wicomico co., SE Md., 13 mi. SW of Salisbury and on Wicomico R.; vegetable cannery. Near by is Green Hill Episcopal Church (1733). **2** Village (pop. 1,311), Shelby co., SW Tenn., at Miss. line just S of Memphis.

Whitehead (hwīt-hĕd'), urban district (1937 pop. 1,279; 1951 census 1,862), E Co. Antrim, Northern Ireland, on N shore of Belfast Lough, near its mouth on the North Channel, 14 mi. NE of Belfast; fishing port and seaside resort. Has remains of anc. Castle Chichester.

Whitehead Island (hwīt'–), Knox co., S Maine, 3.5 mi. NE of Tenants Harbor. Lighthouse here.

White Hill, Czechoslovakia: see WHITE MOUNTAIN.

Whitehill, town and parish (pop. 7,074), E Hampshire, England, 6 mi. ESE of Alton. With adjoining town of Bordon Camp (N) it forms part of an important military training area.

Whitehills, fishing village, N Banffshire, Scotland, on Moray Firth, 3 mi. WNW of Banff; tile mfg. Just N is Knock Head.

Whitehorn Mountain (11,101 ft.), E B.C., near Alta. border, in Rocky Mts., in Mt. Robson Provincial Park, 55 mi. WNW of Jasper.

Whitehorse or **White Horse,** town (pop. 754), S Yukon, on Lewes R. (head of navigation, a name for upper course of Yukon R.), and 90 mi. N of Skagway, on Alaska Highway and at terminus of White Pass and Yukon RR from Skagway; 60°43'N 135°3'W. Distributing center for mining (coal, copper), hunting, trapping region. Has Anglican and R.C. churches, airport, radio and meteorological station; Royal Canadian Mounted Police hq. for S Yukon; hosp. During navigation season (June–Oct.) there is steamer connection with Dawson. In Second World War town was center of the *Canol* oil project, pipe line terminal, and site of oil refinery; all closed down in 1945. During war, population reached c.8,000, including U.S. Army personnel. Town grew as distributing and staging center during the Klondike gold rush, 1897–98. Near by are the Whitehorse Rapids and Miles Canyon of Lewes R.

White Horse Beach, Mass.: see PLYMOUTH.

White Horse Vale or **Vale of the White Horse,** Berkshire, England, extends 15 mi. NE from Wiltshire border to just W of Abingdon. Takes name from large figure of galloping horse on side of White Horse Hill (856 ft.), 6 mi. W of Wantage, just S of village of Uffington. Region is closely associated with Alfred the Great, whose victory (871) at Ashdown, 3 mi. NW of Lambourn, the figure of the white horse commemorates. The figure, of rude outline and 355 ft. long, is visible for miles. There are other "white horses" in Wiltshire, Berkshire, York, and elsewhere.

Whitehouse, minor port, Westmoreland parish, SW Jamaica, 15 mi. SE of Savanna-la-Mar; ships logwood.

Whitehouse, village (pop. 849), Lucas co., NW Ohio, 16 mi. WSW of downtown Toledo; grain, dairy products, fruit; mfg. of auto parts.

Whitehouse Lower (hwīt-hous'), town (pop. 327), N suburb of Belfast, S Co. Antrim, Northern Ireland, on Belfast Lough.

White House Station, village (1940 pop. 519), Hunterdon co., W N.J., 9 mi. NW of Somerville; poultry, grain, fruit, dairy.

Whitehouse Upper (hwīt-hous'), town (pop. 1,129), N suburb of Belfast, S Co. Antrim, Northern Ireland, near Belfast Lough.
White Iron Lake, in Lake and St. Louis counties and Superior Natl. Forest, NE Minn., just SE of Ely; 6 mi. long, 1.5 mi. wide. Fishing, boating, bathing resorts. Fed and drained by South Kawishiwi R.
White Island 38 mi. long, 6–10 mi. wide), E Keewatin Dist., Northwest Territories, in Frozen Strait, off S Melville Peninsula (N), just NW of Southampton Isl.; 65°47'N 84°45'W.
White Island, uninhabited island (1½ mi. long) in Bay of Plenty, N N.Isl., New Zealand, 43 mi. W of Cape Runaway; active volcano (alt. 1,075 ft.) with mineral lake; guano, building stone. Formerly mined for sulphur.
White Island, N.H.: see ISLES OF SHOALS.
White Körös River, Hungary and Rumania: see KÖRÖS RIVER.
White Lake. 1 Resort village, Muskegon co., SW Mich.: see WHITE RIVER. **2** Village (pop. 1,385, with adjacent Seven Harbors), Oakland co., SE Mich., 14 mi. NW of Pontiac. **3** City (pop. 395), Aurora co., S S.Dak., 11 mi. W of Plankinton; dairy products, livestock, poultry, grain. **4** Village (pop. 408), Langlade co., NE Wis., 45 mi. ENE of Wausau; sawmilling.
White Lake. 1 Lake in Vermilion parish, S La., c.40 mi. WSW of New Iberia and near Gulf coast, in marshy region; c.13 mi. long, c.6 mi. wide. Joined by navigable waterways to Grand L. (NW), Gulf Intracoastal Waterway (passing to N), and Vermilion Bay (E). **2** Lake in Sullivan co., SE N.Y., 8 mi. W of Monticello; c.1¼ mi. long. White Lake and Kauneonga Lake (kŏnēŏng'gù), resort villages, are here.
White Land, Russian SFSR: see BELAYA ZEMLYA.
Whiteland, town (pop. 465), Johnson co., central Ind., 16 mi. SSE of Indianapolis, in agr. area.
Whitelaw, village (pop. estimate 300), W Alta., 32 mi. WSW of Peace River; lumbering, mixed farming, wheat.
Whitelick River, central Ind., rises in N Hendricks co., flows c.40 mi. generally S, past Plainfield and Brooklyn, to West Fork of White R. 5 mi. NNE of Martinsville.
White Main (mān), Ger. *Weisser Main* (vī'sûr mīn'), N headstream of the Main, W Germany, rises in the Fichtelgebirge 6 mi. W of Wunsiedel, flows c.30 mi. WNW, past Kulmbach, to Mainleus, where it joins the RED MAIN to form MAIN RIVER.
Whitemark, largest town and port (pop. 139) on Flinders Isl. of Furneaux Isls., Tasmania, on W coast of isl.; center of sheep area.
White Marsh, village, Gloucester co., E Va., 8 mi. N of Yorktown. Near by are "Belroi," birthplace of Walter Reed, and Abingdon Church (1754–55).
White Mere, England: see ELLESMERE.
White Mountain, village (pop. 127), W Alaska, on S Seward Peninsula, 60 mi. E of Nome; fishing; trade center for gold-mining district. Has native school.
White Mountain or **White Hill,** Czech *Bílá Hora* (bē'lä hô'rä), Ger. *Weisserberg* (vī'sûrbĕrk), hill (1,246 ft.), in central Bohemia, Czechoslovakia, within Greater Prague area, 4 mi. ESE of city center. Site of fateful battle (Nov., 1620), when Bohemian armies under Frederick the Winter King (Frederick V) were defeated by imperial army under Tilly, the country passing thereafter to Austria; 1st major engagement of Thirty Years War. Has 16th-cent. star-shaped pavilion.
White Mountains. 1 In E Ariz., in Fort Apache Indian Reservation, E of McNary. Chief peaks are GREENS PEAK (10,115 ft.) and BALDY PEAK (11,590 ft.). **2** In E Calif. and SW Nev., range extending c.55 mi. S from Mineral-Esmeralda co. line in Nev. to N end of Inyo Mts. 13 mi. SE of Bishop, Calif.; mts. partly bound Owens Valley on E. White Mtn. peak (14,242 ft.), 20 mi. NNE of Bishop, is highest point. BOUNDARY PEAK (13,145 ft.), in N, is highest point in Nev.; just S, in Calif., is Montgomery Peak (13,545 ft.). Montgomery Pass crosses range in N. **3** In N.H., glaciated granitic mountain mass (□ c.1,000), part of the Appalachian system, occupying most of N central N.H. from Connecticut R. (W) to W Maine (E); one of leading summer-resort regions of E U.S. Mt. WASHINGTON (6,288 ft.), highest peak in NE U.S., is in the PRESIDENTIAL RANGE here. FRANCONIA MOUNTAINS, separated from the Presidentials by Crawford Notch, rise to 5,249 ft. at Mt. Lafayette. Other ranges: CARTER-MORIAH RANGE (highest peak 4,843 ft.), SANDWICH RANGE (up to 3,993 ft.). Old Man of the Mountain is on Profile (Cannon) Mtn. Among scenic passes (locally called "notches") are Crawford, Dixville (in N outlying range), Franconia, Kinsman, and Pinkham notches. Long famous for scenic beauty (deep ravines, glacial cirques, forests, streams), mts. have been summer-resort region since early-19th cent.; more recently, snow sports have brought winter vacationers. Resorts include Barlett, Bethlehem, Conway, Dixville Notch, Franconia, Gorham, Jackson, Jefferson, North Conway, Randolph, Woodstock. Much of area within White Mtn. Natl. Forest.
Whitemouth, village (pop. estimate 300), SE Man., on Whitemouth R. and 50 mi. E of Winnipeg; dairying; grain.
Whitemud River, SW and S Man., rises S of Riding Mountain Natl. Park, flows 150 mi. E, past Neepawa, Gladstone, and Westbourne, to S end of L. Manitoba 23 mi. NW of Portage la Prairie.
White Nile, former province, Anglo-Egyptian Sudan: see BLUE NILE prov.
White Nile, Arabic *Bahr el Abiad* or *Bahr el Abyad* (bä'hûr ĕl ăb'yăd), left headstream of the main Nile, in E central Anglo-Egyptian Sudan; the White Nile proper, formed in L. No by union of the BAHR EL JEBEL and BAHR EL GHAZAL, flows 600 mi. E then N, past Malakal, Kodok, Kosti (bridge), Ed Dueim, and Jebel Aulia (dam), and joins the Blue Nile at Khartoum to form the Nile proper. Navigable at all seasons. The name White Nile is sometimes also applied to the Bahr el Jebel S to Nimule, 1,200 mi. above Khartoum. Of the 2 principal Nile headstreams, the White Nile has the more regular flow; during flood season it provides but 10% of main Nile flow at Khartoum (while the Blue Nile makes its heavy, but seasonal contribution); at low water the White Nile's contribution is 83% of total Nile volume. The Sobat (chief tributary), in turn, supplies ½ of the White Nile's discharge.
White Oak. 1 Locality, Md.: see SILVER SPRING. **2** Borough (pop. 6,159), Allegheny co., W Pa., near McKeesport. Inc. 1948.
Whiteoak, town (pop. 91), Dunklin co., extreme SE Mo., near St. Francis R., 7 mi. N of Kennett.
White Oak Bayou (bī'ō) or **White Oak Creek,** NE Texas, rises W of Sulphur Springs, flows c.75 mi. generally E to Sulphur R. c.20 mi. ENE of Mount Pleasant.
White Oil Springs, Persian *Naft Safid* (näft' säfēd'), oil town, Sixth Prov., in Khuzistan, SW Iran, 45 mi. NE of Ahwaz and 105 mi. NE of Abadan (linked by pipeline); oil field opened 1945.
White Otter Lake (22 mi. long, 5 mi. wide), W Ont., 120 mi. WNW of Port Arthur; alt. 1,392 ft. Drains S into Seine R.
White Pass, village, NW B.C., on Alaska border, on Skagway R. and 14 mi. NNE of Skagway, on White Pass and Yukon Railway, near summit of White Pass.
White Pass (2,888 ft.), in Coast Range, on border bet. SE Alaska and NW B.C., 14 mi. NE of Skagway; 59°38'N 135°8'W; summit of White Pass and Yukon RR, built (1898–1900), during Klondike gold rush along trail made (1897) as alternate to difficult Chilkoot Pass route. White Pass village, on both sides of border, is frontier station.
White Pigeon, village (pop. 1,113), St. Joseph co., SW Mich., 35 mi. S of Kalamazoo, near Ind. line; mfg. (incubators, paper products, cement blocks); dairying. Settled c.1827, inc. 1837.
White Pine, county (□ 8,893; pop. 9,424), E Nev.; ⊙ Ely. Mtn. region bordering on Utah. Snake and Shell Creek ranges are E of Ely; Egan Range and White Pine Mts. are W. Parts of Nevada Natl. Forest are in S; Lehman Caves Natl. Monument is in SE. Mining (copper, lead, gold, silver), ranching. Formed 1869.
White Pine, town (pop. 780), Jefferson co., E Tenn., near Douglas Reservoir, 37 mi. ENE of Knoxville, in timber and farm region; wood products, hosiery.
White Pine Mine, Mich.: see PORCUPINE MOUNTAINS.
White Pine Mountains, E Nev., in White Pine co., N of Grant Range, in Nevada Natl. Forest. Rise to 10,741 ft. in Mt. Hamilton and 11,493 ft. in Duckwater peak (highest point), 37 mi. SW of Ely.
White Plains, town, Montserrado co., SW Liberia, on St. Paul R. and 12 mi. N of Monrovia (linked by launch); road junction; palm oil and kernels, coffee, cassava, rice.
White Plains. 1 City (pop. 359), Greene co., NE central Ga., 11 mi. SE of Greensboro; textile mfg. **2** Town (pop. 385), Hopkins co., W Ky., 12 mi. SSE of Madisonville, in coal-mining, agr., and timber area; lumber, canned goods. **3** Residential city (pop. 43,466), ⊙ Westchester co., SE N.Y., in New York city metropolitan area, c.25 mi. NNE of downtown Manhattan; produces plumbing and heating equipment, wire, cables, concrete pipe, tile, clothing, dairy foods, textiles, chemicals. Seat of Good Counsel Col., a state institute of applied arts and sciences, and a hosp. for mental diseases. Westchester County Center is near by. Provincial congress met here (1776) and ratified Declaration of Independence. American Revolution battle (1776) on Chatterton Hill here is commemorated by the memorial markers of White Plains Natl. Battlefield Site. Elijah Miller House (1738), where Washington stayed, and other historic bldgs. remain. Settled in late-17th cent.; inc. as village in 1866, as city in 1916.
White Regen River (rā'gùn), Ger. *Weisser Regen* (vī'sûr rā'gùn), Bavaria, Germany, rises on NW slope of the Great Arber, flows 20 mi. W and S, joining Black Regen River SW of Kötzting to form REGEN RIVER.
White River, Alaska and SW Yukon, rises in Alaska in St. Elias Mts. at foot of Mt. Sulzer, flows E, crossing into Yukon, and turns NNE, past Snag, to Yukon R. 60 mi. S of Dawson; c.200 mi. long.
White River, village (pop. estimate 400), central Ont., on White R. and 150 mi. NNW of Sault Ste. Marie; alt. 1,223 ft.; lumbering. Reputedly one of the coldest places in Canada.
White River, N Jamaica, flows c.20 mi. NNW to the coast 3 mi. E of Ocho Rios. Dam and hydroelectric station.
Whiteriver, village (pop. c.300), Navajo co., E Ariz., on White R., in Fort Apache Indian Reservation, and c.55 mi. NE of Globe; alt. c.5,000 ft.; trading point and hq. for Indian reservation. White Mts. near by.
White River, town (pop. 465), ⊙ Mellette co., S S.Dak., 60 mi. SSW of Pierre and on South Fork White R.; trading point for farming and cattle-raising area; wheat, hogs. Hydroelectric plant is here.
White River. 1 E Ariz., formed by confluence of 2 forks near White Mts., flows c.30 mi. W to Black R., forming Salt R. c.40 mi. NE of Globe. **2** In Ark. and Mo., rises in Boston Mts., NW Ark., flows irregularly NE into Mo., then re-enters Ark., flowing SE and S to Mississippi R. 5 mi. N of Rosedale, Miss.; c.690 mi. long; drains □ 28,000. Near its mouth it is joined to Arkansas R. by cutoff channel. Navigable for shallow drafts for 302 mi., to Batesville, Ark. Tributaries are Cache, Little Red, Black, Buffalo, and James rivers, and North Fork (site of Norfork Dam). Bull Shoals Dam (283 ft. high above foundations, 2,256 ft. long; for flood control, power; begun 1947) is c.7 mi. N of Cotter, Ark.; Bull Shoals Reservoir extends 87 mi. upstream. Forsyth Dam impounds L. Taneycomo (tă'nēkō"mō) (c.25 mi. long; hydroelectric plant; lake resorts) c.5 mi. ENE of Bronson, S Mo. **3** In SW Ind., formed NE of Petersburg by confluence of long East and West forks, flows 52 mi. SW to the Wabash opposite Mount Carmel, Ill. West Fork of White R. (sometimes called simply White R.) rises in Randolph co. near Ohio line, flows 255 mi. W and SW, past Winchester, Muncie, Anderson, and Indianapolis. East Fork is formed by confluence of tributaries near Columbus, flows 282 mi. S and SW to junction with West Fork. Upper section of East Fork is sometimes called Driftwood R. **4** In W Mich., rises in Newaygo co., flows c.55 mi. SE, past White Cloud and Hesperia, widening just below Montague into White L. (c.5 mi. long, 1 mi. wide; resort). Lake drains from W end into L. Michigan through short outlet. **5** In Nebr. and S.Dak., rises in NW Nebr. at alt. of 5,000 ft., flows 507 mi. NE, through Badlands of S.Dak., to Missouri R. near Chamberlain. Drainage basin (□ 10,200) has deposits of manganese and fuller's earth. **6** In NW Texas, formed by small headstreams in Hale co., flows c.100 mi. SE to Salt Fork of Brazos R. 25 mi. E of Post; partly intermittent. **7** In E Vt., rises near Granville in Green Mts., flows c.50 mi. SE, receiving First, Second, and Third branches, to the Connecticut at White River Junction. **8** In W Wash., rises on NE slopes of Mt. Rainier, flows c.90 mi. N and NW to junction with Green R. to form Duwamish R. S of Seattle. Stevens Dam (425 ft. high, 700 ft. long; completed 1948; for flood control) is E of Buckley; sometimes called Mud Mtn. Dam. **9** In SE Wis., rises in L. Geneva in Walworth co., flows c.12 mi. NE, past Lake Geneva city, to Fox R. at Burlington; generates power for both cities.
White River Junction, industrial, commercial, and railroad center (pop. 2,365) in HARTFORD town, Windsor co., E Vt., on Connecticut R., at mouth of White R.; wood products, printing; poultry, dairy products. Gateway to Green Mtn. resorts.
White Rock, town (pop. estimate 1,000), SW B.C., near Wash. border, on Strait of Georgia, 20 mi. SE of Vancouver; beach resort; mixed farming, poultry raising.
White Rock. 1 Village, R.I.: see WESTERLY. **2** Town (1940 pop. 141), Richland co., central S.C., 18 mi. NW of Columbia. **3** Town (pop. 113), Roberts co., extreme NE S.Dak., 30 mi. NE of Sisseton and on Bois de Sioux R., which forms Minn. boundary at this point, near N.Dak. line. Near by is Traverse–Boix de Sioux dam, U.S. water-conservation project.
White Rock Lake, N Texas, former water-supply reservoir (c.1,350 acres) in NE Dallas city, impounded by dam in small White Rock Creek, a N tributary of the Trinity; large park here.
White Rock Mountain, peak (13,532 ft.) in Rocky Mts., Gunnison co., W central Colo.
White Russia, USSR: see BELORUSSIA.
Whites, town (pop. 2,101), central Orange Free State, U. of So. Afr., 30 mi. SW of Kroonstad; alt. 4,541 ft.; rail junction; cement-mfg. center.
Whitesail Lake (28 mi. long, 1–3 mi. wide), W central B.C., in Coast Mts., in Tweedsmuir Park, 170 mi. WSW of Prince George, just NW of Eutsuk L. Drains N into Ootsa L.
White Salmon, town (pop. 1,353), Klickitat co., S Wash., 18 mi. E of Stevenson and on Columbia R., opposite Hood River, Oregon; timber, fruit, livestock.
White Salmon River, S Wash., rises in Cascade Range of Mt. Adams, flows c.50 mi. S to Columbia R. near White Salmon.

Whitesand River, SE Sask., issues from small Whitesand L. 50 mi. NW of Yorkton, flows 120 mi. in an arc SE and NE to Assiniboine R. at Kamsack.

Whitesands, New Hebrides: see TANNA.

White Sands National Monument (□ 219.1; established 1933), S N.Mex., in Tularosa Basin bet. San Andres Mts. (W) and Sacramento Mts. (E), 15 mi. WSW of Alamogordo. Great expanse of white gypsum sand with dunes 10–60 ft. high. L. Lucero (lōōsĕr'ō) (3 mi. long, 1.5 mi. wide; in SW) is crystal-encrusted marsh. Plant and animal life shows high degree of adaptation to environment.

White Sands Proving Grounds, N.Mex.: see ALAMOGORDO.

Whitesboro. 1 Village (pop. 3,902), Oneida co., central N.Y., on Mohawk R. and the Barge Canal, and 4 mi. WNW of Utica; baskets, furniture, wood products, heaters. Settled 1784, inc. 1813. **2** Town (pop. 1,854), Grayson co., N Texas, 13 mi. W of Sherman; rail, trade center in cotton, grain area; nursery, poultry hatchery; flour, cottonseed-oil milling.

Whitesburg. 1 Town (pop. 400), Carroll co., W Ga., 11 mi. SE of Carrollton, near Chattahoochee R. **2** Mining town (pop. 1,393), ⊙ Letcher co., SE Ky., in the Cumberlands, on North Fork Kentucky R. and 10 mi. WSW of Jenkins, near Pine Mtn.; bituminous coal. Formerly a lumbering town. Clay, sand, and gravel pits, timber, farms in region. Settled 1840, inc. 1872.

White Sea, Rus. *Beloye More* (byĕ'lŭyŭ mô'ryŭ), inlet (□ 36,680) of Barents Sea, in N European USSR; 365 mi. long. N section (mouth) opens into Barents Sea bet. capes Svyatoi Nos (W) and Kanin Nos (E); connects with main body of sea (S) by a strait or neck, Rus. *gorlo*, 100 mi. long, 30–35 mi. wide. Main basin has rocky, indented shores (W), low shores (E); forms long bays of Kandalaksha (NW; max. depth 1,115 ft.), Onega (S), and Dvina (SE). Mezen Bay is inlet of N part. Receives Mezen, Northern Dvina, and Onega rivers. Freezes (Nov.–May) except in central section. Main ports: Archangel, Kem, Belomorsk (N end of WHITE SEA–BALTIC CANAL), Onega, Mezen, and Kandalaksha. Solovetskiye Isls. are at entrance to Onega Bay. Abounds in fish (herring, cod), seal herds (N). Lumber exports.

White Sea-Baltic Canal, Rus. *Belomorsko-Baltiyskiy Kanal,* in Karelo-Finnish SSR; leaves Onega Bay of White Sea at Belomorsk, passes S along lower canalized Vyg R., through lake Vygozero, and across 246-ft.-high watershed (using 19 locks), to L. Onega at Povenets; 140 mi. long. Waterway to Baltic Sea continues, via L. Onega, Svir R., L. Ladoga, and Neva R., to Leningrad. Freight includes apatite and lumber. Frozen Oct.–May. Built 1931–32. Damaged in Second World War.

White Settlement, residential town (pop. 10,827), Tarrant co., N Texas, a W suburb of Fort Worth. Formerly called Liberator Village or Liberator. Inc. after 1940.

Whiteshed, Point, Alaska: see POINT WHITESHED.

Whiteshill, agr. village and parish (pop. 1,206), central Gloucester, England, 2 mi. NW of Stroud.

Whiteside, county (□ 690; pop. 49,336), NW Ill.; ⊙ Morrison. Bounded NW by the Mississippi; drained by Rock R. and Rock and Elkhorn Creeks. Agr. (livestock, corn, wheat, oats, hay, truck, poultry). Limestone quarries. Processing of farm and dairy products; mfg. of machinery, home appliances, metal and wire products, hardware, gas engines, petroleum products. Hunting areas along the Mississippi. Includes a natl. wildlife refuge. Formed 1836.

Whiteside, town (pop. 93), Lincoln co., E Mo., bet. Mississippi R. and North Fork of Cuivre R., 14 mi. N of Troy.

Whiteside Channel, S extension of Strait of Magellan, bet. main isl. of Tierra del Fuego and Dawson Isl., joining Admiralty Sound; c.50 mi. long.

White Springs, resort town (pop. 700), Hamilton co., N Fla., on Suwannee R. and c.65 mi. W of Jacksonville.

Whitestone, SE N.Y., a residential section of N Queens borough of New York city; some mfg. (X-ray equipment, wood and metal products, boats). Bronx-Whitestone Bridge crosses East R. here.

White Stone or **Whitestone,** village (1940 pop. 916), Lancaster co., E Va., near Rappahannock R. mouth (ferry) on Chesapeake Bay, 45 mi. N of Newport News; fish-oil extracting, vegetable canning. White Stone Beach (resort) is near by.

Whitestown, town (pop. 550), Boone co., central Ind., 15 mi. NW of Indianapolis.

White Sulphur Springs. 1 Town (pop. 32), Meriwether co., W Ga., 15 mi. SE of La Grange. **2** Town (pop. 1,025), ⊙ Meagher co., central Mont., on Smith R. and 55 mi. E of Helena; gold, silver mines; livestock, dairy products, grain. Mineral springs used for medicinal purposes. **3** Town (pop. 2,643), Greenbrier co., SE W.Va., 8 mi. E of Lewisburg, in the Alleghenies; alt. 1,917 ft. Well-known health resort, with mineral springs, since early 1800s. Settled c.1750.

Whitesville. 1 Town (pop. 723), Daviess co., NW Ky., 15 mi. ESE of Owensboro. **2** Village (pop. c.650), Allegany co., W N.Y., 20 mi. SSW of Hornell, near Pa. line; mfg. (dairy products, wood products, feed, furniture); timber; poultry, livestock, potatoes. **3** Town (pop. 1,017), Boone co., SW W.Va., on Coal R. and 17 mi. ESE of Madison; rail junction; trade center for agr. (livestock, truck, fruit, tobacco), bituminous-coal area; lumber milling.

Whitetail, village (pop. c.200), Daniels co., NE Mont., port of entry near Sask. line, 13 mi. NE of Scobey.

White Tank Mountains, range in Maricopa co., SW central Ariz., W of Phoenix, N of Gila R. Rises to 4,200 ft.

White Top Mountain (5,520 ft.), in spur of Iron Mts., S Va., near N.C.-Tenn. border, 15 mi. SSW of Marion. Site of annual music festival. Whitetop village is S.

Whiteville. 1 Town (pop. 4,238) ⊙ Columbus co., S N.C., c.45 mi. W of Wilmington; tobacco market and trade center; mfg. of fertilizer, meat products; lumber milling. Founded 1810. **2** Town (pop. 794), Hardeman co., SW Tenn., 27 mi. SW of Jackson, in cotton-growing area.

White Volta River (vŏl'tŭ) rises in Upper Volta (Fr. W. Africa) N of Ouahigouya, enters Gold Coast NW of Bawku, flows c.550 mi. generally S, through Northern Territories past Yapei (high-water head of canoe traffic), joining the Black Volta 38 mi. NW of Yeji to form VOLTA RIVER. Receives Red Volta R. (right) near Gambaga.

Whitewater. 1 Village (pop. c.150), Mesa co., W Colo., on Gunnison R. and 8 mi. SE of Grand Junction; alt. c.4,660 ft. Livestock-shipping point in irrigated agr. area. **2** Town (pop. 104), Wayne co., E Ind., on East Fork of Whitewater R. and 9 mi. NNE of Richmond, near Ohio line. **3** City (pop. 453), Butler co., S central Kansas, 21 mi. NNE of Wichita, in grain and livestock area; flour milling. **4** Town (pop. 187), Cape Girardeau co., SE Mo., on Whitewater R. and 15 mi. WSW of Cape Girardeau. **5** City (pop. 5,101), Walworth co., SE Wis., on small Whitewater Creek and 17 mi. NE of Janesville, in farm (dairy, poultry, truck, grain) area; mfg. (hardware, steel products, clothing, canned foods, beer). Seat of a state teachers col. Inc. 1885.

Whitewater Baldy, peak (10,892 ft.) in Mogollon Mts., SW N.Mex., c.45 mi. NNW of Silver City.

Whitewater Bay, shallow mangrove-lined inlet (c.15 mi. long, 4–8 mi. wide) of the Gulf of Mexico, in Everglades Natl. Park, extreme S Fla., enclosed S and partly W by Cape Sable; contains many small isls.

Whitewater River. 1 In Ind. and Ohio, formed by headstreams N of Connersville, E Ind., flows generally S and SE, past Brookville (at influx of East Fork, c.55 mi. long), to Great Miami R. in Hamilton co., Ohio, 15 mi. W of Cleveland. Length c.70 mi. **2** In SE Mo., rises in St. Francois co., flows c.50 mi. SE and S, and is diverted into Mississippi flood-plain drainage system in S Cape Girardeau co.

Whitewood, town (pop. 630), SE Sask., 30 mi. WNW of Moosomin; grain elevators, lumbering.

Whitewood, town (pop. 304), Lawrence co., W S.Dak., 7 mi. NNE of Deadwood in Black Hills; dairy products, livestock, grain.

Whitewood, Lake, Kingsbury co., E S.Dak., near L. Preston; 7 mi. long, 1 mi. wide.

Whitewright, town (pop. 1,372), Grayson co., N Texas, 15 mi. SE of Sherman; trade, shipping point in cotton, grain, dairying area. Settled 1877, inc. 1888.

Whitfield, county (□ 281; pop. 34,432), NW Ga.; ⊙ Dalton. Bounded N by Tenn. line, E by Conasauga R. Agr. (cotton, corn, hay, fruit, livestock); bedspread mfg. at Dalton. Part of Chattahoochee Natl. Forest in S. Formed 1851.

Whitford, town and parish (pop. 3,453), Flint, Wales, 3 mi. WNW of Holywell; agr. market.

Whithorn (hwĭt'hôrn), burgh (1931 pop. 951; 1951 census 1,068), SE Wigtown, Scotland, 9 mi. S of Wigtown; agr. market. Site of ruins of 12th-cent. priory church, later a cathedral, reputedly built on site of church founded by St. Ninian. On Wigtown Bay, 4 mi. SE of Whithorn, is small port of Isle of Whithorn, with ruins of 13th-cent. chapel. This site is reputedly also associated with St. Ninian.

Whiting (hwī'tĭng). **1** City (pop. 9,669), Lake co., extreme NW Ind., on L. Michigan, near Ill. line, adjacent to SE Chicago, in the CALUMET industrial region; large chemical plants, oil refineries. Settled 1885, inc. 1903. **2** Town (pop. 663), Monona co., W Iowa, 30 mi. SSE of Sioux City; grain elevators. **3** City (pop. 267), Jackson co., NE Kansas, 5 mi. NNE of Topeka, in livestock and grain region. **4** Town (pop. 354), Washington co., E Maine, on Dennys Bay and 12 mi. SW of Eastport. **5** Town (pop. 282), Addison co., W Vt., on Otter Creek and 10 mi. S of Middlebury; dairying. **6** Village (pop. 854), Portage co., central Wis., just SE of Stevens Point.

Whitingham (hwī'tĭng-ŭm), town (pop. 816), Windham co., SE Vt., 17 mi. WSW of Brattleboro, partly in Green Mtn. Natl. Forest; wood products. Includes Jacksonville village (pop. 220). L. Whitingham (or Davis Bridge Reservoir), here, is formed by Harriman (or Davis Bridge) Dam in Deerfield R. (water power). Brigham Young b. here.

Whitingham, Lake, Vt.: see HARRIMAN DAM.

Whiting River, NW B.C. and SE Alaska, rises in B.C. near 58°20'N 132°58'W, flows 50 mi. SW to Stephens Passage 30 mi. SE of Juneau.

Whitinsville, Mass.: see NORTHBRIDGE.

Whitlash, village, Liberty co., N Mont., port of entry near Alta. line, c.40 mi. NE of Shelby.

Whitley (hwĭt'lē). **1** County (□ 336; pop. 18,828), NE Ind.; ⊙ Columbia City. Agr. area (livestock, grain, truck, poultry, soybeans; dairy products). Some mfg. at Columbia City and South Whitley. Drained by Eel R. Formed 1835. **2** County (□ 460; pop. 31,940), SE Ky.; ⊙ Williamsburg. In the Cumberlands; bounded S by Tenn.; drained by Cumberland and Laurel rivers. Cumberland Natl. Forest, CUMBERLAND FALLS STATE PARK, and Pine Mtn. are partly in co. Bituminous-coal-mining and agr. area (tobacco, corn, oats, Irish potatoes, apples, poultry, cattle, dairy products, lespedeza); gas wells; hardwood timber. Formed 1818.

Whitley Bay, urban district (1931 pop. 24,210; 1951 census 32,257), SE Northumberland, England, seaside resort on North Sea, 9 mi. NE of Newcastle-upon-Tyne; also has paint works. Includes (W) coal-mining town of Monkseaton. Urban dist. was formerly called Whitley and Monkseaton.

Whitley City, village (1940 pop. 1,180), ⊙ McCreary co., S Ky., in the Cumberlands, 26 mi. SSE of Somerset; bituminous-coal mining, lumbering, some agr. Cumberland Falls State Park is near by.

Whitley Home State Park, Ky.: see CRAB ORCHARD.

Whitman, county (□ 2,167; pop. 32,469), SE Wash., on Idaho line; ⊙ Colfax. Plateau region drained by Snake and Palouse rivers. Wheat, barley, oats, hogs, canned peas, flour; lumber milling. Formed 1871.

Whitman, town (pop. 8,413), Plymouth co., E Mass., 20 mi. SSE of Boston, just E of Brockton; mfg., chiefly shoes. Settled c.1670, set off from Abington 1875.

Whitman Knob, W.Va.: see RICH MOUNTAIN.

Whitman National Monument, Wash.: see WALLA WALLA.

Whitmire, town (pop. 3,006), Newberry co., NW central S.C., on Enoree R. and 22 mi. E of Laurens, in agr. area; cotton mills.

Whitmore Lake, village (1940 pop. 573), Washtenaw co., SE Mich., 9 mi. N of Ann Arbor, on small Whitmore L.; resort (fishing, swimming).

Whitnel (hwĭt'nŭl), village (pop. 1,405), Caldwell co., W central N.C., 2 mi. SE of Lenoir.

Whitney. 1 Village (pop. 132), Dawes co., NW Nebr., 13 mi. WSW of Chadron and on White R. Near-by artificial lake used for fishing and irrigation. **2** Town (pop. 3), Baker co., NE Oregon, 23 mi. SW of Baker. **3** Mill village (pop. 1,611), Spartanburg co., NW S.C., just N of Spartanburg; textile finishing. **4** Town (pop. 1,383), Hill co., central Texas, 30 mi. NNW of Waco; farm trade point. About 5 mi. SW is Whitney Dam (begun 1946) in Brazos R.

Whitney, Mount, highest peak (14,495 ft.) in U.S., in the Sierra Nevada, E Calif., at E border of Sequoia Natl. Park, on Inyo-Tulare co. line. Named for Josiah D. Whitney (chief of expedition which discovered it in 1864). First climbed (1873) by A. H. Johnson, C. D. Begole, and J. Lucas. Connected with Death Valley (SE), lowest area in U.S., by scenic highway.

Whitney Dam, central Texas, in Brazos R. c.5 mi. SW of Whitney; 163 ft. high, 1,674 ft. long; for power, flood control; begun 1946. Impounds Whitney Reservoir (capacity 2,017,000 acre-ft.).

Whitney Point, village (pop. 883), Broome co., S N.Y., on Tioughnioga R. at mouth of Otselic R., and 16 mi. N of Binghamton, in farming and dairying area; summer resort; some mfg. (furniture, feed, metal products); timber.

Whitney Reservoir, Texas: see WHITNEY DAM.

Whitneyville, town (pop. 227), Washington co., E Maine, on Machias R. and just above Machias.

Whitrigg, England: see TORPENHOW AND WHITRIGG.

Whitshed, Point, Alaska: see POINT WHITESHED.

Whitstable, urban district (1931 pop. 11,201; 1951 census 17,467), NE Kent, England, on S shore of Thames estuary, near mouth of the Swale, 6 mi. N of Canterbury; bathing resort, with noted oyster fisheries. Terminal of early regular steam railroad service for passengers (1830), linking town with Canterbury.

Whitsunday Island (hwĭt'sŭn'dē), coral island (□ 38) in Coral Sea, bet. Great Barrier Reef and Cape Conway peninsula on E coast of Queensland, Australia; roughly triangular, 11 mi. long, 9 mi. wide; rises to 1,230 ft. Wooded; trochus shell, fish. Tourist resort.

Whittemore, (hwĭ'tŭmôr). **1** town (pop. 678), Kossuth co., N Iowa, 10 mi. W of Algona; dairy products. **2** City (pop. 452), Iosco co., NE Mich., c.45 mi. N of Bay City, in farm area.

Whitten, town (pop. 174), Hardin co., central Iowa, near Iowa R., 8 mi. SSE of Eldora.

Whittier (hwĭ'tēŭr), village (pop. 52), S Alaska, on SE Kenai Peninsula, at head of Port Wells, arm of Prince William Sound, 50 mi. SE of Anchorage; 60°46'N 148°45'W; ice-free seaport, terminus of Alaska RR branch, supply and logging center.

Whittier. **1** City (pop. 23,820), Los Angeles co., S Calif., 12 mi. SE of downtown Los Angeles; oranges, avocados, walnuts, dairy products. Oil fields near by. Makes tools, heaters, clay products, agr. sprays, tile, steel products. Seat of Whittier Col. and Whittier State School for Boys. Has world's largest Quaker church. Founded 1887, inc. 1898. **2** Resort village (pop. c.300), Swain co., W N.C., 5 mi. E of Bryson City and on Tuckasegee R., near Great Smoky Mts. Natl. Park.

Whittingham (hwĭ'tĭnjŭm), agr. parish (pop. 4,403), W central Lancashire, England, 4 mi. NNE of Preston; cattle raising, dairy farming. Has large co. mental hosp.

Whittington, England: see CHESTERFIELD.

Whittle, village and parish (pop. 219), E Northumberland, England, 4 mi. S of Alnwick; coal mining.

Whittle-le-Woods, village and parish (pop. 2,197), W central Lancashire, England, near Leeds-Liverpool Canal 6 mi. SSE of Preston; cotton milling; agr. market.

Whittlesey (hwĭ'tŭlsē), urban district (1931 pop. 8,301; 1951 census 8,609), in Isle of Ely, N Cambridge, England, near Nene R., 5 mi. E of Peterborough; brick mfg. Has church dating from 13th cent., with 15th-cent. tower.

Whittlesford, town and parish (pop. 1,073), S Cambridge, England, on Cam R. and 7 mi. S of Cambridge; agr. market; mfg. of farm implements. Has ruins of 13th-cent. St. John's Hosp., and 13th-cent. church.

Whitwell, town and parish (pop. 4,424), NE Derby, England, 13 mi. ESE of Sheffield; coal mining. Has 12th-cent. church.

Whitwell, village (pop. 1,586), Marion co., SE Tenn., 16 mi. NW of Chattanooga.

Whitwood, former urban district (1931 pop. 6,197), West Riding, S central Yorkshire, England, 4 mi. NE of Wakefield; coal mining, pottery industry. Inc. 1938 in Castleford.

Whitworth, urban district (1931 pop. 8,360; 1951 census 7,442), SE Lancashire, England, 3 mi. N of Rochdale; cotton milling. Site of Rochdale reservoir. In urban dist. is cotton-milling and coal-mining town of Shawforth.

Wholdaia Lake (45 mi. long, 5–20 mi. wide), expansion of Dubawnt R., SE Mackenzie Dist., Northwest Territories, near Keewatin Dist. boundary; 60°45'N 104°20'W.

Whonock (hwŏ'nŭk), village (pop. estimate 300), SW B.C., on Fraser R. and 28 mi. E of Vancouver; lumbering, dairying; fruit, vegetables.

Whyalla (hwīă'lŭ), town and port (pop. 7,845), S South Australia, on NE Eyre Peninsula, 26 mi. NW of Port Pirie across Spencer Gulf; iron smelting; shipyards. Exports iron mined at Iron Knob and Iron Monarch.

Whycocomagh (hwīkō'mŭ), village (pop. estimate 400), NE N.S., central Cape Breton Isl., at head of St. Patrick Channel of Great Bras d'Or, 50 mi. WSW of Sydney; popular resort. Near by is Indian reservation.

Whydah, Fr. West Africa: see OUIDAH.

Wiak, Netherlands East Indies: see BIAK.

Wianno, Mass.: see BARNSTABLE, town.

Wiarton (wī'ûrtŭn), town (pop. 1,749), S Ont., on Saugeen Peninsula, on Colpay Bay (inlet of Georgian Bay), 16 mi. NW of Owen Sound; port; lumber and flour milling, dairying, boatbuilding, furniture mfg. Site of govt. fish hatchery.

Wiawso (wēō'sō), town, Western Prov., SW Gold Coast colony, 50 mi. WNW of Dunkwa; cacao, cassava, corn.

Wiazow (vyō'zōof), Pol. *Wiązów*, Ger. *Wansen* (vän'zŭn), town (1939 pop. 3,153; 1946 pop. 2,598) in Lower Silesia, after 1945 in Wroclaw prov., SW Poland, on Olawa R. and 12 mi. WSW of Brieg (Brzeg); agr. market (grain, sugar beets, potatoes, livestock).

Wibaux (wē'bō), county (□ 889; pop. 1,907), E Mont.; ⊙ Wibaux. Agr. region bordering on N. Dak.; drained by Beaver Creek. Grain, livestock. Formed 1914.

Wibaux, town (pop. 739), ⊙ Wibaux co., E Mont., 26 mi. ESE of Glendive and on Beaver Creek, near N.Dak. line; shipping point in sheep, cattle, and grain region; machine parts. Near-by Anvil Buttes is scenic spot in badlands region.

Wiblingwerde, Germany: see NACHRODT-WIBLINGWERDE.

Wichita (wĭ'chĭtô). **1** County (□ 724; pop. 2,640), W Kansas; ⊙ Leoti. Rolling plain area. Grain, livestock. Formed 1886. **2** County (□ 612; pop. 98,493), N Texas; ⊙ WICHITA FALLS, commercial, shipping, industrial center of wide region. Bounded N by Red R. (Okla. line); drained by Wichita R., small creeks. Includes L. Wichita (irrigation, water supply; fishing). A leading Texas petroleum-producing co.; Wichita Falls, Electra, Burkburnett are oil centers. Agr. (corn, oats, wheat, cotton, corn, hay, fruit, truck; extensive irrigation); livestock (cattle, hogs, sheep, poultry, horses), dairying. Formed 1858.

Wichita, city (1940 pop. 114,966; 1950 pop. 168,279), ⊙ Sedgwick co., S Kansas, on Arkansas R. at mouth of Little Arkansas R., and c.170 mi. SW of Kansas City, Mo.; 37°42'N 97°20'W; alt. 1,283 ft. Largest city in Kansas. Processing and commercial center for wheat and oil region of S Kansas. Chief industries: flour milling, meat packing; grain storage; oil refining; railroad maintenance. Large broomcorn market. Mfg. also of airplanes and airplane supplies; oil-drilling, agr., and automobile equipment; household appliances; dairy products. Has stockyards, railroad repair shops. Municipal airport (Air Force base). City was founded 1868 on Chisholm Trail, having grown up around trading post (established 1864), and was inc. 1871. Boomed as cow town after arrival of railroad (1872); after 1880 became flour-milling center for agr. and stock-raising area. Art mus., municipal auditorium, veterans hosp., and Cathedral of the Immaculate Conception (R.C.) are here. Institutions of education are Friends Univ. (coeducational; 1898) and Municipal Univ. of Wichita (coeducational; 1892).

Wichita, Lake, Texas: see WICHITA RIVER.

Wichita Falls, city (pop. 68,042), ⊙ Wichita co., N Texas, on Wichita R. and c.105 mi. NW of Fort Worth. Commercial, industrial, transportation hub of rich oil, wheat, cattle region; large oil refineries, flour mills, glass plant; also makes foundry products, oil-field machinery and supplies, chemicals, footwear, clothing, cottonseed oil, dairy products. Seat of Hardin Col., a state mental hosp., and Sheppard Air Force Base. L. Wichita (just S), Kemp and Diversion lakes (to SW), impounded by dams in Wichita R., are recreation areas. Settled in 1870s; grew as cow town after coming of railroad, 1882; inc. 1889. Oil development in co. made it a boom town (1918); irrigation developments in region (beginning 1900; continued in 1920s) gave city a balanced oil, agr., livestock-based economy.

Wichita Mountains, SW Okla., low granite range (c.60 mi. long, 25 mi. wide), mainly in Comanche co.; mts. rise to max. alt. of 2,464 ft. A wildlife refuge (buffalo, elk, Texas longhorns, deer, birds), a state park (summer resort), and L. Lawtonka (recreation) are here.

Wichita River or **Big Wichita River,** Texas, rises in intermittent streams on E Llano Estacado, flows c.250 mi. E and NE, past Wichita Falls, to Red R. in Clay co. Main branch (called North Fork in upper course) receives from S the intermittent Middle Fork and South Fork (c.95 mi. long; partly intermittent). W of Wichita Falls, dams impound L. Kemp (c.12 mi. long; capacity 600,000 acre-ft.) and Diversion Reservoir (c.7 mi. long; capacity 45,000 acre-ft.), for water supply, irrigation. Lakes are recreational areas; fishing. Just SW of Wichita Falls is L. Wichita (13,500 acre-ft.; irrigation, water supply; fishing), formed by dam in a small S tributary.

Wick, England: see LITTLEHAMPTON.

Wick, burgh (1931 pop. 7,548; 1951 census 7,161), ⊙ Caithness, Scotland, in E part of co., on Wick Bay of the North Sea, at mouth of Wick R., 80 mi. NE of Inverness; 58°26'N 3°6'W; important herring-fishing center, with exports of fish and farm produce; woolen milling. Airport. Port was built by Telford and includes E suburb of Pulteneytown, center of fishery activity, founded 1808 by the British Fisheries Association. Burgh also includes N suburb of Louisburgh. Just S of town is the "Old Man of Wick," 12th-cent. tower of anc. castle. Promontory of Nass Head, 3 mi. NE of Wick, has ruins of 15th-cent. Castle Girnigoe.

Wickenburg, town (pop. 1,736), Maricopa co., W central Ariz., on Hassayampa R. and 52 mi. NW of Phoenix; winter resort. Gold mines and dude ranches in vicinity.

Wickes (wĭks), town (pop. 401), Polk co., W Ark., 20 mi. SSW of Mena; canning, lumber milling.

Wickett, village (pop. c.900), Ward co., extreme W Texas, in the Pecos valley, 30 mi. ENE of Pecos; trading point for oil field; carbon-black plants.

Wickford, town and parish (pop. 2,979), S central Essex, England, 9 mi. SSE of Chelmsford.

Wickford, resort village (pop. 2,437) in North Kingstown town, Washington co., S central R.I., on inlet of Narragansett Bay and 17 mi. S of Providence; makes elastic braid; agr.; oyster, lobster fisheries. Has many fine 18th-cent. bldgs., including St. Paul's Episcopal Church. State lobster hatchery here. Settled soon after 1650.

Wickham (wĭ'kŭm), W suburb of Newcastle, E New South Wales, Australia.

Wickham, town and parish (pop. 1,358), S Hampshire, England, 9 mi. NNW of Portsmouth; agr. market; flour mills. William of Wykeham b. here.

Wickham Market (wĭ'kŭm), town and parish (pop. 1,210), E Suffolk, England, on Deben R. and 11 mi. NE of Ipswich; agr. market. Has 14th–15th-cent. church.

Wickham West, village (pop. 369), S Que., 9 mi. S of Drummondville; dairying, stock raising.

Wickliffe (wĭ'klĭf). **1** Town (pop. 1,019), ⊙ Ballard co., SW Ky., on the Mississippi just below influx of the Ohio, 9 mi. below Cairo, Ill.; agr. (dark tobacco, corn, potatoes), clay pits, timber; makes pottery, lamp bases. A buried Indian city near by has yielded valuable archaeological material. Hunting, fishing near by. **2** City (pop. 5,002), Lake co., NE Ohio, 13 mi. NE of downtown Cleveland, near L. Erie; petroleum refining; mfg. of machinery, brick. Inc. 1916.

Wicklow (wĭk'lō), Gaelic *Chill Mhantáin*, county (□ 781.6; pop. 60,451), Leinster, SE Ireland; ⊙ Wicklow. Bounded by cos. Wexford (S), Carlow and Kildare (W), Dublin (N), and the Irish Sea (E). Drained by Avoca, Slaney, and Liffey rivers. Except for narrow coastal strip, surface is hilly or mountainous, rising to 3,039 ft. on Lugnaquillia. Valleys, noted for scenic beauty, include Glendalough, Avoca, Glen of the Downs, and Glenmalure. Lough Dan is largest lake. Lead, copper, iron, sulphur pyrites, granite, and slate are worked. Dairying, cattle and sheep raising, and potato growing are carried on. Sea fisheries. Industries include woolen milling, mfg. of agr. implements, explosives. Besides Wicklow, other towns are Arklow, Bray (seaside resort), Greystones, Rathdrum. Shillelagh was famous for its oak forest. Being difficult of access, co. was favorite hideout of fugitives from authority.

Wicklow, Gaelic *Cill Mhantáin*, urban district (pop. 3,183), ⊙ Co. Wicklow, Ireland, on E coast of co., on the Irish Sea, 26 mi. SSE of Dublin; 52°59'N 6°3'W; seaport and agr. market (sheep, cattle; potatoes); agr.-implement mfg. Bog iron is mined in vicinity. There are remains of anc. Black Castle. Near by is promontory of Wicklow Head.

Wicklow Head, promontory on the Irish Sea, E Co. Wicklow, Ireland, 2 mi. ESE of Wicklow; lighthouse (52°58'N 6°W).

Wickrath (vĭk'rät), village (pop. 9,212), in former Prussian Rhine Prov., W Germany, after 1945 in North Rhine-Westphalia, on the Niers and 3 mi. S of Rheydt; stud farm.

Wick River, Caithness, Scotland, rises in Loch Watten, flows 9 mi. SE to the North Sea at Wick.

Wickwar, town and parish (pop. 831), SW Gloucester, England, 13 mi. NE of Bristol; agr. market. Church has 15th-cent. tower.

Wicomico (wĭkŏ'mĭkō), county (□ 380; pop. 39,641), SE Md.; ⊙ Salisbury. On the Eastern Shore (Delmarva Peninsula); bounded N by Del. line, E by Pocomoke R. (fringed by great swamp), SW by Wicomico R., W and NW by Nanticoke R. Tidewater agr. area (fruit, especially strawberries; truck, sweet potatoes, poultry, dairy products), with some timber. Clothing factories, vegetable and fruit canneries, lumber mills (especially at Salisbury). Fishing, muskrat trapping. Formed 1867.

Wicomico River. **1** River in S Md., rises near Charles-Prince Georges co. line, flows c.37 mi. generally S through swamps to the Potomac just below Rock Point. Its estuary (c.2 mi. wide at mouth) is navigable for c.14 mi. **2** River on the Eastern Shore, Md., rises in N Wicomico co. near Del. line, flows c.33 mi. generally SW, past Salisbury (head of navigation), to Monie Bay (a N arm of Tangier Sound).

Wiconisco (wĭkūnĭ'skō), village (pop. 1,549), Dauphin co., E central Pa., just NE of Lykens, in anthracite area.

Wida, Fr. West Africa: see OUIDAH.

Widdern (vĭ'dŭrn), town (pop. 1,243), N Württemberg, Germany, after 1945 in Württemberg-Baden, on the Jagst and 13 mi. NE of Heilbronn; wine.

Widdrington, town and parish (pop. 669), E Northumberland, England, 12 mi. SSE of Alnwick; coal mining.

Widecombe-in-the-Moor (wĭ'dĭkŭm), agr. village and parish (pop. 704), S central Devon, England, 5 mi. NNW of Ashburton. Celebrated fair held here each Sept. Has 15th-cent. church.

Widen, village (pop. 1,274), Clay co., central W.Va., 40 mi. E of Charleston, in coal-mining area.

Widener (wĭd'nûr), town (pop. 187), St. Francis co., E Ark., 6 mi. E of Forrest City and on St. Francis R.

Wideopen, England: see WEETSLADE.

Widnau (vĭd'nou), town (pop. 3,052), St. Gall canton, NE Switzerland, 12 mi. E of St. Gall, near the Rhine and Austrian border; textiles (artificial silk), embroideries, metal products made here and in vicinity.

Widnes (wĭd'nĭs), municipal borough (1931 pop. 40,619; 1951 census 48,795), SW Lancashire, England, on Mersey R. (bridged) opposite Runcorn, and on Manchester Ship Canal, 11 mi. ESE of Liverpool; mfg. of chemicals, soap, paint, pharmaceuticals, steel and sheet-metal products. In borough (NW) is town of Ditton, with metalworking, mfg. of tools, chemicals.

Widze, Belorussian SSR: see VIDZY.

Wiebelskirchen (vē'bŭlskĭr"khŭn), town (pop. 10,704), E Saar, 2 mi. NNE of Neunkirchen; coal.

Wiecbork (vyĕts'bôrk), Pol. *Więcbork*, Ger. *Vandsburg* (vänts'bōork), town (pop. 3,068), Bydgoszcz prov., NW Poland, 27 mi. NW of Bydgoszcz; rail junction; flour milling, sawmilling, mfg. of furniture, bricks.

Wieda (vē'dä), village (pop. 2,251), in Brunswick, NW Germany, after 1945 in Lower Saxony, in the lower Harz, 6 mi. S of Braunlage; metal- and woodworking.

Wieden (vē'dŭn), district (□ .7; pop. 42,335) of Vienna, Austria, just S of city center.

Wiedenbrück (vē"dŭnbrük'), town (pop. 11,016), in former Prussian prov. of Westphalia, NW Germany, after 1945 in North Rhine-Westphalia, on the Ems and 6 mi. SW of Gütersloh; mfg. of electrical machinery and equipment.

Wiederitzsch (vē'dŭrĭch), industrial village (pop. 5,677), Saxony, E central Germany, 5 mi. N of Leipzig city center.

Wied il Ghain, Malta: see MARSA SCALA.

Wiefelstede (vē'fŭl-shtā"dŭ), village (commune pop. 6,210), in Oldenburg, NW Germany, after 1945 in Lower Saxony, 9 mi. NW of Oldenburg city, in peat region.

Wiehe (vē'ŭ), town (pop. 3,148), in former Prussian Saxony prov., central Germany, after 1945 in Saxony-Anhalt, near the Unstrut, 19 mi. WNW of Naumburg; agr. market (grain, sugar beets, potatoes, livestock). Leopold von Ranke b. here.

Wiehen Mountains, Ger. *Wiehengebirge* (vē'ŭngŭbĭr"gŭ), low range of the Weser Mts., NW Germany, extends c.30 mi. W of the Porta Westfalica; rises to 1,050 ft. S of Lübbecke.

Wiehl (vēl), village (pop. 8,810), in former Prussian Rhine Prov., W Germany, after 1945 in North Rhine-Westphalia, 5 mi. SSW of Gummersbach; forestry.

Wiehle (wē'lē), town (1940 pop. 91), Fairfax co., N Va., 19 mi. WNW of Washington, D.C.

Wielbark (vyĕl'bärk), Ger. *Willenberg* (vĭ'lŭnbĕrk), town (1939 pop. 2,600; 1946 pop. 760) in East Prussia, after 1945 in Olsztyn prov., NE Poland, 35 mi. SE of Allenstein (Olsztyn); rail junction; grain and cattle market.

Wielen (vyĕ'lĕnyŭ), Pol. *Wieleń*, Ger. *Filehne* (fē'lā"nŭ), town (1946 pop. 2,851), Poznan prov., W Poland, on Notec R. and 45 mi. NW of Poznan; brick mfg., flour milling.

Wielichowo (vyĕlē-khô'vô), town (1946 pop. ,1514), Poznan prov., W Poland, 31 mi. SW of Poznan, near Obra Canal; mfg. of cement, carpets; distilling, flour milling.

Wieliczka (vyĕlēch'kä), town (pop. 8,191), Krakow prov., S Poland, 7 mi. SE of Cracow; rail spur terminus; rock-salt mining and processing center; flour milling. Mines worked since 11th cent.; deposits estimated at 2,000,000 tons; mines have impressively carved chambers and chapels. During Second World War, under Ger. rule, called Gross Salze.

Wielim, Lake (vyĕ'lĕm), Ger. *Vilm* (fĭlm) (□ 7), in Pomerania, after 1945 in NW Poland, just NE of Szczecinek; 4.5 mi. long, 1–4 mi. wide; drains S into small tributary of Notec R.

Wielun (vyĕ'lōōnyŭ), Pol. *Wieluń*, Rus. *Velyun* or *Velyun'* (both: vyĕ'lūnyŭ), town (pop. 10,357), Lodz prov., S central Poland, 55 mi. SW of Lodz. Rail junction; limestone quarrying, beet-sugar and flour milling, brewing, mfg. of cement products, tanning, sawmilling. During Second World War, under Ger. rule, called Welungen.

Wien, Austria: see VIENNA.

Wiencke Island (wĭng'kē), southernmost isl. of Palmer Archipelago, Antarctica, in the South Pacific just off NW coast of Palmer Peninsula; 64°50'S 63°20'W. Discovered 1898 by Adrien de Gerlache, Belgian explorer.

Wiener Neudorf (vē'nŭr noi'dôrf), town (pop. 2,379), after 1938 in Mödling dist. of Vienna, Austria, 8 mi. SSW of city center; wine.

Wiener Neustadt (–shtät), city (1951 pop. 30,509), Lower Austria, 25 mi. S of Vienna, near Leitha R.; industrial and rail center; mfg. (railroad cars, locomotives, machinery). Emperor Maximilian I b. here. Castle of Babenberg, built 1192, became military acad. 1752. Has late-Gothic church, town hall with collection of antiquities. City heavily damaged by air attacks in Second World War.

Wiener Wald (vēn'ŭr vält") [Ger.,=Vienna forest], forested range of Lower Austria, just W of Vienna, bet. the Danube (N) and Triesting R. (S). Popular recreation area. A low range, the easternmost outlier of the Alps. Summits include: Schöpfl (2,930 ft.), Hoher Lindkogel (2,779 ft.), Kahlenberg (1,585 ft.), Leopoldsberg (1,388 ft.).

Wieniec Zdroj, Poland: see SWIERADOW ZDROJ.

Wieprz River (vyĕpsh). **1** Ger. *Wipper* (vĭ'pŭr), in Pomerania, after 1945 in Koszalin prov., NW Poland, rises 12 mi. E of Miastko, flows c.90 mi. generally NNW, past Slawno and Darlowo, to the Baltic just below Darlowo. **2** Rus. *Vepsh*, Lublin prov., E Poland, rises 3 mi. N of Tomaszow Lubelski, flows NNW past Szczebrzeszyn, Krasnystaw, and Leczna, and W to Vistula R. 12 mi. N of Putawy; 194 mi. long. Main tributaries, Bystrzyca and Tysmienica rivers. In lower course, forms Lublin-Warszawa prov. border.

Wierden (vĕr'dŭn), town (pop. 3,763), Overijssel prov., E Netherlands, 3 mi. W of Almelo; wool weaving and bleaching, meat packing, wooden-shoe mfg.

Wieringen (vē'rĭng-ŭn), former island (□ 9.8) of North Holland prov., NW Netherlands, in the Ijsselmeer, 10 mi. ESE of Helder; 6 mi. long, 1.5 mi. wide; now joined to mainland by reclaimed area Wieringermeer Polder (S). Chief village, DEN OEVER.

Wieringermeer Polder (–ŭrmăr pōl'dŭr), reclaimed area (□ 80), North Holland prov., NW Netherlands, on the Ijsselmeer and 30 mi. N of Amsterdam; joins what was Wieringen isl. (N) to mainland; 12 mi. long, 8 mi. wide. Reclamation completed 1932. Flooded (1945) in Second World War; subsequently reclaimed. Chief town, Medemblik.

Wieruszow (vyĕrōō'shōōf), Pol. *Wieruszów*, Rus. *Verushov* (vyĭrōō'shŭf), town (pop. 3,102), Lodz prov., S central Poland, on Prosna R. and 18 mi. WNW of Wielun; tanning, flour milling.

Wierzbica (vyĕrbē'tsä), village (commune pop. 2,072), Kielce prov., E central Poland, 10 mi. SSW of Radom; large cement plant. Another Wierzbica is located near Chelm in Lublin prov.

Wierzbnik (vyĕzhb'nēk), Rus. *Verzhbnik* (vyĕrsh'bŭnyēk), town (pop. 18,569), Kielce prov., E central Poland, on Kamienna R., on railroad and 25 mi. S of Radom; ironworks; mfg. of agr. tools, glass, porcelain; flour milling, sawmilling; stone quarry.

Wierzbolow, Lithuania: see VIRBALIS.

Wierzyca River (vyĕ-zhĭ'tsä), Ger. *Ferse* (fĕr'zŭ), N Poland, rises 6 mi. E of Koscierzyna, flows c.60 mi. generally SE, past Starogard and Pelplin, to the Vistula at Gniew.

Wiesau (vē'zou), village (pop. 3,857), Upper Palatinate, NE Bavaria, Germany, 7 mi. WNW of Tirschenreuth; rail junction; mfg. of textiles, glass, chemicals; woodworking, tanning. Has mid-17th-cent. church. Just NW is König Otto Bad, with mineral (iron) springs and mud baths.

Wiesbaden (vēs'bä"dŭn, vĭs–), city (1946 pop. 105,953, including suburbs 188,370; 1950 pop. 218,255), in former Prussian prov. of Hesse-Nassau, W Germany, after 1945 ⊙ Hesse, at S foot of the Taunus, on right bank of the Rhine and 20 mi. W of Frankfurt; 50°4'N 8°14'E. One of Europe's leading spas, it is noted for its mineral springs and mild climate. Rail center; airport (E outskirts). Metal and concrete construction; boatbuilding; iron foundries; chemical industry (basic and commercial chemicals, plastics, pharmaceuticals). Portland-cement and pottery works. Textile mfg., food processing, printing. Trades in lumber, sparkling wine, fruit, and vegetables of vicinity. Second World War damage (about 70%) included 19th-cent. castle, town hall, theater, and casino. Large Nassau state library was preserved. Founded in 3d cent. B.C. by Celts, Wiesbaden [anc. *Aquae Mattiacorum*] became a popular Roman spa (remains of water conduits; walls). Chartered in 13th cent. Was ⊙ duchy of Nassau from 1806 (confirmed 1816) until 1866. After First World War, was occupied by Fr., later English, troops; seat (1918–29) of Rhineland Commission. After its capture by U.S. troops (March, 1945), it inc. 2 former right-bank suburbs (Kastel and Kostheim) of Mainz.

Wiescherhöfen (vē"shŭrhû'fŭn), village (pop. 6,641), in former Prussian prov. of Westphalia, W Germany, after 1945 in North Rhine-Westphalia, in the Ruhr, 3 mi. SW of Hamm.

Wiesdorf, Germany: see LEVERKUSEN.

Wiese Island, Russian SFSR: see VIZE ISLAND.

Wieselburg (vē'zŭlbōōrk), town (pop. 2,308), W Lower Austria, 12 mi. E of Amstetten; rail junction; grain, cattle.

Wieselburg, county, Hungary: see GYÖR-MOSON.

Wieselburg, city, Hungary: see MOSONMAGYAROVAR.

Wiesen (vē'zŭn), village (pop. 2,071), Burgenland, E Austria, 6 mi. SE of Wiener Neustadt; sugar beets, fruit.

Wiesenberg, Czechoslovakia: see LOUCNA NAD DESNOU.

Wiesengrund, Czechoslovakia: see DOBRANY.

Wiesensteig (vē'zŭn-shtĭk), town (pop. 2,025), N Württemberg, Germany, after 1945 in Württemberg-Baden, on the Fils (near its source) and 10 mi. WSW of Geislingen; grain, cattle. Has 15th-cent. church.

Wiesental (vē'zŭntäl), village (pop. 5,684), N Baden, Germany, after 1945 in Württemberg-Baden, 8 mi. NNW of Bruchsal, in tobacco area; mfg. of cigars and cigarettes.

Wiesent River (vē'zŭnt), Bavaria, Germany, rises 4 mi. NW of Hollfeld, flows 35 mi. S and SW to the Regnitz at Forchheim.

Wiesloch (vēs'lôkh"), town (pop. 10,339), N Baden, Germany, after 1945 in Württemberg-Baden, 8 mi. S of Heidelberg (linked by tramway), in tobacco and wine region. Mfg. of cigars, cigarettes, fountain pens, paper, shoes; metalworking, food processing (frozen foods, wine). Potteries, brickworks. Lead and zinc mines, clay pits, limestone quarries. Sulphur spring.

Wiessee, Bad, Germany: see BAD WIESSEE.

Wietze (vē'tsŭ), commune (pop., including Steinförde, 4,203), in former Prussian prov. of Hanover, NW Germany, after 1945 in Lower Saxony, 10 mi. WNW of Celle; oil-drilling center; chemical mfg.

Wietzendorf (vē'tsŭndôrf), village (pop. 2,157), in former Prussian prov. of Hanover, NW Germany, after 1945 in Lower Saxony, 7 mi. SE of Soltau; woodworking.

Wiezyca (vyĕ-zhĭ'tsä), Pol. *Wieżyca*, mountain (1,085 ft.) in Gdansk prov., N Poland, 9 mi. NE of Koscierzyna; highest point in Pol. maritime and lake region. Wiezyca rail station is on N slope.

Wifflisburg, Switzerland: see AVENCHES.

Wigan (wĭ'gŭn), county borough (1931 pop. 85,357; 1951 census 84,546), S central Lancashire, England, 17 mi. NE of Liverpool; coal-mining and cotton-textile center; metallurgy, engineering, mfg. of explosives, soap, fertilizer, pharmaceuticals; oil distilling. Formerly a center of bell-founding, pewter, and pottery industries. Its fine Church of All Saints has Norman tower, parts of a Roman altar, and a 14th-cent. altar tomb. The town played an important part in the Civil War, being taken by Parliamentarians in 1643 and 1651. Just WSW is cotton-milling town of Pemberton.

Wigger River (vĭ'gŭr), N central Switzerland, receives its headstream Enziwigger R. at Willisau, flows 25 mi. N to the Aar near Aarburg.

Wiggins. 1 Village (pop. c.300), Morgan co., NE Colo., near S.Platte R., 15 mi. W of Fort Morgan; alt. 4,443 ft. Supply point in livestock and agr. region. Empire Reservoir just W. **2** Town (pop. 1,436), ⊙ Stone co., SE Miss., 34 mi. N of Gulfport; lumber, tung oil, naval stores; makes pickles.

Wight, Isle of, island and administrative county (□ 147.1; 1931 pop. 88,454; 1951 census 95,594), of Hampshire, S England, in English Channel just off the coast, separated from mainland (Southampton) by the Solent (NW) and Spithead (NE); ⊙ Newport. Length E-W, 23.5 mi.; width, 13 mi. Medina R. almost bisects the isl.; row of chalk downs traverses isl. E-W; low hills are in S. Off W coast are The NEEDLES, chalk cliffs. Because of its excellent climate and the beauty of its coastal and inland scenery, Wight has long been a popular resort. Resorts include: Newport, Cowes, Ryde, Sandown, Shanklin, Ventnor, Yarmouth, Freshwater, Carisbrooke. Sheep raising, vegetable and fruit- growing. Yachts and small craft are made. Wight is probably *Vectis* of the Romans.

Wignehies (vēnyē'), town (pop. 2,942), Nord dept., N France, 8 mi. SSE of Avesnes; wool spinning, cloth mfg.

Wigry, Lake (vē'grĭ), Rus. *Vigry* (vē'grĭ) (□ 8), Bialystok prov., NE Poland, 6 mi. SSE of Suwalki; irregularly shaped. The Czarna Hancza flows through.

Wigstadl, Czechoslovakia: see VITKOV.

Wigston or **Wigston Magna**, urban district (1931 pop. 11,389; 1951 census 15,452), central Leicester, England, 4 mi. SSE of Leicester; hosiery and shoe mfg., textile printing. Has 2 churches dating from 14th cent. In urban dist. (WSW) is town of South Wigston, with mfg. of hosiery, shoes, electrical equipment, concrete, biscuits.

Wigton, former urban district (1931 pop. 3,521), NW Cumberland, England, 10 mi. WSW of Carlisle; leather tanning; mfg. of agr. machinery and metal products; agr. market.

Wigtown or **Wigtownshire** (wĭg'tŭn, –shĭr), county (□ 487.5; 1931 pop. 29,331; 1951 census 31,625), SW Scotland, on the North Channel and the Irish Sea; ⊙ Wigtown. Bounded by Ayrshire (N) and Kirkcudbright (E). Drained by Cree R. and several minor streams. Surface is hilly in N, flat and fertile in S and W. Co. forms W part of GALLOWAY dist. Peninsula at W end of co., formed by deep inlets of Luce Bay (S) and Loch Ryan (N), is called the Rhinns of Galloway; at S extremity is the Mull of Galloway. Bet. Luce Bay and Wigtown Bay (E) is the fertile Machers dist. Agr.; cattle, sheep, pig raising; and fishing are chief occupations. Besides Wigtown, other towns are Stranraer (port) and Portpatrick. There are numerous vestiges of anc. occupation, including hill forts, standing stones, and Pictish lake dwellings. Whithorn is associated with early introduction of Christianity into Scotland.

Wigtown, burgh (1931 pop. 1,261; 1951 census 1,376), ⊙ Wigtownshire, Scotland, in E part of co., on W shore of Wigtown Bay of Irish Sea, 37 mi. WSW of Dumfries; agr. market. Has Martyr's Memorial, commemorating drowning (1685) of 2 Covenanters. Wigtown became burgh in 1457. Near by is anc. stone circle of the Standing Stones of Torhouse.

Wigtown Bay, inlet of Irish Sea at mouth of Solway firth bet. Wigtown and Kirkcudbright, Scotland; 11 mi. wide at mouth bet. Burrow Head and Little Ross Isl., and 15 mi. long. Receives Cree R. at its head. Main towns: Wigtown and Creetown.

Wigtownshire, Scotland: see WIGTOWN, county.

Wijchmaal, Belgium: see HERENT.

Wijde Ee (vĭ'dŭ ā'), canal, Friesland prov., N Netherlands; extends 12 mi. E-W, bet. W shore of Bergum L. and Leeuwarden. Connects with the KOLONELSDIEP at Bergum L.; joined by GROUW CANAL at Fonejacht (6 mi. ESE of Leevwarden); connects with the HARLINGER TREKVAART at Leeuwarden.

Wijde Fjord (vē'dŭ, vĭ'dŭ), Nor. *Wijdefjorden*, inlet (70 mi. long, 3–14 mi. wide) of Arctic Ocean, N West Spitsbergen, Spitsbergen group; 78°54'–79°48'N 15°35'E. Near its head is Mt. Newton (5,633 ft.), highest peak of Spitsbergen.

Wijh, Al, Saudi Arabia: see WEJH.

Wijhe or **Wije** (both: vĕ'jŭ), town (pop. 2,626), Overijssel prov., E central Netherlands, on Ijssel R. and 9 mi. N of Deventer; mfg. (linoleum, floor mats, asphalt roofing paper); meat packing. Site of many country houses. Sometimes spelled Wyhe or Wye.

Wijk aan Zee (vĭk' än zā'), village (pop. 2,258), North Holland prov., W Netherlands, on North Sea, 2.5 mi. NNW of Ijmuiden; seaside resort;

agr., truck gardening, cattle raising. Sometimes spelled Wyk aan Zee.

Wijk bij Duurstede (bī dür'stüdů), town (pop. 3,004), Utrecht prov., central Netherlands, 13 mi. SE of Utrecht, where the Lower Rhine branches into Lek R. and Crooked Rhine R.; river locks; brickworks; fruitgrowing, cattle raising. Has 13th-cent. Slot Duurstede, once palace-castle of archbishops of Utrecht, and 15th-cent. church. First mentioned in 7th cent. as Dorestadum; supplanted as trading center by Utrecht in 9th cent. Sometimes spelled Wyk by Duurstede.

Wijnegem (wī'nůkh-ěm), residential town (pop. 5,946), Antwerp prov., N Belgium, on Albert Canal and 5 mi. E of Antwerp.

Wik (vēk), N district of KIEL, NW Germany, on W bank of Kiel Firth, just S of mouth of Kiel Canal; free port, grain harbor. Until 1945, site of major naval installations, including U-boat harbor.

Wil (vēl), town (pop. 7,626), St. Gall canton, NE Switzerland, 16 mi. W of St. Gall; knit goods, embroideries; metalworking, printing. Former palace of abbots of St. Gall and law court (both with museums), 15th-cent. church. Formerly Wyl.

Wilamowice (vēlämôvē'tsě), town (pop. 1,945), Katowice prov., S Poland, 36 mi. WSW of Cracow. Until 1951 in Krakow prov.

Wilbarger (wĭl'bärgůr), county (□ 954; pop. 20,552), N Texas; ⊙ Vernon. Bounded N by Red R. (here the Okla. line); drained by Pease R., small creeks. Rich agr. area in N (cotton, wheat, oats, grain sorghums, corn, fruit, truck); large-scale cattle ranching in S; some dairying, poultry. Large oil production. Clay mining. Formed 1858.

Wilber, city (pop. 1,356), ⊙ Saline co., SE Nebr., 27 mi. SSW of Lincoln and on Big Blue R.; flour; grain, livestock, dairy and poultry produce. Platted 1873, inc. 1879.

Wilberforce, town (1931 pop. 1,386), Sierra Leone colony, on Sierra Leone Peninsula, on railroad and 2 mi. WSW of Freetown; residential area for govt. officials. Has technical school.

Wilberforce, village (pop. c.300), Greene co., S central Ohio, 3 mi. NE of Xenia; seat of Wilberforce Univ. and Col. of Education and Industrial Arts.

Wilborn, village, Lewis and Clark co., W central Mont., 25 mi. NW of Helena; supply point; silver and lead mines; sawmill.

Wilbraham (wĭl'brůhăm″), town (pop. 4,003), Hampden co., S Mass., 7 mi. E of Springfield; paper products, wire, plastics. Has boys' acad., state game farm. Settled 1730, inc. 1763. Includes village of North Wilbraham (1940 pop. 955).

Wilbur, town (pop. 1,043), Lincoln co., E Wash., 25 mi. WNW of Davenport; agr.; ships grain, flour, feed. Settled 1884.

Wilbur Cross Parkway, Conn.: see MERRITT PARKWAY.

Wilbur Park, town (pop. 743), St. Louis co., E Mo.

Wilburton (wĭl'bůrtůn), city (pop. 1,939), ⊙ Latimer co., SE Okla., 26 mi. E of McAlester, near the Ouachita Mts. (S); lumber milling, ranching, coal mining; gas wells; cotton ginning. Seat of Eastern Okla. Agr. and Mechanical Col. A state park, an Indian settlement project, and a colony of veterans of the Spanish-American War are near by. Settled 1890, inc. 1902.

Wilcannia (wĭlkăn'yů), municipality (pop. 799), W central New South Wales, Australia, on Darling R. and 110 mi. ENE of Broken Hill; sheep center.

Wilcox, village (pop. 245), S Sask., 26 mi. S of Regina; wheat.

Wilcox. 1 County (□ 900; pop. 23,476), SW central Ala.; ⊙ Camden. In the Black Belt; drained by Alabama R. Cotton, cattle; lumber milling. Formed 1819. **2** County (□ 383; pop. 10,167), S central Ga.; ⊙ Abbeville. Bounded E by Ocmulgee R.; drained by Alapaha R. Coastal plain agr. (cotton, corn, melons, peanuts) and forestry (lumber, naval stores) area. Formed 1857.

Wilcox. 1 Village (pop. 296), Kearney co., S Nebr., 12 mi. ESE of Holdrege; livestock, grain. **2** Village (1940 pop. 733), Elk co., N Pa., 5 mi. N of Johnsonburg and on Clarion R.; tannery.

Wilczek Land (vĭl'chěk), island in E Franz Josef Land, Russian SFSR, in Arctic Ocean; 50 mi. long, 40 mi. wide; rises to 2,410 ft.; 80°45'N 61°E. First isl. sighted in discovery (1873) of Franz Josef Land by Payer-Weyprecht expedition.

Wild Ammonoosuc River, N.H.: see AMMONOOSUC RIVER.

Wildau (vĭl'dou), town (pop. 5,166), Brandenburg, E Germany, 17 mi. SE of Berlin; mfg. of locomotives, railroad cars, buses, basic chemicals.

Wildbad or **Wildbad im Schwarzwald** (vĭlt'bät ĭm shvärts'vält), town (pop. 4,999), S Württemberg, Germany, after 1945 in Württemberg-Hohenzollern, on the Enz and 12 mi. SW of Pforzheim; after Baden-Baden, the most frequented spa of Black Forest; rail terminus; hot mineral springs. Has 18th-cent. church.

Wildbad Kreuth, Germany: see KREUTH.

Wildberg (vĭlt'běrk), town (pop. 1,406), S Württemberg, Germany, after 1945 in Württemberg-Hohenzollern, in Black Forest, on the Nagold and 5 mi. N of Nagold; summer resort. Has remains of old fortifications; and 15th-cent. town hall.

Wildcat, town (pop. 147), Okmulgee co., E central Okla., 7 mi. NE of Henryetta, in agr. area.

Wildcat Creek, Ind., rises in Tipton co., flows E, NE, and W to Kokomo, thence W to the Wabash 4 mi. N of Lafayette; 81 mi. long. Receives South Fork (c.40 mi. long) near its mouth.

Wildcat Mountain, peak (4,997 ft.) of White Mts., N Carroll co., E N.H., SE of Mt. Washington and just N of Jackson, in recreational area.

Wildcat Peak, Nev.: see TOQUEMA RANGE.

Wilde, town (pop. estimate 5,000) in Greater Buenos Aires, Argentina, adjoining Bernal, 6 mi. SE of Buenos Aires; industrial center; petroleum refineries, paper mills, tanneries, glassworks; mfg. of printing machinery.

Wilde Adler River, Poland and Czechoslovakia: see DIVOCHA ORLICE RIVER.

Wildemann (vĭl'důmän), town (pop. 2,089), in former Prussian prov. of Hanover, W Germany, after 1945 in Lower Saxony, in the upper Harz, on Innerste R. and 3 mi. W of Clausthal-Zellerfeld; summer resort. Stone quarries near by.

Wildenfels (vĭl'dünfěls), town (pop. 2,586), Saxony, E central Germany, at N foot of the Erzgebirge, 7 mi. SE of Zwickau; cotton and paper milling; marble and chalk quarrying. Has old castle.

Wildenschwert, Czechoslovakia: see USTI NAD ORLICI.

Wilder. 1 Village (pop. 555), Canyon co., SW Idaho, 11 mi. W of Caldwell; potatoes, corn, onions. Phosphate, silver, gold mines near by. **2** Village (pop. 118), Jackson co., SW Minn., near Heron L., 18 mi. NW of Jackson; dairy products. **3** Village, Vt.: see HARTFORD.

Wilderness, The, historic locality in Spotsylvania and Orange counties, NE Va., along S bank of Rapidan R., 15 mi. W of Fredericksburg. Scene of Civil War battle of the Wilderness (May 5–6, 1864), a bloody but indecisive engagement bet. Union troops under Grant and Confederates under Lee and Longstreet; Federals, although repulsed, were able to push past Lee's right to attack unsuccessfully at SPOTSYLVANIA and, later, at COLD HARBOR, in final phases of costly Wilderness campaign. Part of battlefield now in Fredericksburg and Spotsylvania Co. Battlefields Memorial (hq. at FREDERICKSBURG).

Wilderness Road, S U.S., pioneer trail (c.220 mi. long) of the Old Southwest, which extended from SW Va. into E Tenn., then through Cumberland Gap into Ky., terminating at present Harrodsburg. Daniel Boone marked the trail in 1775 beyond E Tenn.; for nearly 50 years it was a principal route of westward migration, although it was not made passable for wagons until 1790s. Long deserted in 19th cent., the route was made (1926) a section of U.S. 26, the Dixie Highway.

Wilders, town (pop. 204), Campbell co., N Ky., near Licking R., 6 mi. S of downtown Cincinnati; liquor distilling.

Wilderswil (vĭl'důrsvēl), village (pop. 1,643), Bern canton, central Switzerland, on Lütschine R. and 1 mi. S of Interlaken; resort; watches.

Wildervank (vĭl'důrvängk), town (pop. 4,858), Groningen prov., N Netherlands, 9 mi. SW of Winschoten; potato-flour milling, knitting mills; peat production.

Wildeshausen (vĭl″důs-hou'zůn), town (pop. 8,705), in Oldenburg, NW Germany, after 1945 in Lower Saxony, on the Hunte and 19 mi. SW of Bremen; cigar mfg.

Wilde Weisseritz, Germany: see WILD WEISSERITZ RIVER.

Wildhaus (vĭlt'hous), village (pop. 1,141), St. Gall canton, NE Switzerland, 6 mi. NNE of Wallenstadt; resort (alt. 3,602 ft.) 3 mi. S of the Säntis. Birthplace of Zwingli.

Wildhorn (vĭlt'hôrn), peak (10,664 ft.) in Bernese Alps, SW Switzerland, 8 mi. N of Sion.

Wildhorse Creek, S Okla., rises near Marlow in Stephens co., flows c.55 mi. E to Washita R. just NW of Davis.

Wild Rice River. 1 In Minn., rises in Upper Rice L. in Clearwater co., NW Minn., flows 160 mi. generally W, through White Earth Indian Reservation, past Mahnomen and Twin Valley, to Red River of the North, on N.Dak. line, just S of Halstad. Drains Rice L. (5 mi. long, 1 mi. wide; half dry) in upper course. **2** In N.Dak., rises in Sargent co. near S.Dak. line, meanders E and N c.100 mi. and enters Red River of the North 8 mi. S of Fargo.

Wildrose, city (pop. 430), Williams co., NW N.Dak., 40 mi. NNE of Williston; flour refining, dairying, livestock, poultry.

Wild Rose, village (pop. 582), Waushara co., central Wis., on small Pine R. and 36 mi. WNW of Oshkosh, in agr. area.

Wildspitze (vĭlt'shpĭtsů), highest peak (12,379 ft.) of Ötztal Alps, in Tyrol, W Austria, 25 mi. SSE of Imst.

Wildstein, Czechoslovakia: see VILDSTEJN.

Wildstrubel (vĭlt'shtrōōbůl), mountain in Bernese Alps, S Switzerland. Its highest peak (10,649 ft.), the Grossstrubel, is 8 mi. N of Sierre. Wildstrubel Hütte (9,174 ft.) and Wildstrubel Glacier are SW of the peak.

Wildungen, Bad, Germany: see BAD WILDUNGEN.

Wild Weisseritz River, Ger. *Wilde Weisseritz* (vĭl'dů vī'sůrĭts), E central Germany, rises in the Erzgebirge 6 mi. SE of Frauenstein, flows 25 mi. generally N, past Klingenberg (dam) and Tharandt (hydroelectric station), joining Red Weisseritz R. just above Hainsberg to form the Weisseritz.

Wildwood, village (pop. estimate 300), central Alta., on Chip L. (12 mi. long, 5 mi. wide), 70 mi. W of Edmonton; mixed farming, lumbering.

Wildwood. 1 City (pop. 2,019), Sumter co., central Fla., 24 mi. SSE of Ocala, in agr. area; rail junction with repair shops. **2** Resort city (pop. 5,475), Cape May co., S N.J., on 9-mi.-long barrier isl. (bridged to mainland) off Cape May Peninsula, 33 mi. SW of Atlantic City; seafood, fertilizer, cement blocks, poultry, fruit, truck. Settled 1882, Wildwood borough (inc. 1898) consolidated with Holly Beach City borough and inc. as city 1911.

Wildwood Crest, resort borough (pop. 1,772), Cape May co., S N.J., on barrier isl. off Cape May Peninsula, just S of Wildwood.

Wildwood State Park, N.Y.: see WADING RIVER.

Wilejka, Belorussian SSR: see VILEIKA, city.

Wiley, town (pop. 417), Prowers co., SE Colo., near Arkansas R., 6 mi. NW of Lamar; sugar beets, grain, livestock.

Wilgartswiesen (vĭl'gärtsvē'zůn), village (pop. 1,313), Rhenish Palatinate, W Germany, on the Queich and 11 mi. W of Landau; cattle. Has ruined castle.

Wilge River (vĭl'khů), W Natal and Orange Free State, U. of So. Afr., rises in Drakensberg range NNW of Ladysmith, flows c.250 mi. generally NW, past Harrismith and Frankfort, to Vaal R. at Vaalbank Dam irrigation works, 50 mi. SSE of Johannesburg.

Wilhelm, Mount, New Guinea: see BISMARCK MOUNTAINS.

Wilhelm II Coast (vĭl'hělm), part of Antarctica, on Indian Ocean, bet. 86° and 91°52'E. Discovered 1902 by Erich von Drygalski, German explorer. Formerly Kaiser Wilhelm II Land.

Wilhelmina, Mount (vĭlhělmē'nů), highest peak (c.15,585 ft.) of Orange Range, central New Guinea.

Wilhelmina Canal, North Brabant prov., S Netherlands, extends 34 mi. WNW-ESE, bet. E end of MARK CANAL just W of Oosterhout and the ZUID-WILLEMSVAART just S of Beek; 85 ft. wide, 8 ft. deep. Serves Tilburg and Oirschot. Crosses Donge R. near Dongen.

Wilhelmina Mountains (vĭlhělmē'nů), W central Du. Guiana, N spur of the Guiana Highlands, extending c.70 mi. W-E at c.3°45'N, rising to 4,200 ft. The Tafelberg (3,540 ft.) is at E end.

Wilhelmoya, Spitsbergen: see HINLOPEN STRAIT.

Wilhelmsbad (vĭl'hělmsbät), NW suburb (pop. 224) of Hanau, W Germany; mineral springs.

Wilhelmsburg (vĭl'hělmsbŏŏrk), town (pop. 5,489), central Lower Austria, on Traisen R. and 7 mi. S of Sankt Pölten; grain, cattle, orchards.

Wilhelmsburg, Germany: see HARBURG-WILHELMSBURG.

Wilhelmshaven (vĭl″hělms-hä'fůn), city (1939 pop. 113,686; 1946 pop. 89,717; 1950 pop. 100,926), in Oldenburg, NW Germany, after 1945 in Lower Saxony, in East Friesland, port at mouth of Jade Bay, at E head of Ems-Jade Canal, 40 mi. NW of Bremen; until 1945 chief Ger. naval base on North Sea; 53°32'N 8°8'E. Rail terminus; industrial center; mfg. of structural shapes, cranes, auto chassis, bicycles, agr. and other machinery, electric motors, refrigerators, vacuum cleaners, measuring instruments, furniture, textiles, leather goods. Food processing. Dispatches deep-sea fishing fleet. Has teachers col.; research institutes for marine biology and geology; ornithological station. Founded 1869 on territory acquired (1853–54) by Prussia from Oldenburg for purpose of building a naval base. Scene (Oct. 30, 1918) of sailors' mutiny. Inc. 1937 with neighboring RÜSTRINGEN and returned to Oldenburg. Naval installations were either destroyed by Allied aerial attacks in Second World War or dismantled after 1945, and complete reorientation of industry (hitherto based on naval construction) took place.

Wilhelmshöhe, Germany: see WAHLERSHAUSEN.

Wilhering (vĭl'hārĭng), town (pop. 2,448), N central Upper Austria, on the Danube and 5 mi. W of Linz. Benedictine abbey dates from 12th cent.

Wilja River, Belorussian SSR and Lithuania: see VILIYA RIVER.

Wilkau-Hasslau (vĭl'kou-häs'lou), town (pop. 13,455), Saxony, E central Germany, on the Zwickauer Mulde and 4 mi. SSE of Zwickau; textile and paper milling, woodworking.

Wilkes (wĭlks). **1** County (□ 472; pop. 12,388), NE Ga.; ⊙ Washington. Piedmont agr. (cotton, corn, hay, sweet potatoes, peaches, livestock) and timber area; mfg. at Washington. Formed 1777. **2** County (□ 765; pop. 45,243), NW N.C.; ⊙ Wilkesboro. Mostly in the Blue Ridge; drained by Yadkin R. Agr. (poultry, tobacco, corn), lumbering and sawmilling, mfg. of textiles, furniture. Mtn. resorts. Formed 1777.

Wilkes-Barre (wĭlks'-bă″rů, –bă″rē), industrial city (pop. 76,826), ⊙ Luzerne co., NE central Pa., 16 mi. SW of Scranton and on Susquehanna R. Center of Wyoming Valley anthracite area; railroad shops (locomotive mfg.); mfg. (textiles, clothing, food products, beverages, furniture, machinery, and tobacco, wire, paper, and metal products). Seat of Wilkes Col., King's Col. Settled 1769; burned 1778 by Tories and Indians after Wyoming Valley Massacre; burned again 1784; inc. as borough 1806, as city 1871.

Wilkesboro (wĭlks'bŭrō), town (pop. 1,370), ⊙ Wilkes co., NW N.C., on Yadkin R. (bridged) opposite North Wilkesboro; mfg. of wood and dairy products. Founded c.1777; inc. 1889.

Wilkes Land (wĭlks), part of Antarctica bordering Indian Ocean, S of Australia, bet. Queen Mary Coast and George V Coast; extends from 102° to c.142°20'E. It includes Adélie, Clarie, Banzare, Sabrina, Budd, and Knox coasts. In its E sector is South Magnetic Pole. Named for Charles Wilkes, who led U.S. expedition of 1838–42.

Wilkeson (wĭl'kŭsŭn), town (pop. 386), Pierce co., W central Wash., 22 mi. ESE of Tacoma.

Wilkesville, village (pop. 203), Vinton co., S Ohio, near Raccoon Creek, 21 mi. SW of Athens.

Wilkie, town (pop. 1,425), W Sask., 30 mi. SW of North Battleford; railroad divisional point; grain elevators, lumbering, stock raising.

Wilkin, county (□ 752; pop. 10,567), W Minn.; ⊙ Breckenridge. Agr. area drained by Otter Tail R. and bounded W by Bois de Sioux R. and Red River of the North, which form part of N.Dak. line. Wheat, small grains, potatoes, livestock. Formed 1868.

Wilkins, S.C.: see LADIES ISLAND.

Wilkinsburg, residential borough (pop. 31,418), Allegheny co., SW Pa., adjacent to E Pittsburgh; steel alloys, bricks, pumps, railroad supplies, cement products, tools, beverages. Settled c.1800, inc. 1887.

Wilkinson. 1 County (□ 458; pop. 9,781), central Ga.; ⊙ Irwinton. Bounded NE by Oconee R. Coastal plain agr. (cotton, corn, potatoes, grain, melons, peanuts), kaolin mining, and sawmilling area. Formed 1803. **2** County (□ 675; pop. 14,116), extreme SW Miss.; ⊙ Woodville. Borders S and W on La., with Mississippi R. forming W boundary. Drained by Homochitto R. and short Buffalo Bayou. Agr. (cotton, corn); lumbering; cattle raising. Includes part of Homochitto Natl. Forest. Formed 1802.

Wilkinson, town (pop. 365), Hancock co., central Ind., 31 mi. ENE of Indianapolis, in agr. area.

Wilkinsonville, Mass.: see SUTTON.

Wilkins Strait (80 naut. mi. long, c.20 naut. mi. wide), Antarctica, separates Charcot Isl. from Alexander I Isl., in E Bellingshausen Sea; 70°30'S 72°W. Discovered 1940 by U.S. expedition.

Wilkomierz, Lithuania: see UKMERGE.

Will, county (□ 845; pop. 134,336), NE Ill., bounded by Ind. (E); ⊙ Joliet. Agr. (corn, oats, soybeans, fruit, truck, livestock, poultry; dairy products). Bituminous-coal mines; limestone deposits. Diversified mfg. in industrial region of NE, adjoining Chicago metropolitan area. Crossed by Illinois Waterway; drained by Des Plaines, Du Page, and Kankakee rivers. Formed 1836.

Willacoochee, town (pop. 987), Atkinson co., S Ga., 17 mi. SW of Douglas, in agr. area; sawmilling.

Willacy (wĭ'lŭsē), county (□ 595; pop. 20,920), extreme S Texas; ⊙ Raymondville. Bounded E by Laguna Madre, which is separated from Gulf of Mexico by Padre Isl. and traversed by Gulf Intracoastal Waterway. In rich irrigated agr. region of lower Rio Grande valley (citrus, truck, cotton); also ranching (beef and dairy cattle, sheep, hogs, poultry). Oil wells; salt lakes; also clay, sulphur deposits. Fishing, warm winter climate attract tourists. Formed 1911, reorganized 1921.

Willamette River (wĭlă'mĭt), W Oregon, formed by confluence of Coast Fork and Middle Fork near Eugene, flows 183 mi. N, past Albany, Salem, Oregon City, and Portland to Columbia R. just NW of Portland; from head of Middle Fork, its main tributary, it is c.300 mi. long and drains □ 11,250. Navigable by steamer to Eugene. Fruitgrowing, lumbering, and food processing are important activities in river valley (state's most populous area since 1st settlement in 1830s), which receives hydroelectric power generated by river. U.S. project (begun 1938) includes flood-control works and other improvements designed to facilitate navigation and increase power production. Fern Ridge Dam, on LONG TOM RIVER, and Cottage Grove Dam, on COAST FORK, were completed, respectively, in 1941 and 1942.

Willamina (wĭlumē'nŭ), city (pop. 1,082), Yamhill and Polk counties, NW Oregon, 25 mi. WNW of Salem and on South Yamhill R.; wood, clay products.

Willapa (wĭ'lŭpä", –pŭ), village (pop. c.400), Pacific co., SW Wash., on Willapa R. just SE of Raymond; agr., lumber. **Willapa Bay**, sheltered harbor (c.25 mi. long) bet. mouth of the Columbia and Grays Harbor, is oyster-growing center. Receives **Willapa River**, rising in SW Chehalis co. and flowing c.50 mi. generally NW, past Raymond, to N end of Willapa Bay.

Willard (wĭ'lŭrd). **1** City (pop. 95), Shawnee co., NE Kansas, on Kansas R. and 14 mi. W of Topeka. **2** Town (pop. 124), Carter co., NE Ky., 23 mi. SW of Ashland. **3** Village (pop. 296), Torrance co., central N.Mex., 12 mi. S of Estancia, just NE of Chupadero Mesa; alt. 6,091 ft. Trade center in livestock region; railroad div. point. Laguna del Perro is 4 mi. E. Part of Lincoln Natl. Forest near by. **4** Village (1940 pop. 602), Seneca co., W central N.Y., on E shore of Seneca L., 25 mi. NW of Ithaca. Seat of Willard State Hosp. **5** Village (pop. 4,744), Huron co., N Ohio, 24 mi. NNW of Mansfield, in fruit, truck, and grain area; makes rubber goods, food and dairy products, lumber, burial vaults. **6** City (pop. 548), Box Elder co., N Utah, 7 mi. S of Brigham City, near Great Salt L.; alt. 4,266 ft.

Willards (wĭ'lŭrdz), town (pop. 464), Wicomico co., SE Md., near Pocomoke R. 14 mi. E of Salisbury; strawberry market.

Willaston, town and parish (pop. 1,296), NW Cheshire, England, 7 mi. S of Birkenhead; mfg. of clothing; flour milling.

Willaumez Peninsula (wĭlou'mĕz), N New Britain, Bismarck Archipelago, Territory of New Guinea, SW Pacific; 35 mi. long, 10 mi. wide. Talasea harbor on E coast.

Willcox, town (pop. 1,266), Cochise co., SE Ariz., 65 mi. E of Tucson; alt. 4,163 ft. Ships cattle; dude ranches. Near-by alkali desert known for mirages.

Willebroek (vĭ'lŭbrōōk), town (pop. 14,735), Antwerp prov., N Belgium, on Willebroek Canal and 11 mi. S of Antwerp; coke plants, paper mills; boiler mfg. chemicals (ammonia, superphosphates). Formerly spelled Willebroeck.

Willebroek Canal, central Belgium, runs 21 mi. N-S bet. CHARLEROI-BRUSSELS CANAL at Brussels and RUPEL RIVER just SW of Niel; serves Vilvoorde and Willebroek. Navigable for small seagoing ships.

Willems Canal, Netherlands: see ZUID-WILLEMSVAART.

Willemsdorp (vĭ'lŭmzdôrp), village (pop. 41), South Holland prov., SW Netherlands, on the Hollandschdiep, at mouth of the Dortsche Kil, 6 mi. SSW of Dordrecht, at N end of Moerdijk Bridge.

Willemstad (vĭ'lŭmstät), city (1948 pop. estimate 40,000), ⊙ Dutch Antilles (until 1949 called Curaçao territory), Du. West Indies, port on SW coast of Curaçao isl., 200 mi. ENE of Maracaibo (Venezuela), 500 mi. WNW of Port of Spain; 12°6'N 68°57'W. A free port, with one of the finest harbors in the West Indies, on deepwater Sint Anna Bay, which widens into the sheltered Schottegat. Long a coal-fueling station and entrepôt for passengers and cargoes, it has become a major transshipment and refining center for Venezuelan petroleum (mostly from L. Maracaibo region); also exports Venezuelan coffee. Having a varied trade, and in focus of international sea routes, it serves as warehousing and shopping center for SE Caribbean. Willemstad ranks high as tourist resort, visited by cruise ships. Airport. A neat, distinctly Du. city with quaint old houses, it is protected by historic Fort Amsterdam. Has administrative bldgs., town hall, governor's palace, Protestant church (built 1769), Jewish cemetery (dating from 1650). Punda, its oldest part, is now the shopping dist. Across the channel (W) lies the Otrabanda section. There are several beaches in vicinity. Oil pipe lines link the city with Bullen Bay (NW) and Caracas Bay (SE).

Willemstad, town (pop. 905), North Brabant prov., SW Netherlands, on the Hollandschdiep and 10 mi. N of Roosendaal. Built (1683) as fortress by William the Silent.

Willenberg, Poland: see WIELBARK.

Willenhall. 1 Urban district (1931 pop. 21,150; 1951 census 30,695), S Stafford, England, 3 mi. E of Wolverhampton; coal mining, steel casting, mfg. of light metals, tools, electrical equipment. **2** Residential village and parish (pop. 348), central Warwick, England, 3 mi. SE of Coventry.

Willernie (wĭ'lŭrnē), village (pop. 592), Washington co., E Minn., on White Bear L. and 10 mi. NE of St. Paul.

Willesborough (wĭlz'-), residential town and parish (pop. 4,979), E central Kent, England, just SE of Ashford. Has 13th-cent. church.

Willesden (wĭlz'dŭn), residential municipal borough (1931 pop. 184,434; 1951 census 179,647), Middlesex, England, 6 mi. NW of London; rail center. Site of post office research laboratory. Willesden includes residential areas of Cricklewood (NE; pop. 35,923), Kilburn (E; pop. 40,865), Brondesbury Park (E; pop. 9,788), Harlesden (SW; pop. 16,562), Kensal Rise (S; pop. 13,291).

Willey, town (pop. 94), Carroll co., W central Iowa, 6 mi. SSE of Carroll.

Willey, Mount (4,302 ft.), N central N.H., in White Mts., W of Crawford Notch and SW of Presidential Range.

William, Mount, highest peak (3,828 ft.) of the Grampians, SW central Victoria, Australia, 130 mi. WNW of Melbourne; gold.

William Penn, village (pop. 1,075), Schuylkill co., E central Pa., 10 mi. N of Pottsville.

Williams. 1 County (□ 2,100; pop. 16,442), NW N.Dak.; ⊙ Williston. Agr. area bounded S by Missouri R. Coal mines, oil wells (developed 1951), grain, livestock, dairy products, turkeys. Formed 1873. **2** County (□ 421; pop. 26,202), extreme NW Ohio; ⊙ Bryan. Bounded N by Mich., W by Ind.; intersected by St. Joseph and Tiffin rivers. Livestock, poultry, small grain; diversified mfg., especially at Bryan, Montpelier. Sand, gravel pits. Formed 1824.

Williams. 1 Town (pop. 2,152), Coconino co., N central Ariz., in Kaibab Natl. Forest, 30 mi. W of Flagstaff, S of Grand Canyon, to which it is a gateway; alt. c.6,700 ft.; tourist and lumbering point. Settled 1876–78. Bill Williams Mtn. is just S. **2** Town (pop. 1,134), Colusa co., N central Calif., 8 mi. SW of Colusa; highway junction; ships rice, sheep. **3** Town (pop. 519), Hamilton co., central Iowa, 15 mi. E of Webster City, in agr. area. **4** Village (pop. 414), Lake of the Woods co., NW Minn., 17 mi. WNW of Baudette, near Lake of the Woods, in grain and potato area. State forest near by. **5** Town (pop. 254), Colleton co., S S.C., 15 mi. NW of Walterboro.

Williams, Fort, Maine: see COTTAGE, CAPE.

Williams, Mount (7,250 ft.), in Chugach Mts., S Alaska, 40 mi. NNW of Katalla; 60°44'N 144°55'W.

Williams, Mount, Mass.: see GREYLOCK, MOUNT.

Williams Air Force Base, Ariz.: see CHANDLER.

Williams Bay, resort village (pop. 1,118), Walworth co., SE Wis., on small arm of L. Geneva, 6 mi. WSW of Lake Geneva city. Yerkes Observatory of Univ. of Chicago is here.

Williamsbridge, SE N.Y., a residential section of central Bronx borough of New York city.

Williamsburg, county (□ 931; pop. 43,807), E central S.C.; ⊙ Kingstree. Bounded S by Santee R.; drained by Black R. Agr. area (tobacco, truck, cotton, fruit), hogs, cattle, poultry; timber. Hunting and fishing attract tourists. Formed 1785.

Williamsburg. 1 Town (pop. 65), Fremont co., S central Colo., near Arkansas R., 30 mi. WNW of Pueblo; alt. 5,250 ft. **2** Town (pop. 1,183), Iowa co., E central Iowa, on Old Man Creek and 29 mi. SW of Cedar Rapids; dairy products. Inc. 1884. **3** City (pop. 297), Franklin co., E Kansas, 14 mi. SW of Ottawa; livestock, grain. **4** City (pop. 3,348), ⊙ Whitley co., SE Ky., in the Cumberlands, on Cumberland R. and 27 mi. WNW of Middlesboro, in coal-mining, gas, hardwood-timber, and farm (corn, oats) area; mfg. of coke, soft drinks, clothing; lumber mills. Seat of Cumberland Col. Many Indian artifacts have been found in this area. Cumberland Falls State Park is near by. City established 1817. **5** Village, Dorchester co., E Md., near Marshyhope Creek 15 mi. ENE of Cambridge; vegetable, seafood canneries. **6** Town (pop. 2,056), Hampshire co., W central Mass., on Mill R., in the Berkshires, and 8 mi. NW of Northampton; ornamental hardware. Settled 1735, set off from Hatfield 1771. Includes village of Haydenville. **7** A residential section of NW Brooklyn borough of New York city, SE N.Y. East R. is here crossed by Williamsburg Bridge to Manhattan. **8** Village (pop. 1,490), Clermont co., SW Ohio, 25 mi. E of Cincinnati and on East Fork of Little Miami R.; agr. (corn, wheat, tobacco); mfg. of chairs. Settled 1795, inc. 1800. **9** Borough (pop. 1,792), Blair co., central Pa., on Frankstown Branch of Juniata R. and 11 mi. ESE of Altoona; paper; limestone. Settled 1790, laid out 1795, inc. 1827. **10** Historic city (pop. 6,735), in but independent of James City and York cos., SE Va., on peninsula bet. York and James rivers, 45 mi. ESE of Richmond; co. courthouse is here. City is historic shrine whose restored colonial bldgs. are visited by thousands annually; it is included in COLONIAL NATIONAL HISTORICAL PARK. Settled 1632 as Middle Plantation; laid out and name changed 1699; in 1722, was 1st Va. city to be inc. After burning (1676) of Jamestown in Bacon's Rebellion, became temporary ⊙; was ⊙ Va., 1699–1779. Restoration of city to its colonial aspect was begun 1927; major points of interest are the old capitol (reconstructed), Raleigh Tavern (reconstructed), where Revolutionary patriots often met, old co. courthouse (1770), Bruton Parish Church (1710–15), reconstructed palace of royal governor, the gaol (c.1701), and many other 18th-cent. bldgs. Col. of William and Mary (now coeducational), here, chartered 1693. City holds annual Garden Week. State general assembly meets in old colonial capitol once in each session. Important conventions met in Williamsburg during movement for colonies' independence. A Civil War action was fought here (May 5, 1862) in Peninsular Campaign.

Williamsburg Bridge, in New York city, SE N.Y., across East R. bet. lower Manhattan and Brooklyn; 1,600-ft. suspension span, with vehicular road, rails; built 1903.

Williams Creek, town (pop. 288), Marion co., central Ind., N suburb of Indianapolis, on West Fork of White R.; inc. 1932.

Williamsfield, town (pop. 1,100), Manchester parish, W central Jamaica, on Kingston–Montego Bay RR and 2½ mi. NE of Mandeville, for which it is the rail station; popular mtn. resort (alt. c.2,000 ft.).

Williamsfield, village (pop. 542), Knox co., W central Ill., near Spoon R., 18 mi. E of Galesburg; bituminous-coal mines; grain growing, livestock, poultry raising.

Williamsford, village (pop. 202), W Tasmania, 90 mi. WSW of Launceston; zinc mines.

Williams Lake, village (pop. 540), S central B.C., at foot of Cariboo Mts., on Williams L. (5 mi. long), near Fraser R., 130 mi. S of Prince George; center of Chilcotin cattle-raising dist.; lumbering.

Williamson. 1 County (□ 441; pop. 48,621), S Ill.; ⊙ Marion. Bituminous-coal-mining and agr. area (corn, wheat, livestock, fruit; dairy products). Part of Ill. Ozarks in S. Drained by Big Muddy R., South Fork of Saline R., and Crab Orchard Creek, dammed to form Crab Orchard L. (resorts), one of largest in state. Formed 1839. **2** County (□ 594; pop. 24,307), central Tenn.; ⊙ Franklin. Drained by Harpeth R. Agr. (livestock, tobacco, dairy products); phosphate mining. Mfg. at Franklin. Formed 1799. **3** County (□ 1,126; pop. 38,853), central Texas; ⊙ Georgetown. Drained by San Gabriel R. and its forks. Ranching (sheep, goats, cattle) in hilly W; agr. (cotton, corn, oats, grain sorghums, grain, hay, peanuts, fruit, truck) in rich blackland prairies of E; poultry raising, some dairying, beekeeping. Timber (mainly cedar); limestone quarries, oil wells. Processing, mfg. at Georgetown, Taylor. Hunting, fishing in W. Formed 1848.

Williamson. 1 Town (pop. 211), Pike co., W central Ga., 7 mi. SW of Griffin. **2** Village (pop. 319), Madison co., SW Ill., 16 mi. NE of Edwardsville, in agr. and bituminous-coal area. **3** Town (pop. 294), Lucas co., S Iowa, 5 mi. NNE of Chariton, in coal-mining and stock-raising area. State park near by. **4** Village (pop. 1,520), Wayne co., W N.Y., 21 mi. ENE of Rochester, in fruit and truck region; mfg. (chemicals, paper products, canned foods). **5** City (pop. 8,624), ⊙ Mingo co., SW W.Va., on Tug Fork at Ky. line and 60 mi. SW of Charleston; trade and distribution center for bituminous-coal field (partly in E Ky.); mfg. of gasoline, foundry products, wood products, armatures; railroad shops. Natural-gas and oil wells, timber near by. Inc. 1892.

Williamson, Mount (14,384 ft.), E Calif., in the Sierra Nevada, 6 mi. N of Mt. Whitney and on E boundary of Sequoia Natl. Park.

Williamson River, rises in Klamath Indian Reservation, S Oregon, flows 20 mi. N, then 36 mi. SSW, through marshland, to Upper Klamath L. 20 mi. NNW of Klamath Falls; 56 mi. long. Flow is underground for short distance in lower course. Sprague R. is tributary.

Williams Peak, Colo.: see WILLIAMS RIVER MOUNTAINS.

Williamsport. 1 Town (pop. 1,241), ⊙ Warren co., W Ind., on the Wabash and 24 mi. WSW of Lafayette, in grain-growing area; lumber milling; poultry hatchery. Settled 1829. **2** Town (pop. 1,890), Washington co., W Md., on the Potomac at mouth of Conococheague Creek and 7 mi. WSW of Hagerstown. Makes ribbons, clothing labels, brick; leather tannery; limestone quarries. Laid out c.1786. **3** Village (pop. 631), Pickaway co., S central Ohio, 9 mi. W of Circleville, and on Deer Creek, in agr. area (grain, soybeans). **4** City (pop. 45,047), ⊙ Lycoming co., N central Pa., 75 mi. WSW of Scranton and on West Branch of Susquehanna R. Motors, aircraft parts, heating equipment; wood, wire, and electrical products; leather, furniture, textiles, paper products. Ordnance depot. Seat of Lycoming Col. In 19th cent was lumbering center. Settled 1772, laid out 1795, inc. as borough 1806, as city 1866.

Williams River. 1 In Ariz.: see BILL WILLIAMS RIVER. **2** In N central Colo., formed in Grand co. by confluence of several forks; flows c.30 mi. NNW, bet. Vasquez and Williams River Mts., to Colorado R. just W of Hot Sulphur Springs. **3** In E Vt., rises near Andover, flows c.25 mi. E and SE to the Connecticut near Rockingham.

Williams River Mountains, N central Colo., in Front Range; extend N–S bet. Blue R. and Williams R. Chief peaks: Williams Peak (11,619 ft.), Ute Peak (12,298 ft.), PTARMIGAN PEAK (12,400 ft.).

Williamston. 1 City (pop. 2,051), Ingham co., S central Mich., 14 mi. ESE of Lansing and on Red Cedar R., in farm area; mfg. (brick, tile); clay and soft-coal deposits. Settled c.1835, inc. 1871 as village, as city 1945. **2** Town (pop. 4,975), ⊙ Martin co., E N.C., 40 mi. E of Rocky Mount and on navigable Roanoke R.; tobacco market; fishing and mfg. center (lumber, boxes, fertilizer, peanut products). Inc. 1779. **3** Town (pop. 2,782), Anderson co., NW S.C., on Saluda R. and 17 mi. S of Greenville, in agr. area; textile mill, clothing plant.

Williamstown. 1 Village (pop. 383), SE South Australia, 29 mi. NE of Adelaide; orchards; pottery clay. **2** Municipality and port (pop. 26,471), S Victoria, Australia, 5 mi. SW of Melbourne, on SW shore of Hobson's Bay, in metropolitan area; shipyards, drydock.

Williams Town, town (pop. 163), central Bahama Isl., on Little Exuma Isl., just S of the Tropic of Cancer, 14 mi. ESE of George Town (Great Exuma Isl.); 23°25′N 75°34′W.

Williamstown, village (pop. estimate 550), SE Ont., on North Raisin R. and 12 mi. NE of Cornwall; dairying, mixed farming.

Williamstown. 1 Town (pop. 1,466), ⊙ Grant co., N Ky., 31 mi. S of Covington; trade and shipping center for Bluegrass agr. area (burley tobacco, corn, hay, livestock, poultry, dairy products); makes baseballs; flour and feed mills. Area settled c.1790. **2** Town (pop. 6,194), including Williamstown village (pop. 5,015), Berkshire co., extreme NW Mass., in the Berkshires, on Hoosic R. and 6 mi. W of North Adams; mfg. (wire, photographic paper and film, beverages); dairying, poultry. Seat of Williams Col. Mt. Greylock is just S. Settled 1749, inc. 1765. **3** Village (pop. 2,632), Gloucester co., SW N.J., 6 mi. E of Glassboro; mfg. (clothing, canned goods), agr. (poultry, truck, fruit). Settled before 1800. **4** Village in Williamstown town (1940 pop. 710), Oswego co., central N.Y., 31 mi. E of Oswego; lumber. **5** Borough (pop. 2,332), Dauphin co., E central Pa., 25 mi. NE of Harrisburg; anthracite, hosiery. Laid out 1869. **6** Town (pop. 1,600), Orange co., central Vt., just SW of Barre. Chartered 1781, settled 1784. **7** City (pop. 2,001), Wood co., W W.Va., on the Ohio opposite Marietta, Ohio; trade center for farm region; makes glass. Settled 1787.

Williamsville, village (pop. 439), W Trinidad, B.W.I., on railroad and 6 mi. ENE of San Fernando; sugar growing. Has housing development.

Williamsville. 1 Village (pop. 656), Sangamon co., central Ill., 10 mi. NNE of Springfield; grain, dairy products, livestock. **2** City (pop. 492), Wayne co., SE Mo., in Ozark region, on Black R. and 17 mi. NNW of Popular Bluff. **3** Residential village (pop. 4,649), Erie co., W N.Y., 4 mi. NE of Buffalo; mfg. (wood products, chemicals, gelatin, burial vaults, concrete blocks, cider); agr. (truck, potatoes). Settled c.1800, inc. 1869.

Willich (vĭ′lĭkh), town (pop. 9,630), in former Prussian Rhine Prov., W Germany, after 1945 in North Rhine-Westphalia, 4 mi. S of Krefeld; steel mills.

Willie, town (1940 pop. 192), Liberty co., SE Ga., 34 mi. W of Savannah.

Williford (wĭ′lĭfûrd), town (pop. 213), Sharp co., N Ark., 37 mi. NNE of Batesville and on Spring R.; limestone quarrying.

Willigen River, New Guinea: see ROUFFAER RIVER.

Willimansett, Mass.: see CHICOPEE.

Willimantic (wĭlĭmăn′tĭk). **1** City (pop. 13,586), in Windham town, a ⊙ of Windham co., E central Conn., 24 mi. ESE of Hartford, at junction of Willimantic and Natchaug rivers, which form Shetucket R. Known as the Thread City (cotton spinning since 1822); mfg. (textiles, yarns, metal products, tools, machinery, hardware, airplane parts, optical goods). Inc. 1893. **2** Resort town (pop. 189), Piscataquis co., central Maine, on Sebec L. and 10 mi. NW of Dover-Foxcroft. Includes Sebec Lake village.

Willimantic River, NE Conn., formed by several branches near Stafford Springs; flows c.35 mi. S, joining Natchaug R. to form Shetucket R. at Willimantic. Near South Coventry village is site of flood-control dam.

Willingdon, village (pop. 436), central Alta., 23 mi. N of Vegreville; railroad junction; tanning, mixed farming, dairying.

Willingdon, airport, India: see DELHI, city.

Willingdon, Mount (11,044 ft.), SW Alta., near B.C. border, in Rocky Mts., in Banff Natl. Park, 50 mi. NW of Banff; 51°45′N 116°15′W.

Willingdon Island, India: see COCHIN, city.

Willingham, town and parish (pop. 1,732), central Cambridge; agr. market; mfg. of farm implements. Has noted 14th-cent. church.

Willington. 1 Town, Durham, England: see CROOK AND WILLINGTON. **2** Town, Northumberland, England: see WALLSEND.

Willington, town (pop. 1,462), Tolland co., NE Conn., on Willimantic R. and 23 mi. ENE of Hartford; farming; sawmills. Includes mfg. villages of South Willington (thread) and West Willington (pearl buttons). Inc. 1727.

Willington Quay, England: see WALLSEND.

Willis. 1 City (pop. 140), Brown co., NE Kansas, 35 mi. W of St. Joseph (Mo.), in corn, poultry, livestock, and dairying region. **2** City (pop. 1,164), Montgomery co., E Texas, 20 mi. S of Huntsville, in lumbering area. Inc. 1937.

Willisau (vĭ′lēzou), town (pop. 5,179), Lucerne canton, central Switzerland, at confluence of Enzwigger and Wigger rivers, 15 mi. WNW of Lucerne; farming, metal-and woodworking, foodstuffs. Old castle, early 19th-cent. church. Consists of Willisau-Land and Willisau-Stadt.

Willis Island (3 mi. long, 2 mi. wide), E N.F., in Bonavista Bay, 30 mi. WNW of Cape Bonavista; 48°47′N 53°44′W.

Willis Mountains, volcanic range (c.30 mi. long), central Java, Indonesia, W of Kediri; highest peaks are Mt. Liman (8,409 ft.) and Mt. Dorowati (8,386 ft.).

Williston, town (pop. 1,725), W Cape Prov., U. of So. Afr., on Zak R. (irrigation dam) and 70 mi. E of Calvinia; stock, grain, fruit.

Williston. 1 Town (pop. 1,323), Levy co., N Fla., 34 mi. WNW of Ocala; lumbering; limestone quarrying. **2** City (pop. 7,378), ⊙ Williams co., NW N.Dak., 110 mi. W of Minot and on Missouri R. Trade center for irrigated agr. area and div. hq. of Great Northern RR. Cooperative creamery, grain elevator, stockyards, coal mines. Agr. experiment station is here. Williston Basin oil field, extending into Mont., S.Dak., Sask., and Man., was being developed in early 1950s. Settled c.1880, inc. 1904. **3** Town (pop. 896), Barnwell co., W S.C., 33 mi. WSW of Orangeburg; lumber, wood products. Shipping point for asparagus. **4** Town (pop. 1,182), Chittenden co., NW Vt., on the Winooski and 7 mi. SE of Burlington. Chartered 1763, settled 1774, abandoned in Revolution, inc. 1786.

Williston Park, residential village (pop. 7,505), Nassau co., SE N.Y., on W Long Isl., just N of Mineola; makes paints. Inc. 1926.

Willisville, village (pop. 635), Perry co., SW Ill., 41 mi. SSE of Belleville, in agr. and bituminous-coal-mining area.

Williton, town and parish (pop. 1,204), W Somerset, England, 2 mi. SSE of Watchet; agr. market.

Willits, town (pop. 2,691), Mendocino co., NW Calif., in a valley of the Coast Ranges, c.20 mi. N of Ukiah; railroad shops, sawmills; livestock, poultry, hay, dairy products. Founded c.1865, inc. 1888.

Willmar (wĭl′mûr), city (pop. 9,410), ⊙ Kandiyohi co., SW central Minn., c.90 mi. W of Minneapolis in lake region. Resort, trade center, and railroad div. point with foundries and machine shops; dairy and wood products, beverages. Settled 1856, virtually deserted during Sioux Indian uprising of 1862. Platted 1869, inc. as village 1874, as city 1901. State hosp. for insane is here.

Willoughby, municipality (pop. 51,945), E New South Wales, Australia, 5 mi. N of Sydney, in metropolitan area; mfg. (watches, toys), tanneries.

Willoughby (wĭ′lūbē). **1** City (pop. 5,602), Lake co., NE Ohio, 17 mi. NE of downtown Cleveland, and on Chagrin R., near L. Erie; auto parts, rubber products, furniture, machinery, metal products, chemicals, heating apparatus. Settled c.1800. **2** Village, Vt.: see BARTON.

Willoughby, Cape, easternmost point of Kangaroo Isl., South Australia; 35°51′S 138°8′E.

Willoughby, Lake, NE Vt., scenic resort lake 20 mi. N of St. Johnsbury; c.5 mi. long. Drained by small Willoughby R., flowing c.10 mi. W to Barton R. at Orleans.

Willoughby Spit, SE Va., sandbar extending into Hampton Roads at S side of entrance from Chesapeake Bay, opposite Old Point Comfort (ferry); part of Norfolk city; summer cottages. Shelters Willoughby Bay (W), on whose shore is a U.S. naval base.

Willow, village (1939 pop. 13), S Alaska, near Susitna R., 40 mi. N of Anchorage; supply point for gold-mining region and for sportsmen (trout fishing). Airfield. Formerly sometimes called Willow Station.

Willow, town (pop. 223), Greer co., SW Okla., 12 mi. N of Mangum; cotton ginning.

Willowbrook, industrial suburb (1940 pop. 5,731), Los Angeles co., S Calif., c.10 mi. S of downtown Los Angeles, in mfg. dist.

Willow Bunch, village (pop. 454), S Sask., near Willowbunch L., 24 mi. SE of Assiniboia; coal.

Willowbunch Lake (22 mi. long, 1 mi. wide), S Sask., 17 mi. SE of Assiniboia.

Willow City, city (pop. 595), Bottineau co., N N. Dak., 17 mi. S of Bottineau; grain, wheat, rye, oats.

Willow Creek, N Oregon, rises in Blue Mts., flows 70 mi. generally NW, past Heppner, to Columbia R. 10 mi. NE of Arlington. Used for irrigation.

Willowdale, village (pop. estimate 1,000), S Ont., N suburb of Toronto.

Willow Glen, Calif.: see SAN JOSE.

Willow Grove, village (1940 pop. 4,339), Montgomery co., SE Pa., 13 mi. N of Philadelphia; clothing; agr. Amusement park. Naval air station.

Willow Hill, village (pop. 333), Jasper co., SE Ill., 17 mi. N of Olney, in agr. area.

Willowick (wĭ′lūwĭk″). **1** Village (pop. 2,226), Orange co., S Calif. **2** Residential village (pop. 3,677), Lake co., NE Ohio, on L. Erie, 15 mi. NE of downtown Cleveland. Inc. 1922.

Willow Lake, city (pop. 484), Clark co., E central S.Dak., 18 mi. SSE of Clark; farm trading point; dairy produce, livestock, poultry, grain.

Willowmore, town (pop. 2,532), S Cape Prov., U. of So. Afr., 80 mi. ENE of Oudtshoorn at E end of Great Swartberg range; agr. center (stock, ostriches, wool, mohair, grain). Attacked (1901) unsuccessfully by Boers in South African War.

Willow Palisade, Chinese *Liu-ch'eng* (lyō′chŭng′) or *Liu-ch'iang* (–chyăng′), former stake barrier in S Manchuria, extending from Shanhaikwan to Sungari R. N of Kirin city. Dating from 3d cent. B.C., it was built to protect the old Chinese pale in the Liao valley against Mongol inroads. An Inner Willow Palisade protected Liaotung peninsula on the E. Only isolated traces of the palisades remain.

Willow River, village (pop. 294), Pine co., E Minn., on Kettle R. and c.45 mi. SW of Duluth; dairy products.

Willow Run, residential and industrial suburb (pop. 11,365), Washtenaw co., SE Mich., 4 mi. ENE of Ypsilanti. Automobiles and farm machinery are made here in huge Willow Run plant, which produced bombers in Second World War. Univ. of Mich. has aeronautical research center at airport here.

Willows, city (pop. 3,019), ⊙ Glenn co., N central Calif., in Sacramento Valley, 35 mi. W of Oroville, in agr. area irrigated from Sacramento R.; rice and other grain, livestock, dairy products, poultry. Inc. as town in 1886, as city in 1935.

Willow Springs. 1 Village (pop. 1,314), Cook co., NE Ill., SW suburb of Chicago. Until 1937, called Spring Forest. **2** City (pop. 1,914), Howell co., S Mo., in the Ozarks, at headwaters of Eleven Point R., 75 mi. SE of Springfield; dairy and poultry market. Mark Twain Natl. Forest near by.

Willow Station, Alaska: see WILLOW.

Willsboro, resort village (1940 pop. 946), Essex co., NE N.Y., near mouth of Bouquet R. on L. Champlain, 23 mi. S of Plattsburg; lumber, paper, wood pulp. NW are Long Pond (c.1½ mi. long) and Highlands Forge L. (c.1 mi. long).

Wills Creek. 1 In NE Ala., rises in De Kalb co. near Ga. line, flows SW bet. Sand Mtn. and Lookout Mtn. to Attalla, then ESE to Coosa R. just below Gadsden; 73 mi. long. Also known as Big Wills Creek. **2** In E and central Ohio, formed by junction of small forks near Pleasant City, flows c.65 mi. NW and W, past Cambridge, Kimbolton, and Plainfield, to Muskingum R. 8 mi. S of Coshocton. Flood-control reservoir (capacity 196,000 acre-ft.) is impounded by dam on lower course. **3** In S Pa. and NW Md., rises in W Bedford co., Pa., flows c.35 mi. SSW, bet. Wills Mtn. and Dans Mtn., past Hyndman, Pa., Ellerslie, Corriganville, and Cumberland, Md., to North Branch of the Potomac. Just NW of Cumberland, cuts gorge (Cumberland Narrows) in Wills Mtn.

Willshire (wĭl'shûr), village (pop. 567), Van Wert co., W Ohio, on St. Marys R., at Ind. line, and 14 mi. SW of Van Wert; sawmills.

Wills Mountain, in NW Md. and S Pa., ridge (1,600–2,400 ft.) of the Appalachian system, running c.35 mi. NE from just N of Cresaptown, Md., to Raystown Branch of Juniata R. just W of Bedford, Pa. Just NW of Cumberland, Md., Wills Creek cuts through Cumberland Narrows, beautiful gorge c.1,000 ft. deep, which was discovered 1755 by Braddock's army; a natural E–W gateway across the Appalachians, it was traversed by old Cumberland (or National) Road, and is now followed by U.S. Route 40.

Wills Point, city (pop. 2,030), Van Zandt co., NE Texas, 16 mi. E of Terrell; trade, shipping center in truck, cotton area. Cottonseed oil, lumber, candy, clothing; ships nursery stock.

Willunga (wĭlŭng'gù), village (pop. 549), SE South Australia, 25 mi. S of Adelaide; rail terminus; fruitgrowing, dairying center; roofing slate. Port Willunga on near-by Gulf St. Vincent.

Wilmar (wĭl'mär). **1** Town (pop. 746), Drew co., SE Ark., 8 mi. W of Monticello, in agr. area. **2** Unincorporated town (1940 pop. 11,590), Los Angeles co., S Calif., suburb 8 mi. E of downtown Los Angeles, near San Gabriel; truck, poultry, citrus-fruit farms.

Wilmer, town (pop. 465), Dallas co., N Texas, just SE of Dallas.

Wilmerding (wĭl'mûrdĭng), borough (pop. 5,325), Allegheny co., SW Pa., industrial E suburb of Pittsburgh; railroad equipment, tools; agr. Inc. 1890.

Wilmersdorf (vĭl'mûrsdôrf), residential district (1939 pop. 206,779; 1946 pop. 126,615), W Berlin, Germany, 5 mi. WSW of city center. Includes N part of Grunewald picnic area. After 1945 in British sector.

Wilmette (wĭlmĕt'), residential village (pop. 18,162), Cook co., NE Ill., N suburb of Chicago, on L. Michigan, just N of Evanston. Seat of a Bahaist temple, and Mallinckrodt Col. Inc. 1872.

Wilmington, village (pop. 317), S South Australia, 32 mi. N of Port Pirie; rail terminus; wool, wheat.

Wilmington, residential town and parish (pop. 2,830), NW Kent, England, just SSW of Dartford.

Wilmington. 1 Port and industrial section (pop. c.17,500) of LOS ANGELES city, Los Angeles co., S Calif., on man-made Los Angeles Harbor, 18 mi. S of city's center; has freight and passenger terminals and landing for Santa Catalina Isl. excursion steamers. Oil wells; oil refining and shipping; auto assembly plant. Laid out 1857 as port of New San Pedro, renamed 1863; was military post and supply depot in Civil War. Railroad's coming to harbor dist. (1869) and construction of small jetty (1871) stimulated its growth, as well as San Pedro's; the 2 cities were consolidated (1909) with Los Angeles and modern harbor development followed. **2** City (pop. 110,356), ⊙ New Castle co., N Del., 25 mi. SW of Philadelphia and on Delaware R. (bridged near by), at influx of Brandywine Creek and Christina R.; 39°43'N 75°32'W; alt. 225 ft. Largest city in Del. and industrial, financial, commercial center of state; deepwater port (with municipal marine terminal, and docks along Christina R.) and port of entry; has shipyards, drydocks, railroad-car-building plants. Important industries include mfg. of chemicals (at near-by Edge Moor and Newport), leather, iron and steel products, cork products, rubber, and textiles; oil refining, automobile assembling, meat packing. Served by 3 railroads. Executive offices of Du Pont company are here; its experimental research laboratory is near by. Has Del. Acad. of Medicine and an art center. Settled 1st by Swedes, who built Fort Cristina in 1638 (site is now a state park); Dutch and English followed; William Penn took possession of settlement in 1682. Occupied by Br. troops in Revolution. Inc. as borough 1809, as city 1832. A powder mill, established 1802 by E. I. du Pont de Nemours on the Brandywine, was 1st of many Du Pont enterprises for which Wilmington is hq. Historic sites include Old Swedes Church (1698), town hall (1798), Brandywine Acad. (founded 1798; now a library). On Rodney Square are various public bldgs. **3** Village (pop. 147), Greene co., W central Ill., 22 mi. SW of Jacksonville, in agr. and bituminous-coal area. Formerly Patterson. **4** City (pop. 3,354), Will co., NE Ill., on Kankakee R. (bridged here) and 15 mi. SSW of Joliet; trade center in agr. and bituminous-coal-mining area; mfg. (felt, clothing, fireworks); corn, oats, soybeans, livestock, dairy products, poultry. Island Park in river is resort. Settled c.1839, inc. 1875. **5** Town (pop. 7,039), including Wilmington village (pop. 1,331), Middlesex co., NE Mass., 15 mi. NNW of Boston; dairying, poultry, truck, apples; nursery; patent leather. Settled 1639, inc. 1730. **6** Resort village (pop. c.350), Essex co., NE N.Y., in the Adirondacks, 11 mi. NE of Lake Placid village. Road to Whiteface Mtn. (skiing) starts here. Wilmington Mtn. (3,458 ft.) is NW. **7** City (pop. 45,043), ⊙ New Hanover co., SE N.C., 115 mi. SSE of Raleigh and on Cape Fear R., 30 mi. above its mouth. Chief port and port of entry of N.C.; exports include cotton, tobacco, lumber, naval stores, superphosphates; imports include phosphates, sugar, molasses, petroleum products, creosote. A railroad and mfg. center, with clothing, textile, bromine, fertilizer, lumber, metal, creosoting, shipbuilding, and meat-packing industries. City has many old buildings and natl. cemetery; near by are popular beach resorts. Moores Creek Natl. Military Park is 18 mi. NW. City was hq. for Cornwallis in 1781 and important Confederate port during Civil War. Founded 1730; inc. 1739. **8** City (pop. 7,387), ⊙ Clinton co., SW Ohio, 30 mi. SE of Dayton; trade center for agr. area; mfg. (tools, metal products, electrical goods, machinery, furnaces, food products). Seat of Wilmington Col. Clinton County Air Force Base here. Fort Ancient State Memorial Park is near by. Settled 1810, inc. 1828. **9** Town (pop. 1,169), including Wilmington village (pop. 571), Windham co., S Vt., on Deerfield R. and 15 mi. W of Brattleboro, in Green Mts.; wood products; winter sports. Chartered 1751, settled c.1770.

Wilmington, Lake, Indian River co., central Fla., 31 mi. NW of Fort Pierce; c.5 mi. long, 2 mi. wide.

Wilmington Island, one of the Sea Isls., in Chatham co., SE Ga., just off the coast, 10 mi. ESE of Savannah, bet. two distributaries of Savannah R.; marshy, c.7 mi. long, 4 mi. wide; connected with mainland by causeway.

Wilmington Mountain, N.Y.: see WILMINGTON.

Wilmont, village (pop. 473), Nobles co., SW Minn., 16 mi. NW of Worthington; grain, livestock.

Wilmore. 1 City (pop. 172), Comanche co., S Kansas, 8 mi. NE of Coldwater; shipping point for livestock and grain area. **2** Town (pop. 2,337), Jessamine co., central Ky., near Herrington L., 17 mi. SW of Lexington, in Bluegrass agr. area (burley tobacco, corn, wheat); limestone quarry; flour and feed mills. Seat of Asbury Col., Asbury Theological Seminary. Dix R. Dam is S. **3** Borough (pop. 390), Cambria co., SW central Pa., 11 mi. ENE of Johnstown and on Conemaugh R.

Wilmot, village (pop. 386), N Tasmania, 50 mi. W of Launceston; dairying center; sawmill.

Wilmot (wĭl'mŏt). **1** Town (pop. 721), Ashley co., SE Ark., 33 mi. S of Dermott, near La. line, in cotton-growing area. **2** Town (pop. 370), Merrimack co., S central N.H., 26 mi. NW of Concord; abrasive garnet deposits. **3** Village (pop. 354), Stark co., E central Ohio, 16 mi. SW of Canton; makes cheese. **4** City (pop. 590), Roberts co., NE S.Dak., 20 mi. SSE of Sisseton; resort; diversified farming; dairy produce.

Wilmslow (wĭlmz'lō), urban district (1931 pop. 9,760; 1951 census 19,531), NE Cheshire, England, 6 mi. SSW of Stockport; cotton milling. Has 15th-cent. church.

Wilna or Wilno, Lithuania: see VILNA.

Wilnecote and Castle Liberty (wĭl'nĭkùt, wĭn'kùt), parish (pop. 4,343), N Warwick, England. Includes coal-mining town of Wilnecote, 2 mi. SE of Tamworth.

Wilno (vēl'nô), former province (□ 9,632; 1931 pop. 1,272,851) of NE Poland; ⊙ Vilna. Formed 1921 out of Rus. Vilna govt.; occupied 1939 by USSR, when it became Vileika (after 1944, MOLODECHNO) oblast of Belorussian SSR. W part was ceded (1939–40) to Lithuania.

Wilpshire, residential village and parish (pop. 1,443), central Lancashire, England, 3 mi. N of Blackburn; truck gardening.

Wilrijk (vĭl'rīk), residential town (pop. 26,450), Antwerp prov., N Belgium, 3 mi. S of Antwerp.

Wilsall (wĭl'săl"), village (pop. c.400), Park co., S Mont., on branch of Yellowstone R. and 23 mi. N of Livingston; trade and shipping point; grain, seed peas, livestock.

Wilsden, England: see BINGLEY.

Wilsdruff (vĭls'drŏŏf), town (pop. 4,581), Saxony, E central Germany, 9 mi. W of Dresden; furniture mfg.; market gardening.

Wilsele (vĭl'sùlù), town (pop. 5,044), Brabant prov., central Belgium, just N of Louvain; mfg. of metallic pigments.

Wilsey (wĭl'sē), city (pop. 251), Morris co., E central Kansas, 31 mi. WNW of Emporia; grazing, agr.

Wilsnack, Bad, Germany: see BAD WILSNACK.

Wilson. 1 County (□ 574; pop. 14,815), SE Kansas; ⊙ Fredonia. Dissected plain, watered by Verdigris and Fall rivers. Stock, poultry, and grain raising; dairying. Oil and gas fields. Formed 1865. **2** County (□ 373; pop. 54,506), E central N.C.; ⊙ Wilson. Coastal plain tobacco and timber area, drained by small Contentnea Creek; mfg. at Wilson. Formed 1855. **3** County (□ 580; pop. 26,318), N central Tenn.; ⊙ Lebanon. Bounded N by Cumberland R. Livestock, timber, agr. (corn, tobacco), dairying; mfg. at Lebanon and Watertown. Formed 1799. **4** County (□ 802; pop. 14,672), S Texas; ⊙ Floresville. Drained by San Antonio R. Agr., especially peanuts, watermelons, grain sorghums; also corn, cotton, truck. Livestock (cattle, hogs, poultry). Some oil. Clay mining, tile mfg. Formed 1860.

Wilson. 1 Village (pop. 1,301), Mississippi co., NE Ark., 25 mi. SSW of Blytheville, near Mississippi R.; company-owned hq. for large farm (cotton, alfalfa, corn, soybeans). U.S. farm resettlement project near by. **2** City (pop. 1,039), Ellsworth co., central Kansas, 14 mi. WNW of Ellsworth, near Smoky Hill R., in wheat and livestock region; flour, feed. Oil fields in vicinity. Founded 1871, inc. 1883. **3** Village (pop. 962), Niagara co., W N.Y., on L. Ontario, 30 mi. N of Buffalo; summer resort; mfg. (cider, vinegar, canned fruit, flour); fisheries. Inc. 1858. **4** Town (pop. 23,010), ⊙ Wilson co., E central N.C., 40 mi. E of Raleigh; a leading leaf-tobacco market; processes tobacco; mfg. of cotton textiles, clothing, fertilizer, truck and bus bodies, veneer. Atlantic Christian Col. here. Inc. 1849. **5** City (pop. 1,832), Carter co., S Okla., 17 mi. W of Ardmore, in oil and agr. area (livestock, truck, peanuts, corn, grain); petroleum products; peanut processing. **6** Borough (pop. 8,159), Northampton co., E Pa., just W of Easton; foundries; textiles, paper cups. Inc. 1920. **7** Village (pop. 174), St. Croix co., W Wis., 29 mi. E of Hudson, in dairying region.

Wilson, Mount. 1 Peak (5,750 ft.) in NW Ariz., S of L. Mead; highest peak in Black Mts. **2** Peak (5,710 ft.) of San Gabriel Mts., S Calif., just NE of Pasadena; highway to summit. Site of Mt. Wilson Observatory (established 1904), operated jointly by Carnegie and California institutes of technology. **3** Peak (14,250 ft.) in San Miguel Mts., SW Colo., 12 mi. SW of Telluride. Highest point in range. Known unofficially as Mt. Franklin Roosevelt.

Wilson Creek, town (pop. 337), Grant co., E central Wash., 22 mi. ENE of Ephrata, at junction of Wilson Creek and Crab L., in Columbia basin agr. area; grain, livestock, apples.

Wilson Lake, Franklin co., W central Maine, resort lake near Wilton; 2.25 mi. long. Source of Wilson Stream, which flows c.15 mi. E to Sandy R.

Wilson Dam, NW Ala., on Tennessee R., 2.5 mi. E of Florence, c.15 mi. downstream from Wheeler Dam. Started 1918, completed, except for locks, 1925, opened to navigation 1927; built by U.S. Army Engineers, controlled by TVA since 1933; 137 ft. high, 4,862 ft. long. Designed to supply power and aid navigation; has 2 locks (larger is 300 ft. long, 60 ft. wide; smaller is 292 ft. long, 60 ft. wide), each providing lift of 92 ft. Forms L. Wilson (□ 25; 15.5 mi. long, 1.5 mi. wide; capacity 562,500 acre-ft.) in Colbert and Lauderdale counties. Rapids (MUSCLE SHOALS) in Tennessee R. have been submerged by L. Wilson and Wheeler Reservoir. Small navigation dam, 2.5 mi. below Wilson Dam, has eliminated lesser rapids at Florence.

Wilson Mills, town (pop. 349), Johnston co., central N.C., 21 mi. SE of Raleigh, near Neuse R.

Wilson Peak (14,026 ft.), in Rocky Mts., Dolores co., SW Colo.

Wilson's Promontory, peninsula forming southernmost extremity of Australia, in S Victoria, sheltering Corner Inlet of Bass Strait; 39°8'S 146°25'E. Connected with mainland by low, sandy neck (10 mi. long, 5 mi. wide); 22 mi. long N-S, 8 mi. wide E-W; mountainous, rising to 2,434 ft. (Mt. Latrobe). Site of large natl. park containing native flora and fauna.

Wilsonville. 1 Town (pop. 692), Shelby co., central Ala., on Coosa R. and 27 mi. SE of Birmingham. **2** Village, Conn.: see THOMPSON. **3** Village (pop. 822), Macoupin co., SW Ill., 21 mi. ENE of Alton. **4** Village (pop. 327), Furnas co., S Nebr., 16 mi. W of Beaver City and on Beaver Creek; livestock, grain.

Wilstedt (vĭl'shtĕt), village (pop. 1,453), in former Prussian prov. of Hanover, NW Germany, after 1945 in Lower Saxony, 14 mi. NE of Bremen; building materials.

Wilster (vĭl'stûr), town (pop. 7,290), in Schleswig-Holstein, NW Germany, harbor on small navigable right tributary of the Stör, and 5 mi. W of Itzehoe; mfg. (chemicals, leather goods, machinery). Trade (grain, cattle). Has 18th-cent. church. Chartered 1282.

Wilthen (vĭl'tŭn), village (pop. 5,006), Saxony, E central Germany, in Upper Lusatia, 6 mi. S of Bautzen; cotton and linen milling, mfg. of canvas products.

Wilton. 1 Municipal borough (1931 pop. 2,195; 1951 census 2,857), S Wiltshire, England, on Wylye R. and 3 mi. WNW of Salisbury; agr. market; famous carpet-weaving center since 16th cent. Anc. ⊙ Wessex, residence of Saxon kings, and scene of battle (871) bet. King Arthur and Danes. Until 1050 seat of bishopric. Near by is Wilton House, built by Inigo Jones, where Sir Philip Sidney wrote *Arcadia.* **2** Village, NE North Riding, Yorkshire, England, near North Sea, near mouth of the Tess, 4 mi. S of Redcar; chemical-mfg. center (plastics, synthetic fibers, synthetic gasoline); coal-mining region.

Wilton, Scotland: see HAWICK.

Wilton. 1 Town (pop. 413), Shelby co., central Ala., 30 mi. S of Birmingham. **2** Town (pop. 328), Little River co., extreme SW Ark., 20 mi. NNW of Texarkana; ships truck produce, timber. **3** Residential town (pop. 4,558), Fairfield co., SW Conn., on Norwalk R., just N of Norwalk; agr. (dairy products, fruit, truck); nurseries. Mfg. (golf clubs, wood and metal products) at South Wilton village (1940 pop. 540). Includes residential Cannondale and part of Georgetown village. Settled in early 18th cent., inc. 1801. **4** or **Wilton Junction,** town (pop. 1,446), Muscatine co., SE Iowa, 11 mi. N of Muscatine; dairy products. Inc. 1863. **5** Town (pop. 3,455), including Wilton village (pop. 1,910), Franklin co., W central Maine, 7 mi. SW of Farmington, on Wilson L. (resort); textiles, shoes, canned foods; winter sports center. Settled 1789 as Tyngtown, inc. 1803 as Wilton. **6** Village (pop. 108), Beltrami co., NW central Minn., 6 mi. W of Bemidji, in state forest; grain, potatoes. **7** Town (pop. 1,952), Hillsboro co., S N.H., on the Souhegan and 17 mi. SW of Manchester; mill town (textiles, lumber, mill machinery) with resort villages. Inc. 1762. **8** City (pop. 796), McLean and Burleigh counties, central N.Dak., 25 mi. N of Bismarck, near Missouri R.; lignite mines; dairy products, livestock, poultry, wheat, corn, flax. **9** Village (pop. 533), Monroe co., W central Wis., on Kickapoo R. and 35 mi. E of La Crosse, in dairy and livestock area.

Wilton Manor, town (pop. 883), Broward co., S Fla.

Wiltshire (wĭlt'shĭr, -shûr), county (□ 1,345; 1931 pop. 303,373; 1951 census 387,379), SW England; ⊙ Salisbury. Bounded by Somerset (W), Gloucester (NW and N), Berkshire (E), Hampshire (E and S), and Dorset (S). Drained by Avon, Wylye, and Thames rivers. The chalky SALISBURY PLAIN and Marlborough Downs cover large part of co. Farming and dairying are chief industries; other activities include textile milling and leather mfg. Wilton is noted for carpets. Other important towns are Devizes, Marlborough, Swindon (with large locomotive works and railroad workshops), Trowbridge, and Melksham. Salisbury Plain is army training ground. There are numerous historic associations, including prehistoric monuments of STONEHENGE, Silbury Hill, Avebury, connections with Alfred the Great. Shortened form, Wilts.

Wiltz (vĭlts), town (pop. 1,572), NW Luxembourg, on Wiltz R. and 11 mi. NW of Ettelbruck, in the Ardennes; leather tanning, mfg. (leather products, tanning fluid), beer brewing; market center for rye, oats, potato area. Has 12th-cent. church, old feudal castle. Scene of action during Battle of the Bulge (1944–45) in Second World War. Niederwiltz is NW part (pop. 1,994) of town.

Wiltz River, SE Belgium and W Luxembourg, rises 2 mi. WSW of Bastogne (Belgium), flows 20 mi. E and SE, past Bastogne, thence past Wiltz and Kautenbach (Luxembourg), to Sûre R. at Goebelsmühle. Receives Clerf R. at Kautenbach.

Wiluna (wĭlōō'nŭ), town (pop. 576), central Western Australia, 380 mi. ENE of Geraldton; terminus of railroad from Geraldton; gold-mining center; arsenic-recovery plant.

Wilwerwiltz (vĭl'vŭrvĭlts), village (pop. 236), N Luxembourg, on Clerf R. and 4 mi. ENE of Wiltz, in the Ardennes; rye, oats, potatoes.

Wimauma (wĭmô'mŭ), city (pop. 440), Hillsborough co., W Fla., 20 mi. SSE of Tampa.

Wimberly, village (pop. c.150), Hays co., S central Texas, 11 mi. NW of San Marcos and on Blanco R.; trade point in livestock area.

Wimbledon (wĭm'bŭldŭn), residential municipal borough (1931 pop. 59,524; 1951 census 58,158), N Surrey, England, 8 mi. SW of London. Hq. of All England Lawn Tennis Club, where international matches are held; 1st championship match took place here 1877. Wimbledon is reputed scene of defeat of King Æthelbert of Kent by Ceawlin, king of Wessex (568). The extensive Wimbledon Common has anc. earthworks, called "Caesar's Camp," and British remains. George Eliot lived in Wimbledon.

Wimbledon, village (pop. 449), Barnes co., E central N.Dak., 30 mi. NW of Valley City; creamery; cattle, grain.

Wimblington, agr. village and parish (pop. 1,269), in Isle of Ely, N Cambridge, England, 3 mi. S of March.

Wimborne Minster or **Wimborne** (wĭm'bôrn), urban district (1931 pop. 3,895; 1951 census 4,488), E Dorset, England, on Stour R. and 6 mi. N of Poole; agr. market. Its minster was begun 1120.

Wimereux (vēmrû'), town (pop. 2,355), Pas-de-Calais dept., N France, beach resort on English Channel, 3 mi. N of Boulogne, heavily damaged in Second World War.

Wimico, Lake (wĭmŭkō'), Gulf co., NW Fla., 13 mi. WNW of Apalachicola; c.5 mi. long, 1–2 mi. wide. Forms part of Gulf Intracoastal Waterway bet. Apalachicola R. and St. Andrew Bay.

Wimmera River (wĭ'mŭrŭ), W Victoria, Australia, rises in Great Dividing Range E of Ararat, flows generally NW, past Horsham, and N, past Dimboola and Jeparit, to L. Hindmarsh; 155 mi. long.

Wimpassing (vĭm'päsĭng), village (pop. 1,820), SE Lower Austria, 3 mi. WSW of Neunkirchen; rubber.

Wimpfen, Bad, Germany: see BAD WIMPFEN.

Wimsbach (vĭms'bäkh), town (pop. 2,405), central Upper Austria, 9 mi. SW of Wels; brewery.

Winamac (wĭ'nŭmăk), town (pop. 2,166), ⊙ Pulaski co., NW Ind., on Tippecanoe R. and c.45 mi. NNE of Lafayette; trade center in agr. area (livestock, poultry, grain, soybeans); canned goods, clothing, lumber; ships grain. Settled 1837, inc. 1868.

Winamarca, Lake, Bolivia: see UINAMARCA, LAKE.

Wiñaymarca, Lake, Bolivia: see UINAMARCA, LAKE.

Winborn, village (1940 pop. 109), Benton co., N Miss., 14 mi. SE of Holly Springs, in Holly Springs Natl. Forest.

Winburg (wĭn'bûrg), town (pop. 3,797), central Orange Free State, U. of So. Afr., 65 mi. NE of Bloemfontein; alt. 4,724 ft.; distributing center for stock-raising, grain-growing region.

Winburne, village (pop. 1,085, with adjacent Lanse), Clearfield co., central Pa., 15 mi. ESE of Clearfield.

Wincanton (wĭn-kăn'tŭn), town and parish (pop. 2,047); SE Somerset, England, 13 mi. SSW of Frome; agr. market in dairying region; milk canning, cheese making. Church dates from 14th cent. Scene of 1st skirmish of 1688 rebellion.

Wincham, town and parish (pop. 1,003), N central Cheshire, England, just NE of Northwich; salt refining; mfg. of chemicals and rubber footwear.

Winchcomb (wĭnch'kŭm), town and parish (pop. 2,546), NE Gloucester, England, 6 mi. NE of Cheltenham; agr. market, with paper works. Has 15th-cent. church. In Saxon times it was a walled city. In Middle Ages it was a cloth-making center.

Winchelsea (wĭn'chŭlsē), village (pop. 763), S Victoria, Australia, 60 mi. WSW of Melbourne; flax, agr. products.

Winchelsea, village and parish (pop. 130), E Sussex, England, on the short Brede R., near the Channel, 2 mi. SW of Rye. It is 3 mi. NW of the old town of Winchelsea, a port in Saxon times, which became a shipbuilding center (dockyard established 1238) and as an "ancient town" was added to the CINQUE PORTS under Richard I. Town was destroyed 1287 by encroachment of the sea; parts of the town walls remain. The church of St. Thomas à Becket dates from the 14th cent. Winchelsea is frequented by artists. Near by is Camber Castle (1531).

Winchendon (wĭn'chŭndŭn), town (pop. 6,585), including Winchendon village (pop. 4,019), Worcester co., N Mass., 15 mi. NW of Fitchburg, in wooded country, near N.H. line; wood and paper products; poultry, dairying. Settled 1753, inc. 1764. Includes village of Waterville (1940 pop. 643).

Winchester, village (pop. 1,049), SE Ont., 28 mi. SE of Ottawa; woolen and lumber milling, furniture mfg., dairying.

Winchester (wĭn'chĭstŭr), municipal borough (1931 pop. 22,970; 1951 census 25,710), ⊙ Hampshire, England, in center of co., on the Itchen and 60 mi. SW of London; 51°4'N 1°19'W. It was the *Caer Went* of anc. Britons, the *Venta Belgarum* of the Romans, and, under Saxon name of *Wintecaester*, it became capital of Wessex (519), rivaling London in importance for centuries. A bishopric was established here c.675. Winchester became govt. seat of Alfred the Great, Canute, and William the Conqueror, who was crowned here as well as in London. In 1079 Bishop Walkelin founded the great cathedral, which contains tombs of bishops Edington, Wykeham, Waynflete, of some Danish and Saxon kings, and of Isaac Walton and Jane Austen. Periodically it is scene of performances of *Everyman.* Near the cathedral is Hyde Abbey on site of a minster built by King Alfred, where he and other Saxons were buried and where Edward the Confessor was crowned. Winchester also has 12th-cent. Hosp. of St. Cross, ruins of Wolvesey Castle (bishops' residence), and the Norman Winchester Castle, with "Wheel of Fortune," known as King Arthur's Round Table (the town is sometimes identified with CAMELOT). Of the town walls 2 gates remain. The Anglo-Saxon Chronicle was compiled here. A grammar school, founded in 7th cent. by bishops of Winchester, was transformed into Winchester Col. c.1394 by William of Wykeham, and is the oldest English public school. In medieval times the town was a center of woolen trade and commerce. The town's manufactures include aircraft and pharmaceuticals.

Winchester (wĭn'chĕ"stŭr, wĭn'chĭstŭr). **1** Town (pop. 198), Drew co., SE Ark., 11 mi. NNW of McGehee, near Bayou Bartholomew. **2** Town (pop. 10,535), Litchfield co., NW Conn., in Litchfield Hills, just N of Torrington; includes WINSTED. Highland L. (resorts) here. Settled c.1750, inc. 1771. **3** Village (pop. 488), Lewis co., W Idaho, 19 mi. W of Nezperce; agr. trade center. **4** City (pop. 1,591), ⊙ Scott co., W central Ill., 14 mi. SW of Jacksonville, in agr. area (corn, wheat, oats, poultry); flour mill. Platted 1830, inc. 1843. Has statue of Stephen A. Douglas, who here taught school. Here, too, Lincoln made his 1st speech on the Kansas-Nebraska issue. **5** City (pop. 5,467), ⊙ Randolph co., E Ind., on West Fork of White R. and 20 mi. E of Muncie; shipping center for livestock, grain, poultry, dairy products; mfg. (glass, machine-shop products, furniture, gloves, slippers). Settled 1812. Anc. Indian earthworks are NW. **6** City (pop. 355), Jefferson co., NE Kansas, 29 mi. NE of Topeka, in grain-growing, stock-raising, and general-farming region. **7** City (pop. 9,226), ⊙ Clark co., central Ky., 18 mi. ESE of Lexington, in Bluegrass region. Residential community; commercial and distributing center for agr. (burley tobacco, bluegrass seed, livestock), limestone-quarry area; mfg. of agr. implements and machinery, wood products, clothing, bricks, fertilizer, dairy products, soft drinks, bedding, sheet metal; flour, feed, and lumber mills. Ky. Wesleyan Col. here. Hq. for Cumberland Natl. Forest. In old courthouse here Henry Clay made his 1st and last Ky. speeches. Many fine old estates and homes in vicinity. Inc. 1793. **8** Residential town (pop. 15,509), Middlesex co., E Mass., 8 mi. NNW of Boston; leather, felt, gelatine, watch hands. Settled 1640, inc. 1850. **9** Town (pop. 176), St. Louis co., E Mo., W of St. Louis. **10** Mill town (pop. 2,388), including Winchester village (pop. 1,057), Cheshire co., extreme SW N.H., on the Ashuelot and 12 mi. SSW of Keene; wood products, leather. Settled 1732, inc. 1753. **11** Residential village (1940 pop. 1,165), Erie co., W N.Y., just E of Buffalo. **12** Village (pop. 690), Adams co., S Ohio, 17 mi. S of Hillsboro, in agr. area. **13** Town (pop. 3,974), ⊙ Franklin co., S Tenn., near Elk R., 45 mi. WNW of Chattanooga; trade center for livestock, dairying area; mfg. of clothing, rayon goods, wood products, medicines, processed foods. Near by is Hundred Oaks Monastery. Town founded c.1814. **14** City (pop. 13,841), in but independent of Frederick co., N Va., 60 mi. WNW of Washington, D.C., near N end of Shenandoah Valley. Co. courthouse is here. Trade, processing, shipping center for noted apple-growing region; holds annual Apple Blossom Festival. Mfg. of textiles, hosiery, rubber goods (heels, soles), apple products (vinegar, dried and canned fruit), packing equipment, asbestos products, barrels; flour milling. Seat of Shenandoah Valley Military Acad. Richard E. Byrd and Willa Cather b. here. Oldest Va. city W of the Blue Ridge; settled 1744 in Lord Fairfax's holdings; inc. as town 1779, as city 1874. Here George Washington began his career as a surveyor; he later (1756) built Fort Loudoun here (a remnant is still extant). Gen. Daniel Morgan lived here and raised a company in the Revolution. In Civil War, city changed hands repeatedly; a natl. cemetery and Stonewall cemetery here have graves of men killed in the many engagements fought in the vicinity. Apple culture was developed in region after the Civil War.

Wincobank, town in Sheffield county borough, West Riding, S Yorkshire, England, just NE of Sheffield; has steel mills; produces steam engines, locomotives, heavy machinery.

Windau, Latvia: see VENTSPILS.

Windau River, Latvia and Lithuania: see VENTA RIVER.

Windber (wĭnd'bŭr), borough (pop. 8,010), Somerset co., SW central Pa., 6 mi. SE of Johnstown; bituminous coal; bricks, lumber; agr. Laid out 1897, inc. 1900.

Wind Cave National Park (□ 41.5; established 1903), SW S.Dak., in the Black Hills c.10 mi. N of Hot Springs. Includes game preserve (buffalo, elk, antelope, deer) and limestone cavern (Wind Cave), which contains delicate traceries of calcite crystals and other beautiful formations.

Windecken (vĭn'dĕ"kŭn), town (pop. 2,775), in former Prussian prov. of Hesse-Nassau, W Germany, after 1945 in Hesse, 6 mi. N of Hanau.

Winden (vĭn'dŭn), village (pop. 630), Rhenish Palatinate, W Germany, 7 mi. S of Landau; rail junction; grain, tobacco.

Winder (wĭn'dŭr), city (pop. 4,604), ⊙ Barrow co., NE central Ga., 19 mi. W of Athens; textile center; mfg. (work clothes, blankets, rugs, furniture). Inc. 1893.

[W]indermere (wĭn'dûrmẽr), village (pop. 143), S Ont., in Muskoka lake region, on Rosseau L., 15 mi. NW of Bracebridge; resort.

Windermere, urban district (1931 pop. 5,702; 1951 census 6,306), W Westmorland, England, in the Lake District 7 mi. WNW of Kendal, near E shore of L. Windermere; resort and agr. market. Includes resort village of Bowness-on-Windermere, with 15th-cent. church.

Windermere, town (pop. 317), Orange co., central Fla., 10 mi. WSW of Orlando.

Windermere, Lake, largest lake in England, in wooded hills bet. Lancashire and Westmorland; 10½ mi. long, 1 mi. wide, 210 ft. deep. Fed by Rothay, Brathay, and other small streams; drained by the Leven into Morecambe Bay. Has several small isls. A tourist and fishing resort; steamers ply the lake. Windermere (E) and Ambleside (N) are near by.

Windermere Lake (9 mi. long, 1–2 mi. wide), SE B.C., expansion of Columbia R., on slope of Rocky Mts., 50 mi. SSW of Banff; alt. 2,624 ft. Noted for its scenic beauty; here are resorts of Invermere and Athalmer.

Windfall or **Windfall City,** town (pop. 963), Tipton co., central Ind., 12 mi. SE of Kokomo, in agr. area.

Wind Gap, borough (pop. 1,577), Northampton co., E Pa., 1 mi. SW of Pen Argyl; slate quarries, silk mills. Inc. 1893.

Windham (wĭn'dûm), village (1939 pop. 20), SE Alaska, on bay of Stephens Passage, opposite Admiralty Isl., 60 mi. SE of Juneau; trading post; fur farming.

Windham. 1 County (□ 516; pop. 61,759), NE Conn., on Mass. and R.I. lines; ⊙ Putnam and Willimantic. Agr. area with mfg. centers producing textiles, thread, machinery, cutlery, metal products, clothing, paper and rubber goods, shoes, chemicals, furniture, optical goods, wood products; agr. (dairy products, poultry, truck). Has several state parks and forests; resorts on small lakes. Drained by Quinebaug, Natchaug, Shetucket, Little, Moosup, and French rivers. Constituted 1726. **2** County (□ 793; pop. 28,749), SE Vt., bounded E by the Connecticut and rising to Green Mts. in W; ⊙ Newfane. Dairying, mfg. (wood products, textiles, paper, machinery, shoes, sports equipment), lumbering; resorts. Drained by West and Deerfield rivers; includes part of Green Mtn. Natl. Forest. Organized 1779.

Windham. 1 Town (pop. 15,884), Windham co., E central Conn., at junction of Willimantic and Natchaug rivers to form Shetucket R., 25 mi. ESE of Hartford. Truck farming. Includes industrial WILLIMANTIC, mfg. villages of North Windham and South Windham (paper-milling machinery, mill supplies). Settled c.1688, inc. 1692. **2** Agr. and resort town (pop. 3,434), Cumberland co., SW Maine, on Presumpscot R. and 8 mi. NW of Portland. State reformatory here. Newhall village has explosives plant. Includes part of South Windham village. Settled 1737, inc. 1762. **3** Village (pop. c.150), Judith Basin co., central Mont., on branch of Judith R. and 35 mi. W of Lewistown; trading point in livestock and grain region. **4** Town (pop. 964), Rockingham co., SE N.H., 10 mi. ENE of Nashua. **5** Resort village, Greene co., SE N.Y., in the Catskills, 21 mi. WNW of Catskill. **6** Village (pop. 3,968), Portage co., NE Ohio, 12 mi. W of Warren, in agr. area. **7** Resort town (pop. 146), Windham co., SE Vt., 25 mi. NW of Brattleboro, in Green Mts.; alt. c.2,000 ft.

Windhoek (vĭnt'ho͝ok), town (pop. 14,930), ⊙ South-West Africa, in central part of country, 900 mi. N of Cape Town; 22°34'S 17°5'E; alt. 5,428 ft.; rail junction; distributing and commercial center of South-West Africa. In important dairying region, town has cold-storage and bone-meal plants; brewery. Features are mus. and R.C. cathedral; seat of Anglican and R.C. bishops. Near by are hot springs. Airport. Previously hq. of Hottentot chief Jonker Afrikaner, locality became ⊙ German Southwest Africa 1892, named Windhuk. Occupied (1915) by U. of So. Afr. forces, became seat of administration of the mandate after First World War. Mean temp. ranges from 68.3°F. (June) to 87.4°F. (Nov.); average annual rainfall 14.03 in.

Windisch (vĭn'dĭsh), town (pop. 3,627), Aargau canton, N Switzerland, on the Reuss, near its confluence with the Aar, 1 mi. E of Brugg; cotton textiles, metalworking. On site of Helvetian settlement, near which Romans built (1st cent. A.D.) their camp of Vindonissa, with amphitheater for 10,000 spectators (foundations excavated 1897).

Windisch Büheln, Yugoslavia: see SLOVENSKE GORICE.

Windischeschenbach (–ĕ'shûnbäkh), village (pop. 4,513), Upper Palatinate, NE Bavaria, Germany, at mouth of the Fichtelnab (a branch of the Nab) 9 mi. N of Weiden; mfg. (excelsior, paper, glass). Granite quarried in area.

Windisch-Feistritz, Yugoslavia: see BISTRICA, NE Slovenia.

Windischgarsten (–gärstûn), village (pop. 1,837), SE Upper Austria, in the Sengsengebirge, 22 mi. S of Steyr; scythes; summer resort (alt. 1,970 ft.).

Windischgraz, Yugoslavia: see SLOVENJGRADEC.

Windisch-Matrei, Austria: see MATREI.

Wind Lake, village (pop. 1,067), Racine co., SE Wis., near Waterford.

Windle, agr. parish (pop. 1,341), SW Lancashire, England, just NW of St. Helens.

Windlesham (wĭn'dûlshûm), residential former urban district (1931 pop. 5,257), NW Surrey, England, 6 mi. SW of Egham. Has 17th-cent. church. Just W is town of Bagshot (băg'shŏt) with large park, hunting seat of Stuart kings.

Windmill Point, Mass.: see NANTASKET BEACH.

Wind Mountain (10,190 ft.), SW Alta., near B.C. border, in Rocky Mts., near Banff Natl. Park, 20 mi. SE of Banff; 50°58'N 115°16'W.

Windom (wĭn'dûm). **1** City (pop. 193), McPherson co., central Kansas, 22 mi. N of Hutchinson, in wheat region. **2** City (pop. 3,165), ⊙ Cottonwood co., SW Minn., on Des Moines R. and c.70 mi. WSW of Mankato; trade center for agr. area; dairy products. Heron L. is 10 mi. WSW. Platted 1870, inc. as village 1875, as city 1920. **3** Town (pop. 297), Fannin co., NE Texas, 11 mi. E of Bonham, in agr. area.

Windom Peak (14,091 ft.), SW Colo., in San Juan Mts., 13 mi. SSE of Silverton.

Windorah (wĭndô'rû), village, S central Queensland, Australia, 225 mi. WNW of Charleville; sheep.

Windorf (vĭn'dôrf), village (pop. 1,350), Lower Bavaria, Germany, on the Danube and 11 mi. WNW of Passau; barley, wheat, cattle, horses. Chartered in early 13th cent.

Window Rock, village, Apache co., NE Ariz., near N.Mex. line, 23 mi. NW of Gallup, N.Mex.; alt. 6,850 ft. Central agency hq. for huge Navajo Indian Reservation.

Wind River (wĭnd), W central Wyo., rises in several forks in N tip of Wind River Range, flows c.110 mi. SE, past Dubois, joining Popo Agie R. at Riverton to form Bighorn R. Wind R. diversion dam, 35 mi. NW of Riverton, is part of Riverton power and land-reclamation project; irrigated valley produces grain, beans, sugar beets, fruit.

Wind River Range, in Rocky Mts. of W central Wyo., extends c.120 mi. NNW from Sweetwater R.; constitutes part of Continental Divide. Highest peaks are Atlantic Peak (12,734 ft.), Roberts Mtn. (12,767 ft.), Lizard Head Peak (12,842 ft.), Mt. Hooker (12,900 ft.), Knife Point Mtn. (13,007 ft.), Jackson Peak (13,400 ft.), Wind River Peak (c.13,500 ft.), Chimney Rock Peak (13,340 ft.), Downs Mtn. (13,344 ft.), Mt. Helen (13,600 ft.), Mt. Sacagawea (săkûjôwē'û) (13,607 ft.), Mt. Warren (13,720 ft.), Fremont Peak (13,730 ft.), and Gannett Peak (13,787 ft.; highest point in Wyo.). Historic passes are SOUTH PASS (7,550 ft.) and Washakie Pass (wŏ'shûkē) (11,610 ft.), in S half of range, Indian Pass (12,130 ft.) and Green River Pass (12,222 ft.), near Fremont Peak, and Togwotee Pass (tō'gûtē) (9,658 ft.) and Union Pass (9,210 ft.) in N. Wind R. and its branches flow from E side of range into Bighorn R.; Green R. rises on SW slope. Range includes parts of Bridger and Washakie Natl. Forests and Wind River Indian Reservation.

Windsbach (vĭnts'bäkh), town (pop. 2,963), Middle Franconia, W Bavaria, Germany, on the Franconian Rezat and 12 mi. ESE of Ansbach; brewing, flour and lumber milling. Rye, oats, wheat, hops, horses. Has medieval castle.

Windsheim (vĭnts'hīm), town (pop. 7,074), Middle Franconia, W Bavaria, Germany, on Aisch R. and 15 mi. NNW of Ansbach; machine shops; woodworking, brewing, flour and lumber milling; winegrowing. Mineral springs. Was free imperial city from 1379 to 1803. Gypsum quarries in area.

Windsor (wĭn'zûr). **1** Municipality (pop. 3,853), E New South Wales, Australia, on Hawkesbury R. and 29 mi. NW of Sydney; dairying and fruitgrowing center. **2** N suburb (pop. 14,681) of Brisbane, SE Queensland, Australia; truck gardening.

Windsor. 1 Town (pop. 3,436), W central N.S., on Avon R. on an arm of Minas Basin, and 35 mi. NW of Halifax; furniture, fertilizer, clothing mfg.; trade and shipping center for quarrying (gypsum, anhydrite, limestone) and fruitgrowing region. The original French settlement, known as Piziquid, dates back to 1703. King's Col., 1st English univ. in Canada, founded here 1789, was moved to Halifax in 1923. Fort Edward, known as Fort Piziquid under the French, fell to the English in 1750 and was prominent in the Acadian expulsion. **2** Residential and industrial city (pop. 105,311), ⊙ Essex co., S Ont., on Detroit R. opposite Detroit; port. Industries include steel milling; mfg. of auto engines, machinery, chemicals; salt refining, distilling. Connected with Detroit by bridge, tunnel, and ferries. Suburbs include Walkerville, Sandwich, Riverside, and Tecumseh. Seat of Assumption Col., affiliated with Univ. of Western Ontario. **3** Town (pop. 3,368), S Que., on St. Francis R. and 14 mi. NNW of Sherbrooke; paper milling, lumbering, dairying; hydroelectric plant. Inc. 1899.

Windsor, officially **New Windsor,** municipal borough (1931 pop. 20,287; 1951 census 23,181), E Berkshire, England, on the Thames and 23 mi. W of London. In Elizabethan times some 70 inns enlivened the town and at least one was mentioned in Shakespeare. Nell Gwynn and Jane Seymour lived in Windsor and their residences are still points of interest. Site of Windsor Castle, chief royal residence, built by William the Conqueror and later enlarged. Town hall was built by Wren. St. George's Chapel (15th cent.), where Knights of the Garter are installed, contains tombs of several kings, including Henry VIII and Charles I. Church of St. John the Baptist contains wood carvings by Grinling Gibbons. Castle is in Home Park, which is also site of Frogmore, the royal mausoleum where Queen Victoria and Prince Albert are buried. The Long Walk connects this park with Windsor Great Park (c.2,000 acres). In municipal borough (W) is residential dist. of Clewer (pop. 7,972).

Windsor, county (□ 965; pop. 40,885), E Vt., bounded E by the Connecticut; ⊙ Woodstock. Mfg. (machinery, tools, textiles, wood and metal products, printing, sports equipment, chemicals); lumber, marble; poultry, dairying, maple sugar. Summer and winter resorts. Includes Mt. Ascutney. Drained by Ottauquechee, White, Black, and Williams rivers. Organized 1781.

Windsor. 1 Town (pop. 1,548), Weld co., N Colo., on Cache la Poudre R. and 10 mi. WNW of Greeley, in sugar-beet and grain region; alt. 4,900 ft.; beet sugar. Inc. 1890. **2** Town (pop. 11,833), Hartford co., N Conn., on the Connecticut, at mouth of Farmington R., just above Hartford; agr. (tobacco, potatoes, truck), mfg. (tools, brick, fiber board, canned tomatoes). State agr. experiment station, Loomis school for boys, 17th- and 18th-cent. buildings here. Includes Poquonock village. Settled 1633, 1st English settlement in Conn. **3** or **New Windsor,** village (pop. 569), Mercer co., NW Ill., 17 mi. NNW of Galesburg; dairy products, grain, soybeans. **4** City (pop. 1,008), Shelby co., central Ill., 12 mi. W of Mattoon, in agr. and bituminous-coal area; dairy products, corn, soybeans. Inc. 1865. **5** Town (pop. 740), Kennebec co., S Maine, just E of Augusta. **6** Town (pop. 372), Berkshire co., W Mass., in the Berkshires, 11 mi. ENE of Pittsfield. State forest. **7** City (pop. 2,429), Henry co., W central Mo., 20 mi. SW of Sedalia; shoe factory; agr. trade; coal. Settled 1855, inc. 1873. **8** Village (pop. 822), Broome co., S N.Y., on the Susquehanna and 14 mi. ESE of Binghamton, in dairying area; summer resort. Makes whips. **9** Town (pop. 1,781), ⊙ Bertie co., NE N.C., 45 mi. W of Rocky Mount and on Cashie R. (head of navigation); sawmilling, fishing. Settled 1721; inc. 1776. **10** Borough (pop. 1,126), York co., S Pa., 9 mi. ESE of York. Inc. 1905. **11** Town (1940 pop. 151), Aiken co., W S.C., 12 mi. ESE of Aiken. **12** Town (pop. 4,402), including Windsor village (pop. 3,467), Windsor co., E Vt., on the Connecticut and 24 mi. N of Bellows Falls. Mfg. (machinery, metal, rubber and concrete products, lumber); agr. (dairy products, potatoes, maple sugar); winter sports. State prison here. Town chartered 1761 by N.H., 1772 by N.Y.; settled 1764. State's constitutional convention (1777) and 1st legislature (1778) met here; Old Constitution House, now an inn, is memorial. **13** Town (pop. 451), Isle of Wight co., SE Va., 11 mi. NW of Suffolk. Rail station for Smithfield, 14 mi. NE.

Windsor Heights, town (pop. 1,414), Polk co., central Iowa, just W of Des Moines.

Windsor Lake (□ 4), SE N.F., on NE Avalon Peninsula, 4 mi. NW of St. John's; 3 mi. long, 1 mi. wide. Near E shore is airport.

Windsor Locks, town (pop. 5,221), Hartford co., N Conn., on the Connecticut (here bridged) above Windsor; mfg. (paper, textiles, thread, tinsel, fireworks, machinery, clothing); agr. (tobacco, potatoes, truck). Mfg. developed after canal and locks built around rapids, 1829. Settled 1663, inc. 1854.

Windsorton (wĭn'zûrtûn), town (pop. 1,631), NE Cape Prov., U. of So. Afr., near Orange Free State border, in Griqualand West, on Vaal R. (bridge) and 30 mi. N of Kimberley; center for alluvial diamond diggings.

Windward Islands, S group of the Lesser Antilles, SE West Indies, extending c.300 mi. S from the Leeward Isls. toward NE Venezuela, bet. 12°–15°40'N and 60°48'–61°48'W. Excluding Trinidad and Tobago (at S end of the group) and Barbados (just E), which are in the area but not generally considered part of the Windwards, the principal isls. are, N-S: Fr.-owned MARTINIQUE and the Br. colony of the **Windward Islands** (□ 821; pop. 251,771), consisting of the 4 colonies, DOMINICA, SAINT LUCIA, SAINT VINCENT, and GRENADA, all of which, for administrative purposes, are placed under one governor, though each has a large measure of local govt. SAINT GEORGE'S is ⊙ Windward Isls. The GRENADINES, a small archipelago in the S Windwards, are dependencies of St. Vincent and Grenada, bet. which they are situated. Part of the volcanic formation of the Lesser Antilles, the isls. are remarkably similar in their physical structure. Rugged and generally oval-shaped, they have a wooded, mtn. backbone, intersected by many streams and lakes. The sheltered valleys and level lands are of great fertility. Isls. have equable climate; mean temp. c.80°F.; rainfall, usually sufficient, varies greatly. The isls. are exposed to occasional hurricanes and have been subject to volcanic disturbances. Sugar cane, long its staple crop, has now been largely replaced by cacao, coconuts, sea-island cotton, limes, arrowroot, nutmeg, bananas, and spices, which are exported, as are processed products (rum, molasses, lime juice, vegetable oil, copra). Though the interior lands yield fine timber and the coastal waters abound in fish, these resources have been so far little exploited. Favored by an excellent climate and picturesque scenery, the isls. offer great attractions to tourists. Leading ports and commercial centers are: Roseau (Dominica), Castries (St. Lucia), Kingstown (St. Vincent), St. George's (Grenada). The Windward Isls. were reputedly discovered by Columbus. Because of fierce resistance by the native Caribs, European colonization was started relatively late (early 17th cent.), followed by a continuous struggle bet. England and France for possession of the isls. The Br. colony was constituted in 1855; Dominica, formerly part of Leeward Isls. colony, was joined to it in 1940. The majority of the inhabitants are Negro, while less than 5% are white; some East Indians were introduced in 19th cent. A few Caribs remain in St. Vincent and Dominica. English is generally spoken, though a Fr. patois is still widely used. For further political history, see articles on respective isls.

Windward Islands, in S Pacific: see SOCIETY ISLANDS.

Windward Passage, strait in the West Indies, separating Cuba (W) from Haiti (E), and linking the Atlantic (N) with the Caribbean (S); 50 mi. wide bet. Cape Maisí (Cuba) and Cape St. Nicolas, Haiti. It is on direct shipping route from E coast of U.S. to the Panama Canal.

Windy Lake, trading post, S Keewatin Dist., Northwest Territories, W of Nueltin L.; 60°35′N 99°50′W.

Wine Islands, N Ohio, name sometimes given to islands in L. Erie N and NW of Sandusky; best-known are BASS ISLANDS, KELLEYS ISLAND.

Winesburg, village, Holmes co., central Ohio, 7 mi. NE of Millersburg, in agr. area.

Wine Spring Bald Mountain, N.C.: see NANTAHALA MOUNTAINS.

Winfall (wĭn′fôl), town (pop. 421), Perquimans co., NE N.C., 2 mi. NNE of Hertford; sawmilling.

Winfield, village (pop. estimate 350), S central Alta., 50 mi. SW of Edmonton; farming, dairying.

Winfield. 1 Town (pop. 2,108), Marion co., NW Ala., 65 mi. NW of Birmingham; lumber, cotton milling. Coal mines in vicinity. **2** Village (pop. 714), Du Page co., NE Ill., just W of Wheaton, in dairying area. **3** Town (pop. 888), Henry co., SE Iowa, 28 mi. NW of Burlington; tile factory. **4** City (pop. 10,264), ⊙ Cowley co., S Kansas, on Walnut R. and 36 mi. SSE of Wichita; trade and shipping center in livestock, grain, and oil region; dairying, poultry packing, flour and feed milling; metal products. Gas and power utilities publicly owned. Seat of Southwestern Col. (Methodist; coeducational; 1886) and a jr. col. Co. fair is held here annually in Aug. State school for feebleminded is near by. Laid out 1870, inc. 1872. **5** Town (pop. 474), Lincoln co., E Mo., near Mississippi R., 13 mi. E of Troy. **6** A residential section of W Queens borough of New York city, SE N.Y. **7** Town (pop. 319), Titus co., NE Texas, 8 mi. W of Mt. Pleasant. **8** Town (pop. 346), ⊙ Putnam co., W W.Va., on the Kanawha and 19 mi. NW of Charleston, in agr. and coal-mining area.

Winfield Scott, Fort, Calif.: see SAN FRANCISCO.

Winfred, town (pop. 171), Lake co., E S.Dak., 12 mi. W of Madison.

Wing, agr. village and parish (pop. 1,415), E Buckingham, England, 3 mi. SW of Leighton Buzzard. Has notable Saxon church.

Wing, village (pop. 312), Burleigh co., central N. Dak., 33 mi. NE of Bismarck.

Wingate, town and parish (pop. 12,348), E Durham, England, 9 mi. ESE of Durham; coal-mining center.

Wingate (wĭn′gāt). **1** Town (pop. 400), Montgomery co., W Ind., 14 mi. NW of Crawfordsville, in agr. area. **2** Fishing village (pop. c.300), Dorchester co., E Md., 19 mi. S of Cambridge and on Honga R.; ships seafood, builds boats, cans vegetables. **3** Town (pop. 793), Union co., S N.C., 5 mi. E of Monroe; lumber milling. Seat of Wingate Col.

Wingdale, village, Dutchess co., SE N.Y., near Conn. line, 20 mi. ESE of Poughkeepsie; magnesium plant. Seat of a state hosp. for the insane.

Wingello, village (pop. 347), E New South Wales, Australia, 85 mi. SW of Sydney; iron, bauxite.

Wingene (vĭn′khünů), agr. village (pop. 7,353), West Flanders prov., NW Belgium, 10 mi. SSE of Bruges. Formerly spelled Wynghene.

Winger (wĭng′ůr), village (pop. 283), Polk co., NW Minn., 33 mi. SE of Crookston, in grain, poultry area; dairy products.

Wingfield, airport, SW Cape Prov., U. of So. Afr., 6 mi. E of Cape Town, just E of Maitland.

Wingham (wĭng′ům), municipality (pop. 2,097), E New South Wales, Australia, on Manning R. and 80 mi. NNE of Newcastle; dairying center.

Wingham, town (pop. 2,030), S Ont., on Maitland R. and 22 mi. ENE of Goderich; mfg. of stoves, furnaces, gloves; tanning, woodworking, flour milling, dairying.

Wingles (vēg′lů), town (pop. 8,034), Pas-de-Calais dept., N France, near Haute-Deûle Canal, 5 mi. NNE of Lens, in coal-mining dist.; copper and bronze smelting, glass and ammonia mfg.

Wingo, town (pop. 451), Graves co., SW Ky., 9 mi. SW of Mayfield, in clay-mining and agr. area.

Wingon, China: see TZEKAM.

Wingshun (wĭng′shōōn′), Mandarin *Yungshun* (yōōng′shōōn′), town, ⊙ Wingshun co. (pop. 188,107), S Kwangsi prov., China, 35 mi. E of Nanning and on Yü R.

Wingst (vĭngst), village (pop. 3,042), in former Prussian prov. of Hanover, NW Germany, after 1945 in Lower Saxony, 17 mi. SE of Cuxhaven; woodworking.

Winhall, town (pop. 255), Bennington co., SW Vt., on small Winhall R. and 24 mi. WSW of Springfield, in Green Mts.; includes Bondville village.

Winiec, Poland: see WINSKO.

Winifred, town (pop. 217), Fergus co., central Mont., on branch of Missouri R. and 35 mi. N of Lewistown.

Winifreda (wēnēfrā′dä), town (pop. estimate 1,200), E La Pampa natl. territory, Argentina, 25 mi. N of Santa Rosa; rail terminus; grain, stock center.

Winisk River (wĭ′nĭsk), N Ont., issues from Winisk L., in Patricia dist., flows 300 mi. N and NE to Hudson Bay at Weenusk.

Wink, city (pop. 1,521), Winkler co., W Texas, 30 mi. NE of Pecos; supply center for oil, natural-gas fields. Inc. 1928.

Winkel (vĭng′kůl), village (pop. 3,467), in former Prussian prov. of Hesse-Nassau, W Germany, after 1945 in Hesse, in the Rheingau, on right bank of the Rhine and 12 mi. WSW of Wiesbaden; wine. Has oldest dwelling house (9th cent.?) in Germany; country house of Brentano family, where Goethe frequently visited.

Winkelman (wĭng′kůlmůn), town (pop. 548), Gila co., SE central Ariz., on Gila R., at mouth of San Pedro R., and 28 mi. S of Globe; trade center for copper- and gypsum-mining and agr. area (fruit, cattle, Angora goats).

Winkfield, town and parish (pop. 4,451), E Berkshire, England, 4 mi. SW of Windsor; agr. market. Has 17th-cent. church.

Winkler, village (pop. 1,164), S Man., 60 mi. SW of Winnipeg; grain; mixed farming.

Winkler, county (□ 887; pop. 10,064), W Texas; ⊙ Kermit. High plains, bounded N by N.Mex. line; alt. c.2,700–3,000 ft. W-facing Cap Rock escarpment is in E. Oil, natural-gas fields, large-scale cattle ranching. Formed 1887.

Winlaw, village (pop. estimate 250), S B.C., on Slocan R. and 16 mi. NW of Nelson, in lumbering and mining (gold, silver, tungsten) region.

Winlock, town (pop. 878), Lewis co., SW Wash., 12 mi. S of Chehalis; eggs, poultry, timber.

Winn, parish (□ 950; pop. 16,119), N central La.; ⊙ Winnfield. Bounded W by Saline Bayou, SE by Bayou Castor; intersected by Dugdemona R. Includes part of Kisatchie Natl. Forest; also Saline L. game and fish preserve (camping, fishing). Agr. (corn, cotton, hay, sweet potatoes, truck, peanuts). Salt mines, limestone quarries; lumber. Some mfg. Formed 1852.

Winn, town (pop. 497), Penobscot co., E central Maine, on the Penobscot and c.42 mi. above Old Town; hunting, fishing area.

Winnapaug Pond (wĭ′nůpôg), SW R.I., salt pond c.2.5 mi. long, separated from Block Isl. Sound by sandbar, with inlet just W of Weekapaug.

Winneba (wĭ′nēbů), town (pop. 15,920), Western Prov., S Gold Coast colony, port on Gulf of Guinea, 35 mi. WSW of Accra; fishing center; coconuts, cassava, corn. Exports cacao.

Winnebago (wĭnůbā′gō). **1** County (□ 520; pop. 152,385), N Ill., bordered by Wis. (N); ⊙ ROCKFORD. Drained by Rock, Pecatonica, and Kishwaukee rivers. Dairy, grain, and livestock area; extensive mfg. Formed 1836. **2** County (□ 402; pop. 13,450), N Iowa, on Minn. line; ⊙ Forest City. Prairie agr. area (cattle, hogs, poultry, corn, oats, sugar beets) drained by Lime Creek; sand and gravel pits. Formed 1851. **3** County (□ 454; pop. 91,103), E central Wis.; ⊙ Oshkosh. Bounded E by L. Winnebago; drained by Wolf and Fox rivers; contains Poygan, Rush, and Butte des Morts lakes. Primarily a dairying and farming area with extensive mfg. (especially paper and other wood products) at Oshkosh, Menasha, and Neenah. Formed 1840.

Winnebago. 1 Village (pop. 752), Winnebago co., N Ill., 8 mi. W of Rockford, in agr. area. **2** Village (pop. 2,127), Faribault co., S Minn., near Blue Earth R., 10 mi. N. of Blue Earth city, in grain, livestock, poultry area; dairy products, canned vegetables. Settled before 1865. **3** Village (pop. 684), Thurston co., NE Nebr., 20 mi. S of Sioux City, Iowa, near Missouri R. Here are 2 religious missions, a U.S. hosp. for Indians, and hq. of Omaha, Ponca, Santee, and Winnebago Indian reservations.

Winnebago, Lake, largest lake (□ 215) of Wis., 55 mi. NNW of Milwaukee; c.30 mi. long, 5–10 mi. wide. Fox R. enters the lake at Oshkosh (on W shore), leaves it at Neenah and Menasha (at NW end). Fond du Lac is on S shore. Lake sports.

Winneconne (wĭnůkŏ′nē), village (pop. 1,078), Winnebago co., E central Wis., on L. Winneconne, 10 mi. NW of Oshkosh; dairying; vegetable canning.

Winneconne, Lake, Wis.: see POYGAN, LAKE.

Winnecook, Maine: see BURNHAM.

Winnegance, Maine: see BATH.

Winnemucca (wĭnĭmŭ′ků), city (pop. 2,847), ⊙ Humboldt co., N Nev., on Humboldt R., at N end of Sonoma Range, and c.150 mi. NE of Reno; alt. 4,344 ft.; trade center and livestock-shipping point; smelting, bottling. Gold, silver, copper, tungsten mines near by. Settled 1850 as trading post (French Ford), renamed 1868, inc. 1917.

Winnemucca Lake, W Nev., intermittent lake partly in Pyramid Lake Indian Reservation, E of Pyramid L. and Lake Range; c.25 mi. long, 5 mi. wide.

Winnenden (vĭ′nůndůn), town (pop. 8,021), N Württemberg, Germany, after 1945 in Württemberg-Baden, 5 mi. NE of Waiblingen; wine, grain. Has castle.

Winnepesaukee, Lake, and **Winnepesaukee River,** N.H.: see WINNIPESAUKEE, LAKE.

Winner, city (pop. 3,252), ⊙ Tripp co., S S.Dak., 70 mi. SSE of Pierre; trading center for farming and cattle-raising region, shipping point for turkeys and poultry products; soap, awnings, ice cream, grain, dairy products. Founded after 1908.

Winnersh, agr. village and parish (pop. 1,536), E Berkshire, England, 2 mi. NW of Wokingham.

Winneshiek (wĭ′nůshēk), county (□ 688; pop. 21,639), NE Iowa, on Minn. line; ⊙ Decorah. Prairie agr. area (hogs, cattle, poultry, corn, oats, hay) drained by Upper Iowa and Turkey rivers; many limestone quarries. State parks. Formed 1847.

Winnetka (wĭnĕt′ků), village (pop. 12,105), Cook co., NE Ill., N suburb of Chicago, on L. Michigan, 5 mi. NNW of Evanston; makes pharmaceuticals, cosmetics. Has noted school system. Seat of graduate Teachers Col. Inc. 1869.

Winnetoon (wĭ′nĭtōōn), village (pop. 120), Knox co., NE Nebr., 45 mi. NW of Norfolk.

Winnett (wĭ′nůt), town (pop. 407), ⊙ Petroleum co., central Mont., on branch of Musselshell R. and 50 mi. E of Lewistown; shipping point in wheat region; oil wells; oil products and drilling equipment; livestock.

Winnfield, town (pop. 5,629), ⊙ Winn parish, N central La., c.45 mi. NNW of Alexandria, in pine-woods region; salt mining, lumbering, limestone and gypsum quarrying; mfg. of creosoted products, concrete and wood products, canned foods. Agr. (truck, corn, cotton). Inc. 1855.

Winnibigoshish Lake (wĭ″nĭbĭgō′shĭsh), Itasca and Cass counties, N central Minn., in Greater Leech Lake Indian Reservation and Chippewa Natl. Forest, 31 mi. WNW of Grand Rapids; max. length 13.5 mi.; max. width 10 mi. Hunting, fishing, bathing, boating resorts. Fed and drained by Mississippi R. Village of Bena is on S shore. Since construction of dam on E outlet □ 179; □ 75 in natural state.

Winniki, Ukrainian SSR: see VINNIKI.

Winnington, town and parish (pop. 1,268), N central Cheshire, England, just NW of Northwich; chemical industry.

Winnipauk, Conn.: see NORWALK.

Winnipeg (wĭ′nĭpĕg, wĭ′nůpĕg″), largest city (pop. 229,045) and ⊙ Manitoba, 4th largest city in Canada, in SE part of prov., on Red R. at mouth of Assiniboine R., and c.40 mi. SSW of L. Winnipeg, 60 mi. N of U.S. line; 49°53′N 97°9′W. Midway bet. the Atlantic and the Pacific, it is railroad, commercial, and distributing center for the Prairie Provinces and the largest Amer. wheat market, with grain exchange, major railroad yards and shops, grain elevators, and stockyards. Industries include flour milling, meat packing, automobile assembly; mfg. of agr. machinery, clothing, paper products, gypsum, bricks. Hydroelectric power is supplied from several stations on Winnipeg R. Seat of Univ. of Manitoba and Manitoba Agr. Col. Notable features are legislative bldgs., provincial offices, law courts, city hall, civic auditorium, Cenotaph, La Vérendrye memorial, and remains of Fort Garry. Mean temp. ranges from —2.7°F. (Jan.) to 67°F. (July); average annual rainfall is 51 inches. First settlement was established 1738 near site of present city by La Vérendrye and called Fort Rouge; subsequently abandoned. In early 19th cent. Fort Gibraltar (North West Co.) and Fort Douglas (Hudson's Bay Co.) were built; after 1812 surrounding region was settled by colonists brought from Scotland by the earl of Selkirk. After bitter rivalry, the North West Co. and Hudson's Bay Co. were merged (1821); Fort Gibraltar was renamed Fort Garry (1821) and rebuilt (1835). Settlement grew up around the fort and was inc. 1873 as Winnipeg. Its growth dates from arrival of the Canadian Pacific Railway in 1881 and its completion in 1885. Until early part of 20th cent. Winnipeg's development was slow (1871 pop. 241; 1901 pop. 42,340; 1911 pop. 136,035). Adjoining Winnipeg (E) is city of St. Boniface. A disastrous flood in 1950 forced the evacuation of the city and caused great damage.

Winnipeg, Lake (□ 9,398), S central Man., 40 mi. NNE of Winnipeg; 240 mi. long, 55 mi. wide; alt. 713 ft. Drained N into Hudson Bay by Nelson R., it receives Red, Winnipeg, Berens, Dauphin, and Saskatchewan rivers. It is remnant of glacial L. Agassiz. Shipping and fisheries are important; there are major stands of timber and pulpwood. On S shore are several resorts. Discovered 1733 by Vérendrye expedition.

Winnipeg Beach, town (pop. 318), SE Man., on L. Winnipeg, 45 mi. N of Winnipeg; resort.

Winnipegosis (wĭnĭpĕgō′sĭs), village (pop. 896), W Man., on L. Winnipegosis, at mouth of Mossy R., 35 mi. NNE of Dauphin; pike-fishing center; lumber and flour milling.

Winnipegosis, Lake (□ 2,086), W Man., 35 mi. NNE of Dauphin and W of L. Manitoba; 125 mi. long, 25 mi. wide; alt. 831 ft. Drains SE into L. Manitoba, and thence into L. Winnipeg. Once part of glacial L. Agassiz. Important pike fisheries.

Winnipeg River (wĭ′nĭpĕg, wĭ′nŭpĕg″), NW Ont. and SE Man., issues from N end of L. of the Woods at Kenora, flows in a winding course generally NW, through several lakes, to SE end of L. Winnipeg 60 mi. NE of Winnipeg; 200 mi. long; length from head of Firesteel R., its principal headstream, near W end of L. Superior and near U.S. border, 475 mi. On lower course are numerous rapids; hydroelectric-power centers are Pointe du Bois, Slave Falls, Seven Sisters Falls, McArthur Falls, Great Falls, and Pine Falls. English R. is its principal tributary. Route of early explorers, river was 1st traveled by the sons of La Vérendrye.

Winnipesaukee, Lake (wĭ″nĭpûsô′kē), Belknap and Carroll counties, E central N.H., largest lake (25 mi. long, 12 mi. wide) in N.H., with irregular wooded shores and many isls., largest of which is Long Isl. (3 mi. long, 1.5 mi. wide). Center of resort region, with steamboat service, annual regatta. Its outlet, **Winnipesaukee River**, flows c.20 mi. SW, past The Weirs, Laconia, and Tilton (linking L. Paugus and Winnisquam L.), to junction with Pemigewasset R., forming Merrimack R. at Franklin. Sometimes spelled Winnepesaukee.

Winnisquam Lake (wĭ′nĭskwăm), Belknap co., central N.H., resort lake (7.5 mi. long) just W of Laconia; joined to L. Paugus and Pemigewasset R. by Winnipesaukee R. Winnisquam village is on S shore.

Winnsboro. 1 Town (pop. 3,655), ⊙ Franklin parish, NE La., 33 mi. SE of Monroe and on small Turkey Creek; trade center for rich agr. region (cotton, hay, fruit, livestock, grain); cotton gins and compresses, sawmills; mfg. of wood products, bricks. Founded c.1844, inc. 1902. **2** City (pop. 3,267), ⊙ Fairfield co., N central S.C., 26 mi. N of Columbia, in agr. area; lumber, stone, granite. Settled mid-18th cent., inc. 1785. Textiles, tire cord made at adjacent Winnsboro Mills village (pop. 2,936). **3** Town (pop. 2,512), on Franklin-Wood co. line, NE Texas, c.50 mi. ESE of Greenville; shipping center for truck, dairy products, cotton; lumber milling. Oil wells near.

Winnweiler (vĭn′vī″lŭr), village (pop. 1,703), Rhenish Palatinate, W Germany, 9 mi. NE of Kaiserslautern; ironworks, copper smelters; machinery mfg., brewing.

Winona (wĭnō′nŭ), village (pop. estimate 600), S Ont., on L. Ontario, 11 mi. ESE of Hamilton; fruit.

Winona (wĭnō′nŭ, wī–), county (□ 623; pop. 39,841), SE Minn.; ⊙ Winona. Agr. area bounded E by Mississippi R. and Wis. Dairy products, livestock, poultry, corn, oats, barley, potatoes. Food processing and mfg. at Winona. Formed 1854.

Winona. 1 Village, Coconino co., N central Ariz., 13 mi. E of Flagstaff. Archaeological excavations have been made at Indian ruins here. **2** Village (pop. 1,004), Larimer co., N Colo. **3** City (pop. 382), Logan co., W Kansas, 22 mi. WSW of Oakley, in grain and cattle region. **4** City (pop. 25,031), ⊙ Winona co., SE Minn., on bluffs overlooking Mississippi R. and c.100 mi. SE of St. Paul. Trade and industrial center with railroad repair shops; food processing (dairy products, flour, beverages, feed, candy, canned pickles and kraut), mfg. (bricks, patent medicines, clothing, auto accessories, wood products, drilling equipment); limestone quarrying. Winona State Teachers Col. (1860), St. Mary's Col. (R.C.), and Col. of St. Teresa (R.C.) are here. Settled 1851 as trading and lumbering point, inc. 1857. Grew with increase in river traffic and with arrival of railroad. **5** City (pop. 3,441), ⊙ Montgomery co., central Miss., 26 mi. E of Greenwood, in farming, dairying, stock-raising, and timber region; cottonseed products, lumber, chenille articles, chemicals, dairy products. **6** (also wī′nōnŭ) City (pop. 473), Shannon co., S Mo., in the Ozarks, 35 mi. NE of West Plains; ships livestock, lumber. **7** Village (pop. c.400), Smith co., E Texas, 12 mi. NE of Tyler, near the Sabine; trade, shipping point in agr. area. **8** Village (1940 pop. 1,058), Fayette co., S central W.Va., near New R., 40 mi. SE of Charleston, in agr. and coal-mining area.

Winona, Lake, central Ark., water-supply reservoir (c.4 mi. long), in the Ozarks c.40 mi. W of Little Rock.

Winona Lake, resort town (pop. 1,366), Kosciusko co., N Ind., on Winona L. (c.1 mi. long), just SE of Warsaw. Seat of Grace Theological Seminary. Annual Mid-West Chautauqua held here.

Winooski (wĭnōō′skē), industrial city (pop. 6,734), Chittenden co., NW Vt., on Winooski R., just E of Burlington; textiles, window screens, wood and metal products; lime; fruit. St. Michael's Col. here. Mills built here just after Revolution. City set off from Colchester and inc. 1922. **Winooski River**, N central Vt., rises near Cabot, flows c.90 mi. SW and NW, through Green Mts., past Montpelier, Waterbury, and Winooski, to L. Champlain N of Burlington. Receives North Branch (c.15 mi. long) at Montpelier. Three flood-control dams built (1933–37) on tributaries to prevent recurrence of disastrous 1927 flood.

Winschoten (vĭn′skhōtŭn), town (pop. 13,675), Groningen prov., NE Netherlands, on the Winschoter Diep and 20 mi. ESE of Groningen; trade center; mfg. (agr. machinery, chemicals, bicycles, furniture, strawboard), dairy products, potato-flour milling, meat packing. Has 13th-cent. church.

Winschoter Diep (vĭn′skhōtŭr dēp′), canal, Groningen prov., N Netherlands, extends 23 mi. ESE-WNW, bet. Groningen and a point 2 mi. E of Winschoten; 6.5 feet deep. Serves Hoogezand, Sappemeer, and Winschoten.

Winscombe, town and parish (pop. 1,979), N Somerset, England, 6 mi. ESE of Weston-super-Mare; agr. market in dairy area. Has 15th-cent. church.

Winsen or **Winsen an der Luhe** (vĭn′zŭn än dĕr lōō′ŭ), town (pop. 8,208), in former Prussian prov. of Hanover, NW Germany, after 1945 in Lower Saxony, on Luhe R. (small tributary of the Ilmenau) near its mouth, and 11 mi. NW of Lüneburg; machinery, leather and paper products, chemicals; food processing. Johann Eckermann b. here.

Winsford, urban district (1931 pop. 10,998; 1951 census 12,745), central Cheshire, England, on Weaver R. and 5 mi. S of Northwich; salt-mining and -processing center; mfg. of chemicals; silica and quartz processing. Has 16th-cent. church. Includes industrial suburbs of Wharton (E) and Over (W).

Winside, village (pop. 454), Wayne co., NE Nebr., 8 mi. WSW of Wayne and on branch of Logan Creek; grain.

Winsko (vē′nyŭskô), Pol. *Wińsko*, Ger. *Winzig* (vĭn′tsĭkh), town (1939 pop. 2,078; 1946 pop. 1,334) in Lower Silesia, after 1945 in Wroclaw prov., SW Poland, 30 mi. NW of Breslau (Wroclaw); agr. market (grain, sugar beets, potatoes, livestock). After 1945, briefly called Winiec.

Winslow (wĭnz′lō), town and parish (pop. 1,539), N central Buckingham, England, 9 mi. NNW of Aylesbury; agr. market. Has 14th-cent. church and 18th-cent. mansion designed by Inigo Jones.

Winslow. 1 City (pop. 6,518), Navajo co., E central Ariz., near Little Colorado R., 55 mi. ESE of Flagstaff; alt. 4,856 ft.; rail center (with repair shops) for livestock area; silica works. Founded 1882, inc. 1900. METEOR CRATER is 17 mi. W. Navajo Indian Reservation is N. **2** Town (pop. 248), Washington co., NW Ark., 18 mi. S of Fayetteville, in the Ozarks. Devil's Den State Park (recreational area) is W. **3** Village (pop. 355), Stephenson co., N Ill., on Pecatonica R. (bridged here), near Wis. line, and 16 mi. NNW of Freeport, in agr. area; dairy products. **4** Mining town (pop. 1,322), Pike co., SW Ind., on Patoka R. and 26 mi. SE of Vincennes, in agr. and bituminous-coal area; makes wooden rulers. Clay pits; timber. **5** Town (pop. 4,413), including Winslow village (pop. 2,916), Kennebec co., S Maine, on the Kennebec opposite WATERVILLE, at influx of the Sebasticook; paper, pulp mills. Cassiterite found here. Blockhouse ruins of Fort Halifax (1754). Town inc. 1771. **6** Village (pop. 138), Dodge co., E Nebr., 12 mi. N of Fremont and on Elkhorn R. **7** Town (pop. 637), Kitsap co., W Wash., on Bainbridge Isl. in Puget Sound, 8 mi. W of Seattle.

Winsor Dam, Mass.: see QUABBIN RESERVOIR.

Winstanley, England: see BILLINGE AND WINSTANLEY.

Winsted. 1 City (pop. 8,781) in Winchester town, a ⊙ Litchfield co., NW Conn., on Still R. and 8 mi. N of Torrington. Mfg. (clocks, hosiery, clothing, cutlery, chain-hoists, pins, fishing tackle, electrical equipment, tools, thread, wood and paper boxes, hatters' felt), agr. (truck, dairy products, poultry). Resorts on Highland L. Clock-making here since 1807. Inc. 1917. **2** Village (pop. 941), McLeod co., S central Minn., on small lake and c.40 mi. W of Minneapolis, in grain and livestock area; dairy products, canned corn.

Winster, village and parish (pop. 677), central Derby, England, 4 mi. W of Matlock; manganese mining; former lead-mining center. Has 15th-cent. market house.

Winston. 1 County (□ 633; pop. 18,250), NW Ala.; ⊙ Double Springs. Drained by branches of Sipsey Fork. Wm. B. Bankhead Natl. Forest throughout. Cotton, melons, poultry; lumber milling. Formed 1850. **2** County (□ 606; pop. 22,231), E central Miss.; ⊙ Louisville. Drained by Noxubee R., Lobutcha Creek, and headwaters of Pearl R. Agr. (cotton, corn), dairying; lumbering. Formed 1833.

Winston. 1 Village (pop. 1,870), Polk co., central Fla., just W of Lakeland. Also called Lakeland Junction. **2** Town (pop. 154), Douglas co., NW central Ga., 26 mi. W of Atlanta, in farm area. **3** Town (pop. 278), Daviess co., NW Mo., 38 mi. ENE of St. Joseph; coal. **4** Village (pop. c.150), Broadwater co., W central Mont., near Missouri R., 20 mi. ESE of Helena, in mining region.

Winston Park, city (pop. 588), Kenton co., N Ky., near Licking R., just S of Covington.

Winston-Salem (wĭn″stŭn-sā′lŭm), city (pop. 87,811), ⊙ Forsyth co., N central N.C., 70 mi. NNE of Charlotte, in the piedmont; 36°5′N 80°14′W; state's second-largest city. Port of entry; one of world's chief tobacco centers, with large cigarette and pipe-tobacco factories, stemming and redrying plants, and warehouses; also mfg. of nylon yarn, underwear, hosiery, furniture, and communications equipment. Seat of Salem Col. (women), Winston-Salem Teachers Col. (Negro), and the medical school of Wake Forest Col. Salem was founded 1766 by a Moravian colony, Winston c.1850 as co. seat; consolidated in 1913.

Winstonville, village (pop. 322), Bolivar co., NW Miss., 22 mi. SSW of Clarksdale, in cotton-growing area. Post office name formerly Chambers.

Winsum (vĭn′sŭm), town (pop. 996), Groningen prov., N Netherlands, 8 mi. NNW of Groningen; shipbuilding. One of the Netherlands' oldest towns.

Winteceaster, England: see WINCHESTER.

Winterbach (vĭn′tŭrbäkh), village (pop. 3,091), N Württemberg, Germany, after 1945 in Württemberg-Baden, on the Rems and 2 mi. W of Schorndorf; mfg. of precision instruments.

Winterberg, Czechoslovakia: see VIMPERK.

Winterberg (vĭn′tŭrbĕrk), town (pop. 3,353), in former Prussian prov. of Westphalia, W Germany, after 1945 in North Rhine-Westphalia, at NE foot of the Rothaargebirge, 13 mi. S of Brilon; trades in lumber and woolens. Winter-sports center; summer resort.

Winterberg (–bĕrkh), mountain range, SE Cape Prov., U. of So. Afr., at SW end of Drakensberg range system, extends c.100 mi. E from upper Great Fish R. valley to Swart Kei R., SW of Queenstown; rises to 7,778 ft. on Great Winterberg, 12 mi. N of Adelaide.

Winterbourne, town and parish (pop. 3,554), SW Gloucester, England, 6 mi. NE of Bristol; agr. market. Church dates partly from 12th cent.

Winter Garden, city (pop. 3,503), Orange co., central Fla., 12 mi. W of Orlando, on L. Apopka; packing and shipping center (citrus fruit, truck).

Winter Garden, SW Texas, irrigated year-round agr. region SW of San Antonio, extending E from valley of the Rio Grande. Includes parts of Maverick, Zavala, Frio, La Salle, Dimmit counties; principal shipping, processing centers are Eagle Pass, Crystal City. Irrigation from the Rio Grande and artesian wells. Known for winter vegetables (especially spinach), citrus, other fruit, truck.

Winter Harbor, resort town (pop. 568), Hancock co., S Maine, on peninsula at entrance to Frenchman Bay, opposite Mt. Desert Isl.

Winter Harbour, SE Melville Isl., W Franklin Dist., Northwest Territories, small inlet of Viscount Melville Sound; 74°46′N 110°45′W.

Winterhausen (vĭn″tŭrhou′zŭn), village (pop. 1,482), Lower Franconia, W Bavaria, Germany, on the Main (canalized) and 7 mi. WSW of Kitzingen; wheat, barley, cattle. Has 15th–16th-cent. church; rococo town hall.

Winterhaven, village, Imperial co., S Calif., in Yuma Indian Reservation, on Colorado R., opposite Yuma, Ariz.

Winter Haven, city (pop. 8,605), Polk co., central Fla., 14 mi. E of Lakeland; citrus-fruit shipping center, with large canneries and packing houses; mfg. of concrete products, millwork. Also a boating resort with c.100 lakes in a 5 mi. radius, some 16 of them linked by a navigable channel.

Winterhude (vĭn″tŭrhōō′dŭ), N district of Hamburg, NW Germany, just N of the Aussenalster, separated from Eppendorf (W) by the Alster; site of Hamburg's municipal park.

Winter Park, city (pop. 8,250), Orange co., central Fla., adjacent to Orlando; resort, and citrus-fruit shipping point; has small lakes within city limits. Rollins College is here. Settled in 1850s, inc. 1887.

Winterport, town (pop. 1,694), Waldo co., S Maine, on the Penobscot and 12 mi. below Bangor; food processing, wood products. Inc. 1860.

Winters. 1 Town (pop. 1,265), Yolo co., central Calif., 25 mi. W of Sacramento, in orchard and farm area; ships fruit, wine. Inc. 1898. **2** City (pop. 2,676), Runnels co., W central Texas, 35 mi. SSW of Abilene; shipping, processing point in agr. area; cotton gins; cottonseed-oil, flour mills. Settled c.1890, inc. 1909.

Wintersdorf (vĭn′tŭrsdôrf), village (pop. 4,414), Thuringia, central Germany, on Schnauder R. and 6 mi. NW of Altenburg, in lignite-mining region.

Winterset, city (pop. 3,570), ⊙ Madison co., S central Iowa, near Middle R., 28 mi. SW of Des Moines; ships fruit, grain, livestock; produces hybrid seed corn, feed, concrete, metal products. Limestone quarries near by. State park is SW. The original Delicious apple tree was discovered near here in 1872. Founded 1846, inc. 1876.

Winterslag, Belgium: see GENK.
Winterstown, borough (pop. 298), York co., S Pa., 11 mi. SE of York.
Wintersville, village (pop. 1,950), Jefferson co., E Ohio, just W of Steubenville. Inc. 1947.
Winterswijk (vĭn'tŭrsvĭk), town (pop. 12,883), Gelderland prov., E Netherlands, 34 mi. E of Arnhem, near Ger. border; rail junction and border station; salt and coal mining; mfg. (bricks, tiles, furniture, wheels, woven and knitted cotton goods, wire, machinery), meat products. Sometimes spelled Winterswyk.
Winterthur (vĭn'tŭrtōōr), city (1950 pop. 66,971), Zurich canton, N Switzerland, 12 mi. NE of Zurich; rail, industrial center. Metalworks (locomotives), cotton textiles, knit goods, soap, beer, flour, bakery products; printing. City hall, mus. with library, Gothic church, notable art gall.
Winterton, former urban district (1931 pop. 1,958), Parts of Lindsey, N Lincolnshire, England, 5 mi. NE of Scunthorpe; ironstone quarrying; agr. market. Has church of Norman origin.
Winterville. 1 Town (pop. 453), Clarke co., NE central Ga., 6 mi. E of Athens. **2** Plantation (pop. 373), Aroostook co., NE Maine, on St. Froid L. and 35 mi. NW of Presque Isle, in hunting, fishing area. **3** Town (pop. 870), Pitt co., E N.C., 5 mi. S of Greenville; sawmilling.
Wintham (vĭn'täm), town, Antwerp prov., N Belgium, on Rupel R. and 3 mi. WNW of Boom; ship- and barge-building.
Winthrop. 1 Town (pop. 284), Little River co., extreme SW Ark., 14 mi. S of DeQueen. **2** Town (pop. 604), Buchanan co., E Iowa, near Buffalo Creek, 8 mi. E of Independence; dairy products. **3** Town (pop. 3,026), including Winthrop village (pop. 1,885), Kennebec co., SW Maine, 10 mi. W of Augusta, in lake region of resorts and farms; woolens, oilcloth, linoleum. Settled 1765, inc. 1771. **4** Town (pop. 19,496), Suffolk co., E Mass., on peninsula just NE of Boston; residential suburb. Has several old houses. Settled 1635, inc. 1852. Includes summer resort of Point Shirley. **5** City (pop. 1,251), Sibley co., S Minn., 7 mi. W of Gaylord; agr. trading point in grain, livestock, and poultry area; dairy products, canned corn. Settled 1881, inc. as village 1884, as city 1910. **6** Town (pop. 396), Okanogan co., N Wash., 25 mi. WNW of Okanogan and on Methow R., in hunting, fishing, mining region.
Winthrop Harbor, village (pop. 1,765), Lake co., extreme NE Ill., near Wis. line and L. Michigan, 9 mi. N of Waukegan; dairy products.
Winton, town (pop. 1,351), central Queensland, Australia, 330 mi. SW of Townsville; livestock center.
Winton, England: see BOURNEMOUTH.
Winton, borough (pop. 987), S S.Isl., New Zealand, 20 mi. N of Invercargill; agr. center; winery, dairy products.
Winton, village in Pencaitland parish, W East Lothian, Scotland, 2 mi. SE of Tranent; coal mining. Site of 17th-cent. Winton Castle.
Winton. 1 Resort village (pop. 184), St. Louis co., NE Minn., on Fall L., in Superior Natl. Forest, c.45 mi. NE of Virginia; grain, potatoes. **2** Town (pop. 834), ⊙ Hertford co., NE N.C., 9 mi. SE of Murfreesboro and on Chowan R.; sawmilling. Richard J. Gatling b. here. **3** Industrial borough (pop. 6,280), Lackawanna co., NE Pa., 7 mi. NE of Scranton and on Lackawanna R.; anthracite mines; silk mill. Settled 1849, inc. 1877. **4** Village (pop. c.650), Sweetwater co., SW Wyo., 12 mi. NNE of Rock Springs; alt. 6,945 ft.; coal mines.
Wintzenheim (vēzŭnĕm'), Ger. *Winzenheim* (vĭnts'ŭnhīm), town (pop. 2,638), Haut-Rhin dept., E France, at E foot of the Vosges, 3 mi. W of Colmar; iron founding; clothing, silk fabrics, ink. Winegrowing in area. Damaged in Second World War.
Winwick with Hulme (wĭ'nĭk, hūm), residential parish (pop. 4,659), S Lancashire, England, 3 mi. N of Warrington.
Winyah Bay (wĭn'yô, –yä), S.C., estuary (14 mi. long) c.50 mi. NE of Charleston; receives Waccamaw, Pee Dee, Sampit, and Black rivers (all navigable); traversed by Intracoastal Waterway. Georgetown is at head of bay. North Isl. (c.8 mi. long) extends almost across its mouth; lighthouse at 33°13'N 79°11'W. South Isl. (c.9 mi. long) is at S side of bay entrance.
Winz (vĭnts), village (pop. 6,837), in former Prussian prov. of Westphalia, W Germany, after 1945 in North Rhine-Westphalia, on the Ruhr, just opposite Hattingen.
Winzenheim, France: see WINTZENHEIM.
Winzig, Poland: see WINSKO.
Wiota (wīō'tŭ), town (pop. 227), Cass co., SW Iowa, 7 mi. E of Atlantic, in agr. area.
Wippach, Yugoslavia: see VIPAVA.
Wipperfürth (vĭ"pŭrfürt'), town (pop. 9,924), in former Prussian Rhine Prov., W Germany, after 1945 in North Rhine-Westphalia, on the Wupper (where it is formed by several headstreams, including the Wipper) and 10 mi. SE of Remscheid. Has Romanesque church. Neye dam 1.5 mi. N.
Wipper River (vĭ'pŭr). **1** In central Germany, rises in the lower Harz E of Stolberg, flows 45 mi. E and NE, past Hettstedt, Sandersleben, and Güsten, to the Saxonian Saale 3 mi. SW of Bernburg. **2** In central Germany, rises at S foot of the lower Harz NNE of Worbis, flows 35 mi. E and SE, past Sondershausen, to the Unstrut 6 mi. SSE of Bad Frankenhausen.
Wipper River, Poland: see WIEPRZ RIVER.
Wipptal (vĭp'täl), valley of Tyrol, W Austria, extending 15 mi. along Sill R., from Brenner Pass to Innsbruck, bet. Tuxer Alps (E) and Stubai Alps (W); used by Brenner RR.
Wiraketiya (vĭrŭkä'tĭyŭ), village, Southern Prov., Ceylon, 20 mi. NE of Matara, near large irrigation tank; citronella grass, tomatoes, rice. On isolated rock 2 mi. SW is one of most anc. Buddhist monasteries in Ceylon; honeycombed with caves and temples.
Wirballen, Lithuania: see VIRBALIS.
Wirbeln, Russian SFSR: see ZHAVORONKOVO.
Wirges (vĭr'gŭs), village (pop. 4,019), in former Prussian prov. of Hesse-Nassau, W Germany, after 1945 in Rhineland-Palatinate, 11 mi. NE of Coblenz; glassworks.
Wirksworth, urban district (1931 pop. 3,910; 1951 census 4,886), central Derby, England, 4 mi. S of Matlock; limestone-quarrying center; site of abandoned lead mines (worked since Roman and Saxon times). Has 10th-cent. church with later tower.
Wirrabara (wĭ"rŭbă'rŭ), village (pop. 381), S South Australia, 18 mi. NE of Port Pirie; wheat, wool.
Wirral (wĕr'ŭl), extensive residential urban district (1951 census 17,362), W Cheshire, England, on Dee R. estuary, 7 mi. SW of Birkenhead.
Wirral, peninsula on the Irish Sea, NW Cheshire, England, bet. Mersey R. estuary and Dee R. estuary; 14 mi. long, 8 mi. wide. Lowland protected from sea by embankment. Chief towns: Birkenhead, Wallasey, Hoylake, Wirral.
Wirsitz, Poland: see WYRZYSK.
Wirt (wûrt), county (□ 234; pop. 5,119), W W.Va.; ⊙ Elizabeth. Drained by the Little Kanawha. Agr. (livestock, poultry, dairy products, fruit, truck, tobacco). Formed 1848.
Wirt, village, Carter co., S Okla., 24 mi. W of Ardmore, in oil-producing area; gasoline plant.
Wisbech (wĭz'bēch), municipal borough (1931 pop. 12,006; 1951 census 17,430), in Isle of Ely, N Cambridge, England, on Nene R. and 12 mi. SW of King's Lynn; river port, fruit and vegetable-canning center, with agr.-machinery, paper, printing, and concrete works. There are many Dutch-type houses. Has 14th–16th-cent. church and monument to Thomas Clarkson, b. here. Surrounding fenland area was drained by Dutch engineers.
Wisbech Saint Mary (sŭnt), town and parish (pop. 2,644), in Isle of Ely, in N Cambridge, England, 3 mi. WSW of Wisbech; agr. market in fruitgrowing region. There is a 15th-cent. church. In parish, on Nene R. and 5 mi. SW of Wisbech, is agr. village of Guyhirne.
Wisborough Green (wĭz'bŭrŭ), town and parish (pop. 1,751), W Sussex, England, 5 mi. ENE of Petworth; agr. market. Has medieval church.
Wisby, Sweden: see VISBY.
Wiscasset (wĭskă'sĭt), town (pop. 1,584), ⊙ Lincoln co., S Maine, on Sheepscot R. and 10 mi. NE of Bath; resort and small port; flourishing place in sailing-ship days. Has colonial homes; courthouse (1824) still in use. Settled 1663, inc. 1802.
Wisch, France: see WISCHES.
Wischau, Czechoslovakia: see VYSKOV.
Wisches (vēsh), Ger. *Wisch* (vĭsh), village (pop. 1,068), Bas-Rhin dept., E France, in Bruche R. valley of the E Vosges, and 11 mi. WSW of Mosheim; wood veneer mfg.
Wiscoal, mining village (pop. 1,333, with near by Sassafras), Knott co., E Ky., in Cumberland foothills, 7 mi. E of Hazard; bituminous coal.
Wisconsin (wĭskŏn'sŭn, –sĭn), state (land □ 54,715; with inland waters, but without □ 10,062 of Great Lakes, □ 56,154; 1950 pop. 3,434,575; 1940 pop. 3,137,587), N U.S., bordered N by L. Superior and Mich., E by L. Michigan, S by Ill., W by Iowa and Minn.; 25th in area, 14th in pop.; admitted 1848 as 30th state; ⊙ Madison. The "Badger State"—measuring 300 mi. N-S and 280 mi. E-W at its widest points—is bounded by St. Croix R. and Mississippi R. on W and Menominee R. on NE. It lies in 2 contrasting physiographic provs.: the Laurentian Plateau (N, N center), consisting of Pre-Cambrian crystalline rocks, and the interior lowlands region (E, S, W), underlain by early Paleozoic sedimentary strata. More resistant rocks (limestone, dolomite) of the lowlands section have formed ridges or cuestas, such as Niagara cuesta in the E, of which Door Peninsula bet. L. Michigan and Green Bay is a part; Baraboo Range (S center) is an isolated quartzite outcrop. Surface features and drainage have been greatly affected by continental glaciation. SE and E Wis. consist of a glaciated plain with a variety of moraines, kames, drumlins (notably near Madison), small streams, and lakes, by far the largest of which is L. WINNEBAGO. The SW quarter of the state lies in the unglaciated or Driftless Area (□ c.13,000), where topography is bolder and lakes practically nonexistent. In the center is a fairly level sandstone plain, broken in places by castellated crags, which, from a distance, resemble buttes and mesas. N Wis. comprises a broad upland region (sometimes known as Superior Highlands in extreme N) of moderate relief, containing large forests and woodlands and many lakes and swamps. Here and there are low ridges, e.g., Gogebic Range, and monadnocks, such as Rib Mtn. (1,940 ft.) and Sugarbush Hill (1,951 ft.; highest point in state). In the extreme NW, around Superior, is a lowland of sedimentary rock. Principal rivers within Wis. are Wisconsin, Chippewa, Black, and Rock rivers, flowing generally SSW to the Mississippi, and the Fox and Wolf rivers, emptying into Green Bay. Many streams have falls and rapids, which are utilized for power. Wis. has a continental climate marked by extremes of temp. and an annual rainfall (spring-summer max.) of 30–35 in., slightly less in E and extreme NW. Days with snow cover range from 120 (N) to 60 (S), while the growing season averages 80–170 days (N-S). Green Bay (NE) has mean temp. of 15°F. in Jan., 70°F. in July, and annual rainfall of 28 in.; Madison (S) has mean temp. of 17°F. in Jan., 73°F. in July, and 31 in. of rain. Native vegetation consisted of oak-hickory with some prairie grassland in the S and hardwood (birch, beech, maple, hemlock) and pine (white, Norway, jack) forests in center and N. The large forest area, covering some 16,265,000 acres, is still commercially important, especially for white pine timber; natl. forest reserves comprise 2,019,000 acres. Wis.'s agr. is diversified and highly developed, with marketing and purchasing cooperatives (on Rochdale plan) a notable feature. Farm and range land totals c.23,500,000 acres, of which some 10,500,000 acres are in crops. Principal crops, grown mostly in S half of state, are corn, oats, and hay (Wis. ranks 1st in hay production), as well as much smaller amounts of barley, wheat, rye, potatoes (especially in sandy loam of central plain), and tobacco (largely near Viroqua and SE of Madison). The bulk of the agr. produce supports a flourishing dairy industry, for which the state is known as "America's Dairyland." Wis. has the most milch cows (2,432,000 in 1950), and leads in the production of milk and cheese, with creamery butter also important. Scientific methods of stock breeding are employed in such major dairying areas as the E and S parts. Other livestock include hogs (c.1,650,000; in S corn belt, mainly SW), beef cattle, horses (c.230,000), and sheep (c.260,000). Poultry is raised on most farms. Wis. is a leading producer of peas, sweet corn, beets, beans, cucumbers, and other truck crops, as well as cranberries (chiefly in NW), strawberries, and cherries (notably on Door Peninsula). There are several fur farms (fox, mink, rabbit, badger). Of the state's relatively few mineral resources, building stone (sandstone, granite, dolomite) is the most valuable. Other products are zinc and lead (mined in SW corner); iron ore, around Hurley in Gogebic Range (ore shipped largely from Ashland by lake steamer to Calumet and L. Erie mills); sand and gravel; lime; and pyrite. Favored by a skilled labor supply, good transportation facilities, and access to large Midwestern markets, the mfg. industry produces a wide variety of goods. The principal industries are mfg. of motor vehicles and parts, agr. machinery, fabricated metal products, paper and pulp (sawmills along lower Fox and upper Wisconsin rivers), furniture, malt liquors; meat packing, vegetable and fruit canning; mfg. of household appliances and utensils, leather, and footwear. The chief industrial area is in the SE, centering at Kenosha, Racine, and Milwaukee (by far the state's largest city, noted for its beer and meat-packing industries). Other mfg. centers at Superior, Green Bay, Madison, Sheboygan, Oshkosh, La Crosse, Eau Claire, West Allis, Appleton (1st hydroelectric plant in U.S. built here 1882), Fond du Lac, and Manitowoc. As a recreational area Wis. offers lake resorts, fishing, wild game (as on Apostle Isls.), winter sports (Beloit), and such scenic spots as Dells of the Wisconsin, waterfalls on Black and Bad rivers, and several state parks. Leading educational institutions are Univ. of Wis. (at Madison), Marquette Univ. (at Milwaukee), and Wis. Inst. of Technology (at Platteville). Remains of the Early Mound Builders' culture are found in a number of places. Present-day Indians are mostly Chippewas, Menominees, and Winnebagos living on reservations in the N part of the state. The French were the 1st to open up the area, from the time of Jean Nicolet, who landed at Green Bay in 1634. Then came fur traders, explorers, and missionaries, including Groseilliers and Radisson (1657–59), Father Allouez, who founded a mission at De Pere in 1671, Marquette and Jolliet, who crossed the portage (see PORTAGE, city, Wis.) bet. Fox and Wisconsin rivers in 1673, Father Hennepin (1680), and Perrot, who built fort at PRAIRIE DU CHIEN in 1686. First permanent settlement in Wis. was at Green Bay in 1701. The prosperous fur dominion of New France was ceded to England at conclusion of French and Indian War (1754–63). In 1783 the area was ceded to the U.S.; and, after New England states had relinquished their claims, it formed part of NORTHWEST TERRITORY (1787), Indiana Territory (1800), and Illinois Territory

(1809). However, Amer. control was not fully established until after War of 1812, when forts were built (1816) at Prairie du Chien and Green Bay and Wis. was made part of Michigan Territory (1818). Settlement increased rapidly with the development of lead mining (SW) and the elimination of hostile Indian tribes. In 1836 a separate territorial govt. was organized. Statehood was achieved (1848) in a period of great German and Scandinavian immigration; railroads were extended and wheat farming became important. Strongly antislavery, Wis. supported the Union during the Civil War, although the German farmers resisted conscription. Lumbering soon became the dominant industry (declined after 1910) and beef and dairy cattle were raised in large numbers. Hard times for the farmers gave rise to the Granger organizations in the '70s and '80s, which fought against high prices and railroad monopolies. At the turn of the century Robert La Follette launched his successful campaign of political reform and "experimental" govt., known as the "Wisconsin idea." For many years the Socialist movement, under Victor Berger and Daniel Hoan, dominated Milwaukee's municipal govt. Wis. has been a leader in progressive legislation, and 3 native sons —Frederick Jackson Turner (history), Thorstein Veblen (economics), and Frank Lloyd Wright (architecture)—have been pioneers in their respective fields. See also articles on the cities, towns, geographic features, and the 71 counties: ADAMS, ASHLAND, BARRON, BAYFIELD, BROWN, BUFFALO, BURNETT, CALUMET, CHIPPEWA, CLARK, COLUMBIA, CRAWFORD, DANE, DODGE, DOOR, DOUGLAS, DUNN, EAU CLAIRE, FLORENCE, FOND DU LAC, FOREST, GRANT, GREEN, GREEN LAKE, IOWA, IRON, JACKSON, JEFFERSON, JUNEAU, KENOSHA, KEWAUNEE, LA CROSSE, LAFAYETTE, LANGLADE, LINCOLN, MANITOWOC, MARATHON, MARINETTE, MARQUETTE, MILWAUKEE, MONROE, OCONTO, ONEIDA, OUTAGAMIE, OZAUKEE, PEPIN, PIERCE, POLK, PORTAGE, PRICE, RACINE, RICHLAND, ROCK, RUSK, SAINT CROIX, SAUK, SAWYER, SHAWANO, SHEBOYGAN, TAYLOR, TREMPEALEAU, VERNON, VILAS, WALWORTH, WASHBURN, WASHINGTON, WAUKESHA, WAUPACA, WAUSHARA, WINNEBAGO, WOOD.

Wisconsin, Lake, artificial lake in S central Wis., 7 mi. NE of Prairie du Sac; formed by power dam on Wisconsin R.; c.5 mi. long, c.3 mi. wide.

Wisconsin Dells, city (pop. 1,957), Columbia co., S central Wis., on Wisconsin R. (water power) and 43 mi. NNW of Madison, in agr. area (dairy products; grain, potatoes); produces hardware, pickles, butter; summer resort. Gateway to DELLS OF THE WISCONSIN. State park is near by. Settled c.1850, inc. 1925. Until 1931, called Kilbourn.

Wisconsin Rapids, city (pop. 13,496), ⊙ Wood co., central Wis., on both banks of Wisconsin R. and c.70 mi. WNW of Oshkosh, in agr. area (corn, grain, cranberries); railroad junction and cranberry-shipping center; mfg. (paper, paper products, stoves, paints, varnishes, beverages, clothing). Formed in 1900 by union of Grand Rapids and Centralia. Until 1920, called Grand Rapids.

Wisconsin River, rises in N Wis. in the lake region of Vilas co. near Wis.-Mich. line, flows generally S, past Rhinelander, Tomahawk, Merrill, Wausau, Stevens Point, Wisconsin Rapids, and Wisconsin Dells (site of scenic gorge), to Portage, where it is connected by Portage Canal with Fox R.; thence the Wisconsin flows generally SW to the Mississippi 3 mi. S of Prairie du Chien; c.430 mi. long. Feeds c.50 hydroelectric plants. L. Wisconsin formed by power dam on river near Prairie du Sac. Because of isls. and shifting channels, lower course (up to Portage) is navigable only by small boats.

Wise. 1 County (□ 909; pop. 16,141), N Texas; ⊙ Decatur. Drained by West Fork of Trinity R., here dammed into L. Bridgeport (water supply for Fort Worth; recreation area); also includes part of Eagle Mtn. L. Diversified agr., stock raising; grain, peanuts, corn, cotton, hay, fruit, truck; cattle, horses, mules, goats, sheep, hogs, poultry; extensive dairying. Clay mining, limestone quarrying; some coal. Processing, mfg. at Decatur. Formed 1856. **2** County (□ 414; pop. 56,336), SW Va.; ⊙ Wise. In the Alleghenies, with the Cumberlands NW, along Ky. line; drained by Powell and short Pound rivers; bounded SE by Clinch R. Includes part of Jefferson Natl. Forest. Bituminous-coal fields, iron mines; agr. (grain, livestock, fruit, tobacco, dairy products); timber. Mtn. resorts. Formed 1856.

Wise, town (pop. 1,574), ⊙ Wise co., SW Va., in the Cumberlands near Ky. line, 4 mi. NE of Norton; trade center for bituminous-coal and agr. area. Settled as Big Glades; later named Gladeville; renamed Wise in 1924. Damaged by Union troops in Civil War.

Wiseman, village (1939 pop. 53), N central Alaska, on upper Koyukuk R. and 55 mi. NE of Bettles; 67°25'N 150°7'W; supply center for rich placer gold region; fur-trading post.

Wishaw, Scotland: see MOTHERWELL AND WISHAW.

Wishek (wĭ'shĕk), city (pop. 1,241), McIntosh co., S N.Dak., 18 mi. NNW of Ashley; dairy products, livestock, poultry, wheat.

Wishkah River (wĭsh'kŭ), SW Wash., rises in Olympic Natl. Forest, flows c.40 mi. S to Chehalis R. at Aberdeen.

Wislana, Mierzeja, Poland and USSR: see VISTULA SPIT.

Wislane, Zulawy, Poland: see VISTULA RIVER.

Wislany, Zalew, Poland and USSR: see VISTULA LAGOON.

Wisla River, Poland: see VISTULA RIVER.

Wisloka River (vēswô'kä), Pol. *Wisłoka*, SE Poland, rises in the Carpathians 21 mi. S of Jaslo, on Czechoslovak border; flows c.95 mi. N, past Jaslo, Debica, and Mielec, to Vistula R. 7 mi. SW of Baranow.

Wislok River (vēs'wôk), Pol. *Wisłok*, SE Poland, rises in the Carpathians 17 mi. SW of Sanok, near Czechoslovak border; flows NNW, past Krosno, and generally NE, past Strzyzow and Rzeszow, to San R. 4 mi. NW of Sieniawa; c.60 mi. long.

Wismar, village (pop., including adjoining Christianburg, 1,458), Demerara co., N central Br. Guiana, landing on left bank of Demerara R. and 3 mi. NW of Mackenzie, 55 mi. SSW of Georgetown. Railroad to Rockstone (16 mi. W) on the Essequibo; ships gold and balata to Georgetown.

Wismar (vĭs'mär), city (pop. 42,018), Mecklenburg, N Germany, port on Wismar Bay of the Baltic, 35 mi. E of Lübeck; 53°53'N 11°28'E. Fishing center; shipbuilding, sugar refining, distilling, metalworking; mfg. of railroad cars, machinery, food products. Has several Gothic churches and 15th–17th-cent. warehouses and residences. First mentioned as town in 1229; residence (1256–1306) of princes of Mecklenburg. Was member of Hanseatic League, with important trade in herring and beer. Passed to Sweden under Treaty of Westphalia (1648). Pledged (1803) to Mecklenburg with right of recall within 100 years; Sweden renounced (1903) all rights to city. Captured by British in May, 1945; later occupied by Soviet troops. Second World War destruction about 25%.

Wismar Bay, N Germany, S arm of Mecklenburg Bay of the Baltic, extends 10 mi. inland to Wismar. Entrance (13 mi. wide) sheltered by Poel isl.

Wisner (wĭz'nŭr). **1** Village (pop. 738), Franklin parish, NE La., 45 mi. SE of Monroe, in agr. area; cotton gins, lumber mills. **2** City (pop. 1,233), Cuming co., NE Nebr., 25 mi. E of Norfolk and on Elkhorn R.; livestock center, shipping point in rich agr. region; dairy and poultry produce, grain. Platted 1871.

Wisniowiec, Ukrainian SSR: see VISHNEVETS.

Wisowitz, Czechoslovakia: see VIZOVICE.

Wissahickon Creek (wĭ'sŭhĭ"kŭn), SE Pa., rises near Lansdale in Montgomery co., flows c.40 mi. S, through Philadelphia, to Schuylkill R. In Philadelphia, scenic Wissahickon Valley (c.7 mi. long) is recreational area.

Wissant (vēsā'), village (pop. 860), Pas-de-Calais dept., N France, bathing resort on Strait of Dover near Cape Gris-Nez, 9 mi. WSW of Calais. Atop near-by Cape Blanc-Nez (3 mi. NNE; 440 ft. high) is monument commemorating Allied naval cooperation in First World War.

Wissek, Poland: see WYSOKA.

Wissembourg (vēsäbōōr'), Ger. *Weissenburg* (vī'sŭnbōōrk), town (pop. 4,277), Bas-Rhin dept., E France, on the Lauter and Ger. border, and 32 mi. NNE of Strasbourg, 20 mi. W of Karlsruhe; custom station; road center; food preserving (jams, *pâté de foie gras*), furniture and rubber mfg. Winegrowing on slopes of N Vosges Mts. Grew up around 7th-cent. Benedictine abbey. Became free imperial city in 1255. French were defeated here (1870) in Franco-Prussian War.

Wissen links der Sieg (vĭ'sŭn lĭngks' dĕr sēk'), village (pop. 4,630), in former Prussian Rhine Prov., W Germany, after 1945 in Rhineland-Palatinate, on left bank of the Sieg and 14 mi. WSW of Siegen.

Wissen rechts der Sieg (rĕkhts' dĕr sēk'), village (pop. 4,612), in former Prussian Rhine Prov., W Germany, after 1945 in Rhineland-Palatinate, on right bank of the Sieg and 14 mi. WSW of Siegen.

Wissington, England: see NAYLAND WITH WISSINGTON.

Wissmann Falls (vēsmän'), series of rapids in Kasai R., S Belgian Congo, c.10 mi. SW of Charlesville, circumvented by Charlesville-Makumbi railroad.

Wissota, Lake (wĭsō'tŭ), Chippewa co., W central Wis., just E of Chippewa Falls; formed by backwater from power dam at Chippewa Falls; 4 mi. long, 2 mi. wide.

Wister, town (pop. 729), Le Flore co., SE Okla., 8 mi. SW of Poteau, in agr. area; cotton ginning. Wister Dam is just S, on POTEAU RIVER.

Wiston, agr. village and parish (pop. 568), central Pembroke, Wales, 5 mi. ENE of Haverfordwest.

Wisznia River (vēsh'nyä), Rus. *Vishnya* (vēsh'nyŭ), W Ukrainian SSR and SE Poland, rises 13 mi. N of Sambor (Ukrainian SSR), flows E past Rudki, and NW past Sudovaya Vishnya, into Poland to San R. 12 mi. NNE of Przemysl; c.50 mi. long.

Witbank (wĭt'băngk, Afrikaans vĭt'bängk), town (pop. 12,900), S Transvaal, U. of So. Afr., 65 mi. E of Pretoria; alt. 5,322 ft.; coal-mining center; site of Union's largest electric-power station; carbide, cyanide mfg. Airfield.

Witchampton, town and parish (pop. 455), E Dorset, England, 4 mi. NNW of Wimborne Minster; paper milling. Has 15th-cent. church. Traces of Roman occupation have been found here.

Witham (wĭ'tŭm), urban district (1931 pop. 4,367; 1951 census 8,598), central Essex, near Blackwater R., 9 mi. NE of Chelmsford; agr. market, with chemical works. Has 13th–15th-cent. church.

Witham River (wĭ'dhŭm), Lincolnshire, England, rises in Rutland near the co. boundary, flows N past Grantham to Lincoln, thence E and SE, past Boston to The Wash. Length, 80 mi.

Withee (wĭ'thē), village (pop. 421), Clark co., central Wis., 45 mi. ENE of Eau Claire, in dairying and stock-raising area.

Witherbee (wĭ'dhŭrbē), village (1940 pop. 1,288), Essex co., NE N.Y., in the Adirondacks, near L. Champlain, 18 mi. NNW of Ticonderoga, in iron-mining region.

Withernsea (wĭ'dhŭrnsē, -dhrŭnsē), urban district (1931 pop. 4,251; 1951 census 5,101), East Riding, SE Yorkshire, England, on North Sea 15 mi. E of Hull; seaside resort. Has 15th-cent. church.

Witherspoon, Mount (12,023 ft.), S Alaska, in Chugach Mts., 40 mi. WNW of Valdez; 61°24'N 147°12'W.

Withington, S suburb of Manchester, SE Lancashire, England; has cotton and engineering industries.

Withlacoochee River (wĭth"lŭkōō'chē). **1** In central Fla., rises in Polk co. in swampy area E of Polk City, flows W and N to Dunnellon, then W to Gulf of Mexico near Yankeetown; total length c.160 mi. Receives outlet of L. Panasoffkee. Channel dredged for 85 mi. above mouth. **2** In Ga. and Fla., rises in Tift co., S central Ga., flows c.115 mi. SSE, into Fla., to Suwannee R. 14 mi. SE of Madison, Fla. Receives Little River (c.80 mi. long) just NW of Valdosta, Ga.

Withnell, urban district (1931 pop. 3,040; 1951 census 2,923), central Lancashire, England, 5 mi. SW of Blackburn; cotton milling, paper milling. Site of 3 Liverpool reservoirs.

Withyham (wĭ'dhĭhăm), town and parish (pop. 2,724), NE Sussex, England, 7 mi. E of East Grinstead; agr. market. The 17th-cent. church has tombs of Sackville family.

Witkowitz, Czechoslovakia: see OSTRAVA.

Witkowo (vētkô'vô), town (1946 pop. 2,703), Poznan prov., W central Poland, 10 mi. SE of Gniezno; machine mfg., distilling, sawmilling; trades in cattle, grain.

Witley, residential town and parish (pop. 4,284), SW Surrey, England, 7 mi. SSW of Guildford; agr. market. Church is of Saxon origin. George Eliot lived here.

Witney, urban district (1931 pop. 3,409; 1951 census 6,553), W Oxfordshire, England, 10 mi. WNW of Oxford; agr. market, with woolen mills (blankets). Has Butter Cross (1683), grammar school founded 1663, and medieval church.

Witnica (vētnē'tsä), Ger. *Vietz* (fēts), town (1939 pop. 5,623; 1946 pop. 2,599) in Brandenburg, after 1945 in Zielona Gora prov., W Poland, near the Warta, 15 mi. WSW of Landsberg (Gorzow Wielkopolski); mfg. of agr. implements, furniture, syrup. First mentioned 1262; chartered 1935. In Second World War, c.65% destroyed.

Witt, city (pop. 1,156), Montgomery co., S central Ill., 16 mi. ENE of Litchfield, in agr. and bituminous-coal area. Inc. 1911.

Wittdün (vĭt'dün"), village (pop. 845), in Schleswig-Holstein, NW Germany, harbor at S tip of Amrum isl., 3 mi. SE of Nebel; North Sea resort; fishing.

Witteberge (vĭ'tŭbĕr"khŭ), mountain range, E Cape Prov., U. of So. Afr., part of the Drakensberg, extends c.50 mi. E from Lady Grey; rises to 9,090 ft. on Snowden, 18 mi. NNW of Barkly East.

Wittebergen (vĭ'tŭbĕr"khŭ), mountain range, SW Cape Prov., U. of So. Afr., extends 50 mi. E from Touws River, continued E by Swartberg range. Rises to 5,062 ft. 13 mi. SW of Laingsburg.

Wittelsheim (vētŭlzĕm', Ger. wĭ'tŭls-hīm), commune (pop. 7,145), Haut-Rhin dept., E France, 7 mi. NW of Mulhouse; potash mining.

Witten (vĭ'tŭn), city (1950 pop. 76,351), in former Prussian prov. of Westphalia, W Germany, after 1945 in North Rhine-Westphalia, on the Ruhr (head of navigation), bet. Dortmund (N,E) and Hagen (S); steel-mfg. center; extraction of coal-tar products; glassworks. Second World War destruction c.45%. Chartered 1825.

Witten, S.Dak.: see NEW WITTEN.

Wittenbach (vĭ'tŭnbäkh), town (pop. 2,193), St. Gall canton, NE Switzerland, 2 mi. N of St. Gall; textiles (cotton, silk), embroideries, metalworking.

Wittenberg (wĭ'tŭnbûrg, Ger. vĭ'tŭnbĕrk), city (pop. 41,304), in former Prussian Saxony prov., central Germany, after 1945 in Saxony-Anhalt, on the Elbe and 55 mi. SW of Berlin; 51°52'N 12°39'E. Rail center. On door of 15th-cent. castle church, Luther (buried here) nailed (Oct. 31, 1517) his Ninety-Five Theses, launching 1st phase of the Reformation. In market place, Luther publicly burned (1520) papal bull condemning him. City has 14th-cent. town church; Luther's residence, now mus. Paper milling, distilling; mfg. of machinery, soap, pottery, chocolate, jam. Important chemical works at Piesteritz, just W. First mentioned c.1180. Was capital (1273–1422) of Ascanian dukes of Saxe-Wittenberg (after 1356 electors of SAXONY); then passed to house of Wettin. Univ. founded here in 1502 was absorbed by Univ. of Halle in 1817; among its noted teachers were Luther, Melanchthon, Bugenhagen, and Justus Jonas. Lucas Cranach the Elder here established school of painting. First complete Lutheran Bible printed here in 1534. In Schmalkaldic War, city was captured (1547) by Emperor Charles V after battle of Mühlberg. By the Capitulation of Wittenberg (1547), Albertine line of house of Wettin received all lands of Ernestine line, which retained only the Thuringian duchies. Taken 1813 by French; stormed by Prussians in 1814; passed to Prussia in 1815.

Wittenberg, Russian SFSR: see NIVENSKOYE.

Wittenberg. 1 Town (pop. 54), Perry co., E Mo., on Mississippi R., just NW of Grand Tower, Ill. **2** Village (pop. 961), Shawano co., E central Wis., 25 mi. ESE of Wausau; sawmilling, flour and feed milling, cheese making.

Wittenberg, Mount (3,802 ft.), Ulster co., SE N.Y., in the Catskills.

Wittenberge (vĭ'tůnbĕr"gů), city (pop. 31,485), Brandenburg, E Germany, on the Elbe at mouth of Stepenitz R., and 75 mi. NW of Berlin, 80 mi. SE of Hamburg; 53°N 11°46'E. Rail and commercial center; railroad workshops; woolen milling, metalworking, oil refining, synthetic-fiber mfg. Has 13th-cent. town gate.

Wittenburg (vĭ'tůnbŏŏrk), town (pop. 6,689), Mecklenburg, N Germany, 16 mi. WSW of Schwerin; mfg. of barrels, cloth shoes, chocolate; agr. market (stock, grain, potatoes). Has remains of old town walls and gates. Founded in 13th cent. In Thirty Years War, captured (1642) by Imperial forces.

Wittenheim (vētůněm', Ger. vĭ'tůnhīm), town (pop. 2,104), Haut-Rhin dept., E France, 4 mi. N of Mulhouse; potash mining.

Wittgensdorf (vĭt'gůnsdôrf), village (pop. 7,350), Saxony, E central Germany, 5 mi. NW of Chemnitz; hosiery knitting, cotton milling.

Wittgenstein Island, Tuamotu Isls.: see FAKARAVA.

Wittichenau (vĭ'tĭ-khůnou"), town (pop. 3,362), in former Prussian Lower Silesia prov., E central Germany, after 1945 in Saxony, in Upper Lusatia, on the Black Elster and 10 mi. NE of Kamenz, in lignite-mining region.

Wittingau, Czechoslovakia: see TREBON.

Wittingen (vĭ'tĭng-ůn), town (pop. 4,789), in former Prussian prov. of Hanover, NW Germany, after 1945 in Lower Saxony, 32 mi. NNE of Brunswick; rail junction; food processing (flour products, canned goods, beverages); mfg. of chemicals.

Wittlage (vĭt'lä"gů), village (pop. 517), in former Prussian prov. of Hanover, NW Germany, after 1945 in Lower Saxony, on Ems-Weser Canal and 22 mi. W of Minden.

Wittlich (vĭt'lĭkh), town (pop. 6,994), in former Prussian Rhine Prov., W Germany, after 1945 in Rhineland-Palatinate, 19 mi. NE of Trier; vineyards; tobacco.

Wittmannsgereuth (vĭt'mänsgůroit'), village (pop. 174), Thuringia, central Germany, at foot of Thuringian Forest, 3 mi. WSW of Saalfeld; iron mining.

Wittmund (vĭt'mŏŏnt), town (pop. 4,874), in former Prussian prov. of Hanover, NW Germany, after 1945 in Lower Saxony, in East Friesland, 14 mi. WNW of Wilhelmshaven; woodworking, food processing.

Wittstock (vĭt'shtŏk), town (pop. 9,460), Brandenburg, E Germany, on Dosse R. and 30 mi. WSW of Neustrelitz; woolen milling, woodworking, machinery mfg. Has 13th-cent. church, 14th-cent. chapel, and old town walls. First mentioned 946. Swedes under Banér here defeated (Oct., 1636) Saxon and imperial forces under Hatzfeld.

Witu (wē'tŏŏ), town, Coast Prov., SE Kenya, on road and 9 mi. NW of Kipini; sisal, copra, rice.

Witu Islands, Bismarck Archipelago: see VITU ISLANDS.

Witwatersrand (wĭtwô'tůrzrănd, Afrikaans vĭtvä"tůrsränt') [Afrikaans,=white water ridge] or **The Rand,** region (□ c.1,000; pop. 1,435,093), S Transvaal, U. of So. Afr., on rocky ridge (5–6,000 ft. high) extending c.150 mi. E-W, centered on Johannesburg. Through the almost continuously urban region in central part of ridge runs a gold-bearing reef which produces about one-third of world's gold. Main towns (E-W) are Springs, Brakpan, Benoni, Boksburg, Germiston, Johannesburg, Roodepoort-Maraisburg, Krugersdorp, and Randfontein, all connected by dense railroad network. Apart from gold, refined at central plant at Germiston, coal and manganese are mined in region, which also has numerous ancillary and mfg. industries. Surface gold discovered 1884; Witwatersrand officially proclaimed gold field 1886, when mining operations began and Johannesburg was founded. In 1889, the main reef was reached at depth of 581 ft. Abandonment of gold standard (1931–32) by most European countries and subsequently by U. of So. Afr., and U.S. program of unlimited gold purchases (1934) made mining to depth of c.12,000 ft. profitable and gave important stimulus to the industry.

Witzenhausen (vĭ"tsůnhou'zůn), town (pop. 8,031), in former Prussian prov. of Hesse-Nassau, W Germany, after 1945 in Hesse, on the Werra and 13 mi. NW of Eschwege; cherries. Has 14th-cent. church.

Wiveliscombe (wĭ'vůlĭskům, wĭls'–), former urban district (1931 pop. 1,262), W Somersert, England, 6 mi. NW of Wellington; agr. market; electrical-equipment works, woolen mills, breweries.

Wivelsfield (wĭ'vůlzfēld), town and parish (pop. 2,732), central Sussex, England, 3 mi. S of Haywards Heath; agr. market. Has Norman church with 14th–15th-cent. tower.

Wivenhoe (wĭ'vůnhō), urban district (1931 pop. 2,193; 1951 census 2,381), NE Essex, England, on Colne R. estuary and 3 mi. SE of Colchester; fishing port; fish canneries. Oyster beds near by.

Wizernes (vēzărn'), village (pop. 1,698), Pas-de-Calais dept., N France, on the Aa and 3 mi. SSW of Saint-Omer; paper milling. Damaged in Second World War.

Wkra River (fkrä), NE Poland, rises 4 mi. NW of Nidzica, flows SW past Nidzica and Dzialdowo, and SE to Narew R. 2 mi. ENE of (opposite) Nowy Dwor Mazowiecki; 164 mi. long. In upper course, in former East Prussia, also called Nida, Ger. *Neide,* in middle course Dzialdowka, Pol. *Działdowka.*

Wlaschim, Czechoslovakia: see VLASIM.

Wlen (vlĕ'nyů), Pol. *Wleń,* Ger. *Lähn* (lĕn), town (1939 pop. 1,470; 1946 pop. 1,455) in Lower Silesia, after 1945 in Wroclaw prov., SW Poland, on Bobrawa R. and 9 mi. NNW of Hirschberg (Jelenia Gora); climatic health resort. Has remains of 12th-cent. castle, destroyed (1646) in Thirty Years War by imperial forces. After 1945, briefly called Lenno.

Wlingi (vlĭng'ē), town (pop. 10,383), SE Java, Indonesia, 25 mi. SE of Kediri; trade center for agr. area (coffee, tobacco, rubber, corn, cinchona bark).

Wlochy (vwô'khĭ), Pol. *Włochy,* residential town (pop. 18,105), Warszawa prov., E central Poland, on railroad and 5 mi. WSW of Warsaw city center.

Wloclawek (vwôtswä'vĕk), Pol. *Włocławek,* Rus. *Vlotslavsk* (vlůtsläfsk'), city (1950 pop. 54,650), Bydgoszcz prov., central Poland, on the Vistula and 65 mi. N of Lodz. Chief town of the fertile Kujawy; rail junction; mfg. of machinery, organs, bricks, pottery, paper, cartons, cellulose, tar, fertilizer, dyes, chocolate; sawmilling, tanning, chicory drying, flour milling, distilling. Salt domes, lignite deposits, sulphur springs near by. Founded 12th cent.; became bishopric; sacked (1329, 1431) by Teutonic Knights. Has 14th-cent. Gothic cathedral. In Rus. Poland, 1815–1918, near Prussian frontier. Developed rapidly at end of 19th cent. In Second World War, under Ger. rule, called Leslau.

Wlodawa (vwôdä'vä), Pol. *Włodawa,* Rus. *Vlodava* (vlůdä'vů), town (pop. 4,438), Lublin prov., E Poland, on Bug R. and 50 mi. ENE of Lublin. Pol. frontier station opposite Tomashevka (Belorussian SSR); mfg. of agr. machinery, bricks; tanning, flour milling. Before Second World War, pop. over 50% Jewish.

Wlodzimierz, Ukrainian SSR: see VLADIMIR-VOLYNSKI.

Wlodzimierzec, Ukrainian SSR: see VLADIMIRETS.

Wloszczowa (vwôshchô'vä), Pol. *Włoszczowa,* Rus. *Vloshchova* (vlůshchô'vů), town (pop. 4,683), Kielce prov., S central Poland, 29 mi. W of Kielce; road junction; mfg. of bricks, agr. machinery; flour milling, sawmilling.

Wnion River (ōōn'yŏn), Merioneth, Wales, rises 8 mi. NE of Dolgelley, flows 11 mi. SW, past Dolgelley, to Mawddach R. just NW of Dolgelley.

Wöbbelin (vûbůlēn'), village (pop. 902), Mecklenburg, N Germany, 5 mi. N of Ludwigslust. Poet Theodor Körner, killed (1813) in battle near by, is buried here.

Woburn (wŏŏ'bûrn), town and parish (pop. 951), SW Bedford, England, 5 mi. NNE of Leighton Buzzard; agr. market. Near by is Woburn Abbey, seat of duke of Bedford, with 18th-cent. mansion containing art collection. Built on site of 1145 Cistercian abbey. An agr. experiment station established here 1876. Woburn was site of an Eleanor Cross. For a short time Charles I was prisoner here.

Woburn. 1 (wō'bůrn, wŏŏ'bůrn) Residential city (pop. 20,492), Middlesex co., E Mass., 10 mi. NNW of Boston; mfg. (machinery, leather, food products, fertilizer, tools); floriculture. Settled 1640, inc. as town 1642, as city 1888. **2** (wō'bûrn) Village (pop. 17), Burke co., N N.Dak., 8 mi. W of Bowbells.

Woburn Sands (wō'–), agr. village and parish (pop. 1,156), NE Buckingham, England, 3 mi. NE of Bletchley.

Wocheiner Sau, river, Yugoslavia: see SAVA BOHINJKA RIVER.

Wocheiner See, Yugoslavia: see BOHINJ LAKE.

Woden, town (pop. 272), Hancock co., N Iowa, 20 mi. NE of Algona; livestock, grain.

Wodnian, Czechoslovakia: see VODNANY.

Wodonga (wōdŏng'gů), town (pop. 2,806), NE Victoria, Australia, 160 mi. NE of Melbourne, near Hume Reservoir, in livestock area; wool, dairy products.

Wodzislaw or **Wodzislaw Slaski** (wôjē'swäf shlō'skē), Pol. *Wodzisław Śląski,* Ger. *Loslau* (lô'slou), town (pop. 5,110), Katowice prov., S Poland, 8 mi. SSW of Rybnik; rail junction; mfg. of agr. machinery, cement goods, bricks; tanning, flour milling. Sanatorium.

Woerden (vōōr'důn), town (pop. 9,782), South Holland prov., W Netherlands, on Old Rhine R. and 9 mi. NE of Gouda; rail junction; machinery, metalware, refrigerators, heating installations, organs, lingerie; woodworking; shipbuilding.

Woerth or **Woerth-sur-Sauer** (vârt'-sür-sōär'), Ger. *Wörth* or *Wörth an der Sauer* (vûrt' än dĕr zou'ůr), village (pop. 1,165), Bas-Rhin dept., E France, on the Sauer and 9 mi. N of Haguenau; sawmilling. Here French were defeated (1870) in Franco-Prussian War.

Woëvre (vôĕ'vrů), tableland in Meuse and Meurthe-et-Moselle depts., NE France, bounded by Côtes de Meuse (W) and Côtes de Moselle (E), bet. Verdun, Metz, and Saint-Mihiel. Scene of severe fighting (1915 and 1918) in First World War.

Wohlau, Poland: see WOLOW.

Wohlen (vō'lůn), town (pop. 6,070), Aargau canton, N Switzerland, on Bünz R. and 12 mi. W of Zurich; straw goods, flour, clothes; metalworking.

Wohlen bei Bern (bī bĕrn'), town (pop. 2,811), Bern canton, W central Switzerland, on Wohlensee and 4 mi. WNW of Bern; farming.

Wohlensee (–zā"), lake (□ 1), Bern canton, W central Switzerland, on Aar R., W of Bern; formed 1920 by damming the Aar. Mühleberg hydroelectric plant is on it.

Wohoa Bay (wōhō'ů), Washington co., E Maine, inlet at mouth of Chandler R.; bounded by Jonesport on W, Roque Isl. on E; 7 mi. long, 2 mi. wide. Formerly Chandler Bay.

Woincourt (vwĕkōōr'), village (pop. 1,022), Somme dept., N France, 13 mi. WSW of Abbeville; aluminum and copper founding, locksmithing.

Woinville (vwĕvēl'), village (pop. 147), Meuse dept., NE France, in the Côtes de Meuse, 5 mi. E of Saint-Mihiel.

Woippy (vwäpē'), outer NNW suburb (pop. 1,873) of Metz, Moselle dept., NE France; iron founding, mfg. of electric kitchen ranges; strawberry shipping.

Woischnik, Poland: see WOZNIKI.

Wojnilow, Ukrainian SSR: see VOINILOV.

Wokam, Indonesia: see ARU ISLANDS.

Wokha (vō'kŭ), village, Naga Hills dist., E Assam, India, in Naga Hills, 31 mi. NNE of Kohima; rice, cotton, oranges. Tribal control post for Lhota Nagas.

Woking (wō'kĭng), village (pop. estimate 350), W Alta., near B.C. border, on Saddle R. and 30 mi. N of Grande Prairie; lumbering, farming; wheat.

Woking, residential urban district (1931 pop. 29,931; 1951 census 47,612), central Surrey, England, on Wey R. and 23 mi. SW of London; also makes electrical equipment and has printing industry. There are a church (dating from 12th cent.) and a Mohammedan mosque. Village of Brookwood, 4 mi. WSW, has large cemeteries, including American military cemetery where many soldiers of First World War are buried.

Wokingham (wō'kĭng-ům), municipal borough (1931 pop. 7,294; 1951 census 8,716), E Berkshire, England, 7 mi. ESE of Reading; agr. market, with electrical-appliance works. Rose Inn was frequented by Pope, Swift, and Gay. Has 17th-cent. almshouses and, near by, 17th-cent. hosp. In medieval times there were bell foundries, and in Elizabethan times a silk industry was established here.

Wola (vô'lä), industrial suburb of Warsaw, Warszawa prov., E central Poland, 2 mi. E of city center.

Wolbach (wôl'băk'), village (pop. 442), Greeley co., E central Nebr., 12 mi. SE of Greeley; dairy products, grain.

Wolbrom (vôl'brôm), town (pop. 5,437), Krakow prov., S Poland, on railroad and 24 mi. NNW of Cracow; mfg. of rubber products, enamelware; tanning, flour milling.

Wolcott. 1 (wŏŏl'kůt) Town (pop. 3,553), New Haven co., central Conn., 4 mi. NE of Waterbury; agr. Bronson Alcott b. near by. Settled 1731, inc. 1796. **2** (wŏŏl'kůt) Town (pop. 778), White co., NW central Ind., 36 mi. W of Logansport, in agr. area; tile, brick; limestone quarrying. **3** (wôl'kůt) Village (pop. 1,516), Wayne co., W N.Y., 22 mi. NNW of Auburn; agr. shipping point (fruit, truck, dairy products); mfg. (canned foods, metal products). Summer resort. Inc. 1873. **4** (wôl'kůt) Town (pop. 766), Lamoille co., N central Vt., on Lamoille R. and 23 mi. N of Barre; trade center for agr., lumbering region.

Wolcottville (wŏŏl'kůtvĭl, wŏl'–), town (pop. 672) on Noble-Lagrange co. line, NE Ind., 34 mi. NNW of Fort Wayne, in lake-resort and agr. area.

Wolczyn (vô'ŏŏ-chĭn), Pol. *Wołczyn,* Ger. *Konstadt* (kŏn'shtät), town (1939 pop. 3,777; 1946 pop. 2,072), in Upper Silesia, after 1945 in Opole prov., S Poland, 8 mi. WNW of Kluczbork; flax and hemp growing; yeast mfg.

Woldegk (vôl'dĕk), town (pop. 3,583), Mecklenburg, N Germany, 15 mi. ESE of Neubrandenburg; agr. market (grain, sugar beets, potatoes, stock); sugar refining, brick mfg. Has old town walls and gates.

Woldenberg, Poland: see DOBIEGNIEW.

Wolds (wōldz), range of chalk hills in Lincoln and Yorkshire, England, N and S of Humber R., paralleling the coast; rises to c.800 ft.

Woleai (wōlā-ī′), atoll (pop. 354), Yap dist., W Caroline Isls., W Pacific, 535 mi. W of Truk; 7°24′N 143°52′E; 23 islets. Formerly spelled Uleai.

Woleu-N'Tem, Fr. Equatorial Africa: see OYEM.

Woleu River, Gabon, Fr. Equatorial Africa: see BENITO RIVER.

Wolfach (vôl′fäkh), town (pop. 2,627), S Baden, Germany, in Black Forest, on the Kinzig and 9 mi. NW of Schramberg; metal- and woodworking, lumber milling. Climatic health resort (alt. 863 ft.). Has 17th-cent. castle.

Wolf Creek. 1 In E central Iowa, rises in Grundy co., flows c.60 mi. S, E, and ENE to Cedar R. near La Porte City. **2** In Texas and Okla., rises in Ochiltree co. in N Texas, flows E into Okla., then NE, past Gage, to North Canadian R. at Fort Supply; c.110 mi. long. FORT SUPPLY DAM is near its mouth.

Wolf Creek Dam, S Ky., in Cumberland R., 12 mi. N of Albany. Key unit in program for development of Cumberland R. basin; 240 ft. high, 5,736 ft. long; for flood control and power. Closure effected 1950; dam and hydroelectric plant scheduled for completion in 1951; forms Wolf Creek Reservoir (max. □ 100; capacity 6,089,000 acre-ft.; length 100 mi.).

Wolf Creek Pass, Colo.: see SAN JUAN MOUNTAINS.

Wolfe, county (□ 680; pop. 17,492), S Que., on St. Francis and Nicolet rivers; ⊙ Ham Sud.

Wolfe, county (□ 227; pop. 7,615), E central Ky.; ⊙ Campton. In Cumberland foothills; drained by Red R. and North Fork Kentucky R. Mtn. agr. area (livestock, fruit, tobacco). Includes NATURAL BRIDGE STATE PARK and part of Cumberland Natl. Forest. Formed 1860.

Wolfeboro, town (pop. 2,581), including Wolfeboro village (pop. 1,271), Carroll co., E N.H., on SE L. Winnipesaukee, 13 mi. ENE of Laconia. Summer resort, trade center, lake port; mfg. (wood products, shoes, clothing); lumber, fruit. Winter sports. Seat of Brewster Acad. Settled c.1760.

Wolfe City, town (pop. 1,345), Hunt co., NE Texas, 16 mi. N of Greenville; rail, trade center in cotton, grain, cattle area; flour, cottonseed-oil milling, cotton ginning. Inc. 1873.

Wolfe Island (□ 48), SE Ont., at head of L. Ontario, at entrance to the St. Lawrence, opposite Kingston. Largest of the Thousand Isls.; 18 mi. long, ⅙ mi. wide. Heavily wooded until end of 19th cent., now intensively cultivated; popular resort. Just S is U.S. boundary line.

Wolfen (vôl′fün), town (pop. 11,458), in former Prussian Saxony prov., central Germany, after 1945 in Saxony-Anhalt, 4 mi. NNW of Bitterfeld; lignite mining. Mfg.: photographic film, chemicals (dyes, cellulose, chlorine), rayon, synthetic fertilizer. Power station.

Wolfenbüttel (vôl′fünbü″tül), town (pop. 31,546), in Brunswick, NW Germany, after 1945 in Lower Saxony, on the Oker and 7 mi. S of Brunswick; rail junction; mfg. of agr. machinery, limekilns, soap; canning, distilling. Truck produce (fruit, vegetables). Seat of noted library (founded in mid-17th cent.) containing c.350,000 volumes, 3,000 incunabula, and over 7,000 manuscripts; Lessing was chief librarian here (1770–81). Has 15th–18th-cent. former palace, now housing several schools; 17th-cent. church; Lessing's house, where he wrote *Nathan the Wise;* many 17th-cent., half-timbered houses. Developed around a castle, which became (c.1280) favorite Guelph residence. Chartered 1540. Captured 1542 by Schmalkaldic League. A center of Ger. culture in 17th cent. Residence of dukes of Brunswick-Wolfenbüttel until 1753.

Wölfersheim (vûl′fürs-hīm), village (pop. 2,394), central Hesse, W Germany, in former Upper Hesse prov., 4 mi. NE of Bad Nauheim; lignite-fed power plant.

Wolfgangsee, Austria: see SANKT WOLFGANGSEE.

Wolfhagen (vôlf′hä″gün), town (pop. 5,124), in former Prussian prov. of Hesse-Nassau, W Germany, after 1945 in Hesse, 13 mi. W of Kassel; lumber. Has 15th–18th-cent. castle.

Wolfhalden (–häl″dün), town (pop. 2,159), Appenzell Ausser Rhoden half-canton, NE Switzerland, 9 mi. ENE of St. Gall; silk textiles, embroideries.

Wolf Lake. 1 Village (pop. 1,591), Muskegon co., SW Mich., 8 mi. ENE of Muskegon. **2** Village (pop. 109), Becker co., W Minn., 23 mi. E of Detroit Lakes.

Wolf Lake, in NE Ill. and NW Ind., on state line and partly within SE Chicago; c.3 mi. long. Amusement park, race track here.

Wolf Neck, SW Maine, peninsula extending 3 mi. into Casco Bay, near Freeport; resort area.

Wolford (wŏŏl′fürd), village (pop. 140), Pierce co., N central N.Dak., 16 mi. NE of Rugby.

Wolf Point, city (pop. 2,557), Roosevelt co., NE Mont., on Missouri R. and 20 mi. W of Poplar; wheat-shipping point; coal mines, oil wells; flour, dairy products. Radio broadcasting station and subagency of Fort Peck Indian Reservation are here. Has annual July rodeo. Settled 1878, inc. 1915.

Wolframs-Eschenbach (vôl′främs-ĕ′shünbäkh), town (pop. 1,519), Middle Franconia, W Bavaria, Germany, 8 mi. SE of Ansbach; rye, wheat, cattle, hogs. Has medieval walls; church from 2d half of 13th cent. with late-14th-cent. tower; old paneled town hall (1471), new Renaissance town hall. Home of minnesinger Wolfram von Eschenbach. Chartered 1332, town belonged to Teutonic Knights from mid-13th cent. until 1796. Until 1917, called Eschenbach.

Wolfratshausen (vôl″fräts-hou′zün), village (pop. 4,796), Upper Bavaria, Germany, on the Loisach and 17 mi. SW of Munich; glass mfg. and grinding, metalworking, lumber milling. First mentioned in 8th cent.; chartered 1312.

Wolf River. 1 In S Miss., rises in N Pearl River co., flows c.60 mi. SE and SW to St. Louis Bay of Mississippi Sound. **2** In N Miss. and SW Tenn., rises 11 mi. NE of Ashland, in Benton co., N Miss.; flows WNW across SW corner of Tenn., past Moscow and Rossville, to Mississippi R. at Memphis; c.100 mi. long. **3** In NE Wis., rises in Forest co., flows generally S, past Shawano and New London, widens into L. Poygan, and reaches Fox R. 10 mi. above Oshkosh; c.220 mi. long. Receives Embarrass R. at New London. Formerly important for log driving.

Wolfsberg (vôlfs′bĕrk), town (pop. 8,411), Carinthia, S Austria, on Lavant R. and 29 mi. NE of Klagenfurt; ironworks; leather goods, breweries, flour mills. Summer resort. Large paper mill near by.

Wolfsburg (vôlfs′bŏŏrk), town (pop. 18,924), in former Prussian prov. of Hanover, NW Germany, after 1945 in Lower Saxony, on Weser-Elbe Canal and 16 mi. NE of Brunswick; automobile mfg. (Volkswagen); repair shops; metalworking. Founded 1938.

Wolfsegg (vôlfs′ĕk), town (pop. 2,661), central Upper Austria, 7 mi. N of Vöcklabruck; lignite mined near by.

Wolfshagen (vôlfs″hä′gün), village (pop. 3,074), in Brunswick, NW Germany, after 1945 in Lower Saxony, on N slope of the upper Harz, 5 mi. W of Goslar; woodworking; resort.

Wolfstein (vôlf′shtīn). **1** Village, Bavaria, Germany: see FREYUNG. **2** Town (pop. 1,405), Rhenish Palatinate, W Germany, on the Lauter and 12 mi. NW of Kaiserslautern; apples, pears, plums. Chartered 1257. Roman tombs and remains of bldgs. excavated near by.

Wolfurt (vôl′fŏŏrt), village (pop. 2,282), Vorarlberg, W Austria, on river Bregenzer Ache and 3 mi. S of Bregenz; embroidery.

Wolfville, town (pop. 1,944), N N.S., on SW shore of Minas Basin, at mouth of Cornwallis R., 7 mi. E of Kentville; agr. market in dairying, fruitgrowing region. Site of Acadia Univ. Extending S is the *Evangeline* district celebrated by Longfellow; Grand Pré is near by.

Wolgast (vôl′gäst), town (pop. 10,139), in former Prussian Pomerania prov., N Germany, after 1945 in Mecklenburg, on Peene R. estuary (bridge), opposite Usedom isl., and 16 mi. E of Greifswald; metal- and woodworking, shipbuilding; agr. market (grain, potatoes, stock). Has Gothic church. Chartered 1282; after 1293 residence of dukes of Pomerania-Wolgast. Passed to Sweden in 1648, to Prussia in 1815.

Wolhusen (vōl′hŏŏzün), town (pop. 2,948), Lucerne canton, central Switzerland, on Kleine Emme R. and 12 mi. W of Lucerne; chemicals, paper products, pastry. Consists of Wolhusen-Wiggern and Wolhusen-Markt.

Wolin (vô′lēn), Ger. *Wollin* (vô′lĭn), town (1939 pop. 4,800; 1946 pop. 2,369), in Pomerania, after 1945 in Szczecin prov., NW Poland, on SE shore of Wolin isl., on Dievenow arm of the Oder and 16 mi. ESE of Swinemünde (Swinoujscie); fishing port. In Second World War, c.50% destroyed. Bishopric founded here 1140 and moved (1175) to Kamien Pomorski. Town is one of reputed sites of anc. Wendish trading post of Vineta (also called Julin, Jumneta, or Jomsburg) mentioned (1075) as largest town in Europe; destroyed (1098) by Danes. According to legend, however, city was inundated by flood tide. Other sources locate Vineta at Peenemünde, Germany.

Wolin, Ger. *Wollin,* island (□ 95) in Pomerania, after 1945 in NW Poland, 30 mi. N of Stettin, bet. the Baltic (N) and Stettin Lagoon (S); separated from mainland (E) by the Dievenow (bridges), from Usedom isl. (W) by the Swine; 22 mi. long, 1–13 mi. wide; irregular coast line; generally lowland, with beech forests. Shipping, fisheries, and tourist trade are chief industries. Wolin (SE) is largest town; Miedzyzdroje (N) is main seaside resort. Odra Port (NW) is terminus of train ferry to Trelleborg, Sweden. Isl. passed 1648 to Sweden, 1720 to Prussia; in 1945, came under Pol. administration.

Wolkenstein (vôl′kün-shtīn), town (pop. 2,192), Saxony, E central Germany, in the Erzgebirge, 4 mi. W of Marienberg; woodworking, hosiery knitting, shoe and button mfg. Spa. Has castle, 1st mentioned in 13th cent.

Wolkersdorf (vôl′kürsdôrf), town (pop. 2,734), E Lower Austria, 12 mi. NNE of Vienna; vineyards.

Wolkowysk, Belorussian SSR: see VOLKOVYSK.

Wöllan, Yugoslavia: see VELENJE.

Wollaston (wŏŏ′lŭstŭn). **1** Town and parish (pop. 2,345), E Northampton, England, 3 mi. S of Wellingborough; shoe mfg. Has church dating from 14th cent. **2** Suburb, Worcester, England: see STOURBRIDGE.

Wollaston, Mass.: see QUINCY.

Wollaston, Cape (wŏŏ′lŭstŭn), SW Victoria Isl., SW Franklin Dist., Northwest Territories, on Amundsen Gulf, on S side of entrance of Minto Inlet; 71°4′N 118°8′W.

Wollaston Islands (wŏŏ′lŭstŭn), small group in S Tierra del Fuego, Chile, just N of Cape Horn; largest, Wollaston, rises to 3,200 ft.; 55°40′S 67°30′W.

Wollaston Lake (□ 768), NE Sask., near Man. border, 30 mi. NW of Reindeer L.; 58°N 103°W; 65 mi. long, 35 mi. wide; alt. 1,300 ft. Drains into Churchill and Mackenzie river systems.

Wollaston Peninsula (140 mi. long, 60–70 mi. wide), SW part of Victoria Isl., SW Franklin Dist., Northwest Territories, extending W into Amundsen Gulf bet. Prince Albert Sound (N) and Dolphin and Union Strait (S); Cape Baring (70°1′N 116°58′W) is its W extremity. Named Wollaston Land (1821) by Sir John Franklin, name was changed to Wollaston Peninsula by Geographic Board of Canada.

Wollega, Ethiopia: see WALLAGA.

Wöllersdorf (vûl′ürsdôrf), village (pop. 1,741), E Lower Austria, 5 mi. NW of Wiener Neustadt; rail junction; mfg. of machines.

Wollescote, England: see LYE AND WOLLESCOTE.

Wollin, Poland: see WOLIN.

Wollmeringen, France: see VOLMERANGE-LES-MINES.

Wollo, Ethiopia: see WALLO.

Wollomombi Falls (wŏlŭmŏm′bē) (1,700 ft.), in New South Wales, Australia, on headstream of Macleay R., in New England Range, 22 mi. E of Armidale.

Wollondilly River, Australia: see HAWKESBURY RIVER.

Wollongong (wŏŏ′lŭn-gông, wŭ′–), municipality (pop. 18,116), E New South Wales, Australia, 40 mi. S of Sydney; coal-mining center; steel mills. Its port is near-by Port Kembla.

Wollstein, Poland: see WOLSZTYN.

Wolmar, Latvia: see VALMIERA.

Wolmi Island, Korea: see CHEMULPO.

Wolmirsleben (vôl′mĭrslä″bün), village (pop. 2,764), in former Prussian Saxony prov., central Germany, after 1945 in Saxony-Anhalt, on the Bode and 14 mi. SW of Magdeburg; lignite and potash mining.

Wolmirstedt (vôl′mĭr-shtĕt), town (pop. 7,179), in former Prussian Saxony prov., central Germany, after 1945 in Saxony-Anhalt, on the Ohre and 9 mi. N of Magdeburg; sugar refining, mfg. of leather goods. In Thirty Years War, town was Tilly's hq. (1631) after capture of Magdeburg.

Wolmünster, France: see VOLMUNSTER.

Wolomin (vôwô′mēn), Pol. *Wołomin,* Rus. *Volomin* (vŭlô′myĭn), town (pop. 8,296), Warszawa prov., E central Poland, on railroad and 13 mi. NE of Warsaw; ironworks; mfg. of agr. machinery, glass, beds; tanning, flour milling.

Wolow (vô′wŏŏf), Pol. *Wołów,* Ger. *Wohlau* (vō′lou), town (1939 pop. 7,402; 1946 pop. 2,902) in Lower Silesia, after 1945 in Wroclaw prov., SW Poland, 20 mi. NW of Breslau (Wroclaw); agr. market (grain, sugar beets, potatoes, livestock); woodworking. Heavily damaged in Second World War. In Middle Ages, was ⊙ independent duchy.

Wolozyn, Belorussian SSR: see VOLOZHIN.

Wolseley (wŏŏlz′lē), village (pop. 394), SE South Australia, 165 mi. SE of Adelaide, near Victoria border; rail junction; agr. center; wheat.

Wolseley, town (pop. 901), SE Sask., 60 mi. E of Regina; grain elevators.

Wolsey (wŏŏl′zē), town (pop. 391), Beadle co., E central S.Dak., 12 mi. W of Huron and on branch of James R.; wheat, corn, rye.

Wolsingham (wŏl′sĭng-ŭm, wŏŏl′zĭng–), town and parish (pop. 3,127), W central Durham, England, on Wear R. and 13 mi. WSW of Durham; steel milling, marble quarrying.

Wolstanton United (wŏŏl′stăntŭn, wŏŏl′stŭn), former urban district (1931 pop. 30,525), NW Stafford, England, 3 mi. NW of Stoke-on-Trent; mfg. of pottery and tile; coal mining. Inc. 1932 in Newcastle-under-Lyme.

Wolstenholme (wŏ′stŭnhōm) or **Eric Cove,** trading post, NW Ungava Peninsula, NW Que., on Eric Cove, small inlet of Hudson Strait; 62°32′N 77°24′W; radio station. Cape Wolstenholme, NW extremity of Ungava Peninsula (62°34′N 77°30′W), is 5 mi. NW.

Wolstenholme Fjord (vôl′stŭnhôlmŭ), inlet (20 mi. long, 5–20 mi. wide) of N Baffin Bay, NW Greenland; 76°36′N 68°45′W. Extends E to edge of inland icecap, receiving Great Land Glacier. THULE settlement on S shore. Mouth protected by small Saunders and Wolstenholme isls.

Wolston (wŏŏl′stŭn), town and parish (pop. 918), E central Warwick, England, 5 mi. ESE of Coventry; plastics works. Has remains of 12th-cent. castle and of priory founded c.1090.

Wolsztyn (vôl′shtĭn), Ger. *Wollstein* (vôl′shtīn), town (1946 pop. 4,967), Poznan prov., W Poland, 40 mi. SW of Poznan; rail junction; flour milling, sawmilling, brewing, tanning, mfg. of machinery, copper goods, furniture.

Wolters, Camp, Texas: see Mineral Wells.

Woltersdorf (vôl'tûrsdôrf), village (pop. 5,765), Brandenburg, E Germany, bet. 2 small lakes, 16 mi. ESE of Berlin; excursion resort.

Woltorf (vôl'tôrf), village (pop. 1,885), in former Prussian prov. of Hanover, NW Germany, after 1945 in Lower Saxony, 3.5 mi. ESE of Peine; dairying. Formed Brunswick exclave until 1941.

Woluwe-Saint-Lambert (vôlüvü-sē-läbâr'), Flemish *Sint-Lambrechts-Woluwe* (sĭnt-läm'brĕkhs-vō'lüvü) residential town (pop. 26,504), Brabant prov., central Belgium, E suburb of Brussels. Anc. church has 12th-cent. tower.

Woluwe-Saint-Pierre (-pyâr'), Flemish *Sint-Pieters-Woluwe* (-pē'tûrs-), residential town (pop. 18,801), Brabant prov., central Belgium, ESE suburb of Brussels; site of racecourse.

Wolvega (vôl'väkhä), town (pop. 4,773), Friesland prov., N Netherlands, 7 mi. SE of Heerenveen; dairying center; meat packing; mfg. of rush-bottom chairs, reed furniture.

Wolvercote, England: see Oxford.

Wolverhampton (wŏŏl'vûrhămptûn), county borough (1931 pop. 133,212; 1951 census 162,669), SW Stafford, England, 13 mi. NW of Birmingham, one of the principal centers of the Black Country; industrial center with coal mines and mfg. of automobiles, tires, locomotives, aircraft, hardware, electrical products, rayon. St. Peter's church dates from 13th and 15th cent.; there is a grammar school founded in 16th cent. and a technical col. In the borough is industrial town of Bushbury.

Wolverine, village (pop. 318), Cheboygan co., N Mich., 19 mi. SE of Petoskey and on Sturgeon R., in resort and farm area.

Wolvertem (vôl'vûrtĕm), agr. village (pop. 4,359), Brabant prov., central Belgium, 8 mi. NNW of Brussels. Formerly spelled Wolverthem.

Wolverton (wŏŏl'vûrtûn), urban district (1931 pop. 12,873; 1951 census 13,421), N Buckingham, England, on Ouse R. and 17 mi. N of Aylesbury; has large railroad shops and railroad-personnel school. Medieval church has 14th-cent. tower. In urban dist. (W) is town of Stony Stratford (pop. 3,799), with leather industry; it was the site of an Eleanor Cross.

Wolverton, village (pop. 198), Wilkin co., W Minn., on Red R. and 22 mi. S of Fargo, N.Dak.; dairying.

Wolves, The, group of 5 islets in the Bay of Fundy, SW N.B., off Maine coast, 12 mi. NE of Eastport, 10 mi. NNE of Grand Manan; 44°57'N 66°41'W.

Wolxheim (vôlksĕm', Ger. vôlks'hīm), village (pop. 581), Bas-Rhin dept., E France, at E foot of the Vosges, on the Bruche and 2 mi. N of Molsheim; winegrowing.

Wolyn (vō'wĭnyü), Pol. *Wołyń*, former province (□ 13,795; 1931 pop. 2,081,501) of E Poland; ⊙ Luck. Formed 1921 out of W part of Rus. Volhynia govt.; occupied (1939) by USSR; became part of Rovno and Volyn oblasts of Ukrainian SSR.

Wolznach (vôlts'näkh), village (pop. 3,961), Upper Bavaria, Germany, 16 mi. SE of Ingolstadt; metal- and woodworking. Hops.

Woman Lake, Cass co., central Minn., c.40 mi. SW of Grand Rapids; 4 mi. long, 3 mi. wide. Has small inlet in N; drains into Leech L. Resorts.

Wombali, Belgian Congo: see Banningville.

Wombeyan Caves, Australia: see Taralga.

Wombwell (wŏŏm'bŭl, -wĕl), urban district (1931 pop. 18,367; 1951 census 18,837), West Riding, S Yorkshire, England, 4 mi. ESE of Barnsley; coal mining; has glass industry.

Womelsdorf. 1 (wŏŏ'mŭlzdôrf) Borough (pop. 1,549), Berks co., SE central Pa., 14 mi. W of Reading; textiles, bricks; nurseries. Settled 1723, laid out 1762, inc. 1833. **2** (wŏ'mŭlzdôrf) Town (pop. 407), Randolph co., E W.Va., 7 mi. WSW of Elkins.

Womens Bay, naval and naval air base on NE Kodiak Isl., S Alaska, on Womens Bay, inlet of Chiniak Bay of Gulf of Alaska, 10 mi. SW of Kodiak; 57°42'N 152°31'W.

Wommelgem (vô'mŭl-khŭm), residential town (pop. 5,603), Antwerp prov., N Belgium, 5 mi. E of Antwerp. Has 16th-cent. church.

Wondelgem (wŏn'dŭl-khĕm), town (pop. 5,718), East Flanders prov., NW Belgium, 3 mi. N of Ghent, near Ghent-Terneuzen Canal; chemical industry (sulphuric acid, metallic pigments).

Wonder Lake, village (pop. 1,072), McHenry co., NE Ill.

Wonersh (wŏ'nŭrsh), residential town and parish (pop. 2,190), W central Surrey, England, 3 mi. SSE of Guildford.

Wonewoc (wŏ'nüwŏk), village (pop. 961), Juneau co., S central Wis., on Baraboo R. and 28 mi. NW of Baraboo, in agr. area (dairy products; poultry, fruit); wood products.

Wong Chu, river, Bhutan: see Raidak River.

Wongrowitz, Poland: see Wagrowiec.

Wonju (wŭn'jōō'), Jap. *Genshu*, town (1949 pop. 33,978), Kangwon prov., central Korea, S of 38°N, 55 mi. ESE of Kyongsong; rice, soybeans.

Wonokromo, Indonesia: see Surabaya.

Wononskopomuc, Lake (wŏnŭnskŏ'pŭmŭk), NW Conn., resort lake in Salisbury town, 17 mi. NW of Torrington; c.1 mi. long. Lakeville village here.

Wonosobo or **Wanasaba** (both: wŏnŏsŏ'bŏ), town (pop. 10,701), central Java, Indonesia, 40 mi. NW of Jogjakarta, at foot of Mt. Sumbing; alt. 2,559 ft.; trade center for agr. area (rice, corn, tobacco, peanuts, cassava).

Wonreli, Indonesia: see Kisar.

Wonsan (wŭn'sän'), Jap. *Genzan* (gän'zä) and *Gensan* (gän'sä), city (1944 pop. 112,952), S.Hamgyong prov., N Korea, port on Yonghung Bay (inlet of E.Korea Bay), 90 mi. E of Pyongyang; commercial center for agr. and gold-mining area. Its deep, natural harbor is sheltered by narrow peninsula (site of airfield) opposite city. There are fish canneries, sake breweries, cement factories, railroad shops, and a marine products experiment station. Has agr. col. Exports fish, rice, soybeans, lumber, metalwork, graphite. Port opened 1883 to foreign trade. Heavily bombed in Korean War (1950–51).

Wonthaggi (wŏnthä'gē), municipality (pop. 4,225), Victoria, Australia, 65 mi. SSE of Melbourne, near S coast; rail terminus; chief coal-mining center of state.

Wooburn (wōō'bûrn, ōō'-), town and parish (pop. 4,723), S Buckingham, England, on Wye R. and 4 mi. SE of High Wycombe; paper industry. Has 14th–15th-cent. church. In parish (SW), on the Thames at mouth of the Wye, is town of Bourne End, producing paper and pharmaceuticals.

Woocalla, settlement, S South Australia, 110 mi. NNW of Port Pirie, on Trans-Australian RR; wool, salt.

Wood. 1 County (□ 618; pop. 59,605), NW Ohio; ⊙ Bowling Green. Bounded NW by Maumee R., and intersected by Portage R. Diversified farming (corn, wheat, livestock, poultry, oats, fruit). Mfg. at Bowling Green, North Baltimore, Perrysburg, Rossford. Limestone quarries, clay pits. Formed 1820. **2** County (□ 723; pop. 21,308), NE Texas; ⊙ Quitman. Bounded SW and S by Sabine R., drained by its tributaries. Agr. (especially fruit, truck; also sweet potatoes, corn, legumes, cotton, hay); extensive dairying, poultry raising; also cattle, hogs, horses. Extensive lumbering; large oil production; also natural gas, lignite, clay. Hunting, fishing. Formed 1850. **3** County (□ 368; pop. 66,540), W W.Va.; ⊙ Parkersburg. Bounded W by Ohio R. (Ohio line); drained by Little Kanawha R. Oil and natural-gas wells, bituminous coal, clay; agr. (livestock, tobacco, truck). Extensive mfg. at Parkersburg and Vienna. Formed 1798. **4** County (□ 812; pop. 50,500), central Wis.; ⊙ Wisconsin Rapids. Intersected by Wisconsin R.; also drained by Yellow R. Dairying and general farming area; cranberries; mfg. (chiefly paper and paper products). Formed 1856.

Wood. 1 Town (pop. 128), Franklin co., N central N.C., 15 mi. NE of Louisburg. **2** Town (pop. 260), Mellette co., S S.Dak., 14 mi. ESE of White River; ships grain, livestock.

Wood, Fort Leonard, Mo.: see Newburg.

Wood, Mount (15,880 ft.), SW Yukon, near Alaska border, 200 mi. WNW of Whitehorse; 61°15'N 140°33'W.

Wood, Mount, Mont.: see Beartooth Range.

Woodall Mountain, Tishomingo co., extreme NE Miss., near Iuka; highest point (806 ft.) in the state.

Woodbine. 1 Town (pop. 750), ⊙ Camden co., extreme SE Ga., 18 mi. SW of Brunswick and on Satilla R.; fishing, sawmilling, box mfg. **2** Town (pop. 1,304), Harrison co., W Iowa, on Boyer R. and 34 mi. NNE of Council Bluffs, in agr. area (apples, grain, livestock). Inc. 1877. **3** City (pop. 195), Dickinson co., central Kansas, 16 mi. SE of Abilene; grain, livestock. **4** Village (1940 pop. 628), Whitley co., SE Ky., in the Cumberlands, 3 mi. S of Corbin, in bituminous-coal-mining area. **5** Village (pop. c.175), Carroll co., N Md., on S branch of Patapsco R. and 25 mi. W of Baltimore; wormseed oil, canned vegetables. **6** Borough (pop. 2,417), Cape May co., SE N.J., 23 mi. SW of Atlantic City; mfg. (rubber products, clothing, hats). Belleplain State Forest is W. Inc. 1903. **7** Village (1940 pop. 8,180), Davidson co., central Tenn., SE suburb of Nashville.

Woodbridge, village (pop. 1,044), S Ont., on Humber R. and 12 mi. NW of Toronto; dairying, mixed farming.

Woodbridge, urban district (1931 pop. 4,734; 1951 census 5,310), SE Suffolk, England, on Deben R. estuary and 7 mi. ENE of Ipswich; agr. market. Has 15th-cent. church and many old houses. Edward Fitzgerald, b. in near-by village, spent his last years here.

Woodbridge. 1 Residential town (pop. 2,822), New Haven co., S Conn., just NW of New Haven; dairy products, fruit, truck, poultry. Settled before 1660, inc. 1784. **2** Township (pop. 35,758), Middlesex co., NE N.J., just N of Perth Amboy; mfg. (ceramics, bricks, chemicals, file cabinets, dairy products, carbonated beverages, brewery supplies); clay pits; boat yards. Settled 1665 by colonists from Mass., led by John Woodbridge; inc. 1669. Had sawmill in 1682, printing press in 1751. Includes villages of Fords, Sewaren, Port Reading, Hopelawn, and Keasbey.

Woodbrook, W section of Port of Spain, Trinidad, B.W.I.

Woodbrook, WSW residential suburb of East London, SE Cape Prov., U. of So. Afr., on Buffalo R.

Wood Buffalo National Park (□ 17,300), NE Alta. and S District of Mackenzie, just W of L. Athabaska, bounded E by Athabaska and Slave rivers. Vast unfenced forest region, with open plains and numerous lakes (including L. Claire), crossed by Peace R. Contains large herd of buffalo, as well as bear, beaver, caribou, deer, moose, waterfowl.

Woodburn. 1 Town (pop. 255), Clarke co., S Iowa, 9 mi. E of Osceola, in agr. area. **2** Town (pop. 240), Warren co., S Ky., 12 mi. SSW of Bowling Green, in agr. area. **3** City (pop. 2,395), Marion co., NW Oregon, 17 mi. NE of Salem, in berry-raising dist. of Willamette R. valley; fruit and vegetable canning, woodworking. State training school for boys is here. Inc. 1889.

Woodburn City or **Woodburn,** town (pop. 540), Allen co., NE Ind., 16 mi. ENE of Fort Wayne, near Ohio line. Until 1936, called Shirley City.

Woodburn Hills, village (pop. 2,500), Spartanburg co., NW S.C., residential suburb of Spartanburg.

Woodbury, agr. village and parish (pop. 1,637), SE Devon, England, 7 mi. SE of Exeter; limestone and sandstone quarries. Has 15th-cent. church. Site of Roman camp.

Woodbury, county (□ 866; pop. 103,917), W Iowa; ⊙ Sioux City. Bounded on W by Big Sioux R. (forms S.Dak. line here) and Missouri R. (forms Nebr. line here). Prairie agr. area (hogs, cattle, corn, oats, wheat) drained by Little Sioux and West Fork Little Sioux rivers. Includes state park. Industry at Sioux City. Formed 1851.

Woodbury. 1 Town (pop. 2,564), Litchfield co., W Conn., on Pomperaug R. and 8 mi. W of Waterbury; dairy products, machinery. Fine 18th-cent. houses, several old churches. Settled 1672, chartered 1674. **2** Town (pop. 985), Meriwether co., W Ga., 17 mi. WNW of Thomaston; food canning. **3** Town (pop. 94), Butler co., W central Ky., on Green R., near Barren R. mouth, and 16 mi. NW of Bowling Green. **4** City (pop. 10,391), ⊙ Gloucester co., SW N.J., 9 mi. SSW of Camden and on Woodbury Creek (navigable), c.4 mi. above its mouth on the Delaware; mfg. (luggage, clothing); truck farming. Its 18th-cent. buildings include Cooper and Lawrence houses and Friends' meetinghouse. Settled 1683, inc. as borough 1854, as city 1870. **5** Borough (pop. 254), Bedford co., S Pa., 18 mi. SSE of Altoona. **6** Town (pop. 1,000), ⊙ Cannon co., central Tenn., on East Fork of Stones R. and 19 mi. E of Murfreesboro; makes cheese, shirts. **7** Town (pop. 449), Washington co., N central Vt., 15 mi. NNE of Montpelier; lumber, granite.

Woodbury Heights, borough (pop. 1,373), Gloucester co., SW N.J., S of Woodbury; mfg. (clothing, concrete blocks). Settled c.1770, inc.1915.

Woodchester, town and parish (pop. 767), central Gloucester, England, 2 mi. S of Stroud; leather tanning, machinery mfg. Site of R.C. abbey and theological col. Extensive Roman remains have been found here.

Woodcliff Lake, borough (pop. 1,420), Bergen co., NE N.J., on Woodcliff L. (c.1 mi. long), near N.Y. line, and 10 mi. NNE of Paterson. Inc. 1910.

Woodcock, borough (pop. 130), Crawford co., NW Pa., 8 mi. N of Meadville.

Woodcote, England: see Coulsdon and Purley.

Wood Dale, village (pop. 1,857), Du Page co., NE Ill., WNW of Chicago and 17 mi. ESE of Elgin, in dairying area.

Wooden Ball Island, Maine: see Matinicus Isle.

Woodend, town (pop. 1,118), S central Victoria, Australia, 40 mi. NW of Melbourne, in livestock, agr. area; knitting mill.

Woodfibre, village (pop. estimate 500), SW B.C., on W shore of Howe Sound, 30 mi. N of Vancouver; pulp milling.

Woodford, residential former urban district (1931 pop. 23,946) now in Wanstead and Woodford municipal borough (1948 pop. estimate 61,150), SW Essex, England, on Roding R. and 10 mi. NE of London near Epping Forest; oleomargarine and pharmaceutical works.

Woodford. 1 County (□ 537; pop. 21,335), central Ill.; ⊙ Eureka. Bounded W by L. Peoria, a widening of Illinois R.; drained by Mackinaw R. and small Crow Creek. Agr. (corn, oats, soybeans, wheat, truck, livestock, poultry). Bituminous-coal mines. Mfg. (tile, concrete blocks, dairy and canned food products, feed). Formed 1841. **2** County (□193; pop. 11,212), central Ky.; ⊙ Versailles. In Bluegrass region; bounded W by Kentucky R., N and NE by Elkhorn Creek. Gently rolling upland agr. area (dairy products, livestock, especially horses; poultry, burley tobacco, hemp; bluegrass seed). Fluorspar mines. Some mfg. Formed 1788.

Woodford. 1 Town (pop. 179), Orangeburg co., central S.C., 18 mi. NW of Orangeburg. **2** Town (pop. 198), Bennington co., SW Vt., just E of Bennington, in Green Mts.; lumber. Woodford village (elev. 2,215 ft.) is one of state's highest.

Wood Green, residential municipal borough (1931 pop. 54,181; 1951 census 52,224), Middlesex, England, 7 mi. N of London. Site of Alexandra Palace. Has television station.

Woodhall Spa, urban district (1931 pop. 1,372; 1951 census 1,671), Parts of Lindsey, central Lincolnshire, England, near Witham R. 15 mi. ESE of Lincoln; resort with mineral springs. Just SW is agr. village and parish of Kirkstead (pop. 92), with remains of 13th-cent. Cistercian abbey.

Woodhaven (wŏŏd″hā′vŭn), SE N.Y., a residential section of SW Queens borough of New York city; some mfg. (clothing, metal and food products, optical goods).

Woodhorn Demesne, England: see NEWBIGGIN-BY-THE-SEA.

Woodhull. 1 Village (pop. 718), Henry co., NW Ill., 24 mi. SSE of Moline, in agr. and bituminous-coal area; ships grain; mfg. (dairy products, burial vaults). **2** Village (pop. 332), Steuben co., S N.Y., 19 mi. WSW of Corning; cheese and other dairy products, poultry, grain.

Wood Island, village (pop. 110), NE Kodiak Isl., SW Alaska, 4 mi. SW of Kodiak village, on Chiniak Bay. Village is sometimes confused with Woody Isl., 7 mi. E in Chiniak Bay.

Wood Island (□ 8.5), in Bahía Blanca (bay), SW Buenos Aires prov., Argentina, 34 mi. SSE of Bahía Blanca city, SW of Trinidad Isl.; 6 mi. long, 2 mi. wide.

Wood Island, village, SE P.E.I., near coast, 25 mi. SE of Charlottetown. Near by is terminal of car ferry to Pictou, N.S.

Wood Island, SW Maine, lighthouse isl. at mouth of Saco R.

Wood Lake. 1 Village (pop. 504), Yellow Medicine co., SW Minn., 10 mi. S of Granite Falls, in grain, livestock area; dairy products. **2** Village (pop. 238), Cherry co., N Nebr., 23 mi. SE of Valentine; trade center for ranch region.

Woodlake, city (pop. 2,525), Tulare co., S central Calif., in Sierra Nevada foothills, 12 mi. NE of Visalia, near Sequoia Natl. Park (E); fruit packing. Settled 1914, inc. 1939.

Woodland. 1 City (pop. 9,386), ⊙ Yolo co., central Calif., in Sacramento Valley, 18 mi. NW of Sacramento; trading, shipping, and processing center; stockyards, beet-sugar refineries, vegetable- and fruit-packing plants, rice and olive-oil mills. Seat of Woodland Clinic Hosp. Founded 1855, inc. 1874. **2** Town (pop. 621), Talbot co., W Ga., 16 mi. WSW of Thomaston; crate mfg. **3** Village (pop. 334), Iroquois co., E Ill., 29 mi. SSE of Kankakee, in rich agr. area. **4** Town (pop. 1,292), Aroostook co., NE Maine, 60 mi. NW of Houlton. Inc. 1880. **5** Village (pop. 1,370), in BAILEYVILLE town, Washington co., E Maine. **6** Village (pop. 410), Barry co., SW Mich., 32 mi. SE of Grand Rapids, in farm area. **7** Village (pop. 2,425, with adjacent Southland), Jackson co., S Mich. **8** Village (pop. 411), Hennepin co., E Minn., 12 mi. W of Minneapolis, at E end of L. Minnetonka, in resort area. **9** Village (pop. 133), Chickasaw co., NE central Miss., 38 mi. SSW of Tupelo. **10** Resort village, Ulster co., SE N.Y., in the Catskills, 20 mi. WNW of Kingston. State camp site here. **11** Town (pop. 590), Northampton co., NE N.C., 35 mi. NNE of Tarboro; woodworking. **12** Village (pop. c.1,000), Clearfield co., central Pa., 5 mi. ESE of Clearfield; clay products. **13** Town (pop. 1,292), Cowlitz co., SW Wash., 20 mi. NNW of Vancouver, near confluence of Lewis and Columbia rivers; trade center for agr. area; dairy products, poultry, truck, bulbs; cannery. Settled 1842; inc. 1906.

Woodland Beach. 1 Resort, Del.: see BOMBAY HOOK ISLAND. **2** Resort village (pop. 1,169, with near-by Lees Wharf), Anne Arundel co., central Md., on South R. and 5 mi. SW of Annapolis. **3** Village (pop. 1,966, with adjacent Detroit Beach), Monroe co., SE Mich., near Monroe. **4** Section of New York city, N.Y.: see SOUTH BEACH.

Woodland Hills, suburban section of LOS ANGELES city, Los Angeles co., S Calif., in W San Fernando Valley, 12 mi. SW of San Fernando. Until 1941 called Girard.

Woodland Park, village (pop. 41), S Alaska, near Anchorage.

Woodland Park, town (pop. 391), Teller co., central Colo., in Front Range, 15 mi. NW of Colorado Springs, 10 mi. N of Pikes Peak; alt. 8,500 ft. Shipping point for railroad ties and mine props.

Woodlands, village, N Singapore isl., on railroad and 13 mi. NNW of Singapore, on Johore Strait, at road and rail causeway linking isl. with Johore Bharu on Malay Peninsula. Rail spur to Br. naval base area (E).

Woodlark Island, wooded volcanic island (pop. c.950), part of Territory of Papua, SW Pacific, 175 mi. SE of New Guinea; 9°9′S 152°46′E; 40 mi. long, 10 mi. wide; gold mining. In Second World War, made Allied air base (1943).

Woodlawn. 1 Village (pop. 320), Jefferson co., S Ill., 8 mi. W of Mount Vernon, in agr. area. **2** Town (pop. 339), Campbell co., N Ky., near Newport and Covington, 5 mi. S of Cincinnati. **3** Suburb (pop. 1,053, with near-by Tyler) of Paducah, McCracken co., SW Ky. **4** Hamlet, Nelson co., central Ky., 6 mi. E of Bardstown. **5** A residential section of N Bronx borough of New York city, SE N.Y. Large cemetery here. **6** Village (pop. 1,335), Hamilton co., extreme SW Ohio, suburb 10 mi. N of downtown Cincinnati. Inc. 1941.

Woodlawn Heights, town (pop. 31), Madison co., E central Ind., just NW of Anderson.

Woodlawn Orchards, village (pop. 4,035, with adjacent Knollwood Park), Jackson co., S Mich.

Woodle Island, Gilbert Isls.: see KURIA.

Woodley, town in Bredbury and Romiley urban dist., NE Cheshire, England, 3 mi. NE of Stockport; cotton milling, mfg. of chemicals.

Woodlyn, Pa.: see CRUM LYNNE.

Woodlynne or **Wood-Lynne** (wŏŏd′lĭn″), residential borough (pop. 2,776), Camden co., SW N.J., S suburb of Camden. Laid out 1892, inc. 1901.

Woodman, village (pop. 149), Grant co., extreme SW Wis., on Wisconsin R. and 6 mi. WSW of Boscobel, in farm area.

Woodmansterne, residential town and parish (pop. 1,301), NE Surrey, England, 4 mi. E of Epsom.

Woodmere (wŏŏd′mēr″). **1** Residential village (1940 pop. 6,359), Nassau co., SE N.Y., on SW Long Isl., bet. Cedarhurst and Hewlett; mfg. (candy, costume jewelry). **2** Village (pop. 419), Cuyahoga co., N Ohio, suburb 11 mi. ESE of downtown Cleveland.

Woodmont, Conn.: see MILFORD.

Woodplumpton, village and parish (pop. 1,572), W Lancashire, England, 4 mi. NW of Preston; dairy farming, agr.

Wood-Ridge (wŏŏd′rĭj″), borough (pop. 6,283), Bergen co., NE N.J., just E of Passaic; mfg. (airplane motors, chemicals, tools, emery bags, furniture, nitrocellulose products); printing; truck farming. Settled before the Revolution, inc. 1894.

Woodridge, resort village (pop. 951), Sullivan co., SE N.Y., 7 mi. NE of Monticello.

Wood River. 1 City (pop. 10,190), Madison co., SW Ill., on the Mississippi and 16 mi. NNE of downtown St. Louis, and within its metropolitan area; oil refinery, planing mill, tannery. Founded 1907; inc. as village in 1911, as city in 1923. **2** Village (pop. 858), Hall co., S Nebr., 15 mi. SW of Grand Island and on Wood R.; grain, livestock, sugar beets.

Wood River. 1 In Conn. and R.I., rises in branches in W R.I. and in Windham co., E Conn.; flows c.22 mi. SE and S, through R.I., to Pawcatuck R. NNE of Bradford. **2** In S central Nebr., rises in S Custer co., flows 110 mi. SE and ENE, past Shelton, Wood River, and Grand Island, to Platte R. near Central City.

Woodroffe, Mount, Australia: see MUSGRAVE RANGES.

Woodruff, county (□ 592; pop. 18,957), E central Ark.; ⊙ Augusta. Bounded W by White R.; drained by Cache R. Agr. (cotton, rice, corn, hay, peaches). Mfg. at Augusta, Cotton Plant, and McCrory. Commercial fishing, mussel-shell gathering; timber. Formed 1862.

Woodruff. 1 Mill town (pop. 3,831), Spartanburg co., NW S.C., 16 mi. S of Spartanburg, in agr. area; textiles, grain products; power plant. Inc. 1876. **2** Town (pop. 175), Rich co., N Utah, 10 mi. S of Randolph, near Bear R. and Wyo. line; alt. 6,344 ft.; agr. **3** Resort village, Oneida co., N Wis., 22 mi. NW of Rhinelander, in lake region, near American Legion State Forest.

Woodruff Place, residential town (pop. 1,557), Marion co., central Ind., within the boundaries of Indianapolis. Platted 1872, inc. 1876.

Woods, county (□ 1,271; pop. 14,526), NW Okla.; ⊙ Alva. Bounded N by Kansas line, W and S by Cimarron R.; drained also by Salt Fork of Arkansas R. Agr. (wheat, sorghums, alfalfa), stock-raising, and dairying area. Processing of agr. products at Alva. Sand and gravel pits, salt deposits. Formed 1893.

Woodsboro. 1 Town (pop. 427), Frederick co., N Md., 10 mi. NNE of Frederick; lime kilns; makes clothing, cosmetics. **2** City (pop. 1,836), Refugio co., S Texas, 6 mi. SW of Refugio; trade center in farm, cattle, petroleum area; cotton gins. Inc. 1928.

Woodsburgh, village (pop. 745), Nassau co., SE N.Y., on SW Long Isl., just E of Cedarhurst, in summer-resort area.

Woods Cross, town (pop. 273), Davis co., N Utah, 8 mi. N of Salt Lake City; alt. 4,293 ft.; vegetable canning; oil refining. Great Salt L. is just W.

Woodsfield, village (pop. 2,410), ⊙ Monroe co., E Ohio, 29 mi. NE of Marietta, in agr. area; coal mines, oil and gas wells; hardwood timber. Makes dairy products, vaults, tools. Settled 1815, inc. 1834.

Woods Hole (wŏŏdz″hōl′), village (1940 pop. 549) in FALMOUTH town, Barnstable co., SE Mass., at SW tip of Cape Cod, 16 mi. SE of New Bedford; summer resort with good harbor (boats to Nantucket and Martha's Vineyard). A U.S. fish and wildlife station here includes laboratories, hatcheries, aquarium. Woods Hole is also site of important marine biological inst. and of Oceanographic Institution which maintains research ship *Atlantis*.

Woodside, village (pop. 477), SE South Australia, 17 mi. ESE of Adelaide; dairy products, livestock.

Woodside, England: see CROYDON.

Woodside, Scotland: see ABERDEEN.

Woodside. 1 Residential suburb (pop. c.500), San Mateo co., W Calif., 5 mi. W of Palo Alto. Small Searsville L. (reservoir; swimming, boating resort) is near by. **2** Town (pop. 157), Kent co., central Del., 7 mi. SSW of Dover; shipping point in grain, fruitgrowing area. **3** A residential section of W Queens borough of New York city, SE N.Y.; some mfg. of gloves, chemicals, furniture, optical goods, machine parts, paper and stone products; publishing. **4** Village (pop. 1,422), Luzerne co., E central Pa. **5** Village (pop. 8,471, with adjacent Riverside and City View), Greenville co., NW S.C., just W of Greenville.

Woods Island (□ 3; pop. 442), W N.F., on S side of the Bay of Islands, 15 mi. NW of Corner Brook; 3 mi. long, 2 mi. wide; 49°6′N 58°13′W. Fishing, lobster canning.

Woodson, county (□ 504; pop. 6,711), SE Kansas; ⊙ Yates Center. Dissected plain, crossed in NE by Neosho R., in SW by Verdigris R. Livestock raising, grain growing. There are scattered oil fields. Formed 1855.

Woodson. 1 Village (pop. 211), Morgan co., W central Ill., 6 mi. S of Jacksonville, in agr. area. **2** Village (pop. c.500), Throckmorton co., N Texas, 14 mi. SE of Throckmorton; farm, ranch trade point.

Woodson Terrace, town (pop. 616), St. Louis co., E Mo.

Woods Point, village, S central Victoria, Australia, 75 mi. ENE of Melbourne, in Great Dividing Range; gold mining.

Woodstock. 1 Town (pop. 3,593), ⊙ Carleton co., W N.B., on St. John R. and 45 mi. WNW of Fredericton, near Maine border, in mining (zinc, copper, lead), dairying, and fruitgrowing (apples, plums) region; lumbering; mfg. of furniture, agr. machinery, dairy products. Has agr. col. Former iron-mining center. **2** City (pop. 12,461), ⊙ Oxford co., S Ont., on Thames R. and 80 mi. WSW of Toronto; mfg. of furniture, pianos, organs, hardware, tools, textiles; feed and lumber milling. Center of stock-raising region. Has seminary.

Woodstock, municipal borough (1931 pop. 1,484; 1951 census 1,713), central Oxfordshire, England, on lake formed by the small Glyme R., 8 mi. NW of Oxford; leather industry. On site of castle in which the Black Prince was b. and in which Mary imprisoned Elizabeth. It is reputed site of dwelling built by Henry II for "Fair Rosamond," and is locale of Scott's novel *Woodstock*. Near by is BLENHEIM PARK.

Woodstock. 1 Town (pop. 2,271), Windham co., NE Conn., on Mass. line, 9 mi. SSE of Southbridge, Mass.; agr.; textile milling. Has 18th- and 19th-cent. houses. Settled 1686, inc. 1690. **2** Town (pop. 545), Cherokee co., NW Ga., 24 mi. NNW of Atlanta; clothing mfg. **3** City (pop. 7,192), ⊙ McHenry co., NE Ill., 32 mi. W of Waukegan, in dairy and farm area; mfg. (typewriters, beds, metal products). Todd School for boys (1848) is here. Inc. 1852. **4** Town (pop. 29), Marion co., central Ind., NW suburb of Indianapolis. **5** Town (pop. 971), Oxford co., W Maine, 12 mi. S of Rumford; wood products. Includes Bryant Pond, resort on small lake draining S into Little Androscoggin R. **6** Village (pop. c.300), Howard co., N Md., on Patapsco R. and 14 mi. W of downtown Baltimore. Seat of Woodstock Col. and Seminary (R.C.; for men; opened 1869). **7** Village (pop. 277), Pipestone co., SW Minn., 12 mi. E of Pipestone; corn, oats, barley, potatoes. **8** Resort town (pop. 894), Grafton co., W central N.H., on Pemigewasset R. just S of Franconia Notch; winter sports. North Woodstock village is commercial center of town. **9** Summer-resort village (1940 pop. 1,067), Ulster co., SE N.Y., in the foothills of the Catskills, 10 mi. NW of Kingston. Noted artists' colony and seat of summer school of the Art Students League. **10** Village (pop. 316), Champaign co., W central Ohio, 13 mi. ENE of Urbana, in agr. area. **11** Resort town (pop. 2,613), including Woodstock village (pop. 1,326), ⊙ Windsor co., E Vt., on Ottauquechee R. and 23 mi. E of Rutland. Summer and winter resorts; mfg. (clothing, furniture, building materials), printing; agr. (dairy products, maple sugar). Noted for fine old houses and village green. Hiram Powers, George P. Marsh, John Cotton Dana b. here. Chartered and settled c.1761. **12** Town (pop. 1,816), ⊙ Shenandoah co., NW Va., near North Fork of Shenandoah R., 28 mi. SW of Winchester; trade center in agr., lumber area; ships apples, dairy products, poultry; canning, mfg. of food-packing equipment. On crest of Massanutten Mtn. (E) is observation tower overlooking Shenandoah Valley. Settled 1752; inc. 1872.

Woodston, England: see OLD FLETTON.

Woodston, city (pop. 296), Rooks co., N Kansas, on South Fork Solomon R. and 9 mi. E of Stockton; wheat, livestock.

Woodstown, borough (pop. 2,345), Salem co., SW N.J., on Salem R. and 8 mi. NE of Salem, in agr. region; mfg. (bricks, clothing). Has 18th-cent. Friends' meetinghouse. Quaker center since settlement before 1725; inc. 1882.

Woodsville, village (pop. 1,542), ⊙ Grafton co., W N.H., in Haverhill town, 8 mi. NNE of Haverhill village, at junction of Ammonoosuc and Connecticut rivers, both bridged here. Railroad center; timber, dairy products, poultry.

Woodville, town (pop. 38,592), SE South Australia, 5 mi. NW of Adelaide, in metropolitan area; automobile plants.

Woodville, village (pop. 394), S Ont., 13 mi. W of Lindsay; dairying, farming; fruit.

Woodville, borough (pop. 1,095), ⊙ Woodville co. (□ 156; pop. 1,762), S central N.Isl., New Zealand, 90 mi. NE of Wellington; rail junction; dairying center.

Woodville. 1 Town (pop. 165), Jackson co., NE Ala., 20 mi. SE of Huntsville, near Paint Rock R. **2** Town (pop. 484), Greene co., NE central Ga., 8 mi. NE of Greensboro; sawmilling. **3** Town (pop. 91), Penobscot co., central Maine, on the Penobscot and 18 mi. SE of Millinocket, in agr., lumbering, camping area. **4** Village (pop. 1,926), Jackson co., S Mich., just NW of Jackson. **5** Town (pop. 1,609), ⊙ Wilkinson co., extreme SW Miss., 32 mi. S of Natchez, near La. line, in farming, timber, and cattle-raising area; lumber milling. Inc. 1811. **6** Town (pop. 387), Bertie co., NE N.C., 15 mi. NW of Windsor. **7** Village (pop. 1,358), Sandusky co., N Ohio, 16 mi. SE of Toledo, and on Portage R., in grain and livestock area; limestone quarrying and processing. Founded c.1836. **8** Town (1940 pop. 364), Marshall co., S Okla., on peninsula extending into L. Texoma, 32 mi. SE of Ardmore. **9** Town (pop. 1,863), ⊙ Tyler co., E Texas, near Neches R., c.50 mi. NNW of Beaumont; lumber milling, cotton ginning; nurseries. Settled c.1847, inc. 1929. **10** Village (pop. 410), St. Croix co., W Wis., 23 mi. E of Hudson; trade center for dairying, farming, and stock-raising area.

Woodward (wŏŏd'wûrd, wŏŏ'dûrd), county (□ 1,235; pop. 14,383), NW Okla.; ⊙ Woodward. Intersected by North Canadian and Cimarron rivers; Wolf Creek is impounded here by FORT SUPPLY DAM. Includes a state park. Agr. (wheat, rye, broomcorn, alfalfa, vegetables), cattle raising, dairying. Mfg. at Woodward. Formed 1893.

Woodward. 1 Village (pop. c.750), Jefferson co., N central Ala., just SW of Birmingham; pig-iron, industrial chemicals, tar, coke-oven gas, granulated slag. **2** Town (pop. 908), Dallas co., central Iowa, 24 mi. NW of Des Moines; food processing (corn, oats). Coal mines near by. State hosp. for epileptics and school for feeble-minded adjacent to town. **3** City (pop. 5,915), ⊙ Woodward co., NW Okla., on North Canadian R. and c.85 mi. W of Enid; market and processing center for wheat and cattle area, also producing sorghums, hay, vegetables, poultry, dairy products. Mfg. (brooms, bedding, leather, clothing, furniture, alabaster products). Fuller's-earth pits. Has a jr. col. and a U.S. agr. experiment station. State park near by. Settled 1893.

Woodworth. 1 Village (pop. 392), Rapides parish, central La., 12 mi. S of Alexandria. **2** Village (pop. 207), Stutsman co., central N.Dak., 32 mi. WNW of Jamestown. **3** Village (pop. c.100), Kenosha co., extreme SE Wis., near Des Plaines R., 8 mi. W of Kenosha; mfg. of biologicals and other drug products.

Woody Island, Alaska: see WOOD ISLAND.

Woody Island, Chinese *Yunghing* or *Yung-hsing* (yŏŏng'shĭng'), southernmost and largest of the Amphitrite Group in Paracel Isls., China, in S. China Sea, 200 mi. SE of Hainan; 16°50'N 112°20'E; 1½ mi. long (E-W), 1 mi. wide (S-N). Guano deposits; fisheries. Meteorological and radio station, military post.

Wookey Hole (wŏŏ'kē), cavern, N Somerset, England, on SW slope of Mendip Hills and 2 mi. NW of Wells, consisting of series of natural caves. Prehistoric human skeletons and utensils have been found here. Site of paper mills.

Wool, town and parish (pop. 2,876), S Dorset, England, on Frome R. (15th-cent. bridge) and 5 mi. W of Wareham; agr. market in dairying region. Near by are ruins of 12th-cent. Bindon Abbey.

Wooldale, England: see HOLMFIRTH.

Wooldridge. 1 Town (pop. 137), Cooper co., central Mo., near Missouri R., 13 mi. ESE of Boonville. **2** Mining village (1940 pop. 514), Campbell co., NE Tenn., near Ky. line, 45 mi. NNW of Knoxville, in Cumberland foothills; coal.

Wooler, town and parish (pop. 1,505), N Northumberland, England, 15 mi. NW of Alnwick; agr. market and resort at foot of Cheviot Hills.

Woolfardisworthy, England: see WOOLSERY.

Woolfold, town in Bury borough, SE Lancashire, England; cotton and paper milling.

Woollahra (wŏŏlä'rŭ), municipality (pop. 45,122), SE suburb of Sydney, E New South Wales, Australia.

Woolsery (wŏŏl'zûrē) or **Woolfardisworthy** (wŏŏlfär'dĭswûrdhē, wŏŏl'zûrē), agr. village and parish (pop. 591), NW Devon, England, 9 mi. WSW of Bideford. Has 13th-cent. church.

Woolsey, town (pop. 90), Fayette co., W central Ga., 11 mi. NW of Griffin.

Woolsthorpe (wŏŏlz'thôrp), agr. village in parish of Colsterworth (pop. 824), Parts of Kesteven, S Lincolnshire, England, 7 mi. S of Grantham. Isaac Newton b. here. Just E is agr. village of Colsterworth, which is the site of a church with 14th-cent. tower.

Woolstock, town (pop. 255), Wright co., N central Iowa, 7 mi. N of Webster City, in agr. area.

Woolston with Martinscroft, parish (pop. 530), S Lancashire, England. Includes leather-tanning village of Woolston, 3 mi. ENE of Warrington.

Woolton, England: see MUCH WOOLTON.

Woolwich (wŏŏ'lĭj), metropolitan borough (1931 pop. 146,881; 1951 census 147,824) of London, England, on S bank of the Thames, 11 mi. E of Charing Cross. Here are Royal Military Acad. (founded 1741), Royal Arsenal (with Royal Gun Factory and Royal Laboratories), and hq. of Royal Regiment of Artillery, Royal Army Ordnance Corps, and Royal Naval Ordnance Corps. There are large barracks, warehouses, and a hosp. The dockyards have been used for military traffic only since 1869. The Rotunda (built 1814 by Nash) has military mus. Near Woolwich Common is Shooter's Hill (425 ft.). Borough suffered considerable air-raid damage, 1940–41.

Woolwich (wŏŏl'wĭch), town (pop. 1,344), Sagadahoc co., S Maine, on the Kennebec opposite Bath; boat building, agr. Includes Nequasset village on small Nequasset L. Settled 1638, destroyed in Indian wars, resettled 1734, inc. 1759.

Woomera (wŏŏ'mûrŭ), township (pop. c.1,500), central South Australia, 110 mi. NW of Port Augusta, in arid, sparsely populated area, near Pimba (on transcontinental railroad); site of joint British-Australian base for rocket-launching experiments (the rocket range extending c.1,200 mi. to NW coast of Western Australia). Woomera's supply center is Salisbury; water is piped from Port Augusta. There are 3 airfields. The site was selected in 1945.

Woonasquatucket River (wŏŏnă'skwĭtŭ'kĭt), N R.I., rises SW of Woonsocket, flows c.16 mi. generally SE, through Smithfield town, past mill villages (water power), and through Providence, joining Moshassuck R. just before entering Providence R. Woonasquatucket Reservoir (c.2.5 mi. long) and others are formed by dams.

Woonsocket. 1 (wŏŏnsŏ'kĭt, wŏŏn–) Textile city (pop. 50,211), Providence co., N R.I., on Mass. line, on Blackstone R. (bridged here) and 13 mi. NNW of Providence; woolen center, producing also cotton and rayon goods, rubber, metal, and paper products, glass fabrics, bedding, textile machinery, insulators, leather goods, machine tools, beverages. Seat of Hill Col. Settled before 1675, set off from Cumberland 1867, made a city 1888. Textile industry dates from c.1814. Inhabitants are predominantly of French-Canadian descent. **2** (wŏŏn'sŏkĭt) City (pop. 1,051), ⊙ Sanborn co., SE central S.Dak., 85 mi. WSW of Sioux Falls; trading center for cattle-raising and farming region; dairy products, poultry, grain. Parochial school, hydroelectric plant, and artificial lake are here. Settled 1883, inc. 1888.

Wooster (wŏŏ'stûr), city (pop. 14,005), ⊙ Wayne co., N central Ohio, 30 mi. SW of Akron, and on Killbuck Creek, in dairying and farming area; rubber products, motor vehicles, metal products, mill machinery, paint and varnish, tools, clay products, foodstuffs; oil and gas wells. Seat of Col. of Wooster. Ohio Agr. Experiment Station is near by. Settled 1807, inc. 1817.

Woosung or **Wusung** (both: wōō'sŏŏng'), outer port of Shanghai, S Kiangsu prov., China, 13 mi. N of Shanghai, and on Yangtze R. at mouth of Whangpoo R.; terminus of Shanghai-Woosung RR; cotton, rice, sea food.

Woosung River, China: see SOOCHOW CREEK.

Wootton (wŏŏ'tŭn), town and parish (pop. 1,551), W Bedford, England, 4 mi. SW of Bedford; agr. market. Stewartby, with brickworks, is 2 mi. SE.

Wootton Bassett, town and parish (pop. 2,419), N Wiltshire, England, 5 mi. WSW of Swindon; agr. market in dairying region. Has 13th-cent. church.

Wootton Saint Lawrence, agr. village and parish (pop. 1,114), N Hampshire, England. Has 13th-cent. church.

Wootton Wawen, England: see HENLEY-IN-ARDEN.

Wora Wora (wō'"rä wō'rä), town, S Br. Togoland, administered as part of Eastern Prov., Gold Coast colony, 37 mi. N of Kpandu; road junction; cacao market. Also spelled Worra Worra.

Worb (vôrp), town (pop. 4,645), Bern canton, W central Switzerland, 5 mi. ESE of Bern; linen textiles, flour, beer; metal- and woodworking. Early medieval castle, late-Gothic church.

Worbis (vôr'bĭs), town (pop. 2,896), in former Prussian Saxony prov., central Germany, after 1945 in Thuringia, on Wipper R. and 15 mi. NNW of Mühlhausen; textile milling, tobacco processing.

Worcester or **Worcestershire** (wŏŏ'stûr, –shĭr), county (□ 699.5; 1931 pop. 420,056; 1951 census 522,974), W central England; ⊙ Worcester. Bounded by Hereford (W), Shropshire (NW), Stafford (N), Warwick (E), Gloucester (S and SE), and including, in S, a small enclave of Stafford. Drained by Severn, Avon, Stour, and Arrow rivers. Undulating plain, with hills in SW (Malvern Hills), rising to c.1,400 ft. The SE is an important truck-gardening area, centered on Evesham. There are coal deposits near Dudley, fire clay is quarried near Stourbridge, and brine and salt are obtained in Droitwich area. Other important towns are Worcester, Redditch (needles), Kidderminster (carpets), Dudley (glass), Stourport (steel), and Malvern (spa). In co. are several old abbeys.

Worcester, city and county borough (1931 pop. 50,546; 1951 census 59,700), ⊙ Worcestershire, England, in center of co., on left bank of the Severn and 100 mi. NW of London; 52°12'N 2°13'W; long known for its porcelain products, gloves, and sauce ("Worcestershire sauce"), it also produces machinery and other metal products. Site was occupied in anc. Br. and Roman times and became seat of a bishopric probably in 679. The cathedral (largely 14th cent., with a Norman crypt) was founded in 11th cent. by St. Wulfstan. The Commandery (or St. Wulfstan's Hosp.), founded in 11th cent., is now part of 15th-cent. bldg. There are several old parish churches and many old houses. The last city to yield to Parliament in 1646, it was scene of Cromwell's final victory and the complete rout of Charles II and the Scots, Sept. 3, 1651 (battle of Worcester).

Worcester, town (pop. 19,001), SW Cape Prov., U. of So. Afr., near Breede R., 60 mi. ENE of Cape Town (connected by rail), at foot of Hex River Mts.; winegrowing center; fruit, jam, vegetable canning; mfg. of textiles, furniture, bricks, asbestos-cement products. Has branch of Cape Technical Col. and col. for colored teachers.

Worcester. 1 County (□ 483; pop. 23,148), SE Md.; ⊙ Snow Hill. On the Eastern Shore (Delmarva Peninsula); bounded S by Va. line, SW and NW by Pocomoke R. (flows across co.), N by Del. line. Off its Atlantic shore, a N–S chain of bays forms inland waterway bet. mainland and barrier isls. Tidewater agr. area (truck, potatoes, fruit, dairy products, poultry); large timber stands (mainly softwoods) E of Pocomoke R.; lumber mills, vegetable canneries, clothing factories. Shores have small fishing towns and resorts, best-known of which is Ocean City (noted for deep-sea fishing). Great cypress swamps, including part of Pocomoke State Forest, lie along Pocomoke R. Formed 1742. **2** County (□ 1,532; pop. 546,401), central Mass., bordering on N.H., R.I., and Conn.; ⊙ Worcester and Fitchburg. Drained by Blackstone, Nashua, Assabet, Millers, and Ware rivers; give water power to such industrial centers as Worcester, Fitchburg, Leominster, Milford, Webster. Dairying and truck. Wachusett Mtn. and Reservoir are in co. Includes state forests, resort lakes. Formed 1731.

Worcester. 1 City (pop. 203,486), a ⊙ Worcester co., central Mass., on Blackstone R. and 39 mi. W of Boston; 2d largest city in state; rail and industrial center. Textiles, foundry and machine-shop products, paper, abrasives, printing, electrical supplies, looms, carpets, clothing, shoes. Port of entry. Seat of Clark Univ., Col. of the Holy Cross, state teachers col., Worcester Polytechnic Inst., art mus., and museums of history and natural history. In Memorial Auditorium is held annual music festival begun 1858. Canalization (1828) of the Blackstone marked beginning of city's rapid industrial development. L. Quinsigamond near by. In Shay's Rebellion the courthouse was besieged (1786) by insurgents. First settled 1668; attacked by Indians; permanently settled 1713; inc. as city 1848. **2** Resort village (1940 pop. 980), Otsego co., central N.Y., 12 mi. SE of Cooperstown, in the Catskills. Small lakes near by. Makes gloves, clothing, maple syrup. **3** Town (pop. 445), Washington co., N central Vt., on North Branch Winooski R. and 7 mi. N of Montpelier; lumber.

Worcestershire, England: see WORCESTER, county.

Worcestershire Beacon, England: see MALVERN HILLS.

Worcum, Netherlands: see WOUDRICHEM.

Worden. 1 (wôr'dŭn) Village (pop. 968), Madison co., SW Ill., 27 mi. NE of East St. Louis, in agr. and coal area. Inc. 1877. **2** (wûr'dŭn) Village (pop. c.250), Yellowstone co., S Mont., near Yellowstone R., 20 mi. NE of Billings, in irrigated agr. region; shipping point for sugar beets, livestock.

Worden, Fort, Wash.: see PORT TOWNSEND.

Worden Pond (wûr'dŭn), S R.I., in South Kingstown, 4 mi. W of Wakefield; c.2 mi. long; one of largest bodies of fresh water in state. Receives small Chipuxet R. from N. Source of Pawcatuck R., flowing W.

Worfield, agr. village and parish (pop. 1,416), SE Shropshire, England, 3 mi. NE of Bridgnorth; flour milling. Has church dating from 13th cent.

Wörgl (vûr'gŭl), town (pop. 5,862), Tyrol, W Austria, on Inn R. and 8 mi. SW of Kufstein; rail junction; cellulose mfg.; cement works. Limestone quarry, mineral springs near by.

Wörishofen, Bad, Germany: see BAD WÖRISHOFEN.

Workington, municipal borough (1931 pop. 24,751; 1951 census 28,886), W Cumberland, England, port on Solway Firth at mouth of Derwent R., 30 mi. SW of Carlisle; coal-mining center, with iron mines, steel mills, shipbuilding yards; leather tanning, salmon fishing. Refuge of Mary Queen of Scots in 1568 on her flight to England after battle of Langside.

Worksop (wûrk'sŏp), municipal borough (1931 pop. 26,285; 1951 census 31,038), NW Nottingham, England, on Ryton R. and 15 mi. ESE of Sheffield;

coal-mining center, with metal foundries, chemical works, glassworks. Has remains of Augustinian priory founded 1103. Worksop Manor, built on site of mansion erected in 15th cent., was scene of imprisonment of Mary Queen of Scots, and was burned in 1761.

Workum (vōr'kŭm), town (pop. 4,113), Friesland prov., N Netherlands, on the Ijsselmeer, 10 mi. WSW of Sneek; dairying center. Has 15th-cent. church, 17th-cent. weighhouse and other 17th-cent. buildings.

Worland (wûr'lŭnd). **1** Town (pop. 40), Bates co., W Mo., near Marais des Cygnes R., 15 mi. WSW of Butler. **2** Town (pop. 4,202), ⊙ Washakie co., N central Wyo., on Bighorn R. and 115 mi. NW of Casper; alt. 4,061 ft. Trade center for irrigated sugar-beet and livestock region; terminus of crude-oil pipe line (begun 1950) to St. Louis (via Casper). Beet-sugar and oil refineries; dairy products, grain, beans, timber. State industrial school for boys near by.

World's View, height in Matopo Hills, SW Southern Rhodesia, c.25 mi. S of Bulawayo. Here are buried Cecil Rhodes and Sir Leander Starr Jameson.

Worley (wûr'lē), village (pop. 233), Kootenai co., N Idaho, 20 mi. SSW of Coeur d'Alene, near Wash. line; hay, grain, potatoes.

Wörlitz (vûr'lĭts), town (pop. 3,059), in former Anhalt state, central Germany, after 1945 in Saxony-Anhalt, 4 mi. SSW of Coswig. Has noted 18th-cent. castle with large collection of paintings and antiques; park, botanical gardens.

Wormditt, Poland: see ORNETA.

Worme, Netherlands: see WORMER.

Wormeldange (vôr'mŭldăzh"), village (pop. 679), SE Luxembourg, on Moselle R. and 5 mi. SSW of Grevenmacher, on Ger. border; grape-growing center; plums.

Wormer (vôr'mŭr), town (pop. 5,493), North Holland prov., W Netherlands, 4 mi. N of Zaandam, in Zaanstreek industrial area; shipbuilding, mfg. (industrial belting, synthetic marble and granite, wood products). Sometimes spelled Worme.

Wormerveer (–vār), town (pop. 10,688), North Holland prov., W Netherlands, on Zaan R. and 4 mi. NNW of Zaandam, at N end of Zaanstreek industrial area; paint industry; mfg. (explosives, soap, oils, cacao products, paper, chemicals); shipbuilding.

Wormhill, England: see MILLER'S DALE.

Wormhout (vôrmōō'), agr. village (pop. 1,197), Nord dept., N France, 12 mi. SSE of Dunkirk.

Wormit, Scotland: see NEWPORT.

Wormleysburg (wûrm'lēzbûrg), borough (pop. 1,511), Cumberland co., S central Pa., on Susquehanna R. opposite Harrisburg. Laid out 1815.

Worms, Estonia: see VORMSI.

Worms (wûrmz, Ger. vôrms), city (1939 pop. 58,781; 1946 pop. 47,074; 1950 pop. 51,857), Rhenish Hesse, W Germany, port on the Rhine (2 bridges) and 11 mi. NNW of Mannheim; 49°38'N 8°22'E. Rail junction; a center of Ger. leather industry; mfg. of machinery, chemicals (fertilizer, various substitutes), textiles, furniture, cork goods. Food processing (preserves, sugar, flour, sparkling wine, beer). Noted for its Liebfraumilch wine. Worms suffered greatly in Second World War (destruction about 60%). Completely destroyed were two 18th-cent. Protestant churches and city mus. Heavily damaged were noted Romanesque basilica and churches of St. Paul, St. Andrew, and St. Martin. Romanesque-Gothic synagogue, one of Germany's oldest (founded 1034), was destroyed 1938. Worms, the anc. *Borbetomagus,* is one of Europe's historic centers. Originally a Celtic settlement, it was captured and fortified by Drusus in 14 B.C. Was Burgundian capital in 5th cent., and as such is center of action in the Nibelungenlied. First Ger. town to be created free imperial city (1156). Numerous important meetings were held here: Council of 1076 declared Gregory VII no longer pope; Concordat of Worms (1122) settled the question of investiture; at Diet of 1495, Emperor Maximilian I proclaimed a perpetual land peace, established the supreme judiciary of the Holy Roman Empire, and levied a general tax; and at the so-called Diet of Worms (1521), Luther refused to retract his teachings, for which he was banished by the emperor. City suffered severely in Thirty Years War. The anc. bishopric was secularized 1803. Went to Hesse-Darmstadt in 1815. Occupied 1918–30 by Fr. troops. Captured by Americans in March, 1945; later occupied by French. Right-bank suburb of Rosengarten passed to Hesse in 1945.

Worms Head, cape on Bristol Channel, Glamorgan, Wales, at E end of Carmarthen Bay, 9 mi. SSW of Kidwelly; 51°34'N 4°20'W.

Wörnitz River (vûr'nĭts), Bavaria, Germany, rises S of Schillingsfürst, flows 70 mi. generally S, past Dinkelsbühl, to the Danube at Donauwörth.

Worochta, Ukrainian SSR: see VOROKHTA.

Woronoco, Mass.: see RUSSELL.

Woropajewo, Belorussian SSR: see VOROPAYEVO.

Worplesdon (wôr'pŭldŭn), residential town and parish (pop. 3,494), W Surrey, England, 3 mi. NW of Guildford. Has 15th-cent. church.

Worpswede (vôrps"vā'dŭ), village (pop. 4,393), in former Prussian prov. of Hanover, NW Germany, after 1945 in Lower Saxony, fen colony 10 mi. NE of Bremen; weaving, flour milling.

Worringen (vô'rĭng-ŭn), suburb of Cologne, W Germany, on left bank of the Rhine and 10 mi. NNW of city center; transshipment harbor.

Wörrstadt (vûr'shtät), village (pop. 2,551), Rhenish Hesse, W Germany, 6 mi. N of Alzey; wine.

Worsborough (wûrz'bŭrŭ), urban district (1931 pop. 12,399; 1951 census 14,155), West Riding, S Yorkshire, England, 2 mi. S of Barnsley; coal mining.

Worsley (wûrs'lē), urban district (1931 pop. 14,502; 1951 census 27,363), SE Lancashire, England, on Bridgewater Canal and 6 mi. WNW of Manchester; cotton milling. Has 15th-cent. mansion. In urban dist. are towns of BARTON-UPON-IRWELL, WALKDEN, and (since 1932) LITTLE HULTON.

Worstead (wōō'stĭd), town and parish (pop. 719), NE Norfolk, England, 12 mi. NNE of Norwich; agr. market. In Middle Ages it was a woolen-weaving center, giving its name to worsted materials. Woolen industry introduced in Norman times by group of Flemish weavers. Has church, begun 1379. Center of a peasants' rebellion (1381).

Worsthorne with Hurstwood (wûrst'hôrn), parish (pop. 1,239), NE Lancashire, England. Includes cotton-weaving village of Worsthorne, 2 mi. E of Burnley, site of Burnley reservoir; and, just SE, granite-quarrying village of Hurstwood. Has a 16th-cent. house where Edmund Spenser lived.

Worth, town and parish (pop. 5,085), N Sussex, England, 8 mi. NNW of Haywards Heath; agr. market. Church is of Saxon origin. Just S is Worth Forest, remnant of the great Weald forest; town was one of centers of Weald iron industry.

Wörth, France: see WOERTH.

Wörth (vûrt'). **1** or **Wörth am Main** (äm mīn'), town (pop. 2,954), Lower Franconia, NW Bavaria, Germany, on the Main (canalized) and 12 mi. S of Aschaffenburg; brewing, flour and lumber milling. **2** or **Wörth an der Donau** (än dĕr dō'nou), village (pop. 2,653), Upper Palatinate, E Bavaria, Germany, near the Danube, 14 mi. E of Regensburg; brewing, tanning; winegrowing. Has 16th–17th-cent. castle. **3** or **Wörth am Rhein** (äm rīn'), village (pop. 2,511), Rhenish Palatinate, W Germany, on an arm of the Rhine and 6 mi. WNW of Karlsruhe; rail junction; grain, tobacco.

Worth. 1 County (□ 580; pop. 19,357), S central Ga.; ⊙ Sylvester. Coastal plain agr. (peanuts, cotton, tobacco, corn, melons) and forestry (lumber, naval stores) area. Formed 1853. **2** County (□ 401; pop. 11,068), N Iowa, on Minn. line; ⊙ Northwood. Prairie agr. area (hogs, cattle, poultry, corn, oats, soybeans) drained by Shell Rock R. Formed 1851. **3** County (□ 267; pop. 5,120), NW Mo.; ⊙ Grant City. Borders Iowa on N; drained by Grand R.; agr. region, livestock. Formed 1861.

Worth. 1 Town (1940 pop. 90), Turner co., S central Ga., 15 mi. SSE of Cordele. **2** Village (pop. 1,472), Cook co., NE Ill., SW suburb of Chicago; truck farming. **3** Town (pop. 141), Worth co., NW Mo., on Middle Fork of Grand R. and 22 mi. ENE of Maryville.

Worth, Lake. 1 Lake in Fla.: see LAKE WORTH. **2** Lake in N Texas, impounded by dam (1916) in West Fork of TRINITY RIVER, just NW of Fort Worth; capacity 27,000 acre-ft.; for water supply, irrigation. Recreational area.

Wortham (wûr'dhŭm), town (pop. 1,170), Freestone co., E central Texas, 22 mi. S of Corsicana; trade center in agr. (cotton, corn, cattle) and oil-producing area. Inc. 1910.

Wörthersee (vûrt'ŭrzā), lake (□ 7.49) in Carinthia, S Austria, just W of Klagenfurt; c.11 mi. long, c.1 mi. wide, average depth 130 ft. Site of resorts (Maria Wörth, Velden, Pörtschach).

Worthing, SE residential suburb and seaside resort of Bridgetown, SW Barbados, B.W.I.

Worthing (wûr'dhĭng), residential municipal borough (1931 pop. 46,224; 1951 census 69,375), S Sussex, England, on the Channel 10 mi. W of Brighton; seaside resort with mild climate, protected by the South Downs. Greenhouse cultivation of fruit and flowers is a specialty. Mus. contains remains of Neolithic flint mines worked at near-by Cissbury Ring (N). There are many traces of Roman occupation; at Highdown Hill (W) a complete Roman bath system was excavated in 1937. Town's industries include metalworking and pharmaceutical mfg. In urban dist. are residential sections of Durrington (NW), Goring-by-Sea (W), and Broadwater (N).

Worthing, town (pop. 272), Lincoln co., SE S.Dak., 9 mi. E of Canton; center of wheat-growing area.

Worthington (wûr'dhĭngtŭn). **1** Town (pop. 1,627), Greene co., SW Ind., on West Fork of White R., at influx of Eel R., and 33 mi. SE of Terre Haute, in agr. area (grain, livestock); bituminous-coal mines. **2** Town (pop. 337), Dubuque co., E Iowa, 23 mi. WSW of Dubuque; dairy products. **3** Town (pop. 695), Greenup co., NE Ky., on the Ohio and 7 mi. NW of Ashland. **4** Town (pop. 462), Hampshire co., W central Mass., 17 mi. ESE of Pittsfield; dairying. **5** City (pop. 7,923), ⊙ Nobles co., SW Minn., on Okabena L., near Iowa line, c.90 mi. SW of Mankato. Resort; agr. trade center in grain, livestock, poultry area; dairy products. Junior col. here. Settled 1871. **6** Town (pop. 186), Putnam co., N Mo., on Chariton R. and 16 mi. ESE of Unionville. **7** Village (pop. 2,141), Franklin co., central Ohio, suburb 8 mi. N of downtown Columbus and on Olentangy R. Near by is the Pontifical Col. Josephinum. Laid out 1804. **8** Borough (pop. 800), Armstrong co., W central Pa., 6 mi. WNW of Kittanning; woolens, clay products, asphalt. **9** Town (pop. 544), Marion co., N W.Va., 7 mi. WSW of Fairmont.

Worthville. 1 Town (pop. 308), Carroll co., N Ky., on Eagle Creek near its confluence with Kentucky R. and 9 mi. SE of Carrollton, in outer Bluegrass agr. region. **2** Borough (pop. 73), Jefferson co., W central Pa., 14 mi. NW of Punxsutawney.

Wortley, England: see FARNLEY AND WORTLEY.

Woshm, Saudi Arabia: see WASHM.

Wota (wō'tä), Ital. *Uota,* town (pop. 2,000), Kaffa prov., SW Ethiopia, 40 mi. WSW of Bonga. Trade center (cereals, wax, coffee, hides). Has Coptic church. Formerly Shoa Gimirra.

Wotho (wôt'hô), atoll (□ 1; pop. 31), Ralik Chain, Marshall Isls., W central Pacific, 125 mi. NW of Kwajalein; 13 islets.

Wotitz, Czechoslovakia: see VOTICE.

Wotje (wôt'jĕ), atoll (□ 3; pop. 320), Ratak Chain, Majuro dist., Marshall Isls., W central Pacific, 175 mi. E of Kwajalein; 29 mi. long, 15 mi. wide; 72 islets. Wotje isl. (1 mi. long, ¾ mi. wide), on E side of atoll, is largest islet of Marshall group; Jap. air base during Second World War. Formerly Romanzoff Isls.

Wotton (wŏ'–), village (pop. estimate 500), S Que., 8 mi. ESE of Asbestos; asbestos mining.

Wotton, England: see GLOUCESTER, city.

Wotton-under-Edge, town and parish (pop. 3,121), SW Gloucester, England, 16 mi. NE of Bristol; agr. market. School dates from 1382. John Biddle b. here. Town has 14th–15th-cent. church.

Woudenberg (vou'dŭnbĕrkh), village (pop. 860), Utrecht prov. central Netherlands, 8 mi. E of Zeist; bicycle-parts mfg.; cattle raising, tobacco growing, agr.

Woudrichem (vou'drĭkhŭm), town (pop. 2,022), North Brabant prov., SW Netherlands, at junction of Maas R. and Waal R. (here forming Upper Merwede R.), 17 mi. NW of 's Hertogenbosch; salmon fishing; potatoes, green vegetables. Mentioned in 1186 as a small market town, property of bishopric of Utrecht. Also spelled Worcum.

Wounta, Nicaragua: see HUOUNTA.

Wouri (wōō'rē, vōō'–), administrative region (□ 465; 1950 pop. 102,250), SW Fr. Cameroons, bordering W on Br. Cameroons; ⊙ Douala, the outlet for the Fr. Cameroons hinterland. Covers the shores of Cameroons Estuary and of lower Wouri R. Lies in tropical rain-forest zone. Hardwood lumbering, rubber, palms. Fishing.

Wouri River or **Vouri River,** SW Fr. Cameroons, formed by 2 headstreams 20 mi. NE of Yabassi, flows 100 mi. SW, past Yabassi, to Cameroon R. just below Douala. Navigable for c.40 mi. in its lower course. Also spelled Vuri.

Wouw (vou), village (pop. 1,631), North Brabant prov., SW Netherlands, 5 mi. ENE of Bergen op Zoom; stone quarrying; dairying; cattle, agr.

Wowoni (wōwō'nē), island (21 mi. long, 20 mi. wide; pop. 4,381), Indonesia, just off SE coast of Celebes, near Buton (S); 4°7'S 123°7'E. Largely mountainous, rising to 2,867 ft. Sago, coconuts.

Woy Woy (woi'woi"), town (pop. 1,451), E New South Wales, Australia, on N inlet of Broken Bay, 25 mi. NNE of Sydney; seaside resort.

Wozniki (vŏzhnē'kē), Pol. *Woźniki,* Ger. *Woischnik* (voish'nĭk), town (pop. 2,312), Katowice prov., S Poland, 16 mi. S of Czestochowa; rail spur terminus; brick mfg.

Wrangel Island or **Wrangell Island** (răng'gŭl, Rus. vrän'gĭl), Rus. *Ostrov Vrangelya,* tundra-covered island (□ 1,740) in W Chukchi Sea, 85 mi. off NE Siberia (separated by Long Strait), in Khabarovsk Territory, Russian SFSR; 71°N 180°E; 75 mi. long, 45 mi. wide; rises to nearly 3,000 ft. Govt. arctic station and trading post at Rogers (Rodzhers) Bay on SE shore. Named for F. P. Wrangel (Vrangel'), 19th-cent. Rus. navigator.

Wrangell (răng'gŭl), town (pop. 1,227), SE Alaska, on N tip of Wrangell Isl., in Alexander Archipelago, 30 mi. SE of Petersburg; 56°28'N 132°23'W; lumbering, fishing, fur-farming, fish-processing, and outfitting center (for hunting parties to N British Columbia); port of entry. Wrangell Institute, Federal vocational school for natives, is near by. Town founded c.1835 when Russians built fort here; U.S. military post, 1867–77. Later became outfitting point for miners using Stikine R. route to the Yukon.

Wrangell, Mount (14,005 ft.), S Alaska, active volcano in Wrangell Mts., 95 mi. NE of Valdez; 62°1'N 144°3'W.

Wrangell Island (30 mi. long, 5–14 mi. wide), SE Alaska, in Alexander Archipelago, bet. Etolin Isl. (SW) and mainland (NE); 56°18'N 132°10'W; rises to 3,350 ft. (SW); fishing, fish processing, fur-farming, logging. Occupied 1834 by Russian fur traders who named it for Baron F. P. Wrangel or Wrangell and built fort on site of present town.

Wrangell Mountains, SE Alaska, range (extending 100 mi. NW–SE, 70 mi. wide) of volcanic origin, bounded by St. Elias Mts. (SE), Chitina R. (S), and Copper R. (W), near Yukon line; center near 61°55′N 143°30′W. Highest peak, Mt. Sanford (16,208 ft.); other high peaks are mts. Blackburn (16,140 ft.), Wrangell (14,005 ft.; active volcano), and Regal (13,400 ft.). Central mtn. mass covered by large snowfield.

Wrangell Narrows, SE Alaska, narrow channel bet. Mitkof and Kupreanof Isls., Alexander Archipelago, S of Petersburg; part of the Inside Passage.

Wrath, Cape, promontory at NW extremity of Scotland, in NW Sutherland, 10 mi. WNW of Durness. On high cliffs is site of lighthouse (58°36′N 5°W).

Wraxall (răk′sôl), agr. village and parish (pop. 1,169), N Somerset, England, 6 mi. W of Bristol. Its church is Norman to 14th cent.

Wray (rā), town (pop. 2,198), ⊙ Yuma co., NE Colo., on North Fork, Republican R., near Nebr. line, and 150 mi. ENE of Denver; grain, dairy products. Fish hatchery here. Near by is Beecher Island memorial auditorium, commemorating battle (1868) with Indians. Inc. 1906.

Wraysbury, England: see WYRARDISBURY.

Wreak River (rēk), Leicester, England, rises 7 mi. NE of Melton Mowbray, flows 18 mi. SW, past Melton Mowbray, to Soar R. just E of Rothley.

Wrecclesham, England: see FARNHAM.

Wreck Island, E Va., barrier island and (c.3 mi. long) off Atlantic shore of Northampton co., 12 mi. E of Cape Charles city, S of Cobb Isl. Sand Shoal Inlet is at N end.

Wrekin, The (rē′kĭn), isolated volcanic hill (1,335 ft.), central Shropshire, England, 3 mi. SW of Wellington.

Wren, village (pop. 278), Van Wert co., W Ohio, 11 mi. WSW of Van Wert, near Ind. line, in agr. area.

Wrens (rĕnz), town (pop. 1,380), Jefferson co., E Ga., 28 mi. SW of Augusta; agr. trade center; food processing, sawmilling. Founded 1884.

Wrenshall (rĕn′shŭl), village (pop. 148), Carlton co., E Minn., near St. Louis R. and Wis. line, 17 mi. SW of Duluth; grain, stock.

Wrentham (rĕn′thŭm), town (pop. 5,341), including Wrentham village (pop. 1,119), Norfolk co., SE Mass., 18 mi. NNE of Providence, R.I.; summer resort; mfg. (metal products). Settled 1669, inc. 1673. State school for mentally handicapped children here.

Wreschen, Poland: see WRZESNIA.

Wrexham (rĕk′sŭm), municipal borough (1931 pop. 18,569; 1951 census 30,962), E Denbigh, Wales, 11 mi. SSW of Chester; coal-mining center and livestock market, with metalworking, leatherworking, brick mfg., and bacon and ham curing. St. Giles's Church dates mostly from 16th cent. and has noted peal of bells, one of "Seven Wonders of Wales." Bishop Heber here wrote *From Greenland's Icy Mountains.* Elihu Yale buried here. Wrexham is seat of R.C. bishopric of Menevia, which includes all of Wales except Glamorgan. Municipal borough includes residential districts of Offa and Erdigg.

Wriezen (vrē′tsŭn), town (pop. 4,806), Brandenburg, E Germany, on Old Oder arm of the Oder, at W edge of Oder Marshes, 16 mi. ESE of Eberswalde; agr. market (sugar beets, grain, poultry). Has 15th-cent. church.

Wright, town (1939 pop. 7,244; 1948 municipality pop. 16,717), W Samar isl., Philippines, on Maqueda Bay (small inlet of Samar Sea), 10 mi. E of Catbalogan; agr. center (rice, hemp, coconuts, corn).

Wright. 1 County (□ 577; pop. 19,652), N central Iowa; ⊙ Clarion. Rolling prairie agr. area (livestock, grain) drained by Iowa and Boone rivers. Contains several small lakes. Bituminous-coal deposits (S), sand and gravel pits. Formed 1851. **2** County (□ 671; pop. 27,716), S central Minn.; ⊙ Buffalo. Agr. area bounded N by Mississippi R., on E by Crow R.; watered by small lakes. Dairy products, livestock, poultry, corn, oats, barley. Clearwater L. is in NW, Pelican L. in NE. Co. formed 1855. **3** County (□ 684; pop. 15,834), S central Mo.; ⊙ Hartville. In the Ozarks; drained by Gasconade R. Agr., fruit, poultry, dairying; lumber; lead, zinc mines. Part of Mark Twain Natl. Forest here. Formed 1841.

Wright, village (pop. 199), Carlton co., E Minn., c.40 mi. WSW of Duluth; cheese. State forests in vicinity.

Wright, Fort George, Wash.: see SPOKANE city.

Wright, Fort H. G., N.Y.: see FISHERS ISLAND.

Wright City. 1 Town (pop. 543), Warren co., E central Mo., 7 mi. E of Warrenton. **2** Village (pop. 1,121), McCurtain co., extreme SE Okla., 30 mi. E of Hugo, near Little R., in lumbering and agr. area.

Wrightington, village and parish (pop. 2,000), SW Lancashire, England, 6 mi. NW of Wigan; coal mining; dairy farming, agr.

Wright Patterson Air Force Base, Ohio: see DAYTON.

Wrightson, Mount (9,432 ft.), SE Ariz., 27 mi. NNE of Nogales; highest peak in Santa Rita Mts. Sometimes called Old Baldy.

Wrightstown. 1 Borough (pop. 1,199), Burlington co., central N.J., 15 mi. SE of Trenton. Fort Dix, U.S. army post, and McGuire Air Force Base here; fort (formerly Camp Dix) was built in First World War, renamed and made a permanent garrison in 1939. **2** Village (pop. 761), Brown co., E Wis., on Fox R. and 15 mi. SSW of Green Bay city, in dairying region.

Wrightsville. 1 Village (pop. c.300), Pulaski co., central Ark., 9 mi. SSE of Little Rock, in farm and timber area. Has industrial school for boys. **2** City (pop. 1,750), ⊙ Johnson co., E central Ga., 17 mi. NE of Dublin; vegetable canning, clothes mfg. Inc. 1866. **3** Borough (pop. 2,104), York co., S Pa., on Susquehanna R. opposite Columbia; dolomite quarries. Settled 1730, laid out 1811, inc. 1834.

Wrightsville Beach, resort town (pop. 711), New Hanover co., SE N.C., 8 mi. E of Wilmington, on a narrow isl. (c.5 mi. long) in the Atlantic; connected to mainland by bridge and causeway.

Wrigley village (district pop. 83), SW Mackenzie Dist., Northwest Territories, on Mackenzie R., at mouth of Wrigley R.; 63°16′N 123°37′W; trading post; airfield, radio station. Founded (1877) 25 mi. upstream, it was moved to present site 1904. Sometimes called Fort Wrigley.

Wrington, agr. village and parish (pop. 1,448), N Somerset, England, 9 mi. E of Weston-super-Mare. Has 15th-cent. church. John Locke b. here.

Writtle (rĭ′tŭl), town and parish (pop. 3,194), central Essex, England, 2 mi. W of Chelmsford; agr. market. Has agr. col.

Wrockwardine, town and parish (pop. 1,022), central Shropshire, England, 2 mi. W of Wellington; beet-sugar refining; agr. market. Church is mainly Norman.

Wroclaw (vrôts′wäf), Pol. *Wrocław,* province [Pol. *województwo*] (□ 7,321; pop. 1,768,702), SW Poland; ⊙ BRESLAU (Wroclaw). Borders S on Czechoslovakia, W on Germany. From fertile Oder valley rises (SW) to the Sudetes range; highest peak (5,259 ft.), the Schneekoppe, is in the Riesengebirge. Drained by Oder, Kwisa (Queis), Bobrawa (Bober), and Katzbach rivers. Metalworking, glass mfg., textile and paper milling, machinery mfg. are principal industries, concentrated in Breslau, Waldenburg (Walbrzych), Hirschberg (Jelenia Gora), and Liegnitz (Legnica). Coal mining in Waldenburg and Glatz (Klodzko) regions; galena and tetrahedryte are among other minerals worked. Many popular health and winter-sports resorts; Szklarska Poreba (Schreiberhau; also glass-mfg. center), Karpacz (Krummhübel), and Kudowa Zdroj (Bad Kudowa) are among best-known. Rye, potatoes, oats, wheat, barley, flax are principal crops; livestock. Until 1945, in Ger. Lower SILESIA prov.; subsequently briefly called Slask Dolny, Pol. *Śląsk Dolny.* After 1945, Ger. pop. was expelled and replaced by Poles. In 1950, NW part of prov. transferred to Zielona Gora prov., small SE section to Opole prov.

Wroclaw, city, Poland: see BRESLAU.

Wronki (vrôn′kē), Ger. *Wronke* (vrông′kŭ), town (1946 pop. 4,051), Poznan prov., W Poland, on Warta R. and 31 mi. NW of Poznan; lumbering; brickworks; mfg. of soap, candles.

Wrotham (rōō′tŭm), former urban district (1931 pop. 4,510), W Kent, England, 10 mi. WNW of Maidstone; agr. market. Has 13th-cent. church, formerly part of palace of archbishops of Canterbury (removed to Maidstone in 15th cent.).

Wroughton (rô′tŭn), town and parish (pop. 2,641), NE Wiltshire, England, 3 mi. S of Swindon; agr. market in dairying region. Has 14th-15th-cent. church.

Wroxeter (rŏk′sĭtŭr), village (pop. estimate 450), S Ont., on Maitland R. and 30 mi. ENE of Goderich; dairying, mixed farming.

Wroxeter, agr. village and parish (pop. 539), central Shropshire, England, on Severn R. and 7 mi. ESE of Shrewsbury. Near by are remains of *Uriconium,* 4th largest Roman camp in Britain, on Watling Street.

Wrzesnia (vzhĕsh′nyä), Pol. *Września,* Ger. *Wreschen* (vrĕ′shŭn), town (1946 pop. 9,851), Poznan prov., W central Poland, 28 mi. ESE of Poznan; rail junction; mfg. of machinery, cement, chemicals, liqueur; beet-sugar milling, chicory processing, distilling, brewing; trades in grain, cattle.

Wschowa (fŭs-khô′vä), Ger. *Fraustadt* (frou′shtät), town (1939 pop. 7,740; 1946 pop. 4,075) in Lower Silesia, after 1945 in Zielona Gora prov., W Poland, 11 mi. WSW of Leszno; center of sugar-beet area; sugar refining. Founded c.1150; chartered 1524.

Wsetin, Czechoslovakia: see VSETIN.

Wu, province, China: see KIANGSU.

Wu, river, China: see WU RIVER.

Wualpatanta, Honduras: see GUALPATANTA.

Wuan (wōō′än′), town, ⊙ Wuan co. (pop. 303,163), SW Hopeh prov., China, on highway and 30 mi. SSW of Singtai, near Peking-Hankow RR; wheat, millet, beans. Until 1950 in Honan prov.

Wuchai (wōō′jī′), town, ⊙ Wuchai co. (pop. 74,320), N Shansi prov., China, at foot of Luya Mts., 25 mi. WSW of Ningwu; lumbering center; wheat, millet, beans. Coal mines near by.

Wuchan, China: see WUSI.

Wuchang or **Wu-ch'ang** (wōō′chäng′). **1** City (1946 pop. 174,367; 1947 pop. 199,012; 1948 pop. 204,634), ⊙ Hupeh prov., China, port on right bank of Yangtze R., opposite Hanyang and Hankow, at mouth of Han R.; 30°32′N 114°17′E. Administrative and cultural center of the WUHAN cities; cotton and silk weaving, paper mfg., tanning. Seat of Wuhan and Chunghwa universities, medical and agr. colleges; govt. mint. Commercial suburbs and Hankow-Canton rail terminus extend along Yangtze R., N of walled city. The oldest of the Wuhan cities, Wuchang dates from 3d cent. A.D. In 13th cent. it became ⊙ anc. prov. of Hukwang under the Mongol dynasty, and then ⊙ Hupeh upon its separation from Hukwang in 1660s. It was captured (19th cent.) by the Taipings. Here occurred one of the 1st outbreaks of the Chinese revolution (1911). The city was occupied by the Nationalists in 1927, by the Japanese during 1938–45, and by the Communists in 1949. Wuchang became an independent municipality in 1935, when the seat of Wuchang co. (1946 pop. 198,196) was moved 17 mi. SW on the Yangtze to Kinkow, thereafter also called Wuchang. **2** Town, ⊙ Wuchang co. (pop. 266,347), SW Sungkiang prov., Manchuria, China, on railroad and 65 mi. SSE of Harbin, near Kirin line; lead deposits; beans, wheat, hemp, tobacco.

Wucheng or **Wu-ch'eng** (wōō′chŭng′). **1** Town, ⊙ Wucheng co. (pop. 183,743), S Hopeh prov., China, 70 mi. WNW of Tsinan and on Grand Canal; cotton, wheat, millet, kaoliang, peanuts. **2** Town, N Kiangsi prov., China, 13 mi. ENE of Yungsiu, and on Poyang L. at mouth of Siu R.; mfg. (paper, vegetable oil). **3** Town in E Tibet, 50 mi. N of Paan, across Yangtze R.; wheat, beans, cabbage. Until 1913 called Sanyen.

Wu-chi or **Wu-ch'i,** China: see WUKI.

Wuchi, Formosa: see WUSI.

Wu-ch'ia, China: see ULUGHCHAT.

Wu-chiang or **Wu-ch'iang,** town, China: see WUKIANG.

Wu Chiang, river, China: see WU RIVER.

Wu-ch'iao, China: see WUKIAO.

Wuchih (wōō′jŭ′), town, ⊙ Wuchih co. (pop. 134,638), SW Pingyuan prov., China, on Tsin R. and 30 mi. SW of Sinsiang, near Yellow R. (Honan line); rice, wheat, millet, kaoliang. Until 1949 in Honan prov.

Wuchimiho, Manchuria: see SHANGCHIH.

Wuchi Mountains, Mandarin *Wuchih Shan* (wōō′-jŭ′ shän′) [=five finger mountains], central Hainan, Kwangtung prov., China; rise to 5,118 ft. 35 mi. NE of Aihsien; covered by virgin forest. Inhabited by Li aborigines.

Wu-chin, China: see CHANGCHOW.

Wu-ch'ing, China: see WUTSING.

Wuchow or **Wu-chou** (both: wōō′jō′), city (1946 pop. 206,986), ⊙ but independent of Tsangwu co. (1946 pop. 423,614), E Kwangsi prov., China, port on West R. (head of steamer navigation) at mouth of Kwei R., and 120 mi. W of Canton; trade center of E Kwangsi and silk-processing point; cotton weaving, chemical mfg. (sulphuric acid). Rice, millet, wheat, bamboo. Gold deposits near by. Site of univ. Opened 1897 to foreign trade. Was U.S. air base in Second World War, and was briefly held (1944–45) by Japanese. Called Tsangwu from 1913 until 1946, when it became an independent municipality.

Wu-ch'uan. 1 Town, Kwangtung prov., China: see NGCHÜN. **2** Town, Kweichow prov., China: see WUCHWAN.

Wuchuho, Manchuria: see SHANGCHIH.

Wuchwan or **Wu-ch'uan** (both: wōō′chwän′). **1** Town, Kwangtung prov., China: see NGCHÜN. **2** Town (pop. 3,430), ⊙ Wuchwan co. (pop. 138,526), NE Kweichow prov., China, 30 mi. NW of Szenan; tung-oil processing; timber, millet, wheat, beans. Mercury deposits.

Wudinna, village (pop. 281), S South Australia, on central Eyre Peninsula, 120 mi. NNW of Port Lincoln, on Port Lincoln–Penong RR; wheat.

Wufeng (wōō′fŭng′), town (pop. 8,883), ⊙ Wufeng co. (pop. 85,486), SW Hupeh prov., China, near Hunan line, 50 mi. SW of Ichang; tea, beans. Until 1914 called Changlo.

Wufeng, Jap. *Muho* (mōō′hō), town (1935 pop. 8,235), W central Formosa, 5 mi. S of Taichung and on railroad; banana center; rice, sugar cane, fruit.

Wufu, China: see NANKIAO, Yunnan prov.

Wuhan (wōō′hän′), tri-city area of Hupeh prov., central China, on Yangtze R. at mouth of Han R., consisting of HANKOW (mfg., trade), HANYANG (steelworks), and WUCHANG (administration, education). Wuhan is the economic heart of central China, its greatest urban agglomeration (pop. c.1,000,000) and leading transportation hub at crossing of Peking-Canton RR and Yangtze R.

Wuhing or **Wu-hsing** (both: wōō′shĭng′), town (pop. 45,151), ⊙ Wuhing co. (pop. 604,403), northernmost Chekiang prov., China, 40 mi. N of Hangchow, on S shore of Tai L.; major silk-milling center; mfg. of writing brushes. Last stronghold of Taiping Rebellion (1864). Until 1912, Huchow.

Wuho (wōō′hŭ′), town, ⊙ Wuho co. (pop. 129,053), N Anhwei prov., China, 32 mi. ENE of Pengpu and on Hwai R.; rice, wheat, kaoliang, melon seeds, tobacco; winegrowing.

Wu-hsi. 1 City, Kiangsu prov., China: see WUSIH. **2** Town, Suiyuan prov., China: see WUSI.

Wuhsi, Formosa: see WUSI.

Wu-hsiang, China: see WUSIANG.

Wuhsien, China: see SOOCHOW.

Wu-hsing, China: see WUHING.

Wu-hsüan, China: see MOSÜN.

Wu-hsüeh, China: see WUSÜEH.

Wuhu (wōō'hōō'), city (1947 pop. 203,550), ⊙ South Anhwei, China, port on Yangtze R. and 60 mi. SW of Nanking, and on railroad; leading industrial center of S Anhwei; cotton and silk weaving, tanning, flour milling, egg processing. Trades in rice, cotton, tea. Opened 1877 to foreign trade, it rapidly superseded near-by Taiping (present Tangtu) as the chief commercial hub of S Anhwei. A foreign settlement was founded here in 1905. During Second World War, occupied 1938–45 by Japanese. Passed to Communists in 1949, when it became an independent municipality.

Wu-hua, China: see NGWA.

Wuhutsui, Manchuria: see FUHSIEN.

Wu-i, China: see WUYI.

Wuiñaimarca, Lake, Bolivia: see UINAMARCA, LAKE.

Wui Shan, China: see BOHEA HILLS.

Wujih (wōō'rû'), Jap. *Ujitsu* (ōōjē'tsōō), village (1935 pop. 2,412), W central Formosa, 4 mi. SW of Taichung and on railroad; sugar milling; rice.

Wukang. 1 or **Wu-k'ang** (wōō'käng'), town (pop. 5,562), ⊙ Wukang co. (pop. 52,087), N Chekiang prov., China, 24 mi. NNW of Hangchow, SE of the Mokan Shan; rice, wheat. **2** (wōō'gäng') Town, ⊙ Wukang co. (pop. 805,952), SW Hunan prov., China, 60 mi. SW of Shaoyang; rice, wheat, beans, cotton. Arsenic and coal found near by.

Wukari (wōōk'ärē), town (pop. 7,869), Benue prov., Northern Provinces, E central Nigeria, 90 mi. E of Makurdi; agr. trade center; shea nuts, cassava, durra, yams. Its port on Benue R. is Ibi, 25 mi. N.

Wuki. 1 or **Wu-chi** (wōō'jē'), town, ⊙ Wuki co. (pop. 170, 927), SW Hopeh prov., China, 30 mi. ENE of Shihkiachwang; cotton, kaoliang, millet, beans. **2** or **Wu-ch'i** (wōō'chē'), town (pop. 4,083), ⊙ Wuki co. (pop. 167,163), easternmost Szechwan prov., China, 25 mi. NNE of Fengkieh; tung oil, tobacco, rice, potatoes, medicinal herbs. Sulphur deposits, saltworks near by. Until 1914 called Taning.

Wukia, China: see ULUGHCHAT.

Wukiang. 1 or **Wu-ch'iang** (wōō'chyäng'), town, ⊙ Wukiang co. (pop. 124,989), S Hopeh prov., China, 45 mi. NW of Tehchow; cotton, wheat, kaoliang, millet. **2** or **Wu-chiang** (wōō'jyäng'), town (pop. 55,373), ⊙ Wukiang co. (pop. 477,613), S Kiangsu prov., China, on E shore of Tai L., on railroad and 10 mi. S of Soochow, and on Grand Canal; agr. center in rice region; also silk, hemp, rapeseed, beans.

Wu Kiang, river, China: see WU RIVER.

Wukiao or **Wu-ch'iao** (both: wōō'chyou'), town, ⊙ Wukiao co. (pop. 237,676), NW Shantung prov., China, 15 mi. NE of Tehchow: cotton, wheat, kaoliang, corn. Until 1949 in Hopeh prov.

Wukung (wōō'gōōng'), town (pop. 5,805), ⊙ Wukung co. (pop. 128,435), SW Shensi prov., China, 50 mi. W of Sian and on Lunghai RR; cotton-growing center; cattle raising; wheat, beans, indigo, millet.

Wukung Mountains (wōō'gōōng'), W Kiangsi prov., China, on Hunan border, rise to over 4,500 ft. 25 mi. ESE of Pingsiang. Pingsiang coal mines are at N foot.

Wulai (wōō'lī'), Jap. *Urai* (ōōrī'), village, N Formosa, 13 mi. S of Taipei, in mtn. area; hot springs.

Wu-lan-ch'a-pu, China: see OLANCHAB.

Wu-lan-hao-t'e, Manchuria: see ULAN HOTO.

Wular Lake (vōōlûr'), largest lake (□ 44) in Kashmir, in N Vale of Kashmir, 20 mi. NNW of Srinagar; c.10 mi. long, 6 mi. wide; surrounded by marshes. Traversed E-W by Jhelum R.; area decreasing as result of river silting. Sopur is on SW shore; isl. near NE shore has 15th-cent. ruins.

Wülfrath (vül'frät), town (pop. 14,453), in former Prussian Rhine Prov., W Germany, after 1945 in North Rhine-Westphalia, 4 mi. S of Velbert; iron and steel foundries.

Wu Ling, mountains, China: see NAN LING.

Wuling Mountains (wōō'lĭng'), NW Hunan prov., China, form divide bet. Li and Yüan rivers.

Wulukokiati, China: see ULUGHCHAT.

Wulung (wōō'lōōng'), town (pop. 11,457), ⊙ Wulung co. (pop. 124,548), SE Szechwan prov., China, 30 mi. SE of Fowling and on Kien R.; tung oil, hog bristles, rice, wheat. Until 1941, Siangkow.

Wuming (wōō'mĭng'), town, ⊙ Wuming co. (pop. 248,459), SW central Kwangsi prov., China, 26 mi. N of Nanning; gold deposits. Until 1913 called Wuyüan.

Wun (vōōn), town (pop. 12,225), Yeotmal dist., SW Madhya Pradesh, India, near Wardha R., 60 mi. ESE of Yeotmal, on rail spur serving near-by collieries and limestone quarries; cotton ginning, oilseed milling.

Wundwin (wōōn'dwĭn), village, Meiktila dist., Upper Burma, on railroad (Thedaw station) and 60 mi. S of Mandalay; irrigation headworks.

Wuning (wōō'nĭng'), town (pop. 5,248), ⊙ Wuning co. (pop. 107,457), NW Kiangsi prov., China, 60 mi. NW of Nanchang and on Siu R.; tea-growing center; rice, ramie. Anthracite mining.

Wünnenberg (vü'nûnbĕrk), town (pop. 1,785), in former Prussian prov. of Westphalia, NW Germany, after 1945 in North Rhine-Westphalia, 13 mi. SSW of Paderborn.

Wünschelburg, Poland: see RADKOW.

Wunsiedel (vōōn'zē"dûl), town (pop. 8,535), Upper Franconia, NE Bavaria, Germany, main town in the Fichtelgebirge, 20 mi. ENE of Bayreuth; mfg. of textiles, machinery, glass, porcelain, shoes; brewing, tanning, flour milling. Chartered c.1285. Jean Paul b. here. Tin mines, limestone quarries, and clay pits in area. Alexandersbad, with chalybeate springs, is 1½ mi. SE.

Wunstorf (vōōns'tôrf), town (pop. 10,691), in former Prussian prov. of Hanover, W Germany, after 1945 in Lower Saxony, 13 mi. WNW of Hanover; rail junction; oil refining. Has 12th-cent. church.

Wuntho (wōōn'thō), village, Katha dist., Upper Burma, on railroad and 45 mi. SW of Katha; shipping point for Pinlebu coal mine; gold mining (N). Former ⊙ petty Shan state.

Wupatki National Monument (wōōpăt'kē) (□ 54.7; established 1924), N central Ariz., on Little Colorado R. near San Francisco Peaks, and 28 mi. NNE of Flagstaff. Area of pre-Columbian Indian ruins, including more than 800 home sites. Largest pueblo ruin is Wupatki, which accommodated 150–200 persons at max. occupancy (12th cent.). Settlement of region followed eruption in 11th cent. of near-by Sunset Crater, which produced soil-enriching ash and made farming possible.

Wuping or **Wu-p'ing** (wōō'pĭng'), town (pop. 21,644), ⊙ Wuping co. (pop. 140,477), SW Fukien prov., China, near Kwangtung-Kiangsi line, 45 mi. SSW of Changting; rice, wheat. Manganese and coal mines near by.

Wupper River (vōō'pûr), W Germany, formed at Wipperfürth by several headstreams, flows tortuously c.65 mi. N and SW, past Wuppertal, Remscheid, and Solingen, to the Rhine at Leverkusen. Middle valley highly industrialized.

Wuppertal (vōō'pûrtäl), city (□ 57; 1939 pop. 401,672; 1946 pop. 325,846; 1950 pop. 362,125), in former Prussian Rhine Prov., W Germany, after 1945 in North Rhine-Westphalia, on the Wupper and c.15 mi. E of Düsseldorf, adjoining Solingen (SW) and Remscheid (S). Industrial center, noted for its textiles (cloth, silk, velvet, linen, artificial fiber, ribbons, lace, trimmings, rugs, upholstery materials, hats, caps); iron and steel milling (machinery, tools, wire); other mfg.: chemicals (dyes, colors, pharmaceuticals), organs, pianos, paper, wallpaper. Food processing. City extends c.8 mi. along middle course of the Wupper, in its narrow valley and up its slopes. Has interurban suspension tramway, which follows course of the river. Formed 1929 through incorporation of BARMEN, ELBERFELD, BEYENBURG, CRONENBERG, RONSDORF, and VOHWINKEL. A major seat of I.G. Farben concern and a center of Ger. ball- and roller-bearing mfg., city was subjected to severe aerial attacks in Second World War (destruction c.50%).

Wupu or **Wu-p'u** (wōō'pōō'), town, ⊙ Wupu co. (pop. 36,492), NE Shensi prov., China, 75 mi. SE of Yülin, and on Yellow R. (Shansi line; ferry), opposite Küntu; cotton weaving; wheat, kaoliang.

Würbenthal, Czechoslovakia: see VRBNO.

Wu River (wōō). **1** or **Ou River,** local Chinese *Wu Kiang* or *Wu Chiang* (both: wōō' jyäng'), Mandarin *Ou Chiang* (ō' jyäng'), in Chekiang prov., China, rises in 2 branches which join near Lishui, flows 90 mi. ESE, past Tsingtien and Wenchow, to E.China Sea. Total length, including headstreams, 285 mi. Navigable for junks below Sungyang, for launches below Tsingtien. Sometimes spelled Ngeu. **2** Chinese *Wu Shui* (wōō' shwā'), in S China, rises in S Hunan prov. near Linwu, flows 80 mi. S, into Kwangtung prov., past Pingshek and Lokchong, joining Cheng R. to form NORTH RIVER at Kukong. **3** Chinese *Wu Kiang* or *Wu Chiang* (both: wōō' jyäng'), chief stream of Kweichow prov., China, the upper course of KIEN RIVER.

Würm River (vürm), Bavaria, Germany, rises in the Starnberger See, flows 27 mi. NNE and E to the Isar, 6 mi. NNE of Munich. Canalized in lower course, where it is called Würm Canal.

Würmsee, Germany: see STARNBERGER SEE.

Wurno (wûrnō'), town (pop. 9,333), Sokoto prov., Northern Provinces, NW Nigeria, on Kebbi R. and 20 mi. NE of Sokoto; cotton, millet, rice; cattle, skins. Was capital (with Sokoto) of 19th-cent. Sokoto or Fulah empire.

Würselen (vür'zûlûn), town (pop. 13,165), in former Prussian Rhine Prov., W Germany, after 1945 in North Rhine-Westphalia, 3 mi. NE of Aachen; coal mining; mfg. (needles, cigars, tobacco).

Wurtsboro, resort village (pop. 628), Sullivan co., SE N.Y., 10 mi. NNW of Middletown, at base of the Shawangunk range.

Württemberg (wûr'tûmbûrg, Ger. vür'tûmbĕrk), former state (1939 □ 7,532; 1939 pop. 2,896,920) of SW Germany; ⊙ was Stuttgart. Bounded by Baden (S, W, NW), Bavaria (NE, E, S), and L. of Constance (S; Swiss border); includes (S) partial enclave of Hohenzollern. Mountainous region including Swabian Jura (S) and Black Forest (W); drained by the Neckar. Originally inhabited by Celts; occupied successively by Suebi, Romans, and Alemanni. Conquered (c.500) by Clovis; major portion of territory fell to duchy of SWABIA. From 12th cent. on, Württemberg was ruled by counts, who acquired Swabian territory after dissolution of duchy. Count Eberhard V declared (1482) Württemberg holdings indivisible, and was created duke at Diet of Worms (1495). Reformation was introduced 1534. Duchy was devastated in Thirty Years War, and during invasions of Louis XIV. Duke Frederick II (1797-1816) became (1803) elector and assumed (1806) title of king. As Napoleon's ally he expanded his holdings to their final extent. Joined Allies in Nov., 1813. Constitution granted 1819. R.C. bishopric for Württemberg was established (1817) at ROTTENBURG. Siding with Austria, Württemberg was decisively defeated by Prussia at Tauberbischofsheim (1866); joined (1871) German Empire. With termination of monarchy, state received new constitution and joined Weimar Republic (1919). After its capture (spring, 1945) by U.S. and Fr. troops, Württemberg was divided into 2 parts: N section was united with N BADEN and constituted into state of Württemberg-Baden of U.S. zone of occupation; S portion, together with Hohenzollern, became state of Württemberg-Hohenzollern in Fr. occupation zone.

Württemberg-Baden (–bä'dûn), state (□ 6,062; 1946 pop. 3,607,304, including displaced persons 3,675,237; 1950 pop. 3,884,462), SW Germany; ⊙ Stuttgart. Formed 1945 through union of N WÜRTTEMBERG (□ 4,078; 1950 pop. 2,417,146) and N BADEN (□ 1,984; 1950 pop. 1,467,316). Bounded by Rhenish Palatinate (W), Hesse (NW), Bavaria (NE, E), Württemberg-Hohenzollern (S), and Baden (SW). Hilly except for Rhine plain (W); includes outliers of Black Forest (SW), SWABIAN JURA (SE), and part of the ODENWALD (N). Drained by Rhine (W border), Neckar, Jagst, and Kocher rivers. Fertile region; grows spelt, oats; hops and wine along the Neckar and its tributaries; tobacco growing and processing on Rhine plain; the BERGSTRASSE is noted fruitgrowing region. Navigable NECKAR RIVER supplies numerous industrial centers with raw materials. Secondary industries—notably metal (machinery, electrical and transportation equipment, precision and optical instruments) and textiles—predominate, with centers at STUTTGART, MANNHEIM (harbor at confluence of Rhine and Neckar rivers), AALEN, ESSLINGEN, GEISLINGEN, GÖPPINGEN, HEIDENHEIM, HEILBRONN, KARLSRUHE, LUDWIGSBURG, SCHWÄBISCH GMÜD, and ULM; PFORZHEIM is known for its jewelry; WEINHEIM is leatherworking center. Salt worked at BAD FRIEDRICHSHALL, BAD RAPPENAU, and Heilbronn. BAD CANNSTATT, BAD WIMPFEN, MERGENTHEIM, and SCHWÄBISCH HALL are frequented spas. Noted univ. at HEIDELBERG. Placed 1945 in U.S. occupation zone. New constitution ratified 1946. Joined (1949) the German Federal Republic (West German state).

Württemberg-Hohenzollern (–hō"ûntsô'lûrn), state (with LINDAU, □ 4,018; 1946 pop. 1,108,768, including displaced persons 1,118,812; 1950 pop. 1,240,999), SW Germany; ⊙ TÜBINGEN. Formed 1945 through union of S WÜRTTEMBERG (□ 3,457; 1950 pop. 1,097,166) and former Prussian prov. of HOHENZOLLERN. Bounded by Baden (S, W), Württemberg-Baden (N), Bavaria (E), Austria and Switzerland (S). Hilly region extending from Black Forest (W) to Iller R. (E) and L. of Constance (S); includes SWABIAN JURA (NW); drained by Neckar and Danube rivers. Agr. (spelt, oats) and cattle raising; dairying (S); vineyards on shore of. L. of Constance. Tourism in Black Forest (FREUDENSTADT, WILDBAD). Some industry (textiles, machinery, precision instruments), centering in BIBERACH, FRIEDRICHSHAFEN (home of the Zeppelin), RAVENSBURG, REUTLINGEN, ROTTWEIL, and Tübingen; TUTTLINGEN is known for its surgical instruments. Univ. at Tübingen. Placed (1945) in Fr. occupation zone. New constitution ratified 1947. Württemberg-Hohenzollern joined (1949) the German Federal Republic (West German state).

Wurzach (vōōr'tsäkh), town (pop.1,931), S Württemberg, Germany, after 1945 in Württemberg-Hohenzollern, 15 mi. NE of Ravensburg; has baroque castle.

Wurzbach (vōōrts'bäkh), town (pop. 2,947), Thuringia, central Germany, 15 mi. SE of Saalfeld; slate quarrying; cardboard mfg.

Würzburg (wûrts'bûrg, Ger. vürts'bōōrk), city (1939 pop. 107,515; 1946 pop. 55,604; 1950 pop. 78,195), ⊙ Lower Franconia, NW Bavaria, Germany, on the Main (canalized) and 57 mi. NW of Nuremberg; 49°48'N 9°56'E. Rail junction; viticultural center; mfg. of machine tools, chemicals, textiles; lumber milling, brewing. City was almost completely destroyed in Second World War; all noteworthy bldgs., including Romanesque cathedral, noted baroque residence, and univ. (founded 1582), sustained heavy damage. Created bishopric in 741,

Würzburg, until secularized in 1801, was seat of powerful prince-bishops who bore title of dukes of Eastern Franconia. Röntgen was professor of physics at the univ. when he discovered X rays (1895). City captured by U.S. troops April, 1945.

Wurzen (vo͝or'tsŭn), town (pop. 22,234), Saxony, E central Germany, on the Mulde and 15 mi. E of Leipzig; metalworking; mfg. of agr. machinery, wallpaper, felt, carpets, furniture, biscuits. Hydroelectric power station. Has 12th-cent. basilica; 15th-cent. castle, now courthouse. Anc. German settlement. Fortified in 10th cent.; 1st mentioned as town in 961. In Middle Ages, important river crossing on salt-trade route leading E from Halle.

Wurzen Pass or **Koren Pass** (kō'rŭn) (alt. 3,515 ft.), road over the Karawanken bet. Austria and Yugoslavia, SSW of Villach, Austria.

Wurzner Sau, river, Yugoslavia: see Sava Dolinka River.

Wushan (wo͞o'shän'). **1** Town, ⊙ Wushan co. (pop. 121,337), SE Kansu prov., China, 45 mi. W of Tienshui and on upper Wei R.; alt. 4,757 ft.; wool and ramie weaving; rice. Until 1914 called Ningyüan. **2** Town (pop. 25,502), ⊙ Wushan co. (pop. 215,645), E Szechwan prov., China, near Hupeh border, 22 mi. E of Fengkieh, and on Yangtze R., in central section of its gorges; rice, sweet potatoes, millet. Iron mines, coal and sulphur deposits near.

Wusheng (wo͞o'shŭng'), town (pop. 10,996), ⊙ Wusheng co. (pop. 343,718), central Szechwan prov., China, 18 mi. N of Hochwan and on right bank of Kialing R.; tung-oil processing; rice, sweet potatoes, wheat, beans, sugar. Until 1914, Tingyüan.

Wushih, China: see Uch Turfan.

Wushishi (wo͞oshē'shē), town (pop. 1,997), Niger prov., Northern Provinces, W central Nigeria, on Kaduna R., on railroad, and 8 mi. SW of Zungeru; road junction; shea nuts, cotton, cassava, durra.

Wu Shui, China: see Wu River.

Wusi or **Wu-hsi** (both: wo͞o'shē'), town (pop. 7,046), ⊙ Wusi co. (pop. 116,308), E central Suiyuan prov., China, 25 mi. NNW of Kweisui; cattle raising; oats, wheat. Until 1950 called Wuchan.

Wusi or **Wuhsi** (both: wo͞o'shē'), Jap. *Gosei* (gō'sā), town (1935 pop. 5,413), W central Formosa, minor port on W coast, 2 mi. WNW of Shalu; hatmaking; fishing; rice. Sometimes spelled Wuchi.

Wusiang or **Wu-hsiang** (both: wo͞o'shyäng'), town, ⊙ Wusiang co. (pop. 145,530), SE Shansi prov., China, 50 mi. N of Changchih; wheat, millet, kaoliang. Coal mines near by.

Wusih or **Wu-hsi** (both: wo͞o'shē'), city (1948 pop. 273,346), ⊙ South Kiangsu, China, on Grand Canal, N of Tai L., 26 mi. NW of Soochow, and on Shanghai-Nanking RR; cotton-milling center; machine and needle mfg., rice and flour milling, oil pressing. An old walled market town, it became industrialized in late-19th cent., using modern machine methods, and party supplanted the traditional textile center of Soochow. It is ⊙ Wusih co. (1948 pop. 1,078,070), from which it was separated in 1949 to become an independent municipality.

Wusterhausen (vo͞o"stŭrhou'zŭn), town (pop. 4,040), Brandenburg, E Germany, on Dosse R. and 15 mi. W of Neuruppin; grain, potatoes, livestock; forestry. Has late-Gothic church.

Wustrow (vo͞os'trō). **1** Town (pop. 1,628), in former Prussian prov. of Hanover, NW Germany, after 1945 in Lower Saxony, 5 mi. N of Salzwedel; wood products. **2** or **Ostseebad Wustrow** (ôst'zābät'), village (pop. 1,674), Mecklenburg, N Germany, on SW Darss peninsula, on Mecklenburg Bay of the Baltic, 20 mi. NE of Rostock; seaside resort. **3** Resort, Mecklenburg, Germany: see Rerik.

Wusu (wo͞o'so͞o'), town and oasis (pop. 24,899), N Sinkiang prov., China, in the Dzungaria, 140 mi. WNW of Urumchi, and on highway N of the Tien Shan; petroleum center at junction of roads to Kuldja and Chuguchak.

Wusüeh or **Wu-hsüeh** (both: wo͞o'shüĕ'), town (1922 pop. estimate 50,000), SE Hupeh prov., China, port on left bank of Yangtze R. (Kiangsi line) and 16 mi. S of Kwangtsi; exports ramie, salt. Treaty port of call after 1876.

Wusung, Kiangsu prov., China: see Woosung.

Wutach River (vo͞o'täkh), S Baden, Germany, rises in the Titisee, flows 50 mi. ESE and SSW to the Rhine 2 mi. E of Waldshut. In upper reaches called Gutach.

Wutai or **Wu-t'ai** (wo͞o'tī'), town, ⊙ Wutai co. (pop. 197,804), NE Shansi prov., China, 70 mi. NE of Taiyüan, at SW foot of Wutai Mts.; agr. center (millet, kaoliang, corn, wheat, medicinal herbs). Coal mines at Kiatzewan (S).

Wutai Mountains, Chinese *Wutai Shan* or *Wu-t'ai Shan* (wo͞o'tī' shän'), NE Shansi prov., China, near Chahar-Hopeh line; rise to 9,974 ft. 30 mi. NE of Wutai town. Sacred to the Mongols, the mts. contain lamaseries frequented by pilgrims.

Wutan (wo͞o'dän'), town, ⊙ Wutan co., N Jehol prov., Manchuria, 50 mi. N of Chihfeng; has trade with Inner Mongolia; livestock, furs, skins and hides, medicinal herbs, tobacco. Called Wutancheng until 1949. Also called Chüanning in 1930s.

Wutang Mountains, Chinese *Wutang Shan* (wo͞o'däng' shän'), NW Hupeh prov., China, on right bank of Han R.; rise to 5,250 ft. 30 mi. W of Kwanghwa (Laohokow).

Wutankeng or **Wu-tan-k'eng** (both: wo͞o'dän'kŭng'), Jap. *Butanko* (bo͞otäng'kō), village, N Formosa, 8 mi. ESE of Keelung and on railroad; gold-mining center; also silver and copper.

Wuteh, Mongolia: see Dzamyn Ude.

Wuti (wo͞o'dē), town, ⊙ Wuti co. (pop. 262,536), NW Shantung prov., China, 80 mi. NNE of Tsinan; grain. Fisheries, saltworks on coast near by. Until 1914 called Haifeng.

Wuting (wo͞o'dĭng'). **1** Town, Shantung prov., China: see Hweimin. **2** Town (pop. 3,045), ⊙ Wuting co. (pop. 83,351), N central Yunnan prov., China, 35 mi. NNW of Kunming; alt. 6,193 ft.; rice, wheat, millet, beans. Iron mines near by.

Wutsin, China: see Changchow.

Wutsing or **Wu-ch'ing** (both: wo͞o'chĭng'), town, ⊙ Wutsing co. (pop. 367,019), N Hopeh prov., China, 35 mi. NW of Tientsin; cotton, wheat, kaoliang, corn, chestnuts.

Wutu (wo͞o'do͞o), town, ⊙ Wutu co. (pop. 200,750), SE Kansu prov., China, 95 mi. SW of Tienshui; rice, wheat, sesame. Gold mines near by. Until 1913 called Kiehchow.

Wutung (wo͞o'do͝ong'), town, ⊙ Wuting co., E Suiyuan prov., China, 30 mi. NE of Kweisui and on railroad to Peking; cattle raising; wheat, millet. Coal mines near by. Called Kisiaying until 1949.

Wutungkiao or **Wu-t'ung-ch'iao** (both: wo͞o'to͝ong'-chyou'), town, SW Szechwan prov., China, 15 mi. SE of Loshan and on left bank of Min R.

Wuustwezel (vüst'vāzŭl), town (pop. 6,603), Antwerp prov., N Belgium, near Netherlands border, 15 mi. NE of Antwerp; agr. market; frontier post.

Wuwei (wo͞o'wā'). **1** Town, ⊙ Wuwei co. (pop. 111,504), N Anhwei prov., China, 35 mi. W of Wuhu, bet. Chao L. and Yangtze R.; rice, wheat, rapeseed. **2** Town, ⊙ Wuwei co. (pop. 307,756), central Kansu prov., China, 150 mi. NNW of Lanchow and on Silk Road to Sinkiang; alt. 4,983 ft.; wheat-growing center; wool and cotton weaving, match mfg.; sheepskins, hides, grain, licorice. Coal mines, saltworks near by. Until 1913 Liangchow.

Wuyang (wo͞o'yäng'), town, ⊙ Wuyang co. (pop. 401,935), central Honan prov., China, 28 mi. WSW of Yencheng; wheat, beans, kaoliang.

Wuyi or **Wu-i** (both: wo͞o'yē'). **1** Town (pop. 11,852), ⊙ Wuyi co. (pop. 94,971), SW Chekiang prov., China, on tributary of Tsientang R., on rail spur and 18 mi. SSE of Kinhwa; papermaking; winegrowing; indigo, cotton, tobacco, timber. **2** Town, ⊙ Wuyi co. (pop. 224,009), SW Hopeh prov., China, 35 mi. NE of Tehchow; wheat, beans, kaoliang, peanuts.

Wuyi Shan, China: see Bohea Hills.

Wuyüan (wo͞o'yüän'). **1** Town, ⊙ Wuyüan co. (pop. 143,426), NE Kiangsi prov., China, 35 mi. SW of Tunki; tea, timber. Part of Anhwei prov. until 1934 and again briefly during 1947–49. **2** Town, Kwangsi prov., China: see Wuming. **3** Town (pop. 10,290), ⊙ Wuyüan co. (pop. 40,170), W Suiyuan prov., China, on railroad and 95 mi. WNW of Paotow; center of Howtao irrigated area. Trade in furs, wool, grain, licorice is transacted at Lunghingchang, just SE.

Wuyün (wo͞o'yün'), town, ⊙ Wuyün co. (pop. 6,833), NE Heilungkiang prov., Manchuria, 125 mi. SE of Aigun, on Amur R. (USSR line) opposite Innokentyevka; coal deposits; corn, millet, kaoliang.

Wuyyur, India: see Vuyyuru.

Wyaconda (wīŭkŏn'dŭ), city (pop. 483), Clark co., extreme NE Mo., near Wyaconda R., 11 mi. W of Kahoka.

Wyaconda River (wô'kŭndō", wīŭkŏn'dŭ), in S Iowa and NE Mo., rises in Davis co., Iowa, flows SE c.110 mi. to Mississippi R. at La Grange.

Wyalong, town (pop. 524), S central New South Wales, Australia, 230 mi. W of Sydney; gold-mining center.

Wyalusing (wīŭlo͞o'sĭng), agr. borough (pop. 612), Bradford co., NE Pa., 12 mi. SE of Towanda and on Susquehanna R.

Wyalusing State Park (1,671 acres), Grant co., extreme SW Wis., on bluffs near confluence (on Iowa border) of Wisconsin and Mississippi rivers. Has caves, waterfalls, and curious rock formations. On Sentinel Ridge (590 ft. above the Mississippi) are Indian mounds.

Wyandanch (wī'ŭndănch"), village (1940 pop. 647), Suffolk co., SE N.Y., on central Long Isl., 4 mi. E of Farmingdale; mfg. (bottling gases, cement blocks, aircraft parts). Belmont Lake Park is S.

Wyandot (wī'ŭndŏt, wīn'dŏt), county (□ 406; pop. 19,785), N central Ohio; ⊙ Upper Sandusky. Drained by Sandusky R. and small Broken Sword and Tymochtee creeks. Agr. (livestock, grain, poultry, fruit; dairy products); mfg. at Upper Sandusky and Carey; limestone quarries, gravel pits. Formed 1845.

Wyandotte (wī'ŭndŏt, wīn'dŏt), county (□ 151; pop. 165,318), NE Kansas; ⊙ Kansas City. Rolling to hilly area, bounded N by Missouri R. and Mo., E by Mo.; drained by Kansas R. Dairying, general farming. Gas fields. Industries at Kansas City. Formed 1855.

Wyandotte. 1 City, Kansas: see Kansas City, Kansas. **2** Industrial city (pop. 36,846), Wayne co., SE Mich., on Detroit R. SSW of Detroit, within Detroit metropolitan dist. Salt deposits here are basis of extensive chemical industry. Also mfg. of metal toys, novelties, rubber and dairy products; shipbuilding. Bessemer steel was 1st commercially produced here in 1864. Founded on site of Wyandotte Indian village; inc. as city in 1867. **3** Town (pop. 242), Ottawa co., extreme NE Okla., 24 mi. SSW of Joplin (Mo.), and on an arm of L. of the Cherokees. A U.S. school for Indians is near by.

Wyandotte Cave, Crawford co., S Ind., just N of Ohio R., 25 mi. W of New Albany. Limestone cave (one of largest in North America) has miles of passages on 5 levels and large chambers with notable stone formations.

Wyanet (wīŭnĕt', wīnĕt'), village (pop. 950), Bureau co., N Ill., on old Illinois and Mississippi Canal and 6 mi. W of Princeton. Fish hatchery near by.

Wyangala Dam, village (pop. 116), E central New South Wales, Australia, near Cowra, on Lachlan R. and 130 mi. W of Sydney; site of dam.

Wyatt, town (pop. 345), Mississippi co., extreme SE Mo., near Mississippi R., 7 mi. E of Charleston.

Wychbold, England: see Droitwich.

Wycheproof (wĭch'pro͞of), town (pop. 756), N central Victoria, Australia, 155 mi. NW of Melbourne, in wheat, livestock area.

Wycombe, England: see High Wycombe.

Wycombe Marsh, England: see High Wycombe.

Wye (wī), town and parish (pop. 1,454), E central Kent, England, on Great Stour R. and 4 mi. NE of Ashford; agr. market. South Eastern Agr. Col., in 15th-cent. bldg. here, formerly col. for priests.

Wye, Netherlands: see Wijhe.

Wye East River, Md.: see Wye River.

Wye Island, Md.: see Wye River.

Wye Mills (wī), village, Queen Annes and Talbot counties, E Md., 26 mi. N of Cambridge. In Wye Oak State Park is state tree of Md., a 400-year-old white oak (95 ft. high, 165 ft. across crown), which is one of largest in U.S. Wye Chapel (1721; restored) is here; Wye Plantation (1747) is near.

Wye Oak State Park, Md.: see Wye Mills.

Wye River (wī). **1** In Buckingham, England, rises just NW of West Wycombe, flows 9 mi. SE, past High Wycombe and Loudwater, to the Thames opposite Cookham. **2** In Derby, England, rises near Buxton, flows 20 mi. SE, past Buxton and Bakewell, to Derwent R. 3 mi. SE of Bakewell, at Rowsley. **3** In Wales and England, rises on Plinlimmon Fawr, Wales, flows 130 mi. SE, past Rhayader, Builth Wells, Hay, Hereford, Ross, Monmouth, and Chepstow, to Severn R. estuary just S of Chepstow. Forms boundary bet. Radnor and Brecknock, and bet. Monmouth and Gloucester. Navigable below Hay. Noted for scenic beauty of its valley. Welsh, *Gwy.*

Wye River, Md., an estuary on the Eastern Shore, extends c.13 mi. S from point E of Queenstown to Eastern Bay. A branch, Wye East R. (c.15 mi. long), extends S and SE from near Wye Mills, along Talbot-Queen Annes co. line, to Wye R. near its mouth. Wye Isl. (c.5 mi. long; bridged to mainland) lies bet. branches.

Wyeville (wī'vĭl), village (pop. 195), Monroe co., W central Wis., on Lemonweir R. and 45 mi. ENE of La Crosse, in dairy and livestock area.

Wygmael, Belgium: see Herent.

Wygoda, Ukrainian SSR: see Vygoda.

Wygonowo, Lake, Belorussian SSR: see Vygonovo, Lake.

Wyhe, Netherlands: see Wijhe.

Wyhl (vēl, vül), village (pop. 2,055), S Baden, Germany, near the Rhine, 14 mi. NW of Freiburg; tobacco mfg.

Wyhlen (vē'lŭn, vü'–), village (pop. 2,865), S Baden, Germany, at S foot of Black Forest, near the Rhine (Swiss border), 4 mi. SSE of Lörrach, opposite Augst. Mfg. of chemicals; metal construction. Site of Augst-Wyhlen hydroelectric plant.

Wyk or **Wyk auf Föhr** (vēk' ouf fûr'), town (pop. 5,948), in Schleswig-Holstein, NW Germany, harbor on SE tip of Föhr isl.; North Sea resort; ceramics; shell fishing. Has Romanesque church.

Wyk aan Zee, Netherlands: see Wijk aan Zee.

Wyk auf Föhr, Germany: see Wyk.

Wyk by Duurstede, Netherlands: see Wijk bij Duurstede.

Wyke Regis, England: see Weymouth and Melcombe Regis.

Wykoff (wī'kôf), village (pop. 509), Fillmore co., SE Minn., near Iowa line, 24 mi. SSE of Rochester, in grain, livestock, poultry area; dairy products.

Wyl, Switzerland: see Wil.

Wylam, town and parish (pop. 1,279), S Northumberland, England, on Tyne R. and 8 mi. W of Newcastle-upon-Tyne; coal mining. George Stephenson b. here.

Wylie, town (pop. 1,295), Collin co., N Texas, 21 mi. NE of Dallas, in agr. area.

Wylkowyszki, Lithuania: see Vilkaviskis.

Wylye River (wī'lē), Wiltshire, England, rises 6 mi. SW of Warminster near Somerset border, flows 22 mi. NE and SE, past Wilton, to the Avon at Salisbury.

Wyman Lake, Somerset co., central Maine, artificial lake formed in the Kennebec at Bingham by Wyman Dam (150 ft. high, 2,810 ft. long; for power; completed 1931).

Wymeswold, agr. village and parish (pop. 755), N Leicester, England, 5 mi. ENE of Loughborough; cheese making. Has 14th–15th-cent. church.

Wymondham (wĭ'mŭndŭm, wĭn'dŭm), urban district (1951 census 5,664), central Norfolk, England, 9 mi. SW of Norwich; agr. market. Has church of Norman origin, once part of 14th-cent. abbey. Kett's rebellion (1549) originated here.

Wymore (wī'môr), city (pop. 2,258), Gage co., SE Nebr., 10 mi. SSE of Beatrice and on Big Blue R., near Kansas line; shipping and railroad center; flour, livestock, grain. Founded 1871.

Wynaad (wī'näd), rugged section (□ c.180) of Western Ghats, India, forming SW portion of Deccan Plateau in Nilgiri and Malabar dists., SW Madras; separated from Nilgiri Hills (E) by upper course of Moyar R. Average height, 3,000 ft.; rises to over 6,000 ft. in several peaks and to 7,673 ft. in Camel's Hump or Vavul Mala (S); average annual rainfall, 130 in. Noted for extensive tea, rubber, spice (pepper, ginger), and coffee plantations and rich timber (teak, blackwood) forests; mica quarries. Usually called the Wynaad.

Wynantskill (wī'nŭntskĭl"), village (1940 pop. 1,428), Rensselaer co., E N.Y., just SE of Troy, in dairying area.

Wynberg (wĭn'bûrg, Afrikaans vĭn'bĕrkh), residential town, SW Cape Prov., U. of So. Afr., SSE suburb of Cape Town, on E side of Table Mtn. Site of Battswood Training School, Inc. in Cape Town 1927.

Wyncote (wĭn'kōt), village (1940 pop. 3,301), in CHELTENHAM township, Montgomery co., SE Pa., N suburb of Philadelphia; mfg. (hosiery, cement, ink).

Wyndham (wĭn'dŭm), northernmost port (pop. 458) of Western Australia, at head of Cambridge Gulf, 270 mi. SW of Darwin; 15°28'S 128°6'E. Port for Kimberley Goldfield; meat packing.

Wyndmere (wīnd'mēr), village (pop. 627), Richland co., SE N.Dak., 25 mi. W of Wahpeton.

Wynghene, Belgium: see WINGENE.

Wynigen (vē'nĭgŭn), town (pop. 2,345), Bern canton, NW central Switzerland, 4 mi. NNE of Burgdorf; farming.

Wynne (wĭn), city (pop. 4,142), ⊙ Cross co., E Ark., c.45 mi. W of Memphis (Tenn.), on W slope of Crowley's Ridge; ships peaches, rice, lumber, cotton. Founded 1863.

Wynnedale, town (pop. 75), Marion co., central Ind., NW suburb of Indianapolis.

Wynnewood. 1 or **Wynne Wood** (wĭ'nĭwŏŏd), city (pop. 2,423), Garvin co., S central Okla., 7 mi. SSE of Pauls Valley; trade and shipping point for agr. area (livestock, poultry, cotton, alfalfa, pecans). Mfg. of cottonseed products, asphalt, brooms, lumber, concrete blocks; pecan shelling, oil refining, cotton ginning. **2** Village, Pa.: see LOWER MERION.

Wynnum (wĭ'nŭm), town (pop. 13,528), SE Queensland, Australia, 17 mi. ENE of Brisbane; seaside resort; fruit, poultry.

Wynona (wīnō'nŭ), city (pop. 678), Osage co., N Okla., 8 mi. S of Pawhuska.

Wynoochee River (wīnōō'chē), W Wash., rises in Olympic Natl. Park, flows c.60 mi. S to Chehalis R. W of Montesano.

Wynot (wī'nŏt), village (pop. 233), Cedar co., NE Nebr., 10 mi. NNE of Hartington, near Missouri R. Duck and pheasant hunting in vicinity.

Wynwood, Pa.: see LOWER MERION.

Wynyard (wĭn'yŭrd), town (pop. 1,084), S central Sask., near Quill Lakes, 90 mi. NNE of Regina, at foot of Touchwood Hills; grain elevators. Resort.

Wynyard, town (pop. 1,858), N Tasmania, 80 mi. WNW of Launceston and on Bass Strait; agr. center (wheat, oats, barley, potatoes, flax); butter factories.

Wyocena (wīŭsē'nŭ), village (pop. 714), Columbia co., S central Wis., 8 mi. SE of Portage, in agr. area.

Wyola (wīō'lŭ), village (pop. c.150), Big Horn co., S Mont., on Little Bighorn R., near Wyo. line, and 43 mi. SSE of Hardin; shipping point in livestock area.

Wyoming (wīō'mĭng), village (pop. 523), S Ont., 15 mi. E of Sarnia, in oil-producing region; dairying, mixed farming, flour milling.

Wyoming, state (land □ 97,506; with inland waters □ 97,914; 1950 pop. 290,529; 1940 pop. 250,742), W U.S., bordered N by Mont., E by S.Dak. and Nebr., S by Colo., SW by Utah, W by Idaho; 8th in area, 47th in pop.; admitted 1890 as 44th state; ⊙ Cheyenne. The "Equality State," rectangular, measures c.356 mi. E–W, 278 mi. N–S. Lying in the Rocky Mts. and Great Plains physiographic provs., the state consists of a vast upland (average elevation 5–7,000 ft.), crossed by mtn. ranges, with intervening river basins and rolling plains. From the NW corner to the S central border, the Continental Divide traverses the state along the crests of the Wind River Range and the Sierra Madre (a N extension of the Park Range of Colo.). In the E are the high Great Plains, characterized by broad stretches of grassland, negligible woodland, and low rainfall (10–20 in. annually). The fairly level expanse is broken by the Goshen Hole depression in the SE and by the W slopes of the Black Hills and the noted Devils Tower in the NE. This section lies within the Missouri R. basin and is drained by the Powder, Belle Fourche, Cheyenne, and North Platte rivers. E of the Divide, in the Rockies, the Bighorn Mts. (8–10,000 ft.) and the Absaroka Range (10–13,000 ft.) enclose the broad basin (c.100 mi. N–S, 60 mi. E–W) of the Bighorn R., and, in the S, the Medicine Bow Mts. and Laramie Mts. enclose the Laramie Plains. In the NW corner is the YELLOWSTONE NATIONAL PARK region, a lofty plateau (c.7,000 ft.) surrounded by peaks of 10–11,000 ft. and crossed by the upper course of the Yellowstone R.; Yellowstone L. is the largest in Wyo. To the S, lying W of the Divide and running roughly parallel to the Idaho line, are the Teton (with Grand Teton, 13,766 ft.), Gros Ventre (rising to over 11,000 ft.), and Salt R. (c.10,000 ft.) mtn. ranges. Gannett Peak (13,785 ft.), in the Wind R. Range, is the highest point in the state. The central and SW counties lie in an extensive semiarid tract, commonly called the Wyoming basin, which merges with the Great Plains in the E and the Colorado Plateau in the S and forms a topographical break in the Rocky Mtn. system. It is a region of scrub and sagebrush, with sand dunes, buttes, and low hills, and drained mainly by the Green and Sweetwater rivers. The mostly dry continental climate of Wyo. is marked by severe winters and fairly cool summers with an annual average rainfall of 15 in.; yearly snowfall is c.55 in. Cheyenne has a mean temp. of 25°F. in Jan. and 67°F. in July. The state's total farm land amounts to 33,000,000 acres, most of it devoted to sheep and cattle raising. With over 1,000,000 head of cattle and c.3,500,000 sheep and lambs, Wyo. is a leading livestock region and ranks next to Texas in wool and mutton production. The large sheep and cattle ranches are located in the Great Plains (E) and the intermontane basins of the central and S parts of the state. Horse raising is important, and in some irrigated areas dairying is carried on. Chief stock markets are Cheyenne (Wyo.'s largest city), Casper, Green River, Laramie, and Rawlins. The state's principal agr. crops (grown mostly for livestock feed) are hay, wheat, corn, potatoes, oats, barley, sugar beets, and beans. Dry farming is practiced in the E where a sturdy wheat crop is produced, but elsewhere agr. depends upon irrigation. Reclamation works include PATHFINDER DAM, SEMINOE DAM, GUERNSEY DAM on the North Platte, and other projects on the Bighorn, Shoshone, and Wind rivers. Goshen Hole, Bighorn R. basin, and the Salt R. and Wind R. valleys are intensive farming regions (grain, sugar beets, beans, fruit). Agr.-processing plants (sugar, flour) are at Torrington, Sheridan, Wheatland, and a few other towns. Much of the state is underlain with good quality bituminous coal, said to be the greatest reserves in the country, but so far largely undeveloped. The main coal mines are near Gillette, Rock Springs, Superior, Sheridan, and Hanna. First in value, however, among Wyo.'s mineral resources is petroleum, most of which comes from the Salt Creek, Teapot Dome (naval oil reserve), Big Muddy, Elk Basin, N Bighorn basin, and Lusk-Greybull areas. Oil refineries are located at Casper (one of the most important oil centers in the Rocky Mtn. area), Glenrock, Greybull, Lovell, Thermopolis, Cheyenne, Cody, Worland, and elsewhere. Other important mineral products include natural gas and gasoline, iron ore (mined at Sunrise, near Guernsey, and shipped to smelters at Pueblo, Colo.), phosphate rock (W), gold, clay products, and low-grade copper; deposits of potash, gypsum, and asbestos also occur. Outside of oil refining and beet sugar processing, Wyo.'s mfg. industries are on a small scale. Casper (tents, bricks, torpedoes), Cheyenne (airplane and railway workshops), Laramie (cement), Sheridan, and Rawlins (pistols, soda products) are the chief mfg. centers. Railroad ties are made at Evanston from local timber (fir, pine, spruce forests in mts.), and there are other sawmills. Some 51% of the state's area is in Federal ownership. Its clear mtn. air and abundant sunshine make Wyo. a popular health resort. Besides Yellowstone Natl. Park, the principal sites of interest are GRAND TETON NATIONAL PARK, DEVILS TOWER NATIONAL MONUMENT, SHOSHONE CAVERN NATIONAL MONUMENT, and the mineral hot springs near THERMOPOLIS; dude ranching, hunting (elk, moose, deer, antelope), trout fishing, and mtn. climbing are the main recreational activities. The Univ. of Wyo. is at Laramie. John Colter, a member of the Lewis and Clark expedition, was probably the 1st white man to explore (1807) parts of what is now Wyo.; a trapper himself, he ushered in a period of profitable fur trading. A route to the West across the Continental Divide was opened up in 1812 by the discovery of SOUTH PASS, which was later used by Capt. B. de Bonneville's exploratory expedition (1832) and by the thousands of pioneers moving W along the Oregon Trail during the Calif. gold rush (1849–51). The 1st permanent fur-trading posts were established at FORT LARAMIE (1834) and at FORT BRIDGER (1843). The settlement of Wyo. proceeded rapidly as the Pony Express, railroad, and telegraph facilitated communication with the East and the development of the area's gold and coal deposits. A period (1860–70) of bitterly fought Indian wars failed to stem the tide of immigration. Prior to its organization as a separate territory in 1869, Wyo. formed part of the Oregon, Idaho, Dakota, and Utah territories. The open ranges soon attracted cattlemen, who drove their herds up from Texas; later, sheep were pastured on the public ranges. The late 19th cent. was a turbulent period marked by cattle rustling and cattlemen-sheepmen feuds. The state's economy, already diversified by the introduction of dry farming and irrigated agr., was given a boost c.1912 by the discovery of rich petroleum fields and other valuable mineral resources. Wyo. was the 1st to adopt women's suffrage(1869) and the 1st to elect a woman governor, Mrs. Nellie Tayloe Ross (1925–27). See also articles on the cities, towns, geographic features and the 23 counties: ALBANY, BIG HORN, CAMPBELL, CARBON, CONVERSE, CROOK, FREMONT, GOSHEN, HOT SPRINGS, JOHNSON, LARAMIE, LINCOLN, NATRONA, NIOBRARA, PARK, PLATTE, SHERIDAN, SUBLETTE, SWEETWATER, TETON, UINTA, WASHAKIE, WESTON.

Wyoming. 1 County (□ 598; pop. 32,822), W N.Y.; ⊙ Warsaw. Drained by Genesee R. and Tonawanda and Cattaraugus creeks; includes part of Letchworth State Park, in valley of the Genesee. Dairying and farming area (vegetables, grain, fruit); diversified mfg., especially at Warsaw and Perry. Formed 1841. **2** County (□ 396; pop. 16,766), NE Pa.; ⊙ Tunkhannock. Hilly agr. region drained by scenic Susquehanna R. Settled in 18th cent. by New Englanders. Dairying; flagstone quarrying, sand, gravel; woodworking, lumber, gristmills. Formed 1842. **3** County (□ 504; pop. 37,540), S W.Va.; ⊙ Pineville. On Allegheny Plateau; drained by Guyandot R. and tributaries. An important bituminous and semibituminous coal-producing co.; timber; natural gas, agr. (livestock, poultry, truck, fruit, tobacco). Formed 1850.

Wyoming. 1 Town (pop. 911), Kent co., central Del., 3 mi. SSW of Dover, in fruit and grain area; canning. **2** City (pop. 1,496), Stark co., N central Ill., 14 mi. SSE of Kewanee; corn, oats, wheat. Bituminous-coal mines near by. Inc. 1865. **3** Town (pop. 724), Jones co., E Iowa, 34 mi. ENE of Cedar Rapids; livestock, grain. **4** Village (pop. 325), Chisago co., E Minn., 27 mi. N of St. Paul, in lake region; grain, livestock, poultry. **5** Village (pop. 508), Wyoming co., W N.Y., 15 mi. SSE of Batavia; produces dried apples, canned foods, lumber, textiles. Agr. (apples, beans, hay); timber. **6** City (pop. 5,582), Hamilton co., extreme SW Ohio, a N suburb of Cincinnati. Settled 1865, inc. 1874. **7** Borough (pop. 4,511), Luzerne co., NE central Pa., 4 mi. NNE of Wilkes-Barre and on Susquehanna R.; anthracite; silk, metal products. Wyoming Battle Monument commemorates Wyoming Valley massacre (1778) of settlers by Tories and Indians. Inc. 1885. **8** Village, R.I.: see RICHMOND.

Wyoming Range, in Rocky Mts. of W Wyo., near Idaho line, just E of Salt River Range and Greys R.; extends c.40 mi. N–S. Highest point, Wyoming Peak (11,388 ft.). Includes part of Bridger Natl. Forest.

Wyoming Valley (c.20 mi. long, 3–4 mi. wide), in Luzerne co., NE Pa., along Susquehanna R. below mouth of the Lackawanna; rich anthracite region. Chief settlement, Wilkes-Barre. Pennsylvania disputed title to valley with first settlers from Conn. until Congress decided (1782) in favor of Pa. Wyoming Valley massacre of settlers by Indians and Tories (1778) is commemorated by monument in Wyoming borough.

Wyomissing (wīōmĭ'sĭng), borough (pop. 4,187), Berks co., SE central Pa., 3 mi. WSW of Reading; machinery, textiles, bricks. Seat of Wyomissing Polytechnic Inst. Founded 1896, inc. 1906.

Wyomissing Hills, borough (pop. 646), Berks co., SE central Pa., just NW of Wyomissing.

Wyong (wī'ŏng), town (pop. 1,324), E New South Wales, 45 mi. NNE of Sydney; dairying center; hardwood timber.

Wyrardisbury or **Wraysbury** (both: răz'bŭrē), residential town and parish (pop. 2,093), SE Buckingham, England, near the Thames, 3 mi. NW of Staines; paper mill. Has 13th-cent. church.

Wyre (wīr), island (pop. 44) of the Orkneys, Scotland, just off SE coast of Rousay; 2 mi. long.

Wyre Forest, England: see BEWDLEY.

Wyre River, Lancashire, England, rises in N Lancashire 10 mi. ESE of Lancaster, flows 28 mi. SW, past Garstang and Poulton-le-Fylde, to Morecambe Bay at Fleetwood.

Wyrzysk (vĭ'zhĭsk), Ger. *Wirsitz* (vĭr'zĭts), town (pop. 3,039), Bydgoszcz prov., NW Poland, 30 mi. W of Bydgoszcz; brewing, flour milling, sawmilling.

Wysg, Wales: see USK RIVER.

Wysmierzyce (vĭshmyĕ-zhĭ'tsĕ), Pol. *Wyśmierzyce*, Rus. *Vysmerzhitse* (vĭsmyĭrzhĭ'tsĕ), town (pop. 1,118), Kielce prov., E central Poland, near Pilica R., 17 mi. NW of Radom.

Wysock, Ukrainian SSR; see VYSOTSK, Rovno oblast.

Wysoka (vĭsô'kä), Ger. *Wissek* (vĭ'sĕk), town (pop. 1,321), Bydgoszcz prov., NW Poland, 37 mi. WNW of Bydgoszcz; mfg. of cement, agr. machinery.

Wysoka Gora, Poland: see HOHENFRIEDEBERG.

Wysokie or **Wysokie Mazowieckie** (vĭsô′kyĕ mäzôvyĕts′kyĕ), Rus. *Mazovetsk* (mŭzôv′yĭtsk), town (pop. 2,121), Bialystok prov., NE Poland, 70 mi. NE of Warsaw in an agr. area (grain); brick mfg., flour milling.

Wysokie, Belorussian SSR: see Vysokoye, Brest oblast.

Wyszkow (vĭsh′ko͞of), Pol. *Wyszków*, Rus. *Vyshkov* (vĭsh′kŭf), town (pop. 5,021), Warszawa prov., E central Poland, on Bug R., on railroad and 32 mi. NNE of Warsaw; mfg. of machinery, cement, glass, vegetable oil; flour milling, sawmilling, brewing, tanning.

Wyszogrod (vĭ-shô′gro͞ot), Pol. *Wyszogród*, Rus. *Vyshegrod* (vĭshĭgrôt′), town (pop. 2,267), Warszawa prov., E central Poland, port on the Vistula, opposite Bzura R. mouth, and 35 mi. WNW of Warsaw. Has notable church, which was 1st built 12th–13th cent.

Wythe (wĭth), county (□ 460; pop. 23,327), SW Va.; ⊙ Wytheville. Partly in Great Appalachian Valley traversed by ridges, with the Alleghenies in N and NW, part of Iron Mts. in S; drained by New R. Includes part of Jefferson Natl. Forest. Agr. (especially cabbage; also grain, potatoes); bluegrass pastures support beef, dairy cattle. Lead, zinc mines; timber. Industries at Wytheville, Ivanhoe. Formed 1790.

Wythenshawe (wĭ′dhŭnshô), residential town in Cheadle and Gatley urban dist., N Cheshire, England, 4 mi. E of Altrincham; mfg. of lubricating oil, electrical equipment, biscuits.

Wytheville (wĭth′vĭl), town (pop. 5,513), ⊙ Wythe co., SW Va., 65 mi. WSW of Roanoke. Trade, market, processing point for agr., stock-raising area; mfg. of hosiery, shirts, furniture, textiles; meat packing, flour and lumber milling, rock quarrying. Girls' school. Founded 1792; inc. 1839.

Wytopitlock, village, Maine: see Reed.

Wytopitlock Lake (wĭ″tŭpĭt′lŏk), Aroostook co., E Maine, 27 mi. SW of Houlton; 3 mi. long. Source of **Wytopitlock Stream,** which flows 15 mi. SE to Mattawamkeag R.

Wyzyna Krakowsko-Czestochowska, Poland: see Cracow Jura.

X

Xaghara (shä′gärä) or **Shagra** (shä′grä), Maltese *Xagħara*, town (pop. 4,759), central Gozo, Maltese Isls., 18 mi. NW of Valletta; citrus fruit, grapes; goats.

Xaianga River, Port. Guinea: see Geba River.

Xalitzintla (sälētsēn′tlä), town (pop. 1,616), Puebla, central Mexico, at NE foot of Popocatepetl, 21 mi. W of Puebla; cereals, maguey, livestock.

Xalmimilulco (sälmēmēlo͞ol′kō), town (pop. 3,023), Puebla, central Mexico, 15 mi. NW of Puebla; cereals, fruit, maguey, stock.

Xalostoc or **San Cosme Xalostoc** (sän kōz′mā sälōstōk′), town (pop. 2,107), Tlaxcala, central Mexico, 13 mi. NE of Tlaxcala; cereals, maguey, vegetables, stock.

Xaloxtoc (sälōstōk′), officially San Pedro Xaloxtoc, town (pop. 1,771), Mexico state, central Mexico, 11 mi. N of Mexico city; cereals, maguey, livestock.

Xalpatlahuac (sälpätläwäk′), town (pop. 1,231), Guerrero, SW Mexico, in Sierra Madre del Sur, 7 mi. SW of Tlapa; alt. 5,259 ft.; cereals, fruit, stock.

Xaltocan or **San Martín Xaltocan** (sän märtēn′ sältō′kän), town (pop. 1,373), Tlaxcala, central Mexico, 8 mi. NNE of Tlaxcala; cereals, maguey, stock.

Xammes (säm), village (pop. 162), Meurthe-et-Moselle dept., NE France, 10 mi. WNW of Pont-à-Mousson.

Xanten (zăn′tŭn, Ger. ksän′tŭn), town (pop. 4,042), in former Prussian Rhine Prov., W Germany, after 1945 in North Rhine-Westphalia, in the Ruhr, near left bank of the Rhine, 7 mi. W of Wesel. Noted Gothic collegiate church of St. Victor was severely damaged during heavy fighting here in Second World War (March, 1945). Mentioned in Nibelungenlied as birthplace of Siegfried.

Xanthe or **Xanthi** (both: ksän′thē), nome (□ 667; pop. 98,575), W Thrace, Greece; ⊙ Xanthe. Bordered N by Bulgaria (along the Rhodope Mts.), S by Aegean Sea, and W by Macedonia along Mesta R. Agr.: tobacco, grain, cotton; livestock; fishing. Served by Salonika-Adrianople RR; Xanthe is main center, Porto Lago a potential port. Separated from Rhodope nome after Second World War.

Xanthe or **Xanthi,** city (1951 pop. 27,302), ⊙ Xanthe nome, W Thrace, Greece, on railroad 115 mi. ENE of Salonica; major tobacco center, producing also barley, beans, vegetables, lumber. Linked by road across Rhodope Mts. with Smolyan (Bulgaria). Known as Eskije under Turkish rule (until Balkan Wars, 1912–13), the city developed (1890s) in connection with railroad construction, succeeding old Turkish tobacco center of Yenije (see Genesaia).

Xanthus (zănth′ŭs), anc. city of Lycia, SW Asia Minor, whose site is on Koca R. (anc. Xanthus) 5 mi. from its mouth on the Mediterranean, 22 mi. SE of Fethiye, Turkey. Its rich ruins were explored in mid-19th cent.; many of its fine sculptures are in British Mus.

Xanthus River. 1 River of anc. Lydia, W Asia Minor, also called the Scamander, modern Kucuk Menderes River. **2** River of anc. Lycia, SW Asia Minor, the modern Koca River.

Xapecó, Brazil: see Chapecó.

Xapuri (shŭpo͞orē′), city (pop. 1,288), SE Acre territory, westernmost Brazil, head of navigation and hydroplane landing on Acre R., near Bolivia border, and 65 mi. SW of Rio Branco; rubber, Brazil nuts, hardwood. Formerly spelled Xapury. Gold deposits near by.

Xassengue (shäsĕng′gā), village, Malange prov., N central Angola, on upper Kwango R. and 170 mi. ESE of Malange. Also spelled Chassengue.

Xauen (shä′wĕn) or **Xexauen** (shäshä′wĕn), Fr. *Chechaouene*, town (pop. 14,476), ⊙ Gomara territory (□ 1,510; 1945 pop. 134,494), W central Sp. Morocco, on W slope of Rif Mts., overlooking the upper Uad Lau valley, 28 mi. S of Tetuán; Moslem holy city, founded 15th cent. by Moors expulsed from Granada, and long closed to non-Moslems. It is surrounded by walls and still presents a medieval appearance. Has flourishing handicraft industry. Occupied 1920 by Spaniards, who were forced to abandon it (1924–26) during Rif revolt. Also spelled Chauen, Shishawen.

Xavantes, Brazil: see Chavantes.

Xayacatlán (sīäkätlän′), officially Xayacatlán de Bravo, town (pop. 1,195), Puebla, central Mexico, 5 mi. NE of Acatlán; rice, sugar cane, fruit, stock. San Jerónimo Xayacatlán is 4 mi. E.

Xcalak (skäläk′), town (pop. 227), Quintana Roo, SE Mexico, on E Yucatan Peninsula; small artificial port guarding entrance to Chetumal Bay.

Xenacoj or **Santo Domingo Xenacoj** (sän′tō dōmĕng′gō sänäkōkh′), town (1950 pop. 1,879), Sacatepéquez dept., S central Guatemala, 9 mi. NNE of Antigua; alt. 8,661 ft.; market center; corn, black beans; cattle raising.

Xenia (zē′nēŭ). **1** Village (pop. 643), Clay co., S central Ill., 16 mi. E of Salem, in agr., oil, and natural-gas area. **2** City (pop. 12,877), ⊙ Greene co., S central Ohio, 14 mi. ESE of downtown Dayton, near Little Miami R.; trade center for stock-raising and farming area. Mfg.: rope, twine, furniture, shoes, advertising novelties, electrical equipment, foundry products. Seat of Ohio Soldiers' and Sailors' Orphans' Home. Wilberforce Univ. is at Wilberforce (3 mi. NE). Laid out 1803.

Xerez or **Xeres,** Spain: see Jerez.

Xerias River, Greece: see Titaresios River.

Xerochori, Greece: see Histiaia.

Xeronesi or **Xeronisi** (both: ksĕrônē′sē). **1** One of Petalia Isls., in Gulf of Petalion, Greece, 1 mi. off Euboea; 1.5 mi. long, 1 mi. wide. Also called Xero. **2** Islands in the Sporades, Greece: see Likorema; Peristera.

Xeropotamos or **Xiropotamos** (both: ksĕrôpô′tŭmôs), town (pop. 2,983), Drama nome, E Macedonia, Greece, 3 mi. NW of Drama; tobacco, barley; olive oil. Formerly called Vesotsane, Visotsani, or Vissotsani.

Xeros, Cyprus: see Karavostasi.

Xerovouni (ksĕrôvo͞o′nē), mountain outlier of central Pindus system, S Epirus, Greece, W of Arachthus R.; rises to 5,295 ft. 15 mi. N of Arta.

Xertigny (zĕrtēnyē′), village (pop. 739), Vosges dept., E France, in Monts Faucilles, 9 mi. S of Épinal; brewery, small metalworks; cotton milling.

Xewkija or **Showkija** (both: shōkē′jä), town (pop. 3,079), S Gozo, Maltese Isls., 1½ mi. SE of Victoria; forage, wheat; goats, sheep. Fishing. The near-by Gourgion Tower, notable landmark, was demolished (1942) during Second World War.

Xexauen, Sp. Morocco: see Xauen.

Xichú (sēcho͞o′), town (pop. 523), Guanajuato, central Mexico, at E foot of Sierra Gorda, 30 mi. E of San Luis de la Paz; zinc and lead mining.

Xicoténcatl (sēkōtĕn′kätl), town (pop. 991), Tamaulipas, NE Mexico, 50 mi. SSE of Ciudad Victoria; henequen, stock.

Xicotlán (sēkōtlän′), town (pop. 455), Puebla, central Mexico, 38 mi. S of Matamoros; corn, stock.

Xiengkhouang (syĕng′khwäng′), town, ⊙ Xiengkhouang (or Tranninh) prov. (□ 7,500; 1947 pop. 84,000), N Laos, in Tranninh Plateau at alt. of 3,800 ft., on road and 85 mi. ESE of Luang Prabang; trading center; salt mines. Archaeological remains near by. Until 1830, ⊙ petty Lao state.

Xiengmai, Thailand: see Chiangmai.

Xilitla (hēlēt′lä), town (pop. 2,092), San Luis Potosí, E Mexico, at E foot of Sierra Madre Oriental, 45 mi. S of Valles; coffee-growing center.

Xilokastron, Greece: see Xylokastron.

Xinavane (shēnävä′nā), sugar mill, Sul do Save prov., S Mozambique, on Komati R. and 65 mi. N of Lourenço Marques (linked by rail).

Xingu River (sēng-go͞o′), large right tributary of the Amazon, N and N central Brazil, rises in several branches in central Mato Grosso (Serra do Roncador), flows N into Pará, entering the Amazon at the head of its delta below Pôrto de Moz. Length, 1,230 mi. Navigable in lower 100 mi. Chief tributary, Iriri R. (left). Course is interrupted by rapids and falls, and remains partially unexplored. Formerly spelled Xingú.

Xinias, Lake, Greece: see Xynias, Lake.

Xions, Poland: see Ksiaz.

Xique-Xique (shē′kĭ-shē′kĭ), city (pop. 2,519), NW Bahia, Brazil, on right bank of São Francisco R. (navigable) and 40 mi. NE of Barra; rock-crystal-mining center; gold placers, silver and lead deposits. Ships carnauba wax. Formerly spelled Chique-Chique.

Xirias River, Greece: see Titaresios River.

Xiririca, Brazil: see Eldorado.

Xirohkori, Greece: see Histiaia.

Xiropotamos, Greece: see Xeropotamos.

Xiutetelco (sūtātĕl′kō), officially San Juan Xiutetelco, town (pop. 1,877), Puebla, central Mexico, on Veracruz border, 2 mi. ESE of Teziutlán; corn, coffee, tropical fruit. Anc. pyramids are near by.

Xocchel (sōkchĕl′), town (pop. 1,227), Yucatan, SE Mexico, 30 mi. ESE of Mérida; henequen, sugar cane, corn.

Xochiatipán (sōchyätēpän′), town (pop. 754), Hidalgo, central Mexico, 23 mi. SSE of Huejutla; corn, rice, sugar cane, tobacco, livestock.

Xochicalco, Mexico: see Tetecala.

Xochicoatlán (sōchēkwätlän′), town (pop. 1,245), Hidalgo, central Mexico, 14 mi. NE of Metztitlán; alt. 6,568 ft.; corn, beans, fruit, cotton, tomatoes.

Xochihuehuetlán (sōchēwäwätlän′), town (pop. 2,988), Guerrero, SW Mexico, in Sierra Madre del Sur, near Oaxaca–Puebla border, 55 mi. ENE of Chilapa; cereals, sugar cane, fruit, forest products (rubber, resin, vanilla).

Xochiltepec (sōchēl″tāpĕk′), town (pop. 1,031), Puebla, central Mexico, 9 mi. NE of Matamoros; corn, sugar cane.

Xochimilco (sōchēmēl′kō, shō–, hō–), city (pop. 14,370), Federal Dist., central Mexico, on small L. Xochimilco, 13 mi. S of Mexico city; a picturesque residential suburb, famous for its canals lined with poplars and flowers, and for its "floating gardens." On L. Xochimilco, on rafts covered with soil (called *chinamoas*), Indians raised vegetables, fruits, and flowers, which they transported by La Viga Canal to Mexico city's markets; the rafts became isls. rooted to the lake bottom. Today boating on the canals is a popular diversion for tourists and the people of Mexico city. Xochimilco was home of Aztec nobles in pre-Columbian days.

Xochistlahuaca (sōchēsläwä′kä), town (pop. 1,515), Guerrero, SW Mexico, on S slope of Sierra Madre del Sur, 15 mi. NE of Ometepec; fruit, livestock.

Xochitepec (sōchētāpĕk′), town (pop. 1,532), Morelos, central Mexico, 9 mi. S of Cuernavaca; rice, sugar cane, coffee, fruit, livestock.

Xochitlán (sochētlän′). **1** Town (pop. 1,720), Puebla, central Mexico, 38 mi. SE of Puebla; alt. 6,676 ft.; cereals, maguey, livestock. **2** Officially Xochitlán de Romero Rubio, town (pop. 2,297), Puebla, central Mexico, in SE foothills of Sierra Madre Oriental, 22 mi. ENE of Zacatlán; sugar cane, coffee, tobacco, fruit.

Xoïs, anc. city of Lower Egypt, in middle of the Nile delta, c.20 mi. NW of Busiris; was ⊙ XIV (Xoite) dynasty of c.17th cent. B.C.

Xolotlán, Lake, Nicaragua: see Managua, Lake.

Xonacatlán (sōnäkätlän′), officially San Francisco Xonacatlán, town (pop. 2,490), Mexico state, central Mexico, 25 mi. W of Mexico city; grain, stock.

Xonrupt-Longemer (sõrü′-lõzhmâr′), village (pop. 465), Vosges dept., E France, in the high Vosges 2 mi. NE of Gérardmer, on road to Col de l Schlucht; linen weaving and bleaching. Until 1938 called Xonrupt.

Xoxocotla (shō-shōkōt′lä). **1** Town (pop. 3,081), Morelos, central Mexico, on S slope of central plateau, 17 mi. S of Cuernavaca; rice, sugar cane, fruit, vegetables. **2** Town (pop. 1,189), Veracruz, E Mexico, in Sierra Madre Oriental, on Puebla border, 14 mi. SSW of Orizaba; coffee, fruit.

Xuanloc (swûn′lōk′), town, Bienhoa prov., S Vietnam, on Saigon-Hanoi RR and 40 mi. ENE of Saigon; rubber and forestry center.

Xuí, Brazil: see Chuí.

Xylokastron or **Xilokastron** (both: ksēlô′kästron), town (pop. 3,877), Argolis and Corinthia nome, NE Peloponnesus, Greece, port on Gulf of Corinth, on railroad, and 19 mi. WNW of Corinth; exports Zante currants, trades in citrus fruits, olive oil. Summer resort.

Xynias, Lake, or **Lake Xinias** (both: ksēnēäs′) (□ 10), in Phthiotis nome, central Greece, on Thessalian border, 13 mi. NW of Lamia; 5 mi. long; fisheries. Also called Daukli and Nezeros.

Y

Y, Netherlands: see IJ.
Yaan (yä'än'), town, ⊙ Yaan co. (pop. 131,248) and ⊙ Sikang prov., China, 60 mi. E of Kangting, at Szechwan border; road junction; tea center; bamboo shoots. Until 1913 called Yachow. Before 1938 in Szechwan. Succeeded Kangting as prov. ⊙ in 1950.
Ya'arot ha Carmel or **Yaarot Hacarmel** (both: yäärōt' häkärmĕl'), residential sub urb of Haifa, NW Israel, on Mt. Carmel, 5 mi. S of city center.
Yaba (yä'bä), residential town (pop. 1,240) in Lagos township, Nigeria colony, on mainland, 2.5 mi. NW of Lagos; bricks. Has Higher Col. (opened 1932), hosp., yellow-fever research institute.
Yabalkovo (yä'bŭlkôvô), village (pop. 3,316), Khaskovo dist., S central Bulgaria, on the Maritsa and 11 mi. NNW of Khaskovo; cotton, tobacco, vineyards. Formerly Almalii.
Yabanabat, Turkey: see KIZILCAHAMAM.
Yabase (yä"bä'sā), town (pop. 5,025), Tottori prefecture, SW Honshu, Japan, on Sea of Japan, 20 mi. ENE of Yonago; raw silk, livestock; fishing.
Yabassi (yäbä'sē), village, M'Bam region, W Fr. Cameroons, on Wouri R. and 35 mi. S of N'Kongsamba; native market; hardwood lumbering, coffee, cacao and banana plantations. Has R.C. and Protestant missions, hosp.
Yabebyry (yäbābĕrē', bürü'), town (dist. pop. 3,483), Ñeembucú dept., S Paraguay, on small affluent of the Paraná and 85 mi. ESE of Pilar; agr. center (oranges, cattle).
Yablanitsa, Yugoslavia: see JABLANICA.
Yablochny or **Yablochnyy** (yä'blŭchnē), town (1940 pop. 5,952), S Sakhalin, Russian SFSR, on W coast railroad, 8 mi. N of Kholmsk. Under Jap. rule (1905–45), called Rantomari (räntō'märē).
Yablonitsa Pass (yä'blŭnyĕtsŭ), Czech and Pol. *Jablonica*, pass (alt. 2,332 ft.) in the Carpathians, SW Ukrainian SSR, at SE end of Gorgany Mts., 3 mi. E of Yasinya; highway corridor. Also called Magyar Pass or Tatar Pass.
Yablonoi Range, Russian SFSR: see YABLONOVY RANGE.
Yablonov (yä'blŭnŭf), Pol. *Jabłonów* (yäbwô'nŏŏf), town (1931 pop. 1,790), S Stanislav oblast, Ukrainian SSR, in East Beskids, 10 mi. SSW of Kolomyya; summer resort; flour milling; lumbering.
Yablonovo (yä'blŭnŭvŭ), town (1940 pop. over 500), SW Chita oblast, Russian SFSR, on Trans-Siberian RR (Yablonovaya station) and 30 mi. WSW of Chita, in Yablonovy Range.
Yablonovy Range or **Yablonovyy Range** (–vē), section of watershed bet. Arctic and Pacific drainage areas, in SE Siberian Russian SFSR; extends from upper Ingoda R. NE, past Chita, to Olekma R.; forms divide bet. Khilok and Vitim rivers (W slopes) and Ingoda and Olekma rivers (E slopes). Highest point, Bolshoi Saranakan (5,280 ft.), NNE of Chita. Trans-Siberian RR crosses range WSW of Chita. Also known as Yablonoi or Yablonoy Range.
Yablunovka (yä'blŏŏnŭfkŭ), village (1926 pop. 4,981), S Chernigov oblast, Ukrainian SSR, 13 mi. SW of Priluki; grain. Formerly also Yablonovka.
Yabo (yä'bō), town (pop. 5,650), Sokoto prov., Northern Provinces, NW Nigeria, 28 mi. SW of Sokoto; cotton, millet; cattle, skins.
Yabrud (yäbrōōd'), Fr. *Yabroud*, town (pop. c.5,000), Damascus prov., W Syria, 40 mi. NNE of Damascus, on E slope of Anti-Lebanon mts.; alt. 5,080 ft.; summer resort; orchards. Has Ptolemaic and Roman ruins.
Yabu (yä'bōō), town (pop. 3,783), Hyogo prefecture, S Honshu, Japan, 39 mi. NNE of Himeji, in agr. area (rice, wheat, tea, poultry). Until early 1940s, called Yabuichiba.
Yabucoa (yäbōōkō'ä), town (pop. 5,258), SE Puerto Rico, in hills 8 mi. SW of Humacao; sugar growing and milling; mfg. of cigars, liquor distilling. Its landing Puerto Yabucoa is 3½ mi. E.
Yabuki (yäbōō'kē), town (pop. 6,734), Fukushima prefecture, central Honshu, Japan, 8 mi. NE of Shirakawa; rice growing, horse breeding.
Yabukovats, Yugoslavia: see JABUKOVAC.
Yabuzukahon (yäbōō'zōōkähō'), town (pop. 8,600), Gumma prefecture, just SW of Kiryu, in agr. area. Mineral springs.
Yacanto (yäkän'tō), village (pop. estimate 400), W Córdoba prov., Argentina, at foot of Sierra Grande, 70 mi. SW of Córdoba; resort, with mineral springs, in fruit- and stock-producing area.
Yacaré (yäkärā'), village, Artigas dept., NW Uruguay, on road, and 33 mi. WNW of Artigas; cattle raising; grain.
Yachi (yä'chē), town (pop. 14,829), Yamagata prefecture, N Honshu, Japan, on Mogami R. and 12 mi. N of Yamagata; commercial center for agr. area; sake brewing.
Ya-chiang, China: see YAKIANG.
Yachimata (yächē'mätŭ), town (pop. 19,644), Chiba prefecture, central Honshu, Japan, at base of Chiba Peninsula, 11 mi. ENE of Chiba; agr. center (rice, wheat); raw silk.
Yachow, China: see YAAN.
Yacimientos Petrolíferos or **Yacimientos Petrolíferos Fiscales** (yäsēmyĕn'tōs pātrōlē'fārōs, fēskä'lĕs), town (pop. estimate 5,000), E Comodoro Rivadavia military zone, Argentina, on railroad, on Gulf of San Jorge, and adjoining Comodoro Rivadavia in N. Port for oil tankers. Hosiery and textile factory, oil refinery. Planned as residential suburb for employees of govt.-owned oil industry.
Yaciretá Island (yäsērätä'), Itapúa dept., SE Paraguay, formed by arms of upper Paraná R. (Argentina border), opposite San Cosme; 40 mi. long, 2–7 mi. wide; forested.
Yaco (yä'kō), town (pop. c.4,200), La Paz dept., W Bolivia, at SW foot of Cordillera de Tres Cruces, 18 mi. ESE of Luribay; alt. 11,811 ft.; barley.
Yacolt (yă'kōlt, yăkōlt'), town (pop. 411), Clark co., SW Wash., 20 mi. NE of Vancouver.
Yacuiba (yäkwē'bä), town (pop. c.1,400), ⊙ Gran Chaco prov., Tarija dept., SE Bolivia, 75 mi. ESE of Tarija, on Argentina border. Terminus of railroad from Embarcación (Argentina), with customs station; airport; local trade center. Head of projected railroad to Villa Montes and Santa Cruz.
Yacuma, province, Bolivia: see SANTA ANA, Beni dept.
Yacuma River (yäkōō'mä), Beni dept., N Bolivia, rises in several branches on NE slopes of Cordillera de La Paz 30 mi. SE of Rurrenabaque, flows 160 mi. NE, past Santa Ana, to the Mamoré 28 mi. SSW of Exaltación. Navigable for c.110 mi. below Santa Rosa.
Yadar, Yugoslavia: see JADAR.
Yaddo, N.Y.: see SARATOGA SPRINGS.
Yadgir (yäd'gēr), town (pop. 17,661), Gulbarga dist., SW central Hyderabad state, India, near Bhima R., 45 mi. SSE of Gulbarga; cotton ginning, rice and oilseed milling, biri making, mfg. of caps, tassels. Match mfg. 15 mi. NW, at village of Nalwar. Sometimes called Yadgiri.
Yadkin (yăd'kĭn), county (□ 335; pop. 22,133), NW N.C.; ⊙ Yadkinville. In the piedmont; bounded N and E by Yadkin R. Tobacco growing; lumbering (pine, oak); sawmilling. Formed 1850.
Yadkin College, town (pop. 82), Davidson co., central N.C., 9 mi. NW of Lexington, near Yadkin R.
Yadkin Dam, N.C.: see BADIN.
Yadkin River, N.C.: see PEE DEE RIVER.
Yadkinville, town (pop. 820), ⊙ Yadkin co., NW N.C., 22 mi. W of Winston-Salem; tobacco basket factories, lumber and grain mills.
Yad Mordekhai or **Yad Mordechai** (both: yäd' môrdĕkhī'), settlement (pop. 250), SW Israel, in Judaean Plain, at NW edge of the Negev, near border of Egyptian-held Palestine, 8 mi. NE of Gaza; mixed farming; fruit and vegetable canning. Founded 1943; in 1948 heavily shelled and then briefly occupied by Egyptians.
Yadrin (yä'drĭn), city (1931 pop. 3,065), NW Chuvash Autonomous SSR, Russian SFSR, port on Sura R. and 32 mi. NNW of Shumerlya; food processing (flour, butter, vegetable oil), distilling, woodworking; hog raising near by. Founded 1609.
Yadua, Fiji: see YANDUA.
Yaduda, El, or **Al-Yadudah** (both: ĕl-yădōō'dŭ), village (pop. c.2,000), N central Jordan, 8 mi. SSW of Amman; road junction; grain (barley, wheat).
Yae (yä'ā), town (pop. 5,286), Hiroshima prefecture, SW Honshu, Japan, 20 mi. N of Hiroshima; agr. center (rice, wheat); sake, charcoal, raw silk.
Yaeyama-gunto (yīyä'mä-gōōn'tô) or **Yaeyama-retto** (–rĕ'tô), southernmost island group (□ 247; 1950 pop. 43,973) of Ryukyu Isls., forming part of the Sakishima Isls. Includes Ishigaki-shima, Iriomote-shima, Yonaguni-shima, and Senkaku-gunto.
Yafa, Yafa' (both: yă'fä), or **Yafa'i** (yăfä'ē), tribal area of Western Aden Protectorate, NE of Aden Colony, bet. Fadhli sultanate and Yemen *status quo* line. One of the original Nine Cantons, it consists of Lower Yafa in the foothills and Upper Yafa in the higher hinterland. Agr. (coffee, gums, grain). The **Lower Yafa** is a separate sultanate (pop. 23,300), with ⊙ at Al Qara. Its sultan concluded a protectorate treaty in 1895 and an adviser agreement in 1946. The **Upper Yafa** is a loose confederation (pop. 89,500) of small treaty areas with no central authority. There has been little contact with the British owing to hostile attitude of local tribesmen. The confederation is ruled by an over-all sultan (⊙ Mahjaba) and consists of the sectional treaty (1903) sheikdoms of MAUSATTA, DHUBI, MAFLAHI, and HADHRAMI, as well as the minor nontreaty sheikdoms of Bo'si and Da'udi.
Yagi (yä'gē). **1** Town (pop. 2,847), Kyoto prefecture, S Honshu, Japan, 14 mi. WNW of Kyoto; agr. center; mulberry wine. **2** Town (pop. 5,861), Nara prefecture, S Honshu, Japan, 12 mi. S of Nara; commercial center for agr. area (rice, wheat); raw silk, medicine.
Yagman (yŭgmän'), village (pop. over 500), W Ashkhabad oblast, Turkmen SSR, on NW slope of Greater Balkhan Range, near Trans-Caspian RR, 70 mi. E of Krasnovodsk; coal mining.
Yago (yä'gō), village (pop. 965), Nayarit, W Mexico, on Santiago R. and 26 mi. NNW of Tepic, on railroad; corn, tobacco, tomatoes, bananas. Silver and gold mines near by. Settled by Spanish in 1531; church built in 1603.
Yagodin (yä'gŭdyĭn), Pol. *Jagodzin* (yägô'dzēn), rail station, W Volyn oblast, Ukrainian SSR, near Bug R. (Pol. border), 35 mi. W of Kovel; rail terminus.
Yagodina, Yugoslavia: see SVETOZAREVO.
Yagodny or **Yagodnyy** (yä'gŭdnē), town (1948 pop. over 2,000), N Khabarovsk Territory, Russian SFSR, on Debin R. (small left affluent of Kolyma R.) and 200 mi. NNW of Magadan (linked by highway); 62°33'N 149°39'E. Road center in Kolyma gold-mining region.
Yagotin (yŭgŭtyēn'), town (1926 pop. 6,182), W Poltava oblast, Ukrainian SSR, 55 mi. WNW of Lubny, just N of Lesnyaki; machine shops.
Yagoua (yägōō'ä), village, Nord-Cameroun region, N Fr. Cameroons, near Logone R. (Fr. Equatorial Africa border), 65 mi. ESE of Maroua; customs station and center of native trade; peanuts, millet, cattle; experimental rice cultures.
Yaguachi (yägwä'chē), town (1950 pop. 2,879), Guayas prov., W Ecuador, on Yaguachi R., on railroad to Quito, and 16 mi. ENE of Guayaquil; agr. center (sugar cane, cacao, rice, bananas, coffee) sugar refining, rice milling. Its San Jacinto church is frequented in Aug. by many pilgrims. The old village of Yaguachi is 4 mi. S across the river.
Yaguachi River, Ecuador: see CHIMBO RIVER.
Yaguajay (yägwähī'), town (pop. 4,867), Las Villas prov., central Cuba, near N coast, on railroad and 20 mi. SE of Caibarién; agr. center (sugar cane, tobacco, cattle). Near by are the centrals of Narcisa (NW) and Victoria (NNE). At Caguanes Point (8 mi. NE) are well-known caverns.
Yagual, El, Venezuela: see EL YAGUAL.
Yaguaramas (yägwärä'mäs), town (pop. 849), Las Villas prov., central Cuba, on railroad and 18 mi. WNW of Cienfuegos; charcoal burning, lumbering.
Yaguaraparo (yägwäräpä'rō), town (pop. 1,752), Sucre state, NE Venezuela, on Paria Peninsula (SW), near Gulf of Paria, 36 mi. W of Güiria; coconuts, cacao, sugar cane.
Yaguarí (yägwärē'), village, Rivera dept., NE Uruguay, on the Arroyo Yaguarí, near Brazil border, and 55 mi. SE of Rivera; grain, vegetables, cattle, sheep.
Yaguarí, Arroyo, river, NE Uruguay, rises in the Cuchilla de Santa Ana 15 mi. NNW of Yaguarí, flows 100 mi. SSW, across Rivera dept., past Yaguarí, to the Tacuarembó.
Yaguarón (yägwärōn'), town (dist. pop. 14,248), Central dept., S Paraguay, 32 mi. SE of Asunción; agr. center (rice, tobacco, cotton). Founded 1539 by Franciscan mission. Has fine old church of San Roque, built 1670–1720.
Yaguarón River, Uruguay and Brazil: see JAGUARÃO RIVER.
Yaguarú (yägwärōō'), village (pop. c.600), Santa Cruz dept., E central Bolivia, 90 mi. NW of Concepción; cotton. Franciscan mission until 1938.
Yaguate (yägwä'tā), village (1950 pop. 929), Trujillo prov., S Dominican Republic, near the coast, 22 mi. WSW of Ciudad Trujillo, in agr. region (rice, coffee, fruit).
Yagur (yägōōr'), settlement (pop. 1,500), NW Israel, in Kishon R. valley, at E foot of Mt. Carmel, on railroad and 7 mi. SE of Haifa; mixed farming; textile milling, metalworking, box mfg., marble polishing. Founded 1922.
Yahagi (yä"hä'gē), town (pop. 15,682), Aichi prefecture, central Honshu, Japan, just W of Okazaki; rice-growing center.
Yahara River (yŭhär'ŭ), S Wis., rises in small lake in Dane co., and links the Four Lakes: flows S and SE, through L. Mendota, past Madison, and then through lakes Monona, Waubesa, and Kegonsa, past Stoughton, to Rock R. 9 mi. NW of Janesville. Formerly Catfish R.
Yahata, Japan: see YAWATA, Fukuoka prefecture.
Yahk (yăk), village (pop. estimate 150), S B.C., near Mont. and Idaho borders, 30 mi. SW of Cranbrook; rail junction, N terminal of Spokane International RR; lumbering.
Yahualica (yäwälē'kä). **1** Town (pop. 811), Hidalgo, central Mexico, 12 mi. S of Huejutla; corn, rice, sugar, fruit, livestock. **2** Town (pop. 4,298), Jalisco, central Mexico, 45 mi. NE of Guadalajara; alt. 6,168 ft.; agr. center (corn, wheat, vegetables, fruit, livestock).
Yaichow, China: see AIHSIEN.
Yaihsien, China: see AIHSIEN.
Yaik River, USSR: see URAL RIVER.
Yaila Mountains, Russian SFSR: see CRIMEAN MOUNTAINS.
Yaipan, Uzbek SSR: see BAZAR-YAIPAN.
Yaita (yī'tä), town (pop. 14,802), Tochigi prefecture, central Honshu, Japan, 18 mi. NNE of Utsunomiya; agr. (rice, barley), lumbering, woodworking.

Yaitien (yī'dyĕn'), village, SW Kwangsi prov., China, 20 mi. E of Chennankwan; border post on Vietnam line.
Yaitse, Yugoslavia: see JAJCE.
Yaiva or **Yayva** (yī'vŭ), town (1948 pop. over 500), E central Molotov oblast, Russian SFSR, on Yaiva R., on railroad and 22 mi. NE of Kizel; sawmilling.
Yaiva River or **Yayva River**, in Molotov oblast, Russian SFSR, rises in the central Urals 60 mi. ENE of Solikamsk, flows generally SW, past Yaiva, and NW to Kama R. opposite Orel; 180 mi. long.
Yaiza (yī'thä), village (pop. 623), Lanzarote, Canary Isls., 13 mi. W of Arrecife; cereals, fruit, grapes, tomatoes, onions, livestock. Fishing, hunting. Limestone quarries, limekilns. Just N is the Montaña de Fuego, semiactive volcanoes.
Yaizu (yī'zōō), town (pop. 27,386), Shizuoka prefecture, cental Honshu, Japan, on W shore of Suruga Bay, 8 mi. SW of Shizuoka; major fishing port; dried bonito, bamboo shoots, pears. Fishery school.
Yajalón (yähälōn'), town (pop. 2,023), Chiapas, S Mexico, 26 mi. ENE of Simojovel; corn, sugar, fruit.
Yajima (yä'jĭmä) or **Yashima** (yä'shĭmä), town (pop. 9,810), Akita prefecture, N Honshu, Japan, 12 mi. SSE of Honjo; horse breeding, sugar refining, agr.
Yajur, Israel: see NESHER.
Yakake (yä"kä'kā), town (pop. 6,014), Okayama prefecture, SW Honshu, Japan, 19 mi. W of Okayama, in agr area (rice, wheat, peppermint), livestock; raw silk, charcoal, sake.
Yakalo (yä'kälō) or **Yerkalo** (yĕr'–), Chinese *P'u-ting-ts'un* (pōō'dĭng'tsōōn'), after 1913 *Yentsing* or *Yen-ching* (both: yĕn'jĭng'), town, E Tibet, in Kham prov., 70 mi. SSW of Paan, at Yunnan line. Saltworks near by.
Yakaolang, Afghanistan: see NAIAK.
Yakataga, Cape (yăkŭtä'gŭ), S Alaska, on Gulf of Alaska, 100 mi. WNW of Yakutat; 60°1'N 142°24'W; air base, radio station. Placer gold mining in vicinity.
Yakhorina, mountain, Yugoslavia: see JAHORINA.
Yakhroma (yŭkhrŭmä'), city (1939 pop. over 10,000), N Moscow oblast, Russian SFSR, on E bank of Moscow Canal, 38 mi. N of Moscow; cotton-milling center; lathe mfg. Became city in 1940. During Second World War, briefly held (1941) by Germans in Moscow campaign.
Yakh-Su (yŭkh-sōō'), river in Tadzhik SSR; rises in Darvaza Range, flows c.80 mi. SSW, past Kulyab, to the Kyzyl-Su just below Kolkhozabad.
Yakiang or **Ya-chiang** (both: yä'jyäng'), town, ⊙ Yakiang co. (pop. 4,824), E Sikang prov., China, 60 mi. W of Kangting, and on Yalung R., at road crossing; wheat, millet. Until 1913, Hokow.
Yakima (yă'kŭmô, –mŭ), county (□ 4,273; pop. 135,723), S Wash.; ⊙ Yakima. Mtn. area in Cascade Range, divided by Yakima valley; fertile irrigated agr. region (fruit, truck, dairy products, grain, hay, hops, potatoes, livestock); lumbering. Includes parts of Snoqualmie Natl. Forest and Yakima Indian Reservation. Formed 1865.
Yakima, city (pop. 38,486), ⊙ Yakima co., S Wash., 100 mi. SE of Seattle and on Yakima R. Settled 1861, but moved in 1885 4 mi. NW to Northern Pacific RR site; called North Yakima until 1918. Commercial and industrial center for irrigated Yakima valley; produces fruit, grain, vegetables, sugar beets, hops, livestock; lumber and flour mills, packing plants, canneries. Jr. col. is here; Yakima Indian Reservation is near by.
Yakima River, central and S Wash., rises in Cascade Range near Snoqualmie Pass, flows 203 mi. SE, past Ellensburg and Yakima, to Columbia R. near Kennewick. The river supplies U.S. irrigation project (begun 1905) in Yakima valley, which produces fruit (especially apples), grain, vegetables, and livestock; hydroelectric power.
Yakkabag (yŭkŭbäk'), village (1926 pop. 1,783), NE Kashka-Darya oblast, Uzbek SSR, 10 mi. E of station on Karshi-Kitab RR, 13 mi. S of Kitab; food processing; cotton, rice, fruit.
Yakkaolang, Afghanistan: see NAIAK.
Yako (yä'kō), town (pop. c.5,600), central Upper Volta, Fr. West Africa, 60 mi. NW of Ouagadougou; agr. center (shea nuts, peanuts, millet, rice; livestock). Shea-nut butter processing. Markets. R.C. and Protestant missions.
Yako, Portuguese Timor: see JACO.
Yakoba, Nigeria: see BAUCHI, town.
Yakobi Island (yŭkō'bē) (17 mi. long, 7 mi. wide), SE Alaska, in Alexander Archipelago, W of Chichagof Isl.; 57°58'N 136°28'W; rises to 2,880 ft. Sometimes spelled Jacobi.
Yakoma (yäkō'mä), village, Equator Prov., N Belgian Congo, on left bank of Ubangi R. (Fr. Equatorial Africa border) and 140 mi. NNE of Lisala; customs station and trading center in cotton-growing area; cotton ginning. Capuchin mission. Upper Ubangi R. is navigable bet. here and Banzyville.
Yakoruda (yäkôrōō'dä), village (pop. 5,287), Gorna Ozhumaya dist., SW Bulgaria, on Mesta R. and 18 mi. NE of Razlog; flour milling; truck, livestock.
Yakova, Yugoslavia: see DJAKOVICA.
Yakovlevichi (yä'kŭvlyĭvēchē), town (1939 pop. over 500), S Vitebsk oblast, Belorussian SSR, 14 mi. SSE of Orsha; linen milling.
Yakovlevka (–lyĭfkŭ), village (1926 pop. 895), SW Maritime Territory, Russian SFSR, on Daubikhe R. and 90 mi. NE of Voroshilov, in agr. area (grain, soybeans, rice).
Yakovlevskoye, Russian SFSR: see PRIVOLZHSK.
Yakshanga (yŭkshŭn-gä'), town (1948 pop. over 2,000), E Kostroma oblast, Russian SFSR, on railroad and 15 mi. E of Sharya; sawmilling center.
Yakshur-Bodya (yŭkshōōr'-bŭdyä'), village (1948 pop. over 2,000), central Udmurt Autonomous SSR, Russian SFSR, 24 mi. N of Izhevsk; lumbering. Limestone deposits near by.
Yakubitsa or **Yakupitsa**, mountain, Yugoslavia: see JAKUPICA.
Yakumo (yä"kōō'mō), town (pop. 19,227), SW Hokkaido, Japan, on W shore of Uchiura Bay, 36 mi. W of Muroran; mining (gold, silver, copper, lead); agr., stock raising, fishing.
Yaku-shima (yäkōō'shĭmä), island (□ 208; pop. 19,316, including offshore islets), Kagoshima prefecture, Japan, in E.China Sea 40 mi. S of Cape Sata, Kyushu, just W of Tanega-shima; 18 mi. long, 16 mi. wide; roughly circular; mountainous. Fishing; dried tuna. Japan cedars.
Yakusu (yäkōō'sōō), village, Eastern Prov., N central Belgian Congo, on right bank of Congo R. and 17 mi. W of Stanleyville, in palm-growing region. Has Baptist mission with native teachers' and nurses' schools.
Yakutat (yă'kŭtăt), village (pop. 293), SE Alaska, on Yakutat Bay on Gulf of Alaska, near base of Alaska Panhandle, 200 mi. WNW of Juneau; 59°33'N 139°45'W; fishing, fish processing, fur trapping. Connected by narrow-gauge RR with fishing camps (Situk and Lost River) on Gulf of Alaska. Near by is airfield built in Second World War.
Yakutat Bay, SE Alaska, inlet (75 mi. long, 20 mi. wide at mouth) of Gulf of Alaska, near base of Alaska Panhandle, 40 mi. SE of Mt. Elias, 200 mi. WNW of Juneau; 59°40'N 139°55'W. Contains Khantaak and Knight isls.; Disenchantment Bay, continued by Russell Fiord, is NE arm. Several large glaciers flow into upper bay.
Yakut Autonomous Soviet Socialist Republic (yŭkōōt'), administrative division (□ 1,182, 300; 1946 pop. estimate 450,000; in 1939 census 400,544) of NE Siberian Russian SFSR; ⊙ Yakutsk. Bounded N by Arctic Ocean, S by Stanovoi Range; drained by Lena, Yana, and Indigirka rivers. NE section is mountainous (Verkhoyansk, Cherski ranges). Extreme continental climate: "pole of cold" (near VERKHOYANSK); relatively warm summers. Pop. (80% Yakuts, 10% Russians; Evenki, Lamuts, Yukagirs) settled in river valleys; engaged in fishing, fur trapping, reindeer raising (N), cattle raising, agr. (center), gold mining in Aldan and Allakh-Yun areas (S). Deposits of platinum, nonferrous metals (chiefly tin), coal, iron, salt; extensive forests as yet little exploited because of lack of transportation (the Republic is N of Trans-Siberian RR). Furs, gold, and mammoth ivory are chief exports. Leading cities: Yakutsk, Verkhoyansk, VILYUISK, OLEKMINSK, Sredne-Kolymsk. Formed 1922 as largest autonomous SSR in Russian SFSR.
Yakutsk (–kōōtsk'), city (1926 pop. 10,558; 1939 pop. 52,888), ⊙ Yakut Autonomous SSR, Russian SFSR, on Lena R. and 3,000 mi. ENE of Moscow; 62°1'N 129°43'E. River port and highway center, in agr. area; tannery, brickworks, sawmills, shiprepair docks; power plant. Site of teachers col., several technical schools and institutes, large library. Founded 1632; former political exile center.
Yala (yŭlä'), town (1947 pop. 7,100), ⊙ Yala prov. (□ 1,895; 1947 pop. 81,471), S Thailand, in Malay Peninsula, on Pattani R., on railroad, and 20 mi. S of Pattani; rubber plantations; tin and lead mining at Bannang Sata and Betong (S).
Yalagüina (yälägwē'nä), town (1950 pop. 212), Madríz dept., NW Nicaragua, 6 mi. ESE of Somoto, on Inter-American Highway; road junction; grain-producing center.
Yalchiki or **Yal'chiki** (yäl'chĭkē), village (1939 pop. over 500), E Chuvash Autonomous SSR, Russian SFSR, 33 mi. SE of Kanash; wheat, livestock. Until c.1940, Yalchikovo.
Yalding (yôl'dĭng), town and parish (pop. 2,314), central Kent, England, on Medway R. and 6 mi. SW of Maidstone; agr. market in hop-growing region. Has 15th-cent. bridge,13th-cent. church.
Yale, village (pop. estimate 200), SW B.C., at head of navigation on Fraser R. and 35 mi. NW of Chilliwack; lumbering. Fort Yale, post of Hudson's Bay Co., was established here 1848.
Yale. 1 Village (pop. 153), Jasper co., SE Ill., 28 mi. E of Effingham, in agr. area. **2** Town (pop. 293), Guthrie co., W central Iowa, 14 mi. WSW of Perry, in agr. area. **3** City (pop. 1,641), St. Clair co., E Mich., 21 mi. NW of Port Huron, in grain-growing, and truck- and dairy-farming area; woolen mill, canning plant. Settled 1859; inc. as village 1885, as city 1905. **4** City (pop. 1,359), Payne co., N central Okla., near Cimarron R., 21 mi. E of Stillwater, in oil-producing and agr. area (grain, cotton, livestock); oil refineries; cotton ginning. Inc. 1903. **5** Town (pop. 164), Beadle co., E central S.Dak., 12 mi. ENE of Huron.
Yale, Lake, Lake co., central Fla., 2 mi. NW of Eustis; c.4 mi. long, 1 mi. wide.
Yale, Mount (14,172 ft.), central Colo., in Collegiate Range of Sawatch Mts., 9 mi. W of Buena Vista.
Yale Dam, Wash.: see LEWIS RIVER.
Yale Point (8,050 ft.), NE Ariz., at E end of Black Mesa, 27 mi. WNW of Canyon de Chelly Natl. Monument.
Yalesville, Conn.: see WALLINGFORD.
Yalí or **San Sebastián de Yalí** (sän sābästyän' dā yälē'), town (1950 pop. 575), Jinotega dept., W Nicaragua, 20 mi. NW of Jinotega; coffee, wheat.
Yalinga (yälĭng-gä'), village, E Ubangi-Shari, Fr. Equatorial Africa, 135 mi. NNE of Bangassou; trading post.
Yalkabul Point (yälkäbōōl'), cape on bar off N coast of Yucatan, SE Mexico, 70 mi. ENE of Progreso; 21°32'N 88°37'W.
Yallahs (yă'lŭs), town, St. Thomas parish, SE Jamaica, on coast, 17 mi. ESE of Kingston; bananas, coconuts. Sometimes called Yallahs Bay. Yallahs Point is 2½ mi. SE, adjoining a salt pond.
Yallo Bally Mountains, Calif.: see KLAMATH MOUNTAINS.
Yallourn (yălōōrn'), town (pop. 4,119), S Victoria, Australia, 80 mi. ESE of Melbourne, in Gippsland dist.; lignite mines. Town governed by State Electricity Commission.
Yalobusha (yălŭbōō'shŭ), county (□ 504; pop. 15,191), N central Miss.; ⊙ Coffeeville and Water Valley. Drained by Yocona and Skuna rivers. Agr. (cotton, corn, watermelons), stock raising, dairying. Timber. Formed 1833.
Yalobusha River, central Miss., rises in Chickasaw co., flows S, W, and SW, past Calhoun City and Grenada, joining Tallahatchie R. to form Yazoo R. just N of Greenwood; 165 mi. long. Site of Grenada Dam (for flood control), begun 1947, is just NE of Grenada. Receives Skuna R.
Yalova (yälôvä'), village (pop. 3,608), Istanbul prov., NW Turkey in Asia, on S shore of Gulf of Izmit, 30 mi. SE of Istanbul; hot springs. Sometimes spelled Yaluva.
Yalpug Lagoon or **Yalpukh Lagoon** (yäl'pŏŏk, –pŏŏkh), Rum. *Ialpug* or *Ialpuh* (yäl'pōōg, –pōōkh), SW Izmail oblast, Ukrainian SSR, near the Danube, W of Izmail; 25 mi. long, 4 mi. wide. Coal mining on shore. Receives (N) **Yalpug River**, rising near Chimishliya and flowing 70 mi. S, past Komrat, to the lagoon at Bolgrad.
Yalta (yôl'tŭ, yäl'tŭ, Rus. yäl'tŭ), city (1926 pop. 28,838), S Crimea, Russian SFSR, port on Black Sea, 32 mi. ESE of Sevastopol. Major resort on protected S coast; one of principal spas of USSR; center of the entire Crimea subtropical S coast, with satellite resorts at Alupka, Gurzuf, Koreiz, Livadiya, Massandra, and Simeiz. A wine-making center amid orchards, vineyards, and tobacco fields; fish canning, agr. processing. Has many hotels, sanatoriums, and rest homes, art and regional mus. Originally a Gr. colony named Yalita; passed (14th cent.) to Genoese and (15th cent.) to Turks, when it developed as lumber-trading and shipbuilding center. Declined (late-18th cent.) following deportation of pop. by Russians, but revived later with Rus. settlement of S coast. City suffered in 1927 earthquake. The Yalta Conference (1945) of Roosevelt, Churchill, and Stalin was held in near-by Livadiya.
Yaltra, Greece: see LOUTRA AIDEPSOU.
Yalu (yä'lōō'), town, ⊙ Yalu co. (pop. 43,128), NE Inner Mongolian Autonomous Region, Manchuria, on E slopes of the Great Khingan Mts., on Chinese Eastern RR and 75 mi. NW of Tsitsihar; agr., lumber, and fur trade. Until 1925 called Chalantun, a name revived under Manchukuo govt., when it was ⊙ East Hsingan prov.
Yalung River, Chinese *Yalung Kiang* or *Yalung Chiang* (yä'lōōng' jyäng'), Sikang prov., China, rises in the Bayan Kara Mts. in SE Tsinghai at 34°N 98°E, flows 800 mi. S, past Shihchü, Kantse, and Yakiang (road crossing), in deep gorges, to Yangtze R. on Yunnan border W of Hweili.
Yalu River, Chinese *Yalu Kiang* (or *Chiang*) (yä'lōō' jyäng'), Jap. *Oryokko* (ōryōk'kō), Korean *Amnok-kang* (än'nŭk'-käng'), on Manchuria-Korea border, rises on S slope of Changpai mtn., flows S entirely along international line, past Changpai, then W, past Linkiang, and SW, past Tsian (opposite Manpojin), Supung (Shuifeng; hydroelectric station), and Antung (opposite Sinuiju), to Korea Bay of Yellow Sea at Tatungkow. Total length, 500 mi. Navigable only in lower reaches, it is used mainly for logging. It is frozen from Nov. to March.
Yalusaka (yälōōsä'kä), village, Equator Prov., central Belgian Congo, on Tshuapa R. and 165 mi. ESE of Boende; agr. and hardwood-lumbering center.
Yalutorovsk (yŭlōōtŭrôfsk'), city (1939 pop. over 10,000), SW Tyumen oblast, Russian SFSR, on Tobol R., at mouth of Iset R., on Trans-Siberian RR and 45 mi. S of Tyumen, in agr. area (wheat, oats); flour milling, sawmilling, food canning Founded 1693 on Tatar site.
Yalvac (yälväch'), Turkish *Yalvaç*, town (pop. 8,249), Isparta prov., W central Turkey, 50 mi. NE of Isparta; tannery; wheat, barley, potatoes, opium.
Yam, China: see YAM RIVER.

Yam, Saudi Arabia: see NAJRAN.
Yama (yä'mŭ), town (1939 pop. over 500), NE Stalino oblast, Ukrainian SSR, in the Donbas, 20 mi. N of Artemovsk; rail junction; dolomite quarries.
Yama, river, Russian SFSR: see YAMA RIVER.
Yamabe (yä"mä'bā). **1** Town (pop. 13,103), Tochigi prefecture, central Honshu, Japan, just S of Ashikaga, in agr. area (rice, wheat); silk textiles. **2** or **Yamanobe** (yämä'nōbā), town (pop. 7,906), Yamagata prefecture, N Honshu, Japan, 5 mi. NW of Yamagata; cotton textiles; silk cocoons, rice.
Yamachiche (yămŭshĕsh'), village (pop. 811), ⊙ St. Maurice co., S Que., on Petit Yamachiche R., near its mouth on the St. Lawrence, and 15 mi. WSW of Trois Rivières; dairying, truck gardening.
Yamada (yä"mä'dä). **1** Town (pop. 32,177), Fukuoka prefecture, N Kyushu, Japan, 9 mi. SW of Nogata; agr. center (rice, barley, wheat); raw silk. **2** Town (pop. 8,010), Iwate prefecture, N Honshu, Japan, fishing port on the Pacific, 14 mi. NNE of Kamaishi; rice, soybeans, charcoal. **3** Town (pop. 8,163), Kochi prefecture, S Shikoku, Japan, 9 mi. ENE of Kochi; agr. center (rice, wheat, tea), poultry; raw silk. Has artisan umbrella industry. Stalactite cave near by. Sometimes called Tosa-Yamada.
Yamaga (yä"mä'gä), town (pop. 13,149), Kumamoto prefecture, W Kyushu, Japan, 14 mi. N of Kumamoto; rail terminus; agr. center; rice, lumber. Has artisan fan industry.
Yamagata (yä"mä'gätŏŏ), prefecture [Jap. *ken*] (□ 3,601; 1940 pop. 1,119,338; 1947 pop. 1,335,653), N Honshu, Japan; ⊙ Yamagata. Bounded W by Sea of Japan; largely mountainous, with fertile plains in Mogami R. basin. Chief port, SAKATA. Rice, fruit, wheat, tobacco are principal agr. products. Horse breeding, lumbering, raw-silk culture; mining (iron, gold, silver, copper). Mfg. (textiles, lacquer ware), metalworking. Many hot-springs and ski resorts. Principal centers: Yamagata, Sakata, YONEZAWA, TSURUOKA.
Yamagata, city (1940 pop. 69,184; 1947 pop. 98,632), ⊙ Yamagata prefecture, N Honshu, Japan, 180 mi. NNE of Tokyo; silk-reeling center; mfg. (textiles, lacquer ware), metalworking. Has anc. Shinto shrine and feudal castle.
Yamagawa, Japan: see YAMAKAWA.
Yamaguchi (yä"mŭgōō'chē, yämä'gōōchē), prefecture [Jap. *ken*] (□ 2,348; 1940 pop. 1,294,242; 1947 pop. 1,479,244), SW Honshu, Japan; ⊙ Yamaguchi. Bounded N by Sea of Japan, W by Hibiki Sea, S by Suo Sea (W section of Inland Sea). Includes offshore isls. of O-SHIMA, OMI-SHIMA, HEIGUN-SHIMA, MI-SHIMA, NAGA-SHIMA, TSUNO-SHIMA, and many smaller isls. Chief port and largest city is SHIMONOSEKI. Mountainous terrain with fertile valleys, drained by many small streams. Hot springs in N and central areas; limestone caves in interior. Mining of gold, silver, copper, lead; Ube (S) is coal-mining center. Saltmaking on shores of Inland Sea. Agr. products include rice, tobacco, sweet potatoes, oranges. Extensive sawmilling and livestock raising. Mfg. (textiles, pottery), metalworking. Industrial centers: Shimonoseki, KUDAMATSU, HAGI. Other centers: IWAKUNI, BOFU, TOKUYAMA, ONODA.
Yamaguchi, city (1940 pop. 34,579; 1947 pop. 97,975), ⊙ Yamaguchi prefecture, SW Honshu, Japan, 35 mi. ENE of Shimonoseki and on short Fushino R.; 34°10'N 131°28'E. Commercial center; mfg. (dolls, sake, household furnishings). Commercial school. Hot springs in S part of city. Kameyama Park is on site of anc. villa of Ouchi clan, feudal lords of Yamaguchi. A great castle city, 14th–16th cent. Christian mission established here 1550 by St. Francis Xavier.
Yamakawa (yä"mä'käwŏŏ) or **Yamagawa** (–gäwŏŏ), town (pop. 15,432), Kagoshima prefecture, S Kyushu, Japan, on SE Satsuma Peninsula, on Kagoshima Bay, 26 mi. SSE of Kagoshima; fishing port in agr. area (rice, wheat, raw silk).
Yamakita (yä"mä'kētä), town (pop. 10,839), Kanagawa prefecture, central Honshu, Japan, 9 mi. NW of Odawara; lumbering; wheat, sweet potatoes.
Yam-Alin, Russian SFSR: see BUREYA RANGE.
Yamal-Nenets National Okrug (yŭmäl'-nyĕnyĭts, ô'krŏŏk) administrative division (□ 258,800; 1946 pop. estimate 40,000) of N Tyumen oblast, Siberian Russian SFSR; on Arctic Circle; ⊙ Salekharde. Includes Yamal Peninsula. Drained by Taz and lower Ob rivers; chiefly tundra and, in S, wooded tundra. Main occupations of pop. (Nentsy, Khanty, Komi) are reindeer breeding, fur trapping, fishing. Formed 1930 within former Ural oblast; passed 1934 to Omsk oblast, 1944 to Tyumen oblast.
Yamal Peninsula, Yamal-Nenets Natl. Okrug, Tyumen oblast, Russian SFSR, in NW Siberia, N of Arctic Circle, bet. Kara Sea and Ob Bay (E); c.400 mi. long, up to 140 mi. wide; tundra covered; reindeer breeding.
Yamamah, Saudi Arabia: see KHARJ.
Yaman, Al-: see YEMEN.
Yamanaka (yä"mä'näkä), town (pop. 7,171), Ishikawa prefecture, central Honshu, Japan, 6 mi. SE of Daishoji; hot-springs resort.
Yamanashi (yämä'-nä'shē), prefecture [Jap. *ken*] (□ 1,724; 1940 pop. 663,026; 1947 pop. 807,251), central Honshu, Japan; ⊙ KOFU. Largely mountainous, with mtn. range (of which Mt. Shirane is highest peak) along W border; fertile plains, drained by Fuji R. S area is included in Fuji-Hakone Natl. Park. Prefecture is major producer of raw silk. Chief crops: rice, wheat. Mfg. (silk textiles, crystal glassware), woodworking. Kofu is principal center.
Yamanashi, town (pop. 4,482), Shizuoka prefecture, central Honshu, Japan, 12 mi. NE of Hamamatsu; rice, watermelons.
Yamane, Japan: see MOROYAMA.
Yamankhalinka (yŭmŭnkhä'lyĭn-kŭ), village (1939 pop. over 500), N Guryev oblast, Kazakh SSR, on Ural R. and 40 mi. NNW of Guryev; sheep.
Yamano (yämä'nō), town (pop. 9,711), Kagoshima prefecture, W Kyushu, Japan, 35 mi. N of Kagoshima; mining center (gold, silver); rice, livestock.
Yamanobe, Japan: see YAMABE, Yamagata prefecture.
Yaman-Tau (yä'mŭn-tou'), highest peak (5,377 ft.) in S Urals, Russian SFSR, NW of Beloretsk; 54°14'N. The Yuryuzan (affluent of the Ufa) rises here.
Yama River (yä'mŭ), N Khabarovsk Territory, Russian SFSR, rises in S Kolyma Range, flows 155 mi. SE to Shelekhov Gulf at Yamsk. Lignite and lead-silver deposits along banks.
Yamarovka (yŭmä'rŭfkŭ), town (1939 pop. over 500), SW Chita oblast, Russian SFSR, 50 mi. S of Khilok; health resort; chalybeate and calcareous springs.
Yamasá (yämäsä'), town (1950 pop. 837), Trujillo prov., central Dominican Republic, on S slopes of the Cordillera Central, 22 mi. NNW of Ciudad Trujillo, in agr. region (rice, coffee, cacao, tobacco, fruit, livestock).
Yamasaki (yämä'säkē) or **Yamazaki** (–zäkē), town (pop. 8,962), Hyogo prefecture, S Honshu, Japan, 15 mi. NW of Himeji; distribution center in agr. area (rice, wheat, poultry); mfg. (cutlery, tiles, paper), woodworking.
Yamase (yä"mä'sā), town (pop. 6,706), Tokushima prefecture, NE Shikoku, Japan, 17 mi. W of Tokushima; agr. center (rice, wheat); raw silk. Mulberry groves.
Yamashi (yŭmŭshē'), village (1939 pop. over 500), central Tatar Autonomous SSR, Russian SFSR, on right tributary of Sheshma R. and 45 mi. SE of Chistopol; grain, livestock.
Yamashiro (yä"mä'shĭrō), former province in S Honshu, Japan; now part of Kyoto prefecture.
Yamashiro. 1 Town (pop. 6,766), Ishikawa prefecture, central Honshu, Japan, 3 mi. ESE of Daishoji; hot-springs resort; pottery making. **2** Town (pop. 16,198), Saga prefecture, NW Kyushu, Japan, 11 mi. NE of Sasebo; rice, wheat, raw silk. Coal mines near by. Formerly Nishi-yamashiro.
Yamaska (yŭmă'skŭ), county (□ 365; pop. 16,516), S Que., on the St. Lawrence, St. Francis, Nicolet, and Yamaska rivers; ⊙ St. François du Lac.
Yamaska, village (pop. estimate 800), S Que., on Yamaska R., near its mouth on the St. Lawrence, 10 mi. ESE of Sorel; dairying, pig raising.
Yamaska River, S Que., rises in the Sutton Mts. N of Vt. border, flows NW to Farnham, thence N, past St. Hyacinthe and Yamaska, to L. St. Peter 9 mi. ENE of Sorel; 110 mi. long. Chief tributaries are Centre Yamaska and North Yamaska rivers, which it receives near Farnham.
Yamatae, Japan: see KISHIWADA.
Yamato (yämä'tō), former province in S Honshu, Japan; now Nara prefecture.
Yamato. 1 Town (pop. 12,983), Kanagawa prefecture, central Honshu, Japan, 10 mi. WNW of Yokohama; tea-growing center; silk textiles. **2** Town (pop. 10,563), Saitama prefecture, central Honshu, Japan, 5 mi. WSW of Kawaguchi; agr. (wheat, rice, truck). Formed in early 1940s by combining former villages of Niikura (1940 pop. 2,064) and Shirako (1940 pop. 3,508).
Yamato-suido, Russian SFSR: see KURILE STRAIT.
Yamazaki. 1 Town, Hyogo prefecture, Japan: see YAMASAKI. **2** City, Ishikawa prefecture, Japan: see KANAZAWA.
Yambéré River, Fr. Equatorial Africa: see OMBELLA RIVER.
Yambéring (yämbĕ'rĭng), village, N Fr. Guinea, Fr. West Africa, in Fouta Djallon mts., 40 mi. N of Labé; cattle; rubber.
Yambinga (yämbĭng'gä), village, Equator Prov., N Belgian Congo, on right bank of Congo R., near mouth of Itimbiri R., and 75 mi. E of Lisala; palm-oil milling.
Yambio (yäm'byō), town, Equatoria prov., S Anglo-Egyptian Sudan, near Belgian Congo border, 220 mi. SSE of Wau; road junction. Hq. of Zande dist., site of govt.-sponsored native cotton-growing and processing scheme.
Yambo, Saudi Arabia: see YENBO.
Yambol (yäm'bôl), city (pop. 30,311), ⊙ Yambol dist. (formed 1949), E central Bulgaria, on Tundzha R. and 50 mi. W of Burgas; rail junction; agr., commercial, and mfg. center, producing cotton textiles, metalware, ceramics, furniture; flour and rice milling, tanning, food canning. Has ruins of stone mosque with interesting arabesques, covered Turkish bazaar, and monument to 19th-cent. revolutionary Georgi Drazhev. Known as Diampolis (11th–14th cent.). Called Yamboli under Turkish rule (15th–19th cent.). Sometimes spelled Jambol.
Yambrasbamba (yämbräs-bäm'bä), town (pop. 1,149), Amazonas dept., N Peru, 33 mi. N of Chachapoyas; sugar growing, liquor distilling.
Yamburg, Russian SFSR: see KINGISEPP.
Yambuya (yämbōō'yä), village, Eastern Prov., N Belgian Congo, on Aruwimi R. and 70 mi. NW of Stanleyville; terminus of steam navigation; palm-growing area. From here Stanley departed in 1887 to rescue Emin Pasha from the Mahdists.
Yamchow, China: see YAMHSIEN.
Yamdena, Indonesia: see TANIMBAR ISLANDS.
Yamdrok Tso (yäm'drōk tsō') or **Yamdrog Tsho** (–drōg), Chinese *Yang-cho-yung Hu* (yäng'jô' yōōng' hōō'), irregularly shaped lake (□ 340), S Tibet, S of the Brahmaputra, 40 mi. SE of Lhasa; alt. 14,500 ft. Also called Palti Tso.
Yamethin (yŭmĕ'dhĭn), district (□ 4,201; 1941 pop. 463,189), Mandalay div., Upper Burma; ⊙ Yamethin; bet. Pegu Yoma and Shan hills. Narrow plain bet. barren (W) and jungle-covered (E) hills; N part, in dry zone (annual rainfall 38 in.), is well irrigated and fertile (rice, sugar cane, corn, millet); S part is covered with teak forests. Tungsten and tin mining. Served by Rangoon-Mandalay RR and Pyinmana-Kyaukpadaung RR. Pop. is 90% Burmese; includes Indians and Karens.
Yamethin, town (pop. 9,291), ⊙ Yamethin dist., Upper Burma, on Rangoon-Mandalay RR and 105 mi. S of Mandalay; railroad shops.
Yamhill, county (□ 709; pop. 33,484), NW Oregon; ⊙ McMinnville. Agr. area bounded on E by Willamette R., drained by Yamhill R. Fruit, grain, truck, poultry, dairy products, lumber. Coast Range in W. Formed 1843.
Yamhill, city (pop. 539), Yamhill co., NW Oregon, 25 mi. SW of Portland and on North Yamhill R.; orchards.
Yamhill River, NW Oregon, formed NE of McMinnville by North Yamhill R. (c.25 mi. long) and South Yamhill R. (c.50 mi. long) rising in Coast Range; flows c.12 mi. E to Willamette R. S of Newberg. Used for logging.
Yamhsien (Cantonese yŭm'yŭn'), Mandarin *Ch'inhsien* (chĭn'shyĕn'), town (pop. 16,975), ⊙ Yamhsien co. (pop. 352,763), SW Kwangtung prov., China, port on Yam R., near Gulf of Tonkin, and 60 mi. SSE of Nanning. Gypsum quarries, manganese mines near by. Until 1912 called Yamchow.
Yaminskoye (yä'mĭnskŭyŭ), village (1926 pop. 5,236), E Altai Territory, Russian SFSR, 40 mi. NNE of Bisk; dairy farming.
Yam Kong, China: see YAM RIVER.
Yamm (yäm), town (1939 pop. over 500), NW Pskov oblast, Russian SFSR, on railroad and 40 mi. NNW of Pskov; sawmilling.
Yamma Yamma, Lake, or **Mackillop, Lake** (mŭkĭ'-lŭp), salt lake (□275), SW Queensland, Australia, 280 mi. W of Charleville; 20 mi. long, 18 mi. wide; frequently dry.
Yammune or **Yammunah** (yăm-mōō'nŭ), Fr. *Yammouni*, village, central Lebanon, 35 mi. NE of Beirut, at an alt. of 4,800 ft., overlooking **Lake Yammune** (16 mi. long, less than 1 mi. wide), dry in summer. Ruins of Greco-Roman temple on its shores.
Yamome-iwa, Japan: see LOT'S WIFE.
Yamoto (yämō'tō), town (pop. 11,861), Miyagi prefecture, N Honshu, Japan, 5 mi. W of Ishinomaki; rice and mulberry fields. Until late 1930s, called Takaki.
Yampa, agr. town (pop. 421), Routt co., NW Colo., on headstream of Yampa R., in SW foothills of Park Range, and 23 mi. S of Steamboat Springs; alt. 7,884 ft.
Yampa Canyon, Colo.: see DINOSAUR NATIONAL MONUMENT.
Yamparáez, province, Bolivia: see TARABUCO.
Yamparáez (yämpärä'ĕs), town (pop. c.5,380), Chuquisaca dept., S central Bolivia, 13 mi. W of Tarabuco (connected by railroad); alt. 10,335 ft.; barley, *oca*, quinoa, potatoes.
Yampa River, NW Colo., rises in Rocky Mts. in NE Garfield co., flows N, past Steamboat Springs, and W, past Craig, through Yampa Canyon (c.1,600 ft. deep) in DINOSAUR NATIONAL MONUMENT, to Green R. near Utah line; c.250 mi. long. Tributary, Little Snake R.
Yampol or **Yampol'** (yäm'pŭl). **1** Town (1926 pop. 2,774), W Kamenets-Podolski oblast, Ukrainian SSR, on Goryn R. and 39 mi. WSW of Shepetovka; wheat, sugar beets. **2** Town (1926 pop. 3,431), NE Stalino oblast, Ukrainian SSR, 8 mi. ESE of Krasny Liman. **3** Village (1926 pop. 4,312), N Sumy oblast, Ukrainian SSR, 19 mi. NNW of Glukhov; hemp processing. **4** Town (1926 pop. 6,289), S Vinnitsa oblast, Ukrainian SSR, on Dniester R. (N of Soroki) and 27 mi. SE of Mogilev-Podolski; fruit; flour; metalworks.
Yam River (yŭm), Mandarin *Chin Kiang* or *Ch'in Chiang* (both: chĭn'jyäng'), Cantonese *Yam Kong* (yŭm' gông'), W Kwangtung prov., China, rises on Kwangtung-Kwangsi border near Lingshan, flows 70 mi. SW, past Yamhsien, to Gulf of Tonkin.

Yamsk (yämsk), village (1948 pop. over 500), N Khabarovsk Territory, Russian SFSR, port on Shelekhov Gulf of Sea of Okhotsk, at mouth of Yama R., 110 mi. E of Magadan.

Yamskaya Sloboda (yŭmskī'ŭ slŭbŏdä'), suburb of Kursk, Russian SFSR.

Yamuna River, India: see Jumna River.

Yamura (yä"mōō'rä), town (pop. 14,450), Yamanashi prefecture, central Honshu, Japan, 21 mi. ESE of Kofu; mfg. (dyes, silk goods).

Yamursba, Tanjung, Netherlands New Guinea: see Good Hope, Cape of.

Yana, Bulgaria: see Novoseltsi.

Yana, river, Russian SFSR: see Yana River.

Yanaca (yänä'kä), town (pop. 955), Apurímac dept., S central Peru, in the Andes, 45 mi. SSW of Abancay; grain, potatoes, stock.

Yanacancha (yänakän'chä), village (pop. 475), Cajamarca dept., NW Peru, in Cordillera Occidental, 25 mi. W of Celendín; coal mining.

Yanagawa (yä"nä'gäwŏ). **1** Town (pop. 9,307), Fukuoka prefecture, W Kyushu, Japan, 8 mi. SE of Saga; raw silk, rice; spinning mill. **2** Town (pop. 8,325), Fukushima prefecture, N Honshu, Japan, on Abukuma R. and 11 mi. NE of Fukushima; spinning.

Yanagigaura (yänägē'-gä'ōōrä), town (pop. 4,815), Oita prefecture, N Kyushu, Japan, 26 mi. NW of Oita, near Nagasu, on Suo Sea; rice, wheat, barley, raw silk.

Yanagimoto (yänä'gē'-mōtō), town (pop. 3,760), Nara prefecture, S Honshu, Japan, 8 mi. S of Nara; rice, wheat, raw silk.

Yanahuanca (yänäwäng'kä), town (pop. 476), ⊙ Daniel Carrión prov., Pasco dept., central Peru, in Cordillera Central of the Andes, on Yanahuanca R. (a left branch of the Huallaga) and 22 mi. NW of Cerro de Pasco; barley, potatoes. Thermal springs.

Yanahuara (yänäwä'rä), town (pop. 4,076), Arequipa dept., S Peru, N suburb of Arequipa, in irrigation area (corn, wheat, barley, potatoes, alfalfa, vegetables).

Yanai (yänī'), town (pop. 20,291), Yamaguchi prefecture, SW Honshu, Japan, port on Iyo Sea, 14 mi. SSW of Iwakuni; saltmaking center; soy sauce. Exports tobacco, rice, salt.

Yanaizu (yänī'zōō). **1** Town (pop. 5,934), Fukushima prefecture, N central Honshu, Japan, 11 mi. WNW of Wakamatsu; agr. (rice, raw silk, tobacco); gold mining. **2** Town (pop. 4,149), Miyagi prefecture, N Honshu, Japan, 13 mi. N of Ishinomaki; silk cocoons, rice, charcoal.

Yanam (yŭnŭm'), Fr. *Yanaon* (yänäō'), town and settlement (after 1947, officially "free city"; □ 6; pop. 5,853) of Fr. India, within East Godavari dist., NE Madras, India; port on Bay of Bengal, 15 mi. S of Cocanada, near mouth of Gautami Godavari R. Fertile soil yields rice, sesame, millet, mangoes. Trading post established 1750 by French; occupied 1793 by English; restored to French in 1817.

Yanaoca (yänäō'kä), town (pop. 1,537), ⊙ Canas prov. (□ 1,244; pop. 29,810), Cuzco dept., S Peru, in the Andes, 60 mi. SE of Cuzco, in agr. region (potatoes, grain, coca); ocher mining; alt. 12,870 ft.

Yana River (yä'nŭ), NE Yakut Autonomous SSR, Russian SFSR, rises in central Verkhoyansk Range, flows 667 mi. N, past Verkhoyansk and Kazachye, to Laptev Sea, forming large delta mouth below Ust-Yansk. Navigable below Verkhoyansk during ice-free period (June-Sept.). Chief tributaries: Bytantai (left), Adycha (right) rivers.

Yanas (yä'näs), town (pop. 1,279), Huánuco dept., central Peru, on W slopes of Cordillera Blanca, near Marañón R., 20 mi. NE of Huallanca; barley, potatoes, cattle, sheep.

Yanase (yä"nä'sä), town (pop. 4,601), Hyogo prefecture, S Honshu, Japan, 16 mi. ESE of Toyooka, in agr. area (rice, wheat, flowers), poultry; home industries (woodworking, yarn, cutlery, raw silk).

Yanaul (yŭnŭōōl'), town (1939 pop. over 10,000), NW Bashkir Autonomous SSR, Russian SFSR, on railroad and 115 mi. NNW of Ufa; meat packing, dairying center.

Yanaurcu or **Yana-Urcu** (yä"nä-ōōr'kōō). **1** Andean peak (14,878 ft.), Imbabura prov., N Eucador, 18 mi. NW of Ibarra. **2** Andean peak (13,980 ft.), Imbabura prov., N Ecuador, 19 mi. SSW of Ibarra; has several crater lakes.

Yanbu', Saudi Arabia: see Yenbo.

Yancey (yăn'sē), county (□ 311; pop. 16,306), W N.C.; ⊙ Burnsville. Bounded NW by Tenn., E by Nolichucky R.; traversed by ranges of the Blue Ridge and Black Mts., including Mt. Mitchell (6,684 ft.), highest point E of the Mississippi; Bald Mts. are along Tenn. line. Includes parts of Pisgah Natl. Forest (S, NW). Farming (tobacco, hay, potatoes, corn), stock raising, lumbering, mining (mica, kaolin, feldspar); resorts. Formed 1833.

Yancey, mining village (1940 pop. 1,122), Harlan co., SE Ky., in the Cumberlands, 24 mi. ENE of Middlesboro; bituminous coal.

Yanceyville, village (pop. 1,391), ⊙ Caswell co., N N.C., 15 mi. S of Danville, Va.; textile and lumber mills.

Yancuitlalpan (yäng-kwētläl'pän), town (pop. 1,633), Puebla, central Mexico, 29 mi. SSE of Papantla; corn, coffee, sugar cane, fruit.

Yandabo (yän'dŭbō), village, Myingyan dist., Upper Burma, on left bank of Irrawaddy R. and 60 mi. WSW of Mandalay. Treaty signed here (1826) ended 1st Anglo-Burmese War. Also spelled Yandabu.

Yandoon (yän'dōōn'), town (pop. 9,925), Maubin dist., Lower Burma, on left bank of Irrawaddy R. and 35 mi. WNW of Rangoon.

Yandua or **Yadua** (both: yändōō'ä), island (□ 5; pop. 77), Fiji, SW Pacific, 5 mi. W of Vanua Levu; 4.5 mi. long.

Yanfa (yŭn'fä'), Mandarin *Jen-hua* (rŭn'hwä'), town (pop. 13,514), ⊙ Yanfa co. (pop. 46,992), N Kwangtung prov., China, 25 mi. NE of Kükong; coal mining.

Yang, China: see Yang River.

Yanga (yäng'gä), town (pop. 1,524), Veracruz, E Mexico, in Sierra Madre Oriental, 9 mi. ESE of Córdoba; coffee, fruit. Formerly San Lorenzo.

Yangambi (yäng-gäm'bē), village, Eastern Prov., N Belgian Congo, on right bank of Congo R. and 50 mi. WNW of Stanleyville; center of agr. research, with large botanical gardens, experimental plantations (elaeis palm, coffee, cacao) and laboratories. Also hq. of pedological service of Belgian Congo. Hosp. for Europeans.

Yangcheng or **Yang-ch'eng** (yäng'chŭng'), town, ⊙ Yangcheng co. (pop. 244,583), SE Shansi prov., China, 25 mi. W of Tsincheng; agr. center; sericulture; wheat, beans, corn; pottery making. Coal mines near by.

Yang-chiang, China: see Yeungkong.

Yang-chiao-kou, China: see Yangkiokow.

Yang-ch'i-chen, China: see Yangkichen.

Yangchow or **Yang-chou** (both: yäng'jō'), city (pop. 127,104), ⊙ North Kiangsu, China, 15 mi. N of Chinkiang, and on Grand Canal, just N of Yangtze R.; commercial center; machine mfg.; processing of rice, wheat, beans, kaoliang, corn, cotton. An anc. city, it was ⊙ Yang kingdom under the Sui dynasty (A.D. 581–618). It was reported as Yangiu by Marco Polo, who was named honorary governor of the city (1282–85). Called Kiangtu (1912–49) while ⊙ Kiangtu co. (1948 pop. 1,333,529); became (1949) an independent municipality and was made ⊙ North Kiangsu administrative region.

Yang-cho-yung Hu, Tibet: see Yamdrok Tso.

Yang-ch'ü, China: see Yangkü.

Yangchüan, China: see Pingting.

Yang-ch'un, China: see Yeungchun.

Yangchung (yäng'jōōng'), town (pop. 10,758), ⊙ Yangchung co. (pop. 192,685), S central Kiangsu prov., China, 25 mi. E of Chinkiang, on isl. in Yangtze R.; rice, beans, wheat. Until 1914 called Taiping.

Yangdok (yäng'dŭk'), Jap. *Yotoku,* town (1944 pop. 15,413), S.Pyongan prov., N Korea, 29 mi. W of Wonsan, in lumber area. Hot springs near by.

Yanggeta, Fiji: see Yasawa.

Yang Ho, China: see Yang River.

Yanghsien (yäng'shyĕn'), town (pop. 9,489), ⊙ Yanghsien co. (pop. 174,390), SW Shensi prov., China, 28 mi. NE of Nancheng and on Han R.; agr.

Yang-hsin, China: see Yangsin.

Yangi-Aryk (yŭn-gē"ŭrĭk'), village (1926 pop. 2,370), S Khorezm oblast, Uzbek SSR, on Khiva oasis, 14 mi. S of Urgench; cotton.

Yangi-Bazar (–bŭzär'). **1** Village (1948 pop. over 2,000), SW Talas oblast, Kirghiz SSR, on Chatkal R. and 60 mi. NW of Namangan; wheat, livestock. **2** Town, Tadzhik SSR: see Ordzhonikidzeabad. **3** Village (1939 pop. over 500), central Bukhara oblast, Uzbek SSR, in Bukhara oasis, 20 mi. NNW of Bukhara; cotton, sericulture. **4** Village (pop. over 500), Khorezm oblast, Uzbek SSR, in Khiva oasis, NW of Urgench; cotton, sericulture. **5** Village (1939 pop. over 2,000), N Tashkent oblast, Uzbek SSR, 10 mi. E of Tashkent; rice; metalworks.

Yangi Hissar (yänjē' hĭsär'), Chinese *Yingkisha* or *Ying-chi-sha* (yĭng'jē'shä'), town and oasis (pop. 152,998), SW Sinkiang prov., China, 37 mi. SSE of Kashgar, and on road to Yarkand; 38°56'N 76°9'E. Carpet and cotton-textile mfg.; wheat, rice, cattle.

Yangi-Kishlak (yŭn-gē"-kēshläk'), village (1939 pop. over 500), N Samarkand oblast, Uzbek SSR, on N slope of the Nura-Tau, 55 mi. N of Samarkand; wheat, sheep.

Yangi-Kurgan (–kōōrgän'). **1** Village (1939 pop. over 500), NW Fergana oblast, Uzbek SSR, 10 mi. E of Kokand; cotton, sericulture. **2** Village (1926 pop. 2,481), N Namangan oblast, Uzbek SSR, 12 mi. N of Namangan; cotton; sericulture.

Yangi Shahr (yänjē' shä'hŭr) [Uigur,=new town], Chinese *Shuleh* or *Sulo* (both: shōō'lŭ'), town, ⊙ Yangi Shahr co. (pop. 169,413), SW Sinkiang prov., China, 5 mi. SE of Kashgar; commercial center; trades in grain, cotton, carpets, silk. Opened to foreign trade in 1860. Sometimes called Kashgar Yangi Shahr as opposed to the old town of Kashgar proper.

Yangi-Yul or **Yangi-Yul'** (yŭn-gē"yōōl'), city (1947 pop. estimate 30,000), N Tashkent oblast, Uzbek SSR, on Trans-Caspian RR (Kaufmanskaya station) and 12 mi. SW of Tashkent. Cotton-ginning center; food canning (dairy, flour products), sugar refining, cottonseed-oil extraction, soap mfg.; sugar beets. Until c.1935, Kaunchi.

Yangkao (yäng'gou'), town, ⊙ Yangkao co. (pop. 115,105), SW Chahar prov., China, 33 mi. NE of Tatung and on railroad; flour milling; winegrowing; ramie, millet. Until 1949 in N Shansi.

Yangkichen or **Yang-ch'i-chen** (both: yäng'chē'-chŭn'), town, central Szechwan prov., China, 16 mi. SE of Shehung and on left bank of Fow R.

Yangkiokow or **Yang-chiao-kou** (both: yäng'jou'-gō'), city, N Shantung prov., China, minor port on Gulf of Chihli, on lower Siaoching R. near its mouth, and 110 mi. ENE of Tsinan.

Yangkow or **Yang-k'ou** (both: yäng'kō'), town, N Fukien prov., China, 5 mi. ESE of Shunchang and on Min R.

Yangku (yäng'gōō'), town, ⊙ Yangku co. (pop. 329,443), NE Pingyuan prov., China, 25 mi. SSW of Liaocheng; cotton and silk weaving; wheat, millet, kaoliang, peanuts. Until 1949 in Shantung prov.

Yangkü or **Yang-ch'ü** (both: yäng'chü'), town, ⊙ Yangkü co. (pop. 65,517), N Shansi prov., China, 10 mi. N of Taiyüan and on railroad. The name of Yangkü was applied 1912–47 to Taiyüan.

Yangli (yäng'lē'), town, ⊙ Yangli co. (pop. 80,664), SW Kwangsi prov., China, 55 mi. W of Nanning; wheat, corn, beans, kaoliang.

Yangmei (yäng'mā'), Jap. *Yobai* (yō'bī), town (1935 pop. 4,934), NW Formosa, 14 mi. NE of Sinchu and on railroad; tea-growing and -processing center; sugar refining, rice milling; mfg. of bricks, furniture.

Yangpi or **Yang-p'i** (yäng'pē'), town (pop. 6,919), ⊙ Yangpi co. (pop. 19,694), NW Yunnan prov., China, on Burma Road and 10 mi. WSW of Tali; alt. 6,430 ft.; tung-oil processing; rice, wheat, millet, beans.

Yang River, Chinese *Yang Ho* (yäng' hŭ'), Chahar prov., China, rises on Suiyuan line, flows 60 mi. SE, past Süanhwa, joining Sangkan R. near Cholu to form Yungting R.

Yangshan (yäng'shän'). **1** Town, ⊙ Yangshan co., SE Jehol prov., Manchuria, China, 37 mi. W of Chinchow. **2** Town, Kwangtung prov., China: see Yeungshan.

Yangshuo, China: see Yangso.

Yangsin or **Yang-hsin** (both: yäng'shĭn'). **1** Town (pop. 7,244), ⊙ Yangsin co. (pop. 309,380), SE Hupeh prov., China, near Kiangsi line, 70 mi. SE of Hankow; ramie. Coal mining, copper deposits near by. Until 1912 called Hingkwo. **2** Town, ⊙ Yangsin co. (pop. 238,648), N Shantung prov., China, on road and 12 mi. NNE of Hweimin; cotton, honey, wheat, beans.

Yangso or **Yangshuo** (both: yäng'shwô'), town, ⊙ Yangso co. (pop. 124,982), NE Kwangsi prov., China, 45 mi. SSE of Kweilin and on Kwei R.; rice, sugar cane, corn, wheat, beans.

Yangtze Cape, China: see Pootung.

Yangtze River (yăng'sē', Chinese yäng'dzŭ'), in Chinese commonly *Chang Kiang* or *Ch'ang Chiang* (both: chäng' jyäng') [long river]; in upper course *Kinsha Kiang* or *Chin-sha Chiang* (both: jin'shä) [golden sand river], Tibetan *Dre Chu,* longest river of Asia and China; flows 3,430 mi. from the Tibetan highlands, past central China's great cities of Chungking, Hankow, and Nanking, to the East China Sea of the Pacific near Shanghai. Rising in several headstreams (Murui Ussu, Ulan Muren) at c.16,000 ft. in SW Tsinghai prov. at 34°N 91°E, it flows S through the gorges of the Tahsüeh Mts., past Paan, separating E Tibet from W Sikang and passing within 40 mi. of the canyon-encased upper Mekong and Salween rivers. Its precipitous course continues into N Yunnan, where the high tableland diverts the stream NE in 3 great bends toward Szechwan. The river descends to 1,000 ft. at Ipin, the head of navigation. Its course becomes easterly as it flows through Szechwan's Red Basin, past Luhsien, Chungking, and Wanhsien. Bet. Fengkieh and Ichang, the Yangtze traverses its celebrated gorges on Szechwan-Hupeh border, where rapids endanger navigation. Below Ichang, the head of navigation for ocean-going vessels, the Yangtze passes through the lake-filled central basin of Hupeh, past Shasi and the Wuhan cities (Hankow, Wuchang, Hanyang). It then turns NE at Kiukiang, through Anhwei and Kiangsu, past Anking, Wuhu, Nanking, and Chinkiang (Grand Canal crossing) to the sea. Its mouth of 2 main arms, separated by Tsungming isl., is linked with Shanghai by the Whangpoo R. Its chief tributaries are, on the left, the precipitous Yalung R., the Min, To, and Kialing rivers of the Red Basin, and the Han R.; on the right, the Kien (Wu) R. of Kweichow. The Yüan and Siang rivers of Hunan and the Kan R. of Kiangsi reach the Yangtze through the Tungting and Poyang lake basins. These lakes, connected by numerous channels with the Yangtze, serve as natural overflow reservoirs during the summer flood season. A major E-W trade artery of central China, the Yangtze is navigable for 1,000 mi. for ocean-going ships, and for 1,500 mi. for smaller vessels. It traverses some of China's chief economic regions, among the most densely populated in the world. Named for the early Yang kingdom (c.1000 B.C.) along its lower course, the Yangtze once entered the sea through a S arm traversing Tai L. to Hangchow Bay. Unlike the Yellow R., the Yangtze has no devastating floods threatening agr. and human life. An early foreign name for the Yangtze was Blue R., possibly to differentiate it from the Yellow R.

Yangwu (yäng'wōō'), town, ⊙ Yangwu co. (pop. 121,325), SW Pingyuan prov., China, 20 mi. SSE of Sinsiang, near Yellow R. (Honan line); rice, wheat, beans, kaoliang. Until 1949 in Honan prov.

Yangyang (yäng'yäng'), Jap. *Joyo*, township (1944 pop. 9,991), Kangwon prov., central Korea, N of 38°N, 50 mi. ENE of Chunchon; fishing port on Sea of Japan.

Yangyüan (yäng'yüän'), town, ⊙ Yangyüan co. (pop. 116,820), SW Chahar prov., China, 50 mi. E of Tatung; cattle raising; grain. Called Sining until 1914. Until 1928 in Chihli (Hopeh).

Yani (yä'nē), town, La Paz dept., W Bolivia, at N foot of the Illampu, 13 mi. NNE of Sorata; alt. 11,906 ft. Gold mine near by.

Yanina, Greece: see IOANNINA.

Yanishki, Lithuania: see JONISKIS.

Yaniskoski, Russian SFSR: see PATS RIVER.

Yankalilla (yŏng"kŭlĭ'lŭ), village (pop. 272), SE South Australia, on Gulf St. Vincent and 40 mi. SSW of Adelaide; dairying center; livestock.

Yankee Lake, village (pop. 53), Trumbull co., NE Ohio.

Yankeetown, town (pop. 322), on Levy-Citrus co. line, N central Fla., on Withlacoochee R. near its mouth on the Gulf, and c.50 mi. SSW of Gainesville; sportsmen's resort.

Yankton, county (□ 524; pop. 16,804), SE S.Dak., on Nebr. line; ⊙ Yankton. Farming area drained by James R. and bounded S by Missouri R. Mfg. at Yankton; dairy products, livestock, corn, fruit. Formed 1862.

Yankton, city (pop. 7,709), ⊙ Yankton co., SE S. Dak., 60 mi. SW of Sioux Falls and on Missouri R., near James R. Railroad and shipping center for grain and cattle area; crates, cigars, bricks, cement products, seed, flour, dairy products. State insane asylum, Yankton Col., jr. col. here. City was Dakota territorial ⊙ 1861–83. Settled 1858, platted 1859, inc. 1869.

Yannina, Greece: see IOANNINA.

Yano (yä'nō), town (pop. 9,047), Hiroshima prefecture, SW Honshu, Japan, on Hiroshima Bay, 5 mi. SE of Hiroshima; fishing port.

Yanonge (yänông'gä), village, Eastern Prov., N central Belgian Congo, on Congo R. and 40 mi. W of Stanleyville; agr. center; rubber, coffee, elaeis-palm plantations. R.C. mission.

Yanov, Poland: see JANOW.

Yanov (yä'nŭf). **1** Town, Lvov oblast, Ukrainian SSR: see IVAN-FRANKO. **2** Pol. *Janów* (yä'nōōf), town (1937 pop. estimate 2,500), central Ternopol oblast, Ukrainian SSR, on Seret R. and 6 mi. S of Terebovlya; flour milling; stone quarrying. Has ruins of old castle.

Yanovichi (yä'nŭvēchē), town (1926 pop. 2,155), NE Vitebsk oblast, Belorussian SSR, 21 mi. ENE of Vitebsk; food products.

Yanovka, Ukrainian SSR: see IVANOVKA, Odessa oblast.

Yanping (yän'pĭng'), Mandarin *En-p'ing* (ŭn'pĭng'), town (pop. 3,432), ⊙ Yanping co. (pop. 236,021), SW Kwangtung prov., China, 90 mi. SW of Canton; rice, wheat, potatoes. Extensive gold and tungsten mines near by.

Yanque (yäng'kä), town (pop. 1,229), Arequipa dept., S Peru, in high valley of Cordillera Occidental, 4 mi. SW of Chivay; alfalfa, potatoes, grain, cattle, alpacas.

Yanski or **Yanskiy** (yän'skē), town (1948 pop. over 500), N Yakut Autonomous SSR, Russian SFSR, on Yana R. and 90 mi. N of Verkhoyansk; shipbuilding.

Yantales (yäntä'lĕs), massif (6,725 ft.) of Patagonian Andes, Chiloé prov., S Chile, near the coast, at 43°30'S 72°48'W. Has several peaks and glaciers.

Yantarny or **Yantarnyy** (yŭntär'nē) [Rus. yantar'=amber], town (1939 pop. 3,079), W Kaliningrad oblast, Russian SFSR, on the Baltic, 25 mi. WNW of Kaliningrad; major amber-extracting and -processing center; fisheries. Until 1945, in East Prussia and called Palmnicken (pälm'nĭkŭn).

Yantic (yăn'tĭk), woolen-milling village (1940 pop. 518) in Norwich and Franklin towns, New London co., SE Conn., on **Yantic River,** formed by small streams near Bozrah, SE Conn., and flowing c.12 mi. SE to join Shetucket R., forming the Thames at Norwich.

Yantikovo (yän'tyĭkŭvŭ), village (1939 pop. over 500), E Chuvash Autonomous SSR, Russian SFSR, 12 mi. E of Kanash; grain; limestone quarrying.

Yantra River (yän'trä), N Bulgaria, formed just S of Gabrovo by confluence of 3 streams rising in Shipka Mts.; flows generally NE, past Gabrovo and Tirnovo, and NNW, past Byala, to the Danube 12 mi. E of Svishtov; 168 mi. long. Receives Bregovitsa (right) and Rositsa (left) rivers. Has gold-carrying sand. Sometimes spelled Jantra.

Yanushpol, Ukrainian SSR: see IVANOPOL.

Yanya, Yugoslavia: see JANJA.

Yanyevo, Yugoslavia: see JANJEVO.

Yany-Kurgan (yŭnē"-kōōrgän'), village, SE Kzyl-Orda oblast, Kazakh SSR, on the Syr Darya, on Trans-Caspian RR and 105 mi. SE of Kzyl-Orda; metalworks; Glauber's-salt extraction. Health resort (mud baths).

Yao (yä'ō), town (pop. 23,317), Osaka prefecture, S Honshu, Japan, 5 mi. E of Osaka; poultry and agr. (rice, wheat) center; truck gardening.

Yaoan (you'än'), town, ⊙ Yaoan co. (pop. 110,145), N central Yunnan prov., China, 40 mi. NW of Tsuyung, in mtn. region; timber, rice, millet, beans. Until 1913 called Yaochow.

Yaochow. 1 Town, Shensi prov., China: see YAOHSIEN. **2** Town, Yunnan prov., China: see YAOAN.

Yaohsien (you'shyĕn'), town (pop. 13,744), ⊙ Yaohsien co. (pop. 55,723), central Shensi prov., China, 45 mi. N of Sian and on spur of Lunghai RR; commercial center; silk weaving. Important coal mines at Tungchwan (N). Until 1913, Yaochow.

Yaoka (yä'ôkä) or **Yoka** (yō'kä), town (pop. 8,617), Hyogo prefecture, S Honshu, Japan, 10 mi. NNW of Toyooka, in agr. area (rice, wheat, tea); spinning mills. Produces raw silk, *konnyaku* (paste made from devil's tongue), frozen fish. Sericulture school.

Yaonahuac (younäwäk'), town (pop. 967), Puebla, central Mexico, 8 mi. WNW of Teziutlán; corn, sugar cane, fruit.

Yaonan (you'nän'), town, ⊙ Changshan co. (pop. 250,351), central Shantung prov., China, 7 mi. N of Chowtsun; cotton and silk weaving, straw plaiting; beans, wheat, peanuts, millet, corn. Called Changshan until 1949.

Yao Noi, Ko (kô' you' noi'), island (1937 pop. 1,545), Phangnga prov., S Thailand, smaller of 2 isls. in bay of Andaman Sea bet. Phuket isl. and Malay Peninsula; 7 mi. long, 2 mi. wide.

Yaoshan, town, China: see LUNGYAO.

Yao Shan (you' shän'), mountain in E central Kwangsi prov., China, 50 mi. SE of Liuchow; inhabited by Yao aborigenes.

Yaotsu (yäō'tsōō), town (pop. 7,651), Gifu prefecture, central Honshu, Japan, 10 mi. N of Tajimi; mfg. (sake, soy sauce, silk and rayon textiles).

Yaoundé or **Yaunde** (youn'dā, youndā'), town (pop. estimate c.30,000), ⊙ Fr. Cameroons and of Nyong et Sanaga region, W central Fr. Cameroons, 130 mi. E of the coastal port of Douala; 3°51'N 11°39'E. Commercial center, terminus of railroad from Douala, and road communications hub. Handles a large share of transport to and from Ubangi-Shari (Fr. Equatorial Africa). Manufactures soap, cigarettes, butter, cheese, bricks, tiles, printed matter. Has sawmills and machine shops. Coffee plantations and native cacao fields in vicinity. Seat of vicar apostolic. Airport. Also an educational center for natives, with agr. school, laboratory of entomology and bacteriology, teachers col., mulattoes school. There is a meteorological station, hosp., racecourse, R.C. and Protestant missions. Founded 1888, it became ⊙ Fr. Cameroons after establishment of Fr. mandate; it was replaced as capital temporarily (1940–46) by Douala. Occupied by Belgian colonial troops, 1915.

Yaowan (you'wän'), town, N Kiangsu prov., China, on Grand Canal, and 70 mi. NW of Hwaiyin, near Shantung line; commercial center.

Yao Yai, Ko (kô' you' yī'), Malay *Pulau Panjang*, island (1937 pop. 1,695), Phangnga prov., S Thailand, larger of 2 isls. in bay of Andaman Sea bet. Phuket isl. and Malay Peninsula; 80°N 98°35'E; 15 mi. long, 2 mi. wide; tin deposits; coconuts.

Yap (yăp, yäp), island group (□ 39; pop. 2,744), W CAROLINE ISLANDS, W Pacific, 275 mi. NE of Palau; 9°32'N 138°8'E. Consists of 4 large and 10 small isls. surrounded by coral reef 16 mi. long. Composed of older crystalline rocks, Yap is geologically different from other Carolines. Rull is largest of 4 major isls. (10 mi. long, 3 mi. wide; rising to 984 ft.); others are Tomil, Map, Rumung. Tomil Harbor (12–20 fathoms deep) in SE. Micronesian natives use stone money (large discs of aragonite). Produces copra, dried bonito. Isl. is communication center, with 2 radio stations and a cable station. In Second World War, site of large Jap. air base; naval base at Tomil Harbor. Isl. was surrendered after defeat of Japan. Yap dist. (□ 46; pop. 4,652) includes EAURIPIK, ELATO, FAIS, FARAULEP, GAFERUT, IFALIK, LAMOTREK, NGULU, OLIMARAO, PIKELOT, SATAWAL, SOROL, ULITHI, WEST FAYU, WOLEAI. Formerly spelled Guap.

Yapahuwa (yŭp'ŭhōōvŭ) [Singhalese, =the excellent mountain], ancient rock fortress (alt. 785 ft.), North Western Prov., Ceylon, 2.5 mi. ESE of Maho. Palace ruins (13th cent.) on summit reached by great flight of steps (now partially destroyed). Ruins of 13th-cent. city at foot of rock; was ⊙ Ceylon for 13 years in late-13th cent., after which ⊙ moved to Kurunegala following capture of city by Tamil invaders.

Yapei (yäpā'), village, Northern Territories, N central Gold Coast, 27 mi. SW of Tamale (linked by road), on White Volta R.; canoe port for Tamale.

Yapen Islands, Netherlands New Guinea: see JAPEN ISLANDS.

Yapeyú (yäpĕyōō') or **San Martín** (sän märtēn'), town (pop. estimate 1,000), E Corrientes prov., Argentina, on Uruguay R. (Brazil border) and 80 mi. ESE of Mercedes; farming center (corn, rice, peanuts, oranges). José de San Martín, heroic revolutionist, b. here.

Yaphank (yăp'hăngk"), village (pop. c.350), Suffolk co., SE N.Y., on E central Long Isl., 6 mi. NE of Patchogue; cranberry growing. U.S. Camp Upton here was a U.S. army induction center in both world wars.

Yappen Islands, Netherlands New Guinea: see JAPEN ISLANDS.

Yapurá River, Brazil: see JAPURÁ RIVER.

Yaque del Norte (yä'kā dĕl nôr'tā), river, central and NW Dominican Republic, rises in the Cordillera Central SE of the Pico Trujillo, flows N, past Santiago, where it turns WNW, past Guayubín, through the fertile Cibao region, to the Atlantic 2 mi. W of Monte Cristi; c.125 mi. long. Lower course navigable for small craft in rainy season.

Yaque del Sur (sōōr'), river, W central and SW Dominican Republic, rises in the Cordillera Central SE of the Pico Trujillo, flows c.80 mi. S, past Cabral, to Neiba Bay (Caribbean) 5 mi. N of Barahona. Partly navigable for small craft.

Yaquina Bay (yŭkwē'nŭ, yŭkwĭ'nŭ), W Oregon, sheltered inlet of the Pacific at mouth of Yaquina R., just S of Newport, whose harbor it forms. **Yaquina Head,** coastal promontory 4 mi. N of Yaquina Bay, has a lighthouse. **Yaquina River,** W Oregon, rises NW of Corvallis, flows 50 mi. generally W, past Toledo, to Yaquina Bay at Newport.

Yaqui River (yä'kē), Sonora, NW Mexico, formed 12 mi. N of Sahuaripa in W outliers of Sierra Madre Occidental by Bavispe R. and other affluents, flows c.200 mi. S and SW, through plateaus and alluvial lowlands, past Suaqui, Soyopa, Tónichi, Onavas, Bácum, and Potam, to Gulf of California in large delta 28 mi. SE of Guaymas; length, with longest tributary, c.420 mi. Largest river in Sonora. Used for irrigation, especially along its lower course, where wheat, corn, rice, and fruit are grown. Not navigable.

Yar (yär), town (1948 pop. over 2,000), NW Udmurt Autonomous SSR, Russian SFSR, 22 mi. WNW of Glazov; rail junction; flax processing.

Yara (yä'rä), town (pop. 1,306), Oriente prov., E Cuba, on Central Highway, on railroad, and 11 mi. ESE of Manzanillo. Noted for its tobacco. Site of proclamation of Cuban independence (1868), which led to outbreak of Ten Years War.

Yaracuy (yäräkwē'), state (□ 2,740; 1941 pop. 127,030; 1950 census 132,790), N Venezuela; ⊙ San Felipe. Comprises Yaracuy valley, flanked by Sierra de Aroa (W) and outliers of coastal range (E). Climate is tropical, with heavy rains (June–Dec.). Mineral resources include the Aroa copper mines, which also contain iron pyrite; deposits of lead (Chivacoa), platinum (Albarico), marble (Cocorote), and coal. In fertile Yaracuy valley are grown sugar cane, corn, cacao, tobacco, cotton, rice, yuca, bananas; coffee plantations at higher alt.

Yaracuy River, Yaracuy state, N Venezuela, rises S of Urachiche, flows 75 mi. NE to Triste Gulf of Caribbean Sea, 18 mi. WNW of Puerto Cabello. Its valley produces sugar cane, cacao, cotton, tobacco, corn, rice, yuca, fruit. Separates great Andean spur (W) from coastal range (E) of Venezuela. Navigable for small craft.

Yaraligoz Dag (yärälŭ'gŭz" dä), Turkish *Yaralıgöz Dağ*, peak (6,514 ft.), N Turkey, in Kure Mts., 32 mi. NE of Kastamonu.

Yarangum, Turkey: see TAVAS.

Yaransk (yŭränsk'), city (1948 pop. over 10,000), SW Kirov oblast, Russian SFSR, 45 mi. N of Ioshkar-Ola; distilling, flax processing; agr. implements. Chartered 1584.

Yaras, Las, Peru: see LAS YARAS.

Yarboutenda (yärbōōtĕn'dä) or **Yarbatenda** (yärbä–), village, Fr. enclave in Gambia, West Africa, landing on upper Gambia R. and 180 mi. E of Bathurst; leased to France by Great Britain in 1904.

Yardley, E industrial suburb (pop. 31,467) of Birmingham, NW Warwick, England. Church dates from 10th cent.

Yardley, borough (pop. 1,916), Bucks co., SE Pa., on Delaware R. and 5 mi. WNW of Trenton, N.J.; clothing mfg.; agr. Settled 1682, inc. c.1895.

Yardymly (yŭrdĭm'lē), village (1932 pop. estimate 610), SE Azerbaijan SSR, on forested E slope of Talysh Mts., 33 mi. NW of Lenkoran; livestock, wheat.

Yarega (yŭryĕ'gŭ), town (1944 pop. over 500), central Komi Autonomous SSR, Russian SFSR, near N Pechora RR, 4 mi. SE of Ukhta, in area of oil fields.

Yaremcha (yŭrĭmchä'), Pol. *Jaremcze* (yärĕm'chĕ), town (1931 pop. 760), S Stanislav oblast, Ukrainian SSR, in E Beskids, on Prut R. and 24 mi. WSW of Kolomyya; noted summer resort with mineral springs; lumbering; sheep raising.

Yarensk (yä'ryĭnsk), village (1948 pop. over 2,000), S Archangel oblast, Russian SFSR, on Vychegda R. and 100 mi. NE of Kotlas; dairying.

Yare River (yâr, yâr), Norfolk, England, rises 3 mi. SSE of East Dereham, flows 50 mi. E, past Norwich, to confluence with Waveney R. at BREYDON WATER, 4 mi. WSW of Yarmouth. Receives Wensum R. just below Norwich. Its lower course passes through The BROADS.

Yari-ga-take (yä'rē-gä-tä'kä), peak (10,494 ft.), central Honshu, Japan, on Toyama-Nagano prefecture border, 25 mi. WNW of Nagano. Hot-springs resorts and rest huts on slopes.

Yarim or **Yerim** (both: yĕrēm'), town (pop. 5,000), Ibb prov., S Yemen, 70 mi. S of Sana (linked by motor road), on central plateau; alt. 7,000 ft. Farming and stock-raising center.

Yarí River (yärē'), Caquetá commissary, S Colombia, rises in Cordillera Oriental SE of Neiva, flows c.300 mi. SE through tropical forests to Caquetá R. at 0°25'S 72°16'W. Not navigable. Its lower course is also called Río de los Engaños (ĕngän'yōs).

Yaritagua (yärētä'gwä), town (pop. 5,399), Yaracuy state, N Venezuela, in SW foothills of Sierra de Aroa, on Barquisimeto–Puerto Cabello highway and 12 mi. E of Barquisimeto; sugar-cane center; also corn, cacao, tobacco, fruit. Trading post for N llanos.

Yarkand (yärkänd'), Chinese *Soche* or *So-ch'e* (both: sô'chŭ'), town (pop. 60,000) and oasis (pop. 311,159), SW Sinkiang prov., China, 100 mi. SE of Kashgar, 170 mi. NW of Khotan; 38°24'N 77°16'E. One of Sinkiang's leading trading centers, it is on route to Kashmir, on left bank of Yarkand R., at W edge of Taklamakan Desert. Cotton, silk, and wool weaving; sericulture; embroideries, carpets. Visited c.1275 by Marco Polo.

Yarkand River, major headstream of Tarim R, SW Sinkiang prov., China; rises on N slopes of the main Karakoram range near the peak K² (Mt. Godwin Austen), flows over 500 mi. generally NE, past Yarkand and Merket, joining Aksu R. 50 mi. SE of Aksu to form the Tarim.

Yarkeyevo, Russian SFSR: see VERKHNE-YARKEYEVO.

Yarkovo (yär'kŭvŭ), village (1926 pop. 741), SW Tyumen oblast, Russian SFSR, on Tobol R. (landing) and 55 mi. ENE of Tyumen; grain, livestock.

Yarm, town and parish (pop. 1,714), North Riding, NE Yorkshire, England, on Tees R. and 4 mi. SSW of Stockton; leather tanning and mfg. Was site of 13th-cent. monastery. Has church with 15th-cent. tower.

Yarmolintsy (yŭrmŭlyĕn'tsē), agr. town (1939 pop. over 500), central Kamenets-Podolski oblast, Ukrainian SSR, 16 mi. SSW of Proskurov; road and rail junction; sugar beets.

Yarmouth (yär'mŭth), county (□ 838; pop. 22,415), W N.S., on the Atlantic; ⊙ Yarmouth.

Yarmouth, town (pop. 7,790), ⊙ Yarmouth co., SW N.S., on the Atlantic, at entrance of the Bay of Fundy, 140 mi. WSW of Halifax; 43°49'N 66°7'W; seaport, with shipping lines to Boston, N.Y., and St. John; fishing center, popular summer resort. Fish curing, shipbuilding, cotton milling, woodworking, iron founding; ships Irish moss and strawberries. One of the great shipbuilding centers in days of wooden sailing vessels, it developed in mid-18th cent.

Yarmouth. 1 Town and parish (pop. 823), W Isle of Wight, Hampshire, England, on The Solent, at mouth of the small Yar, 10 mi. WSW of Cowes; small port (ferry to Lymington) and resort. Church rebuilt 1543. **2** Officially **Great Yarmouth,** county borough (1931 pop. 56,771; 1951 census 51,105), E Norfolk, England, on narrow peninsula bet. North Sea and Breydon Water (formed by Yare R. and Waveney R.), 18 mi. E of Norwich; 52°36'N 1°44'E. Port and herring-fishing center, famous for its "bloaters" (cured herring); shipyards, boilerworks, silk and knitting mills, flour mills. Has protected harbor and offshore anchorage in the Roads. Church of St. Nicholas, largest parish church in England, was founded early in 12th cent. by Bishop Losinga. Points of interest: Priory Hall, refectory of 11th-cent. monastery; remains of 14th-cent. Greyfriars' monastery; old tollhouse, now containing mus. and library; and the "rows," or narrow lanes, about 145 in number, many of them only 3–5 ft. wide. Town chartered 1272. Near-by beaches are seaside resorts. In co. borough (S) is industrial suburb of Gorleston.

Yarmouth. 1 Town (pop. 2,669), Cumberland co., SW Maine, 10 mi. NNE of Portland. Mfg. (sporting goods, wood products, bldg. materials); fish canned. Includes resort, fishing village of Yarmouth (pop. 2,189) on Casco Bay. Seat of North Yarmouth Acad. Scene of raids in Indian wars, 17th and 18th cent. Settled 1636, set off from North Yarmouth 1849. **2** Town (pop. 3,297), Barnstable co., SE Mass., extending across middle of Cape Cod, 4 mi. E of Barnstable; summer resort; agr. (cranberries, truck). Important shipping and fishing center in early 19th cent. Includes several resort villages: Bass River; South Yarmouth (pop. 1,185); West Yarmouth (pop. 1,355), on S shore and known for its cranberries; and Yarmouth Port (cranberries, asparagus) on N shore. Settled and inc. 1639.

Yarmouth Island (½ mi. in diameter), SW Maine, off Sebascodegan Isl. in Casco Bay.

Yarmouth Port, Mass.: see YARMOUTH.

Yarmuk River (yärmōōk'), river on Jordan–Syria border, formed NE of Samar by 3 tributaries, flows WNW then SW to the Jordan at Naharayim (hydroelectric plant), c.5 mi. S of Sea of Galilee (L. Tiberias); c.50 mi. long.

Yaroslav, Poland: see JAROSLAW.

Yaroslavl or **Yaroslavl'** (yŭrŭslä'vŭl), oblast (□ 14,250; 1946 pop. estimate 1,500,000) in N central European Russian SFSR; ⊙ Yaroslavl. In wooded level terrain, with Rybinsk Reservoir (NW), Uglich Upland (S), and Danilov Ridge (NE); drained by upper Volga R. Sandy and clayey soils grow mainly flax (N, W), potatoes (SE), truck produce (vegetables, fruit) around Rostov, Yaroslavl, and Shcherbakov; also chicory (SE), wheat (in N flax area and in extreme S). Dairy farming in alluvial meadows. Peat and building stone are only mineral resources. Power stations include hydroelectric plants at Uglich and Shcherbakov, peat-powered plant at Yaroslavl. Old linen-milling industries at Yaroslavl, Tutayev, Gavrilov-Yam, and Rostov; now superseded at Yaroslavl and Shcherbakov by shipbuilding, automobile and machinery mfg., and chemical industries. Fisheries on Rybinsk Reservoir and Volga R. Railroads and Volga R. form excellent transportation network; exports machinery, automobiles, tires, rubber goods, linen, lumber, lacquers; imports metals, petroleum, cotton, grain, alcohol. Formed 1936 out of Ivanovo oblast.

Yaroslavl or **Yaroslavl',** city (1926 pop. 114,282; 1939 pop. 298,065), ⊙ Yaroslavl oblast, Russian SFSR, on Volga R., at mouth of the Kotorosl, and 160 mi. NE of Moscow; 57°31'N 39°55'E. Major industrial center and river port; mfg. (automobiles, spare parts, synthetic rubber and asbestos, tires, rubber footwear, asbestos products, enamels, lacquers, paints, electric motors, brakes, agr. machinery); shipyards. Peat-fed power plant on left bank. In suburbs are large cotton mills of Krasny Perekop (2.5 mi. W) and Krasny Pereval (9 mi. NW of city center), and locomotive and railroad shops at Vspolye (2 mi. W) and at Uroch on left Volga bank. City has 12th-cent. monastery, several 17th-cent. churches, art gall., mus. of natural history and of old Rus. art. Agr., medical, and teachers colleges, technological institute. Site of 1st Rus. theater (founded 1747 by Volkov). City founded 1024 (oldest Rus. city on the Volga) at mouth of Kotorosl R. as N outpost of Rostov domain; became ⊙ principality after 1218 and a rival of Moscow, to which it fell in 1463. Developed (16th–17th cent.) into major trading center on White Sea–Volga R.–Near East route; seat of English trading station which initiated (1564–65) modern Rus. shipbuilding. Rise of St. Petersburg marked decline of Yaroslavl trade and growth of its industries. First Rus. linen mill founded here, 1722. Many historical spots, including old kremlin, were destroyed in revolution, which was followed by shift from textile to new machine-building and chemical industries. In recent years, city has widened considerably along both banks and c.15 mi. along Volga R. from Krasny Pereval (N) to point 5 mi. below city proper. Was ⊙ Yaroslavl govt., inc. 1929 into Ivanovo oblast.

Yaroslavskaya (yŭrŭslăf'skīŭ), village (1926 pop. 9,097), S central Krasnodar Territory, Russian SFSR, 17 mi. E of Maikop; wheat, sunflowers. Sometimes called Yaroslavskoye.

Yaroupi River (yärōōpē'), SE Fr. Guiana, rises in Tumuc-Humac Mts. near Brazil line, flows c.130 mi. NE, through tropical forests, to Oyapock R. at 2°50'N 52°23'W.

Yarovaya (yŭrŭvī'ŭ), town (1926 pop. 2,120), NW Stalino oblast, Ukrainian SSR, 9 mi. WNW of Krasny Liman.

Yarpus, Turkey: see AFSIN.

Yarram (yă'rŭm), town (pop. 1,547), S Victoria, Australia, 105 mi. SE of Melbourne; livestock center; dairy plant. Sometimes called Yarram Yarram.

Yarra River (yă'rŭ), S Victoria, Australia, rises in Great Dividing Range S of Woods Point, flows 115 mi. generally W, past Warburton, Melbourne, and S.Melbourne, to Hobson's Bay of Port Phillip. Navigable 5 mi. by small steamers below Melbourne. Formerly Yarra Yarra R.

Yarrawonga (yă"rŭwŏng'gŭ), town (pop. 2,393), N Victoria, Australia, on Murray R. and 135 mi. NNE of Melbourne, on New South Wales border; agr. (wheat, tobacco); flour mill.

Yarra Yarra River, Australia: see YARRA RIVER.

Yar River, Isle of Wight, Hampshire, England, rises just S of Freshwater, flows 3 mi. N to The Solent at Yarmouth.

Yarrow (yă'rō), village (pop. estimate 300), SW B.C., 8 mi. SW of Chilliwack; lumbering; fruit, hops, tobacco.

Yarrow, agr. village and parish (pop. 459), N central Selkirk, Scotland, on Yarrow Water and 7 mi. W of Selkirk. Has 17th-cent. church (restored).

Yarrow Water, river, Selkirk, Scotland, rises in Moffat Hills near junction of Selkirk, Dumfries, and Peebles border, 11 mi. NE of Moffat, flows 24 mi. ENE through Loch of the Lowes and St. Mary's Loch, past Yarrow, to Ettrick Water 2 mi. SW of Selkirk. Valley is of noted scenic beauty and has been celebrated by Wordsworth, Scott, and Hogg.

Yar-Sale (yär"-sŭlyĕ'), village, N Yamal-Nenets Natl. Okrug, Tyumen oblast, Russian SFSR, on Ob Bay, 140 mi. ENE of Salekhard; trading post.

Yartsevo (yär'tsyĭvŭ). **1** Village (1948 pop. over 2,000), central Krasnoyarsk Territory, Russian SFSR, 140 mi. NNW of Yeniseisk and on Yenisei R.; lumber milling. **2** City (1926 pop. 18,703), central Smolensk oblast, Russian SFSR, 30 mi. NE of Smolensk; cotton-milling center; machine mfg., food processing. Peat works at Pronkino (SE). Became city in 1926.

Yaru (yŭrōō'), village, Quetta-Pishin dist., N Baluchistan, W Pakistan, 20 mi. NNW of Quetta, on railroad; wool factory.

Yarumal (yärōōmäl'), town (pop. 8,693). Antioquia dept., NW central Colombia, in Cordillera Central, 50 mi. NNE of Medellín; alt. 7,546 ft. Gold-mining, dairying, and agr. center (coffee, corn, potatoes, sugar cane, beans, rice, fruit, livestock); cigar mfg. Waterfalls and a natural bridge across small Yarumalito R. are near by.

Yarun or **Yarun'** (yä'rōōnyŭ), town (1939 pop. over 2,000), W Zhitomir oblast, Ukrainian SSR, 7 mi. SW of Novograd-Volynski; flour mill.

Yarvakandi, Estonia: see JARVAKANDI.

Yarva-Yani, Estonia: see JARVA-JANI.

Yaryshev (yä'rĭshĭf), village (1926 pop. 3,492), SW Vinnitsa oblast, Ukrainian SSR, 9 mi. NW of Mogilev-Podolski; wheat, fruit.

Yas (yăs), island in Persian Gulf, off Trucial Coast, belonging to Abu Dhabi sheikdom; 24°20'N 52°35'E. Landing field.

Yasaka (yä"sä'kä), town (pop. 6,056), Osaka prefecture, S Honshu, Japan, just E of Izumi-otsu, in agr. area (rice, wheat). Until early 1940s, called Minami-oji.

Yasawa (yäsä'wä), volcanic group (□ 52; pop. 3,582), Fiji, SW Pacific, NW of Viti Levu; 45-mi. chain of 16 isls., including Naviti (largest isl., 10 mi. long, 3 mi. wide), Yasawa (2d largest, 15 mi. long, 1 mi. wide), Nathula, Matathawa Levu, Yanggeta, Waya, and Waya Lailai. Deposits of silver, lead, zinc on Naviti and Waya.

Yaselda River (yŭsyôl'dŭ), Pol. *Jasiolda* (yäsyôl'dä), in SW Belorussian SSR, rises in Pripet Marshes 12 mi. SW of Ruzhany, flows 150 mi. generally ESE, past Bereza and Motol (head of navigation) to Pripet R. 15 mi. E of Pinsk. Navigable in lower course, where it joins Oginski Canal to form part of Dnieper-Neman waterway. Receives Pina R. (right).

Yasen (yä'sĕn), village (pop. 1,584), Pleven dist., N Bulgaria, on Vit R. and 4 mi. W of Pleven; rail junction; grain, livestock, truck. Formerly Plazigaz.

Yasen or **Yasen'** (yä'sĭnyŭ), town (1926 pop. 701), NE central Bobruisk oblast, Belorussian SSR, 15 mi. NW of Bobruisk; peat works, sawmills.

Yashá or **Yaxhá** (yäshä'), village (pop. 41), Petén dept., N Guatemala, 34 mi. ENE of Flores, on L. Yasha (6 mi. long, 2 mi. wide); airfield for chicle shipments. Also called Laguna de Yaxhá.

Yashalta (yŭshŭltä'), village (1939 pop. over 2,000), S Rostov oblast, Russian SFSR, in Manych Depression, 55 mi. ESE of Salsk; wheat, sunflowers, cattle, sheep. Salt deposits. Until 1943, in Kalmyk Autonomous SSR.

Yasha Tomich, Yugoslavia: see JASA TOMIC.

Yashbum, Aden: see YESHBUM.

Yashchikovo (yä'shchĭkŭvŭ), town (1939 pop. over 500), SW Voroshilovgrad oblast, Ukrainian SSR, in the Donbas, 6 mi. SSW of Voroshilovsk; coal mines.

Yashil-Kul or **Yashil'-Kul'** (yŭshēl"-kōōl'), lake in Gorno-Badakhshan Autonomous Oblast, Tadzhik SSR, in the Pamir, 70 mi. E of Khorog; 12 mi. long; alt. 13,100 ft. Alichur R. enters lake from E and leaves (W) as GUNT RIVER.

Yashima. 1 Town, Akita prefecture, Japan: see YAJIMA. **2** Suburb, Kagawa prefecture, Japan: see TAKAMATSU.

Ya-shima, island, Japan: see NAGA-SHIMA, Yamaguchi prefecture.

Yashiro (yä"shē'rō). **1** Town (pop. 7,746), Hyogo prefecture, S Honshu, Japan, 17 mi. ENE of Himeji; agr. center (rice, wheat, tobacco, poultry); home industries (leather goods, woodworking, paper products). **2** Town (pop. 5,069), Nagano prefecture, central Honshu, Japan, 9 mi. SSW of Nagano; raw silk; spinning.

Yashkino (yäsh'kĭnŭ). **1** Village (1939 pop. over 500), W central Chkalov oblast, Russian SFSR, on right tributary of Sakmara R. and 20 mi. NE of Sorochinsk; wheat, sunflowers, livestock. **2** Town (1939 pop. over 2,000), NW Kemerovo oblast, Russian SFSR, on Trans-Siberian RR and 38 mi. SW of Anzhero-Sudzhensk; cement-milling center; power plant.

Yashkul, Russian SFSR: see PESCHANOYE.

Yasin (yäsēn'), feudatory state (□ 1,200; pop. 9,989) in Gilgit Agency, NW Kashmir; ⊙ Yasin. In trans-Indus extension of N Punjab Himalayas. Held since 1948 by Pakistan.

Yasin, village, ⊙ Yasin state, Gilgit Agency, NW Kashmir, 65 mi. NW of Gilgit.

Yasinovataya (yŭsē"nŭvä'tĭŭ), city (1939 pop. over 10,000), central Stalino oblast, Ukrainian SSR, in the Donbas, 9 mi. NNE of Stalino; rail junction; mfg. of mining equipment; also food-processing industries.

Yasinovka (yŭsē'nŭfkŭ), town (1939 pop. over 500), central Stalino oblast, Ukrainian SSR, in the Donbas, 8 mi. NNW of Makeyevka.

Yasinya (yŭsē'nyŭ), Czech *Jasiňa* or *Jasiňe* (yä'sĭnyä, –nyĕ), Hung. *Kőrösmező* (kû'rûshmĕ"-zû), village (1941 pop. 12,717), E Transcarpathian Oblast, Ukrainian SSR, on Black Tissa R., on railroad and 50 mi. NE of Khust; lumbering and trading center; mfg. of wooden utensils. Woodworking school. Has picturesque old wooden church. A town of Austria-Hungary which passed 1920 to Czechoslovakia, 1938 to Hungary, and 1945 to USSR.

Yaski, Russian SFSR: see LESOGORSKI.

Yasnaya Polyana (yä'snīŭ pŭlyä'nŭ), village (1939 pop. over 500), central Tula oblast, Russian SFSR, 7 mi. S of Tula. Birthplace and home of L. N. Tolstoy, here, is now a mus. Briefly held (1941) and sacked by Germans during Second World War.

Yasnogorka (yŭsnŭgôr'kŭ), town (1939 pop. over 500), N Stalino oblast, Ukrainian SSR, in the Donbas, 3 mi. N of Kramatorsk.

Yasnomorski or **Yasnomorskiy** (yŭsnŭmôr'skē), town (1947 pop. over 500), S Sakhalin, Russian SFSR, on W coast railroad and 6 mi. NNE of Nevelsk; fisheries. Under Jap. rule (1905–45), called Oko.

Yasnoye (yä'snŭyŭ), village (1939 pop. 4,492), N Kaliningrad oblast, Russian SFSR, near main arm of Neman R. delta, 15 mi. NW of Sovetsk; agr. market; sawmilling; limestone quarrying. Elk reserve (SW). Until 1945, in East Prussia where it was called Kaukehmen (kou'kāmŭn) and, later (1938–45), Kuckerneese (kŏŏ'kĭrnāsŭ).

Yasny or **Yasnyy** (–snē), town (1948 pop. over 2,000), central Amur oblast, Russian SFSR, 40 mi. ESE of Zeya; gold mines.

Yasohara, E Pakistan: see JESSORE.

Yasothon (yä'sô'tôn'), village (1937 pop. 9,109), Ubon prov., E Thailand, in Korat Plateau, on Chi R. and 60 mi. NW of Ubon; road center. Also spelled Yasodhor.

Yass (yăs), municipality (pop. 3,254), SE New South Wales, Australia, 35 mi. NNW of Canberra; sheep and agr. center. Silver-lead and bismuth mines near by.

Yass-Canberra, Australia: see AUSTRALIAN CAPITAL TERRITORY.

Yastrebovka (yä'stryĭbŭfkŭ), village (1926 pop. 3,921), E Kursk oblast, Russian SFSR, 16 mi. NW of Stary Oskol; wheat, sunflowers.

Yasu (yä'sōō), town (pop. 7,373), Shiga prefecture, S Honshu, Japan, 16 mi. E of Kyoto across L. Biwa, in agr. area (rice, wheat, tea, market produce); raw silk.

Yasuda (yä"sōō'dä), town (pop. 6,936), Kochi prefecture, S Shikoku, Japan, on Tosa Bay, 27 mi. ESE of Kochi; rice, oranges.

Yasugi (yä"sōō'gē), town and port (pop. 9,908), Shimane prefecture, SW Honshu, Japan, on SE shore of Naka-no-umi (lagoon), 10 mi. ESE of Matsue. Industrial center; mfg. (steel, pig iron); canneries, sake breweries; rice, soy sauce, raw silk. Exports charcoal, lumber (Japan cedar).

Yasuní River (yäsōōnē'), Napo-Pastaza prov., NE Ecuador, minor affluent (c.100 mi. long) of upper Napo R., which it joins at Nueva Rocafuerte.

Yasuoka, Japan: see SHIMONOSEKI.

Yatabe (yä"tä'bā), town (pop. 7,037), Ibaraki prefecture, central Honshu, Japan, 8 mi. WSW of Tsuchiura; cotton textiles, woodworking.

Yatagan (yätän'), Turkish *Yatağan*, village (pop. 2,194), Mugla prov., SW Turkey, 15 mi. NW of Mugla; silver, manganese, and chromium in dist. Formerly Ahikoy or Bozuyuk.

Yataity (yätītē'), town (dist. pop. 4,235), Guairá dept., S Paraguay, 7 mi. NW of Villarrica, in agr. area (sugar cane, tobacco, oranges, cattle); liquor distilling.

Yata River (yä'tä), Beni dept., N Bolivia, rises just N of L. Rogagua, flows 180 mi. NNE to Mamoré R. at Yata, 8 mi. S of Villa Bella. Navigable for 80 mi.

Yate, town and parish (pop. 1,559), SW Gloucester, England, 10 mi. NE of Bristol; electrical-equipment works. The church was rebuilt in 15th cent.

Yaté (yätā'), settlement (dist. pop. c.600), New Caledonia, on SE coast, 32 mi. ENE of Nouméa; nickel smelter; hydroelectric plant.

Yateley, town and parish (pop. 2,157), NE Hampshire, England, 8 mi. NNW of Aldershot; agr. market. Has 14th-cent. church.

Yates, village, W Alta., 5 mi. NE of Edson; pulp mill; power plant.

Yates, county (□ 344; pop. 17,615), W central N.Y.; ⊙ Penn Yan. Situated in Finger Lakes region; bounded E by Seneca L.; includes parts of Keuka and Canandaigua lakes (resorts). Drained by small Flint Creek. Grape-growing area; also truck, other fruit, wheat, potatoes, hay, dry beans. Diversified mfg., especially at Penn Yan. Formed 1823.

Yatesboro, village (pop. 1,264), Armstrong co., W central Pa., 9 mi. E of Kittaning, in bituminous-coal area.

Yates Center, city (pop. 2,178), ⊙ Woodson co., SE Kansas, 18 mi. W of Iola; shipping point for grain area (corn, wheat, oats, hay). Oil wells in vicinity. State park near by. Inc. 1884.

Yates City, village (pop. 623), Knox co., W central Ill., 22 mi. SE of Galesburg, in agr. and bituminous-coal area.

Yates Dam, E Ala., in Tallapoosa R., 3 mi. N of Tallassee. Privately built power dam (87 ft. high, 1,261 ft. long) completed 1928. Formerly known as Upper Tallassee Dam.

Yatesville. 1 Town (pop. 290), Upson co., W central Ga., 11 mi. ENE of Thomaston. **2** Borough (pop. 565), Luzerne co., NE central Pa., 6 mi. ENE of Wilkes-Barre.

Yathkyed Lake (□ 860), S central Keewatin Dist., Northwest Territories; 62°40'N 98°W; 45 mi. long, 5–21 mi. wide. Drained N by Kazan R.

Yathrib, Saudi Arabia: see MEDINA.

Yatiyantota (yŭtĭyŭntō'tŭ), village (pop., including near-by villages, 3,777), Sabaragamuwa Prov., SW central Ceylon, on the Kelani Ganga and 30 mi. SW of Kandy; rubber processing; rubber, vegetables, rice, areca nuts.

Yatomi (yä"tō'mē), town (pop. 8,225), Aichi prefecture, central Honshu, Japan, 11 mi. WSW of Nagoya, in rice-growing area; goldfish breeding.

Yátova (yä'tōvä), village (pop. 2,033), Valencia prov., E Spain, 25 mi. WSW of Valencia; olive-oil processing; lumbering; cereals, wine, tobacco.

Yatsuka (yä'tsōōkä), town (pop. 6,737), Saitama prefecture, central Honshu, Japan, just E of Kawaguchi; rice, wheat.

Yatsuo (yätsōō'ō), town (pop. 7,505), Toyama prefecture, central Honshu, Japan, 9 mi. SW of Toyama; mfg. (cotton textiles, paper), wood- and metalworking.

Yatsushiro (yätsōō'shĭrō), city and port (1940 pop. 35,586; 1947 pop. 48,085), Kumamoto prefecture, W Kyushu, Japan, on Yatsushiro Bay, at mouth of Kuma R., 21 mi. SSW of Kumamoto; rail junction; mfg. center (porcelain ware, paper, cement). Trout fishing; citrus-fruit orchards. Exports porcelain ware. Since 1940, includes former town of Otago.

Yatsushiro Bay, Jap. *Yatsushiro-wan*, inlet of E.China Sea, Japan, bet. Kyushu and Amakusa Isls.; 42 mi. long, 10 mi. wide; unusually phosphorescent water. Yatsushiro and Minamoto on E shore. Sometimes called Shiranuhino-umi.

Yatton, town and parish (pop. 2,280), N Somerset, England, 12 mi. WSW of Bristol; agr. market in dairying region; mfg. (cheese, leather, leather goods). Has 13th–15th-cent. church.

Yatung (yä'tŏŏng), town, S Tibet, in Chumbi Valley, on upper Torsa (Amo Chu) R., on main India-Tibet trade route and 22 mi. ENE of Gangtok; alt. 9,500 ft. Trade (wool, barley, salt, borax, yak tails, wheat, cotton goods) center; residence of Indian trade agent following treaty of 1893. Temporary refuge of the Dalai Lama (1950–51). Also called Shasima.

Yauca (you'kä), town (pop. 596), Arequipa dept., S Peru, Pacific landing at mouth of small Yauca R. (irrigation), on Pan American Highway and 65 mi. S of Nazca; cotton, cereals, fruit, stock.

Yauco (you'kō), town (pop. 9,801), SW Puerto Rico, on small Yauco R., on railroad and 16 mi. W of Ponce; coffee and sugar center; trading and processing; mfg. of cigars, bottling, cotton ginning. Hydroelectric plant. Mainly settled by Corsicans.

Yauhquemehcan or **San Dionisio Yauhquemehcan** (sän dyōnē'syō youkāmā'kän), town (pop. 1,163), Tlaxcala, central Mexico, 7 mi. NE of Tlaxcala; maguey, cereals, alfalfa, stock.

Yauli, province, Peru: see LA OROYA.

Yauli (you'lē), town (pop. 821), Junín dept., central Peru, in Cordillera Occidental, on Yauli R. (right affluent of the Mantaro) and 16 mi. SW of La Oroya (connected by railroad); barley, potatoes; thermal baths. Copper and silver mining near by.

Yaunde, Fr. Cameroons: see YAOUNDÉ.

Yaungulbene, Latvia: see GULBENE.

Yaunyelgava, Latvia: see JAUNJELGAVA.

Yauri, Nigeria: see YELWA.

Yauri (you'rē), town (pop. 1,652), ⊙ Espinar prov. (□1,790; pop. 34,793), Cuzco dept., S Peru, in Cordillera Occidental, 90 mi. SSE of Cuzco, in agr. region (potatoes, grain, stock); alt. 12,946 ft. Some mining (gold, silver, copper, iron, lead, cinnabar, coal, sulphur); mfg. of woolen goods. Has archaeological remains. Sometimes Espinar.

Yauricocha (yourēkō'chä), village (pop. 192), Lima dept., W central Peru, in Cordillera Occidental, 15 mi. ENE of Yauyos; alt. c.15,500 ft.; copper-mining center. Since 1948 served by railroad and aerial tramway.

Yautepec (youtāpĕk'). **1** City (pop. 4,538), Morelos, central Mexico, on railroad and 11 mi. ESE of Cuernavaca; agr. center (rice, wheat, sugar cane, coffee, oranges, vegetables, livestock). **2** or **San Carlos Yautepec** (sän kär'lōs youtāpĕk'),' town (pop. 451), Oaxaca, S Mexico, in Sierra Madre del Sur, 40 mi. SE of Ocotlán; alt. 4,003 ft. Cereals, sugar cane, coffee, fruit, vegetables, livestock.

Yauyos (you'yōs), city (pop. 1,085), ⊙ Yauyos prov. (□3,222; pop. 30,640), Lima dept., W central Peru, in Cordillera Occidental of the Andes, in upper Cañete R. valley, 75 mi. ESE of Lima (connected by road); alt. 9,609 ft. Wheat, corn, potatoes, alfalfa; cattle and sheep raising.

Yava (yŭvä'), village (1926 pop. 3,267), central Leninabad oblast, Tadzhik SSR, near Leninabad; cotton, sericulture.

Yavai Peninsula, Russian SFSR: see GYDA PENINSULA.

Yaval (yä'vŭl), town (pop. 13,705), East Khandesh dist., NE Bombay, India, near S foot of Satpura Range, 13 mi. NE of Jalgaon; market center for cotton and timber (forests N); cotton ginning, handicraft cloth weaving. Sometimes spelled Yawal.

Yavan (yŭvän'), village (1939 pop. over 500), E Stalinabad oblast, Tadzhik SSR, 22 mi. SE of Stalinabad; wheat, cattle, horses.

Yavapai (yä'vŭpī), county (□ 8,091; pop. 24,991), W central Ariz.; ⊙ Prescott. Plateau region with Black Hills in NE and Black Mesa in N. Verde, Santa Maria, and Agua Fria rivers cross co. Includes Montezuma Castle Natl. Monument in NE, and Prescott Natl. Forest. Jerome is mining center. Gold, silver, copper, lead, zinc; livestock, fruit. Formed 1864.

Yavarí River, Brazil and Peru: see JAVARI RIVER.

Yavello (yävĕ'lō), Ital. *Iavello*, town (pop. 1,500), Sidamo-Borana prov., S Ethiopia, on road and 65 mi. N of Mega, in agr. (corn, millet, durra) and cattle-raising region; trade center.

Yavero River, Peru: see PAUCARTAMBO RIVER, Cuzco dept.

Yaví, Argentina: see LA QUIACA.

Yaviza (yävē'sä), village (pop. 787), Darién prov., E Panama, on Chucunaque R. (landing) and 4 mi. NE of El Real; lumbering; stock; corn, rice, beans.

Yavlenka (yŭ'vlyĕn'kŭ), village (1948 pop. over 2,000), S North Kazakhstan oblast, Kazakh SSR, on Ishim R. and 45 mi. SW of Petropavlovsk; wheat, cattle.

Yavne, Israel: see JAMNIA.

Yavneel or **Yavniel** (both: yäv'nĕ-ĕl"), agr. settlement (pop. 650), Lower Galilee, NE Israel, 6 mi. SSW of Tiberias; flour mill. Founded 1901. Irrigation reservoir (□5.5) built 1950.

Yavor Mountains, Yugoslavia: see JAVOR MOUNTAINS.

Yavornik, mountain, Yugoslavia: see JAVORNIK.

Yavorov (yä'vŭrŭf), Pol. *Jaworów* (yävô'rōōf), city (1931 pop. 10,690), W Lvov oblast, Ukrainian SSR, 28 mi. WNW of Lvov; flour milling, sawmilling, woodworking. Has ruins of 17th-cent. castle. Passed (1772) from Poland to Austria; reverted (1919) to Poland; ceded to USSR in 1945.

Yawal, India: see YAVAL.

Yawata (yä"wä'tä). **1** Town (pop. 14,717), Aichi prefecture, central Honshu, Japan, on Chita Peninsula, on Ise Bay, 12 mi. SSW of Nagoya; commercial center for rice-growing area. **2** Town (pop. 6,579), Chiba prefecture, central Honshu, Japan, 4 mi. S of Chiba, agr., poultry raising. **3** or **Yahata** (yä"hä'tä), city (1940 pop. 261,309; 1947 pop. 167,829), Fukuoka prefecture, N Kyushu, Japan, on small inlet of Hibiki Sea, opposite Wakamatsu, 30 mi. NE of Fukuoka, adjacent to Kokura (E) and Tobata (NE). Principal industrial center of Kyushu; steel mills. Coal mines near by. Heavily bombed (1945) during Second World War. **4** Village, Hyogo prefecture, Japan: see HIROHATA. **5** Town (pop. 11,045), Kyoto prefecture, S Honshu, Japan, 11 mi. SSW of Kyoto; commercial center for agr. area (rice, wheat). **6** Town (pop. 4,795), Tokushima prefecture, NE Shikoku, Japan, 14 mi. W of Tokushima; rice, raw silk, corn.

Yawatahama (yäwä'tähämŭ), city (1940 pop. 31,-728; 1947 pop. 37,809), Ehime prefecture, W Shikoku, Japan, on Hoyo Strait, 33 mi. SW of Matsuyama; terminus of railroad from Matsuyama; mfg. center (cotton textiles, sake, dried bonito, canned food); fishing port.

Yawnghwe (yông'hwä), W state (sawbwaship) (□1,393; pop. 126,513), Southern Shan State, Upper Burma; ⊙ Yawnghwe. Contains Inle L. drained by the Nam Pilu. Rice, sugar cane; tungsten deposits; silk and cotton weaving. Served by Shwenyaung-Thazi RR.

Yawnghwe, town (pop. 4,705), ⊙ Yawnghwe state, Southern Shan State, Upper Burma, on N edge of Inle L. and 10 mi. SW of Taunggyi. Center of trade in rice-growing area. Founded 1359 by emigrants from Tavoy.

Yawri Bay (yô'rē), inlet of the Atlantic in SW Sierra Leone, S of Sierra Leone Peninsula; 22 mi. wide (bet. Cape Shilling and Shenge), 10 mi. long.

Yaw River (yô), in Pakokku dist., Upper Burma; rises in Chin Hills NW of Kanpetlet, flows over 150 mi. E and S to the Irrawaddy opposite Chauk. Coal and salt deposits along course.

Yaxartes River, Central Asia: see SYR DARYA, river.

Yaxcabá (yäskäbä'), town (pop. 640), Yucatan, SE Mexico, 15 mi. E of Sotuta; henequen, corn.

Yaxhá, Guatemala: see YASHÁ.

Yaxkukul (yäskōōkōōl'), town (pop. 741), Yucatan, SE Mexico, 17 mi. NE of Mérida; henequen.

Yaxley, town and parish (pop. 1,934), N Huntingdon, England, 4 mi. S of Peterborough; agr. market. Has 13th-cent. church.

Yaya (yä'yŭ), town (1939 pop. over 10,000), N Kemerovo oblast, Russian SFSR, on Trans-Siberian RR, on Yaya R. and 19 mi. ENE of Anzhero-Sudzhensk, in agr. area.

Yaya River, in Kemerovo and Tomsk oblasts, Russian SFSR, rises near Yashkino, flows 125 mi. NE and N, past town of Yaya, to Chulym R. above Asino.

Yayladagi (yĭlä'däŭ), Turkish *Yayladağı*, village (pop. 1,427), Hatay prov., S Turkey, 22 mi. S of Antioch; southernmost town in Turkey, at Syrian line. Also called Ordu.
Yaylak, Turkey: see BOZOVA.
Yaytse, Yugoslavia: see JAJCE.
Yayva, Russian SFSR: see YAIVA.
Yazd, Iran: see YEZD.
Yazoo (yă'zōō), county (□ 938; pop. 35,712), W central Miss.; ⊙ Yazoo City. Bounded E and SE by Big Black R. Intersected by Yazoo and other streams of Yazoo system. Agr. (cotton, corn, hay); lumbering; oil fields. Formed 1823.
Yazoo Basin, Miss.: see YAZOO RIVER.
Yazoo City, city (pop. 9,746), ⊙ Yazoo co., W central Miss., 40 mi. NNW of Jackson and on the Yazoo; cotton market, and trade and processing center in cotton area; cottonseed products, lumber. Oil field near by. Founded 1824, inc. 1830.
Yazoo River, W central Miss., formed just N of Greenwood by junction of Tallahatchie and Yalobusha rivers, meanders 189 mi. generally SSW, along the foot of bluffs bordering the Mississippi-Yazoo flood plain on E, to the Mississippi at Vicksburg, where the larger stream swings E to the base of the bluffs along which the Yazoo flows. The long-delayed junction of the rivers, which flow generally parallel through a common flood plain, is due to aggradation of the Mississippi; observation of this phenomenon gave rise in physiography to the descriptive term "Yazoo type." The flood plain, an alluvial lowland up to 65 mi. wide and extending c.200 mi. bet. Memphis on N and Vicksburg on S, with the Mississippi on W and the Yazoo and its N tributaries (the Coldwater and the Tallahatchie) on E, is traversed by a maze of sluggish streams; it is known variously as the Delta, the Yazoo Delta, and the Yazoo Basin. Chief cities are Greenwood, Clarksdale, Yazoo City. One of richest cotton-growing regions of the South, noted for its long-staple cotton, The Delta is subject to recurrent floods, despite extensive levee systems. Agr. diversification (livestock, feed crops) is increasing. River is navigable for light draughts; timber, gravel, farm products are shipped.
Yazykovo (yŭzĭ'kŭvŭ). **1** Village (1948 pop. over 2,000), central Bashkir Autonomous SSR, Russian SFSR, 40 mi. W of Ufa; wheat, rye, oats, livestock. **2** Town (1939 pop. over 2,000), N Ulyanovsk oblast, Russian SFSR, 40 mi. W of Ulyanovsk; woolen milling.
Ybbs (ĭps), town (pop. 4,436), W Lower Austria, on right bank of the Danube, 10 mi. ENE of Amstetten. Site of hydroelectric plant. Anc. Roman settlement. Castle on opposite shore of Danube.
Ybbsitz (ĭp'sĭts), town (pop. 3,167), W Lower Austria, 5 mi. E of Waidhofen an der Ybbs; rail terminus; scythes, cutlery.
Ybbs River, SW Lower Austria, rises at Styria border, flows 90 mi. W, N, and NE, past Waidhofen and Amstetten, to the Danube just E of Ybbs. Called Ois R. (ois) in its upper course.
Ybycuí (ēbēkwē'), town (dist. pop. 15,791), Paraguarí dept., S Paraguay, 65 mi. SE of Asunción; lumbering and agr. center (oranges, tobacco, cereals, cattle); tanning, extracting of oil of petitgrain. Formerly an iron foundry with ore deposits at Cerro Tabucuá (2,065 ft.) near by.
Ybytimí or **Ybytymí** (ēbētēmē'), town (dist. pop. 7,277), Paraguarí dept., S Paraguay, on railroad and 65 mi. ESE of Asunción; lumbering and agr. center (sugar cane, fruit, livestock); liquor distilling. Founded 1783.
Ydes (ēd), village (pop. 67), Cantal dept., S central France, 10 mi. NNE of Mauriac; coal mining.
Ydra, Greece: see HYDRA.
Ye (yā), village, Amherst dist., Lower Burma, in Tenasserim, on short Ye R. (7 mi. from mouth in Andaman Sea) and 85 mi. S of Moulmein, linked by railroad. Tungsten deposits.
Yea (yā), town (pop. 954), central Victoria, Australia, on Goulburn R. and 45 mi. NNE of Melbourne, in livestock area; dairy plants.
Yeadon (yē'dŭn), borough (pop. 11,068), Delaware co., SE Pa., W suburb of Philadelphia. Inc. 1894.
Yeager (yā'gŭr), town (pop. 180), Hughes co., central Okla., 6 mi. NNE of Holdenville, in agr. area.
Yeagertown (yā'–), village (pop. 1,628), Mifflin co., central Pa., just N of Lewistown.
Yealmpton (yăm'tŭn), village and parish (pop. 869), S Devon, England, on short Yealm R. (yĕlm), near inlet of the Channel, and 6 mi. ESE of Plymouth; fishing; limestone quarrying.
Yebala, territory, Sp. Morocco: see TETUÁN.
Yébenes, Los (lōs yā'vĕnĕs), town (pop. 5,424), Toledo prov., central Spain, 21 mi. SSE of Toledo; agr. center (wheat, grapes, honey, cheese, livestock). Olive-oil pressing, wine making, flour milling, tanning, charcoal burning. The town consists of 2 sections, one Yébenes de San Juan (formerly belonging to San Juan order) and Yébenes de Toledo (formerly belonging to Toledo).
Yebisu, Japan: see RYOTSU.
Yebra (yā'vrä), town (pop. 1,289), Guadalajara prov., central Spain, on railroad and 38 mi. E of Madrid; grapes, cereals, olives, sugar beets. Lumbering. Olive-oil pressing, plaster mfg.
Yecapixtla (yākäpēs'lä), town (pop. 2,205), Morelos, central Mexico, on railroad and 8 mi. NE of Cuautla; sugar cane, grain, fruit, stock. Airfield.
Yechon (yā'chŭn'), Jap. *Reisen,* town (1949 pop. 21,714), N.Kyongsang prov., S Korea, 55 mi. NNW of Taegu; commercial center for agr. area (cotton, rice, wheat); produces cotton textiles.
Yecla (yā'klä), city (pop. 19,906), Murcia prov., SE Spain, 45 mi. N of Murcia; agr. center in irrigated dist. yielding wine, olive oil, cereals, esparto. Mfg. of footwear, furniture, soap, knit goods, tiles; flour milling. Has 16th-cent. church and ruins of old castle. Mineral springs near by.
Yécora (yā'kōrä), town (pop. 483), Sonora, NW Mexico, in W outliers of Sierra Madre Occidental, near Chihuahua border, 130 mi. ESE of Hermosillo; silver, lead, copper mining; stock raising.
Yecuatla (yākwät'lä), town (pop. 1,575), Veracruz, E Mexico, in Sierra Madre Oriental foothills, 27 mi. NNE of Jalapa; corn, sugar cane, coffee, fruit.
Yedashe (yā'däshä), village, Toungoo dist., Lower Burma, on railroad and 15 mi. NNW of Toungoo.
Yedatore, India: see KRISHNARAJNAGAR.
Yeddo, Japan: see TOKYO.
Yedidya or **Yedidia** (both: yĕdēd'yä), settlement (pop. 300), W Israel, in Plain of Sharon, 3 mi. NE of Natanya; farming, citriculture. Founded 1935.
Yedintsy (yĭdyēn'tsē), Rum. *Edineţi* (yĕdēnĕts'), town (1941 pop. 3,969), N Moldavian SSR, 30 mi. SW of Mogilev-Podolski; road junction; agr. center; flour milling; limestone quarry. Until Second World War, pop. largely Jewish.
Yedo, Japan: see TOKYO.
Yedo Bay, Japan: see TOKYO BAY.
Yedzo, Japan: see HOKKAIDO.
Yefimovskaya (yĭfē'mŭfskĭŭ), town (1939 pop. over 500), SE Leningrad oblast, Russian SFSR, near Tikhvin Canal, 40 mi. ESE of Tikhvin; dairying. Sometimes spelled Efimovskaya.
Yefremov (yĭfryĕ'mŭf), city (1939 pop. over 10,000), SE Tula oblast, Russian SFSR, 75 mi. SSE of Tula; synthetic-rubber works; flour milling, distilling. Chartered 1672. During Second World War briefly held (1941) by Germans in Moscow campaign. Sometimes spelled Efremov.
Yefremovo-Stepanovka (–mŭvŭ-styĭpä'nŭfkŭ), village (1926 pop. 3,245), W central Rostov oblast, Russian SFSR, on Kalitva R. and 24 mi. SE of Millerovo; wheat, sunflowers. Flour mill at Kolushino (1939 pop. over 2,000), 6 mi. SE, on river. Sometimes spelled Efremovo-Stepanovka.
Yefris or **Yefrus,** Yemen: see YIFRAS.
Yegendy-Bulak (yĭgyĕn'dē-bōōläk'), village (1939 pop. over 500), NE Karaganda oblast, Kazakh SSR, 90 mi. NE of Karkaralinsk, on dry steppe. Sometimes spelled Egendy-Bulak.
Yeghe Jo, China: see ORDOS DESERT.
Yegorlyk River or **Great Yegorlyk River** (yĭgôr'lĭk), Rus. *Bolshoi Yegorlyk,* in N Caucasus, Russian SFSR, rises in foothills of the Greater Caucasus c.20 mi. S of Stavropol, flows c.175 mi. generally N, past Novo-TROITSKOYE (Stavropol oblast; irrigation reservoir) and Molotovskoye, to Western Manych R. 15 mi. E of Salsk. Linked by NEVINNOMYSSK CANAL with Kuban R.; forms part of Kuban-Yegorlyk irrigation system (developed after Second World War). Sometimes spelled Egorlyk.
Yegorlykskaya (yĭgôr'lĭkskĭŭ), village (1926 pop. 6,822), S Rostov oblast, Russian SFSR, on railroad (Ataman station) and 45 mi. W of Salsk; flour mill, metalworks; wheat, sunflowers, castor beans. Sometimes spelled Egorlykskaya.
Yegorshino, Russian SFSR: see ARTEMOVSKI, Sverdlovsk oblast.
Yegoryevsk or **Yegor'yevsk** (yĭgô'ryĭfsk), city (1939 pop. 56,340), E central Moscow oblast, Russian SFSR, 60 mi. ESE of Moscow; cotton-milling center; clothing mfg., metalworks. Important phosphorite quarries (WSW), with phosphate works at VOSKRESENSK. Has historical mus. Chartered 1778. Sometimes spelled Egorevsk.
Yegoshikha, Russian SFSR: see MOLOTOV, city.
Yegri-Dere, Bulgaria: see ARDINO.
Yegros (yā'grōs), town (dist. pop. 9,316), Caazapá dept., S Paraguay, on railroad and 110 mi. SE of Asunción, S of Caazapá; cattle-raising center; sawmills, liquor distilleries. Ger. settlement.
Yegua Creek (yĕ'gŭ), S central Texas, rises in several branches in Lee co., flows c.30 mi. generally E to the Brazos 12 mi. W of Navasota.
Yeguas, Sierra de (syĕ'rä dhā yä'gwäs), spur of the Cordillera Penibética, in Andalusia, S Spain, runs for c.35 mi. along Málaga-Seville prov. border, N of Antequera; rises to 2,518 ft. The agr. town of Sierra de Yeguas is in its center.
Yeguas Volcano (yā'gwäs) or **San Pedro Volcano** (sän pā'drō), Andean peak (11,500 ft.), Linares prov., S central Chile, 45 mi. ESE of Linares.
Yegüüdzer, Mongolia: see YUGODZYR.
Yegyi (yā-jē'), village, Bassein dist., Lower Burma, on Bassein-Henzada RR and 40 mi. NNE of Bassein.
Yehcheng, China: see KARGHALIK.
Yeh-hsien, China: see YEHSIEN.
Yehposhow or **Yeh-po-shou** (yĕ'bô'shō'), town, ⊙ Yehposhow co., SE Jehol prov., Manchuria, 95 mi. ENE of Chengteh; rail junction for Chihfeng. Sometimes written Yehpaishow.
Yehsien or **Yeh-hsien** (both: yĕ'shyĕn'). **1** Town, ⊙ Yehsien co. (pop. 309,658), central Honan prov., China, 40 mi. W of Yencheng; road junction; wheat, beans, millet. **2** Town (1922 pop. estimate 80,000), ⊙ Yehsien co. (1946 pop. 757,204), NE Shantung prov., China, on road and 80 mi. WSW of Chefoo, near Laichow Bay of Gulf of Chihli; silk weaving, straw plaiting. Formerly one of Shantung's leading towns. Until 1913, Laichow.
Yehualtepec (yāwältāpĕk'), town (pop. 908), Puebla, central Mexico, 40 mi. SE of Puebla; cereals, maguey.
Yei (yā), town, Equatoria prov., S Anglo-Egyptian Sudan, near Belgian Congo and Uganda boundaries, 85 mi. SSW of Juba; road junction; cotton, peanuts, sesame, corn, durra; livestock. Leper settlement.
Yeisk or **Yeysk** (yāsk), city (1926 pop. 38,094), NW Krasnodar Territory, Russian SFSR, fishing port on Taganrog Gulf of Sea of Azov, 75 mi. SW of Rostov, at base of Yeya sandspit, separating Yeya Liman from the sea. Industrial center; fish canning, metalworking, mfg. of agr. implements, machine repair work, agr. processing (flour, vegetable oils, meat). Exports grain, livestock, fish. Health resort (since 1912; sulphur and mud baths). Founded 1848 W of original fortified site of Yeiskoye Ukrepleniye. Sometimes spelled Eisk.
Yeiskoye Ukrepleniye or **Yeyskoye Ukrepleniye** (–skŭyŭ ōōkryĭplyĕ'nyĕŭ), village (1926 pop. 3,927), N Krasnodar Territory, Russian SFSR, on Sea of Azov, at mouth of Yeya R., 15 mi. E of Yeisk (across Yeya Liman); metalworks; wheat, sunflowers, cotton. Sometimes spelled Eiskoye Ukrepleniye.
Yeji (yĕ'jē), town, Northern Territories, central Gold Coast, on Volta R. and 85 mi. SSE of Tamale, on road; millet, durra, yams. Important ferry station; seasonal head of canoe traffic.
Yekabpils, Latvia: see JEKABPILS.
Yekaterina Canal, Russian SFSR: see KELTMA.
Yekaterina Harbor, Russian SFSR: see KOLA GULF.
Yekaterina Strait (yĭkŭtyĭrē'nŭ), Jap. *Kunashiri-kaikyo* (kōōnä'shĭrē-kī'kyō'), in S Kuriles, Russian SFSR; separates Iturup (NE) and Kunashir (SW) isls.; 14 mi. wide.
Yekaterinburg, Russian SFSR: see SVERDLOVSK, city, Sverdlovsk oblast.
Yekaterinenshtadt, Russian SFSR: see MARKS.
Yekaterinodar, Russian SFSR: see KRASNODAR, city.
Yekaterinofeld, Georgian SSR: see BOLNISI.
Yekaterinopol, Ukrainian SSR: see KATERINOPOL.
Yekaterinoslav, Ukrainian SSR: see DNEPROPETROVSK, city.
Yekaterinoslavka (yĭkŭtyĭrē"nŭsläf'kŭ), village (1939 pop. over 2,000), SE Amur oblast, Russian SFSR, on Trans-Siberian RR (Kaganovich station) and 70 mi. E of Blagoveshchensk, in agr. area (grain, soybeans); metalworks. Sometimes spelled Ekaterinoslavka.
Yekaterinovka (–rē'nŭfkŭ), village (1948 pop. over 2,000), NW Saratov oblast, Russian SFSR, on railroad and 27 mi. SE of Rtishchevo; flour milling. Sometimes spelled Ekaterinovka.
Yekaterinovskaya (–nŭfskĭŭ), village (1926 pop. 13,393), N Krasnodar Territory, Russian SFSR, on Yeya R. and 23 mi. SE of Kushchevskaya; flour mill, metalworks; wheat, sunflowers, essential oils. Sometimes spelled Ekaterinovskaya.
Yekimovichi (yĭkē'mŭvēchē), village (1939 pop. over 500), SW Smolensk oblast, Russian SFSR, on Desna R. and 20 mi. NE of Roslavl, on main Moscow highway; flax. Sometimes spelled Ekimovichi.
Yelabuga (yĭlä'bōōgŭ). **1** Village (1948 pop. over 500), S Khabarovsk Territory, Russian SFSR, on Amur R. and 40 mi. NNE of Khabarovsk; fisheries. **2** City (1939 pop. estimate 15,000), NE Tatar Autonomous SSR, Russian SFSR, port on right bank of Kama R. and 110 mi. E of Kazan; agr.-processing (cereals, potatoes, hops), grain-trading center; mfg. of chemicals, fireproof bricks; metal- and woodworking. Teachers col. Noted excavations of Bronze and Iron Age relics near by. Chartered 1780; sometimes spelled Elabuga.
Yelahanka (yĕlŭhŭng'kŭ), town (pop. 4,207), Bangalore dist., E Mysore, India, suburb of Bangalore, 10 mi. N of city center; rail junction; mfg. of firebrick, pottery. Bangalore's airport and civil aviation col. are just S.
Yelan or **Yelan'** (yĭlän'yŭ). **1** Village, Penza oblast, Russian SFSR: see BOLSHAYA YELAN. **2** Village (1926 pop. 13,273), N Stalingrad oblast, Russian SFSR, 45 mi. SE of Balashov; agr. center; flour milling, meat packing, dairying. **3** Village (1948 pop. over 2,000), E central Sverdlovsk oblast, Russian SFSR, on Nitsa R. and 26 mi. E of Irbit; food processing; grain, livestock. Sometimes spelled Elan.
Yelandapahad, India: see YELLANDLAPAD.
Yelandur (yĕlŭn'dōōr), town (pop. 3,637), Mysore dist., S Mysore, India, 30 mi. SE of Mysore; handloom silk weaving. Annual temple-festival market.
Yelanets (yĭlä'nyĭts), village (1926 pop. 3,920), N Nikolayev oblast, Ukrainian SSR, 25 mi. ENE of Voznesensk; flour mill. Sometimes spelled Elanets.
Yelan-Kolenovski or **Yelan'-Kolenovskiy** (yĭlän'yŭ-kŭlyĕ'nŭfskē), town (1926 pop. 8,312), E Voronezh

oblast, Russian SFSR, 37 mi. WSW of Borisoglebsk; metalworks, sugar refinery, flour mill. Formerly Koleno; now also Yelan-Koleno; sometimes spelled Elan-Kolenovski.

Yelantsy (yĭlän'tsĕ), village (1948 pop. over 500), SE Irkutsk oblast, Russian SFSR, 95 mi. NE of Irkutsk, near L. Baikal.

Yelasy (yĭlä'sē), village (1939 pop. over 500), SW Mari Autonomous SSR, Russian SFSR, 30 mi. W of Cheboksary; wheat. Sometimes spelled Elasy.

Yelatma or **Yelat'ma** (yĭlät'yùmŭ), village (pop. 4,720), NE Ryazan oblast, Russian SFSR, on Oka R. and 14 mi. E of Kasimov, in potato and livestock area. Founded in 12th cent. by Mordvinians. Sometimes spelled Elatma.

Yelcho, Lake (yĕl'chō) (□ 42), Chiloé prov., S Chile, surrounded by glaciers and peaks of Patagonian Andes; 18 mi. long, 2–4 mi. wide. Receives Futaleufú R. Outlet: Yelcho R. (50 mi. long, navigable), flowing NW to Gulf of Corcovado. NW of the lake rises Yelcho Volcano (6,625 ft.).

Yele (yĕ'lā), town (pop. 1,700), Northern Prov., central Sierra Leone, on Teye R. (headstream of Jong R.) and 32 mi. NNW of Bo; road junction; palm oil and kernels, cacao, coffee.

Yelena (yĕlĕ'nä), city (pop. 2,706), Gorna Oryakhovitsa dist., N central Bulgaria, on N slope of Yelena Mts., 14 mi. SE of Tirnovo, on road through Tvarditsa Pass (S); health resort; horticulture, winegrowing. Has old houses and church with wood carvings. Handicraft center under Turkish rule. **Yelena Mountains**, E part of central Balkan Mts., E of Tryavna Mts., lie bet. Yelena (N) and Tvarditsa (S); rise to 5,036 ft. in Chumerna peak. Bituminous coal deposits on N slopes. Also called Tvarditsa Mts. Sometimes spelled Elena.

Yelenendorf, Azerbaijan SSR: see KHANLAR, city.

Yelenovka (yĭlyĕ'nŭfkŭ). **1** Town, Armenian SSR: see SEVAN, town. **2** Town (1939 pop. over 500), E Stalino oblast, Ukrainian SSR, in the Donbas, 3 mi. NE (under jurisdiction) of Yenakiyevo. **3** Town (1939 pop. over 2,000), S central Stalino oblast, Ukrainian SSR, in the Donbas, 13 mi. SW of Stalino; fireproof clays. Limestone quarries at Yelenovskiye Karyery, 6 mi. S. **4** Town (1939 pop. over 500), SW Voroshilovgrad oblast, Ukrainian SSR, in the Donbas, 10 mi. SW of Voroshilovsk; coal mines. Sometimes spelled Elenovka.

Yelenski or **Yelenskiy** (yĭlyĕn'skē), town (1926 pop. 751), S Kaluga oblast, Russian SFSR, 34 mi. SE of Zhizdra; glassworks. Sometimes spelled Elenski.

Yeleru River, India: see ELURU RIVER.

Yeleshnitsa (yĕlĕshnē'tsä), village (pop. 2,438), Gorna Dzhumaya dist., SW Bulgaria, on W slope of W Rhodope Mts., 10 mi. E of Razlog; flour milling; livestock. Has thermal springs. Also spelled Eleshnitsa.

Yeleshwaram, India: see ELESVARAM.

Yelets (yĭlyĕts'), city (1939 pop. 50,888), E Orel oblast, Russian SFSR, on Sosna R. and 100 mi. E of Orel; rail junction; agr.-processing center (flour, alcohol, tobacco); tanning, metalworking. Teachers col. Limestone quarries, iron mining near by. Originally founded 1146; northernmost point reached (1395) by Tamerlane; passed (late 15th cent.) to Moscow and became a fortified S outpost in 1592. Important grain center in late-19th cent.; 1st Rus. grain elevator built here (1887). During Second World War, briefly held (1941) by Germans. Sometimes spelled Elets.

Yelgava, Latvia: see JELGAVA.

Yelidere River, Bulgaria: see CHEPINO RIVER.

Yélimané (yĕlĕmä'nä), village (pop. 800), W Fr. Sudan, Fr. West Africa, near Mauritania border, 70 mi. NE of Kayes; stock raising. Dispensary.

Yeliseina or **Yeliseyna** (yĕlĭsä'nä), village (pop. 579), Vratsa dist., NW Bulgaria, on S slope of Vratsa Mts., on Iskar R. and 8 mi. SSW of Vratsa; copper-mining center. Sometimes spelled Eliseina.

Yelizaveta, Cape (yĭlyĕzŭvyĕtŭ), northernmost point of Sakhalin, Russian SFSR, on Sea of Okhotsk; 54°25'N 142°45'E. Also known as Cape Elizabeth; sometimes spelled Elizaveta.

Yelizavetgrad, Ukrainian SSR: see KIROVOGRAD, city.

Yelizavetgradka (yĭlyĕ"zŭvyĭtgrät'kŭ), village (1926 pop. 5,455), N Kirovograd oblast, Ukrainian SSR, 20 mi. NNE of Kirovograd; wheat. Sometimes spelled Elizavetgradka.

Yelizavetpol, Azerbaijan SSR: see KIROVABAD, city.

Yelizovo (yĭlyĕ'zùvŭ). **1** Town (1948 pop. over 2,000), NE Bobruysk oblast, Belorussian SSR, on Berezina R. and 22 mi. NNW of Bobruysk; glassworks; peat bogs. In 1920s, also called Krasnyy Oktyabr. **2** Village (1939 pop. over 500), S Kamchatka oblast, Khabarovsk Territory, Russian SFSR, on Avacha R. and 23 mi. NW of Petropavlovsk; agr.; lumbering. Sometimes spelled Elizovo.

Yelkhovka (yĭlkhôf'kŭ), village (1926 pop. 2,944), W Kuibyshev oblast, Russian SFSR, on Kondurcha R. and 50 mi. NNE of Kuibyshev; wheat, sunflowers, potatoes. Sometimes spelled Elkhovka.

Yelkhovo (yĕlkhô'vô), city (pop. 6,749), Yambol dist., SE Bulgaria, on Tundzha R., on rail spur, and 20 mi. S of Yambol; agr. center; flour milling, vegetable-oil extracting, brickworking. Also spelled Elhovo; until 1925, Kizil-agach.

Yell, island (□ 81.4, including Hascosay isl.; pop. 1,883), 2d largest of the Shetlands, Scotland, 2 mi. NE of NE coast of Mainland isl. across Sound of Yell; 17 mi. long, 6 mi. wide; rises to 672 ft. Chief village is fishing port of Mid Yell, in center of isl., at head of 2-mi.-long sea loch. At SW end of isl. is fishing port of Ulsta, with woolen weaving. Crofting and fishing are chief occupations; there are large peat deposits, and oyster beds.

Yell, county (□ 942; pop. 14,057), W central Ark.; ⊙ Danville and Dardanelle. Bounded NE by Arkansas R.; drained by Petit Jean R. and Fourche La Fave R. Agr. (cotton, corn, hay, livestock, poultry; dairy products). Timber; sand and gravel. Mt. Nebo State Park (recreation) is in N. Nimrod Dam is in co. Formed 1840.

Yellamanchili (yĕlùmŭn'chĭlē) or **Elamanchili** (ĕlùmŭn'chĭlē), town (pop. 9,054), Vizagapatam dist., NE Madras, India, 22 mi. WSW of Vizagapatam; lacquerwork; sugar cane, oilseeds, rice. Sugar milling 8 mi. SW, at village of Etikoppaka. Saltworks S, on Bay of Bengal (Casuarina plantations).

Yellamma Hill, India: see SAUNDATTI.

Yellandlapad (yäl"lŭndlŭpäd') or **Yellandu** (yäl'lŭndōō), town (pop. 15,907), Warangal dist., SE Hyderabad state, India, 55 mi. SE of Warangal; rail spur terminus (Singareni Collieries station); iron-ore, graphite, mica, and marble quarrying, rice and oilseed milling. Site of former coal mines (opened 1886); center of operations moved from here to Kottagudem, 21 mi. ESE, in 1941. Sometimes called Yelandapahad.

Yellapur (yäl-lä'pŏŏr), village (pop. 1,926), Kanara dist., S Bombay, India, 40 mi. ENE of Karwar, in forested area; rice, sugar cane, betel nuts, coconuts.

Yellareddi (yäl'lärädē), village (pop. 4,521), Medak dist., central Hyderabad state, India, 19 mi. NW of Medak; rice milling. Formerly Yellareddipet.

Yelleswaram, India: see ELESVARAM.

Yellow Grass, town (pop. 487), S Sask., 18 mi. NW of Weyburn; grain elevators, mixed farming.

Yellowhead Pass (3,711 ft.), in Rocky Mts. bet. Alta. and B.C., 16 mi. W of Jasper, on Canadian National RR; 52°54'N 118°27'W.

Yellowjacket Mountains, in Lemhi co., E Idaho, just E of Middle Fork of Salmon R.; N extension of Salmon R. Mts. Rise to 10,070 ft. in Mt. McGuire.

Yellowknife, town (pop. estimate 3,450), S Mackenzie Dist., Northwest Territories, on Yellowknife Bay, on N Shore of Great Slave L., at mouth of Yellowknife R.; 62°27'N 114°22'W; gold-mining center; airport, radio and meteorological stations, public school, Royal Canadian Mounted Police post. Largest town of the Northwest Territories, it was founded 1935 after discovery (1934) of rich gold and silver deposits in the vicinity. Con Mine, on W shore of Yellowknife Bay, just S of town, began production 1938, followed (1939) by adjacent Rycon and Negus mines; 3 other mines were in production in 1941, including Thompson Lake, 30 mi. ENE of Yellowknife, and Camlaren, 50 mi. NE of Yellowknife. By 1943 operations ceased, but new deposits were discovered 1944–45, notably at Indin L., 120 mi. NNW of Yellowknife. Transportation to railheads in Alberta is via Hay River (on SW shore of Great Slave L.), thence by road to Grimshaw, or via Res-delta (on S shore of Great Slave L.), thence by Slave and Athabaska rivers to Fort McMurray; air transportation is extensively used. Greyling Falls, on Yellowknife R., 15 mi. N of town, provide hydroelectric power.

Yellow Medicine, county (□ 758; pop. 16,279), SW Minn.; ⊙ Granite Falls. Agr. area bordering S.Dak., bounded NE by Minnesota R.; drained by Lac qui Parle and Yellow Medicine rivers. Corn, oats, barley, livestock. Sioux Indian reservation in NE. Co. formed 1871.

Yellow Medicine River, SW Minn., rises near S.Dak. line, flows c.100 mi. E, past Hanley Falls, to Minnesota R. 8 mi. SE of Granite Falls.

Yellow Mountain, N.C.: see COWEE MOUNTAINS.

Yellow River, Chinese *Hwang Ho*, *Huang Ho*, or *Hoang Ho* (all: hwäng' hō', Chinese hwäng' hŭ'), Mongolian *Kara Muren*, Tibetan *Ma Chu*, 2d-longest river of China; flows 2,900 mi. from the Tibetan highlands in a circuitous course through the loess lands of N China and across the alluvial N China plain to the Gulf of Chihli of Yellow Sea, on N side of the Shantung peninsula. Rising at c.14,000 ft. in S central Tsinghai prov. at 35°N 97°E, the Yellow R. takes its source in 2 lakes (Kyaring Nor and Ngoring Nor). It describes a hairpin bend around the Amne Machin Mts., avoids L. Koko Nor, and enters Kansu prov. Here it flows past Lanchow in a circuitous rocky course, receiving the Sining (left) and the Tao (right) rivers. At the start of its characteristic Ordos bend, the Yellow R. waters the rich Ningsia plain at the foot of the Alashan Mts. It traverses Suiyuan, passing Paotow, and waters the Howtao and Saratsi irrigation areas. In its N-S course through loess lands it forms the border bet. Shansi and Shensi provs., receives the Fen (left) and Wei (right) rivers, and gathers most of the yellow silt to which it owes its color and name. Below the Tungkwan bend, it enters the N China lowland, forming the border bet. Honan and Pingyuan. It receives the Lo R., flows past Kaifeng, and then traverses Pingyuan and Shantung provs. before reaching the Gulf of Chihli. The silt has built up a continually growing delta, which provides fertile soil for grains and cotton, but has also necessitated the building of embankments to contain the elevated river bed. No large cities, except Lanchow and Kaifeng, have developed along the Yellow R., because only short stretches are navigable and disastrous floods are always possible when water pressure breaches the dikes of the lower course. Labelled "China's Sorrow" because of the frequently catastrophic inundations, the Yellow R. has built up the great N China plain as a result of its frequent course changes. Since 2300 B.C., 8 major shifts have been recorded. Most recently, from 1194 on, the Yellow R. entered the East China Sea through N Kiangsu; it returned 1853 to the Gulf of Chihli and 1938 to the E.China Sea, but since 1947 it again flows to the Gulf of Chihli.

Yellow River. 1 In Ala. and Fla., rises E of Dozier in S Ala., flows SW, across NW Fla., into BLACKWATER BAY 6 mi. S of Milton; c.100 mi. long; receives Shoal R. **2** In N central Ga., rises 3 mi. S of Lawrenceville, flows c.45 mi. S, past Porterdale, to LLOYD SHOALS RESERVOIR 9 mi. NE of Jackson. **3** In N and NW Ind., rises in St. Joseph co., flows c.50 mi. SW and W to Kankakee R. c.7 mi. W of Knox. **4** In Barron co., NW Wis., rises in lakes c.20 mi. NW of Rice Lake, flows c.30 mi. SE, past Barron, to Red Cedar R. 10 mi. S of Rice Lake. **5** In central Wis., rises in Clark co., flows c.60 mi. SSE to Wisconsin R. 9 mi. NE of Mauston. **6** In central Wis., rises in Taylor co., flows c.65 mi. generally SW to Chippewa R. at L. Wissota (near Chippewa Falls). Formerly important for log driving. **7** In NW Wis., rises in small lake near Spooner, flows c.55 mi. generally NW, past Spooner, through lake region to St. Croix R. at Danbury.

Yellow Sea, Chinese *Hwang Hai* or *Huang Hai* (both: hwäng' hī'), Korean *Hwang Hae*, arm of Pacific Ocean, bet. China mainland and Korean peninsula, N of East China Sea; 400 mi. wide, 400 mi. long. The Strait of Chihli, bet. the Liaotung (N) and Shantung (S) peninsulas, links the Yellow Sea proper with the Gulf of Chihli and the Gulf of Liaotung. The Yellow Sea receives the Hwai, Yellow, Pai, Liao, and Yalu rivers of China, and the Taedong and Han rivers of Korea. The main ports are Lienyün, Tsingtao, Chefoo, Tientsin, Hulutao, Yingkow, Dairen, and Port Arthur in China; and Chinnampo and Chemulpo (Inchon) in Korea.

Yellow Springs, village (pop. 2,896), Greene co., S central Ohio, 8 mi. NNE of Xenia, in grain, truck, and poultry area. Seat of Antioch Col. Mfg. of bronze products, rubber goods, food products; lithographing and printing. Settled c.1820, inc. 1856.

Yellowstone, county (□ 2,635; pop. 55,875), S Mont.; ⊙ Billings. Agr. area drained by Yellowstone R. Sugar beets, beans, livestock, dairy products, wool; mfg. at Billings. Formed 1883.

Yellowstone Lake, Wyo.: see YELLOWSTONE NATIONAL PARK.

Yellowstone National Park (□ 3,458.1; established 1872), largely in NW Wyo., just N of Grand Teton Natl. Park; narrow strips of park are in Mont. (W and N) and Idaho (W). Largest and oldest of U.S. natl. parks, and world-famous for its geysers and other thermal phenomena, it consists of broad volcanic plateau (average elevation 7–8,000 ft.) of the Rocky Mts., surrounded by ranges rising 2–4,000 ft. above tableland. Drained by headwaters of Madison, Gallatin, Yellowstone, and Snake rivers. Continental Divide crosses park in S; Absaroka Range forms E boundary; part of Gallatin Range is in extreme NW; Washburn Range is in N, just W of Yellowstone R.; Red Mts. are in S, just SW of Yellowstone L. There are c.3,000 geysers and hot springs (remnants of volcanic activity), mostly in W and S central parts of park. Best-known geysers are Old Faithful, whose jet rises to c.140 ft. at intervals of c.65 min., Daisy, and Riverside. Largest lake in park and in Wyo. is Yellowstone L. (□ 139; c.20 mi. long, 14 mi. wide; alt. 7,731 ft.; max. depth 300 ft.), in SE, which is fed and drained by Yellowstone R. Other lakes are Heart L., Lewis L., and Shoshone L. (6 mi. long, up to 4 mi. wide). Largest canyon is Grand Canyon of the Yellowstone (c.15 mi. long, average depth 1,000 ft.), extending N–S through N half of park; at its S end are Upper Falls of Yellowstone R., dropping 109 ft., and Lower Falls of Yellowstone R., 308 ft. high; at N end are Tower Falls, with drop of 132 ft. Park is sanctuary for deer, bears, elk, antelopes, mountain sheep, moose, bison, and more than 200 species of birds; has extensive growth of pine, fir, and spruce. There are facilities for camping and boating. Main artery in road system is Grand Loop Highway (c.140 mi. long). At Mammoth Hot Springs, in N near Mont. line, are park hq., mus. of historical relics, and springs consisting of 5 terraces flooded by steaming water at temp. of c.160°F. Other points of interest are Obsidian Cliff, in NW, and fossil forests, in N. John Colter was probably 1st white man to visit area (1807); the 1st official and detailed exploration of the area took place in 1870.

Yellowstone River, Wyo. Mont., and N.Dak., rises in Absaroka Range, NW Wyo.; flows NNW, through Yellowstone Natl. Park (here forms 3 large falls and Yellowstone L.; traverses Grand Canyon of the Yellowstone), into SW Mont. at Gardiner, past Livingston, thence E and ENE, past Billings, Miles City, and Glendive, into N.Dak. near Fairview, Mont., joining Missouri R. near Mont. line; 671 mi. long; drains □ 70,400. Important tributaries are Bighorn, Tongue, and Powder rivers, all rising in N Wyo. and entering Yellowstone R. in SE Mont. River was developed (1940) to irrigate 236,500 acres. Private irrigation developments are extensive. Bureau of Reclamation projects in Mont. are Huntley project at Huntley, Buffalo Rapids projects at Terry and Glendive, and Lower Yellowstone project at Sidney (including areas in Richland and Dawson counties, Mont., and McKenzie co., N.Dak.). Future development of river is to be coordinated (as part of comprehensive Missouri R. Basin plan) with projects planned for control of Bighorn R.

Yellville, town (pop. 697), ⊙ Marion co., N Ark., 23 mi. E of Harrison, in the Ozarks. Buffalo R. State Park near by.

Yelm, town (pop. 470), Thurston co., W Wash., 15 mi. SE of Olympia; dairy products, poultry, fruit, timber.

Yelniki or **Yel'niki** (yĕl'nyĭkē), village (1926 pop. 4,224), NW Mordvinian Autonomous SSR, Russian SFSR, 13 mi. NNE of Krasnoslobodsk; grain, potatoes. Peat bogs near by. Sometimes spelled Elniki.

Yelnya or **Yel'nya** (yĕl'nyŭ), city (1948 pop. over 10,000), E central Smolensk oblast, Russian SFSR, 45 mi. ESE of Smolensk; distilleries, flax mill, oil press, food-processing plants. Became city in 1926. During Second World War, scene of heavy Rus. defensive fighting (1941); recaptured (1943) by Russians. Sometimes spelled Elnya.

Yelogui River or **Yeloguy River** (yĕlŭgōō'ē), W Krasnoyarsk Territory, Russian SFSR, rises in marshes near Vakh R. source, flows 350 mi. N and NE to Yenisei R. above Verkhne-Imbatskoye; former trade route bet. Ob and Yenisei rivers. Sometimes spelled Elogui.

Yeloixtlahuacán (yāloisläwäkän'), officially San Pedro Yeloixtlahuacán, town (pop. 1,115), Puebla, central Mexico, 6 mi. SSW of Acatlán; sugar cane, corn, fruit, stock. Sometimes Yeloixtlahuacá.

Yelovo (yĭlô'ŭ), village (1948 pop. over 2,000), SW Molotov oblast, Russian SFSR, on left bank of Kama R. (landing) and 35 mi. E of Votkinsk; woodworking, flax processing; grain, livestock. Sometimes spelled Elovo.

Yelshanka, Saratov oblast, Russian SFSR: see SARATOV, city.

Yelsk or **Yel'sk** (yĕlsk), town (1948 pop. over 2,000), S Polesye oblast, Belorussian SSR, 18 mi. SSW of Mozyr; sawmilling. Sometimes spelled Elsk.

Yeltepe, Bulgaria: see VIKHREN.

Yeltsovka or **Yel'tsovka** (yĭltsôf'kŭ), village (1926 pop. 3,042), NE Altai Territory, Russian SFSR, on Chumysh R. and 65 mi. NE of Bisk; dairy farming. Sometimes spelled Eltsovka.

Yeluca (yälōō'kä), peak (3,700 ft.) in N spur of Cordillera Isabelia, N Nicaragua, near Coco R., 40 mi. NW of Bonanza.

Yeluca Mountains, Nicaragua: see ISABELIA, CORDILLERA.

Yelwa (yĕl'wä), town (pop. 2,142), Sokoto prov., Northern Provinces, NW Nigeria, on Niger R. and 155 mi. SSW of Sokoto; agr. trade center (cotton, durra, timber). Was 19th-cent. capital of minor Hausa state of Yauri.

Yemamah, Saudi Arabia: see KHARJ.

Yemanzhelinka (yĕmŭnzhĭlyĕn'kŭ), town (1939 pop. over 10,000), central Chelyabinsk oblast, Russian SFSR, 8 mi. S (under jurisdiction) of Korkino, on rail spur; lignite-mining center; metalworking. Sometimes spelled Emanzhelinka.

Yemanzhelinski or **Yemanzhelinskiy** (–skē), village (1939 pop. under 500), central Chelyabinsk oblast, Russian SFSR, 5 mi. WNW of Yemanzhelinka; rail junction (Yemanzhelinskaya station); wheat, livestock. Sometimes spelled Emanzhelinski.

Yemassee (yĕ'mŭsē), tourist-resort town (pop. 712), Hampton and Beaufort counties, S S.C., 20 mi. NNW of Beaufort, near the Combahee. Good hunting in vicinity.

Yembongo, Belgian Congo: see MOGALE.

Yemelyanovo or **Yemel'yanovo** (yĭmĭlyä'nŭvŭ). **1** Village (1926 pop. 653), S Kalinin oblast, Russian SFSR, 25 mi. SW of Kalinin; flax. **2** Village, S Krasnoyarsk Territory, Russian SFSR, 13 mi. NW of Krasnoyarsk. Sometimes spelled Emelyanovo.

Yemen (yĕ'mŭn), Arabic *Al-Yaman* (ăl yămăn'), kingdom (□ 75,000; 1949 pop. estimate 4,500,000) of SW Arabian Peninsula, on the Red Sea; ⊙ Sana. Bounded N by Asir prov. of Saudi Arabia and S by the Western Aden Protectorate along borders settled in 1934, Yemen merges E along an indeterminate line with the great Arabian desert of Rub' al Khali. Offshore, in the Red Sea, are the Zuqar and Hanish isls., belonging to Yemen, and the Kamaran Isls., a dependency of Aden Colony. Physiographically, Yemen comprises the narrow Tihama coastal plain and the interior highlands. The Tihama, which represents the southern continuation of the Asir coastal lowland, is a desolate, arid belt (up to 50 mi. wide) inhabited by a semipastoral pop. largely of mixed Arab and African origin (Danakils, Somalis, Ethiopians). The Tihama rises abruptly to the maritime range and the central plateau (to 12,336 ft.), which represents the uptilted SW edge of the Arabian platform. Here the pop. approaches the true Arab stock and is settled in highland villages and fortresslike towns. The Yemen highlands, with winter temperatures below 40°F. and cool summers with a well-marked rainy season (about 20 inches), have a climate unusual for the Arabian Peninsula. They represent one of the most extensive cultivated or cultivable areas of the peninsula, producing grain (millet, wheat, barley), fruit (apricots, pomegranates, grapes, citrus fruit), vegetables, and alfalfa. Mocha coffee, apparently introduced from Ethiopia, and the kat (*qat*) shrub, a narcotic stimulant, are characteristic of the highlands. Stock raising (sheep, goats, camels) is important, particularly in the coastal lowlands. Among the chief native highland industries are stone, glass, and metal handicrafts, as well as weaving and tanning. Coffee, hides, and skins are the leading exports, which move via Hodeida, Yemen's chief port, or by overland caravans for shipment from Aden. Trade is active with the neighboring Arab tribal areas of Asir (Saudi Arabia) and the Aden Protectorate, notably the Hadhramaut states. In addition to Hodeida, the chief lowland towns are the lesser ports of Mocha (once the leading coffee-export center) and Loheia, and the inland towns of Bait al Faqih and Zabid in a cotton- and indigo-growing dist. The principal highland centers, in addition to Sana, are Sada (N), and Taiz, Yarim, and Ibb (S). Transportation is by primitive caravan routes, but Sana is linked by motor highways with Yarim and Hodeida, and via Taiz with Aden. Country's highland pop. belongs to the Zaidi (Zeidi) sect of Shiah Islam, founded by Zaid, grandson of Husein. The most tolerant of the Shiite sects, it is closely akin to the Sunnite faith, whose Shafai creed prevails among pop. of the coastal plain and of the E plateau margins bordering on the desert. Most of the Jews, established in Yemen since 4th cent. A.D. and estimated at 50,000, emigrated to Israel in late 1940s. Earliest recorded civilization on the territory of modern Yemen was that of the Minaean kingdom, which flourished during 1200–650 B.C. in the JAUF oasis of the Yemen hinterland. It was succeeded by the Sabaean kingdon (the biblical SHEBA), which lasted until 115 B.C., with its center at MARIB. The Sabaeans were in turn superseded by the Himyarites (⊙ ZAFAR; after 4th cent. A.D., Sana), who inherited the Minaeo-Sabaean culture and its Semitic language (deciphered in 19th cent.). Christianity and Judaism were introduced in 4th cent A.D. Himyaritic rule, which had been marked by a Roman raid (24 B.C.) and a brief Ethiopian occupation (A.D. c.340–378), was ended (A.D. 525) by a 2d Ethiopian conquest. After a Persian period (575–628), Islam came to Yemen (it then included the Hadhramaut), which was reduced to a prov. of the Arab caliphate. At the breakup of the caliphate, Yemen was among the 1st to secede (c.900) and came under the control of the rising Rassite dynasty of the Zaidi sect, which rules to the present day. Through the Middle Ages, control of the Zaidi rulers, known as Imams, was centered at Sada, the original home of the dynasty. It was largely restricted to the highlands, while the Sunnite Tihama lowland, with ⊙ at Zabid, remained independent. In 1538 began the 1st occupation of the country by the Turks, which lasted until 1630. After their departure, the Zaidi rulers moved to Sana and extended a vague suzerainty to the Tihama lowland, where Dutch and French vied for trading rights at the then flourishing coffee port of Mocha. In 18th cent., the tribal chiefs of the present Aden Protectorate, led by the Abdali sultan, declared their independence, thus paving the way for British penetration in 19th cent. Following brief Egyptian control (1819–40) of the coast, the Turks initiated (1849) their 2d occupation of Yemen, extended to Sana by 1872. This lasted until the First World War, during which Turkish troops from Yemen closely threatened Aden. Following Turkish evacuation in 1918, the Zaidi Imams maintained control of the highlands, but their rule in the Tihama lowland was challenged sporadically by the Idrisi rulers of Asir, backed by Ibn Saud. Yemen's present boundaries date from 1934, when treaties were signed with Saudi Arabia and with Britain (for the Aden Protectorate), which also recognized the Imam as king of Yemen. The Aden border, originally delimited (1902–05) and extended inland (1914) by an Anglo-Turkish convention, was modified (1934) by the so-called "Status Quo Line," effective for 40 years. Italian influence existed briefly in Yemen in late 1930s. Although foreign penetration continued to be discouraged, Yemen became more active in world affairs after the Second World War. It joined the Arab League in 1945, established diplomatic relations with the U.S. in 1946, and became a member of the United Nations in 1947. The king is the religious head of the Zaidi sect and his govt. is an absolute monarchy. Administratively, Yemen falls into the provs. of Sana, Hodeida, Taiz, Ibb, Hajja, Sada, and Huth.

Yemetsk (yĭmyĕtsk'), village (1939 pop. over 500), W Archangel oblast, Russian SFSR, on Northern Dvina R., and 80 mi. SE of Archangel; potatoes. Sometimes spelled Emetsk.

Yemilchino or **Yemil'chino** (yĭmēl'chĭnŭ), agr. town (1926 pop. 3,609), W Zhitomir oblast, Ukrainian SSR, 21 mi. NNE of Novograd-Volynski; flax, buckwheat, potatoes. Until 1944, Emilchino.

Yemine, Cape (yĕmē'nĕ), E Bulgaria, on Black Sea, 25 mi. NE of Burgas, at E extremity (Yemine Mts.) of Balkan Mts.; 200 ft. high. Lighthouse. Also spelled Emine.

Yemmiganur (yĕmĭgŭnōōr'), town (pop. 12,670), Bellary dist., N Madras, India, 16 mi. NE of Adoni; cotton ginning, peanut milling, hand-loom cotton and silk weaving. Also spelled Emmiganur or Emmiganuru.

Yemtsa (yĕm'tsŭ), town (1926 pop. 708), W Archangel oblast, Russian SFSR, on railroad and 23 mi. N of Plesetsk; sawmilling. Sometimes spelled Emtsa.

Yen, China: see YEN RIVER.

Yen (yĕn), village (pop. 1,354), W Kedah, Malaya, on Strait of Malacca, 23 mi. S of Alor Star; rice; fisheries.

Yena (yĕ'nŭ), village (1939 pop. under 500), SW Murmansk oblast, Russian SFSR, 45 mi. NW of Kandalaksha; extensive iron deposits. Sometimes spelled Ena.

Yenakiyevo (yĕnŭkē'ŭvŭ), city (1926 pop. 24,329; 1939 pop. 88,246), E Stalino oblast, Ukrainian SSR, in the Donbas, 25 mi. NE of Stalino; major coal and metallurgical center; iron and steel mills, chemical plant. Originally called Yenakiyevo; named Rykovo (c.1928–35) and Ordzhonikidze (1935–43); sometimes spelled Enakiyevo.

Yenan (yĕ'nän'), town, ⊙ Yenan co. (pop. 29,856), N Shensi prov., China, 160 mi. NNE of Sian; commercial center; wool weaving; cattle raising. Was hq. of Chinese Communists (1937–47). Called Fushih, 1913–48.

Yenangyat (yä"nän-jät'), village, Pakokku dist., Upper Burma, on right bank of Irrawaddy R. (opposite Padan) and 25 mi. SW of Pakokku; petroleum center (production begun 1893), in Singu oil field.

Yenangyaung (yä"nän-joung'), town (pop. 11,098), ⊙ Magwe div. and dist., Upper Burma, on left bank of Irrawaddy R. (landing) and 20 mi. N of Magwe. Leading oil-production center in Burma; linked by pipe line with refinery at Syriam (near Rangoon). Worked for many centuries by Burmese; modern exploitation begun 1887. Became administrative center after Second World War, when it was held (1942–45) by Japanese.

Yenanma (yä-nän-mä'), village, Thayetmyo dist., Upper Burma, 35 mi. NW of Thayetmyo. Oil field (production started 1922); linked by pipe line to Minhla (Irrawaddy R. landing).

Yenbay (yĕn'bī'), town (1936 pop. 5,000), ⊙ Yenbay prov. (□ 2,900; 1943 pop. 107,600), N Vietnam, on Red R. and Hanoi-Kunming RR, 75 mi. NW of Hanoi; coffee, cotton; gums and resins; sericulture. Coal deposits.

Yenbo, Yambo, or **Yanbu'** (all: yĕn'bō, yĕm'bō), city (pop. 10,000), N central Hejaz, Saudi Arabia, Red Sea port for Medina and 200 mi. NNW of Jidda; 24°7'N 38°3'E. Second port of Hejaz (after Jidda); some pilgrim trade; exports dates. Sometimes called Yenbo el Bahr [=Yenbo on the sea]. The name Yenbo en Nakhl is applied to an oasis of palm groves 30 mi. ENE.

Yenchang or **Yen-ch'ang** (yĕn'chäng'), town, ⊙ Yenchang co. (pop. 24,812), NE Shensi prov., China, 40 mi. ESE of Yenan, near Yellow R.; petroleum center; refinery.

Yencheng or **Yen-ch'eng** (yĕn'chŭng'). **1** Town, ⊙ Yencheng co. (pop. 333,382), central Honan prov., China, on Sha R. and 80 mi. SSE of Chengchow, and on Peking-Hankow RR; commercial center of central Honan; exports wool, ramie, poultry, hogs; grain growing. **2** Town (1935 pop. 102,036), ⊙ Yencheng co. (1946 pop. 1,162,927), E central Kiangsu prov., China, 65 mi. ESE of Hwaiyin; rice center; wheat, beans, kaoliang, corn, cotton.

Yen-chi, Manchuria: see YENKI.

Yen-chiang, China: see YENKIANG.

Yenchih or **Yen-ch'ih** (yĕn'chû'), town (pop. 6,895), ⊙ Yenchih co. (pop. 22,245), SE Ningsia prov., China, 80 mi. S of Yinchwan; salt-producing center. Until 1950, Weichow. The name Yenchih was applied 1913–48 to Hwamachih (60 mi. NE), and 1948–50 to Hweianpao (12 mi. NE).

Yen-ch'ing, China: see YENKING.

Yen-ching, China: see YENTSING.

Yenchow. 1 Town, Chekiang prov., China: see KIENTEH. **2** Town, Shantung prov., China: see TZEYANG.

Yenchwan or **Yen-ch'uan** (both: yĕn'chwän'), town, ⊙ Yenchwan co. (pop. 40,920), NE Shensi prov., China, 40 mi. NE of Yenan, near Yellow R.; petroleum center.

Yendi (yĕn'dē), town, N Br. Togoland, administered as part of the Northern Territories of the Gold

Coast, 55 mi. E of Tamale; road junction; shea nuts, millet, durra, yams; cattle, skins. Airfield. Hq. of Br. Togoland section of Dagomba dist.

Yenfeng (yĕn'fŭng'), town (pop. 5,216), ⊙ Yenfeng co. (pop. 44,812), N central Yunnan prov., China, 65 mi. NW of Tsuyung; alt. 5,610 ft.; rice, millet, beans. Saltworks near by. Until 1913 called Paiyentsing.

Yengan (yĕng'-gän), W state (ngegunhmu) (□ 359; pop. 8,672), Southern Shan State, Upper Burma, on edge of Shan Plateau; ⊙ Yengan, village 45 mi. NW of Taunggyi. Hilly, forested. Sometimes spelled Ywangan.

Yengema (yĕng-gĕ'mä), town (pop. 931), South-Eastern Prov., E central Sierra Leone, 13 mi. NW of Sefadu; center for alluvial diamond dredging.

Yenhai Tze (yĕn'hī' dzŭ) or **Tayenhai Tze** (dä'–), Mongolian *Dabasun Nor* (däbäsōōn' nōr'), salt lake in N Ordos Desert, Suiyuan prov., China, 90 mi. WSW of Paotow, across Yellow R.; 8 mi. long, 2 mi. wide. Natron extraction.

Yenhing or **Yen-hsing** (both: yĕn'shĭng'), town (pop. 4,370), ⊙ Yenhing co. (pop. 24,719), N central Yunnan prov., China, 25 mi. NNE of Tsuyung, rice, wheat, millet. Saltworks near by.

Yenho (yĕn'hŭ'), town (pop 4,595), ⊙ Yenho co. (pop. 191,614), NE Kweichow prov., China, on Wu R. and 40 mi. NE of Szenan, on Szechwan line; tung-oil center; cotton weaving; lacquer, medicinal herbs. Sulphur mine near by.

Yen Ho, river, China: see YEN RIVER.

Yen-hsing, China: see YENHING.

Yéni (yĕ'nē), village, SW Niger territory, Fr. West Africa, 50 mi. E of Niamey; millet; livestock.

Yenice (yĕnĭjĕ'). **1** Village (pop. 1,291), Canakkale prov., NW Turkey, 50 mi. ESE of Canakkale; cereals, beans. **2** Village (pop. 2,067), Icel prov., S Turkey, 9 mi. ENE of Tarsus; rail junction.

Yenice Irmak, Turkey: see SEYHAN RIVER.

Yenice River, N Turkey, rises in Koroglu Mts., flows 135 mi. ENE and NW to Black Sea 15 mi. NE of Zonguldak. Receives Devrek R. (left) and Arac R. (right). Upper section called Gerede R., center Soganli R., lower Filyos R.

Yenidje or **Yenidje-i-Karasu**, Greece: see GENESAIA.

Yeni-Erivan (yĕ"nyē-ĕrēvän'), suburb (1945 pop. over 500) of Kirovabad, Azerbaijan SSR. Sometimes spelled Eni-Erivan.

Yenihan, Turkey: see YILDIZELI.

Yeni Harput, Turkey: see ELAZIG.

Yenije or **Yenije-i-Karasu**, Greece: see GENESAIA.

Yenije-i-Vardar, Greece: see GIANNITSA.

Yenikale (yĕnyĭkŭlyĕ'), fishing village (1926 pop. 850), E Crimea, Russian SFSR, on Kerch Strait, 6 mi. E of Kerch. Has ruins of anc. Turkish fortress. Sometimes spelled Enikale.

Yenikale Strait, USSR: see KERCH STRAIT.

Yenikol, Turkey: see BORCKA.

Yenikoy, Turkey: see SAVSAT.

Yeni Pazar, Bulgaria: see NOVI PAZAR.

Yeni-Pazar, Yugoslavia: see NOVI PAZAR.

Yenisaia, Greece: see GENESAIA.

Yenisehir (yĕnĭ'shĕhĭr"), Turkish *Yenişehir*. **1** City, Ankara prov., Turkey: see CANKAYA. **2** Town (pop. 7,257), Bursa prov., NW Turkey, 31 mi. E of Bursa; wheat center.

Yenisei Bay or **Yenisey Bay** (yĕnĭsā', Rus. yĕnyĭsyā'), estuary of Yenisei R., NW Krasnoyarsk Territory, Russian SFSR; in S portion are Brekhov Isls. At 71°45'N, near Golchikha, it opens into **Yenisei Gulf**, extending N to Dickson Isl.; up to 90 mi. wide. Sometimes spelled Enisei.

Yenisei Ridge or **Yenisey Ridge**, Rus. *Yeniseiski Kryazh* or *Yeniseyskiy Kryazh*, upland in central Siberian, Russian SFSR; extends 400 mi. N-S, along right bank of Yenisei R., bet. Trans-Siberian RR and Stony Tunguska R.; rises to 3,600 ft. Crystalline schists, gneiss formations. Major gold-mining region. Chief centers: Severo-Yeniseiski, Ayakhta, Pit-Gorodok, Novo-Yerudinski, Yuzhno-Yeniseiski. Sometimes spelled Enisei.

Yenisei River or **Yenisey River**, in central Siberian Russian SFSR, one of the longest (2,364 mi.) rivers of the world. Rises in Eastern Sayan Mts. in E Tuva Autonomous Oblast; called the Greater Yenisei [Rus. *Bolshoi Yenisei*] or Bi-Khem (Bei-Kem) [native name] until its junction with the Lesser Yenisei [Rus. *Maly Yenisei*] or Kaa-Khem [native name] at Kyzyl, where it becomes the Yenisei proper. Flows first W and, after breaking through Western Sayan Mts. and entering Krasnoyarsk Territory, N, past Minusinsk (S.Siberian RR crossing), Krasnoyarsk (Trans-Siberian RR crossing), Yeniseisk, Igarka, and Dudinka, entering Kara Sea via Yenisei Bay and Yenisei Gulf. Upper course is precipitous, with rapids. During ice-free months navigation is possible from Minusinsk (Apr.-Nov.; 1,720 mi. upstream), from Yeniseisk (May-Oct.; 1,195 mi. upstream), and from Igarka (June-Oct.; 270 mi. upstream), for lumber, grain, construction materials. Average width in lower course is 4 mi. Receives Kan, Angara, Stony Tunguska, Lower Tunguska, and Kureika rivers on right (E), Abakan, Yelogui, and Turukhan on left (W) rivers. Forms physical limit bet. E and W Siberia. Joined to Ob R. by OB-YENISEI CANAL SYSTEM. Sometimes spelled Enisei.

Yeniseisk or **Yeniseysk** (yĕnyĭsyäsk'), city (1939 pop. over 10,000), central Krasnoyarsk Territory, Russian SFSR, on Yenisei R. and 150 mi. N of Krasnoyarsk; river port; sawmilling; fur-collecting center. Teachers col. Founded 1618 as fortress; formerly important as shipping and gold-mining point. After construction of Trans-Siberian RR it declined and was supplanted by Krasnoyarsk, which became ⊙ former Yeniseisk govt. (see KRASNOYARSK Territory). Sometimes spelled Eniseisk.

Yeni-Shehr, Greece: see LARISSA.

Yenitsa, Greece: see GIANNITSA.

Yen Kechil (yĕn' kŏchĕl'), village (pop. 1,124), W Kedah, Malaya, 2 mi. NNE of Yen; rice, coconuts.

Yenki. **1** or **Yen-chi** (yĕn'jē'), town (pop. 42,792), ⊙ Yenki co. (pop. 364,617), E Kirin prov., Manchuria, China, on railroad and 160 mi. ESE of Kirin, near Tumen R. (Korea line); industrial and agr. center; mfg. of wood-distillation products, alcohol, sulphuric acid; soybean and flour milling. Developed with rail construction as the political center of CHIENTAO. **2** or **Yen-ch'i** (yĕn'chē'), town and oasis, Sinkiang prov., China: see KARA SHAHR.

Yenkiang or **Yen-chiang** (both: yĕn'jyäng'), town (pop. 3,775), ⊙ Yenkiang co. (pop. 25,800), W Suiyuan prov., China, 25 mi. WNW of Wuyüan, in Howtao oasis; cattle raising; wheat, millet, licorice. Until 1942 called Taerhhu.

Yenking or **Yen-ch'ing** (both: yĕn'chĭng'), town, ⊙ Yenking co. (pop. 110,472), E Chahar prov., China, 60 mi. ESE of Kalgan; cattle raising; beans, ramie. Until 1928 in Chihli (Hopeh).

Yenling (yĕn'lĭng'), town, ⊙ Yenling co. (pop. 158,175), N Honan prov., China, on road and 50 mi. SSW of Kaifeng; wheat, beans, kaoliang, millet.

Yenmen, Yenmenkwan, or **Yen-men-kuan** (yĕn'-mŭn'gwän'), gate in S section of China's Great Wall, on Shansi-Chahar border, 95 mi. N of Taiyüan, and on main highway to Tatung.

Yenne (yĕn), village (pop. 1,002), Savoie dept., SE France, on left bank of Rhone R. and 12 mi. NW of Chambéry; road junction; silk working.

Yenotayevka (yĕnŭtī'ŭfkŭ), village (1926 pop. 3,798), E central Astrakhan oblast, Russian SFSR, on right bank of Volga R. (landing) and 75 mi. NNW of Astrakhan; fruit, cotton, wheat; cattle, sheep. Sometimes spelled Enotayevka.

Yenpien (yĕn'byĕn'), town, ⊙ Yenpien co. (pop. 36,343), SE Sikang prov., China, 45 mi. WNW of Hweili, at Yunnan border; rice, wheat, kaoliang, potatoes; iron mines, saltworks. Until 1938 in Szechwan.

Yenping, China: see NANPING.

Yen River, Chinese *Yen Ho* (yĕn' hŭ'), N Kiangsu prov., China, formed in canals of Hwaiyin area, flows 100 mi. N, past Lienshui and Kwanyün, to Yellow Sea W of Lienyün. Navigable in summer season only. Also called Lien R.

Yenshan (yün'shän'). **1** Town, Shantung prov., China: see KINGYÜAN. **2** Town (pop. 8,820), ⊙ Yenshan co. (pop. 56,958), SE Yunnan prov., China, 15 mi. N of Wenshan, in mtn. region; rice, wheat, millet, beans, sugar cane. Until 1933, Kiangna.

Yenshih (yĕn'shŭ'), town, ⊙ Yenshih co. (pop. 184,120), N Honan prov., China, on Lo R. and 18 mi. E of Loyang, and on Lunghai RR; cotton weaving; agr. products.

Yenshow or **Yen-shou** (both: yĕn'shō'), town, ⊙ Yenshow co. (pop. 163,108), W Sungkiang prov., Manchuria, 85 mi. ESE of Harbin; kaoliang, soybeans, millet, corn, buckwheat, timber. Called Changshow until 1914; and Tungpin, 1914–29.

Yenshui (yĕn'shwā'), Jap. *Ensui* (ān'sōōē), town (1935 pop. 7,433), W central Formosa, 3 mi. WNW of Sinying; sugar-milling center.

Yentai or **Yen-t'ai** (yĕn'tī'). **1** Town, W central Liaotung prov., Manchuria, China, on South Manchuria RR and 25 mi. S of Mukden; coal- and alunite-mining center, with mines on rail spur, 8 mi. E. **2** City, Shantung prov., China: see CHEFOO.

Yentang Mountain, Chinese *Yentang Shan* (yĕn'-däng' shän'), SE Chekiang prov., China, 15 mi. N of Yotsing; rises to 3,400 ft. Monastery on summit dates from Sung dynasty (960–1127).

Yenting or **Yen-t'ing** (yĕn'tĭng'), town (pop. 17,814), ⊙ Yenting co. (pop. 271,644), N Szechwan prov., China, 22 mi. ENE of Santai; cotton textiles; sweet potatoes, rice, wheat, beans, rapeseed, indigo. Saltworks near by.

Yentna River (yĕnt'nŭ), S Alaska, rises in Mt. Dall glacier system near 62°25'N 152°W, flows 100 mi. SE to Susitna R. 2 mi. N of Susitna. Receives Skweena R.

Yentsing or **Yen-ching** (both: yĕn'jĭng'). **1** Town, ⊙ Yentsing co. (pop. 90,605), SW Pingyuan prov., China, 20 mi. SE of Sinsiang; silkgrowing center; grain. Until 1949 in Honan prov. **2** Town, ⊙ Yentsing co. (pop. 84,664), NE Yunnan prov., China, 60 mi. NNE of Chaotung, near Szechwan border; cotton textiles; rice, wheat, timber. Until 1917 called Laoyatan.

Yentsing, Tibet: see YAKALO.

Yentung Shan, China: see SÜANHWA.

Yenukidze, Georgian SSR: see AMBROLAURI.

Yenyüan (yĕn'yüän'), town, ⊙ Yenyüan co. (pop. 58,435), SE Sikang prov., China, 50 mi. SW of Sichang; cotton weaving, tobacco processing; rice, wheat, corn. Gold mines, saltworks near by. Until 1938 in Szechwan.

Yeola (yäō'lŭ), town (pop. 17,817), Nasik dist., E Bombay, India, 45 mi. E of Nasik; road center; cotton and silk handicraft weaving, oilseed pressing, mfg. of gold and silver thread, biris, gur.

Yeoman (yō'mŭn), town (pop. 180), Carroll co., NW central Ind., 20 mi. NNE of Lafayette, near Freeman L.

Yeo River (yō). **1** In Somerset, England, rises in Mendip Hills at Cheddar, flows 20 mi. WNW, past Congresbury, to Bristol Channel 2 mi. SW of Weston-super-Mare. Yeo Reservoir is part of Bristol's water supply. **2** In Somerset and Dorset, England, rises near Milborne Port, flows SW and NW, past Sherborne, Yeovil, and Ilchester, to Parrett R. at Langport; 24 mi. long.

Yeotmal (yä'ōtmäl), district (□ 5,238; pop. 887,738), Berar div., SW Madhya Pradesh, India, on Deccan Plateau; ⊙ Yeotmal. Bordered E by Wardha R., S by the Penganga; undulating highland, drained mainly by numerous tributaries of the Penganga. In major cotton-growing tract; also produces millet, oilseeds, wheat; mangoes, tamarind along rivers. Timber (teak) in dispersed forest areas. Cotton ginning, oilseed milling. Coal mining and limestone quarrying near Wun. Yeotmal is a cotton-trade center. Pop. 80% Hindu, 15% tribal, 6% Moslem.

Yeotmal, town (pop. 26,555), ⊙ Yeotmal dist., SW Madhya Pradesh, India, 80 mi. SW of Nagpur; road and cotton-trade center; terminus of rail spur from Murtazapur (55 mi. WNW); cotton ginning, oilseed milling; sawmills, ice factory. Timber (teak) in near-by forests.

Yeovil (yō'vĭl), municipal borough (1931 pop. 19,077; 1951 census 23,337), S Somerset, England, on Yeo R. and 21 mi. ESE of Taunton; leather and glove center; mfg. (leatherworking machinery, agr. machinery, internal combustion engines); agr. market in dairying region. The notable 15th-cent. Church of St. John, here, is sometimes called "Lantern of the West."

Yepes (yā'pĕs), town (pop. 3,070), Toledo prov., central Spain, 35 mi. S of Madrid; agr. center (cereals, olives, grapes, livestock). Olive-oil pressing, cheese processing. Noted for white wine. Clay and lime quarrying; cement mfg.

Yepifan or **Yepifan'** (yĕpēfän'yŭ.) **1** Village, S Moscow oblast, Russian SFSR, on railroad and 13 mi. ESE of Stalinogorsk; wheat. **2** Town (1926 pop. 2,566), E Tula oblast, Russian SFSR, 17 mi. ENE of Bogoroditsk, on road from Yepifan station and village (N); distilling, flour milling. During Second World War, held (1941) by Germans in Moscow campaign. Lignite mining at Kazanovka (S). Sometimes spelled Epifan.

Yepocapa or **San Pedro Yepocapa** (sän pā'drō yäpōkä'pä), town (1950 pop. 2,263), Chimaltenango dept., S central Guatemala, 15 mi. SSW of Chimaltenango; alt. 3,999 ft.; coffee, sugar, grain.

Yeppoon (yĕp-pōōn'), town (pop. 2,115), Queensland, Australia, on E coast, near Keppel Bay, 23 mi. NE of Rockhampton; banana-growing center.

Yerakhtur (yĕrŭkhtōōr'), village (1926 pop. 4,056), N central Ryazan oblast, Russian SFSR, in Oka R. valley, 19 mi. WSW of Kasimov; potatoes, dairy farming. Sometimes spelled Erakhtur.

Yerakini, Greece: see GERAKINE.

Yerakovouni, Greece: see OTHRYS.

Yerania, Greece: see GERANEIA.

Yerba Buena (yĕr'bä bwā'nä), town (pop. estimate 500), central Tucumán prov., Argentina, on railroad and 6 mi. W of Tucumán; resort at outliers of Nevado del Aconquija; tannery.

Yerba Buena Island (yâr'bŭ bwā'nŭ, yŭr'bŭ) (300 acres), in San Francisco Bay, W Calif., bet. San Francisco and Oakland; midpoint of SAN FRANCISCO-OAKLAND BAY BRIDGE. Causeway connects it with Treasure Isl. (N).

Yerbal Viejo, Argentina: see OBERÁ.

Yerbas Buenas (yĕr'bäs bwā'näs), village (1930 pop. 457), Linares prov., S central Chile, 7 mi. N of Linares; wheat, oats, chick-peas, wine, livestock.

Yerbent (yĭrbyĕnt'), village (1948 pop. over 2,000), central Ashkhabad oblast, Turkmen SSR, in Kara-Kum desert, on Serny Zavod–Ashkhabad highway and 90 mi. N of Ashkhabad. Sometimes spelled Erbent.

Yerbogachen (yĕrbŭgŭchĕn'), village (1948 pop. over 500), N Irkutsk oblast, Russian SFSR, on Lower Tunguska R. and 625 mi. N of Irkutsk, 240 mi. N of Kirensk; agr., lumbering. Sometimes spelled Erbogachen.

Yercaud (yŭrkôd'), village, Salem dist., S central Madras, India, 8 mi. NNE of Salem. Climatic health resort (sanatorium) on scenic wooded plateau in Shevaroy Hills; alt. c.4,500 ft. Fruit orchards; essential-oil (lemon grass) factory. Numerous coffee plantations near by.

Yères River or **Yerres River** (yâr), Seine-et-Marne and Seine-et-Oise depts., N central France, rises above Rozay-en-Brie, flows c.40 mi. W to the Seine at Villeneuve-Saint-Georges.

Yerevan, Armenian SSR: see ERIVAN.

Yergach, Russian SFSR: see KUNGUR.

Yergeni Hills (yĕrgĭnyē'), S continuation of Volga Upland, in S European Russian SFSR; extend c.200

mi. bet. Stalingrad (N) and Manych Depression (S); rise to c.700 ft. SW of Stepnoi; sheep raising; mustard, wheat. Sometimes spelled Ergeni.

Yerim, Yemen: see YARIM.

Yerington, city (pop. 1,157), ⊙ Lyon co., W Nev., on Walker R. and 35 mi. ESE of Carson City; alt. 4,382 ft.; shipping point in mining (copper, gold, silver), livestock, and dairying area. Settled 1860, inc. 1907.

Yerkalo, Tibet: see YAKALO.

Yerkoy (yĕrkoi'), Turkish *Yerköy*, village (pop. 2,621), Yozgat prov., central Turkey, on railroad, on Delice R., and 21 mi. SW of Yozgat; grain silos; mohair goats. Formerly Baglarbasi.

Yermak (yĭrmäk'), village (1939 pop. over 500), central Pavlodar oblast, Kazakh SSR, on Irtysh R. and 15 mi. S of Pavlodar; cattle breeding. Sometimes spelled Ermak.

Yermakovskoye (–mä'kŭfskŭyŭ), village (1926 pop. 3,255), S Krasnoyarsk Territory, Russian SFSR, 40 mi. SE of Minusinsk; dairy farming. Sometimes spelled Ermakovskoye.

Yerma River, Bulgaria and Yugoslavia: see JERMA RIVER.

Yermekeyevo (yĕrmĭkyā'ŭvŭ), village (1948 pop. over 2,000), W Bashkir Autonomous SSR, Russian SFSR, 70 mi. WNW of Sterlitamak; grain, livestock. Sometimes spelled Ermekeyevo.

Yermish or **Yermish'** (yĭrmēsh'), village (1926 pop. 2,750), NE Ryazan oblast, Russian SFSR, 33 mi. NNE of Sasovo; metalworking, flour milling. Sometimes spelled Ermish.

Yermolayevo (yĕrmŭlī'ŭvŭ), village (1948 pop. over 2,000), SW Bashkir Autonomous SSR, Russian SFSR, 60 mi. SSW of Sterlitamak; rail spur terminus; mining center in Babai lignite basin (developed after Second World War); metalworking, distilling. Sometimes spelled Ermolayevo.

Yermolino (yĭrmô'lyĭnŭ), town (1926 pop. 863), NE Kaluga oblast, Russian SFSR, on Protva R. and 5 mi. E of Borovsk; textiles. Sometimes spelled Ermolino.

Yerofei Pavlovich or **Yerofey Pavlovich** (yĕrŭfyā" pä'vlŭvĭch), town (1948 pop. over 10,000), SW Amur oblast, Russian SFSR, on Trans-Siberian RR and 80 mi. W of Skovorodino; railway shops; gold mines. Named for Y. P. Khabarov, 17th-cent. Rus. explorer. Sometimes spelled Erofei Pavlovich.

Yerofeyevka (yĕrŭfyā'ŭfkŭ), town (1945 pop. over 500), NE Kazakhstan oblast, Kazakh SSR, in Altai Mts., 20 mi. S of Leninogorsk. Sometimes spelled Erofeyevka.

Yeroskipou (yĕrôskē'pōō) or **Yeroskipos** (–pôs), village (pop. 1,375), Paphos dist., W Cyprus, 2 mi. SE of Paphos; wheat, tobacco; sheep, cattle. Flax fiber mfg.

Yerraguntla, India: see PRODDATUR.

Yerranderie, village, E New South Wales, Australia, 60 mi. WSW of Sydney; silver mining.

Yerres (yâr), town (pop. 5,455), Seine-et-Oise dept., N central France, on right bank of Yères R. and 12 mi. SE of Paris; metalworks.

Yerres River, France: see YÈRES RIVER.

Yerseke or **Ierseke** (both: ĕr'sŭkŭ), town (pop. 4,522), Zeeland prov., SW Netherlands, on South Beveland isl. 7 mi. E of Goes, on the Eastern Scheldt; center of oyster culture; shell grinding, machinery mfg., woodworking. Also spelled Ijerseke.

Yershichi (yĭrshē'chē), village (1926 pop. 335), SW Smolensk oblast, Russian SFSR, on Iput R. and 18 mi. S of Roslavl; flax. Sometimes spelled Ershichi.

Yershov (yĭrshôf'), town (1944 pop. over 10,000), E central Saratov oblast, Russian SFSR, 95 mi. E of Saratov; rail junction; flour milling, metalworking. Until c.1940, Yershovo; sometimes spelled Ershov.

Yertarskii or **Yertarskiy** (yĭrtär'skē), town (1926 pop. 2,157), SE Sverdlovsk oblast, Russian SFSR, on right tributary of Pyshma R. and 23 mi. SSW of Tugulym; glassworking center. Peat deposits near by. Formerly (until c.1928) called Yertarski Zavod and (1928–40) Yertarskoye; sometimes spelled Ertarski.

Yeruá (yĕrwä'), village (pop. estimate 500), E Entre Ríos prov., Argentina, on railroad and 15 mi. SW of Concordia, in livestock and rice area; apiculture. Agr. research station.

Yerupaja, Cerro (sĕ'rō yärōōpä'hä), Peruvian peak (21,758 ft.) in Cordillera Occidental of the Andes, on Lima-Ancash-Huánuco dept. line, 50 mi. NW of Cerro de Pasco. Until ascent (1950) by U.S. party, highest unclimbed peak of the Americas.

Yeruslan River (yĕrōōslän'), intermittent steppe river in S European Russian SFSR, rises SE of Mokrous, flows SSW, past Krasny Kut (Saratov oblast) and Staraya Poltavka, and W to arm of the Volga above Nikolayevski; 219 mi. long. Sometimes spelled Eruslan.

Yerville (yĕrvēl'), village (pop. 1,003), Seine-Inférieure dept., N France, 18 mi. NNW of Rouen; dairying.

Yerwa, Nigeria: see MAIDUGURI.

Yesa (yä'sä), village (pop. 276), Navarre prov., N Spain, on Aragon R. and 27 mi. ESE of Pamplona. Near by is hydroelectric plant and reservoir feeding irrigation canal.

Yesagyo (yā'zŭjō"), village, Pakokku dist., Upper Burma, 22 mi. NE of Pakokku, on Chindwin R. near its mouth on the Irrawaddy.

Yesan (yä'sän'), Jap. *Reisen*, town (1949 pop. 24,662), S.Chungchong prov., S Korea, 60 mi. S of Seoul; agr. (rice, soybeans, tobacco, hemp), mining (gold, tungsten).

Yesan, Cape, Japan: see ESAN, CAPE.

Yesaulovka (yĕsŭōō'lŭfkŭ), town (1939 pop. over 500), S Voroshilovgrad oblast, Ukrainian SSR, in the Donbas, 4 mi. SSW of Bokovo-Antratsit; coal mines. Sometimes spelled Esaulovka.

Yesca, La, Mexico: see LA YESCA.

Yesenovichi (yĭsyĕ'nŭvĕchē), village (1939 pop. over 500), W central Kalinin oblast, Russian SFSR, 25 mi. SW of Vyshni Volochek; metalworks; dairying, sawmilling. Sometimes Esenovichi.

Yesera (yäsā'rä), town (pop. c.2,000), Tarija dept., S Bolivia, 13 mi. NE of Tarija; vineyards; fruit, grain, livestock.

Yeshbum or **Yashbum** (both: yĕshbōōm'), town, ⊙ Upper Aulaqi sheikdom, Western Aden Protectorate, in upper reaches of the Wadi Meifa'a, 55 mi. N of Ahwar, near boundary line of Eastern Aden Protectorate; market center of agr. area (grain, sesame, jujubes). Noted for its honey. Cotton spinning and dyeing.

Yesil Irmak (yĕ-shĭl' ĭrmäk") or **Yesil River,** Turkish *Yeşil Irmak*, anc. *Iris*, river, N Turkey, rises in the Kizil Dag 15 mi. NNE of Zara, flows 260 mi. WNW, past Tokat, Amasya, and Carsamba, to Black Sea at Cape Civa, 15 mi. E of Samsun. Receives Cekerek R. (left), Kelkit R. (right). Sometimes spelled Yeshil Irmak.

Yesilkoy, Turkey: see SAN STEFANO.

Yesilova (yĕ-shĭl'ôvä), Turkish *Yeşilova*. **1** Village (pop. 1,165), Burdur prov., SW Turkey, 35 mi. WSW of Burdur; wheat, hemp. Formerly Satirlar or Satilar. **2** Village, Yozgat prov., Turkey: see SORGUN.

Yeski Dzhumaya, Bulgaria: see TARGOVISHTE.

Yeski Stambolluk, Bulgaria: see PRESLAV.

Yeski-Zagra, Bulgaria: see STARA ZAGORA, city.

Yessei or **Yessey** (yĭsyā'), village, N Evenki Natl. Okrug, Krasnoyarsk Territory, Russian SFSR, 310 mi. N of Tura, N of Arctic Circle, in reindeer-raising area. Sometimes spelled Essei.

Yessentuki (yĕ"syĭntōōkē'), city (1926 pop. 23,142), S Stavropol Territory, Russian SFSR, in the N Caucasus, on Podkumok R., on railroad and 10 mi. W of Pyatigorsk; major health resort with noted mineral springs; mineral-water bottling, food processing. Consists of old Cossack village (S) and newly developed resort (N). Sometimes spelled Essentuki. During Second World War, held (1942–43) by Germans.

Yesso, Japan: see HOKKAIDO.

Yessod Hamaalah, Israel: see YESUD HAM MA'ALA.

Yessup, Peru: see PUERTO YESSUP.

Yeste (yĕ'stā), town (pop. 2,826), Albacete prov., SE central Spain, 36 mi. WSW of Hellín; wool spinning, perfume mfg., olive-oil processing; esparto, cereals, honey. Reservoir, dam, and hydroelectric plant on Segura R. near by.

Yester, parish (pop. 691), S central East Lothian, Scotland. Includes GIFFORD.

Yes Tor, England: see DARTMOOR.

Yesud ham Ma'ala or **Yessod Hamaalah** (both: yĕsōd' hämä-älä'), settlement (pop. 200), Upper Galilee, NE Israel, on W shore of L. Hula, 9 mi. NE of Safad; fishing, fruitgrowing. Founded 1883. Also spelled Yesud ha Ma'ala, Yesud Hamaala, or Yesod Hamaala.

Yesup, Peru: see PUERTO YESSUP.

Yesvantpur, India: see BANGALORE, city.

Yetkul or **Yetkul'** (yĭtkōōl'), village (1926 pop. 2,705), central Chelyabinsk oblast, Russian SFSR, 22 mi. SSE of Chelyabinsk; grain, livestock. Sometimes spelled Etkul.

Yetminster, agr. village and parish (pop. 438), N Dorset, England, 4 mi. SW of Sherborne. Has 15th-cent. church.

Yetropole (yĕtrôpô'lĕ), city (pop. 3,041), Sofia dist., W central Bulgaria, in Yetropole Mts., at N end of road through Yetropole Pass, on Malki Iskar R. and 35 mi. ENE of Sofia; summer resort; dairying center; butter and cheese exports; furniture mfg., coopering. **Yetropole Mountains,** W part of central Balkan Mts., S of Yetropole, rise to c.5,870 ft. Forested N slopes; lead-silver, copper, and gold deposits. Crossed by **Yetropole Pass,** 5 mi. SW of Yetropole, on road to Sofia. Sometimes spelled Etropole or Etropolje.

Yetter, town (pop. 121), Calhoun co., central Iowa, 17 mi. N of Carroll.

Yeu or **Ye-u** (yā-ōō'), village (pop. 3,739), Shwebo dist., Upper Burma, on Mu R. and 70 mi. NW of Mandalay (linked by railroad), near Yeu irrigation canal (opened 1918; fed by Mu R.); trade center in rice-growing area.

Yeu, Île d' (ēl dyû'), island (□ 9; pop. 4,249), in Bay of Biscay, off Vendée dept., W France, c.27 mi. NW of Les Sables-d'Olonne; 6 mi. long, 2 mi. wide; a granite rock inhabited by fishermen. Attracts tourists. Village of Port-Joinville on NE shore. Pétain imprisoned here 1945.

Yeungchun (yŭrn'tsōōn'), Mandarin *Yang-ch'un* (yäng'chōōn'), town (pop. 11,156), ⊙ Yeungchun co. (pop. 324,607), SW Kwangtung prov., China, 25 mi. NNW of Yeungkong; rice, beans; sericulture. Tin and lead mining near by.

Yeungkong (yŭrng'gông'), Mandarin *Yang-chiang* (yäng'jyäng'), town (pop. 31,002), ⊙ Yeungkong co. (pop. 508,608), SW Kwangtung prov., China, port on S.China Sea, 110 mi. ENE of Chankiang; fishing center; leather products.

Yeungshan (yŭrng'sän'), Mandarin *Yangshan* (yäng'shän'), town (pop. 1,074), ⊙ Yeungshan co. (pop. 204,202), N Kwangtung prov., China, on Linchow R. and 30 mi. SSE of Linhsien; millet, peanuts; extracts tung and peanut oil. Coal, arsenic, tin mining near by.

Yevdakovo, Russian SFSR: see KAMENKA, Voronezh oblast.

Yevdokimovskoye, Russian SFSR: see MOLOTOVSKOYE.

Yevgashchino (yĭvgä'shchĭnŭ), village (1926 pop. 954), E Omsk oblast, Russian SFSR, on Irtysh R. and 110 mi. NNE of Omsk; dairying farming, flour milling; river port.

Yevgenyevka or **Yevgen'yevka,** Russian SFSR: see SPASSK-DALNI.

Yevkandzhinski or **Yevkandzhinskiy** (yĕfkŭnjĕn'skē), town (1940 pop. over 500), SE Yakut Autonomous SSR, Russian SFSR, 17 mi. N of Allakh-Yun; gold-mining center. Sometimes spelled Evkandzhinski.

Yevlakh (yĭvläkh'), city (1944 pop. over 10,000), central Azerbaijan SSR, on Kura R. (head of navigation) and 140 mi. W of Baku; road and rail center, near Mingechaur dam; highways lead N to Nukha and Zakataly, S to Stepanakert and Shusha, E to Baku, and W to Kirovabad; cotton ginning. Sometimes spelled Evlakh.

Yevpatoriya (yĕfpŭtô'rēŭ), anc. *Eupatoria* (ūpŭtô'rēŭ), city (1926 pop. 23,512), W Crimea, Russian SFSR, port on Black Sea, 40 mi. N of Sevastopol; 45°12'N 33°23'E. Agr. center for grain and livestock area; saltworking, fish processing, meat packing, clothing mfg. Has 16th-cent. mosque, mus. of antiquities. City consists of old Tatar town (E), with ruins of anc. fortress, and new Rus. section (W), developed after 1910. Residential and seaside resort dist. (visited chiefly by children) extends 2 mi. W to L. Mainak, a salt lagoon with mud baths. Founded 1st cent. A.D. as Pontic military post; named for Pontic king Eupator. In Middle Ages, became Tatar fortress of Gesleve or Guesleve; flourished through its developing sea trade. Regained its anc. name following Rus. annexation of Crimea. Occupied (1854–56) during Crimean War by allied Br., Fr., and Turkish troops. In 19th cent., also called Kozlov. Sometimes spelled Evpatoriya.

Yèvre River (yĕ'vrŭ), Cher dept., central France, rises near Baugy in Sancerrois Hills, flows 40 mi. W, past Bourges (where it receives the Auron) and Mehunsur-Yèvre, into the Cher at Vierzon. Bet. Bourges and Vierzon followed by part of Berry Canal.

Yevstratovski or **Yevstratovskiy** (yĭfsträ'tŭfskē), town (1939 pop. over 10,000), S Voronezh oblast, Russian SFSR, 3 mi. SE of Rossosh.

Yevsug (yĭfsōōk'), village (1926 pop. 7,301), NE Voroshilovgrad oblast, Ukrainian SSR, 19 mi. E of Starobelsk; wheat.

Yeya River (yä'yŭ), Krasnodar Territory, Russian SFSR, rises S of Novo-Pokrovskaya, flows 125 mi. NW, past Kalnibolotskaya, Kushchevskaya (rail and road bridges), and Staro-Shcherbinovskaya, to Yeva Liman, a lagoon (15 mi. long, 6 mi. wide) of Sea of Azov, just E of Yeisk. Lower course (salt water) frequently dry in summer. Sometimes spelled Eya.

Yeysk, Russian SFSR: see YEISK.

Yezd (yĕzd) or **Yazd** (yäzd), former province (□ 50,000; pop. 325,806) of central Iran; ⊙ was Yezd. Situated largely on central plateau at N foot of the Zagros ranges, it is bounded E by Kerman, S by Fars, W by Isfahan, and N by Samnan and Khurasan (boundary through the desert Dasht-i-Kavir). Some irrigated agr.: mulberry cultivation; grain, opium, madder root; goat and sheep raising. Mining of lead and other nonferrous metals at Anarak, at S edge of the Dasht-i-Kavir. Main centers—Yezd and Nain—are served by road and railroad from Teheran along N foot of Zagros ranges. In 1938, Yezd prov. was joined with Isfahan to form the Tenth Province (□ 100,000; pop. 1,431,762) of Iran.

Yezd or **Yazd,** city (1941 pop. 60,066), Tenth Prov., central Iran, 160 mi. SE of Isfahan; alt. 3,870 ft.; 31°54'N 54°25'E. Road and trade center of Yezd prov., on main Zahidan-Teheran highway; terminus of railroad from Teheran. Located in agr. area (wheat, barley, cotton, opium). Silk-spinning and -weaving center, noted for its hand-woven goods; produces also cotton and woolen textiles and carpets. Has large Zoroastrian colony. Airport. City contains 12th-cent. fort and mosque and a later governor's citadel. Present city dates from 5th cent., became a refuge of Zoroastrians after Arab conquest, and was visited in 1272 by Marco Polo. Withstood Afghan attacks in 18th cent.

Yezd-i-Khast, Iran: see SAMIRUM.

Yezerche (yĕ'zĕrchĕ), village (pop. 3,590), Ruse dist., NE Bulgaria, 11 mi. WNW of Razgrad; wheat, rye, sunflowers. Formerly Yezerets.

Yezerishche or **Yezerishchi** (yĕ'zyĭrĕshchĕ), village (1939 pop. over 500), N Vitebsk oblast, Belorussian SSR, on small Yezerishchi L., 45 mi. N of Vitebsk; flax. Sometimes spelled Ezerishche.

Yezerska Chesma, peak, Yugoslavia: see JEZERSKA CESMA.

Yezhovo-Cherkessk, Russian SFSR: see CHERKESSK.

Yezo, Japan: see HOKKAIDO.

Yezupol, Ukrainian SSR: see ZHOVTEN, Stanislav.

Ygatimí, Paraguay: see IGATIMÍ.

Yhú (ēōō'), town (dist. pop. 4,506), Caaguazú dept., S central Paraguay, 40 mi. NE of Coronel Oviedo; sugar cane, maté, livestock.

Yi, China: see I RIVER.

Yialousa or **Yialoussa** (both: yälōō'sä), village (pop. 2,771), Famagusta dist., NE Cyprus, on Karpas Peninsula, 32 mi. NE of Famagusta; tobacco, olives, carobs; sheep, cattle.

Yiannitsa, Greece: see GIANNITSA.

Yiaros, Greece: see GYAROS.

Yicheng or **I-ch'eng** (both: yē'chŭng'), town, ⊙ Yicheng co. (pop. 99,982), S Shansi prov., China, 28 mi. SSE of Linfen, near railroad; cotton weaving; sesame, wheat, corn, tobacco.

Yichow, China: see YIHSIEN, Hopeh prov.

Yiewsley and West Drayton (yōōz'lē), residential urban district (1931 pop. 13,066; 1951 census 20,488), Middlesex, England, on Colne R. and 15 mi. W of London; chemical industry. Just S, on Colne R., is West Drayton (pop. 2,856), mfg. color film and metal products. Has 15th-cent. church, with 13th-cent. remains. Also in urban dist. (S, on Colne R.) is residential town of Harmondsworth (pop. 3,084), with electrical-equipment works and Ministry of Transport experimental station. Church dates from 12th cent.

Yifras or **Yifrus** (both: yĭ'fräs), town (pop. 1,200), Taiz prov., SW Yemen, 14 mi. SSW of Taiz, in coffeegrowing dist. Also spelled Yefris and Yefrus.

Yigo (yē'gō), village (pop. 411) and municipality (pop. 9,026), NE Guam; coconuts.

Yihe Bogdo, Mongolia: see IKHE BOGDO.

Yihsien or **Ihsien** (both: yē'shyĕn'). **1** Town, ⊙ Yihsien co. (pop. 249,646), NW Hopeh prov., China, 30 mi. N of Paoting and on spur of Peking-Hankow RR; sheep raising; medicinal herbs, tobacco, walnuts. Crystal quarrying. Until 1913 called Yichow or Ichow. **2** Town, ⊙ Yihsien co. (pop. 423,887), SW Shantung prov., China, 45 mi. WSW of Lini and on spur of Tientsin-Pukow RR; coal-mining center with mines at TSAOCHWANG (N).

Yihwang, China: see IHWANG.

Yildirim Dag (yŭldŭrŭm' dä), Turkish *Yıldırım Dağ*, peak (6,522 ft.), N central Turkey, 12 mi. ENE of Kizilcahamam.

Yildiz Dag (yŭldŭz' dä), Turkish *Yıldız Dağ*, peak (8,323 ft.), N central Turkey, 23 mi. SE of Tokat.

Yildizeli (yŭldŭ'zĕlē), Turkish *Yıldızeli*, village (pop. 3,636), Sivas prov., central Turkey, on railroad and 23 mi. WNW of Sivas; lentils, vetch, wheat, barley. Formerly Yenihan.

Yilgarn Goldfield, Australia: see SOUTHERN CROSS.

Yiliang or **Iliang** (both: yē'lyäng'), town, ⊙ Yiliang co. (pop. 100,808), NE Yunnan prov., China, 25 mi. NE of Chaotung and on road to Szechwan; rice, buckwheat, millet. Lead, zinc mines near by.

Yilin or **Ilin** (both: yē'lĭn'), town, N Kiangsu prov., China, 17 mi. SW of Fowning; commercial center.

Yin-chiang, China: see YINKIANG.

Yinchwan or **Yin-ch'uan** (yĭn'chwän'), city (1948 pop. 40,940), ⊙ Ningsia prov., China, near Yellow R. (its port is HUNGCHENG), 530 mi. WSW of Peking, near Great Wall; 38°28'N 106°19'E. Major commercial center; exports cattle, furs, wool, sheepskins, camel's hair, grain, licorice; winegrowing; coal mining. A walled city, it contains a monastery, park, and lake (NW). Visited in 13th cent. by Marco Polo, who reported it as Egrigaia (Irgai), it developed as an early Chinese border city, protected against Mongol areas by 16th-cent. Great Wall. It was in Kansu prov. until made ⊙ Ningsia in 1928. Called Ningsia until 1945, when it became an independent municipality. Passed 1949 to Communist control.

Ying, China: see YING RIVER.

Yingcheng or **Ying-ch'eng** (yĭng'chŭng'), town (pop. 15,891), ⊙ Yingcheng co. (pop. 266,176), E central Hupeh prov., China, 50 mi. WNW of Hankow; salt-mining center; cotton weaving; rice, wheat.

Ying-chi-sha, China: see YANGI HISSAR.

Yingchow. 1 Town, Anhwei prov., China: see FOWYANG. **2** Town, Chahar prov., China: see YINGHSIEN.

Ying Ho, China: see YING RIVER.

Yinghsien (yĭng'shyĕn'), town, ⊙ Yinghsien co. (pop. 108,847), SW Chahar prov., China, 35 mi. S of Tatung; ramie weaving; wheat, kaoliang, potatoes. Called Yingchow until 1912. Until 1949 in N Shansi.

Yingkiang or **Ying-chiang** (both: yĭng'jyäng'), village, ⊙ Yingkiang dist. (pop. 21,010), W Yunnan prov., China, 30 mi. SW of Tengchung, in mtn. region; rice, wheat, millet, beans. Until 1935 called Kanai.

Yingkisha, China: see YANGI HISSAR.

Yingko (yĭng'gŭ'), Jap. *Oka* (ō'kä), town (1935 pop. 4,105), N Formosa, 8 mi. W of Taipei and on railroad; coal mining; clay quarry; distilling; mfg. of pottery, bricks and tiles, rush mats.

Yingkow or **Ying-k'ou** (both: yĭng'kō), city (1947 pop. 158,587), ⊙ but independent of Yingkow co., SW Liaotung prov., Manchuria, port on Gulf of Liaotung, at mouth of Liao R., on railroad and 100 mi. SW of Mukden; 40°40'N 122°13'E. Major port of S Manchuria and natural outlet of the Liao valley, Yingkow is handicapped, however, by bars and a shallow access channel. Mfg. of soybean oil, tobacco products, cotton and silk textiles, wood pulp, matches; shipbuilding; magnesium plant. Called Yingtze until 1836, when lower Liao R. port was transferred here from TIENCHWANGTAI; it developed rapidly as the port of entry to Liao R. valley, supplanting the older NEWCHWANG and becoming a treaty port in 1858. Yingkow decreased in importance with the building of railroads and the rise of Dairen. Its trade—mainly imports and coal, grain, and soybean exports—is restricted to coastal junk shipping. Formerly also called Newchwang.

Yingpankai, China: see PIKIANG.

Ying River, Chinese *Ying Ho* (yĭng'hŭ'), chief left tributary of Hwai R. in central China, rises near Tengfeng in Sung Mts. of NW Honan prov, flows 300 mi. SE, past Yühsien, Linying, Sihwa, Chowkiakow (head of navigation), into NW Anhwei prov., past Taiho, Fowyang, Yingshang, to Hwai R. at Chengyangkwan. Chief tributary is Sha River or Tasha River, which joins it in 2 arms at Chowkiakow and Fowyang. Lower valley of the Ying was used (1938–46) by diverted Yellow R.

Yingshan (yĭng'shän'). **1** Town (pop. 18,910), ⊙ Yingshan co. (pop. 315,167), N Hupeh prov., China, near Honan line, 25 mi. NNE of Anlu; cotton weaving, tobacco processing; wheat, rice, beans. **2** Town (pop. 18,592), ⊙ Yingshan co. (pop. 214,447), E Hupeh prov., China, near Anhwei line, 50 mi. NNE of Kichun; rice, wheat, timber, medicinal herbs. Until 1936 in Anhwei prov. **3** Town (pop. 26,625), ⊙ Yingshan co. (pop. 391,752), N central Szechwan prov., China, 32 mi. NE of Nanchung, near Kialing R.; rice, sweet potatoes, kaoliang, millet, wheat, beans.

Yingshang (yĭng'shäng'), town, ⊙ Yingshang co. (pop. 341,788), N Anhwei prov., China, 32 mi. SE of Fowyang and on Ying R.; wheat, kaoliang, sweet potatoes, cotton.

Yingtak (yĭng'dŭk'), Mandarin *Yinte* (yĭn'dŭ'), town (pop. 9,600), ⊙ Yingtak co. (pop. 300,305), N Kwangtung prov., China, on North R., on Canton-Hankow RR and 45 mi. SSW of Kükong; tin and gold mining.

Yingtze, Manchuria: see YINGKOW.

Yinhsien, China: see NINGPO.

Yinkiang or **Yin-chiang** (both: yĭn'jyäng'), town (pop. 6,842), ⊙ Yinkiang co. (pop. 178,041), NE Kweichow prov., China, 10 mi. ENE of Szenan; lumbering center; cotton weaving, papermaking. Gold deposits near by.

Yinmabin (yĭn'mäbĭn"), village, Lower Chindwin dist., Upper Burma, 15 mi. W of Monywa. Sometimes spelled Yinmabyin.

Yin Mountains, Chinese *Yin Shan* (yĭn' shän'), Inner Mongolia, China, in Suiyuan and Chahar provs., extending E–W at 40–41°N bet. Alashan Mts. in Ningsia (W) and the Great Khingan Mts. in Manchuria (E); rise to c.6,000 ft. in Tatsing Mts. Coal mining on S slopes.

Yinte, China: see YINGTAK.

Yioura, Greece: see GIOURA.

Yirga-Alam (yĭr'gä äläm'), **Ital.** *Irgalem*, **town,** ⊙ Sidamo-Borana prov., S Ethiopia, in Great Rift valley near Mt. Guramba, 165 mi. S of Addis Ababa; 6°39'N 38°33'E; alt. c.8,200 ft. Trade center (hides, coffee, wax). Under Italian administration (1936–41) called Dalle.

Yi River, China: see I RIVER.

Yí River (yē), central Uruguay, rises in the Cuchilla Grande Principal just W of Cerro Chato, flows 140 mi. W, past Sarandí del Yí and Durazno, to the Río Negro 40 mi. WNW of Durazno.

Yirol (yērōl'), village (pop. 700), Bahr el Ghazal prov., S Anglo-Egyptian Sudan, 200 mi. SE of Wau.

Yithion, Greece: see GYTHEION.

Yitu or **Itu** (both: yē'dōō'), town (1922 pop. estimate 60,000), ⊙ Yitu co. (pop. 425,000), central Shantung prov., China, 80 mi. E of Tsinan and on Tsingtao-Tsinan RR; major pongee-weaving center; millet, wheat, eggs, kaoliang, fruit. Until 1913 called Tsingchow.

Yiwu, China: see CHENYÜEH.

Yiyang or **Iyang** (both: yē'yäng'). **1** Town, ⊙ Yiyang co. (pop. 165,808), NW Honan prov., China, on Lo R. and 22 mi. SW of Loyang; tobacco processing; sesame, indigo, kaoliang. **2** Town, ⊙ Yiyang co. (pop. 797,506), N Hunan prov., China, port on Tzu R. delta of Tungting L., 55 mi. NW of Changsha; commercial center of Tzu R. valley; exports tea, rice, cotton, tobacco, hemp.

Yizre'el, Israel: see JEZREEL.

Ykspihlaja (üks'pĭläyä), Swedish *Yxpila* (üks'pĭlä"), suburb and outport of Kokkola, Vaasa co., W Finland, on Gulf of Bothnia, 3 mi. W of Kokkola; foundries.

Ylitornio (ü'lĭtōr"nēō), Swedish *Övertorneå* (û'vûrtōr"nûō), village (commune pop. 8,246), Lapi co., NW Finland, on Torne R. (Swedish border) and 35 mi. NNW of Tornio; agr., lumbering.

Ylivieska (ü'lĭvē"ĕskä), village (commune pop. 9,332), Oulo co., W Finland, on Kala R. and 45 mi. ENE of Kokkola; rail junction; lumbering.

Ylöjärvi (ü'lûyăr"vē), village (commune pop. 7,037), Häme co., SW Finland, near L. Näsi, 5 mi. NW of Tampere; copper and wolfram mines.

Ylst, Netherlands: see IJLST.

Ymer Island (ü'mûr), Dan. *Ymers Ø* (60 mi. long, 3–28 mi. wide), in King Oscar Archipelago, E Greenland, in E part of Franz Josef Fjord, just N of Geographical Society Isl.; 73°15' 24°30'W. E coast deeply indented by 35-mi.-long Dusen Fjord. Mountainous surface rises to 6,282 ft. Whaling station at SE extremity.

Ymir (wī'mĕr), village (pop. estimate 200), SE B.C., in Selkirk Mts., on Salmo R. and 15 mi. S of Nelson; alt. 4,220 ft.; mining (gold, silver, lead, zinc).

Ymuiden, Netherlands: see IJMUIDEN.

Ynykchanski or **Ynykchanskiy** (ĭnĭkchän'skē), town (1940 pop. over 500), SE Yakut Autonomous SSR, Russian SFSR, 60 mi. S of Allakh-Yun; gold.

Ynysawdre (ŭnĭsou'drē), town and parish (pop. 2,260), S Glamorgan, Wales, 3 mi. NNW of Bridgend; coal mining.

Ynyscynhaiarn, Wales: see PORTMADOC.

Ynys Enlli, Wales: see BARDSEY.

Ynys Seiriol, Wales: see PUFFIN.

Ynysybwl (ŭnĭsŭbōōl'), town (pop. 4,849) in Mountain Ash urban dist., NE Glamorgan, Wales; coal mining.

Yo-, for Chinese names beginning thus and not found here: see under YÜEH-.

Yo (yō), town, Bornu prov., Northern Provinces, NE Nigeria, near L. Chad, on Komadugu Yobe R. (Fr. West Africa border) and 50 mi. NNW of Kukawa; millet, cassava, durra; cattle raising; saltworks. Sometimes spelled Yeu.

Yoakum (yō'kŭm), county (□ 830; pop. 4,339), NW Texas; ⊙ Plains. On Llano Estacado, and bordering W on N.Mex.; alt. 3,400–3,900 ft. Formerly entirely a cattle-ranching area, now also produces and refines oil and natural gas; some sheep, goats, horses, hogs, mules; some dairying, poultry raising; agr. (grain sorghums, corn, peanuts, cotton). Formed 1876.

Yoakum, city (pop. 5,231), De Witt and Lavaca counties, S Texas, 35 mi. N of Victoria, in tomato-growing, livestock and poultry-raising area; processing center, with tannery, leather factory, plants producing cottonseed oil, wood products, canned foods, dairy products, packed poultry, and truck; hatcheries. Founded 1887, inc. 1891.

Yobai, Formosa: see YANGMEI.

Yobain (yōbīn'), town (pop. 990), Yucatan, SE Mexico, 37 mi. NE of Mérida; henequen.

Yocalla (yōkä'yä), village (pop. c.1,400), Potosí dept., S central Bolivia, on Pilcomayo R. and 15 mi. NNW of Potosí, on road from Oruro; alt. 11,319 ft.; power plant.

Yo-chia-k'ou, China: see YOKIAKOW.

Yochih or **Yo-ch'ih** (yō'chŭ'), town (pop. 85,380), ⊙ Yochih co. (pop. 560,051), E central Szechwan prov., China, 37 mi. NNE of Hochwan; rice, sweet potatoes, wheat, ramie, beans.

Yochow, China: see YOYANG, Hunan prov.

Yockanookany River (yŏkŭnōō'kŭnē), central Miss., rises in Choctaw co., flows c.65 mi. SW, past Ethel, to Pearl R. 10 mi. WSW of Carthage. Sometimes spelled Yokahockany or Yockahockany (yŏkŭhŏ'kŭnē).

Yoco (yō'kō), town (pop. 1,171), Sucre state, NE Venezuela, on Paria Peninsula, 9 mi. WNW of Güiria; cacao growing.

Yocón (yōkōn'), town (pop. 172), Olancho dept., central Honduras, on upper Yaguale R. (right affluent of Aguán R.), and 10 mi. NNW of Salamá; sugar-milling center; sugar cane, coffee.

Yocona River (yŏ'kŭnŭ), N Miss., rises in W Pontotoc co., flows 130 mi. generally W, past Crowder, to the Tallahatchie (here often called the Little Tallahatchie) in E Quitman co. Enid Dam, to impound reservoir near Enid, was begun in 1947.

Yodda (yŏ'dŭ), gold field in Territory of Papua, SE New Guinea, in valley of small Yodda R., near Kokoda, 60 mi. NE of Port Moresby.

Yoder (yō'dŭr), town (pop. 128), Goshen co., SE Wyo., near Nebr. line, 60 mi. NNE of Cheyenne.

Yodo (yō'dō), town (pop 5,504), Kyoto prefecture, S Honshu, Japan, on Yodo R. and 8 mi. S of Kyoto. Port for Kyoto, exporting lacquer and porcelain ware. Race tracks.

Yodoe (yōdō'ā), town (pop. 5,081), Tottori prefecture, SW Honshu, Japan, on inlet of Sea of Japan, 6 mi. ENE of Yonago, in agr. area (rice, wheat); sake, umbrellas.

Yodo River (yō'dō), Jap. *Yodo-gawa*, S Honshu, Japan, leaves L. Biwa, of which it is the only outlet; flows S, past Seta (where it is called Seta R.), W, past Uji (hydroelectric plants; here called Uji R.) and Yodo (port for Kyoto), then SW to Osaka Bay at Osaka; 47 mi. long. Largest tributary, Kizu R. (28 mi. long).

Yoe, borough (pop. 681), York co., S Pa., 7 mi. SE of York.

Yoff (yôf), village, W Senegal, Fr. West Africa, on Cape Verde peninsula, 10 mi. NNW of Dakar. Modern international airport.

Yoho National Park (yō'hō) (□ 507), SE B.C., on Alta. border, in Rocky Mts., W of Banff Natl. Park; established 1886, later enlarged. Centered on town of Field. With several peaks over 10,000 ft. high (mts. Gordon, Stephen, Goodsir, and Vaux), it is a mtn.-climbing center. Takakkaw Falls here.

Yo-hsi, China: see YOSI.

Yoichi (yōē'chē), town (pop. 24,885), W Hokkaido, Japan, on Ishikari Bay, 11 mi. W of Otaru; mining (gold, silver, copper); apple growing, fishing.

Yoita (yōē'tä), town (pop. 7,380), Niigata prefecture, central Honshu, Japan, on Shinano R. and 6 mi. NNW of Nagaoka; rice, raw silk, tobacco.

Yojoa, Lake (yōhō'ä), largest inland lake of Honduras, on Cortés–Santa Bárbara–Comayagua dept. border, 70 mi. NW of Tegucigalpa; 12 mi. long, 4 mi. wide; alt. 2,133 ft. Volcanic in origin, surrounded by steep hills; empties S into Jaitique R., a tributary of Ulúa R. A popular tourist resort on route bet. Tegucigalpa and Caribbean coast. Ferry service connects former road termini of Pito Solo (S) and El Jaral (N), linked since early 1940s by road skirting E shore.

Yoju (yŭ'jōō'), Jap. *Reishu*, town (1949 pop. 14,083), Kyonggi prov., central Korea, S of 38°N, on Han R. and 40 mi. SE of Seoul, in gold-mining area; rail terminus.

Yoka, Japan: see YAOKA.

Yokadouma (yōkädōō'mä), village, Lom et Kadéï region, SE Fr. Cameroons, near Fr. Equatorial Africa border, 80 mi. SE of Batouri; coffee plantations.

Yokahockany River, Miss.: see YOCKANOOKANY RIVER.

Yokaichi (yō'-kī'chē), town (pop. 9,649), Shiga prefecture, S Honshu, Japan, 26 mi. ENE of Kyoto; commercial center for agr. area (rice, tea, wheat, market produce); raw silk.

Yokaichiba (yō'-kī'chĭbä), town (pop. 10,423), Chiba prefecture, central Honshu, Japan, at base of Chiba Peninsula, 16 mi. W of Choshi; commercial center for area producing rice, raw silk, poultry.

Yokata (yōkä'tä), town (pop. 4,601), Toyama prefecture, central Honshu, Japan, on S shore of Toyama Bay, 4 mi. NW of Toyama; fishing port; patent medicines.

Yokiakow or **Yo-chia-k'ou** (both: yō'jyä'kō'), town, S central Hupeh prov., China, 70 mi. W of Hankow and on right bank of Han R.; commercial center; cotton weaving; rice, wheat, beans, millet.

Yokkaichi (yōk-kī'chē). **1** City (1940 pop. 63,732; 1947 pop. 112,433), Mie prefecture, S Honshu, Japan, port on NW shore of Ise Bay, 20 mi. SW of Nagoya; mfg. center; makes Banko ware (a kind of porcelain), cotton textiles, rubber goods, plate glass; green-tea processing. Exports cotton textiles, ceramic products, Portland cement. Includes (since early 1940s) former towns of Tomita (1940 pop. 10,749) and Tomisuhara (1940 pop. 14,616). Sometimes spelled Yokkaiti. **2** Town (pop. 6,464), Oita prefecture, N Kyushu, Japan, 26 mi. NW of Oita; rice, wheat, barley.

Yokneam, Israel: see JOKNEAM.

Yoko (yō'kō), village, M'Bam region, W central Fr. Cameroons, 100 mi. NE of Bafia. Protestant mission.

Yokogawa, Japan: see YOKOKAWA.

Yokohama (yō"kähä'mä, yōkä'hämŭ), city (□ 153; 1940 pop. 968,091; 1947 pop. 814,379), ⊙ Kanagawa prefecture, central Honshu, Japan, on Kwanto plain; major foreign-trade port, on W shore of Tokyo Bay, 17 mi. W of Tokyo, bet. Kawasaki (N) and Yokosuka (S); forms part of urban belt. Traversed by a network of canals and divided into 3 general sections: industrial (N), principal dock area (central), commercial (S). Steel, chemical, and automobile plants, shipyards, oil refineries. Major part of Japan's silk-export trade is here. Other exports: canned fish, rayon goods. Ports of Yokohama and Tokyo are collectively called Keihin (kā'hēn). City visited 1854 by Perry; opened 1859 to foreign trade as 1st open port. The U.S.-Japanese treaty of 1858 had named Kanagawa (just N of city; included in Yokohama since 1901) as the original trading port, but it was never used as such. Virtually destroyed in earthquake of 1923, city was completely reconstructed. Extensive harbor improvements were made, and city was greatly expanded by reclamation of bay area. Heavily bombed (1945) in Second World War. Includes former towns of Kanazawa (since 1936), Totsuka (since 1938), and Kawawa (since 1939).

Yokokawa (yōkō'käwŭ) or **Yokogawa** (–gäwŭ), town (pop. 11,559), Kagoshima prefecture, S Kyushu, Japan, 23 mi. NNE of Kagoshima; mining center (gold, silver); rice, raw silk; charcoal, lumber.

Yokoshiba (yōkō'shĭbä), town (pop. 6,568), Chiba prefecture, central Honshu, Japan, at N base of Chiba Peninsula, 5 mi. SW of Yokaichiba; rice, wheat, raw silk, poultry.

Yokosuka (yō"kŭsōō'kŭ, yōkō'sōōkä). **1** Town (pop. 14,598), Aichi prefecture, central Honshu, Japan, on NE shore of Ise Bay, 10 mi. S of Nagoya; rice-growing center. Important port in anc. times. **2** City (1940 pop. 193,358; 1947 pop. 252,923), Kanagawa prefecture, central Honshu, Japan, on SW shore of Tokyo Bay, just S of Yokohama; site of important naval base (established 1884). Shipyards, arsenals, ironworks. Navigation schools. The city proper (N of naval base) produces livestock, fish, agr. products. Since early 1940s, includes former towns of Uraga (1940 pop. 28,073), Zushi (1940 pop. 24,119; known as summer resort), Ogusu (1940 pop. 5,749), Nagai (1940 pop. 5,686). **3** Town (pop. 8,576), Shizuoka prefecture, central Honshu, Japan, on Philippine Sea, 15 mi. ESE of Hamamatsu; tea, rice.

Yokota (yōkō'tä), town (pop. 4,441), Shimane prefecture, SW Honshu, Japan, 20 mi. S of Matsue, in agr. area (rice, wheat); raw silk, sake, charcoal. Agr. school.

Yokote (yōkō'tā), town (pop. 26,993), Akita prefecture, N Honshu, Japan, 37 mi. SE of Akita; mfg. (cotton textiles, dyes), woodworking, sake brewing.

Yola (yō'lä), town (pop. 5,310), ⊙ Adamawa prov., Northern Provinces, E Nigeria, on Benue R. (navigable in flood season), near Fr. Cameroons frontier, and 260 mi. ESE of Jos; alt. 850 ft.; 9°13'N 12°29'E. Agr. center; peanuts, millet, durra, cassava, yams; cattle. Airfield. A former Fulah capital.

Yolaina, Cordillera de (kôrdĭyā'rä dā yōlī'nä), SE Nicaragua, E spur of main continental divide; extends c.60 mi. E toward Mico Point; forms left watershed of Punta Gorda R.; rises over 2,000 ft.

Yoli Pass (yō'lē) (alt. 18,000 ft.), in the E Hindu Kush, on Afghanistan-China line, at easternmost point of Wakhan panhandle; 37°17'N 74°45'E.

Yolla, village (pop. 212), N Tasmania, 75 mi. WNW of Launceston; dairying center.

Yolla Bolly Mountains, Calif.: see KLAMATH MOUNTAINS.

Yolo (yō'lō), county (□ 1,034; pop. 40,640), central Calif.; ⊙ Woodland. In Sacramento Valley, co. is bounded E by Sacramento R., and rises to foothills in W. Drained by Cache and Putah creeks. Year-round agr. (sugar beets, tomatoes, asparagus, alfalfa, rice, fruit, olives, beans, grain); stock raising (sheep, beef cattle), dairying. Sand, gravel, quicksilver; natural gas. Processing industries (beet sugar, canned and dried fruit, dairy products). Has suburbs of Sacramento in E. Formed 1850.

Yolombó (yōlōmbō'), town (pop. 2,681), Antioquia dept., N central Colombia, in Cordillera Central, 45 mi. NE of Medellín; alt. 4,872 ft.; coffee, sugar cane, rice, cacao, yucca, cattle; gold mining.

Yolyn (yō'lĭn), town (1940 pop. 245), Logan co., SW W.Va., 7 mi. SE of Logan; bituminous-coal area.

Yom River (yôm), one of headstreams of the Chao Phraya R., N Thailand, rises in Phi Pan Nam Mts., near Laos frontier, at 19°20'N 100°40'E, flows over 400 mi. S, past Phrae, Sawankalok (head of navigation), and Sukhothai, forming (in lower course) a common flood plain with Nan R. The combined stream joins Ping R. just above Nakhon Sawan to form the Chao Phraya.

Yona (yô'nyă), village (pop. 997) and municipality (pop. 1,386), SE Guam; coconut plantations.

Yonabaru (yōnä'bärōō), town (1950 pop. 6,573), on Okinawa, in the Ryukyus, 5 mi. E of Naha, on E coast; fishing port.

Yonago (yōnä'gō), city (1940 pop. 47,051; 1947 pop. 55,836), Tottori prefecture, SW Honshu, Japan, port on SE shore of lagoon Naka-no-umi, 60 mi. NNW of Okayama. Transportation center; tobacco factory, spinning mills; salted fish, soy sauce, sake. Ferry to Matsue.

Yonaguni-shima (yōnä'gōōnē-shĭmä) or **Yonakuni-shima** (–kōōnē–), westernmost island (□ 12; 1950 pop. 6,158) of Sakishima Isls., in Ryukyu Isls., lying bet. E.China Sea (N) and Philippine Sea (S), 70 mi. E of Formosa; 6 mi. long, 2.5 mi. wide. Generally low, rising to 750 ft.; volcanic; rice.

Yonaizawa (yōnī'zäwŭ), town (pop. 6,607), Akita prefecture, N Honshu, Japan, 19 mi. ESE of Noshiro; rice, silk cocoons.

Yonakuni-shima, Ryukyus: see YONAGUNI-SHIMA.

Yonan (yŭn'än'), Jap. *Enan*, town (1949 pop. 29,743), Hwanghae prov., central Korea, S of 38°N, 26 mi. ESE of Haeju, in gold-mining area. Near by are hot springs.

Yonava, Lithuania: see JONAVA.

Yoncalla (yônkă'lŭ), city (pop. 626), Douglas co., W Oregon, 33 mi. SSW of Eugene.

Yondó (yōndo'), village (pop. 220), Antioquia dept., N central Colombia, on Magdalena R. and 7 mi. SW of Barrancabermeja (Santander dept.). Site of petroleum field.

Yoneda (yōnā'dä), town (pop. 8,229), Hyogo prefecture, S Honshu, Japan, 7 mi. ESE of Himeji, in agr. area (tobacco, rice, wheat, flowers); raw silk, lumber.

Yonezawa (yōnā'zäwŭ), city (1940 pop. 48,816; 1947 pop. 55,344), Yamagata prefecture, N Honshu, Japan, 27 mi. SW of Yamagata; textile center (silk, rayon); soybean processing, woodworking. Hot springs near by.

Yongampo (yông'äm'pô), Jap. *Ryugampo*, township (1944 pop. 17,873), N.Pyongan prov., N Korea, at mouth of Yalu R., 12 mi. SSW of Sinuiju; port (ice-free) for Sinuiju; gold refining. Exports lumber, paper, agr. and marine products.

Yongchon (yŭng'chŭn'), Jap. *Eisen*, town (1949 pop. 26,638), N.Kyongsang prov., S Korea, 20 mi. ENE of Taegu; rail junction; soybeans, cotton.

Yongdong (yŭng'dông'), Jap. *Eido*, town (1949 pop. 21,387), N.Chungchong prov., S Korea, 22 mi. SE of Taejon, in agr. area (rice, wheat, soybeans, cotton). Gold is mined near by.

Yonghung (yŭng'hōōng'), Jap. *Eiko*, township (1944 pop. 18,445), S.Hamgyong prov., N Korea, 28 mi. SW of Hungnam; lumbering, stock raising, agr. (soybeans, grains, hemp). Graphite is mined near by.

Yonghung Bay, Jap. *Eiko-wan*, Korean *Yonghung-man*, inlet of E. Korea Bay, S.Hamgyong prov., N Korea, sheltered by 2 narrow peninsulas; c.10 mi. N-S, 8 mi. E-W. Wonsan is on S shore. Formerly sometimes called Port Lazarev.

Yongju (yŭng'jōō'), Jap. *Eishu*, town (1949 pop. 22,771), N.Kyongsang prov., S Korea, 65 mi. N of Taegu; agr. center (rice, soybeans, cotton, hemp, ramie); produces raw silk.

Yong Peng (yōng" pĕng'), town (pop. 1,678), W central Johore, Malaya, 15 mi. NE of Bandar Penggaram; iron and bauxite mining (SW).

Yong Sata or **Tanyong Sata** (tän'yōng' sŭtä'), Malay *Tanyong Star* (tän'yông' stär'), village (1937 pop. 1,944), Trang prov., S Thailand, minor port on W coast of Malay Peninsula, 25 mi. S of Trang.

Yongwol (yŭng'wŭl'), Jap. *Neietsu*, township (1946 pop. 12,763), Kangwon prov., central Korea, S of 38°N, on Han R. and 23 mi. NE of Chungju; anthracite mining.

Yonibana (yōnēbä'nä), town (pop. 2,700), Northern Prov., W central Sierra Leone, on railroad and 30 mi. NE of Bauya; palm oil and kernels, piassava, kola nuts. Has mission school.

Yonishkis, Lithuania: see JONISKIS.

Yonkers (yŏng'kŭrz), residential and mfg. city (pop. 152,798), Westchester co., SE N.Y., on E bank of the Hudson, in hilly region just N of the Bronx borough of New York city, of whose metropolitan area it is a part; carpet-, elevator-, and cable-mfg. plants; sugar refinery. Also makes hats, clothing, knit goods, chemicals, food products; printing. Ferry to Alpine, N.J. Yonkers is seat of Boyce Thompson Inst. for Plant Research and of St. Joseph's Seminary and Col. Here is a manor house (c.1682) of PHILIPSE MANOR. Tibbetts Brook Park (recreational center) and Empire City race track are here. Settled in land grant made (1646) by Dutch West India Company to Adriaen van der Donck; became part of Frederick Philipse's manor, which was chartered in 1693 and confiscated (1779) in the Revolution. Inc. as village in 1855, as city in 1872.

Yonne (yôn), department (□ 2,881; pop. 266,014), N central France, occupying parts of old Burgundy, Champagne, and Orléanais; ⊙ Auxerre. Abutting SE on the Morvan, it slopes gently toward Paris Basin; drained S-N by the navigable Yonne and its tributaries (Cure, Serein, Armançon). Predominantly agr., with central winegrowing belt (especially around CHABLIS) and calf-fattening region (W of Sens); wheat, oats, potatoes, sugar beets, apples (for cider). Numerous limestone and ocher quarries. Lignite deposits near Dixmont. Industries: paint and dye mfg., wood- and metal-working (agr. machines, cutlery), distilling. Important trade in wines and building materials. Chief towns: Auxerre, Sens, Avallon.

Yonne River, central and N central France, rises in the Morvan on N slope of Mont Beuvray, flows 182 mi. NNW, past Clamecy, Auxerre (head of navigation), Joigny, and Sens, to the Seine at Montereau-Faut-Yonne. Paralleled by Nivernais Canal bet. Corbigny and Auxerre. Picturesque course. Until 19th cent. extensively used for lumber floating. Receives Cure, Serein, and Armançon rivers (right). N terminus of Burgundy Canal at Laroche-Saint-Cydroine on the Yonne.

Yono (yō'nō), town (pop. 26,518), Saitama prefecture, central Honshu, Japan, just W of Omiya; agr. center (rice, wheat); raw silk.

Yonsanpo (yŭn'sän'pō'), Jap. *Eizanho*, town (1949 pop. 22,209), S.Cholla prov., Korea, 23 mi. NE of Mokpo; rice, cotton.

Yopuho, China: see YUPURGA.

Yorba Linda (yôr'bŭ lĭn'dŭ), village (1940 pop. 1,141), Orange co., S Calif., 10 mi. N of Santa Ana; oil fields; citrus-fruit and avocado groves, truck farms.

Yore River, England: see URE RIVER.

Yorii (yōrē'), town (pop. 12,401), Saitama prefecture, central Honshu, Japan, 11 mi. W of Kumagaya; wheat, raw silk, sake.

Yorishima (yōrē'shĭmä), town (pop. 8,887), Okayama prefecture, SW Honshu, Japan, on Hiuchi Sea, 21 mi. WSW of Okayama, in agr. area (rice, wheat, persimmons, peppermint); raw silk, sake.

Yorito (yōrē'tō), town (pop. 541), Yoro dept., N Honduras, in Sierra de Sulaco, on upper Aguán R. and 10 mi. SSW of Yoro; mfg. (palm hats, ceramics); coffee, tobacco.

York, municipality (pop. 1,623), SW Western Australia, 55 mi. E of Perth and on Avon R.; rail junction; agr. center (citrus fruit, grain).

York. 1 County (□ 3,545; pop. 36,447), W central N.B., extending NE from Maine border; ⊙ Fredericton. Drained by St. John R. 2 County (□ 882; pop. 951,549), S Ont., on L. Ontario; ⊙ Toronto.

York, town, Ont., former name of TORONTO.

York or **Yorkshire** (-shĭr), county (□ 6,079.7; 1931 pop. 4,389,679; 1951 census 4,516,362), NE England, largest English co.; ⊙ York. Bounded by Lincolnshire, Nottingham, and Derby (S), Cheshire (SW), Lancashire and Westmorland (W), Durham (N), and the North Sea (E). Drained by Ouse, Humber, Aire, Don, Calder, Derwent, Wharfe, Swale, and Tees rivers. The North Sea coast is rocky from Tees estuary to Flamborough Head; thence there is flat agr. land, including Holderness Peninsula. Behind the coast lie the Cleveland Hills and the Wolds, sheltering a central N–S valley, bounded W by the Pennines. The county is divided into the administrative areas of East Riding (□ 1,172; 1931 pop. 483,058; 1951 census 510,800), ⊙ Beverley; North Riding (□ 2,127.4; 1931 pop. 469,389; 1951 census 525,496), ⊙ Northallerton; and West Riding (□ 2,780.2; 1931 pop. 3,352,208; 1951 census 3,480,066), ⊙ Wakefield. York city, a co. of itself, is not included in any of the ridings. Important coal deposits in the West Riding (Doncaster, Wakefield, Rotherham), iron mining in Cleveland Hills, and some lead mining in the Pennines. Chief industries are woolen milling (Huddersfield, Bradford, Leeds, Halifax), steel mfg. (Sheffield, Rotherham, Redcar, Middlesbrough), cotton milling (near Lancashire border), leather, chemical, clothing, machinery industries. Other towns are Hull (chief port), Scarborough (resort), and Dewsbury. Highest elevation is Mickle Fell, in the Pennines.

York, anc. *Erboracum*, county borough (1931 pop. 84,813; 1951 census 105,336) and city, ⊙ Yorkshire, England, on Ouse R. at mouth of Foss R., 200 mi. N of London; 53°57'N 1°5'W. It is not included administratively in any of the 3 ridings of Yorkshire. Mfg. of chocolate and cocoa, leather, gloves, glass, machinery and other metal products, flour, beet sugar. York may have been an old Br. settlement. As Eboracum, it was chief station of the Br. province of the Roman Empire. The emperors Severus and Constantius Chlorus died here, and Constantine was crowned here. In 314 a bishop of York is mentioned, and in 7th cent. Paulinus, the 1st archbishop, was consecrated. York is ecclesiastical center of the north of England, 2d only to Canterbury in the Church of England. York was in 8th cent. one of the most famous centers of education in Europe. Alcuin, b. here c.735, became headmaster of St. Peter's School, now one of the oldest schools in England. In York are: Cathedral of St. Peter, commonly known as York Minster, dating from Saxon and Norman period; Abbey of St. Mary (Benedictine; dates from the 11th cent.); York Castle (13th cent.), with Clifford's Tower, near the river, on site of castle built by William the Conqueror in 1068; old city walls dating in part from Norman times, but mainly of 14th cent. (4 gates, including Micklegate and Monk Bar, remain); the Roman Multangular Tower; the medieval guildhall; St. William's Col. (1453); palace of the archbishops of York. Council of the North was established 1537 in York after suppression of the Pilgrimage of Grace; city was taken 1644 by Parliamentarians after battle of Marston Moor. In Second World War the town sustained air-raid damage, including the gutting of the guildhall.

York, town (1931 pop. 1,052), Sierra Leone colony, minor port on Sierra Leone Peninsula, 15 mi. S of Freetown; fishing. Platinum mining (N).

York. 1 County (□ 1,000; pop. 93,541), southernmost in Maine, bet. N.H. line and coast; ⊙ Alfred. Mfg. (textiles, wood products, shoes, machinery) at Biddeford and Saco; truck gardening, dairying, lumbering, fishing, food canning. Drained by Salmon Falls and Piscataqua (on N.H. line), Saco, Mousam, and Ossippee rivers. Summer resorts on coast and lakes. Oldest co. in state; named Yorkshire 1658; Cumberland and Lincoln counties set off 1670. 2 County (□ 577; pop. 14,346), SE Nebr.; ⊙ York. Agr. region drained by branches of Big Blue R. Livestock, grain, dairy and poultry produce. Formed 1870. 3 County (□ 914; pop. 202,737), S Pa.; ⊙ York. Mfg. and agr. area; bounded E by Susquehanna R., S by Md. Part of South Mtn. lies in NW. Apple orchards; limestone; mfg. (machinery, grist-mill products, textiles, shoes, metal products). Formed 1749. 4 County (□ 685; pop. 71,596), N S.C.; ⊙ York. Bounded W by Broad R., E by Catawba R., N by N.C.; contains lower end of Catawba L., formed by dam N of Rock Hill. Part of Kings Mtn. Natl. Military Park in NW. Fertile agr. area (cotton, grain, peaches), truck, poultry, dairy products; timber; mfg. (especially textiles) at Rock Hill and York and in mill villages. Formed 1785. 5 County (□ 123; pop. 11,750), SE Va.; ⊙ YORKTOWN, which is included in COLONIAL NATIONAL HISTORICAL PARK. In tidewater region, on NE (York R.) shore of peninsula bounded SW by James R., S by Hampton Roads, E by Chesapeake Bay. Truck farming, some general agr. (including tobacco), stock raising; fishing, oystering. Formed 1634.

York. 1 Town (pop. 1,774), Sumter co., W Ala., 25 mi. ENE of Meridian, Miss.; farm trade, lumbering; railroad repair shops. 2 Town (pop. 3,256), York co., SW Maine, on the coast NE of Kittery; its villages include York (formerly York Village), summer resorts York Beach and York Harbor. Settled 1624 as Agamenticus; chartered 1641 as Gorgeana, 1st English city chartered in America; inc. 1652 as York. Nearly destroyed (1692) in Indian wars. Many colonial bldgs.; stone jail (1653) is historical mus. Has pre-Revolutionary pile drawbridge, rebuilt 1933. 3 City (pop. 6,178), ⊙ York co., SE Nebr., 45 mi. W of Lincoln and on branch of Big Blue R.; trade center for farming region. Metal castings, bricks, agr. implements; serum, feed, dairy products, grain. York Col. and orphans' home here. State reformatory for women near by. Platted 1869, inc. 1872. 4 City (pop. 59,953), ⊙ York co., S Pa., on small Codorus Creek (kŭdô'rŭs) and 21 mi. SSE of Harrisburg; mfg. (refrigerating equipment, chains, building materials, agr. machinery, food products). Has a jr. col. Congress met here, 1777–78. Munitions center during Revolution. Occupied 1863 by Confederates. Laid out 1741, inc. as borough 1787, as city 1887. 5 Town (pop. 4,181), ⊙ York co., N S.C., 13 mi. WNW of Rock Hill; rail junction; processing center for agr. area; textiles, rugs, lumber and grain products. Winter home of a circus; a Gretna Green for N.C. Settled in 1750s.

York, Cape, northernmost point of Australia, in Torres Strait; forms N end of CAPE YORK PENINSULA, Queensland, and E side of entrance to Gulf of Carpentaria; 10°41'S 142°32'E. Rises to 372 ft.; densely wooded.

York, Cape, NW tip of Baffin Isl., E Franklin Dist., Northwest Territories, on Lancaster Sound, at N end of Prince Regent Inlet; 73°52'N 86°45'W.

York, Cape, NW Greenland, on Baffin Bay, at W end of Melville Bay; 75°54'N 66°25'W. A breeding center of the little auk, it is site of the Cape York meteorites, discovered by Peary, who brought largest (c.100) tons to Mus. of Natural History in New York. Site of monument (1932) to Peary.

Yorkana (yôrkă'nŭ), borough (pop. 229), York co., S Pa., 8 mi. E of York.

York Beach, Maine: see YORK.

Yorke Peninsula, S South Australia, bet. Spencer Gulf (W) and Gulf St. Vincent (E), N of Investigator Strait; 160 mi. long (from Cape Spencer to Port Pirie), 35 mi. wide; rises to 400 ft. S foot projects W. Regular coastline. Chief ports: Port Pirie, Wallaroo. Principally agr. area. Sometimes called Yorke's Peninsula.

Yorketown, town (pop. 555), S South Australia, on SE central Yorke Peninsula and 130 mi. SSW of Port Pirie; agr. center; salt; wheat, barley.

York Factory, village, NE Man., on Hudson Bay, at mouth of Hayes R., 140 mi. SE of Churchill; 57°1'N 92°20'W; Hudson's Bay Co. post. First post in region was established in late 17th cent. Site subsequently changed hands frequently bet. Great Britain and France; French post was called Fort Bourbon, British post Fort Nelson. Present post was built 1788–90.

York Harbor, resort village of York town, York co., SW Maine, NE of Kittery, at mouth of York R.

York Haven, borough (pop. 743), York co., S Pa., 10 mi. N of York and on Susquehanna R.

York Island (1931 pop. 706), Sierra Leone colony, in Sherbro R. E of Sherbro Isl., off Bonthe; 2 mi. long, 1 mi. wide. Part of Bonthe harbor.

Yorklyn, village (pop. c.400), New Castle co., N Del., 5 mi. NW of Wilmington; makes snuff, vulcanized fiber. Annual trapshooting tournament held here.

York River. 1 In SW Maine, tidal stream flowing c.6 mi. SE to the Atlantic at York Harbor. 2 In E Va., estuary (1–2½ mi. wide) receiving Pamunkey and Mattaponi rivers at West Point and running 40 mi. SE to Chesapeake Bay 17 mi. N of Newport News. Navigable; trade in lumber, wood products; shellfishing. Yorktown, other historic places are on its banks.

Yorkshire, England: see YORK, county.

Yorkshire, village (pop. 142), Darke co., W Ohio, 17 mi. NNE of Greenville, in agr. area; makes tile.

York Sound, inlet of Timor Sea, NE Western Australia, bet. Montague Sound (E) and Brunswick Bay (W); 20 mi. long, 10 mi. wide; leads into Prince Frederick Harbour (30 mi. long, 5 mi. wide). Bigge Isl. near entrance.

York Springs, borough (pop. 413), Adams co., S Pa., 23 mi. SSW of Harrisburg; orchards.

Yorkton, city (pop. 5,714), SE Sask., on Yorkton R. and 110 mi. ENE of Regina; railroad and distributing center for E Sask., with grain elevators; lumbering, tanning, dairying, brick mfg. S of city are York, Roussay, Leech, and Crescent lakes.

Yorktown. 1 Town (pop. 1,109), Delaware co., E central Ind., on West Fork of White R. and 6 mi. W of Muncie, in agr. area. 2 Town (pop. 146), Page co., SW Iowa, 7 mi. W of Clarinda, in agr. region. 3 Town (pop. 2,596), De Witt co., S Texas, 33 mi. WNW of Victoria; trade, shipping center in agr. area; ships livestock, packed poultry; cotton ginning, cottonseed- and peanut-oil milling, dairying; hatcheries. Laid out 1848, inc. 1871. 4 Historic town (pop. 384), ⊙ York co., SE Va., on York R. and 11 mi. ESE of Williamsburg. Scene of Cornwallis's surrender after Yorktown Campaign at end of the Revolution, town is included in COLONIAL NATIONAL HISTORICAL PARK (hq. here). Points of interest: restored customhouse (built c.1706); Grace Church (1697); Moore house, where Cornwallis's surrender was negotiated; Yorktown Monument (1881); natl. cemetery (2.91 acres; established 1866). Settled 1631; laid out 1691; became an important port of entry before the Revolution. Besieged and taken (1862) by Federals in Peninsular Campaign of Civil War.

Yorktown Heights, residential village (1940 pop. 1,076), Westchester co., SE N.Y., 8 mi. E of Peekskill, in apple- and peach-growing area.

York Village, Maine: see YORK.

Yorkville. 1 Village (pop. 632), ⊙ Kendall co., NE Ill., on Fox R. (bridged here) and 10 mi. SW of Aurora, in rich agr. area; ships grain. 2 District of N Manhattan borough of New York city, SE N.Y., lying approximately bet. 72d and 96th streets E of 3d Ave. 3 Village (pop. 3,528), Oneida co., central N.Y., on Mohawk R. and the Barge Canal, just W of Utica. Henry Inman b. here. Settled before 1800, inc. 1902. 4 Village (pop. 1,854), on Jefferson-Belmont co. line, E Ohio, on Ohio R. and 7 mi. N of Wheeling, W.Va.; steel mills.

Yoro (yō'rō), department (□ 4,030; 1950 pop. 108,569), N Honduras; ⊙ Yoro. Bounded SW by Sulaco and Comayagua rivers, W by Ulúa R.; Sierra de Nombre de Dios on N border; drained by Aguán R. Largely mountainous, except for Sula (W) and Olanchito (E) valleys, which are major banana zones. Agr. in highlands (coffee, sugar cane, grain), livestock. Hardwood, especially mahogany) lumbering; palm-hat mfg., sugar milling, ceramics. Main centers: Yoro (in highlands), Progreso and Olanchito (in banana zones; served by plantation railroads). Formed 1825.

Yoro, city (pop. 1,471), ⊙ Yoro dept., N Honduras, 70 mi. N of Tegucigalpa; 15°8'N 87°8'W; alt. 1,837 ft. Commercial center in agr. area; coffee, tobacco, stock; sugar milling, ceramics. Has city hall, market, R.C. church. Airfield. First mentioned 1684.

Yoroberikunda (yōrō"bĕrĕkōōn'dä), village (pop. 482), MacCarthy Isl. div., central Gambia, on left bank of Gambia R. and 3 mi. SSE of Georgetown; dairying, butter making. Also Yoro-Beri-Kunda.

Yoron-jima (yōrō'-jĭmä), island (□ 8; 1950 pop. 8,141) of isl. group Amami-gunto, in Ryukyu Isls., lying bet. E.China Sea (W) and Philippine Sea (E), 13 mi. N of Okinawa; 3.5 mi. long, 3 mi. wide. Rice, wheat, raw silk, livestock; fishing.

Yöröö Gol, Mongolia: see IRO RIVER.

Yoruba (yô'rōōbä), name referring to a former native state in W Africa (now in SW Nigeria) inhabited by the predominantly Moslem Yorubes, who speak a Sudanic language. Pop. is concentrated in large urban centers such as Lagos, Ibadan, Iwo, Ede, Oyo, Oshogbo, Ogbomosho.

Yose (yō'sä), town (pop. 3,190), Kanagawa prefecture, central Honshu, Japan, 9 mi. WSW of Hachioji; wheat, raw silk.

Yosemite National Park (yōsĕ'mĭtē) (□ 1,182.8; established 1890), E central Calif., on W slope of Sierra Nevada, c.150 mi. E of San Francisco. Spectacular mtn. region with deep canyons, towering peaks and cliffs, lofty waterfalls, many lakes, parklike meadows, and enormous trees. Outstanding feature is Yosemite Valley (7 mi. long, average width 1 mi.; ½ mi. deep) of Merced R.; valley is steep-walled U-shaped canyon formed by glaciation and stream erosion. Prominent summits overlooking valley (all more than 3,000 ft. above valley floor) are Liberty Cap (7,072 ft.), Taft Point (7,503 ft.), Profile Cliff (7,503 ft.), North Dome (7,531 ft.), El Capitan (ĕl kăpĭtăn') (7,564 ft.; precipitous cliff on N side of valley), Basket Dome (7,602 ft.), Eagle Peak (7,773 ft.), Sentinel Dome (8,117 ft.), Half Dome (8,852 ft.; huge split monolith with 2,000-ft. vertical face), Clouds Rest peak (9,929 ft.), Cathedral Rocks and adjoining Cathedral Spires, which overlook valley opposite El Capitan. Park's world-famous cataracts are formed by small streams falling into Yosemite Valley over rims of hanging tributary valleys; they are Upper Yosemite Fall (1,430 ft.) and Lower Yosemite Fall (320 ft.), with total drop, including intermediate cascades, of 2,425 ft.; Ribbon Fall (1,612 ft.), one of highest single cataracts in world; Silver Strand Fall (1,170 ft.), Bridalveil Fall (620 ft.), Nevada Fall (594 ft.), Illilouette Fall (ĭ"lĭlōō-ĕt') (370 ft.), and Vernal Fall (317 ft.). Best view is obtained from Glacier Point, 3,254 ft. above valley floor. Other features of scenic interest are Tuolumne Meadows (tōō-ŏ'lŭmē) (alt. c.8,600 ft.; 10 mi. long, 2 mi. wide), in E, and Grand Canyon of the Tuolumne (1 mi. deep in places), extending E–W across N half of park and including HETCH HETCHY VALLEY, which is overlooked by Hetch Hetchy Dome (6,200 ft.) in W. There are 3 groves of sequoia trees (*Sequoia gigantea*): Merced and Tuolumne groves, in W, and Mariposa Grove (with 200 trees, including famous tunnel tree, Wawona, through which an opening 11 ft. wide and 8 ft. high has been cut), in S. Chief peaks are on or near E boundary, extending along crest of Sierra Nevada; highest are Mount Dana, 13,055 ft., and Mount Lyell (lī'ŭl), 13,095 ft. Facilities for winter sports in SW at Badger Pass. Year-round tourist accommodations; c.700 mi. of trails. John Muir Trail extends SE to Mt. Whitney, in Sequoia Natl. Park.

Yoshanichka Banya, Yugoslavia: see JOSANICKA BANJA.

Yoshida (yō'shĭdä). **1** Town (pop. 9,542), Aichi prefecture, central Honshu, Japan, on Atsumi Bay, 13 mi. SSW of Okazaki; fishing port. **2** Town (pop. 9,565), Ehime prefecture, W Shikoku, Japan, on Hoyo Strait, 4 mi. NNW of Uwajima; agr. center (sweet potatoes, wheat); vegetable wax, raw silk. Exports oranges, raw silk, cattle. Fishery. **3** Town (pop. 4,836), Hiroshima prefecture, SW Honshu, Japan, 23 mi. NE of Hiroshima; sake, floor mats, charcoal; raw silk. **4** Town (pop. 9,447), Niigata prefecture, central Honshu, Japan, 6 mi. NW of Sanjo; rice, raw silk, charcoal. **5** Town (pop. 4,974), Saitama prefecture, central Honshu, Japan, 4 mi. NW of Chichibu; lumbering, agr. (rice, wheat), raw-silk production. **6** Town, Shimane prefecture, Japan: see MASUDA. **7** Town, Yamanashi prefecture, Japan: see SHIMO-YOSHIDA.

Yoshihama (yōshē'hämŭ), town (pop. 5,406), Kanagawa prefecture, central Honshu, Japan, on Sagami Sea, 8 mi. SSW of Odawara; potatoes, wheat.

Yoshii (yōshē'). **1** Town (pop. 6,089), Fukuoka prefecture, N central Kyushu, Japan, 14 mi. E of Kurume; rice, wheat, barley. **2** Town (pop. 9,464), Gumma prefecture, central Honshu, Japan, 5 mi. SSW of Takahashi; wheat, rice, raw silk. **3** Town (pop. 6,427), Okayama prefecture, SW Honshu, Japan, 10 mi. NNE of Fukuyama, in agr. area (rice, wheat, peppermint); raw silk, charcoal, sake.

Yoshikawa (yōshē'käwŭ), town (pop. 7,322), Saitama prefecture, central Honshu, Japan, 11 mi. E of Urawa; rice, wheat, raw silk.

Yoshino (yōshē'nō). **1** Town (pop. 1,127), Kanagawa prefecture, central Honshu, Japan, 10 mi. WSW of Hachioji; wheat, raw silk. **2** Town (pop. 5,567), Nara prefecture, S Honshu, Japan, on N central Kii Peninsula, 22 mi. S of Nara; rice, wheat, raw silk; medicine. In Yoshino-kumano Natl. Park; known for cherry blossoms. Sometimes spelled Yosino.

Yoshino-kumano National Park, Japan: see KII PENINSULA.

Yoshino River (yōshē'nō), Jap. *Yoshino-gawa*, largest river of Shikoku, Japan; rises in mts. SE of Saijo in Ehime prefecture; flows 146 mi. generally ENE, past Motoyama, Ikeda, Mino, and Waki, to Kii Channel at Tokushima; wide delta mouth. Drains agr. area.

Yoshioka (yōshē'ōkä), town (pop. 5,094), Miyagi prefecture, N Honshu, Japan, 13 mi. N of Sendai; rice; horse breeding.

Yoshitomi, Japan: see HIGASHI-YOSHITOMI.

Yoshiwara (yōshē'wärŭ), town (pop. 31,152), Shizuoka prefecture, central Honshu, Japan, 22 mi. NE of Shizuoka, in rice-growing area; textiles.

Yoshkar-Ola, Russian SFSR: see IOSHKAR-OLA.

Yosi or **Yo-hsi** (both: yō'shē), town, ⊙ Yosi co. (pop. 195,950), SW Anhwei prov., China, 32 mi. S of Hwoshan, in Tapieh Mts.; rice, tea, tung oil, lacquer; vegetable-tallow processing (soap, candles). Sometimes written Yüehsi (or Yüeh-hsi).

Yosino, Japan: see YOSHINO, Nara prefecture.

Yösön Bulag, Mongolia: see YUSUN BULAK.

Yost, town (pop. 107), Box Elder co., NW Utah, near Idaho line, 90 mi. WNW of Logan.

Yosu (yŭ'sōō'), Jap. *Reisui*, town (1949 pop. 60,251), S.Cholla prov., S Korea, port on inlet of Korea Strait, 75 mi. WSW of Pusan, on small peninsula; fishing center. Rice refineries, boatyards, rubber-goods factories. Exports rice, raw silk, fish, edible seaweed.

Yotala (yōtä'lä), town (pop. c.3,960), ⊙ Oropeza prov., Chuquisaca dept., S central Bolivia, on Potosí-Sucre RR and 8 mi. S of Sucre, in agr. area (wheat, barley, vegetables, fruit). Sometimes called Villa Oropeza.

Yotaú (yōtäōō'), village (pop. c.500), Santa Cruz dept., E central Bolivia, 65 mi. WNW of Concepción; cotton. Mission.

Yotoco (yōtō'kō), town (pop. 1,622), Valle del Cauca dept., W Colombia, near Cauca R., 7 mi. WSW of Buga; coffee, tobacco, sugar cane, fruit, livestock.

Yotoku, Korea: see YANGDOK.

Yotsing (yō'chĭng'), Mandarin *Lotsing* or *Lo-ch'ing* (both: lō'chĭng'), town (pop. 10,162), ⊙ Yotsing co. (pop. 363,177), SE Chekiang prov., China, 20 mi. ENE of Wenchow, on Yotsing Bay (sheltered by Yühwan isl.) of E.China Sea; rice, wheat, tea, cotton.

Yotsukura (yōtsōōkōō'rä), town (pop. 9,744), Fukushima prefecture, central Honshu, Japan, on the Pacific, 6 mi. NE of Taira; rice growing, fishing; cement making.

Youbou (yōō'bō), village (pop. estimate 250), SW B.C., on S Vancouver Isl., on Cowichan L., 25 mi. WNW of Duncan; lumbering.

Youghal (yôl), Gaelic *Eochaill*, urban district (pop. 4,809), SE Co. Cork, Ireland, on Youghal Bay of the Atlantic, at mouth of the Blackwater, 28 mi. E of Cork; 51°57'N 7°50'W; fishing port and seaside resort, noted also for its mfg. of fine lace and earthenware. Features are the Clock Gate (1771) and the parish church, incorporating part of collegiate church founded 1464. Myrtle Grove, here, was residence (1584–97) of Sir Walter Ralegh, who traditionally here planted 1st potato in Ireland. Town, of anc. origin, was chartered 1209 by King John and later became stronghold of the Fitzgeralds. It suffered siege during 1579 Desmond rebellion; in 1641 it was fortified by the earl of Cork; and in 1649 it was visited by Cromwell. Just N of Youghal are ruins of Dominican North Abbey (1268); there are no remains of the Franciscan South Abbey (1224). Near-by St. John's Abbey (remains), founded in 14th cent., was converted into munitions depot under Charles II. Entrance to Youghal harbor is marked by lighthouse.

Youghiogheny River (yŏkŭgā'nē), in W.Va., Md., and Pa., rises in Preston co., W.Va. at Backbone Mtn., near W border of Md.; flows c.135 mi. NNW, past Connellsville, Pa., to Monongahela R. at McKeesport; navigable for c.20 mi. above mouth. Youghiogheny Dam (184 ft. high, 1,610 ft. long; completed 1944; for flood control, pollution abatement) impounds Youghiogheny Reservoir above Confluence, Pa. Somerfield, Pa., where there was a famous pioneer ford, was inundated by reservoir.

Youkounkoun (yōōkōōnkōōn'), village (pop. c.700), N Fr. Guinea, Fr. West Africa, at N foot of Fouta Djallon massif, near Senegal border, 50 mi. NNE of Gaoual; peanuts, rubber; cattle. R.C. mission; customhouse.

Young, municipality (pop. 4,656), S central New South Wales, Australia, 80 mi. NW of Canberra; fruitgrowing and agr. center. Gold mines near by.

Young, village (pop. 352), S central Sask., 45 mi. SE of Saskatoon; grain elevators, lumbering, dairying.

Young, county (□ 899; pop. 16,810), N Texas; ⊙ Graham. Drained by Brazos R., here receiving its Clear Fork and tributary creeks; includes part of Possum Kingdom L. Agr. (wheat, cotton, grain sorghums, oats, barley, fruit, truck); dairying, livestock (cattle, poultry, horses, sheep, hogs). Oil, natural-gas fields; clay, sand; large coal deposits (some mining). Processing, mfg. at Graham, Olney, Newcastle. Formed 1856.

Young, town (pop. 2,500), Río Negro dept., W Uruguay, in the Cuchilla de Haedo, on highway and railroad, and 50 mi. NE of Fray Bentos; trade and shipping center; cattle raising.

Young America, village (pop. 365), Carver co., S central Minn., 35 mi. WSW of Minneapolis; corn, oats, barley, potatoes, livestock, poultry.

Young Harris, town (pop. 450), Towns co., NE Ga., 37 mi. NW of Toccoa, in the Blue Ridge. Jr. col. and agricultural experiment station here.

Young Island (19 naut. mi. long, 5 naut. mi. wide), Antarctica, off Victoria Land; one of the Balleny Isls.; 66°25'S 162°30'E. Rises to 4,000 ft. Discovered 1839 by John Balleny, Br. sealer.

Young's Island, islet off S St. Vincent, B.W.I., facing Calliaqua, 2 mi. SE of Kingstown. Quarantine station.

Youngstown, village (pop. 235), SE Alta., 30 mi. ESE of Hanna; railroad junction; grain elevators, flour mills; stock.

Youngstown. 1 Village (pop. 932), Niagara co., W N.Y., on Niagara R. near its mouth on L. Ontario, and 25 mi. N of Buffalo. U.S. coast guard station here. Just N is Fort NIAGARA (restored). **2** City (□ 33; pop. 168,330), on Mahoning-Trumbull co. line, NE Ohio, on Mahoning R., near Pa. line, and 55 mi. NNW of Pittsburgh. It is one of largest U.S. pig-iron and steelmaking centers, and heart of a metropolitan dist. (1940 pop. 372,428; 1947 pop. estimate 380,897) which includes steel-milling cities of the Mahoning and Shenango valleys (Warren, Niles, Campbell, Struthers, and Girard, Ohio; Sharon and Farrell, Pa.; and other communities). City also produces fabricated steel, bronze and other metal products, electrical equipment, motor vehicles, rubber tires, furniture, coke, chemicals, cement. Limestone quarries. Seat of Butler Art Inst. and Youngstown Col. Founded 1797; local coal and iron resources were used early in 19th cent.; city grew rapidly after opening (1839) of Pennsylvania-Ohio Canal and coming of railroad (1853). Steel plants were established in 1890s; city's present steelmaking importance is result of its favorable location for utilization of L. Superior iron ore, Appalachian coal. **3** Borough (pop. 577), Westmoreland co., SW central Pa., just SSE of Latrobe.

Youngsville. 1 Village (pop. 769), Lafayette parish, S La., 10 mi. S of Lafayette; cotton ginning, sugar refining. **2** Resort village, Sullivan co., SE N.Y., 7 mi. W of Liberty; dairying. **3** Town (pop. 619), Franklin co., N central N.C., 19 mi. NNE of Raleigh; sawmilling. **4** Borough (pop. 1,944), Warren co., NW Pa., 8 mi. W of Warren and on branch of Allegheny R.; furniture, mirrors, bricks; oil wells. Settled 1795.

Youngwood, borough (pop. 2,720), Westmoreland co., SW Pa., 25 mi. SE of Pittsburgh; scientific instruments; railroad shops. Inc. 1902.

Yountville (yount'vĭl), village (1940 pop. 517), Napa co., W Calif., 7 mi. NNW of Napa. State veterans' home and state game farm near by.

Yovkovo (yôf'kôvô), village (pop. 473) Stalin dist., E Bulgaria, on Provadiya R. and 14 mi. W of Stalin; rail junction; winegrowing, horticulture.

Yoyang (yō'yäng'). **1** Town, ⊙ Yoyang co. (pop. 415,656), NE Hunan prov., China, on Tungting L. and on short canal linking it with Yangtze R., 85 mi. NNE of Changsha, and on railroad; commercial port; exports rice, wheat, tea, tung oil. Opened to foreign trade in 1899. Until 1913 called Yochow. Sometimes written Yüehyang. Yangtze port of Chenglingki is 5 mi. NE. **2** Town, Shansi prov., China: see ANTSEH.

Yoyema (yōyĕ'mä), village (pop. 150), South-Western Prov., SW Sierra Leone, on railroad and 4 mi. W of Moyamba; palm oil and kernels, piassava.

Yozgat (yôzgät'), province (□ 5,291; 1950 pop. 323,-506), central Turkey; ⊙ Yozgat. On SE are Ak Mts. Drained by Delice and Cekerek rivers. Well forested. Produces lead, gum tragacanth, mohair, wool, grain.

Yozgat, town (1950 pop. 12,032), ⊙ Yozgat prov., Turkey, 105 mi. E of Ankara, in a mtn. valley; alt. 4,360 ft.; wheat, barley, mohair goats, horses.

Ypacaraí or **Ypacaray** (ēpäkäräē'), town (dist. pop. 9,140), La Cordillera dept., S central Paraguay, near S shore of L. Ypacaraí, on railroad and 28 mi. ESE of Asunción; trading, mfg., and agr. center (tobacco, cotton, fruit, livestock); cotton ginning, tobacco processing, tanning; ceramics, glass, and soap mfg. Founded 1887. Agr. school near by.

Ypacaraí, Lake, S Paraguay, 18 mi. E of Asunción; 12 mi. long NW–SE, 2–4 mi. wide; pleasure resort. Navigable for small craft. San Bernardino on E shore. Along the lake, fossils of primitive men have been found.

Ypané (ēpänā'), town (dist. pop. 5,384), Central dept., S Paraguay, 15 mi. SE of Asunción, in agr. area (rice, bananas); vegetable-oil mfg. Founded 1538.

Ypané River, E central Paraguay, rises in Sierra de Amambay (Brazil border), flows c.150 mi. SW, along San Pedro and Concepción dept. border, past Tacuatí and Belén, to Paraguay R. 5 mi. S of Concepción; navigable for c.20 mi. Many cataracts on its upper course.

Ypati, Greece: see HYPATE.

Ypé-jhú (ēpā'-hōō', ŭpā'-hō'), town (dist. pop. 1,780), Caaguazú dept., E central Paraguay, in Cordillera de Mbaracayú, on Brazil border, 170 mi. NE of Asunción; lumber, maté.

Ypiranga, Brazil: see IPIRANGA.

Ypoá, Lake (ēpwä'), S Paraguay, 40 mi. SSE of Asunción, largest in Paraguay; 28 mi. long NE–SW. Irregular, narrowing to a few hundred yards and widening to 10 mi. Navigable for small craft. The name Ypoá is sometimes restricted to its N part, while its central part is called Laguna Paranamí and its S part Laguna Verá.

Yporanga, Brazil: see IPORANGA.

Yport (ēpôr'), village (pop. 1,569), Seine-Inférieure dept., N France, on English Channel, 3 mi. SW of Fécamp; resort and fishing port.

Ypres (ē'prù; colloquially, in First World War, wī'pŭrz), Flemish *Ieper* (ē'pŭr), town (pop. 17,073), West Flanders prov., W Belgium, 30 mi. SSW of Bruges; textile industry; agr. market. Textile center in Middle Ages; importance declined in 16th cent. Frequently besieged in 16th, 17th, and 18th cent. Site of 3 major battles (1914, 1915, 1917) in First World War, when town was almost entirely destroyed; since rebuilt. American Memorial near by commemorates fighting.

Ypsilanti (ĭpsĭlăn'tē), city (pop. 18,302), Washtenaw co., SE Mich., 30 mi. WSW of Detroit and on Huron R. Industrial, commercial, and farm-trade center; mfg. (paper, stoves, aircraft and auto parts, foundry products, ladders, tents, awnings, clothing, chemicals). Huge WILLOW RUN plant is near. Ypsilanti is seat of Mich. State Normal Col. and a business col. Many Indian trails crossed this site, and an Indian village and a Fr. trading post (1809–c.1819) were located here. Settled 1823; inc. as village 1832, as city 1858.

Ypsilon Mountain, Colo.: see MUMMY RANGE.

Yr Eifel, Wales: see NEVIN.

Yreka (wīrē'kŭ) or **Yreka City,** town (pop. 3,227), ⊙ Siskiyou co., N Calif., in valley bet. Klamath Mts. (W) and Cascade Range (E), near Oregon line, in agr., mining, and resort area; alt. c.2,600 ft. Hq. for Klamath Natl. Forest. Boomed as gold-mining town of Shasta Butte City in 1851; renamed 1852; inc. 1857.

Ysabel, Solomon Isls.: see SANTA ISABEL.

Ysabel Channel, Bismarck Archipelago, SW Pacific, bet. Mussau (N) and Lavongai (S); 50 mi. wide.

Ysceifiog (ŭskīv'yôg), agr. village and parish (pop. 1,040), Flint, Wales, 4 mi. SWof Holywell.

Ysel River, Netherlands: see IJSSEL RIVER.

Yser River (ēzâr'), N France and W Belgium, rises 5 mi. NNE of Saint-Omer, flows ENE across Nord dept., then in an arc across W Flanders prov. to North Sea 2 mi. below Nieuport; 48 mi. long. Connects network of canals. Ger. advance on Calais was stopped along Yser R. in 1914.

Ysleta (ĭslĕ'tŭ), village (pop. 4,782), El Paso co., extreme W Texas, 10 mi. SE of El Paso, near the Rio Grande; port of entry and shipping point in irrigated farm area. Oldest settlement in state; founded near mission (modern mission bldg. on its site) established 1681 or 1682 by refugees from Pueblo revolt in N.Mex.

Ysselmeer, Netherlands: see IJSSELMEER.
Ysselmonde, Netherlands: see IJSSELMONDE.
Yssel River, Netherlands: see IJSSEL RIVER.
Ysselstein, Netherlands: see IJSSELSTEIN.
Yssingeaux (ēsē-zhō'), town (pop. 2,695), Haute-Loire dept., S central France, 13 mi. ENE of Le Puy; road center and agr. market; lumber trade; mfg. of silk ribbons, lace, and agr. tools.
Ystad (ü'städ), city (1950 pop. 13,002), Malmohus co., S Sweden, Baltic seaport, 35 mi. ESE of Malmo; steel milling, milk canning; mfg. of machinery, furniture, soap. Bathing beach just E. Has 12th-cent. church of St. Mary, 13th-cent. church of St. Peter, 14th-cent. town hall, and remains of 14th-cent. Franciscan monastery. Founded in 12th cent., city was known to Hanseatic merchants for its herring fisheries. Burned (1569) by Charles IX.
Ystalyfera (ŭstăluvĕ'rä), town in Llangiwg (lăng-gē'ōōg) parish (pop. 21,350), NW Glamorgan, Wales, on Tawe R. and 7 mi. N of Neath; coal-mining center.
Ystradgynlais (ŭstrădgŭn'līs), town in parish of Ystradgynlais Lower (pop. 10,099), SW Brecknock, Wales, 9 mi. NNE of Neath; coal mining. Near by are caves with stalagmites and stalactites.
Ystradgynlais Higher, Wales: see GLYNTAWE.
Ystrad Mynach (ŭ'străd mŭ'näkh), town (pop. 5,838) in Caerphilly urban district, E Glamorgan, Wales, on Rhymney R.; coal mining.
Ystrad Rhondda, Wales: see RHONDDA.
Ystradyfodwg, Wales: see RHONDDA.
Ystwyth River or **Ystwith River** (ŭst'wĭth), Cardigan, Wales, rises 8 mi. WSW of Llanidloes, flows 25 mi. SW and NW to Cardigan Bay of Irish Sea at Aberystwyth.
Ytapé, Paraguay: see ITAPÉ.
Ythan River, (ī'thŭn), Aberdeen, Scotland, rises 7 mi. E of Huntly, flows 35 mi. SE, past Fyvie, Methlick, Ellon, and Newburgh, to the North Sea just SE of Newburgh.
Ytre Arna (üt'rü är'nä), village (pop. 1,678) in Haus canton, Hordaland co., SW Norway, on Sor Fjord, 2 mi. W of Haus; textile mill.
Ytre Sandsvaer, Norway: see HVITTINGFOSS.
Ytteran (ü'tŭrōn"), Swedish *Ytterån*, village (pop. 608), Jamtland co., W central Sweden, on NW shore of Stor L., 18 mi. NW of Ostersund; lumbering, dairying; hydroelectric station.
Ytú, Brazil: see ITU.
Ytyk-Kel or **Ytyk-Kel'** (ĭtĭk"-kyôl'), village (1948 pop. over 500), E Yakut Autonomous SSR, Russian SFSR, 140 mi. ENE of Yakutsk, in agr. area; livestock raising. Formerly spelled Ytyk-Kyuyel.
Yü, China: see YÜ RIVER.
Yu or **Yuu** (both: yōō), town (pop. 6,393), Yamaguchi prefecture, SW Honshu, Japan, on Iyo Sea, 8 mi. S of Iwakuni; commercial center for agr. area.
Yüan 1 River, Hunan prov., China: see YÜAN RIVER. **2** River, Kiangsi prov., China: see YÜAN RIVER. **3** River, Yunnan prov., China: see RED RIVER.
Yüanan (yüăn'ăn'), town (pop. 12,957), ⊙ Yüanan co. (pop. 110,562), W central Hupeh prov., China, 30 mi. NNE of Ichang; rice, wheat near by.
Yüan-chiang, town, China: see YÜANKIANG.
Yüan Chiang. 1 River, Hunan prov., China: see YÜAN RIVER. **2** River, Yunnan prov., China: see RED RIVER.
Yüanchow. 1 Town, Hunan prov., China: see CHIHKIANG. **2** Town, Kiangsi prov., China: see ICHUN.
Yüan-chü, China: see YÜANKÜ.
Yüankiang or **Yüan-chiang** (both: yüăn'jyăng'). **1** Town, ⊙ Yüankiang co. (pop. 294,685), N Hunan prov., China, on Tungting L. at Tzu R. delta, 65 mi. NW of Changsha; rice, wheat, beans, corn, cotton. Fisheries. **2** Town, ⊙ Yüankiang co. (pop. 83,271), S Yunnan prov., China, on right bank of Red R. and 110 mi. SW of Kunming, and on road to Burma; medicinal plants, indigo, timber, rice, sugar cane.
Yüan Kiang. 1 River, Hunan prov., China: see YÜAN RIVER. **2** River, Yunnan prov., China: see RED RIVER.
Yüankü or **Yüan-chü** (both: yüăn'jü'), town, ⊙ Yüankü co. (pop. 61,917), S Shansi prov., China, on Yellow R. and 55 mi. E of Anyi, at Honan-Pingyuan border; cotton weaving; millet, wheat, beans.
Yüanli (yüăn'lē'), Jap. *Enri* (ăn'rē), town (1935 pop. 7,287), NW Formosa, on W coast, 13 mi. SW of Miaoli, and on railroad; rice, wheat, sweet potatoes.
Yüanlin (yüăn'lĭn'), Jap. *Inrin* (ēn'rēn), officially **Taichung** (dī'jōōng'), town (1935 pop. 10,869), W central Formosa, on railroad and 14 mi. SW of Taichung; agr. center (oranges, pineapples, bananas, rice, sugar cane); pineapple canning.
Yüanling (yüăn'lĭng'), town, ⊙ Yüanling co. (pop. 391,820), NW Hunan prov., China, on Yüan R. and 90 mi. SW of Changteh. Gold and tin mining near by. Until 1913 called Shenchow.
Yüanmow or **Yüan-mou** (both: yüăn'mō'), town, ⊙ Yüanmow co. (pop. 42,239), N central Yunnan prov., China, 60 mi. NW of Kunming, near Yangtze R. (Sikang border); alt. 4,101 ft.; cotton-textiles; tung-oil processing; rice, millet, beans, peanuts.
Yüan River (yüăn'). **1** Chinese *Yüan Kiang* or *Yüan Chiang* (both: yüăn' jyăng'), river in NW Hunan prov., China, rises in W Kweichow prov., flows 540 mi. E and NE, past Chenyüan (head of navigation), Kienyang, and Yüanling, to Tungting L. below Changteh. Rapids above Changteh restrict navigation to small vessels. Valley is a major Hunan-Kweichow trade route. **2** Chinese *Yüan Shui* (yüăn' shwā'), river in W Kiangsi prov., China, rises E of Pingsiang, flows 120 mi. ENE, past Ichun and Sinyü, to Kan R. near Tsingkiang.
Yüanshan (yüăn'shăn'), town (pop. 7,592), ⊙ Yüanshan co. (pop. 137,125), NW Kiangsi prov., China, near Fukien line, 20 mi. SSW of Shangjao, in the Bohea Hills; tea, rice, wheat, beans, cotton; mfg. of bamboo and straw paper. Anthracite mining near by.
Yüanshih (yüăn'shû'), town, ⊙ Yüanshih co. (pop. 151,179), SW Hopeh prov., China, 20 mi. S of Shihkiachwang and on Peking-Hankow RR; wheat, kaoliang, millet.
Yüan Shui. 1 River, Kiangsi prov., China: see YÜAN RIVER. **2** River, Kwangtung prov., China: see CHENG RIVER.
Yüanwu (yüăn'wōō'), town, ⊙ Yüanwu co. (pop. 68,406), SW Pingyuan prov., China, 22 mi. SSW of Sinsiang, near Yellow R. (Honan line); wheat, rice, kaoliang, beans. Until 1949 in Honan prov.
Yuasa (yōōä'sä), town (pop. 13,555), Wakayama prefecture, S Honshu, Japan, port on Kii Channel, on W Kii Peninsula, 13 mi. S of Wakayama; agr. center (rice, citrus fruit); fishery; mfg. (drugs, cotton textiles, soy sauce). Exports fish.
Yuba (yōō'bŭ), county (□ 638; pop. 24,420), N central Calif.; ⊙ Marysville. Extends NE from Feather R. through Sacramento Valley to lower W slope of the Sierra Nevada; also drained by Yuba and Bear rivers. Includes parts of Plumas and Tahoe natl. forests. Gold dredging. Orchards (peaches, pears, grapes, figs, prunes, olives, nuts); farming (hops, rice, barley and other grain, alfalfa, truck), dairying, stock raising (cattle, sheep, hogs, poultry). Pine, fir, cedar timber. Mining of platinum and silver, quarrying of sand and gravel. Hunting, fishing. Formed 1850.
Yuba, village (pop. 119), Richland co., S central Wis., on Pine R. and 14 mi. N of Richland Center, in dairying region.
Yuba City, town (pop. 7,861), ⊙ Sutter co., N central Calif., in Sacramento Valley, on Feather R., opposite Marysville; trade, shipping, and processing center (canned and dried fruit, especially peaches; wine, dairy products, vegetables, rice). Laid out 1849, town boomed in the gold rush; inc. 1878.
Yuba Pass, Sierra co., NE Calif., highway pass (alt. 6,700 ft.) across the Sierra Nevada, E of Downieville.
Yubara, Japan: see YUHARA.
Yubari (yōō'bärē), city (1940 pop. 64,998; 1947 pop. 82,123), W central Hokkaido, Japan, 32 mi. E of Sapporo; coal-mining center in mtn. area drained by Ishikari R. Principal center of important Yubari (or Ishikari) coal field (□ c.770), a narrow belt 50–60 mi. long.
Yuba River (yōō'bŭ), N central Calif., formed in Sierra Nevada foothills c.30 mi. NE of Marysville by junction of the North Yuba (c.55 mi. long) and the Middle Yuba (c.45 mi. long), flows c.35 mi. SW, through Upper Narrows Reservoir, to Feather R. just SW of Marysville. Receives South Yuba R. (c.55 mi. long) in lower course. In South Yuba R. are: L. Spaulding (3 mi. long), formed by Lake Spaulding Dam (275 ft. high, 800 ft. long; completed 1919; for power); and L. Van Norden (1½ mi. long), impounded by power dam near Norden. Upper Narrows Dam on lower course is 260 ft. high and 1,142 ft. long; completed 1941 for debris control. North Yuba R. is site of New Bullards Bar Dam and reservoir of CENTRAL VALLEY project, replacing Bullards Bar Dam (completed 1924). River and headstreams yielded much gold after 1848.
Yubdo (yōōb'dō), Ital. *Iubdo*, town (pop. 2,000), Wallaga prov., W central Ethiopia, in Birbir valley, on road and 25 mi. WSW of Gimbi; 8°56'N 35°26'E; major placer mining (platinum, gold).
Yubi, Cape, Sp. West Africa: see JUBY, CAPE.
Yucaipa (yōōkī'pŭ), village (pop. 1,515), San Bernardino co., S Calif., in foothills of San Bernardino Mts., 15 mi. ESE of San Bernardino; apples, truck, poultry.
Yucatan (yōō"kŭtăn', yōō'kŭtăn"), Sp. *Yucatán* (yōōkätän'), state (□ 14,868; 1940 pop. 418,210; 1950 pop. 515,256), on N Yucatan Peninsula, SE Mexico; ⊙ MÉRIDA. Bordering N on Gulf of Mexico, it is bounded by Campeche (W and SW) and Quintana Roo (SE and E). It consists entirely of lowlands made up of porous limestone formations, except for narrow ridge in SW. Long narrow bars, separated from mainland by channel called El Río or La Ciénaga, extend along its coast. Though entirely devoid of rivers, it has ample water from subterranean wells. Tropical climate, relieved by cool breezes; has rainy season (May–August). Covered by abundant forests, with savannas in drier NW; forests yield dyewood and hardwood. Principal industry is cultivation and preparation of henequen (sisal), processed principally at Mérida and exported mainly from the port of Progreso, mostly to the U.S. Produces also corn, rice, beans, sugar cane, chicle, tobacco, coffee, tropical fruit, chili, indigo. Turtle and sponge fishing along the coast. The region was settled by Mayas as early as the 6th cent. and the remarkable ruins of CHICHÉN ITZÁ and UXMAL bear witness to their cultural achievements. Yucatan became a state in 1821, but was in state of secession 1839–43. It was the scene of violent Indian uprisings (1847 and 1910). Quintana Roo was established 1902 as a separate territory.
Yucatan Channel, strait bet. Yucatan and Cuba, connecting Gulf of Mexico and Caribbean Sea; 135 mi. wide (W–E) bet. Cape Catoche (Mexico) and Cape San Antonio (Cuba).
Yucatan Peninsula (□ c.70,000), mostly in SE Mexico, separating the Caribbean from the Gulf of Mexico. Comprises states of Yucatan and Campeche, territory of Quintana Roo, British Honduras, and part of Petén, Guatemala. Almost entirely a low, flat, limestone tableland, rising to c.500 ft. at the interior drainage basin of Petén. To the N and W the plain continues as the Campeche Bank, stretching under shallow water c.150 mi. from the low, sandy shoreline. N part of E coast of the peninsula rises in low cliffs, and S part is indented by bays and paralleled by isls. and cays. Short, transverse ranges of hills cross the peninsula at scattered intervals. The only rivers are those flowing E and NW from Petén. In N half of the tableland, where rainfall is light and absorbed by the porous limestone, water for the inhabitants, who are predominantly Mayan, and for livestock comes from underground rivers and wells (*cenotes*) and surface pools (*aguadas*). Cold winds blow from the N in winter, and the land has the tropical dry and rainy seasons (Aug.–Sept.); but generally in N the climate is hot and dry, and in S hot and humid. Most of the N half, though covered with only a few inches of subsoil, is one of the most important henequen-raising regions of the world. The territory of Quintana Roo is a chicle-growing center. The uncultivated area lies under a dense growth of scrub, cactus, sapote wood, and mangrove thickets. Corn, sugar cane, tobacco, cotton, and coffee are also grown. Magnificent forests of mahogany, cabinet woods, vanilla, rubber, logwood, and dyewood are in SW Campeche, Petén, and British Honduras; and this area teems with tropicopolitan life—from jaguar, armadillo, and iguana to the ocellated turkey, which is found nowhere else in the world. Centuries before the Spanish came Yucatan was the seat of a great civilization having its origin in Guatemala. Probably the first white men to arrive were the survivors of a Sp. caravel that foundered off Jamaica in 1511. Later (1524–25) Cortés made his epic march across the base of the peninsula to Honduras. Francisco Fernández de Córdoba had already led an expedition of discovery in 1517, skirting the coast from Cape Catoche to the Bay of Campeche. The following year Juan de Grijalva explored the same coast. The conquest of the Maya was begun 1527 by Francisco de Montejo but was not completed until 1546, when his son, Francisco the younger, crushed the revolt of a coalition of Mayan tribes.
Yucay (yōōkī'), town (pop. 2,303), Cuzco dept., S central Peru, on Urubamba R. and 19 mi. NNW of Cuzco; agr. center (cereals, potatoes). There are anc. Inca remains.
Yucca House National Monument (yŭ'kŭ) (9.6 acres established 1919), SW Colo., 10 mi. SW of Cortez. Ruins of pre-Columbian Indian village.
Yücheng or **Yü-ch'eng** (yü'chŭng'). **1** Town, ⊙ Yücheng co. (pop. 161,927), NE Honan prov., China, 20 mi. NE of Shangkiu, on Pingyuan line; rice, wheat, millet, beans. **2** Town, ⊙ Yucheng co. (pop. 226,000), NW Shantung prov., China, 30 mi. NW of Tsinan and on Tientsin-Pukow RR; grain, peanuts.
Yü-ch'i and **Yu-ch'i**, China: see YUKI; YUKI.
Yü-chiang, town, China: see YÜKIANG.
Yü Chiang, river, China: see YÜ RIVER.
Yü-ch'ien, China: see YÜTSIEN.
Yüchih or **Yü-ch'ih** (both: yü'chû'), Jap. *Gyochi* (gyō'chē), village (1935 pop. 2,605), W central Formosa, 23 mi. SE of Taichung; black tea, bananas, rice; lumber, bamboo. Jihyüeh L. is S.
Yü-ch'ing, China: see YÜKING.
Yüchow. 1 Town, Chahar prov., China: see YÜHSIEN. **2** Town, Chekiang prov., China: see YÜTSIEN. **3** Town, Honan prov., China: see FANGCHENG.
Yüchung (yü'jōōng'), town, ⊙ Yüchung co. (pop. 82,889), SE Kansu prov., China, 25 mi. SE of Lanchow; tobacco processing; gold deposits. Until 1912 called Kinhsien; and 1912–19, Kincheng.
Yucuyácua, Cerro (sĕ'rō yōōkwëä'kwä), peak (11,076 ft.) in Oaxaca, S Mexico, in Sierra Madre del Sur, 60 mi. W of Oaxaca.
Yudino (yōō'dyĭnŭ). **1** City, Kurgan oblast, Russian SFSR: see PETUKHOVO. **2** Town (1932 pop. estimate 3,680), W Tatar Autonomous SSR, Russian SFSR, near Volga R., on railroad and 8 mi. W of Kazan; metalworking center.
Yue (yōō'ä), town (pop. 7,788), Nagasaki prefecture, W Kyushu, Japan, on S Hizen Peninsula, 19 mi. NE of Nagasaki, on inlet of the Ariakeno-umi; agr. center (rice, wheat, soybeans).

Yüeh-, for Chinese names beginning thus and not found here: see under Yo-.
Yüeh, province, China: see CHEKIANG; KWANGTUNG.
Yüeh, river, China: see CANTON RIVER.
Yüeh Chiang, China: see CANTON RIVER.
Yüeh-hsi, China: see YOSI.
Yüeh Kiang, China: see CANTON RIVER.
Yüehlaichen, Manchuria: see HWACHWAN.
Yüehsi. 1 (yüĕ'shē') Town, Anhwei prov., China: see YOSI. **2** or **Yüehsui** (yüĕ'swā'), town, ⊙ Yüehsi co. (pop. 70,975), SE Sikang prov., China, 55 mi. NNE of Sichang; trades in cotton cloth, tobacco, wine, salt. Until 1938 in Szechwan.
Yüehyang, China: see YOYANG, Hunan prov.
Yüen-, for Chinese names beginning thus and not found here: see under YÜAN-.
Yug (yŏŏk), town (1926 pop. 7,357), S central Molotov oblast, Russian SFSR, 20 mi. S of Molotov; woodworking, leather products. Until 1943, Yugovskoi or Yugovskoi Zavod.
Yug, river, Russian SFSR: see YUG RIVER.
Yuganets (yŏŏgŭnyĕts'), town (1946 pop. over 500), W Gorki oblast, Russian SFSR, near Volodary.
Yugawara (yōōgä'wärŭ), town (pop. 9,824), Kanagawa prefecture, central Honshu, Japan, 9 mi. SW of Odawara; wheat, sweet potatoes. Hot springs.
Yuge (yōō'gā), town (pop. 4,534), Okayama prefecture, SW Honshu, Japan, 18 mi. N of Okayama, in agr. area (rice, wheat, persimmons); charcoal, raw silk, sake.
Yugodzyr or **Yegüüdzer** (both: yŭ'gŭdzĕr), village, Sukhe Bator aimak, SE Mongolian People's Republic, on road, and 160 mi. SSE of Choibalsan, near China line; coal mining. Formerly called Chonoin Gol.
Yugo-Kamski or **Yugo-Kamskiy** (yōō"gŭ-käm'skē), town (1926 pop. 3,807), W central Molotov oblast, Russian SFSR, near Kama R., 7 mi. E of Okhansk; metalworking center; mfg. of agr. machinery. Until 1929, Yugokamski Zavod.
Yugo-Osokino (–ŭsô'kēnŭ), village (1926 pop. 5,328), S central Molotov oblast, Russian SFSR, 33 mi. ENE of Osa; lumbering; wheat, rye, clover, livestock. Sometimes called Yugo-Osokinskoye.
Yugor Peninsula (yōōgôr'), N European Russian SFSR, bet. Barents and Kara seas; separated from Vaigach Isl. by strait Yugorski Shar. Pai-Khoi mtn. range in center.
Yugorski Shar or **Yugorskiy Shar** (–skē shär"), strait joining Barents and Kara seas, Russian SFSR, bet. Vaigach Isl. (N) and Yugor Peninsula (S); 25 mi. long, 5 mi. wide. Khabarovo village on S shore. Also called Yugor Strait.
Yugoslavia (yōō"gōslä'vēŭ, –slă'vēŭ), Serbo-Croatian *Jugoslavija* (yōō"gōslä'vēä) [=land of the South Slavs], federal republic (□ 99,069; 1948 pop. 15,751,953), SE Europe, on the Adriatic, largest country of the Balkans, occupying NW part of the peninsula; ⊙ BELGRADE. Borders on 7 countries: NW on Italy and the Free Territory of TRIESTE, N on Austria and Hungary, E on Rumania and Bulgaria, S on Greece and Albania. One of the physiographically and ethnically most complex of countries, it consists under 1946 constitution of 6 "people's republics" corresponding roughly to the old historic divisions (for detailed information on history and economy see separate articles on these units): SERBIA (E), ⊙ Belgrade; CROATIA (N and W), ⊙ ZAGREB; SLOVENIA (N), ⊙ LJUBLJANA; BOSNIA AND HERZEGOVINA (W), ⊙ SARAJEVO; MACEDONIA (S), ⊙ SKOPLJE; MONTENEGRO (S central), ⊙ TITOGRAD (formerly called Podgorica). VOJVODINA territory (⊙ NOVI SAD) and Kosovo-METOHIJA oblast (⊙ PRISTINA) represent autonomous sections in N and SW Serbia respectively. SLAVONIA and DALMATIA survive as regional concepts within Croatia. Serbia, Croatia, Slovenia, Macedonia, and Bosnia and Herzegovina are administratively divided into oblasts since 1949. With an Adriatic coast line paralleling that of the Italian peninsula for c.450 mi., mountainous Yugoslavia is crossed NW–SE by the densely wooded, calcareous DINARIC ALPS, which tower above the picturesque Dalmatian littoral. Beyond the rugged ridges, among the most inhospitable of the continent, covering more than ⅓ of entire area, lie in the NE the fertile Danubian lowlands, contiguous with the Alföld and Banat of Hungary. In this region are the principal centers of pop., and here the bulk of crops and livestock of predominantly agr. Yugoslavia is raised. Thus the country is oriented at least as much towards the Balkan interior as towards its maritime frontage on the Adriatic. Communication bet. the coast and the transmontane plain is still inadequate. In the N are spurs of the Alps, among them the KARAWANKEN and JULIAN ALPS. Triglav Peak (c.9,395 ft.), in the Julians, is country's highest summit. The KARST is in NNW, the jumbled NORTH ALBANIAN ALPS in S. The BALKAN MOUNTAINS of Bulgaria enter SE. Heavily forested (beech, oak, fir)—c.30% of Yugoslavia is wooded—these ranges yield much timber for export, and their mineral riches are enormous. Livestock is grazed on the slopes. Only the river valleys and the depressions or *polyes*—such as that of Kosovo—are agriculturally productive, while the low peneplains of the S, e.g., ZETA plain of Montenegro and the Macedonian Vardar R. valley (S section of the great Morava-Vardar furrow), grow all kinds of Mediterranean and even subtropical crops (tobacco, cotton, figs, olives, sesame, poppy, citrus, etc.). More favorable conditions prevail in the maritime region of ISTRIA and Dalmatia, a land of a mild, equable climate, unsurpassed in scenic beauty. Some of the parallel ridges split off near here in numerous enchanting isls., such as Krk, Cres, Brac, Hvar, Korcula. Along the coast are many ports and resorts, some famed since antiquity and once disputing the sway of Venice, among them RIJEKA (Fiume), OPATIJA (Abbazia), CRIKVENICA, ZADAR (Zara), SIBENIK, SPLIT, DUBROVNIK (Ragusa), KOTOR, BUDVA, ULCINJ. Fishing (sardines, tunny, lobster) is highly developed, and there are canneries. Shipyards at Rijeka, Split, and Dubrovnik service Yugoslavia's merchant fleet. Of the rivers flowing to the Adriatic, only the navigable NERETVA RIVER (used for hydroelectric power) is of importance. All major streams of Yugoslavia (apart from the Vardar, which flows to the Aegean) drain to the Black Sea as tributaries of the great Danube, a primary shipping route traversing the NE for c.370 mi. These are the SAVA RIVER, DRAVA RIVER, MORAVA RIVER, and TISZA RIVER. The agr. heartland in the fork of these rivers has a rigorous continental climate with cold winters and hot summers, sometimes harassed by droughts. About ⅔ of Yugoslavia's arable land—an estimated 60% of total area—is planted with cereals, chiefly corn and wheat, followed by barley, oats, and rye; also rice, potatoes, onions, beans, peas, peppers, and other vegetables. Industrial crops include tobacco, grapes, sugar beets, hemp, flax, hops, sunflowers, cotton, sesame, rape, chicory. Fruitgrowing—plums, apples, pears, walnuts, chestnuts, etc.—is important for foreign trade, as is the growing of medicinal and aromatic plants (camomile, thyme, wormwood, salvia). The brandies and wines, particularly Dalmatian red wines, are held in high repute. Yugoslavia is a notable stock-breeding country whose livestock (cattle, sheep, hogs, horses), meat, dairy products, and eggs are a valuable export in normal times. Both sericulture and apiculture are widely practised. From its rich mineral resources few of the minerals used in modern industry are lacking. Economically most prominent are bauxite (Istria, BAR), lead (TREPCA, MEZICA, LITIJA), antimony (PODRINJE), mercury IDRIJA), copper (BOR, MAYDANPEC), and zinc (Kosovo valley). There are scattered iron mines (VARESH, LYUBIYA, PRIEDOR SANSKI, MOST, TOPUSKO), coal and lignite (RASA, SIVERIC, FRUSCA GORA, ARANDJELOVAC, KOSTOLAC, TRBOVLJE), petroleum (DONLJA LENDAVA, MEDRUMURJE, TUZLA, BUJAVICA, GOILO), natural gas (Bujavica, Goilo), sulphur (KRAPINA); also magnesite, chromite, pyrite, molybdenum, silver, gold, asphalt, gypsum, limestone, marble, granite, salt. The country abounds in spas, e.g., VRNJACKA BANJA, VRANJSKA BANJA, KOVILJACA in Serbia; Topusko, LIPIK, DARUVAR, VARAZDIN in Croatia; LASKO, RIMSKE TOPLICE, DOBRNA, ROGASKA SLATINA, SLATINA RADENCI in Slovenia. Lake resorts such as BLED are internationally renowned, as are the grottoes of POSTOJNA (Adelsberg) in the Karst. Among other lake dists. dotting the countryside are those of the large border lakes SCUTARI, OHRID, and PRESPANA; high in the mts. are the lakes PLITVICE, DURMITOR, and TRIGLAV. The great hydroelectric potential has been increasingly developed since 1947. Industrialization has also made great progress, but processing industries still take the lead. These are concentrated in the chief trading and administrative centers: Belgrade, a key to the Balkans, turning out electrical equipment, machine tools, automobiles, and aircraft (ZELEZNIK, RAKOVICA, and ZEMUN suburbs); Zagreb, the republic's progressive 2d city, with a famous fair; Ljubljana, on railroad from Trieste; SUBOTICA and Novi Sad in Tisza plain; NIS (Nish), a Balkan rail center with repair shops; MARIBOR on Zagreb-Vienna RR, mfg. of automobiles; OSIJEK, chief city of Slavonia, with petroleum refinery; KRAGUJEVAC, economic and cultural center of the SUMADIJA, with munition plants; semi-oriental Sarajevo, renowned for its jewelry and carpets; Skoplje, Macedonian tobacco and cigarette capital; CETINJE, former ⊙ Montenegro. There are metallurgical plants at VALJEVO, SMEDEREVO, PALANKA, SISAK, Tuzla, and KRUSEVAC. Cement made at Split and other centers has become a major export, but textiles, iron and steel products, vehicles, machinery, and coal still have to be imported. Though the country lost, during Second World War, 86% of its rolling stock and more than half of its bridges, its communication system has made great strides. To its existing railroad net (4,315 mi.) 645 mi. were added bet. 1946 and 1948. There are universities at Belgrade, Zagreb, Ljubljana, and Skoplje. New medical schools were installed at Sarajevo and Skoplje. The Yugoslav people consist of roughly 4 groups—the Serbs (43%), Croats (34%), Slovenes (7%), and Macedonians (7%); the remaining minorities are chiefly Rumanians, Albanians (concentrated in Kosovo-Metohija), Germans, Bulgarians, Czechoslovaks, Turks, Italians, and Ruthenians. Linguistically, the 4 natl. groups are very closely related, but historic, cultural, and religious factors have long kept them apart and still cause tensions and rivalries. There are 3 official Slav languages, Slovene, Macedonian, and Serbo-Croat. The latter is the lingua franca, but Serbs print in Cyrillic characters, while the more westernized Croats prefer the Latin alphabet, as do the Slovenes. A majority (47%) belong to Orthodox Eastern Church. The Catholics (36%) are mostly in Croatia, the Moslems (11%) in Bosnia and Herzegovina. After the First World War, which broke out here as an immediate result of the assassination of Austrian Archduke Francis Ferdinand (June 28, 1914) at Sarajevo, modern Yugoslavia emerged as a separate state. Of the country's 6 components only Serbia (which then included the Yugoslav part of Macedonia) and Montenegro were independent kingdoms. Croatia, Slovenia, and Bosnia and Herzegovina belonged to the Austro-Hungarian Monarchy. On Dec. 4, 1918, the "Kingdom of Serbs, Croats, and Slovenes," to be headed by Serbia, was formally proclaimed. Its name was changed to Yugoslavia in 1929. Recognized (1919) by the Paris Peace Conference, its territory was enlarged at the expense of Austria and Hungary. Fiume or Rijeka, seized (1919) by an Italian free corps under d'Annunzio, caused friction with Italy, which also claimed the Dalmatian coast, while Yugoslav nationalists demanded on ethnic grounds parts of Venezia Giulia, including Trieste. Dissension of the different Slav sections who were refused autonomous rights was a permanent cause of internal turmoil, and led King Alexander to establish (1929) a personal dictatorship. Troubles with Croatian and Macedonian nationalists continued, culminating (1934) in Alexander's assassination at Marseilles. His infant son Peter II succeeded him under the regency of Prince Paul, who pursued the same policy, though gradually drifting into the Axis camp. In March, 1941, Yugoslavia signed a pact with the Axis powers, but 2 days later a bloodless coup d'état ousted the regent. The new govt. repudiated the treaty. The country was promptly invaded (April, 1941) by German troops, assisted by Bulgarian, Hungarian, and Italian forces to share the spoils. Though organized resistance was broken within a week, the Yugoslavs continued a heroic guerrilla war. The Germans set up a Croatian puppet state. Dalmatia, Montenegro, and Slovenia were divided among Italy, Hungary, and Germany. Serbian Macedonia was awarded to Bulgaria, while Serbia itself became a German-controlled satellite. Peter II and his ministers established a govt. in exile in London, whilst the irregulars, entrenched in the mtn. strongholds, stiffened their resistance. Most important among these were at first the *Chetniks* under Mikhailovich, but in 1942 the "Army of National Liberation" under the Communist Josip Broz (Tito) was organized in Bosnia and had gained the upper hand by 1943. Tito's spectacular successes won him eventually the support of Great Britain. In Sept., 1944, Russian and Allied forces made contact with the guerrillas and by late Oct. the Germans had been expelled from Yugoslavia, which had lost during the hostilities more than 10% of its people, besides suffering great material losses. Tito, who became premier in March, 1945, won the Nov., 1945, elections. The constitutional assembly of the same year proclaimed a "Federal People's Republic," largely modeled along Soviet lines. Wide autonomy was granted to the 6 newly created republics, though actual political power was vested in Tito and the Communist People's Front, a coalition of all "legal" parties. The Allied peace treaty (1947) with Italy awarded Yugoslavia the eastern part of VENEZIA GIULIA, the Dalmatian town of Zadar with adjacent isls., and PELAGRUZ ISLANDS (Pelagosa) in central Adriatic Sea. Trieste, also claimed by Yugoslavia, became a free territory. Marshal Tito's regime seemed initially in close harmony with the USSR, towards which its economy was oriented. The newly created *Cominform* had its hq. in Belgrade. A 5-year plan was inaugurated in 1947. Opposition of religious and political groups was crushed mercilessly. In summer of 1948 a breach bet. the Yugoslav and Russian Communist parties came into the open. Tito accused Russia of trying to dominate Yugoslavia, while the USSR accused him of reactionary heresies. Consequently relations with Russia, Hungary, Rumania, Bulgaria, and Albania became increasingly strained. Yugoslavia sought a rapprochement with the Western powers, without, however, altering its domestic policy. For further information see individual entries on regions, physical features, towns, and cities.
Yugovskoi, Russian SFSR: see YUG, town.
Yug River (yōōk'), N European Russian SFSR, rises in the Northern Urals NE of Nikolsk, flows S, W, and generally N, past Nikolsk (head of navigation; 190 mi. above mouth), Kichmengski Gorodok, and Podosinovets, joining Sukhona R. at Veliki Ustyug to form Lesser Northern Dvina R.; 305 mi. long.
Yühang (yü'häng'), town (pop. 12,795), ⊙ Yühang co. (pop. 112,619), N Chekiang prov., China, 14 mi. W of Hangchow; mfg. of silk, paper; trade in bamboo, timber.

Yuhara (yōōhä'rä) or **Yubara** (–bä'rä) town (pop. 5,158), Okayama prefecture, SW Honshu, Japan, 18 mi. NW of Tsuyama; hot-springs resort; agr. (rice, wheat, persimmons); charcoal, sake.

Yü-hsiang, China: see YÜSIANG.

Yühsien (yü'shyĕn'). **1** Town, ⊙ Yühsien co. (pop. 299,358), S Chahar prov., China, 70 mi. SSW of Kalgan; coal-mining center; cattle raising; trades in wool, furs, beans, ramie, buckwheat. Called Yüchow until 1913. Until 1928 in Chihli (Hopeh). **2** Town, ⊙ Yühsien co. (pop. 392,040), N Honan prov., China, on Ying R. and 45 mi. SSW of Chengchow; porcelain mfg.; medicinal herbs, grain. **3** Town, ⊙ Yühsien co. (pop. 196,196), E Shansi prov., China, 25 mi. NW of Pingting; wheat, corn, kaoliang.

Yuhsien (yō'shyĕn'), town, ⊙ Yuhsien co. (pop. 325,436), E Hunan prov., China, 50 mi. ENE of Hengyang; rice, wheat.

Yühwan or **Yü-huan** (both: yü'hwän'), main town (pop. 8,768) of Yühwan isl. (pop. 191,765) in East China Sea, SE Chekiang prov., China, off Yotsing and 35 mi. ENE of Wenchow; mfg. (furniture, paper umbrellas); fisheries, saltworks. Yühwan isl. shelters Yotsing Bay (W).

Yui (yōō'ē), town (pop. 13,861), Shizuoka prefecture, central Honshu, Japan, on N shore of Suruga Bay, adjacent to Kambara, 8 mi. NE of Shimizu; seaside resort. Orange orchards.

Yukamenskoye (yōōkä'myĭnskŭyŭ), village (1939 pop. under 500), NW Udmurt Autonomous SSR, Russian SFSR, 25 mi. SW of Glazov; flax.

Yükan (yü'gän'), town (pop. 13,112), ⊙ Yükan co. (pop. 244,785), N Kiangsi prov., China, 50 mi. E of Nanchang, near SE shore of Poyang L.; rice, cotton, indigo, ramie. Coal, kaolin deposits.

Yukhmachi (yōōkhmŭchē'), village (1926 pop. 1,574), S Tatar Autonomous SSR, Russian SFSR, 37 mi. SE of Kuibyshev; grain, livestock.

Yukhnov (yōōkh'nŭf), city (1926 pop. 2,032), NW Kaluga oblast, Russian SFSR, on Ugra R. and 40 mi. WNW of Kaluga; metalworks, sawmilling, veneering. Chartered 1777.

Yüki or **Yü-ch'i** (both: yü'chē'). **1** Town, N Anhwei prov., China, 10 mi. NNW of Wuhu, across Yangtze R.; terminus of Hwainan RR from Tienkiaan. **2** Town (pop. 6,106), ⊙ Yüki co. (pop. 117,862), E central Yunnan prov., China, 50 mi. SSW of Kunming; alt. 5,449 ft.; cotton-weaving center; iron smelting; rice, wheat, millet, beans. Until 1913 called Sinsing; and 1913–16, Siuna.

Yuki or **Yu-ch'i** (both: yō'chē'), town (pop. 4,273), ⊙ Yuki co. (pop. 147,678), central Fukien prov., China, 30 mi. S of Nanping and on the Yu Ki (tributary of Min R.); rice, sweet potatoes, wheat.

Yuki (yōō'kē). **1** Town (pop. 4,852), Hiroshima prefecture, SW Honshu, Japan, 20 mi. NNW of Fukuyama; commercial center for livestock, rice-growing area; sake, *konnyaku* (paste made from devil's tongue), charcoal, raw silk. **2** Town (pop. 21,289), Ibaraki prefecture, central Honshu, Japan, 10 mi. SE of Tochigi; agr. center (rice, wheat, pears, gourds); silk and cotton textiles.

Yuki, Korea: see UNGGI.

Yükiang or **Yü-chiang** (both: yü'jyäng'), town (pop. 10,811), ⊙ Yükiang co. (pop. 121,097), E central Kiangsi prov., China, 60 mi. ESE of Nanchang and on Kwangsin R.; rice, indigo. Coal and kaolin deposits. Until 1914 called Anjen.

Yü Kiang, river, China: see YÜ RIVER.

Yüking or **Yü-ch'ing** (both: yü'chĭng'), town (pop. 4,118), ⊙ Yuking co. (pop. 72,162), E Kweichow prov., China, 80 mi. NE of Kweiyang; cotton weaving, tung-oil processing; rice, wheat, tea, tobacco.

Yukon (yōō'kŏn), territory (land area □ 205,346, total □ 207,076; 1941 pop. 4,914; 1948 estimate 8,000), NW Canada, bet. Alaska and the Northwest Territories, bordered S by British Columbia and touching N on Beaufort Sea of the Arctic Ocean; ⊙ Dawson. A plateau region, it slopes NE from St. Elias Mts. at Alaska line; near S end of Alaska border is Mt. Logan (19,850 ft.), highest peak of Canada. Other high mts. in this region are mts. St. Elias (18,008 ft.), Lucania (17,150 ft.), King (17,130 ft.), Steele (16,439), and Wood (15,880). E and S parts of territory are crossed by the Mackenzie and Pelly mtn. ranges of the Rocky Mts. S Yukon is drained by Yukon R. system (Pelly, Lewes, Teslin, Stewart, and Klondike rivers); N Yukon by Peel R. of Mackenzie R. system. Largest lakes are Teslin, Kluane, Aishihik, Kusawa, Laberge, and Frances lakes. Territory has arctic climate, with long, cold winters, and short warm summers, when there are sometimes 24 hours of sunshine a day. Average summer temp. at Dawson is 50–60°F.; mean Jan. temp. is -21°F. Average annual precipitation is 9-13 inches per year. Lowest temperature for territory (-81°F.) was recorded (Feb., 1947) at Snag. Some grain and root crops are grown; dairying and truck gardening are carried on near large settlements. Fur trade and fishing are important. Mining (gold, silver, lead, coal) is primary industry; gold mining is centered on Klondike region, scene of the gold rush of 1897–98. Besides Dawson, Whitehorse (terminus of railroad from Skagway) is only other town. Villages and trading posts are Carcross, Forty Mile, Old Crow, Fort Selkirk (established 1848 by Hudson's Bay Co.), Mayo Landing, and Keno Hill. SW portion of territory is served by Alaska Highway, and air transportation is important. Yukon R. system is major highway below Whitehorse. The area was an unorganized part of the Northwest Territories until 1895; Yukon-Alaska border was defined by treaty (1825) bet. Great Britain and Russia. Yukon Territory, organized 1895 within Northwest Territories, was placed under separate administration (1898) when the Klondike gold rush, resulting from discovery of gold at Bonanza Creek (Aug. 17, 1896), was at its height (1901 pop. of Yukon, 27,219). W border was fixed (1903) by the Alaska Boundary Tribunal. During Second World War Yukon was important link on the Northwest Staging Route; Whitehorse became a center of the *Canol* oil-supply project (oil refinery, pipeline terminal). Several new airfields were built. *Canol* project was closed down, 1945. Alaska Highway has opened new commercial and tourist transportation route.

Yukon. 1 City (pop. 1,990), Canadian co., central Okla., 13 mi. WNW of Oklahoma City, in agr. area; flour-milling center; cotton ginning, dairying. Laid out 1891. **2** Village (pop. 1,099), Westmoreland co., SW Pa., 9 mi. SW of Greensburg.

Yukon Flats, E Alaska, series of channels and adjoining swamp region in Yukon R., roughly bet. Circle and Fort Yukon; c.60 mi. long, c.20 mi. wide.

Yukon River, Yukon and Alaska, one of the longest rivers of North America. Its headstreams rise at B.C. line, but Yukon proper is formed by confluence of Pelly and Lewes (upper Yukon) rivers at Fort Selkirk (Yukon); flows N past Dawson (c.½ mi. wide here), and turns NW, flowing past Forty Mile, crossing into Alaska to Fort Yukon, thence W and SW, past Stevens, Tanana, Kokrines, Ruby, Galena, Koyukuk, Nulato, Kaltag, Anvik, Holy Cross, and Pilot Station, to the Bering Sea, which it enters through several channels (only one of which is navigable) near Hamilton and Akulurak. It is 1,979 mi. long to head of Nisutlin R., near B.C. border, including Teslin and Lewes rivers; length in Alaska is 1,265 mi. Its chief tributaries are White, Stewart, Klondike, Porcupine, Innoko, Koyukuk, Tanana, and Chandalar rivers. Whitehorse (c.1,700 mi. upstream), on Lewes R., is head of navigation. Lower course was explored (1836–37) by Glazunov and (1843) by Zagoskin; in 1843 Robert Campbell explored upper reaches of river. During 1897–98 Klondike gold rush it was a major transportation route to Dawson gold-mining region.

Yuksekkum, Turkey: see KOYCEGIZ.

Yuksekova (yüksĕ'kôvä), Turkish *Yüksekova*, village (pop. 1,212), Hakari prov., SE Turkey, 29 mi. E of Hakari; grain. Formerly Gevar and Dize.

Yukuhashi (yōōkōō'-hä'shē) or **Yukubashi** (–bä'shē), town (pop. 15,675), Fukuoka prefecture, N Kyushu, Japan, 14 mi. SE of Yawata; rail junction; commercial center for rice, wheat, barley area.

Yuldybayevo (yōōldĭbī'ŭvŭ), village (1939 pop. over 500), S Bashkir Autonomous SSR, Russian SFSR, in the S Urals, on Sakmara R. and 25 mi. SW of Baimak; lumbering.

Yule Island, small island off Papua coast of SE Guinea, 90 mi. NW of Port Moresby; coconut plantations. R.C. mission at Kairuku.

Yüli (yü'lē'), Jap. *Tamazato* (tämä'zätō), town (1935 pop. 5,500), E central Formosa, 45 mi. SW of Hwalien and on railroad; lignite, copper mining; rice, sugar cane, camphor, camphor oil, coffee.

Yülin (yü'lĭn'). **1** Town, Kwangsi prov., China: see WATLAM. **2** Town, S Hainan, Kwangtung prov., China, on S coast, 135 mi. SSW of Kiungshan, on land-locked Yülin Bay (5 mi. wide, 6 mi. long). Visited 1904 by Russian fleet on route to Tsushima Strait. With near-by SAMA, it was developed by Japanese during Second World War as a major air and naval base and port of the Tientu and Shekluk iron mines. **3** Town, ⊙ Yülin co. (pop. 137,428), N Shensi prov., China, 115 mi. N of Yenan, at the Great Wall (Suiyuan line), at edge of Ordos Desert; commercial center of N Shensi, trading with Mongol areas (N) in tea, cotton goods, hides, wool, cattle, horses.

Yuma, town, Dominican Republic: see SAN RAFAEL DEL YUMA.

Yuma (yōō'mŭ). **1** County (□ 9,985; pop. 28,006), SW Ariz.; ⊙ Yuma. Agr. area bounded N by Bill Williams R., W by Colorado R. (forming Calif. line), S by Mexico; drained by Gila R. Colorado River Indian Reservation is in NW, Trigo Mts. in W; Cocopah Indian Reservation, Gila Mts., and Yuma Desert are in SW. Yuma irrigation project is reclaimed section (69,000 acres) of Yuma Desert in vicinity of Yuma; receives water through irrigation canals proceeding from ALL-AMERICAN CANAL. Cotton, alfalfa, citrus fruits, truck products, and pecans are raised in project area. Co. formed 1864. **2** County (□ 2,383; pop. 10,827), NE Colo.; ⊙ Wray. Agr. area, bordering on Kansas and Nebr.; drained by Arikaree R. Grain, livestock, dairy and poultry products. Formed 1889.

Yuma. 1 City (pop. 9,145), ⊙ Yuma co., SW Ariz., on Colorado R. (forming Calif. line), at mouth of Gila R., and c.160 mi. WSW of Phoenix, near Mexico; alt. c.140 ft. Located in warm, dry area (annual rainfall 3.4 in.; average high temp. 86.3°F., average low 57.5°F.). City is railroad center (with repair shops) and trading point in agr. region developed by Yuma Irrigation Project (see YUMA, county). Experiment station of state univ. col. of agr. is here. Gold mines in vicinity. Yuma Indian Reservation is on opposite bank of Colorado R., in Calif.; Gila Mts. are ESE. Laid out 1854 as Colorado City, renamed Arizona City c.1862 and Yuma 1873; inc. 1871. **2** Town (pop. 1,908), Yuma co., NE Colo., 27 mi. W of Wray, in grain and livestock area; alt. 4,128 ft. Flour, dairy and poultry products. Inc. 1887.

Yuma Desert, SW Ariz., large semiarid region extending into Sonora, NW Mexico, and lying bet. Gila Mts. (E) and Colorado R. (W). Yuma irrigation project is reclaimed area in vicinity of Yuma, Ariz.

Yumaguzino (yōōmŭgōō'zĭnŭ), village (1948 pop. over 2,000), SW Bashkir Autonomous SSR, Russian SFSR, 55 mi. SSE of Sterlitamak; grain, stock.

Yumbel (yōōmbĕl'), town (1940 pop. 2,099), ⊙ Yumbel dept. (□742; 1940 pop. 39,040), Concepción prov., S central Chile, 30 mi. SE of Concepción; agr. center (grain, vegetables, potatoes, livestock); flour milling, lumbering. Sometimes called Yumbel Nuevo [Sp.,=new Yumbel] as opposed to near-by Yumbel Viejo (1940 pop. 600), the descendant of an old town destroyed in 17th-cent. earthquake. Its railroad station (1930 pop. 542) is 5 mi. SE.

Yumbi (yōōm'bē), village, Leopoldville prov., W Belgian Congo, on left bank of Congo R. (Fr. Equatorial Africa border) and 130 mi. W of Inongo; palm products, coffee.

Yumbo (yōōm'bō), town (pop. 2,471), Valle del Cauca dept., W Colombia, in Cauca valley, on railroad and 10 mi. N of Cali; coffee, sugar cane, tobacco, cacao, cereals, livestock. Coal mines in vicinity.

Yümen (yü'mŭn') [Chinese,=jade gate], town, ⊙ Yümen co. (pop. 28,396), NW Kansu prov., China, on Silk Road to Sinkiang, on Shuleh R. and 75 mi. WNW of Kiuchuan; alt. 5,177 ft.; China's leading petroleum center; cattle raising. Named for anc. Jade Gate in Great Wall near by.

Yümin (yü'mĭn'), town, ⊙ Yümin co. (pop. 14,159), N Sinkiang prov., China, 35 mi. S of Chuguchak, near USSR border; cattle raising; agr. products.

Yumoto (yōōmō'tō). **1** Town (pop. 24,829), Fukushima prefecture, central Honshu, Japan, 4 mi. SW of Taira; coal-mining center. Hot springs. **2** Town (pop. 3,916), Kanagawa prefecture, central Honshu, Japan, 4 mi. WSW of Odawara; hot-springs resort.

Yumrukchal, peak, Bulgaria: see BOTEV PEAK.

Yumura, Japan: see ONSEN.

Yumurí River (yōōmōōrē'), Matanzas prov., W Cuba, flows c.10 mi. through Matanzas to Matanzas Bay. Along its course—outside the city—is a gorge and the Yumurí Valley, celebrated for its beauty, and one of Cuba's finest sights.

Yunak (yōōnäk'), village (pop. 450), Stalin dist., E Bulgaria, on Provadiya R. and 16 mi. WSW of Stalin; rail junction; fruitgrowing. Sawmilling in near-by woodland. Formerly Oruch-gaazi.

Yünan, China; see WATNAM.

Yuna River (yōō'nä), central Dominican Republic, rises in the Cordillera Central S of Monseñor Nouel, flows c.100 mi. NE and E, past Villa Rivas, to Samaná Bay 3 mi. SW of Sánchez. Lower course is being canalized; navigable for smaller craft. Main affluent, Camú R. Its valley forms E section of fertile La Vega Real valley.

Yunchara (yōōnchä'rä) town (pop. c.1,100), Tarija dept., S Bolivia, 30 mi. SW of Tarija; road center; corn, fruit, sheep.

Yüncheng or **Yün-ch'eng** (both: yün'chŭng'). **1** Town, ⊙ Yüncheng co. (pop. 489,654), E Pingyuan prov., China, 40 mi. NE of Hotseh; tobacco processing; peanuts, wheat, millet. Until 1949 in Shantung prov. **2** Town, Shansi prov., China: see ANYI.

Yunchow, China: see YUNHSIEN, Yunnan prov.

Yuncler (yōōng-klĕr'), town (pop. 1,093), Toledo prov., central Spain, 27 mi. SSW of Madrid; olive and grain growing; olive-oil extracting.

Yunclillos (yōōng-klē'lyōs), town (pop. 925), Toledo prov., central Spain, 12 mi. NNE of Toledo; cereals, grapes, truck produce, cattle, sheep.

Yuncos (yōōng'kōs), town (pop. 1,095), Toledo prov., central Spain, 25 mi. SSW of Madrid; cereals, grapes, olives. Olive-oil extracting, flour milling, tile mfg.

Yundum (yōōn'dōōm), village (pop. 381), Western Div., Gambia, in Kombo North, 10 mi. SW of Bathurst; tomato and truck gardening. Large-scale poultry farm (producing chickens and eggs for export to England) established 1948 failed by 1951. Yundum airport (just ESE at 13°21'N 16°39'W) was built as a major air base during Second World War.

Yün-fou, China: see WANFOW.

Yung-, for Chinese names beginning thus and not found here: see under JUNG-.

Yüng. 1 River, Chekiang prov., China: see YUNG RIVER. **2** River, Kwangsi prov., China: see JUNG RIVER.

Yungaburra (yŭng″gŭbo͞o′rŭ), village (pop. 545), NE Queensland, Australia, 30 mi. SSW of Cairns; livestock, dairy products.
Yungan (yo͝ong′än′). **1** Town (pop. 11,782), ⊙ Yungan co. (pop. 78,774), W central Fukien prov., China, 70 mi. SW of Nanping and on Sha R. (tributary of Min R.); rice, sweet potatoes, sugar cane. Chemical industry; printing. Coal mines near by. **2** Town, Kwangsi prov., China: see MENGSHAN.
Yungas (yo͞ong′gäs), region of W Bolivia, in La Paz dept., on NE slopes (5,–8,000 ft.) of Cordillera de La Paz, bet. Zongo and La Paz rivers; watered by Coroico and Tamampaya rivers. Humid subtropical climate; coca, coffee, cacao, tobacco, fruit (citrus, bananas) are typical agr. products. Main centers: Coroico, Chulumani, Coripata, Irupana. A railroad from La Paz has been completed as far as Hichuloma. The term *yungas* is also applied to all valleys and slopes of Eastern Cordillera of the Andes at an alt. of 5–8,000 ft.
Yungas, Nor, province, Bolivia: see COROICO.
Yungas, Sud, province, Bolivia: see CHULUMANI.
Yungay (yo͞ong-gī′), town (pop. 3,671), ⊙ Yungay dept. (□1,751; pop. 38,031), Ñuble prov., S central Chile, in the central valley, 40 mi. S of Chillán; agr. center (wheat, corn, oats, wine, fruit, lentils, potatoes, livestock). Flour milling, dairying, lumbering. Sometimes spelled Yungai.
Yungay, city (pop. 2,755), ⊙ Yungay prov. (□ 577; pop. 32,335), Ancash dept., W central Peru, in the Callejón de Huaylas, on Santa R. and 30 mi. NNW of Huarás (connected by road); alt. 8,481 ft. Wheat, corn, livestock. Airport.
Yungchang or **Yung-ch'ang** (yo͝ong′chäng′). **1** Town, ⊙ Yungchang co. (pop. 49,858), central Kansu prov., China, on Silk Road to Sinkiang, and 45 mi. NE of Wuwei; alt. 6,037 ft.; coal-mining center. Petroleum wells near by. **2** Town, Yunnan prov., China: see PAOSHAN.
Yungcheng or **Yung-ch'eng** (yo͝ong′chŭng′), town, ⊙ Yungcheng co. (pop. 550,684), NW Anhwei prov., China, on road and 55 mi. WSW of Süchow; fruitgrowing center; grain. Until 1949 in Honan.
Yüng-chi, China: see YÜNGTSI.
Yung Chiang. 1 River, Chekiang prov., China: see YUNG RIVER. **2** River, Kwangsi prov., China: see JUNG RIVER.
Yung-ching or **Yung-ch'ing,** China: see YUNGTSING.
Yungching, Formosa: see YUNGTSING.
Yungchow, China: see LINGLING.
Yung-ch'uan, China: see YUNGCHWAN.
Yungchun or **Yung-ch'un** (yo͝ong′cho͞on′), town (pop. 39,218), ⊙ Yungchun co. (pop. 199,918), S Fukien prov., China, 55 mi. WSW of Putien; rice, sweet potatoes, tobacco; food processing, printing; mfg. of chemicals, cotton textiles. Coal and iron mines, and kaolin quarrying near by.
Yungchwan or **Yung-ch'uan** (both: yo͝ong′chwän′), town (pop. 18,780), ⊙ Yungchwan co. (pop. 276,318), S Szechwan prov., China, on railroad to Chengtu and 45 mi. WSW of Chungking city; rice, wheat, kaoliang, rapeseed. Coal mines near by.
Yungfeng (yo͝ong′fŭng′). **1** Town, central Hunan prov., China, 28 mi. SW of Siangsiang; coal-mining center. **2** Town (pop. 5,959), ⊙ Yungfeng co. (pop. 133,523), central Kiangsi prov., China, 25 mi. NE of Kian; tea, rice, wheat, beans; paper mfg. Anthracite and iron deposits.
Yungfu (yo͝ong′fo͞o′). **1** Town, Fukien prov., China: see YUNGTAI. **2** Town, ⊙ Yungfu co. (pop. 56,739), NW Kwangsi prov., China, 30 mi. SW of Kweilin and on railroad; rice, bananas, timber (pine).
Yunghing or **Yung-hsing** (both: yo͝ong′shĭng′), town, ⊙ Yunghing co. (pop. 216,248), SE Hunan prov., China, on Lei R., near Hankow-Canton RR, and 65 mi. SE of Hengyang; rice, wheat. Coal mining.
Yunghing Island, China: see WOODY ISLAND.
Yungho (yo͝ong′hŭ′). **1** Town, ⊙ Yungho co. (pop. 74,071), SW Shansi prov., China, 35 mi. NW of Anyi, near Yellow R. (Shensi border); cotton weaving; wheat, persimmons. Sometimes written Jungho. **2** Town, ⊙ Yungho co. (pop. 19,476), W Shansi prov., China, 70 mi. NW of Linfen, near Yellow R. (Shensi border); millet, kaoliang, beans.
Yunghsien, China: see JUNGHSIEN.
Yung-hsin, China: see YUNGSIN.
Yung-hsing, town, China: see YUNGHING.
Yung-hsing Island, China: see WOODY ISLAND.
Yung-hsiu, China: see YUNGSIU.
Yungjen (yo͝ong′rŭn′), town, ⊙ Yungjen co. (pop. 65,106), N Yunnan prov., China, 70 mi. N of Tsuyung, near Yangtze R. (Sikang line); alt. 4,199 ft.; rice, millet, beans. Coal mines near by. Until 1929 called Chüchüeh.
Yungkang or **Yung-k'ang** (yo͝ong′käng′). **1** Town (pop. 11,547), ⊙ Yungkang co. (pop. 267,508), S central Chekiang prov., China, 25 mi. SE of Kinhwa and on tributary of Tsientang R.; rice, wheat, peanuts, tea, sugar. **2** Town, Kwangsi prov., China: see TUNGCHENG.
Yungki, Manchuria: see KIRIN, city.
Yungkia, China: see WENCHOW.
Yung Kiang. 1 River, Chekiang prov., China: see YUNG RIVER. **2** River, Kwangsi prov., China: see JUNG RIVER.
Yunglo, China: see CRESCENT GROUP.
Yungming (yo͝ong′mĭng′), town, ⊙ Yungming co. (pop. 101,730), S Hunan prov., China, near Kwangsi line 65 mi. SSW of Lingling; rice, wheat, corn. Tin and coal mining near by.
Yungnien (yo͝ong′nyĕn′), town, ⊙ Yungnien co. (pop. 308,830), SW Hopeh prov., China, 30 mi. SSE of Singtai; cotton, wheat, millet, kaoliang. Until 1913 called Kwangping, it was formerly a flourishing town that declined when by-passed by railroad. The name Kwangping is now applied to a town 20 mi. SE.
Yungning (yo͝ong′nĭng′). **1** Town, Honan prov., China: see LONING. **2** Town, Kiangsi prov., China: see NINGKANG. **3** City, Kwangsi prov., China: see NANNING. **4** Town, Kwangsi prov., China: see POSHOW. **5** Town, ⊙ Yungning co. (pop. 77,192), SE Ningsia prov., China, 10 mi. S of Yinchwan and on Yellow R.; cattle raising; grain. Until 1942 called Yanghopao. **6** Town, Shansi prov., China: see LISHIH. **7** Town, Szechwan prov., China: see SÜYUNG.
Yungpeh, China: see YUNGSHENG.
Yungping or **Yung-p'ing** (yo͝ong′pĭng′). **1** Town, Hopeh prov., China: see LULUNG. **2** Town, ⊙Yungping co. (pop. 35,379), W Yunnan prov., China, on Burma Road and 30 mi. NE of Paoshan; rice, wheat, millet, beans.
Yung River. 1 Chinese *Yung Kiang* or *Yung Chiang* (both: yo͝ong′ jyäng′), river in Chekiang prov., China, rises in 2 branches which join at Ningpo, flows 13 mi. NE, past Chinhai, to outer Hangchow Bay. Also called Ningpo R. **2** River, Kwangsi prov., China: see JUNG RIVER.
Yungshan (yo͝ong′shän′), town (pop. 9,041), ⊙ Yungshan co. (pop. 103,056), NE Yunnan prov., China, 34 mi. N of Chaotung, near Yangtze R.; alt. 6,362 ft.; rice, millet, cotton, timber. Coal mines near by.
Yungsheng (yo͝ong′shŭng′), town (pop. 4,895), ⊙ Yungsheng co. (pop. 78,166), N Yunnan prov., China, 34 mi. ESE of Likiang; alt. 7,283 ft.; silk- and cotton-textile mfg., tung-oil processing; rice, millet, beans. Iron mining, kaolin quarrying near by. Until 1913 called Yungpeh.
Yungshow or **Yung-shou** (both: yo͝ong′shō′), town (pop. 5,720), ⊙ Yungshow co. (pop. 58,501), SW Shensi prov., China, 60 mi. NW of Sian and on road to Lanchow; millet, buckwheat, kaoliang. Called Kienkünchen until c.1940, when co. seat was moved here from old Yungshow, 10 mi. NW.
Yungshun (yo͝ong′sho͞on′). **1** Town, ⊙ Yungshun co. (pop. 199,325), NW Hunan prov., China, 45 mi. NW of Yüanling; rice, wheat, beans. **2** Town, Kwangsi prov., China: see WINGSHUN.
Yungsin or **Yung-hsin** (both: yo͝ong′shĭn′), town (pop. 12,244), ⊙ Yungsin co. (pop. 202,099), W Kiangsi prov., China, 35 mi. WSW of Kian; tea, rice, wheat. Coal and iron mining; gypsum deposits.
Yungsiu or **Yung-hsiu** (both: yo͝ong′shyō′), town (pop. 7,030), ⊙ Yungsiu co. (pop. 41,847), N Kiangsi prov., China, on Siu R., on Kiukiang-Nanchang RR and 32 mi. NNW of Nanchang; rice, cotton, ramie, wheat.
Yungsui (yo͝ong′swā′), town, ⊙ Yungsui co. (pop. 121,627), NW Hunan prov., China, near Szechwan line, 80 mi. NNW of Chihkiang; rice, wheat. Lead and zinc mining (S); gold deposits. Pop. is 85% Miao.
Yungtai or **Yung-t'ai** (yo͝ong′tī′), town (pop. 23,946), ⊙ Yungtai co. (pop. 135,895), 35 mi. SW of Foochow; rice, wheat, sweet potatoes. Silver-lead and molybdenum mines, iron deposits near by. Until 1941, Inghok (Mandarin *Yungfu*).
Yungteng (yo͝ong′dŭng′), town, ⊙ Yungteng co. (pop. 100,680), central Kansu prov., China, 50 mi. NW of Lanchow, at the Great Wall; alt. 6,791 ft.; gold, oil, and iron deposits. Saltworks near by. Until 1928 called Pingfan.
Yungting. 1 Town, Fukien prov., China: see ENGTENG. **2** Town, Hunan prov., China: see TAYUNG.
Yungting River, Chinese *Yungting Ho* (yo͝ong′dĭng′ hŭ′), N China, formed near Cholu in Chahar prov. by union of Yang (left) and Sangkan (right) rivers, flows 150 mi. into Hopeh to Tientsin area, where it joins Pai R. Sometimes called Hun R. (Chinese *Hun Ho*).
Yüngtsi or **Yüng-chi** (both: yüng′jē′), town, ⊙ Yüngtsi co. (pop. 119,336), SW Shansi prov., China, on railroad and 20 mi. N of Tungkwan, and on Yellow R. (Shensi border), opposite Pingmin; cotton-milling center; wheat, pears. Until 1912 called Puchow.
Yungtsing. 1 or **Yung-ch'ing** (yo͝ong′chĭng′), town, ⊙ Yungtsing co. (pop. 168,775), N Hopeh prov., China, 40 mi. WNW of Tientsin and on Yungting R.; willow plaiting; pears, apricots, grain. **2** or **Yung-ching** (yo͝ong′jĭng′), town, ⊙ Yungtsing co. (pop. 84,944), SE Kansu prov., China, 40 mi. WSW of Lanchow and on Yellow R.
Yungtsing, Yungching, or **Yung-ch'ing** (all: yo͝ong′-chĭng′), Jap. *Eisei* (ā′sā), village (1935 pop. 3,127), W central Formosa, 3 mi. SW of Yüanlin; rice, sugar cane, tobacco, fruit.
Yunguyo (yo͞ong-go͞o′yō), town (pop. 1,484), Puno dept., SE Peru, on L. Titicaca, at neck of Copacabana Peninsula, on Bolivian border, 55 mi. SE of Puno; potatoes, barley, livestock.
Yungyün (yo͝ong′yün′), Mandarin *Wengyüan* (wŭng′-yüän′), town (pop. 4,139), ⊙ Yungyün co. (pop. 140,957), N Kwangtung prov., China, 45 mi. ESE of Kukong; rice, wheat, beans, sugar cane. Tungsten mining near by. The name Yungyün was applied until 1947 to town (now called Old Yungyün) 25 mi. W. Present Yungyün was called Lungsinhü or Lunghsien until it became co. ⊙ in 1947.
Yün Ho, China: see GRAND CANAL.
Yünho, China: see YÜNHWO.
Yün-hsi, China: see YÜNSI.
Yün-hsiao, China: see YÜNSIAO.
Yünhsien (yün′shyĕn′). **1** Town (pop. 20,016), ⊙ Yünhsien co. (pop. 338,688), northwesternmost Hupeh prov., China, 90 mi. NW of Siangyang and on left bank of Han R.; lacquer-producing center; tobacco and tung-oil processing, silk and ramie weaving, tanning. Until 1912 called Yünyang. **2** Town, ⊙ Yünhsien co. (pop. 59,869), W central Yunnan prov., China, 75 mi. SE of Paoshan; alt. 3,799 ft.; cotton textiles; rice, millet, wheat, beans. Until 1913 called Yünchow.
Yünhwo or **Yün-huo** (both: yün′hwô′), town (pop. 3,453), ⊙ Yünhwo co. (pop. 51,565), SW Chekiang prov., China, 30 mi. SW of Lishui; tung-oil and tea-oil processing; rice, wheat, tea. Iron mines near by. Sometimes written Yünho.
Yün-lien, China: see KÜNLIEN.
Yünlung (yün′lo͝ong′), town, ⊙ Yünlung co. (pop. 62,356), NW Yunnan prov., China, 50 mi. WNW of Tali, near Mekong R.; timber, rice, millet, beans. Iron mines and saltworks near by.
Yünmeng (yün′mŭng′), town (pop. 23,295), ⊙ Yünmeng co. (pop. 225,512), E central Hupeh prov., China, 45 mi. NW of Hankow; cotton, indigo, rice.
Yunnan, Yünnan, or **Yün-nan** (yo͞onăn′, yün′nän′) [Chinese,=south of the clouds], province (□ 160,000; pop. 10,000,000) of SW China; ⊙ Kunming. Bounded W by Burma, S by Laos and by N Vietnam, E by Kwangsi and Kweichow, and N by Szechwan and Sikang, the prov. forms part of the dissected tableland of SW China. It consists of so-called lower Yunnan (NE) along Yangtze R., a sparsely settled region of malarial climate; of a NW region of high ranges and precipitous gorges of Salween, Mekong, and Yangtze rivers; and of the E, lake-studded plateaus (average alt. 6,000 ft.), with healthy, mild climate, which constitute the chief section of Yunnan. Here the temperate climate has a dry season (Nov.–April) and a wet and warm monsoon season (April–Aug.); average yearly rainfall is 45 in. Agr. is restricted to the few upland plains, open valleys, and terraced hillsides. Rice is the leading summer crop, along with corn, barley, and millet; while wheat, oilseed, and opium are grown in the winter. Tea (from Ningerh), tobacco, fruit, and nuts are exported. Mules and buffaloes, sheep and goats are extensively raised. Kütsing is noted for its hams. Yunnan prov. is China's leading tin producer (mines at Kokiu); copper at Hweitseh was a source of early Chinese copper coins. Coal (Iliang), antimony (Kaiyüan), salt (Pinchwan), iron, and lead-zinc are other mineral resources. The prov. is served by the Burma Road and the railroad from Kunming to Hanoi, partly dismantled after Second World War. Rail lines are planned to extend to Szechwan and Kweichow. Leading cities are: Kunming, on lake Tien Chih; Tali, a marble-producing center on lake Erh Hai; Mengtsz, an old treaty port; and Paoshan, a road center on W Burma Road. The Chinese pop., settled here since Ming and Ching dynasties, is concentrated in access corridor extending from Szechwan SW to Kunming. Among the non-Chinese minorities are the Lolos, the Moso (NW), and the Laos and Shans along the W and S borders. Conquered by the Mongol Yüan dynasty and long tributary to the Manchus, Yunnan was inc. into China in 1681. It was ravaged by a Moslem revolt (1855–72). During Sino-Japanese War, Yunnan became a major center of Chinese resistance, though occupied (1942–44) in extreme W (up to Salween R.) by Japanese who invaded from Burma. Prov. passed to Communist control in 1950. Yunnan has traditionally been known as Tien (or T'ien), so named for the lake Tien Chih.
Yunnan. 1 City, Yunnan prov., China: see KUNMING. **2** Town, Yunnan prov., China: see SIANGYÜN.
Yunnanfu, China: see KUNMING.
Yuno (yo͞o′nō), town (pop. 5,641), Fukushima prefecture, N Honshu, Japan, 5 mi. N of Fukushima; hot-springs resort.
Yunohira (yo͞onō′hĭrä), village (pop. 3,009), Oita prefecture, E Kyushu, Japan, 13 mi. WSW of Oita; rice, raw silk, soybeans. Hot springs.
Yunokawa, Japan: see HAKODATE.
Yunomae (yo͞onō′mäā), town (pop. 8,348), Kumamoto prefecture, S central Kyushu, Japan, 39 mi. SSE of Kumamoto; terminus of railroad from Hitoyoshi; agr. center (rice, wheat, sweet potatoes).
Yunotsu (yo͞onō′tso͞o), town (pop. 4,638), Shimane prefecture, SW Honshu, Japan, on Sea of Japan, 30 mi. SW of Izumo; radioactive hot-springs resort; salt- and sake making, charcoal. Fishing port.
Yunque, El, or **El Yunque de Baracoa** (ĕl yo͞ong′kā dā bärä kō′ä), flat summit (1,932 ft.), Oriente prov., E Cuba, in hills 5 mi. W of Baracoa.

Yunque, El, peak (3,497 ft.), NE Puerto Rico, in the Sierra de Luquillo, 23 mi. ESE of San Juan; 18°19′N 65°47′W. One of the isl.'s best-known peaks, a tourist resort with observation tower in Luquillo unit of Caribbean Natl. Forest. The La Mina recreational area is at its S foot.

Yunque de Baracoa, El, Cuba: see YUNQUE, EL.

Yunquera (yōōng-kā′rä), town (pop. 3,469), Málaga prov., S Spain, in spur of the Cordillera Penibética, 28 mi. W of Málaga; agr. center (olives, oranges, figs, grapes, potatoes, chestnuts, livestock). Liquor distilling, olive-oil extracting, mfg. of woolen goods. The Las Máquinas textile factory is 2 mi. SW.

Yunquera de Henares (dhā ānä′rĕs), town (pop. 1,403), Guadalajara prov., central Spain, near Henares R., 9 mi. N of Guadalajara; grain, grapes, potatoes. Flour milling, tile mfg.

Yünsi or **Yün-hsi** (both: yün′shē′), town (pop. 17,693), ⊙ Yünsi co. (pop. 191,440), northwesternmost Hupeh prov., China, near Shensi line, 30 mi. NW of Yünhsien; lacquer processing; exports mushrooms; millet, wheat.

Yünsiao or **Yün-hsiao** (both: yün′shyou′), town (pop. 17,664), ⊙ Yünsiao co. (pop. 108,944), S Fukien prov., China, 60 mi. WSW of Amoy, near S.China Sea; rice, sweet potatoes, wheat.

Yüntsao or **Yün-ts'ao** (yün′tsou′), town, N Anhwei prov., China, 20 mi. WNW of Wuhu, near railroad; commercial center.

Yünyang (yün′yäng′). **1** Town, Hupeh prov., China: see YÜNHSIEN. **2** Town (pop. 12,019), ⊙ Yünyang co. (pop. 473,590), E Szechwan prov., China, 30 mi. ENE of Wanhsien and on left bank of Yangtze R.; sugar-milling center; tung oil, rice, sweet potatoes, beans, wheat, rapeseed. Iron mines, coal and sulphur deposits, saltworks near by.

Yunykh Kommunarov, Imeni (ē′mĭnyē yōō′nĭkh kŭmōōnä′rŭf), town (1926 pop. 5,187), E Stalino oblast, Ukrainian SSR, in the Donbas, 4 mi. ESE of Yenakiyevo; coal mines. Formerly Bunge Rudnik.

Yunzalin River (yōōn′zŭlĭn″), Salween dist., Lower Burma, rises in Karenni Hills 40 mi. ESE of Toungoo, flows c.140 mi. SE and S, past Papun, to Salween R. at Kamamaung.

Yuodkrante, Lithuania: see JUODKRANTE.

Yupiltepeque (yōōpēltāpā′kā), town (1950 pop. 915), Jutiapa dept., SE Guatemala, in highlands, 11 mi. SE of Jutiapa; corn, beans, livestock.

Yüping or **Yü-p'ing** (yü′pĭng′), town (pop. 3,058), ⊙ Yüping co. (pop. 62,005), E Kweichow prov., China, 30 mi. NE of Chenyüan, on Hunan line; mercury-mining center; paper, tung oil, lacquer.

Yupurga (yōōpōōrgä′), Chinese *Yopuho* or *Yo-p'u-ho* (both: yō′pōō′hŭ), town ⊙ Yupurga co. (pop. 46,704), SW Sinkiang prov., China, 40 mi. ESE of Kashgar; cattle raising; agr. products.

Yuquerí (yōōkärē′), village (pop. estimate 500), E Entre Ríos prov., Argentina, on railroad and 6 mi. W of Concordia; stock-raising and meat-packing center.

Yur (yōōr), town (1942 pop. over 500), SE Yakut Autonomous SSR, Russian SFSR, 75 mi. S of Allakh-Yun; gold mines.

Yura (yōō′rä), town (pop. c.4,400), Potosí dept., SW Bolivia, on headstream of Tumusla R. and 50 mi. NE of Uyuni (linked by road); corn, fruit, vegetables.

Yura (yōō′rä). **1** Town (pop. 9,125) on SE Awajishima, Hyogo prefecture, Japan, on channel bet. Osaka Bay and Kii Channel, 4 mi. SE of Sumoto, in agr. area (rice, wheat). **2** Town (pop. 5,205), Tottori prefecture, S Honshu, Japan, on Sea of Japan, 27 mi. W of Tottori; raw silk, timber; agr. (rice, wheat).

Yura, town (pop. 165), Arequipa dept., S Peru, at W foot of the Nevado de Chachani, on affluent of Vitor R. and 18 mi. NW of Arequipa; alt. 9,183 ft. Health resort, with thermal springs containing sulphur and iron. Sulphur deposits near by. Its railroad station (pop. 248) is 3 mi. SSE.

Yuratishki (yōōrŭtyĕsh′kē), Pol. *Juraciszki*, village (1939 pop. over 500), SW Molodechno oblast, Belorussian SSR, 8 mi. NE of Ivye; lumbering.

Yurbarkas, Lithuania: see JURBARKAS.

Yurécuaro (yōōrā′kwärō), town (pop. 8,956), Michoacán, central Mexico, on Lerma R. (Jalisco border), on central plateau, and 15 mi. W of La Piedad; rail junction, agr. center (corn, wheat, beans, oranges, cattle, hogs); tanning, dairying. Airfield.

Yurga (yōōr′gŭ), city (1939 pop. over 2,000), NW Kemerovo oblast, Russian SFSR, on Trans-Siberian RR and 50 mi. NW of Kemerovo; junction for branch railroad to Stalinsk; rail center with repair shops; truck produce.

Yurgamysh (yōōrgŭmĭsh′), town (1948 pop. over 2,000), central Kurgan oblast, Russian SFSR, on Trans-Siberian RR and 35 mi. W of Kurgan; dairy.

Yurginskoye (yōōrgēn′skŭyŭ), village (1948 pop. over 2,000), SW Tyumen oblast, Russian SFSR, 40 mi. NE of Yalutorovsk, in agr. area (grain, livestock).

Yuriage (yōōrē′ägä), town (pop. 8,706), Miyagi prefecture, N Honshu, Japan, on the Pacific, 6 mi. SE of Sendai; fishing, agr. (rice, wheat).

Yurimaguas (yōōrēmä′gwäs), town (pop. 5,918), ⊙ Alto Amazonas prov. (in 1940: □ 13,500; enumerated pop. 23,977, plus estimated 50,000 Indians) Loreto dept., N central Peru, port on Huallaga R., at W edge of the Amazon basin and 60 mi. E of Moyobamba (linked by road); 5°54′S 76°5′W. Distributing center in fertile agr. region (sugar cane, cotton, bananas, yucca); pottery. Launch and air service to Iquitos.

Yurino (yōō′rēnŭ), town (1932 pop. estimate 4,590), SW Mari Autonomous SSR, Russian SFSR, on Volga R., near mouth of Vetluga R., 38 mi. WNW of Cheboksary; mfg. center (felt-boots, mittens).

Yuriria (yōōrēr′yä), city (pop. 5,698), Guanajuato, central Mexico, on S shore of L. Yuriria, 30 mi. SW of Celaya; alt. 5,695 ft.; grain, sugar cane, vegetables, fruit, stock. Anc. Tarascan Indian city.

Yuriria, Lake (□ 44; alt. 5,695 ft.), in Guanajuato, central Mexico, on central plateau, in Lerma R. basin, 25 mi. SW of Celaya. Linked with L. Cuizleo, 12 mi. S. Lake was artificially created (1548) by Father Diego de Chávez y Alvarado, by damming a stream.

Yü River, Chinese *Yü Kiang* or *Yü Chiang* (both: yü′ jyäng′), main navigable headstream (right) of West R., S China, rises in Yunnan-Kwangsi border region in 2 branches with confluence at Poseh (head of junk navigation), flows c.500 mi. generally E through S Kwangsi, past Tientung, Nanning, and Kweihsien, joining Hungshui R. at Kweiping to form Sün R. section of West R. Receives Li R. (right). Yü R. sometimes called Siang.

Yurla (yōōrlä′), village (1932 pop. estimate 2,400), S central Komi-Permyak Natl. Okrug, Molotov oblast, Russian SFSR, 26 mi. NNW of Kudymkar; food processing; wheat, livestock.

Yurlovka (yōōr′lŭfkŭ), village (1926 pop. 2,151), W Tambov oblast, Russian SFSR, 14 mi. SE of Michurinsk; grain, potatoes.

Yurma (yōōr′mŭ), peak (3,392 ft.) in Urals, Russian SFSR, at junction of central and S Urals, NE of Zlatoust; 55°30′N.

Yurovski or **Yurovskiy** (yōō′rŭfskē), town (1939 pop. over 500), S Kostroma oblast, Russian SFSR, on Unzha R., just S of Manturovo; sawmilling. Oil-shale deposits.

Yuruari River (yōōrwä′rē), Bolívar state, SE Venezuela, rises in N outliers of Guiana Highlands, flows 145 mi. E and S, past El Callao, to minor affluent of Cuyuni R. 3 mi. W of El Dorado. Important gold placers along its course.

Yurya or **Yur'ya** (yōō′ryŭ), village (1948 pop. over 2,000), N Kirov oblast, Russian SFSR, 35 mi. NNW of Kirov; grain.

Yuryev, Estonia: see TARTU.

Yuryevets or **Yur'yevets** (yōō′ryĭvyĭts), city (1939 pop. over 10,000), NE Ivanovo oblast, Russian SFSR, on Volga R., opposite mouth of the Unzha, and 80 mi. ENE of Ivanovo; linen-milling center. Sawmilling at Novaya Slobodka, across Volga R. Remains of old city wall and moat. Founded 1225; passed 1393 to Moscow. Formerly also called Yuryevets-Povolski, Yuryevets-Povolzhski.

Yuryevka or **Yur'yevka** (yōō′ryĭfkŭ). **1** Village (1926 pop. 2,669), NE Dnepropetrovsk oblast, Ukrainian SSR, 15 mi. NNE of Pavlograd; flour mill. **2** Town (1939 pop. over 500), S Voroshilovgrad oblast, Ukrainian SSR, in the Donbas, 9 mi. E of Voroshilovsk; coal mining.

Yuryev-Polski or **Yur'yev-Pol'skiy** (yōō′ryĭf-pôl′skē), city (1939 pop. over 10,000), NW Vladimir oblast, Russian SFSR, on left affluent of Klyazma R. and 38 mi. NW of Vladimir; cotton-milling center; food processing. Has kremlin with monastery (1234), art and cultural mus. Founded 1152; became ⊙ principality; inc. (c.1341) into Muscovite state.

Yuryuzan or **Yuryuzan'** (yōōryōōzän′yŭ), city (1939 pop. over 10,000), W Chelyabinsk oblast, Russian SFSR, in the S Urals, on Yuryuzan R. and 50 mi. SW of Zlatoust, on railroad; metalworking center; iron founding, sawmilling, charcoal burning. Became city in 1943. Formerly Yuryuzanski Zavod.

Yuryuzan River or **Yuryuzan' River**, E European Russian SFSR, rises in the S Urals, on NE slope of Yamantan mtn.; flows NNE and generally NW, past Yuryuzan, Vyazovaya, Ust-Katav, and Maloyaz, to Ufa R. 7 mi. S of Karaidel; 265 mi. long. Lumber floating.

Yusa (yōō′sä), town (pop. 3,058), Yamagata prefecture, N Honshu, Japan, 8 mi. NNE of Sakata; rice growing, lumbering.

Yuscarán (yōōskärän′), city (pop. 1,189), ⊙ El Paraíso dept., S Honduras, at E foot of Mt. Monserrat (site of silver mines), on road and 30 mi. ESE of Tegucigalpa; 13°50′N 86°48′W; alt. 3,379 ft. Commercial center in grain and fruit area. Has civic bldgs., old residences. Airfield. Founded 1744 following discovery of silver and gold. Mining, abandoned in 19th cent., resumed in 1940s.

Yüshan (yü′shän′), town (pop. 16,364), ⊙ Yüshan co. (pop. 212,430), NW Kiangsi prov., China, 23 mi. NE of Shangjao; tea, tobacco, rice, wheat. Coal mines and limestone quarries.

Yü Shan, Formosa: see MORRISON, MOUNT.

Yüshe (yü′shŭ′), town, ⊙ Yüshe co. (pop. 59,081), E Shansi prov., China, 55 mi. SE of Taiyüan; wheat, millet, cattle.

Yüshih (yü′shû′), town, ⊙ Yüshih co. (pop. 80,534), N Honan prov., China, on road and 30 mi. SSW of Kaifeng; wheat, kaoliang, cotton. Sometimes written Weishih.

Yüshu (yü′shōō′). **1** Town, ⊙ Yüshu co. (pop. 604,650), N Kirin prov., Manchuria, China, 70 mi. N of Kirin; soybeans, kaoliang, millet, rye, hemp, tobacco, indigo. **2** Town, Tsinghai prov., China: see JYEKUNDO.

Yüsiang or **Yü-hsiang** (both: yü′shyäng′), town, ⊙ Yüsiang co. (pop. 52,505), SW Shansi prov., China, 16 mi. E of Yüngtsi and on railroad; cotton weaving; cattle raising; wheat, persimmons, pears.

Yusong (yōō′sŭng′), Jap. *Jujo*, township (1946 pop. 10,895), S.Chungchong prov., S Korea, 6 mi. WNW of Taejon; agr., paper milling, pottery making. Near by are hot springs.

Yuste, San Jerónimo de (sän′ hārō′nēmō dhā yōō′stā), former Hieronymite monastery, Cáceres prov., W Spain, in Estremadura, 20 mi. ENE of Plasencia, picturesquely situated in a fertile valley (La Vera). Founded in 1402, it is chiefly noted as the residence (1556–58) of Emperor Charles V from his abdication until his death. His palace adjoins the S side of the monastery's church. Heavily damaged (1809) in the Peninsular War by the French, the bldgs. are now partly restored.

Yusufeli (yōōsōō′fĕlĕ), village (pop. 686), Coruh prov., NE Turkey, on Coruh R. and 38 mi. SSW of Artvin; grain. Formerly Ogdem.

Yusun Bulak or **Yösön Bulag** (both: yü′sŭn bōō′läkh), town (pop. over 2,000), ⊙ Gobi Altai aimak, SW Mongolian People's Republic, in the Gobi Altai mts., 100 mi. SSW of Uliassutai. Until 1931, administrative hq. of tribe of Dzasaktu Khan (Dzasag Haan) or Khan Taishirin Khure (Haan Tayshiriin Hüryee).

Yusva or **Yus'va** (yōōs′vŭ), village (1932 pop. estimate 1,200), S Komi-Permyak Natl. Okrug, Molotov oblast, Russian SFSR, 12 mi. SE of Kudymkar; flax processing; wheat, livestock.

Yütai or **Yü-t'ai** (yü′tī′), town, ⊙ Yütai co. (pop. 215,874), SE Pingyuan prov., China, 60 mi. ESE of Hotseh, on Shantung line; rice, beans, kaoliang, fruit. Until 1949 in Shantung prov.

Yutan (ū′tăn), village (pop. 287), Saunders co., E Nebr., 23 mi. W of Omaha and on Platte R.

Yutaza (yōōtŭzä′), village (1948 pop. over 2,000), SE Tatar Autonomous SSR, Russian SFSR, on railroad and 17 mi. ENE of Bugulma; wheat, livestock.

Yütien or **Yü-t'ien** (both: yü′tyĕn′). **1** Town, ⊙ Yütien co. (pop. 335,095), NE Hopeh prov., China, 30 mi. NW of Tangshan; straw plaiting; cotton, rice, wheat. **2** Town and oasis, Sinkiang prov., China: see KERIYA.

Yutien, Yunnan prov., China: see CHANGNING.

Yuto (yōō′tō), town (pop. estimate 500), E Jujuy prov., Argentina, on San Francisco R., on railroad and 65 mi. NE of Jujuy; agr. (oranges, tomatoes, pepper, vegetables, livestock) and lumbering center; tannin extracting; sawmills.

Yütsien or **Yü-ch'ien** (both: yü′chyĕn′), town (pop. 6,688), ⊙ Yütsien co. (pop. 64,735), NW Chekiang prov., China, S of Tienmu Mts., 45 mi. W of Hangchow; rice, wheat, medicinal herbs. Until 1912 called Yüchow.

Yütu (yü′dōō′), town (pop. 16,164), ⊙ Yütu co. (pop. 220,857), S Kiangsi prov., China, 23 mi. ENE of Kanchow and on Kung R.; rice, sugar, paper, tobacco, timber. Anthracite, gold, and tungsten mining; limestone quarrying.

Yuty (yōōtē′), town (dist. pop. 20,206), Caazapá dept., S Paraguay, 120 mi. SE of Asunción, 55 mi. SSE of Villarrica; lumber and cattle center. Founded 1610 by a Franciscan friar. Its rail station is 3 mi. W.

Yütze or **Yü-tz'u** (both: yü′tsŭ′), town, ⊙ Yütze co. (pop. 139,314), N central Shansi prov., China, 15 mi. SE of Taiyüan; rail junction and cotton-milling center; exports wheat, cotton, kaoliang, beans.

Yuu, Japan: see YU.

Yüweng Island (yü′wŭng′), Chinese *Yü-weng Tao* (dou), Jap. *Gyoo-to* (gyō′-tō), one of the Pescadores, W of Penghu Isl.; 6 mi. long.

Yuyang (yō′yäng′), town (pop. 18,385), ⊙ Yuyang co. (pop. 500,525), southernmost Szechwan prov., China, 70 mi. NNE of Szenan, near Kweichow border, in mtn. region; millet center; rice, sweet potatoes, wheat, beans, rapeseed.

Yüyao (yü′you′), town (pop. 26,253), ⊙ Yüyao co. (pop. 672,658), NE Chekiang prov., China, 25 mi. WNW of Ningpo and on railroad; cotton growing.

Yuyü (yō′yü′), town, ⊙ Yuyü co. (pop. 82,806), SW Chahar prov., China, 40 mi. W of Tatung, near Great Wall (Suiyuan border); cattle raising; wool-textile weaving. Called Shoping until 1911. Until 1949 in N Shansi.

Yüyüan (Cantonese yü′yün′), Mandarin *Juyüan* (rōō′yüăn′), town (pop. 3,060), ⊙ Yüyüan co. (pop. 82,251), N Kwangtung prov., China, 30 mi. W of Kukong; antimony and coal mining; rice, wheat, tea, timber.

Yuzawa (yōō′zäwŭ), town (pop. 16,880), Akita prefecture, N Honshu, Japan, 11 mi. SSW of Yokote; sake, woodworking, silk cocoons. Sericulture experiment station.

Yuzha (yōō'zhŭ), city (1926 pop. 12,889), SE Ivanovo oblast, Russian SFSR, on railroad and 30 mi. SE of Shuya, in wooded area; cotton-milling center; supplies thread to Shuya weaving industry; peat works. Became city in 1925.
Yuzhkuzbassgres, Russian SFSR: see OSINNIKI.
Yuzhni Brod, Yugoslavia: see BROD, Macedonia.
Yuzhno-Kazakhstan, Kazakh SSR: see SOUTH KAZAKHSTAN.
Yuzhno-Kurilsk or **Yuzhno-Kuril'sk** (yōō"zhnŭ-kōōrēlsk'), village on Kunashir Isl., S Kuriles, Russian SFSR, on E coast; fishing port; canning center. Under Jap. rule (until 1945), called Furukamappu (fōōrōō'kämäp'pōō).
Yuzhno-Sakhalinsk (–sŭkhŭlyĕnsk'), city (1940 pop. 38,606), ⊙ (since 1947) Sakhalin oblast, Russian SFSR, on E coast railroad and 275 mi. S of Aleksandrovsk; 46°58'N 142°44'E. Rail junction (branch to Kholmsk) in agr. area (grain, potatoes, sugar beets, livestock); industrial center; pulp and paper milling, mfg. of plastic footwear, fur processing, sugar refining, brewing. Airport; teachers col. Originally called Vladimirovka; later, under Jap. rule (1905–45), Toyohara (tōyō'härŏŏ). Succeeded Otomari (Korsakov) as ⊙ Karafuto.
Yuzhno-Yeniseiski or **Yuzhno-Yeniseyskiy** (–yĕnyĭsyä'skē), town (1939 pop. over 2,000), central Krasnoyarsk Territory, Russian SFSR, 190 mi. NNE of Krasnoyarsk; gold mines.
Yuzhny or **Yuzhnyy** (yōōzh'nē). **1** Town, Tula oblast, Russian SFSR: see SKURATOVSKI. **2** Town (1926 pop. 2,092), N central Kharkov oblast, Ukrainian SSR, 10 mi. SW of Kharkov city center.
Yuzhny Alamyshik or **Yuzhnyy Alamyshik** (ŭlŭmĭshēk'), town (1947 pop. over 500), SE Andizhan oblast, Uzbek SSR, c.15 mi. SE of Andizhan; oil fields.
Yuzhny Bug River, Ukrainian SSR: see BUG RIVER (Southern Bug).
Yuzovka, Ukrainian SSR: see STALINO, city.
Yverdon (ēvĕrdō'), Ger. *Iferten* (ē'fŭrtŭn), town (1950 pop. 12,306), Vaud canton, W Switzerland, resort on S L. of Neuchâtel, at mouth of Thièle R.; typewriters, flour, fats, pastry, tobacco; woodworking. Railroad shops. An old town (anc. *Eburodunum*), it has relics of walls of Roman castrum, castle (once seat of Pestalozzi's school) with historical mus., church and town hall (both 18th cent.).
Yves-Gomezée (ēv-gōmzā'), town (pop. 1,332), Namur prov., S Belgium, 4 mi. NNW of Philippeville; steel foundries, rolling mills.
Yvetot (ēvtō'), town (pop. 5,789), Seine-Inférieure dept., N France, 20 mi. NW of Rouen; textile center (clothing, lingerie, shirts, felt hats); apple brandy distilling, mustard mfg., printing. Town center damaged in Second World War. Became known through Beranger's popular song (translated into English by Thackeray) entitled "The King of Yvetot."
Yvoir (ēvwär'), town (pop. 1,971), Namur prov., S Belgium, on Meuse R. and 5 mi. N of Dinant; granite quarries; limekilns.
Yvoire (ēvwär'), village (pop. 242), Haute-Savoie dept., SE France, on S shore of L. Geneva, 7 mi. W of Thonon-les-Bains. Preserves medieval fortifications.
Yvorne (ēvôrn'), village (pop. 723), Vaud canton, SW Switzerland, in valley of the Rhone, N of Aigle; excellent wine.
Ywangan, Burma: see YENGAN.
Y Wyddgrug, Wales: see MOLD.
Yxpila, Finland: see YKSPIHLAJA.
Yyarvakandi, Estonia: see JARVAKANDI.
Yyarva-Yani, Estonia: see JARVA-JANI.
Yygeva, Estonia: see JOGEVA.
Yykhvi, Estonia: see JOHVI.
Yzendyke, Netherlands: see IJZENDIJKE.
Yzeure (ēzûr'), E suburb (pop. 2,383) of Moulins, Allier dept., central France; mfg. (perfumes, pottery, drainage pipes).

Z

Zaachila (säche'lä), town (pop. 4,513), Oaxaca, S Mexico, in Sierra Madre del Sur, on railroad, and 7 mi. S of Oaxaca; cereals, sugar cane, tobacco, fruit. Pre-Columbian ruins are near by. As Teozapotlán, it was once capital of powerful Zapotec people.
Zaalaiski Khrebet, Tadzhik SSR: see TRANS-ALAI RANGE.
Zaamin (zä-ŭmēn'), village (1926 pop. 1,282), NE Samarkand oblast, Uzbek SSR, 30 mi. WSW of Dzhizak; cotton, metalworks.
Zaamslag (zäm'släkh), village (pop. 1,403), Zeeland prov., SW Netherlands, on Flanders mainland 4.5 mi. ESE of Terneuzen; stone quarrying; flax growing.
Zaandam (zändäm'), city (pop. 41,698), North Holland prov., W Netherlands, on Zaan R., near junction with North Sea Canal, and 6 mi. NNW of Amsterdam, in low-lying meadows. Center of ZAANSTREEK industrial area; rail junction; lumber industry, with sawmills; dye mfg. Peter the Great stayed here (1697) to learn shipbuilding, then a flourishing local industry.
Zaandijk (zändīk'), town (pop. 4,467), North Holland prov., W Netherlands, on Zaan R. and 2.5 mi. NNW of Zaandam, in Zaanstreek industrial area; mfg. of cacao products, candy, flour products, oleomargarine, dairy products, oil and feed cakes, paints, dyes, metal products. Sometimes spelled Zaandyk.
Zaan River (zän), North Holland prov., NW Netherlands, rises in Alkmaar L. 13 mi. NNW of Amsterdam, flows 10 mi. S, past Wormerveer, Zaandijk, Koog aan de Zaan, and Zaandam, to NORTH SEA CANAL 4 mi. NW of Amsterdam. Most of its course is canalized; forms transportation artery of the Zaanstreek industrial area. Entire length navigable.
Zaanstreek (zän'sträk), industrial area in North Holland prov., W Netherlands, extending S along Zaan R. from Wormerveer, 9 mi. NW of Amsterdam, to junction of Zaan R. and North Sea Canal, 4 mi. NW of Amsterdam. Industries, centered on ZAANDAM, include lumber and paper milling, oil extracting, rice milling, flour milling and allied industries, cacao processing, linoleum mfg.
Zab, Great, or **Zab River** (zäb), Arabic *Zab al Kabir* (zăb älkăbēr'), Turkish *Zap* (zäp), anc. *Lycus*, rises in Turkish Kurdistan, in Hakari Mts. near Iranian line, flows SSW for 115 mi. in Turkey, passing Colemerik, crosses into Iraq, and continues 150 mi. generally S to the Tigris near the site of anc. Calah, 25 mi. SSE of Mosul; total length, c.265 mi.
Zab, Little, Arabic *Zab al Asfal* (äl äs'fäl), anc. *Caprus*, river of Iran and Iraq, rising in Persian Azerbaijan and flowing c.250 mi. SW to the Tigris 75 mi. SSE of Mosul, 50 mi. S of mouth of the Great Zab.
Zabadani, Syria: see ZEBDANI.
Zabaikalye, Russian USSR: see TRANSBAIKALIA.
Zabalj, Zhabal, or **Zhabal'** (all: zhä'bäl), Serbo-Croatian *Žabalj*, Hung. *Zsablya* (zhŏb'yŏ), village (pop. 5,967), Vojvodina, N Serbia, Yugoslavia, on railroad and 14 mi. ENE of Novi Sad, in the Backa.
Zabari or **Zhabari** (zhä'bärē), Serbo-Croatian *Žabari*, village, E central Serbia, Yugoslavia, 18 mi. S of Pozarevac.
Zabbar (zäb-bär'), Maltese *Żabbar*, town (pop., including adjacent landing Marsa Scala, 11,726), SE Malta, 2 mi. SE of Valletta. Parish grows tomatoes, blackberries, citrus fruit. Contains megalithic remains and several 16th- and 17th-cent. churches.
Zabczyce, Belorussian SSR: see ZHABCHITSY.
Zabeln, Latvia: see SABILE.
Zabern, France: see SAVERNE.
Zabid or **Zebid** (both: zĕbēd'), town (pop. 8,000), Hodeida prov., W Yemen, on Tihama coastal plain, 50 mi. SSE of Hodeida; former capital and spiritual center of Sunni pop. of Tihama lowland; noted for its univ. (c.1500) and Sunni col. in the Great Mosque. Agr. center of cotton and indigo dist.; weaving, dyeing, tanning. A walled quadrilaterial town, it has 4 gates; large bazaar. Founded 9th cent.; was seat of lowland dynasty through the Middle Ages; often independent of Sana.
Zabie, Ukrainian SSR: see ZHABYE.
Zabinka, Belorussian SSR: see ZHABINKA.
Zabitui or **Zabituy** (zŭbētōō'ē), town (1948 pop. over 500), W Ust-Orda Buryat-Mongol Natl. Okrug, Irkutsk oblast, Russian SFSR, on Trans-Siberian RR and 15 mi. NW of Cheremkhovo; coal mining.
Zabkowice or **Zabkowice Slaskie** (zōpkôvē'tsĕ shlō'skyĕ), Pol. *Ząbkowice Śląskie*, Ger. *Frankenstein* (fräng'kŭn-shtīn), town (1939 pop. 10,857; 1946 pop. 10,127) in Lower Silesia, after 1945 in Wroclaw prov., SW Poland, near E foot of the Eulengebirge, 40 mi. SSW of Breslau (Wroclaw); nickel mining and smelting, woolen milling, mfg. of electrical equipment, tar paper; grain market. Has 14th-cent. church with leaning tower, remains of old castle and fortifications. Founded c.1260.
Zabljak or **Zhablyak** (both: zhäb'lyäk), Serbo-Croatian *Žabljak*, village, N Montenegro, Yugoslavia, near Tara R., 14 mi. N of Savnik. The Durmitor rises 5 mi. to the WSW.
Zablocie, Ukrainian SSR: see ZABOLOTYE.
Zablotce, Ukrainian SSR: see ZABOLOTTSY.
Zablotow, Ukrainian SSR: see ZABOLOTOV.
Zablotye, Ukrainian SSR: see ZABOLOTYE.
Zabludow (zäbwōō'dōōf), Pol. *Zabłudów*, Rus. *Zabludov* (zŭblōō'dŭf), town (pop. 1,220), Bialystok prov., NE Poland, 11 mi. SE of Bialystok; mfg. of bricks, caps, sawmilling, tanning, flour milling.
Zab Mountains (zäb), low range of the Saharan Atlas, N central Algeria, forming S limit of the Hodna depression, bet. Ouled-Naïl Mts. (W) and the Aurès massif (NE). Rise to 3,566 ft.
Zabno (zhäb'nô), Pol. *Żabno*, town (pop. 2,178), Krakow prov., S Poland, near Dunajec R., 8 mi. NNW of Tarnow; brickworks; flour milling; rail junction linked (1951–52) by railroad with Kielce.
Zaboishchik, Russian SFSR: see KURGANOVKA.
Zabol, Iran: see ZABUL.
Zabolotov (zŭbŭlô'tŭf), Pol. *Zabłotów* (zäbwô'tōōf), town (1931 pop. 6,541), E Stanislav oblast, Ukrainian SSR, on Prut R. and 12 mi. ESE of Kolomyya; tobacco mfg., flour milling.
Zabolottsy (zŭbŭlô'tsē), Pol. *Zabłotce* (zäbwô'tsĕ), village (1939 pop. over 500), E Lvov oblast, Ukrainian SSR, 8 mi. WSW of Brody; stone quarry; wheat, rye, oats.
Zabolotye or **Zabolot'ye** (zŭbŭlô'tyĭ), village (1939 pop. over 500), NW Volyn oblast, Ukrainian SSR, on lake in Pripet Marshes, 11 mi. WSW of Ratno; flax, potatoes; lumbering. Until 1944, Zablotye, Pol. *Zabłocie* (zäbwô'tsyĕ).
Zabrat (zŭbrät') town (1939 pop. over 10,000) in Lenin dist. of Greater Baku, Azerbaijan SSR, on central Apsheron Peninsula, 10 mi. NE of Baku, on electric railroad; machine mfg.
Zabreh (zä'bŭrzhĕ), Czech *Zábřeh*, Ger. *Hohenstadt* (hō'ŭnshtät), town (pop. 5,487), NW Moravia, Czechoslovakia, 26 mi. NW of Olomouc, in oat-growing dist.; rail junction; textile industry, including dyeing of cotton goods; mfg. of machinery, sewing articles, stoneware, earthenware. Noted for 18th-cent. castle. Remains of 13th-cent. Hostejn castle are 4 mi. W.
Zab River, Iraq and Turkey: see ZAB, GREAT.
Zabrze, Poland: see HINDENBURG.
Zabul or **Zabol** (both: zäbōl'), town (1940 pop. 15,966), Eighth Prov., in Seistan, SE Iran, 115 mi. NNE of Zahidan, near Afghanistan line; chief town of Iranian Seistan, one of Iran's important wheat-growing regions; flour milling. Military post. Founded c.1870, it was originally called Nasirabad, later Nasratabad; now also known as Shahr Zabul or Shahr-i-Zabul. Ruins of anc. ZAHIDAN are 12 mi. ESE.
Zacapa (säkä'pä), department (□ 1,039; 1950 pop. 69,391), E Guatemala; ⊙ Zacapa. In Motagua R. valley, bet. Sierra de las Minas (N) and E highlands (S); dry, warm climate. Irrigated agr. (corn, beans, tobacco, sugar cane); livestock raising, dairying. Coffee growing on lower slopes. Main centers are Zacapa and Gualán, served by Guatemala–Puerto Barrios RR.
Zacapa, city (1950 pop. 8,282), ⊙ Zacapa dept., E Guatemala, on Chiquimula R. and 70 mi. ENE of Guatemala; 14°59'N 89°31'W; alt. 738 ft. Rail center (branch to San Salvador); dairying industry; corn, beans, sugar cane; livestock. Developed rapidly after building of railroad (1896).
Zacapa or **San Pedro Zacapa** (sän pā'drō), town (pop. 1,466), Santa Bárbara dept., W Honduras, 12 mi. SE of Santa Bárbara; mfg. of harvest hats; corn, beans, tobacco.
Zacapala (säkäpä'lä), town (pop. 825), Puebla, central Mexico, on affluent of Atoyac R. and 33 mi. SSE of Puebla; corn, sugar cane.
Zacapoaxtla (säkäpwä'slä), city (pop. 2,163), Puebla, central Mexico, on plateau, 25 mi. ESE of Zacatlán; agr. center (corn, coffee, fruit, vegetables).
Zacapu (säkä'pōō), officially Zacapu de Mier, town (pop. 6,169), Michoacán, central Mexico, on central plateau, 40 mi. WNW of Morelia; alt. 6,516 ft. Rail junction; agr. center (cereals, vegetables, sugar cane, fruit, tobacco, stock). Tarasco Indian ruins are near by.
Zacatecas (säkätä'käs), state (□ 28,125; 1940 pop. 565,437; 1950 pop. 664,394), N central Mexico; ⊙ Zacatecas. Bounded by Coahuila (N), Durango (W), Jalisco and Aguascalientes (S), San Luis Potosí (E). Forms N part of large central plateau (average alt. 8,000 ft.), being traversed NW–SE by Sierra Madre Occidental. Arid area intersected by Aguanaval R. (N) and Juchipila R. (S). Climate varies with alt.: hot and humid in SE, colder in highlands. Since early colonial days Zacatecas has been known for its rich silver deposits. The economy of the state depends almost entirely on the extensive mineral output in silver, gold, lead, zinc, copper, iron, tin, antimony, manganese, bismuth, and mercury; mining is centered at Concepción del Oro, Mazapil, Fresnillo, Zacatecas, Villa Hidalgo, Sombrerete, and other towns. Agr. crops (center and S) include wheat, barley, corn, chick-peas, alfalfa, chili, sugar cane, tobacco, maguey, citrus fruit, bananas, and guayule rubber. Stock raising (cattle, sheep, horses, mules) ranks second as source of income. Processing industries concentrated at Zacatecas, Fresnillo, García, Concepción del Oro. An early habitat of the Aztecs, Zacatecas formerly also included Aguascalientes. The area had been opened (1530) by the Spanish but not colonized. An expedition (1546) to conquer the In-

dians was followed by the discovery of silver, which caused a "silver rush."

Zacatecas, city (pop. 21,846), ⊙ Zacatecas, N central Mexico, in a ravine of the interior plateau, 155 mi. NNE of Guadalajara, 375 mi. NW of Mexico city; 22°46′N 102°35′W; alt. 8,075 ft. Rail junction. Trading, mining (silver, gold, lead, copper, zinc), processing, and agr. center (grain, maguey, fruit, vegetables, livestock); iron foundry, flour mills, distilleries (tequila, mescal); mfg. of rubber, cigars, serapes, furniture. Airfield. Has old colonial bldgs., cathedral in churrigueresque manner, Santo Domingo church. La Bufa ridge (with observatory and church), where a revolutionary army was defeated (1871) by Juárez, is NE. City was founded 1548 as silver-mining center.

Zacatecoluca (säkätäkōlōō′kä), city (pop. 11,684), ⊙ La Paz dept., S Salvador, on railroad and road, 27 mi. SE of San Salvador; alt. 564 ft.; 13°28′N 88°51′W. Commercial center; produces cotton goods, baskets, and mangrove bark; grain, coffee, livestock raising. Trades in salt and lumber. Almost destroyed by earthquake, 1932.

Zacate Grande Island (säkä′tā grän′dā), largest island in Gulf of Fonseca, in Valle dept., S Honduras, bet. mainland (separated by narrow channel) and Tigre Isl. (S); 6 mi. long, 4 mi. wide. Volcanic in origin; rises to 2,247 ft. Agr. (grain, sugar cane, coffee, cacao).

Zacatelco (säkätĕl′kō), officially Santa Inés Zacatelco, town (pop. 7,029), Tlaxcala, central Mexico, on central plateau, 12 mi. N of Puebla; agr. center (corn, wheat, beans, alfalfa, maguey, stock); flour milling, pulque distilling.

Zacatepec (säkätāpĕk′), town (pop. 1,917), Morelos, central Mexico, 45 mi. SE of Cuernavaca; sugar-refining center.

Zacatlán (säkätlän′), city (pop. 3,804), Puebla, central Mexico, on central plateau, 65 mi. NNE of Puebla; agr. center (corn, coffee, tobacco, sugar cane, fruit); noted for apples and cider. Iron and silver deposits. Pre-Columbian pyramids near by.

Zacazonapan (säkäsōnä′pän), town (pop. 496), Mexico state, central Mexico, 40 mi. SW of Toluca; coffee, sugar cane.

Zaccar, Djebel (je′bĕl zäkär), mountain of the Tell Atlas, in Alger dept., N central Algeria, overlooking the Chéliff valley. Rises to 5,180 ft. in W summit; to 5,029 ft. in E summit. Iron mining. Town of Miliana on S slope.

Zachan, Poland: see SUCHAN.

Zacharo or **Zakharo** (both: zŭkhä′rô), town (pop. 3,094), Elis nome, W Peloponnesus, Greece, port on Gulf of Kyparissia, on railroad and 16 mi SE of Pyrgos; fisheries; Zante currants, wine, livestock. Sulphur baths on L. Kaiapha or Kaiafa (both: käyä′fŭ), a coastal lagoon (NW).

Zachary (ză′kūrē), town (pop. 1,542), East Baton Rouge parish, SE central La., 14 mi. N of Baton Rouge; agr.; metalworking.

Zachepilovka (zŭchĭpē′lŭfkŭ), village (1926 pop. 4,268), SW Kharkov oblast, Ukrainian SSR, 15 mi. SW of Krasnograd; wheat, sunflowers.

Zacler (zhäts′lärsh), Czech *Žacléř*, Ger. *Schatzlar* (shäts′lär), village (pop. 2,347), NE Bohemia, Czechoslovakia, 16 mi. NNE of Dvur Kralove, near Pol. border; rail terminus; important coal mines (Zacler-Svatonovice bituminous coal field, part of Lower Silesian bed). Zacler pass (alt. 1,692 ft.) is at SE end of the Riesengebirge.

Zacoalco or **Zacoalco de Torres** (säkwäl′kō dā tô′rĕs), town (pop. 6,227), Jalisco, W Mexico, on L. Zacoalco and 35 mi. SSW of Guadalajara, on railroad; alt. 4,432 ft. Agr. center (grain, beans, alfalfa, fruit, livestock).

Zacualpa (säkwäl′pä), town (1950 pop. 705), Quiché dept., W central Guatemala, in Sierra de Chuacús, 20 mi. ENE of Quiché; alt. 7,782 ft.; livestock raising.

Zacualpan (säkwäl′pän), **1** Town (pop. 2,221), Mexico state, central Mexico, 40 mi. SSW of Toluca; silver, gold, lead, copper mining. **2** Town (pop. 1,602), Veracruz, E Mexico, in Sierra Madre Oriental, 33 mi. NE of Pachuca; alt. 5,922 ft.; cereals, sugar cane, tobacco, coffee.

Zacualpan de Amilpas (dā ämēl′päs), town (pop. 1,213), Morelos, central Mexico, 13 mi. E of Cuautla; sugar cane, coffee, fruit, livestock.

Zacualtipán (säkwältēpän′), city (pop. 3,516), Hidalgo, central Mexico, in Sierra Madre Oriental, 40 mi. N of Pachuca; alt. 6,627 ft.; agr. center (corn, beans, fruit, stock); tanning, leather goods.

Zacynthus, Greece: see ZANTE.

Zadar (zä′där), Ital. *Zara* (dzä′rä), anc. *Diadora* (Slavic *Iadera* or *Jadera*), town (pop. 14,847), W Croatia, Yugoslavia, major port on Zadar Channel (bet. Uljan Isl. and mainland) of Adriatic Sea, 120 mi. SSW of Zagreb, in Dalmatia. Tourist center; seaside resort; liqueur mfg. (maraschino), marasca growing. Zemunik airport is 7 mi. E. Town has many parks and Roman remains. It is a R.C. archiepiscopal see, made a bishopric in 950 and an archbishopric in 1154. Its 9th-cent. church (now a mus.) was built on ruins of Roman temple. Has 2 Romanesque churches (13th cent.), 5 fountains (built 1574), Venetian clock tower. Former Croatian and Serbian cultural center. Pop. includes Italians, Croats, and Serbs. A Roman colony from time of Augustus, it was settled by the South Slavs in 7th cent. and was conquered by Venice in 1000. The city having been seized by the Hungarians, the doge Enrico Dandolo of Venice persuaded the leaders of the 4th Crusade to reconquer it for Venice. The crusaders took it in Nov., 1202, after a 5-day siege, and sacked the city, an act for which they were condemned by Pope Innocent III. Hungary continued to dispute the city with Venice, which obtained permanent possession of the city only in 1409. The Treaty of Campo Formio (1797) gave it to the Hapsburg monarchy, and from 1815 to 1918 it was ⊙ Austrian crownland of Dalmatia. Passed (1920) to Italy, where it constituted (with Lastovo Isl.) Zara prov. (□ 42; 1936 pop. 22,000) of Venezia Giulia; ceded (1947) to Yugoslavia. Almost entirely destroyed in Second World War; rapidly rebuilt.

Zadonsk (zŭdônsk′), city (1926 pop. 7,575), E Orel oblast, Russian SFSR, on Don R. (head of navigation) and 23 mi. SE of Yelets; fruit- and vegetable-canning center.

Zadonye or **Zadon'ye** (zŭdô′nyĭ), town (1939 pop. over 2,000), S Moscow oblast, Russian SFSR, 3 mi. NW of Donskoi; lignite-mining center.

Zadorra River (thä-dhō′rä), Álava prov., N Spain, rises NE of Vitoria, flows c.60 mi. SSW to the Ebro 4 mi. below Mirando de Ebro.

Zadvarje, Yugoslavia: see SESTANOVAC.

Zafar, Oman: see DHOFAR.

Zafar, Jabal (jă′băl zăfär′), hill of S Yemen, 5 mi. W of Yarim. Here stood **Zafar** (anc. *Sapphar*), capital of Himyaritic kingdom (115 B.C.–A.D. 300) which superseded the Sabaean capital of Marib.

Zafarabad (zŭfŭr″äbäd′), town (pop. 2,962), Jaunpur dist., SE Uttar Pradesh, India, on the Gumti and 5 mi. SE of Jaunpur; rail junction; barley, rice, corn, wheat. Moslem fort ruins, 14th cent. mosque. Under Kanauj kingdom, 11th–12th cents.; under Tughlaks in 14th cent.

Zafargarh (zŭfŭr′gŭr) or **Zafargadh** (–gŭd), town (pop. 5,177), Warangal dist., E Hyderabad state, India, 17 mi. SSW of Warangal; rice, oilseeds. Also called Zafargudh and Valabgonda.

Zafarin Islands, Spain: see CHAFARINAS ISLANDS.

Zafarraya (thäfärī′ä), town (pop. 1,818), Granada prov., S Spain, 14 mi. S of Loja; sheep raising; cereals, vegetables.

Zaffarano, Cape (zäf″färä′nô), point on NW coast of Sicily, at SE end of Gulf of Palermo, 9 mi. E of Palermo; 38°7′N 13°32′E.

Zaffarine Islands, Spain: see CHAFARINAS ISLANDS.

Zaffelare (zä′fŭlärŭ), village (pop. 3,265), East Flanders prov., NW Belgium, 9 mi. NE of Ghent; agr., truck gardening. Formerly spelled Saffelaere.

Zafra (thä′frä), city (pop. 7,740), Badajoz prov., W Spain, in Estremadura, on railroad and 44 mi. SE of Badajoz; trading and processing center in agr. region (cereals, grapes, vegetables, fruit, olives, chick-peas, livestock). Olive-oil pressing, flour milling, liquor distilling, tanning, sawmilling; mfg. of plaster, tiles, ceramics, paper bags, soft drinks; iron foundries. Coal deposits near by. Known for its cattle fairs. A picturesque city of outstanding architectural landmarks, it has an imposing alcazar, a parochial church with Renaissance portal, and several other fine religious bldgs. Of Celtic origin, and successively seized by Romans and Visigoths, Zafra was taken from the Moors in 1240.

Zafra de Záncara (dhā thäng′kärä), town (pop. 910), Cuenca prov., E central Spain, 26 mi. SW of Cuenca; grain, sheep.

Zafrane (zäfrän′), agr. village, Le Kef dist., NW central Tunisia, on railroad and 6 mi. ESE of Le Kef.

Zagan, Poland: see SAGAN.

Zagare or **Zhagare** (zhägärā′), Lith. *Žagarė*, Pol. *Żagory*, city (pop. 5,443), N Lithuania, 15 mi. NW of Joniskis, on Latvian border; shoe-mfg. center; brewing. First mentioned in 12th cent.; in Rus. Kovno govt. until 1920.

Zagarolo (zägärô′lô), village (pop. 4,840), Roma prov., Latium, central Italy, 3 mi. W of Palestrina; wine making. Damaged in Second World War.

Zagazig (ză′gă′zēg), **Zaqaziq** (ză′kă′zēk), **El Zagazig, Ez Zagazig,** or **Al-Zaqaziq** (all: ĕz), town (pop. 82,912), ⊙ Sharqiya prov., SE Lower Egypt, 40 mi. NNE of Cairo; 30°35′N 31°30′E. Rail and canal center; important cotton and grain market; cotton ginning. Two mi. SE are ruins of anc. BUBASTIS.

Zages, Georgian SSR: see ZEMO-AVCHALA.

Zaghartah, Lebanon: see ZGHARTA.

Zagheh (zăgĕ′), town, Sixth Prov., in Luristan, SW Iran, 18 mi. E of Khurramabad.

Zaghouan (zägwän′, Fr. zägwã′), town (pop. 4,436), ⊙ Zaghouan dist. (□ 971; pop. 60,764), NE Tunisia, at foot of the Djebel Zaghouan, 27 mi. S of Tunis; market center (olives, fruits, cereals). Lead and zinc mines near by. Scene of fighting (1943) in Second World War.

Zaghouan, Djebel (jĕ′bĕl), mountain (alt. 4,249 ft.) of NE Tunisia, overlooking Zaghouan, 30 mi. S of Tunis; lead and zinc mines. Its waters were conveyed to Carthage (35 mi. N) by means of a Roman aqueduct still in use. A Roman temple guards the spring.

Zaglik (zŭglyēk′), village (1939 pop. over 2,000), W Azerbaijan SSR, 20 mi. SW of Kirovabad; alunite-mining center, supplying Erivan aluminum works.

Zagliverion, Greece: see ZANGLIVERION.

Zagnando (zänyän′dō), village, S Dahomey, Fr. West Africa, on railroad and 55 mi. NNW of Porto Novo; palm kernels, palm oil, coffee. R.C. mission.

Zagora (zŭgôrä′), town (pop. 3,223), Magnesia nome, SE Thessaly, Greece, near Aegean Sea, 10 mi. NE of Volos, across the Pelion. Olive oil, tobacco; sheep and goat raising. Was important commercial and industrial center in 14th cent., exporting cloth fabrics.

Zagora, mountain, Greece: see HELICON.

Zagora (zägôrä′), village and Saharan oasis (pop. 667), Marrakesh region, S Fr. Morocco, on the Oued Dra and 75 mi. SE of Ouarzazate; 30°19′N 5°50′W; date palms.

Zagora (zä′gôrä), region, W Croatia, Yugoslavia, bet. Dinara mtn. range and Adriatic Sea, in Dalmatia. Bauxite deposits. Chief village, SINJ.

Zagorje or **Zagorje ob Savi** (zä′gôryĕ ôp sä′vē), Ger. *Sagor* (zä′gôr), village, central Slovenia, Yugoslavia, on Sava R., on railroad and 24 mi. E of Ljubljana; brown-coal mining; hollow-glass mfg. Until 1918, in Carniola.

Zagorow (zägōō′rōōf), Pol. *Zagórów*, Rus. *Zagurov* (zŭgōō′rŭf), town (pop. 3,034), Poznan prov., W central Poland, 45 mi. ESE of Poznan, near Warta R.; flour milling, tanning; trades in cattle, swine.

Zagorsk (zŭgôrsk′), city (1926 pop. 21,563), NE Moscow oblast, Russian SFSR, 40 mi. NNE of Moscow; handicraft center; produces home-made toys. Has handicraft art mus., toy-research institute, teachers col. Chemical works near by, at Krasnozavodsk. Site of Troitsko-Sergiyevskaya Lavra, one of most famous former Rus. monasteries (now a mus.), founded 1340; contains Troitski cathedral (1427), 16th-cent. Uspenski cathedral (tomb of Boris Godunov), treasure chamber with rich tapestries and other church art objects. Chartered 1762; known as Sergiyevski Posad until the revolution, and, until c.1930, as Sergiyev.

Zagorski or **Zagorskiy** (–skē). **1** Town, Moscow oblast, Russian SFSR; see KRASNOZAVODSK. **2** Town (1947 pop. over 500), S Sakhalin, Russian SFSR, in Naiba R. valley, near Dolinsk; coal mining. Under Japanese rule (1905–45) called Nishi-naibuchi.

Zagreb (zä′grĕb), Ger. *Agram* (ä′gräm), Hung. *Zágráb* (zä′gräb), city (pop. 290,417), ⊙ Croatia and Zagreb oblast (formed 1949), Yugoslavia, on Sava R., on Belgrade-Ljubljana highway (constructed 1947–50) and 230 mi. WNW of Belgrade; 45°49′N 15°58′E. Second-largest city of Yugoslavia; rail and road junction; airport; major industrial center; mfg. of machinery, woolen textiles, leather and leather goods, paper, furniture, bricks, asbestos goods, paints and varnishes, pharmaceuticals, confectionery, cigars; meat and vegetable packing, flour milling, distilling, brewing. Wine-growing and vegetable raising near by. Has univ. (1669), music (1829) and art (1907) academies, teachers' (1919), economic and commercial (1920), and public health colleges, several museums and galleries, theaters, opera, botanic and zoological gardens, and parks. Seat of R.C. and Orthodox Eastern archbishops, Protestant bishop. City consists of: Kaptol (NE), the old ecclesiastical town, with Gothic cathedral (begun 1093; present edifice dates from early-17th cent.) and archbishop's palace (1723–48) protected by walls and towers; old Gornji Grad [Serbo-Croatian, =upper town] (N) with palaces of former Croat nobility and remnants of town walls; Donji Grad [Serbo-Croatian, =lower town] (S) developed entirely since beginning of 19th cent. The MEDVEDNICA, which overlooks Zagreb on N, is pierced by tunnel linking the city with Krapina R. valley. First mentioned on occasion of erection (1093) of bishopric by Hungary, Zagreb developed through gradual merger of the Kaptol and the upper town (formerly called Gradec; made a free royal city in 1242); became capital of Croatia and Slavonia in 1867. Damaged by earthquakes (1880, 1901). The Catholic see of Zagreb was left vacant after the imprisonment (1946) of Archbishop Stepinac.

Zagreb Mountain, Yugoslavia: see MEDVEDNICA.

Zagros (ză′grŏs), major mountain system of Iran, forming W and S limits of Iranian plateau, and extending from Azerbaijan, along the Turkish and Iraq frontiers and along the Persian Gulf, to Iranian Baluchistan; it rises to 14–15,000 ft. The NW Zagros in Azerbaijan underwent faulting and other tectonic movements which resulted in the creation of large basins (Lake Urmia), horst blocks separated by deeply incised river valleys, and numerous volcanic cones (Savalon, Sahand). In the central Zagros, folding is the main feature, with a series of well-defined parallel ridges separated by deep valleys and cut by river gorges known as *tangs*. The central Zagros is noted for its curious salt domes or plugs rising to 5,000 ft., and for several closed lowland basins with salt marshes in their lowest part. The SE Zagros trends E-W, unlike the NW-SE direction of the remainder of the system, and presents an irregular, desolate landscape of rock or sand dunes. Pop. is relatively dense in NW valleys where wheat, barley, tobacco, cotton, and fruit are raised. Tribal pastoral pop. resides in central section; and in arid SE, dates are the principal agr. product. The Zagros is crossed by Trans-Iranian RR bet. Arak and Andimishk and by roads to the Persian Gulf ports of Bushire and Bandar Abbas. Iran's great oil production stems from the Khuzistan foothills of the central Zagros. The name Zagros is sometimes restricted to the NW and central sections of the system in W Iran.

Zagubica or **Zhagubitsa** (both: zhä'gŏŏbētsä), Serbo-Croatian *Žagubica*, village (pop. 3,253), E Serbia, Yugoslavia, on Mlava R. and 40 mi. SE of Pozarevac.

Zagurov, Poland: see ZAGOROW.

Zagyvapalfalva (zŏ'dyŭvŏpälfŏlvŏ), Hung. *Zagyvapálfalva*, town (pop. 4,286), Nograd-Hont co., N Hungary, on branch of Zagyva R. and 3 mi. S of Salgotarjan; glass mfg.; rye, potatoes, sheep.

Zagyvarekas (zŏ'dyŭvŏrākŏsh), Hung. *Zagyvarékas*, town (pop. 4,854), Jasz-Nagykun-Szolnok co., central Hungary, on Zagyva R. and 7 mi. NNW of Szolnok; wheat, corn, hogs.

Zagyva River (zŏ'dyŭvŏ), N Hungary, rises near Czechoslovak border NNE of Salgotarjan, flows 100 mi. S, past Zagyvarona, Paszto, Hatvan, and Jaszbereny, to the Tisza at Szolnok.

Zagyvarona (zŏ'dyŭvŏ"rōnŏ), Hung. *Zagyvaróna*, town (pop. 2,529), Nograd-Hont co., N Hungary, on Zagyva R. and 4 mi. NE of Salgotarjan; potatoes, rye, hogs.

Zahara (thä-ä'rä), town (pop. 1,651), Cádiz prov., SW Spain, 14 mi. NW of Ronda, in agr. region (cereals, olives, truck produce, fruit, livestock); timber. Old Moorish town taken (1483) by Ferdinand V. Has old castle. Another Zahara village is on Atlantic coast 31 mi. SE of Cádiz.

Zahidan or **Zahedan** (both: zähĕdän'), town (1933 pop. 5,000), Eighth Prov., in Baluchistan, SE Iran, 230 mi. ESE of Kerman, near Pakistan line; major transit center; rail terminus (since 1919) of line to Quetta; airfield. Formerly called Duzdab, it was renamed (1930s) for anc. capital of Seistan, whose ruins (12 mi. ESE of Zabul) date from its destruction (1383) by Tamerlane.

Zahinos (thäē'nōs), town (pop. 3,352), Badajoz prov., W Spain, 10 mi. W of Jerez de los Caballeros; flour milling; grain, livestock.

Zahirabad (zŭhē'räbäd), town (pop. 8,020), Bidar dist., central Hyderabad state, India, 12 mi. SSE of Bidar; cotton ginning, rice and oilseed milling. Formerly called Ekeli.

Zahirah, Oman: see DHAHIRA.

Zahle or **Zahlah** (both: zä'lŭ), Fr. *Zahlé*, town (pop. 25,153), ⊙ Bekaa prov., central Lebanon, on Beirut-Damascus RR, and 25 mi. ESE of Beirut; alt. 3,100 ft. Popular summer resort, with a fine climate; overlooks the fertile BEKAA valley. Vineyards cover the mtn. slopes here. Well-known arrack is distilled in Zahle.

Zahna (tsä'nä), town (pop. 5,992), in former Prussian Saxony prov., central Germany, after 1945 in Saxony-Anhalt, 7 mi. NE of Wittenberg; paper and cardboard milling.

Zahony (zä'hônyŭ), Hung. *Záhony*, frontier town (pop. 1,383), Szabolcs co., NE Hungary, on the Tisza and 37 mi. NE of Nyiregyhaza, just opposite Chop, USSR; rail junction; lumber mill; potatoes, rye, hogs.

Zahran, Saudi Arabia: see DHAHRAN.

Zähringen (tsâ'rĭng-ŭn), N suburb of FREIBURG, S Baden, Germany, with ruins of ancestral castle of the powerful dynasty of Zähringen.

Zai, river, Russian SFSR: see ZAI RIVER.

Zaidín (thī-dhēn'), town (pop. 1,833), Huesca prov., NE Spain, near Cinca R., 20 mi. W of Lérida; olive-oil processing; cereals, figs. Has remains of medieval castle and walls.

Zaidiya or **Zaydiyah** (zädē'yŭ), town (pop. 5,000), Hodeida prov., Yemen, 35 mi. N of Hodeida, on Tihama coastal plain; cotton weaving, tanning. Sometimes spelled Zeydiyeh.

Zaidpur (zīd'pŏŏr), town (pop. 8,785), Bara Banki dist., central Uttar Pradesh, India, 11 mi. SE of Nawabganj; hand-loom cotton weaving; trades in rice, gram, wheat, oilseeds, barley. Founded 15th cent. by a Sayid.

Zaigrayevo (zŭēgrī'ŭvŭ), village (1948 pop. over 500), S Buryat-Mongol Autonomous SSR, Russian SFSR, on Trans-Siberian RR and 25 mi. E of Ulan-Ude, in agr. area (wheat, livestock).

Zaikovo or **Zaykovo** (zī'kŭvŭ), village (1926 pop. 786), SE central Sverdlovsk oblast, Russian SFSR, on Irbit R. (right tributary of Nitsa R.) and 14 mi. SW of Irbit, on railroad; food processing; wheat, livestock.

Zailiski Ala-Tau, Zailiiski Ala-Tau, or **Zailiyskiy Ala-Tau,** Kazakh SSR: see TRANS-ILI ALA-TAU.

Zaindeh River (zīndĕ'), **Zayandeh River,** or **Zayendeh River** (both: zīyĕndĕ'), central Iran, rises on the Kuh-i-Rang in the Bakhtiari country S of Khunsar, flows 250 mi. E in lowland bet. 2 Zagros ranges, through Linjan agr. dist., and past Isfahan, to Gavkhaneh (Gavkhuni) salt marsh 70 mi. ESE of Isfahan. Used for irrigation along entire course. Hydroelectric project involves connection in upper reaches with Karun R.

Zainsk (zī'ĭnsk), village (1926 pop. 4,337), E central Tatar Autonomous SSR, Russian SFSR, on Zai R. and 55 mi. E of Chistopol; wheat, livestock.

Zaio (thä'yō), village (pop. 577), Kert territory, E Sp. Morocco, near the Muluya (Fr. Morocco border), on road and 27 mi. SE of Melilla; olive and palm trees. Military post.

Zaire, Angola: see SANTO ANTÓNIO DO ZAIRE.

Zai River or **Zay River** (zī), Tatar Autonomous SSR, Russian SFSR, rises c.10 mi. SW of Bugulma as Stepnoi Zai R., flows generally NNW, past Aktash and Zainsk (here becoming Zai R.), to Kama R. 14 mi. SE of Mamadysh; length, including Stepnoi Zai R., 100 mi. Receives Lesnoi Zai R. (right).

Zaisan or **Zaysan** (zīsän'), city (1926 pop. 8,245), SW East Kazakhstan oblast, Kazakh SSR, bet. L. Zaisan (N) and China frontier, 200 mi. SE of Ust-Kamenogorsk; wheat, cattle; opium fields. Founded 1868 as Rus. military post.

Zaisan, Lake, or **Lake Zaysan** (□ 700), S East Kazakhstan oblast, Kazakh SSR, near China border, 120 mi. SE of Ust-Kamenogorsk, in large depression bet. Narym Range of Altai Mts. (N) and Tarbagatai Range (S); 60 mi. long. 30 ft. deep; receives the Black-Irtysh R. (E) and Kenderlyk R. (S); gives rise to Irtysh R.; fisheries.

Zaiton, China: see TSINKIANG.

Zaitsevo or **Zaytsevo** (zī'tsyĭvŭ), town (1926 pop. 4,967), central Stalino oblast, Ukrainian SSR, in the Donbas, 6 mi. N of Gorlovka; dolomite quarries.

Zaitun, China: see TSINKIANG.

Zajecar or **Zayechar** (both: zäyĕ'chär), Serbo-Croatian *Zaječar*, town (pop. 12,300), ⊙ Timak oblast (formed 1949), E Serbia, Yugoslavia, on the Crna Reka, just above its confluence with Beli Timok R. and 110 mi. SE of Belgrade, near Bulg. border. Rail junction; glassworks, brewery; antimony mine and smelter. High-grade bituminous coal mines in vicinity.

Zajecice, Czechoslovakia: see JIRKOV.

Zaka (zä'kä), village, Victoria prov., SE Southern Rhodesia, in Mashonaland, 45 mi. ESE of Fort Victoria; livestock; corn. Hq. of native commissioner for Ndanga dist. Police post.

Zakamsk, Russian SFSR: see MOLOTOV, city.

Zakarovce, Czechoslovakia: see KROMPACHY.

Zakarpatskaya Oblast, Ukrainian SSR: see TRANSCARPATHIAN OBLAST.

Zakataly (zŭkŭtä'lē), city (1932 pop. estimate 6,380), N Azerbaijan SSR, on S slope of the Greater Caucasus, on highway from Yevlakh and 40 mi. NW of Nukha; fruit, nuts, vegetable canning; tobacco products; subtropical agr. Founded 1830 as Rus. fortress. Was ⊙ separate okrug until 1920.

Zakharo, Greece: see ZACHARO.

Zakharovka, Ukrainian SSR: see FRUNZOVKA.

Zakharovo (zŭkhä'rŭvŭ), village (1939 pop. over 500), W Ryazan oblast, Russian SFSR, 20 mi. SW of Ryazan; grain, wheat.

Zakhmatabad (zŭkhmät"ŭbät'), village (1939 pop. over 500), S Leninabad oblast, Tadzhik SSR, on Zerafshan R., on Leninabad-Stalinabad highway and 40 mi. SSW of Ura-Tyube; wheat, goats; gold placers.

Zakinthos, Greece: see ZANTE.

Zakopane (zäkôpä'nĕ), town (pop. 13,752), Krakow prov., S Poland, 50 mi. S of Cracow, in the Podhale, at N foot of the High Tatra. Rail spur terminus; principal Pol. mtn. health resort (alt. 2,919 ft.) and winter-sports center; many sanatoria, hotels, and pensions; lumbering; hydroelectric plant. Development began in late-19th cent.

Zakovce, Czechoslovakia: see POPRAD, town.

Zak River or **Sak River** (both: säk), W Cape Prov., U. of So. Afr., rises on the Great Karroo NNW of Beaufort West, flows 350 mi. generally N, past Williston, through several swamp areas, to confluence with small Mottels R. 7 mi. SE of Kenhardt, forming Hartebeest R.

Zakroczym (zäkrô'chĭm), Rus. *Zakrochim* (zŭkrô'-chĭm), town (pop. 3,358), Warszawa prov., E central Poland, port on the Vistula and 22 mi. NW of Warsaw; flour milling, chicory processing.

Zakrzow, Poland: see SAKRAU.

Zakupy (zä'kŏŏpĭ), Czech *Zákupy*, Ger. *Reichstadt* (rīkh'shtät), (pop. 1,937), N Bohemia, Czechoslovakia, on railroad and 27 mi. E of Usti nad Labem; agr. center. Forestry school. Noted for its castle, from which son of Napoleon I took his title of duke of Reichstadt.

Zakynthos, Greece: see ZANTE.

Zala (zŏ'lŏ), county (□ 1,763; pop. 356,533), W Hungary; ⊙ Zalaegerszeg. Hilly, heavily forested central area; drained by Zala and Mura rivers; borders E on L. Balaton. Wheat, rye, corn, potatoes, grapes, honey; truck farming; livestock. Vineyards near L. Balaton produce fine wines. Mfg. at Nagykanizsa. Formerly the co. included a small region (MEDJUMURJE), now in Yugoslavia.

Zalaapati (zŏ'lŏ-ôpätē), Hung. *Zalaapáti*, town (pop. 2,081), Zala co., W Hungary, on Zala R. and 14 mi. SE of Zalaegerszeg; rye, corn, cattle.

Zalaegerszeg (zŏ'lŏĕ"gĕrsĕg), city (pop. 13,967), ⊙ Zala co., SW Hungary, on Zala R. and 52 mi. WSW of Veszprem; rail center; brickworks. Truck farming (eggs, plums, apples, pears), cattle, hogs; wheat, rye, corn grown in vicinity.

Zalalövö (zŏ'lŏlûvû), Hung. *Zalalövő*, town (pop. 3,356), Zala co., W Hungary, on Zala R. and 12 mi. W of Zalaegerszeg; rail junction; sawmills; grain, hogs, sheep.

Zalamea de la Serena (thälämā'ä dhā lä sārā'nä), town (pop. 8,451), Badajoz prov., SW Spain, in Estremadura, on La Serena plain, 40 mi. E of Almendralejo; agr. center (cereals, grapes, olives, livestock); mfg. of tiles, shoes, cheese, flour. Granite quarries near by. Chiefly noted for its cultural associations, the anc. town has a splendid parochial church, whose steeple is a relic of an arch built by Trajan. Also has a Moorish castle, Druid altars, and the house where the mayor of Zalamea (immortalized by Calderón's play) supposedly lived.

Zalamea la Real (lä rääl'), town (pop. 3,834), Huelva prov., SW Spain, on railroad and 33 mi. NE of Huelva; copper, manganese, and pyrite mining. Produces also cereals, acorns, timber, livestock. Liquor distilling, mfg. of meat products.

Zalari (zŭlŭrē'), village (1926 pop. 2,220), S Irkutsk oblast, Russian SFSR, on Trans-Siberian RR and 45 mi. NW of Cheremkhovo; coal mining; metalworking, distilling.

Zala River (zŏ'lŏ), W Hungary, rises near Yugoslavian border, flows E, past Zalaegerszeg, thence NE and S, past Zalaszentgrot to L. Balaton 6 mi. S of Keszthely. Length, 70 mi.

Zalaszanto (zŏ'lŏsäntō), Hung. *Zalaszántó*, town (pop. 2,459), Zala co., W Hungary, 18 mi. E of Zalaegerszeg; rye, wheat, cattle.

Zalaszentgrot (zŏ'lŏsĕndgrōt), Hung. *Zalaszentgrót*, town (pop. 2,516), Zala co., W Hungary, on Zala R. and 13 mi. NE of Zalaegerszeg; rye, corn, sheep.

Zalatna, Rumania: see ZLATNA.

Zalau (zŭlû'ŏŏ), Rum. *Zălău*, Hung. *Zilah* (zē'lŏkh), town (1948 pop. 11,652), Cluj prov., NW Rumania, in Transylvania, on railroad and 250 mi. NW of Bucharest; trading center for agr. produce (grain, livestock, fruit); flour milling, tanning; mfg. of edible oils, bricks. Predominantly Magyar pop. In Hungary, 1940–45.

Zalawad (zŭ'lŭväd), district, N Saurashtra, India; ⊙ Surendranagar.

Zaldivia (thäldē'vyä), town (pop. 1,622), Guipúzcoa prov., N Spain, 7 mi. SSW of Tolosa; flour milling, cheese processing; lumbering; cereals, apples, chestnuts, livestock.

Zalegoshch or **Zalegoshch'** (zŭlyĕ'gŭshch), village (1939 pop. over 500), central Orel oblast, Russian SFSR, 33 mi. E of Orel; hemp.

Zaleshchiki (zŭlyĕ'shchĭkē), Pol. *Zaleszczyki* (zälĕshchĭ'kē), city (1931 pop. 4,114), S Ternopol oblast, Ukrainian SSR, on the Dniester and 25 mi. S of Chortkov; summer resort; winegrowing center; distilling, flour milling; fruit, truck. Passed to Austria (1772). Reverted to Poland (1919); developed as frontier town on Rum. border. Ceded to USSR in 1945.

Zaleski (zŭlĕ'skē), village (pop. 388), Vinton co., S Ohio, 30 mi. E of Chillicothe, and on Raccoon Creek, in forested area.

Zalesovo (zŭlyĕ'sŭvŭ), village (1926 pop. 2,379), NE Altai Territory, Russian SFSR, 60 mi. NE of Barnaul, in agr. area.

Zalesye or **Zales'ye** (zŭlyĕ'syĭ), village (1939 pop. 4,089), N central Kaliningrad oblast, Russian SFSR, 18 mi. NW of Chernyakhovsk, in marshy wooded dist. Until 1945, in East Prussia where it was called Mehlauken (mā'loukŭn) and, later (1938–45), Liebenfelde (lē'bŭnfĕldŭ).

Zaleszczyki, Ukrainian SSR: see ZALESHCHIKI.

Zalingei (zä'lĭng-gā), town, Darfur prov., W Anglo-Egyptian Sudan, in Marra Mts., 140 mi. WSW of El Fasher; trade center (gum arabic, peanuts, sesame).

Zalma (zăl'mŭ), town (pop. 137), Bollinger co., SE Mo., on Castor R. and 32 mi. WSW of Cape Girardeau.

Zalozhtsy (zŭlôsh'tsē), Pol. *Założce* (zäwôsh'tsĕ), village (1931 pop. 5,891), NW Ternopol oblast, Ukrainian SSR, on Seret R. (here forms artificial lake) and 20 mi. NW of Ternopol; flour milling, distilling; bricks. Has ruins of 16th-cent. castle.

Zaltbommel (zält'bômŭl), town (pop. 4,774), Gelderland prov., central Netherlands, on Bommelwaard isl., on Waal R. (bridges) and 9 mi. N of 's Hertogenbosch; mfg. (metalware, buttons, lighting fixtures, tobacco products); tin-coating and printing plants; shipbuilding. Formerly a fortified place; attacked by Spaniards (1599) and French (1672). Sometimes called Bommel.

Zaluchye or **Zaluch'ye** (zŭlŏŏ'chyĭ), village (1926 pop. 351), SW Novgorod oblast, Russian SFSR, 27 mi. SE of Staraya Russa; flax.

Zalukokoazhe (zŭlŏŏ"kŭkŭä'zhĕ), village (1939 pop. over 500), NW Kabardian Autonomous SSR, Russian SFSR, on Pyatigorsk-Nalchik road and 11 mi. SE of Pyatigorsk; wheat, corn, sunflowers; horse breeding.

Zalun (zŭlŏŏn'), village, Henzada dist., Lower Burma, on right bank of Irrawaddy R. (ferry) and 13 mi. SSE of Henzada; celebrated brass image of Buddha.

Zaluzi (zä'lŏŏzhē), Czech *Záluží*, village (pop. 3,182), NW Bohemia, Czechoslovakia; 3 mi. NW of Most; site of major synthetic-fuel plant; coal and peat mining.

Zama, Tunisia: see JAMA.

Zamalka (zămăl'kă), village (pop. c.1,500), Damascus prov., SW Syria, 2 mi. ENE of Damascus, in the fertile Ghuta valley; pears, walnuts.

Zamami-shima (zä"mä'mē-shĭmä), island (□ 8; 1950 pop. 1,179, including offshore islets) of Kerama-retto, Okinawa Isls., in Ryukyu Islands, in E. China Sea, 20 mi. W of Okinawa; 3 mi. long, 1.5 mi. wide. Rice, sweet potatoes, sugar cane.

Zamania (zŭmän'yŭ), town (pop. 6,183), Ghazipur dist., E Uttar Pradesh, India, on the Ganges and 12 mi. S of Ghazipur; rice, barley, gram, sugar cane. Founded 1560 by a governor of Akbar.

Zamanti River, Turkey: see SEYHAN RIVER.

Zamarramala (thämä"rämä'lä), village (pop. 521), Segovia prov., central Spain, 1 mi. NW of Segovia; grain, chick-peas, livestock. Its parochial church once belonged to Knights Templars.

Zambales (sämbä'läs), province (□ 1,408; 1948 pop. 138,536), central Luzon, Philippines, bounded W by S. China Sea, S by Subic Bay; ⊙ IBA. Largely mountainous; rises to 6,683 ft. in High Peak. Extensive rice growing on low coastal strip. Zambales is chief chromite center of Philippines; chrome ore was discovered here in 1922.

Zamberk (zhäm'bĕrk), Czech *Žamberk*, Ger. *Senftenberg* (zĕnf'tŭnbĕrk), town (pop. 3,085), E Bohemia, Czechoslovakia, on Divocha Orlice R., on railroad and 29 mi. ESE of Hradec Kralove; oats; textiles (notably cotton), smoked meats. Lace-making school. Has large castle with park.

Zambesi River, Africa: see ZAMBEZI RIVER.

Zambézia (zămbē'zhŭ, Port. zămbĕz'yä), province (□ 38,804; 1950 pop. 1,164,182), central Mozambique; ⊙ Quelimane. Bounded W by Nyasaland, SW by lower Shire and Zambezi rivers, and SE by Mozambique Channel of Indian Ocean. Coastal plain (c.80 mi. wide) rises to an undulating highland (NW) above which tower isolated higher peaks (especially Namuli Mts., 7,936 ft.). Commercial agr. consists of sugar (near mouth of Zambezi R.) and of sisal and cotton (especially in Mocuba area). Coconut palms grow along coast. A short railroad links Mocuba with Quelimane (prov.'s only good port); roads lead N and NW into Nyasaland. Zambézia prov. is coextensive with Quelimane dist.

Zambezia or **Zambesia,** name which was formerly given to drainage basin of Zambezi R. in S central and SE Africa, within limits of Rhodesia.

Zambezi River or **Zambesi River** (both: zămbē'zē), Port. *Zambeze*, one of Africa's great rivers, in S central and SE Africa, rises in northwesternmost Northern Rhodesia (near 11°20'S 24°E), flows in a vast S-curve whose general trend is SE, across Rhodesia and Mozambique to the Mozambique Channel of Indian Ocean 130 mi. NE of Beira; estimated length, 1,600–1,650 mi. From its source river flows S, across easternmost section of Angola, traverses Barotseland, and, turning SE and E, forms (for over 80 mi.) border bet. Northern Rhodesia and South-West Africa's Caprivi Strip. Beyond Kasungula it marks the entire border bet. Northern and Southern Rhodesia. In this section are the world-famous VICTORIA FALLS and, 200 mi. further, the Kariba Gorge (hydroelectric, irrigation, and industrial scheme is planned). At Zumbo the Zambezi enters Mozambique, and beyond the Quebrabasa Rapids turns SE, flowing past Tete (head of steamboat navigation) and Sena (site of Trans-Zambezia RR bridge) to Mozambique Channel in a marshy delta. The Chinde mouth is used for navigation. The upper Zambezi and its largest tributaries are navigable for barges in stretches bet. falls and rapids, but large-scale commercial navigation is impossible. Chief affluents are on right—the Lungwebungu and Luanginga from Angola, the Chobe from N Bechuanaland's marshes, the Shangani and Sanyati from Southern Rhodesia's high veld, and the Mazoe; on left are the Kafue and Luangwa, draining Northern Rhodesia, and the Shire (outlet of L. Nyasa). The Zambezi's middle course was explored by Livingstone 1851–56, but little further information was gathered until end of 19th cent.

Zamboanga (sämbōäng'gä), province (□ 6,517; 1948 pop. 521,941), Philippines, occupying a long peninsula at extreme W part of Mindanao; ⊙ Zamboanga. Includes a number of offshore isls., notably BASILAN ISLAND, off S tip 10 mi. across Basilan Strait. Borders W on Sulu Sea (Sulu Archipelago extends to SW), S on Sibuguey Bay and Moro Gulf, SE on Illana Bay. Mtn. chain traverses its length, rising to 8,620 ft. in Mt. Dapiak (N). Moros inhabit much of the prov. and engage in fishing. Heavily forested. Copra, abacá, rice, corn. Most of Philippine rubber comes from Zamboanga. Coal mined at Malangas. Chief town, besides Zamboanga, are Pagadian, Dapitan, Dipolog, Kabasalan, Katipunan, Liloy, Sindañgan.

Zamboanga, city (1939 pop. 12,469; 1948 dist. pop. 103,317), ⊙ Zamboanga prov., Philippines, at SW tip of Mindanao, on Basilan Strait across from Basilan Isl., 550 mi. S of Manila; 6°55'N 122°5'E. Port, trade center, and chief city of Mindanao. Exports copra, desiccated coconut, timber, rubber, agr. produce, abacá. Founded 1635 as colonial fort. The city is part of the "City of Zamboanga," which is really a vast district, equivalent to a county; besides the S part of the peninsula, it formerly also included Basilan Isl. Zamboanga, a Jap. stronghold in Second World War, was taken by U.S. forces in March, 1945. The badly damaged port facilities have been repaired.

Zamboanguita (sämbōäng-gē'tä), town (1939 pop. 3,126; 1948 municipality pop. 9,922), Negros Oriental prov., SE Negros isl., Philippines, on Mindanao Sea, 16 mi. SW of Dumaguete; agr. center (coconuts, sugar cane.).

Zambrano (sämbrä'nō), town (pop. 2,901), Bolívar dept., N Colombia, minor river port on the Magdalena and 36 mi. S of Calamar; tobacco and cattle center. Picturesque Jesús del Río (häsōōs'dĕl rē'ō) settlement is 8 mi. NW.

Zambrow (zäm'brōōf), Pol. *Zambrów*, Rus. *Zambrov* (zäm'brŭf), town (pop. 4,150), Bialystok prov., NE Poland, 15 mi. SSE of Lomza; mfg. of rack wagons, tanning, flour milling. Before Second World War, pop. was 1/3 Jewish.

Zamfara River (zämfä'rä), NW Nigeria, rises S of Gusau, flows 225 mi. W, past Gummi and Jega, to Kebbi R. 30 mi. SSW of Birnin Kebbi. Gold deposits in valley. Also called Gindi R.

Zamfira (zäm'fērä), village (pop. 526), Prahova prov., S central Rumania, 9 mi. N of Ploesti. Site of convent with 18th- and 19th-cent. churches.

Zami River, Burma: see ATARAN RIVER.

Zamora (sämō'rä), town (1950 pop. 485), Santiago-Zamora prov., SE Ecuador, at E foot of the Cordillera de Zamora, on Zamora R. 35 mi. ESE of Loja.

Zamora, city (pop. 15,447), Michoacán, central Mexico, on central plateau, on railroad and 85 mi. SE of Guadalajara, 75 mi. WNW of Morelia; alt. 5,141 ft. Industrial and agr. center (grain, sugar cane, tobacco, fruit, vegetables, stock); dairying, flour milling, tanning, lumbering; mfg. of cigars, textile goods, sweets, forest products (resins). President Lázaro Cárdenas b. here.

Zamora (thämō'rä), province (□ 4,089; pop. 298,722), NW Spain, in Leon, bordering on Portugal; ⊙ Zamora. Consists mostly of tableland (part of Spain's central plateau), except for mountainous area in NW. Drained by Duero (Douro) R. and its tributaries (Esla, Valderaduey). Land mostly poor and dry, with few irrigated tracts (new projects under construction). Chief crop, cereals; vineyards and fruit orchards in river valleys and Tierra del Vino dist. (SE). Potato and flax growing, sheep and cattle raising, lumbering. Some tungsten and tin mines. Unfavorable climate, landlord absenteeism, sparse pop., primitive agr. methods, and poor communications have all hampered development. Chief industries are flour milling and food processing (wine, dairy products, meat). Brandy distilling, tanning, and other mfg. (woolen textiles, blankets, soap, candy) are limited to a few larger towns: Zamora, Toro, Benavente.

Zamora, city (pop. 29,036), ⊙ Zamora prov., NW Spain, in Leon, on rocky hill above the Duero (Douro), 130 mi. NW of Madrid, 40 mi. N of Salamanca; 41°30'N 5°45'W. Communications and agr.-trade center (wine and cereals); flour milling, meat processing; mfg. of cement, woolen and cotton textiles, blankets, soap, wax, candy. Episcopal see. City is circled by anc. walls and towers, and its narrow, irregular streets preserve medieval aspect. Has 12th-cent. Romanesque cathedral, church of Santa Magdalena (12th cent.; formerly of the Knights Templars), palace of Sanabria in Mudejar style, and other fine mansions. Bridge on Roman foundations span Duero R. Of pre-Roman origin, the city was occupied by Moors (8th cent.) and, as an important stronghold, was repeatedly taken and lost by Christians in 10th cent. It was bone of contention bet. kings of Leon and Castile (11th cent.); occupied by Portuguese (1474–76), and by French (1808–13).

Zamora (sämō'rä), former state of Venezuela, bordering S on Apure R.; now the states of Portuguesa and Cojedes.

Zamora, Cordillera de (kôrdĭyā'rä dā sämō'rä), Andean range, S Ecuador, E of Loja city; c.30 mi. N-S; rises to over 9,500 ft.

Zamora River, S and SE Ecuador, rises in the Andes S of Loja city, flows c.150 mi. E and N through tropical forests to join Paute (Namangoza) R., forming the Santiago at 3°S.

Zamosc (zä'môshch), Pol. *Zamość*, Rus. *Zamostye* or *Zamost'ye* (both: zŭmôs'tyĕ), city (pop. 20,899), Lublin prov., E Poland, on railroad and 45 mi. SE of Lublin. Trade center; mfg. of furniture, cigarette cases, marmalade, soap, concrete blocks, bricks; flour milling, sawmilling, chicory drying, brewing, distilling. Airport. Has castle, cathedral, town hall. Founded 1579 by Jan Zamoski, who established a univ. (1595–1783); built in chesslike pattern and reconstructed 1937 in accordance with original plans. Situated on crossroads, it became a fortress defending Pol. E marshes. Passed (1772) to Austria and (1815) to Rus. Poland; returned to Poland in 1921. Before Second World War, pop. 50% Jewish.

Zamostye or **Zamost'ye** (zŭmô'styĭ), town (1926 pop. 2,313), central Kharkov oblast, Ukrainian SSR, 17 mi. S of Kharkov; woodworking, fruit canning. Inc. 1948 into Zmiyev city.

Zanaga (zänägä'), village, central Middle Congo territory, Fr. Equatorial Africa, 125 mi. NE of Dolosie, in gold, lead, and zinc mining region.

Zaña River, Peru: see SAÑA RIVER.

Záncara River (thäng'kärä), New Castile, central Spain, rises W of Cuenca, flows c.125 mi. S and W, partly along Albacete-Cuenca prov. border, to join the Gigüela 8 mi. SW of Alcázar de San Juan (Ciudad Real prov.). The united stream, called Záncara or Gigüela, flows c.25 mi. SW to swamps from which emerges the Guadiana.

Zancle, Sicily: see MESSINA, city.

Zande, district, Anglo-Egyptian Sudan: see YAMBIO.

Zanderij or **Zanderij I** (zändŭrī'), locality, Surinam dist., N Du. Guiana, on railroad and 25 mi. S of Paramaribo; airport. Another village, Zanderij II, is 10 mi. SSW. Sometimes spelled Sanderey.

Zandkreek (zänt'krāk), SW Netherlands, channel (11 mi. long), bet. the Veersche Gat (W) and the Eastern Scheldt (E); separates North Beveland and South Beveland isls. Kortgene is on it.

Zandvoorde (zänd'vōrdŭ), town (pop. 1,515), West Flanders prov., W Belgium, 3 mi. SE of Ostend; coke ovens; electric-power station.

Zandvoort (zänt'vōrt), village (pop. 8,475), North Holland prov., W Netherlands, on North Sea, 5 mi. W of Haarlem; seaside resort for Amsterdam. Terminal of North Sea cables to Lowestoft and Benacre, England. Looted in Second World War.

Zanesfield (zānz'fēld), village (pop. 288), Logan co., W central Ohio, 5 mi. ESE of Bellefontaine, and on Mad R., in agr. area.

Zanesville (zānz'vĭl), city (pop. 40,517), ⊙ Muskingum co., central Ohio, c.50 mi. E of Columbus, and on Muskingum R. at its junction with Licking R. (both bridged); trade and industrial center for region rich in clay, coal, oil, gas, limestone, and sand. Mfg.: glass, tile, pottery, electrical apparatus, foundry products, clothing, meat products. Has an art institute. Zane Grey was b. here. Platted 1799.

Zanga River (zŭn'gŭ), central Armenian SSR, rises in L. SEVAN (alt. 6,285 ft.), near town of Sevan (site of Ozernaya hydroelectric station); flows 68 mi. SSW, past Gyumush (power station), Kanaker (power station), and Erivan, to Aras R. (alt. 2,790 ft.) Used for irrigation in lower course. Also called Razdan.

Zangezur Range (zŭn-gyĭzōōr'), in the Lesser Caucasus, extends from E of L. Sevan c.100 mi. S, through SE Armenian SSR, to Aras R.; abounds in copper (at Kafan) and molybdenum (at Kadzharan) ores; rises to 12,850 ft.

Zangibasar (zŭn-gēbŭzär'), village (1939 pop. over 2,000), S Armenian SSR, near Ulukhanlu rail junction, 8 mi. SSW of Erivan; cotton, wheat; marble quarries. Formerly called Ulukhanlu.

Zangliverion or **Zagliverion** (both: zäng-glēvĕ'rēôn), village (pop. 2,718), Salonika nome, Macedonia, Greece, 20 mi. ESE of Salonika, on Chalcidice peninsula.

Zangwan Katab, Nigeria: see ZUNGON KATAB.

Zani (zä'nē), village, Eastern Prov., NE Belgian Congo, on Kibali R. and 90 mi. NE of Irumu; cattle raising for the needs of Kilo-Moto goldfields here and at Kerekere (2 mi. NE). Also gold mining.

Zaniemysl (zänyĕ'mĭ-shŭl), Pol. *Zaniemyśl*, Ger. *Santomischel* (zän'tōmĭ"shŭl), town (1946 pop. 1,384), Poznan prov., W central Poland, 20 mi. SSE of Poznan; rail spur terminus; trades in horses, cattle.

Zanjan, Iran: see ZENJAN.

Zanjón River (sänhōn'), San Juan prov., Argentina, rises as the Río Blanco in the Andes near Cerro del Potro in La Rioja prov., flows S, becoming the Jachal (hächäl') in mid-course, and flows intermittently SE as the Zanjón to Bermejo R. 50 mi. ENE of San Juan; total length, c.300 mi.

Zankalun, El, Ez Zankalun, or **Al-Zankalun** (all: ĕz-zănkălōōn'), village (pop. 6,488), Sharqiya prov., Lower Egypt, on railroad and 4 mi. WSW of Zagazig; cotton.

Zanow, Poland: see SIANOW.

Zanskar Range, Kashmir, Tibet, and India: see ZASKAR RANGE.

Zante (zăn'tē), Gr. *Zakynthos* or *Zakinthos* (both: (zä'kĭnthôs), Lat. *Zacynthus* (zŭsĭn'thŭs), southernmost main island (□ 157; pop. 41,154) of Ionian Isls., Greece, in Ionian Sea, off NW Peloponnesus (separated by 12-mi.-wide Zante Strait) and 10 mi. S of Cephalonia; forms with the Strophades and other islets a nome (□ 158; pop. 41,165) of W central Greece; ⊙ Zante (37°47'N 20°53'E). Limestone hills (W) rise to 2,724 ft.; densely settled lowland (E); 23 mi. long, 10 mi. wide. Mild climate; annual rainfall 45 in. Agr.: currants, wine, olive oil, citrus fruit. Gypsum deposits; mineral pitch at Keri. Main economic center is Zante. Traditionally a dependency of Ulysses, king of Ithaca, it was settled, in historical times, by Achaea and Arcadia. It was used by Athens as a naval base in late 5th cent. B.C., was conquered 211 B.C. by Macedon, and passed 191 B.C. to Rome. Ravaged 5th cent. by Gaiseric, king of the Vandals, it was ruled (11th cent.) by the Normans of Sicily, later by the rulers of Cephalonia, and passed 1482 to Venice, sharing the later history of the Ionian Isls. Frequently subjected to earthquakes.

Zante, Gr. *Zakynthos* or *Zakinthos*, Lat. *Zacynthus*, city (pop. 11,315), ⊙ Zante nome, Greece, on SE coast of Zante isl., 75 mi. SW of Patras; agr. trade center (currants, olive oil, citrus fruit); mfg. of soap, flour milling. Of Italian appearance, it is seat of Gr. metropolitan and has ruins of Venetian castle. Anc. Zacynthus (N; no remains) was traditionally founded by Zacynthus, son of Arcadian chief Dardanus.

Zanzibar (zăn'zĭbär), island (□ 640, including offshore islets; pop. 149,377) in Indian Ocean, just off E coast of Africa, separated from mainland (Tanganyika) by Zanzibar Channel (22½ mi. wide); 6°S 39°E; 53 mi. long, 24 mi. wide. With near-by PEMBA isl. and adjacent islets it forms the Br. protectorate (□ 1,020; pop. 264,236) of Zanzibar. Zanzibar isl., of coral limestone, rises to 390 ft. in Masingini Ridge. Has tropical monsoon climate, tempered by sea breezes; Dec. to March is hot and dry, April and May have heavy rains. Annual rainfall, 58 in. Mean high and low temperatures are 84.4° F. and 76.6°F. A fertile isl., nearly entirely under cultivation. Main agr. products are cloves (introduced early 19th cent. from Réunion or Mauritius), coconuts, citrus and other fruit, chillies, tobacco, and mangrove bark. Cattle raised on E coast (hides and skins are exported). Industry: clove-oil distilling, coconut-oil pressing, soap mfg., lime burning, coir-fiber and rope making. The world's leading clove exporter, Zanzibar ships dried clove buds and clove oil (60% of total exports), copra and coconut oil, and mangrove bark. Pop. includes Africans (Bantu Swahili; 80%), Omani Arabs (13%), Indians (Gujarati, Khoja, Goans; 6%). Main centers are Zanzibar town and Mkokotoni. The history of Zanzibar reflects its position as a springboard to coast of E Africa, and from ancient times it has been closely connected with India and with lands bordering the Red Sea and the Persian Gulf. Peopled by Bantu settlers from mainland (in 1st 5 centuries A.D.) Shiraz Persians, and Arabs, Zanzibar embraced Islam c.10th cent. Became part of Zenj Empire (founded 975 by Persians), until occupied (c.1500) by Portuguese as a base for their territorial acquisitions on mainland. Port. domination was followed (17th cent.) by Omani Arab rule. With the weakening of the widespread domain of Oman, the Sayid of Muscat transferred his capital to Zanzibar in 1832. Zanzibar's independence from Oman (1861) was followed (1885) by Ger. annexation of most of its holdings on E African mainland, and by a great-power struggle for control of the isl. which further reduced the Sultan's possessions. Br. protectorate over Zanzibar was declared in 1890 (Germany's claim was satisfied by Br. cession of Helgoland), and strengthened in 1906. A 10-mi.-wide strip along the Kenya coast (including Mombasa isl.) remains nominally a part of the Sultan's dominion but is administered by Kenya against payment (since 1895) of a yearly rental to the Sultan. The Br. resident is assisted by an executive council (presided over by the Sultan) and by a legislative council. Justice is administered both by Br. and Sultan's courts.

Zanzibar, town (pop. 45,275), ⊙ Zanzibar protectorate, on W coast of Zanzibar isl., facing Tanganyika coast across Zanzibar Channel (here 25 mi. wide), and 45 mi. N of Dar es Salaam; 6°10'S 39°11'E. Administrative and commercial center, long a leading entrepôt for E African trade. Residence of Sultan of Zanzibar and of Br. resident. The world's leading clove exporter; also ships copra, mangrove bark, chillies, and citrus fruit. Chief industries: clove-oil distilling, coconut-oil pressing, soap mfg. Handicraft industries. Kisauni airport is 4 mi. SE. Zanzibar consists of the Stone Town (pop. 13,308; W) directly on Zanzibar Channel, with Br. residency, Sultan's palace, govt. offices, hosp., and bazaar, Arab and Indian quarters, R.C. and Anglican cathedrals, and modern concrete wharf. The inner town, E, known as Ngambo (ŭngäm'bō), is mainly the native quarter. Founded 16th cent. as a Port. trading depot, town remained insignificant until transfer here (1832) of Omani capital from Muscat. It then achieved commercial and political preeminence, only to decline in early 20th cent. with the rise of competing ports (Mombasa, Dar es Salaam) on the adjacent mainland, and with the assumption (1906) of more direct Br. control.

Zanzur (zänzōōr'), village (pop. 600), W Tripolitania, Libya, 10 mi. WSW of Tripoli, on highway and railroad, in an oasis on Mediterranean coast; olive-oil pressing, flour milling, tunny fishing.

Zaokskoye (zŭôk'skŭyŭ), village (1939 pop. over 500), NW Tula oblast, Russian SFSR, on railroad (Tarusskaya station) and 38 mi. NNW of Tula; clothing mfg.

Zaorejas (thourā'häs), town (pop. 880), Guadalajara prov., central Spain, near the Tagus, 50 mi. ENE of Guadalajara; wheat, forage, livestock; resins. Flour milling.

Zaozerny or **Zaozernyy** (zä-ŭzyôr'nē), city (1939 pop. over 2,000), SE Krasnoyarsk Territory, Russian SFSR, on Trans-Siberian RR and 75 mi. E of Krasnoyarsk; metalworks.

Zaozerye or **Zaozer'ye** (zä-ŭzyô'ryĭ), town (1939 pop. under 500), S central Molotov oblast, Russian SFSR, port on left bank of Kama R., opposite Chusovaya R. mouth and Levshino section of Molotov city; shipbuilding.

Zap, river, Turkey and Iraq: see ZAB, GREAT.

Zap, village (pop. 425), Mercer co., central N.Dak., 65 mi. NW of Bismarck and on Spring Creek. Near by is lignite mine.

Zapadna Morava River, Yugoslavia: see WESTERN MORAVA RIVER.

Zapadnaya Dvina (zä'pŭdnŭ dvēnä'), city (1926 pop. 2,029), E central Velikiye Luki oblast, Russian SFSR, on Western Dvina R. and 60 mi. E of Velikiye Luki; sawmilling center; mfg. of prefabricated houses.

Zapadnaya Dvina River, USSR and Latvia: see DVINA RIVER (Western Dvina).

Zapadnaya Litsa, Bolshaya, or **Bol'shaya Zapadnaya Litsa** (bŭlshī'ŭ, lyētsä'), village, NW Murmansk oblast, Russian SFSR, on bay of Mostovka Gulf, at mouth of Zapadnaya Litsa R. (50 mi. long), 35 mi. NW of Murmansk; fisheries. Village of Malaya Zapadnaya Litsa is 9 mi. ENE, at mouth of bay.

Zapadno-Gruppski, Ukrainian SSR: see KATYK.

Zapadno-Kazakhstan, Kazakh SSR: see WEST KAZAKHSTAN.

Zapadnyy Bug River, USSR and Poland: see BUG RIVER.

Zapala (säpä'lä), town (1947 pop. 3,385), ⊙ Zapala dept., central Neuquén natl. territory, Argentina, 110 mi. W of Neuquén; rail terminus; stock-raising (sheep, cattle, goats) and trading center. Outlet for Plaza Huincul oilfields. Chalk deposits near by. Point of departure for tourists to Nahuel Huapí lake dist. Seismographic station.

Zapaleri, Cerro (sĕ'rō säpälā'rē) (18,514 ft.), in the Andes, at S end of Cordillera de Lípez, at junction of Bolivia-Chile-Argentina border, 65 mi. E of San Pedro de Atacama (Chile); 22°49'S 67°12'W. Sometimes spelled Sapaleri.

Zapallar, Argentina: see EL ZAPALLAR.

Zapallar (säpäyär'), village (1930 pop. 499), Aconcagua prov., central Chile, on the coast, 15 mi. SW of La Ligua; beach resort.

Zapallo, El, Chile: see EL ZAPALLO.

Zapaluta, Mexico: see LA TRINITARIA.

Zapara Island (säpä'rä), Zulia state, NW Venezuela, across N entrance of Tablazo Bay on Gulf of Venezuela, on the passage to L. Maracaibo, 25 mi. N of Maracaibo; 3 mi. long.

Zapata (zŭpă'tŭ), county (□ 1,080; pop. 4,405), extreme S Texas; ⊙ Zapata. Bounded W by the Rio Grande (here the Mex. border); drained by its small tributaries. Ranching area (cattle, sheep); some agr. (corn, grain sorghums, feeds, cotton); some dairying. Oil, natural gas; exports gas by pipeline to Mexico. Formed 1858.

Zapata, village (pop. 1,409), ⊙ Zapata co., extreme S Texas, c.45 mi. SSE of Laredo and on the Rio Grande, bridged near by to Guerrero, Mexico; trade center in ranch area. Settled in 18th cent. from old Mex. town across the river.

Zapata, Ciénaga de (syā'nägä dā säpä'tä), swamps, W Cuba, N of Zapata Peninsula, extending c.100 mi. NW–SE in S Havana, Matanzas, and Las Villas provs. An unhealthful region abounding in tropical timber and wild birds. Commonly divided into Ciénga Occidental de Zapata (W) and Ciénaga Oriental de Zapata (E). Sometimes called Gran Ciénaga de Zapata.

Zapata, Sierra de (syĕ'rä dā), subandean mountain range in S Catamarca prov., Argentina, W and SW of Belén; rises to c.9,000 ft. Rich in mineral deposits, mainly tin and tungsten.

Zapata Peninsula, Las Villas prov., SW Cuba, shoe-shaped extension of Ciénaga de Zapata marshland (N), 50 mi. W of Cienfuegos; bounded by the Gulf of Matamanó (NW), Gulf of Batabanó (W), Jardines Bank (S), Cochinos Bay (E). It is c.60 mi. long E–W, up to 20 mi. wide. An unhealthful region of swamps, largely covered by tropical forests (hardwood), and abounding in wildlife. Off its coast are numerous coral keys.

Zapatas, Valle de las, Nicaragua: see VALLE DE LAS ZAPATAS.

Zapatera Island (säpätā'rä), SW Nicaragua, in NW L. Nicaragua, c.2 mi. offshore, 13 mi. SSE of Granada; 5 mi. long, 3 mi. wide. Rises to 2,428 ft. in volcano Zapatera. A place sacred to Indians, isl. contains many stone idols.

Zapatoca (säpätō'kä), town (pop. 4,617), Santander dept., N central Colombia, in W Cordillera Oriental, near Sogamoso R., on road to Barrancabermeja, and 23 mi. SSW of Bucaramanga; alt. 5,699 ft. Agr. center (sugar cane, coffee, corn, tobacco, anise, vegetables, fruit, cattle, goats); mfg. (tobacco products, straw hats, wine).

Zapatosa, Ciénaga de (syā'nägä dā säpätō'sä), lake in Magdalena dept., N Colombia, in Magdalena basin, 8 mi. NE of El Banco; 19 mi. long NE–SW, c.6 mi. wide. Dotted with isls. Through it flows César R., linking it with the Magdalena. Rich fishing ground.

Zapicán (säpēkän'), town (pop. 1,500), Lavalleja dept., SE Uruguay, in E outlier of the Cuchilla Grande Principal, on railroad and 9 mi. ESE of José Batlle y Ordóñez; traffic center; grain, cattle.

Zapiga (säpē'gä), village (pop. 219), Tarapacá prov., N Chile, on railroad and 15 mi. ESE of Pisagua, in nitrate area.

Zapla (sä'plä), village (pop. estimate 500), SE Jujuy prov., Argentina, at SE foot of Sierra de Zapla, 10 mi. SE of Jujuy, in agr. area. Its iron deposits supply blast furnace of near-by Palpalá.

Zapla, Sierra de (syĕ'rä dā), subandean mountain range in SE Jujuy prov., Argentina, 15 mi. E of Jujuy; 20 mi. N–S; rises to c.3,500 ft. Iron deposits.

Zapokrovski or **Zapokrovskiy** (zŭpŭkrôf'skē), town (1940 pop. over 500), SE Chita oblast, Russian SFSR, near Argun R., 120 mi. ENE of Borzya; silver and lead mines.

Zapopan (säpō'pän), town (pop. 3,685), Jalisco, central Mexico, 4 mi. NW of Guadalajara; alt. 5,216 ft. Agr. center (grain, sugar cane, cotton, fruit, vegetables, peanuts, livestock). Has 17th-cent. church, site of pilgrimage.

Zaporozhe, Zaporozhye, or **Zaporozh'ye** (zŭpŭrô'-zhyĭ), oblast (□ 10,400; 1946 pop. estimate 1,300,000), SE Ukrainian SSR; ⊙ Zaporozh. Bet. Dnieper R. and Sea of Azov, in Black Sea Lowland; rises to 1,007 ft. in Azov Upland (E); flat steppe region (S and W). Rich agr. area, with emphasis on cotton (S) and wheat (N); other crops include sunflowers and castor beans (N), vineyards (SE, near Osipenko), and fruit (near Melitopol and Kamenka); truck produce in Zaporozhe metropolitan area (chief industrial dist.). Other mfg. centers include Osipenko (main port), Melitopol, and Bolshoi Tokmak. Formed 1939.

Zaporozhe, Zaporozhye, or **Zaporozh'ye,** city (1926 pop. 55,744; 1939 pop. 289,188), ⊙ Zaporozhe oblast, Ukrainian SSR, on left bank of Dnieper R., opposite Khortitsa Isl., and 40 mi. S of Dnepropetrovsk, 280 mi. SE of Kiev; 47°50'N 35°8'E. Major rail, industrial, and hydroelectric center; site of DNEPROGES dam and power station, supplying steel industry (ferroalloys, special steels); coking plants, aluminum and magnesium works. Mfg. of agr. machinery, metal wire; meat packing; locomotive repair shops. River-rail transfer point for Dnieper R.–Donbas traffic. Has agr. and teachers colleges, trade schools (agr. machine construction, aviation). Founded 1770 as fort, city consists of old Zaporozhe (SE; called Aleksandrovsk until 1921), and new industrial Zaporozhe (NW; developed in 1930s) adjoining Dneproges installations and the port of Zaporozhe (Port Imeni Lenina). In Second World War, city held (1941–43) by Germans.

Zapotal (säpōtäl'), village, Los Ríos prov., W central Ecuador, on highway to Guayaquil, on affluent of the Guayas system, and 38 mi. NE of Vinces, in fertile agr. region (cacao, rice, sugar cane, tropical fruit); rice milling.

Zapotal, El, Mexico: see EL ZAPOTAL.

Zapotiltic (säpōtēltēk'), town (pop. 5,522), Jalisco, W Mexico, in W outliers of Sierra Madre Occidental, on railroad and 6 mi. SE of Guzmán; alt. 4,301 ft. Corn-growing center; alfalfa, sugar cane, beans, livestock.

Zapotitlán (säpōtētlän'). **1** Town (pop. 2,218), Federal Dist., central Mexico, 11 mi. SSE of Mexico city; cereals, fruit, vegetables, livestock. **2** Town (pop. 1,925), Guerrero, SW Mexico, in Sierra Madre del Sur, 30 mi. SE of Chilapa; cereals, sugar cane, fruit, livestock. **3** Town (pop. 2,009), Jalisco, W Mexico, in W outliers of Sierra Madre Occidental, 21 mi. SW of Guzmán; agr. center (corn, alfalfa, sugar cane, beans, fruit, livestock). **4** Officially Zapotitlán de Méndez, town (pop. 1,354), Puebla, central Mexico, 25 mi. SE of Huauchinango; sugar cane, fruit; saltworks. **5** or **Zapotitlán Salinas** (sälē'näs), town (pop. 726), Puebla, central Mexico, 11 mi. SW of Tehuacán; corn, sugar, livestock.

Zapotitlán Point, Veracruz, SE Mexico, on Gulf of Campeche, 28 mi. ENE of San Andrés Tuxtla; 18°33'N 94°48'W.

Zapotlán (säpōtlän'), officially Zapotlán de Juárez, town (pop. 1,845), Hidalgo, central Mexico, 17 mi. SW of Pachuca; corn, maguey, livestock.

Zapotlán del Rey (dĕl rā'), town (pop. 1,640), Jalisco, central Mexico, 32 mi. ESE of Guadalajara; alt. 5,790 ft.; grain, vegetables, fruit, stock.

Zapotlanejo (säpōtlänā'hō), town (pop. 3,712), Jalisco, central Mexico, 19 mi. E of Guadalajara; alt. 5,236 ft.; agr. center (grain, beans, sugar cane, fruit, stock).

Zapotlán el Grande, Mexico: see GUZMÁN.

Zapovednoye (zŭpŭvyĕd'nŭyŭ), village (1939 pop. 1,488), N Kaliningrad oblast, Russian SFSR, 20 mi. W of Sovetsk, in marshy, wooded Neman R. delta. Elk reserve near by. Until 1945, in East Prussia and called Seckenburg (sĕ'kŭnbōōrk).

Zapresic (zä'prĕshĭts), Serbo-Croatian *Zaprešić*, village, N Croatia, Yugoslavia, 9 mi. WNW of Zagreb, near Krapina R. mouth; rail junction.

Zap River, Turkey and Iraq: see ZAB, GREAT.

Zaprudnya (zŭprōōd'nyŭ), town (1939 pop. over 2,000), N Moscow oblast, Russian SFSR, near Moscow Canal, 15 mi. NNW of Dmitrov; glassworks.

Zaqaziq, Egypt: see ZAGAZIG.

Zar, Czechoslovakia: see ZDIAR.

Zara (zä'rŭ), town, Audhali sultanate, Western Aden Protectorate, 35 mi. NNE of Shuqra and 3 mi. SSW of Lodar, in agr. area; radio station. Sultan's residence.

Zara (zärä'), town (pop. 6,109), Sivas prov., central Turkey, on the Kizil Irmak and 40 mi. ENE of Sivas; wheat, barley, vetch. Formerly Kocgiri.

Zara, Yugoslavia: see ZADAR.

Zarabi, El, Ez Zarabi, or **Al-Zarabi** (all: ĕz-zärä'bē), village (pop. 9,970), Asyut prov., central Upper Egypt, 5 mi. SW of Abu Tig; cereals, dates, sugar.

Zaradros, river, Asia: see SUTLEJ RIVER.

Zaragosa, Philippines: see ZARAGOZA.

Zaragoza (särägō'sä), town (pop. 1,052), Antioquia dept., NW central Colombia, on navigable Nechí R., connected by highway with Remedios 35 mi. SSE, 100 mi. NE of Medellín; gold mining. Coal deposits are also near by.

Zaragoza, town (1950 pop. 2,817), Chimaltenango dept., S central Guatemala, on Inter-American Highway and 3 mi. W of Chimaltenango; alt. 6,630 ft.; wheat, corn, avocados.

Zaragoza. 1 Village (pop. 1,653), Chihuahua, N Mexico, on the Rio Grande near Ciudad Juárez; cotton, grain, alfalfa, cattle. Cooperative settlement. **2** City (pop. 3,510), Coahuila, N Mexico, on railroad and 28 mi. SW of Piedras Negras (Texas border); cereals, livestock, istle fibers; flour milling. **3** Town, Durango, Mexico: see TLAHUALILO DE ZARAGOZA. **4** Town (pop. 567), Nuevo León, N Mexico, in Sierra Madre Oriental, 60 mi. NE of Matehuala (Zacatecas); alt. 4,498 ft.; silver, lead, copper, iron, zinc mining. **5** Town (pop. 1,426), Puebla, central Mexico, on railroad and 13 mi. WSW of Teziutlán; alt. 7,579 ft.; sugar cane, corn, coffee, fruit. **6** Town (pop. 1,539), San Luis Potosí, N central Mexico, in Sierra Madre Oriental, 18 mi. SE of San Luis Potosí; alt. 6,434 ft.; corn, cotton, fruit, livestock. **7** Town (pop. 1,802), Veracruz, SE Mexico, on Isthmus of Tehuantepec, 6 mi. WSW of Minatitlán; rice, fruit, coffee, livestock. Sometimes San Isidro de Zaragoza.

Zaragoza or **Zaragosa** (both: särägō'sä), town (1939 pop. 1,391; 1948 municipality pop. 14,088), Nueva Ecija prov., central Luzon, Philippines, 7 mi. WSW of Cabanatuan; rice-growing center.

Zaragoza, Spain: see SARAGOSSA.

Zaraguro, Ecuador: see SARAGURO.

Zaraisk or **Zaraysk** (zŭrīsk'), city (1926 pop. 11,766), SE Moscow oblast, Russian SFSR, 23 mi. SSE of Kolomna; cotton textiles, clothing articles. Chartered 1531.

Zaraka, Lake, Greece: see STYMPHALIA, LAKE.

Zarand (zärănd'), town (1942 pop. 4,493), Eighth Prov., in Kerman, SE Iran, 45 mi. NW of Kerman; grain, cotton, pistachios.

Zaranj, Iran: see SEISTAN.

Zarasai or **Zarasay** (zäräsī'), Rus. *Novoaleksandrovsk,* city (pop. 4,534), NE Lithuania, on highway and 15 mi. SW of Daugavpils; resort in lake dist.; sawmilling; mfg. of wooden boxes, barrels; oilseed pressing, flour milling. In Rus. Kovno govt. until 1920. During Second World War, held (1941–44) and called Ossersee by Germans.

Zaratán (thärätän'), town (pop. 1,435), Valladolid prov., N central Spain, 3 mi. W of Valladolid; wine processing; grain, mules.

Zárate (sä'rätā), city (pop. 32,070), ⊙ Zárate dist. (□ 218; pop. 43,621), N Buenos Aires prov., Argentina, port on S (Paraná de las Palmas) arm of Paraná R. delta, and 50 mi. NW of Buenos Aires, in agr. region (wheat, alfalfa, flax, potatoes, livestock). Meat packing, paper milling, dairying. Connected by ferry with Ibicuy (railhead in Entre Ríos prov.). Called General José F. Uriburu or General Uriburu (1930–c.1945).

Zárate River, N Tucumán prov., Argentina, rises as Tacanas R. at NE foot of Cumbres Calchaquíes, flows 30 mi. E to the Río Salí 8 mi. SE of Trancas.

Zarauz (thärouth'), town (pop. 4,140), Guipúzcoa prov., N Spain, on Bay of Biscay, 10 mi. WSW of San Sebastián; metalworking, cotton and woolen milling, furniture mfg. *Chacolí* wine, cattle, lumber. Popular bathing resort. Copper mines near by.

Zaravecchia, Yugoslavia: see BIOGRAD.

Zaraza (särä'sä), town (pop. 4,476), Guárico state, N central Venezuela, on Unare R. and 70 mi. SW of Barcelona; cattle-grazing center; corn, sugar cane.

Zarcero (särsā'rō), city (pop. 451), ⊙ Alfaro Ruíz canton, Alajuela prov., W central Costa Rica, in Zarcero depression W of Poás volcano, 15 mi. NW of Alajuela; potatoes, corn, garden crops; lumber milling. Gateway to San Carlos lowland.

Zardézas Dam, Algeria: see SAF-SAF, OUED.

Zardob (zŭrdôp'), village (1926 pop. 512), central Azerbaijan SSR, on Kura R. and 40 mi. SE of Yevlakh; silk, cotton growing; metalworks.

Zarechnoye (zŭryĕch'nŭyŭ), Pol. *Zarzeczny,* village (1939 pop. over 500), NW Rovno oblast, Ukrainian SSR, in Pripet Marshes, 22 mi. S of Pinsk; potatoes, flax; lumbering.

Zarek, Poland: see BREMBERG.

Zarembo Island (zŭrĕm'bō) (14 mi. long, 9 mi. wide), SE Alaska, in Alexander Archipelago, 12 mi. W of Wrangell; 56°21'N 132°50'W; rises to 2,500 ft.; fishing.

Zarephath (ză'rĕfăth) or **Sarepta** (sŭrĕp'tŭ), anc. town, SW Syria, on the coast bet. Sidon and Tyre, c.9 mi. S of Sidon. Elijah stayed here in the drought.

Zaria (zä'rēä), province (□ 16,488; pop. 428,142), Northern Provinces, N Nigeria; ⊙ Zaria. Kagoro Hills in SE; drained by Kaduna R.; savanna vegetation. Mainly agr. (cotton, peanuts, ginger, durra); beeswax. Tin mining at Kagarko (S), Kagoro and Leri (SE). Main centers: Zaria, Kaduna.

Zaria, town (pop. 21,953), ⊙ Zaria prov., Northern Provinces, N central Nigeria, 90 mi. SW of Kano; 11°2'N 7°4'E. Important rail junction (rail line serves the near-by tin-mining area); agr. center in cotton area; cotton ginning; peanuts, ginger, durra; beeswax. Hq. of Agr. Dept. of N Nigeria; experimental farm stations. Site of leper settlement, sleeping-sickness research institute. Airfield. Founded in 16th cent.

Zarineh River or **Zarrineh River** (zärēnē'), in Azerbaijan, NW Iran, rises in the Zagros mts. on Iraq line NW of Sanandaj, flows 150 mi. N, past Shahin Dezh and Miyanduab, to S shore of L. Urmia in swampy delta. Formerly called Jaghatu.

Zarmast Pass (zŭrmŭst') (alt. 7,774 ft.), in the Paropamisus Mts., NW Afghanistan, 40 mi. ENE of Herat and on road to Afghan Turkestan.

Zarnesti (zûrnĕsht'), Rum. *Zărneşti,* Hung. *Zernest* (zĕr'nĕsht), village (pop. 5,890), Stalin prov., central Rumania, on NE slopes of the Transylvanian Alps, 15 mi. SW of Stalin (Brasov); rail terminus; mfg. of paper and cellulose, flour milling, limestone quarrying. Has 16th-cent. church.

Zarqa', Jordan: see ZERQA'.

Zarqa, El, Ez Zarqa, or **Al-Zarqah** (all: ĕz-zär'kŭ), village (pop. 6,069), Daqahliya prov., Lower Egypt, on Damietta branch of the Nile and 13 mi. NE of Mansura; cotton, cereals.

Zarrentin (tsärĕntēn'), town (pop. 3,796), Mecklenburg, N Germany, at S tip of Schaal L., 21 mi. WSW of Schwerin, 5 mi. SE of Hollenbek; agr. market (stock, grain, potatoes); tourist resort. Has bldgs. of former Cistercian convent (founded 1246; secularized 1552).

Zarrineh River, Iran: see ZARINEH RIVER.

Zarubino (zŭrōō'bēnŭ). **1** Town, SW Maritime Territory, Russian SFSR, on Posyet Bay, 55 mi. SSW of Vladivostok; fish cannery. **2** Town (1939 pop. over 500), central Novgorod oblast, Russian SFSR, near Msta R., 28 mi. NNW of Borovichi; lignite mining.

Zaruma (särōō'mä), town (1950 pop. 3,855), El Oro prov., S Ecuador, in the Andes, 39 mi. SE of Machala; alt. 3,943 ft.; gold-mining center; also silver and copper deposits.

Zarumilla (särōōmē'yä), town (pop. 1,738), ⊙ Zarumilla prov. (formed 1942), Tumbes dept., NW Peru, on coastal plain, on Pan American Highway and 13 mi. ENE of Tumbes, near short Zarumilla R. (Peru–Ecuador boundary). Saltworks; cattle raising. Customs station, military post. In 1941 it was the site of military action during border conflict bet. Peru and Ecuador. Sometimes Sarumilla.

Zarusat, Turkey: see ARPACAY.

Zary, Poland: see SORAU.

Zarza, La (lä thär'thä), copper mines, Huelva prov., SW Spain, 31 mi. N of Huelva (linked by rail).

Zarza-Capilla (thär'thä-käpē'lyä), town (pop. 1,565), Badajoz prov., W Spain, 37 mi. ESE of Villanueva de la Serena; olives, sheep, goats. Tile mfg.

Zarza de Alange (dhä älän'hä), town (pop. 4,516), Badajoz prov., W Spain, 10 mi. SE of Mérida; agr. center (cereals, olives, chick-peas, livestock). Olive-oil pressing, flour milling, dairying, tile mfg. Kaolin quarrying.

Zarza de Granadilla (gränä-dhē'lyä), village (pop. 1,696), Cáceres prov., W Spain, 15 mi. N of Plasencia; cereals, olive oil, pepper; stock raising.

Zarza de Montánchez (mōntän'chĕth), town (pop. 1,957), Cáceres prov., W Spain, 24 mi. SE of Cáceres; olive oil, cereals, figs; stock raising.

Zarza de Tajo (tä'hō), town (pop. 954), Cuenca prov., E central Spain, 24 mi. E of Aranjuez; potatoes, beans, chick-peas, cereals, truck, olives, grapes, livestock. Lumbering; olive-oil extracting. Saltpeter and quartz deposits.

Zarzal (särsäl'), town (pop. 4,287), Valle del Cauca dept., W Colombia, on Manizales-Cali RR and highway, and 26 mi. SSW of Cartago; communication and agr. center (tobacco, sugar cane, coffee, cacao, cereals, fruit, livestock).

Zarza la Mayor (thär'thä lä mīôr'), town (pop. 4,233), Cáceres prov., W Spain, near Port. border, 36 mi. NW of Cáceres; agr. trade center (olive oil, cereals, livestock). Chocolate mfg., flour- and sawmilling. Mineral springs and phosphate-rock mines near by.

Zarzalejo (thär-thälā'hō), town (pop. 658), Madrid prov., central Spain, on railroad and 28 mi. WNW of Madrid; grain, grapes, livestock; apiculture. Stone quarries.

Zarzeczny, Ukrainian SSR: see ZARECHNOYE.

Zarzis (zärzēs'), town and oasis (pop. 9,160), Southern Territories, SE Tunisia, small port on the central Mediterranean, 65 mi. ESE of Gabès; 33°30'N 11°5'E. Olive-oil processing, tuna and sponge fishing. Saltworks just S. Roman ruins near by.

Zarzuela (thärthwā'lä), village (pop. 714), Cuenca prov., E central Spain, 12 mi. N of Cuenca; cereals, resins, timber.

Zarzuela del Monte (dhĕl mōn'tā), town (pop. 915), Segovia prov., central Spain, 14 mi. SW of Segovia; grain growing.

Zarzuela del Pinar (pēnär'), town (pop. 936), Segovia prov., central Spain, 22 mi. N of Segovia; grain, naval stores.

Zasenbeck (tsä'zŭnbĕk), village (pop. 644), in former Prussian prov. of Hanover, NW Germany, after 1945 in Lower Saxony, 6 mi. SE of Wittingen, 6 mi. WSW of Rohrberg; grain, cattle.

Zashchita (zŭshchē'tŭ), village (1939 pop. over 500), N East Kazakhstan oblast, Kazakh SSR, on railroad and 4 mi. NW of Ust-Kamenogorsk.

Zasheyek (zŭshā'ŭk), town (1939 pop. over 2,000), SW central Murmansk oblast, Russian SFSR, on S L. Imandra, at outlet of Niva R., on Murmansk RR and 15 mi. N of Kandalaksha; sawmilling.

Zashiversk (zŭshē'vyĭrsk), village (1948 pop. over 500), NE Yakut Autonomous SSR, Russian SFSR, on Indigirka R. and 240 mi. E of Verkhoyansk, in reindeer-raising area. Founded 1639.

Zasieki (zäsyĕ'kē), town (1946 pop. 110), Zielona Gora prov., W Poland, before 1945 part of FORST, E Germany, on right bank of the Lusatian Neisse. Chartered after 1945 and briefly called Barsc, Pol. *Barść.*

Zaskar Range or **Zanskar Range** (both: zŭns'kŭr), N lateral Himalayan range in Kashmir, Tibet, and India, astride Sutlej R., in Punjab Himalayas (NW) and Kumaun Himalayas (SE); from Suru R. extends c.400 mi. SE to upper Karnali (Gogra) R.; rises to Kamet peak (25,447 ft.) in SE. Separated from Ladakh Range by Indus R. Contains important Shipki, Lipu La, and Mana passes. Deosai Mts., a W section of Punjab Himalayas, are sometimes regarded as a trans-Suru extension of Zaskar Range, which is often restricted to the section W of the Sutlej.

Zaslavl or **Zaslavl'** (zŭslä'vŭl). **1** Town (1926 pop. 1,645), W Minsk oblast, Belorussian SSR, 15 mi. NW of Minsk, near former Pol. border; metalworks. **2** City, Kamenets-Podolski oblast, Ukrainian SSR: see IZYASLAV.

Zastavka (zä'stäfkä), Czech *Zastávka,* village (pop. 1,596), S Moravia, Czechoslovakia, 11 mi. W of Brno; local rail junction; bituminous coal mines.

Zastavna (zŭstäv'nŭ), town (1941 pop. 5,000), N Chernovtsy oblast, Ukrainian SSR, in N Bukovina, 16 mi. NNW of Chernovtsy; flour, oilseed.

Zastron (ză'strŭn), town (pop. 3,986), SW Orange Free State, U. of So. Afr., near Basutoland border, 40 mi. NE of Aliwal North; alt. 5,515 ft.; stock, grain. Airfield.

Zasulye or **Zasul'ye** (zŭsōō'lyĭ), town (1926 pop. 7,402), SW Sumy oblast, Ukrainian SSR, on Sula R., opposite Romny; flour milling.

Zatec (zhä'tĕts), Czech *Žatec,* Ger. *Saaz* (zäts), town (pop. 12,620), NW Bohemia, Czechoslovakia, on Ohre R. and 34 mi. WNW of Prague; rail junction; center of Bohemian trade in quality hop growing (world-wide export); outlet for agr. region producing, beside hops, sugar beets, wheat, vegetables, fruit. Has 16th-cent. town hall, 14th-cent. church, remains of fortifications.

Zatobolsk or **Zatobol'sk** (zŭtŭbôlsk'), E suburb (1939 pop. over 2,000) of Kustanai, Kustanai oblast, Kazakh SSR, on right bank of Tobol R.

Zator (zä'tôr), town (pop. 1,844), Krakow prov., Poland, on Skawa R., on railroad and 22 mi. WSW of Cracow; mfg. (soap, tiles, flour).

Zatsarevo (zŭtsä'ryĭvŭ), SW suburb (1926 pop. 2,433) of Astrakhan, Astrakhan oblast, Russian SFSR, on left bank of Balchtemir arm of Volga R., on Tsarev channel opposite Astrakhan; fisheries; truck.

Zaturtsy (zŭtōōr'tsē), Pol. *Zaturce,* village (1939 pop. over 500), S Volyn oblast, Ukrainian SSR, 19 mi. W of Vladimir-Volynski; grain, livestock.

Zaucejo, Spain: see PERALEDA DE ZAUCEJO.

Zauckerode, Germany: see FREITAL.

Zauia, Tripolitania: see ZAVIA.

Zaule (zou'lā), S suburb of Trieste, Free Territory of Trieste, on E shore of Muggia Bay; industrial port (built after Second World War); petroleum refinery, vegetable-oil mill.

Zaur, Az, Kuwait: see FAILAKA ISLAND.

Zauran, Tadzhik SSR: see TAKFAN.

Zautla (sout'lä), officially Santiago Zautla, town (pop. 858), Puebla, central Mexico, 25 mi. SE of Zacatlán; silver, gold, copper mining.

Zavala (zŭvă'lŭ), county (□ 1,292; pop. 11,201), SW Texas; ⊙ Crystal City. Drained by Nueces and Leona rivers. Partly in irrigated Winter Garden area (spinach, other vegetables, citrus); also grain sorghums, corn, oats, peanuts, hay, pecans; livestock (cattle, hogs, poultry); dairying. Asphalt mining. Formed 1858.

Zavalla (sävä'yä), town (pop. estimate 1,000), S Santa Fe prov., Argentina, 13 mi. WSW of Rosario; agr. center (corn, wheat, alfalfa, livestock); dairy industry.

Zavalla (zŭvă'lŭ), village (1940 pop. 690), Angelina co., E Texas, 22 mi. SE of Lufkin, in Angelina Natl. Forest; trade point in lumbering area.

Zavelstein (tsä'vŭl-shtīn), town (pop. 271), S Württemberg, Germany, after 1945 in Württemberg-Hohenzollern, in Black Forest, 2.5 mi. SW of Calw; climatic health resort (alt. 1,832 ft.). Has ruined castle.

Zaventem (zä'vŭntĕm), town (pop. 7,690), Brabant prov., central Belgium, 6 mi. NE of Brussels; leather tanning, mfg. (tanning fluid, paper products). Formerly spelled Saventhem.
Zavertse, Poland: see ZAWIERCE.
Zavet (zä'vĕt), village (pop. 3,914), Ruse dist., NE Bulgaria, 34 mi. E of Ruse; wheat, rye, sunflowers.
Zavetnoye (zŭvyĕt'nŭyŭ), village (1926 pop. 5,679), SE Rostov oblast, Russian SFSR, near Sal R., 50 mi. SE of Kotelnikovski; flour milling, dairying.
Zavia (zävē'ä) or **Zauia** (zäwē'ä), town (pop. c.3,000; 1950 dist. pop. 36,000), W Tripolitania, Libya, 28 mi. WSW of Tripoli, on coastal highway and railroad, in an oasis (dates, olives, cereals, tobacco); olive oil, flour, native beverages; limekilns.
Zavidovici or **Zavidovichi** (both: zä'vēdôvĕchē), Serbo-Croatian *Zavidovići*, village (pop. 4,264), central Bosnia, Yugoslavia, on Bosna R., at Krivaja R. mouth, and 40 mi. N of Sarajevo; rail junction; lumber center.
Zavikhost, Poland: see ZAWICHOST.
Zavitaya (zŭvētī'ŭ), town (1948 pop. over 10,000), SE Amur oblast, Russian SFSR, on Trans-Siberian RR and 85 mi. E of Blagoveshchensk; junction for railroad to Poyarkovo; agr. center; flour milling, dairying.
Zavodo-Petrovski or **Zavodo-Petrovskiy** (zŭvô'-dŭ-pētrôf'skē), town (1926 pop. 2,516), SW Tyumen oblast, Russian SFSR, 20 mi. NE of Yalutorovsk; glassworks.
Zavodoukovski or **Zavodoukovskiy** (zŭvô"dōōō'-kŭfskē), town (1948 pop. over 2,000), SW Tyumen oblast, Russian SFSR, on Tobol R., on Trans-Siberian RR and 10 mi. SSE of Yalutorovsk.
Zavodouspenskoye (-ōōspyĕn'skŭyŭ), town (1941 pop. over 500), SE Sverdlovsk oblast, Russian SFSR, near Pyshma R., 19 mi. SE of Tugulym; paper mfg.
Zavolzhye or **Zavolzh'ye** (zŭvôl'zhyĭ), town (1939 pop. over 10,000), NE Ivanovo oblast, Russian SFSR, on Volga R., opposite Kineshma; phosphate fertilizer works, lumber mills.
Zavrsnica River (zä'vŭrshnētsä), Slovenian *Završnica*, NW Slovenia, Yugoslavia, rises in the Karawanken, flows c.5 mi. WSW to Sava Dolinka R. 3 mi. N of Bled; hydroelectric plant.
Zavyalovo or **Zav'yalovo** (zŭvyä'lŭvŭ). **1** Village (1926 pop. 3,217), central Altai Territory, Russian SFSR, on Siberian RR and 80 mi. WNW of Aleisk, in agr. area. **2** Village (1926 pop. 1,225), E Udmurt Autonomous SSR, Russian SFSR, 8 mi. SE of Izhevsk; dairying, truck gardening.
Zawgyi River (zôjē'), central Upper Burma, rises near Pangtara, S Shan State, at alt. of c.4,000 ft.; flows c.150 mi. N and W through Kyaukse dist. to Myitnge R. S of Mandalay. Used for irrigation.
Zawi (zä'wē), village, Salisbury prov., W Southern Rhodesia, in Mashonaland, 15 mi. NW of Sinoia; rail terminus; tobacco, cotton, peanuts; livestock. Gold deposits.
Zawichost (zävē'khôst), Rus. *Zavikhost* (zŭvyē'-khŭst), town (pop. 1,554), Kielce prov., SE Poland, port on the Vistula and 10 mi. NNE of Sandomierz; starch mfg., stone quarrying.
Zawidow (zävē'dōōf), Pol. *Zawidów*, Ger. *Seidenberg* (zī'dŭnbĕrk), town (1939 pop. 2,645; 1946 pop. 2,405) in Lower Silesia, after 1945 in Wroclaw prov., SW Poland, in Upper Lusatia, 10 mi. SSE of Görlitz, near E Germany border, in lignite-mining region. Frontier station on Czechoslovak border, opposite Frydlant; woolen milling, metal-working, agr.-machinery mfg.
Zawiercie (zävyĕr'chĕ), Rus. *Zavertse* (zŭvyĕr'tsyĕ), city (pop. 21,225), Katowice prov., S Poland, on Warta R. and 26 mi. SSE of Czestochowa; mfg. of glassware, metal products, textiles, chemicals; flour milling, sawmilling. Passed (1795) to Prussia and (1815) to Rus. Poland; returned to Poland after First World War. During Second World War, under Ger. rule, called Warthenau.
Zayandeh River, Iran: see ZAINDEH RIVER.
Zayarsk (zŭyärsk'), town (1948 pop. over 10,000), central Irkutsk oblast, Russian SFSR, on Angara R. and 40 mi. ENE of Bratsk; on projected Baikal-Amur rail line; flour milling.
Zaydiyah, Yemen: see ZAIDIYA.
Zayechar, Yugoslavia: see ZAJECAR.
Zayendeh River, Iran: see ZAINDEH RIVER.
Zaykovo, Russian SFSR: see ZAIKOVO.
Zay River, Russian SFSR: see ZAI RIVER.
Zaysan, Kazakh SSR: see ZAISAN.
Zayton, China: see TSINKIANG.
Zaytsevo, Ukrainian SSR: see ZAITSEVO.
Zayukovo (zŭyōō'kŭvŭ), village (1926 pop. 4,185), W central Kabardian SSR, Russian SFSR, on Baksan R. and 15 mi. WNW of Nalchik; grain, livestock.
Zayul River, China: see LUHIT RIVER, India.
Zaza, village, Cuba: see TUNAS DE ZAZA.
Zaza del Medio (sä'sä dĕl mā'dyō), town (pop. 3,473), Las Villas prov., central Cuba, on railroad and 6 mi. NE of Sancti-Spíritus; sugar cane, tobacco, livestock.
Zaza River (sä'sä), Las Villas prov., central Cuba, rises E of Placetas, flows c.60 mi. S, past Zaza del Medio, to the Caribbean near Tunas de Zaza.
Zazuar (thä'thwär'), town (pop. 951), Burgos prov., N Spain, on affluent of the Douro, (Duero) and 7 mi. E of Aranda de Duero; cereals, vegetables, grapes; resins; flour milling.
Zazzega (zäz'zĕgä), village, Asmara div., central Eritrea, near railroad and 10 mi. W of Asmara, in agr. (grain, fruit, vegetable) and livestock region.
Zbarazh (zbŭräsh'), Pol. *Zbaraż* (ŭzbä'räsh), city (1931 pop. 7,673), central Ternopol oblast, Ukrainian SSR, on left tributary of the Seret and 11 mi. NE of Ternopol; flour milling, distilling, tile mfg. Has old monastery, ruins of 16th-cent. castle. Originally known as Slavic settlement of Stary Zbaraz; scene of Pol.-Ruthenian battles in early 13th cent.; passed to Poland in 14th cent.; frequently pillaged and finally destroyed by Tatars. Rebuilt in 16th cent. on its present site. Assaulted (1649) by Cossack hetman Bogdan Chmielnicki (Khmelnitski); sacked (1676) by Turks. Passed to Austria (1772); reverted to Poland (1919); ceded to USSR in 1945.
Zbaszyn (zbō'shĭnyŭ), Pol. *Zbąszyń*, Ger. *Bentschen* (bĕn'chŭn), town (1946 pop. 4,042), Poznan prov., W Poland, on Obra R. and 45 mi. WSW of Poznan; rail junction; sawmilling, brewing, liqueur mfg., tanning, flour milling. From 1919 to 1939 frontier station on Ger. border, E of Zbaszynck (Neu Bentschen), on main Berlin-Warsaw line.
Zbaszynek (zbō-shĭ'nĕk), Pol. *Zbąszynek*, Ger. *Neu Bentschen* (noi" bĕn'chŭn), town (1939 pop. 1,812; 1946 pop. 2,091) in Brandenburg, after 1945 in Zielona Gora prov., W Poland, 25 mi. NNE of Grünberg (Zielona Gora); agr. market (grain, potatoes, livestock). From 1919 to 1939, Ger. frontier station Pol. border, 4 mi. W of Zbaszyn, on main Berlin-Warsaw line. Chartered after 1945.
Zbiroh (zbĭ'rô), town (pop. 1,630), W Bohemia, Czechoslovakia, 19 mi. NE of Pilsen, in iron-mining region. Old castle.
Zborov (zbô'rôf), Hung. *Zboró* (zbô'rō), village (pop. 1,551), NE Slovakia, Czechoslovakia, 7 mi. N of Bardejov; lumbering. Old castle remains. Heavy fighting here and in both World Wars.
Zborov (zbô'rŭf), Pol. *Zborów* (ŭzbô'rōōf), city (1931 pop. 5,182), W Ternopol oblast, Ukrainian SSR, on Strypa R. and 22 mi. WNW of Ternopol; food processing (flour, sweets, liquor); brick mfg. Has old palace and churches. Site of battle (1649), followed by alliance bet. Cossack hetman Bogdan Chmielnicki (Khmelnitski) and Pol. king John II Casimir. Passed to Austria (1772); reverted to Poland (1919); ceded to USSR in 1945.
Zbraslav (zbrä'släf), town (pop. 4,643), S central Bohemia, Czechoslovakia, on Vltava R., on railroad and 7 mi. S of Prague; popular summer resort. Has 13th-cent. castle, old monastery.
Zbruch River (zbrōōch'), Pol. *Zbrucz* (zbrōōch'), W Ukrainian SSR, rises N of Volochisk in Volyn-Podolian Upland, flows 120 mi. S, past Satanov and Gusyatin, to Dniester R. NW of Khotin. Formed frontier bet. Austria-Hungary and Russia prior to First World War; was Poland-USSR border from 1921 to 1939.
Zbysov (zbē'shôf), Czech *Zbýšov*, village (pop. 2,151), S Moravia, Czechoslovakia, 12 mi. WSW of Brno; local rail terminus; coking and ironworks (rolling stock, machinery); coal mines.
Zdanice (zdä'nyĭtsĕ), Czech *Ždánice*, town (pop. 2,165), S Moravia, Czechoslovakia, 20 mi. ESE of Brno, in sugar-beet and wheat dist.; rail terminus.
Zdar, Czech *Žd'ár* or *Město Žd'ár* (myĕ'stô zhdyär), Ger. *Saar* or *Saar in Mähren* (zär'ĭn mâ'rŭn), town (pop. 3,532), W Moravia, Czechoslovakia, in Bohemian-Moravian Heights, on railroad and 19 mi. NE of Jihlava; tourist center; tanning, shoe mfg.
Zdiar (zhdyär), Slovak *Ždiar*, Hung. *Zár* (zär), village (pop. 1,103), N Slovakia, Czechoslovakia, on NE slope (alt. 2,965 ft.) of the High Tatra, 15 mi. N of Poprad; oats; lumbering. Part of Vysoke Tatry commune.
Zdice (zdyĭ'tsĕ), village (pop. 3,037), W central Bohemia, Czechoslovakia, on railroad and 23 mi. SW of Prague; iron mining. Has 18th-cent. church. A peace treaty signed here, 1193, bet. Bohemian princes.
Zdolbunov (zdŭlbōōnôf'), Pol. *Zdołbunów* (zdôw-bōō'nōōf), city (1931 pop. 10,228), S Rovno oblast, Ukrainian SSR, 7 mi. S of Rovno; rail junction (repair shops); cement mfg., iron smelting, agr. (grain, fruit, vegetables) processing, tanning, sawmilling; slate works. Passed from Russia to Poland in 1921; ceded to USSR in 1945.
Zdounky (zdōn'kĭ), town (pop. 1,423), S central Moravia, Czechoslovakia, on railroad and 5 mi. SSW of Kromeriz, in agr. area (sugar beets, wheat, oats, barley).
Zdunska Wola (zdōō'nyŭskä vô'lä), Pol. *Zduńska Wola*, Rus. *Zdunskaya Volya* or *Zdun'skaya Volya* (both: zdōō'nyŭskŭ"yŭ vôl'yŭ), town (pop. 14,601), Lodz prov., central Poland, 25 mi. WSW of Lodz. Rail junction; ironworks; weaving, flour milling, brewing, mfg. of leather goods, sawmilling. Before Second World War, pop. 50% Jewish.
Zduny (zdōō'nĭ), town (1946 pop. 2,555), Poznan prov., W central Poland, 4 mi. SSW of Krotoszyn; beet-sugar and flour milling, tanning. Monastery.
Zdvinsk (zdvēnsk'), village (1939 pop. over 2,000), SW Novosibirsk oblast, Russian SFSR, on Kargat R. and 45 mi. S of Barabinsk; dairy farming.
Zdzieciol, Belorussian SSR: see DYATLOVO.
Zea, Greece: see KEA.
Zea (sä'ä), town (pop. 521), Mérida state, W Venezuela, in Andean spur, 45 mi. WSW of Mérida; alt. 4,806 ft.; sugar cane, coffee, grain; gold mining.
Zealand (zē'lŭnd), Dan. *Sjælland*, (shĕ'län), Ger. *Seeland*, island (□2,709; pop. 1,482,978), largest (80 mi. long) of Denmark, bet. the Kattegat and Baltic Sea; separated from Sweden by the Oresund, from Fyn isl. by the Great Belt. Divided into 5 amts: Copenhagen, Frederiksborg, Holbaek, Soro, Praesto. Chief cities: Copenhagen, Roskilde, Helsingor. Largest lake, Arreso. Highest point, Gyldenloves Height (413 ft.) in NE Soro amt. N shore broken by many-branched ISE FJORD. Sus R. (52 mi. long), most important river. Grain and dairy farming, cattle breeding, fisheries.
Zealand, Netherlands: see ZEELAND.
Zealand, forest camp area, Coos co., N central N.H., in Zealand Notch recreational region of White Mtn. Natl. Forest, NW of Crawford Notch, near Ammonoosuc R.
Zealandia (zēlăn'dēŭ), town (pop. 156), SE central Sask., 60 mi. SW of Saskatoon; grain elevators.
Zearing (zēr'ĭng), town (pop. 514), Story co., central Iowa, 20 mi. ENE of Ames; livestock, grain.
Zebak or **Zibak** (zä'bŭk), town (pop. 5,000), Afghan Badakhshan, NE Afghanistan, on highway and 60 mi. SE of Faizabad, and on Kokcha R.; trades in lapis lazuli, gold, emeralds, and rubies; precious-stone handicrafts.
Zeballos (zĕbă'lŭs), village (pop. estimate 650), SW B.C., on NW Vancouver Isl., on Zeballos Arm (7 mi. long) of Esperanza Inlet, at mouth of Zeballos R. (20 mi. long), 40 mi. S of Alert Bay; gold- and silver-mining center. Mines extend along Zeballos R.
Zeballos-cué (säbä'yōs-kwā'), NE suburb of Asunción, Paraguay, on Paraguay R.; meat-packing center.
Zebbug or **Zebbuj** (both: zĕb-bōōj'), Maltese *Żebbuġ*, town (parish pop. 7,493), central Malta, 4 mi. WSW of Valletta; olive oil, flowers, citrus fruit; goats. Furniture mfg. Has several churches, a fortified tower, Roman arch, bishop's palace.
Zebdani or **Zabadani** (both: zĕbdä'nē), Fr. *Zébédani*, town (pop. c.5,000), Damascus prov., SW Syria, on Barada R., on Damascus-Beirut RR, and 19 mi. NW of Damascus in the Anti-Lebanon mts.; alt. 3,980 ft.; health and summer resort; also noted for its apple orchards.
Zébé (zĕ'bā), village, S Fr. Togoland, just NE of Anécho, of which it is the govt. and residential suburb. Hosp., missions. Formerly spelled Sebbe.
Zébédani, Syria: see ZEBDANI.
Zebediela (zĕbĭdē'lŭ), village, N central Transvaal, U. of So. Afr., in Strydpoort Mts., 30 mi. SSW of Pietersburg; orange-growing center.
Zeberged, Egypt: see SAINT JOHN'S ISLAND.
Zebib, Ras (räs' zĕbēb'), cape on the Mediterranean coast of N Tunisia, 10 mi. E of Bizerte; 37°16'N 10°5'E.
Zebid, Yemen: see ZABID.
Zebirget, Egypt: see SAINT JOHN'S ISLAND.
Zebrak (zhĕ'bräk), Czech *Žebrák*, village (pop. 1,245), W central Bohemia, Czechoslovakia, 27 mi. SW of Prague. Has historical mus. Picturesque remains of 12th-cent. Zebrak castle and 14th-cent. Tocnik castle (both associated with Wenceslaus IV), are just NNW.
Zebreira (zĭbrā'rŭ), town (pop. 2,608), Castelo Branco dist., central Portugal, 24 mi. E of Castelo Branco, near Sp. border; grain, corn, beans, livestock.
Zebulon (zĕ'byŭlŭn). **1** City (pop. 539), ⊙ Pike co., W central Ga., 11 mi. SSW of Griffin; food canning. **2** Town (pop. 1,378), Wake co., central N.C., 18 mi. E of Raleigh; fertilizer and lumber mills, tobacco warehouses.
Zebulun Valley (zĕ'byŭlŭn, –byōō–) or **Zevulun Valley** (zĕvōōlōōn'), NW Israel, extends c.10 mi. NNE from Haifa along Bay of Acre of the Mediterranean. Densely populated, it is site of many residential settlements, economically dependent upon Haifa's industries. In biblical times a division of Palestine.
Zedelgem (zä'dŭl-khĕm), village (pop. 3,655), West Flanders prov., NW Belgium, 6 mi. SSW of Bruges; metal industry; agr. Formerly spelled Zedelghem.
Zeebrugge (zā'brŭ"khŭ), seaport in Bruges commune, West Flanders prov., NW Belgium, on North Sea, at N end of Bruges-Zeebrugge Canal, and 9 mi. N of Bruges city; port and terminal of train ferry to Harwich (England). Developed about the turn of the cent. as port for Bruges. Has coke ovens; mfg. of window glass. Ger. naval base in First World War, its harbor was sealed (1918) by Br. naval force which sank concrete-filled blockships at entrance.
Zeehan (zē'ŭn), town (pop. 767), W Tasmania, 100 mi. WSW of Launceston; sawmills. Silver-lead and zinc mines near by.
Zeeland (zē'lŭnd, Du. zä'länt), province (□ 650.7 pop. 260,800), SW Netherlands; ⊙ Middelburg. Bounded by the Krammer, S arm of Maas R. estuary (N), North Brabant prov. (E), Belgium (S), North Sea (W). Comprises mainland area contiguous with Belgium, and isls. of Walcheren,

North and South Beveland, Schouwen-Duiveland, Tholen, and Sint Philipsland. Drained by Scheldt R. estuary (the Eastern and Western Scheldt). Extensive growing of wheat, oats, vegetables, flax, potatoes, fruit. Coke production and allied coal-tar chemical industries (Terneuzen and Sluiskil), shipbuilding (Flushing), flax spinning and other small industries; oyster culture (centered on Kruiningen), mussel and shrimp fishing and processing; dairying. Main towns: Middelburg, Flushing (chief port), Goes, Terneuzen, Sas van Gent. In Middle Ages possession of Zeeland was disputed by Counts of Holland and Flanders; annexed to Holland (1323) by Count William III; united with remainder of country during reign of Stadholder William III (1672–1702). Formerly also spelled Zealand.

Zeeland. **1** City (pop. 3,075), Ottawa co., SW Mich., 20 mi. SW of Grand Rapids, near Black R., in farm area (livestock, truck, grain, corn, hay; dairy products); ships chicks. Mfg. (furniture, brick, caskets, clocks). Settled 1847 by Dutch; inc. as village 1875, as city 1907. **2** Village (pop. 484), McIntosh co., S N.Dak., 22 mi. W of Ashley.

Zeelandia (zēlăn'dēŭ), village (pop. 710), Essequibo co., N Br. Guiana, on NW tip of Wakenaam Isl., 24 mi. WNW of Georgetown; rice, coconuts.

Zeelandia, Fort, Formosa: see ANPING.

Zeerust (zē'rŭst, Afrikaans sē'rûst), town (pop. 5,104), W Transvaal, U. of So. Afr., near Cape Prov. and Bechuanaland Protectorate border, 35 mi. NE of Mafeking; agr. center (fruit, wheat, oats, cotton); in mining region (zinc, lead, fluorspar).

Zeesen (tsā'zŭn), village (pop. 2,567), Brandenburg, E Germany, just SSE of Königs Wusterhausen; until 1945, site of major short-wave broadcasting transmitters.

Zehden, Poland: see CEDYNIA.

Zehdenick (tsā'dŭnĭk), town (pop. 13,246), Brandenburg, E Germany, on the Havel, at N end of Voss Canal, and 30 mi. N of Berlin; mfg. of chemicals, flour milling. Ruins of Cistercian monastery (founded 1250) now form part of convent (established 1541).

Zehlendorf (tsā'lŭndôrf), residential district (1939 pop. 81,141; 1946 pop. 76,432), SW Berlin, Germany, on the Havel and 9 mi. SW of city center. Includes S part of Grunewald picnic area. After 1945 in U.S. sector.

Zeidab or **Ez Zeidab** (ĕz zādăb'), town, Northern Prov., N Anglo-Egyptian Sudan, on right bank of the Nile, on railroad, and 10 mi. S of Ed Damer; cotton center.

Zeiden, Rumania: see CODLEA.

Zeier River, Yugoslavia: see SORA RIVER.

Zeigler (zī'glŭr), city (pop. 2,516), Franklin co., S Ill., 6 mi. N of Herrin; bituminous-coal mines; fruit, dairy products, livestock. Inc. 1914.

Zeil (tsīl), town (pop. 3,386), Lower Franconia, N Bavaria, Germany, near the Main, 15 mi. NW of Bamberg; spinning, weaving, brewing, flour and lumber milling. Sand- and grindstone quarries near by.

Zeil, Mount, Australia: see MACDONNELL RANGES.

Zeila or **Zeilah** (zā'lä), town, W Br. Somaliland, port on Gulf of Aden, 25 mi. ESE of Djibouti (Fr. Somaliland); roadhead to livestock-raising region; exports sheep, hides and skins, gums. Transit trade from Ethiopia. Pearl fisheries; salines. A flourishing slave-trade depot until end of 19th cent. Formerly spelled Zeyla.

Zeist (zīst), town (pop. 34,891; commune pop. 40,590), Utrecht prov., central Netherlands, 5 mi. E of Utrecht; residential area; mfg. (pharmaceuticals, soap, furniture, gold- and silverware); agr., truck gardening. Moravian settlement established here 1746.

Zeitin, Cape, Greece: see MALEA, CAPE.

Zeitun, Greece: see LAMIA.

Zeitun, Malta: see ZEJTUN.

Zeitun, Turkey: see ZEYTUN.

Zeitz (tsīts), city (pop. 39,581), in former Prussian Saxony prov., central Germany, after 1945 in Saxony-Anhalt, on the White Elster and 25 mi. SW of Leipzig; 51°3'N 12°8'E. Lignite and clay mining; woolen and cotton milling, sugar refining, metal- and woodworking; mfg. of machinery, chemicals, pianos, baby carriages, food products. Power station. Has 10th-cent. church, rebuilt in 13th cent.; and 17th-cent. Moritzburg castle. Originally a Slav settlement. Bishopric, founded 968 by Otto I, was moved 1028 to Naumburg. Was ⊙ duchy of Saxe-Zeitz (1563–1718). Passed to Prussia in 1815.

Zejtun or **Zeitun** (both: zā'tōōn), Maltese *Żejtun*, town (parish pop. 11,980), SE Malta, 3 mi. S of Valletta, in agr. region (wheat, vegetables, citrus fruit). Has several fine churches, notably St. Gregory (1436, restored 1492), among isl.'s oldest; Trigona palace, fortifications, handsome houses.

Zela, Turkey: see ZILE.

Zelandia, Fort, Formosa: see ANPING.

Zelaya (sälī'ä), largest department (□ 27,145; 1950 pop. 71,662, including territory of CABO GRACIAS A DIOS) of Nicaragua, on Caribbean Sea; ⊙ Bluefields. Extends from N Nicaragua border S to Costa Rica along entire Atlantic littoral; drained by Coco, Huahua, Prinzapolka rivers, Rio Grande, and Escondido and San Juan rivers. Includes E sections of Cordillera Isabelia and Huapi Mts., Cordillera de Yolaina, and CORN ISLANDS. Largely covered by tropical forest, with hardwood (NE); has low swampy coast. Interior is inhabited mainly by Mosquito (Miskitto) and Zumo Indians. Gold mining at Siuna and Bonanza. Lumbering. Exports bananas and coconuts. Some agr. (rice, corn, beans, sugar cane). Chief ports: Bluefields (and its outer port El Bluff), Puerto Cabezas, Prinzapolka, Rama (on Escondido R.). Formed 1894 out of autonomous Indian reserve (until 1860 a Br. protectorate) of MOSQUITO COAST. Formerly called Bluefields. The territory (□675) of San Juan del Norte, formerly in Zelaya, became (1949) part of dept. of Río San Juan.

Zelazowa Wola (zhĕläzô'vä vô'lä), Pol. *Żelazowa Wola*, village, Warszawa prov., E central Poland, 30 mi. W of Warsaw, 5 mi. ENE of Sochaczew. Chopin b. here. Mus.

Zele (zā'lù), town (pop. 16,363), East Flanders prov., N Belgium, 4 mi. NW of Dendermonde; textiles; agr. market.

Zelechow (zhĕlĕ'khōōf), Pol. *Żelechów*, Rus. *Zhelekhov* (zhĕ'lyĭ-khŭf), town (pop. 3,892), Warszawa prov., E central Poland, 50 mi. SE of Warsaw; mfg. of shoes, vegetable oil; tanning, flour milling.

Zelenchuk (zĕlyĭnchōōk'), name of two parallel left affluents of Kuban R., in Stavropol Territory, Russian SFSR. **Zelenchuk River** proper or **Great Zelenchuk River,** Rus. *Bolshoi Zelenchuk*, rises in the Greater Caucasus on peak Pshish, flows 73 mi. NNE, past Zelenchukskaya and Ersakon, to Kuban R. at Nevinnomyssk. **Little Zelenchuk River,** Rus. *Maly Zelenchuk*, is formed by 3 headstreams joining NE of Zelenchukskaya; flows 76 mi. (including longest headstream), parallel (8 mi. E) with the Great Zelenchuk, past Khabez and Ikon-Khalk, to Kuban R. above Nevinnomyssk. Typical mtn. streams.

Zelenchukskaya (–skīŭ), village (1926 pop. 8,889), SW Stavropol Territory, Russian SFSR, in the W Greater Caucasus, on Great Zelenchuk R. and 35 mi. SW of Cherkessk, in grain dist.; flour milling, sawmilling. Until 1943, in Karachai Autonomous Oblast.

Zelenga (zĕlyĭn-gä'), village (1926 pop. 1,683), E Astrakhan oblast, Russian SFSR, on arm of Volga R. delta mouth and 30 mi. ESE of Astrakhan; fisheries; fruit, cotton.

Zelenika (zĕlĕ'nĭkä), village, SW Montenegro, Yugoslavia, on NE shore of Bay of Topla (inlet of Gulf of Kotor), 2 mi. E of Herceg Novi; small seaport; terminus of narrow-gauge railway to Sarajevo; summer resort.

Zelenodolsk or **Zelenodol'sk** (zĭlyĕ"nŭdôlsk'), city (1926 pop. 1,083; 1948 pop. estimate 32,200), W Tatar Autonomous SSR, Russian SFSR, port on left bank of Volga R. and 25 mi. W of Kazan; rail junction; woodworking center (furniture, plywood, rail ties); shipbuilding; mfg. of agr. machinery, shoes, knitwear, porcelain, food processing. Became city in 1932. Until c.1940, Zeleny Dol.

Zelenogorsk (–gôrsk'), former city, N Leningrad oblast, Russian SFSR; since 1946, within Leningrad city limits, on Gulf of Finland and 27 mi. NW of city center; major bathing and health resort; summer residences. Called Terijoki (tĕ'rēôkē) while in Finland (until 1940) and, until 1948, in USSR.

Zelenogradsk (–grätsk'), town (1939 pop. 5,079), W Kaliningrad oblast, Russian SFSR, on the Baltic, at S end of Courland Spit, 17 mi. N of Kaliningrad; leading Baltic seaside resort; mudbaths; fisheries. Founded 1816. Until 1945, in East Prussia and called Cranz or Kranz (kränts).

Zelenoye (zĭlyô'nŭyŭ), town (1939 pop. over 500), SW Dnepropetrovsk oblast, Ukrainian SSR, on right bank of Ingulets R. and 12 mi. SSW of Krivoi Rog; iron mining.

Zelensk, Uzbek SSR: see LENINSK, Andizhan oblast.

Zeleny Dol, Russian SFSR: see ZELENODOLSK.

Zelezna Ruda (zhĕ'lĕznä rōō'dä), Czech *Železná Ruda*, Ger. *Eisenstein* or *Böhmisch-Eisenstein* (bû'mĭsh ī'zŭnshtīn), village (pop. 1,322), SW Bohemia, Czechoslovakia, in Bohemian Forest, on railroad and 18 mi. SSW of Klatovy, on Ger. border opposite Bayrisch Eisenstein; popular summer and winter-sports resort; lace making. Has 18th-cent. Greek-style cathedral.

Zeleznice (zhĕ'lĕznyĭtsĕ), Czech *Železnice*, village (pop. 1,082), N Bohemia, Czechoslovakia, on railroad and 3 mi. NNE of Jicin; health resort.

Zeleznik or **Zheleznik** (zhĕ'lyĕznĭk), Serbo-Croatian *Železnik*, village, N central Serbia, Yugoslavia, 8 mi. SSW of Belgrade; mfg. of machine tools.

Zelezny Brod (zhĕ'lĕznē brôt"), Czech *Železný Brod*, Ger. *Eisenbrod* (ī'zŭnbrōt), town (pop. 2,837), N Bohemia, Czechoslovakia, on Jizera R. and 12 mi. SE of Liberec; rail junction; known for its glass industry (notably glass jewelry and comic glass figures); mfg. of pianos, rope, cloth, knitwear. Glass-makers' and glass-jewelers' schools. Has picturesque wooden bldgs., glass-art mus. Manganese mined at Vrat (vrät), Czech *Vrát*, Ger. *Wrat* (vrät), just SW.

Zelhem (zĕl'hĕm), village (pop. 1,085), Gelderland prov., E Netherlands, 4 mi. NE of Doetinchem; wood products; agr.

Zeliachova, Greece: see NEA ZICHNA.

Zelienople (zē"lēnō'pŭl), borough (pop. 2,981), Butler co., W Pa., 25 mi. NNW of Pittsburgh; metal and clay products; bituminous coal. Settled by Germans; laid out c.1802, inc. 1840.

Zeliezovce (zhĕ'lyĕzôftsĕ), Slovak *Želiezovce*, town (pop. 3,748), S Slovakia, Czechoslovakia, on railroad, on Hron R. and 32 mi. SW of Nitra; wheat, grapes, tobacco.

Zelina (zĕ'lēnä), village (pop. 2,025), N Croatia, Yugoslavia, 17 mi. NE of Zagreb, near Lonja R.; center of winegrowing region. Castle. Until 1948, Sveti Ivan Zelina.

Zell (tsĕl'). **1** or **Zell am Harmersbach** (äm här'mŭrsbäkh), village (pop. 2,172), S Baden, Germany, in Black Forest, 10 mi. SSE of Offenburg; ceramics and machinery mfg., lumber milling. Summer resort. Has pilgrimage church. **2** or **Zell im Wiesental** (ĭm vē'zŭntäl), town (pop. 3,412), S Baden, Germany, in Black Forest, 11 mi. NE of Lörrach; mfg. of textiles, machinery, cellulose; paper milling. **3** Town, Baden, Germany: see RADOLFZELL. **4** or **Zell am Main** (äm mīn'), village (pop. 2,772), Lower Franconia, NW Bavaria, Germany, on the Main (canalized) and 2 mi. WNW of Würzburg; brewing. In near-by former monastery, Friedrich König invented the steam printing press (1810). Sometimes called Zell über Würzburg (übŭr vürts'bŏŏrk). **5** Town (pop. 2,723), in former Prussian Rhine Prov., W Germany, after 1945 in Rhineland-Palatinate, on the Mosel and 30 mi. SW of Coblenz; wine. Has 16th-cent. castle.

Zell (tsĕl), town (pop. 2,646), Zurich canton, N Switzerland, 6 mi. SE of Winterthur; cotton textiles.

Zella (dzĕl'lä), Saharan oasis (1950 pop. 2,500), SE Tripolitania, Libya, 105 mi. ESE of Hun; caravan center and road terminus; dates, figs, barley; livestock.

Zella-Mehlis (tsĕ'lä-mā'lĭs), town (pop. 17,352), Thuringia, central Germany, in Thuringian Forest, at W foot of the Beerberg, 20 mi. S of Gotha; machinery, typewriter, calculating-machine, metal- and woodworking plants. Noted formerly as small-arms-mfg. center. Formed 1919 through incorporation of Zella Sankt Blasii (which developed around 12th-cent. chapel) and Mehlis.

Zell am Harmersbach, Germany: see ZELL, Baden.

Zell am Main, Germany: see ZELL, Bavaria.

Zell am See (tsĕl' äm zā'), town (pop. 6,320), Salzburg, W central Austria, on the Zeller See and 20 mi. WSW of Bischofshofen; rail junction; tourist center, resort (alt. 2,486 ft.); copper works, tannery. Suspension railway to Schmittenhöhe, with excellent view.

Zell an der Pram (än dĕr präm'), town (pop. 2,506), W Upper Austria, 13 mi. SE of Schärding; hogs, potatoes.

Zella Sankt Blasii, Germany: see ZELLA-MEHLIS.

Zell bei Zellhof (bī tsĕl'hōf), town (pop. 2,288), NE Upper Austria, 18 mi. ENE of Linz, N of the Danube; vineyards.

Zellerfeld, Germany: see CLAUSTHAL-ZELLERFELD.

Zeller See (tsĕl'ŭrzā). **1** Small lake (□ 1.81) in Salzburg, W central Austria, 20 mi. WSW of Bischofshofen, c.2 mi. long, 1 mi. wide, average depth 120 ft., alt. 2,460 ft. Resort of Zell am See is on W shore. Noted view of the Hohe Tauern from center of lake. **2** Small lake in Upper Austria: see MONDSEE.

Zeller See, Germany: see UNTERSEE.

Zell im Wiesental, Germany: see ZELL, Baden.

Zell über Würzburg, Germany: see ZELL, Bavaria.

Zell-Weierbach (tsĕl'-vī'ŭrbäkh), village (pop. 2,101), S Baden, Germany, on W slope of Black Forest, 2 mi. E of Offenburg; noted for its red wine.

Zellwood, resort village (1940 pop. 600), Orange co., central Fla., 18 mi. NW of Orlando; citrus-fruit packing and canning, ramie milling.

Zelman, Russian SFSR: see ROVNOYE, Saratov.

Zeltweg (tsĕlt'vĕk), town (pop. 5,529), Styria, S central Austria, on Mur R. and 5 mi. ENE of Judenburg; rail junction; iron- and steelworks.

Zeluán (thĕlwän'), village (pop. 476), Kert territory, E Sp. Morocco, on railroad and 15 mi. S of Melilla; road center; olives, barley, sheep. Military post.

Zelva or **Zel'va** (zyĕl'vŭ), Pol. *Zelwa* (zĕl'vä), town (1937 pop. 2,700), SE Grodno oblast, Belorussian SSR, 15 mi. E of Volkovysk; dairying, flour milling, sawmilling; lime- and brickworks.

Zelzate (zĕl'zätŭ), town (pop. 10,038), East Flanders prov., NW Belgium, on Ghent-Terneuzen Canal and 11 mi. NNE of Ghent; coke plants; chemical industry. Formerly spelled Selzaete.

Zembra (zĕmbrä'), Arabic *Djamour el Kebir*, anc. *Aegimures*, uninhabited island (□ 1.5) in Gulf of Tunis (Mediterranean sea), off tip of Cape Bon Peninsula, 40 mi. NE of Tunis. Islet of Zembretta is 3 mi. ESE.

Zemen (zĕ'mĕn), village (pop. 1,786), Sofia dist., W Bulgaria, on Struma R. and 12 mi. SW of Radomir; fruit, truck. Has medieval monastery with 14th-cent. frescoes and paintings. Formerly Belovo, sometimes spelled Bjelovo.

Zemetchino (zĭmyĕ'chĭnŭ), town (1926 pop. 5,342), NW Penza oblast, Russian SFSR, 33 mi. ENE of Molshansk, in sugar-beet area; sugar milling.

Zemgale (zĕm'gälĕ), **Zemgalia**, or **Zemgallia** (zĕmgăl'yŭ,-ēŭ), former province (□ 5,259; 1935 pop. 299,369) of S Latvia; ⊙ Jelgava. Originally ruled by Livonian Knights; became (1561–1795) part of duchy of Courland, which passed in 1795 to Russia and in 1920 to independent Latvia. Sometimes spelled Semgallia or Semigallia.

Zemgale, village, SE Latvia, in Zemgale, on railroad and 11 mi. S of Daugavpils; frontier station on Lith. (formerly, 1921–39, Pol.) border.

Zemio (zĕmyō'), village, SE Ubangi-Shari, Fr. Equatorial Africa, on Bomu R. (Belgian Congo border) and 170 mi. ENE of Bangassou; customs station. Has Protestant mission and leprosarium.

Zemlyansk (zĭmlyänsk'), village (1926 pop. 1,781), NW Voronezh oblast, Russian SFSR, 25 mi. NW of Voronezh; wheat.

Zemmora (zĕmôrä'), village (pop. 2,269), Oran dept., NW Algeria, on railroad and 12 mi. E of Relizane; brick mfg.; sheep raising.

Zemo-Avchala (zyĕ"mŭ-ŭfchŭlä'), village, E central Georgian SSR, on Kura R., on railroad and 8 mi. N of Tiflis; site of hydroelectric station supplying Tiflis.

Zempelburg, Poland: see SEPOLNO.

Zemple, village (pop. 87), Itasca co., N central Minn., near Mississippi R., 14 mi. WNW of Grand Rapids, in lake and forest region; grain, potatoes.

Zemplen (zĕmp'lān), Hung. *Zemplén*, county (□ 682; pop. 155,291), NE Hungary; ⊙ Satoraljaujhely. Level agr. area (BODROGKÖZ) in E, mountainous in W (HEGYALJA), drained by Tisza and Bodrog rivers. Fruit (grapes, nuts, plums), cattle, hogs. Industry at Satoraljaujhely, Sarospatak, and Tokaj. Excellent Tokay wine produced here.

Zempoala (sĕmpwä'lä), town (pop. 1,749), Hidalgo, central Mexico, on railroad and 17 mi. SSE of Pachuca; cereals, maguey, livestock.

Zempoaltépetl (sĕmpwätä'pĕtŭl), peak (11,142 ft.), Oaxaca, S Mexico, 50 mi. E of Oaxaca; situated at E end of Sierra Madre del Sur, where it converges with unified Sierra Madre of S Mexico and Central America. Also Zempoaltépec or Cempoaltépetl.

Zemst (zĕmst), agr. village (pop. 3,681), Brabant prov., central Belgium, 10 mi. NNE of Brussels. Formerly spelled Sempst.

Zemsz, Poland: see LUBSKO.

Zemtsy (zĕm'tsē), village (1926 pop. 223), E Velikiye Luki oblast, Russian SFSR, 12 mi. E of Zapadnaya Dvina; rail junction; mfg. of prefabricated houses.

Zemu Glacier (zāmōō'), largest glacier in Sikkim, India, in Singalila Range of E Nepal Himalayas; only accessible glacier descending from Kanchenjunga mtn. Flows c.16 mi. NE; gives rise to upper branch of the Tista; 650 ft. deep; daily velocity, 9 in. Remarkable for trenches occurring along glacial sides, bet. lateral moraine and mtn. side.

Zemun (zĕ'mōōn), Ger. *Semlin* (zĕm'lĭn), Hung. *Zimony* (zĭm'ônyŭ), section of Belgrade, N central Serbia, Yugoslavia, in the Srem; port on the Danube, across Sava R. mouth, and 3 mi. NW of city center, on railroad. Internatl. airport; mfg. of aircraft, woolen textiles, leather belting, penicillin, glue, asbestos products. Ruins of castle of John Hunyady (died here 1456). Formerly a separate city; remains seat of Zemun co. of Vojvodina.

Zemunik (zĕmōō'nĭk), village, W Croatia, Yugoslavia, 7 mi. E of Zadar; airport for Zadar.

Zenda, city (pop. 226), Kingman co., S Kansas, 16 mi. SSW of Kingman, in wheat region.

Zendoji (zāndō'jē), town (pop. 4,639), Fukuoka prefecture, N central Kyushu, Japan, 5 mi. E of Kurume and on Chikugo R.; rice, wheat, barley, millet, sweet potatoes.

Zeng Abad, Iraq: see KIFRI.

Zengg, Yugoslavia: see SENJ, Croatia.

Zengövar, Mount, Hungary: see MECSEK MOUNTAINS.

Zenica or **Zenitsa** (both: zĕ'nĭtsä), town (pop. 16,827), central Bosnia, Yugoslavia, on Bosna R., on railroad and 35 mi. NW of Sarajevo, in Sarajevo coal area; brown-coal mine; iron- and steelworks, paper mills.

Zenjan (zĕnjän'), **Zinjan** (zĭn–), or **Zanjan** (zän–), town (1941 pop. 39,450), First Prov., N Iran, on highway and railroad to Tabriz and 180 mi. NW of Teheran, and on Zenjan R. (tributary of the Qizil Uzun); main center of former Khamseh prov., in agr. area (grapes, raisins, wheat, fruit). Rug weaving; hand-woven cotton goods, cutlery, matches. Airfield. Pop. is largely Turkic. Town was former stronghold of Babism.

Zenka, Formosa: see SHANHWA.

Zenkoji, Japan: see NAGANO, Nagano prefecture.

Zenkov or **Zen'kov** (zĕn'yŭkŭf), city (1926 pop. 10,926), NE Poltava oblast, Ukrainian SSR, 40 mi. NNW of Poltava; dairying, metalworking.

Zenkovka Russian SFSR: see CHKALOVSKOYE, Maritime Territory.

Zenkovo or **Zen'kovo** (–kŭvŭ), S suburb of Prokopyevsk, Kemerovo oblast, Russian SFSR, in Kuznetsk Basin; coal mines; limestone works.

Zenon Park (zĕ'nŭn), village (pop. 300), E Sask., 20 mi. NE of Tisdale; dairying, wheat.

Zenon Pereyra (sā'nōn pĕrä'rä), town (pop. estimate 1,200), S central Santa Fe prov., Argentina, 70 mi. W of Santa Fe; wheat, flax, corn, livestock; mfg. of harvesters, dairy products.

Zenra-hokudo, Korea: see NORTH CHOLLA.

Zenra-nando, Korea: see SOUTH CHOLLA.

Zenshu, Korea: see CHONJU.

Zenson di Piave (zĕntsôn' dē pyä'vĕ), village (pop. 390), Treviso prov., Veneto, N Italy, on Piave R. and 12 mi. E of Treviso; alcohol distillery, mfg. (agr. machinery, stoves).

Zensyu, Korea: see CHONJU.

Zenta, Yugoslavia: see SENTA.

Zentsuji (zäntsōō'jē), town (pop. 21,827), Kagawa prefecture, N Shikoku, Japan, 4 mi. SSW of Marugame, in agr. area. Site of 8th-cent. Buddhist temple. Birthplace of Kobo-Daishi, founder of Shingon sect of Buddhism.

Zepce or **Zhepche** (both: zhĕp'chĕ), Serbo-Croatian *Žepče*, village, central Bosnia, Yugoslavia, on Bosna R., on railroad and 45 mi. NNW of Sarajevo. Fruitgrowing, mineral springs in vicinity. Seat of Bosnian kings in late-14th cent.

Zepernick (tsā'pŭrnĭk), village (pop. 9,769), Brandenburg, E Germany, 12 mi. NNE of Berlin; market gardening.

Zephyr (zĕ'fŭr), village (pop. c.750), Brown co., central Texas, 11 mi. E of Brownwood, in farm area.

Zephyrhills, town (pop. 1,826), Pasco co., W central Fla., 25 mi. NE of Tampa; lumber, food products. Founded c.1911, inc. 1914.

Zeraf, Bahr el, Anglo-Egyptian Sudan: see BAHR EL ZERAF.

Zera'im, Israel: see GILBOA.

Zéralda (zäräldä'), village (pop. 3,008), Alger dept., N central Algeria, near the Mediterranean, 13 mi. SW of Algiers; vineyards, truck gardens, citrus groves.

Zeramedine or **Zéramdine** (zārämdēn'), village, Sousse dist., E Tunisia, 18 mi. SSE of Sousse; olive groves. Lignite mines.

Zeran (zhĕ'rānyŭ), Pol. *Żerań*, industrial suburb of Warsaw, Warszawa prov., E central Poland, port on right bank of the Vistula and 4 mi. N of city center; automobile plant.

Zeravshan (zyĕrŭfshän'), former oblast (1924–26) of Uzbek SSR, corresponding to Bukhara oasis.

Zeravshan Range (zyĕrŭfshän'), branch of Tien Shan mountain system in W Tadzhik SSR; extends from Alai Range c.200 mi. W, along S watershed of Zeravshan R.; rises to 18,480 ft. Extensive coal, antimony, and tungsten deposits. Sometimes considered part of Pamir-Alai system.

Zeravshan River, in Tadzhik and Uzbek SSR, rises in E Turkestan Range, flows W, past Matcha, Zakhmatabad, and Pendzhikent, through irrigated cotton area, splitting into 2 arms, the Kara Darya (N) and the Ak Darya (S), bet. Samarkand and Khatyrchi, past Kermine, and SW, past Bukhara, to disappear in desert near the Amu Darya, N of Chardzhou; 460 mi. long. Reservoir on Kara Darya arm, near Katta-Kurgan. Called Matcha R. in upper course.

Zerbst (tsĕrpst), city (pop. 19,237), in former Anhalt state, central Germany, after 1945 in Saxony-Anhalt, 11 mi. NW of Dessau; 51°58'N 12°6'E. Mfg. of machinery, leather goods; brewing. Asparagus market. Entire Old City destroyed in heavy air raids during Second World War. Was ⊙ duchy of Anhalt-Zerbst (1603–1793). Empress Catherine II of Russia spent her youth here.

Zerenda (zyĕryĭndä'), village (1948 pop. over 2,000), S Kokchetav oblast, Kazakh SSR, 25 mi. S of Kokchetav, in cattle area; metalworks.

Zerenik, Turkey: see OVACIK.

Zergjan or **Zergjani**, Albania: see ZERQAN.

Zerhoun (zĕgōōn'), isolated limestone massif in N central Fr. Morocco, c.10 mi. N of Meknès; rises to 2,650 ft. Noted for its sheer cliffs and deep gorges. Its slopes are covered with olive and lemon groves, orchards (apples, pears), and vineyards. Moulay Idris and the ruins of VOLUBILIS are at W foot.

Zeria Mountain, Greece: see KYLLENE MOUNTAINS.

Zerka', Jordan: see ZERQA'.

Zerkow (zhĕr'kōōf), Pol. *Żerków*, town (1946 pop. 1,574), Poznan prov., W central Poland, 36 mi. SE of Poznan; machine mfg., flour milling, sawmilling. Monastery.

Zermagna River, Yugoslavia: see ZRMANJA RIVER.

Zermatt (tsĕr'mät), village (pop. 1,148), Valais canton, S Switzerland, on Mattervisp R. and 24 mi. SE of Sion; resort (alt. 5,315 ft.), 5 mi. NE of the Matterhorn and 8 mi. NW of the Dufourspitze, commanding one of finest views in Switzerland. Especially popular among sportsmen (notably Alpinists), Zermatt is frequented in summer (season of main traffic) and winter. Rack-and-pinion railway leads to Gornergrat, passing the Rifflehorn.

Zernest, Rumania: see ZARNESTI.

Zernovoi or **Zernovoy** (zyĕrnŭvoi'), town (1939 pop. over 500), S Rostov oblast, Russian SFSR, on railroad (Verblyud station) and 8 mi. NW of Mechetinskaya, in grain area; mfg. of farm implements. Hq. of Azov–Black Sea institute for agr. mechanization.

Zerqa', El, Es Zerqa', El Zerka', or **Al-Zarqa'** (all: ĕz-zär'kä), village (pop. c.3,000), N central Jordan, on Hejaz RR and 12 mi. NE of Amman; airfield and road junction. Power plant; phosphate deposits (S). Extraction of yellow ochre near by.

Zerqa', Wadi, Wadi Zerka', or **Wadi Zarqa'** (all: wä'dē zär'kä), river in N Jordan, rising in hills W of Amman, flows NE past Amman to El Zerqa' village, where it turns to flow NW and W to the Jordan just NW of Damiya; 80 mi. long. It is the anc. Jabbok.

Zerqan (zĕr'kyän) or **Zerqani** (zĕr'kyänē), village (1930 pop. 597), E central Albania, 14 mi. SSW of Peshkopi. Sometimes spelled Zergjan or Zergjani.

Zestafoni (zyĕstŭfô'nyē), city (1939 pop. over 10,000), W Georgian SSR, on Kvirila R., on railroad and 20 mi. ESE of Kutaisi; ferromanganese works (supplied by Chiatura manganese), wineries, distillery. Has tree nursery, viticulture experiment station. Called Kvirily until 1924; formerly also known as Dzhugeli.

Zeta (zĕ'tä), fertile lowland in Dinaric Alps, S Montenegro, Yugoslavia; bounded by L. Scutari (S), lower Moraca R. (W, NW), and North Albanian Alps (E, NE). Includes TITOGRAD and PLAVNICA; crossed by narrow-gauge railway. Corn, wheat, cotton, rice, tobacco. Marsh draining (1947–51).

Zeta River, S Montenegro, Yugoslavia, rises in 2 branches joining 4 mi. N of Niksic, flows c.50 mi. SSE, past Danilov Grad and Spuz, to Moraca R. 2 mi. N of Titograd. Flows underground S of Niksic for 4 mi. The BJELOPAVLICI extends along its course. Its valley separates the Brda from Montenegro proper.

Zetland, Scotland: see SHETLAND.

Zeughari, Cape (zĕvgä'rē), SW Cyprus, at SW tip of Akrotiri Peninsula, washed by Episkopi Bay (NW), 10 mi. SW of Limassol. Sometimes spelled Cape Zevghari.

Zeulenroda (tsoi"lŭnrō'dä), town (pop. 14,039), Thuringia, central Germany, 13 mi. NW of Plauen; mfg. of machine tools, chemicals, wire and rubber products; textile milling.

Zeuthen (tsoi'tŭn), village (pop. 4,166), Brandenburg, E Germany, on Seddin L., 14 mi. SE of Berlin; glass mfg.

Zeven (tsā'vŭn), town (pop. 5,625), in former Prussian prov. of Hanover, NW Germany, after 1945 in Lower Saxony, 23 mi. NE of Bremen; metal- and woodworking, dairying. Has Romanesque church of former Benedictine nunnery (founded 1141). After his defeat at Hastenbeck, duke of Cumberland here concluded (1757) the convention of Kloster-Zeven (Closter-Seven), abandoning Hanover to the French.

Zevenaar (zā'vŭnär), village (pop. 3,273), Gelderland prov., E Netherlands, 8 mi. ESE of Arnhem, near Ger. frontier; border station; brick mfg. Its possession disputed by the Netherlands and Prussia until 1816, when it was awarded to the Netherlands.

Zevenbergen (zā'vŭnbĕr'khŭn), town (pop. 4,704), North Brabant prov., SW Netherlands, 8 mi. NW of Breda; beet-sugar-refining center; processing of flax, linseed oil, edible fats; woodworking, mfg. of mattresses, machinery.

Zevghari, Cape, Cyprus: see ZEUGHARI, CAPE.

Zevgolation, Greece: see HELICE.

Zevio (zā'vyô), town (pop. 3,232), Verona prov., Veneto, N Italy, on Adige R. and 8 mi. SE of Verona; canned foods, wine.

Zevulun Valley, Israel: see ZEBULUN VALLEY.

Zeya (zā'ä, Rus. zyā'ŭ), city (1948 pop. over 10,000), central Amur oblast, Russian SFSR, on Zeya R. and 140 mi. E of Skovorodino; gold mining, lumbering. Chartered 1878.

Zeya-Bureya Plain (–bōōrā'ŭ), fertile agr. area in Amur oblast, Russian SFSR, bet. Amur R. and its left affluents, Zeya and Bureya rivers. Heavily populated (2/3 Russian, 1/3 Ukrainian); wheat, rye, oats, buckwheat. Trans-Siberian RR crosses area NW–SE. Main centers: Blagoveshchensk, Kuibyshevka, Svobodny.

Zeya River, Amur oblast, Russian SFSR, rises in SE Stanovoi Range, flows 750 mi. SE and S, past Bomnak, Zeya, and Svobodny, to Amur R. at Blagoveshchensk. Navigable below Bomnak, April–Oct. Receives Selemdzha R. (left). Lower course flows through rich agr. area. Gold found along upper reaches.

Zeyawaddy (zäyä'wŭdē), village, Toungoo dist., Lower Burma, on Rangoon-Mandalay RR and 25 mi. S of Toungoo; sugar factory. Also Zeyawadi.

Zeydiyeh, Yemen: see ZAIDIYA.

Zeyla, Br. Somaliland: see ZEILA.

Zeytun (zātōōn') or **Suleymanli** (sülā'mänlŭ"), Turkish *Süleymanlı*, village (pop. 696), Maras prov., S central Turkey, 21 mi. NNW of Maras; iron mines. Also spelled Zeitun.

Zêzere River (zā'zĭrĭ), N central Portugal, rises in the Serra da Estrêla, flows c.130 mi. generally SW, past Belmonte and Pedrogão Grande, to the Tagus at Constância (Santarém dist.).

Zgerzh, Poland: see ZGIERZ.

Zgharta or **Zaghartah** (both: zŭgär'tŭ), Fr. *Zgnorta*, town (pop. 9,553), N Lebanon, near the coast, 4 mi. SE of Tripoli; cotton, sericulture, cereals, oranges.

Zgierz (zgyĕsh), Rus. *Zgerzh* (zgyĕrsh), city (pop. 21,690), Lodz prov., central Poland, on Bzura R. and 7 mi. NNW of Lodz city center. Rail junction; industrial center; mfg. of textiles, explosives, sulphur and nitrogen acids, dyes, metal products; flour milling, brewing.

Zgonik, Free Territory of Trieste: see SGONICO.
Zgorzelec (zgô-zhĕ'lĕts), town (1946 pop. 5,621), Wroclaw prov., SW Poland, before 1945 E suburb of GORLITZ, E Germany, on right bank of the Lusatian Neisse; woolen milling, lignite mining, glass mfg. Chartered after 1945 and briefly called Zgorzelica. Includes SE suburb of Zgorzelec Ujazd, Ger. *Moys.*
Zgosca or **Zgoshcha** (both: sgôsh'chä), Serbo-Croatian *Zgošća,* village (pop. 6,390), central Bosnia, Yugoslavia, 11 mi. NNW of Visoko.
Zguritsa (sgōō'rĭtsŭ), Rum. *Zgurița* (zgōō'rētsä), village (1941 pop. 959), N Moldavian SSR, 13 mi. WSW of Soroki; flour and oilseed milling. Pop. largely Jewish until Second World War.
Zgurovka (ŭzgōō'rŭfkŭ), village (1926 pop. 5,452), NE Poltava oblast, Ukrainian SSR, 27 mi. WSW of Priluki; sugar refining.
Zhabal, Yugoslavia: see ZABALJ.
Zhabari, Yugoslavia: see ZABARI.
Zhabchitsy (zhäp'chĕtsē), Pol. *Żabczyce,* village (1939 pop. over 500), S Pinsk oblast, Belorussian SSR, 7 mi. WNW of Pinsk; potatoes, flax.
Zhabinka (zhä'bēn-kŭ), Pol. *Żabinka,* village (1939 pop. over 500), W central Brest oblast, Belorussian SSR, on Mukhavets R. and 16 mi. ENE of Brest; rail junction; flour milling, sawmilling.
Zhablyak, Yugoslavia: see ZABLJAK.
Zhabye or **Zhab'ye** (zhä'byĭ), Pol. *Żabie* (zhä'byĕ), village (1939 pop. over 2,000), S Stanislav oblast, Ukrainian SSR, in the Chernagora, 29 mi. SSW of Kolomyya; summer resort; cultural center of Guzuls; wood carving, brassworking, carpet weaving; sheep raising.
Zhadovka (zhä"dŭfkŭ), village (1926 pop. 3,093), W Ulyanovsk oblast, Russian SFSR, 10 mi. SW of Barysh; hemp, woolen, and paper milling, metalworking.
Zhagare, Lithuania: see ZAGARE.
Zhagubitsa, Yugoslavia: see ZAGUBICA.
Zhalanash (zhŭlŭnäsh'), village (1939 pop. over 500), SE Alma-Ata oblast, Kazakh SSR, 90 mi. E of Alma-Ata; sheep.
Zhana-Arka, Kazakh SSR: see ATASUSKI.
Zhanasemei or **Zhanasemey** (zhŭnŭsĭmyā'), S suburb of Semipalatinsk, Semipalatinsk oblast, Kazakh SSR, on Turksib RR; sawmilling.
Zhangis-Tobe (zhŭn-gēs"-tŭbyĕ'), town (1948 pop. over 2,000), E Semipalatinsk oblast, Kazakh SSR, on Turksib RR and 90 mi. SE of Semipalatinsk, in gold-mining area.
Zharkamys (zhŭrkŭmĭs'), village, W Aktyubinsk oblast, Kazakh SSR, on Emba R. and 180 mi. E of Guryev, in petroleum area.
Zharkovski or **Zharkovskiy** (zhär'kŭfskē), town (1939 pop. over 500), SE Velikiye Luki oblast, Russian SFSR, 25 mi. W of Bely; flax.
Zharma (zhŭrmä'), town (1948 pop. over 2,000), central Semipalatinsk oblast, Kazakh SSR, on Turksib RR and 115 mi. S of Semipalatinsk. Formerly Dzharma.
Zharyk (zhŭrĭk'), railroad station, central Karaganda oblast, Kazakh SSR, 65 mi. S of Karaganda; junction of Trans-Kazakhstan RR and branch line to Baikonur.
Zhashkov (zhäsh'kŭf), town (1926 pop. 4,497), SW Kiev oblast, Ukrainian SSR, 37 mi. N of Uman; sugar-refining center.
Zhatai or **Zhatay** (zhŭtī'), town (1948 pop. over 5,000), central Yakut Autonomous SSR, Russian SFSR, on Lena R., near Yakutsk; shipbuilding; construction materials.
Zhavoronkovo (zhä'vŭrŭn-kŭvŭ), village (1939 pop. 364), central Kaliningrad oblast, Russian SFSR, 10 mi. WNW of Chernyakhovsk, on lumber railroad. Until 1945, in East Prussia and called Wirbeln (vĭr'bŭln).
Zhdanov (zhdä'nŭf), city (1926 pop. 63,920; 1939 pop. 222,427), S Stalino oblast, Ukrainian SSR, port on Sea of Azov, at Kalmius R. mouth, 60 mi. SSW of Stalino. Major industrial center; Azovstal steel mills (on left bank), metallurgical works (steel pipes; at Sartana station, just N of city); mfg. (machinery, chemicals, netting, clothing), shipbuilding; fish canning. City has small fishing and steamer port at Kalmius R. mouth; principal freight docks (4 mi. SW of city center) export coal, salt, grain. Has metallurgical institute, Gk. cathedral, regional mus. Pop. includes Jews and Greeks. Founded by Crimean Greeks in 1880s. Called Mariupol until 1948; renamed Zhdanov for Soviet statesman b. here.
Zhdanovsk (zhdä'nŭfsk), town (1948 pop. over 2,000), S Azerbaijan SSR, on Mili Steppe, 45 mi. WSW of Sabirabad; agr. (cotton). Developed in late 1930s. Rail station and ginning center is ORDZHONIKIDZE.
Zhelaniye, Cape (zhĭlä'nyēŭ), NE extremity of N isl. of Novaya Zemlya, Russian SFSR; 76°58'N 68°30'E. Site of govt. observation station. Formerly called Cape Mauritius.
Zhelekhov, Poland: see ZELECHOW.
Zhelezinka (zhĭlyĕ'zēn-kŭ), village (1939 pop. over 500), N Pavlodar oblast, Kazakh SSR, on Irtysh R. and 110 mi. NNW of Pavlodar, in agr. area. Formerly Zheleznenka. Founded 1717 as Rus. frontier post.
Zheleznaya (–lyĕz'nĭŭ), laccolithic mountain (2,795 ft.) of the N Caucasus foothills, Russian SFSR, overlooking (N) Zheleznovodsk.
Zheleznaya Balka (bäl'kŭ), town (1939 pop. over 500), central Stalino oblast, Ukrainian SSR, in the Donbas, 2 mi. W of Gorlovka; coal mines.
Zheleznenka, Kazakh SSR: see ZHELEZINKA.
Zheleznik, Yugoslavia: see ZELEZNIK.
Zheleznodorozhny or **Zheleznodorozhnyy** (zhĭlyĕ" znŭdŭrôzh'nē). **1** Town (1939 pop. 5,118), S Kaliningrad oblast, Russian SFSR, 40 mi. SE of Kaliningrad, on Polish line; rail junction (repair shops); woodworking, mfg. (bricks, beer, malt). Remains of 14th-cent. castle. Until 1945, in East Prussia and called Gerdauen (gĕrdou'ŭn). **2** Town (1941 pop. over 500), W Komi Autonomous SSR, Russian SFSR, on N. Pechora RR, on left bank of Vym R. and 60 mi. N of Syktyvkar; railroad shops. Developed c.1941 opposite village of Knyazhpogost. **3** Town (1926 pop. 982), central Moscow oblast, Russian SFSR, 15 mi. E of Moscow; railroad shops. Until 1939, Obiralovka.
Zheleznovodsk (zhĭlyĕznŭvôtsk'), city (1926 pop. 2,053), S Stavropol Territory, Russian SFSR, in the N Caucasus, at S foot of Zheleznaya mtn., 7 mi. NNW of Pyatigorsk, on rail spur; major health resort on wooded mtn. site; mineral springs, sanatoria. Mineral-water bottling; dairying.
Zheleznoye (zhĭlyĕz'nŭyŭ), town (1926 pop. 4,967), central Stalino oblast, Ukrainian SSR, in the Donbas, on railroad (Fenolnaya station) and 4 mi. S of Dzerzhinsk; site (with adjacent town of Imeni Kirova) of chemical and food industries.
Zheleznyakov Island, Russian SFSR: see NEW SIBERIAN ISLANDS.
Zhelnino (zhĕlnyĭnô'), town (1942 pop. over 500), W Gorki oblast, Russian SFSR, on Oka R. and 5 mi. SW of Dzerzhinsk.
Zheltaya Reka (zhôl'tĭŭ ryĭkä'), town (1939 pop. over 2,000), W Dnepropetrovsk oblast, Ukrainian SSR, on rail spur and 10 mi. SW of Pyatikhatki, in Krivoi Rog iron dist.; iron mining. Until 1939, called Rudnik Imeni Shvartsa.
Zheltukhino (zhĭltōō'khēnŭ), village (1939 pop. over 500), W central Ryazan oblast, Russian SFSR, 11 mi. WNW of Ryazhsk; wheat, tobacco.
Zheludok (zhĭlōō'dŭk), Pol. *Żołudek* (zhôwōō'dĕk), town (1931 pop. 1,550), E Grodno oblast, Belorussian SSR, 24 mi. SSW of Lida; tanning, woolen weaving, flour milling, distilling, brick mfg.
Zhelyabova, Imeni (ē'mĭnyē zhĭlyä'bŭvŭ), town (1945 pop. over 500), SW Vologda oblast, Russian SFSR, on Mologa R. and 10 mi. SW of Ustyuzhna; shipyards.
Zhepche, Yugoslavia: see ZEPCE.
Zherdevka (zhĭrdyĕf'kŭ), village (1926 pop. 574), S Tambov oblast, Russian SFSR, 40 mi. NW of Borisoglebsk; sunflower-oil press, meat-packing plant.
Zhicha, Yugoslavia: see ZICA.
Zhidachov (zhĭdä'chŭf), Pol. *Żydaczów* (zhĭdä'chōōf), city (1,931 pop. 4,514), E Drogobych oblast, Ukrainian SSR, on Stry R. and 16 mi. NE of Stry; agr. processing, mfg. (cement, bricks). Old Pol. town; scene of battle (1390) during Polish-Hungarian War; suffered severely from Tatar assaults (14th–15th cent.). Passed to Austria (1772); reverted to Poland (1919); ceded to USSR in 1945.
Zhigalovo (zhĭgä'lŭvŭ), town (1939 pop. over 2,000), S Irkutsk oblast, Russian SFSR, on Lena R. and 175 mi. N of Irkutsk; river port; transit point on highways from Tyret and Irkutsk; shipbuilding, flour milling.
Zhigansk (zhĭgänsk'), village N Yakut Autonomous SSR, Russian SFSR, N of Arctic Circle, on Lena R. and 375 mi. NNW of Yakutsk; river port; coal deposits, reindeer raising. Founded 1632.
Zhigulevsk (zhēgōōlyôfsk'), town (1949 pop. over 1,000), W Kuibyshev oblast, Russian SFSR, on right bank of the Volga, on Samara Bend and 30 mi. WNW of Kuibyshev; petroleum-extracting center (pipe line to Kuibyshev). Asphalt mining near by (ESE). Brewery. Developed during Second World War through urbanization of villages of Morkvashi (limestone quarrying) and Otvazhnoye. Site of hydroelectric station of Kuibyshev Dam; reached 1951 by rail from Syzran. Called Otvazhny 1946–49.
Zhiguli Mountains (zhēgōōlyē'), in Samara Bend of the Volga, W Kuibyshev oblast, Russian SFSR; extend c.35 mi. bet. Usa R. (W) and the Volga (E; opposite Kuibyshev city); rise to 1,217 ft. Mineral resources include petroleum (Zhigulevsk; pipe line to Kuibyshev), dolomite, limestone, asphalt, gypsum, and sulphur. Karstlike formation, coniferous forests, and mild climate attract tourists.
Zhikatse, Tibet: see SHIGATSE.
Zhikhlin, Poland: see ZYCHLIN.
Zhikhor or **Zhikhor'** (zhē'khŭr), S suburb (1926 pop. 4,898) of Kharkov, Kharkov oblast, Ukrainian SSR, 5 mi. S of city center; woodworking.
Zhilaya Kosa (zhĭlĭ'ŭ kŭsä'), village, N Guryev oblast, Kazakh SSR, port on Caspian Sea, 65 mi. SE of Guryev; fisheries.
Zhilkino (zhēl'kēnŭ), N suburb (1920 pop. 400; 1947 pop. 9,000) of Irkutsk, Irkutsk oblast, Russian SFSR, on left bank of Angara R.; food industries (meat, flour); soap, livestock feed. Site of former monastery.
Zhirardov, Poland: see ZYRARDOW.
Zhiryatino (zhĭryä'tyĭnŭ), village (1926 pop. 640), central Bryansk oblast, Russian SFSR, 25 mi. W of Bryansk; distilling.
Zhitkovats, Yugoslavia: see ZITKOVAC.
Zhitkovichi (zhĭtkô'vēchē), town (1926 pop. 2,976), W Polesye oblast, Belorussian SSR, 60 mi. WNW of Mozyr; sawmilling, wood cracking.
Zhitkur (zhĭtkōōr'), village (1926 pop. 3,494), E Stalingrad oblast, Russian SFSR, 80 mi. ENE of Stalingrad, SW of L. Elton; wheat, mustard; cattle, sheep raising.
Zhitomir (zhĭtô'mēr), oblast (□ 11,600; 1946 pop. estimate 1,800,000), W Ukrainian SSR, in Volhynia; ⊙ Zhitomir. On N edge of Volyn-Podolian Upland, extending (N) into Pripet Marshes. Forested area (N) yields lumber, clay, kaolin, granite, quartzite; S area chiefly agr. (sugar beets, wheat); potatoes, flax, buckwheat, hops grown towards N; dairy farming. Main centers: Zhitomir, Berdichev, Novograd-Volynski, Korosten. Sugar refining, distilling, flour milling (S); glass and ceramics industry, paper milling (N). Formed 1937. In Second World War, held (1941–43) by Germans.
Zhitomir, city (1939 pop. 95,090), ⊙ Zhitomir oblast, Ukrainian SSR, on Teterev R. and 85 mi. WSW of Kiev; 50°15'N 28°40'E. Road and rail center (lumber, grain trade); mfg. of furniture, clothing; distilling; metalworks. Agr. and teachers colleges. Dates from 1240; passed (14th cent.) to Lithuania and in 1569 to Poland. Annexed 1793 to Russia; became ⊙ Volhynia govt. (abolished 1925) and an important commercial center. Until Second World War, when it was held (1941–43) by Germans, pop. was 40% Jewish.
Zhivkovo (zhēf'kôvô), village (pop. 1,246), Sofia dist., W central Bulgaria, in Ikhtiman Basin, 4 mi. WNW of Ikhtiman; hardy grain, livestock, potatoes; talc quarrying. Formerly Avli-koi.
Zhiyevo, mountains, Yugoslavia: see ZIJEVO.
Zhizdra (zhēz'drŭ), city (1926 pop. 9,371), S Kaluga oblast, Russian SFSR, on Zhizdra R. and 38 mi. NNE of Bryansk; sawmilling, brickworking. Woodworking handicrafts near by. Chartered 1777.
Zhizdra River, Kaluga oblast, Russian SFSR, rises E of Lyudinovo, flows generally E, past Zhizdra, and NNE, past Kozelsk, to Oka R. at Peremyshl; 150 mi. long.
Zhlobin (zhlô'bĭn), city (1926 pop. 11,030), NW Gomel oblast, Belorussian SSR, on Dnieper R. and 125 mi. SE of Minsk; rail junction; railroad shops, metalworks; fruit cannery, meat plant.
Zhlyeb, peak, Yugoslavia: see MOKRA PLANINA.
Zhmerinka (zhmĕ'rēn-kŭ), city (1926 pop. 22,241), W Vinnitsa oblast, Ukrainian SSR, 20 mi. SW of Vinnitsa; rail junction; metalworks, tobacco factory.
Zhob (zhōb), district (□ 10,478; 1951 pop. 66,000), NE Baluchistan, W Pakistan; ⊙ Fort Sandeman. Bordered NW by Afghanistan, NE by Sulaiman Range; crossed NE–SW by Toba-Kakar Range; drained by seasonal streams and Zhob R. (S, E). Agr. (wheat, rice); handicrafts (felts, felt coats, saddlebags, woolen carpets). Chromite mines and asbestos deposits near Hindubagh. Disturbances among Pathan tribes in late-19th cent. caused British to set up military posts at Fort Sandeman and along Afghanistan border. Pop. 91% Moslem, 7% Hindu, 2% Sikh.
Zhob River, in Zhob dist., NE Baluchistan, W Pakistan, rises near Kand peak in Toba-Kakar Range, flows E, past Hindubagh, and NE to Gumal R. 55 mi. NNE of Fort Sandeman; c.230 mi. long. Receives drainage of central and N Toba-Kakar Range; seasonal.
Zholkva (zhôlk'vŭ), city (1931 pop. 10,348), central Lvov oblast, Ukrainian SSR, 14 mi. N of Lvov; agr. processing (cereals, vegetables), tanning, tile and brick mfg., glassworks. Lignite deposits near by. Has medieval town walls and gates, several old churches and monuments; notable 17th-cent. castle, monastery, and synagogue. Fortified and chartered in 1602. Developed as trade center under Pol. king John III Sobieski, when it was subjected to several Cossack and Tatar assaults. Destroyed (1705) by Swedes; passed (1772) from Poland to Austria; reverted (1919) to Poland; ceded to USSR in 1945. Called Zholkev, Pol. *Żółkiew* (zhôw'kyĕf), until 1941.
Zholymbet (zhŭlĭmbyĕt'), town (1948 pop. over 2,000), NE Akmolinsk oblast, Kazakh SSR, 30 mi. E of Shortandy.
Zhovten or **Zhovten'** (zhôf'tyĭnyŭ). **1** Village (pop. over 2,000), central Odessa oblast, Ukrainian SSR, 55 mi. NNW of Odessa; flour mill. Until c.1928, Petroverovka; later sometimes called Oktyabrskoye. **2** Town (1931 pop. 3,010), N Stanislav oblast, Ukrainian SSR, on Bystritsa R. and 8 mi. NNE of Stanislav; flour milling, tile and brick mfg. Has ruins of 16th-cent. monastery. Until 1940, called Yezupol, Pol. *Jezupol* (yĕzōō'pôl).
Zhukovka (zhōō'kŭfkŭ), town (1948 pop. over 10,000), N Bryansk oblast, Russian SFSR, 32 mi. NW of Bryansk; rail junction (spur to Kletnya); car-building works, woodworking plant.
Zhukovski or **Zhukovskiy** (zhōōkôf'skē), city (1939 pop. over 2,000), central Moscow oblast, Russian SFSR, 3 mi. NW of Ramenskoye; sawmilling cen-

ter. Called Otdykh until 1938; later Stakhanovo until 1947, when it became a city.

Zhupa, county, Yugoslavia: see ZUPA.

Zhupanovo (zhōōpä'nůvů), village, Kamchatka oblast, Khabarovsk Territory, Russian SFSR, on SE Kamchatka Peninsula, 60 mi. NNE of Petropavlovsk, on Kronotski Gulf of Pacific Ocean; fish canneries.

Zhuravichi (zhōōrä'vēchē), village (1926 pop. 2,138), N Gomel oblast, Belorussian SSR, 45 mi. S of Mogilev, in potato region; hemp processing.

Zhuravlevka (zhōōrůvlyôf'ků), village (1948 pop. over 2,000), N Akmolinsk oblast, Kazakh SSR, 80 mi. NW of Akmolinsk; cattle, horses. Bauxite deposits near by.

Zhuravno (zhōōräv'nů), Pol. *Żurawno* (zhōōräv'nô), village (1931 pop. 3,860), E Drogobych oblast, Ukrainian SSR, on Dniester R. and 20 mi. E of Stry; alabaster and brick mfg., flour milling.

Zhuromin, Poland: see ZUROMIN.

Zhvanets (zhvä'nyĭts), village (1926 pop. 3,445), S Kamenets-Podolski oblast, Ukrainian SSR, on Dniester R. and 10 mi. SSW of Kamenets-Podolski; wheat, corn, sugar beets, fruit, tobacco.

Zia, Greece: see KEA.

Zia (zē'ů), pueblo (□ 96.9), Sandoval co., NW central N.Mex. Zia village (1948 pop. 269) is on Jemez Creek and 30 mi. NNW of Albuquerque; alt. c.5,400 ft. Pueblo Indians make pottery and raise grain and chili. Mission of Nuestra Señora de la Asunción dates from 1692. Annual fiesta takes place in Aug. Village participated in Pueblo revolt of 1680.

Ziama-Mansouriah (zyämä'-mänsōōryä'), village (pop. 768), Constantine dept., NE Algeria, on the Gulf of Bougie, 23 mi. E of Bougie; cork processing, zinc mining; winegrowing.

Zianchurino, Russian SFSR: see ZIYANCHURINO.

Ziarat (zyä'rŭt), village, Sibi dist., NE central Baluchistan, W Pakistan, in N Central Brahui Range, 42 mi. ENE of Quetta; hill resort (alt. c.8,030 ft.); summer hq. of Baluchistan govt. Formerly called Gwashki.

Zib or **Ez Zib,** Palestine: see ACHZIB.

Zibak, Afghanistan: see ZEBAK.

Ziban or **Zibane** (zēbän'), arid region in NE Algeria, at S foot of the Aurès massif (Saharan Atlas), surrounding Biskra, its chief oasis. It is traversed N–S by Biskra-Touggourt RR. Principal oases (fed by artesian waters, and by intermittent streams) are Tolga, Ourlal, Sidi Okba. Chief product: dates.

Zibirjat, Egypt: see SAINT JOHN'S ISLAND.

Ziça or **Zhicha** (both: zhē'chä), Serbo-Croatian *Žiča*, monastery, central Serbia, Yugoslavia, 3 mi. SW of Rankovicevo, town, near Ibar R. Founded c.1207. Coronation church of medieval kings of Serbia and 1st seat of its archbishops.

Zicavo (zēkä'vō), village (pop. 1,524), S central Corsica, 20 mi. E of Ajaccio; alt. 2,395 ft.

Zichem (zĭ'khům), town (pop. 4,162), Brabant prov., N central Belgium, 4 mi. WNW of Diest; agr. market. Trade center in Middle Ages. Formerly spelled Sichem.

Zichenau, Poland: see CIECHANOW.

Zichron Yaakov, Israel: see ZIKHRON YA'AQOV.

Zichy Land (tsĭ'khē), name formerly applied to central section of Franz Josef Land, Russian SFSR, in Arctic Ocean, bet. British Channel (W) and Austrian Sound (E). Included Jackson and Payer isls. (N), Zeigler and Salisbury isls. (center), Luigi and Champ isls. (S).

Zictepec (sēktāpĕk'), officially San Pedro Zictepec, town (pop. 1,828), Mexico state, central Mexico, 19 mi. SSE of Toluca; cereals, fruit, livestock.

Zidani Most (zē'dänē môst'), Ger. *Steinbrück* (shtīn'brük), village, central Slovenia, Yugoslavia, on Sava R., at Savinja R. mouth, and 11 mi. SSW of Celje; rail junction; cement plant. Until 1918, in Styria.

Ziddy (zēdĭ'), village (1939 pop. over 500), N Stalinabad oblast, Tadzhik SSR, in Gissar Range, on Leninabad-Stalinabad highway and 35 mi. N of Stalinabad (linked by narrow-gauge railroad); coal mining.

Zidki or **Zid'ki,** Ukrainian SSR: see ZYEZDKI.

Zidlochovice (zhĕd'lôkhôvĭtsĕ), Czech *Židlochovice*, Ger. *Seelowitz* (zā'lōvĭts), town (pop. 2,486), S Moravia, Czechoslovakia, on Svratka R. and 11 mi. S. of Brno, in wheat and sugar-beet dist.; rail terminus; sugar refining. Has noted castle (occasional residence of Czechoslovak president).

Zidon, Lebanon: see SAIDA.

Ziebach (zē'bäk), county (□ 1,982; pop. 2,606), NW central S.Dak.; ⊙ Dupree. Agr. and cattle-raising area bounded S by Cheyenne R. and drained by Moreau R. Cheyenne River Indian Reservation in S. Small farms and ranches; livestock, dairy products, grain. Formed 1911.

Ziebice (zhĕbē'tsĕ), Pol. *Ziębice*, Ger. *Münsterberg* (mün'stûrbĕrk), town (1939 pop. 8,923; 1946 pop. 8,184) in Lower Silesia, after 1945 in Wroclaw prov., SW Poland, on Olawa R. and 35 mi. S of Breslau (Wroclaw); mfg. of ceramics, cement; textile milling. Has 13th-cent. church. In early-14th cent. became ⊙ duchy under branch of Pol. Piast princes; passed 1454 to Bohemia. Was (1654–1791) ⊙ principality of Münsterberg.

Ziebingen, Poland: see CYBINKA.

Ziegelhausen (tsē"gůlhou'zůn), village (pop. 6,704), N Baden, Germany, after 1945 in Württemberg-Baden, at SW foot of the Odenwald, on the canalized Neckar and 3 mi. ENE of Heidelberg; mfg. of chemicals, woodworking.

Ziegenhain (tsē'gůnhīn), town (pop. 3,375), in former Prussian prov. of Hesse-Nassau, W Germany, after 1945 in Hesse, 20 mi. WNW of Hersfeld; lumber milling. Castle (fortifications razed 1807) houses, since 1842, a prison.

Ziegenhals, Poland: see GLUCHOLAZY.

Ziegenrück (tsē'gůnrük"), town (pop. 1,714), in former Prussian Saxony prov. exclave, central Germany, after 1945 in Thuringia, on the Thuringian Saale and 13 mi. ESE of Saalfeld; woolen and paper milling, woodworking; resort. Hydroelectric power station near by.

Zielenzig, Poland: see SULECIN.

Zielona Gora (zhĕlô'nä gōō'rä), Pol. *Zielona Góra*, province [Pol. *województwo*] (□ 5,744; pop. 347,024), W Poland; ⊙ Grünberg (Zielona Gora). In Upper Lusatia; borders W on the Oder and Lusatian Neisse (Ger. line). Low, rolling surface has fertile soil; drained by Oder, Lusatian Neisse, and Bobrawa (Bober) rivers. Stock raising, fruitgrowing, viticulture; metalworking, glass mfg. Principal cities: Grünberg, Sorau (Zary), Sprottau (Szprotawa). Until 1945, in Ger. Brandenburg and Lower Silesia provs.; following transfer to Poland, it was (until 1950) part of Poznan and Wroclaw provs. Ger. pop. expelled after 1945 and replaced by Poles.

Zielona Gora, town, Poland: see GRÜNBERG.

Zierenberg (tsē'rünbĕrk), town (pop. 2,920), in former Prussian prov. of Hesse-Nassau, W Germany, after 1945 in Hesse, 9 mi. WNW of Kassel; lumber. Has 15th-cent. church.

Zierikzee or **Zieriksee** (both: zē'rĭksā), town (pop. 6,964), Zeeland prov., SW Netherlands, on Schouwen-Duiveland isl., 18 mi. NE of Middelburg, on the Eastern Scheldt; market center; mfg. (biscuits, jellies, fruit wines, candy, bicycle tires, cigars). Has 15th-cent. church dedicated to an Irish apostle of Zeeland, 16th-cent. town hall, many other 14th-, 15th-, and 16th-cent. buildings. Important medieval trade center; member of Hanseatic League. Scene of heavy fighting (1576) when taken by Spaniards.

Ziesar (tsē'zär), town (pop. 3,598), in former Prussian Saxony prov., central Germany, after 1945 in Saxony-Anhalt, 15 mi. SW of Brandenburg; dairying; mfg. of starch, pottery. Has remains of former castle of bishops of Brandenburg.

Zifta (zĭf'tä), town (pop. 26,520), Gharbiya prov., Lower Egypt, on Damietta branch of the Nile and 15 mi. ESE of Tanta; cotton center; also cereals, rice, fruits. Just S is irrigation barrage.

Zigazinski or **Zigazinskiy** (zēgä'zĭnskē), town (1939 pop. over 2,000), central Bashkir Autonomous SSR, Russian SFSR, in the S Urals, on S.Siberian RR and 40 mi. WSW of Beloretsk; mining center in Komarovo-Zigazinski iron dist.

Zighen (zēgĕn'), village (pop. 280), central Fezzan, Libya, 30 mi. NE of Sebha, in an oasis; date growing. Has mosques and ruins of Turkish fort.

Zigon (zē'gōn"), town (pop. 6,338), Tharrawaddy dist., Lower Burma, on Rangoon-Prome RR and 40 mi. SSE of Prome.

Zigos, Greece: see ARAKYNTHOS.

Ziguei (zēgā'), military outpost, W Chad territory, Fr. Equatorial Africa, 90 mi. NW of Moussoro.

Ziguinchor (zēgēshôr'), town (pop. c.15,200), SW Senegal, Fr. West Africa, port on left bank of Casamance R. (c.40 mi. from mouth), near Port. Guinea boundary, and 160 mi. SSE of Dakar. Ships chiefly peanuts; also wood, beeswax, honey, gum, titanium, zirconium. Fishing. The surrounding Casamance region produces rice, millet, corn, manioc, potatoes. Main industry is vegetable-oil extracting. Airport.

Zihl Canal, Switzerland: see THIÈLE CANAL.

Zijevo or **Zhiyevo** (both: zhē'yĕvô), Serbo-Croatian *Žijevo*, mountain in Dinaric Alps, E Montenegro, Yugoslavia, near Albania border; highest point (6,986 ft.) is 14 mi. NE of Titograd.

Zijpe, Netherlands: see MASTGAT.

Zikawei, Sicawei, or **Siccawei** (all: sĭ'kůwā"), Mandarin *Hsü-chia-hui* (shü'jyä'hwā'), outlying SW district of Shanghai, China; noted observatory.

Zikhron Ya'aqov or **Zichron Yaakov** (both: zēkhrōn' yä-äkōv'), settlement (pop. 2,000), NW Israel, at N end of Plain of Sharon, 25 mi. S of Haifa; center of important wine-growing region. Resort frequented by artists; scene of music and dance festivals, art exhibitions. Founded 1882.

Ziki or **Zikki,** Oman: see IZKI.

Zilah, Rumania: see ZALAU.

Zilair (zēlīēr'), village (1926 pop. 5,624), S Bashkir Autonomous SSR, Russian SFSR, in the S Urals, on Zilair R. (right tributary of Sakmara R.) and 105 mi. SSW of Magnitogorsk; dairying; livestock, grain.

Zile (zĭlĕ'), anc. *Zela* (zē'lů), town (1950 pop. 17,121), Tokat prov., N central Turkey, near railroad, 35 mi. W of Tokat; wheat, tobacco. Julius Caesar here in anc. Pontus defeated Pharnaces II of Pontus in 47 B.C., recording his famous "Veni, vidi, vici" [I came, I saw, I conquered].

Zilfi (zĭl'fē), town, N central Nejd, Saudi Arabia, in Sudair dist., 170 mi. NW of Riyadh; 26°14'N 44°49'E. Trading center; grain (wheat, sorghum), dates, vegetables; mfg. of woolen cloth; stock.

Ziliakhova, Greece: see NEA ZICHNA.

Zilina (zhĭ'lĭnä), Slovak *Žilina*, Ger. *Sillein* (zĭ'līn), Hung. *Zsolna* (zhôl'nŏ), town (pop. 16,450), ⊙ Zilina prov. (□ 3,193; pop. 509,403), NW Slovakia, Czechoslovakia, on Vah R. and 110 mi. NE of Bratislava; 49°13'N 18°44'E. Important rail junction (workshops, switchyard); trade and industrial center; woodworking (matches, cellulose, paper), mfg. (liqueurs, fertilizers, cement, woolen textiles, linen goods), fish canning. Has 14th-cent. church, arcaded square, large military cemetery of Second World War. Important center for treatment of eye diseases here.

Zilis, Sp. Morocco: see ARCILA.

Zillah (zĭ'lů), town (pop. 911), Yakima co., S Wash., 18 mi. SE of Yakima and on Yakima R.; fruit.

Zillebeke (zĭlůbā'ků), village (pop. 1,644), West Flanders prov., Belgium, near Ypres; scene of many attacks in battles of Ypres in First World War.

Ziller River (tsĭ'lůr), in Tyrol, W Austria, rises in Zillertal Alps near Salzburg border, flows 30 mi. NW and N, past Mayrhofen, to Inn R. 2 mi. SW of Brixlegg. Its 15-mi. lower valley, the *Zillertal* (tsĭ'lůrtäl), bordered by the Zillertal Alps, is noted for its magnificent scenery. Wheat, corn, fine breed of cattle raised.

Zillertal Alps (tsĭ'lůrtäl), Ger. *Zillertaler Alpen*, Ital. *Alpi Aurine*, range of Eastern Alps astride Austro-Ital. border, extend 35 mi. NE, into Tyrol, Austria, W of the Hohe Tauern. Rise to 11,555 ft. in the Hochfeiler, on Austro-Ital. line. Brenner Pass (W) separates range from Ötztal Alps. Noted for its glaciers and beautiful scenery.

Zilling Tso (zĭl'lĭng tsō), **Goring Tso,** or **Goring Tsho** (gō'rĭng), salt lake (□ 720), E central Tibet, on Chang Tang plateau, at 31°45'N 89°E; alt. 14,760 ft. Formerly spelled Selling Tso.

Zilly (tsĭ'lē), village (pop. 1,719), in former Prussian Saxony prov., central Germany, after 1945 in Saxony-Anhalt, 8 mi. N of Wernigerode; phosphorite mining.

Zilovo-Aksenovo, Russian SFSR: see AKSENOVO-ZILOVSKOYE.

Zilupe (zē'lōōpä), Ger. *Rosenhof*, city (pop. 1,566), E Latvia, in Latgale, 32 mi. ESE of Rezekne, on Russian SFSR border. In Rus. Vitebsk govt. until 1920; USSR-Latvian frontier station (1920–40).

Zilwaukee (zĭl"wô'kē), village (1940 pop. 1,037), Saginaw co., E central Mich., 3 mi. N of Saginaw and on Saginaw R.

Zima (zēmä'), city (1933 pop. estimate 15,100), S Irkutsk oblast, Russian SFSR, on Trans-Siberian RR, on Oka R. and 70 mi. NW of Cheremkhovo; lumber industry (prefabricated houses); metalworks, railroad shops.

Zimapán (sēmäpän'), city (pop. 3,217), Hidalgo, central Mexico, in Sierra Madre Occidental, 60 mi. NW of Pachuca; alt. 5,961 ft. Mining center (silver, gold, lead, copper, mercury, antimony). Picturesque Indian town.

Zimatlán (sēmätlän'), officially Zimatlán de Alvarez, town (pop. 3,970), Oaxaca, S Mexico, in Atoyac R. valley, on railroad, and 14 mi. SSW of Oaxaca; agr. center (sugar cane, cereals, coffee, tobacco, fruit, livestock). Silver and gold deposits. Sometimes Villa Alvarez.

Zimba (zēm'bä), town (pop. 77), Southern Prov., Northern Rhodesia, on railroad and 40 mi. NNE of Livingstone; tobacco, wheat, corn.

Zimbabwe (zēmbä'bwä) [Bantu, =stone houses], site of ruined city, SE Southern Rhodesia, in Mashonaland, 15 mi. SE of Fort Victoria (nearest railhead). Rediscovered c.1870. Structures (probably dating from 15th cent.) appear to have been the work of a Bantu people. Ruins include a massive wall, a "temple," a citadel, and near-by dwellings. Overlooking the main group of ruins (Great Zimbabwe) is a modern hotel. Remains of more recent origin (Little Zimbabwe) are 8 mi. away.

Zimella (zēmĕl'lä), village (pop. 1,301), Verona prov., Veneto, N Italy, 20 mi. SE of Verona; mfg. of wine presses.

Zimmerman or **Lake Fremont,** village (pop. 169), Sherburne co., E Minn., 37 mi. NNW of Minneapolis, in grain area.

Zimnicea (zēm'nēchä), Bulg. *Zimnitsa* (zēm'nēt-sä), town (1948 pop. 11,056), Teleorman prov., S Rumania, in Walachia, port on left bank of the Danube opposite Svishtov (Bulgaria), and 25 mi. E of Turnu-Magurele; trades in grain and livestock; produces edible oils and carbonated drinks. Former ⊙ Teleorman dept.

Zimnitsa (zēm'nĭtsä), village (pop. 2,003), Yambol dist., E Bulgaria, 9 mi. NNE of Yambol; rail junction; grain, vineyards. Formerly Kashla-koi.

Zimnyatski or **Zimnyatskiy** (zēmnyät'skē), village (1939 pop. over 500), W Stalingrad oblast, Russian SFSR, near Medveditsa R., 33 mi. W of Frolovo; wheat, fruit.

Zimony, Yugoslavia: see ZEMUN.

Zimovniki (zēmôv'nyĭkē), village (1926 pop. 2,885), SE central Rostov oblast, Russian SFSR, on railroad and 65 mi. NE of Salsk; flour mill, metalworks; wheat, cotton, livestock.

Zimrovice, Czechoslovakia: see OPAVA.
Zinacantán (sēnäkäntän'), town (pop. 664), Chiapas, S Mexico, in Sierra de Hueytepec, 4 mi. WNW of San Cristóbal de las Casas; wheat, fruit.
Zinacantepec (sēnäkäntäpěk'), officially San Miguel Zinacantepec, town (pop. 2,871), Mexico state, central Mexico, on railroad and 5 mi. W of Toluca; agr. center (cereals, livestock); dairying.
Zinacatepec (sēnäkätäpěk'), officially San Sebastián Zinacatepec, town (pop. 4,131), Puebla, central Mexico, on railroad and 13 mi. SE of Tehuacán; alt. 3,766 ft. Agr. center (corn, sugar cane, fruit, livestock).
Zinal (Fr. zēnäl', Ger. tsē'näl), hamlet, Valais canton, S Switzerland, in the Val de Zinal, 10 mi. NNW of Zermatt; summer resort (alt. 5,504 ft.). The peaks **Zinalrothorn** (13,860 ft.) and Pointe de Zinal (12,448 ft.) are S.
Zinantécatl, Mexico: see TOLUCA, NEVADO DE.
Zináparo (sēnä'pärō), town (pop. 891), Michoacán, central Mexico, 13 mi. SSW of La Piedad; cereals, livestock.
Zinapécuaro (sēnäpā'kwärō), officially Zinapécuaro de Figueroa, town (pop. 3,533), Michoacán, central Mexico, 26 mi. NE of Morelia; agr. center (cereals, fruit, stock).
Zinc, town (pop. 99), Boone co., N Ark., 11 mi. ENE of Harrison, in the Ozarks.
Zincirlihoyuk, Turkey: see SENJIRLI.
Zinder (zĭn'dûr), town (pop. c.13,200), S Niger territory, Fr. West Africa, near Nigeria border, 620 mi. NE of Lagos and 450 mi. E of Niamey. Trading and agr. center, chiefly for peanuts; also millet, wheat, manioc, beans; sheep, cattle. Has airport, meteorological station, R.C. and Protestant missions, garrison. Occupied by French in 1899, it was former ⊙ Niger territory.
Zingst or Zingst am Darss (tsĭngst' äm därs'), village (pop. 3,238), in former Prussian Pomerania prov., N Germany, after 1945 in Mecklenburg, on Darss peninsula, on the Baltic, 18 mi. NW of Stralsund; popular seaside resort; fishing port.
Zinjan, Iran: see ZENJAN.
Zinkgruvan (sĭngk'grü"vän), village (pop. 758), Orebro co., S central Sweden, 19 mi. N of Motala; zinc mines.
Zinnik, Belgium: see SOIGNIES.
Zinnowitz (tsĭ'nōvĭts), village (pop. 3,803), in former Prussian Pomerania prov., N Germany, after 1945 in Mecklenburg, on N Usedom isl., on the Baltic, 6 mi. ENE of Wolgast; seaside resort.
Zinnwald, Czechoslovakia: see CINVALD.
Zinnwald (tsĭn'vält), village (pop. 643), Saxony, E central Germany, in the Erzebirge, on Red Weisseritz R. and 18 mi. SSW of Pirna; frontier point on Czechoslovak border, opposite Cinvald; mining (bismuth, tungsten). Winter-sports center. Mining begun in 15th cent.
Zinovyevsk, Ukrainian SSR: see KIROVOGRAD, city.
Zinsen, Korea: see CHEMULPO.
Zinten, Russian SFSR: see KORNEVO.
Zintenhof, Estonia: see SINDI.
Zintu River, Japan: see JINTSU RIVER.
Zintzuntzan, Mexico: see TZINTZUNTZAN.
Zinvié (zēnvyā'), village, S Dahomey, Fr. West Africa, 20 mi. WNW of Porto-Novo; palm kernels, palm oil. Market.
Zion (zī'ŭn) or **Sion** (sī'ŭn), part of Jerusalem. It is defined in the Bible as the City of David (2 Sam. 5.7). Tradition names the SW hill of the city as Zion, but there is controversy about the identity. The name is symbolic of Jerusalem, of the Promised Land, of the Messianic hope of Israel, and, among Christians, of heaven.
Zion. **1** City (pop. 8,950), Lake co., extreme NE Ill., on L. Michigan, 6 mi. N of Waukegan, in dairy and farm area; mfg. (bakery goods, lace curtains, candy, wicker furniture, underwear). Founded 1901 by John Alexander Dowie of the Christian Catholic Apostolic Church; inc. 1902; had a theocratic govt. until 1935. The tabernacle here burned in 1937. Passion play presented annually. **2** Town, (1940 pop. 216), Marion co., E S.C., 26 mi. ENE of Florence.
Zion National Park (□ 147.2; established 1919), SW Utah, c.35 mi. ENE of St. George. Area of deep canyons, lofty cliffs and mesas, noted for scenic grandeur of its spectacular rock formations and vivid colors. Outstanding feature is Zion Canyon (½ mi. deep; c.15 mi. long), brilliantly colored gorge (predominantly vermilion) cut by North Fork Virgin R. and extending N-S through park. S entrance of canyon is dominated by 2 gigantic rock masses, the Watchman (6,555 ft.) on E rim, and the West Temple (7,795 ft.; rising c.3,800 ft. above canyon floor; highest point in park). Other magnificent formations are found throughout lower course of canyon. Zion–Mt. Carmel Highway is 25-mi. scenic route, passing through Zion–Mt. Carmel Tunnel (5,607 ft. long). Campgrounds, lodge, riding and hiking trails. Canyon discovered 1858, park area first set aside (1909) as Mukuntuweap Natl. Monument; established as Zion Natl. Park in 1919. Zion National Monument (□ 53; established 1937) is undeveloped area adjoining park on NW; includes part of Kolob Terrace (kŏ'lŭb) and colorful Kolob Canyon (1,500–2,500 ft. deep).
Zionsville, town (pop. 1,536), Boone co., central Ind., on small Eagle Creek and 14 mi. NNW of Indianapolis, in dairying and farming area; makes pharmaceuticals.
Zipaquirá (sēpäkērä'), town (pop. 6,955), Cundinamarca dept., central Colombia, in Sabana de Bogotá of Cordillera Oriental, on railroad and highway, and 30 mi. N of Bogotá; alt. 8,694 ft. Salt-mining center in rich cattle-farming region. There are immense deposits of rock salt. Caustic soda plant. Coal, sulphur, and lead deposits near by.
Zips, region, Czechoslovakia and Poland: see SPIS.
Zips, castle, Czechoslovakia: see SPISSKE PODHRADIE.
Zipsendorf (tsĭp'sŭndôrf), town (pop. 3,408), in former Prussian Saxony prov., central Germany, after 1945 in Saxony-Anhalt, 7 mi. E of Zeitz; lignite-mining center. Mfg. of rubber products.
Zira (zē'rŭ), town (pop. 5,963), Ferozepore dist., W Punjab, India, 22 mi. E of Ferozepore; wheat, gram, oilseeds.
Zirab (zēräb'), village, Second Prov., in E Mazanderan, N Iran, in Elburz mts., on railroad and 20 mi. S of Shahi, in lumbering area; coal mining.
Zirabulak, Uzbek SSR: see AKTASH, Samarkand oblast.
Ziracuaretiro (sērākwärātē'rō), town (pop. 1,532), Michoacán, central Mexico, 9 mi. ESE of Uruapan; sugar cane, coffee, cereals, fruit.
Zirándaro (sērän'därō), town (pop. 1,192), Guerrero, SW Mexico, on Río de las Balsas (Michoacán border) and 10 mi. SSW of Huetamo; cereals, sugar cane, cotton, sesame, fruit.
Zirate, Cerro (sě'rō sērä'tā), peak (10,958 ft.), Michoacán, central Mexico, on N shore of L. Pátzcuaro, 25 mi. W of Morelia.
Zirc (zĭrts), town (pop. 3,062), Veszprem co., NW central Hungary, 11 mi. N of Veszprem; flour mills; wheat, corn, cattle, hogs.
Ziria Mountains, Greece: see KYLLENE MOUNTAINS.
Zir'in, Israel: see JEZREEL.
Zirje Island or **Zirije Island** (zhēr'yě, zhē'rēyě), Serbo-Croatian *Žirje* or *Žirije*, Ital. *Zuri* (dzōō'rē), Dalmatian island in Adriatic Sea, W Croatia, Yugoslavia, 13 mi. WSW of Sibenic; 7.5 mi. long, up to 1.5 mi. wide. Chief village, Zirje.
Zirke, Poland: see SIERAKOW.
Zirkel, Mount (zûr'kŭl) (12,220 ft.), N Colo., in Park Range, 20 mi. WNW of Walden.
Zirknitz, Yugoslavia: see CERKNICA.
Zirknitzer See, Yugoslavia: see CIRKNISKO JEZERO.
Zirl (tsĭrl), town (pop. 2,815), Tyrol, W Austria, on Inn R. and 7 mi. W of Innsbruck; summer resort. Near by is the Martinswand, small mtn. appearing in legends of Maximilian I.
Zirndorf (tsĭrn'dôrf), town (pop. 10,018), Middle Franconia, N central Bavaria, Germany, just SW of Fürth; mfg. of machinery, precision instruments, toys, paper, textiles, glass; printing, brewing.
Zirnovon, Greece: see KATO NEUROKOPION.
Zirona Grande; **Zirona Piccola**, Yugoslavia: see VELIKI DRVENIK ISLAND.
Zirovnice (zhĭ'rôvnyĭtsě), Czech *Žirovnice*, village (pop. 2,379), SE Bohemia, Czechoslovakia, in Bohemian-Moravian Heights, on railroad and 11 mi. NE of Jindrichuv Hradec; center of mother-of-pearl industries, notably buttons, buckles, clasps.
Zirreh, Gaud-i-, Afghanistan: see GAUD-I-ZIRREH.
Zistersdorf (tsĭs'tŭrsdôrf), town (pop. 3,044), NE Lower Austria, 28 mi. NNE of Vienna; rail junction; wine. Large oil fields in vicinity.
Zitácuaro (sētä'kwärō), city (pop. 11,434), Michoacán, central Mexico, in valley of central plateau, on railroad and 50 mi. SE of Morelia; alt. 6,549 ft. Lumbering and agr. center (cereals, vegetables, fruit, stock); sawmilling, tanning, soapmaking, vegetable-oil extracting, resin processing. The spa of Purua or San José Pura, with radioactive mineral waters, is 9 mi. WNW.
Zitkovac or **Zhitkovats** (both: zhēt'kôväts), Serbo-Croatian *Žitkovac*, village, E central Serbia, Yugoslavia, on the Southern Morava opposite Aleksinac, on railroad and 19 mi. ESE of Krusevac.
Zitlala (sētlä'lä), town (pop. 2,044), Guerrero, SW Mexico, on N slopes of Sierra del Sur, 19 mi. ENE of Chilpancingo; cereals, sugar cane, coffee, fruit, forest products (rubber, resin, vanilla).
Zitlaltepec (sētlältäpěk'). **1** Officially San Juan Zitlaltepec, town (pop. 3,821), Mexico state, central Mexico, 27 mi. N of Mexico city; cereals, maguey, livestock. **2** Officially San Pablo Zitlaltepec, town (pop. 2,587), Tlaxcala, central Mexico, at W foot of Malinche volcano, 22 mi. NE of Puebla; corn, barley, alfalfa, maguey, livestock.
Zittau (tsĭ'tou), town (pop. 45,084), Saxony, E Germany, frontier station near Czechoslovak-Pol. border, opposite Hradek nad Nisou (Czechoslovakia), in Lusatian Mts., near the Lusatian Neisse, 19 mi. SSW of Görlitz. Rail junction; textile-milling center (linen, cotton, woolen, felt); metal- and woodworking, mfg. of automobiles, machinery, bicycles, musical instruments, food products. Has 12th-cent. church. Originally Slav settlement of Sitowir; mentioned as city in 1255 when it belonged to Bohemia. Joined Lusatian League in 1346. Captured by Saxony in 1620.
Zituni, Greece: see LAMIA.
Zitzio, Mexico: see TZITZIO.
Ziyanchurino (zēŭnchōō'rēnŭ), village (1939 pop. over 500), N Chkalov oblast, Russian SFSR, on Sakmara R. and 18 mi. WNW of Mednogorsk, near railroad; wheat, livestock. Sometimes Zianchurino.
Ziyautdin, Uzbek SSR: see PAKHTAKOR.
Ziz, Oued (wěd' zēz'), desert stream in SE Fr. Morocco, rises on S slope of the Djebel Ayachi (High Atlas), flows c.175 mi. S, past Rich and Ksar-es-Souk, through the Tafilalet oasis, and, considerably depleted, joins the Oued Ghéris at 30°35'N to form the Oued ed Daoura, which loses itself in the Algerian Sahara near lat. 29°N.
Zizkov (zhĭsh'kôf), Czech *Žižkov*, E suburb (pop. 92,012) of Prague, Czechoslovakia, S of Zizkov heights, so-called to commemorate Zizka's victory (1420) over Emperor Sigismund's armies. Industrial and mfg. dist.; formerly an independent town. Has Natl. Liberation Memorial with military mus.
Zlabings, Czechoslovakia: see SLAVONICE.
Zlata Koruna (zlä'tä kô'rōōnä), Czech *Zlatá Koruna*, village (pop. 401), S Bohemia, Czechoslovakia, in foothills of Bohemian Forest, on Vltava R. and 4 mi. NE of Cesky Krumlov. Noted for its 13th-cent. Gothic cloister (part of former Cistercian abbey founded by Premysl Ottocar II) and 13th-cent. Gothic church.
Zlatar (zlä'tär), village (pop. 2,694), N Croatia, Yugoslavia, 19 mi. SW of Varazdin; local trade center; small gold deposits. Coal mine near by.
Zlataritsa (zlätä'rētsä), village (pop. 4,268), Gorna Oryakhovitsa dist., N Bulgaria, 12 mi. E of Tirnovo; horticulture, sheep and goat raising.
Zlate Hory (zlä'tä hô'rĭ), Czech *Zlaté Hory*, formerly *Cukmantl*, Ger. *Zuckmantel* (tsŏŏk'mäntŭl), village (pop. 2,190), NW Silesia, Czechoslovakia, 9 mi. ENE of Jesenik; rail terminus; health resort (alt. 1,574 ft.) in NE foothills of the Jeseniky; mfg. of linen and cotton textiles.
Zlate Moravce (mô'räftsě), Slovak *Zlaté Moravce*, Hung. *Aranyosmarót* (ŏ'rŏnyôsh-mŏ'rōt), town (pop. 4,003), SW Slovakia, Czechoslovakia, 15 mi. ENE of Nitra; rail junction; agr. center (wheat, barley) noted for orchards and vineyards. Near-by Mlynany (mlĭ'nyänĭ), Slovak *Mlyňany*, 4 mi. SSW, has subtropical gardens.
Zlatibor (zlä'tēbôr), mountain in Dinaric Alps, W Serbia, Yugoslavia; highest point (3,864 ft.) is 5 mi. SW of Cajetina. Climatic resort.
Zlati-dol, Bulgaria: see SIMEONOVGRAD.
Zlatitsa (zlätē'tsä), city (pop. 2,776), Sofia dist., W central Bulgaria, on S slope of Teteven Mts., 42 mi. E of Sofia; summer resort and market center in Zlatitsa Basin; dairying, truck gardening.
Zlatitsa Basin, valley (□ 47; average alt. 2,500 ft.) in W central Bulgaria, bet. central Balkan Mts. (N) and Sredna Gora (S). Access is provided by Galabets Pass (W). Koznitsa Pass (E), and Zlatitsa Pass (NW). Drained by Topolnitsa R. Livestock, sheep raising. Main centers: Zlatitsa, Pirdop. Also called Pirdop Basin.
Zlatitsa Mountains, Bulgaria: see TETEVEN MOUNTAINS.
Zlatitsa Pass (alt. 4,513 ft.), W central Bulgaria, in Teteven Mts., 3 mi. NW of Zlatitsa, on road to Yetropole (N).
Zlatna (zlät'nä), Ger. *Klein-Schlatten* (klīn'-shlä'-tŭn), Hung. *Zalatna* (zŏ'lŏtnŏ), anc. *Ampelum*, village (pop. 4,142), Hunedoara prov., central Rumania, in Transylvania, in S part of the Muntii Metalici, 16 mi. W of Alba-Iulia; rail terminus and noted gold-mining center, with reduction works; mfg. of sulphuric acid. Tellurium is also mined in vicinity.
Zlatograd (zlä'tôgrät), city (pop. 4,169), Plovdiv dist., S Bulgaria, in SE Rhodope Mts., on right branch of Arda R. and 23 mi. SW of Kirdzhali; agr. center (tobacco, rye, potatoes, livestock). Scattered lead, copper, and zinc deposits near by; mined in Boyevo (N; pop. 573). Until 1934, Dara Dere, sometimes spelled Daridere.
Zlatopol or **Zlatopol'** (zlŭtŭpôl'), town (1926 pop. 6,256), NW Kirovograd oblast, Ukrainian SSR, 34 mi. NW of Kirovograd; food processing; metalworks.
Zlatoust (zlŭtŭōōst'), city (1926 pop. 48,261; 1939 pop. 99,272), W central Chelyabinsk oblast, Russian SFSR, in the S Urals, in Ai R. gorge, 65 mi. W of Chelyabinsk, on railroad. Major metallurgical center, based on Bakal iron mines, Ural chromium, nickel, and tungsten alloys, and charcoal; produces quality steels and precision castings; mfg. of lathes, agr. machinery, cutlery, chemicals, bricks; flour milling, sawmilling, distilling, brewing. Has teachers col., mus., and old churches. Founded 1754 as iron- and copper-working settlement; destroyed 1774 by peasant rebels under Yemelyan Pugachev. Developed as armament and sword mfg. center during Napoleonic invasion; chartered 1835. Metallurgical plants, established in 19th cent., were reconstructed and modernized in 1930s.
Zlatoustovsk (-ōō'stŭfsk), town (1942 pop. over 500), NE Amur oblast, Russian SFSR, near Selemdzha R., 40 mi. E of Ekimchan; gold mining. Developed during Second World War.
Zleby (zhlě'bĭ), Czech *Žleby*, village (pop. 1,441), E Bohemia, Czechoslovakia, on railroad and 10 mi. SE of Kutna Hora; summer resort. Has 13th-cent. castle-mus., 17th-cent. church.

Zletovo (zlĕ'tôvô), village, N Macedonia, Yugoslavia, on Zletovo R. and 40 mi. E of Skoplje, at W foot of Osogov Mts.; lead, zinc, and copper mines. Nearest railroad station at Kocane, 10 mi. SE.

Zletovo River, Serbo-Croatian *Zletovska Reka* (zlĕ'-tôfskä rĕ'kä), N Macedonia, Yugoslavia, rises in Osogov Mts. 6 mi. SSE of Kriva Palanka, flows c.30 mi. SSW, past Zletovo, to Bregalnica R. 9 mi. NNE of Stip.

Zliechov (zlyĕ'khôf), Hung. *Zsolt* (zhôlt), village (pop. 1,261), W Slovakia, Czechoslovakia, 18 mi. ENE of Trencin; noted for well-preserved regional costumes and customs.

Zlin, Czechoslovakia: see GOTTWALDOV.

Zliten (zlētĕn'), town (pop. 4,000), Tripolitania, Libya, in an oasis on Mediterranean coast, on highway and 22 mi. ESE of Homs; commercial center (dates, barley, olives, vegetables, chickens); olive-oil pressing, barracan weaving. Has mosque. Its port, Zliten Marina (tunny fishing), is 2 mi. N.

Zljeb, peak, Yugoslavia: see MOKRA PLANINA.

Zlocieniec (zwôtsyĕ'nyĕts), Pol. *Złocieniec*, Ger. Falkenburg (fäl'kŏonbŏork), town (1939 pop. 8,620; 1946 pop. 2,553) in Pomerania, after 1945 in Koszalin prov., NW Poland, on Drawa R. and 35 mi. S of Bialogard; woolen milling, blanket mfg.

Zloczew (zwô'chĕf), Pol. *Złoczew*, Rus. *Zlochev* (zlô'-chĭf), town (pop. 2,948), Lodz prov., central Poland, 14 mi. N of Wielun; tanning, sawmilling, mfg. of caps. Monastery.

Zloczow, Ukrainian SSR: see ZOLOCHEV, Lvov oblast.

Zlokuchen (zlôkŏo'chĕn), village (pop. 3,397), Kolarovgrad dist., E Bulgaria, on Golyama Kamchiya R. and 11 mi. SSE of Kolarovgrad; vineyards, livestock. Formerly Kopryu-koi.

Zlot (zlôt), village (pop. 5,313), E Serbia, Yugoslavia, 7 mi. SW of Bor; gold mines produce auriferous copper pyrites.

Zlota Lipa River, Ukrainian SSR: ZOLOTAYA LIPA RIVER.

Zlotniki, Ukrainian SSR: see ZOLOTNIKI.

Zlotoryja (zwôtôrĭ'yä), Pol. *Złotoryja*, Ger. *Goldberg* (gôlt'bĕrk), town (1939 pop. 7,860; 1946 pop. 4,613) in Lower Silesia, after 1945 in Wroclaw prov., SW Poland, on the Katzbach and 12 mi. WSW of Liegnitz (Legnica); copper mining and smelting. Has 13th-cent. church, remains of anc. fortifications. Known as gold-mining center from 10th to mid-13th cent. Chartered 1211.

Zlotostockie, Gory, Poland: see REICHENSTEIN MOUNTAINS.

Zlotow (zwô'tŏof), Pol. *Złotów*, Ger. *Flatow* (flä'tō), town (1939 pop. 7,494; 1946 pop. 5,275) in Pomerania, after 1945 in Koszalin prov., NW Poland, on small lake, 20 mi. NE of Schneidemühl (Pila); agr. market (grain, sugar beets, potatoes, livestock); sawmilling. Until 1938, in former Prussian prov. of Grenzmark Posen-Westpreussen.

Zloty Stok (zwô'tĭ stôk'), Pol. *Złoty Stok*, Ger. *Reichenstein* (rī'khŭn-shtīn), town (1939 pop. 2,609; 1946 pop. 3,388) in Lower Silesia, after 1945 in Wroclaw prov., SW Poland, on Czechoslovak border, at N foot of Reichenstein Mts., 10 mi. E of Glatz (Klodzko); mining (tin, lead, arsenic), mfg. (chemicals, matches); summer resort. After 1945, briefly called Rowne, Pol. *Równe*.

Zlutice (zhlŏo'tyĭtsĕ), Czech *Žlutice*, Ger. *Luditz* (lŏo'dĭts), town (pop. 1,265), W Bohemia, Czechoslovakia, on railroad and 25 mi. NNW of Pilsen; coal mining.

Zlynka (zlĭn'kŭ), city (1926 pop. 6,444), SW Bryansk oblast, Russian SFSR, on rail spur and 10 mi. SW of Novozybkov; match-mfg. center; sawmilling, woodworking, distilling.

Zmajevo or **Zmayevo** (both: zmä'yĕvô), Hung. *Óker* (ō'kĕr), village, Vojvodina, N Serbia, Yugoslavia, on railroad and 16 mi. NNW of Novi Sad, in the Backa; mineral waters. Until 1947, called Pasicevo or Pashichevo, Serbo-Croatian *Pašićevo*.

Zmeika or **Zmeyka** (zmä'kŭ), laccolithic mountain (3,261 ft.) of the N Caucasus foothills, Russian SFSR, 3 mi. SSW of Mineralnye Vody.

Zmeinogorsk (zmăēn"ŭgôrsk'), town (1948 pop. over 10,000), S Altai Territory, Russian SFSR, 50 mi. SE of Rubtsovsk; distillery, dairy plant. Mining of lead, zinc, semi-precious stones, marble, and barite near by. Former silver-mining center.

Zmigrod (zhmē'grŏot), Pol. *Żmigród*, Ger. *Trachenberg* (trä'khŭnbĕrk), town (1939 pop. 4,570; 1946 pop. 1,881) in Lower Silesia, after 1945 in Wroclaw prov., SW Poland, near Barycz R., 30 mi. N of Breslau (Wroclaw); linen, hemp, and jute milling. First mentioned 1155; chartered 1253. Long the property of prince-bishops of Breslau. From 1919 to 1939, Ger. frontier station near Pol. border.

Zmiyev (zmēyôf'), city (1926 pop. 6,006), central Kharkov oblast, Ukrainian SSR, on the Northern Donets and 20 mi. S of Kharkov; sawmilling, distilling.

Zmiyevka (–kŭ), village (1926 pop. 3,066), central Orel oblast, Russian SFSR, 20 mi. SSE of Orel; metalworking, starch and hemp processing, distilling.

Zmutt Glacier (tsmŏot), in the Alps of Valais canton, S Switzerland, descends E along N foot of the Matterhorn to the Zmuttbach, a headstream of the Mattervisp. Hamlet of Zmutt is SW of Zermatt.

Znaim, Czechoslovakia: see ZNOJMO.

Znamenity or **Znamenityy** (znŭmĭnyē'tē), town (1948 pop. over 2,000), N Khakass Autonomous Oblast, Krasnoyarsk Territory, Russian SFSR, 105 mi. NW of Abakan; gold mines.

Znamenka (znä'myĭnkŭ). **1** Village (1926 pop. 2,909), W Altai Territory, Russian SFSR, on N Kulunda L., 35 mi. E of Slavgorod; metalworks, dairy plant. **2** village (1939 pop. over 500), E Smolensk oblast, Russian SFSR, on Ugra R. and 23 mi. SSE of Vyazma; flax. **3** Village (1939 pop. over 500), central Tambov oblast, Russian SFSR, 20 mi. S of Tambov; wheat, sunflowers. **4** or **Znamenka I**, city (1939 pop. over 10,000), central Kirovograd oblast, Ukrainian SSR, 23 mi. NE of Kirovograd; rail junction; metalworking, flour milling. **Znamenka II** is a town 5 mi. from here.

Znamensk (znä'myĭnsk), town (1939 pop. 8,463), W central Kaliningrad oblast, Russian SFSR, on the Pregel, at mouth of Lyna R., on railroad and 30 mi. E of Kaliningrad; paper mfg., flour milling; horse fair. By treaty concluded here (1657) with Brandenburg, Poland renounced its suzerainty over duchy of Prussia. Until 1945, in East Prussia and called Wehlau (vā'lou).

Znamenskoye (–skŭyŭ). **1** Village (1939 pop. over 500), N Omsk oblast, Russian SFSR, on Osha R., near its mouth, and 28 mi. NW of Tara; metalworks. **2** Village (1939 pop. over 500), W Orel oblast, Russian SFSR, 25 mi. NW of Orel; hemp processing.

Znauri (znŭŏo'rē), village (1932 pop. estimate 220), SW South Ossetian Autonomous Oblast, Georgian SSR, 10 mi. WSW of Stalinir; orchards, grain. Until c.1945, Znaur-Kau.

Znepole Basin, Bulgaria: see TRIN.

Znin (zhnēn), Pol. *Żnin*, town (pop. 5,615), Bydgoszcz prov., W central Poland, on small lake, 22 mi. SSW of Bydgoszcz; rail junction; brewing, sugar and flour milling, mfg. of bricks, machinery, engines.

Znob-Novgorodskaya or **Znob'-Novgorodskaya** (znôp"-nŭvgŭrôt'skē), village (1939 pop. over 500), N Sumy oblast, Ukrainian SSR, 40 mi. NNW of Glukhov; hemp, potatoes.

Znojmo (znoi'mô), Ger. *Znaim* (znīm), city (pop. 19,695), S Moravia, Czechoslovakia, on Dyje R. and 35 mi. SW of Brno; rail junction; mfg. center (pottery, stoneware, furniture, machinery); noted for fruit- and vegetable-processing industry. Orchards, vineyards, cucumber fields in vicinity. Founded in 1226 by Ottocar I. Has 13th-cent. Romanesque castle chapel with old frescoes, 14th-cent. Gothic church, 15th-cent. town hall with tower. Armistice bet. France and Austria signed here, 1809, after battle of Wagram.

Zoan, Egypt: see TANIS.

Zoar (zôr, zō'ŭr), village (pop. 200), Tuscarawas co., E Ohio, 8 mi. N of New Philadelphia and on Tuscarawas R.; makes refractories.

Zoar, Lake, Conn.: see HOUSATONIC RIVER.

Zöblitz (tsû'blĭts), town (pop. 3,054), Saxony, E central Germany, in the Erzgebirge, 6 mi. W of Olbernhau, near Czechoslovak border; toy mfg.; stone quarrying.

Zobten, Poland: see SOBOTKA.

Zodhia, Kato (kä'tō zôdhyä), village (pop. 1,712), Nicosia dist., N Cyprus, 20 mi. W of Nicosia; wheat, barley, oats, watermelons; sheep, hogs. Adjoined by Pano Zodhia.

Zoetermeer (zŏo'tŭrmär), town (pop. 4,346), South Holland prov., W Netherlands, 8 mi. E of The Hague; milk products.

Zoeterwoude (zŏo'tŭrvou"dŭ), town (pop. 1,374), South Holland prov., W Netherlands, 2.5 mi. S of Leiden; shipbuilding; pottery, cement, musical instruments, woodworking.

Zofingen (tsō'fĭng-ŭn), town (pop. 6,502), Aargau canton, N Switzerland, on Wigger R. and 5 mi. SSE of Olten; printing; cotton textiles, chemicals, knit goods, flour, beer. Late-Gothic church, mus. with old library. Römer-Bad (S of town) has mineral spring, Roman relics.

Zofit, Israel: see TSOFIT.

Zogno (zô'nyō), village (pop. 1,590), Bergamo prov., Lombardy, N Italy, on Brembo R. and 7 mi. N of Bergamo; paper mill, rayon and lace factories.

Zohreh River, Iran: see ZUHREH RIVER.

Zoji La (zōjē' lä'), important pass (alt. 11,578 ft.) in Punjab Himalayas, W central Kashmir, 40 mi. ENE of Srinagar, on main Srinagar-Leh road.

Zola Predosa (zô'lä prĕdô'zä), village (pop. 697), Bologna prov., Emilia-Romagna, N central Italy, 6 mi. W of Bologna; mfg. (cement, fertilizer, agr. machinery).

Zolder (zôl'dŭr), town (pop. 7,285), Limburg prov., NE Belgium, 6 mi. N of Hasselt; coal mining.

Zolfo Springs, town (pop. 334), Hardee co., central Fla., 4 mi. S of Wauchula. Large sulphur spring near by.

Zoliborz (zhôlē'bŏozh), Pol. *Żoliborz*, residential suburb of Warsaw, Warszawa prov., E central Poland, on left bank of the Vistula, 2 mi. N of city center.

Zolkiew, Ukrainian SSR: see ZHOLKVA.

Zolla, Yugoslavia: see COL.

Zollfeld (tsôl'fĕlt), region in Carinthia, S Austria, bet. Sankt Veit and Maria Saal, drained by Glan R. Agr. (wheat, rye), livestock (cattle, horses). Marshy in parts. Many Roman remains have been excavated here.

Zollikofen (tsô'lēkôfŭn), town (pop. 2,653), Bern canton, W central Switzerland, 3 mi. NNE of Bern; knit goods, beer, flour, tiles.

Zollikon (tsô'lēkôn), town (pop. 5,910), Zurich canton, N Switzerland, on L. of Zurich, 2 mi. SSE of Zurich.

Zolochev (zŭ'lŭchôf'). **1** Town (1932 pop. estimate 11,080), N Kharkov oblast, Ukrainian SSR, 20 mi. NNW of Kharkov; flour milling, metalworking. **2** Pol. *Złoczów* (zwô'chŏof), city (1931 pop. 13,265), E Lvov oblast, Ukrainian SSR, on E slope of the Gologory, 39 mi. E of Lvov; mfg. and lignite-mining center (mine at near-by Trostyanets); metalworking, cardboard mfg., sawmilling, tanning, agr. processing (cereals, fruits, vegetables). Founded in 1630; passed (1772) from Poland to Austria; reverted (1919) to Poland; ceded to USSR in 1945.

Zolotarevka (zŭlŭtŭryôf'kŭ), town (1948 pop. over 2,000), central Penza oblast, Russian SFSR, 15 mi. SE of Penza; woolen-milling center.

Zolotaya Lipa River (zŭlŭtī"ŭlyē'pŭ), Pol. *Złota Lipa* (zlô'tä lyē'pä), W Ukrainian SSR, rises S of Zolochev in the Gologory, flows 78 mi. S, past Pomoryany and Berezhany, to Dniester R. 5 mi. WNW of Koropets.

Zolotaya Sopka, Russian SFSR: see TROITSK.

Zolotkovo (zŭlŭtkô'vŭ), town (1939 pop. over 500), S Vladimir oblast, Russian SFSR, 17 mi. ESE of Gus-Khrustalny; glassworking, woodworking.

Zolotniki (zŭlŭtnyĭkē'), Pol. *Złotniki*, village (1939 pop. over 500), central Ternopol oblast, Ukrainian SSR, on Strypa R. and 15 mi. W of Terebovlya; wheat, barley, tobacco.

Zolotogorski or **Zolotogorskiy** (zŭlŭtŭgôr'skē), town (1940 pop. over 500), NW Khakass Autonomous Oblast, Krasnoyarsk Territory, Russian SFSR, 110 mi. NW of Abakan; gold mines.

Zolotoi Potok or **Zolotoy Potok** (zŭlŭtoi' pŭtôk'), Pol. *Potok Złoty* (pô'tôk zwô'tē), (1937 pop. estimate 3,500), SW Ternopol oblast, Ukrainian SSR, 22 mi. WSW of Chortkov; flour milling; grain, tobacco. Has 17th-cent. castle.

Zolotonosha (zŭ"lŭtŭnô'shŭ), city (1926 pop. 15,482), SW Poltava oblast, Ukrainian SSR, 15 mi. N of Cherkassy; rail junction; flour milling, distilling, dairying, metalworking.

Zolotoye (zŭlŭtoi'ŭ). **1** Village (1926 pop. 5,583), S Saratov oblast, Russian SFSR, on right bank of Volga R. (landing) and 50 mi. S of Saratov, in apple and cherry dist.; flour milling. **2** City (1926 pop. 2,974), W Voroshilovgrad oblast, Ukrainian SSR, in the Donbas, 7 mi. NE of Popasnaya; coal-mining center. Formerly Zolotoi Rudnik.

Zolotukhino (zŭlŭtŏo'khēnŭ), village (1939 pop. over 500), N Kursk oblast, Russian SFSR, 25 mi. NNE of Kursk; vegetable drying, hemp processing.

Zoludek, Belorussian SSR: see ZHELUDOK.

Zolyom, Czechoslovakia: see ZVOLEN.

Zomba (zôm'bŏ), town (pop. 2,914), Tolna co., SW central Hungary, 8 mi. NW of Szekszard; wheat, potatoes.

Zomba (zŏm'bä), town (pop. 6,850), ⊙ Nyasaland, in Southern Prov., on Shire Highlands, 37 mi. NE of Blantyre (road) and 300 mi. NNW of Beira, Mozambique; 15°23'S 35°20'E; alt. c.2,900 ft. Administrative center; has Anglican, Scottish, and R.C. churches, European and African hospitals, agr. experimental station, military cantonment. Founded as planters' settlement in 1880s. Zomba plateau (c.7,000 ft.) is just N; cool summer resort.

Zombor, Yugoslavia: see SOMBOR.

Zomergem (zō'mŭr-khŭm), town (pop. 5,939), East Flanders prov., NW Belgium, 9 mi. NW of Ghent; textile industry; flower growing. Formerly spelled Somerghem.

Zonalnaya or **Zonal'naya** (zŭnäl'nīŭ), village (1939 pop. over 500), central Altai Territory, Russian SFSR, on railroad and 15 mi. NW of Bisk, in agr. area.

Zonda (sōn'dä), village, ⊙ Zonda dist. (pop. 1,536; created c.1947), S San Juan prov., Argentina, in San Juan valley (irrigation), 13 mi. W of San Juan; hydroelectric station and dam.

Zongo (zông'gō), village, Equator Prov., NW Belgian Congo, on Ubangi R. (Fr. Equatorial Africa border), opposite Bangui, and 250 mi. NW of Lisala; customs station, trading post in cotton region.

Zongo (sōng'gō), village (pop. 1,140), La Paz dept., W Bolivia, at N foot of Eastern Cordillera of the Andes, on Zongo R. (branch of Coroico R.) and 27 mi. NNE of La Paz; alt. 6,725 ft.; coffee, cacao, rice, vineyards.

Zongolica (sōng-gōlē'kä), city (pop. 1,296), Veracruz, E Mexico, in Sierra Madre Oriental, 16 mi. SSW of Córdoba; coffee, corn, fruit.

Zongozotla (sōng-gōsōt'lä), town (pop. 1,489), Puebla, central Mexico, 18 mi. ENE of Zacatlán; corn, coffee, tobacco.

Zonguldak (zôn"gŏoldäk'), province (□ 2,876; 1950 pop. 425,974), N Turkey, on Black Sea; ⊙ Zonguldak. Bordered S by Bolu Mts.; drained by Yenice, Arac, and Devrek rivers. Its important and extensive coal deposits extend throughout the prov., with some manganese and asbestos in W near Eregli. Also grain, hemp, flax.

Zonguldak, city (1950 pop. 35,631), ⊙ Zonguldak prov., N Turkey, coal-shipping port on Black Sea, 120 mi. NNW of Ankara; center for distribution of all coal mined in prov.; manufactures artificial anthracite; grain, flax, hemp.

Zons (tsōns), town (pop. 3,706), in former Prussian Rhine Prov., W Germany, after 1945 in North Rhine-Westphalia, on left bank of the Rhine and 7 mi. S of Düsseldorf. Has medieval fortifications.

Zontecomatlán (sōntākōmätlän'), town (pop. 1,324), Veracruz, E Mexico, in Sierra Madre Oriental, 17 mi. SW of Chicontepec; corn, sugar cane, coffee.

Zontehuitz, Cerro, Mexico: see HUEYTEPEC, SIERRA DE.

Zonza (zōzä', It. zôn'tsä), village (pop. 1,074), S central Corsica, 14 mi. NE of Sartène; alt. 2,600 ft. Resort. Chestnuts.

Zoppot, Poland: see SOPOT.

Zoquiapan (sōkyä'pän), town (pop. 1,510), Puebla, central Mexico, 32 mi. ESE of Huauchinango; cereals, coffee, fruit.

Zoquitlán (sōkētlän'), town (pop. 2,926), Puebla, central Mexico, in Sierra Madre, 28 mi. ESE of Tehuacán; agr. center (corn, sugar, fruit, stock).

Zor (tsōr', zōr'), former region of Turkey along the middle Euphrates; now divided bet. Syria and Turkey; ⊙ was DEIR EZ ZOR, in modern Syria.

Zor, Az, Kuwait: see FAILAKA ISLAND.

Zorbatiya (zôrbätē'yü), village, Kut prov., E Iraq, near Iran line, c.60 mi. NNE of Kut; cotton, dates.

Zörbig (tsûr'bĭkh), town (pop. 6,806), in former Prussian Saxony prov., central Germany, after 1945 in Saxony-Anhalt, 8 mi. W of Bitterfeld, in lignite-mining region; sugar refining, paper milling.

Zorge (tsôr'gù), village (pop. 1,904), in Brunswick, NW Germany, after 1945 in Lower Saxony, in the lower Harz, 6.5 mi. S of Braunlage; foundry.

Zorita (thōrē'tä), town (pop. 5,630), Cáceres prov., W Spain, 16 mi. SE of Trujillo; agr. trade center and road junction; olive-oil processing, flour milling. Wine, fruit, livestock, lumbering area.

Zor-Kul or **Zor-Kul'** (zôr"-kōōl'), lake in the Pamir, on USSR-Afghanistan border, 110 mi. E of Khorog; alt. 13,295 ft.; 8 mi. long. Source of Pamir R., a headstream of the Panj. Also called L. Victoria.

Zorleni (zôrlān'), village (pop. 3,143), Barlad prov., E Rumania, on Barlad R. and 5 mi. NE of Barlad; rail junction and agr. center, notably for corn.

Zorndorf (tsôrn'dôrf), Pol. *Sarbinowo* (särbēnô'vô), village (1939 pop. 860) in Brandenburg, after 1945 in Zielona Gora prov., W Poland, 5 mi. NNE of Küstrin. Scene (Aug. 25, 1758) of victory of Prussians under Frederick the Great over Russians.

Zorn River (zôrn), Bas-Rhin dept., E France, rises in the Vosges S of Dabo, flows c.45 mi. generally E, through Saverne Gap, past Saverne, Hochfelden, and Brumath, to the Moder just below Herrlisheim. Followed, through most of its course, by Marne-Rhine Canal.

Zoro, Belgian Congo: see WATSA.

Zoroa, Syria: see IZRA'.

Zorritos (sōrē'tōs), town (pop. 1,593), ⊙ Contralmirante Villar prov. (formed 1942), Tumbes dept., NW Peru, port on the Pacific, on Pan American Highway and 15 mi. WSW of Tumbes, in oil fields; petroleum-refining center; fisheries.

Zory (zô'rĭ), Pol. *Żory*, Ger. *Sohrau* (zō'rou), town (pop. 4,730), Katowice prov., S Poland, 7 mi. ESE of Rybnik; rail junction; metalworks; flour milling, sawmilling, paper mfg.

Zorzor (zôrzôr'), town, Western Prov., NW Liberia, 50 mi. SSE of Vonjama, near Fr. Guinea border; palm oil and kernels, cotton, pineapples; cattle. Mission station.

Zossen (tsō'sùn), town (pop. 5,958), Brandenburg, E Germany, 20 mi. S of Berlin; market gardening.

Zottegem (zô'tù-khùm), town (pop. 6,127), East Flanders prov., W central Belgium, 13 mi. SSE of Ghent; textiles, leather, shoes; agr. market. Formerly spelled Sottegem.

Zouanké, Fr. Equatorial Africa: see SOUANKÉ.

Zouar (zwär), village, N Chad territory, Fr. Equatorial Africa, in the Tibesti, 250 mi. NW of Largeau, near Fr. West Africa border; customs station and military outpost on trans-Saharan track.

Zoufftgen (zōōfgē'), Ger. *Suftgen* (zōōft'gùn), village (pop. 345), Moselle dept., NE France, 7 mi. NNW of Thionville; customs station near Luxembourg border opposite Bettembourg.

Zouila, Fezzan: see ZUILA.

Zoute, Het, or **Le Zoute,** Belgium: see KNOKKE.

Zoutleeuw (zout'lāōō), Fr. *Léau* (lā-ō'), town (pop. 2,269), Brabant prov., central Belgium, 8 mi. E of Tirlemont; agr. market. Has 12th-cent. church, 14th-cent. cloth hall, Renaissance town hall. Town dates from 7th cent.

Zoutpansberg (sout'pänsbĕrkh"), mountain range, N Transvaal, U. of So. Afr., extends 100 mi. E–W, N of Louis Trichardt and S of Limpopo R.; rises to 5,714 ft. 30 mi. W of Louis Trichardt.

Zoyatlán (soiätlän'), officially Zoyatlán de Juárez, town (pop. 750), Guerrero, SW Mexico, in Sierra Madre del Sur, 7 mi. SE of Tlapa; cereals, fruit. Sometimes Soyatlán.

Zozocolco (sōsōkōl'kō), officially Zozocolco de Hidalgo, town (pop. 2,268), Veracruz, E Mexico, in Sierra Madre Oriental foothills, 28 mi. SW of Papantla; corn, sugar cane, coffee, fruit.

Zrenjanin or **Zrenyanin** (both: zrĕn'yänĭn), city (pop. 40,517), Vojvodina, N Serbia, Yugoslavia, port on canalized Begej R. and 26 mi. ENE of Novi Sad, in the Banat. Rail center on Belgrade-Kikinda RR, with lines to Rumania; mfg. of agr. machinery, dairy products, sugar, molasses, dried beet pulp; flour milling, vegetable canning, brewing. Carpet making in vicinity. Until 1930s, called Veliki Beckerek or Veliki Bechkerek, Serbo-Croatian *Veliki Bečkerek*, Hung. *Nagybecskerek*, and after, until c.1947, Petrovgrad.

Zriba (zrēbä'), agr. village, Zaghouan dist., NE Tunisia, 33 mi. S of Tunis; hot springs near by.

Zrinska Gora (zrēn'skä gô'rä), mountain in Dinaric Alps, N Croatia, Yugoslavia; highest point, Priseka (3,117 ft.), is 14 mi. SE of Glina.

Zrmanja River (zûr'mänyä), Ital. *Zermagna* (dzĕrmä'nyä), W Croatia, Yugoslavia, mostly in Dalmatia; rises 13 mi. NNW of Knin, flows 33 mi. W, past Obrovac, to Adriatic Sea 5 mi. W of Obrovac. Navigable for 9 mi. Asphalt deposits in valley.

Zsabalya, Yugoslavia: see ZABALJ.

Zsadany (zhŏ'dänyü), Hung. *Zsadány*, town (pop. 3,479), Bihar co., E Hungary, 13 mi. NNE of Sarkad; hemp, tobacco, cattle.

Zsaka (zhä'kō), Hung. *Zsáka*, town (pop. 3,473), Bihar co., E Hungary, 8 mi. SW of Berettyoujfalu; flour mill.

Zsambek (zhäm'bāk), Hung. *Zsámbék*, town (pop. 4,525), Pest-Pilis-Solt-Kiskun co., N central Hungary, 17 mi. W of Budapest; textile, button factories; flour mills. Church is half 12th-cent. Romanesque, half late-13th-cent. Gothic.

Zschachwitz (chäkh'vĭts), residential village (pop. 7,968), Saxony, E central Germany, on the Elbe and 6 mi. ESE of Dresden.

Zscherndorf (chĕrn'dôrf), village (pop. 4,104), in former Prussian Saxony prov., central Germany, after 1945 in Saxony-Anhalt, 2 mi. W of Bitterfeld; lignite mining; mfg. of chemicals and fertilizer.

Zschopau (chō'pou), town (pop. 8,983), Saxony, E central Germany, in the Erzgebirge, on Zschopau R. and 9 mi. SE of Chemnitz; automobile mfg., hosiery knitting; cotton, woolen, and paper milling. Old Wildeck castle overlooks town. First mentioned 1292. Was important river crossing on medieval Prague-Chemnitz trade route.

Zschopau River, E central Germany, rises in the Erzgebirge on the Fichtelberg, flows 60 mi. N, past Zschopau, Frankenberg, and Waldheim (dam), to the Freiberger Mulde 3 mi. W of Döbeln.

Zschorlau (chôr'lou), village (pop. 5,118), Saxony, E central Germany, in the Erzgebirge, 4 mi. WSW of Aue; uranium, wolframite, antimony mining and smelting; woodworking.

Zschornegosda, Germany: see SCHWARZHEIDE.

Zschornewitz (chôr'nùvĭts), village (pop. 5,125), in former Prussian Saxony prov., central Germany, after 1945 in Saxony-Anhalt, 8 mi. NE of Bitterfeld; lignite mining; machinery mfg. Major power station, located bet. Zschornewitz and Golpa (2 mi. W), supplies Berlin and Leipzig; completed 1918.

Zsibo, Rumania: see JIBON.

Zsilyvajdejvulkan, Rumania: see VULCAN.

Zsolna, Czechoslovakia: see ZILINA.

Zsombolya, Rumania: see JIMBOLIA.

Zuai, lake, Ethiopia: see ZWAI, LAKE.

Zuara (zwä'rä), town (pop. 8,408), W Tripolitania, Libya, port on Mediterranean Sea, on coastal highway and 65 mi. W of Tripoli, in an oasis (cereals, dates, olives, vegetables, esparto grass); rail terminus; sponge fishing, olive-oil pressing, flour milling; camel breeding.

Zuarungu (zwärōōng'gōō), village, Northern Territories, N Gold Coast, on road and 95 mi. N of Tamale; millet, durra; livestock.

Zubair, Al, Az Zubair, or **Al-Zubayr** (all: äz-zōōbīr'), town, Basra prov., SE Iraq, just SE of the lake Hor al Hammar, on railroad and 10 mi. SW of Basra; dates, rice, corn, millet. Oil well begun 1947 began producing in 1949; pipe line to FAO, marine loading terminal. Town is on original site (7th cent.) of Basra.

Zubia (thōō'vyä), town (pop. 4,640), Granada prov., S Spain, 5 mi. SSE of Granada; olive-oil, sugar beets, hemp, truck produce.

Zubova Polyana (zōō'bùvù pŭlyä"nù), village (1926 pop. 867), SW Mordvinian Autonomous SSR, Russian SFSR, on railroad and 85 mi. W of Ruzayevka, in lumbering area; woodworking, mfg. of building materials.

Zubovka (zōō'bùfkù), village (1926 pop. 2,181), N Kuibyshev oblast, Russian SFSR, on Kondurcha R. and 22 mi. N of Sergiyevsk; distilling; wheat, sunflowers.

Zubovo (zōō'bùvù), village, W Vologda oblast, Russian SFSR, on Shola R. (right affluent of the Kovzha) and 32 mi. NW of Belozersk; coarse grain. Sawmill at Sholski Zavod (SE).

Zubtsov (zōōptsôf'), city (1926 pop. 3,663), S Kalinin oblast, Russian SFSR, on Volga R. (landing) and 12 mi. SE of Rzhev; marble quarries; hemp processing. Summer resort. Formerly an important grain river port. Chartered 1216; passed 1486 to Moscow.

Zuchwil (tsōōkh'vēl), industrial town (pop. 3,391), Solothurn canton, NW Switzerland, adjacent to and SE of Solothurn.

Zuckerhütl (tsōō'kûrhütùl), Ital. *Pan di Zucchero*, highest peak (11,519 ft.) of Stubai Alps, on Austro-Ital. border, 20 mi. SSW of Innsbruck, at head of Stubai Valley.

Zuckmantel, Czechoslovakia: see ZLATE HORY.

Zudañez (sōōdänyĕs'), town (pop. c.5,300), ⊙ Zudañez prov., Chuquisaca dept., S central Bolivia, on projected Sucre-Camiri RR and 35 mi. E of Sucre, on Camiri-Tintín oil pipe line; vegetables, potatoes, fruit, corn. Until 1900s, Tacopaya.

Zuénoula (zwĕnōō'lä), village (pop. c.1,200), central Ivory Coast, Fr. West Africa, 70 mi. W of Bouaké; cacao, coffee, palm kernels.

Zuera (thwā'rä), town (pop. 3,190), Saragossa prov., NE Spain, on the Gállego and 15 mi. NNE of Saragossa; agr. trade center (cereals, sugar beets, alfalfa); lumbering, sheep raising.

Zuetina (zwĕtē'nä), village (pop. 1,500), W Cyrenaica, Libya, port on Gulf of Sidra, 80 mi. S of Benghazi; fishing, stock raising (sheep, goats), fruit and vegetable growing.

Zuffenhausen (tsōō"fùnhou'zùn), industrial N suburb of Stuttgart, Germany, 4 mi. N of city center.

Zufre (thōō'frā), town (pop. 2,013), Huelva prov., SW Spain, in Sierra Morena, 50 mi. NE of Huelva; olives, cereals, cork, livestock. Iron mining.

Zug (tsōōk), Fr. *Zoug* (zōōg), canton (□ 93; 1950 pop. 42,268), N central Switzerland; smallest in country; ⊙ Zug. Land of meadows, forests, some pastures and cultivated fields, numerous orchards; industry limited to towns of Zug, Baar, Cham, Unterägeri. Pop. is German-speaking and Roman Catholic.

Zug, town (1950 pop. 14,601), ⊙ Zug canton, N central Switzerland, on shore of L. of Zug, 14 mi. S of Zurich; metalware, electrical apparatus, tiles, fats; woodworking, printing. Fine views of mts. to S and SW. Zug retains, in the Oberstadt and the Altstadt, and in its remnants of old fortifications, a partially medieval appearance. Points of interest: cantonal bldgs. (1869), town hall (1505), clock tower (1480), mus. (mainly historical), churches of St. Oswald (late Gothic) and of St. Michael (1902), Capuchin monastery (1597) with church (1676).

Zug, Lake of, Ger. *Zugersee* (tsōō'gûrzā), N central Switzerland, bordering on cantons of Zug, Schwyz, and Lucerne; c.9 mi. long, □ 15, alt. 1,357 ft., max. depth 649 ft. Kiemen promontory juts out from W shore. Lorze R. flows through lake in N. The Rigi (S), Zugerberg (E), and Rossberg (E) rise on its shores. Zug (NE) is main town on lake.

Zugdidi (zōōgdyĭdyē'), city (1939 pop. over 10,000), W Georgian SSR, on rail spur, near Ingur R., and 45 mi. NW of Kutaisi; trading center; tea, wines, cognac; mfg. (bricks, tiles), metalworks. Has 14th-cent. church, botanic garden, and Mingrelian mus. (1921). Large paper and pulp mill near by, on Ingur R. Dates from c.1500; developed in 17th cent.; was ⊙ Mingrelia. Formerly spelled Zugdidy.

Zugerberg (tsōō'gûrbĕrk), mountain (over 3,000 ft.) in the Alps, N central Switzerland, 3 mi. S of Zug; ascended by cable railway; fine views; winter sports.

Zugersee, Switzerland: see ZUG, LAKE OF.

Zugliget (zōō'glĭgĕt), residential area of Budapest, N central Hungary, in Buda Mts.

Zugres (zōōgrĕs'), city (1939 pop. over 2,000), E central Stalino oblast, Ukrainian SSR, in the Donbas, 5 mi. ESE of Khartsyzsk; has large power plant, using anthracite dust.

Zugspitze (tsōōk'shpĭ"tsù), highest peak (9,721 ft.) of Germany, in the Wettersteingebirge of the Bavarian Alps, on Austrian border; glaciers. Meteorological observatory. On NE slope is rack-and-pinion railroad from Garmisch-Partenkirchen; on W slope is aerial tramway from Ehrwald, Austria.

Zuheros (thōōā'rōs), town (pop. 2,198), Córdoba prov., S Spain, 5 mi. S of Baena; hose mfg., olive-oil processing. Cereals, almonds, wine, livestock. Gypsum quarries.

Zuhreh River or **Zohreh River** (both: zōrē'), or **Tab River** (täb), SW Iran, in Fars and Khuzistan, rises in the Zagros mts. 90 mi. NW of Shiraz, flows 200 mi. W and S, past Hindijan, to head of Persian Gulf 80 mi. ESE of Abadan.

Zuid Beveland, Netherlands: see SOUTH BEVELAND.

Zuidbroek (zoid'brōōk), town (pop. 900), Groningen prov., NE Netherlands, on the Winschoter Diep and 12 mi. E of Groningen; rail junction; potato-flour mfg., dairying. Has 13th-cent. church.

Zuider Zee or **Zuyder Zee** (both: zī'dùr, Du. zoid'ùr) [Du.,=southern sea], anc. *Flevo Lacus*, former shallow inlet (80 mi. long) of North Sea, in N and central Netherlands. Once a lake; in 13th cent. a great flood joined it to North Sea, leaving a string of isls. across its mouth. Vast drainage project, begun in 1920, split old Zuider Zee into 2 main areas: the IJSSELMEER, where reclamation has made vast strides, and the WADDENZEE.

Zuidholland, Netherlands: see SOUTH HOLLAND.

Zuidhorn (zoit"hôrn'), town (pop. 1,863), Groningen prov., N Netherlands, near the Hoendiep, 7 mi. W of Groningen; cement mfg., dairying.

Zuidlaren (zoit"lä'rùn), town (pop. 1,991), Drenthe prov., N Netherlands, near a small lake, 8 mi. NNE of Assen; cattle and horse market (known since 13th cent.). Lunatic asylum near by.

Zuid Natoena Islands, Indonesia: see SOUTH NATUNA ISLANDS.

Zuid-Willemsvaart (zoit-wĭ'lŭmsvärt) or **Willems Canal,** S central Netherlands and NE Belgium, extends 76 mi. generally SSE from Dieze R. at 's Hertogenbosch to ALBERT CANAL near Maastricht, entering Belgium 6 mi. WSW of Weert, reentering the Netherlands near Maastricht. Serves Veghel (via 1½-mi. branch canal), Helmond, Weert, Lanaken (Belgium), and Maastricht. Joined by WILHELMINA CANAL 1 mi. S of Beek, by WESSEM-NEDERWEERD CANAL 3 mi. NE of Weert, and by Scheldt-Meuse Junction Canal S of Hamont (Belgium). Built 1822-26.

Zuiho, Formosa: see JUIFANG.

Zuila or **Zouila** (zwē'lä), village (pop. 527), central Fezzan, Libya, 70 mi. SE of Sebha, near a Saharan oasis (dates, cereals, vegetables). Has ruined fort and anc. mausoleums (c.11th cent.).

Zuilen (zoi'lŭn), town (pop. 22,251), Utrecht prov., W central Netherlands, on Vecht R. and 4 mi. NW of Utrecht; oil refining; mfg. (railroad supplies, machinery, bricks, roofing tiles); dairying.

Zuisan, Korea: see SOSAN.

Zújar (thōō'här), town (pop. 3,372), Granada prov., S Spain, 5 mi. NW of Baza; olive-oil processing, flour milling, cement mfg. Cereals, sugar beets, esparto; sheep raising. Mineral springs near by.

Zújar River, W Spain, rises in the Sierra Morena W of Fuenteovejuna, flows along Córdoba-Badajoz prov. border, then enters Badajoz prov. and, turning N and W, joins Guadiana R. 3 mi. N of Villanueva de la Serena; c.100 mi. long.

Zula (zōō'lä), village (pop. 500), Massawa div., central Eritrea, near Gulf of Zula (formerly Annesley Bay), an inlet (30 mi. long; 5-20 mi. wide) of the Red Sea, 30 mi. SSE of Massawa, in irrigated region; cereals, sesame, cotton. Near by are ruins of anc. *Adulis*, a major Axumite seaport.

Zulfiqar (zōōlfĭkär'), frontier post, Herat prov., northwesternmost Afghanistan, 100 mi. NW of Herat, and on the Hari Rud (Iran line), at USSR border; 35°34'N 61°17'E.

Zulia (sōō'lyä), state (□ 24,360; 1941 pop. 345,667; 1950 census 523,568), NW Venezuela, on Gulf of Venezuela (Caribbean Sea); ⊙ MARACAIBO. Borders W (Sierra de Perijá) on Colombia, and occupies narrow S strip of Guajira peninsula. Apart from Andean outliers in W and S, it consists of lowlands grouped like a horseshoe around the vast expanse of L. MARACAIBO, which receives the rivers Catatumbo, Zulia, Escalante, Chama, and Motatán. S lowlands are extremely hot and humid (rainy periods May-July and Sept.-Nov.), N is arid. One of the richest oil-producing regions in the world. Most of the petroleum fields (Campo Ambrosio, La Rosa, Tía Juana, Lagunillas, Bachaquero) stretch along the lake, and many derricks are built in the water. In S basin sugar cane, cacao, cotton, coconuts, and fruit are grown, and cattle raised, on large scale; goat grazing in N. Forests yield fine construction timber (rosewood, mahogany, ebony). Fishing in L. Maracaibo and Gulf of Venezuela. Leading petroleum producing centers are Cabimas, Lagunillas, San Lorenzo. The oil industry is centered at Maracaibo, 2d largest city of Venezuela, whence oil is transshipped. With development of the oil wells after the First World War, the entire economy of Venezuela was changed.

Zulia, Mount (zōō'lyä), at meeting point of Kenya, Uganda, and Anglo-Egyptian Sudan boundaries; 4°10'N 34°E. Rises to 6,325 ft.

Zulia River (sōō'lyä), in Venezuela and Colombia, rises in Cordillera Oriental W of Pamplona (Norte de Santander dept., Colombia), flows c.150 mi. N, past Puerto Villamizar, and across international line, to Catatumbo R. in Maracaibo basin 4 mi. W of Encontrados. Barco petroleum fields along its upper course. Receives Pamplonita R.

Züllichau, Poland: see SULECHOW.

Zülpich (tsül'pĭkh), town (pop. 3,719), in former Prussian Rhine Prov., W Germany, after 1945 in North Rhine-Westphalia, 6 mi. WNW of Euskirchen; distilling. Noted 11th-12th-cent. Romanesque basilica and 15th-cent. town gates were heavily damaged in Second World War.

Zulueta (sōōlwā'tä), town (pop. 4,337), Las Villas prov., central Cuba, on railroad and 22 mi. E of Santa Clara; sugar cane, tobacco, livestock.

Zululand (zōō'lōōlănd), district (□ 10,427; total pop. 398,460; native pop. 386,633), NE Natal, U. of So. Afr., on Indian Ocean, bounded by Mozambique (N), Swaziland (NW), and Buffalo and Tugela rivers (S); ⊙ Eshowe. Surface rises from fertile coastal plain to plateau and hills at foot of Drakensberg range. The land, crown property, is made up mostly of native reserves. Administered by European commissioner with some administrative and judicial powers delegated to native chiefs. Cotton and sugar growing, stock raising are main occupations. Zululand includes Hluhluwe Game Reserve (□ c.62), in NE part of dist., near Indian Ocean, 80 mi. NE of Eshowe; and Amatongaland or Tongaland, a region on Mozambique border annexed to Natal 1897 and merged with Zululand 1898. Voortrekkers under Piet Retief arrived in Zululand 1838; after negotiations with Zulu chief Dingaan, Retief and his men were murdered at Dingaans Kraal. Subsequently (1838) Zulus massacred other Boer advance parties in Weenen dist. Andries Pretorius defeated Dingaan at battle of Blood River (Dec. 16, 1838); the new chief, Mpanda, became vassal of Boer republic of Natal. In 1878 British demanded that Cetewayo, the Zulu chief, accept British rule; this went unanswered and in Jan., 1879, force under Lord Chelmsford invaded Zululand. British troops were almost annihilated at Iswandhlawa, and the Zulus besieged other forces at Eshowe and at Rorkesdrift, but the Zulus were finally defeated at Ulundi (July 3, 1879) and Cetewayo was captured (Aug., 1879). Zululand was proclaimed British territory (1887) and annexed to Natal (1897). Chief Dinizulu staged revolt in 1888; disturbances continued until 1907. The Zulus, noted for their physical development, their bravery, and their powers in battle, are chiefly a pastoral people.

Zülz, Poland: see BIALA, Opole prov.

Zumarraga, Philippines: see BUAD ISLAND.

Zumárraga (thōōmä'rägä), town (pop. 2,669), Guipúzcoa prov., N Spain, 10 mi. WSW of Tolosa; metalworking, mfg. of rattan and willow articles. Cereals and cattle in area.

Zumaya (thōōmī'ä), town (pop. 2,828), Guipúzcoa prov., N Spain, fishing port on Bay of Biscay, 14 mi. W of San Sebastián; metalworking (marine motors, boilers); fish processing, boatbuilding, cement mfg. Bathing resort.

Zumba (sōōm'bä), town, Santiago-Zamora prov., SE Ecuador, on E slopes on the Andes, near Chinchipe R., in selvas; 4°52'S 79°7'W.

Zumberak Mountains (zhōōm'bĕräk), Serbo-Croatian *Žumberak*, or **Uskok Mountains** (ōō'skôk), Serbo-Croatian *Uskočke Planine*, or **Gorjanci** (gôr'yäntsĕ), in Dinaric Alps, Yugoslavia, along Croatia-Slovenia border; highest peak (3,874 ft.) rises 8 mi. ESE of Novo Mesto.

Zumbo (zōōm'bō), village, Manica and Sofala prov., northwesternmost Mozambique, on left bank of Zambezi R. at Northern Rhodesia border opposite Feira, and 220 mi. W of Tete; ships rice, beans, corn, manioc. Coal deposits.

Zumbro Falls (zŭm'brō), village (pop. 172), Wabasha co., SE Minn., at falls of Zumbro R., 18 mi. N of Rochester, in grain, livestock, and poultry area; dairy products.

Zumbro River, SE Minn., formed by confluence of North Branch (50 mi. long) and South Branch (60 mi. long) just W of Zumbro Falls, flows 50 mi. E to Mississippi R. SE of Wabasha. Drains rich agr. area. Dammed for power near Zumbro Falls.

Zumbrota (zŭmbrō'tŭ), village (pop. 1,686), Goodhue co., SE Minn., on Zumbro R. and 20 mi. NNW of Rochester, in grain, livestock, and poultry area; dairy products, tile.

Zumpango (sōōmpäng'gō). **1** Officially Zumpango del Río, town (pop. 3,266), Guerrero, SW Mexico, on affluent of Mezcala R. (Río de las Balsas system) and 7 mi. N of Chilpancingo; cereals, sugar cane, tobacco, coffee, fruit, forest products (rubber, resin, vanilla). **2** Officially Zumpango de Ocampo, town (pop. 5,583), Mexico state, central Mexico, on railroad and 25 mi. N of Mexico city; cattle-raising center; cereals, maguey, fruit.

Zumpango, Lake, Mexico state, central Mexico, in depression of Valley of Mexico, just W of Zumpango; 4 mi. long, 2-3 mi. wide; now mostly dry. Linked through canalized Cuautitlán R. with Pánuco R. system.

Zundert (zŭn'dŭrt), village (pop. 2,603), North Brabant prov., SW Netherlands, 10 mi. SSW of Breda; frontier post near Belg. border; cigar mfg.

Zung, Tadzhik SSR: see VAKHAN.

Zungaria, China: see DZUNGARIA.

Zungeru (zōōng-gĕrōō'), town (pop. 1,661), Niger prov., Northern Provinces, W central Nigeria, on Kaduna R., on railroad and 30 mi. WNW of Minna; communications center; lumber milling (roofing timber, railway sleepers); shea nuts, cotton. Was ⊙ N Nigeria (1902-14) after transfer from Jebba.

Zungon Katab (zŭng-gwôn' kŭtäb'), town (pop. 294), Zaria prov., Northern Provinces, central Nigeria, 15 mi. NNE of Kafanchan; tin mining. Sometimes spelled Zangwan Katab.

Zuni (zōō'nē), Pueblo Indian village (pop. 2,563), McKinley co., W N.Mex., on Zuni R., in Zuni Indian Reservation (□ 627.9), 33 mi. S of Gallup; alt. c.6,300 ft. Inhabitants are chiefly Pueblo Indians of distinct linguistic family (Zuñi). They farm irrigated land and are noted for basketry, pottery, turquoise jewelry, weaving, and native dances. Chief festival, Shalako, in late Nov. or early Dec., represents Zuñi deities in act of blessing new homes. Present village built c.1695. Earlier Zuni pueblos ("Seven Cities of Cibola") were attacked (1540) by Coronado expedition under false impression that Indians possessed vast stores of gold. Zuni Reservoir near by, Zuni Mts. E.

Zunil (sōōnēl'), town (1950 pop. 1,876), Quezaltenango dept., SW Guatemala, on Samalá R. (hydroelectric station) and 5 mi. SSW of Quezaltenango, at NW foot of volcano Zunil; alt. 7,598 ft. Market center; coffee, grain. Flour milling near by. On N slopes of volcano Santo Tomás, near Zunil, are hot-spring resorts of Aguas Amargas (3 mi. S) and Fuentes Georginas (5 mi. SE).

Zunil, inactive volcano (11,591 ft.), SW Guatemala, on Quezaltenango-Sololá-Suchitepéquez dept. border, 9 mi. SE of Quezaltenango.

Zunilito (sōōnēlē'tō), town (1950 pop. 259), Suchitepéquez dept., SW Guatemala, in Pacific piedmont, on S slope of volcano Santo Tomás, 9 mi. NNE of Mazatenango; coffee, grain, tobacco. Transferred 1944 from Quezaltenango dept.

Zuni Mountains (zōō'nē), domed uplift (c.70 mi. long, 30 mi. wide) W N.Mex., in Valencia and McKinley counties, near Ariz. line, SE of Gallup, on Colorado Plateau. Highest point, Lookout Mtn. (9,110 ft.). Extensive lava beds S and SE.

Zuni River, W N.Mex., rises in McKinley co., flows c.90 mi. SW, past Zuni Pueblo Indian village, through Zuni Indian Reservation, to Little Colorado R. in Apache co., E Ariz. Dam at head forms Zuni Reservoir. Intermittent flow.

Zupa or **Zhupa** (zhōō'pä), Serbo-Croatian *Župa*, county (pop. 28,248), S central Yugoslavia; ⊙ Aleksandrovac; winegrowing.

Zupanja (zhōō'pänyä), Serbo-Croatian *Županja*, village (pop. 4,826), N Croatia, Yugoslavia, on Sava R. (Bosnia border) and 16 mi. S of Vinkovci, in Slavonia; rail terminus; Sugar and tannin mfg.

Zuqar Island (zōōkär'), in Red Sea, 50 mi. SSW of Hodeida, belonging to Yemen; 14°N 42°45'E; 11 mi. long, 7 mi. wide.

Zura (zōōrä'), village (1926 pop. 1,175), central Udmurt Autonomous SSR, Russian SFSR, 45 mi. SE of Glazov; wheat, rye, oats, livestock.

Zuran, Yemen: see DHORAN.

Zurawno, Ukrainian SSR: see ZHURAVNO.

Zuri, island, Yugoslavia: see ZIRJE ISLAND.

Zurich (zōōr'ĭk), village (pop. estimate 550), S Ont., near L. Huron, 22 mi. S of Goderich; jam making, lumbering, flax milling, dairying.

Zurich (zü'rĭkh), town (pop. 275), Friesland prov., N Netherlands, on the Waddenzee, 13 mi. WNW of Sneek; dairy center.

Zurich (zōō'rĭk), Ger. *Zürich* (tsü'rĭkh), canton (□ 668· 1950 pop. 772,617), N Switzerland; ⊙ Zurich. Forests, meadows, fertile fields (cereals); orchards in S, some gardens and vineyards. Mfg. (mainly metal products and textiles) in Zurich and Winterthur. Hydroelectric plants on the Rhine. Pop. German speaking and Protestant.

Zurich, Ger. *Zürich*, city (1950 pop. 386,485), ⊙ Zurich canton, N Switzerland, on N shore of L. of Zurich, at mouth of Limmat and Sihl rivers; 47°22'N 8°22'E; alt. 1,350 ft. Largest city in Switzerland and most important economically. Its site occupied by lake dwellers as early as the New Stone Age. Settled by the Helvetii; conquered (58 B.C.) by Romans and developed into a Roman settlement (*Turicum*) in 1st cent. A.D. Became a free imperial city in 1218, joined the Swiss Confederation in 1351, and in 16th cent. became center of Swiss Reformation. It remains an international intellectual center. Residential section extends along banks of lake and at foot of Zürichberg and Ütliberg mts. Industry centers in N; cars, radios, clothes, paper, canned products, beer, flour, pastry, fats, silk and woolen textiles, cement, chemicals, tobacco, woodworking; it is a printing and publishing center. Also a large tourist resort (served by Kloten and Dübendorf airports). Zurich is noted for the Grossmünster (11th-13th cent.; Romanesque) and the Fraumünster (13th-15th cent.), both Protestant churches, Univ. of Zurich (1832), Technical Acad. (1855), Swiss Natl. Mus. (mainly historical), art gall., Industrial Art Mus., Central Library, and city hall (1693-98). Has botanical and zoölogical gardens, several parks.

Zurich. 1 City (pop. 186), Rooks co., N central Kansas, 23 mi. ESE of Hill City. **2** Village, Blaine co., N Mont., on Milk R. and 10 mi. E of Chinook; trading and shipping point in sugar-beet region.

Zurich, Lake of, Ger. *Zürichsee* (tsü'rĭkhzā"), or *Zürichersee* (tsü'rĭkhŭrzā"), N Switzerland, bordering on cantons of Zurich, Schwyz, and St. Gall; c.25 mi. long, □ 34, alt. 1,332 ft., max. depth 469 ft.; long and narrow in shape. Causeway (1,017 yds. long) with swing bridge connects Rapperswil (N shore) with Hurden (S shore) and is used by railway and other traffic; E of causeway lake is called Obersee. Linth R. enters lake (E) through Linth Canal, which connects it with L. of Wallenstadt; emerges as Limmat R. in N, at Zurich. Fine views of the Alps (S). Its shores rise in gentle slopes, covered with vineyards and orchards, to wooded hills; they are dotted with houses, villas, and factories. ZURICH (N) is only large town on lake. Ufenau, an isl. SW of Rapperswil, has belonged since 965 to the monastery of Einsiedeln; Ulrich von Hutten sought refuge here in 1523.

Zurite, Peru: see SURITE.

Zurmi (zōōr'mē), town (pop. 11,154), Sokoto prov., Northern Provinces, NW Nigeria, 20 mi. NE of Kaura Namoda; agr. trade center (cotton, millet, peanuts, cattle, skins).

Zuromin (zhōōrô'mēn), Pol. *Żuromin*, Rus. *Zhuromin* (zhōōrô'myĭn), town (pop. 2,235), Warszawa prov., N central Poland, 20 mi. W of Mlawa; flour and groat milling.

Zurrieq (zōōr-ryĕk') or **Zurrico** (dzōōr-rē'kō), Maltese *Żurrieq*, village (parish pop. 5,359), S Malta, 5 mi. SSW of Valletta, in agr. region (citrus fruit,

grapes; goats). Has 16th-cent. houses and large palace. Environs are rich in megalithic remains.
Zürs (tsürs), village, Vorarlberg, W Austria, 26 mi. E of Feldkirch; popular winter resort (alt. 5,320 ft.) in the Arlberg.
Zuru (zōō'rōō), town (pop. 4,716), Sokoto prov., Northern Provinces, NW Nigeria, 115 mi. S of Sokoto; agr. trade (cotton, durra, cattle, skins).
Zurulum, Turkey: see CORLU.
Zurumuato, Mexico: see PASTOR ORTIZ.
Zurzach (tsōōr'tsäkh), town (pop. 2,025), Aargau canton, N Switzerland, on the Rhine (Ger. border; bridge) and 21 mi. NNW of Zurich; mfg. (soda, shoes), woodworking. Brine baths. Near by are Klingnau (W), Rekingen (SE), and Beznau (SW) hydroelectric plants.
Zurzuna, Turkey: see CILDIR.
Züschen (tsü'shün), town (pop. 1,006), in former Prussian prov. of Hesse-Nassau, W Germany, after 1945 in Hesse, 15 mi. SW of Kassel; mfg. of chemicals. Until 1929 in former Waldeck principality.
Zushi, Japan: see YOKOSUKA, Kanagawa prefecture.
Zutphen (zût'fün), town (pop. 21,714), Gelderland prov., E central Netherlands, at junction of Ijssel and Berkel rivers, near W end of Twente Canal, and 16 mi. NE of Arnhem; rail junction; dairy and lumber center; mfg. (bricks, soap, glue, furniture, clothing), machine shops, tobacco processing, meat packing, printing. Has 12th-cent. Gothic church, 17th-cent. Stadswijnhuis (town winehouse), 18th-cent. town hall. Sometimes spelled Zutfen.
Zuurbrak (sür'bräk), village (pop. 1,357), SW Cape Prov., U. of So. Afr., on Buffeljagts R. and 12 mi. E of Swellendam, at foot of Langeberg range; mission station; wheat, fruit, feed crops.
Zuviría, Argentina: see FACUNDO ZUVIRÍA.
Zuya (zōō'yü), village (1926 pop. 1,600), central Crimea, Russian SFSR, 12 mi. NE of Simferopol; flour mill; wheat, orchards.
Zuyder Zee, Netherlands: see ZUIDER ZEE; IJSSELMEER.
Zuyevka (zōō'yĭfkŭ). **1** City (1939 pop. over 10,000), E Kirov oblast, Russian SFSR, on railroad, near Cheptsa R., and 55 mi. E of Kirov; paper-milling center. Became city in 1944. **2** Town (1926 pop. 2,487), E central Stalino oblast, Ukrainian SSR, in the Donbas, 4 mi. ENE of Khartsyzsk; anthracite mines.
Zuyevo, Russian SFSR: see OREKHOVO-ZUYEVO.
Zvanka, Russian SFSR: see VOLKHOV, city.
Zvecan or **Zvechan** (both: zvĕ'chän), Serbo-Croatian *Zvečan*, village (pop. 5,423), S Serbia, Yugoslavia, on railroad and 4 mi. NW of Mitrovica, within bend of Ibar R., in the Kosovo. Produces concentrates of lead, zinc, pyrite, and copper ores. Has lead smelter. Aerial ropeway to TREPCA mine.
Zvenigorod (zvĭnyē'gŭrŭt), city (1926 pop. 3,144), central Moscow oblast, Russian SFSR, on Moskva R. and 30 mi. W of Moscow; resort and excursion center; knitting and lumber mills, metalworks. Has remains of fortress (11th-14th cent.) and Uspenski cathedral (1393), with frescoes. Chartered 1328. During Second World War, reached (1941) by advance Ger. units in Moscow campaign.
Zvenigorodka (zvĕ"nyĕgŭrôt'kŭ), city (1926 pop. 18,018), S Kiev oblast, Ukrainian SSR, 40 mi. ENE of Uman, in lignite-mining region; flour milling, fruit canning, dairying.
Zvenigovo (zvĭnyē'gŭvŭ), town (1948 pop. over 10,000), S Mari Autonomous SSR, Russian SFSR, on left bank of Volga R. and 40 mi. WNW of Kazan; ship repair yards; metalworking. Until c.1940, Zvenigovski Zaton.
Zverevo (zvĕ'ryĭvŭ), town (1926 pop. 2,388), W Rostov oblast, Russian SFSR, 22 mi. S of Kamensk; rail junction; metalworks.
Zverinogolovskoye (zvĭrē"nŭgŭlôf'skŭyŭ), village (1926 pop. 5,133), S Kurgan oblast, Russian SFSR, near Kazakh SSR border, on Tobol R., just below mouth of the Ubagan, and 65 mi. S of Kurgan; metalworks, dairy plant. A Rus. frontier post in 18th cent.
Zvijezda or **Zviyezda** (both: zvēyĕz'dä), mountain in Dinaric Alps, E Bosnia, Yugoslavia; highest point (4,428 ft.) is 4 mi. W of Vares.
Zvikov, Czechoslovakia: see PISEK.
Zviyezda, mountain, Yugoslavia: see ZVIJEZDA.
Zvolen (zvô'lĕn), Ger. *Altsohl* (ält'zōl), Hung. *Zólyom* (zō'yôm), town (pop. 12,641), S central Slovakia, Czechoslovakia, on Hron R. and 11 mi. S of Banska Bystrica; rail junction; trade center; mfg. (porcelain, glass), woodworking, cheese making. Has remains of 14th-cent. castle, former seat of Slovak Hussites. Health resort (alt. 1,180 ft.) of Sliac (slyäts), Slovak *Sliač*, Hung. *Szliácsfürdő*, with ferruginous arsenic and carbonic thermal springs (baths and wells), is 2 mi. NNE; exports table waters. Kovacova (kô'vächôvä), Slovak *Kováčova* (alt. 1,551 ft.), with radioactive and thermal springs, is 2 mi. NW.
Zvolen, Poland: see ZWOLEN.
Zvornik (zvôr'nĭk), town (pop. 3,974), E Bosnia, Yugoslavia, on Drina R. (Serbia border) and 23 mi. ESE of Tuzla; local trade center. Hydroelectric plant planned (1947) here. Has 11-span stone bridge (16th cent.) and ruins of medieval fortress. Seat of Orthodox Eastern metropolitan under Turkish rule. Formerly Turkish *Izvornik*.
Zwai, Lake (zwī), Ital. *Zuai* (□ c.150), S central Ethiopia, northernmost of chain of lakes in Great Rift Valley, 65 mi. S of Addis Ababa; 8°N 38°50'E; alt. 6,056 ft.; 20 mi. long, 12 mi. wide. Has outlet (S) to L. Hora Abyata. Contains 5 inhabited isls. and several islets. Largest (2 mi. long) is Tulugudu (pop. 300).
Zwalmen, Netherlands: see SWALMEN.
Zwartberg (zvärt'bĕrkh), town, Limburg prov., NE Belgium, 3 mi. NE of Genk; coal mining.
Zwartberg, U. of So. Afr.: see SWARTBERG.
Zwartewater (zvärt'ŭvätŭr), river, Overijssel prov., N central Netherlands; branches from Ijssel R. near Zwolle; flows 14 mi. NNW, past Hasselt and Zwartsluis, to the Ijsselmeer 2.5 mi. W of Zwartsluis. Joined by Overijssel Canal at Zwolle, by Vecht R. 3 mi. N of Zwolle, by the Meppelerdiep at Zwartsluis.
Zwartkop (svärt'kôp), airport, S central Transvaal, U. of So. Afr., 7 mi. SSW of Pretoria; 25°50'S 28°10'E; alt. 4,770 ft.
Zwartkops (–kôps), N residential suburb of Port Elizabeth, S Cape Prov., U. of So. Afr., on Algoa Bay at mouth of short Zwartkops R.; resort.
Zwartruggens (svärt'rŭ"khŭns), town (pop. 2,097), SW Transvaal, U. of So. Afr., 35 mi. W of Rustenburg, at foot of NW Witwatersrand; alt. 4,099 ft.; fruit, wheat, oats, cotton.
Zwartsluis (zvärtslois'), town (pop. 2,940), Overijssel prov., N central Netherlands, on the Meppelerdiep and 9 mi. N of Zwolle; coffee-extract mfg.; chalk quarrying.
Zweibrücken (tsvī"brü'kŭn), Fr. *Deux-Ponts* (dû-pō'), city (1939 pop. 30,714; 1946 pop. 23,099; 1950 pop. 25,725), Rhenish Palatinate, W Germany, 22 mi. SW of Kaiserslautern, on Saar border; 49°15'N 7°22'E. Rail junction. Second World War destruction (c.80%) severely curtailed industrial (metal, leather, textile, wood) activity. Brickworks. Noted 15th-, 18th-, and 19th-cent. churches were destroyed. Baroque ducal castle was heavily damaged. First mentioned 1170. Chartered 1352. Passed to Wittelsbachs in 1385. Was ⊙ independent duchy of Pfalz-Zweibrücken from 1410 until Elector Maximilian united all Wittelsbach holdings (see BAVARIA). Captured by U.S. troops in March, 1945.
Zweisimmen (tsvī'zĭmŭn), town (pop. 2,492), Bern canton, SW central Switzerland, at confluence of Simme and Kleine Simme rivers, 18 mi. SW of Thun; year-round resort. Medieval church.
Zwenkau (tsĕng'kou), town (pop. 11,821), Saxony, E central Germany, on the White Elster and 9 mi. SSW of Leipzig; brick and shoe mfg., brewing.
Zwentendorf (tsvĕnt'ŭndôrf), town (pop. 2,316), central Lower Austria, on the Danube and 6 mi. W of Tulln; grain, orchards.
Zwettl Stadt (tsvĕt'ŭl shtät), town (pop. 4,019), NW Lower Austria, on Kamp R. and 23 mi. NW of Krems; mfg. of fustian. Has Cistercian abbey with 12th-cent. Romanesque church.
Zwevegem (zwā'vŭ-khŭm), town (pop. 8,653), West Flanders prov., W Belgium, 3 mi. ESE of Courtrai, in flax-growing area; electric-power station. Formerly spelled Sweveghem.
Zwevezele (zwā'vŭzālŭ), agr. village (pop. 5,021), West Flanders prov., W Belgium, 10 mi. S of Bruges. Formerly spelled Swevezeele.
Zwickau, Czechoslovakia: see CVIKOV.
Zwickau (tsvĭ'kou), city (pop. 122,862), Saxony, E central Germany, on the Zwickauer Mulde and 40 mi. S of Leipzig, in major coal-mining region; 50°43'N 12°30'E. Rail junction; cotton and woolen milling and knitting, paper milling; mfg. of machinery, automobiles, tractors, chemicals, storage batteries, electrical and mining equipment, china, bricks, pianos. Has 15th-cent. basilica, 14th-cent. church of St. Catherine, and 15th-cent. town hall. Robert Schumann b. here. Founded in 11th cent.; chartered 1212. Was free imperial city from 1290 to 1323, then passed to margraves of Meissen. Thomas Münzer here founded Anabaptist movement. Repeatedly plundered during Thirty Years War. Bombed in Second World War.
Zwickauer Mulde (tsvĭ'kou"ŭr mōōl'dŭ), river in E central Germany, rises in the Erzegebirge 2 mi. E of Schöneck near Czechoslovak border, flows c.80 mi. generally N, past Aue, Zwickau, and Glauchau, joining the FREIBERGER MULDE 2 mi. N of Colditz to form MULDE RIVER. Receives Chemnitz R.
Zwiesel (tsvē'zŭl), town (pop. 9,102), Lower Bavaria, Germany, in Bohemian Forest, on the Black Regen and 18 mi. NE of Deggendorf; rail junction; mfg. of cut glass, lenses, precision instruments, machinery; brewing, woodworking, lumber milling. Winter-sports center (alt. 1,899 ft.). Has glassworking school. Chartered 1471.
Zwijnaarde (zwīn'ärdŭ), town (pop. 4,923), East Flanders prov., NW Belgium, on Scheldt R. and 4 mi. S of Ghent; artificial-silk mfg. Formerly spelled Zwynaerde.
Zwijndrecht (zwīn'drĕkht), town (pop. 7,232), Antwerp prov., N Belgium, 4 mi. W of Antwerp; agr. market. Sometimes spelled Zwyndrecht.
Zwijndrecht (zvīn'drĕkht), town (pop. 12,524), South Holland prov., W Netherlands, on the Old Maas and 1 mi. NW of Dordrecht; mfg. (chemicals, synthetic fertilizer, edible fats); salt and rice processing, jute spinning; shipbuilding; fruit and vegetable market.
Zwingenberg (tsvĭng'ŭnbĕrk), village (pop. 3,148), S Hesse, W Germany, in former Starkenburg prov., on the Bergstrasse, at W foot of the Odenwald, 2.5 mi. N of Bensheim, at W foot of the Malchen; fruit; vineyards.
Zwingle (zwĭng'gŭl), town (pop. 132), on Dubuque-Jackson co. line, E Iowa, 14 mi. S of Dubuque; dairying.
Zwischenahn or **Bad Zwischenahn** (bät" tsvĭ'-shŭnän), village (commune pop. 16,471), in Oldenburg, NW Germany, after 1945 in Lower Saxony, on S shore of the Zwischenahner Meer (lake), 9 mi. NW of Oldenburg city; mfg. of wool; food processing (ham, sausage, preserves). Resort.
Zwischenwässern, Yugoslavia: see MEDVODE.
Zwittau, Czechoslovakia: see SVITAVY.
Zwolen (zvô'lĕnyŭ), Pol. *Zwoleń*, Rus. *Zvolen* or *Zvolen'* (both: zvô'lyĭnyŭ), town (pop. 4,813), Kielce prov., E central Poland, 19 mi. E of Radom; brick mfg., tanning, flour milling.
Zwolle (zvô'lŭ), town (pop. 47,462), ⊙ Overijssel prov., N central Netherlands, on the Zwartewater, on Overijssel Canal and 18 mi. N of Deventer; 52°31'N 6°6'E. Rail junction; chemicals, metal products, clothing, edible fats, dairy products; printing industry. Site of 15th-cent. Gothic church of St. Michael, 15th-cent. town hall and town gate, many other Renaissance buildings. On near-by Agnietenberg is 14th-cent. monastery, residence (1407–71) of Thomas à Kempis.
Zwolle (zwŏ'lē), town (pop. 1,555), Sabine parish, W La., 60 mi. S of Shreveport, near Texas line; oil industry (since 1928) has replaced lumber in importance. Settled 1896.
Zwönitz (tsvû'nĭts), town (pop. 7,500), Saxony, E central Germany, at N foot of the Erzgebirge, 15 mi. SSW of Chemnitz; hosiery knitting, cotton milling, metalworking; mfg. of shoes, electrical equipment.
Zwynaerde, Belgium: see ZWIJNAARDE.
Zwyndrecht, Belgium: see ZWIJNDRECHT.
Zychlin (zhĭkh'lēn), Pol. *Żychlin*, Rus. *Zhikhlin* (zhĭkh'lēn), town (pop. 6,019), Lodz prov., central Poland, 10 mi. E of Kutno; mfg. of machinery, beet-sugar and flour milling.
Zydaczow, Ukrainian SSR: see ZHIDACHOV.
Zyezdki or **Z"yezdki** (zyĕst'kē), town (1939 pop. over 500), central Kharkov oblast, Ukrainian SSR, near Zmiyev, 18 mi. S of Kharkov. Also called Zidki or Zid'ki.
Zygos, Greece: see ARAKYNTHOS.
Zykh (zĭkh), town (pop. over 2,000), in Kaganovich dist. of Greater Baku, Azerbaijan SSR, on S Apsheron Peninsula, 7 mi. E of Baku; oil wells; textile and food industries.
Zyohen, Japan: see JOHEN.
Zyohozi, Japan: see JOHOJI.
Zyosin, Korea: see SONGJIN.
Zyrardow (zhĭrär'dōōf), Pol. *Żyrardów*, Rus. *Zhirardov* (zhĭrär'dŭf), city (pop. 20,186), Warszawa prov., E central Poland, on railroad and 27 mi. WSW of Warsaw. Textile (cotton, linen) center; mfg. of railroad cars, clothing; tanning, distilling, brewing, flour milling. Brown-coal deposits near by. Named after F. Girard, founder of a weaving mill which was moved here in 1833.
Zyrian (or **Zyryan**) **Autonomous Oblast**, Russian SFSR: see KOMI AUTONOMOUS SOVIET SOCIALIST REPUBLIC.
Zyrnovon, Greece: see KATO NEUROKOPION.
Zyryanka (zĭryän'kŭ), town (1940 pop. over 500), NE Yakut Autonomous SSR, Russian SFSR, on Kolyma R., at mouth of Zyryanka R., and 135 mi. S of Sredne-Kolymsk; coal-mining center. Developed in 1930s just N of Verkhne-Kolymsk, an old Siberian colonization center dating from 17th cent.
Zyryanka River, NE Yakut Autonomous SSR, Russian SFSR, rises in Cherski Range, flows c.125 mi. NNE to Kolyma R. at Zyryanka. Lignite deposits along its course.
Zyryanovsk (zĭryä'nŭfsk), city (1939 pop. over 10,000), E East Kazakhstan oblast, Kazakh SSR, near Bukhtarma R., 70 mi. ESE of Ust-Kamenogorsk; silver-lead- and zinc-mining center.
Zyryanovski or **Zyryanovskiy** (–skē), town (1941 pop. over 500), central Sverdlovsk oblast, Russian SFSR, on Neiva R. and 8 mi. SSW (under jurisdiction) of Alapayevsk; iron-mining center.
Zyryanskoye (–skŭyŭ), village (1926 pop. 1,558), SE Tomsk oblast, Russian SFSR, on Chulym R., at mouth of Kiya R., and 65 mi. ENE of Tomsk, in agr. area.
Zyukaika or **Zyukayka** (zyōōkī'kŭ), town (1943 pop. over 500), W Molotov oblast, Russian SFSR, 8 mi. N of Vereshchagino; mfg. of transportation equipment, metalworking. Flax processing near by.
Zyuzelski or **Zyuzel'skiy** (zyōōzĕl'skē), town (1938 pop. over 500), S Sverdlovsk oblast, Russian SFSR, in the central Urals, 4 mi. NNW of Polevskoi; pyrite and copper mining.
Zywiec (zhĭ'vyĕts), Pol. *Żywiec*, Ger. *Saybusch* (zī'bōōsh), town (pop. 5,500), Krakow prov., S Poland, on Sola R. and 40 mi. SW of Cracow; rail junction; brewing, tanning, mfg. of paper, machinery. Hydroelectric plant. Castle with art works.

1961 SUPPLEMENT

Edited by CAROL WAGNER

with the assistance of

RUSSELL FREEDMAN and DAVID HAYDEN

SUPP.

NEW NATIONS AND MAJOR GEOGRAPHICAL CHANGES

Since the Gazetteer was published in 1952, the world has been in turmoil. New nations have been carved out of colonies formerly belonging to European states; some trusteeship territories and protectorates have been promoted to independence; boundaries have been changed; the status of governments and populations in various regions has been adjusted or even revolutionized. This brief Supplement attempts to note the most important of these alterations. Inevitably, then, the articles are largely concerned with political shifts and political creations, with some attention to social conditions. The sole criterion for selecting the headings has been usefulness to the reader.

Severe limitations were, therefore, placed upon the compilers of the Supplement. Many countries that have played an important part, even a dominant part, in events of the period 1952–1961, have of necessity been ignored. Since the Supplement is not a record of events, many notable events appear not at all. Some countries with major roles in world history are represented only by notes on administrative or territorial changes; the United States and the USSR are examples.

So brief a survey cannot supply exhaustive information, nor would it have been possible to collect reliable data on many of the areas where conditions are in flux. Neither space nor time will permit lengthy lists bristling with reservations about the facts. The aim has been simplicity.

The Supplement is in no sense a revision of the book itself. Instead it is intended as a compilation of true supplementary material to be read along with the articles in the original printing of the book. If, for example, no significant change has been made in the area of a unit when it has changed from a colonial possession to an independent republic, the area given in the Gazetteer itself is not repeated. Though population figures are given for every new nation, the figures are not given for long-established states or regions, where unless the figure has altered by a large percent, the population figure is not repeated and the reader is left to find it in the original Gazetteer. As a consequence the entries may show a seeming, though not a real inconsistency, thus for Ghana both area and population are given, but for some of the neighboring states only the population appears.

The Supplement has a very few and insignificant variations from the usual style practices of the Gazetteer proper. Names of countries are usually given in fuller form, because those in the Supplement are usually much more unfamiliar than those of the original book, and the longer form is much more rapidly communicated to readers. In some cases, the fuller form is useful to distinguish a political unit from a region or a former territory sharing the name in part, for instance, Republic of Sudan, as distinct from Sudan (region), Anglo-Egyptian Sudan (predecessor state), French Sudan (former colony) and the Sudanese Republic (now the Republic of Mali). In another case, an arbitrary distinction has been made. The former French Congo is called Congo Republic; the former Belgian Congo is called Republic of the Congo. This device seemed much less unwieldy than Congo (Brazzaville) and Congo (Leopoldville).

Abbreviations are used more sparingly in the Supplement than in the original book—again for ease of comprehension. Otherwise the Supplement will offer no surprises in style to the users of the Gazetteer.

The compilers have, of course, done their best to obtain and present the most accurate and usable data available. Official publications have been studied with some care. Information officers of various countries have been questioned to the point of their annoyance. It has been necessary to augment the statements of governments and private agencies by perusal of the newspapers and some periodicals. No detail has been too small for attention, though some of the information proved of no value for so compressed a listing. Area and population figures have been mostly derived from official sources. Where, as in the case of India, a census report has been made available, those figures have been used. In general official estimates have supplied the needed figures. We are greatly indebted to various officials and workers at the UN for giving us information and for checking some materials.

The Census of the United States for 1960 has been canvassed, and a separate section of the Supplement is devoted to listing the figures for all places with a population of more than 1,000.

The information gathered takes the reader through Dec. 31, 1961. Obtaining up-to-the-minute data has offered many difficulties and even literally headaches. Since the situations across the world are fluid, surety has not always been possible. There may be errors and in some cases the information obtained may be outdated even before this Supplement has come from the press. We regret possible deficiencies and hope that the Supplement may prove useful.

Abidjan, capital of the Republic of the Ivory Coast; until 1958 capital of the French overseas territory of Ivory Coast.

Accra, capital of Ghana; until 1957 capital of the British colony of the Gold Coast.

Alaska, the 49th state of the United States, admitted Jan. 3, 1959; formerly a U.S. territory. An important provision of the State Enabling Act (July, 1958) gave Alaska the right to select 103,550,000 acres of unappropriated public lands in order to establish an adequate tax base; lands in areas of strategic importance for national security were to remain under Federal control. Citizens of the territory approved statehood in a special referendum in Aug., 1959; in November they elected state officials and representatives to Congress. The first new state to be admitted to the United States since the entry of Arizona and New Mexico in 1912, Alaska ranks last among the states in population and first in area.

Algeria, region of N Africa (1959 est. pop. 10,930,000); since 1959 divided into 13 departments—Algiers (Alger), Tizi-Ouzou, Orléansville, Médéa, Oran, Tlemcen, Mostaganem, Tiaret, Constantine, Bône, Sétif, Batna, and Saida—besides the two SAHARAN DEPARTMENTS. Tension between the French administration and Moslem nationalists flared into the open revolt of the nationalists in Nov., 1954. Years of violence followed, with guerrilla warfare, riots, murder, and terrorism, and Algeria was a center of attention for all the world. The struggle was three-cornered with the French government opposing on the one hand the Moslem nationalists, and on the other the European colonists backed by the army and some rightest Moslems in an effort to keep Algeria French. The extremist right forces of the European Algerians rebelled in May, 1958, opposing attempts to conciliate the nationalist Moslems. This revolt precipitated the downfall of the Fourth Republic of France, which was succeeded by the Fifth Republic, with Gen. Charles de Gaulle as its head (first as premier, then as president). The rightists again rioted in Jan., 1960, with no success and in April, 1961, an Army revolt against Gen. de Gaulle failed. Yet the dissident elements, aided by rightists in France, had created the Secret Army Organization (OAS) to oppose by terrorism any conciliation of the Moslem nationalists. The French government sought to reach agreement with the Moslem provisional government set up in Tunisia, and after open parleys fell through, secret negotiations went on. Moslem rebel forces of the National Liberal Front (FLN) continued intermittent warfare. On Dec. 29, 1961, President de Gaulle voiced hope of a settlement under terms of Algerian independence and withdrawal of French troops from Algeria, but the year ended with violence still dominant.

Anglo-Egyptian Sudan: see SUDAN, REPUBLIC OF THE.

Angola or **Portuguese West Africa.** Protests by nationalists against Portuguese rule resulted in 1961 in raids against the whites and in open rebellion. The uprising was quelled by force, and the UN Security Council censured Portuguese methods of repression and proposed that a UN commission be sent to investigate conditions. Portugal rejected all UN action. The promises of gradual approaches to freedom for all the peoples of Angola, made earlier, were not rescinded.

Antarctica. In 1959, partly as a result of international scientific cooperation during the International Geophysical Year (1957-58), twelve nations—the United States, Great Britain, France, the USSR., Belgium, Australia, Argentina, Chile, Japan, Norway, Union of South Africa, and New Zealand—signed a treaty defining the political status of the antarctic continent; the treaty went into force in 1961 after ratification by the signatories. Under its terms, the entire continent is opened freely to scientific and technical teams; all territorial claims are suspended (but not renounced) for a period of 34 years and the signatories agree not to make new claims during that period; military installations and nuclear testing and stockpiling are banned; the signatories are guaranteed unlimited inspection and overflight rights in all areas to insure that the agreement is not being violated. One of the major findings to have emerged from recent exploration of the Antarctic was evidence suggesting that the continent is divided into three distinct land masses, wholly or partially separated by two deep, ice-filled channels. Other findings included discoveries of mountain ranges with peaks rising to 17,000 ft. above sea level; small valleys within 300 mi. of the South Pole almost entirely free of ice and snow; numerous minerals suggesting the possible existence of large and potentially valuable mineral deposits.

Ashkhabad, oblast, W Turkmen SSR, was dissolved in 1960.

Austria, recognized as a sovereign, independent state with the signing (May 15, 1955) of the Austrian State Treaty by the four occupying powers and the Second Republic of Austria (est. 1945). The peace treaty went into effect in July, 1955, and the last occupation troops left the country in October. As a condition of the treaty, Austria agreed to remain permanently neutral. Austria was admitted to the UN in 1955.

Baden-Württemberg, state of West Germany (German Federal Republic); ⊙ Stuttgart. The state was formed (1952) by a merger of the states Baden, Württemberg-Baden, and Württemberg-Hohenzollern, all of which were formed in 1945. The merger was approved by the electorate of the three states in a plebiscite held in Dec., 1951.

Bamako, capital of the Mali Republic; formerly (1958-1960) capital of the Sudanese Republic and, prior to that, capital of the French overseas territory of French Sudan.

Bangui, capital of the Central African Republic; until 1958 capital of the French overseas territory of Ubangi-Shari.

Belgian Congo: see CONGO, REPUBLIC OF THE.

Brasília, city (1961 pop. 130,968), ⊙ Brazil, inaugurated 1960. W central Brazil; occupies W central section of newly created Federal District (□c.2,260) within SW Goiás state; 575 mi. NW of Rio de Janeiro; 15°48′S 47°53′W. A plan was approved by Congress in 1956 to move the federal capital from Rio de Janeiro in the coastal area to a site on Brazil's high central plateau (alt. c.3,500 ft.), a

Area in square miles is indicated by the symbol □, capital city by the symbol ⊙.

region of low humidity, little temperature variation (average winter temp. 66°; summer 72°), and ample surface water supplies. In March, 1957, an international jury selected a plan for Brasília submitted by Brazilian architect Lucio Costa. By the time of the official inauguration (April, 1960) a substantial city had emerged from virtual wilderness. Costa's unconventional plan and the ultramodern architecture of Oscar Niemeyer (who designed all the civic buildings) combined to fashion a city striking and unique, distinguished throughout by broad avenues, promenades, and open areas; all industry was to be relegated to outlying suburbs. Planned to accommodate a population in excess of 500,000 by the mid-1960s, Brasília was created partly in the hope of spurring development of Brazil's sparsely-populated and little-exploited central region.

Brazzaville, capital of the Congo Republic; until 1958 capital of French Equatorial Africa.

British Cameroons, until 1961 a UN trust territory administered by Great Britain through Nigeria. After long negotiations and changes in organization, separate plebiscites were held in the northern and southern sections. The northern section voted to join the Federation of Nigeria and the southern section voted to merge with the Cameroon Republic.

British Commonwealth of Nations. The attainment of independence by former British colonies after 1949 added the following self-governing member-states to the Commonwealth: Ghana (1957); Federation of Malaya (1957); Federation of Nigeria (1960); Cyprus (1961); Sierra Leone (1961). The relationship between Commonwealth members and the Crown of the United Kingdom varies. India, Pakistan, and Ghana were formerly dominions recognizing the sovereignty of the crown; in 1950, 1956, and 1960 respectively they became republics with their own heads of state and acknowledged the British monarch merely as head of the Commonwealth. Cyprus joined the Commonwealth as a republic. Malaya, while not a republic, has its own head of state and also accepts the Queen as head of the Commonwealth. Nigeria and Sierra Leone formally recognize the Queen (represented by a governor-general) as their head of state. In 1961 the Union of South Africa became a republic and subsequently withdrew from the Commonwealth.

British Somaliland, merged with Italian Somaliland to form SOMALIA in 1960.

Cambodia, attained full sovereignty in 1954. Previously, as an associated state within the French Union, Cambodia had limited autonomy; France controlled the state's foreign affairs and retained authority in certain military, police, judicial, economic and other matters. Transfer of police and judicial powers from France to Cambodia in Aug., 1953, was followed by transfer of authority over the Cambodian armed forces on Nov. 9 (which Cambodia considers its effective date of independence). Transfer of full sovereignty was completed when remaining economic and financial ties with France were severed under an agreement signed in Dec., 1954. Earlier in 1954 Cambodia had been drawn into the final stages of the Indochinese war with the invasion of Communist Vietminh troops from neighboring Vietnam; these troops were aided by Cambodian rebel guerrilla bands organized as the Khmer Issarak. The Geneva agreements (July, 1954) ending the war provided for the withdrawal of both Vietminh and French Union troops, demobilization of Khmer Issarak forces, and free elections which were to be open to all Cambodian citizens, including members of former dissident groups. The elections called for by the Geneva agreements were held in Sept., 1955; supporters of Prince Norodom Sihanouk (who as king had led the country's independence movement) won all 91 seats in the national assembly. Prince Sihanouk thereafter served as premier of several governments; whatever his official position at any given time, however, he remained the dominant force in Cambodian politics and followed a rigidly neutral course in foreign affairs, accepting economic aid from both Western and Communist powers. By the end of 1961 his policies had kept Cambodia relatively free of the armed internal opposition and external pressures which were threatening the regimes in neighboring Laos and South Vietnam. Cambodia was admitted to the UN in 1955.

Cameroon Republic, independent state (□ 193,681; 1959 est. pop. 3,225,000), W Africa; ⊙ Yaoundé; formerly French Cameroons, a UN trust territory under French administration. It borders W on the Gulf of Guinea, NW on Nigeria, N on Lake Chad, E on the Republic of Chad and the Central African Republic, S on the Congo Republic, Gabon, and Río Muni (Spanish Guinea). From 1955 into 1960 the progress of the French Cameroons toward independence was marked by an unrest stemming partly from agitations of nationalists and partly from conflicts within tribal and regional groups. An active anti-French and nationalist minority party, Union of the Peoples of the Cameroons, demanded immediate independence after special elections; its exiled leaders directed bands of guerrilla fighters and terrorists within the French Cameroons. In 1957 France granted the territory extensive self-government, and in Jan., 1959, full autonomy passed to the territorial government headed by Premier Ahmadou Adhijo. In March the UN voted to terminate the trusteeship, and on Jan. 1, 1960, independence was proclaimed. As terrorism abated toward the close of 1960, educational and other reforms designed to unify the country were introduced. The discovery of oil and bauxite promised to strengthen the nation's economy. The southern section of the British Cameroons joined with the Cameroon Republic as a self-governing province in Oct., 1961. Cameroon was admitted to the UN in 1960.

Cameroons: see BRITISH CAMEROONS; CAMEROON REPUBLIC

Central African Republic, independent state (1959 est. pop. 1,185,000), central Africa; ⊙ Bangui; formerly the French overseas territory of Ubangi-Shari. It borders S on the Republic of the Congo and the Congo Republic, E on Sudan, N on Chad, W on Cameroon. In June, 1956, France granted to the territory universal direct suffrage and more extensive internal self-government. In the French constitutional referendum of Sept. 28, 1958, Ubangi-Shari voted to join the FRENCH COMMUNITY, and in Dec., 1958, the territorial assembly proclaimed the establishment of the Central African Republic as an autonomous member of the Community. Independence was attained in 1960, the republic becoming a member of the remodeled Community. The republic in 1959 joined in a customs union with the Congo Republic, Chad, and Gabon. In May, 1960, together with the Congo Republic and Chad, the Central African Republic formed an organization for the coordination of the members' foreign affairs and of their policies relating to money and credit. The Central African Republic was admitted to the UN in 1960.

Chad, Republic of, independent state (1958 est. pop. 2,600,000), central Africa; ⊙ Fort-Lamy; formerly the French overseas territory of Chad. It borders S on the Central African Republic, E on Sudan, N on Libya, W on Niger, Cameroon, and (along Lake Chad) Nigeria. In June, 1956, France granted the territory universal direct suffrage and more self-government. In the French constitutional referendum of Sept. 28, 1958, Chad voted to join the FRENCH COMMUNITY, and in Nov., 1958, the territorial assembly, acting as a constituent assembly, proclaimed the Republic of Chad as an autonomous member of the Community. After the French constitution was amended in June, 1960, Chad initialed agreements by which France transferred to Chad the control of those common affairs under the jurisdiction of the Community. Initialed at the same time were agreements of cooperation between the two states within the framework of the remodeled Community. In Aug., 1960, both sets of these agreements were signed and Chad received its independence. In Jan., 1959, Chad formed a customs union with the other former members of French Equatorial Africa (Republic of Gabon, Central African Republic, Congo Republic), and in May, 1960, together with the Congo Republic and the Central African Republic, signed a charter establishing an organization for coordinating the members' policies on foreign affairs and on the control of money and credit. Chad was admitted to the UN in 1960.

Chechen-Ingush Autonomous Soviet Socialist Republic, reestablished as an ASSR in 1957 after having been abolished in 1944 following the collaboration of its peoples with the Germans during the Second World War. (For history prior to 1944, see main body of the Gazetteer, p. 380.)

Ciudad Trujillo, city, Dominican Republic: see SANTO DOMINGO.

Conakry, capital of the Republic of Guinea; until 1958 capital of the French overseas territory of French Guinea.

Congo, Republic of the, independent state (1959 est. pop. 13,821,000), S central Africa; ⊙ Leopoldville; formerly the Belgian colony of the Belgian Congo. It borders N on the Central African Republic and Sudan, E on Uganda, Ruanda-Urundi, and Lake Tanganyika, SE and S on Northern Rhodesia, SW on Angola, W on the Atlantic, the Cabinda enclave of Angola, and the Congo Republic. Vigorous nationalist agitation brought concessions from Belgium, and in 1957, popular elections for councilmen were held in the larger cities of the Congo. Yet Belgian attempts to suppress the nationalists led to riots in Leopoldville and elsewhere. A plan offered (1959) by Belgium provided for Congolese autonomy by 1964; it had little or no effect. Finally, the Brussels Conference was held Jan.–Feb., 1960; Belgian and Congolese leaders agreed on a specific program leading to immediate independence. Elections for national and provincial legislatures were held in May and June. On the eve of its independence, the Congo appeared little prepared to enter the society of nations. Belgian rule had left the land with few able native administrators; the mass of the people lived under primitive conditions with no modern political organization; the economy had been seriously undermined by flights of foreign capital; the political scene was crowded with over 200 parties, with rivalries based on personal, tribal, and regional loyalties. Independence was formally proclaimed June 30, 1960. Almost immediately the new state fell prey to fierce tribal warfare, based on long-standing hostilities and giving rise to political and social upheavals (all the principal figures in the new Congo were tribal as well as political leaders). Riots, massacres, and pillage were the rule of the day. Army mutinies aggravated the situation. Against this background political rivalries were violent. Many provinces threatened secession. Chief among the politicians of the central Congolese government were Joseph Kasavubu, head of state (president), and Patrice Lumumba, premier of the new republic. Their quarrels were supplemented by the ambitions of other leaders. Weakness of authority, lack of trained administrators, and social disorganization aggravated the disorder. The rebellious secessionist states caused disruption. The withdrawal of the mineral-rich KATANGA was of particular importance and drew world-wide attention and concern. Both Kasavubu and Lumumba appealed to the United Nations for help in ousting foreign troops and restoring order in the Congo, and a UN resolution authorized (July, 1961) a UN force. When the force was gathered in the Congo and charged with nonintervention and removal of foreign soldiers from all the Congo, it had skirmishes with both factions of the central government, but settled down to the Katanga problem. Fiery Lumumba reviled the UN for not producing order and unity by giving aid to him. He was encouraged by the USSR, other nations of the Communist bloc, and some countries of Africa and Asia. His drive to power was halted for a time by a military coup led by Colonel Joseph Mobutu in Sept., 1960, which put the army in power. Lumumba was seized but was immediately freed and built a huge popular following with control of several provinces. On Dec. 1, he was arrested. Later he was moved to Katanga for imprisonment but before Feb. 12, 1961, he was murdered—allegedly after he escaped and was in flight. Chief among those who later claimed leadership of the Lumumba faction was the leftist Antoine Gizenga, who from Stanleyville held sway over much of the Congo. Bloody struggles continued through 1961, punctuated by unsuccessful efforts to knit the provinces together, impose some sort of order, and prepare for some development out of chaos.

Congo Republic, independent state (1959 est. pop. 795,000), W Africa; ⊙ Brazzaville; formerly the French overseas territory of Middle Congo. It is S of the African bulge and borders E and S on the Republic of the Congo, SW on Cabinda, W on the Atlantic and Gabon, NW on Cameroon, NE on the Central African Republic. In 1956 France granted the territory universal direct suffrage and more self-government. In the French constitutional referendum of Sept. 28, 1958, the Middle Congo voted to join the FRENCH COMMUNITY, and in Nov., 1958, the territorial assembly proclaimed the establishment of the Congo Republic as an autonomous member of the Community. In July, 1960, following negotiations, France agreed to transfer to the republic control over those external affairs previously under the jurisdiction of the Community. At the same time bilateral agreements were initialed to govern cooperation between France and the Congo Republic within the framework of the remodeled Community. The independence of the Congo Republic was formally proclaimed on Aug. 15, 1960. The Congo Republic formed a customs union with the other former members of French Equatorial Africa (Chad, Gabon, Central African Republic) in 1959, and in 1960, together with the Central African Republic and Chad signed a charter for an organization for the coordination of the members' policies in foreign affairs and in the control of money and credit. The Congo Republic was admitted to the UN in 1960.

Crimea, oblast in the Ukrainian SSR; until 1954 in the RSFSR.

Cyprus, Republic of, independent state, on the isl. of Cyprus; (1960 est. pop. 563,000); ⊙ Nicosia; formerly the British colony of Cyprus. The years following the Second World War were marked by mounting demands by the Greek Cypriot majority for independence and eventual union with Greece, and by opposing demands by the Turkish minority for protection against Greek domination. Various constitutional reforms proposed by the British were rejected or failed to gain approval of all parties. In 1955 Greek Cypriots launched a campaign of terror against British forces on the island, against the Turkish community, and eventually against Greek Cypriot "traitors." Early in 1959, after repeated appeals to the UN on the part of the Greek government, the prime ministers of Greece and Turkey met in Zurich in an attempt to reach a settlement. This meeting resulted in an agreement signed (Feb., 1959) by Turkey, Greece, and Britain, and declared acceptable by representatives of the Greek and Turkish Cypriots. The agreement provided for the establishment of a Cypriot republic with a government composed of a Greek president and a Turkish vice president, elected by the Greek and Turkish communities respectively; a council of ministers composed of seven Greek and three Turkish members, designated jointly by the president and vice president; and a legislature composed of 70 percent Greek and 30 percent Turkish representatives, elected by their respective communities. Negotiations continued, however, until Britain was granted sovereignty over areas containing its military bases. By July, 1960, agreement had been reached on all outstanding issues, and the following month the Republic was proclaimed as a sovereign state. Cyprus was admitted to the UN in 1960, and in March, 1961, became a member of the British Commonwealth of Nations.

Dahomey, Republic of, independent state (1959 est. pop. 2,000,000), W Africa; ⊙ Porto-Novo; formerly the French overseas territory of Dahomey. On the S coast of the African bulge; it borders S on the Gulf of Guinea, E on Nigeria, N on Niger and Upper Volta, W on Togo. In June, 1956, France granted universal direct suffrage and more self-government to the territory. In the French constitutional referendum of Sept. 28, 1958, Dahomey voted to join the FRENCH COMMUNITY. In Dec., 1958, the territorial assembly, acting as a constituent assembly, proclaimed the establishment of the Republic of Dahomey as an autonomous member of the Community. In May, 1959, Dahomey joined Ivory Coast, Niger, and Upper Volta to form a cooperative economic organization (the Council of the Entente). Following amendments to the French constitution in June, 1960, agreements were made by Dahomey and France for transfer to Dahomey of the control over those affairs maintained under the jurisdiction of the Community. On Aug. 1, 1960, the agreements were signed and the independence of Dahomey proclaimed. Dahomey was admitted to the UN in 1960.

Dakar, capital of the Republic of Senegal; formerly (1959–60) capital of the Mali Federation and, prior to 1959, capital of French West Africa.

Damão, India: see PORTUGUESE INDIA.

Diu, India: see PORTUGUESE INDIA.

Donetsk, city, Ukrainian SSR; formerly called Stalino.

East Germany: see GERMANY.

Egypt, republic (1959 est. pop. 25,365,000), NE Africa; ⊙ Cairo; formerly a kingdom, and, from 1958 to 1961, the Southern (Egyptian) region of the United Arab Republic. In Jan., 1952, a riot in Cairo expressed popular discontent with corruption and inefficiency in the government, and in July, 1952, Gen. Mohammed Naguib by a coup d'état forced the abdication of the King Farouk in favor of his infant son. Naguib was made president, but power was actually in the hands of a military junta, which in June, 1953, abolished the monarchy and declared Egypt a republic. A shifting of forces in the junta in 1954 brought Colonel Gamal Abdel Nasser to the fore. In June, 1956, a new constitution was approved by a referendum, which also made Nasser president. The constitution provided for a single political party (the National Union Party) committed to the establishment of a socialist, democratic society. Realization of this goal was blocked by Egypt's perennial problems, overpopulation and wide-spread poverty. A key project in Nasser's reform program was the construction at Aswan of a new, mammoth dam to increase arable land. Egyptian trouble with Israel over the Gaza region caused the United States and Great Britain to withdraw financial support for the dam, and Nasser in July, 1956, nationalized the Suez Canal. Israel promptly invaded Gaza and Sinai Peninsula. Great Britain and France attacked Egypt. International pressure forced all the invaders out, and Egypt agreed to pay indemnities to shareholders in the old Suez Canal Company. In Feb., 1958, in partial fulfillment of Nasser's pan-Arabist dreams, Syria and Egypt united to form the United Arab Republic. Increasing dominance of Egypt in the combined state, and Nasser's attempts to extend its program of socialization into Syria caused Syrians to revolt. Syria withdrew from the United Arab Republic in Sept., 1961. In October of that year Nasser acknowledged the dissolution of the union, while retaining the title United Arab Republic for the Egyptian region.

Eritrea, in 1952 federated with ETHIOPIA.

Ethiopia, in 1952 federated with Eritrea. The Imperial Government of Ethiopia was to control the defense, economic, and foreign policy of the federation, while Eritrea was to keep responsibility for its own internal self-government.

Fort-Lamy, capital of the Republic of Chad; until 1958 capital of the French overseas territory of Chad.

France. During the Fourth Republic (1946–58), the French political scene was marked by the rise and fall of 25 cabinets. Governmental instability, in part the result of the comparatively simple procedure required for the overthrow of cabinets, was aggravated by periodic crises in the colonial possessions in the French Union. Paramount among France's colonial problems was that of ALGERIA, which since the beginning of the Moslem nationalist revolt in Nov., 1954, had embroiled France in massive military operations in North Africa. In May, 1958, a rightist-military coup d'état in Algeria threatened to spread to France. In the ensuing crisis the cabinet fell, and in June General Charles de Gaulle was called to assume the premiership. The National Assembly accepted his demand that he be granted emergency powers for six months, the right to found a presidential republic, and the power to establish a new relationship between France and its possessions. On Sept. 28, 1958, General de Gaulle submitted to the members of the French Union the Constitution of the French Fifth Republic. The Constitution provided for improved governmental stability through the creation of a strong executive department under the leadership of a president; it also provided for alleviation of France's colonial problems through the replacing of the FRENCH UNION by the FRENCH COMMUNITY. Approval was secured and the Fifth Republic was proclaimed on Oct. 5, 1958.

French Cameroons: see CAMEROON REPUBLIC.

French Community, est. 1958, remodeled 1960. The original Community, superseding the French Union, was a quasi-political organization authorized by the Constitution of the French Fifth Republic. On Sept. 28, 1958, this constitution was submitted to the members remaining in the French Union at that date. Approval of the constitution permitted each territory the choice of one of three relationships to France: continuance of its existing status; establishment as a department of France; autonomy within the Community. Nonapproval entailed exclusion from the Community. Twelve territories—Chad, Middle Congo, Dahomey, Gabon, Ivory Coast, Madagascar, Niger, Mauritania, Senegal, Upper Volta, Ubangi-Shari, and French Sudan—opted for autonomy within the Community. French Guinea, the only nonapproving territory, was given independence immediately. The remainder of the Community (constituting the French Republic) comprises France, the Algerian departments (see ALGERIA) and SAHARAN DEPARTMENTS, the overseas departments of Martinique, Guadeloupe, Réunion, and Guiana, and the five overseas territories which voted to retain their status: French Polynesia, Comoro Islands, French Somaliland, New Caledonia, and St. Pierre and Miquelon. Wallis and Futuna Island became an overseas territory within the Community in 1960. Special status in relation to the Community was accorded to the Anglo-French condominium of New Hebrides and to the French Southern and Antarctic Lands. Two multinational units, the MALI FEDERATION and the Council of the Entente (comprising the republics of Dahomey, the Ivory Coast, the Niger, the Upper Volta), were formed in accordance with the provisions of the constitution establishing the Community. Members of the Community maintained their internal autonomy while submitting to the jurisdiction of the Community certain common concerns, such as foreign policy, economic policy, and defense. At the end of 1959, the autonomous members began to press for complete independence. The result was the remodeled Community. This came into existence after the French government amended the constitution (June, 1960), to allow nations assuming complete sovereignty to remain in the Community. Relationships within the remodeled Community were established through specific bilateral and multilateral agreements of the member states with France. Before the close of 1960, the 12 autonomous republics secured their independence. Those choosing to remain in the remodeled Community were the Central African Republic, the Congo Republic, Malagasy, Chad, Gabon, and Senegal.

French Equatorial Africa, four French overseas territories until the end of 1958, when the territories became autonomous republics. See CHAD, REPUBLIC OF; CONGO REPUBLIC; GABON, REPUBLIC OF; CENTRAL AFRICAN REPUBLIC.

French Guinea: see GUINEA, REPUBLIC OF.

French India. The settlements of Pondicherry, Karikal, Mahé, and Yanam were formally ceded by France to India in 1956.

French Sudan: see MALI, REPUBLIC OF.

French Union. In the period 1954–1958, a gradual withering away of the territories of the Union took place. The remaining French settlements in India (Pondicherry, Karikal, Mahé, and Yanam) were ceded formally to India in 1956. The associate states of Vietnam, Laos, and Cambodia withdrew from the Union in 1954, although the latter two retained representation in the assembly of the organization until 1958. The protectorates of Tunisia and Morocco left the Union when they were granted independence in 1956. In 1958, after the establishment of the French Fifth Republic, the French Union was superseded by the FRENCH COMMUNITY.

French West Africa, eight French overseas territories until 1958, when seven of the territories entered the French Community as autonomous republics and the eighth became independent. See DAHOMEY, REPUBLIC OF; GUINEA, REPUBLIC OF; IVORY COAST, REPUBLIC OF THE; MALI, REPUBLIC OF; MAURITANIA, ISLAMIC REPUBLIC OF; NIGER, REPUBLIC OF THE; SENEGAL, REPUBLIC OF; UPPER VOLTA, REPUBLIC OF THE.

Gabon, Republic of, independent state (1959 est. pop. 420,000), W central Africa; ⊙ Libreville; formerly the French overseas territory of Gabon. It borders SW and W on the Gulf of Guinea, NW on Río Muni (Spanish Guinea), N on Cameroon, E and S on the Congo Republic. In 1956 France extended universal direct suffrage and more extensive self-government to the territory. In the French constitutional referendum of Sept. 28, 1958, Gabon voted to join the FRENCH COMMUNITY. Gabon attained complete internal self-government in Nov., 1958, when the territorial assembly proclaimed the Republic of Gabon as an autonomous member of the Community. Following amendments to the French constitution in June, 1960, Gabon initialed agreements with France for the transfer to Gabon of those concerns previously under the jurisdiction of the Community. On Aug. 17, 1960, independence was proclaimed, the republic becoming a member of the remodeled Community. In Jan., 1959, Gabon joined an "economic, technical, and customs union" with Chad, the Congo Republic, and the Central African Republic, the other former members of French Equatorial Africa. The Republic of Gabon was admitted to the UN in 1960.

Germany. The 1949 political division of Germany prevented the signing of a peace treaty with a central authority representing a unified German state. Nevertheless, the technical state of war with Germany was terminated by the Western powers in 1951, and by the USSR in 1955. The future of the divided country and the status of Berlin gave rise to prolonged controversy between the Soviet Union and the Western powers. In 1958 the USSR repudiated wartime agreements among the four occupying powers concerning the control of Germany. Russia demanded that the four powers join in signing separate peace treaties with the two Germanies and that West Berlin be made a demilitarized "free city." The USSR declared that if the West refused to join in such an agreement, Russia would sign a unilateral peace treaty with East Germany and transfer to that government control of Western access routes to Berlin. The Western powers opposed any unilateral action on the part of Russia; their basic position was a commitment to German reunification on the basis of self-determination and free elections in all parts of Germany and in Berlin; and they insisted also that the Western Allies had legal right to remain in West Berlin as guarantors of the city's freedom pending a final settlement of the German question. In 1960 the USSR declared that the four-power occupation of Berlin was no longer in effect and transferred to East Germany control of movement between the two Berlins; the Western Allies claimed that they, with the USSR, were sole authorities over this phase of the city's life. In 1961 the USSR repeatedly threatened to sign an East German peace treaty abrogating Western occupation rights in Berlin; the Western Allies asserted that they would maintain their occupation rights by force, if necessary, and that these rights were not negotiable with the East German government. **East Germany** or German Democratic Republic, est. 1949 (□41,635; 1959 est. pop. 16,213,000); ⊙ East Berlin. In Oct., 1949, the People's Chamber of the Soviet-occupied zone of Germany adopted the constitution of the German Democratic Republic. The Allied High Commission, however, declared that the government of East Germany had been imposed by the USSR without popular approval and was not a valid government. In June, 1953, after Soviet troops had suppressed an uprising in East Germany, the USSR ended East Germany's reparation payments, lowered certain occupation costs, and granted other financial assistance. A Soviet–East German treaty signed in 1955 gave East Germany authority to decide all questions of domestic and foreign policy, including its relations with West Germany and other states. Thereafter East Germany repeatedly demanded recognition by the West; in support of its claims to sovereignty, the East German government in 1960 placed restrictions on travel between the two sectors of Berlin and in 1961 sealed the border between the sectors. Attempts have been made to develop East Germany as an independent economic unit despite the scarcity of raw materials, the large-scale flight of East German workers to the West, and the effects of Soviet dismantling of industry after the war. **West Germany** or German Federal Republic, est. 1949, (□95,913; 1960 est. pop. 53,373,000; both figures include West Berlin); ⊙ Bonn. In 1948 the US, Britain, and France agreed on a central government for the three occupation zones; the Basic Law of May 23, 1949, was to serve as a constitution until a peace treaty would permit establishment of a unified government for the whole of Germany. General elections were held and the Federal Republic officially came into existence on Sept. 21, 1949, under the Occupation Statute which reduced the responsibilities of the occupation authorities. Subsequent agreements authorized the Federal Republic to establish diplomatic relations with foreign countries and to become a member of international organizations. The Federal Republic became a sovereign independent state on May 5,

1955, when the Occupation Statute was superseded by the London and Paris treaties (signed 1954) which stipulated that: West German rearmament would be under international western control; the Western occupying powers would retain formal control in West Berlin, which was administratively united with the Federal Republic; the occupation powers would retain authority over a final peace settlement and reunification of the country. In 1957 the politically autonomous Saar was integrated with the Federal Republic as the state of Saarland. Since the war the Federal Republic has emerged as a leading industrial power; reconstruction of the country's economy, with considerable aid from Western nations, brought living standards and purchasing power which were in 1961 among the highest in Europe.

Ghana, republic (□92,100; 1960 est. pop. 6,691,000), W Africa; ⊙ Accra; a member of the British Commonwealth. It comprises the former British colony of the Gold Coast, together with the protectorates of Ashanti and the Northern Territories, and the UN trusteeship territory of British Togoland. On the S coast of the African bulge, it borders W on Ivory Coast, N and NW on Mali and Upper Volta, E on Togo. After the Second World War a nationalist movement grew and gave rise to unrest, particularly riots in Accra (1948). The British, after investigating the problem of constitutional reform in the colony and holding conferences with native leaders, in 1951 agreed to a constitution providing for some home rule to be exercised by a body of popularly elected representatives. Amendments to the constitution in 1954 made the colony virtually self-governing. In 1956 the Legislative Assembly requested independence, and on March 6, 1957, the sovereign state of Ghana was proclaimed as a dominion of the British Commonwealth of Nations. The nationalist leader, Kwame Nkrumah, was made premier. On July 1, 1960, Ghana became a republic (retaining membership in the Commonwealth). Nkrumah became president. The first African colony to gain independence after the Second World War, Ghana became a symbol of success for other African colonies aspiring to self-rule. A program of agricultural reform and increased education slowly began to improve economic and social conditions. Nkrumah maintained friendly relations with the USSR and other states of the Communist bloc. He advocated West African political unity, and in 1960 Ghana, Guinea, and Mali signed an agreement for coordination of the defense, economic, and foreign policies of the three republics. Ghana was admitted to the UN in 1957.

Goa, India: see PORTUGUESE INDIA.

Gold Coast: see GHANA.

Greenland. Under the 1953 Danish constitution, Greenland (formerly a Danish colony) was granted the same rights and same measure of self-government as other political subdivisions of Denmark. The island elects two representatives to the Danish parliament; local administration rests with a popularly elected council.

Guinea, Republic of, independent state (1960 est. pop. 3,000,000), W Africa; ⊙ Conakry; formerly the French overseas territory of French Guinea. On the SW coast of the African bulge, it borders NW on Portuguese Guinea, N on Senegal and Mali, E on Ivory Coast, S on Liberia and Sierra Leone. In 1957 France extended universal suffrage and greater self-government to the territory. In the French constitutional referendum of Sept. 28, 1958, French Guinea rejected the French Fifth Republic and gained immediate independence (proclaimed Oct. 2, 1958). Economic ties with France were cut and French administrators, technicians and professionals withdrawn. Loans of teachers from Senegal and of money from Ghana gave some immediate relief, but not enough. By the end of 1959 Guinea had obtained arms, farm equipment, and technicians from E European states and substantial loans from the USSR, and had negotiated barter and trade agreements with Communist China. Meanwhile, increasing exploitation of bauxite and iron reserves broadened the country's economy. An advocate of a political union of West African states, Guinea in 1960 signed a trilateral agreement with Ghana and Mali for the coordination of the three countries' defense, economic, and foreign policies. Guinea was admitted to the UN in 1958.

Hanoi, capital of North Vietnam since 1954.

Hawaii, the 50th state of the United States, admitted on Aug. 21, 1959; formerly a U.S. territory (see the main body of the Gazetteer under Hawaiian Islands, p. 767). Longstanding efforts to gain statehood for the territory finally succeeded with the enactment of the State Enabling Act in March, 1959. Boundaries of the new state were set to include the entire area within the territory except for privately owned Palmyra Island. In June, 1959, voters in the territory approved statehood; elections for state and federal offices were held in July. Hawaii ranks 44th in population among the states and 47th in area.

India. In 1956 the constituent states of the Indian union were reorganized, generally according to linguistic regions, into 14 states and six federally administered territories. Some former states remained intact; others disappeared or underwent extensive territorial changes resulting in the creation of new states. Constitutional distinctions between the states, which previously had varying degrees of provincial autonomy, were eliminated. After 1960, when Bombay was divided into two states, Punjab remained the only bilingual state. India thereafter was composed of the following 15 states: Andhra Pradesh (pop. 35,980,000; created from the Telugu-speaking area of Madras State, later absorbed the Telugu districts of former Hyderabad State); Assam (pop. 11,860,000); Bihar (pop. 46,460,000; certain areas transferred to West Bengal); Gujarat (pop. 20,620,000; created from the predominantly Gujarati-speaking sections of former Bombay State); Jammu and Kashmir (pop. 3,580,000); Kerala (pop. 16,880,000; created from former state of Travancore-Cochin and part of Madras State); Madhya Pradesh (pop. 32,390,000; added former states of Bhopal, Madhya Bharat, and Vindhya Pradesh and an area of Rajasthan State, lost Marathi-speaking districts); Madras (pop. 33,650,000; transferred areas to Kerala and Mysore, absorbed areas of former state of Travencore-Cochin); Maharashtra (pop. 39,500,000; created from predominantly Marathi-speaking section of former Bombay State); Mysore (pop. 23,550,000; absorbed Kanarese-speaking areas of Madras state and former states of Bombay, Coorg, and Hyderabad); Orissa (pop. 17,560,000); Punjab (pop. 20,300,000; absorbed former state of the Patiala and East Punjab States Union); Rajasthan (pop. 20,150,000; absorbed former state of Ajmer and areas of former states of Bombay and Madhya Bharat; transferred an area to Madhya Pradesh); Uttar Pradesh (pop. 73,750,000); West Bengal (pop. 34,970,000; absorbed certain areas of Bihar State). India set out to incorporate the enclaves still possessed by European powers. The French settlements of Pondicherry, Karikal, Mahé, and Yanam were formally ceded to India in 1956; Portuguese India was seized by force in 1961. Meanwhile, Communist China pushed claims to some 50,000 square miles of territory along the Indian border in KASHMIR (see also LADAKH), the North East Province Agency of Assam, and elsewhere. The borders of Bhutan, Sikkim, and Nepal were also threatened by China.

Indochina or **French Indochina,** until 1954 three states associated with France within the French Union. See CAMBODIA; LAOS; VIETNAM.

Iraq, republic (1959 est. pop. 6,952,000), ⊙ Baghdad; formerly a kingdom. In July, 1958, following an army coup d'état in which the king and other members of the royal family were slain, a regime under the leadership of General Abdul Karim Kassim issued a provisional republican constitution proclaiming Iraq an independent, sovereign state and "an integral part of the Arab nation." The country was thereafter ruled by General Kassim, acting as premier, and an appointed cabinet. Ambitious economic development programs emphasizing industrialization were announced (1958, 1961) and an agrarian reform law designed to break up large landholdings was issued (1958). Kassim, meanwhile, was confronted with strong pressures from internal political factions, including Communists and adherents of the pan-Arabist policies of Egypt's President Nasser. Sporadic anti-government unrest was reported in various parts of the country (1959–62) and in Nov., 1959, Kassim was wounded in the second assassination attempt since he had assumed power. However, political parties were again allowed to function in Jan., 1959; elections were promised for the future but had not yet been held by Nov., 1961.

Islamabad, W Pakistan: see RAWALPINDI.

Israel. The population of the republic continued to grow after 1950 and in 1960 was estimated at 2,114,000. Trouble with neighboring Arab states reached a climax in 1956 after the SUEZ CANAL was nationalized and Israeli ships were forbidden its use. Israeli troops invaded and occupied the Gaza strip and the Sinai peninsula, but were forced by international pressure to withdraw. Israel continued its intensive program for land reclamation, diversification of farming, and development of mineral resources and general industry.

Italian Somaliland, merged with British Somaliland to form SOMALIA in 1960.

Ivory Coast, Republic of the, independent state (1960 est. pop. 3,200,000), W Africa; ⊙ Abidjan; formerly the French overseas territory of Ivory Coast. On the S coast of the African bulge, it borders S on the Gulf of Guinea, E on Ghana, N on Mali and Upper Volta, NW on Guinea, W on Liberia. In 1956 France granted the territory universal direct suffrage and increased self-government. In the French constitutional referendum of Sept. 28, 1958, Ivory Coast voted to join the FRENCH COMMUNITY. In December of that year, the territorial assembly proclaimed itself a constituent assembly and voted to establish the Republic of the Ivory Coast as an autonomous member of the Community. In Aug., 1960, the Republic proclaimed itself a sovereign nation and withdrew from the Community. However, like Dahomey, Niger, and Upper Volta, the other members of the Council of the Entente (an economic organization established in 1959), the nation signed (1961) bilateral agreements with France. The Republic of the Ivory Coast was admitted to the UN in 1960.

Jamaica, West Indies. In Oct., 1961, Britain announced that Jamaica would be granted independence apart from The West Indies federation early in 1962.

Japan, regained her sovereignty on April 28, 1952, when the San Francisco Peace Treaty went into effect. The treaty, signed in Sept., 1951, by Japan and 48 countries (excluding the USSR and China), was ratified the following month by the Japanese Diet. In 1956 the technical state of war between Japan and the USSR was terminated by mutual agreement. In the same year Japan was admitted to the UN.

Kabardinian-Balkar Autonomous Soviet Socialist Republic, reestablished as an ASSR in 1957; formerly the Kabardin-Balkar ASSR, which was broken up in 1944 with the resettlement of the Balkar peoples for collaboration with the Germans during the Second World War. (For history prior to 1944, see the main body of the Gazetteer under Kabardian Autonomous Soviet Socialist Republic, p. 891.)

Kalmyk (or **Kalmuck**) **Autonomous Soviet Socialist Republic,** reestablished as an ASSR in 1957 after having been abolished in 1943 following the collaboration of its people with the Germans during the Second World War. (For history prior to 1943, see main body of the Gazetteer, p. 899.)

Karachai-Cherkess Autonomous Oblast, established in 1957 as an autonomous oblast in the RSFSR when the rehabilitated Karachai people, who had been resettled and had had their oblast dissolved in 1944 for collaboration with the Germans during the Second World War, were joined to the Cherkess Autonomous Oblast. (See main body of the Gazetteer, pp. 384 and 910, for separate articles on component oblasts.)

Karachi, city, W Pakistan; former capital of Pakistan, replaced as seat of government by RAWALPINDI in 1959. The federal area comprising Karachi and its surrounding territory (□566), still under federal jurisdiction in 1961, was scheduled to become an administrative division of West Pakistan.

Karelia or **Karelo-Finnish Soviet Socialist Republic,** ASSR in the RSFSR; until 1956 a constituent republic of the USSR.

Kashka-Darya or **Kashka-Dar'ya,** oblast, SE Uzbek SSR, was dissolved in 1960.

Kashmir, region, extreme N India and NE West Pakistan. After the fighting between India and Pakistan over Kashmir was ended by a UN cease-fire in 1948, the area remained divided along the cease-fire line. Indian Kashmir, with its capital at Srinagar, occupied about three quarters of the region, and Azad Kashmir (Pakistani), with the capital at Muzaffarabad, occupied the remainder. Tension over the control of the whole territory was strong. Projects for a plebiscite were blocked by the Indian government because the population is predominantly Moslem. A constituent assembly in Indian Kashmir voted in 1953 for incorporation into India, but this move was voided by continued Pakistani-Indian discussion and disapproval by the UN of the annexation without a plebiscite. A new vote by the assembly in 1956 led (despite Pakistani protests) to integration of Kashmir as an Indian state (Jammu and Kashmir). Further talk of a plebiscite under UN auspices came to nothing. Another claimant to territory in NE Kashmir was China. Chinese troops occupied Ladakh and neighboring areas, and there were short clashes in 1958. Talks between India and China came to nothing. China rejected all protests and in 1961 still held the territory.

Katanga, former province of the Belgian Congo and secessionist state, S Central Africa in the S and SE Congo region; ⊙ Elisabethville. Soon after the independence of the Republic of the Congo was proclaimed (June 30, 1960), Katanga, the richest of the provinces, demanded a large share in a federalized government and on July 11, 1960, seceded from the new republic. Under the leadership of Premier Moise Tshombe, the province was proclaimed a republic with Tshombe as president. To protect his state from armed attack by the central Congolese government, Tshombe obtained Belgian aid. With disorder rampant throughout the Congo, rival leaders of the central government asked for help from the UN. A UN force was gathered. Tshombe reluctantly allowed Secretary General Dag Hammarskjold and a small group to enter Katanga Aug. 14, 1960. Later a considerable force of UN troops were stationed in Katanga committed to a policy of nonintervention and of overseeing withdrawal of foreign troops. The Belgian troops were slowly withdrawn, but white mercenary officers continued to command in the army of the Katanga. There was recurrent trouble between the UN forces and the Katangese. Attempts at reconciliation with the central government were pointless. Premier Patrice Lumumba planned a full-scale attack on Katanga and reviled the UN for not supporting his efforts at unity; he was echoed by vituperation of Hammarskjold in the UN from the USSR and the Communist countries (as well as some African and Asian nations). The situation grew steadily worse and was not improved after the murder of Lumumba in Katanga early in 1961. Further conferences with Congolese leaders failed. Tshombe, briefly held under arrest (June, 1961) after quitting a meeting with Congolese leaders, kept to his independent way. Opposition between the UN and Katangan forces grew to regular warfare late in the summer, and the UN was set back. A cease-fire agreement in October was promptly violated. Under a new UN mandate the international force undertook a vigorous campaign in Dec., and succeeded in taking control of the capital and other strong points. Tshombe met with the Congolese premier, Cyrille Adoula, at Kitona and arrived at an agreement (Dec., 1961) for reintegration of the rebellious state into the Congo. Still the Katangan government protested the Kitona pact and, though some delegates were sent to the parliament of the central government, matters were not settled at the end of 1961. Hopes for a federated republic were strong, yet violence still held sway in parts of Katanga.

Khartoum, capital of the Republic of the Sudan; until 1956 capital of the Anglo-Egyptian Sudan.

Korea. The Korean truce talks lasted for two years; although this period was punctuated by bitter fighting, the front remained generally stabilized just north of the 38th parallel. A truce was signed in July, 1953, and a political conference followed in Geneva (April–June, 1954) but adjourned without agreement. After a transfer of some frontier districts in Aug., 1954, the boundary between North and South followed a line running from the Han estuary NE across the 38th parallel. **North Korea** or Democratic People's Republic of Korea (□c.47,861; 1959 est. pop. 8,100,000); ⊙ Pyongyang. Since its establishment in 1948, the Communist-dominated government of North Korea has used the rich mineral and power resources of its territory as the basis for an ambitious program of industrialization (the North after the Second World War had 90 percent of undivided Korea's power, 70 percent of its heavy industry, and 70 percent of its coal). A five-year plan announced in 1958 emphasized development of heavy industry; it was sharply curtailed in 1959 because of acute shortages of food, housing, and essential consumer goods. However, with rigid planning and the aid of Soviet-bloc nations, North Korea has managed to make substantial economic progress. **South Korea** or Republic of Korea (□c.37,425; 1959 est. pop. 23,848,000); ⊙ Seoul. Traditionally the agricultural region of the Korean peninsula, South Korea (est. as a nation in 1948) faced severe economic problems after partition. Attempts to establish an adequate industrial base were hampered by limited resources and an acute lack of power, most of which, prior to 1948, had been supplied by the industrial North. Intensive efforts improved the power supply and expanded the economy until about one third of the working force was engaged in industry. However, war damage and continued maintenance of a large military establishment made it impossible to put South Korea on a self-sustaining basis. The country was dependent upon foreign aid, primarily from the US and the UN, and the economy was characterized by recurrent inflation, highly unfavorable trade balances, and mass unemployment. Much of its manufacturing continued to be provided by small factories and handicraft methods, and was confined largely to products for home consumption. In 1960 a political crisis focused on the authoritarian policies of President Syngman Rhee, who had dominated the Republic since its inception. The elections of March, 1960, in which Rhee won a fourth term, were marked by widespread violence and accusations by Rhee's opponents of government fraud and police intimidation. Following the elections, student-led protest demonstrations sparked a wave of uprisings across the country. The government capitulated, and Rhee resigned and went into exile. Constitutional amendments subsequently set up a Second Republic of Korea, which, following new elections in July, was led by Dr. John M. Chang as premier. In May, 1961, the South Korean armed forces revolted and seized power; a military junta decreed a military government. Power was held by a small group of officers who announced their opposition to Communism and promised to restore civilian government after reconstructing South Korea as "a genuine democratic republic" and overcoming "the national crisis resulting from corruption, injustices, and poverty."

Kuala Lumpur, capital of the independent Federation of Malaya; until 1957 capital of the British-protected Federation of Malaya.

Kuwait. In 1961 British protection over the oil-rich state ended, and Kuwait was proclaimed a fully independent nation. A treaty, however, guaranteed British armed assistance at Kuwait's request. When Iraq in 1961 renewed its claims to the territory, the ruler of Kuwait appealed to Great Britain for aid.

Ladakh, district, E Kashmir. Once part of the kingdom of W Tibet, Ladakh was annexed to Kashmir in the 19th cent., but Tibet did not acknowledge its loss, and after Tibet was occupied by the Chinese Communists, China took up Tibetan claims. There were fierce clashes between Chinese and Indian troops in 1958. In 1961 the Chinese held a considerable strip of territory.

Lagos, capital of the Federation of Nigeria; until 1954 capital of the British colony and the protectorate of Nigeria.

Laos, attained full sovereignty in 1954. Previously, as an associated state within the French Union, Laos had limited autonomy; France retained ultimate control of Laotian foreign affairs and maintained jurisdiction in certain trade, currency, judicial, and military matters. The signing of a French-Laotian treaty in 1953 and of subsequent agreements in 1954 completed the gradual transfer of full sovereignty to Laos; under these agreements Laos in effect withdrew from the French Union. Meanwhile, in 1953, with the invasion of Communist Vietminh troops from Vietnam (aided by the guerrilla forces of the Pathet Lao, a Communist-supported Laotian nationalist movement), Laos became a major battleground. Under agreements signed at a nine-nation conference in Geneva (July, 1954), Vietminh and French Union forces withdrew from the country; Pathet Lao forces were permitted to retain control of two northern provinces pending a political settlement with the established government. Negotiations between the Laotian premier, Prince Souvanna Phouma, and the leader of the Pathet Lao, Prince Souphanouvong, led in 1957 to an agreement which provided for the reestablishment of government authority in the north, partial integration of Pathet Lao troops into the Laotian army, and Pathet Lao participation in the government. In 1959 the breakdown of the compromise agreement and the arrest of some Pathet Lao political leaders led to renewed hostilities in the northern provinces. A succession of coups resulted (1960) in a three-way struggle for power. Neutralist Premier Souvanna Phouma remained in the administrative capital of Vientiane and maneuvered in vain to set up a unified government. In the south, General Phoumi Nosavan (controlling the bulk of the Laotian army) denounced Premier Souvanna Phouma's regime as illegal and proclaimed a revolutionary pro-western government headed by Prince Boun Oum. In the northern provinces, Prince Souphanouvong again led the Pathet Lao rebels. The power struggle was climaxed by civil war in Dec., 1960, when General Phoumi marched on Vientiane and took the city. Premier Souvanna Phouma fled to neighboring Cambodia; Pathet Lao forces, allied with pro-neutralist Laotian troops (loyal to Souvanna Phouma), continued fighting in the north. The government of Boun Oum, installed in Vientiane, was recognized by the United States and other Western countries. The Soviet bloc continued to recognize the deposed government of Souvanna Phouma. In May, 1961, with Pathet Lao and neutralist forces in control of about half the country, a cease-fire was arranged and a fourteen-nation conference was convened in Geneva to secure the neutrality of Laos under a unified government. In October the three contending princes—Souvanna Phouma, Boun Oum, and Souphanouvong—agreed that Souvanna Phouma would become premier of a new government including all factions. Guerrilla warfare continued, however, and the agreement had not been implemented by Dec., 1961. Laos was admitted to the UN in 1955.

Leopoldville, capital of the Republic of the Congo; until 1960 capital of the Belgian colony of the Belgian Congo.

Libreville, capital of the Republic of Gabon; until 1958 capital of the French overseas territory of Gabon.

Libya, kingdom (1959 est. pop. 1,172,000); ⊙ Benghazi and Tripoli. The independence of the United Kingdom of Libya was proclaimed by King Idris I on Dec. 24, 1951, in accordance with prior UN decisions. At that time the temporary British and French administrations in Tripolitania, Cyrenaica, and Fezzan relinquished their authority. Since independence Libya has been reliant on economic and technical assistance from the UN and foreign states and on revenue from US and British military bases. However, discovery of substantial oil reserves in the late 1950s increased the country's promise of achieving some degree of economic self-sufficiency. Libya was admitted to the UN in 1955.

Lomé, capital of the Republic of Togo; until 1960 capital of the UN trusteeship territory of French Togoland.

Madagascar: see Malagasy Republic.

Malagasy Republic, independent state (1959 est. pop. 5,287,000), coextensive with the island of Madagascar; ⊙ Tananarive; formerly the French overseas territory of Madagascar. Developments on the island from 1951 to 1958 centered on the extension of the economic base through extensive investment of French capital and (after 1956) on the increased self-government and extension of universal direct suffrage granted by the French government. In the French constitutional referendum of Sept. 28, 1958, Madagascar voted to join the French Community. On Oct. 14, 1958, the territorial assembly proclaimed the Malagasy Republic as an autonomous member of the Community. Following amendments to the French constitution in June, 1960, agreements were signed (June 26) between Malagasy and France providing for the former's independence and its membership in the remodeled community. Creation of Diégo-Suarez province in 1957 brought the number of provinces to six. The island state was admitted to the UN in 1960.

Malaya, Federation of, independent state (1959 est. pop. 6,698,000), on the Malay Peninsula; a member of the British Commonwealth of Nations; ⊙ Kuala Lumpur; formerly a federation of nine British-protected Malay states and two settlements (Panang and Malacca). After the formation of the Federation in 1948, the British administration helped to promote plans for Malayan home rule and eventual independence. The first federal elections were held in 1955. In 1956 Malayan and British representatives approved a constitution providing for a parliamentary form of government, with executive power vested in a cabinet chosen by a prime minister. The Paramount Ruler, or monarch, was to be elected for a five-year term by (and from among) the hereditary rulers of the nine Malay states. The constitution went into effect in 1957. The nation opted for dominion status within the British Commonwealth of Nations. Meanwhile a state of emergency declared in 1948 to combat a Communist terrorist campaign continued. Until their suppression in 1960, the Communist underground and rebel guerrillas based in the Malayan jungles reduced the Federation to chaos. Yet the flourishing economy, traditionally based on the export of tin and rubber, was being expanded by industrialization and rural development. In 1961 the prime ministers of Singapore and the Federation of Malaya initiated plans for a merger of the two states by 1963 into the Federation of Malaysia, to which the British areas on Borneo (Sarawak, Brunei, and North Borneo) were being asked to adhere. Malaya was admitted to the UN in 1957.

Mali, Republic of, independent state (1959 est. pop. 4,300,000), NW Africa; ⊙ Bamako; from 1958 to 1960 the Sudanese Republic and, earlier, the French overseas territory of French Sudan. It borders N on the Saharan Departments, W on Mauritania, SW on Senegal, S on Guinea and Ivory Coast, SE on Upper Volta, E on Niger. In June, 1956, France extended to the territory universal direct suffrage and greater self-government. In the French constitutional referendum of Sept. 28, 1958, French Sudan voted to join the French Community. On Nov. 28, 1958, the territorial assembly, acting as a constituent assembly, proclaimed the establishment of the Sudanese Republic as an autonomous member of the Community. In April, 1959, the Sudan joined Senegal to form the Mali Federation; this union was dissolved in Aug., 1960. On Sept. 22, 1960, the Sudanese Republic, under the name Mali Republic, obtained full independence from France and severed its ties with the Community. In 1960 Mali signed a trilateral agreement with Ghana and Guinea for the coordination of the three countries' defense, economic, and foreign policies. Mali was admitted to the UN in 1960.

Mali Federation, political union of the Republic of Senegal and the Sudanese Republic, est. 1959, dissolved 1960; ⊙ Dakar. In early 1959, the Sudanese Republic, Dahomey, Senegal, and Upper Volta drafted a constitution for a federal political union within the French Community. Senegal and the Sudanese Republic ratified it (April, 1959) and formed the Mali Federation. The Senegalese wanted a loose federal government, the Sudanese wanted a strong federal government and a tight federation, nevertheless the union remained in force for over a year. It was made independent on June 20, 1960, and joined the remodeled Community. Yet tensions continued, and in Aug., 1960, Senegal withdrew from the union. France's attempts to mediate proved futile, and Senegal's full independence was acknowledged. A month later the Sudanese Republic formally conceded the dissolution of the Federation and, in Sept., 1960, secured its own independence as the Republic of Mali.

Mauritania, Islamic Republic of, independent state (1958 est. pop. 640,000), NW Africa; ⊙ Nouakchott; formerly the French overseas territory of Mauritania. It borders W on the Atlantic, NW on Spanish Sahara, N on the Saharan dept. of the Saoura, E and S on Mali, SW on Senegal (along the Senegal river). In 1956 the French government granted to the territory universal direct suffrage and more self-government. In the French constitutional referendum of Sept. 28, 1958, Mauritania voted to join the French Community, and in November the territorial assembly proclaimed the Islamic Republic of Mauritania as an autonomous member of the Community. The republic became independent on Nov. 28, 1960, and, though expressing a desire to retain close ties with France, left the French Community. In 1958, Mauritania began an intensive building program to provide a new capital at Nouakchott and an improved seaport at Port-Etienne. Attention was also given to the country's lack of an internal transportation system. In the early 1950s iron and copper were discovered; these resources were extensively exploited by the French on a profit-sharing basis with the Mauritanian government. Oil deposits were found in the late 1950s. Mauritania was admitted to the UN in 1961.

Middle Congo: see CONGO REPUBLIC.

Mogadishu, capital of Somalia; until 1960 capital of Italian Somaliland.

Molotov, city and oblast, RSFSR: see PERM.

Morocco, kingdom (□c. 450,000; 1960 est. pop. 11,598,000), NW Africa; ⊙ Rabat. The kingdom includes the former protectorate of French Morocco and Spanish Morocco; the former international zone of Tangier; and the former Southern Protectorate of Morocco (Spanish). Its boundaries in the E and the S are not finally delimited, but it borders on both the Atlantic and the Mediterranean, E on Algeria, SE on the Saharan dept. of the Saoura, S on Spanish Sahara, W on the enclave of Ifni. Moroccan nationalists, led by the Istiqlal party, demonstrated against French rule, and after riots in Casablanca in 1952, France outlawed the party. Sultan Mohammed V (Sidi Mohammed) was in 1953 imprisoned because of his sympathy with the rebels. A wave of riots, terrorism, and guerrilla warfare followed. In 1955 the sultan was restored. In March, 1956, France relinquished its rights in Morocco; in April, the Spanish surrendered their protectorate; in October, TANGIER was given to Morocco by international agreement. Spanish cession of the Southern Protectorate (but not Ifni) rounded out the territory of Morocco in 1958. Already Mohammed V had in 1957 changed his title to king. After his death (Feb. 26, 1961), his son Hassan II ascended the throne of the constitutional monarchy. The newly independent nation faced many problems: need of capital for industrialization; scantiness of economic resources for an increasing population; difficulty in drawing administrators from a largely illiterate population. Morocco was admitted to the UN in 1956.

Namangan, oblast, E Uzbek SSR, was dissolved in 1960.

Netherlands New Guinea: see NEW GUINEA, WEST.

New Guinea, West or **Netherlands New Guinea.** Possession of the territory was a cause of continuing friction between Indonesia and the Netherlands from 1950 through 1961. Negotiations between the countries failed in 1955, and the UN could not solve the problem. Efforts at settlement with the United States and the UN acting as intermediaries continued. Indonesia refused in 1961 to negotiate without a prior agreement that the territory would be given to Indonesia and threatened forcible seizure of West New Guinea (called West Irian by the Indonesians).

Niamey, capital of the Republic of the Niger; until 1958 capital of the French overseas territory of Niger.

Niger, Republic of the independent state (1960 est. pop. 2,850,000), N central Africa; ⊙ Niamey; formerly the French overseas territory of Niger. It borders N on Libya and the Saharan dept. of the Oases, W on Mali, SW on Upper Volta and Dahomey, S on Nigeria, E on Chad. In 1956 France granted the territory universal suffrage and more extensive self-government. In the French constitutional referendum of Sept. 28, 1958, Niger voted to join the FRENCH COMMUNITY, and in December of that year the territorial assembly proclaimed the Republic of the Niger as an autonomous state within the Community. On Aug. 3, 1960, Niger was proclaimed independent. Like Dahomey, Ivory Coast, and Upper Volta, the other members of the Council of the Entente (a cooperative economic organization established in 1959), Niger did not join the remodeled Community. It chose instead to sign bilateral agreements with France covering economic and defense matters. The Republic of the Niger was admitted to the UN in 1960.

Nigeria, Federation of, independent state (□356,669; 1960 est. pop. 34,296,000), W Africa; a member of the British Commonwealth of Nations; ⊙ Lagos; formerly divided as a British colony and a British protectorate. In 1954 the protectorate (Northern Region, Eastern Region, Western Region) and the colony (Lagos municipality and surrounding territory) became a federation under a constitution providing for limited self-government. Complete independence under a new constitution was proclaimed on Oct. 1, 1960. Under the constitution, executive authority is vested in a prime minister responsible to the legislature; a governor-general represents the British sovereign. In June, 1961, the northern section of the British Cameroons was incorporated into Nigeria's Northern Region. In contrast to some African nations, Nigeria at the time of its independence had well-developed political institutions, disciplined police and military forces, and an efficient civil service staffed by thousands of British-educated nationals. Its high degree of political stability, its status as Africa's most populous nation, and several other factors indicated that Nigeria would become an influential leader among the young African nations. The other factors were a prosperous agricultural economy, rich natural resources (oil, tin, lead), and an extensive system of public education, bringing rapidly expanding literacy. Nigeria was admitted to the UN in 1960.

Northern Rhodesia: see RHODESIA AND NYASALAND, FEDERATION OF.

North Korea: see KOREA.

North Vietnam: see VIETNAM.

Nouakchott, city, since 1958 capital of the Islamic Republic of Mauritania (formerly the French overseas territory Mauritania, with extraterritorial capital at Saint-Louis in Senegal). Transformation of the rural village into a suitable administrative center began in 1958 as part of Mauritania's preparations for independence.

Novo Kuznetsk, city, RSFSR; formerly known as Stalinsk.

Nyasaland: see RHODESIA AND NYASALAND, FEDERATION OF.

Oman or **Muscat and Oman.** In 1958 Oman sold the port and enclave of Gwadar on the Baluchistan coast to Pakistan. A revolt against the sultan lasted some two years before it was put down by the troops of the sultan and the British.

Ouagadougou, capital of the Republic of the Upper Volta; until 1958 capital of the French overseas territory of Upper Volta.

Pakistan, country (1959 est. pop. 80,823,000), of the Indian subcontinent; interim ⊙ Rawalpindi; proclaimed in 1956 an "Islamic Republic"; under military government since 1958. A dominion of the British Commonwealth of Nations from 1947 to 1956, it became in 1956 an independent republic retaining membership in the Commonwealth. In 1955, former provinces and princely states were consolidated into two units, West Pakistan and East Pakistan. West Pakistan administratively has ten Divisions; East Pakistan has three Divisions. The federal district around Karachi was in 1961 still a separate unit, but it presumably will be made a Division of West Pakistan. The president of the new republic, Iskander Mirza, with army support abrogated the constitution, dissolved the national and provincial legislatures, abolished all political parties, and declared martial law throughout the country. (Membership in the British Commonwealth was not affected.) Presidential authority was transferred to General Mohammad Ayub Khan, commander-in-chief of the armed forces, who thereafter ruled by decree. The military regime took vigorous steps to end the political and economic chaos which had for years plagued the underdeveloped, predominately illiterate (c.80 percent) nation. In 1959, President Ayub, declaring his intention of preparing Pakistan for effective representative government, set up a system of local councils comprising both elected and appointed members. In 1960 the president appointed a commission to draft a constitution which would provide for a strong central government, indirect election of a president and national assembly through the local councils, and gradual elimination of appointed members from the councils. Despite the considerable success of the military regime's program, Pakistan continued to face problems which were aggravated by a rate of population growth which threatened to outstrip the country's economic development. In 1958 Pakistan purchased the port and surrounding enclave of Gwadar from Oman. Pakistan intended to develop Gwadar as a second port for West Pakistan, at that time served only by Karachi. The dispute with India over KASHMIR continued, though Pakistan tried repeatedly to have it settled by a UN plebiscite. Chinese claims to Kashmir also affected Pakistan.

Perm, city and oblast, RSFSR; formerly called Molotov.

Port of Spain, capital of The WEST INDIES federation; until 1958 capital of Trinidad and Tobago, crown colony in the British West Indies.

Porto-Novo, capital of the Republic of Dahomey; until 1958 capital of the French overseas territory of Dahomey.

Portuguese India. When India gained its independence, Portugal still held three enclaves in India: Goa, Damão, and Diu. Strong nationalistic sentiment in India led to many anti-Portuguese demonstrations. In 1954 two small segments of the Damão enclave were detached as independent, and in 1961 they were absorbed into India. In 1955 a group of armed Indians marched into Goa and were dispersed by Portuguese gunfire. Diplomatic negotiations between India and Portugal were broken. Threats of forcible annexation grew, and there were border incidents. In Dec., 1961, India took a strong hand. Indian troops invaded Goa and gained complete control. Damão and Diu also fell to India.

Portuguese West Africa: see ANGOLA.

Rabat, capital of Morocco; until 1956 capital of French Morocco.

Rawalpindi, city, West Pakistan; after 1959 interim ⊙ of Pakistan. In 1958 a presidential commission recommended transfer of the capital from Karachi to an area on the Potwar Plateau at the foot of the Himalayas, c.750 mi. N of Karachi. Reasons for the transfer included Karachi's humid climate paucity of water, and commercial influences. Rawalpindi was designated as interim capital pending construction of a permanent capital, to be called Islamabad, at a site c.8 mi. north of Rawalpindi. The master plan for Islamabad provided for construction by 1965 of a presidential palace; buildings for the supreme court, parliament, and secretariat with offices for 9,000 civil servants; and housing for an initial population of c.36,000. Islamabad was expected to be the functioning seat of government by 1963.

Rhodesia and Nyasaland, Federation of, political union of three units of S central Africa; ⊙ Salisbury. The units are the British self-governing territory of Southern Rhodesia, and the British protectorates of Northern Rhodesia and Nyasaland; all retain their pre-federation constitutional status. The Federation borders NW on the Republic of the Congo, NE on Tanganyika, E on Mozambique, S on the Republic of South Africa, SW on Bechuanaland protectorate and South-West Africa, W on Angola. Conceived as a means of developing the disparate economic resources of the three areas, the Federation was established on Oct. 23, 1953. The United Kingdom maintained jurisdiction chiefly over the Federation's foreign relations, constitutional changes, and discrimination against Africans; the Federal government was made mainly responsible for the Federation's economic and internal affairs; the territorial assemblies were made responsible for local government. Despite marked economic progress, the history of the Federation was marred by tension between the politically dominant white minority and the numerically dominant native population. After native riots in Nyasaland (1959), a British investigative commission predicted that the future of the Federation depended on the extension of majority rule to the African natives. By the end of 1961 equal political rights had not been granted to the native population, and it appeared that racial antagonisms might either alter or destroy the Federation. **Northern Rhodesia** (1960 est. pop. 2,430,000, of which 76,000 are Europeans), with its extensive copper deposits, is the economic backbone of the Federation. Under a 1958 charter providing for extension of the franchise to natives, Africans were for the first time permitted the direct election of members of their own race to the protectorate's legislative council. Prior to the first elections held under the charter (March, 1959), the nationalist party of Kenneth Kaunda, which demanded majority rule and advocated boycott of the elections, was outlawed by the Federal government for fear of an outbreak of nationalist riots such as had already occurred in Nyasaland. In Feb., 1961, the Federal government adamantly opposed a constitution proposed by the British Colonial Office to increase African legislative representation in Northern Rhodesia; from then to the end of 1961 the political scene in the protectorate was disturbed by nationalist-inspired unrest. **Southern Rhodesia** (1960 est. pop. 3,070,000, of which 223,000 are Europeans), dominates the Federation. Its economy, though based largely on agriculture, has some commerce and industry. In 1953, when the Federation was founded, there was considerable feeling in favor of white supremacy in the colony and it was believed that eventually white-settler control would establish itself in the protectorates and that the Federation would attain dominion status in the Commonwealth. Instead, the British Colonial Office's policy of extension of rights to Africans led to the creation of a special voters roll for Africans (1957) and to an agreement (1961) to expand the legislative assembly to 65, with 15 seats reserved for directly elected Africans. Despite these concessions, at the end of 1961 nationalist organization was growing within the Federation's white stronghold. **Nyasaland** (1960 est. pop. 2,830,000, of which 9,000 are Europeans), although a poor country, is a source of manpower for the Federation and is believed to possess considerable untapped natural resources. In 1958, under the leadership of Dr. Hastings Banda, nationalism became an effective force in the protectorate. Nationalist demands for universal suffrage and majority rule caused an eruption of violence in the protectorate in Feb., 1959. Talks between Dr. Banda and the British colonial secretary in 1960 led to a constitutional agreement providing for the territory's eventual self-government under an African majority government. After the victory of his party in elections held (1961) under the new constitution, Dr. Banda demanded immediate independence for Nyasaland.

Rio de Janeiro, city, former capital of Brazil. With the inauguration of the new capital, BRASÍLIA, in April, 1960, the area comprising the Federal District around Rio became the state of Guanabara, with Rio as capital.

Ruanda-Urundi, United Nations trust territories, administered by Belgium (formerly through the Belgian Congo). After long-drawn discussion of projects for gradual concession of autonomy, Belgium in 1960 made plans for popular elections in the territories on the question of independence. The UN agreed, and elections were held. The vote for independence, however, did not lead immediately to the change. Ruanda and Urundi both favored separation, and the matter was scheduled to be settled in 1962. The choice of the official name or names after independence had not been decided by the end of 1961.

Saarland, state of West Germany (German Federal Republic); until 1957 the Saar or Saar Territory. German claims to the Saar after the Second World War led to a French-German agreement (1954) which provided for continued maintenance of the Saar's economic links with France and her political autonomy under a neutral commissioner. Rejection of this arrangement in a plebiscite held in 1955 resulted in a new agreement (1956) under which the territory became a state of the German Federal Republic on Jan. 1, 1957. France was permitted to extract coal from the Warndt deposit until 1981. In July, 1959, the customs union with France was dissolved and Saarland was economically integrated with the rest of Germany.

Saharan Departments. In 1957 the former Southern Territories (i.e., S of Algeria) were officially constituted as the departments of the Oases (eastern part of the territory). and the Saoura (western part of the territory). NW Africa; border N on Algeria, NE on Tunisia, E on Libya, SE on Niger, SW on Mali and Mauritania, W on Río Oro, NW on Morocco. In 1956 large deposits of oil and natural gas were discovered in Oases. The departments were an important factor in negotiations for a settlement between the French government and the Algerian nationalists.

Saigon, capital of South Vietnam; until 1954 capital of Vietnam.

Saint-Louis, former joint capital of the French overseas territories of Mauritania and Senegal; replaced by Nouakchott and Dakar respectively.

Salisbury, capital of the Federation of Rhodesia and Nyasaland and of Southern Rhodesia territory.

Samoa, Western: see WESTERN SAMOA, TERRITORY OF.

Santo Domingo, city, capital of the Dominican Republic. The old name of the capital came into use in place of Ciudad Trujillo in 1961.

Senegal, Republic of, independent republic (1958 est. pop. 2,300,000), W Africa; ⊙ Dakar; formerly the French overseas territory of Senegal. On the W coast of the African bulge, it borders N on Mauritania, E on Mali, S on Portuguese Guinea and the Republic of Guinea, W on Gambia (an enclave). In June, 1956, France established in Senegal universal direct suffrage and more extensive self-government. In the French constitutional referendum of Sept. 28, 1958, Senegal voted to join the FRENCH COMMUNITY, and in Nov., 1958, the territorial assembly proclaimed the Republic of Senegal as an autonomous member of the Community. In April, 1959, Senegal joined the Sudanese Republic to form the MALI FEDERATION, but in Aug., 1960, withdrew from the Federation and declared its independence. Senegal was admitted to the UN in 1960.

Sierra Leone, independent state (1959 est. pop. 2,400,000), E Africa; a member of the British Commonwealth of Nations; ⊙ Freetown; formerly a British colony and protectorate. Constitutional advances during the 1950s brought about a greater degree of self-government and led to the first general elections in 1957. Further constitutional changes in 1958 provided for an all-African executive council (cabinet) and an elected legislature. Early in 1960 all political parties agreed to work for Sierra Leone's independence as a member of the Commonwealth and to form a coalition in order to achieve an effecient administration after independence. Later in 1960 the date for complete independence (April 27, 1961) was set at a constitutional conference in London. Under the new constitution, the British sovereign is formally recognized as head of state and is represented in Sierra Leone by a governor-general; executive authority, however, is vested in a prime minister responsible to the legislature. Sierra Leone was admitted to the UN in 1961.

Singapore, self-governing state; on Singapore isl. at the tip of the Malay Peninsula; ⊙ Singapore; formerly a British crown colony. In 1957 British officials and representatives of the colony signed an agreement to establish a state of Singapore under home rule and to create a Singapore citizenship. Britain, however, retained absolute control over defense and foreign affairs (except those involving economic and cultural matters) and also reserved the right to suspend the constitution under certain circumstances. Executive power was vested in a prime minister responsible to an elected legislature. For the former colonial governor was substituted a Malayan-born head of state, also appointed by the Crown but having little political responsibility. Internal security of the state was placed under control of a council with three British and three Singapore members and one member from the Federation of Malaya. In 1961 the prime ministers of Singapore and the Federation of Malaya initiated plans for a merger of the two states to which the British areas on Borneo (Sarawak, Brunei, and North Borneo) were being asked to adhere.

Somalia, independent republic (□c.262,000; 1959 est. pop. 490,000), E Africa; ⊙ Mogadishu. It borders NW on French Somaliland, N on the Gulf of Aden, E on the Indian Ocean, W on Kenya; formed by a combination of the UN trust territory of Italian Somaliland and the protectorate of British Somaliland. In accordance with the UN decisions to grant Italian Somaliland independence, the territory was given autonomy in 1956, with independence scheduled for 1960. In British Somaliland, meanwhile, all political parties pledged themselves to seek independence and unification with Italian Somaliland. The British speeded up the program of Somali self-government. Independence was proclaimed in British Somaliland June 26, 1960. On July 1, 1960, Italian Somaliland was declared independent, and the legislatures of the two areas adopted an act of union, establishing Somalia. The nation was admitted to the UN later that year.

Somaliland. In 1960 British Somaliland and Italian Somaliland merged to form SOMALIA. French Somaliland voted in a referendum (1958) to become an overseas territory of the French Community. The Ogaden region remained part of Ethiopia.

South Africa, Republic of, independent state, S Africa; formerly a dominion of the British Commonwealth of Nations. In a referendum held in 1960, the electorate voted that South Africa should assume the status of a republic with its own chief of state. The Dutch-descended Afrikaaners (c.1,700,000), who dominated the country politically, were generally in favor of the change; the white, English-speaking minority (c.1,300,000) was mostly opposed; the country's 11 million nonwhites were barred from voting. At the Commonwealth conference in London in March, 1961, South Africa applied for readmission to the Commonwealth as a republic, a status held by India and other members. This application was withdrawn when the heads of state of other Commonwealth nations expressed firm opposition to South Africa's policy of apartheid, (rigid racial segregation and disenfranchisement of the nonwhite population). On May 31, 1961, South Africa formally became a republic and severed its association with the Commonwealth.

Southern Rhodesia: see RHODESIA AND NYASALAND, FEDERATION OF.

Southern Territories, Algeria: see SAHARAN DEPARTMENTS.

South Korea: see KOREA.

South Vietnam: see VIETNAM.

Spanish West Africa. The Southern Protectorate of Morocco was transferred to Morocco in 1958.

Stalingrad, city, RSFSR: see VOLGOGRAD.

Stalino, city, Ukranian SSR: see DONETSK.

Stalinsk, city,RSFSR: see NOVO KUZNETSK.

Sudan, French: see MALI, REPUBLIC OF.

Sudan, Republic of the, independent state (1960 est. pop. 11,615,000); ⊙ Khartoum; formerly the territory of Anglo-Egyptian Sudan, under joint British-Egyptian rule. NE Africa; borders N on Egypt, NW on Libya, W on Chad and the Central African Republic, S on the Republic of the Congo, Uganda, and Kenya, E on Ethiopia and the Red Sea. In 1951, differences between the joint powers resulted in a decision to grant the Sudan self-government. Proposals for home rule submitted by the Sudanese government to the joint powers in 1952 were accepted by the United Kingdom and Egypt and amplified in an agreement signed in 1953. The first all-Sudanese government took office in Jan., 1954. On Jan. 1, 1956, on the basis of a popular vote and with the approval of the joint powers, the Sudan assumed the status of a sovereign republic. In Nov., 1958, the interim government (authorized under a provisional constitution) collapsed when the army, led by General Ibrahim Abboud, assumed power in a bloodless coup. The virtual dictatorship that emerged under the military regime greatly stabilized the Sudan's political and economic situation. Nevertheless, the Sudan still faced three longstanding problems: reconciliation of the predominantly Arab population of the N part of the country with the Negroid population of the S part; agitation for union with Egypt; controversy with Egypt over control of Nile waters and the related problem of the irrigation of nonarable lands. The Republic of the Sudan was accepted into the UN in 1956.

Sudanese Republic: see MALI, REPUBLIC OF.

Suez Canal. The desire of Egypt to gain control of the Canal with withdrawal of British troops from the Canal Zone caused disputes and some threat of violence until 1954, when the British agreed to the withdrawal, which was completed in 1956. In that year, however, tension between Egypt and the Western powers grew because of the border struggles between Egypt and Israel. Britain and the United States withdrew their offers of financial help to Egypt for construction of the new Aswan Dam. On July 26, 1956 President Nasser of Egypt proclaimed nationalization of the Canal. Late in Oct., 1956, Israeli ships were barred passage. A few days afterward the British and French sent a military expedition against Egypt. Protests came from the United States, the USSR, other countries, and the UN. The British and French withdrew their forces in Dec., 1956, and in 1957 Israeli troops left the border territories they had conquered. Egypt in 1958 promised to pay compensation (over a six-year period) to shareholders in the nationalized Suez Canal Company.

Syria, republic (1959 est. pop. 4,537,000), SW Asia. The early years of the 1950s were marked by border disputes. Syria drew closer to Egypt and in 1958 joined EGYPT in the UNITED ARAB REPUBLIC. As partner in this new state, Syria steadily lost control of its internal affairs. Syrian officials were replaced by Egyptians, and the Republic-sponsored immigration of peasants into Syria aggravated a Syrian economy weakened by a succession of bad harvests. In the summer of 1961, Syrian resentment against Egyptian dominance was intensified by the extension of President Nasser's program of socialization to the Syrian region. Finally, the transfer to Cairo of the government of the Syrian region in Sept., 1961, crystallized Syrian opposition (especially among business interests and the military) to Egyptian control. After a military coup, a civilian government was installed. Syria withdrew from the United Arab Republic and proclaimed its independence. In Oct., 1961, Syria reassumed its seat in the UN.

Taldy-Kurgan, oblast, SE Kazakh SSR, was dissolved in 1960.

Tananarive, capital of the Malagasy Republic; until 1958 capital of the French overseas territory of Madagascar.

Tanganyika, independent state (1960 est. pop. 9,238,000) within the British Commonwealth of Nations; ⊙ Dar es Salaam; formerly a UN trust territory administered by Britain. Tanganyika made rapid strides toward independence after 1957, when the UN asked Britain to accelerate the progress of self-government in the territory. The first general election was held in 1958, and in 1960 the legislature became primarily an elected body. In April, 1961, after a constitutional conference held in Dar es Salaam, the UN endorsed Britain's plans to end the trusteeship in December and recommended Tanganyika's subsequent admission to the UN. The following month the territory achieved complete internal self-government, with Britain retaining control of defense and foreign affairs. Full independence was proclaimed on Dec. 9, 1961. The constitution recognized the British sovereign (represented by a governor general) as head of state; executive authority was vested in a prime minister responsible to the legislature.

Tangier, former international zone, NW Africa. In 1956 it was by internal agreement transferred to MOROCCO. In 1960 its privileges as a free trade zone were abolished.

Tibet. After Chinese conquest and creation of the autonomous province by an agreement in 1951, there was much complaint in Tibet that true autonomy was not granted; complaint increased under the government set up in 1953. Discontent rose and led to a rebellion, which reached a climax in March, 1959. The Dalai Lama fled to India, and the Chinese made the Panchen Lama nomina ruler in Tibet. The rebellion was soon put down, though some sporadic fighting recurred in 1960. China took over Tibetan border claims and clashed with India in KASHMIR (see also LADAKH). The Tibetan border with Nepal was at least temporarily settled in 1956.

Togo, Republic of, independent state (1959 est. pop. 1,442,000), W Africa; formerly the UN trusteeship territory of French Togoland under French administration. On the S coast of the African bulge, it borders N on Upper Volta, E on Dahomey, S on the Gulf of Guinea, W on Ghana. France in 1956 undertook to end the trusteeship and by a constitution approved by a territorial referendum to make French Togoland an autonomous state within the French Union. In Jan., 1957, the UN disallowed this action. New elections (April, 1958) were held under UN supervision to choose an assembly, which decided the status of the territory. The National Unity Party, under Sylvanus Olympio, won and negotiated with France. On April 27, 1960, Togo's complete independence was proclaimed. The republic was admitted to the UN in 1960.

Togoland, formerly two UN trusteeship territories, British Togoland and French Togoland. In accordance with a plebiscite held in May, 1956, British Togoland merged with Ghana when Ghana became independent in 1957. French Togoland became an independent republic in 1960 (see TOGO, REPUBLIC OF).

Trieste, city, formerly capital of the Free Territory of Trieste. Part of Italy since 1954, it has been maintained as a free port.

Trieste, Free Territory of, divided between Italy and Yugoslavia in 1954; formerly a free state under protection of the UN Security Council. Military government in the Free Territory was terminated under an agreement (Oct., 1954) signed by the U.S., Britain, Italy, and Yugoslavia. Administration of almost the entire Anglo-American Zone "A" (including the city of Trieste) was transferred to the Italian government; the Yugoslav Zone "B" (and a small strip of land from Zone "A") passed to the civil administration of Yugoslavia. Italy agreed to preserve Trieste city as a free port.

Tunisia, republic (1959 est. pop. 3,935,000), N Africa; ⊙ Tunis; formerly a French protectorate. After the Second World War nationalist demands for home rule were strongly advanced by the Neo-Destour (New Constitution) party, headed by Habib Bourgiba. Terrorism and small-scale guerrilla warfare struck hard at the European colonists, who opposed the nationalist demands. Attempts by the French government to reach a compromise with the nationalists had little result. Negotiations, however, ended in 1955 with the grant of a considerable amount of autonomy. On March 20, 1956, Tunisia achieved independence, though France retained the right to maintain troops in the country and some French-Tunisian economic interdependence was instituted. A constituent assembly empowered to draw up a constitution on July 25, 1957, deposed the bey and set up a republic. Bourgiba, who already was premier, was made president. His policy of friendship for the Western powers was somewhat shaken by troubles with France. Tunisia favored the Moslem nationalists of Algeria, who had in Tunisia their base for a provisional (revolutionary) government and for the National Liberal Front (FLN), which conducted guerrilla warfare against the French in Algeria. The French in 1958 bombed a Tunisian border town, and there was considerable discontent in Tunisia over affairs in the Saharan region. The real center of trouble was, however, the French naval and air base at Bizerte. Bourgiba's government insisted that the French withdraw, and France refused. In July, 1961, a Tunisian "peaceful siege" of the base led to a week of fierce conflict. Tunisia referred the question to the UN, and the UN Assembly adopted a resolution supporting the Tunisian claims. At the end of 1961, however, the withdrawal of French armed forces was not yet scheduled.

Ubangi-Shari: see CENTRAL AFRICAN REPUBLIC.

Uganda, British protectorate; scheduled to become independent in Oct., 1962.

Union of South Africa: see SOUTH AFRICA, REPUBLIC OF.

Union of Soviet Socialist Republics. Since 1956 the Soviet Union has comprised 15 republics. In 1956, the Karelo-Finnish Soviet Socialist Republic became the Karelian Autonomous Soviet Socialist Republic within the Russian Soviet Federated Socialist Republic. In 1954, the Crimean Oblast of the RSFSR passed to the Ukrainian SSR. The rehabilitation (1957) of some peoples deported during the Second World War from their native lands for having collaborated with the Germans led to formation of the following ASSRs: Chechen-Ingush, Kalmyck, and the Kabardinian-Balkar, all in the RSFSR. In addition, the Karachai-Cherkess Autonomous Oblast was created. Other oblast changes since 1956 are the abolition of Ashkhabad, Kashka-Darya, Namangan, and Taldy-Kurgan oblasts and their absorption by other oblasts. Also since 1956, major and minor cities have suffered name changes relating to the political eclipse of persons after which they were named, for example: Molotov (RSFSR) changed to Perm, and Voroshilov (RSFSR) changed to Ussuriysk. In 1961, as a result of a high-level party speech (1956) denouncing Stalin, those place names connected with him were changed; the major changes were Stalingrad (RSFSR) to Volgograd, Stalino (Ukraine) to Donetsk, and Stalinsk (Asiatic RSFSR) to Novo Kuznetsk.

United Arab Republic, political union of Egypt and Syria into a single state, 1958–61. Its capital was Cairo. The constitution of Feb., 1958, set up a "presidential democracy" with two regions, the Northern (Syria) and the Southern (Egypt). The kingdom of Yemen was joined with the new republic by a federation called the United Arab States. The president of the United Arab Republic was given wide powers, and President Gamal Abdel Nasser used them for advancing a program of socialist reform and nationalization. His imposition of Egyptian officials and Egyptian power in Syria led to a Syrian revolt and dissolution of the union in Sept., 1961. In Dec., 1961, Nasser denounced Yemen, and the United Arab States came to an end.

United States. The number of states was increased to 50 when the former territories of Alaska and Hawaii became states in 1959.

Upper Volta, Republic of the, independent state (1959 est. pop. 3,534,000, excluding non-indigenous pop.), NW Africa; ⊙ Ouagadougou; formerly the French overseas territory of Upper Volta. It borders N and W on Mali, SW on Ivory Coast, S on Ghana and Togo, SE on Dahomey, E on Niger. In June, 1956, France granted to the territory universal direct suffrage and more self-government. In the French constitutional referendum of Sept. 28, 1958, Upper Volta voted to join the FRENCH COMMUNITY, and in Dec., 1958, the territorial assembly, acting as a constituent assembly, proclaimed the Voltaic Republic as an autonomous member of the Community. In 1959 it was renamed Republic of the Upper Volta. In May, 1959, Upper Volta joined Dahomey, Niger, and Ivory Coast in a cooperative economic organization (the Council of the Entente). Following amendments to the French constitution in June, 1960, agreements were made by Upper Volta and France for transferring to Upper Volta control over those matters maintained under jurisdiction of the Community. The agreements were signed and the independence of the republic was proclaimed on Aug. 5, 1960. The Republic of the Upper Volta was admitted to the UN in 1960.

Ussuriysk, city, RSFSR; formerly called Voroshilov.

Vietnam, partitioned since 1954 as South Vietnam and North Vietnam. Hostilities between French Union and Vietminh forces in Vietnam continued until the spring of 1954, when the war was climaxed by the successful Vietminh siege of Dienbienphu. Agreements signed at a nine-nation conference in Geneva (July, 1954) ended the war and provided for provisional partition of the country on a line approximating the 17th parallel; at the same time, general elections designed to bring about the unification of Vietnam were scheduled for July, 1956. In the interim, the southern zone was placed under administration of the French-sponsored government of Bao Dai, recognized by the Western powers; the north was placed under control of the Vietminh government, recognized by the Soviet bloc. The South Vietnam delegation refused to sign the Geneva accords. Consequently, the elections provided for under the agreements did not take place, and Vietnam remained divided into two separate states. **North Vietnam** (Democratic Republic of Vietnam), ⊙ Hanoi. Following the 1954 partition of Vietnam, the premier of the Democratic Republic (which had a majority of the Vietnamese population) vainly called for elections to unify the country. These demands were turned down by South Vietnam. North Vietnam meanwhile cooperated closely with the Communist-bloc states, and initiated a gradual program of socialization; in 1960, however, less than half of the agriculture and the industry had been collectivized. By late 1961, North Vietnam had been repeatedly charged with aggression by the neighboring states of Laos and South Vietnam and had been accused of aiding with arms, equipment, and reinforcements the guerrilla forces which were threatening to take over those states. **South Vietnam** (Republic of Vietnam), ⊙ Saigon; attained full sovereignty in 1954. Previously, as an associated state within the French Union, the Vietnamese government of Bao Dai had limited autonomy; France controlled foreign affairs and maintained jurisdiction in certain military, judicial, economic, and other matters. Transfer of complete sovereignty took place with the signing of agreements in October and December of 1954; under these agreements South Vietnam, in effect, withdrew from the French Union. In a referendum held in Oct., 1955, the electorate voted for deposition of Bao Dai as chief of state and for the establishment of a republic with nationalist Premier Ngo Dinh Diem as president. The republic, proclaimed on Oct. 26, 1955, was recognized as the legal government of Vietnam by the United States, France, Britain, and other Western powers. The following years saw increasing criticism by some political leaders of President Ngo's authoritarian policies, specifically rigid press censorship, alleged interference with elections, and restriction of opposition parties. In 1960 Ngo crushed an armed revolt whose leaders had protested his "totalitarian" methods while declaring their aim to strengthen the country in its battle against Communism. Despite rural development and land reform programs, buttressed by aid from the U.S. and other countries, by late 1961 Communist guerrilla forces (the Viet Cong) had won control of virtually half the country with little local opposition. In Oct., 1961, Ngo placed South Vietnam in a "state of emergency" and accused North Vietnam of arming and reinforcing the Viet Cong guerrilla bands.

Volgograd, city, RSFSR; formerly called Stalingrad.

Voltaic Republic: see UPPER VOLTA, REPUBLIC OF THE.

Voroshilov, city, RSFSR: see USSURIYSK.

Western Samoa, Territory of, UN trusteeship, administered by New Zealand. In 1947 New Zealand started training the population for self-government, which was formally introduced in 1959. The territory was scheduled to become independent Jan. 1, 1962.

West Germany: see GERMANY.

West Indies, The, union of former British territories (□c. 8,000; 1960 est. pop. 3,115,000), in the West Indies, commonly called the West Indies Federation. Under the founding constitution (Jan. 3, 1958) Britain granted limited self-government to the Federation, which provisionally included 10 territories: Jamaica; Trinidad and Tobago; Barbadoes; three of the Leeward Isls., Antigua, Monserrat, and St. Kitts–Nevis–Anguilla; and four of the Windward Isls., Dominica, Grenada, St. Lucia, and St. Vincent. This constitution gave control of international relations, defense, and financial stability to Great Britain. In June, 1961, a constitutional conference held in London set May 31, 1962, as the date for independence of the Federation and recorded the desire of the Federation to become a member of the British Commonwealth of Nations. However, hopes for the future were darkened when in a referendum in Sept., 1961, the people of Jamaica, with approximately half the population and half the land area of the island union, voted to secede from the Federation and were later promised independence apart.

West Irian: see NEW GUINEA, WEST.

Württemberg-Baden: see BADEN-WÜRTTEMBERG.

Württemberg-Hohenzollern: see BADEN-WÜRTTEMBERG.

Yaoundé, capital of the Cameroon Republic; until 1960 capital of the UN trusteeship territory of French Cameroons.

Yemen. In 1958 Yemen and the United Arab Republic formed a loose confederation called the United Arab States. This was dissolved in 1961 by President Nasser of the United Arab Republic (by then reduced to Egypt).

CENSUS OF THE UNITED STATES, 1960

The list includes all places, incorporated or unincorporated, which had a population of 1,000 or more in 1960.

UNITED STATES, 179,323,175

ALABAMA, 3,266,740

Abbeville, 2,524
Adamsville, 2,095
Alabaster, 1,623
Albertville, 8,250
Alexander City, 13,140
Aliceville, 3,194
Andalusia, 10,263
Anniston, 33,657
Arab, 2,989
Ashford, 1,511
Ashland, 1,610
Athens, 9,330
Atmore, 8,173
Attalla, 8,257
Auburn, 16,261
Bay Minette, 5,197
Bayou La Batre, 2,572
Bay View, 1,081
Bessemer, 33,054
Birmingham, 340,887
Boaz, 4,654
Brantley, 1,014
Brent, 1,879
Brewton, 6,309
Bridgeport, 2,906
Brighton, 2,884
Brundidge, 2,523
Butler, 1,765
Calera, 1,928
Camden, 1,121
Camp Hill, 1,270
Carbon Hill, 1,944
Carrville, 1,081
Carver Court, 1,818
Centre, 2,392
Centreville, 1,981
Cherokee, 1,349
Chickasaw, 10,002
Childersburg, 4,884
Citronelle, 1,918
Clanton, 5,683
Clayton, 1,313
Collinsville, 1,199
Columbiana, 2,264
Cordova, 3,184
Cullman, 10,883
Dadeville, 2,940
Daphne, 1,527
Decatur, 29,217
Demopolis, 7,377
Dora, 1,776
Dothan, 31,440
East Brewton, 2,511
Elba, 4,321
Enterprise, 11,410
Eufaula, 8,357
Eutaw, 2,784
Evergreen, 3,703
Fairfax, 3,107
Fairfield, 15,816
Fairhope, 4,858
Fayette, 4,227
Flat Creek–Wegra, 1,140
Flomaton, 1,454
Florala, 3,011
Florence, 31,649
Foley, 2,889
Fort Deposit, 1,466
Fort Payne, 7,029
Frisco City, 1,177
Fultondale, 2,001
Gadsden, 58,088
Gardendale, 4,712
Geneva, 3,840
Georgiana, 2,093
Glencoe, 2,592
Goodwater, 2,023
Gordo, 1,714
Graysville, 2,870
Greensboro, 3,081
Greenville, 6,894
Greenwood, 3,561
Grove Hill, 1,834
Guin, 1,462
Guntersville, 6,592
Haleyville, 3,740
Hamilton, 1,934
Hanceville, 1,174
Hartford, 1,956
Hartselle, 5,000
Headland, 2,650
Heflin, 2,400
Hokes Bluff, 1,619
Homewood, 20,289
Hueytown, 5,997
Huntsville, 72,365
Hurtsboro, 1,056
Irondale, 3,501
Jackson, 4,959
Jacksonville, 5,678
Jasper, 10,799
Lafayette, 2,605
Lanett, 7,674
Langdale, 2,528
Leeds, 6,162
Leighton, 1,158
Linden, 2,516
Lineville, 1,612
Lipscomb, 2,811
Livingston, 1,544
Luverne, 2,238
Madison, 1,435
Marion, 3,807
Midfield, 3,556
Mignon, 2,271
Mobile, 202,779
Monroeville, 3,632
Montevallo, 2,755
Montgomery, 134,393
Moulton, 1,716
Mountain Brook, 12,680
Mount Pinson, 1,121
Muscle Shoals, 4,084
New Brockton, 1,093
Northport, 5,245
Oneonta, 4,136
Opelika, 15,678
Opp, 5,535
Oxford, 3,603
Ozark, 9,534
Parrish, 1,608
Pell City, 4,165
Phenix City, 27,630
Piedmont, 4,794
Pleasant Grove, 3,097
Prattville, 6,616
Prichard, 47,371
Ragland, 1,166
Rainbow City, 1,625
Red Bay, 1,954
Reform, 1,241
River View, 1,171
Roanoke, 5,288
Robertsdale, 1,474
Russellville, 6,628
Samson, 1,932
Saraland, 4,595
Satsuma, 1,491
Scottsboro, 6,449
Selma, 28,385
Shawmut, 1,898
Sheffield, 13,491
Slocomb, 1,368
Southwest Lanett, 2,189
Stevenson, 1,456
Sulligent, 1,346
Sumiton, 1,287
Sylacauga, 12,857
Talladega, 17,742
Tallassee, 4,934
Tarrant City, 7,810
Thomasville, 3,182
Troy, 10,234
Trussville, 2,510
Tuscaloosa, 63,370
Tuscumbia, 8,994
Tuskegee, 1,750
Union Springs, 3,704
Uniontown, 1,993
Vernon, 1,492
Vestavia Hills, 4,029
Vincent, 1,402
Warrior, 2,448
Weaver, 1,401
West Blocton, 1,156
West End Anniston, 5,485
Wetumpka, 3,672
Winfield, 2,907
York, 2,932

ALASKA, 226,167

Anchorage, 44,237
Barrow, 1,314
Bethel, 1,258
College, 1,755
Cordova, 1,128
Douglas, 1,042
Fairbanks, 13,311
Graehl Hamilton Acres, 2,162
Homer, 1,247
Juneau, 6,797
Ketchikan, 6,483
Kodiak, 2,628
Kotzebue, 1,290
Lemeta Johnston, 1,227
Mount Edgecumbe, 1,884
Nome, 2,316
Nunaka Valley, 1,442
Palmer, 1,181
Petersburg, 1,502
Seward, 1,891
Sitka, 3,237
Spenard, 9,074
Wrangell, 1,315

ARIZONA, 1,302,161

Ajo, 7,049
Avondale, 6,151
Bagdad, 1,462
Benson, 2,494
Bisbee, 9,914
Buckeye, 2,286
Casa Grande, 8,311
Central Heights, 2,486
Chandler, 9,531
Clarkdale, 1,095
Claypool, 2,505
Clifton, 4,191
Coolidge, 4,990
Cottonwood-Clemenceau, 1,879
Douglas, 11,925
El Mirage, 1,723
Eloy, 4,899
Flagstaff, 18,214
Florence, 2,143
Gila Bend, 1,813
Gilbert, 1,833
Glendale, 15,696
Globe, 6,217
Goodyear, 1,654
Hayden, 1,760
Holbrook, 3,438
Huachuca, 1,330
Kingman, 4,525
McNary, 1,608
Mammoth, 1,913
Mesa, 33,772
Miami, 3,350
Morenci, 2,431
Nogales, 7,286
Page, 2,960
Parker, 1,642
Peoria, 2,593
Phoenix, 439,170
Plantsite, 1,552
Prescott, 12,861
Ray, 1,468
Safford, 4,648
St. Johns, 1,310
San Manuel, 4,524
Scottsdale, 10,026
Show Low, 1,625
Sierra Vista, 3,121
Somerton, 1,613
Sonora, 1,244
South Tucson, 7,004
Stargo, 1,075
Superior, 4,875
Tanque Verde, 1,053
Tempe, 24,897
Thatcher, 1,581
Tolleson, 3,886
Tombstone, 1,283
Tucson, 212,892
West Yuma, 2,781
Wickenburg, 2,445
Willcox, 2,441
Williams, 3,559
Winkelman, 1,123
Winslow, 8,862
Yuma, 23,974

ARKANSAS, 1,786,272

Alma, 1,370
Arkadelphia, 8,069
Ashdown, 2,725
Atkins, 1,391
Augusta, 2,272
Bald Knob, 1,705
Batesville, 6,207
Bearden, 1,268
Beebe, 1,697
Benton, 10,399
Bentonville, 3,649
Berryville, 1,999
Blytheville, 20,797
Booneville, 2,690
Brinkley, 4,636
Cabot, 1,321
Camden, 15,823
Cammack Village, 1,355
Carlisle, 1,514
Charleston, 1,036
Clarendon, 2,293
Clarksville, 3,919
Conway, 9,791
Corning, 2,192
Cotton Plant, 1,704
Crossett, 5,370
Dardanelle, 2,098
De Queen, 2,859
Dermott, 3,665
Des Arc, 1,482
De Witt, 3,019
Dierks, 1,276
Dumas, 3,540
Earle, 2,391
El Dorado, 25,292
England, 2,861
Euclid Heights, 2,030
Eudora, 3,598
Eureka Springs, 1,437
Fayetteville, 20,274
Fordyce, 3,890
Forrest City, 10,544
Fort Smith, 52,991
Gould, 1,210
Green Forest, 1,038
Greenwood, 1,558
Gurdon, 2,166
Hamburg, 2,904
Hampton, 1,011
Harrisburg, 1,481
Harrison, 6,580
Hazen, 1,456
Heber Springs, 2,265
Helena, 11,500
Hope, 8,399
Hot Springs, 28,337
Hoxie, 1,886
Hughes, 1,960
Huntsville, 1,050
Jacksonville, 14,488
Jonesboro, 21,418
Lake Village, 2,998
Leachville, 1,507
Lepanto, 1,157
Lewisville, 1,373
Little Rock, 107,813
Lonoke, 2,359
Luxora, 1,236
McCrory, 1,053
McGehee, 4,448
Magnolia, 10,651
Malvern, 9,566
Manila, 1,753
Marianna, 5,134
Marked Tree, 3,216
Marshall, 1,095
Marvell, 1,690
Mena, 4,388
Monticello, 4,412
Morrilton, 5,997
Mountain Home, 2,105
Mountain Pine, 1,279
Murfreesboro, 1,096
Nashville, 3,579
Newport, 7,007
New Rocky Comfort, 1,001
North Little Rock, 58,032
Osceola, 6,189
Ozark, 1,965
Paragould, 9,947
Paris, 3,007
Parkin, 1,489
Piggott, 2,776
Pine Bluff, 44,037
Pine Bluff Southeast, 2,679
Pocahontas, 3,665
Prairie Grove, 1,056
Prescott, 3,533
Rector, 1,757
Rogers, 5,700
Russellville, 8,921
Searcy, 7,272
Sheridan, 1,938
Sherwood, 1,222
Siloam Springs, 3,953
Smackover, 2,434
Springdale, 10,076
Stamps, 2,591
Star City, 1,573
Stephens, 1,275
Stuttgart, 9,661
Texarkana, 19,788
Trumann, 4,511
Tuckerman, 1,539
Van Buren, 6,787
Waldo, 1,722
Waldron, 1,619
Walnut Ridge, 3,547
Warren, 6,752
West End, 2,208
West Helena, 8,385
West Memphis, 19,374
Wilson, 1,191
Wynne, 4,922

CALIFORNIA, 15,717,204

Airport, 3,689
Alameda, 61,316
Alamo, 1,791
Albany, 14,804
Alhambra, 54,807
Alisal, 16,473
Alpine, 1,044
Altadena, 40,568
Alta Hill, 1,078
Alturas, 2,819
Alum Rock, 18,942
Alviso, 1,174
Anaheim, 104,184
Anderson, 4,492
Angels, 1,121
Antioch, 17,305
Arcadia, 41,005
Arcata, 5,235
Arden Arcade, 73,352
Armona, 1,302
Arroyo Grande, 3,291
Artesia, 9,993
Arvin, 5,310
Atascadero, 5,983
Atherton, 7,717
Atwater, 7,318
Auburn, 5,586
Avalon, 1,536
Avenal, 3,147
Azusa, 20,497
Bakersfield, 56,848
Baldwin Park, 33,951
Banning, 10,250
Barstow, 11,644
Bayview-Rosewood, 2,980
Beaumont, 4,288
Bell, 19,450
Bellflower, 44,846
Bell Gardens, 26,467
Belmont, 15,996
Belvedere, 2,148
Benicia, 6,070
Ben Lomond, 1,814
Berkeley, 111,268
Beverly Hills, 30,817
Big Bear Lake, 1,562
Bishop, 2,875
Blue Lake, 1,234
Bly, 1,554
Blythe, 6,023
Bonnyville, 4,686
Boulder Creek, 1,306
Boyes Springs, 2,462
Brawley, 12,703
Brea, 8,487
Brentwood, 2,186
Buena Park, 46,401
Burbank, 90,155
Burlingame, 24,036
Burney, 1,294
Burton, 4,635
Calexico, 7,992
Calipatria, 2,548
Calistoga, 1,514
Camarillo, 2,359
Camarillo Heights, 1,704
Campbell, 11,863
Capistrano Beach, 2,026
Capitola, 2,021
Carlsbad, 9,253
Carmel-by-the-Sea, 4,580
Carmel Valley, 1,143
Carmel Woods, 1,043
Carmichael, 20,455
Carpinteria, 4,998
Carson, 38,059
Castro Valley, 37,120
Castroville, 2,838
Cathedral City, 1,855
Central Valley, 2,854
Ceres, 4,406
Ceres Northwest, 1,126
Chemeketa Park–Redwood Estates, 1,284
Chester, 1,553
Chico, 14,757
Chico Vecino, 4,688
Chino, 10,305
Chowchilla, 4,525
Chrisman, 3,923
Chula Vista, 42,034
Claremont, 12,633
Cloverdale, 2,848
Clovis, 5,546
Coachella, 4,854
Coalinga, 5,965
College Gardens, 4,132
Colton, 18,666
Colusa, 3,518
Commerce, 9,555
Compton, 71,812
Concord, 36,208
Corcoran, 4,976
Corning, 3,006
Corona, 13,336
Coronado, 18,039
Corte Madera, 5,962
Costa Mesa, 37,550
Cotati, 1,852
Covina, 20,124
Crescent City, 2,958
Crescent City Northwest, 3,086
Crestline, 1,290
Crowley, 3,950
Culver City, 32,163
Cupertino, 3,664
Cutler, 2,191
Cutten, 1,572
Cypress, 1,753
Dairy Valley, 3,508
Daly City, 44,791
Dana Point, 1,186
Danville, 3,585
Davis, 8,910
Delano, 11,913
Delhi, 1,175
Del Mar, 3,124
Del Monte Heights, 1,174
Del Monte Park, 2,177
Del Paso Heights–Robla, 11,495
Del Rey Oaks, 1,831
Desert Hot Springs, 1,472
Diablo, 2,096
Dinuba, 6,103
Dixon, 2,970
Dos Palos, 2,028
Downey, 82,505
Duarte, 13,962
Dunsmuir, 2,873
Earlimart, 2,897
East Los Angeles, 104,270
East Modesto, 2,084
East Porterville, 3,538
East Tulare, 1,342
East Whittier, 19,884
Edgemont, 1,628
El Cajon, 37,618
El Centro, 16,811
El Cerrito, 25,437
Elk Grove, 2,205
El Monte, Contra Costa co., 4,186
El Monte, Los Angeles co., 13,163
El Paso de Robles, 6,677
El Rio, 6,966
El Segundo, 14,219
Elsinore, 2,432
El Verano, 1,236
Emeryville, 2,686
Empire, 1,635
Encinitas, 2,786
Enterprise, 4,946
Escalon, 1,763
Escondido, 16,377
Eureka, 28,137
Exeter, 4,264
Fairfax, 5,813
Fairfield, 14,968
Fair Oaks, 1,622
Fairview, 3,586
Fallbrook, 4,814
Farmersville, 3,101
Felton, 1,380
Ferndale, 1,116
Fillmore, 4,808
Firebaugh, 2,070
Florence-Graham, 38,164
Folsom, 3,925
Fontana, 14,659
Ford City, 3,926
Fort Bragg, 4,433
Fortuna, 3,523
Fountain Valley, 2,068
Fowler, 1,892
Freedom, 4,206
Fremont, 43,790
Fresno, 133,929
Fullerton, 56,180
Galt, 1,868
Gardena, 35,943
Garden Grove, 84,238
Gilroy, 7,348
Glen Avon Heights, 3,416
Glendale, 119,442
Glendora, 20,752
Gonzales, 2,138
Goshen, 1,061
Grass Valley, 4,876
Graton, 1,055
Greenfield, 1,207
Greenville, 1,140
Gridley, 3,343
Grover, 5,210
Guadalupe, 2,614
Gustine, 2,300
Hagginwood, 11,469
Half Moon Bay, 1,957
Hanford, 10,133
Hanford Northwest, 1,364
Hatton Fields, 2,362
Hawthorne, 33,035
Hayward, 72,700
Healdsburg, 4,816
Hemet, 5,416
Hemet East, 1,936
Hermosa Beach, 16,115
Highway City, 1,381
Hillgrove, 14,669
Hillsborough, 7,554
Hollister, 6,071
Holtville, 3,080
Home Gardens, 1,541
Hughson, 1,898
Huntington Beach, 11,492
Huntington Park, 29,920
Huron, 1,269
Imperial, 2,658
Imperial Beach, 17,773
Indio, 9,745
Inglewood, 63,390
Ione, 1,118
Irwindale, 1,518
Isleton, 1,039
Ivanhoe, 1,616
Jackson, 1,852
Kamondorski, 1,006
Kerman, 1,970
Keyes, 1,546
King City, 2,937
Kingsburg, 3,093
La Canada–Flintridge, 18,338
Lafayette, 7,114
Laguna Beach, 9,288
La Habra, 25,136
Lakeland Village, 3,539
Lakeport, 2,303
Lakewood, 67,126
La Mesa, 30,441
Lamont, 6,177
Lancaster, 26,012
La Puente, 24,723
Larkspur, 5,710
Lathrop, 1,123
Laton, 1,052
La Verne, 6,516
Lawndale, 21,740
Lemon Grove, 19,348
Lemoore, 2,561
Lennox, 31,224
Lenwood, 2,407
Leucadia, 5,665
Lincoln, 3,197
Linda, 6,129
Lindsay, 5,397
Live Oak, Santa Cruz co., 3,518
Live Oak, Sutter co., 2,276
Livermore, 16,058
Livingston, 2,188
Lodi, 22,229
Lomita, 14,983
Lompoc, 14,415
Lone Pine, 1,310
Long Beach, 344,168
Los Alamitos, 4,312
Los Altos, 19,696
Los Altos Hills, 3,412
Los Angeles City, 2,479,015
Los Banos, 5,272
Los Gatos, 9,036
Lynwood, 31,614
McCloud, 2,140
McFarland, 3,686
McMillan Manor, 1,193
Madera, 14,430
Manhattan Beach, 33,934
Manteca, 8,242
Marina, 3,310
Martinez, 9,604
Martinez East, 3,958
Marysville, 9,553
Maywood, 14,588
Meiners Oaks, 3,513
Mendota, 2,099
Menlo Park, 26,957
Merced, 20,068
Merritt–Peck Colonies, 1,299
Millbrae, 15,873
Mill Valley, 10,411
Milpitas, 6,572
Mirada Hills, 22,444
Mira Loma, 3,982
Mirro Beach, 1,907
Modesto, 36,585
Mojave, 1,845
Monrovia, 27,079
Montalvo, 2,028
Montclair, 13,546
Montebello, 32,097
Monterey, 22,618
Monterey Park, 37,821
Monte Sereno, 1,506
Moorpark, 2,902
Morada, 2,156
Morgan Hill, 3,151
Morro Bay, 3,692
Mountain View, 30,889
Mount Shasta, 1,936
Mulberry, 2,643
Napa, 22,170
National City, 32,771
Needles, 4,590
Nevada City, 2,353
Newark, 9,884
Newhall, 4,705
Newman, 2,148
Newport Beach, 26,564
Norco, 4,964
Northcrest, 1,945
North Highlands, 21,271
North Sacramento, 12,922
North Turlock, 2,535
Norwalk, 88,739
Novato, 17,881
Nyeland Acres, 1,619
Oakdale, 4,980
Oakland, 367,548
Oak View, 2,448
Oceano, 1,317
Oceanside, 24,971
Ojai, 4,495
Olivehurst, 4,835
Ontario, 46,617
Opal Cliffs, 3,825
Orange, 26,444
Orange Cove, 2,885
Orcutt, 1,414
Orinda, 4,712
Orinda Village, 5,568
Orland, 2,534
Orosi, 1,048
Oroville, 6,115
Oxnard, 40,265
Pacheco, 1,518
Pacifica, 20,995
Pacific Grove, 12,121
Pajaro, 1,273
Palmdale, 11,522
Palm Desert, 1,295
Palm Springs, 13,468
Palo Alto, 52,287
Palos Verdes Estates, 9,564
Paradise, Butte co., 8,268
Paradise, Stanislaus co., 5,616
Paramount, 27,249
Parlier, 1,366
Pasadena, 116,407

California (cont.)
Patterson, 2,246
Perris, 2,950
Petaluma, 14,035
Pico Rivera, 49,150
Piedmont, 11,117
Pinole, 6,064
Pismo Beach, 1,762
Pittsburg, 19,062
Pittsburg East, 1,977
Pittsburg West, 5,188
Pixley, 1,327
Placentia, 5,861
Placerville, 4,439
Planada, 1,704
Pleasant Hill, 23,844
Pleasanton, 4,203
Pomona, 67,157
Poplar, 1,478
Port Chicago, 1,746
Porterville, 7,991
Port Hueneme, 11,067
Portola, 1,874
Poway, 1,921
Quartz Hill, 3,325
Quincy–East Quincy, 2,723
Ramona, 2,449
Rancho Cordova, 7,429
Red Bluff, 7,202
Redding, 12,773
Redlands, 26,829
Redondo Beach, 46,986
Redwood City, 46,290
Reedley, 5,850
Rialto, 18,567
Richmond, 71,854
Ridgecrest, 5,099
Rio Dell, 3,222
Rio Linda, 2,189
Rio Vista, 2,616
Ripon, 1,894
Riverbank, 2,786
Riverdale, 1,012
Riverside, 84,332
Rocklin, 1,495
Rohnerville, 2,268
Rolling Hills, 1,664
Rolling Hills Estates, 3,941
Roseland, 4,510
Rosemead, 15,476
Roseville, 13,421
Ross, 2,551
Ryans Slough, 3,634
Sacramento, 191,667
St. Helena, 2,722
Salida, 1,109
Salinas, 28,957
San Andreas, 1,416
San Anselmo, 11,584
San Bernardino, 91,922
San Bruno, 29,063
San Buenaventura, 29,114
San Carlos, 21,370
San Clemente, 8,527
San Diego, 573,224
San Fernando, 16,093
San Francisco, 742,855
San Gabriel, 2,561
Sanger, 8,072
San Jacinto, 2,553
San Jose, 204,196
San Juan Bautista, 1,046
San Juan Capistrano, 1,120
San Leandro, 65,962
San Lorenzo, 23,773
San Luis Obispo, 20,437
San Marino, 13,658
San Martin, 1,162
San Mateo, 69,870
San Pablo, 19,687
San Rafael, 20,460
Santa Ana, 100,350
Santa Barbara, 58,768
Santa Clara, 58,880
Santa Cruz, 25,596
Santa Fe Springs, 16,342
Santa Maria, 20,027
Santa Monica, 83,249
Santa Paula, 13,279
Santa Rosa, 31,027
Santa Susana, 2,310
Saranap, 6,450
Saratoga, 14,861
Saticoy, 2,283
Sausalito, 5,331
Scotia, 1,122
Seal Beach, 6,994
Seaside, 19,353
Sebastopol, 2,694
Selma, 6,934
Shafter, 4,576
Shell Beach, 1,820
Shore Acres, 3,093
Sierra Madre, 9,732
Signal Hill, 4,627
Silver Strand, 1,192
Simi, 2,107
Soledad, 2,837
Solvang, 1,325
Sonoma, 3,023
Sonora, 2,725
South El Monte, 4,850
South Gate, 53,831
South Laguna, 2,000
South Modesto, 5,465
South Oroville, 3,704
South Park, 3,261
South Pasadena, 19,706
South Sacramento–Fruitridge, 16,443
South San Francisco, 39,418
South San Gabriel, 26,213
South Taft, 1,910
South Turlock, 1,577
South Yuba, 3,200
Stanton, 11,163
Stockton, 86,321
Strathmore, 1,095
Suisun City, 2,470
Suncrest–La Cresta, 1,166
Sunnymead, 3,404
Sunnyvale, 52,898
Susanville, 5,598
Sutter, 1,219
Sutter Creek, 1,161
Taft, 3,822
Taft Heights, 2,661
Tehachapi, 3,161
Temple City, 31,838
Thousand Oaks, 2,934
Torrance, 100,991
Tracy, 11,289
Trona, 1,138
Tulare, 13,824
Tuolumne, 1,403
Turlock, 9,116
Tustin, 2,006
Twin Lakes, 1,849
Ukiah, 9,900
Union City, 6,618
Upland, 15,918
Vacaville, 10,898
Vallejo, 60,877
Visalia, 15,791
Vista, 14,795
Walnut Creek, 9,903
Walnut Heights, 5,080
Wasco, 6,841
Waterford, 1,780
Watsonville, 13,293
Weaverville, 1,736
Weed, 3,223
West Covina, 50,645
Westgate-Waverly-Park, 2,191
West Hollywood, 28,870
Westminster, 25,750
West Modesto, 1,897
Westmorland, 1,404
Westwood, 1,209
Whittier, 33,663
Williams, 1,370
Willits, 3,410
Willows, 4,139
Winters, 1,700
Woodlake, 2,623
Woodland, 13,524
Woodside, 3,592
Woodville, 1,045
Yorba Linda, 1,198
Yreka City, 4,759
Yuba City, 11,507

COLORADO, 1,753,947
Akron, 1,890
Alamosa, 6,205
Antonito, 1,045
Arvada, 19,242
Aspen, 1,101
Aurora, 48,548
Berthoud, 1,014
Boulder, 37,718
Brighton, 7,055
Broomfield Heights, 4,535
Brush, 3,621
Buena Vista, 1,806
Burlington, 2,090
Canon City, 8,973
Castle Rock, 1,152
Center, 1,600
Cherry Hills Village, 1,931
Cheyenne Wells, 1,020
Climax, 1,609
Colorado Springs, 70,194
Commerce Town, 8,970
Cortez, 6,764
Craig, 3,984
Del Norte, 1,856
Delta, 3,832
Denver, 493,887
Derby, 10,124
Durango, 10,530
East Canon, 1,101
Eaton, 1,267
Edgewater, 4,314
Englewood, 33,398
Estes Park, 1,175
Evans, 1,453
Fleming, 1,903
Florence, 2,821
Fort Collins, 25,027
Fort Collins West, 1,569
Fort Lupton, 2,194
Fort Morgan, 7,379
Fountain, 1,602
Fowler, 1,240
Fruita, 1,830
Glenwood Springs, 3,637
Golden, 7,118
Grand Junction, 18,694
Greeley, 26,314
Gunnison, 3,477
Holly, 1,108
Holyoke, 1,555
Idaho Springs, 1,480
Ivywild, 11,065
Julesburg, 1,840
Lafayette, 2,612
La Junta, 8,026
Lakewood, 19,338
Lamar, 7,369
La Salle, 1,070
Las Animas, 3,402
Leadville, 4,008
Limon, 1,811
Lincoln Park, 2,085
Littleton, 13,670
Longmont, 11,489
Louisville, 2,073
Loveland, 9,734
Manitou Springs, 3,626
Meeker, 1,655
Merino, 1,222
Monte Vista, 3,385
Montrose, 5,044
Orchard City, 1,021
Orchard Mesa, 4,956
Ordway, 1,254
Pagosa Springs, 1,374
Paonia, 1,083
Pueblo, 91,181
Rangely, 1,464
Rifle, 2,135
Rocky Ford, 4,929
Salida, 4,560
Security, 9,017
Sheridan, 3,559
Springfield, 1,791
Steamboat Springs, 1,843
Sterling, 10,751
Thornton, 11,353
Trinidad, 10,691
Uravan, 1,005
Walsenburg, 5,071
Westminster, 13,850
Wheat Ridge, 21,619
Windsor, 1,509
Wray, 2,082
Yuma, 1,919

CONNECTICUT, 2,535,234
Ansonia, 19,819
Baltic, 1,366
Bethel, 5,624
Branford, 2,371
Bridgeport, 156,748
Bristol, 45,499
Broad Brook, 1,389
Canaan, 1,146
Cheshire, 4,072
Chester, 1,414
Clinton, 2,693
Colchester, 2,260
Collinsville, 1,682
Conning Towers, 3,457
Cromwell, 2,889
Danbury, 22,928
Danielson, 4,642
Deep River, 2,166
Derby, 12,132
East Brooklyn, 1,213
East Hampton, 1,574
East Hartford, 43,977
East Haven, 21,388
Enfield, 31,464
Essex, 1,470
Fairfield, 46,183
Germantown, 2,893
Greenwich, 53,793
Groton, 10,111
Guilford, 2,420
Hamden, 41,056
Hartford, 162,178
Jewett City, 3,608
Lake Pocotopang, 1,314
Litchfield, 1,363
Madison, 1,416
Manchester, 42,102
Meriden, 51,850
Middletown, 33,250
Milford, 41,662
Montville, 1,060
Moodus, 1,103
Moosup, 2,760
Morningside Park, 3,181
Mystic, 2,536
Naugatuck, 19,511
New Britain, 82,201
New Hartford, 1,034
New Haven, 152,048
New London, 34,182
New Milford, 3,023
Newtown, 1,261
Niantic, 2,788
Noank, 1,116
North Grosvenor Dale, 1,874
Norwalk, 67,775
Norwich, 38,506
Old Saybrook, 1,671
Pawcatuck, 4,389
Plainfield, 2,044
Plantsville, 2,793
Pleasure Beach, 1,264
Portland, 5,587
Putnam, 6,952
Quaker Hill, 1,671
Ridgefield, 2,954
Rockville, 9,478
Shelton, 18,190
Simsbury, 2,745
South Coventry, 3,568
Southington, 9,952
Stafford Springs, 3,322
Stamford, 92,713
Stonington, 1,622
Storrs, 6,054
Stratford, 45,012
Suffield, 1,069
Terryville, 5,231
Thomaston, 3,579
Torrington, 30,045
Uncasville, 1,381
Unionville, 2,246
Wallingford, 29,920
Warehouse Point, 1,936
Waterbury, 107,130
West Hartford, 62,382
West Haven, 43,002
West Mystic, 3,268
Wethersfield, 20,561
Willimantic, 13,881
Winsted, 8,136
Woodbury, 3,910

DELAWARE, 446,292
Bellefonte, 1,536
Bridgeville, 1,469
Camden, 1,125
Clayton, 1,028
Delaware City, 1,658
Dover, 7,250
Elsmere, 7,319
Georgetown, 1,765
Harrington, 2,495
Laurel, 2,709
Lewes, 3,025
Middletown, 2,191
Milford, 5,795
Milton, 1,617
Newark, 11,404
New Castle, 4,469
Newport, 1,239
Rehoboth Beach, 1,507
Seaford, 4,430
Selbyville, 1,080
Smyrna, 3,241
Wilmington, 95,827
Wyoming, 1,172

DISTRICT OF COLUMBIA
(Washington city), 763,956

FLORIDA, 4,951,560
Alachua, 1,974
Altamonte Springs, 1,212
Apalachicola, 3,099
Apopka, 3,578
Arcadia, 5,889
Atlantic Beach, 3,125
Auburndale, 5,595
Avon Park, 6,073
Baldwin, 1,272
Bartow, 12,849
Bay Harbor Islands, 3,249
Bayshore Gardens, 2,297
Bee Ridge, 2,043
Belleair, 2,456
Belle Glade, 11,273
Belle Isle, 2,344
Bellglade Camp, 1,658
Bend–South City, 1,148
Biscayne Park, 2,911
Blountstown, 2,375
Boca Raton, 6,961
Bonifay, 2,222
Bowling Green, 1,171
Boynton Beach, 10,467
Bradenton, 19,380
Bradenton Beach, 1,124
Bradenton South, 3,400
Bradley Junction, 1,035
Brandon, 1,665
Brooksville, 3,301
Brownsville, 38,417
Bunnell, 1,860
Cantonment, 2,499
Carol City, 21,749
Carrabelle, 1,146
Casselberry, 2,463
Cedar Hammock, 3,089
Century, 2,046
Chattahoochee, 9,699
Chiefland, 1,459
Chipley, 3,159
Chosen, 1,858
Clearwater, 34,653
Clermont, 3,313
Clewiston, 3,114
Cocoa, 12,294
Cocoa Beach, 3,475
Cocoa West, 3,975
Combee Settlement, 2,697
Coral Gables, 34,793
Crescent City, 1,629
Crestview, 7,467
Cross City, 1,857
Crystal River, 1,423
Cutler Ridge, 7,005
Dade, 4,759
Dania, 7,065
Davenport, 1,209
Daytona Beach, 37,395
Debary, 2,362
Deerfield Beach, 9,573
De Funiak Springs, 5,282
De Land, 10,775
Delray Beach, 12,230
Dundee, 1,554
Dunedin, 8,444
Dunnellon, 1,079
Eagle Lake, 1,364
East Palatka, 1,133
Eau Gallie, 12,300
Edgewater, 2,051
Eloise, 3,256
El Portal, 2,079
Englewood, 2,877
Ensley, 1,836
Eustis, 6,189
Fernandina Beach, 7,276
Florida City, 4,114
Fort Lauderdale, 83,648
Fort Meade, 4,014
Fort Myers, 22,523
Fort Myers Beach, 2,463
Fort Pierce, 25,256
Fort Walton Beach, 12,147
Frostproof, 2,664
Fruitville, 2,131
Gainesville, 29,701
Gainesville East, 2,393
Gainesville North, 4,290
Gainesville West, 2,725
Gibsonton, 1,673
Goulds, 5,124
Gifford, 3,509
Graceville, 2,307
Greenacres City, 1,026
Green Cove Springs, 4,233
Greenville, 1,318
Groveland, 1,747
Gulfport, 9,730
Haines City, 9,135
Hallandale, 10,483
Harlem, 1,256
Havana, 2,090
Hawthorn, 1,167
Hayden, 5,471
Hialeah, 66,972
Highland City, 1,020
High Springs, 2,329
Hilliard, 1,075
Holly Hill, 4,182
Hollywood, 35,237
Holmes Beach, 1,143
Homestead, 9,152
Immokalee, 3,224
Indialantic, 1,653
Indian Rocks Beach, 1,940
Indiantown, 1,411
Inverness, 1,878
Jacksonville, 201,030
Jacksonville Beach, 12,049
Jasper, 2,103
June Park, 1,484
Jupiter, 1,058
Kenneth City, 2,114
Kensington Park, 2,969
Key West, 33,956
Kissimmee, 6,845
La Belle, 1,262
Lacoochee, 1,523
Lake Alfred, 2,191
Lake Butler, 1,311
Lake, 9,465
Lake Clarke Shores, 1,297
Lake Helen, 1,096
Lake Holloway, 3,172
Lakeland, 41,350
Lake Park, 3,589
Lake Placid, 1,007
Lake Wales, 8,346
Lake Worth, 20,758
Lantana, 5,021
Largo, 5,302
Lauderdale by-the-Sea, 1,327
Leesburg, 11,172
Leisure City, 3,001
Lighthouse Point, 2,453
Live Oak, 6,544
Longboat Key, 1,000
Longwood, 1,689
Lynn Haven, 3,078
Macclenny, 2,671
Maderia Beach, 3,943
Madison, 3,239
Maitland, 3,570
Margate, 2,646
Marianna, 7,152
Melbourne, 11,982
Melbourne Beach, 1,004
Memphis, 2,647
Merritt Island, 3,554
Miami, 291,688
Miami Beach, 63,145
Miami Shores, 8,865
Miami Springs, 11,229
Midway-Canaan, 1,897
Milton, 4,108
Mims, 1,307
Miramar, 5,485
Monticello, 2,490
Mount Dora, 3,756
Mulberry, 2,922
Nakomis Laurel, 2,253
Naples, 4,655
Naranja, 2,509
Neptune Beach, 2,868
Newberry, 1,105
New Port Richey, 3,520
New Smyrna Beach, 8,781
Niceville, 4,517
North Bay, 2,006
North Miami, 28,708
North Miami Beach, 21,405
North Palm Beach, 2,684
North Peninsula, 3,476
Oakland Park, 5,331
Ocala, 13,598
Oceanway, 1,271
Ocoee, 2,628
Okeechobee, 2,947
Oneco, 1,530
Opa-Locka, 9,810
Orange City, 1,598
Orange Park, 2,624
Orlando, 88,135
Ormond Beach, 8,658
Oviedo, 1,926
Pahokee, 4,709
Palatka, 11,028
Palm Bay, 2,808
Palm Beach, 6,055
Palmetto, 5,556
Palm Springs, 2,503
Panama City, 33,275
Parker, 2,669
Pembroke Pines, 1,429
Pensacola, 56,752
Perrine, 6,424
Perry, 8,030
Pinellas Park, 10,848
Plantation, 4,772
Plant City, 15,711
Pompano Beach, 15,992
Port Charlotte, 3,197
Port Orange, 1,801
Port Richey, 1,931
Port St. Joe, 4,217
Port Tampa, 1,764
Princeton, 1,719
Punta Gorda, 3,157
Quincy, 8,874
Redington Beach, 1,368
Richmond Heights, 4,311
Riviera Beach, 13,046
Rockledge, 3,481
Rosedale, 4,085
Ruskin, 1,894
Safety Harbor, 1,787
St. Augustine, 14,734
St. Cloud, 4,353
St. Petersburg, 181,298
St. Petersburg Beach, 6,268
Samoset, 4,824
Sanford, 19,175
Sarasota, 34,083
Sebring, 6,939
Sneads, 1,399
Solano, 1,309
South Apopka, 2,484
South Bay, 1,631
South Daytona, 1,954
South Miami, 9,846
South Peninsula, 3,741
Springfield, 4,628
Starke, 4,806
Stuart, 4,791
Sunland Gardens, 1,417
Sunnyland, 4,761
Surfside, 3,157
Sylvan Shores, 1,214
Taft, 1,214
Tallahassee, 48,174
Tampa, 274,970
Tarpon Springs, 6,768
Tavares, 2,724
Temple Terrace, 3,812
Tice, 4,377
Titusville, 6,410
Trailer Estates, 1,562
Treasure Island, 3,506
Umatilla, 1,717
Valparaiso, 5,975
Venice, 3,444
Vero Beach, 8,849
Virginia Gardens, 2,159
Wahneta, 1,796
Ward Ridge, 1,886
Warrington, 16,752
Watertown, 2,109
Wauchula, 3,411
Waverly, 1,160
West End, 3,124
West Melbourne, 2,266
West Miami, 5,296
West Palm Beach, 56,208
West Winter Haven, 5,050
Westwood Lakes, 22,517
Wewahitchka, 1,436
Wildwood, 2,170
Williston, 1,582
Wilton Manor, 8,257
Winston, 3,323
Winter Garden, 5,513
Winter Haven, 16,277
Winter Park, 17,162
Zephyrhills, 2,887

GEORGIA, 3,943,116
Acworth, 2,359
Adairsville, 1,026
Adel, 4,321
Albany, 55,890
Alma, 3,515
Alpharetta, 1,349
Alto Park, 2,526
Americus, 13,472
Aragon, 1,023
Arlington, 1,462
Ashburn, 3,291
Athens, 31,355
Atlanta, 487,455
Augusta, 70,626
Austell, 1,867
Avondale Estates, 1,646
Bainbridge, 12,714
Barnesville, 4,919
Baxley, 4,268
Bibb City, 1,213
Blackshear, 2,482
Blakely, 3,580
Bloomfield Gardens, 4,381
Blue Ridge, 1,406
Boston, 1,357
Bowdon, 1,548
Bremen, 3,132
Brunswick, 21,703
Buena Vista, 1,574
Buford, 4,168
Butler, 1,346
Byron, 1,138
Cairo, 7,427
Calhoun, 3,587
Camilla, 4,753
Canton, 2,411
Carrollton, 10,973
Cartersville, 8,668
Cave Springs, 1,153
Cedartown, 9,340
Celanese Village, 1,500
Chamblee, 6,635
Chatsworth, 1,184
Chickamauga, 1,824
Clarkesville, 1,352
Clarkston, 1,524
Claxton, 2,672
Clayton, 1,507
Cochran, 4,714
College Park, 23,469
Colquitt, 1,556
Columbus, 116,779
Commerce, 3,551
Conyers, 2,881
Cordele, 10,609
Cornelia, 2,936
Covington, 8,167
Cumming, 1,561
Cuthbert, 4,300
Dahlonega, 2,604
Dallas, 2,065
Dalton, 17,868
Darien, 1,569
Dawson, 5,062
Decatur, 22,026
Demorest, 1,029
Denton, 1,726
Dock Junction, 5,417
Doerun, 1,037
Donalsonville, 2,621
Doraville, 4,437
Douglas, 8,736
Douglasville, 4,462
Dublin, 13,814
Duluth, 1,483
East Dublin, 1,677
East Griffin, 1,715
Eastman, 5,118
East Point, 35,633
East Thomaston, 2,237
Eatonton, 3,612
Edison, 1,232
Elberton, 7,107
Elizabeth, 1,620
Ellijay, 1,320
Experiment, 2,497
Fairburn, 2,470
Fair Oaks, 7,969
Fayetteville, 1,389
Fitzgerald, 8,781
Folkston, 1,810
Forest Park, 14,201
Forsyth, 3,697
Fort Gaines, 1,320
Fort Oglethorpe, 2,251
Fort Valley, 8,310
Gainesville, 16,523
Gainesville Cotton Mills, 2,207
Garden City, 5,451
Glennville, 2,791
Gordon, 1,793
Grantville, 1,158
Gray, 1,320
Greensboro, 2,773
Griffin, 21,735
Grovetown, 1,396
Hahira, 1,297
Hampton, 1,253
Hapeville, 10,082
Harlem, 1,423
Hartwell, 4,599
Hawkinsville, 3,967
Hazlehurst, 3,699
Hebardville, 2,758
Helena, 1,290
Hinesville, 3,174
Hogansville, 3,658
Homerville, 2,634
Jackson, 2,545
Jasper, 1,036
Jefferson, 1,746
Jeffersonville, 1,013
Jesup, 7,304
Jonesboro, 3,014
Kennesaw, 1,507
Kingsland, 1,536
La Fayette, 5,588
La Grange, 23,632
Lake, 1,042
Lakeland, 2,236
Lavonia, 2,088
Lawrenceville, 3,804
Lincoln Park, 1,840
Lincolnton, 1,450
Lindale–Silver Creek, 2,800
Lithonia, 1,667
Louisville, 2,413
Ludowici, 1,578
Lumber City, 1,360
Lumpkin, 1,348
Lyons, 3,219
McCaysville, 1,871
McDonough, 2,224

McRae, 2,738
Mableton, 7,127
Macon, 69,764
Madison, 2,680
Manchester, 4,115
Marietta, 25,565
Marietta East, 4,535
Marshallville, 1,308
Meigs, 1,236
Metter, 2,362
Midway-Hardwick, 16,909
Milledgeville, 11,117
Millen, 3,633
Milstead, 1,047
Monroe, 6,826
Montezuma, 3,744
Monticello, 1,931
Moultrie, 15,764
Mount Vernon, 1,166
Nashville, 4,070
Newnan, 12,169
Norcross, 1,605
North Atlanta, 12,661
North Canton, 1,996
Ocilla, 3,217
Oglethorpe, 1,169
Oxford, 1,047
Palmetto, 1,466
Pearson, 1,615
Pelham, 4,609
Pembroke, 1,450
Perry, 6,032
Phillipsburg, 2,037
Pooler, 1,073
Porterdale, 2,365
Port Wentworth, 3,705
Quitman, 5,071
Reidsville, 1,229
Reynolds, 1,087
Richland, 1,472
Rincon, 1,057
Ringgold, 1,311
Riverdale, 1,045
Rochelle, 1,235
Rockmart, 3,938
Rome, 32,226
Rossville, 4,665
Roswell, 2,983
Royston, 2,333
St. Marys, 3,272
St. Simons, 3,199
Sandersville, 5,425
Savannah, 149,245
Savannah Beach, 1,385
Screven, 1,010
Shannon, 1,629
Shellman, 1,050
Smyrna, 10,157
Social Circle, 1,780
Soperton, 2,317
Sparks, 1,158
Sparta, 1,921
Statesboro, 8,356
Stockbridge, 1,201
Stone Mountain, 1,976
Sugar Hill, 1,175
Summerville, 4,706
Swainsboro, 5,943
Sylvania, 3,469
Sylvester, 3,610
Talbotton, 1,163
Tallapoosa, 2,744
Tennille, 1,837
Thomaston, 9,336
Thomasville, 18,246
Thomson, 4,522
Thunderbolt, 1,925
Tifton, 9,903
Toccoa, 7,303
Trenton, 1,301
Trion, 2,227
Twin City, 1,095
Unadilla, 1,304
Union City, 2,118
Union Point, 1,615
Unionville, 1,607
Valdosta, 30,652
Vidalia, 7,569
Vienna, 2,099
Villa Rica, 3,450
Wadley, 1,898
Warner Robins, 18,633
Warrenton, 1,770
Washington, 4,440
Waycross, 20,944
Waynesboro, 5,359
West Point, 4,610
Willacoochee, 1,061
Winder, 5,555
Woodbury, 1,230
Wrens, 1,628
Wrightsville, 2,056

HAWAII, 632,772

Aiea, 11,826
Captain Cook, 1,687
Ewa, 3,257
Ewa Beach, 2,459
Haleiwa, 2,504
Hanapepe, 1,383
Hilo, 25,966
Honokaa, 1,247
Honolulu, 294,179
Kahaluu, 1,125
Kahuku, 1,238
Kahului, 4,223
Kailua-Lanikai, 25,622
Kalaheo, 1,185
Kaneohe, 14,414
Kapaa, 3,439
Keaau, 1,334
Kekaha, 2,082
Koloa, 1,426
Kurtistown, 1,025
Lahaina, 3,423
Laie, 1,767
Lanai City, 2,056
Lihue, 3,908
Lualualei-Maili, 5,045
Nanakuli, 2,745
Paauilo, 1,059
Pahala, 1,392
Pahoa, 1,046
Paia, 2,149
Papaikou, 1,591
Puunene, 3,054
Wahiawa, 15,512
Waialua, 2,689
Waianae-Makaha, 6,844
Wailua Houselots, 1,129
Wailuku, 6,969
Waimanalo, 3,011
Waimea, 1,312
Waipio Acres, 1,158
Whitmore, 1,820

IDAHO, 667,191

Aberdeen, 1,484
Alameda, 10,660
American Falls, 2,123
Ammon, 1,882
Arco, 1,562
Ashton, 1,242
Blackfoot, 7,378
Boise City, 34,481
Bonners Ferry, 1,921
Buhl, 3,059
Burley, 7,508
Caldwell, 12,230
Chubbuck, 1,590
Coeur D'Alene, 14,291
Collister, 5,436
Cottonwood, 1,081
Dalton Gardens, 1,083
Emmett, 3,769
Filer, 1,249
Franklin, 7,222
Garden City, 1,681
Glenns Ferry, 1,374
Gooding, 2,750
Grangeville, 3,642
Hailey, 1,185
Homedale, 1,381
Idaho Falls, 33,161
Jerome, 4,761
Kamiah, 1,245
Kellogg, 5,061
Kimberly, 1,298
Lewiston, 12,691
Lewiston Orchards, 9,680
McCall, 1,423
Malad City, 2,274
Meridian, 2,081
Montpelier, 3,146
Moscow, 11,183
Mountain Home, 9,344
Mountain View, 4,898
Mullan, 1,477
Nampa, 18,013
Orofino, 2,471
Osburn, 1,788
Parma, 1,295
Payette, 4,451
Pinehurst, 1,432
Pocatello, 28,534
Post Falls, 1,983
Preston, 3,640
Priest River, 1,749
Rexburg, 4,767
Rigby, 2,281
Rupert, 4,153
St. Anthony, 2,700
St. Maries, 2,435
Salmon, 2,944
Sandpoint, 4,355
Shelley, 2,612
Shoshone, 1,416
Smelterville, 1,127
Soda Springs, 2,424
South Boise, 1,452
Twin Falls, 20,126
Wallace, 2,412
Weiser, 4,208
Wendell, 1,232
Whitney, 13,603

ILLINOIS, 10,081,158

Abingdon, 3,469
Addison, 6,741
Albion, 2,025
Aledo, 3,080
Algonquin, 2,014
Alorton, 3,282
Alsir, 3,770
Altamont, 1,656
Alton, 43,047
Alton North, 1,505
Amboy, 2,067
Anna, 4,280
Antioch, 2,268
Arcola, 2,273
Arlington Heights, 27,878
Arthur, 2,120
Ashland, 1,064
Ashton, 1,024
Assumption, 1,439
Astoria, 1,206
Athens, 1,035
Atlanta, 1,568
Atwood, 1,258
Auburn, 2,209
Aurora, 63,715
Barrington, 5,434
Barrington Hills, 1,391
Barry, 1,422
Bartlett, 1,540
Bartonville, 7,253
Batavia, 7,496
Beardstown, 6,294
Beckemeyer, 1,056
Beecher, 1,367
Belleville, 37,264
Bellevue, 1,561
Bellwood, 20,729
Belvidere, 11,223
Bement, 1,558
Benld, 1,848
Bensenville, 9,141
Benton, 7,023
Berkeley, 5,792
Berwyn, 54,224
Bethalto, 3,235
Bethany, 1,118
Bloomingdale, 1,262
Bloomington, 36,271
Blue Island, 19,618
Blue Mound, 1,038
Bourbonnais, 3,336
Bradley, 8,082
Braidwood, 1,944
Breese, 2,461
Bridgeport, 2,260
Bridge View, 7,334
Brighton, 1,248
Broadview, 8,588
Brookfield, 29,429
Brooklyn, 1,922
Brookport, 1,154
Buffalo Grove, 1,492
Bunker Hill, 1,524
Burnham, 2,478
Bushnell, 3,710
Byron, 1,578
Cahokia, 15,829
Cairo, 9,348
Calumet City, 25,000
Calumet Park, 8,448
Cambridge, 1,665
Camp Point, 1,092
Canton, 13,588
Carbon Cliff, 1,268
Carbondale, 14,670
Carlinville, 5,440
Carlyle, 2,903
Carmi, 6,152
Carpentersville, 17,424
Carrier Mills, 2,006
Carrollton, 2,558
Carterville, 2,643
Carthage, 3,325
Cary, 2,530
Casey, 2,890
Caseyville, 2,455
Catlin, 1,263
Central City, 1,422
Centralia, 13,904
Central Park, 2,676
Centreville, 12,769
Cerro Gordo, 1,067
Champaign, 49,583
Channel Lake, 1,969
Charleston, 10,505
Chatham, 1,069
Chatsworth, 1,330
Chenoa, 1,523
Chester, 4,460
Chicago, 3,550,404
Chicago Heights, 34,331
Chicago Ridge, 5,748
Chillicothe, 3,054
Chrisman, 1,221
Christopher, 2,854
Cicero, 69,130
City Park, 1,133
Clarendon Hills, 5,885
Clay City, 1,144
Clifton, 1,018
Clinton, 7,355
Coal City, 2,852
Colchester, 1,495
Collinsville, 14,217
Columbia, 3,174
Cottage Hills, 3,976
Coulterville, 1,022
Country Club Hills, 3,421
Crest Hill, 5,887
Crestwood, 1,213
Crete, 3,463
Creve Coeur, 6,684
Crystal Lake, 8,314
Cuba, 1,380
Dallas City, 1,276
Danville, 41,856
Decatur, 78,004
Deerfield, 11,786
De Kalb, 18,486
Delavan, 1,377
Depue, 1,920
Des Plaines, 34,886
Dewey-Park, 1,747
Dixmoor, 3,076
Dixon, 19,565
Dolton, 18,746
Downers Grove, 21,154
Dupo, 2,937
Du Quoin, 6,558
Dwight, 3,086
Earlville, 1,420
East Alton, 7,630
East Chicago Heights, 3,270
East Dubuque, 2,082
East Dundee, 2,221
East Hazelcrest, 1,457
East Moline, 16,732
East Peoria, 12,310
Eastside Galesburg, 1,147
East St. Louis, 81,712
East Streator, 1,517
Edinburg, 1,003
Edwardsville, 9,996
Effingham, 8,172
Eldorado, 3,573
Elgin, 49,447
Elk Grove Village, 6,608
Elmhurst, 36,991
Elmwood, 1,882
Elmwood Park, 23,866
El Paso, 1,964
Erie, 1,215
Eureka, 2,538
Evanston, 79,283
Evergreen Park, 24,178
Fairbury, 2,937
Fairfield, 6,362
Fairmont City, 2,688
Farmer City, 1,838
Farmington, 2,831
Fisher, 1,155
Flora, 5,331
Flossmoor, 4,624
Forest Homes, 2,025
Forest Park, 14,452
Forest View, 1,042
Forrest, 1,220
Forreston, 1,153
Fox Lake, 3,700
Fox River Grove, 1,866
Frankfort, 1,135
Franklin Park, 18,322
Freeburg, 1,908
Freeport, 26,628
Fulton, 3,387
Gages Lake, 3,395
Galena, 4,410
Galesburg, 37,243
Galva, 3,060
Gardner, 1,041
Geneseo, 5,169
Geneva, 7,646
Genoa, 2,330
Georgetown, 3,544
Gibson City, 3,453
Gillespie, 3,569
Gilman, 1,704
Girard, 1,734
Glasford, 1,012
Glen Carbon, 1,241
Glencoe, 10,472
Glen Ellyn, 15,972
Glenview, 18,132
Godfrey, 1,231
Grafton, 1,084
Grandview, 2,214
Granite City, 40,073
Granville, 1,048
Grayslake, 3,762
Grayville, 2,280
Greenfield, 1,064
Green Rock, 2,677
Greenup, 1,477
Greenville, 4,569
Griggsville, 1,240
Gurnee, 1,831
Hamilton, 2,228
Hampshire, 1,309
Hanna City, 1,056
Hanover, 1,396
Harrisburg, 9,171
Hartford, 2,355
Harvard, 4,248
Harvey, 29,071
Harwood Heights, 5,688
Havana, 4,363
Hazel Crest, 6,205
Hegeler, 1,640
Henry, 2,278
Herrin, 9,474
Heyworth, 1,196
Hickory Hills, 2,707
Highland, 4,943
Highland Park, 25,532
Highwood, 4,499
Hillsboro, 4,232
Hillside, 7,794
Hinsdale, 12,859
Hodgkins, 1,126
Homer, 1,276
Hometown, 7,479
Homewood, 13,371
Hoopeston, 6,606
Huntley, 1,143
Island Lake, 1,639
Itasca, 3,564
Jacksonville, 21,690
Jerome, 1,666
Jerseyville, 7,420
Johnston City, 3,891
Joliet, 66,780
Jonesboro, 1,636
Justice, 2,803
Kankakee, 27,666
Kenilworth, 2,959
Kewanee, 16,324
Kincaid, 1,544
Klondike Lotus Point, 1,402
Knoxville, 2,560
Lacon, 2,175
Ladd, 1,255
La Grange, 15,285
La Grange Park, 13,793
La Harpe, 1,322
Lake Bluff, 3,494
Lake Forest, 10,687
Lake in the Hills, 2,046
Lake Zurich, 3,458
Lanark, 1,473
Lansing, 18,098
La Salle, 11,897
Lawrenceville, 5,492
Lebanon, 2,863
Leland Grove, 1,731
Lemont, 3,397
Lena, 1,552
Leroy, 2,088
Lewistown, 2,603
Lexington, 1,244
Libertyville, 8,560
Lincoln, 16,890
Lincolnwood, 11,744
Lindenhurst, 1,259
Lisle, 4,219
Litchfield, 7,330
Lockport, 7,560
Lombard, 22,561
Long Lake, 3,502
Loves Park, 9,086
Lovington, 1,200
Lyons, 9,936
McHenry, 3,336
McLeansboro, 2,951
Mackinaw, 1,163
Macomb, 12,135
Macon, 1,229
Madison, 6,861
Mahomet, 1,367
Manhattan, 1,117
Manito, 1,093
Manteno, 2,225
Marengo, 3,568
Marion, 11,274
Marissa, 1,722
Markham, 11,704
Maroa, 1,235
Marquette Heights, 2,517
Marseilles, 4,347
Marshall, 3,270
Martinsville, 1,351
Mascoutah, 3,625
Mason City, 2,160
Matteson, 3,225
Mattoon, 19,088
Maywood, 27,330
Melrose Park, 22,291
Mendota, 6,154
Meredosia, 1,034
Merrionette Park, 2,354
Metamora, 1,808
Metropolis, 7,339
Midlothian, 6,605
Milan, 3,065
Milford, 1,699
Milledgeville, 1,208
Millstadt, 1,830
Minonk, 2,001
Mokena, 1,332
Moline, 42,705
Momence, 2,949
Monmouth, 10,372
Montgomery, 2,122
Monticello, 3,219
Morris, 7,935
Morrison, 4,159
Morrisonville, 1,129
Morton, 5,325
Morton Grove, 20,533
Mound City, 1,669
Mounds, 1,835
Mount Carmel, 8,594
Mount Carroll, 2,056
Mount Morris, 3,075
Mount Olive, 2,295
Mount Prospect, 18,906
Mount Pulaski, 1,689
Mount Sterling, 2,262
Mount Vernon, 15,566
Moweaqua, 1,614
Mundelein, 10,526
Murphysboro, 8,673
Naperville, 12,933
Nashville, 2,606
Nauvoo, 1,039
Neoga, 1,145
New Athens, 1,923
New Baden, 1,464
New Lenox, 1,750
Newman, 1,097
Newton, 2,901
Niles, 20,393
Nokomis, 2,476
Normal, 13,357
Norridge, 14,087
Norris City, 1,243
North Aurora, 2,088
Northbrook, 11,635
North Chicago, 20,517
North Chillicothe, 2,259
Northfield, 4,005
Northlake, 12,318
North Pekin, 2,025
North Quincy, 2,256
North Riverside, 7,989
North Utica, 1,014
Oakbrook Terrace, 1,121
Oak Forest, 3,724
Oak Lawn, 27,471
Oak Park, 61,093
Oblong, 1,817
Odin, 1,242
O'Fallon, 4,018
Oglesby, 4,215
Olney, 8,780
Olympia Fields, 1,503
Onarga, 1,397
Oquawka, 1,090
Oregon, 3,732
Orion, 1,269
Orland Park, 2,592
Oswego, 1,510
Ottawa, 19,408
Palatine, 11,504
Palestine, 1,564
Palos Heights, 3,775
Palos Hills, 3,766
Palos Park, 2,169
Pana, 6,432
Paris, 9,823
Park, 1,408
Park Forest, 29,993
Park Ridge, 32,659
Pawnee, 1,517
Paxton, 4,370
Pecatonica, 1,659
Pekin, 28,146
Peoria, 103,162
Peoria Heights, 7,064
Peotone, 1,788
Peru, 10,460
Petersburg, 2,359
Phoenix, 4,203
Pinckneyville, 3,085
Pittsfield, 4,089
Plainfield, 2,183
Plano, 3,343
Polo, 2,551
Pontiac, 8,435
Port Byron, 1,153
Posen, 4,517
Princeton, 6,250
Princeville, 1,281
Prophetstown, 1,802
Quincy, 43,793
Rantoul, 22,116
Red Bud, 1,942
Ridgway, 1,055
Riverdale, 12,008
River Forest, 12,695
River Grove, 8,464
Riverside, 9,750
Riverton, 1,536
Roanoke, 1,821
Robbins, 7,511
Robinson, 7,226
Rochelle, 7,008
Rockdale, 1,272
Rock Falls, 10,261
Rockford, 126,706
Rock Island, 51,863
Rockton, 1,833
Rolling Meadows, 10,879
Rome, 1,347
Romeoville, 3,574
Roodhouse, 2,352
Roselle, 3,581
Roseville, 1,065
Rosewood Heights, 4,572
Rosiclare, 1,700
Rossville, 1,470
Round Lake Beach, 5,011
Round Lake Park, 2,565
Roxana, 2,090
Royalton, 1,225
Rushville, 2,819
St. Anne, 1,378
St. Charles, 9,269
St. Elmo, 1,503
St. Francisville, 1,040
St. Joseph, 1,210
Salem, 6,165
Sandoval, 1,356
Sandwich, 3,842
San Jose, 1,093
Sauk, 4,687
Savanna, 4,950
Schiller Park, 5,687
Seneca, 1,719
Sesser, 1,764
Shawneetown, 1,280
Sheffield, 1,078
Shelbyville, 4,821
Sheldon, 1,137
Silvis, 3,973
Skokie, 59,364
South Beloit, 3,781
South Chicago Heights, 4,043
South Elgin, 2,624
Southern View, 1,485
South Holland, 10,412
South Jacksonville, 2,340
South Pekin, 1,007
South Roxana, 2,010
South Streator, 1,923
Sparta, 3,452
Springfield, 83,271
Spring Valley, 5,371
Staunton, 4,228
Steeleville, 1,569
Steger, 6,432
Sterling, 15,688
Stickney, 6,239
Stockton, 1,800
Stone Park, 3,038
Stonington, 1,076
Streamwood, 4,821
Streator, 16,868
Sullivan, 3,946
Summit, 10,374
Sumner, 1,035
Swansea, 3,018
Sycamore, 6,961
Taylorville, 8,801
Teutopolis, 1,140
Thornton, 2,895
Tilton, 2,598
Tinley Park, 6,392
Tolono, 1,539
Toluca, 1,352
Toulon, 1,213
Tremont, 1,558
Trenton, 1,866
Troy, 1,778
Tuscola, 3,875
Urbana, 27,294
Valley View, 1,741
Vandalia, 5,537
Venetian Village, 2,084
Venice, 5,380
Vermilion Heights, 1,568
Vienna, 1,094
Villa Grove, 2,308
Villa Park, 20,391
Virden, 3,309
Virginia, 1,669
Walnut, 1,192
Wamac, 1,394
Warren, 1,470
Warrenville, 3,134
Warsaw, 1,938
Washburn, 1,064
Washington, 5,919
Washington Park, 6,601
Waterloo, 3,739
Watseka, 5,219
Wauconda, 3,227
Waukegan, 55,719
Waverly, 1,375
Wenona, 1,005
Westchester, 18,092
West Chicago, 6,854
West Dundee, 2,530
Western Springs, 10,838
West Frankfort, 9,027
West Kankakee, 3,197
Westmont, 5,997
West Sterling, 1,430
Westville, 3,497
Wheaton, 24,312
Wheeling, 7,169
White Hall, 3,012
Willow Springs, 2,348
Wilmette, 28,268
Wilmington, 4,210
Winchester, 1,657
Windmere, 1,268
Windsor, Shelby co., 1,021
Winfield, 1,575
Winnebago, 1,059
Winnetka, 13,368
Winthrop Harbor, 3,848
Witt, 1,101
Wonder Lake, 3,543
Wood Dale, 3,071
Wood River, 11,694
Woodstock, 8,897
Worden, 1,060
Worth, 8,196
Wyoming, 1,559
Yorkville, 1,568
Zeigler, 2,133
Zion, 11,941

INDIANA, 4,662,498

Albany, 2,132
Albion, 1,325
Alexandria, 5,582
Anderson, 49,061
Anderson East Side, 3,778
Andrews, 1,132
Angola, 4,746
Arcadia, 1,271
Argos, 1,339
Attica, 4,341
Auburn, 6,350
Aurora, 4,119
Austin, 3,838
Batesville, 3,349
Bedford, 13,024
Beech Grove, 10,973
Berne, 2,644
Bicknell, 3,878
Bloomfield, 2,224
Bloomington, 31,357
Bluffside, 1,372
Bluffton, 6,238
Boonville, 4,801
Bourbon, 1,522
Brazil, 8,853
Bremen, 3,062
Broadview, 1,865
Brookston, 1,202
Brookville, 2,596
Brownsburg, 4,478
Brownstown, 2,140
Bunker Hill, 1,049
Butler, 2,176
Cambridge City, 2,569
Cannelton, 1,829
Carmel, 1,442
Carthage, 1,043
Cedar Lake, 5,766
Centerville, 2,378
Chandler, 1,784
Charlestown, 5,726
Chesterfield, 2,588
Chesterton, 4,335
Churubusco, 1,284
Cicero, 1,284
Clarksville, 8,088
Clermont, 1,058
Clinton, 5,843
Columbia City, 4,803
Columbus, 20,778
Connersville, 17,698
Converse, 1,044
Corydon, 2,701
Covington, 2,759
Crawfordsville, 14,231
Crestlawn, 2,194
Crothersville, 1,449
Crown Point, 8,443
Culver, 1,558
Daleville, 1,548
Danville, 3,287
Decatur, 8,327
Delphi, 2,517
Dublin, 1,021
Dugger, 1,062
Dunkirk, 3,117
Dunlap, 1,935
Dyer, 3,993
East Chicago, 57,669
East Columbus, 1,912

Indiana (cont.)
East Gary, 9,309
Eaton, 1,529
Edgewood, 2,119
Edinburg, 3,664
Elkhart, 40,274
Ellettsville, 1,222
Elmhurst, 1,046
Elwood, 11,793
Englewood, 1,232
Evansville, 141,543
Fairmount, 3,080
Fairview Park, 1,039
Farmersburg, 1,027
Farmland, 1,102
Ferdinand, 1,427
Flora, 1,742
Fort Branch, 1,983
Fortville, 2,209
Fort Wayne, 161,776
Fowler, 2,491
Francesville, 1,002
Frankfort, 15,302
Franklin, 9,453
Frankton, 1,445
French Lick, 1,954
Galveston, 1,111
Garrett, 4,364
Gary, 178,320
Gas City, 4,469
Geneva, 1,053
Goodland, 1,202
Goshen, 13,718
Greencastle, 8,506
Greendale, 2,861
Greenfield, 9,049
Greensburg, 6,605
Greentown, 1,266
Greenwood, 7,169
Griffith, 9,483
Hagerstown, 1,730
Hammond, 111,698
Hanover, 1,170
Hartford City, 8,053
Haubstadt, 1,029
Hebron, 1,401
Highland, 16,284
Hobart, 18,680
Home Corner, 2,636
Hope, 1,489
Huntingburg, 4,146
Huntington, 16,185
Hymera, 1,015
Independence Hill, 1,824
Indianapolis, 476,258
Jasonville, 2,436
Jasper, 6,737
Jeffersonville, 19,522
Jonesboro, 2,260
Kendallville, 6,765
Kentland, 1,783
Kingsford Heights, 1,276
Knightstown, 2,496
Knox, 3,458
Kokomo, 47,197
Kouts, 1,007
Lafayette, 42,330
Lagrange, 1,990
Lapel, 1,772
LaPorte, 21,157
Lawrence, 10,103
Lawrenceburg, 5,004
Lebanon, 9,523
Liberty, 1,745
Ligonier, 2,595
Linton, 5,736
Logansport, 21,106
Long Beach, 2,007
Loogootee, 2,858
Lowell, 2,270
Lydick, 1,217
Lynn, 1,260
Madison, 10,097
Marion, 37,854
Martinsville, 7,525
Meridian Hills, 1,807
Michigan City, 36,653
Middletown, 2,033
Milan, 1,174
Milford, 1,167
Mishawaka, 33,361
Mitchell, 3,552
Monon, 1,417
Monroeville, 1,294
Montezuma, 1,231
Monticello, 4,035
Montpelier, 1,954
Mooresville, 3,856
Morocco, 1,341
Mount Vernon, 5,970
Mulberry, 1,062
Muncie, 68,603
Munster, 10,313
Nappanee, 3,895
New Albany, 37,812
Newburgh, 1,450
New Carlisle, 1,376
New Castle, 20,349
New Chicago, 2,312
New Harmony, 1,121
New Haven, 3,396
New Whiteland, 3,488
Noblesville, 7,664
North Judson, 1,942
North Liberty, 1,241
North Manchester, 4,377
North Vernon, 4,062
Oakland City, 3,016
Odon, 1,192
Oolitic, 1,140
Orleans, 1,659
Osceola, 1,350
Osgood, 1,434
Ossian, 1,108
Owensville, 1,121
Oxford, 1,108
Paoli, 2,754
Parker City, 1,181
Pendleton, 2,472
Peru, 14,453
Petersburg, 2,939
Pierceton, 1,186
Plainfield, 5,460
Plymouth, 7,558
Portage, 11,822
Porter, 2,189
Portland, 6,999
Princeton, 7,906
Redkey, 1,746
Remington, 1,207
Rensselaer, 4,740
Richmond, 44,149
Rising Sun, 2,230
Rochester, 4,883
Rockport, 2,474
Rockville, 2,756
Rushville, 7,264
Russiaville, 1,064
St. John, 1,128
Salem, 4,546
Schererville, 2,875
Scottsburg, 3,810
Seelyville, 1,114
Sellersburg, 2,679
Seymour, 11,629
Shelburn, 1,299
Shelbyville, 14,317
Sheridan, 2,165
Shirley, 1,038
Shoals, 1,022
South Bend, 132,445
South Whitley, 1,325
Speedway, 9,624
Spencer, 2,557
Sullivan, 4,979
Summitville, 1,048
Syracuse, 1,595
Tell City, 6,609
Terre Haute, 72,500
Thorntown, 1,486
Tipton, 5,604
Trail Creek, 1,552
Tri Lakes, 1,089
Union City, 4,047
Upland, 1,999
Valparaiso, 15,227
Veedersburg, 1,762
Versailles, 1,158
Vevay, 1,503
Vincennes, 18,046
Wabash, 12,621
Wakarusa, 1,145
Walkerton, 2,044
Walton, 1,079
Warren, 1,241
Warsaw, 7,234
Washington, 10,846
Waterloo, 1,432
Westfield, 1,217
West Lafayette, 12,680
West Terre Haute, 3,006
Whiteland, 1,368
Whiting, 8,137
Williamsport, 1,353
Winamac, 2,375
Winchester, 5,742
Windfall City, 1,135
Winona Lake, 1,928
Winslow, 1,089
Woodruff Place, 1,501
Worthington, 1,635
Yorktown, 1,137
Zionsville, 1,822

IOWA, 2,757,537
Ackley, 1,731
Adel, 2,060
Akron, 1,351
Albia, 4,582
Algona, 5,702
Alta, 1,393
Alton, 1,048
Altoona, 1,458
Ames, 27,003
Anamosa, 4,616
Anita, 1,233
Ankeny, 2,964
Atlantic, 6,890
Audubon, 2,928
Avoca, 1,540
Bancroft, 1,000
Bedford, 1,807
Belle Plaine, 2,923
Bellevue, 2,181
Belmond, 2,506
Bettendorf, 11,534
Bloomfield, 2,771
Boone, 12,468
Britt, 2,042
Brooklyn, 1,415
Buffalo, 1,088
Buffalo Center, 1,140
Burlington, 32,430
Camanche, 2,225
Carlisle, 1,317
Carroll, 7,682
Carter Lake, 2,287
Cascade, 1,601
Cedar Falls, 21,195
Cedar Rapids, 92,035
Center Point, 1,236
Centerville, 6,629
Central City, 1,087
Chariton, 5,042
Charles City, 9,964
Cherokee, 7,724
Clarinda, 4,903
Clarion, 3,232
Clarksville, 1,328
Clear Lake, 6,158
Clinton, 33,589
Colfax, 2,331
Columbus Junction, 1,016
Coon Rapids, 1,560
Coralville, 2,357
Corning, 2,041
Corydon, 1,687
Council Bluffs, 54,361
Cresco, 3,809
Creston, 7,667
Dallas Center, 1,083
Davenport, 88,981
Decorah, 6,435
Denison, 4,930
Des Moines, 208,982
DeWitt, 3,224
Dubuque, 56,606
Dunlap, 1,254
Durant, 1,266
Dyersville, 2,818
Dysart, 1,197
Eagle Grove, 4,381
Eddyville, 1,014
Eldon, 1,386
Eldora, 3,225
Elgin, 1,123
Elkader, 1,526
Elk Run Heights, 1,124
Emmetsburg, 3,887
Estherville, 7,927
Evansdale, 5,738
Exira, 1,111
Fairfield, 8,054
Fayette, 1,597
Fonda, 1,026
Forest City, 2,930
Fort Dodge, 28,399
Fort Madison, 15,247
Garner, 1,990
George, 1,200
Glenwood, 4,783
Gowrie, 1,127
Greene, 1,427
Greenfield, 2,243
Grinnell, 7,367
Griswold, 1,207
Grundy Center, 2,403
Guthrie Center, 2,071
Guttenberg, 2,087
Hamburg, 1,647
Hampton, 4,501
Harlan, 4,350
Hartley, 1,738
Hawarden, 2,544
Hiawatha, 1,336
Holstein, 1,413
Hudson, 1,085
Hull, 1,289
Humboldt, 4,031
Ida Grove, 2,265
Independence, 7,069
Indianola, 7,062
Iowa City, 33,443
Iowa Falls, 5,565
Jefferson, 4,570
Jesup, 1,488
Jewell, 1,113
Kalona, 1,235
Keokuk, 16,316
Keosauqua, 1,023
Keota, 1,096
Kingsley, 1,044
Knoxville, 7,817
Lake City, 2,114
Lake Mills, 1,758
Lake View, 1,165
Lamoni, 2,173
Lansing, 1,325
La Porte City, 1,953
Laurens, 1,799
Le Claire, 1,546
Le Mars, 6,767
Lenox, 1,178
Leon, 2,004
Lisbon, 1,227
Logan, 1,605
McGregor, 1,040
Madrid, 2,286
Malvern, 1,193
Manchester, 4,402
Manly, 1,425
Manning, 1,676
Manson, 1,789
Mapleton, 1,686
Maquoketa, 5,909
Marcus, 1,307
Marengo, 2,264
Marion, 10,882
Marshalltown, 22,521
Mason City, 30,642
Mechanicsville, 1,010
Mediapolis, 1,040
Milford, 1,476
Missouri Valley, 3,567
Monona, 1,346
Monroe, 1,366
Montezuma, 1,416
Monticello, 3,190
Mount Ayr, 1,738
Mount Pleasant, 7,339
Moville, 1,156
Mt. Vernon, 2,593
Muscatine, 20,997
Nashua, 1,737
Nevada, 4,227
New Hampton, 3,456
New London, 1,694
New Sharon, 1,063
Newton, 15,381
Nora Springs, 1,275
North English, 1,004
Northwood, 1,768
Norwalk, 1,328
Oakland, 1,340
Odebolt, 1,331
Oelwein, 8,282
Ogden, 1,525
Onawa, 3,176
Orange City, 2,707
Osage, 3,753
Osceola, 3,350
Oskaloosa, 11,053
Ottumwa, 33,871
Panora, 1,019
Parkersburg, 1,468
Paullina, 1,329
Pella, 5,198
Perry, 6,442
Pleasantville, 1,025
Pocahontas, 2,011
Postville, 1,554
Red Oak, 6,421
Reinbeck, 1,621
Remsen, 1,338
Rock Rapids, 2,780
Rock Valley, 1,693
Rockwell City, 2,313
Sac City, 3,354
St. Ansgar, 1,014
Sanborn, 1,323
Seymour, 1,117
Sheffield, 1,156
Sheldon, 4,251
Shell Rock, 1,112
Shenandoah, 6,567
Sibley, 2,852
Sidney, 1,057
Sigourney, 2,387
Sioux Center, 2,275
Sioux City, 89,159
Spencer, 8,864
Spirit Lake, 2,685
State Center, 1,142
Storm Lake, 7,728
Story City, 1,773
Strawberry Point, 1,303
Stuart, 1,486
Sumner, 2,170
Tama, 2,925
Tipton, 2,862
Toledo, 2,850
Traer, 1,623
Tripoli, 1,179
Urbandale, 5,821
Villisca, 1,690
Vinton, 4,781
Wapello, 1,745
Washington, 6,037
Waterloo, 71,755
Waukon, 3,639
Waverly, 6,357
Webster City, 8,520
Wellman, 1,085
West Branch, 1,053
West Burlington, 2,560
West Des Moines, 11,949
West Liberty, 2,042
West Union, 2,551
Williamsburg, 1,342
Wilton, 1,750
Windsor Heights, 5,906
Winterset, 3,639
Woodbine, 1,304

KANSAS, 2,178,611
Abilene, 6,746
Anthony, 2,744
Arkansas City, 14,262
Arma, 1,296
Ashland, 1,312
Atchison, 12,529
Atwood, 1,906
Augusta, 6,434
Baldwin City, 1,877
Baxter Springs, 4,498
Belle Plaine, 1,579
Belleville, 2,940
Beloit, 3,837
Blue Rapids, 1,426
Bonner Springs, 3,171
Burlingame, 1,151
Burlington, 2,113
Caldwell, 1,788
Caney, 2,682
Chanute, 10,849
Chapman, 1,095
Cheney, 1,101
Cherryvale, 2,783
Chetopa, 1,538
Cimarron, 1,115
Clay Center, 4,613
Clearwater, 1,073
Clyde, 1,025
Coffeyville, 17,382
Colby, 4,210
Coldwater, 1,164
Columbus, 3,395
Concordia, 7,022
Conway Springs, 1,057
Council Grove, 2,664
Derby, 6,458
De Soto, 1,271
Dighton, 1,526
Dodge City, 13,520
Douglass, 1,058
Downs, 1,206
Eastborough, 1,001
El Dorado, 12,523
Elkhart, 1,780
Ellinwood, 2,729
Ellis, 2,218
Ellsworth, 2,361
Elwood, 1,191
Emporia, 18,190
Enterprise, 1,015
Erie, 1,309
Eudora, 1,526
Eureka, 4,055
Fairway, 5,398
Fort Scott, 9,410
Frankfort, 1,106
Fredonia, 3,233
Frontenac, 1,713
Galena, 3,827
Garden City, 11,811
Gardner, 1,619
Garnett, 3,034
Girard, 2,350
Goodland, 4,459
Great Bend, 16,670
Greensburg, 1,988
Halstead, 1,598
Harper, 1,899
Hays, 11,947
Haysville, 5,836
Herington, 3,702
Hesston, 1,103
Hiawatha, 3,391
Hill City, 2,421
Hillsboro, 2,441
Hoisington, 4,248
Holmdel Gardens, 1,436
Holton, 3,028
Horton, 2,361
Howard, 1,017
Hoxie, 1,289
Hugoton, 2,912
Humboldt, 2,285
Hutchinson, 37,574
Independence, 11,222
Iola, 6,885
Jetmore, 1,028
Junction City, 18,700
Kansas City, 121,901
Kingman, 3,582
Kinsley, 2,263
Kiowa, 1,674
La Crosse, 1,767
Lakin, 1,432
Lansing, 1,264
Larned, 5,001
Lawrence, 32,858
Leavenworth, 22,052
Leawood, 7,466
Lenexa, 2,487
Leoti, 1,401
Liberal, 13,813
Lincoln Center, 1,717
Lindsborg, 2,609
Lyons, 4,592
McPherson, 9,996
Madison, 1,105
Manhattan, 22,993
Mankato, 1,231
Marion, 2,169
Marysville, 4,143
Meade, 2,019
Medicine Lodge, 3,072
Merriam, 5,084
Minneapolis, 2,024
Mission, 4,626
Mission Hills, 3,621
Moundridge, 1,214
Mulvane, 2,981
Neodesha, 3,594
Ness City, 1,653
Newton, 14,877
Nickerson, 1,091
Norton, 3,345
Oakley, 2,190
Oberlin, 2,337
Ogden, 1,780
Olathe, 10,987
Osage City, 2,213
Osawatomie, 4,622
Osborne, 2,049
Oswego, 2,027
Ottawa, 10,673
Overland Park, 21,110
Paola, 4,784
Park City, 2,687
Parsons, 13,929
Peabody, 1,309
Phillipsburg, 3,233
Pittsburg, 18,678
Plainville, 3,104
Pleasanton, 1,098
Prairie Village, 25,356
Pratt, 8,156
Roeland Park, 8,949
Russell, 6,113
Sabetha, 2,318
St. Francis, 1,594
St. John, 1,753
St. Marys, 1,509
Salina, 43,202
Scott City, 3,555
Sedan, 1,677
Sedgwick, 1,095
Seneca, 2,072
Shawnee, 9,072
Smith Center, 2,379
Solomon, 1,008
South Hutchinson, 1,672
Stafford, 1,862
Sterling, 2,303
Stockton, 2,073
Sublette, 1,077
Syracuse, 1,888
Tonganoxie, 1,354
Topeka, 119,484
Towanda, 1,031
Tribune, 1,036
Troy, 1,051
Ulysses, 3,157
Valley Center, 2,570
Valley Falls, 1,193
Victoria, 1,170
Wa Keeney, 2,808
Wamego, 2,363
Washington, 1,506
Wellington, 8,809
Westwood, 2,040
Wichita, 254,698
Winfield, 11,117
Yates Center, 2,080

KENTUCKY, 3,038,156
Albany, 1,887
Alexandria, 1,318
Anchorage, 1,170
Ashland, 31,283
Auburn, 1,013
Audubon Park, 1,867
Augusta, 1,458
Barbourville, 3,211
Bardstown, 4,798
Bardwell, 1,067
Beattyville, 1,048
Beaver Dam, 1,648
Beechwood, 1,903
Bellevue, 9,336
Benham, 1,874
Benton, 3,074
Berea, 4,302
Bowling Green, 28,338
Brandenburg, 1,542
Burkesville, 1,688
Cadiz, 1,980
Calvert, 1,505
Campbellsville, 6,966
Carlisle, 1,601
Carrollton, 3,218
Catlettsburg, 3,874
Cave City, 1,418
Central, 3,694
Clay, 1,343
Clinton, 1,647
Cloverport, 1,334
Cold Spring, 1,095
Columbia, 2,255
Corbin, 7,119
Covington, 60,376
Cumberland, 4,271
Cynthiana, 5,641
Danville, 9,010
Dawson Springs, 3,002
Dayton, 9,050
Earlington, 2,786
East Somerset, 3,645
Eddyville, 1,858
Edgewood, 1,100
Elizabethtown, 9,641
Elkhorn City, 1,085
Elkton, 1,448
Elsmere, 4,607
Eminence, 1,958
Erlanger, 7,072
Evarts, 1,473
Falmouth, 2,568
Flatwoods, 3,741
Flemingsburg, 2,067
Florence, 5,837
Fort Thomas, 14,896
Fort Wright, 2,184
Frankfort, 18,365
Franklin, 5,319
Fullerton, 1,082
Fulton, 3,265
Georgetown, 6,986
Glasgow, 10,069
Grayson, 1,692
Greensburg, 2,334
Greenup, 1,240
Greenville, 3,198
Guthrie, 1,211
Hardinsburg, 1,377
Harlan, 4,177
Harrodsburg, 6,061
Hartford, 1,618
Hazard, 5,958
Henderson, 16,892
Hickman, 1,537
Highland Heights, 3,491
Hodgenville, 1,985
Hopkinsville, 19,465
Horse Cave, 1,780
Irvine, 2,955
Irvington, 1,190
Jackson, 1,852
Jeffersontown, 3,431
Jenkins, 3,202
Junction City, 1,047
La Grange, 2,168
Lakeside Park, 2,214
Lancaster, 3,021
Lawrenceburg, 2,523
Leatherwood, 1,283
Lebanon, 4,813
Lebanon Junction, 1,527
Leitchfield, 2,982
Lexington, 62,810
Liberty, 1,578
Livermore, 1,506
London, 4,035
Lone Oak, 2,104
Lothair, 1,082
Louisa, 2,071
Louisville, 390,639
Loyall, 1,260
Ludlow, 6,233
Lynch, 3,810
Lynnview, 1,711
McRoberts, 1,363
Madisonville, 13,110
Manchester, 1,868
Marion, 2,468
Mayfield, 10,762
Maysville, 8,484
Middlesborough, 12,607
Middletown, 2,764
Midway, 1,044
Monticello, 2,940
Morehead, 4,170
Morganfield, 3,741
Morgantown, 1,318
Mortons Gap, 1,308
Mount Sterling, 5,370
Mount Vernon, 1,177
Mount Washington, 1,173
Muldraugh, 1,743
Munfordville, 1,157
Murray, 9,303
New Haven, 1,009
Newport, 30,070
Nicholasville, 4,275
Olive Hill, 1,398
Owensboro, 42,471
Owensboro East, 2,244
Owensboro West, 1,366
Owenton, 1,376
Owingsville, 1,040
Paducah, 34,479
Paintsville, 4,025
Paris, 7,791
Park Hills, 4,076
Pikeville, 4,754
Pineville, 3,181
Pleasure Ridge Park, 10,612
Prestonsburg, 3,133
Princeton, 5,618
Providence, 3,771
Raceland, 1,115
Radcliff, 3,384
Richmond, 12,168
Russell, 1,458
Russell Springs, 1,125
Russellville, 5,861
St. Matthews, 8,738
St. Regis Park, 1,179
Salyersville, 1,173
Scottsville, 3,324
Sebree, 1,139
Shelbyville, 4,525
Shepherdsville, 1,525
Shively, 15,155
Silver Grove, 1,207
Somerset, 7,112
South Fort Mitchell, 4,086
Southgate, 2,070
South Williamson, 1,097
Springfield, 2,382
Stanford, 2,019
Sturgis, 2,209
Tompkinsville, 2,091
Uniontown, 1,255
Valley Station, 10,553
Vanceburg, 1,881
Versailles, 4,060
Vine Grove, 2,435
Walton, 1,530
Wayland, 1,340
West Liberty, 1,165
West Point, 1,957
Wheelwright, 1,518
Whitesburg, 1,774
Whitley City, 1,034
Williamsburg, 3,478
Williamstown, 1,611
Wilmore, 2,773
Winchester, 10,187
Windy Hills, 1,371
Woodlawn, 1,688
Woodlawn Park, 1,137
Worthington, 1,235

LOUISIANA, 3,257,022
Abbeville, 10,414
Alexandria, 40,279
Alexandria Southwest, 2,782
Allemands, 1,167
Amite City, 3,316
Anandale, 2,827
Arcadia, 2,547
Arnaudville, 1,184
Baker, 4,823
Baldwin, 1,548
Basile, 1,932
Bastrop, 15,193
Baton Rouge, 152,419
Bayou Cane, 3,173
Benton, 1,336
Bernice, 1,641
Berwick, 3,880
Bogalusa, 21,423
Bossier City, 32,776
Boyce, 1,094
Breaux Bridge, 3,303
Broussard, 1,600
Bunkie, 5,188
Buras-Triumph, 4,908
Campti, 1,045
Carencro, 1,519
Cheneyville, 1,037
Church Point, 3,606
Clinton, 1,568
Colfax, 1,934
Columbia, 1,021
Cottonport, 1,581
Cotton Valley, 1,145
Coushatta, 1,663
Covington, 6,754
Crowley, 15,617
Cullen, 2,194
Daigleville, 5,906
Delcambre, 1,857
Delhi, 2,514
Denham Springs, 5,991
De Quincy, 3,928
De Ridder, 7,188
Donaldsonville, 6,082
Doyline, 1,061
Dubach, 1,013
Duson, 1,033
Elizabeth, 1,030
Elton, 1,595
Erath, 2,019

Eunice, 11,326
Farmerville, 2,727
Ferriday, 4,563
Franklin, 8,673
Franklinton, 3,141
Garyville, 2,389
Gibsland, 1,150
Glenmora, 1,447
Golden Meadow, 3,097
Gonzales, 3,252
Goosport, 16,778
Grambling, 3,144
Gramercy, 2,094
Grand Coteau, 1,165
Grand Isle, 2,074
Gretna, 21,967
Gueydan, 2,156
Hahnville, 1,297
Hammond, 10,563
Hammond East, 1,462
Harahan, 9,275
Haynesville, 3,031
Hollywood, 1,750
Homer, 4,665
Houma, 22,561
Independence, 1,941
Iota, 1,245
Iowa, 1,857
Jackson, 1,824
Jeanerette, 5,568
Jefferson Heights, 19,353
Jena, 2,098
Jennings, 11,887
Jonesboro, 3,848
Jonesville, 2,347
Kaplan, 5,267
Kenner, 17,037
Kentwood, 2,607
Kinder, 2,299
Krotz Springs, 1,057
Lafayette, 40,400
Lafayette Southwest, 6,682
Lake Arthur, 3,541
Lake Charles, 63,392
Lake Providence, 5,781
Laplace, 3,541
Larose, 2,796
Lecompte, 1,485
Leesville, 4,689
Livingston, 1,183
Lockport, 2,221
Logansport, 1,371
Luling, 2,122
Lutcher, 3,274
Mamou, 2,928
Mandeville, 1,740
Mansfield, 5,839
Mansura, 1,579
Many, 3,164
Maplewood, 2,432
Maringouin, 1,168
Marksville, 4,257
Melville, 1,939
Merryville, 1,232
Minden, 12,785
Monroe, 52,219
Morgan City, 13,540
Napoleonville, 1,148
Natchitoches, 13,924
Newellton, 1,453
New Iberia, 29,062
New Orleans, 627,525
New Roads, 3,965
New Sarpy, 1,259
Norco, 4,682
North Shreveport, 7,701
Oakdale, 6,618
Oak Grove, 1,797
Oberlin, 1,794
Oil City, 1,430
Olla, 1,246
Opelousas, 17,417
Patterson, 2,923
Pineville, 8,636
Pineville Junction, 1,233
Plain Dealing, 1,357
Plaquemine, 7,689
Plaquemine Southwest, 1,272
Ponchatoula, 4,727
Port Allen, 5,026
Port Barre, 1,876
Port Sulphur, 2,868
Raceland, 3,666
Rayne, 8,634
Rayville, 4,052
Remy, 1,014
Reserve, 5,297
Roseland, 1,254
Ruston, 13,991
St. Francisville, 1,661
St. Joseph, 1,653
St. Martinsville, 6,468
St. Rose, 1,099
Samtown, 4,008
Seymourville, 1,788
Shreveport, 164,372
Simmesport, 2,125
Slidell, 6,356
Sorrento, 1,151
Springhill, 6,437
Sulphur, 11,429
Sulphur South, 1,351
Sun, 1,125
Sunset, 1,307
Tallulah, 9,413
Thibodaux, 13,403
Urania, 1,063
Vidalia, 4,313
Ville Platte, 7,512
Vinton, 2,987
Vivian, 2,624
Wardville, 1,086
Washington, 1,291
Waterproof, 1,412
Weeks Island, 1,138
Welsh, 3,332
Westlake, 3,311
West Monroe, 15,215
Westwego, 9,815
White Castle, 2,253
Winnfield, 7,022
Winnsboro, 4,437
Wisner, 1,254
Zachary, 3,268
Zwolle, 1,326

MAINE, 969,265

Auburn, 24,449
Augusta, 21,680
Bangor, 38,912
Bar Harbor, 2,444
Bath, 10,717
Belfast, 6,140
Berwick, 1,557
Bethel, 1,117
Biddeford, 19,255
Bingham, 1,180
Boothbay Harbor, 2,252
Brewer, 9,009
Bridgton, 1,715
Brunswick, 9,444
Bucksport, 2,327
Calais, 4,223
Camden, 3,523
Caribou, 8,305
Chisholm, 1,193
Dexter, 2,720
Dixfield, 1,334
Dover-Foxcroft, 2,481
East Millinocket, 2,295
Eastport, 2,537
Ellsworth, 4,444
Fairfield, 3,766
Falmouth Foreside, 1,062
Farmington, 2,749
Fort Fairfield, 3,082
Fort Kent, 2,787
Freeport, 1,801
Gardiner, 6,897
Gorham, 2,322
Greenville, 1,893
Guilford, 1,372
Hallowell, 3,169
Hartland, 1,016
Houlton, 5,976
Howland, 1,313
Jonesport–West Jonesport, 1,339
Kennebunk, 2,804
Kittery, 8,051
Kittery Point, 1,259
Lewiston, 40,804
Limestone, 1,772
Lincoln, 3,616
Lisbon, 1,542
Lisbon Falls, 2,640
Livermore Falls, 2,882
Lubec, 1,289
Machias, 1,523
Madawaska, 4,035
Madison, 2,761
Mars Hill, 1,458
Mechanic Falls, 1,992
Mexico, 3,951
Millinocket, 7,318
Milo, 1,802
Newport, 1,589
North Berwick, 1,295
Norway, 2,654
Oakland, 1,880
Old Orchard Beach, 4,431
Old Town, 8,626
Orono, 3,234
Patten, 1,099
Pittsfield, 3,232
Portland, 72,566
Presque Isle, 12,886
Randolph, 1,585
Richmond, 1,412
Rockland, 8,769
Rumford, 7,233
Saco, 10,515
Sanford, 10,936
Skowhegan, 6,667
South Berwick, 1,773
South Eliot, 1,730
South Paris, 2,063
South Portland, 22,788
South Windham, 1,142
Springvale, 2,379
Thomaston, 2,342
Topsham, 2,240
Van Buren, 3,589
Washburn, 1,055
Waterville, 18,695
Webster, 4,747
Westbrook, 13,820
Wilton, 1,761
Winslow, 3,640
Winthrop, 2,260
Woodland, 1,393
Yarmouth, 2,913

MARYLAND, 3,100,689

Aberdeen, 9,679
Annapolis, 23,385
Arbutus-Halethorpe-Relay, 22,402
Baltimore, 939,024
Bel Air, 4,300
Berlin, 2,046
Berwyn Heights, 2,376
Bethesda, 56,527
Bladensburg, 3,103
Boonsboro, 1,211
Bowie, 1,489
Brentwood, 3,693
Brunswick, 3,555
Cambridge, 12,239
Capitol Heights, 3,138
Carrollton, 3,385
Catonsville, 37,372
Centreville, 1,863
Chesapeake City, 1,104
Chestertown, 3,602
Cheverly, 5,223
Chevy Chase, 2,405
Chevy Chase Section Four, 2,243
Clinton, 1,578
Cockeysville, 2,582
College Park, 18,482
Colmar Manor, 1,772
Cottage City, 1,099
Cresaptown, 1,680
Crisfield, 3,540
Cumberland, 33,415
Delmar, 1,291
Denton, 1,938
District Heights, 7,524
Dundalk, 82,428
Easton, 6,337
Edgewood, 1,670
Edmonston, 1,197
Elkton, 5,989
Emmitsburg, 1,369
Essex, 35,205
Fairmont Heights, 2,308
Federalsburg, 2,060
Forest Heights, 3,524
Frederick, 21,744
Frostburg, 6,722
Fruitland, 1,147
Gaithersburg, 3,847
Glenarden, 1,336
Glynden-Reistertown, 4,216
Greenbelt, 7,479
Green Haven, 1,302
Greensboro, 1,160
Hagerstown, 36,660
Halfway, 4,256
Hancock, 2,004
Havre de Grace, 8,510
Hillcrest Heights, 15,295
Hurlock, 1,035
Hyattsville, 15,168
Kensington, 2,175
Landover Hills, 1,850
Langley Park, 11,510
Lansdowne–Baltimore Highlands, 13,134
La Plata, 1,214
Laurel, 8,503
Lavale–Narrows Park, 4,031
Leonardtown, 1,281
Lexington Park, 7,039
Loch Raven, 23,278
Lonaconing, 2,077
Manchester, 1,108
Middle River, 10,825
Middletown, 1,036
Morningside, 1,708
Mount Airy, 1,352
Mount Ranier, 9,855
Mount Savage, 1,639
North East, 1,628
Oakland, 1,977
Odenton, 1,914
Oliver Beach–Twin River Beach, 1,426
Orchard Beach, 1,691
Overlea, 10,795
Owings Mills, 3,810
Parkville-Carney, 27,236
Pikesville, 18,737
Pocomoke City, 3,329
Potomac Park, 1,016
Princess Anne, 1,351
Riverdale, 4,389
Riviera Beach, 4,902
Rock Hall, 1,073
Rockville, 26,090
St. Michaels, 1,484
Salisbury, 16,302
Savage, 1,341
Seat Pleasant, 5,365
Severna Park–Round Bay, 3,728
Silver Spring, 66,348
Snow Hill, 2,311
Somerset, 1,444
Sparrows Point–Fort Howard–Edgemere, 11,775
Stoneleigh–Rodgers Forge, 15,645
Suitland–Silver Hills, 10,300
Sykesville, 1,196
Takoma Park, 16,799
Taneytown, 1,519
Thurmont, 2,802
Timonium-Lutherville, 12,265
Towson, 19,090
University Park, 3,098
Waldorf, 1,048
Walkersville, 1,020
Westernport, 3,559
Westminster, 6,123
Wheaton, 54,635
Williamsport, 1,853
Woodland Beach, 1,855
Woodlawn–Rockdale–Millford Mills, 19,254

MASSACHUSETTS, 5,148,578

Adams, 11,949
Amesbury, 9,625
Amherst, 10,306
Arlington, 49,953
Athol, 10,161
Attleboro, 27,118
Ayer, 3,323
Baldwinville, 1,631
Barre, 1,065
Belmont, 28,715
Beverly, 36,108
Boston, 697,197
Braintree, 31,069
Bridgewater, 4,296
Brockton, 72,813
Brookline, 54,044
Buzzards Bay, 2,170
Cambridge, 107,716
Chatham, 1,479
Chelsea, 33,749
Cheshire, 1,078
Chicopee, 61,553
Clinton, 12,848
Cohasset, 2,748
Concord, 3,188
Danvers, 21,926
Dedham, 23,869
Dennis Port, 1,271
Duxbury, 1,069
East Brookfield, 1,150
East Douglas, 1,695
East Falmouth, 1,655
Edgartown, 1,181
Everett, 43,544
Fall River, 99,942
Falmouth, 3,308
Farnumsville, 1,041
Fitchburg, 43,021
Forge Village, 1,191
Foxborough, 3,169
Framingham, 44,526
Franklin, 6,391
Gardner, 19,038
Georgetown, 2,005
Gilbertville, 1,202
Gloucester, 25,789
Great Barrington, 2,943
Greenfield, 14,389
Groton, 1,178
Hatfield, 1,330
Haverhill, 46,346
Holden, 1,704
Holliston, 2,447
Holyoke, 52,689
Hopedale, 2,904
Hopkinton, 2,754
Housatonic, 1,370
Hudson, 7,897
Hull, 7,055
Hyannis, 5,139
Ipswich, 4,617
Kingston, 1,301
Lawrence, 70,933
Lee, 3,078
Leicester, 1,750
Lenox, 1,713
Leominster, 27,929
Lexington, 27,691
Littleton Common, 2,277
Lowell, 92,107
Lynn, 94,478
Malden, 57,676
Mansfield, 4,674
Marblehead, 18,521
Marion, 1,160
Marlborough, 18,819
Mattapoisett, 1,640
Maynard, 7,695
Medfield, 2,424
Medford, 64,971
Medway, 1,602
Melrose, 29,619
Merino Village, 3,099
Methuen, 28,114
Middleborough, 6,003
Milford, 13,722
Millers Falls, 1,199
Millis-Clicquot, 2,588
Millville, 1,141
Milton, 26,375
Monson, 2,413
Nabnasset, 1,381
Nahant, 3,960
Nantucket, 2,804
Natick, 28,831
Needham, 25,793
New Bedford, 102,477
Newburyport, 14,004
Newton, 92,384
North Adams, 19,905
North Amherst, 1,009
Northampton, 30,058
Northborough, 2,516
Northbridge, 2,128
North Brookfield, 2,615
North Dighton, 1,167
Northfield, 1,179
North Oxford, 1,466
North Plymouth, 3,467
North Scituate, 3,421
North Uxbridge, 1,882
Norton, 1,501
Norwood, 24,898
Oak Bluffs, 1,027
Onset, 1,714
Orange, 3,689
Osterville, 1,094
Oxford, 6,985
Palmer, 3,888
Peabody, 32,202
Pigeon Cove, 1,064
Pinehurst, 1,991
Pittsfield, 57,879
Plymouth, 6,488
Provincetown, 3,346
Quincy, 87,409
Randolph, 18,900
Reading, 19,259
Revere, 40,080
Rochdale, 1,058
Rockport, 3,511
Rowley, 1,223
Rutland, 1,774
Salem, 39,211
Sandwich, 1,099
Saugus, 20,666
Scituate, 3,229
Sharon, 5,888
Shelburne Falls, 2,097
Shirley, 1,762
Shore Acres–Sand Hill, 1,778
Silver Lake, 4,654
Somerset, 12,196
Somerville, 94,697
South Acton, 1,114
Southborough, 1,114
Southbridge, 15,889
South Deerfield, 1,253
South Lancaster, 1,891
Southwick, 1,242
South Yarmouth, 2,029
Spencer, 5,593
Springfield, 174,463
Stoneham, 17,821
Swampscott, 13,294
Taunton, 41,132
Tewksbury, 1,151
Three Rivers, 3,082
Townsend Center, 1,101
Turner Falls, 4,917
Upton–West Upton, 1,991
Uxbridge, 3,377
Vineyard Haven, 1,701
Wakefield, 24,295
Waltham, 55,413
Ware, 6,650
Wareham–Wareham Center, 1,739
Warren, 1,616
Watertown, 39,092
Webster, 12,072
Wellesley, 26,071
Westborough, 4,011
West Brookfield, 1,250
West Concord, 1,556
Westfield, 26,302
West Medway, 1,818
Westminster, 1,047
West Warren, 1,124
West Yarmouth, 1,365
Weymouth, 48,177
Whitinsville, 5,102
Whitman, 10,485
Williamstown, 5,428
Wilmington, 2,250
Winchendon, 3,839
Winchester, 19,376
Winthrop, 20,303
Woburn, 31,214
Worcester, 186,587
Wrentham, 1,790

MICHIGAN, 7,823,194

Adrian, 20,347
Albion, 12,749
Algonac, 3,190
Allegan, 4,822
Allen Park, 37,052
Alma, 8,978
Almont, 1,279
Alpena, 14,682
Anchor Bay Gardens, 1,830
Ann Arbor, 67,340
Armada, 1,111
Auburn, 1,497
Austin Lake, 3,520
Bad Axe, 2,998
Bangor, 2,109
Battle Creek, 44,169
Bay City, 53,604
Bayport Park–Lakeside, 1,569
Beechwood, 2,323
Belding, 4,887
Belleville, 1,921
Belleville North, 1,128
Bellevue, 1,277
Benton Harbor, 19,136
Benton Heights, 6,112
Berkley, 23,275
Berrien Springs, 1,953
Bessemer, 3,304
Beverly Hills, 8,633
Big Rapids, 8,686
Birmingham, 25,525
Blissfield, 2,653
Bloomfield Hills, 2,378
Boyne, 2,797
Breckenridge, 1,131
Bridgeport, 1,326
Bridgman, 1,454
Brighton, 2,282
Bronson, 2,267
Brownlee Park, 3,307
Buchanan, 5,341
Bunny Run, 1,058
Cadillac, 10,112
Calumet, 1,139
Capac, 1,235
Carleton, 1,379
Caro, 3,534
Carson City, 1,201
Caspian, 1,493
Cass City, 1,945
Cassopolis, 2,027
Cedar Springs, 1,768
Center Line, 10,164
Charlevoix, 2,751
Charlotte, 7,657
Cheboygan, 5,859
Chelsea, 3,355
Chesaning, 2,770
Clair Haven, 1,365
Clare, 2,442
Clawson, 14,795
Clinton, 1,481
Clio, 2,212
Coldwater, 8,880
Coleman, 1,264
Coloma, 1,473
Colon, 1,055
Constantine, 1,710
Coopersville, 1,584
Corunna, 2,764
Croswell, 1,817
Crystal Falls, 2,203
Davison, 3,761
Dearborn, 112,007
Decatur, 1,827
Detroit, 1,670,144
Detroit Beach, 1,571
De Witt, 1,238
Dexter, 1,702
Dowagiac, 7,208
Dundee, 2,377
Durand, 3,312
East Detroit, 45,756
East Grand Rapids, 10,924
East Jordan, 1,919
East Kingsford, 1,063
East Lansing, 30,198
Eastlawn, 17,652
East Tawas, 2,462
Eaton Rapids, 4,052
Ecorse, 17,328
Edmore, 1,234
Elk Rapids, 1,015
Elkton, 1,014
Escanaba, 15,391
Essexville, 4,590
Euclid Center, 2,343
Evart, 1,775
Fair Plain, 7,998
Farmington, 6,881
Fenton, 6,142
Ferndale, 31,347
Ferrysburg, 2,590
Flat Rock, 4,696
Flint, 196,940
Flushing, 3,761
Fowlerville, 1,674
Frankenmuth, 1,728
Frankfort, 1,690
Franklin, 2,262
Fraser, 7,027
Fremont, 3,384
Fruitport, 1,037
Galesburg, 1,410
Garden City, 38,017
Gaylord, 2,568
Gibraltar, 2,196
Gladstone, 5,267
Gladwin, 2,226
Grand Blanc, 1,565
Grand Haven, 11,066
Grand Ledge, 5,165
Grand Rapids, 177,313
Grandville, 7,975
Grass Lake, 1,037
Grayling, 2,015
Greenville, 7,440
Grosse Pointe, 6,631
Grosse Pointe Farms, 12,172
Grosse Pointe Park, 15,457
Grosse Pointe Shores, 2,301
Grosse Pointe Woods, 18,580
Gwinn, 1,009
Hamtramck, 34,137
Hancock, 5,022
Harbor Beach, 2,282
Harbor Springs, 1,433
Harper Woods, 19,995
Harrison, 1,072
Hart, 1,990
Hartford, 2,305
Hastings, 6,375
Hazel Park, 25,631
Highland Park, 38,063
Hillsdale, 7,629
Holland, 24,777
Holly, 3,269
Holt, 4,818
Homer, 1,629
Houghton, 3,393
Houghton Lake Heights, 1,195
Howard City, 1,004
Howell, 4,861
Hubbell, 1,429
Hudson, 2,546
Hudsonville, 2,649
Huntington Woods, 8,746
Imlay City, 1,968
Inkster, 39,097
Ionia, 6,754
Iron Mountain, 9,299
Iron River, 3,754
Ironwood, 10,265
Ishpeming, 8,857
Ithaca, 2,611
Jackson, 50,720
Jonesville, 1,896
Kalamazoo, 82,089
Kalkaska, 1,321
Keego Harbor, 2,761
Kingsford, 5,084
Laingsburg, 1,057
Lake Linden, 1,314
Lake Michigan, 1,092
Lake Odessa, 1,806
Lake Orion, 2,698
Lake Orion Heights, 1,918
Lakeview, Calhoun Co., 10,384
Lakeview, Montcalm Co., 1,126
Lakewood, 1,815
Lambertville, 1,168
L'Anse, 2,397
Lansing, 107,807
Lapeer, 6,160
Lathrup Village, 3,556
Laurium, 3,058
Lawton, 1,402
Leslie, 1,807
Level Park–Oak Park, 3,017
Lincoln Park, 53,933
Linden, 1,146
Livonia, 66,702
Lowell, 2,545
Ludington, 9,421
Madison Heights, 33,343
Mancelona, 1,141
Manchester, 1,568
Manistee, 8,324
Manistique, 4,875
Manitou Beach–Devils Lake, 1,544
Manton, 1,050
Marcellus, 1,073
Marine City, 4,404
Marlette, 1,640
Marquette, 19,824
Marshall, 6,736
Marysville, 4,065
Mason, 4,522
Melvindale, 13,089
Menominee, 11,289
Michigan Center, 4,611
Middleville, 1,196
Midland, 27,779
Milan, 3,616
Milford, 4,323
Millington, 1,159
Monroe, 22,968
Montague, 2,366
Montrose, 1,466
Morenci, 2,053
Mount Clemens, 21,016
Mount Morris, 3,484
Mount Pleasant, 14,875
Munising, 4,228
Muskegon, 46,485
Muskegon Heights, 19,552
Nashville, 1,525
Negaunee, 6,126
Newaygo, 1,447
New Baltimore, 3,159
Newberry, 2,612
New Buffalo, 2,128
New Haven, 1,198
Niles, 13,842
North Muskegon, 3,855
Northville, 3,967
Norway, 3,171
Novi, 6,390
Oak Park, 36,632
Olivet, 1,185
Onaway, 1,388
Ontonagon, 2,358
Orchard Lake, 1,127
Otsego, 4,142
Ovid, 1,505
Owosso, 17,006
Oxford, 2,357
Parchment, 1,565
Patterson Gardens, 1,747
Paw Paw, 2,970
Paw Paw Lake, 3,518
Pearl Beach, 1,224
Pentwater, 1,030
Perry, 1,370
Petersburg, 1,018
Petoskey, 6,138
Pigeon, 1,191
Pinconning, 1,329
Plainwell, 3,125
Pleasant Ridge, 3,807
Plymouth, 8,766
Pontiac, 82,233
Port Huron, 36,084
Portland, 3,330
Potterville, 1,028
Quincy, 1,602
Ramsay, 1,158
Reading, 1,128
Reed City, 2,184
Richmond, 2,667
River Rouge, 18,147
Riverview, 7,237
Rochester, 5,431
Rockford, 2,074
Rockwood, 2,026
Rogers City, 4,722
Romeo, 3,327
Romulus, 1,798
Roosevelt Park, 2,578
Roseville, 50,195
Royal Oak, 80,612
Saginaw, 98,265
St. Charles, 1,959
St. Clair, 4,538
St. Clair Shores, 76,657
St. Ignace, 3,334
St. Johns, 5,629
St. Joseph, 11,755
St. Louis, 3,808
Saline, 2,334
Sandusky, 2,066
Saranac, 1,081

Michigan (cont.)
Sault Ste. Marie, 18,722
Schoolcraft, 1,205
Scottville, 1,245
Sebewaing, 2,026
Shelby, 1,603
Shepherd, 1,293
Shorewood Hills–Flower Hills, 1,330
Southfield, 31,501
Southgate, 29,404
South Haven, 6,149
South Lyon, 1,753
South Monroe, 2,919
South Rockwood, 1,337
Sparlingville, 1,877
Sparta, 2,749
Springfield, 4,605
Springfield Place, 5,136
Spring Lake, 2,063
Stambaugh, 1,876
Standish, 1,214
Stanton, 1,139
Stockbridge, 1,097
Sturgis, 8,915
Sunrise Heights, 1,569
Swartz Creek, 3,006
Sylvan Lake, 2,004
Tawas City, 1,810
Tecumseh, 7,045
Temperance, 2,215
Three Oaks, 1,763
Three Rivers, 7,092
Traverse, 18,432
Trenton, 18,439
Troy, 19,058
Union City, 1,669
Utica, 1,454
Vassar, 2,680
Verona Park, 1,884
Vicksburg, 2,224
Wakefield, 3,231
Walled Lake, 3,550
Warren, 89,246
Watervliet, 1,818
Wayland, 2,019
Wayne, 16,034
West Branch, 2,025
White Cloud, 1,001
Whitehall, 2,590
White Lake Seven Harbors, 2,748
White Pigeon, 1,399
Williamston, 2,214
Wixom, 1,531
Wolf Lake, 2,525
Wolverine Lake, 2,404
Woodland Beach, 1,944
Wyandotte, 43,519
Wyoming, 45,829
Yale, 1,621
Ypsilanti, 20,957
Zeeland, 3,702

MINNESOTA, 3,413,864
Ada, 2,064
Adrian, 1,215
Aitkin, 1,829
Albany, 1,375
Albert Lea, 17,108
Alexandria, 6,713
Anoka, 10,562
Appleton, 2,172
Arden Hills, 3,930
Arlington, 1,601
Aurora, 2,799
Austin, 27,908
Babbitt, 2,587
Bagley, 1,385
Barnesville, 1,632
Baudette, 1,597
Baxter, 1,037
Bayport, 3,205
Belle Plaine, 1,931
Bemidji, 9,958
Benson, 3,678
Bird Island, 1,384
Biwabik, 1,836
Blaine, 7,570
Blooming Prairie, 1,778
Bloomington, 50,498
Blue Earth, 4,200
Bovey, 1,086
Brainerd, 12,898
Breckenridge, 4,335
Brooklyn Center, 24,356
Brooklyn Park, 10,197
Browns Valley, 1,033
Buffalo, 2,322
Buhl, 1,526
Caledonia, 2,563
Cambridge, 2,728
Canby, 2,146
Cannon Falls, 2,055
Cass Lake, 1,586
Champlin, 1,271
Chaska, 2,501
Chatfield, 1,841
Chisholm, 7,144
Circle Pines, 2,789
Clara City, 1,358
Clarkfield, 1,100
Cloquet, 9,013
Cokato, 1,356
Cold Spring, 1,760
Coleraine, 1,346
Columbia Heights, 17,533
Coon Rapids, 14,931
Corcoran, 1,237
Crookston, 8,546
Crosby, 2,629
Crystal, 24,283
Dawson, 1,766
Deephaven, 3,286
Delano, 1,612
Detroit Lakes, 5,633
Dilworth, 2,102
Dodge Center, 1,441
Duluth, 106,884
East Grand Forks, 6,998
Edgerton, 1,019
Edina, 28,501
Elbow Lake, 1,521
Elk River, 1,763
Elmore, 1,078
Ely, 5,438
Eveleth, 5,721
Excelsior, 2,020
Fairfax, 1,489
Fairmont, 9,745
Falcon Heights, 5,927
Faribault, 16,926
Farmington, 2,300
Fergus Falls, 13,733
Foley, 1,112
Forest Lake, 2,347
Fosston, 1,704
Frazee, 1,083
Fridley, 15,173
Fulda, 1,202
Gaylord, 1,631
Gilbert, 2,591
Glencoe, 3,216
Glenwood, 2,631
Golden Hill, 2,190
Golden Valley, 14,559
Goodview, 1,348
Grand Marais, 1,301
Grand Rapids, 7,265
Granite Falls, 2,728
Hallock, 1,527
Harmony, 1,214
Hastings, 8,965
Hawley, 1,270
Hector, 1,297
Hibbing, 17,731
Hopkins, 11,370
Houston, 1,082
Howard Lake, 1,007
Hoyt Lakes, 3,186
Hutchinson, 6,207
Independence, 1,446
International Falls, 6,778
Jackson, 3,370
Janesville, 1,426
Jordan, 1,479
Kasson, 1,732
Keewatin, 1,651
Kenyon, 1,624
La Crescent, 2,624
Lake City, 3,494
Lake Crystal, 1,652
Lakefield, 1,789
Lanesboro, 1,063
Lauderdale, 1,676
Le Center, 1,597
Le Sueur, 3,310
Lexington, 1,457
Lino Lakes, 2,329
Litchfield, 5,078
Little Canada, 3,512
Little Falls, 7,551
Long Prairie, 2,414
Luverne, 4,249
Madelia, 2,190
Madison, 2,380
Mahnomen, 1,462
Mahtomedi, 2,127
Mankato, 23,797
Maple Grove, 2,213
Maple Lake, 1,018
Mapleton, 1,107
Maplewood, 18,519
Marshall, 6,681
Medina, 1,472
Melrose, 2,135
Mendota Heights, 5,028
Milaca, 1,821
Minneapolis, 482,872
Minneota, 1,297
Minnetonka, 25,037
Montevideo, 5,693
Montgomery, 2,118
Monticello, 1,477
Moorhead, 22,934
Moose Lake, 1,514
Mora, 2,329
Morningside, 1,981
Morris, 4,199
Mound, 5,440
Mounds View, 6,416
Mountain Iron, 1,808
Mountain Lake, 1,943
Nashwauk, 1,712
New Brighton, 6,448
New Hope, 3,552
Newport, 2,349
New Prague, 2,533
New Richland, 1,046
New Ulm, 11,114
Northfield, 8,707
North Mankato, 5,927
North St. Paul, 8,520
Olivia, 2,355
Orono, 5,643
Ortonville, 2,674
Osakis, 1,396
Osseo, 2,104
Owatonna, 13,409
Park Rapids, 3,047
Paynesville, 1,754
Pelican Rapids, 1,693
Perham, 2,019
Pine City, 1,972
Pine Island, 1,308
Pipestone, 5,324
Plainview, 1,833
Plymouth, 9,576
Preston, 1,491
Princeton, 2,353
Proctor, 2,963
Red Lake Falls, 1,520
Red Wing, 10,528
Redwood Falls, 4,285
Renville, 1,373
Richfield, 42,523
Robbinsdale, 16,381
Rochester, 40,663
Roseau, 2,146
Rosemount, 1,068
Roseville, 23,997
Rush City, 1,108
Rushford, city, 1,335
St. Anthony, Hennepin co., 5,084
St. Charles, 1,882
St. Cloud, 33,815
St. James, 4,174
St. Joseph, 1,487
St. Louis Park, 43,310
St. Paul, 313,411
St. Paul Park, 3,267
St. Peter, 8,484
Sandstone, 1,552
Sauk Centre, 3,573
Sauk Rapids, 4,038
Savage, 1,094
Scanlon, 1,126
Shakopee, 5,201
Sherburn, 1,227
Shoreview, 7,157
Shorewood, 3,197
Silver Bay, 3,723
Slayton, 2,487
Sleepy Eye, 3,492
South International Falls Villa, 2,479
South St. Paul, 22,032
Springfield, 2,701
Spring Grove, 1,342
Spring Lake Park, 3,260
Spring Valley, 2,628
Staples, 2,706
Starbuck, 1,099
Stewartville, 1,670
Stillwater, 8,310
Thief River Falls, 7,151
Tonka Bay, 1,204
Tracy, 2,862
Truman, 1,256
Two Harbors, 4,695
Tyler, 1,138
Vadnais Heights, 2,459
Virginia, 14,034
Wabasha, 2,500
Waconia, 2,048
Wadena, 4,381
Waite Park, 2,016
Walker, 1,180
Warren, 2,007
Warroad, 1,309
Waseca, 5,898
Watertown, 1,046
Waterville, 1,623
Wayzata, 3,219
Wells, 2,897
Westbrook, 1,012
West St. Paul, 13,101
Wheaton, 2,102
White Bear Lake, 12,849
Willmar, 10,417
Windom, 3,691
Winnebago, 2,088
Winona, 24,895
Winsted, 1,163
Winthrop, 1,381
Worthington, 9,015
Zumbrota, 1,830

MISSISSIPPI, 2,178,141
Aberdeen, 6,450
Ackerman, 1,382
Amory, 6,474
Baldwyn, 2,023
Batesville, 3,284
Bay St. Louis, 5,073
Bay Springs, 1,544
Belzoni, 4,142
Biloxi, 44,053
Booneville, 3,480
Brandon, 2,139
Brookhaven, 9,885
Bruce, 1,698
Bude, 1,185
Calhoun City, 1,714
Canton, 9,707
Carthage, 2,442
Centreville, 1,229
Charleston, 2,528
Clarksdale, 21,105
Cleveland, 10,172
Clinton, 3,438
Coldwater, 1,264
Collins, 1,537
Columbia, 7,117
Columbus, 24,771
Corinth, 11,453
Crenshaw, 1,382
Crystal Springs, 4,496
Decatur, 1,340
D'Iberville, 3,005
Drew, 2,143
Durant, 2,617
Eastside, 4,304
Edwards, 1,206
Ellisville, 4,592
Escatawpa, 1,464
Eupora, 1,468
Fayette, 1,626
Forest, 3,917
Friars Point, 1,029
Fulton, 1,706
Gloster, 1,369
Greenville, 41,502
Greenville North, 2,516
Greenwood, 20,436
Grenada, 7,914
Gulfport, 30,204
Handsboro, 1,577
Hattiesburg, 34,989
Hazlehurst, 3,400
Heidelberg, 1,049
Hernando, 1,898
Hollandale, 2,646
Holly Springs, 5,621
Houston, 2,577
Indianola, 6,714
Inverness, 1,039
Itta Bena, 1,914
Iuka, 2,010
Jackson, 144,422
Kosciusko, 6,800
Kreole, 1,870
Lambert, 1,181
Laurel, 27,889
Leakesville, 1,014
Leland, 6,295
Lexington, 2,839
Long Beach, 4,770
Louisville, 5,066
Lucedale, 1,977
Lumberton, 2,108
McComb, 12,020
McComb South, 1,865
Macon, 2,432
Magee, 2,039
Magnolia, 2,083
Marks, 2,572
Mendenhall, 1,946
Meridian, 49,374
Mississippi City, 4,169
Monticello, 1,432
Moorhead, 1,754
Morton, 2,260
Moss Point, 6,631
Mound Bayou, 1,354
Natchez, 23,791
Nettleton, 1,389
New Albany, 5,151
Newton, 3,178
Ocean Springs, 5,025
Okolona, 2,622
Oxford, 5,283
Pascagoula, 17,139
Pass Christian, 3,881
Pearl, 5,081
Pelahatchie, 1,066
Petal, 4,007
Philadelphia, 5,017
Picayune, 7,834
Pontotoc, 2,108
Poplarville, 2,136
Port Gibson, 2,861
Prentiss, 1,321
Purvis, 1,614
Quitman, 2,030
Raymond, 1,381
Richton, 1,089
Ripley, 2,668
Rolling Fork, 1,619
Rosedale, 2,339
Ruleville, 1,902
Sardis, 2,098
Senatobia, 3,259
Shaw, 2,062
Shelby, 2,384
Starkville, 9,041
Stonewall, 1,126
Summit, 1,663
Taylorsville, 1,132
Tie Plant, 1,491
Tunica, 1,445
Tunica North, 1,025
Tupelo, 17,221
Tylertown, 1,532
Union, 1,726
University, 3,597
Vicksburg, 29,130
Water Valley, 3,206
Waveland, 1,106
Waynesboro, 3,892
Wesson, 1,157
West Gulfport, 3,323
West Point, 8,550
Wiggins, 1,591
Winona, 4,282
Woodville, 1,856
Yazoo City, 11,236

MISSOURI, 4,319,813
Adrian, 1,082
Albany, 1,662
Appleton City, 1,075
Arbor Terrace, 1,225
Aurora, 4,683
Ava, 1,581
Ballwin, 5,710
Belle, 1,016
Bellefontaine Neighbors, 13,650
Bel-Nor, 2,388
Bel-Ridge, 4,395
Belton, 4,897
Berkeley, 18,676
Bernie, 1,578
Bethany, 2,771
Bismarck, 1,237
Bloomfield, 1,330
Blue Springs, 2,555
Bolivar, 3,512
Bonne Terre, 3,219
Boonville, 7,090
Bowling Green, 2,650
Branson, 1,887
Breckenridge Hills, 6,299
Brentwood, 12,250
Bridgeton, 7,820
Brookfield, 5,694
Brunswick, 1,493
Buckner, 1,198
Buffalo, 1,477
Butler, 3,791
Cabool, 1,284
California, 2,788
Calverton Park, 1,714
Camdenton, 1,405
Cameron, 3,674
Campbell, 1,964
Canton, 2,562
Cape Girardeau, 24,947
Carl Junction, 1,220
Carrollton, 4,554
Carterville, 1,443
Carthage, 11,264
Caruthersville, 8,643
Cassville, 1,451
Centralia, 3,200
Chaffee, 2,862
Charlack, 1,493
Charleston, 5,911
Chillicothe, 9,236
Clarence, 1,103
Clarkton, 1,049
Claycomo, 1,423
Clayton, 15,245
Clinton, 6,925
Columbia, 36,650
Concordia, 1,471
Cool Valley, 1,492
Country Club Hills, 1,763
Crestwood, 11,106
Creve Coeur, 5,122
Crystal City, 3,678
Cuba, 1,672
Dellwood, 4,720
Desloge, 2,308
De Soto, 5,804
Des Peres, 4,362
Dexter, 5,519
Dixon, 1,473
Doniphan, 1,421
East Prairie, 3,449
Edina, 1,457
Edmundson, 1,428
Eldon, 3,158
Eldorado Springs, 2,864
Ellisville, 2,732
Elsberry, 1,491
Elvins, 1,818
Esther, 1,033
Eureka, 1,134
Excelsior Springs, 6,473
Farmington, 5,618
Fayette, 3,294
Ferguson, 22,149
Festus, 7,021
Flat River, 4,515
Flordell Hills, 1,119
Florissant, 38,166
Fredericktown, 3,484
Frontenac, 3,089
Fulton, 11,131
Gallatin, 1,658
Gideon, 1,411
Gladstone, 14,502
Glasgow, 1,200
Glendale, 7,048
Granby, 1,808
Grandview, 6,027
Grant City, 1,061
Greendale, 1,107
Greenfield, 1,172
Hamilton, 1,701
Hanley Hills, 3,308
Hannibal, 20,028
Harrisonville, 3,510
Hayti, 3,737
Hazelwood, 6,045
Herculaneum, 1,767
Hermann, 2,536
Higginsville, 4,003
Hillsdale, 2,788
Holden, 1,951
Houston, 1,660
Huntsville, 1,526
Illmo, 1,174
Independence, 62,328
Ironton, 1,310
Jackson, 4,875
Jefferson City, 28,228
Jennings, 19,965
Joplin, 38,958
Kahoka, 2,160
Kansas City, 475,539
Kennett, 9,098
King, 1,009
Kinloch, 6,501
Kirksville, 13,123
Kirkwood, 29,421
Knob Noster, 2,292
Ladue, 9,466
La Grange, 1,347
Lake Lotawana, 1,499
Lamar, 3,608
La Plata, 1,365
Lathrop, 1,006
Leadwood, 1,343
Lebanon, 8,220
Lees Summit, 8,267
Lexington, 4,845
Liberty, 8,909
Lilbourn, 1,216
Linn, 1,050
Louisiana, 4,286
Macon, 4,547
Malden, 5,007
Manchester, 2,021
Maplewood, 12,552
Marceline, 2,872
Marionville, 1,251
Marshall, 9,572
Marshfield, 2,221
Marvin Terrace, 1,260
Maryville, 7,807
Memphis, 2,106
Mexico, 12,889
Milan, 1,670
Moberly, 13,170
Moline Acres, 3,132
Monett, 5,359
Monroe, 2,337
Montgomery City, 1,918
Morehouse, 1,417
Mound City, 1,249
Mountain Grove, 3,176
Mount Vernon, 2,381
Neosho, 7,452
Nevada, 8,416
New Franklin, 1,096
New Haven, 1,223
New Madrid, 2,867
Normandy, 4,452
North Kansas City, 5,657
Northwoods, 4,701
Oak Grove, 1,100
Oakland, 1,552
Odessa, 2,034
O'Fallon, 3,770
Olivette, 8,257
Oran, 1,090
Osceola, 1,066
Overland, 22,763
Owensville, 2,379
Ozark, 1,536
Pacific, 2,795
Pagedale, 5,106
Palmyra, 2,933
Paris, 1,393
Parkville, 1,229
Parma, 1,060
Pasadena Hills, 1,315
Perryville, 5,117
Piedmont, 1,555
Pierce City, 1,006
Pine Lawn, 5,943
Platte City, 1,188
Plattsburg, 1,663
Pleasant Hill, 2,689
Pleasant Valley, 1,109
Poplar Bluff, 15,926
Portageville, 2,505
Potosi, 2,805
Princeton, 1,443
Raytown, 17,083
Republic, 1,519
Rich Hill, 1,699
Richland, 1,662
Richmond, 4,604
Richmond Heights, 15,622
Riverside, 1,315
Riverview, 3,706
Rock Hill, 6,523
Rockport, 1,310
Rolla, 11,132
St. Ann, 12,155
St. Charles, 21,189
St. Clair, 2,711
Ste. Genevieve, 4,443
St. George, 1,323
St. James, 2,384
St. John, 7,342
St. Joseph, 79,673
St. Louis, 750,026
Salem, 3,870
Salisbury, 1,787
Sarcoxie, 1,056
Savannah, 2,455
Scott City, 1,963
Sedalia, 23,874
Senath, 1,369
Seneca, 1,478
Seymour, 1,046
Shelbina, 2,067
Shrewsbury, 4,730
Sikeston, 13,765
Slater, 2,767
Smithville, 1,254
Springfield, 95,865
Stanberry, 1,409
Steele, 2,301
Steelville, 1,127
Sugar Creek, 2,663
Sullivan, 4,098
Sunset Hills, 3,525
Sweet Springs, 1,452
Tarkio, 2,160
Thayer, 1,713
Tipton, 1,639
Town and Country, 1,440
Trenton, 6,262
Troy, 1,779
Union, 3,937
Unionville, 1,896
University City, 51,249
Valley Park, 3,452
Vandalia, 3,055
Velda Village Hills, 1,365
Versailles, 2,047
Vinita Park, 2,204
Warrensburg, 9,689
Warrenton, 1,869
Warsaw, 1,054
Warson Woods, 1,746
Washington, 7,961
Waynesville, 2,377
Webb City, 6,740
Webster Groves, 28,990
Wellston, 7,979
Wellsville, 1,523
Wentzville, 2,742
Weston, 1,057
West Plains, 5,836
Willow Springs, 1,913
Winchester, 1,299
Windsor, 2,714
Woodson Terrace, 6,048

MONTANA, 674,767
Anaconda, 12,054
Baker, 2,365
Belgrade, 1,057
Big Timber, 1,660
Billings, 52,851
Boulder, 1,394
Bozeman, 13,361
Browning, 2,011
Butte, 27,877
Centerville–Dublin Gulch, 3,398
Chester, 1,158
Chinook, 2,326
Choteau, 1,966
Circle, 1,117
Columbia Falls, 2,132
Columbus, 1,281
Conrad, 2,665
Cut Bank, 4,539
Deer Lodge, 4,681
Dillon, 3,690
East Helena, 1,490
Eureka, 1,229
Fairview, 1,006
Floral Park, 4,079
Forsyth, 2,032
Fort Benton, 1,887
Glasgow, 6,398
Glendive, 7,058
Great Falls, 55,357
Hamilton, 2,475
Hardin, 2,789
Harlem, 1,267
Harlowton, 1,734
Havre, 10,740
Helena, 20,227
Kalispell, 10,151
Laurel, 4,601
Lewistown, 7,408
Libby, 2,828
Livingston, 8,229
Malta, 2,239
Meaderville-McQueen, 1,345
Miles City, 9,665
Missoula, 27,090
Missoula Southwest, 3,817
North Havre, 1,168
Orchard Homes, 2,019
Philipsburg, 1,107
Plentywood, 2,121
Polson, 2,314
Poplar, 1,565
Red Lodge, 2,278
Ronan, 1,334
Roundup, 2,842
Scobey, 1,726
Shelby, 4,017
Sidney, 4,564
Silver Bow Park, 4,798
Superior, 1,242
Terry, 1,140
Thompson Falls, 1,274
Three Forks, 1,161
Townsend, 1,528
Walkerville, 1,453
Whitefish, 2,965
White Sulphur Springs, 1,519
Wolf Point, 3,585

NEBRASKA, 1,411,330
Ainsworth, 1,982
Albion, 1,982
Alliance, 7,845
Alma, 1,342
Arapahoe, 1,084
Ashland, 1,989
Atkinson, 1,324
Auburn, 3,229
Aurora, 2,576
Bassett, 1,023
Bayard, 1,519
Beatrice, 12,132
Bellevue, 8,831
Benkelman, 1,400
Blair, 4,931
Bloomfield, 1,349
Bridgeport, 1,645
Broken Bow, 3,482
Burwell, 1,425
Cambridge, 1,090
Central City, 2,406
Chadron, 5,079
Chappell, 1,280
Columbus, 12,476
Cozad, 3,184
Crawford, 1,588
Creighton, 1,388
Crete, 3,546
David City, 2,304
Fairbury, 5,572
Falls City, 5,598
Franklin, 1,194
Fremont, 19,698
Friend, 1,069
Fullerton, 1,475
Geneva, 2,352
Genoa, 1,009
Gering, 4,585
Gibbon, 1,083
Gordon, 2,223
Gothenburg, 3,050
Grand Island, 25,742
Grant, 1,166
Hartington, 1,648
Harvard, 1,261
Hastings, 21,412
Hebron, 1,920
Holdrege, 5,226
Humboldt, 1,322
Imperial, 1,423
Kearney, 14,210
Kimball, 4,384
Lexington, 5,572

Lincoln, 128,521
Louisville, 1,194
Loup City, 1,415
McCook, 8,301
Madison, 1,513
Milford, 1,462
Millard, 1,014
Minden, 2,383
Mitchell, 1,920
Nebraska City, 7,252
Neligh, 1,776
Norfolk, 13,111
North Bend, 1,174
North Platte, 17,184
Oakland, 1,429
Ogallala, 4,250
Omaha, 301,598
O'Neill, 3,181
Ord, 2,413
Oshkosh, 1,025
Oxford, 1,090
Papillion, 2,235
Pawnee City, 1,343
Pell–Lincoln Hwy., 1,709
Pender, 1,165
Peru, 1,151
Pierce, 1,216
Plainview, 1,467
Plattsmouth, 6,244
Ralston, 2,977
Randolph, 1,063
Ravenna, 1,417
Red Cloud, 1,525
Rushville, 1,228
St. Paul, 1,714
Schuyler, 3,096
Scottsbluff, 13,377
Scribner, 1,021
Seward, 4,208
Sidney, 8,004
South Sioux City, 7,200
Stanton, 1,317
Stromsburg, 1,244
Superior, 2,935
Sutton, 1,252
Syracuse, 1,261
Tecumseh, 1,887
Tekamah, 1,788
Valentine, 2,875
Valley, 1,452
Wahoo, 3,610
Wakefield, 1,068
Wayne, 4,217
Weeping Water, 1,048
West Point, 2,921
Wilber, 1,358
Wisner, 1,192
Wymore, 1,975
York, 6,173

NEVADA, 285,278

Babbitt, 2,159
Boulder City, 4,059
Carlin, 1,023
Carson City, 5,163
East Ely, 1,796
Elko, 6,298
Ely, 4,018
Fallon, 2,734
Hawthorne, 2,838
Henderson, 12,525
Las Vegas, 64,405
Lovelock, 1,948
McGill, 2,195
North Las Vegas, 18,422
Reno, 51,470
Sparks, 16,618
Tonopah, 1,679
Weed Heights, 1,092
Wells, 1,071
Winnemucca, 3,453
Yerington, 1,764

NEW HAMPSHIRE, 606,921

Ashland, 1,237
Berlin, 17,821
Blodgett, 1,489
Bristol, 1,054
Charlestown, 1,173
Claremont, 13,563
Colebrook, 1,550
Concord, 28,991
Conway, 1,143
Dover, 19,131
Durham, 4,688
Enfield, 1,121
Exeter, 5,896
Farmington, 2,241
Franklin, 6,742
Goffstown, 1,052
Gorham, 1,945
Greenville, 1,251
Groveton, 2,004
Hampton, 3,281
Hanover, 5,649
Hillsborough, 1,645
Hinsdale, 1,235
Hudson, 3,651
Jaffrey, 1,648
Keene, 17,562
Laconia, 15,288
Lancaster, 2,392
Lebanon, 9,299
Lisbon, 1,220
Littleton, 3,355
Manchester, 88,282
Marlborough, 1,097
Milford, 3,916
Nashua, 39,096
New London, 1,007
Newmarket, 2,745
Newport, 3,222
North Conway, 1,104
Northfield, 1,243
Peterborough, 1,931
Pittsfield, 1,407
Plymouth, 2,244
Portsmouth, 25,833
Rochester, 15,927
Salem Depot, 2,523
Salmon Falls, 1,210
Somersworth, 8,529
Suncook, 2,318
Tilton, 1,129
West Derry, 4,468
Whitefield, 1,244
Wilton, 1,425
Wolfeboro, 1,557
Woodsville, 1,596

NEW JERSEY, 6,066,782

Absecon, 4,320
Allendale, 4,092
Allentown, 1,393
Alpha, 2,406
Asbury Park, 17,366
Atlantic City, 59,544
Atlantic Highlands, 4,119
Audubon, 10,440
Audubon Park, 1,713
Avon-by-the-Sea, 1,707
Barrington, 7,943
Basking Ridge, 2,438
Bayonne, 74,215
Beach Haven, 1,041
Beachwood, 2,765
Belleville, 35,005
Bellmawr, 11,853
Belmar, 5,190
Belvidere, 2,636
Bergenfield, 27,203
Berlin, 3,578
Bernardsville, 5,515
Beverly, 3,400
Blansingburg, 1,702
Bloomfield, 51,867
Bloomingdale, 5,293
Bogota, 7,965
Boonton, 7,981
Bordentown, 4,974
Bound Brook, 10,263
Bradley Beach, 4,204
Branchburg Park, 1,468
Breton Woods, 1,292
Bridgeton, 20,966
Brielle, 2,619
Brigantine, 4,201
Brooklawn, 2,504
Budd Lake, 1,520
Buena, 3,243
Burlington, 12,687
Butler, 5,414
Caldwell, 6,942
Camden, 117,159
Cape May, 4,477
Cape May Court House, 1,749
Carlstadt, 6,042
Carteret, 20,502
Cedar Grove, 14,603
Cedarville, 1,095
Cedarwood Park, 1,052
Chatham, 9,517
Chester, 1,074
Clark, 12,195
Clayton, 4,711
Clementon, 3,766
Cliffside Park, 17,642
Clifton, 82,084
Clinton, 1,158
Closter, 7,767
Collingswood, 17,370
Cranbury, 1,038
Cranford, 26,424
Cresskill, 7,290
Deal, 1,889
Delaware, 31,522
Demarest, 4,231
Dover, 13,034
Dumont, 18,882
Dunellen, 6,840
East Newark, 1,872
East Orange, 77,259
East Paterson, 19,344
East Rutherford, 7,769
Eatontown, 10,334
Edgewater, 4,113
Edison, 44,799
Egg Harbor City, 4,416
Elizabeth, 107,698
Elmer, 1,505
Emerson, 6,849
Englewood, 26,057
Englewood Cliffs, 2,913
Englishtown, 1,143
Espanong, 1,107
Essex Fells, 2,174
Ewing, 26,628
Fair Haven, 5,678
Fair Lawn, 36,421
Fairview, 9,399
Fanwood, 7,963
Flemington, 3,232
Florence, 4,215
Florham Park, 7,222
Fort Lee, 21,815
Franklin, 3,624
Franklin Lakes, 3,316
Freehold, 9,140
Frenchtown, 1,340
Garfield, 29,253
Garwood, 5,426
Gibbsboro, 2,141
Gibbstown, 2,820
Gilford Park, 1,560
Glassboro, 10,253
Glen Ridge, 8,322
Glen Rock, 12,896
Gloucester City, 15,511
Guttenberg, 5,118
Hackensack, 30,521
Hackettstown, 5,276
Haddon, 17,099
Haddonfield, 13,201
Haddon Heights, 9,260
Haledon, 6,161
Hamburg, 1,532
Hamilton, 65,035
Hammonton, 9,854
Hampton, 1,135
Harrington Park, 3,581
Harrison, 11,743
Hasbrouck Heights, 13,046
Haworth, 3,215
Hawthorne, 17,735
High Bridge, 2,148
Highland Park, 11,049
Highlands, 3,536
Hightstown, 4,317
Hillcrest, 1,922
Hillsdale, 8,734
Hillside, 22,304
Hoboken, 48,441
Hohokus, 3,988
Hopatcong, 3,391
Hopewell, 1,928
Huntington, 1,879
Interlaken, 1,168
Irvington, 59,379
Island Heights, 1,150
Jamesburg, 2,853
Jersey City, 276,101
Keansburg, 6,854
Kearny, 37,472
Kenilworth, 8,379
Keyport, 6,440
Kinnelon, 4,431
Lakehurst, 2,780
Lake Mohawk, 4,647
Lakewood, 13,004
Lambertville, 4,269
Laurel Springs, 2,028
Lawnside, 2,155
Leonia, 8,384
Levittown, 11,861
Lincoln Park, 6,048
Linden, 39,931
Lindenwold, 7,335
Linwood, 3,847
Little Falls, 9,730
Little Ferry, 6,175
Little Silver, 5,202
Livingston, 23,124
Lodi, 23,502
Long Branch, 26,228
Longport, 1,077
Long Valley, 1,220
Lyndhurst, 21,867
Madison, 15,122
Magnolia, 4,199
Manasquan, 4,022
Manville, 10,995
Maple Shade, 12,947
Maplewood, 23,977
Margate City, 9,474
Matawan, 5,097
Mays Landing, 1,404
Maywood, 11,460
Medford, 1,480
Medford Lakes, 2,876
Mendham, 2,371
Merchantville, 4,075
Metuchen, 14,041
Middlesex, 10,520
Middletown, 39,675
Midland Park, 7,543
Milford, 1,114
Millburn, 18,799
Millington, 1,182
Milltown, 5,435
Millville, 19,096
Monmouth Beach, 1,363
Montclair, 43,129
Montvale, 3,699
Moonachie, 3,052
Morris Plains, 4,703
Morristown, 17,712
Mountain Lakes, 4,037
Mountainside, 6,325
Mount Arlington, 1,246
Mount Ephraim, 5,447
Mount Freedom, 1,328
Mount Holly, 13,271
National Park, 3,380
Neptune, 21,487
Neptune City, 4,013
Netcong, 2,765
Newark, 405,220
New Brunswick, 40,139
New Egypt, 1,737
Newfield, 1,299
New Hanover, 28,528
New Milford, 18,810
New Providence, 10,243
New Shrewsbury, 7,313
Newton, 6,563
North Arlington, 17,477
North Bergen, 42,387
North Caldwell, 4,163
Northfield, 5,849
North Haledon, 6,026
North Plainfield, 16,993
North Princeton, 4,506
Northvale, 2,892
North Wildwood, 3,598
Norwood, 2,852
Nutley, 29,513
Oakhurst, 4,374
Oakland, 9,446
Oaklyn, 4,778
Ocean City, 7,618
Oceanport, 4,937
Ogdensburg, 1,212
Old Tappan, 2,330
Oradell, 7,487
Orange, 35,789
Palisades Park, 11,943
Palmyra, 7,036
Paramus, 23,238
Park Ridge, 6,389
Parsippany–Troy Hills, 25,557
Passaic, 53,963
Paterson, 143,663
Paulsboro, 8,121
Peapack-Gladstone, 1,804
Pemberton, 1,250
Pennington, 2,063
Pennsauken, 33,771
Penns Grove, 6,176
Perth Amboy, 38,007
Phillipsburg, 18,502
Pine Hill, 3,939
Pitman, 8,644
Plainfield, 45,330
Pleasantville, 15,172
Point Pleasant, 10,182
Point Pleasant Beach, 3,873
Pompton Lakes, 9,445
Port Norris, 1,789
Princeton, 11,890
Prospect Park, 5,201
Rahway, 27,699
Ramsey, 9,527
Raritan, borough, 6,137
Raritan, 15,334
Red Bank, 12,482
Ridgefield, 10,788
Ridgefield Park, 12,701
Ridgewood, 25,391
Ringwood, 4,182
Riverdale, 2,596
River Edge, 13,264
Riverside, 8,474
Riverton, 3,324
Rochelle Park, 6,119
Rockaway, 5,413
Roebling, 3,272
Roseland, 2,804
Roselle, 21,032
Roselle Park, 12,546
Rumson, 6,405
Runnemede, 8,396
Rutherford, 20,473
Saddle Brook, 13,834
Saddle River, 1,776
Salem, 8,941
Sayreville, 22,553
Scotch Plains, 18,491
Sea Bright, 1,138
Seabrook Farms, 1,798
Sea Girt, 1,798
Sea Isle City, 1,393
Seaside Park, 1,054
Seacaucus, 12,154
Shore Hills, 1,068
Shrewsbury, 3,222
Somerdale, 4,839
Somers Point, 4,504
Somerville, 12,458
South Amboy, 8,422
South Belmar, 1,537
South Bound Brook, 3,626
South Orange, 16,175
South Plainfield, 17,879
South River, 13,397
South Toms River, 1,603
Spotswood, 5,788
Springfield, 14,467
Spring Lake, 2,922
Spring Lake Heights, 3,309
Stanhope, 1,814
Stirling, 1,382
Stratford, 4,308
Summit, 23,677
Sussex, 1,656
Swedesboro, 2,449
Teaneck, 42,085
Tenafly, 14,264
Toms River, 6,062
Totowa, 10,897
Trenton, 114,167
Tuckerton, 1,536
Union City, 52,180
Union, 51,499
Union Beach, 5,862
Upper Saddle River, 3,570
Vail Homes, 1,204
Ventnor City, 8,688
Verona, 13,782
Victory Gardens, 1,085
Villas, 2,085
Vineland, 37,685
Waldwick, 10,495
Wallington, 9,261
Wanamassa, 3,928
Wanaque, 7,126
Washington, 5,723
Watchung, 3,312
Wayne, 29,353
Weehawken, 13,504
Wenonah, 2,100
West Belmar, 2,511
West Caldwell, 8,314
West Cape May, 1,030
Westfield, 31,447
West Long Branch, 5,337
West New York, 35,547
West Orange, 39,895
West Paterson, 7,602
Westville, 4,951
Westwood, 9,046
Wharton, 5,006
Wildwood, 4,690
Wildwood Crest, 3,011
Williamstown, 2,722
Woodbine, 2,823
Woodbridge, 78,846
Woodbury, 12,453
Woodbury Heights, 1,723
Woodcliff Lake, 2,742
Wood-Lynne, 3,128
Wood-Ridge, 7,964
Woodstown, 2,942
Wrightstown, 4,846
Wyckoff, 11,205

NEW MEXICO, 951,023

Alamogordo, 21,723
Albuquerque, 201,189
Artesia, 12,000
Aztec, 4,137
Bayard, 2,327
Belen, 5,031
Bernalillo, 2,574
Bloomfield, 1,292
Carlsbad, 25,541
Carrizozo, 1,546
Central, 1,075
Clayton, 3,314
Clovis, 23,713
Deming, 6,764
Espanola, 1,976
Eunice, 3,531
Farmington, 23,786
Fort Sumner, 1,809
Gallup, 14,089
Grants, 10,274
Hagerman, 1,144
Hobbs, 26,275
Hurley, 1,851
Jal, 3,051
Las Cruces, 29,367
Las Vegas, city, 7,790
Las Vegas, town, 6,028
Lordsburg, 3,436
Los Alamos, 12,584
Los Lunas, 1,186
Loving, 1,646
Lovington, 9,660
Magdalena, 1,211
Mesilla, 1,264
Milan, 2,658
Mountainair, 1,605
Portales, 9,695
Ranchos de Taos, 1,668
Raton, 8,146
Roswell, 39,593
Ruidoso, 1,557
San Felipe, 1,034
Santa Fe, 34,676
Santa Rita, 1,772
Santa Rosa, 2,220
Silver City, 6,972
Socorro, 5,271
Springer, 1,564
State College–Mesilla Park, 4,387
Taos, 2,163
Tatum, 1,168
Truth or Consequences, 4,269
Tucumcari, 8,143
Tularosa, 3,200
Vaughn, 1,170
Zuni Pueblo, 3,585

NEW YORK, 16,782,304

Adams, 1,914
Addison, 2,185
Akron, 2,841
Albany, 129,726
Albion, 5,182
Alden, 2,042
Alexandria Bay, 1,583
Alfred, 2,807
Allegany, 2,064
Altamont, 1,365
Amagansett, 1,095
Amityville, 8,318
Amsterdam, 28,772
Andover, 1,247
Angola, 2,499
Arcade, 1,930
Ardsley, 3,991
Arlington, 8,317
Athens, 1,754
Attica, 2,758
Auburn, 35,249
Ausable Forks, 2,026
Avoca, 1,086
Avon, 2,772
Babylon, 11,062
Bainbridge, 1,712
Baldwin, 30,204
Baldwinsville, 5,985
Ballston Spa, 4,991
Balmuille, 1,538
Batavia, 18,210
Bath, 6,166
Bayville, 3,962
Beacon, 13,922
Bellerose, 1,083
Bellmore, 12,784
Bellport, 2,461
Belmont, 1,146
Bethpage–Old Bethpage, 20,515
Binghamton, 75,941
Black River, 1,237
Blasdell, 3,909
Bolivar, 1,405
Boonville, 2,403
Brentwood, 15,387
Brewster, 1,714
Briarcliff Manor, 5,105
Brightwaters, 3,193
Broadalbin, 1,438
Brockport, 5,256
Brocton, 1,416
Bronxville, 6,744
Brookville, 1,468
Brownville, 1,082
Buchanan, 2,019
Buffalo, 532,759
Caledonia, 1,917
Cambridge, 1,748
Camden, 2,694
Camillus, 1,416
Canajoharie, 2,681
Canadaigua, 9,370
Canastota, 4,896
Canisteo, 2,731
Canton, 5,046
Carthage, 4,216
Castile, 1,146
Castleton-on-Hudson, 1,752
Catskill, 5,825
Cattaraugus, 1,258
Cayuga Heights, 2,788
Cazenovia, 2,584
Cedarhurst, 6,954
Celoron, 1,507
Centereach, 8,524
Center Moriches, 2,521
Centerport, 3,628
Champlain, 1,549
Chateaugay, 1,097
Chatham, 2,426
Cheektowaga-North-west, 52,362
Cheektowaga-South-west, 12,766
Chester, 1,492
Chittenango, 3,180
Churchville, 1,003
Clarence, 1,456
Clark Mills, 1,148
Clayton, 1,996
Clifton Springs, 1,953
Clinton, 1,855
Clyde, 2,693
Cobleskill, 3,471
Cohoes, 20,129
Cold Spring, 2,083
Cold Spring Harbor, 1,705
Colonie, 6,992
Commack, 9,613
Cooperstown, 2,553
Copiague, 14,081
Corinth, 3,193
Corning, 17,085
Cornwall, 2,785
Cornwall Southwest, 2,824
Cortland, 19,181
Coxsackie, 2,849
Croton-on-Hudson, 6,812
Cuba, 1,949
Dannemora, 4,835
Dansville, 5,460
Deer Park, 16,726
Delhi, 2,307
Depew, 13,580
Deposit, 2,025
Dexter, 1,009
Dobbs Ferry, 9,260
Dolgeville, 3,058
Dryden, 1,263
Dundee, 1,468
Dunkirk, 18,205
Earlville, 1,004
East Aurora, 6,791
East Greenbush, 1,325
East Hampton, 1,772
East Herkimer, 1,068
East Hills, 7,184
East Massapequa, 14,779
East Meadow, 46,036
East Middletown, 1,752
East Moriches, 1,210
East Neck, 3,789
East Northport, 8,381
East Rochester, 8,152
East Rockaway, 10,721
East Setauket, 1,127
East Syracuse, 4,708
East Williston, 2,940
Eden, 2,366
Eggertsville, 44,807
Ellenville, 5,003
Ellicottville, 1,150
Elmira, 46,517
Elmira Heights, 5,157
Elmira Southeast, 6,698
Elmont, 30,138
Elmsford, 3,795
Endicott, 18,775
Fairport, 5,507
Fairview, 8,626
Falconer, 3,343
Farmingdale, 6,128
Farmingville, 2,134
Fayetteville, 4,311
Fernwood, 2,108
Fishkill, 1,033
Flanders, 1,248
Floral Park, 17,499
Florida, 1,550
Flower Hill, 4,594
Fonda, 1,004
Fort Edward, 3,737
Fort Plain, 2,809
Frankfort, 3,872
Franklin Square, 32,483
Franklinville, 2,124
Fredonia, 8,477
Freeport, 34,419
Freetown, 1,365
Frewsburg, 1,623
Friendship, 1,231
Fulton, 14,261
Garden City, 23,948
Garden City Park–Herricks, 15,364
Geneseo, 3,284
Geneva, 17,286
Glen Cove, 23,817
Glens Falls, 18,580
Glenwood Park, 1,317
Gloversville, 21,741
Goshen, 3,906
Gouverneur, 4,946
Gowanda, 3,352
Granville, 2,715
Great Neck, 10,171
Great Neck Estates, 3,262
Great Neck Plaza, 4,948
Greene, 2,051
Green Island, 3,533
Greenlawn, 5,422
Greenport, 2,608
Greenwich, 2,263
Greenwood Lake, 1,236
Groton, 2,123
Hagaman, 1,292
Halesite, 2,857
Hamburg, 9,145
Hamburg–Lake Shore, 11,527
Hamilton, 3,348
Hammondsport, 1,176
Hampton Bays, 1,431
Hancock, 1,830
Harris Hill, 3,944
Hastings-on-Hudson, 8,979
Haverstraw, 5,771
Hempstead, 34,641
Henrietta Northeast, 6,403
Herkimer, 9,396
Hewlett Harbor, 1,610
Hicksville, 50,405
Highland, 2,931
Highland Falls, 4,469
Hillburn, 1,114
Hilton, 1,334
Holbrook, 3,441
Holley, 1,788
Homer, 3,622
Honeoye Falls, 2,143
Hoosick Falls, 4,023
Hornell, 13,907
Horseheads, 7,207
Hudson, 11,075
Hudson Falls, 7,752
Huntington, 11,255
Huntington Bay, 1,267
Huntington Station, 23,438
Hyde Park, 1,979
Ilion, 10,199
Inwood, 10,362
Irvington, 5,494
Island Park, 3,846
Ithaca, 28,799
Jamestown, 41,818
Jericho, 10,795
Johnson City, 19,118
Johnstown, 10,390
Jordan, 1,390
Keeseville, 2,213
Kenmore, 21,261
Kensington, 1,166
Kinderhook, 1,078
Kings Park, 4,949
Kings Point, 5,410
Kingston, 29,260
Lackawanna, 29,564
Lake Carmel, 2,735
Lake Erie Beach, 2,117
Lake George, 1,026
Lake Katrine, 1,149
Lake Placid, 2,998
Lake Ronkonkoma, 4,841
Lake Shenorock, 1,402
Lake Success, 2,954
Lakewood, 3,933
Lancaster, 12,254
Larchmont, 6,789
Lattingtown, 1,461
Lawrence, 5,907
Le Roy, 4,662
Levittown, 65,276
Lewiston, 3,320
Liberty, 4,704
Lima, 1,366
Lincoln Park, 2,707
Lindenhurst, 20,905
Little Falls, 8,935
Little Valley, 1,244
Liverpool, 3,487
Livingston Manor, 2,080
Lloyd Harbor, 2,521
Lockport, 26,443
Locust Grove, 11,558
Long Beach, 26,473
Lowville, 3,616
Lynbrook, 19,881
Lyons, 4,673
McGraw, 1,276
Mahopac, 1,337
Malone, 8,737
Malverne, 9,968
Mamaroneck, 17,673
Manchester, 1,344
Manlius, 1,997
Manorhaven, 3,566
Marathon, 1,079

New York (cont.)
Marcellus, 1,697
Marlboro, 1,733
Massapequa, 32,900
Massapequa Park, 19,904
Massena, 15,478
Mastic Beach, 3,035
Mastic Shirley, 3,397
Mattituck, 1,274
Maybrook, 1,348
Mayville, 1,619
Mechanicville, 6,831
Medina, 6,681
Melrose Park, 2,058
Menands, 2,314
Merrick, 18,789
Mexico, 1,465
Middleburg, 1,317
Middleport, 1,882
Middletown, 23,475
Millbrook, 1,717
Millerton, 1,027
Mineola, 20,519
Mineville, 1,181
Minoa, 1,838
Mohawk, 3,533
Monroe, 3,323
Montgomery, 1,312
Monticello, 5,222
Montour Falls, 1,533
Moravia, 1,575
Morrisville, 1,304
Mount Kisco, 6,805
Mount Morris, 3,250
Mount Vernon, 76,010
Munsey Park, 2,847
Muttontown, 1,265
Naples, 1,237
Nassau, 1,248
Nesconset, 1,964
Newark, 12,868
Newark Valley, 1,234
New Berlin, 1,262
Newburgh, 30,979
Newfane, 1,423
New Hartford, 2,468
New Hyde Park, 10,808
New Paltz, 3,041
New Rochelle, 76,812
New Windsor, 4,041
New York City, 7,781,984
New York Mills, 3,788
Niagara Falls, 102,394
Norfolk, 1,353
North Bellmore, 19,639
North Collins, 1,574
North Merrick, 12,976
North New Hyde Park, 17,929
North Pelham, 5,326
Northport, 5,972
North Syracuse, 7,412
North Tarrytown, 8,818
North Tonawanda, 34,757
North Valley Stream, 17,239
Northville, 1,156
Norwich, 9,175
Norwood, 2,200
Nunda, 1,224
Nyack, 6,062
Oakfield, 2,070
Oceanside, 30,448
Ogdensburg, 16,122
Olcott, 1,215
Old Brookville, 1,126
Old Westbury, 2,064
Olean, 21,868
Oneida, 11,677
Oneonta, 13,412
Orchard Park, 3,278
Oriskany, 1,580
Ossining, 18,662
Oswego, 22,155
Owego, 5,417
Oxford, 1,871
Painted Post, 2,570
Palmyra, 3,476
Patchogue, 8,838
Pawling, 1,734
Peekskill, 18,737
Pelham, 1,964
Pelham Manor, 6,114
Penn Yan, 5,770
Perry, 4,629
Phelps, 1,887
Philmont, 1,750
Phoenix, 2,408
Piermont, 1,906
Pine Bush, 1,016
Pittsford, 1,749
Plainedge, 21,973
Plainview, 27,710
Plandome, 1,379
Plandome Heights, 1,025
Plattsburgh, 20,172
Pleasantville, 5,877
Port Byron, 1,201
Port Chester, 24,960
Port Dickinson, 2,295
Port Ewen, 2,622
Port Henry, 1,767
Port Jefferson, 2,336
Port Jefferson Station, 1,041
Port Jervis, 9,268
Portville, 1,336
Port Washington, 15,657
Potsdam, 7,765
Poughkeepsie, 38,330
Pulaski, 2,256
Randolph, 1,414
Ravena, 2,410
Red Hook, 1,719
Rensselaer, 10,506
Rhinebeck, 2,093
Richfield Springs, 1,630
Ripley, 1,247
Riverhead, 5,830
Riverside, 1,030
Rochdale, 1,800
Rochester, 318,611
Rockville Centre, 26,355
Rocky Point, 2,261
Rome, 51,646
Ronkonkoma, 4,220
Ronkonkoma West, 1,446
Roosevelt, 12,883
Rosendale, 1,033
Roslyn, 2,681
Roslyn Estates, 1,289
Rotterdam, 16,871
Rouses Point, 2,160
Russell Gardens, 1,156
Rye, 14,225
Sackets Harbor, 1,279
Saddle Rock, 1,109
Sag Harbor, 2,346
St. James, 3,524
St. Johnsville, 2,196
Salamanca, 8,480
Salem, 1,076
Sands Point, 2,161
San Remo, 11,996
Saranac Lake, 6,421
Saratoga Springs, 16,630
Saugerties, 4,286
Sauquoit, 1,715
Scarsdale, 17,968
Schenectady, 81,682
Schoharie, 1,168
Schuylerville, 1,361
Scotia, 7,625
Scottsville, 1,863
Scranton, 1,078
Sea Cliff, 5,669
Seaford, 14,718
Selden, 1,604
Seneca Falls, 7,439
Setauket, 1,207
Sherburne, 1,647
Sherrill, 2,922
Shortsville, 1,382
Shrub Oak, 1,874
Sidney, 5,157
Silver Creek, 3,310
Skaneateles, 2,921
Sloan, 5,803
Sloatsburg, 2,565
Smithtown Branch, 1,986
Sodus, 1,645
Solvay, 8,732
Sound Beach, 1,625
Southampton, 4,582
South Corning, 1,448
South Fallsburgh, 1,290
South Farmingdale, 16,318
South Floral Park, 1,090
South Glens Falls, 4,129
South Huntington, 7,084
South Nyack, 3,113
South Westbury, 11,977
Spencerport, 2,461
Spring Valley, 6,538
Springville, 3,852
Stamford, 1,166
Stewart Manor, 2,422
Stillwater, 1,398
Stony Brook, 3,548
Stony Point, 3,330
Stottville, 1,040
Suffern, 5,094
Syracuse, 216,038
Tarrytown, 11,109
Thomaston, 2,767
Ticonderoga, 3,568
Tonawanda, city, 21,561
Tonawanda, 83,771
Troy, 67,492
Trumansburg, 1,768
Tuckahoe, 6,423
Tupper Lake, 5,200
Unadilla, 1,586
Uniondale, 20,041
Union Springs, 1,066
Upper Brookville, 1,045
Upper Nyack, 1,833
Utica, 100,410
Valatie, 1,237
Valley Stream, 38,629
Vernon Valley, 5,998
Victor, 1,180
Victory Heights, 2,528
Voorheesville, 1,228
Walden, 4,851
Wallkill, 1,215
Walton, 3,855
Wantagh, 34,172
Wappingers Falls, 4,447
Warrensburg, 2,240
Warsaw, 3,653
Warwick, 3,218
Washington Heights, 1,231
Washingtonville, 1,178
Waterford, 2,915
Waterloo, 5,098
Watertown, 33,306
Waterville, 1,901
Watervliet, 13,917
Watkins Glen, 2,813
Waverly, 5,950
Wayland, 2,003
Webster, 3,060
Weedsport, 1,731
Wellsville, 5,967
Westbury, 14,757
West Carthage, 2,167
West Elmira, 5,763
West End, 1,436
Westfield, 3,878
West Glens Falls, 2,725
Westhampton Beach, 1,460
West Haverstraw, 5,020
West Hempstead–Lakeview, 24,783
West Seneca, 23,138
Whitehall, 4,016
White Plains, 50,485
Whitesboro, 4,784
Whitney Point, 1,049
Williamson, 1,690
Williamsville, 6,316
Williston Park, 8,255
Wilson, 1,320
Windsor, 1,026
Winona Lakes, 1,655
Wolcott, 1,641
Woodmere, 14,011
Woodridge, 1,034
Yonkers, 190,634
Yorktown, 3,576
Yorktown Heights, 2,478
Yorkville, 3,749
Youngstown, 1,848

NORTH CAROLINA, 4,556,155
Aberdeen, 1,531
Ahoskie, 4,583
Albemarle, 12,261
Andrews, 1,404
Angier, 1,249
Apex, 1,368
Archdale, 1,520
Asheboro, 9,449
Asheboro South, 1,515
Asheboro West, 1,228
Asheville, 60,192
Aulander, 1,083
Ayden, 3,108
Badin, 1,905
Balfour, 1,106
Balfours, 3,805
Bannertown, 1,096
Barker Heights, 2,184
Beaufort, 2,922
Belhaven, 2,386
Belmont, 5,007
Belmont–South Rosemary, 2,043
Benson, 2,355
Bessemer City, 4,017
Bethel, 1,578
Beulaville, 1,062
Biltmore Forest, 1,004
Biscoe, 1,053
Black Mountain, 1,313
Boger City, 1,728
Boiling Springs, 1,311
Bonnie Doone, 4,481
Boone, 3,686
Brevard, 4,857
Bryson City, 1,084
Burgaw, 1,750
Burlington, 33,199
Burnsville, 1,388
Canton, 5,068
Caroleen, 1,168
Carolina Beach, 1,192
Carrboro, 1,997
Carthage, 1,190
Cary, 3,356
Chadbourn, 2,323
Chapel Hill, 12,573
Charlotte, 201,564
Cherryville, 3,607
China Grove, 1,500
Clayton, 3,302
Cliffside, 1,275
Clinton, 7,461
Coats, 1,049
Columbia, 1,099
Concord, 17,799
Concord North, 2,199
Conover, 2,281
Cooleemee, 1,609
Cornelius, 1,444
Cramerton, 3,123
Dallas, 3,270
Daniels-Rhyne, 1,285
Davidson, 2,573
Draper, 3,382
Drexel, 1,146
Druid Hills, 1,207
Dunn, 7,566
Durham, 78,302
East Fayetteville, 2,797
East Gastonia, 3,326
East Marion, 2,442
East Rockingham, 3,211
East Spencer, 2,171
East Wilmington, 5,520
Edenton, 4,458
Elizabeth City, 14,062
Elizabethtown, 1,625
Elkin, 2,868
Elon College, 1,284
Enfield, 2,978
Erwin, 3,183
Fair Bluff, 1,030
Fairmont, 2,286
Farmville, 3,997
Fayetteville, 47,106
Fayetteville North, 3,071
Flat Rock, 1,808
Forest City, 6,556
Four Oaks, 1,010
Franklin, 2,173
Franklinton, 1,513
Fremont, 1,609
Fuquay Springs, 3,389
Garner, 3,451
Gaston, 1,214
Gastonia, 37,276
Gibsonville, 1,784
Glen Raven, 2,418
Goldsboro, 28,873
Graham, 7,723
Granite Falls, 2,644
Granite Quarry, 1,059
Greensboro, 119,574
Greenville, 22,860
Grifton, 1,816
Hamlet, 4,460
Harkers Island, 1,362
Havelock, 2,433
Haw River, 1,410
Hazelwood, 1,925
Henderson, 12,740
Hendersonville, 5,911
Hertford, 2,068
Hickory, 19,328
Hickory East, 3,274
Hickory North, 1,541
High Point, 62,063
Hillsboro, 1,349
Hope Mills, 1,109
Hudson, 1,536
Huntersville, 1,004
Jacksonville, 13,491
James City, 1,474
Jamestown, 1,247
Jonesville, 1,895
Kannapolis, 34,647
Kenly, 1,147
Kernersville, 2,942
Kings Mountain, 8,008
Kinston, 24,819
La Grange, 2,133
Landis, 1,763
Landis Northeast, 1,517
Laurinburg, 8,242
Leaksville, 6,427
Lenoir, 10,257
Lexington, 16,093
Liberty, 1,438
Lillington, 1,242
Lincolnton, 5,699
Littleton, 1,024
Longhurst, 1,546
Longview, 2,997
Longwood Park, 1,144
Louisburg, 2,862
Lowell, 2,784
Lumberton, 15,305
Madison, 1,912
Maiden, 2,039
Marion, 3,345
Mars Hill, 1,574
Marshville, 1,360
Maxton, 1,755
Mayodan, 2,366
Mebane, 2,364
Midstate Mill, 1,090
Midway Park, 4,164
Mocksville, 2,379
Monroe, 10,882
Mooresville, 6,918
Morehead City, 5,583
Morganton, 9,186
Mount Airy, 7,055
Mount Gilead, 1,229
Mount Holly, 4,037
Mount Olive, 4,673
Mount Pleasant, 1,041
Murfreesboro, 2,643
Murphy, 2,235
Nashville, 1,423
New Bern, 15,717
Newton, 6,658
North Belmont, 8,328
North Henderson, 1,995
North Wilkesboro, 4,197
Norwood, 1,844
Owens, 5,207
Oxford, 6,978
Pembroke, 1,372
Phillipsville, 1,311
Pilot Mountain, 1,310
Pinehurst, 1,124
Pinetops, 1,372
Pineville, 1,514
Pittsboro, 1,215
Plymouth, 4,666
Raeford, 3,058
Raleigh, 93,931
Ramseur, 1,258
Randleman, 2,232
Red Springs, 2,767
Reidsville, 14,267
Rex, 1,515
Richlands, 1,079
Richmond Hill, 2,943
Rich Square, 1,134
Roanoke Rapids, 13,320
Robbins, 1,294
Robersonville, 1,684
Rockingham, 5,512
Rocky Mount, 32,147
Roseboro, 1,354
Rose Hill, 1,292
Rowan Mill, 1,089
Rowland, 1,408
Roxboro, 5,147
Rural Hall, 1,503
Rutherfordton, 3,392
St. Pauls, 2,249
Salisbury, 21,297
Salisbury West, 1,323
Sanford, 12,253
Scotland Neck, 2,974
Selma, 3,102
Shelby, 17,698
Siler City, 4,455
Smithfield, 6,117
Smyre, 1,197
Snow Hill, 1,043
South Belmont, 2,286
Southern Pines, 5,198
South Fayetteville, 3,411
South Gastonia, 3,762
South Henderson, 2,017
Southport, 2,034
South Salisbury, 3,065
South Wilmington, 2,238
Sparta, 1,047
Spencer, 2,904
Spindale, 4,082
Spray, 4,565
Spring Hope, 1,336
Spring Lake, 4,110
Spruce Pine, 2,504
Stanley, 1,980
Stanleyville, 1,138
Statesville, 19,844
Stony Point, 1,015
Swannanoa, 2,189
Swansboro, 1,104
Sylva, 1,564
Tabor City, 2,338
Tarboro, 8,411
Taylorsville, 1,470
Thomasville, 15,190
Toast, 2,023
Troy, 2,346
Tryon, 2,223
Valdese, 2,941
Wadesboro, 3,744
Wake Forest, 2,664
Walkertown, 1,240
Wallace, 2,285
Walnut Cove, 1,288
Warrenton, 1,124
Warsaw, 2,221
Washington, 9,939
Waynesville, 6,159
Weaverville, 1,041
Weldon, 2,165
Wendell, 1,620
West Concord, 5,510
West Hillsboro, 1,065
West Jefferson, 1,000
West Marion, 2,335
West Rockingham, 1,128
Whitakers, 1,004
Whiteville, 4,683
Whitnel, 1,232
Wilkesboro, 1,568
Williamston, 6,924
Wilmington, 44,013
Wilson, 28,753
Windsor, 1,813
Wingate, 1,304
Winston-Salem, 111,135
Winterville, 1,418
Yadkinville, 1,644
Yanceyville, 1,113
Zebulon, 1,534

NORTH DAKOTA, 632,446
Ashley, 1,419
Beach, 1,460
Belfield, 1,064
Beulah, 1,318
Bismarck, 27,670
Bottineau, 2,613
Bowman, 1,730
Cando, 1,566
Carrington, 2,438
Casselton, 1,394
Cavalier, 1,423
Cooperstown, 1,424
Crosby, 1,759
Devils Lake, 6,299
Dickinson, 9,971
Dunseith, 1,017
Ellendale, 1,800
Enderlin, 1,596
Fargo, 46,662
Garrison, 1,794
Glen Ullin, 1,210
Grafton, 5,885
Grand Forks, 34,451
Hankinson, 1,285
Harvey, 2,365
Hazen, 1,222
Hebron, 1,340
Hettinger, 1,769
Hillsboro, 1,278
Jamestown, 15,163
Kenmare, 1,696
Lakota, 1,066
La Moure, 1,068
Langdon, 2,151
Larimore, 1,714
Lidgerwood, 1,081
Linton, 1,826
Lisbon, 2,093
Mandan, 10,525
Mayville, 2,168
Minot, 30,604
Mott, 1,463
Napoleon, 1,078
New England, 1,095
New Rockford, 2,177
New Town, 1,586
Northwood, 1,195
Oakes, 1,650
Park River, 1,813
Parshall, 1,216
Ray, 1,049
Riverdale, 1,055
Rolla, 1,398
Rugby, 2,972
South West Fargo, 3,328
Stanley, 1,795
Tioga, 2,087
Valley, 7,809
Velva, 1,330
Wahpeton, 5,876
Walhalla, 1,432
Watford City, 1,865
Williston, 11,866
Wishek, 1,290

OHIO, 9,706,397
Ada, 3,918
Addyston, 1,376
Adena, 1,317
Akron, 290,351
Alger, 1,068
Alliance, 28,362
Amberley, 2,951
Amherst, 6,750
Andover, 1,116
Ansonia, 1,002
Antwerp, 1,465
Arcanum, 1,678
Archbold, 2,348
Arlington Heights, 1,355
Ashland, 17,419
Ashtabula, 24,559
Ashville, 1,639
Athens, 16,470
Aurora, 4,049
Avon Lake, 9,403
Bainbridge, 1,001
Ballville, 1,424
Baltimore, 2,116
Barberton, 33,805
Barnesville, 4,425
Batavia, 1,729
Bay, 14,489
Beach City, 1,151
Beachwood, 6,089
Bedford, 15,223
Bedford Heights, 5,275
Bellaire, 11,502
Bellefontaine, 11,424
Bellevue, 8,286
Bellville, 1,621
Belpre, 5,418
Berea, 16,592
Bethel, 2,019
Bethesda, 1,178
Beverly, 1,194
Bexley, 14,319
Blanchester, 2,944
Blue Ash, 8,341
Bluffton, 2,591
Bowling Green, 13,574
Bradford, 2,148
Bratenahl, 1,332
Brecksville, 5,435
Bremen, 1,417
Brewster, 2,025
Bridgeport, 3,824
Brilliant, 2,174
Broadview Heights, 6,209
Brooklyn, 10,733
Brooklyn Heights, 1,449
Brook Park, 12,856
Brookville, 3,184
Brunswick, 6,453
Bryan, 7,361
Buckeye Lake, 2,129
Bucyrus, 12,276
Burton, 1,085
Byesville, 2,447
Cadiz, 3,259
Calcutta, 2,221
Caldwell, 1,999
Cambridge, 14,562
Camden, 1,308
Campbell, 13,406
Canal Fulton, 1,555
Canal Winchester, 1,976
Canfield, 3,252
Canton, 113,631
Cardington, 1,613
Carey, 3,722
Carrollton, 2,786
Cedarville, 1,702
Celina, 7,659
Centerville, 3,490
Chagrin Falls, 3,458
Chardon, 3,154
Chesapeake, 1,396
Cheviot, 10,701
Chillicothe, 24,957
Cincinnati, 502,550
Circleville, 11,059
Cleveland, 876,050
Cleveland Heights, 61,813
Cleves, 2,076
Clyde, 4,826
Coal Grove, 2,961
Coldwater, 2,766
Columbiana, 4,164
Columbus, 471,316
Columbus Grove, 2,104
Conneaut, 10,557
Continental, 1,147
Corning, 1,065
Cortland, 1,957
Coshocton, 13,106
Covington, 2,473
Craig Beach, 1,139
Crestline, 5,521
Creston, 1,522
Cridersville, 1,053
Crooksville, 2,958
Crystal Lakes, 1,569
Cuyahoga Falls, 47,922
Dalton, 1,067
Dayton, 262,332
Deer Park, 8,423
Defiance, 14,553
Delaware, 13,282
Delphos, 6,961
Delta, 2,376
Dennison, 4,158
Deshler, 1,824
Dillonvale, 1,232
Dover, 11,300
Doylestown, 1,873
Dresden, 1,338
Dunkirk, 1,006
East Alliance, 1,275
East Ashtabula, 4,179
East Canton, 1,521
East Cleveland, 37,991
Eastlake, 12,467
East Liverpool, 22,306
East Palestine, 5,232
Eaton, 5,034
Eaton Estates, 1,733
Edgerton, 1,566
Elida, 1,215
Elmore, 1,302
Elmwood Place, 3,813
Elyria, 43,782
Englewood, 1,515
Enon, 1,227
Euclid, 62,998
Fairborn, 19,453
Fairfax, 2,430
Fairfield, 9,734
Fairport, 4,267
Fairview Park, 14,624
Fayette, 1,090
Findlay, 30,344
Flushing, 1,189
Forest, 1,314
Fort Recovery, 1,336
Fostoria, 15,732
Franklin, 7,917
Fredericktown, 1,531
Fremont, 17,573
Gahanna, 2,717
Galion, 12,650
Gallipolis, 8,775
Gambier, 1,148
Garfield Heights, 38,455
Garrettsville, 1,662
Gates Mills, 1,588
Geneva, 5,677
Genoa, 1,957
Georgetown, 2,674
Germantown, 3,399
Gibsonburg, 2,540
Girard, 12,997
Glendale, 2,823
Glouster, 2,255
Gnadenhutten, 1,257
Golf Manor, 4,648
Grafton, 1,683
Grandview Heights, 8,270
Granville, 2,868
Greenfield, 5,422
Greenhills, 5,407
Green Springs, 1,262
Greenville, 10,585
Greenwich, 1,371
Grove City, 8,107
Groveport, 2,043
Hamden, 1,035
Hamilton, 72,354
Harrison, 3,878
Hartville, 1,353
Heath, 2,426
Hebron, 1,260
Hicksville, 3,116
Highland Heights, 2,929
Hilliard, 5,633
Hillsboro, 5,474
Hiram, 1,011
Holgate, 1,374
Hubbard, 7,137
Hudson, 2,438
Huron, 5,197
Independence, 6,868
Indian Hill, 4,526
Ironton, 15,745
Jackson, 6,980
Jamestown, 1,730
Jefferson, Ashtabula co., 2,116
Jefferson, Madison co., 2,774
Johnstown, 2,881
Kent, 17,836
Kenton, 8,747
Kettering, 54,462
Kingston, 1,066
Lagrange, 1,007
Lakemore, 2,765
Lakeview, 1,008
Lakeville, 4,181
Lakewood, 66,154
Lancaster, 29,916
Lebanon, 5,993
Leetonia, 2,543
Leipsic, 1,802
Lewisburg, 1,415
Lexington, 1,311
Lima, 51,037
Lincoln Heights, Richland co., 8,004
Lincoln Heights, Hamilton co., 7,798
Lisbon, 3,579
Liverpool North, 1,575
Lockland, 5,292

Lodi, 2,213
Logan, 6,417
London, 6,379
Lorain, 68,932
Loudonville, 2,611
Louisville, 5,116
Loveland, 5,008
Lowellville, 2,055
Lucasville, 1,277
Lynchburg, 1,022
Lyndhurst, 16,805
McArthur, 1,529
McComb, 1,176
McConnelsville, 2,257
McDonald, 2,727
Madeira, 6,744
Madison, 1,347
Magnolia, 1,596
Malvern, 1,320
Manchester, 2,172
Mansfield, 47,325
Mansfield Southeast, 2,961
Mantua, 1,194
Maple Heights, 31,667
Mariemont, 4,120
Marietta, 16,847
Marion, 37,079
Martins Ferry, 11,919
Marysville, 4,952
Mason, 4,727
Massillon, 31,236
Masury, 2,512
Maumee, 12,063
Mayfield, Butler co., 2,747
Mayfield, Cuyahoga co., 1,977
Mayfield Heights, 13,478
Mechanicsburg, 1,810
Medina, 8,235
Mentor, 4,354
Mentor-on-the-Lake-Village, 3,290
Miamisburg, 9,893
Middleburg Heights, 7,282
Middlefield, 1,467
Middleport, 3,373
Middletown, 42,115
Milan, 1,309
Milford, 4,131
Millersburg, 3,101
Minerva, 3,833
Minerva Park, 1,169
Mingo Junction, 4,987
Minster, 2,193
Mogadore, 3,851
Monroe, 1,475
Monroeville, 1,371
Montgomery, 3,075
Montpelier, 4,131
Moraine, 2,262
Moreland Hills, 2,188
Morrow, 1,477
Mount Gilead, 2,788
Mount Healthy, 6,553
Mount Orab, 1,058
Mount Sterling, 1,338
Mount Vernon, 13,284
Munroe Falls, 1,828
Napoleon, 6,739
Navarre, 1,698
Nelsonville, 4,834
Newark, 41,790
New Boston, 3,984
New Bremen, 1,972
Newburgh Hts., 3,512
New Carlisle, 4,107
Newcomerstown, 4,273
New Concord, 2,127
New Lebanon, 1,459
New Lexington, 4,514
New London, 2,392
New Miami, 2,360
New Paris, 1,679
New Philadelphia, 14,241
New Richmond, 2,834
New Straitsville, 1,019
Newton Falls, 5,038
Newtown, 1,750
New Washington, 1,162
Niles, 19,545
North Baltimore, 3,011
North Canton, 7,727
North College Hill, 12,035
Northfield, 1,055
North Kingsville, 1,854
North Mount Vernon, 1,465
North Olmsted, 16,290
North Royalton, 9,290
North Zanesville, 2,201
Norwalk, 12,900
Norwood, 34,580
Oak Harbor, 2,903
Oak Hill, 1,748
Oakwood, Montgomery co., 10,493
Oakwood, Cuyahoga co., 3,283
Oberlin, 8,198
Obetz, 1,984
Olmsted Falls, 2,144
Oneida–Rolling Mill Park, 6,504
Ontario, 3,049
Orange, 2,006
Oregon, 13,319
Orrville, 6,511
Ottawa, 3,245
Ottawa Hills, 3,870
Oxford, 7,828
Painesville, 16,116
Painesville Northeast, 1,267
Parkview, 2,018
Parma, 82,845
Parma Heights, 18,100
Pataskala, 1,046
Paulding, 2,936
Payne, 1,287
Peebles, 1,601
Pemberville, 1,237
Pepper Pike, 3,217
Perrysburg, 5,519
Piketon, 1,244
Piqua, 19,219
Plain City, 2,146
Pleasant Hill, 1,060
Plymouth, 1,822
Poland, 2,766
Pomeroy, 3,345
Port Clinton, 6,870
Portsmouth, 33,637
Powhatan Point, 2,147
Prospect, 1,067
Ravenna, 10,918
Reading, 12,832
Reynoldsburg, 7,793
Richmond Hts., 5,068
Richwood, 2,137
Ripley, 2,174
Rittman, 5,410
Rockford, 1,155
Rocky River, 18,097
Rosedale, 8,204
Roseville, 1,749
Rossford, 4,406
Russells Point, 1,111
Sabina, 2,313
St. Bernard, 6,778
St. Clairsville, 3,865
St. Marys, 7,737
St. Paris, 1,460
Salem, 13,854
Salineville, 1,898
Sandusky, 31,989
Sandusky South, 4,724
Scio, 1,135
Sciotodale, 1,113
Sebring, 4,439
Seven Hills, 5,708
Seville, 1,190
Shadyside, 5,028
Shaker Heights, 36,460
Sharonville, 3,890
Sharon West, 3,365
Shawnee, 1,000
Sheffield, 1,664
Sheffield Lake, 6,884
Shelby, 9,106
Shreve, 1,617
Sidney, 14,663
Silver Lake, 2,655
Silverton, 6,682
Smithfield, 1,312
Smithville, 1,024
Solon, 6,333
Somerset, 1,361
South Amherst, 1,657
South Charleston, 1,505
South Euclid, 27,569
South Lebanon, 2,720
South Mount Vernon, 1,420
South Point, 1,663
South Russell, 1,276
South Zanesville, 1,557
Spencerville, 2,061
Springdale, 3,556
Springfield, 82,723
Steubenville, 32,495
Story Prairie, 1,720
Stow, 12,194
Strasburg, 1,687
Strongsville, 8,504
Struthers, 15,631
Stryker, 1,205
Sunbury, 1,360
Swanton, 2,306
Sylvania, 5,187
Tallmadge, 10,246
Terrace Park, 2,023
The Plains, 1,148
Tiffin, 21,478
Tiltonsville, 2,454
Tipp City, 4,267
Toledo, 318,003
Toronto, 7,780
Trenton, 3,064
Trotwood, 4,992
Troy, 13,685
Twinsburg, 4,098
Uhrichsville, 6,201
Union, 1,072
Union City, 1,657
Uniontown, 1,668
University Heights, 16,641
Upper Arlington, 28,486
Upper Sandusky, 4,941
Urbana, 10,461
Urbancrest, 1,029
Utica, 1,854
Valley View, 1,221
Vandalia, 6,342
Van Wert, 11,323
Vermilion, 4,785
Vermilion-on-the-Lake, 1,273
Versailles, 2,159
Wadsworth, 10,635
Walbridge, 2,142
Walton Hills, 1,776
Wapakoneta, 6,756
Warren, 59,648
Warrensville Heights, 10,609
Washington, 12,388
Waterville, 1,856
Wauseon, 4,311
Waverly, 3,830
Waynesburg, 1,442
Waynesville, 1,298
Wellington, 3,599
Wellston, 5,728
Wellsville, 7,117
West Alexandria Village, 1,524
West Ausdale, 1,354
West Carrollton, 4,749
Westerville, 7,011
West Lafayette, 1,476
Westlake, 12,906
West Liberty, 1,522
West Milton, 2,972
Weston, 1,075
West Portsmouth, 3,100
West Salem, 1,017
West Union, 1,762
West Unity, 1,192
West View, 1,303
Wheelersburg, 2,682
Whitehall, 20,818
Whitehouse, 1,135
Wickliffe, 15,760
Willard, 5,457
Williamsburg, 1,956
Willoughby, 15,058
Willoughby Hills, 4,241
Willowick, 18,749
Wilmington, 8,915
Windham, 3,777
Wintersville, 3,597
Withamsville, 2,811
Woodlawn, 3,007
Woodsfield, 2,956
Woodville, 1,700
Wooster, 17,046
Worthington, 9,239
Wyoming, 7,736
Xenia, 20,445
Yellow Springs, 4,167
Yorkville, 1,801
Youngstown, 166,689
Zanesville, 39,077

OKLAHOMA, 2,328,284

Ada, 14,347
Afton, 1,111
Allen, 1,005
Altus, 21,225
Alva, 6,258
Anadarko, 6,299
Antlers, 2,085
Apache, 1,455
Ardmore, 20,184
Arkoma, 1,862
Atoka, 2,877
Barnsdall, 1,663
Bartlesville, 27,893
Beaver, 2,087
Beggs, 1,114
Bethany, 12,342
Bixby, 1,711
Blackwell, 9,588
Blanchard, 1,377
Boise City, 1,978
Bristow, 4,795
Broken Arrow, 5,928
Broken Bow, 2,087
Buffalo, 1,618
Burns Flat, 2,280
Cache, 1,003
Carnegie, 1,500
Chandler, 2,524
Checotah, 2,614
Chelsea, 1,541
Cherokee, 2,410
Chickasha, 14,866
Claremore, 6,639
Cleveland, 2,519
Clinton, 9,617
Coalgate, 1,689
Collinsville, 2,526
Comanche, 2,082
Commerce, 2,378
Coweta, 1,858
Crescent, 1,264
Cushing, 8,619
Cyril, 1,284
Davis, 2,203
Del City, 12,934
Dewey, 3,994
Drumright, 4,190
Duncan, 20,009
Durant, 10,467
Edmond, 8,577
Elk City, 8,196
El Reno, 11,015
Enid, 38,859
Erick, 1,342
Eufaula, 2,382
Fairfax, 2,076
Fairview, 2,213
Fort Gibson, 1,407
Frederick, 5,879
Geary, 1,416
Grandfield, 1,606
Guthrie, 9,502
Guymon, 5,768
Hartshorne, 1,903
Haskell, 1,887
Healdton, 2,898
Heavener, 1,891
Hennessey, 1,228
Henryetta, 6,551
Hobart, 5,132
Holdenville, 5,712
Hollis, 3,006
Hominy, 2,866
Hooker, 1,684
Hugo, 6,287
Idabel, 4,967
Jay, 1,120
Jenks, 1,734
Kingfisher, 3,249
Konawa, 1,555
Krebs, 1,342
Laverne, 1,937
Lawton, 61,697
Lexington, 1,216
Lindsay, 4,258
McAlester, 17,419
Madill, 3,084
Mangum, 3,950
Marietta, 1,933
Marlow, 4,027
Maud, 1,137
Maysville, 1,530
Medford, 1,223
Miami, 12,869
Midway, 2,292
Midwest City, 36,058
Minco, 1,021
Moore, 1,783
Muldrow, 1,137
Muskogee, 38,059
New Cordell, 3,589
Newkirk, 2,092
Nichols Hills, 4,897
Nicoma Park, 1,263
Norman, 33,412
Nowata, 4,163
Oilton, 1,100
Okeene, 1,164
Okemah, 2,836
Oklahoma City, 324,253
Okmulgee, 15,951
Owasso, 2,032
Pauls Valley, 6,856
Pawhuska, 5,414
Pawnee, 2,303
Perry, 5,210
Picher, 2,553
Ponca City, 24,411
Poteau, 4,428
Prague, 1,545
Prattville, 2,530
Pryor Creek, 6,476
Purcell, 3,729
Ringling, 1,170
Rush Springs, 1,303
Sallisaw, 3,351
Sand Springs, 7,754
Sapulpa, 14,282
Sayre, 2,913
Seminole, 11,464
Sentinel, 1,154
Shattuck, 1,625
Shawnee, 24,326
Skiatook, 2,503
Snyder, 1,663
Spencer, 1,189
Spiro, 1,450
Stigler, 1,923
Stillwater, 23,965
Stilwell, 1,916
Stratford, 1,058
Stroud, 2,456
Sulphur, 4,737
Tahlequah, 5,840
Talihina, 1,048
Tecumseh, 2,630
Temple, 1,282
The Village, 12,118
Thomas, 1,211
Tipton, 1,117
Tishomingo, 2,381
Tonkawa, 3,415
Tulsa, 261,685
Valley Brook, 1,378
Vinita, 6,027
Wagoner, 4,469
Walters, 2,825
Warr Acres, 7,135
Watonga, 3,252
Waurika, 1,933
Waynoka, 1,794
Weatherford, 4,499
Weleetka, 1,231
Wetumka, 1,798
Wewoka, 5,954
Wilburton, 1,772
Wilson, 1,647
Woodward, 7,747
Wright City, 1,161
Wynnewood, 2,509
Yale, 1,369
Yukon, 3,076

OREGON, 1,768,687

Albany, 12,926
Altamont, 10,811
Ashland, 9,119
Astoria, 11,239
Baker, 9,986
Bandon, 1,653
Barnes, 5,076
Beaverton, 5,937
Bend, 11,936
Brookings, 2,637
Bunker Hill, 1,655
Burns, 3,523
Canby, 2,168
Canyonville, 1,089
Central Point, 2,289
Condon, 1,149
Coos Bay, 7,084
Coquille, 4,730
Cornelius, 1,146
Corvallis, 20,669
Cottage Grove, 3,895
Dallas, 5,072
Dalles, 10,493
Drain, 1,052
Eastside, 1,380
Elgin, 1,315
Empire, 3,781
Englewood, 1,382
Enterprise, 1,932
Eugene, 50,977
Florence, 1,642
Forest Grove, 5,628
Four Corners, 4,743
Fruitdale, 2,158
Garibaldi, 1,163
Gladstone, 3,854
Gold Beach, 1,765
Grants Pass, 10,118
Gresham, 3,944
Hayesville, 4,568
Heppner, 1,661
Hermiston, 4,402
Hillsboro, 8,232
Hines, 1,207
Hood River, 3,657
Independence, 1,930
Jacksonville, 1,172
John Day, 1,520
Junction City, 1,614
Keizer, 5,288
Klamath Falls, 16,949
La Grande, 9,014
Lakeview, 3,260
Lebanon, 5,858
McMinnville, 7,656
Madras, 1,515
May Park, 1,071
Medford, 24,425
Mill City, 1,289
Milton-Freewater, 4,110
Milwaukie, 9,099
Molalla, 1,501
Monmouth, 2,229
Mount Angel, 1,428
Myrtle Creek, 2,231
Myrtle Point, 2,886
Newberg, 4,204
Newport, 5,344
North Bend, 7,512
Nyssa, 2,611
Oakridge, 1,973
Oceanlake, 1,342
Ontario, 5,101
Oregon City, 7,996
Oswego, 8,906
Pendleton, 14,434
Philomath, 1,359
Pilot Rock, 1,695
Portland, 372,676
Port Orford, 1,171
Powers, 1,366
Prineville, 3,263
Prineville Southeast, 1,299
Rainier, 1,152
Redmond, 3,340
Reedsport, 2,998
Roseburg, 1,467
St. Helens, 5,022
Salem, 49,142
Salem Heights, 10,770
Sandy, 1,147
Seaside, 3,877
Sheridan, 1,763
Silverton, 3,081
South Medford, 2,306
Springfield, 19,616
Stayton, 2,108
Sutherlin, 2,452
Sweet Home, 3,353
Tillamook, 4,244
Toledo, 3,053
Union, 1,490
Vale, 1,491
Vernonia, 1,089
Warrenton, 1,717
West Linn, 3,933
Winston, 2,395
Woodburn, 3,120

PENNSYLVANIA, 11,319,366

Abington, 55,831
Adamstown, 1,190
Akron, 2,167
Albion, 1,630
Alburtis, 1,086
Aldan, 4,324
Aliquippa, 26,369
Allentown, 108,347
Allison, 1,285
Altoona, 69,407
Ambler, 6,765
Ambridge, 13,865
Annville, 4,264
Apollo, 2,694
Archbald, 5,471
Arlington Heights–Pocono Park, 1,569
Arnold, 9,437
Ashland, 5,237
Ashley, 4,258
Aspinwall, 3,727
Aston, 10,595
Athens, 4,515
Atlas, 1,574
Avalon, 6,859
Avella, 1,310
Avis, 1,262
Avoca, 3,562
Avon, 1,212
Avondale, 1,016
Avonmore, 1,351
Baden, 6,109
Bakerton, 1,057
Baldwin, borough, 24,489
Baldwin, 3,004
Bally, 1,033
Bangor, 5,766
Barnesboro, 3,035
Bath, 1,736
Beaver, 6,160
Beaverdale-Lloydell, 1,862
Beaver Falls, 16,240
Beaver Meadows, 1,392
Bedford, 3,696
Bellefonte, 6,088
Belle Vernon, 1,784
Belleville, 1,539
Bellevue, 11,412
Bellwood, 2,330
Ben Avon, 2,553
Bentleyville, 3,160
Berlin, 1,600
Berwick, 13,353
Bessemer, 1,491
Bethel, 23,650
Bethlehem, 75,408
Big Beaver, 2,381
Birdsboro, 3,025
Blairsville, 4,930
Blakely, 6,374
Blawnox, 2,085
Bloomsburg, 10,655
Blossburg, 1,956
Bobtown, 1,167
Boiling Springs, 1,182
Borough, 2,917
Boswell, 1,508
Boyertown, 4,067
Brackenridge, 5,697
Braddock, 12,337
Braddock Hills, 2,414
Bradford, 15,061
Brentwood, 13,706
Bridgeport, 5,306
Bridgeville, 7,112
Bridgewater 1,292
Bristol, borough, 12,364
Bristol, 59,298
Brockway, 2,563
Brookhaven, 5,280
Brookville, 4,620
Brownstown, 1,379
Brownsville, 6,055
Bryn Athyn, 1,057
Burgettstown, 2,383
Burnham, 2,755
Butler, 20,975
Cairnbrook, 1,100
California, 5,978
Calumet, 1,241
Cambridge Springs, 2,031
Campbelltown, 1,061
Camp Hill, 8,559
Canonsburg, 11,877
Canton, 2,102
Carbondale, 13,595
Carlisle, 16,623
Carnegie, 11,887
Carrolltown, 1,525
Castle Shannon, 11,836
Catasauqua, 5,062
Catawissa, 1,824
Centerville, Washington co., 5,088
Central City, 1,604
Centralia, 1,435
Centre Hall, 1,109
Chalfant, 1,414
Chalfont, 1,410
Chambersburg, 17,670
Charleroi, 8,148
Chatwood, 3,621
Cheltenham, 35,990
Chester, city, 63,658
Chester, 3,602
Cheswick, 2,734
Chevy Chase Heights, 1,160
Chicora, 1,156
Christiana, 1,069
Churchill, 3,428
Clairton, 18,389
Clarion, 4,958
Clarks Green, 1,256
Clarks Summit, 3,693
Claysburg, 1,439
Clearfield, 9,270
Cleona, 1,988
Clifton Heights, 8,005
Clymer, 2,251
Coaldale, Schuylkill co., 3,949
Coaltown, 1,033
Coatesville, 12,971
Cochranton, 1,139
Collegeville, 2,254
Collingdale, 10,268
Columbia, 12,075
Colver, 1,261
Colwyn, 3,074
Conneautville, 1,100
Connellsville, 12,814
Conshohocken, 10,259
Conway, 1,926
Conyngham, 1,163
Coopersburg, 1,800
Coplay, 3,701
Coraopolis, 9,643
Cornwall, 1,934
Corry, 7,744
Coudersport, 2,889
Crafton, 8,418
Crescent Heights-Daisytown, 1,396
Cresson, 2,659
Cressona, 1,854
Crucible, 1,064
Curtisville, 1,376
Curwensville, 3,231
Dale, 2,807
Dallas, 2,586
Dallastown, 3,615
Dalton, 1,227
Danville, 6,889
Darby, borough, 14,059
Darby, 12,598
Denver, 1,875
Derry, 3,426
Dickson City, 7,738
Dillsburg, 1,322
Donora, 11,131
Dormont, 13,098
Downingtown, 5,598
Doylestown, 5,917
Dravosburg, 3,458
Du Bois, 10,667
Duboistown, 1,358
Dunbar, 1,536
Duncannon, 1,800
Duncansville, 1,396
Dunmore, 18,917
Dupont, 3,669
Duquesne, 15,019
Duryea, 5,626
East Berlin, 1,037
East Berwick, 1,258
East Brady, 1,282
East Butler, 1,007
East Conemaugh, 3,334
East Deer, 2,865
East Faxon, 3,641
East Greenville, 1,931
East Lansdowne, 3,224
East McKeesport, 3,470
Easton, 31,955
East Petersburg, 2,053
East Pittsburgh, 4,122
East Rochester, 1,025
East Stroudsburg, 7,674
East Uniontown, 2,424
East Vandergrift, 1,388
East Washington, 2,483
East Weissport, 2,057
Ebensburg, 4,111
Economy, 5,925
Eddystone, 3,006
Edgewood, Allegheny co., 5,124
Edgewood, Northumberland co., 3,399
Edgeworth, 2,030
Edinboro, 1,703
Edwardsville, 5,711
Eldred, 1,107
Elizabeth, 2,597
Elizabethtown, 6,780
Elizabethville, 1,455
Elkland, 2,189
Ellport, 1,458
Ellsworth, 1,456
Ellwood City, 12,413
Elysburg, 1,100
Emmaus, 10,262
Emporium, 3,397
Emsworth, 3,341
Ephrata, 7,688
Erie, 138,440
Espy, 1,375
Etna, 5,519
Evans City, 1,825
Everett, 2,279
Everson, 1,304
Exeter, 4,747
Export, 1,518
Fairbank, 1,361
Fairchance, 2,120
Fairhope–Arnold City, 2,803
Fairview, Erie co., 1,399
Fairview, Northampton co., 1,146
Fairview-Ferndale, 4,067
Falls, 29,082
Falls Creek, 1,344
Farrell, 13,793
Faxon, 1,841
Fayette City, 1,159
Ferndale, 2,717
Fleetwood, 2,647
Flemington, 1,608
Florin, 1,518
Folcroft, 7,013
Ford City, 5,440
Forest City, 2,651
Forest Hills, 8,796
Forty Fort, 6,431
Fountain Hill, 5,428
Fox Chapel, 3,302
Frackville, 5,654
Franklin, Cambria co., 1,352
Franklin, Venango co., 9,586
Fredericksburg, 1,169
Fredericktown, 1,270
Freedom, 2,895
Freeland, 5,068
Freemansburg, 1,652
Freeport, 2,439
Frisco, 1,578
Galeton, 1,646
Gallitzin, 2,783
Garden View, 2,418
Geistown, 3,186
Gettysburg, 7,960
Gibsonia, 1,150
Gilberton, 1,712
Girard, 2,451
Girardville, 2,958
Glassport, 8,418
Glen Lyon, 4,173
Glenolden, 7,249
Glen Rock, 1,546
Greencastle, 2,988
Greensburg, 17,383
Green Tree, 5,226
Greenville, 8,765
Grindstone, 1,094
Grove City, 8,368

Pennsylvania (cont.)
Hallam, 1,234
Hallstead, 1,580
Hamburg, 3,747
Hanover, 15,538
Harmony, Beaver co., 5,106
Harmony, Butler co., 1,142
Harrisburg, 79,697
Harrison, 15,710
Hastings, 1,751
Hatboro, 7,315
Hatfield, 1,941
Haverford, 54,019
Hawley, 1,433
Hazleton, 32,056
Heidelberg, 2,118
Hellertown, 6,716
Hempfield, 29,704
Herminie, 1,571
Hershey, 6,851
Highfield, 2,471
Highland Park, 1,534
Highspire, 2,999
Hillcrest, 3,541
Hiller, 1,746
Hollidaysburg, 6,475
Homeacre, 3,508
Homer City, 2,471
Homestead, 7,502
Honesdale, 5,569
Honey Brook, 1,023
Hooversville, 1,120
Hopwood, 1,615
Houston, 1,865
Houtzdale, 1,239
Hughestown, 1,615
Hughesville, 2,218
Hummelstown, 4,474
Huntingdon, 7,234
Hyndman, 1,124
Imperial, 1,592
Indiana, 13,005
Industry, 2,338
Ingram, 4,730
Irwin, 4,270
Jeannette, 16,565
Jefferson, Allegheny co., 8,280
Jenkintown, 5,017
Jermyn, 2,568
Jerome, 1,241
Jersey Shore, 5,613
Jim Thorpe, 5,945
Johnsonburg, 4,966
Johnstown, 53,949
Kane, 5,380
Kenhorst, 2,815
Kennett Square, 4,355
Kingston, 20,261
Kittanning, 6,793
Knox, 1,247
Koppel, 1,389
Kulpmont, 4,288
Kutztown, 3,312
Lake City, 1,722
Lancaster, city, 61,055
Lancaster, 10,020
Landisville, 1,690
Langeloth, 1,112
Langhorne, 1,461
Langhorne Manor, 1,506
Lansdale, 12,612
Lansdowne, 12,601
Lansford, 5,958
Larksville, 4,390
Latrobe, 11,932
Laureldale, 4,051
Lawrence Hills, 1,048
Lawrence Park, 4,403
Lebanon, 30,045
Leechburg, 3,545
Leetsdale, 2,153
Lehighton, 6,318
Leith, 1,622
Lemont, 1,153
Lemoyne, 4,662
Lewisburg, 5,523
Lewistown, 12,640
Lewistown Junction, 1,428
Liberty, Allegheny co., 3,624
Ligonier, 2,276
Lilly, 1,642
Lincoln, 1,686
Linesville, 1,255
Linntown, 1,628
Lititz, 5,987
Littlestown, 2,756
Lock Haven, 11,748
Lorain, 1,324
Loretto, 1,338
Lower Burrell, 11,952
Lower Chichester, 4,460
Lower Merion, 59,420
Lower Southampton, 12,619
Lucerne, 1,524
Luzerne, 5,118
Lykens, 2,527
Lyndora, 3,232
Lynnwood, 2,230
McAdoo, 3,560
McChesneytown-Loyalhanna, 3,138
McClure, 1,001
McConnellsburg, 1,245
McDonald, 3,141
McKeesport, 45,489
McKees Rocks, 13,185
McSherrystown, 2,839
Macungie, 1,266
Mahanoy City, 8,536
Malvern, 2,268
Manchester, 1,454
Manheim, 4,790
Manor, 1,136
Mansfield, 2,678
Marcus Hook, 3,299
Marianna, 1,088
Marietta, 2,385
Marion Heights, 1,132
Marple, 19,722
Mars, 1,522
Marshallton, 2,316
Martinsburg, 1,772
Marysville, 2,580
Masontown, 4,730
Matamoras, 2,087
Mather, 1,033
Mayfield, 1,996
Meadowlands, 1,967
Meadville, 16,671
Mechanicsburg, 8,123
Mechanicsville, Montour co., 1,758
Media, 5,803
Mercer, 2,800
Mercersburg, 1,759
Meridian, 1,649
Meyersdale, 2,901
Middleburg, 1,366
Middletown, Bucks co., 26,894
Middletown, Dauphin co., 11,182
Midland, Beaver co., 6,425
Midland, Washington co., 1,317
Midway, Adams co., 1,568
Midway, Washington co., 1,012
Mifflinburg, 2,476
Mifflinville, 1,027
Milford, 1,198
Millcreek, 28,441
Millersburg, 2,984
Millersville, 3,883
Mill Hall, 1,891
Millsboro, 1,179
Millvale, 6,624
Milroy, 1,666
Milton, 7,972
Minersville, 6,606
Mocanaqua, 1,104
Mohnton, 2,223
Monaca, 8,394
Monessen, 18,424
Monongahela, 8,388
Monroeville, 22,446
Mont Alto, 1,039
Mont Clare, 1,124
Montgomery, 2,150
Montoursville, 5,211
Montrose, 2,363
Moosic, 4,243
Morrisville, 7,790
Morton, 2,207
Moscow, 1,212
Mount Carmel, 10,760
Mount Holly Springs, 1,840
Mount Jewett, 1,226
Mount Joy, 3,292
Mount Lebanon, 35,361
Mount Oliver, 5,980
Mount Penn, 3,574
Mount Pleasant, 6,107
Mount Union, 4,091
Mountville, 1,411
Mount Wolf, 1,514
Muncy, 2,830
Munhall, 17,312
Muse, 1,386
Myerstown, 3,268
Nanticoke, 15,601
Nanty-Glo, 4,608
Narberth, 5,109
Nazareth, 6,209
Nemacolin, 1,404
Nescopeck, 1,934
Nesquehoning, 2,714
Nether Providence, 10,380
New Berlinville, 1,151
New Bethlehem, 1,599
New Brighton, 8,397
New Britain, 1,109
New Castle, 44,790
New Castle Northwest, 2,007
New Cumberland, 9,257
New Eagle, 2,670
New Freedom, 1,395
New Holland, 3,425
New Kensington, 23,485
Newmanstown, 1,459
New Milford, 1,129
New Oxford, 1,407
New Philadelphia, 1,702
Newport, 1,861
New Salem, West-moreland co., 1,313
New Salem–Buffington, 1,834
Newtown, 2,323
Newville, 1,656
New Wilmington, 2,203
Noblestown-Sturgeon, 1,709
Norristown, 38,925
Northampton, 8,866
North Apollo, 1,741
North Belle Vernon 3,148
North Braddock, 13,204
North Catasauqua, 2,805
North Charleroi, 2,259
North East, 4,217
North Irwin, 1,143
Northumberland, 4,156
North Vandergrift, 1,827
North Versailles, 13,583
North Wales, 3,673
North Warren, 1,458
North York, 2,290
Norvelt, 1,211
Norwood, 6,729
Oakdale, 1,695
Oakland, Lawrence co., 2,303
Oakmont, 7,504
Oakwood, 3,303
Oil City, 17,692
Old Forge, 8,928
Oliver, 3,015
Olyphant, 5,864
Orwigsburg, 2,131
Osceola, 1,777
Oxford, 3,376
Paint, 1,275
Palmer Heights, 2,597
Palmerton, 5,942
Palmyra, 6,999
Palo Alto, 1,445
Parkesburg, 2,759
Parkside, 2,426
Parkville, 4,516
Patton, 2,880
Paxtang, 1,916
Pen Argyl, 3,693
Penbrook, 3,671
Penndel, 2,158
Penn Hills, 51,512
Pennsburg, 1,698
Perkasie, 4,650
Perryopolis, 1,799
Philadelphia, 2,002,512
Philipsburg, 3,872
Phoenixville, 13,797
Pine Grove, 2,267
Pitcairn, 5,383
Pittsburgh, 604,332
Pittston, 12,407
Pleasant Gap, 1,389
Pleasant Hills, 8,573
Plum, 10,241
Plymouth, 10,401
Plymptonville, 1,822
Point Marion, 1,853
Polk, 3,574
Pomeroy, 1,085
Portage, 3,933
Port Allegany, 2,742
Port Carbon, 2,775
Port Vue, 6,635
Pottstown, 26,144
Pottsville, 21,659
Pricedale-Sanfield, 1,548
Primrose, 1,416
Pringle, 1,418
Prospect Park, Delaware co., 6,596
Prospect Park, Northampton co., 1,305
Punxsutawney, 8,805
Quakertown, 6,305
Quarryville, 1,427
Radnor, 21,697
Rankin, 5,164
Ranshaw, 1,078
Reading, 98,177
Red Hill, 1,086
Red Lion, 5,594
Renovo, 3,316
Republic, 1,921
Reserve, 4,230
Reynoldsville, 3,158
Richland, 1,276
Ridgway, 6,387
Ridley, 35,738
Ridley Park, 7,387
Rimersburg, 1,323
Riverside, 1,580
Roaring Spring, 2,937
Robesonia, 1,579
Rochester, 5,952
Rockledge, 2,587
Rockwood, 1,101
Rocky Grove, 3,168
Roscoe, 1,315
Roseto, 1,630
Ross, 25,952
Royalton, 1,128
Royersford, 3,969
Russellton, 1,613
Saegertown, 1,131
St. Clair, 5,159
St. Marys, 8,065
St. Michael, 1,292
Saltsburg, 1,054
Sandy, 2,070
Sayre, 7,917
Scalp Level, 1,445
Schuylkill Haven, 6,470
Scott, 19,094
Scottdale, 6,244
Scranton, 111,443
Selinsgrove, 3,948
Sellersville, 2,497
Sewickley, 6,157
Shaler, 24,939
Shamokin, 13,674
Shamokin Dam, 1,093
Sharon, 25,267
Sharon Hill, 7,123
Sharon North, 1,192
Sharpsburg, 6,096
Sharpsville, 6,061
Sheffield, 1,971
Shenandoah, 11,073
Shenandoah, Heights, 1,721
Shickshinny, 1,843
Shillington, 5,639
Shinglehouse, 1,298
Shippensburg, 6,138
Shiremanstown, 1,212
Shoemakersville, 1,464
Sinking Spring, 2,244
Slatington, 4,316
Slippery Rock, 2,563
Slovan, 1,018
Smethport, 1,725
Smithfield–Crooked Creek, 1,320
Smock, 1,012
Somerset, 6,347
Souderton, 5,381
South Coatesville, 2,032
South Connellsville, 2,434
South Fork, 2,053
South Greensburg, 3,058
Southmont, 2,857
South Pottstown, 1,850
South Uniontown, 3,603
South Waverly, 1,382
Southwest Greensburg 3,264
South Williamsport, 6,972
Spangler, 2,658
Speers, 1,479
Spring City, 3,162
Springdale, 5,602
Springfield, Delaware co., 26,733
Springfield, Montgomery co., 20,652
Spring Garden, 11,387
Spring Grove, 1,675
Spring Hill, 1,127
Star Junction, 1,142
State College, 22,409
Steelton, 11,266
Stewartstown, 1,164
Stoneboro, 1,267
Stowe, Allegheny co., 11,730
Stowe, Montgomery co., 2,765
Strabane, 3,036
Strasburg, 1,416
Stroudsburg, 6,070
Sugar Notch, 1,524
Summit Hill, 4,386
Sunbury, 13,687
Susquehanna Depot, 2,591
Swarthmore, 5,753
Swissvale, 15,089
Swoyersville, 6,751
Sykesville, 1,479
Tamaqua, 10,173
Tarentum, 8,232
Taylor, 6,148
Telford, 2,763
Temple, 1,633
Terre Hill, 1,129
Throop, 4,732
Titusville, 8,356
Topton, 1,684
Towanda, 4,293
Tower City, 1,968
Trafford, 4,330
Trainer, 2,358
Trappe, 1,264
Tremont, 1,893
Tresckow, 1,145
Trevorton, 2,597
Troy, 1,478
Tullytown, 2,452
Tunkhannock, 2,297
Turtle Creek, 10,607
Tyrone, 7,792
Union City, 3,819
Uniontown, Fayette co., 17,942
Uniontown, Northumberland co., 1,085
United, 2,044
Upland, 4,343
Upper Darby, 93,158
Upper Moreland, 21,032
Valley View, 1,540
Vandergrift, 8,742
Verona, 4,032
Versailles, 2,297
Wall, 1,493
Walnutport, 1,609
Wampum, 1,085
Warminster, 15,994
Warren, 14,505
Washington, Washington co., 23,545
Washington North, 2,077
Washington West, 3,951
Waterford, 1,390
Watsontown, 2,431
Waymart, 1,106
Waynesboro, 10,427
Waynesburg, 5,188
Weatherly, 2,591
Wellsboro, 4,369
Wernersville, 1,462
Wesleyville, 3,534
West Brownsville, 1,907
West Chester, 15,705
West Conshohocken, 2,254
West Derry, 1,237
West Easton, 1,228
West Fairview, 1,718
Westfield, 1,333
West Grove, 1,607
West Hazleton, 6,278
West Homestead, 4,155
West Kittanning, 1,101
West Lawn, 2,059
West Lebanon, 2,301
West Leechburg, 1,323
West Mayfield, 2,201
West Middlesex, 1,301
West Mifflin, 27,289
Westmont, 6,573
West Newton, 3,982
West Norriton, 8,342
West Pittston, 6,998
West Reading, 4,938
West View, 8,079
West Wyoming, 3,166
West York, 5,526
Wheatland, 1,813
Whitaker, 2,130
Whitehall, 16,075
White Haven, 1,778
White Oak, 9,047
Wiconisco, 1,402
Wilden, 1,787
Wilkes-Barre, city, 63,551
Wilkes-Barre, 4,319
Wilkins, 8,272
Wilkinsburg, 30,066
Williamsburg, 1,792
Williamsport, 41,967
Williamstown, 2,097
Wilmerding, 4,349
Wilson, 8,465
Windber, 6,994
Wind Gap, 1,930
Windsor, 1,029
Winton, 5,456
Womelsdorf, 1,471
Woodside-Drifton, 1,293
Wormleysburg, 1,794
Wrightsville, 2,345
Wyoming, 4,127
Wyomissing, 5,044
Wyomissing Hills, 1,644
Yardley, 2,271
Yeadon, 11,610
Yeagertown, 1,349
York, 54,504
Youngsville, 2,211
Youngwood, 2,813
Yukon, 1,062
Zelienople, 3,284

RHODE ISLAND, 859,488

Ashaway, 1,298
Barrington, 13,826
Bristol, 14,570
Central Falls, 19,858
Cranston, 66,766
East Providence, 41,955
Harrisville, 1,024
Island Park, 1,147
Jamestown, 1,843
Kingston, 2,616
Narragansett, 1,741
Newport, 47,049
Newport East, 2,643
North Providence, 18,220
Pascoag, 2,983
Pawtucket, 81,001
Providence, 207,498
Wakefield-Peacedale, 5,569
Warwick, 68,504
Westerly, 9,698
West Warwick, 21,414
Wickford, 2,934
Woonsocket, 47,080

SOUTH CAROLINA, 2,382,594

Abbeville, 5,436
Aiken, 11,243
Aiken South, 2,980
Aiken West, 2,602
Allendale, 3,114
Anderson, 41,316
Andrews, 2,995
Arcadia, 2,458
Arkwright, 1,656
Baldwin–Aragon Mills, 1,201
Bamberg, 3,081
Barnwell, 4,568
Batesburg, 3,806
Bath, 1,419
Beaufort, 6,298
Belton, 5,106
Bendale, 1,544
Bennettsville, 6,963
Bennettsville Southwest, 1,022
Bishopville, 3,586
Blacksburg, 2,174
Blackville, 1,901
Bowman, 1,106
Branchville, 1,182
Buffalo, 1,209
Calhoun Falls, 2,525
Camden, 6,842
Cayce, 8,517
Central, 1,473
Charleston, 65,925
Cheraw, 5,171
Chesnee, 1,045
Chester, 6,906
Chesterfield, 1,532
City View, 2,475
Clearwater, 1,450
Clemson, 1,587
Clifton, 1,249
Clinton, 7,937
Clover, 3,500
College Heights, 1,330
Columbia, 97,433
Conway, 8,563
Cowpens, 2,038
Darlington, 6,710
Denmark, 3,221
Dillon, 6,173
Doneraile, 1,043
Drayton, 1,128
Due West, 1,166
Duncan, 1,186
Easley, 8,283
East Gaffney, 4,779
Edgefield, 2,876
Elloree, 1,031
Estill, 1,865
Eureka, 1,423
Fairfax, 1,814
Florence, 24,722
Folly Beach, 1,137
Forest Acres, 3,842
Fort Mill, 3,315
Fountain Inn, 2,385
Gaffney, 10,435
Georgetown, 12,261
Gloverville, 1,551
Graniteville, 1,017
Great Falls, 3,030
Greenville, 66,188
Greenwood, 16,644
Greer, 8,967
Hampton, 2,486
Hartsville, 6,392
Holly Hill, 1,235
Honea Path 3,453
Industrial–Aragon Mills, 1,656
Inman, 1,714
Inman Mills, 1,769
Irwin, 1,113
Isle of Palms, 1,186
Iva, 1,357
Jackson, 1,746
Joanna, 1,831
Johnston, 2,119
Jonesville, 1,439
Kershaw, 1,567
Kingstree, 3,847
Lake City, 6,059
Lamar, 1,121
Lancaster, 7,999
Lancaster Mills, 3,274
Landrum, 1,930
Langley, 1,216
Latta, 1,901
Laurens, 9,598
Leesville, 1,619
Lexington, 1,127
Liberty, 2,657
Lone Oak, 1,435
Loris, 1,702
Lydia Mills, 1,177
Lyman, 1,261
McColl, 2,479
McCormick, 1,998
Madison, 1,904
Manning, 3,917
Marion, 7,174
Mauldin, 1,462
Monarch Mills, 1,990
Moncks Corner, 2,030
Mount Pleasant, 5,116
Mullins, 6,229
Myrtle Beach, 7,834
Newberry, 8,208
New Ellenton, 2,309
Ninety-Six, 1,435
North, 1,047
North Augusta, 10,348
North Hartsville, 1,899
Orangeburg, 13,852
Pacolet, 1,252
Pacolet Mills, 1,476
Pageland, 2,020
Pelzer North, 1,400
Pendleton, 2,358
Pickens, 2,198
Piedmont, 2,108
Pinehurst–Sheppard Park, 1,708
Ridgeland, 1,192
Rock Hill, 29,404
St. George, 1,833
St. Matthews, 2,433
St. Stephen, 1,462
Saluda, 2,089
Saxon, 3,917
Seneca, 5,227
Shannontown, 7,064
Simpsonville, 2,282
South Bennettsville, 1,025
South Greenwood, 2,520
Spartanburg, 44,352
Springdale, Lancaster co., 2,981
Springdale, Lexington co., 1,002
Spring Mills, 1,069
Sullivans Island, 1,358
Summerton, 1,504
Summerville, 3,633
Sumter, 23,062
Taylor, 1,071
Timmonsville, 2,178
Travelers Rest, 1,973
Union, 10,191
Utica, 1,294
Varnville, 1,461
Victor Mills, 2,018
Walhalla, 3,431
Walterboro, 5,417
Ware Shoals, 2,671
Warrenville, 1,128
Watts Mills, 1,438
Wellford, 1,040
West Columbia, 6,410
West Hartsville, 2,427
Westminster, 2,413
Whitmire, 2,663
Whitney, 2,502
Williamston, 3,721
Williston, 2,722
Windy Hill, 2,201
Winnsboro, 3,479
Winnsboro Mills, 2,411
Woodruff, 3,679
York, 4,758

SOUTH DAKOTA, 680,514

Aberdeen, 23,073
Belle Fourche, 4,087
Beresford, 1,794
Britton, 1,442
Brookings, 10,558
Canton, 2,511
Chamberlain, 2,598
Clark, 1,484
Clear Lake, 1,137
Custer, 2,105
Deadwood, 3,045
Dell Rapids, 1,863
De Smet, 1,324
Edgemont, 1,772
Elk Point, 1,378
Eureka, 1,555
Faulkton, 1,051
Flandreau, 2,129
Fort Pierre, 2,649
Freeman, 1,140
Gettysburg, 1,950
Gregory, 1,478
Groton, 1,063
Highmore, 1,078
Hot Springs, 4,943
Howard, 1,208
Huron, 14,180
Ipswich, 1,131
Lake Andes, 1,097
Lead, 6,211
Lemmon, 2,412
Lennox, 1,353
Madison, 5,420
Martin, 1,184
Milbank, 3,500
Miller, 2,081
Mitchell, 12,555
Mobridge, 4,391
Parker, 1,142
Parkston, 1,514
Philip, 1,114
Pierre, 10,088
Pine Ridge, 1,256
Platte, 1,167
Rapid City, 42,399
Redfield, 2,952
Salem, 1,188
Scotland, 1,077
Sioux Falls, 65,466
Sisseton, 3,218
Spearfish, 3,682
Springfield, 1,194
Sturgis, 4,639
Tyndall, 1,262
Vermillion, 6,102
Wagner, 1,586
Watertown, 14,077
Webster, 2,409
Wessington Springs, 1,488
Winner, 3,705
Woonsocket, 1,035
Yankton, 9,279

TENNESSEE, 3,567,089

Adamsville, 1,046
Alamo, 1,665
Alcoa, 6,395
Ashland City, 1,400
Athens, 12,103
Banner Hill, 2,132
Belle Meade, 3,082
Bells, 1,233
Bemis, 3,127
Berry Hill, 1,551
Bolivar, 3,338
Briceville, 1,217
Bristol, 17,582
Brownsville, 5,424
Bruceton, 1,158
Camden, 2,774
Carthage, 2,021
Celina, 1,228
Centerville, 1,678
Chattanooga, 130,009
Clarksville, 22,021
Cleveland, 16,196
Clinton, 4,943
Collierville, 2,020
Colonial Heights, 2,312
Columbia, 17,624
Cookeville, 7,805
Covington, 5,298
Cowan, 1,979

Crossville, 4,668
Daisy, 1,508
Dayton, 3,500
Decherd 1,704
Dickson, 5,028
Donelson, 17,195
Dresden, 1,510
Dunlap, 1,026
Dupontonia, 1,896
Dyer, 1,909
Dyersburg, 12,499
Eagleton Village, 5,068
East Cleveland, 1,452
East Ridge, 19,570
Elizabethton, 10,896
Embreeville Junction, 1,204
Englewood, 1,574
Erin, 1,097
Erwin, 3,210
Etowah, 3,223
Fairview, 1,017
Fayetteville, 6,804
Forest Hills 2,101
Fountain City, 10,365
Franklin, 6,977
Gainesboro, 1,021
Gallatin, 7,901
Gatlinburg, 1,764
Germantown, 1,104
Goodlettsville, 3,163
Greenbrier, 1,238
Greeneville, 11,759
Greenfield, 1,779
Halls, 1,890
Hampton, 1,048
Harriman, 5,931
Hartsville, 1,712
Henderson, 2,691
Hohenwald, 2,194
Humboldt, 8,482
Huntingdon, 2,119
Inglewood, 26,527
Jackson, 33,849
Jamestown, 1,727
Jasper, 1,450
Jefferson City, 4,550
Jellico, 2,210
Johnson City, 29,892
Johnson City Southeast, 2,435
Jonesboro, 1,148
Kenton, 1,095
Kingsport, 26,314
Kingston, 2,010
Knoxville, 111,827
Lafayette, 1,590
La Follette, 6,204
Lake City, 1,914
Lawrenceburg, 8,042
Lebanon, 10,512
Lenoir City, 4,979
Lewisburg, 6,338
Lexington, 3,943
Linden, 1,086
Livingston, 2,817
Long Island, 1,925
Lookout Mt., 1,817
Loudon, 3,812
Lynn Garden, 5,261
McKenzie, 3,780
McMinnville, 9,013
Madison, 13,583
Madisonville, 1,812
Manchester, 3,930
Martin, 4,750
Maryville, 10,348
Memphis, 497,524
Milan, 5,208
Millington, 6,059
Monterey, 2,069
Morrison City, 2,426
Morristown, 21,267
Mountain City, 1,379
Mount Pleasant, 2,921
Munford, 1,014
Murfreesboro, 18,991
Nashville, 170,874
Newbern, 1,695
Newport, 6,448
New Providence, 4,451
Norris, 1,389
Oak Hill, 4,490
Oak Ridge, 27,169
Obion, 1,097
Oliver Springs, 1,163
Oneida, 2,480
Palmer, 1,069
Paris, 9,325
Parsons, 1,859
Plainfield, 2,127
Portland, 2,424
Providence, 3,830
Pulaski, 6,616
Red Bank–White Oak, 10,777
Ridgely, 1,464
Ripley, 3,782
Rockwood, 5,345
Rogersville, 3,121
Savannah, 4,315
Selmer, 1,897
Sevierville, 2,890
Sewanee, 1,464
Shelbyville, 10,466
Signal Mountain, 3,413
Smithville, 2,348
Smyrna, 3,612
Soddy, 2,206
Somerville, 1,820
South Cleveland, 1,512
South Clinton, 1,356
South Fulton, 2,512
South Harriman, 2,884
South Pittsburg, 4,130
Sparta, 4,510
Spring City, 1,800
Springfield, 9,221
Sweetwater, 4,145
Tazewell, 1,264
Tiftona, 3,520
Tiptonville, 2,068
Tracy City, 1,577
Trenton, 4,225
Tullahoma, 12,242
Tusculum, 1,433
Union City, 8,837
Waverly, 2,891
Waynesboro, 1,343
West View Park, 4
Whitehaven, 13,89
White Pine, 1,035
Whitwell, 1,857
Winchester, 4,760
Woodbine–Radnor Glencliff, 14,485
Woodbury, 1,562
Woodmont–Green Hills–Glendale, 23,161

TEXAS, 9,579,67
Abernathy, 2,491
Abilene, 90,368
Alamo, 4,121
Alamo Heights, 72
Albany, 2,174
Alice, 20,861
Alice Southwest, 13
Alpine, 4,740
Alta Loma, 1,020
Alvarado, 1,907
Alvin, 5,643
Amarillo, 137,96
Anahuac, 1,985
Andrews, 11,135
Angleton, 7,312
Anson, 2,890
Anthony, 1,082
Anton, 1,068
Aransas Pass, 6,
Archer City, 1,9
Arlington, 44,77
Asherton, 1,890
Aspermont, 1,28
Athens, 7,086
Atlanta, 4,076
Austin, 186,545
Azle, 2,969
Bacliff, 1,707
Baird, 1,633
Balch Springs, 61
Ballinger, 5,043
Barrett, 2,364
Bartlett, 1,540
Bastrop, 3,001
Bay City, 11,65
Baytown, 28,15
Beaumont, 119,
Bedford, 2,706
Beeville, 13,811
Bellaire, 19,872
Bellmead, 5,127
Bellville, 2,218
Belton, 8,163
Benavides, 2,45
Benbrook, 3,254
Beverly Hills, 1,8
Big Lake, 2,668
Big Spring, 31,2
Bishop, 3,722
Bloomington, 1,
Blue Mound, 1,2
Boerne, 2,169
Bogata, 1,112
Bonham, 7,357
Borger, 20,911
Bovina, 1,029
Bowie, 4,566
Brackettville, 1,6
Brady, 5,338
Brazoria, 1,291
Breckenridge, 6,2
Brenham, 7,740
Bridge City, 4,67
Bridgeport, 3,218
Brookshire, 1,339
Brownfield, 10,28
Brownsville, 48,04
Brownwood, Oran co., 1,286
Brownwood, Brow co., 16,974
Bryan, 27,542
Buffalo, 1,108
Bunker Hill, 2,216
Burkburnett, 7,621
Burleson, 2,345
Burnet, 2,214
Caldwell 2,204
Calvert, 2,073
Camden, 1,131
Cameron, 5,640
Canadian, 2,239
Canton, 1,114
Canutillo, 1,377
Canyon, 5,864
Carrizo Springs, ,699
Carrollton, 4,242
Carthage, 5,262
Castle Hills, 2,62
Castroville, 1,508
Cedar Hill, 1,848
Celina, 1,204
Center, 4,510
Charlotte, 1,465
Childress, 6,399
Chillicothe, 1,161
Cisco, 4,499
Clarendon, 2,172
Clarksville, 3,851
Cleburne, 15,381
Cleveland, 5,838
Clifton, 2,335
Clute City, 4,501
Clyde, 1,116
Coahoma 1,239
Cockrell Hill, 3,104
Coleman, 6,371
College Station, 11,396
Colleyville, 1,491
Colorado City, 6,457
Columbus, 3,656
Comanche, 3,415
Commerce, 5,789
Conroe, 9,192
Cooper, 2,213
Copperas Cove, 4,567
Corpus Christi, 167,690
Corsicana, 20,344
Cotulla, 3,960
Cove City, 1,749
Crane, 3,796
Crockett, 5,356
Crosbyton, 2,088
Cross Plains, 1,168
Crowell, 1,703
Crystal City, 9,101
Cuero, 7,338
Daingerfield, 3,133
Daisetta, 1,500
Dalhart, 5,160
Dallas, 679,684
Dayton, 3,367
Decatur, 3,563
Deer Park, 4,865
De Kalb, 2,042
De Leon, 2,022
Del Rio, 18,612
Denison, 22,748
Denton, 26,844
Denver City, 4,302
De Soto, 1,969
Devine, 2,522
Diboll, 2,506
Dickinson, 4,715
Dilley, 2,118
Dimmitt, 2,935
Donna, 7,522
Dublin, 2,443
Dumas, 8,477
Duncanville, 3,774
Eagle Lake, 3,565
Eagle Pass, 12,094
Earth, 1,104
Eastland, 3,292
Edcouch, 2,814
Eden, 1,486
Edinburg, 18,706
Edna, 5,038
El Campo, 7,700
El Campo North, 1,086
El Campo South, 1,884
Eldorado, 1,815
Electra, 4,759
Elgin, 3,511
El Paso, 276,687
Elsa, 3,847
Ennis, 9,347
Euless, 2,062
Everman, 1,076
Fabens, 3,134
Fairfield, 1,781
Falfurrias, 6,515
Farmers Branch, 13,441
Farmersville, 2,021
Farwell, 1,009
Ferris, 1,807
Flatonia, 1,009
Floresville, 2,126
Floydada, 3,769
Forest Hill, 3,221
Forney, 1,544
Fort Stockton, 6,373
Fort Worth, 356,268
Franklin, 1,065
Fredericksburg, 4,629
Freeport, 11,619
Freer, 2,724
Friona, 2,048
Frisco, 1,184
Fritch, 1,846
Fruitdale, 1,418
Gainesville, 13,083
Galena Park, 10,852
Galveston, 67,175
Ganado, 1,626
Garland, 38,501
Gatesville, 4,626
Georgetown, 5,218
George West, 1,878
Giddings, 2,821
Gilmer, 4,312
Gladewater, 5,742
Glen Rose, 1,422
Goldthwaite, 1,383
Goliad, 1,782
Gonzales, 5,829
Gorman, 1,142
Graham, 8,505
Granbury, 2,227
Grandfalls, 1,012
Grand Prairie, 30,386
Grand Saline, 2,006
Granger, 1,339
Grapeland, 1,113
Grapevine, 2,821
Greenville, 19,087
Gregory, 1,970
Griffing Park, 2,267
Groesbeck, 2,498
Groves, 17,304
Groveton, 1,148
Grulla, 1,436
Gruver, 1,030
Hale Center, 2,196
Hallettsville, 2,808
Haltom City, 23,133
Hamilton, 3,106
Hamlin, 3,791
Harlingen, 41,207
Haskell, 4,016
Hearne, 5,072
Hebbronville, 3,987
Hedwig, 1,182
Hempstead, 1,505
Henderson, 9,666
Henrietta, 3,062
Hereford, 7,652
Hico, 1,020
Hidalgo, 1,078
Highland Park, 10,411
Highlands, 4,336
Highway Village, 1,927
Hillsboro, 7,402
Hitchcock, 5,216
Holliday, 1,139
Hondo, 4,992
Honey Grove, 2,071
Hooks, 2,048
Houston, 938,219
Hubbard, 1,628
Hughes Springs, 1,813
Humble, 1,711
Hunters Creek Village, 2,478
Huntington, 1,009
Huntsville, 11,999
Hurst, 10,165
Hutchins, 1,100
Idalou 1,274
Ingleside, 3,022
Iowa Park, 3,295
Iraan, 1,255
Irving, 45,985
Italy, 1,183
Itasca, 1,383
Jacinto City, 9,547
Jacksboro, 3,816
Jacksonville, 9,590
Jasper, 4,889
Jefferson, 3,082
Jourdanton, 1,504
Junction, 2,441
Karnes City, 2,693
Katy, 1,569
Kaufman, 3,087
Keene, 1,532
Keltys, 1,056
Kenedy, 4,301
Kennedale, 1,521
Kerens, 1,123
Kermit, 10,465
Kerrville, 8,901
Kilgore, 10,092
Kilgore East, 1,236
Killeen, 23,377
Kingsville, 25,297
Kirbyville, 1,660
Kleburg, 3,572
Knox City, 1,805
Kountze, 1,768
Kyle, 1,023
Lacy-Lakeview, 2,272
La Feria, 3,047
La Grange, 3,623
Lake Jackson, 9,651
Lakeview, 3,849
Lakewood, 1,882
Lake Worth Village, 3,833
La Marque, 13,969
Lamesa, 12,438
Lampasas, 5,061
Lancaster, 7,501
La Porte, 4,512
Laredo, 60,678
La Villa, 1,261
League City, 2,622
Legion, 1,691
Leonard, 1,117
Levelland, 10,153
Lewisville, 3,956
Liberty, 6,127
Lindale, 1,285
Linden, 1,832
Littlefield, 7,236
Livingston, 3,398
Llano, 2,656
Lockhart, 6,084
Lockney, 2,141
Lone Star, 1,513
Longview, 40,050
Lorenzo, 1,188
Los Fresnos, 1,289
Lubbock, 128,691
Lufkin, 17,641
Luling, 4,412
Lyford, 1,554
McAllen, 32,728
McCamey, 3,375
McGregor, 4,642
McKinney, 13,763
McLean, 1,330
McNair, 1,880
Madisonville, 2,324
Malakoff, 1,657
Mansfield, 1,375
Marble Falls, 2,161
Marfa, 2,799
Marlin, 6,918
Marshall, 23 846
Marshall Northeast, 1,192
Mart, 2,197
Mason, 1,910
Matador, 1,217
Mathis, 6,075
Memphis, 3,332
Menard, 1,914
Mercedes, 10,943
Merkel, 2,312
Mesquite, 27,526
Mexia, 6,121
Midland, 62,625
Midlothian, 1,521
Mineola, 3,810
Mineral Wells, 11,053
Mission, 14,081
Monahans, 8,567
Moody, 1,074
Morton, 2,731
Mount Pleasant, 8,027
Mount Vernon, 1,338
Muenster, 1,190
Muleshoe, 3,871
Munday, 1,978
Nacogdoches, 12,674
Naples, 1,692
Nash, 1,124
Natalia, 1,154
Navasota, 4,937
Nederland, 12,036
New Boston, 2,773
New Braunfels, 15,631
Newgulf, 1,419
Newton, 1,233
Nixon, 1,751
Nocona, 3,127
North Pleasanton, 1,018
North Richland Hills, 8,662
Odem, 2,088
Odessa, 80,338
O'Donnell, 1,356
Olmos Park, 2,457
Olney 3,872
Olton, 1,917
Orange, 25,605
Orange Grove, 1,109
Overton, 1,950
Ozona, 3,361
Paducah, 2,392
Palacios, 3,676
Palestine, 13,974
Pampa, 24,664
Panhandle, 1,958
Paris, 20,977
Pasadena, 58,737
Pearland, 1,497
Pear Ridge, 3,470
Pearsall, 4,957
Pecos, 12,728
Perryton, 7,903
Petersburg, 1,400
Pharr, 14,106
Phillips, 3,605
Philrich, 2,067
Pilot Point, 1,254
Pinehurst, 1,703
Pineland, 1,236
Piney Point, 1,790
Pittsburg, 3,796
Plains, 1,195
Plainview, 18,735
Plano, 3,695
Pleasanton, 3,467
Point Comfort, 1,453
Port Arthur, 66,676
Port Isabel, 3,575
Portland, 2,538
Port Lavaca, 8,864
Port Neches, 8,696
Post, 4,663
Poteet, 2,811
Poth, 1,119
Prairie View, 2,326
Premont, 3,049
Presidio, 1,062
Primera, 1,066
Quanah, 4,564
Queen City, 1,081
Quitman, 1,237
Ralls, 2,229
Ranger, 3,313
Rankin, 1,214
Raymondville, 9,385
Reese Village, 1,433
Refugio, 4,944
Richardson, 16,810
Richland Hills, 7,804
Richmond, 3,668
Rio Grande City, 5,835
Rio Hondo, 1,344
River Oaks, 8,444
Robinson, 2,111
Robstown, 10,266
Rockdale, 4,481
Rockport, 2,989
Rocksprings, 1,182
Rockwall, 2,166
Roma–Los Saenz, 1,496
Roscoe, 1,490
Rosebud, 1,644
Rosenberg, 9,698
Rotan, 2,788
Round Rock, 1,878
Rowlett, 1,015
Royse City, 1,274
Rule, 1,347
Runge, 1,036
Rusk, 4,900
Sabinal, 1,747
Saginaw, 1,001
San Angelo, 58,815
San Antonio, 587,718
San Augustine, 2,584
San Benito, 16,422
Sanderson, 2,189
San Diego, 4,351
San Elizario, 1,064
Sanger, 1,190
San Juan, 4,371
San Marcos, 12,713
San Pedro, 7,634
San Saba, 2,728
Sansom Park Village, 4,175
Santa Anna, 1,320
Santa Rosa, 1,572
Schertz, 2,281
Schulenburg, 2,207
Seadrift, 1,082
Seagoville, 3,745
Seagraves, 2,307
Sealy, 2,328
Seguin, 14,299
Seminole, 5,737
Seth Ward, 1,328
Seymour, 3,789
Shallowater, 1,001
Shamrock, 3,113
Sherman, 24,988
Shiner, 1,945
Silsbee, 6,277
Silverton, 1,098
Sinton, 6,008
Slaton, 6,568
Smithville, 2,933
Snyder, 13,850
Somerville, 1,177
Sonora, 2,619
Sour Lake, 1,602
South Houston, 7,523
Southlake, 1,023
South Side Place, 1,282
Spearman, 3,555
Spring Valley, 3,004
Spur, 2,170
Stafford, 1,485
Stamford, 5,259
Stanton, 2,228
Stephenville, 7,359
Stinnett, 2,695
Stockdale, 1,111
Stratford, 1,380
Sudan, 1,235
Sugar Land, 2,802
Sulphur Springs, 9,160
Sundown, 1,186
Sunray, 1,967
Sunrise, 1,708
Sweeny, 3,087
Sweetwater, 13,914
Taft, 3,463
Taft Southwest, 1,927
Tahoka, 3,012
Talco, 1,024
Taylor, 9,434
Teague, 2,728
Temple, 30,419
Tenaha, 1,097
Terrell, 13,803
Terrell Hills, 5,572
Texarkana, 30,218
Texas City, 32,065
Three Rivers, 1,932
Throckmorton, 1,299
Timpson, 1,120
Tomball, 1,713
Trinity, 1,787
Troup, 1,667
Tulia, 4,410
Tyler, 51,230
University Park, 23,202
Uvalde, 10,293
Valley Mills, 1,061
Van, 1,103
Van Alstyne, 1,608
Van Horn, 1,953
Vernon, 12,141
Victoria, 33,047
Vidor, 4,938
Waco, 97,808
Waelder, 1,270
Wake Village, 1,140
Waskom, 1,336
Waxahachie, 12,749
Weatherford, 9,759
Weimar, 2,006
Wellington, 3,137
Weslaco, 15,649
Weslaco North, 1,049
West, 2,352
West Columbia, 2,947
West Orange, 4,848
West University Place, 14,628
Westworth, 3,321
Wharton, 5,734
Wharton West, 1,609
Wheeler, 1,174
White Deer, 1,057
White Oak, 1,250
Whitesboro, 2,485
White Settlement, 11,513
Whitewright, 1,315
Whitney, 1,050
Wichita Falls, 101,724
Wills Point, 2,281
Wilmer, 1,785
Wink, 1,863
Winnie, 1,114
Winnsboro, 2,675
Winters, 3,266
Wolfe City, 1,317
Woodsboro, 2,081
Woodville, 1,920
Woodway, 1,244
Wortham, 1,087
Wylie, 1,804
Yoakum, 5,761
Yorktown, 2,527
Zapata, 2,031

UTAH, 890,627
American Fork, 6,373
Beaver, 1,548
Bingham Canyon, 1,516
Blanding, 1,805
Bountiful, 17,039
Brigham City, 11,728
Cedar City, 7,543
Centerville, 2,361
Clearfield, 8,833
Clinton, 1,025
Delta, 1,576
Dragerton, 2,959
Ephraim, 1,801
Farmington, 1,951
Fillmore, 1,602
Garland, 1,119
Grantsville, 2,166
Green River, 1,075
Gunnison, 1,059
Heber, 2,936
Helper, 2,459
Hurricane, 1,251
Hyrum, 1,728
Kanab, 1,645
Kaysville, 3,608
Kearns, 17,172
Layton, 9,027
Lehi, 4,377
Lewiston, 1,336
Lindon, 1,150
Logan, 18,731
Magna, 6,442
Manti, 1,739
Mapleton, 1,516
Midvale, 5,802
Milford, 1,471
Moab, 4,682
Monticello, 1,845
Morgan City, 1,299
Mount Pleasant, 1,572
Murray, 16,806
Nephi, 2,566
North Ogden, 2,621
North Salt Lake, 1,655
Ogden, 70,197
Orem, 18,394
Panguitch, 1,435
Park City, 1,366
Parowan, 1,486
Payson, 4,237
Plain City, 1,152
Pleasant Grove, 4,772
Price, 6,802
Providence, 1,189
Provo, 36,047
Richfield, 4,412
Riverdale, 1,848
Riverton, 1,993
Roosevelt, 1,812
Roy, 9,239
St. George, 5,130
Salina, 1,618
Salt Lake City, 189,454
Sandy City, 3,322
Santaquin, 1,183
Smithfield, 2,512
South Jordan, 1,354
South Ogden, 7,405
South Salt Lake, 9,520
Spanish Fork City, 6,472
Springville, 7,913
Sunnyside, 1,740
Sunset, 4,235
Syracuse, 1,061
Tooele, 9,133
Tremonton, 2,115
Vernal, 3,655
Washington Terrace, 6,441
Wellington, 1,066
Wellsville, 1,106
West Jordan, 3,009
Woods Cross, 1,098

VERMONT, 389,881
Arlington, 1,111
Barre, 10,387
Barton, 1,169
Bellows Falls, 3,831
Bennington, 8,023
Brandon, 1,675
Brattleboro, 9,315
Bristol, 1,421
Burlington, 35,531
Enosburg Falls, 1,321
Essex Junction, 5,340
Hardwick, 1,521
Island Pond, 1,319
Ludlow, 1,658
Lyndonville, 1,477
Manchester Depot, 1,387
Middlebury, 3,688
Montpelier, 8,782
Morrisville, 2,047
Newport, 5,019
North Bennington, 1,437
Northfield, 2,159
Orleans, 1,240
Poultney, 1,810
Proctor, 1,978
Randolph, 2,122
Richford, 1,663
Rutland, 18,325
St. Albans, 8,806
St. Johnsbury, 6,809
Shelburne Road Section, 2,037
Springfield, 6,600
Swanton, 2,390
Vergennes, 1,921
Waterbury, 2,984
West Rutland, 1,991
White River Junction, 2,546
Wilder, 1,322
Williston Road Section, 3,259
Windsor, 3,256
Winooski, 7,420
Woodstock, 1,415

VIRGINIA, 3,966,949
Abingdon, 4,758
Acredale, 1,022
Alexandria, 91,023
Altavista, 3,299

Virginia (cont.)
Amherst, 1,200
Appalachia, 2,456
Appomattox, 1,184
Arlington County, 163,401
Ashland, 2,773
Bassett, 3,148
Bay Colony–North Linkhorn Park, 1,151
Bedford, 5,921
Berryville, 1,645
Big Stone Gap, 4,688
Blacksburg, 7,070
Blackstone, 3,659
Bluefield, 4,235
Bridgewater, 1,815
Bristol, 17,144
Brookneal, 1,070
Buchanan, 1,349
Buena Vista, 6,300
Cape Charles, 2,041
Charlottesville, 29,427
Chase City, 3,207
Chatham, 1,822
Chester, 1,290
Chilhowie, 1,169
Chincoteague, 2,131
Christiansburg, 3,653
Clarksville, 1,530
Clifton Forge, 5,268
Clintwood, 1,400
Coeburn, 2,471
Collinsville, 3,586
Colonial Beach, 1,769
Colonial Heights, 9,587
Covington, 11,062
Crewe, 2,012
Culpeper, 2,412
Damascus, 1,485
Dante, 1,436
Danville, 46,577
Dublin, 1,427
Dumfries, 1,368
Elkton, 1,506
Emporia, 5,535
Ettrick, 2,998
Exmore, 1,566
Fairfax, 13,585
Fairlawn, 1,325
Falls Church, 10,192
Falmouth, 1,478
Farmville, 4,293
Fieldale, 1,499
Franklin, 7,264
Fredericksburg, 13,639
Fries, 1,039
Front Royal, 7,949
Galax, 5,254
Gate City, 2,142
Glade Spring, 1,407
Glasgow, 1,091
Glenwood, 1,857
Gordonsville, 1,109
Grundy, 2,287
Hampton, 89,258
Harmon Maxie, 1,071
Harrisonburg, 11,916
Herndon, 1,960
Hopewell, 17,895
Jericho, 2,300
Kenbridge, 1,188
Lawrenceville, 1,941
Lebanon, 2,085
Leesburg, 2,869
Lenox, 1,520
Lewis Gardens, 1,380
Lexington, 7,537
Lloyd Place, 2,282
Londonbridge, 1,061
Luray, 3,014
Lynchburg, 54,790
Manassas, 3,555
Manassas Park, 5,342
Marion, 8,385
Martinsville, 18,798
Narrows, 2,508
Newport News, 113,662
Norfolk, 305,872
North Pulaski, 1,156
North Virginia Beach, 2,587
Norton, 4,996
Oceana, 2,448
Onancock, 1,759
Orange, 2,955
Pearisburg, 2,268
Pembroke, 1,038
Pennington Gap, 1,799
Petersburg, 36,750
Pleasant Hill, 2,636
Pocahontas, 1,313
Poquoson, 4,278
Portsmouth, 114,773
Pound, 1,135
Pulaski, 10,469
Purcellville, 1,419
Quantico, 1,015
Radford, 9,371
Richlands, 4,963
Richmond, 219,958
Roanoke, 97,110
Rocky Mount, 1,412
St. Paul, 1,156
Salem, 16,058
Saltville, 2,844
Saratoga Place, 1,478
Seatack, 3,120
Shenandoah, 1,839
South Boston, 5,974
South Hill, 2,569
South Norfolk, 22,035
Springfield, 10,783
Stanley, 1,039
Staunton, 22,232
Strasburg, 2,428
Suffolk, 12,609
Tappahannock, 1,086
Tazewell, 3,000
Triangle, 2,948
Victoria, 1,737
Vienna, 11,440
Vinton, 3,432
Virginia Beach, 8,091
Wakefield, 1,015
Warrenton, 3,522
Waverly, 1,601
Waynesboro, 15,694
Weber City, 1,274
West Point, 1,678
Williamsburg, 6,832
Winchester, 15,110
Wise, 2,614
Woodstock, 2,083
Wytheville, 5,634

WASHINGTON, 2,853,214
Aberdeen, 18,741
Algona, 1,311
Anacortes, 8,414
Annapolis, 1,472
Arlington, 2,025
Auburn, 11,933
Beacon Hill, 1,019
Bellevue, 12,809
Bellingham, 34,688
Benton City, 1,210
Black Diamond, 1,026
Blaine, 1,735
Bothell, 2,237
Bremerton, 28,922
Buckley, 3,538
Burlington, 2,968
Camas, 5,666
Cashmere, 1,891
Castle Rock, 1,424
Centralia, 8,586
Central Park, 1,622
Chehalis, 5,199
Chelan, 2,402
Cheney, 3,173
Chewelah, 1,525
Clarkston, 6,209
Cle Elum, 1,816
Clyde Hill, 1,871
Colfax, 2,860
College Place, 4,031
Columbia Heights, 2,227
Colville, 3,806
Cosmopolis, 1,312
Coulee Dam, 1,344
Darrington, 1,272
Davenport, 1,494
Dayton, 2,913
Deer Park, 1,333
Des Moines, 1,987
East Wenatchee Bench, 2,327
Edmonds, 8,016
Ellensburg, 8,625
Elma, 1,811
Enetai, 2,539
Enumclaw, 3,269
Ephrata, 6,548
Everett, 40,304
Fairmont, 1,227
Fairview, 2,758
Ferndale, 1,442
Fife, 1,463
Fircrest, 3,565
Fords Prairie, 1,404
Forks, 1,156
Fruitvale, 3,345
Garrett, 1,641
Gig Harbor, 1 094
Goldendale, 2,536
Grand Coulee, 1,058
Grandview, 3,366
Granger, 1·424
Green Acres, 2,074
Hoquiam, 10,762
Houghton, 2,426
Intercity, 1,475
Issaquah, 1,870
Kalama, 1,088
Kelso, 8,379
Kennewick, 14,244
Kent, 9,017
Kirkland, 6,025
Lacey, 6,630
Lake Stevens, 1,538
Leavenworth, 1,480
Longview 23,349
Lowell, 1,086
Lynden, 2,542
Lynnwood, 7,207
McCleary, 1,115
Marysville, 3,117
Medical Lake, 4,765
Medina, 2,285
Millwood, 1,776
Milton, 2,218
Monroe, 1,901
Montesano, 2,486
Morton, 1,183
Moses Lake, 11,299
Mountlake Terrace, 9,122
Mount Vernon, 7,921
Mukilteo, 1,128
Navy Yard City, 3,341
Newport, 1,513
Normandy Park, 3,224
Oak Harbor 3,942
Odessa, 1,231
Okanogan, 2,001
Olympia, 18,273
Omak, 4,068
Opportunity, 12,465
Oroville, 1,437
Orting, 2,697
Othello, 2,669
Pacific, 1,577
Pasco, 14,522
Pasco West, 2,894
Pinehurst, 3,989
Pomeroy, 1,677
Port Angeles, 12,653
Port Angeles East, 1,283
Port Orchard, 2,778
Port Townsend, 5,074
Poulsbo, 1,505
Prosser, 2,763
Pullman, 12,957
Puyallup, 12,063
Quincy, 3,269
Raymond, 3,301
Redmond, 1,426
Renton, 18,453
Republic, 1,064
Richland, 23,548
Ritzville, 2,173
Rocky Point–Marine Drive, 2,733
Roslyn, 1,283
Seattle, 557,087
Sedro-Woolley, 3,705
Selah, 2,824
Sequim, 1,164
Shelton, 5,651
Shoultes, 3,159
Snohomish, 3,894
Snoqualmie, 1,216
Soap Lake, 1, 591
South Bend, 1,671
South Broadway, 3,661
Spokane, 181, 608
Steilacoom, 1,569
Sumach, 1,345
Sumner, 5,874
Sunnyside, 6,208
Tacoma, 147,979
Toppenish, 5,667
Trentwood, 1,387
Tukwila, 1,804
Tumwater, 3,885
Union Gap, 2,100
Vancouver, 32,464
Waitsburg, 1,010
Walla Walla, 24,536
Walla Walla East, 1,557
Wapato, 3,137
Washougal, 2,672
Waterville, 1,013
Wenatchee, 16,726
West Clarkston–Highland, 2,851
West Richland, 1,347
West Wenatchee, 2,518
White Salmon, 1,590
Wilbur, 1,138
Woodland, 1,336
Yakima, 43,284
Zillah, 1,059

WASHINGTON, city, see DISTRICT OF COLUMBIA

WEST VIRGINIA, 1,860,421
Addison, 1,132
Alderson, 1,225
Amherstdale-Robinette, 1,716
Anawalt, 1,062
Anmoore, 1,050
Ansted, 1,511
Athens, 1,086
Barboursville, 2,331
Bath, 1,138
Beckley, 18,642
Belington, 1,528
Benwood, 2,850
Bethlehem, 2,308
Bluefield, 19,256
Boomer-Harewood, 1,657
Bramwell, 1,195
Bridgeport, 4,199
Buckhannon, 6,386
Cameron, 1,652
Cannelton-Carbondale, 1,044
Caretta, 1,092
Cedar Grove, 1,569
Ceredo, 1,387
Chapmanville, 1,241
Charleston, 85,796
Charles Town, 3,329
Chesapeake, 2,699
Chester, 3,787
Clarksburg, 28,112
Clendenin, 1,510
Coalwood, 1,199
Colored Hill, 1,115
Corrinne, 1,273
Crab Orchard, 1,953
Davy, 1,331
Delbarton, 1,122
Despard, 1,763
Dunbar, 11,006
East Bank, 1,023
East Rainelle, 1,244
East View, 1,704
Eccles, 1,145
Eckman, 1,125
Elkins, 8,307
Fairmont, 27,477
Falls View–Charlton Heights, 1,127
Fayetteville, 1,848
Follansbee, 4,052
Gary, 1,393
Gassaway, 1,223
Glendale, 1,905
Glen Hedrick, 1,230
Glen Jean–Hilltop, 1,665
Glenville, 1,828
Grafton, 5,791
Grant Town, 1,105
Harrisville, 1,428
Henlawson, 1,670
Hinton, 5,197
Holden-Beebe, 1,900
Hopewell, 1,230
Huntington, 83,627
Hurricane, 1,970
Kenova, 4,577
Keyser, 6,192
Keystone, 1,457
Kimball, 1,175
Kingwood, 2,530
Kistler, 1,084
Lewisburg, 2,259
Lilly Grove, 1,255
Logan, 4,185
Lumberport, 1,031
McDowell, 1,109
McMechen, 2,999
Mabscott, 1,591
MacArthur, 1,418
Madison, 2,215
Mallory, 1,133
Man, 1,486
Mannington, 2,996
Marlinton, 1,586
Marmet, 2,500
Martinsburg, 15,179
Mason, 1,005
Maybeury-Switchback 1,423
Milton, 1,714
Minden, 1,114
Monongah, 1,321
Montgomery, 3,000
Moorefield, 1,434
Morgantown, 22,487
Moundsville, 15,163
Mt. Gay, 3,386
Mount Hope, 2,000
Mullens, 3,544
New Cumberland, 2,076
Newell, 1,842
New Haven, 1,314
New Martinsville, 5,607
Nitro, 6,894
Nutter Fort, 2,440
Oak Hill, 4,711
Oceana, 1,303
Paden City, 3,137
Parkersburg, 44,797
Parsons, 1,798
Pennsboro, 1,660
Petersburg, 2,079
Philippi, 2,228
Piedmont, 2,307
Pineville, 1,137
Point Pleasant, 5,785
Powellton, 1,256
Princeton, 8,393
Ranson, 1,974
Ravenswood, 3,410
Richwood, 4,110
Ridgeley, 1,229
Ripley, 2,756
Rivesville, 1,191
Roderfield, 1,020
Romney, 2,203
Ronceverte, 1,882
St. Albans, 15,103
St. Marys, 2,443
Salem, 2,366
Shepherdstown, 1,328
Shinnston, 2,724
Sistersville, 2,331
Smithers, 1,696
Sophia, 1,284
South Charleston, 19,180
Spencer, 2,660
Sprague, 3,073
Star City, 1,236
Stonewood, 2,202
Summersville, 2,008
Switzer, 1,131
Terra Alta, 1,504
Thorpe, 1,102
Verdunville, 2,260
Vienna, 9,381
War, 3,006
Ward, 1,109
Wayne, 1,274
Weirton, 28,201
Welch, 5,313
Wellsburg, 5,514
Weston, 8,754
Westover, 4,749
West Union, 1,186
Wharton, 1,055
Wheeling, 53,400
White Sulphur Springs, 2,676
Williamson, 6,746
Williamstown, 2,632

WISCONSIN, 3,951,777
Abbotsford, 1,171
Adams, 1,301
Algoma, 3,855
Alma, 1,008
Altoona, 2,114
Amery, 1,769
Antigo, 9,691
Appleton, 48,411
Arcadia, 2,084
Ashland, 10,132
Augusta, 1,338
Baldwin, 1,184
Baraboo, 6,672
Barron, 2,338
Barton, 1,569
Bayside, 3,181
Beaver Dam, 13,118
Beloit, 32,846
Beloit West 1,092
Berlin, 4,838
Black River Falls, 3,195
Bloomer, 2,834
Boscobel, 2,608
Brillion, 1,783
Brodhead, 2,444
Brookfield, 19,812
Brown Deer, 11,280
Burlington, 5,856
Butler, 2,274
Campbellsport, 1,472
Cassville, 1,290
Cedarburg, 5,191
Cedar Grove, 1,175
Chetek, 1,729
Chilton, 2,578
Chippewa Falls, 11,708
Clinton, 1,274
Clintonville, 4,778
Colby, 1,085
Columbus, 3,467
Combined Locks, 1,421
Cornell, 1,685
Cottage Grove, 1,195
Crandon, 1,679
Cross Plains, 1,066
Cuba City, 1,673
Cudahy, 17,975
Cumberland, 1,860
Darlington, 2,349
De Forest, 1,223
Delafield, 2,334
Delavan, 4,846
Delavan Lake, 1,884
Denmark, 1,106
De Pere, 10,045
Dodgeville, 2,911
Durand, 2,039
Eagle River, 1,367
East Troy, 1,455
Eau Claire, 37,987
Edgerton, 4,000
Elkhorn, 3,586
Ellsworth, 1,701
Elm Grove, 4,994
Elroy, 1,505
Evansville, 2,858
Fennimore, 1,747
Fond du Lac, 32,719
Fontana on Geneva Lake, 1,326
Fort Atkinson, 7,908
Fox Lake 1,181
Fox Point, 7,315
Franklin, 10,000
Galesville, 1,199
Genoa City, 1,005
Gillett, 1,374
Glendale, 9,537
Grafton, 3,748
Grand Avenue Park, 1,070
Green Bay, 62,888
Greendale, 6,843
Greenfield, 17,636
eenwood, 1,041
les Corners, 5,549
rtford, 5,627
rtland, 2,088
yward, 1,540
rrington, 2,405
lsboro, 1,366
ricon, 2,996
rtonville, 1,366
ward, 3,485
dson, 4,325
rley, 2,763
esville, 35,164
erson, 4,548
eau, 1,718
lkauna, 10,096
losha, 67,899
Jaskum, 1,572
Jaunee, 2,772
I, 2,524
Iberly, 5,322
Ier, 1,524
Lrosse, 47,575
Lsmith, 3,584
L Geneva, 4,929
L Mills, 2,951
Laster, 3,703
Lon, 1,084
Le Chute, 5,099
L 1,620
Ll, 1,146
Marland, 1,272
Mson, 126,706
Mawa, 1,037
Mtowoc, 32,275
Me Bluff, 1,565
Mthon, 1,022
Mhette, 13,329
Mon, 1,200
Mesan, 1,060
Mafield, 14,153
Mton, 3,531
Mille, 3,607
Mmanie, 1,069
Mord, 3,260
Ma, 1,182
Msha, 14,647
Memonee Falls, 176
Menonie, 8,624
Meon, 8,543
Mel, 9,451
Mieton, 4,410
Mil, 1,671
Mil Junction, 1,433
Milukee, 741,324
Minl Point, 2,385
Moovi, 2,320
Moa, 8,178
Moe, 8,050
Mollo, 1,021
Moeal, 1,361
Moee, 2,067
Mo Horeb, 1,991
Muonago, 1,877
Neeh, 18,057
Neiille, 2,728
Neksa, 2,515
Nec, 1,359
Neverlin, 15,788
Nevlarus, 1,468
Nevlolstein, 2,401
Nevisbon, 1,337
Nevondon, 5,288
NevRichmond, 3,316
Niara, 2,098
Nor Fond du Lac, 2,9
Nor Hudson, 1,019
Oakreek, 9,372
Ocomowoc, 6,682
Ocoo, 4,805
Ocoo Falls, 2,331
Okahee, 1,879
Om, 1,991
Onaska, 3,161
Oosurg, 1,065
Oren, 1,701
Oshosh, 45,110
Oss, 1,144
Owe, 1,098
Palyra, 1,000
Pareeville, 1,331
Par Falls, 2,919
Perrgo Place, 4,475
Pestigo, 2,504
Pewukee, 2,484
Philps, 1,524
Plateville, 6,957
Plyouth, 5,128
Porage, 7,822
Por Edwards, 1,849
Por Washington, 5,984
Poyette, 1,090
Prarie lu Chien, 5,649
Prarie lu Sac, 1,676
Prescot, 1,536
Princeton, 1,509
Pulash, 1,540
Racin, 89,144
Randdph, 1,507
Reedsurg, 4,371
Rhineander, 8,790
Rice lake, 7,303
Richlnd Center, 4,746
Ripor, 6,163
River Falls, 4,857
River Hills, 1,257
Rothschild, 2,550
St. Croix Falls, 1,249
St. Francis, 10,065
Sauk City, 2,095
Saukville, 1,038
Schofield, 3,038
Seymour, 2,045
Sharon, 1,167
Shawano, 6,103
Sheboygan, 45,747
Sheboygan Falls, 4,061
Shell Lake, 1,016
Shorewood, 15,990
Shorewood Hills, 2,320
Shullsburg, 1,324
Silver Lake, 1,077
Slinger, 1,141
Smiths Garden–Fairview, 1,302
South Milwaukee, 20,307
Southwest Wausau, 4,105
South Wisconsin Rapids, 1,464
Sparta, 6,080
Spooner, 2,398
Spring Green, 1,146
Stanley, 2,014
Stevens Point, 17,837
Stoughton, 5,555
Stratford, 1,106
Sturgeon Bay, 7,353
Sturtevant, 1,488
Sun Prairie, 4,008
Superior, 33,563
Sussex, 1,087
Thiensville, 2,507
Thorp, 1,496
Tomah, 5,321
Tomahawk, 3,348
Twin Lakes, 1,497
Two Rivers, 12,393
Union Grove, 1,970
Verona, 1,471
Viroqua, 3,926
Walworth, 1,494
Washburn, 1,896
Waterford, 1,500
Waterloo, 1,947
Watertown, 13,943
Waukesha, 30,004
Waunakee, 1,611
Waupaca, 3,984
Waupun, 7,935
Wausau, 31,943
Wautoma, 1,466
Wauwatosa, 56,923
West Allis, 68,157
West Bend, 9,969
Westby, 1,544
West La Crosse, 1,440
West Milwaukee, 5,043
West Salem, 1,707
Weyauwega, 1,239
Whitefish Bay, 18,390
Whitehall, 1,446
Whitewater, 6,380
Whiting, 1,193
Williams Bay, 1,347
Wind Lake, 1,305
Winneconne, 1,273
Wisconsin Dells, 2,105
Wisconsin Rapids, 15,042

WYOMING, 330,066
Afton, 1,337
Basin, 1,319
Buffalo, 2,907
Casper, 38,930
Cheyenne, 43,505
Cody, 4,838
Douglas, 2,822
Evanston, 4,901
Fox Farm, 1,371
Gillette, 3,580
Glenrock, 1,584
Green River, 3,497
Greybull, 2,286
Jackson, 1,437
Kemmerer, 2,028
Lander, 4,182
Laramie, 17,520
Lovell, 2,451
Lusk, 1,890
Mills, 1,477
Mountain View, 1,721
Newcastle, 4,345
Orchard Valley, 1,449
Pine Bluffs, 1,121
Powell, 4,740
Rawlins, 8,968
Riverton, 6,845
Rock Springs, 10,371
Saratoga, 1,133
Sheridan, 11,651
Thermopolis, 3,955
Torrington, 4,188
Upton, 1,224
Wheatland, 2,350
Worland, 5,806